INTERNATIONAL MONETARY FUND

Balance of
Payments Statistics

Part I: Country Tables

Yearbook 2011

BALANCE OF PAYMENTS STATISTICS YEARBOOK

Volume 62, Part 1: Country Tables, 2011
Prepared by the IMF Statistics Department
Adelheid Burgi-Schmelz, Director, Statistics Department

For information related to this publication, please:
   fax the Statistics Department at (202) 623-6460,
   or write   Statistics Department
                  International Monetary Fund
                  Washington, D.C. 20431
   or e-mail your query to **StatisticsQuery@imf.org**
For copyright inquiries, please fax the Editorial Division at (202) 623-6579.
For purchases only, please contact Publication Services (see information below).

Balance of Payments Statistics Yearbook (BOPSY): Issued in three parts, this annual publication contains balance of payments and international investment position data. Part I provides detailed tables on balance of payments statistics for approximately 179 countries and international investment position data for 127countries. Part 2 presents tables of regional and world totals of major balance of payments components, net International Investment Position (IIP), plus Total Assets and Total Liabilities for the IIP. Part 3 contains description of methodologies, compilation practices, and data sources used by reporting countries.

Cutoff date: August 22, 2011

Address orders to:
International Monetary Fund
Attention: Publication Services
Washington, D.C. 20431
U.S.A.
Telephone: (202) 623-7430
Telefax: (202) 623-7201
E-mail: publications@imf.org
Internet: http://www.imf.org

ISSN 0252-3035
ISBN 978-1-61635-147-2

CONTENTS

Country Tables

"Country" in this publication does not always refer to a territorial entity that is a state as understood by international law and practice; the term also covers the euro area, the Eastern Caribbean Currency Union, and some nonsovereign territorial entities, for which statistical data are provided internationally on a separate basis.

SELECTION OF STATISTICAL PUBLICATIONS

International Financial Statistics (IFS)

Acknowledged as a standard source of statistics on all aspects of international and domestic finance, *IFS* publishes, for most countries of the world, current data on exchange rates, international liquidity, international banking, money and banking, interest rates, prices, production, international transactions (including balance of payments and international investment position), government finance, and national accounts. Information is presented in tables for specific countries and in tables for area and world aggregates. *IFS* is published monthly and annually. *Price:* Subscription price is US$847 a year (US$550 to university faculty and students) for twelve monthly issues and the yearbook. Single copy price is US$109 for a monthly issue and US$172 for a yearbook issue.

Balance of Payments Statistics Yearbook (BOPSY)

Issued in three parts, this annual publication contains balance of payments and international investment position data. Part 1 provides detailed tables on balance of payments statistics for approximately 177 countries and international investment position data for 123 countries. Part 2 presents tables of regional and world totals of major balance of payments components, net International Investment Position (IIP), plus Total Assets and Total Liabilities for the IIP. Part 3 contains descriptions of methodologies, compilation practices, and data sources used by reporting countries. *Price:* US$153.

Direction of Trade Statistics (DOTS)

Quarterly issues of this publication provide, for 160 countries, tables with current data (or estimates) on the value of imports from and exports to their most important trading partners. In addition, similar summary tables for the world, industrial countries, and developing countries are included. The yearbook provides, for the most recent seven years, detailed trade data by country for approximately 184 countries, the world, and major areas. *Price:* Subscription price is US$247 a year (US$212 to university faculty and students) for the quarterly issues and the yearbook. Price for a quarterly issue only is US$41 and the yearbook only is US$110.

Government Finance Statistics Yearbook (GFSY)

This annual publication provides detailed data on transactions in revenue, expense, net acquisition of assets and liabilities, other economic flows, and balances of assets and liabilities of general government and its subsectors. The data are compiled according to the framework of the 2001 *Government Finance Statistics Manual*, which provides for several summary measures of government fiscal performance. *Price:* US$102.

CD-ROM Subscriptions

International Financial Statistics (IFS), Balance of Payments Statistics (BOPS), Direction of Trade Statistics (DOTS), and *Government Finance Statistics (GFS)* are available on CD-ROM by annual subscription. The CD-ROMs incorporate a Windows-based browser facility, as well as a flat file of the database in scientific notation. *Price of each subscription:* US$690 a year for single-user PC license (US$414 for university faculty and students). Network and redistribution licenses are negotiated on a case-by-case basis. Please visit www.imfbookstore.org/onlineServicePricing.asp for information.

Subscription Packages

Combined Subscription Package

The combined subscription package includes all issues of *IFS, DOTS, GFS,* and *BOPSY. Combined subscription price:* US$1,349 a year (US$1,017 for university faculty and students). Expedited delivery available at additional cost; please inquire.

Combined Statistical Yearbook Subscription

This subscription comprises *BOPSY, IFSY, GFSY,* and *DOTSY* at a combined rate of US$537. Because of different publication dates of the three yearbooks, it may take up to one year to service an order. Expedited delivery available at additional cost; please inquire.

IFS, BOPS, DOTS, GFS on the Internet

The Statistics Department of the Fund is pleased to make available to subscribers the *International Financial Statistics (IFS), Balance of Payments Statistics (BOPS), Direction of Trade Statistics (DOTS),* and *Government Finance Statistics (GFS)* databases through the new, easy-to-use IMF eLibrary Data online service. New features include Data Reports, which provides quick access to predefined tables and charts aimed at satisfying many common data searches. From your data report, you can download to Excel, PDF, and Word. IMF eLibrary Data lets you create a basic custom-built data query in well under a minute, using the Query Builder tool and it offers greater flexibility to create larger and more complex queries. Once you have defined your query, you can structure the table the way you want it, and then convert your data into a chart or download it. A number of personalization options are available in the "My Data" section such as accessing your favorites and saved queries. Free registration for My Data can be obtained by clicking on the Sign In or Register link on the IMF eLibrary Data home page. Single user license price for each of the *IFS, BOP, DOTS, GFS Online Service* is $690, and $414 for academic users. Dependent on certain criteria, a range of scaled discounts is available. For full details of qualification for these discounts and online payment, please visit http://www.imfbookstore.org/statistical.asp or e-mail us directly at publications@imf.org.

Address orders to

Publication Services, International Monetary Fund, PO Box 92780, Washington, DC 20090, USA
Telephone: (202) 623-7430   Fax: (202) 623-7201   E-mail: publications@imf.org
Internet: http://www.imfbookstore.org

Note: Prices include the cost of delivery by surface mail. Expedited delivery is available for an additional charge.

INTRODUCTION[1]

Volume 62 of the *Balance of Payments Statistics Yearbook*, published by the International Monetary Fund (the Fund), contains balance of payments and international investment position (IIP) data that member countries have reported to the Fund. The Fund is grateful to these countries for their cooperation in providing these data. For some of these countries, some data have been supplemented by details Fund economists have derived from other sources.

The *Yearbook* consists of three parts. Part 1 presents balance of payments and IIP data of individual countries. Part 2 contains regional and world totals for major components of the balance of payments. Part 3 provides technical descriptions for most reporting countries. Part 1 is separately bound, and Parts 2 and 3 are bound together.

This volume of the *Yearbook* continues the features introduced in Volumes 46 through 61. As in Volume 46, balance of payments data are presented in accordance with the standard components of the fifth edition of the *Balance of Payments Manual (BPM5)*.[2] However, the standard components have changed with the publication of *Financial Derivatives, a Supplement to the Fifth Edition (1993) of the Balance of Payments Manual*, published in 2000 and amended in 2002. Thereafter, references to *BPM5* include the supplement and its addendum. In conformity with the recommendations in the addendum, this *Yearbook* reflects the decision of the IMF Committee on Balance of Payments Statistics (BOPCOM) that the financial derivative transactions involving affiliated enterprises should be included in the financial derivatives component of the balance of payments statistics and the IIP. Similarly, as in Volume 47, IIP data also are presented in the *BPM5* format, and Part 3 of the *Yearbook* publishes detailed reviews of the methodologies, compilation practices, and sources of data for most of the countries included in the volume.

The *BPM5*[3] introduced a number of methodological changes in the compilation of balance of payments data. Chapter I of the *BPM5* describes these changes in detail. Since Volume 46, a set of data codes has accompanied data presented in this *Yearbook* under the standard components of the *BPM5*. These data codes were developed jointly by the Fund, the Organisation for Economic Cooperation and Development (OECD), and the Statistical Office of the European Union (Eurostat). An annex to this introduction explains the structure of the codes. In addition, beginning with Volume 46, the *Yearbook* no longer presents quarterly balance of payments data for those countries that report quarterly balance of payments statistics to the Fund. Such quarterly data are published in the monthly Fund publication *International Financial Statistics (IFS)* and are available on the Balance of Payments Statistics CD-ROM, and on the Internet (BOP Online).

Data conversion work undertaken by the Fund staff has made possible the presentation in the *BPM5* format of both historical data from the Fund's database and more recent statistics reported by those member countries who are still compiling their data in the format of the fourth edition of the *Balance of Payments Manual (BPM4)*. In 1995, the Fund staff developed formulas to transform reported balance of payments data for each country in the Fund's database to approximate the *BPM5* methodology and presentation. Converted data for each reporting country were sent to the respective authorities for review, and their comments were incorporated in the new *BPM5* database. In l996, the Fund staff, in collaboration with country authorities, completed a similar conversion of the *BPM4* IIP data into the *BPM5* presentation. In principle, the IIP of a country is a balance sheet of its stock of external financial assets and liabilities.

The technical descriptions of reporting countries' methodologies, compiling practices, and data sources, shown in Part 3 of the *Yearbook*, are largely based on information that the countries provide to the Fund. The descriptions are intended to enhance users' understanding of the coverage, as well as of the limitations, of individual country data published in this *Yearbook*. They are also designed to inform compilers of data sources and practices used by their counterparts in other countries.

The balance of this introduction is organized as follows:

- Section I describes essential features of the tables published in Part 1 of this volume

---

[1]French and Spanish translations of this introduction appear after the annexes; data on individual countries follow immediately thereafter.

[2]Volume 1 of the yearbook, published in 1949, was based on the first edition of the Fund's *Balance of Payments Manual*, issued in 1948; Volumes 2-12 were compiled pursuant to the second edition of the manual, issued in 1950; Volumes 13-23 were based on the third edition of the manual, issued in 1961; and Volumes 24-29 were associated with that edition as well as the *Balance of Payments Manual: Supplement to Third Edition*, issued in 1973. Volumes 30-45 followed the guidance of the fourth edition of the manual, published in 1977.

[3]International Monetary Fund, *Balance of Payments Manual*, fifth edition, Washington, D.C., September 1993, and *Financial Derivatives, A Supplement to the Fifth Edition (1993) of the Balance of Payments Manual*, 2000.

of the *Yearbook*. (Readers can find details on coverage for Parts 2 and 3 in the separately bound publication.)

•   Section II offers information on the accessibility of the Fund's balance of payments data on CD-ROM and BOP Online.

•   There are six annexes. Annex I shows an analytic presentation of balance of payments components (and related data codes) arranged in a summary form. Annex II presents the standard components of the *BPM5* (and related data codes). Annex III explains the data coding scheme. Annex IV presents the standard components for IIP as shown in the *BPM5*. Annex V provides the conceptual framework of the balance of payments and IIP. Annex VI explains the coverage of major components of the balance of payments accounts, as set forth in the *BPM5*.

I. Part 1 of the Yearbook: Individual Country Data

Part 1 of the *Yearbook* presents country pages alphabetically. "Country" in this publication does not always refer to a territorial entity that is a state as understood by international law and practice; the term also covers the euro area, the Eastern Caribbean Currency Union, and some nonsovereign territorial entities for which statistical data are provided internationally on a separate basis.

For most countries, balance of payments data are presented in two tables. Table 1 is an analytical summary of the more detailed data of Table 2. This table provides an array of balance of payments components to highlight the financing items (the reserves and related items). (See also Annex I.) Table 2 displays data in the standard components described in the *BPM5*. (See also Annex II.)

For countries for which IIP statistics are available, Table 3 presents those data. Tables 1, 2, and 3 present data for the years 2003–2010 for each country. Unless otherwise indicated, the tables report figures for calendar years.

Analytic Presentation

In the analytic presentation, shown in Table 1, balance of payments components are classified into five major data categories (groups A through E), which the Fund regards as useful for analyzing balance of payments developments uniformly. The selected groups, however, should not be considered to reflect the Fund's recommendation about the analytic approach appropriate for every country. Other analytical presentations could be arrayed by regrouping the standard components of Table 2 in other ways to take account of the special cir-

cumstances of a specific country or to serve particular analytical requirements.

Note that the figures shown in Tables 1 and 2 differ for some countries for balances of the current account, the capital account, and the financial account. This is because in Table 1 certain transactions under these accounts are excluded and reclassified as "exceptional financing" under reserves and related items. "Exceptional financing" refers to transactions undertaken by the authorities to finance balance of payments needs, including such items as external borrowing, payment arrears, and debt forgiveness. Exceptional financing does not include reserves.

Standard Presentation

The standard components of *BPM5*, shown in Table 2, list a more detailed classification of goods and services than appears in *BPM4*. The designated "capital and financial account" has separate components for the "capital" and the "financial account." Under the "financial account," components are classified by types of investment (i.e., direct investment, portfolio investment, financial derivatives,[4] other investment, and reserve assets), assets/liabilities, domestic sectors (monetary authorities, general government, banks, and other sectors), and original maturity.

International Investment Position

IIP data, as shown in Table 3, are arrayed in accordance with the standard components for IIP, as set forth in the *BPM5*. (See also Annex IV.)

Although the classification of the IIP components in Table 3 is consistent with that of the financial account of the balance of payments as shown in Table 2, there are several differences between the two tables. As mentioned earlier, IIP data reflect a country's external financial assets and liabilities at a specific point in time. Table 3, therefore, provides the basic presentation of the IIP components under two general categories, namely, assets and liabilities, as opposed to the functional types of investment (direct investment, portfolio investment, financial derivatives, other investment, and reserve assets) shown in Table 2. Also, the data in Table 3 reflect a country's IIP at the end of the reporting period, as opposed to transactions during the period shown in Table 2. Furthermore, unlike Table 2, which shows

---

[4]Owing to the unique nature of financial derivatives, and the manner in which some institutions record transactions, some countries can only provide net transactions data. By convention, these net transactions are generally included under liabilities in the *Yearbook*. In some cases, countries have requested to classify the net transactions only under Financial Derivatives, Net.

Box. International Investment Position

IIP statements for reporting countries are shown as Table 3 in the country pages. A country's IIP statement should be read in conjunction with the notes included in Part 3—Methodologies, Compilation Practices, and Data Sources—for that particular country. As countries collect more IIP data, the coverage of the IIP will be expanded in subsequent volumes of the *Yearbook*.

Readers may refer to Chapter XXIII of the *BPM5* for a full discussion of the concept of international investment position.

External debt is not a separate component of the IIP but can be derived by summing up the non-equity liability components of the IIP (i.e., all recorded liabil-

ities other than equity securities, direct investment equity capital [including reinvested earnings], and financial derivatives). Such a view is in general concordance with the core definition of gross external debt in the *External Debt Statistics: Guide for Compilers and Users*, prepared by the Inter-Agency Task Force on Finance Statistics. The Task Force was chaired by the IMF, and the work on the Guide involved representatives from the Bank for International Settlements, the Commonwealth Secretariat, the European Central Bank, Eurostat, the IMF, the OECD, the Paris Club Secretariat, the United Nations Conference on Trade and Development, and the World Bank.

Key Components [1]

A. Assets

1. Direct investment
    1.1 Equity capital and
        reinvested earnings
    1.2 Other capital[2]

2. Portfolio investment
    2.1 Equity securities
    2.2 Debt securities[4]

3. Financial derivatives
    3.1 Monetary authorities
    3.2 General government
    3.3 Banks
    3.4 Other sectors

4. Other investment
    4.1 Trade credits
    4.2 Loans
    4.3 Currency and deposits
    4.4 Other assets

5. Reserve assets
    5.1 Monetary gold
    5.2 SDRs
    5.3 Reserve position in the Fund
    5.4 Foreign exchange
    5.5 Other claims

B. Liabilities

1. Direct investment
    1.1 Equity capital and
        reinvested earnings
    1.2 Other capital[3]

2. Portfolio investment
    2.1 Equity securities
    2.2 Debt securities[4]

3. Financial derivatives
    3.1 Monetary authorities
    3.2 General government
    3.3 Banks
    3.4 Other sectors

4. Other investment
    4.1 Trade credits
    4.2 Loans
    4.3 Currency and deposits
    4.4 Other liabilities[5]

---

[1] Not all components are shown, such as those broken down by sector (monetary authorities, general government, banks, and other) and, in some cases, by maturity. If a country reports IIP data with major subcomponents missing, totals may not be published.

[2] Liabilities to affiliated enterprises, a component of other capital, are included in external debt.

[3] Liabilities to direct investors, a component of other capital, are included in external debt.

[4] Includes bonds, notes, and money market instruments.

[5] Includes SDR allocations to monetary authorities.

the value of financial transactions over a period, the valuation of a country's IIP shown in Table 3 reflects the value of financial transactions, valuation changes, and other adjustments at the end of the reporting period. The net IIP shown in Table 3 is derived by taking the difference between the value of reported external financial assets and that of reported external financial liabilities.

Data Codes

Tables 1, 2, and 3 show codes for each data category and component. As mentioned earlier, these codes were developed jointly by the Fund, the OECD, and Eurostat and are intended to facilitate international data reporting. The codes are designed for the standard components of balance of payments and international investment position data as defined in the *BPM5*, as well as for the OECD/Eurostat components for trade in services.

There are six digits/characters for each code shown in the *Yearbook*. The first digit designates credit/debit/net, with the number "2" assigned to credit, "3" to debit, and "4" to net (the difference between credit and debit). The next three digits are used to classify balance of payments components. For example the current account is coded 993, the capital account, 994, and the financial account, 995. Readers may refer to Annex III for details of the coding scheme.

The fifth and sixth digits/characters of the code shown in the *Yearbook* denote special features about specific data components. For example, in Table 1, the fifth character Z indicates that the component excludes exceptional financing; W is used to show where exceptional financing and use of Fund credit and loans from the Fund are excluded. Letters A, B, C, and D in Table 1 differentiate the various domestic sectors.

Credits and Debits

In Tables 1 and 2, the transactions data are shown as gross credit or gross debit entries in the current and capital accounts. In the financial account, they are shown as net credit or net debit entries (to reflect net changes in liabilities and net changes in assets). Credit entries, gross or net, are positive (but without a plus sign), and debit entries, gross or net, are negative (with a minus sign). Thus, decreases in assets and increases in liabilities (credits) are shown as positive, and increases in assets and decreases in liabilities (debits) are shown as negative.

Nil, Unavailable Entries, or Confidential Data

It is often difficult to discern in data reported by countries whether missing numbers are not available, zero or insignificant, or confidential. In the *Yearbook* tables, dots (....) indicate that data are either not available, zero or insignificant, or confidential. In cases where data for one or more given subcomponent(s) cannot be revealed due to confidentiality reasons, the nondisclosed value(s) will be either (i) added to a generic subcomponent (such as "other") within the relevant data component; or (ii) omitted without adjusting a generic subcomponent. In either instance, the reported total remains unchanged.

A Note on the Components of *Income* and *Other Investment*

In Table 2, Standard Presentation, the data reported by certain countries under "income" and "other investment" are at a level of aggregation that does not allow all the individual components within this category to be separately identified. In these cases, therefore, the aggregate data for certain subcategories cannot be derived by summing the components for these subcategories. The same principle applies to "other investment" shown in Table 3, International Investment Position.

Previously, in Volumes 46 through 49, the tables showed data for "other investment" (assets and liabilities) under "long-term" and "short-term." Beginning with volume 50, tables now show the data for "other investment" (assets and liabilities) for monetary authorities, general government, banks, and other sectors as totals (of long- and short-term financing) and as "of which: short-term." (For "loans, monetary authorities," tables show the data as totals, as "of which: use of Fund credit and loans from the Fund," and as "of which: short-term.")

Rounding of Figures

Most data in the tables are expressed in units of one million; users should not assume that any table showing smaller units necessarily contains more accurate figures. The unit is chosen to present the figures conveniently. Because of the calculation routines used, there may be rounding differences between an aggregate and the sum of its components.

Currency Conversion

Most of the balance of payments data reported to the Fund are expressed in national currencies or in U.S. dollars, although some countries report certain data in SDRs. To ease comparisons among countries, all balance of payments statements published in the *Yearbook* are expressed in U.S. dollars. In addition, all countries' reported data on transactions with the Fund and transactions in SDRs are replaced with data obtained from the Fund records, which are kept in SDRs. This information is, in turn, converted to U.S. dollars.

For countries that do not report in U.S. dollars, balance of payments data are converted using the country conversion rates shown at the bottom of Table 1. These rates are normally the average exchange rates for a country for the relevant period taken from the *IFS*. For example, the *IFS* pages for the Euro Area contain line "rf," giving average rates for euros per U.S. dollar. Conversions of transactions data from SDRs into U.S. dollars are made at the rates shown in line "sb" of the *IFS* pages for the United States. For countries reporting quarterly data in national currencies, annual U.S. dollar totals are obtained by aggregating the quarterly U.S. dollar figures.

For countries that do not report IIP data in U.S. dollars, data are converted using the country conversion rates shown at the bottom of Table 3. These rates are normally the end-of- period exchange rates for a country (line "ae") for the relevant period taken from *IFS*.

Readers may find more information on the exchange rates that are used in the introduction to *IFS*, Section 2.

II. CD-ROM and Internet Versions

Statistics published in the *Yearbook* are also available on CD-ROM and on the Internet (Balance of Payments Statistics Online—BOP online). In this electronic version, the number of countries and time series covered is slightly larger than that appearing in the printed version of the *Yearbook*, as is the number of periods for which data observations of time series are given. Also, quarterly data reported by countries are available, and updates and revisions of the data are included as they become available. Inquiries about the CD-ROM and BOP Online should be addressed to:

Publication Services
International Monetary Fund
Washington, D.C. 20431, U.S.A.
Telephone (202) 623-7430
Telefax   (202) 623-7201
E-mail   publications@imf.org
Internet   http://www.imf.org

ANNEX I. ANALYTIC PRESENTATION

	Data Codes
A. CURRENT ACCOUNT[1]	4 993 Z .
Goods: exports f.o.b.	2 100 ..
Goods: imports f.o.b.	3 100 ..
Balance on Goods	4 100 ..
Services: credit	2 200 ..
Services: debit	3 200 ..
Balance on Goods and Services	4 991 ..
Income: credit	2 300 ..
Income: debit	3 300 ..
Balance on Goods, Services, and Income	4 992 ..
Current transfers: credit	2 379 Z .
Current transfers: debit	3 379 ..
B. CAPITAL ACCOUNT[1]	4 994 Z .
Capital account: credit	2 994 Z .
Capital account: debit	3 994 ..
Total, Groups A plus B	4 981 ..
C. FINANCIAL ACCOUNT[1]	4 995W .
Direct investment abroad	4 505 ..
Direct investment in reporting economy	4 555 Z .
Portfolio investment assets	4 602 ..
Equity securities	4 610 ..
Debt securities	4 619 ..
Portfolio investment liabilities	4 652 Z .
Equity securities	4 660 ..
Debt securities	4 669 Z .
Financial derivatives	4 910 ..
Financial derivatives assets	4 900
Financial derivatives liabilities	4 905
Other investment assets	4 703 ..
Monetary authorities	4 701 ..
General government	4 704 ..
Banks	4 705 ..
Other sectors	4 728 ..
Other investment liabilities[2]	4 753W .
Monetary authorities	4 753WA
General government	4 753 ZB
Banks	4 753 ZC
Other sectors	4 753 ZD
Total, Groups A through C	4 983 ..
D. NET ERRORS AND OMISSIONS	4 998 ..
Total, Groups A through D	4 984 ..
E. RESERVES AND RELATED ITEMS	4 802 A .
Reserve assets	4 802 ..
Use of Fund credit and loans	4 766 ..
Exceptional financing	4 920 ..
CONVERSION RATES: CURRENCY PER U.S. DOLLAR	0 101 ..

---

[1]Excludes components that have been classified in the categories of Group E.

[2]Includes SDR allocations to monetary authorities.

ANNEX II. STANDARD PRESENTATION

	Data Codes
CURRENT ACCOUNT	4 993 ..
A. GOODS	4 100 ..
Credit	2 100 ..
General merchandise: exports f.o.b.	2 110 ..
Goods for processing: exports f.o.b.	2 150 ..
Repairs on goods	2 160 ..
Goods procured in ports by carriers	2 170 ..
Nonmonetary gold	2 180 ..
Debit	3 100 ..
General merchandise: imports f.o.b.	3 110 ..
Goods for processing: imports f.o.b.	3 150 ..
Repairs on goods	3 160 ..
Goods procured in ports by carriers	3 170 ..
Nonmonetary gold	3 180 ..
B. SERVICES	4 200 ..
Total Credit	2 200 ..
Total Debit	3 200 ..
Transportation services, credit	2 205 ..
Passenger	2 850 ..
Freight	2 851 ..
Other	2 852 ..
Sea transport, passenger	2 207 ..
Sea transport, freight	2 208 ..
Sea transport, other	2 209 ..
Air transport, passenger	2 211 ..
Air transport, freight	2 212 ..
Air transport, other	2 213 ..
Other transport, passenger	2 215 ..
Other transport, freight	2 216 ..
Other transport, other	2 217 ..
Transportation services, debit	3 205 ..
Passenger	3 850 ..
Freight	3 851 ..
Other	3 852 ..
Sea transport, passenger	3 207 ..
Sea transport, freight	3 208 ..
Sea transport, other	3 209 ..
Air transport, passenger	3 211 ..
Air transport, freight	3 212 ..
Air transport, other	3 213 ..
Other transport, passenger	3 215 ..
Other transport, freight	3 216 ..
Other transport, other	3 217 ..
Travel, credit	2 236 ..
Business travel	2 237 ..
Personal travel	2 240 ..
Travel, debit	3 236 ..
Business travel	3 237 ..
Personal travel	3 240 ..

	Data Codes
Other services, credit	2 200 BA
Communications	2 245 ..
Construction	2 249 ..
Insurance	2 253 ..
Financial	2 260 ..
Computer and information	2 262 ..
Royalties and license fees	2 266 ..
Other business services	2 268 ..
Personal, cultural, and recreational	2 287 ..
Government, n.i.e.	2 291 ..
Other services, debit	3 200 BA
Communications	3 245 ..
Construction	3 249 ..
Insurance	3 253 ..
Financial	3 260 ..
Computer and information	3 262 ..
Royalties and license fees	3 266 ..
Other business services	3 268 ..
Personal, cultural, and recreational	3 287 ..
Government, n.i.e.	3 291 ..
C. INCOME	4 300 ..
Total Credit	2 300 ..
Total Debit	3 300 ..
Compensation of employees, credit	2 310 ..
Compensation of employees, debit	3 310 ..
Investment income, credit	2 320 ..
Direct investment income	2 330 ..
Dividends and distributed branch profits	2 332 ..
Reinvested earnings and undistributed branch profits	2 333 ..
Income on debt (interest)	2 334 ..
Portfolio investment income	2 339 ..
Income on equity	2 340 ..
Income on bonds and notes	2 350 ..
Income on money market instruments	2 360 ..
Other investment income	2 370 ..
Investment income, debit	3 320 ..
Direct investment income	3 330 ..
Dividends and distributed branch profits	3 332 ..
Reinvested earnings and undistributed branch profits	3 333 ..
Income on debt (interest)	3 334 ..
Portfolio investment income	3 339 ..
Income on equity	3 340 ..
Income on bonds and notes	3 350 ..
Income on money market instruments	3 360 ..
Other investment income	3 370 ..
D. CURRENT TRANSFERS	4 379 ..
Credit	2 379 ..
General government	2 380 ..
Other sectors	2 390 ..
Workers' remittances	2 391 ..
Other current transfers	2 392 ..

Data Codes

Debit	3 379 ..
General government	3 380 ..
Other sectors	3 390 ..
Workers' remittances	3 391 ..
Other current transfers	3 392 ..
CAPITAL AND FINANCIAL ACCOUNT	4 996 ..
CAPITAL ACCOUNT	4 994 ..
Total Credit	2 994 ..
Total Debit	3 994 ..
Capital transfers, credit	2 400 ..
General government	2 401 ..
Debt forgiveness	2 402 ..
Other capital transfers	2 410 ..
Other sectors	2 430 ..
Migrants' transfers	2 431 ..
Debt forgiveness	2 432 ..
Other capital transfers	2 440 ..
Capital transfers, debit	3 400 ..
General government	3 401 ..
Debt forgiveness	3 402 ..
Other capital transfers	3 410 ..
Other sectors	3 430 ..
Migrants' transfers	3 431 ..
Debt forgiveness	3 432 ..
Other capital transfers	3 440 ..
Nonproduced nonfinancial assets, credit	2 480 ..
Nonproduced nonfinancial assets, debit	3 480 ..
FINANCIAL ACCOUNT	4 995 ..
A. **DIRECT INVESTMENT**	4 500 ..
Direct investment abroad	4 505 ..
Equity capital	4 510 ..
Claims on affiliated enterprises	4 515 ..
Liabilities to affiliated enterprises	4 520 ..
Reinvested earnings	4 525 ..
Other capital	4 530 ..
Claims on affiliated enterprises	4 535 ..
Liabilities to affiliated enterprises	4 540 ..
Direct investment in reporting economy	4 555 ..
Equity capital	4 560 ..
Claims on direct investors	4 565 ..
Liabilities to direct investors	4 570 ..
Reinvested earnings	4 575 ..
Other capital	4 580 ..
Claims on direct investors	4 585 ..
Liabilities to direct investors	4 590 ..

	Data Codes
B. PORTFOLIO INVESTMENT	4 600 ..
Assets	4 602 ..
Equity securities	4 610 ..
Monetary authorities	4 611 ..
General government	4 612 ..
Banks	4 613 ..
Other sectors	4 614 ..
Debt securities	4 619 ..
Bonds and notes	4 620 ..
Monetary authorities	4 621 ..
General government	4 622 ..
Banks	4 623 ..
Other sectors	4 624 ..
Money market instruments	4 630 ..
Monetary authorities	4 631 ..
General government	4 632 ..
Banks	4 633 ..
Other sectors	4 634 ..
Liabilities	4 652 ..
Equity securities	4 660 ..
Banks	4 663 ..
Other sectors	4 664 ..
Debt securities	4 669 ..
Bonds and notes	4 670 ..
Monetary authorities	4 671 ..
General government	4 672 ..
Banks	4 673 ..
Other sectors	4 674 ..
Money market instruments	4 680 ..
Monetary authorities	4 681 ..
General government	4 682 ..
Banks	4 683 ..
Other sectors	4 684 ..
C. FINANCIAL DERIVATIVES	4 910 ..
Monetary authorities	4 911 ..
General government	4 912 ..
Banks	4 913 ..
Other sectors	4 914 ..
Assets	4 900 ..
Monetary authorities	4 901 ..
General government	4 902 ..
Banks	4 903 ..
Other sectors	4 904 ..
Liabilities	4 905 ..
Monetary authorities	4 906 ..
General government	4 907 ..
Banks	4 908 ..
Other sectors	4 909 ..
D. OTHER INVESTMENT	4 700 ..
Assets	4 703 ..
Trade credits	4 706 ..
General government	4 707 ..
of which: short-term	4 709 ..
Other sectors	4 710 ..
of which: short-term	4 712 ..

	Data Codes	
Loans	4 714	..
Monetary authorities	4 715	..
of which: short-term	4 718	..
General government	4 719	..
of which: short-term	4 721	..
Banks	4 722	..
of which: short-term	4 724	..
Other sectors	4 725	..
of which: short-term	4 727	..
Currency and deposits	4 730	..
Monetary authorities	4 731	..
General government	4 732	..
Banks	4 733	..
Other sectors	4 734	..
Other assets	4 736	..
Monetary authorities	4 737	..
of which: short-term	4 739	..
General government	4 740	..
of which: short-term	4 742	..
Banks	4 743	..
of which: short-term	4 745	..
Other sectors	4 746	..
of which: short-term	4 748	..
Liabilities	4 753	..
Trade credits	4 756	..
General government	4 757	..
of which: short-term	4 759	..
Other sectors	4 760	..
of which: short-term	4 762	..
Loans	4 764	..
Monetary authorities	4 765	..
of which: Use of Fund credit and loans from the Fund	4 766	..
of which: short-term	4 768	..
General government	4 769	..
of which: short-term	4 771	..
Banks	4 772	..
of which: short-term	4 774	..
Other sectors	4 775	..
of which: short-term	4 777	..
Currency and deposits	4 780	..
Monetary authorities	4 781	..
General government	4 782	..
Banks	4 783	..
Other sectors	4 784	..
Other liabilities[1]	4 786	..
Monetary authorities	4 787	..
of which: short-term	4 789	..
General government	4 790	..
of which: short-term	4 792	..
Banks	4 793	..
of which: short-term	4 795	..
Other sectors	4 796	..
of which: short-term	4 798	..
E. RESERVE ASSETS	4 802	..
Monetary gold	4 812	..
SDRs	4 811	..
Reserve position in the Fund	4 810	..
Foreign exchange	4 803	..
Other claims	4 813	..
NET ERRORS AND OMISSIONS	4 998	..

---

[1]Includes SDR allocations to monetary authorities.

ANNEX III. IMF/OECD/EUROSTAT CODING SYSTEM FOR BALANCE OF PAYMENTS, INTERNATIONAL INVESTMENT POSITION, AND TRADE IN SERVICES[1]

This coding system incorporates all the standard components and supplementary information lines of the fifth edition of the *Balance of Payments Manual,* as well as the components and memorandum items of the OECD-Eurostat classification for international trade in services.

The code consists of three components or sections as follows:

<position>   one decimal digit (selected from the range of 1 to 8) that describes the position of the subject in the international investment position (IIP)/balance of payments (BOP) accounts;

<BOP topic>   three decimal digits (selected from the range of integers from 100 to 998) that identify all the BOP, IIP, trade-in-services, and selected supplementary information components; and

<tag>   a user-defined component that may be of any length.

The complete code would take the form <position><topic><tag>. However, the tag component is optional. In contrast, the position and the topic components of the code are always required. Thus, a common implementation of the code will take the form <position><topic>.

The first section of the code describes the position in the IIP and BOP accounts and is defined as follows:

Code	Position in IIP/BOP Accounts
1	stock at the beginning of the period
2	credit flows
3	debit flows
4	net flows
5	price valuation adjustment
6	exchange rate valuation adjustment
7	other adjustments
8	stock at the end of the period
0	other

The first digit of the topic component identifies the section of the balance of payments or the IIP as follows:

Code	Section of the accounts
1	goods
2	services
3	income and current transfers
4	capital account
5	direct investment
6	portfolio investment
7	other investment
8	reserves
9	aggregates, financial derivatives and supplementary information

The second and third digits of the component are generally sequential counts of the components with some gaps to allow for the possibility of additional codes being included at a later time. In addition, with the exception of the direct investment accounts, the second digit of the topic component takes the numbers 0, 1, 2, 3, or 4 for assets and 5, 6, 7, 8, or 9 for liabilities in the financial accounts.

Examples of data codes for "Other Investment" of the financial account are shown below.

Topic	Single Field			Multiple Field		
	Credit	Debit	Net	Credit	Debit	Net
Other investment	2700	3700	4700	2700	3700	4700
Liabilities	2750	3750	4750	2750	3750	4750
Loans	2762	3762	4762	2762	3762	4762
General govt.	2767	3767	4767	2767	3767	4767
Long-term	2768	3768	4768	2768	3768	4768
Short-term	2769	3769	4769	2769	3769	4769
Banks	2770	3770	4770	2770	3770	4770
Long-term	2771	3771	4771	2771	3771	4771
Short-term	2772	3772	4772	2772	3772	4772
Other sectors	2773	3773	4773	2773	3773	4773
Long-term	2774	3774	4774	2774	3774	4774
Short-term	2775	3775	4775	2775	3775	4775

When considering credits and debits for loans, the language that is commonly used is drawings and repayments. The *BPM5* recommends reporting of all drawings and repayments for long-term loans as a supplementary classification. Most other financial account items are presently collected by the Fund on a net basis. Nevertheless, the coding system provides for the identification of all flows on a credit, debit, and net basis.

---

[1] This is adopted from International Monetary Fund, "Balance of Payments Codes for Standard Components and Additional Items," Washington, D.C., March 3, 1995.

Data Codes

A. ASSETS	8 995 C .
Direct investment abroad	8 505 ..
Equity capital and reinvested earnings	8 506 ..
Claims on affiliated enterprises	8 507 ..
Liabilities to affiliated enterprises	8 508 ..
Other capital	8 530 ..
Claims on affiliated enterprises	8 535 ..
Liabilities to affiliated enterprises	8 540 ..
Portfolio investment	8 602 ..
Equity securities	8 610 ..
Monetary authorities	8 611 ..
General government	8 612 ..
Banks	8 613 ..
Other sectors	8 614 ..
Debt securities	8 619 ..
Bonds and notes	8 620 ..
Monetary authorities	8 621 ..
General government	8 622 ..
Banks	8 623 ..
Other sectors	8 624 ..
Money market instruments	8 630 ..
Monetary authorities	8 631 ..
General government	8 632 ..
Banks	8 633 ..
Other sectors	8 634 ..
Financial derivatives	8 900 ..
Monetary authorities	8 901 ..
General government	8 902 ..
Banks	8 903 ..
Other sectors	8 904 ..
Other investment	8 703 ..
Trade credits	8 706 ..
General government	8 707 ..
of which: short-term	8 709 ..
Other sectors	8 710 ..
of which: short-term	8 712 ..
Loans	8 714 ..
Monetary authorities	8 715 ..
of which: short-term	8 718 ..
General government	8 719 ..
of which: short-term	8 721 ..
Banks	8 722 ..
of which: short-term	8 724 ..
Other sectors	8 725 ..
of which: short-term	8 727 ..
Currency and deposits	8 730 ..
Monetary authorities	8 731 ..
General government	8 732 ..
Banks	8 733 ..
Other sectors	8 734 ..

Data Codes

Other assets	8 736 ..
Monetary authorities	8 737 ..
of which: short-term	8 739 ..
General government	8 740 ..
of which: short-term	8 742 ..
Banks	8 743 ..
of which: short-term	8 745 ..
Other sectors	8 746 ..
of which: short-term	8 748 ..
Reserve assets	8 802 ..
Monetary gold	8 812 ..
SDRs	8 811 ..
Reserve position in the Fund	8 810 ..
Foreign exchange	8 803 ..
Other claims	8 813 ..
B. LIABILITIES	8 995 D .
Direct investment in reporting economy	8 555 ..
Equity capital and reinvested earnings	8 556 ..
Claims on direct investors	8 557 ..
Liabilities to direct investors	8 558 ..
Other capital	8 580 ..
Claims on direct investors	8 585 ..
Liabilities to direct investors	8 590 ..
Portfolio investment	8 652 ..
Equity securities	8 660 ..
Banks	8 663 ..
Other sectors	8 664 ..
Debt securities	8 669 ..
Bonds and notes	8 670 ..
Monetary authorities	8 671 ..
General government	8 672 ..
Banks	8 673 ..
Other sectors	8 674 ..
Money market instruments	8 680 ..
Monetary authorities	8 681 ..
General government	8 682 ..
Banks	8 683 ..
Other sectors	8 684 ..
Financial derivatives	8 905 ..
Monetary authorities	8 906 ..
General government	8 907 ..
Banks	8 908 ..
Other sectors	8 909 ..
Other investment	8 753 ..
Trade credits	8 756 ..
General government	8 757 ..
of which: short-term	8 759 ..
Other sectors	8 760 ..
of which: short-term	8 762 ..

	Data Codes
Loans	8 764 ..
Monetary authorities	8 765 ..
of which: Use of Fund credit and loans from the Fund	8 766 ..
of which: short-term	8 768 ..
General government	8 769 ..
of which: short-term	8 771 ..
Banks	8 772 ..
of which: short-term	8 774 ..
Other sectors	8 775 ..
of which: short-term	8 777 ..
Currency and deposits	8 780 ..
Monetary authorities	8 781 ..
General government	8 782 ..
Banks	8 783 ..
Other sectors	8 784 ..
Other liabilities[1]	8 786 ..
Monetary authorities	8 787 ..
of which: short-term	8 789 ..
General government	8 790 ..
of which: short-term	8 792 ..
Banks	8 793 ..
of which: short-term	8 795 ..
Other sectors	8 796 ..
of which: short-term	8 798 ..
NET INTERNATIONAL INVESTMENT POSITION	8 995 ..
Conversion rates (end of period)	0 102 ..

[1]Includes SDR allocations to monetary authorities.

This annex is reproduced from Chapter II of the BPM5. Please note that paragraph and page numbers cited in this annex refer to those that appear in the BPM5.

Definitions

12. Part one of this *Manual* deals with the conceptual framework of balance of payments accounts and the international investment position. Part one covers their relationship to national accounts; to concepts of residence, valuation, and time of recording; and to the unit of account and conversion.

13. The balance of payments is a statistical statement that systematically summarizes, for a specific time period, the economic transactions of an economy with the rest of the world. Transactions, for the most part between residents and nonresidents,[1] consist of those involving goods, services, and income; those involving financial claims on, and liabilities to, the rest of the world; and those (such as gifts) classified as transfers, which involve offsetting entries to balance—in an accounting sense—one-sided transactions. (See paragraph 28.)[2] A transaction itself is defined as an economic flow that reflects the creation, transformation, exchange, transfer, or extinction of economic value and involves changes in ownership of goods and/or financial assets, the provision of services, or the provision of labor and capital.

14. Closely related to the flow-oriented balance of payments framework is the stock-oriented international investment position. Compiled at a specified date such as year end, this investment position is a statistical statement of (i) the value and composition of the stock of an economy's financial assets or the economy's claims on the rest of the world, and (ii) the value and composition of the stock of an economy's liabilities to the rest of the world. In some instances, it may be of analytic interest to compute the difference between the two sides of the balance sheet. The calculation would provide a measure of the net position, and the measure would be equivalent to that portion of an economy's net worth attributable to, or derived from, its relationship with the rest of the world. A change in stocks during any defined period can be attributable to transactions (flows); to valuation changes reflecting changes in exchange rates, prices, etc.; or to other adjustments (e.g., uncompensated seizures). By contrast, balance of payments accounts reflect only transactions.

---

[1]The exceptions to the resident/nonresident basis of the balance of payments are the exchange of transferable foreign financial assets between resident sectors and, to a lesser extent, the exchange of transferable foreign financial liabilities between nonresidents. (See paragraph 318.)

[2]The definitions and classifications of international accounts presented in this *Manual* are intended to facilitate reporting of data on international transactions to the Fund. These definitions and classifications do not purport to give effect to, or interpret, various provisions (which pertain to the legal characterization of official action or inaction in relation to such transactions) of the *Articles of Agreement of the International Monetary Fund.*

Principles and Concepts

15. The remainder of this chapter deals with the conceptual framework of international accounts, that is, the set of underlying principles and conventions that ensure the systematized and coherent recording of international transactions and stocks of foreign assets and liabilities. Relevant aspects of these principles, together with practical considerations and limitations, will be thoroughly discussed in subsequent chapters.

Double Entry System

16. The basic convention applied in constructing a balance of payments statement is that every recorded transaction is represented by two entries with equal values. One of these entries is designated a credit with a positive arithmetic sign; the other is designated a debit with a negative sign. In principle, the sum of all credit entries is identical to the sum of all the debit entries, and the net balance of all entries in the statement is zero.

17. In practice, however, the accounts frequently do not balance. Data for balance of payments estimates often are derived independently from different sources; as a result, there may be a summary net credit or net debit (i.e., net errors and omissions in the accounts). A separate entry, equal to that amount with the sign reversed, is then made to balance the accounts. Because inaccurate or missing estimates may be offsetting, the size of the net residual cannot be taken as an indicator of the relative accuracy of the balance of payments statement. Nonetheless, a large, persistent residual that is not reversed should cause concern. Such a residual impedes analysis or interpretation of estimates and diminishes the credibility of both. A large net residual may also have implications for interpretation of the investment position statement. (See the discussion in Chapter XXIII.)

18. Most entries in the balance of payments refer to transactions in which economic values are provided or received in exchange for other economic values; those values consist of real resources (goods, services, and income) and financial items. Therefore, the offsetting credit and debit entries called for by the recording system are often the result of equal amounts having been entered for the two items exchanged. When items are given away rather than exchanged, or when a recording is one-sided for other reasons, special types of entries—referred to as *transfers*—are made as the required offsets. (The various kinds of entries that may be made in the balance of payments are discussed in paragraphs 26 through 31.)

19. Under the conventions of the system, a compiling economy records credit entries (i) for real resources denoting exports and (ii) for financial items reflecting reductions in an economy's foreign assets or increases in an economy's foreign liabilities. Conversely, a compiling economy records debit entries (i) for real resources denoting imports and (ii) for financial items reflecting increases in assets or decreases in liabilities. In other words, for assets—whether real or financial—a positive figure (credit) represents a decrease in holdings, and a negative figure (debit) represents an increase. In contrast, for liabilities, a positive figure shows an increase, and a negative figure shows a decrease. Transfers are shown as credits when the entries to which they provide the offsets are debits and as debits when those entries are credits.

20. The content or coverage of a balance of payments statement depends somewhat on whether transactions are treated on a gross or on a net basis. The recommendations in this *Manual* specify which transactions should be recorded gross or net. The recommendations are appropriately reflected in the list of standard components and in suggested supplementary presentations.

Concepts of Economic Territory, Residence, and Center of Economic Interest

21. Identical concepts of economic territory, residence, and center of economic interest are used in this *Manual* and in the *SNA*. (These concepts are discussed fully in Chapter IV.) Economic territory may not be identical with boundaries recognized for political purposes. A country's economic territory consists of a geographic territory administered by a government; within this geographic territory, persons, goods, and capital circulate freely. For maritime countries, geographic territory includes any islands subject to the same fiscal and monetary authorities as the mainland.

22. An institutional unit has a center of economic interest and is a resident unit of a country when, from some location (dwelling, place of production, or other premises) within the economic territory of the country, the unit engages and intends to continue engaging (indefinitely or for a finite period) in economic activities and transactions on a significant scale. (One year or more may be used as a guideline but not as an inflexible rule.)

Principles for Valuation and Time of Recording

23. A uniform basis of valuation for the international accounts (both real resources and financial claims and liabilities) is necessary for compiling, on a consistent basis, any aggregate of individual transactions and an asset/liability position consistent with such transactions. This *Manual* generally uses, as the basis of transaction valuations, actual market prices agreed upon by transactors. (This practice is consistent with that of the *SNA*.) Conceptually, all stocks of assets and liabilities are valued at market prices prevailing at the time to which the international investment position relates. A full exposition of valuation principles; recommended practices; limitations; and the valuation of transfers, financial items, and stocks of assets and liabilities appears in Chapter V. (The exposition includes cases in which conditions may not allow for the existence or assumption of market prices.)

24. In the *Manual* and the *SNA*, the principle of accrual accounting governs the *time of recording* for transactions. Therefore, transactions are recorded when economic value

is created, transformed, exchanged, transferred, or extinguished. Claims and liabilities arise when there is a change in ownership. The change may be legal or physical (economic). In practice, when a change in ownership is not obvious, the change may be proxied by the time that parties to a transaction record it in their books or accounts. (The recommended timing and conventions for various balance of payments entries, together with exceptions to and departures from the change of ownership principle, are covered in Chapter VI.)

Concept and Types of Transactions

25. Broadly speaking, changes in economic relationships registered by the balance of payments stem primarily from dealings between two parties. These parties are, with one exception (see footnote 1), a resident and a nonresident, and all dealings of this kind are covered in the balance of payments. Recommendations for specific entries are embodied in the list of standard components (see Chapter VIII) and are spelled out in detail from Chapter IX onward.

26. Despite the connotation, the balance of payments is not concerned with *payments*, as that term is generally understood, but with *transactions*. A number of international transactions that are of interest in a balance of payments context may not involve the payment of money, and some are not paid for in any sense. The inclusion of these transactions, in addition to those matched by actual payments, constitutes a principal difference between a balance of payments statement and a record of foreign payments.

Exchanges

27. The most numerous and important transactions found in the balance of payments may be characterized as *exchanges*. A transactor (economic entity) provides an economic value to another transactor and receives in return an equal value. The economic values provided by one economy to another may be categorized broadly as real resources (goods, services, income) and financial items. The parties that engage in the exchange are residents of different economies, except in the case of an exchange of foreign financial items between resident sectors. The provision of a financial item may involve not only a change in the ownership of an existing claim or liability but also the creation of a new claim or liability or the cancellation of existing ones. Moreover, the terms of a contract pertaining to a financial item (e.g., contractual maturity) may be altered by agreement between the parties. Such a case is equivalent to fulfillment of the original contract and replacement by a contract with different terms. All exchanges of these kinds are covered in the balance of payments.

Transfers

28. Transactions involving *transfers* differ from exchanges in that one transactor provides an economic value to another transactor but does not receive a quid pro quo on which, according to the conventions and rules adopted for the system, economic value is placed. This absence of value on one side is represented by an entry referred to as a *transfer*. Such transfers (economic value provided and received without a quid pro quo) are shown in the balance of payments. **Current transfers** are included in the **current account** (see Chapter XV) and *capital transfers* appear in the **capital account**. (See Chapter XVII.)

Migration

29. Because an economy is defined in terms of the economic entities associated with its territory, the scope of an economy is likely to be affected by changes in entities associated with the economy.

30. Migration occurs when the residence of an individual changes from one economy to another because the person moves his or her abode. Certain movable, tangible assets owned by the migrant are, in effect, imported into the new economy. The migrant's immovable assets and certain movable, tangible assets located in the old economy become claims of the new economy on the old economy. The migrant's claims on, or liabilities to, residents of an economy other than the new economy become foreign claims or liabilities of the new economy. The migrant's claims on, or liabilities to, residents of the new economy cease to be claims on, or liabilities to, the rest of the world for any economy. The net sum of all these shifts is equal to the net worth of the migrant, and his or her net worth must also be recorded as an offset if the other shifts are recorded. These entries are made in the balance of payments where the offset is conventionally included with transfers.

Other imputed transactions

31. In some instances, transactions may be imputed and entries may be made in balance of payments accounts when no actual flow occurs. Attribution of reinvested earnings to foreign direct investors is an example. The earnings of a foreign subsidiary or branch include earnings attributable to a direct investor. The earnings, whether distributed or reinvested in the enterprise, are proportionate to the direct investor's equity share in the enterprise. Reinvested earnings are recorded as part of direct investment income. An offset-

ting entry, with opposite sign, is made in the *financial account*, under direct investment, reinvested earnings, to reflect the direct investor's increased investment in the foreign subsidiary or branch. (Reinvested earnings are discussed in Chapters XIV and XVIII.)

Changes Other Than Transactions

Reclassification of claims and liabilities

32. The classification of financial items in the *Manual* reflects characteristics designed to reveal the motivation of creditor or debtor. Changes in motivation affect the characteristics, and financial items are subject to reclassification in accordance with such changes. A case in point is the distinction drawn between *direct investment* and other types of investment. For example, several independent holders of *portfolio investment* (in the form of corporate equities issued by a single enterprise abroad) may form an associated group to have a lasting, effective voice in the management of the enterprise. Their holdings will then meet the criteria for *direct investment*, and the change in the status of the investment could be recorded as a reclassification. Such a reclassification would be reflected, at the end of the period during which it occurred, in the international investment position but not in the balance of payments. Similarly, claims on nonresidents can come under, or be released from, the control of resident monetary authorities. In such cases, there are reclassifications between *reserve assets* and assets other than reserves.

Valuation changes

33. The values of real resources and financial items are constantly subject to change stemming from either or both of two causes: (i) The price at which transactions in a certain type of item customarily take place may undergo alteration in terms of the currency in which that price is quoted. (ii) The exchange rate for the currency in which the price is quoted may change in relation to the unit of account that is being used. Valuation changes are not included in the balance of payments but are included in the international investment position.

Except for the discussion of special drawing rights (SDRs), this annex is consistent with Chapter VIII of the BPM5. Please note that paragraph and page numbers cited in this annex refer to those that appear in the BPM5. The discussion of SDRs is drawn from BPM6.

Structure and Classification

139. Part two of this *Manual* deals with the structure and classification of balance of payments accounts and the international investment position. Part two encompasses the standard components of both sets of accounts and contains discussions and elaboration of the ***current account***, the ***capital and financial account***, selected supplementary information, and the international investment position.

140. Balance of payments statistics must be arranged within a coherent structure to facilitate their utilization and adaptation for multiple purposes—policy formulation, analytical studies, projections, bilateral comparisons of particular components or total transactions, regional and global aggregations, etc. (See paragraph 7.)

141. The standard classification and the list of components reflect conceptual and practical considerations, take into account views expressed by national balance of payments experts, and are in general concordance with the *SNA* and with harmonization of the expanded classification of international transactions in services with the Central Product Classification (CPC). (See Appendix III.)

142. The scheme also reflects efforts to link the structure of the ***Financial account*** to income accounts and to the international investment position classification. The scheme is designed as a flexible framework to be used by many countries in the long-term development of external statistics. Some countries may not be able to provide data for many items; other countries may be able to provide additional data.

Standard Components

143. The determination of standard components (see list at end of this chapter) is based on a number of considerations. Those that have been given the greatest weight are:

The item should exhibit distinctive behavior. The economic factor or factors that influence the item should be different from those that influence other items, or the item should respond differently to the same factor or combination. This response to economic influences is what the balance of payments purports to make evident.

The item should be important for a number of countries. Importance may be defined as a function of behavior (unusual variability, for example) or as absolute size.

It should be possible to collect statistics for the item without undue difficulty. However, the desirability of collection should be evaluated according to the two previous criteria.

The item should be needed on a separate basis for other purposes, such as incorporation into, or reconciliation with, the national accounts. The list of standard components should not be unduly long. A large number of countries, including many that are statistically less advanced, are asked to report uniformly on the components.

To the extent practicable, standard components should be in concordance with, and apply to, other IMF statistical systems, the *SNA*, and, for ***services*** in particular, the CPC.

144. The list of standard components carries no implication that recommendations made in this *Manual* are intended to inhibit countries from compiling and publishing additional data of national importance. IMF requests for information will not be limited to standard components when further details are needed to understand the circumstances of particular countries or to analyze new developments. Supplementary information can also be most useful for verifying and reconciling the statistics of partner countries and, for example, analyzing exceptional financing transactions. (See the table entitled *Selected Supplementary Information* at the end of this chapter.) IMF staff will, from time to time, consult with countries to decide on the reporting of additional details.

145. Few countries are likely to have significant information to report for every standard component. Furthermore, several components may be available only in combination, or a minor component may be grouped with one that is more significant. The standard components should nevertheless be reported to the IMF as completely and accurately as possible. National compilers are in better positions than IMF staff to make estimates and adjustments for those components that do not exactly correspond to the basic series of the compiling economy.

Net Errors and Omissions

146. Application of the principles recommended in this *Manual* should result in a consistent body of positive and negative entries with a net (conceptual) total of zero. In practice, however, when all actual entries are totaled, the resulting balance will almost inevitably show a net credit or a net debit. That balance is the result of errors and omissions in compilation of statements. Some of the errors and omissions may be related to recommendations for practical approximation to principles.

147. In balance of payments statements, the standard practice is to show separately an item for net errors and omissions. Labeled by some compilers as a balancing item or statistical discrepancy, that item is intended as an offset to the overstatement or understatement of the recorded components. Thus, if the balance of those components is a credit, the item for net errors and omissions will be shown as a debit of equal value, and vice versa.

148. Some of the errors and omissions that occur in the course of compilation usually offset one another. Therefore, the size of the residual item does not necessarily provide any indication of the overall accuracy of the statement. Nonetheless, interpretation of the statement is hampered by a large net residual.

Major Classifications

149. The standard components, which are listed at the end of this chapter, are comprised of two main groups of accounts:

> The **current account** refers to *goods and services, income,* and **current transfers**.

> The **capital and financial account** refers to (i) *capital transfers* and *acquisition/disposal of non-produced, nonfinancial assets* and (ii) financial assets and liabilities.

This arrangement is based on common historical usage in most countries and on a major change introduced in this *Manual*. The former capital account has been relabeled **capital and financial account**. Reflecting harmonization with the *SNA*, this change introduces that system's distinction between *capital transfers* and **current transfers** in balance of payments accounts and concordance of the account with *SNA* capital and financial accounts.

150. Current account entries for most items in the list of standard components should show gross debits and credits. Most **capital and financial account** entries should be made on a net basis; that is, each component is shown only as a credit or a debit. (The recommended treatments for specific items and exceptions are discussed in appropriate chapters.) Inflows of real resources, increases in financial assets, and decreases in liabilities should be shown as debits; outflows of real resources, decreases in financial assets, and increases in liabilities should be shown as credits. Transfers, both in sections 1.C and 2.A, should be numerically equal with opposite sign to the entries for which they provide offsets.

Detailed Classifications

151. The following classifications of standard components have been developed in accordance with the criteria set out in paragraph 143. The structure and characteristics of the **current account** and the **capital and financial account** and significant changes from the fourth to the fifth edition of the *Manual* are discussed in chapters IX and XVI, respectively. The standard components of the **current account** are described fully in chapters X through XV, and those of the **capital and financial account** are covered in chapters XVII through XXI, and in *Financial Derivatives, A Supplement to the Fifth Edition (1993) of the Balance of Payments Manual,* 2000.

Current Account (1.)

152. Covered in the **current account** are all transactions (other than those in financial items) that involve economic values and occur between resident and non-resident entities. Also covered are offsets to current economic values provided or acquired without a quid pro quo. Specifically, the major classifications are **goods and services, income,** and **current transfers**.

Goods and services (1.A.)

Goods (1.A.a.)

153. *General merchandise* covers most movable goods that are exported to, or imported from, non-residents by residents and that, with a few specified exceptions, undergo changes in ownership (actual or imputed).

154. *Goods for processing* cover exports (or imports, in the compiling economy) of goods crossing the frontier for processing abroad and subsequent reimport (or export, in the compiling economy) of the goods, which are valued on a gross basis before and after processing. This item is an exception to the change of ownership principle.

155. *Repairs on goods* cover repair activity on goods provided to or received from nonresidents on ships, aircraft, etc. Although the physical movement of these goods is similar to that described in paragraph 154, the repairs are valued at the prices (fees paid or received) of the repairs and not at the gross values of the goods before and after repairs are made.

156. *Goods procured in ports by carriers* cover all goods (such as fuels, provisions, stores, and supplies) that resident/nonresident carriers—air, shipping, etc.—procure abroad (in the compiling economy). The classification does not cover the provision of auxiliary services (towing, maintenance, etc.), which are covered under *transportation*.

157. *Nonmonetary gold* covers exports and imports of all gold that is not held as a reserve asset (monetary gold) by the authorities. *Nonmonetary gold* is treated the same as any other commodity and is subdivided, when feasible, into gold held as a store of value and other (industrial) gold.

Services (1.A.b.)

158. *Transportation* covers most of the services, performed by residents for nonresidents and vice versa, that were included in shipment and other transportation in the fourth edition of the *Manual*. However, freight insurance is now included with *insurance services* rather than with *transportation*. *Transportation* includes freight and passenger transportation by all modes of transportation and other distributive and auxiliary services, including rentals of transportation equipment with crew. Certain exceptions are noted in chapters X, XI, and XIII.

159. *Travel* covers goods and services—including those related to health and education—acquired from an economy by nonresident travelers (including excursionists) for business purposes and personal use during their visits (of less than one year) in that economy. *Travel* excludes international passenger services, which are included in *transportation*. Students and medical patients are treated as travelers, regardless of their length of stay. Certain others—military and embassy personnel and nonresident workers—are not regarded as travelers. However, expenditures by nonresident workers are included in *travel*, while those of military and embassy personnel are included in *government services, n.i.e.* These cases are noted in chapters XII and XIII.

160. *Communications services* cover communications transactions between residents and nonresidents. Such services comprise postal, courier, and telecommunications services (transmission of sound, images, and other information by various modes and associated maintenance provided by/for residents by/for nonresidents).

161. *Construction services* cover construction and installation project work that is, on a temporary basis, performed abroad/in the compiling economy or in extraterritorial enclaves by resident/nonresident enterprises and their personnel. Such work does not include that undertaken by a foreign affiliate of a resident enterprise or by an unincorporated site office that, if it meets certain criteria, is equivalent to a foreign affiliate. Such residency aspects are covered in chapters IV and XIII.

162. *Insurance services* cover the provision of insurance to nonresidents by resident insurance enterprises and vice versa. This item comprises services provided for freight insurance (on goods exported and imported), services provided for other types of direct insurance (including life and non-life), and services provided for reinsurance. (For the method of calculating the value of insurance services, see paragraphs 256 and 257.)

163. *Financial services* (other than those related to insurance enterprises and pension funds) cover financial intermediation services and auxiliary services conducted between residents and nonresidents. Included are commissions and fees for letters of credit, lines of credit, financial leasing services, foreign exchange transactions, consumer and business credit services, brokerage services, underwriting services, arrangements for various forms of hedging instruments, etc. Auxiliary services include financial market operational and regulatory services, security custody services, etc.

164. *Computer and information services* cover resident/nonresident transactions related to hardware consultancy, software implementation, information services (data processing, database, news agency), and maintenance and repair of computers and related equipment.

165. *Royalties and license fees* cover receipts (exports) and payments (imports) of residents and nonresidents for: (i) the authorized use of intangible nonproduced, nonfinancial assets and proprietary rights such as trademarks, copyrights, patents, processes, techniques, designs, manufacturing rights, franchises,

etc. and (ii) the use, through licensing agreements, of produced originals or prototypes, such as manuscripts, films, etc.

166. *Other business services* provided by residents to nonresidents and vice versa cover merchanting and other trade-related services; operational leasing services; and miscellaneous business, professional, and technical services. (See the table on *Selected Supplementary Information* following this chapter and paragraphs 261 through 264 for details.)

167. *Personal, cultural, and recreational services* cover (i) audiovisual and related services and (ii) other cultural services provided by residents to nonresidents and vice versa. Included under (i) are services associated with the production of motion pictures on films or video tape, radio and television programs, and musical recordings. (Examples of these services are rentals and fees received by actors, producers, etc. for productions and for distribution rights sold to the media.) Included under (ii) are other personal, cultural, and recreational services, such as those associated with libraries, museums, and other cultural and sporting activities.

168. *Government services, n.i.e.* cover all services (such as expenditures of embassies and consulates) associated with government sectors or international and regional organizations and not classified under other items.

Income (1.B.)

169. *Compensation of employees* covers wages, salaries, and other benefits, in cash or in kind, and includes those of border, seasonal, and other nonresident workers (e.g., local staff of embassies).

170. *Investment income* covers receipts and payments of income associated, respectively, with holdings of external financial assets by residents and with liabilities to nonresidents. *Investment income* consists of direct investment income, portfolio investment income, and other investment income. The direct investment component is broken down into income on equity (dividends, branch profits, and reinvested earnings) and income on debt (interest); portfolio investment income is broken down into income on equity (dividends) and income on debt (interest); other investment income covers interest earned on other capital (loans, etc.) and, in principle, imputed income to households from net equity in life insurance reserves and in pension funds.

Current transfers (1.C.)

171. **Current transfers** are distinguished from *capital transfers*, which are included in the **capital and financial account** in accordance with the *SNA* treatment of transfers. Transfers are the offsets to changes, which take place between residents and nonresidents, in ownership of real resources or financial items and, whether the changes are voluntary or compulsory, do not involve a quid pro quo in economic value. ***Current transfers*** consist of all transfers that **do not involve** (i) transfers of ownership of fixed assets; (ii) transfers of funds linked to, or conditioned upon, acquisition or disposal of fixed assets; (iii) forgiveness, without any counterparts being received in return, of liabilities by creditors. All of these are *capital transfers*. **Current transfers** include those of general government (e.g., current international cooperation between different governments, payments of current taxes on income and wealth, etc.) and other transfers (e.g., workers' remittances, premiums—less service charges, and claims on non-life insurance). A full discussion of the distinction between **current transfers** and *capital transfers* appears in Chapter XV; see also paragraphs 175 and 344.

Capital and Financial Account (2.)

172. The **capital and financial account** has two major components—the ***capital account*** and the ***financial account***—that are in concordance with those same accounts in the *SNA*. Assets represent claims on nonresidents, and liabilities represent indebtedness to nonresidents. The two parties to a transaction in assets or liabilities are usually a resident and a nonresident but, in some instances, both parties may both be residents or nonresidents. (See paragraph 318.)

173. All valuation and other changes in foreign assets and liabilities, which do not reflect transactions (see paragraph 310), are excluded from the **capital and financial account** but are reflected in the international investment position. Supplementary statements identify certain items that are of analytical interest and that affect various accounts. Examples of such items are liabilities constituting foreign authorities' reserves and exceptional financing transactions, which are discussed in Chapter XXII.

174. Classification of the ***financial account*** and the income components of the **current account** are interrelated and must be consistent to facilitate analysis, to form an effective link between the balance of payments and the international investment position, and to be compatible with the *SNA* and other IMF statistical systems.

Capital account (2.A.)

175. The major components of the ***capital account*** are *capital transfers* and *acquisition/disposal of nonproduced, nonfinancial assets. Capital transfers* consist of those involving transfers of ownership of fixed assets; transfers of funds linked to, or conditional upon, acquisition or disposal of fixed assets; or cancellation, without any counterparts being received in return, of liabilities by creditors. *Capital transfers* include two components: (i) general government, subdivided into debt forgiveness and other, and (ii) other, subdivided into migrants' transfers, debt forgiveness, and other

transfers. (See Chapter XV for discussion of the distinction between *capital transfers* and **current transfers**. *Acquisition/disposal of nonproduced, nonfinancial assets* largely covers intangibles, such as patented entities, leases or other transferable contracts, goodwill, etc. This item does not cover land in a specific economic territory but may include the purchase or sale of land by a foreign embassy. (See paragraph 312.)

Financial account (2.B.)

176. The classification of standard components in the ***financial account*** is based on these criteria:

All components are classified according to type of investment or by functional breakdown (*direct investment, portfolio investment, financial derivatives, other investment, reserve assets*).

For the category of *direct investment*, there are directional distinctions (abroad or in the reporting economy) and for the equity capital, other capital.

For the categories of *portfolio investment, financial derivatives,* and *other investment*, there are the customary asset/liability distinctions.

Particularly significant for *portfolio investment* and *other investment* is the distinction by type of instrument (equity or debt securities, trade credits, loans, currency and deposits, other assets or liabilities). In this *Manual*, traditional and new money market and other financial instruments are included in *portfolio investment*.

For *portfolio investment, financial derivatives,* and *other investment*, there are distinctions by sector of the domestic creditor for assets or by sector of the domestic debtor for liabilities. These distinctions serve to facilitate links with the income accounts, the international investment position, the *SNA*, and other statistical systems.

The traditional distinction, which is based on original contractual maturity of more than one year or one year or less, between long- and short-term assets and liabilities applies only to *other investment*. In recent years, the significance of this distinction has clearly diminished for many domestic and international transactions. Consequently, the long- and short-term distinction is accorded less importance in the *SNA* and in this *Manual* than in previous editions. However, because the maturity factor remains important for specific purposes—analysis of external debt, for example—it is retained in the *Manual* for *other investment*.

177. *Direct investment*—reflecting the lasting interest of a resident entity in one economy (direct investor) in an entity resident in another economy (direct investment enterprise)—covers all transactions between direct investors and direct investment enterprises. That is, *direct investment* covers the initial transaction between the two and all subsequent transactions between them and among affiliated enterprises, both incorporated and unincorporated. Direct investment transactions occurring abroad and in the reporting economy are subclassified into equity capital, reinvested earnings, and other capital (intercompany debt transactions). For equity capital and other capital, claims on and liabilities to affiliated enterprises and to direct investors are distinguished. Transactions between affiliated banks and between other affiliated financial intermediaries are limited to equity and permanent debt capital. (See paragraph 372 of the fifth edition of the *Balance of Payments Manual.*)

178. *Portfolio investment* covers transactions in equity securities and debt securities; the latter are subclassified, into bonds and notes and money market instruments. Various new financial instruments, other than financial derivatives, are covered under appropriate instrument classifications. (Transactions covered under *direct investment* and *reserve assets* are excluded.)

179. The *financial derivatives* category covers financial instruments that are linked to other specific financial instruments, indicators, or commodities and through which specific financial risks (such as interest rate risk, foreign exchange risk, equity and commodity price risks, credit risk. etc.) can, in their own right, be traded in financial markets. Transactions in financial derivatives should be treated as separate transactions rather than as integral parts of the values of the underlying transactions to which they are linked.

180. *Other investment* covers short- and long-term trade credits; loans (including use of Fund credit, loans from the Fund, and loans associated with financial leases); currency and deposits (transferable and other—such as savings and term deposits, savings and loan shares, shares in credit unions, etc.); and other assets and liabilities (including SDR allocations). (Transactions covered under *direct investment* are excluded.)

181. *Reserve assets* cover transactions in those assets that are considered, by the monetary authorities of an economy, to be available for use in meeting balance of payments and, in some instances, other needs. Such availability is not closely linked in principle to formal criteria such as ownership or currency of denomination. The items covered are monetary gold, SDRs, reserve position in the Fund, foreign exchange assets (currency, deposits, and securities), and other claims.

182. Coverage and identification of *reserve asset* components are linked to an analytic concept, are in part judgmental, and are not always amenable to application of objective, formal criteria or clear rankings as to conditionality and other considerations. In contrast to the treatment in the fourth edition of the *Manual*, valuation changes in *reserve assets* are excluded, along with counterparts to such changes, in the fifth edition. Data in the current volume include the allocation of SDRs and counterpart entries. These changes are reflected in the international investment position.

INTRODUCTION

Le volume 62 du *Balance of Payments Statistics Yearbook* (Annuaire de statistiques de balance des paiements) (l'annuaire), publié par le Fonds monétaire international (FMI), présente les données de balance des paiements et de position extérieure globale (PEG) que ses pays membres lui ont communiquées. Le FMI est reconnaissant à ces derniers d'avoir collaboré au présent ouvrage en lui fournissant ces informations. Pour certains pays, les données sont parfois complétées par des renseignements que les économistes ont tirées d'autres sources.

Le présent volume de l'annuaire se compose de trois parties. La première présente les données de la balance des paiements et de la PEG pour les divers pays. La deuxième contient des totaux régionaux et mondiaux pour les principales composantes de la balance des paiements. La troisième partie fournit une description technique des méthodes de la plupart des pays qui ont communiqué les données. La première partie constitue une publication distincte, et les deuxième et troisième parties sont reliées ensemble.

Les caractéristiques introduites dans les volumes 46 à 61 sont conservées dans le présent ouvrage. Comme dans le volume 46, les données de balance des paiements sont présentées conformément à la classification des composantes types adoptées dans la cinquième édition du *Manuel de la balance des paiements (MBP5)*[1]. Il convient toutefois de noter que les composantes types ont été modifiées par suite de la publication, en 2000, puis de la modification en 2002, de l'ouvrage intitulé *«Dérivés financiers — Supplément à la cinquième édition (1993) du Manuel de la balance des paiements»* (le Supplément). À compter de cette date, toute référence au *MBP5* renvoie également au Supplément et à son addendum. Conformément aux recommandations formulées dans l'addendum, le présent annuaire rend compte de la décision prise par le Comité d'experts de la balance des paiements créé sous les auspices du FMI (Comité d'experts) qui préconise d'inclure les trans

actions sur dérivés financiers effectuées par les entreprises apparentées dans la composante dérivés financiers de la balance des paiements et de la position extérieure globale (PEG). Parallèlement, comme pour le volume 47, les données sur la PEG sont elles aussi présentées conformément au *MBP5*, et la troisième partie de l'annuaire présente une analyse détaillée des méthodologies, méthodes de calcul et sources de données utilisées par la plupart des pays compris dans l'annuaire. Le *MBP5*[2] apporte un certain nombre de changements à la méthodologie utilisée pour l'établissement des données de balance des paiements. Ces changements sont décrits en détail au chapitre I du *MBP5*. Depuis la publication du volume 46, une série de codes accompagne les données présentées dans le présent Annuaire conformément à la classification des composantes types du *MBP5*. Ces codes ont été mis au point conjointement par le FMI, l'Organisation de coopération et de développement économiques (OCDE) et l'Office statistique de l'Union européenne (Eurostat). La structure de ces codes est décrite en annexe. En outre, à partir du volume 46, l'annuaire ne présente plus de données trimestrielles de balance des paiements pour les pays qui communiquent ce type de statistiques au FMI. Ces données trimestrielles sont publiées dans l'édition mensuelle de *Statistiques financières internationales (SFI)*, et sont également disponibles sur le CD-ROM de balance des paiements ainsi que sur la version Internet en ligne (BOP Online).

La conversion des données par les services du FMI a permis de présenter, selon la classification retenue dans le *MBP5*, les statistiques de la base de données du FMI qui se rapportent à des périodes antérieures, ainsi que les données communiquées pour des périodes plus récentes par les pays membres qui continuent à suivre les recommandations de la quatrième édition du *Manuel de la balance des paiements*. En 1995, les services du FMI ont mis au point des formules de conversion permettant de mettre sous une forme à peu près conforme à la méthodologie et à la présentation retenues dans la cinquième édition les données de balance des paiements reçues de chaque pays et figurant dans la base de données du FMI. Une fois converties, les données ont été soumises à l'examen des autorités des pays en question, et les observations formulées ont été incorporées dans la nouvelle base de données du *MBP5*. En 1996, avec la collaboration des autorités nationales, les services du FMI ont procédé d'une manière analogue pour présenter conformément au *MBP5* les données sur la PEG établies selon les recommandations de la quatrième édition. En principe, la PEG d'un pays est un relevé du stock de ses avoirs et engagements financiers extérieurs.

---

[1]Le volume 1 de l'annuaire, paru en 1949, était fondé sur la première édition du Manuel de la balance des paiements du FMI, publiée en 1948; les volumes 2 à 12, sur la deuxième édition du Manuel, publiée en 1950; les volumes 13 à 23, sur la troisième édition du Manuel, publiée en 1961; et les volumes 24 à 29, sur la troisième édition, ainsi que sur le Manuel de la balance des paiements : supplément à la troisième édition, paru en 1973. Les volumes 30 à 45 ont été établis sur la base des directives de la quatrième édition du Manuel, publiée en 1977.

[2]Fonds monétaire international, Manuel de la balance des paiements, cinquième édition, Washington, Septembre 1993, et Dérivés financiers — Supplément à la cinquième édition (1993) du Manuel de la balance des paiements, Washington, 2000.

La troisième partie présente une description technique des méthodologies, méthodes de calcul et sources de données qui se fonde en grande partie sur les renseignements que les pays transmettent au FMI. Les descriptions ont pour but de mieux renseigner les utilisateurs sur la couverture et les limitations des données publiées pour les différents pays dans cet annuaire, de même que les statisticiens sur les sources de données et méthodes utilisées par leurs homologues étrangers.

Le reste de la présente introduction s'articule comme suit :

• La section I décrit les caractéristiques fondamentales des tableaux publiés dans la première partie du présent volume de l'annuaire. (Les lecteurs trouveront dans les deuxième et troisième parties des précisions sur le champ d'application des données.)

• La section II donne des indications sur l'abonnement aux données de balance des paiements du FMI sur disques optiques compacts (CD-ROM et BOP Online).

• Il y a six annexes. L'annexe I contient une présentation analytique des composantes de la balance des paiements (accompagnées des codes correspondants) sous forme résumée. L'annexe II présente les composantes types définies dans le *MBP5* (et les codes correspondants). L'annexe III explique le système de codage des données. L'annexe IV présente les composantes types de la PEG, telles qu'elles ressortent du *MBP5*. L'annexe V est consacrée au cadre conceptuel de la balance des paiements et de la PEG. L'annexe VI décrit le champ couvert par les principales composantes de la balance des paiements, telles qu'elles sont définies dans le *MBP5*.

I. Première partie de l'annuaire : données relatives aux pays

La première partie de l'annuaire présente les pages consacrées aux divers pays suivant un ordre alphabétique. Il convient de noter toutefois que, dans la présente publication, le terme «pays» ne désigne pas toujours une entité territoriale constituant un État tel qu'il est défini selon l'usage et le droit internationaux; ce terme recouvre également la zone euro, l'Union monétaire des Caraïbes orientales et certaines entités territoriales qui ne sont pas des États souverains mais sur lesquelles des données statistiques sont disponibles séparément au niveau international.

Pour la plupart des pays, les données de balance des paiements se présentent sous la forme de deux tableaux. Le tableau 1 constitue un résumé analytique des données plus détaillées contenues au tableau 2, et présente toute une série de composantes de la balance des paiements de manière à mettre en relief les postes de financement (réserves et postes apparentés). (Voir aussi l'annexe I). Le tableau 2 présente des données correspondant aux composantes types décrites dans le *MBP5*. (Voir aussi l'annexe II). Dans le cas des pays pour lesquels on dispose de statistiques sur la PEG, ces dernières figurent au tableau 3. Les tableaux 1, 2 et 3 présentent, pour chaque pays, des données pour les années 2003 à 2010. Sauf indication contraire, les chiffres portent sur l'année civile.

Présentation analytique

Dans la présentation analytique, qui fait l'objet du tableau 1, les composantes de la balance des paiements sont réparties entre cinq grandes catégories (groupes A à E), que le FMI juge utiles à une analyse homogène de l'évolution de la balance des paiements. Cependant, le choix des groupes ne saurait être considéré comme découlant de la recommandation du FMI quant à l'approche analytique à retenir pour chaque pays. Il existe d'autres types de présentation analytique, qui consisteraient à regrouper les composantes types du tableau 2 d'une manière différente, soit pour tenir compte de la situation particulière d'un pays donné, soit pour répondre à des besoins analytiques précis.

Il convient de noter que les données présentées au tableau 1 sur le solde du compte des transactions courantes, du compte de capital et du compte d'opérations financières de certains pays ne concordent pas avec les données correspondantes du tableau 2. Cela tient au fait que, dans le tableau 1, certaines transactions relevant de ces comptes en sont exclues et sont reclassées en tant que «financement exceptionnel» à la rubrique des réserves et postes apparentés. Le «financement exceptionnel» se rapporte aux transactions que les autorités effectuent pour répondre aux besoins de financement de la balance des paiements et prend notamment la forme d'emprunts extérieurs, d'arriérés de paiements et de remises de dette. Le financement exceptionnel ne comprend pas les réserves.

Présentation type

Comme le montre le tableau 2, la liste des composantes types du *MBP5* présentée au tableau 2 fait apparaître une classification plus détaillée des biens et services que celle qui figure dans la quatrième édition. Le compte dénommé «compte de capital et d'opérations financières» comporte deux volets distincts, qui sont le «compte de capital» et le «compte d'opérations financières». Les composantes du «compte d'opérations financières» sont classées selon plusieurs critères : type d'investissement (c'est-à-dire investissements directs,

Encadré – Position extérieure globale

Les relevés de la PEG des pays déclarants font l'objet du tableau 3 aux pages par pays. Il convient, pour chaque pays donné, de lire le relevé de la PEG en consultant simultanément les notes de la troisième partie — Méthodologies, méthodes de calcul et sources de données — qui se rapportent au pays concerné. Au fur et à mesure que les pays recueilleront davantage de données pour la PEG, la couverture des données de la PEG sera élargie dans les éditions ultérieures de l'Annuaire.

Voir le chapitre XXIII du *MBP5* pour une étude exhaustive du concept de position extérieure globale.

La dette extérieure ne constitue pas une composante distincte de la PEG, mais elle peut être calculée par addition des composantes de la PEG autres que le capital social (c'est-à-dire tous les engagements autres que les titres de participation, le capital social correspondant à des investissements directs [y compris les bénéfices réinvestis] et les dérivés financiers). Cette conception cadre dans l'ensemble avec la définition de référence de la dette extérieure brute qui est retenue dans l'ouvrage intitulé Statistiques de la dette extérieure : Guide du statisticien et de l'utilisateur (External Debt Statistics : Guide for Compilers and Users), mis au point par l'Équipe spéciale interinstitutions des statistiques financières. L'Équipe spéciale était présidée par le FMI et des représentants de la Banque centrale européenne, de la Banque mondiale, de la Banque des Règlements internationaux, de la CNUCED, d'Eurostat, du FMI, de l'OCDE, du Secrétariat du Club de Paris et du Secrétariat du Commonwealth ont pris part aux travaux du Guide.

Position extérieure globale : composantes types[1]

A. Avoirs

1. Investissements directs
    1.1 Capital social et
           bénéfices réinvestis
    1.2 Autres capitaux[2]

2. Investissements de portefeuille
    2.1 Titres de participation
    2.2 Titres de créance[4]

3. Dérivés financiers
    3.1 Autorités monétaires
    3.2 Administrations publiques
    3.3 Banques
    3.4 Autres secteurs

4. Autres investissements
    4.1 Crédits commerciaux
    4.2 Prêts
    4.3 Monnaie fiduciaire et dépôts
    4.4 Autres avoirs

5. Avoirs de réserve
    5.1 Or monétaire
    5.2 Droits de tirage spéciaux
    5.3 Position de réserve au FMI
    5.4 Devises étrangères
    5.5 Autres créances

B. Engagements

1. Investissements directs
    1.1 Capital social et
           bénéfices réinvestis
    1.2 Autres capitaux[3]

2. Investissements de portefeuille
    2.1 Titres de participation
    2.2 Titres d'engagement[4]

3. Dérivés financiers
    3.1 Autorités monétaires
    3.2 Administrations publiques
    3.3 Banques
    3.4 Autres secteurs

4. Autres investissements
    4.1 Crédits commerciaux
    4.2 Prêts
    4.3 Monnaie fiduciaire et dépôts
    4.4 Autres engagements[5]

---

[1] Les composantes ne sont pas toutes présentées, comme par exemple celles qui sont ventilées par secteur (autorités monétaires, administrations publiques, banques, autres secteurs) ou, dans certains cas, par échéance. Si un pays fournit des données de PEG dont des composantes majeures sont manquantes, les totaux peuvent ne pas être publiés.

[2] Les passifs à l'égard des entreprises apparentées, qui entrent dans la composition des «Autres capitaux», sont inclus dans la dette extérieure.

[3] Les passifs envers les investisseurs directs, qui entrent dans la composition des «Autres capitaux», sont inclus dans la dette extérieure.

[4] Ce poste comprend les obligations, les effets et les instruments du marché monétaire.

[5] Y compris allocations de DTS aux autorités monétaires.

investissements de portefeuille, dérivés financiers[3], autres investissements et avoirs de réserve), avoirs et engagements, secteurs intérieurs (autorités monétaires, administrations publiques, banques et autres secteurs) et échéances initiales (long terme et court terme).

Position extérieure globale

Comme le montre le tableau 3, les données de la PEG sont disposées conformément à la classification des composantes types de la PEG retenue dans le *MBP5*. (Voir aussi l'annexe IV.)

La classification des composantes de la PEG présentée au tableau 3 correspond à celle des composantes du compte d'opérations financières de la balance des paiements figurant au tableau 2, mais plusieurs différences apparaissent toutefois entre les deux tableaux. Comme indiqué précédemment, la PEG est un relevé des avoirs et engagements extérieurs d'un pays à un moment précis. Par conséquent, au tableau 3, la présentation de base des composantes de la PEG comporte deux catégories générales, celles des avoirs et des engagements, par opposition à la classification fonctionnelle des investissements retenue au tableau 2 (investissements directs, investissements de portefeuille, dérivés financiers, autres investissements et avoirs de réserve). En outre, le tableau 3 présente la PEG d'un pays à la fin de la période considérée, alors que le tableau 2 retrace les transactions effectuées pendant cette période. Par ailleurs, contrairement au tableau 2, qui indique la valeur des transactions financières pendant une période, le tableau 3 présente de la PEG d'un pays une évaluation qui reflète les transactions financières, réévaluations et autres ajustements opérés à la fin de la période considérée. La PEG nette indiquée au tableau 3 est égale à la différence entre la valeur des avoirs financiers extérieurs recensés et celle des engagements financiers extérieurs recensés.

Codage des données

Aux tableaux 1, 2 et 3, chaque catégorie de données et chaque composante s'accompagnent d'un code. Comme indiqué plus haut, ces codes ont été établis conjointement par le FMI, l'OCDE et Eurostat en vue de faciliter la communication des statistiques au niveau international. Les codes s'appliquent aux composantes types de la balance des paiements et de

la position extérieure globale, telles qu'elles sont définies dans le *MBP5*, ainsi qu'aux composantes de la classification OCDE/Eurostat pour le commerce des services.

Chaque code figurant dans l'annuaire est un code alphanumérique à six composantes. Le chiffre placé en première position indique s'il s'agit d'un crédit, d'un débit ou d'un solde; le chiffre «2» désigne un crédit, «3» un débit et «4» un solde (différence entre crédit et débit). Les trois chiffres suivants correspondent au code attribué à la composante de la balance des paiements. Par exemple, le compte des transactions courantes a pour code 993, le compte de capital, 994, et le compte d'opérations financières, 995. Pour plus de précisions sur le système de codage, les lecteurs pourront se référer à l'annexe III.

Les cinquième et sixième chiffres ou lettres du code figurant dans l'annuaire signalent l'existence de caractéristiques particulières à certaines composantes. Par exemple, dans le tableau 1, la lettre Z, placée en cinquième position, indique que la composante exclut le financement exceptionnel; W signifie que, outre le financement exceptionnel, les données excluent l'utilisation des crédits et les prêts du FMI. Au tableau 1, les lettres A, B, C et D différencient les divers secteurs intérieurs.

Écritures passées au crédit et au débit

Aux tableaux 1 et 2, les données sur les transactions sont présentées sous forme de chiffres bruts inscrits au crédit ou au débit du compte des transactions courantes et du compte de capital. Au compte d'opérations financières, les données sont présentées en chiffres nets au crédit ou au débit (pour rendre compte des variations nettes des passifs et des actifs). Les montants inscrits au crédit, qu'ils soient bruts ou nets, sont positifs (mais ne sont pas accompagnés du signe plus) et les montants portés au débit, bruts ou nets, sont négatifs (ils sont affectés du signe moins). En conséquence, la diminution des avoirs et l'augmentation des engagements (crédit) sont indiquées par des chiffres positifs, et l'accroissement des avoirs et la diminution des engagements (débit), par des chiffres négatifs.

Montants nuls, non disponibles, ou données confidentielles

Lorsqu'il manque des chiffres dans les statistiques communiquées par les pays, il est souvent difficile de savoir si ces données font défaut parce qu'elles ne sont pas disponibles, ou parce qu'il s'agit de montants nuls ou négligeables, ou confidentiels. Dans les tableaux de l'annuaire, le symbole (....) indique que les données ne sont pas disponibles, ou que les montants sont nuls ou négligeables, ou que les données sont confidentielles. Au cas où les données pour une ou plusieurs sous-composantes ne peuvent être publiées pour des raisons de confiden-

---

[3]Compte tenu de la nature unique des produits financiers dérivés et de la manière dont certaines institutions enregistrent les transactions, certains ne sont en mesure de communiquer que les données des transactions nettes. Par convention, les transactions nettes sont généralement incluses dans les passifs dans l'annuaire. Dans certains cas, les pays ont demandé que les transactions nettes soient classées dans la catégorie Produits financiers dérivés, net.

tialité, les valeurs non déclarées seront i) ajoutées à une sous-composante générique (telle que "autres") au sein de la composante correspondante ou ii) omises sans ajustement d'une sous-composante générique. Dans un cas comme dans l'autre, le total déclaré reste inchangé.

Note sur les composantes du *Revenu* et des *Autres investissements*

Au tableau 2, Standard Presentation (Présentation type), les chiffres que certains pays communiquent pour les postes "Income" (Revenu) et "Other Investment" (Autres investissements) présentent un niveau d'agrégation qui ne permet pas d'identifier séparément chaque composante de la catégorie intéressée. En pareil cas, il n'est donc pas possible de faire la somme des composantes de certaines sous-catégories pour calculer le total agrégé de ces mêmes sous-catégories. Il en va de même pour le poste "Other Investment" (Autres investissements) du tableau 3, International Investment Position (Position extérieure globale).

Auparavant, dans les volumes 46 à 49, les données concernant les «Autres investissements» (avoirs et engagements) étaient ventilées sous les rubriques «long terme» et «court terme». Depuis la publication du volume 50, les tableaux présentent dorénavant les chiffres des «autres investissements» (actifs et passifs) pour les autorités monétaires, les administrations publiques, les banques et les autres secteurs sous forme de totaux (du financement à long terme et du financement à court terme), avec une rubrique «dont : court terme». (Au poste «prêts, autorités monétaires», les chiffrent sont présentés sous forme de totaux, avec une rubrique «dont : utilisation des crédits et des prêts du FMI» et une rubrique «dont : court terme»).

Présentation de chiffres arrondis

La plupart des chiffres des tableaux sont exprimés en millions; les utilisateurs ne doivent pas présumer qu'un tableau présentant des chiffres exprimés en unités plus petites fournit nécessairement des données plus exactes. L'unité est choisie pour des raisons de commodité. Compte tenu des pratiques couramment utilisées pour le calcul, il peut exister un écart, dû au fait que les chiffres ont été arrondis, entre le total indiqué et la somme de ses composantes.

Méthodes de conversion

La plupart des données de balance des paiements communiquées au FMI sont exprimées en monnaie nationale ou en dollars E.U., bien que quelques pays fournissent certaines données en DTS. Pour faciliter les comparaisons entre pays, tous les états de balance des paiements publiés dans l'annuaire sont exprimés en dollars E.U. En outre, dans tous les cas, les données que les pays communiquent sur leurs tran-

sactions avec le FMI et sur leurs transactions en DTS sont remplacées par des données tirées des registres du FMI, qui sont exprimées en DTS; celles-ci sont à leur tour converties en dollars E.U.

Pour les pays qui communiquent des données de la balance des paiments exprimées en unités autres que le dollar E.U., les chiffres sont convertis à l'aide des taux de conversion figurant au bas du tableau 1. Ces taux de conversion sont normalement les taux de change moyens de la monnaie du pays pour la période considérée publiés dans *SFI*. Par exemple, les pages consacrées à la zone euro dans *SFI* comportent la ligne «rf», qui présente le taux moyen du dollar en euros. Les données de flux exprimées en DTS sont converties en dollars E.U. à l'aide des taux indiqués à la ligne «sb» de la page consacrée aux États-Unis dans *SFI*. Pour les pays qui transmettent des données trimestrielles exprimées en monnaie nationale, le total annuel en dollars E.U. est égal à la somme des données trimestrielles en dollars E.U.

Pour les pays qui communiquent des données de position extérieure globale dans des unités autres que le dollar EU, les chiffres sont convertis à partir des taux de conversion figurant au bas du tableau 3. Ces taux sont normalement les taux de change en vigueur en fin de période (ligne "ae"), pour la période considérée, publiés dans SFI.

Les lecteurs trouveront à la section 2 de l'introduction de *International Financial Statistics (IFS)* de plus amples renseignements sur les taux de change retenus.

II. Versions CD-ROM et Internet

Les statistiques publiées dans l'annuaire sont également disponibles sur CD-ROM et sur l'Internet (Balance of Payments Statistics Online—BOP Online). Dans cette version électronique, le nombre de pays et de séries chronologiques est légèrement supérieur à celui de la version imprimée de l'annuaire; il en est de même pour le nombre de périodes auxquelles se rapportent les séries chronologiques. Elle contient également les données trimestrielles communiquées par les pays, et fournit en outre les révisions et les mises à jour dès que les données actualisées sont disponibles. Les demandes de renseignements concernant les CD-ROM et BOP Online doivent être adressées à :

Publication Services
International Monetary Fund
Washington, DC 20431, U.S.A.
Téléphone : (202) 623–7430
Télécopie : (202) 623–7201
Messagerie électronique : publications@imf.org
Internet : http://www.imf.org

ANNEXE I. PRÉSENTATION ANALYTIQUE

		Codes
A.	**COMPTE DES TRANSACTIONS COURANTES**[1]	4 993 Z .
	Biens : exportations, f.à.b.	2 100 ..
	Biens : importations, f.à.b.	3 100 ..
	Solde au titre des biens	4 100 ..
	Services : crédit	2 200 ..
	Services : débit	3 200 ..
	Solde au titre des biens et services	4 991 ..
	Revenus : crédit	2 300 ..
	Revenus : débit	3 300 ..
	Solde au titre des biens, services et revenus	4 992 ..
	Transferts courants : crédit	2 379 Z .
	Transferts courants : débit	3 379 ..
B.	**COMPTE DE CAPITAL**[1]	4 994 Z .
	Compte de capital : crédit	2 994 Z .
	Compte de capital : débit	3 994 ..
	Total, groupes A plus B	4 981 ..
C.	**COMPTE D'OPÉRATIONS FINANCIÈRES**[1]	4 995W .
	Investissements directs à l'étranger	4 505 ..
	Investissements directs dans l'économie	4 555 Z .
	Investissements de portefeuille : avoirs	4 602 ..
	Titres de participation	4 610 ..
	Titres de créance	4 619 ..
	Investissements de portefeuille : engagements	4 652 Z .
	Titres de participation	4 660 ..
	Titres d'engagement	4 669 Z .
	Dérivés financiers	4 910 ..
	Dérivés financiers (actifs)	4 900 ..
	Dérivés financiers (passifs)	4 905 ..
	Autres investissements : avoirs	4 703 ..
	Autorités monétaires	4 701 ..
	Administrations publiques	4 704 ..
	Banques	4 705 ..
	Autres secteurs	4 728 ..
	Autres investissements : engagements[2]	4 753W .
	Autorités monétaires	4 753WA
	Administrations publiques	4 753 ZB
	Banques	4 753 ZC
	Autres secteurs	4 753 ZD
	Total, groupes A à C inclus	4 983 ..
D.	**ERREURS ET OMISSIONS NETTES**	4 998 ..
	Total, groupes A à D inclus	4 984 ..
E.	**RÉSERVES ET POSTES APPARENTÉS**	4 802.A.
	Avoirs de réserve	4 802 ..
	Utilisation des crédits et prêts du FMI	4 766 ..
	Financements exceptionnels	4 920 ..
TAUX DE CONVERSION : MONTANT D'UNITÉS MONÉTAIRES POUR UN DOLLAR E.U.		0 101 ..

[1]Non compris les composantes qui font partie des catégories du groupe E.

[2]Y compris allocations de DTS aux autorités monétaires.

ANNEXE II. COMPOSANTES TYPES

	Codes
COMPTE DES TRANSACTIONS COURANTES	4 993 ..
A. BIENS	4 100 ..
Crédit	2 100 ..
Marchandises générales : exportations, f.à.b.	2 110 ..
Biens exportés pour transformation, f.à.b.	2 150 ..
Réparations de biens	2 160 ..
Achats de biens dans les ports par les transporteurs	2 170 ..
Or non monétaire	2 180 ..
Débit	3 100 ..
Marchandises générales : importations, f.à.b.	3 110 ..
Biens importés pour transformation, f.à.b.	3 150 ..
Réparations de biens	3 160 ..
Achats de biens dans les ports par les transporteurs	3 170 ..
Or non monétaire	3 180 ..
B. SERVICES	4 200 ..
Total, crédit	2 200 ..
Total, débit	3 200 ..
Services de transport, crédit	2 205 ..
Passagers	2 850 ..
Fret	2 851 ..
Autres	2 852 ..
Transports maritimes, passagers	2 207 ..
Transports maritimes, fret	2 208 ..
Transports maritimes, autres	2 209 ..
Transports aériens, passagers	2 211 ..
Transports aériens, fret	2 212 ..
Transports aériens, autres	2 213 ..
Autres transports, passagers	2 215 ..
Autres transports, fret	2 216 ..
Autres transports, autres	2 217 ..
Services de transport, débit	3 205 ..
Passagers	3 850 ..
Fret	3 851 ..
Autres	3 852 ..
Transports maritimes, passagers	3 207 ..
Transports maritimes, fret	3 208 ..
Transports maritimes, autres	3 209 ..
Transports aériens, passagers	3 211 ..
Transports aériens, fret	3 212 ..
Transports aériens, autres	3 213 ..
Autres transports, passagers	3 215 ..
Autres transports, fret	3 216 ..
Autres transports, autres	3 217 ..
Voyages, crédit	2 236 ..
Voyages à titre professionnel	2 237 ..
Voyages à titre personnel	2 240 ..
Voyages, débit	3 236 ..
Voyages à titre professionnel	3 237 ..
Voyages à titre personnel	3 240 ..

	Codes
Autres services, crédit	2 200 BA
Services de communication	2 245 ..
Services de bâtiment et travaux publics	2 249 ..
Services d'assurance	2 253 ..
Services financiers	2 260 ..
Services d'informatique et d'information	2 262 ..
Redevances et droits de licence	2 266 ..
Autres services aux entreprises	2 268 ..
Services personnels, culturels et relatifs aux loisirs	2 287 ..
Services fournis ou reçus par les administrations publiques, n.c.a.	2 291 ..
Autres services, débit	3 200 BA
Services de communication	3 245 ..
Services de bâtiment et travaux publics	3 249 ..
Services d'assurance	3 253 ..
Services financiers	3 260 ..
Services d'informatique et d'information	3 262 ..
Redevances et droits de licence	3 266 ..
Autres services aux entreprises	3 268 ..
Services personnels, culturels et relatifs aux loisirs	3 287 ..
Services fournis ou reçus par les administrations publiques, n.c.a.	3 291 ..
C. REVENUS	4 300 ..
Total, crédit	2 300 ..
Total, débit	3 300 ..
Rémunération des salariés, crédit	2 310 ..
Rémunération des salariés, débit	3 310 ..
Revenu des investissements, crédit	2 320 ..
Revenu des investissements directs	2 330 ..
Dividendes et bénéfices distribués des succursales	2 332 ..
Bénéfices réinvestis et bénéfices non distribués des succursales	2 333 ..
Revenu des titres de créance (intérêts)	2 334 ..
Revenu des investissements de portefeuille	2 339 ..
Revenu des titres de participation	2 340 ..
Revenu des obligations et autres titres d'emprunt	2 350 ..
Revenu des instruments du marché monétaire	2 360 ..
Revenu des autres investissements	2 370 ..
Revenu des investissements, débit	3 320 ..
Revenu des investissements directs	3 330 ..
Dividendes et bénéfices distribués des succursales	3 332 ..
Bénéfices réinvestis et bénéfices non distribués des succursales	3 333 ..
Revenu des titres de créance (intérêts)	3 334 ..
Revenu des investissements de portefeuille	3 339 ..
Revenu des titres de participation	3 340 ..
Revenu des obligations et autres titres d'emprunt	3 350 ..
Revenu des instruments du marché monétaire	3 360 ..
Revenu des autres investissements	3 370 ..
D. TRANSFERTS COURANTS	4 379 ..
Crédit	2 379 ..
Administrations publiques	2 380 ..
Autres secteurs	2 390 ..
Envois de fonds des travailleurs	2 391 ..
Autres transferts courants	2 392 ..

	Codes
Débit	3 379 . .
Administrations publiques	3 380 . .
Autres secteurs	3 390 . .
Envois de fonds des travailleurs	3 391 . .
Autres transferts courants	3 392 . .
COMPTE DE CAPITAL ET D'OPÉRATIONS FINANCIÈRES	4 996 . .
COMPTE DE CAPITAL	4 994 . .
Total, crédit	2 994 . .
Total, débit	3 994 . .
Transferts de capital, crédit	2 400 . .
Administrations publiques	2 401 . .
Remise de dettes	2 402 . .
Autres transferts de capital	2 410 . .
Autres secteurs	2 430 . .
Transferts des migrants	2 431 . .
Remise de dettes	2 432 . .
Autres transferts de capital	2 440 . .
Transferts de capital, débit	3 400 . .
Administrations publiques	3 401 . .
Remise de dettes	3 402 . .
Autres transferts de capital	3 410 . .
Autres secteurs	3 430 . .
Transferts des migrants	3 431 . .
Remise de dettes	3 432 . .
Autres transferts de capital	3 440 . .
Acquisitions et cessions d'actifs non financiers non produits, crédit	2 480 . .
Acquisitions et cessions d'actifs non financiers non produits, débit	3 480 . .
COMPTE D'OPÉRATIONS FINANCIÈRES	4 995 . .
A. **INVESTISSEMENTS DIRECTS**	4 500 . .
De l'économie à l'étranger	4 505 . .
Capital social	4 510 . .
Créances sur les entreprises apparentées	4 515 . .
Engagements envers les entreprises apparentées	4 520 . .
Bénéfices réinvestis	4 525 . .
Autres transactions	4 530 . .
Créances sur les entreprises apparentées	4 535 . .
Engagements envers les entreprises apparentées	4 540 . .
De l'étranger dans l'économie	4 555 . .
Capital social	4 560 . .
Créances sur les investisseurs directs	4 565 . .
Engagements envers les investisseurs directs	4 570 . .
Bénéfices réinvestis	4 575 . .
Autres transactions	4 580 . .
Créances sur les investisseurs directs	4 585 . .
Engagements envers les investisseurs directs	4 590 . .

		Codes
B.	**INVESTISSEMENTS DE PORTEFEUILLE**	4 600
	Avoirs	4 602
	Titres de participation	4 610
	Autorités monétaires	4 611
	Administrations publiques	4 612
	Banques	4 613
	Autres secteurs	4 614
	Titres de créance	4 619
	Obligations et autres titres d'emprunt	4 620
	Autorités monétaires	4 621
	Administrations publiques	4 622
	Banques	4 623
	Autres secteurs	4 624
	Instruments du marché monétaire	4 630
	Autorités monétaires	4 631
	Administrations publiques	4 632
	Banques	4 633
	Autres secteurs	4 634
	Engagements	4 652
	Titres de participation	4 660
	Banques	4 663
	Autres secteurs	4 664
	Titres d'engagement	4 669
	Obligations et autres titres d'emprunt	4 670
	Autorités monétaires	4 671
	Administrations publiques	4 672
	Banques	4 673
	Autres secteurs	4 674
	Instruments du marché monétaire	4 680
	Autorités monétaires	4 681
	Administrations publiques	4 682
	Banques	4 683
	Autres secteurs	4 684
C.	**DÉRIVÉS FINANCIERS**	4 910
	Autorités monétaires	4 911
	Administrations publiques	4 912
	Banques	4 913
	Autres secteurs	4 914
	Avoirs	4 900
	Autorités monétaires	4 901
	Administrations publiques	4 902
	Banques	4 903
	Autres secteurs	4 904
	Engagements	4 905
	Autorités monétaires	4 906
	Administrations publiques	4 907
	Banques	4 908
	Autres secteurs	4 909
D.	**AUTRES INVESTISSEMENTS**	4 700
	Avoirs	4 703
	Crédits commerciaux	4 706
	Administrations publiques	4 707
	dont : court terme	4 709
	Autres secteurs	4 710
	dont : court terme	4 712

	Codes
Prêts	4 714 ..
Autorités monétaires	4 715 ..
dont : court terme	4 718 ..
Administrations publiques	4 719 ..
dont : court terme	4 721 ..
Banques	4 722 ..
dont : court terme	4 724 ..
Autres secteurs	4 725 ..
dont : court terme	4 727 ..
Monnaie fiduciaire et dépôts	4 730 ..
Autorités monétaires	4 731 ..
Administrations publiques	4 732 ..
Banques	4 733 ..
Autres secteurs	4 734 ..
Autres avoirs	4 736 ..
Autorités monétaires	4 737 ..
dont : court terme	4 739 ..
Administrations publiques	4 740 ..
dont : court terme	4 742 ..
Banques	4 743 ..
dont : court terme	4 745 ..
Autres secteurs	4 746 ..
dont : court terme	4 748 ..
Engagements	4 753 ..
Crédits commerciaux	4 756 ..
Administrations publiques	4 757 ..
dont : court terme	4 759 ..
Autres secteurs	4 760 ..
dont : court terme	4 762 ..
Prêts	4 764 ..
Autorités monétaires	4 765 ..
dont : utilisation des crédits et prêts du FMI	4 766 ..
dont : court terme	4 768 ..
Administrations publiques : long terme	4 769 ..
dont : court terme	4 771 ..
Banques	4 772 ..
dont : court terme	4 774 ..
Autres secteurs	4 775 ..
dont : court terme	4 777 ..
Monnaie fiduciaire et dépôts	4 780 ..
Autorités monétaires	4 781 ..
Administrations publiques	4 782 ..
Banques	4 783 ..
Autres secteurs	4 784 ..
Autres engagements[1]	4 786 ..
Autorités monétaires	4 787 ..
dont : court terme	4 789 ..
Administrations publiques	4 790 ..
dont : court terme	4 792 ..
Banques	4 793 ..
dont : court terme	4 795 ..
Autres secteurs	4 796 ..
dont : court terme	4 798 ..
E. AVOIRS DE RÉSERVE	4 802 ..
Or monétaire	4 812 ..
DTS	4 811 ..
Position de réserve au FMI	4 810 ..
Avoirs en devises	4 803 ..
Autres créances	4 813 ..
ERREURS ET OMISSIONS NETTES	4 998 ..

---

[1]Y compris allocations de DTS aux autorités monétaires.

ANNEXE III. SYSTÈME DE CODAGE FMI/OCDE/EUROSTAT APPLICABLE À LA BALANCE DES PAIEMENTS, À LA POSITION EXTÉRIEURE GLOBALE ET AU COMMERCE INTERNATIONAL DE SERVICES[1]

Le système de codage examiné ici s'applique à toutes les composantes types et aux postes complémentaires définis dans la cinquième édition du *Manuel de la balance des paiements*; il s'applique également aux composantes et postes pour mémoire de la classification OCDE-Eurostat des données sur le commerce international de services.

Le code a trois composantes ou sections, qui sont :

\<position\>	un nombre à un chiffre (compris entre 1 et 8) décrivant la position du poste dans les comptes de la position extérieure globale (PEG) ou de la balance des paiements (BP);
\<sujet\>	un nombre à trois chiffres (choisi parmi les nombres entiers compris entre 100 et 998) permettant d'identifier toutes les composantes de la balance des paiements, de la position extérieure globale et de la classification du commerce international des services et certains postes complémentaires;
\<sous-code\>	une composante définie par l'utilisateur et de longueur illimitée.

Le code complet comprendrait ces trois éléments dans l'ordre suivant : \<position\>\<sujet\>\<sous-code\>. Cependant, le sous-code est fa-cultatif, contrairement au code de la position et au code du sujet. En conséquence, le code comportera, sous sa forme couramment utilisée, les composantes suivantes : \<position\>\<sujet\>.

La première composante du code indique la position du poste dans les comptes de la position extérieure globale (PEG) et de la balance des paiements (BP); elle est définie comme suit :

Code	Position dans les comptes de la PEG et de la BP
1	Stock au début de la période
2	Flux, crédit
3	Flux, débit
4	Flux nets
5	Ajustement de la valeur en fonction des variations du prix
6	Ajustement de la valeur en fonction des variations du taux de change
7	Autres ajustements
8	Stock à la fin de la période
0	Autres

Le premier chiffre de la composante indicative du sujet correspond à la rubrique de la balance des paiements ou de la position extérieure globale, c'est-à-dire :

Code	Rubrique de la BP
1	Biens
2	Services
3	Revenus et transferts courants
4	Compte de capital
5	Investissements directs
6	Investissements de portefeuille
7	Autres investissements
8	Avoirs de réserve
9	Principaux agrégats, dérivés financiers et détails complémentaires

Les deuxième et troisième chiffres de la composante sont généralement attribués dans un ordre consécutif et sont séparés par des espaces permettant l'inclusion ultérieure de codes additionnels, le cas échéant. En outre, dans le compte d'opérations financières, à l'exception des comptes des investissements directs, le deuxième chiffre de cette composante est 0, 1, 2, 3 ou 4 pour les avoirs et 5, 6, 7, 8 ou 9 pour les engagements.

Un exemple des codes appliqués aux «Autres investissements» dans le compte d'opérations financières est donné ci-après.

Sujet	Champ unique			Champ multiple		
	Crédit	Débit	Net	Crédit	Débit	Net
Autres investissements	2700	3700	4700	2700	3700	4700
Engagements	2750	3750	4750	2750	3750	4750
Prêts	2762	3762	4762	2762	3762	4762
Administrations publiques	2767	3767	4767	2767	3767	4767
Long terme	2768	3768	4768	2768	3768	4768
Court terme	2769	3769	4769	2769	3769	4769
Banques	2770	3770	4770	2770	3770	4770
Long terme	2771	3771	4771	2771	3771	4771
Court terme	2772	3772	4772	2772	3772	4772
Autres secteurs	2773	3773	4773	2773	3773	4773
Long terme	2774	3774	4774	2774	3774	4774
Court terme	2775	3775	4775	2775	3775	4775

Pour les prêts, les écritures passées au crédit et au débit servent à comptabiliser les transactions communément dénommées tirages et remboursements. La cinquième édition du *Manuel* recommande de classer tous les tirages sur prêts à long terme et tous les remboursements de ces prêts parmi les postes complémentaires. À l'heure actuelle, le FMI recueille des données nettes sur la plupart des autres postes du compte d'opérations financières. Néanmoins, le système de codage permet d'identifier tous les flux, qu'il s'agisse de transactions nettes ou de transactions inscrites au crédit ou au débit.

---

[1] Tiré de l'ouvrage du FMI intitulé «Balance des paiements : codes utilisés pour les composantes types et les postes complémentaires», Washington, DC, 3 mars 1995.

ANNEXE IV. POSITION EXTÉRIEURE GLOBALE : COMPOSANTES TYPES

	Codes
A. AVOIRS	8 995 C
Investissements directs à l'étranger	8 505
Capital social et bénéfices réinvestis	8 506
Créances sur les entreprises apparentées	8 507
Engagements envers les entreprises apparentées	8 508
Autres capitaux	8 530
Créances sur les entreprises apparentées	8 535
Engagements envers les entreprises apparentées	8 540
Investissements de portefeuille	8 602
Titres de participation	8 610
Autorités monétaires	8 611
Administrations publiques	8 612
Banques	8 613
Autres secteurs	8 614
Titres de créances	8 619
Obligations et autres titres d'emprunt	8 620
Autorités monétaires	8 621
Administrations publiques	8 622
Banques	8 623
Autres secteurs	8 624
Instruments du marché monétaire	8 630
Autorités monétaires	8 631
Administrations publiques	8 632
Banques	8 633
Autres secteurs	8 634
Dérivés financiers	8 900
Autorités monétaires	8 901
Administrations publiques	8 902
Banques	8 903
Autres secteurs	8 904
Autres investissements	8 703
Crédits commerciaux	8 706
Administrations publiques	8 707
dont : court terme	8 709
Autres secteurs	8 710
dont : court terme	8 712
Prêts	8 714
Autorités monétaires	8 715
dont : court terme	8 718
Administrations publiques	8 719
dont : court terme	8 721
Banques	8 722
dont : court terme	8 724
Autres secteurs	8 725
dont : court terme	8 727
Monnaie fiduciaire et dépôts	8 730
Autorités monétaires	8 731
Administrations publiques	8 732
Banques	8 733
Autres secteurs	8 734

	Codes
Autres avoirs	8 736 ..
Autorités monétaires	8 737 ..
dont : court terme	8 739 ..
Administrations publiques	8 740 ..
dont : court terme	8 742 ..
Banques	8 743 ..
dont : court terme	8 745 ..
Autres secteurs	8 746 ..
dont : court terme	8 748 ..
Avoirs de réserve	8 802 ..
Or monétaire	8 812 ..
DTS	8 811 ..
Position de réserve au FMI	8 810 ..
Devises étrangères	8 803 ..
Autres créances	8 813 ..
B. ENGAGEMENTS	8 995 D.
Investissements directs de l'étranger dans l'économie	8 555 ..
Capital social et bénéfices réinvestis	8 556 ..
Créances sur les investisseurs directs	8 557 ..
Engagements envers les investisseurs directs	8 558 ..
Autres capitaux	8 580 ..
Créances sur les investisseurs directs	8 585 ..
Engagements envers les investisseurs directs	8 590 ..
Investissements de portefeuille	8 652 ..
Titres de participation	8 660 ..
Banques	8 663 ..
Autres secteurs	8 664 ..
Titres d'engagement	8 669 ..
Obligations et autres titres d'emprunt	8 670 ..
Autorités monétaires	8 671 ..
Administrations publiques	8 672 ..
Banques	8 673 ..
Autres secteurs	8 674 ..
Instruments du marché monétaire	8 680 ..
Autorités monétaires	8 681 ..
Administrations publiques	8 682 ..
Banques	8 683 ..
Autres secteurs	8 684 ..
Dérivés financiers	8 905 ..
Autorités monétaires	8 906 ..
Administrations publiques	8 907 ..
Banques	8 908 ..
Autres secteurs	8 909 ..
Autres investissements	8 753 ..
Crédits commerciaux	8 756 ..
Administrations publiques	8 757 ..
dont : court terme	8 759 ..
Autres secteurs	8 760 ..
dont : court terme	8 762 ..

	Codes
Prêts	8 764 ..
Autorités monétaires	8 765 ..
dont : utilisation des crédits et des prêts du FMI	8 766 ..
dont : court terme	8 768 ..
Administrations publiques	8 769 ..
dont : court terme	8 771 ..
Banques	8 772 ..
dont : court terme	8 774 ..
Autres secteurs	8 775 ..
dont : court terme	8 777 ..
Monnaie fiduciaire et dépôts	8 780 ..
Autorités monétaires	8 781 ..
Administrations publiques	8 782 ..
Banques	8 783 ..
Autres secteurs	8 784 ..
Autres engagements[1]	8 786 ..
Autorités monétaires	8 787 ..
dont : court terme	8 789 ..
Administrations publiques	8 790 ..
dont : court terme	8 792 ..
Banques	8 793 ..
dont : court terme	8 795 ..
Autres secteurs	8 796 ..
dont : court terme	8 798 ..
POSITION EXTÉRIEURE GLOBALE NETTE	8 995 ..
Taux de conversion (fin de période)	0 102 ..

---

[1]Y compris allocations de DTS aux autorités monétaires.

ANNEXE V. CADRE CONCEPTUEL DE LA BALANCE DES PAIEMENTS ET DE LA POSITION EXTÉRIEURE GLOBALE

La présente annexe reprend le texte du chapitre II de la cinquième édition du Manuel. *Il convient de noter que les numéros de paragraphe et page cités dans cette annexe sont ceux du* Manuel.

Définitions

12. La première partie du présent *Manuel* décrit le cadre conceptuel de la balance des paiements et de la position extérieure globale. Elle traite de leur relation avec la comptabilité nationale, du concept de résidence, des principes d'évaluation et de chronologie, enfin des notions d'unité de compte et de conversion.

13. La balance des paiements est un état statistique où sont systématiquement résumées, pour une période donnée, les transactions économiques d'une économie avec le reste du monde. Les transactions, pour la plupart entre résidents et non-résidents[1], sont celles qui portent sur les biens, services et revenus; celles qui font naître des créances financières sur le reste du monde ou des engagements financiers envers celui-ci; et celles qui, telles les donations, sont considérées comme des transferts, pour lesquels il y a lieu de passer des contre-écritures de manière à solder — au sens comptable du terme — les transactions à sens unique (voir paragraphe 28)[2]. Une transaction se définit comme un flux économique découlant de la création, de la transformation, de l'échange, du transfert ou de l'extinction d'une valeur économique et faisant intervenir le transfert de propriété de biens ou d'actifs financiers, la prestation de services ou la fourniture de travail et de capital.

14. De même que la balance des paiements retrace des flux, la position extérieure globale est un relevé de stocks. C'est un état statistique qui présente, à une date donnée, par exemple en fin d'année, i) la valeur et la composition du stock des actifs financiers d'une économie ou de ses créances sur le reste du monde, ainsi que ii) la valeur et la composition du stock de ses engagements envers le reste du monde. Dans certains cas, il peut être utile, pour les besoins de l'analyse, de calculer la différence entre avoirs et engagements extérieurs de ce bilan pour évaluer la position nette de l'économie, qui équivaut à la partie de la valeur nette de son patrimoine attribuable à ses relations avec le reste du monde ou en résultant. Une variation des stocks pendant une période définie peut être attribuable soit à des transactions (flux), soit à des réévaluations (qui rendent compte des variations des taux de change, des prix, etc.), soit à d'autres ajustements (des confiscations sans dédommagement, par exemple). Au contraire, la balance des paiements n'enregistre que des transactions.

[1]Sauf dans le cas d'échanges d'avoirs financiers extérieurs transférables entre secteurs résidents et, dans une moindre mesure, d'engagements financiers extérieurs entre non-résidents (voir paragraphe 318).
[2]Les définitions et classifications des comptes internationaux contenues dans le présent *Manuel* visent à faciliter la communication au FMI des données sur les transactions internationales, et non à donner effet ou à interpréter les diverses dispositions des statuts du Fonds monétaire international qui ont trait aux aspects juridiques de l'action (ou du manque d'action) officielle concernant ces transactions.

Principes et concepts

15. Le reste du présent chapitre est consacré au cadre conceptuel des comptes internationaux — c'est-à-dire l'ensemble de conventions et principes sous-jacents qui assurent l'enregistrement systématisé et cohérent des transactions internationales et des stocks d'avoirs et engagements extérieurs. Les aspects pertinents de ces principes, ainsi que les considérations et contraintes pratiques qui s'y rapportent, seront examinés en détail dans les chapitres suivants.

Système d'enregistrement en partie double

16. La convention de base à respecter pour l'établissement d'un état de balance des paiements est que toute transaction enregistrée doit donner lieu à deux inscriptions de montants égaux. L'un de ces montants est inscrit en crédit et est affecté du signe plus, tandis que l'autre est inscrit en débit et affecté du signe moins. En théorie, donc, la somme des montants inscrits en crédit est censée être identique à celle des montants inscrits en débit et le solde de toutes les inscriptions est égal à zéro.

17. Dans la pratique, toutefois, il arrive fréquemment que les comptes ne s'équilibrent pas. Les données servant à établir les estimations pour la balance des paiements sont souvent obtenues séparément de sources différentes. C'est pourquoi le solde peut être un crédit net ou un débit net, qui correspond au montant net des erreurs et omissions. Une écriture distincte, de montant égal mais de signe contraire, doit alors être passée pour équilibrer les comptes. Comme les estimations erronées ou manquantes peuvent s'annuler, on ne peut juger du degré d'exactitude de l'état de balance des paiements d'après le montant de la différence entre la somme des crédits et celle des débits. Néanmoins, il y a lieu de s'inquiéter lorsqu'il subsiste une différence non négligeable qui n'est pas corrigée, car cela gêne l'analyse ou l'interprétation des estimations et en mine la crédibilité (il peut en aller de même pour l'interprétation de l'état de la position extérieure globale dont il sera question au chapitre XXIII).

18. La plupart des inscriptions à la balance des paiements se rapportent à des transactions dans lesquelles des valeurs économiques sont fournies ou reçues en échange d'autres valeurs économiques; ces valeurs sont soit des ressources réelles (biens, services et revenus), soit des actifs financiers. Les écritures compensatoires en crédit et en débit que requiert le système d'enregistrement résultent donc souvent de l'inscription de montants égaux pour les deux éléments échangés. Dans le cas où il y a don, et non échange, ou quand, pour d'autres raisons, la transaction donne lieu à un enregistrement unique, et non à deux enregistrements, une écriture — dénommée *transfert* — spécifiquement conçue pour assurer la compensation nécessaire doit être passée. (Les diverses sortes d'inscriptions qui peuvent être faites à la balance des paiements sont décrites aux paragraphes 26 à 31.)

19. Par convention de ce système, les inscriptions effectuées en crédit par l'économie qui établit sa balance des paiements reflètent i) des exportations lorsqu'il s'agit de ressources réelles et ii) soit une diminution des avoirs extérieurs de l'économie, soit une augmentation de ses engagements extérieurs, lorsqu'il s'agit d'actifs financiers. Parallèlement, les inscriptions faites en débit par l'économie qui établit les données reflètent i) des importations lorsqu'il s'agit de ressources réelles et ii) soit une augmentation des avoirs, soit une diminution des engagements lorsqu'il s'agit d'actifs financiers. En d'autres termes, pour les avoirs — qu'ils soient réels ou financiers —, un chiffre positif (crédit) dénote une baisse, tandis qu'un chiffre négatif (débit) correspond à une hausse. Par contre, pour les engagements, un chiffre positif indique une augmentation et un chiffre négatif une diminution. Les transferts sont portés au crédit lorsque les inscriptions qu'ils compensent sont faites en débit et ils sont portés au débit lorsque ces inscriptions sont effectuées en crédit.

20. La teneur ou la composition d'un état de balance des paiements varie quelque peu selon que les transactions sont enre-gistrées sur une base brute ou sur une base nette; les recommandations énoncées dans le présent *Manuel* indiquent quelles transactions sont à enregistrer sur une base brute et lesquelles sont à comptabiliser sur une base nette. Les inscriptions qu'il est recommandé d'effectuer sont énumérées dans la liste des composantes types de la balance des paiements et des renseignements complémentaires qui peuvent être présentés séparément.

Concepts de territoire économique, de résidence et de pôle d'intérêt économique

21. Les concepts de territoire économique, de résidence et de pôle d'intérêt économique utilisés dans le présent *Manuel* sont identiques à ceux qui ont été adoptés dans le *SCN* et seront exa-minés en détail au chapitre IV. Le territoire économique ne corres-pond pas forcément à la zone délimitée par les frontières reconnues sur le plan politique. Il recouvre un territoire géographique admi-nistré par un gouvernement. À l'intérieur de ce territoire géographique circulent librement des personnes, des biens et des ca-pitaux. Dans le cas de pays maritimes, le territoire géographique comprend toutes les îles régies par les mêmes autorités fiscales et monétaires que le territoire principal.

22. Une unité institutionnelle a son pôle d'intérêt économique dans un pays et est résidente dudit pays lorsqu'il existe, sur le territoire économique de celui-ci, un endroit (domicile, lieu de production ou locaux à autre usage) auquel ou à partir duquel elle exerce et a l'intention de continuer à exercer des activités économiques et effectue ou a l'intention de continuer à effectuer des transactions sur une grande échelle, que ce soit pendant une période de temps indéfinie ou déterminée — en principe d'un an au moins, mais c'est là un critère indicatif et non une règle absolue.

Principes d'évaluation et de chronologie

23. Il est nécessaire d'utiliser une base d'évaluation uniforme pour l'ensemble des transactions internationales (qu'elles portent sur des ressources réelles ou sur des créances et engagements financiers) afin de pouvoir établir de façon systématique et cohérente la somme des transactions individuelles et une position des avoirs et des

engagements qui corresponde bien à ces transactions. La base d'évaluation des transactions retenue dans le présent *Manuel* — comme dans le *SCN* — est généralement le prix de marché effectif convenu entre les agents. En théorie, tous les stocks d'avoirs et engagements doivent être évalués aux prix en vigueur sur le marché à la date à laquelle se rapporte la position extérieure globale. Les principes d'évaluation, les pratiques recommandées et leurs limites sont décrits au chapitre V, de même que la méthode d'évaluation des transferts, des actifs financiers et des stocks d'avoirs et engagements. (On y traitera aussi des cas où un prix de marché ne peut ni exister, ni être présumé.)

24. Dans le *Manuel* comme dans le *SCN*, c'est le principe de la comptabilité sur la base des faits générateurs (des droits constatés) qui régit le *moment de l'enregistrement* des transactions. Elles sont donc enregistrées au moment où une valeur économique est créée, transformée, échangée, transférée ou éteinte. Des créances et des engagements se créent lorsqu'il y a transfert de propriété. Le transfert peut être soit juridique, soit matériel (économique). Dans la pratique, lorsque le transfert de propriété n'est pas manifeste, on peut considérer comme une approximation raisonnable de cette date celle à laquelle les parties à une transaction l'enregistrent dans leurs livres ou dans leurs comptes. (Les principes de chronologie et les conventions qu'il est recommandé de respecter pour les diverses inscriptions à la balance des paiements, ainsi que les cas où il est possible de faire exception à la règle du transfert de propriété ou de s'en écarter, sont traités au chapitre VI.)

Le concept et les différents types de transactions

25. En général, les modifications des rapports économiques qu'enregistre la balance des paiements résultent principalement de la relation qui se noue entre deux parties, c'est-à-dire, à une exception près (voir la note 1), entre un résident et un non-résident, et toutes les transactions de cet ordre sont comptabilisées à la ba-lance des paiements. Les inscriptions spécifiques qu'il est recommandé d'effectuer sont celles qui figurent dans la liste des composantes types (voir le chapitre VIII) et elles sont décrites en détail dans les chapitres IX et suivants.

26. En dépit de son appellation, la balance des paiements ne rend pas compte des *paiements*, au sens usuel du terme, mais des *transactions*. Un certain nombre de transactions internationales qui ont leur place à la balance des paiements peuvent ne pas donner lieu à un paiement moné-taire et certaines ne comportent même aucun type de paiement. L'enregistrement de ces transactions, en plus de celles qui ont un paiement pour contrepartie, constitue la principale différence entre un état de balance des paiements et un relevé des paiements extérieurs.

Échanges

27. Parmi les transactions qui figurent à la balance des paiements, les plus nombreuses et les plus importantes sont celles qui peuvent être dénommées *échanges*. Un agent économique (entité économique) fournit une valeur économique à un autre et reçoit en échange une valeur égale. Les valeurs économiques fournies par une économie à une autre appartiennent à deux grandes catégories : les ressources réelles (biens, services, revenus), d'une part, et les instruments financiers, d'autre part. Les deux parties à l'échange sont des résidents d'économies différentes, sauf lorsqu'il s'agit d'échanges d'actifs financiers extérieurs entre secteurs résidents. Il se peut que la fourniture d'un instrument financier fasse intervenir non seulement le transfert de propriété d'une créance ou d'un engagement existant, mais aussi la création d'un nouvel avoir ou engagement ou l'annulation d'un avoir ou engagement existant. En outre, les modalités d'un contrat afférent à un instrument financier (par exemple son échéance) peuvent être modifiées par accord entre les parties; on considère dans ce cas que le contrat initial a été exécuté et est remplacé par un autre, assorti de modalités différentes. Tous les échanges de cet ordre doivent être enregistrés à la balance des paiements.

Transferts

28. Les transactions donnant lieu à un *transfert* diffèrent des échanges en ce qu'un agent économique fournit une valeur économique à un autre agent économique sans en recevoir une contrepartie qui, d'après les conventions et règles adoptées aux fins de ce système, a une valeur économique. La valeur qui fait défaut d'un côté de la transaction est représentée par une inscription dénommée *transfert*. Les transferts (valeurs économiques fournies et reçues sans réciprocité) doivent figurer à la balance des paiements. Les **transferts courants** figurent au **compte des transactions courantes** (voir le chapitre XV), tandis que les *transferts de capital* sont classés dans le **compte de capital** (voir le chapitre XVII).

Migration

29. Comme une économie se définit en fonction des entités économiques qui sont associées à son territoire, il est probable que toute modification touchant ces entités influera sur le champ que recouvre l'économie.

30. Il y a migration lorsqu'un particulier devient résident d'une nouvelle économie parce qu'il y transfère son lieu d'habitation principal. Certains avoirs mobiliers corporels appartenant au migrant sont effectivement importés dans la nouvelle économie; les avoirs immobiliers du migrant et certains de ses avoirs mobiliers corporels qui sont situés sur le territoire de l'ancienne économie deviennent des créances de la nouvelle économie sur l'ancienne; les créances du migrant sur les résidents d'une économie autre que la nouvelle ou ses engagements envers ceux-ci deviennent des créances ou engagements extérieurs de la nouvelle économie; et les créances du migrant sur les résidents de la nouvelle économie ou ses engagements envers ceux-ci cessent d'être des créances d'une économie, quelle qu'elle soit, sur le reste du monde, ou des engagements de cette économie envers celui-ci. La somme nette de tous ces changements est égale à la valeur nette du patrimoine du migrant, qui doit être inscrite en contrepartie si les autres changements sont enregistrés; ces inscriptions doivent être effectuées à la balance des paiements, où, par convention, la contre-écriture est passée sous la rubrique des transferts.

Autres transactions imputées

31. Dans quelques autres cas, des transactions peuvent être imputées et des inscriptions faites à la balance des paiements sans que des flux aient été effectivement engendrés. L'attribution des bénéfices réinvestis aux investisseurs directs étrangers en constitue un exemple. Les bénéfices d'une filiale ou succursale étrangère comprennent les bénéfices attribuables à l'investisseur direct. Ces bénéfices, qu'ils soient distribués ou réinvestis dans l'entreprise, sont proportionnels à sa participation au capital de l'entreprise. Les bénéfices réinvestis sont classés parmi les revenus des investissements directs. Un montant affecté du signe contraire est inscrit en contrepartie au poste investissement direct du *compte d'opérations financières* et représente l'augmentation de la participation des investisseurs directs étrangers au capital de la filiale ou succursale étrangère. (Les bénéfices réinvestis sont traités aux chapitres XIV et XVIII.)

Modifications non dues aux transactions

Reclassement des créances et engagements

32. Dans le *Manuel*, la classification des actifs financiers est établie en fonction de caractéristiques choisies de manière à révéler les intentions du créancier ou du débiteur. Les changements d'intentions influent sur les caractéristiques retenues, et il y a lieu de reclasser les actifs financiers en conséquence. L'un des cas ty-piques est celui de la distinction qui est faite entre les *investissements directs* et les autres catégories d'opérations financières. Par exemple, plusieurs détenteurs indépendants d'*investissements de portefeuille* (sous forme d'actions émises par une même entreprise à l'étranger) peuvent s'associer de manière à avoir, de façon durable, un pouvoir de décision effectif dans la gestion de l'entreprise. Leurs avoirs répondront alors à la définition de l'*investissement direct*, et la modification de la nature de l'investissement pourrait être assimilée à un reclassement. Ce reclassement se reflétera, à la fin de la période pendant laquelle il aura eu lieu, dans la position extérieure globale, mais non dans la balance des paiements. De même, les créances sur les non-résidents peuvent être soumises, ou cesser d'être assujetties, au contrôle des autorités monétaires résidentes. En pareil cas, il y aura reclassement entre les *actifs de réserve* et les actifs autres que les réserves.

Réévaluations

33. La valeur des ressources réelles et des actifs financiers est constamment sujette à variation. Cette variation peut être due à l'une ou à l'autre des causes suivantes, ou aux deux à la fois : i) le prix auquel les transactions sur une certaine sorte d'avoirs s'effectuent habituellement peut subir des variations qui sont liées à la monnaie dans laquelle le prix est exprimé; ii) le taux de change de la monnaie dans laquelle le prix est exprimé peut varier par rapport à l'unité de compte utilisée. Les réévaluations ne doivent pas être reportées à la balance des paiements, mais doivent figurer dans la position extérieure globale.

ANNEXE VI. CLASSIFICATION ET COMPOSANTES TYPES DE LA BALANCE DES PAIEMENTS

Sauf pour la discussion des droits de tirage spéciaux (DTS), cette annexe est conforme au chapitre VIII de la cinquième édition du Manuel. Il convient de noter que les numéros de paragraphe et de page cités dans cette annexe sont ceux du Manuel. La discussion des DTS est tirée du MBP6.

Structure et classification

139. La deuxième partie de ce *Manuel* a trait à la structure et à la classification des comptes de la balance des paiements et de la position extérieure globale. À l'examen des composantes types de ces deux séries de comptes succéderont l'analyse et la description détaillée du **compte des transactions courantes**, du **compte de capital et d'opérations financières**, des renseignements complémentaires qui peuvent être requis sur certains postes et de la position extérieure globale.

140. Il importe d'ordonner les statistiques de la balance des paiements selon une structure cohérente afin d'en faciliter l'utilisation et l'adaptation à des fins multiples : élaboration de politiques, études analytiques, projections, comparaisons bilatérales de telle ou telle composante ou de l'ensemble des transactions, agrégations régionales ou mondiales, etc. (Voir paragraphe 7.)

141. La classification et la liste des composantes types reposent sur des considérations théoriques et pratiques qui tiennent compte des opinions exprimées par les experts nationaux de la balance des paiements; elles concordent en général avec les définitions que donne le *SCN*. La classification élargie des transactions internationales au titre des services est conforme aux principes de la Classification centrale des produits (CCP). (Voir l'appendice III.)

142. Le système de classification est aussi le résultat d'efforts entrepris pour rattacher la structure du **compte d'opérations financières** aux comptes de revenu et à la classification de la position extérieure globale. Il a été conçu de manière à offrir un cadre flexible pouvant être utilisé par de nombreux pays pour développer au fil des années leurs statistiques extérieures. Certains pays ne sont peut-être pas en mesure de communiquer des chiffres pour de nombreux postes. D'autres sont peut-être en mesure de fournir des données supplémentaires.

Composantes types

143. Le choix des composantes types (dont la liste figure à la fin du présent chapitre) est fonction d'un certain nombre de considérations; celles qui suivent ont été jugées primordiales.

Le poste doit manifester un comportement distinct. Il doit être influencé par un facteur économique ou un ensemble de facteurs différents de ceux qui influent sur les autres postes, ou réagir différemment au même facteur ou ensemble de facteurs. C'est cette réaction aux facteurs économiques que la balance des paiements cherche à mettre en évidence.

Le poste doit revêtir de l'importance pour plusieurs pays; cette importance peut être fonction soit de son compor-tement (par exemple une variabilité exceptionnelle), soit de son ordre de grandeur.

Les données relatives à ce poste ne doivent pas être excessivement difficiles à obtenir. L'utilité qu'il présente doit cependant être évaluée à la lumière des deux considérations qui précèdent.

Le poste doit être utilisable séparément à d'autres fins, par exemple pouvoir être incorporé dans la comptabilité nationale ou servir au rapprochement avec cette dernière. La liste des composantes types ne doit pas être trop longue. En effet, un très grand nombre de pays, dont beaucoup ne disposent pas d'un système statistique très développé, sont censés utiliser les mêmes catégories lorsqu'ils communiquent leurs données.

Dans la mesure du possible, les composantes types doivent être conformes et applicables aux autres systèmes statistiques du FMI et au *SCN* et concorder, pour les *services* en particulier, avec la CCP.

144. La liste type n'implique nullement que les recommandations formulées dans ce *Manuel* empêchent les pays d'établir et de publier d'autres données qu'ils jugent importantes. En fait, lorsque de plus amples détails sont nécessaires pour comprendre les circonstances particulières à tel ou tel pays ou pour analyser les situations nouvelles, les demandes de renseignements que le FMI adresse à ses pays membres ne se limitent pas aux composantes types. Des renseignements complémentaires peuvent être aussi très utiles pour vérifier et rapprocher les statistiques de pays partenaires, et, par exemple, pour analyser les financements exceptionnels. (Voir, à la fin du chapitre, le tableau intitulé *Renseignements complémentaires qui peuvent être requis sur certains postes*.) De temps en temps, les services du FMI tiennent des consultations avec les pays membres afin de déterminer avec eux quelles données complémentaires ils devraient lui communiquer.

145. Rares sont les pays qui ont des renseignements signifi-catifs à communiquer pour chacune des composantes types. Il se peut aussi que certaines des composantes n'existent que regroupées ou qu'une composante mineure soit incluse dans une composante plus importante. Les composantes types doivent néanmoins être communiquées au FMI de manière aussi complète et exacte que pos-sible. Les statisticiens nationaux sont incontestablement mieux placés que les services du FMI pour estimer et ajuster les composantes qui ne correspondent pas exactement aux séries de base de l'économie établissant ses statistiques.

Erreurs et omissions nettes

146. L'application des principes recommandés dans le présent *Manuel* devrait donner un ensemble cohérent d'inscriptions positives et négatives dont la somme est (en principe) égale à zéro. Or, en pratique, si l'on additionne toutes les inscriptions effectuées, on obtient presque inévitablement un crédit net ou un débit net. Ce solde est le résultat d'erreurs et d'omissions dont certaines peuvent être liées aux méthodes d'approximation recommandées pour la mise en pratique des principes.

147. La balance des paiements comprend normalement un poste distinct réservé aux erreurs et omissions nettes, appelé par certains statisticiens «solde» ou «écart statistique». Ce poste vise à compenser la surévaluation ou la sous-évaluation des composantes enregistrées. Ainsi donc, si ces composantes se soldent par un crédit, le poste des erreurs et omissions nettes constituera un débit de valeur égale et vice versa.

148. Certaines erreurs et omissions qui se produisent au cours de l'établissement des données se neutralisent habituellement. C'est pourquoi le montant du solde ne renseigne pas nécessairement sur la précision globale du relevé. Cependant, l'interprétation du relevé devient difficile si ce solde est considérable.

Classification générale

149. Les composantes types, dont la liste est donnée à la fin du présent chapitre, sont réparties en deux principales sections :

Le compte des transactions courantes, qui se subdivise en : *biens et services*, *revenus* et *transferts courants*.

Le **compte de capital et d'opérations financières**, qui enregistre i) les *transferts de capital* et les *acquisitions ou cessions d'actifs non financiers non produits*, et ii) les opérations portant sur des avoirs et engagements financiers.

Cette répartition correspond à la pratique suivie par la plupart des pays depuis de longues années et dénote un changement important apporté dans le présent *Manuel*. L'ancien compte des mouvements de capitaux a été rebaptisé **compte de capital et d'opérations financières**. Dicté par un souci d'harmonisation avec le *SCN*, ce changement consiste à adopter pour la balance des paiements la distinction que le *SCN* établit entre les *transferts de capital* et les *transferts courants* et à faire concorder le nouveau compte avec le compte de capital et le compte financier du *SCN*.

150. Les inscriptions à la plupart des rubriques du **compte des transactions courantes** doivent faire apparaître les crédits ou débits bruts. La plupart des inscriptions au **compte de capital et d'opérations financières** doivent être effectuées sur une base nette, c'est-à-dire que chaque composante ne doit y figurer que comme un crédit ou un débit (le mode de traitement recommandé pour certains postes spécifiques et les exceptions seront examinés dans les chapitres correspondants). Les entrées de ressources réelles et les augmentations d'avoirs financiers (ou diminutions d'engagements) seront enregistrées au débit; les sorties de ressources réelles et les diminutions d'avoirs financiers (ou augmentations d'engagements) seront enregistrées au crédit. Les transferts, dans les sections 1.C et 2.A, doivent avoir la même valeur numérique, mais affectée du signe opposé, que les inscriptions dont ils sont la contre-écriture.

Classification détaillée

151. La classification des composantes types qui suit a été mise au point conformément aux critères exposés au paragraphe 143. La structure et les caractéristiques du **compte des transactions courantes** et du **compte de capital et d'opérations financières**, sensiblement modifiées par rapport à la quatrième édition du *Manuel*, sont exposées aux chapitres IX et XVI, respectivement. Les composantes types du **compte des transactions courantes** sont décrites en détail aux chapitres X à XV, celles du **compte de capital et d'opérations financières** aux chapitres XVII à XXI et dans *Dérivés financiers — Supplément à la cinquième édition (1993) du Manuel de la balance des paiements*, Washington, 2000.

Transactions courantes (1.)

152. Sont incluses dans le **compte des transactions courantes** toutes les transactions portant sur des valeurs économiques (autres que des actifs financiers) entre entités résidentes et non résidentes. On y inscrit aussi les contreparties des valeurs économiques courantes qui sont fournies ou acquises sans réciprocité. Les grandes subdivisions (postes) sont les *biens et services*, les *revenus* et les *transferts courants*.

Biens et services (1.A)
Biens (1.A.a.)

153. La rubrique *marchandises générales* recouvre la plupart des biens meubles que les résidents exportent à destination de non-résidents ou qu'ils importent en provenance de non-résidents et qui, à quelques exceptions près, font l'objet d'un transfert de propriété (effectif ou présumé).

154. La rubrique *biens importés ou exportés pour transformation* recouvre les exportations (ou importations dans l'économie établissant sa balance des paiements) de biens franchissant une frontière pour faire l'objet à l'étranger d'une transformation, suivie d'une réimportation (ou exportation) des biens, dont la valeur est établie sur une base brute avant et après la transformation. Cette rubrique fait exception au principe du transfert de propriété.

155. La rubrique *réparations de biens* recouvre les travaux de réparation de biens — bateaux, avions, etc. — fournis à des non-résidents ou reçus de non-résidents. Bien que le mouvement physique de ces biens soit analogue à celui qui est décrit au paragraphe 154, la valeur de la réparation correspond à son prix (c'est-à-dire au montant payé ou reçu pour cette réparation) et non à la valeur brute des biens avant et après la réparation.

156. La rubrique *achats de biens dans les ports par les transporteurs* recouvre tous les biens, tels que carburants, vivres, approvisionnements et fournitures, que les transporteurs résidents ou non résidents — aériens ou maritimes, par exemple — ont achetés à l'étranger (ou dans l'économie établissant sa balance des paiements). Cette rubrique n'enregistre pas les services auxiliaires fournis (remorquage, entretien, etc.), qui sont inclus dans les services de *transports*.

157. La rubrique *or non monétaire* recouvre les exportations et importations de tout or non détenu sous la forme d'avoir de réserve (or monétaire) par les autorités. L'*or non monétaire* est traité comme n'importe quel autre produit et se décompose, lorsque cela est possible, en or détenu à titre de réserve de valeur et or détenu à d'autres fins (industrielles).

Services (1.A.b.)

158. La rubrique *transports* recouvre la plupart des services fournis par les résidents aux non-résidents et vice versa, qui étaient précédemment classés aux rubriques *expéditions* et *autres transports* dans la quatrième édition du *Manuel*. Cependant, l'assurance du fret ne figure pas ici, mais à la rubrique des *services d'assu-rance*. Sous la rubrique *transports*, on enregistre le transport de marchandises et de passagers, quel qu'en soit le mode, ainsi que les autres services de distribution et services auxiliaires, y compris l'affrètement de véhicules de transport avec leur équipage. Certaines exceptions sont signalées aux chapitres X, XI et XIII.

159. La rubrique *voyages* recouvre les biens et les services acquis dans une économie par les voyageurs non résidents (y compris les excursionnistes), à des fins professionnelles ou personnelles — notamment pour des raisons de santé ou à titre éducatif —, au cours de leur séjour (de moins d'un an) sur le territoire de cette économie. Cette rubrique exclut les services internationaux fournis aux passagers, qui sont inclus dans les *transports*. Les étudiants et les personnes en traitement médical sont consi-dérés comme étant des voyageurs, quelle que soit la durée de leur séjour, contrairement à certaines autres catégories — militaires, personnel des ambassades et travailleurs non résidents. Les dépenses des travailleurs non résidents sont toutefois comprises dans les *voyages*, tandis que celles des militaires et du personnel des ambassades sont incluses dans les *services fournis ou reçus par les administrations publiques, n.c.a.* Ces cas sont signalés aux chapitres XII et XIII.

160. La rubrique *services de communication* recouvre les opérations de communication entre résidents et non-résidents. Ce sont les services postaux (y compris les messageries) et les services de télécommuni-cation (transmission du son, des images et d'autres types d'information par divers moyens et entretien des installations correspondantes, assuré par des résidents pour le compte de non-résidents et vice versa).

161. La rubrique *services de bâtiment et travaux publics (BTP)* recouvre les travaux de construction et d'installation effectués à l'étranger (ou dans l'économie qui établit sa balance des paiements) ou dans les enclaves extraterritoriales, à titre temporaire, par les entreprises résidentes (ou non résidentes) et leur personnel mais qui ne sont effectués ni par une entreprise étrangère apparentée à une entreprise résidente, ni par un bureau sur place non constitué en société qui, dans certaines conditions, équivaut à une entreprise étrangère apparentée. Ces aspects de la résidence sont traités aux chapitres IV et XIII.

162. La rubrique *services d'assurance* recouvre les assurances fournies aux non-résidents par des compagnies d'assurances résidentes et vice versa. On entend par là l'assurance du fret (pour les biens exportés ou importés) et les autres types d'assurance directe (notamment l'assurance-vie et autres formes d'assurances), ainsi que la réassurance. (Pour la méthode de calcul de la valeur des services d'assurance, voir paragraphes 256 et 257.)

163. La rubrique *services financiers* (autres que ceux qui sont offerts par les compagnies d'assurances et les caisses de retraite) recouvre les services d'intermédiation financière et les services auxiliaires entre résidents et non-résidents. Sont inclus les commissions et les frais ayant trait aux services suivants : lettres de crédit, lignes de crédit, crédit-bail, opérations de change, services de crédit aux consommateurs et aux entreprises, opérations de courtage, souscriptions de titres, différentes formes de couverture des opérations à terme, etc. Les services auxiliaires se rapportent à l'administration et à la réglementation des marchés financiers, à la garde de titres, etc.

164. La rubrique *services d'informatique et d'information* recouvre les transactions entre résidents et non-résidents concernant le conseil en matériel, l'installation de logiciels, les services d'information (traitement de données, banques de données, agences de presse) et l'entretien et la réparation des ordinateurs et du matériel connexe.

165. La rubrique *redevances et droits de licence* recouvre les recettes (exportations) et paiements (importations) des résidents et non-résidents se rapportant à i) l'exploitation d'actifs incorporels non financiers non produits et de droits de propriété — marques, droits d'auteur, brevets, procédés, techniques, dessins, licences de fabrication, franchises, etc. — et à ii) l'utilisation, dans le cadre d'accords de licence, de brevets, d'oeuvres originales ou de prototypes, tels que les manuscrits, films, etc.

166. La rubrique *autres services aux entreprises* recouvre les services fournis par des résidents à des non-résidents et vice versa : le négoce international et les autres services liés au commerce, la location-exploitation et divers services aux entreprises, spécialisés et techniques. (Voir, à la fin du chapitre, le tableau des *Renseignements complémentaires qui peuvent être requis sur certains postes*, et les paragraphes 261 à 264 pour de plus amples détails.)

167. La rubrique *services personnels, culturels et relatifs aux loisirs* recouvre i) les services audio-visuels et connexes et ii) les autres services culturels fournis par des résidents à des non-résidents et vice versa. Sont compris dans la catégorie i) les services qui ont trait à la production de films cinématographiques (films ou bandes vidéo), d'émissions de radio ou de télévision et d'enre-gistrements musicaux, par exemple les droits de location, les redevances perçues par les acteurs, producteurs etc., pour les productions et pour les droits de distribution cédés aux médias. Dans la catégorie ii) figurent les autres services personnels, culturels et relatifs aux loisirs tels que ceux qui ont associés aux bibliothèques, musées et autres activités culturelles ou sportives.

168. La rubrique *services fournis ou reçus par les administrations publiques, n.c.a.* recouvre tous les services (auxquels corres-pondent par exemple les dépenses des ambassades et consulats) fournis ou reçus par le secteur public ou les organisations internationales ou régionales et non classés ailleurs.

Revenus (1.B.)

169. La rubrique *rémunération des salariés* recouvre les salaires, traitements et autres émoluments versés, en espèces ou en nature, aux travailleurs frontaliers, saisonniers et autres travailleurs non résidents, (par exemple le personnel local des ambassades).

170. La rubrique *revenus des investissements* recouvre les recettes et paiements se rapportant respectivement à la détention d'avoirs financiers extérieurs par les résidents et aux engagements envers les non-résidents. Cela comprend les revenus des investissements directs, les revenus des investissements de portefeuille et les autres revenus d'investissement. La composante investissements directs se subdivise en revenus des participations au capital (dividendes, bénéfices des succursales et bénéfices réinvestis) et en revenus des titres de créance (intérêts); les revenus des investissements de portefeuille se subdivisent en revenus des participations au capital (dividendes) et en revenus des titres de créance (intérêts); les autres revenus d'investissement recouvrent les intérêts provenant d'autres opérations financières (prêts, etc.) et, en principe, les droits nets des ménages sur les réserves techniques d'assurance-vie et les réserves des caisses de retraite.

Transferts courants (1.C.)

171. À l'instar du *SCN*, le *Manuel* distingue les **transferts courants** des *transferts de capital* (ces derniers sont enregistrés au **compte de capital et d'opérations financières**). Les transferts sont la contrepartie des transferts de propriété, volontaires ou forcés, de ressources réelles ou d'actifs financiers entre résidents et non-résidents, qui ne reçoivent pas en échange une valeur économique. Les *transferts courants* sont tous ceux qui **ne font pas intervenir** i) le transfert de propriété d'un actif fixe, ii) le transfert de fonds lié ou subordonné à l'acquisition ou à la cession d'un actif fixe, ni iii) la remise, sans contrepartie, d'une dette par un créancier (toutes ces opérations sont des *transferts de capital*). Les **transferts courants** comprennent ceux des administrations publiques — par exemple la coopération internationale courante (entre des administrations publiques appartenant à différentes économies), les paiements des impôts courants sur le revenu et sur la fortune, etc. — et les autres transferts, tels que les envois de fonds des travailleurs, les primes (moins les commissions de service) et les indemnités au titre des assurances autres que l'assu-rance-vie, etc. La distinction entre les *transferts courants* et les *transferts de capital* fait l'objet d'un examen approfondi au chapitre XV (voir également les paragraphes 175 et 344).

Le compte de capital et d'opérations financières (2.)

172. Le **compte de capital et d'opérations financières** a deux principales composantes — le *compte de capital* correspond au compte de capital du *SCN* et le *compte d'opérations financières* au compte financier du *SCN*. Les avoirs (ou actifs) sont des créances sur les non-résidents et les engagements (ou passifs) des dettes envers les non-résidents. Les deux parties à une transaction portant sur des avoirs ou des engagements sont en général un résident et un non-résident mais, dans certains cas, il peut s'agir de deux résidents ou de deux non-résidents. (Voir paragraphe 318.)

173. Toutes les réévaluations et toutes les autres variations d'actifs et de passifs extérieurs qui ne sont pas dues à des transactions (voir paragraphe 310) sont exclues du **compte de capital et d'opérations financières** mais apparaissent dans la position extérieure globale. Des relevés complémentaires identifient certains postes qui présentent un intérêt pour l'analyse et qui relèvent de plusieurs comptes. C'est le cas, par exemple, des engagements qui constituent des réserves pour les autorités étrangères et des financements exceptionnels, dont il est question au chapitre XXII.

174. La classification des *opérations financières* et celle des composantes des revenus dans les **transactions courantes** sont liées et doivent être cohérentes pour faciliter l'analyse, permettre le rapprochement effectif entre la balance des paiements et la position extérieure globale, et assurer la compatibilité avec le *SCN* et avec les autres systèmes statistiques du FMI.

Compte de capital (2.A.)

175. Les grandes subdivisions du **compte de capital** sont les *transferts de capital* et les *acquisitions et cessions d'actifs non financiers non produits*. Les *transferts de capital* sont ceux qui font intervenir le transfert de propriété d'un actif fixe; le transfert de fonds lié ou subordonné à l'acquisition ou à la cession d'un actif fixe; ou la remise, sans contrepartie, d'une dette par un créancier. Ils se subdivisent en deux catégories : i) les transferts des adminis-trations publiques, qui se décomposent en remises de dettes et autres transferts et ii) les autres transferts, qui se subdivisent en transferts des migrants, remises de dettes et autres transferts. (Voir le chapitre XV, qui traite de la distinction entre les *transferts de capital* et les **transferts courants**). Les *acquisitions et cessions d'actifs non financiers non produits* se rapportent généralement aux avoirs incorporels tels que les brevets, les contrats de location et autres contrats transférables, la marque, etc. Ce poste ne recouvre pas les propriétés non bâties situées sur le territoire d'une économie donnée mais peut inclure l'achat (ou la vente) de terrains par une ambassade étrangère. (Voir paragraphe 312.)

Compte d'opérations financières (2.B.)

176. La classification des composantes types comprises sous ce poste est fondée sur les critères suivants :

La nature des investissements ou leur ventilation fonctionnelle (*investissements directs, investissements de portefeuille, dérivés financiers, autres investissements* et *avoirs de réserve*).

Dans le cas des *investissements directs*, la distinction en fonction du sens des mouvements de capitaux — entre l'étranger et l'économie qui établit sa balance des paiements — étant entendu que, dans chaque sous-catégorie, les avoirs sont distingués des engagements.

Pour ce qui est des *investissements de portefeuille,* des *dérivés financiers* et des *autres investissements,* la distinction traditionnelle entre avoirs et engagements.

La nature de l'instrument est particulièrement importante pour les *investissements de portefeuille* et les *autres investissements* (titres de participation ou d'engagement, crédits commerciaux, prêts, monnaie et dépôts, autres avoirs ou engagements). Le présent *Manuel* regroupe dans les *investissements de portefeuille* les instruments du marché monétaire, ainsi que les autres instruments financiers, tant traditionnels que nouveaux.

Pour ce qui est des *investissements de portefeuille,* des *dérivés financiers,* et des *autres investissements,* on distingue le secteur dont relève le créancier intérieur en ce qui concerne les avoirs et le secteur dont relève le débiteur intérieur en ce

qui concerne les engagements. Cette distinction facilite les rapprochements avec les comptes de revenu et la position extérieure globale ainsi qu'avec le *SCN* et les autres systèmes statistiques;

La distinction habituelle entre les avoirs et engagements à long et à court terme, le long terme étant défini par une échéance contractuelle initiale de plus d'un an et le court terme par une échéance ne dépassant pas un an, n'est faite que pour les *autres investissements*. Depuis quelques années, cette distinction a perdu à l'évidence beaucoup de son utilité pour de nombreuses transactions, intérieures ou internationales. C'est pourquoi la différenciation du long et du court terme a moins d'importance dans le présent *Manuel* — et dans le *SCN* — que dans les éditions précédentes. Cependant, parce qu'elle est importante à certains égards, par exemple pour l'analyse de la dette extérieure, elle est retenue dans le présent *Manuel* pour les *autres investissements*.

177. La rubrique *investissements directs* — lesquels témoignent d'un intérêt durable de la part d'une entité résidente d'une économie (l'investisseur direct) pour une entité résidente d'une autre économie (l'entreprise d'investissement direct) — recouvre toutes les transactions entre les investisseurs directs et les entreprises d'investissement direct. Les *investissements directs* recouvrent donc la transaction initiale entre les uns et les autres et toutes les transactions ultérieures entre eux, ainsi que les transactions entre les entreprises apparentées, constituées ou non en sociétés. Les opérations d'investissement direct effectuées à l'étranger et dans l'économie déclarante se décomposent en capital social, bénéfices réinvestis et autres opérations en capital (transactions liées aux dettes entre entreprises d'un même groupe). En ce qui concerne le capital social et les autres capitaux, les créances et les engagements à l'égard des entreprises affiliées et à l'égard des investisseurs directs sont ventilés séparément. Les transactions entre banques apparentées et entre autres intermédiaires financiers apparentés se limitent aux transactions portant sur des titres de participation (capital social) et des dettes/créances permanentes. (Voir paragraphe 372 de la cinquième édition du *Manuel de la balance des paiements*).

178. Les investissements de portefeuille comprennent les titres de participation et les titres de créance; ces derniers se subdivisent en obligations et autres titres d'emprunt, et instruments du marché monétaire. Divers nouveaux instruments financiers, autres que les dérivés financiers, sont classés dans les catégories d'instruments appropriées. (Les opérations classées parmi les investissements directs et les avoirs de réserve sont exclues.)

179. La catégorie des *dérivés financiers* recouvre les instruments financiers qui sont liés à un autre instrument ou indicateur financier ou produit de base spécifique et par le biais desquels des risques financiers spécifiques (de taux d'intérêt, de taux de change, de participation ou de prix des produits de base, de crédit, etc.) peuvent être négociés en tant que tels sur les marchés financiers. Les opérations sur dérivés financiers doivent être traitées en tant qu'opérations distinctes et non comme faisant partie intégrante de la valeur des opérations sous-jacentes auxquelles elles sont liées.

180. La rubrique *autres investissements* recouvre les crédits commerciaux et les prêts à court et à long terme (y compris l'utilisation des crédits et des prêts du FMI, ainsi que les prêts/emprunts au titre de la location-vente; la monnaie fiduciaire et les dépôts (transférables et autres, tels que les dépôts d'épargne et les dépôts à terme, les parts des associations d'épargne et de prêt, des associations de crédit mutuel, etc.); et les autres avoirs et engagements (y compris les allocations de DTS). (Les transactions classées parmi les *investissements directs* sont exclues de la présente rubrique.)

181. La rubrique *avoirs de réserve* recouvre les transactions portant sur les avoirs dont les autorités monétaires d'une économie considèrent qu'elles disposent pour répondre aux besoins de financement de la balance des paiements et, dans certains cas, à d'autres besoins; en principe, cette disponibilité n'est pas étroitement liée à des critères formels tels que la propriété des avoirs ou la monnaie dans laquelle ils sont libel-lés. Les rubriques incluses sous ce poste sont l'or monétaire, les DTS, la position de réserve au FMI, les avoirs en devises (monnaie fiduciaire et dépôts, et valeurs mobilières) et les autres créances.

182. Le champ couvert par les composantes des *avoirs de réserve* et leur définition répondent aux besoins de l'analyse, comportent un élément d'appréciation et ne se prêtent pas toujours à l'application de critères objectifs formels ou de systèmes de classement précis fondés sur la conditionnalité ou sur d'autres facteurs. Contrairement à la quatrième édition du *Manuel*, la cinquième édition prescrit d'exclure de ce poste les réévaluations des *avoirs de réserve*, ainsi que leurs contreparties. Les données dans le volume actuel comprennent l'allocation des DTS et les inscriptions de contrepartie. Ces variations apparaissent dans la position extérieure globale.

INTRODUCCIÓN

El volumen 62 de *Balance of Payments Statistics Yearbook* (anuario) que publica el Fondo Monetario Internacional (FMI) presenta las estadísticas de balanza de pagos y la posición de inversión internacional (PII) declaradas por los países miembros al FMI. El FMI agradece a los países miembros su cooperación en la declaración de estos datos. En el caso de algunos países, esta información se complementa con detalles que los economistas de la institución obtienen de diferentes fuentes.

El anuario consta de tres partes. En la parte 1 se presentan datos de balanza de pagos y PII de cada país. En la parte 2 figuran los totales regionales y mundiales de los componentes principales de la balanza de pagos. En la parte 3 se presentan descripciones técnicas sobre la majoría de países declarantes. La parte 1 se publica en un tomo separado y las partes 2 y 3 en un mismo tomo.

En este volumen del anuario se mantienen las características introducidas en los volúmenes 46 al 61 inclusive. Como en el volumen 46, los datos de balanza de pagos se desglosan conforme a los componentes normalizados de la quinta edición del *Manual de Balanza de Pagos (Manual)*[1]. No obstante, se han modificado los componentes normalizados tras la publicación de *Instrumentos financieros derivados: Suplemento a la quinta edición (1993) del* Manual de Balanza de Pagos, en 2000 y las modificaciones de dicha publicación en 2002. Por consiguiente, las referencias a la quinta edición del *Manual* incluyen el suplemento y el apéndice. De conformidad con las recomendaciones del suplemento y el apéndice, el presente anuario refleja la decisión del Comité del FMI de Estadísticas de Balanza de Pagos en el sentido de que las transacciones de instrumentos financieros derivados relacionadas con empresas afiliadas deben incluirse en el componente correspondiente a los instrumentos financieros derivados de las estadísticas de balanza de pagos y de la posición de inversión in

ternacional. Además, como en el volumen 47, se incluyen los datos sobre la posición de inversión internacional en el formato de la quinta edición del *Manual*, y en la parte 3 del anuario, se publican descripciones detalladas de las metodologías, los procedimientos de compilación y las fuentes de datos que se utilizan en la mayoría de los países incluidos en el presente volumen. En el *Manual*[2], se introducen varios cambios metodológicos en la compilación de los datos de balanza de pagos, cambios que se describen con detalle en el capítulo I del *Manual*. A partir del volumen 46, en este anuario los datos presentados conforme a los componentes normalizados del *Manual* están acompañados de una lista de códigos, preparada conjuntamente por el FMI, la Organización de Cooperación y Desarrollo Económicos (OCDE) y la Oficina Estadística de las Comunidades Europeas (Eurostat). La estructura de estos códigos se explica en un anexo de esta introducción. Además, a partir del volumen 46, no se presentan datos trimestrales de balanza de pagos en el caso de los países que declaran estadísticas trimestrales de balanza de pagos al FMI. Estos datos trimestrales se publican en las ediciones mensuales de la publicación del FMI *International financial statistics (IFS)* y también se presentan en el CD-ROM y en Internet (Balanza de Pagos en Línea).

La conversión de los datos realizada por el personal del FMI ha permitido presentar en el formato de la quinta edición los datos históricos extraídos de la base de datos del FMI, así como los datos más recientes declarados por los países miembros en el formato de la cuarta edición del *Manual de Balanza de Pagos*. En 1995, el personal del FMI elaboró fórmulas para transformar la información de balanza de pagos de cada país incluida en la base de datos del FMI a fin de adaptarla a la metodología y presentación que se establecen en la quinta edición. Seguidamente se enviaron los datos convertidos a las autoridades de los respectivos países para su revisión y se incorporaron los comentarios recibidos a la nueva base de datos. En 1996, el personal del FMI, en colaboración con las autoridades de los países, convirtió en forma similar los datos sobre la posición de inversión internacional declarados en el formato de la cuarta edición a la presentación de la quinta edición. En principio, la posición de inversión internacional de un país es un balance general de las tenencias de activos y pasivos financieros frente al exterior.

En la parte 3 del anuario se incluyen las descripciones técnicas de la metodología, los procedimientos de compilación y las fuentes de datos que utilizan los países que declaran datos. Las descripciones

---

[1]El volumen 1 del anuario, publicado en 1949, se basó en la primera edición del Manual de Balanza de Pagos del FMI, publicado en 1948; los volúmenes 2–12 se basaron en la segunda edición del manual, publicada en 1950; los volúmenes 13–23 se basaron en la tercera edición, publicada en 1961, y los volúmenes 24–29 se basaron en esa edición así como en el Ma-nual de Balanza de Pagos: Suplemento a la tercera edición, que apareció en 1973. Desde el volumen 30 al 45, las presentaciones siguieron las recomendaciones de la cuarta edición del manual, publicada en 1977.

[2]Fondo Monetario Internacional, *Manual de Balanza de Pagos*, quinta edición, Washington, septiembre de 1993, e *Instrumentos financieros derivados: Suplemento a la quinta edición (1993) del* Manual de Balanza de Pagos, 2000.

se basan en gran medida en la información que los países suministran al FMI. Se incluyen estas descripciones para que los usuarios comprendan mejor la cobertura de los datos de los distintos países publicados en el anuario, así como sus limitaciones, y para informar a los compiladores sobre las fuentes de datos y los métodos utilizados por los compiladores de otros países.

El resto de esta introducción se ha organizado de la siguiente manera:

- En la sección I se describen las características básicas de los cuadros que se publican en la parte 1 del anuario. (Pueden consultarse los detalles sobre cobertura de los datos de las partes 2 y 3 en el segundo tomo.)

- La sección II contiene información sobre la manera de acceder a la información del FMI sobre balanza de pagos en CD-ROM y en Internet (Balanza de Pagos en Línea).

- Se han incluido seis anexos. En el anexo I se incluye una presentación analítica sucinta de los componentes de la balanza de pagos (y los códigos correspondientes). En el anexo II se presentan los componentes normalizados (con sus respectivos códigos) de la quinta edición del *Manual*. En el anexo III se explica el sistema de codificación empleado. En el anexo IV se presentan los componentes normalizados de la posición de inversión internacional que figuran en la quinta edición del *Manual*. En el anexo V se describe el marco conceptual de la balanza de pagos y la PII, en el anexo VI, se explica la cobertura de los componentes principales de las cuentas de la balanza de pagos conforme a las directrices establecidas en la quinta edición del *Manual*.

I. Parte 1 del anuario: Datos de cada país

En la parte 1 del anuario se presentan las páginas de países en orden alfabético. Debe hacerse la salvedad de que el término "país", según se emplea en esta publicación, no siempre se refiere a una entidad territorial que constituya un Estado conforme al derecho y la práctica internacionales; el término también abarca la zona del euro, la Unión Monetaria del Caribe Oriental y ciertas entidades territoriales que no son Estados soberanos, sobre las cuales también se facilitan datos estadísticos a nivel internacional en forma separada.

Los datos de balanza de pagos de la mayoría de los países se presentan en dos cuadros. El cuadro 1 es un resumen analítico de los datos más detallados que se presentan en el cuadro 2. En el cuadro 1 se presentan los componentes de la balanza de pagos que están ordenados de tal manera que se destacan

las partidas de financiamiento (reservas y partidas conexas). (Véase también el anexo I.) El cuadro 2 presenta los datos correspondientes a los componentes normalizados que se describen en la quinta edición del *Manual*. (Véase también el anexo II.) En el caso de los países sobre los que se dispone de información relativa a la posición de inversión internacional, los datos se presentan en el cuadro 3. En los cuadros 1, 2 y 3, los datos corresponden al período 2003–2010 para cada país. Los datos que figuran en los cuadros se declaran en base a los años calendario, salvo indicación contraria.

Presentación analítica

En la presentación analítica, que figura en el cuadro 1, los componentes de la balanza de pagos se clasifican en cinco categorías principales de datos (grupos A a E) que el FMI considera útiles para analizar de manera uniforme la evolución de la balanza de pagos. No obstante, no debe interpretarse que esta división en grupos refleja una recomendación del FMI sobre el enfoque analítico más apropiado para todos los países. Los componentes normalizados del cuadro 2 podrían agruparse conforme a una presentación analítica diferente en función de las circunstancias especiales de determinado país o de ciertos requisitos analíticos.

Obsérvese que las cifras que aparecen en los cuadros 1 y 2 en lo que respecta a los saldos de la cuenta corriente, la cuenta de capital y la cuenta financiera difieren en el caso de algunos países. Esto se debe a que en el cuadro 1 se excluyen ciertas transacciones que se clasifican en estas cuentas porque han sido reclasificadas como "financiamiento excepcional" en reservas y partidas conexas. El "financiamiento excepcional" se refiere a las transacciones efectuadas por las autoridades para financiar su balanza de pagos, e incluye la obtención de recursos en préstamo del exterior, los atrasos en los pagos y la condonación de deudas, pero no incluye las reservas.

Presentación normalizada

Los componentes normalizados conforme a la quinta edición del *Manual*, que figuran en el cuadro 2, ofrecen una clasificación más detallada de los bienes y servicios que en la cuarta edición. La llamada "cuenta de capital y financiera" agrupa diferentes componentes bajo la "cuenta de capital" y la "cuenta

---

[3] Debido a la naturaleza única de los instrumentos financieros derivados, y a la forma en que algunas instituciones registran las transacciones, algunos países solamente pueden declarar datos en cifras netas. Por convención, en el presente anuario estas transacciones en cifras netas se incluyen, por lo general, en la categoría de pasivos. En algunos casos, los países han solicitado clasificar las transacciones en cifras netas únicamente en la categoría de instrumentos financieros derivados (netos).

Recuadro. Posición de inversión internacional

Las declaraciones de la posición de inversión internacional de los países declarantes figuran como cuadro 3 en las páginas de países. Las declaraciones sobre la posición de inversión internacional de algunos países deben interpretarse teniendo en cuenta las notas que figuran en la parte 3 en la que se presentan las metodologías, los procedimientos de compilación y las fuentes de datos que utilizan estos países. A medida que los países sigan recopilando datos más completos, se publicará una presentación más extensa de los datos sobre la posición de inversión internacional en volúmenes subsiguientes del anuario.

Véase el capítulo XXIII de la quinta edición del *Manual* en el que se presenta un análisis detallado del concepto de posición de inversión internacional.

Deuda externa no es un componente aparte de la posición de inversión internacional sino que se deriva mediante la suma de los componentes del pasivo de la posición de inversión internacional que no corresponden a capital (es decir, todos los pasivos registrados que no sean títulos de participación en el capital, ni acciones y otras participaciones de capital mediante inversión directa, incluidas las utilidades reinvertidas, y los instrumentos financieros derivados). Esta opinión concuerda, en general, con la definición básica de la deuda externa bruta adoptada en la publicación *Estadísticas de la deuda externa: Guía para compiladores y usuarios (Guía)* realizada por el Grupo de tareas interinstitucional sobre estadísticas financieras. Este grupo de tareas, que se reunió bajo la presidencia del FMI, se encargó de la elaboración de la *Guía* en la que participaron representantes del Banco de Pagos Internacionales (BPI), la Secretaría del Commonwealth, el Banco Central Europeo, Eurostat, el FMI, la OCDE, la Secretaría del Club de París, la Conferencia de las Naciones Unidas sobre Comercio y Desarrollo (UNCTAD) y el Banco Mundial.

Posición de inversión internacional: Componentes clave[1]

A. Activos

1. Inversión directa
    1.1 Acciones y otras participaciones de capital y utilidades reinvertidas
    1.2 Otro capital[2]

2. Inversión de cartera
    2.1 Títulos de participación en el capital
    2.2 Títulos de deuda[4]

3. Instrumentos financieros derivados
    3.1 Autoridades monetarias
    3.2 Gobierno general
    3.3 Bancos
    3.4 Otros sectores

4. Otra inversión
    4.1 Créditos comerciales
    4.2 Préstamos
    4.3 Moneda y depósitos
    4.4 Otros activos

5. Activos de reserva
    5.1 Oro monetario
    5.2 Derechos especiales de giro
    5.3 Posición de reserva en el FMI
    5.4 Divisas
    5.5 AOtros activos

B. Pasivos

1. Inversión directa
    1.1 Acciones y otras participaciones de capital y utilidades reinvertidas
    1.2 Otro capital[3]

2. Inversión de cartera
    2.1 Títulos de participación en el capital
    2.2 Títulos de deuda[4]

3. Instrumentos financieros derivados
    3.1 Autoridades monetarias
    3.2 Gobierno general
    3.3 Bancos
    3.4 Otros sectores

4. Otra inversión
    4.1 Créditos comerciales
    4.2 Préstamos
    4.3 Moneda y depósitos
    4.4 Otros pasivos[5]

---

[1] No se indican todos los componentes, por ejemplo, los que están desglosados por sectores (autoridades monetarias, gobierno general, bancos y otros) y, en algunos casos, por vencimientos. Un país que reporte datos de la PII omitiendo los principales subcomponentes, los totales podrían no ser publicados.
[2] Los pasivos frente a empresas filiales, componentes de otro capital, se incluyen en la deuda externa.
[3] Los pasivos frente a inversionistas directos, componentes de otro capital, se incluyen en la deuda externa.
[4] Incluye bonos, pagarés e instrumentos del mercado de dinero.
[5] Incluye asignaciones de DEG a autoridades monetarias.

financiera". En esta última se clasifican los componentes según la clase de inversión (es decir, inversión directa, inversión de cartera, instrumentos finan-cieros derivados[3], otra inversión y activos de reserva),

activos/pasivos, sectores internos (autoridades monetarias, gobierno general, bancos y otros sectores) y vencimiento original.

Posición de inversión internacional

Los datos sobre la posición de inversión internacional, que figuran en el cuadro 3, se agrupan conforme a los componentes normalizados de la posición de inversión internacional que se establecen en la quinta edición del *Manual*. (Véase también el anexo IV.)

La clasificación de los componentes de la posición de inversión internacional en el cuadro 3 coincide con la de la cuenta financiera de la balanza de pagos que figura en el cuadro 2. Sin embargo, hay varias diferencias entre los dos cuadros. Como se mencionó anteriormente, los datos sobre la posición de inversión internacional reflejan los activos y pasivos financieros de un país frente al exterior en un momento determinado. Por lo tanto, en el cuadro 3 los componentes de la posición de inversión internacional se agrupan en la presentación básica en dos categorías generales, a saber, activos y pasivos, a diferencia de la clasificación funcional de la inversión (es decir, inversión directa, inversión de cartera, instrumentos financieros derivados, otra inversión y activos de reserva) que figura en el cuadro 2. Además, los datos del cuadro 3 reflejan la posición de inversión internacional de un país al final del período de declaración de datos, a diferencia de las transacciones que tuvieron lugar durante el período, que se presentan en el cuadro 2. Asimismo, a diferencia del cuadro 2, en el que se indica el valor de las transacciones a lo largo de un período, la valoración de la posición de inversión internacional de un país, que se presenta en el cuadro 3, refleja el valor de las transacciones financieras, las variaciones por valoración y otros ajustes al final del período de declaración. La posición de inversión internacional neta, que figura en el cuadro 3, se calcula como diferencia entre el valor de los activos financieros externos declarados y el de los pasivos financieros externos declarados.

Códigos de datos

En los cuadros 1, 2 y 3 se indican los códigos de cada categoría y componente. Como se señaló anteriormente, los códigos fueron elaborados conjuntamente por el FMI, la OCDE y Eurostat, a efectos de facilitar la declaración de datos a nivel internacional. Los códigos corresponden a los componentes normalizados de la balanza de pagos y de la posición de inversión internacional según se definen en la quinta edición del *Manual*, así como a los componentes de la clasificación conjunta OCDE/Eurostat para el comercio de servicios.

Cada uno de los códigos que figuran en el anuario está formado por seis dígitos/caracteres. El primer dígito indica si se trata de un crédito, un débito o del valor neto (el número "2" corresponde a un crédito, el "3" a un débito y el "4" al valor neto, es decir, la diferencia entre créditos y débitos). Los tres dígitos siguientes se utilizan para clasificar los componentes de la balanza de pagos. Por ejemplo, para la cuenta corriente se utiliza el código 993, para la cuenta de capital 994 y para la cuenta financiera 995. Los detalles del sistema de codificación figuran en el anexo III.

Los dígitos/caracteres que ocupan los lugares quinto y sexto de los códigos que figuran en el anuario se reservan para indicar características especiales de ciertos componentes específicos. Por ejemplo, en el cuadro 1, la Z del quinto carácter señala que se excluye de ese componente el financiamiento excepcional; la W indica que se excluyen esta misma partida y el uso del crédito del FMI y préstamos del FMI. Las letras A, B, C y D del cuadro 1 indican los distintos sectores internos.

Créditos y débitos

En los cuadros 1 y 2, los datos sobre transacciones figuran como asientos de crédito bruto o débito bruto en la cuenta corriente y la cuenta de capital. En la cuenta financiera se presentan como asientos de crédito neto o débito neto (para reflejar variaciones netas de los pasivos y de los activos) en la cuenta financiera. Los asientos de crédito, bruto o neto, representan valores positivos (aunque no se indica el signo) y los asientos de débito, bruto o neto, son negativos (y sí se indica el signo). Por lo tanto, toda disminución de los activos y todo aumento de los pasivos (crédito) figuran como valores positivos y todo aumento de los activos y toda disminución de los pasivos (débito) aparecen con signo negativo.

Asientos nulos, carencia de datos, o datos confidenciales

Con frecuencia es difícil discernir en la información declarada por los países si faltan cifras porque no se dispone de datos, porque el valor de esa partida es cero o insignificante, o porque son datos confidenciales. La inclusión de tres puntos (....) en los cuadros del anuario significa que no se dispone de datos o bien que el valor es cero o insignificante, o confidencial. En caso de que los datos de uno o más subcomponentes no puedan ser revelados debido a razones de confidencialidad, los valores en cuestión (i) se añadirán a un subcomponente genérico (por ejemplo, "otros") dentro del componente que corresponda, o (ii) se omitirán sin ajustar ningún subcomponente genérico. En ambos casos, el total declarado permanece invariable.

Nota sobre los componentes de renta y otra inversión

En el cuadro 2 relativo a la presentación normalizada, los datos declarados por algunos países en las categorías de "renta" y "otra inversión" presentan un grado de agregación que no permite identificar por separado cada uno de los componentes que figuran en esta categoría. Por consiguiente, en estos casos, los datos agregados de ciertas subcategorías no pueden obtenerse sumando los componentes de estas subcategorías. Lo mismo ocurre en el caso de los datos relativos a "otra inversión" que figuran en el cuadro 3 relativo a la posición de inversión internacional.

Anteriormente, en los volúmenes 46 al 49, en los cuadros se presentaban los datos correspondientes a "otra inversión" (activos y pasivos) desglosados en "a largo plazo" y "a corto plazo". Desde el Volumen 50, en los cuadros se presentan los datos correspondientes a "otra inversión" (activos y pasivos) de las autoridades monetarias, el gobierno general, los bancos y otros sectores en cifras totales (del financiamiento a largo plazo y a corto plazo) y en partidas "de los cuales: a corto plazo". (En el caso de los préstamos, autoridades monetarias, los datos se indican en cifras totales, desglosados en "de los cuales: uso del crédito del FMI y préstamos del FMI" y "de los cuales: a corto plazo".)

Redondeo de las cifras

La mayor parte de las cifras de los cuadros se expresan en unidades de un millón; no debe suponerse que los cuadros que incluyen unidades más pequeñas representan, necesariamente, cifras más exactas. La unidad se elige con el fin de presentar las cifras de una manera práctica. Debido al redondeo en el cálculo de las cifras, puede haber diferencias entre un total y la suma de sus componentes.

Conversión de monedas

La mayoría de los datos de balanza de pagos declarados al FMI se expresan en unidades de moneda nacional o en dólares de EE.UU., pero algunos países declaran ciertos datos en DEG. Para facilitar la comparación de datos entre los países, todos los estados de balanza de pagos publicados en el anuario se expresan en dólares de EE.UU. Además, los datos sobre transacciones con el FMI y sobre transacciones en DEG declarados por todos los países se remplazan por los datos que figuran en los registros del FMI, expresados en DEG. Esta información se convierte, a su vez, a dólares de EE.UU.

En el caso de los países que no declaran sus estadísticas en dólares de EE.UU., los datos se convierten utilizando el tipo de cambio que figura al pie del cuadro 1 para cada país, que normalmente es el tipo promedio vigente en el país en el período correspondiente y se obtiene de *IFS*. Por ejemplo, en las páginas de *IFS* correspondientes a la zona del euro figura la línea "rf", en la que se indica el tipo de cambio promedio del euro frente al dólar de EE.UU. La conversión de los datos sobre transacciones de DEG a dólares de EE.UU. se efectúa a los tipos de cambio que se indican en la línea "sb" de las páginas de *IFS* correspondientes a Estados Unidos. En lo que respecta a los países que declaran datos trimestrales en unidades de moneda nacional, los totales anuales en dólares de EE.UU. se obtienen sumando los montos trimestrales en dólares de EE.UU.

En el caso de los países que no declaran datos sobre posición de inversión internacional en dólares de EE.UU., los datos se convierten utilizando las tasas de conversión para el país que figuran en la parte inferior del cuadro 3. Estas tasas son normalmente las del fin del período basado en los datos de IFS pertinente para el país (linea "ae").

En la introducción de *IFS*, sección 2, se presenta mayor información sobre los tipos de cambio empleados.

II. Versiones en CD-ROM e Internet

Las estadísticas publicadas en el anuario también se presentan en CD-ROM y en Internet, (Estadísticas de Balanza de Pagos en Línea). En esta versión electrónica, el número de países y las series cronológicas son ligeramente mayores que en la versión impresa del anuario, así como el número de períodos sobre los cuales se incluyen observaciones estadísticas en las series cronológicas. También se incluyen los datos trimestrales declarados por los países y los datos actualizados y corregidos a medida que se dispone de los mismos. Para mayor información sobre el CD-ROM y Estadísticas de Balanza de Pagos en Línea, sírvase dirigirse a:

Publication Services
International Monetary Fund
Washington, D.C. 20431, EE.UU.
Teléfono: (202) 623–7430
Fax: (202) 623–7201
Correo electrónico: publications@imf.org
Internet: http://www.imf.org

ANEXO I. PRESENTACIÓN ANALÍTICA

	Códigos
A. CUENTA CORRIENTE[1]	4 993 Z .
Bienes: exportaciones f.o.b.	2 100 . .
Bienes: importaciones f.o.b.	3 100 . .
Balanza de bienes	4 100 . .
Servicios: crédito	2 200 . .
Servicios: débito	3 200 . .
Balanza de bienes y servicios	4 991 . .
Renta: crédito	2 300 . .
Renta: débito	3 300 . .
Balanza de bienes, servicios y renta	4 992 . .
Transferencias corrientes: crédito	2 379 Z .
Transferencias corrientes: débito	3 379 . .
B. CUENTA DE CAPITAL[1]	4 994 Z .
Cuenta de capital: crédito	2 994 Z .
Cuenta de capital: débito	3 994 . .
Total, grupos A más B	4 981 . .
C. CUENTA FINANCIERA[1]	4 995W .
Inversión directa en el extranjero	4 505 . .
Inversión directa en la economía declarante	4 555 Z .
Activos de inversión de cartera	4 602 . .
Títulos de participación en el capital	4 610 . .
Títulos de deuda	4 619 . .
Pasivos de inversión de cartera	4 652 Z .
Títulos de participación en el capital	4 660 . .
Títulos de deuda	4 669 Z .
Instrumentos financieros derivados	4 910 . .
Activos financieros derivados	4 900 . .
Pasivos financieros derivados	4 905 . .
Activos de otra inversión	4 703 . .
Autoridades monetarias	4 701 . .
Gobierno general	4 704 . .
Bancos	4 705 . .
Otros sectores	4 728 . .
Pasivos de otra inversión[2]	4 753W .
Autoridades monetarias	4 753WA
Gobierno general	4 753 ZB
Bancos	4 753 ZC
Otros sectores	4 753 ZD
Total, grupos A a C	4 983 . .
D. ERRORES Y OMISIONES NETOS	4 998 . .
Total, grupos A a D	4 984 . .
E. RESERVAS Y PARTIDAS CONEXAS	4 802 A .
Activos de reserva	4 802 . .
Uso del crédito del FMI y préstamos del FMI	4 766 . .
Financiamiento excepcional	4 920 . .
TIPOS DE CONVERSIÓN: MONEDA DEL PAÍS POR DÓLAR DE EE.UU.	0 101 . .

---

[1]Excluidos los componentes que se han clasificado en las categorías del Grupo E.

[2]Incluye asignaciones de DEG a autoridades monetarias.

ANEXO II. PRESENTACIÓN NORMALIZADA

		Códigos
CUENTA CORRIENTE		4 993 ..
A.	**BIENES**	4 100 ..
	Crédito	2 100 ..
	Mercancías generales: exportaciones f.o.b.	2 110 ..
	Bienes para transformación: exportaciones f.o.b.	2 150 ..
	Reparaciones de bienes	2 160 ..
	Bienes adquiridos en puerto por medios de transporte	2 170 ..
	Oro no monetario	2 180 ..
	Débito	3 100 ..
	Mercancías generales: importaciones f.o.b.	3 110 ..
	Bienes para transformación: importaciones f.o.b.	3 150 ..
	Reparaciones de bienes	3 160 ..
	Bienes adquiridos en puerto por medios de transporte	3 170 ..
	Oro no monetario	3 180 ..
B.	**SERVICIOS**	4 200 ..
	Crédito total	2 200 ..
	Débito total	3 200 ..
	Servicios de transportes, crédito	2 205 ..
	Pasajeros	2 850 ..
	Fletes	2 851 ..
	Otros	2 852 ..
	Transporte marítimo, pasajeros	2 207 ..
	Transporte marítimo, fletes	2 208 ..
	Transporte marítimo, otros	2 209 ..
	Transporte aéreo, pasajeros	2 211 ..
	Transporte aéreo, fletes	2 212 ..
	Transporte aéreo, otros	2 213 ..
	Otros transportes, pasajeros	2 215 ..
	Otros transportes, fletes	2 216 ..
	Otros transportes, otros	2 217 ..
	Servicios de transportes, débito	3 205 ..
	Pasajeros	3 850 ..
	Fletes	3 851 ..
	Otros	3 852 ..
	Transporte marítimo, pasajeros	3 207 ..
	Transporte marítimo, fletes	3 208 ..
	Transporte marítimo, otros	3 209 ..
	Transporte aéreo, pasajeros	3 211 ..
	Transporte aéreo, fletes	3 212 ..
	Transporte aéreo, otros	3 213 ..
	Otros transportes, pasajeros	3 215 ..
	Otros transportes, fletes	3 216 ..
	Otros transportes, otros	3 217 ..
	Viajes, crédito	2 236 ..
	De negocios	2 237 ..
	Personales	2 240 ..
	Viajes, débito	3 236 ..
	De negocios	3 237 ..
	Personales	3 240 ..

		Códigos
B.	**INVERSIÓN DE CARTERA**	4 600 ..
	Activos	4 602 ..
	Títulos de participación en el capital	4 610 ..
	Autoridades monetarias	4 611 ..
	Gobierno general	4 612 ..
	Bancos	4 613 ..
	Otros sectores	4 614 ..
	Títulos de deuda	4 619 ..
	Bonos y pagarés	4 620 ..
	Autoridades monetarias	4 621 ..
	Gobierno general	4 622 ..
	Bancos	4 623 ..
	Otros sectores	4 624 ..
	Instrumentos del mercado monetario	4 630 ..
	Autoridades monetarias	4 631 ..
	Gobierno general	4 632 ..
	Bancos	4 633 ..
	Otros sectores	4 634 ..
	Pasivos	4 652 ..
	Títulos de participación en el capital	4 660 ..
	Bancos	4 663 ..
	Otros sectores	4 664 ..
	Títulos de deuda	4 669 ..
	Bonos y pagarés	4 670 ..
	Autoridades monetarias	4 671 ..
	Gobierno general	4 672 ..
	Bancos	4 673 ..
	Otros sectores	4 674 ..
	Instrumentos del mercado monetario	4 680 ..
	Autoridades monetarias	4 681 ..
	Gobierno general	4 682 ..
	Bancos	4 683 ..
	Otros sectores	4 684 ..
C.	**INSTRUMENTOS FINANCIEROS DERIVADOS**	4 910 ..
	Autoridades monetarias	4 911 ..
	Gobierno general	4 912 ..
	Bancos	4 913 ..
	Otros sectores	4 914 ..
	Activos	4 900 ..
	Autoridades monetarias	4 901 ..
	Gobierno general	4 902 ..
	Bancos	4 903 ..
	Otros sectores	4 904 ..
	Pasivos	4 905 ..
	Autoridades monetarias	4 906 ..
	Gobierno general	4 907 ..
	Bancos	4 908 ..
	Otros sectores	4 909 ..
D.	**OTRA INVERSIÓN**	4 700 ..
	Activos	4 703 ..
	Créditos comerciales	4 706 ..
	Gobierno general	4 707 ..
	de la cual: a corto plazo	4 709 ..
	Otros sectores	4 710 ..
	de la cual: a corto plazo	4 712 ..

	Códigos
Préstamos	4 714 ..
Autoridades monetarias	4 715 ..
de la cual: a corto plazo	4 718 ..
Gobierno general	4 719 ..
de la cual: a corto plazo	4 721 ..
Bancos	4 722 ..
de la cual: a corto plazo	4 724 ..
Otros sectores	4 725 ..
de la cual: a corto plazo	4 727 ..
Moneda y depósitos	4 730 ..
Autoridades monetarias	4 731 ..
Gobierno general	4 732 ..
Bancos	4 733 ..
Otros sectores	4 734 ..
Otros pasivos	4 736 ..
Autoridades monetarias	4 737 ..
de la cual: a corto plazo	4 739 ..
Gobierno general	4 740 ..
de la cual: a corto plazo	4 742 ..
Bancos	4 743 ..
de la cual: a corto plazo	4 745 ..
Otros sectores	4 746 ..
de la cual: a corto plazo	4 748 ..
Pasivos	4 753 ..
Créditos comerciales	4 756 ..
Gobierno general	4 757 ..
de la cual: a corto plazo	4 759 ..
Otros sectores	4 760 ..
de la cual: a corto plazo	4 762 ..
Préstamos	4 764 ..
Autoridades monetarias: otros	4 765 ..
de la cual: uso del crédito del FMI y préstamos del FMI	4 766 ..
de la cual: a corto plazo	4 768 ..
Gobierno general	4 769 ..
de la cual: a corto plazo	4 771 ..
Bancos	4 772 ..
de la cual: a corto plazo	4 774 ..
Otros sectores	4 775 ..
de la cual: a corto plazoo	4 777 ..
Moneda y depósitos	4 780 ..
Autoridades monetarias	4 781 ..
Gobierno general	4 782 ..
Bancos	4 783 ..
Otros sectores	4 784 ..
Otros pasivos[1]	4 786 ..
Autoridades monetarias	4 787 ..
de la cual: a corto plazo	4 789 ..
Gobierno general	4 790 ..
de la cual: a corto plazo	4 792 ..
Bancos	4 793 ..
de la cual: a corto plazo	4 795 ..
Otros sectores	4 796 ..
de la cual: a co°rto plazo	4 798 ..
D. ACTIVOS DE RESERVA	4 802 ..
Oro monetario	4 812 ..
Derechos especiales de giro	4 811 ..
Posición de reserva en el FMI	4 810 ..
Divisas	4 803 ..
Otros activos	4 813 ..
ERRORES Y OMISIONES NETOS	4 998 ..

[1]Incluye asignaciones de DEG a autoridades monetarias.

Anexo III. Sistema de codificación FMI/OCDE/Eurostat para la balanza de pagos, la posición de inversión internacional y el comercio de servicios[1]

Este sistema de codificación incorpora todos los componentes normalizados y las líneas de información suplementaria de la quinta edición del *Manual de Balanza de Pagos*, así como los componentes y partidas informativas de la clasificación OCDE/Eurostat para el comercio internacional de servicios.

El código consta de tres partes:

\<posición\>	Un dígito (del 1 al 8) que describe la posición de la partida en las cuentas de la posición de inversión internacional o de la balanza de pagos.
\<tema\>	Tres dígitos (del 100 al 998) que identifican todos los componentes de la balanza de pagos, de la posición de inversión internacional, del comercio de servicios y de información suplementaria seleccionada.
\<sufijo\>	Serie de caracteres definidos por el usuario; puede ser de cualquier longitud.

El código completo deberá tener la siguiente configuración: \<posición\>\<tema\>\<sufijo\>, aunque el sufijo es optativo. Los dígitos de posición y tema, en cambio, son obligatorios. Por esa razón, en la mayoría de los casos, la configuración del código es \<posición\>\<tema\>.

El primer dígito del código describe la posición de la partida en las cuentas de la posición de inversión internacional y de la balanza de pagos, a saber:

Código	Posición en las cuentas de la posición de inversión internacional y la balanza de pagos
1	Posición al comienzo del período
2	Flujos de crédito
3	Flujos de débito
4	Flujos netos
5	Ajuste por variaciones de precios
6	Ajuste por variaciones de tipos de cambio
7	Otros ajustes
8	Posición al final del período
0	Otros

El primer dígito del tema identifica la sección de la balanza de pagos o de la posición de inversión internacional, a saber:

Código	Sección de las cuentas
1	Bienes
2	Servicios
3	Renta y transferencias corrientes
4	Cuenta de capital
5	Inversión directa
6	Inversión de cartera
7	Otra inversión
8	Activos de reserva
9	Agregados principales, instrumentos financieros e información suplementaria

El segundo y tercer dígito del tema corresponden al orden consecutivo de los componentes con interrupciones para poder incluir códigos adicionales posteriormente. Además, en la cuenta financiera, salvo las cuentas de inversión directa, el segundo dígito del tema puede ser 0, 1, 2, 3 ó 4 en el caso de los activos y 5, 6, 7, 8 ó 9 en el caso de los pasivos.

A continuación se presentan ejemplos de códigos para "Otra inversión" en la cuenta financiera.

Tema	Campo único			Campo múltiple		
	Crédito	Débito	Neto	Crédito	Débito	Neto
Otra inversión	2700	3700	4700	2700	3700	4700
Pasivos	2750	3750	4750	2750	3750	4750
Préstamos	2762	3762	4762	2762	3762	4762
Gobierno general	2767	3767	4767	2767	3767	4767
A largo plazo	2768	3768	4768	2768	3768	4768
A corto plazo	2769	3769	4769	2769	3769	4769
Bancos	2770	3770	4770	2770	3770	4770
A largo plazo	2771	3771	4771	2771	3771	4771
A corto plazo	2772	3772	4772	2772	3772	4772
Otros sectores	2773	3773	4773	2773	3773	4773
A largo plazo	2774	3774	4774	2774	3774	4774
A corto plazo	2775	3775	4775	2775	3775	4775

Tratándose de créditos y débitos correspondientes a préstamos, los términos que se emplean comúnmente son giros y rembolsos. La quinta edición del *Manual* recomienda declarar todos los giros y rembolsos de los préstamos a largo plazo en una clasificación suplementaria. Actualmente, el FMI recopila la mayoría de las demás partidas de la cuenta financiera en cifras netas. No obstante, el sistema de co-dificación permite identificar todos los flujos como créditos, débitos o flujos netos.

---

[1] Adoptado de "Balance of Payments Codes for Standard Components and Additional Items", FMI, Washington, 3 de marzo de 1995.

	Códigos
Otros activos	8 736 ..
Autoridades monetarias	8 737 ..
de la cual: a corto plazo	8 739 ..
Gobierno general	8 740 ..
de la cual: a corto plazo	8 742 ..
Bancos	8 743 ..
de la cual: a corto plazo	8 745 ..
Otros sectores	8 746 ..
de la cual: a corto plazo	8 748 ..
Activos de reserva	8 802 ..
Oro monetario	8 812 ..
Derechos especiales de giro	8 811 ..
Posición de reserva en el FMI	8 810 ..
Divisas	8 803 ..
Otros activos	8 813 ..
B. PASIVOS	8 995 D.
Inversión directa en la economía declarante	8 555 ..
Acciones y otras participaciones de capital y utilidades reinvertidas	8 556 ..
Activos frente a inversionistas directos	8 557 ..
Pasivos frente a inversionistas directos	8 558 ..
Otro capital	8 580 ..
Activos frente a inversionistas directos	8 585 ..
Pasivos frente a inversionistas directos	8 590 ..
Inversión de cartera	8 652 ..
Títulos de participación en el capital	8 660 ..
Bancos	8 663 ..
Otros sectores	8 664 ..
Títulos de deuda	8 669 ..
Bonos y pagarés	8 670 ..
Autoridades monetarias	8 671 ..
Gobierno general	8 672 ..
Bancos	8 673 ..
Otros sectores	8 674 ..
Instrumentos del mercado monetario	8 680 ..
Autoridades monetarias	8 681 ..
Gobierno general	8 682 ..
Bancos	8 683 ..
Otros sectores	8 684 ..
Instrumentos financieros derivados	8 905 ..
Autoridades monetarias	8 906 ..
Gobierno general	8 907 ..
Bancos	8 908 ..
Otros sectores	8 909 ..
Otra inversión	8 753 ..
Créditos comerciales	8 756 ..
Gobierno general	8 757 ..
de la cual: a corto plazo	8 759 ..
Otros sectores	8 760 ..
de la cual: a corto plazo	8 762 ..

	Códigos
Préstamos	8 764 ..
Autoridades monetarias	8 765 ..
de la cual: uso del crédito del FMI y préstamos del FMI	8 766 ..
de la cual: a corto plazo	8 768 ..
Gobierno general	8 769 ..
de la cual: a corto plazo	8 771 ..
Bancos	8 772 ..
de la cual: a corto plazo	8 774 ..
Otros sectores	8 775 ..
de la cual: a corto plazo	8 777 ..
Moneda y depósitos	8 780 ..
Autoridades monetarias	8 781 ..
Gobierno general	8 782 ..
Bancos	8 783 ..
Otros sectores	8 784 ..
Otros pasivos[1]	8 786 ..
Autoridades monetarias	8 787 ..
de la cual: a corto plazo	8 789 ..
Gobierno general	8 790 ..
de la cual: a corto plazo	8 792 ..
Bancos	8 793 ..
de la cual: a corto plazo	8 795 ..
Otros sectores	8 796 ..
de la cual: a corto plazo	8 798 ..
POSICIÓN DE INVERSIÓN INTERNACIONAL NETA	8 995 ..
Tipos de conversión (fin de período)	0 102 ..

[1]Incluye asignaciones de DEG a autoridades monetarias.

Este anexo es la reproducción del capítulo II del Manual de Balanza de Pagos, 5a. edición. *Los párrafos y los números de página citados en este anexo corresponden a los del* Manual.

Definiciones

12. La primera parte de este *Manual* abarca el marco conceptual de las cuentas de la balanza de pagos y de la posición de inversión internacional, examinándose su relación con las cuentas nacionales y con los conceptos de residencia, valoración, momento de re-gistro, unidad de cuenta y conversión.

13. La balanza de pagos es un estado estadístico que resume sistemáticamente, para un período específico dado, las transacciones económicas entre una economía y el resto del mundo. Las transacciones, que en su mayoría tienen lugar entre residentes y no residentes[1], comprenden las que se refieren a bienes, servicios y renta, las que entrañan activos y pasivos financieros frente al resto del mundo y las que se clasifican como transferencias (como los regalos), en las que se efectúan asientos compensatorios para equilibrar —desde el punto de vista contable— las transacciones unilaterales (véase el párrafo 28)[2]. Una transacción en sí se define como un flujo económico que refleja la creación, transformación, intercambio, transferencia o extinción de un valor económico y entraña traspasos de propiedad de bienes y/o activos financieros, la prestación de servicios o el suministro de mano de obra y capital.

14. En estrecha relación con el marco de la balanza de pagos, basado en los flujos, se encuentra la posición de inversión internacional, definida por las tenencias de recursos financieros. Esta última, que corresponde a una fecha específica como el fin del año, es un estado estadístico que representa i) el valor y la composición de las tenencias de activos financieros de una economía, o de los créditos adquiridos por una economía frente al resto del mundo, y ii) el valor y la composición de las tenencias de pasivos de una economía a favor del resto del mundo. En algunos casos, puede ser de interés analítico calcular la diferencia entre los dos lados del balance para tener una medida de la posición neta. Dicha medida sería equivalente a la porción del patrimonio de una economía atribuible a su relación con el resto del mundo, o derivado de ella. Toda variación de las tenencias en cualquier período definido puede atribuirse a transacciones (flujos), a variaciones de valoración debidas a fluctuaciones del tipo de cambio, precios, etc., o a otros ajustes (por ejemplo, confiscaciones sin indemnización). En cambio, las cuentas de la balanza de pagos sólo reflejan transacciones.

Criterios y conceptos

15. El resto de este capítulo se refiere al marco conceptual de las cuentas internacionales, vale decir, al conjunto de criterios y convenciones básicos que permite el registro sistematizado y coherente de las transacciones internacionales y de las tenencias de activos y pasivos sobre el exterior. En los capítulos subsiguientes se analizarán detenidamente los aspectos sobresalientes de estos criterios, así como sus consideraciones y limitaciones prácticas.

Método de contabilidad por partida doble

16. El criterio básico aplicado a la preparación del estado de balanza de pagos es que toda transacción registrada está representada por dos asientos de igual valor. Uno de ellos se denomina crédito y tiene signo aritmético positivo. El otro se llama débito y tiene signo negativo. En principio, la suma de todos los asientos de crédito es igual a la suma de todos los asientos de débito y el saldo neto de la totalidad de los asientos del estado es igual a cero.

17. En la práctica, sin embargo, las cuentas no suelen estar en equilibrio. A menudo, los datos empleados para estimar la balanza de pagos suelen derivarse en forma independiente de diferentes fuentes; en consecuencia, puede haber un crédito neto o débito neto agregado (es decir, errores y omisiones netos en las cuentas). Para equilibrar las cuentas, se deberá efectuar un asiento separado por un monto equivalente pero de signo contrario. Debe observarse que, como hay estimaciones imprecisas o faltantes de signo contrario que suelen compensarse mutuamente, la magnitud del residuo neto no es indicativa de la exactitud relativa del estado de balanza de pagos. No obstante, la existencia de un residuo significativo y persistente que no se corrige debe ser motivo de preocupación, porque esta situación impide el análisis o la interpretación de las estimaciones y les resta credibilidad. Por otra parte, un residuo neto elevado también puede afectar a la interpretación del estado de la posición de inversión internacional. (Véase la explicación en el capítulo XXIII.)

18. La mayoría de los asientos de la balanza de pagos se refieren a transacciones en las que se entregan o reciben valores económicos a cambio de otros. Dichos valores comprenden recursos reales (bienes, servicios y renta) y financieros. Así, los asientos compensatorios de crédito y débito que exige el método de re-gistro suelen resultar del hecho de que se han anotado montos iguales para los dos recursos que se han intercambiado. Si en vez de ser intercambiados se ceden gratuitamente, o si el registro es unilateral por otras razones, se efectúan asientos especiales —llamados transferencias— para saldarlos. En los párrafos 26 a 31 se describen las distintas clases de asientos que pueden figurar en la balanza de pagos.

---

[1]En la balanza de pagos, las únicas transacciones que no se efectúan entre residentes y no residentes son el intercambio de activos financieros sobre el exterior transferibles entre sectores residentes y, en menor medida, el intercambio de pasivos financieros sobre el exterior transferibles entre no residentes. (Véase el párrafo 318.)

[2]Cabe destacar que las definiciones y clasificaciones de las cuentas internacionales que se presentan en este Manual tienen por objeto facilitar a los países miembros la tarea de declarar al FMI la información sobre transacciones internacionales y no pretenden hacer efectivas ni interpretar las disposiciones del Convenio Constitutivo del Fondo Monetario Internacional que se refieren al carácter jurídico de la acción (o falta de acción) oficial en relación con dichas transacciones.

19. Conforme a las convenciones del método contable, una economía compiladora registra asientos de crédito i) para los recursos reales que denotan exportaciones y ii) para los recursos financieros que indican reducciones de sus activos sobre el exterior o aumentos de sus pasivos sobre el exterior. A su vez, registra asientos de débito i) para los recursos reales que denotan importaciones y ii) para los recursos financieros que indican aumentos de los activos o disminuciones de los pasivos. En otras palabras, en los activos —reales o financieros— una cifra con signo positivo (crédito) representa una disminución de las tenencias y una cifra con signo negativo (débito) indica un incremento. En cambio, en los pasivos, una cifra con signo positivo significa un aumento, y una cifra con signo negativo, una disminución. Las transferencias aparecen como créditos si compensan asientos de débito, y como débitos si saldan asientos de crédito.

20. El contenido o la cobertura del estado de balanza de pagos depende, en cierto modo, de que las transacciones sean tratadas en base a valores brutos o netos. Las recomendaciones de este *Ma-nual* especifican cuáles deberán registrarse en valores brutos y cuáles en valores netos, como se refleja en la lista de componentes normalizados y en las presentaciones suplementarias sugeridas.

Conceptos de territorio económico, residencia y centro de interés económico

21. Los conceptos de territorio económico, residencia y centro de interés económico que se utilizan en este *Manual* son idénticos a los del *SCN* y se describen detalladamente en el capítulo IV. El territorio económico puede no coincidir con las fronteras políticas reconocidas. El territorio económico de un país comprende el terri-torio geográfico administrado por un gobierno dentro del cual circulan libremente personas, bienes y capital. En el caso de países marítimos, incluye también las islas que están sujetas a las mismas autoridades fiscales y monetarias que el territorio continental.

22. Una unidad institucional tiene un centro de interés económico y es residente de un país cuando desde algún lugar (vivienda, planta de producción u otro establecimiento), ubicado dentro del territorio económico del país, dicha unidad realiza e intenta seguir realizando (indefinidamente o durante un período finito) actividades económicas y transacciones en gran escala. (Se sugiere emplear un año o más como referencia, aunque no se trata de una regla inflexible.)

Criterios de valoración y momento de registro

23. Para compilar de manera uniforme cualquier agregado de transacciones individuales y registrar la posición de los activos y pasivos que les corresponden, es necesario contar con una base uniforme de valoración de las cuentas internacionales (tanto los recursos reales como los activos y pasivos financieros). En general, en este *Manual* se utiliza como base para la valoración de las transacciones el precio efectivo de mercado acordado por las partes que intervienen en la transacción. (Este criterio coincide con el adoptado en el *SCN*.) Desde el punto de vista conceptual, todas las tenencias de activos y pasivos deberán valorarse de acuerdo a los precios de mercado vigentes en el momento al cual se refiere la posición de inversión internacional. En el capítulo V se presenta una exposición completa de los criterios de valoración, las prácticas recomendadas, las limitaciones y la valoración de transferencias, recursos financieros y tenencias de activos y pasivos. (Se incluyen también casos en que no existe un precio de mercado o no es posible suponerlo.)

24. En el *Manual* y en el *SCN*, el criterio que se aplica con res-pecto al *momento de registro* de las transacciones es el de contabilidad en valores devengados. Por lo tanto, las transacciones deben registrarse con referencia al momento en que se crea, transforma, intercambia, transfiere o extingue un valor económico. Se crean activos y pasivos cuando tiene lugar un traspaso de propiedad, ya sea de índole legal o física (económica). En la práctica, cuando no sea evidente el traspaso de propiedad, el momento en que éste ocurre puede determinarse de una forma aproximada utilizando la fecha en que las partes de una transacción la registran en sus libros o en sus cuentas. (El capítulo VI trata sobre los momentos de registro y convenciones recomendados para diferentes asientos de la balanza de pagos, e incluye excepciones y desviaciones del criterio de traspaso de propiedad.)

Concepto y clase de transacción

25. En general, las variaciones de las relaciones económicas que se registran en la balanza de pagos provienen básicamente de las transacciones realizadas entre dos partes. Dichas partes son, con una excepción (véase la nota 1), un residente y un no residente, y todas las transacciones de esta clase aparecen en la balanza de pagos. Las recomendaciones sobre los asientos específicos necesarios se hallan incorporadas en la lista de componentes normalizados (véase el capítulo VIII) y se detallan a partir del capítulo IX.

26. A pesar de su nombre, la balanza de pagos no se refiere a *pagos* en su acepción común, sino a *transacciones*. Algunas transacciones internacionales que revisten interés a efectos de la balanza de pagos pueden no entrañar un pago en efectivo y algunas no se pagan en ningún sentido. La inclusión de estas transacciones, además de las que tienen como contrapartida un pago, constituye la diferencia principal entre un estado de balanza de pagos y un registro de pagos externos.

Intercambios

27. Las transacciones más comunes e importantes de la balanza de pagos pueden caracterizarse como *intercambios*. Una parte (entidad económica) suministra un valor económico a otra y recibe a cambio un valor igual. Los valores económicos suministrados por una economía a otra pueden clasificarse en términos generales como recursos reales (bienes, servicios, renta) y recursos financieros. Las partes que intervienen en la transacción son residentes de distintas economías, salvo en el caso de intercambio de recursos financieros externos entre sectores residentes. El sumi-nistro de un recurso financiero puede suponer no sólo un traspaso de propiedad de un activo o de un pasivo existente sino también la creación de uno nuevo o la cancelación de uno existente. Es más, las condiciones de un contrato relativo a un recurso financiero (por ejemplo, el plazo de vencimiento contractual) pueden modificarse por acuerdo entre las partes, en cuyo caso se da por cumplido el primer contrato y se considera que éste ha sido remplazado por otro con condiciones distintas. Todos estos intercambios se deberán incluir en la balanza de pagos.

Transferencias

28. Las transacciones que comprenden *transferencias* difieren de los intercambios porque una de las partes entrega un valor económico a la otra sin recibir un quid pro quo que, según las normas y reglas adoptadas en el sistema, tiene valor económico. Esta ausencia de valor por un lado de la transacción está representado por un asiento denominado *transferencia*. Las transferencias de esta clase (valores económicos suministrados y recibidos sin quid pro quo) se registran en la balanza de pagos. Las **transferencias corrientes** se incluyen en la **cuenta corriente** (véase el capítulo XV), en tanto que las *transferencias de capital* aparecen en la **cuenta de capital** (véase el capítulo XVII).

Migración

29. Como una economía se define en función de las entidades económicas vinculadas a su territorio, su ámbito posiblemente se vea afectado por los cambios que tengan lugar en las entidades vinculadas a ella.

30. Se produce una migración cuando la residencia de una persona se traslada de una economía a otra por haber cambiado su domicilio. Ciertos bienes muebles del emigrante se importan, de hecho, a la nueva economía. Sus bienes inmuebles y ciertos bienes muebles que se encuentran en la economía anterior se transforman en activos de la nueva economía frente a la anterior. Sus activos o pasivos frente a residentes de otra economía distinta de la nueva pasan a ser activos o pasivos sobre el exterior de la nueva economía. Sus activos o pasivos frente a residentes de la nueva economía dejan de ser activos o pasivos de una economía frente al resto del mundo. La suma neta de todas estas variaciones es igual al patrimonio del emigrante, que también debe registrarse como asiento compensatorio, si se registran los demás cambios. Estos asientos se efectúan en la balanza de pagos donde, por norma, se incluyen en las transferencias.

Otras transacciones imputadas

31. En algunos casos, las transacciones pueden ser imputadas y pueden efectuarse asientos en las cuentas de la balanza de pagos cuando no exista un flujo efectivo. Cabe citar como ejemplo la atribución de las utilidades reinvertidas a inversionistas directos extranjeros. Las utilidades de una filial o sucursal extranjera incluyen utilidades atribuibles a un inversionista directo residente. Dichas utilidades, independientemente de que se hayan distribuido o reinvertido en la empresa, son proporcionales a la participación del inversionista directo residente en el capital de la empresa. Las utilidades reinvertidas se registran como parte de la renta de la inversión directa. Se efectúa un asiento compensatorio, con signo contrario, en el rubro inversión directa de la *cuenta financiera* para reflejar el hecho de que aumentó la inversión del inversionista directo extranjero en la filial o sucursal extranjera. (En los capítulos XIV y XVIII se trata el tema de las utilidades reinvertidas.)

Otras variaciones que no entrañan transacciones

Reclasificación de activos y pasivos

32. En este *Manual*, la clasificación de los recursos financieros se basa en características que revelan los motivos del acreedor o del deudor. Si cambian los motivos, varían también dichas características, de modo que los recursos financieros quedan sujetos a reclasificación en función de dichos cambios. Cabe destacar la diferencia que se establece entre la *inversión directa* y otras clases de inversión. Por ejemplo, varios tenedores independientes de *inversiones de cartera* (en forma de acciones y otras participaciones de capital social emitidas por una sola empresa en el extranjero) pueden asociarse para adquirir una participación efectiva duradera en la dirección de la empresa. Sus tenencias reúnen así las condiciones de una *inversión directa* y el cambio de situación de la inversión puede registrarse como reclasificación. Dicha reclasificación se reflejará, al final del período en el que tuvo lugar, en la posición de inversión internacional, pero no en la balanza de pagos. Análogamente, ciertos activos frente a no residentes pueden pasar al control de las autoridades monetarias residentes o quedar fuera de su control, lo cual da lugar a una reclasificación entre *activos de reserva* y activos que no constituyen reservas.

Variaciones de valoración

33. El valor de los recursos reales y financieros está sujeto a constantes cambios, que pueden atribuirse a una de las dos, o a las dos, causas siguientes: i) el precio habitual al que se efectúan transacciones de ciertos tipos de recursos puede variar en relación con la moneda en que se cotiza dicho precio; ii) el tipo de cambio de la moneda en que se cotiza el precio puede variar en relación con la unidad de cuenta utilizada. Las variaciones de valoración no se registran en la balanza de pagos, pero sí en la posición de inversión internacional.

Con excepción de las explicaciones correspondientes a los derechos especiales de giro (DEG), este anexo es congruente con el capítulo VIII del Manual de Balanza de Pagos, 5ª edición. Los párrafos y los números de página citados en este anexo corresponden a los del Manual. Las explicaciones correspondientes a los DEG se han obtenido del MBP6.

Estructura y clasificación

139. En la segunda parte de este *Manual* se definen la estructura y la clasificación de las cuentas de la balanza de pagos y de la posición de inversión internacional. Abarca, asimismo, los componentes normalizados de ambos grupos de cuentas; se examina y explica la forma de preparar la **cuenta corriente**, la **cuenta de capital y financiera**, la información suplementaria seleccionada y la posición de inversión internacional.

140. Las estadísticas de balanza de pagos deben organizarse dentro de una estructura coherente para facilitar su utilización y adaptación para diferentes fines, tales como formulación de la política económica, estudios analíticos, proyecciones, comparaciones bilaterales de componentes específicos o transacciones totales, agregados regionales y mundiales, etc. (Véase el párrafo 7.)

141. La clasificación y la lista de componentes normalizados reflejan consideraciones de índole conceptual y práctica, toman en cuenta opiniones expresadas por expertos nacionales en balanza de pagos y, en general, concuerdan con el *SCN* y con la armonización entre la nueva clasificación de las transacciones internacionales de servicios y la Clasificación Central de Productos (CCP). (Véase el apéndice III.)

142. Se ha hecho todo lo posible para vincular la estructura de la **cuenta financiera** a las cuentas de renta y a la clasificación de la posición de inversión internacional. El objetivo es que muchos países puedan utilizarla como marco flexible para desarrollar a largo plazo sus estadísticas del sector externo. Si bien puede ocurrir que algunos países no puedan proporcionar datos para muchas partidas, este marco permitirá a otros países declarar da-tos adicionales.

Componentes normalizados

143. La determinación de los componentes normalizados (véase la lista al final de este capítulo) depende de una serie de factores, considerándose los más importantes los siguientes:

La partida debe exhibir un comportamiento característico, que indique que influyen en ella un factor o una combinación de factores económicos distintos de los que influyen en las demás partidas o que responde de dife-rente manera ante el mismo factor o combinación de factores. En la balanza de pagos se trata precisamente de poner de manifiesto esta respuesta ante las influencias económicas.

La partida debe ser importante para una serie de países, ya sea en función de su comportamiento (por ejemplo, varia-bilidad excepcional) o de su valor absoluto.

Deberá ser posible obtener los datos estadísticos de la partida sin demasiada dificultad, aunque cabe tener en cuenta la conveniencia de recopilarlos en razón de las dos pri-meras consideraciones citadas.

La partida deberá también ser necesaria para otros fines, por ejemplo, para incluirla en las cuentas nacionales o conciliarla con éstas. La lista de componentes normalizados no debe ser demasiado larga, dado el gran número de países, entre ellos muchos con sistemas estadísticos menos adelantados, a los cuales se solicita que presenten esos datos de manera uniforme.

En la medida en que sea posible, los componentes norma-lizados deberán ser compatibles con otros sistemas estadísticos del FMI, el *SCN* y, en el caso específico de los **servicios**, con la CCP.

144. La presentación de una lista de componentes normalizados no significa que las recomendaciones formuladas en este *Manual* tengan por objeto disuadir a los países de compilar y publicar otros datos de importancia nacional. Si se requieren mayores datos para comprender las circunstancias que rodean a determinados países o para analizar nuevas situaciones que puedan surgir, la información que solicite el FMI a los países miembros no se limitará a la lista de componentes normalizados. La información suplementaria también puede ser sumamente útil para verificar y conciliar las estadísticas de países que comercian entre sí y, por ejemplo, para analizar transacciones de financiamiento excepcional. (Véase el cuadro *Información suplementaria seleccionada* al final de este capítulo.) El personal del FMI consultará periódicamente con los países para decidir qué otros datos deberán presentar.

145. Es probable que sean pocos los países que cuentan con información significativa sobre todos los componentes normalizados. Tal vez los datos sobre varios de los componentes sólo puedan obtenerse en combinación con otros, o quizás un componente de menor importancia esté agrupado con otro más importante. No obstante, los componentes normalizados deberán declararse al FMI de la manera más completa y exacta que sea posible. En este sentido, los compiladores nacionales se encuentran en mejores condiciones que el personal del FMI para estimar y ajustar los componentes que no correspondan exactamente a los datos básicos de la economía declarante.

Errores y omisiones netos

146. Al aplicar los criterios recomendados en este *Manual*, se obtiene un conjunto coherente de asientos con signo positivo y negativo cuyo total neto es teóricamente igual a cero. En la práctica, sin embargo, una vez sumados todos los asientos, la balanza de pagos casi siempre arroja un crédito neto o un débito neto. Este saldo se debe a errores y omisiones en la compilación de las estadísticas, algunos de los cuales pueden tener relación con recomendaciones para una aproximación práctica a los criterios establecidos.

147. Por regla general, en el estado de balanza de pagos se presenta una partida separada de errores y omisiones netos, que algunos compiladores denominan partida equilibradora o discre-pancia estadística, para compensar toda sobrestimación o subestimación de los componentes registrados. Así, si el saldo de estos componentes refleja un crédito, la partida de errores y omisiones netos aparece como un débito de igual valor, y viceversa.

148. Como algunos de los errores y omisiones que se producen al compilar los datos suelen compensarse entre sí, la magnitud de la partida residual no es necesariamente un indicio de la exactitud global del estado. Aun así, cuando el residuo neto es grande, es difícil interpretar un estado.

Clasificaciones principales

149. Los componentes normalizados, cuya lista figura al final de este capítulo, se clasifican en dos grupos principales de cuentas:

La **cuenta corriente**, que comprende *bienes y servicios, renta* y *transferencias corrientes*.

La **cuenta de capital y financiera**, que se refiere a i) *transferencias de capital y adquisición/enajenación de activos no financieros no producidos* y ii) *activos y pasivos financieros*.

Esta presentación general refleja el uso común adoptado en la mayoría de los países en el transcurso de los años y un importante cambio que se introduce en este *Manual*. La cuenta de capital se denomina ahora **cuenta de capital y financiera**. A efectos de mantener la uniformidad con el *SCN*, se hace la distinción entre *transferencias de capital* y **transferencias corrientes** en las cuentas de la balanza de pagos, y se procura la concordancia con la cuenta de capital y la cuenta financiera del *SCN*.

150. Los asientos de la mayoría de las partidas de la lista de componentes normalizados de la **cuenta corriente** deberán mostrar créditos y débitos en cifras brutas. La mayoría de los asientos de la **cuenta de capital y financiera** deberán registrarse en cifras netas, es decir, cada componente se indicará únicamente como un crédito o como un débito. (Los tratamientos recomendados para determinadas partidas y las excepciones se describen en los capítulos correspondientes.) Las entradas de recursos reales, los aumentos de activos financieros y las disminuciones de pasivos deberán aparecer como débitos, en tanto que las salidas de recursos reales, las disminuciones de activos financieros y los aumentos de pasivos deberán figurar como créditos. Las transferencias de las secciones 1.C. y 2.A. deben ser numéricamente iguales, pero con signo contrario, a los asientos que saldan.

Clasificaciones detalladas

151. De acuerdo con los criterios establecidos en el párrafo 143, se han determinado las siguientes clasificaciones de los componentes normalizados. En los

capítulos IX y XVI, respectivamente, se analizan la estructura y las características de la **cuenta corriente** y de la **cuenta de capital y financiera**, mencionándose los cambios significativos con respecto a la cuarta edición. En los capítulos X al XV se describen detalladamente los componentes normalizados de la **cuenta corriente**, y en los capítulos XVII al XXI, los de la **cuenta de capital y financiera** e *Instrumentos financieros derivados: Suplemento a la quinta edición (1993) del* Manual de Balanza de Pagos, 2000.

Cuenta corriente (1.)

152. En la **cuenta corriente** se registran todas las transacciones en valores económicos, salvo recursos financieros, que tienen lugar entre entidades residentes y no residentes; asimismo se re-gistran los asientos compensatorios de los valores económicos co-rrientes que se suministren o adquieran sin un quid pro quo. Con-cretamente, las clasificaciones principales son *bienes y servicios, renta* y *transferencias corrientes*.

Bienes y servicios (1.A.)

Bienes (1.A.a.)

153. *Mercancías generales* comprende la mayoría de los bienes muebles que los residentes exportan a no residentes, o importan de ellos, dando lugar, salvo algunas excepciones especificadas, a un traspaso de propiedad (efectivo o imputado).

154. *Bienes para transformación* comprende la exportación (o importación, en la economía compiladora) de bienes que cruzan la frontera para ser transformados en el extranjero y la reimportación (o exportación, en la economía compiladora) subsiguiente de dichos bienes, valorados en cifras brutas antes y después de su transformación. Esta partida constituye una excepción al criterio de traspaso de propiedad.

155. *Reparaciones de bienes* comprende las reparaciones de bienes efectuadas para no residentes o recibidas de ellos en embarcaciones, aeronaves, etc. Si bien el movimiento físico de estos bienes es similar al descrito en el párrafo 154, las reparaciones deben valorarse según el precio (derechos pagados o recibidos) de las mismas y no según el valor bruto de los bienes antes y después de las reparaciones.

156. *Bienes adquiridos en puerto por medios de transporte* comprende todos los bienes (como combustibles, víveres, pertrechos y suministros) que las empresas residentes/no residentes de transporte —aéreo, marítimo, etc.— adquieren en el extranjero/en la economía compiladora. Esta clasificación no cubre los servicios auxiliares prestados (remolque, mantenimiento, etc.), que se clasifican en la categoría *transportes*.

157. *Oro no monetario* comprende las exportaciones e importaciones de todo el oro que no esté en poder de las autoridades como activo de reserva (oro monetario). El *oro no monetario* se trata como cualquier otra mercancía y se subdivide, toda vez que sea posible, en oro que se mantiene como reserva de valor y oro para otros usos (industrial).

Servicios (1.A.b.)

158. *Transportes* abarca la mayoría de los servicios prestados por residentes a no residentes, y viceversa, que se incluían en las partidas embarques y otros transportes en la cuarta edición del *Manual*. En esta edición se excluye el seguro de fletes, que ahora forma parte de *servicios de seguros*. *Transportes* incluye el transporte de carga y de pasajeros por todos los medios, así como otros servicios de distribución y auxiliares, incluido el arrendamiento de equipo de transporte tripulado, con ciertas excepciones indicadas en los capítulos X, XI y XIII.

159. *Viajes* comprende bienes y servicios —incluidos los relacionados con salud y educación— adquiridos en una economía por viajeros no residentes (incluidos los excursionistas) para fines de negocios y para uso personal durante su estancia (inferior a un año) en esa economía. En *viajes* no se incluyen los servicios de transporte internacional de pasajeros, que forman parte de *transportes*. Los estudiantes y las personas que están bajo tratamiento médico se tratan como viajeros, independientemente de la duración de su estancia, en tanto que otros individuos —personal militar y de embajadas y trabajadores no residentes— no se consideran viajeros. No obstante, los gastos incurridos por los trabajadores no residentes se incluyen en *viajes*, mientras que los del personal militar y de embajadas se incluyen en *servicios del gobierno, n.i.o.p.* Estos casos se tratan en los capítulos XII y XIII.

160. *Servicios de comunicaciones* abarca las transacciones de comunicaciones entre residentes y no residentes, incluidos los servicios postales, de mensajería y de telecomunicaciones (transmisión de sonido, imagen y otra información por diferentes medios, así como el mantenimiento pertinente proporcionado por residentes a no residentes y viceversa).

161. *Servicios de construcción* incluye las obras de proyectos de construcción e instalación realizadas, con carácter temporal, en el extranjero/en la economía compiladora o en enclaves extraterritoriales por empresas residentes/no residentes y su personal. En este concepto no se incluyen las obras realizadas por una filial extranjera de una empresa residente o una oficina local no constituida en sociedad que sea equivalente siempre y cuando satisfaga ciertos criterios a una filial extranjera. En los capítulos IV y XIII se explica lo relativo a la residencia de esta clase de empresas.

162. *Servicios de seguros* comprende la contratación de seguros de no residentes con aseguradoras residentes y viceversa, incluidos los seguros de fletes (de bienes exportados e importados), los servicios correspondientes a otras clases de seguros directos (de vida y otros) y los servicios correspondientes a reaseguros. (En los párrafos 256 y 257 se describe el método que se emplea para calcular el valor de los servicios de seguros.)

163. *Servicios financieros* (salvo los relacionados con las empresas aseguradoras y las cajas de pensiones) abarca los servicios de intermediación financiera y los servicios auxiliares entre residentes y no residentes. Se incluyen las comisiones y derechos relacionados con cartas de crédito, líneas de crédito, arrendamiento financiero, transacciones en divisas, crédito al consumidor y a las empresas, corretaje, colocación y suscripción de valores, instrumentos de coberturas de riesgo de diferentes clases, etc. En los servicios auxiliares se incluyen los servicios de operación y reglamentación de los mercados financieros, servicios de custodia de valores, etc.

164. *Servicios de informática y de información* abarca las transacciones entre residentes y no residentes relacionadas con el asesoramiento en soporte técnico (*hardware*), aplicación de soporte lógico (*software*), servicios de información (procesamiento de datos, bases de datos, agencias noticiosas), y mantenimiento y reparación de computadores y equipo conexo.

165. *Regalías y derechos de licencia* comprende ingresos (exportación) y pagos (importación) de residentes y no residentes por: i) el uso autorizado de activos intangibles no financieros no producidos y derechos de propiedad como marcas registradas, derechos de autor, patentes, procesos, técnicas, diseños, derechos de fabricación, concesiones, etc., y ii) el uso, mediante convenios de licencia, de originales o prototipos producidos, como manuscritos, películas, etc.

166. *Otros servicios empresariales* prestados por residentes a no residentes y viceversa se refiere a servicios de compraventa y otros servicios relacionados con el comercio, servicios de arrendamiento de explotación y servicios empresariales, profesionales y técnicos varios. (Para información más detallada, véase el cuadro *Información suplementaria seleccionada* al final de este capítulo y los párrafos 261 a 264.)

167. *Servicios personales, culturales y recreativos* abarca i) servicios audiovisuales y conexos y ii) otros servicios culturales prestados por residentes a no residentes y viceversa. En el inciso i) se incluyen servicios relacionados con la producción de películas cinematográficas o videocintas, programas de radio y televisión y grabaciones musicales. (Ejemplos de estos servicios son los alquileres y honorarios percibidos por artistas, productores, etc. por sus producciones y por la venta de derechos de distribución a los medios de comunicación.) En el inciso ii) se incluyen otros servicios personales, culturales y recreativos, como los relacionados con bibliotecas, museos y otras actividades culturales y deportivas.

168. *Servicios del gobierno, n.i.o.p.* incluye todos los servicios (como los gastos incurridos por embajadas y consulados) relacionados con sectores gubernamentales u organismos internacionales y regionales y no clasificados en otras partidas.

Renta (1.B.)

169. *Remuneración de empleados* abarca los salarios, sueldos y otras prestaciones, en efectivo o en especie, incluidos los de los trabajadores fronterizos, de temporada y otros no residentes (por ejemplo, personal local de embajadas).

170. *Renta de la inversión* comprende los ingresos y pagos de la renta derivados, respectivamente, de las tenencias de activos financieros de residentes frente al exterior y de pasivos frente a no residentes, y se divide en renta de la inversión directa, renta de la inversión de cartera y renta de otra inversión. El componente inversión directa se desglosa en renta procedente de acciones y otras participaciones de capital (dividendos, utilidades de sucursales y utilidades reinvertidas) y en renta procedente de la deuda (intereses); la renta de la inversión de cartera se desglosa también en renta procedente de acciones y otras participaciones de capital (dividendos) y renta procedente de la deuda (intereses); en renta de otra inversión se registran los intereses devengados por otra inversión (préstamos, etc.) y, en principio, la renta imputada a las unidades familiares procedente de su parti-cipación neta de capital en las reservas de los seguros de vida y en las cajas de pensiones.

Transferencias corrientes (1.C.)

171. Las **transferencias corrientes** se distinguen de las *transfe-rencias de capital*, que se incluyen en la **cuenta de capital y financiera** para guardar la uniformidad con el tratamiento de las transferencias que hace el *SCN*. Las transferencias son los asientos compensatorios de los traspasos de propiedad de recursos reales o financieros entre residentes y no residentes, ya sea en forma voluntaria u obligatoria, que no entrañan un quid pro quo en valor económico. Las **transferencias corrientes** comprenden todas aquellas en las que **no tiene lugar**: i) un **traspaso** de propiedad de activos fijos; ii) un traspaso de fondos vinculados o condicionados a la adquisición o enajenación de activos fijos; iii) una condonación de un pasivo por parte de un acreedor, sin que se reciba a cambio una contrapartida. Todas éstas son *transferencias de capital*. En las **transferencias corrientes** se distinguen las del gobierno general (por ejemplo, cooperación internacional corriente entre diferentes go-biernos, pagos de impuestos corrientes sobre la renta y el patrimonio, etc.) y otras transferencias (por ejemplo, remesas de trabajadores, primas —menos cargos por servicio— e indemnizaciones de seguros excepto los de vida). En el capítulo XV se examina en forma detallada la distinción entre **transferencias corrientes** y *transferencias de capital*; véanse también los párrafos 175 y 344.

Cuenta de capital y financiera (2.)

172. Esta cuenta tiene dos componentes principales —la **cuenta de capital** y la **cuenta financiera**— coincidiendo así con la clasificación adoptada en el *SCN*. Los activos representan créditos frente a no residentes y los pasivos representan deudas contraídas con no residentes. Las dos partes de una transacción de activos o pasivos son, generalmente, un residente y un no residente pero, en algunos casos, ambas partes pueden ser residentes o bien no residentes. (Véase el párrafo 318.)

173. Todas las variaciones de valoración y de otra índole de los activos y pasivos frente al exterior que no reflejen transacciones (véase el párrafo 310) se excluyen de la **cuenta de capital y financiera** pero figuran en la posición de inversión internacional. Los estados suplementarios identifican ciertas partidas que tienen interés analítico y que afectan a varias cuentas, como los pasivos que constituyen reservas de autoridades extranjeras y las transacciones de financiamiento excepcional, que se describen en el capítulo XXII.

174. La clasificación de la **cuenta financiera** y de los componentes de renta de la **cuenta corriente** están interrelacionadas y deben ser coherentes para facilitar el análisis, permitir una vinculación eficaz de la balanza de pagos con la posición de inversión internacional y mantener la compatibilidad con el *SCN* y con otros sistemas estadísticos del FMI.

Cuenta de capital (2.A.)

175. Los componentes principales de la **cuenta de capital** son las *transferencias de capital* y la *adquisición/enajenación de activos no financieros no producidos*. Las *transferencias de capital* son aquéllas en las que tiene lugar un traspaso de propiedad de un activo fijo, un traspaso de fondos vinculado o condicionado a la adquisición o enajenación de un activo fijo, o la cancelación de un pasivo por parte de un acreedor sin que se reciba a cambio una contrapartida. Las *transferencias de capital* se dividen en: i) las del gobierno general, que a su vez se subdividen en condonación de deudas y otras y ii) las de otros sectores, haciéndose el desglose en transferencias de emigrantes, condonación de deudas y otras. (Véase el capítulo XV, donde se explica la diferencia entre las *transferencias de capital* y las **transferencias corrientes**.) La *adquisición/enajenación de activos no financieros no producidos* abarca, en general, los factores intangibles, como las patentes, arrendamientos u otros contratos transferibles, el buen nombre, etc. En esta partida no se incluyen las tierras situadas en un territorio económico específico, pero puede incluirse la compra o venta de tierras por una embajada. (Véase el párrafo 312.)

Cuenta financiera (2.B.)

176. La clasificación de los componentes normalizados de la cuenta financiera se basa en los siguientes criterios:

Todos los componentes se clasifican según la clase de inversión o haciéndose un desglose funcional (*inversión directa, inversión de cartera, instrumentos financieros derivados, otra inversión, activos de reserva*).

Para la categoría *inversión directa*, se hace la distinción según la dirección (en el extranjero o en la economía declarante); para los componentes acciones y otras participaciones de capital, otro capital.

En *inversión de cartera, instrumentos financieros derivados* y *otra inversión* se hace la distinción habitual entre activos y pasivos.

Cobra particular importancia en *inversión de cartera* y *otra inversión* la distinción por clases de instrumentos (títulos de participación en el capital, títulos de deuda, créditos comerciales, préstamos, moneda y depósitos, otros activos o pasivos). En este *Manual*, se incluyen en *inversión de cartera* los instrumentos tradicionales y nuevos del mercado monetario y otros instrumentos financieros básicos.

La distinción tradicional entre activos y pasivos a largo y a corto plazo, basada en un plazo contractual original de más de un año o de un año o menos, se efectúa solamente en *otra inversión*. En los últimos años, este desglose ha perdido importancia para muchas transacciones internas e internacionales. En consecuencia, tanto en el *SCN* como en este *Manual*, se da menos importancia a la diferencia entre largo y corto plazo que en ediciones previas. Sin embargo, debido a que el vencimiento sigue siendo importante para fines específicos —el análisis de la deuda externa, por ejemplo—, esta distinción se mantiene en el *Manual* para *otra inversión*.

177. *Inversión directa*, categoría que refleja el interés duradero de una entidad residente de una economía (inversionista directo) en una entidad residente de otra economía (empresa de inversión directa), abarca todas las transacciones entre inversionistas directos y empresas de inversión directa. Es decir, la *inversión directa* abarca la transacción inicial entre las dos partes y todas las transacciones subsiguientes que tienen lugar entre ellas y entre empresas filiales, constituidas o no en sociedad. Las transacciones de inversión directa (en el extranjero y en la economía declarante) se subclasifican en acciones y otras participaciones de capital, utilidades reinvertidas y otro capital (transacciones entre empresas afiliadas). En el caso de las acciones y otras participaciones de capital y otro capital, se hace la distinción entre activos y pasivos frente a empresas filiales y frente a inversionistas directos. Las transacciones entre bancos filiales y entre otros intermediarios financieros filiales se limitan al capital en acciones y al que está relacionado con la deuda permanente. (Véase el párrafo 372 de la quinta edición del *Manual de Balanza de Pagos*.)

178. *Inversión de cartera* comprende las transacciones en títulos de participación en el capital y títulos de deuda. Los títulos de deuda están subdivididos en bonos y pagarés e instrumentos del mercado monetario. Se incluyen, asimismo, varios instrumentos financieros nuevos, además de los derivados financieros, en las clasificaciones de instrumentos pertinentes.(Se excluyen las transacciones clasificadas como *inversión directa* y *activos de reserva*.)

179. La categoría de instrumentos financieros derivados abarca los instrumentos financieros vinculados a otros instrumentos financieros específicos o indicadores o productos primarios, a través de los cuales pueden negociarse en los mercados financieros, por derecho propio, riesgos financieros específicos (como riesgos de variaciones de tasas de interés, riesgo cambiario, riesgos de variaciones de las cotizaciones bursátiles y de los precios de los productos primarios, riesgo de crédito, etc.). Las transacciones de instrumentos financieros derivados deberán tratarse por separado y no como parte integral del valor de las transacciones a las que estén vinculadas.

180. *Otra inversión* incluye créditos comerciales a corto y largo plazo; préstamos (entre ellos, el uso de crédito del FMI, préstamos del FMI y préstamos relacionados con arrendamientos financieros); moneda y depósitos (transferibles y otros, como depósitos de ahorro y a plazo, acciones de asociaciones de ahorro y préstamo, acciones de cooperativas de crédito, etc.); y otros activos y pasivos (incluidas asignaciones de DEG). (Se excluyen las transacciones clasificadas como *inversión directa*.)

181. *Activos de reserva* comprende las transacciones de aque-llos activos que las autoridades monetarias de una economía consideran disponibles para atender necesidades de financiamiento de la balanza de pagos y, en algunos casos, otras necesidades. Tal disponibilidad, en principio, no guarda estrecha relación con criterios formales tales como los de propiedad o moneda de denominación. Esta categoría se divide en oro monetario, DEG, posición de reserva en el FMI, activos en divisas (moneda, depósitos y va-lores) y otros activos.

182. La cobertura e identificación de los componentes de los *activos de reserva* están relacionadas con un concepto analítico, son en parte resultado de una decisión razonada y no siempre se prestan a la aplicación de criterios objetivos y formales ni a clasificaciones bien delimitadas respecto a la condicionalidad y otras consideraciones. A diferencia de la cuarta edición del *Manual*, en la quinta edición se excluyen las variaciones de valoración de los *activos de reserva* y sus contrapartidas. Los datos en este volumen incluyen las asignaciones de DEG y los asientos de contrapartida. Estas variaciones figuran en la posición de inversión internacional.

COUNTRY TABLES

Table 1. ANALYTIC PRESENTATION, 2003–2010

(Millions of U.S. dollars)

	Code	2003	2004	2005	2006	2007	2008	2009	2010
A. Current Account[1]	4 993 Z.	−406.8	−357.9	−571.5	−670.9	−1,150.8	−2,018.7	−1,838.0	−1,403.9
Goods: exports f.o.b.	2 100 ..	447.2	603.3	656.3	792.9	1,078.7	1,355.6	1,048.0	1,547.9
Goods: imports f.o.b.	3 100 ..	−1,783.5	−2,194.9	−2,477.6	−2,915.6	−3,978.3	−4,907.4	−4,264.1	−4,305.3
Balance on Goods	4 100 ..	*−1,336.3*	*−1,591.6*	*−1,821.3*	*−2,122.7*	*−2,899.6*	*−3,551.7*	*−3,216.1*	*−2,757.5*
Services: credit	2 200 ..	719.7	1,003.5	1,164.6	1,504.0	1,945.9	2,478.2	2,482.8	2,243.2
Services: debit	3 200 ..	−802.6	−1,054.8	−1,382.9	−1,584.8	−1,926.0	−2,379.4	−2,231.2	−2,010.3
Balance on Goods and Services	4 991 ..	*−1,419.2*	*−1,642.9*	*−2,039.6*	*−2,203.5*	*−2,879.7*	*−3,452.9*	*−2,964.6*	*−2,524.6*
Income: credit	2 300 ..	194.8	203.7	226.7	332.1	382.4	473.0	377.2	377.6
Income: debit	3 300 ..	−24.4	−28.3	−52.6	−69.1	−85.1	−418.1	−557.5	−478.7
Balance on Goods, Services, and Income	4 992 ..	*−1,248.8*	*−1,467.5*	*−1,865.5*	*−1,940.5*	*−2,582.4*	*−3,398.1*	*−3,144.9*	*−2,625.7*
Current transfers: credit	2 379 Z.	924.2	1,200.2	1,519.2	1,426.3	1,673.6	1,643.2	1,528.1	1,426.3
Current transfers: debit	3 379 ..	−82.3	−90.6	−225.1	−156.7	−242.0	−263.8	−221.2	−204.5
B. Capital Account[1]	4 994 Z.	**157.0**	**132.4**	**122.9**	**179.8**	**123.6**	**115.3**	**118.7**	**112.3**
Capital account: credit	2 994 Z.	157.0	132.4	122.9	179.8	123.6	195.5	213.6	210.3
Capital account: debit	3 994 ..	....	....	....	....	....	−80.1	−94.9	−98.0
Total, Groups A Plus B	4 981 ..	*−249.9*	*−225.5*	*−448.6*	*−491.1*	*−1,027.2*	*−1,903.3*	*−1,719.3*	*−1,291.7*
C. Financial Account[1]	4 995 W.	**200.6**	**396.3**	**392.6**	**523.4**	**857.8**	**1,493.7**	**662.8**	**816.4**
Direct investment abroad	4 505 ..	....	−13.6	−4.1	−10.6	−14.9	−84.2	−39.2	−.2
Direct investment in Albania	4 555 Z.	178.0	341.3	262.5	325.3	662.3	958.7	963.7	1,109.6
Portfolio investment assets	4 602 ..	−22.5	−3.6	−5.7	34.2	25.8	−83.5	18.7	−118.4
Equity securities	4 610 ..	....	....	....	....	....	....	.6	
Debt securities	4 619 ..	−22.5	−3.6	−5.7	34.2	25.8	−83.5	18.1	−118.4
Portfolio investment liabilities	4 652 Z.	....	....	....	....	....	45.7	8.5	421.0
Equity securities	4 660 ..	....	....	....	....	....	23.3	2.6	7.9
Debt securities	4 669 Z.	....	....	....	....	....	22.4	5.9	413.1
Financial derivatives	4 910 ..	....	....	....	....	....	....	....	....
Financial derivatives assets	4 900 ..	....	....	....	....	....	....	....	....
Financial derivatives liabilities	4 905 ..	....	....	....	....	....	....	....	....
Other investment assets	4 703 ..	−71.6	−113.8	6.6	−210.7	−88.1	286.8	62.1	−212.6
Monetary authorities	4 701 ..	.3	....	....	−.6	−6.0	7.8	−9.1	....
General government	4 704 ..	....	....	....	....	....	....	....	....
Banks	4 705 ..	−45.3	−112.1	8.5	−212.5	−78.2	283.6	74.6	−203.8
Other sectors	4 728 ..	−26.7	−1.7	−1.9	2.4	−3.9	−4.6	−3.5	−8.8
Other investment liabilities	4 753 W.	116.7	186.1	133.2	385.2	272.8	370.3	−351.0	−383.0
Monetary authorities	4 753 WA	−1.0	−1.2	−1.5	−1.3	−.9	−.3	72.3	−.3
General government	4 753 ZB	96.6	106.4	50.4	51.9	−44.0	−49.7	−60.5	−323.9
Banks	4 753 ZC	19.8	.3	20.7	244.1	311.7	442.8	−329.3	−24.3
Other sectors	4 753 ZD	1.4	80.6	63.6	90.5	5.9	−22.5	−33.5	−34.5
Total, Groups A Through C	4 983 ..	*−49.2*	*170.8*	*−56.0*	*32.2*	*−169.3*	*−409.6*	*−1,056.5*	*−475.3*
D. Net Errors and Omissions	4 998 ..	**147.4**	**115.3**	**203.8**	**237.0**	**189.0**	**14.2**	**415.8**	**411.0**
Total, Groups A Through D	4 984 ..	*98.1*	*286.1*	*147.8*	*269.2*	*19.7*	*−395.4*	*−640.7*	*−64.3*
E. Reserves and Related Items	4 802 A.	**−98.1**	**−286.1**	**−147.8**	**−269.2**	**−19.7**	**395.4**	**640.7**	**64.3**
Reserve assets	4 802 ..	−99.6	−288.4	−150.7	−265.1	−202.3	−262.1	34.4	−236.3
Use of Fund credit and loans	4 766 ..	1.5	2.4	3.0	−4.1	−7.0	−7.4	−10.3	−12.3
Exceptional financing	4 920 ..	....	....	....	....	189.7	664.9	616.6	312.9
Conversion rates: leks per U.S. dollar	0 101 ..	**121.86**	**102.78**	**99.87**	**98.10**	**90.43**	**83.89**	**94.98**	**103.94**

[1] Excludes components that have been classified in the categories of Group E.

Table 2. STANDARD PRESENTATION, 2003–2010

(Millions of U.S. dollars)

	Code	2003	2004	2005	2006	2007	2008	2009	2010
CURRENT ACCOUNT..	4 993 ..	**−406.8**	**−357.9**	**−571.5**	**−670.9**	**−1,150.8**	**−2,018.7**	**−1,838.0**	**−1,403.9**
A. GOODS...	4 100 ..	**−1,336.3**	**−1,591.6**	**−1,821.3**	**−2,122.7**	**−2,899.6**	**−3,551.7**	**−3,216.1**	**−2,757.5**
Credit..	2 100 ..	**447.2**	**603.3**	**656.3**	**792.9**	**1,078.7**	**1,355.6**	**1,048.0**	**1,547.9**
General merchandise: exports f.o.b.................	2 110 ..	100.7	149.0	194.1	233.1	359.5	542.9	398.5	720.8
Goods for processing: exports f.o.b..............	2 150 ..	346.5	454.3	462.2	559.8	719.3	812.7	649.6	827.1
Repairs on goods..	2 160 ..	....	....	....	....	....	....	....	....
Goods procured in ports by carriers...............	2 170 ..	....	....	....	....	....	....	....	....
Nonmonetary gold...	2 180 ..	....	....	....	....	....	....	....	....
Debit..	3 100 ..	**−1,783.5**	**−2,194.9**	**−2,477.6**	**−2,915.6**	**−3,978.3**	**−4,907.4**	**−4,264.1**	**−4,305.3**
General merchandise: imports f.o.b................	3 110 ..	−1,463.3	−1,837.9	−2,117.5	−2,499.8	−3,419.7	−4,359.2	−3,793.0	−3,775.1
Goods for processing: imports f.o.b..............	3 150 ..	−320.1	−357.0	−360.1	−415.8	−558.6	−548.2	−471.2	−530.3
Repairs on goods..	3 160 ..	....	....	....	....	....	....	....	....
Goods procured in ports by carriers...............	3 170 ..	....	....	....	....	....	....	....	....
Nonmonetary gold...	3 180 ..	....	....	....	....	....	....	....	....
B. SERVICES..	4 200 ..	**−82.9**	**−51.4**	**−218.3**	**−80.8**	**19.9**	**98.8**	**251.5**	**232.9**
Total credit..	2 200 ..	*719.7*	*1,003.5*	*1,164.6*	*1,504.0*	*1,945.9*	*2,478.2*	*2,482.8*	*2,243.2*
Total debit..	3 200 ..	*−802.6*	*−1,054.8*	*−1,382.9*	*−1,584.8*	*−1,926.0*	*−2,379.4*	*−2,231.2*	*−2,010.3*
Transportation services, credit................	2 205 ..	**68.8**	**98.2**	**126.1**	**163.2**	**158.2**	**211.7**	**257.9**	**248.6**
Passenger...	2 850 ..	*15.4*	*21.1*	*26.4*	*44.5*	*101.0*	*135.1*	*184.9*	*166.7*
Freight...	2 851 ..	*51.8*	*64.8*	*72.7*	*86.0*	*56.5*	*75.6*	*63.7*	*80.9*
Other..	2 852 ..	*1.6*	*12.2*	*27.0*	*32.7*	*.8*	*1.0*	*9.3*	*1.1*
Sea transport, passenger...............................	2 207 ..	6.1	8.5	10.6	17.8	16.7	22.4	28.0	32.9
Sea transport, freight.....................................	2 208 ..	46.6	58.4	65.4	77.4	34.2	45.8	38.0	46.2
Sea transport, other.......................................	2 209 ..	.8	6.1	13.5	16.4	.3	.4	4.0	.5
Air transport, passenger.................................	2 211 ..	9.2	12.7	15.8	26.7	82.0	109.7	155.1	133.4
Air transport, freight......................................	2 212 ..	5.2	6.5	7.3	8.6	1.7	2.3	2.3	3.4
Air transport, other..	2 213 ..	.8	6.1	13.5	16.4	.1	.2	4.1	.3
Other transport, passenger............................	2 215 ..	....	....	....	....	2.2	3.0	1.9	.4
Other transport, freight..................................	2 216 ..	....	....	....	....	20.5	27.5	23.3	31.2
Other transport, other....................................	2 217 ..	....	....	....	....	.3	.4	1.1	.3
Transportation services, debit................	3 205 ..	**−156.3**	**−204.1**	**−226.6**	**−250.0**	**−245.8**	**−349.7**	**−325.5**	**−316.0**
Passenger...	3 850 ..	*−18.2*	*−26.5*	*−21.5*	*−24.1*	*−62.6*	*−89.1*	*−106.5*	*−92.2*
Freight...	3 851 ..	*−124.4*	*−154.6*	*−173.8*	*−205.1*	*−175.1*	*−249.2*	*−213.7*	*−216.7*
Other..	3 852 ..	*−13.8*	*−23.0*	*−31.2*	*−20.8*	*−8.1*	*−11.5*	*−5.2*	*−7.0*
Sea transport, passenger...............................	3 207 ..	−7.3	−10.6	−8.6	−9.7	−20.8	−29.6	−22.0	−21.4
Sea transport, freight.....................................	3 208 ..	−111.9	−139.1	−156.4	−184.6	−106.0	−150.8	−127.5	−123.6
Sea transport, other.......................................	3 209 ..	−6.9	−11.5	−15.6	−10.4	−3.5	−5.0	−3.3	−4.8
Air transport, passenger.................................	3 211 ..	−10.9	−15.9	−12.9	−14.5	−40.0	−57.0	−84.2	−70.0
Air transport, freight......................................	3 212 ..	−12.4	−15.5	−17.4	−20.5	−5.4	−7.6	−7.7	−9.2
Air transport, other..	3 213 ..	−6.9	−11.5	−15.6	−10.4	−3.1	−4.4	−.9	−.7
Other transport, passenger............................	3 215 ..	....	....	....	....	−1.7	−2.5	−.3	−.8
Other transport, freight..................................	3 216 ..	....	....	....	....	−63.8	−90.8	−78.6	−83.9
Other transport, other....................................	3 217 ..	....	....	....	....	−1.4	−2.0	−1.0	−1.6
Travel, credit..	2 236 ..	**522.1**	**735.3**	**853.9**	**1,012.1**	**1,378.3**	**1,713.5**	**1,827.4**	**1,612.8**
Business travel..	2 237 ..	212.4	332.4	211.5	233.9	251.6	320.6	416.9	330.3
Personal travel..	2 240 ..	309.7	402.9	642.4	778.2	1,126.7	1,392.9	1,410.5	1,282.5
Travel, debit...	3 236 ..	**−489.1**	**−641.5**	**−786.1**	**−964.6**	**−1,268.1**	**−1,555.1**	**−1,584.6**	**−1,361.5**
Business travel..	3 237 ..	−170.8	−217.9	−167.9	−191.8	−325.4	−278.5	−412.1	−485.2
Personal travel..	3 240 ..	−318.2	−423.6	−618.3	−772.8	−942.6	−1,276.5	−1,172.5	−876.4
Other services, credit.............................	2 200 BA ..	**128.8**	**169.9**	**184.6**	**328.6**	**409.3**	**553.0**	**397.5**	**381.8**
Communications...	2 245 ..	48.1	75.1	71.4	52.8	67.9	149.8	148.6	101.8
Construction...	2 249 ..	3.3	3.4	2.7	2.3	7.8	24.5	37.7	32.5
Insurance..	2 253 ..	3.1	6.5	5.7	3.6	6.9	5.3	3.8	1.7
Financial...	2 260 ..	20.6	10.9	16.0	25.8	42.5	69.2	20.0	2.9
Computer and information..............................	2 262 ..	1.2	.6	3.1	1.3	2.8	19.1	17.4	5.5
Royalties and licence fees..............................	2 266 ..	5.3	15.4	.5	.7	7.5	39.2	17.1	.7
Other business services..................................	2 268 ..	17.5	43.9	56.6	161.0	184.4	174.1	66.1	146.7
Personal, cultural, and recreational................	2 287 ..	4.5	7.8	18.1	58.3	67.5	13.4	17.6	38.5
Government, n.i.e..	2 291 ..	25.1	6.3	10.4	22.9	22.0	58.4	69.2	51.5
Other services, debit..............................	3 200 BA ..	**−157.3**	**−209.2**	**−370.2**	**−370.2**	**−412.2**	**−474.6**	**−321.1**	**−332.8**
Communications...	3 245 ..	−21.2	−20.9	−14.6	−7.4	−5.9	−80.1	−48.9	−45.1
Construction...	3 249 ..	−1.8	−.7	−1.6	−2.0	−28.6	−5.6	−18.8	−8.5
Insurance..	3 253 ..	−21.1	−26.1	−30.5	−35.9	−65.5	−120.0	−84.6	−78.7
Financial...	3 260 ..	−5.3	−5.4	−17.4	−20.2	−25.2	−30.0	−23.2	−15.6
Computer and information..............................	3 262 ..	−1.8	−1.6	−3.4	−3.4	−15.2	−23.2	−10.0	−9.0
Royalties and licence fees..............................	3 266 ..	−8.4	−4.9	−4.2	−6.8	−11.9	−12.4	−14.4	−12.2
Other business services..................................	3 268 ..	−20.9	−55.7	−129.2	−149.0	−157.4	−145.0	−67.9	−104.3
Personal, cultural, and recreational................	3 287 ..	−8.2	−30.4	−104.0	−112.9	−70.1	−39.9	−36.6	−41.1
Government, n.i.e..	3 291 ..	−68.6	−63.4	−65.2	−32.6	−32.6	−18.4	−16.7	−18.2

Table 2 (Continued). STANDARD PRESENTATION, 2003–2010

(Millions of U.S. dollars)

	Code	2003	2004	2005	2006	2007	2008	2009	2010
C. INCOME	4 300	**170.4**	**175.4**	**174.1**	**263.0**	**297.3**	**54.9**	**−180.4**	**−101.1**
Total credit	2 300	*194.8*	*203.7*	*226.7*	*332.1*	*382.4*	*473.0*	*377.2*	*377.6*
Total debit	3 300	*−24.4*	*−28.3*	*−52.6*	*−69.1*	*−85.1*	*−418.1*	*−557.5*	*−478.7*
Compensation of employees, credit	2 310	**110.6**	**132.3**	**129.0**	**183.9**	**163.5**	**269.5**	**227.1**	**231.7**
Compensation of employees, debit	3 310	**−4.1**	**−4.9**	**−6.5**	**−26.5**	**−9.9**	**−15.9**	**−8.6**	**−15.3**
Investment income, credit	2 320	**84.1**	**71.4**	**97.7**	**148.2**	**219.0**	**203.5**	**150.1**	**145.9**
Direct investment income	2 330	....	....	.4	13.3	18.8	35.6	45.2	18.1
Dividends and distributed branch profits	2 332	....	....	.4	13.3	18.8	4.1	25.9	14.7
Reinvested earnings and undistributed branch profits	2 333	....	....	....	....	....	31.4	10.7	−.6
Income on debt (interest)	2 334	....	....	....	....	....	.1	8.7	4.0
Portfolio investment income	2 339	31.2	25.8	37.0	51.4	88.5	35.5	20.5	47.3
Income on equity	2 340	....	....	7.9	22.4	18.8	21.6	.4	.2
Income on bonds and notes	2 350	31.2	25.8	29.2	29.0	69.8	13.9	20.1	40.2
Income on money market instruments	2 360	....	....	....	....	....	....	....	6.9
Other investment income	2 370	53.0	45.7	60.2	83.6	111.7	132.4	84.4	80.5
Investment income, debit	3 320	**−20.2**	**−23.5**	**−46.1**	**−42.6**	**−75.2**	**−402.2**	**−548.9**	**−463.5**
Direct investment income	3 330	−1.0	−.2	−2.1	−4.6	−8.6	−301.2	−435.8	−362.3
Dividends and distributed branch profits	3 332	−1.0	−.2	−2.1	−4.6	−8.6	−13.9	−127.4	−109.7
Reinvested earnings and undistributed branch profits	3 333	....	....	....	....	....	−278.8	−307.6	−241.9
Income on debt (interest)	3 334	....	....	....	....	....	−8.5	−.9	−10.7
Portfolio investment income	3 339	....	....	−11.3	−1.9	−8.6	−5.8	−4.6	−7.9
Income on equity	3 340	....	....	−10.8	−1.2	−8.6	−5.6	−2.9	−4.4
Income on bonds and notes	3 350	....	....	−.4	−.8	....	....	−.1	....
Income on money market instruments	3 360	....	....	....	....	....	−.2	−1.6	−3.5
Other investment income	3 370	−19.3	−23.3	−32.7	−36.1	−58.1	−95.2	−108.6	−93.3
D. CURRENT TRANSFERS	4 379	**841.9**	**1,109.6**	**1,294.0**	**1,269.6**	**1,431.6**	**1,379.4**	**1,306.9**	**1,221.8**
Credit	2 379	**924.2**	**1,200.2**	**1,519.2**	**1,426.3**	**1,673.6**	**1,643.2**	**1,528.1**	**1,426.3**
General government	2 380	61.1	75.7	80.2	62.3	82.9	46.1	37.9	68.4
Other sectors	2 390	863.1	1,124.5	1,439.0	1,364.1	1,590.7	1,597.1	1,490.3	1,357.9
Workers' remittances	2 391	778.1	1,028.3	1,160.7	1,175.6	1,304.6	1,225.6	1,090.4	924.3
Other current transfers	2 392	85.0	96.1	278.3	188.5	286.1	371.5	399.9	433.6
Debit	3 379	**−82.3**	**−90.6**	**−225.1**	**−156.7**	**−242.0**	**−263.8**	**−221.2**	**−204.5**
General government	3 380	−.9	....	−4.7	−9.5	−.6	....	....	−10.2
Other sectors	3 390	−81.4	−90.6	−220.5	−147.3	−241.4	−263.8	−221.2	−194.3
Workers' remittances	3 391	....	....	....	....	....	....	−1.4	−8.9
Other current transfers	3 392	−81.4	−90.6	−220.5	−147.2	−241.4	−263.8	−219.8	−185.4
CAPITAL AND FINANCIAL ACCOUNT	4 996	**259.5**	**242.6**	**367.7**	**433.9**	**961.8**	**2,004.4**	**1,422.3**	**992.9**
CAPITAL ACCOUNT	4 994	**157.0**	**132.4**	**122.9**	**179.8**	**123.6**	**115.3**	**118.7**	**112.3**
Total credit	2 994	*157.0*	*132.4*	*122.9*	*179.8*	*123.6*	*195.5*	*213.6*	*210.3*
Total debit	3 994	....	....	....	....	....	*−80.1*	*−94.9*	*−98.0*
Capital transfers, credit	2 400	**157.0**	**132.4**	**122.9**	**179.8**	**123.6**	**195.5**	**213.6**	**210.3**
General government	2 401	157.0	132.4	122.9	179.8	46.7	42.6	45.1	29.8
Debt forgiveness	2 402	....	....	....	....	....	....	....	....
Other capital transfers	2 410	157.0	132.4	122.9	179.8	46.7	42.6	45.1	29.8
Other sectors	2 430	....	....	....	....	77.0	152.8	168.5	180.5
Migrants' transfers	2 431	....	....	....	....	....	....	....	....
Debt forgiveness	2 432	....	....	....	....	....	....	....	....
Other capital transfers	2 440	....	....	....	....	77.0	152.8	168.5	180.5
Capital transfers, debit	3 400	....	....	....	....	....	**−80.1**	**−94.9**	**−98.0**
General government	3 401	....	....	....	....	....	−5.8	−1.2	−.3
Debt forgiveness	3 402	....	....	....	....	....	....	....	....
Other capital transfers	3 410	....	....	....	....	....	−5.8	−1.2	−.3
Other sectors	3 430	....	....	....	....	....	−74.3	−93.7	−97.7
Migrants' transfers	3 431	....	....	....	....	....	....	....	....
Debt forgiveness	3 432	....	....	....	....	....	....	....	....
Other capital transfers	3 440	....	....	....	....	....	−74.3	−93.7	−97.7
Nonproduced nonfinancial assets, credit	2 480	....	....	....	....	....	....	....	....
Nonproduced nonfinancial assets, debit	3 480	....	....	....	....	....	....	....	....

Table 2 (Continued). STANDARD PRESENTATION, 2003–2010

(Millions of U.S. dollars)

	Code	2003	2004	2005	2006	2007	2008	2009	2010
FINANCIAL ACCOUNT..........................	4 995 ..	**102.5**	**110.2**	**244.8**	**254.1**	**838.2**	**1,889.1**	**1,303.5**	**880.7**
A. DIRECT INVESTMENT......................	4 500 ..	**178.0**	**327.7**	**258.4**	**314.6**	**647.4**	**874.5**	**924.5**	**1,109.4**
Direct investment abroad.................	4 505 ..	....	**–13.6**	**–4.1**	**–10.6**	**–14.9**	**–84.2**	**–39.2**	**–.2**
Equity capital............................	4 510 ..	....	–13.6	–4.1	–10.6	–14.7	–50.1	–25.8	2.0
Claims on affiliated enterprises..........	4 515 ..	....	–13.6	–4.1	–10.5	–4.9	–51.1	–26.3	–6.9
Liabilities to affiliated enterprises......	4 520 ..	....	....	....	–.1	–9.8	1.0	.5	8.9
Reinvested earnings......................	4 525 ..	....	....	....	....	....	–31.4	–10.7	.6
Other capital............................	4 530 ..	....	....	....	....	–.2	–2.7	–2.7	–2.8
Claims on affiliated enterprises..........	4 535 ..	....	....	....	....	....	–2.7	–3.3	–3.7
Liabilities to affiliated enterprises......	4 540 ..	....	....	....	....	–.2	....	.6	.9
Direct investment in Albania..............	4 555 ..	**178.0**	**341.3**	**262.5**	**325.3**	**662.3**	**958.7**	**963.7**	**1,109.6**
Equity capital............................	4 560 ..	178.0	341.3	262.5	75.8	470.1	590.3	703.2	863.2
Claims on direct investors................	4 565 ..	....	....	....	....	....	–11.5	–2.2	–81.3
Liabilities to direct investors............	4 570 ..	178.0	341.3	262.5	75.8	470.1	601.8	705.5	944.5
Reinvested earnings......................	4 575 ..	....	....	....	....	....	278.8	307.6	241.9
Other capital............................	4 580 ..	....	....	....	249.5	192.2	89.6	–47.1	4.5
Claims on direct investors................	4 585 ..	....	....	....	....	....	–270.1	–192.8	–69.8
Liabilities to direct investors............	4 590 ..	....	....	....	249.5	192.2	359.7	145.6	74.2
B. PORTFOLIO INVESTMENT...................	4 600 ..	**–22.5**	**–3.6**	**–5.7**	**34.2**	**25.8**	**–37.9**	**27.3**	**302.6**
Assets...................................	4 602 ..	**–22.5**	**–3.6**	**–5.7**	**34.2**	**25.8**	**–83.5**	**18.7**	**–118.4**
Equity securities........................	4 610 ..	....	....	....	....	....	....	.6	....
Monetary authorities.....................	4 611 ..	....	....	....	....	....	....	....	....
General government......................	4 612 ..	....	....	....	....	....	....	....	....
Banks....................................	4 613 ..	....	....	....	....	....	....	.6	....
Other sectors............................	4 614 ..	....	....	....	....	....	....	....	....
Debt securities..........................	4 619 ..	–22.5	–3.6	–5.7	34.2	25.8	–83.5	18.1	–118.4
Bonds and notes.........................	4 620 ..	–22.5	–3.6	–5.7	34.2	25.8	–83.0	27.6	–118.4
Monetary authorities.....................	4 621 ..	....	....	....	....	....	....	....	....
General government......................	4 622 ..	....	....	....	....	....	....	....	....
Banks....................................	4 623 ..	–22.5	–3.6	–5.7	34.2	25.8	–83.0	27.7	–118.4
Other sectors............................	4 624 ..	....	....	....	....	....	....	–.1	....
Money market instruments...............	4 630 ..	....	....	....	....	....	–.5	–9.4	....
Monetary authorities.....................	4 631 ..	....	....	....	....	....	....	....	....
General government......................	4 632 ..	....	....	....	....	....	....	....	....
Banks....................................	4 633 ..	....	....	....	....	....	....	–9.3	....
Other sectors............................	4 634 ..	....	....	....	....	....	–.5	–.1	....
Liabilities..............................	4 652 ..	....	....	....	....	....	**45.7**	**8.5**	**421.0**
Equity securities........................	4 660 ..	....	....	....	....	....	23.3	2.6	7.9
Banks....................................	4 663 ..	....	....	....	....	....	16.9	–4.4	.5
Other sectors............................	4 664 ..	....	....	....	....	....	6.4	7.1	7.4
Debt securities..........................	4 669 ..	....	....	....	....	....	22.4	5.9	413.1
Bonds and notes.........................	4 670 ..	....	....	....	....	....	22.4	5.9	413.1
Monetary authorities.....................	4 671 ..	....	....	....	....	....	....	....	....
General government......................	4 672 ..	....	....	....	....	....	....	....	407.1
Banks....................................	4 673 ..	....	....	....	....	....	....	....	....
Other sectors............................	4 674 ..	....	....	....	....	....	22.4	5.9	6.0
Money market instruments...............	4 680 ..	....	....	....	....	....	....	....	....
Monetary authorities.....................	4 681 ..	....	....	....	....	....	....	....	....
General government......................	4 682 ..	....	....	....	....	....	....	....	....
Banks....................................	4 683 ..	....	....	....	....	....	....	....	....
Other sectors............................	4 684 ..	....	....	....	....	....	....	....	....
C. FINANCIAL DERIVATIVES...................	4 910 ..	....	....	....	....	....	....	....	....
Monetary authorities.....................	4 911 ..	....	....	....	....	....	....	....	....
General government......................	4 912 ..	....	....	....	....	....	....	....	....
Banks....................................	4 913 ..	....	....	....	....	....	....	....	....
Other sectors............................	4 914 ..	....	....	....	....	....	....	....	....
Assets...................................	4 900 ..	....	341.3	262.5	325.3	662.3	958.7	....	....
Monetary authorities.....................	4 901 ..	....	....	....	....	....	....	....	....
General government......................	4 902 ..	....	....	....	....	....	....	....	....
Banks....................................	4 903 ..	....	....	....	....	....	....	....	....
Other sectors............................	4 904 ..	....	....	....	....	....	....	....	....
Liabilities..............................	4 905 ..	....	....	....	....	....	....	....	....
Monetary authorities.....................	4 906 ..	....	....	....	....	....	....	....	....
General government......................	4 907 ..	....	....	....	....	....	....	....	....
Banks....................................	4 908 ..	....	....	....	....	....	....	....	....
Other sectors............................	4 909 ..	....	....	....	....	....	....	....	....

Table 2 (Concluded). STANDARD PRESENTATION, 2003–2010

(Millions of U.S. dollars)

	Code	2003	2004	2005	2006	2007	2008	2009	2010
D. OTHER INVESTMENT	4 700	**46.6**	**74.6**	**142.8**	**170.4**	**367.3**	**1,314.6**	**317.4**	**−295.0**
Assets	4 703	**−71.6**	**−113.8**	**6.6**	**−210.7**	**−88.1**	**286.8**	**62.1**	**−212.6**
Trade credits	4 706	....	....	....	....	....	....	....	....
General government	4 707	....	....	....	....	....	....	....	....
of which: Short-term	4 709	....	....	....	....	....	....	....	....
Other sectors	4 710	....	....	....	....	....	....	....	....
of which: Short-term	4 712	....	....	....	....	....	....	....	....
Loans	4 714	....		....	....	5.6	−9.4	−109.6	−38.2
Monetary authorities	4 715	....				....	....	....	....
of which: Short-term	4 718	....				....	....	....	....
General government	4 719					....	....	....	....
of which: Short-term	4 721					....	....	....	....
Banks	4 722	....			....	5.6	−9.4	−109.6	−38.2
of which: Short-term	4 724					5.6	−9.4	−54.7	−36.9
Other sectors	4 725	....				....	....	....	....
of which: Short-term	4 727	....				....	....	....	....
Currency and deposits	4 730	−70.4	−110.5	63.2	−219.9	−100.5	290.6	174.5	−162.6
Monetary authorities	4 731	.3	....	....	−.6	−6.0	....	....	....
General government	4 732								
Banks	4 733	−44.0	−108.7	65.2	−225.2	−93.3	293.3	175.0	−156.0
Other sectors	4 734	−26.7	−1.7	−1.9	5.9	−1.2	−2.7	−.5	−6.6
Other assets	4 736	−1.3	−3.4	−56.6	9.2	6.8	5.6	−2.9	−11.8
Monetary authorities	4 737	....	....	....	....	....	7.9	−9.1	....
of which: Short-term	4 739	....	....	....	....	....	....	....	....
General government	4 740	....	....	....	....	....	....	....	....
of which: Short-term	4 742	....	....	....	....	....	....	....	....
Banks	4 743	−1.3	−3.4	−56.6	12.7	9.5	−.3	9.2	−9.6
of which: Short-term	4 745	−1.3	−3.4	−56.6	12.7	9.5	−.3	9.2	−9.6
Other sectors	4 746	....	....	....	−3.5	−2.7	−1.9	−3.0	−2.2
of which: Short-term	4 748	....	....	....	−3.5	−2.7	−1.9	−3.0	−2.2
Liabilities	4 753	**118.2**	**188.4**	**136.2**	**381.1**	**455.4**	**1,027.8**	**255.4**	**−82.4**
Trade credits	4 756	11.1	23.1	9.6	9.7	18.9	22.9	7.4	16.9
General government	4 757	....	....	....	....	....	....	....	....
of which: Short-term	4 759	....	....	....	....	....	....	....	....
Other sectors	4 760	11.1	23.1	9.6	9.7	18.9	22.9	7.4	16.9
of which: Short-term	4 762	11.1	23.1	9.6	9.7	18.9	22.9	7.4	16.9
Loans	4 764	118.9	193.2	134.0	124.6	296.4	1,010.7	163.1	−218.7
Monetary authorities	4 765	.5	1.2	1.5	−5.4	−7.9	−7.7	−10.6	−12.6
of which: Use of Fund credit and loans from the Fund.	4 766	1.5	2.4	3.0	−4.1	−7.0	−7.4	−10.3	−12.3
of which: Short-term	4 768	....	....	....	....	....	....	....	....
General government	4 769	96.6	106.4	50.4	51.9	87.4	445.2	416.8	−107.8
of which: Short-term	4 771	....	....	....	....	....	....	....	....
Banks	4 772	....	....	....	−.7	175.2	445.7	−345.0	−141.6
of which: Short-term	4 774	....	....	....	....	175.6	445.9	−479.4	−141.6
Other sectors	4 775	21.8	85.7	82.1	78.8	41.7	127.6	101.8	43.3
of which: Short-term	4 777	....	....	....	....	....	....	.2	2.2
Currency and deposits	4 780	19.7	3.4	−36.9	163.6	207.1	−3.5	24.9	129.8
Monetary authorities	4 781	....	....	....	....	....	....	....	....
General government	4 782	....	....	....	....	....	....	....	....
Banks	4 783	19.7	3.4	−36.9	163.6	207.1	−3.5	24.6	129.8
Other sectors	4 784	....	....	....	....	....	....	.3	....
Other liabilities	4 786	−31.4	−31.4	29.5	83.3	−67.0	−2.3	60.0	−10.4
Monetary authorities	4 787	....	....	....	....	....	....	72.7	....
of which: Short-term	4 789	....	....	....	....	....	....	....	....
General government	4 790	....	....	....	....	.3	....	....	....
of which: Short-term	4 792	....	....	....	....	.3	....	....	....
Banks	4 793	.1	−3.1	57.5	81.2	−70.5	.7	−8.9	−12.5
of which: Short-term	4 795	.1	−3.1	57.5	81.2	−70.5	.7	−8.9	−12.5
Other sectors	4 796	−31.5	−28.3	−28.1	2.1	3.3	−2.9	−3.7	2.2
of which: Short-term	4 798	−31.5	−28.3	−28.1	2.1	3.3	−2.9	−3.7	2.2
E. RESERVE ASSETS	4 802	**−99.6**	**−288.4**	**−150.7**	**−265.1**	**−202.3**	**−262.1**	**34.4**	**−236.3**
Monetary gold	4 812	....	....	....	....	....	....	....	....
Special drawing rights	4 811	−1.2	−5.8	82.1	4.2	7.4	−5.7	−71.6	−.3
Reserve position in the Fund	4 810	....	....	....	....	....	....	....	....
Foreign exchange	4 803	−98.4	−282.7	−232.8	−269.3	−209.7	−256.5	105.9	−236.0
Other claims	4 813	....	....	....	....	....	....	....	....
NET ERRORS AND OMISSIONS	4 998	**147.4**	**115.3**	**203.8**	**237.0**	**189.0**	**14.2**	**415.8**	**411.0**

Table 3. INTERNATIONAL INVESTMENT POSITION (End-period stocks), 2003–2010

(Millions of U.S. dollars)

	Code	2003	2004	2005	2006	2007	2008	2009	2010
ASSETS..	8 995 C.	....	....	....	....	**3,565.4**	**3,558.8**	**3,518.8**	....
Direct investment abroad..............	8 505 ..	....	....	....	....	**74.4**	**147.4**	**166.6**	....
Equity capital and reinvested earnings..............	8 506 ..	....	....	....	....	74.4	145.0	161.6	....
Claims on affiliated enterprises.................	8 507 ..	....	....	....	....	77.0	153.8	170.2	....
Liabilities to affiliated enterprises.............	8 508 ..	....	....	....	....	−2.6	−8.8	−8.6	....
Other capital.............................	8 530 ..	....	....	....	....	....	2.5	5.0	....
Claims on affiliated enterprises.................	8 535 ..	....	....	....	....	....	2.5	5.7	....
Liabilities to affiliated enterprises.............	8 540 ..	....	....	....	....	....	....	−.7	....
Portfolio investment.......................	8 602 ..	....	....	....	....	**89.9**	**154.6**	**149.0**	....
Equity securities..........................	8 610 ..	....	....	....	....	....	1.0	.4	....
Monetary authorities.....................	8 611 ..	....	....	....	....	....	....	....	....
General government......................	8 612 ..	....	....	....	....	....	....	....	....
Banks.................................	8 613 ..	....	....	....	....	....	.9	.3	....
Other sectors..........................	8 614 ..	....	....	....	....	....	.1	.1	....
Debt securities............................	8 619 ..	....	....	....	....	89.9	153.6	148.6	....
Bonds and notes........................	8 620 ..	....	....	....	....	89.9	153.2	138.8	....
Monetary authorities..................	8 621 ..	....	....	....	....	....	....	....	....
General government...................	8 622 ..	....	....	....	....	....	....	....	....
Banks...............................	8 623 ..	....	....	....	....	89.9	153.2	138.7	....
Other sectors.........................	8 624 ..	....	....	....	....	....	....	.1	....
Money market instruments..............	8 630 ..	....	....	....	....	....	.4	9.8	....
Monetary authorities..................	8 631 ..	....	....	....	....	....	....	....	....
General government...................	8 632 ..	....	....	....	....	....	....	....	....
Banks...............................	8 633 ..	....	....	....	....	....	....	9.3	....
Other sectors.........................	8 634 ..	....	....	....	....	....	.4	.5	....
Financial derivatives.......................	8 900 ..	....	....	....	....	....	....	....	....
Monetary authorities.....................	8 901 ..	....	....	....	....	....	....	....	....
General government......................	8 902 ..	....	....	....	....	....	....	....	....
Banks.................................	8 903 ..	....	....	....	....	....	....	....	....
Other sectors..........................	8 904 ..	....	....	....	....	....	....	....	....
Other investment..........................	8 703 ..	....	....	....	....	**1,256.3**	**897.4**	**832.5**	....
Trade credits.............................	8 706 ..	....	....	....	....	....	....	....	....
General government......................	8 707 ..	....	....	....	....	....	....	....	....
of which: Short-term..................	8 709 ..	....	....	....	....	....	....	....	....
Other sectors..........................	8 710 ..	....	....	....	....	....	....	....	....
of which: Short-term..................	8 712 ..	....	....	....	....	....	....	....	....
Loans...................................	8 714 ..	....	....	....	....	39.5	48.2	157.0	....
Monetary authorities.....................	8 715 ..	....	....	....	....	....	....	....	....
of which: Short-term..................	8 718 ..	....	....	....	....	....	....	....	....
General government......................	8 719 ..	....	....	....	....	....	....	....	....
of which: Short-term..................	8 721 ..	....	....	....	....	....	....	....	....
Banks.................................	8 722 ..	....	....	....	....	39.5	48.2	157.0	....
of which: Short-term..................	8 724 ..	....	....	....	....	*25.5*	*34.9*	*89.6*	....
Other sectors..........................	8 725 ..	....	....	....	....	....	....	....	....
of which: Short-term..................	8 727 ..	....	....	....	....	....	....	....	....
Currency and deposits.....................	8 730 ..	....	....	....	....	1,108.9	751.8	581.3	....
Monetary authorities.....................	8 731 ..	....	....	....	....	....	....	.1	....
General government......................	8 732 ..	....	....	....	....	....	....	....	....
Banks.................................	8 733 ..	....	....	....	....	1,103.4	744.7	574.2	....
Other sectors..........................	8 734 ..	....	....	....	....	5.5	7.0	7.0	....
Other assets.............................	8 736 ..	....	....	....	....	107.9	97.4	94.2	....
Monetary authorities.....................	8 737 ..	....	....	....	....	83.6	71.9	75.3	....
of which: Short-term..................	8 739 ..	....	....	....	....	....	....	....	....
General government......................	8 740 ..	....	....	....	....	....	....	....	....
of which: Short-term..................	8 742 ..	....	....	....	....	....	....	....	....
Banks.................................	8 743 ..	....	....	....	....	22.8	22.3	12.9	....
of which: Short-term..................	8 745 ..	....	....	....	....	*22.8*	*22.3*	*12.9*	....
Other sectors..........................	8 746 ..	....	....	....	....	1.5	3.3	6.0	....
of which: Short-term..................	8 748 ..	....	....	....	....	*1.5*	*3.3*	*6.0*	....
Reserve assets............................	8 802 ..	....	....	....	....	**2,144.7**	**2,359.4**	**2,370.7**	....
Monetary gold............................	8 812 ..	....	....	....	....	42.3	43.9	55.8	....
Special drawing rights.....................	8 811 ..	90.6	100.8	12.5	9.0	1.9	7.2	79.0	78.1
Reserve position in the Fund...............	8 810 ..	5.0	5.2	4.8	5.0	5.3	5.2	5.3	5.2
Foreign exchange.........................	8 803 ..	....	....	....	....	2,095.1	2,303.0	2,230.6	....
Other claims.............................	8 813 ..	....	....	....	....	....	....	....	....

Table 3 (Concluded). INTERNATIONAL INVESTMENT POSITION (End-period stocks), 2003–2010

(Millions of U.S. dollars)

	Code	2003	2004	2005	2006	2007	2008	2009	2010
LIABILITIES	8 995 D.	....	....	....	....	**5,615.8**	**6,955.5**	**7,606.4**	....
Direct investment in Albania	8 555 ..	....	....	....	....	**2,666.7**	**3,055.5**	**3,329.5**	....
Equity capital and reinvested earnings	8 556 ..	....	....	....	....	2,389.2	2,705.7	3,177.3	....
Claims on direct investors	8 557 ..	....	....	....	....	....	−10.7	−12.0	....
Liabilities to direct investors	8 558 ..	....	....	....	....	2,389.2	2,716.4	3,189.3	....
Other capital	8 580 ..	....	....	....	....	277.5	349.7	152.2	....
Claims on direct investors	8 585 ..	....	....	....	....	−121.1	−373.1	−530.2	....
Liabilities to direct investors	8 590 ..	....	....	....	....	398.6	722.8	682.4	....
Portfolio investment	8 652 ..	....	....	....	....	**158.2**	**191.1**	**203.5**	....
Equity securities	8 660 ..	....	....	....	....	85.2	99.7	104.0	....
Banks	8 663 ..	....	....	....	....	12.1	23.5	18.7	....
Other sectors	8 664 ..	....	....	....	....	73.1	76.2	85.2	....
Debt securities	8 669 ..	....	....	....	....	73.0	91.4	99.5	....
Bonds and notes	8 670 ..	....	....	....	....	73.0	91.4	99.5	....
Monetary authorities	8 671 ..	....	....	....	....	....	....	....	....
General government	8 672 ..	....	....	....	....	....	....	....	....
Banks	8 673 ..	....	....	....	....	....	....	....	....
Other sectors	8 674 ..	....	....	....	....	73.0	91.4	99.5	....
Money market instruments	8 680 ..	....	....	....	....	....	....	....	....
Monetary authorities	8 681 ..	....	....	....	....	....	....	....	....
General government	8 682 ..	....	....	....	....	....	....	....	....
Banks	8 683 ..	....	....	....	....	....	....	....	....
Other sectors	8 684 ..	....	....	....	....	....	....	....	....
Financial derivatives	8 905 ..	....	....	....	....	....	....	....	....
Monetary authorities	8 906 ..	....	....	....	....	....	....	....	....
General government	8 907 ..	....	....	....	....	....	....	....	....
Banks	8 908 ..	....	....	....	....	....	....	....	....
Other sectors	8 909 ..	....	....	....	....	....	....	....	....
Other investment	8 753 ..	....	....	....	....	**2,790.9**	**3,708.9**	**4,073.3**	....
Trade credits	8 756 ..	....	....	....	....	129.5	142.8	138.2	....
General government	8 757 ..	....	....	....	....	....	....	....	....
of which: Short-term	8 759 ..	....	....	....	....	....	....	....	....
Other sectors	8 760 ..	....	....	....	....	129.5	142.8	138.2	....
of which: Short-term	8 762 ..	....	....	....	....	129.5	142.8	138.2	....
Loans	8 764 ..	....	....	....	....	2,367.4	3,293.8	3,575.9	....
Monetary authorities	8 765 ..	....	....	....	....	104.2	93.7	84.6	....
of which: Use of Fund credit and loans from the Fund	8 766 ..	90.4	97.0	91.9	92.6	90.1	80.5	71.5	57.8
of which: Short-term	8 768 ..	....	....	....	....	....	....	....	....
General government	8 769 ..	....	....	....	....	1,450.9	1,864.3	2,369.2	....
of which: Short-term	8 771 ..	....	....	....	....	....	....	....	....
Banks	8 772 ..	....	....	....	....	333.0	744.6	410.3	....
of which: Short-term	8 774 ..	....	....	....	....	322.8	735.0	255.8	....
Other sectors	8 775 ..	....	....	....	....	479.4	591.2	711.7	....
of which: Short-term	8 777 ..	....	....	....	....	....	....	.2	....
Currency and deposits	8 780 ..	....	....	....	....	244.8	227.9	255.3	....
Monetary authorities	8 781 ..	....	....	....	....	....	....	....	....
General government	8 782 ..	....	....	....	....	....	....	....	....
Banks	8 783 ..	....	....	....	....	244.4	227.5	254.8	....
Other sectors	8 784 ..	....	....	....	....	.4	.4	.6	....
Other liabilities	8 786 ..	....	....	....	....	49.2	44.4	103.9	....
Monetary authorities	8 787 ..	....	....	....	....	....	....	72.8	....
of which: Short-term	8 789 ..	....	....	....	....	....	....	....	....
General government	8 790 ..	....	....	....	....	....	....	....	....
of which: Short-term	8 792 ..	....	....	....	....	....	....	....	....
Banks	8 793 ..	....	....	....	....	35.3	33.8	25.2	....
of which: Short-term	8 795 ..	....	....	....	....	35.3	33.8	25.2	....
Other sectors	8 796 ..	....	....	....	....	13.9	10.6	5.9	....
of which: Short-term	8 798 ..	....	....	....	....	13.9	10.6	5.9	....
NET INTERNATIONAL INVESTMENT POSITION	8 995 ..	....	....	....	....	**−2,050.4**	**−3,396.6**	**−4,087.6**	....
Conversion rates: leks per U.S. dollar (end of period)	0 102 ..	**106.5800**	**92.6400**	**103.5800**	**94.1400**	**82.8900**	**87.9100**	**95.8100**	**104.0000**

Table 1. ANALYTIC PRESENTATION, 2003–2010
(Millions of U.S. dollars)

	Code	2003	2004	2005	2006	2007	2008	2009	2010
A. Current Account[1]	4 993 Z.	....	....	**21,084.0**	**28,824.0**	**30,425.0**	**34,231.0**	**160.0**	....
Goods: exports f.o.b.	2 100 ..	....	....	46,334.0	54,741.0	60,591.0	78,590.0	45,186.0	....
Goods: imports f.o.b.	3 100 ..	....	....	−19,857.0	−20,561.0	−26,413.0	−38,070.0	−37,402.0	....
Balance on Goods	4 100 ..	....	....	*26,477.0*	*34,180.0*	*34,178.0*	*40,520.0*	*7,784.0*	....
Services: credit	2 200 ..	....	....	2,507.0	2,563.0	2,833.0	3,490.0	2,985.0	....
Services: debit	3 200 ..	....	....	−4,782.0	−4,796.0	−6,767.0	−11,082.0	−11,680.0	....
Balance on Goods and Services	4 991 ..	....	....	*24,202.0*	*31,947.0*	*30,244.0*	*32,928.0*	*−911.0*	....
Income: credit	2 300 ..	....	....	1,427.0	2,417.0	3,806.0	5,132.0	4,746.0	....
Income: debit	3 300 ..	....	....	−6,515.0	−7,052.0	−5,638.0	−6,394.0	−6,065.0	....
Balance on Goods, Services, and Income	4 992 ..	....	....	*19,114.0*	*27,312.0*	*28,412.0*	*31,666.0*	*−2,230.0*	....
Current transfers: credit	2 379 Z.	....	....	2,250.0	1,959.0	2,420.0	2,789.0	2,690.0	....
Current transfers: debit	3 379 ..	....	....	−280.0	−447.0	−407.0	−224.0	−300.0	....
B. Capital Account[1]	4 994 Z.	....	....	**−3.0**	**−5.0**	**−1.0**	**−1.0**	....	....
Capital account: credit	2 994 Z.	....	....	....	....	1.0	....	....	....
Capital account: debit	3 994 ..	....	....	−3.0	−5.0	−2.0	−1.0	....	....
Total, Groups A Plus B	4 981 ..	....	....	*21,081.0*	*28,819.0*	*30,424.0*	*34,230.0*	*160.0*	....
C. Financial Account[1]	4 995 W.	....	....	**−4,769.0**	**−9,869.0**	**−663.0**	**5,981.0**	**5,676.2**	....
Direct investment abroad	4 505 ..	....	....	20.0	−34.0	−295.0	−318.0	−215.0	....
Direct investment in Algeria	4 555 Z.	....	....	1,081.0	1,796.0	1,662.0	2,595.0	2,760.0	....
Portfolio investment assets	4 602 ..	....	....	....	....	....	....	....	....
Equity securities	4 610 ..	....	....	....	....	....	....	....	....
Debt securities	4 619 ..	....	....	....	....	....	....	....	....
Portfolio investment liabilities	4 652 Z.	....	....	....	....	....	....	....	....
Equity securities	4 660 ..	....	....	....	....	....	....	....	....
Debt securities	4 669 Z.	....	....	....	....	....	....	....	....
Financial derivatives	4 910 ..	....	....	....	....	....	....	....	....
Financial derivatives assets	4 900 ..	....	....	....	....	....	....	....	....
Financial derivatives liabilities	4 905 ..	....	....	....	....	....	....	....	....
Other investment assets	4 703 ..	....	....	−1,687.0	30.0	−1,509.0	2,780.0	−7.0	....
Monetary authorities	4 701 ..	....	....	5.0	378.0	−314.0	−284.0	−266.0	....
General government	4 704 ..	....	....	....	115.0	175.0	5.0	195.0	....
Banks	4 705 ..	....	....	130.0	−407.0	49.0	50.0	−10.0	....
Other sectors	4 728 ..	....	....	−1,822.0	−56.0	−1,419.0	3,009.0	74.0	....
Other investment liabilities	4 753 W.	....	....	−4,183.0	−11,661.0	−521.0	924.0	3,138.2	....
Monetary authorities	4 753 WA	....	....	−3,149.0	−12,058.0	−252.0	−323.0	1,539.2	....
General government	4 753 ZB	....	....	....	....	....	....	....	....
Banks	4 753 ZC	....	....	....	....	....	....	....	....
Other sectors	4 753 ZD	....	....	−1,034.0	397.0	−269.0	1,247.0	1,599.0	....
Total, Groups A Through C	4 983 ..	....	....	*16,312.0*	*18,950.0*	*29,761.0*	*40,211.0*	*5,836.2*	....
D. Net Errors and Omissions	4 998 ..	....	....	**−190.2**	**−1,693.9**	**−602.7**	**−3,609.6**	**−2,319.6**	....
Total, Groups A Through D	4 984 ..	....	....	*16,121.8*	*17,256.1*	*29,158.3*	*36,601.4*	*3,516.6*	....
E. Reserves and Related Items	4 802 A.	....	....	**−16,121.8**	**−17,256.1**	**−29,158.3**	**−36,601.4**	**−3,516.6**	....
Reserve assets	4 802 ..	....	....	−16,303.7	−17,736.1	−29,547.3	−36,997.4	−3,859.6	....
Use of Fund credit and loans	4 766 ..	....	....	−600.1	....	....	....	....	....
Exceptional financing	4 920 ..	....	....	782.0	480.0	389.0	396.0	343.0	....
Conversion rates: Algerian dinars per U.S. dollar	0 101 ..	**77.4**	**72.1**	**73.3**	**72.6**	**69.3**	**64.6**	**72.6**	**74.4**

[1] Excludes components that have been classified in the categories of Group E.

Table 2. STANDARD PRESENTATION, 2003–2010

(Millions of U.S. dollars)

	Code	2003	2004	2005	2006	2007	2008	2009	2010
CURRENT ACCOUNT	4 993	....	....	**21,181.0**	**28,923.0**	**30,631.0**	**34,440.0**	**402.0**	....
A. GOODS	4 100	....	....	**26,477.0**	**34,180.0**	**34,178.0**	**40,520.0**	**7,784.0**	....
Credit	2 100	....	....	**46,334.0**	**54,741.0**	**60,591.0**	**78,590.0**	**45,186.0**	....
General merchandise: exports f.o.b.	2 110	....	....	46,334.0	54,740.0	60,591.0	78,590.0	45,186.0	
Goods for processing: exports f.o.b.	2 150	....	....	....	....	....	....	....	
Repairs on goods	2 160	....	....	....	1.0	....	....	....	
Goods procured in ports by carriers	2 170	....	....	....	....	....	....	....	
Nonmonetary gold	2 180	....	....	....	....	....	....	....	
Debit	3 100	....	....	**−19,857.0**	**−20,561.0**	**−26,413.0**	**−38,070.0**	**−37,402.0**	....
General merchandise: imports f.o.b.	3 110	....	....	−19,817.0	−20,520.0	−26,376.0	−38,013.0	−37,388.0	
Goods for processing: imports f.o.b.	3 150	....	....	....	....	−9.0	....	−3.0	
Repairs on goods	3 160	....	....	−40.0	−41.0	−28.0	−57.0	−11.0	
Goods procured in ports by carriers	3 170	....	....	....	....	....	....	....	
Nonmonetary gold	3 180	....	....	....	....	....	....	....	
B. SERVICES	4 200	....	....	**−2,275.0**	**−2,233.0**	**−3,934.0**	**−7,592.0**	**−8,695.0**	....
Total credit	2 200	....	....	*2,507.0*	*2,563.0*	*2,833.0*	*3,490.0*	*2,985.0*	....
Total debit	3 200	....	....	*−4,782.0*	*−4,796.0*	*−6,767.0*	*−11,082.0*	*−11,680.0*	....
Transportation services, credit	2 205	....	....	**836.0**	**784.0**	**876.0**	**945.0**	**770.0**	....
Passenger	2 850	....	....	*293.0*	*173.0*	*113.0*	*150.0*	*115.0*	
Freight	2 851	....	....	*348.0*	*304.0*	*307.0*	*276.0*	*143.0*	
Other	2 852	....	....	*195.0*	*307.0*	*456.0*	*519.0*	*512.0*	
Sea transport, passenger	2 207	....	....	81.0	56.0	61.0	89.0	73.0	
Sea transport, freight	2 208	....	....	119.0	120.0	91.0	116.0	24.0	
Sea transport, other	2 209	....	....	144.0	156.0	182.0	198.0	198.0	
Air transport, passenger	2 211	....	....	201.0	99.0	25.0	20.0	10.0	
Air transport, freight	2 212	....	....	11.0	5.0	1.0	1.0	1.0	
Air transport, other	2 213	....	....	51.0	151.0	274.0	321.0	314.0	
Other transport, passenger	2 215	....	....	11.0	18.0	27.0	41.0	32.0	
Other transport, freight	2 216	....	....	218.0	179.0	215.0	159.0	118.0	
Other transport, other	2 217	....	....	....	....	....	....	....	
Transportation services, debit	3 205	....	....	**−1,800.0**	**−1,634.0**	**−2,149.0**	**−3,120.0**	**−2,946.0**	....
Passenger	3 850	....	....	*−290.0*	*−65.0*	*−128.0*	*−148.0*	*−119.0*	
Freight	3 851	....	....	*−1,222.0*	*−1,236.0*	*−1,571.0*	*−2,268.0*	*−2,235.0*	
Other	3 852	....	....	*−288.0*	*−333.0*	*−450.0*	*−704.0*	*−592.0*	
Sea transport, passenger	3 207	....	....	−4.0	−5.0	−8.0	−51.0	−18.0	
Sea transport, freight	3 208	....	....	−1,200.0	−1,221.0	−1,566.0	−2,254.0	−2,226.0	
Sea transport, other	3 209	....	....	−180.0	−220.0	−286.0	−414.0	−325.0	
Air transport, passenger	3 211	....	....	−284.0	−59.0	−78.0	−96.0	−100.0	
Air transport, freight	3 212	....	....	−15.0	−3.0	−4.0	−5.0	−5.0	
Air transport, other	3 213	....	....	−108.0	−113.0	−164.0	−290.0	−267.0	
Other transport, passenger	3 215	....	....	−2.0	−1.0	−42.0	−1.0	−1.0	
Other transport, freight	3 216	....	....	−7.0	−12.0	−1.0	−9.0	−4.0	
Other transport, other	3 217	....	....	....	....	....	....	....	
Travel, credit	2 236	....	....	**184.0**	**220.0**	**219.0**	**324.0**	**267.0**	....
Business travel	2 237	....	....	1.0	....	1.0	1.0	3.0	
Personal travel	2 240	....	....	183.0	220.0	218.0	323.0	264.0	
Travel, debit	3 236	....	....	**−370.0**	**−349.0**	**−376.0**	**−469.0**	**−456.0**	....
Business travel	3 237	....	....	−50.0	−58.0	−42.0	−49.0	−39.0	
Personal travel	3 240	....	....	−320.0	−291.0	−334.0	−420.0	−417.0	
Other services, credit	2 200 BA	....	....	**1,487.0**	**1,559.0**	**1,738.0**	**2,221.0**	**1,948.0**	....
Communications	2 245	....	....	101.0	123.0	220.0	156.0	88.0	
Construction	2 249	....	....	167.0	265.0	298.0	312.0	185.0	
Insurance	2 253	....	....	479.0	60.0	72.0	137.0	67.0	
Financial	2 260	....	....	48.0	50.0	88.0	143.0	184.0	
Computer and information	2 262	....	....	10.0	24.0	23.0	18.0	17.0	
Royalties and licence fees	2 266	....	....	....	2.0	1.0	3.0	2.0	
Other business services	2 268	....	....	637.0	979.0	976.0	1,376.0	1,210.0	
Personal, cultural, and recreational	2 287	....	....	4.0	4.0	8.0	6.0	4.0	
Government, n.i.e.	2 291	....	....	41.0	52.0	52.0	70.0	191.0	
Other services, debit	3 200 BA	....	....	**−2,612.0**	**−2,813.0**	**−4,242.0**	**−7,493.0**	**−8,278.0**	....
Communications	3 245	....	....	−123.0	−62.0	−70.0	−120.0	−104.0	
Construction	3 249	....	....	−548.0	−603.0	−1,477.0	−2,658.0	−3,023.0	
Insurance	3 253	....	....	−127.0	−125.0	−169.0	−188.0	−182.0	
Financial	3 260	....	....	−40.0	−37.0	−79.0	−213.0	−68.0	
Computer and information	3 262	....	....	−39.0	−47.0	−58.0	−80.0	−81.0	
Royalties and licence fees	3 266	....	....	−2.0	−15.0	−11.0	−10.0	−17.0	
Other business services	3 268	....	....	−1,448.0	−1,612.0	−1,932.0	−3,593.0	−4,308.0	
Personal, cultural, and recreational	3 287	....	....	−4.0	−8.0	−13.0	−22.0	−18.0	
Government, n.i.e.	3 291	....	....	−281.0	−304.0	−433.0	−609.0	−477.0	

Table 2 (Continued). STANDARD PRESENTATION, 2003–2010

(Millions of U.S. dollars)

	Code	2003	2004	2005	2006	2007	2008	2009	2010
C. INCOME	4 300	....	....	**−5,088.0**	**−4,635.0**	**−1,832.0**	**−1,262.0**	**−1,319.0**	....
Total credit	2 300	....	....	*1,427.0*	*2,417.0*	*3,806.0*	*5,132.0*	*4,746.0*	....
Total debit	3 300	....	....	*−6,515.0*	*−7,052.0*	*−5,638.0*	*−6,394.0*	*−6,065.0*	....
Compensation of employees, credit	2 310	....	....	**1.0**	....	**62.0**	**59.0**	**77.0**	....
Compensation of employees, debit	3 310	....	....	**−2.0**	....	....	....	....	....
Investment income, credit	2 320	....	....	**1,426.0**	**2,417.0**	**3,744.0**	**5,073.0**	**4,669.0**	....
Direct investment income	2 330	....	....	9.0	26.0	40.0	617.0	111.0	....
Dividends and distributed branch profits	2 332	....	....	9.0	26.0	40.0	617.0	111.0	....
Reinvested earnings and undistributed branch profits	2 333	....	....	....	....	....	....	....	....
Income on debt (interest)	2 334	....	....	....	....	....	....	....	....
Portfolio investment income	2 339	....	....	....	....	....	....	....	....
Income on equity	2 340	....	....	....	....	....	....	....	....
Income on bonds and notes	2 350	....	....	....	....	....	....	....	....
Income on money market instruments	2 360	....	....	....	....	....	....	....	....
Other investment income	2 370	....	....	1,417.0	2,391.0	3,704.0	4,456.0	4,558.0	....
Investment income, debit	3 320	....	....	**−6,513.0**	**−7,052.0**	**−5,638.0**	**−6,394.0**	**−6,065.0**	....
Direct investment income	3 330	....	....	−5,485.0	−6,295.0	−5,405.0	−6,206.0	−5,892.0	....
Dividends and distributed branch profits	3 332	....	....	−5,485.0	−6,295.0	−5,405.0	−6,206.0	−5,892.0	....
Reinvested earnings and undistributed branch profits	3 333	....	....	....	....	....	....	....	....
Income on debt (interest)	3 334	....	....	....	....	....	....	....	....
Portfolio investment income	3 339	....	....	....	....	....	....	....	....
Income on equity	3 340	....	....	....	....	....	....	....	....
Income on bonds and notes	3 350	....	....	....	....	....	....	....	....
Income on money market instruments	3 360	....	....	....	....	....	....	....	....
Other investment income	3 370	....	....	−1,028.0	−757.0	−233.0	−188.0	−173.0	....
D. CURRENT TRANSFERS	4 379	....	....	**2,067.0**	**1,611.0**	**2,219.0**	**2,774.0**	**2,632.0**	....
Credit	2 379	....	....	**2,347.0**	**2,058.0**	**2,626.0**	**2,998.0**	**2,932.0**	....
General government	2 380	....	....	97.0	99.0	206.0	209.0	242.0	....
Other sectors	2 390	....	....	2,250.0	1,959.0	2,420.0	2,789.0	2,690.0	....
Workers' remittances	2 391	....	....	169.0	189.0	36.0	45.0	73.0	....
Other current transfers	2 392	....	....	2,081.0	1,770.0	2,384.0	2,744.0	2,617.0	....
Debit	3 379	....	....	**−280.0**	**−447.0**	**−407.0**	**−224.0**	**−300.0**	....
General government	3 380	....	....	−135.0	−181.0	−94.0	−102.0	−36.0	....
Other sectors	3 390	....	....	−145.0	−266.0	−313.0	−122.0	−264.0	....
Workers' remittances	3 391	....	....	−25.0	−35.0	−48.0	−27.0	−46.0	....
Other current transfers	3 392	....	....	−120.0	−231.0	−265.0	−95.0	−218.0	....
CAPITAL AND FINANCIAL ACCOUNT	4 996	....	....	**−20,990.8**	**−27,229.1**	**−30,028.3**	**−30,830.4**	**1,917.6**	....
CAPITAL ACCOUNT	4 994	....	....	**−3.0**	**−5.0**	**−1.0**	**−1.0**	....	....
Total credit	2 994	....	....	....	....	*1.0*	....	....	....
Total debit	3 994	....	....	*−3.0*	*−5.0*	*−2.0*	*−1.0*	....	....
Capital transfers, credit	2 400	....	....	....	....	**1.0**	....	....	....
General government	2 401	....	....	....	....	....	....	....	....
Debt forgiveness	2 402	....	....	....	....	....	....	....	....
Other capital transfers	2 410	....	....	....	....	....	....	....	....
Other sectors	2 430	....	....	....	....	1.0	....	....	....
Migrants' transfers	2 431	....	....	....	....	....	....	....	....
Debt forgiveness	2 432	....	....	....	....	....	....	....	....
Other capital transfers	2 440	....	....	....	....	1.0	....	....	....
Capital transfers, debit	3 400	....	....	**−3.0**	**−5.0**	**−2.0**	**−1.0**	....	....
General government	3 401	....	....	....	....	....	....	....	....
Debt forgiveness	3 402	....	....	....	....	....	....	....	....
Other capital transfers	3 410	....	....	....	....	....	....	....	....
Other sectors	3 430	....	....	−3.0	−5.0	−2.0	−1.0	....	....
Migrants' transfers	3 431	....	....	....	....	....	....	....	....
Debt forgiveness	3 432	....	....	....	....	....	....	....	....
Other capital transfers	3 440	....	....	−3.0	−5.0	−2.0	−1.0	....	....
Nonproduced nonfinancial assets, credit	2 480	....	....	....	....	....	....	....	....
Nonproduced nonfinancial assets, debit	3 480	....	....	....	....	....	....	....	....

Table 2 (Continued). STANDARD PRESENTATION, 2003–2010

(Millions of U.S. dollars)

	Code	2003	2004	2005	2006	2007	2008	2009	2010
FINANCIAL ACCOUNT............................	4 995 ..	....	....	**−20,987.8**	**−27,224.1**	**−30,027.3**	**−30,829.4**	**1,917.6**	....
A. DIRECT INVESTMENT.........................	4 500 ..	....	....	**1,101.0**	**1,762.0**	**1,367.0**	**2,277.0**	**2,545.0**	....
Direct investment abroad....................	4 505 ..	....	....	**20.0**	**−34.0**	**−295.0**	**−318.0**	**−215.0**	....
Equity capital..	4 510 ..	....	....	20.0	−34.0	−295.0	−318.0	−215.0	....
Claims on affiliated enterprises................	4 515 ..	....	....	20.0	−74.0	−304.0	−63.0	−124.0	....
Liabilities to affiliated enterprises............	4 520 ..	....	....	....	40.0	9.0	−255.0	−91.0	....
Reinvested earnings...................................	4 525 ..	....	....	....	....	....	....	....	....
Other capital..	4 530 ..	....	....	....	....	....	....	....	....
Claims on affiliated enterprises................	4 535 ..	....	....	....	....	....	....	....	....
Liabilities to affiliated enterprises............	4 540 ..	....	....	....	....	....	....	....	....
Direct investment in Algeria...............	4 555 ..	....	....	**1,081.0**	**1,796.0**	**1,662.0**	**2,595.0**	**2,760.0**	....
Equity capital..	4 560 ..	....	....	1,081.0	1,735.0	1,610.0	2,470.0	2,846.0	....
Claims on direct investors.........................	4 565 ..	....	....	1,081.0	1,735.0	1,610.0	2,470.0	2,846.0	....
Liabilities to direct investors....................	4 570 ..	....	....	....	....	....	....	....	....
Reinvested earnings...................................	4 575 ..	....	....	....	....	....	....	....	....
Other capital..	4 580 ..	....	....	....	61.0	52.0	125.0	−86.0	....
Claims on direct investors.........................	4 585 ..	....	....	....	66.0	126.0	148.0	99.0	....
Liabilities to direct investors....................	4 590 ..	....	....	....	−5.0	−74.0	−23.0	−185.0	....
B. PORTFOLIO INVESTMENT..................	4 600 ..	....	....	....	....	....	....	....	....
Assets...	4 602 ..	....	....	....	....	....	....	....	....
Equity securities..	4 610 ..	....	....	....	....	....	....	....	....
Monetary authorities................................	4 611 ..	....	....	....	....	....	....	....	....
General government..................................	4 612 ..	....	....	....	....	....	....	....	....
Banks..	4 613 ..	....	....	....	....	....	....	....	....
Other sectors...	4 614 ..	....	....	....	....	....	....	....	....
Debt securities..	4 619 ..	....	....	....	....	....	....	....	....
Bonds and notes..	4 620 ..	....	....	....	....	....	....	....	....
Monetary authorities................................	4 621 ..	....	....	....	....	....	....	....	....
General government..................................	4 622 ..	....	....	....	....	....	....	....	....
Banks..	4 623 ..	....	....	....	....	....	....	....	....
Other sectors...	4 624 ..	....	....	....	....	....	....	....	....
Money market instruments......................	4 630 ..	....	....	....	....	....	....	....	....
Monetary authorities................................	4 631 ..	....	....	....	....	....	....	....	....
General government..................................	4 632 ..	....	....	....	....	....	....	....	....
Banks..	4 633 ..	....	....	....	....	....	....	....	....
Other sectors...	4 634 ..	....	....	....	....	....	....	....	....
Liabilities...	4 652 ..	....	....	....	....	....	....	....	....
Equity securities..	4 660 ..	....	....	....	....	....	....	....	....
Banks..	4 663 ..	....	....	....	....	....	....	....	....
Other sectors...	4 664 ..	....	....	....	....	....	....	....	....
Debt securities..	4 669 ..	....	....	....	....	....	....	....	....
Bonds and notes..	4 670 ..	....	....	....	....	....	....	....	....
Monetary authorities................................	4 671 ..	....	....	....	....	....	....	....	....
General government..................................	4 672 ..	....	....	....	....	....	....	....	....
Banks..	4 673 ..	....	....	....	....	....	....	....	....
Other sectors...	4 674 ..	....	....	....	....	....	....	....	....
Money market instruments......................	4 680 ..	....	....	....	....	....	....	....	....
Monetary authorities................................	4 681 ..	....	....	....	....	....	....	....	....
General government..................................	4 682 ..	....	....	....	....	....	....	....	....
Banks..	4 683 ..	....	....	....	....	....	....	....	....
Other sectors...	4 684 ..	....	....	....	....	....	....	....	....
C. FINANCIAL DERIVATIVES..................	4 910 ..	....	....	....	....	....	....	....	....
Monetary authorities................................	4 911 ..	....	....	....	....	....	....	....	....
General government..................................	4 912 ..	....	....	....	....	....	....	....	....
Banks..	4 913 ..	....	....	....	....	....	....	....	....
Other sectors...	4 914 ..	....	....	....	....	....	....	....	....
Assets...	4 900 ..	....	....	....	....	....	....	....	....
Monetary authorities................................	4 901 ..	....	....	....	....	....	....	....	....
General government..................................	4 902 ..	....	....	....	....	....	....	....	....
Banks..	4 903 ..	....	....	....	....	....	....	....	....
Other sectors...	4 904 ..	....	....	....	....	....	....	....	....
Liabilities...	4 905 ..	....	....	....	....	....	....	....	....
Monetary authorities................................	4 906 ..	....	....	....	....	....	....	....	....
General government..................................	4 907 ..	....	....	....	....	....	....	....	....
Banks..	4 908 ..	....	....	....	....	....	....	....	....
Other sectors...	4 909 ..	....	....	....	....	....	....	....	....

Table 2 (Concluded). STANDARD PRESENTATION, 2003–2010

(Millions of U.S. dollars)

	Code	2003	2004	2005	2006	2007	2008	2009	2010
D. OTHER INVESTMENT............................	4 700 ..	....	....	**−5,785.1**	**−11,250.0**	**−1,847.0**	**3,891.0**	**3,232.2**	....
Assets...	4 703 ..	....	....	**−1,687.0**	**30.0**	**−1,509.0**	**2,780.0**	**−7.0**	....
Trade credits...........................	4 706 ..	....	....	−1,495.0	−48.0	−1,306.0	3,152.0	134.0	....
General government...............	4 707 ..	....	....	....	....	....	....	....	....
of which: Short-term..........	4 709 ..	....	....	....	....	....	....	....	....
Other sectors.........................	4 710 ..	....	....	−1,495.0	−48.0	−1,306.0	3,152.0	134.0	....
of which: Short-term..........	4 712 ..	....	....	*−1,553.0*	*−54.0*	*−1,336.0*	*3,119.0*	*140.0*	....
Loans.....................................	4 714 ..	....	....	....	115.0	175.0	5.0	193.0	....
Monetary authorities.............	4 715 ..	....	....	....	....	....	....	....	....
of which: Short-term..........	4 718 ..	....	....	....	....	....	....	....	....
General government...............	4 719 ..	....	....	....	115.0	175.0	5.0	195.0	....
of which: Short-term..........	4 721 ..	....	....	....	....	....	....	....	....
Banks.....................................	4 722 ..	....	....	....	....	....	....	....	....
of which: Short-term..........	4 724 ..	....	....	....	....	....	....	....	....
Other sectors.........................	4 725 ..	....	....	....	....	....	....	−2.0	....
of which: Short-term..........	4 727 ..	....	....	....	....	....	....	....	....
Currency and deposits...............	4 730 ..	....	....	−225.0	−298.0	−294.0	−125.0	−128.0	....
Monetary authorities.............	4 731 ..	....	....	−28.0	117.0	−230.0	−32.0	−60.0	....
General government...............	4 732 ..	....	....	....	....	....	....	....	....
Banks.....................................	4 733 ..	....	....	130.0	−407.0	49.0	50.0	−10.0	....
Other sectors.........................	4 734 ..	....	....	−327.0	−8.0	−113.0	−143.0	−58.0	....
Other assets.............................	4 736 ..	....	....	33.0	261.0	−84.0	−252.0	−206.0	....
Monetary authorities.............	4 737 ..	....	....	33.0	261.0	−84.0	−252.0	−206.0	....
of which: Short-term..........	4 739 ..	....	....	*33.0*	*261.0*	*−84.0*	*−252.0*	*−206.0*	....
General government...............	4 740 ..	....	....	....	....	....	....	....	....
of which: Short-term..........	4 742 ..	....	....	....	....	....	....	....	....
Banks.....................................	4 743 ..	....	....	....	....	....	....	....	....
of which: Short-term..........	4 745 ..	....	....	....	....	....	....	....	....
Other sectors.........................	4 746 ..	....	....	....	....	....	....	....	....
of which: Short-term..........	4 748 ..	....	....	....	....	....	....	....	....
Liabilities...................................	4 753 ..	....	....	**−4,098.1**	**−11,280.0**	**−338.0**	**1,111.0**	**3,239.2**	....
Trade credits...........................	4 756 ..	....	....	−595.0	−447.0	−432.0	46.0	14.0	....
General government...............	4 757 ..	....	....	....	....	....	....	....	....
of which: Short-term..........	4 759 ..	....	....	....	....	....	....	....	....
Other sectors.........................	4 760 ..	....	....	−595.0	−447.0	−432.0	46.0	14.0	....
of which: Short-term..........	4 762 ..	....	....	*66.0*	*−23.0*	*161.0*	*568.0*	*271.0*	....
Loans.....................................	4 764 ..	....	....	−3,128.1	−11,705.0	−244.0	−216.0	−169.0	....
Monetary authorities.............	4 765 ..	....	....	−3,358.1	−11,916.0	−134.0	−215.0	−57.0	....
of which: Use of Fund credit and loans from the Fund..	4 766 ..	....	....	*−600.1*	....	....	....	....	....
of which: Short-term..........	4 768 ..	....	....	....	....	....	....	....	....
General government...............	4 769 ..	....	....	....	....	....	....	....	....
of which: Short-term..........	4 771 ..	....	....	....	....	....	....	....	....
Banks.....................................	4 772 ..	....	....	....	....	....	....	....	....
of which: Short-term..........	4 774 ..	....	....	....	....	....	....	....	....
Other sectors.........................	4 775 ..	....	....	230.0	211.0	−110.0	−1.0	−112.0	....
of which: Short-term..........	4 777 ..	....	....	....	....	....	....	....	....
Currency and deposits...............	4 780 ..	....	....	−375.0	872.0	338.0	1,281.0	1,723.0	....
Monetary authorities.............	4 781 ..	....	....	....	....	....	....	....	....
General government...............	4 782 ..	....	....	....	....	....	....	....	....
Banks.....................................	4 783 ..	....	....	....	....	....	....	....	....
Other sectors.........................	4 784 ..	....	....	−375.0	872.0	338.0	1,281.0	1,723.0	....
Other liabilities........................	4 786 ..	....	....	....	....	....	....	1,671.2	....
Monetary authorities.............	4 787 ..	....	....	....	....	....	....	1,671.2	....
of which: Short-term..........	4 789 ..	....	....	....	....	....	....	....	....
General government...............	4 790 ..	....	....	....	....	....	....	....	....
of which: Short-term..........	4 792 ..	....	....	....	....	....	....	....	....
Banks.....................................	4 793 ..	....	....	....	....	....	....	....	....
of which: Short-term..........	4 795 ..	....	....	....	....	....	....	....	....
Other sectors.........................	4 796 ..	....	....	....	....	....	....	....	....
of which: Short-term..........	4 798 ..	....	....	....	....	....	....	....	....
E. RESERVE ASSETS...............................	4 802 ..	....	....	**−16,303.7**	**−17,736.1**	**−29,547.3**	**−36,997.4**	**−3,859.6**	....
Monetary gold...........................	4 812 ..	....	....	....	....	....	....	....	....
Special drawing rights................	4 811 ..	....	....	−3.7	−1.1	1.7	−7.4	−1,670.6	....
Reserve position in the Fund.......	4 810 ..	....	....	....	....	....	....	....	....
Foreign exchange.......................	4 803 ..	....	....	−16,315.0	−17,650.0	−28,267.0	−36,527.0	−2,278.0	....
Other claims.............................	4 813 ..	....	....	15.0	−85.0	−1,282.0	−463.0	89.0	....
NET ERRORS AND OMISSIONS...........................	4 998 ..	....	....	**−190.2**	**−1,693.9**	**−602.7**	**−3,609.6**	**−2,319.6**	....

Table 1. ANALYTIC PRESENTATION, 2003–2010

(Millions of U.S. dollars)

	Code	2003	2004	2005	2006	2007	2008	2009	2010
A. Current Account[1]	4 993 Z.	**−719.6**	**681.2**	**5,137.9**	**10,689.8**	**10,581.3**	**7,194.2**	**−7,571.7**	**7,421.1**
Goods: exports f.o.b.	2 100 ..	9,508.2	13,475.0	24,109.4	31,862.2	44,396.2	63,913.9	40,827.9	50,594.9
Goods: imports f.o.b.	3 100 ..	−5,480.1	−5,831.8	−8,353.2	−8,777.6	−13,661.5	−20,982.2	−22,659.9	−16,666.9
Balance on Goods	4 100 ..	*4,028.1*	*7,643.2*	*15,756.2*	*23,084.6*	*30,734.7*	*42,931.8*	*18,168.0*	*33,928.0*
Services: credit	2 200 ..	201.1	322.8	176.8	1,484.2	310.7	329.5	623.1	856.9
Services: debit	3 200 ..	−3,321.1	−4,802.7	−6,791.0	−7,511.2	−12,643.2	−22,139.3	−19,169.4	−18,754.4
Balance on Goods and Services	4 991 ..	*908.0*	*3,163.3*	*9,142.0*	*17,057.7*	*18,402.2*	*21,121.9*	*−378.2*	*16,030.5*
Income: credit	2 300 ..	12.3	33.0	25.8	145.0	622.6	422.3	131.3	134.0
Income: debit	3 300 ..	−1,738.7	−2,521.6	−4,056.6	−6,322.9	−8,221.6	−14,139.8	−6,954.5	−8,305.8
Balance on Goods, Services, and Income	4 992 ..	*−818.5*	*674.7*	*5,111.1*	*10,879.8*	*10,803.2*	*7,404.3*	*−7,201.3*	*7,858.7*
Current transfers: credit	2 379 Z.	186.2	124.4	172.5	59.5	45.7	154.5	56.8	58.4
Current transfers: debit	3 379 ..	−87.3	−117.9	−145.8	−249.5	−267.6	−364.5	−427.1	−496.1
B. Capital Account[1]	4 994 Z.	....	....	....	....	**6.9**	**6.5**	**4.1**	**.9**
Capital account: credit	2 994 Z.	....	....	....	....	6.9	6.5	4.1	.9
Capital account: debit	3 994 ..	....	....	....	....	....	....	....	....
Total, Groups A Plus B	4 981 ..	*−719.6*	*681.2*	*5,137.9*	*10,689.8*	*10,588.1*	*7,200.8*	*−7,567.5*	*7,422.0*
C. Financial Account[1]	4 995 W.	**1,535.7**	**993.2**	**−3,126.0**	**−3,982.9**	**−5,842.2**	**1,218.7**	**2,123.5**	**−1,511.6**
Direct investment abroad	4 505 ..	−23.6	−35.2	−219.4	−190.6	−911.8	−2,569.6	−6.8	−1,340.4
Direct investment in Angola	4 555 Z.	3,504.7	1,449.2	−1,303.8	−37.7	−893.3	1,679.0	2,205.3	−3,227.2
Portfolio investment assets	4 602 ..	1.0	−2.7	−1,267.0	−1,439.5	−2,015.4	−1,757.5	−558.1	−273.5
Equity securities	4 610 ..	....	−3.3	−1,264.0	−1,491.0	−1,965.9	−1,757.5	−558.1	−273.5
Debt securities	4 619 ..	1.0	.6	−3.0	51.5	−49.5	....	....	....
Portfolio investment liabilities	4 652 Z.	....	....	....	....	....	....	68.0	3.0
Equity securities	4 660 ..	....	....	....	....	....	....	....	....
Debt securities	4 669 Z.	....	....	....	....	....	....	68.0	3.0
Financial derivatives	4 910 ..	....	....	....	....	....	....	....	....
Financial derivatives assets	4 900 ..	....	....	....	....	....	....	....	....
Financial derivatives liabilities	4 905 ..	....	....	....	....	....	....	....	....
Other investment assets	4 703 ..	120.0	−1,951.5	−1,850.1	−1,633.1	−4,854.9	−2,709.2	−1,369.0	97.6
Monetary authorities	4 701 ..	....	....	....	....	....	....	....	....
General government	4 704 ..	....	....	....	....	....	....	....	....
Banks	4 705 ..	75.0	−68.2	−371.0	−1,444.3	42.2	−2,634.0	1,463.8	−139.7
Other sectors	4 728 ..	45.0	−1,883.3	−1,479.1	−188.7	−4,897.1	−75.2	−2,832.8	237.2
Other investment liabilities	4 753 W.	−2,066.4	1,533.4	1,514.3	−682.1	2,833.3	6,576.1	1,784.1	3,228.9
Monetary authorities	4 753 WA	−38.0	−2.2	.1	10.0	.1	364.2	237.4	1,289.3
General government	4 753 ZB	475.6	1,430.4	−1,127.3	−992.6	1,404.6	1,526.5	1,297.6	39.7
Banks	4 753 ZC	−11.5	18.4	29.7	133.0	615.1	2,967.3	834.2	458.4
Other sectors	4 753 ZD	−2,492.5	86.9	2,611.8	167.4	813.4	1,718.1	−585.1	1,441.5
Total, Groups A Through C	4 983 ..	*816.1*	*1,674.5*	*2,011.9*	*6,706.9*	*4,746.0*	*8,419.4*	*−5,444.0*	*5,910.4*
D. Net Errors and Omissions	4 998 ..	**−821.9**	**282.2**	**−574.2**	**266.5**	**−1,641.0**	**−1,235.9**	**454.7**	**−1,730.0**
Total, Groups A Through D	4 984 ..	*−5.8*	*1,956.7*	*1,437.7*	*6,973.4*	*3,105.0*	*7,183.5*	*−4,989.3*	*4,180.3*
E. Reserves and Related Items	4 802 A.	**5.8**	**−1,956.7**	**−1,437.7**	**−6,973.4**	**−3,105.0**	**−7,183.5**	**4,989.3**	**−4,180.3**
Reserve assets	4 802 ..	−262.8	−780.3	−1,817.3	−5,401.7	−3,019.1	−6,672.6	5,003.8	−5,148.6
Use of Fund credit and loans	4 766 ..	....	....	....	....	....	....	....	877.6
Exceptional financing	4 920 ..	268.6	−1,176.4	379.6	−1,571.7	−85.9	−510.9	−14.5	90.6
Conversion rates: kwanzas per U.S. dollar	0 101 ..	**74.606**	**83.541**	**87.159**	**80.368**	**76.706**	**75.033**	**79.328**	**91.906**

[1] Excludes components that have been classified in the categories of Group E.

Table 2. STANDARD PRESENTATION, 2003–2010

(Millions of U.S. dollars)

	Code	2003	2004	2005	2006	2007	2008	2009	2010
CURRENT ACCOUNT	4 993	**−719.6**	**681.2**	**5,137.9**	**10,689.8**	**10,581.3**	**7,194.2**	**−7,571.7**	**7,421.1**
A. GOODS	4 100	**4,028.1**	**7,643.2**	**15,756.2**	**23,084.6**	**30,734.7**	**42,931.8**	**18,168.0**	**33,928.0**
Credit	2 100	**9,508.2**	**13,475.0**	**24,109.4**	**31,862.2**	**44,396.2**	**63,913.9**	**40,827.9**	**50,594.9**
General merchandise: exports f.o.b.	2 110	9,508.2	13,475.0	24,109.4	31,862.2	44,396.2	63,913.9	40,827.9	50,594.9
Goods for processing: exports f.o.b.	2 150	....	....	....	....	....	....	....	....
Repairs on goods	2 160	....	....	....	....	....	....	....	....
Goods procured in ports by carriers	2 170	....	....	....	....	....	....	....	....
Nonmonetary gold	2 180	....	....	....	....	....	....	....	....
Debit	3 100	**−5,480.1**	**−5,831.8**	**−8,353.2**	**−8,777.6**	**−13,661.5**	**−20,982.2**	**−22,659.9**	**−16,666.9**
General merchandise: imports f.o.b.	3 110	−5,480.1	−5,831.8	−8,353.2	−8,777.6	−13,661.5	−20,982.2	−22,659.9	−16,666.9
Goods for processing: imports f.o.b.	3 150	....	....	....	....	....	....	....	....
Repairs on goods	3 160	....	....	....	....	....	....	....	....
Goods procured in ports by carriers	3 170	....	....	....	....	....	....	....	....
Nonmonetary gold	3 180	....	....	....	....	....	....	....	....
B. SERVICES	4 200	**−3,120.1**	**−4,480.0**	**−6,614.2**	**−6,027.0**	**−12,332.5**	**−21,809.9**	**−18,546.2**	**−17,897.5**
Total credit	2 200	*201.1*	*322.8*	*176.8*	*1,484.2*	*310.7*	*329.5*	*623.1*	*856.9*
Total debit	3 200	*−3,321.1*	*−4,802.7*	*−6,791.0*	*−7,511.2*	*−12,643.2*	*−22,139.3*	*−19,169.4*	*−18,754.4*
Transportation services, credit	2 205	**15.8**	**17.7**	**18.1**	**20.2**	**16.7**	**14.5**	**32.0**	**42.7**
Passenger	2 850	*13.7*	*16.0*	*15.4*	*15.7*	*11.1*	*8.4*	*20.1*	*7.1*
Freight	2 851	....	....	*.7*	*.6*	*.4*	....	*.5*	*.5*
Other	2 852	*2.1*	*1.7*	*2.0*	*3.9*	*5.3*	*6.1*	*11.4*	*35.1*
Sea transport, passenger	2 207	....	....	....	....	....	....	....	....
Sea transport, freight	2 208	....	....	....	....	....	....	....	....
Sea transport, other	2 209	....	....	....	....	....	....	....	....
Air transport, passenger	2 211	13.7	16.0	15.4	15.7	11.1	8.4	20.1	7.1
Air transport, freight	2 212	....	....	.7	.6	.4	....	.5	.5
Air transport, other	2 213	2.1	1.7	2.0	3.9	5.3	6.1	11.4	35.1
Other transport, passenger	2 215	....	....	....	....	....	....	....	....
Other transport, freight	2 216	....	....	....	....	....	....	....	....
Other transport, other	2 217	....	....	....	....	....	....	....	....
Transportation services, debit	3 205	**−758.6**	**−877.4**	**−1,320.2**	**−1,626.7**	**−2,505.0**	**−3,720.9**	**−4,155.5**	**−3,088.5**
Passenger	3 850	*−36.6*	*−47.0*	*−61.0*	*−245.2*	*−261.5*	*−192.6*	*−136.8*	*−127.5*
Freight	3 851	*−695.6*	*−795.0*	*−1,217.7*	*−1,331.9*	*−2,187.2*	*−3,486.7*	*−3,964.0*	*−2,913.8*
Other	3 852	*−26.5*	*−35.5*	*−41.6*	*−49.7*	*−56.3*	*−41.6*	*−54.7*	*−47.2*
Sea transport, passenger	3 207	....	....	....	....	....	....	....	....
Sea transport, freight	3 208	−695.6	−786.5	−1,216.0	−1,330.3	−2,185.2	−3,485.2	−3,962.7	−2,912.5
Sea transport, other	3 209	....	....	....	....	....	....	....	....
Air transport, passenger	3 211	−36.6	−47.0	−61.0	−245.2	−261.5	−192.6	−136.8	−127.5
Air transport, freight	3 212	....	−8.5	−1.7	−1.6	−2.0	−1.5	−1.3	−1.3
Air transport, other	3 213	−26.5	−35.5	−41.6	−49.7	−56.3	−41.6	−54.7	−47.2
Other transport, passenger	3 215	....	....	....	....	....	....	....	....
Other transport, freight	3 216	....	....	....	....	....	....	....	....
Other transport, other	3 217	....	....	....	....	....	....	....	....
Travel, credit	2 236	**49.0**	**65.8**	**88.2**	**74.9**	**224.9**	**284.9**	**534.1**	**719.1**
Business travel	2 237	49.0	65.8	88.2	74.9	160.8	207.2	322.1	500.8
Personal travel	2 240	....	....	....	....	64.1	77.8	212.0	218.3
Travel, debit	3 236	**−12.1**	**−38.8**	**−74.0**	**−147.7**	**−211.9**	**−254.1**	**−132.5**	**−148.1**
Business travel	3 237	−12.1	−38.2	−24.1	−29.3	−102.4	−119.7	−76.3	−83.8
Personal travel	3 240	....	−.6	−49.9	−118.4	−109.5	−134.4	−56.2	−64.3
Other services, credit	2 200 BA	**136.3**	**239.3**	**70.5**	**1,389.1**	**69.0**	**30.1**	**57.1**	**95.1**
Communications	2 245	....	....	14.0	10.7	....	....	34.0	35.1
Construction	2 249	....	....	....	....	....	.3	....	29.7
Insurance	2 253	−.3	....	....	....	....	....	....	....
Financial	2 260	....	....	....	....	....	....	....	....
Computer and information	2 262	....	....	....	....	....	....	−.1	....
Royalties and licence fees	2 266	....	226.8	49.4	1,339.6	12.0	12.0	....	....
Other business services	2 268	135.5	9.6	2.5	32.4	47.9	4.6	8.5	15.3
Personal, cultural, and recreational	2 287	1.1	2.9	4.6	6.4	9.1	13.1	14.6	15.0
Government, n.i.e.	2 291	....	....	....	....	....	....	....	....
Other services, debit	3 200 BA	**−2,550.4**	**−3,886.4**	**−5,396.7**	**−5,736.7**	**−9,926.3**	**−18,164.4**	**−14,881.3**	**−15,517.7**
Communications	3 245	−9.1	−16.9	−23.3	−19.0	−48.1	−88.3	−607.8	−362.2
Construction	3 249	−149.9	−866.4	−1,323.2	−1,475.7	−2,633.7	−5,007.2	−4,676.4	−4,643.1
Insurance	3 253	−157.5	−174.4	−103.4	−296.9	−414.2	−1,498.1	−329.2	−257.3
Financial	3 260	−9.4	−59.0	−16.2	−123.5	−154.0	−537.1	−444.8	−830.1
Computer and information	3 262	−1.9	−7.7	−17.8	−11.8	−23.3	−26.9	−37.7	−65.5
Royalties and licence fees	3 266	....	−2.5	−3.4	−1.4	−1.2	−.5	....	−6.4
Other business services	3 268	−1,665.1	−2,212.8	−3,264.6	−3,092.5	−5,906.7	−9,197.3	−7,679.8	−6,470.2
Personal, cultural, and recreational	3 287	−10.8	−28.5	−44.9	−64.7	−99.1	−121.2	−146.4	−156.2
Government, n.i.e.	3 291	−546.8	−518.2	−599.8	−651.2	−645.8	−1,687.8	−959.0	−2,726.7

Table 2 (Continued). STANDARD PRESENTATION, 2003–2010

(Millions of U.S. dollars)

	Code	2003	2004	2005	2006	2007	2008	2009	2010
C. INCOME	4 300 ..	**−1,726.5**	**−2,488.6**	**−4,030.9**	**−6,177.9**	**−7,599.0**	**−13,717.5**	**−6,823.1**	**−8,171.8**
Total credit	2 300 ..	*12.3*	*33.0*	*25.8*	*145.0*	*622.6*	*422.3*	*131.3*	*134.0*
Total debit	3 300 ..	*−1,738.7*	*−2,521.6*	*−4,056.6*	*−6,322.9*	*−8,221.6*	*−14,139.8*	*−6,954.5*	*−8,305.8*
Compensation of employees, credit	2 310 ..	....	....	....	....	....	11.0	....	....
Compensation of employees, debit	3 310 ..	−141.9	−178.6	−97.7	−240.8	−374.4	−447.0	−320.9	−303.9
Investment income, credit	2 320 ..	12.3	33.0	25.8	145.0	622.6	411.3	131.3	134.0
Direct investment income	2 330 ..	....	....	17.9	....	....	....	....	....
Dividends and distributed branch profits	2 332 ..	....	....	....	....	....	....	....	....
Reinvested earnings and undistributed branch profits	2 333 ..	....	....	17.9	....	....	....	....	....
Income on debt (interest)	2 334 ..	....	....	....	....	....	....	....	....
Portfolio investment income	2 339 ..	....	....	....	....	....	....	....	....
Income on equity	2 340 ..	....	....	....	....	....	....	....	....
Income on bonds and notes	2 350 ..	....	....	....	....	....	....	....	....
Income on money market instruments	2 360 ..	....	....	....	....	....	....	....	....
Other investment income	2 370 ..	12.3	33.0	7.9	145.0	622.6	411.3	131.3	134.0
Investment income, debit	3 320 ..	**−1,596.8**	**−2,343.0**	**−3,958.9**	**−6,082.2**	**−7,847.2**	**−13,692.8**	**−6,633.6**	**−8,001.9**
Direct investment income	3 330 ..	−1,263.9	−1,955.1	−3,405.9	−5,278.4	−7,268.2	−13,184.6	−6,130.1	−7,525.7
Dividends and distributed branch profits	3 332 ..	−574.4	−896.0	−2,264.2	−2,361.3	−4,025.4	−7,918.6	−3,386.9	−4,199.2
Reinvested earnings and undistributed branch profits	3 333 ..	−679.6	−1,057.8	−1,139.7	−2,915.7	−3,242.7	−5,266.0	−2,743.2	−3,325.6
Income on debt (interest)	3 334 ..	−9.9	−1.3	−1.9	−1.4	....	....	....	−1.0
Portfolio investment income	3 339 ..	....	....	....	....	....	....	....	....
Income on equity	3 340 ..	....	....	....	....	....	....	....	....
Income on bonds and notes	3 350 ..	....	....	....	....	....	....	....	....
Income on money market instruments	3 360 ..	....	....	....	....	....	....	....	....
Other investment income	3 370 ..	−332.9	−387.9	−553.1	−803.7	−579.0	−508.3	−503.5	−476.1
D. CURRENT TRANSFERS	4 379 ..	**98.9**	**6.5**	**26.8**	**−190.0**	**−221.9**	**−210.1**	**−370.3**	**−437.7**
Credit	2 379 ..	**186.2**	**124.4**	**172.5**	**59.5**	**45.7**	**154.5**	**56.8**	**58.4**
General government	2 380 ..	186.2	124.4	172.5	59.5	45.7	83.4	56.7	40.5
Other sectors	2 390 ..	....	....	....	....	....	71.1	.2	18.0
Workers' remittances	2 391 ..	....	....	....	....	....	71.0	.2	18.0
Other current transfers	2 392 ..	....	....	....	....	....	....	....	....
Debit	3 379 ..	**−87.3**	**−117.9**	**−145.8**	**−249.5**	**−267.6**	**−364.5**	**−427.1**	**−496.1**
General government	3 380 ..	....	....	−28.4	−35.8	−37.7	−142.1	−30.1	−83.4
Other sectors	3 390 ..	−87.3	−117.9	−117.3	−213.7	−229.9	−222.5	−397.1	−412.7
Workers' remittances	3 391 ..	−87.9	−117.5	−117.2	−171.9	−228.3	−222.4	−395.1	−410.5
Other current transfers	3 392 ..	.6	−.4	−.1	−41.8	−1.6	....	−2.0	−2.2
CAPITAL AND FINANCIAL ACCOUNT	4 996 ..	**1,541.4**	**−963.5**	**−4,563.7**	**−10,956.3**	**−8,940.3**	**−5,958.3**	**7,116.9**	**−5,691.0**
CAPITAL ACCOUNT	4 994 ..	**22.0**	**440.0**	**7.8**	**1.4**	**7.2**	**12.9**	**11.3**	**.9**
Total credit	2 994 ..	*22.0*	*440.0*	*7.8*	*1.4*	*7.2*	*12.9*	*11.3*	*.9*
Total debit	3 994 ..	....	....	....	....	....	....	....	....
Capital transfers, credit	2 400 ..	**22.0**	**440.0**	**7.8**	**1.4**	**7.2**	**12.9**	**11.3**	**.9**
General government	2 401 ..	22.0	440.0	7.8	1.4	7.2	12.9	11.3	.9
Debt forgiveness	2 402 ..	22.0	440.0	7.8	1.4	.3	6.4	7.1	....
Other capital transfers	2 410 ..	....	....	....	....	6.9	6.5	4.1	.9
Other sectors	2 430 ..	....	....	....	....	....	....	....	....
Migrants' transfers	2 431 ..	....	....	....	....	....	....	....	....
Debt forgiveness	2 432 ..	....	....	....	....	....	....	....	....
Other capital transfers	2 440 ..	....	....	....	....	....	....	....	....
Capital transfers, debit	3 400 ..	....	....	....	....	....	....	....	....
General government	3 401 ..	....	....	....	....	....	....	....	....
Debt forgiveness	3 402 ..	....	....	....	....	....	....	....	....
Other capital transfers	3 410 ..	....	....	....	....	....	....	....	....
Other sectors	3 430 ..	....	....	....	....	....	....	....	....
Migrants' transfers	3 431 ..	....	....	....	....	....	....	....	....
Debt forgiveness	3 432 ..	....	....	....	....	....	....	....	....
Other capital transfers	3 440 ..	....	....	....	....	....	....	....	....
Nonproduced nonfinancial assets, credit	2 480 ..	....	....	....	....	....	....	....	....
Nonproduced nonfinancial assets, debit	3 480 ..	....	....	....	....	....	....	....	....

Table 2 (Continued). STANDARD PRESENTATION, 2003–2010

(Millions of U.S. dollars)

	Code	2003	2004	2005	2006	2007	2008	2009	2010
FINANCIAL ACCOUNT..	4 995 ..	**1,519.5**	**−1,403.5**	**−4,571.5**	**−10,957.8**	**−8,947.4**	**−5,971.2**	**7,105.7**	**−5,692.0**
A. DIRECT INVESTMENT...................................	4 500 ..	**3,481.1**	**1,414.0**	**−1,523.2**	**−228.3**	**−1,805.1**	**−890.7**	**2,198.5**	**−4,567.6**
Direct investment abroad..................................	4 505 ..	**−23.6**	**−35.2**	**−219.4**	**−190.6**	**−911.8**	**−2,569.6**	**−6.8**	**−1,340.4**
Equity capital..	4 510 ..	....	....	....	....	−80.5	−593.8	−.1	−85.0
Claims on affiliated enterprises............................	4 515 ..	....	....	....	....	−80.5	−593.8	−.1	−85.0
Liabilities to affiliated enterprises........................	4 520 ..	....	....	....	....	....	....	....	....
Reinvested earnings.......................................	4 525 ..	....	....	−17.9	....	....	....	....	....
Other capital..	4 530 ..	−23.6	−35.2	−201.5	−190.6	−831.3	−1,975.8	−6.7	−1,255.4
Claims on affiliated enterprises............................	4 535 ..	−23.6	−35.2	−201.5	−190.6	−831.3	−1,975.8	−6.7	−1,255.4
Liabilities to affiliated enterprises........................	4 540 ..	....	....	....	....	....	....	....	....
Direct investment in Angola.............................	4 555 ..	**3,504.7**	**1,449.2**	**−1,303.8**	**−37.7**	**−893.3**	**1,679.0**	**2,205.3**	**−3,227.2**
Equity capital..	4 560 ..	....	−748.0	....	....	....	....	....	....
Claims on direct investors.................................	4 565 ..	....	−748.0	....	....	....	....	....	....
Liabilities to direct investors..............................	4 570 ..	....	....	....	....	....	....	....	....
Reinvested earnings.......................................	4 575 ..	679.6	1,057.9	1,139.7	2,915.7	3,242.7	5,266.0	2,743.2	3,325.6
Other capital..	4 580 ..	2,825.1	1,139.4	−2,443.6	−2,953.5	−4,136.1	−3,587.0	−537.9	−6,552.8
Claims on direct investors.................................	4 585 ..	−72.3	....	....	....	....	....	....	....
Liabilities to direct investors..............................	4 590 ..	2,897.4	1,139.4	−2,443.6	−2,953.5	−4,136.1	−3,587.0	−537.9	−6,552.8
B. PORTFOLIO INVESTMENT............................	4 600 ..	**1.0**	**−2.7**	**−1,267.0**	**−1,439.5**	**−2,015.4**	**−1,757.5**	**−490.1**	**−270.5**
Assets..	4 602 ..	**1.0**	**−2.7**	**−1,267.0**	**−1,439.5**	**−2,015.4**	**−1,757.5**	**−558.1**	**−273.5**
Equity securities...	4 610 ..	....	−3.3	−1,264.0	−1,491.0	−1,965.9	−1,757.5	−558.1	−273.5
Monetary authorities......................................	4 611 ..	....	....	....	....	....	....	....	....
General government......................................	4 612 ..	....	....	....	....	....	....	....	....
Banks..	4 613 ..	....	....	....	....	....	....	....	....
Other sectors...	4 614 ..	....	−3.3	−1,264.0	−1,491.0	−1,965.9	−1,757.5	−558.1	−273.5
Debt securities..	4 619 ..	1.0	.6	−3.0	51.5	−49.5	....	....	....
Bonds and notes..	4 620 ..	....	.6	−3.0	51.5	−49.5	....	....	....
Monetary authorities.....................................	4 621 ..	....	....	....	....	....	....	....	....
General government.....................................	4 622 ..	....	....	....	....	....	....	....	....
Banks..	4 623 ..	....	.6	−3.0	51.5	−49.5	....	....	....
Other sectors...	4 624 ..	....	....	....	....	....	....	....	....
Money market instruments................................	4 630 ..	1.0	....	....	....	....	....	....	....
Monetary authorities.....................................	4 631 ..	....	....	....	....	....	....	....	....
General government.....................................	4 632 ..	....	....	....	....	....	....	....	....
Banks..	4 633 ..	1.0	....	....	....	....	....	....	....
Other sectors...	4 634 ..	....	....	....	....	....	....	....	....
Liabilities..	4 652 ..	....	....	....	....	....	....	**68.0**	**3.0**
Equity securities...	4 660 ..	....	....	....	....	....	....	....	....
Banks..	4 663 ..	....	....	....	....	....	....	....	....
Other sectors...	4 664 ..	....	....	....	....	....	....	....	....
Debt securities..	4 669 ..	....	....	....	....	....	....	68.0	3.0
Bonds and notes..	4 670 ..	....	....	....	....	....	....	68.0	3.0
Monetary authorities.....................................	4 671 ..	....	....	....	....	....	....	....	....
General government.....................................	4 672 ..	....	....	....	....	....	....	68.0	3.0
Banks..	4 673 ..	....	....	....	....	....	....	....	....
Other sectors...	4 674 ..	....	....	....	....	....	....	....	....
Money market instruments................................	4 680 ..	....	....	....	....	....	....	....	....
Monetary authorities.....................................	4 681 ..	....	....	....	....	....	....	....	....
General government.....................................	4 682 ..	....	....	....	....	....	....	....	....
Banks..	4 683 ..	....	....	....	....	....	....	....	....
Other sectors...	4 684 ..	....	....	....	....	....	....	....	....
C. FINANCIAL DERIVATIVES............................	4 910 ..	....	....	....	....	....	....	....	....
Monetary authorities..	4 911 ..	....	....	....	....	....	....	....	....
General government..	4 912 ..	....	....	....	....	....	....	....	....
Banks...	4 913 ..	....	....	....	....	....	....	....	....
Other sectors..	4 914 ..	....	....	....	....	....	....	....	....
Assets..	4 900 ..	....	....	....	....	....	....	....	....
Monetary authorities..	4 901 ..	....	....	....	....	....	....	....	....
General government..	4 902 ..	....	....	....	....	....	....	....	....
Banks...	4 903 ..	....	....	....	....	....	....	....	....
Other sectors..	4 904 ..	....	....	....	....	....	....	....	....
Liabilities..	4 905 ..	....	....	....	....	....	....	....	....
Monetary authorities..	4 906 ..	....	....	....	....	....	....	....	....
General government..	4 907 ..	....	....	....	....	....	....	....	....
Banks...	4 908 ..	....	....	....	....	....	....	....	....
Other sectors..	4 909 ..	....	....	....	....	....	....	....	....

Table 2 (Concluded). STANDARD PRESENTATION, 2003–2010

(Millions of U.S. dollars)

	Code	2003	2004	2005	2006	2007	2008	2009	2010
D. OTHER INVESTMENT...........................	4 700 ..	**−1,699.8**	**−2,034.5**	**36.0**	**−3,888.3**	**−2,107.8**	**3,349.6**	**393.4**	**4,294.8**
Assets...	4 703 ..	**120.0**	**−1,951.5**	**−1,850.1**	**−1,633.1**	**−4,854.9**	**−2,709.2**	**−1,369.0**	**97.6**
Trade credits................................	4 706 ..	45.0	−251.1	−1,366.1	138.3	−2,751.7	2,791.0	−2,263.1	−1,478.1
General government....................	4 707 ..	....	....	....	....	....	....	....	....
of which: Short-term.................	4 709 ..	....	....	....	....	....	....	....	....
Other sectors..............................	4 710 ..	45.0	−251.1	−1,366.1	138.3	−2,751.7	2,791.0	−2,263.1	−1,478.1
of which: Short-term.................	4 712 ..	*45.0*	*−251.1*	*−1,366.1*	*138.3*	*−2,751.7*	*2,791.0*	*−2,263.1*	*−1,478.1*
Loans...	4 714 ..	−12.6	−.1	9.2	−7.0	7.1	−7.0	−6.7	....
Monetary authorities..................	4 715 ..	....	....	....	....	....	....	....	....
of which: Short-term.................	4 718 ..	....	....	....	....	....	....	....	....
General government....................	4 719 ..	....	....	....	....	....	....	....	....
of which: Short-term.................	4 721 ..	....	....	....	....	....	....	....	....
Banks..	4 722 ..	−12.6	−.1	9.2	−7.0	7.1	−7.0	−6.7	....
of which: Short-term.................	4 724 ..	*−12.6*	*−.1*	*9.2*	*−7.0*	*7.1*	*−7.0*	*−6.7*	....
Other sectors..............................	4 725 ..	....	....	....	....	....	....	....	....
of which: Short-term.................	4 727 ..	....	....	....	....	....	....	....	....
Currency and deposits.....................	4 730 ..	100.6	−1,679.1	−511.4	−1,783.5	−2,107.9	−5,439.4	937.9	3,829.0
Monetary authorities..................	4 731 ..	....	....	....	....	....	....	....	....
General government....................	4 732 ..	....	....	....	....	....	....	....	....
Banks..	4 733 ..	100.6	−46.9	−398.4	−1,456.5	37.6	−2,573.1	1,507.6	2,113.6
Other sectors..............................	4 734 ..	....	−1,632.2	−113.0	−327.0	−2,145.4	−2,866.2	−569.7	1,715.4
Other assets.................................	4 736 ..	−13.0	−21.1	18.2	19.2	−2.5	−53.9	−37.1	−2,253.3
Monetary authorities..................	4 737 ..	....	....	....	....	....	....	....	....
of which: Short-term.................	4 739 ..	....	....	....	....	....	....	....	....
General government....................	4 740 ..	....	....	....	....	....	....	....	....
of which: Short-term.................	4 742 ..	....	....	....	....	....	....	....	....
Banks..	4 743 ..	−13.0	−21.1	18.2	19.2	−2.5	−53.9	−37.1	−2,253.3
of which: Short-term.................	4 745 ..	*−13.0*	*−21.1*	*18.2*	*19.2*	*−2.5*	*−53.9*	*−37.1*	*−2,253.3*
Other sectors..............................	4 746 ..	....	....	....	....	....	....	....	....
of which: Short-term.................	4 748 ..	....	....	....	....	....	....	....	....
Liabilities..	4 753 ..	**−1,819.8**	**−83.0**	**1,886.1**	**−2,255.2**	**2,747.1**	**6,058.8**	**1,762.4**	**4,197.2**
Trade credits................................	4 756 ..	....	....	−6.8	406.9	−198.1	−372.0	199.9	−611.2
General government....................	4 757 ..	....	....	....	....	....	....	....	....
of which: Short-term.................	4 759 ..	....	....	....	....	....	....	....	....
Other sectors..............................	4 760 ..	....	....	−6.8	406.9	−198.1	−372.0	199.9	−611.2
of which: Short-term.................	4 762 ..	....	....	*−6.8*	*406.9*	*−198.1*	*−372.0*	*199.9*	*−611.2*
Loans...	4 764 ..	−2,040.2	1,510.6	1,473.8	−1,128.9	2,532.2	5,029.8	2,638.3	1,496.4
Monetary authorities..................	4 765 ..	−38.0	−2.2	.1	10.0	.1	364.2	−121.7	1,749.5
of which: Use of Fund credit and loans from the Fund..	4 766 ..	....	....	....	....	....	....	....	*877.6*
of which: Short-term.................	4 768 ..	*−38.0*	*−2.2*	*.1*	*10.0*	*.1*	*364.2*	*−121.7*	*871.9*
General government....................	4 769 ..	475.6	1,430.4	−1,127.3	−992.6	1,425.8	1,593.9	1,297.6	39.7
of which: Short-term.................	4 771 ..	....	....	....	....	....	....	*−219.0*	*−57.5*
Banks..	4 772 ..	−3.1	20.6	−17.5	93.2	94.7	981.6	2,247.3	−2,345.6
of which: Short-term.................	4 774 ..	*−2.1*	*20.6*	*−17.5*	*21.2*	*7.4*	*832.3*	*2,199.4*	*−2,183.5*
Other sectors..............................	4 775 ..	−2,474.7	61.9	2,618.5	−239.5	1,011.5	2,090.1	−784.9	2,052.7
of which: Short-term.................	4 777 ..	*−1,828.8*	*17.4*	*−5.9*	*50.9*	....	....	*−33.7*	*−29.2*
Currency and deposits.....................	4 780 ..	75.0	.4	42.7	44.4	519.1	1,983.0	−1,482.0	2,494.3
Monetary authorities..................	4 781 ..	....	....	....	....	....	....	−68.0	−3.0
General government....................	4 782 ..	....	....	....	....	....	....	....	....
Banks..	4 783 ..	8.0	.4	42.7	44.4	519.1	1,983.0	−1,414.0	2,497.3
Other sectors..............................	4 784 ..	67.0	....	....	....	....	....	....	....
Other liabilities............................	4 786 ..	145.4	−1,594.0	376.3	−1,577.6	−106.1	−582.0	406.2	817.7
Monetary authorities..................	4 787 ..	....	−3.6	....	....	....	....	427.0	420.4
of which: Short-term.................	4 789 ..	....	*−3.6*	....	....	....	....	....	....
General government....................	4 790 ..	245.6	−1,612.9	337.1	−1,149.5	−26.3	−601.7	−124.6	102.5
of which: Short-term.................	4 792 ..	*245.6*	*−1,612.9*	*337.1*	*−1,149.5*	*−26.3*	*−601.7*	*−124.6*	*102.5*
Banks..	4 793 ..	−15.4	−2.6	4.5	−3.6	2.9	19.7	57.8	344.7
of which: Short-term.................	4 795 ..	*−15.4*	*−2.6*	*4.5*	*−3.6*	*2.9*	*19.7*	*57.8*	*344.7*
Other sectors..............................	4 796 ..	−84.8	25.0	34.7	−424.5	−82.8	−.1	46.1	−49.9
of which: Short-term.................	4 798 ..	*−84.8*	*25.0*	*34.7*	*−424.5*	*−82.8*	*−.1*	*46.1*	*−49.9*
E. RESERVE ASSETS...........................	4 802 ..	**−262.8**	**−780.3**	**−1,817.3**	**−5,401.7**	**−3,019.1**	**−6,672.6**	**5,003.8**	**−5,148.6**
Monetary gold.............................	4 812 ..	....	....	....	....	....	....	....	....
Special drawing rights...................	4 811 ..	....	....	....	....	....	....	−424.4	8.0
Reserve position in the Fund...........	4 810 ..	....	....	....	....	....	....	....	....
Foreign exchange..........................	4 803 ..	−262.8	−780.2	−1,817.3	−5,401.7	−3,019.0	−6,672.6	5,428.2	−5,156.6
Other claims.................................	4 813 ..	....	....	....	....	....	....	....	....
NET ERRORS AND OMISSIONS...............	4 998 ..	**−821.9**	**282.2**	**−574.2**	**266.5**	**−1,641.0**	**−1,235.9**	**454.7**	**−1,730.0**

Table 3. INTERNATIONAL INVESTMENT POSITION (End-period stocks), 2003–2010

(Millions of U.S. dollars)

	Code	2003	2004	2005	2006	2007	2008	2009	2010
ASSETS..............	8 995 C.	**3,362.0**	**5,845.6**	**9,414.4**	**18,217.5**	**25,846.1**	**48,959.4**	**45,968.4**	**49,669.5**
Direct investment abroad................	8 505 ..	**23.6**	**23.9**	**24.4**	**215.0**	**1,126.8**	**3,502.3**	**3,509.1**	**4,849.5**
Equity capital and reinvested earnings.........	8 506 ..	....	....	....	....	....	....	....	....
Claims on affiliated enterprises.............	8 507 ..	....	....	....	....	....	....	....	....
Liabilities to affiliated enterprises..........	8 508 ..	....	....	....	....	....	....	....	....
Other capital.........	8 530 ..	....	....	....	....	....	....	....	....
Claims on affiliated enterprises.............	8 535 ..	....	....	....	....	....	....	....	....
Liabilities to affiliated enterprisess.........	8 540 ..	....	....	....	....	....	....	....	....
Portfolio investment.................	8 602 ..	**47.2**	**49.8**	**1,316.8**	**2,756.3**	**4,771.7**	**6,529.2**	**6,536.0**	**6,809.5**
Equity securities......................	8 610 ..	....	....	1,316.8	2,756.3	4,771.7	6,529.2	6,536.0	6,809.5
Monetary authorities..................	8 611 ..	....	....	....	....	....	....	....	....
General government...................	8 612 ..	....	....	....	....	....	....	....	....
Banks..............................	8 613 ..	....	....	....	....	....	....	....	....
Other sectors.......................	8 614 ..	....	....	1,316.8	2,756.3	4,771.7	6,529.2	6,536.0	6,809.5
Debt securities.......................	8 619 ..	....	....	....	....	....	....	....	....
Bonds and notes....................	8 620 ..	....	....	....	....	....	....	....	....
Monetary authorities..............	8 621 ..	....	....	....	....	....	....	....	....
General government...............	8 622 ..	....	....	....	....	....	....	....	....
Banks..........................	8 623 ..	....	....	....	....	....	....	....	....
Other sectors....................	8 624 ..	....	....	....	....	....	....	....	....
Money market instruments...........	8 630 ..	....	....	....	....	....	....	....	....
Monetary authorities..............	8 631 ..	....	....	....	....	....	....	....	....
General government...............	8 632 ..	....	....	....	....	....	....	....	....
Banks..........................	8 633 ..	....	....	....	....	....	....	....	....
Other sectors....................	8 634 ..	....	....	....	....	....	....	....	....
Financial derivatives.................	8 900 ..	....	....	....	....	....	....	....	....
Monetary authorities..................	8 901 ..	....	....	....	....	....	....	....	....
General government...................	8 902 ..	....	....	....	....	....	....	....	....
Banks..............................	8 903 ..	....	....	....	....	....	....	....	....
Other sectors.......................	8 904 ..	....	....	....	....	....	....	....	....
Other investment.................	8 703 ..	**2,691.9**	**4,392.3**	**4,876.3**	**6,647.6**	**8,750.8**	**21,422.2**	**23,043.9**	**19,990.1**
Trade credits........................	8 706 ..	....	....	....	....	....	7,184.3	9,447.4	7,969.3
General government................	8 707 ..	....	....	....	....	....	....	....	....
of which: Short-term............	8 709 ..	....	....	....	....	....	....	....	....
Other sectors.....................	8 710 ..	....	....	....	....	....	7,184.3	9,447.4	7,969.3
of which: Short-term............	8 712 ..	....	....	....	....	....	*7,184.3*	*9,447.4*	*7,969.3*
Loans..............................	8 714 ..	14.3	14.4	5.2	12.2	5.1	12.1	18.8	18.8
Monetary authorities...............	8 715 ..	....	....	....	....	....	....	....	....
of which: Short-term............	8 718 ..	....	....	....	....	....	....	....	....
General government................	8 719 ..	....	....	....	....	....	....	....	....
of which: Short-term............	8 721 ..	....	....	....	....	....	....	....	....
Banks............................	8 722 ..	14.3	14.4	5.2	12.2	5.1	12.1	18.8	18.8
of which: Short-term............	8 724 ..	....	....	....	....	....	....	....	....
Other sectors.....................	8 725 ..	....	....	....	....	....	....	....	....
of which: Short-term............	8 727 ..	....	....	....	....	....	....	....	....
Currency and deposits................	8 730 ..	2,645.1	4,324.2	4,835.6	6,619.1	8,727.0	14,145.9	13,516.8	9,687.8
Monetary authorities...............	8 731 ..	....	....	....	....	....	....	....	....
General government................	8 732 ..	....	....	....	....	....	....	....	....
Banks............................	8 733 ..	1,169.1	1,216.0	1,614.4	3,070.9	3,033.3	5,586.0	4,387.2	2,273.7
Other sectors.....................	8 734 ..	1,476.0	3,108.2	3,221.2	3,548.2	5,693.6	8,559.9	9,129.6	7,414.2
Other assets........................	8 736 ..	32.5	53.7	35.5	16.3	18.8	79.9	61.0	2,314.2
Monetary authorities...............	8 737 ..	....	....	....	....	....	....	....	....
of which: Short-term............	8 739 ..	....	....	....	....	....	....	....	....
General government................	8 740 ..	....	....	....	....	....	....	....	....
of which: Short-term............	8 742 ..	....	....	....	....	....	....	....	....
Banks............................	8 743 ..	32.5	53.7	35.5	16.3	18.8	79.9	61.0	2,314.2
of which: Short-term............	8 745 ..	....	....	*35.5*	*16.3*	*18.8*	*79.9*	*61.0*	*2,314.2*
Other sectors.....................	8 746 ..	....	....	....	....	....	....	....	....
of which: Short-term............	8 748 ..	....	....	....	....	....	....	....	....
Reserve assets.................	8 802 ..	**599.3**	**1,379.6**	**3,196.9**	**8,598.6**	**11,196.8**	**17,505.7**	**12,879.4**	**18,020.4**
Monetary gold......................	8 812 ..	....	....	....	....	....	....	....	....
Special drawing rights................	8 811 ..	.2	.2	.2	.2	.3	.3	425.7	410.1
Reserve position in the Fund..........	8 810 ..	....	....	....	....	....	....	....	....
Foreign exchange....................	8 803 ..	599.1	1,379.4	3,196.6	8,598.4	11,196.5	17,505.5	12,453.7	17,610.3
Other claims.......................	8 813 ..	....	....	....	....	....	....	....	....

Table 3 (Concluded). INTERNATIONAL INVESTMENT POSITION (End-period stocks), 2003–2010

(Millions of U.S. dollars)

	Code	2003	2004	2005	2006	2007	2008	2009	2010
LIABILITIES	8 995 D.	**20,521.3**	**22,547.2**	**22,487.4**	**20,274.7**	**21,948.7**	**30,314.8**	**35,419.8**	**36,274.3**
Direct investment in Angola	8 555	**11,987.5**	**13,436.7**	**12,132.9**	**12,095.1**	**11,201.8**	**12,880.8**	**15,086.1**	**11,858.9**
Equity capital and reinvested earnings	8 556	....	....	....	....	....	....	....	....
Claims on direct investors	8 557	....	....	....	....	....	....	....	....
Liabilities to direct investors	8 558	....	....	....	....	....	....	....	....
Other capital	8 580	....	....	....	....	....	....	....	....
Claims on direct investors	8 585	....	....	....	....	....	....	....	....
Liabilities to direct investors	8 590	....	....	....	....	....	....	....	....
Portfolio investment	8 652	....	....	....	....	....	....		
Equity securities	8 660	....	....	....	....	....	....		
Banks	8 663	....	....	....	....	....	....		
Other sectors	8 664	....	....	....	....	....	....		
Debt securities	8 669	....	....	....	....	....	....		
Bonds and notes	8 670	....	....	....	....	....	....		
Monetary authorities	8 671	....	....	....	....	....	....		
General government	8 672	....	....	....	....	....	....		
Banks	8 673	....	....	....	....	....	....		
Other sectors	8 674	....	....	....	....	....	....		
Money market instruments	8 680	....	....	....	....	....	....		
Monetary authorities	8 681	....	....	....	....	....	....		
General government	8 682	....	....	....	....	....	....		
Banks	8 683	....	....	....	....	....	....		
Other sectors	8 684	....	....	....	....	....	....		
Financial derivatives	8 905	....	....	....	....	....	....		....
Monetary authorities	8 906	....	....	....	....	....	....		
General government	8 907	....	....	....	....	....	....		
Banks	8 908	....	....	....	....	....	....		
Other sectors	8 909	....	....	....	....	....	....		
Other investment	8 753	**8,533.8**	**9,110.5**	**10,354.6**	**8,179.6**	**10,746.9**	**17,434.0**	**20,333.8**	**24,415.4**
Trade credits	8 756	6.8	6.8	....	406.9	208.8	....	36.7	....
General government	8 757	....	....	....	....	....	....	....	....
of which: Short-term	8 759	....	....	....	....	....	....	....	....
Other sectors	8 760	6.8	6.8	....	406.9	208.8	....	36.7	....
of which: Short-term	8 762	....	....	....	*406.9*	*208.8*	....	*36.7*	....
Loans	8 764	6,529.8	6,987.3	7,819.1	6,770.4	9,122.9	14,615.5	18,284.3	19,518.6
Monetary authorities	8 765	21.8	7.1	7.2	17.3	12.0	369.8	276.3	2,029.9
of which: Use of Fund credit and loans from the Fund	8 766	....	....	....	....	....	....	....	*881.8*
of which: Short-term	8 768	....	....	*7.2*	*17.3*	*12.0*	*369.8*	*276.3*	*1,148.1*
General government	8 769	5,523.3	5,929.3	4,219.7	3,321.6	4,595.9	6,642.8	8,788.7	8,828.4
of which: Short-term	8 771	....	....	....	....	....	....	....	....
Banks	8 772	56.8	80.1	62.6	174.3	293.0	1,296.6	3,782.2	1,170.3
of which: Short-term	8 774	....	....	....	....	....	....	....	....
Other sectors	8 775	927.9	970.8	3,529.6	3,257.2	4,222.0	6,306.3	5,437.2	7,489.9
of which: Short-term	8 777	....	....	....	....	....	....	....	....
Currency and deposits	8 780	14.4	14.8	57.5	101.8	620.9	2,604.4	1,258.4	3,752.7
Monetary authorities	8 781	....	....	....	....	....	....	....	....
General government	8 782	....	....	....	....	....	....	68.0	65.0
Banks	8 783	14.4	14.8	57.5	101.8	620.9	2,604.4	1,190.4	3,687.7
Other sectors	8 784	....	....	....	....	....	....	....	....
Other liabilities	8 786	1,982.8	2,101.7	2,478.0	900.4	794.3	214.1	754.4	1,144.2
Monetary authorities	8 787	.2	....	....	....	....	....	428.0	420.4
of which: Short-term	8 789	....	....	....	....	....	....	....	....
General government	8 790	1,451.1	1,547.7	1,884.8	735.3	709.0	107.4	29.0	157.0
of which: Short-term	8 792	....	....	....	....	....	....	....	....
Banks	8 793	15.3	12.7	17.3	13.7	16.6	38.2	75.6	414.9
of which: Short-term	8 795	....	....	....	....	....	....	....	....
Other sectors	8 796	516.2	541.2	575.9	151.4	68.7	68.6	221.9	151.8
of which: Short-term	8 798	....	....	....	....	....	....	....	....
NET INTERNATIONAL INVESTMENT POSITION	8 995	**−17,159.2**	**−16,701.6**	**−13,073.0**	**−2,057.3**	**3,897.4**	**18,644.6**	**10,548.5**	**13,395.2**
Conversion rates: kwanzas per U.S. dollar (end of period)	0 102	79.081	85.988	80.780	80.264	75.023	75.169	89.398	92.643

Table 1. ANALYTIC PRESENTATION, 2003–2010

(Millions of U.S. dollars)

	Code	2003	2004	2005	2006	2007	2008	2009	2010
A. Current Account[1]	4 993 Z.	**−39.87**	**−47.40**	**−52.05**	**−144.58**	**−184.00**	**−211.25**	**−93.64**	**−68.37**
Goods: exports f.o.b.	2 100 ..	4.26	6.03	15.02	12.27	9.21	11.50	23.22	12.65
Goods: imports f.o.b.	3 100 ..	−67.60	−90.18	−114.30	−197.12	−218.20	−239.19	−148.72	−138.57
Balance on Goods	4 100 ..	*−63.34*	*−84.16*	*−99.29*	*−184.84*	*−208.99*	*−227.69*	*−125.50*	*−125.92*
Services: credit	2 200 ..	72.70	77.89	98.56	123.85	133.87	117.46	110.12	128.91
Services: debit	3 200 ..	−43.51	−46.56	−56.27	−91.55	−102.93	−86.73	−67.24	−67.55
Balance on Goods and Services	4 991 ..	*−34.15*	*−52.82*	*−57.00*	*−152.54*	*−178.06*	*−196.96*	*−82.62*	*−64.56*
Income: credit	2 300 ..	1.87	7.66	11.68	14.98	12.63	6.82	6.47	6.36
Income: debit	3 300 ..	−7.81	−6.88	−7.71	−7.18	−10.95	−15.13	−12.58	−12.92
Balance on Goods, Services, and Income	4 992 ..	*−40.09*	*−52.05*	*−53.02*	*−144.74*	*−176.38*	*−205.27*	*−88.73*	*−71.12*
Current transfers: credit	2 379 Z.	10.40	14.37	10.74	14.34	10.79	9.07	7.88	15.32
Current transfers: debit	3 379 ..	−10.17	−9.71	−9.77	−14.19	−18.41	−15.05	−12.79	−12.57
B. Capital Account[1]	4 994 Z.	**7.83**	**7.56**	**12.81**	**17.88**	**13.76**	**16.37**	**11.50**	**16.21**
Capital account: credit	2 994 Z.	9.20	8.93	14.19	19.28	15.19	17.83	12.99	17.66
Capital account: debit	3 994 ..	−1.38	−1.38	−1.38	−1.40	−1.43	−1.46	−1.49	−1.45
Total, Groups A Plus B	4 981 ..	*−32.04*	*−39.84*	*−39.24*	*−126.70*	*−170.24*	*−194.88*	*−82.14*	*−52.16*
C. Financial Account[1]	4 995 W.	**45.91**	**42.24**	**47.24**	**132.71**	**173.37**	**186.46**	**78.07**	**57.12**
Direct investment abroad	4 505 ..	....	....	....	....	....	....	....	....
Direct investment in Anguilla	4 555 Z.	29.39	86.73	117.31	142.00	118.88	98.71	46.32	73.41
Portfolio investment assets	4 602 ..	....	....	....	−.18	−.11	....	−5.59	....
Equity securities	4 610 ..	....	....	....	....	....	....	....	....
Debt securities	4 619 ..	....	....	....	....	....	....	....	....
Portfolio investment liabilities	4 652 Z.	−.22	1.17	.59	3.69	−.18	5.43	2.11	2.18
Equity securities	4 660 ..	....	....	....	....	....	....	....	....
Debt securities	4 669 Z.	....	....	....	....	....	....	....	....
Financial derivatives	4 910 ..	....	....	....	....	....	....	....	....
Financial derivatives assets	4 900 ..	....	....	....	....	....	....	....	....
Financial derivatives liabilities	4 905 ..	....	....	....	....	....	....	....	....
Other investment assets	4 703 ..	−13.15	−63.20	−72.77	−15.64	−24.59	−25.29	−16.97	−73.76
Monetary authorities	4 701 ..	....	....	....	....	....	....	....	....
General government	4 704 ..	....	....	....	....	....	....	....	....
Banks	4 705 ..	....	−48.57	−62.48	−1.79	....	....	....	−56.42
Other sectors	4 728 ..	−13.15	−14.64	−10.30	−13.85	−24.59	−25.29	−16.97	−17.34
Other investment liabilities	4 753 W.	29.89	17.55	2.12	2.83	79.37	107.61	52.20	55.30
Monetary authorities	4 753 WA	−.21	.34	−.78	.21	.96	6.57	−.35	46.84
General government	4 753 ZB	....	....	....	....	....	....	....	....
Banks	4 753 ZC	10.32	....	....	....	51.96	83.59	41.88	....
Other sectors	4 753 ZD	19.79	17.20	2.89	2.63	26.45	17.45	10.68	8.46
Total, Groups A Through C	4 983 ..	*13.87*	*2.40*	*8.00*	*6.00*	*3.12*	*−8.42*	*−4.07*	*4.97*
D. Net Errors and Omissions	4 998 ..	**−6.79**	**−1.43**	**−2.55**	**−3.89**	**−.07**	**4.55**	**.53**	**−2.53**
Total, Groups A Through D	4 984 ..	*7.08*	*.97*	*5.45*	*2.12*	*3.05*	*−3.87*	*−3.54*	*2.43*
E. Reserves and Related Items	4 802 A.	**−7.08**	**−.97**	**−5.45**	**−2.12**	**−3.05**	**3.87**	**3.54**	**−2.43**
Reserve assets	4 802 ..	−7.08	−.97	−5.45	−2.12	−3.05	3.87	3.54	−2.43
Use of Fund credit and loans	4 766 ..	....	....	....	....	....	....	....	....
Exceptional financing	4 920 ..	....	....	....	....	....	....	....	....
Conversion rates: Eastern Caribbean dollars per U.S. dollar	0 101 ..	**2.7000**	**2.7000**	**2.7000**	**2.7000**	**2.7000**	**2.7000**	**2.7000**	**2.7000**

[1] Excludes components that have been classified in the categories of Group E.

Table 2. STANDARD PRESENTATION, 2003–2010

(Millions of U.S. dollars)

	Code	2003	2004	2005	2006	2007	2008	2009	2010
CURRENT ACCOUNT.....................................	4 993 ..	**−39.87**	**−47.40**	**−52.05**	**−144.58**	**−184.00**	**−211.25**	**−93.64**	**−68.37**
A. GOODS...	4 100 ..	**−63.34**	**−84.16**	**−99.29**	**−184.84**	**−208.99**	**−227.69**	**−125.50**	**−125.92**
Credit..	2 100 ..	**4.26**	**6.03**	**15.02**	**12.27**	**9.21**	**11.50**	**23.22**	**12.65**
General merchandise: exports f.o.b.	2 110 ..	4.25	5.75	14.74	12.25	9.19	11.47	23.07	12.59
Goods for processing: exports f.o.b.	2 150 ..	....	....	....	....	....	....	....	....
Repairs on goods..................................	2 160 ..	....	....	....	....	....	....	....	....
Goods procured in ports by carriers...............	2 170 ..	.01	.27	.27	.02	.02	.02	.14	.06
Nonmonetary gold..................................	2 180 ..	....	....	....	....	....	....	....	....
Debit...	3 100 ..	**−67.60**	**−90.18**	**−114.30**	**−197.12**	**−218.20**	**−239.19**	**−148.72**	**−138.57**
General merchandise: imports f.o.b.	3 110 ..	−67.56	−90.15	−114.27	−197.08	−218.16	−239.14	−148.67	−138.52
Goods for processing: imports f.o.b.	3 150 ..	....	....	....	....	....	....	....	....
Repairs on goods..................................	3 160 ..	....	....	....	....	....	....	....	....
Goods procured in ports by carriers...............	3 170 ..	−.04	−.04	−.04	−.04	−.04	−.05	−.05	−.05
Nonmonetary gold..................................	3 180 ..	....	....	....	....	....	....	....	....
B. SERVICES..	4 200 ..	**29.20**	**31.34**	**42.29**	**32.30**	**30.93**	**30.73**	**42.88**	**61.36**
Total credit	2 200 ..	*72.70*	*77.89*	*98.56*	*123.85*	*133.87*	*117.46*	*110.12*	*128.91*
Total debit	3 200 ..	*−43.51*	*−46.56*	*−56.27*	*−91.55*	*−102.93*	*−86.73*	*−67.24*	*−67.55*
Transportation services, credit............	2 205 ..	**1.52**	**1.80**	**1.91**	**2.39**	**3.41**	**3.29**	**5.30**	**5.46**
Passenger	2 850 ..	....	....	....	....	....	....	....	....
Freight	2 851 ..	....	....	....	....	....	....	....	....
Other	2 852 ..	....	....	....	....	....	....	....	....
Sea transport, passenger.........................	2 207 ..	....	....	....	....	....	....	....	....
Sea transport, freight............................	2 208 ..	....	....	....	....	....	....	....	....
Sea transport, other..............................	2 209 ..	....	....	....	....	....	....	....	....
Air transport, passenger..........................	2 211 ..	....	....	....	....	....	....	....	....
Air transport, freight............................	2 212 ..	....	....	....	....	....	....	....	....
Air transport, other..............................	2 213 ..	....	....	....	....	....	....	....	....
Other transport, passenger........................	2 215 ..	....	....	....	....	....	....	....	....
Other transport, freight..........................	2 216 ..	....	....	....	....	....	....	....	....
Other transport, other............................	2 217 ..	....	....	....	....	....	....	....	....
Transportation services, debit.............	3 205 ..	**−11.30**	**−13.23**	**−16.38**	**−27.14**	**−32.43**	**−33.03**	**−22.57**	**−21.10**
Passenger	3 850 ..	....	....	....	....	....	....	....	....
Freight	3 851 ..	....	....	....	....	....	....	....	....
Other	3 852 ..	....	....	....	....	....	....	....	....
Sea transport, passenger.........................	3 207 ..	....	....	....	....	....	....	....	....
Sea transport, freight............................	3 208 ..	....	....	....	....	....	....	....	....
Sea transport, other..............................	3 209 ..	....	....	....	....	....	....	....	....
Air transport, passenger..........................	3 211 ..	....	....	....	....	....	....	....	....
Air transport, freight............................	3 212 ..	....	....	....	....	....	....	....	....
Air transport, other..............................	3 213 ..	....	....	....	....	....	....	....	....
Other transport, passenger........................	3 215 ..	....	....	....	....	....	....	....	....
Other transport, freight..........................	3 216 ..	....	....	....	....	....	....	....	....
Other transport, other............................	3 217 ..	....	....	....	....	....	....	....	....
Travel, credit................................	2 236 ..	**64.42**	**69.22**	**85.90**	**107.37**	**114.52**	**102.08**	**92.77**	**111.69**
Business travel....................................	2 237 ..	....	....	....	....	....	....	....	....
Personal travel....................................	2 240 ..	....	....	....	....	....	....	....	....
Travel, debit.................................	3 236 ..	**−8.88**	**−9.05**	**−9.79**	**−12.58**	**−15.39**	**−17.39**	**−16.11**	**−15.69**
Business travel....................................	3 237 ..	....	....	....	....	....	....	....	....
Personal travel....................................	3 240 ..	....	....	....	....	....	....	....	....
Other services, credit.......................	2 200 BA ..	**6.76**	**6.87**	**10.74**	**14.10**	**15.93**	**12.09**	**12.04**	**11.76**
Communications....................................	2 245 ..	1.18	1.10	1.21	1.28	2.72	2.92	2.69	2.62
Construction......................................	2 249 ..	....	....	....	....	....	....	....	....
Insurance...	2 253 ..	1.06	1.13	.99	1.31	1.94	1.97	1.26	1.12
Financial...	2 260 ..	....	....	....	....	....	....	....	....
Computer and information..........................	2 262 ..	....	....	....	....	....	....	....	....
Royalties and licence fees........................	2 266 ..	....	....	....	....	....	....	....	....
Other business services...........................	2 268 ..	3.21	3.44	7.10	9.86	9.56	5.10	5.85	5.70
Personal, cultural, and recreational..............	2 287 ..	....	....	....	....	....	....	....	....
Government, n.i.e.................................	2 291 ..	1.31	1.20	1.44	1.65	1.71	2.08	2.25	2.32
Other services, debit........................	3 200 BA ..	**−23.32**	**−24.28**	**−30.10**	**−51.83**	**−55.11**	**−36.31**	**−28.56**	**−30.75**
Communications....................................	3 245 ..	−.92	−.78	−1.85	−1.94	−2.59	−2.66	−1.95	−2.01
Construction......................................	3 249 ..	−2.86	−5.48	−4.26	−21.67	−23.46	−3.95	−1.26	−4.19
Insurance...	3 253 ..	−2.05	−2.95	−3.06	−4.98	−5.66	−6.03	−3.83	−3.58
Financial...	3 260 ..	....	....	....	....	....	....	....	....
Computer and information..........................	3 262 ..	....	....	−.07	−.09	−.05	−.03	−.02	−.02
Royalties and licence fees........................	3 266 ..	−.21	−.23	−.39	−.40	−.50	−.99	−.52	−.51
Other business services...........................	3 268 ..	−14.83	−13.19	−20.16	−21.94	−22.77	−22.64	−20.88	−20.33
Personal, cultural, and recreational..............	3 287 ..	....	....	....	....	....	....	....	....
Government, n.i.e.................................	3 291 ..	−2.44	−1.66	−.32	−.82	−.09	−.01	−.11	−.12

Table 2 (Continued). STANDARD PRESENTATION, 2003–2010

(Millions of U.S. dollars)

	Code	2003	2004	2005	2006	2007	2008	2009	2010
C. INCOME	4 300	**−5.95**	**.77**	**3.97**	**7.80**	**1.68**	**−8.31**	**−6.11**	**−6.56**
Total credit	2 300	*1.87*	*7.66*	*11.68*	*14.98*	*12.63*	*6.82*	*6.47*	*6.36*
Total debit	3 300	*−7.81*	*−6.88*	*−7.71*	*−7.18*	*−10.95*	*−15.13*	*−12.58*	*−12.92*
Compensation of employees, credit	2 310	**.48**	**3.83**	**2.98**	**3.71**	**3.83**	**4.10**	**4.07**	**4.19**
Compensation of employees, debit	3 310	....	....	....	....	**−3.91**	**−1.97**	**−.63**	**−.61**
Investment income, credit	2 320	**1.38**	**3.82**	**8.70**	**11.28**	**8.80**	**2.72**	**2.40**	**2.17**
Direct investment income	2 330	....	....	....	....	....	.17	.15	....
Dividends and distributed branch profits	2 332	....	....	....	....	....	....	....	....
Reinvested earnings and undistributed branch profits	2 333	....	....	....	....	....	....	....	....
Income on debt (interest)	2 334	....	....	....	....	....	.17	.15	....
Portfolio investment income	2 339	.17	.71	.87	2.09	.59	.84	1.01	1.01
Income on equity	2 340	.17	.71	.87	2.09	.59	.84	1.01	1.01
Income on bonds and notes	2 350	....	....	....	....	....	....	....	....
Income on money market instruments	2 360	....	....	....	....	....	....	....	....
Other investment income	2 370	1.21	3.11	7.84	9.18	8.21	1.71	1.24	1.16
Investment income, debit	3 320	**−7.81**	**−6.88**	**−7.71**	**−7.18**	**−7.04**	**−13.15**	**−11.95**	**−12.31**
Direct investment income	3 330	−6.47	−4.57	−4.46	−4.17	−3.89	−10.91	−9.50	−9.66
Dividends and distributed branch profits	3 332	−1.24	−1.74	−2.75	−.51	−.72	−1.07	−1.35	−1.31
Reinvested earnings and undistributed branch profits	3 333	−5.06	−2.66	−1.60	−3.56	−3.01	−8.62	−7.23	−7.44
Income on debt (interest)	3 334	−.17	−.17	−.11	−.11	−.17	−1.21	−.93	−.90
Portfolio investment income	3 339	....	....	....	....	....	....	....	....
Income on equity	3 340	....	....	....	....	....	....	....	....
Income on bonds and notes	3 350	....	....	....	....	....	....	....	....
Income on money market instruments	3 360	....	....	....	....	....	....	....	....
Other investment income	3 370	−1.35	−2.31	−3.25	−3.01	−3.15	−2.25	−2.45	−2.65
D. CURRENT TRANSFERS	4 379	**.23**	**4.65**	**.97**	**.15**	**−7.62**	**−5.98**	**−4.90**	**2.76**
Credit	2 379	**10.40**	**14.37**	**10.74**	**14.34**	**10.79**	**9.07**	**7.88**	**15.32**
General government	2 380	4.33	7.94	3.90	7.08	3.39	1.98	1.01	8.25
Other sectors	2 390	6.07	6.42	6.84	7.26	7.40	7.09	6.87	7.08
Workers' remittances	2 391	6.02	6.22	6.39	6.59	6.76	6.83	6.61	6.81
Other current transfers	2 392	.06	.20	.45	.67	.63	.26	.26	.27
Debit	3 379	**−10.17**	**−9.71**	**−9.77**	**−14.19**	**−18.41**	**−15.05**	**−12.79**	**−12.57**
General government	3 380	−.63	−.63	−.48	−.75	−.86	−.53	−.42	−.52
Other sectors	3 390	−9.54	−9.09	−9.29	−13.44	−17.55	−14.52	−12.37	−12.05
Workers' remittances	3 391	−6.54	−6.87	−7.22	−10.82	−13.78	−11.91	−8.83	−8.60
Other current transfers	3 392	−3.00	−2.22	−2.08	−2.62	−3.77	−2.60	−3.54	−3.45
CAPITAL AND FINANCIAL ACCOUNT	4 996	**46.66**	**48.82**	**54.60**	**148.47**	**184.07**	**206.71**	**93.11**	**70.90**
CAPITAL ACCOUNT	4 994	**7.83**	**7.56**	**12.81**	**17.88**	**13.76**	**16.37**	**11.50**	**16.21**
Total credit	2 994	*9.20*	*8.93*	*14.19*	*19.28*	*15.19*	*17.83*	*12.99*	*17.66*
Total debit	3 994	*−1.38*	*−1.38*	*−1.38*	*−1.40*	*−1.43*	*−1.46*	*−1.49*	*−1.45*
Capital transfers, credit	2 400	**9.20**	**8.93**	**14.19**	**19.28**	**15.19**	**17.83**	**12.99**	**17.66**
General government	2 401	1.23	.56	1.64	5.48	....	3.40	....	4.28
Debt forgiveness	2 402	....	....	....	....	....	....	....	....
Other capital transfers	2 410	1.23	.56	1.64	5.48	....	3.40	....	4.28
Other sectors	2 430	7.97	8.37	12.55	13.81	15.19	14.43	12.99	13.38
Migrants' transfers	2 431	7.97	8.37	12.55	13.81	15.19	14.43	12.99	13.38
Debt forgiveness	2 432	....	....	....	....	....	....	....	....
Other capital transfers	2 440	....	....	....	....	....	....	....	....
Capital transfers, debit	3 400	**−1.38**	**−1.38**	**−1.38**	**−1.40**	**−1.43**	**−1.46**	**−1.49**	**−1.45**
General government	3 401	....	....	....	....	....	....	....	....
Debt forgiveness	3 402	....	....	....	....	....	....	....	....
Other capital transfers	3 410	....	....	....	....	....	....	....	....
Other sectors	3 430	−1.38	−1.38	−1.38	−1.40	−1.43	−1.46	−1.49	−1.45
Migrants' transfers	3 431	−1.38	−1.38	−1.38	−1.40	−1.43	−1.46	−1.49	−1.45
Debt forgiveness	3 432	....	....	....	....	....	....	....	....
Other capital transfers	3 440	....	....	....	....	....	....	....	....
Nonproduced nonfinancial assets, credit	2 480	....	....	....	....	....	....	....	....
Nonproduced nonfinancial assets, debit	3 480	....	....	....	....	....	....	....	....

Table 2 (Continued). STANDARD PRESENTATION, 2003–2010
(Millions of U.S. dollars)

	Code	2003	2004	2005	2006	2007	2008	2009	2010
FINANCIAL ACCOUNT	4 995	38.83	41.27	41.79	130.59	170.31	190.33	81.61	54.69
A. DIRECT INVESTMENT	4 500	29.39	86.73	117.31	142.00	118.88	98.71	46.32	73.41
Direct investment abroad	4 505	....	....	....	....	....	....	....	....
Equity capital	4 510	....	....	....	....	....	....	....	....
Claims on affiliated enterprises	4 515	....	....	....	....	....	....	....	....
Liabilities to affiliated enterprises	4 520	....	....	....	....	....	....	....	....
Reinvested earnings	4 525	....	....	....	....	....	....	....	....
Other capital	4 530	....	....	....	....	....	....	....	....
Claims on affiliated enterprises	4 535	....	....	....	....	....	....	....	....
Liabilities to affiliated enterprises	4 540	....	....	....	....	....	....	....	....
Direct investment in Anguilla	4 555	29.39	86.73	117.31	142.00	118.88	98.71	46.32	73.41
Equity capital	4 560	6.34	21.47	89.93	72.25	78.20	39.48	22.56	41.88
Claims on direct investors	4 565	....	....	....	....	....	....	....	....
Liabilities to direct investors	4 570	6.34	21.47	89.93	72.25	78.20	39.48	22.56	41.88
Reinvested earnings	4 575	5.06	2.66	1.60	3.56	3.01	8.62	7.23	7.44
Other capital	4 580	17.99	62.59	25.77	66.19	37.67	50.61	16.53	24.09
Claims on direct investors	4 585	....	....	....	....	....	....	....	....
Liabilities to direct investors	4 590	17.99	62.59	25.77	66.19	37.67	50.61	16.53	24.09
B. PORTFOLIO INVESTMENT	4 600	−.22	1.17	.59	3.51	−.29	5.43	−3.48	2.18
Assets	4 602	....	....	....	−.18	−.11	....	−5.59	....
Equity securities	4 610	....	....	....	....	....	....	....	....
Monetary authorities	4 611	....	....	....	....	....	....	....	....
General government	4 612	....	....	....	....	....	....	....	....
Banks	4 613	....	....	....	....	....	....	....	....
Other sectors	4 614	....	....	....	....	....	....	....	....
Debt securities	4 619	....	....	....	....	....	....	....	....
Bonds and notes	4 620	....	....	....	....	....	....	....	....
Monetary authorities	4 621	....	....	....	....	....	....	....	....
General government	4 622	....	....	....	....	....	....	....	....
Banks	4 623	....	....	....	....	....	....	....	....
Other sectors	4 624	....	....	....	....	....	....	....	....
Money market instruments	4 630	....	....	....	....	....	....	....	....
Monetary authorities	4 631	....	....	....	....	....	....	....	....
General government	4 632	....	....	....	....	....	....	....	....
Banks	4 633	....	....	....	....	....	....	....	....
Other sectors	4 634	....	....	....	....	....	....	....	....
Liabilities	4 652	−.22	1.17	.59	3.69	−.18	5.43	2.11	2.18
Equity securities	4 660	....	....	....	....	....	....	....	....
Banks	4 663	....	....	....	....	....	....	....	....
Other sectors	4 664	....	....	....	....	....	....	....	....
Debt securities	4 669	....	....	....	....	....	....	....	....
Bonds and notes	4 670	....	....	....	....	....	....	....	....
Monetary authorities	4 671	....	....	....	....	....	....	....	....
General government	4 672	....	....	....	....	....	....	....	....
Banks	4 673	....	....	....	....	....	....	....	....
Other sectors	4 674	....	....	....	....	....	....	....	....
Money market instruments	4 680	....	....	....	....	....	....	....	....
Monetary authorities	4 681	....	....	....	....	....	....	....	....
General government	4 682	....	....	....	....	....	....	....	....
Banks	4 683	....	....	....	....	....	....	....	....
Other sectors	4 684	....	....	....	....	....	....	....	....
C. FINANCIAL DERIVATIVES	4 910	....	....	....	....	....	....	....	....
Monetary authorities	4 911	....	....	....	....	....	....	....	....
General government	4 912	....	....	....	....	....	....	....	....
Banks	4 913	....	....	....	....	....	....	....	....
Other sectors	4 914	....	....	....	....	....	....	....	....
Assets	4 900	....	....	....	....	....	....	....	....
Monetary authorities	4 901	....	....	....	....	....	....	....	....
General government	4 902	....	....	....	....	....	....	....	....
Banks	4 903	....	....	....	....	....	....	....	....
Other sectors	4 904	....	....	....	....	....	....	....	....
Liabilities	4 905	....	....	....	....	....	....	....	....
Monetary authorities	4 906	....	....	....	....	....	....	....	....
General government	4 907	....	....	....	....	....	....	....	....
Banks	4 908	....	....	....	....	....	....	....	....
Other sectors	4 909	....	....	....	....	....	....	....	....

Table 2 (Concluded). STANDARD PRESENTATION, 2003–2010

(Millions of U.S. dollars)

	Code	2003	2004	2005	2006	2007	2008	2009	2010
D. OTHER INVESTMENT	4 700 ..	**16.74**	**−45.66**	**−70.66**	**−12.80**	**54.78**	**82.32**	**35.24**	**−18.47**
Assets	4 703 ..	−13.15	−63.20	−72.77	−15.64	−24.59	−25.29	−16.97	−73.76
Trade credits	4 706 ..	....	....	....	....	....	....	....	....
General government	4 707 ..	....	....	....	....	....	....	....	....
of which: Short-term	4 709 ..	....	....	....	....	....	....	....	....
Other sectors	4 710 ..	....	....	....	....	....	....	....	....
of which: Short-term	4 712 ..	....	....	....	....	....	....	....	....
Loans	4 714 ..	....	−48.57	−62.48	−1.79	....	....	....	−56.42
Monetary authorities	4 715 ..	....	....	....	....	....	....	....	....
of which: Short-term	4 718 ..	....	....	....	....	....	....	....	....
General government	4 719 ..	....	....	....	....	....	....	....	....
of which: Short-term	4 721 ..	....	....	....	....	....	....	....	....
Banks	4 722 ..	....	−48.57	−62.48	−1.79	....	....	....	−56.42
of which: Short-term	4 724 ..	....	....	....	....	....	....	....	....
Other sectors	4 725 ..	....	....	....	....	....	....	....	....
of which: Short-term	4 727 ..	....	....	....	....	....	....	....	....
Currency and deposits	4 730 ..	....	....	....	....	....	....	....	....
Monetary authorities	4 731 ..	....	....	....	....	....	....	....	....
General government	4 732 ..	....	....	....	....	....	....	....	....
Banks	4 733 ..	....	....	....	....	....	....	....	....
Other sectors	4 734 ..	....	....	....	....	....	....	....	....
Other assets	4 736 ..	−13.15	−14.64	−10.30	−13.85	−24.59	−25.29	−16.97	−17.34
Monetary authorities	4 737 ..	....	....	....	....	....	....	....	....
of which: Short-term	4 739 ..	....	....	....	....	....	....	....	....
General government	4 740 ..	....	....	....	....	....	....	....	....
of which: Short-term	4 742 ..	....	....	....	....	....	....	....	....
Banks	4 743 ..	....	....	....	....	....	....	....	....
of which: Short-term	4 745 ..	....	....	....	....	....	....	....	....
Other sectors	4 746 ..	−13.15	−14.64	−10.30	−13.85	−24.59	−25.29	−16.97	−17.34
of which: Short-term	4 748 ..	....	....	....	....	....	....	....	....
Liabilities	4 753 ..	**29.89**	**17.55**	**2.12**	**2.83**	**79.37**	**107.61**	**52.20**	**55.30**
Trade credits	4 756 ..	....	....	....	....	....	....	....	....
General government	4 757 ..	....	....	....	....	....	....	....	....
of which: Short-term	4 759 ..	....	....	....	....	....	....	....	....
Other sectors	4 760 ..	....	....	....	....	....	....	....	....
of which: Short-term	4 762 ..	....	....	....	....	....	....	....	....
Loans	4 764 ..	−.21	.34	−.78	.21	.96	6.57	−.35	46.84
Monetary authorities	4 765 ..	−.21	.34	−.78	.21	.96	6.57	−.35	46.84
of which: Use of Fund credit and loans from the Fund	4 766 ..	....	....	....	....	....	....	....	....
of which: Short-term	4 768 ..	....	....	....	....	....	....	....	....
General government	4 769 ..	....	....	....	....	....	....	....	....
of which: Short-term	4 771 ..	....	....	....	....	....	....	....	....
Banks	4 772 ..	....	....	....	....	....	....	....	....
of which: Short-term	4 774 ..	....	....	....	....	....	....	....	....
Other sectors	4 775 ..	....	....	....	....	....	....	....	....
of which: Short-term	4 777 ..	....	....	....	....	....	....	....	....
Currency and deposits	4 780 ..	....	....	....	....	....	....	....	....
Monetary authorities	4 781 ..	....	....	....	....	....	....	....	....
General government	4 782 ..	....	....	....	....	....	....	....	....
Banks	4 783 ..	....	....	....	....	....	....	....	....
Other sectors	4 784 ..	....	....	....	....	....	....	....	....
Other liabilities	4 786 ..	30.11	17.20	2.89	2.63	78.41	101.04	52.56	8.46
Monetary authorities	4 787 ..	....	....	....	....	....	....	....	....
of which: Short-term	4 789 ..	....	....	....	....	....	....	....	....
General government	4 790 ..	....	....	....	....	....	....	....	....
of which: Short-term	4 792 ..	....	....	....	....	....	....	....	....
Banks	4 793 ..	10.32	....	....	....	51.96	83.59	41.88	....
of which: Short-term	4 795 ..	....	....	....	....	....	....	....	....
Other sectors	4 796 ..	19.79	17.20	2.89	2.63	26.45	17.45	10.68	8.46
of which: Short-term	4 798 ..	....	....	....	....	....	....	....	....
E. RESERVE ASSETS	4 802 ..	**−7.08**	**−.97**	**−5.45**	**−2.12**	**−3.05**	**3.87**	**3.54**	**−2.43**
Monetary gold	4 812 ..	....	....	....	....	....	....	....	....
Special drawing rights	4 811 ..	....	....	....	....	....	....	....	....
Reserve position in the Fund	4 810 ..	....	....	....	....	....	....	....	....
Foreign exchange	4 803 ..	....	....	....	....	....	....	....	....
Other claims	4 813 ..	−7.08	−.97	−5.45	−2.12	−3.05	3.87	3.54	−2.43
NET ERRORS AND OMISSIONS	4 998 ..	**−6.79**	**−1.43**	**−2.55**	**−3.89**	**−.07**	**4.55**	**.53**	**−2.53**

Table 1. ANALYTIC PRESENTATION, 2003–2010
(Millions of U.S. dollars)

	Code	2003	2004	2005	2006	2007	2008	2009	2010
A. Current Account[1]	4 993 Z.	−79.06	−95.10	−171.49	−291.76	−385.55	−357.60	−241.92	−112.69
Goods: exports f.o.b.	2 100 ..	71.15	57.13	82.74	74.03	59.35	57.61	35.25	34.75
Goods: imports f.o.b.	3 100 ..	−360.21	−402.36	−455.35	−559.70	−648.91	−669.89	−527.86	−439.56
Balance on Goods	4 100 ..	*−289.06*	*−345.23*	*−372.62*	*−485.67*	*−589.56*	*−612.27*	*−492.61*	*−404.81*
Services: credit	2 200 ..	417.91	476.84	462.53	477.44	525.28	563.32	513.64	511.00
Services: debit	3 200 ..	−182.47	−189.98	−227.37	−258.71	−283.46	−273.20	−238.86	−222.42
Balance on Goods and Services	4 991 ..	*−53.61*	*−58.37*	*−137.45*	*−266.95*	*−347.74*	*−322.15*	*−217.83*	*−116.23*
Income: credit	2 300 ..	8.61	11.54	17.96	26.71	25.79	16.11	13.11	13.24
Income: debit	3 300 ..	−47.31	−56.62	−60.00	−73.45	−78.46	−76.40	−63.93	−45.37
Balance on Goods, Services, and Income	4 992 ..	*−92.31*	*−103.45*	*−179.49*	*−313.69*	*−400.41*	*−382.44*	*−268.65*	*−148.36*
Current transfers: credit	2 379 Z.	29.46	25.10	26.17	41.08	44.01	43.89	40.48	48.98
Current transfers: debit	3 379 ..	−16.21	−16.75	−18.17	−19.15	−29.15	−19.04	−13.75	−13.32
B. Capital Account[1]	4 994 Z.	10.19	21.30	214.33	31.57	11.11	14.81	4.20	8.45
Capital account: credit	2 994 Z.	10.19	21.30	214.33	31.57	11.11	14.81	4.20	8.45
Capital account: debit	3 994 ..	....	....	....	....	....	....	....	....
Total, Groups A Plus B	4 981 ..	*−68.87*	*−73.80*	*42.83*	*−260.19*	*−374.44*	*−342.78*	*−237.72*	*−104.25*
C. Financial Account[1]	4 995 W.	110.77	122.90	138.93	310.37	383.81	333.68	212.92	−14.24
Direct investment abroad	4 505 ..	....	....	....	....	....	....	....	....
Direct investment in Antigua & Barbuda	4 555 Z.	166.32	80.37	220.96	358.82	338.20	174.19	118.05	57.50
Portfolio investment assets	4 602 ..	−.03	−1.38	.47	....	−.02	....	....	−.17
Equity securities	4 610 ..	....	....	....	....	....	....	....	....
Debt securities	4 619 ..	....	....	....	....	....	....	....	....
Portfolio investment liabilities	4 652 Z.	2.67	13.48	10.06	24.78	−1.21	10.80	−6.11	1.33
Equity securities	4 660 ..	....	....	....	....	....	....	....	....
Debt securities	4 669 Z.	....	....	....	....	....	....	....	....
Financial derivatives	4 910 ..	....	....	....	....	....	....	....	....
Financial derivatives assets	4 900 ..	....	....	....	....	....	....	....	....
Financial derivatives liabilities	4 905 ..	....	....	....	....	....	....	....	....
Other investment assets	4 703 ..	−120.01	−37.93	−143.18	−149.76	−82.01	−80.09	−46.25	−108.88
Monetary authorities	4 701 ..	....	....	....	....	....	....	....	....
General government	4 704 ..	....	....	....	....	....	....	....	....
Banks	4 705 ..	−99.49	....	−18.26	−64.54	....	....	....	....
Other sectors	4 728 ..	−20.52	−37.93	−124.92	−85.23	−82.01	−80.09	−46.25	−108.88
Other investment liabilities	4 753 W.	61.82	68.37	50.62	76.53	128.84	228.78	147.23	35.97
Monetary authorities	4 753 WA	....	....	....	....	....	....	19.55	....
General government	4 753 ZB	....	....	....	....	....	....	....	....
Banks	4 753 ZC	....	16.05	....	....	15.42	119.03	33.54	6.97
Other sectors	4 753 ZD	61.82	52.32	50.62	76.53	113.43	109.75	94.15	29.00
Total, Groups A Through C	4 983 ..	*41.91*	*49.10*	*181.77*	*50.18*	*9.37*	*−9.10*	*−24.80*	*−118.49*
D. Net Errors and Omissions	4 998 ..	−15.75	−42.68	−174.53	−34.92	−9.05	3.28	14.58	100.33
Total, Groups A Through D	4 984 ..	*26.15*	*6.42*	*7.24*	*15.26*	*.32*	*−5.83*	*−10.21*	*−18.16*
E. Reserves and Related Items	4 802 A.	−26.15	−6.42	−7.24	−15.26	−.32	5.83	10.21	18.16
Reserve assets	4 802 ..	−26.15	−6.42	−7.24	−15.26	−.32	5.83	10.21	−11.89
Use of Fund credit and loans	4 766 ..	....	....	....	....	....	....	....	30.05
Exceptional financing	4 920 ..	....	....	....	....	....	....	....	....
Conversion rates: Eastern Caribbean dollars per U.S. dollar	0 101 ..	2.7000	2.7000	2.7000	2.7000	2.7000	2.7000	2.7000	2.7000

[1] Excludes components that have been classified in the categories of Group E.

Table 2. STANDARD PRESENTATION, 2003–2010

(Millions of U.S. dollars)

	Code	2003	2004	2005	2006	2007	2008	2009	2010
CURRENT ACCOUNT	4 993 ..	−79.06	−95.10	−171.49	−291.76	−385.55	−357.60	−241.92	−112.69
A. GOODS	4 100 ..	−289.06	−345.23	−372.62	−485.67	−589.56	−612.27	−492.61	−404.81
Credit	2 100 ..	71.15	57.13	82.74	74.03	59.35	57.61	35.25	34.75
General merchandise: exports f.o.b.	2 110 ..	44.73	21.42	35.45	23.30	25.21	27.01	23.55	22.98
Goods for processing: exports f.o.b.	2 150 ..	....	....	....	....	....	....	....	....
Repairs on goods	2 160 ..	....	.07	.07	.03	.07	.07	.07	.07
Goods procured in ports by carriers	2 170 ..	26.42	35.64	47.22	50.70	34.08	30.54	11.63	11.69
Nonmonetary gold	2 180 ..	....	....	....	....	....	....	....	....
Debit	3 100 ..	−360.21	−402.36	−455.35	−559.70	−648.91	−669.89	−527.86	−439.56
General merchandise: imports f.o.b.	3 110 ..	−352.29	−393.56	−444.36	−547.86	−639.77	−651.39	−517.52	−429.54
Goods for processing: imports f.o.b.	3 150 ..	....	....	....	....	....	....	....	....
Repairs on goods	3 160 ..	....	....	....	....	....	....	....	....
Goods procured in ports by carriers	3 170 ..	−7.92	−8.80	−11.00	−11.84	−9.15	−18.49	−10.34	−10.02
Nonmonetary gold	3 180 ..	....	....	....	....	....	....	....	....
B. SERVICES	4 200 ..	235.45	286.86	235.16	218.73	241.82	290.12	274.78	288.58
Total credit	2 200 ..	*417.91*	*476.84*	*462.53*	*477.44*	*525.28*	*563.32*	*513.64*	*511.00*
Total debit	3 200 ..	*−182.47*	*−189.98*	*−227.37*	*−258.71*	*−283.46*	*−273.20*	*−238.86*	*−222.42*
Transportation services, credit	2 205 ..	74.60	79.75	84.63	80.15	96.02	135.78	135.79	138.95
Passenger	2 850 ..	....	....	....	....	....	....	....	....
Freight	2 851 ..	....	....	....	....	....	....	....	....
Other	2 852 ..	....	....	....	....	....	....	....	....
Sea transport, passenger	2 207 ..	....	....	....	....	....	....	....	....
Sea transport, freight	2 208 ..	....	....	....	....	....	....	....	....
Sea transport, other	2 209 ..	....	....	....	....	....	....	....	....
Air transport, passenger	2 211 ..	....	....	....	....	....	....	....	....
Air transport, freight	2 212 ..	....	....	....	....	....	....	....	....
Air transport, other	2 213 ..	....	....	....	....	....	....	....	....
Other transport, passenger	2 215 ..	....	....	....	....	....	....	....	....
Other transport, freight	2 216 ..	....	....	....	....	....	....	....	....
Other transport, other	2 217 ..	....	....	....	....	....	....	....	....
Transportation services, debit	3 205 ..	−61.39	−66.09	−78.02	−87.85	−102.33	−93.49	−77.93	−74.13
Passenger	3 850 ..	....	....	....	....	....	....	....	....
Freight	3 851 ..	....	....	....	....	....	....	....	....
Other	3 852 ..	....	....	....	....	....	....	....	....
Sea transport, passenger	3 207 ..	....	....	....	....	....	....	....	....
Sea transport, freight	3 208 ..	....	....	....	....	....	....	....	....
Sea transport, other	3 209 ..	....	....	....	....	....	....	....	....
Air transport, passenger	3 211 ..	....	....	....	....	....	....	....	....
Air transport, freight	3 212 ..	....	....	....	....	....	....	....	....
Air transport, other	3 213 ..	....	....	....	....	....	....	....	....
Other transport, passenger	3 215 ..	....	....	....	....	....	....	....	....
Other transport, freight	3 216 ..	....	....	....	....	....	....	....	....
Other transport, other	3 217 ..	....	....	....	....	....	....	....	....
Travel, credit	2 236 ..	299.82	337.32	309.45	326.75	337.85	333.97	305.12	300.77
Business travel	2 237 ..	....	....	....	....	....	....	....	....
Personal travel	2 240 ..	....	....	....	....	....	....	....	....
Travel, debit	3 236 ..	−34.82	−37.50	−40.05	−45.34	−51.80	−58.36	−54.44	−51.47
Business travel	3 237 ..	....	....	....	....	....	....	....	....
Personal travel	3 240 ..	....	....	....	....	....	....	....	....
Other services, credit	2 200 BA	43.50	59.78	68.45	70.54	91.42	93.57	72.73	71.28
Communications	2 245 ..	8.83	8.06	8.06	8.06	18.77	18.90	15.20	14.72
Construction	2 249 ..	....	....	....	....	....	....	....	....
Insurance	2 253 ..	5.69	13.85	15.50	10.98	13.90	18.81	13.51	13.09
Financial	2 260 ..	....	....	....	....	....	....	....	....
Computer and information	2 262 ..	....	....	....	....	....	....	....	....
Royalties and licence fees	2 266 ..	....	....	....	....	....	....	....	....
Other business services	2 268 ..	23.77	31.47	36.45	39.53	46.75	43.72	32.36	31.54
Personal, cultural, and recreational	2 287 ..	....	....	....	....	....	....	....	....
Government, n.i.e.	2 291 ..	5.21	6.40	8.43	11.97	12.00	12.15	11.66	11.93
Other services, debit	3 200 BA	−86.25	−86.39	−109.29	−125.52	−129.33	−121.35	−106.48	−96.82
Communications	3 245 ..	−5.29	−5.03	−5.03	−5.03	−6.98	−6.65	−5.22	−5.34
Construction	3 249 ..	−3.47	−1.44	−17.82	−25.09	−23.02	−10.66	−7.70	−2.22
Insurance	3 253 ..	−31.18	−31.63	−36.48	−44.89	−48.99	−56.57	−52.56	−49.39
Financial	3 260 ..	....	....	....	....	....	....	....	....
Computer and information	3 262 ..	−.02	....	....	....	....	....	....	....
Royalties and licence fees	3 266 ..	−.51	−.53	−.58	−.77	−.81	−1.89	−1.09	−1.06
Other business services	3 268 ..	−37.63	−39.69	−40.44	−40.34	−37.20	−33.61	−29.55	−28.62
Personal, cultural, and recreational	3 287 ..	....	....	....	....	....	....	....	....
Government, n.i.e.	3 291 ..	−8.14	−8.08	−8.95	−9.40	−12.34	−11.97	−10.35	−10.19

Table 2 (Continued). STANDARD PRESENTATION, 2003–2010

(Millions of U.S. dollars)

	Code	2003	2004	2005	2006	2007	2008	2009	2010
C. INCOME	4 300	**−38.70**	**−45.09**	**−42.04**	**−46.74**	**−52.67**	**−60.29**	**−50.82**	**−32.13**
Total credit	2 300	*8.61*	*11.54*	*17.96*	*26.71*	*25.79*	*16.11*	*13.11*	*13.24*
Total debit	3 300	*−47.31*	*−56.62*	*−60.00*	*−73.45*	*−78.46*	*−76.40*	*−63.93*	*−45.37*
Compensation of employees, credit	2 310	**5.22**	**6.16**	**6.56**	**7.22**	**8.37**	**9.29**	**8.55**	**8.75**
Compensation of employees, debit	3 310	....	....	....	....	....	....	....	....
Investment income, credit	2 320	**3.39**	**5.38**	**11.40**	**19.49**	**17.42**	**6.81**	**4.56**	**4.49**
Direct investment income	2 330	....	....	....	....	....	....	....	....
Dividends and distributed branch profits	2 332	....	....	....	....	....	....	....	....
Reinvested earnings and undistributed branch profits	2 333	....	....	....	....	....	....	....	....
Income on debt (interest)	2 334	....	....	....	....	....	....	....	....
Portfolio investment income	2 339	.69	.05	.08	1.50	2.72	1.80	1.45	1.49
Income on equity	2 340	.69	.05	.08	1.50	2.72	1.80	1.45	1.49
Income on bonds and notes	2 350	....	....	....	....	....	....	....	....
Income on money market instruments	2 360	....	....	....	....	....	....	....	....
Other investment income	2 370	2.70	5.33	11.32	17.99	14.70	5.01	3.10	3.00
Investment income, debit	3 320	**−47.31**	**−56.62**	**−60.00**	**−73.45**	**−78.46**	**−76.40**	**−63.93**	**−45.37**
Direct investment income	3 330	−23.88	−24.68	−30.69	−41.55	−43.81	−40.64	−35.53	−29.22
Dividends and distributed branch profits	3 332	−11.60	−11.04	−15.57	−29.69	−27.70	−25.51	−25.85	−19.85
Reinvested earnings and undistributed branch profits	3 333	−9.00	−11.27	−12.86	−8.59	−12.14	−11.68	−4.93	−4.77
Income on debt (interest)	3 334	−3.27	−2.37	−2.26	−3.27	−3.98	−3.46	−4.76	−4.61
Portfolio investment income	3 339	....	....	....	−1.14	−.52	−.97	−.94	−.42
Income on equity	3 340	....	....	....	−1.14	−.52	−.97	−.94	−.42
Income on bonds and notes	3 350	....	....	....	....	....	....	....	....
Income on money market instruments	3 360	....	....	....	....	....	....	....	....
Other investment income	3 370	−23.43	−31.94	−29.31	−30.76	−34.12	−34.78	−27.46	−15.72
D. CURRENT TRANSFERS	4 379	**13.25**	**8.35**	**8.00**	**21.93**	**14.86**	**24.84**	**26.73**	**35.66**
Credit	2 379	**29.46**	**25.10**	**26.17**	**41.08**	**44.01**	**43.89**	**40.48**	**48.98**
General government	2 380	4.70	4.24	5.01	7.22	8.99	7.72	5.96	13.66
Other sectors	2 390	24.76	20.86	21.15	33.86	35.02	36.17	34.52	35.32
Workers' remittances	2 391	11.16	11.45	11.74	12.11	12.41	12.53	12.14	12.42
Other current transfers	2 392	13.60	9.42	9.41	21.75	22.61	23.64	22.38	22.90
Debit	3 379	**−16.21**	**−16.75**	**−18.17**	**−19.15**	**−29.15**	**−19.04**	**−13.75**	**−13.32**
General government	3 380	−3.56	−3.59	−4.22	−5.27	−13.56	−5.02	−2.36	−2.29
Other sectors	3 390	−12.65	−13.17	−13.95	−13.88	−15.59	−14.03	−11.39	−11.03
Workers' remittances	3 391	−1.49	−1.57	−1.67	−1.84	−2.13	−2.37	−2.30	−2.22
Other current transfers	3 392	−11.16	−11.60	−12.28	−12.04	−13.46	−11.66	−9.10	−8.81
CAPITAL AND FINANCIAL ACCOUNT	4 996	**94.81**	**137.78**	**346.02**	**326.68**	**394.60**	**354.32**	**227.34**	**12.36**
CAPITAL ACCOUNT	4 994	**10.19**	**21.30**	**214.33**	**31.57**	**11.11**	**14.81**	**4.20**	**8.45**
Total credit	2 994	*10.19*	*21.30*	*214.33*	*31.57*	*11.11*	*14.81*	*4.20*	*8.45*
Total debit	3 994	....	....	....	....	....	....	....	....
Capital transfers, credit	2 400	**10.19**	**21.30**	**214.33**	**31.57**	**11.11**	**14.81**	**4.20**	**8.45**
General government	2 401	6.86	17.97	210.62	27.87	7.41	11.11	.46	4.83
Debt forgiveness	2 402	....	....	....	....	....	....	....	....
Other capital transfers	2 410	6.86	17.97	210.62	27.87	7.41	11.11	.46	4.83
Other sectors	2 430	3.33	3.33	3.70	3.70	3.70	3.70	3.74	3.62
Migrants' transfers	2 431	3.33	3.33	3.70	3.70	3.70	3.70	3.74	3.62
Debt forgiveness	2 432	....	....	....	....	....	....	....	....
Other capital transfers	2 440	....	....	....	....	....	....	....	....
Capital transfers, debit	3 400	....	....	....	....	....	....	....	....
General government	3 401	....	....	....	....	....	....	....	....
Debt forgiveness	3 402	....	....	....	....	....	....	....	....
Other capital transfers	3 410	....	....	....	....	....	....	....	....
Other sectors	3 430	....	....	....	....	....	....	....	....
Migrants' transfers	3 431	....	....	....	....	....	....	....	....
Debt forgiveness	3 432	....	....	....	....	....	....	....	....
Other capital transfers	3 440	....	....	....	....	....	....	....	....
Nonproduced nonfinancial assets, credit	2 480	....	....	....	....	....	....	....	....
Nonproduced nonfinancial assets, debit	3 480	....	....	....	....	....	....	....	....

Table 2 (Continued). STANDARD PRESENTATION, 2003–2010

(Millions of U.S. dollars)

	Code	2003	2004	2005	2006	2007	2008	2009	2010
FINANCIAL ACCOUNT	4 995 ..	**84.62**	**116.48**	**131.70**	**295.11**	**383.49**	**339.51**	**223.14**	**3.91**
A. DIRECT INVESTMENT	4 500 ..	**166.32**	**80.37**	**220.96**	**358.82**	**338.20**	**174.19**	**118.05**	**57.50**
Direct investment abroad	4 505 ..	....	....	....	....	....	....	....	....
Equity capital	4 510 ..	....	....	....	....	....	....	....	....
Claims on affiliated enterprises	4 515 ..	....	....	....	....	....	....	....	....
Liabilities to affiliated enterprises	4 520 ..	....	....	....	....	....	....	....	....
Reinvested earnings	4 525 ..	....	....	....	....	....	....	....	....
Other capital	4 530 ..	....	....	....	....	....	....	....	....
Claims on affiliated enterprises	4 535 ..	....	....	....	....	....	....	....	....
Liabilities to affiliated enterprises	4 540 ..	....	....	....	....	....	....	....	....
Direct investment in Antigua & Barbuda	4 555 ..	**166.32**	**80.37**	**220.96**	**358.82**	**338.20**	**174.19**	**118.05**	**57.50**
Equity capital	4 560 ..	34.74	14.37	178.22	272.37	254.56	106.24	74.43	22.22
Claims on direct investors	4 565 ..	....	....	....	....	....	....	....	....
Liabilities to direct investors	4 570 ..	34.74	14.37	178.22	272.37	254.56	106.24	74.43	22.22
Reinvested earnings	4 575 ..	9.00	11.27	12.86	8.59	12.14	11.68	4.93	4.77
Other capital	4 580 ..	122.57	54.73	29.88	77.85	71.51	56.26	38.70	30.51
Claims on direct investors	4 585 ..	....	....	....	....	....	....	....	....
Liabilities to direct investors	4 590 ..	122.57	54.73	29.88	77.85	71.51	56.26	38.70	30.51
B. PORTFOLIO INVESTMENT	4 600 ..	**2.64**	**12.10**	**10.53**	**24.78**	**−1.23**	**10.80**	**−6.11**	**1.16**
Assets	4 602 ..	−.03	−1.38	.47	....	−.02	....	....	−.17
Equity securities	4 610 ..	....	....	....	....	....	....	....	....
Monetary authorities	4 611 ..	....	....	....	....	....	....	....	....
General government	4 612 ..	....	....	....	....	....	....	....	....
Banks	4 613 ..	....	....	....	....	....	....	....	....
Other sectors	4 614 ..	....	....	....	....	....	....	....	....
Debt securities	4 619 ..	....	....	....	....	....	....	....	....
Bonds and notes	4 620 ..	....	....	....	....	....	....	....	....
Monetary authorities	4 621 ..	....	....	....	....	....	....	....	....
General government	4 622 ..	....	....	....	....	....	....	....	....
Banks	4 623 ..	....	....	....	....	....	....	....	....
Other sectors	4 624 ..	....	....	....	....	....	....	....	....
Money market instruments	4 630 ..	....	....	....	....	....	....	....	....
Monetary authorities	4 631 ..	....	....	....	....	....	....	....	....
General government	4 632 ..	....	....	....	....	....	....	....	....
Banks	4 633 ..	....	....	....	....	....	....	....	....
Other sectors	4 634 ..	....	....	....	....	....	....	....	....
Liabilities	4 652 ..	**2.67**	**13.48**	**10.06**	**24.78**	**−1.21**	**10.80**	**−6.11**	**1.33**
Equity securities	4 660 ..	....	....	....	....	....	....	....	....
Banks	4 663 ..	....	....	....	....	....	....	....	....
Other sectors	4 664 ..	....	....	....	....	....	....	....	....
Debt securities	4 669 ..	....	....	....	....	....	....	....	....
Bonds and notes	4 670 ..	....	....	....	....	....	....	....	....
Monetary authorities	4 671 ..	....	....	....	....	....	....	....	....
General government	4 672 ..	....	....	....	....	....	....	....	....
Banks	4 673 ..	....	....	....	....	....	....	....	....
Other sectors	4 674 ..	....	....	....	....	....	....	....	....
Money market instruments	4 680 ..	....	....	....	....	....	....	....	....
Monetary authorities	4 681 ..	....	....	....	....	....	....	....	....
General government	4 682 ..	....	....	....	....	....	....	....	....
Banks	4 683 ..	....	....	....	....	....	....	....	....
Other sectors	4 684 ..	....	....	....	....	....	....	....	....
C. FINANCIAL DERIVATIVES	4 910 ..	....	....	....	....	....	....	....	....
Monetary authorities	4 911 ..	....	....	....	....	....	....	....	....
General government	4 912 ..	....	....	....	....	....	....	....	....
Banks	4 913 ..	....	....	....	....	....	....	....	....
Other sectors	4 914 ..	....	....	....	....	....	....	....	....
Assets	4 900 ..	....	....	....	....	....	....	....	....
Monetary authorities	4 901 ..	....	....	....	....	....	....	....	....
General government	4 902 ..	....	....	....	....	....	....	....	....
Banks	4 903 ..	....	....	....	....	....	....	....	....
Other sectors	4 904 ..	....	....	....	....	....	....	....	....
Liabilities	4 905 ..	....	....	....	....	....	....	....	....
Monetary authorities	4 906 ..	....	....	....	....	....	....	....	....
General government	4 907 ..	....	....	....	....	....	....	....	....
Banks	4 908 ..	....	....	....	....	....	....	....	....
Other sectors	4 909 ..	....	....	....	....	....	....	....	....

Table 2 (Concluded). STANDARD PRESENTATION, 2003–2010

(Millions of U.S. dollars)

	Code	2003	2004	2005	2006	2007	2008	2009	2010
D. OTHER INVESTMENT	4 700	**−58.19**	**30.44**	**−92.56**	**−73.24**	**46.83**	**148.69**	**100.98**	**−42.86**
Assets	4 703	**−120.01**	**−37.93**	**−143.18**	**−149.76**	**−82.01**	**−80.09**	**−46.25**	**−108.88**
Trade credits	4 706	....	....	....	....	....	....	....	....
General government	4 707	....	....	....	....	....	....	....	....
of which: Short-term	4 709	....	....	....	....	....	....	....	....
Other sectors	4 710	....	....	....	....	....	....	....	....
of which: Short-term	4 712	....	....	....	....	....	....	....	....
Loans	4 714	−99.49	....	−18.26	−64.54	....	....	....	....
Monetary authorities	4 715	....	....	....	....	....	....	....	....
of which: Short-term	4 718	....	....	....	....	....	....	....	....
General government	4 719	....	....	....	....	....	....	....	....
of which: Short-term	4 721	....	....	....	....	....	....	....	....
Banks	4 722	−99.49	....	−18.26	−64.54	....	....	....	....
of which: Short-term	4 724	....	....	....	....	....	....	....	....
Other sectors	4 725	....	....	....	....	....	....	....	....
of which: Short-term	4 727	....	....	....	....	....	....	....	....
Currency and deposits	4 730	....	....	....	....	....	....	....	....
Monetary authorities	4 731	....	....	....	....	....	....	....	....
General government	4 732	....	....	....	....	....	....	....	....
Banks	4 733	....	....	....	....	....	....	....	....
Other sectors	4 734	....	....	....	....	....	....	....	....
Other assets	4 736	−20.52	−37.93	−124.92	−85.23	−82.01	−80.09	−46.25	−108.88
Monetary authorities	4 737	....	....	....	....	....	....	....	....
of which: Short-term	4 739	....	....	....	....	....	....	....	....
General government	4 740	....	....	....	....	....	....	....	....
of which: Short-term	4 742	....	....	....	....	....	....	....	....
Banks	4 743	....	....	....	....	....	....	....	....
of which: Short-term	4 745	....	....	....	....	....	....	....	....
Other sectors	4 746	−20.52	−37.93	−124.92	−85.23	−82.01	−80.09	−46.25	−108.88
of which: Short-term	4 748	....	....	....	....	....	....	....	....
Liabilities	4 753	**61.82**	**68.37**	**50.62**	**76.53**	**128.84**	**228.78**	**147.23**	**66.02**
Trade credits	4 756	....	....	....	....	....	....	....	....
General government	4 757	....	....	....	....	....	....	....	....
of which: Short-term	4 759	....	....	....	....	....	....	....	....
Other sectors	4 760	....	....	....	....	....	....	....	....
of which: Short-term	4 762	....	....	....	....	....	....	....	....
Loans	4 764	....	....	....	....	....	....	....	30.05
Monetary authorities	4 765	....	....	....	....	....	....	....	30.05
of which: Use of Fund credit and loans from the Fund	4 766	....	....	....	....	....	....	....	*30.05*
of which: Short-term	4 768	....	....	....	....	....	....	....	....
General government	4 769	....	....	....	....	....	....	....	....
of which: Short-term	4 771	....	....	....	....	....	....	....	....
Banks	4 772	....	....	....	....	....	....	....	....
of which: Short-term	4 774	....	....	....	....	....	....	....	....
Other sectors	4 775	....	....	....	....	....	....	....	....
of which: Short-term	4 777	....	....	....	....	....	....	....	....
Currency and deposits	4 780	....	....	....	....	....	....	....	....
Monetary authorities	4 781	....	....	....	....	....	....	....	....
General government	4 782	....	....	....	....	....	....	....	....
Banks	4 783	....	....	....	....	....	....	....	....
Other sectors	4 784	....	....	....	....	....	....	....	....
Other liabilities	4 786	61.82	68.37	50.62	76.53	128.84	228.78	147.23	35.97
Monetary authorities	4 787	....	....	....	....	....	....	19.55	....
of which: Short-term	4 789	....	....	....	....	....	....	....	....
General government	4 790	....	....	....	....	....	....	....	....
of which: Short-term	4 792	....	....	....	....	....	....	....	....
Banks	4 793	....	16.05	....	....	15.42	119.03	33.54	6.97
of which: Short-term	4 795	....	....	....	....	....	....	....	....
Other sectors	4 796	61.82	52.32	50.62	76.53	113.43	109.75	94.15	29.00
of which: Short-term	4 798	....	....	....	....	....	....	....	....
E. RESERVE ASSETS	4 802	**−26.15**	**−6.42**	**−7.24**	**−15.26**	**−.32**	**5.83**	**10.21**	**−11.89**
Monetary gold	4 812	....	....	....	....	....	....	....	....
Special drawing rights	4 811	....	....	....	....	....	....	−19.55	19.14
Reserve position in the Fund	4 810	−.01	....	....	....	....	....	....	−.04
Foreign exchange	4 803	−.03	−.05	−.05	.05	.90	....	....	−3.16
Other claims	4 813	−26.11	−6.37	−7.18	−15.31	−1.21	5.83	29.76	−27.84
NET ERRORS AND OMISSIONS	4 998	**−15.75**	**−42.68**	**−174.53**	**−34.92**	**−9.05**	**3.28**	**14.58**	**100.33**

Table 1. ANALYTIC PRESENTATION, 2003–2010

(Millions of U.S. dollars)

	Code	2003	2004	2005	2006	2007	2008	2009	2010
A. Current Account[1]	4 993 Z.	**8,140**	**3,212**	**5,275**	**7,767**	**7,354**	**6,755**	**8,405**	**3,082**
Goods: exports f.o.b.	2 100 ..	29,939	34,576	40,387	46,546	55,980	70,019	55,672	68,134
Goods: imports f.o.b.	3 100 ..	−13,134	−21,311	−27,300	−32,588	−42,525	−54,596	−37,146	−53,868
Balance on Goods	4 100 ..	*16,805*	*13,265*	*13,087*	*13,958*	*13,456*	*15,423*	*18,526*	*14,266*
Services: credit	2 200 ..	4,500	5,288	6,634	8,023	10,363	12,156	11,058	13,214
Services: debit	3 200 ..	−5,693	−6,619	−7,626	−8,523	−10,876	−13,440	−12,214	−14,066
Balance on Goods and Services	4 991 ..	*15,612*	*11,934*	*12,095*	*13,458*	*12,943*	*14,138*	*17,369*	*13,414*
Income: credit	2 300 ..	3,104	3,721	4,313	5,685	6,625	5,619	3,524	2,731
Income: debit	3 300 ..	−11,080	−13,004	−11,617	−11,835	−12,567	−13,173	−12,535	−12,704
Balance on Goods, Services, and Income	4 992 ..	*7,636*	*2,651*	*4,791*	*7,308*	*7,001*	*6,585*	*8,358*	*3,441*
Current transfers: credit	2 379 Z.	942	1,110	1,225	1,409	1,628	1,867	1,876	1,866
Current transfers: debit	3 379 ..	−438	−549	−741	−950	−1,274	−1,698	−1,829	−2,226
B. Capital Account[1]	4 994 Z.	**70**	**196**	**89**	**97**	**121**	**181**	**74**	**67**
Capital account: credit	2 994 Z.	77	201	93	107	141	202	82	80
Capital account: debit	3 994 ..	−7	−4	−4	−9	−20	−21	−8	−12
Total, Groups A Plus B	4 981 ..	*8,210*	*3,408*	*5,364*	*7,864*	*7,476*	*6,936*	*8,479*	*3,149*
C. Financial Account[1]	4 995 W.	**−15,860**	**−10,949**	**1,898**	**5,178**	**4,055**	**−11,565**	**−8,510**	**9,193**
Direct investment abroad	4 505 ..	−774	−676	−1,311	−2,439	−1,504	−1,391	−712	−964
Direct investment in Argentina	4 555 Z.	1,652	4,125	5,265	5,537	6,473	9,726	4,017	6,337
Portfolio investment assets	4 602 ..	−95	−77	1,368	−1	−2	−12	−2	1,261
Equity securities	4 610 ..	−34	−72	−4	6	13	1	....	....
Debt securities	4 619 ..	−61	−5	1,373	−7	−14	−12	−2	1,261
Portfolio investment liabilities	4 652 Z.	−7,663	−9,339	−1,731	7,921	7,098	−7,062	−3,144	9,099
Equity securities	4 660 ..	65	−86	−48	707	1,785	−531	−212	−208
Debt securities	4 669 Z.	−7,728	−9,253	−1,683	7,215	5,313	−6,531	−2,932	9,307
Financial derivatives	4 910 ..	....	....	....	−127	−565	−935	−1,248	712
Financial derivatives assets	4 900 ..	....	....	....	....	....	....	....	....
Financial derivatives liabilities	4 905 ..	....	....	....	−127	−565	−935	−1,248	712
Other investment assets	4 703 ..	−4,400	−2,347	1,956	−4,501	−11,729	−14,651	−6,825	−9,318
Monetary authorities	4 701 ..	....	....	....	....	....	....	....	....
General government	4 704 ..	−74	−191	−59	52	−445	−451	−456	−612
Banks	4 705 ..	447	240	−129	−505	−1,272	133	1,625	225
Other sectors	4 728 ..	−4,773	−2,395	2,143	−4,048	−10,012	−14,332	−7,994	−8,931
Other investment liabilities	4 753 W.	−4,580	−2,636	−3,649	−1,214	4,283	2,760	−596	2,065
Monetary authorities	4 753 WA	−633	54	−10	−1,173	−199	−693	−252	−3,650
General government	4 753 ZB	−98	−1,054	−1,374	−1,431	1	−1,093	1,425	586
Banks	4 753 ZC	−2,917	−916	−1,304	−31	952	−425	−1,407	−30
Other sectors	4 753 ZD	−932	−719	−961	1,421	3,529	4,971	−361	5,160
Total, Groups A Through C	4 983 ..	*−7,650*	*−7,541*	*7,262*	*13,042*	*11,530*	*−4,629*	*−31*	*12,342*
D. Net Errors and Omissions	4 998 ..	**−1,428**	**548**	**383**	**1,192**	**39**	**1,344**	**−435**	**−1,591**
Total, Groups A Through D	4 984 ..	*−9,077*	*−6,993*	*7,644*	*14,234*	*11,569*	*−3,285*	*−466*	*10,751*
E. Reserves and Related Items	4 802 A.	**9,077**	**6,993**	**−7,644**	**−14,234**	**−11,569**	**3,285**	**466**	**−10,751**
Reserve assets	4 802 ..	−3,497	−5,283	−9,088	−3,458	−13,075	−24	−1,327	−4,212
Use of Fund credit and loans	4 766 ..	−151	−2,038	−3,582	−9,630	....	....	....	....
Exceptional financing	4 920 ..	12,725	14,314	5,026	−1,146	1,505	3,309	1,793	−6,538
Conversion rates: Argentine pesos per U.S. dollar	0 101 ..	**2.90063**	**2.92330**	**2.90366**	**3.05431**	**3.09565**	**3.14416**	**3.71011**	**3.89630**

[1] Excludes components that have been classified in the categories of Group E.

Table 2. STANDARD PRESENTATION, 2003–2010

(Millions of U.S. dollars)

	Code	2003	2004	2005	2006	2007	2008	2009	2010
CURRENT ACCOUNT.....................................	4 993 ..	**8,140**	**3,212**	**5,275**	**7,767**	**7,354**	**6,755**	**8,405**	**3,082**
A. GOODS...	4 100 ..	**16,805**	**13,265**	**13,087**	**13,958**	**13,456**	**15,423**	**18,526**	**14,266**
Credit..	2 100 ..	**29,939**	**34,576**	**40,387**	**46,546**	**55,980**	**70,019**	**55,672**	**68,134**
General merchandise: exports f.o.b..........	2 110 ..	29,500	34,069	39,636	45,249	54,818	68,466	54,836	64,960
Goods for processing: exports f.o.b..........	2 150 ..	....	....	....	....	....	....	....	....
Repairs on goods...............................	2 160 ..	....	....	....	....	....	....	....	....
Goods procured in ports by carriers........	2 170 ..	328	372	608	750	875	1,354	836	1,160
Nonmonetary gold............................	2 180 ..	111	135	143	547	287	199	....	2,014
Debit...	3 100 ..	**−13,134**	**−21,311**	**−27,300**	**−32,588**	**−42,525**	**−54,596**	**−37,146**	**−53,868**
General merchandise: imports f.o.b..........	3 110 ..	−13,055	−21,218	−27,162	−32,443	−42,358	−54,370	−36,936	−53,565
Goods for processing: imports f.o.b..........	3 150 ..	....	....	....	....	....	....	....	....
Repairs on goods...............................	3 160 ..	....	....	....	....	....	....	....	....
Goods procured in ports by carriers........	3 170 ..	−80	−94	−138	−145	−167	−226	−210	−303
Nonmonetary gold............................	3 180 ..	....	....	....	....	....	....	....	....
B. SERVICES......................................	4 200 ..	**−1,193**	**−1,331**	**−992**	**−501**	**−513**	**−1,284**	**−1,157**	**−852**
Total credit......................................	2 200 ..	*4,500*	*5,288*	*6,634*	*8,023*	*10,363*	*12,156*	*11,058*	*13,214*
Total debit......................................	3 200 ..	*−5,693*	*−6,619*	*−7,626*	*−8,523*	*−10,876*	*−13,440*	*−12,214*	*−14,066*
Transportation services, credit...............	2 205 ..	**932**	**1,140**	**1,264**	**1,408**	**1,666**	**1,771**	**1,575**	**2,021**
Passenger.....................................	2 850 ..	*300*	*425*	*480*	*555*	*670*	*650*	*516*	*687*
Freight..	2 851 ..	*224*	*256*	*237*	*241*	*293*	*272*	*284*	*430*
Other..	2 852 ..	*408*	*459*	*547*	*612*	*703*	*849*	*775*	*905*
Sea transport, passenger......................	2 207 ..	4	3	....	....	....	....	....	....
Sea transport, freight.........................	2 208 ..	106	90	55	39	40	43	38	48
Sea transport, other..........................	2 209 ..	280	299	348	412	467	543	467	563
Air transport, passenger......................	2 211 ..	287	410	463	533	643	614	487	648
Air transport, freight..........................	2 212 ..	8	10	10	9	9	10	7	9
Air transport, other...........................	2 213 ..	128	160	198	199	236	306	308	342
Other transport, passenger...................	2 215 ..	9	12	17	23	27	36	29	39
Other transport, freight.......................	2 216 ..	110	156	172	193	244	219	239	372
Other transport, other........................	2 217 ..	....	....	....	....	....	....	....	....
Transportation services, debit...............	3 205 ..	**−1,126**	**−1,600**	**−1,958**	**−2,278**	**−2,997**	**−3,911**	**−2,693**	**−3,704**
Passenger.....................................	3 850 ..	*−486*	*−604*	*−764*	*−939*	*−1,142*	*−1,401*	*−1,272*	*−1,497*
Freight..	3 851 ..	*−529*	*−869*	*−1,078*	*−1,196*	*−1,713*	*−2,325*	*−1,250*	*−2,009*
Other..	3 852 ..	*−111*	*−127*	*−116*	*−143*	*−142*	*−185*	*−171*	*−198*
Sea transport, passenger......................	3 207 ..	−17	−26	−31	−33	−43	−61	−65	−65
Sea transport, freight.........................	3 208 ..	−337	−550	−729	−809	−1,242	−1,736	−848	−1,452
Sea transport, other..........................	3 209 ..	−17	−16	−11	−8	−8	−15	−12	−9
Air transport, passenger......................	3 211 ..	−461	−569	−723	−897	−1,089	−1,330	−1,191	−1,410
Air transport, freight..........................	3 212 ..	−104	−177	−191	−200	−242	−323	−200	−279
Air transport, other...........................	3 213 ..	−94	−111	−105	−135	−134	−170	−159	−189
Other transport, passenger...................	3 215 ..	−8	−10	−10	−10	−10	−10	−16	−22
Other transport, freight.......................	3 216 ..	−88	−142	−158	−187	−229	−266	−203	−278
Other transport, other........................	3 217 ..	....	....	....	....	....	....	....	....
Travel, credit...................................	2 236 ..	**2,005**	**2,235**	**2,729**	**3,344**	**4,314**	**4,646**	**3,960**	**4,942**
Business travel.................................	2 237 ..	669	445	504	520	684	693	620	796
Personal travel.................................	2 240 ..	1,337	1,790	2,226	2,824	3,630	3,953	3,340	4,146
Travel, debit....................................	3 236 ..	**−2,511**	**−2,604**	**−2,790**	**−3,099**	**−3,921**	**−4,561**	**−4,494**	**−4,878**
Business travel.................................	3 237 ..	−598	−936	−1,030	−1,120	−1,515	−1,415	−1,134	−1,373
Personal travel.................................	3 240 ..	−1,914	−1,668	−1,760	−1,979	−2,405	−3,146	−3,360	−3,505
Other services, credit..........................	2 200 BA	**1,562**	**1,913**	**2,641**	**3,271**	**4,383**	**5,738**	**5,523**	**6,251**
Communications...............................	2 245 ..	146	162	210	273	314	363	318	335
Construction...................................	2 249 ..	41	61	46	20	38	30	18	63
Insurance......................................	2 253 ..	....	....	....	....	....	12	11	10
Financial.......................................	2 260 ..	1	2	4	6	9	8	6	7
Computer and information....................	2 262 ..	166	193	238	378	655	894	1,059	1,248
Royalties and licence fees.....................	2 266 ..	52	61	51	71	106	105	108	135
Other business services.......................	2 268 ..	953	1,194	1,774	2,140	2,816	3,690	3,531	3,910
Personal, cultural, and recreational..........	2 287 ..	122	153	203	258	314	486	336	356
Government, n.i.e..............................	2 291 ..	81	86	115	124	130	151	136	186
Other services, debit...........................	3 200 BA	**−2,056**	**−2,415**	**−2,878**	**−3,146**	**−3,958**	**−4,968**	**−5,028**	**−5,484**
Communications...............................	3 245 ..	−228	−223	−269	−309	−362	−438	−384	−381
Construction...................................	3 249 ..	−37	−31	−2	−1	−17	−28	−18	−4
Insurance......................................	3 253 ..	−149	−158	−230	−283	−375	−449	−442	−540
Financial.......................................	3 260 ..	−113	−105	−210	−78	−87	−84	−94	−101
Computer and information....................	3 262 ..	−139	−160	−195	−226	−310	−378	−422	−463
Royalties and licence fees.....................	3 266 ..	−403	−521	−651	−806	−1,042	−1,463	−1,454	−1,538
Other business services.......................	3 268 ..	−648	−827	−896	−990	−1,250	−1,512	−1,561	−1,745
Personal, cultural, and recreational..........	3 287 ..	−108	−143	−165	−172	−208	−249	−289	−357
Government, n.i.e..............................	3 291 ..	−231	−246	−262	−281	−307	−367	−365	−356

Table 2 (Continued). STANDARD PRESENTATION, 2003–2010

(Millions of U.S. dollars)

	Code	2003	2004	2005	2006	2007	2008	2009	2010
C. INCOME	4 300	**−7,976**	**−9,283**	**−7,304**	**−6,150**	**−5,942**	**−7,553**	**−9,011**	**−9,973**
Total credit	2 300	*3,104*	*3,721*	*4,313*	*5,685*	*6,625*	*5,619*	*3,524*	*2,731*
Total debit	3 300	*−11,080*	*−13,004*	*−11,617*	*−11,835*	*−12,567*	*−13,173*	*−12,535*	*−12,704*
Compensation of employees, credit	2 310	**38**	**42**	**51**	**56**	**65**	**92**	**92**	**106**
Compensation of employees, debit	3 310	**−63**	**−81**	**−102**	**−115**	**−137**	**−150**	**−161**	**−169**
Investment income, credit	2 320	**3,066**	**3,679**	**4,262**	**5,630**	**6,559**	**5,528**	**3,432**	**2,625**
Direct investment income	2 330	450	859	1,020	1,635	1,485	1,322	1,290	939
Dividends and distributed branch profits	2 332	148	217	277	310	355	305	392	158
Reinvested earnings and undistributed branch profits	2 333	302	643	744	1,325	1,130	1,017	898	780
Income on debt (interest)	2 334	....	....	....	....	....	....	....	....
Portfolio investment income	2 339	99	173	122	382	954	760	265	55
Income on equity	2 340	1	2	2	2	2	2	2	1
Income on bonds and notes	2 350	97	171	120	380	951	758	263	53
Income on money market instruments	2 360	....	....	....	....	....	....	....	....
Other investment income	2 370	2,518	2,647	3,119	3,612	4,120	3,446	1,877	1,631
Investment income, debit	3 320	**−11,017**	**−12,923**	**−11,515**	**−11,720**	**−12,430**	**−13,023**	**−12,375**	**−12,535**
Direct investment income	3 330	−1,626	−3,712	−5,456	−7,112	−7,283	−7,902	−8,360	−8,516
Dividends and distributed branch profits	3 332	−1,865	−3,066	−3,755	−3,446	−4,645	−6,957	−4,991	−5,816
Reinvested earnings and undistributed branch profits	3 333	808	−71	−1,156	−3,108	−2,050	−396	−2,894	−2,273
Income on debt (interest)	3 334	−568	−575	−545	−558	−588	−548	−475	−427
Portfolio investment income	3 339	−6,181	−6,542	−3,396	−2,423	−2,696	−2,793	−2,391	−2,450
Income on equity	3 340	−27	−12	−6	−23	−33	−64	−34	−10
Income on bonds and notes	3 350	−6,154	−6,530	−3,390	−2,400	−2,662	−2,729	−2,356	−2,440
Income on money market instruments	3 360	....	....	....	....	....	....	....	....
Other investment income	3 370	−3,209	−2,668	−2,663	−2,185	−2,451	−2,328	−1,624	−1,570
D. CURRENT TRANSFERS	4 379	**504**	**561**	**484**	**459**	**353**	**170**	**46**	**−360**
Credit	2 379	**942**	**1,110**	**1,225**	**1,409**	**1,628**	**1,867**	**1,876**	**1,866**
General government	2 380	255	315	357	430	556	734	842	919
Other sectors	2 390	687	795	868	980	1,071	1,133	1,033	947
Workers' remittances	2 391	236	270	381	486	541	606	529	535
Other current transfers	2 392	451	525	486	494	530	527	504	412
Debit	3 379	**−438**	**−549**	**−741**	**−950**	**−1,274**	**−1,698**	**−1,829**	**−2,226**
General government	3 380	−71	−86	−84	−107	−118	−114	−105	−119
Other sectors	3 390	−366	−462	−658	−843	−1,156	−1,584	−1,724	−2,107
Workers' remittances	3 391	−117	−154	−212	−240	−325	−481	−595	−825
Other current transfers	3 392	−249	−309	−446	−602	−831	−1,103	−1,129	−1,282
CAPITAL AND FINANCIAL ACCOUNT	4 996	**−6,712**	**−3,760**	**−5,658**	**−8,959**	**−7,394**	**−8,099**	**−7,970**	**−1,490**
CAPITAL ACCOUNT	4 994	**70**	**196**	**89**	**97**	**121**	**181**	**74**	**67**
Total credit	2 994	*77*	*201*	*93*	*107*	*141*	*202*	*82*	*80*
Total debit	3 994	*−7*	*−4*	*−4*	*−9*	*−20*	*−21*	*−8*	*−12*
Capital transfers, credit	2 400	....	**149**	....	**35**	....	....	....	....
General government	2 401	....	....	....	....	....	....	....	....
Debt forgiveness	2 402	....	....	....	....	....	....	....	....
Other capital transfers	2 410	....	....	....	....	....	....	....	....
Other sectors	2 430	....	149	....	35	....	....	....	....
Migrants' transfers	2 431	....	....	....	....	....	....	....	....
Debt forgiveness	2 432	....	149	....	35	....	....	....	....
Other capital transfers	2 440	....	....	....	....	....	....	....	....
Capital transfers, debit	3 400	....	....	....	....	....	....	....	....
General government	3 401	....	....	....	....	....	....	....	....
Debt forgiveness	3 402	....	....	....	....	....	....	....	....
Other capital transfers	3 410	....	....	....	....	....	....	....	....
Other sectors	3 430	....	....	....	....	....	....	....	....
Migrants' transfers	3 431	....	....	....	....	....	....	....	....
Debt forgiveness	3 432	....	....	....	....	....	....	....	....
Other capital transfers	3 440	....	....	....	....	....	....	....	....
Nonproduced nonfinancial assets, credit	2 480	**77**	**52**	**93**	**72**	**141**	**202**	**82**	**80**
Nonproduced nonfinancial assets, debit	3 480	**−7**	**−4**	**−4**	**−9**	**−20**	**−21**	**−8**	**−12**

Table 2 (Continued). STANDARD PRESENTATION, 2003–2010

(Millions of U.S. dollars)

	Code	2003	2004	2005	2006	2007	2008	2009	2010
FINANCIAL ACCOUNT	4 995	**−6,782**	**−3,956**	**−5,747**	**−9,056**	**−7,515**	**−8,280**	**−8,044**	**−1,558**
A. DIRECT INVESTMENT	4 500	**878**	**3,449**	**3,954**	**3,099**	**4,969**	**8,335**	**3,306**	**5,372**
Direct investment abroad	4 505	**−774**	**−676**	**−1,311**	**−2,439**	**−1,504**	**−1,391**	**−712**	**−964**
Equity capital	4 510	−228	−44	−567	−1,114	−374	−374	186	−184
Claims on affiliated enterprises	4 515	−228	−44	−567	−1,114	−374	−374	186	−184
Liabilities to affiliated enterprises	4 520	....	....	....	....	....	....	....	....
Reinvested earnings	4 525	−302	−643	−744	−1,325	−1,130	−1,017	−898	−780
Other capital	4 530	−243	11	....	....	....	....	....	....
Claims on affiliated enterprises	4 535	−243	11	....	....	....	....	....	....
Liabilities to affiliated enterprises	4 540	....	....	....	....	....	....	....	....
Direct investment in Argentina	4 555	**1,652**	**4,125**	**5,265**	**5,537**	**6,473**	**9,726**	**4,017**	**6,337**
Equity capital	4 560	2,975	3,025	4,590	2,166	2,578	4,553	2,133	2,043
Claims on direct investors	4 565	....	....	....	....	....	....	....	....
Liabilities to direct investors	4 570	2,975	3,025	4,590	2,166	2,578	4,553	2,133	2,043
Reinvested earnings	4 575	−808	71	1,156	3,108	2,050	396	2,894	2,273
Other capital	4 580	−515	1,029	−481	263	1,846	4,777	−1,010	2,021
Claims on direct investors	4 585	....	....	....	....	....	....	....	....
Liabilities to direct investors	4 590	−515	1,029	−481	263	1,846	4,777	−1,010	2,021
B. PORTFOLIO INVESTMENT	4 600	**−7,758**	**−9,416**	**−387**	**7,823**	**7,069**	**−8,028**	**−3,149**	**10,361**
Assets	4 602	**−95**	**−77**	**1,368**	**−1**	**−2**	**−12**	**−2**	**1,261**
Equity securities	4 610	−34	−72	−4	6	13	1	....	....
Monetary authorities	4 611	....	....	....	....	....	....	....	....
General government	4 612	....	....	....	....	....	....	....	....
Banks	4 613	−34	−72	−4	6	13	1	....	....
Other sectors	4 614	....	....	....	....	....	....	....	....
Debt securities	4 619	−61	−5	1,373	−7	−14	−12	−2	1,261
Bonds and notes	4 620	−61	−5	1,373	−7	−14	−12	−2	1,261
Monetary authorities	4 621	....	....	....	....	....	....	....	....
General government	4 622	−63	−68	1,373	−7	−8	−8	−9	1,269
Banks	4 623	1	64	....	....	−6	−4	8	−8
Other sectors	4 624	....	....	....	....	....	....	....	....
Money market instruments	4 630	....	....	....	....	....	....	....	....
Monetary authorities	4 631	....	....	....	....	....	....	....	....
General government	4 632	....	....	....	....	....	....	....	....
Banks	4 633	....	....	....	....	....	....	....	....
Other sectors	4 634	....	....	....	....	....	....	....	....
Liabilities	4 652	**−7,663**	**−9,339**	**−1,755**	**7,824**	**7,070**	**−8,017**	**−3,148**	**9,099**
Equity securities	4 660	65	−86	−48	707	1,785	−531	−212	−208
Banks	4 663	28	−45	−13	439	151	−223	15	137
Other sectors	4 664	38	−41	−35	268	1,634	−308	−227	−344
Debt securities	4 669	−7,728	−9,253	−1,707	7,118	5,285	−7,486	−2,936	9,307
Bonds and notes	4 670	−7,728	−9,253	−1,707	7,118	5,285	−7,486	−2,936	9,307
Monetary authorities	4 671	....	....	−24	−97	−27	−955	−4	....
General government	4 672	−5,463	−8,172	−139	7,639	6,007	−5,215	−1,544	9,671
Banks	4 673	−978	455	−514	69	−160	−383	−339	−438
Other sectors	4 674	−1,287	−1,536	−1,031	−492	−534	−934	−1,049	74
Money market instruments	4 680	....	....	....	....	....	....	....	....
Monetary authorities	4 681	....	....	....	....	....	....	....	....
General government	4 682	....	....	....	....	....	....	....	....
Banks	4 683	....	....	....	....	....	....	....	....
Other sectors	4 684	....	....	....	....	....	....	....	....
C. FINANCIAL DERIVATIVES	4 910	....	....	....	**−127**	**−565**	**−935**	**−1,248**	**712**
Monetary authorities	4 911	....	....	....	....	....	....	....	....
General government	4 912	....	....	....	−243	−535	−877	−1,207	....
Banks	4 913	....	....	....	....	....	....	....	....
Other sectors	4 914	....	....	....	116	−30	−58	−41	712
Assets	4 900	....	....	....	....	....	....	....	....
Monetary authorities	4 901	....	....	....	....	....	....	....	....
General government	4 902	....	....	....	....	....	....	....	....
Banks	4 903	....	....	....	....	....	....	....	....
Other sectors	4 904	....	....	....	....	....	....	....	....
Liabilities	4 905	....	....	....	**−127**	**−565**	**−935**	**−1,248**	**712**
Monetary authorities	4 906	....	....	....	....	....	....	....	....
General government	4 907	....	....	....	−243	−535	−877	−1,207	....
Banks	4 908	....	....	....	....	....	....	....	....
Other sectors	4 909	....	....	....	116	−30	−58	−41	712

Argentina 213

Table 2 (Concluded). STANDARD PRESENTATION, 2003–2010

(Millions of U.S. dollars)

	Code	2003	2004	2005	2006	2007	2008	2009	2010
D. OTHER INVESTMENT	4 700	**3,595**	**7,294**	**−225**	**−16,393**	**−5,913**	**−7,628**	**−5,625**	**−13,790**
Assets	4 703	**−4,400**	**−2,347**	**1,956**	**−4,501**	**−11,729**	**−14,651**	**−6,825**	**−9,318**
Trade credits	4 706	....	....	....	....	....	....	....	....
General government	4 707	....	....	....	....	....	....	....	....
of which: Short-term	4 709	....	....	....	....	....	....	....	....
Other sectors	4 710	....	....	....	....	....	....	....	....
of which: Short-term	4 712	....	....	....	....	....	....	....	....
Loans	4 714	838	−456	85	−342	−1,021	−329	1,279	−267
Monetary authorities	4 715	....	....	....	....	....	....	....	....
of which: Short-term	4 718	....	....	....	....	....	....	....	....
General government	4 719	−40	−102	−95	−124	−212	−464	−390	−305
of which: Short-term	4 721	....	....	....	....	....	....	....	....
Banks	4 722	877	−354	180	−218	−810	135	1,669	38
of which: Short-term	4 724	*877*	*−354*	*180*	*−218*	*−810*	*135*	*1,669*	*38*
Other sectors	4 725	....	....	....	....	....	....	....	....
of which: Short-term	4 727	....	....	....	....	....	....	....	....
Currency and deposits	4 730	−419	562	−236	−12	−642	162	−58	120
Monetary authorities	4 731	....	....	....	....	....	....	....	....
General government	4 732	11	−31	72	275	−180	164	−14	−67
Banks	4 733	−430	594	−309	−287	−462	−2	−44	187
Other sectors	4 734	....	....	....	....	....	....	....	....
Other assets	4 736	−4,819	−2,453	2,107	−4,147	−10,065	−14,484	−8,047	−9,171
Monetary authorities	4 737	....	....	....	....	....	....	....	....
of which: Short-term	4 739	....	....	....	....	....	....	....	....
General government	4 740	−46	−58	−36	−99	−53	−152	−53	−240
of which: Short-term	4 742	....	....	....	....	....	....	....	....
Banks	4 743	....	....	....	....	....	....	....	....
of which: Short-term	4 745	....	....	....	....	....	....	....	....
Other sectors	4 746	−4,773	−2,395	2,143	−4,048	−10,012	−14,332	−7,994	−8,931
of which: Short-term	4 748	....	....	....	....	....	....	....	....
Liabilities	4 753	**7,995**	**9,640**	**−2,181**	**−11,893**	**5,815**	**7,023**	**1,200**	**−4,473**
Trade credits	4 756	810	1,144	571	1,547	2,323	3,272	711	3,867
General government	4 757	....	....	....	....	....	....	....	....
of which: Short-term	4 759	....	....	....	....	....	....	....	....
Other sectors	4 760	810	1,144	571	1,547	2,323	3,272	711	3,867
of which: Short-term	4 762	*810*	*1,144*	*571*	*1,547*	*2,323*	*3,272*	*711*	*3,867*
Loans	4 764	−5,182	−6,391	−7,457	−12,040	2,579	3,478	−1,477	−985
Monetary authorities	4 765	−774	−2,038	−2,882	−10,330	1,520	2,770	−1,380	−2,910
of which: Use of Fund credit and loans from the Fund	4 766	*−151*	*−2,038*	*−3,582*	*−9,630*	....	....	....	....
of which: Short-term	4 768	....	....	*700*	*−700*	*1,520*	*2,770*	*−1,380*	*−2,910*
General government	4 769	−87	−1,263	−1,460	−1,416	8	−1,086	1,417	538
of which: Short-term	4 771	....	....	....	....	....	....	....	....
Banks	4 772	−2,579	−1,227	−1,583	−168	−155	96	−442	94
of which: Short-term	4 774	*−2,519*	*−1,376*	*−1,571*	*−174*	*11*	*86*	*−500*	*126*
Other sectors	4 775	−1,742	−1,863	−1,532	−126	1,206	1,698	−1,072	1,293
of which: Short-term	4 777	....	....	....	....	....	....	....	....
Currency and deposits	4 780	−31	17	80	279	194	−168	−145	−121
Monetary authorities	4 781	....	....	....	....	....	....	....	....
General government	4 782	....	....	....	....	....	....	....	....
Banks	4 783	−31	17	80	279	194	−168	−145	−121
Other sectors	4 784	....	....	....	....	....	....	....	....
Other liabilities	4 786	12,398	14,870	4,625	−1,678	719	441	2,112	−7,234
Monetary authorities	4 787	−135	54	−10	−73	1	7	2,638	....
of which: Short-term	4 789	*−136*	*53*	*−11*	*−73*	*1*	*7*	*−20*	....
General government	4 790	11,447	15,500	4,588	−887	−67	833	304	−7,236
of which: Short-term	4 792	*11,447*	*15,500*	*4,588*	*−887*	*−67*	*833*	*304*	*−7,236*
Banks	4 793	466	−941	80	−128	929	−352	−820	−3
of which: Short-term	4 795	*466*	*−941*	*80*	*−128*	*929*	*−352*	*−820*	*−3*
Other sectors	4 796	621	257	−33	−591	−144	−47	−10	5
of which: Short-term	4 798	*621*	*257*	*−33*	*−591*	*−144*	*−47*	*−10*	*5*
E. RESERVE ASSETS	4 802	**−3,497**	**−5,283**	**−9,088**	**−3,458**	**−13,075**	**−24**	**−1,327**	**−4,212**
Monetary gold	4 812	−1	−765	−139	−207	−353	−57	−408	−564
Special drawing rights	4 811	−824	168	−3,794	4,022	....	....	−2,657	....
Reserve position in the Fund	4 810	....	....	....	....	....	....	....	....
Foreign exchange	4 803	−2,673	−4,685	−5,155	−6,918	−12,784	−13	1,744	−3,452
Other claims	4 813	....	....	....	−355	62	46	−5	−197
NET ERRORS AND OMISSIONS	4 998	**−1,428**	**548**	**383**	**1,192**	**39**	**1,344**	**−435**	**−1,591**

Table 3. INTERNATIONAL INVESTMENT POSITION (End-period stocks), 2003–2010

(Millions of U.S. dollars)

	Code	2003	2004	2005	2006	2007	2008	2009	2010
ASSETS	8 995 C.	**144,822**	**154,673**	**165,855**	**177,994**	**206,097**	**210,703**	**223,735**	**238,442**
Direct investment abroad	8 505 ..	**21,500**	**21,804**	**23,340**	**25,897**	**27,543**	**28,789**	**29,445**	**29,841**
Equity capital and reinvested earnings	8 506 ..	21,500	21,804	23,340	25,897	27,543	28,789	29,445	29,841
Claims on affiliated enterprises	8 507 ..	21,500	21,804	23,340	25,897	27,543	28,789	29,445	29,841
Liabilities to affiliated enterprises	8 508 ..	....	....	....	....	....	....	....	....
Other capital	8 530 ..	....	....	....	....	....	....	....	....
Claims on affiliated enterprises	8 535 ..	....	....	....	....	....	....	....	....
Liabilities to affiliated enterprises	8 540 ..	....	....	....	....	....	....	....	....
Portfolio investment	8 602 ..	**939**	**1,016**	**192**	**192**	**195**	**1,431**	**1,684**	**420**
Equity securities	8 610 ..	64	73	77	70	58	57	57	64
Monetary authorities	8 611 ..	....	....	....	....	....	....	....	....
General government	8 612 ..	....	....	....	....	....	....	....	....
Banks	8 613 ..	64	73	77	70	58	57	57	64
Other sectors	8 614 ..	....	....	....	....	....	....	....	....
Debt securities	8 619 ..	875	943	115	122	137	1,374	1,627	356
Bonds and notes	8 620 ..	875	943	115	122	137	1,374	1,627	356
Monetary authorities	8 621 ..	....	....	....	....	....	....	....	....
General government	8 622 ..	874	942	114	121	129	1,363	1,624	352
Banks	8 623 ..	1	1	1	1	8	11	3	4
Other sectors	8 624 ..	....	....	....	....	....	....	....	....
Money market instruments	8 630 ..	....	....	....	....	....	....	....	....
Monetary authorities	8 631 ..	....	....	....	....	....	....	....	....
General government	8 632 ..	....	....	....	....	....	....	....	....
Banks	8 633 ..	....	....	....	....	....	....	....	....
Other sectors	8 634 ..	....	....	....	....	....	....	....	....
Financial derivatives	8 900 ..	....	....	....	....	....	....	....	
Monetary authorities	8 901 ..	....	....	....	....	....	....	....	
General government	8 902 ..	....	....	....	....	....	....	....	
Banks	8 903 ..	....	....	....	....	....	....	....	
Other sectors	8 904 ..	....	....	....	....	....	....	....	
Other investment	8 703 ..	**107,256**	**111,330**	**109,811**	**119,387**	**132,186**	**134,098**	**144,639**	**155,993**
Trade credits	8 706 ..	4,830	4,934	2,761	3,239	4,190	3,846	3,382	5,086
General government	8 707 ..	....	....	....	....	....	....	....	....
of which: Short-term	8 709 ..	....	....	....	....	....	....	....	....
Other sectors	8 710 ..	4,830	4,934	2,761	3,239	4,190	3,846	3,382	5,086
of which: Short-term	8 712 ..	*4,830*	*4,934*	*2,761*	*3,239*	*4,190*	*3,846*	*3,382*	*5,086*
Loans	8 714 ..	....	....	....	....	....	....	....	....
Monetary authorities	8 715 ..	....	....	....	....	....	....	....	....
of which: Short-term	8 718 ..	....	....	....	....	....	....	....	....
General government	8 719 ..	....	....	....	....	....	....	....	....
of which: Short-term	8 721 ..	....	....	....	....	....	....	....	....
Banks	8 722 ..	....	....	....	....	....	....	....	....
of which: Short-term	8 724 ..	....	....	....	....	....	....	....	....
Other sectors	8 725 ..	....	....	....	....	....	....	....	....
of which: Short-term	8 727 ..	....	....	....	....	....	....	....	....
Currency and deposits	8 730 ..	1,446	841	1,149	1,436	1,898	1,900	1,944	1,757
Monetary authorities	8 731 ..	....	....	....	....	....	....	....	....
General government	8 732 ..	....	....	....	....	....	....	....	....
Banks	8 733 ..	1,446	841	1,149	1,436	1,898	1,900	1,944	1,757
Other sectors	8 734 ..	....	....	....	....	....	....	....	....
Other assets	8 736 ..	100,979	105,555	105,900	114,712	126,097	128,353	139,313	149,150
Monetary authorities	8 737 ..	....	....	....	....	....	....	....	....
of which: Short-term	8 739 ..	....	....	....	....	....	....	....	....
General government	8 740 ..	6,334	6,842	7,111	7,197	7,916	8,900	8,497	9,663
of which: Short-term	8 742 ..	....	....	....	....	....	....	....	....
Banks	8 743 ..	1,247	1,601	1,421	1,639	2,449	2,314	645	607
of which: Short-term	8 745 ..	....	....	....	....	....	....	....	....
Other sectors	8 746 ..	93,398	97,112	97,368	105,875	115,732	117,139	130,171	138,880
of which: Short-term	8 748 ..	....	....	....	....	....	....	....	....
Reserve assets	8 802 ..	**15,128**	**20,523**	**32,513**	**32,520**	**46,173**	**46,385**	**47,966**	**52,188**
Monetary gold	8 812 ..	4	769	908	1,115	1,468	1,524	1,932	2,497
Special drawing rights	8 811 ..	1,008	877	4,437	482	507	494	3,170	3,114
Reserve position in the Fund	8 810 ..	....	....	....	....	....	....	....	....
Foreign exchange	8 803 ..	14,149	18,881	27,178	30,914	44,030	44,181	42,817	46,318
Other claims	8 813 ..	−34	−4	−10	8	169	185	46	259

Table 3 (Concluded). INTERNATIONAL INVESTMENT POSITION (End-period stocks), 2003–2010

(Millions of U.S. dollars)

	Code	2003	2004	2005	2006	2007	2008	2009	2010
LIABILITIES..	8 995 D.	**145,594**	**151,541**	**144,567**	**156,104**	**171,653**	**152,887**	**168,816**	**192,241**
Direct investment in Argentina........................	8 555 ..	**48,262**	**52,507**	**55,139**	**60,253**	**67,574**	**77,066**	**79,871**	**86,685**
Equity capital and reinvested earnings....................	8 556 ..	33,456	36,897	40,694	46,276	50,922	55,586	60,461	64,615
Claims on direct investors.............................	8 557 ..	....	....	....	....	....	....	....	....
Liabilities to direct investors.........................	8 558 ..	33,456	36,897	40,694	46,276	50,922	55,586	60,461	64,615
Other capital..	8 580 ..	14,806	15,610	14,445	13,977	16,652	21,481	19,410	22,070
Claims on direct investors.............................	8 585 ..	....	....	....	....	....	....	....	....
Liabilities to direct investors.........................	8 590 ..	14,806	15,610	14,445	13,977	16,652	21,481	19,410	22,070
Portfolio investment..	8 652 ..	**30,456**	**36,122**	**33,794**	**46,352**	**48,971**	**17,984**	**29,141**	**41,199**
Equity securities...	8 660 ..	2,127	2,371	2,497	4,843	6,786	2,510	3,494	5,375
Banks...	8 663 ..	529	658	622	1,616	1,377	426	927	2,029
Other sectors...	8 664 ..	1,598	1,713	1,875	3,227	5,409	2,084	2,567	3,346
Debt securities..	8 669 ..	28,329	33,751	31,297	41,509	42,186	15,473	25,647	35,823
Bonds and notes..	8 670 ..	28,329	33,751	31,297	41,509	42,186	15,473	25,647	35,823
Monetary authorities................................	8 671 ..	....	....	97	872	2,239	254	1	....
General government.................................	8 672 ..	18,455	22,569	19,831	28,902	29,804	9,689	18,806	29,465
Banks..	8 673 ..	1,376	1,858	2,165	2,474	1,812	670	1,202	1,123
Other sectors.......................................	8 674 ..	8,497	9,324	9,205	9,261	8,332	4,861	5,637	5,235
Money market instruments.............................	8 680 ..	....	....	....	....	....	....	....	....
Monetary authorities................................	8 681 ..	....	....	....	....	....	....	....	....
General government.................................	8 682 ..	....	....	....	....	....	....	....	....
Banks..	8 683 ..	....	....	....	....	....	....	....	....
Other sectors.......................................	8 684 ..	....	....	....	....	....	....	....	....
Financial derivatives..............................	8 905 ..	....	....	**1,832**	**5,323**	**4,641**	**1,178**	**2,283**	**6,669**
Monetary authorities......................................	8 906 ..	....	....	....	....	....	....	....	....
General government.......................................	8 907 ..	....	....	1,832	5,323	4,641	1,178	2,283	6,669
Banks...	8 908 ..	....	....	....	....	....	....	....	....
Other sectors...	8 909 ..	....	....	....	....	....	....	....	....
Other investment..	8 753 ..	**66,876**	**62,913**	**53,802**	**44,176**	**50,467**	**56,660**	**57,521**	**57,688**
Trade credits..	8 756 ..	6,902	7,649	7,319	8,456	10,675	12,641	13,235	14,375
General government.....................................	8 757 ..	181	108	12	9	32	22	16	31
of which: Short-term.................................	8 759 ..	....	....	....	....	....	....	....	....
Other sectors...	8 760 ..	6,721	7,541	7,307	8,447	10,643	12,619	13,220	14,344
of which: Short-term.................................	8 762 ..	*5,646*	*5,128*	*3,434*	*4,378*	*5,002*	*4,583*	*5,643*	*6,636*
Loans..	8 764 ..	57,060	51,979	41,855	29,871	33,494	36,910	34,003	32,814
Monetary authorities....................................	8 765 ..	15,523	14,091	10,213	....	1,520	4,290	2,910	....
of which: Use of Fund credit and loans from the Fund....	8 766 ..	*15,523*	*14,091*	*9,513*	....	....	....	....	....
of which: Short-term.................................	8 768 ..	....	....	700	....	*1,520*	*4,290*	*2,910*	....
General government.....................................	8 769 ..	21,920	21,180	18,234	17,059	17,179	16,212	17,555	18,087
of which: Short-term.................................	8 771 ..	....	....	....	....	....	....	....	....
Banks...	8 772 ..	5,428	4,122	2,760	2,451	3,209	2,953	1,691	1,782
of which: Short-term.................................	8 774 ..	*2,985*	*1,113*	*580*	*564*	*834*	*906*	*516*	*696*
Other sectors...	8 775 ..	14,189	12,586	10,648	10,361	11,585	13,455	11,848	12,945
of which: Short-term.................................	8 777 ..	*6,527*	*6,419*	*3,727*	*3,150*	*4,982*	*6,862*	*3,995*	*3,874*
Currency and deposits......................................	8 780 ..	119	136	217	495	689	521	376	255
Monetary authorities....................................	8 781 ..	....	....	....	....	....	....	....	....
General government.....................................	8 782 ..	....	....	....	....	....	....	....	....
Banks...	8 783 ..	119	136	217	495	689	521	376	255
Other sectors...	8 784 ..	....	....	....	....	....	....	....	....
Other liabilities..	8 786 ..	2,795	3,148	4,411	5,354	5,608	6,588	9,906	10,244
Monetary authorities....................................	8 787 ..	....	....	80	....	....	7	3,167	3,111
of which: Short-term.................................	8 789 ..	....	....	80	....	....	7	....	....
General government.....................................	8 790 ..	1,742	3,022	4,271	5,354	5,608	6,581	6,739	7,133
of which: Short-term.................................	8 792 ..	*1,742*	*3,022*	*4,271*	*5,354*	*5,608*	*6,581*	*6,739*	*7,133*
Banks...	8 793 ..	1,054	127	61	....	....	....	....	....
of which: Short-term.................................	8 795 ..	*1,054*	*127*	*61*	....	....	....	....	....
Other sectors...	8 796 ..	....	....	....	....	....	....	....	....
of which: Short-term.................................	8 798 ..	....	....	....	....	....	....	....	....
NET INTERNATIONAL INVESTMENT POSITION........	8 995 ..	**−772**	**3,131**	**21,288**	**21,890**	**34,444**	**57,816**	**54,919**	**46,201**
Conversion rates: Argentine pesos per U.S. dollar (end of period)............................	0 102 ..	**2.90500**	**2.95900**	**3.01200**	**3.04200**	**3.12900**	**3.43300**	**3.78000**	**3.95600**

Armemia, Republic of   911

Table 1. ANALYTIC PRESENTATION, 2003–2010

(Millions of U.S. dollars)

	Code	2003	2004	2005	2006	2007	2008	2009	2010
A. Current Account[1]	4 993 Z.	**−189.44**	**−19.63**	**−51.71**	**−117.13**	**−589.60**	**−1,382.85**	**−1,369.48**	**−1,373.19**
Goods: exports f.o.b.	2 100 ..	696.13	738.31	1,004.85	1,025.45	1,196.66	1,112.02	748.85	1,175.42
Goods: imports f.o.b.	3 100 ..	−1,130.21	−1,196.26	−1,592.78	−1,921.30	−2,796.91	−3,775.55	−2,830.13	−3,207.95
Balance on Goods	4 100 ..	*−434.08*	*−457.95*	*−587.93*	*−895.86*	*−1,600.25*	*−2,663.53*	*−2,081.28*	*−2,032.53*
Services: credit	2 200 ..	207.36	332.60	411.09	484.74	580.10	644.97	589.50	761.52
Services: debit	3 200 ..	−275.70	−431.53	−531.05	−615.13	−792.60	−973.12	−857.62	−1,003.80
Balance on Goods and Services	4 991 ..	*−502.42*	*−556.89*	*−707.89*	*−1,026.25*	*−1,812.75*	*−2,991.68*	*−2,349.40*	*−2,274.81*
Income: credit	2 300 ..	165.97	397.46	457.51	624.26	810.75	994.43	715.16	959.75
Income: debit	3 300 ..	−71.48	−290.04	−324.99	−409.09	−532.36	−523.23	−549.16	−621.08
Balance on Goods, Services, and Income	4 992 ..	*−407.93*	*−449.47*	*−575.37*	*−811.08*	*−1,534.36*	*−2,520.48*	*−2,183.40*	*−1,936.14*
Current transfers: credit	2 379 Z.	245.01	514.82	603.52	791.67	1,024.77	1,239.46	894.79	783.71
Current transfers: debit	3 379 ..	−26.53	−84.98	−79.86	−97.71	−80.01	−101.83	−80.87	−220.76
B. Capital Account[1]	4 994 Z.	**89.94**	**41.34**	**73.25**	**86.38**	**142.75**	**148.88**	**89.10**	**107.92**
Capital account: credit	2 994 Z.	92.14	47.23	76.06	91.94	160.13	165.86	102.55	123.14
Capital account: debit	3 994 ..	−2.20	−5.89	−2.81	−5.56	−17.38	−16.98	−13.45	−15.22
Total, Groups A Plus B	4 981 ..	*−99.51*	*21.71*	*21.54*	*−30.74*	*−446.85*	*−1,233.97*	*−1,280.38*	*−1,265.27*
C. Financial Account[1]	4 995 W.	**174.45**	**16.62**	**162.73**	**434.12**	**1,008.44**	**1,006.27**	**1,425.77**	**974.17**
Direct investment abroad	4 505 ..	−.36	−2.25	−6.72	−3.08	2.14	−10.21	−52.72	−8.25
Direct investment in Armenia	4 555 Z.	120.87	247.86	239.38	453.17	698.82	935.43	777.50	570.06
Portfolio investment assets	4 602 ..	.05	−.48	−2.72	−.18	.52	2.61	−10.56	−1.48
Equity securities	4 610 ..	.05	−.11	−.20	.41	−.14	.05	−.55	−.11
Debt securities	4 619 ..	....	−.37	−2.52	−.59	.66	2.56	−10.01	−1.37
Portfolio investment liabilities	4 652 Z.	.21	−2.39	1.13	9.40	−9.74	5.72	6.69	12.23
Equity securities	4 660 ..	.05	1.37	1.33	−.60	.18	−.70	.51	.44
Debt securities	4 669 Z.	.16	−3.77	−.20	10.00	−9.92	6.42	6.19	11.79
Financial derivatives	4 910 ..	....	....	....	....	....	....	....	....
Financial derivatives assets	4 900 ..	....	....	....	....	....	....	....	....
Financial derivatives liabilities	4 905 ..	....	....	....	....	....	....	....	....
Other investment assets	4 703 ..	−63.59	−315.80	−170.65	−175.67	−257.83	−580.64	−478.00	−245.62
Monetary authorities	4 701 ..	−.10	−1.46	2.55	.70	−.04	.64	−2.36	−.23
General government	4 704 ..	2.18	−19.89	−58.71	84.24	−2.18	−2.81	−.11	−1.69
Banks	4 705 ..	−52.71	−62.90	42.10	−7.68	−18.60	−71.98	−202.99	−4.68
Other sectors	4 728 ..	−12.95	−231.56	−156.59	−252.94	−237.01	−506.48	−272.54	−239.02
Other investment liabilities	4 753 W.	117.27	89.69	102.31	150.48	574.54	653.34	1,182.85	647.23
Monetary authorities	4 753 WA	.24	5.25	.87	−.55	9.32	7.37	170.87	4.33
General government	4 753 ZB	24.68	38.46	36.05	68.67	181.12	144.95	885.76	194.34
Banks	4 753 ZC	10.51	32.85	24.16	34.05	331.69	365.23	−42.43	257.30
Other sectors	4 753 ZD	81.84	13.13	41.23	48.32	52.41	135.79	168.65	191.26
Total, Groups A Through C	4 983 ..	*74.95*	*38.33*	*184.27*	*403.38*	*561.59*	*−227.70*	*145.39*	*−291.10*
D. Net Errors and Omissions	4 998 ..	**−1.56**	**−5.53**	**2.37**	**−16.12**	**−1.95**	**13.70**	**20.12**	**17.63**
Total, Groups A Through D	4 984 ..	*73.39*	*32.81*	*186.64*	*387.26*	*559.64*	*−214.00*	*165.51*	*−273.47*
E. Reserves and Related Items	4 802 A.	**−73.39**	**−32.81**	**−186.64**	**−387.26**	**−559.64**	**214.00**	**−165.51**	**273.47**
Reserve assets	4 802 ..	−47.36	−26.40	−161.89	−365.90	−546.12	233.43	−600.24	111.45
Use of Fund credit and loans	4 766 ..	1.78	−6.41	−24.75	−21.36	−13.52	−19.43	435.01	161.91
Exceptional financing	4 920 ..	−27.81	....	....	....	....	....	−.29	.10
Conversion rates: drams per U.S. dollar	0 101 ..	**578.76**	**533.45**	**457.69**	**416.04**	**342.08**	**305.97**	**363.28**	**373.66**

[1] Excludes components that have been classified in the categories of Group E.

Table 2. STANDARD PRESENTATION, 2003–2010

(Millions of U.S. dollars)

	Code	2003	2004	2005	2006	2007	2008	2009	2010
CURRENT ACCOUNT...	4 993 ..	**−189.44**	**−19.63**	**−51.71**	**−117.13**	**−589.60**	**−1,382.85**	**−1,369.48**	**−1,373.19**
A. GOODS...	4 100 ..	**−434.08**	**−457.95**	**−587.93**	**−895.86**	**−1,600.25**	**−2,663.53**	**−2,081.28**	**−2,032.53**
Credit..	2 100 ..	**696.13**	**738.31**	**1,004.85**	**1,025.45**	**1,196.66**	**1,112.02**	**748.85**	**1,175.42**
General merchandise: exports f.o.b........	2 110 ..	685.60	722.91	973.92	991.95	1,162.55	1,065.91	726.88	1,144.66
Goods for processing: exports f.o.b.......	2 150 ..	1.03	1.30	1.29	1.33	1.89	1.74	1.34	1.52
Repairs on goods.......................................	2 160 ..	....	....	....	....	....	....	....	....
Goods procured in ports by carriers.......	2 170 ..	9.50	14.10	29.65	32.17	32.22	44.37	20.64	29.24
Nonmonetary gold.....................................	2 180 ..	....	....	....	....	....	....	....	....
Debit...	3 100 ..	**−1,130.21**	**−1,196.26**	**−1,592.78**	**−1,921.30**	**−2,796.91**	**−3,775.55**	**−2,830.13**	**−3,207.95**
General merchandise: imports f.o.b........	3 110 ..	−1,115.86	−1,173.06	−1,556.11	−1,883.73	−2,755.97	−3,719.69	−2,793.66	−3,161.50
Goods for processing: imports f.o.b.......	3 150 ..	−.89	−.92	−.93	−.84	−.87	−.78	−.70	−.28
Repairs on goods.......................................	3 160 ..	....	....	....	....	....	....	....	....
Goods procured in ports by carriers.......	3 170 ..	−13.46	−22.29	−35.75	−36.73	−40.07	−55.08	−35.77	−46.17
Nonmonetary gold.....................................	3 180 ..	....	....	....	....	....	....	....	....
B. SERVICES..	4 200 ..	**−68.34**	**−98.93**	**−119.96**	**−130.39**	**−212.50**	**−328.15**	**−268.12**	**−242.28**
Total credit..	2 200 ..	*207.36*	*332.60*	*411.09*	*484.74*	*580.10*	*644.97*	*589.50*	*761.52*
Total debit...	3 200 ..	*−275.70*	*−431.53*	*−531.05*	*−615.13*	*−792.60*	*−973.12*	*−857.62*	*−1,003.80*
Transportation services, credit..........	2 205 ..	**73.00**	**73.56**	**92.16**	**102.31**	**133.01**	**137.65**	**108.66**	**156.43**
Passenger...	2 850 ..	*17.24*	*16.89*	*19.54*	*35.60*	*38.31*	*45.79*	*40.46*	*48.13*
Freight...	2 851 ..	*46.21*	*43.21*	*58.02*	*59.19*	*83.31*	*76.82*	*52.78*	*91.51*
Other...	2 852 ..	*9.55*	*13.46*	*14.59*	*7.52*	*11.39*	*15.05*	*15.42*	*16.79*
Sea transport, passenger..........................	2 207 ..	....	....	....	....	....	....	....	....
Sea transport, freight...............................	2 208 ..	....	....	....	....	....	....	....	....
Sea transport, other..................................	2 209 ..	....	....	....	....	....	....	....	....
Air transport, passenger...........................	2 211 ..	14.18	12.99	15.18	30.32	31.98	38.51	33.06	35.92
Air transport, freight.................................	2 212 ..	1.31	.75	.80	.88	.88	1.08	.83	4.06
Air transport, other...................................	2 213 ..	9.49	13.38	14.34	6.59	9.37	12.56	12.00	13.48
Other transport, passenger......................	2 215 ..	3.06	3.89	4.36	5.28	6.33	7.28	7.40	12.21
Other transport, freight............................	2 216 ..	44.90	42.46	57.22	58.30	82.51	75.74	51.95	87.45
Other transport, other..............................	2 217 ..	.07	.08	.25	.92	2.02	2.49	3.43	3.31
Transportation services, debit..........	3 205 ..	**−151.33**	**−178.66**	**−211.56**	**−231.90**	**−361.32**	**−468.74**	**−382.41**	**−448.25**
Passenger...	3 850 ..	*−29.98*	*−37.26*	*−48.13*	*−34.57*	*−51.26*	*−59.25*	*−53.31*	*−62.44*
Freight...	3 851 ..	*−116.57*	*−118.28*	*−147.18*	*−183.93*	*−267.81*	*−369.00*	*−288.48*	*−330.23*
Other...	3 852 ..	*−4.78*	*−23.11*	*−16.25*	*−13.40*	*−42.25*	*−40.49*	*−40.63*	*−55.58*
Sea transport, passenger..........................	3 207 ..	....	....	....	....	....	....	....	....
Sea transport, freight...............................	3 208 ..	−14.81	−24.31	−33.44	−36.65	−54.57	−74.08	−55.39	−64.28
Sea transport, other..................................	3 209 ..	....	....	....	....	....	....	....	....
Air transport, passenger...........................	3 211 ..	−24.59	−30.85	−36.18	−26.79	−42.77	−49.31	−45.73	−51.98
Air transport, freight.................................	3 212 ..	−1.26	−1.38	−1.36	−4.45	−1.09	−1.13	−2.86	−11.51
Air transport, other...................................	3 213 ..	−4.57	−22.40	−14.26	−10.21	−37.05	−33.50	−32.03	−46.04
Other transport, passenger......................	3 215 ..	−5.40	−6.42	−11.95	−7.78	−8.49	−9.94	−7.58	−10.46
Other transport, freight............................	3 216 ..	−100.50	−92.59	−112.38	−142.82	−212.15	−293.79	−230.23	−254.44
Other transport, other..............................	3 217 ..	−.21	−.71	−1.99	−3.20	−5.20	−7.00	−8.60	−9.54
Travel, credit..	2 236 ..	**72.69**	**171.45**	**219.97**	**270.73**	**304.91**	**330.51**	**334.11**	**408.19**
Business travel...	2 237 ..	35.06	60.01	98.99	111.00	108.91	115.99	116.84	145.15
Personal travel...	2 240 ..	37.64	111.44	120.99	159.73	196.00	214.52	217.27	263.04
Travel, debit...	3 236 ..	**−67.00**	**−178.85**	**−236.34**	**−286.04**	**−294.31**	**−324.00**	**−325.86**	**−403.95**
Business travel...	3 237 ..	−33.58	−77.24	−126.49	−134.73	−95.83	−121.26	−79.90	−119.27
Personal travel...	3 240 ..	−33.42	−101.61	−109.85	−151.31	−198.48	−202.75	−245.96	−284.68
Other services, credit..........................	2 200 BA	**61.66**	**87.59**	**98.95**	**111.70**	**142.18**	**176.81**	**146.73**	**196.90**
Communications...	2 245 ..	16.70	23.75	28.19	22.88	41.33	62.14	51.70	64.57
Construction..	2 249 ..	7.91	11.95	10.56	9.94	11.17	14.34	7.61	8.31
Insurance...	2 253 ..	7.42	9.24	11.89	14.77	14.68	15.49	10.54	13.10
Financial..	2 260 ..	1.58	2.70	3.23	3.60	4.15	3.88	5.03	7.07
Computer and information........................	2 262 ..	11.01	17.64	22.45	33.03	43.62	50.38	43.23	63.48
Royalties and licence fees.........................	2 266 ..	....	....	....	....	....	....	....	....
Other business services............................	2 268 ..	6.72	9.15	9.53	12.44	12.14	13.98	12.69	9.63
Personal, cultural, and recreational.........	2 287 ..	2.28	4.93	4.78	5.42	5.88	7.15	6.49	18.92
Government, n.i.e.......................................	2 291 ..	8.04	8.23	8.34	9.61	9.21	9.44	9.44	11.82
Other services, debit...........................	3 200 BA	**−57.37**	**−74.03**	**−83.15**	**−97.19**	**−136.97**	**−180.37**	**−149.35**	**−151.60**
Communications...	3 245 ..	−10.95	−12.86	−13.90	−16.51	−17.16	−20.14	−16.95	−20.83
Construction..	3 249 ..	−3.08	−3.32	−2.77	−3.21	−3.76	−5.23	−3.81	−2.53
Insurance...	3 253 ..	−15.36	−18.37	−23.70	−28.68	−48.95	−72.78	−51.50	−57.08
Financial..	3 260 ..	−1.06	−2.16	−1.89	−2.65	−4.99	−6.83	−9.44	−9.04
Computer and information........................	3 262 ..	−.78	−1.42	−1.52	−2.61	−3.87	−6.78	−4.83	−4.89
Royalties and licence fees.........................	3 266 ..	....	....	....	....	....	....	....	....
Other business services............................	3 268 ..	−8.81	−17.06	−18.30	−21.24	−29.68	−36.14	−35.02	−27.21
Personal, cultural, and recreational.........	3 287 ..	−5.17	−6.06	−6.66	−7.32	−7.97	−10.85	−9.37	−11.65
Government, n.i.e.......................................	3 291 ..	−12.18	−12.78	−14.41	−14.97	−20.59	−21.62	−18.44	−18.37

Table 2 (Continued). STANDARD PRESENTATION, 2003–2010

(Millions of U.S. dollars)

	Code	2003	2004	2005	2006	2007	2008	2009	2010
C. INCOME	4 300	**94.49**	**107.41**	**132.52**	**215.17**	**278.39**	**471.20**	**166.00**	**338.67**
Total credit	2 300	*165.97*	*397.46*	*457.51*	*624.26*	*810.75*	*994.43*	*715.16*	*959.75*
Total debit	3 300	*−71.48*	*−290.04*	*−324.99*	*−409.09*	*−532.36*	*−523.23*	*−549.16*	*−621.08*
Compensation of employees, credit	2 310	**152.87**	**381.81**	**428.75**	**575.95**	**742.66**	**929.18**	**676.96**	**918.86**
Compensation of employees, debit	3 310	**−19.12**	**−122.29**	**−132.99**	**−129.63**	**−166.08**	**−168.96**	**−130.16**	**−148.09**
Investment income, credit	2 320	**13.10**	**15.65**	**28.76**	**48.30**	**68.09**	**65.25**	**38.20**	**40.89**
Direct investment income	2 330	....	....	.43	1.41	1.01	1.20	−.26	.07
Dividends and distributed branch profits	2 332	....	....	....	.72	....	....	....	....
Reinvested earnings and undistributed branch profits	2 333	....	....	.43	.69	1.01	1.20	−.26	.07
Income on debt (interest)	2 334	....	....	....	....	....	....	....	....
Portfolio investment income	2 339	1.80	3.41	6.95	8.64	14.82	34.53	18.75	21.20
Income on equity	2 340	....	....	....	....	....	.01	....	....
Income on bonds and notes	2 350	....	....	6.91	8.60	14.78	34.51	18.75	21.20
Income on money market instruments	2 360	1.80	3.41	.04	.04	.04	.02	....	....
Other investment income	2 370	11.30	12.24	21.38	38.26	52.26	29.52	19.71	19.62
Investment income, debit	3 320	**−52.35**	**−167.75**	**−192.00**	**−279.46**	**−366.28**	**−354.28**	**−419.00**	**−472.99**
Direct investment income	3 330	−34.81	−146.53	−169.91	−244.37	−332.23	−279.18	−331.63	−363.91
Dividends and distributed branch profits	3 332	−7.64	−38.93	−14.19	−49.26	−81.02	−58.44	−49.88	−101.63
Reinvested earnings and undistributed branch profits	3 333	−27.17	−107.60	−155.24	−193.90	−250.22	−208.10	−265.07	−258.26
Income on debt (interest)	3 334	....	....	−.47	−1.22	−.99	−12.65	−16.67	−4.02
Portfolio investment income	3 339	−.45	−.22	−.58	−.85	−1.20	−.30	−.97	−2.21
Income on equity	3 340	....	....	....	−.30	−.37	−.07	−.14	−.41
Income on bonds and notes	3 350	−.05	−.05	−.31	−.54	−.83	−.23	−.83	−1.74
Income on money market instruments	3 360	−.40	−.17	−.27	....	....	....	....	−.06
Other investment income	3 370	−17.10	−21.00	−21.52	−34.24	−32.85	−74.79	−86.41	−106.87
D. CURRENT TRANSFERS	4 379	**218.48**	**429.84**	**523.66**	**693.95**	**944.76**	**1,137.63**	**813.92**	**562.95**
Credit	2 379	**245.01**	**514.82**	**603.52**	**791.67**	**1,024.77**	**1,239.46**	**894.79**	**783.71**
General government	2 380	62.03	62.96	68.49	81.95	97.22	78.19	84.04	89.48
Other sectors	2 390	182.99	451.86	535.02	709.71	927.55	1,161.27	810.75	694.23
Workers' remittances	2 391	9.32	42.54	57.99	74.38	94.36	123.57	85.79	71.91
Other current transfers	2 392	173.66	409.32	477.03	635.33	833.19	1,037.70	724.96	622.32
Debit	3 379	**−26.53**	**−84.98**	**−79.86**	**−97.71**	**−80.01**	**−101.83**	**−80.87**	**−220.76**
General government	3 380	−1.84	−2.01	−2.42	−2.00	−2.76	−2.95	−3.35	−3.68
Other sectors	3 390	−24.69	−82.98	−77.44	−95.71	−77.25	−98.88	−77.52	−217.08
Workers' remittances	3 391	−5.59	−10.02	−16.04	−18.53	−5.32	−10.93	−10.97	−3.97
Other current transfers	3 392	−19.11	−72.95	−61.40	−77.18	−71.93	−87.95	−66.56	−213.11
CAPITAL AND FINANCIAL ACCOUNT	4 996	**191.01**	**25.16**	**49.35**	**133.25**	**591.55**	**1,369.14**	**1,349.36**	**1,355.56**
CAPITAL ACCOUNT	4 994	**89.94**	**41.34**	**73.25**	**86.38**	**142.75**	**148.88**	**89.10**	**107.92**
Total credit	2 994	*92.14*	*47.23*	*76.06*	*91.94*	*160.13*	*165.86*	*102.55*	*123.14*
Total debit	3 994	*−2.20*	*−5.89*	*−2.81*	*−5.56*	*−17.38*	*−16.98*	*−13.45*	*−15.22*
Capital transfers, credit	2 400	**92.14**	**47.23**	**76.06**	**91.94**	**160.13**	**165.86**	**102.55**	**123.14**
General government	2 401	86.63	13.08	18.03	24.51	62.42	52.83	25.47	37.36
Debt forgiveness	2 402	....	....	....	....	....	....	....	....
Other capital transfers	2 410	86.63	13.08	18.03	24.51	62.42	52.83	25.47	37.36
Other sectors	2 430	5.52	34.15	58.03	67.43	97.71	113.03	77.08	85.78
Migrants' transfers	2 431	5.52	10.21	11.32	7.81	8.84	9.36	6.70	5.00
Debt forgiveness	2 432	....	....	....	....	....	....	....	....
Other capital transfers	2 440	....	23.95	46.71	59.62	88.87	103.67	70.37	80.78
Capital transfers, debit	3 400	**−2.20**	**−5.89**	**−2.81**	**−5.56**	**−17.38**	**−16.98**	**−13.45**	**−15.22**
General government	3 401	....	....	....	....	....	....	....	....
Debt forgiveness	3 402	....	....	....	....	....	....	....	....
Other capital transfers	3 410	....	....	....	....	....	....	....	....
Other sectors	3 430	−2.20	−5.89	−2.81	−5.56	−17.38	−16.98	−13.45	−15.22
Migrants' transfers	3 431	−2.20	−5.89	−2.81	−5.56	−4.74	−5.26	−4.02	−4.58
Debt forgiveness	3 432	....	....	....	....	....	....	....	....
Other capital transfers	3 440	....	....	....	....	−12.64	−11.72	−9.43	−10.64
Nonproduced nonfinancial assets, credit	2 480	....	....	....	....	....	....	....	....
Nonproduced nonfinancial assets, debit	3 480	....	....	....	....	....	....	....	....

Table 2 (Continued). STANDARD PRESENTATION, 2003–2010

(Millions of U.S. dollars)

	Code	2003	2004	2005	2006	2007	2008	2009	2010
FINANCIAL ACCOUNT..	4 995 ..	**101.07**	**−16.19**	**−23.90**	**46.86**	**448.80**	**1,220.27**	**1,260.26**	**1,247.64**
A. DIRECT INVESTMENT..................................	4 500 ..	**120.51**	**245.61**	**232.66**	**450.09**	**700.96**	**925.22**	**724.78**	**561.81**
Direct investment abroad..............................	4 505 ..	**−.36**	**−2.25**	**−6.72**	**−3.08**	**2.14**	**−10.21**	**−52.72**	**−8.25**
Equity capital..	4 510 ..	−.36	−2.25	−6.29	−2.39	3.15	−9.01	−43.49	−8.18
Claims on affiliated enterprises..................	4 515 ..	−.36	−2.25	−6.29	−2.39	3.15	−9.01	−43.49	−8.18
Liabilities to affiliated enterprises..............	4 520 ..	. . . .	. . . .	. . . .	. . . .	. . . .	. . . .	. . . .	. . . .
Reinvested earnings.......................................	4 525 ..	. . . .	. . . .	−.43	−.69	−1.01	−1.20	.26	−.07
Other capital...	4 530 ..	. . . .	. . . .	. . . .	. . . .	. . . .	. . . .	−9.48	. . . .
Claims on affiliated enterprises..................	4 535 ..	. . . .	. . . .	. . . .	. . . .	. . . .	. . . .	−9.48	
Liabilities to affiliated enterprises..............	4 540 ..	. . . .	. . . .	. . . .	. . . .	. . . .	. . . .		
Direct investment in Armenia...........................	4 555 ..	**120.87**	**247.86**	**239.38**	**453.17**	**698.82**	**935.43**	**777.50**	**570.06**
Equity capital..	4 560 ..	75.20	117.63	74.06	216.73	207.46	819.82	470.52	143.17
Claims on direct investors............................	4 565 ..	. . . .	. . . .	. . . .	. . . .	. . . .	. . . .	. . . .	. . . .
Liabilities to direct investors......................	4 570 ..	75.20	117.63	74.06	216.73	207.46	819.82	470.52	143.17
Reinvested earnings.......................................	4 575 ..	27.17	107.60	155.24	193.90	250.22	208.10	265.07	258.26
Other capital...	4 580 ..	18.51	22.63	10.08	42.54	241.14	−92.48	41.91	168.63
Claims on direct investors............................	4 585 ..	. . . .	. . . .	. . . .	. . . .	. . . .	. . . .	. . . .	. . . .
Liabilities to direct investors......................	4 590 ..	18.51	22.63	10.08	42.54	241.14	−92.48	41.91	168.63
B. PORTFOLIO INVESTMENT.............................	4 600 ..	**.26**	**−2.88**	**−1.59**	**9.22**	**−9.22**	**8.33**	**−3.86**	**10.75**
Assets...	4 602 ..	**.05**	**−.48**	**−2.72**	**−.18**	**.52**	**2.61**	**−10.56**	**−1.48**
Equity securities..	4 610 ..	.05	−.11	−.20	.41	−.14	.05	−.55	−.11
Monetary authorities.....................................	4 611 ..	. . . .	. . . .	. . . .	. . . .	. . . .	. . . .	. . . .	. . . .
General government.......................................	4 612 ..	. . . .	. . . .	. . . .	. . . .	. . . .	. . . .	. . . .	. . . .
Banks...	4 613 ..	.05	−.01	−.10	.41	−.14	.05	−.05	−.02
Other sectors..	4 614 ..	. . . .	−.10	−.10	. . . .	. . . .	. . . .	−.49	−.09
Debt securities..	4 619 ..	. . . .	−.37	−2.52	−.59	.66	2.56	−10.01	−1.37
Bonds and notes..	4 620 ..	.02	.01	−2.40	−.83	.94	2.25	−10.01	−.69
Monetary authorities.................................	4 621 ..	. . . .	. . . .	. . . .	. . . .	. . . .	. . . .	−10.05	−.72
General government....................................	4 622 ..	. . . .	. . . .	. . . .	. . . .	. . . .	. . . .	. . . .	. . . .
Banks..	4 623 ..	.02	.01	−2.40	−.83	.94	2.25	.06	.03
Other sectors..	4 624 ..	. . . .	. . . .	. . . .	. . . .	. . . .	. . . .	−.02	. . . .
Money market instruments...........................	4 630 ..	−.02	−.38	−.12	.24	−.28	.32	. . . .	−.68
Monetary authorities.................................	4 631 ..	. . . .	. . . .	. . . .	. . . .	. . . .	. . . .	. . . .	. . . .
General government....................................	4 632 ..	. . . .	. . . .	. . . .	. . . .	. . . .	. . . .	. . . .	. . . .
Banks..	4 633 ..	−.02	−.38	−.12	.24	−.28	.32	. . . .	−.68
Other sectors..	4 634 ..	. . . .	. . . .	. . . .	. . . .	. . . .	. . . .	. . . .	. . . .
Liabilities..	4 652 ..	**.21**	**−2.39**	**1.13**	**9.40**	**−9.74**	**5.72**	**6.69**	**12.23**
Equity securities..	4 660 ..	.05	1.37	1.33	−.60	.18	−.70	.51	.44
Banks...	4 663 ..	.05	1.37	1.33	−.60	.18	−.70	.45	.44
Other sectors..	4 664 ..	. . . .	. . . .	. . . .	. . . .	. . . .	. . . .	.06	. . . .
Debt securities..	4 669 ..	.16	−3.77	−.20	10.00	−9.92	6.42	6.19	11.79
Bonds and notes..	4 670 ..	.37	−.62	. . . .	. . . .	−10.00	6.58	6.15	10.57
Monetary authorities.................................	4 671 ..	. . . .	. . . .	. . . .	. . . .	. . . .	. . . .	. . . .	. . . .
General government....................................	4 672 ..	.37	−.62	. . . .	. . . .	. . . .	. . . .	. . . .	.02
Banks..	4 673 ..	. . . .	. . . .	. . . .	. . . .	−10.00	6.58	6.15	10.55
Other sectors..	4 674 ..	. . . .	. . . .	. . . .	. . . .	. . . .	. . . .	. . . .	. . . .
Money market instruments...........................	4 680 ..	−.21	−3.15	−.20	10.00	.08	−.16	.04	1.22
Monetary authorities.................................	4 681 ..	. . . .	. . . .	. . . .	. . . .	. . . .	. . . .	. . . .	. . . .
General government....................................	4 682 ..	. . . .	−3.11	−.20	. . . .	. . . .	. . . .	. . . .	1.26
Banks..	4 683 ..	−.21	−.04	. . . .	10.00	.08	−.07	.04	−.04
Other sectors..	4 684 ..	. . . .	. . . .	. . . .	. . . .	. . . .	−.08	. . . .	. . . .
C. FINANCIAL DERIVATIVES.............................	4 910 ..	. . . .	. . . .	. . . .	. . . .	. . . .	. . . .	. . . .	. . . .
Monetary authorities...	4 911 ..	. . . .	. . . .	. . . .	. . . .	. . . .	. . . .	. . . .	. . . .
General government...	4 912 ..	. . . .	. . . .	. . . .	. . . .	. . . .	. . . .	. . . .	. . . .
Banks...	4 913 ..	. . . .	. . . .	. . . .	. . . .	. . . .	. . . .	. . . .	. . . .
Other sectors...	4 914 ..	. . . .	. . . .	. . . .	. . . .	. . . .	. . . .	. . . .	. . . .
Assets...	4 900 ..	. . . .	. . . .	. . . .	. . . .	. . . .	. . . .	. . . .	. . . .
Monetary authorities.....................................	4 901 ..	. . . .	. . . .	. . . .	. . . .	. . . .	. . . .	. . . .	. . . .
General government.......................................	4 902 ..	. . . .	. . . .	. . . .	. . . .	. . . .	. . . .	. . . .	. . . .
Banks...	4 903 ..	. . . .	. . . .	. . . .	. . . .	. . . .	. . . .	. . . .	. . . .
Other sectors..	4 904 ..	. . . .	. . . .	. . . .	. . . .	. . . .	. . . .	. . . .	. . . .
Liabilities..	4 905 ..	. . . .	. . . .	. . . .	. . . .	. . . .	. . . .	. . . .	. . . .
Monetary authorities.....................................	4 906 ..	. . . .	. . . .	. . . .	. . . .	. . . .	. . . .	. . . .	. . . .
General government.......................................	4 907 ..	. . . .	. . . .	. . . .	. . . .	. . . .	. . . .	. . . .	. . . .
Banks...	4 908 ..	. . . .	. . . .	. . . .	. . . .	. . . .	. . . .	. . . .	. . . .
Other sectors..	4 909 ..	. . . .	. . . .	. . . .	. . . .	. . . .	. . . .	. . . .	. . . .

Table 2 (Concluded). STANDARD PRESENTATION, 2003–2010

(Millions of U.S. dollars)

	Code	2003	2004	2005	2006	2007	2008	2009	2010
D. OTHER INVESTMENT	4 700 ..	**27.66**	**−232.52**	**−93.09**	**−46.55**	**303.19**	**53.28**	**1,139.58**	**563.62**
Assets	4 703 ..	**−63.59**	**−315.80**	**−170.65**	**−175.67**	**−257.83**	**−580.64**	**−478.00**	**−245.62**
Trade credits	4 706 ..	−23.36	−22.05	−24.35	−23.25	−22.06	−18.27	−8.78	−12.49
General government	4 707 ..	....	....	....	....	....	....	....	....
of which: Short-term	4 709 ..	....	....	....	....	....	....	....	....
Other sectors	4 710 ..	−23.36	−22.05	−24.35	−23.25	−22.06	−18.27	−8.78	−12.49
of which: Short-term	4 712 ..	−23.36	−22.05	−24.35	−23.25	−22.06	−18.27	−8.78	−12.49
Loans	4 714 ..	4.17	−19.93	1.13	−4.09	8.95	−33.50	−120.18	−72.30
Monetary authorities	4 715 ..	....	....	....	....	....	....	....	....
of which: Short-term	4 718 ..	....	....	....	....	....	....	....	....
General government	4 719 ..	....	....	1.35	.83	.15	.09	.20	.25
of which: Short-term	4 721 ..	....	....	....	....	....	....	....	....
Banks	4 722 ..	4.17	−.78	−7.87	3.84	6.80	−12.20	−104.97	−57.51
of which: Short-term	4 724 ..	8.11	−1.07	−8.62	4.50	6.98	−8.25	−106.22	−49.57
Other sectors	4 725 ..	....	−19.15	7.65	−8.75	2.00	−21.38	−15.41	−15.04
of which: Short-term	4 727 ..	....	−4.15	14.15	−8.00	3.00	−20.78	−13.81	−13.04
Currency and deposits	4 730 ..	−45.79	−270.68	−145.18	−148.36	−228.73	−537.07	−307.82	−150.93
Monetary authorities	4 731 ..	−.02	−.04	−.04	.12	....	....	....	....
General government	4 732 ..	2.18	−19.89	−57.45	85.56	....	−.01	.01	....
Banks	4 733 ..	−58.36	−60.40	52.20	−13.10	−11.71	−70.42	−67.47	52.62
Other sectors	4 734 ..	10.41	−190.35	−139.89	−220.94	−217.02	−466.63	−240.36	−203.55
Other assets	4 736 ..	1.39	−3.13	−2.25	.02	−15.99	8.19	−41.22	−9.90
Monetary authorities	4 737 ..	−.08	−1.42	2.59	.58	−.04	.64	−2.36	−.23
of which: Short-term	4 739 ..	−.08	−1.42	2.59	.58	−.04	.64	−2.36	−.23
General government	4 740 ..	....	....	−2.61	−2.14	−2.33	−2.89	−.32	−1.94
of which: Short-term	4 742 ..	....	....	−2.61	−2.14	−2.33	−2.89	....	....
Banks	4 743 ..	1.47	−1.72	−2.23	1.58	−13.69	10.65	−30.55	.21
of which: Short-term	4 745 ..	1.47	−1.72	−2.23	1.58	−13.69	10.65	−30.55	.21
Other sectors	4 746 ..	....	....	....	....	.07	−.21	−7.99	−7.94
of which: Short-term	4 748 ..	....	....	....	....	−.08	−.21	.01	−1.35
Liabilities	4 753 ..	**91.24**	**83.28**	**77.57**	**129.13**	**561.02**	**633.91**	**1,617.58**	**809.24**
Trade credits	4 756 ..	46.15	23.76	−10.62	−39.45	−80.48	2.93	49.93	14.16
General government	4 757 ..	....	....	....	....	....	....	....	....
of which: Short-term	4 759 ..	....	....	....	....	....	....	....	....
Other sectors	4 760 ..	46.15	23.76	−10.62	−39.45	−80.48	2.93	49.93	14.16
of which: Short-term	4 762 ..	34.94	17.74	−2.14	−.42	−63.72	−7.61	18.70	5.91
Loans	4 764 ..	57.46	43.73	93.52	179.67	538.66	485.17	1,377.19	715.98
Monetary authorities	4 765 ..	1.78	−.83	−24.75	−21.36	−4.92	−11.10	468.29	166.79
of which: Use of Fund credit and loans from the Fund..	4 766 ..	1.78	−6.41	−24.75	−21.36	−13.52	−19.43	435.01	161.91
of which: Short-term	4 768 ..	....	....	....	....	....	....	....	....
General government	4 769 ..	24.68	38.46	36.05	68.67	181.12	144.95	885.76	194.34
of which: Short-term	4 771 ..	....	....	....	....	....	....	....	....
Banks	4 772 ..	−1.14	7.76	15.66	38.90	243.59	228.06	−89.78	190.60
of which: Short-term	4 774 ..	2.09	−1.14	−1.42	17.80	107.37	−65.44	−38.43	40.26
Other sectors	4 775 ..	32.14	−1.67	66.56	93.46	118.87	123.26	112.92	164.25
of which: Short-term	4 777 ..	20.02	5.46	6.06	37.89	24.14	−2.96	−4.16	9.18
Currency and deposits	4 780 ..	12.07	17.74	12.23	−2.43	76.33	140.68	52.60	54.37
Monetary authorities	4 781 ..	.03	−.06	.88	−.50	.55	−.73	−.07	.02
General government	4 782 ..	....	....	....	....	....	....	....	....
Banks	4 783 ..	12.04	17.79	11.16	−1.93	75.78	141.40	52.67	54.35
Other sectors	4 784 ..	....	....	.19	....	....	....	....	....
Other liabilities	4 786 ..	−24.43	−1.94	−17.57	−8.66	26.51	5.14	137.85	24.73
Monetary authorities	4 787 ..	.21	−.28	....	−.05	.17	−.23	137.66	−.57
of which: Short-term	4 789 ..	....	−.28	....	−.05	.17	−.23	.03	−.57
General government	4 790 ..	−27.81	....	....	....	....	....	....	....
of which: Short-term	4 792 ..	−27.81	....	....	....	....	....	....	....
Banks	4 793 ..	−.39	7.29	−2.66	−2.92	12.32	−4.23	−5.32	12.35
of which: Short-term	4 795 ..	−.39	7.29	−2.66	−2.92	12.32	−4.23	−5.32	12.35
Other sectors	4 796 ..	3.56	−8.95	−14.90	−5.69	14.02	9.60	5.51	12.95
of which: Short-term	4 798 ..	2.45	−6.95	.49	−2.74	11.79	5.60	−.39	1.36
E. RESERVE ASSETS	4 802 ..	**−47.36**	**−26.40**	**−161.89**	**−365.90**	**−546.12**	**233.43**	**−600.24**	**111.45**
Monetary gold	4 812 ..	15.68	....	....	....	....	....	....	....
Special drawing rights	4 811 ..	12.81	7.30	1.07	−3.16	4.69	5.89	−121.07	88.62
Reserve position in the Fund	4 810 ..	....	....	....	....	....	....	....	....
Foreign exchange	4 803 ..	−75.85	−33.61	−163.07	−363.05	−547.44	225.15	−479.42	22.82
Other claims	4 813 ..	−.01	−.09	.11	.31	−3.37	2.40	.26	.01
NET ERRORS AND OMISSIONS	4 998 ..	**−1.56**	**−5.53**	**2.37**	**−16.12**	**−1.95**	**13.70**	**20.12**	**17.63**

Armenia, Republic of   911

Table 3. INTERNATIONAL INVESTMENT POSITION (End-period stocks), 2003–2010

(Millions of U.S. dollars)

	Code	2003	2004	2005	2006	2007	2008	2009	2010
ASSETS	8 995 C.	**786.85**	**1,141.46**	**1,427.93**	**1,982.46**	**2,822.65**	**3,113.15**	**4,222.57**	**4,331.67**
Direct investment abroad	8 505 ..	**.39**	**2.67**	**10.27**	**15.54**	**14.34**	**24.49**	**76.71**	**85.48**
Equity capital and reinvested earnings	8 506 ..	.39	2.67	10.27	15.54	14.34	24.49	67.23	76.00
Claims on affiliated enterprises	8 507 ..	.39	2.67	10.27	15.54	14.34	24.49	67.23	76.00
Liabilities to affiliated enterprises	8 508 ..	....	....	....	....	....	....	....	....
Other capital	8 530 ..	....	....	....	....	....	....	9.48	9.48
Claims on affiliated enterprises	8 535 ..	....	....	....	....	....	....	9.48	9.48
Liabilities to affiliated enterprises	8 540 ..	....	....	....	....	....	....	....	....
Portfolio investment	8 602 ..	**4.45**	**4.62**	**5.94**	**5.26**	**4.89**	**2.19**	**14.15**	**15.48**
Equity securities	8 610 ..	4.39	4.49	3.29	2.04	2.18	2.08	3.89	3.45
Monetary authorities	8 611 ..	....	....	....	....	....	....	....	....
General government	8 612 ..	....	....	....	....	....	....	....	....
Banks	8 613 ..	.45	.47	.58	.22	.36	.34	1.64	1.12
Other sectors	8 614 ..	3.94	4.02	2.71	1.82	1.82	1.73	2.25	2.34
Debt securities	8 619 ..	.06	.13	2.64	3.22	2.71	.11	10.26	12.03
Bonds and notes	8 620 ..	....	.01	2.41	3.22	2.32	.09	10.26	11.37
Monetary authorities	8 621 ..	....	....	....	....	....	....	10.22	11.37
General government	8 622 ..	....	....	....	....	....	....	....	....
Banks	8 623 ..	....	.01	2.41	3.22	2.32	.09	.03	....
Other sectors	8 624 ..	....	....	....	....	....	....	.01	....
Money market instruments	8 630 ..	.06	.12	.24	....	.39	.02	....	.66
Monetary authorities	8 631 ..	....	....	....	....	....	....	....	....
General government	8 632 ..	....	....	....	....	....	....	....	....
Banks	8 633 ..	.07	.12	.24	−.01	.30	.02	....	.66
Other sectors	8 634 ..	....	....	....	....	.09	....	....	....
Financial derivatives	8 900 ..	....	**−.01**	**.01**	**.01**	....	....	....	....
Monetary authorities	8 901 ..	....	....	....	....	....	....	....	....
General government	8 902 ..	....	....	....	....	....	....	....	....
Banks	8 903 ..	....	....	....	....	....	....	....	....
Other sectors	8 904 ..	....	....	....	....	....	....	....	....
Other investment	8 703 ..	**277.95**	**584.23**	**737.96**	**889.73**	**1,144.32**	**1,676.75**	**2,128.10**	**2,364.88**
Trade credits	8 706 ..	65.98	73.10	85.08	72.07	76.00	54.61	39.94	52.43
General government	8 707 ..	....	....	....	....	....	....	....	....
of which: Short-term	8 709 ..	....	....	....	....	....	....	....	....
Other sectors	8 710 ..	65.98	73.10	85.08	72.07	76.00	54.61	39.94	52.43
of which: Short-term	8 712 ..	*65.98*	*73.10*	*85.08*	*72.07*	*76.00*	*54.61*	*39.94*	*52.43*
Loans	8 714 ..	29.22	49.83	48.84	52.50	44.84	77.25	194.98	268.74
Monetary authorities	8 715 ..	....	....	....	....	....	....	....	....
of which: Short-term	8 718 ..	....	....	....	....	....	....	....	....
General government	8 719 ..	19.59	19.59	18.49	17.66	17.51	17.42	17.22	16.97
of which: Short-term	8 721 ..	....	....	....	....	....	....	....	....
Banks	8 722 ..	9.63	10.93	18.80	15.94	10.40	21.48	124.00	182.97
of which: Short-term	8 724 ..	*5.57*	*6.97*	*15.55*	*11.96*	*5.98*	*13.13*	*117.43*	*168.40*
Other sectors	8 725 ..	....	19.31	11.56	18.90	16.93	38.35	53.76	68.80
of which: Short-term	8 727 ..	....	*4.15*	*−10.05*	*−2.87*	*−5.87*	*14.91*	*28.72*	*41.76*
Currency and deposits	8 730 ..	180.84	455.94	596.42	756.50	997.09	1,527.47	1,836.28	1,978.39
Monetary authorities	8 731 ..	.03	.08	.12	....	....	....	....	....
General government	8 732 ..	8.21	28.10	85.56	....	....	.01	....	....
Banks	8 733 ..	169.82	234.63	177.92	194.95	215.15	278.35	346.79	285.60
Other sectors	8 734 ..	2.78	193.13	332.82	561.55	781.94	1,249.11	1,489.49	1,692.78
Other assets	8 736 ..	1.92	5.36	7.61	8.66	26.39	17.43	56.90	65.31
Monetary authorities	8 737 ..	.68	2.41	.01	.46	.68	.06	2.19	2.48
of which: Short-term	8 739 ..	*.68*	*2.41*	*.01*	*.46*	*.68*	*.06*	*2.19*	*2.48*
General government	8 740 ..	....	....	2.61	4.75	7.08	9.97	10.29	10.91
of which: Short-term	8 742 ..	....	....	*2.61*	*4.75*	*7.08*	*9.97*	....	....
Banks	8 743 ..	1.23	2.96	4.99	3.45	17.59	6.14	36.80	37.81
of which: Short-term	8 745 ..	*1.23*	*2.96*	*4.99*	*3.45*	*17.59*	*6.14*	*36.80*	*37.81*
Other sectors	8 746 ..	....	....	....	....	1.04	1.26	7.62	14.12
of which: Short-term	8 748 ..	....	....	....	....	*1.04*	*1.26*	*1.03*	*.95*
Reserve assets	8 802 ..	**504.06**	**549.96**	**673.76**	**1,071.92**	**1,659.10**	**1,409.73**	**2,003.61**	**1,865.82**
Monetary gold	8 812 ..	....	....	....	....	....	2.93	....	....
Special drawing rights	8 811 ..	18.83	11.96	10.18	13.96	9.60	2.91	124.64	33.48
Reserve position in the Fund	8 810 ..	....	....	....	....	....	....	....	....
Foreign exchange	8 803 ..	485.22	537.89	663.58	1,057.95	1,647.21	1,403.83	1,878.96	1,832.34
Other claims	8 813 ..	.01	.11	....	....	2.29	.06	.01	....

Table 3 (Concluded). INTERNATIONAL INVESTMENT POSITION (End-period stocks), 2003–2010

(Millions of U.S. dollars)

	Code	2003	2004	2005	2006	2007	2008	2009	2010
LIABILITIES	8 995 D.	2,363.90	2,703.32	2,899.76	3,528.98	4,912.35	6,580.22	8,301.66	10,259.16
Direct investment in Armenia	8 555	793.38	1,037.93	1,298.29	1,774.37	2,485.76	3,520.86	3,628.22	4,338.18
Equity capital and reinvested earnings	8 556	605.39	830.45	1,070.11	1,503.53	1,986.93	3,129.30	3,272.49	3,707.33
Claims on direct investors	8 557	....	....	....	....	....	....	....	....
Liabilities to direct investors	8 558	605.39	830.45	1,070.11	1,503.53	1,986.93	3,129.30	3,272.49	3,707.33
Other capital	8 580	187.99	207.48	228.17	270.84	498.83	391.57	355.73	630.85
Claims on direct investors	8 585	....	....	....	....	....	....	....	....
Liabilities to direct investors	8 590	187.99	207.48	228.17	270.84	498.83	391.57	355.73	630.85
Portfolio investment	8 652	6.38	4.87	5.47	15.96	9.36	18.27	20.92	33.62
Equity securities	8 660	2.95	4.84	5.48	5.97	9.28	11.67	8.35	9.15
Banks	8 663	2.75	4.68	5.32	5.81	9.17	11.56	8.20	8.99
Other sectors	8 664	.20	.16	.16	.16	.11	.11	.15	.15
Debt securities	8 669	3.43	.03	−.01	9.99	.08	6.60	12.57	24.48
Bonds and notes	8 670	.41	−.15	−.01	10.00	....	6.58	12.53	23.15
Monetary authorities	8 671	....	....	....	....	....	....	....	....
General government	8 672	.55	....						.06
Banks	8 673	....	....	....	10.00	....	6.58	12.53	23.09
Other sectors	8 674	−.14	−.14	....					
Money market instruments	8 680	3.02	.18			.08	.02	.04	1.33
Monetary authorities	8 681	....	....						
General government	8 682	2.99	.18						1.33
Banks	8 683	.04	....			.08	.02	.04	....
Other sectors	8 684	....	....						
Financial derivatives	8 905	....	....	....	....	....	....	....	....
Monetary authorities	8 906	....	....	....	....	....	....	....	....
General government	8 907	....	....	....	....	....	....	....	....
Banks	8 908	....	....	....	....	....	....	....	....
Other sectors	8 909	....	....	....	....	....	....	....	....
Other investment	8 753	1,564.14	1,660.51	1,596.00	1,738.65	2,417.23	3,041.09	4,652.52	5,887.36
Trade credits	8 756	229.68	208.58	161.92	93.74	7.33	10.56	60.49	74.65
General government	8 758	....	....	....	....	....	....	....	....
of which: Short-term	8 759	....	....	....	....	....	....	....	....
Other sectors	8 760	229.68	208.58	161.92	93.74	7.33	10.56	60.49	74.65
of which: Short-term	8 762	162.77	137.99	113.59	80.82	7.44	.07	18.77	24.68
Loans	8 764	1,194.25	1,294.23	1,290.17	1,516.10	2,165.44	2,642.43	4,020.17	5,171.72
Monetary authorities	8 765	229.86	240.45	196.23	185.79	191.67	175.32	661.62	816.70
of which: Use of Fund credit and loans from the Fund	8 766	214.64	217.63	176.40	163.67	157.90	134.77	586.71	740.77
of which: Short-term	8 768	....	....	....	....	....	....	....	....
General government	8 769	860.23	942.49	903.15	1,021.20	1,259.79	1,403.80	2,313.01	2,742.27
of which: Short-term	8 771	....	....	....	....	....	....	....	....
Banks	8 772	14.58	22.23	37.88	83.85	333.90	561.04	464.20	654.20
of which: Short-term	8 774	4.35	3.09	1.67	29.55	137.45	71.50	32.80	73.09
Other sectors	8 775	89.59	89.06	152.92	225.27	380.08	502.28	581.34	958.55
of which: Short-term	8 777	29.97	35.72	40.47	76.76	107.17	105.91	99.01	157.63
Currency and deposits	8 780	78.75	98.25	109.50	108.26	194.94	336.54	382.41	432.91
Monetary authorities	8 781	.03	.01	.88	.59	1.22	.48	.19	.21
General government	8 782	....	....	....	....	....	....	....	....
Banks	8 783	78.57	98.25	108.43	107.48	193.72	336.05	382.22	432.70
Other sectors	8 784	.15	....	.19	.19	....	....	....	....
Other liabilities	8 786	61.45	59.44	34.41	20.55	49.52	51.56	189.45	208.06
Monetary authorities	8 787	.54	.10	.12	.17	.38	.17	138.68	135.69
of which: Short-term	8 789	.36	.28	.30	.35	.38	.17	.74	.19
General government	8 790	....	....	....	....	....	....	....	....
of which: Short-term	8 792	....	....	....	....	....	....	....	....
Banks	8 793	1.48	8.87	6.08	3.51	16.01	11.14	5.48	17.86
of which: Short-term	8 795	1.48	8.87	6.08	3.51	16.01	11.14	5.48	17.86
Other sectors	8 796	59.44	50.48	28.21	16.87	33.13	40.25	45.29	54.51
of which: Short-term	8 798	29.67	22.72	17.19	13.66	28.64	31.76	30.90	8.35
NET INTERNATIONAL INVESTMENT POSITION	8 995	−1,577.04	−1,561.85	−1,471.83	−1,546.52	−2,089.70	−3,467.06	−4,079.09	−5,927.49
Conversion rates: drams per U.S. dollar (end of period)	0 102	566.00	485.84	450.19	363.50	304.22	306.73	377.89	363.44

Table 1. ANALYTIC PRESENTATION, 2003–2010

(Millions of U.S. dollars)

	Code	2003	2004	2005	2006	2007	2008	2009	2010
A. Current Account[1]	4 993 Z.	**−166.1**	**11.6**	**−197.8**	**−25.3**	**−88.3**	**−164.8**	**131.0**	**−410.2**
Goods: exports f.o.b.	2 100 ..	2,051.8	2,736.4	3,483.3	3,667.1	2,690.9	3,705.2	1,434.3	265.8
Goods: imports f.o.b.	3 100 ..	−2,400.7	−3,004.3	−3,461.8	−3,786.2	−2,852.8	−4,201.0	−1,911.4	−1,343.0
Balance on Goods	4 100 ..	*−348.9*	*−267.9*	*21.5*	*−119.1*	*−161.9*	*−495.8*	*−477.1*	*−1,077.3*
Services: credit	2 200 ..	1,048.1	1,252.7	1,307.5	1,308.6	1,469.1	1,594.2	1,516.6	1,532.5
Services: debit	3 200 ..	−724.1	−792.5	−922.1	−987.4	−914.9	−1,041.3	−767.9	−689.9
Balance on Goods and Services	4 991 ..	*−24.9*	*192.3*	*406.9*	*202.1*	*392.2*	*57.0*	*271.6*	*−234.7*
Income: credit	2 300 ..	32.5	35.7	42.7	62.6	89.7	71.9	57.2	49.2
Income: debit	3 300 ..	−85.9	−112.3	−520.8	−167.1	−468.4	−179.9	−119.7	−157.2
Balance on Goods, Services, and Income	4 992 ..	*−78.3*	*115.7*	*−71.3*	*97.6*	*13.6*	*−50.9*	*209.1*	*−342.7*
Current transfers: credit	2 379 Z.	40.8	44.7	50.9	53.9	57.2	67.0	69.5	68.3
Current transfers: debit	3 379 ..	−128.6	−148.8	−177.5	−176.8	−159.0	−180.8	−147.6	−135.8
B. Capital Account[1]	4 994 Z.	**100.3**	**16.9**	**18.6**	**21.1**	**18.9**	**157.0**	**34.1**	**6.9**
Capital account: credit	2 994 Z.	122.8	28.9	26.8	29.5	28.2	167.2	39.8	12.2
Capital account: debit	3 994 ..	−22.5	−12.0	−8.2	−8.4	−9.2	−10.2	−5.8	−5.4
Total, Groups A Plus B	4 981 ..	*−65.8*	*28.6*	*−179.2*	*−4.2*	*−69.3*	*−7.8*	*165.0*	*−403.4*
C. Financial Account[1]	4 995 W.	**6.5**	**−33.7**	**139.4**	**68.5**	**107.5**	**243.7**	**−117.4**	**387.2**
Direct investment abroad	4 505 ..	3.2	10.3	8.9	12.8	−29.5	−2.8	−1.5	−4.0
Direct investment in Aruba	4 555 Z.	154.5	133.9	100.8	564.9	−126.4	200.3	73.4	160.8
Portfolio investment assets	4 602 ..	−30.7	−34.3	−18.4	−84.0	−26.1	−2.6	−11.1	−.1
Equity securities	4 610 ..	−19.4	−26.2	−3.3	−75.4	−39.1	−12.3	14.4	2.2
Debt securities	4 619 ..	−11.3	−8.1	−15.2	−8.6	13.0	9.7	−25.5	−2.2
Portfolio investment liabilities	4 652 Z.	66.4	60.6	40.2	35.8	85.4	47.4	12.1	10.9
Equity securities	4 660 ..	....	....	....	....	....	....	....	....
Debt securities	4 669 Z.	66.4	60.6	40.2	35.8	85.4	47.4	12.1	10.9
Financial derivatives	4 910 ..	.1	−1.4	1.6	−2.6	1.1	−10.3	−.9	....
Financial derivatives assets	4 900 ..	.1	.2	2.6	1.2	2.8	.1	.6	....
Financial derivatives liabilities	4 905 ..	....	−1.6	−1.0	−3.9	−1.8	−10.4	−1.6	....
Other investment assets	4 703 ..	−82.9	−103.9	51.5	−423.1	205.3	75.0	−129.1	231.1
Monetary authorities	4 701 ..	....	....	....	....	....	....	....	....
General government	4 704 ..	.2	....	....	....	....	....	....	....
Banks	4 705 ..	−73.7	48.7	−7.8	−2.4	−55.2	−50.8	−57.5	86.4
Other sectors	4 728 ..	−9.4	−152.6	59.3	−420.7	260.5	125.8	−71.6	144.7
Other investment liabilities	4 753 W.	−104.2	−98.9	−45.1	−35.3	−2.3	−63.4	−60.3	−11.6
Monetary authorities	4 753 WA	....	....	....	....	....	....	....	....
General government	4 753 ZB	−160.1	−13.0	−3.2	−13.7	−12.5	−25.0	−10.2	−13.7
Banks	4 753 ZC	78.2	−51.5	−10.9	29.9	47.5	−14.7	−22.9	−4.4
Other sectors	4 753 ZD	−22.2	−34.4	−31.1	−51.5	−37.4	−23.6	−27.2	6.5
Total, Groups A Through C	4 983 ..	*−59.3*	*−5.1*	*−39.8*	*64.3*	*38.1*	*236.0*	*47.6*	*−16.1*
D. Net Errors and Omissions	4 998 ..	**23.0**	**6.7**	**17.6**	**−9.2**	**5.1**	**−10.7**	**−13.4**	**5.6**
Total, Groups A Through D	4 984 ..	*−36.4*	*1.6*	*−22.2*	*55.1*	*43.2*	*225.3*	*34.2*	*−10.6*
E. Reserves and Related Items	4 802 A.	**36.4**	**−1.6**	**22.2**	**−55.1**	**−43.2**	**−225.3**	**−34.2**	**10.6**
Reserve assets	4 802 ..	36.4	−1.6	22.2	−55.1	−43.2	−225.3	−34.2	10.6
Use of Fund credit and loans	4 766 ..	....	....	....	....	....	....	....	....
Exceptional financing	4 920 ..	....	....	....	....	....	....	....	....
Conversion rates: florins per U.S. dollar	0 101 ..	**1.7900**	**1.7900**	**1.7900**	**1.7900**	**1.7900**	**1.7900**	**1.7900**	**1.7900**

[1] Excludes components that have been classified in the categories of Group E.

Table 2. STANDARD PRESENTATION, 2003–2010

(Millions of U.S. dollars)

	Code	2003	2004	2005	2006	2007	2008	2009	2010
CURRENT ACCOUNT	4 993 ..	**−166.1**	**11.6**	**−197.8**	**−25.3**	**−88.3**	**−164.8**	**131.0**	**−410.2**
A. GOODS	4 100 ..	**−348.9**	**−267.9**	**21.5**	**−119.1**	**−161.9**	**−495.8**	**−477.1**	**−1,077.3**
Credit	2 100 ..	**2,051.8**	**2,736.4**	**3,483.3**	**3,667.1**	**2,690.9**	**3,705.2**	**1,434.3**	**265.8**
General merchandise: exports f.o.b.	2 110 ..	60.6	54.0	58.6	74.0	72.1	88.0	87.0	116.0
Goods for processing: exports f.o.b.	2 150 ..	1,892.5	2,516.5	3,311.7	3,504.1	2,548.6	3,521.5	1,303.9	90.8
Repairs on goods	2 160 ..	....	....	....	....	....	....	....	....
Goods procured in ports by carriers	2 170 ..	98.7	165.9	113.0	89.0	70.2	95.8	43.4	58.9
Nonmonetary gold	2 180 ..	....	....	....	....	....	....	....	....
Debit	3 100 ..	**−2,400.7**	**−3,004.3**	**−3,461.8**	**−3,786.2**	**−2,852.8**	**−4,201.0**	**−1,911.4**	**−1,343.0**
General merchandise: imports f.o.b.	3 110 ..	−1,066.4	−939.2	−1,092.3	−1,185.6	−1,143.9	−1,335.4	−1,016.3	−1,030.9
Goods for processing: imports f.o.b.	3 150 ..	−1,334.3	−2,065.0	−2,369.5	−2,600.4	−1,708.2	−2,863.1	−894.9	−312.0
Repairs on goods	3 160 ..	....	−.1	....	−.2	−.4	−1.8	−.1	....
Goods procured in ports by carriers	3 170 ..	....	....	....	−.1	−.4	−.6	−.1	−.2
Nonmonetary gold	3 180 ..	....	....	....	....	....	....	....	....
B. SERVICES	4 200 ..	**324.0**	**460.2**	**385.4**	**321.2**	**554.1**	**552.8**	**748.7**	**842.6**
Total credit	*2 200 ..*	*1,048.1*	*1,252.7*	*1,307.5*	*1,308.6*	*1,469.1*	*1,594.2*	*1,516.6*	*1,532.5*
Total debit	*3 200 ..*	*−724.1*	*−792.5*	*−922.1*	*−987.4*	*−914.9*	*−1,041.3*	*−767.9*	*−689.9*
Transportation services, credit	2 205 ..	**38.8**	**53.1**	**56.4**	**53.4**	**56.9**	**56.9**	**60.7**	**50.9**
Passenger	*2 850 ..*	*.1*	*....*	*....*	*.1*	*.3*	*.8*	*.6*	*2.8*
Freight	*2 851 ..*	*....*	*....*	*....*	*....*	*....*	*....*	*....*	*....*
Other	*2 852 ..*	*38.7*	*53.1*	*56.4*	*53.3*	*56.6*	*56.1*	*60.1*	*48.1*
Sea transport, passenger	2 207 ..	....	....	....	....	....	....	....	....
Sea transport, freight	2 208 ..	....	....	....	....	....	....	....	....
Sea transport, other	2 209 ..	....	....	....	....	....	....	....	....
Air transport, passenger	2 211 ..	....	....	....	....	....	....	....	....
Air transport, freight	2 212 ..	....	....	....	....	....	....	....	....
Air transport, other	2 213 ..	....	....	....	....	....	....	....	....
Other transport, passenger	2 215 ..	....	....	....	....	....	....	....	....
Other transport, freight	2 216 ..	....	....	....	....	....	....	....	....
Other transport, other	2 217 ..	....	....	....	....	....	....	....	....
Transportation services, debit	3 205 ..	**−266.0**	**−331.1**	**−370.9**	**−402.1**	**−304.1**	**−442.0**	**−211.7**	**−153.0**
Passenger	*3 850 ..*	*−24.8*	*−30.2*	*−24.4*	*−23.0*	*−18.8*	*−21.9*	*−20.6*	*−18.7*
Freight	*3 851 ..*	*−240.1*	*−300.4*	*−346.2*	*−378.9*	*−285.3*	*−420.1*	*−191.1*	*−134.3*
Other	*3 852 ..*	*−1.1*	*−.4*	*−.3*	*−.1*	*−.1*	*−.1*	*....*	*....*
Sea transport, passenger	3 207 ..	....	....	....	....	....	....	....	....
Sea transport, freight	3 208 ..	....	....	....	....	....	....	....	....
Sea transport, other	3 209 ..	....	....	....	....	....	....	....	....
Air transport, passenger	3 211 ..	....	....	....	....	....	....	....	....
Air transport, freight	3 212 ..	....	....	....	....	....	....	....	....
Air transport, other	3 213 ..	....	....	....	....	....	....	....	....
Other transport, passenger	3 215 ..	....	....	....	....	....	....	....	....
Other transport, freight	3 216 ..	....	....	....	....	....	....	....	....
Other transport, other	3 217 ..	....	....	....	....	....	....	....	....
Travel, credit	2 236 ..	**858.1**	**1,056.5**	**1,097.4**	**1,063.6**	**1,211.1**	**1,343.0**	**1,211.0**	**1,238.8**
Business travel	2 237 ..	....	....	....	....	....	....	....	....
Personal travel	2 240 ..	....	....	....	....	....	....	....	....
Travel, debit	3 236 ..	**−187.7**	**−217.9**	**−226.0**	**−217.8**	**−250.7**	**−258.2**	**−245.1**	**−244.8**
Business travel	3 237 ..	....	....	....	....	....	....	....	....
Personal travel	3 240 ..	....	....	....	....	....	....	....	....
Other services, credit	2 200 BA	**151.1**	**143.1**	**153.7**	**191.6**	**201.1**	**194.2**	**244.8**	**242.8**
Communications	2 245 ..	10.4	13.5	10.4	14.5	15.0	16.5	14.2	16.4
Construction	2 249 ..	.1	....	.1	1.5	9.3	3.4	6.2	7.2
Insurance	2 253 ..	.3	.1	....	.2	.8	.8	.6	.2
Financial	2 260 ..	3.2	3.0	3.9	5.2	5.1	7.2	7.6	11.2
Computer and information	2 262 ..	.2	....	.1	.3	.4	.4	1.4	.6
Royalties and licence fees	2 266 ..	.2	....	....	....	....	....	....	....
Other business services	2 268 ..	122.5	110.8	122.4	150.5	151.7	149.1	194.8	191.8
Personal, cultural, and recreational	2 287 ..	....	....	....	....	....	....	....	....
Government, n.i.e.	2 291 ..	14.2	15.7	16.9	19.4	18.8	16.7	19.9	15.3
Other services, debit	3 200 BA	**−270.4**	**−243.4**	**−325.3**	**−367.6**	**−360.1**	**−341.1**	**−311.0**	**−292.1**
Communications	3 245 ..	−21.5	−19.3	−19.5	−22.5	−26.6	−36.0	−42.3	−44.9
Construction	3 249 ..	−25.9	−25.3	−26.2	−50.7	−49.4	−47.3	−16.2	−13.7
Insurance	3 253 ..	−.2	−.2	−.3	−.3	−.9	−1.4	−.2	−.2
Financial	3 260 ..	−7.0	−7.4	−11.1	−13.4	−14.1	−14.3	−11.5	−11.9
Computer and information	3 262 ..	−12.5	−5.8	−17.3	−15.8	−12.8	−16.7	−16.9	−12.3
Royalties and licence fees	3 266 ..	−4.2	−4.5	−6.8	−10.3	−9.8	−11.9	−13.2	−14.1
Other business services	3 268 ..	−164.9	−148.5	−216.4	−220.9	−212.1	−178.4	−168.3	−156.5
Personal, cultural, and recreational	3 287 ..	....	....	....	....	....	....	....	....
Government, n.i.e.	3 291 ..	−34.1	−32.3	−27.8	−33.6	−34.4	−35.1	−42.3	−38.4

Table 2 (Continued). STANDARD PRESENTATION, 2003–2010

(Millions of U.S. dollars)

	Code	2003	2004	2005	2006	2007	2008	2009	2010
C. INCOME	4 300	**−53.4**	**−76.6**	**−478.2**	**−104.5**	**−378.7**	**−107.9**	**−62.5**	**−108.0**
Total credit	2 300	*32.5*	*35.7*	*42.7*	*62.6*	*89.7*	*71.9*	*57.2*	*49.2*
Total debit	3 300	*−85.9*	*−112.3*	*−520.8*	*−167.1*	*−468.4*	*−179.9*	*−119.7*	*−157.2*
Compensation of employees, credit	2 310	**.2**	**.6**	**.8**	**.9**	**4.8**	**4.7**	**4.9**	**2.4**
Compensation of employees, debit	3 310	**−1.1**	**−1.2**	**−3.2**	**−9.2**	**−9.6**	**−5.2**	**−1.6**	**−1.9**
Investment income, credit	2 320	**32.3**	**35.1**	**41.9**	**61.6**	**84.9**	**67.2**	**52.3**	**46.8**
Direct investment income	2 330	1.2	2.9	5.1	15.8	15.0	17.3	11.2	11.3
Dividends and distributed branch profits	2 332	....	....	....	....	....	....	....	....
Reinvested earnings and undistributed branch profits	2 333	....	....	....	....	....	....	....	....
Income on debt (interest)	2 334	....	....	....	....	....	....	....	....
Portfolio investment income	2 339	17.0	20.0	20.7	25.5	37.2	27.8	29.1	26.3
Income on equity	2 340	2.5	4.5	4.7	4.8	12.0	7.5	3.8	3.1
Income on bonds and notes	2 350	....	....	....	....	....	....	....	....
Income on money market instruments	2 360	....	....	....	....	....	....	....	....
Other investment income	2 370	14.1	12.2	16.1	20.3	32.7	22.2	12.0	9.2
Investment income, debit	3 320	**−84.8**	**−111.2**	**−517.6**	**−157.9**	**−458.8**	**−174.7**	**−118.1**	**−155.3**
Direct investment income	3 330	−33.8	−48.9	−451.2	−96.9	−392.2	−107.7	−52.7	−99.1
Dividends and distributed branch profits	3 332	....	....	....	....	....	....	....	....
Reinvested earnings and undistributed branch profits	3 333	....	....	....	....	....	....	....	....
Income on debt (interest)	3 334	....	....	....	....	....	....	....	....
Portfolio investment income	3 339	−21.1	−27.7	−32.5	−31.1	−32.0	−33.2	−38.2	−36.0
Income on equity	3 340	....	−.1	−.1	−.5	....	....	....	....
Income on bonds and notes	3 350	....	....	....	....	....	....	....	....
Income on money market instruments	3 360	....	....	....	....	....	....	....	....
Other investment income	3 370	−29.9	−34.6	−33.9	−29.9	−34.6	−33.8	−27.3	−20.2
D. CURRENT TRANSFERS	4 379	**−87.8**	**−104.1**	**−126.5**	**−123.0**	**−101.8**	**−113.9**	**−78.2**	**−67.5**
Credit	2 379	**40.8**	**44.7**	**50.9**	**53.9**	**57.2**	**67.0**	**69.5**	**68.3**
General government	2 380	13.6	15.2	17.8	14.9	14.2	17.7	15.4	12.8
Other sectors	2 390	27.2	29.5	33.2	38.9	43.0	49.3	54.1	55.5
Workers' remittances	2 391	....	.9	....	.1	.4	2.5	4.9	3.9
Other current transfers	2 392	27.2	28.6	33.2	38.9	42.6	46.8	49.2	51.6
Debit	3 379	**−128.6**	**−148.8**	**−177.5**	**−176.8**	**−159.0**	**−180.8**	**−147.6**	**−135.8**
General government	3 380	−9.5	−4.7	−11.1	−8.0	−9.3	−9.8	−5.2	−3.4
Other sectors	3 390	−119.1	−144.1	−166.4	−168.8	−149.7	−171.0	−142.4	−132.4
Workers' remittances	3 391	−46.6	−47.9	−58.7	−62.7	−63.5	−70.2	−69.5	−62.1
Other current transfers	3 392	−72.5	−96.2	−107.7	−106.1	−86.2	−100.8	−72.9	−70.3
CAPITAL AND FINANCIAL ACCOUNT	4 996	**143.1**	**−18.3**	**180.2**	**34.5**	**83.2**	**175.4**	**−117.6**	**404.6**
CAPITAL ACCOUNT	4 994	**100.3**	**16.9**	**18.6**	**21.1**	**18.9**	**157.0**	**34.1**	**6.9**
Total credit	2 994	*122.8*	*28.9*	*26.8*	*29.5*	*28.2*	*167.2*	*39.8*	*12.2*
Total debit	3 994	*−22.5*	*−12.0*	*−8.2*	*−8.4*	*−9.2*	*−10.2*	*−5.8*	*−5.4*
Capital transfers, credit	2 400	**122.7**	**28.9**	**26.8**	**29.5**	**28.2**	**167.2**	**39.8**	**12.2**
General government	2 401	112.9	17.3	15.9	18.5	19.1	158.7	28.3	2.8
Debt forgiveness	2 402	95.9	....	....	....	....	....	....	....
Other capital transfers	2 410	17.0	17.3	15.9	18.5	19.1	158.7	28.3	2.8
Other sectors	2 430	9.8	11.6	10.9	11.0	9.1	8.6	11.6	9.4
Migrants' transfers	2 431	9.8	11.6	10.8	11.0	8.7	8.2	11.6	9.3
Debt forgiveness	2 432	....	....	.1	....	....	....	....	....
Other capital transfers	2 440	....	....	....	....	.4	.4	....	.1
Capital transfers, debit	3 400	**−22.5**	**−12.0**	**−8.2**	**−8.4**	**−9.2**	**−10.2**	**−5.8**	**−5.4**
General government	3 401	−10.0	....	....	....	....	....	....	....
Debt forgiveness	3 402	....	....	....	....	....	....	....	....
Other capital transfers	3 410	−10.0	....	....	....	....	....	....	....
Other sectors	3 430	−12.5	−12.0	−8.2	−8.4	−9.2	−10.2	−5.8	−5.4
Migrants' transfers	3 431	−12.5	−12.0	−8.2	−8.4	−9.2	−10.2	−5.8	−5.4
Debt forgiveness	3 432	....	....	....	....	....	....	....	....
Other capital transfers	3 440	....	....	....	....	....	....	....	....
Nonproduced nonfinancial assets, credit	2 480	....	....	....	....	....	....	....	....
Nonproduced nonfinancial assets, debit	3 480	....	....	....	....	....	....	....	....

Table 2 (Continued). STANDARD PRESENTATION, 2003–2010

(Millions of U.S. dollars)

	Code	2003	2004	2005	2006	2007	2008	2009	2010
FINANCIAL ACCOUNT	4 995	**42.9**	**−35.2**	**161.6**	**13.4**	**64.3**	**18.4**	**−151.6**	**397.8**
A. DIRECT INVESTMENT	4 500	**157.8**	**144.2**	**109.7**	**577.7**	**−155.9**	**197.5**	**72.0**	**156.8**
Direct investment abroad	4 505	**3.2**	**10.3**	**8.9**	**12.8**	**−29.5**	**−2.8**	**−1.5**	**−4.0**
Equity capital	4 510	−4.2	−.1	−.4	.9	1.5	−3.8	−.4	−4.4
Claims on affiliated enterprises	4 515	....	....	....	....	....	....	....	....
Liabilities to affiliated enterprises	4 520	....	....	....	....	....	....	....	....
Reinvested earnings	4 525	....	....	....	....	....	....	....	....
Other capital	4 530	7.5	10.4	9.3	11.8	−30.9	1.0	−1.1	.4
Claims on affiliated enterprises	4 535	....	....	....	....	....	....	....	....
Liabilities to affiliated enterprises	4 540	....	....	....	....	....	....	....	....
Direct investment in Aruba	4 555	**154.5**	**133.9**	**100.8**	**564.9**	**−126.4**	**200.3**	**73.4**	**160.8**
Equity capital	4 560	95.8	104.5	112.1	266.9	69.4	215.4	173.2	32.2
Claims on direct investors	4 565	....	....	....	....	....	....	....	....
Liabilities to direct investors	4 570	....	....	....	....	....	....	....	....
Reinvested earnings	4 575	....	....	....	....	....	....	....	....
Other capital	4 580	58.8	29.4	−11.2	298.0	−195.9	−15.1	−99.8	128.5
Claims on direct investors	4 585	....	....	....	....	....	....	....	....
Liabilities to direct investors	4 590	....	....	....	....	....	....	....	....
B. PORTFOLIO INVESTMENT	4 600	**35.7**	**26.4**	**21.8**	**−48.1**	**59.3**	**44.8**	**.9**	**10.9**
Assets	4 602	**−30.7**	**−34.3**	**−18.4**	**−84.0**	**−26.1**	**−2.6**	**−11.1**	**−.1**
Equity securities	4 610	−19.4	−26.2	−3.3	−75.4	−39.1	−12.3	14.4	2.2
Monetary authorities	4 611	....	....	....	....	....	....	....	....
General government	4 612	....	....	....	....	....	....	....	....
Banks	4 613	....	....	....	....	....	....	....	....
Other sectors	4 614	−19.4	−26.2	−3.3	−75.4	−39.1	−12.3	14.4	2.2
Debt securities	4 619	−11.3	−8.1	−15.2	−8.6	13.0	9.7	−25.5	−2.2
Bonds and notes	4 620	−1.2	−4.6	−8.4	....	20.3	7.8	−16.5	−5.8
Monetary authorities	4 621	....	....	....	....	....	....	....	....
General government	4 622	....	....	....	....	....	....	....	....
Banks	4 623	−6.5	−6.6	10.9	−3.6	15.7	1.3	−.4	.8
Other sectors	4 624	5.3	2.0	−19.3	3.6	4.6	6.5	−16.1	−6.6
Money market instruments	4 630	−10.1	−3.4	−6.7	−8.6	−7.3	1.9	−9.0	3.5
Monetary authorities	4 631	....	....	....	....	....	....	....	....
General government	4 632	....	....	....	....	....	....	....	....
Banks	4 633	....	....	....	....	....	....	....	....
Other sectors	4 634	−10.1	−3.4	−6.7	−8.6	−7.3	1.9	−9.0	3.5
Liabilities	4 652	**66.4**	**60.6**	**40.2**	**35.8**	**85.4**	**47.4**	**12.1**	**10.9**
Equity securities	4 660	....	....	....	....	....	....	....	....
Banks	4 663	....	....	....	....	....	....	....	....
Other sectors	4 664	....	....	....	....	....	....	....	....
Debt securities	4 669	66.4	60.6	40.2	35.8	85.4	47.4	12.1	10.9
Bonds and notes	4 670	64.9	59.9	42.4	35.8	85.4	47.4	12.1	10.9
Monetary authorities	4 671	....	....	....	....	....	....	....	....
General government	4 672	46.5	66.0	32.6	46.4	29.5	52.6	23.3	44.5
Banks	4 673	....	....	19.0	....	....	−19.0	....	....
Other sectors	4 674	18.4	−6.1	−9.2	−10.6	55.9	13.8	−11.2	−33.5
Money market instruments	4 680	1.5	.7	−2.1	....	....	....	....	....
Monetary authorities	4 681	....	....	....	....	....	....	....	....
General government	4 682	1.5	.7	−2.1	....	....	....	....	....
Banks	4 683	....	....	....	....	....	....	....	....
Other sectors	4 684	....	....	....	....	....	....	....	....
C. FINANCIAL DERIVATIVES	4 910	**.1**	**−1.4**	**1.6**	**−2.6**	**1.1**	**−10.3**	**−.9**	**....**
Monetary authorities	4 911	....	....	....	....	....	....	....	....
General government	4 912	....	....	....	....	....	....	....	....
Banks	4 913	....	....	....	....	....	....	....	....
Other sectors	4 914	....	....	....	....	....	....	....	....
Assets	4 900	**.1**	**.2**	**2.6**	**1.2**	**2.8**	**.1**	**.6**	**....**
Monetary authorities	4 901	....	....	....	....	....	....	....	....
General government	4 902	....	....	....	....	....	....	....	....
Banks	4 903	....	....	....	....	....	....	....	....
Other sectors	4 904	....	....	....	....	....	....	....	....
Liabilities	4 905	**....**	**−1.6**	**−1.0**	**−3.9**	**−1.8**	**−10.4**	**−1.6**	**....**
Monetary authorities	4 906	....	....	....	....	....	....	....	....
General government	4 907	....	....	....	....	....	....	....	....
Banks	4 908	....	....	....	....	....	....	....	....
Other sectors	4 909	....	....	....	....	....	....	....	....

Table 2 (Concluded). STANDARD PRESENTATION, 2003–2010

(Millions of U.S. dollars)

	Code	2003	2004	2005	2006	2007	2008	2009	2010
D. OTHER INVESTMENT............................	4 700 ..	**−187.1**	**−202.8**	**6.3**	**−458.4**	**203.0**	**11.7**	**−189.4**	**219.5**
Assets...	4 703 ..	**−82.9**	**−103.9**	**51.5**	**−423.1**	**205.3**	**75.0**	**−129.1**	**231.1**
Trade credits...................................	4 706 ..	....	....	....	....	....	....	....	....
General government.......................	4 707 ..	....	....	....	....	....	....	....	....
of which: Short-term.................	4 709 ..	....	....	....	....	....	....	....	....
Other sectors................................	4 710 ..	....	....	....	....	....	....	....	....
of which: Short-term.................	4 712 ..	....	....	....	....	....	....	....	....
Loans..	4 714 ..	−12.5	3.7	7.9	19.3	1.0	−6.1	−10.3	−.1
Monetary authorities......................	4 715 ..	....	....	....	....	....	....	....	....
of which: Short-term.................	4 718 ..	....	....	....	....	....	....	....	....
General government.......................	4 719 ..	....	....	....	....	....	....	....	....
of which: Short-term.................	4 721 ..	....	....	....	....	....	....	....	....
Banks...	4 722 ..	−7.9	5.1	11.4	16.8	−4.5	−4.6	−5.9	5.3
of which: Short-term.................	4 724 ..	....	....	....	....	....	....	....	....
Other sectors................................	4 725 ..	−4.6	−1.5	−3.5	2.5	5.5	−1.5	−4.4	−5.4
of which: Short-term.................	4 727 ..	....	....	....	....	....	....	....	....
Currency and deposits.....................	4 730 ..	−80.8	−98.5	46.1	−444.4	194.2	85.1	−156.8	255.6
Monetary authorities......................	4 731 ..	....	....	....	....	....	....	....	....
General government.......................	4 732 ..	.2	....	....	....	....	....	....	....
Banks...	4 733 ..	−79.8	47.7	−18.4	−22.1	−46.4	−47.7	−56.0	80.7
Other sectors................................	4 734 ..	−1.2	−146.3	64.5	−422.3	240.6	132.8	−100.8	174.9
Other assets..................................	4 736 ..	10.5	−9.1	−2.6	2.0	10.1	−4.0	38.0	−24.5
Monetary authorities......................	4 737 ..	....	....	....	....	....	....	....	....
of which: Short-term.................	4 739 ..	....	....	....	....	....	....	....	....
General government.......................	4 740 ..	....	....	....	....	....	....	....	....
of which: Short-term.................	4 742 ..	....	....	....	....	....	....	....	....
Banks...	4 743 ..	14.0	−4.2	−.8	2.8	−4.4	1.5	4.4	.3
of which: Short-term.................	4 745 ..	....	....	....	....	....	....	....	....
Other sectors................................	4 746 ..	−3.5	−4.9	−1.8	−.8	14.5	−5.5	33.6	−24.8
of which: Short-term.................	4 748 ..	....	....	....	....	....	....	....	....
Liabilities....................................	4 753 ..	**−104.2**	**−98.9**	**−45.1**	**−35.3**	**−2.3**	**−63.4**	**−60.3**	**−11.6**
Trade credits...................................	4 756 ..	....	....	....	....	....	....	....	....
General government.......................	4 757 ..	....	....	....	....	....	....	....	....
of which: Short-term.................	4 759 ..	....	....	....	....	....	....	....	....
Other sectors................................	4 760 ..	....	....	....	....	....	....	....	....
of which: Short-term.................	4 762 ..	....	....	....	....	....	....	....	....
Loans..	4 764 ..	88.1	−63.7	−38.4	−39.4	−49.7	−28.8	−13.4	27.9
Monetary authorities......................	4 765 ..	....	....	....	....	....	....	....	....
of which: Use of Fund credit and loans from the Fund..	4 766 ..	....	....	....	....	....	....	....	....
of which: Short-term.................	4 768 ..	....	....	....	....	....	....	....	....
General government.......................	4 769 ..	45.8	−13.0	−3.2	−13.7	−12.5	−25.0	−10.2	−13.7
of which: Short-term.................	4 771 ..	....	....	....	....	....	....	....	....
Banks...	4 772 ..	54.3	−31.2	−14.9	8.8	−6.9	.7	−2.7	11.4
of which: Short-term.................	4 774 ..	....	....	....	....	....	....	....	....
Other sectors................................	4 775 ..	−12.0	−19.4	−20.3	−34.5	−30.3	−4.6	−.5	30.2
of which: Short-term.................	4 777 ..	....	....	....	....	....	....	....	....
Currency and deposits.....................	4 780 ..	49.3	−25.6	2.5	22.7	54.4	−19.8	−13.6	−16.0
Monetary authorities......................	4 781 ..	....	....	....	....	....	....	....	....
General government.......................	4 782 ..	....	....	....	....	....	....	....	....
Banks...	4 783 ..	49.3	−25.6	2.5	22.7	54.4	−19.8	−13.6	−16.0
Other sectors................................	4 784 ..	....	....	....	....	....	....	....	....
Other liabilities...............................	4 786 ..	−241.6	−9.6	−9.2	−18.5	−7.0	−14.7	−33.3	−23.5
Monetary authorities......................	4 787 ..	....	....	....	....	....	....	....	....
of which: Short-term.................	4 789 ..	....	....	....	....	....	....	....	....
General government.......................	4 790 ..	−205.9							
of which: Short-term.................	4 792 ..	....	....	....	....	....	....	....	....
Banks...	4 793 ..	−25.4	5.4	1.6	−1.6	....	4.3	−6.6	.2
of which: Short-term.................	4 795 ..	....	....	....	....	....	....	....	....
Other sectors................................	4 796 ..	−10.2	−15.0	−10.7	−17.0	−7.0	−19.1	−26.7	−23.7
of which: Short-term.................	4 798 ..	....	....	....	....	....	....	....	....
E. RESERVE ASSETS.............................	4 802 ..	**36.4**	**−1.6**	**22.2**	**−55.1**	**−43.2**	**−225.3**	**−34.2**	**10.6**
Monetary gold...............................	4 812 ..	....	....	....	....	....	....	....	....
Special drawing rights......................	4 811 ..	....	....	....	....	....	....	....	....
Reserve position in the Fund.............	4 810 ..	....	....	....	....	....	....	....	....
Foreign exchange............................	4 803 ..	36.4	−1.6	22.2	−55.1	−43.2	−225.3	−34.2	10.6
Other claims..................................	4 813 ..	....	....	....	....	....	....	....	....
NET ERRORS AND OMISSIONS..............	4 998 ..	**23.0**	**6.7**	**17.6**	**−9.2**	**5.1**	**−10.7**	**−13.4**	**5.6**

Table 3. INTERNATIONAL INVESTMENT POSITION (End-period stocks), 2003–2010

(Millions of U.S. dollars)

	Code	2003	2004	2005	2006	2007	2008	2009	2010
ASSETS...	8 995 C.	1,470.6	1,594.5	1,542.4	2,130.2	2,016.6	2,051.9	2,295.9	2,133.8
Direct investment abroad............................	8 505 ..	359.1	348.0	337.9	324.2	310.9	313.5	312.6	316.1
Equity capital and reinvested earnings............................	8 506 ..	....	....	....	....	....	....	....	....
Claims on affiliated enterprises............................	8 507 ..	....	....	....	....	....	....	....	....
Liabilities to affiliated enterprises............................	8 508 ..	....	....	....	....	....	....	....	....
Other capital............................	8 530 ..	....	....	....	....	....	....	....	....
Claims on affiliated enterprises............................	8 535 ..	....	....	....	....	....	....	....	....
Liabilities to affiliated enterprises............................	8 540 ..	....	....	....	....	....	....	....	....
Portfolio investment............................	8 602 ..	344.6	382.5	409.6	508.1	524.7	404.3	485.7	545.7
Equity securities............................	8 610 ..	236.4	261.0	279.1	342.8	374.4	278.2	326.7	344.8
Monetary authorities............................	8 611 ..	....	....	....	....	....	....	....	....
General government............................	8 612 ..	....	....	....	....	....	....	....	....
Banks............................	8 613 ..	....	....	....	....	....	....	....	....
Other sectors............................	8 614 ..	236.4	261.0	279.1	342.8	374.4	278.2	326.7	344.8
Debt securities............................	8 619 ..	108.2	121.5	130.6	165.3	150.3	126.1	158.9	200.9
Bonds and notes............................	8 620 ..	89.3	83.5	104.4	97.0	119.7	94.3	110.6	166.9
Monetary authorities............................	8 621 ..	....	....	....	....	....	....	....	....
General government............................	8 622 ..	....	....	....	....	....	....	....	....
Banks............................	8 623 ..	15.5	12.7	8.7	2.8	.4	.4	.4	.4
Other sectors............................	8 624 ..	73.8	70.9	95.7	94.2	119.3	94.0	110.2	166.6
Money market instruments............................	8 630 ..	18.9	38.0	26.2	68.3	30.6	31.8	48.4	34.0
Monetary authorities............................	8 631 ..	....	....	....	....	....	....	....	....
General government............................	8 632 ..	....	....	....	....	....	....	....	....
Banks............................	8 633 ..	6.4	15.9	9.0	18.4	5.2	3.9	4.4	3.5
Other sectors............................	8 634 ..	12.6	22.1	17.2	49.9	25.4	27.9	44.0	30.5
Financial derivatives............................	8 900 ..	....	....	....	....	....	....	....	....
Monetary authorities............................	8 901 ..	....	....	....	....	....	....	....	....
General government............................	8 902 ..	....	....	....	....	....	....	....	....
Banks............................	8 903 ..	....	....	....	....	....	....	....	....
Other sectors............................	8 904 ..	....	....	....	....	....	....	....	....
Other investment............................	8 703 ..	425.3	519.9	464.4	889.5	715.9	633.1	796.5	547.4
Trade credits............................	8 706 ..	....	....	....	....	....	....	....	....
General government............................	8 707 ..	....	....	....	....	....	....	....	....
of which: Short-term............................	8 709 ..	....	....	....	....	....	....	....	....
Other sectors............................	8 710 ..	....	....	....	....	....	....	....	....
of which: Short-term............................	8 712 ..	....	....	....	....	....	....	....	....
Loans............................	8 714 ..	96.8	90.8	73.3	57.3	62.4	74.7	83.0	79.5
Monetary authorities............................	8 715 ..	....	....	....	....	....	....	....	....
of which: Short-term............................	8 718 ..	....	....	....	....	....	....	....	....
General government............................	8 719 ..	....	....	....	....	....	....	....	....
of which: Short-term............................	8 721 ..	....	....	....	....	....	....	....	....
Banks............................	8 722 ..	75.0	69.9	58.5	41.7	46.1	50.7	56.6	51.4
of which: Short-term............................	8 724 ..	*36.2*	*29.5*	*20.6*	*12.3*	*14.5*	*13.7*	*19.7*	*14.1*
Other sectors............................	8 725 ..	21.8	20.9	14.8	15.7	16.3	24.0	26.4	28.2
of which: Short-term............................	8 727 ..	*1.9*	*1.7*	*3.6*	*3.5*	*1.5*	*1.5*	*1.5*	*1.5*
Currency and deposits............................	8 730 ..	319.5	415.8	377.1	821.1	638.0	544.2	703.9	448.4
Monetary authorities............................	8 731 ..	....	....	....	....	....	....	....	....
General government............................	8 732 ..	....	....	....	....	....	....	....	....
Banks............................	8 733 ..	270.5	222.8	241.2	263.3	309.7	357.2	413.4	332.6
Other sectors............................	8 734 ..	49.0	193.0	135.9	557.7	328.3	187.0	290.5	115.8
Other assets............................	8 736 ..	9.1	13.2	14.0	11.2	15.6	14.2	9.6	19.5
Monetary authorities............................	8 737 ..	....	....	....	....	....	....	....	....
of which: Short-term............................	8 739 ..	....	....	....	....	....	....	....	....
General government............................	8 740 ..	....	....	....	....	....	....	....	....
of which: Short-term............................	8 742 ..	....	....	....	....	....	....	....	....
Banks............................	8 743 ..	9.1	13.2	14.0	11.2	15.4	14.2	9.6	9.2
of which: Short-term............................	8 745 ..	*3.7*	*7.8*	*8.6*	*5.7*	*10.0*	*8.8*	*4.2*	*3.9*
Other sectors............................	8 746 ..	....	....	....	....	.2	....	....	10.2
of which: Short-term............................	8 748 ..	....	....	....	....	....	....	....	*10.2*
Reserve assets............................	8 802 ..	341.6	344.1	330.5	408.4	465.0	701.0	701.1	724.5
Monetary gold............................	8 812 ..	46.4	48.7	57.0	70.6	92.9	96.1	122.9	157.0
Special drawing rights............................	8 811 ..	....	....	....	....	....	....	....	....
Reserve position in the Fund............................	8 810 ..	....	....	....	....	....	....	....	....
Foreign exchange............................	8 803 ..	293.7	294.0	271.5	335.6	369.7	601.0	574.5	564.7
Other claims............................	8 813 ..	1.5	1.4	2.0	2.3	2.4	3.9	3.7	2.8

Table 3 (Concluded). INTERNATIONAL INVESTMENT POSITION (End-period stocks), 2003–2010

(Millions of U.S. dollars)

	Code	2003	2004	2005	2006	2007	2008	2009	2010
LIABILITIES	8 995 D.	**2,304.0**	**2,377.6**	**2,431.1**	**3,188.2**	**3,128.9**	**3,427.5**	**3,448.9**	**3,633.6**
Direct investment in Aruba	8 555	**1,000.4**	**1,114.9**	**1,217.0**	**1,825.2**	**1,709.0**	**1,959.4**	**2,039.3**	**2,207.9**
Equity capital and reinvested earnings	8 556	....	....	....	....	....	....	....	....
Claims on direct investors	8 557	....	....	....	....	....	....	....	....
Liabilities to direct investors	8 558	....	....	....	....	....	....	....	....
Other capital	8 580	....	....	....	....	....	....	....	....
Claims on direct investors	8 585	....	....	....	....	....	....	....	....
Liabilities to direct investors	8 590	....	....	....	....	....	....	....	....
Portfolio investment	8 652	**317.2**	**379.2**	**422.1**	**514.5**	**549.7**	**613.7**	**633.6**	**600.8**
Equity securities	8 660	....	....	....	....	....	....	....	....
Banks	8 663	....	....	....	....	....	....	....	....
Other sectors	8 664	....	....	....	....	....	....	....	....
Debt securities	8 669	317.2	379.2	422.1	514.5	549.7	613.7	633.6	600.8
Bonds and notes	8 670	317.2	379.2	422.1	514.5	549.7	613.7	633.6	600.8
Monetary authorities	8 671	....	....	....	....	....	....	....	....
General government	8 672	219.2	286.0	316.4	362.8	392.3	444.9	468.2	512.7
Banks	8 673	....	....	19.0	19.0	19.0	....	....	....
Other sectors	8 674	98.0	93.2	86.7	132.6	138.4	168.8	165.4	88.1
Money market instruments	8 680	....	....	....	....	....	....	....	....
Monetary authorities	8 681	....	....	....	....	....	....	....	....
General government	8 682	....	....	....	....	....	....	....	....
Banks	8 683	....	....	....	....	....	....	....	....
Other sectors	8 684	....	....	....	....	....	....	....	....
Financial derivatives	8 905	....	....	....	....	....	....	....	....
Monetary authorities	8 906	....	....	....	....	....	....	....	....
General government	8 907	....	....	....	....	....	....	....	....
Banks	8 908	....	....	....	....	....	....	....	....
Other sectors	8 909	....	....	....	....	....	....	....	....
Other investment	8 753	**986.4**	**883.5**	**792.0**	**848.5**	**870.2**	**854.4**	**776.0**	**824.9**
Trade credits	8 756	....	....	....	35.3	29.1	13.4	11.2	12.9
General government	8 757	....	....	....	35.3	29.1	13.4	11.2	12.9
of which: Short-term	8 759	....	....	....	*4.9*	*2.4*	*.6*	*2.8*	*1.5*
Other sectors	8 760	....	....	....	....	....	....	....	....
of which: Short-term	8 762	....	....	....	....	....	....	....	....
Loans	8 764	657.7	579.2	475.1	471.9	431.9	432.2	409.5	428.5
Monetary authorities	8 765	....	....	....	....	....	....	....	....
of which: Use of Fund credit and loans from the Fund	8 766	....	....	....	....	....	....	....	....
of which: Short-term	8 768	....	....	....	....	....	....	....	....
General government	8 769	185.4	181.2	162.3	158.8	156.4	138.9	127.6	106.6
of which: Short-term	8 771	....	....	....	....	....	....	....	....
Banks	8 772	58.7	27.5	12.6	21.4	14.5	15.2	12.4	23.8
of which: Short-term	8 774	*54.2*	*21.3*	*6.4*	*15.2*	*11.1*	*11.8*	*9.0*	*20.4*
Other sectors	8 775	413.6	370.5	300.2	291.7	261.1	278.1	269.5	298.1
of which: Short-term	8 777	....	....	....	....	....	....	....	....
Currency and deposits	8 780	266.3	240.1	242.7	274.0	321.3	303.2	287.1	270.0
Monetary authorities	8 781	1.5	.8	1.7	9.6	2.5	4.2	1.7	.7
General government	8 782	....	....	....	....	....	....	....	....
Banks	8 783	264.8	239.2	241.1	264.4	318.8	299.0	285.3	269.3
Other sectors	8 784	....	....	....	....	....	....	....	....
Other liabilities	8 786	62.4	64.2	74.1	67.3	87.9	105.6	68.3	113.5
Monetary authorities	8 787	34.9	36.4	44.2	59.2	79.7	88.6	56.9	92.0
of which: Short-term	8 789	....	....	....	....	....	....	....	....
General government	8 790	....	....	....	....	....	....	....	....
of which: Short-term	8 792	....	....	....	....	....	....	....	....
Banks	8 793	1.8	7.1	9.2	7.1	7.1	11.4	4.8	5.0
of which: Short-term	8 795	*1.8*	*7.1*	*9.2*	*7.1*	*7.1*	*11.4*	*4.8*	*5.0*
Other sectors	8 796	25.7	20.6	20.7	1.1	1.2	5.6	6.5	16.5
of which: Short-term	8 798	*25.7*	*20.6*	*20.7*	*1.1*	*1.2*	*5.6*	*6.5*	*16.5*
NET INTERNATIONAL INVESTMENT POSITION	8 995	**−833.4**	**−783.1**	**−888.7**	**−1,057.9**	**−1,112.3**	**−1,375.6**	**−1,153.0**	**−1,499.8**
Conversion rates: florins per U.S. dollar (end of period)	0 102	**1.7900**	**1.7900**	**1.7900**	**1.7900**	**1.7900**	**1.7900**	**1.7900**	**1.7900**

Table 1. ANALYTIC PRESENTATION, 2003–2010

(Millions of U.S. dollars)

	Code	2003	2004	2005	2006	2007	2008	2009	2010
A. Current Account[1]	4 993 Z.	**−28,684**	**−38,854**	**−41,032**	**−41,504**	**−58,032**	**−47,786**	**−43,891**	**−31,990**
Goods: exports f.o.b.	2 100 ..	70,522	87,166	107,011	124,913	142,421	189,057	154,788	212,850
Goods: imports f.o.b.	3 100 ..	−85,861	−105,230	−120,383	−134,509	−160,205	−193,972	−159,003	−194,670
Balance on Goods	4 100 ..	*−15,339*	*−18,064*	*−13,372*	*−9,596*	*−17,784*	*−4,915*	*−4,215*	*18,180*
Services: credit	2 200 ..	23,747	28,485	31,047	33,088	40,496	45,240	41,589	48,490
Services: debit	3 200 ..	−21,940	−27,943	−30,505	−32,219	−39,908	−48,338	−42,121	−51,470
Balance on Goods and Services	4 991 ..	*−13,532*	*−17,521*	*−12,830*	*−8,727*	*−17,196*	*−8,013*	*−4,747*	*15,200*
Income: credit	2 300 ..	10,487	14,311	16,445	21,748	32,655	37,320	27,923	38,587
Income: debit	3 300 ..	−25,456	−35,327	−44,166	−54,131	−73,202	−76,719	−65,998	−84,390
Balance on Goods, Services, and Income	4 992 ..	*−28,501*	*−38,537*	*−40,552*	*−41,110*	*−57,743*	*−47,412*	*−42,822*	*−30,603*
Current transfers: credit	2 379 Z.	2,743	3,114	3,333	3,698	4,402	4,431	5,069	6,063
Current transfers: debit	3 379 ..	−2,926	−3,431	−3,813	−4,092	−4,690	−4,805	−6,138	−7,451
B. Capital Account[1]	4 994 Z.	**889**	**1,076**	**1,252**	**1,737**	**1,632**	**1,994**	**−313**	**−213**
Capital account: credit	2 994 Z.	1,664	1,979	2,009	2,467	2,639	3,244	21	64
Capital account: debit	3 994 ..	−775	−904	−757	−731	−1,008	−1,250	−334	−278
Total, Groups A Plus B	4 981 ..	*−27,795*	*−37,778*	*−39,780*	*−39,767*	*−56,400*	*−45,792*	*−44,204*	*−32,204*
C. Financial Account[1]	4 995 W.	**34,694**	**39,373**	**47,617**	**49,901**	**20,248**	**49,114**	**54,180**	**32,940**
Direct investment abroad	4 505 ..	−17,216	−11,055	33,940	−23,933	−19,966	−38,110	−15,721	−24,526
Direct investment in Australia	4 555 Z.	8,024	36,827	−35,601	26,415	41,076	47,281	27,246	30,576
Portfolio investment assets	4 602 ..	−8,168	−24,579	−21,271	−43,866	−77,304	3,035	−70,990	−42,407
Equity securities	4 610 ..	−3,419	−11,071	−8,383	−22,156	−49,543	3,941	−37,958	−19,353
Debt securities	4 619 ..	−4,749	−13,509	−12,888	−21,710	−27,761	−905	−33,032	−23,055
Portfolio investment liabilities	4 652 Z.	49,389	40,018	58,979	97,180	60,227	30,397	145,696	109,561
Equity securities	4 660 ..	12,209	−25,221	8,127	13,933	13,706	19,408	33,402	9,974
Debt securities	4 669 Z.	37,180	65,239	50,852	83,248	46,520	10,989	112,294	99,587
Financial derivatives	4 910 ..	−520	250	−38	2,452	−13,258	123	−6,385	316
Financial derivatives assets	4 900 ..	7,910	19,397	16,498	13,378	673	2,289	39,021	28,039
Financial derivatives liabilities	4 905 ..	−8,430	−19,147	−16,536	−10,925	−13,931	−2,167	−45,407	−27,723
Other investment assets	4 703 ..	−4,603	−5,844	−3,188	−16,736	−11,107	−55,611	−27,787	−13,544
Monetary authorities	4 701 ..	110	....	....	....	....	....	....	....
General government	4 704 ..	−104	−147	−274	−549	−241	−321	....	....
Banks	4 705 ..	−4,823	−6,241	−1,457	−16,566	−8,244	−47,453	....	....
Other sectors	4 728 ..	214	544	−1,457	379	−2,623	−7,837	....	....
Other investment liabilities	4 753 W.	7,788	3,757	14,796	8,389	40,580	62,000	2,122	−27,035
Monetary authorities	4 753 WA	37	7	10	18	230	26,159	....	....
General government	4 753 ZB	....	−27	....	....	....	....	....	....
Banks	4 753 ZC	9,455	670	1,668	5,899	51,363	29,736	....	....
Other sectors	4 753 ZD	−1,704	3,108	13,118	2,472	−11,013	6,106	....	....
Total, Groups A Through C	4 983 ..	*6,899*	*1,595*	*7,837*	*10,134*	*−36,152*	*3,322*	*9,976*	*737*
D. Net Errors and Omissions	4 998 ..	**−22**	**−429**	**−581**	**−412**	**1,004**	**370**	**−1,426**	**−303**
Total, Groups A Through D	4 984 ..	*6,877*	*1,166*	*7,256*	*9,722*	*−35,148*	*3,692*	*8,550*	*434*
E. Reserves and Related Items	4 802 A.	**−6,877**	**−1,166**	**−7,256**	**−9,722**	**35,148**	**−3,692**	**−8,550**	**−434**
Reserve assets	4 802 ..	−6,877	−1,166	−7,256	−9,722	35,148	−3,692	−8,550	−434
Use of Fund credit and loans	4 766 ..	....	....	....	....	....	....	....	....
Exceptional financing	4 920 ..	....	....	....	....	....	....	....	....
Conversion rates: Australian dollars per U.S. dollar	0 101 ..	1.5419	1.3598	1.3095	1.3280	1.1951	1.1922	1.2822	1.0902

[1] Excludes components that have been classified in the categories of Group E.

Table 2. STANDARD PRESENTATION, 2003–2010

(Millions of U.S. dollars)

	Code	2003	2004	2005	2006	2007	2008	2009	2010
CURRENT ACCOUNT...	4 993 ..	**−28,684**	**−38,854**	**−41,032**	**−41,504**	**−58,032**	**−47,786**	**−43,891**	**−31,990**
A. GOODS...	4 100 ..	**−15,339**	**−18,064**	**−13,372**	**−9,596**	**−17,784**	**−4,915**	**−4,215**	**18,180**
Credit...	2 100 ..	**70,522**	**87,166**	**107,011**	**124,913**	**142,421**	**189,057**	**154,788**	**212,850**
General merchandise: exports f.o.b.	2 110 ..	64,896	81,460	100,692	115,415	131,154	174,690	....	....
Goods for processing: exports f.o.b.	2 150 ..	67	105	137	387	300	366	....	....
Repairs on goods...	2 160 ..	50	40	64	54	81	92	....	....
Goods procured in ports by carriers...........	2 170 ..	503	685	925	1,100	1,171	1,513	....	....
Nonmonetary gold...	2 180 ..	5,007	4,875	5,193	7,956	9,715	12,397	....	....
Debit...	3 100 ..	**−85,861**	**−105,230**	**−120,383**	**−134,509**	**−160,205**	**−193,972**	**−159,003**	**−194,670**
General merchandise: imports f.o.b.	3 110 ..	−83,217	−102,370	−116,938	−128,646	−153,350	−183,353	....	....
Goods for processing: imports f.o.b.	3 150 ..	−48	−126	−130	−507	−178	−429	....	....
Repairs on goods...	3 160 ..	−157	−125	−135	−82	−111	−114	....	....
Goods procured in ports by carriers...........	3 170 ..	−533	−689	−936	−1,134	−1,217	−1,780	....	....
Nonmonetary gold...	3 180 ..	−1,907	−1,920	−2,244	−4,140	−5,349	−8,296	....	....
B. SERVICES...	4 200 ..	**1,807**	**543**	**542**	**869**	**588**	**−3,098**	**−532**	**−2,980**
Total credit...	2 200 ..	*23,747*	*28,485*	*31,047*	*33,088*	*40,496*	*45,240*	*41,589*	*48,490*
Total debit...	3 200 ..	*−21,940*	*−27,943*	*−30,505*	*−32,219*	*−39,908*	*−48,338*	*−42,121*	*−51,470*
Transportation services, credit...........	2 205 ..	**4,722**	**5,792**	**6,170**	**6,358**	**7,258**	**7,923**	....	....
Passenger...	2 850 ..	*4,209*	*5,239*	*5,698*	*5,875*	*4,218*	*3,408*	....	....
Freight...	2 851 ..	*513*	*553*	*472*	*483*	*524*	*568*	....	....
Other...	2 852 ..	....	....	....	....	*2,516*	*3,947*	....	....
Sea transport, passenger...........................	2 207 ..	....	....	....	....	....	....	....	....
Sea transport, freight...............................	2 208 ..	....	....	....	....	....	....	....	....
Sea transport, other...................................	2 209 ..	....	....	....	....	....	....	....	....
Air transport, passenger...........................	2 211 ..	....	....	....	....	....	....	....	....
Air transport, freight...............................	2 212 ..	....	....	....	....	....	....	....	....
Air transport, other...................................	2 213 ..	....	....	....	....	....	....	....	....
Other transport, passenger.......................	2 215 ..	....	....	....	....	....	....	....	....
Other transport, freight...........................	2 216 ..	....	....	....	....	....	....	....	....
Other transport, other...............................	2 217 ..	....	....	....	....	....	....	....	....
Transportation services, debit...........	3 205 ..	**−7,231**	**−9,681**	**−10,759**	**−11,334**	**−13,072**	**−14,820**	....	....
Passenger...	3 850 ..	*−2,865*	*−3,982*	*−4,340*	*−4,703*	*−5,758*	*−6,174*	....	....
Freight...	3 851 ..	*−3,845*	*−5,082*	*−5,781*	*−6,023*	*−6,858*	*−8,165*	....	....
Other...	3 852 ..	*−520*	*−617*	*−637*	*−608*	*−456*	*−480*	....	....
Sea transport, passenger...........................	3 207 ..	....	....	....	....	....	....	....	....
Sea transport, freight...............................	3 208 ..	....	....	....	....	....	....	....	....
Sea transport, other...................................	3 209 ..	....	....	....	....	....	....	....	....
Air transport, passenger...........................	3 211 ..	....	....	....	....	....	....	....	....
Air transport, freight...............................	3 212 ..	....	....	....	....	....	....	....	....
Air transport, other...................................	3 213 ..	....	....	....	....	....	....	....	....
Other transport, passenger.......................	3 215 ..	....	....	....	....	....	....	....	....
Other transport, freight...........................	3 216 ..	....	....	....	....	....	....	....	....
Other transport, other...............................	3 217 ..	....	....	....	....	....	....	....	....
Travel, credit...	2 236 ..	**12,438**	**15,214**	**16,868**	**17,854**	**22,415**	**25,062**	....	....
Business travel...	2 237 ..	1,093	1,313	1,446	1,721	2,179	2,347	....	....
Personal travel...	2 240 ..	11,345	13,901	15,423	16,133	20,236	22,715	....	....
Travel, debit...	3 236 ..	**−7,270**	**−10,241**	**−11,253**	**−11,690**	**−14,853**	**−18,729**	....	....
Business travel...	3 237 ..	−1,500	−1,830	−1,864	−1,951	−2,306	−2,786	....	....
Personal travel...	3 240 ..	−5,770	−8,412	−9,389	−9,739	−12,547	−15,942	....	....
Other services, credit...........................	2 200 BA	**6,587**	**7,480**	**8,009**	**8,876**	**10,823**	**12,255**	....	....
Communications...	2 245 ..	627	601	625	646	599	795	....	....
Construction...	2 249 ..	63	78	95	98	67	66	....	....
Insurance...	2 253 ..	441	505	530	530	599	626	....	....
Financial...	2 260 ..	652	740	764	756	856	901	....	....
Computer and information...........................	2 262 ..	769	939	886	1,060	1,290	1,418	....	....
Royalties and licence fees...........................	2 266 ..	430	517	552	621	691	703	....	....
Other business services...............................	2 268 ..	2,615	3,035	3,451	4,013	5,500	6,347	....	....
Personal, cultural, and recreational...........	2 287 ..	469	421	438	502	510	671	....	....
Government, n.i.e.	2 291 ..	521	644	668	650	710	727	....	....
Other services, debit...........................	3 200 BA	**−7,440**	**−8,020**	**−8,493**	**−9,195**	**−11,983**	**−14,790**	....	....
Communications...	3 245 ..	−797	−682	−625	−643	−764	−978	....	....
Construction...	3 249 ..	....	....	....	....	....	....	....	....
Insurance...	3 253 ..	−563	−643	−677	−678	−768	−812	....	....
Financial...	3 260 ..	−365	−399	−408	−452	−512	−540	....	....
Computer and information...........................	3 262 ..	−696	−782	−802	−935	−1,242	−1,313	....	....
Royalties and licence fees...........................	3 266 ..	−1,503	−1,743	−2,005	−2,190	−2,808	−3,026	....	....
Other business services...............................	3 268 ..	−2,427	−2,423	−2,607	−2,827	−4,243	−6,155	....	....
Personal, cultural, and recreational...........	3 287 ..	−625	−781	−774	−851	−934	−1,240	....	....
Government, n.i.e.	3 291 ..	−465	−566	−596	−619	−711	−725	....	....

Table 2 (Continued). STANDARD PRESENTATION, 2003–2010

(Millions of U.S. dollars)

	Code	2003	2004	2005	2006	2007	2008	2009	2010
C. INCOME	4 300	**−14,969**	**−21,015**	**−27,721**	**−32,383**	**−40,547**	**−39,399**	**−38,075**	**−45,803**
Total credit	2 300	*10,487*	*14,311*	*16,445*	*21,748*	*32,655*	*37,320*	*27,923*	*38,587*
Total debit	3 300	*−25,456*	*−35,327*	*−44,166*	*−54,131*	*−73,202*	*−76,719*	*−65,998*	*−84,390*
Compensation of employees, credit	2 310	**695**	**868**	**982**	**1,018**	**1,213**	**1,475**	**1,340**	**1,601**
Compensation of employees, debit	3 310	**−1,192**	**−1,530**	**−1,686**	**−2,190**	**−2,225**	**−2,170**	**−2,524**	**−3,011**
Investment income, credit	2 320	**9,792**	**13,444**	**15,463**	**20,730**	**31,442**	**35,845**	**26,583**	**36,986**
Direct investment income	2 330	6,054	8,273	9,058	11,800	17,235	19,422	10,538	15,502
Dividends and distributed branch profits	2 332	1,499	1,529	1,979	3,490	3,357	3,197	2,603	3,818
Reinvested earnings and undistributed branch profits	2 333	4,466	6,662	7,084	8,394	13,852	16,149	7,417	10,948
Income on debt (interest)	2 334	90	83	−5	−84	26	76	518	736
Portfolio investment income	2 339	2,874	3,884	4,728	6,264	10,747	14,164	14,243	19,702
Income on equity	2 340	1,154	1,558	1,738	2,153	3,327	4,609	7,235	10,602
Income on bonds and notes	2 350	1,720	2,327	2,990	4,111	7,420	9,555	6,983	9,032
Income on money market instruments	2 360	....	....	....	....	....	....	25	67
Other investment income	2 370	864	1,286	1,677	2,666	3,460	2,259	1,802	1,783
Investment income, debit	3 320	**−24,264**	**−33,796**	**−42,480**	**−51,941**	**−70,977**	**−74,549**	**−63,474**	**−81,379**
Direct investment income	3 330	−12,301	−16,956	−21,893	−24,185	−33,006	−34,412	−25,816	−38,739
Dividends and distributed branch profits	3 332	−5,301	−6,102	−7,462	−10,008	−11,350	−10,544	−5,414	−8,436
Reinvested earnings and undistributed branch profits	3 333	−6,119	−9,649	−13,465	−12,747	−18,785	−20,686	−17,235	−26,013
Income on debt (interest)	3 334	−881	−1,204	−966	−1,430	−2,872	−3,181	−3,167	−4,289
Portfolio investment income	3 339	−10,504	−15,211	−18,236	−24,186	−33,716	−36,028	−34,736	−40,051
Income on equity	3 340	−2,695	−3,903	−4,720	−6,158	−7,865	−7,316	−8,818	−10,959
Income on bonds and notes	3 350	−7,042	−10,508	−12,615	−15,854	−22,736	−26,682	−24,982	−28,442
Income on money market instruments	3 360	−767	−800	−901	−2,174	−3,115	−2,030	−936	−650
Other investment income	3 370	−1,459	−1,629	−2,351	−3,570	−4,254	−4,109	−2,922	−2,590
D. CURRENT TRANSFERS	4 379	**−183**	**−317**	**−480**	**−394**	**−288**	**−374**	**−1,069**	**−1,388**
Credit	2 379	**2,743**	**3,114**	**3,333**	**3,698**	**4,402**	**4,431**	**5,069**	**6,063**
General government	2 380	721	817	938	1,316	1,725	1,653	1,350	1,560
Other sectors	2 390	2,022	2,297	2,395	2,382	2,677	2,778	3,718	4,503
Workers' remittances	2 391	....	....	....	....	....	....	....	....
Other current transfers	2 392	2,022	2,297	2,395	2,382	2,677	2,778	3,718	4,503
Debit	3 379	**−2,926**	**−3,431**	**−3,813**	**−4,092**	**−4,690**	**−4,805**	**−6,138**	**−7,451**
General government	3 380	−558	−629	−643	−658	−759	−769	−1,456	−1,741
Other sectors	3 390	−2,368	−2,802	−3,170	−3,434	−3,931	−4,036	−4,682	−5,710
Workers' remittances	3 391	....	....	....	....	....	....	−649	−766
Other current transfers	3 392	−2,368	−2,802	−3,170	−3,434	−3,931	−4,036	−4,032	−4,944
CAPITAL AND FINANCIAL ACCOUNT	4 996	**28,706**	**39,283**	**41,613**	**41,916**	**57,027**	**47,416**	**45,317**	**32,293**
CAPITAL ACCOUNT	4 994	**889**	**1,076**	**1,252**	**1,737**	**1,632**	**1,994**	**−313**	**−213**
Total credit	2 994	*1,664*	*1,979*	*2,009*	*2,467*	*2,639*	*3,244*	*21*	*64*
Total debit	3 994	*−775*	*−904*	*−757*	*−731*	*−1,008*	*−1,250*	*−334*	*−278*
Capital transfers, credit	2 400	**1,631**	**1,969**	**2,008**	**2,112**	**2,613**	**3,238**	....	....
General government	2 401	....	....	....	....	....	....	....	....
Debt forgiveness	2 402	....	....	....	....	....	....	....	....
Other capital transfers	2 410	....	....	....	....	....	....	....	....
Other sectors	2 430	1,631	1,969	2,008	2,112	2,613	3,238	....	....
Migrants' transfers	2 431	1,631	1,969	2,008	2,112	2,613	3,238	....	....
Debt forgiveness	2 432	....	....	....	....	....	....	....	....
Other capital transfers	2 440	....	....	....	....	....	....	....	....
Capital transfers, debit	3 400	**−715**	**−844**	**−799**	**−729**	**−952**	**−1,077**	....	....
General government	3 401	−127	−121	−111	−105	−154	−198	....	....
Debt forgiveness	3 402	....	....	....	....	....	....	....	....
Other capital transfers	3 410	−127	−121	−111	−105	−154	−198	....	....
Other sectors	3 430	−587	−723	−689	−625	−799	−879	....	....
Migrants' transfers	3 431	−587	−723	−689	−625	−799	−879	....	....
Debt forgiveness	3 432	....	....	....	....	....	....	....	....
Other capital transfers	3 440	....	....	....	....	....	....	....	....
Nonproduced nonfinancial assets, credit	2 480	**33**	**10**	**2**	**355**	**26**	**5**	**21**	**64**
Nonproduced nonfinancial assets, debit	3 480	**−61**	**−60**	**42**	**−1**	**−56**	**−173**	....	....

Table 2 (Continued). STANDARD PRESENTATION, 2003–2010

(Millions of U.S. dollars)

	Code	2003	2004	2005	2006	2007	2008	2009	2010
FINANCIAL ACCOUNT	4 995	**27,817**	**38,208**	**40,361**	**40,179**	**55,396**	**45,422**	**45,630**	**32,507**
A. DIRECT INVESTMENT	4 500	**−9,192**	**25,771**	**−1,661**	**2,482**	**21,110**	**9,170**	**11,525**	**6,050**
Direct investment abroad	4 505	**−17,216**	**−11,055**	**33,940**	**−23,933**	**−19,966**	**−38,110**	**−15,721**	**−24,526**
Equity capital	4 510	−13,298	−2,832	43,388	−10,340	−4,564	−15,652	−701	−11,020
Claims on affiliated enterprises	4 515	....	....	....	....	....	....	....	....
Liabilities to affiliated enterprises	4 520	....	....	....	....	....	....	....	....
Reinvested earnings	4 525	−4,466	−6,662	−7,084	−8,394	−13,852	−16,149	−7,417	−10,948
Other capital	4 530	548	−1,562	−2,364	−5,199	−1,550	−6,310	−7,603	−2,558
Claims on affiliated enterprises	4 535	−802	−1,641	−497	−7,562	−2,438	−4,091	....	....
Liabilities to affiliated enterprises	4 540	1,350	79	−1,866	2,363	887	−2,219	....	....
Direct investment in Australia	4 555	**8,024**	**36,827**	**−35,601**	**26,415**	**41,076**	**47,281**	**27,246**	**30,576**
Equity capital	4 560	2,401	26,043	−50,570	5,037	10,095	8,419	12,435	4,308
Claims on direct investors	4 565	....	....	....	....	....	....	....	....
Liabilities to direct investors	4 570	....	....	....	....	....	....	....	....
Reinvested earnings	4 575	6,119	9,649	13,465	12,747	18,785	20,686	17,235	26,013
Other capital	4 580	−496	1,134	1,504	8,631	12,196	18,176	−2,424	255
Claims on direct investors	4 585	−1,949	−676	−776	−1,651	−2,746	187	....	....
Liabilities to direct investors	4 590	1,452	1,810	2,280	10,282	14,942	17,988	....	....
B. PORTFOLIO INVESTMENT	4 600	**41,222**	**15,439**	**37,707**	**53,314**	**−17,077**	**33,432**	**74,705**	**67,154**
Assets	4 602	**−8,168**	**−24,579**	**−21,271**	**−43,866**	**−77,304**	**3,035**	**−70,990**	**−42,407**
Equity securities	4 610	−3,419	−11,071	−8,383	−22,156	−49,543	3,941	−37,958	−19,353
Monetary authorities	4 611	....	....	....	....	....	....	....	....
General government	4 612	....	....	....	....	....	....	....	....
Banks	4 613	19	....	....	....	....	....	....	....
Other sectors	4 614	−3,437	....	....	....	....	....	....	....
Debt securities	4 619	−4,749	−13,509	−12,888	−21,710	−27,761	−905	−33,032	−23,055
Bonds and notes	4 620	−5,073	−11,884	−14,087	−19,676	−29,710	−170	−33,226	−22,284
Monetary authorities	4 621	....	....	....	....	....	....	....	....
General government	4 622	....	....	....	....	....	−1,705	−9,962	−3,748
Banks	4 623	−1,807	−2,770	2,359	−3,743	−4,963	1,612	−3,087	−3,320
Other sectors	4 624	−3,265	−9,113	−16,446	−15,933	−24,747	−77	−20,176	−15,216
Money market instruments	4 630	323	−1,625	1,199	−2,034	1,949	−735	194	−771
Monetary authorities	4 631	....	....	....	....	....	....	....	....
General government	4 632	....	....	....	....	....	−68	−7	−130
Banks	4 633	411	−1,541	1,421	−1,223	−74	−763	−135	−750
Other sectors	4 634	−88	−84	−222	−811	2,023	96	336	109
Liabilities	4 652	**49,389**	**40,018**	**58,979**	**97,180**	**60,227**	**30,397**	**145,696**	**109,561**
Equity securities	4 660	12,209	−25,221	8,127	13,933	13,706	19,408	33,402	9,974
Banks	4 663	1,207	505	622	−2,117	−66	4,901	9,859	−5,684
Other sectors	4 664	11,002	−25,727	7,505	16,050	13,772	14,507	23,543	15,659
Debt securities	4 669	37,180	65,239	50,852	83,248	46,520	10,989	112,294	99,587
Bonds and notes	4 670	36,913	61,678	38,449	57,043	61,678	25,005	101,959	77,511
Monetary authorities	4 671	....	....	....	....	....	....	....	....
General government	4 672	2,623	4,374	3,363	−215	7,744	485	26,080	43,948
Banks	4 673	18,549	35,976	21,695	34,080	24,775	20,127	65,565	27,473
Other sectors	4 674	15,742	21,328	13,390	23,179	29,159	4,392	10,314	6,090
Money market instruments	4 680	267	3,561	12,403	26,204	−15,158	−14,016	10,335	22,076
Monetary authorities	4 681	....	....	....	....	....	....	....	....
General government	4 682	−592	....	....	....	....	....	1,786	6,673
Banks	4 683	3,148	4,332	10,294	21,890	−17,785	−10,954	12,367	11,824
Other sectors	4 684	−2,290	−770	2,109	4,315	2,627	−3,062	−3,818	3,580
C. FINANCIAL DERIVATIVES	4 910	**−520**	**250**	**−38**	**2,452**	**−13,258**	**123**	**−6,385**	**316**
Monetary authorities	4 911	....	....	....	....	....	....	....	....
General government	4 912	....	....	....	....	....	....	2,028	5,209
Banks	4 913	−1,692	−974	−52	−1,187	−11,591	5,547	−11,762	−723
Other sectors	4 914	1,173	1,224	14	3,639	−1,667	−5,424	3,349	−4,170
Assets	4 900	**7,910**	**19,397**	**16,498**	**13,378**	**673**	**2,289**	**39,021**	**28,039**
Monetary authorities	4 901	....	....	....	....	....	....	....	....
General government	4 902	....	....	....	....	....	....	3,068	6,035
Banks	4 903	6,004	17,819	15,925	8,938	1,394	3,911	34,580	24,029
Other sectors	4 904	1,905	1,579	572	4,440	−721	−1,621	1,373	−2,025
Liabilities	4 905	**−8,430**	**−19,147**	**−16,536**	**−10,925**	**−13,931**	**−2,167**	**−45,407**	**−27,723**
Monetary authorities	4 906	....	....	....	....	....	....	....	....
General government	4 907	....	....	....	....	....	....	−1,040	−827
Banks	4 908	−7,697	−18,793	−15,978	−10,125	−12,985	1,637	−46,343	−24,752
Other sectors	4 909	−733	−355	−558	−800	−945	−3,803	1,976	−2,145

Table 2 (Concluded). STANDARD PRESENTATION, 2003–2010

(Millions of U.S. dollars)

	Code	2003	2004	2005	2006	2007	2008	2009	2010
D. OTHER INVESTMENT	4 700 ..	**3,185**	**−2,087**	**11,608**	**−8,347**	**29,473**	**6,389**	**−25,665**	**−40,579**
Assets	4 703 ..	**−4,603**	**−5,844**	**−3,188**	**−16,736**	**−11,107**	**−55,611**	**−27,787**	**−13,544**
Trade credits	4 706 ..	481	−645	−1,501	−929	−660	−3,355	....	....
General government	4 707 ..	−104	−147	−274	−549	−241	−321	....	....
of which: Short-term	4 709 ..	....	....	....	....	....	....		
Other sectors	4 710 ..	584	−498	−1,227	−380	−420	−3,035	....	....
of which: Short-term	4 712 ..	463	−479	....	....	....	....		
Loans	4 714 ..	−3,209	−4,591	−4,604	−16,721	6,068	−29,211		
Monetary authorities	4 715 ..	110	....	....	....	....	....		
of which: Short-term	4 718 ..	....	....	....	....	....	....		
General government	4 719 ..	....	....	....	....	....	....		
of which: Short-term	4 721 ..	....	....	....	....	....	....		
Banks	4 722 ..	−3,207	−5,188	−4,697	−17,634	6,556	−27,567		
of which: Short-term	4 724 ..	−1,547	244	−3,118	−11,365	−3,397	−16,623		
Other sectors	4 725 ..	−113	597	94	913	−489	−1,645		
of which: Short-term	4 727 ..	−165	....	....	....	....	....		
Currency and deposits	4 730 ..	−1,368	−907	2,974	1,296	−13,349	−20,796		
Monetary authorities	4 731 ..	....	....	....	....	....	....		
General government	4 732 ..	....	....	....	....	....	....		
Banks	4 733 ..	−928	−1,214	3,315	1,427	−12,015	−18,915		
Other sectors	4 734 ..	−440	307	−341	−131	−1,334	−1,881		
Other assets	4 736 ..	−506	299	−57	−383	−3,166	−2,248		
Monetary authorities	4 737 ..	....	....	....	....	....	....		
of which: Short-term	4 739 ..	....	....	....	....	....	....		
General government	4 740 ..	....	....	....	....	....	....		
of which: Short-term	4 742 ..	....	....	....	....	....	....		
Banks	4 743 ..	−688	161	−74	−359	−2,785	−972		
of which: Short-term	4 745 ..	−654	....	....	....	....	....		
Other sectors	4 746 ..	182	138	17	−23	−380	−1,277		
of which: Short-term	4 748 ..	172	306	43	−9	−302	−1,039	....	....
Liabilities	4 753 ..	**7,788**	**3,757**	**14,796**	**8,389**	**40,580**	**62,000**	**2,122**	**−27,035**
Trade credits	4 756 ..	−707	−11	−10	348	−193	1,965		
General government	4 757 ..	....	....	....	....	....	....		
of which: Short-term	4 759 ..	....	....	....	....	....	....		
Other sectors	4 760 ..	−707	−11	−10	348	−193	1,965		
of which: Short-term	4 762 ..	−692	23	−33	....	....	....		
Loans	4 764 ..	−1,806	7,027	9,046	7,803	20,422	30,439		
Monetary authorities	4 765 ..	....	....	....	....	....	....		
of which: Use of Fund credit and loans from the Fund	4 766 ..	....	....	....	....	....	....		
of which: Short-term	4 768 ..	....	....	....	....	....	....		
General government	4 769 ..	....	−27	....	....	....	....		
of which: Short-term	4 771 ..	....	....	....	....	....	....		
Banks	4 772 ..	−1,092	3,610	−4,556	4,997	31,184	27,558		
of which: Short-term	4 774 ..	−2,733	4,415	−1,925	2,564	28,831	19,751		
Other sectors	4 775 ..	−714	3,444	13,602	2,806	−10,761	2,880		
of which: Short-term	4 777 ..	−533	4,307	2,580	547	−12,038	2,496	....	
Currency and deposits	4 780 ..	10,314	−3,747	5,697	1,759	16,394	27,911		
Monetary authorities	4 781 ..	37	7	10	18	230	26,159		
General government	4 782 ..	....	....	....	....	....	....		
Banks	4 783 ..	10,277	−3,754	5,687	1,741	16,164	1,752		
Other sectors	4 784 ..	....	....	....	....	....	....		
Other liabilities	4 786 ..	−13	488	63	−1,521	3,956	1,685	4,080	....
Monetary authorities	4 787 ..	....	....	....	....	....	....	4,080	
of which: Short-term	4 789 ..	....	....	....	....	....	....		
General government	4 790 ..	....	....	....	....	....	....		
of which: Short-term	4 792 ..	....	....	....	....	....	....		
Banks	4 793 ..	270	814	537	−839	4,015	425		
of which: Short-term	4 795 ..	270	814	537	−900	4,016	440		
Other sectors	4 796 ..	−283	−325	−474	−682	−59	1,260		
of which: Short-term	4 798 ..	−279	....	....	....	....	....		
E. RESERVE ASSETS	4 802 ..	**−6,877**	**−1,166**	**−7,256**	**−9,722**	**35,148**	**−3,692**	**−8,550**	**−434**
Monetary gold	4 812 ..	....	....	....	....	....	−2	....	....
Special drawing rights	4 811 ..	−20	−17	−14	4	17	14	−4,672	6
Reserve position in the Fund	4 810 ..	63	418	813	377	106	−310	−423	−29
Foreign exchange	4 803 ..	−6,920	−1,567	−8,055	−10,102	35,026	−3,395	−3,455	−411
Other claims	4 813 ..	....	....	....	....	....	....	....	....
NET ERRORS AND OMISSIONS	4 998 ..	**−22**	**−429**	**−581**	**−412**	**1,004**	**370**	**−1,426**	**−303**

Table 3. INTERNATIONAL INVESTMENT POSITION (End-period stocks), 2003–2010

(Millions of U.S. dollars)

	Code	2003	2004	2005	2006	2007	2008	2009	2010
ASSETS...................................	8 995 C.	**415,442**	**513,502**	**501,939**	**660,497**	**883,738**	**702,956**	**1,045,622**	**1,238,025**
Direct investment abroad.........................	8 505 ..	**161,948**	**204,347**	**178,481**	**227,531**	**289,516**	**196,488**	**338,747**	**400,706**
Equity capital and reinvested earnings..................	8 506 ..	162,278	202,968	174,516	217,687	284,630	188,299	284,521	340,011
Claims on affiliated enterprises...................	8 507 ..	....	....	....	....	....	....	....	....
Liabilities to affiliated enterprises...............	8 508 ..	....	....	....	....	....	....	....	....
Other capital..............	8 530 ..	−330	1,379	3,965	9,844	4,886	8,190	54,226	60,694
Claims on affiliated enterprises...................	8 535 ..	9,491	11,577	11,864	20,674	28,682	28,699	....	....
Liabilities to affiliated enterprises...............	8 540 ..	−9,821	−10,199	−7,899	−10,830	−23,796	−20,510	....	....
Portfolio investment.........................	8 602 ..	**129,982**	**167,066**	**187,209**	**249,684**	**395,221**	**259,444**	**386,183**	**468,042**
Equity securities...............	8 610 ..	92,613	114,438	126,870	164,800	262,517	159,291	238,793	285,050
Monetary authorities..............	8 611 ..	....	....	....	....	....	....	260	292
General government..............	8 612 ..	....	....	....	....	....	....	21,683	34,329
Banks..............	8 613 ..	190	....	....	....	....	....	....	....
Other sectors..............	8 614 ..	92,423	....	....	....	....	....	....	....
Debt securities..............	8 619 ..	37,369	52,628	60,339	84,884	132,705	100,153	147,389	182,992
Bonds and notes..............	8 620 ..	35,527	48,916	57,967	80,731	128,948	96,787	145,357	178,722
Monetary authorities..............	8 621 ..	....	....	....	−1	....	....	....	....
General government..............	8 622 ..	....	....	....	....	....	1,550	12,557	16,565
Banks..............	8 623 ..	5,539	8,602	5,408	9,203	14,620	9,385	14,596	19,306
Other sectors..............	8 624 ..	29,988	40,314	52,559	71,529	114,328	85,852	118,203	142,852
Money market instruments..............	8 630 ..	1,842	3,712	2,373	4,154	3,756	3,366	2,032	4,269
Monetary authorities..............	8 631 ..	....	....	....	−1	....	....	....	....
General government..............	8 632 ..	....	....	....	....	....	62	84	211
Banks..............	8 633 ..	1,481	3,154	1,635	2,800	2,753	2,734	1,405	2,887
Other sectors..............	8 634 ..	361	558	738	1,355	1,003	570	543	1,171
Financial derivatives.........................	8 900 ..	**33,139**	**38,960**	**27,696**	**41,156**	**64,970**	**78,428**	**80,893**	**102,593**
Monetary authorities..............	8 901 ..	....	....	....	....	....	....	....	....
General government..............	8 902 ..	....	....	....	....	....	....	1,539	4,782
Banks..............	8 903 ..	31,901	36,119	24,802	40,124	63,484	71,083	70,163	85,563
Other sectors..............	8 904 ..	1,238	2,841	2,894	1,033	1,485	7,346	9,191	12,248
Other investment.........................	8 703 ..	**57,116**	**66,202**	**65,296**	**87,045**	**107,123**	**135,672**	**198,057**	**224,414**
Trade credits..............	8 706 ..	6,049	7,101	8,093	9,121	10,289	11,309	....	....
General government..............	8 707 ..	2,111	2,225	2,401	3,063	3,198	3,560	....	....
of which: Short-term..............	8 709 ..	....	....	....	....	....	....	....	....
Other sectors..............	8 710 ..	3,938	4,876	5,693	6,057	7,091	7,748	....	....
of which: Short-term..............	8 712 ..	*3,917*	*4,834*	....	....	....	....	....	....
Loans..............	8 714 ..	33,983	40,471	42,563	63,054	63,656	76,677	....	....
Monetary authorities..............	8 715 ..	....	....	....	....	....	....	....	....
of which: Short-term..............	8 718 ..	....	....	....	....	....	....	....	....
General government..............	8 719 ..	....	....	....	....	....	....	....	....
of which: Short-term..............	8 721 ..	....	....	....	....	....	....	....	....
Banks..............	8 722 ..	30,286	37,323	39,628	60,946	60,420	72,528	....	....
of which: Short-term..............	8 724 ..	*12,482*	*12,998*	*15,328*	*28,026*	*34,073*	*42,760*	....	....
Other sectors..............	8 725 ..	3,697	3,147	2,936	2,108	3,235	4,149	....	....
of which: Short-term..............	8 727 ..	*701*	....	....	....	....	....	....	....
Currency and deposits..............	8 730 ..	11,024	12,720	9,251	8,693	23,501	38,499	....	....
Monetary authorities..............	8 731 ..	....	....	....	....	....	....	....	....
General government..............	8 732 ..	....	....	....	....	....	....	....	....
Banks..............	8 733 ..	8,751	10,682	6,929	5,985	19,110	33,750	....	....
Other sectors..............	8 734 ..	2,273	2,037	2,322	2,709	4,391	4,748	....	....
Other assets..............	8 736 ..	6,061	5,911	5,388	6,178	9,677	9,188	....	....
Monetary authorities..............	8 737 ..	....	....	....	....	....	....	....	....
of which: Short-term..............	8 739 ..	....	....	....	....	....	....	....	....
General government..............	8 740 ..	3,572	3,710	3,494	3,768	4,198	3,299	....	....
of which: Short-term..............	8 742 ..	....	....	....	....	....	....	....	....
Banks..............	8 743 ..	1,037	942	960	1,454	4,515	3,998	....	....
of which: Short-term..............	8 745 ..	*999*	....	....	....	....	....	....	....
Other sectors..............	8 746 ..	1,453	1,260	934	956	964	1,891	....	....
of which: Short-term..............	8 748 ..	*1,448*	*1,084*	*787*	*781*	*690*	*1,790*	....	....
Reserve assets.........................	8 802 ..	**33,258**	**36,927**	**43,257**	**55,080**	**26,908**	**32,923**	**41,743**	**42,269**
Monetary gold..............	8 812 ..	1,070	1,123	1,316	1,631	2,140	2,233	2,792	3,609
Special drawing rights..............	8 811 ..	170	195	193	200	193	174	4,856	4,764
Reserve position in the Fund..............	8 810 ..	2,053	1,706	776	428	339	649	1,092	1,102
Foreign exchange..............	8 803 ..	29,966	33,903	40,972	52,822	24,237	29,867	33,002	32,794
Other claims..............	8 813 ..	....	....	....	....	....	....	....	....

Table 3 (Concluded). INTERNATIONAL INVESTMENT POSITION (End-period stocks), 2003–2010

(Millions of U.S. dollars)

	Code	2003	2004	2005	2006	2007	2008	2009	2010
LIABILITIES..	8 995 D.	**741,249**	**889,588**	**891,451**	**1,138,776**	**1,458,342**	**1,202,092**	**1,740,594**	**2,032,909**
Direct investment in Australia.............................	8 555 ..	**199,340**	**261,552**	**207,952**	**249,963**	**341,656**	**270,830**	**425,819**	**514,424**
Equity capital and reinvested earnings............	8 556 ..	165,779	225,358	171,650	203,071	269,971	192,925	297,554	372,858
Claims on direct investors............................	8 557 ..	....	....	....	....	....	....	....	....
Liabilities to direct investors.......................	8 558 ..	....	....	....	....	....	....	....	....
Other capital...	8 580 ..	33,562	36,193	36,302	46,892	71,685	77,905	128,265	141,566
Claims on direct investors............................	8 585 ..	−11,706	−12,662	−12,648	−15,618	−17,715	−14,903	....	....
Liabilities to direct investors.......................	8 590 ..	45,268	48,855	48,950	62,510	89,400	92,807	....	....
Portfolio investment.............................	8 652 ..	**401,381**	**482,548**	**537,752**	**714,026**	**871,567**	**646,501**	**988,830**	**1,165,066**
Equity securities...	8 660 ..	138,854	146,415	176,266	244,206	320,673	169,547	331,283	386,495
Banks..	8 663 ..	29,607	35,001	40,324	48,132	50,533	28,315	69,325	66,755
Other sectors...	8 664 ..	109,247	111,413	135,942	196,074	270,140	141,232	261,958	319,740
Debt securities..	8 669 ..	262,526	336,134	361,486	469,820	550,893	476,954	657,546	778,571
Bonds and notes..	8 670 ..	208,749	276,443	293,280	367,160	454,985	416,002	570,556	663,898
Monetary authorities.................................	8 671 ..	....	....	....	....	....	....	....	....
General government..................................	8 672 ..	18,998	23,874	25,315	25,879	35,206	31,419	64,555	120,013
Banks..	8 673 ..	91,174	129,049	140,666	187,161	225,085	223,388	307,059	332,796
Other sectors..	8 674 ..	98,577	123,520	127,299	154,120	194,694	161,195	198,941	211,090
Money market instruments..........................	8 680 ..	53,777	59,691	68,206	102,660	95,908	60,952	86,990	114,673
Monetary authorities.................................	8 681 ..	....	....	....	....	....	....	....	....
General government..................................	8 682 ..	....	....	....	....	....	....	1,993	9,670
Banks..	8 683 ..	49,076	55,748	62,425	92,549	83,036	52,446	76,908	92,700
Other sectors..	8 684 ..	4,702	3,943	5,781	10,111	12,872	8,506	8,089	12,303
Financial derivatives.............................	8 905 ..	**36,584**	**37,712**	**27,899**	**43,960**	**62,147**	**75,194**	**70,786**	**105,908**
Monetary authorities......................................	8 906 ..	....	....	....	....	....	....	....	....
General government..	8 907 ..	....	....	....	....	....	....	1,080	3,491
Banks..	8 908 ..	35,031	36,094	26,137	41,339	57,868	69,261	59,931	88,343
Other sectors..	8 909 ..	1,553	1,618	1,762	2,621	4,278	5,933	9,775	14,074
Other investment.................................	8 753 ..	**103,944**	**107,776**	**117,848**	**130,826**	**182,973**	**209,566**	**255,160**	**247,512**
Trade credits..	8 756 ..	1,852	2,229	2,035	2,560	2,347	3,447	....	....
General government......................................	8 757 ..	....	....	....	....	....	....	....	....
of which: Short-term..................................	8 759 ..	....	....	....	....	....	....	....	....
Other sectors..	8 760 ..	1,852	2,229	2,035	2,560	2,347	3,447	....	....
of which: Short-term..................................	8 762 ..	*1,823*	*2,198*	*1,975*	....	....	....	....	....
Loans...	8 764 ..	46,073	53,030	59,604	68,971	97,309	107,107	....	....
Monetary authorities....................................	8 765 ..	....	....	....	....	....	....	....	....
of which: Use of Fund credit and loans from the Fund....	8 766 ..	....	....	....	....	....	....	....	....
of which: Short-term..................................	8 768 ..	....	....	....	....	....	....	....	....
General government......................................	8 769 ..	29	....	....	....	....	....	....	....
of which: Short-term..................................	8 771 ..	*29*	....	....	....	....	....	....	....
Banks..	8 772 ..	33,713	37,142	31,132	36,173	71,906	84,019	....	....
of which: Short-term..................................	8 774 ..	*25,626*	*29,786*	*26,547*	*28,722*	*58,697*	*64,353*	....	....
Other sectors..	8 775 ..	12,332	15,888	28,473	32,798	25,403	23,088	....	....
of which: Short-term..................................	8 777 ..	*5,143*	*9,578*	*11,878*	*13,989*	*2,722*	*4,496*	....	....
Currency and deposits..................................	8 780 ..	53,423	49,279	52,902	57,174	76,394	92,045	....	....
Monetary authorities....................................	8 781 ..	81	91	93	119	373	24,466	....	....
General government......................................	8 782 ..	....	....	....	....	....	....	....	....
Banks..	8 783 ..	53,342	49,188	52,809	57,054	76,021	67,580	....	....
Other sectors..	8 784 ..	....	....	....	....	....	....	....	....
Other liabilities...	8 786 ..	2,596	3,238	3,308	2,121	6,922	6,967	....	....
Monetary authorities....................................	8 787 ..	....	....	....	....	....	....	....	....
of which: Short-term..................................	8 789 ..	....	....	....	....	....	....	....	....
General government......................................	8 790 ..	60	62	59	63	71	55	....	....
of which: Short-term..................................	8 792 ..	....	....	....	....	....	....	....	....
Banks..	8 793 ..	462	1,330	1,921	1,579	5,862	5,169	....	....
of which: Short-term..................................	8 795 ..	*462*	*1,330*	*1,921*	*1,514*	*5,797*	*5,161*	....	....
Other sectors..	8 796 ..	2,074	1,846	1,328	480	990	1,743	....	....
of which: Short-term..................................	8 798 ..	*2,061*	....	....	....	....	....	....	....
NET INTERNATIONAL INVESTMENT POSITION........	8 995 ..	**−325,807**	**−376,087**	**−389,513**	**−478,279**	**−574,604**	**−499,136**	**−694,972**	**−794,884**
Conversion rates: Australian dollars per U.S. dollar (end of period).............................	0 102 ..	**1.3333**	**1.2837**	**1.3630**	**1.2637**	**1.1343**	**1.4434**	**1.1150**	**.9840**

Table 1. ANALYTIC PRESENTATION, 2003–2010

(Millions of U.S. dollars)

	Code	2003	2004	2005	2006	2007	2008	2009	2010
A. Current Account[1]	4 993 Z.	**4,186**	**6,074**	**6,245**	**7,807**	**13,189**	**20,127**	**10,291**	**11,461**
Goods: exports f.o.b.	2 100 ..	88,105	109,875	119,228	133,844	162,899	179,201	135,100	147,710
Goods: imports f.o.b.	3 100 ..	−89,799	−110,905	−120,977	−133,419	−161,089	−179,794	−138,511	−151,993
Balance on Goods	4 100 ..	*−1,694*	*−1,029*	*−1,750*	*426*	*1,810*	*−592*	*−3,412*	*−4,283*
Services: credit	2 200 ..	32,455	37,945	42,589	46,112	54,308	63,728	54,531	54,706
Services: debit	3 200 ..	−23,738	−27,986	−30,730	−33,514	−39,131	−42,894	−37,070	−37,041
Balance on Goods and Services	4 991 ..	*7,023*	*8,930*	*10,109*	*13,024*	*16,987*	*20,241*	*14,050*	*13,383*
Income: credit	2 300 ..	16,514	20,193	25,914	28,027	42,909	44,478	34,625	36,522
Income: debit	3 300 ..	−17,611	−21,403	−27,957	−31,701	−45,107	−42,093	−36,214	−35,785
Balance on Goods, Services, and Income	4 992 ..	*5,926*	*7,720*	*8,066*	*9,350*	*14,789*	*22,627*	*12,460*	*14,120*
Current transfers: credit	2 379 Z.	2,954	3,449	3,949	4,290	5,001	5,411	4,877	4,498
Current transfers: debit	3 379 ..	−4,693	−5,096	−5,770	−5,833	−6,601	−7,911	−7,046	−7,156
B. Capital Account[1]	4 994 Z.	**8**	**−342**	**−237**	**−1,009**	**274**	**−70**	**161**	**517**
Capital account: credit	2 994 Z.	897	764	739	586	1,027	726	1,103	1,407
Capital account: debit	3 994 ..	−888	−1,105	−976	−1,595	−752	−796	−942	−889
Total, Groups A Plus B	4 981 ..	*4,194*	*5,732*	*6,008*	*6,799*	*13,464*	*20,057*	*10,452*	*11,978*
C. Financial Account[1]	4 995 W.	**−2,515**	**−2,823**	**−917**	**−6,862**	**−13,508**	**−22,792**	**−14,465**	**−2,467**
Direct investment abroad	4 505 ..	−7,143	−8,425	−81,842	−5,527	−71,582	−29,536	−11,908	20,378
Direct investment in Austria	4 555 Z.	7,098	3,892	81,648	2,477	63,972	6,602	11,523	−25,636
Portfolio investment assets	4 602 ..	−18,654	−33,024	−44,004	−32,900	−16,078	11,996	−4,788	−8,800
Equity securities	4 610 ..	−2,762	−4,067	−5,690	−8,420	−582	8,126	−6,167	−9,714
Debt securities	4 619 ..	−15,893	−28,957	−38,314	−24,480	−15,496	3,870	1,379	913
Portfolio investment liabilities	4 652 Z.	23,440	31,695	30,525	47,725	46,373	25,298	−5,858	−1,099
Equity securities	4 660 ..	2,431	6,926	5,999	10,550	3,625	−6,808	284	−385
Debt securities	4 669 Z.	21,009	24,769	24,526	37,176	42,748	32,106	−6,142	−714
Financial derivatives	4 910 ..	−742	−669	153	−1,029	−913	635	790	343
Financial derivatives assets	4 900 ..	....	....	....	....	....	....	....	....
Financial derivatives liabilities	4 905 ..	....	....	....	....	....	....	....	....
Other investment assets	4 703 ..	−16,648	−21,440	−30,098	−68,095	−51,646	−58,927	30,363	19,455
Monetary authorities	4 701 ..	362	−147	−29	....	1,566	695	−4,818	−10,713
General government	4 704 ..	−243	−541	−135	....	−446	−10,144	8,537	635
Banks	4 705 ..	−12,756	−16,666	−27,618	....	−62,272	−47,318	28,094	32,939
Other sectors	4 728 ..	−4,011	−4,086	−2,317	....	9,506	−2,161	−1,450	−3,406
Other investment liabilities	4 753 W.	10,135	25,147	42,701	50,485	16,366	21,141	−34,586	−7,108
Monetary authorities	4 753 WA	960	12,470	8,774	....	5,959	12,475	−19,671	11,265
General government	4 753 ZB	53	1,420	5,032	939	1,587	−1,643	1,916	1,097
Banks	4 753 ZC	7,500	9,372	25,852	....	18,971	1,527	−12,547	−17,856
Other sectors	4 753 ZD	1,621	1,884	3,042	....	−10,150	8,782	−4,285	−1,614
Total, Groups A Through C	4 983 ..	*1,679*	*2,909*	*5,091*	*−64*	*−44*	*−2,735*	*−4,013*	*9,511*
D. Net Errors and Omissions	4 998 ..	**−3,703**	**−4,758**	**−5,841**	**−797**	**2,569**	**1,895**	**2,962**	**−8,076**
Total, Groups A Through D	4 984 ..	*−2,023*	*−1,849*	*−750*	*−861*	*2,525*	*−840*	*−1,050*	*1,435*
E. Reserves and Related Items	4 802 A.	**2,023**	**1,849**	**750**	**861**	**−2,525**	**840**	**1,050**	**−1,435**
Reserve assets	4 802 ..	2,023	1,849	750	861	−2,525	840	1,050	−1,435
Use of Fund credit and loans	4 766 ..	....	....	....	....	....	....	....	....
Exceptional financing	4 920 ..	....	....	....	....	....	....	....	....
Conversion rates: euros per U.S. dollar	0 103 ..	**.8860**	**.8054**	**.8041**	**.7971**	**.7306**	**.6827**	**.7198**	**.7550**

[1] Excludes components that have been classified in the categories of Group E.

Table 2. STANDARD PRESENTATION, 2003–2010

(Millions of U.S. dollars)

	Code	2003	2004	2005	2006	2007	2008	2009	2010
CURRENT ACCOUNT..	4 993 ..	**4,186**	**6,074**	**6,245**	**7,807**	**13,189**	**20,127**	**10,291**	**11,461**
A. GOODS...	4 100 ..	**−1,694**	**−1,029**	**−1,750**	**426**	**1,810**	**−592**	**−3,412**	**−4,283**
Credit...	2 100 ..	**88,105**	**109,875**	**119,228**	**133,844**	**162,899**	**179,201**	**135,100**	**147,710**
General merchandise: exports f.o.b............................	2 110 ..	83,653	102,648	111,320	133,844	153,270	168,749	127,425	140,714
Goods for processing: exports f.o.b.........................	2 150 ..	3,096	3,679	3,375	....	3,950	4,408	3,227	4,077
Repairs on goods..	2 160 ..	1,205	3,400	4,276	....	5,305	5,055	3,410	2,018
Goods procured in ports by carriers.........................	2 170 ..	38	39	96	....	85	145	66	97
Nonmonetary gold..	2 180 ..	113	110	160	....	290	843	971	805
Debit...	3 100 ..	**−89,799**	**−110,905**	**−120,977**	**−133,419**	**−161,089**	**−179,794**	**−138,511**	**−151,993**
General merchandise: imports f.o.b..........................	3 110 ..	−85,163	−103,964	−113,119	−133,419	−151,434	−170,142	−132,185	−145,241
Goods for processing: imports f.o.b.........................	3 150 ..	−3,319	−3,638	−3,365	....	−4,140	−4,584	−2,848	−4,253
Repairs on goods..	3 160 ..	−1,273	−3,277	−4,468	....	−5,441	−4,972	−3,275	−2,222
Goods procured in ports by carriers.........................	3 170 ..	....	....	....	....	....	....	....	....
Nonmonetary gold..	3 180 ..	−44	−26	−25	....	−74	−96	−203	−277
B. SERVICES..	4 200 ..	**8,717**	**9,959**	**11,859**	**12,598**	**15,177**	**20,834**	**17,461**	**17,665**
Total credit...	2 200 ..	*32,455*	*37,945*	*42,589*	*46,112*	*54,308*	*63,728*	*54,531*	*54,706*
Total debit..	3 200 ..	*−23,738*	*−27,986*	*−30,730*	*−33,514*	*−39,131*	*−42,894*	*−37,070*	*−37,041*
Transportation services, credit......................	2 205 ..	**6,544**	**8,169**	**8,969**	**10,291**	**12,082**	**15,074**	**12,002**	**12,883**
Passenger...	2 850 ..	*1,821*	*2,101*	*2,228*	*2,376*	*2,529*	*2,716*	*2,061*	*2,173*
Freight...	2 851 ..	*4,051*	*5,279*	*5,846*	*6,849*	*8,304*	*10,945*	*8,707*	*9,397*
Other...	2 852 ..	*672*	*789*	*895*	*1,066*	*1,249*	*1,414*	*1,234*	*1,312*
Sea transport, passenger...	2 207 ..	7	6	9	16	10	10	14	7
Sea transport, freight...	2 208 ..	289	369	437	545	668	760	500	643
Sea transport, other...	2 209 ..	13	31	29	23	10	16	12	11
Air transport, passenger...	2 211 ..	1,636	1,924	2,023	2,146	2,305	2,472	1,846	1,950
Air transport, freight..	2 212 ..	267	340	351	367	406	430	312	367
Air transport, other..	2 213 ..	289	346	378	409	485	599	490	508
Other transport, passenger......................................	2 215 ..	178	171	196	214	214	234	201	216
Other transport, freight..	2 216 ..	3,494	4,569	5,059	5,936	7,230	9,755	7,895	8,388
Other transport, other..	2 217 ..	371	412	489	634	755	799	732	794
Transportation services, debit........................	3 205 ..	**−5,639**	**−7,588**	**−8,661**	**−10,201**	**−12,139**	**−13,726**	**−10,698**	**−12,161**
Passenger...	3 850 ..	*−1,138*	*−1,575*	*−1,761*	*−2,093*	*−2,264*	*−2,561*	*−1,954*	*−2,090*
Freight...	3 851 ..	*−3,979*	*−5,391*	*−6,230*	*−7,214*	*−8,999*	*−10,136*	*−7,896*	*−9,101*
Other...	3 852 ..	*−522*	*−622*	*−669*	*−895*	*−876*	*−1,029*	*−848*	*−970*
Sea transport, passenger...	3 207 ..	−14	−16	−17	−16	−16	−25	−24	−23
Sea transport, freight...	3 208 ..	−606	−796	−953	−1,141	−1,330	−1,548	−1,056	−1,538
Sea transport, other...	3 209 ..	−64	−81	−72	−58	−43	−40	−29	−45
Air transport, passenger...	3 211 ..	−1,009	−1,411	−1,580	−1,919	−2,087	−2,347	−1,754	−1,879
Air transport, freight..	3 212 ..	−476	−568	−545	−486	−506	−564	−374	−428
Air transport, other..	3 213 ..	−325	−396	−447	−638	−621	−739	−589	−678
Other transport, passenger......................................	3 215 ..	−116	−148	−164	−157	−161	−188	−176	−189
Other transport, freight..	3 216 ..	−2,897	−4,028	−4,732	−5,586	−7,162	−8,024	−6,466	−7,135
Other transport, other..	3 217 ..	−132	−145	−150	−199	−213	−249	−230	−246
Travel, credit..	2 236 ..	**13,307**	**15,150**	**16,243**	**16,510**	**18,559**	**21,630**	**19,159**	**18,758**
Business travel..	2 237 ..	2,112	2,487	2,881	3,053	3,642	3,705	3,021	2,877
Personal travel..	2 240 ..	11,195	12,663	13,362	13,458	14,916	17,926	16,137	15,881
Travel, debit..	3 236 ..	**−8,623**	**−9,237**	**−9,316**	**−9,626**	**−10,561**	**−11,432**	**−10,813**	**−10,125**
Business travel..	3 237 ..	−1,830	−2,029	−1,957	−1,958	−2,249	−2,344	−1,773	−1,728
Personal travel..	3 240 ..	−6,793	−7,208	−7,359	−7,669	−8,312	−9,087	−9,040	−8,397
Other services, credit......................................	2 200 BA	**12,604**	**14,626**	**17,377**	**19,312**	**23,667**	**27,024**	**23,370**	**23,065**
Communications..	2 245 ..	684	672	1,010	1,416	1,663	1,757	1,563	1,389
Construction..	2 249 ..	1,043	1,174	985	969	1,382	1,710	1,411	1,169
Insurance...	2 253 ..	647	775	797	756	1,315	1,290	1,187	1,147
Financial..	2 260 ..	429	524	913	804	1,494	1,565	1,055	1,125
Computer and information..	2 262 ..	657	899	1,234	1,503	1,833	2,160	2,016	2,012
Royalties and licence fees...	2 266 ..	347	372	391	540	742	905	751	646
Other business services..	2 268 ..	8,254	9,618	11,423	12,635	14,362	16,659	14,454	14,763
Personal, cultural, and recreational..........................	2 287 ..	177	219	236	251	274	365	309	269
Government, n.i.e..	2 291 ..	365	373	388	437	600	612	624	545
Other services, debit..	3 200 BA	**−9,475**	**−11,161**	**−12,753**	**−13,687**	**−16,431**	**−17,737**	**−15,558**	**−14,755**
Communications..	3 245 ..	−624	−664	−824	−1,132	−1,305	−1,330	−1,190	−1,091
Construction..	3 249 ..	−942	−1,000	−840	−773	−1,212	−1,532	−1,107	−902
Insurance...	3 253 ..	−534	−660	−913	−1,105	−1,730	−1,078	−1,147	−1,016
Financial..	3 260 ..	−420	−337	−745	−613	−723	−738	−402	−413
Computer and information..	3 262 ..	−667	−857	−949	−1,080	−1,451	−1,741	−1,604	−1,584
Royalties and licence fees...	3 266 ..	−1,118	−1,249	−1,334	−1,328	−1,481	−1,598	−1,280	−1,403
Other business services..	3 268 ..	−4,610	−5,614	−6,314	−6,799	−7,560	−8,637	−7,834	−7,298
Personal, cultural, and recreational..........................	3 287 ..	−467	−693	−728	−750	−845	−955	−876	−935
Government, n.i.e..	3 291 ..	−93	−88	−106	−107	−124	−127	−119	−114

Table 2 (Continued). STANDARD PRESENTATION, 2003–2010

(Millions of U.S. dollars)

	Code	2003	2004	2005	2006	2007	2008	2009	2010
C. INCOME	4 300	**−1,097**	**−1,210**	**−2,043**	**−3,674**	**−2,198**	**2,386**	**−1,589**	**737**
Total credit	2 300	*16,514*	*20,193*	*25,914*	*28,027*	*42,909*	*44,478*	*34,625*	*36,522*
Total debit	3 300	*−17,611*	*−21,403*	*−27,957*	*−31,701*	*−45,107*	*−42,093*	*−36,214*	*−35,785*
Compensation of employees, credit	2 310	**1,608**	**1,865**	**1,917**	**1,880**	**2,172**	**2,398**	**2,186**	**2,122**
Compensation of employees, debit	3 310	**−856**	**−1,121**	**−1,316**	**−1,406**	**−1,594**	**−1,913**	**−1,826**	**−1,829**
Investment income, credit	2 320	**14,906**	**18,328**	**23,997**	**26,147**	**40,737**	**42,080**	**32,438**	**34,400**
Direct investment income	2 330	3,494	5,214	8,770	8,541	15,943	12,923	10,874	14,190
Dividends and distributed branch profits	2 332	1,886	2,429	4,893	4,151	6,187	8,938	9,789	8,774
Reinvested earnings and undistributed branch profits	2 333	1,537	2,736	3,811	3,368	8,525	2,137	−98	4,142
Income on debt (interest)	2 334	71	50	66	1,022	1,231	1,848	1,183	1,273
Portfolio investment income	2 339	6,641	8,049	9,425	11,145	14,521	15,154	11,680	11,162
Income on equity	2 340	486	637	798	....	1,390	1,233	1,320	1,504
Income on bonds and notes	2 350	6,060	7,302	8,450	....	12,477	13,708	10,232	9,570
Income on money market instruments	2 360	94	110	177	....	654	213	128	88
Other investment income	2 370	4,771	5,064	5,802	6,461	10,273	14,004	9,884	9,048
Investment income, debit	3 320	**−16,755**	**−20,282**	**−26,641**	**−30,295**	**−43,513**	**−40,180**	**−34,387**	**−33,956**
Direct investment income	3 330	−3,731	−5,006	−9,233	−9,278	−13,902	−6,406	−9,581	−11,467
Dividends and distributed branch profits	3 332	−2,805	−3,363	−5,070	−5,555	−6,109	−7,194	−9,056	−7,509
Reinvested earnings and undistributed branch profits	3 333	−902	−1,618	−4,147	−2,642	−5,638	3,765	2,110	−2,380
Income on debt (interest)	3 334	−24	−25	−16	−1,080	−2,154	−2,977	−2,635	−1,578
Portfolio investment income	3 339	−9,792	−11,353	−12,178	−13,929	−18,717	−20,776	−17,401	−15,605
Income on equity	3 340	−352	−536	−740	....	−1,724	−1,968	−1,530	−1,300
Income on bonds and notes	3 350	−9,242	−10,684	−11,204	....	−15,710	−17,752	−15,491	−14,217
Income on money market instruments	3 360	−198	−132	−234	....	−1,283	−1,056	−380	−88
Other investment income	3 370	−3,232	−3,922	−5,230	−7,088	−10,893	−12,998	−7,406	−6,884
D. CURRENT TRANSFERS	4 379	**−1,740**	**−1,646**	**−1,821**	**−1,543**	**−1,600**	**−2,500**	**−2,169**	**−2,658**
Credit	2 379	**2,954**	**3,449**	**3,949**	**4,290**	**5,001**	**5,411**	**4,877**	**4,498**
General government	2 380	687	776	880	883	892	1,012	1,040	953
Other sectors	2 390	2,267	2,674	3,069	3,407	4,109	4,400	3,837	3,545
Workers' remittances	2 391	340	383	398	418	467	519	508	458
Other current transfers	2 392	1,926	2,291	2,672	2,990	3,642	3,881	3,328	3,087
Debit	3 379	**−4,693**	**−5,096**	**−5,770**	**−5,833**	**−6,601**	**−7,911**	**−7,046**	**−7,156**
General government	3 380	−2,444	−2,896	−3,291	−3,273	−3,504	−3,892	−3,972	−4,189
Other sectors	3 390	−2,249	−2,200	−2,479	−2,560	−3,098	−4,019	−3,074	−2,967
Workers' remittances	3 391	−694	−789	−804	−839	−1,058	−1,209	−1,070	−1,058
Other current transfers	3 392	−1,555	−1,411	−1,675	−1,721	−2,040	−2,809	−2,004	−1,909
CAPITAL AND FINANCIAL ACCOUNT	4 996	**−483**	**−1,316**	**−404**	**−7,010**	**−15,759**	**−22,022**	**−13,253**	**−3,385**
CAPITAL ACCOUNT	4 994	**8**	**−342**	**−237**	**−1,009**	**274**	**−70**	**161**	**517**
Total credit	2 994	*897*	*764*	*739*	*586*	*1,027*	*726*	*1,103*	*1,407*
Total debit	3 994	*−888*	*−1,105*	*−976*	*−1,595*	*−752*	*−796*	*−942*	*−889*
Capital transfers, credit	2 400	**857**	**577**	**684**	**487**	**911**	**596**	**995**	**1,308**
General government	2 401	135	145	175	125	533	196	145	116
Debt forgiveness	2 402	....	....	....	....	....	....	....	....
Other capital transfers	2 410	135	145	175	125	533	196	145	116
Other sectors	2 430	722	432	509	361	378	400	849	1,192
Migrants' transfers	2 431	548	273	294	341	373	400	406	462
Debt forgiveness	2 432	44	35	66	....	....	....	443	727
Other capital transfers	2 440	131	125	149	20	5	....	....	4
Capital transfers, debit	3 400	**−878**	**−916**	**−906**	**−1,323**	**−454**	**−454**	**−457**	**−481**
General government	3 401	−50	−37	−3	−879	....	....	....	....
Debt forgiveness	3 402	....	....	....	−575	....	....	....	....
Other capital transfers	3 410	−50	−37	−3	−304	....	....	....	....
Other sectors	3 430	−828	−879	−903	−443	−454	−454	−457	−481
Migrants' transfers	3 431	−324	−317	−447	−330	−356	−382	−382	−467
Debt forgiveness	3 432	−380	−418	−313	−104	−94	−72	−14	−9
Other capital transfers	3 440	−124	−144	−143	−9	−3	....	−61	−5
Nonproduced nonfinancial assets, credit	2 480	**39**	**186**	**55**	**99**	**116**	**130**	**109**	**99**
Nonproduced nonfinancial assets, debit	3 480	**−10**	**−189**	**−70**	**−272**	**−299**	**−342**	**−485**	**−408**

Table 2 (Continued). STANDARD PRESENTATION, 2003–2010

(Millions of U.S. dollars)

	Code	2003	2004	2005	2006	2007	2008	2009	2010
FINANCIAL ACCOUNT............................	4 995 ..	**–491**	**–974**	**–168**	**–6,002**	**–16,033**	**–21,952**	**–13,414**	**–3,902**
A. DIRECT INVESTMENT..........................	4 500 ..	**–45**	**–4,533**	**–194**	**–3,050**	**–7,610**	**–22,934**	**–385**	**–5,258**
Direct investment abroad....................	4 505 ..	**–7,143**	**–8,425**	**–81,842**	**–5,527**	**–71,582**	**–29,536**	**–11,908**	**20,378**
Equity capital..................................	4 510 ..	–4,925	–6,062	–76,979	–1,573	–64,987	–21,681	–12,839	25,052
Claims on affiliated enterprises.........	4 515 ..	....	....	....	....	....	....	....	....
Liabilities to affiliated enterprises......	4 520 ..	....	....	....	....	....	....	....	....
Reinvested earnings........................	4 525 ..	–1,537	–2,736	–3,811	–3,368	–8,525	–2,137	98	–4,142
Other capital..................................	4 530 ..	–681	373	–1,052	–586	1,930	–5,719	833	–532
Claims on affiliated enterprises.........	4 535 ..	–612	375	–726	–701	–706	–4,828	–1,668	–382
Liabilities to affiliated enterprises......	4 540 ..	–70	–2	–327	115	2,636	–890	2,501	–150
Direct investment in Austria..............	4 555 ..	**7,098**	**3,892**	**81,648**	**2,477**	**63,972**	**6,602**	**11,523**	**–25,636**
Equity capital..................................	4 560 ..	3,139	1,876	79,299	–2,881	38,832	9,833	6,941	–30,908
Claims on direct investors................	4 565 ..	....	....	....	....	....	....	....	....
Liabilities to direct investors.............	4 570 ..	....	....	....	....	....	....	....	....
Reinvested earnings........................	4 575 ..	902	1,618	4,147	2,642	5,638	–3,765	–2,110	2,380
Other capital..................................	4 580 ..	3,058	398	–1,798	2,716	19,502	534	6,691	2,892
Claims on direct investors................	4 585 ..	641	2	34	–171	–1,503	590	–620	–483
Liabilities to direct investors.............	4 590 ..	2,417	396	–1,832	2,887	21,005	–56	7,311	3,376
B. PORTFOLIO INVESTMENT...................	4 600 ..	**4,786**	**–1,329**	**–13,479**	**14,826**	**30,295**	**37,294**	**–10,646**	**–9,899**
Assets...	4 602 ..	**–18,654**	**–33,024**	**–44,004**	**–32,900**	**–16,078**	**11,996**	**–4,788**	**–8,800**
Equity securities.............................	4 610 ..	–2,762	–4,067	–5,690	–8,420	–582	8,126	–6,167	–9,714
Monetary authorities.......................	4 611 ..	–99	–186	–176	....	–129	–346	–83	–674
General government........................	4 612 ..	2	–41	–33	....	–35	–22	21	–78
Banks...	4 613 ..	–138	–414	–543	....	725	749	535	188
Other sectors.................................	4 614 ..	–2,526	–3,426	–4,938	....	–1,144	7,745	–6,641	–9,151
Debt securities...............................	4 619 ..	–15,893	–28,957	–38,314	–24,480	–15,496	3,870	1,379	913
Bonds and notes............................	4 620 ..	–19,880	–27,639	–37,552	–26,706	–14,474	2,685	815	85
Monetary authorities.....................	4 621 ..	–2,122	1,074	–982	....	–2,688	–920	–4,424	–9,071
General government......................	4 622 ..	209	–85	32	....	–27	–115	–7	201
Banks..	4 623 ..	–7,375	–17,763	–17,179	....	–11,691	2,511	7,587	9,397
Other sectors...............................	4 624 ..	–10,592	–10,864	–19,423	....	–67	1,209	–2,340	–443
Money market instruments...............	4 630 ..	3,987	–1,318	–761	2,226	–1,023	1,185	563	828
Monetary authorities.....................	4 631 ..	1,837	–1,676	772	....	–488	575	88	–32
General government......................	4 632 ..	1,521	818	–1,008	....	1,089	–13	12	–3
Banks..	4 633 ..	610	–614	244	....	–1,256	394	–254	1,073
Other sectors...............................	4 634 ..	20	153	–769	....	–368	229	717	–209
Liabilities......................................	4 652 ..	**23,440**	**31,695**	**30,525**	**47,725**	**46,373**	**25,298**	**–5,858**	**–1,099**
Equity securities.............................	4 660 ..	2,431	6,926	5,999	10,550	3,625	–6,808	284	–385
Banks...	4 663 ..	1,390	437	–2,832	....	–755	–1,340	1,577	637
Other sectors.................................	4 664 ..	1,040	6,489	8,831	....	4,380	–5,469	–1,293	–1,021
Debt securities...............................	4 669 ..	21,009	24,769	24,526	37,176	42,748	32,106	–6,142	–714
Bonds and notes............................	4 670 ..	20,263	23,167	23,193	29,208	39,895	20,129	7,474	1,054
Monetary authorities.....................	4 671 ..	....	....	....	....	....	....	....	....
General government......................	4 672 ..	10,701	8,184	5,618	....	9,371	6,703	4,399	12,384
Banks..	4 673 ..	5,549	11,290	12,899	....	25,464	11,580	–1,431	–13,395
Other sectors...............................	4 674 ..	4,013	3,693	4,676	....	5,060	1,846	4,506	2,065
Money market instruments...............	4 680 ..	746	1,601	1,333	7,967	2,853	11,977	–13,616	–1,768
Monetary authorities.....................	4 681 ..	....	....	....	....	....	....	....	....
General government......................	4 682 ..	265	320	224	....	–213	9,628	–2,826	–2,686
Banks..	4 683 ..	452	1,306	1,170	....	3,048	2,566	–10,866	456
Other sectors...............................	4 684 ..	29	–24	–61	....	19	–217	77	462
C. FINANCIAL DERIVATIVES...................	4 910 ..	**–742**	**–669**	**153**	**–1,029**	**–913**	**635**	**790**	**343**
Monetary authorities........................	4 911 ..	–23	12	8	....	....	–498	275	42
General government.........................	4 912 ..	449	1,124	1,584	....	–382	2,868	–1,221	145
Banks..	4 913 ..	–620	–1,062	–1,215	....	–1,224	–2,923	1,324	28
Other sectors..................................	4 914 ..	–548	–743	–223	....	694	1,189	412	128
Assets...	4 900 ..	....	....	....	....	....	....	....	....
Monetary authorities........................	4 901 ..	....	....	....	....	....	....	....	....
General government.........................	4 902 ..	....	....	....	....	....	....	....	....
Banks..	4 903 ..	....	....	....	....	....	....	....	....
Other sectors..................................	4 904 ..	....	....	....	....	....	....	....	....
Liabilities......................................	4 905 ..	....	....	....	....	....	....	....	....
Monetary authorities........................	4 906 ..	....	....	....	....	....	....	....	....
General government.........................	4 907 ..	....	....	....	....	....	....	....	....
Banks..	4 908 ..	....	....	....	....	....	....	....	....
Other sectors..................................	4 909 ..	....	....	....	....	....	....	....	....

Table 2 (Concluded). STANDARD PRESENTATION, 2003–2010

(Millions of U.S. dollars)

	Code	2003	2004	2005	2006	2007	2008	2009	2010
D. OTHER INVESTMENT	4 700	**−6,513**	**3,707**	**12,602**	**−17,610**	**−35,280**	**−37,786**	**−4,223**	**12,347**
Assets	4 703	−16,648	−21,440	−30,098	−68,095	−51,646	−58,927	30,363	19,455
Trade credits	4 706	52	−490	−728	−1,720	....	−369	532	−1,215
General government	4 707	....	−647	−99	....	54	139	491	....
of which: Short-term	4 709	....	....	....	....	....	....	....	....
Other sectors	4 710	52	157	−629	....	−54	−507	41	−1,215
of which: Short-term	4 712	*52*	*157*	*−629*	....	....	*−477*	*−38*	*−1,204*
Loans	4 714	−14,568	−8,104	−15,237	−17,303	−36,014	−33,765	7,736	4,358
Monetary authorities	4 715	....	....	−1	....	....	....	....	....
of which: Short-term	4 718	....	....	*−1*	....	....	....	....	....
General government	4 719	30	7	−4	....	....	−4,783	2,877	282
of which: Short-term	4 721	....	*11*	....	....	....	*−4,772*	*2,890*	*1,068*
Banks	4 722	−12,973	−5,916	−14,212	....	−29,353	−27,429	4,906	7,610
of which: Short-term	4 724	*−894*	*6,017*	*−6,272*	....	*−8,181*	*2,897*	*4,177*	*3,239*
Other sectors	4 725	−1,625	−2,194	−1,021	....	−6,661	−1,553	−47	−3,535
of which: Short-term	4 727	*−1,327*	*−516*	*−353*	....	*−5,038*	*−478*	*−394*	*−4,731*
Currency and deposits	4 730	−2,089	−12,002	−13,670	−48,879	−14,878	−23,362	25,130	18,567
Monetary authorities	4 731	362	−150	−28	....	1,567	695	−4,825	−10,669
General government	4 732	−192	192	78	....	−548	−5,156	6,004	883
Banks	4 733	−147	−10,685	−13,283	....	−32,469	−19,274	25,161	26,827
Other sectors	4 734	−2,112	−1,359	−438	....	16,571	372	−1,211	1,527
Other assets	4 736	−43	−844	−464	−193	−753	−1,431	−3,035	−2,255
Monetary authorities	4 737	....	3	....	....	−1	....	7	−43
of which: Short-term	4 739	....	....	....	....	....	....	....	....
General government	4 740	−82	−93	−111	....	48	−344	−835	−530
of which: Short-term	4 742	....	....	....	....	*312*	*−32*	*−381*	*−81*
Banks	4 743	364	−64	−123	....	−451	−615	−1,973	−1,498
of which: Short-term	4 745	*385*	*−30*	*−91*	....	*−451*	*−615*	*−1,973*	*−1,498*
Other sectors	4 746	−326	−689	−230	....	−349	−472	−233	−183
of which: Short-term	4 748	*−185*	*−121*	*118*	....	*−48*	*−136*	*102*	*105*
Liabilities	4 753	**10,135**	**25,147**	**42,701**	**50,485**	**16,366**	**21,141**	**−34,586**	**−7,108**
Trade credits	4 756	171	507	117	1,071	224	581	−382	915
General government	4 757	....	....	....	....	....	....	....	....
of which: Short-term	4 759	....	....	....	....	....	....	....	....
Other sectors	4 760	171	507	117	....	224	581	−382	915
of which: Short-term	4 762	*171*	*507*	*117*	....	*−244*	*383*	*154*	*915*
Loans	4 764	940	2,545	7,431	18,695	−10,560	8,196	−2,697	−442
Monetary authorities	4 765	....	....	....	....	....	....	....	....
of which: Use of Fund credit and loans from the Fund	4 766	....	....	....	....	....	....	....	....
of which: Short-term	4 768	....	....	....	....	....	....	....	....
General government	4 769	−256	1,641	5,074	939	528	218	2,195	743
of which: Short-term	4 771	....	*−1*	*−1*	....	....	....	....	....
Banks	4 772	....	....	....	....	....	....	....	....
of which: Short-term	4 774	....	....	....	....	....	....	....	....
Other sectors	4 775	1,196	904	2,358	....	−11,088	7,978	−4,892	−1,186
of which: Short-term	4 777	*260*	*736*	*1,414*	....	*−4,196*	*4,262*	*−3,093*	*−1,106*
Currency and deposits	4 780	8,200	21,803	34,252	29,954	24,930	14,001	−34,650	−6,591
Monetary authorities	4 781	960	12,470	8,774	....	5,959	12,475	−22,104	11,265
General government	4 782	....	....	....	....	....	....	....	....
Banks	4 783	7,240	9,332	25,478	....	18,971	1,527	−12,547	−17,856
Other sectors	4 784	....	....	....	....	....	....	....	....
Other liabilities	4 786	824	292	901	765	1,772	−1,637	3,143	−990
Monetary authorities	4 787	....	....	....	....	....	....	2,433	....
of which: Short-term	4 789	....	....	....	....	....	....	....	....
General government	4 790	310	−221	−41	....	1,059	−1,861	−279	354
of which: Short-term	4 792	*310*	*−221*	*−41*	....	*1,059*	*−1,861*	*−279*	*354*
Banks	4 793	260	40	374	....	....	....	....	....
of which: Short-term	4 795	*249*	*8*	*253*	....	....	....	....	....
Other sectors	4 796	254	473	568	....	713	224	990	−1,344
of which: Short-term	4 798	*54*	*−43*	*50*	....	*408*	*22*	*−336*	*−87*
E. RESERVE ASSETS	4 802	**2,023**	**1,849**	**750**	**861**	**−2,525**	**840**	**1,050**	**−1,435**
Monetary gold	4 812	....	140	70	219	187	....	....	....
Special drawing rights	4 811	20	28	1	−36	−32	−78	−2,425	5
Reserve position in the Fund	4 810	−90	251	477	163	61	−168	−214	−142
Foreign exchange	4 803	2,095	1,430	202	515	−2,741	1,085	3,689	−1,297
Other claims	4 813	−2	1	....	....	....	....	....	....
NET ERRORS AND OMISSIONS	4 998	**−3,703**	**−4,758**	**−5,841**	**−797**	**2,569**	**1,895**	**2,962**	**−8,076**

Table 3. INTERNATIONAL INVESTMENT POSITION (End-period stocks), 2003–2010

(Millions of U.S. dollars)

	Code	2003	2004	2005	2006	2007	2008	2009	2010
ASSETS	8 995 C.	443,661	548,839	650,836	853,539	1,089,040	1,044,770	1,103,480	1,041,078
Direct investment abroad	8 505 ..	58,295	70,997	149,146	184,116	270,722	273,606	290,350	274,939
Equity capital and reinvested earnings	8 506 ..	54,918	67,809	139,611	175,597	261,848	260,685	283,682	267,031
Claims on affiliated enterprises	8 507 ..	....	....	....	....	....	....	....	....
Liabilities to affiliated enterprises	8 508 ..	....	....	....	....	....	....	....	....
Other capital	8 530 ..	3,377	3,187	9,535	8,519	8,874	12,921	6,668	7,908
Claims on affiliated enterprises	8 535 ..	4,117	4,153	....	....	....	....	....	....
Liabilities to affiliated enterprises	8 540 ..	−740	....	....	....	....	....	....	....
Portfolio investment	8 602 ..	207,035	264,539	284,173	352,401	404,424	320,767	358,148	353,562
Equity securities	8 610 ..	44,149	54,935	63,566	87,890	100,308	54,174	74,252	86,595
Monetary authorities	8 611 ..	1,839	2,194	2,072	2,322	2,758	2,888	3,115	3,609
General government	8 612 ..	57	95	125	171	199	136	131	208
Banks	8 613 ..	2,229	2,818	3,469	4,481	4,482	2,643	2,427	2,112
Other sectors	8 614 ..	40,024	49,827	57,900	80,915	92,869	48,507	68,579	80,666
Debt securities	8 619 ..	162,885	209,604	220,607	264,511	304,116	266,593	283,896	266,967
Bonds and notes	8 620 ..	159,650	204,408	216,173	261,190	298,076	262,359	280,251	264,410
Monetary authorities	8 621 ..	9,073	7,972	7,517	8,380	12,144	12,549	17,688	25,070
General government	8 622 ..	448	569	448	743	1,156	1,116	1,136	901
Banks	8 623 ..	59,716	84,584	91,075	115,493	136,801	120,665	118,813	104,909
Other sectors	8 624 ..	90,412	111,282	117,132	136,574	147,975	128,029	142,614	133,530
Money market instruments	8 630 ..	3,236	5,196	4,434	3,321	6,040	4,234	3,645	2,558
Monetary authorities	8 631 ..	951	2,700	1,606	64	698	72	....	27
General government	8 632 ..	414	7	....	....	....	1	....	2
Banks	8 633 ..	1,282	2,095	1,686	1,504	3,000	2,181	2,459	1,192
Other sectors	8 634 ..	589	395	1,143	1,752	2,342	1,980	1,186	1,337
Financial derivatives	8 900 ..	....	....	....	4,632	9,969	19,775	16,344	14,294
Monetary authorities	8 901 ..	....	....	....	4	3	1,032	55	....
General government	8 902 ..	....	....	....	....	3,832	689	734	846
Banks	8 903 ..	....	....	....	4,476	6,065	17,876	15,174	12,798
Other sectors	8 904 ..	....	....	....	152	69	179	380	651
Other investment	8 703 ..	165,602	201,115	205,685	299,479	385,704	413,919	420,588	375,999
Trade credits	8 706 ..	6,912	7,994	7,675	10,701	12,404	12,281	12,589	13,244
General government	8 707 ..	....	....	....	....	....	....	....	....
of which: Short-term	8 709 ..	....	....	....	....	....	....	....	....
Other sectors	8 710 ..	6,912	7,994	7,675	10,701	....	....	....	....
of which: Short-term	8 712 ..	....	....	....	....	....	....	....	....
Loans	8 714 ..	101,343	81,990	86,122	113,912	162,700	185,035	183,482	171,293
Monetary authorities	8 715 ..	....	....	3	....	....	....	....	....
of which: Short-term	8 718 ..	....	....	....	....	....	....	....	....
General government	8 719 ..	82	78	19	21	472	5,075	2,513	2,251
of which: Short-term	8 721 ..	....	....	....	....	....	....	....	....
Banks	8 722 ..	85,604	62,614	68,374	88,685	126,863	144,416	143,591	130,302
of which: Short-term	8 724 ..	*20,238*	*9,531*	*14,312*	*19,257*	*27,923*	*22,774*	*19,328*	*14,816*
Other sectors	8 725 ..	15,657	19,299	17,726	25,206	35,365	35,544	37,379	38,740
of which: Short-term	8 727 ..	....	....	....	....	....	....	....	....
Currency and deposits	8 730 ..	49,443	101,937	107,775	169,243	203,842	209,432	214,302	180,122
Monetary authorities	8 731 ..	2,023	2,327	2,144	3,091	2,411	1,632	26,136	34,995
General government	8 732 ..	1,106	1,302	683	263	1,575	6,931	1,008	214
Banks	8 733 ..	40,849	90,865	102,297	145,483	194,522	195,173	176,626	136,535
Other sectors	8 734 ..	5,464	7,444	2,652	20,406	5,334	5,697	10,532	8,378
Other assets	8 736 ..	7,904	9,193	4,113	5,623	6,757	7,171	10,214	11,341
Monetary authorities	8 737 ..	149	159	137	153	173	163	161	193
of which: Short-term	8 739 ..	....	....	....	....	....	....	....	....
General government	8 740 ..	2,158	2,428	2,052	2,024	1,900	1,508	1,899	1,747
of which: Short-term	8 742 ..	....	....	....	....	....	....	....	....
Banks	8 743 ..	3,886	4,247	1,834	1,811	2,476	2,945	5,070	6,357
of which: Short-term	8 745 ..	....	....	....	....	....	....	....	....
Other sectors	8 746 ..	1,710	2,359	89	1,635	2,208	2,555	3,084	3,045
of which: Short-term	8 748 ..	....	....	....	....	....	....	....	....
Reserve assets	8 802 ..	12,729	12,188	11,832	12,911	18,222	16,702	18,051	22,283
Monetary gold	8 812 ..	4,259	4,330	4,989	5,901	7,530	7,787	9,938	12,695
Special drawing rights	8 811 ..	181	160	147	190	233	306	2,744	2,691
Reserve position in the Fund	8 810 ..	1,145	935	394	247	195	362	589	723
Foreign exchange	8 803 ..	7,144	6,763	6,302	6,573	10,263	8,248	4,780	6,173
Other claims	8 813 ..	....	....	....	....	....	....	....	....

Table 3 (Concluded). INTERNATIONAL INVESTMENT POSITION (End-period stocks), 2003–2010

(Millions of U.S. dollars)

	Code	2003	2004	2005	2006	2007	2008	2009	2010
LIABILITIES	8 995 D.	**480,881**	**610,289**	**711,981**	**923,406**	**1,162,449**	**1,111,345**	**1,137,909**	**1,081,201**
Direct investment in Austria	8 555 ..	**56,529**	**65,842**	**157,301**	**192,199**	**283,953**	**269,014**	**298,611**	**273,271**
Equity capital and reinvested earnings	8 556 ..	49,901	58,863	148,271	180,770	246,375	233,446	256,657	231,748
Claims on direct investors	8 557 ..	....	....	....	....	....	....	....	....
Liabilities to direct investors	8 558 ..	....	....	....	....	....	....	....	....
Other capital	8 580 ..	6,628	6,978	9,030	11,429	37,578	35,569	41,954	41,523
Claims on direct investors	8 585 ..	−2,140	−2,307	....	....	....	....	....	....
Liabilities to direct investors	8 590 ..	8,768	....	....	....	....	....	....	....
Portfolio investment	8 652 ..	**281,670**	**348,127**	**350,616**	**447,308**	**535,240**	**496,746**	**519,035**	**505,199**
Equity securities	8 660 ..	26,470	45,181	59,237	92,957	105,127	46,805	60,308	62,660
Banks	8 663 ..	5,459	9,536	7,517	13,970	13,061	5,209	7,573	10,787
Other sectors	8 664 ..	21,011	35,645	51,720	78,987	92,066	41,596	52,735	51,873
Debt securities	8 669 ..	255,201	302,946	291,379	354,351	430,113	449,941	458,726	442,540
Bonds and notes	8 670 ..	247,486	293,229	280,804	336,306	408,996	418,407	440,965	426,768
Monetary authorities	8 671 ..	....	....	....	....	....	....	....	....
General government	8 672 ..	129,146	149,902	137,275	156,711	179,845	183,905	195,223	199,565
Banks	8 673 ..	89,921	108,405	118,005	152,011	193,951	199,585	203,163	184,205
Other sectors	8 674 ..	28,420	34,922	25,524	27,584	35,200	34,917	42,579	42,997
Money market instruments	8 680 ..	7,714	9,717	10,575	18,045	21,118	31,535	17,761	15,772
Monetary authorities	8 681 ..	....	....	....	....	....	....	....	....
General government	8 682 ..	788	1,143	1,174	1,087	1,098	10,367	7,726	4,752
Banks	8 683 ..	6,858	8,505	9,326	16,839	19,846	21,156	9,929	10,458
Other sectors	8 684 ..	68	69	76	120	174	12	107	562
Financial derivatives	8 905 ..	....	....	....	**4,651**	**11,110**	**14,952**	**10,398**	**10,687**
Monetary authorities	8 906 ..	....	....	....	....	....	....	....	....
General government	8 907 ..	....	....	....	1,221	4,245	4,773	3,760	2,389
Banks	8 908 ..	....	....	....	3,331	6,699	10,073	6,408	8,077
Other sectors	8 909 ..	....	....	....	99	167	107	230	221
Other investment	8 753 ..	**142,681**	**196,321**	**204,063**	**279,248**	**332,145**	**330,632**	**309,865**	**292,044**
Trade credits	8 756 ..	3,936	4,801	4,510	7,973	10,038	11,349	12,964	13,414
General government	8 757 ..	....	....	....	....	....	....	....	....
of which: Short-term	8 759 ..	....	....	....	....	....	....	....	....
Other sectors	8 760 ..	3,936	4,801	4,510	7,973	....	....	....	....
of which: Short-term	8 762 ..	....	....	....	....	....	....	....	....
Loans	8 764 ..	38,981	45,007	29,495	53,895	55,797	61,319	61,883	60,107
Monetary authorities	8 765 ..	566	....	....	....	....	....	....	....
of which: Use of Fund credit and loans from the Fund	8 766 ..	....	....	....	....	....	....	....	....
of which: Short-term	8 768 ..	....	....	....	....	....	....	....	....
General government	8 769 ..	3,741	5,786	10,000	12,108	14,697	14,255	16,940	16,479
of which: Short-term	8 771 ..	....	....	....	....	....	....	....	....
Banks	8 772 ..	15,236	16,424	....	....	....	....	....	....
of which: Short-term	8 774 ..	*5,072*	*6,422*	....	....	....	....	....	....
Other sectors	8 775 ..	19,439	22,797	19,495	41,787	41,101	47,064	44,943	43,628
of which: Short-term	8 777 ..	....	....	....	....	....	....	....	....
Currency and deposits	8 780 ..	94,880	141,530	167,503	213,096	258,629	252,288	225,327	210,175
Monetary authorities	8 781 ..	−1,934	12,262	18,533	28,544	38,424	49,687	28,289	36,709
General government	8 782 ..	....	....	....	....	....	....	....	....
Banks	8 783 ..	96,814	129,267	148,970	184,552	220,205	202,601	197,038	173,466
Other sectors	8 784 ..	....	....	....	....	....	....	....	....
Other liabilities	8 786 ..	4,884	4,983	2,555	4,283	7,681	5,676	9,690	8,348
Monetary authorities	8 787 ..	....	....	....	....	....	....	2,722	2,674
of which: Short-term	8 789 ..	....	....	....	....	....	....	....	....
General government	8 790 ..	1,450	1,249	1,721	1,617	3,030	1,026	728	1,052
of which: Short-term	8 792 ..	....	....	....	....	....	....	....	....
Banks	8 793 ..	980	1,187	....	....	....	....	....	....
of which: Short-term	8 795 ..	....	....	....	....	....	....	....	....
Other sectors	8 796 ..	2,454	2,547	835	2,666	4,651	4,650	6,240	4,622
of which: Short-term	8 798 ..	....	....	....	....	....	....	....	....
NET INTERNATIONAL INVESTMENT POSITION	8 995 ..	**−37,220**	**−61,450**	**−61,144**	**−69,867**	**−73,409**	**−66,575**	**−34,428**	**−40,123**
Conversion rates: euros per U.S. dollar (end of period)	0 104 ..	**.7918**	**.7342**	**.8477**	**.7593**	**.6793**	**.7185**	**.6942**	**.7484**

Table 1. ANALYTIC PRESENTATION, 2003–2010

(Millions of U.S. dollars)

	Code	2003	2004	2005	2006	2007	2008	2009	2010
A. Current Account[1]	4 993 Z.	**−2,020.9**	**−2,589.2**	**167.3**	**3,707.6**	**9,018.9**	**16,452.8**	**10,174.9**	**15,040.4**
Goods: exports f.o.b.	2 100 ..	2,624.6	3,743.0	7,649.0	13,014.6	21,269.3	30,586.3	21,096.8	26,476.0
Goods: imports f.o.b.	3 100 ..	−2,723.1	−3,581.7	−4,349.9	−5,269.3	−6,045.0	−7,574.7	−6,513.9	−6,745.6
Balance on Goods	4 100 ..	*−98.5*	*161.3*	*3,299.1*	*7,745.3*	*15,224.3*	*23,011.7*	*14,582.9*	*19,730.4*
Services: credit	2 200 ..	432.0	492.0	683.0	939.9	1,247.5	1,547.9	1,778.9	2,113.9
Services: debit	3 200 ..	−2,046.5	−2,730.4	−2,653.0	−2,863.2	−3,378.6	−3,891.2	−3,389.5	−3,846.0
Balance on Goods and Services	4 991 ..	*−1,713.0*	*−2,077.1*	*1,329.1*	*5,821.9*	*13,093.3*	*20,668.4*	*12,972.3*	*17,998.4*
Income: credit	2 300 ..	52.6	65.3	201.8	280.0	327.8	595.1	551.4	675.5
Income: debit	3 300 ..	−494.7	−765.9	−1,847.4	−2,960.6	−5,407.2	−5,861.2	−4,070.6	−4,142.6
Balance on Goods, Services, and Income	4 992 ..	*−2,155.0*	*−2,777.7*	*−316.6*	*3,141.3*	*8,013.9*	*15,402.4*	*9,453.2*	*14,531.3*
Current transfers: credit	2 379 Z.	225.1	262.6	626.2	748.2	1,313.4	1,500.1	1,292.4	1,420.4
Current transfers: debit	3 379 ..	−90.9	−74.1	−142.3	−182.0	−308.4	−449.7	−570.7	−911.3
B. Capital Account[1]	4 994 Z.	**−23.1**	**−4.1**	**40.9**	**−3.8**	**−2.8**	**10.6**	**5.4**	**14.3**
Capital account: credit	2 994 Z.	15.0	24.0	70.2	25.0	28.0	36.0	19.1	22.1
Capital account: debit	3 994 ..	−38.1	−28.1	−29.3	−28.9	−30.8	−25.3	−13.7	−7.8
Total, Groups A Plus B	4 981 ..	*−2,044.0*	*−2,593.4*	*208.2*	*3,703.8*	*9,016.1*	*16,463.4*	*10,180.2*	*15,054.7*
C. Financial Account[1]	4 995 W.	**2,279.7**	**2,960.2**	**78.0**	**−2,105.3**	**−6,874.1**	**−13,158.9**	**−9,682.0**	**−12,695.0**
Direct investment abroad	4 505 ..	−933.3	−1,204.8	−1,220.8	−705.5	−285.6	−555.6	−326.1	−232.0
Direct investment in Azerbaijan	4 555 Z.	3,285.0	3,556.1	1,679.9	−584.0	−4,748.9	14.8	473.3	563.1
Portfolio investment assets	4 602 ..	....	−18.1	−47.8	−34.4	−110.9	−320.8	−84.3	−163.3
Equity securities	4 610 ..	....	1.9	....	−3.1	−11.9	−21.4	−3.5	9.8
Debt securities	4 619 ..	....	−20.0	−47.8	−31.3	−99.0	−299.5	−80.8	−173.1
Portfolio investment liabilities	4 652 Z.	....	....	78.3	22.3	84.5	−26.6	−54.5	24.5
Equity securities	4 660 ..	....	....	....	.8	2.0	....	....	.6
Debt securities	4 669 Z.	....	....	78.3	21.6	82.5	−26.6	−54.5	23.9
Financial derivatives	4 910 ..	....	....	....	....	....	....	....	....
Financial derivatives assets	4 900 ..	....	....	....	....	....	....	....	....
Financial derivatives liabilities	4 905 ..	....	....	....	....	....	....	....	....
Other investment assets	4 703 ..	−169.2	−360.4	−1,365.3	−1,416.7	−2,687.8	−13,197.5	−9,326.4	−14,698.0
Monetary authorities	4 701 ..	....	1.8	....	....	....	....	....	....
General government	4 704 ..	−109.4	−123.5	−475.7	−408.7	−1,153.6	−9,612.2	−3,672.7	−9,103.7
Banks	4 705 ..	−16.7	20.1	−83.7	−58.5	−246.9	−903.6	−112.5	−545.8
Other sectors	4 728 ..	−43.2	−258.8	−806.0	−949.5	−1,287.2	−2,681.7	−5,541.2	−5,048.5
Other investment liabilities	4 753 W.	97.2	987.4	953.7	612.9	874.6	926.9	−364.0	1,810.6
Monetary authorities	4 753 WA	34.4	....	−1.0	16.9	−1.4	....	240.2	....
General government	4 753 ZB	32.4	34.8	37.5	80.5	139.1	166.2	277.4	456.6
Banks	4 753 ZC	−.2	−16.4	46.7	336.1	742.2	185.2	−279.1	732.4
Other sectors	4 753 ZD	30.5	969.0	870.4	179.5	−5.2	575.5	−602.5	621.6
Total, Groups A Through C	4 983 ..	*235.7*	*366.9*	*286.2*	*1,598.4*	*2,142.0*	*3,304.6*	*498.2*	*2,359.7*
D. Net Errors and Omissions	4 998 ..	**−111.8**	**−49.9**	**−125.7**	**−255.9**	**−360.6**	**−845.1**	**−1,461.2**	**−989.7**
Total, Groups A Through D	4 984 ..	*123.8*	*317.0*	*160.5*	*1,342.6*	*1,781.3*	*2,459.5*	*−963.0*	*1,370.0*
E. Reserves and Related Items	4 802 A.	**−123.8**	**−317.0**	**−160.5**	**−1,342.6**	**−1,781.3**	**−2,459.5**	**963.0**	**−1,370.0**
Reserve assets	4 802 ..	−82.0	−257.2	−132.0	−1,305.5	−1,744.8	−2,437.7	981.5	−1,355.4
Use of Fund credit and loans	4 766 ..	−41.8	−59.8	−28.5	−37.1	−36.5	−21.8	−18.5	−14.6
Exceptional financing	4 920 ..	....	....	....	....	....	....	....	....
Conversion rates: manat per U.S. dollar	0 101 ..	**.9821**	**.9827**	**.9454**	**.8934**	**.8581**	**.8216**	**.8038**	**.8027**

[1] Excludes components that have been classified in the categories of Group E.

Table 2. STANDARD PRESENTATION, 2003–2010

(Millions of U.S. dollars)

	Code	2003	2004	2005	2006	2007	2008	2009	2010
CURRENT ACCOUNT.....................................	4 993 ..	−2,020.9	−2,589.2	167.3	3,707.6	9,018.9	16,452.8	10,174.9	15,040.4
A. GOODS...	4 100 ..	−98.5	161.3	3,299.1	7,745.3	15,224.3	23,011.7	14,582.9	19,730.4
Credit..	2 100 ..	2,624.6	3,743.0	7,649.0	13,014.6	21,269.3	30,586.3	21,096.8	26,476.0
General merchandise: exports f.o.b..............	2 110 ..	2,529.9	3,538.1	7,383.0	12,729.3	20,822.0	30,143.0	20,498.4	25,379.1
Goods for processing: exports f.o.b..............	2 150 ..	12.1	151.1	241.7	248.5	340.0	342.5	398.1	632.5
Repairs on goods.................................	2 160 ..	1.5	5.0	9.2	11.7	27.6	23.3	40.3	102.4
Goods procured in ports by carriers.............	2 170 ..	81.2	48.8	15.1	25.1	79.7	77.6	150.2	280.3
Nonmonetary gold.................................	2 180 ..	....	....	....	....	....	....	9.8	81.8
Debit..	3 100 ..	−2,723.1	−3,581.7	−4,349.9	−5,269.3	−6,045.0	−7,574.7	−6,513.9	−6,745.6
General merchandise: imports f.o.b..............	3 110 ..	−2,701.3	−3,459.7	−4,146.4	−4,948.7	−5,866.2	−7,284.5	−6,100.1	−6,297.9
Goods for processing: imports f.o.b..............	3 150 ..	−18.6	−112.0	−193.3	−236.9	−159.1	−244.5	−116.4	−355.2
Repairs on goods.................................	3 160 ..	−.5	−5.4	−5.0	−78.6	−9.2	−25.1	−284.0	−83.5
Goods procured in ports by carriers.............	3 170 ..	−2.7	−4.6	−5.2	−5.2	−10.5	−20.5	−13.3	−9.0
Nonmonetary gold.................................	3 180 ..	....	....	....	....	....	....	....	....
B. SERVICES..	4 200 ..	−1,614.5	−2,238.4	−1,970.0	−1,923.4	−2,131.0	−2,343.3	−1,610.6	−1,732.0
Total credit.....................................	2 200 ..	*432.0*	*492.0*	*683.0*	*939.9*	*1,247.5*	*1,547.9*	*1,778.9*	*2,113.9*
Total debit......................................	3 200 ..	*−2,046.5*	*−2,730.4*	*−2,653.0*	*−2,863.2*	*−3,378.6*	*−3,891.2*	*−3,389.5*	*−3,846.0*
Transportation services, credit.................	2 205 ..	198.2	205.7	239.2	407.7	604.7	793.9	662.1	644.0
Passenger.......................................	2 850 ..	*11.6*	*14.0*	*21.8*	*83.9*	*139.4*	*191.5*	*166.2*	*134.7*
Freight..	2 851 ..	*144.7*	*112.1*	*143.8*	*208.9*	*320.9*	*375.5*	*294.2*	*335.7*
Other...	2 852 ..	*41.9*	*79.6*	*73.6*	*114.8*	*144.3*	*227.0*	*201.6*	*173.5*
Sea transport, passenger.........................	2 207 ..	....	....	....	2.8	.4	.5	1.0	1.0
Sea transport, freight............................	2 208 ..	....	....	....	57.0	72.7	108.2	132.9	117.9
Sea transport, other..............................	2 209 ..	....	....	....	29.8	41.6	66.4	75.8	47.2
Air transport, passenger..........................	2 211 ..	....	....	....	78.6	127.4	173.1	136.2	122.9
Air transport, freight.............................	2 212 ..	....	....	....	29.8	58.6	93.1	39.4	79.5
Air transport, other..............................	2 213 ..	....	....	....	82.2	98.1	148.3	120.7	120.8
Other transport, passenger.......................	2 215 ..	....	....	....	2.6	11.7	17.8	29.0	10.8
Other transport, freight...........................	2 216 ..	....	....	....	122.1	189.7	174.2	122.0	138.3
Other transport, other............................	2 217 ..	....	....	....	2.8	4.6	12.2	5.0	5.5
Transportation services, debit..................	3 205 ..	−190.0	−289.4	−378.9	−509.2	−547.6	−682.5	−801.4	−800.7
Passenger.......................................	3 850 ..	*−8.8*	*−13.6*	*−24.0*	*−54.9*	*−116.8*	*−113.1*	*−82.3*	*−74.3*
Freight..	3 851 ..	*−140.7*	*−206.3*	*−270.1*	*−361.4*	*−340.1*	*−446.7*	*−591.3*	*−631.7*
Other...	3 852 ..	*−40.5*	*−69.5*	*−84.9*	*−92.9*	*−90.7*	*−122.7*	*−127.8*	*−94.7*
Sea transport, passenger.........................	3 207 ..	....	....	....	....	−.2	−.1	....	....
Sea transport, freight............................	3 208 ..	....	....	....	−73.5	−12.0	−31.1	−34.1	−42.9
Sea transport, other..............................	3 209 ..	....	....	....	−25.4	−32.4	−48.4	−44.1	−20.4
Air transport, passenger..........................	3 211 ..	....	....	....	−54.6	−115.7	−111.7	−81.1	−74.1
Air transport, freight.............................	3 212 ..	....	....	....	−46.6	−39.7	−42.5	−76.9	−49.3
Air transport, other..............................	3 213 ..	....	....	....	−57.4	−37.4	−42.0	−46.5	−55.7
Other transport, passenger.......................	3 215 ..	....	....	....	−.3	−.9	−1.2	−1.1	−.1
Other transport, freight...........................	3 216 ..	....	....	....	−241.3	−288.4	−373.1	−480.3	−539.4
Other transport, other............................	3 217 ..	....	....	....	−10.0	−20.9	−32.3	−37.3	−18.6
Travel, credit....................................	2 236 ..	57.7	65.3	77.7	116.9	177.8	191.2	378.7	657.4
Business travel...................................	2 237 ..	6.1	11.3	16.3	29.7	59.0	74.2	156.2	208.0
Personal travel...................................	2 240 ..	51.6	54.0	61.3	87.3	118.7	117.1	222.4	449.4
Travel, debit.....................................	3 236 ..	−111.4	−126.2	−164.0	−201.4	−263.6	−342.8	−405.6	−781.5
Business travel...................................	3 237 ..	−10.9	−15.5	−18.5	−22.2	−18.2	−27.1	−61.3	−194.3
Personal travel...................................	3 240 ..	−100.5	−110.7	−145.5	−179.2	−245.4	−315.7	−344.3	−587.2
Other services, credit...........................	2 200 BA	176.0	221.1	366.1	415.2	465.1	562.7	738.1	812.6
Communications..................................	2 245 ..	22.4	36.5	35.6	31.0	34.0	46.9	72.0	75.6
Construction.....................................	2 249 ..	3.8	9.8	9.4	45.8	45.8	109.1	174.3	152.7
Insurance..	2 253 ..	4.5	7.5	7.8	13.7	7.8	4.9	4.8	11.4
Financial...	2 260 ..	....	....	.1	1.4	.1	.1	.3	.3
Computer and information.......................	2 262 ..	....	....	.1	2.7	4.2	8.4	9.5	9.5
Royalties and licence fees........................	2 266 ..	....	....	....	.1	....	....	1.8	.1
Other business services..........................	2 268 ..	102.5	126.1	251.7	219.2	294.3	296.5	367.7	416.8
Personal, cultural, and recreational..............	2 287 ..	2.5	2.6	3.0	3.0	3.2	3.9	27.3	49.0
Government, n.i.e................................	2 291 ..	40.4	38.5	58.3	98.4	75.6	92.9	80.5	97.1
Other services, debit.............................	3 200 BA	−1,745.1	−2,314.9	−2,110.1	−2,152.7	−2,567.4	−2,865.9	−2,182.4	−2,263.8
Communications..................................	3 245 ..	−12.7	−16.5	−12.2	−10.8	−10.4	−28.0	−46.5	−53.0
Construction.....................................	3 249 ..	−1,023.2	−1,373.6	−1,498.8	−1,300.3	−1,471.1	−1,440.8	−773.7	−325.3
Insurance..	3 253 ..	−24.4	−31.6	−40.6	−70.9	−66.5	−52.8	−73.4	−110.9
Financial...	3 260 ..	−.1	−5.2	−10.4	−48.0	−121.7	−12.5	−15.4	−8.9
Computer and information.......................	3 262 ..	....	....	−.3	−7.3	−8.3	−11.5	−19.1	−21.3
Royalties and licence fees........................	3 266 ..	−.1	....	....	−1.3	−4.7	−4.8	−19.2	−16.5
Other business services..........................	3 268 ..	−660.0	−854.8	−514.9	−629.7	−825.2	−1,245.5	−1,142.7	−1,595.7
Personal, cultural, and recreational..............	3 287 ..	−5.1	−5.0	−5.0	−5.0	−5.4	−6.6	−31.8	−48.2
Government, n.i.e................................	3 291 ..	−19.4	−28.2	−27.9	−79.4	−54.1	−63.4	−60.8	−84.0

Table 2 (Continued). STANDARD PRESENTATION, 2003–2010

(Millions of U.S. dollars)

	Code	2003	2004	2005	2006	2007	2008	2009	2010
C. INCOME	4 300	**−442.0**	**−700.6**	**−1,645.6**	**−2,680.6**	**−5,079.4**	**−5,266.0**	**−3,519.2**	**−3,467.1**
Total credit	2 300	*52.6*	*65.3*	*201.8*	*280.0*	*327.8*	*595.1*	*551.4*	*675.5*
Total debit	3 300	*−494.7*	*−765.9*	*−1,847.4*	*−2,960.6*	*−5,407.2*	*−5,861.2*	*−4,070.6*	*−4,142.6*
Compensation of employees, credit	2 310	**1.8**	**12.3**	**133.0**	**127.9**	**75.6**	**102.3**	**72.9**	**72.5**
Compensation of employees, debit	3 310	**−53.6**	**−107.6**	**−112.2**	**−124.9**	**−131.1**	**−168.3**	**−115.7**	**−113.6**
Investment income, credit	2 320	**50.8**	**53.1**	**68.8**	**152.1**	**252.2**	**492.8**	**478.5**	**603.1**
Direct investment income	2 330	.2	....	.4	.5	.1	10.4	12.1	31.1
Dividends and distributed branch profits	2 332	.2	....	....	....	.1	10.4	12.1	31.1
Reinvested earnings and undistributed branch profits	2 333	....	....	....	....	....	....	....	....
Income on debt (interest)	2 334	....	....	....	....	....	....	....	....
Portfolio investment income	2 339	....	....	....	2.0	6.5	22.1	231.0	514.5
Income on equity	2 340	....	....	....	....	....	....	....	....
Income on bonds and notes	2 350	....	....	....	2.0	6.5	22.1	231.0	514.5
Income on money market instruments	2 360	....	....	....	....	....	....	....	....
Other investment income	2 370	50.6	53.1	68.4	149.6	245.6	460.3	235.4	57.5
Investment income, debit	3 320	**−441.1**	**−658.4**	**−1,735.2**	**−2,835.7**	**−5,276.1**	**−5,692.8**	**−3,954.9**	**−4,029.1**
Direct investment income	3 330	−422.3	−581.2	−1,581.7	−2,624.4	−4,995.3	−5,401.4	−3,663.7	−3,815.0
Dividends and distributed branch profits	3 332	....	....	....	−2,493.0	−4,920.9	−5,357.3	−3,615.2	−3,622.9
Reinvested earnings and undistributed branch profits	3 333	....	....	....	−131.3	−74.4	−44.1	−48.5	−192.1
Income on debt (interest)	3 334	....	....	....	....	....	....	....	....
Portfolio investment income	3 339	....	....	....	....	−4.2	−10.9	−6.9	−2.0
Income on equity	3 340	....	....	....	....	....	....	....	....
Income on bonds and notes	3 350	....	....	....	....	−4.2	−10.9	−6.9	−2.0
Income on money market instruments	3 360	....	....	....	....	....	....	....	....
Other investment income	3 370	−18.8	−77.2	−153.5	−211.4	−276.6	−280.5	−284.3	−212.0
D. CURRENT TRANSFERS	4 379	**134.1**	**188.5**	**483.9**	**566.3**	**1,005.0**	**1,050.5**	**721.7**	**509.1**
Credit	2 379	**225.1**	**262.6**	**626.2**	**748.2**	**1,313.4**	**1,500.1**	**1,292.4**	**1,420.4**
General government	2 380	62.6	63.3	122.3	69.2	103.2	67.7	65.4	70.8
Other sectors	2 390	162.4	199.3	503.9	679.0	1,210.2	1,432.4	1,226.9	1,349.7
Workers' remittances	2 391	154.1	191.3	490.2	662.3	1,192.1	1,416.1	1,181.7	1,337.8
Other current transfers	2 392	8.3	8.0	13.6	16.7	18.1	16.3	45.2	11.8
Debit	3 379	**−90.9**	**−74.1**	**−142.3**	**−182.0**	**−308.4**	**−449.7**	**−570.7**	**−911.3**
General government	3 380	−6.0	−5.8	−7.3	−7.2	−9.0	−16.3	−20.3	−31.9
Other sectors	3 390	−84.9	−68.3	−135.0	−174.8	−299.4	−433.4	−550.4	−879.4
Workers' remittances	3 391	−77.7	−64.7	−127.2	−149.5	−273.4	−399.0	−522.4	−840.0
Other current transfers	3 392	−7.2	−3.5	−7.9	−25.3	−26.0	−34.4	−28.0	−39.4
CAPITAL AND FINANCIAL ACCOUNT	4 996	**2,132.7**	**2,639.1**	**−41.6**	**−3,451.7**	**−8,658.2**	**−15,607.7**	**−8,713.7**	**−14,050.7**
CAPITAL ACCOUNT	4 994	**−23.1**	**−4.1**	**40.9**	**−3.8**	**−2.8**	**10.6**	**5.4**	**14.3**
Total credit	2 994	*15.0*	*24.0*	*70.2*	*25.0*	*28.0*	*36.0*	*19.1*	*22.1*
Total debit	3 994	*−38.1*	*−28.1*	*−29.3*	*−28.9*	*−30.8*	*−25.3*	*−13.7*	*−7.8*
Capital transfers, credit	2 400	**15.0**	**24.0**	**70.2**	**22.3**	**19.5**	**36.0**	**19.1**	**22.1**
General government	2 401	....	....	....	....	....	....	....	....
Debt forgiveness	2 402	....	....	....	....	....	....	....	....
Other capital transfers	2 410	....	....	....	....	....	....	....	....
Other sectors	2 430	15.0	24.0	70.2	22.3	19.5	36.0	19.1	22.1
Migrants' transfers	2 431	15.0	24.0	70.2	22.3	19.5	36.0	19.1	22.1
Debt forgiveness	2 432	....	....	....	....	....	....	....	....
Other capital transfers	2 440	....	....	....	....	....	....	....	....
Capital transfers, debit	3 400	**−38.1**	**−28.1**	**−29.3**	**−26.6**	**−30.8**	**−25.3**	**−13.7**	**−7.8**
General government	3 401	−.1	−.1	−.1	−.1	....	....	....	....
Debt forgiveness	3 402	....	....	....	....	....	....	....	....
Other capital transfers	3 410	....	....	....	....	....	....	....	....
Other sectors	3 430	−38.0	−28.0	−29.2	−26.4	−30.8	−25.3	−13.7	−7.8
Migrants' transfers	3 431	−38.0	−28.0	−29.2	−26.4	−30.8	−25.3	−13.7	−7.8
Debt forgiveness	3 432	....	....	....	....	....	....	....	....
Other capital transfers	3 440	....	....	....	....	....	....	....	....
Nonproduced nonfinancial assets, credit	2 480	....	....	....	2.7	8.5	....	....	....
Nonproduced nonfinancial assets, debit	3 480	....	....	....	−2.3	....	....	....	....

Table 2 (Continued). STANDARD PRESENTATION, 2003–2010

(Millions of U.S. dollars)

	Code	2003	2004	2005	2006	2007	2008	2009	2010
FINANCIAL ACCOUNT	4 995	2,155.8	2,643.2	−82.5	−3,447.9	−8,655.4	−15,618.4	−8,719.1	−14,065.0
A. DIRECT INVESTMENT	4 500	2,351.7	2,351.3	459.2	−1,289.5	−5,034.5	−540.8	147.2	331.2
Direct investment abroad	4 505	−933.3	−1,204.8	−1,220.8	−705.5	−285.6	−555.6	−326.1	−232.0
Equity capital	4 510	−933.3	−1,204.8	−1,220.8	−705.5	−516.0	−380.0	−321.9	−232.0
Claims on affiliated enterprises	4 515	−933.3	−1,204.8	−1,220.8	−705.5	−516.9	−380.2	−321.9	−235.7
Liabilities to affiliated enterprises	4 520	....	....	....	....	.9	.2	....	3.7
Reinvested earnings	4 525	....	....	....	....				....
Other capital	4 530	....	....	....	....	230.4	−175.6	−4.2	....
Claims on affiliated enterprises	4 535	....	....	....	....	....	−175.6	−4.2	
Liabilities to affiliated enterprises	4 540	....	....	....	....			....	
Direct investment in Azerbaijan	4 555	3,285.0	3,556.1	1,679.9	−584.0	−4,748.9	14.8	473.3	563.1
Equity capital	4 560	3,285.0	3,556.1	1,679.9	−897.2	−5,101.2	−495.2	49.4	371.0
Claims on direct investors	4 565	−722.3	−1,163.0	−2,796.5	−5,069.4	−9,105.1	−3,971.7	−2,426.7	−2,786.2
Liabilities to direct investors	4 570	4,007.3	4,719.1	4,476.4	4,172.1	4,003.9	3,476.5	2,476.1	3,157.2
Reinvested earnings	4 575	....	....	....	131.3	74.4	44.1	48.5	192.1
Other capital	4 580	....	....	....	182.0	277.9	465.9	375.4	
Claims on direct investors	4 585	....	....	....	−.6	−3.1	−.1	....	....
Liabilities to direct investors	4 590	....	....	....	182.5	281.0	466.0	375.4	....
B. PORTFOLIO INVESTMENT	4 600	....	−18.1	30.5	−12.0	−26.4	−347.4	−138.8	−138.8
Assets	4 602	....	−18.1	−47.8	−34.4	−110.9	−320.8	−84.3	−163.3
Equity securities	4 610	....	1.9	....	−3.1	−11.9	−21.4	−3.5	9.8
Monetary authorities	4 611	....	....	....	....	....	....	....	....
General government	4 612	....	....	....	−3.0	....	....	....	....
Banks	4 613	....	1.9	....	....	....	....	....	....
Other sectors	4 614	....	....	....	−.1	−11.9	−21.4	−3.5	9.8
Debt securities	4 619	....	−20.0	−47.8	−31.3	−99.0	−299.5	−80.8	−173.1
Bonds and notes	4 620	....	−20.0	−47.8	−31.3	−99.0	−299.5	−80.8	−173.1
Monetary authorities	4 621	....	....	....	....	....	....	....	....
General government	4 622	....	....	....	....	−2.7	....	24.9	....
Banks	4 623	....	−19.8	....	−31.3	−28.6	−22.0	−15.5	....
Other sectors	4 624	....	−.2	....	....	−67.7	−277.4	−90.2	−173.1
Money market instruments	4 630	....	....	....	....	....	....	....	....
Monetary authorities	4 631	....	....	....	....	....	....	....	....
General government	4 632	....	....	....	....	....	....	....	....
Banks	4 633	....	....	....	....	....	....	....	....
Other sectors	4 634	....	....	....	....	....	....	....	....
Liabilities	4 652	....	....	78.3	22.3	84.5	−26.6	−54.5	24.5
Equity securities	4 660	....	....	....	.8	2.0	....	....	.6
Banks	4 663	....	....	....	.8	....	....	....	.6
Other sectors	4 664	....	....	....	....	2.0	....	....	....
Debt securities	4 669	....	....	78.3	21.6	82.5	−26.6	−54.5	23.9
Bonds and notes	4 670	....	....	78.3	21.6	82.5	−26.6	−54.5	23.9
Monetary authorities	4 671	....	....	....	....	....	....	....	....
General government	4 672	....	....	....	....	62.0	−35.4	....	....
Banks	4 673	....	....	78.3	32.1	14.0	18.5	−49.5	−9.7
Other sectors	4 674	....	....	....	−10.5	6.6	−9.7	−5.1	33.6
Money market instruments	4 680	....	....	....	....	....	....	....	....
Monetary authorities	4 681	....	....	....	....	....	....	....	....
General government	4 682	....	....	....	....	....	....	....	....
Banks	4 683	....	....	....	....	....	....	....	....
Other sectors	4 684	....	....	....	....	....	....	....	....
C. FINANCIAL DERIVATIVES	4 910	....	....	....	....	....	....	....	....
Monetary authorities	4 911	....	....	....	....	....	....	....	....
General government	4 912	....	....	....	....	....	....	....	....
Banks	4 913	....	....	....	....	....	....	....	....
Other sectors	4 914	....	....	....	....	....	....	....	....
Assets	4 900	....	....	....	....	....	....	....	....
Monetary authorities	4 901	....	....	....	....	....	....	....	....
General government	4 902	....	....	....	....	....	....	....	....
Banks	4 903	....	....	....	....	....	....	....	....
Other sectors	4 904	....	....	....	....	....	....	....	....
Liabilities	4 905	....	....	....	....	....	....	....	....
Monetary authorities	4 906	....	....	....	....	....	....	....	....
General government	4 907	....	....	....	....	....	....	....	....
Banks	4 908	....	....	....	....	....	....	....	....
Other sectors	4 909	....	....	....	....	....	....	....	....

Table 2 (Concluded). STANDARD PRESENTATION, 2003–2010

(Millions of U.S. dollars)

	Code	2003	2004	2005	2006	2007	2008	2009	2010
D. OTHER INVESTMENT........................	4 700 ..	−113.9	567.2	−440.2	−840.9	−1,849.7	−12,292.5	−9,708.9	−12,902.0
Assets..................................	4 703 ..	−169.2	−360.4	−1,365.3	−1,416.7	−2,687.8	−13,197.5	−9,326.4	−14,698.0
Trade credits..........................	4 706 ..	−42.9	−57.9	−766.4	−948.5	−1,257.2	−1,984.3	−1,077.1	−1,471.6
General government................	4 707 ..	....	....	....	....	....	....	....	....
of which: Short-term	4 709 ..	....	....	....	....	....	....	....	....
Other sectors.......................	4 710 ..	−42.9	−57.9	−766.4	−948.5	−1,257.2	−1,984.3	−1,077.1	−1,471.6
of which: Short-term	4 712 ..	*−42.9*	*−57.9*	*−766.4*	*−948.5*	*−1,257.2*	*−1,984.3*	*−1,077.1*	*−1,471.6*
Loans..................................	4 714 ..	.2	....	−12.6	−42.0	−142.3	−731.2	−301.4	−266.6
Monetary authorities.............	4 715 ..	....	....	....	....	....	....	....	....
of which: Short-term	4 718 ..	....	....	....	....	....	....	....	....
General government................	4 719 ..	....	....	....	2.1	....	....	....	....
of which: Short-term	4 721 ..	....	....	....	....	....	....	....	....
Banks................................	4 722 ..	....	....	−9.5	−43.0	−112.3	−40.4	9.2	−84.8
of which: Short-term	4 724 ..	....	....	....	....	....	....	....	....
Other sectors.......................	4 725 ..	.2	....	−3.1	−1.1	−30.0	−690.8	−310.6	−181.8
of which: Short-term	4 727 ..	*.2*	....	....	*−1.1*	....	....	....	....
Currency and deposits................	4 730 ..	−138.3	−307.8	−549.9	−426.3	−1,288.2	−10,482.1	−7,947.9	−12,959.8
Monetary authorities.............	4 731 ..	....	....	....	....	....	....	....	....
General government................	4 732 ..	−123.4	−127.0	−475.7	−410.8	−1,153.6	−9,612.2	−3,672.7	−9,103.7
Banks................................	4 733 ..	−14.9	20.1	−74.2	−15.5	−134.6	−863.2	−121.7	−461.0
Other sectors.......................	4 734 ..	....	−200.9	....	....	....	−6.6	−4,153.5	−3,395.1
Other assets..........................	4 736 ..	11.8	5.3	−36.4	....	....	....	....	....
Monetary authorities.............	4 737 ..	....	1.8	....	....	....	....	....	....
of which: Short-term	4 739 ..	....	*1.8*	....	....	....	....	....	....
General government................	4 740 ..	14.0	3.5	....	....	....	....	....	....
of which: Short-term	4 742 ..	....	....	....	....	....	....	....	....
Banks................................	4 743 ..	−1.8	....	....	....	....	....	....	....
of which: Short-term	4 745 ..	*−1.8*	....	....	....	....	....	....	....
Other sectors.......................	4 746 ..	−.5	....	−36.4	....	....	....	....	....
of which: Short-term	4 748 ..	*−.5*	....	....	....	....	....	....	....
Liabilities.............................	4 753 ..	**55.4**	**927.7**	**925.1**	**575.9**	**838.1**	**905.1**	**−382.5**	**1,796.0**
Trade credits..........................	4 756 ..	−169.9	−89.9	−97.4	−302.2	163.1	42.3	75.6	523.4
General government................	4 757 ..	....	....	....	....	....	....	....	....
of which: Short-term	4 759 ..	....	....	....	....	....	....	....	....
Other sectors.......................	4 760 ..	−169.9	−89.9	−97.4	−302.2	163.1	42.3	75.6	523.4
of which: Short-term	4 762 ..	*−169.9*	*−89.9*	*−97.4*	*−302.2*	*163.1*	*42.3*	*75.6*	*523.4*
Loans..................................	4 764 ..	210.3	1,038.1	1,179.6	701.4	597.9	759.9	−548.6	1,316.9
Monetary authorities.............	4 765 ..	−7.4	−59.8	−29.5	−20.2	−37.9	−21.8	−18.5	−14.6
of which: Use of Fund credit and loans from the Fund..	4 766 ..	*−41.8*	*−59.8*	*−28.5*	*−37.1*	*−36.5*	*−21.8*	*−18.5*	*−14.6*
of which: Short-term	4 768 ..	....	....	....	....	....	....	....	....
General government................	4 769 ..	32.4	34.8	37.5	80.5	139.1	166.2	277.4	456.6
of which: Short-term	4 771 ..	....	....	....	....	....	....	....	....
Banks................................	4 772 ..	−.2	4.1	31.9	159.4	665.1	82.3	−129.3	776.7
of which: Short-term	4 774 ..	....	....	....	....	....	....	....	....
Other sectors.......................	4 775 ..	185.5	1,058.9	1,139.7	481.8	−168.3	533.2	−678.2	98.2
of which: Short-term	4 777 ..	....	....	....	....	....	....	....	....
Currency and deposits................	4 780 ..	....	−20.5	14.8	176.7	77.1	102.9	−149.8	−44.3
Monetary authorities.............	4 781 ..	....	....	....	....	....	....	....	....
General government................	4 782 ..	....	....	....	....	....	....	....	....
Banks................................	4 783 ..	....	−20.5	14.8	176.7	77.1	102.9	−149.8	−44.3
Other sectors.......................	4 784 ..	....	....	....	....	....	....	....	....
Other liabilities.......................	4 786 ..	15.0	....	−171.9	....	....	....	240.2	....
Monetary authorities.............	4 787 ..	....	....	....	....	....	....	240.2	....
of which: Short-term	4 789 ..	....	....	....	....	....	....	....	....
General government................	4 790 ..	....	....	....	....	....	....	....	....
of which: Short-term	4 792 ..	....	....	....	....	....	....	....	....
Banks................................	4 793 ..	....	....	....	....	....	....	....	....
of which: Short-term	4 795 ..	....	....	....	....	....	....	....	....
Other sectors.......................	4 796 ..	15.0	....	−171.9	....	....	....	....	....
of which: Short-term	4 798 ..	*15.0*	....	*−171.9*	....	....	....	....	....
E. RESERVE ASSETS............................	4 802 ..	**−82.0**	**−257.2**	**−132.0**	**−1,305.5**	**−1,744.8**	**−2,437.7**	**981.5**	**−1,355.4**
Monetary gold...........................	4 812 ..	....	....	....	....	....	....	....	....
Special drawing rights..................	4 811 ..	−17.0	3.6	−.4	−1.4	5.5	8.5	−235.6	−2.9
Reserve position in the Fund..........	4 810 ..	....	....	....	....	−.1	....	−.1	....
Foreign exchange.......................	4 803 ..	−65.0	−260.8	−131.6	−1,304.2	−1,750.2	−2,446.2	1,217.2	−1,352.5
Other claims............................	4 813 ..	....	....	....	....	....	....	....	....
NET ERRORS AND OMISSIONS............................	4 998 ..	**−111.8**	**−49.9**	**−125.7**	**−255.9**	**−360.6**	**−845.1**	**−1,461.2**	**−989.7**

Table 3. INTERNATIONAL INVESTMENT POSITION (End-period stocks), 2003–2010

(Millions of U.S. dollars)

	Code	2003	2004	2005	2006	2007	2008	2009	2010
ASSETS	8 995 C.	**3,154.6**	**4,937.3**	**7,456.4**	**10,180.5**	**14,187.4**	**28,548.6**	....	....
Direct investment abroad	8 505 ..	**1,259.7**	**2,464.5**	**3,685.3**	**4,390.8**	**4,676.4**	**5,232.0**	....	....
Equity capital and reinvested earnings	8 506 ..	1,259.7	2,464.5	3,685.3	4,390.8	4,910.5	5,465.8	....	....
Claims on affiliated enterprises	8 507 ..	1,259.7	2,464.5	3,685.3	4,390.8	4,910.5	5,465.8	....	....
Liabilities to affiliated enterprises	8 508 ..	....	....	....	....	....	....	....	....
Other capital	8 530 ..	....	....	....	....	−234.1	−233.8	....	....
Claims on affiliated enterprises	8 535 ..	....	....	....	....	....	....	....	....
Liabilities to affiliated enterprises	8 540 ..	....	....	....	....	−234.1	−233.8	....	....
Portfolio investment	8 602 ..	**.4**	**20.4**	**84.6**	**119.0**	**229.9**	**550.7**	....	....
Equity securities	8 610 ..	....	....	....	....	....	....	....	....
Monetary authorities	8 611 ..	....	....	....	....	....	....	....	....
General government	8 612 ..	....	....	....	....	....	....	....	....
Banks	8 613 ..	....	....	....	....	....	....	....	....
Other sectors	8 614 ..	....	....	....	....	....	....	....	....
Debt securities	8 619 ..	.4	20.4	84.6	119.0	229.9	550.7	....	....
Bonds and notes	8 620 ..	.4	20.4	84.6	119.0	229.9	550.7	....	....
Monetary authorities	8 621 ..	....	....	....	....	....	....	....	....
General government	8 622 ..	....	....	....	....	....	....	....	....
Banks	8 623 ..	.4	20.4	84.6	119.0	229.9	550.7	....	....
Other sectors	8 624 ..	....	....	....	....	....	....	....	....
Money market instruments	8 630 ..	....	....	....	....	....	....	....	....
Monetary authorities	8 631 ..	....	....	....	....	....	....	....	....
General government	8 632 ..	....	....	....	....	....	....	....	....
Banks	8 633 ..	....	....	....	....	....	....	....	....
Other sectors	8 634 ..	....	....	....	....	....	....	....	....
Financial derivatives	8 900 ..	....	....	....	....	....	....	....	....
Monetary authorities	8 901 ..	....	....	....	....	....	....	....	....
General government	8 902 ..	....	....	....	....	....	....	....	....
Banks	8 903 ..	....	....	....	....	....	....	....	....
Other sectors	8 904 ..	....	....	....	....	....	....	....	....
Other investment	8 703 ..	**1,091.7**	**1,376.4**	**2,508.8**	**3,170.4**	**5,008.0**	**16,298.6**	....	....
Trade credits	8 706 ..	....	....	824.3	948.5	1,257.2	1,984.3	....	....
General government	8 707 ..	....	....	....	....	....	....	....	....
of which: Short-term	8 709 ..	....	....	....	....	....	....	....	....
Other sectors	8 710 ..	....	....	824.3	948.5	1,257.2	1,984.3	....	....
of which: Short-term	8 712 ..	....	....	*824.3*	*948.5*	*1,257.2*	*1,984.3*	....	....
Loans	8 714 ..	....	....	15.3	62.5	219.3	841.7	....	....
Monetary authorities	8 715 ..	....	....	....	....	....	....	....	....
of which: Short-term	8 718 ..	....	....	....	....	....	....	....	....
General government	8 719 ..	....	....	....	....	14.5	14.5	....	....
of which: Short-term	8 721 ..	....	....	....	....	....	....	....	....
Banks	8 722 ..	....	....	12.2	58.3	170.6	102.2	....	....
of which: Short-term	8 724 ..	....	....	....	....	....	....	....	....
Other sectors	8 725 ..	....	....	3.1	4.2	34.2	725.0	....	....
of which: Short-term	8 727 ..	....	....	*3.1*	....	....	....	....	....
Currency and deposits	8 730 ..	1,039.4	1,376.4	1,669.2	2,159.4	3,531.5	13,472.6	....	....
Monetary authorities	8 731 ..	....	....	....	....	....	....	....	....
General government	8 732 ..	815.6	971.8	1,394.0	1,868.7	3,106.2	12,088.2	....	....
Banks	8 733 ..	223.8	203.7	275.2	290.7	425.3	1,377.8	....	....
Other sectors	8 734 ..	....	200.9	....	....	....	6.6	....	....
Other assets	8 736 ..	52.3	....	....	....	....	....	....	....
Monetary authorities	8 737 ..	....	....	....	....	....	....	....	....
of which: Short-term	8 739 ..	....	....	....	....	....	....	....	....
General government	8 740 ..	....	....	....	....	....	....	....	....
of which: Short-term	8 742 ..	....	....	....	....	....	....	....	....
Banks	8 743 ..	....	....	....	....	....	....	....	....
of which: Short-term	8 745 ..	....	....	....	....	....	....	....	....
Other sectors	8 746 ..	52.3	....	....	....	....	....	....	....
of which: Short-term	8 748 ..	*52.3*	....	....	....	....	....	....	....
Reserve assets	8 802 ..	**802.8**	**1,076.0**	**1,177.7**	**2,500.3**	**4,273.1**	**6,467.3**	....	....
Monetary gold	8 812 ..	....	....	....	....	....	....	....	....
Special drawing rights	8 811 ..	18.0	14.5	13.9	15.4	10.1	1.6	237.8	236.6
Reserve position in the Fund	8 810 ..	....	....	....	....	.1	.1	.2	.2
Foreign exchange	8 803 ..	784.8	1,061.5	1,163.8	2,484.9	4,262.9	6,465.6	....	....
Other claims	8 813 ..	....	....	....	....	....	....	....	....

Table 3 (Concluded). INTERNATIONAL INVESTMENT POSITION (End-period stocks), 2003–2010

(Millions of U.S. dollars)

	Code	2003	2004	2005	2006	2007	2008	2009	2010
LIABILITIES	8 995 D.	10,903.6	14,395.4	16,805.1	17,247.0	13,555.6	15,945.6	....	....
Direct investment in Azerbaijan	8 555 ..	8,639.1	11,482.4	12,757.5	11,346.5	6,597.6	6,611.7	....	....
Equity capital and reinvested earnings	8 556 ..	8,639.1	11,482.4	12,757.5	11,346.5	6,597.6	6,611.7	....	....
Claims on direct investors	8 557 ..	−2,995.8	−4,158.8	−7,360.1	−13,257.0	−22,365.3	−26,337.1	....	....
Liabilities to direct investors	8 558 ..	11,634.9	15,641.2	20,117.6	24,603.5	28,962.9	32,948.8	....	....
Other capital	8 580 ..	....	....	....	....	....	....		
Claims on direct investors	8 585 ..	....	....	....	....	....	....		
Liabilities to direct investors	8 590 ..	....	....	....	....	....	....		
Portfolio investment	8 652 ..	....	....	97.1	119.4	203.9	177.3	....	....
Equity securities	8 660 ..	....	....	....	....	....	....		
Banks	8 663 ..	....	....	....	....	....	....		
Other sectors	8 664 ..	....	....	....	....	....	....		
Debt securities	8 669 ..	....	....	97.1	119.4	203.9	177.3		
Bonds and notes	8 670 ..	....	....	97.1	119.4	203.9	177.3		
Monetary authorities	8 671 ..	....	....	....	....	....	....		
General government	8 672 ..	....	....	....	....	....	....		
Banks	8 673 ..	....	....	97.1	119.4	203.9	177.3		
Other sectors	8 674 ..	....	....	....	....	....	....		
Money market instruments	8 680 ..	....	....	....	....	....	....		
Monetary authorities	8 681 ..	....	....	....	....	....	....		
General government	8 682 ..	....	....	....	....	....	....		
Banks	8 683 ..	....	....	....	....	....	....		
Other sectors	8 684 ..	....	....	....	....	....	....		
Financial derivatives	8 905 ..	....	....	....	....	....	....		
Monetary authorities	8 906 ..	....	....	....	....	....	....		
General government	8 907 ..	....	....	....	....	....	....		
Banks	8 908 ..	....	....	....	....	....	....		
Other sectors	8 909 ..	....	....	....	....	....	....		
Other investment	8 753 ..	2,264.5	2,913.0	3,950.5	5,781.1	6,754.1	9,156.6	....	....
Trade credits	8 756 ..	....	....	....	....	163.1	42.3	....	....
General government	8 757 ..	....	....	....	....	....	....		
of which: Short-term	8 759 ..	....	....	....	....	....	....		
Other sectors	8 760 ..	....	....	....	....	163.1	42.3	....	....
of which: Short-term	8 762 ..	....	....	....	....	*163.1*	*42.3*	....	....
Loans	8 764 ..	1,730.5	2,825.4	3,889.3	5,543.2	6,276.0	7,758.0	....	....
Monetary authorities	8 765 ..	476.9	455.0	392.2	393.3	375.0	345.2	....	....
of which: Use of Fund credit and loans from the Fund	8 766 ..	*259.3*	*208.4*	*163.6*	*134.2*	*103.0*	*79.2*	*61.8*	*45.8*
of which: Short-term	8 768 ..	....	....	....	....	....	....		
General government	8 769 ..	131.4	237.0	351.9	1,007.1	1,210.4	1,489.1	....	....
of which: Short-term	8 771 ..	....	....	....	....	....	....		
Banks	8 772 ..	4.4	8.5	40.4	258.0	923.1	1,654.8	....	....
of which: Short-term	8 774 ..	*4.4*	....	....	....	....	....		
Other sectors	8 775 ..	1,117.8	2,124.9	3,104.8	3,884.8	3,767.5	4,268.9	....	....
of which: Short-term	8 777 ..	....	....	....	....	....	....		
Currency and deposits	8 780 ..	108.1	87.6	61.2	237.9	315.0	1,356.3	....	....
Monetary authorities	8 781 ..	....	....	....	....	....	....		
General government	8 782 ..	....	....	....	....	....	....		
Banks	8 783 ..	108.1	87.6	61.2	237.9	315.0	1,356.3	....	....
Other sectors	8 784 ..	....	....	....	....	....	....		
Other liabilities	8 786 ..	425.9	....	....	....	....	....		
Monetary authorities	8 787 ..	....	....	....	....	....	....		
of which: Short-term	8 789 ..	....	....	....	....	....	....		
General government	8 790 ..	....	....	....	....	....	....		
of which: Short-term	8 792 ..	....	....	....	....	....	....		
Banks	8 793 ..	....	....	....	....	....	....		
of which: Short-term	8 795 ..	....	....	....	....	....	....		
Other sectors	8 796 ..	425.9	....	....	....	....	....		
of which: Short-term	8 798 ..	*425.9*	....	....	....	....	....		
NET INTERNATIONAL INVESTMENT POSITION	8 995 ..	−7,748.9	−9,458.0	−9,348.7	−7,066.5	631.8	12,603.0	....	....
Conversion rates: manat per U.S. dollar (end of period)	0 102 ..	.9846	.9806	.9186	.8714	.8453	.8010	.8031	.7979

Table 1. ANALYTIC PRESENTATION, 2003–2010

(Millions of U.S. dollars)

	Code	2003	2004	2005	2006	2007	2008	2009	2010
A. Current Account[1].....................	4 993 Z.	**−473.5**	**−307.1**	**−700.6**	**−1,403.7**	**−1,315.1**	**−1,222.1**	**−893.3**	**−899.9**
Goods: exports f.o.b....................	2 100 ..	426.5	477.5	549.1	703.5	801.9	955.8	710.7	702.4
Goods: imports f.o.b....................	3 100 ..	−1,758.6	−1,906.8	−2,377.4	−2,766.5	−2,956.9	−3,199.0	−2,535.3	−2,590.6
Balance on Goods....................	4 100 ..	*−1,332.0*	*−1,429.4*	*−1,828.3*	*−2,063.0*	*−2,155.0*	*−2,243.2*	*−1,824.7*	*−1,888.2*
Services: credit........................	2 200 ..	2,054.7	2,244.1	2,510.9	2,436.1	2,599.3	2,533.9	2,266.1	2,405.7
Services: debit........................	3 200 ..	−1,092.4	−1,231.3	−1,286.4	−1,610.9	−1,579.6	−1,402.9	−1,196.0	−1,181.1
Balance on Goods and Services....................	4 991 ..	*−369.8*	*−416.6*	*−603.8*	*−1,237.8*	*−1,135.3*	*−1,112.2*	*−754.6*	*−663.6*
Income: credit........................	2 300 ..	79.1	79.7	97.0	119.4	121.3	113.4	57.7	38.8
Income: debit........................	3 300 ..	−231.6	−221.1	−279.1	−337.4	−352.9	−198.6	−209.9	−272.5
Balance on Goods, Services, and Income....................	4 992 ..	*−522.2*	*−557.9*	*−785.9*	*−1,455.8*	*−1,366.9*	*−1,197.5*	*−906.8*	*−897.3*
Current transfers: credit....................	2 379 Z.	59.8	264.7	103.3	66.4	71.0	75.9	96.6	99.3
Current transfers: debit....................	3 379 ..	−11.1	−13.9	−18.1	−14.3	−19.2	−100.5	−83.1	−101.9
B. Capital Account[1].....................	4 994 Z.	**−37.4**	**−47.9**	**−60.4**	**−63.5**	**−75.7**	**−16.8**	**−7.2**	**−3.6**
Capital account: credit....................	2 994 Z.	....	....	....	....	....	....	....	....
Capital account: debit....................	3 994 ..	−37.4	−47.9	−60.4	−63.5	−75.7	−16.8	−7.2	−3.6
Total, Groups A Plus B....................	4 981 ..	*−510.9*	*−355.0*	*−761.1*	*−1,467.2*	*−1,390.8*	*−1,238.9*	*−900.5*	*−903.5*
C. Financial Account[1].....................	4 995 W.	**535.5**	**358.5**	**822.1**	**1,280.2**	**1,030.6**	**1,223.4**	**1,120.2**	**1,123.4**
Direct investment abroad....................	4 505 ..	....	....	....	....	....	....	....	....
Direct investment in The Bahamas....................	4 555 Z.	190.2	273.6	563.4	706.4	713.4	860.2	664.0	861.5
Portfolio investment assets....................	4 602 ..	....	....	....	−18.8	−7.2	−21.9	−16.7	−25.4
Equity securities....................	4 610 ..	....	....	....	....	−4.1	−12.5	−4.2	−13.0
Debt securities....................	4 619 ..	....	....	....	−18.8	−3.1	−9.4	−12.5	−12.4
Portfolio investment liabilities....................	4 652 Z.	....	....	....	....	....	....	....	....
Equity securities....................	4 660 ..	....	....	....	....	....	....	....	....
Debt securities....................	4 669 Z.	....	....	....	....	....	....	....	....
Financial derivatives....................	4 910 ..	....	....	....	....	....	....	....	....
Financial derivatives assets....................	4 900 ..	....	....	....	....	....	....	....	....
Financial derivatives liabilities....................	4 905 ..	....	....	....	....	....	....	....	....
Other investment assets....................	4 703 ..	46,576.8	19,293.4	−11,064.2	−9,016.7	−15,801.8	−4,830.6	25,373.1	4,969.8
Monetary authorities....................	4 701 ..	....	....	....	....	....	....	....	....
General government....................	4 704 ..	....	....	....	....	....	....	....	....
Banks....................	4 705 ..	46,576.8	19,293.4	−11,064.2	−9,016.7	−15,801.8	−4,830.6	25,373.1	4,969.8
Other sectors....................	4 728 ..	....	....	....	....	....	....	....	....
Other investment liabilities....................	4 753 W.	−46,231.5	−19,208.5	11,322.9	9,609.3	16,126.3	5,215.8	−24,900.1	−4,682.4
Monetary authorities....................	4 753 WA	....	....	....	....	....	....	178.5	....
General government....................	4 753 ZB	52.6	−20.6	−8.5	−3.5	−6.4	106.4	323.6	148.4
Banks....................	4 753 ZC	−46,679.2	−19,358.0	11,111.7	9,159.8	15,715.2	4,866.9	−25,395.0	−4,946.2
Other sectors....................	4 753 ZD	395.1	170.1	219.7	453.0	417.4	242.6	−7.2	115.4
Total, Groups A Through C....................	4 983 ..	*24.6*	*3.5*	*61.1*	*−187.1*	*−360.2*	*−15.5*	*219.8*	*220.0*
D. Net Errors and Omissions....................	4 998 ..	**85.5**	**179.8**	**−149.2**	**107.5**	**313.9**	**124.7**	**32.5**	**−172.2**
Total, Groups A Through D....................	4 984 ..	*110.1*	*183.3*	*−88.1*	*−79.5*	*−46.3*	*109.2*	*252.3*	*47.7*
E. Reserves and Related Items....................	4 802 A.	**−110.1**	**−183.3**	**88.1**	**79.5**	**46.3**	**−109.2**	**−252.3**	**−47.7**
Reserve assets....................	4 802 ..	−110.1	−183.3	88.1	79.5	46.3	−109.2	−252.3	−47.7
Use of Fund credit and loans....................	4 766 ..	....	....	....	....	....	....	....	....
Exceptional financing....................	4 920 ..	....	....	....	....	....	....	....	....
Conversion rates: Bahamian dollars per U.S. dollar....................	0 101 ..	**1.0000**	**1.0000**	**1.0000**	**1.0000**	**1.0000**	**1.0000**	**1.0000**	**1.0000**

[1] Excludes components that have been classified in the categories of Group E.

Table 2. STANDARD PRESENTATION, 2003–2010

(Millions of U.S. dollars)

	Code	2003	2004	2005	2006	2007	2008	2009	2010
CURRENT ACCOUNT	4 993 ..	**−473.5**	**−307.1**	**−700.6**	**−1,403.7**	**−1,315.1**	**−1,222.1**	**−893.3**	**−899.9**
A. GOODS	4 100 ..	**−1,332.0**	**−1,429.4**	**−1,828.3**	**−2,063.0**	**−2,155.0**	**−2,243.2**	**−1,824.7**	**−1,888.2**
Credit	2 100 ..	**426.5**	**477.5**	**549.1**	**703.5**	**801.9**	**955.8**	**710.7**	**702.4**
General merchandise: exports f.o.b.	2 110 ..	340.4	363.6	388.1	454.4	502.5	560.0	465.7	459.2
Goods for processing: exports f.o.b.	2 150 ..	....	....	....	....	....	....	....	....
Repairs on goods	2 160 ..	....	....	....	....	....	....	....	....
Goods procured in ports by carriers	2 170 ..	86.2	113.9	161.0	249.1	299.4	395.8	244.9	243.3
Nonmonetary gold	2 180 ..	....	....	....	....	....	....	....	....
Debit	3 100 ..	**−1,758.6**	**−1,906.8**	**−2,377.4**	**−2,766.5**	**−2,956.9**	**−3,199.0**	**−2,535.3**	**−2,590.6**
General merchandise: imports f.o.b.	3 110 ..	−1,755.5	−1,903.6	−2,374.3	−2,763.3	−2,948.7	−3,193.5	−2,522.6	−2,575.3
Goods for processing: imports f.o.b.	3 150 ..	....	....	....	....	....	....	....	....
Repairs on goods	3 160 ..	....	....	....	....	....	....	....	....
Goods procured in ports by carriers	3 170 ..	−3.1	−3.2	−3.1	−3.2	−8.3	−5.6	−12.7	−15.3
Nonmonetary gold	3 180 ..	....	....	....	....	....	....	....	....
B. SERVICES	4 200 ..	**962.2**	**1,012.8**	**1,224.5**	**825.2**	**1,019.8**	**1,131.0**	**1,070.0**	**1,224.6**
Total credit	2 200 ..	*2,054.7*	*2,244.1*	*2,510.9*	*2,436.1*	*2,599.3*	*2,533.9*	*2,266.1*	*2,405.7*
Total debit	3 200 ..	*−1,092.4*	*−1,231.3*	*−1,286.4*	*−1,610.9*	*−1,579.6*	*−1,402.9*	*−1,196.0*	*−1,181.1*
Transportation services, credit	2 205 ..	**56.7**	**55.3**	**55.6**	**57.4**	**57.5**	**52.7**	**79.2**	**118.2**
Passenger	2 850 ..	*13.0*	*13.0*	*9.7*	*9.9*	*10.7*	*11.2*	*10.7*	*11.7*
Freight	2 851 ..	....	....	....	....	....	....	....	....
Other	2 852 ..	*43.7*	*42.3*	*45.9*	*47.6*	*46.8*	*41.6*	*68.5*	*106.6*
Sea transport, passenger	2 207 ..	....	....	....	....	....	....	....	....
Sea transport, freight	2 208 ..	....	....	....	....	....	....	....	....
Sea transport, other	2 209 ..	31.7	26.8	26.9	31.4	31.4	26.2	21.9	19.4
Air transport, passenger	2 211 ..	13.0	13.0	9.7	9.9	10.7	11.2	10.7	11.7
Air transport, freight	2 212 ..	....	....	....	....	....	....	....	....
Air transport, other	2 213 ..	12.1	15.5	19.0	16.2	15.5	15.3	46.6	87.1
Other transport, passenger	2 215 ..	....	....	....	....	....	....	....	....
Other transport, freight	2 216 ..	....	....	....	....	....	....	....	....
Other transport, other	2 217 ..	....	....	....	....	....	....	....	....
Transportation services, debit	3 205 ..	**−244.2**	**−304.6**	**−366.4**	**−358.5**	**−373.3**	**−360.7**	**−346.8**	**−342.0**
Passenger	3 850 ..	*−98.9*	*−153.0*	*−183.7*	*−156.1*	*−161.2*	*−154.7*	*−146.4*	*−141.2*
Freight	3 851 ..	*−132.4*	*−138.4*	*−166.5*	*−185.2*	*−193.3*	*−182.6*	*−167.1*	*−169.3*
Other	3 852 ..	*−12.9*	*−13.2*	*−16.2*	*−17.3*	*−18.7*	*−23.4*	*−33.4*	*−31.5*
Sea transport, passenger	3 207 ..	....	....	....	....	....	....	....	....
Sea transport, freight	3 208 ..	−105.9	−110.7	−133.1	−148.1	−154.7	−146.1	−133.7	−135.5
Sea transport, other	3 209 ..	−2.2	−2.6	−3.0	−4.1	−4.5	−4.2	−3.8	−1.8
Air transport, passenger	3 211 ..	−98.9	−153.0	−183.7	−156.1	−161.2	−154.7	−146.4	−141.2
Air transport, freight	3 212 ..	−26.5	−27.7	−33.4	−37.0	−38.7	−36.5	−33.4	−33.9
Air transport, other	3 213 ..	−10.6	−10.6	−13.2	−13.2	−14.3	−19.2	−29.6	−29.8
Other transport, passenger	3 215 ..	....	....	....	....	....	....	....	....
Other transport, freight	3 216 ..	....	....	....	....	....	....	....	....
Other transport, other	3 217 ..	....	....	....	....	....	....	....	....
Travel, credit	2 236 ..	**1,757.4**	**1,884.5**	**2,070.5**	**2,056.4**	**2,187.2**	**2,143.8**	**1,929.4**	**2,058.4**
Business travel	2 237 ..	....	....	....	....	....	....	....	....
Personal travel	2 240 ..	1,757.4	1,884.5	2,070.5	2,056.4	2,187.2	2,143.8	1,929.4	2,058.4
Travel, debit	3 236 ..	**−304.7**	**−315.6**	**−344.3**	**−385.2**	**−377.4**	**−304.5**	**−240.4**	**−227.5**
Business travel	3 237 ..	−46.6	−39.5	−38.9	−52.9	−39.2	−36.9	−26.0	−32.9
Personal travel	3 240 ..	−258.1	−276.1	−305.4	−332.3	−338.3	−267.6	−214.4	−194.7
Other services, credit	2 200 BA	**240.6**	**304.3**	**384.8**	**322.2**	**354.6**	**337.5**	**257.5**	**229.0**
Communications	2 245 ..	....	....	....	....	....	....	....	....
Construction	2 249 ..	....	....	....	....	....	....	....	....
Insurance	2 253 ..	....	....	....	....	....	....	....	....
Financial	2 260 ..	....	....	....	....	....	....	....	....
Computer and information	2 262 ..	....	....	....	....	....	....	....	....
Royalties and licence fees	2 266 ..	....	....	....	....	....	....	....	....
Other business services	2 268 ..	214.1	271.0	333.6	289.4	321.7	296.9	217.8	191.6
Personal, cultural, and recreational	2 287 ..	....	....	....	....	....	....	....	....
Government, n.i.e.	2 291 ..	26.5	33.3	51.2	32.9	32.9	40.6	39.6	37.4
Other services, debit	3 200 BA	**−543.6**	**−611.1**	**−575.7**	**−867.1**	**−828.9**	**−737.7**	**−608.8**	**−611.5**
Communications	3 245 ..	−1.0	−1.0	−1.0	−1.0	−1.0	−1.1	−1.0	−1.0
Construction	3 249 ..	−37.8	−23.2	−40.7	−214.4	−176.2	−34.3	−20.7	−15.7
Insurance	3 253 ..	−105.7	−81.6	−96.9	−120.7	−107.0	−106.6	−92.6	−165.3
Financial	3 260 ..	....	....	....	....	....	....	....	....
Computer and information	3 262 ..	....	....	....	....	....	....	....	....
Royalties and licence fees	3 266 ..	−14.6	−18.5	−16.1	−17.7	−19.7	−17.9	−17.5	−10.6
Other business services	3 268 ..	−298.7	−422.3	−341.3	−410.0	−445.2	−479.0	−348.5	−338.0
Personal, cultural, and recreational	3 287 ..	−2.0	−2.0	−2.0	−2.0	−2.0	−2.0	−2.0	−.5
Government, n.i.e.	3 291 ..	−83.8	−62.5	−77.8	−101.3	−77.7	−96.9	−126.6	−80.5

Table 2 (Continued). STANDARD PRESENTATION, 2003–2010

(Millions of U.S. dollars)

	Code	2003	2004	2005	2006	2007	2008	2009	2010
C. INCOME	4 300	**−152.4**	**−141.3**	**−182.1**	**−218.0**	**−231.6**	**−85.3**	**−152.2**	**−233.8**
Total credit	2 300	*79.1*	*79.7*	*97.0*	*119.4*	*121.3*	*113.4*	*57.7*	*38.8*
Total debit	3 300	*−231.6*	*−221.1*	*−279.1*	*−337.4*	*−352.9*	*−198.6*	*−209.9*	*−272.5*
Compensation of employees, credit	2 310	....	....	....	....	....	....	....	....
Compensation of employees, debit	3 310	**−56.3**	**−63.3**	**−73.2**	**−92.8**	**−84.7**	**−26.9**	**−11.8**	**−27.4**
Investment income, credit	2 320	**79.1**	**79.7**	**97.0**	**119.4**	**121.3**	**113.4**	**57.7**	**38.8**
Direct investment income	2 330	....	....	....	....	....	....	....	....
Dividends and distributed branch profits	2 332	....	....	....	....	....	....	....	....
Reinvested earnings and undistributed branch profits	2 333	....	....	....	....	....	....	....	....
Income on debt (interest)	2 334	....	....	....	....	....	....	....	....
Portfolio investment income	2 339	....	....	....	....	....	....	....	....
Income on equity	2 340	....	....	....	....	....	....	....	....
Income on bonds and notes	2 350	....	....	....	....	....	....	....	....
Income on money market instruments	2 360	....	....	....	....	....	....	....	....
Other investment income	2 370	79.1	79.7	97.0	119.4	121.3	113.4	57.7	38.8
Investment income, debit	3 320	**−175.3**	**−157.8**	**−205.9**	**−244.6**	**−268.2**	**−171.7**	**−198.0**	**−245.1**
Direct investment income	3 330	....	....	....	....	....	....	....	....
Dividends and distributed branch profits	3 332	....	....	....	....	....	....	....	....
Reinvested earnings and undistributed branch profits	3 333	....	....	....	....	....	....	....	....
Income on debt (interest)	3 334	....	....	....	....	....	....	....	....
Portfolio investment income	3 339	....	....	....	....	....	....	....	....
Income on equity	3 340	....	....	....	....	....	....	....	....
Income on bonds and notes	3 350	....	....	....	....	....	....	....	....
Income on money market instruments	3 360	....	....	....	....	....	....	....	....
Other investment income	3 370	−175.3	−157.8	−205.9	−244.6	−268.2	−171.7	−198.0	−245.1
D. CURRENT TRANSFERS	4 379	**48.7**	**250.8**	**85.2**	**52.0**	**51.8**	**−24.6**	**13.5**	**−2.6**
Credit	2 379	**59.8**	**264.7**	**103.3**	**66.4**	**71.0**	**75.9**	**96.6**	**99.3**
General government	2 380	58.6	65.5	66.3	65.2	69.8	74.7	95.4	98.1
Other sectors	2 390	1.2	199.2	37.0	1.2	1.2	1.2	1.2	1.2
Workers' remittances	2 391	....	....	....	....	....	....	....	....
Other current transfers	2 392	1.2	199.2	37.0	1.2	1.2	1.2	1.2	1.2
Debit	3 379	**−11.1**	**−13.9**	**−18.1**	**−14.3**	**−19.2**	**−100.5**	**−83.1**	**−101.9**
General government	3 380	−4.6	−5.8	−7.3	−6.8	−8.9	−11.8	−8.7	−10.8
Other sectors	3 390	−6.5	−8.1	−10.8	−7.5	−10.3	−88.7	−74.5	−91.1
Workers' remittances	3 391	−6.5	−8.1	−10.8	−7.5	−10.3	−39.0	−51.5	−60.7
Other current transfers	3 392	....	....	....	....	....	−49.7	−23.0	−30.5
CAPITAL AND FINANCIAL ACCOUNT	4 996	**388.0**	**127.3**	**849.8**	**1,296.2**	**1,001.2**	**1,097.4**	**860.8**	**1,072.1**
CAPITAL ACCOUNT	4 994	**−37.4**	**−47.9**	**−60.4**	**−63.5**	**−75.7**	**−16.8**	**−7.2**	**−3.6**
Total credit	2 994	....	....	....	....	....	....	....	....
Total debit	3 994	*−37.4*	*−47.9*	*−60.4*	*−63.5*	*−75.7*	*−16.8*	*−7.2*	*−3.6*
Capital transfers, credit	2 400	....	....	....	....	....	....	....	....
General government	2 401	....	....	....	....	....	....	....	....
Debt forgiveness	2 402	....	....	....	....	....	....	....	....
Other capital transfers	2 410	....	....	....	....	....	....	....	....
Other sectors	2 430	....	....	....	....	....	....	....	....
Migrants' transfers	2 431	....	....	....	....	....	....	....	....
Debt forgiveness	2 432	....	....	....	....	....	....	....	....
Other capital transfers	2 440	....	....	....	....	....	....	....	....
Capital transfers, debit	3 400	**−37.4**	**−47.9**	**−60.4**	**−63.5**	**−75.7**	**−16.8**	**−7.2**	**−3.6**
General government	3 401	....	....	....	....	....	....	....	....
Debt forgiveness	3 402	....	....	....	....	....	....	....	....
Other capital transfers	3 410	....	....	....	....	....	....	....	....
Other sectors	3 430	−37.4	−47.9	−60.4	−63.5	−75.7	−16.8	−7.2	−3.6
Migrants' transfers	3 431	−37.4	−47.9	−60.4	−63.5	−75.7	−16.8	−7.2	−3.6
Debt forgiveness	3 432	....	....	....	....	....	....	....	....
Other capital transfers	3 440	....	....	....	....	....	....	....	....
Nonproduced nonfinancial assets, credit	2 480	....	....	....	....	....	....	....	....
Nonproduced nonfinancial assets, debit	3 480	....	....	....	....	....	....	....	....

Table 2 (Continued). STANDARD PRESENTATION, 2003–2010

(Millions of U.S. dollars)

	Code	2003	2004	2005	2006	2007	2008	2009	2010
FINANCIAL ACCOUNT	4 995	**425.4**	**175.2**	**910.3**	**1,359.7**	**1,076.9**	**1,114.2**	**867.9**	**1,075.7**
A. DIRECT INVESTMENT	4 500	**190.2**	**273.6**	**563.4**	**706.4**	**713.4**	**860.2**	**664.0**	**861.5**
Direct investment abroad	4 505	....	....	....	....	....	....	....	....
Equity capital	4 510	....	....	....	....	....	....	....	....
Claims on affiliated enterprises	4 515	....	....	....	....	....	....	....	....
Liabilities to affiliated enterprises	4 520	....	....	....	....	....	....	....	....
Reinvested earnings	4 525	....	....	....	....	....	....	....	....
Other capital	4 530	....	....	....	....	....	....	....	....
Claims on affiliated enterprises	4 535	....	....	....	....	....	....	....	....
Liabilities to affiliated enterprises	4 540	....	....	....	....	....	....	....	....
Direct investment in The Bahamas	4 555	**190.2**	**273.6**	**563.4**	**706.4**	**713.4**	**860.2**	**664.0**	**861.5**
Equity capital	4 560	44.7	90.2	219.8	233.9	356.0	285.8	201.4	148.3
Claims on direct investors	4 565	....	....	....	....	....	....	....	....
Liabilities to direct investors	4 570	44.7	90.2	219.8	233.9	356.0	285.8	201.4	148.3
Reinvested earnings	4 575	....	....	....	....	....	....	....	....
Other capital	4 580	145.5	183.4	343.6	472.5	357.4	574.4	462.5	713.2
Claims on direct investors	4 585	....	....	....	....	....	....	....	....
Liabilities to direct investors	4 590	145.5	183.4	343.6	472.5	357.4	574.4	462.5	713.2
B. PORTFOLIO INVESTMENT	4 600	....	....	....	**–18.8**	**–7.2**	**–21.9**	**–16.7**	**–25.4**
Assets	4 602	....	....	....	**–18.8**	**–7.2**	**–21.9**	**–16.7**	**–25.4**
Equity securities	4 610	....	....	....	....	–4.1	–12.5	–4.2	–13.0
Monetary authorities	4 611	....	....	....	....	....	....	....	....
General government	4 612	....	....	....	....	....	....	....	....
Banks	4 613	....	....	....	....	....	....	....	....
Other sectors	4 614	....	....	....	....	–4.1	–12.5	–4.2	–13.0
Debt securities	4 619	....	....	....	–18.8	–3.1	–9.4	–12.5	–12.4
Bonds and notes	4 620	....	....	....	–18.8	–3.1	....	–6.3	....
Monetary authorities	4 621	....	....	....	....	....	....	....	....
General government	4 622	....	....	....	....	....	....	....	....
Banks	4 623	....	....	....	....	....	....	....	....
Other sectors	4 624	....	....	....	–18.8	–3.1	....	–6.3	....
Money market instruments	4 630	....	....	....	....	....	–9.4	–6.3	–12.4
Monetary authorities	4 631	....	....	....	....	....	....	....	....
General government	4 632	....	....	....	....	....	....	....	....
Banks	4 633	....	....	....	....	....	....	....	....
Other sectors	4 634	....	....	....	....	....	–9.4	–6.3	–12.4
Liabilities	4 652	....	....	....	....	....	....	....	....
Equity securities	4 660	....	....	....	....	....	....	....	....
Banks	4 663	....	....	....	....	....	....	....	....
Other sectors	4 664	....	....	....	....	....	....	....	....
Debt securities	4 669	....	....	....	....	....	....	....	....
Bonds and notes	4 670	....	....	....	....	....	....	....	....
Monetary authorities	4 671	....	....	....	....	....	....	....	....
General government	4 672	....	....	....	....	....	....	....	....
Banks	4 673	....	....	....	....	....	....	....	....
Other sectors	4 674	....	....	....	....	....	....	....	....
Money market instruments	4 680	....	....	....	....	....	....	....	....
Monetary authorities	4 681	....	....	....	....	....	....	....	....
General government	4 682	....	....	....	....	....	....	....	....
Banks	4 683	....	....	....	....	....	....	....	....
Other sectors	4 684	....	....	....	....	....	....	....	....
C. FINANCIAL DERIVATIVES	4 910	....	....	....	....	....	....	....	....
Monetary authorities	4 911	....	....	....	....	....	....	....	....
General government	4 912	....	....	....	....	....	....	....	....
Banks	4 913	....	....	....	....	....	....	....	....
Other sectors	4 914	....	....	....	....	....	....	....	....
Assets	4 900	....	....	....	....	....	....	....	....
Monetary authorities	4 901	....	....	....	....	....	....	....	....
General government	4 902	....	....	....	....	....	....	....	....
Banks	4 903	....	....	....	....	....	....	....	....
Other sectors	4 904	....	....	....	....	....	....	....	....
Liabilities	4 905	....	....	....	....	....	....	....	....
Monetary authorities	4 906	....	....	....	....	....	....	....	....
General government	4 907	....	....	....	....	....	....	....	....
Banks	4 908	....	....	....	....	....	....	....	....
Other sectors	4 909	....	....	....	....	....	....	....	....

Table 2 (Concluded). STANDARD PRESENTATION, 2003–2010

(Millions of U.S. dollars)

	Code	2003	2004	2005	2006	2007	2008	2009	2010
D. OTHER INVESTMENT	4 700	**345.3**	**84.9**	**258.7**	**592.6**	**324.5**	**385.1**	**473.0**	**287.3**
Assets	4 703	46,576.8	19,293.4	−11,064.2	−9,016.7	−15,801.8	−4,830.6	25,373.1	4,969.8
Trade credits	4 706	....	....	....	....	....	....	....	....
General government	4 707	....	....	....	....	....	....	....	....
of which: Short-term	4 709	....	....	....	....	....	....	....	....
Other sectors	4 710	....	....	....	....	....	....	....	....
of which: Short-term	4 712	....	....	....	....	....	....	....	....
Loans	4 714	....	....	....	....	....	....	....	....
Monetary authorities	4 715	....	....	....	....	....	....	....	....
of which: Short-term	4 718	....	....	....	....	....	....	....	....
General government	4 719	....	....	....	....	....	....	....	....
of which: Short-term	4 721	....	....	....	....	....	....	....	....
Banks	4 722	....	....	....	....	....	....	....	....
of which: Short-term	4 724	....	....	....	....	....	....	....	....
Other sectors	4 725	....	....	....	....	....	....	....	....
of which: Short-term	4 727	....	....	....	....	....	....	....	....
Currency and deposits	4 730	46,576.8	19,293.4	−11,064.2	−9,016.7	−15,801.8	−4,830.6	25,373.1	4,969.8
Monetary authorities	4 731	....	....	....	....	....	....	....	....
General government	4 732	....	....	....	....	....	....	....	....
Banks	4 733	46,576.8	19,293.4	−11,064.2	−9,016.7	−15,801.8	−4,830.6	25,373.1	4,969.8
Other sectors	4 734	....	....	....	....	....	....	....	....
Other assets	4 736	....	....	....	....	....	....	....	....
Monetary authorities	4 737	....	....	....	....	....	....	....	....
of which: Short-term	4 739	....	....	....	....	....	....	....	....
General government	4 740	....	....	....	....	....	....	....	....
of which: Short-term	4 742	....	....	....	....	....	....	....	....
Banks	4 743	....	....	....	....	....	....	....	....
of which: Short-term	4 745	....	....	....	....	....	....	....	....
Other sectors	4 746	....	....	....	....	....	....	....	....
of which: Short-term	4 748	....	....	....	....	....	....	....	....
Liabilities	4 753	**−46,231.5**	**−19,208.5**	**11,322.9**	**9,609.3**	**16,126.3**	**5,215.8**	**−24,900.1**	**−4,682.4**
Trade credits	4 756	....	....	....	....	....	....	....	....
General government	4 757	....	....	....	....	....	....	....	....
of which: Short-term	4 759	....	....	....	....	....	....	....	....
Other sectors	4 760	....	....	....	....	....	....	....	....
of which: Short-term	4 762	....	....	....	....	....	....	....	....
Loans	4 764	447.7	149.5	211.3	449.5	411.1	348.9	316.4	263.8
Monetary authorities	4 765	....	....	....	....	....	....	....	....
of which: Use of Fund credit and loans from the Fund	4 766	....	....	....	....	....	....	....	....
of which: Short-term	4 768	....	....	....	....	....	....	....	....
General government	4 769	52.6	−20.6	−8.5	−3.5	−6.4	106.4	323.6	148.4
of which: Short-term	4 771	....	....	....	....	....	....	....	....
Banks	4 772	....	....	....	....	....	....	....	....
of which: Short-term	4 774	....	....	....	....	....	....	....	....
Other sectors	4 775	395.1	170.1	219.7	453.0	417.4	242.6	−7.2	115.4
of which: Short-term	4 777	....	....	....	....	....	....	....	....
Currency and deposits	4 780	−46,679.2	−19,358.0	11,111.7	9,159.8	15,715.2	4,866.9	−25,395.0	−4,946.2
Monetary authorities	4 781	....	....	....	....	....	....	....	....
General government	4 782	....	....	....	....	....	....	....	....
Banks	4 783	−46,679.2	−19,358.0	11,111.7	9,159.8	15,715.2	4,866.9	−25,395.0	−4,946.2
Other sectors	4 784	....	....	....	....	....	....	....	....
Other liabilities	4 786	....	....	....	....	....	....	178.5	....
Monetary authorities	4 787	....	....	....	....	....	....	178.5	....
of which: Short-term	4 789	....	....	....	....	....	....	....	....
General government	4 790	....	....	....	....	....	....	....	....
of which: Short-term	4 792	....	....	....	....	....	....	....	....
Banks	4 793	....	....	....	....	....	....	....	....
of which: Short-term	4 795	....	....	....	....	....	....	....	....
Other sectors	4 796	....	....	....	....	....	....	....	....
of which: Short-term	4 798	....	....	....	....	....	....	....	....
E. RESERVE ASSETS	4 802	**−110.1**	**−183.3**	**88.1**	**79.5**	**46.3**	**−109.2**	**−252.3**	**−47.7**
Monetary gold	4 812	....	....	....	....	....	....	....	....
Special drawing rights	4 811	.1	....	....	....	−.1	....	−178.4	....
Reserve position in the Fund	4 810	....	....	....	....	....	....	....	....
Foreign exchange	4 803	−110.2	−183.2	88.1	79.5	46.4	−109.2	−73.9	−47.8
Other claims	4 813	....	....	....	....	....	....	....	....
NET ERRORS AND OMISSIONS	4 998	**85.5**	**179.8**	**−149.2**	**107.5**	**313.9**	**124.7**	**32.5**	**−172.2**

Table 1. ANALYTIC PRESENTATION, 2003–2010

(Millions of U.S. dollars)

	Code	2003	2004	2005	2006	2007	2008	2009	2010
A. Current Account[1]	4 993 Z.	**200.4**	**471.6**	**1,474.2**	**2,187.4**	**2,906.6**	**2,256.9**	**560.0**	**770.1**
Goods: exports f.o.b.	2 100 ..	6,720.6	7,660.3	10,348.7	12,339.8	13,790.2	17,491.2	12,051.9	13,833.2
Goods: imports f.o.b.	3 100 ..	−5,298.4	−6,922.6	−8,870.7	−9,953.8	−10,925.4	−14,246.3	−9,613.0	−11,190.4
Balance on Goods	4 100 ..	*1,422.2*	*737.7*	*1,477.9*	*2,386.0*	*2,864.8*	*3,244.9*	*2,438.8*	*2,642.8*
Services: credit	2 200 ..	1,260.1	2,676.4	3,048.3	3,322.4	3,524.2	3,740.2	3,652.9	4,047.1
Services: debit	3 200 ..	−906.7	−1,247.8	−1,416.2	−1,605.2	−1,700.9	−2,030.1	−1,741.0	−1,905.1
Balance on Goods and Services	4 991 ..	*1,775.6*	*2,166.3*	*3,110.0*	*4,103.2*	*4,688.0*	*4,955.1*	*4,350.8*	*4,784.8*
Income: credit	2 300 ..	1,266.6	2,544.3	5,015.8	7,633.7	10,373.6	7,088.0	1,680.1	1,467.6
Income: debit	3 300 ..	−1,759.6	−3,119.1	−5,428.1	−8,018.6	−10,672.3	−8,011.7	−4,080.0	−3,840.6
Balance on Goods, Services, and Income	4 992 ..	*1,282.6*	*1,591.5*	*2,697.6*	*3,718.3*	*4,389.3*	*4,031.4*	*1,950.9*	*2,411.8*
Current transfers: credit	2 379 Z.	....	....	....	....	....	....	....	....
Current transfers: debit	3 379 ..	−1,082.2	−1,119.9	−1,223.4	−1,530.9	−1,482.8	−1,774.5	−1,391.0	−1,641.8
B. Capital Account[1]	4 994 Z.	**50.0**	**50.0**	**50.0**	**75.0**	**50.0**	**50.0**	**50.0**	**50.0**
Capital account: credit	2 994 Z.	50.0	50.0	50.0	75.0	50.0	50.0	50.0	50.0
Capital account: debit	3 994 ..	....	....	....	....	....	....	....	....
Total, Groups A Plus B	4 981 ..	*250.4*	*521.6*	*1,524.2*	*2,262.4*	*2,956.6*	*2,306.9*	*610.0*	*820.1*
C. Financial Account[1]	4 995 W.	**493.1**	**−390.8**	**−1,380.0**	**−1,451.4**	**−1,552.2**	**−2,570.8**	**−478.4**	**352.4**
Direct investment abroad	4 505 ..	−741.4	−1,035.6	−1,135.4	−980.1	−1,669.1	−1,620.5	1,791.5	−334.0
Direct investment in Bahrain	4 555 Z.	516.7	865.3	1,048.6	2,914.7	1,756.3	1,794.0	257.1	155.8
Portfolio investment assets	4 602 ..	−3,095.7	−3,892.6	−7,036.2	−10,527.3	−9,890.1	6,286.8	6,710.1	2,051.6
Equity securities	4 610 ..	−489.0	−1,999.0	−2,219.7	−2,200.7	−3,368.1	−793.2	1,641.6	253.1
Debt securities	4 619 ..	−2,606.7	−1,893.6	−4,816.5	−8,326.7	−6,522.0	7,079.9	5,068.5	1,798.5
Portfolio investment liabilities	4 652 Z.	688.4	387.7	2,421.9	1,696.1	1,330.2	2,990.1	1,565.5	2,704.2
Equity securities	4 660 ..	238.5	20.9	1,801.1	133.8	138.8	156.4	−487.2	1,652.7
Debt securities	4 669 Z.	449.9	366.8	620.8	1,562.3	1,191.5	2,833.7	2,052.8	1,051.5
Financial derivatives	4 910 ..	....	....	....	....	....	....	....	....
Financial derivatives assets	4 900 ..	....	....	....	....	....	....	....	....
Financial derivatives liabilities	4 905 ..	....	....	....	....	....	....	....	....
Other investment assets	4 703 ..	−20,786.6	−9,779.9	−11,562.4	−30,234.9	−38,504.7	−3,264.6	18,123.8	2,739.7
Monetary authorities	4 701 ..	....	....	....	....	....	....	....	....
General government	4 704 ..	−10.4	−5.1	−4.5	−11.4	−10.6	−2.7	−39.9	−9.3
Banks	4 705 ..	−20,777.7	−9,777.2	−11,562.2	−30,226.6	−38,497.3	−3,265.2	18,160.5	2,745.8
Other sectors	4 728 ..	1.6	2.3	4.3	3.2	3.2	3.2	3.2	3.2
Other investment liabilities	4 753 W.	23,911.6	13,064.3	14,883.6	35,680.1	45,425.2	−8,756.6	−28,926.4	−6,964.8
Monetary authorities	4 753 WA	....	....	....	....	....	....	184.7	....
General government	4 753 ZB	168.5	24.7	39.7	22.7	46.3	60.0	19.9	−61.9
Banks	4 753 ZC	23,793.4	13,004.7	14,797.4	35,613.3	45,331.6	−8,869.8	−29,184.2	−6,956.1
Other sectors	4 753 ZD	−50.3	35.0	46.5	44.1	47.3	53.2	53.2	53.2
Total, Groups A Through C	4 983 ..	*743.5*	*130.7*	*144.2*	*811.1*	*1,404.4*	*−263.9*	*131.5*	*1,172.4*
D. Net Errors and Omissions	4 998 ..	**−699.8**	**27.2**	**149.9**	**10.9**	**10.3**	**−30.3**	**−250.0**	**107.1**
Total, Groups A Through D	4 984 ..	*43.7*	*157.9*	*294.2*	*822.0*	*1,414.7*	*−294.2*	*−118.5*	*1,279.5*
E. Reserves and Related Items	4 802 A.	**−43.7**	**−157.9**	**−294.2**	**−822.0**	**−1,414.7**	**294.2**	**118.5**	**−1,279.5**
Reserve assets	4 802 ..	−43.7	−157.9	−294.2	−822.0	−1,414.7	294.2	118.5	−1,279.5
Use of Fund credit and loans	4 766 ..	....	....	....	....	....	....	....	....
Exceptional financing	4 920 ..	....	....	....	....	....	....	....	....
Conversion rates: Bahrain dinar per U.S. dollar	0 101 ..	**.3760**	**.3760**	**.3760**	**.3760**	**.3760**	**.3760**	**.3760**	**.3760**

[1] Excludes components that have been classified in the categories of Group E.

Table 2. STANDARD PRESENTATION, 2003–2010

(Millions of U.S. dollars)

	Code	2003	2004	2005	2006	2007	2008	2009	2010
CURRENT ACCOUNT..........................	4 993 ..	**200.4**	**471.6**	**1,474.2**	**2,187.4**	**2,906.6**	**2,256.9**	**560.0**	**770.1**
A. GOODS..	4 100 ..	**1,422.2**	**737.7**	**1,477.9**	**2,386.0**	**2,864.8**	**3,244.9**	**2,438.8**	**2,642.8**
Credit...	2 100 ..	**6,720.6**	**7,660.3**	**10,348.7**	**12,339.8**	**13,790.2**	**17,491.2**	**12,051.9**	**13,833.2**
General merchandise: exports f.o.b............	2 110 ..	6,631.4	7,558.2	10,242.0	12,200.0	13,633.5	17,315.7	11,873.7	13,647.1
Goods for processing: exports f.o.b...........	2 150 ..	....	....	....	....	....	....	....	....
Repairs on goods......................................	2 160 ..	89.2	102.1	106.6	139.8	156.6	175.5	178.2	186.2
Goods procured in ports by carriers...........	2 170 ..	....	....	....	....	....	....	....	....
Nonmonetary gold....................................	2 180 ..	....	....	....	....	....	....	....	....
Debit...	3 100 ..	**−5,298.4**	**−6,922.6**	**−8,870.7**	**−9,953.8**	**−10,925.4**	**−14,246.3**	**−9,613.0**	**−11,190.4**
General merchandise: imports f.o.b............	3 110 ..	−5,298.4	−6,922.6	−8,870.7	−9,953.8	−10,925.4	−14,246.3	−9,613.0	−11,190.4
Goods for processing: imports f.o.b...........	3 150 ..	....	....	....	....	....	....	....	....
Repairs on goods......................................	3 160 ..	....	....	....	....	....	....	....	....
Goods procured in ports by carriers...........	3 170 ..	....	....	....	....	....	....	....	....
Nonmonetary gold....................................	3 180 ..	....	....	....	....	....	....	....	....
B. SERVICES....................................	4 200 ..	**353.4**	**1,428.6**	**1,632.0**	**1,717.2**	**1,823.3**	**1,710.1**	**1,912.0**	**2,142.0**
Total credit..	2 200 ..	*1,260.1*	*2,676.4*	*3,048.3*	*3,322.4*	*3,524.2*	*3,740.2*	*3,652.9*	*4,047.1*
Total debit...	3 200 ..	*−906.7*	*−1,247.8*	*−1,416.2*	*−1,605.2*	*−1,700.9*	*−2,030.1*	*−1,741.0*	*−1,905.1*
Transportation services, credit..........	2 205 ..	**486.4**	**640.4**	**683.0**	**737.5**	**749.2**	**761.2**	**755.3**	**801.1**
Passenger...	2 850 ..	*486.4*	*640.4*	*683.0*	*737.5*	*749.2*	*761.2*	*755.3*	*801.1*
Freight..	2 851 ..	....	....	....	....	....	....	....	....
Other..	2 852 ..	....	....	....	....	....	....	....	....
Sea transport, passenger..........................	2 207 ..	....	....	....	....	....	....	....	....
Sea transport, freight................................	2 208 ..	....	....	....	....	....	....	....	....
Sea transport, other.................................	2 209 ..	....	....	....	....	....	....	....	....
Air transport, passenger...........................	2 211 ..	486.4	640.4	683.0	737.5	749.2	761.2	755.3	801.1
Air transport, freight.................................	2 212 ..	....	....	....	....	....	....	....	....
Air transport, other..................................	2 213 ..	....	....	....	....	....	....	....	....
Other transport, passenger.......................	2 215 ..	....	....	....	....	....	....	....	....
Other transport, freight............................	2 216 ..	....	....	....	....	....	....	....	....
Other transport, other..............................	2 217 ..	....	....	....	....	....	....	....	....
Transportation services, debit...........	3 205 ..	**−442.8**	**−557.0**	**−630.2**	**−689.3**	**−698.4**	**−905.3**	**−715.0**	**−757.7**
Passenger...	3 850 ..	*−119.7*	*−141.2*	*−160.1*	*−184.0*	*−192.3*	*−201.1*	*−189.1*	*−177.9*
Freight..	3 851 ..	*−323.2*	*−415.7*	*−470.1*	*−505.2*	*−506.1*	*−704.2*	*−525.9*	*−579.7*
Other..	3 852 ..	....	....	....	....	....	....	....	....
Sea transport, passenger..........................	3 207 ..	....	....	....	....	....	....	....	....
Sea transport, freight................................	3 208 ..	−323.2	−415.7	−470.1	−505.2	−506.1	−704.2	−525.9	−579.7
Sea transport, other.................................	3 209 ..	....	....	....	....	....	....	....	....
Air transport, passenger...........................	3 211 ..	−119.7	−141.2	−160.1	−184.0	−192.3	−201.1	−189.1	−177.9
Air transport, freight.................................	3 212 ..	....	....	....	....	....	....	....	....
Air transport, other..................................	3 213 ..	....	....	....	....	....	....	....	....
Other transport, passenger.......................	3 215 ..	....	....	....	....	....	....	....	....
Other transport, freight............................	3 216 ..	....	....	....	....	....	....	....	....
Other transport, other..............................	3 217 ..	....	....	....	....	....	....	....	....
Travel, credit..................................	2 236 ..	**720.0**	**864.2**	**919.8**	**1,047.7**	**1,105.1**	**1,166.0**	**1,118.1**	**1,361.7**
Business travel...	2 237 ..	....	....	....	....	....	....	....	....
Personal travel...	2 240 ..	....	....	....	....	....	....	....	....
Travel, debit...................................	3 236 ..	**−371.8**	**−386.8**	**−413.8**	**−455.3**	**−478.7**	**−503.2**	**−407.7**	**−505.6**
Business travel...	3 237 ..	....	....	....	....	....	....	....	....
Personal travel...	3 240 ..	....	....	....	....	....	....	....	....
Other services, credit.......................	2 200 BA ..	**53.6**	**1,171.8**	**1,445.5**	**1,537.2**	**1,669.9**	**1,813.0**	**1,779.5**	**1,884.3**
Communications......................................	2 245 ..	....	632.4	637.5	634.3	666.5	699.7	740.4	799.5
Construction..	2 249 ..	....	....	....	....	....	....	....	....
Insurance...	2 253 ..	....	394.9	655.1	732.7	819.1	915.7	851.3	905.9
Financial..	2 260 ..	....	....	....	....	....	....	....	....
Computer and information........................	2 262 ..	....	....	....	....	....	....	....	....
Royalties and licence fees........................	2 266 ..	....	....	....	....	....	....	....	....
Other business services............................	2 268 ..	53.6	144.4	152.9	170.2	184.3	197.6	187.8	179.0
Personal, cultural, and recreational...........	2 287 ..	....	....	....	....	....	....	....	....
Government, n.i.e.....................................	2 291 ..	....	....	....	....	....	....	....	....
Other services, debit........................	3 200 BA ..	**−92.0**	**−304.0**	**−372.2**	**−460.7**	**−523.8**	**−621.6**	**−618.3**	**−641.8**
Communications......................................	3 245 ..	....	−5.3	−11.2	−16.2	−23.7	−34.6	−40.4	−47.3
Construction..	3 249 ..	....	....	....	....	....	....	....	....
Insurance...	3 253 ..	−35.9	−177.3	−234.1	−305.6	−352.0	−429.0	−417.5	−431.7
Financial..	3 260 ..	....	....	....	....	....	....	....	....
Computer and information........................	3 262 ..	....	....	....	....	....	....	....	....
Royalties and licence fees........................	3 266 ..	....	....	....	....	....	....	....	....
Other business services............................	3 268 ..	−56.1	−121.4	−126.9	−138.8	−148.1	−158.0	−160.4	−162.8
Personal, cultural, and recreational...........	3 287 ..	....	....	....	....	....	....	....	....
Government, n.i.e.....................................	3 291 ..	....	....	....	....	....	....	....	....

Table 2 (Continued). STANDARD PRESENTATION, 2003–2010

(Millions of U.S. dollars)

	Code	2003	2004	2005	2006	2007	2008	2009	2010
C. INCOME..	4 300 ..	**−493.0**	**−574.8**	**−412.4**	**−384.9**	**−298.7**	**−923.7**	**−2,399.9**	**−2,373.0**
Total credit....................................	2 300 ..	*1,266.6*	*2,544.3*	*5,015.8*	*7,633.7*	*10,373.6*	*7,088.0*	*1,680.1*	*1,467.6*
Total debit....................................	3 300 ..	*−1,759.6*	*−3,119.1*	*−5,428.1*	*−8,018.6*	*−10,672.3*	*−8,011.7*	*−4,080.0*	*−3,840.6*
Compensation of employees, credit..............	2 310 ..	....	....	....	....	....	....	....	....
Compensation of employees, debit..............	3 310 ..	....	....	....	....	....	....	....	....
Investment income, credit....................	2 320 ..	**1,266.6**	**2,544.3**	**5,015.8**	**7,633.7**	**10,373.6**	**7,088.0**	**1,680.1**	**1,467.6**
Direct investment income........................	2 330 ..	257.5	346.5	470.8	607.0	724.6	924.9	1,305.9	1,055.1
Dividends and distributed branch profits.........	2 332 ..	103.0	138.6	188.3	242.8	289.9	370.0	522.4	422.1
Reinvested earnings and undistributed branch profits.....	2 333 ..	154.5	207.9	282.5	364.2	434.8	555.0	783.6	633.1
Income on debt (interest)........................	2 334 ..	....	....	....	....	....	....	....	....
Portfolio investment income......................	2 339 ..	254.9	515.1	1,120.1	1,754.9	2,297.1	1,291.5	54.2	63.0
Income on equity...............................	2 340 ..	47.4	73.8	191.1	296.0	401.1	239.3	10.8	13.8
Income on bonds and notes......................	2 350 ..	207.5	441.3	929.0	1,458.8	1,896.1	1,052.2	43.4	49.2
Income on money market instruments.............	2 360 ..	....	....	....	....	....	....	....	....
Other investment income........................	2 370 ..	754.1	1,682.7	3,424.9	5,271.8	7,351.8	4,871.6	320.0	349.4
Investment income, debit.....................	3 320 ..	**−1,759.6**	**−3,119.1**	**−5,428.1**	**−8,018.6**	**−10,672.3**	**−8,011.7**	**−4,080.0**	**−3,840.6**
Direct investment income........................	3 330 ..	−943.9	−1,006.0	−1,158.0	−1,445.7	−1,914.9	−2,198.7	−1,600.6	−3,143.3
Dividends and distributed branch profits.........	3 332 ..	−379.0	−393.1	−453.3	−640.3	−826.4	−938.3	−699.1	−1,316.2
Reinvested earnings and undistributed branch profits.....	3 333 ..	−564.9	−612.9	−704.6	−805.4	−1,088.5	−1,260.4	−901.5	−1,827.2
Income on debt (interest)........................	3 334 ..	....	....	....	....	....	....	....	....
Portfolio investment income......................	3 339 ..	−13.2	−48.9	−92.5	−164.3	−242.8	−204.6	−38.2	−105.7
Income on equity...............................	3 340 ..	....	....	....	....	....	....	....	....
Income on bonds and notes......................	3 350 ..	−13.2	−48.9	−92.5	−164.3	−242.8	−204.6	−38.2	−105.7
Income on money market instruments.............	3 360 ..	....	....	....	....	....	....	....	....
Other investment income........................	3 370 ..	−802.5	−2,064.1	−4,177.6	−6,408.6	−8,514.6	−5,608.3	−2,441.1	−591.6
D. CURRENT TRANSFERS.......................	4 379 ..	**−1,082.2**	**−1,119.9**	**−1,223.4**	**−1,530.9**	**−1,482.8**	**−1,774.5**	**−1,391.0**	**−1,641.8**
Credit...	2 379 ..	....	....	....	....	....	....	....	....
General government.............................	2 380 ..	....	....	....	....	....	....	....	....
Other sectors...................................	2 390 ..	....	....	....	....	....	....	....	....
Workers' remittances...........................	2 391 ..	....	....	....	....	....	....	....	....
Other current transfers.........................	2 392 ..	....	....	....	....	....	....	....	....
Debit...	3 379 ..	**−1,082.2**	**−1,119.9**	**−1,223.4**	**−1,530.9**	**−1,482.8**	**−1,774.5**	**−1,391.0**	**−1,641.8**
General government.............................	3 380 ..	....	....	....	....	....	....	....	....
Other sectors...................................	3 390 ..	−1,082.2	−1,119.9	−1,223.4	−1,530.9	−1,482.8	−1,774.5	−1,391.0	−1,641.8
Workers' remittances...........................	3 391 ..	−1,082.2	−1,119.9	−1,223.4	−1,530.9	−1,482.8	−1,774.5	−1,391.0	−1,641.8
Other current transfers.........................	3 392 ..	....	....	....	....	....	....	....	....
CAPITAL AND FINANCIAL ACCOUNT............	4 996 ..	**499.4**	**−498.8**	**−1,624.1**	**−2,198.3**	**−2,916.9**	**−2,226.6**	**−310.0**	**−877.2**
CAPITAL ACCOUNT.............................	4 994 ..	**50.0**	**50.0**	**50.0**	**75.0**	**50.0**	**50.0**	**50.0**	**50.0**
Total credit....................................	2 994 ..	*50.0*	*50.0*	*50.0*	*75.0*	*50.0*	*50.0*	*50.0*	*50.0*
Total debit....................................	3 994 ..	....	....	....	....	....	....	....	....
Capital transfers, credit.......................	2 400 ..	**50.0**	**50.0**	**50.0**	**75.0**	**50.0**	**50.0**	**50.0**	**50.0**
General government.............................	2 401 ..	50.0	50.0	50.0	75.0	50.0	50.0	50.0	50.0
Debt forgiveness...............................	2 402 ..	....	....	....	....	....	....	....	....
Other capital transfers..........................	2 410 ..	50.0	50.0	50.0	75.0	50.0	50.0	50.0	50.0
Other sectors...................................	2 430 ..	....	....	....	....	....	....	....	....
Migrants' transfers.............................	2 431 ..	....	....	....	....	....	....	....	....
Debt forgiveness...............................	2 432 ..	....	....	....	....	....	....	....	....
Other capital transfers..........................	2 440 ..	....	....	....	....	....	....	....	....
Capital transfers, debit........................	3 400 ..	....	....	....	....	....	....	....	....
General government.............................	3 401 ..	....	....	....	....	....	....	....	....
Debt forgiveness...............................	3 402 ..	....	....	....	....	....	....	....	....
Other capital transfers..........................	3 410 ..	....	....	....	....	....	....	....	....
Other sectors...................................	3 430 ..	....	....	....	....	....	....	....	....
Migrants' transfers.............................	3 431 ..	....	....	....	....	....	....	....	....
Debt forgiveness...............................	3 432 ..	....	....	....	....	....	....	....	....
Other capital transfers..........................	3 440 ..	....	....	....	....	....	....	....	....
Nonproduced nonfinancial assets, credit............	2 480 ..	....	....	....	....	....	....	....	....
Nonproduced nonfinancial assets, debit.............	3 480 ..	....	....	....	....	....	....	....	....

Table 2 (Continued). STANDARD PRESENTATION, 2003–2010

(Millions of U.S. dollars)

	Code	2003	2004	2005	2006	2007	2008	2009	2010
FINANCIAL ACCOUNT..............................	4 995 ..	**449.4**	**−548.8**	**−1,674.1**	**−2,273.3**	**−2,966.9**	**−2,276.6**	**−360.0**	**−927.2**
A. DIRECT INVESTMENT............................	4 500 ..	**−224.7**	**−170.3**	**−86.8**	**1,934.6**	**87.2**	**173.5**	**2,048.6**	**−178.3**
Direct investment abroad..........................	4 505 ..	**−741.4**	**−1,035.6**	**−1,135.4**	**−980.1**	**−1,669.1**	**−1,620.5**	**1,791.5**	**−334.0**
Equity capital..	4 510 ..	−586.8	−827.7	−852.9	−615.8	−1,234.4	−1,065.5	2,575.1	299.0
Claims on affiliated enterprises..................	4 515 ..	−586.8	−827.7	−852.9	−615.8	−1,234.4	−1,065.5	2,575.1	299.0
Liabilities to affiliated enterprises..............	4 520 ..	....	....	....	....	....	....	....	....
Reinvested earnings..................................	4 525 ..	−154.5	−207.9	−282.5	−364.2	−434.8	−555.0	−783.6	−633.1
Other capital...	4 530 ..	....	....	....	....	....	....	....	....
Claims on affiliated enterprises..................	4 535 ..	....	....	....	....	....	....	....	....
Liabilities to affiliated enterprises..............	4 540 ..	....	....	....	....	....	....	....	....
Direct investment in Bahrain.......................	4 555 ..	**516.7**	**865.3**	**1,048.6**	**2,914.7**	**1,756.3**	**1,794.0**	**257.1**	**155.8**
Equity capital..	4 560 ..	−48.2	252.4	344.0	2,109.3	667.8	533.6	−644.4	−1,671.4
Claims on direct investors.........................	4 565 ..	....	....	....	....	....	....	....	....
Liabilities to direct investors.....................	4 570 ..	−48.2	252.4	344.0	2,109.3	667.8	533.6	−644.4	−1,671.4
Reinvested earnings..................................	4 575 ..	564.9	612.9	704.6	805.4	1,088.5	1,260.4	901.5	1,827.2
Other capital...	4 580 ..	....	....	....	....	....	....	....	....
Claims on direct investors.........................	4 585 ..	....	....	....	....	....	....	....	....
Liabilities to direct investors.....................	4 590 ..	....	....	....	....	....	....	....	....
B. PORTFOLIO INVESTMENT..........................	4 600 ..	**−2,407.3**	**−3,504.9**	**−4,614.3**	**−8,831.2**	**−8,559.9**	**9,276.9**	**8,275.6**	**4,755.8**
Assets...	4 602 ..	**−3,095.7**	**−3,892.6**	**−7,036.2**	**−10,527.3**	**−9,890.1**	**6,286.8**	**6,710.1**	**2,051.6**
Equity securities.....................................	4 610 ..	−489.0	−1,999.0	−2,219.7	−2,200.7	−3,368.1	−793.2	1,641.6	253.1
Monetary authorities..............................	4 611 ..	....	....	....	....	....	....	....	....
General government...............................	4 612 ..	....	....	....	....	....	....	....	....
Banks...	4 613 ..	−301.8	−1,668.6	−1,103.7	−1,342.0	−2,183.6	1,421.4	115.0	−318.4
Other sectors..	4 614 ..	−187.2	−330.4	−1,116.0	−858.6	−1,184.5	−2,214.5	1,526.6	571.5
Debt securities.......................................	4 619 ..	−2,606.7	−1,893.6	−4,816.5	−8,326.7	−6,522.0	7,079.9	5,068.5	1,798.5
Bonds and notes....................................	4 620 ..	−2,606.7	−1,893.6	−4,816.5	−8,326.7	−6,522.0	7,079.9	5,068.5	1,798.5
Monetary authorities..............................	4 621 ..	....	....	....	....	....	....	....	....
General government...............................	4 622 ..	....	....	....	....	....	....	....	....
Banks...	4 623 ..	−2,559.9	−1,812.3	−4,538.8	−8,113.1	−6,226.9	7,861.4	4,199.3	1,912.1
Other sectors..	4 624 ..	−46.8	−81.3	−277.7	−213.6	−295.1	−781.5	869.2	−113.6
Money market instruments.......................	4 630 ..	....	....	....	....	....	....	....	....
Monetary authorities..............................	4 631 ..	....	....	....	....	....	....	....	....
General government...............................	4 632 ..	....	....	....	....	....	....	....	....
Banks...	4 633 ..	....	....	....	....	....	....	....	....
Other sectors..	4 634 ..	....	....	....	....	....	....	....	....
Liabilities..	4 652 ..	**688.4**	**387.7**	**2,421.9**	**1,696.1**	**1,330.2**	**2,990.1**	**1,565.5**	**2,704.2**
Equity securities.....................................	4 660 ..	238.5	20.9	1,801.1	133.8	138.8	156.4	−487.2	1,652.7
Banks...	4 663 ..	....	....	....	....	....	....	....	....
Other sectors..	4 664 ..	238.5	20.9	1,801.1	133.8	138.8	156.4	−487.2	1,652.7
Debt securities.......................................	4 669 ..	449.9	366.8	620.8	1,562.3	1,191.5	2,833.7	2,052.8	1,051.5
Bonds and notes....................................	4 670 ..	449.9	366.8	620.8	1,562.3	1,191.5	2,833.7	2,052.8	1,051.5
Monetary authorities..............................	4 671 ..	....	....	....	....	....	....	....	....
General government...............................	4 672 ..	500.0	....	....	....	....	−500.0	750.0	1,250.0
Banks...	4 673 ..	−50.1	366.8	620.8	1,562.3	1,191.5	3,333.7	1,302.8	−198.5
Other sectors..	4 674 ..	....	....	....	....	....	....	....	....
Money market instruments.......................	4 680 ..	....	....	....	....	....	....	....	....
Monetary authorities..............................	4 681 ..	....	....	....	....	....	....	....	....
General government...............................	4 682 ..	....	....	....	....	....	....	....	....
Banks...	4 683 ..	....	....	....	....	....	....	....	....
Other sectors..	4 684 ..	....	....	....	....	....	....	....	....
C. FINANCIAL DERIVATIVES..........................	4 910 ..	....	....	....	....	....	....	....	....
Monetary authorities................................	4 911 ..	....	....	....	....	....	....	....	....
General government.................................	4 912 ..	....	....	....	....	....	....	....	....
Banks...	4 913 ..	....	....	....	....	....	....	....	....
Other sectors...	4 914 ..	....	....	....	....	....	....	....	....
Assets...	4 900 ..	....	....	....	....	....	....	....	....
Monetary authorities................................	4 901 ..	....	....	....	....	....	....	....	....
General government.................................	4 902 ..	....	....	....	....	....	....	....	....
Banks...	4 903 ..	....	....	....	....	....	....	....	....
Other sectors...	4 904 ..	....	....	....	....	....	....	....	....
Liabilities..	4 905 ..	....	....	....	....	....	....	....	....
Monetary authorities................................	4 906 ..	....	....	....	....	....	....	....	....
General government.................................	4 907 ..	....	....	....	....	....	....	....	....
Banks...	4 908 ..	....	....	....	....	....	....	....	....
Other sectors...	4 909 ..	....	....	....	....	....	....	....	....

Table 2 (Concluded). STANDARD PRESENTATION, 2003–2010

(Millions of U.S. dollars)

	Code	2003	2004	2005	2006	2007	2008	2009	2010
D. OTHER INVESTMENT	4 700 ..	**3,125.0**	**3,284.4**	**3,321.2**	**5,445.2**	**6,920.5**	**−12,021.2**	**−10,802.7**	**−4,225.2**
Assets	4 703 ..	**−20,786.6**	**−9,779.9**	**−11,562.4**	**−30,234.9**	**−38,504.7**	**−3,264.6**	**18,123.8**	**2,739.7**
Trade credits	4 706 ..	....	....	....	....	....	....	....	....
General government	4 707 ..	....	....	....	....	....	....	....	....
of which: Short-term	4 709 ..	....	....	....	....	....	....	....	....
Other sectors	4 710 ..	....	....	....	....	....	....	....	....
of which: Short-term	4 712 ..	....	....	....	....	....	....	....	....
Loans	4 714 ..	−2,854.0	−3,798.1	−8,409.7	−15,644.6	−24,544.4	−16,368.7	12,051.9	7,820.2
Monetary authorities	4 715 ..	....	....	....	....	....	....	....	....
of which: Short-term	4 718 ..	....	....	....	....	....	....	....	....
General government	4 719 ..	....	....	....	....	....	....	....	....
of which: Short-term	4 721 ..	....	....	....	....	....	....	....	....
Banks	4 722 ..	−2,854.0	−3,798.1	−8,409.7	−15,644.6	−24,544.4	−16,368.7	12,051.9	7,820.2
of which: Short-term	4 724 ..	....	....	....	....	....	....	....	....
Other sectors	4 725 ..	....	....	....	....	....	....	....	....
of which: Short-term	4 727 ..	....	....	....	....	....	....	....	....
Currency and deposits	4 730 ..	−17,923.7	−5,979.1	−3,152.5	−14,582.0	−13,952.9	13,103.5	6,108.6	−5,074.4
Monetary authorities	4 731 ..	....	....	....	....	....	....	....	....
General government	4 732 ..	....	....	....	....	....	....	....	....
Banks	4 733 ..	−17,923.7	−5,979.1	−3,152.5	−14,582.0	−13,952.9	13,103.5	6,108.6	−5,074.4
Other sectors	4 734 ..	....	....	....	....	....	....	....	....
Other assets	4 736 ..	−8.8	−2.7	−.3	−8.2	−7.4	.5	−36.7	−6.1
Monetary authorities	4 737 ..	....	....	....	....	....	....	....	....
of which: Short-term	4 739 ..	....	....	....	....	....	....	....	....
General government	4 740 ..	−10.4	−5.1	−4.5	−11.4	−10.6	−2.7	−39.9	−9.3
of which: Short-term	4 742 ..	....	....	....	....	....	....	....	....
Banks	4 743 ..	....	....	....	....	....	....	....	....
of which: Short-term	4 745 ..	....	....	....	....	....	....	....	....
Other sectors	4 746 ..	1.6	2.3	4.3	3.2	3.2	3.2	3.2	3.2
of which: Short-term	4 748 ..	....	....	....	....	....	....	....	....
Liabilities	4 753 ..	**23,911.6**	**13,064.3**	**14,883.6**	**35,680.1**	**45,425.2**	**−8,756.6**	**−28,926.4**	**−6,964.8**
Trade credits	4 756 ..	1.0	3.1	−11.3	−5.6	−7.7	−7.7	−7.7	−7.7
General government	4 757 ..	....	....	....	....	....	....	....	....
of which: Short-term	4 759 ..	....	....	....	....	....	....	....	....
Other sectors	4 760 ..	1.0	3.1	−11.3	−5.6	−7.7	−7.7	−7.7	−7.7
of which: Short-term	4 762 ..	....	....	....	....	....	....	....	....
Loans	4 764 ..	117.4	57.2	97.9	80.9	109.8	129.4	89.3	7.5
Monetary authorities	4 765 ..	....	....	....	....	....	....	....	....
of which: Use of Fund credit and loans from the Fund	4 766 ..	....	....	....	....	....	....	....	....
of which: Short-term	4 768 ..	....	....	....	....	....	....	....	....
General government	4 769 ..	168.5	24.7	39.7	22.7	46.3	60.0	19.9	−61.9
of which: Short-term	4 771 ..	....	....	....	....	....	....	....	....
Banks	4 772 ..	....	....	....	....	....	....	....	....
of which: Short-term	4 774 ..	....	....	....	....	....	....	....	....
Other sectors	4 775 ..	−51.1	32.4	58.2	58.2	63.6	69.4	69.4	69.4
of which: Short-term	4 777 ..	....	....	....	....	....	....	....	....
Currency and deposits	4 780 ..	23,793.4	13,004.7	14,797.4	35,613.3	45,331.6	−8,869.8	−29,184.2	−6,956.1
Monetary authorities	4 781 ..	....	....	....	....	....	....	....	....
General government	4 782 ..	....	....	....	....	....	....	....	....
Banks	4 783 ..	23,793.4	13,004.7	14,797.4	35,613.3	45,331.6	−8,869.8	−29,184.2	−6,956.1
Other sectors	4 784 ..	....	....	....	....	....	....	....	....
Other liabilities	4 786 ..	−.3	−.6	−.5	−8.5	−8.5	−8.5	176.1	−8.5
Monetary authorities	4 787 ..	....	....	....	....	....	....	184.7	....
of which: Short-term	4 789 ..	....	....	....	....	....	....	....	....
General government	4 790 ..	....	....	....	....	....	....	....	....
of which: Short-term	4 792 ..	....	....	....	....	....	....	....	....
Banks	4 793 ..	....	....	....	....	....	....	....	....
of which: Short-term	4 795 ..	....	....	....	....	....	....	....	....
Other sectors	4 796 ..	−.3	−.6	−.5	−8.5	−8.5	−8.5	−8.5	−8.5
of which: Short-term	4 798 ..	....	....	....	....	....	....	....	....
E. RESERVE ASSETS	4 802 ..	**−43.7**	**−157.9**	**−294.2**	**−822.0**	**−1,414.7**	**294.2**	**118.5**	**−1,279.5**
Monetary gold	4 812 ..	....	....	....	....	....	....	....	....
Special drawing rights	4 811 ..	.1	.1	−1.6	−3.1	−4.1	−4.2	−185.2	−.3
Reserve position in the Fund	4 810 ..	−1.5	−1.7	−.5	....	....	....	....	....
Foreign exchange	4 803 ..	−42.3	−156.4	−292.0	−818.9	−1,410.6	298.4	303.7	−1,279.3
Other claims	4 813 ..	....	....	....	....	....	....	....	....
NET ERRORS AND OMISSIONS	4 998 ..	**−699.8**	**27.2**	**149.9**	**10.9**	**10.3**	**−30.3**	**−250.0**	**107.1**

Table 3. INTERNATIONAL INVESTMENT POSITION (End-period stocks), 2003–2010

(Millions of U.S. dollars)

	Code	2003	2004	2005	2006	2007	2008	2009	2010
ASSETS...	8 995 C.	**89,800.2**	**104,666.0**	**124,680.7**	**167,239.0**	**218,712.8**	**217,015.2**	**190,238.9**	**187,046.4**
Direct investment abroad.................................	8 505 ..	**2,899.5**	**3,935.1**	**5,070.5**	**6,050.5**	**7,719.7**	**9,340.1**	**7,548.7**	**7,882.7**
Equity capital and reinvested earnings..............................	8 506 ..	2,899.5	3,935.1	5,070.5	6,050.5	7,719.7	9,340.1	7,548.7	7,882.7
Claims on affiliated enterprises..............................	8 507 ..	2,899.5	3,935.1	5,070.5	6,050.5	7,719.7	9,340.1	7,548.7	7,882.7
Liabilities to affiliated enterprises..............................	8 508 ..	....	....	....	....	....	....	....	....
Other capital..............................	8 530 ..	....	....	....	....	....	....	....	....
Claims on affiliated enterprises..............................	8 535 ..	....	....	....	....	....	....	....	....
Liabilities to affiliated enterprises..............................	8 540 ..	....	....	....	....	....	....	....	....
Portfolio investment..	8 602 ..	**22,402.9**	**26,295.5**	**33,331.7**	**43,859.0**	**53,749.1**	**47,463.4**	**40,754.4**	**38,702.8**
Equity securities..	8 610 ..	3,861.7	5,860.7	8,080.4	10,281.1	13,649.2	14,442.4	12,800.8	12,547.6
Monetary authorities..	8 611 ..	....	....	....	....	....	....	....	....
General government..	8 612 ..	....	....	....	....	....	....	....	....
Banks..	8 613 ..	2,361.3	4,029.9	5,133.6	6,475.6	8,659.2	7,237.8	7,122.8	7,441.3
Other sectors..	8 614 ..	1,500.4	1,830.8	2,946.9	3,805.5	4,990.0	7,204.5	5,677.9	5,106.4
Debt securities..	8 619 ..	18,541.2	20,434.8	25,251.2	33,577.9	40,099.9	33,021.0	27,953.7	26,155.2
Bonds and notes..	8 620 ..	18,541.2	20,434.8	25,251.2	33,577.9	40,099.9	33,021.0	27,953.7	26,155.2
Monetary authorities..	8 621 ..	....	....	....	....	....	....	....	....
General government..	8 622 ..	....	....	....	....	....	....	....	....
Banks..	8 623 ..	18,196.9	20,009.2	24,548.0	32,661.1	38,888.0	31,026.6	26,827.4	24,915.3
Other sectors..	8 624 ..	344.3	425.5	703.2	916.8	1,211.9	1,994.4	1,126.3	1,239.9
Money market instruments..	8 630 ..	....	....	....	....	....	....	....	....
Monetary authorities..	8 631 ..	....	....	....	....	....	....	....	....
General government..	8 632 ..	....	....	....	....	....	....	....	....
Banks..	8 633 ..	....	....	....	....	....	....	....	....
Other sectors..	8 634 ..	....	....	....	....	....	....	....	....
Financial derivatives...	8 900 ..	....	....	....	....	....	....	....	....
Monetary authorities...	8 901 ..	....	....	....	....	....	....	....	....
General government...	8 902 ..	....	....	....	....	....	....	....	....
Banks...	8 903 ..	....	....	....	....	....	....	....	....
Other sectors...	8 904 ..	....	....	....	....	....	....	....	....
Other investment...	8 703 ..	**62,959.2**	**72,734.1**	**84,291.9**	**114,515.3**	**153,009.4**	**156,274.5**	**138,114.3**	**135,365.3**
Trade credits...	8 706 ..	....	....	....	....	....	....	....	....
General government...	8 707 ..	....	....	....	....	....	....	....	....
of which: Short-term...	8 709 ..	....	....	....	....	....	....	....	....
Other sectors...	8 710 ..	....	....	....	....	....	....	....	....
of which: Short-term...	8 712 ..	....	....	....	....	....	....	....	....
Loans...	8 714 ..	18,324.5	22,122.6	30,532.3	46,176.9	70,721.2	87,089.9	75,038.1	67,218.0
Monetary authorities...	8 715 ..	....	....	....	....	....	....	....	....
of which: Short-term...	8 718 ..	....	....	....	....	....	....	....	....
General government...	8 719 ..	....	....	....	....	....	....	....	....
of which: Short-term...	8 721 ..	....	....	....	....	....	....	....	....
Banks...	8 722 ..	18,324.5	22,122.6	30,532.3	46,176.9	70,721.2	87,089.9	75,038.1	67,218.0
of which: Short-term...	8 724 ..	....	....	....	....	....	....	....	....
Other sectors...	8 725 ..	....	....	....	....	....	....	....	....
of which: Short-term...	8 727 ..	....	....	....	....	....	....	....	....
Currency and deposits...	8 730 ..	44,616.9	50,596.0	53,748.5	68,330.5	82,283.3	69,179.9	63,071.4	68,145.7
Monetary authorities...	8 731 ..	....	....	....	....	....	....	....	....
General government...	8 732 ..	....	....	....	....	....	....	....	....
Banks...	8 733 ..	44,616.9	50,596.0	53,748.5	68,330.5	82,283.3	69,179.9	63,071.4	68,145.7
Other sectors...	8 734 ..	....	....	....	....	....	....	....	....
Other assets...	8 736 ..	17.8	15.4	11.2	8.0	4.8	4.8	4.8	1.6
Monetary authorities...	8 737 ..	....	....	....	....	....	....	....	....
of which: Short-term...	8 739 ..	....	....	....	....	....	....	....	....
General government...	8 740 ..	....	....	....	....	....	....	....	....
of which: Short-term...	8 742 ..	....	....	....	....	....	....	....	....
Banks...	8 743 ..	....	....	....	....	....	....	....	....
of which: Short-term...	8 745 ..	....	....	....	....	....	....	....	....
Other sectors...	8 746 ..	17.8	15.4	11.2	8.0	4.8	4.8	4.8	1.6
of which: Short-term...	8 748 ..	....	....	....	....	....	....	....	....
Reserve assets..	8 802 ..	**1,538.6**	**1,701.4**	**1,986.6**	**2,814.1**	**4,234.6**	**3,937.2**	**3,821.5**	**5,095.6**
Monetary gold..	8 812 ..	6.6	6.6	6.6	6.6	6.6	6.6	6.6	6.6
Special drawing rights..	8 811 ..	1.0	.9	2.4	5.7	10.2	14.0	200.0	196.8
Reserve position in the Fund..	8 810 ..	103.6	110.0	101.8	107.1	112.5	109.7	111.6	109.7
Foreign exchange..	8 803 ..	1,427.4	1,583.8	1,875.8	2,694.7	4,105.3	3,806.9	3,503.2	4,782.4
Other claims..	8 813 ..	....	....	....	....	....	....	....	....

Table 3 (Concluded). INTERNATIONAL INVESTMENT POSITION (End-period stocks), 2003–2010

(Millions of U.S. dollars)

	Code	2003	2004	2005	2006	2007	2008	2009	2010
LIABILITIES	8 995 D.	**84,599.9**	**98,670.6**	**116,845.5**	**157,067.8**	**205,545.3**	**201,560.1**	**174,386.1**	**170,277.3**
Direct investment in Bahrain	8 555 ..	**6,719.8**	**7,354.0**	**8,276.1**	**11,190.7**	**12,947.0**	**14,741.0**	**14,998.2**	**15,154.0**
Equity capital and reinvested earnings	8 556 ..	6,719.8	7,354.0	8,276.1	11,190.7	12,947.0	14,741.0	14,998.2	15,154.0
Claims on direct investors	8 557 ..	....	....	....	....	....	....	....	....
Liabilities to direct investors	8 558 ..	6,719.8	7,354.0	8,276.1	11,190.7	12,947.0	14,741.0	14,998.2	15,154.0
Other capital	8 580 ..	....	....	....	....	....	....	....	....
Claims on direct investors	8 585 ..	....	....	....	....	....	....	....	....
Liabilities to direct investors	8 590 ..	....	....	....	....	....	....	....	....
Portfolio investment	8 652 ..	**2,188.9**	**2,576.6**	**4,998.4**	**6,694.6**	**8,024.8**	**11,014.9**	**12,580.4**	**15,284.6**
Equity securities	8 660 ..	631.5	652.4	2,453.5	2,587.3	2,726.1	2,882.4	2,395.2	4,047.9
Banks	8 663 ..	....	....	....	....	....	....	....	....
Other sectors	8 664 ..	631.5	652.4	2,453.5	2,587.3	2,726.1	2,882.4	2,395.2	4,047.9
Debt securities	8 669 ..	1,557.4	1,924.2	2,545.0	4,107.3	5,298.7	8,132.4	10,185.2	11,236.7
Bonds and notes	8 670 ..	1,557.4	1,924.2	2,545.0	4,107.3	5,298.7	8,132.4	10,185.2	11,236.7
Monetary authorities	8 671 ..	....	....	....	....	....	....	....	....
General government	8 672 ..	500.0	500.0	500.0	500.0	500.0	....	750.0	2,000.0
Banks	8 673 ..	1,057.4	1,424.2	2,045.0	3,607.3	4,798.7	8,132.4	9,435.2	9,236.7
Other sectors	8 674 ..	....	....	....	....	....	....	....	....
Money market instruments	8 680 ..	....	....	....	....	....	....	....	....
Monetary authorities	8 681 ..	....	....	....	....	....	....	....	....
General government	8 682 ..	....	....	....	....	....	....	....	....
Banks	8 683 ..	....	....	....	....	....	....	....	....
Other sectors	8 684 ..	....	....	....	....	....	....	....	....
Financial derivatives	8 905 ..	....	....	....	....	....	....	....	....
Monetary authorities	8 906 ..	....	....	....	....	....	....	....	....
General government	8 907 ..	....	....	....	....	....	....	....	....
Banks	8 908 ..	....	....	....	....	....	....	....	....
Other sectors	8 909 ..	....	....	....	....	....	....	....	....
Other investment	8 753 ..	**75,691.2**	**88,740.0**	**103,570.9**	**139,182.5**	**184,573.4**	**175,804.2**	**146,807.5**	**139,838.8**
Trade credits	8 756 ..	5.4	8.5	−2.7	−8.2	.5	.5	.5	−8.2
General government	8 757 ..	....	....	....	....	....	....	....	....
of which: Short-term	8 759 ..	....	....	....	....	....	....	....	....
Other sectors	8 760 ..	5.4	8.5	−2.7	−8.2	.5	.5	.5	−8.2
of which: Short-term	8 762 ..	....	....	....	....	....	....	....	....
Loans	8 764 ..	653.0	694.7	739.9	752.4	811.5	912.1	904.3	912.4
Monetary authorities	8 765 ..	....	....	....	....	....	....	....	....
of which: Use of Fund credit and loans from the Fund....	8 766 ..	....	....	....	....	....	....	....	....
of which: Short-term	8 768 ..	....	....	....	....	....	....	....	....
General government	8 769 ..	653.0	694.7	739.9	752.4	811.5	912.1	904.3	912.4
of which: Short-term	8 771 ..	....	....	....	....	....	....	....	....
Banks	8 772 ..	....	....	....	....	....	....	....	....
of which: Short-term	8 774 ..	....	....	....	....	....	....	....	....
Other sectors	8 775 ..	....	....	....	....	....	....	....	....
of which: Short-term	8 777 ..	....	....	....	....	....	....	....	....
Currency and deposits	8 780 ..	75,025.0	88,029.6	102,827.0	138,440.2	183,771.8	174,902.0	145,718.1	138,762.0
Monetary authorities	8 781 ..	....	....	....	....	....	....	....	....
General government	8 782 ..	....	....	....	....	....	....	....	....
Banks	8 783 ..	75,025.0	88,029.6	102,827.0	138,440.2	183,771.8	174,902.0	145,718.1	138,762.0
Other sectors	8 784 ..	....	....	....	....	....	....	....	....
Other liabilities	8 786 ..	7.8	7.2	6.6	−1.9	−10.4	−10.4	184.6	172.6
Monetary authorities	8 787 ..	....	....	....	....	....	....	194.9	191.5
of which: Short-term	8 789 ..	....	....	....	....	....	....	....	....
General government	8 790 ..	....	....	....	....	....	....	....	....
of which: Short-term	8 792 ..	....	....	....	....	....	....	....	....
Banks	8 793 ..	....	....	....	....	....	....	....	....
of which: Short-term	8 795 ..	....	....	....	....	....	....	....	....
Other sectors	8 796 ..	7.8	7.2	6.6	−1.9	−10.4	−10.4	−10.4	−18.9
of which: Short-term	8 798 ..	....	....	....	....	....	....	....	....
NET INTERNATIONAL INVESTMENT POSITION	8 995 ..	**5,200.3**	**5,995.4**	**7,835.2**	**10,171.2**	**13,167.5**	**15,455.1**	**15,852.8**	**16,769.1**
Conversion rates: Bahrain dinar per U.S. dollar (end of period)	0 102 ..	.3760	.3760	.3760	.3760	.3760	.3760	.3760	.3760

Table 1. ANALYTIC PRESENTATION, 2003–2010

(Millions of U.S. dollars)

	Code	2003	2004	2005	2006	2007	2008	2009	2010
A. Current Account[1]	4 993 Z.	**131.6**	**−278.7**	**−176.2**	**1,196.1**	**856.9**	**926.2**	**3,556.1**	**2,502.4**
Goods: exports f.o.b.	2 100 ..	7,050.1	8,150.7	9,302.5	11,553.7	12,474.3	15,501.8	15,072.6	19,238.7
Goods: imports f.o.b.	3 100 ..	−9,492.0	−11,157.1	−12,501.6	−14,443.4	−16,669.2	−21,505.9	−19,677.7	−24,723.4
Balance on Goods	4 100 ..	*−2,441.9*	*−3,006.5*	*−3,199.1*	*−2,889.7*	*−4,194.9*	*−6,004.1*	*−4,605.1*	*−5,484.6*
Services: credit	2 200 ..	1,011.7	1,083.0	1,249.0	1,333.8	1,616.8	1,995.9	1,976.1	2,414.2
Services: debit	3 200 ..	−1,711.5	−1,931.4	−2,206.7	−2,340.5	−2,884.8	−3,664.4	−3,396.3	−4,352.5
Balance on Goods and Services	4 991 ..	*−3,141.7*	*−3,854.9*	*−4,156.8*	*−3,896.3*	*−5,462.8*	*−7,672.6*	*−6,025.3*	*−7,422.9*
Income: credit	2 300 ..	56.5	102.6	116.6	177.4	244.1	192.3	49.1	112.5
Income: debit	3 300 ..	−361.3	−473.9	−910.2	−1,018.1	−1,212.0	−1,211.2	−1,448.4	−1,518.9
Balance on Goods, Services, and Income	4 992 ..	*−3,446.4*	*−4,226.2*	*−4,950.4*	*−4,737.0*	*−6,430.8*	*−8,691.6*	*−7,424.6*	*−8,829.3*
Current transfers: credit	2 379 Z.	3,586.2	3,960.4	4,785.0	5,941.3	7,297.4	9,768.0	11,246.7	11,702.5
Current transfers: debit	3 379 ..	−8.2	−12.9	−10.8	−8.2	−9.8	−150.3	−265.9	−370.7
B. Capital Account[1]	4 994 Z.	**386.7**	**142.1**	**261.7**	**152.5**	**715.4**	**490.5**	**474.9**	**470.9**
Capital account: credit	2 994 Z.	386.7	142.1	261.7	152.5	715.4	490.5	474.9	470.9
Capital account: debit	3 994 ..	....	....	....	....	....	....	....	....
Total, Groups A Plus B	4 981 ..	*518.4*	*−136.6*	*85.5*	*1,348.6*	*1,572.3*	*1,416.6*	*4,031.1*	*2,973.4*
C. Financial Account[1]	4 995 W.	**289.0**	**665.0**	**142.4**	**120.2**	**680.0**	**−268.3**	**951.4**	**−1,626.4**
Direct investment abroad	4 505 ..	−2.8	−4.1	−1.9	....	....	....	....	−.2
Direct investment in Bangladesh	4 555 Z.	268.3	448.9	813.3	697.2	652.8	1,009.6	713.4	967.6
Portfolio investment assets	4 602 ..	....	....	−.1	−2.6	−12.9	−57.6	−11.7	−778.6
Equity securities	4 610 ..	....	....	−.1	−2.6	−12.9	−4.2	−4.3	28.5
Debt securities	4 619 ..	....	....	....	....	....	−53.4	−7.3	−807.0
Portfolio investment liabilities	4 652 Z.	1.6	4.3	19.5	30.8	153.9	19.2	43.3	165.9
Equity securities	4 660 ..	1.6	4.3	19.5	30.8	153.4	−48.3	−152.6	−.2
Debt securities	4 669 Z.	....	....	....	....	.5	67.5	195.9	166.1
Financial derivatives	4 910 ..	....	....	....	....	....	....	....	....
Financial derivatives assets	4 900 ..	....	....	....	....	....	....	....	....
Financial derivatives liabilities	4 905 ..	....	....	....	....	....	....	....	....
Other investment assets	4 703 ..	−693.6	−495.1	−865.3	−1,352.8	−1,004.2	−2,188.1	−1,336.1	−2,657.4
Monetary authorities	4 701 ..	....	....	....	....	....	....	....	....
General government	4 704 ..	....	....	....	....	....	....	....	....
Banks	4 705 ..	136.2	−7.9	−61.8	−90.6	−14.6	−22.4	−53.1	−279.7
Other sectors	4 728 ..	−829.8	−487.2	−803.5	−1,262.2	−989.6	−2,165.8	−1,282.9	−2,377.8
Other investment liabilities	4 753 W.	715.5	711.0	176.8	747.6	890.4	948.6	1,542.4	676.3
Monetary authorities	4 753 WA	37.9	55.1	−50.6	58.9	122.2	14.7	741.6	424.3
General government	4 753 ZB	728.2	664.9	73.0	602.4	827.4	869.5	934.7	272.9
Banks	4 753 ZC	−188.4	−35.4	96.5	72.3	−82.3	152.8	−40.1	179.1
Other sectors	4 753 ZD	137.9	26.4	57.9	14.0	23.1	−88.4	−93.8	−200.0
Total, Groups A Through C	4 983 ..	*807.4*	*528.5*	*227.9*	*1,468.8*	*2,252.3*	*1,148.3*	*4,982.5*	*1,347.0*
D. Net Errors and Omissions	4 998 ..	**81.1**	**−25.0**	**−643.9**	**−603.5**	**−879.5**	**−129.6**	**−647.8**	**−395.5**
Total, Groups A Through D	4 984 ..	*888.5*	*503.4*	*−416.1*	*865.3*	*1,372.8*	*1,018.8*	*4,334.6*	*951.5*
E. Reserves and Related Items	4 802 A.	**−888.5**	**−503.4**	**416.1**	**−865.3**	**−1,372.8**	**−1,018.8**	**−4,334.6**	**−951.5**
Reserve assets	4 802 ..	−886.3	−649.8	318.6	−1,012.0	−1,372.8	−1,229.4	−4,311.5	−906.3
Use of Fund credit and loans	4 766 ..	−2.2	146.3	97.5	146.7	....	210.6	−23.2	−45.2
Exceptional financing	4 920 ..	....	....	....	....	....	....	....	....
Conversion rates: taka per U.S. dollar	0 101 ..	**58.150**	**59.513**	**64.327**	**68.933**	**68.875**	**68.598**	**69.039**	**69.649**

[1] Excludes components that have been classified in the categories of Group E.

Table 2. STANDARD PRESENTATION, 2003–2010

(Millions of U.S. dollars)

	Code	2003	2004	2005	2006	2007	2008	2009	2010
CURRENT ACCOUNT	4 993 ..	**131.6**	**−278.7**	**−176.2**	**1,196.1**	**856.9**	**926.2**	**3,556.1**	**2,502.4**
A. GOODS	4 100 ..	**−2,441.9**	**−3,006.5**	**−3,199.1**	**−2,889.7**	**−4,194.9**	**−6,004.1**	**−4,605.1**	**−5,484.6**
Credit	2 100 ..	**7,050.1**	**8,150.7**	**9,302.5**	**11,553.7**	**12,474.3**	**15,501.8**	**15,072.6**	**19,238.7**
General merchandise: exports f.o.b.	2 110 ..	6,804.2	7,966.5	9,038.8	11,200.9	12,098.1	15,224.1	15,008.8	19,122.7
Goods for processing: exports f.o.b.	2 150 ..	234.5	171.7	246.7	317.9	332.6	201.4	22.3	36.5
Repairs on goods	2 160 ..	1.3	1.2	1.3	2.0	4.3	2.0	....	....
Goods procured in ports by carriers	2 170 ..	10.1	11.3	15.7	32.9	39.2	74.3	41.5	79.5
Nonmonetary gold	2 180 ..	....	....	....	....	....	....	....	....
Debit	3 100 ..	**−9,492.0**	**−11,157.1**	**−12,501.6**	**−14,443.4**	**−16,669.2**	**−21,505.9**	**−19,677.7**	**−24,723.4**
General merchandise: imports f.o.b.	3 110 ..	−9,340.7	−11,013.8	−12,345.9	−14,242.8	−16,469.4	−21,380.3	−19,675.4	−24,689.9
Goods for processing: imports f.o.b.	3 150 ..	−133.5	−115.8	−131.3	−143.0	−184.0	−93.0	....	....
Repairs on goods	3 160 ..	−5.5	−20.1	−26.5	−54.7	−15.4	−1.8	....	....
Goods procured in ports by carriers	3 170 ..	−12.2	−7.5	2.2	−2.9	−.4	−30.7	−2.4	−33.5
Nonmonetary gold	3 180 ..	....	....	....	....	....	....	....	....
B. SERVICES	4 200 ..	**−699.8**	**−848.4**	**−957.7**	**−1,006.6**	**−1,267.9**	**−1,668.6**	**−1,420.2**	**−1,938.3**
Total credit	2 200 ..	*1,011.7*	*1,083.0*	*1,249.0*	*1,333.8*	*1,616.8*	*1,995.9*	*1,976.1*	*2,414.2*
Total debit	3 200 ..	*−1,711.5*	*−1,931.4*	*−2,206.7*	*−2,340.5*	*−2,884.8*	*−3,664.4*	*−3,396.3*	*−4,352.5*
Transportation services, credit	2 205 ..	**71.9**	**77.4**	**113.0**	**88.7**	**80.0**	**114.7**	**142.7**	**173.6**
Passenger	2 850 ..	*1.7*	*8.6*	*8.5*	*.2*			*7.1*	*21.6*
Freight	2 851 ..	*7.9*	*10.5*	*24.5*	*18.9*	*16.1*	*18.0*	*16.2*	*29.4*
Other	2 852 ..	*62.3*	*58.3*	*80.0*	*69.6*	*63.8*	*96.7*	*119.4*	*122.7*
Sea transport, passenger	2 207 ..	....	....	....	....	....	....	....	....
Sea transport, freight	2 208 ..	3.3	9.2	24.5	18.9	16.1	17.3	10.7	29.1
Sea transport, other	2 209 ..	54.1	55.7	77.0	65.5	61.9	89.9	106.9	104.9
Air transport, passenger	2 211 ..	1.7	8.6	8.5	.2	....	....	7.1	21.6
Air transport, freight	2 212 ..	4.6	1.3	....	....	.1	.8	5.5	.3
Air transport, other	2 213 ..	8.2	2.7	3.0	4.0	1.9	4.5	6.7	12.4
Other transport, passenger	2 215 ..	....	....	....	....	....	....	....	....
Other transport, freight	2 216 ..	....	....	....	....	....	....	....	....
Other transport, other	2 217 ..	....	....	....	....	....	2.3	5.8	5.4
Transportation services, debit	3 205 ..	**−1,203.5**	**−1,418.2**	**−1,544.7**	**−1,607.5**	**−2,150.7**	**−3,032.1**	**−2,646.3**	**−3,401.3**
Passenger	3 850 ..	*−223.9*	*−281.3*	*−239.4*	*−303.5*	*−374.2*	*−551.2*	*−402.1*	*−573.7*
Freight	3 851 ..	*−949.3*	*−1,127.6*	*−1,304.9*	*−1,303.9*	*−1,776.1*	*−2,474.8*	*−2,236.9*	*−2,821.7*
Other	3 852 ..	*−30.3*	*−9.2*	*−.4*	*−.1*	*−.5*	*−6.1*	*−7.3*	*−5.8*
Sea transport, passenger	3 207 ..	....	....	....	....	....	....	....	....
Sea transport, freight	3 208 ..	−949.3	−1,127.5	−1,286.9	−1,276.1	−1,745.9	−2,445.8	−2,224.7	−2,809.1
Sea transport, other	3 209 ..	−2.8	−1.0	−.4	−.1	−.1	−.4	−.6	−.4
Air transport, passenger	3 211 ..	−223.9	−281.3	−239.4	−303.5	−374.2	−551.2	−402.1	−573.7
Air transport, freight	3 212 ..	....	−.2	−18.0	−27.8	−30.1	−29.0	−12.2	−12.7
Air transport, other	3 213 ..	−27.5	−8.2	....	....	−.4	−3.6	−3.7	−1.3
Other transport, passenger	3 215 ..	....	....	....	....	....	....	....	....
Other transport, freight	3 216 ..	....	....	....	....	....	....	....	....
Other transport, other	3 217 ..	....	....	....	....	....	−2.1	−3.0	−4.2
Travel, credit	2 236 ..	**56.9**	**66.9**	**70.0**	**80.3**	**76.4**	**74.6**	**69.6**	**81.2**
Business travel	2 237 ..	.9	1.5	2.1	1.8	1.8	.6	.8	1.1
Personal travel	2 240 ..	56.0	65.4	67.9	78.6	74.6	73.9	68.8	80.1
Travel, debit	3 236 ..	**−164.9**	**−160.7**	**−136.3**	**−139.6**	**−155.8**	**−183.6**	**−249.1**	**−260.9**
Business travel	3 237 ..	−26.0	−29.2	−24.3	−25.8	−24.4	−24.0	−21.8	−28.8
Personal travel	3 240 ..	−138.9	−131.6	−112.0	−113.8	−131.3	−159.5	−227.3	−232.2
Other services, credit	2 200 BA	**882.9**	**938.7**	**1,066.0**	**1,164.8**	**1,460.5**	**1,806.6**	**1,763.8**	**2,159.4**
Communications	2 245 ..	71.5	55.7	23.9	62.4	76.5	110.6	188.7	277.6
Construction	2 249 ..	2.8	2.4	14.2	22.4	29.9	7.4	3.9	6.9
Insurance	2 253 ..	3.8	3.9	5.0	8.0	10.6	11.5	10.9	6.8
Financial	2 260 ..	28.5	15.1	18.0	26.2	20.6	30.1	41.5	40.8
Computer and information	2 262 ..	5.1	10.2	18.7	31.2	16.0	30.1	35.3	37.8
Royalties and licence fees	2 266 ..	.3	.1	.3	.3	....	....	.3	.5
Other business services	2 268 ..	152.9	187.9	210.0	280.5	374.2	519.0	453.7	586.3
Personal, cultural, and recreational	2 287 ..	4.0	.5	1.1	2.6	1.2	1.1	1.7	1.6
Government, n.i.e.	2 291 ..	614.0	662.8	774.8	731.3	931.4	1,096.8	1,027.9	1,201.0
Other services, debit	3 200 BA	**−343.1**	**−352.5**	**−525.7**	**−593.3**	**−578.3**	**−448.8**	**−501.0**	**−690.3**
Communications	3 245 ..	−9.7	−12.2	−20.6	−11.9	−23.9	−16.3	−21.1	−20.2
Construction	3 249 ..	−7.4	−.7	−1.1	−1.4	−.3	−.3	−.3	−9.3
Insurance	3 253 ..	−114.3	−135.1	−150.6	−175.0	−153.5	−18.8	−24.4	−26.3
Financial	3 260 ..	−7.7	−8.8	−13.3	−20.3	−21.7	−25.3	−31.0	−45.2
Computer and information	3 262 ..	−1.0	−1.5	−4.3	−2.6	−3.9	−5.2	−6.1	−5.4
Royalties and licence fees	3 266 ..	−3.7	−5.1	−2.7	−5.2	−7.7	−21.9	−8.4	−24.3
Other business services	3 268 ..	−82.6	−92.7	−137.7	−147.4	−155.7	−191.9	−197.9	−306.1
Personal, cultural, and recreational	3 287 ..	−.2	−.1	....	−.4	−.2	−.2	−.4	−.2
Government, n.i.e.	3 291 ..	−116.5	−96.1	−195.3	−229.1	−211.3	−168.9	−211.4	−253.3

Table 2 (Continued). STANDARD PRESENTATION, 2003–2010

(Millions of U.S. dollars)

	Code	2003	2004	2005	2006	2007	2008	2009	2010
C. INCOME	4 300	**−304.8**	**−371.3**	**−793.6**	**−840.7**	**−967.9**	**−1,018.9**	**−1,399.3**	**−1,406.4**
Total credit	2 300	*56.5*	*102.6*	*116.6*	*177.4*	*244.1*	*192.3*	*49.1*	*112.5*
Total debit	3 300	*−361.3*	*−473.9*	*−910.2*	*−1,018.1*	*−1,212.0*	*−1,211.2*	*−1,448.4*	*−1,518.9*
Compensation of employees, credit	2 310	**11.7**	**11.6**	**12.1**	**9.9**	**9.2**	**15.3**	**13.0**	**14.2**
Compensation of employees, debit	3 310	**−2.9**	**−3.1**	**−2.9**	**−1.5**	**−.8**	**−8.6**	**−1.9**	**−1.9**
Investment income, credit	2 320	**44.8**	**90.9**	**104.5**	**167.6**	**234.9**	**177.0**	**36.0**	**98.3**
Direct investment income	2 330	2.7	3.0	2.1	10.7	12.2	.2	1.0	1.5
Dividends and distributed branch profits	2 332	1.7	1.0	2.1	10.7	12.2	.2	1.0	1.5
Reinvested earnings and undistributed branch profits	2 333	1.1	2.0	....	....	....	....	....	....
Income on debt (interest)	2 334	....	....	....	....	....	....	....	....
Portfolio investment income	2 339	....	.1	....	....	.3	....	.1	....
Income on equity	2 340	....	.1	....	....	.3	....	.1	....
Income on bonds and notes	2 350	....	....	....	....	....	....	....	....
Income on money market instruments	2 360	....	....	....	....	....	....	....	....
Other investment income	2 370	42.1	87.9	102.4	156.9	222.3	176.8	34.9	96.7
Investment income, debit	3 320	**−358.4**	**−470.8**	**−907.3**	**−1,016.6**	**−1,211.2**	**−1,202.7**	**−1,446.5**	**−1,516.9**
Direct investment income	3 330	−177.7	−246.7	−661.4	−764.9	−903.3	−839.7	−1,104.9	−1,164.5
Dividends and distributed branch profits	3 332	−95.2	−77.7	−418.6	−460.6	−697.8	−559.4	−799.5	−842.2
Reinvested earnings and undistributed branch profits	3 333	−82.5	−168.2	−242.8	−304.2	−205.5	−280.3	−305.4	−322.1
Income on debt (interest)	3 334	....	−.7	....	....	....	....	....	−.2
Portfolio investment income	3 339	−.1	−.9	−.7	−1.0	−1.1	−25.2	−64.9	−80.2
Income on equity	3 340	−.1	−.9	−.7	−1.0	−1.1	−2.4	−3.9	−5.7
Income on bonds and notes	3 350	....	....	....	....	....	−22.8	−61.0	−74.5
Income on money market instruments	3 360	....	....	....	....	....	....	....	....
Other investment income	3 370	−180.7	−223.3	−245.3	−250.7	−306.8	−337.8	−276.6	−272.2
D. CURRENT TRANSFERS	4 379	**3,578.1**	**3,947.5**	**4,774.2**	**5,933.1**	**7,287.7**	**9,617.8**	**10,980.8**	**11,331.7**
Credit	2 379	**3,586.2**	**3,960.4**	**4,785.0**	**5,941.3**	**7,297.4**	**9,768.0**	**11,246.7**	**11,702.5**
General government	2 380	69.5	23.7	37.8	11.6	168.4	66.5	106.6	73.3
Other sectors	2 390	3,516.7	3,936.7	4,747.1	5,929.6	7,129.0	9,701.6	11,140.0	11,629.2
Workers' remittances	2 391	3,180.0	3,572.2	4,302.4	5,417.7	6,553.1	8,925.3	10,507.6	10,837.7
Other current transfers	2 392	336.7	364.5	444.7	512.0	575.9	776.2	632.4	791.4
Debit	3 379	**−8.2**	**−12.9**	**−10.8**	**−8.2**	**−9.8**	**−150.3**	**−265.9**	**−370.7**
General government	3 380	−.6	−1.0	−1.0	−.8	−1.6	−.9	....	−.2
Other sectors	3 390	−7.6	−11.9	−9.8	−7.4	−8.2	−149.4	−265.9	−370.5
Workers' remittances	3 391	−4.2	−4.7	−2.6	−1.8	−2.1	−5.8	−5.9	−7.5
Other current transfers	3 392	−3.4	−7.3	−7.2	−5.6	−6.1	−143.6	−260.1	−363.1
CAPITAL AND FINANCIAL ACCOUNT	4 996	**−212.8**	**303.7**	**820.2**	**−592.5**	**22.7**	**−796.6**	**−2,908.3**	**−2,106.9**
CAPITAL ACCOUNT	4 994	**386.7**	**142.1**	**261.7**	**152.5**	**715.4**	**490.5**	**474.9**	**470.9**
Total credit	2 994	*386.7*	*142.1*	*261.7*	*152.5*	*715.4*	*490.5*	*474.9*	*470.9*
Total debit	3 994	....	....	....	....	....	....	....	....
Capital transfers, credit	2 400	**386.7**	**142.1**	**261.7**	**152.5**	**715.4**	**490.5**	**474.9**	**470.9**
General government	2 401	386.7	142.1	261.7	152.5	715.0	490.3	474.9	470.9
Debt forgiveness	2 402	86.0	....	....	....	....	....	....	....
Other capital transfers	2 410	300.7	142.1	261.7	152.5	715.0	490.3	474.9	470.9
Other sectors	2 430	....	....	....	....	.5	.1	....	....
Migrants' transfers	2 431	....	....	....	....	....	....	....	....
Debt forgiveness	2 432	....	....	....	....	....	....	....	....
Other capital transfers	2 440	....	....	....	....	.5	.1	....	....
Capital transfers, debit	3 400	....	....	....	....	....	....	....	....
General government	3 401	....	....	....	....	....	....	....	....
Debt forgiveness	3 402	....	....	....	....	....	....	....	....
Other capital transfers	3 410	....	....	....	....	....	....	....	....
Other sectors	3 430	....	....	....	....	....	....	....	....
Migrants' transfers	3 431	....	....	....	....	....	....	....	....
Debt forgiveness	3 432	....	....	....	....	....	....	....	....
Other capital transfers	3 440	....	....	....	....	....	....	....	....
Nonproduced nonfinancial assets, credit	2 480	....	....	....	....	....	....	....	....
Nonproduced nonfinancial assets, debit	3 480	....	....	....	....	....	....	....	....

Table 2 (Continued). STANDARD PRESENTATION, 2003–2010

(Millions of U.S. dollars)

	Code	2003	2004	2005	2006	2007	2008	2009	2010
FINANCIAL ACCOUNT	4 995	**−599.5**	**161.6**	**558.4**	**−745.1**	**−692.7**	**−1,287.1**	**−3,383.2**	**−2,577.9**
A. DIRECT INVESTMENT	4 500	**265.5**	**444.8**	**811.4**	**697.2**	**652.8**	**1,009.6**	**713.4**	**967.4**
Direct investment abroad	4 505	**−2.8**	**−4.1**	**−1.9**	....	....	....	....	**−.2**
Equity capital	4 510	−1.7	−2.1	−1.9	....	....	....	....	−.2
Claims on affiliated enterprises	4 515	−1.7	−2.1	....	....	....	....	....	−.2
Liabilities to affiliated enterprises	4 520	....	....	....	....	....	....	....	....
Reinvested earnings	4 525	−1.1	−2.0	....	....	....	....	....	....
Other capital	4 530	....	....	....	....	....	....	....	....
Claims on affiliated enterprises	4 535	....	....	....	....	....	....	....	....
Liabilities to affiliated enterprises	4 540	....	....	....	....	....	....	....	....
Direct investment in Bangladesh	4 555	**268.3**	**448.9**	**813.3**	**697.2**	**652.8**	**1,009.6**	**713.4**	**967.6**
Equity capital	4 560	138.4	183.9	417.8	361.2	347.8	685.5	336.5	629.4
Claims on direct investors	4 565	....	....	....	....	....	....	−19.4	−1.3
Liabilities to direct investors	4 570	138.4	183.9	417.8	361.2	347.8	685.5	355.9	630.7
Reinvested earnings	4 575	82.5	168.2	242.8	304.2	205.5	280.3	305.4	322.1
Other capital	4 580	47.4	96.7	152.8	31.8	99.5	43.8	71.5	16.2
Claims on direct investors	4 585	....	....	....	....	....	....	....	....
Liabilities to direct investors	4 590	47.4	96.7	152.8	31.8	99.5	43.8	71.5	16.2
B. PORTFOLIO INVESTMENT	4 600	**1.6**	**4.3**	**19.4**	**28.2**	**141.0**	**−38.4**	**31.7**	**−612.7**
Assets	4 602	....	....	**−.1**	**−2.6**	**−12.9**	**−57.6**	**−11.7**	**−778.6**
Equity securities	4 610	....	....	−.1	−2.6	−12.9	−4.2	−4.3	28.5
Monetary authorities	4 611	....	....	....	....	....	....	....	....
General government	4 612	....	....	....	....	....	....	....	....
Banks	4 613	....	....	....	....	....	−4.3	−4.3	26.8
Other sectors	4 614	....	....	−.1	−2.6	−12.9	.1	....	1.7
Debt securities	4 619	....	....	....	....	....	−53.4	−7.3	−807.0
Bonds and notes	4 620	....	....	....	....	....	....	....	....
Monetary authorities	4 621	....	....	....	....	....	....	....	....
General government	4 622	....	....	....	....	....	....	....	....
Banks	4 623	....	....	....	....	....	....	....	....
Other sectors	4 624	....	....	....	....	....	....	....	....
Money market instruments	4 630	....	....	....	....	....	−53.4	−7.3	−807.0
Monetary authorities	4 631	....	....	....	....	....	....	....	....
General government	4 632	....	....	....	....	....	....	....	....
Banks	4 633	....	....	....	....	....	6.2	44.9	−567.0
Other sectors	4 634	....	....	....	....	....	−59.7	−52.3	−240.0
Liabilities	4 652	**1.6**	**4.3**	**19.5**	**30.8**	**153.9**	**19.2**	**43.3**	**165.9**
Equity securities	4 660	1.6	4.3	19.5	30.8	153.4	−48.3	−152.6	−.2
Banks	4 663	....	....	....	3.6	29.9	28.9	7.5	65.3
Other sectors	4 664	1.6	4.3	19.5	27.2	123.4	−77.1	−160.2	−65.5
Debt securities	4 669	....	....	....	....	.5	67.5	195.9	166.1
Bonds and notes	4 670	....	....	....	....	.5	67.5	195.9	166.1
Monetary authorities	4 671	....	....	....	....	....	....	....	....
General government	4 672	....	....	....	....	....	67.5	195.9	166.1
Banks	4 673	....	....	....	....	....	....	....	....
Other sectors	4 674	....	....	....	....	.5	....	....	....
Money market instruments	4 680	....	....	....	....	....	....	....	....
Monetary authorities	4 681	....	....	....	....	....	....	....	....
General government	4 682	....	....	....	....	....	....	....	....
Banks	4 683	....	....	....	....	....	....	....	....
Other sectors	4 684	....	....	....	....	....	....	....	....
C. FINANCIAL DERIVATIVES	4 910	....	....	....	....	....	....	....	....
Monetary authorities	4 911	....	....	....	....	....	....	....	....
General government	4 912	....	....	....	....	....	....	....	....
Banks	4 913	....	....	....	....	....	....	....	....
Other sectors	4 914	....	....	....	....	....	....	....	....
Assets	4 900	....	....	....	....	....	....	....	....
Monetary authorities	4 901	....	....	....	....	....	....	....	....
General government	4 902	....	....	....	....	....	....	....	....
Banks	4 903	....	....	....	....	....	....	....	....
Other sectors	4 904	....	....	....	....	....	....	....	....
Liabilities	4 905	....	....	....	....	....	....	....	....
Monetary authorities	4 906	....	....	....	....	....	....	....	....
General government	4 907	....	....	....	....	....	....	....	....
Banks	4 908	....	....	....	....	....	....	....	....
Other sectors	4 909	....	....	....	....	....	....	....	....

Table 2 (Concluded). STANDARD PRESENTATION, 2003–2010

(Millions of U.S. dollars)

	Code	2003	2004	2005	2006	2007	2008	2009	2010
D. OTHER INVESTMENT	4 700 ..	**19.7**	**362.2**	**−590.9**	**−458.5**	**−113.8**	**−1,028.9**	**183.2**	**−2,026.3**
Assets	4 703 ..	**−693.6**	**−495.1**	**−865.3**	**−1,352.8**	**−1,004.2**	**−2,188.1**	**−1,336.1**	**−2,657.4**
Trade credits	4 706 ..	−713.5	−310.1	−621.3	−842.4	−444.3	−1,669.4	−649.7	−1,856.1
General government	4 707 ..	....	....	....	....	....	....	....	....
of which: Short-term	4 709 ..	....	....	....	....	....	....	....	....
Other sectors	4 710 ..	−713.5	−310.1	−621.3	−842.4	−444.3	−1,669.4	−649.7	−1,856.1
of which: Short-term	4 712 ..	*−713.5*	*−310.1*	*−621.3*	*−842.4*	*−464.6*	*−1,669.4*	*−649.7*	*−1,856.1*
Loans	4 714 ..	....	....	....	....	....	25.7	.8	....
Monetary authorities	4 715 ..	....	....	....	....	....	....	....	....
of which: Short-term	4 718 ..	....	....	....	....	....	....	....	....
General government	4 719 ..	....	....	....	....	....	....	....	....
of which: Short-term	4 721 ..	....	....	....	....	....	....	....	....
Banks	4 722 ..	....	....	....	....	....	....	....	....
of which: Short-term	4 724 ..	....	....	....	....	....	....	....	....
Other sectors	4 725 ..	....	....	....	....	....	25.7	.8	....
of which: Short-term	4 727 ..	....	....	....	....	....	....	....	....
Currency and deposits	4 730 ..	136.2	−7.9	−61.8	−90.6	−14.6	−22.4	−53.1	−279.7
Monetary authorities	4 731 ..	....	....	....	....	....	....	....	....
General government	4 732 ..	....	....	....	....	....	....	....	....
Banks	4 733 ..	136.2	−7.9	−61.8	−90.6	−14.6	−22.4	−53.1	−279.7
Other sectors	4 734 ..	....	....	....	....	....	....	....	....
Other assets	4 736 ..	−116.3	−177.0	−182.1	−419.8	−545.3	−522.0	−634.1	−521.6
Monetary authorities	4 737 ..	....	....	....	....	....	....	....	....
of which: Short-term	4 739 ..	....	....	....	....	....	....	....	....
General government	4 740 ..	....	....	....	....	....	....	....	....
of which: Short-term	4 742 ..	....	....	....	....	....	....	....	....
Banks	4 743 ..	....	....	....	....	....	....	....	....
of which: Short-term	4 745 ..	....	....	....	....	....	....	....	....
Other sectors	4 746 ..	−116.3	−177.0	−182.1	−419.8	−545.3	−522.0	−634.1	−521.6
of which: Short-term	4 748 ..	*−95.1*	*−123.0*	*−157.4*	*−123.7*	*−429.6*	*−522.0*	*−634.1*	*−521.6*
Liabilities	4 753 ..	**713.3**	**857.4**	**274.4**	**894.3**	**890.4**	**1,159.2**	**1,519.3**	**631.1**
Trade credits	4 756 ..	147.4	63.7	78.7	18.8	....	....	....	....
General government	4 757 ..	....	....	....	....	....	....	....	....
of which: Short-term	4 759 ..	....	....	....	....	....	....	....	....
Other sectors	4 760 ..	147.4	63.7	78.7	18.8	....	....	....	....
of which: Short-term	4 762 ..	*147.4*	*63.7*	*78.7*	*18.8*	....	....	....	....
Loans	4 764 ..	722.6	777.6	157.1	748.3	810.9	1,036.5	887.1	164.0
Monetary authorities	4 765 ..	−2.2	146.3	97.5	146.7	....	210.6	−23.2	−45.2
of which: Use of Fund credit and loans from the Fund	4 766 ..	*−2.2*	*146.3*	*97.5*	*146.7*	....	*210.6*	*−23.2*	*−45.2*
of which: Short-term	4 768 ..	....	....	....	....	....	....	....	....
General government	4 769 ..	728.2	664.9	73.0	602.4	827.4	869.5	934.7	272.9
of which: Short-term	4 771 ..	*222.1*	*173.9*	*−209.8*	*296.7*	*188.6*	*−105.8*	....	....
Banks	4 772 ..	6.1	3.7	7.4	3.9	−39.6	44.8	69.3	136.3
of which: Short-term	4 774 ..	....	....	....	....	*−34.1*	*39.1*	*72.9*	*137.2*
Other sectors	4 775 ..	−9.5	−37.3	−20.9	−4.7	23.1	−88.4	−93.8	−200.0
of which: Short-term	4 777 ..	....	....	....	....	....	*.3*	*20.0*	*−57.5*
Currency and deposits	4 780 ..	−195.7	−39.1	89.1	68.4	−42.8	108.0	−109.4	42.8
Monetary authorities	4 781 ..	−1.2	....	....	....	....	....	....	....
General government	4 782 ..	....	....	....	....	....	....	....	....
Banks	4 783 ..	−194.5	−39.1	89.1	68.4	−42.8	108.0	−109.4	42.8
Other sectors	4 784 ..	....	....	....	....	....	....	....	....
Other liabilities	4 786 ..	39.1	55.1	−50.6	58.9	122.2	14.7	741.6	424.3
Monetary authorities	4 787 ..	39.1	55.1	−50.6	58.9	122.2	14.7	741.6	424.3
of which: Short-term	4 789 ..	*39.1*	*55.1*	*−50.6*	*58.9*	*122.2*	*14.7*	*17.6*	*424.3*
General government	4 790 ..	....	....	....	....	....	....	....	....
of which: Short-term	4 792 ..	....	....	....	....	....	....	....	....
Banks	4 793 ..	....	....	....	....	....	....	....	....
of which: Short-term	4 795 ..	....	....	....	....	....	....	....	....
Other sectors	4 796 ..	....	....	....	....	....	....	....	....
of which: Short-term	4 798 ..	....	....	....	....	....	....	....	....
E. RESERVE ASSETS	4 802 ..	**−886.3**	**−649.8**	**318.6**	**−1,012.0**	**−1,372.8**	**−1,229.4**	**−4,311.5**	**−906.3**
Monetary gold	4 812 ..	....	....	....	....	....	....	....	−420.5
Special drawing rights	4 811 ..	−.6	2.0	.2	−.4	.6	−1.5	−714.0	45.7
Reserve position in the Fund	4 810 ..	....	....	....	....	....	....	....	−.2
Foreign exchange	4 803 ..	−885.7	−651.8	318.3	−1,011.6	−1,373.3	−1,227.8	−3,597.5	−531.3
Other claims	4 813 ..	....	....	....	....	....	....	....	....
NET ERRORS AND OMISSIONS	4 998 ..	**81.1**	**−25.0**	**−643.9**	**−603.5**	**−879.5**	**−129.6**	**−647.8**	**−395.5**

Table 3. INTERNATIONAL INVESTMENT POSITION (End-period stocks), 2003–2010

(Millions of U.S. dollars)

	Code	2003	2004	2005	2006	2007	2008	2009	2010
ASSETS..............................	8 995 C.	**3,452.1**	**4,100.7**	**3,779.6**	**5,026.8**	**7,159.4**	**7,730.9**	**12,406.1**	**13,308.5**
Direct investment abroad..............	8 505 ..	**95.5**	**94.7**	**93.9**	**97.2**	**112.3**	**79.9**	**121.1**	**102.1**
Equity capital and reinvested earnings...........	8 506 ..	63.4	61.3	60.2	62.3	65.3	60.3	73.3	80.5
Claims on affiliated enterprises.........	8 507 ..	63.4	61.3	60.2	62.3	65.3	60.3	73.3	80.5
Liabilities to affiliated enterprises........	8 508 ..	....	....	....	....	....	....	....	....
Other capital............................	8 530 ..	32.1	33.4	33.6	34.8	47.0	19.6	47.8	21.5
Claims on affiliated enterprises.........	8 535 ..	32.1	33.4	33.6	34.8	47.0	19.6	47.8	21.5
Liabilities to affiliated enterprises........	8 540 ..	....	....	....	....	....	....	....	....
Portfolio investment...................	8 602 ..	**28.3**	**26.9**	**25.3**	**26.6**	**1,120.1**	**1,184.6**	**1,189.7**	**2,095.6**
Equity securities........................	8 610 ..	28.3	26.9	25.3	26.6	27.1	27.4	32.4	38.8
Monetary authorities..................	8 611 ..	....	....	....	....	....	....	....	....
General government..................	8 612 ..	....	....	....	....	....	....	....	....
Banks................................	8 613 ..	27.3	26.5	25.1	26.4	27.1	27.4	32.4	38.8
Other sectors........................	8 614 ..	1.0	.4	.2	.2	....	....	....	....
Debt securities.........................	8 619 ..	....	....	....	....	1,093.0	1,157.3	1,157.3	2,056.8
Bonds and notes......................	8 620 ..	....	....	....	....	....	....	....	....
Monetary authorities..............	8 621 ..	....	....	....	....	....	....	....	....
General government..............	8 622 ..	....	....	....	....	....	....	....	....
Banks............................	8 623 ..	....	....	....	....	....	....	....	....
Other sectors....................	8 624 ..	....	....	....	....	....	....	....	....
Money market instruments.............	8 630 ..	....	....	....	....	1,093.0	1,157.3	1,157.3	2,056.8
Monetary authorities..............	8 631 ..	....	....	....	....	....	....	....	....
General government..............	8 632 ..	....	....	....	....	....	....	....	....
Banks............................	8 633 ..	....	....	....	....	534.5	549.3	455.7	875.5
Other sectors....................	8 634 ..	....	....	....	....	558.5	608.0	701.6	1,181.3
Financial derivatives..................	8 900 ..	....	....	....	....	....	....	....	....
Monetary authorities....................	8 901 ..	....	....	....	....	....	....	....	....
General government.....................	8 902 ..	....	....	....	....	....	....	....	....
Banks...................................	8 903 ..	....	....	....	....	....	....	....	....
Other sectors...........................	8 904 ..	....	....	....	....	....	....	....	....
Other investment.....................	8 703 ..	**750.5**	**806.6**	**893.1**	**1,097.5**	**649.0**	**677.8**	**752.8**	**980.3**
Trade credits...........................	8 706 ..	....	....	....	....	110.0	141.8	142.6	142.5
General government..................	8 707 ..	....	....	....	....	....	....	....	....
of which: Short-term..............	8 709 ..	....	....	....	....	....	....	....	....
Other sectors........................	8 710 ..	....	....	....	....	110.0	141.8	142.6	142.5
of which: Short-term..............	8 712 ..	....	....	....	....	*110.0*	*141.8*	*142.6*	*142.5*
Loans..................................	8 714 ..	389.4	436.3	457.3	573.6	....	....	....	....
Monetary authorities..................	8 715 ..	....	....	....	....	....	....	....	....
of which: Short-term..............	8 718 ..	....	....	....	....	....	....	....	....
General government..................	8 719 ..	....	....	....	....	....	....	....	....
of which: Short-term..............	8 721 ..	....	....	....	....	....	....	....	....
Banks................................	8 722 ..	389.4	436.3	457.3	573.6	....	....	....	....
of which: Short-term..............	8 724 ..	*389.4*	*436.3*	*457.3*	*573.6*	....	....	....	....
Other sectors........................	8 725 ..	....	....	....	....	....	....	....	....
of which: Short-term..............	8 727 ..	....	....	....	....	....	....	....	....
Currency and deposits...................	8 730 ..	356.1	364.5	429.8	517.9	532.0	528.8	599.9	817.4
Monetary authorities..................	8 731 ..	....	....	....	....	....	....	....	....
General government..................	8 732 ..	....	....	....	....	....	....	....	....
Banks................................	8 733 ..	356.1	364.5	429.8	517.9	532.0	528.8	599.9	817.4
Other sectors........................	8 734 ..	....	....	....	....	....	....	....	....
Other assets...........................	8 736 ..	5.0	5.9	6.1	6.1	7.0	7.1	10.3	20.5
Monetary authorities..................	8 737 ..	5.0	5.9	6.1	6.1	7.0	7.1	10.3	20.5
of which: Short-term..............	8 739 ..	....	....	....	....	....	....	....	....
General government..................	8 740 ..	....	....	....	....	....	....	....	....
of which: Short-term..............	8 742 ..	....	....	....	....	....	....	....	....
Banks................................	8 743 ..	....	....	....	....	....	....	....	....
of which: Short-term..............	8 745 ..	....	....	....	....	....	....	....	....
Other sectors........................	8 746 ..	....	....	....	....	....	....	....	....
of which: Short-term..............	8 748 ..	....	....	....	....	....	....	....	....
Reserve assets.......................	8 802 ..	**2,577.8**	**3,172.4**	**2,767.2**	**3,805.6**	**5,278.0**	**5,788.6**	**10,342.5**	**10,130.6**
Monetary gold..........................	8 812 ..	....	....	....	....	94.6	99.3	124.4	613.2
Special drawing rights...................	8 811 ..	3.2	1.2	.9	1.3	.8	2.1	718.5	659.6
Reserve position in the Fund.............	8 810 ..	.3	.3	.3	.4	.4	.5	.5	.6
Foreign exchange.......................	8 803 ..	2,574.3	3,170.8	2,766.0	3,803.9	5,182.2	5,686.7	9,499.1	8,857.1
Other claims...........................	8 813 ..	....	....	....	....	....	....	....	....

Table 3 (Concluded). INTERNATIONAL INVESTMENT POSITION (End-period stocks), 2003–2010

(Millions of U.S. dollars)

	Code	2003	2004	2005	2006	2007	2008	2009	2010
LIABILITIES	8 995 D.	**21,484.3**	**22,551.5**	**23,650.9**	**25,717.7**	**27,557.6**	**29,661.7**	**31,895.4**	**33,945.9**
Direct investment in Bangladesh	8 555 ..	**2,973.1**	**2,830.1**	**3,701.8**	**4,247.7**	**4,458.2**	**4,912.4**	**5,369.6**	**6,494.0**
Equity capital and reinvested earnings	8 556 ..	2,465.9	2,573.0	3,181.2	3,870.6	4,177.3	4,567.4	4,900.3	5,729.5
Claims on direct investors	8 557 ..	....	....	....	....	....	....	....	....
Liabilities to direct investors	8 558 ..	2,465.9	2,573.0	3,181.2	3,870.6	4,177.3	4,567.4	4,900.3	5,729.5
Other capital	8 580 ..	507.2	257.2	520.6	377.1	280.9	345.0	469.3	764.5
Claims on direct investors	8 585 ..	−45.1	−41.8	−51.5	−81.7	−80.4	−89.6	−207.5	−141.4
Liabilities to direct investors	8 590 ..	552.3	299.0	572.1	458.7	361.3	434.7	676.8	905.9
Portfolio investment	8 652 ..	**36.0**	**87.2**	**81.7**	**105.4**	**420.0**	**1,071.1**	**1,327.3**	**1,936.5**
Equity securities	8 660 ..	34.0	85.3	81.6	105.4	419.9	395.3	460.9	996.8
Banks	8 663 ..	.4	1.6	2.3	10.4	262.1	168.8	88.9	558.6
Other sectors	8 664 ..	33.6	83.7	79.3	94.9	157.8	226.5	372.1	438.2
Debt securities	8 669 ..	2.0	1.9	....	....	.1	675.7	866.3	939.7
Bonds and notes	8 670 ..	2.0	1.9	....	....	.1	675.7	866.3	939.7
Monetary authorities	8 671 ..	....	....	....	....	....	....	....	....
General government	8 672 ..	....	....	....	....	....	675.0	865.4	939.1
Banks	8 673 ..	....	....	....	....	....	.7	.9	.4
Other sectors	8 674 ..	2.0	1.9	....	....	....	....	....	.2
Money market instruments	8 680 ..	....	....	....	....	....	....	....	....
Monetary authorities	8 681 ..	....	....	....	....	....	....	....	....
General government	8 682 ..	....	....	....	....	....	....	....	....
Banks	8 683 ..	....	....	....	....	....	....	....	....
Other sectors	8 684 ..	....	....	....	....	....	....	....	....
Financial derivatives	8 905 ..	**....**	**....**	**....**	**....**	**....**	**....**	**....**	**....**
Monetary authorities	8 906 ..	....	....	....	....	....	....	....	....
General government	8 907 ..	....	....	....	....	....	....	....	....
Banks	8 908 ..	....	....	....	....	....	....	....	....
Other sectors	8 909 ..	....	....	....	....	....	....	....	....
Other investment	8 753 ..	**18,475.2**	**19,634.2**	**19,867.4**	**21,364.6**	**22,679.5**	**23,678.2**	**25,198.5**	**25,515.3**
Trade credits	8 756 ..	....	....	....	....	....	....	....	....
General government	8 757 ..	....	....	....	....	....	....	....	....
of which: Short-term	8 759 ..	....	....	....	....	....	....	....	....
Other sectors	8 760 ..	....	....	....	....	....	....	....	....
of which: Short-term	8 762 ..	....	....	....	....	....	....	....	....
Loans	8 764 ..	17,978.0	19,116.3	19,341.7	20,674.2	21,859.6	22,737.5	23,547.4	23,416.3
Monetary authorities	8 765 ..	73.6	230.6	308.4	476.5	500.5	685.6	674.5	616.9
of which: Use of Fund credit and loans from the Fund	8 766 ..	*73.6*	*230.6*	*308.4*	*476.5*	*500.5*	*685.6*	*674.5*	*616.9*
of which: Short-term	8 768 ..	....	....	....	....	....	....	....	....
General government	8 769 ..	17,139.5	18,186.3	18,260.8	19,176.3	19,568.3	20,040.4	20,850.8	20,515.3
of which: Short-term	8 771 ..	....	....	....	....	....	....	....	....
Banks	8 772 ..	210.5	171.0	196.7	235.5	160.0	199.1	219.0	294.5
of which: Short-term	8 774 ..	*158.6*	*125.0*	*144.8*	*178.1*	*96.1*	*134.4*	*160.0*	*213.9*
Other sectors	8 775 ..	554.4	528.3	575.8	785.9	1,630.8	1,812.4	1,803.1	1,989.7
of which: Short-term	8 777 ..	....	....	....	....	*552.0*	*527.4*	*535.6*	*844.0*
Currency and deposits	8 780 ..	270.7	210.4	261.6	362.0	369.9	473.3	365.6	403.4
Monetary authorities	8 781 ..	....	....	....	....	....	.1	....	.8
General government	8 782 ..	....	....	....	....	....	....	....	....
Banks	8 783 ..	270.7	210.4	261.6	362.0	369.9	473.2	365.6	402.5
Other sectors	8 784 ..	....	....	....	....	....	....	....	....
Other liabilities	8 786 ..	226.6	307.5	264.1	328.4	449.9	467.4	1,285.5	1,695.6
Monetary authorities	8 787 ..	226.6	307.5	264.1	328.4	449.9	467.4	1,285.5	1,695.6
of which: Short-term	8 789 ..	*226.6*	*307.5*	*264.1*	*328.4*	*449.9*	*467.4*	*485.4*	*909.6*
General government	8 790 ..	....	....	....	....	....	....	....	....
of which: Short-term	8 792 ..	....	....	....	....	....	....	....	....
Banks	8 793 ..	....	....	....	....	....	....	....	....
of which: Short-term	8 795 ..	....	....	....	....	....	....	....	....
Other sectors	8 796 ..	....	....	....	....	....	....	....	....
of which: Short-term	8 798 ..	....	....	....	....	....	....	....	....
NET INTERNATIONAL INVESTMENT POSITION	8 995 ..	**−18,032.2**	**−18,450.8**	**−19,871.3**	**−20,690.9**	**−20,398.2**	**−21,930.8**	**−19,489.3**	**−20,637.3**
Conversion rates: taka per U.S. dollar (end of period)	0 102 ..	**58.782**	**60.742**	**66.210**	**69.065**	**68.576**	**68.920**	**69.267**	**70.750**

Table 1. ANALYTIC PRESENTATION, 2003–2010
(Millions of U.S. dollars)

	Code	2003	2004	2005	2006	2007	2008	2009	2010
A. Current Account[1]	4 993 Z.	−241.5	−413.6	−510.4	−408.8	−311.2	−437.2	−312.0	....
Goods: exports f.o.b.	2 100 ..	251.8	278.4	361.5	441.6	489.9	489.6	381.0	....
Goods: imports f.o.b.	3 100 ..	−1,065.6	−1,260.2	−1,431.5	−1,452.6	−1,527.7	−1,731.9	−1,293.9	....
Balance on Goods	4 100 ..	*−813.7*	*−981.7*	*−1,070.0*	*−1,011.0*	*−1,037.8*	*−1,242.3*	*−912.8*	....
Services: credit	2 200 ..	1,088.1	1,137.3	1,317.0	1,452.8	1,640.7	1,556.1	1,415.8	....
Services: debit	3 200 ..	−515.9	−550.8	−676.4	−727.8	−816.0	−650.5	−604.0	....
Balance on Goods and Services	4 991 ..	*−241.6*	*−395.3*	*−429.4*	*−286.0*	*−213.1*	*−336.7*	*−101.1*	....
Income: credit	2 300 ..	92.9	98.2	111.5	101.6	198.9	164.2	242.6	....
Income: debit	3 300 ..	−185.0	−202.1	−260.1	−301.5	−299.6	−255.1	−450.7	....
Balance on Goods, Services, and Income	4 992 ..	*−333.8*	*−499.2*	*−578.0*	*−485.9*	*−313.8*	*−427.6*	*−309.1*	....
Current transfers: credit	2 379 Z.	126.5	123.8	134.8	133.5	113.7	84.1	76.3	....
Current transfers: debit	3 379 ..	−34.2	−38.2	−67.2	−56.4	−111.1	−93.7	−79.2	....
B. Capital Account[1]	4 994 Z.	....	....	....	....	....	....	....	....
Capital account: credit	2 994 Z.	....	....	....	....	....	....	....	
Capital account: debit	3 994 ..	....	....	....	....	....	....	....	
Total, Groups A Plus B	4 981 ..	*−241.5*	*−413.6*	*−510.4*	*−408.8*	*−311.2*	*−437.2*	*−312.0*	
C. Financial Account[1]	4 995 W.	**10.0**	**221.3**	**409.3**	**223.4**	**333.5**	**353.1**	**179.3**	....
Direct investment abroad	4 505 ..	−.5	−3.9	−9.1	−13.8	−197.2	−63.4	−80.1	....
Direct investment in Barbados	4 555 Z.	58.3	−12.1	62.0	104.8	233.2	285.8	298.2	....
Portfolio investment assets	4 602 ..	−23.0	−29.9	−89.5	22.6	−190.6	−161.6	28.6	....
Equity securities	4 610 ..	−23.2	−44.7	−53.2	−14.9	−7.3	−44.2	−36.9	....
Debt securities	4 619 ..	.2	14.8	−36.3	37.5	−183.4	−117.4	65.5	....
Portfolio investment liabilities	4 652 Z.	−104.5	−12.5	125.0	60.7	−19.2	−6.9	98.3	....
Equity securities	4 660 ..	−94.5	....	....	−4.3	1.1	10.7	−8.7	....
Debt securities	4 669 Z.	−10.0	−12.5	125.0	65.0	−20.3	−17.7	107.0	....
Financial derivatives	4 910 ..	....	....	6.6	....	....	.6	.5	....
Financial derivatives assets	4 900 ..	....	....	1.6	....	....	....	....	....
Financial derivatives liabilities	4 905 ..	....	....	5.0	....	.1	.6	.5	....
Other investment assets	4 703 ..	−82.9	31.3	−238.5	−280.9	−605.3	−124.5	238.4	....
Monetary authorities	4 701 ..	....	....	....	....	....	....	.5	....
General government	4 704 ..	−4.2	−3.6	−.2	3.3	−3.2	−2.5	1.8	....
Banks	4 705 ..	−87.9	−26.0	−155.0	−137.4	−630.4	140.9	460.3	....
Other sectors	4 728 ..	9.2	60.8	−83.2	−146.8	28.3	−263.0	−224.2	....
Other investment liabilities	4 753 W.	162.6	248.4	552.9	329.9	1,112.5	423.1	−404.8	....
Monetary authorities	4 753 WA	....	....	....	....	....	....	88.0	....
General government	4 753 ZB	4.8	−10.8	−6.8	−9.1	−25.1	7.9	15.3	....
Banks	4 753 ZC	−41.1	49.2	247.2	59.7	618.8	25.7	−395.1	....
Other sectors	4 753 ZD	198.9	210.0	312.4	279.3	518.7	389.5	−113.0	....
Total, Groups A Through C	4 983 ..	*−231.5*	*−192.3*	*−101.1*	*−185.5*	*22.3*	*−84.1*	*−132.7*	....
D. Net Errors and Omissions	4 998 ..	**267.5**	**26.2**	**128.8**	**162.4**	**141.3**	**−25.4**	**188.1**	....
Total, Groups A Through D	4 984 ..	*35.9*	*−166.1*	*27.6*	*−23.1*	*163.6*	*−109.6*	*55.4*	
E. Reserves and Related Items	4 802 A.	**−35.9**	**166.1**	**−27.6**	**23.1**	**−163.6**	**109.6**	**−55.4**	....
Reserve assets	4 802 ..	−36.5	165.6	−29.3	21.6	−165.6	94.9	−65.5	....
Use of Fund credit and loans	4 766 ..	....	....	....	....	....	....	....	....
Exceptional financing	4 920 ..	.6	.6	1.7	1.5	2.0	14.6	10.0	....
Conversion rates: Barbados dollars per U.S. dollar	0 101 ..	**2.0000**	**2.0000**	**2.0000**	**2.0000**	**2.0000**	**2.0000**	**2.0000**	**2.0000**

[1] Excludes components that have been classified in the categories of Group E.

Table 2. STANDARD PRESENTATION, 2003–2010

(Millions of U.S. dollars)

	Code	2003	2004	2005	2006	2007	2008	2009	2010
CURRENT ACCOUNT	4 993	−240.9	−413.1	−508.8	−407.3	−309.2	−422.6	−301.9	....
A. GOODS	4 100	−813.7	−981.7	−1,070.0	−1,011.0	−1,037.8	−1,242.3	−912.8	....
Credit	2 100	251.8	278.4	361.5	441.6	489.9	489.6	381.0	....
General merchandise: exports f.o.b.	2 110	198.7	211.2	266.7	327.6	373.2	369.1	312.4	....
Goods for processing: exports f.o.b.	2 150	....	....	....	....	....	....	....	....
Repairs on goods	2 160	.1	....	....	.1	1.2	.1	.8	....
Goods procured in ports by carriers	2 170	53.0	67.3	94.8	114.0	115.6	120.3	67.8	....
Nonmonetary gold	2 180	....	....	....	....	....	....	....	....
Debit	3 100	−1,065.6	−1,260.2	−1,431.5	−1,452.6	−1,527.7	−1,731.9	−1,293.9	....
General merchandise: imports f.o.b.	3 110	−1,065.5	−1,260.0	−1,431.4	−1,452.6	−1,525.6	−1,710.4	−1,293.6	....
Goods for processing: imports f.o.b.	3 150	....	−.1	....	....	....	....	....	....
Repairs on goods	3 160	....	....	....	....	−2.1	−21.5	−.3	....
Goods procured in ports by carriers	3 170	−.1	−.1	....	....	....	....	....	....
Nonmonetary gold	3 180	....	....	....	....	....	....	....	....
B. SERVICES	4 200	572.2	586.5	640.6	725.0	824.7	905.6	811.8	....
Total credit	2 200	*1,088.1*	*1,137.3*	*1,317.0*	*1,452.8*	*1,640.7*	*1,556.1*	*1,415.8*	....
Total debit	3 200	*−515.9*	*−550.8*	*−676.4*	*−727.8*	*−816.0*	*−650.5*	*−604.0*	....
Transportation services, credit	2 205	23.2	25.9	25.3	27.3	36.7	30.7	40.8	....
Passenger	2 850	*8.6*	*8.5*	*7.6*	*7.2*	*6.6*	*6.5*	*9.6*	....
Freight	2 851	*4.6*	*4.8*	*5.9*	*7.2*	*7.6*	*7.0*	*5.5*	....
Other	2 852	*10.1*	*12.6*	*11.9*	*13.0*	*22.5*	*17.2*	*25.7*	....
Sea transport, passenger	2 207	3.6	3.8	3.3	3.1	5.8	5.4	2.5	....
Sea transport, freight	2 208	....	....	....	....	....	....	....	....
Sea transport, other	2 209	.1	4.3	3.9	4.1	10.9	4.8	8.3	....
Air transport, passenger	2 211	.8	.5	.5	.4	....	....	....	....
Air transport, freight	2 212	....	....	....	....	....	....	....	....
Air transport, other	2 213	3.0	3.1	3.4	3.5	6.7	7.4	9.6	....
Other transport, passenger	2 215	4.3	4.3	3.8	3.6	.8	1.1	7.1	....
Other transport, freight	2 216	4.6	4.8	5.9	7.2	7.6	7.0	5.5	....
Other transport, other	2 217	7.0	5.3	4.6	5.4	5.0	5.0	7.8	....
Transportation services, debit	3 205	−169.8	−197.4	−218.3	−225.4	−251.7	−158.6	−143.9	....
Passenger	3 850	*−49.1*	*−54.9*	*−56.5*	*−61.7*	*−78.0*	*−74.1*	*−77.0*	....
Freight	3 851	*−119.5*	*−141.3*	*−160.4*	*−162.9*	*−171.0*	*−81.5*	*−65.0*	....
Other	3 852	*−1.2*	*−1.2*	*−1.3*	*−.8*	*−2.6*	*−3.0*	*−1.9*	....
Sea transport, passenger	3 207	−.1	−.1	....	....	....	....	−2.9	....
Sea transport, freight	3 208	−95.6	−113.0	−128.4	−130.3	−136.8	−78.6	−59.3	....
Sea transport, other	3 209	....	....	....	....	−.1	−.6	−.8	....
Air transport, passenger	3 211	−49.0	−54.9	−56.5	−61.7	−78.0	−74.1	−74.1	....
Air transport, freight	3 212	−23.9	−28.3	−32.1	−32.6	−34.2	−3.0	−5.7	....
Air transport, other	3 213	−.6	−.7	−.7	....	−2.5	−2.4	−1.1	....
Other transport, passenger	3 215	....	....	....	....	....	....	....	....
Other transport, freight	3 216	....	....	....	....	....	....	....	....
Other transport, other	3 217	−.6	−.6	−.7	−.7	....	....	....	....
Travel, credit	2 236	757.8	775.3	897.2	1,056.8	1,199.1	1,194.4	1,068.0	....
Business travel	2 237	2.9	3.1	3.5	3.1	2.1	.5	.7	....
Personal travel	2 240	755.0	772.3	893.7	1,053.7	1,197.0	1,193.9	1,067.3	....
Travel, debit	3 236	−104.5	−107.8	−95.7	−104.4	−98.9	−80.4	−70.6	....
Business travel	3 237	−32.6	−32.6	−27.4	−30.8	−29.6	−18.2	−15.7	....
Personal travel	3 240	−71.9	−75.2	−68.3	−73.6	−69.4	−62.2	−54.9	....
Other services, credit	2 200 BA	307.1	336.0	394.4	368.8	404.9	331.0	307.0	....
Communications	2 245	32.2	32.3	32.5	27.2	13.4	5.5	26.3	....
Construction	2 249	3.6	3.8	3.6	3.5	13.0	2.4	11.9	....
Insurance	2 253	90.1	91.0	101.9	92.1	125.2	63.1	69.0	....
Financial	2 260	13.3	18.9	37.1	38.1	77.4	43.8	42.8	....
Computer and information	2 262	18.1	19.9	22.7	20.6	11.5	7.8	11.8	....
Royalties and licence fees	2 266	.9	2.3	1.7	4.2	.4	3.9	2.5	....
Other business services	2 268	123.7	141.3	167.4	158.3	129.5	173.3	112.5	....
Personal, cultural, and recreational	2 287	.8	....	.3	.1	.8	.5	.1	....
Government, n.i.e.	2 291	24.7	26.7	27.5	24.7	33.7	30.8	30.2	....
Other services, debit	3 200 BA	−241.7	−245.6	−362.5	−398.1	−465.4	−411.5	−389.5	....
Communications	3 245	−11.2	−12.5	−11.8	−10.4	−14.9	−2.2	−2.6	....
Construction	3 249	−3.0	−3.0	−3.3	−2.9	−12.4	−9.5	−12.1	....
Insurance	3 253	−123.1	−121.1	−194.1	−215.4	−226.9	−156.8	−115.4	....
Financial	3 260	−5.3	−5.5	−5.8	−5.6	−13.6	−59.9	−64.2	....
Computer and information	3 262	−6.9	−7.2	−8.2	−5.7	−10.9	−12.9	−36.6	....
Royalties and licence fees	3 266	−25.0	−20.0	−29.1	−34.4	−26.0	−31.8	−33.3	....
Other business services	3 268	−43.4	−42.9	−66.0	−74.9	−98.4	−81.1	−67.0	....
Personal, cultural, and recreational	3 287	−.1	−1.4	−.2	−.1	−.9	−.2	−.3	....
Government, n.i.e.	3 291	−23.9	−32.2	−44.0	−48.8	−61.5	−57.1	−58.0	....

Table 2 (Continued). STANDARD PRESENTATION, 2003–2010

(Millions of U.S. dollars)

	Code	2003	2004	2005	2006	2007	2008	2009	2010
C. INCOME	4 300	−92.2	−104.0	−148.6	−199.9	−100.7	−90.9	−208.1	....
Total credit	2 300	*92.9*	*98.2*	*111.5*	*101.6*	*198.9*	*164.2*	*242.6*	....
Total debit	3 300	*−185.0*	*−202.1*	*−260.1*	*−301.5*	*−299.6*	*−255.1*	*−450.7*	....
Compensation of employees, credit	2 310	**33.6**	**30.5**	**32.3**	**32.3**	**51.4**	**45.9**	**56.0**	....
Compensation of employees, debit	3 310	**−6.0**	**−2.5**	**−6.5**	**−4.7**	**−5.0**	**−9.7**	**−10.6**	....
Investment income, credit	2 320	**59.3**	**67.7**	**79.3**	**69.3**	**147.5**	**118.3**	**186.5**	....
Direct investment income	2 330	6.8	22.1	30.5	33.7	63.0	13.0	143.9	....
Dividends and distributed branch profits	2 332	6.1	20.4	26.9	32.1	41.7	−2.8	130.8	....
Reinvested earnings and undistributed branch profits	2 333	.7	1.7	3.6	1.7	21.3	14.3	13.0	....
Income on debt (interest)	2 334	....	....	....	....	....	1.5	....	....
Portfolio investment income	2 339	52.3	45.6	48.5	35.1	61.8	70.4	37.5	....
Income on equity	2 340	17.8	17.8	21.1	13.9	10.3	11.5	6.3	....
Income on bonds and notes	2 350	34.5	27.8	27.4	21.2	51.5	58.9	31.1	....
Income on money market instruments	2 360	....	....	....	....	....	....	....	....
Other investment income	2 370	.3	....	.3	.4	22.7	34.9	5.2	....
Investment income, debit	3 320	**−179.1**	**−199.6**	**−253.6**	**−296.8**	**−294.6**	**−245.3**	**−440.0**	....
Direct investment income	3 330	−17.8	−20.0	−28.9	−50.0	−55.3	−95.1	−297.8	....
Dividends and distributed branch profits	3 332	−6.6	−6.6	−6.6	−6.6	−6.6	−46.6	−149.8	....
Reinvested earnings and undistributed branch profits	3 333	−11.3	−13.5	−22.3	−43.5	−48.8	−44.7	−130.2	....
Income on debt (interest)	3 334	....	....	....	....	....	−3.8	−17.8	....
Portfolio investment income	3 339	−156.6	−118.7	−171.9	−164.4	−172.8	−89.0	−91.1	....
Income on equity	3 340	−46.6	−46.6	−48.5	−63.8	−72.3	−2.7	−10.7	....
Income on bonds and notes	3 350	−110.0	−72.1	−123.4	−100.5	−100.5	−86.4	−80.5	....
Income on money market instruments	3 360	....	....	....	....	....	....	....	....
Other investment income	3 370	−4.7	−61.0	−52.9	−82.4	−66.6	−61.2	−51.1	....
D. CURRENT TRANSFERS	4 379	**92.8**	**86.1**	**69.2**	**78.6**	**4.7**	**5.0**	**7.2**	....
Credit	2 379	**127.1**	**124.3**	**136.4**	**135.0**	**115.7**	**98.7**	**86.4**	....
General government	2 380	3.3	.7	14.3	12.8	5.9	17.3	11.6	....
Other sectors	2 390	123.8	123.6	122.1	122.2	109.8	81.4	74.8	....
Workers' remittances	2 391	96.9	100.0	102.6	106.3	89.8	55.2	57.2	....
Other current transfers	2 392	26.9	23.6	19.6	16.0	20.0	26.2	17.5	....
Debit	3 379	**−34.2**	**−38.2**	**−67.2**	**−56.4**	**−111.1**	**−93.7**	**−79.2**	....
General government	3 380	−7.9	−10.9	−8.9	−9.3	−12.8	−18.1	−17.2	....
Other sectors	3 390	−26.4	−27.3	−58.3	−47.2	−98.2	−75.6	−62.0	....
Workers' remittances	3 391	−15.8	−15.8	−37.0	−28.5	−48.6	−29.3	−29.4	....
Other current transfers	3 392	−10.6	−11.5	−21.3	−18.7	−49.6	−46.3	−32.5	....
CAPITAL AND FINANCIAL ACCOUNT	4 996	**−26.5**	**386.9**	**380.0**	**245.0**	**167.8**	**448.0**	**113.8**	....
CAPITAL ACCOUNT	4 994	....	....	....	....	....	....	....	....
Total credit	2 994	....	....	....	....	....	....	....	....
Total debit	3 994	....	....	....	....	....	....	....	....
Capital transfers, credit	2 400	....	....	....	....	....	....	....	....
General government	2 401	....	....	....	....	....	....	....	....
Debt forgiveness	2 402	....	....	....	....	....	....	....	....
Other capital transfers	2 410	....	....	....	....	....	....	....	....
Other sectors	2 430	....	....	....	....	....	....	....	....
Migrants' transfers	2 431	....	....	....	....	....	....	....	....
Debt forgiveness	2 432	....	....	....	....	....	....	....	....
Other capital transfers	2 440	....	....	....	....	....	....	....	....
Capital transfers, debit	3 400	....	....	....	....	....	....	....	....
General government	3 401	....	....	....	....	....	....	....	....
Debt forgiveness	3 402	....	....	....	....	....	....	....	....
Other capital transfers	3 410	....	....	....	....	....	....	....	....
Other sectors	3 430	....	....	....	....	....	....	....	....
Migrants' transfers	3 431	....	....	....	....	....	....	....	....
Debt forgiveness	3 432	....	....	....	....	....	....	....	....
Other capital transfers	3 440	....	....	....	....	....	....	....	....
Nonproduced nonfinancial assets, credit	2 480	....	....	....	....	....	....	....	....
Nonproduced nonfinancial assets, debit	3 480	....	....	....	....	....	....	....	....

Table 2 (Continued). STANDARD PRESENTATION, 2003–2010

(Millions of U.S. dollars)

	Code	2003	2004	2005	2006	2007	2008	2009	2010
FINANCIAL ACCOUNT.............................	4 995 ..	**−26.5**	**386.9**	**380.0**	**245.0**	**167.8**	**448.0**	**113.8**	....
A. DIRECT INVESTMENT.............................	4 500 ..	**57.8**	**−16.0**	**52.8**	**91.0**	**36.1**	**222.5**	**218.1**	....
Direct investment abroad....................	4 505 ..	**−.5**	**−3.9**	**−9.1**	**−13.8**	**−197.2**	**−63.4**	**−80.1**	....
Equity capital................................	4 510 ..	−.1	−.3	−.5	....	−148.7	19.9	−11.0	....
Claims on affiliated enterprises....................	4 515 ..	....	....	....	....	....	19.9	−11.0	....
Liabilities to affiliated enterprises................	4 520 ..	....	....	....	....	....	....	....	....
Reinvested earnings............................	4 525 ..	−.7	−1.7	−3.6	−1.7	−21.3	−14.3	−13.0	....
Other capital.................................	4 530 ..	.3	−1.9	−5.1	−12.1	−27.2	−68.9	−56.1	....
Claims on affiliated enterprises....................	4 535 ..	....	....	....	....	....	....	8.4	....
Liabilities to affiliated enterprises................	4 540 ..	....	....	....	....	....	....	−64.4	....
Direct investment in Barbados........................	4 555 ..	**58.3**	**−12.1**	**62.0**	**104.8**	**233.2**	**285.8**	**298.2**	....
Equity capital................................	4 560 ..	21.5	−25.6	4.4	5.0	138.2	106.1	235.7	....
Claims on direct investors....................	4 565 ..	....	....	....	....	....	....	7.2	....
Liabilities to direct investors................	4 570 ..	21.5	−25.6	4.4	5.0	138.2	106.1	228.5	....
Reinvested earnings............................	4 575 ..	11.3	13.5	22.3	43.5	48.8	44.7	130.2	....
Other capital.................................	4 580 ..	25.5	....	35.3	56.4	46.3	135.0	−67.7	....
Claims on direct investors....................	4 585 ..	....	....	....	....	....	....	29.0	....
Liabilities to direct investors................	4 590 ..	....	....	....	....	....	....	−96.7	....
B. PORTFOLIO INVESTMENT.........................	4 600 ..	**−127.5**	**−42.4**	**35.5**	**83.4**	**−209.8**	**−168.5**	**126.9**	....
Assets..	4 602 ..	**−23.0**	**−29.9**	**−89.5**	**22.6**	**−190.6**	**−161.6**	**28.6**	....
Equity securities..........................	4 610 ..	−23.2	−44.7	−53.2	−14.9	−7.3	−44.2	−36.9	....
Monetary authorities.......................	4 611 ..	....	....	....	....	....	....	....	....
General government.......................	4 612 ..	−.2	−3.2	....	....	....	....	....	....
Banks.................................	4 613 ..	....	....	....	....	....	....	....	....
Other sectors...........................	4 614 ..	−23.0	−41.5	−53.2	−14.9	−7.3	−44.2	−36.9	....
Debt securities............................	4 619 ..	.2	14.8	−36.3	37.5	−183.4	−117.4	65.5	....
Bonds and notes.........................	4 620 ..	.2	9.1	−29.8	30.1	−148.0	−102.9	68.2	....
Monetary authorities.....................	4 621 ..	....	....	....	....	....	....	....	....
General government.....................	4 622 ..	....	5.7	−6.6	7.5	−35.4	−47.9	69.7	....
Banks...............................	4 623 ..	....	....	....	....	....	....	....	....
Other sectors...........................	4 624 ..	.1	3.4	−23.2	22.6	−112.7	−55.0	−1.5	....
Money market instruments.................	4 630 ..	....	5.7	−6.6	7.5	−35.4	−14.5	−2.7	....
Monetary authorities.....................	4 631 ..	....	....	....	....	....	....	....	....
General government.....................	4 632 ..	....	....	....	....	....	....	....	....
Banks...............................	4 633 ..	....	....	....	....	....	....	....	....
Other sectors...........................	4 634 ..	....	5.7	−6.6	7.5	−35.4	−14.5	−2.7	....
Liabilities....................................	4 652 ..	**−104.5**	**−12.5**	**125.0**	**60.7**	**−19.2**	**−6.9**	**98.3**	....
Equity securities..........................	4 660 ..	−94.5	....	....	−4.3	1.1	10.7	−8.7	....
Banks.................................	4 663 ..	....	....	....	....	....	....	....	....
Other sectors...........................	4 664 ..	−94.5	....	....	−4.3	1.1	10.7	−8.7	....
Debt securities............................	4 669 ..	−10.0	−12.5	125.0	65.0	−20.3	−17.7	107.0	....
Bonds and notes.........................	4 670 ..	−10.0	−12.5	125.0	65.0	−20.3	−19.5	106.9	....
Monetary authorities.....................	4 671 ..	....	....	....	....	....	....	....	....
General government.....................	4 672 ..	−10.0	−12.5	125.0	65.0	−20.3	−19.5	111.8	....
Banks...............................	4 673 ..	....	....	....	....	....	....	....	....
Other sectors...........................	4 674 ..	....	....	....	....	....	....	−4.8	....
Money market instruments.................	4 680 ..	....	....	....	....	....	1.9	....	....
Monetary authorities.....................	4 681 ..	....	....	....	....	....	....	....	....
General government.....................	4 682 ..	....	....	....	....	....	....	....	....
Banks...............................	4 683 ..	....	....	....	....	....	....	....	....
Other sectors...........................	4 684 ..	....	....	....	....	....	1.9	....	....
C. FINANCIAL DERIVATIVES...........................	4 910 ..	....	....	**6.6**	....	....	**.6**	**.5**	....
Monetary authorities.........................	4 911 ..	....	....	....	....	....	....	....	....
General government.........................	4 912 ..	....	....	....	....	....	....	....	....
Banks...................................	4 913 ..	....	....	....	....	....	....	....	....
Other sectors..............................	4 914 ..	....	....	6.6	....	....	.6	.5	....
Assets..	4 900 ..	....	**−1.1**	**1.6**	....	....	....	....	....
Monetary authorities.........................	4 901 ..	....	....	....	....	....	....	....	....
General government.........................	4 902 ..	....	....	....	....	....	....	....	....
Banks...................................	4 903 ..	....	....	....	....	....	....	....	....
Other sectors..............................	4 904 ..	....	....	1.6	....	....	....	....	....
Liabilities....................................	4 905 ..	....	....	**5.0**	....	**.1**	**.6**	**.5**	....
Monetary authorities.........................	4 906 ..	....	....	....	....	....	....	....	....
General government.........................	4 907 ..	....	....	....	....	....	....	....	....
Banks...................................	4 908 ..	....	....	....	....	....	....	....	....
Other sectors..............................	4 909 ..	....	....	5.0	....	.1	.6	.5	....

Table 2 (Concluded). STANDARD PRESENTATION, 2003–2010

(Millions of U.S. dollars)

	Code	2003	2004	2005	2006	2007	2008	2009	2010
D. OTHER INVESTMENT.....................................	4 700 ..	**79.7**	**279.7**	**314.4**	**49.0**	**507.2**	**298.5**	**−166.4**	....
Assets..	4 703 ..	**−82.9**	**31.3**	**−238.5**	**−280.9**	**−605.3**	**−124.5**	**238.4**	....
Trade credits..	4 706 ..	.5	39.5	−101.2	−102.9	−113.3	−38.4	−35.6	....
General government.............................	4 707 ..	....	....	....	....	....	....	....	
of which: Short-term........................	4 709 ..	....	....	....	....	....	....	....	
Other sectors.....................................	4 710 ..	.5	39.5	−101.2	−102.9	−113.3	−38.4	−35.6	
of which: Short-term........................	4 712 ..	−10.3	28.5	−81.8	−76.6	−98.0	−25.0	−33.1	....
Loans..	4 714 ..	−1.3	−3.3	−6.1	....	−74.9	−94.2	−10.0	....
Monetary authorities...........................	4 715 ..	....	....	....	....	....	....	.5	
of which: Short-term........................	4 718 ..	....	....	....	....	....	....		
General government.............................	4 719 ..	−.7	−.7	−.2	....	....	....	....	
of which: Short-term........................	4 721 ..	−.7	−.7	−.2	....	....	....	....	
Banks..	4 722 ..	....	....	....	....	....	....	....	
of which: Short-term........................	4 724 ..	....	....	....	....	....	....	....	
Other sectors.....................................	4 725 ..	−.7	−2.7	−5.9	....	−74.9	−94.2	−10.5	....
of which: Short-term........................	4 727 ..	....	....	....	....	....	....	....	
Currency and deposits............................	4 730 ..	−5.4	−3.8	−20.0	−6.0	−9.0	−21.4	−41.6	
Monetary authorities...........................	4 731 ..	....	....	....	....	....	....	....	
General government.............................	4 732 ..	....	....	....	....	....	....	....	
Banks..	4 733 ..	−5.4	−3.8	−20.0	−6.0	−9.0	....	....	
Other sectors.....................................	4 734 ..	....	....	....	....	....	−21.4	−41.6	
Other assets..	4 736 ..	−76.7	−1.1	−111.2	−171.9	−408.1	29.5	325.6	....
Monetary authorities...........................	4 737 ..	....	....	....	....	....	....	....	
of which: Short-term........................	4 739 ..	....	....	....	....	....	....	....	
General government.............................	4 740 ..	−3.6	−2.9	....	3.3	−3.2	−2.5	1.8	
of which: Short-term........................	4 742 ..	−2.0	−1.4	....	3.3	−1.5	−1.0	.9	
Banks..	4 743 ..	−82.5	−22.2	−135.0	−131.4	−621.5	140.9	460.3	
of which: Short-term........................	4 745 ..	....	....	....	....	....	....	....	
Other sectors.....................................	4 746 ..	9.4	24.0	23.9	−43.9	216.5	−108.9	−136.5	....
of which: Short-term........................	4 748 ..	8.2	20.7	25.8	−41.6	39.0	−39.2	−2.1	....
Liabilities..	4 753 ..	**162.6**	**248.4**	**552.9**	**329.9**	**1,112.5**	**423.1**	**−404.8**	....
Trade credits..	4 756 ..	79.5	156.0	298.1	−17.0	−278.0	160.9	−3.4	
General government.............................	4 757 ..	.9	−1.8	−1.2	....	....	....	....	
of which: Short-term........................	4 759 ..	....	....	....	....	....	....	....	
Other sectors.....................................	4 760 ..	78.6	157.7	299.2	−17.0	−278.0	160.9	−3.4	
of which: Short-term........................	4 762 ..	64.7	99.8	225.2	−108.1	−290.6	145.3	−3.2	....
Loans..	4 764 ..	51.5	−27.1	4.1	222.8	174.9	137.9	−148.6	....
Monetary authorities...........................	4 765 ..	....	....	....	....	....	....	....	
of which: Use of Fund credit and loans from the Fund..	4 766 ..	....	....	....	....	....	....	....	
of which: Short-term........................	4 768 ..	....	....	....	....	....	....	....	
General government.............................	4 769 ..	3.9	−9.0	−5.6	−9.1	−25.1	7.9	15.3	
of which: Short-term........................	4 771 ..	....	....	....	....	....	....	....	
Banks..	4 772 ..	....	....	....	....	....	....	....	
of which: Short-term........................	4 774 ..	....	....	....	....	....	....	....	
Other sectors.....................................	4 775 ..	47.6	−18.1	9.7	231.9	199.9	130.0	−163.9	
of which: Short-term........................	4 777 ..	....	....	....	....	....	....	....	
Currency and deposits............................	4 780 ..	....	....	....	....	....	....	....	
Monetary authorities...........................	4 781 ..	....	....	....	....	....	....	....	
General government.............................	4 782 ..	....	....	....	....	....	....	....	
Banks..	4 783 ..	....	....	....	....	....	....	....	
Other sectors.....................................	4 784 ..	....	....	....	....	....	....	....	
Other liabilities....................................	4 786 ..	31.6	119.6	250.7	124.2	1,215.6	124.3	−252.8	
Monetary authorities...........................	4 787 ..	....	....	....	....	....	....	88.0	
of which: Short-term........................	4 789 ..	....	....	....	....	....	....	....	
General government.............................	4 790 ..	....	....	....	....	....	....	....	
of which: Short-term........................	4 792 ..	....	....	....	....	....	....	....	
Banks..	4 793 ..	−41.1	49.2	247.2	59.7	618.8	25.7	−395.1	
of which: Short-term........................	4 795 ..	....	....	....	....	....	....	....	
Other sectors.....................................	4 796 ..	72.7	70.3	3.5	64.4	596.8	98.6	54.3	
of which: Short-term........................	4 798 ..	25.6	40.2	1.1	22.4	146.6	32.9	16.0	....
E. RESERVE ASSETS................................	4 802 ..	**−36.5**	**165.6**	**−29.3**	**21.6**	**−165.6**	**94.9**	**−65.5**	....
Monetary gold.......................................	4 812 ..	....	....	....	....	....	....	....	
Special drawing rights............................	4 811 ..	.1	....	....	....	−.1	....	−88.0	
Reserve position in the Fund....................	4 810 ..	−.2	−.2	−.2	−.2	−.2	−.1	−.1	....
Foreign exchange...................................	4 803 ..	−36.4	165.8	−29.1	21.8	−165.4	95.0	22.7	
Other claims..	4 813 ..	....	....	....	....	....	....	....	
NET ERRORS AND OMISSIONS...........................	4 998 ..	**267.5**	**26.2**	**128.8**	**162.4**	**141.3**	**−25.4**	**188.1**	....

Table 3. INTERNATIONAL INVESTMENT POSITION (End-period stocks), 2003–2010

(Millions of U.S. dollars)

	Code	2003	2004	2005	2006	2007	2008	2009	2010
ASSETS.........	8 995 C.	....	....	....	....	....	**31,993.3**	**30,350.1**	....
Direct investment abroad.........	8 505 ..	....	....	....	....	....	**3,035.9**	**3,280.4**	....
Equity capital and reinvested earnings.........	8 506 ..	....	....	....	....	....	3,421.8	3,564.8	....
Claims on affiliated enterprises.........	8 507 ..	....	....	....	....	....	3,441.8	3,584.8	....
Liabilities to affiliated enterprises.........	8 508 ..	....	....	....	....	....	−20.0	−20.0	....
Other capital.........	8 530 ..	....	....	....	....	....	−385.9	−284.3	....
Claims on affiliated enterprises.........	8 535 ..	....	....	....	....	....	120.0	137.2	....
Liabilities to affiliated enterprises.........	8 540 ..	....	....	....	....	....	−505.9	−421.5	....
Portfolio investment.........	8 602 ..	....	....	....	....	....	**19,873.7**	**18,368.5**	....
Equity securities.........	8 610 ..	....	....	....	....	....	1,910.9	2,792.2	....
Monetary authorities.........	8 611 ..	....	....	....	....	....	....	....	....
General government.........	8 612 ..	....	....	....	....	....	3.1	2.2	....
Banks.........	8 613 ..	....	....	....	....	....	3.5	4.0	....
Other sectors.........	8 614 ..	....	....	....	....	....	1,904.3	2,786.0	....
Debt securities.........	8 619 ..	....	....	....	....	....	17,962.8	15,576.3	....
Bonds and notes.........	8 620 ..	....	....	....	....	....	4,013.3	6,103.6	....
Monetary authorities.........	8 621 ..	....	....	....	....	....	....	....	....
General government.........	8 622 ..	....	....	....	....	....	216.1	146.4	....
Banks.........	8 623 ..	....	....	....	....	....	4.9	2.2	....
Other sectors.........	8 624 ..	....	....	....	....	....	3,792.4	5,955.0	....
Money market instruments.........	8 630 ..	....	....	....	....	....	13,949.5	9,472.7	....
Monetary authorities.........	8 631 ..	....	....	....	....	....	....	....	....
General government.........	8 632 ..	....	....	....	....	....	....	....	....
Banks.........	8 633 ..	....	....	....	....	....	419.9	419.2	....
Other sectors.........	8 634 ..	....	....	....	....	....	13,529.6	9,053.5	....
Financial derivatives.........	8 900 ..	....	....	....	....	....	**165.5**	**140.4**	....
Monetary authorities.........	8 901 ..	....	....	....	....	....	....	....	....
General government.........	8 902 ..	....	....	....	....	....	....	....	....
Banks.........	8 903 ..	....	....	....	....	....	....	....	....
Other sectors.........	8 904 ..	....	....	....	....	....	165.5	140.4	....
Other investment.........	8 703 ..	....	....	....	....	....	**8,042.9**	**7,642.3**	....
Trade credits.........	8 706 ..	....	....	....	....	....	169.7	134.2	....
General government.........	8 707 ..	....	....	....	....	....	....	....	....
of which: Short-term.........	8 709 ..	....	....	....	....	....	....	....	....
Other sectors.........	8 710 ..	....	....	....	....	....	169.7	134.2	....
of which: Short-term.........	8 712 ..	....	....	....	....	....	*161.0*	*127.9*	....
Loans.........	8 714 ..	....	....	....	....	....	4,181.7	4,211.7	....
Monetary authorities.........	8 715 ..	....	....	....	....	....	....	....	....
of which: Short-term.........	8 718 ..	....	....	....	....	....	....	....	....
General government.........	8 719 ..	....	....	....	....	....	....	....	....
of which: Short-term.........	8 721 ..	....	....	....	....	....	....	....	....
Banks.........	8 722 ..	....	....	....	....	....	64.0	111.2	....
of which: Short-term.........	8 724 ..	....	....	....	....	....	....	....	....
Other sectors.........	8 725 ..	....	....	....	....	....	4,117.7	4,100.5	....
of which: Short-term.........	8 727 ..	....	....	....	....	....	*27.4*	*69.4*	....
Currency and deposits.........	8 730 ..	....	....	....	....	....	516.2	235.7	....
Monetary authorities.........	8 731 ..	....	....	....	....	....	....	....	....
General government.........	8 732 ..	....	....	....	....	....	....	....	....
Banks.........	8 733 ..	....	....	....	....	....	516.2	235.7	....
Other sectors.........	8 734 ..	....	....	....	....	....	....	....	....
Other assets.........	8 736 ..	....	....	....	....	....	3,175.3	3,060.8	....
Monetary authorities.........	8 737 ..	....	....	....	....	....	....	....	....
of which: Short-term.........	8 739 ..	....	....	....	....	....	....	....	....
General government.........	8 740 ..	....	....	....	....	....	2.6	1.7	....
of which: Short-term.........	8 742 ..	....	....	....	....	....	*2.6*	*1.7*	....
Banks.........	8 743 ..	....	....	....	....	....	660.1	61.0	....
of which: Short-term.........	8 745 ..	....	....	....	....	....	....	....	....
Other sectors.........	8 746 ..	....	....	....	....	....	2,512.6	2,998.2	....
of which: Short-term.........	8 748 ..	....	....	....	....	....	....	....	....
Reserve assets.........	8 802 ..	....	....	....	....	....	**875.3**	**918.5**	....
Monetary gold.........	8 812 ..	....	....	....	....	....	....	....	....
Special drawing rights.........	8 811 ..	....	.1	....	....	.1	.1	88.3	86.7
Reserve position in the Fund.........	8 810 ..	7.5	8.0	7.6	8.2	8.8	8.7	9.0	8.9
Foreign exchange.........	8 803 ..	....	....	....	....	....	866.3	821.0	....
Other claims.........	8 813 ..	....	....	....	....	....	.2	.2	....

Table 3 (Concluded). INTERNATIONAL INVESTMENT POSITION (End-period stocks), 2003–2010

(Millions of U.S. dollars)

	Code	2003	2004	2005	2006	2007	2008	2009	2010
LIABILITIES................................	8 995 D.	....	....	....	....	....	**21,398.0**	**20,519.0**	....
Direct investment in Barbados............................	8 555 ..	....	....	....	....	....	**2,123.7**	**2,213.6**	....
Equity capital and reinvested earnings...........	8 556 ..						933.4	1,074.1	....
Claims on direct investors...............	8 557 ..	....	....	....	....	....	−191.2	−227.5	....
Liabilities to direct investors..............	8 558 ..	....	....	....	....	....	1,124.6	1,301.6	....
Other capital............................	8 580 ..	....	....	....	....	....	1,190.3	1,139.5	....
Claims on direct investors...............	8 585 ..	....	....	....	....	....	−31.5	−69.5	....
Liabilities to direct investors..............	8 590 ..	....	....	....	....	....	1,221.8	1,209.0	....
Portfolio investment.............................	8 652 ..	....	....	....	....	....	**741.9**	**847.6**	....
Equity securities................................	8 660 ..	....	....	....	....	....	68.0	60.4	....
Banks..	8 663 ..	....	....	....	....	....	....	....	....
Other sectors...............................	8 664 ..	....	....	....	....	....	68.0	60.4	....
Debt securities..............................	8 669 ..	....	....	....	....	....	673.9	787.2	....
Bonds and notes...........................	8 670 ..	....	....	....	....	....	538.2	645.2	....
Monetary authorities...................	8 671 ..	....	....	....	....	....	....	....	....
General government...................	8 672 ..	....	....	....	....	....	498.7	610.5	....
Banks...................................	8 673 ..	....	....	....	....	....	....	....	....
Other sectors...........................	8 674 ..	....	....	....	....	....	39.5	34.7	....
Money market instruments................	8 680 ..	....	....	....	....	....	135.7	142.0	....
Monetary authorities...................	8 681 ..	....	....	....	....	....	....	....	....
General government...................	8 682 ..	....	....	....	....	....	....	....	....
Banks...................................	8 683 ..	....	....	....	....	....	1.4	1.5	....
Other sectors...........................	8 684 ..	....	....	....	....	....	134.3	140.5	....
Financial derivatives........................	8 905 ..	....	....	....	....	....	.1	....	....
Monetary authorities.........................	8 906 ..	....	....	....	....	....	....	....	....
General government.........................	8 907 ..	....	....	....	....	....	....	....	....
Banks...	8 908 ..	....	....	....	....	....	....	....	....
Other sectors................................	8 909 ..	....	....	....	....	....	.1	....	....
Other investment.............................	8 753 ..	....	....	....	....	....	**18,532.3**	**17,457.9**	....
Trade credits................................	8 756 ..	....	....	....	....	....	60.5	57.0	....
General government.......................	8 757 ..	....	....	....	....	....	16.0	16.0	....
of which: Short-term.................	8 759 ..	....	....	....	....	....	....	....	....
Other sectors...............................	8 760 ..	....	....	....	....	....	44.5	41.0	....
of which: Short-term.................	8 762 ..	....	....	....	....	....	*36.3*	*33.0*	....
Loans...	8 764 ..	....	....	....	....	....	3,397.4	3,026.6	....
Monetary authorities........................	8 765 ..	....	....	....	....	....	....	....	....
of which: Use of Fund credit and loans from the Fund....	8 766 ..	....	....	....	....	....	....	....	....
of which: Short-term.................	8 768 ..	....	....	....	....	....	....	....	....
General government.......................	8 769 ..	....	....	....	....	....	332.0	347.4	....
of which: Short-term.................	8 771 ..	....	....	....	....	....	....	....	....
Banks...	8 772 ..	....	....	....	....	....	379.4	238.8	....
of which: Short-term.................	8 774 ..	....	....	....	....	....	....	....	....
Other sectors...............................	8 775 ..	....	....	....	....	....	2,685.9	2,440.5	....
of which: Short-term.................	8 777 ..	....	....	....	....	....	....	....	....
Currency and deposits.......................	8 780 ..	....	....	....	....	....	1,117.6	745.7	....
Monetary authorities........................	8 781 ..	....	....	....	....	....	....	....	....
General government.......................	8 782 ..	....	....	....	....	....	....	....	....
Banks...	8 783 ..	....	....	....	....	....	1,117.6	745.7	....
Other sectors...............................	8 784 ..	....	....	....	....	....	....	....	....
Other liabilities..............................	8 786 ..	....	....	....	....	....	13,956.8	13,628.6	....
Monetary authorities........................	8 787 ..	....	....	....	....	....	.1	100.9	....
of which: Short-term.................	8 789 ..	....	....	....	....	....	....	....	....
General government.......................	8 790 ..	....	....	....	....	....	....	....	....
of which: Short-term.................	8 792 ..	....	....	....	....	....	....	....	....
Banks...	8 793 ..	....	....	....	....	....	72.0	11.4	....
of which: Short-term.................	8 795 ..	....	....	....	....	....	....	....	....
Other sectors...............................	8 796 ..	....	....	....	....	....	13,884.8	13,516.3	....
of which: Short-term.................	8 798 ..	....	....	....	....	....	....	....	....
NET INTERNATIONAL INVESTMENT POSITION........	8 995 ..	....	....	....	....	....	**10,595.3**	**9,831.1**	....
Conversion rates: Barbados dollars per U.S. dollar (end of period).............................	0 102 ..	**2.0000**	**2.0000**	**2.0000**	**2.0000**	**2.0000**	**2.0000**	**2.0000**	**2.0000**

Table 1. ANALYTIC PRESENTATION, 2003–2010

(Millions of U.S. dollars)

	Code	2003	2004	2005	2006	2007	2008	2009	2010
A. Current Account[1]	4 993 Z.	**−426.2**	**−1,193.3**	**435.5**	**−1,448.4**	**−3,032.2**	**−4,988.1**	**−6,177.8**	**−8,316.8**
Goods: exports f.o.b.	2 100 ..	10,076.1	13,942.2	16,108.8	19,834.7	24,361.7	32,804.7	21,360.7	25,405.1
Goods: imports f.o.b.	3 100 ..	−11,397.3	−16,214.0	−16,746.4	−22,103.7	−28,403.5	−39,041.5	−28,317.7	−34,482.7
Balance on Goods	4 100 ..	*−1,321.2*	*−2,271.8*	*−637.6*	*−2,269.0*	*−4,041.8*	*−6,236.8*	*−6,957.0*	*−9,077.6*
Services: credit	2 200 ..	1,499.9	1,746.9	2,072.7	2,400.8	3,263.8	4,258.0	3,504.3	4,504.0
Services: debit	3 200 ..	−841.2	−970.4	−1,093.3	−1,663.3	−2,033.6	−2,629.5	−2,115.8	−2,884.5
Balance on Goods and Services	4 991 ..	*−662.5*	*−1,495.3*	*341.8*	*−1,531.5*	*−2,811.6*	*−4,608.3*	*−5,568.5*	*−7,458.1*
Income: credit	2 300 ..	126.3	157.6	168.4	246.6	275.5	633.6	476.3	491.3
Income: debit	3 300 ..	−112.1	−158.5	−239.4	−367.4	−686.6	−1,184.2	−1,359.7	−1,654.1
Balance on Goods, Services, and Income	4 992 ..	*−648.3*	*−1,496.2*	*270.8*	*−1,652.3*	*−3,222.7*	*−5,158.9*	*−6,451.9*	*−8,620.9*
Current transfers: credit	2 379 Z.	291.7	390.6	266.8	316.6	350.2	400.6	505.5	951.0
Current transfers: debit	3 379 ..	−69.6	−87.7	−102.1	−112.7	−159.7	−229.8	−231.4	−646.9
B. Capital Account[1]	4 994 Z.	**68.9**	**49.3**	**40.5**	**74.3**	**92.2**	**137.0**	**159.8**	**144.9**
Capital account: credit	2 994 Z.	133.2	130.4	134.7	165.0	199.9	272.9	264.2	237.8
Capital account: debit	3 994 ..	−64.3	−81.1	−94.2	−90.7	−107.7	−135.9	−104.4	−92.9
Total, Groups A Plus B	4 981 ..	*−357.3*	*−1,144.0*	*476.0*	*−1,374.1*	*−2,940.0*	*−4,851.1*	*−6,018.0*	*−8,171.9*
C. Financial Account[1]	4 995 W.	**428.9**	**1,151.7**	**−64.9**	**1,690.9**	**5,199.5**	**4,025.9**	**5,259.0**	**6,140.2**
Direct investment abroad	4 505 ..	−1.5	−1.3	−2.5	−3.0	−15.2	−30.6	−102.2	−50.4
Direct investment in Belarus	4 555 Z.	171.8	163.8	305.0	354.0	1,785.2	2,180.6	1,884.4	1,402.8
Portfolio investment assets	4 602 ..	.8	3.2	−2.9	−1.7	−41.2	4.8	16.5	−59.4
Equity securities	4 610 ..	−1.1	.6	....	−5.6	−5.8	.9	−1.8	−.2
Debt securities	4 619 ..	1.9	2.6	−2.9	3.9	−35.4	3.9	18.3	−59.2
Portfolio investment liabilities	4 652 Z.	5.3	59.6	−38.6	−24.7	2.4	.5	2.3	1,245.0
Equity securities	4 660 ..	3.3	.5	.6	−1.2	4.5	.7	1.2	.7
Debt securities	4 669 Z.	2.0	59.1	−39.2	−23.5	−2.1	−.2	1.1	1,244.3
Financial derivatives	4 910 ..	....	....	−.2	−12.9	....	....	....	....
Financial derivatives assets	4 900 ..	....	....	1.6	.1	....	....	....	....
Financial derivatives liabilities	4 905 ..	....	....	−1.8	−13.0	....	....	....	....
Other investment assets	4 703 ..	18.4	−151.4	−492.1	−165.7	−1,931.7	−477.0	−507.7	−1,178.4
Monetary authorities	4 701 ..	−10.0	231.5	72.8	−15.4	−185.4	−20.7	227.7	−667.9
General government	4 704 ..	....	....	....	....	−7.3	−198.5	101.2	101.1
Banks	4 705 ..	−61.1	−120.5	−232.5	257.7	−775.3	−74.7	−186.5	−47.8
Other sectors	4 728 ..	89.5	−262.4	−332.4	−408.0	−963.7	−183.1	−650.1	−563.8
Other investment liabilities	4 753 W.	234.1	1,077.8	166.4	1,544.9	5,400.0	2,347.6	3,965.7	4,780.6
Monetary authorities	4 753 WA	13.4	−194.9	−65.7	....	589.9	−155.9	574.7	1,449.6
General government	4 753 ZB	−43.2	122.1	116.5	3.4	1,419.9	1,397.1	1,326.3	−139.6
Banks	4 753 ZC	118.4	218.8	214.4	534.5	1,075.1	530.8	483.0	2,296.0
Other sectors	4 753 ZD	145.5	931.8	−98.8	1,007.0	2,315.1	575.6	1,581.7	1,174.6
Total, Groups A Through C	4 983 ..	*71.6*	*7.7*	*411.1*	*316.8*	*2,259.5*	*−825.2*	*−759.0*	*−2,031.7*
D. Net Errors and Omissions	4 998 ..	**−13.2**	**270.3**	**108.9**	**−300.6**	**477.0**	**−300.4**	**300.3**	**593.9**
Total, Groups A Through D	4 984 ..	*58.4*	*278.0*	*520.0*	*16.2*	*2,736.5*	*−1,125.6*	*−458.7*	*−1,437.8*
E. Reserves and Related Items	4 802 A.	**−58.4**	**−278.0**	**−520.0**	**−16.2**	**−2,736.5**	**1,125.6**	**458.7**	**1,437.8**
Reserve assets	4 802 ..	13.8	−255.8	−539.2	1.4	−2,778.1	1,001.8	−2,441.5	808.4
Use of Fund credit and loans	4 766 ..	−32.3	−17.3	−8.9	....	....	....	2,855.9	668.9
Exceptional financing	4 920 ..	−40.0	−4.9	28.1	−17.6	41.6	123.8	44.3	−39.6
Conversion rates: rubels per U.S. dollar	0 101 ..	**2,051.3**	**2,160.3**	**2,153.8**	**2,144.6**	**2,146.1**	**2,136.4**	**2,793.0**	**2,978.5**

[1] Excludes components that have been classified in the categories of Group E.

Table 2. STANDARD PRESENTATION, 2003–2010
(Millions of U.S. dollars)

	Code	2003	2004	2005	2006	2007	2008	2009	2010
CURRENT ACCOUNT	4 993	−426.2	−1,193.3	435.5	−1,448.4	−3,032.2	−4,988.1	−6,177.8	−8,316.8
A. GOODS	4 100	−1,321.2	−2,271.8	−637.6	−2,269.0	−4,041.8	−6,236.8	−6,957.0	−9,077.6
Credit	2 100	10,076.1	13,942.2	16,108.8	19,834.7	24,361.7	32,804.7	21,360.7	25,405.1
General merchandise: exports f.o.b.	2 110	9,177.7	13,009.3	15,197.9	18,876.7	23,244.1	31,447.5	20,546.8	24,427.4
Goods for processing: exports f.o.b.	2 150	830.5	873.9	821.6	870.9	987.6	1,058.7	686.5	783.9
Repairs on goods	2 160	59.8	46.1	65.6	45.0	38.3	88.3	54.6	93.9
Goods procured in ports by carriers	2 170	8.1	12.9	23.7	42.1	91.7	210.2	72.8	99.9
Nonmonetary gold	2 180	....	....	....	....	....	....	....	....
Debit	3 100	−11,397.3	−16,214.0	−16,746.4	−22,103.7	−28,403.5	−39,041.5	−28,317.7	−34,482.7
General merchandise: imports f.o.b.	3 110	−10,727.8	−15,484.5	−16,052.2	−21,336.0	−27,552.2	−38,092.7	−27,697.4	−33,756.8
Goods for processing: imports f.o.b.	3 150	−621.4	−670.3	−624.2	−679.8	−733.1	−793.9	−505.6	−569.3
Repairs on goods	3 160	−25.6	−27.9	−22.7	−23.2	−32.7	−59.5	−42.4	−53.5
Goods procured in ports by carriers	3 170	−22.5	−31.3	−47.3	−64.7	−85.5	−95.4	−72.3	−103.1
Nonmonetary gold	3 180	....	....	....	....	....	....	....	....
B. SERVICES	4 200	658.7	776.5	979.4	737.5	1,230.2	1,628.5	1,388.5	1,619.5
Total credit	2 200	*1,499.9*	*1,746.9*	*2,072.7*	*2,400.8*	*3,263.8*	*4,258.0*	*3,504.3*	*4,504.0*
Total debit	3 200	*−841.2*	*−970.4*	*−1,093.3*	*−1,663.3*	*−2,033.6*	*−2,629.5*	*−2,115.8*	*−2,884.5*
Transportation services, credit	2 205	856.3	1,025.5	1,337.5	1,710.2	2,349.5	2,991.5	2,288.7	3,006.8
Passenger	2 850	*71.8*	*92.4*	*92.5*	*115.3*	*155.4*	*221.7*	*193.1*	*225.2*
Freight	2 851	*728.2*	*855.1*	*1,147.5*	*1,460.5*	*2,015.9*	*2,536.5*	*1,912.8*	*2,567.0*
Other	2 852	*56.3*	*78.0*	*97.5*	*134.4*	*178.2*	*233.3*	*182.8*	*214.6*
Sea transport, passenger	2 207	....	....	....	....	....	....	....	....
Sea transport, freight	2 208	....	2.2	4.7	147.1	325.9	431.0	187.4	453.3
Sea transport, other	2 209	1.1	4.5	3.6	....	.1	.5	.1	....
Air transport, passenger	2 211	31.8	44.7	37.9	44.6	64.3	95.1	89.1	103.7
Air transport, freight	2 212	9.6	10.6	13.1	21.5	18.2	22.1	15.8	20.0
Air transport, other	2 213	26.6	37.7	48.8	52.2	66.9	83.6	75.0	82.2
Other transport, passenger	2 215	40.0	47.7	54.6	70.7	91.1	126.6	104.0	121.5
Other transport, freight	2 216	718.6	842.3	1,129.7	1,291.9	1,671.8	2,083.4	1,709.6	2,093.7
Other transport, other	2 217	28.6	35.8	45.1	82.2	111.2	149.2	107.7	132.4
Transportation services, debit	3 205	−191.0	−248.6	−308.8	−677.5	−904.5	−1,262.9	−825.7	−1,390.9
Passenger	3 850	*−36.9*	*−50.1*	*−68.3*	*−88.6*	*−117.8*	*−143.8*	*−113.4*	*−126.8*
Freight	3 851	*−94.5*	*−135.1*	*−183.7*	*−489.9*	*−667.9*	*−942.5*	*−580.9*	*−1,062.7*
Other	3 852	*−59.6*	*−63.4*	*−56.8*	*−99.0*	*−118.8*	*−176.6*	*−131.4*	*−201.4*
Sea transport, passenger	3 207	....	....	....	....	....	....	....	....
Sea transport, freight	3 208	−4.7	−6.6	−15.1	−130.6	−301.0	−459.6	−189.0	−440.1
Sea transport, other	3 209	−33.8	−34.6	−20.6	−22.7	−38.6	−64.4	−33.8	−69.3
Air transport, passenger	3 211	−17.3	−24.4	−29.9	−35.8	−48.9	−60.4	−49.5	−54.9
Air transport, freight	3 212	−3.1	−2.6	−2.5	−3.6	−4.8	−10.8	−6.7	−10.2
Air transport, other	3 213	−9.7	−11.8	−13.4	−18.8	−26.0	−30.1	−32.6	−41.0
Other transport, passenger	3 215	−19.6	−25.7	−38.4	−52.8	−68.9	−83.4	−63.9	−71.9
Other transport, freight	3 216	−86.7	−125.9	−166.1	−355.7	−362.1	−472.1	−385.2	−612.4
Other transport, other	3 217	−16.1	−17.0	−22.8	−57.5	−54.2	−82.1	−65.0	−91.1
Travel, credit	2 236	266.9	270.0	253.1	286.3	323.6	362.9	369.8	437.0
Business travel	2 237	107.4	112.7	104.9	110.9	119.3	136.2	134.5	135.8
Personal travel	2 240	159.5	157.3	148.2	175.4	204.3	226.7	235.3	301.2
Travel, debit	3 236	−399.3	−449.9	−447.6	−586.4	−606.0	−716.4	−638.5	−611.4
Business travel	3 237	−105.9	−110.2	−97.9	−127.3	−133.6	−206.9	−186.8	−158.1
Personal travel	3 240	−293.4	−339.7	−349.7	−459.1	−472.4	−509.5	−451.7	−453.3
Other services, credit	2 200 BA	376.7	451.4	482.1	404.3	590.7	903.6	845.8	1,060.2
Communications	2 245	70.3	82.4	94.0	105.5	124.2	146.5	153.2	173.2
Construction	2 249	60.3	79.9	60.1	47.7	82.1	96.4	69.3	125.4
Insurance	2 253	1.0	1.3	1.2	4.3	3.7	2.5	1.8	2.0
Financial	2 260	1.5	2.6	2.8	5.3	6.4	16.1	9.0	11.9
Computer and information	2 262	17.4	17.5	26.4	49.4	96.9	160.5	163.2	221.4
Royalties and licence fees	2 266	1.4	1.7	3.1	5.9	3.1	4.7	9.5	8.5
Other business services	2 268	200.2	242.6	274.7	165.1	246.5	427.8	393.5	468.1
Personal, cultural, and recreational	2 287	1.8	2.5	2.4	4.9	7.8	12.7	14.8	16.1
Government, n.i.e.	2 291	22.8	20.9	17.4	16.2	20.0	36.4	31.5	33.6
Other services, debit	3 200 BA	−250.9	−271.9	−336.9	−399.4	−523.1	−650.2	−651.6	−882.2
Communications	3 245	−63.8	−65.4	−71.7	−73.7	−77.4	−85.9	−75.6	−104.0
Construction	3 249	−28.0	−17.7	−19.9	−27.4	−52.5	−41.0	−84.4	−168.0
Insurance	3 253	−2.4	−4.0	−5.3	−5.3	−6.2	−5.2	−2.6	−3.1
Financial	3 260	−4.9	−12.4	−18.4	−30.1	−52.1	−75.8	−72.2	−76.3
Computer and information	3 262	−7.0	−13.6	−12.5	−21.2	−19.7	−35.5	−44.0	−52.9
Royalties and licence fees	3 266	−5.5	−9.1	−19.5	−50.5	−52.5	−75.2	−76.0	−100.5
Other business services	3 268	−113.3	−115.0	−141.7	−155.4	−219.6	−291.9	−268.6	−343.8
Personal, cultural, and recreational	3 287	−5.2	−6.8	−11.1	−15.5	−20.9	−26.8	−18.5	−26.7
Government, n.i.e.	3 291	−20.8	−27.9	−36.8	−20.3	−22.2	−12.9	−9.7	−6.9

Table 2 (Continued). STANDARD PRESENTATION, 2003–2010

(Millions of U.S. dollars)

	Code	2003	2004	2005	2006	2007	2008	2009	2010
C. INCOME	4 300	**14.2**	**−.9**	**−71.0**	**−120.8**	**−411.1**	**−550.6**	**−883.4**	**−1,162.8**
Total credit	2 300	*126.3*	*157.6*	*168.4*	*246.6*	*275.5*	*633.6*	*476.3*	*491.3*
Total debit	3 300	*−112.1*	*−158.5*	*−239.4*	*−367.4*	*−686.6*	*−1,184.2*	*−1,359.7*	*−1,654.1*
Compensation of employees, credit	2 310	**89.2**	**126.3**	**120.1**	**175.4**	**156.6**	**413.8**	**333.7**	**353.3**
Compensation of employees, debit	3 310	**−.7**	**−.5**	**−.3**	**−2.5**	**−5.0**	**−11.3**	**−10.0**	**−11.9**
Investment income, credit	2 320	**37.1**	**31.3**	**48.3**	**71.2**	**118.9**	**219.8**	**142.6**	**138.0**
Direct investment income	2 330	1.1	1.0	1.3	1.0	1.9	7.3	67.4	56.4
Dividends and distributed branch profits	2 332	1.1	1.0	1.3	1.0	1.8	7.0	61.8	52.9
Reinvested earnings and undistributed branch profits	2 333	....	....	....	....	.1	.3	5.6	3.5
Income on debt (interest)	2 334	....	....	....	....	....	....	....	....
Portfolio investment income	2 339	.5	.8	.7	1.6	.9	3.5	17.0	12.5
Income on equity	2 340	.5	.7	.6	1.3	.9	3.2	13.7	8.5
Income on bonds and notes	2 350	....	....	....	.3	....	.3	.1	.1
Income on money market instruments	2 360	....	.1	....	....	....	....	3.2	3.9
Other investment income	2 370	35.5	29.5	46.3	68.6	116.1	209.0	58.2	69.1
Investment income, debit	3 320	**−111.4**	**−158.0**	**−239.1**	**−364.9**	**−681.6**	**−1,172.9**	**−1,349.7**	**−1,642.2**
Direct investment income	3 330	−37.5	−75.7	−134.9	−236.3	−434.8	−682.1	−871.5	−1,039.1
Dividends and distributed branch profits	3 332	−25.2	−52.1	−91.6	−166.3	−234.0	−398.4	−433.2	−539.0
Reinvested earnings and undistributed branch profits	3 333	−12.3	−23.6	−32.6	−58.4	−185.2	−261.1	−417.7	−473.1
Income on debt (interest)	3 334	....	....	−10.7	−11.6	−15.6	−22.6	−20.6	−27.0
Portfolio investment income	3 339	−1.1	−2.2	−4.0	−1.8	−4.0	−2.8	−5.8	−5.0
Income on equity	3 340	−1.0	−2.2	−4.0	−1.7	−4.0	−2.8	−2.8	−1.3
Income on bonds and notes	3 350	−.1	....	....	−.1	....	....	−.9	−.7
Income on money market instruments	3 360	....	....	....	....	....	....	−2.1	−3.0
Other investment income	3 370	−72.8	−80.1	−100.2	−126.8	−242.8	−488.0	−472.4	−598.1
D. CURRENT TRANSFERS	4 379	**222.1**	**302.9**	**164.7**	**203.9**	**190.5**	**170.8**	**274.1**	**304.1**
Credit	2 379	**291.7**	**390.6**	**266.8**	**316.6**	**350.2**	**400.6**	**505.5**	**951.0**
General government	2 380	60.8	58.2	59.1	100.5	112.9	102.9	135.5	537.4
Other sectors	2 390	230.9	332.4	207.7	216.1	237.3	297.7	370.0	413.6
Workers' remittances	2 391	....	....	....	....	....	....	....	....
Other current transfers	2 392	230.9	332.4	207.7	216.1	237.3	297.7	370.0	413.6
Debit	3 379	**−69.6**	**−87.7**	**−102.1**	**−112.7**	**−159.7**	**−229.8**	**−231.4**	**−646.9**
General government	3 380	−25.5	−17.0	−15.0	−7.3	−10.4	−7.2	−11.7	−372.5
Other sectors	3 390	−44.1	−70.7	−87.1	−105.4	−149.3	−222.6	−219.7	−274.4
Workers' remittances	3 391	....	....	....	....	....	....	....	....
Other current transfers	3 392	−44.1	−70.7	−87.1	−105.4	−149.3	−222.6	−219.7	−274.4
CAPITAL AND FINANCIAL ACCOUNT	4 996	**439.4**	**923.0**	**−544.4**	**1,749.0**	**2,555.2**	**5,288.5**	**5,877.5**	**7,722.9**
CAPITAL ACCOUNT	4 994	**68.9**	**49.3**	**40.5**	**74.3**	**92.2**	**137.0**	**159.8**	**144.9**
Total credit	2 994	*133.2*	*130.4*	*134.7*	*165.0*	*199.9*	*272.9*	*264.2*	*237.8*
Total debit	3 994	*−64.3*	*−81.1*	*−94.2*	*−90.7*	*−107.7*	*−135.9*	*−104.4*	*−92.9*
Capital transfers, credit	2 400	**133.2**	**130.4**	**134.5**	**164.5**	**197.7**	**266.5**	**255.1**	**235.9**
General government	2 401	....	....	....	....	....	....	....	....
Debt forgiveness	2 402	....	....	....	....	....	....	....	....
Other capital transfers	2 410	....	....	....	....	....	....	....	....
Other sectors	2 430	133.2	130.4	134.5	164.5	197.7	266.5	255.1	235.9
Migrants' transfers	2 431	133.2	130.4	134.5	164.4	197.6	266.0	255.1	235.9
Debt forgiveness	2 432	....	....	....	....	....	....	....	....
Other capital transfers	2 440	....	....	....	.1	.1	.5	....	....
Capital transfers, debit	3 400	**−64.3**	**−81.1**	**−94.2**	**−90.2**	**−104.2**	**−129.7**	**−102.4**	**−92.2**
General government	3 401	....	....	....	....	....	....	....	....
Debt forgiveness	3 402	....	....	....	....	....	....	....	....
Other capital transfers	3 410	....	....	....	....	....	....	....	....
Other sectors	3 430	−64.3	−81.1	−94.2	−90.2	−104.2	−129.7	−102.4	−92.2
Migrants' transfers	3 431	−64.3	−81.1	−94.2	−90.2	−104.2	−129.7	−102.4	−92.2
Debt forgiveness	3 432	....	....	....	....	....	....	....	....
Other capital transfers	3 440	....	....	....	....	....	....	....	....
Nonproduced nonfinancial assets, credit	2 480	....	....	.2	.5	2.2	6.4	9.1	1.9
Nonproduced nonfinancial assets, debit	3 480	....	....	....	−.5	−3.5	−6.2	−2.0	−.7

Table 2 (Continued). STANDARD PRESENTATION, 2003–2010

(Millions of U.S. dollars)

	Code	2003	2004	2005	2006	2007	2008	2009	2010
FINANCIAL ACCOUNT	4 995	370.5	873.7	−584.9	1,674.7	2,463.0	5,151.5	5,717.7	7,578.0
A. DIRECT INVESTMENT	4 500	170.3	162.5	302.5	351.0	1,770.0	2,150.0	1,782.2	1,352.4
Direct investment abroad	4 505	−1.5	−1.3	−2.5	−3.0	−15.2	−30.6	−102.2	−50.4
Equity capital	4 510	−1.3	−1.3	−2.9	−2.4	−13.5	−27.0	−63.1	−54.2
Claims on affiliated enterprises	4 515	−1.3	−1.3	−2.9	−2.4	−13.5	−27.0	−63.1	−54.2
Liabilities to affiliated enterprises	4 520	....	....	....	....	....	....	....	....
Reinvested earnings	4 525	....	....	....	....	−.1	−.3	−5.6	−3.5
Other capital	4 530	−.2	....	.4	−.6	−1.6	−3.3	−33.5	7.3
Claims on affiliated enterprises	4 535	−.2	....	.4	−.6	−1.6	−3.3	−33.5	7.3
Liabilities to affiliated enterprises	4 540	....	....	....	....	....	....	....	....
Direct investment in Belarus	4 555	171.8	163.8	305.0	354.0	1,785.2	2,180.6	1,884.4	1,402.8
Equity capital	4 560	136.1	120.3	281.1	304.9	1,438.5	1,755.1	1,404.8	874.0
Claims on direct investors	4 565	....	....	....	....	....	....	....	....
Liabilities to direct investors	4 570	136.1	120.3	281.1	304.9	1,438.5	1,755.1	1,404.8	874.0
Reinvested earnings	4 575	12.3	23.6	32.6	58.4	185.2	261.1	417.7	473.1
Other capital	4 580	23.4	19.9	−8.7	−9.3	161.5	164.4	61.9	55.7
Claims on direct investors	4 585	....	....	....	....	....	....	....	....
Liabilities to direct investors	4 590	23.4	19.9	−8.7	−9.3	161.5	164.4	61.9	55.7
B. PORTFOLIO INVESTMENT	4 600	6.1	62.8	−41.5	−26.4	−38.8	5.3	18.8	1,185.6
Assets	4 602	.8	3.2	−2.9	−1.7	−41.2	4.8	16.5	−59.4
Equity securities	4 610	−1.1	.6	....	−5.6	−5.8	.9	−1.8	−.2
Monetary authorities	4 611	....	....	....	....	....	....	....	....
General government	4 612	....	....	....	....	....	....	−.1	....
Banks	4 613	....	.5	....	−1.2	−.5	.4	−1.3	.4
Other sectors	4 614	−1.1	.1	....	−4.4	−5.3	.5	−.4	−.6
Debt securities	4 619	1.9	2.6	−2.9	3.9	−35.4	3.9	18.3	−59.2
Bonds and notes	4 620	....	....	....	....	....	....	....	....
Monetary authorities	4 621	....	....	....	....	....	....	....	....
General government	4 622	....	....	....	....	....	....	....	....
Banks	4 623	....	....	....	....	....	....	....	....
Other sectors	4 624	....	....	....	....	....	....	....	....
Money market instruments	4 630	1.9	2.6	−2.9	3.9	−35.4	3.9	18.3	−59.2
Monetary authorities	4 631	....	....	....	....	....	....	....	....
General government	4 632	....	....	....	....	....	....	....	....
Banks	4 633	2.1	6.1	−2.4	7.5	−29.2	10.1	18.8	−59.4
Other sectors	4 634	−.2	−3.5	−.5	−3.6	−6.2	−6.2	−.5	.2
Liabilities	4 652	5.3	59.6	−38.6	−24.7	2.4	.5	2.3	1,245.0
Equity securities	4 660	3.3	.5	.6	−1.2	4.5	.7	1.2	.7
Banks	4 663	2.6	....	1.1	−1.3	3.6	−.4	....	.1
Other sectors	4 664	.7	.5	−.5	.1	.9	1.1	1.2	.6
Debt securities	4 669	2.0	59.1	−39.2	−23.5	−2.1	−.2	1.1	1,244.3
Bonds and notes	4 670	.1	4.1	−4.0	−1.6	−.8	−.1	1.1	1,244.3
Monetary authorities	4 671	....	....	....	....	....	....	....	....
General government	4 672	.1	3.8	−1.3	−1.6	−.5	−.2	.1	1,229.6
Banks	4 673	....	.1	....	....	....	.1	1.0	14.7
Other sectors	4 674	....	.2	−2.7	....	−.3	....	....	....
Money market instruments	4 680	1.9	55.0	−35.2	−21.9	−1.3	−.1	....	....
Monetary authorities	4 681	−1.0	−5.1	.1	....	....	−.1	....	....
General government	4 682	2.1	51.7	−31.9	−21.9	−1.2	....	....	....
Banks	4 683	.8	4.5	−3.4	....	....	....	....	....
Other sectors	4 684	....	3.9	....	....	−.1	....	....	....
C. FINANCIAL DERIVATIVES	4 910	....	....	−.2	−12.9	....	....	....	....
Monetary authorities	4 911	....	....	−.2	−12.9	....	....	....	....
General government	4 912	....	....	....	....	....	....	....	....
Banks	4 913	....	....	....	....	....	....	....	....
Other sectors	4 914	....	....	....	....	....	....	....	....
Assets	4 900	....	....	1.6	.1	....	....	....	....
Monetary authorities	4 901	....	....	1.6	.1	....	....	....	....
General government	4 902	....	....	....	....	....	....	....	....
Banks	4 903	....	....	....	....	....	....	....	....
Other sectors	4 904	....	....	....	....	....	....	....	....
Liabilities	4 905	....	....	−1.8	−13.0	....	....	....	....
Monetary authorities	4 906	....	....	−1.8	−13.0	....	....	....	....
General government	4 907	....	....	....	....	....	....	....	....
Banks	4 908	....	....	....	....	....	....	....	....
Other sectors	4 909	....	....	....	....	....	....	....	....

Table 2 (Concluded). STANDARD PRESENTATION, 2003–2010

(Millions of U.S. dollars)

	Code	2003	2004	2005	2006	2007	2008	2009	2010
D. OTHER INVESTMENT	4 700	**180.2**	**904.2**	**−306.5**	**1,361.6**	**3,509.9**	**1,994.4**	**6,358.2**	**4,231.5**
Assets	4 703	**18.4**	**−151.4**	**−492.1**	**−165.7**	**−1,931.7**	**−477.0**	**−507.7**	**−1,178.4**
Trade credits	4 706	119.3	−261.8	−300.6	−410.0	−806.9	−95.4	−620.5	−527.2
General government	4 707	....	....	....	....	....	....	....	....
of which: Short-term	4 709	....	....	....	....	....	....	....	....
Other sectors	4 710	119.3	−261.8	−300.6	−410.0	−806.9	−95.4	−620.5	−527.2
of which: Short-term	4 712	119.3	−261.8	−300.6	−410.0	−806.9	−95.4	−620.5	−527.2
Loans	4 714	12.6	6.0	6.8	−43.5	−174.0	140.5	−5.4	68.2
Monetary authorities	4 715	14.7	15.0	−5.0	....	....	30.0	....	....
of which: Short-term	4 718	14.7	15.0	....	....	....	....	....	....
General government	4 719	....	....	....	....	....	....	....	....
of which: Short-term	4 721	....	....	....	....	....	....	....	....
Banks	4 722	−2.1	−9.2	13.2	−24.6	−71.1	85.8	−19.7	−15.9
of which: Short-term	4 724	−1.9	−8.6	12.5	−21.8	−69.6	96.9	−18.2	−15.7
Other sectors	4 725	....	.2	−1.4	−18.9	−102.9	24.7	14.3	84.1
of which: Short-term	4 727	....	....	−1.2	−17.6	−104.1	27.4	15.2	81.5
Currency and deposits	4 730	−58.0	133.9	−189.5	258.9	−785.7	−300.6	152.0	−765.3
Monetary authorities	4 731	17.0	245.5	22.0	−15.5	−185.4	−50.5	227.7	−667.9
General government	4 732	....	....	....	....	....	....	....	....
Banks	4 733	−59.8	−112.6	−213.9	278.7	−595.8	−246.5	−55.3	−103.0
Other sectors	4 734	−15.2	1.0	2.4	−4.3	−4.5	−3.6	−20.4	5.6
Other assets	4 736	−55.5	−29.5	−8.8	28.9	−165.1	−221.5	−33.8	45.9
Monetary authorities	4 737	−41.7	−29.0	55.8	.1	....	−.2	....	....
of which: Short-term	4 739	−41.7	−29.0	55.8	.1	....	−.2	....	....
General government	4 740	....	....	....	....	−7.3	−198.5	101.2	101.1
of which: Short-term	4 742	....	....	....	....	−1.5	1.5	....	....
Banks	4 743	.8	1.3	−31.8	3.6	−108.4	86.0	−111.5	71.1
of which: Short-term	4 745	.8	1.3	−31.8	3.6	−108.4	86.0	−111.5	71.1
Other sectors	4 746	−14.6	−1.8	−32.8	25.2	−49.4	−108.8	−23.5	−126.3
of which: Short-term	4 748	−14.6	−1.8	−32.8	25.2	−49.4	−108.8	−23.5	−126.3
Liabilities	4 753	**161.8**	**1,055.6**	**185.6**	**1,527.3**	**5,441.6**	**2,471.4**	**6,865.9**	**5,409.9**
Trade credits	4 756	63.4	852.6	−245.1	567.5	1,497.1	384.5	1,277.5	1,095.5
General government	4 757	....	....	....	....	....	....	....	....
of which: Short-term	4 759	....	....	....	....	....	....	....	....
Other sectors	4 760	63.4	852.6	−245.1	567.5	1,497.1	384.5	1,277.5	1,095.5
of which: Short-term	4 762	63.4	852.6	−245.1	567.5	1,497.1	384.5	1,277.5	1,095.5
Loans	4 764	59.7	191.7	299.1	1,171.2	3,714.6	1,944.3	4,326.6	3,464.2
Monetary authorities	4 765	−19.9	−183.8	−61.8	....	440.0	−161.0	2,655.0	1,327.4
of which: Use of Fund credit and loans from the Fund	4 766	−32.3	−17.3	−8.9	....	....	....	2,855.9	668.9
of which: Short-term	4 768	−5.1	....	....	....	200.0	....	−200.0	146.3
General government	4 769	−43.2	122.1	116.5	3.4	1,419.9	1,397.1	1,326.3	−139.6
of which: Short-term	4 771	....	....	32.0	53.6	−95.7	....	....	....
Banks	4 772	40.7	174.2	98.1	728.3	1,036.7	517.1	41.1	2,197.3
of which: Short-term	4 774	40.7	174.2	98.1	452.3	671.9	1.4	−235.4	1,241.3
Other sectors	4 775	82.1	79.2	146.3	439.5	818.0	191.1	304.2	79.1
of which: Short-term	4 777	84.7	116.6	111.6	177.8	438.2	−303.6	413.6	−268.0
Currency and deposits	4 780	78.7	16.2	103.5	−226.7	172.8	44.9	219.6	1,118.1
Monetary authorities	4 781	1.0	−28.4	−12.8	....	144.6	9.9	199.3	791.1
General government	4 782	....	....	....	....	....	....	....	....
Banks	4 783	77.7	44.6	116.3	−226.7	28.2	35.0	20.3	327.0
Other sectors	4 784	....	....	....	....	....	....	....	....
Other liabilities	4 786	−40.0	−4.9	28.1	15.3	57.1	97.7	1,042.2	−267.9
Monetary authorities	4 787	....	....	....	....	5.3	−4.8	576.3	....
of which: Short-term	4 789	....	....	....	....	5.3	−4.8	−.3	....
General government	4 790	21.0	−20.8	−.5	....	....	....	....	....
of which: Short-term	4 792	21.0	−20.8	−.5	....	....	....	....	....
Banks	4 793	.3	.8	5.5	32.9	10.2	−21.3	421.6	−228.3
of which: Short-term	4 795	.3	.8	5.5	32.9	10.2	−21.3	421.6	−228.3
Other sectors	4 796	−61.3	15.1	23.1	−17.6	41.6	123.8	44.3	−39.6
of which: Short-term	4 798	−61.3	15.1	23.1	−17.6	41.6	123.8	44.3	−39.6
E. RESERVE ASSETS	4 802	**13.8**	**−255.8**	**−539.2**	**1.4**	**−2,778.1**	**1,001.8**	**−2,441.5**	**808.4**
Monetary gold	4 812	35.7	−35.9	−90.4	−80.1	34.8	−5.8	−295.4	−538.2
Special drawing rights	4 811	.2	....	....	....	....	−1.0	−576.0	....
Reserve position in the Fund	4 810	....	....	....	....	....	....	....	....
Foreign exchange	4 803	−22.1	−220.4	−448.2	81.9	−2,728.8	1,004.1	82.4	569.0
Other claims	4 813	....	.5	−.6	−.4	−84.1	4.5	−1,652.5	777.6
NET ERRORS AND OMISSIONS	4 998	**−13.2**	**270.3**	**108.9**	**−300.6**	**477.0**	**−300.4**	**300.3**	**593.9**

Table 3. INTERNATIONAL INVESTMENT POSITION (End-period stocks), 2003–2010

(Millions of U.S. dollars)

	Code	2003	2004	2005	2006	2007	2008	2009	2010
ASSETS	8 995 C.	**1,811.4**	**2,240.7**	**3,289.1**	**3,583.4**	**8,592.2**	**7,771.2**	**11,001.9**	**11,681.9**
Direct investment abroad	8 505 ..	**6.2**	**8.2**	**13.9**	**18.5**	**46.3**	**72.4**	**144.6**	**204.8**
Equity capital and reinvested earnings	8 506 ..	5.2	7.1	12.4	16.6	36.6	66.4	137.7	193.1
Claims on affiliated enterprises	8 507 ..	5.2	7.1	12.4	16.6	36.6	66.4	137.7	193.1
Liabilities to affiliated enterprises	8 508 ..	....	....	....	....	....	....	....	....
Other capital	8 530 ..	1.0	1.1	1.5	1.9	9.7	6.0	6.9	11.7
Claims on affiliated enterprises	8 535 ..	1.0	1.1	1.5	1.9	9.7	6.0	6.9	11.7
Liabilities to affiliated enterprises	8 540 ..	....	....	....	....	....	....	....	....
Portfolio investment	8 602 ..	**16.3**	**9.1**	**21.3**	**23.0**	**65.8**	**61.5**	**43.5**	**101.7**
Equity securities	8 610 ..	1.8	.3	.3	5.9	13.1	12.9	13.1	12.8
Monetary authorities	8 611 ..	....	....	....	....	....	....	....	....
General government	8 612 ..	....	....	....	....	....	....	.1	.1
Banks	8 613 ..	.5	.1	.1	1.3	2.1	1.4	2.7	2.3
Other sectors	8 614 ..	1.3	.2	.2	4.6	11.0	11.5	10.3	10.4
Debt securities	8 619 ..	14.5	8.8	21.0	17.1	52.7	48.6	30.4	88.9
Bonds and notes	8 620 ..	....	....	....	....	....	....	....	....
Monetary authorities	8 621 ..	....	....	....	....	....	....	....	....
General government	8 622 ..	....	....	....	....	....	....	....	....
Banks	8 623 ..	....	....	....	....	....	....	....	....
Other sectors	8 624 ..	....	....	....	....	....	....	....	....
Money market instruments	8 630 ..	14.5	8.8	21.0	17.1	52.7	48.6	30.4	88.9
Monetary authorities	8 631 ..	....	....	....	....	....	....	....	....
General government	8 632 ..	....	....	....	....	....	....	....	....
Banks	8 633 ..	14.3	8.6	20.3	13.1	42.5	32.3	13.5	72.3
Other sectors	8 634 ..	.2	.2	.7	4.0	10.2	16.3	16.9	16.6
Financial derivatives	8 900 ..	**....**	**2.0**	**....**	**....**	**....**	**....**	**....**	**....**
Monetary authorities	8 901 ..	....	2.0	....	....	....	....	....	....
General government	8 902 ..	....	....	....	....	....	....	....	....
Banks	8 903 ..	....	....	....	....	....	....	....	....
Other sectors	8 904 ..	....	....	....	....	....	....	....	....
Other investment	8 703 ..	**1,289.9**	**1,451.2**	**1,957.3**	**2,158.9**	**4,297.8**	**4,576.2**	**5,161.3**	**6,344.6**
Trade credits	8 706 ..	431.9	687.8	988.5	1,398.5	2,205.4	2,300.9	2,921.3	3,448.5
General government	8 707 ..	....	....	....	....	....	....	....	....
of which: Short-term	8 709 ..	....	....	....	....	....	....	....	....
Other sectors	8 710 ..	431.9	687.8	988.5	1,398.5	2,205.4	2,300.9	2,921.3	3,448.5
of which: Short-term	8 712 ..	*431.9*	*687.8*	*988.5*	*1,398.5*	*2,205.4*	*2,300.9*	*2,921.3*	*3,448.5*
Loans	8 714 ..	51.7	47.4	40.5	90.0	257.9	102.9	164.1	80.7
Monetary authorities	8 715 ..	40.0	25.0	30.0	30.0	30.0	....	....	....
of which: Short-term	8 718 ..	*15.0*	....	....	....	....	....	....	....
General government	8 719 ..	....	....	....	....	....	....	....	....
of which: Short-term	8 721 ..	....	....	....	....	....	....	....	....
Banks	8 722 ..	11.5	20.8	7.6	32.6	105.1	20.0	40.7	56.5
of which: Short-term	8 724 ..	*11.3*	*19.9*	*7.3*	*29.6*	*100.5*	*4.3*	*23.6*	*39.9*
Other sectors	8 725 ..	.2	1.6	2.9	27.4	122.8	82.9	123.4	24.2
of which: Short-term	8 727 ..	....	*1.2*	*2.4*	*22.8*	*120.3*	*78.6*	*118.0*	*20.7*
Currency and deposits	8 730 ..	599.6	468.7	734.8	504.6	1,502.4	1,619.8	1,490.9	2,279.9
Monetary authorities	8 731 ..	277.1	38.3	96.3	132.8	522.1	416.9	226.7	966.3
General government	8 732 ..	....	....	....	....	....	....	....	....
Banks	8 733 ..	297.8	413.8	624.8	352.8	954.9	1,176.1	1,216.9	1,273.6
Other sectors	8 734 ..	24.7	16.6	13.7	19.0	25.4	26.8	47.3	40.0
Other assets	8 736 ..	206.7	247.3	193.5	165.8	332.1	552.6	585.0	535.5
Monetary authorities	8 737 ..	84.0	118.3	.2	.1	.3	.3	.3	....
of which: Short-term	8 739 ..	*84.0*	*118.3*	*.2*	*.1*	*.3*	*.3*	*.3*	....
General government	8 740 ..	....	....	....	....	7.3	205.8	104.6	3.6
of which: Short-term	8 742 ..	....	....	....	....		*1.5*	....	....
Banks	8 743 ..	2.6	1.2	32.8	30.5	139.9	53.2	164.3	89.8
of which: Short-term	8 745 ..	*2.6*	*1.2*	*32.8*	*30.5*	*139.9*	*53.2*	*164.3*	*89.8*
Other sectors	8 746 ..	120.1	127.8	160.5	135.2	184.6	293.3	315.8	442.1
of which: Short-term	8 748 ..	*120.1*	*127.8*	*160.5*	*135.2*	*184.6*	*293.3*	*315.8*	*442.1*
Reserve assets	8 802 ..	**499.0**	**770.2**	**1,296.6**	**1,383.0**	**4,182.3**	**3,061.1**	**5,652.5**	**5,030.8**
Monetary gold	8 812 ..	37.4	79.4	190.0	314.4	230.0	374.1	821.1	1,599.8
Special drawing rights	8 811 ..	....	....	....	....	....	1.0	578.4	567.7
Reserve position in the Fund	8 810 ..	....	....	....	....	....			
Foreign exchange	8 803 ..	460.7	690.4	1,105.6	1,067.2	3,866.2	2,605.5	2,519.9	1,907.7
Other claims	8 813 ..	.8	.4	.9	1.3	86.0	80.5	1,733.1	955.5

Table 3 (Concluded). INTERNATIONAL INVESTMENT POSITION (End-period stocks), 2003–2010

(Millions of U.S. dollars)

	Code	2003	2004	2005	2006	2007	2008	2009	2010
LIABILITIES	8 995 D.	**5,794.2**	**6,674.9**	**7,184.9**	**9,200.6**	**16,500.9**	**21,160.5**	**29,846.7**	**37,507.3**
Direct investment in Belarus	8 555 ..	**1,898.6**	**2,057.0**	**2,382.8**	**2,734.3**	**4,483.0**	**6,682.7**	**8,536.7**	**9,904.2**
Equity capital and reinvested earnings	8 556 ..	1,605.6	1,718.8	2,030.9	2,337.9	3,981.2	5,977.2	7,751.6	9,081.7
Claims on direct investors	8 557 ..	....	....	....	....	....	....	....	....
Liabilities to direct investors	8 558 ..	1,605.6	1,718.8	2,030.9	2,337.9	3,981.2	5,977.2	7,751.6	9,081.7
Other capital	8 580 ..	293.0	338.2	351.9	396.4	501.8	705.5	785.1	822.5
Claims on direct investors	8 585 ..	....	....	....	....	....	....	....	....
Liabilities to direct investors	8 590 ..	293.0	338.2	351.9	396.4	501.8	705.5	785.1	822.5
Portfolio investment	8 652 ..	**24.9**	**87.8**	**50.7**	**27.2**	**30.0**	**35.9**	**32.2**	**1,276.8**
Equity securities	8 660 ..	11.7	16.9	18.7	18.6	23.2	29.2	24.4	24.7
Banks	8 663 ..	9.7	9.8	10.9	9.6	13.2	12.8	12.8	12.9
Other sectors	8 664 ..	2.0	7.1	7.8	9.0	10.0	16.4	11.6	11.8
Debt securities	8 669 ..	13.2	70.9	32.0	8.6	6.8	6.7	7.8	1,252.1
Bonds and notes	8 670 ..	....	....	....	....	....	....	.5	1,230.1
Monetary authorities	8 671 ..	....	....	....	....	....	....	....	....
General government	8 672 ..	....	....	....	....	....	....	.5	1,230.1
Banks	8 673 ..	....	....	....	....	....	....	....	....
Other sectors	8 674 ..	....	....	....	....	....	....	....	....
Money market instruments	8 680 ..	13.2	70.9	32.0	8.6	6.8	6.7	7.3	22.0
Monetary authorities	8 681 ..	5.1	....	.1	.1	.1	....	....	....
General government	8 682 ..	3.0	58.5	25.7	2.3	.6	.5	....	....
Banks	8 683 ..	5.1	9.7	6.2	6.1	6.1	6.2	7.3	22.0
Other sectors	8 684 ..	....	2.7	....	.1	....	....	....	....
Financial derivatives	8 905 ..	**....**	**3.7**	**7.1**	**....**	**....**	**....**	**....**	**....**
Monetary authorities	8 906 ..	....	3.7	7.1	....	....	....	....	....
General government	8 907 ..	....	....	....	....	....	....	....	....
Banks	8 908 ..	....	....	....	....	....	....	....	....
Other sectors	8 909 ..	....	....	....	....	....	....	....	....
Other investment	8 753 ..	**3,870.7**	**4,526.4**	**4,744.3**	**6,439.1**	**11,987.9**	**14,441.9**	**21,277.8**	**26,326.3**
Trade credits	8 756 ..	1,259.5	2,161.7	1,966.2	2,533.7	4,031.5	4,416.1	5,693.2	6,788.6
General government	8 757 ..	....	....	....	....	....	....	....	....
of which: Short-term	8 759 ..	....	....	....	....	....	....	....	....
Other sectors	8 760 ..	1,259.5	2,161.7	1,966.2	2,533.7	4,031.5	4,416.1	5,693.2	6,788.6
of which: Short-term	8 762 ..	*1,259.5*	*2,161.7*	*1,966.2*	*2,533.7*	*4,031.5*	*4,416.1*	*5,693.2*	*6,788.6*
Loans	8 764 ..	1,817.2	1,608.5	1,942.6	3,278.4	7,089.2	9,036.6	13,355.3	16,496.1
Monetary authorities	8 765 ..	238.8	63.5	....	....	440.0	279.1	2,949.5	4,229.6
of which: Use of Fund credit and loans from the Fund....	8 766 ..	*26.0*	*9.1*	....	....	....	....	*2,871.4*	*3,495.1*
of which: Short-term	8 768 ..	....	....	....	....	*200.0*	*200.0*	....	*146.3*
General government	8 769 ..	319.4	433.1	581.1	586.7	2,035.7	3,596.7	4,923.6	4,764.8
of which: Short-term	8 771 ..	....	....	*32.0*	*85.6*	....	....	....	....
Banks	8 772 ..	216.8	390.9	595.4	1,324.8	2,368.3	2,875.0	2,915.7	5,013.2
of which: Short-term	8 774 ..	*216.8*	*390.9*	*149.8*	*603.2*	*1,281.9*	*1,275.0*	*1,039.4*	*2,246.1*
Other sectors	8 775 ..	1,042.2	721.0	766.1	1,366.9	2,245.2	2,285.8	2,566.5	2,488.5
of which: Short-term	8 777 ..	*187.8*	*122.5*	*283.0*	*523.7*	*977.8*	*683.6*	*950.9*	*493.5*
Currency and deposits	8 780 ..	215.7	233.0	336.2	110.6	289.4	321.4	530.4	1,625.8
Monetary authorities	8 781 ..	41.8	13.4	.6	.6	150.8	150.3	345.4	1,120.8
General government	8 782 ..	....	....	....	....	....	....	....	....
Banks	8 783 ..	173.9	219.6	335.6	110.0	138.6	171.1	185.0	505.0
Other sectors	8 784 ..	....	....	....	....	....	....	....	....
Other liabilities	8 786 ..	578.3	523.2	499.3	516.4	577.8	667.8	1,698.9	1,415.8
Monetary authorities	8 787 ..	....	....	....	....	5.3	.5	578.1	567.7
of which: Short-term	8 789 ..	....	....	....	....	*5.3*	*.5*	*.2*	....
General government	8 790 ..	21.5	.5	....	....	....	....	....	....
of which: Short-term	8 792 ..	*21.5*	*.5*	....	....	....	....	....	....
Banks	8 793 ..	4.9	5.6	11.1	45.8	57.8	28.8	445.0	211.9
of which: Short-term	8 795 ..	*4.9*	*5.6*	*11.1*	*45.8*	*57.8*	*28.8*	*445.0*	*211.9*
Other sectors	8 796 ..	551.9	517.1	488.2	470.6	514.7	638.5	675.8	636.2
of which: Short-term	8 798 ..	*551.9*	*517.1*	*488.2*	*470.6*	*514.7*	*638.5*	*675.8*	*636.2*
NET INTERNATIONAL INVESTMENT POSITION	8 995 ..	**−3,982.9**	**−4,434.1**	**−3,895.8**	**−5,617.2**	**−7,908.7**	**−13,389.3**	**−18,844.7**	**−25,825.5**
Conversion rates: rubels per U.S. dollar (end of period)	0 102 ..	**2,156.0**	**2,170.0**	**2,152.0**	**2,140.0**	**2,150.0**	**2,200.0**	**2,863.0**	**3,000.0**

Table 1. ANALYTIC PRESENTATION, 2003–2010

(Millions of U.S. dollars)

	Code	2003	2004	2005	2006	2007	2008	2009	2010
A. Current Account[1]	4 993 Z.	**10,790**	**11,426**	**7,703**	**7,545**	**7,041**	**−7,110**	**−7,817**	**6,349**
Goods: exports f.o.b.	2 100 ..	184,638	220,131	240,245	260,379	299,406	332,384	249,748	279,701
Goods: imports f.o.b.	3 100 ..	−175,801	−211,538	−236,569	−257,507	−298,791	−348,507	−256,433	−284,431
Balance on Goods	4 100 ..	*8,837*	*8,593*	*3,676*	*2,872*	*615*	*−16,123*	*−6,685*	*−4,730*
Services: credit	2 200 ..	44,711	52,713	56,144	59,516	74,643	88,447	84,420	87,153
Services: debit	3 200 ..	−42,860	−49,027	−51,172	−53,252	−68,869	−83,286	−76,280	−78,609
Balance on Goods and Services	4 991 ..	*10,688*	*12,279*	*8,648*	*9,135*	*6,388*	*−10,962*	*1,455*	*3,815*
Income: credit	2 300 ..	40,212	48,893	59,028	74,277	100,086	107,886	73,355	69,102
Income: debit	3 300 ..	−33,731	−43,269	−53,604	−69,325	−93,075	−95,143	−73,612	−58,144
Balance on Goods, Services, and Income	4 992 ..	*17,169*	*17,903*	*14,072*	*14,087*	*13,399*	*1,781*	*1,198*	*14,772*
Current transfers: credit	2 379 Z.	6,515	7,949	9,356	8,810	9,885	11,150	10,709	11,315
Current transfers: debit	3 379 ..	−12,894	−14,427	−15,725	−15,353	−16,243	−20,041	−19,724	−19,738
B. Capital Account[1]	4 994 Z.	**−1,021**	**−497**	**−894**	**−405**	**−1,882**	**−2,619**	**−1,811**	**−857**
Capital account: credit	2 994 Z.	267	399	399	984	284	839	844	772
Capital account: debit	3 994 ..	−1,288	−896	−1,293	−1,389	−2,166	−3,458	−2,655	−1,629
Total, Groups A Plus B	4 981 ..	*9,769*	*10,928*	*6,809*	*7,140*	*5,159*	*−9,729*	*−9,627*	*5,492*
C. Financial Account[1]	4 995 W.	**−12,518**	**−10,660**	**−11,397**	**−7,514**	**−6,255**	**10,153**	**15,746**	**−5,846**
Direct investment abroad	4 505 ..	−39,043	−34,682	−32,545	−50,140	−83,492	−213,613	−6,633	−47,867
Direct investment in Belgium	4 555 Z.	34,544	44,415	33,684	58,828	96,588	184,842	60,933	72,914
Portfolio investment assets	4 602 ..	−6,046	−35,558	−43,491	−26,529	−80,503	−295	18,624	7,879
Equity securities	4 610 ..	−5,508	−8,037	−20,449	−19,980	−20,401	31,861	3,152	−4,994
Debt securities	4 619 ..	−538	−27,520	−23,043	−6,548	−60,102	−32,156	15,472	12,873
Portfolio investment liabilities	4 652 Z.	6,628	5,070	−1,215	17,348	37,481	48,102	21,625	−9,025
Equity securities	4 660 ..	3,182	4,092	5,712	4,588	3,360	8,818	−3,242	−1,837
Debt securities	4 669 Z.	3,446	978	−6,927	12,760	34,121	39,285	24,867	−7,188
Financial derivatives	4 910 ..	−3,626	−5,586	−5,448	3,372	1,424	5,809	728	1,800
Financial derivatives assets	4 900 ..	−7,195	−8,648	−9,647	−1,497	....	....	....	....
Financial derivatives liabilities	4 905 ..	3,570	3,063	4,199	4,870	....	....	....	....
Other investment assets	4 703 ..	−75,625	−64,685	−87,399	−91,915	−158,361	73,479	116,669	10,186
Monetary authorities	4 701 ..	−107	−853	−130	242	−840	−58	538	−549
General government	4 704 ..	878	−403	19	−297	1,265	−66	−70	−757
Banks	4 705 ..	−69,263	−64,840	−92,342	−80,317	−148,883	75,373	123,324	22,544
Other sectors	4 728 ..	−7,133	1,412	5,055	−11,542	−9,902	−1,770	−7,124	−11,052
Other investment liabilities	4 753 W.	70,649	80,365	125,017	81,520	180,608	−88,171	−196,200	−41,732
Monetary authorities	4 753 WA	6,663	15,366	5,639	13,562	25,081	65,454	−78,738	−37,199
General government	4 753 ZB	−632	−786	−296	−2,736	139	599	−1,326	2,514
Banks	4 753 ZC	57,497	57,694	119,771	64,658	147,477	−181,514	−104,481	−2,048
Other sectors	4 753 ZD	7,121	8,092	−97	6,036	7,911	27,291	−11,656	−4,999
Total, Groups A Through C	4 983 ..	*−2,749*	*268*	*−4,588*	*−375*	*−1,096*	*424*	*6,119*	*−353*
D. Net Errors and Omissions	4 998 ..	**1,024**	**−992**	**2,413**	**530**	**2,322**	**−1,741**	**849**	**1,172**
Total, Groups A Through D	4 984 ..	*−1,725*	*−723*	*−2,176*	*156*	*1,226*	*−1,316*	*6,968*	*819*
E. Reserves and Related Items	4 802 A.	**1,725**	**723**	**2,176**	**−156**	**−1,226**	**1,316**	**−6,968**	**−819**
Reserve assets	4 802 ..	1,725	723	2,176	−156	−1,226	1,316	−6,968	−819
Use of Fund credit and loans	4 766 ..	....	....	....	....	....	....	....	....
Exceptional financing	4 920 ..	....	....	....	....	....	....	....	....
Conversion rates: euros per U.S. dollar	0 103 ..	**.88603**	**.80537**	**.80412**	**.79714**	**.73064**	**.68267**	**.71984**	**.75504**

[1] Excludes components that have been classified in the categories of Group E.

Table 2. STANDARD PRESENTATION, 2003–2010

(Millions of U.S. dollars)

	Code	2003	2004	2005	2006	2007	2008	2009	2010
CURRENT ACCOUNT	4 993	10,790	11,426	7,703	7,545	7,041	−7,110	−7,817	6,349
A. GOODS	4 100	8,837	8,593	3,676	2,872	615	−16,123	−6,685	−4,730
Credit	2 100	184,638	220,131	240,245	260,379	299,406	332,384	249,748	279,701
General merchandise: exports f.o.b.	2 110	168,921	203,731	223,961	242,272	279,340	311,287	234,469	263,561
Goods for processing: exports f.o.b.	2 150	13,868	14,190	13,636	14,861	17,251	17,519	11,785	12,645
Repairs on goods	2 160	248	280	387	402	628	600	624	583
Goods procured in ports by carriers	2 170	1,288	1,645	1,777	2,013	1,639	2,306	2,084	2,032
Nonmonetary gold	2 180	313	286	483	831	549	673	786	880
Debit	3 100	−175,801	−211,538	−236,569	−257,507	−298,791	−348,507	−256,433	−284,431
General merchandise: imports f.o.b.	3 110	−162,586	−197,756	−223,222	−242,682	−283,927	−332,826	−246,193	−273,428
Goods for processing: imports f.o.b.	3 150	−12,363	−12,809	−12,137	−13,189	−13,049	−13,108	−8,428	−8,746
Repairs on goods	3 160	−191	−211	−259	−305	−331	−406	−148	−214
Goods procured in ports by carriers	3 170	−475	−531	−627	−768	−1,282	−1,705	−1,075	−1,185
Nonmonetary gold	3 180	−186	−231	−323	−564	−203	−462	−589	−858
B. SERVICES	4 200	1,851	3,686	4,972	6,264	5,773	5,161	8,140	8,544
Total credit	2 200	44,711	52,713	56,144	59,516	74,643	88,447	84,420	87,153
Total debit	3 200	−42,860	−49,027	−51,172	−53,252	−68,869	−83,286	−76,280	−78,609
Transportation services, credit	2 205	9,948	13,048	13,872	15,664	23,370	27,727	21,731	25,397
Passenger	2 850	655	881	1,036	1,314	1,354	1,318	1,246	1,196
Freight	2 851	6,836	9,235	9,551	10,327	14,067	17,806	12,850	15,721
Other	2 852	2,457	2,931	3,285	4,022	7,948	8,603	7,636	8,481
Sea transport, passenger	2 207	4	3	6	4	1	4	6	8
Sea transport, freight	2 208	3,625	5,257	5,244	5,541	8,341	10,568	7,634	9,112
Sea transport, other	2 209	1,099	1,448	1,850	2,201	3,003	2,989	2,501	3,339
Air transport, passenger	2 211	569	791	907	1,172	1,323	1,295	1,200	1,149
Air transport, freight	2 212	375	490	541	588	1,335	1,637	1,079	638
Air transport, other	2 213	591	673	529	432	919	1,075	957	821
Other transport, passenger	2 215	82	88	123	138	30	19	40	39
Other transport, freight	2 216	2,836	3,488	3,766	4,198	4,392	5,602	4,137	5,971
Other transport, other	2 217	767	811	907	1,389	4,026	4,539	4,177	4,321
Transportation services, debit	3 205	−9,036	−11,065	−12,265	−13,041	−19,212	−22,490	−16,833	−19,639
Passenger	3 850	−1,192	−1,500	−1,823	−2,317	−1,709	−1,586	−1,747	−1,879
Freight	3 851	−6,631	−8,165	−8,702	−8,932	−11,505	−15,550	−10,487	−12,726
Other	3 852	−1,213	−1,400	−1,740	−1,792	−5,998	−5,354	−4,599	−5,034
Sea transport, passenger	3 207	−27	−28	−40	−30	−7	−9	−6	−5
Sea transport, freight	3 208	−4,117	−5,124	−5,244	−5,183	−5,681	−6,978	−4,717	−6,028
Sea transport, other	3 209	−334	−401	−629	−776	−1,989	−2,130	−1,979	−2,320
Air transport, passenger	3 211	−1,093	−1,375	−1,659	−2,162	−1,674	−1,571	−1,698	−1,813
Air transport, freight	3 212	−370	−458	−736	−906	−1,638	−2,234	−1,472	−1,279
Air transport, other	3 213	−588	−775	−883	−721	−545	−544	−463	−431
Other transport, passenger	3 215	−72	−97	−124	−124	−28	−6	−43	−61
Other transport, freight	3 216	−2,144	−2,583	−2,723	−2,842	−4,187	−6,339	−4,298	−5,419
Other transport, other	3 217	−291	−225	−228	−295	−3,464	−2,680	−2,158	−2,283
Travel, credit	2 236	8,193	9,208	9,845	10,311	11,017	11,788	10,202	10,235
Business travel	2 237	1,467	1,676	1,773	1,936	2,303	2,763	2,358	2,369
Personal travel	2 240	6,726	7,533	8,071	8,375	8,714	9,025	7,843	7,866
Travel, debit	3 236	−12,210	−13,956	−14,948	−15,574	−17,506	−19,859	−20,432	−18,679
Business travel	3 237	−1,394	−2,394	−2,129	−2,292	−2,835	−3,088	−2,953	−2,797
Personal travel	3 240	−10,816	−11,562	−12,819	−13,281	−14,671	−16,771	−17,479	−15,882
Other services, credit	2 200 BA	26,570	30,457	32,428	33,541	40,256	48,933	52,487	51,520
Communications	2 245	1,862	2,230	2,206	2,028	3,639	3,944	4,001	4,051
Construction	2 249	1,965	1,890	1,906	2,230	1,087	1,568	1,511	1,540
Insurance	2 253	744	854	829	933	1,096	1,260	1,254	1,108
Financial	2 260	2,545	2,976	3,397	3,613	3,706	3,968	3,946	3,332
Computer and information	2 262	2,133	2,441	2,581	2,869	2,982	3,698	4,194	4,010
Royalties and licence fees	2 266	883	1,022	1,360	1,542	1,679	1,167	2,466	2,138
Other business services	2 268	14,714	16,502	17,577	17,462	23,342	30,566	32,625	32,913
Personal, cultural, and recreational	2 287	368	454	518	558	484	589	592	613
Government, n.i.e.	2 291	1,356	2,088	2,052	2,307	2,241	2,173	1,897	1,814
Other services, debit	3 200 BA	−21,613	−24,006	−23,958	−24,638	−32,151	−40,937	−39,015	−40,291
Communications	3 245	−1,453	−1,598	−1,321	−1,593	−2,895	−3,034	−3,153	−3,191
Construction	3 249	−983	−1,124	−849	−939	−800	−972	−1,260	−1,247
Insurance	3 253	−643	−619	−511	−551	−806	−1,111	−1,105	−1,167
Financial	3 260	−2,693	−3,214	−3,506	−3,451	−2,658	−3,341	−1,986	−1,894
Computer and information	3 262	−1,606	−2,003	−1,867	−1,985	−2,206	−2,736	−3,046	−2,865
Royalties and licence fees	3 266	−983	−1,038	−1,050	−1,077	−1,998	−1,876	−2,015	−1,904
Other business services	3 268	−12,111	−13,152	−13,621	−13,680	−20,028	−26,793	−25,515	−27,027
Personal, cultural, and recreational	3 287	−443	−494	−470	−498	−566	−797	−705	−764
Government, n.i.e.	3 291	−698	−765	−764	−864	−195	−277	−231	−232

Table 2 (Continued). STANDARD PRESENTATION, 2003–2010

(Millions of U.S. dollars)

	Code	2003	2004	2005	2006	2007	2008	2009	2010
C. INCOME	4 300	**6,481**	**5,624**	**5,424**	**4,952**	**7,011**	**12,743**	**–257**	**10,958**
Total credit	2 300	*40,212*	*48,893*	*59,028*	*74,277*	*100,086*	*107,886*	*73,355*	*69,102*
Total debit	3 300	*–33,731*	*–43,269*	*–53,604*	*–69,325*	*–93,075*	*–95,143*	*–73,612*	*–58,144*
Compensation of employees, credit	2 310	**5,753**	**6,539**	**6,868**	**7,239**	**8,879**	**10,278**	**10,299**	**10,141**
Compensation of employees, debit	3 310	**–1,762**	**–1,997**	**–2,012**	**–2,135**	**–2,727**	**–3,463**	**–3,544**	**–3,457**
Investment income, credit	2 320	**34,459**	**42,355**	**52,160**	**67,038**	**91,206**	**97,608**	**63,056**	**58,961**
Direct investment income	2 330	9,189	13,862	17,287	25,321	33,038	27,190	23,158	23,373
Dividends and distributed branch profits	2 332	4,120	4,693	6,226	8,908	12,005	12,815	11,978	12,680
Reinvested earnings and undistributed branch profits	2 333	1,610	3,814	4,659	8,576	9,657	1,569	4,437	4,277
Income on debt (interest)	2 334	3,459	5,354	6,402	7,837	11,375	12,807	6,743	6,417
Portfolio investment income	2 339	18,775	19,759	22,468	23,616	26,670	29,030	22,401	22,381
Income on equity	2 340	3,622	4,025	4,966	5,635	6,083	7,300	6,824	7,225
Income on bonds and notes	2 350	14,888	15,485	17,238	17,715	19,898	20,852	15,115	14,736
Income on money market instruments	2 360	266	249	264	266	690	878	462	419
Other investment income	2 370	6,495	8,734	12,405	18,101	31,499	41,387	17,497	13,207
Investment income, debit	3 320	**–31,969**	**–41,272**	**–51,593**	**–67,191**	**–90,348**	**–91,680**	**–70,068**	**–54,687**
Direct investment income	3 330	–12,090	–17,260	–22,522	–30,804	–36,627	–31,074	–42,579	–34,304
Dividends and distributed branch profits	3 332	–9,961	–11,105	–14,210	–15,742	–19,103	–25,685	–28,566	–20,254
Reinvested earnings and undistributed branch profits	3 333	569	–3,711	–5,078	–11,247	–13,185	–314	–11,869	–11,623
Income on debt (interest)	3 334	–2,698	–2,445	–3,234	–3,815	–4,339	–5,075	–2,143	–2,427
Portfolio investment income	3 339	–10,116	–11,452	–12,261	–12,840	–16,262	–17,004	–14,229	–11,777
Income on equity	3 340	–730	–884	–1,245	–1,593	–2,213	–2,787	–3,098	–2,196
Income on bonds and notes	3 350	–8,242	–9,051	–9,395	–9,213	–11,596	–11,467	–9,970	–8,312
Income on money market instruments	3 360	–1,143	–1,517	–1,620	–2,034	–2,453	–2,750	–1,161	–1,269
Other investment income	3 370	–9,763	–12,560	–16,810	–23,547	–37,459	–43,602	–13,260	–8,606
D. CURRENT TRANSFERS	4 379	**–6,379**	**–6,478**	**–6,369**	**–6,542**	**–6,358**	**–8,891**	**–9,015**	**–8,423**
Credit	2 379	**6,515**	**7,949**	**9,356**	**8,810**	**9,885**	**11,150**	**10,709**	**11,315**
General government	2 380	1,905	2,514	3,297	3,010	2,159	2,559	2,383	2,136
Other sectors	2 390	4,610	5,435	6,059	5,800	7,725	8,591	8,326	9,179
Workers' remittances	2 391	20	19	20	27	114	139	137	123
Other current transfers	2 392	4,590	5,416	6,040	5,774	7,611	8,452	8,189	9,055
Debit	3 379	**–12,894**	**–14,427**	**–15,725**	**–15,353**	**–16,243**	**–20,041**	**–19,724**	**–19,738**
General government	3 380	–6,505	–7,278	–8,018	–8,325	–8,411	–9,910	–9,339	–9,231
Other sectors	3 390	–6,389	–7,148	–7,707	–7,027	–7,831	–10,131	–10,385	–10,506
Workers' remittances	3 391	–333	–343	–416	–429	–476	–585	–614	–594
Other current transfers	3 392	–6,056	–6,805	–7,292	–6,598	–7,356	–9,546	–9,771	–9,912
CAPITAL AND FINANCIAL ACCOUNT	4 996	**–11,814**	**–10,434**	**–10,115**	**–8,075**	**–9,363**	**8,850**	**6,967**	**–7,522**
CAPITAL ACCOUNT	4 994	**–1,021**	**–497**	**–894**	**–405**	**–1,882**	**–2,619**	**–1,811**	**–857**
Total credit	2 994	*267*	*399*	*399*	*984*	*284*	*839*	*844*	*772*
Total debit	3 994	*–1,288*	*–896*	*–1,293*	*–1,389*	*–2,166*	*–3,458*	*–2,655*	*–1,629*
Capital transfers, credit	2 400	**241**	**342**	**391**	**226**	**47**	**273**	**538**	**348**
General government	2 401	....	6	4	....	47	273	259	348
Debt forgiveness	2 402	....	....	....	....	....	....	....	....
Other capital transfers	2 410	....	6	4	....	47	273	259	348
Other sectors	2 430	241	336	388	226	....	....	278	....
Migrants' transfers	2 431	216	308	354	222	....	....	....	....
Debt forgiveness	2 432	....	....	....	....	....	....	....	....
Other capital transfers	2 440	25	28	33	4	....	....	278	....
Capital transfers, debit	3 400	**–1,104**	**–655**	**–1,024**	**–721**	**–825**	**–885**	**–886**	**–1,241**
General government	3 401	–131	–160	–201	–208	–722	–785	–780	–690
Debt forgiveness	3 402	....	–20	–25	–50	–166	–41	–22	–21
Other capital transfers	3 410	–131	–140	–176	–158	–556	–744	–757	–668
Other sectors	3 430	–973	–495	–824	–512	–103	–100	–106	–552
Migrants' transfers	3 431	–233	–277	–327	–136	....	....	....	....
Debt forgiveness	3 432	–714	–185	–449	–357	–103	–100	–106	–552
Other capital transfers	3 440	–26	–34	–48	–20	....	....	....	....
Nonproduced nonfinancial assets, credit	2 480	**26**	**57**	**7**	**758**	**238**	**567**	**306**	**425**
Nonproduced nonfinancial assets, debit	3 480	**–184**	**–241**	**–268**	**–668**	**–1,341**	**–2,573**	**–1,769**	**–388**

Table 2 (Continued). STANDARD PRESENTATION, 2003–2010

(Millions of U.S. dollars)

	Code	2003	2004	2005	2006	2007	2008	2009	2010
FINANCIAL ACCOUNT	4 995 ..	**−10,793**	**−9,937**	**−9,221**	**−7,670**	**−7,481**	**11,469**	**8,778**	**−6,665**
A. DIRECT INVESTMENT	4 500 ..	**−4,499**	**9,733**	**1,139**	**8,688**	**13,096**	**−28,771**	**54,300**	**25,047**
Direct investment abroad	4 505 ..	**−39,043**	**−34,682**	**−32,545**	**−50,140**	**−83,492**	**−213,613**	**−6,633**	**−47,867**
Equity capital	4 510 ..	−14,392	−17,428	−21,001	−16,778	−44,648	−23,806	−19,391	10,913
Claims on affiliated enterprises	4 515 ..	....	....	....	....	....	....	....	....
Liabilities to affiliated enterprises	4 520 ..	....	....	....	....	....	....	....	....
Reinvested earnings	4 525 ..	−1,610	−3,814	−4,659	−8,576	−9,657	−1,569	−4,437	−4,277
Other capital	4 530 ..	−23,041	−13,439	−6,884	−24,785	−29,187	−188,238	17,196	−54,503
Claims on affiliated enterprises	4 535 ..	....	....	....	....	....	....	....	....
Liabilities to affiliated enterprises	4 540 ..	....	....	....	....	....	....	....	....
Direct investment in Belgium	4 555 ..	**34,544**	**44,415**	**33,684**	**58,828**	**96,588**	**184,842**	**60,933**	**72,914**
Equity capital	4 560 ..	26,653	32,590	30,357	53,791	66,690	147,109	49,789	73,633
Claims on direct investors	4 565 ..	....	....	....	....	....	....	....	....
Liabilities to direct investors	4 570 ..	....	....	....	....	....	....	....	....
Reinvested earnings	4 575 ..	−569	3,711	5,078	11,247	13,185	314	11,869	11,623
Other capital	4 580 ..	8,460	8,114	−1,751	−6,211	16,713	37,418	−726	−12,342
Claims on direct investors	4 585 ..	....	....	....	....	....	....	....	....
Liabilities to direct investors	4 590 ..	....	....	....	....	....	....	....	....
B. PORTFOLIO INVESTMENT	4 600 ..	**582**	**−30,488**	**−44,706**	**−9,181**	**−43,023**	**47,807**	**40,249**	**−1,146**
Assets	4 602 ..	**−6,046**	**−35,558**	**−43,491**	**−26,529**	**−80,503**	**−295**	**18,624**	**7,879**
Equity securities	4 610 ..	−5,508	−8,037	−20,449	−19,980	−20,401	31,861	3,152	−4,994
Monetary authorities	4 611 ..	....	....						
General government	4 612 ..	....	....	....	....	−1,504	727	1,073	89
Banks	4 613 ..	−707	467	−974	−900	−2,690	6,551	218	−324
Other sectors	4 614 ..	−4,801	−8,504	−19,475	−19,081	−16,207	24,584	1,862	−4,759
Debt securities	4 619 ..	−538	−27,520	−23,043	−6,548	−60,102	−32,156	15,472	12,873
Bonds and notes	4 620 ..	−6,123	−28,319	−28,680	−14,411	−52,128	−29,931	8,667	14,447
Monetary authorities	4 621 ..	−888	−872	55	−52	−11,516	−456	−2,345	−3,797
General government	4 622 ..	....	....	....	....	....	....	....	−3
Banks	4 623 ..	−12,248	−21,297	−19,118	3,912	4,679	−5,254	28,593	17,649
Other sectors	4 624 ..	7,013	−6,150	−9,617	−18,271	−45,290	−24,221	−17,581	597
Money market instruments	4 630 ..	5,585	799	5,638	7,863	−7,974	−2,225	6,805	−1,573
Monetary authorities	4 631 ..	....	....	....	....	....	....	433	−230
General government	4 632 ..	....	....						
Banks	4 633 ..	819	−241	2,302	2,837	−6,028	540	4,127	1,169
Other sectors	4 634 ..	4,766	1,040	3,336	5,026	−1,946	−2,766	2,246	−2,513
Liabilities	4 652 ..	**6,628**	**5,070**	**−1,215**	**17,348**	**37,481**	**48,102**	**21,625**	**−9,025**
Equity securities	4 660 ..	3,182	4,092	5,712	4,588	3,360	8,818	−3,242	−1,837
Banks	4 663 ..	−126	141	−31	1,295	....	....	−224	221
Other sectors	4 664 ..	3,307	3,951	5,742	3,293	3,360	8,818	−3,018	−2,057
Debt securities	4 669 ..	3,446	978	−6,927	12,760	34,121	39,285	24,867	−7,188
Bonds and notes	4 670 ..	9,592	−2,144	−1,450	13,847	27,657	12,759	12,600	2,345
Monetary authorities	4 671 ..	....	....	....	....	....	....	....	....
General government	4 672 ..	10,279	−1,946	−498	6,733	22,041	5,045	6,702	5,337
Banks	4 673 ..	−922	−430	266	2,102	3,821	5,580	1,588	−7,507
Other sectors	4 674 ..	235	231	−1,218	5,013	1,796	2,133	4,309	4,515
Money market instruments	4 680 ..	−6,146	3,122	−5,476	−1,087	6,464	26,526	12,267	−9,533
Monetary authorities	4 681 ..	....	....	....	....	....	....	....	....
General government	4 682 ..	256	3,929	−659	1,357	3,898	24,936	−1,726	−521
Banks	4 683 ..	−453	2,066	−2,035	−116	2,419	2,222	13,989	−6,717
Other sectors	4 684 ..	−5,948	−2,874	−2,782	−2,328	146	−631	3	−2,295
C. FINANCIAL DERIVATIVES	4 910 ..	**−3,626**	**−5,586**	**−5,448**	**3,372**	**1,424**	**5,809**	**728**	**1,800**
Monetary authorities	4 911 ..	....	....	....	....	....	342	20	142
General government	4 912 ..	890	16	−551	−342	287	−340	−66	−797
Banks	4 913 ..	−1,774	−2,579	−4,909	1,160	−555	−2,332	−958	620
Other sectors	4 914 ..	−2,742	−3,023	12	2,555	1,692	8,138	1,732	1,835
Assets	4 900 ..	**−7,195**	**−8,648**	**−9,647**	**−1,497**	**....**	**....**	**....**	**....**
Monetary authorities	4 901 ..	....	....	....	....	....	....	....	....
General government	4 902 ..	890	16	−551	−342	....	....	....	....
Banks	4 903 ..	−1,774	−2,579	−4,909	1,160	....	....	....	....
Other sectors	4 904 ..	−6,312	−6,085	−4,188	−2,315	....	....	....	....
Liabilities	4 905 ..	**3,570**	**3,063**	**4,199**	**4,870**	**....**	**....**	**....**	**....**
Monetary authorities	4 906 ..	....	....	....	....	....	....	....	....
General government	4 907 ..	....	....	....	....	....	....	....	....
Banks	4 908 ..	....	....	....	....	....	....	....	....
Other sectors	4 909 ..	3,570	3,063	4,199	4,870	....	....	....	....

Table 2 (Concluded). STANDARD PRESENTATION, 2003–2010

(Millions of U.S. dollars)

	Code	2003	2004	2005	2006	2007	2008	2009	2010
D. OTHER INVESTMENT	4 700	**−4,976**	**15,680**	**37,619**	**−10,394**	**22,248**	**−14,692**	**−79,531**	**−31,547**
Assets	4 703	**−75,625**	**−64,685**	**−87,399**	**−91,915**	**−158,361**	**73,479**	**116,669**	**10,186**
Trade credits	4 706	−352	−1,110	−1,930	−1,784	−1,212	1,694	305	−6,295
General government	4 707	....	....	....	....	....	....	....	....
of which: Short-term	4 709	....	....	....	....	....	....	....	....
Other sectors	4 710	−352	−1,110	−1,930	−1,784	−1,212	1,694	305	−6,295
of which: Short-term	4 712	....	....	....	....	....	....	....	....
Loans	4 714	−2,435	−6,332	−32,894	−11,635	−318	−32,612	−15,433	−399
Monetary authorities	4 715	....	....	....	....	....	....	....	....
of which: Short-term	4 718	....	....	....	....	....	....	....	....
General government	4 719	22	−629	58	64	92	24	−224	−921
of which: Short-term	4 721	....	....	11	....	....	....	....	....
Banks	4 722	−2,414	−5,512	−32,522	−9,036	1,644	−25,613	−16,371	1,157
of which: Short-term	4 724	−40	82	9	37	27	49	−18	−20
Other sectors	4 725	−43	−191	−430	−2,663	−2,053	−7,023	1,162	−635
of which: Short-term	4 727	....	....	....	....	−1,613	−2,904	1,235	4,990
Currency and deposits	4 730	−72,754	−56,988	−52,702	−78,419	−153,430	121,283	101,767	22,985
Monetary authorities	4 731	−107	−529	−83	242	−834	−58	499	−495
General government	4 732	897	355	186	127	446	−7	20	8
Banks	4 733	−66,849	−59,328	−59,820	−71,281	−144,421	119,777	111,039	27,559
Other sectors	4 734	−6,695	2,515	7,016	−7,507	−8,621	1,570	−9,792	−4,087
Other assets	4 736	−84	−254	127	−77	−3,401	−16,886	30,030	−6,105
Monetary authorities	4 737	....	−324	−48	....	−7	....	39	−54
of which: Short-term	4 739	....	....	....	....	....	....	....	....
General government	4 740	−41	−129	−224	−488	727	−84	134	156
of which: Short-term	4 742	....	....	....	....	....	....	....	....
Banks	4 743	....	....	....	....	−6,105	−18,791	28,656	−6,171
of which: Short-term	4 745	....	....	....	....	−6,614	−18,480	29,069	−4,147
Other sectors	4 746	−43	198	399	412	1,984	1,988	1,201	−35
of which: Short-term	4 748	....	....	....	....	1,965	1,891	1,027	114
Liabilities	4 753	**70,649**	**80,365**	**125,017**	**81,520**	**180,608**	**−88,171**	**−196,200**	**−41,732**
Trade credits	4 756	610	691	1,150	1,050	2,975	1,822	−303	7,213
General government	4 757	....	....	....	....	....	....	....	....
of which: Short-term	4 759	....	....	....	....	....	....	....	....
Other sectors	4 760	610	691	1,150	1,050	2,975	1,822	−303	7,213
of which: Short-term	4 762	610	691	1,150	1,050	2,975	1,822	−303	7,213
Loans	4 764	4,771	2,116	1,793	17,078	15,708	45,407	−14,216	6,189
Monetary authorities	4 765	....	....	....	....	....	....	....	....
of which: Use of Fund credit and loans from the Fund..	4 766	....	....	....	....	....	....	....	....
of which: Short-term	4 768	....	....	....	....	....	....	....	....
General government	4 769	−632	−786	−296	−2,736	−591	1,226	−1,451	2,168
of which: Short-term	4 771	−406	−585	131	−2,537	−238	1,237	−655	2,216
Banks	4 772	2,072	−143	1,948	15,127	10,670	17,354	−1,998	15,716
of which: Short-term	4 774	....	....	....	....	....	....	....	....
Other sectors	4 775	3,330	3,045	140	4,686	5,629	26,827	−10,767	−11,695
of which: Short-term	4 777	623	725	182	2,372	1,863	5,581	7	−8,003
Currency and deposits	4 780	62,088	73,202	123,461	63,093	151,859	−152,171	−157,153	−52,479
Monetary authorities	4 781	6,663	15,366	5,639	13,562	25,079	65,449	−84,729	−37,198
General government	4 782	....	....	....	....	....	....	....	....
Banks	4 783	55,425	57,836	117,823	49,531	126,780	−217,620	−72,424	−15,281
Other sectors	4 784	....	....	....	....	....	....	....	....
Other liabilities	4 786	3,180	4,356	−1,388	299	10,066	16,772	−24,528	−2,656
Monetary authorities	4 787	....	....	....	....	1	4	5,991	−1
of which: Short-term	4 789	....	....	....	....	1	4	−4	−1
General government	4 790	....	....	....	....	730	−627	125	346
of which: Short-term	4 792	....	....	....	....	730	−627	125	346
Banks	4 793	....	....	....	....	10,027	18,753	−30,059	−2,484
of which: Short-term	4 795	....	....	....	....	9,595	18,339	−30,290	−3,934
Other sectors	4 796	3,180	4,356	−1,388	299	−692	−1,357	−585	−517
of which: Short-term	4 798	2,922	4,016	−1,496	....	−711	−1,455	−760	−368
E. RESERVE ASSETS	4 802	**1,725**	**723**	**2,176**	**−156**	**−1,226**	**1,316**	**−6,968**	**−819**
Monetary gold	4 812	1	2	417	....	3	....	....	....
Special drawing rights	4 811	−37	314	10	−214	−36	24	−6,313	−4
Reserve position in the fund	4 810	−69	495	1,027	534	167	−514	−179	−642
Foreign exchange	4 803	1,830	−89	721	−476	−1,360	1,806	−477	−173
Other claims	4 813	....	....	....	....	....	....	....	....
NET ERRORS AND OMISSIONS	4 998	**1,024**	**−992**	**2,413**	**530**	**2,322**	**−1,741**	**849**	**1,172**

Table 3. INTERNATIONAL INVESTMENT POSITION (End-period stocks), 2003–2010

(Millions of U.S. dollars)

	Code	2003	2004	2005	2006	2007	2008	2009	2010
ASSETS..	8 995 C.	**1,243,816**	**1,500,462**	**1,557,568**	**1,892,378**	**2,452,421**	**2,345,201**	**2,344,129**	**2,226,976**
Direct investment abroad...........................	8 505 ..	**313,938**	**369,230**	**378,158**	**481,356**	**621,095**	**745,041**	**764,634**	**736,725**
Equity capital and reinvested earnings............................	8 506 ..	170,645	203,559	225,815	290,647	374,309	309,386	309,552	256,342
Claims on affiliated enterprises..........................	8 507 ..	....	....	....	....	....	....	....	....
Liabilities to affiliated enterprises....................	8 508 ..	....	....	....	....	....	....	....	....
Other capital...	8 530 ..	143,292	165,671	152,343	190,708	246,786	435,655	455,083	480,383
Claims on affiliated enterprises..........................	8 535 ..	....	....	....	....	....	461,343	472,788	489,780
Liabilities to affiliated enterprises....................	8 540 ..	....	....	....	....	....	−25,688	−17,705	−9,397
Portfolio investment..	8 602 ..	**455,923**	**534,074**	**554,645**	**643,194**	**837,345**	**735,516**	**777,158**	**739,977**
Equity securities................................	8 610 ..	146,643	172,164	204,560	248,210	313,728	209,828	239,712	241,939
Monetary authorities.......................	8 611 ..	....	....	....	....	....	....	....	....
General government........................	8 612 ..	743	836	751	944	2,601	1,745	627	509
Banks..	8 613 ..	3,519	3,281	3,828	5,128	8,392	1,356	1,111	1,438
Other sectors................................	8 614 ..	142,382	168,046	199,980	242,137	302,734	206,727	237,974	239,992
Debt securities....................................	8 619 ..	309,280	361,910	350,085	394,984	523,617	525,688	537,446	498,038
Bonds and notes............................	8 620 ..	296,233	347,391	343,071	374,867	505,484	503,827	521,349	481,850
Monetary authorities...................	8 621 ..	4,489	5,793	4,952	5,458	19,126	19,283	22,547	23,815
General government...................	8 622 ..	....	....	88	43	50	19	17	19
Banks..	8 623 ..	158,402	193,365	186,113	202,502	205,719	199,509	174,815	145,289
Other sectors.............................	8 624 ..	133,342	148,233	151,917	166,864	280,590	285,016	323,969	312,727
Money market instruments................	8 630 ..	13,047	14,519	7,014	20,117	18,133	21,861	16,097	16,188
Monetary authorities...................	8 631 ..	....	....	....	....	....	544	148	159
General government...................	8 632 ..	1	....	6	....	....	....	....	....
Banks..	8 633 ..	7,313	8,081	5,034	2,490	8,740	8,036	4,332	2,324
Other sectors.............................	8 634 ..	5,733	6,437	1,975	17,627	9,393	13,281	11,617	13,705
Financial derivatives.............................	8 900 ..	**611**	**1,667**	**3,635**	**10,561**	**21,739**	**24,872**	**20,827**	**11,196**
Monetary authorities...........................	8 901 ..	....	131	....	....	....	2,065	108	....
General government............................	8 902 ..	....	....	365	71	....	95	192	974
Banks...	8 903 ..	1	672	2,136	8,985	19,383	17,700	14,932	4,885
Other sectors.....................................	8 904 ..	610	865	1,134	1,505	2,355	5,013	5,595	5,337
Other investment.............................	8 703 ..	**458,896**	**581,502**	**609,135**	**743,831**	**955,737**	**824,124**	**757,528**	**712,171**
Trade credits..................................	8 706 ..	9,387	11,466	11,447	12,673	15,482	12,133	29,102	35,317
General government.......................	8 707 ..	....	....	....	....	....	....	....	....
of which: Short-term.................	8 709 ..	....	....	....	....	....	....	....	....
Other sectors..............................	8 710 ..	9,387	11,466	11,447	12,673	15,482	12,133	29,102	35,317
of which: Short-term.................	8 712 ..	....	....	....	....	....	....	....	....
Loans..	8 714 ..	340,061	430,462	480,901	604,402	800,197	678,086	603,330	551,319
Monetary authorities........................	8 715 ..	418	349	621	391	470	1,180	886	1,629
of which: Short-term.................	8 718 ..	*418*	*349*	*621*	*391*	*470*	*1,180*	*886*	*1,629*
General government.........................	8 719 ..	650	753	1,532	1,636	1,665	1,555	1,745	2,610
of which: Short-term.................	8 721 ..	....	....	....	....	....	....	....	....
Banks..	8 722 ..	338,483	428,455	477,548	598,247	791,417	634,898	562,596	508,564
of which: Short-term.................	8 724 ..	*310,756*	*392,715*	*414,443*	*519,979*	*709,707*	*533,809*	*441,483*	*394,409*
Other sectors................................	8 725 ..	510	904	1,200	4,127	6,645	40,454	38,104	38,516
of which: Short-term.................	8 727 ..	....	....	....	....	....	....	....	....
Currency and deposits.......................	8 730 ..	77,037	96,467	66,523	72,199	87,895	60,515	83,761	78,173
Monetary authorities........................	8 731 ..	....	....	....	....	....	....	....	....
General government.........................	8 732 ..	....	....	....	....	....	....	....	....
Banks..	8 733 ..	....	....	851	948	1,265	1,222	1,344	1,141
Other sectors................................	8 734 ..	77,037	96,467	65,673	71,251	86,630	59,293	82,417	77,032
Other assets.....................................	8 736 ..	32,411	43,108	50,263	54,557	52,164	73,390	41,335	47,362
Monetary authorities........................	8 737 ..	1,990	2,129	1,843	2,057	2,307	2,181	2,214	2,107
of which: Short-term.................	8 739 ..	....	....	....	....	....	....	....	....
General government.........................	8 740 ..	183	....	130	884	240	266	146	60
of which: Short-term.................	8 742 ..	....	....	....	....	....	....	....	....
Banks..	8 743 ..	28,974	37,083	45,192	48,672	48,520	69,009	38,045	41,580
of which: Short-term.................	8 745 ..	....	....	....	....	....	....	....	....
Other sectors................................	8 746 ..	1,263	3,896	3,099	2,943	1,097	1,934	931	3,614
of which: Short-term.................	8 748 ..	....	....	....	....	....	....	....	....
Reserve assets................................	8 802 ..	**14,449**	**13,988**	**11,996**	**13,436**	**16,505**	**15,646**	**23,983**	**26,908**
Monetary gold.................................	8 812 ..	3,459	3,629	3,755	4,653	6,121	6,328	8,076	10,315
Special drawing rights.......................	8 811 ..	645	350	314	545	609	570	6,907	6,789
Reserve position in the Fund...............	8 810 ..	2,693	2,296	1,112	620	477	982	1,199	1,831
Foreign exchange.............................	8 803 ..	7,651	7,714	6,815	7,619	9,298	7,767	7,801	7,973
Other claims....................................	8 813 ..	....	....	....	....	....	....	....	....

Table 3 (Concluded). INTERNATIONAL INVESTMENT POSITION (End-period stocks), 2003–2010

(Millions of U.S. dollars)

	Code	2003	2004	2005	2006	2007	2008	2009	2010
LIABILITIES..	8 995 D.	**1,116,151**	**1,387,972**	**1,437,556**	**1,772,064**	**2,309,522**	**2,195,258**	**2,133,115**	**1,831,067**
Direct investment in Belgium............................	8 555 ..	**357,137**	**471,071**	**478,183**	**618,532**	**784,576**	**822,699**	**862,503**	**670,013**
Equity capital and reinvested earnings....................	8 556 ..	287,840	387,166	406,455	549,247	674,481	640,410	711,309	513,412
Claims on direct investors..........................	8 557 ..	....	....	....	....	....	....	....	....
Liabilities to direct investors......................	8 558 ..	....	....	....	....	....	....	....	....
Other capital....................................	8 580 ..	69,297	83,905	71,728	69,285	110,095	182,289	151,194	156,601
Claims on direct investors..........................	8 585 ..	....	....	....	....	....	−80,904	−89,085	−88,231
Liabilities to direct investors......................	8 590 ..	....	....	....	....	....	263,193	240,279	244,832
Portfolio investment.............................	8 652 ..	**223,877**	**259,902**	**244,761**	**285,067**	**396,669**	**400,917**	**467,632**	**421,575**
Equity securities................................	8 660 ..	27,885	44,251	43,015	57,745	72,900	47,648	69,444	58,119
Banks......................................	8 663 ..	....	....	....	3	3	1,531	1,443	1,971
Other sectors..............................	8 664 ..	27,885	44,251	43,015	57,743	72,897	46,117	68,001	56,148
Debt securities..................................	8 669 ..	195,992	215,652	201,745	227,322	323,769	353,269	398,188	363,456
Bonds and notes..............................	8 670 ..	158,514	170,333	156,350	174,551	258,844	282,507	309,771	290,821
Monetary authorities......................	8 671 ..	....	....	....	....	....	....	....	....
General government........................	8 672 ..	137,760	149,000	135,673	149,468	211,703	234,270	252,105	237,079
Banks..................................	8 673 ..	4,885	3,851	3,379	5,901	10,453	14,975	16,988	8,163
Other sectors............................	8 674 ..	15,868	17,483	17,299	19,182	36,688	33,262	40,678	45,579
Money market instruments....................	8 680 ..	37,478	45,318	45,395	52,771	64,925	70,762	88,417	72,634
Monetary authorities......................	8 681 ..	....	....	....	....	....	....	....	....
General government........................	8 682 ..	18,152	23,540	23,162	28,105	35,938	41,999	44,422	40,711
Banks..................................	8 683 ..	6,200	8,213	5,303	5,783	12,516	13,120	27,902	20,238
Other sectors............................	8 684 ..	13,126	13,565	16,930	18,883	16,471	15,644	16,093	11,685
Financial derivatives...........................	8 905 ..	**....**	**16**	**3,381**	**9,776**	**22,704**	**19,413**	**16,872**	**4,385**
Monetary authorities............................	8 906 ..	....	....	....	....	....	167	137	19
General government.............................	8 907 ..	....	....	....	....	240	4	13	....
Banks..	8 908 ..	....	16	3,329	9,343	21,660	18,471	15,302	2,175
Other sectors...................................	8 909 ..	....	....	52	433	804	771	1,420	2,191
Other investment...............................	8 753 ..	**535,137**	**656,982**	**711,232**	**858,689**	**1,105,572**	**952,229**	**786,108**	**735,093**
Trade credits....................................	8 756 ..	5,982	6,396	6,748	7,448	11,278	11,875	21,370	25,672
General government.........................	8 757 ..	....	....	....	....	....	....	....	....
of which: Short-term.....................	8 759 ..	....	....	....	....	....	....	....	....
Other sectors..............................	8 760 ..	5,982	6,396	6,748	7,448	11,278	11,875	21,370	25,672
of which: Short-term.....................	8 762 ..	....	....	....	....	....	....	....	....
Loans..	8 764 ..	338,763	389,984	431,653	553,501	684,999	434,315	379,277	378,487
Monetary authorities........................	8 765 ..	....	....	....	....	....	....	....	....
of which: Use of Fund credit and loans from the Fund....	8 766 ..	....	....	....	....	....	....	....	....
of which: Short-term.....................	8 768 ..	....	....	....	....	....	....	....	....
General government........................	8 769 ..	681	734	3,950	4,362	4,221	4,299	4,034	5,645
of which: Short-term.....................	8 771 ..	....	....	*190*	*287*	*40*	*356*	*765*	*2,659*
Banks..................................	8 772 ..	299,994	354,414	401,473	515,421	637,569	369,541	323,756	316,446
of which: Short-term.....................	8 774 ..	*279,694*	*334,261*	*384,181*	*492,052*	*617,667*	*336,591*	*287,996*	*273,789*
Other sectors............................	8 775 ..	38,088	34,836	26,231	33,718	43,209	60,475	51,487	56,396
of which: Short-term.....................	8 777 ..	*14,151*	*12,704*	*10,410*	*14,052*	*17,637*	*21,932*	*21,978*	....
Currency and deposits..........................	8 780 ..	156,088	205,373	218,911	240,371	336,213	402,517	308,942	242,538
Monetary authorities........................	8 781 ..	24,266	42,799	42,790	61,235	93,684	148,963	64,804	21,088
General government........................	8 782 ..	....	....	....	....	....	....	....	....
Banks..................................	8 783 ..	131,822	162,575	176,121	179,136	242,528	253,554	244,138	221,450
Other sectors............................	8 784 ..	....	....	....	....	....	....	....	....
Other liabilities................................	8 786 ..	34,304	55,228	53,919	57,370	73,082	103,522	76,519	88,396
Monetary authorities........................	8 787 ..	....	....	....	1	3	6	6,778	6,658
of which: Short-term.....................	8 789 ..	....	....	....	*1*	*3*	*6*	....	....
General government........................	8 790 ..	4,103	4,360	3,100	3,279	4,310	3,528	3,514	3,864
of which: Short-term.....................	8 792 ..	....	....	....	....	....	....	....	....
Banks..................................	8 793 ..	29,854	40,636	44,515	46,923	61,765	92,296	59,200	63,424
of which: Short-term.....................	8 795 ..	....	....	....	....	....	....	....	....
Other sectors............................	8 796 ..	347	10,232	6,304	7,166	7,004	7,692	7,027	14,450
of which: Short-term.....................	8 798 ..	....	....	....	....	....	....	....	....
NET INTERNATIONAL INVESTMENT POSITION........	8 995 ..	**127,665**	**112,490**	**120,012**	**120,314**	**142,899**	**149,943**	**211,015**	**395,909**
Conversion rates: euros per U.S. dollar (end of period)...................................	0 104 ..	**.79177**	**.73416**	**.84767**	**.75930**	**.67930**	**.71855**	**.69416**	**.74839**

Table 1. ANALYTIC PRESENTATION, 2003–2010

(Millions of U.S. dollars)

	Code	2003	2004	2005	2006	2007	2008	2009	2010
A. Current Account[1]	4 993 Z.	**−184.3**	**−154.9**	**−151.2**	**−25.4**	**−52.1**	**−144.9**	**−82.8**	**−45.7**
Goods: exports f.o.b.	2 100 ..	315.5	308.4	325.2	427.1	425.6	480.1	383.9	475.7
Goods: imports f.o.b.	3 100 ..	−522.3	−480.7	−556.2	−611.9	−642.0	−788.2	−620.5	−647.2
Balance on Goods	4 100 ..	*−206.8*	*−172.3*	*−231.0*	*−184.8*	*−216.4*	*−308.2*	*−236.6*	*−171.5*
Services: credit	2 200 ..	212.1	235.3	301.8	362.9	398.1	386.5	344.4	353.8
Services: debit	3 200 ..	−141.0	−147.1	−158.8	−152.2	−168.2	−169.6	−161.7	−162.4
Balance on Goods and Services	4 991 ..	*−135.7*	*−84.1*	*−88.0*	*25.9*	*13.5*	*−91.2*	*−54.0*	*20.0*
Income: credit	2 300 ..	5.5	4.3	6.8	10.1	7.0	5.9	4.5	4.6
Income: debit	3 300 ..	−95.0	−121.1	−121.2	−135.4	−165.9	−171.1	−112.7	−162.1
Balance on Goods, Services, and Income	4 992 ..	*−225.2*	*−200.8*	*−202.4*	*−99.4*	*−145.5*	*−256.4*	*−162.2*	*−137.6*
Current transfers: credit	2 379 Z.	59.1	60.8	68.4	92.2	136.6	141.1	101.9	114.8
Current transfers: debit	3 379 ..	−18.3	−14.9	−17.1	−18.2	−43.2	−29.5	−22.5	−22.9
B. Capital Account[1]	4 994 Z.	**4.2**	**9.8**	**3.0**	**9.1**	**4.1**	**9.0**	**18.5**	**5.6**
Capital account: credit	2 994 Z.	5.1	10.6	3.9	10.2	5.1	10.4	18.8	6.7
Capital account: debit	3 994 ..	−.9	−.8	−1.0	−1.1	−1.0	−1.3	−.3	−1.1
Total, Groups A Plus B	4 981 ..	*−180.1*	*−145.1*	*−148.3*	*−16.2*	*−48.0*	*−135.8*	*−64.3*	*−40.1*
C. Financial Account[1]	4 995 W.	**204.3**	**117.4**	**144.3**	**74.1**	**109.7**	**205.5**	**145.0**	**27.0**
Direct investment abroad	4 505 ..	−.4	−.1	−1.0	−.6	−1.0	−2.8	−.5	−1.1
Direct investment in Belize	4 555 Z.	−10.9	111.5	126.9	108.8	140.4	169.7	108.8	96.4
Portfolio investment assets	4 602 ..	−.2	−.2	−.2	−.3	−.4	2.9	−4.5	−2.2
Equity securities	4 610 ..	−.2	−.2	−.2	−.3	−.4	2.9	−.5	−.1
Debt securities	4 619 ..	....	....	....	....	....	....	−4.0	−2.1
Portfolio investment liabilities	4 652 Z.	79.4	76.9	18.1	−21.4	79.1	−2.7	−5.1	−5.6
Equity securities	4 660 ..	....	....	....	4.0	....	2.0	....	....
Debt securities	4 669 Z.	79.4	76.9	18.1	−25.4	79.1	−4.7	−5.1	−5.6
Financial derivatives	4 910 ..	.7	.5	−5.3	....	....	....	....	....
Financial derivatives assets	4 900 ..	.7	.5	.3	....	....	....	....	....
Financial derivatives liabilities	4 905 ..	....	....	−5.6	....	....	....	....	....
Other investment assets	4 703 ..	−9.9	−4.4	−39.1	−13.6	4.7	−13.8	13.5	−13.1
Monetary authorities	4 701 ..	....	....	−30.6	12.1	18.5	.1	.1	....
General government	4 704 ..	....	....	.1	3.4	−1.9	−2.0	−2.5	−2.3
Banks	4 705 ..	−2.6	−5.3	−9.2	−16.4	−11.4	−16.1	15.8	−11.3
Other sectors	4 728 ..	−7.3	.9	.6	−12.8	−.5	4.2	.1	.5
Other investment liabilities	4 753 W.	145.6	−66.8	45.0	1.1	−113.1	52.2	32.8	−47.4
Monetary authorities	4 753 WA	−2.6	−4.0	−1.3	−.2	....	.4	61.7	1.0
General government	4 753 ZB	76.4	−53.0	45.1	32.0	−87.9	−8.0	25.3	−.4
Banks	4 753 ZC	28.5	.4	3.2	−32.3	−29.3	36.4	−33.0	−14.7
Other sectors	4 753 ZD	43.3	−10.2	−2.1	1.5	4.0	23.4	−21.2	−33.3
Total, Groups A Through C	4 983 ..	*24.2*	*−27.7*	*−3.9*	*57.9*	*61.7*	*69.7*	*80.7*	*−13.0*
D. Net Errors and Omissions	4 998 ..	**−35.0**	**−3.7**	**−7.6**	**−8.5**	**−39.3**	**−11.5**	**−40.7**	**18.0**
Total, Groups A Through D	4 984 ..	*−10.8*	*−31.4*	*−11.5*	*49.3*	*22.4*	*58.2*	*40.0*	*5.0*
E. Reserves and Related Items	4 802 A.	**10.8**	**31.4**	**11.5**	**−49.3**	**−22.4**	**−58.2**	**−40.0**	**−5.0**
Reserve assets	4 802 ..	30.8	31.4	11.5	−49.3	−22.4	−58.2	−47.0	−5.0
Use of Fund credit and loans	4 766 ..	....	....	....	....	....	....	7.0	....
Exceptional financing	4 920 ..	−20.0	....	....	....	....	....	....	....
Conversion rates: Belize dollars per U.S. dollar	0 101 ..	**2.0000**	**2.0000**	**2.0000**	**2.0000**	**2.0000**	**2.0000**	**2.0000**	**2.0000**

[1] Excludes components that have been classified in the categories of Group E.

Table 2. STANDARD PRESENTATION, 2003–2010

(Millions of U.S. dollars)

	Code	2003	2004	2005	2006	2007	2008	2009	2010
CURRENT ACCOUNT	4 993 ..	**−184.3**	**−154.9**	**−151.2**	**−25.4**	**−52.1**	**−144.9**	**−82.8**	**−45.7**
A. GOODS	4 100 ..	**−206.8**	**−172.3**	**−231.0**	**−184.8**	**−216.4**	**−308.2**	**−236.6**	**−171.5**
Credit	2 100 ..	**315.5**	**308.4**	**325.2**	**427.1**	**425.6**	**480.1**	**383.9**	**475.7**
General merchandise: exports f.o.b.	2 110 ..	294.7	285.3	301.4	401.2	407.0	469.2	379.0	470.7
Goods for processing: exports f.o.b.	2 150 ..	15.4	18.6	17.3	18.3	9.4	.2	....	.1
Repairs on goods	2 160 ..	....	....	....	....	....	....	....	....
Goods procured in ports by carriers	2 170 ..	5.3	4.5	6.5	7.7	9.1	10.7	4.9	4.9
Nonmonetary gold	2 180 ..	....	....	....	....	....	....	....	....
Debit	3 100 ..	**−522.3**	**−480.7**	**−556.2**	**−611.9**	**−642.0**	**−788.2**	**−620.5**	**−647.2**
General merchandise: imports f.o.b.	3 110 ..	−510.5	−465.1	−544.2	−597.9	−634.7	−788.2	−620.5	−647.2
Goods for processing: imports f.o.b.	3 150 ..	−11.9	−15.6	−12.0	−14.1	−7.3	....	....	....
Repairs on goods	3 160 ..	....	....	....	....	....	....	....	....
Goods procured in ports by carriers	3 170 ..	....	....	....	....	....	....	....	....
Nonmonetary gold	3 180 ..	....	....	....	....	....	....	....	....
B. SERVICES	4 200 ..	**71.1**	**88.2**	**143.0**	**210.7**	**229.9**	**216.9**	**182.6**	**191.4**
Total credit	2 200 ..	*212.1*	*235.3*	*301.8*	*362.9*	*398.1*	*386.5*	*344.4*	*353.8*
Total debit	3 200 ..	*−141.0*	*−147.1*	*−158.8*	*−152.2*	*−168.2*	*−169.6*	*−161.7*	*−162.4*
Transportation services, credit	2 205 ..	**22.1**	**27.4**	**29.7**	**28.5**	**29.9**	**25.0**	**16.8**	**19.3**
Passenger	2 850 ..	....	....	....	....	....	....	....	....
Freight	2 851 ..	....	....	....	....	....	....	....	....
Other	2 852 ..	*22.1*	*27.4*	*29.7*	*28.5*	*29.9*	*25.0*	*16.8*	*19.3*
Sea transport, passenger	2 207 ..	....	....	....	....	....	....	....	....
Sea transport, freight	2 208 ..	....	....	....	....	....	....	....	....
Sea transport, other	2 209 ..	18.8	22.1	24.1	21.9	23.3	18.2	10.4	12.9
Air transport, passenger	2 211 ..	....	....	....	....	....	....	....	....
Air transport, freight	2 212 ..	....	....	....	....	....	....	....	....
Air transport, other	2 213 ..	3.4	5.3	5.7	6.6	6.6	6.8	6.4	6.4
Other transport, passenger	2 215 ..	....	....	....	....	....	....	....	....
Other transport, freight	2 216 ..	....	....	....	....	....	....	....	....
Other transport, other	2 217 ..	....	....	....	....	....	....	....	....
Transportation services, debit	3 205 ..	**−39.7**	**−44.6**	**−50.1**	**−54.6**	**−56.9**	**−69.4**	**−55.0**	**−57.8**
Passenger	3 850 ..	*−4.1*	*−3.7*	*−3.1*	*−2.3*	*−2.6*	*−3.2*	*−2.3*	*−2.6*
Freight	3 851 ..	*−35.6*	*−40.9*	*−47.0*	*−52.2*	*−54.3*	*−66.3*	*−52.7*	*−55.2*
Other	3 852 ..	....	....	....	....	....	....	....	....
Sea transport, passenger	3 207 ..	....	....	....	....	....	....	....	....
Sea transport, freight	3 208 ..	−35.6	−40.9	−47.0	−52.2	−54.3	−66.3	−52.7	−55.2
Sea transport, other	3 209 ..	....	....	....	....	....	....	....	....
Air transport, passenger	3 211 ..	−4.1	−3.7	−3.1	−2.3	−2.6	−3.2	−2.3	−2.6
Air transport, freight	3 212 ..	....	....	....	....	....	....	....	....
Air transport, other	3 213 ..	....	....	....	....	....	....	....	....
Other transport, passenger	3 215 ..	....	....	....	....	....	....	....	....
Other transport, freight	3 216 ..	....	....	....	....	....	....	....	....
Other transport, other	3 217 ..	....	....	....	....	....	....	....	....
Travel, credit	2 236 ..	**149.7**	**168.1**	**213.6**	**260.1**	**288.6**	**278.5**	**256.2**	**264.5**
Business travel	2 237 ..	8.3	8.8	10.3	17.7	17.1	16.8	15.5	16.1
Personal travel	2 240 ..	141.4	159.3	203.3	242.4	271.5	261.7	240.8	248.3
Travel, debit	3 236 ..	**−45.8**	**−42.6**	**−41.6**	**−41.1**	**−42.7**	**−40.8**	**−40.7**	**−36.5**
Business travel	3 237 ..	−3.4	−2.9	−2.5	−2.0	−2.0	−2.1	−2.0	−1.9
Personal travel	3 240 ..	−42.4	−39.7	−39.2	−39.1	−40.8	−38.6	−38.7	−34.6
Other services, credit	2 200 BA	**40.3**	**39.9**	**58.4**	**74.3**	**79.5**	**83.0**	**71.3**	**70.1**
Communications	2 245 ..	6.1	5.7	8.0	9.1	12.6	11.7	16.0	14.5
Construction	2 249 ..	....	....	1.6	3.6	....	....	....	....
Insurance	2 253 ..	.1	.1	.1	.1	.1	.1	.1	.9
Financial	2 260 ..	.5	.5	.7	.7	.7	2.2	5.2	6.2
Computer and information	2 262 ..	....	....	....	....	....	....	....	....
Royalties and licence fees	2 266 ..	....	....	....	....	....	....	....	....
Other business services	2 268 ..	17.5	21.7	30.3	36.9	37.0	38.0	23.0	20.0
Personal, cultural, and recreational	2 287 ..	....	....	....	....	....	....	....	....
Government, n.i.e.	2 291 ..	16.1	11.9	17.8	23.8	29.1	31.0	26.9	28.5
Other services, debit	3 200 BA	**−55.5**	**−59.9**	**−67.0**	**−56.5**	**−68.5**	**−59.4**	**−66.0**	**−68.1**
Communications	3 245 ..	−1.3	−1.4	−1.8	−2.0	−2.5	−3.2	−6.1	−2.9
Construction	3 249 ..	....	....	....	....	....	....	−.3	....
Insurance	3 253 ..	−18.8	−18.5	−28.3	−24.1	−32.9	−21.9	−23.9	−24.4
Financial	3 260 ..	−7.6	−13.7	−6.6	−2.1	−8.6	−3.5	−2.1	−2.0
Computer and information	3 262 ..	−.6	−.4	−.5	−.4	−.8	−1.1	−2.3	−2.2
Royalties and licence fees	3 266 ..	−.2	−.4	−.4	−.4	−.9	−.7	−1.1	−1.4
Other business services	3 268 ..	−13.2	−16.9	−17.7	−18.5	−13.2	−19.7	−21.8	−25.9
Personal, cultural, and recreational	3 287 ..	−.1	−.4	−.2	−.3	−.4	−.5	−.2	−.4
Government, n.i.e.	3 291 ..	−13.7	−8.2	−11.6	−8.9	−9.2	−8.7	−8.2	−8.8

Table 2 (Continued). STANDARD PRESENTATION, 2003–2010

(Millions of U.S. dollars)

	Code	2003	2004	2005	2006	2007	2008	2009	2010
C. INCOME..	4 300 ..	**−89.5**	**−116.7**	**−114.4**	**−125.3**	**−159.0**	**−165.2**	**−108.3**	**−157.5**
Total credit..	2 300 ..	*5.5*	*4.3*	*6.8*	*10.1*	*7.0*	*5.9*	*4.5*	*4.6*
Total debit...	3 300 ..	*−95.0*	*−121.1*	*−121.2*	*−135.4*	*−165.9*	*−171.1*	*−112.7*	*−162.1*
Compensation of employees, credit..................	2 310 ..	**2.5**	**2.4**	**3.8**	**6.0**	**2.4**	**2.4**	**2.4**	**2.4**
Compensation of employees, debit...................	3 310 ..	**−5.4**	**−6.2**	**−5.9**	**−5.7**	**−5.2**	**−6.3**	**−5.9**	**−5.7**
Investment income, credit................................	2 320 ..	**3.0**	**1.9**	**3.0**	**4.1**	**4.6**	**3.6**	**2.1**	**2.2**
Direct investment income.....................................	2 330 ..	.4	.4	.5	.5	.5	.6	.4	.4
Dividends and distributed branch profits.......................	2 332 ..	.4	.4	.5	.5	.5	.6	.4	.4
Reinvested earnings and undistributed branch profits.....	2 333 ..	....	....	....	....	....	....	....	....
Income on debt (interest)...................................	2 334 ..	....	....	....	....	....	....	....	....
Portfolio investment income..................................	2 339 ..	....	....	....	....	....	.1	.4	.6
Income on equity...	2 340 ..	....	....	....	....	....			
Income on bonds and notes..................................	2 350 ..	....	....	....	....	....	.1	.4	.6
Income on money market instruments........................	2 360 ..	....	....	....	....	....			
Other investment income.....................................	2 370 ..	2.6	1.5	2.5	3.6	4.1	2.9	1.3	1.2
Investment income, debit................................	3 320 ..	**−89.5**	**−114.9**	**−115.3**	**−129.7**	**−160.7**	**−164.8**	**−106.9**	**−156.4**
Direct investment income.....................................	3 330 ..	−31.0	−42.4	−34.9	−51.6	−86.6	−106.5	−56.1	−102.4
Dividends and distributed branch profits.......................	3 332 ..	−18.3	−21.7	−16.3	−26.3	−56.6	−85.8	−33.2	−87.3
Reinvested earnings and undistributed branch profits.....	3 333 ..	−12.1	−20.7	−18.6	−25.2	−30.0	−20.7	−22.9	−15.1
Income on debt (interest)...................................	3 334 ..	−.5	....	....	−.1	....	....	....	....
Portfolio investment income..................................	3 339 ..	−30.5	−36.6	−50.3	−39.0	−36.8	−25.7	−25.1	−29.4
Income on equity...	3 340 ..	....	....	....	....	....	....	....	....
Income on bonds and notes..................................	3 350 ..	−26.8	−33.1	−47.2	−36.2	−34.4	−23.6	−23.4	−28.2
Income on money market instruments........................	3 360 ..	−3.7	−3.4	−3.1	−2.8	−2.4	−2.1	−1.6	−1.1
Other investment income.....................................	3 370 ..	−28.1	−35.9	−30.1	−39.1	−37.3	−32.6	−25.7	−24.6
D. CURRENT TRANSFERS..................................	4 379 ..	**40.9**	**45.9**	**51.2**	**74.0**	**93.4**	**111.5**	**79.4**	**91.8**
Credit...	2 379 ..	**59.1**	**60.8**	**68.4**	**92.2**	**136.6**	**141.1**	**101.9**	**114.8**
General government..	2 380 ..	.8	10.4	5.5	10.9	41.0	28.2	2.2	1.1
Other sectors...	2 390 ..	58.3	50.4	62.8	81.2	95.6	112.8	99.7	113.7
Workers' remittances...	2 391 ..	29.7	31.2	40.9	57.8	70.8	74.1	76.2	75.8
Other current transfers...	2 392 ..	28.6	19.2	21.9	23.4	24.8	38.7	23.4	37.9
Debit..	3 379 ..	**−18.3**	**−14.9**	**−17.1**	**−18.2**	**−43.2**	**−29.5**	**−22.5**	**−22.9**
General government..	3 380 ..	−3.2	−2.3	−2.4	−2.4	−25.2	−5.7	−3.8	−4.4
Other sectors...	3 390 ..	−15.1	−12.6	−14.8	−15.8	−18.0	−23.9	−18.7	−18.6
Workers' remittances...	3 391 ..	−14.3	−11.8	−13.5	−14.9	−16.2	−21.7	−16.7	−16.3
Other current transfers...	3 392 ..	−.8	−.8	−1.3	−.8	−1.8	−2.1	−2.0	−2.2
CAPITAL AND FINANCIAL ACCOUNT.....................	4 996 ..	**219.3**	**158.7**	**158.8**	**33.9**	**91.4**	**156.3**	**123.5**	**27.7**
CAPITAL ACCOUNT...	4 994 ..	**6.6**	**9.8**	**3.0**	**9.1**	**4.1**	**9.0**	**18.5**	**5.6**
Total credit..	2 994 ..	*7.5*	*10.6*	*3.9*	*10.2*	*5.1*	*10.4*	*18.8*	*6.7*
Total debit...	3 994 ..	*−.9*	*−.8*	*−1.0*	*−1.1*	*−1.0*	*−1.3*	*−.3*	*−1.1*
Capital transfers, credit....................................	2 400 ..	**7.5**	**10.6**	**3.9**	**10.2**	**5.1**	**10.4**	**18.8**	**6.7**
General government..	2 401 ..	5.8	9.3	2.6	8.0	3.4	8.4	17.1	5.3
Debt forgiveness...	2 402 ..	2.4	3.0	.7	4.6	....	....	2.5	....
Other capital transfers...	2 410 ..	3.4	6.3	1.9	3.5	3.4	8.4	14.6	5.3
Other sectors...	2 430 ..	1.7	1.3	1.4	2.2	1.7	2.0	1.7	1.4
Migrants' transfers...	2 431 ..	1.7	1.3	1.4	1.7	1.7	1.6	1.7	1.4
Debt forgiveness...	2 432 ..	....	....	....	....	....	....	....	....
Other capital transfers...	2 440 ..	....	....	....	.5	....	.3	....	....
Capital transfers, debit.....................................	3 400 ..	**−.9**	**−.8**	**−1.0**	**−1.1**	**−1.0**	**−1.3**	**−.3**	**−1.1**
General government..	3 401 ..	....	....	....	....	....	....	....	....
Debt forgiveness...	3 402 ..	....	....	....	....	....	....	....	....
Other capital transfers...	3 410 ..	....	....	....	....	....	....	....	....
Other sectors...	3 430 ..	−.9	−.8	−1.0	−1.1	−1.0	−1.3	−.3	−1.1
Migrants' transfers...	3 431 ..	−.9	−.8	−1.0	−1.1	−1.0	−1.3	−.3	−1.1
Debt forgiveness...	3 432 ..	....	....	....	....	....	....	....	....
Other capital transfers...	3 440 ..	....	....	....	....	....	....	....	....
Nonproduced nonfinancial assets, credit.............	2 480 ..	....	....	....	....	....	....	....	....
Nonproduced nonfinancial assets, debit.............	3 480 ..	....	....	....	....	....	....	....	....

Table 2 (Continued). STANDARD PRESENTATION, 2003–2010

(Millions of U.S. dollars)

	Code	2003	2004	2005	2006	2007	2008	2009	2010
FINANCIAL ACCOUNT	4 995	**212.7**	**148.8**	**155.8**	**24.8**	**87.3**	**147.3**	**105.0**	**22.1**
A. DIRECT INVESTMENT	4 500	**–11.3**	**111.4**	**125.9**	**108.3**	**139.4**	**166.9**	**108.4**	**95.3**
Direct investment abroad	4 505	**–.4**	**–.1**	**–1.0**	**–.6**	**–1.0**	**–2.8**	**–.5**	**–1.1**
Equity capital	4 510	–.4	–.1	–1.0	–.6	–1.0	–2.8	–.5	–1.1
Claims on affiliated enterprises	4 515	–.4	–.1	–1.0	–.6	–1.0	–2.8	–.5	–1.1
Liabilities to affiliated enterprises	4 520	....	....	....	....	....	....	....	....
Reinvested earnings	4 525	....	....	....	....	....	....	....	....
Other capital	4 530	....	....	....	....	....	....	....	....
Claims on affiliated enterprises	4 535	....	....	....	....	....	....	....	....
Liabilities to affiliated enterprises	4 540	....	....	....	....	....	....	....	....
Direct investment in Belize	4 555	**–10.9**	**111.5**	**126.9**	**108.8**	**140.4**	**169.7**	**108.8**	**96.4**
Equity capital	4 560	–34.2	77.3	87.7	98.3	97.3	141.3	79.5	79.2
Claims on direct investors	4 565	....	....	....	....	....	....	....	....
Liabilities to direct investors	4 570	–34.2	77.3	87.7	98.3	97.3	141.3	79.5	79.2
Reinvested earnings	4 575	12.1	20.7	18.6	25.2	30.0	20.7	22.9	15.1
Other capital	4 580	11.1	13.5	20.7	–14.7	13.1	7.6	6.4	2.1
Claims on direct investors	4 585	....	....	....	....	....	....	....	....
Liabilities to direct investors	4 590	11.1	13.5	20.7	–14.7	13.1	7.6	6.4	2.1
B. PORTFOLIO INVESTMENT	4 600	**79.2**	**76.6**	**17.8**	**–21.6**	**78.7**	**.2**	**–9.7**	**–7.8**
Assets	4 602	**–.2**	**–.2**	**–.2**	**–.3**	**–.4**	**2.9**	**–4.5**	**–2.2**
Equity securities	4 610	–.2	–.2	–.2	–.3	–.4	2.9	–.5	–.1
Monetary authorities	4 611	....	....	....	....	....	....		
General government	4 612	....	....	....	....	....	....		
Banks	4 613	....	....				3.3		
Other sectors	4 614	–.2	–.2	–.2	–.3	–.4	–.4	–.5	–.1
Debt securities	4 619	....	....	....	....	....	....	–4.0	–2.1
Bonds and notes	4 620	....	....	....	....	....	....	–4.0	–2.1
Monetary authorities	4 621	....	....	....	....	....	....	–4.0	–2.1
General government	4 622	....	....	....	....	....	....		
Banks	4 623	....	....	....	....	....	....		
Other sectors	4 624	....	....	....	....	....	....		
Money market instruments	4 630	....	....	....	....	....	....		
Monetary authorities	4 631	....	....	....	....	....	....		
General government	4 632	....	....	....	....	....	....		
Banks	4 633	....	....	....	....	....	....		
Other sectors	4 634	....	....	....	....	....	....		
Liabilities	4 652	**79.4**	**76.9**	**18.1**	**–21.4**	**79.1**	**–2.7**	**–5.1**	**–5.6**
Equity securities	4 660	....	....	....	4.0	....	2.0	....	....
Banks	4 663	....	....	....	....	....	2.0		
Other sectors	4 664	....	....	....	4.0	....	....		
Debt securities	4 669	79.4	76.9	18.1	–25.4	79.1	–4.7	–5.1	–5.6
Bonds and notes	4 670	92.9	144.7	21.7	–21.4	83.4	....	....	....
Monetary authorities	4 671	–3.0	....	....	....	....	....		
General government	4 672	95.9	144.7	21.7	–21.4	83.4	....		
Banks	4 673	....	....	....	....	....	....		
Other sectors	4 674	....	....	....	....	....	....		
Money market instruments	4 680	–13.6	–67.8	–3.6	–4.0	–4.3	–4.7	–5.1	–5.6
Monetary authorities	4 681	....	....	....	....	....	....	....	....
General government	4 682	–13.6	–67.8	–3.6	–4.0	–4.3	–4.7	–5.1	–5.6
Banks	4 683	....	....	....	....	....	....		
Other sectors	4 684	....	....	....	....	....	....		
C. FINANCIAL DERIVATIVES	4 910	**.7**	**.5**	**–5.3**	....	....	....	....	....
Monetary authorities	4 911	....	....	....	....	....	....		
General government	4 912	.7	.5	–5.3	....	....	....		
Banks	4 913	....	....	....	....	....	....		
Other sectors	4 914	....	....	....	....	....	....		
Assets	4 900	**.7**	**.5**	**.3**	....	....	....	....	....
Monetary authorities	4 901	....	....	....	....	....	....		
General government	4 902	.7	.5	.3	....	....	....		
Banks	4 903	....	....	....	....	....	....		
Other sectors	4 904	....	....	....	....	....	....		
Liabilities	4 905	....	....	**–5.6**	....	....	....	....	....
Monetary authorities	4 906	....	....	....	....	....	....		
General government	4 907	....	....	–5.6	....	....	....		
Banks	4 908	....	....	....	....	....	....		
Other sectors	4 909	....	....	....	....	....	....		

Table 2 (Concluded). STANDARD PRESENTATION, 2003–2010

(Millions of U.S. dollars)

	Code	2003	2004	2005	2006	2007	2008	2009	2010
D. OTHER INVESTMENT	4 700 ..	**113.2**	**−71.2**	**5.9**	**−12.6**	**−108.4**	**38.4**	**53.3**	**−60.5**
Assets	4 703 ..	**−9.9**	**−4.4**	**−39.1**	**−13.6**	**4.7**	**−13.8**	**13.5**	**−13.1**
Trade credits	4 706 ..	−.2	−.1	−.3	−1.2	−1.3	.7	−.8	−.4
General government	4 707 ..	....	....	....	....	....	....	....	....
of which: Short-term	4 709 ..	....	....	....	....	....	....	....	....
Other sectors	4 710 ..	−.2	−.1	−.3	−1.2	−1.3	.7	−.8	−.4
of which: Short-term	4 712 ..	*−.2*	*−.1*	*−.3*	*−1.2*	*−1.3*	*.7*	*−.8*	*−.4*
Loans	4 714 ..	....	....	....	....	....	....	....	....
Monetary authorities	4 715 ..	....	....	....	....	....	....	....	....
of which: Short-term	4 718 ..	....	....	....	....	....	....	....	....
General government	4 719 ..	....	....	....	....	....	....	....	....
of which: Short-term	4 721 ..	....	....	....	....	....	....	....	....
Banks	4 722 ..	....	....	....	....	....	....	....	....
of which: Short-term	4 724 ..	....	....	....	....	....	....	....	....
Other sectors	4 725 ..	....	....	....	....	....	....	....	....
of which: Short-term	4 727 ..	....	....	....	....	....	....	....	....
Currency and deposits	4 730 ..	−9.8	−4.3	−38.8	−10.9	7.9	−12.6	16.7	−10.4
Monetary authorities	4 731 ..	....	....	−30.6	12.1	18.5	.1	.1	....
General government	4 732 ..	....	....	.1	5.0	....	....	....	....
Banks	4 733 ..	−2.6	−5.3	−9.2	−16.4	−11.4	−16.1	15.8	−11.3
Other sectors	4 734 ..	−7.2	1.0	.9	−11.6	.8	3.4	.9	.9
Other assets	4 736 ..	....	....	....	−1.6	−1.9	−2.0	−2.5	−2.3
Monetary authorities	4 737 ..	....	....	....	....	....	....	....	....
of which: Short-term	4 739 ..	....	....	....	....	....	....	....	....
General government	4 740 ..	....	....	....	−1.6	−1.9	−2.0	−2.5	−2.3
of which: Short-term	4 742 ..	....	....	....	....	....	....	....	....
Banks	4 743 ..	....	....	....	....	....	....	....	....
of which: Short-term	4 745 ..	....	....	....	....	....	....	....	....
Other sectors	4 746 ..	....	....	....	....	....	....	....	....
of which: Short-term	4 748 ..	....	....	....	....	....	....	....	....
Liabilities	4 753 ..	**123.2**	**−66.8**	**45.0**	**1.1**	**−113.1**	**52.2**	**39.8**	**−47.4**
Trade credits	4 756 ..	4.9	2.6	−1.3	−.2	1.6	.6	1.4	−1.2
General government	4 757 ..	....	....	....	....	....	....	....	....
of which: Short-term	4 759 ..	....	....	....	....	....	....	....	....
Other sectors	4 760 ..	4.9	2.6	−1.3	−.2	1.6	.6	1.4	−1.2
of which: Short-term	4 762 ..	*4.9*	*2.6*	*−1.3*	*−.2*	*1.6*	*.6*	*1.4*	*−1.2*
Loans	4 764 ..	125.8	−72.3	47.7	62.1	−111.8	64.3	−5.5	−30.6
Monetary authorities	4 765 ..	−2.5	−2.5	−1.3	....	....	....	13.9	....
of which: Use of Fund credit and loans from the Fund	4 766 ..	....	....	....	....	....	....	7.0	....
of which: Short-term	4 768 ..	....	....	....	....	....	....	....	....
General government	4 769 ..	51.5	−52.7	43.7	34.8	−87.9	−8.0	27.8	−.4
of which: Short-term	4 771 ..	*80.0*	*−79.0*	....	....	....	....	....	....
Banks	4 772 ..	33.3	−7.0	2.1	23.2	−29.5	36.1	−33.7	−14.7
of which: Short-term	4 774 ..	*33.3*	*−7.0*	*2.1*	*23.2*	*−29.5*	*36.1*	*−33.7*	*−14.7*
Other sectors	4 775 ..	43.5	−10.2	3.1	4.1	5.6	36.2	−13.5	−15.5
of which: Short-term	4 777 ..	*−.2*	....	....	*−.2*	*−1.4*	*−2.5*	....	*−.6*
Currency and deposits	4 780 ..	−7.1	3.7	−.6	−60.8	−2.9	−11.8	−11.9	−15.1
Monetary authorities	4 781 ..	−.1	−1.5	....	−.2	....	.4	−1.1	1.0
General government	4 782 ..	2.4	−.3	1.4	−2.8	....	....	−2.5	....
Banks	4 783 ..	−4.8	7.3	1.1	−55.5	.3	.3	.7	....
Other sectors	4 784 ..	−4.7	−1.9	−3.1	−2.4	−3.1	−12.4	−9.1	−16.2
Other liabilities	4 786 ..	−.4	−.7	−.8	....	−.1	−1.0	55.8	−.4
Monetary authorities	4 787 ..	....	....	....	....	....	....	55.8	....
of which: Short-term	4 789 ..	....	....	....	....	....	....	....	....
General government	4 790 ..	....	....	....	....	....	....	....	....
of which: Short-term	4 792 ..	....	....	....	....	....	....	....	....
Banks	4 793 ..	....	....	....	....	....	....	....	....
of which: Short-term	4 795 ..	....	....	....	....	....	....	....	....
Other sectors	4 796 ..	−.4	−.7	−.8	....	−.1	−1.0	....	−.4
of which: Short-term	4 798 ..	*−.4*	*−.7*	*−.8*	....	*−.1*	*−1.0*	....	*−.4*
E. RESERVE ASSETS	4 802 ..	**30.8**	**31.4**	**11.5**	**−49.3**	**−22.4**	**−58.2**	**−47.0**	**−5.0**
Monetary gold	4 812 ..	....	....	....	....	....	....	....	....
Special drawing rights	4 811 ..	−.1	−.1	−.2	−.3	−.3	−.3	−27.9	.1
Reserve position in the Fund	4 810 ..	....	....	....	....	....	....	....	....
Foreign exchange	4 803 ..	30.9	31.5	12.0	−48.8	−21.5	−56.9	−21.9	−4.7
Other claims	4 813 ..	.1	.1	−.3	−.2	−.6	−1.0	2.8	−.4
NET ERRORS AND OMISSIONS	4 998 ..	**−35.0**	**−3.7**	**−7.6**	**−8.5**	**−39.3**	**−11.5**	**−40.7**	**18.0**

Table 1. ANALYTIC PRESENTATION, 2003–2010

(Millions of U.S. dollars)

	Code	2003	2004	2005	2006	2007	2008	2009	2010
A. Current Account[1]	4 993 Z.	**−348.6**	**−316.5**	**−270.3**	**−327.3**	**−652.1**	**−618.6**	**−755.8**	....
Goods: exports f.o.b.	2 100 ..	540.8	568.6	578.3	735.5	1,046.9	1,282.2	1,224.8	....
Goods: imports f.o.b.	3 100 ..	−818.7	−842.0	−865.7	−1,045.7	−1,602.0	−1,889.7	−1,737.8	....
Balance on Goods	4 100 ..	*−277.9*	*−273.5*	*−287.4*	*−310.3*	*−555.1*	*−607.5*	*−513.0*	....
Services: credit	2 200 ..	172.3	215.6	193.8	217.1	301.5	348.0	220.9	....
Services: debit	3 200 ..	−253.9	−287.1	−279.1	−352.2	−500.5	−510.0	−496.1	....
Balance on Goods and Services	4 991 ..	*−359.5*	*−345.0*	*−372.7*	*−445.4*	*−754.0*	*−769.5*	*−788.2*	....
Income: credit	2 300 ..	22.8	22.9	25.4	23.8	37.6	44.9	43.1	....
Income: debit	3 300 ..	−60.9	−59.9	−43.2	−54.0	−86.1	−56.2	−76.1	....
Balance on Goods, Services, and Income	4 992 ..	*−397.6*	*−382.0*	*−390.5*	*−475.6*	*−802.5*	*−780.8*	*−821.2*	....
Current transfers: credit	2 379 Z.	56.6	73.4	152.8	205.5	258.8	235.1	137.8	....
Current transfers: debit	3 379 ..	−7.5	−7.9	−32.6	−57.2	−108.4	−72.9	−72.5	....
B. Capital Account[1]	4 994 Z.	**34.4**	**51.6**	**99.0**	**82.9**	**163.6**	**96.5**	**152.8**	....
Capital account: credit	2 994 Z.	34.9	52.2	105.3	89.0	170.7	110.6	158.9	....
Capital account: debit	3 994 ..	−.5	−.6	−6.3	−6.1	−7.1	−14.0	−6.1	....
Total, Groups A Plus B	4 981 ..	*−314.1*	*−264.9*	*−171.3*	*−244.4*	*−488.4*	*−522.1*	*−603.0*	....
C. Financial Account[1]	4 995 W.	**32.1**	**−23.7**	**110.9**	**−899.6**	**239.2**	**372.3**	**186.1**	....
Direct investment abroad	4 505 ..	−.3	1.3	.4	1.7	6.1	4.0	−31.2	....
Direct investment in Benin	4 555 Z.	44.7	63.8	53.0	53.2	255.2	169.8	134.3	....
Portfolio investment assets	4 602 ..	−7.2	2.5	14.7	6.0	−57.7	−10.7	−27.6	....
Equity securities	4 610 ..	.3	.5	1.4	.3	−5.7	1.3	−2.8	....
Debt securities	4 619 ..	−7.5	2.0	13.3	5.7	−52.0	−12.0	−24.8	....
Portfolio investment liabilities	4 652 Z.	−.4	−2.9	2.3	.3	4.9	15.0	106.2	....
Equity securities	4 660 ..	−.4	−2.9	2.3	.3	4.9	−1.8	9.0	....
Debt securities	4 669 Z.	....	....	....	....	....	16.7	97.2	....
Financial derivatives	4 910 ..	−.2	−.5	−.3	....	−.1	−.7	.4	....
Financial derivatives assets	4 900 ..	−.2	−.5	−.3	....	−.1	−.7	.4	....
Financial derivatives liabilities	4 905 ..	....	....	....	....	....	....	....	....
Other investment assets	4 703 ..	25.7	−19.3	6.7	−51.4	−97.6	−43.6	−245.6	....
Monetary authorities	4 701 ..	....	....	....	....	....	....	....	....
General government	4 704 ..	.1	−.3	.2	−.3	.2	....	....	....
Banks	4 705 ..	22.6	−32.4	1.1	−72.7	−69.7	11.2	−108.7	....
Other sectors	4 728 ..	3.1	13.4	5.4	21.5	−28.1	−54.8	−136.9	....
Other investment liabilities	4 753 W.	−30.2	−68.6	34.1	−909.4	128.4	238.6	249.8	....
Monetary authorities	4 753 WA	4.5	18.4	−7.1	5.6	−8.9	7.0	86.4	....
General government	4 753 ZB	−46.2	−40.2	−34.3	−1,026.7	−35.4	−18.6	−19.9	....
Banks	4 753 ZC	32.4	.4	18.8	4.2	−5.1	18.9	−21.9	....
Other sectors	4 753 ZD	−20.9	−47.3	56.7	107.5	177.8	231.3	205.2	....
Total, Groups A Through C	4 983 ..	*−282.0*	*−288.6*	*−60.4*	*−1,144.0*	*−249.2*	*−149.7*	*−416.9*	....
D. Net Errors and Omissions	4 998 ..	**182.0**	**−10.1**	**8.8**	**28.0**	**71.9**	**1.4**	**−4.4**	....
Total, Groups A Through D	4 984 ..	*−100.0*	*−298.7*	*−51.6*	*−1,116.0*	*−177.3*	*−148.4*	*−421.3*	....
E. Reserves and Related Items	4 802 A.	**100.0**	**298.7**	**51.6**	**1,116.0**	**177.3**	**148.4**	**421.3**	....
Reserve assets	4 802 ..	−6.2	126.9	−111.7	−171.5	−176.4	−126.4	72.1	....
Use of Fund credit and loans	4 766 ..	−6.6	−10.6	−7.6	−50.8	1.3	19.3	15.8	....
Exceptional financing	4 920 ..	112.8	182.5	170.9	1,338.4	352.4	255.5	333.5	....
Conversion rates: CFA francs per U.S. dollar	0 101 ..	**581.20**	**528.28**	**527.47**	**522.89**	**479.27**	**447.81**	**472.19**	**495.28**

[1] Excludes components that have been classified in the categories of Group E.

Table 2. STANDARD PRESENTATION, 2003–2010

(Millions of U.S. dollars)

	Code	2003	2004	2005	2006	2007	2008	2009	2010
CURRENT ACCOUNT............................	4 993 ..	**−331.2**	**−288.5**	**−226.1**	**−217.0**	**−534.1**	**−536.0**	**−648.9**	....
A. GOODS.....................................	4 100 ..	**−277.9**	**−273.5**	**−287.4**	**−310.3**	**−555.1**	**−607.5**	**−513.0**	....
Credit.......................................	2 100 ..	**540.8**	**568.6**	**578.3**	**735.5**	**1,046.9**	**1,282.2**	**1,224.8**	....
General merchandise: exports f.o.b..........	2 110 ..	532.1	555.9	563.1	722.7	1,029.7	1,237.1	1,197.7	....
Goods for processing: exports f.o.b...........	2 150 ..	....	....	....	....	....	....	....	....
Repairs on goods...........................	2 160 ..	....	....	....	....	....	....	....	....
Goods procured in ports by carriers........	2 170 ..	8.8	12.7	15.2	12.8	17.2	45.1	27.1	....
Nonmonetary gold..........................	2 180 ..	....	....	....	....	....	....	....	....
Debit..	3 100 ..	**−818.7**	**−842.0**	**−865.7**	**−1,045.7**	**−1,602.0**	**−1,889.7**	**−1,737.8**	....
General merchandise: imports f.o.b..........	3 110 ..	−818.5	−839.3	−863.4	−1,041.9	−1,601.6	−1,889.7	−1,737.7	....
Goods for processing: imports f.o.b..........	3 150 ..	....	....	....	....	....	....	....	....
Repairs on goods...........................	3 160 ..	−.2	−2.3	−2.3	−3.8	−.4	....	....	....
Goods procured in ports by carriers........	3 170 ..	....	−.5	....	−.1	....	....	....	....
Nonmonetary gold..........................	3 180 ..	....	....	....	....	....	....	....	....
B. SERVICES.................................	4 200 ..	**−81.6**	**−71.5**	**−85.3**	**−135.2**	**−198.9**	**−162.0**	**−275.2**	....
Total credit...................................	2 200 ..	*172.3*	*215.6*	*193.8*	*217.1*	*301.5*	*348.0*	*220.9*	....
Total debit...................................	3 200 ..	*−253.9*	*−287.1*	*−279.1*	*−352.2*	*−500.5*	*−510.0*	*−496.1*	....
Transportation services, credit...........	2 205 ..	**14.4**	**33.7**	**32.8**	**29.2**	**12.6**	**13.0**	**17.9**	....
Passenger....................................	2 850 ..	*1.9*	*2.9*	*4.7*	*5.6*	*.3*	*.4*	*.4*	....
Freight......................................	2 851 ..	*6.0*	*8.1*	*8.4*	*.2*	....	....	*.2*	....
Other..	2 852 ..	*6.4*	*22.7*	*19.7*	*23.4*	*12.3*	*12.6*	*17.4*	....
Sea transport, passenger...................	2 207 ..	....	....	....	....	....	....	....	....
Sea transport, freight.....................	2 208 ..	....	....	....	....	....	....	.2	....
Sea transport, other......................	2 209 ..	5.2	21.0	19.7	15.1	2.7	2.1	7.5	....
Air transport, passenger..................	2 211 ..	.1	.5	2.2	5.4	....	....	....	....
Air transport, freight.....................	2 212 ..	....	....	....	.1	....	....	....	....
Air transport, other......................	2 213 ..	1.2	1.6	....	3.0	1.9	2.4	1.7	....
Other transport, passenger...............	2 215 ..	1.8	2.4	2.5	.2	.3	.3	.4	....
Other transport, freight..................	2 216 ..	6.0	8.1	8.4	.1	....	....	....	....
Other transport, other...................	2 217 ..	....	....	....	5.3	7.6	8.2	8.1	....
Transportation services, debit...........	3 205 ..	**−170.6**	**−173.3**	**−174.2**	**−216.8**	**−295.8**	**−310.1**	**−290.2**	....
Passenger....................................	3 850 ..	*−32.1*	*−30.0*	*−30.5*	*−36.9*	*−34.8*	*−38.5*	*−35.4*	....
Freight......................................	3 851 ..	*−134.7*	*−135.9*	*−136.8*	*−168.5*	*−257.9*	*−269.6*	*−252.8*	....
Other..	3 852 ..	*−3.9*	*−7.4*	*−6.9*	*−11.4*	*−3.1*	*−2.1*	*−2.1*	....
Sea transport, passenger...................	3 207 ..	....	....	....	....	....	....	....	....
Sea transport, freight.....................	3 208 ..	−104.3	−105.2	−105.9	−126.8	−205.9	−210.3	−198.0	....
Sea transport, other......................	3 209 ..	−2.6	−5.7	−5.4	−9.6	−1.3	−1.8	−.9	....
Air transport, passenger..................	3 211 ..	−30.8	−28.6	−28.9	−36.9	−34.8	−38.5	−35.4	....
Air transport, freight.....................	3 212 ..	−26.1	−26.3	−26.4	−31.8	−52.0	−52.6	−46.9	....
Air transport, other......................	3 213 ..	−1.2	−1.7	−1.5	−1.8	−1.8	−.2	−1.2	....
Other transport, passenger...............	3 215 ..	−1.3	−1.4	−1.6	....	....	....	....	....
Other transport, freight..................	3 216 ..	−4.3	−4.4	−4.5	−9.9	....	−6.7	−7.9	....
Other transport, other...................	3 217 ..	....	....	....	....	....	....	....	....
Travel, credit...............................	2 236 ..	**106.4**	**118.5**	**103.4**	**116.3**	**206.5**	**235.7**	**131.2**	....
Business travel.............................	2 237 ..	29.8	39.9	38.1	44.2	67.3	99.2	49.3	....
Personal travel.............................	2 240 ..	76.6	78.6	65.3	72.0	139.2	136.5	82.0	....
Travel, debit...............................	3 236 ..	**−21.2**	**−29.1**	**−26.9**	**−34.2**	**−71.7**	**−63.8**	**−52.5**	....
Business travel.............................	3 237 ..	−6.8	−11.5	−10.2	−16.8	−29.1	−28.1	−18.9	....
Personal travel.............................	3 240 ..	−14.4	−17.6	−16.6	−17.5	−42.7	−35.7	−33.6	....
Other services, credit.....................	2 200 BA	**51.6**	**63.5**	**57.6**	**71.6**	**82.4**	**99.4**	**71.8**	....
Communications...........................	2 245 ..	4.2	5.2	5.4	11.2	1.6	2.3	.4	....
Construction...............................	2 249 ..	....	2.7	.1	.1	.1	.3	.7	....
Insurance....................................	2 253 ..	.2	2.3	1.2	.6	4.2	5.9	3.3	....
Financial.....................................	2 260 ..	.6	.8	2.9	4.2	1.9	1.4	1.7	....
Computer and information.................	2 262 ..	....	....	....	.6	.7	....	....	....
Royalties and licence fees..................	2 266 ..	.1	....	....	....	....	....	....	....
Other business services....................	2 268 ..	36.8	40.8	33.5	34.3	53.2	69.7	48.2	....
Personal, cultural, and recreational........	2 287 ..	....	....	....	....	.1	....	....	....
Government, n.i.e..........................	2 291 ..	9.6	11.7	14.6	20.6	20.6	19.7	17.4	....
Other services, debit......................	3 200 BA	**−62.1**	**−84.8**	**−78.0**	**−101.2**	**−133.0**	**−136.1**	**−153.4**	....
Communications...........................	3 245 ..	−6.7	−14.3	−16.4	−17.2	−3.8	−8.3	−12.9	....
Construction...............................	3 249 ..	....	−1.8	−.1	−10.4	−13.0	−18.0	−9.9	....
Insurance....................................	3 253 ..	−29.7	−27.4	−27.3	−31.6	−45.2	−21.6	−18.6	....
Financial.....................................	3 260 ..	−3.1	−3.5	−2.8	−2.3	−3.0	−2.6	−5.0	....
Computer and information.................	3 262 ..	−1.3	−1.8	−3.1	−4.4	−3.8	−6.8	−6.3	....
Royalties and licence fees..................	3 266 ..	−1.9	−2.3	−1.9	−1.6	−2.0	−2.8	−3.0	....
Other business services....................	3 268 ..	−9.3	−19.9	−14.5	−23.5	−50.9	−65.0	−90.0	....
Personal, cultural, and recreational........	3 287 ..	....	−.1	−.1	−.2	−1.9	−1.0	....	....
Government, n.i.e..........................	3 291 ..	−10.1	−13.7	−11.9	−10.0	−9.5	−10.0	−7.7	....

Table 2 (Continued). STANDARD PRESENTATION, 2003–2010

(Millions of U.S. dollars)

	Code	2003	2004	2005	2006	2007	2008	2009	2010
C. INCOME..	4 300 ..	**−38.1**	**−37.0**	**−17.8**	**−30.2**	**−48.5**	**−11.3**	**−33.0**	....
Total credit..	2 300 ..	*22.8*	*22.9*	*25.4*	*23.8*	*37.6*	*44.9*	*43.1*	....
Total debit...	3 300 ..	*−60.9*	*−59.9*	*−43.2*	*−54.0*	*−86.1*	*−56.2*	*−76.1*	....
Compensation of employees, credit..................	2 310 ..	**5.8**	**8.9**	**9.8**	**9.3**	**6.3**	**7.4**	**3.3**	....
Compensation of employees, debit....................	3 310 ..	**−1.4**	**−2.8**	**−3.0**	**−8.7**	**−5.1**	**−6.5**	**−3.1**	....
Investment income, credit..............................	2 320 ..	**16.9**	**14.0**	**15.6**	**14.5**	**31.3**	**37.5**	**39.8**	....
Direct investment income...............................	2 330 ..	.9	.8	−.3	1.1	2.5	1.3	1.8	....
Dividends and distributed branch profits.................	2 332 ..	.3	.5	....	1.7	.5	.4	1.3	....
Reinvested earnings and undistributed branch profits.....	2 333 ..	.2	....	−.9	−1.1	−.2	....	−.1	
Income on debt (interest)...........................	2 334 ..	.5	.3	.6	.5	2.2	.8	.6	
Portfolio investment income............................	2 339 ..	3.9	5.6	5.6	3.9	7.9	5.9	12.9	....
Income on equity.......................................	2 340 ..	.1	.2	1.0	.1	.4	.6	.2	
Income on bonds and notes...........................	2 350 ..	3.2	4.9	3.9	3.3	4.0	3.9	12.0	
Income on money market instruments............	2 360 ..	.7	.5	.7	.5	3.4	1.5	.7	
Other investment income.................................	2 370 ..	12.1	7.5	10.4	9.6	21.0	30.3	25.1	....
Investment income, debit..............................	3 320 ..	**−59.5**	**−57.1**	**−40.1**	**−45.4**	**−80.9**	**−49.7**	**−72.9**	....
Direct investment income...............................	3 330 ..	−22.4	−13.5	−9.0	−14.8	−52.9	−29.5	−31.5	
Dividends and distributed branch profits.................	3 332 ..	−8.1	−5.2	−7.0	−11.7	−13.0	−24.4	−22.7	
Reinvested earnings and undistributed branch profits.....	3 333 ..	−13.3	−6.6	.7	−3.1	−39.2	−5.2	−8.2	
Income on debt (interest)...........................	3 334 ..	−1.1	−1.7	−2.7	....	−.7	....	−.6	
Portfolio investment income............................	3 339 ..	−7.2	−17.6	−8.4	−8.5	−7.2	−6.9	−15.4	
Income on equity.......................................	3 340 ..	−2.1	−7.8	−1.5	−1.7	−2.1	−1.4	−3.4	
Income on bonds and notes...........................	3 350 ..	−5.1	−9.5	−6.9	−6.8	−4.0	−5.5	−3.8	
Income on money market instruments............	3 360 ..	....	−.3	....	....	−1.1	....	−8.1	
Other investment income.................................	3 370 ..	−29.9	−26.0	−22.7	−22.0	−20.9	−13.4	−26.0	
D. CURRENT TRANSFERS.............................	4 379 ..	**66.4**	**93.5**	**164.4**	**258.6**	**268.4**	**244.8**	**172.2**	....
Credit..	2 379 ..	**73.9**	**101.4**	**197.0**	**315.8**	**376.8**	**317.7**	**244.7**	....
General government......................................	2 380 ..	17.4	28.0	44.2	110.3	118.0	82.6	106.9	
Other sectors...	2 390 ..	56.6	73.4	152.8	205.5	258.8	235.1	137.8	
Workers' remittances..................................	2 391 ..	49.5	54.1	137.1	186.2	234.2	199.6	122.6	
Other current transfers...............................	2 392 ..	7.1	19.3	15.7	19.3	24.6	35.5	15.2	
Debit...	3 379 ..	**−7.5**	**−7.9**	**−32.6**	**−57.2**	**−108.4**	**−72.9**	**−72.5**	....
General government......................................	3 380 ..	−2.3	−2.9	−.5	−3.2	−3.0	−1.7	−3.3	
Other sectors...	3 390 ..	−5.3	−5.0	−32.2	−54.0	−105.3	−71.2	−69.2	
Workers' remittances..................................	3 391 ..	−3.9	−2.9	−30.5	−52.1	−102.4	−67.8	−66.8	
Other current transfers...............................	3 392 ..	−1.4	−2.2	−1.7	−1.9	−2.9	−3.4	−2.4	
CAPITAL AND FINANCIAL ACCOUNT...................	4 996 ..	**149.2**	**298.6**	**217.3**	**189.0**	**462.2**	**534.7**	**653.4**	....
CAPITAL ACCOUNT.....................................	4 994 ..	**63.6**	**80.4**	**121.9**	**1,154.8**	**176.0**	**108.0**	**161.1**	....
Total credit..	2 994 ..	*64.1*	*81.1*	*128.2*	*1,160.9*	*183.1*	*122.0*	*167.2*	....
Total debit...	3 994 ..	*−.5*	*−.6*	*−6.3*	*−6.1*	*−7.1*	*−14.0*	*−6.1*	....
Capital transfers, credit..............................	2 400 ..	**64.1**	**81.1**	**128.2**	**1,160.9**	**183.1**	**122.0**	**167.2**	....
General government......................................	2 401 ..	61.3	74.8	98.1	1,127.7	138.8	71.7	140.1	
Debt forgiveness..	2 402 ..	29.2	28.9	22.8	1,071.9	12.3	11.5	8.3	
Other capital transfers................................	2 410 ..	32.1	45.9	75.3	55.8	126.4	60.2	131.7	
Other sectors...	2 430 ..	2.8	6.3	30.1	33.2	44.3	50.4	27.2	
Migrants' transfers....................................	2 431 ..	.1	....	25.8	28.5	41.1	44.3	24.0	
Debt forgiveness......................................	2 432 ..	....	....	....	....	....	....	....	
Other capital transfers..............................	2 440 ..	2.7	6.3	4.2	4.6	3.2	6.1	3.2	
Capital transfers, debit...............................	3 400 ..	**−.4**	**−.6**	**−6.3**	**−6.1**	**−7.0**	**−14.0**	**−6.0**	....
General government......................................	3 401 ..	....	....	....	....	....	....	....	
Debt forgiveness..	3 402 ..	....	....	....	....	....	....	....	
Other capital transfers................................	3 410 ..	....	....	....	....	....	....	....	
Other sectors...	3 430 ..	−.4	−.6	−6.3	−6.1	−7.0	−14.0	−6.0	
Migrants' transfers....................................	3 431 ..	−.4	−.6	−6.3	−6.1	−7.0	−14.0	−6.0	
Debt forgiveness......................................	3 432 ..	....	....	....	....	....	....	....	
Other capital transfers..............................	3 440 ..	....	....	....	....	....	....	....	
Nonproduced nonfinancial assets, credit............	2 480 ..	....	....	....	....	....	....	....	
Nonproduced nonfinancial assets, debit..............	3 480 ..	....	....	....	....	−.1	−.1	−.1	....

Table 2 (Continued). STANDARD PRESENTATION, 2003–2010

(Millions of U.S. dollars)

	Code	2003	2004	2005	2006	2007	2008	2009	2010
FINANCIAL ACCOUNT	4 995	**85.6**	**218.2**	**95.4**	**−965.8**	**286.2**	**426.7**	**492.2**	....
A. DIRECT INVESTMENT	4 500	**44.4**	**65.2**	**53.4**	**54.9**	**261.3**	**173.8**	**103.1**	....
Direct investment abroad	4 505	−.3	1.3	.4	1.7	6.1	4.0	−31.2	....
Equity capital	4 510	−1.9	−.8	7.8	....	1.6	−1.5	−26.3	....
Claims on affiliated enterprises	4 515	....	1.5	8.9	3.2	3.9	1.8	.8	....
Liabilities to affiliated enterprises	4 520	−1.9	−2.3	−1.1	−3.2	−2.3	−3.3	−27.1	....
Reinvested earnings	4 525	−.2	....	.9	1.1	.2	....	.1	....
Other capital	4 530	1.7	2.1	−8.3	.7	4.3	5.5	−5.0	....
Claims on affiliated enterprises	4 535	1.9	8.0	2.3	−2.6	....	.4	−7.2	....
Liabilities to affiliated enterprises	4 540	−.2	−5.9	−10.6	3.2	4.3	5.0	2.2	....
Direct investment in Benin	4 555	**44.7**	**63.8**	**53.0**	**53.2**	**255.2**	**169.8**	**134.3**	....
Equity capital	4 560	28.6	71.2	23.9	14.6	87.8	76.8	113.9	....
Claims on direct investors	4 565	34.7	92.7	52.6	65.8	118.1	127.3	127.0	....
Liabilities to direct investors	4 570	−6.1	−21.5	−28.7	−51.2	−30.3	−50.5	−13.2	....
Reinvested earnings	4 575	13.3	6.6	−.7	3.1	39.2	5.2	8.2	....
Other capital	4 580	2.8	−14.0	29.9	35.5	128.2	87.9	12.2	....
Claims on direct investors	4 585	−2.6	3.7	−2.5	−.3	.1	−3.8	1.1	....
Liabilities to direct investors	4 590	5.4	−17.7	32.4	35.7	128.1	91.7	11.2	....
B. PORTFOLIO INVESTMENT	4 600	**−8.2**	**−.7**	**16.7**	**14.6**	**18.3**	**8.9**	**91.5**	....
Assets	4 602	**−7.2**	**2.5**	**14.7**	**6.0**	**−57.7**	**−10.7**	**−27.6**	....
Equity securities	4 610	.3	.5	1.4	.3	−5.7	1.3	−2.8	....
Monetary authorities	4 611	....	....	....	....	....	....	....	....
General government	4 612	....	....	....	....	....	....	....	....
Banks	4 613	.5	4.1	....	.3	.2	....	−.6	....
Other sectors	4 614	−.2	−3.6	1.4	....	−5.9	1.3	−2.3	....
Debt securities	4 619	−7.5	2.0	13.3	5.7	−52.0	−12.0	−24.8	....
Bonds and notes	4 620	−8.8	−.6	7.2	2.0	−36.7	−13.5	−24.8	....
Monetary authorities	4 621	....	....	....	....	....	....	....	....
General government	4 622	....	....	....	....	....	....	−51.6	....
Banks	4 623	−7.6	.9	7.9	6.4	−38.7	−11.9	3.7	....
Other sectors	4 624	−1.1	−1.5	−.7	−4.3	2.1	−1.7	23.1	....
Money market instruments	4 630	1.3	2.7	6.1	3.7	−15.4	1.5	....	....
Monetary authorities	4 631	....	....	....	....	....	....	....	....
General government	4 632	....	....	....	....	....	....	....	....
Banks	4 633	1.5	2.7	4.7	3.7	−15.4	1.5	....	....
Other sectors	4 634	−.2	....	1.4	....	....	....	....	....
Liabilities	4 652	**−.9**	**−3.2**	**2.0**	**8.5**	**76.0**	**19.7**	**119.2**	....
Equity securities	4 660	−.4	−2.9	2.3	.3	4.9	−1.8	9.0	....
Banks	4 663	−.6	−2.9	.2	−1.1	4.7	−2.4	9.0	....
Other sectors	4 664	.2	....	2.1	1.4	.2	.6	....	....
Debt securities	4 669	−.6	−.3	−.3	8.3	71.1	21.4	110.2	....
Bonds and notes	4 670	−.6	−.3	−.3	8.3	71.1	4.7	13.0	....
Monetary authorities	4 671	....	....	....	....	....	....	....	....
General government	4 672	−.3	....	....	....	64.5	....	12.7	....
Banks	4 673	−.3	−.8	−.3	−.5	−.3	....	.3	....
Other sectors	4 674	....	.5	−.1	8.8	6.9	4.7	.1	....
Money market instruments	4 680	....	....	....	....	....	16.7	97.2	....
Monetary authorities	4 681	....	....	....	....	....	....	....	....
General government	4 682	....	....	....	....	....	....	....	....
Banks	4 683	....	....	....	....	....	....	....	....
Other sectors	4 684	....	....	....	....	....	16.7	97.2	....
C. FINANCIAL DERIVATIVES	4 910	**−.2**	**−.5**	**−.3**	....	**−.1**	**−.7**	**.4**	....
Monetary authorities	4 911	....	....	....	....	....	....	....	....
General government	4 912	....	....	....	....	....	....	....	....
Banks	4 913	....	....	....	....	....	....	....	....
Other sectors	4 914	−.2	−.5	−.3	....	−.1	−.7	.4	....
Assets	4 900	**−.2**	**−.5**	**−.3**	....	**−.1**	**−.7**	**.4**	....
Monetary authorities	4 901	....	....	....	....	....	....	....	....
General government	4 902	....	....	....	....	....	....	....	....
Banks	4 903	....	....	....	....	....	....	....	....
Other sectors	4 904	−.2	−.5	−.3	....	−.1	−.7	.4	....
Liabilities	4 905	....	....	....	....	....	....	....	....
Monetary authorities	4 906	....	....	....	....	....	....	....	....
General government	4 907	....	....	....	....	....	....	....	....
Banks	4 908	....	....	....	....	....	....	....	....
Other sectors	4 909	....	....	....	....	....	....	....	....

Table 2 (Concluded). STANDARD PRESENTATION, 2003–2010

(Millions of U.S. dollars)

	Code	2003	2004	2005	2006	2007	2008	2009	2010
D. OTHER INVESTMENT	4 700	**55.8**	**27.3**	**137.3**	**−863.8**	**183.1**	**371.0**	**225.2**	....
Assets	4 703	**25.7**	**−19.3**	**6.7**	**−51.4**	**−97.6**	**−43.6**	**−245.6**	....
Trade credits	4 706	−2.0	12.4	−3.3	17.2	14.9	−77.6	−93.8	....
General government	4 707	....	....	....	....	....	....	....	....
of which: Short-term	4 709	....	....	....	....	....	....	....	....
Other sectors	4 710	−2.0	12.4	−3.3	17.2	14.9	−77.6	−93.8	....
of which: Short-term	4 712	−2.0	12.4	−3.3	17.2	14.9	−77.6	−93.8	....
Loans	4 714	20.8	−22.9	8.6	−32.7	−80.1	9.5	−34.0	....
Monetary authorities	4 715	....	....	....	....	....	....	....	....
of which: Short-term	4 718	....	....	....	....	....	....	....	....
General government	4 719	....	....	....	....	....	....	....	....
of which: Short-term	4 721	....	....	....	....	....	....	....	....
Banks	4 722	20.8	−22.9	8.6	−32.5	−65.3	−6.1	−33.8	....
of which: Short-term	4 724	20.8	10.0	−8.1	−40.4	−28.0	1.5	60.4	....
Other sectors	4 725	....	....	....	−.2	−14.8	15.7	−.2	....
of which: Short-term	4 727	....	....	....	....	....	....	....	....
Currency and deposits	4 730	−.6	−1.1	−8.3	−40.5	−8.3	44.0	−117.3	....
Monetary authorities	4 731	....	....	....	....	....	....	....	....
General government	4 732	.1	−.3	....	−.1	....	....	....	....
Banks	4 733	1.8	−6.0	−10.2	−39.5	−4.7	17.0	−73.0	....
Other sectors	4 734	−2.5	5.2	1.9	−.8	−3.6	27.0	−44.3	....
Other assets	4 736	7.5	−7.8	9.6	4.7	−24.1	−19.6	−.5	....
Monetary authorities	4 737	....	....	....	....	....	....	....	....
of which: Short-term	4 739	....	....	....	....	....	....	....	....
General government	4 740	....	....	.2	−.2	.2	....	....	....
of which: Short-term	4 742	....	....	.2	−.2	.2	....	....	....
Banks	4 743	....	−3.6	2.7	−.6	.3	.3	−1.9	....
of which: Short-term	4 745	....	−3.6	2.7	−.6	.3	.3	−1.9	....
Other sectors	4 746	7.6	−4.2	6.8	5.4	−24.6	−19.9	1.4	....
of which: Short-term	4 748	−5.7	−4.2	6.8	42.6	−24.6	−19.9	1.4	....
Liabilities	4 753	**30.0**	**46.7**	**130.6**	**−812.4**	**280.7**	**414.6**	**470.8**	....
Trade credits	4 756	−26.5	−34.6	35.6	95.5	45.1	66.6	133.5	....
General government	4 757	....	....	....	....	....	....	....	....
of which: Short-term	4 759	....	....	....	....	....	....	....	....
Other sectors	4 760	−26.5	−34.6	35.6	95.5	45.1	66.6	133.5	....
of which: Short-term	4 762	....	....	....	....	....	....	....	....
Loans	4 764	11.8	65.3	76.1	−928.0	191.5	259.1	207.1	....
Monetary authorities	4 765	−6.6	−10.6	−7.6	−50.8	1.3	19.3	15.8	....
of which: Use of Fund credit and loans from the Fund	4 766	−6.6	−10.6	−7.6	−50.8	1.3	19.3	15.8	....
of which: Short-term	4 768	....	....	....	....	....	....	....	....
General government	4 769	19.0	75.3	66.0	−901.4	103.9	127.9	139.1	....
of which: Short-term	4 771	....	....	....	....	....	....	....	....
Banks	4 772	.3	9.9	2.2	21.5	−12.8	−6.7	25.9	....
of which: Short-term	4 774	−1.6	....	....	13.5	−24.5	−.4	−20.3	....
Other sectors	4 775	−.9	−9.2	15.5	2.8	99.1	118.5	26.4	....
of which: Short-term	4 777	....	−6.5	17.5	−4.4	94.2	....	17.3	....
Currency and deposits	4 780	34.7	4.9	22.0	5.5	22.2	32.1	14.3	....
Monetary authorities	4 781	.7	3.7	2.2	1.3	2.8	−.2	14.1	....
General government	4 782	....	....	....	....	....	....	....	....
Banks	4 783	34.0	1.3	19.8	4.2	19.4	32.3	.2	....
Other sectors	4 784	....	....	....	....	....	....	....	....
Other liabilities	4 786	10.1	11.0	−3.1	14.7	21.9	56.9	115.8	....
Monetary authorities	4 787	3.8	14.8	−9.3	4.3	−11.7	7.2	72.4	....
of which: Short-term	4 789	....	....	....	....	....	....	....	....
General government	4 790	....	....	....	....	....	....	....	....
of which: Short-term	4 792	....	....	....	....	....	....	....	....
Banks	4 793	−.2	−.3	.6	1.1	....	3.5	−1.8	....
of which: Short-term	4 795	−.2	−.3	.6	1.1	....	3.5	−1.8	....
Other sectors	4 796	6.4	−3.5	5.6	9.2	33.6	46.2	45.2	....
of which: Short-term	4 798	6.4	−3.5	5.6	9.2	33.6	46.2	45.2	....
E. RESERVE ASSETS	4 802	**−6.2**	**126.9**	**−111.7**	**−171.5**	**−176.4**	**−126.4**	**72.1**	....
Monetary gold	4 812	....	....	....	....	....	....	....	....
Special drawing rights	4 811	−.1	.2	−.2	.1	−.1	....	−77.5	....
Reserve position in the Fund	4 810	....	....	....	....	....	....	....	....
Foreign exchange	4 803	−6.2	126.7	−111.5	−171.6	−176.4	−126.4	149.6	....
Other claims	4 813	....	....	....	....	....	....	....	....
NET ERRORS AND OMISSIONS	4 998	**182.0**	**−10.1**	**8.8**	**28.0**	**71.9**	**1.4**	**−4.4**	....

Table 3. INTERNATIONAL INVESTMENT POSITION (End-period stocks), 2003–2010

(Millions of U.S. dollars)

	Code	2003	2004	2005	2006	2007	2008	2009	2010
ASSETS	8 995 C.	1,224.0	1,147.1	1,093.8	1,512.9	2,053.2	2,070.2	2,357.9	....
Direct investment abroad	8 505 ..	19.7	9.3	19.6	14.5	29.7	24.3	57.5	....
Equity capital and reinvested earnings	8 506 ..	15.6	18.1	16.2	15.7	20.1	20.4	48.3	....
Claims on affiliated enterprises	8 507 ..	15.6	18.1	16.2	15.7	20.1	20.4	48.3	....
Liabilities to affiliated enterprises	8 508 ..	....	....	....	....	....	....	....	....
Other capital	8 530 ..	4.1	−8.8	3.4	−1.2	9.6	3.9	9.2	....
Claims on affiliated enterprises	8 535 ..	4.1	....	3.4	....	9.6	3.9	9.2	....
Liabilities to affiliated enterprises	8 540 ..	....	−8.8	....	−1.2				
Portfolio investment	8 602 ..	95.5	114.6	99.5	102.1	189.7	134.5	206.3	....
Equity securities	8 610 ..	1.4	4.5	1.6	.8	7.2	4.6	6.9	....
Monetary authorities	8 611 ..	....	....	....	....	....	....	....	
General government	8 612 ..	....	....	....	....	....	....	....	
Banks	8 613 ..	1.0	.3	.1	.1	....	1.1	1.1	
Other sectors	8 614 ..	.5	4.2	1.5	.7	7.1	3.5	5.8	
Debt securities	8 619 ..	94.1	110.1	98.0	101.3	182.5	129.9	199.4	
Bonds and notes	8 620 ..	74.4	98.4	91.3	90.6	176.3	102.3	170.3	
Monetary authorities	8 621 ..	....	....	....	....	....	....	....	
General government	8 622 ..	....	....	....	....	....	....	....	
Banks	8 623 ..	65.6	71.7	51.6	44.4	105.9	34.1	108.4	
Other sectors	8 624 ..	8.8	26.7	39.7	46.2	70.5	68.2	61.9	
Money market instruments	8 630 ..	19.7	11.8	6.7	10.7	6.2	27.6	29.2	
Monetary authorities	8 631 ..	....	....	....	....	....	....	....	
General government	8 632 ..	....	....	....	....	....	....	....	
Banks	8 633 ..	19.7	11.8	5.3	10.7	6.2	27.6	29.2	
Other sectors	8 634 ..	....	....	1.4	....	....	....	....	
Financial derivatives	8 900 ..	.5	1.1	1.1	.1	.2	.8	.2	....
Monetary authorities	8 901 ..	....	....	....	....	....	....	....	
General government	8 902 ..	....	....	....	....	....	....	....	
Banks	8 903 ..	....	....	....	....	....	....	....	
Other sectors	8 904 ..	.5	1.1	1.1	.1	.2	.8	.2	
Other investment	8 703 ..	390.3	387.2	317.5	484.1	624.4	647.3	864.1	....
Trade credits	8 706 ..	119.4	93.8	68.7	94.7	121.9	41.5	110.7	....
General government	8 707 ..	....	....	....	....	....	....	....	
of which: Short-term	8 709 ..	....	....	....	....	....	....	....	
Other sectors	8 710 ..	119.4	93.8	68.7	94.7	121.9	41.5	110.7	....
of which: Short-term	8 712 ..	*119.4*	*93.8*	*68.7*	*94.7*	*121.9*	*41.5*	*110.7*	
Loans	8 714 ..	115.4	136.2	109.3	156.4	256.0	231.7	274.7	
Monetary authorities	8 715 ..	....	....	....	....	....	....	....	
of which: Short-term	8 718 ..	....	....	....	....	....	....	....	
General government	8 719 ..	....	....	....	....	....	....	....	
of which: Short-term	8 721 ..	....	....	....	....	....	....	....	
Banks	8 722 ..	115.4	136.2	109.3	156.2	240.1	231.6	274.3	....
of which: Short-term	8 724 ..	*77.2*	*58.9*	*58.3*	*112.9*	*151.6*	*140.3*	*82.6*	....
Other sectors	8 725 ..	....	....	....	.2	15.9	.1	.3	....
of which: Short-term	8 727 ..	....	....	....	....	....	....	....	
Currency and deposits	8 730 ..	135.2	142.6	129.3	185.0	213.5	361.6	465.3	....
Monetary authorities	8 731 ..	....	....	....	....	....	....	....	
General government	8 732 ..	....	.3	.2	.3	....	....	....	
Banks	8 733 ..	116.8	132.5	124.5	180.5	206.8	179.4	261.4	
Other sectors	8 734 ..	18.4	9.8	4.6	4.2	6.7	182.2	203.9	
Other assets	8 736 ..	20.3	14.5	10.2	48.0	33.0	12.4	13.4	
Monetary authorities	8 737 ..	....	....	....	....	....	....	....	
of which: Short-term	8 739 ..	....	....	....	....	....	....	....	
General government	8 740 ..	.3	.3	.1	.3	....	....	....	
of which: Short-term	8 742 ..	*.3*	*.3*	*.1*	*.3*	....	....	....	
Banks	8 743 ..	....	3.9	.9	1.6	1.4	1.1	3.1	
of which: Short-term	8 745 ..	....	*3.9*	*.9*	*1.6*	*1.4*	*1.1*	*3.1*	
Other sectors	8 746 ..	20.0	10.3	9.2	46.1	31.5	11.4	10.3	
of which: Short-term	8 748 ..	*20.0*	*10.3*	*9.2*	*46.1*	*31.5*	*11.4*	*10.3*	
Reserve assets	8 802 ..	717.9	634.9	656.0	912.2	1,209.2	1,263.4	1,229.8	....
Monetary gold	8 812 ..	....	....	....	....	....	....	....	
Special drawing rights	8 811 ..	.2	....	.2	.1	.1	.1	77.9	76.6
Reserve position in the Fund	8 810 ..	3.3	3.4	3.1	3.3	3.5	3.4	3.4	3.4
Foreign exchange	8 803 ..	714.4	631.5	652.7	908.9	1,205.6	1,259.9	1,148.5	....
Other claims	8 813 ..	....	....	....	....	....	....	....	....

Table 3 (Concluded). INTERNATIONAL INVESTMENT POSITION (End-period stocks), 2003–2010

(Millions of U.S. dollars)

	Code	2003	2004	2005	2006	2007	2008	2009	2010
LIABILITIES	8 995 D.	2,253.6	2,622.7	2,460.3	2,164.3	2,006.9	2,455.3	3,188.5	....
Direct investment in Benin	8 555 ..	231.2	269.0	284.3	384.5	556.3	602.4	762.8	....
Equity capital and reinvested earnings	8 556 ..	132.1	194.6	182.4	210.1	280.7	300.8	437.9	....
Claims on direct investors	8 557 ..	....	....	....	....	....	....	....	....
Liabilities to direct investors	8 558 ..	132.1	194.6	182.4	210.1	280.7	300.8	437.9	....
Other capital	8 580 ..	99.1	74.4	102.0	174.4	275.6	301.6	324.9	
Claims on direct investors	8 585 ..	....	....	....	....	....	....	....	
Liabilities to direct investors	8 590 ..	99.1	74.4	102.0	174.4	275.6	301.6	324.9	....
Portfolio investment	8 652 ..	15.9	13.6	14.0	33.8	25.3	36.6	202.5	....
Equity securities	8 660 ..	11.1	8.8	12.3	12.9	17.5	9.2	18.5	....
Banks	8 663 ..	9.7	7.3	9.0	9.8	16.0	7.7	17.2	....
Other sectors	8 664 ..	1.4	1.5	3.3	3.2	1.5	1.6	1.3	....
Debt securities	8 669 ..	4.7	4.8	1.7	20.9	7.8	27.4	184.0	....
Bonds and notes	8 670 ..	4.7	3.2	1.7	20.9	7.8	11.5	66.7	....
Monetary authorities	8 671 ..	....	....	....	....	....	....		
General government	8 672 ..	....	....	....	....	....	....	56.9	
Banks	8 673 ..	2.2	....	1.1	.6	.4	....	....	
Other sectors	8 674 ..	2.5	3.2	.7	20.2	7.4	11.5	9.7	....
Money market instruments	8 680 ..	....	1.5	....	....	....	15.9	117.3	
Monetary authorities	8 681 ..	....	....	....	....	....	....		
General government	8 682 ..	....	....	....	....	....	15.9		
Banks	8 683 ..	....	1.5	....	....	....	....	117.3	
Other sectors	8 684 ..	....	....	....	....	....	....		
Financial derivatives	8 905 ..	....	....	....	....	....	....	....	....
Monetary authorities	8 906 ..	....	....	....	....	....	....		
General government	8 907 ..	....	....	....	....	....	....		
Banks	8 908 ..	....	....	....	....	....	....		
Other sectors	8 909 ..	....	....	....	....	....	....		
Other investment	8 753 ..	2,006.5	2,340.1	2,161.9	1,746.0	1,425.4	1,816.3	2,223.2	....
Trade credits	8 756 ..	105.8	229.6	228.5	343.0	228.4	279.2	427.5	....
General government	8 757 ..	....	....	....	....	....	....		
of which: Short-term	8 759 ..	....	....	....	....	....	....		
Other sectors	8 760 ..	105.8	229.6	228.5	343.0	228.4	279.2	427.5	
of which: Short-term	8 762 ..	*105.8*	*229.6*	*228.5*	*343.0*	*228.4*	*279.2*	*427.5*	
Loans	8 764 ..	1,727.9	1,871.6	1,763.4	1,197.1	938.3	1,256.6	1,380.1	
Monetary authorities	8 765 ..	73.1	65.3	52.8	2.6	4.2	22.4	38.8	....
of which: Use of Fund credit and loans from the Fund	8 766 ..	*73.1*	*65.3*	*52.8*	*2.6*	*4.2*	*22.4*	*38.8*	*54.5*
of which: Short-term	8 768 ..	....	....	....	....	....	....		
General government	8 769 ..	1,585.0	1,696.1	1,653.6	1,043.6	672.7	880.7	1,017.4	....
of which: Short-term	8 771 ..	....	....	....	....	....	....		
Banks	8 772 ..	19.6	32.0	29.8	55.8	48.6	39.6	67.8	
of which: Short-term	8 774 ..	*14.8*	*27.7*	*27.1*	*44.5*	*23.4*	*21.7*	*1.4*	
Other sectors	8 775 ..	50.2	78.2	27.3	95.1	212.9	313.9	256.0	....
of which: Short-term	8 777 ..	*32.1*	*58.7*	....	*70.6*	*180.3*	*170.4*	....	
Currency and deposits	8 780 ..	132.5	145.5	149.6	176.5	211.6	226.1	254.9	
Monetary authorities	8 781 ..	2.0	6.0	7.3	9.4	13.2	10.8	25.8	
General government	8 782 ..	....	....	....	....	....	....		
Banks	8 783 ..	130.5	139.5	142.3	167.1	198.5	215.3	229.1	
Other sectors	8 784 ..	....	....	....	....	....	....		
Other liabilities	8 786 ..	40.4	93.4	20.4	29.4	47.1	54.5	160.9	
Monetary authorities	8 787 ..	4.8	21.4	9.7	15.3	4.6	11.1	98.7	
of which: Short-term	8 789 ..	....	....	....	....	....	....		
General government	8 790 ..	....	....	....	....	....	....		
of which: Short-term	8 792 ..	....	....	....	....	....	....		
Banks	8 793 ..	....	....	....	....	....	....		
of which: Short-term	8 795 ..	....	....	....	....	....	....		
Other sectors	8 796 ..	35.6	72.0	10.8	14.1	42.5	43.3	62.1	
of which: Short-term	8 798 ..	....	....	....	....	....	....		
NET INTERNATIONAL INVESTMENT POSITION	8 995 ..	−1,029.6	−1,475.6	−1,366.5	−651.5	46.3	−385.1	−830.7	....
Conversion rates: CFA francs per U.S. dollar (end of period)	0 102 ..	519.36	481.58	556.04	498.07	445.59	471.34	455.34	490.91

2011, International Monetary Fund: *Balance of Payments Statistics Yearbook*

Table 1. ANALYTIC PRESENTATION, 2003–2010

(Millions of U.S. dollars)

	Code	2003	2004	2005	2006	2007	2008	2009	2010
A. Current Account[1]	4 993 Z.	....	....	....	1,252.4	1,267.1	1,239.2	578.9	829.0
Goods: exports f.o.b.	2 100 ..	....	....	....	25.8	25.1	24.9	28.7	27.5
Goods: imports f.o.b.	3 100 ..	....	....	....	−1,094.3	−1,167.1	−1,160.1	−1,066.6	−969.4
Balance on Goods	4 100 ..	....	....	....	*−1,068.6*	*−1,141.9*	*−1,135.2*	*−1,037.9*	*−941.9*
Services: credit	2 200 ..	....	....	....	1,592.0	1,650.8	1,580.1	1,328.0	1,426.5
Services: debit	3 200 ..	....	....	....	−861.9	−1,105.3	−1,042.2	−983.7	−1,007.1
Balance on Goods and Services	4 991 ..	....	....	....	*−338.5*	*−596.4*	*−597.3*	*−693.6*	*−522.4*
Income: credit	2 300 ..	....	....	....	1,920.5	2,338.8	2,402.2	1,656.7	1,688.5
Income: debit	3 300 ..	....	....	....	−322.8	−514.5	−575.0	−370.8	−310.2
Balance on Goods, Services, and Income	4 992 ..	....	....	....	*1,259.2*	*1,227.9*	*1,230.0*	*592.2*	*855.9*
Current transfers: credit	2 379 Z.	....	....	....	126.9	193.9	167.6	169.1	189.6
Current transfers: debit	3 379 ..	....	....	....	−133.7	−154.8	−158.4	−182.5	−216.5
B. Capital Account[1]	4 994 Z.	....	....	....	....	....	....	....	....
Capital account: credit	2 994 Z.	....	....	....	....	....	....	....	....
Capital account: debit	3 994 ..	....	....	....	....	....	....	....	....
Total, Groups A Plus B	4 981 ..	....	....	....	*1,252.4*	*1,267.1*	*1,239.2*	*578.9*	*829.0*
C. Financial Account[1]	4 995 W.	....	....	....	1,606.6	755.6	−1,021.0	286.1	−762.9
Direct investment abroad	4 505 ..	....	....	....	−371.7	381.0	−467.2	−123.6	−193.6
Direct investment in Bermuda	4 555 Z.	....	....	....	171.6	176.2	52.5	35.2	404.1
Portfolio investment assets	4 602 ..	....	....	....	511.9	586.7	1,947.0	−1,587.8	−1,407.8
Equity securities	4 610 ..	....	....	....	−49.9	130.9	−27.0	−62.3	5.1
Debt securities	4 619 ..	....	....	....	561.8	455.8	1,974.0	−1,525.4	−1,412.9
Portfolio investment liabilities	4 652 Z.	....	....	....	76.6	−5.3	889.8	−79.4	470.6
Equity securities	4 660 ..	....	....	....	63.8	−8.5	33.6	43.9	241.1
Debt securities	4 669 Z.	....	....	....	12.8	3.2	856.2	−123.2	229.5
Financial derivatives	4 910 ..	....	....	....	−1.0	−102.5	55.3	−161.9	−78.8
Financial derivatives assets	4 900 ..	....	....	....	44.2	−28.1	135.1	−53.5	−78.8
Financial derivatives liabilities	4 905 ..	....	....	....	−45.2	−74.5	−79.8	−108.4	.1
Other investment assets	4 703 ..	....	....	....	743.0	−650.8	−1,878.9	2,366.2	−603.7
Monetary authorities	4 701 ..	....	....	....	....	....	....	....	....
General government	4 704 ..	....	....	....	−3.4	1.0	−1.4	−3.6	3.7
Banks	4 705 ..	....	....	....	741.4	−958.4	117.6	342.8	−217.3
Other sectors	4 728 ..	....	....	....	5.0	306.5	−1,995.1	2,027.0	−390.1
Other investment liabilities	4 753 W.	....	....	....	476.2	370.3	−1,619.5	−162.7	646.2
Monetary authorities	4 753 WA	....	....	....	....	....	....	....	....
General government	4 753 ZB	....	....	....	....	....	....	....	....
Banks	4 753 ZC	....	....	....	510.3	398.3	−1,098.1	−311.3	801.0
Other sectors	4 753 ZD	....	....	....	−34.2	−28.0	−521.4	148.6	−154.9
Total, Groups A Through C	4 983 ..	....	....	....	*2,859.0*	*2,022.6*	*218.2*	*864.9*	*66.0*
D. Net Errors and Omissions	4 998 ..	....	....	....	−2,848.7	−2,015.4	−228.8	−847.1	−62.9
Total, Groups A Through D	4 984 ..	....	....	....	*10.3*	*7.3*	*−10.6*	*17.8*	*3.1*
E. Reserves and Related Items	4 802 A.	....	....	....	−10.3	−7.3	10.6	−17.8	−3.1
Reserve assets	4 802 ..	....	....	....	−10.3	−7.3	10.6	−17.8	−3.1
Use of Fund credit and loans	4 766 ..	....	....	....	....	....	....	....	....
Exceptional financing	4 920 ..	....	....	....	....	....	....	....	....
Conversion rates: Bermuda dollars per U.S. dollar	0 101 ..	1.00	1.00	1.00	1.00	1.00	1.00	....	....

[1] Excludes components that have been classified in the categories of Group E.

Table 2. STANDARD PRESENTATION, 2003–2010
(Millions of U.S. dollars)

	Code	2003	2004	2005	2006	2007	2008	2009	2010
CURRENT ACCOUNT............................	4 993 ..	....	....	....	**1,252.4**	**1,267.1**	**1,239.2**	**578.9**	**829.0**
A. GOODS................................	4 100 ..	....	....	....	**−1,068.6**	**−1,141.9**	**−1,135.2**	**−1,037.9**	**−941.9**
Credit.............................	2 100 ..	....	....	....	**25.8**	**25.1**	**24.9**	**28.7**	**27.5**
General merchandise: exports f.o.b...........	2 110 ..				22.0	20.6	18.8	24.9	24.6
Goods for processing: exports f.o.b.........	2 150 ..	....	....	....	....	....	.1	....	.8
Repairs on goods.............................	2 160 ..	....	....	....	.3	....	....	....	.2
Goods procured in ports by carriers.........	2 170 ..	....	....	....	3.4	4.5	6.0	3.7	2.0
Nonmonetary gold............................	2 180 ..				....	....	....	....	
Debit................................	3 100 ..	....	....	....	**−1,094.3**	**−1,167.1**	**−1,160.1**	**−1,066.6**	**−969.4**
General merchandise: imports f.o.b..........	3 110 ..	....	....	....	−1,089.9	−1,163.1	−1,155.0	−1,061.4	−963.1
Goods for processing: imports f.o.b.........	3 150 ..								
Repairs on goods.............................	3 160 ..	....	....	....	....	−1.3	−.9	−2.3	−3.5
Goods procured in ports by carriers.........	3 170 ..				−4.5	−2.7	−4.2	−2.9	−2.7
Nonmonetary gold............................	3 180 ..				....	....	....	....	....
B. SERVICES.............................	4 200 ..	....	....	....	**730.1**	**545.5**	**538.0**	**344.3**	**419.4**
Total credit................................	2 200 ..	....	....	....	*1,592.0*	*1,650.8*	*1,580.1*	*1,328.0*	*1,426.5*
Total debit................................	3 200 ..	....	....	....	*−861.9*	*−1,105.3*	*−1,042.2*	*−983.7*	*−1,007.1*
Transportation services, credit...........	2 205 ..	....	....	....	**37.2**	**45.2**	**42.8**	**33.2**	**33.2**
Passenger..................................	2 850 ..				....	....	....	....	....
Freight....................................	2 851 ..				*.4*	....	....	*.1*	*6.0*
Other......................................	2 852 ..				*36.8*	*45.1*	*42.7*	*33.2*	*27.1*
Sea transport, passenger....................	2 207 ..				....	....	....	....	....
Sea transport, freight......................	2 208 ..				.4	....	....	.1	6.0
Sea transport, other........................	2 209 ..				11.0	14.7	16.8	12.2	10.5
Air transport, passenger....................	2 211 ..				....	....	....	....	....
Air transport, freight......................	2 212 ..				....	....	....	....	....
Air transport, other........................	2 213 ..				25.8	30.4	25.9	21.0	16.6
Other transport, passenger..................	2 215 ..				....	....	....	....	....
Other transport, freight....................	2 216 ..				....	....	....	....	....
Other transport, other......................	2 217 ..				....	....	....	....	....
Transportation services, debit...........	3 205 ..	....	....	....	**−308.3**	**−376.0**	**−348.1**	**−274.6**	**−268.8**
Passenger..................................	3 850 ..				*−126.0*	*−164.6*	*−151.7*	*−112.4*	*−116.1*
Freight....................................	3 851 ..				*−137.5*	*−164.1*	*−154.1*	*−138.3*	*−128.1*
Other......................................	3 852 ..				*−44.9*	*−47.4*	*−42.3*	*−24.0*	*−24.7*
Sea transport, passenger....................	3 207 ..				....	....	....	....	....
Sea transport, freight......................	3 208 ..				−133.9	−156.5	−146.9	−134.1	−125.8
Sea transport, other........................	3 209 ..				−32.7	−34.8	−33.8	−19.3	−19.3
Air transport, passenger....................	3 211 ..				−126.0	−164.6	−151.7	−112.4	−116.1
Air transport, freight......................	3 212 ..				−3.6	−7.5	−7.3	−4.2	−2.3
Air transport, other........................	3 213 ..				−12.2	−12.6	−8.5	....	....
Other transport, passenger..................	3 215 ..				....	....	....	....	....
Other transport, freight....................	3 216 ..				....	....	....	....	....
Other transport, other......................	3 217 ..				....	....	....	−4.6	−5.3
Travel, credit...........................	2 236 ..	....	....	....	**494.6**	**568.7**	**430.5**	**362.8**	**422.4**
Business travel..............................	2 237 ..				99.1	123.0	108.8	79.7	97.5
Personal travel..............................	2 240 ..				395.5	445.7	321.8	283.0	324.9
Travel, debit............................	3 236 ..	....	....	....	**−268.5**	**−288.4**	**−306.6**	**−294.6**	**−301.0**
Business travel..............................	3 237 ..				−10.1	−12.4	−15.2	−10.9	−11.8
Personal travel..............................	3 240 ..				−258.4	−276.0	−291.4	−283.7	−289.2
Other services, credit...................	2 200 BA	....	....	....	**1,060.2**	**1,037.0**	**1,106.8**	**932.0**	**970.9**
Communications..............................	2 245 ..				77.5	86.2	91.9	75.1	68.3
Construction................................	2 249 ..				64.2	44.6	49.0	34.3	34.7
Insurance...................................	2 253 ..				39.5	91.4	75.9	46.5	42.9
Financial...................................	2 260 ..				206.6	249.3	243.4	175.0	216.1
Computer and information....................	2 262 ..				57.9	48.5	52.0	43.5	37.2
Royalties and licence fees..................	2 266 ..				.2	....	.1	....	....
Other business services.....................	2 268 ..				512.1	483.3	540.8	502.4	510.4
Personal, cultural, and recreational........	2 287 ..				....	2.4	1.0	1.6	1.8
Government, n.i.e............................	2 291 ..				102.0	31.3	52.7	53.6	59.7
Other services, debit....................	3 200 BA	....	....	....	**−285.1**	**−440.9**	**−387.5**	**−414.6**	**−437.2**
Communications..............................	3 245 ..				−13.6	−23.3	−28.7	−28.4	−30.5
Construction................................	3 249 ..				....	....	−3.3	−1.4	−16.6
Insurance...................................	3 253 ..				−77.0	−137.9	−92.9	−116.5	−92.9
Financial...................................	3 260 ..				−15.3	−22.0	−34.9	−30.6	−45.1
Computer and information....................	3 262 ..				−31.4	−28.0	−44.3	−55.2	−66.3
Royalties and licence fees..................	3 266 ..				−4.7	−4.7	−8.7	−9.3	−8.8
Other business services.....................	3 268 ..				−117.8	−200.6	−153.6	−155.3	−158.5
Personal, cultural, and recreational........	3 287 ..				−.1	−.1	−.1	−.1	....
Government, n.i.e............................	3 291 ..				−25.3	−24.4	−20.9	−17.8	−18.6

Table 2 (Continued). STANDARD PRESENTATION, 2003–2010

(Millions of U.S. dollars)

	Code	2003	2004	2005	2006	2007	2008	2009	2010
C. INCOME	4 300	....	....	....	**1,597.7**	**1,824.3**	**1,827.2**	**1,285.9**	**1,378.3**
Total credit	2 300	....	....	....	*1,920.5*	*2,338.8*	*2,402.2*	*1,656.7*	*1,688.5*
Total debit	3 300	....	....	....	*–322.8*	*–514.5*	*–575.0*	*–370.8*	*–310.2*
Compensation of employees, credit	2 310	....	....	....	**1,182.5**	**1,452.1**	**1,594.2**	**1,345.5**	**1,356.3**
Compensation of employees, debit	3 310	....	....	....	**–67.0**	**–70.4**	**–68.5**	**–70.9**	**–85.7**
Investment income, credit	2 320	....	....	....	**738.0**	**886.8**	**808.0**	**311.2**	**332.2**
Direct investment income	2 330	....	....	....	191.6	215.2	311.8	102.5	88.4
Dividends and distributed branch profits	2 332	....	....	....	133.7	136.1	208.8	89.5	105.3
Reinvested earnings and undistributed branch profits	2 333	....	....	....	55.5	75.2	98.9	10.4	–19.2
Income on debt (interest)	2 334	....	....	....	2.4	3.8	4.1	2.6	2.2
Portfolio investment income	2 339	....	....	....	464.9	586.5	443.1	181.8	220.7
Income on equity	2 340	....	....	....	82.2	161.2	104.1	47.3	97.0
Income on bonds and notes	2 350	....	....	....	247.6	291.5	213.1	98.5	88.4
Income on money market instruments	2 360	....	....	....	135.1	133.8	125.8	36.0	35.3
Other investment income	2 370	....	....	....	81.5	85.1	53.2	26.9	23.1
Investment income, debit	3 320	....	....	....	**–255.8**	**–444.1**	**–506.5**	**–299.9**	**–224.5**
Direct investment income	3 330	....	....	....	–45.7	–194.1	–282.6	–176.3	–159.9
Dividends and distributed branch profits	3 332	....	....	....	–16.4	–171.0	–257.7	–166.9	–155.5
Reinvested earnings and undistributed branch profits	3 333	....	....	....	–22.6	–.7	–.2	....	–.1
Income on debt (interest)	3 334	....	....	....	–6.7	–22.4	–24.7	–9.4	–4.4
Portfolio investment income	3 339	....	....	....	–84.6	–118.0	–155.6	–91.2	–18.7
Income on equity	3 340	....	....	....	–18.4	–21.3	–63.7	–57.0	–1.9
Income on bonds and notes	3 350	....	....	....	–14.4	–29.3	–14.8	–16.1	–13.2
Income on money market instruments	3 360	....	....	....	–51.8	–67.3	–77.1	–18.2	–3.6
Other investment income	3 370	....	....	....	–125.6	–132.1	–68.4	–32.4	–45.9
D. CURRENT TRANSFERS	4 379	....	....	....	**–6.8**	**39.1**	**9.3**	**–13.4**	**–26.9**
Credit	2 379	....	....	....	**126.9**	**193.9**	**167.6**	**169.1**	**189.6**
General government	2 380	....	....	....	86.9	107.2	123.4	125.0	148.5
Other sectors	2 390	....	....	....	40.0	86.7	44.2	44.1	41.0
Workers' remittances	2 391	....	....	....	....	....	....	....	....
Other current transfers	2 392	....	....	....	40.0	86.7	44.2	44.1	41.0
Debit	3 379	....	....	....	**–133.7**	**–154.8**	**–158.4**	**–182.5**	**–216.5**
General government	3 380	....	....	....	–1.9	–2.8	–6.1	–4.9	–2.9
Other sectors	3 390	....	....	....	–131.8	–152.0	–152.3	–177.6	–213.6
Workers' remittances	3 391	....	....	....	–104.6	–108.6	–113.7	–115.8	–116.5
Other current transfers	3 392	....	....	....	–27.2	–43.4	–38.5	–61.7	–97.1
CAPITAL AND FINANCIAL ACCOUNT	4 996	....	....	....	**1,596.3**	**748.3**	**–1,010.4**	**268.2**	**–766.1**
CAPITAL ACCOUNT	4 994	....	....	....	....	....	....	....	....
Total credit	2 994	....	....	....	....	....	....	....	....
Total debit	3 994	....	....	....	....	....	....	....	....
Capital transfers, credit	2 400	....	....	....	....	....	....	....	....
General government	2 401	....	....	....	....	....	....	....	....
Debt forgiveness	2 402	....	....	....	....	....	....	....	....
Other capital transfers	2 410	....	....	....	....	....	....	....	....
Other sectors	2 430	....	....	....	....	....	....	....	....
Migrants' transfers	2 431	....	....	....	....	....	....	....	....
Debt forgiveness	2 432	....	....	....	....	....	....	....	....
Other capital transfers	2 440	....	....	....	....	....	....	....	....
Capital transfers, debit	3 400	....	....	....	....	....	....	....	....
General government	3 401	....	....	....	....	....	....	....	....
Debt forgiveness	3 402	....	....	....	....	....	....	....	....
Other capital transfers	3 410	....	....	....	....	....	....	....	....
Other sectors	3 430	....	....	....	....	....	....	....	....
Migrants' transfers	3 431	....	....	....	....	....	....	....	....
Debt forgiveness	3 432	....	....	....	....	....	....	....	....
Other capital transfers	3 440	....	....	....	....	....	....	....	....
Nonproduced nonfinancial assets, credit	2 480	....	....	....	....	....	....	....	....
Nonproduced nonfinancial assets, debit	3 480	....	....	....	....	....	....	....	....

Table 2 (Continued). STANDARD PRESENTATION, 2003–2010

(Millions of U.S. dollars)

	Code	2003	2004	2005	2006	2007	2008	2009	2010
FINANCIAL ACCOUNT....................	4 995 ..	....	....	....	**1,596.3**	**748.3**	**−1,010.4**	**268.2**	**−766.1**
A. DIRECT INVESTMENT................	4 500 ..	....	....	....	**−200.1**	**557.2**	**−414.7**	**−88.5**	**210.6**
Direct investment abroad............	4 505 ..	....	....	....	**−371.7**	**381.0**	**−467.2**	**−123.6**	**−193.6**
Equity capital.............................	4 510 ..	....	....	....	−42.8	−38.7	−196.3	−34.5	23.6
Claims on affiliated enterprises........	4 515 ..	....	....	....	−41.9	−31.1	−196.3	−34.4	23.6
Liabilities to affiliated enterprises......	4 520 ..	....	....	....	−.9	−7.7	....	−.1	....
Reinvested earnings.....................	4 525 ..	....	....	....	−55.5	−75.2	−98.9	−10.4	19.2
Other capital.............................	4 530 ..	....	....	....	−273.4	494.9	−172.0	−78.8	−236.3
Claims on affiliated enterprises........	4 535 ..	....	....	....	−45.7	−23.3	−29.5	45.7	6.5
Liabilities to affiliated enterprises......	4 540 ..	....	....	....	−227.7	518.2	−142.5	−124.4	−242.8
Direct investment in Bermuda........	4 555 ..	....	....	....	**171.6**	**176.2**	**52.5**	**35.2**	**404.1**
Equity capital.............................	4 560 ..	....	....	....	149.1	188.5	39.5	45.7	404.6
Claims on direct investors.............	4 565 ..	....	....	....	31.2	40.9	−.7	−11.8	−35.0
Liabilities to direct investors..........	4 570 ..	....	....	....	117.9	147.6	40.2	57.5	439.6
Reinvested earnings.....................	4 575 ..	....	....	....	22.6	.7	.2	....	.1
Other capital.............................	4 580 ..	....	....	....	....	−12.9	12.8	−10.5	−.5
Claims on direct investors.............	4 585 ..	....	....	....	....	....	....	....	....
Liabilities to direct investors..........	4 590 ..	....	....	....	....	−12.9	12.8	−10.5	−.5
B. PORTFOLIO INVESTMENT............	4 600 ..	....	....	....	**588.5**	**581.4**	**2,836.8**	**−1,667.1**	**−937.2**
Assets.............................	4 602 ..	....	....	....	**511.9**	**586.7**	**1,947.0**	**−1,587.8**	**−1,407.8**
Equity securities........................	4 610 ..	....	....	....	−49.9	130.9	−27.0	−62.3	5.1
Monetary authorities..................	4 611 ..	....	....	....					
General government...................	4 612 ..	....	....	....	−12.0	....	....	−34.0	−30.0
Banks.................................	4 613 ..	....	....	....	10.2	−17.6	5.8	7.8	16.8
Other sectors.........................	4 614 ..	....	....	....	−48.2	148.5	−32.9	−36.1	18.3
Debt securities..........................	4 619 ..	....	....	....	561.8	455.8	1,974.0	−1,525.4	−1,412.9
Bonds and notes......................	4 620 ..	....	....	....	171.2	374.6	409.6	620.4	−380.1
Monetary authorities................	4 621 ..	....	....	....	....	....	....	....	....
General government.................	4 622 ..	....	....	....					
Banks...............................	4 623 ..	....	....	....	203.8	367.7	443.6	581.5	−380.8
Other sectors.......................	4 624 ..	....	....	....	−32.6	7.0	−34.0	38.9	.7
Money market instruments............	4 630 ..	....	....	....	390.6	81.2	1,564.4	−2,145.8	−1,032.8
Monetary authorities................	4 631 ..	....	....	....	....	....	....	....	....
General government.................	4 632 ..	....	....	....					
Banks...............................	4 633 ..	....	....	....	394.2	77.7	1,567.0	−2,138.6	−947.6
Other sectors.......................	4 634 ..	....	....	....	−3.6	3.5	−2.6	−7.2	−85.2
Liabilities...........................	4 652 ..	....	....	....	**76.6**	**−5.3**	**889.8**	**−79.4**	**470.6**
Equity securities........................	4 660 ..	....	....	....	63.8	−8.5	33.6	43.9	241.1
Banks.................................	4 663 ..	....	....	....	55.9	−8.4	35.8	41.8	227.4
Other sectors.........................	4 664 ..	....	....	....	7.9	−.1	−2.2	2.1	13.8
Debt securities..........................	4 669 ..	....	....	....	12.8	3.2	856.2	−123.2	229.5
Bonds and notes......................	4 670 ..	....	....	....	12.8	3.2	2.5	−.1	3.7
Monetary authorities................	4 671 ..	....	....	....	....	....	....	....	....
General government.................	4 672 ..	....	....	....	....	....	....	....	....
Banks...............................	4 673 ..	....	....	....	12.8	2.9	2.8	−.1	3.5
Other sectors.......................	4 674 ..	....	....	....	....	.3	−.3	....	.3
Money market instruments............	4 680 ..	....	....	....	.1	....	853.7	−123.2	225.7
Monetary authorities................	4 681 ..	....	....	....					
General government.................	4 682 ..	....	....	....	....				
Banks...............................	4 683 ..	....	....	....	.1	....	853.7	−123.2	225.7
Other sectors.......................	4 684 ..	....	....	....	....	....	....	....	....
C. FINANCIAL DERIVATIVES............	4 910 ..	....	....	....	**−1.0**	**−102.5**	**55.3**	**−161.9**	**−78.8**
Monetary authorities.....................	4 911 ..	....	....	....	....	....	....	....	....
General government......................	4 912 ..	....	....	....	....	....	....	....	....
Banks....................................	4 913 ..	....	....	....	....	−.1	9.7	−11.5	2.1
Other sectors............................	4 914 ..	....	....	....	−1.0	−102.5	45.6	−150.4	−80.9
Assets.............................	4 900 ..	....	....	....	**44.2**	**−28.1**	**135.1**	**−53.5**	**−78.8**
Monetary authorities....................	4 901 ..	....	....	....	....	....	....	....	....
General government.....................	4 902 ..	....	....	....	....	....	....	....	....
Banks...................................	4 903 ..	....	....	....	45.2	74.4	89.5	98.1	3.2
Other sectors...........................	4 904 ..	....	....	....	−1.0	−102.5	45.6	−151.6	−82.1
Liabilities...........................	4 905 ..	....	....	....	**−45.2**	**−74.5**	**−79.8**	**−108.4**	**.1**
Monetary authorities....................	4 906 ..	....	....	....	....	....	....	....	....
General government.....................	4 907 ..	....	....	....	....	....	....	....	....
Banks...................................	4 908 ..	....	....	....	−45.2	−74.5	−79.8	−109.6	−1.1
Other sectors...........................	4 909 ..	....	....	....	....	....	....	1.2	1.2

Table 2 (Concluded). STANDARD PRESENTATION, 2003–2010

(Millions of U.S. dollars)

	Code	2003	2004	2005	2006	2007	2008	2009	2010
D. OTHER INVESTMENT	4 700	....	....	....	1,219.2	−280.5	−3,498.4	2,203.5	42.5
Assets	4 703	....	....	....	743.0	−650.8	−1,878.9	2,366.2	−603.7
Trade credits	4 706	....	....	....	....	−.2	−.8	.3	−.5
General government	4 707	....	....	....	....	....	....	....	....
of which: Short-term	4 709	....	....	....	....	....	....	....	....
Other sectors	4 710	....	....	....	....	−.2	−.8	.3	−.5
of which: Short-term	4 712	....	....	....	....	−.2	−.8	.3	−.5
Loans	4 714	....	....	....	−45.5	342.4	−2,022.8	1,972.3	−375.0
Monetary authorities	4 715	....	....	....	....	....	....	....	....
of which: Short-term	4 718	....	....	....	....	....	....	....	....
General government	4 719	....	....	....	....	....	....	....	....
of which: Short-term	4 721	....	....	....	....	....	....	....	....
Banks	4 722	....	....	....	....	....	....	....	....
of which: Short-term	4 724	....	....	....	....	....	....	....	....
Other sectors	4 725	....	....	....	−45.5	342.4	−2,022.8	1,972.3	−375.0
of which: Short-term	4 727	....	....	....	−33.6	344.9	−2,021.3	1,995.0	−359.7
Currency and deposits	4 730	....	....	....	737.6	−958.7	114.4	339.1	−229.3
Monetary authorities	4 731	....	....	....	....	....	....	....	....
General government	4 732	....	....	....	−3.4	1.0	−1.4	−3.6	3.7
Banks	4 733	....	....	....	741.4	−958.4	117.6	342.8	−217.3
Other sectors	4 734	....	....	....	−.4	−1.3	−1.8	−.2	−15.7
Other assets	4 736	....	....	....	50.9	−34.4	30.3	54.6	1.0
Monetary authorities	4 737	....	....	....	....	....	....	....	....
of which: Short-term	4 739	....	....	....	....	....	....	....	....
General government	4 740	....	....	....	....	....	....	....	....
of which: Short-term	4 742	....	....	....	....	....	....	....	....
Banks	4 743	....	....	....	....	....	....	....	....
of which: Short-term	4 745	....	....	....	....	....	....	....	....
Other sectors	4 746	....	....	....	50.9	−34.4	30.3	54.6	1.0
of which: Short-term	4 748	....	....	....	53.5	−30.5	31.4	55.6	−.1
Liabilities	4 753	....	....	....	476.2	370.3	−1,619.5	−162.7	646.2
Trade credits	4 756	....	....	....	....	....	4.8	....	−.4
General government	4 757	....	....	....	....	....	....	....	....
of which: Short-term	4 759	....	....	....	....	....	....	....	....
Other sectors	4 760	....	....	....	....	....	4.8	....	−.4
of which: Short-term	4 762	....	....	....	....	....	4.8	....	−.4
Loans	4 764	....	....	....	−16.3	59.2	−478.3	158.9	−133.8
Monetary authorities	4 765	....	....	....	....	....	....	....	....
of which: Use of Fund credit and loans from the Fund	4 766	....	....	....	....	....	....	....	....
of which: Short-term	4 768	....	....	....	....	....	....	....	....
General government	4 769	....	....	....	....	....	....	....	....
of which: Short-term	4 771	....	....	....	....	....	....	....	....
Banks	4 772	....	....	....	....	....	....	....	....
of which: Short-term	4 774	....	....	....	....	....	....	....	....
Other sectors	4 775	....	....	....	−16.3	59.2	−478.3	158.9	−133.8
of which: Short-term	4 777	....	....	....	−.1	13.1	.7	−1.5	.6
Currency and deposits	4 780	....	....	....	493.3	405.7	−1,101.9	−314.8	801.0
Monetary authorities	4 781	....	....	....	....	....	....	....	....
General government	4 782	....	....	....	....	....	....	....	....
Banks	4 783	....	....	....	510.3	398.3	−1,098.1	−311.3	801.0
Other sectors	4 784	....	....	....	−17.0	7.4	−3.9	−3.5	....
Other liabilities	4 786	....	....	....	−.9	−94.6	−44.0	−6.7	−20.6
Monetary authorities	4 787	....	....	....	....	....	....	....	....
of which: Short-term	4 789	....	....	....	....	....	....	....	....
General government	4 790	....	....	....	....	....	....	....	....
of which: Short-term	4 792	....	....	....	....	....	....	....	....
Banks	4 793	....	....	....	....	....	....	....	....
of which: Short-term	4 795	....	....	....	....	....	....	....	....
Other sectors	4 796	....	....	....	−.9	−94.6	−44.0	−6.7	−20.6
of which: Short-term	4 798	....	....	....	3.1	−88.6	−37.6	−9.8	−16.6
E. RESERVE ASSETS	4 802	....	....	....	−10.3	−7.3	10.6	−17.8	−3.1
Monetary gold	4 812	....	....	....	....	....	....	....	....
Special drawing rights	4 811	....	....	....	....	....	....	....	....
Reserve position in the Fund	4 810	....	....	....	....	....	....	....	....
Foreign exchange	4 803	....	....	....	−10.3	−7.3	10.6	−17.8	−3.1
Other claims	4 813	....	....	....	....	....	....	....	....
NET ERRORS AND OMISSIONS	4 998	....	....	....	−2,848.7	−2,015.4	−228.8	−847.1	−62.9

Table 1. ANALYTIC PRESENTATION, FISCAL YEARS 2003–2010 ENDING JUNE 30

(Millions of U.S. dollars)

	Code	2003	2004	2005	2006	2007	2008	2009	2010
A. Current Account[1]	4 993 Z.	....	....	....	−79.1	143.4	−28.1	−20.2	−139.4
Goods: exports f.o.b.	2 100 ..	....	....	....	312.0	573.3	598.8	516.1	544.5
Goods: imports f.o.b.	3 100 ..	....	....	....	−479.7	−526.6	−671.2	−606.6	−843.3
Balance on Goods	4 100 ..	....	....	....	*−167.6*	*46.7*	*−72.4*	*−90.5*	*−298.8*
Services: credit	2 200 ..	....	....	....	51.7	60.2	54.7	56.5	68.7
Services: debit	3 200 ..	....	....	....	−61.0	−57.1	−93.4	−75.4	−90.5
Balance on Goods and Services	4 991 ..	....	....	....	*−176.9*	*49.8*	*−111.1*	*−109.4*	*−320.5*
Income: credit	2 300 ..	....	....	....	18.2	24.5	34.6	21.2	16.3
Income: debit	3 300 ..	....	....	....	−25.2	−26.5	−68.8	−57.8	−77.1
Balance on Goods, Services, and Income	4 992 ..	....	....	....	*−183.9*	*47.8*	*−145.3*	*−146.0*	*−381.3*
Current transfers: credit	2 379 Z.	....	....	....	163.5	147.9	168.4	161.5	277.5
Current transfers: debit	3 379 ..	....	....	....	−58.7	−52.2	−51.2	−35.7	−35.6
B. Capital Account[1]	4 994 Z.	....	....	....	**39.1**	**25.2**	**15.7**	**29.6**	**79.7**
Capital account: credit	2 994 Z.	....	....	....	39.1	25.2	15.7	29.6	79.7
Capital account: debit	3 994 ..	....	....	....	....	....	....	....	....
Total, Groups A Plus B	4 981 ..	....	....	....	*−40.0*	*168.6*	*−12.4*	*9.4*	*−59.7*
C. Financial Account[1]	4 995 W.	....	....	....	**91.5**	**90.7**	**42.3**	**79.4**	**104.8**
Direct investment abroad	4 505 ..	....	....	....	....	....	....	....	....
Direct investment in Bhutan	4 555 Z.	....	....	....	6.1	73.8	3.1	6.5	19.0
Portfolio investment assets	4 602 ..	....	....	....	....	....	....	....	....
Equity securities	4 610 ..	....	....	....	....	....	....	....	....
Debt securities	4 619 ..	....	....	....	....	....	....	....	....
Portfolio investment liabilities	4 652 Z.	....	....	....	....	....	....	....	....
Equity securities	4 660 ..	....	....	....	....	....	....	....	....
Debt securities	4 669 Z.	....	....	....	....	....	....	....	....
Financial derivatives	4 910 ..	....	....	....	....	....	....	....	....
Financial derivatives assets	4 900 ..	....	....	....	....	....	....	....	....
Financial derivatives liabilities	4 905 ..	....	....	....	....	....	....	....	....
Other investment assets	4 703 ..	....	....	....	....	....	1.6	−.2	−.2
Monetary authorities	4 701 ..	....	....	....	....	....	.8	−.5	....
General government	4 704 ..	....	....	....	....	....	....	....	....
Banks	4 705 ..	....	....	....	....	....	.8	−.1	.3
Other sectors	4 728 ..	....	....	....	....	....	.1	.4	−.5
Other investment liabilities	4 753 W.	....	....	....	85.4	16.9	37.6	73.1	86.0
Monetary authorities	4 753 WA	....	....	....	....	....	55.2	−20.3	21.0
General government	4 753 ZB	....	....	....	77.7	17.7	−12.8	87.8	61.2
Banks	4 753 ZC	....	....	....	....	....	−2.9	6.5	6.0
Other sectors	4 753 ZD	....	....	....	7.8	−.9	−1.8	−.8	−2.1
Total, Groups A Through C	4 983 ..	....	....	....	*51.6*	*259.2*	*30.0*	*88.8*	*45.1*
D. Net Errors and Omissions	4 998 ..	....	....	....	**64.9**	**−136.5**	**30.6**	**25.8**	**61.4**
Total, Groups A Through D	4 984 ..	....	....	....	*116.5*	*122.7*	*60.6*	*114.6*	*106.5*
E. Reserves and Related Items	4 802 A.	....	....	....	**−116.5**	**−122.7**	**−60.6**	**−114.6**	**−106.5**
Reserve assets	4 802 ..	....	....	....	−116.5	−122.7	−60.6	−114.6	−106.5
Use of Fund credit and loans	4 766 ..	....	....	....	....	....	....	....	....
Exceptional financing	4 920 ..	....	....	....	....	....	....	....	....
Conversion rates: ngultrum per U.S. dollar	0 101 ..	**47.9308**	**45.4116**	**44.6086**	**44.7401**	**44.1904**	**40.3660**	**47.7769**	**46.6527**

[1] Excludes components that have been classified in the categories of Group E.

Table 2. STANDARD PRESENTATION, FISCAL YEARS 2003–2010 ENDING JUNE 30

(Millions of U.S. dollars)

	Code	2003	2004	2005	2006	2007	2008	2009	2010
CURRENT ACCOUNT	4 993	....	....	....	**−79.1**	**143.4**	**−28.1**	**−20.2**	**−139.4**
A. GOODS	4 100	....	....	....	**−167.6**	**46.7**	**−72.4**	**−90.5**	**−298.8**
Credit	2 100	....	....	....	**312.0**	**573.3**	**598.8**	**516.1**	**544.5**
General merchandise: exports f.o.b.	2 110	....	....	....	312.0	573.3	598.8	516.1	544.5
Goods for processing: exports f.o.b.	2 150	....	....	....	....	....	....	....	....
Repairs on goods	2 160	....	....	....	....	....	....	....	....
Goods procured in ports by carriers	2 170	....	....	....	....	....	....	....	....
Nonmonetary gold	2 180	....	....	....	....	....	....	....	....
Debit	3 100	....	....	....	**−479.7**	**−526.6**	**−671.2**	**−606.6**	**−843.3**
General merchandise: imports f.o.b.	3 110	....	....	....	−452.8	−519.2	−661.3	−598.2	−836.4
Goods for processing: imports f.o.b.	3 150	....	....	....	....	....	....	....	....
Repairs on goods	3 160	....	....	....	....	....	....	....	....
Goods procured in ports by carriers	3 170	....	....	....	−26.9	−7.4	−9.9	−8.4	−6.8
Nonmonetary gold	3 180	....	....	....	....	....	....	....	....
B. SERVICES	4 200	....	....	....	**−9.3**	**3.1**	**−38.7**	**−18.9**	**−21.8**
Total credit	2 200	....	....	....	*51.7*	*60.2*	*54.7*	*56.5*	*68.7*
Total debit	3 200	....	....	....	*−61.0*	*−57.1*	*−93.4*	*−75.4*	*−90.5*
Transportation services, credit	2 205	....	....	....	**12.5**	**18.6**	**10.2**	**8.6**	**23.6**
Passenger	2 850	....	....	....	*12.5*	*18.6*	*10.2*	*8.6*	*23.5*
Freight	2 851	....	....	....	....	....	....	....	*.1*
Other	2 852	....	....	....	....	....	....	....	....
Sea transport, passenger	2 207	....	....	....	....	....	....	....	....
Sea transport, freight	2 208	....	....	....	....	....	....	....	....
Sea transport, other	2 209	....	....	....	....	....	....	....	....
Air transport, passenger	2 211	....	....	....	12.5	18.6	10.2	8.6	23.5
Air transport, freight	2 212	....	....	....	....	....	....	....	.1
Air transport, other	2 213	....	....	....	....	....	....	....	....
Other transport, passenger	2 215	....	....	....	....	....	....	....	....
Other transport, freight	2 216	....	....	....	....	....	....	....	....
Other transport, other	2 217	....	....	....	....	....	....	....	....
Transportation services, debit	3 205	....	....	....	**−2.2**	**−3.6**	**−4.9**	**−4.6**	**−4.9**
Passenger	3 850	....	....	....	....	....	*−.8*	*−1.2*	*−1.6*
Freight	3 851	....	....	....	*−.1*	*−.2*	*−.2*	....	*−.1*
Other	3 852	....	....	....	*−2.1*	*−3.4*	*−3.9*	*−3.3*	*−3.2*
Sea transport, passenger	3 207	....	....	....	....	....	....	....	....
Sea transport, freight	3 208	....	....	....	....	....	....	....	....
Sea transport, other	3 209	....	....	....	....	....	....	....	....
Air transport, passenger	3 211	....	....	....	....	....	−.8	−1.2	−1.6
Air transport, freight	3 212	....	....	....	....	....	....	....	....
Air transport, other	3 213	....	....	....	−2.1	−3.4	−3.9	−3.3	−3.2
Other transport, passenger	3 215	....	....	....	....	....	....	....	....
Other transport, freight	3 216	....	....	....	−.1	−.2	−.2	....	−.1
Other transport, other	3 217	....	....	....	....	....	....	....	....
Travel, credit	2 236	....	....	....	**23.0**	**28.3**	**36.4**	**42.3**	**39.9**
Business travel	2 237	....	....	....	....	....	....	....	....
Personal travel	2 240	....	....	....	23.0	28.2	36.4	42.3	39.9
Travel, debit	3 236	....	....	....	**−22.4**	**−26.0**	**−64.5**	**−33.0**	**−41.3**
Business travel	3 237	....	....	....	−3.7	−4.7	−34.9	−5.9	−6.0
Personal travel	3 240	....	....	....	−18.7	−21.3	−29.6	−27.0	−35.3
Other services, credit	2 200 BA	....	....	....	**16.2**	**13.4**	**8.0**	**5.5**	**5.2**
Communications	2 245	....	....	....	1.1	1.0	1.1	.9	.6
Construction	2 249	....	....	....	....	....	....	....	....
Insurance	2 253	....	....	....	5.2	1.4	1.7	1.6	1.5
Financial	2 260	....	....	....	....	....	....	....	1.0
Computer and information	2 262	....	....	....	....	....	....	....	....
Royalties and licence fees	2 266	....	....	....	.2	.1	.2	....	....
Other business services	2 268	....	....	....	....	2.5	1.1	....	....
Personal, cultural, and recreational	2 287	....	....	....	....	....	....	....	....
Government, n.i.e.	2 291	....	....	....	9.7	8.4	4.0	3.0	2.0
Other services, debit	3 200 BA	....	....	....	**−36.3**	**−27.5**	**−23.9**	**−37.9**	**−44.3**
Communications	3 245	....	....	....	−.7	−.7	−1.1	−1.6	−1.8
Construction	3 249	....	....	....	−27.6	−17.2	−16.0	−22.0	−22.1
Insurance	3 253	....	....	....	−1.9	−.4	−.8	−.9	−1.7
Financial	3 260	....	....	....	....	−.1	....	−.3	−.1
Computer and information	3 262	....	....	....	−.1	−.1	−.2	−.6	−.5
Royalties and licence fees	3 266	....	....	....	....	−.1	−.1	−.4	−.2
Other business services	3 268	....	....	....	−2.8	−5.6	−2.5	−8.0	−13.1
Personal, cultural, and recreational	3 287	....	....	....	....	....	....	....	....
Government, n.i.e.	3 291	....	....	....	−3.2	−3.3	−3.2	−4.1	−5.0

Table 2 (Continued). STANDARD PRESENTATION, FISCAL YEARS 2003–2010 ENDING JUNE 30

(Millions of U.S. dollars)

	Code	2003	2004	2005	2006	2007	2008	2009	2010
C. INCOME	4 300	....	....	....	**−7.0**	**−2.0**	**−34.2**	**−36.6**	**−60.8**
Total credit	2 300	....	....	....	*18.2*	*24.5*	*34.6*	*21.2*	*16.3*
Total debit	3 300	....	....	....	*−25.2*	*−26.5*	*−68.8*	*−57.8*	*−77.1*
Compensation of employees, credit	2 310	....	....	....	**1.0**	**1.3**	**1.6**	**1.8**	**1.5**
Compensation of employees, debit	3 310	....	....	....	**−16.4**	**−10.9**	**−13.1**	**−20.7**	**−27.3**
Investment income, credit	2 320	....	....	....	**17.2**	**23.1**	**33.0**	**19.4**	**14.8**
Direct investment income	2 330	....	....	....	....	....	....	....	....
Dividends and distributed branch profits	2 332	....	....	....	....	....	....	....	....
Reinvested earnings and undistributed branch profits	2 333	....	....	....	....	....	....	....	....
Income on debt (interest)	2 334	....	....	....	....	....	....	....	....
Portfolio investment income	2 339	....	....	....	....	....	....	....	....
Income on equity	2 340	....	....	....	....	....	....	....	....
Income on bonds and notes	2 350	....	....	....	....	....	....	....	....
Income on money market instruments	2 360	....	....	....	....	....	....	....	....
Other investment income	2 370	....	....	....	17.2	23.1	33.0	19.4	14.8
Investment income, debit	3 320	....	....	....	**−8.8**	**−15.6**	**−55.7**	**−37.1**	**−49.8**
Direct investment income	3 330	....	....	....	−.4	−1.1	−3.1	.8	−4.0
Dividends and distributed branch profits	3 332	....	....	....	−.4	−.4	−1.4	−.2	....
Reinvested earnings and undistributed branch profits	3 333	....	....	....		−.7	−1.7	1.1	−4.0
Income on debt (interest)	3 334	....	....	....	....	....	....	....	....
Portfolio investment income	3 339	....	....	....	....	....	....	....	....
Income on equity	3 340	....	....	....	....	....	....	....	....
Income on bonds and notes	3 350	....	....	....	....	....	....	....	....
Income on money market instruments	3 360	....	....	....	....	....	....	....	....
Other investment income	3 370	....	....	....	−8.4	−14.5	−52.6	−37.9	−45.8
D. CURRENT TRANSFERS	4 379	....	....	....	**104.7**	**95.6**	**117.2**	**125.8**	**241.9**
Credit	2 379	....	....	....	**163.5**	**147.9**	**168.4**	**161.5**	**277.5**
General government	2 380	....	....	....	160.5	144.4	165.0	156.5	265.4
Other sectors	2 390	....	....	....	3.0	3.5	3.4	5.0	12.1
Workers' remittances	2 391	....	....	....	1.2	1.6	1.9	3.1	4.1
Other current transfers	2 392	....	....	....	1.7	1.9	1.4	1.9	8.0
Debit	3 379	....	....	....	**−58.7**	**−52.2**	**−51.2**	**−35.7**	**−35.6**
General government	3 380	....	....	....	....	....	....	....	....
Other sectors	3 390	....	....	....	−58.7	−52.2	−51.2	−35.7	−35.6
Workers' remittances	3 391	....	....	....	−58.7	−49.6	−47.9	−33.3	−34.5
Other current transfers	3 392	....	....	....	−.1	−2.6	−3.3	−2.4	−1.2
CAPITAL AND FINANCIAL ACCOUNT	4 996	....	....	....	**14.2**	**−6.9**	**−2.5**	**−5.7**	**78.0**
CAPITAL ACCOUNT	4 994	....	....	....	**39.1**	**25.2**	**15.7**	**29.6**	**79.7**
Total credit	2 994	....	....	....	*39.1*	*25.2*	*15.7*	*29.6*	*79.7*
Total debit	3 994	....	....	....	....	....	....	....	....
Capital transfers, credit	2 400	....	....	....	**39.1**	**25.2**	**15.7**	**29.6**	**79.7**
General government	2 401	....	....	....	39.1	25.2	15.7	29.6	79.7
Debt forgiveness	2 402	....	....	....	....	....	....	....	....
Other capital transfers	2 410	....	....	....	39.1	25.2	15.7	29.6	79.7
Other sectors	2 430	....	....	....	....	....	....	....	....
Migrants' transfers	2 431	....	....	....	....	....	....	....	....
Debt forgiveness	2 432	....	....	....	....	....	....	....	....
Other capital transfers	2 440	....	....	....	....	....	....	....	....
Capital transfers, debit	3 400	....	....	....	....	....	....	....	....
General government	3 401	....	....	....	....	....	....	....	....
Debt forgiveness	3 402	....	....	....	....	....	....	....	....
Other capital transfers	3 410	....	....	....	....	....	....	....	....
Other sectors	3 430	....	....	....	....	....	....	....	....
Migrants' transfers	3 431	....	....	....	....	....	....	....	....
Debt forgiveness	3 432	....	....	....	....	....	....	....	....
Other capital transfers	3 440	....	....	....	....	....	....	....	....
Nonproduced nonfinancial assets, credit	2 480	....	....	....	....	....	....	....	....
Nonproduced nonfinancial assets, debit	3 480	....	....	....	....	....	....	....	....

Table 2 (Continued). STANDARD PRESENTATION, FISCAL YEARS 2003–2010 ENDING JUNE 30

(Millions of U.S. dollars)

	Code	2003	2004	2005	2006	2007	2008	2009	2010
FINANCIAL ACCOUNT	4 995	....	....	....	−24.9	−32.1	−18.2	−35.2	−1.7
A. DIRECT INVESTMENT	4 500	....	....	....	6.1	73.8	3.1	6.5	19.0
Direct investment abroad	4 505	....	....	....	....	....	....	....	....
Equity capital	4 510	....	....	....	....	....	....	....	....
Claims on affiliated enterprises	4 515	....	....	....	....	....	....	....	....
Liabilities to affiliated enterprises	4 520	....	....	....	....	....	....	....	....
Reinvested earnings	4 525	....	....	....	....	....	....	....	....
Other capital	4 530	....	....	....	....	....	....	....	....
Claims on affiliated enterprises	4 535	....	....	....	....	....	....	....	....
Liabilities to affiliated enterprises	4 540	....	....	....	....	....	....	....	....
Direct investment in Bhutan	4 555	....	....	....	6.1	73.8	3.1	6.5	19.0
Equity capital	4 560	....	....	....	2.8	1.0	.7	7.6	15.0
Claims on direct investors	4 565	....	....	....	....	....	....	....	....
Liabilities to direct investors	4 570	....	....	....	2.8	1.0	.7	7.6	15.0
Reinvested earnings	4 575	....	....	....	....	.7	1.7	−1.1	4.0
Other capital	4 580	....	....	....	3.3	72.1	.7	....	....
Claims on direct investors	4 585	....	....	....	....	....	....	....	....
Liabilities to direct investors	4 590	....	....	....	3.3	72.1	.7	....	....
B. PORTFOLIO INVESTMENT	4 600	....	....	....	....	....	....	....	....
Assets	4 602	....	....	....	....	....	....	....	....
Equity securities	4 610	....	....	....	....	....	....	....	....
Monetary authorities	4 611	....	....	....	....	....	....	....	....
General government	4 612	....	....	....	....	....	....	....	....
Banks	4 613	....	....	....	....	....	....	....	....
Other sectors	4 614	....	....	....	....	....	....	....	....
Debt securities	4 619	....	....	....	....	....	....	....	....
Bonds and notes	4 620	....	....	....	....	....	....	....	....
Monetary authorities	4 621	....	....	....	....	....	....	....	....
General government	4 622	....	....	....	....	....	....	....	....
Banks	4 623	....	....	....	....	....	....	....	....
Other sectors	4 624	....	....	....	....	....	....	....	....
Money market instruments	4 630	....	....	....	....	....	....	....	....
Monetary authorities	4 631	....	....	....	....	....	....	....	....
General government	4 632	....	....	....	....	....	....	....	....
Banks	4 633	....	....	....	....	....	....	....	....
Other sectors	4 634	....	....	....	....	....	....	....	....
Liabilities	4 652	....	....	....	....	....	....	....	....
Equity securities	4 660	....	....	....	....	....	....	....	....
Banks	4 663	....	....	....	....	....	....	....	....
Other sectors	4 664	....	....	....	....	....	....	....	....
Debt securities	4 669	....	....	....	....	....	....	....	....
Bonds and notes	4 670	....	....	....	....	....	....	....	....
Monetary authorities	4 671	....	....	....	....	....	....	....	....
General government	4 672	....	....	....	....	....	....	....	....
Banks	4 673	....	....	....	....	....	....	....	....
Other sectors	4 674	....	....	....	....	....	....	....	....
Money market instruments	4 680	....	....	....	....	....	....	....	....
Monetary authorities	4 681	....	....	....	....	....	....	....	....
General government	4 682	....	....	....	....	....	....	....	....
Banks	4 683	....	....	....	....	....	....	....	....
Other sectors	4 684	....	....	....	....	....	....	....	....
C. FINANCIAL DERIVATIVES	4 910	....	....	....	....	....	....	....	....
Monetary authorities	4 911	....	....	....	....	....	....	....	....
General government	4 912	....	....	....	....	....	....	....	....
Banks	4 913	....	....	....	....	....	....	....	....
Other sectors	4 914	....	....	....	....	....	....	....	....
Assets	4 900	....	....	....	....	....	....	....	....
Monetary authorities	4 901	....	....	....	....	....	....	....	....
General government	4 902	....	....	....	....	....	....	....	....
Banks	4 903	....	....	....	....	....	....	....	....
Other sectors	4 904	....	....	....	....	....	....	....	....
Liabilities	4 905	....	....	....	....	....	....	....	....
Monetary authorities	4 906	....	....	....	....	....	....	....	....
General government	4 907	....	....	....	....	....	....	....	....
Banks	4 908	....	....	....	....	....	....	....	....
Other sectors	4 909	....	....	....	....	....	....	....	....

Table 2 (Concluded). STANDARD PRESENTATION, FISCAL YEARS 2003–2010 ENDING JUNE 30

(Millions of U.S. dollars)

	Code	2003	2004	2005	2006	2007	2008	2009	2010
D. OTHER INVESTMENT	4 700	....	....	....	85.4	16.9	39.2	72.8	85.8
Assets	4 703	....	....	....	....	....	1.6	−.2	−.2
Trade credits	4 706	....	....	....	....	....	....	....	....
General government	4 707	....	....	....	....	....	....	....	....
of which: Short-term	4 709	....	....	....	....	....	....	....	....
Other sectors	4 710	....	....	....	....	....	....	....	....
of which: Short-term	4 712	....	....	....	....	....	....	....	....
Loans	4 714	....	....	....	....	....	....	....	....
Monetary authorities	4 715	....	....	....	....	....	....	....	....
of which: Short-term	4 718	....	....	....	....	....	....	....	....
General government	4 719	....	....	....	....	....	....	....	....
of which: Short-term	4 721	....	....	....	....	....	....	....	....
Banks	4 722	....	....	....	....	....	....	....	....
of which: Short-term	4 724	....	....	....	....	....	....	....	....
Other sectors	4 725	....	....	....	....	....	....	....	....
of which: Short-term	4 727	....	....	....	....	....	....	....	....
Currency and deposits	4 730	....	....	....	....	....	.9	.3	−.2
Monetary authorities	4 731	....	....	....	....	....	....	....	....
General government	4 732	....	....	....	....	....	....	....	....
Banks	4 733	....	....	....	....	....	.8	−.1	.3
Other sectors	4 734	....	....	....	....	....	.1	.4	−.5
Other assets	4 736	....	....	....	....	....	.8	−.5	....
Monetary authorities	4 737	....	....	....	....	....	.8	−.5	....
of which: Short-term	4 739	....	....	....	....	....	.8	−.5	....
General government	4 740	....	....	....	....	....	....	....	....
of which: Short-term	4 742	....	....	....	....	....	....	....	....
Banks	4 743	....	....	....	....	....	....	....	....
of which: Short-term	4 745	....	....	....	....	....	....	....	....
Other sectors	4 746	....	....	....	....	....	....	....	....
of which: Short-term	4 748	....	....	....	....	....	....	....	....
Liabilities	4 753	....	....	....	85.4	16.9	37.6	73.1	86.0
Trade credits	4 756	....	....	....	....	....	....	....	....
General government	4 757	....	....	....	....	....	....	....	....
of which: Short-term	4 759	....	....	....	....	....	....	....	....
Other sectors	4 760	....	....	....	....	....	....	....	....
of which: Short-term	4 762	....	....	....	....	....	....	....	....
Loans	4 764	....	....	....	85.4	16.9	40.4	66.6	70.7
Monetary authorities	4 765	....	....	....	....	....	55.1	−20.3	11.6
of which: Use of Fund credit and loans from the Fund	4 766	....	....	....	....	....	....	....	....
of which: Short-term	4 768	....	....	....	....	....	55.1	−20.3	11.6
General government	4 769	....	....	....	77.7	17.7	−12.8	87.8	61.2
of which: Short-term	4 771	....	....	....	....	....	....	....	....
Banks	4 772	....	....	....	....	....	....	....	....
of which: Short-term	4 774	....	....	....	....	....	....	....	....
Other sectors	4 775	....	....	....	7.8	−.9	−1.8	−.8	−2.1
of which: Short-term	4 777	....	....	....	....	....	....	....	....
Currency and deposits	4 780	....	....	....	....	....	−2.9	6.5	6.0
Monetary authorities	4 781	....	....	....	....	....	....	....	....
General government	4 782	....	....	....	....	....	....	....	....
Banks	4 783	....	....	....	....	....	−2.9	6.5	6.0
Other sectors	4 784	....	....	....	....	....	....	....	....
Other liabilities	4 786	....	....	....	....	....	.1	....	9.4
Monetary authorities	4 787	....	....	....	....	....	.1	....	9.4
of which: Short-term	4 789	....	....	....	....	....	....	....	....
General government	4 790	....	....	....	....	....	....	....	....
of which: Short-term	4 792	....	....	....	....	....	....	....	....
Banks	4 793	....	....	....	....	....	....	....	....
of which: Short-term	4 795	....	....	....	....	....	....	....	....
Other sectors	4 796	....	....	....	....	....	....	....	....
of which: Short-term	4 798	....	....	....	....	....	....	....	....
E. RESERVE ASSETS	4 802	....	....	....	−116.5	−122.7	−60.6	−114.6	−106.5
Monetary gold	4 812	....	....	....	....	....	....	....	....
Special drawing rights	4 811	....	....	....	....	−.1	−.1	....	−9.4
Reserve position in the Fund	4 810	....	....	....	....	....	....	....	....
Foreign exchange	4 803	....	....	....	−116.4	−122.7	−60.5	−114.6	−97.1
Other claims	4 813	....	....	....	....	....	....	....	....
NET ERRORS AND OMISSIONS	4 998	....	....	....	64.9	−136.5	30.6	25.8	61.4

Table 3. INTERNATIONAL INVESTMENT POSITION (End-June stocks), 2003-2010

(Millions of U.S. dollars)

	Code	2003	2004	2005	2006	2007	2008	2009	2010
ASSETS	8 995 C.	....	....	....	....	598.1	653.1	766.6	853.2
Direct investment abroad	8 505 ..	....	....	....	....	....	....	....	....
Equity capital and reinvested earnings	8 506 ..	....	....	....	....	....	....	....	....
Claims on affiliated enterprises	8 507 ..	....	....	....	....	....	....	....	....
Liabilities to affiliated enterprises	8 508 ..	....	....	....	....	....	....	....	....
Other capital	8 530 ..	....	....	....	....	....	....	....	....
Claims on affiliated enterprises	8 535 ..	....	....	....	....	....	....	....	....
Liabilities to affiliated enterprises	8 540 ..	....	....	....	....	....	....	....	....
Portfolio investment	8 602 ..	....	....	....	....	....	....	....	....
Equity securities	8 610 ..	....	....	....	....	....	....	....	....
Monetary authorities	8 611 .	....	....	....	....	....	....	....	....
General government	8 612 ..	....	....	....	....	....	....	....	....
Banks	8 613 ..	....	....	....	....	....	....	....	....
Other sectors	8 614 ..	....	....	....	....	....	....	....	....
Debt securities	8 619 ..	....	....	....	....	....	....	....	....
Bonds and notes	8 620 ..	....	....	....	....	....	....	....	....
Monetary authorities	8 621 .	....	....	....	....	....	....	....	....
General government	8 622 ..	....	....	....	....	....	....	....	....
Banks	8 623 ..	....	....	....	....	....	....	....	....
Other sectors	8 624 ..	....	....	....	....	....	....	....	....
Money market instruments	8 630 ..	....	....	....	....	....	....	....	....
Monetary authorities	8 631 .	....	....	....	....	....	....	....	....
General government	8 632 ..	....	....	....	....	....	....	....	....
Banks	8 633 ..	....	....	....	....	....	....	....	....
Other sectors	8 634 ..	....	....	....	....	....	....	....	....
Financial derivatives	8 900 ..	....	....	....	....	....	....	....	....
Monetary authorities	8 901 ..	....	....	....	....	....	....	....	....
General government	8 902 ..	....	....	....	....	....	....	....	....
Banks	8 903 ..	....	....	....	....	....	....	....	....
Other sectors	8 904 ..	....	....	....	....	....	....	....	....
Other investment	8 703 ..	....	....	....	....	62.2	66.4	63.1	62.4
Trade credits	8 706 ..	....	....	....	....	....	....	....	....
General government	8 707 ..	....	....	....	....	....	....	....	....
of which: Short-term	8 709 ..	....	....	....	....	....	....	....	....
Other sectors	8 710 ..	....	....	....	....	....	....	....	....
of which: Short-term	8 712 ..	....	....	....	....	....	....	....	....
Loans	8 714 ..	....	....	....	....	....	....	....	....
Monetary authorities	8 715 ..	....	....	....	....	....	....	....	....
of which: Short-term	8 718 ..	....	....	....	....	....	....	....	....
General government	8 719 ..	....	....	....	....	....	....	....	....
of which: Short-term	8 721 ..	....	....	....	....	....	....	....	....
Banks	8 722 ..	....	....	....	....	....	....	....	....
of which: Short-term	8 724 ..	....	....	....	....	....	....	....	....
Other sectors	8 725 ..	....	....	....	....	....	....	....	....
of which: Short-term	8 727 ..	....	....	....	....	....	....	....	....
Currency and deposits	8 730 ..	....	....	....	....	62.1	65.7	62.9	62.3
Monetary authorities	8 731 ..	....	....	....	....	60.7	63.6	60.8	59.9
General government	8 732 ..	....	....	....	....	....	....	....	....
Banks	8 733 ..	....	....	....	....	1.1	1.8	1.4	2.2
Other sectors	8 734 ..	....	....	....	....	.3	.3	.7	.2
Other assets	8 736 ..	....	....	....	....	....	.7	.2	.2
Monetary authorities	8 737 ..	....	....	....	....	....	.7	.2	.2
of which: Short-term	8 739 ..	....	....	....	....	....	.7	.2	.2
General government	8 740 ..	....	....	....	....	....	....	....	....
of which: Short-term	8 742 ..	....	....	....	....	....	....	....	....
Banks	8 743 ..	....	....	....	....	....	....	....	....
of which: Short-term	8 745 ..	....	....	....	....	....	....	....	....
Other sectors	8 746 ..	....	....	....	....	....	....	....	....
of which: Short-term	8 748 ..	....	....	....	....	....	....	....	....
Reserve assets	8 802 ..	....	....	....	....	535.9	586.6	703.5	790.8
Monetary gold	8 812 ..	.3	....	....	....	....	....	....	....
Special drawing rights	8 811 ..	.3	.4	.4	.5	.5	.7	.7	9.5
Reserve position in the Fund	8 810 ..	1.4	1.5	1.5	1.5	1.5	1.7	1.6	1.5
Foreign exchange	8 803 ..	....	....	....	....	533.8	584.3	701.3	779.8
Other claims	8 813 ..	....	....	....	....	....	....	....	....

Table 3 (Concluded). INTERNATIONAL INVESTMENT POSITION (End-June stocks), 2003-2010

(Millions of U.S. dollars)

	Code	2003	2004	2005	2006	2007	2008	2009	2010
LIABILITIES	8 995 D.	....	....	....	....	**886.5**	**879.0**	**903.3**	**998.9**
Direct investment in Bhutan	8 555 ..	....	....	....	....	**17.9**	**20.6**	**26.7**	**45.7**
Equity capital and reinvested earnings	8 556 ..	....	....	....	....	15.8	18.0	24.3	43.2
Claims on direct investors	8 557 ..	....	....	....	....	....	....	....	....
Liabilities to direct investors	8 558 ..	....	....	....	....	15.8	18.0	24.3	43.2
Other capital	8 580 ..	....	....	....	....	2.1	2.6	2.4	2.4
Claims on direct investors	8 585 ..	....	....	....	....	....	....	....	....
Liabilities to direct investors	8 590 ..	....	....	....	....	2.1	2.6	2.4	2.4
Portfolio investment	8 652 ..	....	....	....	....	....	....	....	....
Equity securities	8 660 ..	....	....	....	....	....	....	....	....
Banks	8 663 ..	....	....	....	....	....	....	....	....
Other sectors	8 664 ..	....	....	....	....	....	....	....	....
Debt securities	8 669 ..	....	....	....	....	....	....	....	....
Bonds and notes	8 670 ..	....	....	....	....	....	....	....	....
Monetary authorities	8 671 ..	....	....	....	....	....	....	....	....
General government	8 672 ..	....	....	....	....	....	....	....	....
Banks	8 673 ..	....	....	....	....	....	....	....	....
Other sectors	8 674 ..	....	....	....	....	....	....	....	....
Money market instruments	8 680 ..	....	....	....	....	....	....	....	....
Monetary authorities	8 681 ..	....	....	....	....	....	....	....	....
General government	8 682 ..	....	....	....	....	....	....	....	....
Banks	8 683 ..	....	....	....	....	....	....	....	....
Other sectors	8 684 ..	....	....	....	....	....	....	....	....
Financial derivatives	8 905 ..	....	....	....	....	....	....	....	....
Monetary authorities	8 906 ..	....	....	....	....	....	....	....	....
General government	8 907 ..	....	....	....	....	....	....	....	....
Banks	8 908 ..	....	....	....	....	....	....	....	....
Other sectors	8 909 ..	....	....	....	....	....	....	....	....
Other investment	8 753 ..	....	....	....	....	**868.7**	**858.4**	**876.6**	**953.2**
Trade credits	8 756 ..	....	....	....	....	....	....	....	....
General government	8 757 ..	....	....	....	....	....	....	....	....
of which: Short-term	8 759 ..	....	....	....	....	....	....	....	....
Other sectors	8 760 ..	....	....	....	....	....	....	....	....
of which: Short-term	8 762 ..	....	....	....	....	....	....	....	....
Loans	8 764 ..	....	....	....	....	785.5	775.2	793.3	855.7
Monetary authorities	8 765 ..	....	....	....	....	....	42.6	19.2	32.2
of which: Use of Fund credit and loans from the Fund	8 766 ..	....	....	....	....	....	....	....	....
of which: Short-term	8 768 ..	....	....	....	....	....	*42.6*	*19.2*	*32.2*
General government	8 769 ..	....	....	....	....	765.7	717.4	759.6	810.7
of which: Short-term	8 771 ..	....	....	....	....	....	....	....	....
Banks	8 772 ..	....	....	....	....	....	....	....	....
of which: Short-term	8 774 ..	....	....	....	....	....	....	....	....
Other sectors	8 775 ..	....	....	....	....	19.9	15.2	14.6	12.9
of which: Short-term	8 777 ..	....	....	....	....	....	....	....	....
Currency and deposits	8 780 ..	....	....	....	....	82.6	82.5	83.3	88.6
Monetary authorities	8 781 ..	....	....	....	....	60.7	63.6	60.8	59.9
General government	8 782 ..	....	....	....	....	....	....	....	....
Banks	8 783 ..	....	....	....	....	21.8	18.9	22.5	28.7
Other sectors	8 784 ..	....	....	....	....	....	....	....	....
Other liabilities	8 786 ..	....	....	....	....	.6	.6	....	8.9
Monetary authorities	8 787 ..	....	....	....	....	.6	.6	....	8.9
of which: Short-term	8 789 ..	....	....	....	....	....	....	....	....
General government	8 790 ..	....	....	....	....	....	....	....	....
of which: Short-term	8 792 ..	....	....	....	....	....	....	....	....
Banks	8 793 ..	....	....	....	....	....	....	....	....
of which: Short-term	8 795 ..	....	....	....	....	....	....	....	....
Other sectors	8 796 ..	....	....	....	....	....	....	....	....
of which: Short-term	8 798 ..	....	....	....	....	....	....	....	....
NET INTERNATIONAL INVESTMENT POSITION	8 995 ..	....	....	....	....	−288.5	−225.9	−136.7	−145.6
Conversion rates: ngultrum per U.S. dollar (end of period)	0 102 ..	**46.4700**	**45.9750**	**43.5150**	**45.0850**	**40.7550**	**42.9500**	**47.8800**	**46.6000**

Table 1. ANALYTIC PRESENTATION, 2003–2010

(Millions of U.S. dollars)

	Code	2003	2004	2005	2006	2007	2008	2009	2010
A. Current Account[1]	4 993 Z.	**75.6**	**337.5**	**622.4**	**1,317.5**	**1,591.2**	**1,992.7**	**813.5**	**873.7**
Goods: exports f.o.b.	2 100 ..	1,597.8	2,146.0	2,791.1	3,874.5	4,458.3	6,526.5	4,917.6	6,290.5
Goods: imports f.o.b.	3 100 ..	−1,497.4	−1,724.7	−2,182.6	−2,632.1	−3,243.5	−4,764.1	−4,143.6	−5,006.8
Balance on Goods	4 100 ..	*100.5*	*421.3*	*608.5*	*1,242.4*	*1,214.8*	*1,762.4*	*774.0*	*1,283.7*
Services: credit	2 200 ..	363.9	416.4	488.8	476.6	499.4	499.7	515.5	549.6
Services: debit	3 200 ..	−551.2	−606.7	−682.5	−826.6	−899.7	−1,017.2	−1,015.3	−1,151.9
Balance on Goods and Services	4 991 ..	*−86.9*	*231.1*	*414.8*	*892.5*	*814.5*	*1,245.0*	*274.2*	*681.4*
Income: credit	2 300 ..	71.1	76.0	121.2	235.4	369.8	346.4	232.7	81.7
Income: debit	3 300 ..	−373.7	−460.6	−497.6	−632.7	−859.3	−882.8	−906.4	−970.6
Balance on Goods, Services, and Income	4 992 ..	*−389.5*	*−153.6*	*38.4*	*495.2*	*325.1*	*708.6*	*−399.6*	*−207.5*
Current transfers: credit	2 379 Z.	510.9	542.6	648.7	895.1	1,344.9	1,391.0	1,315.4	1,187.6
Current transfers: debit	3 379 ..	−45.7	−51.5	−64.7	−72.9	−78.7	−106.9	−102.3	−106.3
B. Capital Account[1]	4 994 Z.	....	....	**8.7**	**1,813.2**	**1,180.2**	**9.7**	**110.5**	**−7.2**
Capital account: credit	2 994 Z.	....	....	8.7	1,813.2	1,180.2	9.7	110.5	−7.2
Capital account: debit	3 994 ..	....	....	....	....	....	....	....	....
Total, Groups A Plus B	4 981 ..	*75.6*	*337.5*	*631.1*	*3,130.7*	*2,771.4*	*2,002.4*	*924.1*	*866.6*
C. Financial Account[1]	4 995 W.	**36.3**	**360.5**	**180.6**	**−1,588.6**	**−794.6**	**370.3**	**69.7**	**860.1**
Direct investment abroad	4 505 ..	−2.8	−2.8	−3.0	−3.0	−3.0	−3.0	−3.0	28.8
Direct investment in Bolivia	4 555 Z.	197.4	65.4	−238.6	280.8	366.3	512.3	423.0	622.0
Portfolio investment assets	4 602 ..	−68.2	−35.4	−153.4	25.1	−29.9	−208.1	−153.6	90.1
Equity securities	4 610 ..	....	1.2	....	....	....	....	....	....
Debt securities	4 619 ..	−68.2	−36.6	−153.4	25.1	−29.9	−208.1	−153.6	90.1
Portfolio investment liabilities	4 652 Z.	....	....	....	....	....	....	....	....
Equity securities	4 660 ..	....	....	....	....	....	....	....	....
Debt securities	4 669 Z.	....	....	....	....	....	....	....	....
Financial derivatives	4 910 ..	....	....	....	....	....	....	....	....
Financial derivatives assets	4 900 ..	....	....	....	....	....	....	....	....
Financial derivatives liabilities	4 905 ..	....	....	....	....	....	....	....	....
Other investment assets	4 703 ..	−462.9	94.3	123.8	−262.4	100.8	−222.8	−425.8	−32.3
Monetary authorities	4 701 ..	....	....	....	....	....	....	....	....
General government	4 704 ..	−17.7	−15.7	−12.1	1.5	−14.5	−6.4	−6.4	−18.3
Banks	4 705 ..	46.3	5.6	−131.7	−105.2	137.2	−84.9	−238.0	18.5
Other sectors	4 728 ..	−491.5	104.4	267.6	−158.7	−21.9	−131.5	−181.4	−32.4
Other investment liabilities	4 753 W.	372.7	239.0	451.8	−1,629.1	−1,228.8	291.9	229.1	151.4
Monetary authorities	4 753 WA	−2.8	.1	.9	1.2	....	....	214.6	....
General government	4 753 ZB	280.1	200.8	132.4	−1,632.5	−1,132.7	176.1	83.6	172.1
Banks	4 753 ZC	−80.9	20.1	−1.9	−20.5	−57.8	109.9	−34.9	−117.5
Other sectors	4 753 ZD	176.4	18.0	320.5	22.7	−38.3	5.8	−34.2	96.8
Total, Groups A Through C	4 983 ..	*111.9*	*698.0*	*811.7*	*1,542.1*	*1,976.8*	*2,372.7*	*993.8*	*1,726.7*
D. Net Errors and Omissions	4 998 ..	**−173.5**	**−625.4**	**−374.5**	**−103.3**	**−111.7**	**1.5**	**−453.6**	**−802.3**
Total, Groups A Through D	4 984 ..	*−61.6*	*72.6*	*437.2*	*1,438.8*	*1,865.1*	*2,374.2*	*540.2*	*924.3*
E. Reserves and Related Items	4 802 A.	**61.6**	**−72.6**	**−437.2**	**−1,438.8**	**−1,865.1**	**−2,374.2**	**−540.2**	**−924.3**
Reserve assets	4 802 ..	−152.0	−157.2	−463.4	−1,286.3	−1,937.7	−2,374.2	−540.2	−924.3
Use of Fund credit and loans	4 766 ..	60.0	14.3	−39.2	−232.9	−14.6	....	....	....
Exceptional financing	4 920 ..	153.5	70.3	65.3	80.4	87.3	....	....	....
Conversion rates: bolivianos per U.S. dollar	0 101 ..	**7.6592**	**7.9363**	**8.0661**	**8.0116**	**7.8512**	**7.2383**	**7.0200**	**7.0167**

[1] Excludes components that have been classified in the categories of Group E.

Table 2. STANDARD PRESENTATION, 2003–2010

(Millions of U.S. dollars)

	Code	2003	2004	2005	2006	2007	2008	2009	2010
CURRENT ACCOUNT	4 993	**75.6**	**337.5**	**622.4**	**1,317.5**	**1,591.2**	**1,992.7**	**813.5**	**873.7**
A. GOODS	4 100	**100.5**	**421.3**	**608.5**	**1,242.4**	**1,214.8**	**1,762.4**	**774.0**	**1,283.7**
Credit	2 100	**1,597.8**	**2,146.0**	**2,791.1**	**3,874.5**	**4,458.3**	**6,526.5**	**4,917.6**	**6,290.5**
General merchandise: exports f.o.b.	2 110	1,406.7	2,002.7	2,528.8	3,518.2	4,114.7	6,100.0	4,569.3	6,007.8
Goods for processing: exports f.o.b.	2 150	96.1	94.9	159.2	187.9	194.9	254.6	206.9	159.9
Repairs on goods	2 160	8.8	6.6	9.2	22.9	....	....	....	....
Goods procured in ports by carriers	2 170	14.4	8.1	16.2	19.4	25.7	29.8	25.0	27.6
Nonmonetary gold	2 180	71.8	33.7	77.8	126.1	123.0	142.2	116.5	95.2
Debit	3 100	**−1,497.4**	**−1,724.7**	**−2,182.6**	**−2,632.1**	**−3,243.5**	**−4,764.1**	**−4,143.6**	**−5,006.8**
General merchandise: imports f.o.b.	3 110	−1,497.4	−1,724.7	−2,182.6	−2,632.1	−3,243.5	−4,764.1	−4,143.6	−5,006.8
Goods for processing: imports f.o.b.	3 150	....	....	....	....	....	....	....	....
Repairs on goods	3 160	....	....	....	....	....	....	....	....
Goods procured in ports by carriers	3 170	....	....	....	....	....	....	....	....
Nonmonetary gold	3 180	....	....	....	....	....	....	....	....
B. SERVICES	4 200	**−187.4**	**−190.3**	**−193.7**	**−350.0**	**−400.3**	**−517.5**	**−499.8**	**−602.3**
Total credit	2 200	*363.9*	*416.4*	*488.8*	*476.6*	*499.4*	*499.7*	*515.5*	*549.6*
Total debit	3 200	*−551.2*	*−606.7*	*−682.5*	*−826.6*	*−899.7*	*−1,017.2*	*−1,015.3*	*−1,151.9*
Transportation services, credit	2 205	**100.9**	**116.9**	**143.2**	**111.4**	**65.4**	**63.0**	**64.2**	**66.4**
Passenger	2 850	*77.0*	*91.4*	*106.0*	*86.0*	*34.1*	*27.0*	*27.3*	*29.1*
Freight	2 851	*7.9*	*8.4*	*13.3*	*8.9*	*11.9*	*12.2*	*12.8*	*13.4*
Other	2 852	*16.0*	*17.1*	*23.9*	*16.5*	*19.4*	*23.8*	*24.1*	*23.9*
Sea transport, passenger	2 207	....	....	....	....	....	....	....	....
Sea transport, freight	2 208	....	....	....	....	....	....	....	....
Sea transport, other	2 209	....	....	....	....	....	....	....	....
Air transport, passenger	2 211	74.4	88.6	102.7	82.8	29.1	21.0	19.6	20.2
Air transport, freight	2 212	1.4	1.9	4.0	.6	....	....	....	....
Air transport, other	2 213	15.8	17.0	23.8	16.4	19.3	22.3	22.2	21.7
Other transport, passenger	2 215	2.6	2.8	3.2	3.2	5.0	6.0	7.7	8.9
Other transport, freight	2 216	6.5	6.5	9.2	8.3	11.9	12.2	12.8	13.4
Other transport, other	2 217	.2	.1	.1	.2	.1	1.5	2.0	2.2
Transportation services, debit	3 205	**−187.5**	**−195.6**	**−233.7**	**−274.0**	**−303.2**	**−400.5**	**−381.5**	**−464.7**
Passenger	3 850	*−58.9*	*−68.1*	*−70.7*	*−87.1*	*−81.1*	*−99.8*	*−97.5*	*−107.7*
Freight	3 851	*−84.3*	*−95.2*	*−121.1*	*−137.0*	*−169.4*	*−251.3*	*−234.1*	*−305.8*
Other	3 852	*−44.3*	*−32.3*	*−41.8*	*−50.0*	*−52.8*	*−49.4*	*−49.9*	*−51.2*
Sea transport, passenger	3 207	....	....	....	....	....	....	....	....
Sea transport, freight	3 208	−59.7	−40.1	−43.9	−46.6	−76.1	−118.7	−96.9	−141.4
Sea transport, other	3 209	−13.9	−2.6	−2.1	−4.6	−5.1	−4.6	−4.4	−6.3
Air transport, passenger	3 211	−56.1	−65.2	−68.8	−82.3	−76.7	−95.4	−90.6	−98.8
Air transport, freight	3 212	−4.1	−9.7	−7.0	−7.5	−10.2	−13.4	−12.3	−15.7
Air transport, other	3 213	−26.0	−25.5	−35.3	−36.8	−39.6	−29.5	−32.7	−29.6
Other transport, passenger	3 215	−2.8	−2.9	−2.0	−4.8	−4.3	−4.4	−6.9	−8.9
Other transport, freight	3 216	−20.5	−45.4	−70.2	−82.8	−83.1	−119.2	−125.0	−148.7
Other transport, other	3 217	−4.4	−4.2	−4.5	−8.6	−8.1	−15.2	−12.8	−15.3
Travel, credit	2 236	**166.5**	**191.6**	**238.6**	**244.1**	**292.0**	**274.9**	**279.0**	**309.7**
Business travel	2 237	40.1	48.4	68.4	65.0	75.3	79.1	89.9	93.6
Personal travel	2 240	126.4	143.2	170.2	179.1	216.7	195.8	189.1	216.1
Travel, debit	3 236	**−138.5**	**−164.4**	**−186.4**	**−272.6**	**−303.6**	**−281.1**	**−289.6**	**−312.8**
Business travel	3 237	−44.3	−51.0	−46.7	−83.0	−101.9	−119.9	−114.0	−110.0
Personal travel	3 240	−94.2	−113.4	−139.7	−189.5	−201.7	−161.2	−175.7	−202.8
Other services, credit	2 200 BA	**96.5**	**107.9**	**107.0**	**121.1**	**142.0**	**161.8**	**172.3**	**173.5**
Communications	2 245	26.9	33.3	36.7	42.9	56.6	61.1	64.1	64.1
Construction	2 249	.3	.4	.4	.4	.4	.5	.5	.5
Insurance	2 253	37.6	41.5	35.4	40.0	41.0	49.0	56.7	56.8
Financial	2 260	5.6	6.0	7.0	9.2	11.5	13.1	11.8	10.4
Computer and information	2 262	.4	.4	.4	.4	.5	.7	.7	.7
Royalties and licence fees	2 266	1.7	1.8	1.9	1.8	2.0	2.3	2.5	2.8
Other business services	2 268	7.5	7.4	7.6	10.4	13.1	16.2	16.5	16.6
Personal, cultural, and recreational	2 287	1.2	1.3	1.4	1.2	1.3	1.5	1.5	1.7
Government, n.i.e.	2 291	15.4	15.7	16.2	14.9	15.6	17.5	17.9	19.9
Other services, debit	3 200 BA	**−225.2**	**−246.7**	**−262.5**	**−280.0**	**−292.8**	**−335.6**	**−344.2**	**−374.4**
Communications	3 245	−12.6	−13.2	−13.1	−13.3	−19.8	−22.5	−24.7	−25.2
Construction	3 249	−5.0	−6.2	−7.4	−10.0	−15.6	−17.6	−18.5	−18.9
Insurance	3 253	−106.2	−116.8	−120.7	−120.0	−108.2	−127.9	−127.7	−145.7
Financial	3 260	−2.2	−1.7	−1.9	−2.0	−2.1	−2.6	−2.8	−3.0
Computer and information	3 262	−8.0	−9.5	−10.9	−13.1	−15.7	−16.6	−18.0	−20.5
Royalties and licence fees	3 266	−8.0	−9.7	−11.2	−14.4	−16.2	−17.8	−18.7	−19.8
Other business services	3 268	−61.7	−67.1	−72.6	−81.4	−89.2	−99.0	−101.1	−106.1
Personal, cultural, and recreational	3 287	−4.5	−5.4	−6.0	−7.6	−9.4	−10.2	−10.4	−11.4
Government, n.i.e.	3 291	−17.2	−17.2	−18.7	−18.3	−16.6	−21.3	−22.4	−23.8

Table 2 (Continued). STANDARD PRESENTATION, 2003–2010

(Millions of U.S. dollars)

	Code	2003	2004	2005	2006	2007	2008	2009	2010
C. INCOME	4 300	**−302.6**	**−384.7**	**−376.4**	**−397.2**	**−489.4**	**−536.4**	**−673.8**	**−888.9**
Total credit	2 300	*71.1*	*76.0*	*121.2*	*235.4*	*369.8*	*346.4*	*232.7*	*81.7*
Total debit	3 300	*−373.7*	*−460.6*	*−497.6*	*−632.7*	*−859.3*	*−882.8*	*−906.4*	*−970.6*
Compensation of employees, credit	2 310	**31.5**	**32.3**	**33.5**	**33.5**	**34.9**	**37.5**	**35.0**	**20.9**
Compensation of employees, debit	3 310	**−7.2**	**−7.4**	**−7.4**	**−7.4**	**−7.4**	**−7.4**	**−7.3**	**−1.9**
Investment income, credit	2 320	**39.6**	**43.7**	**87.7**	**202.0**	**334.9**	**308.9**	**197.7**	**60.8**
Direct investment income	2 330	3.2	2.8	3.0	3.0	3.0	3.0	3.0	−28.8
Dividends and distributed branch profits	2 332	.4	....	....	....	....	....	....	....
Reinvested earnings and undistributed branch profits	2 333	2.8	2.8	3.0	3.0	3.0	3.0	3.0	−28.8
Income on debt (interest)	2 334	....	....	....	....	....	....	....	....
Portfolio investment income	2 339	36.4	40.9	84.7	199.0	331.9	305.9	194.7	89.6
Income on equity	2 340	....	....	....	....	....	....	....	....
Income on bonds and notes	2 350	5.3	5.0	18.3	....	....	....	....	....
Income on money market instruments	2 360	31.1	35.9	66.5	199.0	331.9	305.9	194.7	89.6
Other investment income	2 370	....	....	....	....	....	....	....	....
Investment income, debit	3 320	**−366.5**	**−453.2**	**−490.2**	**−625.3**	**−851.9**	**−875.4**	**−899.2**	**−968.8**
Direct investment income	3 330	−233.6	−291.9	−270.7	−391.5	−643.9	−680.7	−768.9	−863.3
Dividends and distributed branch profits	3 332	−81.1	−200.4	−177.0	−49.8	−292.6	−248.5	−144.6	....
Reinvested earnings and undistributed branch profits	3 333	−96.9	−38.5	−30.3	−266.1	−271.8	−407.0	−509.3	−772.3
Income on debt (interest)	3 334	−55.7	−52.9	−63.4	−75.6	−79.5	−25.2	−115.0	−91.0
Portfolio investment income	3 339	....	....	....	....	....	....	....	....
Income on equity	3 340	....	....	....	....	....	....	....	....
Income on bonds and notes	3 350	....	....	....	....	....	....	....	....
Income on money market instruments	3 360	....	....	....	....	....	....	....	....
Other investment income	3 370	−132.9	−161.3	−219.5	−233.8	−208.0	−194.7	−130.3	−105.4
D. CURRENT TRANSFERS	4 379	**465.1**	**491.1**	**584.0**	**822.3**	**1,266.2**	**1,284.1**	**1,213.2**	**1,081.3**
Credit	2 379	**510.9**	**542.6**	**648.7**	**895.1**	**1,344.9**	**1,391.0**	**1,315.4**	**1,187.6**
General government	2 380	351.6	327.9	309.2	297.4	231.1	199.2	197.2	153.1
Other sectors	2 390	159.2	214.8	339.5	597.8	1,113.8	1,191.8	1,118.2	1,034.5
Workers' remittances	2 391	126.7	178.3	303.5	569.5	1,020.5	1,097.2	1,023.0	939.3
Other current transfers	2 392	32.6	36.5	36.0	28.3	93.3	94.5	95.2	95.1
Debit	3 379	**−45.7**	**−51.5**	**−64.7**	**−72.9**	**−78.7**	**−106.9**	**−102.3**	**−106.3**
General government	3 380	−5.4	−5.4	−2.2	−3.3	−2.5	−4.0	−2.5	−2.7
Other sectors	3 390	−40.4	−46.2	−62.5	−69.6	−76.2	−102.9	−99.7	−103.5
Workers' remittances	3 391	−38.6	−43.2	−59.3	−65.8	−71.5	−98.5	−96.2	−99.9
Other current transfers	3 392	−1.8	−3.0	−3.1	−3.8	−4.7	−4.4	−3.5	−3.6
CAPITAL AND FINANCIAL ACCOUNT	4 996	**97.9**	**287.9**	**−248.0**	**−1,214.2**	**−1,479.5**	**−1,994.2**	**−360.0**	**−71.4**
CAPITAL ACCOUNT	4 994	**7.0**	**8.0**	**8.7**	**1,813.2**	**1,180.2**	**9.7**	**110.5**	**−7.2**
Total credit	2 994	*7.0*	*8.0*	*8.7*	*1,813.2*	*1,180.2*	*9.7*	*110.5*	*−7.2*
Total debit	3 994	....	....	....	....	....	....	....	....
Capital transfers, credit	2 400	**7.0**	**8.0**	**8.7**	**1,813.2**	**1,180.2**	**9.7**	**110.5**	**−7.2**
General government	2 401	7.0	8.0	....	1,804.3	1,171.0	....	77.3	....
Debt forgiveness	2 402	7.0	8.0	....	1,804.3	1,171.0	....	77.3	....
Other capital transfers	2 410	....	....	....	....	....	....	....	....
Other sectors	2 430	....	....	8.7	8.9	9.2	9.7	33.2	−7.2
Migrants' transfers	2 431	....	....	8.7	8.9	9.2	9.7	10.7	−7.2
Debt forgiveness	2 432	....	....	....	....	....	....	22.5	....
Other capital transfers	2 440	....	....	....	....	....	....	....	....
Capital transfers, debit	3 400	....	....	....	....	....	....	....	....
General government	3 401	....	....	....	....	....	....	....	....
Debt forgiveness	3 402	....	....	....	....	....	....	....	....
Other capital transfers	3 410	....	....	....	....	....	....	....	....
Other sectors	3 430	....	....	....	....	....	....	....	....
Migrants' transfers	3 431	....	....	....	....	....	....	....	....
Debt forgiveness	3 432	....	....	....	....	....	....	....	....
Other capital transfers	3 440	....	....	....	....	....	....	....	....
Nonproduced nonfinancial assets, credit	2 480	....	....	....	....	....	....	....	....
Nonproduced nonfinancial assets, debit	3 480	....	....	....	....	....	....	....	....

Table 2 (Continued). STANDARD PRESENTATION, 2003–2010

(Millions of U.S. dollars)

	Code	2003	2004	2005	2006	2007	2008	2009	2010
FINANCIAL ACCOUNT	4 995	**90.9**	**279.9**	**−256.6**	**−3,027.4**	**−2,659.7**	**−2,003.9**	**−470.5**	**−64.2**
A. DIRECT INVESTMENT	4 500	**194.6**	**62.6**	**−241.6**	**277.8**	**363.3**	**509.3**	**420.0**	**650.8**
Direct investment abroad	4 505	**−2.8**	**−2.8**	**−3.0**	**−3.0**	**−3.0**	**−3.0**	**−3.0**	**28.8**
Equity capital	4 510	....	....	....	....	....	....	....	....
Claims on affiliated enterprises	4 515	....	....	....	....	....	....	....	....
Liabilities to affiliated enterprises	4 520	....	....	....	....	....	....	....	....
Reinvested earnings	4 525	−2.8	−2.8	−3.0	−3.0	−3.0	−3.0	−3.0	28.8
Other capital	4 530	....	....	....	....	....	....	....	....
Claims on affiliated enterprises	4 535	....	....	....	....	....	....	....	....
Liabilities to affiliated enterprises	4 540	....	....	....	....	....	....	....	....
Direct investment in Bolivia	4 555	**197.4**	**65.4**	**−238.6**	**280.8**	**366.3**	**512.3**	**423.0**	**622.0**
Equity capital	4 560	24.7	37.9	−121.6	−40.8	−120.2	−126.8	−4.5	1.3
Claims on direct investors	4 565	....	....	....	....	....	....	....	....
Liabilities to direct investors	4 570	24.7	37.9	−121.6	−40.8	−120.2	−126.8	−4.5	1.3
Reinvested earnings	4 575	96.9	38.5	30.3	266.1	271.8	407.0	509.3	772.3
Other capital	4 580	75.8	−11.0	−147.3	55.5	214.7	232.2	−81.7	−151.7
Claims on direct investors	4 585	....	....	....	....	....	....	....	....
Liabilities to direct investors	4 590	75.8	−11.0	−147.3	55.5	214.7	232.2	−81.7	−151.7
B. PORTFOLIO INVESTMENT	4 600	**−68.2**	**−35.4**	**−153.4**	**25.1**	**−29.9**	**−208.1**	**−153.6**	**90.1**
Assets	4 602	**−68.2**	**−35.4**	**−153.4**	**25.1**	**−29.9**	**−208.1**	**−153.6**	**90.1**
Equity securities	4 610	....	1.2	....	....	....	....	....	....
Monetary authorities	4 611	....	....	....	....	....	....	....	....
General government	4 612	....	....	....	....	....	....	....	....
Banks	4 613	....	....	....	....	....	....	....	....
Other sectors	4 614	....	1.2	....	....	....	....	....	....
Debt securities	4 619	−68.2	−36.6	−153.4	25.1	−29.9	−208.1	−153.6	90.1
Bonds and notes	4 620	....	....	....	....	....	....	....	....
Monetary authorities	4 621	....	....	....	....	....	....	....	....
General government	4 622	....	....	....	....	....	....	....	....
Banks	4 623	....	....	....	....	....	....	....	....
Other sectors	4 624	....	....	....	....	....	....	....	....
Money market instruments	4 630	−68.2	−36.6	−153.4	25.1	−29.9	−208.1	−153.6	90.1
Monetary authorities	4 631	....	....	....	....	....	....	....	....
General government	4 632	....	....	....	....	....	....	....	....
Banks	4 633	6.9	17.7	−84.0	28.5	−10.2	−65.8	−264.0	17.9
Other sectors	4 634	−75.1	−54.3	−69.5	−3.4	−19.7	−142.3	110.3	72.3
Liabilities	4 652	....	....	....	....	....	....	....	....
Equity securities	4 660	....	....	....	....	....	....	....	....
Banks	4 663	....	....	....	....	....	....	....	....
Other sectors	4 664	....	....	....	....	....	....	....	....
Debt securities	4 669	....	....	....	....	....	....	....	....
Bonds and notes	4 670	....	....	....	....	....	....	....	....
Monetary authorities	4 671	....	....	....	....	....	....	....	....
General government	4 672	....	....	....	....	....	....	....	....
Banks	4 673	....	....	....	....	....	....	....	....
Other sectors	4 674	....	....	....	....	....	....	....	....
Money market instruments	4 680	....	....	....	....	....	....	....	....
Monetary authorities	4 681	....	....	....	....	....	....	....	....
General government	4 682	....	....	....	....	....	....	....	....
Banks	4 683	....	....	....	....	....	....	....	....
Other sectors	4 684	....	....	....	....	....	....	....	....
C. FINANCIAL DERIVATIVES	4 910	....	....	....	....	....	....	....	....
Monetary authorities	4 911	....	....	....	....	....	....	....	....
General government	4 912	....	....	....	....	....	....	....	....
Banks	4 913	....	....	....	....	....	....	....	....
Other sectors	4 914	....	....	....	....	....	....	....	....
Assets	4 900	....	....	....	....	....	....	....	....
Monetary authorities	4 901	....	....	....	....	....	....	....	....
General government	4 902	....	....	....	....	....	....	....	....
Banks	4 903	....	....	....	....	....	....	....	....
Other sectors	4 904	....	....	....	....	....	....	....	....
Liabilities	4 905	....	....	....	....	....	....	....	....
Monetary authorities	4 906	....	....	....	....	....	....	....	....
General government	4 907	....	....	....	....	....	....	....	....
Banks	4 908	....	....	....	....	....	....	....	....
Other sectors	4 909	....	....	....	....	....	....	....	....

Table 2 (Concluded). STANDARD PRESENTATION, 2003–2010

(Millions of U.S. dollars)

	Code	2003	2004	2005	2006	2007	2008	2009	2010
D. OTHER INVESTMENT..................................	4 700 ..	**116.5**	**409.8**	**601.8**	**−2,043.9**	**−1,055.3**	**69.1**	**−196.7**	**119.1**
Assets..................................	4 703 ..	**−462.9**	**94.3**	**123.8**	**−262.4**	**100.8**	**−222.8**	**−425.8**	**−32.3**
Trade credits..................................	4 706 ..	....	....	....	....	....	....	....	....
General government..................................	4 707 ..	....	....	....	....	....	....	....	....
of which: Short-term..................................	4 709 ..	....	....	....	....	....	....	....	....
Other sectors..................................	4 710 ..	....	....	....	....	....	....	....	....
of which: Short-term..................................	4 712 ..	....	....	....	....	....	....	....	....
Loans..................................	4 714 ..	....	....	....	....	....	....	....	....
Monetary authorities..................................	4 715 ..	....	....	....	....	....	....	....	....
of which: Short-term..................................	4 718 ..	....	....	....	....	....	....	....	....
General government..................................	4 719 ..	....	....	....	....	....	....	....	....
of which: Short-term..................................	4 721 ..	....	....	....	....	....	....	....	....
Banks..................................	4 722 ..	....	....	....	....	....	....	....	....
of which: Short-term..................................	4 724 ..	....	....	....	....	....	....	....	....
Other sectors..................................	4 725 ..	....	....	....	....	....	....	....	....
of which: Short-term..................................	4 727 ..	....	....	....	....	....	....	....	....
Currency and deposits..................................	4 730 ..	−442.7	110.6	141.3	−261.4	117.2	−213.9	−421.3	−6.7
Monetary authorities..................................	4 731 ..	....	....	....	....	....	....	....	....
General government..................................	4 732 ..	....	....	....	....	....	....	....	....
Banks..................................	4 733 ..	46.3	5.6	−131.7	−105.2	137.2	−84.9	−238.0	18.5
Other sectors..................................	4 734 ..	−489.0	105.0	273.0	−156.2	−20.0	−129.0	−183.3	−25.2
Other assets..................................	4 736 ..	−20.2	−16.3	−17.5	−1.0	−16.4	−8.9	−4.5	−25.5
Monetary authorities..................................	4 737 ..	....	....	....	....	....	....	....	....
of which: Short-term..................................	4 739 ..	....	....	....	....	....	....	....	....
General government..................................	4 740 ..	−17.7	−15.7	−12.1	1.5	−14.5	−6.4	−6.4	−18.3
of which: Short-term..................................	4 742 ..	....	....	....	....	....	....	....	....
Banks..................................	4 743 ..	....	....	....	....	....	....	....	....
of which: Short-term..................................	4 745 ..	....	....	....	....	....	....	....	....
Other sectors..................................	4 746 ..	−2.5	−.6	−5.4	−2.5	−1.9	−2.5	1.9	−7.2
of which: Short-term..................................	4 748 ..	*−2.5*	*−.6*	*−5.4*	*−2.5*	*−1.9*	*−2.5*	*1.9*	*−7.2*
Liabilities..................................	4 753 ..	**579.3**	**315.6**	**478.0**	**−1,781.5**	**−1,156.2**	**291.9**	**229.1**	**151.4**
Trade credits..................................	4 756 ..	....	....	....	....	....	....	....	....
General government..................................	4 757 ..	....	....	....	....	....	....	....	....
of which: Short-term..................................	4 759 ..	....	....	....	....	....	....	....	....
Other sectors..................................	4 760 ..	....	....	....	....	....	....	....	....
of which: Short-term..................................	4 762 ..	....	....	....	....	....	....	....	....
Loans..................................	4 764 ..	579.2	313.6	476.4	−1,783.4	−1,156.2	291.9	14.6	151.4
Monetary authorities..................................	4 765 ..	57.2	12.4	−39.9	−233.6	−14.6	....	....	....
of which: Use of Fund credit and loans from the Fund..	4 766 ..	*60.0*	*14.3*	*−39.2*	*−232.9*	*−14.6*	....	....	....
of which: Short-term..................................	4 768 ..	....	....	....	....	....	....	....	....
General government..................................	4 769 ..	426.6	263.1	197.7	−1,552.1	−1,045.5	176.1	83.6	172.1
of which: Short-term..................................	4 771 ..	....	*−25.0*	*5.5*	*22.0*	*17.0*	....	....	....
Banks..................................	4 772 ..	−80.9	20.1	−1.9	−20.5	−57.8	109.9	−34.9	−117.5
of which: Short-term..................................	4 774 ..	*−60.2*	*5.0*	*−19.1*	*−6.5*	*5.7*	*4.6*	*−10.3*	*4.4*
Other sectors..................................	4 775 ..	176.4	18.0	320.5	22.7	−38.3	5.8	−34.2	96.8
of which: Short-term..................................	4 777 ..	*44.1*	*−39.6*	*−60.3*	*22.0*	*−26.8*	*−10.7*	*11.2*	*119.7*
Currency and deposits..................................	4 780 ..	....	....	....	....	....	....	....	....
Monetary authorities..................................	4 781 ..	....	....	....	....	....	....	....	....
General government..................................	4 782 ..	....	....	....	....	....	....	....	....
Banks..................................	4 783 ..	....	....	....	....	....	....	....	....
Other sectors..................................	4 784 ..	....	....	....	....	....	....	....	....
Other liabilities..................................	4 786 ..	.1	2.0	1.6	1.9	....	....	214.6	....
Monetary authorities..................................	4 787 ..	.1	2.0	1.6	1.9	....	....	214.6	....
of which: Short-term..................................	4 789 ..	*.1*	*2.0*	*1.6*	*1.9*	....	....	....	....
General government..................................	4 790 ..	....	....	....	....	....	....	....	....
of which: Short-term..................................	4 792 ..	....	....	....	....	....	....	....	....
Banks..................................	4 793 ..	....	....	....	....	....	....	....	....
of which: Short-term..................................	4 795 ..	....	....	....	....	....	....	....	....
Other sectors..................................	4 796 ..	....	....	....	....	....	....	....	....
of which: Short-term..................................	4 798 ..	....	....	....	....	....	....	....	....
E. RESERVE ASSETS..................................	4 802 ..	**−152.0**	**−157.2**	**−463.4**	**−1,286.3**	**−1,937.7**	**−2,374.2**	**−540.2**	**−924.3**
Monetary gold..................................	4 812 ..	....	−.1	....	.2	−.2	−.3	−.4	−246.0
Special drawing rights..................................	4 811 ..	.3	.9	−.3	....	−.1	−1.1	−214.6	....
Reserve position in the Fund..................................	4 810 ..	....	....	....	....	....	....	....	....
Foreign exchange..................................	4 803 ..	−142.1	−154.0	−459.3	−1,284.5	−1,936.4	−2,373.7	−325.0	−677.1
Other claims..................................	4 813 ..	−10.2	−3.9	−3.8	−2.0	−1.0	.9	−.2	−1.2
NET ERRORS AND OMISSIONS..................................	4 998 ..	**−173.5**	**−625.4**	**−374.5**	**−103.3**	**−111.7**	**1.5**	**−453.6**	**−802.3**

Table 3. INTERNATIONAL INVESTMENT POSITION (End-period stocks), 2003–2010

(Millions of U.S. dollars)

	Code	2003	2004	2005	2006	2007	2008	2009	2010
ASSETS	8 995 C.	**2,984.9**	**3,110.4**	**3,990.4**	**6,196.9**	**8,459.7**	**12,029.7**	**13,407.1**	**14,144.3**
Direct investment abroad	8 505 ..	**83.4**	**84.2**	**87.2**	**90.2**	**94.2**	**63.8**	**49.5**	**20.7**
Equity capital and reinvested earnings	8 506 ..	24.2	26.1	29.1	32.1	36.1	43.1	28.8	....
Claims on affiliated enterprises	8 507 ..	24.2	26.1	29.1	32.1	36.1	43.1	28.8	....
Liabilities to affiliated enterprises	8 508 ..	....	....	....	....	....	....	....	....
Other capital	8 530 ..	59.2	58.1	58.1	58.1	58.1	20.7	20.7	20.7
Claims on affiliated enterprises	8 535 ..	59.2	58.1	58.1	58.1	58.1	20.7	20.7	20.7
Liabilities to affiliated enterprises	8 540 ..	....	....	....	....	....	....	....	....
Portfolio investment	8 602 ..	**398.4**	**433.8**	**587.2**	**562.2**	**484.8**	**583.8**	**885.6**	**782.4**
Equity securities	8 610 ..	....	....	....	....	....	....	....	....
Monetary authorities	8 611 ..	....	....	....	....	....	....	....	....
General government	8 612 ..	....	....	....	....	....	....	....	....
Banks	8 613 ..	....	....	....	....	....	....	....	....
Other sectors	8 614 ..	....	....	....	....	....	....	....	....
Debt securities	8 619 ..	398.4	433.8	587.2	562.2	484.8	583.8	885.6	782.4
Bonds and notes	8 620 ..								
Monetary authorities	8 621 ..								
General government	8 622 ..								
Banks	8 623 ..	....	....						
Other sectors	8 624 ..	....	....						
Money market instruments	8 630 ..	398.4	433.8	587.2	562.2	484.8	583.8	885.6	782.4
Monetary authorities	8 631 ..								
General government	8 632 ..								
Banks	8 633 ..	211.5	193.8	277.8	249.2	259.4	325.2	589.2	571.3
Other sectors	8 634 ..	186.9	240.0	309.5	312.9	225.4	258.6	296.4	211.1
Financial derivatives	8 900 ..	....	....	....	....	....	....	....	....
Monetary authorities	8 901 ..	....	....	....	....	....	....	....	....
General government	8 902 ..	....	....	....	....	....	....	....	....
Banks	8 903 ..	....	....	....	....	....	....	....	....
Other sectors	8 904 ..	....	....	....	....	....	....	....	....
Other investment	8 703 ..	**1,250.2**	**1,160.6**	**1,356.6**	**2,352.2**	**2,561.7**	**3,660.2**	**3,890.6**	**3,611.2**
Trade credits	8 706 ..	....	....	....	....	....	....	....	....
General government	8 707 ..	....	....	....	....	....	....	....	....
of which: Short-term	8 709 ..	....	....	....	....	....	....	....	....
Other sectors	8 710 ..	....	....	....	....	....	....	....	....
of which: Short-term	8 712 ..	....	....	....	....	....	....	....	....
Loans	8 714 ..	....	....	....	....	....	....	....	....
Monetary authorities	8 715 ..								
of which: Short-term	8 718 ..								
General government	8 719 ..								
of which: Short-term	8 721 ..								
Banks	8 722 ..								
of which: Short-term	8 724 ..								
Other sectors	8 725 ..								
of which: Short-term	8 727 ..	....	....						
Currency and deposits	8 730 ..	968.6	858.0	1,024.7	1,849.9	2,046.7	2,657.6	2,736.6	2,416.1
Monetary authorities	8 731 ..	....	....	....	....	....	....	....	....
General government	8 732 ..	....	....	....	....	....	....	....	....
Banks	8 733 ..	332.6	327.0	458.7	563.9	426.7	511.6	749.6	731.1
Other sectors	8 734 ..	636.0	531.0	566.0	1,286.0	1,620.0	2,146.0	1,987.0	1,685.0
Other assets	8 736 ..	281.6	302.6	331.9	502.3	515.0	1,002.6	1,154.0	1,195.0
Monetary authorities	8 737 ..	152.1	164.4	170.4	331.8	343.7	355.2	364.9	392.0
of which: Short-term	8 739 ..	....	....	....	....	....	....	....	....
General government	8 740 ..	119.7	127.6	145.6	152.1	150.9	157.7	157.9	155.4
of which: Short-term	8 742 ..	....	....	....	....	....	....	....	....
Banks	8 743 ..	....	....	....	....	....	....	....	....
of which: Short-term	8 745 ..	....	....	....	....	....	....	....	....
Other sectors	8 746 ..	9.9	10.5	15.9	18.4	20.4	489.7	631.2	647.6
of which: Short-term	8 748 ..	*9.9*	*10.5*	*15.9*	*18.4*	*20.4*	*489.7*	*631.2*	*647.6*
Reserve assets	8 802 ..	**1,252.9**	**1,431.9**	**1,959.3**	**3,192.4**	**5,319.0**	**7,721.8**	**8,581.4**	**9,730.0**
Monetary gold	8 812 ..	379.4	399.4	470.6	577.6	764.3	794.5	997.6	1,596.2
Special drawing rights	8 811 ..	40.3	41.2	38.2	40.2	42.3	42.3	258.5	254.0
Reserve position in the Fund	8 810 ..	13.2	13.8	12.7	13.4	14.0	13.7	13.9	13.7
Foreign exchange	8 803 ..	663.3	817.3	1,276.7	2,561.2	4,497.7	6,871.4	7,311.4	7,866.2
Other claims	8 813 ..	156.7	160.1	161.1	....	.7	....	....	....

Table 3 (Concluded). INTERNATIONAL INVESTMENT POSITION (End-period stocks), 2003–2010

(Millions of U.S. dollars)

	Code	2003	2004	2005	2006	2007	2008	2009	2010
LIABILITIES....................................	8 995 D.	**10,956.9**	**10,905.5**	**11,209.1**	**9,820.7**	**9,148.7**	**9,875.3**	**10,374.1**	**11,011.1**
Direct investment in Bolivia............	8 555 ..	**4,782.0**	**4,816.6**	**4,904.5**	**5,118.9**	**5,485.0**	**5,998.0**	**6,421.1**	**6,869.1**
Equity capital and reinvested earnings............	8 556 ..	3,284.0	3,360.4	3,506.4	3,635.2	3,580.4	3,859.9	4,263.2	5,035.1
Claims on direct investors................	8 557 ..	....	....	....	....	....	....	....	....
Liabilities to direct investors............	8 558 ..	3,284.0	3,360.4	3,506.4	3,635.2	3,580.4	3,859.9	4,263.2	5,035.1
Other capital............................	8 580 ..	1,498.0	1,456.2	1,398.1	1,483.7	1,904.6	2,138.1	2,157.8	1,834.0
Claims on direct investors................	8 585 ..	−175.0	−205.9	−209.7	....	....	....	....	....
Liabilities to direct investors............	8 590 ..	1,673.0	1,662.1	1,607.8	1,483.7	1,904.6	2,138.1	2,157.8	1,834.0
Portfolio investment........................	8 652 ..	**48.2**	**41.8**	**41.8**	**41.8**	**127.3**	**37.5**	**32.6**	**29.7**
Equity securities........................	8 660 ..	46.8	40.9	40.9	40.9	126.5	36.6	32.6	29.7
Banks..................................	8 663 ..	10.5	8.5	9.0	9.2	28.0	15.4	15.6	16.1
Other sectors.........................	8 664 ..	36.3	32.5	31.9	31.8	98.5	21.3	17.1	13.6
Debt securities.........................	8 669 ..	1.4	.9	.9	.9	.9	.9	....	....
Bonds and notes......................	8 670 ..	....	....	....	....	....	....	....	....
Monetary authorities................	8 671 ..	....	....	....	....	....	....	....	....
General government.................	8 672 ..	....	....	....	....	....	....	....	....
Banks...............................	8 673 ..	....	....	....	....	....	....	....	....
Other sectors.......................	8 674 ..	....	....	....	....	....	....	....	....
Money market instruments............	8 680 ..	1.4	.9	.9	.9	.9	.9	....	....
Monetary authorities................	8 681 ..	....	....	....	....	....	....	....	....
General government.................	8 682 ..	....	....	....	....	....	....	....	....
Banks...............................	8 683 ..	....	....	....	....	....	....	....	....
Other sectors.......................	8 684 ..	1.4	.9	.9	.9	.9	.9	....	....
Financial derivatives.......................	8 905 ..	....	....	....	....	....	....	....	....
Monetary authorities....................	8 906 ..	....	....	....	....	....	....	....	....
General government.....................	8 907 ..	....	....	....	....	....	....	....	....
Banks..................................	8 908 ..	....	....	....	....	....	....	....	....
Other sectors...........................	8 909 ..	....	....	....	....	....	....	....	....
Other investment............................	8 753 ..	**6,126.7**	**6,047.2**	**6,262.8**	**4,660.0**	**3,536.4**	**3,839.8**	**3,920.4**	**4,112.3**
Trade credits............................	8 756 ..	....	....	....	....	....	....	....	....
General government....................	8 757 ..	....	....	....	....	....	....	....	....
of which: Short-term.................	8 759 ..	....	....	....	....	....	....	....	....
Other sectors.........................	8 760 ..	....	....	....	....	....	....	....	....
of which: Short-term.................	8 762 ..	....	....	....	....	....	....	....	....
Loans..................................	8 764 ..	6,071.7	5,986.2	6,225.3	4,619.0	3,491.9	3,791.9	3,663.1	3,859.5
Monetary authorities...................	8 765 ..	395.0	321.2	257.1	27.3	....	....	....	....
of which: Use of Fund credit and loans from the Fund....	8 766 ..	*278.7*	*307.0*	*243.8*	*14.5*	....	....	....	....
of which: Short-term.................	8 768 ..	....	....	....	....	....	....	....	....
General government....................	8 769 ..	4,455.2	4,409.5	4,408.1	2,975.8	2,089.7	2,275.0	2,443.1	2,713.7
of which: Short-term.................	8 771 ..	*25.0*	....	*5.3*	*27.2*	*42.2*	*62.5*	*127.6*	*161.6*
Banks.................................	8 772 ..	306.4	318.5	312.5	291.5	139.0	198.6	152.0	152.8
of which: Short-term.................	8 774 ..	*31.1*	*36.0*	*17.0*	*10.4*	*16.1*	*20.6*	*10.3*	*14.7*
Other sectors.........................	8 775 ..	915.2	937.1	1,247.5	1,324.4	1,263.2	1,318.2	1,068.0	993.0
of which: Short-term.................	8 777 ..	*276.0*	*236.4*	*160.3*	*188.3*	*164.6*	*186.6*	*171.6*	*155.4*
Currency and deposits..................	8 780 ..	....	....	....	....	....	....	....	....
Monetary authorities...................	8 781 ..	....	....	....	....	....	....	....	....
General government....................	8 782 ..	....	....	....	....	....	....	....	....
Banks.................................	8 783 ..	....	....	....	....	....	....	....	....
Other sectors.........................	8 784 ..	....	....	....	....	....	....	....	....
Other liabilities.......................	8 786 ..	55.0	60.9	37.6	41.0	44.4	48.0	257.3	252.8
Monetary authorities...................	8 787 ..	29.2	35.1	37.6	41.0	44.4	48.0	257.3	252.8
of which: Short-term.................	8 789 ..	....	....	....	....	....	....	....	....
General government....................	8 790 ..	....	....	....	....	....	....	....	....
of which: Short-term.................	8 792 ..	....	....	....	....	....	....	....	....
Banks.................................	8 793 ..	....	....	....	....	....	....	....	....
of which: Short-term.................	8 795 ..	....	....	....	....	....	....	....	....
Other sectors.........................	8 796 ..	25.9	25.9	....	....	....	....	....	....
of which: Short-term.................	8 798 ..	....	....	....	....	....	....	....	....
NET INTERNATIONAL INVESTMENT POSITION........	8 995 ..	**−7,972.0**	**−7,795.1**	**−7,218.7**	**−3,623.7**	**−689.0**	**2,154.3**	**3,033.0**	**3,133.2**
Conversion rates: bolivianos per U.S. dollar (end of period)....................	0 102 ..	**7.8300**	**8.0500**	**8.0400**	**7.9800**	**7.6200**	**7.0200**	**7.0200**	**6.9900**

Table 1. ANALYTIC PRESENTATION, 2003–2010

(Millions of U.S. dollars)

	Code	2003	2004	2005	2006	2007	2008	2009	2010
A. Current Account[1]................................	4 993 Z.	**−1,631.0**	**−1,639.3**	**−1,844.4**	**−998.1**	**−1,647.7**	**−2,604.6**	**−1,074.9**	**−1,008.5**
Goods: exports f.o.b..................................	2 100 ..	1,477.5	2,086.7	2,555.3	3,381.4	4,243.3	5,194.0	4,079.9	4,937.0
Goods: imports f.o.b..................................	3 100 ..	−5,636.8	−6,656.4	−7,454.2	−7,679.4	−9,946.9	−12,291.3	−8,833.7	−9,230.2
Balance on Goods.................................	4 100 ..	*−4,159.3*	*−4,569.7*	*−4,898.9*	*−4,298.0*	*−5,703.5*	*−7,097.3*	*−4,753.8*	*−4,293.2*
Services: credit...	2 200 ..	721.0	863.5	989.0	1,139.7	1,457.7	1,672.3	1,443.9	1,283.6
Services: debit..	3 200 ..	−383.6	−432.2	−435.6	−466.7	−579.2	−692.3	−646.6	−588.5
Balance on Goods and Services..............	4 991 ..	*−3,821.9*	*−4,138.4*	*−4,345.5*	*−3,624.9*	*−4,825.1*	*−6,117.4*	*−3,956.4*	*−3,598.0*
Income: credit...	2 300 ..	653.9	674.6	682.3	732.6	1,026.6	1,174.8	836.0	598.5
Income: debit..	3 300 ..	−120.6	−170.1	−212.8	−340.1	−566.8	−502.6	−257.5	−267.3
Balance on Goods, Services, and Income........	4 992 ..	*−3,288.6*	*−3,633.9*	*−3,876.0*	*−3,232.5*	*−4,365.3*	*−5,445.2*	*−3,378.0*	*−3,266.8*
Current transfers: credit............................	2 379 Z.	1,780.8	2,204.2	2,171.9	2,399.1	2,917.1	3,080.4	2,531.7	2,497.2
Current transfers: debit.............................	3 379 ..	−123.2	−209.6	−140.3	−164.7	−199.5	−239.9	−228.6	−238.9
B. Capital Account[1]..................................	4 994 Z.	**465.6**	**300.8**	**281.3**	**294.1**	**305.4**	**296.7**	**255.4**	**212.5**
Capital account: credit..............................	2 994 Z.	465.6	300.8	281.3	294.1	305.4	296.7	255.4	212.5
Capital account: debit...............................	3 994 ..	....	....	....	....	....	....	....	....
Total, Groups A Plus B...........................	4 981 ..	*−1,165.4*	*−1,338.5*	*−1,563.1*	*−704.0*	*−1,342.3*	*−2,308.0*	*−819.5*	*−796.0*
C. Financial Account[1]...............................	4 995 W.	**1,055.9**	**1,388.9**	**1,827.9**	**1,299.5**	**2,123.0**	**1,993.8**	**292.3**	**474.9**
Direct investment abroad..........................	4 505 ..	....	−1.5	−.4	−4.1	−28.5	−16.4	−5.5	−43.7
Direct investment in Bosnia and Herzegovina....	4 555 Z.	381.8	709.8	607.8	768.3	2,070.8	981.8	240.1	231.5
Portfolio investment assets.......................	4 602 ..	....	−2.8	2.6	−.4	−.8	−8.8	−188.8	−91.3
Equity securities...................................	4 610 ..	....	....	....	....	....	....	....	....
Debt securities.....................................	4 619 ..	....	−2.8	2.6	−.4	−.8	−8.8	−188.8	−91.3
Portfolio investment liabilities..................	4 652 Z.	....	....	....	....	....	....	....	....
Equity securities...................................	4 660 ..	....	....	....	....	....	....	....	....
Debt securities.....................................	4 669 Z.	....	....	....	....	....	....	....	....
Financial derivatives.................................	4 910 ..	....	....	....	....	....	....	....	....
Financial derivatives assets.......................	4 900 ..	....	....	....	....	....	....	....	....
Financial derivatives liabilities..................	4 905 ..	....	....	....	....	....	....	....	....
Other investment assets............................	4 703 ..	101.0	296.4	305.1	21.1	−1,102.0	−510.8	−206.0	344.5
Monetary authorities.............................	4 701 ..	....	....	....	....	....	....	....	....
General government..............................	4 704 ..	....	....	....	....	....	−167.1	97.7	58.2
Banks..	4 705 ..	−56.8	−225.8	−126.0	−150.4	−834.9	373.3	117.4	332.4
Other sectors..	4 728 ..	157.8	522.2	431.0	171.5	−267.2	−717.1	−421.1	−46.1
Other investment liabilities........................	4 753 W.	573.2	387.0	912.9	514.7	1,183.5	1,548.0	452.5	33.9
Monetary authorities.............................	4 753 WA	−.1	....	....	....	....	....	219.3	.3
General government..............................	4 753 ZB	33.2	99.3	59.8	5.7	46.7	96.9	190.1	345.6
Banks..	4 753 ZC	382.4	6.5	395.3	197.8	634.4	824.5	−486.7	−770.8
Other sectors..	4 753 ZD	157.7	281.3	457.7	311.3	502.5	626.6	529.9	458.9
Total, Groups A Through C......................	4 983 ..	*−109.4*	*50.4*	*264.8*	*595.5*	*780.6*	*−314.2*	*−527.2*	*−321.0*
D. Net Errors and Omissions......................	4 998 ..	**323.2**	**408.8**	**226.6**	**165.3**	**−13.5**	**34.7**	**59.5**	**76.2**
Total, Groups A Through D......................	4 984 ..	*213.7*	*459.2*	*491.4*	*760.8*	*767.1*	*−279.5*	*−467.7*	*−244.9*
E. Reserves and Related Items..................	4 802 A.	**−213.7**	**−459.2**	**−491.4**	**−760.8**	**−767.1**	**279.5**	**467.7**	**244.9**
Reserve assets..	4 802 ..	−196.6	−433.0	−461.4	−789.6	−876.1	261.6	43.6	−155.7
Use of Fund credit and loans.....................	4 766 ..	−17.1	−29.7	−39.4	−44.1	−18.3	−2.4	283.4	239.1
Exceptional financing................................	4 920 ..	....	3.5	9.3	72.9	127.2	20.2	140.7	161.5
Conversion rates: convertible marka per U.S. dollar................	0 101 ..	**1.7329**	**1.5752**	**1.5727**	**1.5591**	**1.4290**	**1.3352**	**1.4079**	**1.4767**

[1] Excludes components that have been classified in the categories of Group E.

Table 2. STANDARD PRESENTATION, 2003–2010

(Millions of U.S. dollars)

	Code	2003	2004	2005	2006	2007	2008	2009	2010
CURRENT ACCOUNT	4 993 ..	**−1,631.0**	**−1,639.3**	**−1,844.4**	**−998.1**	**−1,647.7**	**−2,604.6**	**−1,074.9**	**−1,008.5**
A. GOODS	4 100 ..	**−4,159.3**	**−4,569.7**	**−4,898.9**	**−4,298.0**	**−5,703.5**	**−7,097.3**	**−4,753.8**	**−4,293.2**
Credit	2 100 ..	**1,477.5**	**2,086.7**	**2,555.3**	**3,381.4**	**4,243.3**	**5,194.0**	**4,079.9**	**4,937.0**
General merchandise: exports f.o.b.	2 110 ..	1,477.5	2,086.7	2,555.3	3,381.4	4,243.3	5,194.0	4,079.9	4,937.0
Goods for processing: exports f.o.b.	2 150 ..	....	....	....	....	....	....	....	....
Repairs on goods	2 160 ..	....	....	....	....	....	....	....	....
Goods procured in ports by carriers	2 170 ..	....	....	....	....	....	....	....	....
Nonmonetary gold	2 180 ..	....	....	....	....	....	....	....	....
Debit	3 100 ..	**−5,636.8**	**−6,656.4**	**−7,454.2**	**−7,679.4**	**−9,946.9**	**−12,291.3**	**−8,833.7**	**−9,230.2**
General merchandise: imports f.o.b.	3 110 ..	−5,636.8	−6,656.4	−7,454.2	−7,679.4	−9,946.9	−12,291.3	−8,833.7	−9,230.2
Goods for processing: imports f.o.b.	3 150 ..	....	....	....	....	....	....	....	....
Repairs on goods	3 160 ..	....	....	....	....	....	....	....	....
Goods procured in ports by carriers	3 170 ..	....	....	....	....	....	....	....	....
Nonmonetary gold	3 180 ..	....	....	....	....	....	....	....	....
B. SERVICES	4 200 ..	**337.4**	**431.3**	**553.4**	**673.0**	**878.4**	**980.0**	**797.3**	**695.2**
Total credit	2 200 ..	*721.0*	*863.5*	*989.0*	*1,139.7*	*1,457.7*	*1,672.3*	*1,443.9*	*1,283.6*
Total debit	3 200 ..	*−383.6*	*−432.2*	*−435.6*	*−466.7*	*−579.2*	*−692.3*	*−646.6*	*−588.5*
Transportation services, credit	2 205 ..	**44.3**	**51.4**	**108.0**	**128.4**	**275.7**	**341.9**	**300.9**	**296.7**
Passenger	2 850 ..	*26.5*	*26.4*	*38.1*	*51.3*	*79.8*	*93.6*	*84.9*	*80.5*
Freight	2 851 ..	*17.7*	*25.0*	*69.9*	*77.1*	*149.9*	*175.2*	*147.1*	*143.1*
Other	2 852 ..	....	....	....	....	*45.9*	*73.1*	*68.9*	*73.2*
Sea transport, passenger	2 207 ..	....	....	....	....	....	....	....	....
Sea transport, freight	2 208 ..	....	....	....	....	....	....	.1	....
Sea transport, other	2 209 ..	....	....	....	....	....	....	....	....
Air transport, passenger	2 211 ..	20.1	16.9	27.5	37.7	52.5	60.3	58.4	54.4
Air transport, freight	2 212 ..	....	....	....	....	18.8	23.7	18.5	3.2
Air transport, other	2 213 ..	....	....	....	....	.9	1.0	4.0	10.5
Other transport, passenger	2 215 ..	6.5	9.5	10.5	13.6	27.4	33.3	26.5	26.0
Other transport, freight	2 216 ..	17.7	25.0	69.9	77.1	131.2	151.5	128.4	139.9
Other transport, other	2 217 ..	....	....	....	....	45.0	72.0	64.9	62.6
Transportation services, debit	3 205 ..	**−168.5**	**−195.3**	**−199.5**	**−164.0**	**−228.0**	**−257.3**	**−219.8**	**−225.9**
Passenger	3 850 ..	*−39.3*	*−44.8*	*−36.4*	*−40.4*	*−54.4*	*−56.0*	*−49.8*	*−49.8*
Freight	3 851 ..	*−129.2*	*−150.5*	*−163.1*	*−121.2*	*−136.3*	*−156.7*	*−115.4*	*−121.0*
Other	3 852 ..	....	....	....	*−2.5*	*−37.3*	*−44.6*	*−54.6*	*−55.1*
Sea transport, passenger	3 207 ..	....	....	....	−3.8	−4.4	−4.8	−.6	−1.9
Sea transport, freight	3 208 ..	....	....	....	−.5	−.5	−.6	−.6	−1.1
Sea transport, other	3 209 ..	....	....	....	−.7	−.9	−.9	−1.0	−.9
Air transport, passenger	3 211 ..	−35.5	−40.0	−31.6	−29.7	−41.6	−41.4	−41.8	−40.4
Air transport, freight	3 212 ..	....	....	....	....	....	....	−4.2	−2.0
Air transport, other	3 213 ..	....	....	....	....	−1.3	−1.3	−15.4	−21.8
Other transport, passenger	3 215 ..	−3.8	−4.9	−4.7	−7.0	−8.4	−9.8	−7.3	−7.5
Other transport, freight	3 216 ..	−129.2	−150.5	−163.1	−120.7	−135.8	−156.1	−110.6	−117.9
Other transport, other	3 217 ..	....	....	....	−1.7	−35.1	−42.4	−38.2	−32.4
Travel, credit	2 236 ..	**377.3**	**481.2**	**518.6**	**606.9**	**729.1**	**830.4**	**687.0**	**587.4**
Business travel	2 237 ..	36.2	43.8	44.9	44.7	48.8	52.2	45.1	41.5
Personal travel	2 240 ..	341.1	437.3	473.7	562.2	680.3	778.2	641.9	545.9
Travel, debit	3 236 ..	**−106.1**	**−117.1**	**−122.5**	**−170.0**	**−203.3**	**−281.5**	**−231.1**	**−193.7**
Business travel	3 237 ..	−31.5	−34.2	−32.1	−34.0	−41.1	−40.8	−35.0	−30.8
Personal travel	3 240 ..	−74.6	−82.9	−90.4	−136.0	−162.1	−240.6	−196.1	−162.9
Other services, credit	2 200 BA	**299.4**	**331.0**	**362.4**	**404.4**	**452.9**	**500.0**	**456.0**	**399.5**
Communications	2 245 ..	91.7	104.1	118.7	123.3	129.1	145.3	136.0	128.5
Construction	2 249 ..	112.3	130.3	149.6	205.2	217.8	231.3	208.6	168.9
Insurance	2 253 ..	6.2	9.4	5.1	8.8	10.6	13.3	10.9	13.0
Financial	2 260 ..	19.0	21.7	23.7	2.0	2.2	2.7	2.5	2.5
Computer and information	2 262 ..	....	....	....	....	....	....	....	....
Royalties and licence fees	2 266 ..	....	....	....	3.7	4.3	4.8	12.4	15.1
Other business services	2 268 ..	68.3	63.2	63.0	59.0	85.3	98.8	81.5	68.2
Personal, cultural, and recreational	2 287 ..	....	....	....	....	....	....	....	....
Government, n.i.e.	2 291 ..	1.9	2.2	2.3	2.4	3.4	3.8	4.1	3.3
Other services, debit	3 200 BA	**−109.0**	**−119.8**	**−113.6**	**−132.7**	**−147.9**	**−153.6**	**−195.7**	**−168.9**
Communications	3 245 ..	−47.2	−46.8	−59.7	−56.2	−58.3	−66.0	−73.7	−71.5
Construction	3 249 ..	−9.2	−10.5	−8.7	−13.1	−15.4	−15.9	−15.3	−21.4
Insurance	3 253 ..	−37.2	−44.2	−22.6	−24.2	−27.0	−25.1	−20.5	−21.1
Financial	3 260 ..	−6.3	−8.6	−11.8	−12.3	−16.9	−11.8	−7.5	−10.6
Computer and information	3 262 ..	....	....	....	−3.8	−4.4	−4.9	−8.6	−10.7
Royalties and licence fees	3 266 ..	....	....	....	−8.3	−9.6	−10.8	−6.0	−5.5
Other business services	3 268 ..	....	....	....	−6.1	−7.6	−9.1	−54.8	−20.4
Personal, cultural, and recreational	3 287 ..	....	....	....	....	....	....	....	....
Government, n.i.e.	3 291 ..	−9.1	−9.8	−10.7	−8.7	−8.7	−9.9	−9.3	−7.8

Table 2 (Continued). STANDARD PRESENTATION, 2003–2010

(Millions of U.S. dollars)

	Code	2003	2004	2005	2006	2007	2008	2009	2010
C. INCOME	4 300	**533.3**	**504.5**	**469.5**	**392.4**	**459.8**	**672.2**	**578.5**	**331.2**
Total credit	2 300	*653.9*	*674.6*	*682.3*	*732.6*	*1,026.6*	*1,174.8*	*836.0*	*598.5*
Total debit	3 300	*−120.6*	*−170.1*	*−212.8*	*−340.1*	*−566.8*	*−502.6*	*−257.5*	*−267.3*
Compensation of employees, credit	2 310	**594.6**	**579.2**	**570.4**	**560.0**	**739.0**	**827.7**	**695.3**	**541.4**
Compensation of employees, debit	3 310	**−10.5**	**−13.3**	**−12.3**	**−13.6**	**−15.2**	**−17.0**	**−15.1**	**−12.6**
Investment income, credit	2 320	**59.3**	**95.4**	**111.9**	**172.5**	**287.7**	**347.0**	**140.7**	**57.1**
Direct investment income	2 330	....	....	....	....	.6	5.4	8.6	2.4
Dividends and distributed branch profits	2 332	....	....	....	....	....	....	....	....
Reinvested earnings and undistributed branch profits	2 333	....	....	....	....	.6	....	....	−.3
Income on debt (interest)	2 334	....	....	....	....	....	5.4	8.6	2.7
Portfolio investment income	2 339	....	....	....	....	....	....	....	....
Income on equity	2 340	....	....	....	....	....	....	....	....
Income on bonds and notes	2 350	....	....	....	....	....	....	....	....
Income on money market instruments	2 360	....	....	....	....	....	....	....	....
Other investment income	2 370	59.3	95.4	111.9	172.5	287.1	341.7	132.1	54.7
Investment income, debit	3 320	**−110.1**	**−156.8**	**−200.5**	**−326.6**	**−551.6**	**−485.6**	**−242.4**	**−254.7**
Direct investment income	3 330	−10.0	−59.0	−96.9	−175.3	−344.2	−187.1	70.1	−26.6
Dividends and distributed branch profits	3 332	....	−10.3	−24.3	−27.1	−145.9	−154.7	−272.6	−171.5
Reinvested earnings and undistributed branch profits	3 333	....	−32.4	−33.0	−119.2	−141.8	−17.8	389.8	181.5
Income on debt (interest)	3 334	....	−16.3	−39.6	−29.0	−56.6	−14.7	−47.1	−36.7
Portfolio investment income	3 339	....	....	....	....	....	....	....	....
Income on equity	3 340	....	....	....	....	....	....	....	....
Income on bonds and notes	3 350	....	....	....	....	....	....	....	....
Income on money market instruments	3 360	....	....	....	....	....	....	....	....
Other investment income	3 370	−100.1	−97.8	−103.7	−151.3	−207.5	−298.4	−312.6	−228.0
D. CURRENT TRANSFERS	4 379	**1,657.6**	**1,994.6**	**2,031.6**	**2,234.4**	**2,717.6**	**2,840.6**	**2,303.1**	**2,258.3**
Credit	2 379	**1,780.8**	**2,204.2**	**2,171.9**	**2,399.1**	**2,917.1**	**3,080.4**	**2,531.7**	**2,497.2**
General government	2 380	338.0	323.3	312.0	297.7	265.8	273.8	232.0	182.3
Other sectors	2 390	1,442.7	1,880.9	1,859.9	2,101.4	2,651.3	2,806.6	2,299.6	2,314.9
Workers' remittances	2 391	1,143.5	1,474.0	1,467.3	1,588.9	1,947.5	1,899.4	1,431.7	1,363.4
Other current transfers	2 392	299.3	406.9	392.5	512.5	703.8	907.2	867.9	951.4
Debit	3 379	**−123.2**	**−209.6**	**−140.3**	**−164.7**	**−199.5**	**−239.9**	**−228.6**	**−238.9**
General government	3 380	....	....	....	....	....	....	....	....
Other sectors	3 390	−123.2	−209.6	−140.3	−164.7	−199.5	−239.9	−228.6	−238.9
Workers' remittances	3 391	−9.5	−48.7	−27.7	−40.9	−50.2	−51.8	−45.7	−41.2
Other current transfers	3 392	−113.7	−160.9	−112.5	−123.8	−149.3	−188.1	−182.9	−197.7
CAPITAL AND FINANCIAL ACCOUNT	4 996	**1,307.9**	**1,230.5**	**1,617.8**	**832.8**	**1,661.2**	**2,569.9**	**1,015.4**	**932.3**
CAPITAL ACCOUNT	4 994	**465.6**	**300.8**	**281.3**	**294.1**	**305.4**	**296.7**	**255.4**	**212.5**
Total credit	2 994	*465.6*	*300.8*	*281.3*	*294.1*	*305.4*	*296.7*	*255.4*	*212.5*
Total debit	3 994	....	....	....	....	....	....	....	....
Capital transfers, credit	2 400	**465.6**	**300.8**	**281.3**	**294.1**	**305.4**	**296.7**	**255.4**	**212.5**
General government	2 401	180.8	151.0	156.1	148.7	143.7	156.3	142.2	115.5
Debt forgiveness	2 402	....	....	....	....	....	....	....	....
Other capital transfers	2 410	180.8	151.0	156.1	148.7	143.7	156.3	142.2	115.5
Other sectors	2 430	284.8	149.8	125.1	145.4	161.7	140.3	113.2	97.0
Migrants' transfers	2 431	10.9	18.8	4.9	7.9	13.5	7.8	5.8	1.6
Debt forgiveness	2 432	....	....	....	....	....	....	....	....
Other capital transfers	2 440	273.9	131.0	120.3	137.5	148.2	132.5	107.4	95.4
Capital transfers, debit	3 400	....	....	....	....	....	....	....	....
General government	3 401	....	....	....	....	....	....	....	....
Debt forgiveness	3 402	....	....	....	....	....	....	....	....
Other capital transfers	3 410	....	....	....	....	....	....	....	....
Other sectors	3 430	....	....	....	....	....	....	....	....
Migrants' transfers	3 431	....	....	....	....	....	....	....	....
Debt forgiveness	3 432	....	....	....	....	....	....	....	....
Other capital transfers	3 440	....	....	....	....	....	....	....	....
Nonproduced nonfinancial assets, credit	2 480	....	....	....	....	....	....	....	....
Nonproduced nonfinancial assets, debit	3 480	....	....	....	....	....	....	....	....

Table 2 (Continued). STANDARD PRESENTATION, 2003–2010

(Millions of U.S. dollars)

	Code	2003	2004	2005	2006	2007	2008	2009	2010
FINANCIAL ACCOUNT..................................	4 995 ..	**842.2**	**929.7**	**1,336.5**	**538.8**	**1,355.9**	**2,273.3**	**760.0**	**719.8**
A. DIRECT INVESTMENT.................................	4 500 ..	**381.8**	**708.3**	**607.4**	**764.1**	**2,042.3**	**965.4**	**234.6**	**187.9**
Direct investment abroad........................	4 505 ..	....	−1.5	−.4	−4.1	−28.5	−16.4	−5.5	−43.7
Equity capital..	4 510 ..	....	−.7	.7	−2.8	−21.5	−11.6	1.6	−43.1
Claims on affiliated enterprises...............	4 515 ..	....	−.7	.7	−2.8	−21.5	−11.6	1.6	−43.1
Liabilities to affiliated enterprises..........	4 520 ..	....	....	....	....	....	....	....	....
Reinvested earnings................................	4 525 ..	....	....	....	....	−.6	....	....	−.3
Other capital...	4 530 ..	....	−.9	−1.2	−1.3	−6.4	−4.7	−7.1	−.3
Claims on affiliated enterprises...............	4 535 ..	....	−.9	−1.2	−1.3	−6.4	−4.7	−7.1	−.3
Liabilities to affiliated enterprises..........	4 540 ..	....	....	....	....	....	....	....	....
Direct investment in Bosnia and Herzegovina....	4 555 ..	**381.8**	**709.8**	**607.8**	**768.3**	**2,070.8**	**981.8**	**240.1**	**231.5**
Equity capital..	4 560 ..	381.8	429.0	281.1	420.3	1,518.8	570.6	221.6	246.6
Claims on direct investors......................	4 565 ..	....	−98.4	....	....	....	....	....	....
Liabilities to direct investors.................	4 570 ..	381.8	527.4	281.1	420.3	1,518.8	570.6	221.6	246.6
Reinvested earnings................................	4 575 ..	....	32.4	33.0	119.2	141.8	17.8	−389.8	−181.5
Other capital...	4 580 ..	....	248.5	293.8	228.7	410.2	393.3	408.3	166.4
Claims on direct investors......................	4 585 ..	....	−81.3	−16.0	−77.7	−36.2	−23.1	98.2	−32.7
Liabilities to direct investors.................	4 590 ..	....	329.8	309.8	306.4	446.4	416.4	310.0	199.1
B. PORTFOLIO INVESTMENT............................	4 600 ..	....	**−2.8**	**2.6**	**−.4**	**−.8**	**−8.8**	**−188.8**	**−91.3**
Assets...	4 602 ..	....	**−2.8**	**2.6**	**−.4**	**−.8**	**−8.8**	**−188.8**	**−91.3**
Equity securities....................................	4 610 ..	....	....	....	....	....	....	....	....
Monetary authorities............................	4 611 ..	....	....	....	....	....	....	....	....
General government.............................	4 612 ..	....	....	....	....	....	....	....	....
Banks...	4 613 ..	....	....	....	....	....	....	....	....
Other sectors......................................	4 614 ..	....	....	....	....	....	....	....	....
Debt securities......................................	4 619 ..	....	−2.8	2.6	−.4	−.8	−8.8	−188.8	−91.3
Bonds and notes.................................	4 620 ..	....	−1.8	2.5	−.5	−2.1	−1.0	−102.2	−39.7
Monetary authorities.........................	4 621 ..	....	....	....	....	....	....	....	....
General government..........................	4 622 ..	....	....	....	....	....	....	....	....
Banks...	4 623 ..	....	−1.8	2.5	−.5	−2.1	−1.0	−102.2	−39.7
Other sectors......................................	4 624 ..	....	....	....	....	....	....	....	....
Money market instruments...................	4 630 ..	....	−1.0	....	.1	1.3	−7.8	−86.6	−51.6
Monetary authorities.........................	4 631 ..	....	....	....	....	....	....	....	....
General government..........................	4 632 ..	....	....	....	....	....	....	....	....
Banks...	4 633 ..	....	−1.0	....	.1	1.3	−7.8	−86.6	−51.6
Other sectors......................................	4 634 ..	....	....	....	....	....	....	....	....
Liabilities..	4 652 ..	....	....	....	....	....	....	....	....
Equity securities....................................	4 660 ..	....	....	....	....	....	....	....	....
Banks...	4 663 ..	....	....	....	....	....	....	....	....
Other sectors......................................	4 664 ..	....	....	....	....	....	....	....	....
Debt securities......................................	4 669 ..	....	....	....	....	....	....	....	....
Bonds and notes.................................	4 670 ..	....	....	....	....	....	....	....	....
Monetary authorities.........................	4 671 ..	....	....	....	....	....	....	....	....
General government..........................	4 672 ..	....	....	....	....	....	....	....	....
Banks...	4 673 ..	....	....	....	....	....	....	....	....
Other sectors......................................	4 674 ..	....	....	....	....	....	....	....	....
Money market instruments...................	4 680 ..	....	....	....	....	....	....	....	....
Monetary authorities.........................	4 681 ..	....	....	....	....	....	....	....	....
General government..........................	4 682 ..	....	....	....	....	....	....	....	....
Banks...	4 683 ..	....	....	....	....	....	....	....	....
Other sectors......................................	4 684 ..	....	....	....	....	....	....	....	....
C. FINANCIAL DERIVATIVES............................	4 910 ..	....	....	....	....	....	....	....	....
Monetary authorities...............................	4 911 ..	....	....	....	....	....	....	....	....
General government................................	4 912 ..	....	....	....	....	....	....	....	....
Banks..	4 913 ..	....	....	....	....	....	....	....	....
Other sectors...	4 914 ..	....	....	....	....	....	....	....	....
Assets...	4 900 ..	....	....	....	....	....	....	....	....
Monetary authorities............................	4 901 ..	....	....	....	....	....	....	....	....
General government.............................	4 902 ..	....	....	....	....	....	....	....	....
Banks...	4 903 ..	....	....	....	....	....	....	....	....
Other sectors......................................	4 904 ..	....	....	....	....	....	....	....	....
Liabilities..	4 905 ..	....	....	....	....	....	....	....	....
Monetary authorities............................	4 906 ..	....	....	....	....	....	....	....	....
General government.............................	4 907 ..	....	....	....	....	....	....	....	....
Banks...	4 908 ..	....	....	....	....	....	....	....	....
Other sectors......................................	4 909 ..	....	....	....	....	....	....	....	....

Table 2 (Concluded). STANDARD PRESENTATION, 2003–2010

(Millions of U.S. dollars)

	Code	2003	2004	2005	2006	2007	2008	2009	2010
D. OTHER INVESTMENT	4 700	**657.1**	**657.3**	**1,187.9**	**564.6**	**190.4**	**1,055.0**	**670.6**	**778.9**
Assets	4 703	**101.0**	**296.4**	**305.1**	**21.1**	**–1,102.0**	**–510.8**	**–206.0**	**344.5**
Trade credits	4 706	–20.6	–35.6	–157.7	–145.6	–149.3	–224.7	–133.3	49.7
General government	4 707	....	....	....	....	....	....	....	....
of which: Short-term	4 709	....	....	....	....	....	....	....	....
Other sectors	4 710	–20.6	–35.6	–157.7	–145.6	–149.3	–224.7	–133.3	49.7
of which: Short-term	4 712	–20.6	–35.6	–157.7	–145.6	–149.3	–224.7	–133.3	49.7
Loans	4 714	....	....	....	–7.8	–9.0	–10.5	–11.1	–10.6
Monetary authorities	4 715	....	....	....	....	....	....	....	....
of which: Short-term	4 718	....	....	....	....	....	....	....	....
General government	4 719	....	....	....	....	....	....	....	....
of which: Short-term	4 721	....	....	....	....	....	....	....	....
Banks	4 722	....	....	....	....	....	....	....	....
of which: Short-term	4 724	....	....	....	....	....	....	....	....
Other sectors	4 725	....	....	....	–7.8	–9.0	–10.5	–11.1	–10.6
of which: Short-term	4 727	....	....	....	....	....	....	....	....
Currency and deposits	4 730	100.2	361.6	475.0	195.7	–906.5	–269.4	–131.1	337.1
Monetary authorities	4 731	....	....	....	....	....	....	....	....
General government	4 732	....	....	....	....	....	–167.1	97.7	58.2
Banks	4 733	–78.3	–195.2	–117.7	–128.2	–801.7	386.6	49.2	364.1
Other sectors	4 734	178.4	556.8	592.7	323.9	–104.9	–488.9	–278.0	–85.2
Other assets	4 736	21.4	–29.6	–12.2	–21.2	–37.2	–6.2	69.5	–31.7
Monetary authorities	4 737	....	....	....	....	....	....	....	....
of which: Short-term	4 739	....	....	....	....	....	....	....	....
General government	4 740	....	....	....	....	....	....	....	....
of which: Short-term	4 742	....	....	....	....	....	....	....	....
Banks	4 743	21.4	–30.6	–8.2	–22.2	–33.2	–13.2	68.2	–31.7
of which: Short-term	4 745	24.4	–31.7	–.7	–10.6	–7.5	–7.6	42.0	–31.0
Other sectors	4 746	....	1.0	–4.0	1.0	–4.0	7.0	1.3	....
of which: Short-term	4 748	....	1.0	–4.0	1.0	–4.0	7.0	1.3	....
Liabilities	4 753	**556.1**	**360.8**	**882.8**	**543.6**	**1,292.5**	**1,565.9**	**876.6**	**434.5**
Trade credits	4 756	70.5	118.7	246.9	221.4	325.1	415.6	380.0	321.3
General government	4 757	....	....	....	....	....	....	....	....
of which: Short-term	4 759	....	....	....	....	....	....	....	....
Other sectors	4 760	70.5	118.7	246.9	221.4	325.1	415.6	380.0	321.3
of which: Short-term	4 762	70.5	118.7	246.9	221.4	325.1	415.6	380.0	321.3
Loans	4 764	260.5	–37.8	337.9	183.1	577.1	732.0	648.1	466.5
Monetary authorities	4 765	–17.1	–29.7	–39.4	–44.1	–18.3	–2.4	283.4	239.1
of which: Use of Fund credit and loans from the Fund	4 766	–17.1	–29.7	–39.4	–44.1	–18.3	–2.4	283.4	239.1
of which: Short-term	4 768	....	....	....	....	....	....	....	....
General government	4 769	33.2	99.3	59.8	5.7	46.7	96.9	190.1	345.6
of which: Short-term	4 771	....	....	....	....	....	....	....	....
Banks	4 772	157.2	–260.0	57.0	57.7	216.2	411.3	–170.1	–235.9
of which: Short-term	4 774	–6.8	–1.4	–13.0	3.8	–5.1	–1.6	82.5	–15.6
Other sectors	4 775	87.2	152.6	260.5	163.8	332.5	226.2	344.6	117.8
of which: Short-term	4 777	....	–1.4	1.1	14.5	110.2	–20.3	–51.9	–10.8
Currency and deposits	4 780	222.5	259.3	341.0	139.3	406.3	351.3	–233.7	–408.6
Monetary authorities	4 781	–.1	....	....	....	....	....	–.1	.3
General government	4 782	....	....	....	....	....	....	....	....
Banks	4 783	222.5	259.3	340.9	139.3	406.4	351.3	–233.7	–408.5
Other sectors	4 784	....	....	....	....	....	....	.1	–.4
Other liabilities	4 786	2.7	20.6	–42.9	–.2	–16.0	66.9	82.3	55.3
Monetary authorities	4 787	....	....	....	....	....	....	219.3	....
of which: Short-term	4 789	....	....	....	....	....	....	....	....
General government	4 790	....	....	....	....	....	....	....	....
of which: Short-term	4 792	....	....	....	....	....	....	....	....
Banks	4 793	2.7	7.2	–2.6	.7	11.8	61.9	–.2	–1.8
of which: Short-term	4 795	2.7	7.2	–2.4	.6	10.0	–11.9	–.3	–1.5
Other sectors	4 796	....	13.5	–40.3	–1.0	–27.8	5.0	–136.8	57.1
of which: Short-term	4 798	....	13.5	–40.3	–1.0	–27.8	5.0	–136.8	57.1
E. RESERVE ASSETS	4 802	**–196.6**	**–433.0**	**–461.4**	**–789.6**	**–876.1**	**261.6**	**43.6**	**–155.7**
Monetary gold	4 812	....	....	....	....	....	....	–38.3	12.1
Special drawing rights	4 811	....	2.9	.1	....	.1	....	–1.6	4.0
Reserve position in the Fund	4 810	....	....	....	....	....	....	–.1	....
Foreign exchange	4 803	–196.7	–429.6	–458.6	–774.9	–855.6	237.1	50.1	–171.6
Other claims	4 813	....	–6.4	–2.9	–14.7	–20.6	24.5	33.5	–.3
NET ERRORS AND OMISSIONS	4 998	**323.2**	**408.8**	**226.6**	**165.3**	**–13.5**	**34.7**	**59.5**	**76.2**

Table 3. INTERNATIONAL INVESTMENT POSITION (End-period stocks), 2003–2010

(Millions of U.S. dollars)

	Code	2003	2004	2005	2006	2007	2008	2009	2010
ASSETS	8 995 C.	....	4,507.1	4,641.2	6,339.0	9,189.3	8,605.4	8,792.5	7,927.4
Direct investment abroad	8 505 ..	....	58.1	50.8	61.0	98.3	105.8	102.1	139.1
Equity capital and reinvested earnings	8 506 ..		53.1	45.2	53.4	83.2	89.6	91.4	127.3
Claims on affiliated enterprises	8 507 ..	....	53.1	45.2	53.4	83.2	89.6	91.4	127.3
Liabilities to affiliated enterprises	8 508 ..	....	....	....	....	....	....	....	....
Other capital	8 530 ..	....	5.1	5.5	7.6	15.1	16.1	10.7	11.8
Claims on affiliated enterprises	8 535 ..	....	5.1	5.5	7.6	15.1	16.1	10.7	11.8
Liabilities to affiliated enterprises	8 540 ..	....	....	....	....	....	....	....	....
Portfolio investment	8 602 ..	....	11.2	5.9	8.7	10.6	18.8	205.0	278.4
Equity securities	8 610 ..	....	2.5	.9	2.7	3.1	3.3	2.4	2.0
Monetary authorities	8 611 ..	....	....	....	....	....	....	....	....
General government	8 612 ..	....	....	....	....	....	....	....	....
Banks	8 613 ..	....	2.5	.9	2.7	3.1	3.3	2.4	2.0
Other sectors	8 614 ..	....	....	....	....	....	....	....	....
Debt securities	8 619 ..	....	8.7	5.0	6.0	7.5	15.5	202.6	276.3
Bonds and notes	8 620 ..	....	7.0	3.6	4.5	7.3	7.6	109.9	140.6
Monetary authorities	8 621 ..	....	....	....	....	....	....	....	....
General government	8 622 ..	....	....	....	....	....	....	....	....
Banks	8 623 ..	....	7.0	3.6	4.5	7.3	7.6	109.9	140.6
Other sectors	8 624 ..	....	....	....	....	....	....	....	....
Money market instruments	8 630 ..	....	1.7	1.4	1.5	.3	8.0	92.7	135.7
Monetary authorities	8 631 ..	....	....	....	....	....	....	....	....
General government	8 632 ..	....	....	....	....	....	....	....	....
Banks	8 633 ..	....	1.7	1.4	1.5	.3	8.0	92.7	135.7
Other sectors	8 634 ..	....	....	....	....	....	....	....	....
Financial derivatives	8 900 ..	....	....	....	....	....	....	....	....
Monetary authorities	8 901 ..	....	....	....	....	....	....	....	....
General government	8 902 ..	....	....	....	....	....	....	....	....
Banks	8 903 ..	....	....	....	....	....	....	....	....
Other sectors	8 904 ..	....	....	....	....	....	....	....	....
Other investment	8 703 ..	....	1,973.6	1,997.8	2,550.4	3,982.1	3,944.5	3,889.3	3,079.0
Trade credits	8 706 ..	....	186.1	222.4	308.1	560.4	824.3	937.3	726.7
General government	8 707 ..	....	....	....	....	....	....	....	....
of which: Short-term	8 709 ..	....	....	....	....	....	....	....	....
Other sectors	8 710 ..	....	186.1	222.4	308.1	560.4	824.3	937.3	726.7
of which: Short-term	8 712 ..	....	*186.1*	*222.4*	*308.1*	*560.4*	*824.3*	*937.3*	*726.7*
Loans	8 714 ..	....	....	....	8.2	18.9	27.6	39.6	47.2
Monetary authorities	8 715 ..	....	....	....	....	....	....	....	....
of which: Short-term	8 718 ..	....	....	....	....	....	....	....	....
General government	8 719 ..	....	....	....	....	....	....	....	....
of which: Short-term	8 721 ..	....	....	....	....	....	....	....	....
Banks	8 722 ..	....	....	....	....	....	....	....	....
of which: Short-term	8 724 ..	....	....	....	....	....	....	....	....
Other sectors	8 725 ..	....	....	....	8.2	18.9	27.6	39.6	47.2
of which: Short-term	8 727 ..	....	....	....	....	....	....	....	....
Currency and deposits	8 730 ..	....	1,711.2	1,697.4	2,126.1	3,246.6	2,931.9	2,797.0	2,169.8
Monetary authorities	8 731 ..	....	....	....	....	....	....	....	....
General government	8 732 ..	....	32.2	102.8	206.2	260.5	321.8	271.1	200.2
Banks	8 733 ..	....	1,243.5	1,186.6	1,457.9	2,504.1	2,034.6	2,050.7	1,530.9
Other sectors	8 734 ..	....	435.5	408.0	462.0	481.9	575.5	475.2	438.7
Other assets	8 736 ..	....	76.2	78.0	108.1	156.2	160.7	115.4	135.4
Monetary authorities	8 737 ..	....	....	....	....	....	....	....	....
of which: Short-term	8 739 ..	....	....	....	....	....	....	....	....
General government	8 740 ..	....	....	....	....	....	....	....	....
of which: Short-term	8 742 ..	....	....	....	....	....	....	....	....
Banks	8 743 ..	....	75.2	73.0	104.0	148.2	154.1	93.4	117.0
of which: Short-term	8 745 ..	....	*69.2*	*60.5*	*78.1*	*91.8*	*95.5*	*59.2*	*84.6*
Other sectors	8 746 ..	....	1.0	5.0	4.0	8.0	6.5	22.0	18.4
of which: Short-term	8 748 ..	....	*1.0*	*5.0*	*4.0*	*8.0*	*5.5*	*19.2*	*14.4*
Reserve assets	8 802 ..	....	2,464.2	2,586.8	3,718.9	5,098.3	4,536.3	4,596.2	4,430.9
Monetary gold	8 812 ..	....	21.9	21.9	29.2	35.6	36.7	46.6	45.7
Special drawing rights	8 811 ..	3.4	.5	.3	.4	.3	.3	4.2	....
Reserve position in the Fund	8 810 ..	....	....	....	....	....	....	.1	.1
Foreign exchange	8 803 ..	....	2,415.9	2,540.1	3,652.2	5,032.2	4,348.3	4,466.1	4,315.2
Other claims	8 813 ..	....	25.8	24.4	37.1	30.2	151.0	79.1	69.9

Table 3 (Concluded). INTERNATIONAL INVESTMENT POSITION (End-period stocks), 2003–2010

(Millions of U.S. dollars)

	Code	2003	2004	2005	2006	2007	2008	2009	2010
LIABILITIES..	8 995 D.	....	**7,988.3**	**8,165.5**	**10,204.6**	**14,586.1**	**16,858.0**	**18,810.7**	**17,620.3**
Direct investment in Bosnia and Herzegovina......	8 555 ..	....	**2,286.5**	**2,301.6**	**3,202.6**	**5,396.8**	**6,065.6**	**6,804.4**	**6,520.4**
Equity capital and reinvested earnings............................	8 556 ..	....	1,976.7	1,988.2	2,839.9	4,880.6	5,187.9	5,454.6	5,104.1
Claims on direct investors...............................	8 557 ..	....	....	....	....	....	....	....	....
Liabilities to direct investors...........................	8 558 ..	....	1,976.7	1,988.2	2,839.9	4,880.6	5,187.9	5,454.6	5,104.1
Other capital...	8 580 ..	....	309.7	313.4	362.8	516.2	877.6	1,349.8	1,416.3
Claims on direct investors..............................	8 585 ..	....	−2.8	−18.2	−104.3	−158.1	−171.0	−71.3	−97.4
Liabilities to direct investors..........................	8 590 ..	....	312.5	331.6	467.1	674.3	1,048.7	1,421.1	1,513.7
Portfolio investment................................	8 652 ..	....	**41.1**	**47.9**	**73.2**	**93.0**	**99.3**	**105.7**	**97.8**
Equity securities..	8 660 ..	....	41.1	47.9	73.2	92.7	98.8	105.3	97.5
Banks..	8 663 ..	....	41.1	47.9	73.2	92.7	98.8	105.3	97.5
Other sectors...	8 664 ..	....	....	....	....				
Debt securities...	8 669 ..	....	....	....	....	.3	.5	.4	.3
Bonds and notes...	8 670 ..	....	....	....	....	.3	.5	.4	.3
Monetary authorities................................	8 671 ..	....				....	....	....	....
General government.................................	8 672 ..	....				....	....	....	....
Banks..	8 673 ..	....				.3	.5	.4	.3
Other sectors..	8 674 ..	....							
Money market instruments.............................	8 680 ..	....							
Monetary authorities................................	8 681 ..	....							
General government.................................	8 682 ..	....							
Banks..	8 683 ..	....							
Other sectors..	8 684 ..	....							
Financial derivatives..............................	8 905 ..	....	....	....	....	....	....	....	....
Monetary authorities.....................................	8 906 ..	....	....	....	....	....	....	....	....
General government.......................................	8 907 ..	....	....	....	....	....	....	....	....
Banks..	8 908 ..	....	....	....	....	....	....	....	....
Other sectors..	8 909 ..	....	....	....	....	....	....	....	....
Other investment..................................	8 753 ..	....	**5,660.7**	**5,816.0**	**6,928.8**	**9,096.2**	**10,693.1**	**11,900.6**	**11,002.1**
Trade credits..	8 756 ..	....	450.8	417.2	516.3	616.8	780.6	1,152.0	1,344.0
General government.......................................	8 757 ..	....	....	....	....	....	....	....	....
of which: Short-term................................	8 759 ..	....	....	....	....	....	....	....	....
Other sectors..	8 760 ..	....	450.8	417.2	516.3	616.8	780.6	1,152.0	1,344.0
of which: Short-term................................	8 762 ..	....	*450.8*	*417.2*	*516.3*	*616.8*	*780.6*	*1,152.0*	*1,344.0*
Loans..	8 764 ..	....	3,966.0	4,021.3	4,740.2	6,165.5	7,197.0	7,454.7	7,094.4
Monetary authorities.....................................	8 765 ..	....	108.7	62.0	20.3	2.4	....	286.3	520.8
of which: Use of Fund credit and loans from the Fund....	8 766 ..	*133.9*	*108.7*	*62.0*	*20.3*	*2.4*	....	*286.3*	*520.8*
of which: Short-term................................	8 768 ..	....							
General government.......................................	8 769 ..	....	2,514.6	2,397.7	2,551.7	2,797.9	2,853.3	3,089.2	3,363.0
of which: Short-term................................	8 771 ..	....	....	....	....	....	....	....	....
Banks..	8 772 ..	....	894.3	989.0	1,284.0	1,812.3	2,021.4	1,767.2	1,398.7
of which: Short-term................................	8 774 ..	....	*17.7*	*2.1*	*6.5*	*2.0*	*.2*	*80.7*	*62.0*
Other sectors...	8 775 ..	....	448.3	572.6	884.2	1,552.9	2,322.3	2,311.9	1,811.9
of which: Short-term................................	8 777 ..	....	....	....	*1.8*	*8.5*	*6.7*	*4.5*	*9.2*
Currency and deposits....................................	8 780 ..	....	938.8	1,149.1	1,420.9	2,012.7	2,384.9	2,378.5	1,789.9
Monetary authorities.....................................	8 781 ..	....	.7	.6	.7	.7	.7	.6	.9
General government.......................................	8 782 ..	....	....	....	....	....	....	....	....
Banks..	8 783 ..	....	938.1	1,148.5	1,420.3	2,012.0	2,384.2	2,377.9	1,789.0
Other sectors...	8 784 ..	....	....	....	....	....	....	....	....
Other liabilities..	8 786 ..	....	305.1	228.4	251.4	301.2	330.6	915.4	773.8
Monetary authorities.....................................	8 787 ..	....	31.8	29.2	30.8	32.6	31.1	252.2	247.8
of which: Short-term................................	8 789 ..	....	....	....	....	....	....	....	....
General government.......................................	8 790 ..	....	182.4	154.8	169.3	181.4	164.0	479.7	409.4
of which: Short-term................................	8 792 ..	....	....	....	....	....	....	....	....
Banks..	8 793 ..	....	13.9	9.4	11.3	25.2	84.2	88.1	79.4
of which: Short-term................................	8 795 ..	....	*13.5*	*9.4*	*11.2*	*23.2*	*10.3*	*11.5*	*8.7*
Other sectors...	8 796 ..	....	77.1	35.0	40.0	62.1	51.3	95.5	37.2
of which: Short-term................................	8 798 ..	....	*77.1*	*35.0*	*40.0*	*62.1*	*51.3*	*95.5*	*37.2*
NET INTERNATIONAL INVESTMENT POSITION........	8 995 ..	....	**−3,481.2**	**−3,524.3**	**−3,865.6**	**−5,396.7**	**−8,252.6**	**−10,018.2**	**−9,692.9**
Conversion rates: convertible marka per U.S. dollar (end of period)..	0 102 ..	1.5486	1.4359	1.6579	1.4851	1.3286	1.4054	1.3576	1.4637

Table 1. ANALYTIC PRESENTATION, 2003–2010
(Millions of U.S. dollars)

	Code	2003	2004	2005	2006	2007	2008	2009	2010
A. Current Account[1]	4 993 Z.	**462.3**	**418.6**	**1,562.3**	**1,945.7**	**2,015.4**	**867.8**	**−521.3**	**45.9**
Goods: exports f.o.b.	2 100 ..	3,024.3	3,695.9	4,444.7	4,521.5	5,163.1	4,800.1	3,435.0	4,633.3
Goods: imports f.o.b.	3 100 ..	−2,127.2	−2,864.0	−2,688.9	−2,618.5	−3,460.8	−4,364.9	−4,003.2	−4,841.7
Balance on Goods	4 100 ..	*897.2*	*831.9*	*1,755.8*	*1,903.0*	*1,702.3*	*435.1*	*−568.3*	*−208.5*
Services: credit	2 200 ..	643.2	748.2	833.8	778.6	800.9	871.8	496.0	394.5
Services: debit	3 200 ..	−652.4	−798.6	−863.8	−834.8	−980.8	−783.0	−952.2	−876.6
Balance on Goods and Services	4 991 ..	*888.0*	*781.5*	*1,725.8*	*1,846.9*	*1,522.4*	*524.0*	*−1,024.5*	*−690.6*
Income: credit	2 300 ..	382.6	327.2	462.0	528.7	438.1	474.7	352.4	413.0
Income: debit	3 300 ..	−1,098.4	−1,216.3	−1,297.9	−1,301.3	−1,176.3	−1,171.3	−455.0	−655.6
Balance on Goods, Services, and Income	4 992 ..	*172.2*	*−107.5*	*889.8*	*1,074.3*	*784.3*	*−172.7*	*−1,127.1*	*−933.2*
Current transfers: credit	2 379 Z.	538.3	743.0	886.0	1,073.4	1,494.2	1,399.3	1,153.5	1,396.2
Current transfers: debit	3 379 ..	−248.2	−216.8	−213.6	−202.0	−263.1	−358.9	−547.6	−417.2
B. Capital Account[1]	4 994 Z.	**22.5**	**31.8**	**67.4**	**5.7**	**88.9**	**76.3**	**89.2**	**19.0**
Capital account: credit	2 994 Z.	42.5	53.0	89.1	26.5	110.0	98.8	114.8	41.1
Capital account: debit	3 994 ..	−20.0	−21.2	−21.7	−20.7	−21.1	−22.5	−25.6	−22.1
Total, Groups A Plus B	4 981 ..	*484.7*	*450.4*	*1,629.7*	*1,951.5*	*2,104.3*	*944.0*	*−432.0*	*64.9*
C. Financial Account[1]	4 995 W.	**−270.6**	**−112.7**	**−395.7**	**−812.9**	**−954.0**	**83.0**	**20.5**	**−634.6**
Direct investment abroad	4 505 ..	−210.8	37.2	−55.9	−49.9	−51.0	91.1	−65.2	−.3
Direct investment in Botswana	4 555 Z.	770.5	748.1	492.4	750.8	647.3	902.4	824.1	265.0
Portfolio investment assets	4 602 ..	−315.9	−392.2	−174.4	−593.0	−226.0	322.9	347.8	396.8
Equity securities	4 610 ..	−451.6	−415.1	−289.4	−593.0	−326.5	319.2	456.5	405.0
Debt securities	4 619 ..	135.7	22.9	115.0	....	100.5	3.7	−108.7	−8.1
Portfolio investment liabilities	4 652 Z.	66.8	−29.2	−18.2	36.2	13.7	−29.5	17.7	17.8
Equity securities	4 660 ..	10.2	.6	27.2	36.0	9.4	−36.7	17.2	18.0
Debt securities	4 669 Z.	56.6	−29.8	−45.4	.2	4.3	7.2	.6	−.2
Financial derivatives	4 910 ..	....	....	....	....	....	....	....	....
Financial derivatives assets	4 900 ..	....	....	....	....	....	....	....	....
Financial derivatives liabilities	4 905 ..	....	....	....	....	....	....	....	....
Other investment assets	4 703 ..	−444.6	−474.3	−781.6	−1,053.1	−1,276.7	−1,194.6	−1,142.6	−1,217.8
Monetary authorities	4 701 ..	....	....	....	....	....	....	....	....
General government	4 704 ..	−271.0	−360.6	−513.9	−645.4	−929.3	−897.3	−901.9	−905.1
Banks	4 705 ..	−124.0	−62.0	−36.7	−148.7	−144.3	−268.0	−160.4	−221.9
Other sectors	4 728 ..	−49.7	−51.7	−231.1	−259.0	−203.1	−29.3	−80.2	−90.8
Other investment liabilities	4 753 W.	−136.6	−2.3	142.0	96.1	−61.3	−9.3	38.6	−96.2
Monetary authorities	4 753 WA	....	....	....	....	....	....	82.9	....
General government	4 753 ZB	−8.9	−13.3	−10.9	−40.4	−16.2	−13.5	12.8	−5.4
Banks	4 753 ZC	37.6	−2.2	143.7	10.6	−31.1	9.2	−57.1	−90.8
Other sectors	4 753 ZD	−165.3	13.2	9.2	125.9	−14.0	−5.0	....	....
Total, Groups A Through C	4 983 ..	*214.1*	*337.7*	*1,233.9*	*1,138.6*	*1,150.3*	*1,027.0*	*−411.5*	*−569.8*
D. Net Errors and Omissions	4 998 ..	**−160.7**	**−292.9**	**72.6**	**398.6**	**570.2**	**144.0**	**699.9**	**609.5**
Total, Groups A Through D	4 984 ..	*53.4*	*44.7*	*1,306.5*	*1,537.2*	*1,720.6*	*1,171.0*	*288.5*	*39.8*
E. Reserves and Related Items	4 802 A.	**−53.4**	**−44.7**	**−1,306.5**	**−1,537.2**	**−1,720.6**	**−1,171.0**	**−288.5**	**−39.8**
Reserve assets	4 802 ..	−171.5	37.5	−1,363.5	−1,748.4	−1,739.0	−1,077.6	624.3	957.6
Use of Fund credit and loans	4 766 ..	....	....	....	....	....	....	....	....
Exceptional financing	4 920 ..	118.1	−82.2	57.0	211.2	18.5	−93.5	−912.8	−997.3
Conversion rates: pula per U.S. dollar	0 101 ..	**4.9499**	**4.6929**	**5.1104**	**5.8366**	**6.1388**	**6.8269**	**7.1551**	**6.7936**

[1] Excludes components that have been classified in the categories of Group E.

Table 2. STANDARD PRESENTATION, 2003–2010

(Millions of U.S. dollars)

	Code	2003	2004	2005	2006	2007	2008	2009	2010
CURRENT ACCOUNT	4 993	**462.3**	**418.6**	**1,562.3**	**1,945.7**	**2,015.4**	**867.8**	**−521.3**	**45.9**
A. GOODS	4 100	**897.2**	**831.9**	**1,755.8**	**1,903.0**	**1,702.3**	**435.1**	**−568.3**	**−208.5**
Credit	2 100	**3,024.3**	**3,695.9**	**4,444.7**	**4,521.5**	**5,163.1**	**4,800.1**	**3,435.0**	**4,633.3**
General merchandise: exports f.o.b.	2 110	3,024.3	3,695.9	4,443.5	4,520.8	5,163.0	4,799.8	3,434.9	4,632.7
Goods for processing: exports f.o.b.	2 150	....	....	....	....	....	....	....	....
Repairs on goods	2 160	....	....	1.1	.3	....	.3	.1	.6
Goods procured in ports by carriers	2 170	....	....	....	.3	....	....	....	....
Nonmonetary gold	2 180	....	....	....	....	....	....	....	....
Debit	3 100	**−2,127.2**	**−2,864.0**	**−2,688.9**	**−2,618.5**	**−3,460.8**	**−4,364.9**	**−4,003.2**	**−4,841.7**
General merchandise: imports f.o.b.	3 110	−2,127.2	−2,864.0	−2,686.0	−2,616.5	−3,458.1	−4,362.9	−3,997.9	−4,837.3
Goods for processing: imports f.o.b.	3 150	....	....	....	....	....	....	....	....
Repairs on goods	3 160	....	....	−2.5	−2.0	−2.7	−2.0	−5.4	−4.4
Goods procured in ports by carriers	3 170	....	....	−.3	....	....	....	....	....
Nonmonetary gold	3 180	....	....	....	....	....	....	....	....
B. SERVICES	4 200	**−9.2**	**−50.4**	**−30.0**	**−56.1**	**−179.8**	**88.8**	**−456.2**	**−482.1**
Total credit	2 200	*643.2*	*748.2*	*833.8*	*778.6*	*800.9*	*871.8*	*496.0*	*394.5*
Total debit	3 200	*−652.4*	*−798.6*	*−863.8*	*−834.8*	*−980.8*	*−783.0*	*−952.2*	*−876.6*
Transportation services, credit	2 205	**69.1**	**83.0**	**85.0**	**81.2**	**83.0**	**83.6**	**60.6**	**37.5**
Passenger	2 850	*1.8*	*1.0*	*.8*	*2.2*	*2.8*	*2.2*	*2.3*	*4.1*
Freight	2 851	*24.1*	*31.5*	*33.1*	*27.5*	*47.5*	*21.1*	*21.1*	*32.9*
Other	2 852	*43.1*	*50.5*	*51.1*	*51.5*	*32.7*	*60.3*	*37.1*	*.5*
Sea transport, passenger	2 207	....	....	....	....	....	....	....	....
Sea transport, freight	2 208	....	....	....	....	....	....	....	....
Sea transport, other	2 209	....	....	....	....	....	....	....	....
Air transport, passenger	2 211	1.8	1.0	.8	2.2	2.4	1.1	1.6	2.1
Air transport, freight	2 212	....	....	....	....	....	....	....	....
Air transport, other	2 213	....	....	....	....	....	....	....	....
Other transport, passenger	2 215	....	....	....	....	.3	1.2	.7	2.1
Other transport, freight	2 216	24.1	31.5	33.1	27.5	47.5	21.1	21.1	32.9
Other transport, other	2 217	43.1	50.5	51.1	51.5	32.7	60.3	37.1	.5
Transportation services, debit	3 205	**−248.1**	**−291.1**	**−340.1**	**−322.0**	**−351.1**	**−221.5**	**−427.2**	**−441.1**
Passenger	3 850	*−4.6*	*−4.3*	*−19.4*	*−7.6*	*−2.8*	*−1.5*	*−.9*	*−1.0*
Freight	3 851	*−243.5*	*−286.9*	*−320.7*	*−314.4*	*−348.3*	*−219.9*	*−426.3*	*−440.1*
Other	3 852	....	....	....	....	....	....	....	....
Sea transport, passenger	3 207	....	....	....	....	....	....	....	....
Sea transport, freight	3 208	....	....	....	....	....	....	....	....
Sea transport, other	3 209	....	....	....	....	....	....	....	....
Air transport, passenger	3 211	−3.8	....	−.4	−3.1	−1.5	−.6	−.6	−.5
Air transport, freight	3 212	−31.4	−24.1	−22.6	−51.5	−52.7	−15.0	−27.6	−31.8
Air transport, other	3 213	....	....	....	....	....	....	....	....
Other transport, passenger	3 215	−.9	−4.3	−19.0	−4.5	−1.4	−1.0	−.3	−.5
Other transport, freight	3 216	−212.1	−262.8	−298.1	−262.8	−295.6	−204.9	−398.7	−408.3
Other transport, other	3 217	....	....	....	....	....	....	....	....
Travel, credit	2 236	**456.7**	**549.2**	**561.9**	**537.2**	**497.7**	**552.7**	**228.1**	**218.4**
Business travel	2 237	160.5	192.2	196.7	188.0	148.3	192.8	72.5	22.0
Personal travel	2 240	296.2	357.0	365.2	349.2	349.4	359.9	155.6	196.3
Travel, debit	3 236	**−229.5**	**−276.1**	**−282.5**	**−276.5**	**−281.1**	**−237.7**	**−230.0**	**−25.4**
Business travel	3 237	−55.1	−66.3	−67.8	−66.4	−70.5	−68.1	−62.3	31.1
Personal travel	3 240	−174.4	−209.9	−214.7	−210.2	−210.5	−169.7	−167.7	−56.5
Other services, credit	2 200 BA	**117.5**	**115.9**	**186.9**	**160.2**	**220.2**	**235.5**	**207.3**	**138.6**
Communications	2 245	8.3	7.9	21.8	16.1	23.0	26.4	26.6	20.1
Construction	2 249	8.7	8.4	8.1	8.1	7.5	11.3	7.0	4.2
Insurance	2 253	33.8	48.5	53.9	19.6	26.1	29.2	28.1	4.2
Financial	2 260	1.9	3.7	5.2	2.4	4.5	4.2	4.2	1.0
Computer and information	2 262	1.4	.4	1.2	1.4	6.0	.7	.9	1.5
Royalties and licence fees	2 266	3.4	5.4	.5	.3	.2	.5	.5	.1
Other business services	2 268	42.5	36.1	83.9	104.6	139.9	154.1	130.2	97.7
Personal, cultural, and recreational	2 287	....	....	....	....	....	....	....	....
Government, n.i.e.	2 291	17.6	5.5	12.4	7.6	12.8	9.0	9.8	9.7
Other services, debit	3 200 BA	**−174.8**	**−231.3**	**−241.1**	**−236.2**	**−348.6**	**−323.8**	**−295.0**	**−410.2**
Communications	3 245	−14.3	−21.4	−36.7	−14.4	−46.9	−32.3	−32.3	−45.2
Construction	3 249	−8.2	−10.7	−10.4	−16.9	−9.6	−11.7	−9.1	−33.7
Insurance	3 253	−21.5	−46.9	−34.5	−27.6	−39.9	−45.8	−44.7	−26.2
Financial	3 260	−5.5	−5.7	−3.0	−1.9	−2.2	−2.0	−1.9	−13.5
Computer and information	3 262	−6.1	−7.2	−9.0	−4.3	−7.2	−10.2	−9.8	−7.9
Royalties and licence fees	3 266	−11.8	−11.0	−12.3	−7.3	−11.4	−12.7	−11.6	−11.4
Other business services	3 268	−106.4	−119.0	−117.9	−162.8	−230.9	−208.2	−184.9	−263.2
Personal, cultural, and recreational	3 287	....	....	....	....	....	....	....	....
Government, n.i.e.	3 291	−.9	−9.4	−17.2	−1.0	−.5	−1.0	−.7	−9.1

Table 2 (Continued). STANDARD PRESENTATION, 2003–2010

(Millions of U.S. dollars)

	Code	2003	2004	2005	2006	2007	2008	2009	2010
C. INCOME	4 300	−715.8	−889.1	−836.0	−772.6	−738.1	−696.6	−102.6	−242.6
Total credit	2 300	*382.6*	*327.2*	*462.0*	*528.7*	*438.1*	*474.7*	*352.4*	*413.0*
Total debit	3 300	*−1,098.4*	*−1,216.3*	*−1,297.9*	*−1,301.3*	*−1,176.3*	*−1,171.3*	*−455.0*	*−655.6*
Compensation of employees, credit	2 310	27.3	27.9	35.5	25.2	12.2	20.3	14.0	19.5
Compensation of employees, debit	3 310	−82.4	−89.0	−91.0	−87.1	−88.5	−81.9	−41.9	−36.3
Investment income, credit	2 320	355.3	299.4	426.4	503.5	426.0	454.4	338.4	393.5
Direct investment income	2 330	117.4	41.3	194.4	150.0	39.3	48.0	44.9	11.3
Dividends and distributed branch profits	2 332	112.6	39.8	194.3	149.9	38.9	47.7	44.7	10.9
Reinvested earnings and undistributed branch profits	2 333	4.7	1.6	....	.2	.4	.3	.2	.3
Income on debt (interest)	2 334	....	....	....	....	....	....	....	....
Portfolio investment income	2 339	238.0	209.2	232.1	353.5	386.7	406.4	293.5	382.2
Income on equity	2 340	176.0	188.8	211.1	285.1	381.3	406.4	293.5	382.2
Income on bonds and notes	2 350	....	....	....	....	....	....	....	....
Income on money market instruments	2 360	61.9	20.4	20.9	68.4	5.3	....	....	....
Other investment income	2 370	....	48.9						
Investment income, debit	3 320	−1,016.0	−1,127.3	−1,206.9	−1,214.2	−1,087.8	−1,089.4	−413.1	−619.3
Direct investment income	3 330	−1,003.5	−1,089.4	−1,065.7	−1,042.5	−988.8	−1,056.9	−377.4	−597.7
Dividends and distributed branch profits	3 332	−651.0	−732.3	−851.5	−778.2	−836.0	−682.6	−125.8	−332.8
Reinvested earnings and undistributed branch profits	3 333	−352.6	−357.0	−213.8	−264.4	−152.7	−374.3	−251.6	−265.0
Income on debt (interest)	3 334	....	....	−.4	....	−.1	....	....	....
Portfolio investment income	3 339	....	....	−89.6	−58.0	−37.6	−32.4	−35.8	−21.6
Income on equity	3 340	....	....						
Income on bonds and notes	3 350	....	....	−89.6	−58.0	−37.6	−32.4	−35.8	−21.6
Income on money market instruments	3 360	....	....						
Other investment income	3 370	−12.5	−37.9	−51.6	−113.6	−61.4	....	....	....
D. CURRENT TRANSFERS	4 379	290.1	526.1	672.5	871.4	1,231.1	1,040.4	605.9	979.1
Credit	2 379	538.3	743.0	886.0	1,073.4	1,494.2	1,399.3	1,153.5	1,396.2
General government	2 380	510.8	662.5	798.9	955.9	1,398.1	1,302.0	1,079.8	1,334.2
Other sectors	2 390	27.5	80.5	87.2	117.5	96.1	97.3	73.7	62.1
Workers' remittances	2 391	....	50.8	82.4	78.7	80.0	81.0	61.6	12.1
Other current transfers	2 392	27.5	29.7	4.8	38.8	16.1	16.3	12.2	49.9
Debit	3 379	−248.2	−216.8	−213.6	−202.0	−263.1	−358.9	−547.6	−417.2
General government	3 380	−145.1	−206.6	−197.1	−192.0	−253.0	−318.2	−508.9	−379.1
Other sectors	3 390	−103.2	−10.2	−16.5	−10.0	−10.2	−40.6	−38.8	−38.0
Workers' remittances	3 391	−103.2	−10.2	−16.5	−10.0	−10.2	−40.6	−38.8	−38.0
Other current transfers	3 392	....	....	....	....	....	....	....	....
CAPITAL AND FINANCIAL ACCOUNT	4 996	−301.6	−125.7	−1,634.9	−2,344.3	−2,585.7	−1,011.8	−178.7	−655.4
CAPITAL ACCOUNT	4 994	22.5	31.8	67.4	5.7	88.9	76.3	89.2	19.0
Total credit	2 994	*42.5*	*53.0*	*89.1*	*26.5*	*110.0*	*98.8*	*114.8*	*41.1*
Total debit	3 994	*−20.0*	*−21.2*	*−21.7*	*−20.7*	*−21.1*	*−22.5*	*−25.6*	*−22.1*
Capital transfers, credit	2 400	42.5	53.0	89.1	26.5	110.0	98.8	114.8	41.1
General government	2 401	30.9	40.1	75.9	13.9	97.2	85.9	80.4	10.1
Debt forgiveness	2 402	....	....	....	....	....	....	....	....
Other capital transfers	2 410	30.9	40.1	75.9	13.9	97.2	85.9	80.4	10.1
Other sectors	2 430	11.6	12.8	13.1	12.6	12.8	12.9	34.4	30.9
Migrants' transfers	2 431	11.6	12.8	13.1	12.6	12.8	12.9	34.4	30.9
Debt forgiveness	2 432	....	....	....	....	....	....	....	....
Other capital transfers	2 440	....	....	....	....	....	....	....	....
Capital transfers, debit	3 400	−20.0	−21.2	−21.7	−20.7	−21.1	−22.5	−25.6	−22.1
General government	3 401	....	....	....	....	....	....	....	....
Debt forgiveness	3 402	....	....	....	....	....	....	....	....
Other capital transfers	3 410	....	....	....	....	....	....	....	....
Other sectors	3 430	−20.0	−21.2	−21.7	−20.7	−21.1	−22.5	−25.6	−22.1
Migrants' transfers	3 431	−20.0	−21.2	−21.7	−20.7	−21.1	−22.5	−25.6	−22.1
Debt forgiveness	3 432	....	....	....	....	....	....	....	....
Other capital transfers	3 440	....	....	....	....	....	....	....	....
Nonproduced nonfinancial assets, credit	2 480	....	....	....	....	....	....	....	....
Nonproduced nonfinancial assets, debit	3 480	....	....	....	....	....	....	....	....

Table 2 (Continued). STANDARD PRESENTATION, 2003–2010
(Millions of U.S. dollars)

	Code	2003	2004	2005	2006	2007	2008	2009	2010
FINANCIAL ACCOUNT	4 995	**−324.0**	**−157.5**	**−1,702.3**	**−2,350.1**	**−2,674.6**	**−1,088.1**	**−267.9**	**−674.4**
A. DIRECT INVESTMENT	4 500	**559.8**	**785.3**	**436.5**	**700.9**	**596.2**	**993.5**	**758.9**	**264.7**
Direct investment abroad	4 505	**−210.8**	**37.2**	**−55.9**	**−49.9**	**−51.0**	**91.1**	**−65.2**	**−.3**
Equity capital	4 510	−206.2	49.8	−52.2	−28.8	−29.3	102.7	−74.1	....
Claims on affiliated enterprises	4 515	−206.2	49.8	−52.2	−28.8	−29.3	102.7	−74.1	....
Liabilities to affiliated enterprises	4 520	....	....	....	....	....	....	....	....
Reinvested earnings	4 525	−4.7	−1.6	....	−.2	−.4	−.3	−.2	−.3
Other capital	4 530	.2	−11.0	−3.7	−21.0	−21.3	−11.3	9.1	....
Claims on affiliated enterprises	4 535	.2	−11.0	−3.7	−21.0	−21.3	−11.3	9.1	....
Liabilities to affiliated enterprises	4 540	....	....	....	....	....	....	....	....
Direct investment in Botswana	4 555	**770.5**	**748.1**	**492.4**	**750.8**	**647.3**	**902.4**	**824.1**	**265.0**
Equity capital	4 560	417.9	414.6	210.8	490.9	499.2	520.9	572.5	....
Claims on direct investors	4 565	....	....	....	....	....	....	....	....
Liabilities to direct investors	4 570	417.9	414.6	210.8	490.9	499.2	520.9	572.5	....
Reinvested earnings	4 575	352.6	357.0	213.8	264.4	152.7	374.3	251.6	265.0
Other capital	4 580	.1	−23.5	67.8	−4.5	−4.6	7.2	....	....
Claims on direct investors	4 585	....	....	....	....	....	....	....	....
Liabilities to direct investors	4 590	.1	−23.5	67.8	−4.5	−4.6	7.2	....	....
B. PORTFOLIO INVESTMENT	4 600	**−249.1**	**−421.4**	**−192.6**	**−556.7**	**−212.2**	**293.4**	**365.6**	**414.6**
Assets	4 602	**−315.9**	**−392.2**	**−174.4**	**−593.0**	**−226.0**	**322.9**	**347.8**	**396.8**
Equity securities	4 610	−451.6	−415.1	−289.4	−593.0	−326.5	319.2	456.5	405.0
Monetary authorities	4 611	....	....	....	....	....	....	....	....
General government	4 612	....	....	....	....	....	....	....	....
Banks	4 613	....	....	....	....	....	....	....	....
Other sectors	4 614	−451.6	−415.1	−289.4	−593.0	−326.5	319.2	456.5	405.0
Debt securities	4 619	135.7	22.9	115.0	....	100.5	3.7	−108.7	−8.1
Bonds and notes	4 620	135.7	22.9	115.0	....	100.5	3.7	−108.7	−8.1
Monetary authorities	4 621	....	....	....	....	....	....	....	....
General government	4 622	....	....	....	....	....	....	....	....
Banks	4 623	....	....	....	....	....	....	....	....
Other sectors	4 624	135.7	22.9	115.0	....	100.5	3.7	−108.7	−8.1
Money market instruments	4 630	....	....	....	....	....	....	....	....
Monetary authorities	4 631	....	....	....	....	....	....	....	....
General government	4 632	....	....	....	....	....	....	....	....
Banks	4 633	....	....	....	....	....	....	....	....
Other sectors	4 634	....	....	....	....	....	....	....	....
Liabilities	4 652	**66.8**	**−29.2**	**−18.2**	**36.2**	**13.7**	**−29.5**	**17.7**	**17.8**
Equity securities	4 660	10.2	.6	27.2	36.0	9.4	−36.7	17.2	18.0
Banks	4 663	....	....	....	....	....	....	....	....
Other sectors	4 664	10.2	.6	27.2	36.0	9.4	−36.7	17.2	18.0
Debt securities	4 669	56.6	−29.8	−45.4	.2	4.3	7.2	.6	−.2
Bonds and notes	4 670	56.6	−29.8	−45.4	.2	4.3	7.2	.6	−.2
Monetary authorities	4 671	....	....	....	....	....	....	....	....
General government	4 672	56.6	−29.8	−45.4	.2	4.3	7.2	.6	−.2
Banks	4 673	....	....	....	....	....	....	....	....
Other sectors	4 674	....	....	....	....	....	....	....	....
Money market instruments	4 680	....	....	....	....	....	....	....	....
Monetary authorities	4 681	....	....	....	....	....	....	....	....
General government	4 682	....	....	....	....	....	....	....	....
Banks	4 683	....	....	....	....	....	....	....	....
Other sectors	4 684	....	....	....	....	....	....	....	....
C. FINANCIAL DERIVATIVES	4 910	....	....	....	....	....	....	....	....
Monetary authorities	4 911	....	....	....	....	....	....	....	....
General government	4 912	....	....	....	....	....	....	....	....
Banks	4 913	....	....	....	....	....	....	....	....
Other sectors	4 914	....	....	....	....	....	....	....	....
Assets	4 900	....	....	....	....	....	....	....	....
Monetary authorities	4 901	....	....	....	....	....	....	....	....
General government	4 902	....	....	....	....	....	....	....	....
Banks	4 903	....	....	....	....	....	....	....	....
Other sectors	4 904	....	....	....	....	....	....	....	....
Liabilities	4 905	....	....	....	....	....	....	....	....
Monetary authorities	4 906	....	....	....	....	....	....	....	....
General government	4 907	....	....	....	....	....	....	....	....
Banks	4 908	....	....	....	....	....	....	....	....
Other sectors	4 909	....	....	....	....	....	....	....	....

Table 2 (Concluded). STANDARD PRESENTATION, 2003–2010

(Millions of U.S. dollars)

	Code	2003	2004	2005	2006	2007	2008	2009	2010
D. OTHER INVESTMENT	4 700	**−463.2**	**−558.8**	**−582.6**	**−745.8**	**−1,319.5**	**−1,297.3**	**−2,016.7**	**−2,311.3**
Assets	4 703	**−444.6**	**−474.3**	**−781.6**	**−1,053.1**	**−1,276.7**	**−1,194.6**	**−1,142.6**	**−1,217.8**
Trade credits	4 706	−24.2	−25.8	−115.5	−129.5	−101.5	−14.6	−80.2	−90.8
General government	4 707	....	....	....	....	....	....	....	....
of which: Short-term	4 709	....	....	....	....	....	....	....	....
Other sectors	4 710	−24.2	−25.8	−115.5	−129.5	−101.5	−14.6	−80.2	−90.8
of which: Short-term	4 712	*−24.2*	*−25.8*	*−115.5*	*−129.5*	*−101.5*	*−14.6*	*−80.2*	*−90.8*
Loans	4 714	−24.2	−25.8	−115.5	−129.5	−101.5	−14.6	....	....
Monetary authorities	4 715	....	....	....	....	....	....	....	....
of which: Short-term	4 718	....	....	....	....	....	....	....	....
General government	4 719	....	....	....	....	....	....	....	....
of which: Short-term	4 721	....	....	....	....	....	....	....	....
Banks	4 722	....	....	....	....	....	....	....	....
of which: Short-term	4 724	....	....	....	....	....	....	....	....
Other sectors	4 725	−24.2	−25.8	−115.5	−129.5	−101.5	−14.6	....	....
of which: Short-term	4 727	....	....	....	....	....	....	....	....
Currency and deposits	4 730	−124.0	−62.0	−36.7	−148.7	−144.3	−268.0	−160.4	−221.9
Monetary authorities	4 731	....	....	....	....	....	....	....	....
General government	4 732	....	....	....	....	....	....	....	....
Banks	4 733	−124.0	−62.0	−36.7	−148.7	−144.3	−268.0	−160.4	−221.9
Other sectors	4 734	....	....	....	....	....	....	....	....
Other assets	4 736	−272.1	−360.6	−513.9	−645.4	−929.3	−897.3	−901.9	−905.1
Monetary authorities	4 737	....	....	....	....	....	....	....	....
of which: Short-term	4 739	....	....	....	....	....	....	....	....
General government	4 740	−271.0	−360.6	−513.9	−645.4	−929.3	−897.3	−901.9	−905.1
of which: Short-term	4 742	....	....	....	....	....	....	....	....
Banks	4 743	....	....	....	....	....	....	....	....
of which: Short-term	4 745	....	....	....	....	....	....	....	....
Other sectors	4 746	−1.2	....	....	....	....	....	....	....
of which: Short-term	4 748	....	....	....	....	....	....	....	....
Liabilities	4 753	**−18.5**	**−84.5**	**199.0**	**307.3**	**−42.8**	**−102.7**	**−874.2**	**−1,093.5**
Trade credits	4 756	8.3	13.2	9.2	....	17.4	....	....	....
General government	4 757	8.3	13.2	9.2	....	17.4	....	....	....
of which: Short-term	4 759	*8.3*	*13.2*	*9.2*	....	*−11.3*	....	....	....
Other sectors	4 760	....	....	....	....	....	....	....	....
of which: Short-term	4 762	....	....	....	....	....	....	....	....
Loans	4 764	−43.7	−49.8	−18.9	−72.5	−51.6	−35.0	−912.8	−997.3
Monetary authorities	4 765	....	....	....	....	....	....	....	....
of which: Use of Fund credit and loans from the Fund	4 766	....	....	....	....	....	....	....	....
of which: Short-term	4 768	....	....	....	....	....	....	....	....
General government	4 769	−43.7	−49.8	−18.9	−72.5	−51.6	−35.0	−912.8	−997.3
of which: Short-term	4 771	....	....	....	....	....	....	....	....
Banks	4 772	....	....	....	....	....	....	....	....
of which: Short-term	4 774	....	....	....	....	....	....	....	....
Other sectors	4 775	....	....	....	....	....	....	....	....
of which: Short-term	4 777	....	....	....	....	....	....	....	....
Currency and deposits	4 780	32.4	−2.2	143.7	10.6	−31.1	9.2	−57.1	−90.8
Monetary authorities	4 781	....	....	....	....	....	....	....	....
General government	4 782	....	....	....	....	....	....	....	....
Banks	4 783	32.4	−2.2	143.7	10.6	−31.1	9.2	−57.1	−90.8
Other sectors	4 784	....	....	....	....	....	....	....	....
Other liabilities	4 786	−15.6	−45.7	64.9	369.2	22.4	−76.9	95.7	−5.4
Monetary authorities	4 787	....	....	....	....	....	....	82.9	....
of which: Short-term	4 789	....	....	....	....	....	....	....	....
General government	4 790	4.6	−1.5	−10.7	−9.3	−4.9	−13.5	12.8	−5.4
of which: Short-term	4 792	....	....	....	....	....	....	....	....
Banks	4 793	5.2	....	....	....	....	....	....	....
of which: Short-term	4 795	*5.2*	....	....	....	....	....	....	....
Other sectors	4 796	−25.4	−44.1	75.7	378.5	27.3	−63.4	....	....
of which: Short-term	4 798	*−25.4*	*−44.1*	*75.7*	*378.5*	*27.3*	*−63.4*	....	....
E. RESERVE ASSETS	4 802	**−171.5**	**37.5**	**−1,363.5**	**−1,748.4**	**−1,739.0**	**−1,077.6**	**624.3**	**957.6**
Monetary gold	4 812	....	....	....	....	....	....	....	....
Special drawing rights	4 811	−1.2	−1.3	−1.7	−2.0	−2.3	−1.8	−83.3	−.2
Reserve position in the Fund	4 810	−9.1	14.7	19.0	1.7	2.7	−6.0	−4.4	−3.5
Foreign exchange	4 803	1,254.3	−147.8	−2,041.2	−2,280.9	−1,714.9	−1,456.7	1,570.2	1,042.2
Other claims	4 813	−1,415.4	172.0	660.3	532.7	−24.5	386.9	−858.2	−81.0
NET ERRORS AND OMISSIONS	4 998	**−160.7**	**−292.9**	**72.6**	**398.6**	**570.2**	**144.0**	**699.9**	**609.5**

Table 3. INTERNATIONAL INVESTMENT POSITION (End-period stocks), 2003–2010

(Millions of U.S. dollars)

	Code	2003	2004	2005	2006	2007	2008	2009	2010
ASSETS..	8 995 C.	**8,286.0**	**8,809.7**	**9,957.1**	**12,618.6**	**14,897.5**	**12,873.4**	**12,707.8**	**12,386.1**
Direct investment abroad........................	8 505 ..	**1,446.6**	**950.1**	**796.0**	**757.9**	**1,322.6**	**545.3**	**399.3**	**448.4**
Equity capital and reinvested earnings...........	8 506 ..	1,446.1	941.9	776.7	732.2	1,046.3	544.3	399.3	448.4
Claims on affiliated enterprises.................	8 507 ..	1,446.1	941.9	776.7	732.2	1,046.3	544.3	399.3	448.4
Liabilities to affiliated enterprises.............	8 508 ..	....	....	....	....	....	....	....	....
Other capital...	8 530 ..	.6	8.2	19.3	25.7	276.3	1.0	....	....
Claims on affiliated enterprises.................	8 535 ..	.6	8.2	19.3	25.7	276.3	1.0	....	....
Liabilities to affiliated enterprises.............	8 540 ..	....	....	....	....	....	....	....	....
Portfolio investment.................................	8 602 ..	**1,583.0**	**2,093.5**	**2,607.3**	**3,119.1**	**3,480.0**	**2,412.4**	**2,928.1**	**3,311.2**
Equity securities.......................................	8 610 ..	1,013.5	1,485.4	1,819.4	2,368.5	2,798.2	1,864.5	2,427.3	2,783.7
Monetary authorities..............................	8 611 ..	....	....	....	....	....	....	....	....
General government...............................	8 612 ..	....	....	....	....	....	....	....	....
Banks...	8 613 ..	....	....	....	....	....	....	....	....
Other sectors...	8 614 ..	1,013.5	1,485.4	1,819.4	2,368.5	2,798.2	1,864.5	2,427.3	2,783.7
Debt securities..	8 619 ..	569.5	608.2	787.8	750.6	681.8	548.0	500.9	527.5
Bonds and notes....................................	8 620 ..	569.5	608.2	787.8	750.6	681.8	548.0	500.9	527.5
Monetary authorities..........................	8 621 ..	....	....	....	....	....	....	....	....
General government...........................	8 622 ..	....	....	....	....	....	....	....	....
Banks..	8 623 ..	....	....	....	....	....	....	....	....
Other sectors......................................	8 624 ..	569.5	608.2	787.8	750.6	681.8	548.0	500.9	527.5
Money market instruments.....................	8 630 ..	....	....	....	....	....	....	....	....
Monetary authorities..........................	8 631 ..	....	....	....	....	....	....	....	....
General government...........................	8 632 ..	....	....	....	....	....	....	....	....
Banks..	8 633 ..	....	....	....	....	....	....	....	....
Other sectors......................................	8 634 ..	....	....	....	....	....	....	....	....
Financial derivatives................................	8 900 ..	....	....	....	....	....	....	....	....
Monetary authorities................................	8 901 ..	....	....	....	....	....	....	....	....
General government..................................	8 902 ..	....	....	....	....	....	....	....	....
Banks..	8 903 ..	....	....	....	....	....	....	....	....
Other sectors..	8 904 ..	....	....	....	....	....	....	....	....
Other investment....................................	8 703 ..	**459.0**	**451.7**	**472.2**	**800.6**	**344.6**	**787.0**	**701.6**	**722.5**
Trade credits...	8 706 ..	45.4	83.8	114.4	138.1	71.3	19.4	4.2	....
General government...............................	8 707 ..	....	....	....	....	....	....	....	....
of which: Short-term............................	8 709 ..	....	....	....	....	....	....	....	....
Other sectors...	8 710 ..	45.4	83.8	114.4	138.1	71.3	19.4	4.2	....
of which: Short-term............................	8 712 ..	*45.4*	*83.8*	*114.4*	*138.1*	*71.3*	*19.4*	*4.2*	....
Loans...	8 714 ..	....	1.7	45.1	129.8	11.1	28.4	82.0	84.9
Monetary authorities..............................	8 715 ..	....	....	....	....	....	....	....	....
of which: Short-term............................	8 718 ..	....	....	....	....	....	....	....	....
General government...............................	8 719 ..	....	....	....	....	....	....	....	....
of which: Short-term............................	8 721 ..	....	....	....	....	....	....	....	....
Banks...	8 722 ..	....	....	....	....	....	....	....	....
of which: Short-term............................	8 724 ..	....	....	....	....	....	....	....	....
Other sectors...	8 725 ..	....	1.7	45.1	129.8	11.1	28.4	82.0	84.9
of which: Short-term............................	8 727 ..	....	*1.7*	*45.1*	*129.8*	*11.1*	*28.4*	*82.0*	*84.9*
Currency and deposits................................	8 730 ..	413.6	366.1	312.7	532.7	262.2	739.1	615.5	637.6
Monetary authorities..............................	8 731 ..	....	....	....	....	....	....	....	....
General government...............................	8 732 ..	....	....	....	....	....	....	....	....
Banks...	8 733 ..	413.6	366.1	312.7	532.7	262.2	739.1	615.5	637.6
Other sectors...	8 734 ..	....	....	....	....	....	....	....	....
Other assets...	8 736 ..	....	....	....	....	....	....	....	....
Monetary authorities..............................	8 737 ..	....	....	....	....	....	....	....	....
of which: Short-term............................	8 739 ..	....	....	....	....	....	....	....	....
General government...............................	8 740 ..	....	....	....	....	....	....	....	....
of which: Short-term............................	8 742 ..	....	....	....	....	....	....	....	....
Banks...	8 743 ..	....	....	....	....	....	....	....	....
of which: Short-term............................	8 745 ..	....	....	....	....	....	....	....	....
Other sectors...	8 746 ..	....	....	....	....	....	....	....	....
of which: Short-term............................	8 748 ..	....	....	....	....	....	....	....	....
Reserve assets...	8 802 ..	**4,797.4**	**5,314.4**	**6,081.6**	**7,941.0**	**9,750.2**	**9,128.6**	**8,678.8**	**7,904.1**
Monetary gold..	8 812 ..	....	....	....	....	....	....	....	....
Special drawing rights................................	8 811 ..	49.8	53.5	50.8	55.5	60.7	60.9	145.6	143.2
Reserve position in the Fund......................	8 810 ..	45.0	31.8	10.6	9.4	7.0	13.1	17.8	20.9
Foreign exchange.......................................	8 803 ..	4,702.5	5,229.1	6,020.2	7,876.1	9,682.5	9,054.6	8,515.4	7,740.0
Other claims..	8 813 ..	....	....	....	....	....	....	....	....

Table 3 (Concluded). INTERNATIONAL INVESTMENT POSITION (End-period stocks), 2003–2010

(Millions of U.S. dollars)

	Code	2003	2004	2005	2006	2007	2008	2009	2010
LIABILITIES	8 995 D.	**2,645.4**	**2,452.1**	**2,504.4**	**2,618.5**	**3,290.7**	**1,840.5**	**3,790.3**	**2,297.7**
Direct investment in Botswana	8 555 ..	**1,167.2**	**982.1**	**806.2**	**805.1**	**1,046.2**	**884.6**	**1,405.3**	....
Equity capital and reinvested earnings	8 556 ..	1,079.9	926.6	691.0	732.2	1,008.4	869.6	951.9	....
Claims on direct investors	8 557 ..	....	....	....	....	....	....	....	....
Liabilities to direct investors	8 558 ..	1,079.9	926.6	691.0	732.2	1,008.4	869.6	951.9	....
Other capital	8 580 ..	87.3	55.5	115.2	72.9	37.8	15.0	453.3	....
Claims on direct investors	8 585 ..	....	....	....	....	....	....	....	....
Liabilities to direct investors	8 590 ..	87.3	55.5	115.2	72.9	37.8	15.0	453.3	....
Portfolio investment	8 652 ..	**111.9**	**94.9**	**70.7**	**23.4**	**104.0**	**43.5**	**68.6**	**70.2**
Equity securities	8 660 ..	86.7	69.7	54.6	8.5	89.1	38.1	61.9	63.4
Banks	8 663 ..	....	....	....	....	....	....	....	....
Other sectors	8 664 ..	86.7	69.7	54.6	8.5	89.1	38.1	61.9	63.4
Debt securities	8 669 ..	25.1	25.3	16.0	14.8	14.8	5.5	6.7	6.8
Bonds and notes	8 670 ..	25.1	25.3	16.0	14.8	14.8	5.5	6.7	6.8
Monetary authorities	8 671 ..	....	....	....	....	....	....	....	....
General government	8 672 ..	25.1	25.3	16.0	14.6	14.8	5.5	6.7	6.8
Banks	8 673 ..	....	....	....	....	....	....	....	....
Other sectors	8 674 ..	....	....	....	.2	....	....	....	....
Money market instruments	8 680 ..	....	....	....	....	....	....	....	....
Monetary authorities	8 681 ..	....	....	....	....	....	....	....	....
General government	8 682 ..	....	....	....	....	....	....	....	....
Banks	8 683 ..	....	....	....	....	....	....	....	....
Other sectors	8 684 ..	....	....	....	....	....	....	....	....
Financial derivatives	8 905 ..	....	....	....	....	....	....	....	....
Monetary authorities	8 906 ..	....	....	....	....	....	....	....	....
General government	8 907 ..	....	....	....	....	....	....	....	....
Banks	8 908 ..	....	....	....	....	....	....	....	....
Other sectors	8 909 ..	....	....	....	....	....	....	....	....
Other investment	8 753 ..	**1,366.3**	**1,375.0**	**1,627.6**	**1,790.1**	**2,140.5**	**912.4**	**2,316.5**	**2,227.5**
Trade credits	8 756 ..	89.3	181.5	151.1	275.9	161.3	190.7	232.6	.9
General government	8 757 ..	....	....	9.6	8.4	5.9	3.1	5.3	.9
of which: Short-term	8 759 ..	....	....	....	....	....	....	....	....
Other sectors	8 760 ..	89.3	181.5	141.5	267.5	155.4	187.6	227.3	....
of which: Short-term	8 762 ..	*89.3*	*181.5*	*141.5*	*267.5*	*155.4*	*187.6*	*227.3*	....
Loans	8 764 ..	639.1	557.4	569.1	525.4	1,046.0	395.1	1,595.4	1,757.3
Monetary authorities	8 765 ..	....	....	....	....	....	....	....	....
of which: Use of Fund credit and loans from the Fund	8 766 ..	....	....	....	....	....	....	....	....
of which: Short-term	8 768 ..	....	....	....	....	....	....	....	....
General government	8 769 ..	493.8	464.7	397.1	355.4	317.4	235.6	1,310.7	1,442.1
of which: Short-term	8 771 ..	....	....	....	....	....	....	....	....
Banks	8 772 ..	....	....	....	....	....	....	....	....
of which: Short-term	8 774 ..	....	....	....	....	....	....	....	....
Other sectors	8 775 ..	145.2	92.7	171.9	170.0	728.6	159.5	284.6	315.2
of which: Short-term	8 777 ..	....	....	....	....	....	....	....	....
Currency and deposits	8 780 ..	....	34.5	213.1	197.0	36.9	37.7	54.6	....
Monetary authorities	8 781 ..	....	....	....	....	....	....	....	....
General government	8 782 ..	....	....	....	....	....	....	....	....
Banks	8 783 ..	....	34.5	213.1	197.0	36.9	37.7	54.6	....
Other sectors	8 784 ..	....	....	....	....	....	....	....	....
Other liabilities	8 786 ..	637.9	601.7	694.3	791.8	896.3	288.8	433.9	469.3
Monetary authorities	8 787 ..	6.4	6.7	6.2	6.6	6.9	6.7	90.0	88.4
of which: Short-term	8 789 ..	....	....	....	....	....	....	....	....
General government	8 790 ..	....	....	....	....	....	....	....	....
of which: Short-term	8 792 ..	....	....	....	....	....	....	....	....
Banks	8 793 ..	....	....	....	....	....	....	....	....
of which: Short-term	8 795 ..	....	....	....	....	....	....	....	....
Other sectors	8 796 ..	631.5	595.0	688.0	785.2	889.4	282.1	343.9	380.9
of which: Short-term	8 798 ..	*486.3*	*490.0*	*516.1*	*606.8*	*160.8*	*188.0*	*229.2*	*253.8*
NET INTERNATIONAL INVESTMENT POSITION	8 995 ..	**5,640.7**	**6,357.7**	**7,452.7**	**10,000.1**	**11,606.8**	**11,032.9**	**8,917.5**	**10,088.4**
Conversion rates: pula per U.S. dollar (end of period)	0 102 ..	**4.4425**	**4.2808**	**5.5127**	**6.0314**	**6.0060**	**7.5191**	**6.6730**	**6.4412**

Table 1. ANALYTIC PRESENTATION, 2003–2010

(Millions of U.S. dollars)

	Code	2003	2004	2005	2006	2007	2008	2009	2010
A. Current Account[1]	4 993 Z.	**4,177**	**11,738**	**13,984**	**13,620**	**1,551**	**−28,192**	**−24,302**	**−47,365**
Goods: exports f.o.b.	2 100 ..	73,084	96,475	118,308	137,807	160,649	197,942	152,995	201,915
Goods: imports f.o.b.	3 100 ..	−48,290	−62,809	−73,606	−91,350	−120,617	−173,107	−127,705	−181,694
Balance on Goods	4 100 ..	*24,794*	*33,666*	*44,703*	*46,458*	*40,032*	*24,836*	*25,290*	*20,221*
Services: credit	2 200 ..	10,447	12,584	16,047	19,462	23,954	30,451	27,728	31,821
Services: debit	3 200 ..	−15,378	−17,260	−24,356	−29,116	−37,173	−47,140	−46,974	−62,628
Balance on Goods and Services	4 991 ..	*19,863*	*28,990*	*36,394*	*36,804*	*26,813*	*8,146*	*6,044*	*−10,586*
Income: credit	2 300 ..	3,339	3,199	3,194	6,438	11,493	12,511	8,826	7,353
Income: debit	3 300 ..	−21,891	−23,719	−29,162	−33,927	−40,784	−53,073	−42,510	−46,919
Balance on Goods, Services, and Income	4 992 ..	*1,311*	*8,469*	*10,427*	*9,315*	*−2,478*	*−32,416*	*−27,640*	*−50,152*
Current transfers: credit	2 379 Z.	3,132	3,582	4,050	4,846	4,972	5,317	4,736	4,661
Current transfers: debit	3 379 ..	−265	−314	−493	−541	−943	−1,093	−1,398	−1,873
B. Capital Account[1]	4 994 Z.	**498**	**339**	**663**	**869**	**756**	**1,055**	**1,129**	**1,119**
Capital account: credit	2 994 Z.	535	764	906	1,084	1,089	1,506	1,429	1,453
Capital account: debit	3 994 ..	−37	−425	−243	−215	−333	−451	−300	−335
Total, Groups A Plus B	4 981 ..	*4,675*	*12,077*	*14,647*	*14,489*	*2,307*	*−27,137*	*−23,174*	*−46,246*
C. Financial Account[1]	4 995 W.	**−157**	**−3,333**	**13,144**	**15,113**	**88,330**	**28,297**	**70,160**	**98,543**
Direct investment abroad	4 505 ..	−249	−9,471	−2,517	−28,202	−7,067	−20,457	10,084	−11,519
Direct investment in Brazil	4 555 Z.	10,144	18,166	15,066	18,782	34,585	45,058	25,949	48,438
Portfolio investment assets	4 602 ..	179	−755	−1,771	523	286	1,900	4,125	−4,784
Equity securities	4 610 ..	−258	−121	−831	−915	−1,413	257	2,582	6,211
Debt securities	4 619 ..	437	−633	−940	1,438	1,699	1,643	1,542	−10,995
Portfolio investment liabilities	4 652 Z.	5,129	−3,996	6,655	9,051	48,104	−767	46,159	67,795
Equity securities	4 660 ..	2,973	2,081	6,451	7,716	26,217	−7,565	37,071	37,684
Debt securities	4 669 Z.	2,156	−6,076	204	1,335	21,887	6,798	9,087	30,111
Financial derivatives	4 910 ..	−151	−677	−40	383	−710	−312	156	−112
Financial derivatives assets	4 900 ..	683	467	508	482	88	298	322	133
Financial derivatives liabilities	4 905 ..	−834	−1,145	−548	−99	−799	−610	−166	−245
Other investment assets	4 703 ..	−9,483	−2,196	−5,035	−8,914	−18,552	−5,269	−30,376	−42,575
Monetary authorities	4 701 ..	....	....	....	2	....	−13,023	12,488	535
General government	4 704 ..	−1,101	−1,227	−229	17	−328	−407	1,023	−44
Banks	4 705 ..	−6,999	1,122	−2,211	−3,323	−11,316	15,257	−15,500	1,789
Other sectors	4 728 ..	−1,383	−2,091	−2,595	−5,610	−6,907	−7,096	−28,387	−44,854
Other investment liabilities	4 753 W.	−5,724	−4,404	785	23,491	31,683	8,143	14,064	41,301
Monetary authorities	4 753 WA	−162	−163	−164	−250	−209	−91	3,879	−91
General government	4 753 ZB	−1,561	−2,633	−1,637	−384	−618	403	−772	3,461
Banks	4 753 ZC	348	1,385	841	3,426	17,897	−7,834	−1,131	24,165
Other sectors	4 753 ZD	−4,350	−2,993	1,745	20,699	14,612	15,666	12,088	13,765
Total, Groups A Through C	4 983 ..	*4,519*	*8,744*	*27,791*	*29,602*	*90,636*	*1,160*	*46,986*	*52,297*
D. Net Errors and Omissions	4 998 ..	**−933**	**−2,145**	**−225**	**967**	**−3,152**	**1,810**	**591**	**−3,217**
Total, Groups A Through D	4 984 ..	*3,586*	*6,599*	*27,566*	*30,569*	*87,484*	*2,969*	*47,578*	*49,080*
E. Reserves and Related Items	4 802 A.	**−3,586**	**−6,599**	**−27,566**	**−30,569**	**−87,484**	**−2,969**	**−47,578**	**−49,080**
Reserve assets	4 802 ..	−8,479	−2,238	−4,324	−30,571	−87,484	−2,969	−47,578	−49,080
Use of Fund credit and loans	4 766 ..	4,893	−4,362	−23,243	....	....	....	....	....
Exceptional financing	4 920 ..	....	....	....	2	....	....	....	....
Conversion rates: reais per U.S. dollar	0 101 ..	**3.07748**	**2.92512**	**2.43439**	**2.17533**	**1.94706**	**1.83377**	**1.99943**	**1.75936**

[1] Excludes components that have been classified in the categories of Group E.

Table 2. STANDARD PRESENTATION, 2003–2010

(Millions of U.S. dollars)

	Code	2003	2004	2005	2006	2007	2008	2009	2010
CURRENT ACCOUNT............................	4 993 ..	**4,177**	**11,738**	**13,985**	**13,621**	**1,551**	**−28,192**	**−24,302**	**−47,365**
A. GOODS..	4 100 ..	**24,794**	**33,666**	**44,703**	**46,458**	**40,032**	**24,836**	**25,290**	**20,221**
Credit..	2 100 ..	**73,084**	**96,475**	**118,308**	**137,807**	**160,649**	**197,942**	**152,995**	**201,915**
General merchandise: exports f.o.b.	2 110 ..	71,636	96,091	117,850	137,149	157,059	192,304	148,983	201,915
Goods for processing: exports f.o.b.	2 150 ..	....	....	....	....	....	....	....	....
Repairs on goods............................	2 160 ..	....	....	....	....	....	....	....	....
Goods procured in ports by carriers	2 170 ..	1,121	281	....	....	2,799	4,606	2,611	....
Nonmonetary gold..........................	2 180 ..	327	104	459	659	791	1,033	1,401	....
Debit...	3 100 ..	**−48,290**	**−62,809**	**−73,606**	**−91,350**	**−120,617**	**−173,107**	**−127,705**	**−181,694**
General merchandise: imports f.o.b.	3 110 ..	−47,809	−62,348	−73,140	−91,349	−120,617	−173,106	−127,705	−181,694
Goods for processing: imports f.o.b.	3 150 ..	−481	−461	−466	....	....	....	....	....
Repairs on goods............................	3 160 ..	....	....	....	....	....	....	....	....
Goods procured in ports by carriers	3 170 ..	....	....	....	....	....	....	....	....
Nonmonetary gold..........................	3 180 ..	....	....	....	....	....	−1	....	....
B. SERVICES......................................	4 200 ..	**−4,931**	**−4,677**	**−8,309**	**−9,654**	**−13,219**	**−16,690**	**−19,245**	**−30,807**
Total credit.....................................	2 200 ..	*10,447*	*12,584*	*16,047*	*19,462*	*23,954*	*30,451*	*27,728*	*31,821*
Total debit......................................	3 200 ..	*−15,378*	*−17,260*	*−24,356*	*−29,116*	*−37,173*	*−47,140*	*−46,974*	*−62,628*
Transportation services, credit........	2 205 ..	**1,822**	**2,467**	**3,139**	**3,439**	**4,119**	**5,411**	**4,040**	**4,931**
Passenger.....................................	2 850 ..	*194*	*167*	*307*	*261*	*331*	*324*	*330*	*261*
Freight...	2 851 ..	*659*	*936*	*1,032*	*1,160*	*1,516*	*1,744*	*1,494*	*1,983*
Other...	2 852 ..	*969*	*1,364*	*1,799*	*2,017*	*2,272*	*3,342*	*2,216*	*2,687*
Sea transport, passenger.................	2 207 ..	....	....	....	....	....	....	1	....
Sea transport, freight.....................	2 208 ..	553	792	861	979	1,161	1,325	1,161	1,517
Sea transport, other.......................	2 209 ..	889	1,286	1,740	1,918	2,186	3,251	2,122	2,544
Air transport, passenger.................	2 211 ..	193	165	306	260	330	323	329	260
Air transport, freight......................	2 212 ..	61	76	90	77	247	282	222	291
Air transport, other........................	2 213 ..	64	62	47	89	72	70	61	95
Other transport, passenger.............	2 215 ..	1	2	1	1	1	1	1	1
Other transport, freight..................	2 216 ..	44	69	81	104	108	137	112	176
Other transport, other....................	2 217 ..	16	15	12	10	15	21	33	48
Transportation services, debit.........	3 205 ..	**−3,412**	**−4,452**	**−5,089**	**−6,565**	**−8,503**	**−10,405**	**−7,966**	**−11,337**
Passenger.....................................	3 850 ..	*−613*	*−881*	*−1,185*	*−1,737*	*−2,223*	*−2,307*	*−1,999*	*−2,918*
Freight...	3 851 ..	*−1,247*	*−1,613*	*−1,897*	*−2,296*	*−3,068*	*−4,343*	*−3,234*	*−4,606*
Other...	3 852 ..	*−1,552*	*−1,957*	*−2,007*	*−2,531*	*−3,213*	*−3,755*	*−2,733*	*−3,812*
Sea transport, passenger.................	3 207 ..	−2	−8	−8	−1	−2	−2	−1	−1
Sea transport, freight.....................	3 208 ..	−1,119	−1,438	−1,699	−2,055	−2,755	−3,898	−2,906	−4,110
Sea transport, other.......................	3 209 ..	−939	−1,342	−1,587	−2,127	−2,772	−3,485	−2,473	−3,501
Air transport, passenger.................	3 211 ..	−611	−873	−1,178	−1,736	−2,222	−2,305	−1,997	−2,917
Air transport, freight......................	3 212 ..	−69	−97	−109	−130	−166	−234	−161	−231
Air transport, other........................	3 213 ..	−612	−615	−418	−403	−437	−267	−256	−299
Other transport, passenger.............	3 215 ..	....	....	....	....	....	....	....	....
Other transport, freight..................	3 216 ..	−59	−78	−90	−111	−146	−211	−167	−265
Other transport, other....................	3 217 ..	−1	−1	−1	−1	−3	−2	−5	−12
Travel, credit.................................	2 236 ..	**2,479**	**3,222**	**3,861**	**4,316**	**4,953**	**5,785**	**5,305**	**5,919**
Business travel...............................	2 237 ..	46	51	68	63	70	84	70	89
Personal travel...............................	2 240 ..	2,433	3,171	3,794	4,253	4,883	5,701	5,235	5,830
Travel, debit..................................	3 236 ..	**−2,261**	**−2,871**	**−4,720**	**−5,764**	**−8,211**	**−10,962**	**−10,898**	**−16,422**
Business travel...............................	3 237 ..	−198	−236	−291	−319	−370	−508	−375	−513
Personal travel...............................	3 240 ..	−2,063	−2,635	−4,429	−5,444	−7,841	−10,454	−10,524	−15,909
Other services, credit......................	2 200 BA	**6,146**	**6,895**	**9,047**	**11,708**	**14,882**	**19,255**	**18,383**	**20,971**
Communications.............................	2 245 ..	449	243	239	205	276	466	353	435
Construction..................................	2 249 ..	10	3	8	23	17	23	14	29
Insurance.......................................	2 253 ..	124	105	134	324	543	828	373	416
Financial..	2 260 ..	363	423	507	738	1,090	1,238	1,570	2,073
Computer and information..............	2 262 ..	29	53	88	102	161	189	209	210
Royalties and licence fees...............	2 266 ..	108	114	102	150	319	465	434	397
Other business services...................	2 268 ..	4,133	4,938	6,722	8,568	11,064	14,331	13,867	15,776
Personal, cultural, and recreational..	2 287 ..	54	47	56	81	73	86	80	108
Government, n.i.e...........................	2 291 ..	877	969	1,192	1,517	1,340	1,628	1,483	1,527
Other services, debit.......................	3 200 BA	**−9,705**	**−9,937**	**−14,547**	**−16,788**	**−20,458**	**−25,773**	**−28,109**	**−34,869**
Communications.............................	3 245 ..	−366	−70	−112	−102	−96	−299	−166	−271
Construction..................................	3 249 ..	....	−1	....	−4	−4	−9	−4	−6
Insurance.......................................	3 253 ..	−560	−649	−702	−755	−1,308	−1,665	−1,815	−1,529
Financial..	3 260 ..	−745	−499	−737	−861	−807	−1,145	−1,612	−1,679
Computer and information..............	3 262 ..	−1,063	−1,281	−1,713	−2,005	−2,273	−2,787	−2,795	−3,505
Royalties and licence fees...............	3 266 ..	−1,228	−1,197	−1,404	−1,664	−2,259	−2,697	−2,512	−2,850
Other business services...................	3 268 ..	−4,379	−4,682	−7,480	−8,898	−10,586	−13,556	−15,348	−20,873
Personal, cultural, and recreational..	3 287 ..	−337	−409	−451	−533	−651	−869	−958	−1,271
Government, n.i.e...........................	3 291 ..	−1,028	−1,149	−1,947	−1,967	−2,473	−2,744	−2,899	−2,883

Table 2 (Continued). STANDARD PRESENTATION, 2003–2010

(Millions of U.S. dollars)

	Code	2003	2004	2005	2006	2007	2008	2009	2010
C. INCOME	4 300	**−18,552**	**−20,520**	**−25,967**	**−27,489**	**−29,291**	**−40,562**	**−33,684**	**−39,567**
Total credit	2 300	*3,339*	*3,199*	*3,194*	*6,438*	*11,493*	*12,511*	*8,826*	*7,353*
Total debit	3 300	*−21,891*	*−23,719*	*−29,162*	*−33,927*	*−40,784*	*−53,073*	*−42,510*	*−46,919*
Compensation of employees, credit	2 310	**269**	**354**	**325**	**397**	**497**	**730**	**665**	**565**
Compensation of employees, debit	3 310	**−160**	**−173**	**−111**	**−220**	**−49**	**−185**	**−62**	**−66**
Investment income, credit	2 320	**3,070**	**2,845**	**2,869**	**6,041**	**10,996**	**11,781**	**8,160**	**6,788**
Direct investment income	2 330	886	1,061	733	1,073	2,202	1,997	1,287	1,080
Dividends and distributed branch profits	2 332	760	916	641	928	1,152	1,526	1,186	888
Reinvested earnings and undistributed branch profits	2 333	....	....	...	....	....	....	....	...
Income on debt (interest)	2 334	126	145	92	145	1,050	472	100	193
Portfolio investment income	2 339	1,323	733	785	3,049	6,955	8,695	5,827	4,875
Income on equity	2 340	3	4	10	21	13	15	44	1
Income on bonds and notes	2 350	1,320	729	717	3,024	6,656	8,680	5,783	4,874
Income on money market instruments	2 360	....	....	58	4	286	....	...	...
Other investment income	2 370	861	1,051	1,351	1,919	1,839	1,088	1,046	833
Investment income, debit	3 320	**−21,731**	**−23,546**	**−29,050**	**−33,707**	**−40,735**	**−52,888**	**−42,448**	**−46,853**
Direct investment income	3 330	−5,984	−6,860	−11,035	−13,884	−19,692	−28,773	−21,029	−26,584
Dividends and distributed branch profits	3 332	−4,836	−5,853	−9,783	−12,359	−17,898	−26,874	−18,951	−24,479
Reinvested earnings and undistributed branch profits	3 333	...	....	....	....	....	....	....	...
Income on debt (interest)	3 334	−1,148	−1,007	−1,253	−1,525	−1,794	−1,898	−2,077	−2,106
Portfolio investment income	3 339	−10,066	−11,173	−12,563	−14,101	−14,020	−16,734	−15,041	−14,919
Income on equity	3 340	−1,568	−2,404	−3,554	−4,945	−5,702	−8,542	−7,497	−6,785
Income on bonds and notes	3 350	−8,499	−8,768	−9,009	−9,156	−8,318	−8,192	−7,543	−8,135
Income on money market instruments	3 360	....	....	...	....	....	....	...	...
Other investment income	3 370	−5,681	−5,514	−5,452	−5,723	−7,024	−7,381	−6,378	−5,350
D. CURRENT TRANSFERS	4 379	**2,867**	**3,268**	**3,558**	**4,306**	**4,029**	**4,224**	**3,338**	**2,788**
Credit	2 379	**3,132**	**3,582**	**4,051**	**4,847**	**4,972**	**5,317**	**4,736**	**4,661**
General government	2 380	48	54	81	86	139	146	61	132
Other sectors	2 390	3,084	3,529	3,969	4,761	4,833	5,170	4,675	4,529
Workers' remittances	2 391	2,018	2,459	2,480	2,890	2,809	2,913	2,224	2,076
Other current transfers	2 392	1,066	1,070	1,490	1,871	2,024	2,258	2,451	2,454
Debit	3 379	**−265**	**−314**	**−493**	**−541**	**−943**	**−1,093**	**−1,398**	**−1,873**
General government	3 380	−68	−86	−140	−122	−129	−109	−270	−317
Other sectors	3 390	−197	−228	−353	−419	−813	−983	−1,128	−1,557
Workers' remittances	3 391	−136	−167	−263	−309	−514	−628	−669	−855
Other current transfers	3 392	−61	−61	−91	−110	−299	−355	−459	−701
CAPITAL AND FINANCIAL ACCOUNT	4 996	**−3,245**	**−9,593**	**−13,760**	**−14,589**	**1,601**	**26,382**	**23,711**	**50,582**
CAPITAL ACCOUNT	4 994	**498**	**339**	**663**	**869**	**756**	**1,055**	**1,129**	**1,119**
Total credit	2 994	*535*	*764*	*906*	*1,084*	*1,089*	*1,506*	*1,429*	*1,453*
Total debit	3 994	*−37*	*−425*	*−243*	*−215*	*−333*	*−451*	*−300*	*−335*
Capital transfers, credit	2 400	**535**	**763**	**905**	**1,083**	**1,077**	**1,483**	**1,427**	**1,403**
General government	2 401	....	....	....	....	....	....	....	....
Debt forgiveness	2 402	....	....	....	....	....	....	....	....
Other capital transfers	2 410	....	....	....	....	....	....	....	....
Other sectors	2 430	535	763	905	1,082	1,077	1,483	1,427	1,403
Migrants' transfers	2 431	535	763	735	966	1,077	1,446	1,345	1,359
Debt forgiveness	2 432	....	....	....	....	....	....	....	....
Other capital transfers	2 440	....	....	170	117	....	37	82	44
Capital transfers, debit	3 400	**−37**	**−425**	**−243**	**−213**	**−333**	**−451**	**−300**	**−306**
General government	3 401	....	−364	....	....	....	....	....	....
Debt forgiveness	3 402	....	−364	....	....	....	....	....	....
Other capital transfers	3 410	....	....	....	....	....	....	....	....
Other sectors	3 430	−37	−61	−243	−213	−333	−451	−300	−306
Migrants' transfers	3 431	−37	−61	−124	−161	−333	−378	−272	−276
Debt forgiveness	3 432	....	....	−85	....	....	....	....	....
Other capital transfers	3 440	....	....	−34	−52	....	−73	−28	−30
Nonproduced nonfinancial assets, credit	2 480	**1**	**2**	**1**	**1**	**12**	**22**	**2**	**50**
Nonproduced nonfinancial assets, debit	3 480	....	....	....	−1	....	....	....	−29

Table 2 (Continued). STANDARD PRESENTATION, 2003–2010

(Millions of U.S. dollars)

	Code	2003	2004	2005	2006	2007	2008	2009	2010
FINANCIAL ACCOUNT	4 995	**−3,743**	**−9,932**	**−14,423**	**−15,458**	**845**	**25,327**	**22,583**	**49,463**
A. DIRECT INVESTMENT	4 500	**9,894**	**8,695**	**12,550**	**−9,420**	**27,518**	**24,601**	**36,033**	**36,919**
Direct investment abroad	4 505	**−249**	**−9,471**	**−2,517**	**−28,202**	**−7,067**	**−20,457**	**10,084**	**−11,519**
Equity capital	4 510	−62	−6,640	−2,695	−23,413	−10,091	−13,859	−4,545	−26,782
Claims on affiliated enterprises	4 515	−62	−6,640	−2,695	−23,413	−10,091	−13,859	−4,545	−26,782
Liabilities to affiliated enterprises	4 520	....	....	....	....	....	....	....	....
Reinvested earnings	4 525	....	....	....	....	....	....	....	....
Other capital	4 530	−187	−2,831	178	−4,789	3,025	−6,598	14,629	15,263
Claims on affiliated enterprises	4 535	−187	−2,834	103	−4,773	−5,823	−12,349	10,119	10,401
Liabilities to affiliated enterprises	4 540	....	3	75	−16	8,848	5,751	4,510	4,862
Direct investment in Brazil	4 555	**10,144**	**18,166**	**15,066**	**18,782**	**34,585**	**45,058**	**25,949**	**48,438**
Equity capital	4 560	9,320	18,570	15,045	15,373	26,074	30,064	19,906	40,117
Claims on direct investors	4 565	....	....	....	....	....	....	....	....
Liabilities to direct investors	4 570	9,320	18,570	15,045	15,373	26,074	30,064	19,906	40,117
Reinvested earnings	4 575	....	....	....	....	....	....	....	....
Other capital	4 580	823	−405	21	3,409	8,510	14,994	6,042	8,321
Claims on direct investors	4 585	21	−12	−319	−612	−1,147	93	−1,022	−45
Liabilities to direct investors	4 590	803	−392	340	4,021	9,657	14,901	7,064	8,366
B. PORTFOLIO INVESTMENT	4 600	**5,308**	**−4,750**	**4,885**	**9,573**	**48,390**	**1,133**	**50,283**	**63,011**
Assets	4 602	**179**	**−755**	**−1,771**	**523**	**286**	**1,900**	**4,125**	**−4,784**
Equity securities	4 610	−258	−121	−831	−915	−1,413	257	2,582	6,211
Monetary authorities	4 611	....	....	....	....	....	....	....	....
General government	4 612	....	....	....	....	....	....	....	....
Banks	4 613	−155	−71	−383	−811	−1,409	−15	475	340
Other sectors	4 614	−103	−50	−448	−104	−5	272	2,107	5,871
Debt securities	4 619	437	−633	−940	1,438	1,699	1,643	1,542	−10,995
Bonds and notes	4 620	437	−633	−519	858	1,789	1,523	1,541	−10,995
Monetary authorities	4 621	....	....	....	....	140	45	1,099	....
General government	4 622	359	8	....	846	....	....	....	....
Banks	4 623	−66	−144	−891	−235	998	417	1,069	−2,751
Other sectors	4 624	143	−496	372	248	652	1,061	−627	−8,244
Money market instruments	4 630	....	....	−421	579	−90	120	1	....
Monetary authorities	4 631	....	....	....	....	....	....	....	....
General government	4 632	....	....	....	....	....	....	....	....
Banks	4 633	....	....	....	....	−90	120	1	....
Other sectors	4 634	....	....	−421	579	....	....	....	....
Liabilities	4 652	**5,129**	**−3,996**	**6,655**	**9,051**	**48,104**	**−767**	**46,159**	**67,795**
Equity securities	4 660	2,973	2,081	6,451	7,716	26,217	−7,565	37,071	37,684
Banks	4 663	989	278	1,380	2,085	3,459	−881	8,720	4,169
Other sectors	4 664	1,983	1,803	5,071	5,631	22,759	−6,684	28,351	33,515
Debt securities	4 669	2,156	−6,076	204	1,335	21,887	6,798	9,087	30,111
Bonds and notes	4 670	1,721	−6,513	−506	−2,827	11,302	9,262	9,256	23,493
Monetary authorities	4 671	27	16	69	43	....	....	....	....
General government	4 672	1,154	192	2,976	−6,614	5,878	10,803	9,716	9,819
Banks	4 673	541	−2,913	−101	3,130	4,542	−846	−2,533	11,016
Other sectors	4 674	−1	−3,808	−3,450	614	882	−695	2,073	2,658
Money market instruments	4 680	435	436	710	4,161	10,585	−2,464	−168	6,618
Monetary authorities	4 681	17	10	44	28	....	....	....	....
General government	4 682	91	54	232	4,043	6,934	1,471	404	1,207
Banks	4 683	−233	−310	577	805	3,765	−4,043	−897	4,445
Other sectors	4 684	560	682	−142	−714	−114	108	325	966
C. FINANCIAL DERIVATIVES	4 910	**−151**	**−677**	**−40**	**383**	**−710**	**−312**	**156**	**−112**
Monetary authorities	4 911	....	....	....	....	....	....	....	....
General government	4 912	....	....	....	....	....	....	....	....
Banks	4 913	71	58	206	362	−196	97	−38	11
Other sectors	4 914	−222	−735	−246	21	−514	−409	194	−123
Assets	4 900	**683**	**467**	**508**	**482**	**88**	**298**	**322**	**133**
Monetary authorities	4 901	....	....	....	....	....	....	....	....
General government	4 902	....	....	....	....	....	....	....	....
Banks	4 903	623	814	411	134	37	113	−2	23
Other sectors	4 904	59	−347	97	348	51	185	325	110
Liabilities	4 905	**−834**	**−1,145**	**−548**	**−99**	**−799**	**−610**	**−166**	**−245**
Monetary authorities	4 906	....	....	....	....	....	....	....	....
General government	4 907	....	....	....	....	....	....	....	....
Banks	4 908	−552	−757	−205	228	−234	−16	−36	−12
Other sectors	4 909	−282	−388	−343	−327	−565	−595	−130	−233

Table 2 (Concluded). STANDARD PRESENTATION, 2003–2010

(Millions of U.S. dollars)

	Code	2003	2004	2005	2006	2007	2008	2009	2010
D. OTHER INVESTMENT....................	4 700 ..	**−10,314**	**−10,962**	**−27,493**	**14,577**	**13,131**	**2,875**	**−16,312**	**−1,274**
Assets....................	4 703 ..	**−9,483**	**−2,196**	**−5,035**	**−8,914**	**−18,552**	**−5,269**	**−30,376**	**−42,575**
Trade credits....................	4 706 ..	....	....	....	....	....	....	−25,103	−37,078
General government....................	4 707 ..	....	....	....	....	....	....	....	....
of which: Short-term....................	4 709 ..	....	....	....	....	....	....	....	....
Other sectors....................	4 710 ..	....	....	....	....	....	....	−25,103	−37,078
of which: Short-term....................	4 712 ..	....	....	....	....	....	....	−25,103	−37,078
Loans....................	4 714 ..	−541	−1,599	−1,840	−5,015	−1,773	−4,818	−196	510
Monetary authorities....................	4 715 ..	....	....	....	....	....	−13,023	12,488	535
of which: Short-term....................	4 718 ..	....	....	....	....	....	−13,023	12,488	535
General government....................	4 719 ..	−910	−1,183	....	....	....	....	....	....
of which: Short-term....................	4 721 ..	43	56	....	....	....	....	....	....
Banks....................	4 722 ..	8	−279	−1,014	−1,600	−592	11,770	−12,558	−315
of which: Short-term....................	4 724 ..	8	−279	−12	−11	−305	13,184	−12,558	−322
Other sectors....................	4 725 ..	361	−137	−825	−3,414	−1,182	−3,565	−126	291
of which: Short-term....................	4 727 ..	73	−48	44	−25	122	58	5	328
Currency and deposits....................	4 730 ..	−8,579	−668	−2,930	−3,241	−16,112	−2,232	−4,966	−4,855
Monetary authorities....................	4 731 ..	....	....	....	....	....	....	....	....
General government....................	4 732 ..	−115	20	−198	17	−328	−405	1,038	45
Banks....................	4 733 ..	−7,009	1,407	−1,187	−1,732	−10,691	3,430	−2,936	2,117
Other sectors....................	4 734 ..	−1,455	−2,096	−1,546	−1,526	−5,093	−5,257	−3,068	−7,016
Other assets....................	4 736 ..	−363	72	−265	−658	−666	1,781	−112	−1,152
Monetary authorities....................	4 737 ..	....	....	....	2	....	....	....	....
of which: Short-term....................	4 739 ..	....	....	....	....	....	....	....	....
General government....................	4 740 ..	−76	−64	−32	....	....	−1	−15	−89
of which: Short-term....................	4 742 ..	−3	....	....	....	....	−1	−11	−4
Banks....................	4 743 ..	1	−6	−10	10	−33	57	−6	−12
of which: Short-term....................	4 745 ..	1	−6	−10	10	−33	57	−6	−12
Other sectors....................	4 746 ..	−288	142	−223	−670	−633	1,725	−90	−1,051
of which: Short-term....................	4 748 ..	−284	116	−86	−470	−373	1,691	−108	−929
Liabilities....................	4 753 ..	**−831**	**−8,766**	**−22,458**	**23,491**	**31,683**	**8,143**	**14,064**	**41,301**
Trade credits....................	4 756 ..	−34	1,156	3,585	12,314	17,371	4,462	4,100	−823
General government....................	4 757 ..	....	....	....	....	....	....	....	....
of which: Short-term....................	4 759 ..	....	....	....	....	....	....	....	....
Other sectors....................	4 760 ..	−34	1,156	3,585	12,314	17,371	4,462	4,100	−823
of which: Short-term....................	4 762 ..	926	2,542	4,526	13,155	17,238	3,966	5,145	−291
Loans....................	4 764 ..	−1,425	−10,440	−26,725	9,753	13,694	5,172	4,926	41,158
Monetary authorities....................	4 765 ..	4,768	−4,493	−23,374	−138	−138	....	....	−4
of which: Use of Fund credit and loans from the Fund..	4 766 ..	4,893	−4,362	−23,243	....	....	....	....	....
of which: Short-term....................	4 768 ..	....	....	....	....	....	....	....	....
General government....................	4 769 ..	−1,561	−2,633	−1,637	−384	−618	403	−772	3,461
of which: Short-term....................	4 771 ..	....	....	....	....	....	....	....	....
Banks....................	4 772 ..	−316	835	127	1,889	17,214	−6,434	−2,289	23,114
of which: Short-term....................	4 774 ..	−89	−130	−398	153	13,806	−9,710	−2,315	18,069
Other sectors....................	4 775 ..	−4,316	−4,149	−1,840	8,387	−2,764	11,203	7,987	14,586
of which: Short-term....................	4 777 ..	−1,354	−1,054	−661	−669	−39	1,561	65	4,043
Currency and deposits....................	4 780 ..	625	517	567	1,419	607	−1,495	1,092	964
Monetary authorities....................	4 781 ..	−37	−31	−33	−112	−70	−91	−70	−87
General government....................	4 782 ..	....	....	....	....	....	....	....	....
Banks....................	4 783 ..	662	549	600	1,532	672	−1,406	1,161	1,049
Other sectors....................	4 784 ..	....	....	....	−1	5	1	1	3
Other liabilities....................	4 786 ..	3	1	115	5	11	5	3,946	2
Monetary authorities....................	4 787 ..	....	....	....	....	....	....	3,950	....
of which: Short-term....................	4 789 ..	....	....	....	....	....	....	....	....
General government....................	4 790 ..	....	....	....	....	....	....	....	....
of which: Short-term....................	4 792 ..	....	....	....	....	....	....	....	....
Banks....................	4 793 ..	3	1	115	5	11	5	−4	2
of which: Short-term....................	4 795 ..	....	....	115	5	11	5	−4	2
Other sectors....................	4 796 ..	....	....	....	....	....	....	....	....
of which: Short-term....................	4 798 ..	....	....	....	....	....	....	....	....
E. RESERVE ASSETS....................	4 802 ..	**−8,479**	**−2,238**	**−4,324**	**−30,571**	**−87,484**	**−2,969**	**−47,578**	**−49,080**
Monetary gold....................	4 812 ..	43	14	51	76	129	−535	....	....
Special drawing rights....................	4 811 ..	278	3	−30	21	6	1	−4,503	−3
Reserve position in the Fund....................	4 810 ..	....	....	....	....	....	....	−946	−1,088
Foreign exchange....................	4 803 ..	−8,776	−2,283	−4,308	−30,665	−87,631	−2,459	−42,153	−47,932
Other claims....................	4 813 ..	−24	28	−37	−3	11	24	25	−57
NET ERRORS AND OMISSIONS....................	4 998 ..	**−933**	**−2,145**	**−225**	**967**	**−3,152**	**1,810**	**591**	**−3,217**

Table 3. INTERNATIONAL INVESTMENT POSITION (End-period stocks), 2003–2010

(Millions of U.S. dollars)

	Code	2003	2004	2005	2006	2007	2008	2009	2010
ASSETS	8 995 C.	**134,223**	**148,536**	**168,182**	**238,874**	**379,789**	**408,203**	**479,105**	**616,254**
Direct investment abroad	8 505 ..	**54,892**	**69,196**	**79,259**	**113,925**	**139,886**	**155,668**	**164,523**	**189,222**
Equity capital and reinvested earnings	8 506 ..	44,769	54,027	65,418	97,465	111,339	113,755	132,413	169,066
Claims on affiliated enterprises	8 507 ..	44,769	54,027	65,418	97,465	111,339	113,755	132,413	169,066
Liabilities to affiliated enterprises	8 508 ..	....	....	....	....	....	....	....	....
Other capital	8 530 ..	10,123	15,169	13,842	16,460	28,547	41,914	32,110	20,156
Claims on affiliated enterprises	8 535 ..	10,123	15,169	13,842	16,460	28,547	41,914	32,110	20,156
Liabilities to affiliated enterprises	8 540 ..	....	....	....	....	....	....	....	....
Portfolio investment	8 602 ..	**6,950**	**9,353**	**10,834**	**14,429**	**19,515**	**14,910**	**16,519**	**37,630**
Equity securities	8 610 ..	2,596	2,352	2,809	3,754	6,644	4,828	8,641	14,731
Monetary authorities	8 611 ..	....	....	....	....	....	....	....	....
General government	8 612 ..	....	....	....	....	....	....	....	....
Banks	8 613 ..	140	170	143	1,100	3,348	955	4,070	7,810
Other sectors	8 614 ..	2,456	2,182	2,666	2,654	3,296	3,873	4,571	6,921
Debt securities	8 619 ..	4,354	7,001	8,026	10,675	12,871	10,082	7,877	22,899
Bonds and notes	8 620 ..	2,496	4,028	4,850	6,185	5,132	5,540	5,326	8,392
Monetary authorities	8 621 ..	1,004	1,129	1,249	....	1,054	1,038		
General government	8 622 ..	....	....	....	....	....	....	....	....
Banks	8 623 ..	291	772	1,265	4,361	1,825	3,066	4,469	7,331
Other sectors	8 624 ..	1,200	2,127	2,336	1,824	2,253	1,436	858	1,060
Money market instruments	8 630 ..	1,859	2,973	3,176	4,490	7,739	4,542	2,551	14,508
Monetary authorities	8 631 ..	....	....	....	....	....	....	....	....
General government	8 632 ..	....	....	....	....	....	....	....	....
Banks	8 633 ..	340	862	580	1,994	5,275	2,813	1,972	1,525
Other sectors	8 634 ..	1,519	2,111	2,596	2,496	2,464	1,729	579	12,983
Financial derivatives	8 900 ..	**81**	**109**	**119**	**113**	**142**	**609**	**426**	**797**
Monetary authorities	8 901 ..	....	....	....	....	....	....	....	....
General government	8 902 ..	....	....	....	....	....	....	....	....
Banks	8 903 ..	3	30	....	....	9	84	36	79
Other sectors	8 904 ..	78	79	119	113	133	525	390	718
Other investment	8 703 ..	**23,004**	**16,943**	**24,171**	**24,567**	**39,912**	**43,232**	**59,098**	**100,031**
Trade credits	8 706 ..	186	68	98	70	99	123	16,005	51,813
General government	8 707 ..	....	....	....	....	....	....	....	....
of which: Short-term	8 709 ..	....	....	....	....	....	....	....	....
Other sectors	8 710 ..	186	68	98	70	99	123	16,005	51,813
of which: Short-term	8 712 ..	*160*	*51*	*76*	*49*	*58*	*73*	*15,938*	*51,719*
Loans	8 714 ..	687	631	727	562	10,566	11,143	12,378	13,446
Monetary authorities	8 715 ..	....	....	....	....	....	....	....	....
of which: Short-term	8 718 ..	....	....	....	....	....	....	....	....
General government	8 719 ..	....	....	....	....	2,728	2,491	2,269	2,061
of which: Short-term	8 721 ..	....	....	....	....	....	....	....	....
Banks	8 722 ..	5	1	3	2	7,054	7,994	9,238	10,536
of which: Short-term	8 724 ..	....	....	....	....	....	....	....	....
Other sectors	8 725 ..	683	630	724	560	784	658	871	850
of which: Short-term	8 727 ..	*52*	*70*	*159*	*102*	*236*	*106*	*126*	....
Currency and deposits	8 730 ..	16,412	10,418	17,077	17,200	22,543	24,107	23,070	27,026
Monetary authorities	8 731 ..	....	....	....	....	57	57	89	82
General government	8 732 ..	....	....	....	....	....	....	....	....
Banks	8 733 ..	10,740	6,824	12,334	10,477	13,664	11,750	10,890	12,707
Other sectors	8 734 ..	5,672	3,594	4,743	6,723	8,823	12,301	12,092	14,237
Other assets	8 736 ..	5,718	5,826	6,269	6,736	6,704	7,859	7,645	7,745
Monetary authorities	8 737 ..	1,230	1,230	1,363	1,072	1,088	1,326	1,327	1,414
of which: Short-term	8 739 ..	....	....	....	....	....	....	....	....
General government	8 740 ..	....	....	....	32	....	....	....	....
of which: Short-term	8 742 ..	....	....	....	....	....	....	....	....
Banks	8 743 ..	90	1	1	219	....	....	19	45
of which: Short-term	8 745 ..	*2*	....	....	*5*	....	....	....	....
Other sectors	8 746 ..	4,398	4,596	4,874	5,445	5,616	6,533	6,298	6,286
of which: Short-term	8 748 ..	*215*	*274*	*979*	*1,523*	*489*	....	....	....
Reserve assets	8 802 ..	**49,296**	**52,935**	**53,799**	**85,839**	**180,334**	**193,783**	**238,539**	**288,575**
Monetary gold	8 812 ..	186	195	225	277	366	940	1,175	1,519
Special drawing rights	8 811 ..	2	4	29	8	2	1	4,527	4,450
Reserve position in the Fund	8 810 ..	....	....	....	....	....	....	950	2,037
Foreign exchange	8 803 ..	49,051	52,707	53,479	85,484	179,908	192,809	231,879	280,504
Other claims	8 813 ..	57	29	66	69	58	34	9	66

Table 3 (Concluded). INTERNATIONAL INVESTMENT POSITION (End-period stocks), 2003–2010

(Millions of U.S. dollars)

	Code	2003	2004	2005	2006	2007	2008	2009	2010
LIABILITIES	8 995 D.	**406,778**	**446,229**	**484,775**	**607,735**	**920,284**	**691,588**	**1,079,898**	**1,293,657**
Direct investment in Brazil	8 555 ..	**132,818**	**161,259**	**181,344**	**220,621**	**309,668**	**287,697**	**400,808**	**472,576**
Equity capital and reinvested earnings	8 556 ..	112,334	142,451	162,807	193,838	262,392	223,127	321,436	377,438
Claims on direct investors	8 557 ..	....	....	....	....	....	....	....	....
Liabilities to direct investors	8 558 ..	112,334	142,451	162,807	193,838	262,392	223,127	321,436	377,438
Other capital	8 580 ..	20,484	18,808	18,537	26,783	47,276	64,570	79,372	95,137
Claims on direct investors	8 585 ..	....	....	....	....	....	....	....	....
Liabilities to direct investors	8 590 ..	20,484	18,808	18,537	26,783	47,276	64,570	79,372	95,137
Portfolio investment	8 652 ..	**166,095**	**184,758**	**232,352**	**303,583**	**509,648**	**287,533**	**561,848**	**656,284**
Equity securities	8 660 ..	53,138	77,261	125,532	191,513	363,999	149,608	376,463	430,234
Banks	8 663 ..	....	....	....	....	....	....	....	....
Other sectors	8 664 ..	53,138	77,261	125,532	191,513	363,999	149,608	376,463	430,234
Debt securities	8 669 ..	112,957	107,497	106,820	112,070	145,650	137,925	185,385	226,051
Bonds and notes	8 670 ..	111,343	107,253	105,919	110,282	139,711	134,396	182,013	217,657
Monetary authorities	8 671 ..	....	....	....	....	....	....	....	....
General government	8 672 ..	....	....	....	....	....	....	....	....
Banks	8 673 ..	....	....	....	....	....	....	....	....
Other sectors	8 674 ..	111,343	107,253	105,919	110,282	139,711	134,396	182,013	217,657
Money market instruments	8 680 ..	1,614	244	901	1,788	5,939	3,529	3,372	8,393
Monetary authorities	8 681 ..	....	....	....	....	....	....	....	....
General government	8 682 ..	....	....	....	....	....	....	....	....
Banks	8 683 ..	....	....	....	....	....	....	....	....
Other sectors	8 684 ..	1,614	244	901	1,788	5,939	3,529	3,372	8,393
Financial derivatives	8 905 ..	**125**	**320**	**219**	**445**	**1,771**	**2,450**	**3,413**	**3,781**
Monetary authorities	8 906 ..	....	....	....	....	....	....	....	....
General government	8 907 ..	....	....	....	....	....	....	....	....
Banks	8 908 ..	....	....	....	....	....	....	....	....
Other sectors	8 909 ..	125	320	219	445	1,771	2,450	3,413	3,781
Other investment	8 753 ..	**107,740**	**99,892**	**70,859**	**83,087**	**99,197**	**113,908**	**113,829**	**161,016**
Trade credits	8 756 ..	5,465	4,728	4,772	5,216	5,197	6,241	3,306	3,133
General government	8 757 ..	....	....	....	....	....	....	....	....
of which: Short-term	8 759 ..	....	....	....	....	....	....	....	....
Other sectors	8 760 ..	5,465	4,728	4,772	5,216	5,197	6,241	3,306	3,133
of which: Short-term	8 762 ..	*428*	*314*	*349*	*347*	*134*	*335*	*167*	*138*
Loans	8 764 ..	99,436	92,216	62,729	73,466	89,003	103,463	100,793	145,905
Monetary authorities	8 765 ..	28,857	25,477	301	157	14	10	3	....
of which: Use of Fund credit and loans from the Fund	8 766 ..	*28,317*	*25,029*	....	....	....	....	....	....
of which: Short-term	8 768 ..	....	....	....	....	....	....	....	....
General government	8 769 ..	....	....	....	....	....	....	....	....
of which: Short-term	8 771 ..	....	....	....	....	....	....	....	....
Banks	8 772 ..	5,768	7,161	5,012	4,348	7,801	8,017	6,793	15,611
of which: Short-term	8 774 ..	*5,768*	*7,161*	*5,012*	*4,348*	*7,801*	*8,017*	*6,793*	*15,611*
Other sectors	8 775 ..	64,811	59,578	57,416	68,962	81,188	95,436	93,997	130,294
of which: Short-term	8 777 ..	*12,384*	*11,025*	*12,514*	*13,840*	*25,026*	*24,563*	*20,640*	*33,165*
Currency and deposits	8 780 ..	2,839	2,948	3,358	4,405	4,996	4,204	5,205	7,531
Monetary authorities	8 781 ..	108	100	111	83	73	104	69	57
General government	8 782 ..	....	....	....	....	....	....	....	....
Banks	8 783 ..	2,731	2,848	3,246	4,321	4,923	4,101	5,135	7,474
Other sectors	8 784 ..	....	....	....	....	....	....	....	....
Other liabilities	8 786 ..	....	....	....	....	....	....	4,526	4,446
Monetary authorities	8 787 ..	....	....	....	....	....	....	4,526	4,446
of which: Short-term	8 789 ..	....	....	....	....	....	....	....	....
General government	8 790 ..	....	....	....	....	....	....	....	....
of which: Short-term	8 792 ..	....	....	....	....	....	....	....	....
Banks	8 793 ..	....	....	....	....	....	....	....	....
of which: Short-term	8 795 ..	....	....	....	....	....	....	....	....
Other sectors	8 796 ..	....	....	....	....	....	....	....	....
of which: Short-term	8 798 ..	....	....	....	....	....	....	....	....
NET INTERNATIONAL INVESTMENT POSITION	8 995 ..	**−272,555**	**−297,693**	**−316,592**	**−368,862**	**−540,495**	**−283,385**	**−600,792**	**−677,403**
Conversion rates: reais per U.S. dollar (end of period)	0 102 ..	**2.88840**	**2.65360**	**2.33990**	**2.13720**	**1.77050**	**2.33620**	**1.74040**	**1.66540**

Table 1. ANALYTIC PRESENTATION, 2003–2010

(Millions of U.S. dollars)

	Code	2003	2004	2005	2006	2007	2008	2009	2010
A. Current Account¹	4 993 Z.	**2,484**	**2,882**	**4,033**	**5,229**	**4,828**	**6,939**	**3,977**	....
Goods: exports f.o.b.	2 100 ..	4,424	5,069	6,241	7,627	7,692	10,698	7,172	....
Goods: imports f.o.b.	3 100 ..	−1,258	−1,338	−1,412	−1,588	−1,992	−2,858	−2,282	....
Balance on Goods	4 100 ..	*3,166*	*3,731*	*4,829*	*6,039*	*5,700*	*7,840*	*4,889*	....
Services: credit	2 200 ..	436	544	616	745	813	867	915	....
Services: debit	3 200 ..	−1,034	−1,076	−1,110	−1,214	−1,317	−1,403	−1,434	....
Balance on Goods and Services	4 991 ..	*2,569*	*3,200*	*4,335*	*5,570*	*5,196*	*7,305*	*4,370*	....
Income: credit	2 300 ..	214	236	263	248	268	304	316	....
Income: debit	3 300 ..	−201	−200	−190	−183	−206	−249	−264	....
Balance on Goods, Services, and Income	4 992 ..	*2,581*	*3,236*	*4,408*	*5,635*	*5,259*	*7,359*	*4,422*	....
Current transfers: credit	2 379 Z.	....	....	....	....	....	....	....	....
Current transfers: debit	3 379 ..	−97	−354	−376	−405	−430	−420	−445	....
B. Capital Account¹	4 994 Z.	**−1**	**−11**	**−8**	**−7**	**−7**	**−8**	**−11**	....
Capital account: credit	2 994 Z.	....	....	....	....	....	....	....	....
Capital account: debit	3 994 ..	−1	−11	−8	−7	−7	−8	−11	....
Total, Groups A Plus B	4 981 ..	*2,483*	*2,871*	*4,024*	*5,222*	*4,821*	*6,931*	*3,966*	....
C. Financial Account¹	4 995 W.	**−622**	**−1,652**	**−82**	**603**	**1,167**	**1,346**	**1,607**	....
Direct investment abroad	4 505 ..	....	−42	....	−17	....	....	....	....
Direct investment in Brunei Darussalam	4 555 Z.	124	113	175	88	258	222	326	....
Portfolio investment assets	4 602 ..	60	−45	22	−90	358	88	139	....
Equity securities	4 610 ..	68	−56	13	−90	358	88	139	....
Debt securities	4 619 ..	−7	11	9	....	....	....	....	....
Portfolio investment liabilities	4 652 Z.	....	....	....	....	....	....	....	....
Equity securities	4 660 ..	....	....	....	....	....	....	....	....
Debt securities	4 669 Z.	....	....	....	....	....	....	....	....
Financial derivatives	4 910 ..	....	....	....	....	....	....	....	....
Financial derivatives assets	4 900 ..	....	....	....	....	....	....	....	....
Financial derivatives liabilities	4 905 ..	....	....	....	....	....	....	....	....
Other investment assets	4 703 ..	−605	−1,569	−493	356	1,009	749	644	....
Monetary authorities	4 701 ..	....	....	....	....	....	....	....	....
General government	4 704 ..	−1	−1	−1	−1	2	−1	−4	....
Banks	4 705 ..	−529	−997	−648	648	1,269	984	741	....
Other sectors	4 728 ..	−76	−571	155	−292	−262	−234	−93	....
Other investment liabilities	4 753 W.	−201	−110	214	267	−458	287	498	....
Monetary authorities	4 753 WA	....	....	....	....	....	....	318	....
General government	4 753 ZB	....	....	....	....	....	....	....	....
Banks	4 753 ZC	−73	−22	209	216	−433	228	312	....
Other sectors	4 753 ZD	−129	−88	6	51	−25	59	−133	....
Total, Groups A Through C	4 983 ..	*1,861*	*1,219*	*3,942*	*5,825*	*5,988*	*8,277*	*5,574*	....
D. Net Errors and Omissions	4 998 ..	**−1,838**	**−1,190**	**−4,006**	**−5,796**	**−5,846**	**−8,233**	**−5,420**	....
Total, Groups A Through D	4 984 ..	*23*	*29*	*−63*	*29*	*142*	*45*	*154*	....
E. Reserves and Related Items	4 802 A.	**−23**	**−29**	**63**	**−29**	**−142**	**−45**	**−154**	....
Reserve assets	4 802 ..	−23	−29	63	−29	−142	−45	−154	....
Use of Fund credit and loans	4 766 ..	....	....	....	....	....	....	....	....
Exceptional financing	4 920 ..	....	....	....	....	....	....	....	....
Conversion rates: Brunei Dollars per U.S. dollar	0 101 ..	**1.7422**	**1.6902**	**1.6644**	**1.5889**	**1.5071**	**1.4172**	**1.4546**	**1.3635**

¹ Excludes components that have been classified in the categories of Group E.

Table 2. STANDARD PRESENTATION, 2003–2010
(Millions of U.S. dollars)

	Code	2003	2004	2005	2006	2007	2008	2009	2010
CURRENT ACCOUNT	4 993	**2,484**	**2,882**	**4,033**	**5,229**	**4,828**	**6,939**	**3,977**	....
A. GOODS	4 100	**3,166**	**3,731**	**4,829**	**6,039**	**5,700**	**7,840**	**4,889**	....
Credit	2 100	**4,424**	**5,069**	**6,241**	**7,627**	**7,692**	**10,698**	**7,172**	....
General merchandise: exports f.o.b.	2 110	4,424	5,069	6,241	7,627	7,692	10,698	7,172	....
Goods for processing: exports f.o.b.	2 150	....	....	....	....	....	....	....	....
Repairs on goods	2 160	....	....	....	....	....	....	....	....
Goods procured in ports by carriers	2 170	....	....	....	....	....	....	....	....
Nonmonetary gold	2 180	....	....	....	....	....	....	....	....
Debit	3 100	**−1,258**	**−1,338**	**−1,412**	**−1,588**	**−1,992**	**−2,858**	**−2,282**	....
General merchandise: imports f.o.b.	3 110	−1,258	−1,338	−1,412	−1,588	−1,992	−2,858	−2,282	....
Goods for processing: imports f.o.b.	3 150	....	....	....	....	....	....	....	....
Repairs on goods	3 160	....	....	....	....	....	....	....	....
Goods procured in ports by carriers	3 170	....	....	....	....	....	....	....	....
Nonmonetary gold	3 180	....	....	....	....	....	....	....	....
B. SERVICES	4 200	**−597**	**−531**	**−494**	**−469**	**−503**	**−535**	**−519**	....
Total credit	2 200	*436*	*544*	*616*	*745*	*813*	*867*	*915*	....
Total debit	3 200	*−1,034*	*−1,076*	*−1,110*	*−1,214*	*−1,317*	*−1,403*	*−1,434*	....
Transportation services, credit	2 205	**247**	**285**	**313**	**381**	**406**	**429**	**452**	....
Passenger	2 850	....	....	....	....	....	....	....	....
Freight	2 851	....	....	....	....	....	....	....	....
Other	2 852	....	....	....	....	....	....	....	....
Sea transport, passenger	2 207	....	....	....	....	....	....	....	....
Sea transport, freight	2 208	....	....	....	....	....	....	....	....
Sea transport, other	2 209	....	....	....	....	....	....	....	....
Air transport, passenger	2 211	....	....	....	....	....	....	....	....
Air transport, freight	2 212	....	....	....	....	....	....	....	....
Air transport, other	2 213	....	....	....	....	....	....	....	....
Other transport, passenger	2 215	....	....	....	....	....	....	....	....
Other transport, freight	2 216	....	....	....	....	....	....	....	....
Other transport, other	2 217	....	....	....	....	....	....	....	....
Transportation services, debit	3 205	**−229**	**−297**	**−321**	**−369**	**−398**	**−421**	**−445**	....
Passenger	3 850	....	....	....	....	....	....	....	....
Freight	3 851	....	....	....	....	....	....	....	....
Other	3 852	....	....	....	....	....	....	....	....
Sea transport, passenger	3 207	....	....	....	....	....	....	....	....
Sea transport, freight	3 208	....	....	....	....	....	....	....	....
Sea transport, other	3 209	....	....	....	....	....	....	....	....
Air transport, passenger	3 211	....	....	....	....	....	....	....	....
Air transport, freight	3 212	....	....	....	....	....	....	....	....
Air transport, other	3 213	....	....	....	....	....	....	....	....
Other transport, passenger	3 215	....	....	....	....	....	....	....	....
Other transport, freight	3 216	....	....	....	....	....	....	....	....
Other transport, other	3 217	....	....	....	....	....	....	....	....
Travel, credit	2 236	**124**	**181**	**191**	**224**	**233**	**242**	**254**	....
Business travel	2 237	....	....	....	....	....	....	....	....
Personal travel	2 240	....	....	....	....	....	....	....	....
Travel, debit	3 236	**−469**	**−382**	**−374**	**−408**	**−430**	**−459**	**−477**	....
Business travel	3 237	....	....	....	....	....	....	....	....
Personal travel	3 240	....	....	....	....	....	....	....	....
Other services, credit	2 200 BA	**66**	**77**	**112**	**140**	**174**	**196**	**209**	....
Communications	2 245	4	7	10	13	18	21	22	....
Construction	2 249	....	....	....	....	....	....	....	....
Insurance	2 253	4	6	7	10	13	13	13	....
Financial	2 260	....	....	....	....	....	....	....	....
Computer and information	2 262	....	....	....	....	....	....	....	....
Royalties and licence fees	2 266	....	....	....	....	....	....	....	....
Other business services	2 268	58	65	95	116	142	162	174	....
Personal, cultural, and recreational	2 287	....	....	....	....	....	....	....	....
Government, n.i.e.	2 291	....	....	....	....	....	....	....	....
Other services, debit	3 200 BA	**−336**	**−397**	**−415**	**−436**	**−489**	**−522**	**−512**	....
Communications	3 245	−2	−3	−5	−8	−13	−15	−16	....
Construction	3 249	....	....	....	....	....	....	....	....
Insurance	3 253	−8	−9	−10	−11	−14	−14	−14	....
Financial	3 260	−1	−2	−3	−5	−6	−7	−7	....
Computer and information	3 262	....	....	....	....	....	....	....	....
Royalties and licence fees	3 266	−3	−3	−4	−6	−7	−7	−8	....
Other business services	3 268	−174	−225	−223	−228	−247	−258	−249	....
Personal, cultural, and recreational	3 287	....	....	....	....	....	....	....	....
Government, n.i.e.	3 291	−147	−154	−170	−179	−202	−221	−219	....

Table 2 (Continued). STANDARD PRESENTATION, 2003–2010

(Millions of U.S. dollars)

	Code	2003	2004	2005	2006	2007	2008	2009	2010
C. INCOME	4 300 ..	**12**	**36**	**73**	**65**	**62**	**54**	**52**	....
Total credit	2 300 ..	*214*	*236*	*263*	*248*	*268*	*304*	*316*	....
Total debit	3 300 ..	*–201*	*–200*	*–190*	*–183*	*–206*	*–249*	*–264*	....
Compensation of employees, credit	2 310 ..	....	....	....	....	....	....	....	....
Compensation of employees, debit	3 310 ..	....	....	....	....	....	....	....	....
Investment income, credit	2 320 ..	**214**	**236**	**263**	**248**	**268**	**304**	**316**	....
Direct investment income	2 330 ..	....	....	....	....	....	....	....	....
Dividends and distributed branch profits	2 332 ..	....	....	....	....	....	....	....	....
Reinvested earnings and undistributed branch profits	2 333 ..	....	....	....	....	....	....	....	....
Income on debt (interest)	2 334 ..	....	....	....	....	....	....	....	....
Portfolio investment income	2 339 ..	....	....	....	....	....	....	....	....
Income on equity	2 340 ..	....	....	....	....	....	....	....	....
Income on bonds and notes	2 350 ..	....	....	....	....	....	....	....	....
Income on money market instruments	2 360 ..	....	....	....	....	....	....	....	....
Other investment income	2 370 ..	214	236	263	248	268	304	316	....
Investment income, debit	3 320 ..	**–201**	**–200**	**–190**	**–183**	**–206**	**–249**	**–264**	....
Direct investment income	3 330 ..	....	....	....	....	....	....	....	....
Dividends and distributed branch profits	3 332 ..	....	....	....	....	....	....	....	....
Reinvested earnings and undistributed branch profits	3 333 ..	....	....	....	....	....	....	....	....
Income on debt (interest)	3 334 ..	....	....	....	....	....	....	....	....
Portfolio investment income	3 339 ..	....	....	....	....	....	....	....	....
Income on equity	3 340 ..	....	....	....	....	....	....	....	....
Income on bonds and notes	3 350 ..	....	....	....	....	....	....	....	....
Income on money market instruments	3 360 ..	....	....	....	....	....	....	....	....
Other investment income	3 370 ..	–201	–200	–190	–183	–206	–249	–264	....
D. CURRENT TRANSFERS	4 379 ..	**–97**	**–354**	**–376**	**–405**	**–430**	**–420**	**–445**	....
Credit	2 379 ..	....	....	....	....	....	....	....	....
General government	2 380 ..	....	....	....	....	....	....	....	....
Other sectors	2 390 ..	....	....	....	....	....	....	....	....
Workers' remittances	2 391 ..	....	....	....	....	....	....	....	....
Other current transfers	2 392 ..	....	....	....	....	....	....	....	....
Debit	3 379 ..	**–97**	**–354**	**–376**	**–405**	**–430**	**–420**	**–445**	....
General government	3 380 ..	....	....	....	....	....	....	....	....
Other sectors	3 390 ..	–97	–354	–376	–405	–430	–420	–445	....
Workers' remittances	3 391 ..	–97	–354	–376	–405	–430	–420	–445	....
Other current transfers	3 392 ..	....	....	....	....	....	....	....	....
CAPITAL AND FINANCIAL ACCOUNT	4 996 ..	**–646**	**–1,692**	**–27**	**566**	**1,017**	**1,294**	**1,443**	....
CAPITAL ACCOUNT	4 994 ..	**–1**	**–11**	**–8**	**–7**	**–7**	**–8**	**–11**	....
Total credit	2 994 ..	....	....	....	....	....	....	....	....
Total debit	3 994 ..	*–1*	*–11*	*–8*	*–7*	*–7*	*–8*	*–11*	....
Capital transfers, credit	2 400 ..	....	....	....	....	....	....	....	....
General government	2 401 ..	....	....	....	....	....	....	....	....
Debt forgiveness	2 402 ..	....	....	....	....	....	....	....	....
Other capital transfers	2 410 ..	....	....	....	....	....	....	....	....
Other sectors	2 430 ..	....	....	....	....	....	....	....	....
Migrants' transfers	2 431 ..	....	....	....	....	....	....	....	....
Debt forgiveness	2 432 ..	....	....	....	....	....	....	....	....
Other capital transfers	2 440 ..	....	....	....	....	....	....	....	....
Capital transfers, debit	3 400 ..	....	....	....	....	....	....	....	....
General government	3 401 ..	....	....	....	....	....	....	....	....
Debt forgiveness	3 402 ..	....	....	....	....	....	....	....	....
Other capital transfers	3 410 ..	....	....	....	....	....	....	....	....
Other sectors	3 430 ..	....	....	....	....	....	....	....	....
Migrants' transfers	3 431 ..	....	....	....	....	....	....	....	....
Debt forgiveness	3 432 ..	....	....	....	....	....	....	....	....
Other capital transfers	3 440 ..	....	....	....	....	....	....	....	....
Nonproduced nonfinancial assets, credit	2 480 ..	....	....	....	....	....	....	....	....
Nonproduced nonfinancial assets, debit	3 480 ..	....	....	....	....	....	....	....	....

Table 2 (Continued). STANDARD PRESENTATION, 2003–2010

(Millions of U.S. dollars)

	Code	2003	2004	2005	2006	2007	2008	2009	2010
FINANCIAL ACCOUNT	4 995 ..	**−645**	**−1,680**	**−19**	**573**	**1,025**	**1,302**	**1,454**	....
A. DIRECT INVESTMENT	4 500 ..	**124**	**72**	**175**	**70**	**258**	**222**	**326**	....
Direct investment abroad	4 505 ..	....	**−42**	....	**−17**	....	....	....	....
Equity capital	4 510 ..	....	....	....	....	....	....	....	
Claims on affiliated enterprises	4 515 ..	....	....	....	....	....	....	....	
Liabilities to affiliated enterprises	4 520 ..	....	....	....	....	....	....	....	
Reinvested earnings	4 525 ..	....	....	....	....	....	....	....	
Other capital	4 530 ..	....	....	....	....	....	....	....	
Claims on affiliated enterprises	4 535 ..	....	....	....	....	....	....	....	
Liabilities to affiliated enterprises	4 540 ..	....	....	....	....	....	....	....	
Direct investment in Brunei Darussalam	4 555 ..	**124**	**113**	**175**	**88**	**258**	**222**	**326**	....
Equity capital	4 560 ..	114	111	153	85	240	....	....	
Claims on direct investors	4 565 ..	....	....	....	....	....	....	....	
Liabilities to direct investors	4 570 ..	....	....	....	....	....	....	....	
Reinvested earnings	4 575 ..	....	....	....	....	....	....	....	
Other capital	4 580 ..	10	2	22	3	18	222	326	
Claims on direct investors	4 585 ..	....	....	....	....	....	....	....	
Liabilities to direct investors	4 590 ..	....	....	....	....	....	....	....	
B. PORTFOLIO INVESTMENT	4 600 ..	**60**	**−45**	**22**	**−90**	**358**	**88**	**139**	....
Assets	4 602 ..	**60**	**−45**	**22**	**−90**	**358**	**88**	**139**	....
Equity securities	4 610 ..	68	−56	13	−90	358	88	139	
Monetary authorities	4 611 ..	....	....	....	....	....	....	....	
General government	4 612 ..	....	....	....	....	....	....	....	
Banks	4 613 ..	....	....	....	....	....	....	....	
Other sectors	4 614 ..	....	....	....	....	....	....	....	
Debt securities	4 619 ..	−7	11	9	....	....	....	....	
Bonds and notes	4 620 ..	....	....	....	....	....	....	....	
Monetary authorities	4 621 ..	....	....	....	....	....	....	....	
General government	4 622 ..	....	....	....	....	....	....	....	
Banks	4 623 ..	....	....	....	....	....	....	....	
Other sectors	4 624 ..	....	....	....	....	....	....	....	
Money market instruments	4 630 ..	....	....	....	....	....	....	....	
Monetary authorities	4 631 ..	....	....	....	....	....	....	....	
General government	4 632 ..	....	....	....	....	....	....	....	
Banks	4 633 ..	....	....	....	....	....	....	....	
Other sectors	4 634 ..	....	....	....	....	....	....	....	
Liabilities	4 652 ..	....	....	....	....	....	....	....	....
Equity securities	4 660 ..	....	....	....	....	....	....	....	
Banks	4 663 ..	....	....	....	....	....	....	....	
Other sectors	4 664 ..	....	....	....	....	....	....	....	
Debt securities	4 669 ..	....	....	....	....	....	....	....	
Bonds and notes	4 670 ..	....	....	....	....	....	....	....	
Monetary authorities	4 671 ..	....	....	....	....	....	....	....	
General government	4 672 ..	....	....	....	....	....	....	....	
Banks	4 673 ..	....	....	....	....	....	....	....	
Other sectors	4 674 ..	....	....	....	....	....	....	....	
Money market instruments	4 680 ..	....	....	....	....	....	....	....	
Monetary authorities	4 681 ..	....	....	....	....	....	....	....	
General government	4 682 ..	....	....	....	....	....	....	....	
Banks	4 683 ..	....	....	....	....	....	....	....	
Other sectors	4 684 ..	....	....	....	....	....	....	....	
C. FINANCIAL DERIVATIVES	4 910 ..	....	....	....	....	....	....	....	....
Monetary authorities	4 911 ..	....	....	....	....	....	....	....	
General government	4 912 ..	....	....	....	....	....	....	....	
Banks	4 913 ..	....	....	....	....	....	....	....	
Other sectors	4 914 ..	....	....	....	....	....	....	....	
Assets	4 900 ..	....	....	....	....	....	....	....	....
Monetary authorities	4 901 ..	....	....	....	....	....	....	....	
General government	4 902 ..	....	....	....	....	....	....	....	
Banks	4 903 ..	....	....	....	....	....	....	....	
Other sectors	4 904 ..	....	....	....	....	....	....	....	
Liabilities	4 905 ..	....	....	....	....	....	....	....	....
Monetary authorities	4 906 ..	....	....	....	....	....	....	....	
General government	4 907 ..	....	....	....	....	....	....	....	
Banks	4 908 ..	....	....	....	....	....	....	....	
Other sectors	4 909 ..	....	....	....	....	....	....	....	

Table 2 (Concluded). STANDARD PRESENTATION, 2003–2010

(Millions of U.S. dollars)

	Code	2003	2004	2005	2006	2007	2008	2009	2010
D. OTHER INVESTMENT	4 700	**−806**	**−1,678**	**−279**	**623**	**551**	**1,036**	**1,142**	....
Assets	4 703	**−605**	**−1,569**	**−493**	**356**	**1,009**	**749**	**644**	....
Trade credits	4 706	....	....	....	....	....	....	....	....
General government	4 707	....	....	....	....	....	....	....	....
of which: Short-term	4 709	....	....	....	....	....	....	....	....
Other sectors	4 710	....	....	....	....	....	....	....	....
of which: Short-term	4 712	....	....	....	....	....	....	....	....
Loans	4 714	−163	−762	−454	931	−792	−349	−194	....
Monetary authorities	4 715	....	....	....	....	....	....	....	....
of which: Short-term	4 718	....	....	....	....	....	....	....	....
General government	4 719	....	....	....	....	....	....	....	....
of which: Short-term	4 721	....	....	....	....	....	....	....	....
Banks	4 722	−163	−762	−454	931	−792	−349	−194	....
of which: Short-term	4 724	....	....	....	....	....	....	....	....
Other sectors	4 725	....	....	....	....	....	....	....	....
of which: Short-term	4 727	....	....	....	....	....	....	....	....
Currency and deposits	4 730	−442	−807	−39	−575	1,798	1,099	842	....
Monetary authorities	4 731	....	....	....	....	....	....	....	....
General government	4 732	....	....	....	....	....	....	....	....
Banks	4 733	−366	−235	−194	−283	2,060	1,333	935	....
Other sectors	4 734	−76	−571	155	−292	−262	−234	−93	....
Other assets	4 736	−1	−1	−1	−1	2	−1	−4	....
Monetary authorities	4 737	....	....	....	....	....	....	....	....
of which: Short-term	4 739	....	....	....	....	....	....	....	....
General government	4 740	−1	−1	−1	−1	2	−1	−4	....
of which: Short-term	4 742	....	....	....	....	....	....	....	....
Banks	4 743	....	....	....	....	....	....	....	....
of which: Short-term	4 745	....	....	....	....	....	....	....	....
Other sectors	4 746	....	....	....	....	....	....	....	....
of which: Short-term	4 748	....	....	....	....	....	....	....	....
Liabilities	4 753	**−201**	**−110**	**214**	**267**	**−458**	**287**	**498**	....
Trade credits	4 756	−7	−67	69	71	18	75	219	....
General government	4 757	....	....	....	....	....	....	....	....
of which: Short-term	4 759	....	....	....	....	....	....	....	....
Other sectors	4 760	−7	−67	69	71	18	75	219	....
of which: Short-term	4 762	....	....	....	....	....	....	....	....
Loans	4 764	−122	−21	−63	−20	−43	−16	−352	....
Monetary authorities	4 765	....	....	....	....	....	....	....	....
of which: Use of Fund credit and loans from the Fund..	4 766	....	....	....	....	....	....	....	....
of which: Short-term	4 768	....	....	....	....	....	....	....	....
General government	4 769	....	....	....	....	....	....	....	....
of which: Short-term	4 771	....	....	....	....	....	....	....	....
Banks	4 772	....	....	....	....	....	....	....	....
of which: Short-term	4 774	....	....	....	....	....	....	....	....
Other sectors	4 775	−122	−21	−63	−20	−43	−16	−352	....
of which: Short-term	4 777	....	....	....	....	....	....	....	....
Currency and deposits	4 780	−73	−22	209	216	−433	228	312	....
Monetary authorities	4 781	....	....	....	....	....	....	....	....
General government	4 782	....	....	....	....	....	....	....	....
Banks	4 783	−73	−22	209	216	−433	228	312	....
Other sectors	4 784	....	....	....	....	....	....	....	....
Other liabilities	4 786	....	....	....	....	....	....	318	....
Monetary authorities	4 787	....	....	....	....	....	....	318	....
of which: Short-term	4 789	....	....	....	....	....	....	....	....
General government	4 790	....	....	....	....	....	....	....	....
of which: Short-term	4 792	....	....	....	....	....	....	....	....
Banks	4 793	....	....	....	....	....	....	....	....
of which: Short-term	4 795	....	....	....	....	....	....	....	....
Other sectors	4 796	....	....	....	....	....	....	....	....
of which: Short-term	4 798	....	....	....	....	....	....	....	....
E. RESERVE ASSETS	4 802	**−23**	**−29**	**63**	**−29**	**−142**	**−45**	**−154**	....
Monetary gold	4 812	....	....	....	....	....	....	....	....
Special drawing rights	4 811	−1	−1	−2	−2	−1	−1	−318	....
Reserve position in the Fund	4 810	−9	....	38	11	15	1	....	....
Foreign exchange	4 803	−13	−28	28	−39	−156	−45	165	....
Other claims	4 813	....	....	....	....	....	....	....	....
NET ERRORS AND OMISSIONS	4 998	**−1,838**	**−1,190**	**−4,006**	**−5,796**	**−5,846**	**−8,233**	**−5,420**	....

Table 1. ANALYTIC PRESENTATION, 2003–2010

(Millions of U.S. dollars)

	Code	2003	2004	2005	2006	2007	2008	2009	2010
A. Current Account[1]	4 993 Z.	−1,022.2	−1,671.1	−3,347.0	−5,863.2	−11,437.0	−11,845.5	−4,258.5	−578.0
Goods: exports f.o.b.	2 100 ..	7,081.4	9,931.2	11,754.1	15,101.4	19,469.0	22,484.2	16,377.6	20,608.2
Goods: imports f.o.b.	3 100 ..	−9,657.3	−13,619.1	−17,204.4	−22,129.5	−30,041.0	−35,107.7	−22,152.9	−23,825.6
Balance on Goods	4 100 ..	*−2,575.9*	*−3,688.0*	*−5,450.3*	*−7,028.1*	*−10,572.0*	*−12,623.5*	*−5,775.3*	*−3,217.4*
Services: credit	2 200 ..	2,961.4	4,029.4	4,404.1	5,289.4	6,829.1	7,991.1	6,896.1	6,909.9
Services: debit	3 200 ..	−2,447.1	−3,238.4	−3,403.8	−4,105.6	−5,202.3	−5,957.7	−5,043.1	−4,472.1
Balance on Goods and Services	4 991 ..	*−2,061.6*	*−2,896.9*	*−4,450.0*	*−5,844.4*	*−8,945.2*	*−10,590.1*	*−3,922.3*	*−779.6*
Income: credit	2 300 ..	1,297.7	1,539.3	1,515.6	1,581.7	1,189.4	1,450.1	1,118.0	840.0
Income: debit	3 300 ..	−953.9	−1,235.9	−1,426.0	−2,444.8	−4,665.4	−4,028.9	−2,779.2	−2,674.8
Balance on Goods, Services, and Income	4 992 ..	*−1,717.8*	*−2,593.5*	*−4,360.4*	*−6,707.5*	*−12,421.2*	*−13,168.9*	*−5,583.5*	*−2,614.4*
Current transfers: credit	2 379 Z.	865.5	1,121.0	1,238.0	1,065.7	1,813.1	2,421.1	2,164.9	2,766.7
Current transfers: debit	3 379 ..	−169.8	−198.6	−224.7	−221.5	−828.9	−1,097.7	−839.8	−730.4
B. Capital Account[1]	4 994 Z.	**−.2**	**204.0**	**289.7**	**228.5**	**−852.6**	**419.6**	**654.9**	**391.3**
Capital account: credit	2 994 Z.	....	204.1	293.6	228.5	563.2	419.7	657.4	574.4
Capital account: debit	3 994 ..	−.2	−.1	−3.9	....	−1,415.8	....	−2.5	−183.0
Total, Groups A Plus B	4 981 ..	*−1,022.4*	*−1,467.1*	*−3,057.3*	*−5,634.7*	*−12,289.6*	*−11,425.9*	*−3,603.6*	*−186.7*
C. Financial Account[1]	4 995 W.	**2,738.0**	**3,428.1**	**6,903.1**	**8,910.1**	**20,135.6**	**17,601.6**	**2,555.0**	**−41.1**
Direct investment abroad	4 505 ..	−26.5	217.0	−307.6	−174.9	−311.5	−792.4	136.2	−236.0
Direct investment in Bulgaria	4 555 Z.	2,096.8	2,662.2	4,312.4	7,757.6	13,214.5	9,979.1	3,389.2	2,167.5
Portfolio investment assets	4 602 ..	−78.6	9.6	29.1	−364.7	−242.2	−399.9	−774.7	−738.8
Equity securities	4 610 ..	−15.7	−7.2	−6.0	−129.2	−204.4	−40.1	−211.5	−223.6
Debt securities	4 619 ..	−62.9	16.7	35.1	−235.6	−37.8	−359.8	−563.1	−515.2
Portfolio investment liabilities	4 652 Z.	−36.2	57.9	584.5	759.3	−227.8	−241.4	−93.0	−19.9
Equity securities	4 660 ..	−23.2	21.5	449.0	147.6	88.6	−105.5	7.6	8.7
Debt securities	4 669 Z.	−13.0	36.4	135.5	611.7	−316.4	−135.9	−100.6	−28.7
Financial derivatives	4 910 ..	−1.1	−85.9	−112.0	−143.0	−98.6	−75.6	−27.8	−32.9
Financial derivatives assets	4 900 ..	....	−85.9	−112.5	−168.0	−146.1	−132.5	−55.2	−29.6
Financial derivatives liabilities	4 905 ..	−1.1	....	.5	25.1	47.5	56.9	27.5	−3.3
Other investment assets	4 703 ..	250.9	−1,784.5	15.7	−2,968.9	590.3	198.5	−903.3	482.7
Monetary authorities	4 701 ..	....	....	....	....	....	....	....	....
General government	4 704 ..	2.9	−723.5	703.5	−265.9	1,442.5	367.5	70.5	112.5
Banks	4 705 ..	263.2	−763.2	−470.4	−1,780.1	−489.2	115.6	−379.7	409.1
Other sectors	4 728 ..	−15.2	−297.8	−217.4	−923.0	−363.0	−284.6	−594.1	−38.9
Other investment liabilities	4 753 W.	532.7	2,351.9	2,381.0	4,044.7	7,210.7	8,933.2	828.4	−1,663.7
Monetary authorities	4 753 WA	....	....	....	....	....	....	955.5	....
General government	4 753 ZB	−99.9	−45.6	−122.2	−366.1	22.6	−505.8	348.1	31.9
Banks	4 753 ZC	445.2	1,096.4	1,178.4	1,091.1	3,499.5	5,233.9	−849.8	−2,084.5
Other sectors	4 753 ZD	187.5	1,301.1	1,324.8	3,319.6	3,688.6	4,205.2	374.6	388.8
Total, Groups A Through C	4 983 ..	*1,715.6*	*1,961.0*	*3,845.8*	*3,275.4*	*7,846.0*	*6,175.7*	*−1,048.6*	*−227.8*
D. Net Errors and Omissions	4 998 ..	**−889.0**	**370.8**	**−1,219.4**	**−985.7**	**−3,045.2**	**−4,272.1**	**1,055.8**	**−377.5**
Total, Groups A Through D	4 984 ..	*826.6*	*2,331.8*	*2,626.4*	*2,289.7*	*4,800.8*	*1,903.6*	*7.2*	*−605.3*
E. Reserves and Related Items	4 802 A.	**−826.6**	**−2,331.8**	**−2,626.4**	**−2,289.7**	**−4,800.8**	**−1,903.6**	**−7.2**	**605.3**
Reserve assets	4 802 ..	−929.9	−1,846.4	−415.0	−1,924.2	−4,099.1	−1,469.1	−169.5	603.5
Use of Fund credit and loans	4 766 ..	36.4	−55.2	−436.2	−341.4	−344.2	....	....	....
Exceptional financing	4 920 ..	66.9	−430.1	−1,775.2	−24.1	−357.6	−434.5	162.3	1.8
Conversion rates: leva per U.S. dollar	0 101 ..	**1.7327**	**1.5751**	**1.5741**	**1.5593**	**1.4291**	**1.3371**	**1.4067**	**1.4774**

[1] Excludes components that have been classified in the categories of Group E.

Table 2. STANDARD PRESENTATION, 2003–2010

(Millions of U.S. dollars)

	Code	2003	2004	2005	2006	2007	2008	2009	2010
CURRENT ACCOUNT	4 993	**−1,022.2**	**−1,671.1**	**−3,347.0**	**−5,863.2**	**−11,437.0**	**−11,845.5**	**−4,258.5**	**−578.0**
A. GOODS	4 100	**−2,575.9**	**−3,688.0**	**−5,450.3**	**−7,028.1**	**−10,572.0**	**−12,623.5**	**−5,775.3**	**−3,217.4**
Credit	2 100	**7,081.4**	**9,931.2**	**11,754.1**	**15,101.4**	**19,469.0**	**22,484.2**	**16,377.6**	**20,608.2**
General merchandise: exports f.o.b.	2 110	7,081.4	9,931.2	11,754.1	15,101.4	19,469.0	22,484.2	16,377.6	20,608.2
Goods for processing: exports f.o.b.	2 150	....	....	....	....	....	....	....	....
Repairs on goods	2 160	....	....	....	....	....	....	....	....
Goods procured in ports by carriers	2 170	....	....	....	....	....	....	....	....
Nonmonetary gold	2 180	....	....	....	....	....	....	....	....
Debit	3 100	**−9,657.3**	**−13,619.1**	**−17,204.4**	**−22,129.5**	**−30,041.0**	**−35,107.7**	**−22,152.9**	**−23,825.6**
General merchandise: imports f.o.b.	3 110	−9,657.3	−13,619.1	−17,204.4	−22,129.5	−30,041.0	−35,107.7	−22,152.9	−23,825.6
Goods for processing: imports f.o.b.	3 150	....	....	....	....	....	....	....	....
Repairs on goods	3 160	....	....	....	....	....	....	....	....
Goods procured in ports by carriers	3 170	....	....	....	....	....	....	....	....
Nonmonetary gold	3 180	....	....	....	....	....	....	....	....
B. SERVICES	4 200	**514.3**	**791.0**	**1,000.3**	**1,183.8**	**1,626.8**	**2,033.4**	**1,853.0**	**2,437.8**
Total credit	2 200	*2,961.4*	*4,029.4*	*4,404.1*	*5,289.4*	*6,829.1*	*7,991.1*	*6,896.1*	*6,909.9*
Total debit	3 200	*−2,447.1*	*−3,238.4*	*−3,403.8*	*−4,105.6*	*−5,202.3*	*−5,957.7*	*−5,043.1*	*−4,472.1*
Transportation services, credit	2 205	**778.0**	**1,020.8**	**1,194.1**	**1,589.9**	**1,584.4**	**1,825.5**	**1,412.2**	**1,467.3**
Passenger	2 850	*429.9*	*594.5*	*650.9*	*705.2*	*468.3*	*546.0*	*496.6*	*464.4*
Freight	2 851	*348.1*	*426.3*	*543.2*	*774.3*	*967.1*	*1,066.1*	*757.2*	*841.2*
Other	2 852	....	....	....	*110.5*	*148.9*	*213.4*	*158.4*	*161.6*
Sea transport, passenger	2 207	....	....	32.5	35.3	1.2	1.4	1.3	1.3
Sea transport, freight	2 208	....	29.3	47.8	63.3	79.8	63.5	24.0	30.4
Sea transport, other	2 209	....	....	....	11.8	17.0	21.4	23.2	35.8
Air transport, passenger	2 211	....	....	130.2	141.0	456.8	532.5	484.4	452.7
Air transport, freight	2 212	....	7.7	23.1	25.8	29.8	33.2	17.0	21.5
Air transport, other	2 213	....	....	....	98.6	125.9	187.7	127.6	123.7
Other transport, passenger	2 215	....	....	488.1	528.9	10.4	12.2	10.8	10.5
Other transport, freight	2 216	....	389.2	472.3	685.1	857.6	969.3	716.2	789.4
Other transport, other	2 217	....	....	....	.1	6.1	4.4	7.6	2.1
Transportation services, debit	3 205	**−748.6**	**−1,082.3**	**−1,094.9**	**−1,313.1**	**−1,227.9**	**−1,461.4**	**−1,118.1**	**−1,237.3**
Passenger	3 850	*−433.9*	*−572.3*	*−549.0*	*−620.6*	*−262.4*	*−291.0*	*−200.4*	*−149.9*
Freight	3 851	*−314.7*	*−510.0*	*−545.9*	*−630.3*	*−880.1*	*−1,108.1*	*−882.8*	*−1,010.6*
Other	3 852	....	....	....	*−62.2*	*−85.4*	*−62.3*	*−35.0*	*−76.7*
Sea transport, passenger	3 207	....	....	−43.9	−49.6	....	....	....	....
Sea transport, freight	3 208	....	−234.6	−337.2	−410.8	−580.7	−751.0	−576.2	−705.8
Sea transport, other	3 209	....	....	....	−25.7	−39.5	−21.4	−18.0	−20.1
Air transport, passenger	3 211	....	....	−164.7	−186.2	−205.4	−225.6	−151.8	−115.1
Air transport, freight	3 212	....	−38.3	−36.1	−33.0	−33.2	−40.6	−33.6	−37.2
Air transport, other	3 213	....	....	....	−35.1	−44.7	−38.8	−16.1	−56.1
Other transport, passenger	3 215	....	....	−340.4	−384.8	−57.0	−65.4	−48.6	−34.8
Other transport, freight	3 216	....	−237.2	−172.7	−186.6	−266.1	−316.5	−273.0	−267.6
Other transport, other	3 217	....	....	....	−1.4	−1.3	−2.1	−.8	−.6
Travel, credit	2 236	**1,620.6**	**2,201.8**	**2,411.8**	**2,611.7**	**3,712.5**	**4,306.1**	**3,775.7**	**3,571.2**
Business travel	2 237	169.8	230.0	273.9	291.4	893.0	1,013.7	898.9	893.9
Personal travel	2 240	1,450.8	1,971.9	2,137.9	2,320.3	2,819.5	3,292.4	2,876.8	2,677.3
Travel, debit	3 236	**−1,033.1**	**−1,363.3**	**−1,308.9**	**−1,477.5**	**−1,879.7**	**−2,310.9**	**−1,755.1**	**−1,231.6**
Business travel	3 237	−784.6	−1,042.6	−943.4	−1,069.1	−686.0	−826.2	−564.5	−367.7
Personal travel	3 240	−248.6	−320.6	−365.5	−408.4	−1,193.7	−1,484.7	−1,190.6	−863.9
Other services, credit	2 200 BA	**562.8**	**806.8**	**798.2**	**1,087.7**	**1,532.1**	**1,859.5**	**1,708.2**	**1,871.4**
Communications	2 245	44.8	81.8	145.8	150.6	171.6	259.8	223.3	216.6
Construction	2 249	78.2	122.7	102.8	168.5	278.6	249.0	421.8	171.6
Insurance	2 253	18.0	27.4	30.0	37.5	50.9	58.2	134.6	146.3
Financial	2 260	18.0	38.7	18.3	34.5	34.5	47.7	38.4	28.9
Computer and information	2 262	14.8	28.3	32.6	55.9	124.1	187.1	164.5	385.0
Royalties and licence fees	2 266	4.7	7.1	5.0	10.5	10.9	11.4	9.3	33.6
Other business services	2 268	307.0	413.1	409.0	571.4	775.6	966.3	657.9	839.8
Personal, cultural, and recreational	2 287	37.0	42.4	39.3	56.3	82.8	76.9	54.4	44.9
Government, n.i.e.	2 291	40.3	45.3	15.5	2.4	3.1	3.1	4.0	4.7
Other services, debit	3 200 BA	**−665.4**	**−792.8**	**−1,000.1**	**−1,314.9**	**−2,094.7**	**−2,185.4**	**−2,169.9**	**−2,003.2**
Communications	3 245	−35.7	−52.5	−47.8	−79.9	−119.6	−132.9	−114.1	−116.3
Construction	3 249	−28.7	−67.7	−77.4	−59.9	−481.4	−359.1	−566.0	−185.2
Insurance	3 253	−77.2	−85.8	−93.6	−116.9	−161.4	−135.9	−247.0	−157.5
Financial	3 260	−18.5	−32.9	−33.1	−66.9	−138.7	−123.1	−158.3	−78.3
Computer and information	3 262	−18.2	−23.2	−39.6	−54.4	−74.2	−66.6	−73.4	−190.2
Royalties and licence fees	3 266	−24.4	−30.5	−80.6	−69.4	−77.6	−95.2	−117.2	−118.5
Other business services	3 268	−422.3	−459.3	−589.3	−839.5	−1,001.6	−1,240.8	−862.4	−1,104.9
Personal, cultural, and recreational	3 287	−17.3	−15.1	−16.5	−19.3	−30.9	−19.6	−25.2	−51.3
Government, n.i.e.	3 291	−22.9	−25.7	−22.3	−8.8	−9.2	−12.3	−6.3	−1.0

Table 2 (Continued). STANDARD PRESENTATION, 2003–2010

(Millions of U.S. dollars)

	Code	2003	2004	2005	2006	2007	2008	2009	2010
C. INCOME	4 300	**343.8**	**303.4**	**89.6**	**−863.1**	**−3,476.0**	**−2,578.8**	**−1,661.2**	**−1,834.8**
Total credit	2 300	*1,297.7*	*1,539.3*	*1,515.6*	*1,581.7*	*1,189.4*	*1,450.1*	*1,118.0*	*840.0*
Total debit	3 300	*−953.9*	*−1,235.9*	*−1,426.0*	*−2,444.8*	*−4,665.4*	*−4,028.9*	*−2,779.2*	*−2,674.8*
Compensation of employees, credit	2 310	**1,037.2**	**1,286.5**	**1,151.0**	**1,296.8**	**788.2**	**893.9**	**592.9**	**382.3**
Compensation of employees, debit	3 310	**−12.6**	**−11.1**	**−13.8**	**−28.6**	**−69.2**	**−128.4**	**−87.5**	**−15.8**
Investment income, credit	2 320	**260.5**	**252.8**	**364.7**	**284.9**	**401.2**	**556.2**	**525.1**	**457.7**
Direct investment income	2 330	1.1	−2.3	−1.8	4.1	5.8	57.4	6.6	46.9
Dividends and distributed branch profits	2 332	1.1	.4	1.0	2.3	7.2	32.1	15.6	16.7
Reinvested earnings and undistributed branch profits	2 333	....	−1.0	6.6	1.6	−7.7	20.5	−13.4	18.0
Income on debt (interest)	2 334	....	−1.6	−9.5	.1	6.2	4.8	4.3	12.2
Portfolio investment income	2 339	172.7	140.7	245.9	125.6	158.1	283.1	409.6	339.5
Income on equity	2 340	2.3	....	....	.1	.8	1.2	2.5	3.7
Income on bonds and notes	2 350	169.7	140.2	245.3	124.6	156.5	281.7	400.2	334.1
Income on money market instruments	2 360	.7	.5	.6	.9	.9	.1	7.0	1.6
Other investment income	2 370	86.7	114.4	120.6	155.3	237.3	215.7	108.9	71.3
Investment income, debit	3 320	**−941.3**	**−1,224.8**	**−1,412.2**	**−2,416.2**	**−4,596.2**	**−3,900.5**	**−2,691.7**	**−2,659.0**
Direct investment income	3 330	−550.6	−755.5	−912.1	−1,856.8	−3,742.1	−2,722.2	−1,822.0	−1,963.5
Dividends and distributed branch profits	3 332	−253.8	−140.3	−316.2	−408.3	−862.0	−1,826.1	−1,209.1	−836.8
Reinvested earnings and undistributed branch profits	3 333	−249.8	−548.1	−509.0	−1,203.8	−2,228.2	263.1	377.2	−276.8
Income on debt (interest)	3 334	−47.0	−67.0	−86.9	−244.8	−651.9	−1,159.2	−990.1	−850.0
Portfolio investment income	3 339	−222.7	−232.3	−220.9	−161.9	−168.8	−143.6	−99.0	−111.4
Income on equity	3 340	−.5	....	....	....	....	....	....	....
Income on bonds and notes	3 350	−220.1	−232.2	−220.9	−161.9	−168.8	−143.6	−99.0	−111.4
Income on money market instruments	3 360	−2.2	....	....	....	....	....	....	....
Other investment income	3 370	−168.0	−237.1	−279.2	−397.4	−685.3	−1,034.7	−770.7	−584.1
D. CURRENT TRANSFERS	4 379	**695.6**	**922.4**	**1,013.4**	**844.2**	**984.2**	**1,323.4**	**1,325.0**	**2,036.4**
Credit	2 379	**865.5**	**1,121.0**	**1,238.0**	**1,065.7**	**1,813.1**	**2,421.1**	**2,164.9**	**2,766.7**
General government	2 380	169.8	104.5	109.5	175.0	381.4	830.6	846.4	1,593.6
Other sectors	2 390	695.7	1,016.5	1,128.5	890.7	1,431.7	1,590.5	1,318.4	1,173.2
Workers' remittances	2 391	681.2	436.3	462.0	419.7	905.4	1,024.7	998.9	1,005.0
Other current transfers	2 392	14.5	580.2	666.6	471.1	526.4	565.7	319.5	168.1
Debit	3 379	**−169.8**	**−198.6**	**−224.7**	**−221.5**	**−828.9**	**−1,097.7**	**−839.8**	**−730.4**
General government	3 380	−31.6	−32.4	−38.0	−24.4	−507.3	−652.3	−619.1	−628.9
Other sectors	3 390	−138.3	−166.2	−186.7	−197.1	−321.6	−445.3	−220.7	−101.5
Workers' remittances	3 391	....	−18.3	−21.6	−21.0	−33.4	−33.4	−13.7	−9.2
Other current transfers	3 392	−138.3	−147.9	−165.0	−176.1	−288.2	−411.9	−207.0	−92.2
CAPITAL AND FINANCIAL ACCOUNT	4 996	**1,911.2**	**1,300.4**	**4,566.3**	**6,848.9**	**14,482.2**	**16,117.7**	**3,202.7**	**955.5**
CAPITAL ACCOUNT	4 994	**−.2**	**204.0**	**289.7**	**228.5**	**−852.6**	**419.6**	**654.9**	**391.3**
Total credit	2 994	....	*204.1*	*293.6*	*228.5*	*563.2*	*419.7*	*657.4*	*574.4*
Total debit	3 994	*−.2*	*−.1*	*−3.9*	....	*−1,415.8*	....	*−2.5*	*−183.0*
Capital transfers, credit	2 400	....	**204.1**	**293.6**	**228.5**	**563.2**	**419.7**	**657.4**	**529.9**
General government	2 401	....	179.2	220.3	222.4	551.2	418.8	652.2	517.5
Debt forgiveness	2 402	....	....	....	....	....	....	....	....
Other capital transfers	2 410	....	179.2	220.3	222.4	551.2	418.8	652.2	517.5
Other sectors	2 430	....	24.9	73.3	6.2	12.0	.9	5.2	12.4
Migrants' transfers	2 431	....	....	....	....	....	....	....	....
Debt forgiveness	2 432	....	24.9	73.1	5.9	12.0	.9	4.4	12.2
Other capital transfers	2 440	....	....	.1	.3	....	....	.8	.2
Capital transfers, debit	3 400	**−.2**	**−.1**	**−3.9**	....	**−1,415.8**	....	**−.2**	**−182.7**
General government	3 401	....	....	....	....	−1,415.8	....	....	−182.2
Debt forgiveness	3 402	....	....	....	....	−1,405.8	....	....	....
Other capital transfers	3 410	....	....	....	....	−10.0	....	....	−182.2
Other sectors	3 430	−.2	−.1	−3.9	....	−.1	....	−.2	−.5
Migrants' transfers	3 431	....	....	....	....	....	....	....	....
Debt forgiveness	3 432	....	....	−2.4	....	....	....	....	....
Other capital transfers	3 440	−.2	−.1	−1.5	....	....	....	−.2	−.5
Nonproduced nonfinancial assets, credit	2 480	....	....	....	....	....	....	....	**44.5**
Nonproduced nonfinancial assets, debit	3 480	....	....	....	....	....	....	**−2.3**	**−.3**

Table 2 (Continued). STANDARD PRESENTATION, 2003–2010

(Millions of U.S. dollars)

	Code	2003	2004	2005	2006	2007	2008	2009	2010
FINANCIAL ACCOUNT	4 995	1,911.4	1,096.3	4,276.7	6,620.4	15,334.7	15,698.0	2,547.9	564.2
A. DIRECT INVESTMENT	4 500	2,070.3	2,879.2	4,004.8	7,582.8	12,903.1	9,186.7	3,525.4	1,931.5
Direct investment abroad	4 505	−26.5	217.0	−307.6	−174.9	−311.5	−792.4	136.2	−236.0
Equity capital	4 510	−24.0	−33.1	−65.8	−97.2	−302.2	−834.8	187.4	−129.6
Claims on affiliated enterprises	4 515	−24.0	−33.1	−65.8	−97.2	−302.2	−834.8	187.4	−129.6
Liabilities to affiliated enterprises	4 520	....	....	....	....	....	....	....	....
Reinvested earnings	4 525	....	1.0	−6.6	−1.6	7.7	−20.5	13.4	−18.0
Other capital	4 530	−2.5	249.0	−235.2	−76.0	−17.0	62.9	−64.6	−88.5
Claims on affiliated enterprises	4 535	−2.5	−7.5	−10.3	−75.2	−42.3	−38.9	−61.5	−85.9
Liabilities to affiliated enterprises	4 540	....	256.6	−224.9	−.8	25.4	101.8	−3.1	−2.5
Direct investment in Bulgaria	4 555	2,096.8	2,662.2	4,312.4	7,757.6	13,214.5	9,979.1	3,389.2	2,167.5
Equity capital	4 560	1,233.7	1,554.5	1,508.3	4,078.8	4,892.0	6,085.2	2,633.8	1,971.4
Claims on direct investors	4 565	....	....	....	....	....	....	....	....
Liabilities to direct investors	4 570	1,233.7	1,554.5	1,508.3	4,078.8	4,892.0	6,085.2	2,633.8	1,971.4
Reinvested earnings	4 575	249.8	548.1	509.0	1,203.8	2,228.2	−263.1	−377.2	276.8
Other capital	4 580	613.3	559.6	2,295.1	2,475.0	6,094.4	4,157.0	1,132.6	−80.7
Claims on direct investors	4 585	....	−153.8	−10.6	−117.7	−635.4	−199.9	−474.6	−463.0
Liabilities to direct investors	4 590	613.3	713.3	2,305.7	2,592.7	6,729.7	4,357.0	1,607.2	382.4
B. PORTFOLIO INVESTMENT	4 600	−211.8	−521.0	−1,304.1	363.4	−836.5	−1,080.3	−753.8	−843.7
Assets	4 602	−78.6	9.6	29.1	−364.7	−242.2	−399.9	−774.7	−738.8
Equity securities	4 610	−15.7	−7.2	−6.0	−129.2	−204.4	−40.1	−211.5	−223.6
Monetary authorities	4 611	....	....	....	....	....	....	....	....
General government	4 612	....	....	....	....	....	....	....	....
Banks	4 613	−9.2	−.7	−.3	−.2	−1.5	.4	.1	.1
Other sectors	4 614	−6.6	−6.5	−5.7	−128.9	−202.9	−40.5	−211.6	−223.7
Debt securities	4 619	−62.9	16.7	35.1	−235.6	−37.8	−359.8	−563.1	−515.2
Bonds and notes	4 620	−87.0	70.3	136.7	−316.1	−78.8	−246.4	−508.4	−322.0
Monetary authorities	4 621	....	....	....	....	....	....	....	....
General government	4 622	−11.7	255.2	....	....	....	....	....	....
Banks	4 623	−74.5	−181.5	153.6	−249.0	179.5	44.4	208.5	8.0
Other sectors	4 624	−.8	−3.4	−16.9	−67.2	−258.3	−290.8	−716.9	−330.1
Money market instruments	4 630	24.1	−53.6	−101.7	80.6	41.0	−113.4	−54.7	−193.2
Monetary authorities	4 631	....	....	....	....	....	....	....	....
General government	4 632	21.9	25.7	....	....	....	....	....	....
Banks	4 633	2.2	−80.4	−103.4	88.1	34.1	−65.1	−44.6	−225.7
Other sectors	4 634	....	1.1	1.7	−7.5	6.8	−48.3	−10.1	32.5
Liabilities	4 652	−133.2	−530.6	−1,333.2	728.2	−594.4	−680.4	20.8	−104.9
Equity securities	4 660	−23.2	21.5	449.0	147.6	88.6	−105.5	7.6	8.7
Banks	4 663	−4.4	−4.3	4.6	36.7	82.0	−60.2	−18.4	3.0
Other sectors	4 664	−18.8	25.8	444.4	110.9	6.6	−45.3	25.9	5.7
Debt securities	4 669	−110.0	−552.1	−1,782.2	580.6	−682.9	−574.9	13.3	−113.6
Bonds and notes	4 670	−110.5	−552.1	−1,782.2	352.7	−424.0	−574.9	13.3	−113.6
Monetary authorities	4 671	....	....	....	....	....	....	....	....
General government	4 672	−113.2	−588.5	−1,917.7	−31.1	−366.5	−439.1	113.8	−84.9
Banks	4 673	3.2	4.9	123.1	42.7	−13.7	−122.1	−6.4	−1.4
Other sectors	4 674	−.4	31.6	12.3	341.1	−43.7	−13.8	−94.1	−27.2
Money market instruments	4 680	.5	....	....	227.9	−259.0	....	....	....
Monetary authorities	4 681	....	....	....	....	....	....	....	....
General government	4 682	....	....	....	....	....	....	....	....
Banks	4 683	....	....	....	....	....	....	....	....
Other sectors	4 684	.5	....	....	227.9	−259.0	....	....	....
C. FINANCIAL DERIVATIVES	4 910	−1.1	−85.9	−112.0	−143.0	−98.6	−75.6	−27.8	−32.9
Monetary authorities	4 911	....	....	....	....	....	....	....	....
General government	4 912	....	....	....	....	....	−5.0	−1.7	−.8
Banks	4 913	−1.1	−2.7	−2.9	−.8	10.6	.6	.7	....
Other sectors	4 914	....	−83.3	−109.1	−142.2	−109.2	−71.3	−26.7	−32.1
Assets	4 900	....	−85.9	−112.5	−168.0	−146.1	−132.5	−55.2	−29.6
Monetary authorities	4 901	....	....	....	....	....	....	....	....
General government	4 902	....	....	....	....	....	....	....	....
Banks	4 903	....	−2.7	−3.0	−.6	.1	.6	.6	....
Other sectors	4 904	....	−83.3	−109.5	−167.4	−146.2	−133.2	−55.9	−29.6
Liabilities	4 905	−1.1	....	.5	25.1	47.5	56.9	27.5	−3.3
Monetary authorities	4 906	....	....	....	....	....	....	....	....
General government	4 907	....	....	....	....	....	−5.0	−1.7	−.8
Banks	4 908	−1.1	....	....	−.2	10.4	....	....	....
Other sectors	4 909	....	....	.4	25.3	37.0	61.8	29.1	−2.4

Table 2 (Concluded). STANDARD PRESENTATION, 2003–2010

(Millions of U.S. dollars)

	Code	2003	2004	2005	2006	2007	2008	2009	2010
D. OTHER INVESTMENT	4 700	**984.0**	**670.5**	**2,103.0**	**741.4**	**7,465.9**	**9,136.4**	**−26.5**	**−1,094.3**
Assets	4 703	**250.9**	**−1,784.5**	**15.7**	**−2,968.9**	**590.3**	**198.5**	**−903.3**	**482.7**
Trade credits	4 706	....	−185.8	−38.8	−155.7	−170.5	−253.2	−166.8	−244.9
General government	4 707	....	....	....	....	....	....	....	....
of which: Short-term	4 709	....	....	....	....	....	....	....	....
Other sectors	4 710	....	−185.8	−38.8	−155.7	−170.5	−253.2	−166.8	−244.9
of which: Short-term	4 712	....	−185.8	−38.8	−155.7	−170.5	−253.2	−166.8	−244.9
Loans	4 714	−35.1	−57.3	−85.0	−167.8	−243.9	−362.4	10.8	−155.1
Monetary authorities	4 715	....	....	....	....	....	....	....	....
of which: Short-term	4 718	....	....	....	....	....	....	....	....
General government	4 719	....	....	....	....	....	....	....	....
of which: Short-term	4 721	....	....	....	....	....	....	....	....
Banks	4 722	−36.9	−42.5	−53.2	−22.5	−162.6	−138.8	25.6	−84.3
of which: Short-term	4 724	−20.4	−17.1	7.3	−15.8	3.6	−55.0	34.4	4.4
Other sectors	4 725	1.8	−14.7	−31.8	−145.3	−81.3	−223.6	−14.8	−70.8
of which: Short-term	4 727	.2	−7.2	−12.3	−48.8	−76.6	−218.6	−11.2	−43.2
Currency and deposits	4 730	294.3	−790.0	−540.1	−2,654.4	−255.7	486.0	−740.0	853.4
Monetary authorities	4 731	....	....	....	....	....	....	....	....
General government	4 732	....	22.5	−1.7	−246.3	71.8	27.9	67.6	55.9
Banks	4 733	311.3	−715.1	−391.6	−1,786.3	−216.5	265.0	−410.5	518.1
Other sectors	4 734	−17.0	−97.4	−146.9	−621.8	−111.0	193.1	−397.1	279.5
Other assets	4 736	−8.4	−751.5	679.6	8.9	1,260.5	328.1	−7.4	29.3
Monetary authorities	4 737	....	....	....	....	....	....	....	....
of which: Short-term	4 739	....	....	....	....	....	....	....	....
General government	4 740	2.9	−746.0	705.2	−19.7	1,370.7	339.7	2.9	56.6
of which: Short-term	4 742	2.9	−746.0	705.2	−19.7	1,370.7	339.7	2.9	76.8
Banks	4 743	−11.2	−5.6	−25.6	28.7	−110.0	−10.7	5.2	−24.7
of which: Short-term	4 745	−11.2	−5.6	−25.6	28.7	−110.0	−10.7	5.2	−24.7
Other sectors	4 746	....	.1	....	−.1	−.2	−.8	−15.5	−2.6
of which: Short-term	4 748	....	.1	....	−.1	−.2	−.8	−15.5	−2.6
Liabilities	4 753	**733.1**	**2,455.1**	**2,087.3**	**3,710.4**	**6,875.5**	**8,937.9**	**876.9**	**−1,577.0**
Trade credits	4 756	−103.4	107.8	282.0	405.8	382.9	285.7	47.3	−135.9
General government	4 757	....	....	....	....	....	....	....	....
of which: Short-term	4 759	....	....	....	....	....	....	....	....
Other sectors	4 760	−103.4	107.8	282.0	405.8	382.9	285.7	47.3	−135.9
of which: Short-term	4 762	−103.4	107.8	282.0	405.8	382.9	285.7	47.3	−135.9
Loans	4 764	429.7	1,723.4	1,269.1	2,643.7	3,265.2	5,506.4	746.2	−639.5
Monetary authorities	4 765	36.4	−55.2	−436.2	−341.4	−344.2	....	....	....
of which: Use of Fund credit and loans from the Fund	4 766	36.4	−55.2	−436.2	−341.4	−344.2	....	....	....
of which: Short-term	4 768	....	....	....	....	....	....	....	....
General government	4 769	64.0	105.4	14.6	−366.1	22.6	−505.8	348.1	31.9
of which: Short-term	4 771	....	....	....	....	....	....	....	....
Banks	4 772	62.1	479.8	647.9	437.3	281.0	2,092.8	70.8	−1,196.1
of which: Short-term	4 774	−2.2	119.0	421.4	261.3	−475.8	732.0	128.0	−445.6
Other sectors	4 775	267.1	1,193.3	1,042.7	2,913.8	3,305.7	3,919.5	327.3	524.7
of which: Short-term	4 777	140.1	280.9	493.4	1,336.2	2,207.1	1,721.5	−71.4	469.6
Currency and deposits	4 780	303.1	650.4	499.9	633.4	3,204.4	3,161.7	−829.9	−921.1
Monetary authorities	4 781	....	....	....	....	....	....	....	....
General government	4 782	....	....	....	....	....	....	....	....
Banks	4 783	303.1	650.4	499.9	633.4	3,204.4	3,161.7	−829.9	−921.1
Other sectors	4 784	....	....	....	....	....	....	....	....
Other liabilities	4 786	103.8	−26.4	36.2	27.4	23.0	−16.0	913.2	119.5
Monetary authorities	4 787	....	....	....	....	....	....	955.5	....
of which: Short-term	4 792	....	....	....	....	....	....	....	....
General government	4 790	....	....	....	....	....	....	....	....
of which: Short-term	4 792	....	....	....	....	....	....	....	....
Banks	4 793	80.0	−33.8	30.4	20.4	14.1	−19.6	−74.7	64.0
of which: Short-term	4 795	80.0	−33.8	30.4	20.4	14.1	−19.6	−74.7	64.0
Other sectors	4 796	23.8	7.4	5.8	7.0	9.0	3.6	32.5	55.5
of which: Short-term	4 798	23.8	7.4	5.8	7.0	9.0	3.6	32.5	55.5
E. RESERVE ASSETS	4 802	**−929.9**	**−1,846.4**	**−415.0**	**−1,924.2**	**−4,099.1**	**−1,469.1**	**−169.5**	**603.5**
Monetary gold	4 812	....	....	....	....	....	....	....	....
Special drawing rights	4 811	−60.1	54.1	11.7	.1	.1	−5.8	−948.8	....
Reserve position in the Fund	4 810	....	−.2	−.2	−.2	−.3	−.3	−.3	−.3
Foreign exchange	4 803	−869.9	−1,900.3	−426.5	−1,924.2	−4,098.9	−1,463.0	779.7	603.8
Other claims	4 813	....	....	....	....	....	....	....	....
NET ERRORS AND OMISSIONS	4 998	**−889.0**	**370.8**	**−1,219.4**	**−985.7**	**−3,045.2**	**−4,272.1**	**1,055.8**	**−377.5**

Table 3. INTERNATIONAL INVESTMENT POSITION (End-period stocks), 2003–2010

(Millions of U.S. dollars)

	Code	2003	2004	2005	2006	2007	2008	2009	2010
ASSETS	8 995 C.	**12,016.6**	**16,546.3**	**15,657.9**	**23,028.9**	**29,085.4**	**29,955.7**	**31,932.8**	**30,635.9**
Direct investment abroad	8 505 ..	**102.6**	**−175.8**	**123.5**	**453.3**	**811.6**	**1,457.3**	**1,342.7**	**1,477.1**
Equity capital and reinvested earnings	8 506 ..	106.1	85.0	120.8	371.8	683.8	1,396.6	1,221.2	1,281.2
Claims on affiliated enterprises	8 507 ..	106.1	85.0	120.8	371.8	683.8	1,396.6	1,221.2	1,281.2
Liabilities to affiliated enterprises	8 508 ..	....	....	....	....	....	....	....	....
Other capital	8 530 ..	−3.5	−260.8	2.7	81.5	127.9	60.7	121.6	195.9
Claims on affiliated enterprises	8 535 ..	5.6	17.3	30.3	110.6	157.8	184.5	244.8	321.0
Liabilities to affiliated enterprises	8 540 ..	−9.1	−278.2	−27.6	−29.1	−29.9	−123.8	−123.2	−125.1
Portfolio investment	8 602 ..	**803.3**	**904.5**	**790.5**	**1,250.3**	**1,538.6**	**1,575.8**	**2,592.1**	**3,538.3**
Equity securities	8 610 ..	2.7	19.4	23.2	166.8	409.9	181.6	480.7	865.2
Monetary authorities	8 611 ..	....	....	....	....	....	....	....	....
General government	8 612 ..	....	....	....	....	....	....	....	....
Banks	8 613 ..	1.4	1.3	1.4	1.8	3.4	2.8	2.8	2.5
Other sectors	8 614 ..	1.2	18.0	21.7	165.1	406.5	178.8	477.9	862.7
Debt securities	8 619 ..	800.6	885.2	767.4	1,083.5	1,128.7	1,394.2	2,111.5	2,673.1
Bonds and notes	8 620 ..	765.4	706.3	591.6	964.3	1,053.0	1,201.5	1,850.2	2,229.3
Monetary authorities	8 621 ..	....	....	....	....	....	....	....	....
General government	8 622 ..	239.9	....						
Banks	8 623 ..	519.6	559.9	574.1	877.6	717.7	612.5	455.9	490.9
Other sectors	8 624 ..	5.9	146.4	17.5	86.7	335.4	589.1	1,394.3	1,738.5
Money market instruments	8 630 ..	35.2	178.8	175.8	119.2	75.7	192.7	261.3	443.7
Monetary authorities	8 631 ..	....	....	....	....	....	....	....	....
General government	8 632 ..	26.6	....						
Banks	8 633 ..	7.3	173.9	175.8	111.3	73.9	140.5	196.2	410.3
Other sectors	8 634 ..	1.3	4.9	....	7.9	1.8	52.2	65.1	33.5
Financial derivatives	8 900 ..	**....**	**97.6**	**28.6**	**265.9**	**151.7**	**129.4**	**39.4**	**30.9**
Monetary authorities	8 901 ..	....	....	....	....	....	....	....	....
General government	8 902 ..	....	....	....	....	....	....	....	....
Banks	8 903 ..	....	2.9	2.7	.6	.8	.2	.7	.5
Other sectors	8 904 ..	....	94.6	25.9	265.2	150.9	129.2	38.7	30.3
Other investment	8 703 ..	**4,284.2**	**6,383.6**	**6,020.5**	**9,303.3**	**9,046.1**	**8,870.4**	**9,431.8**	**8,356.6**
Trade credits	8 706 ..	249.1	464.5	516.9	730.6	931.6	1,101.9	1,262.5	1,181.2
General government	8 707 ..	....	....	....	....	....	....	....	....
of which: Short-term	8 709 ..	....	....	....	....	....	....	....	....
Other sectors	8 710 ..	249.1	464.5	516.9	730.6	931.6	1,101.9	1,262.5	1,181.2
of which: Short-term	8 712 ..	*249.1*	*464.5*	*516.9*	*730.6*	*931.6*	*1,101.9*	*1,262.5*	*1,181.2*
Loans	8 714 ..	63.6	129.1	192.7	382.5	635.2	950.9	926.7	1,028.4
Monetary authorities	8 715 ..	....	....	....	....	....	....	....	....
of which: Short-term	8 718 ..	....	....	....	....	....	....	....	....
General government	8 719 ..	....	....	....	....	....	....	....	....
of which: Short-term	8 721 ..	....	....	....	....	....	....	....	....
Banks	8 722 ..	57.2	106.5	142.7	174.9	331.3	424.3	395.2	458.0
of which: Short-term	8 724 ..	*32.6*	*26.9*	*14.9*	*33.4*	*31.1*	*81.9*	*48.5*	*43.6*
Other sectors	8 725 ..	6.3	22.6	50.1	207.7	303.9	526.6	531.5	570.4
of which: Short-term	8 727 ..	*4.6*	*12.8*	*23.7*	*74.1*	*162.7*	*381.6*	*365.3*	*386.6*
Currency and deposits	8 730 ..	1,804.9	2,771.2	3,038.1	5,998.3	6,543.8	5,882.7	6,740.7	5,693.4
Monetary authorities	8 731 ..	....	....	....	....	....	....	....	....
General government	8 732 ..	....	10.7	10.8	282.1	247.1	206.8	138.4	74.0
Banks	8 733 ..	1,350.9	2,183.5	2,383.3	4,408.2	4,734.7	4,267.9	4,744.3	3,905.9
Other sectors	8 734 ..	454.0	577.0	644.0	1,308.0	1,562.0	1,408.0	1,858.0	1,713.5
Other assets	8 736 ..	2,166.7	3,018.7	2,272.7	2,191.8	935.4	934.9	501.9	453.6
Monetary authorities	8 737 ..	.5	16.0	13.5	16.0	....	....	....	....
of which: Short-term	8 739 ..	....	....	....	....	....	....	....	....
General government	8 740 ..	2,135.9	2,965.1	2,205.8	2,147.6	759.4	742.3	363.2	306.4
of which: Short-term	8 742 ..	*2,135.9*	*2,907.5*	*2,147.9*	*2,086.7*	*695.4*	*679.1*	*300.1*	*223.3*
Banks	8 743 ..	30.3	37.5	53.5	28.2	176.0	192.6	138.6	147.1
of which: Short-term	8 745 ..	*30.3*	*37.5*	*53.5*	*28.2*	*176.0*	*192.6*	*138.6*	*147.1*
Other sectors	8 746 ..	....	....	....	....	....	....	....	....
of which: Short-term	8 748 ..	....	....	....	....	....	....	....	....
Reserve assets	8 802 ..	**6,826.5**	**9,336.4**	**8,694.8**	**11,756.1**	**17,537.4**	**17,922.7**	**18,526.7**	**17,233.0**
Monetary gold	8 812 ..	535.5	560.1	654.2	813.1	1,059.5	1,107.8	1,399.5	1,812.5
Special drawing rights	8 811 ..	67.7	13.1	1.0	1.1	1.0	6.5	957.7	940.8
Reserve position in the Fund	8 810 ..	48.7	51.0	47.2	49.9	52.7	51.6	52.9	52.2
Foreign exchange	8 803 ..	6,051.4	8,582.8	7,891.7	10,790.3	16,424.2	16,756.8	16,116.8	14,427.5
Other claims	8 813 ..	123.2	129.4	100.7	101.7	....	....	....	....

Table 3 (Concluded). INTERNATIONAL INVESTMENT POSITION (End-period stocks), 2003–2010

(Millions of U.S. dollars)

	Code	2003	2004	2005	2006	2007	2008	2009	2010
LIABILITIES	8 995 D.	**18,022.4**	**24,892.9**	**27,759.1**	**43,244.5**	**65,764.7**	**78,677.7**	**83,899.7**	**78,302.2**
Direct investment in Bulgaria	8 555	**6,247.0**	**10,107.9**	**13,869.2**	**23,482.7**	**37,860.9**	**44,564.9**	**48,951.0**	**47,676.7**
Equity capital and reinvested earnings	8 556	4,634.0	7,924.8	9,342.7	15,659.3	23,141.4	26,763.5	29,650.0	30,287.7
Claims on direct investors	8 557	....	....	....	....	....	....	....	....
Liabilities to direct investors	8 558	4,634.0	7,924.8	9,342.7	15,659.3	23,141.4	26,763.5	29,650.0	30,287.7
Other capital	8 580	1,613.1	2,183.1	4,526.5	7,823.4	14,719.5	17,801.3	19,301.1	17,389.0
Claims on direct investors	8 585	−78.2	−371.0	−328.5	−394.9	−1,046.9	−1,135.8	−1,387.1	−2,071.3
Liabilities to direct investors	8 590	1,691.3	2,554.1	4,855.0	8,218.3	15,766.4	18,937.1	20,688.2	19,460.4
Portfolio investment	8 652	**4,559.6**	**4,193.6**	**2,646.7**	**3,620.9**	**3,499.0**	**2,545.8**	**2,508.0**	**2,197.8**
Equity securities	8 660	31.1	290.6	439.7	675.0	1,018.4	711.3	668.4	548.0
Banks	8 663	26.3	34.4	30.6	99.0	243.9	178.2	135.9	99.3
Other sectors	8 664	4.8	256.1	409.1	576.0	774.5	533.1	532.5	448.7
Debt securities	8 669	4,528.5	3,903.1	2,207.0	2,945.9	2,480.6	1,834.4	1,839.6	1,649.9
Bonds and notes	8 670	4,528.5	3,903.1	2,207.0	2,710.2	2,480.6	1,834.4	1,839.6	1,649.9
Monetary authorities	8 671	....	....	....	....	....	....	....	....
General government	8 672	4,524.8	3,891.2	2,037.4	2,113.2	1,832.5	1,363.2	1,465.0	1,332.8
Banks	8 673	....	7.9	125.8	186.5	194.6	62.8	57.2	51.6
Other sectors	8 674	3.7	4.0	43.8	410.5	453.5	408.5	317.4	265.5
Money market instruments	8 680	....	....	....	235.7	....	....	....	....
Monetary authorities	8 681	....	....	....	....	....	....	....	....
General government	8 682	....	....	....	....	....	....	....	....
Banks	8 683	....	....	....	....	....	....	....	....
Other sectors	8 684	....	....	....	235.7	....	....	....	....
Financial derivatives	8 905	**....**	**216.2**	**38.6**	**84.2**	**49.9**	**77.8**	**44.6**	**11.2**
Monetary authorities	8 906	....	....	....	....	....	....	....	....
General government	8 907	....	216.2	23.3	31.6	31.4	18.8	9.9	8.1
Banks	8 908	....	....	....	....	4.2	....	....	....
Other sectors	8 909	....	....	15.3	52.6	14.3	59.0	34.7	3.1
Other investment	8 753	**7,215.8**	**10,375.3**	**11,204.7**	**16,056.7**	**24,354.8**	**31,489.2**	**32,396.1**	**28,416.4**
Trade credits	8 756	826.2	1,088.4	1,262.1	1,892.6	2,330.2	2,475.1	2,315.0	1,798.0
General government	8 757	....	....	....	....	....	....	....	....
of which: Short-term	8 759	....	....	....	....	....	....	....	....
Other sectors	8 760	826.2	1,088.4	1,262.1	1,892.6	2,330.2	2,475.1	2,315.0	1,798.0
of which: Short-term	8 762	*826.2*	*1,088.4*	*1,262.1*	*1,892.6*	*2,330.2*	*2,475.1*	*2,315.0*	*1,798.0*
Loans	8 764	5,640.2	7,835.6	8,172.8	11,508.6	16,083.9	20,441.1	21,357.2	19,270.8
Monetary authorities	8 765	1,187.5	1,183.3	660.1	340.9	....	....	....	....
of which: Use of Fund credit and loans from the Fund	8 766	*1,187.5*	*1,183.3*	*660.1*	*340.9*	....	....	....	....
of which: Short-term	8 768	....	....	....	....	....	....	....	....
General government	8 769	2,668.3	2,859.2	2,558.3	2,421.7	2,721.4	2,197.1	2,589.6	2,482.6
of which: Short-term	8 771	....	....	....	....	....	....	....	....
Banks	8 772	249.3	782.4	1,262.5	1,832.6	2,343.2	4,154.3	4,190.3	2,654.8
of which: Short-term	8 774	*12.2*	*137.0*	*497.2*	*791.8*	*418.0*	*1,101.8*	*1,243.8*	*705.0*
Other sectors	8 775	1,535.1	3,010.6	3,691.9	6,913.4	11,019.3	14,089.7	14,577.3	14,133.4
of which: Short-term	8 777	*339.0*	*683.7*	*1,112.0*	*2,534.0*	*5,098.2*	*6,373.7*	*6,354.7*	*6,369.2*
Currency and deposits	8 780	627.4	1,360.5	1,647.6	2,502.4	5,759.1	8,423.0	7,720.8	6,324.5
Monetary authorities	8 781	....	....	....	....	....	....	....	....
General government	8 782	....	....	....	....	....	....	....	....
Banks	8 783	627.4	1,360.5	1,647.6	2,502.4	5,759.1	8,423.0	7,720.8	6,324.5
Other sectors	8 784	....	....	....	....	....	....	....	....
Other liabilities	8 786	121.9	90.7	122.2	153.1	181.6	150.1	1,003.1	1,023.1
Monetary authorities	8 787	....	....	....	....	....	....	957.7	940.8
of which: Short-term	8 789	....	....	....	....	....	....	....	....
General government	8 790	.8	.5	.5	.5	.2	.4	.2	.2
of which: Short-term	8 792	*.8*	*.5*	*.5*	*.5*	*.2*	*.4*	*.2*	*.2*
Banks	8 793	121.1	90.3	121.8	152.6	181.4	149.7	45.3	82.2
of which: Short-term	8 795	*121.1*	*90.3*	*121.8*	*152.6*	*181.4*	*149.7*	*45.3*	*82.2*
Other sectors	8 796	....	....	....	....	....	....	....	....
of which: Short-term	8 798	....	....	....	....	....	....	....	....
NET INTERNATIONAL INVESTMENT POSITION	8 995	**−6,005.8**	**−8,346.6**	**−12,101.2**	**−20,215.6**	**−36,679.3**	**−48,722.0**	**−51,966.9**	**−47,666.4**
Conversion rates: leva per U.S. dollar (end of period)	0 102	**1.5486**	**1.4359**	**1.6579**	**1.4851**	**1.3312**	**1.3873**	**1.3641**	**1.4728**

Table 1. ANALYTIC PRESENTATION, 2003–2010

(Millions of U.S. dollars)

	Code	2003	2004	2005	2006	2007	2008	2009	2010
A. Current Account[1]...............	4 993 Z.	**−550.4**	**−685.9**	**−818.6**	**−720.6**	**−851.2**	**−1,248.0**	**−766.4**	....
Goods: exports f.o.b..............	2 100 ..	320.5	492.5	483.4	607.1	656.7	851.7	900.4	....
Goods: imports f.o.b..............	3 100 ..	−685.3	−955.7	−1,039.7	−1,093.8	−1,254.6	−1,748.0	−1,382.4	....
Balance on Goods..............	4 100 ..	*−364.8*	*−463.2*	*−556.3*	*−486.6*	*−598.0*	*−896.3*	*−482.0*	....
Services: credit..............	2 200 ..	45.8	68.6	67.6	63.9	91.4	132.2	152.6	....
Services: debit..............	3 200 ..	−233.4	−297.0	−359.8	−360.1	−454.3	−604.7	−559.4	....
Balance on Goods and Services..............	4 991 ..	*−552.4*	*−691.6*	*−848.5*	*−782.8*	*−960.9*	*−1,368.8*	*−888.8*	....
Income: credit..............	2 300 ..	22.6	22.2	38.0	60.5	63.4	85.3	87.4	....
Income: debit..............	3 300 ..	−48.4	−52.9	−58.6	−60.9	−65.7	−89.0	−92.9	....
Balance on Goods, Services, and Income..............	4 992 ..	*−578.1*	*−722.3*	*−869.0*	*−783.2*	*−963.2*	*−1,372.4*	*−894.3*	....
Current transfers: credit..............	2 379 Z.	99.7	107.3	124.1	140.5	196.7	216.1	219.8	....
Current transfers: debit..............	3 379 ..	−72.0	−70.9	−73.7	−77.9	−84.6	−91.7	−91.9	....
B. Capital Account[1]...............	4 994 Z.	**163.3**	**153.8**	**209.0**	**1,565.8**	**292.5**	**190.9**	**281.5**	....
Capital account: credit..............	2 994 Z.	163.3	153.8	209.1	1,565.8	292.5	191.8	281.5	....
Capital account: debit..............	3 994 ..	....	....	−.1	−.1	....	−1.0	....	....
Total, Groups A Plus B..............	4 981 ..	*−387.1*	*−532.1*	*−609.6*	*845.2*	*−558.7*	*−1,057.1*	*−485.0*	....
C. Financial Account[1]...............	4 995 W.	**36.8**	**190.7**	**149.4**	**−905.5**	**422.7**	**504.3**	**172.1**	....
Direct investment abroad..............	4 505 ..	−4.7	5.8	−17.5	−39.7	−33.2	−48.6	−34.1	....
Direct investment in Burkina Faso..............	4 555 Z.	30.8	3.8	32.0	74.2	370.1	152.5	105.2	....
Portfolio investment assets..............	4 602 ..	−1.9	−6.8	−8.7	−11.5	−47.3	−63.2	−42.4	....
Equity securities..............	4 610 ..	−.7	−7.7	−.6	....	.7	6.0	1.0	....
Debt securities..............	4 619 ..	−1.3	.8	−8.1	−11.5	−48.0	−69.2	−43.4	....
Portfolio investment liabilities..............	4 652 Z.	2.1	3.9	−4.3	1.4	−.9	−2.3	....	....
Equity securities..............	4 660 ..	2.1	3.9	−4.3	1.4	−.9	−2.3	....	....
Debt securities..............	4 669 Z.	....	....	....	....	....	....	....	....
Financial derivatives..............	4 910 ..	2.0	....	....	....	....	....	....	....
Financial derivatives assets..............	4 900 ..	2.0	....	....	....	....	....	....	....
Financial derivatives liabilities..............	4 905 ..	....	....	....	....	....	....	....	....
Other investment assets..............	4 703 ..	−18.6	−32.7	−73.8	−148.7	−200.5	385.7	91.8	....
Monetary authorities..............	4 701 ..	....	....	....	....	....	....	....	....
General government..............	4 704 ..	....	−9.0	....	−8.2	.5	−1.7	2.5	....
Banks..............	4 705 ..	−9.4	−.5	41.0	−11.0	−58.2	47.4	−165.4	....
Other sectors..............	4 728 ..	−9.2	−23.2	−114.8	−129.5	−142.7	340.1	254.6	....
Other investment liabilities..............	4 753 W.	27.2	216.8	221.7	−781.1	334.5	80.3	51.7	....
Monetary authorities..............	4 753 WA	2.7	−6.1	−11.9	63.2	100.8	29.6	116.0	....
General government..............	4 753 ZB	....	179.3	181.1	−950.4	−31.7	....	....	....
Banks..............	4 753 ZC	9.0	−4.9	−9.8	−2.3	6.1	38.3	−44.1	....
Other sectors..............	4 753 ZD	15.5	48.5	62.3	108.4	259.2	12.3	−20.3	....
Total, Groups A Through C..............	4 983 ..	*−350.3*	*−341.4*	*−460.2*	*−60.3*	*−136.0*	*−552.9*	*−312.9*	....
D. Net Errors and Omissions...............	4 998 ..	**−4.0**	**2.3**	**−5.4**	**−7.9**	**5.5**	**−2.8**	**−48.4**	....
Total, Groups A Through D..............	4 984 ..	*−354.3*	*−339.0*	*−465.5*	*−68.2*	*−130.5*	*−555.7*	*−361.3*	....
E. Reserves and Related Items...............	4 802 A.	**354.3**	**339.0**	**465.5**	**68.2**	**130.5**	**555.7**	**361.3**	....
Reserve assets..............	4 802 ..	−54.0	137.7	146.2	−65.7	−383.7	48.1	−326.3	....
Use of Fund credit and loans..............	4 766 ..	−12.9	−15.0	−1.8	−70.9	.8	18.2	55.5	....
Exceptional financing..............	4 920 ..	421.2	216.3	321.2	204.9	513.5	489.3	632.0	....
Conversion rates: CFA francs per U.S. dollar..........	0 101 ..	**581.20**	**528.28**	**527.47**	**522.89**	**479.27**	**447.81**	**472.19**	**495.28**

[1] Excludes components that have been classified in the categories of Group E.

Table 2. STANDARD PRESENTATION, 2003–2010

(Millions of U.S. dollars)

	Code	2003	2004	2005	2006	2007	2008	2009	2010
CURRENT ACCOUNT	4 993	−367.4	−531.0	−634.3	−543.5	−560.0	−963.1	−380.0	....
A. GOODS	4 100	−364.8	−463.2	−556.3	−486.6	−598.0	−896.3	−482.0	....
Credit	2 100	320.5	492.5	483.4	607.1	656.7	851.7	900.4	....
General merchandise: exports f.o.b.	2 110	311.7	479.3	468.5	588.3	623.0	693.1	517.2	....
Goods for processing: exports f.o.b.	2 150	....	....	....	....	.1	.1	.2	....
Repairs on goods	2 160	....	....	....	....	....	....	.1	
Goods procured in ports by carriers	2 170	....	....	....	....	....	1.8	2.1	
Nonmonetary gold	2 180	8.8	13.3	14.9	18.9	33.6	156.8	380.9	....
Debit	3 100	−685.3	−955.7	−1,039.7	−1,093.8	−1,254.6	−1,748.0	−1,382.4	....
General merchandise: imports f.o.b.	3 110	−676.7	−946.3	−1,026.9	−1,084.7	−1,247.0	−1,736.5	−1,371.5	
Goods for processing: imports f.o.b.	3 150	....	....	−3.3	−3.3	−.2	−.2	−.2	
Repairs on goods	3 160	−.9	−.9	−1.9	−.6	....	−1.8	−1.2	
Goods procured in ports by carriers	3 170	−7.7	−8.5	−7.6	−5.1	−7.4	−9.5	−9.5	
Nonmonetary gold	3 180	....	....	....	....	....	....	....	
B. SERVICES	4 200	−187.6	−228.4	−292.2	−296.2	−362.9	−472.5	−406.8	....
Total credit	2 200	*45.8*	*68.6*	*67.6*	*63.9*	*91.4*	*132.2*	*152.6*	
Total debit	3 200	*−233.4*	*−297.0*	*−359.8*	*−360.1*	*−454.3*	*−604.7*	*−559.4*	
Transportation services, credit	2 205	**13.8**	**12.4**	**1.3**	**2.1**	**4.9**	**21.0**	**36.7**	....
Passenger	2 850	*13.5*	*12.2*	*1.3*	*2.1*	*4.8*	*20.0*	*33.1*	
Freight	2 851	*.2*	*.1*	....	....	*.1*	*.5*	*1.1*	
Other	2 852	*.1*	*.1*	....	....	....	*.5*	*2.5*	
Sea transport, passenger	2 207	....	....				....		
Sea transport, freight	2 208	....	....				....		
Sea transport, other	2 209	....	....				....	1.8	
Air transport, passenger	2 211	13.4	11.9	.9	1.1	2.2	20.0	29.8	
Air transport, freight	2 212	.2	.1	....	....	.1	.5	.9	
Air transport, other	2 213	....	.1	....	....	....	.5	.8	
Other transport, passenger	2 215	.2	.3	.4	1.0	2.6	....	3.3	
Other transport, freight	2 216	....	....				....	.2	
Other transport, other	2 217	....	....				....		
Transportation services, debit	3 205	**−137.6**	**−172.4**	**−209.0**	**−222.5**	**−257.2**	**−332.8**	**−303.6**	....
Passenger	3 850	*−19.4*	*−27.7*	*−28.2*	*−29.4*	*−34.7*	*−47.4*	*−46.6*	
Freight	3 851	*−116.7*	*−141.9*	*−176.4*	*−189.3*	*−215.1*	*−280.8*	*−245.8*	
Other	3 852	*−1.4*	*−2.7*	*−4.5*	*−3.8*	*−7.5*	*−4.7*	*−11.3*	
Sea transport, passenger	3 207	....	....				....		
Sea transport, freight	3 208	−80.9	−94.7	−123.1	−135.1	−165.7	−244.5	−180.5	
Sea transport, other	3 209	....	−.2	....	....	....	....	....	
Air transport, passenger	3 211	−17.6	−21.2	−21.5	−22.1	−34.7	−42.8	−45.7	
Air transport, freight	3 212	−21.4	−33.2	−36.2	−43.6	−41.2	−23.9	−57.2	
Air transport, other	3 213	−1.4	−2.5	−4.5	−3.8	−2.5	−4.7	−11.3	
Other transport, passenger	3 215	−1.7	−6.6	−6.6	−7.3	....	−4.6	−.9	
Other transport, freight	3 216	−14.5	−14.1	−17.1	−10.6	−8.2	−12.4	−8.1	
Other transport, other	3 217	....	....	....	....	−4.9	....	....	
Travel, credit	2 236	**24.5**	**39.9**	**44.7**	**52.6**	**56.1**	**62.3**	**66.5**	....
Business travel	2 237	13.4	21.4	25.4	30.4	31.8	35.2	36.1	
Personal travel	2 240	11.1	18.6	19.4	22.2	24.3	27.2	30.4	
Travel, debit	3 236	**−30.9**	**−38.6**	**−45.7**	**−54.8**	**−57.9**	**−62.7**	**−64.1**	....
Business travel	3 237	−18.1	−20.5	−27.2	−30.0	−36.5	−38.5	−37.3	
Personal travel	3 240	−12.8	−18.2	−18.5	−24.7	−21.4	−24.2	−26.8	
Other services, credit	2 200 BA	**7.6**	**16.3**	**21.6**	**9.2**	**30.5**	**48.9**	**49.4**	....
Communications	2 245	.8	....	.4	.4	2.2	13.9	27.3	
Construction	2 249	....	....	....	....	2.0	....	1.5	
Insurance	2 253	....	....	....	.1	.5	.5	.2	
Financial	2 260	1.0	1.0	11.0	1.0	11.1	1.8	2.0	
Computer and information	2 262	....	....	....	....	....	....	....	
Royalties and licence fees	2 266	....	1.0	....	.1	.1	....	....	
Other business services	2 268	4.2	10.2	5.4	2.4	7.0	18.8	6.7	
Personal, cultural, and recreational	2 287	....	....	....	....	....	2.6	.8	
Government, n.i.e.	2 291	1.5	4.1	4.8	5.2	7.5	11.3	10.9	
Other services, debit	3 200 BA	**−65.0**	**−86.0**	**−105.0**	**−82.9**	**−139.3**	**−209.2**	**−191.6**	....
Communications	3 245	−3.3	−3.6	−1.2	−2.4	−3.4	−10.8	−2.2	
Construction	3 249	−.2	−.2	−28.7	−.2	−36.1	−8.2	−8.2	
Insurance	3 253	−28.9	−36.6	−44.8	−56.6	−66.7	−92.4	−75.2	
Financial	3 260	−2.6	−.9	−3.0	−1.8	−2.8	−3.5	−3.2	
Computer and information	3 262	−1.8	−3.8	−1.7	−2.4	−1.5	−11.6	−9.0	
Royalties and licence fees	3 266	−4.0	−4.1	−4.2	....	−.2	−.2	−.5	
Other business services	3 268	−16.1	−22.7	−8.3	−5.1	−16.2	−60.8	−78.9	
Personal, cultural, and recreational	3 287	....	−1.1	−.1	....	....	−5.5	....	
Government, n.i.e.	3 291	−8.1	−12.9	−13.0	−14.3	−12.5	−16.4	−14.4	

Table 2 (Continued). STANDARD PRESENTATION, 2003–2010

(Millions of U.S. dollars)

	Code	2003	2004	2005	2006	2007	2008	2009	2010
C. INCOME	4 300	**−25.7**	**−30.7**	**−20.6**	**−.4**	**−2.3**	**−3.7**	**−5.5**	....
Total credit	2 300	*22.6*	*22.2*	*38.0*	*60.5*	*63.4*	*85.3*	*87.4*	....
Total debit	3 300	*−48.4*	*−52.9*	*−58.6*	*−60.9*	*−65.7*	*−89.0*	*−92.9*	....
Compensation of employees, credit	2 310	**8.2**	**4.5**	**7.2**	**7.3**	**7.9**	**14.3**	**12.0**	....
Compensation of employees, debit	3 310	**−10.2**	**−11.4**	**−14.0**	**−14.8**	**−15.8**	**−15.6**	**−16.6**	....
Investment income, credit	2 320	**14.5**	**17.7**	**30.8**	**53.2**	**55.4**	**71.0**	**75.4**	....
Direct investment income	2 330	3.0	3.4	17.9	40.0	33.3	49.1	26.9	....
Dividends and distributed branch profits	2 332	.2	.2	.2	.5	.4	.2	1.2	....
Reinvested earnings and undistributed branch profits	2 333	2.8	3.2	17.7	39.5	33.0	48.9	25.6	....
Income on debt (interest)	2 334	....	....	....	....	....	....	....	....
Portfolio investment income	2 339	3.6	6.1	7.1	7.7	7.7	5.0	15.2	....
Income on equity	2 340	.3	.3	.1	.3	1.1	.9	1.3	....
Income on bonds and notes	2 350	3.3	5.9	3.8	5.3	4.1	2.9	8.4	....
Income on money market instruments	2 360	....	....	3.2	2.0	2.5	1.2	5.4	....
Other investment income	2 370	7.9	8.2	5.8	5.5	14.4	16.9	33.4	....
Investment income, debit	3 320	**−38.2**	**−41.5**	**−44.5**	**−46.1**	**−49.9**	**−73.3**	**−76.3**	....
Direct investment income	3 330	−10.8	−8.7	−6.7	−7.1	−11.2	−38.2	−34.7	....
Dividends and distributed branch profits	3 332	−3.1	−5.5	−5.1	−5.3	−5.7	−3.3	−10.8	....
Reinvested earnings and undistributed branch profits	3 333	−7.2	−3.1	−1.5	−1.3	−2.3	−31.1	−16.8	....
Income on debt (interest)	3 334	−.6	−.1	−.2	−.5	−3.2	−3.8	−7.1	....
Portfolio investment income	3 339	−3.5	−4.0	−6.9	−9.1	−14.7	−7.8	−9.3	....
Income on equity	3 340	−1.9	−1.6	−3.8	−4.2	−2.4	−1.8	−.9	....
Income on bonds and notes	3 350	−1.6	−2.3	−3.0	−4.9	−12.3	−6.0	−8.5	....
Income on money market instruments	3 360	....	−.1	....	....	....	....	....	....
Other investment income	3 370	−23.9	−28.9	−30.9	−29.9	−24.0	−27.4	−32.3	....
D. CURRENT TRANSFERS	4 379	**210.7**	**191.3**	**234.7**	**239.8**	**403.3**	**409.3**	**514.2**	....
Credit	2 379	**282.8**	**262.1**	**308.4**	**317.7**	**487.9**	**501.0**	**606.1**	....
General government	2 380	183.0	154.8	184.3	177.1	291.2	284.9	386.4	....
Other sectors	2 390	99.7	107.3	124.1	140.5	196.7	216.1	219.8	....
Workers' remittances	2 391	45.6	39.9	49.5	60.6	76.4	85.0	84.0	....
Other current transfers	2 392	54.1	67.4	74.7	79.9	120.3	131.1	135.8	....
Debit	3 379	**−72.0**	**−70.9**	**−73.7**	**−77.9**	**−84.6**	**−91.7**	**−91.9**	....
General government	3 380	−3.5	−1.4	−2.3	−2.6	−2.7	−2.9	−4.5	....
Other sectors	3 390	−68.5	−69.5	−71.3	−75.3	−81.9	−88.8	−87.4	....
Workers' remittances	3 391	−67.0	−67.8	−69.8	−71.3	−77.4	−84.0	−82.7	....
Other current transfers	3 392	−1.5	−1.7	−1.5	−4.0	−4.5	−4.8	−4.6	....
CAPITAL AND FINANCIAL ACCOUNT	4 996	**371.4**	**528.7**	**639.7**	**551.4**	**554.5**	**965.9**	**428.4**	....
CAPITAL ACCOUNT	4 994	**205.7**	**201.5**	**209.0**	**1,565.8**	**292.5**	**190.9**	**281.5**	....
Total credit	2 994	*205.7*	*201.5*	*209.1*	*1,565.8*	*292.5*	*191.8*	*281.5*	....
Total debit	3 994	....	....	*−.1*	*−.1*	....	*−1.0*	....	....
Capital transfers, credit	2 400	**205.7**	**201.5**	**209.1**	**1,565.8**	**292.5**	**191.8**	**281.5**	....
General government	2 401	196.8	180.7	185.6	1,523.7	239.3	131.1	184.2	....
Debt forgiveness	2 402	42.5	47.7	45.7	1,308.9	....	....	....	....
Other capital transfers	2 410	154.3	133.0	139.9	214.8	239.3	131.1	184.2	....
Other sectors	2 430	8.9	20.8	23.5	42.1	53.2	60.8	97.3	....
Migrants' transfers	2 431	....	....	....	....	....	....	14.6	....
Debt forgiveness	2 432	....	....	....	....	....	....	....	....
Other capital transfers	2 440	8.9	20.8	23.5	42.1	53.2	60.8	82.7	....
Capital transfers, debit	3 400	....	....	....	....	....	....	....	....
General government	3 401	....	....	....	....	....	....	....	....
Debt forgiveness	3 402	....	....	....	....	....	....	....	....
Other capital transfers	3 410	....	....	....	....	....	....	....	....
Other sectors	3 430	....	....	....	....	....	....	....	....
Migrants' transfers	3 431	....	....	....	....	....	....	....	....
Debt forgiveness	3 432	....	....	....	....	....	....	....	....
Other capital transfers	3 440	....	....	....	....	....	....	....	....
Nonproduced nonfinancial assets, credit	2 480	....	....	....	....	....	....	....	....
Nonproduced nonfinancial assets, debit	3 480	....	....	−.1	−.1	....	−1.0	....	....

Table 2 (Continued). STANDARD PRESENTATION, 2003–2010

(Millions of U.S. dollars)

	Code	2003	2004	2005	2006	2007	2008	2009	2010
FINANCIAL ACCOUNT	4 995 ..	**165.7**	**327.2**	**430.7**	**−1,014.4**	**262.0**	**775.1**	**147.0**	....
A. DIRECT INVESTMENT	4 500 ..	**25.0**	**23.3**	**34.3**	**34.5**	**336.9**	**103.8**	**71.1**	....
Direct investment abroad	4 505 ..	**−4.7**	**5.8**	**−17.5**	**−39.7**	**−33.2**	**−48.6**	**−34.1**	....
Equity capital	4 510 ..	−1.9	....	−.5	−.6	−.9	1.8	−7.3	....
Claims on affiliated enterprises	4 515 ..	....	....	−.5	−.6	−.9	5.2	.5	....
Liabilities to affiliated enterprises	4 520 ..	−1.9	....	....	....	....	−3.4	−7.8	....
Reinvested earnings	4 525 ..	−2.8	−3.2	−17.7	−39.5	−33.0	−48.9	−25.6	....
Other capital	4 530 ..	....	9.0	.7	.4	.6	−1.6	−1.2	....
Claims on affiliated enterprises	4 535 ..	....	−.4	.4	−1.4	−1.1	.1	−1.2	....
Liabilities to affiliated enterprises	4 540 ..	....	9.4	.3	1.8	1.8	−1.7	....	....
Direct investment in Burkina Faso	4 555 ..	**29.7**	**17.5**	**51.8**	**74.2**	**370.1**	**152.5**	**105.2**	....
Equity capital	4 560 ..	13.8	12.9	19.8	71.8	350.2	114.4	41.0	....
Claims on direct investors	4 565 ..	14.9	−.8	....	−6.7	350.2	114.4	41.0	....
Liabilities to direct investors	4 570 ..	−1.1	13.7	19.9	78.5	....	....	....	....
Reinvested earnings	4 575 ..	7.2	3.1	1.5	1.3	2.3	31.1	16.8	....
Other capital	4 580 ..	8.8	1.6	30.5	1.1	17.6	7.0	47.4	....
Claims on direct investors	4 585 ..	−.2	....	....	−1.0	....	....	....	....
Liabilities to direct investors	4 590 ..	9.0	1.6	30.5	2.1	17.6	7.0	47.4	....
B. PORTFOLIO INVESTMENT	4 600 ..	**.1**	**−3.0**	**−5.3**	**−10.2**	**−55.8**	**−68.8**	**−39.3**	....
Assets	4 602 ..	**−1.9**	**−6.8**	**−8.7**	**−11.5**	**−47.3**	**−63.2**	**−42.4**	....
Equity securities	4 610 ..	−.7	−7.7	−.6	....	.7	6.0	1.0	....
Monetary authorities	4 611 ..	....	....	....	....	....	....	....	....
General government	4 612 ..	....	....	....	....	....	....	....	....
Banks	4 613 ..	−.1	−7.7	−.6	....	.7	−.2	−.2	....
Other sectors	4 614 ..	−.6	....	....	....	....	6.2	1.2	....
Debt securities	4 619 ..	−1.3	.8	−8.1	−11.5	−48.0	−69.2	−43.4	....
Bonds and notes	4 620 ..	−1.3	.8	−6.2	−13.5	−25.6	−53.0	−11.0	....
Monetary authorities	4 621 ..	....	....	....	....	....	....	....	....
General government	4 622 ..	....	....	....	....	−1.9	2.1	−3.2	....
Banks	4 623 ..	−1.3	.9	−3.4	−10.3	−22.9	−52.1	−20.9	....
Other sectors	4 624 ..	....	−.1	−2.7	−3.2	−.8	−2.9	13.0	....
Money market instruments	4 630 ..	....	....	−1.9	2.0	−22.4	−16.3	−32.4	....
Monetary authorities	4 631 ..	....	....	....	....	....	....	....	....
General government	4 632 ..	....	....	....	....	....	....	....	....
Banks	4 633 ..	....	....	−1.9	....	−24.0	−12.8	−31.8	....
Other sectors	4 634 ..	....	....	....	2.0	1.6	−3.5	−.6	....
Liabilities	4 652 ..	**2.1**	**3.9**	**3.4**	**1.4**	**−8.6**	**−5.5**	**3.1**	....
Equity securities	4 660 ..	2.1	3.9	−4.3	1.4	−.9	−2.3	....	....
Banks	4 663 ..	2.0	3.9	−4.8	1.2	−1.0	.7	−.1	....
Other sectors	4 664 ..	....	....	.5	.2	.1	−3.0	.1	....
Debt securities	4 669 ..	....	....	7.7	....	−7.6	−3.2	3.1	....
Bonds and notes	4 670 ..	....	....	7.7	....	9.1	4.9	7.4	....
Monetary authorities	4 671 ..	....	....	....	....	....	....	....	....
General government	4 672 ..	....	....	....	....	....	....	....	....
Banks	4 673 ..	....	....	7.6	....	.5	−5.4	1.7	....
Other sectors	4 674 ..	....	....	.1	....	8.5	10.2	5.7	....
Money market instruments	4 680 ..	....	....	....	....	−16.7	−8.1	−4.2	....
Monetary authorities	4 681 ..	....	....	....	....	....	....	....	....
General government	4 682 ..	....	....	....	....	....	....	....	....
Banks	4 683 ..	....	....	....	....	−16.7	−8.1	−4.2	....
Other sectors	4 684 ..	....	....	....	....	....	....	....	....
C. FINANCIAL DERIVATIVES	4 910 ..	**2.0**	....	....	....	....	....	....	....
Monetary authorities	4 911 ..	....	....	....	....	....	....	....	....
General government	4 912 ..	....	....	....	....	....	....	....	....
Banks	4 913 ..	....	....	....	....	....	....	....	....
Other sectors	4 914 ..	2.0	....	....	....	....	....	....	....
Assets	4 900 ..	**2.0**	....	....	....	....	....	....	....
Monetary authorities	4 901 ..	....	....	....	....	....	....	....	....
General government	4 902 ..	....	....	....	....	....	....	....	....
Banks	4 903 ..	....	....	....	....	....	....	....	....
Other sectors	4 904 ..	2.0	....	....	....	....	....	....	....
Liabilities	4 905 ..	....	....	....	....	....	....	....	....
Monetary authorities	4 906 ..	....	....	....	....	....	....	....	....
General government	4 907 ..	....	....	....	....	....	....	....	....
Banks	4 908 ..	....	....	....	....	....	....	....	....
Other sectors	4 909 ..	....	....	....	....	....	....	....	....

Table 2 (Concluded). STANDARD PRESENTATION, 2003–2010

(Millions of U.S. dollars)

	Code	2003	2004	2005	2006	2007	2008	2009	2010
D. OTHER INVESTMENT............................	4 700 ..	**192.5**	**169.1**	**255.4**	**−973.0**	**364.7**	**691.9**	**441.5**	....
Assets..............................	4 703 ..	**−18.6**	**−32.7**	**−73.8**	**−148.7**	**−200.5**	**385.7**	**91.8**	....
Trade credits..............................	4 706 ..	−8.2	−11.2	−31.8	−122.0	7.3	17.7	35.7	....
General government..........................	4 707 ..	....	....	....	....	....	....	....	....
of which: Short-term..................	4 709 ..	....	....	....	....	....	....	....	....
Other sectors..............................	4 710 ..	−8.2	−11.2	−31.8	−122.0	7.3	17.7	35.7	....
of which: Short-term..................	4 712 ..	....	....	*−31.8*	*−122.0*	*7.3*	*17.7*	*35.7*	....
Loans..............................	4 714 ..	−8.1	−14.6	25.4	5.6	−29.7	5.3	−171.8	....
Monetary authorities..........................	4 715 ..	....	....	....	....	....	....	....	....
of which: Short-term..................	4 718 ..	....	....	....	....	....	....	....	....
General government..........................	4 719 ..	....	....	....	....	....	....	....	....
of which: Short-term..................	4 721 ..	....	....	....	....	....	....	....	....
Banks..............................	4 722 ..	−8.1	−14.6	25.4	5.6	−29.7	5.3	−171.8	....
of which: Short-term..................	4 724 ..	*−6.7*	*−.6*	*17.9*	*−.6*	*−13.0*	*9.5*	*−58.1*	....
Other sectors..............................	4 725 ..	....	....	....	....	....	....	....	....
of which: Short-term..................	4 727 ..	....	....	....	....	....	....	....	....
Currency and deposits..............................	4 730 ..	.2	−3.3	−53.5	−40.3	−27.1	252.1	187.6	....
Monetary authorities..........................	4 731 ..	....	....	....	....	....	....	....	....
General government..........................	4 732 ..	....	−3.2	....	−4.0	−.6	−.8	.1	....
Banks..............................	4 733 ..	.2	11.4	27.8	−32.1	−28.0	40.0	6.4	....
Other sectors..............................	4 734 ..	....	−11.6	−81.3	−4.3	1.5	212.9	181.2	....
Other assets..............................	4 736 ..	−2.5	−3.6	−13.9	8.0	−151.0	110.6	40.2	....
Monetary authorities..........................	4 737 ..	....	....	....	....	....	....	....	....
of which: Short-term..................	4 739 ..	....	....	....	....	....	....	....	....
General government..........................	4 740 ..	....	−5.8	....	−4.2	1.0	−.9	2.4	....
of which: Short-term..................	4 742 ..	....	*−5.8*	....	....	....	....	....	....
Banks..............................	4 743 ..	−1.5	2.7	−12.2	15.5	−.5	2.0	.1	....
of which: Short-term..................	4 745 ..	*−1.5*	*2.7*	*−12.2*	*15.5*	*−.5*	*2.0*	*.1*	....
Other sectors..............................	4 746 ..	−1.0	−.5	−1.7	−3.3	−151.6	109.5	37.8	....
of which: Short-term..................	4 748 ..	....	....	*−1.7*	....	....	....	....	....
Liabilities..............................	4 753 ..	**211.1**	**201.8**	**329.2**	**−824.3**	**565.2**	**306.2**	**349.7**	....
Trade credits..............................	4 756 ..	15.5	16.2	41.9	43.4	172.5	−105.6	−77.2	....
General government..........................	4 757 ..	....	....	....	....	....	....	....	....
of which: Short-term..................	4 759 ..	....	....	....	....	....	....	....	....
Other sectors..............................	4 760 ..	15.5	16.2	41.9	43.4	172.5	−105.6	−77.2	....
of which: Short-term..................	4 762 ..	*15.5*	....	*41.9*	*43.4*	*172.5*	*−105.6*	*−77.2*	....
Loans..............................	4 764 ..	183.1	118.8	323.3	−1,084.3	274.9	248.9	353.1	....
Monetary authorities..........................	4 765 ..	−12.9	−15.0	−1.8	−70.9	.8	18.2	55.5	....
of which: Use of Fund credit and loans from the Fund..	4 766 ..	*−12.9*	*−15.0*	*−1.8*	*−70.9*	*.8*	*18.2*	*55.5*	....
of which: Short-term..................	4 768 ..	....	....	....	....	....	....	....	....
General government..........................	4 769 ..	175.8	179.3	251.3	−922.7	195.2	228.5	232.0	....
of which: Short-term..................	4 771 ..	....	....	*−1.5*	*27.7*	*−12.0*	....	....	....
Banks..............................	4 772 ..	29.9	−6.5	42.2	−28.6	−13.3	−20.8	10.5	....
of which: Short-term..................	4 774 ..	*.6*	*−3.2*	*39.2*	*−27.0*	*3.1*	*1.5*	*−37.9*	....
Other sectors..............................	4 775 ..	−9.7	−39.0	31.6	−62.1	92.2	23.0	55.0	....
of which: Short-term..................	4 777 ..	....	*−.6*	....	....	....	....	....	....
Currency and deposits..............................	4 780 ..	11.6	2.4	−12.0	29.6	22.6	35.1	−48.7	....
Monetary authorities..........................	4 781 ..	2.7	.9	.7	3.4	.2	−3.2	−4.6	....
General government..........................	4 782 ..	....	....	....	....	....	....	....	....
Banks..............................	4 783 ..	9.0	1.5	−12.7	26.2	22.5	38.3	−44.1	....
Other sectors..............................	4 784 ..	....	....	....	....	....	....	....	....
Other liabilities..............................	4 786 ..	.9	64.4	−23.9	187.0	95.2	127.7	122.5	....
Monetary authorities..........................	4 787 ..	.8	−7.1	−12.6	59.7	100.7	32.8	120.6	....
of which: Short-term..................	4 789 ..	*.8*	*−7.1*	....	....	....	....	....	....
General government..........................	4 790 ..	....	....	....	....	....	....	....	....
of which: Short-term..................	4 792 ..	....	....	....	....	....	....	....	....
Banks..............................	4 793 ..	....	.1	−.1	....	....	....	....	....
of which: Short-term..................	4 795 ..	....	*.1*	*−.1*	....	....	....	....	....
Other sectors..............................	4 796 ..	.1	71.3	−11.2	127.2	−5.5	94.9	1.9	....
of which: Short-term..................	4 798 ..	*.1*	....	*−11.2*	*127.2*	*−5.5*	....	....	....
E. RESERVE ASSETS..............................	4 802 ..	**−54.0**	**137.7**	**146.2**	**−65.7**	**−383.7**	**48.1**	**−326.3**	....
Monetary gold..............................	4 812 ..	....	....	....	....	....	....	....	....
Special drawing rights..............................	4 811 ..	.1	.1	....	.2	−.1	....	−75.0	....
Reserve position in the Fund..............................	4 810 ..	....	....	....	−.1	....	−.1	....	....
Foreign exchange..............................	4 803 ..	−54.1	137.6	146.2	−65.8	−383.6	48.2	−251.2	....
Other claims..............................	4 813 ..	....	....	....	....	....	....	....	....
NET ERRORS AND OMISSIONS..............................	4 998 ..	**−4.0**	**2.3**	**−5.4**	**−7.9**	**5.5**	**−2.8**	**−48.4**	....

Table 3. INTERNATIONAL INVESTMENT POSITION (End-period stocks), 2003–2010

(Millions of U.S. dollars)

	Code	2003	2004	2005	2006	2007	2008	2009	2010
ASSETS	8 995 C.	678.1	1,016.6	793.3	847.0	1,604.0	1,372.2	1,913.5	....
Direct investment abroad	8 505 ..	3.4	3.6	7.4	8.4	9.8	3.9	11.9	....
Equity capital and reinvested earnings	8 506 ..	2.6	12.6	15.4	17.5	20.7	12.6	10.6	....
Claims on affiliated enterprises	8 507 ..	2.6	12.6	15.4	17.5	20.7	12.6	10.6	....
Liabilities to affiliated enterprises	8 508 ..	....	....	....	....	....	....	....	....
Other capital	8 530 ..	.8	−9.0	−8.0	−9.1	−10.9	−8.7	1.3	....
Claims on affiliated enterprises	8 535 ..	.8	....	....	....	....	....	....	....
Liabilities to affiliated enterprises	8 540 ..	....	−9.0	−8.0	−9.1	−10.9	−8.7	1.3	....
Portfolio investment	8 602 ..	49.9	64.5	47.5	16.7	100.1	164.0	216.7	....
Equity securities	8 610 ..	3.5	3.2	6.8	6.8	10.2	4.7	5.4	....
Monetary authorities	8 611 ..	1.9	....	....	....	....	....	....	....
General government	8 612 ..	....	....	....	....	....	....	....	....
Banks	8 613 ..	1.6	1.8	5.6	5.4	3.8	3.3	3.6	....
Other sectors	8 614 ..	....	1.4	1.2	1.4	6.4	1.4	1.7	....
Debt securities	8 619 ..	46.4	61.3	40.7	9.9	89.9	159.3	211.3	....
Bonds and notes	8 620 ..	46.1	60.4	40.7	7.8	75.9	105.4	111.9	....
Monetary authorities	8 621 ..	....	....	....	....	....	....	....	....
General government	8 622 ..	.8	....	....	....	....	....	....	....
Banks	8 623 ..	45.3	60.4	36.7	4.1	63.6	98.5	95.4	....
Other sectors	8 624 ..	....	....	4.0	3.7	12.3	6.9	16.5	....
Money market instruments	8 630 ..	.3	.9	....	2.1	14.0	53.8	99.5	....
Monetary authorities	8 631 ..	....	....	....	....	....	....	99.5	....
General government	8 632 ..	....	....	....	2.1	....	....	....	....
Banks	8 633 ..	.3	....	....	....	9.9	49.1	....	....
Other sectors	8 634 ..	....	.9	....	....	4.1	4.7	....	....
Financial derivatives	8 900 ..	....	....	....	....	.9	5.7	....	....
Monetary authorities	8 901 ..	....	....	....	....	....	....	....	....
General government	8 902 ..	....	....	....	....	....	....	....	....
Banks	8 903 ..	....	....	....	....	.9	5.7	....	....
Other sectors	8 904 ..	....	....	....	....	....	....	....	....
Other investment	8 703 ..	188.1	288.7	305.0	269.7	463.9	271.0	389.1	....
Trade credits	8 706 ..	20.3	17.8	39.3	143.9	100.0	69.7	19.2	....
General government	8 707 ..	....	17.8	39.3	143.9	100.0	69.7	....	....
of which: Short-term	8 709 ..	....	*17.8*	*39.3*	*143.9*	*100.0*	*69.7*	....	....
Other sectors	8 710 ..	20.3	....	....	....	....	....	19.2	....
of which: Short-term	8 712 ..	....	....	....	....	....	....	*19.2*	....
Loans	8 714 ..	33.6	52.2	21.2	17.8	51.8	43.9	223.6	....
Monetary authorities	8 715 ..	....	....	....	....	....	....	....	....
of which: Short-term	8 718 ..	....	....	....	....	....	....	....	....
General government	8 719 ..	....	....	....	....	....	....	....	....
of which: Short-term	8 721 ..	....	....	....	....	....	....	....	....
Banks	8 722 ..	33.6	52.2	21.2	17.8	51.8	43.9	223.6	....
of which: Short-term	8 724 ..	*25.8*	*28.4*	*7.6*	*9.1*	*24.2*	*13.8*	*74.6*	....
Other sectors	8 725 ..	....	....	....	....	....	....	....	....
of which: Short-term	8 727 ..	....	....	....	....	....	....	....	....
Currency and deposits	8 730 ..	116.6	206.1	226.1	97.0	137.4	99.1	130.6	....
Monetary authorities	8 731 ..	....	....	....	....	....	....	....	....
General government	8 732 ..	....	3.5	....	4.2	5.3	5.7	5.8	....
Banks	8 733 ..	116.2	89.6	51.2	90.8	131.7	86.5	82.9	....
Other sectors	8 734 ..	.4	113.0	174.9	2.0	.4	6.9	41.9	....
Other assets	8 736 ..	17.6	12.5	18.4	11.0	174.7	58.3	15.7	....
Monetary authorities	8 737 ..	....	....	....	....	....	....	....	....
of which: Short-term	8 739 ..	....	....	....	....	....	....	....	....
General government	8 740 ..	....	6.4	....	4.4	3.8	4.5	2.2	....
of which: Short-term	8 742 ..	....	....	....	....	....	....	....	....
Banks	8 743 ..	7.4	5.1	15.9	1.5	2.2	.2	.1	....
of which: Short-term	8 745 ..	*7.4*	*5.1*	*15.9*	*1.5*	*2.2*	*.2*	....	....
Other sectors	8 746 ..	10.1	1.0	2.5	5.1	168.7	53.5	13.3	....
of which: Short-term	8 748 ..	*10.1*	....	....	....	....	....	....	....
Reserve assets	8 802 ..	436.7	659.8	433.4	552.2	1,029.2	927.6	1,295.8	....
Monetary gold	8 812 ..	....	....	....	....	.1	....	....	....
Special drawing rights	8 811 ..	.3	.2	.2	....	.1	.1	75.4	74.2
Reserve position in the Fund	8 810 ..	10.8	11.3	10.5	11.1	11.7	11.4	11.7	11.5
Foreign exchange	8 803 ..	425.6	648.2	422.7	541.0	1,017.4	916.1	1,208.8	....
Other claims	8 813 ..	....	....	....	....	....	....	....	....

Table 3 (Concluded). INTERNATIONAL INVESTMENT POSITION (End-period stocks), 2003–2010

(Millions of U.S. dollars)

	Code	2003	2004	2005	2006	2007	2008	2009	2010
LIABILITIES	8 995 D.	**2,092.6**	**2,516.1**	**2,524.4**	**1,945.7**	**3,207.2**	**2,954.3**	**3,311.9**	....
Direct investment in Burkina Faso	8 555 ..	**51.9**	**48.8**	**75.4**	**169.6**	**559.5**	**325.6**	**571.4**	....
Equity capital and reinvested earnings	8 556 ..	45.0	47.1	45.8	136.0	440.6	206.5	146.2	....
Claims on direct investors	8 557 ..	....	....	....	....	....	....	....	....
Liabilities to direct investors	8 558 ..	45.0	47.1	45.8	136.0	440.6	206.5	146.2	....
Other capital	8 580 ..	6.9	1.7	29.6	33.5	118.9	119.0	425.2	....
Claims on direct investors	8 585 ..	....	....	....	....	....	....	....	....
Liabilities to direct investors	8 590 ..	6.9	1.7	29.6	33.5	118.9	119.0	425.2	....
Portfolio investment	8 652 ..	**5.1**	**9.5**	**1.9**	**2.9**	**54.6**	**9.5**	**15.1**	....
Equity securities	8 660 ..	2.8	6.8	1.8	2.9	10.0	7.2	6.8	....
Banks	8 663 ..	2.6	6.6	1.1	2.5	1.8	2.4	1.9	....
Other sectors	8 664 ..	.2	.2	.6	.4	8.2	4.8	4.9	....
Debt securities	8 669 ..	2.2	2.7	.1	....	44.7	2.3	8.3	....
Bonds and notes	8 670 ..	....	2.7	.1	....	44.7	2.3	8.3	....
Monetary authorities	8 671 ..	....	....	....	....	....	....	....	....
General government	8 672 ..	....	....	....	....	....	....	....	....
Banks	8 673 ..	....	2.7	....	....	3.6	2.3	8.3	....
Other sectors	8 674 ..	....	....	.1	....	41.1	....	....	....
Money market instruments	8 680 ..	2.2	....	....	....	....	....	....	....
Monetary authorities	8 681 ..	....	....	....	....	....	....	....	....
General government	8 682 ..	....	....	....	....	....	....	....	....
Banks	8 683 ..	2.2	....	....	....	....	....	....	....
Other sectors	8 684 ..	....	....	....	....	....	....	....	....
Financial derivatives	8 905 ..	....	....	....	....	....	....	....	....
Monetary authorities	8 906 ..	....	....	....	....	....	....	....	....
General government	8 907 ..	....	....	....	....	....	....	....	....
Banks	8 908 ..	....	....	....	....	....	....	....	....
Other sectors	8 909 ..	....	....	....	....	....	....	....	....
Other investment	8 753 ..	**2,035.6**	**2,457.8**	**2,447.1**	**1,773.3**	**2,593.1**	**2,619.2**	**2,725.4**	....
Trade credits	8 756 ..	22.9	85.6	54.2	73.6	289.3	167.0	52.2	....
General government	8 757 ..	....	....	....	....	....	....	....	....
of which: Short-term	8 759 ..	....	....	....	....	....	....	....	....
Other sectors	8 760 ..	22.9	85.6	54.2	73.6	289.3	167.0	52.2	....
of which: Short-term	8 762 ..	*22.9*	*85.6*	*54.2*	*73.6*	*289.3*	*167.0*	*52.2*	....
Loans	8 764 ..	1,907.0	2,182.6	2,263.1	1,311.5	1,696.0	1,960.4	2,186.1	....
Monetary authorities	8 765 ..	124.7	114.7	103.5	34.9	37.5	54.3	110.3	....
of which: Use of Fund credit and loans from the Fund	8 766 ..	*124.7*	*114.7*	*103.5*	*34.9*	*37.5*	*54.3*	*110.3*	*128.7*
of which: Short-term	8 768 ..	....	....	....	....	....	....	....	....
General government	8 769 ..	1,725.9	2,018.7	2,021.7	1,177.2	1,481.8	1,740.3	1,837.3	....
of which: Short-term	8 771 ..	....	....	*26.1*	....	....	....	....	....
Banks	8 772 ..	44.8	41.2	75.7	54.5	46.6	24.3	36.0	....
of which: Short-term	8 774 ..	*23.0*	*21.2*	*55.5*	*33.6*	*40.9*	*40.1*	*2.2*	....
Other sectors	8 775 ..	11.7	8.0	62.2	44.9	130.1	141.5	202.5	....
of which: Short-term	8 777 ..	*11.0*	*1.7*	*15.4*	....	....	....	....	....
Currency and deposits	8 780 ..	93.6	107.4	81.2	138.6	226.5	220.8	118.7	....
Monetary authorities	8 781 ..	3.6	4.9	4.5	8.6	9.7	6.2	6.0	....
General government	8 782 ..	....	....	....	....	....	....	....	....
Banks	8 783 ..	90.1	102.5	76.8	130.0	216.7	214.6	112.7	....
Other sectors	8 784 ..	....	....	....	....	....	....	....	....
Other liabilities	8 786 ..	12.1	82.2	48.5	249.6	381.3	271.0	368.4	....
Monetary authorities	8 787 ..	10.8	3.9	−8.6	53.2	167.7	189.7	331.0	....
of which: Short-term	8 789 ..	*10.8*	....	....	....	....	....	....	....
General government	8 790 ..	....	....	....	....	....	....	....	....
of which: Short-term	8 792 ..	....	....	....	....	....	....	....	....
Banks	8 793 ..	....	....	....	....	....	....	....	....
of which: Short-term	8 795 ..	....	....	....	....	....	....	....	....
Other sectors	8 796 ..	1.2	78.2	57.1	196.5	213.6	81.3	37.3	....
of which: Short-term	8 798 ..	*1.2*	....	....	....	....	....	....	....
NET INTERNATIONAL INVESTMENT POSITION	8 995 ..	**−1,414.5**	**−1,499.5**	**−1,731.1**	**−1,098.7**	**−1,603.2**	**−1,582.2**	**−1,398.4**	....
Conversion rates: CFA francs per U.S. dollar (end of period)	0 102 ..	519.36	481.58	556.04	498.07	445.59	471.34	455.34	490.91

Table 1. ANALYTIC PRESENTATION, 2003–2010

(Millions of U.S. dollars)

	Code	2003	2004	2005	2006	2007	2008	2009	2010
A. Current Account[1]	4 993 Z.	**−131.0**	**−165.5**	**−222.0**	**−324.0**	**−268.1**	**−353.3**	**−261.9**	**−323.1**
Goods: exports f.o.b.	2 100 ..	37.5	48.5	60.8	58.7	58.8	69.6	66.0	101.2
Goods: imports f.o.b.	3 100 ..	−130.0	−145.4	−188.9	−244.7	−254.1	−335.5	−343.0	−438.4
Balance on Goods	4 100 ..	*−92.5*	*−96.9*	*−128.1*	*−186.0*	*−195.3*	*−265.8*	*−277.0*	*−337.2*
Services: credit	2 200 ..	7.3	15.8	34.8	34.5	30.8	83.3	49.9	79.5
Services: debit	3 200 ..	−45.3	−86.6	−134.1	−202.2	−178.9	−258.8	−176.6	−168.2
Balance on Goods and Services	4 991 ..	*−130.5*	*−167.8*	*−227.4*	*−353.8*	*−343.3*	*−441.3*	*−403.7*	*−425.9*
Income: credit	2 300 ..	1.3	1.3	3.2	4.6	8.7	10.9	1.4	1.1
Income: debit	3 300 ..	−18.6	−20.5	−20.9	−13.4	−14.6	−15.2	−18.4	−12.0
Balance on Goods, Services, and Income	4 992 ..	*−147.8*	*−187.0*	*−245.2*	*−362.6*	*−349.2*	*−445.6*	*−420.7*	*−436.8*
Current transfers: credit	2 379 Z.	20.3	24.3	26.5	41.3	81.6	94.3	162.1	127.2
Current transfers: debit	3 379 ..	−3.5	−2.8	−3.3	−2.7	−.5	−2.0	−3.2	−13.6
B. Capital Account[1]	4 994 Z.	**−.9**	**17.9**	**24.4**	**46.3**	**79.4**	**67.0**	**82.2**	**75.7**
Capital account: credit	2 994 Z.	....	18.9	25.3	47.4	80.7	72.5	85.5	84.3
Capital account: debit	3 994 ..	−.9	−.9	−.9	−1.1	−1.3	−5.5	−3.3	−8.6
Total, Groups A Plus B	4 981 ..	*−132.0*	*−147.6*	*−197.6*	*−277.7*	*−188.7*	*−286.3*	*−179.7*	*−247.4*
C. Financial Account[1]	4 995 W.	**−50.3**	**−23.3**	**−10.9**	**−15.5**	**−58.2**	**−7.5**	**−747.3**	**63.4**
Direct investment abroad	4 505 ..	....	....	....	....	....	−.6	....	....
Direct investment in Burundi	4 555 Z.	....	....	.6	....	.5	3.8	.3	.8
Portfolio investment assets	4 602 ..	....	....	....	....	....	....	....	....
Equity securities	4 610 ..	....	....	....	....	....	....	....	....
Debt securities	4 619 ..	....	....	....	....	....	....	....	....
Portfolio investment liabilities	4 652 Z.	....	....	....	....	....	....	....	....
Equity securities	4 660 ..	....	....	....	....	....	....	....	....
Debt securities	4 669 Z.	....	....	....	....	....	....	....	....
Financial derivatives	4 910 ..	....	....	....	....	....	....	....	....
Financial derivatives assets	4 900 ..	....	....	....	....	....	....	....	....
Financial derivatives liabilities	4 905 ..	....	....	....	....	....	....	....	....
Other investment assets	4 703 ..	−19.9	−22.0	−7.8	−30.2	−34.2	−30.8	−28.9	−43.6
Monetary authorities	4 701 ..	....	....	....	....	....	....	....	....
General government	4 704 ..	....	−.1	....	....	−1.9	....	−.6	....
Banks	4 705 ..	−22.2	−10.2	−4.5	−15.0	−22.0	−23.2	−24.4	−5.8
Other sectors	4 728 ..	2.3	−11.7	−3.4	−15.2	−10.3	−7.6	−4.0	−37.8
Other investment liabilities	4 753 W.	−30.4	−1.4	−3.6	14.7	−24.5	20.0	−718.8	106.2
Monetary authorities	4 753 WA	....	....	....	....	....	....	93.9	−1.1
General government	4 753 ZB	−41.0	−18.0	−14.2	−35.4	−26.1	−29.3	−938.9	−3.5
Banks	4 753 ZC	9.7	15.3	.6	6.0	5.8	−1.1	2.8	9.5
Other sectors	4 753 ZD	.9	1.3	10.0	44.0	−4.1	50.5	123.4	101.2
Total, Groups A Through C	4 983 ..	*−182.3*	*−170.9*	*−208.5*	*−293.2*	*−246.9*	*−293.8*	*−927.0*	*−184.0*
D. Net Errors and Omissions	4 998 ..	**−13.8**	**−19.5**	**−84.3**	**3.8**	**−26.1**	**57.8**	**−103.6**	**8.1**
Total, Groups A Through D	4 984 ..	*−196.1*	*−190.3*	*−292.7*	*−289.3*	*−273.0*	*−236.1*	*−1,030.6*	*−175.9*
E. Reserves and Related Items	4 802 A.	**196.1**	**190.3**	**292.7**	**289.3**	**273.0**	**236.1**	**1,030.6**	**175.9**
Reserve assets	4 802 ..	−9.6	−2.0	−33.9	−18.2	−63.1	−108.5	−57.0	−20.0
Use of Fund credit and loans	4 766 ..	13.6	10.7	21.3	21.3	10.8	22.1	−26.2	20.2
Exceptional financing	4 920 ..	192.2	181.7	305.3	286.3	325.3	322.5	1,113.8	175.7
Conversion rates: Burundi francs per U.S. dollar	0 101 ..	**1,082.62**	**1,100.90**	**1,081.58**	**1,028.68**	**1,081.87**	**1,185.69**	**1,230.18**	**1,230.75**

[1] Excludes components that have been classified in the categories of Group E.

Table 2. STANDARD PRESENTATION, 2003–2010

(Millions of U.S. dollars)

	Code	2003	2004	2005	2006	2007	2008	2009	2010
CURRENT ACCOUNT................	4 993 ..	**−24.0**	**−32.4**	**−5.7**	**−133.5**	**−108.0**	**−259.4**	**−163.6**	**−300.9**
A. GOODS................	4 100 ..	**−92.5**	**−96.9**	**−128.1**	**−186.0**	**−195.3**	**−265.8**	**−277.0**	**−337.2**
Credit................	2 100 ..	**37.5**	**48.5**	**60.8**	**58.7**	**58.8**	**69.6**	**66.0**	**101.2**
General merchandise: exports f.o.b....	2 110 ..	37.5	48.5	60.8	58.7	58.8	69.6	66.0	101.2
Goods for processing: exports f.o.b....	2 150 ..	....	....	....	....	....	....	....	....
Repairs on goods................	2 160 ..	....	....	....	....	....	....	....	....
Goods procured in ports by carriers....	2 170 ..	....	....	....	....	....	....	....	....
Nonmonetary gold................	2 180 ..	....	....	....	....	....	....	....	....
Debit................	3 100 ..	**−130.0**	**−145.4**	**−188.9**	**−244.7**	**−254.1**	**−335.5**	**−343.0**	**−438.4**
General merchandise: imports f.o.b....	3 110 ..	−130.0	−145.4	−188.9	−244.7	−254.1	−335.5	−343.0	−438.4
Goods for processing: imports f.o.b....	3 150 ..	....	....	....	....	....	....	....	....
Repairs on goods................	3 160 ..	....	....	....	....	....	....	....	....
Goods procured in ports by carriers....	3 170 ..	....	....	....	....	....	....	....	....
Nonmonetary gold................	3 180 ..	....	....	....	....	....	....	....	....
B. SERVICES................	4 200 ..	**−38.0**	**−70.9**	**−99.3**	**−167.7**	**−148.1**	**−175.5**	**−126.7**	**−88.7**
Total credit................	2 200 ..	*7.3*	*15.8*	*34.8*	*34.5*	*30.8*	*83.3*	*49.9*	*79.5*
Total debit................	3 200 ..	*−45.3*	*−86.6*	*−134.1*	*−202.2*	*−178.9*	*−258.8*	*−176.6*	*−168.2*
Transportation services, credit....	2 205 ..	**.7**	**1.4**	**1.7**	**.8**	**1.4**	**.9**	**.5**	**.7**
Passenger................	2 850 ..	*.5*	*.6*	*.4*	*.3*	*1.0*	*.3*	*.2*	*.3*
Freight................	2 851 ..	*.2*	....	....	....	....	....	....	....
Other................	2 852 ..	....	*.8*	*1.3*	*.5*	*.4*	*.6*	*.4*	*.4*
Sea transport, passenger........	2 207 ..	....	....	....	....	....	....	....	....
Sea transport, freight..........	2 208 ..	.2	....	....	....	....	....	....	....
Sea transport, other............	2 209 ..	....	.8	1.3	.5	.4	.6	.4	.4
Air transport, passenger........	2 211 ..	.5	.6	.4	.3	1.0	.3	.2	.3
Air transport, freight..........	2 212 ..	....	....	....	....	....	....	....	....
Air transport, other............	2 213 ..	....	....	....	....	....	....	....	....
Other transport, passenger......	2 215 ..	....	....	....	....	....	....	....	....
Other transport, freight........	2 216 ..	....	....	....	....	....	....	....	....
Other transport, other..........	2 217 ..	....	....	....	....	....	....	....	....
Transportation services, debit....	3 205 ..	**−20.9**	**−38.3**	**−43.9**	**−55.4**	**−55.5**	**−80.7**	**−84.1**	**−110.9**
Passenger................	3 850 ..	....	*−6.3*	*−2.4*	*−1.2*	*−2.5*	*−6.8*	*−8.7*	*−14.6*
Freight................	3 851 ..	*−20.9*	*−31.9*	*−41.5*	*−54.1*	*−52.5*	*−73.8*	*−75.5*	*−96.2*
Other................	3 852 ..	....	....	....	*−.1*	*−.6*	*−.1*	....	....
Sea transport, passenger........	3 207 ..	....	....	....	....	....	....	....	....
Sea transport, freight..........	3 208 ..	−20.9	−6.4	−8.3	−10.8	−11.3	−14.8	−15.1	−19.2
Sea transport, other............	3 209 ..	....	....	....	−.1	−.6	−.1	....	....
Air transport, passenger........	3 211 ..	....	−6.3	−2.4	−1.2	−2.5	−6.8	−8.7	−14.6
Air transport, freight..........	3 212 ..	....	−4.8	−6.2	−8.1	−8.5	−11.1	−11.3	−14.4
Air transport, other............	3 213 ..	....	....	....	....	....	....	....	....
Other transport, passenger......	3 215 ..	....	....	....	....	....	....	....	....
Other transport, freight........	3 216 ..	....	−20.8	−27.0	−35.2	−32.7	−47.9	−49.1	−62.6
Other transport, other..........	3 217 ..	....	....	....	....	....	....	....	....
Travel, credit................	2 236 ..	**.7**	**1.2**	**1.5**	**1.3**	**1.3**	**1.3**	**1.5**	**1.8**
Business travel................	2 237 ..	....	....	....	....	....	....	....	....
Personal travel................	2 240 ..	.7	1.2	1.5	1.3	1.3	1.3	1.5	1.8
Travel, debit................	3 236 ..	**−14.5**	**−23.5**	**−60.3**	**−125.2**	**−103.6**	**−144.2**	**−62.2**	**−19.8**
Business travel................	3 237 ..	....	−20.1	−54.3	−120.5	−98.6	−133.9	−52.9	−11.7
Personal travel................	3 240 ..	−14.5	−3.3	−6.0	−4.6	−5.0	−10.3	−9.3	−8.1
Other services, credit........	2 200 BA	**5.9**	**13.2**	**31.7**	**32.4**	**28.1**	**81.1**	**47.9**	**77.0**
Communications................	2 245 ..	....	....	....	....	....	....	....	....
Construction................	2 249 ..	....	....	....	....	....	....	....	....
Insurance................	2 253 ..	....	....	....	....	....	.1	.4	1.0
Financial................	2 260 ..	....	....	....	....	....	.1	....	.6
Computer and information........	2 262 ..	....	....	....	....	....	....	....	....
Royalties and licence fees......	2 266 ..	....	....	....	....	....	....	....	....
Other business services........	2 268 ..	.8	1.4	3.4	3.4	3.8	.8	....	3.2
Personal, cultural, and recreational....	2 287 ..	....	....	....	....	....	....	....	....
Government, n.i.e................	2 291 ..	5.1	11.8	28.3	28.9	24.2	80.1	47.5	72.2
Other services, debit........	3 200 BA	**−9.9**	**−24.9**	**−29.9**	**−21.6**	**−19.7**	**−33.9**	**−30.3**	**−37.5**
Communications................	3 245 ..	−1.0	....	....	....	....	....	....	....
Construction................	3 249 ..	....	....	....	....	....	....	....	....
Insurance................	3 253 ..	−1.5	−2.6	−2.0	−2.5	−1.3	−3.4	−2.6	−2.6
Financial................	3 260 ..	....	−1.7	−2.4	−2.2	−1.9	−4.0	−1.9	−1.4
Computer and information........	3 262 ..	....	....	....	....	....	....	....	....
Royalties and licence fees......	3 266 ..	....	....	....	....	....	....	....	....
Other business services........	3 268 ..	−.2	−8.9	−16.1	−8.2	−7.2	−8.2	−9.2	−21.7
Personal, cultural, and recreational....	3 287 ..	....	....	....	....	....	....	....	....
Government, n.i.e................	3 291 ..	−7.1	−11.7	−9.4	−8.7	−9.3	−18.3	−16.5	−11.9

Table 2 (Continued). STANDARD PRESENTATION, 2003–2010

(Millions of U.S. dollars)

	Code	2003	2004	2005	2006	2007	2008	2009	2010
C. INCOME	4 300	**−17.3**	**−19.2**	**−17.8**	**−8.8**	**−5.9**	**−4.3**	**−17.0**	**−10.9**
Total credit	2 300	*1.3*	*1.3*	*3.2*	*4.6*	*8.7*	*10.9*	*1.4*	*1.1*
Total debit	3 300	*−18.6*	*−20.5*	*−20.9*	*−13.4*	*−14.6*	*−15.2*	*−18.4*	*−12.0*
Compensation of employees, credit	2 310	....	....	....	....	....	....	....	....
Compensation of employees, debit	3 310	**−3.3**	....	....	....	....	....	....	....
Investment income, credit	2 320	**1.3**	**1.3**	**3.2**	**4.6**	**8.7**	**10.9**	**1.4**	**1.1**
Direct investment income	2 330	....	....	....	....	....	....	....	....
Dividends and distributed branch profits	2 332	....	....	....			....	....	....
Reinvested earnings and undistributed branch profits	2 333	....	....	....			....	....	
Income on debt (interest)	2 334	....	....	....			....	....	....
Portfolio investment income	2 339	....	....				....		....
Income on equity	2 340	....	....				....	....	....
Income on bonds and notes	2 350	....	....				....		
Income on money market instruments	2 360	....	....	....	....	....	....	....	....
Other investment income	2 370	1.3	1.3	3.2	4.6	8.7	10.9	1.4	1.1
Investment income, debit	3 320	**−15.3**	**−20.5**	**−20.9**	**−13.4**	**−14.6**	**−15.2**	**−18.4**	**−12.0**
Direct investment income	3 330	−4.7	−6.0	−2.1	−3.4	−4.8	−5.3	−8.1	−10.1
Dividends and distributed branch profits	3 332	−4.7	−6.0	−2.1	−3.4	−4.8	−5.3	−8.1	−10.1
Reinvested earnings and undistributed branch profits	3 333	....	....	....	....	....	....	....	....
Income on debt (interest)	3 334	....	....	....	....	....	....	....	....
Portfolio investment income	3 339	....	....	....	....	....	....	....	....
Income on equity	3 340	....	....	....	....	....	....	....	....
Income on bonds and notes	3 350	....	....	....	....	....	....	....	....
Income on money market instruments	3 360	....	....	....	....	....	....	....	....
Other investment income	3 370	−10.7	−14.5	−18.8	−10.1	−9.8	−9.9	−10.3	−1.9
D. CURRENT TRANSFERS	4 379	**123.8**	**154.6**	**239.5**	**229.0**	**241.2**	**186.2**	**257.1**	**135.9**
Credit	2 379	**127.3**	**157.4**	**242.8**	**231.8**	**241.7**	**188.2**	**260.4**	**149.5**
General government	2 380	118.9	144.2	223.2	200.2	160.0	93.9	98.3	22.2
Other sectors	2 390	8.4	13.2	19.5	31.6	81.6	94.3	162.1	127.2
Workers' remittances	2 391	....	....	.1	....	.2	3.6	28.2	34.5
Other current transfers	2 392	8.4	13.2	19.5	31.6	81.5	90.6	133.9	92.7
Debit	3 379	**−3.5**	**−2.8**	**−3.3**	**−2.7**	**−.5**	**−2.0**	**−3.2**	**−13.6**
General government	3 380	−2.0	−1.1	−1.6	−.2	−.2	....	....	−.9
Other sectors	3 390	−1.4	−1.7	−1.7	−2.5	−.2	−2.0	−3.2	−12.7
Workers' remittances	3 391	....	−.3	−.2	−.2	−.2	−.2	−1.1	−5.0
Other current transfers	3 392	−1.4	−1.4	−1.5	−2.3	....	−1.7	−2.1	−7.7
CAPITAL AND FINANCIAL ACCOUNT	4 996	**37.8**	**51.9**	**90.0**	**129.7**	**134.1**	**201.6**	**267.2**	**292.8**
CAPITAL ACCOUNT	4 994	**−.9**	**17.9**	**31.8**	**62.0**	**128.0**	**140.7**	**1,025.3**	**77.9**
Total credit	2 994	....	*18.9*	*32.7*	*63.1*	*129.3*	*146.2*	*1,028.7*	*86.5*
Total debit	3 994	*−.9*	*−.9*	*−.9*	*−1.1*	*−1.3*	*−5.5*	*−3.3*	*−8.6*
Capital transfers, credit	2 400	....	**18.9**	**32.7**	**63.1**	**129.3**	**146.2**	**1,028.7**	**86.5**
General government	2 401		18.9	32.7	63.1	129.3	146.2	1,028.7	86.5
Debt forgiveness	2 402	....	....	7.4	15.7	48.6	73.7	943.1	2.2
Other capital transfers	2 410	....	18.9	25.3	47.4	80.7	72.5	85.5	84.3
Other sectors	2 430	....	....	....	....	....	....	....	....
Migrants' transfers	2 431	....	....	....	....	....	....	....	....
Debt forgiveness	2 432	....	....	....	....	....	....	....	....
Other capital transfers	2 440	....	....	....	....	....	....	....	....
Capital transfers, debit	3 400	**−.9**	**−.9**	**−.9**	**−1.1**	**−1.3**	**−5.5**	**−3.3**	**−8.6**
General government	3 401	....	−.3	−.7	−1.1	−1.3	−5.5	−3.3	−7.8
Debt forgiveness	3 402	....	....	....	....	....	....	....	....
Other capital transfers	3 410	....	−.3	−.7	−1.1	−1.3	−5.5	−3.3	−7.8
Other sectors	3 430	−.9	−.6	−.1	....	....	....	−.1	−.8
Migrants' transfers	3 431	−.9	−.6	−.1	....	....	....	−.1	−.8
Debt forgiveness	3 432	....	....	....	....	....	....	....	....
Other capital transfers	3 440	....	....	....	....	....	....	....	....
Nonproduced nonfinancial assets, credit	2 480	....	....	....	....	....	....	....	....
Nonproduced nonfinancial assets, debit	3 480	....	....	....	....	....	....	....	....

Table 2 (Continued). STANDARD PRESENTATION, 2003–2010

(Millions of U.S. dollars)

	Code	2003	2004	2005	2006	2007	2008	2009	2010
FINANCIAL ACCOUNT	4 995 ..	**38.8**	**33.9**	**58.2**	**67.7**	**6.1**	**60.9**	**−758.1**	**214.9**
A. DIRECT INVESTMENT	4 500 ..	....	....	.6	....	.5	3.3	.3	.8
Direct investment abroad	4 505 ..	....	....	....	....	....	−.6	....	....
Equity capital	4 510 ..	....	....	....	....	....	−.6	....	....
Claims on affiliated enterprises	4 515 ..	....	....	....	....	....	−.6	....	....
Liabilities to affiliated enterprises	4 520 ..	....	....	....	....	....	....	....	....
Reinvested earnings	4 525 ..	....	....	....	....	....	....	....	....
Other capital	4 530 ..	....	....	....	....	....	....	....	....
Claims on affiliated enterprises	4 535 ..	....	....	....	....	....	....	....	....
Liabilities to affiliated enterprises	4 540 ..	....	....	....	....	....	....	....	....
Direct investment in Burundi	4 555 ..	....	....	.6	....	.5	3.8	.3	.8
Equity capital	4 560 ..	....	....	.6	....	.5	3.8	.3	.8
Claims on direct investors	4 565 ..	....	....	....	....	....	....	....	....
Liabilities to direct investors	4 570 ..	....	....	.6	....	.5	3.8	.3	.8
Reinvested earnings	4 575 ..	....	....	....	....	....	....	....	....
Other capital	4 580 ..	....	....	....	....	....	....	....	....
Claims on direct investors	4 585 ..	....	....	....	....	....	....	....	....
Liabilities to direct investors	4 590 ..	....	....	....	....	....	....	....	....
B. PORTFOLIO INVESTMENT	4 600 ..	....	....	....	....	....	....	....	....
Assets	4 602 ..	....	....	....	....	....	....	....	....
Equity securities	4 610 ..	....	....	....	....	....	....	....	....
Monetary authorities	4 611 ..	....	....	....	....	....	....	....	....
General government	4 612 ..	....	....	....	....	....	....	....	....
Banks	4 613 ..	....	....	....	....	....	....	....	....
Other sectors	4 614 ..	....	....	....	....	....	....	....	....
Debt securities	4 619 ..	....	....	....	....	....	....	....	....
Bonds and notes	4 620 ..	....	....	....	....	....	....	....	....
Monetary authorities	4 621 ..	....	....	....	....	....	....	....	....
General government	4 622 ..	....	....	....	....	....	....	....	....
Banks	4 623 ..	....	....	....	....	....	....	....	....
Other sectors	4 624 ..	....	....	....	....	....	....	....	....
Money market instruments	4 630 ..	....	....	....	....	....	....	....	....
Monetary authorities	4 631 ..	....	....	....	....	....	....	....	....
General government	4 632 ..	....	....	....	....	....	....	....	....
Banks	4 633 ..	....	....	....	....	....	....	....	....
Other sectors	4 634 ..	....	....	....	....	....	....	....	....
Liabilities	4 652 ..	....	....	....	....	....	....	....	....
Equity securities	4 660 ..	....	....	....	....	....	....	....	....
Banks	4 663 ..	....	....	....	....	....	....	....	....
Other sectors	4 664 ..	....	....	....	....	....	....	....	....
Debt securities	4 669 ..	....	....	....	....	....	....	....	....
Bonds and notes	4 670 ..	....	....	....	....	....	....	....	....
Monetary authorities	4 671 ..	....	....	....	....	....	....	....	....
General government	4 672 ..	....	....	....	....	....	....	....	....
Banks	4 673 ..	....	....	....	....	....	....	....	....
Other sectors	4 674 ..	....	....	....	....	....	....	....	....
Money market instruments	4 680 ..	....	....	....	....	....	....	....	....
Monetary authorities	4 681 ..	....	....	....	....	....	....	....	....
General government	4 682 ..	....	....	....	....	....	....	....	....
Banks	4 683 ..	....	....	....	....	....	....	....	....
Other sectors	4 684 ..	....	....	....	....	....	....	....	....
C. FINANCIAL DERIVATIVES	4 910 ..	....	....	....	....	....	....	....	....
Monetary authorities	4 911 ..	....	....	....	....	....	....	....	....
General government	4 912 ..	....	....	....	....	....	....	....	....
Banks	4 913 ..	....	....	....	....	....	....	....	....
Other sectors	4 914 ..	....	....	....	....	....	....	....	....
Assets	4 900 ..	....	....	....	....	....	....	....	....
Monetary authorities	4 901 ..	....	....	....	....	....	....	....	....
General government	4 902 ..	....	....	....	....	....	....	....	....
Banks	4 903 ..	....	....	....	....	....	....	....	....
Other sectors	4 904 ..	....	....	....	....	....	....	....	....
Liabilities	4 905 ..	....	....	....	....	....	....	....	....
Monetary authorities	4 906 ..	....	....	....	....	....	....	....	....
General government	4 907 ..	....	....	....	....	....	....	....	....
Banks	4 908 ..	....	....	....	....	....	....	....	....
Other sectors	4 909 ..	....	....	....	....	....	....	....	....

Table 2 (Concluded). STANDARD PRESENTATION, 2003–2010

(Millions of U.S. dollars)

	Code	2003	2004	2005	2006	2007	2008	2009	2010
D. OTHER INVESTMENT	4 700	**48.4**	**35.9**	**91.5**	**85.8**	**68.7**	**166.2**	**−701.4**	**234.1**
Assets	4 703	**−19.9**	**−22.0**	**−7.8**	**−30.2**	**−34.2**	**−30.8**	**−28.9**	**−43.6**
Trade credits	4 706	....	−11.7	−3.4	−15.2	−10.3	−7.6	−4.0	−37.8
General government	4 707	....	....	....	....	....	....	....	....
of which: Short-term	4 709	....	....	....	....	....	....	....	....
Other sectors	4 710	....	−11.7	−3.4	−15.2	−10.3	−7.6	−4.0	−37.8
of which: Short-term	4 712	....	−11.7	−3.4	−15.2	−10.3	−7.6	−4.0	−37.8
Loans	4 714	3.1	....	....	....	....	....	....	....
Monetary authorities	4 715	....	....	....	....	....	....	....	....
of which: Short-term	4 718	....	....	....	....	....	....	....	....
General government	4 719	....	....	....	....	....	....	....	....
of which: Short-term	4 721	....	....	....	....	....	....	....	....
Banks	4 722	....	....	....	....	....	....	....	....
of which: Short-term	4 724	....	....	....	....	....	....	....	....
Other sectors	4 725	3.1	....	....	....	....	....	....	....
of which: Short-term	4 727	3.1	....	....	....	....	....	....	....
Currency and deposits	4 730	−23.0	−10.2	−4.5	−15.0	−22.0	−23.2	−24.4	−5.8
Monetary authorities	4 731	....	....	....	....	....	....	....	....
General government	4 732	....	....	....	....	....	....	....	....
Banks	4 733	−22.2	−10.2	−4.5	−15.0	−22.0	−23.2	−24.4	−5.8
Other sectors	4 734	−.8	....	....	....	....	....	....	....
Other assets	4 736	....	−.1	....	....	−1.9	....	−.6	....
Monetary authorities	4 737	....	....	....	....	....	....	....	....
of which: Short-term	4 739	....	....	....	....	....	....	....	....
General government	4 740	....	−.1	....	....	−1.9	....	−.6	....
of which: Short-term	4 742	....	....	....	....	....	....	....	....
Banks	4 743	....	....	....	....	....	....	....	....
of which: Short-term	4 745	....	....	....	....	....	....	....	....
Other sectors	4 746	....	....	....	....	....	....	....	....
of which: Short-term	4 748	....	....	....	....	....	....	....	....
Liabilities	4 753	**68.3**	**57.9**	**99.3**	**116.1**	**103.0**	**197.0**	**−672.5**	**277.7**
Trade credits	4 756	....	.9	10.0	44.5	−4.3	50.5	124.6	100.9
General government	4 757	....	....	....	....	....	....	....	....
of which: Short-term	4 759	....	....	....	....	....	....	....	....
Other sectors	4 760	....	.9	10.0	44.5	−4.3	50.5	124.6	100.9
of which: Short-term	4 762	....	1.6	11.4	46.5	−2.2	52.1	126.2	101.0
Loans	4 764	30.4	41.7	88.8	65.6	101.4	147.6	−893.8	167.2
Monetary authorities	4 765	13.6	10.7	21.3	21.3	10.8	22.1	−26.2	19.1
of which: Use of Fund credit and loans from the Fund	4 766	13.6	10.7	21.3	21.3	10.8	22.1	−26.2	20.2
of which: Short-term	4 768	....	....	....	....	....	....	....	....
General government	4 769	16.8	30.6	67.4	44.7	90.5	125.5	−866.5	147.8
of which: Short-term	4 771	....	17.5	6.4	1.4	3.1	2.4	....	....
Banks	4 772	....	....	....	....	....	....	....	....
of which: Short-term	4 774	....	....	....	....	....	....	....	....
Other sectors	4 775	....	.4	.1	−.4	.2	−.1	−1.2	.4
of which: Short-term	4 777	....	.4	.1	−.4	.2	−.1	−1.2	.4
Currency and deposits	4 780	9.7	15.3	.6	6.0	5.8	−1.1	2.8	9.5
Monetary authorities	4 781	....	....	....	....	....	....	....	....
General government	4 782	....	....	....	....	....	....	....	....
Banks	4 783	9.7	15.3	.6	6.0	5.8	−1.1	2.8	9.5
Other sectors	4 784	....	....	....	....	....	....	....	....
Other liabilities	4 786	28.2	....	....	....	....	....	93.9	....
Monetary authorities	4 787	....	....	....	....	....	....	93.9	....
of which: Short-term	4 789	....	....	....	....	....	....	....	....
General government	4 790	27.3	....	....	....	....	....	....	....
of which: Short-term	4 792	27.3	....	....	....	....	....	....	....
Banks	4 793	....	....	....	....	....	....	....	....
of which: Short-term	4 795	....	....	....	....	....	....	....	....
Other sectors	4 796	.9	....	....	....	....	....	....	....
of which: Short-term	4 798	1.0	....	....	....	....	....	....	....
E. RESERVE ASSETS	4 802	**−9.6**	**−2.0**	**−33.9**	**−18.2**	**−63.1**	**−108.5**	**−57.0**	**−20.0**
Monetary gold	4 812	−.1	....	....	−.1	−.3	−.1	−.2	−.3
Special drawing rights	4 811	....	−.2	.1	....	....	.2	−103.8	−10.0
Reserve position in the Fund	4 810	....	....	....	....	....	....	....	....
Foreign exchange	4 803	−9.6	−.7	−35.0	−18.4	−62.0	−108.6	47.0	−9.7
Other claims	4 813	....	−1.1	1.0	.4	−.8	....	....	....
NET ERRORS AND OMISSIONS	4 998	**−13.8**	**−19.5**	**−84.3**	**3.8**	**−26.1**	**57.8**	**−103.6**	**8.1**

Table 3. INTERNATIONAL INVESTMENT POSITION (End-period stocks), 2003–2010

(Millions of U.S. dollars)

	Code	2003	2004	2005	2006	2007	2008	2009	2010
ASSETS..	8 995 C.	**119.6**	**136.1**	**197.6**	**246.8**	**314.5**	**419.4**	**507.4**	**568.6**
Direct investment abroad.........................	8 505 ..	**.2**	**.9**	**1.0**	**1.0**	**.9**	**1.4**	**1.4**	**1.4**
Equity capital and reinvested earnings.................	8 506 ..	.2	.9	1.0	1.0	.9	1.4	1.4	1.4
Claims on affiliated enterprises.................	8 507 ..	.2	.9	1.0	1.0	.9	1.4	1.4	1.4
Liabilities to affiliated enterprises.............	8 508 ..	....	....	....	....	....	....	....	....
Other capital...	8 530 ..	....	....	....	....	....	....	....	....
Claims on affiliated enterprises.................	8 535 ..	....	....	....	....	....	....	....	....
Liabilities to affiliated enterprises.............	8 540 ..	....	....	....	....	....	....	....	....
Portfolio investment.................................	8 602 ..	....	....	....	....	....	....	....	....
Equity securities.......................................	8 610 ..	....	....	....	....	....	....	....	....
Monetary authorities.................................	8 611 ..	....	....	....	....	....	....	....	....
General government..................................	8 612 ..	....	....	....	....	....	....	....	....
Banks..	8 613 ..	....	....	....	....	....	....	....	....
Other sectors..	8 614 ..	....	....	....	....	....	....	....	....
Debt securities...	8 619 ..	....	....	....	....	....	....	....	....
Bonds and notes..	8 620 ..	....	....	....	....	....	....	....	....
Monetary authorities.............................	8 621 ..	....	....	....	....	....	....	....	....
General government..............................	8 622 ..	....	....	....	....	....	....	....	....
Banks...	8 623 ..	....	....	....	....	....	....	....	....
Other sectors...	8 624 ..	....	....	....	....	....	....	....	....
Money market instruments........................	8 630 ..	....	....	....	....	....	....	....	....
Monetary authorities.............................	8 631 ..	....	....	....	....	....	....	....	....
General government..............................	8 632 ..	....	....	....	....	....	....	....	....
Banks...	8 633 ..	....	....	....	....	....	....	....	....
Other sectors...	8 634 ..	....	....	....	....	....	....	....	....
Financial derivatives...............................	8 900 ..	....	....	....	....	....	....	....	....
Monetary authorities.................................	8 901 ..	....	....	....	....	....	....	....	....
General government..................................	8 902 ..	....	....	....	....	....	....	....	....
Banks..	8 903 ..	....	....	....	....	....	....	....	....
Other sectors..	8 904 ..	....	....	....	....	....	....	....	....
Other investment.....................................	8 703 ..	**45.6**	**66.7**	**82.7**	**113.3**	**134.5**	**151.5**	**181.0**	**224.2**
Trade credits...	8 706 ..	6.2	17.8	23.4	39.0	44.9	48.0	52.1	89.8
General government..................................	8 707 ..	....	....	....	....	....	....	....	....
of which: Short-term.............................	8 709 ..	....	....	....	....	....	....	....	....
Other sectors..	8 710 ..	6.2	17.8	23.4	39.0	44.9	48.0	52.1	89.8
of which: Short-term.............................	8 712 ..	*6.2*	*17.8*	*23.4*	*39.0*	*44.9*	*48.0*	*52.1*	*89.8*
Loans..	8 714 ..	....	....	....	....	....	....	....	....
Monetary authorities.................................	8 715 ..	....	....	....	....	....	....	....	....
of which: Short-term.............................	8 718 ..	....	....	....	....	....	....	....	....
General government..................................	8 719 ..	....	....	....	....	....	....	....	....
of which: Short-term.............................	8 721 ..	....	....	....	....	....	....	....	....
Banks..	8 722 ..	....	....	....	....	....	....	....	....
of which: Short-term.............................	8 724 ..	....	....	....	....	....	....	....	....
Other sectors..	8 725 ..	....	....	....	....	....	....	....	....
of which: Short-term.............................	8 727 ..	....	....	....	....	....	....	....	....
Currency and deposits...............................	8 730 ..	39.3	48.9	59.2	74.3	87.8	101.8	126.6	132.2
Monetary authorities.................................	8 731 ..	....	....	....	....	....	....	....	....
General government..................................	8 732 ..	....	....	....	....	....	....	....	....
Banks..	8 733 ..	39.3	48.9	59.2	74.3	87.8	101.8	126.6	132.2
Other sectors..	8 734 ..	....	....	....	....	....	....	....	....
Other assets..	8 736 ..	....	.1	.1	.1	1.9	1.7	2.2	2.2
Monetary authorities.................................	8 737 ..	....	....	....	....	....	....	....	....
of which: Short-term.............................	8 739 ..	....	....	....	....	....	....	....	....
General government..................................	8 740 ..	....	.1	.1	.1	1.9	1.7	2.2	2.2
of which: Short-term.............................	8 742 ..	....	*.1*	*.1*	*.1*	*1.9*	*1.7*	*2.2*	*2.2*
Banks..	8 743 ..	....	....	....	....	....	....	....	....
of which: Short-term.............................	8 745 ..	....	....	....	....	....	....	....	....
Other sectors..	8 746 ..	....	....	....	....	....	....	....	....
of which: Short-term.............................	8 748 ..	....	....	....	....	....	....	....	....
Reserve assets...	8 802 ..	**73.8**	**68.5**	**113.9**	**132.5**	**179.0**	**266.5**	**325.0**	**343.0**
Monetary gold...	8 812 ..	.4	.4	.5	.6	.8	.8	1.1	1.4
Special drawing rights................................	8 811 ..	.1	.4	.3	.3	.4	.1	104.5	112.8
Reserve position in the Fund......................	8 810 ..	.5	.6	.5	.5	.6	.6	.6	.6
Foreign exchange.......................................	8 803 ..	72.7	67.2	112.7	131.0	177.3	265.0	218.9	228.3
Other claims..	8 813 ..	....	....	....	....	....	....	....	....

Table 3 (Concluded). INTERNATIONAL INVESTMENT POSITION (End-period stocks), 2003–2010

(Millions of U.S. dollars)

	Code	2003	2004	2005	2006	2007	2008	2009	2010
LIABILITIES..	8 995 D.	**1,313.2**	**1,406.9**	**1,382.5**	**1,506.0**	**1,561.0**	**1,526.6**	**816.6**	**1,032.0**
Direct investment in Burundi......................	8 555 ..	....	....	**.7**	**.7**	**1.1**	**4.7**	**5.1**	**5.8**
Equity capital and reinvested earnings..............	8 556 ..	....	....	.7	.7	1.1	4.7	5.1	5.8
Claims on direct investors.........................	8 557 ..	....	....	....	....	....	....	....	....
Liabilities to direct investors.....................	8 558 ..	....	....	.7	.7	1.1	4.7	5.1	5.8
Other capital..	8 580 ..	....	....	....	....	....	....	....	....
Claims on direct investors.........................	8 585 ..	....	....	....	....	....	....	....	....
Liabilities to direct investors.....................	8 590 ..	....	....	....	....	....	....	....	....
Portfolio investment...............................	8 652 ..	....	....	....	....	....	....	....	....
Equity securities....................................	8 660 ..	....	....	....	....	....	....	....	....
Banks..	8 663 ..	....	....	....	....	....	....	....	....
Other sectors......................................	8 664 ..	....	....	....	....	....	....	....	....
Debt securities......................................	8 669 ..	....	....	....	....	....	....	....	....
Bonds and notes...................................	8 670 ..	....	....	....	....	....	....	....	....
Monetary authorities............................	8 671 ..	....	....	....	....	....	....	....	....
General government.............................	8 672 ..	....	....	....	....	....	....	....	....
Banks..	8 673 ..	....	....	....	....	....	....	....	....
Other sectors....................................	8 674 ..	....	....	....	....	....	....	....	....
Money market instruments.........................	8 680 ..	....	....	....	....	....	....	....	....
Monetary authorities............................	8 681 ..	....	....	....	....	....	....	....	....
General government.............................	8 682 ..	....	....	....	....	....	....	....	....
Banks..	8 683 ..	....	....	....	....	....	....	....	....
Other sectors....................................	8 684 ..	....	....	....	....	....	....	....	....
Financial derivatives..............................	8 905 ..	....	....	....	....	....	....	....	....
Monetary authorities...............................	8 906 ..	....	....	....	....	....	....	....	....
General government................................	8 907 ..	....	....	....	....	....	....	....	....
Banks...	8 908 ..	....	....	....	....	....	....	....	....
Other sectors.......................................	8 909 ..	....	....	....	....	....	....	....	....
Other investment.................................	8 753 ..	**1,313.2**	**1,406.9**	**1,381.9**	**1,505.3**	**1,559.9**	**1,521.9**	**811.6**	**1,026.2**
Trade credits..	8 756 ..	....	.9	11.8	57.4	47.2	91.3	216.2	316.6
General government................................	8 757 ..	....	....	....	....	....	....	....	....
of which: Short-term...........................	8 759 ..	....	....	....	....	....	....	....	....
Other sectors......................................	8 760 ..	....	.9	11.8	57.4	47.2	91.3	216.2	316.6
of which: Short-term...........................	8 762 ..	....	*.9*	*11.8*	*57.4*	*47.2*	*91.3*	*216.2*	*316.6*
Loans...	8 764 ..	1,282.5	1,354.9	1,305.6	1,404.8	1,465.3	1,386.5	547.1	537.8
Monetary authorities..............................	8 765 ..	28.6	41.0	58.2	82.7	98.2	116.9	90.9	109.6
of which: Use of Fund credit and loans from the Fund....	8 766 ..	*28.6*	*41.0*	*58.2*	*82.7*	*98.2*	*116.9*	*90.9*	*109.6*
of which: Short-term...........................	8 768 ..	....	....	....	....	....	....	....	....
General government.............................	8 769 ..	1,253.9	1,313.9	1,247.4	1,322.1	1,367.1	1,269.6	456.2	428.2
of which: Short-term...........................	8 771 ..	....	....	....	....	....	....	....	....
Banks..	8 772 ..	....	....	....	....	....	....	....	....
of which: Short-term...........................	8 774 ..	....	....	....	....	....	....	....	....
Other sectors....................................	8 775 ..	....	....	....	....	....	....	....	....
of which: Short-term...........................	8 777 ..	....	....	....	....	....	....	....	....
Currency and deposits..............................	8 780 ..	30.6	33.3	37.6	15.4	19.4	16.5	19.4	28.9
Monetary authorities..............................	8 781 ..	....	....	....	....	....	....	....	....
General government.............................	8 782 ..	....	....	....	....	....	....	....	....
Banks..	8 783 ..	30.6	33.3	37.6	15.4	19.4	16.5	19.4	28.9
Other sectors....................................	8 784 ..	....	....	....	....	....	....	....	....
Other liabilities....................................	8 786 ..	.1	17.8	26.8	27.7	27.9	27.5	28.8	142.8
Monetary authorities..............................	8 787 ..	....	....	....	....	....	....	....	113.7
of which: Short-term...........................	8 789 ..	....	....	....	....	....	....	....	....
General government.............................	8 790 ..	....	....	....	....	....	....	....	....
of which: Short-term...........................	8 792 ..	....	....	....	....	....	....	....	....
Banks..	8 793 ..	....	....	....	....	....	....	....	....
of which: Short-term...........................	8 795 ..	....	....	....	....	....	....	....	....
Other sectors....................................	8 796 ..	.1	17.8	26.8	27.7	27.9	27.5	28.8	29.1
of which: Short-term...........................	8 798 ..	*.1*	*17.8*	*26.8*	*27.7*	*27.9*	*27.5*	*28.8*	*29.1*
NET INTERNATIONAL INVESTMENT POSITION........	8 995 ..	**−1,193.6**	**−1,270.8**	**−1,184.9**	**−1,259.2**	**−1,246.5**	**−1,107.2**	**−309.2**	**−463.5**
Conversion rates: Burundi francs per U.S. dollar (end of period)...............................	0 102 ..	**1,093.00**	**1,109.51**	**997.78**	**1,002.47**	**1,119.54**	**1,234.98**	**1,230.50**	**1,232.50**

Cambodia   522

Table 1. ANALYTIC PRESENTATION, 2003–2010
(Millions of U.S. dollars)

	Code	2003	2004	2005	2006	2007	2008	2009	2010
A. Current Account[1]	4 993 Z.	**−233.4**	**−182.9**	**−306.7**	**−262.2**	**−480.7**	**−1,050.8**	**−930.9**	**−879.2**
Goods: exports f.o.b.	2 100 ..	2,086.8	2,588.9	2,910.3	3,692.4	4,088.5	4,708.0	4,196.2	5,143.2
Goods: imports f.o.b.	3 100 ..	−2,668.1	−3,269.5	−3,918.3	−4,771.2	−5,431.9	−6,508.4	−5,830.5	−6,790.7
Balance on Goods	4 100 ..	*−581.3*	*−680.6*	*−1,008.0*	*−1,078.9*	*−1,343.4*	*−1,800.4*	*−1,634.2*	*−1,647.5*
Services: credit	2 200 ..	548.0	804.9	1,118.1	1,296.3	1,547.5	1,645.1	1,624.9	1,743.9
Services: debit	3 200 ..	−433.9	−514.4	−642.5	−804.0	−915.4	−1,035.8	−1,018.4	−1,088.0
Balance on Goods and Services	4 991 ..	*−467.2*	*−390.1*	*−532.4*	*−586.5*	*−711.3*	*−1,191.1*	*−1,027.8*	*−991.6*
Income: credit	2 300 ..	43.7	48.6	67.7	90.0	112.2	108.4	55.6	55.4
Income: debit	3 300 ..	−223.0	−269.6	−362.4	−396.1	−476.2	−583.0	−532.8	−588.5
Balance on Goods, Services, and Income	4 992 ..	*−646.5*	*−611.1*	*−827.1*	*−892.7*	*−1,075.2*	*−1,665.7*	*−1,505.0*	*−1,524.7*
Current transfers: credit	2 379 Z.	425.3	443.7	541.1	655.0	620.3	642.8	595.5	666.9
Current transfers: debit	3 379 ..	−12.2	−15.5	−20.7	−24.5	−25.8	−27.9	−21.3	−21.4
B. Capital Account[1]	4 994 Z.	**66.2**	**68.1**	**82.6**	**295.0**	**258.3**	**232.7**	**311.6**	**331.0**
Capital account: credit	2 994 Z.	119.5	141.3	138.1	348.1	325.6	292.5	367.8	418.4
Capital account: debit	3 994 ..	−53.3	−73.2	−55.5	−53.2	−67.2	−59.8	−56.2	−87.4
Total, Groups A Plus B	4 981 ..	*−167.3*	*−114.8*	*−224.1*	*32.8*	*−222.4*	*−818.0*	*−619.3*	*−548.3*
C. Financial Account[1]	4 995 W.	**243.7**	**219.1**	**310.5**	**212.9**	**681.6**	**1,375.7**	**715.2**	**747.0**
Direct investment abroad	4 505 ..	−9.7	−10.2	−6.3	−8.4	−1.1	−20.5	−18.8	−20.6
Direct investment in Cambodia	4 555 Z.	84.0	131.4	381.2	483.2	867.3	815.2	539.1	782.6
Portfolio investment assets	4 602 ..	−7.7	−8.0	−7.2	−8.2	−6.3	−11.6	−7.6	−36.7
Equity securities	4 610 ..	−7.7	−8.0	−7.2	−8.2	−6.5	−11.6	−7.6	−9.4
Debt securities	4 619 ..	....	....	....	....	.1	....	....	−27.2
Portfolio investment liabilities	4 652 Z.	....	....	....	....	....	....	....	....
Equity securities	4 660 ..	....	....	....	....	....	....	....	....
Debt securities	4 669 Z.	....	....	....	....	....	....	....	....
Financial derivatives	4 910 ..	....	....	....	....	....	....	....	....
Financial derivatives assets	4 900 ..	....	....	....	....	....	....	....	....
Financial derivatives liabilities	4 905 ..	....	....	....	....	....	....	....	....
Other investment assets	4 703 ..	−127.0	−91.3	−327.2	−539.6	−780.6	−97.6	−358.8	−643.2
Monetary authorities	4 701 ..	6.3	−66.9	68.6	−70.8	−213.6	50.6	−444.1	−242.8
General government	4 704 ..	....	....	....	....	....	....	....	....
Banks	4 705 ..	−78.5	−34.1	−94.7	−139.6	−353.7	310.2	−155.6	−165.6
Other sectors	4 728 ..	−54.9	9.7	−301.2	−329.1	−213.3	−458.3	241.0	−234.7
Other investment liabilities	4 753 W.	304.1	197.2	270.0	285.8	602.4	690.2	561.3	664.8
Monetary authorities	4 753 WA	....	....	....	....	....	....	106.9	....
General government	4 753 ZB	148.6	154.4	144.0	122.1	199.6	234.7	153.1	244.9
Banks	4 753 ZC	34.3	−3.2	8.3	23.9	183.8	333.8	−284.1	103.8
Other sectors	4 753 ZD	121.2	46.0	117.8	139.8	219.0	121.8	585.4	316.1
Total, Groups A Through C	4 983 ..	*76.5*	*104.3*	*86.4*	*245.7*	*459.2*	*557.7*	*95.9*	*198.7*
D. Net Errors and Omissions	4 998 ..	**−40.0**	**−45.8**	**−11.9**	**−42.6**	**−36.0**	**−35.3**	**6.3**	**−48.4**
Total, Groups A Through D	4 984 ..	*36.5*	*58.5*	*74.5*	*203.1*	*423.2*	*522.4*	*102.2*	*150.3*
E. Reserves and Related Items	4 802 A.	**−36.5**	**−58.5**	**−74.5**	**−203.1**	**−423.2**	**−522.4**	**−102.2**	**−150.3**
Reserve assets	4 802 ..	−47.5	−61.0	−78.4	−133.7	−436.0	−535.2	−115.0	−163.0
Use of Fund credit and loans	4 766 ..	−1.7	−10.3	−8.8	−82.2	....	....	....	....
Exceptional financing	4 920 ..	12.8	12.8	12.8	12.8	12.8	12.8	12.8	12.8
Conversion rates: riels per U.S. dollar	0 101 ..	**3,973.3**	**4,016.3**	**4,092.5**	**4,103.3**	**4,056.2**	**4,054.2**	**4,139.3**	**4,184.9**

[1] Excludes components that have been classified in the categories of Group E.

Table 2. STANDARD PRESENTATION, 2003–2010

(Millions of U.S. dollars)

	Code	2003	2004	2005	2006	2007	2008	2009	2010
CURRENT ACCOUNT	4 993	−233.4	−182.9	−306.7	−262.2	−480.7	−1,050.8	−930.9	−879.2
A. GOODS	4 100	−581.3	−680.6	−1,008.0	−1,078.9	−1,343.4	−1,800.4	−1,634.2	−1,647.5
Credit	2 100	2,086.8	2,588.9	2,910.3	3,692.4	4,088.5	4,708.0	4,196.2	5,143.2
General merchandise: exports f.o.b.	2 110	2,076.7	2,575.0	2,898.6	3,677.6	4,071.9	4,687.3	4,175.3	5,125.1
Goods for processing: exports f.o.b.	2 150	....	....	....	....	....	....	....	....
Repairs on goods	2 160	....	....	....	....	....	....	....	....
Goods procured in ports by carriers	2 170	8.2	9.6	10.8	14.4	16.4	15.9	15.3	18.1
Nonmonetary gold	2 180	2.0	4.2	.8	.3	.1	4.8	5.5	....
Debit	3 100	−2,668.1	−3,269.5	−3,918.3	−4,771.2	−5,431.9	−6,508.4	−5,830.5	−6,790.7
General merchandise: imports f.o.b.	3 110	−2,645.0	−3,232.1	−3,899.7	−4,757.4	−5,421.6	−6,519.6	−5,846.0	−6,768.1
Goods for processing: imports f.o.b.	3 150	....	....	....	....	....	....	....	....
Repairs on goods	3 160	....	....	....	....	....	....	....	....
Goods procured in ports by carriers	3 170	−9.7	−12.3	−13.9	−15.9	−11.2	−17.2	−16.9	−22.6
Nonmonetary gold	3 180	−13.4	−25.0	−4.7	2.0	.8	28.3	32.4	....
B. SERVICES	4 200	114.1	290.5	475.6	492.3	632.1	609.4	606.4	655.9
Total credit	2 200	*548.0*	*804.9*	*1,118.1*	*1,296.3*	*1,547.5*	*1,645.1*	*1,624.9*	*1,743.9*
Total debit	3 200	*−433.9*	*−514.4*	*−642.5*	*−804.0*	*−915.4*	*−1,035.8*	*−1,018.4*	*−1,088.0*
Transportation services, credit	2 205	**84.3**	**104.8**	**126.9**	**166.8**	**209.7**	**238.5**	**191.5**	**226.0**
Passenger	2 850	*52.4*	*69.8*	*88.7*	*116.6*	*149.4*	*179.1*	*126.6*	*152.2*
Freight	2 851	*4.0*	*5.5*	*5.3*	*6.7*	*10.4*	*7.3*	*5.0*	*5.2*
Other	2 852	*28.0*	*29.5*	*32.9*	*43.5*	*49.8*	*52.1*	*59.9*	*68.6*
Sea transport, passenger	2 207	.3	....	....	....	.1	....	....	....
Sea transport, freight	2 208	.1	.2	.2	.2	.3	.6	1.0	.5
Sea transport, other	2 209	14.3	12.5	13.8	17.9	21.1	22.4	21.4	21.5
Air transport, passenger	2 211	52.0	69.6	88.6	116.6	149.3	179.1	126.6	152.2
Air transport, freight	2 212	3.6	5.1	5.0	6.4	7.1	5.6	3.6	4.2
Air transport, other	2 213	12.9	16.4	18.5	21.2	24.2	22.9	22.5	30.2
Other transport, passenger	2 215	....	.2	.1	....	.1	....	....	....
Other transport, freight	2 216	.2	.3	.2	.1	3.0	1.1	.3	.5
Other transport, other	2 217	.7	.6	.6	4.5	4.6	6.8	16.0	16.9
Transportation services, debit	3 205	**−241.4**	**−298.4**	**−360.3**	**−440.0**	**−511.4**	**−607.9**	**−538.4**	**−617.7**
Passenger	3 850	*−24.1*	*−32.2*	*−40.9*	*−53.8*	*−70.6*	*−82.7*	*−58.6*	*−70.3*
Freight	3 851	*−207.9*	*−253.8*	*−306.5*	*−372.0*	*−424.8*	*−506.6*	*−452.9*	*−519.6*
Other	3 852	*−9.3*	*−12.4*	*−12.9*	*−14.2*	*−16.0*	*−18.6*	*−27.0*	*−27.8*
Sea transport, passenger	3 207	−.1	....	....	....	−1.8	−.2	−.1	−.2
Sea transport, freight	3 208	−201.3	−245.9	−299.2	−362.9	−413.0	−495.1	−444.6	−508.2
Sea transport, other	3 209	....	....	....	....	−.1	−.1	−.2	−.1
Air transport, passenger	3 211	−24.0	−32.1	−40.9	−53.8	−68.8	−82.5	−58.3	−70.1
Air transport, freight	3 212	−5.7	−7.1	−6.7	−9.1	−11.2	−10.7	−7.8	−9.1
Air transport, other	3 213	−8.3	−10.6	−11.9	−13.6	−15.5	−14.7	−14.5	−19.4
Other transport, passenger	3 215	....	....	....	....	....	....	−.1	−.1
Other transport, freight	3 216	−.9	−.8	−.6	....	−.6	−.8	−.4	−2.2
Other transport, other	3 217	−1.0	−1.8	−.9	−.5	−.4	−3.8	−12.3	−8.3
Travel, credit	2 236	**389.0**	**603.5**	**839.5**	**963.2**	**1,134.8**	**1,218.8**	**1,184.6**	**1,260.0**
Business travel	2 237	50.4	46.1	64.2	80.8	96.3	109.2	92.3	98.9
Personal travel	2 240	338.6	557.4	775.3	882.4	1,038.5	1,109.6	1,092.3	1,161.1
Travel, debit	3 236	**−36.2**	**−47.6**	**−96.9**	**−122.2**	**−122.7**	**−96.8**	**−103.5**	**−197.7**
Business travel	3 237	−33.5	−43.9	−89.2	−114.3	−113.7	−87.2	−95.4	−188.7
Personal travel	3 240	−2.7	−3.8	−7.7	−7.9	−9.0	−9.6	−8.1	−9.0
Other services, credit	2 200 BA	**74.6**	**96.7**	**151.6**	**166.3**	**203.0**	**187.9**	**248.8**	**257.9**
Communications	2 245	38.7	40.7	42.7	40.3	45.8	45.4	105.9	96.1
Construction	2 249	1.2	1.9	2.0	2.5	3.4	7.6	7.2	10.5
Insurance	2 253	.3	1.1	.8	.9	3.9	.4	6.6	1.0
Financial	2 260	1.6	2.7	10.6	13.4	9.1	6.2	.1	3.6
Computer and information	2 262	....	.2	.1	....	1.6	1.0	....	.3
Royalties and licence fees	2 266	.4	....	.4	.1	.1	.5	....	.3
Other business services	2 268	24.5	31.7	39.1	54.7	100.4	92.2	94.3	71.9
Personal, cultural, and recreational	2 287	1.1	1.2	1.4	1.6	1.8	2.0	2.0	1.0
Government, n.i.e.	2 291	6.8	17.2	54.5	52.7	37.1	32.5	32.7	73.2
Other services, debit	3 200 BA	**−156.3**	**−168.4**	**−185.4**	**−241.8**	**−281.3**	**−331.0**	**−376.5**	**−272.6**
Communications	3 245	−33.1	−33.9	−32.6	−36.4	−41.0	−50.1	−101.3	−45.7
Construction	3 249	−43.6	−41.9	−38.3	−58.4	−63.4	−75.1	−79.9	−103.6
Insurance	3 253	−20.9	−25.0	−28.9	−33.0	−40.0	−44.0	−38.9	−44.3
Financial	3 260	−.2	−.9	−14.4	−12.1	−7.7	−4.2	−5.5	−21.1
Computer and information	3 262	−.5	−1.3	−.4	−.1	−1.2	−2.2	−.7	−.9
Royalties and licence fees	3 266	−6.0	−6.4	−7.3	−7.0	−10.2	−6.4	−8.4	−6.3
Other business services	3 268	−40.1	−42.4	−48.5	−46.5	−68.2	−42.6	−53.3	−41.9
Personal, cultural, and recreational	3 287	−3.2	−4.2	−4.2	−4.7	−5.4	−5.4	−5.6	−5.3
Government, n.i.e.	3 291	−8.6	−12.4	−10.9	−43.6	−44.3	−101.1	−82.9	−3.6

Table 2 (Continued). STANDARD PRESENTATION, 2003–2010

(Millions of U.S. dollars)

	Code	2003	2004	2005	2006	2007	2008	2009	2010
C. INCOME.........	4 300 ..	**−179.3**	**−221.0**	**−294.7**	**−306.1**	**−363.9**	**−474.6**	**−477.2**	**−533.1**
Total credit..........	2 300 ..	*43.7*	*48.6*	*67.7*	*90.0*	*112.2*	*108.4*	*55.6*	*55.4*
Total debit...........	3 300 ..	*−223.0*	*−269.6*	*−362.4*	*−396.1*	*−476.2*	*−583.0*	*−532.8*	*−588.5*
Compensation of employees, credit...............	2 310 ..	**3.2**	**3.4**	**3.7**	**3.7**	**4.0**	**4.5**	**4.5**	**4.5**
Compensation of employees, debit...............	3 310 ..	**−46.2**	**−44.2**	**−112.6**	**−100.2**	**−94.4**	**−146.6**	**−139.8**	**−151.0**
Investment income, credit.................	2 320 ..	**40.5**	**45.2**	**64.0**	**86.3**	**108.2**	**103.9**	**51.1**	**50.9**
Direct investment income........	2 330 ..	7.1	7.5	7.8	8.3	8.5	9.0	6.1	6.4
Dividends and distributed branch profits.........	2 332 ..	7.1	7.5	7.8	8.3	8.5	9.0	6.1	6.4
Reinvested earnings and undistributed branch profits.....	2 333 ..	....	....	....	....	....	....	....	....
Income on debt (interest)........	2 334 ..	....	....	....	....	....	....	....	....
Portfolio investment income........	2 339 ..	9.9	10.5	11.2	12.1	12.4	12.9	8.3	8.6
Income on equity........	2 340 ..	9.9	10.5	11.2	12.1	12.4	12.9	8.3	8.6
Income on bonds and notes........	2 350 ..	....	....	....	....	....	....	....	....
Income on money market instruments........	2 360 ..	....	....	....	....	....	....	....	....
Other investment income........	2 370 ..	23.5	27.1	45.0	65.9	87.4	82.0	36.7	35.9
Investment income, debit.................	3 320 ..	**−176.8**	**−225.4**	**−249.8**	**−295.9**	**−381.8**	**−436.4**	**−393.0**	**−437.6**
Direct investment income........	3 330 ..	−159.8	−205.4	−227.1	−270.2	−353.0	−403.5	−357.7	−399.1
Dividends and distributed branch profits.........	3 332 ..	−158.2	−185.4	−193.6	−225.3	−265.4	−301.7	−325.6	−366.1
Reinvested earnings and undistributed branch profits.....	3 333 ..	11.9	−6.5	−20.0	−31.4	−74.0	−88.2	−18.6	−19.5
Income on debt (interest)........	3 334 ..	−13.5	−13.5	−13.6	−13.6	−13.6	−13.6	−13.6	−13.6
Portfolio investment income........	3 339 ..	....	....	....	....	....	....	....	....
Income on equity........	3 340 ..	....	....	....	....	....	....	....	....
Income on bonds and notes........	3 350 ..	....	....	....	....	....	....	....	....
Income on money market instruments........	3 360 ..	....	....	....	....	....	....	....	....
Other investment income........	3 370 ..	−17.0	−19.9	−22.6	−25.7	−28.8	−32.9	−35.2	−38.4
D. CURRENT TRANSFERS.................	4 379 ..	**413.1**	**428.2**	**520.4**	**630.5**	**594.5**	**614.9**	**574.2**	**645.5**
Credit.................	2 379 ..	**425.3**	**443.7**	**541.1**	**655.0**	**620.3**	**642.8**	**595.5**	**666.9**
General government........	2 380 ..	216.8	209.5	291.9	376.5	310.0	404.5	418.0	478.0
Other sectors........	2 390 ..	208.5	234.2	249.2	278.5	310.3	238.3	177.5	188.9
Workers' remittances........	2 391 ..	125.0	144.0	160.0	180.0	183.6	187.3	140.5	151.0
Other current transfers........	2 392 ..	83.5	90.2	89.2	98.5	126.7	51.0	37.1	37.9
Debit.................	3 379 ..	**−12.2**	**−15.5**	**−20.7**	**−24.5**	**−25.8**	**−27.9**	**−21.3**	**−21.4**
General government........	3 380 ..	−.3	−.3	−.3	−.3	−.3	−.3	−.3	−.3
Other sectors........	3 390 ..	−11.9	−15.2	−20.4	−24.3	−25.5	−27.6	−21.1	−21.1
Workers' remittances........	3 391 ..	−10.0	−12.0	−16.0	−20.0	−24.0	−24.0	−19.2	−19.8
Other current transfers........	3 392 ..	−1.9	−3.2	−4.4	−4.3	−1.5	−3.6	−1.9	−1.3
CAPITAL AND FINANCIAL ACCOUNT.................	4 996 ..	**273.4**	**228.7**	**318.6**	**304.8**	**516.7**	**1,086.0**	**924.6**	**927.6**
CAPITAL ACCOUNT.................	4 994 ..	**66.2**	**68.1**	**82.6**	**295.0**	**258.3**	**232.7**	**311.6**	**331.0**
Total credit........	2 994 ..	*119.5*	*141.3*	*138.1*	*348.1*	*325.6*	*292.5*	*367.8*	*418.4*
Total debit........	3 994 ..	*−53.3*	*−73.2*	*−55.5*	*−53.2*	*−67.2*	*−59.8*	*−56.2*	*−87.4*
Capital transfers, credit.................	2 400 ..	**119.5**	**141.3**	**138.1**	**348.1**	**325.6**	**292.5**	**367.8**	**418.4**
General government........	2 401 ..	109.4	111.3	102.1	234.4	160.6	159.1	174.9	252.8
Debt forgiveness........	2 402 ..	....	....	....	....	....	....	....	....
Other capital transfers........	2 410 ..	109.4	111.3	102.1	234.4	160.6	159.1	174.9	252.8
Other sectors........	2 430 ..	10.1	30.0	36.0	113.7	165.0	133.5	192.9	165.6
Migrants' transfers........	2 431 ..	10.1	30.0	36.0	113.7	165.0	133.5	192.9	165.6
Debt forgiveness........	2 432 ..	....	....	....	....	....	....	....	....
Other capital transfers........	2 440 ..	....	....	....	....	....	....	....	....
Capital transfers, debit.................	3 400 ..	**−53.3**	**−73.2**	**−55.5**	**−53.2**	**−67.2**	**−59.8**	**−56.2**	**−87.4**
General government........	3 401 ..	....	....	....	....	....	....	....	....
Debt forgiveness........	3 402 ..	....	....	....	....	....	....	....	....
Other capital transfers........	3 410 ..	....	....	....	....	....	....	....	....
Other sectors........	3 430 ..	−53.3	−73.2	−55.5	−53.2	−67.2	−59.8	−56.2	−87.4
Migrants' transfers........	3 431 ..	−53.3	−73.2	−55.5	−53.2	−67.2	−59.8	−56.2	−87.4
Debt forgiveness........	3 432 ..	....	....	....	....	....	....	....	....
Other capital transfers........	3 440 ..	....	....	....	....	....	....	....	....
Nonproduced nonfinancial assets, credit.............	2 480 ..	....	....	....	....	....	....	....	....
Nonproduced nonfinancial assets, debit.............	3 480 ..	....	....	....	....	....	....	....	....

Table 2 (Continued). STANDARD PRESENTATION, 2003–2010

(Millions of U.S. dollars)

	Code	2003	2004	2005	2006	2007	2008	2009	2010
FINANCIAL ACCOUNT...........................	4 995 ..	**207.3**	**160.6**	**236.1**	**9.8**	**258.4**	**853.3**	**613.0**	**596.7**
A. DIRECT INVESTMENT........................	4 500 ..	**74.3**	**121.2**	**374.9**	**474.8**	**866.2**	**794.7**	**520.3**	**762.0**
Direct investment abroad.................	4 505 ..	**−9.7**	**−10.2**	**−6.3**	**−8.4**	**−1.1**	**−20.5**	**−18.8**	**−20.6**
Equity capital..	4 510 ..	−9.7	−10.2	−6.3	−8.4	−1.1	−20.5	−18.8	−20.6
Claims on affiliated enterprises..........	4 515 ..	−9.7	−10.2	−6.3	−8.4	−1.1	−20.5	−18.8	−20.6
Liabilities to affiliated enterprises......	4 520 ..	....	....	....	....	....	....	....	....
Reinvested earnings..............................	4 525 ..	....	....	....	....	....	....	....	....
Other capital..	4 530 ..	....	....	....	....	....	....	....	....
Claims on affiliated enterprises..........	4 535 ..	....	....	....	....	....	....	....	....
Liabilities to affiliated enterprises......	4 540 ..	....	....	....	....	....	....	....	....
Direct investment in Cambodia.........	4 555 ..	**84.0**	**131.4**	**381.2**	**483.2**	**867.3**	**815.2**	**539.1**	**782.6**
Equity capital..	4 560 ..	93.5	124.9	359.2	451.9	793.3	726.9	520.5	763.1
Claims on direct investors....................	4 565 ..	....	....	....	....	....	....	....	....
Liabilities to direct investors..............	4 570 ..	93.5	124.9	359.2	451.9	793.3	726.9	520.5	763.1
Reinvested earnings..............................	4 575 ..	−11.9	6.5	20.0	31.4	74.0	88.2	18.6	19.5
Other capital..	4 580 ..	2.4	....	2.0	....	....	....	....	....
Claims on direct investors....................	4 585 ..	2.4	....	2.0	....	....	....	....	....
Liabilities to direct investors..............	4 590 ..	....	....	....	....	....	....	....	....
B. PORTFOLIO INVESTMENT.................	4 600 ..	**−7.7**	**−8.0**	**−7.2**	**−8.2**	**−6.3**	**−11.6**	**−7.6**	**−36.7**
Assets...	4 602 ..	**−7.7**	**−8.0**	**−7.2**	**−8.2**	**−6.3**	**−11.6**	**−7.6**	**−36.7**
Equity securities....................................	4 610 ..	−7.7	−8.0	−7.2	−8.2	−6.5	−11.6	−7.6	−9.4
Monetary authorities............................	4 611 ..	....	....	....	....	....	....	....	....
General government..............................	4 612 ..	....	....	....	....	....	....	....	....
Banks..	4 613 ..	....	....	....	....	....	....	....	....
Other sectors..	4 614 ..	−7.7	−8.0	−7.2	−8.2	−6.5	−11.6	−7.6	−9.4
Debt securities.......................................	4 619 ..	....	....	....	....	.1	....	....	−27.2
Bonds and notes....................................	4 620 ..	....	....	....	....	.1	....	....	−27.2
Monetary authorities............................	4 621 ..	....	....	....	....	....	....	....	....
General government..............................	4 622 ..	....	....	....	....	....	....	....	....
Banks..	4 623 ..	....	....	....	....	.1	....	....	−27.2
Other sectors..	4 624 ..	....	....	....	....	....	....	....	....
Money market instruments..................	4 630 ..	....	....	....	....	....	....	....	....
Monetary authorities............................	4 631 ..	....	....	....	....	....	....	....	....
General government..............................	4 632 ..	....	....	....	....	....	....	....	....
Banks..	4 633 ..	....	....	....	....	....	....	....	....
Other sectors..	4 634 ..	....	....	....	....	....	....	....	....
Liabilities.......................................	4 652 ..	....	....	....	....	....	....	....	....
Equity securities....................................	4 660 ..	....	....	....	....	....	....	....	....
Banks..	4 663 ..	....	....	....	....	....	....	....	....
Other sectors..	4 664 ..	....	....	....	....	....	....	....	....
Debt securities.......................................	4 669 ..	....	....	....	....	....	....	....	....
Bonds and notes....................................	4 670 ..	....	....	....	....	....	....	....	....
Monetary authorities............................	4 671 ..	....	....	....	....	....	....	....	....
General government..............................	4 672 ..	....	....	....	....	....	....	....	....
Banks..	4 673 ..	....	....	....	....	....	....	....	....
Other sectors..	4 674 ..	....	....	....	....	....	....	....	....
Money market instruments..................	4 680 ..	....	....	....	....	....	....	....	....
Monetary authorities............................	4 681 ..	....	....	....	....	....	....	....	....
General government..............................	4 682 ..	....	....	....	....	....	....	....	....
Banks..	4 683 ..	....	....	....	....	....	....	....	....
Other sectors..	4 684 ..	....	....	....	....	....	....	....	....
C. FINANCIAL DERIVATIVES.................	4 910 ..	....	....	....	....	....	....	....	....
Monetary authorities............................	4 911 ..	....	....	....	....	....	....	....	....
General government..............................	4 912 ..	....	....	....	....	....	....	....	....
Banks..	4 913 ..	....	....	....	....	....	....	....	....
Other sectors..	4 914 ..	....	....	....	....	....	....	....	....
Assets...	4 900 ..	....	....	....	....	....	....	....	....
Monetary authorities............................	4 901 ..	....	....	....	....	....	....	....	....
General government..............................	4 902 ..	....	....	....	....	....	....	....	....
Banks..	4 903 ..	....	....	....	....	....	....	....	....
Other sectors..	4 904 ..	....	....	....	....	....	....	....	....
Liabilities.......................................	4 905 ..	....	....	....	....	....	....	....	....
Monetary authorities............................	4 906 ..	....	....	....	....	....	....	....	....
General government..............................	4 907 ..	....	....	....	....	....	....	....	....
Banks..	4 908 ..	....	....	....	....	....	....	....	....
Other sectors..	4 909 ..	....	....	....	....	....	....	....	....

Table 2 (Concluded). STANDARD PRESENTATION, 2003–2010

(Millions of U.S. dollars)

	Code	2003	2004	2005	2006	2007	2008	2009	2010
D. OTHER INVESTMENT	4 700 ..	**188.1**	**108.4**	**−53.2**	**−323.2**	**−165.5**	**605.4**	**215.3**	**34.4**
Assets	4 703 ..	**−127.0**	**−91.3**	**−327.2**	**−539.6**	**−780.6**	**−97.6**	**−358.8**	**−643.2**
Trade credits	4 706 ..	−95.1	−47.0	−145.2	−168.9	−190.4	−.2	10.0	−367.0
General government	4 707 ..	....	....	....	....	....	....	....	....
of which: Short-term	4 709 ..	....	....	....	....	....	....	....	....
Other sectors	4 710 ..	−95.1	−47.0	−145.2	−168.9	−190.4	−.2	10.0	−367.0
of which: Short-term	4 712 ..	*−95.1*	*−47.0*	*−145.2*	*−168.9*	*−190.4*	*−.2*	*10.0*	*−367.0*
Loans	4 714 ..	....	....	....	....	....	....	....	....
Monetary authorities	4 715 ..	....	....	....	....	....	....	....	....
of which: Short-term	4 718 ..	....	....	....	....	....	....	....	....
General government	4 719 ..	....	....	....	....	....	....	....	....
of which: Short-term	4 721 ..	....	....	....	....	....	....	....	....
Banks	4 722 ..	....	....	....	....	....	....	....	....
of which: Short-term	4 724 ..	....	....	....	....	....	....	....	....
Other sectors	4 725 ..	....	....	....	....	....	....	....	....
of which: Short-term	4 727 ..	....	....	....	....	....	....	....	....
Currency and deposits	4 730 ..	−25.0	−35.6	−177.4	−362.2	−582.4	−90.3	−364.4	−247.3
Monetary authorities	4 731 ..	6.3	−66.9	68.6	−70.8	−213.6	50.6	−444.1	−242.8
General government	4 732 ..	....	....	....	....	....	....	....	....
Banks	4 733 ..	−78.0	−32.1	−96.9	−139.9	−353.7	310.2	−155.6	−141.8
Other sectors	4 734 ..	46.7	63.3	−149.1	−151.5	−15.1	−451.0	235.3	137.4
Other assets	4 736 ..	−6.9	−8.8	−4.6	−8.5	−7.8	−7.1	−4.4	−28.9
Monetary authorities	4 737 ..	....	....	....	....	....	....	....	....
of which: Short-term	4 739 ..	....	....	....	....	....	....	....	....
General government	4 740 ..	....	....	....	....	....	....	....	....
of which: Short-term	4 742 ..	....	....	....	....	....	....	....	....
Banks	4 743 ..	−.4	−2.1	2.2	.3	....	....	....	−23.8
of which: Short-term	4 745 ..	*−.4*	*−2.1*	*2.2*	*.3*	....	....	....	*−23.8*
Other sectors	4 746 ..	−6.5	−6.7	−6.9	−8.7	−7.8	−7.1	−4.4	−5.1
of which: Short-term	4 748 ..	*−6.5*	*−6.7*	*−6.9*	*−8.7*	*−7.8*	*−7.1*	*−4.4*	*−5.1*
Liabilities	4 753 ..	**315.2**	**199.8**	**274.0**	**216.4**	**615.1**	**703.0**	**574.1**	**677.6**
Trade credits	4 756 ..	117.2	43.0	107.8	96.8	192.0	119.1	583.4	316.1
General government	4 757 ..	....	....	....	....	....	....	....	....
of which: Short-term	4 759 ..	....	....	....	....	....	....	....	....
Other sectors	4 760 ..	117.2	43.0	107.8	96.8	192.0	119.1	583.4	316.1
of which: Short-term	4 762 ..	*117.2*	*43.0*	*107.8*	*96.8*	*192.0*	*119.1*	*583.4*	*316.1*
Loans	4 764 ..	163.0	175.7	149.5	88.4	212.3	652.4	−192.9	198.4
Monetary authorities	4 765 ..	−1.7	−10.3	−8.8	−82.2	....	....	....	....
of which: Use of Fund credit and loans from the Fund..	4 766 ..	*−1.7*	*−10.3*	*−8.8*	*−82.2*	....	....	....	....
of which: Short-term	4 768 ..	....	....	....	....	....	....	....	....
General government	4 769 ..	148.6	154.4	144.0	122.1	199.6	234.7	153.1	244.9
of which: Short-term	4 771 ..	....	....	....	....	....	....	....	....
Banks	4 772 ..	12.1	28.6	4.3	5.5	−14.3	415.0	−348.0	−46.5
of which: Short-term	4 774 ..	....	....	....	....	....	....	....	....
Other sectors	4 775 ..	4.0	3.0	10.0	43.0	27.0	2.7	2.0	....
of which: Short-term	4 777 ..	....	....	....	....	....	....	....	....
Currency and deposits	4 780 ..	22.2	−31.8	4.0	18.4	198.0	−81.2	63.9	150.3
Monetary authorities	4 781 ..	....	....	....	....	....	....	....	....
General government	4 782 ..	....	....	....	....	....	....	....	....
Banks	4 783 ..	22.2	−31.8	4.0	18.4	198.0	−81.2	63.9	150.3
Other sectors	4 784 ..	....	....	....	....	....	....	....	....
Other liabilities	4 786 ..	12.8	12.8	12.8	12.8	12.8	12.8	119.7	12.8
Monetary authorities	4 787 ..	....	....	....	....	....	....	106.9	....
of which: Short-term	4 789 ..	....	....	....	....	....	....	....	....
General government	4 790 ..	12.8	12.8	12.8	12.8	12.8	12.8	12.8	12.8
of which: Short-term	4 792 ..	*12.8*	*12.8*	*12.8*	*12.8*	*12.8*	*12.8*	*12.8*	*12.8*
Banks	4 793 ..	....	....	....	....	....	....	....	....
of which: Short-term	4 795 ..	....	....	....	....	....	....	....	....
Other sectors	4 796 ..	....	....	....	....	....	....	....	....
of which: Short-term	4 798 ..	....	....	....	....	....	....	....	....
E. RESERVE ASSETS	4 802 ..	**−47.5**	**−61.0**	**−78.4**	**−133.7**	**−436.0**	**−535.2**	**−115.0**	**−163.0**
Monetary gold	4 812 ..	....	....	....	....	....	....	....	....
Special drawing rights	4 811 ..	.5	.1	−.2	.1	....	.1	−106.8	.1
Reserve position in the Fund	4 810 ..	....	....	....	....	....	....	....	....
Foreign exchange	4 803 ..	−48.0	−61.1	−78.2	−133.7	−436.0	−535.3	−8.2	−163.1
Other claims	4 813 ..	....	....	....	....	....	....	....	....
NET ERRORS AND OMISSIONS	4 998 ..	**−40.0**	**−45.8**	**−11.9**	**−42.6**	**−36.0**	**−35.3**	**6.3**	**−48.4**

Table 3. INTERNATIONAL INVESTMENT POSITION (End-period stocks), 2003–2010

(Millions of U.S. dollars)

	Code	2003	2004	2005	2006	2007	2008	2009	2010
ASSETS	8 995 C.	**3,348.0**	**3,558.4**	**4,033.4**	**4,588.0**	**5,761.4**	**6,448.7**	**7,045.0**	**8,014.2**
Direct investment abroad	8 505 ..	**241.5**	**255.6**	**267.0**	**279.0**	**283.8**	**308.0**	**325.6**	**349.9**
Equity capital and reinvested earnings	8 506 ..	241.5	255.6	267.0	279.0	283.8	308.0	325.6	349.9
Claims on affiliated enterprises	8 507 ..	241.5	255.6	267.0	279.0	283.8	308.0	325.6	349.9
Liabilities to affiliated enterprises	8 508 ..	....	....	....	....	....	....	....	....
Other capital	8 530 ..	....	....	....	....	....	....	....	....
Claims on affiliated enterprises	8 535 ..	....	....	....	....	....	....	....	....
Liabilities to affiliated enterprises	8 540 ..	....	....	....	....	....	....	....	....
Portfolio investment	8 602 ..	**253.8**	**270.3**	**286.4**	**312.8**	**332.3**	**345.6**	**355.2**	**395.5**
Equity securities	8 610 ..	228.5	243.3	257.8	281.6	299.1	311.1	319.7	331.4
Monetary authorities	8 611 ..	....	....	....	....	....	....	....	....
General government	8 612 ..	....	....	....	....	....	....	....	....
Banks	8 613 ..	....	....	....	....	....	....	....	....
Other sectors	8 614 ..	228.5	243.3	257.8	281.6	299.1	311.1	319.7	331.4
Debt securities	8 619 ..	25.4	27.0	28.6	31.3	33.2	34.6	35.5	64.1
Bonds and notes	8 620 ..	25.4	27.0	28.6	31.3	33.2	34.6	35.5	64.1
Monetary authorities	8 621 ..	....	....	....	....	....	....	....	....
General government	8 622 ..	....	....	....	....	....	....	....	....
Banks	8 623 ..	....	....	....	....	....	....	....	....
Other sectors	8 624 ..	25.4	27.0	28.6	31.3	33.2	34.6	35.5	64.1
Money market instruments	8 630 ..	....	....	....	....	....	....	....	....
Monetary authorities	8 631 ..	....	....	....	....	....	....	....	....
General government	8 632 ..	....	....	....	....	....	....	....	....
Banks	8 633 ..	....	....	....	....	....	....	....	....
Other sectors	8 634 ..	....	....	....	....	....	....	....	....
Financial derivatives	8 900 ..	....	....	....	....	....	....	....	....
Monetary authorities	8 901 ..	....	....	....	....	....	....	....	....
General government	8 902 ..	....	....	....	....	....	....	....	....
Banks	8 903 ..	....	....	....	....	....	....	....	....
Other sectors	8 904 ..	....	....	....	....	....	....	....	....
Other investment	8 703 ..	**1,989.4**	**2,096.8**	**2,438.2**	**2,905.5**	**3,529.7**	**3,631.6**	**3,997.0**	**4,654.1**
Trade credits	8 706 ..	623.1	670.1	815.3	983.8	1,039.5	1,039.7	1,029.7	1,396.7
General government	8 707 ..	....	....	....	....	....	....	....	....
of which: Short-term	8 709 ..	....	....	....	....	....	....	....	....
Other sectors	8 710 ..	623.1	670.1	815.3	983.8	1,039.5	1,039.7	1,029.7	1,396.7
of which: Short-term	8 712 ..	*623.1*	*670.1*	*815.3*	*983.8*	*1,039.5*	*1,039.7*	*1,029.7*	*1,396.7*
Loans	8 714 ..	....	....	....	....	....	....	....	....
Monetary authorities	8 715 ..	....	....	....	....	....	....	....	....
of which: Short-term	8 718 ..	....	....	....	....	....	....	....	....
General government	8 719 ..	....	....	....	....	....	....	....	....
of which: Short-term	8 721 ..	....	....	....	....	....	....	....	....
Banks	8 722 ..	....	....	....	....	....	....	....	....
of which: Short-term	8 724 ..	....	....	....	....	....	....	....	....
Other sectors	8 725 ..	....	....	....	....	....	....	....	....
of which: Short-term	8 727 ..	....	....	....	....	....	....	....	....
Currency and deposits	8 730 ..	1,213.5	1,262.0	1,450.7	1,734.0	2,290.7	2,384.5	2,754.2	3,012.6
Monetary authorities	8 731 ..	244.8	311.7	243.1	313.9	570.7	520.1	964.3	1,207.1
General government	8 732 ..	....	....	....	....	....	....	....	....
Banks	8 733 ..	427.5	459.5	556.4	696.3	853.7	543.5	699.1	841.0
Other sectors	8 734 ..	541.3	490.8	651.2	723.7	866.4	1,320.8	1,090.8	964.5
Other assets	8 736 ..	152.7	164.7	172.1	187.7	199.4	207.4	213.1	244.8
Monetary authorities	8 737 ..	....	....	....	....	....	....	....	....
of which: Short-term	8 739 ..	....	....	....	....	....	....	....	....
General government	8 740 ..	....	....	....	....	....	....	....	....
of which: Short-term	8 742 ..	....	....	....	....	....	....	....	....
Banks	8 743 ..	.4	2.5	.3	....	....	....	....	23.8
of which: Short-term	8 745 ..	*.4*	*2.5*	*.3*	....	....	....	....	*23.8*
Other sectors	8 746 ..	152.3	162.2	171.9	187.7	199.4	207.4	213.1	220.9
of which: Short-term	8 748 ..	*152.3*	*162.2*	*171.9*	*187.7*	*199.4*	*207.4*	*213.1*	*220.9*
Reserve assets	8 802 ..	**863.2**	**935.7**	**1,041.7**	**1,090.7**	**1,615.6**	**2,163.5**	**2,367.3**	**2,614.7**
Monetary gold	8 812 ..	166.4	177.9	205.6	253.4	336.3	349.0	437.3	523.6
Special drawing rights	8 811 ..	.2	.1	.2	.2	.2	.1	107.4	105.4
Reserve position in the Fund	8 810 ..	....	....	....	....	....	....	....	....
Foreign exchange	8 803 ..	696.6	757.7	835.9	837.1	1,279.1	1,814.4	1,822.6	1,985.7
Other claims	8 813 ..	....	....	....	....	....	....	....	....

Table 3 (Concluded). INTERNATIONAL INVESTMENT POSITION (End-period stocks), 2003–2010

(Millions of U.S. dollars)

	Code	2003	2004	2005	2006	2007	2008	2009	2010
LIABILITIES..	8 995 D.	**4,122.6**	**4,457.8**	**5,105.6**	**5,706.2**	**7,456.8**	**8,753.7**	**9,278.0**	**10,735.8**
Direct investment in Cambodia..........................	8 555 ..	**1,958.4**	**2,089.8**	**2,471.0**	**2,954.2**	**3,821.5**	**4,636.7**	**5,175.8**	**5,958.4**
Equity capital and reinvested earnings................	8 556 ..	1,282.7	1,414.1	1,793.3	2,276.5	3,143.8	3,959.0	4,498.1	5,280.7
Claims on direct investors...........................	8 557 ..	....	....	....	....	....	....	....	....
Liabilities to direct investors........................	8 558 ..	1,282.7	1,414.1	1,793.3	2,276.5	3,143.8	3,959.0	4,498.1	5,280.7
Other capital...	8 580 ..	675.7	675.7	677.7	677.7	677.7	677.7	677.7	677.7
Claims on direct investors...........................	8 585 ..	....	....	....	....	....	....	....	....
Liabilities to direct investors........................	8 590 ..	675.7	675.7	677.7	677.7	677.7	677.7	677.7	677.7
Portfolio investment...............................	8 652 ..	....	....	....	....	....	....	....	....
Equity securities..	8 660 ..	....	....	....	....	....	....	....	....
Banks..	8 663 ..	....	....	....	....	....	....	....	....
Other sectors...	8 664 ..	....	....	....	....	....	....	....	....
Debt securities..	8 669 ..	....	....	....	....	....	....	....	....
Bonds and notes.....................................	8 670 ..	....	....	....	....	....	....	....	....
Monetary authorities.............................	8 671 ..	....	....	....	....	....	....	....	....
General government.............................	8 672 ..	....	....	....	....	....	....	....	....
Banks..	8 673 ..	....	....	....	....	....	....	....	....
Other sectors.....................................	8 674 ..	....	....	....	....	....	....	....	....
Money market instruments........................	8 680 ..	....	....	....	....	....	....	....	....
Monetary authorities.............................	8 681 ..	....	....	....	....	....	....	....	....
General government.............................	8 682 ..	....	....	....	....	....	....	....	....
Banks..	8 683 ..	....	....	....	....	....	....	....	....
Other sectors.....................................	8 684 ..	....	....	....	....	....	....	....	....
Financial derivatives..............................	8 905 ..	....	....	....	....	....	....	....	....
Monetary authorities...................................	8 906 ..	....	....	....	....	....	....	....	....
General government.....................................	8 907 ..	....	....	....	....	....	....	....	....
Banks..	8 908 ..	....	....	....	....	....	....	....	....
Other sectors..	8 909 ..	....	....	....	....	....	....	....	....
Other investment...................................	8 753 ..	**2,164.2**	**2,368.0**	**2,634.6**	**2,752.0**	**3,635.3**	**4,117.0**	**4,102.2**	**4,777.4**
Trade credits...	8 756 ..	809.6	852.7	960.4	957.2	1,417.5	1,315.4	1,285.2	1,601.3
General government...................................	8 757 ..	....	....	....	....	....	....	....	....
of which: Short-term...............................	8 759 ..	....	....	....	....	....	....	....	....
Other sectors..	8 760 ..	809.6	852.7	960.4	957.2	1,417.5	1,315.4	1,285.2	1,601.3
of which: Short-term...............................	8 762 ..	*809.6*	*852.7*	*960.4*	*957.2*	*1,417.5*	*1,315.4*	*1,285.2*	*1,601.3*
Loans...	8 764 ..	1,029.0	1,208.8	1,350.9	1,440.3	1,652.6	2,305.0	2,112.1	2,310.5
Monetary authorities................................	8 765 ..	103.6	97.4	81.2	....	....	....	....	....
of which: Use of Fund credit and loans from the Fund....	8 766 ..	*103.6*	*97.4*	*81.2*	....	....	....	....	....
of which: Short-term.............................	8 768 ..	....	....	....	....	....	....	....	....
General government.................................	8 769 ..	885.9	1,040.3	1,184.3	1,306.4	1,511.0	1,745.7	1,898.8	2,143.7
of which: Short-term.............................	8 771 ..	....	....	....	....	....	....	....	....
Banks..	8 772 ..	18.5	47.1	51.4	56.9	42.6	457.6	109.7	63.2
of which: Short-term.............................	8 774 ..	....	....	....	....	....	....	....	....
Other sectors...	8 775 ..	21.0	24.0	34.0	77.0	99.0	101.7	103.7	103.7
of which: Short-term.............................	8 777 ..	....	....	....	....	....	....	....	....
Currency and deposits..................................	8 780 ..	57.4	25.6	29.6	48.0	246.1	164.8	228.7	379.0
Monetary authorities................................	8 781 ..	....	....	....	....	....	....	....	....
General government.................................	8 782 ..	....	....	....	....	....	....	....	....
Banks..	8 783 ..	57.4	25.6	29.6	48.0	246.1	164.8	228.7	379.0
Other sectors...	8 784 ..	....	....	....	....	....	....	....	....
Other liabilities..	8 786 ..	268.1	280.9	293.7	306.4	319.1	331.8	476.2	486.6
Monetary authorities................................	8 787 ..	....	....	....	....	....	....	131.6	129.2
of which: Short-term.............................	8 789 ..	....	....	....	....	....	....	....	....
General government.................................	8 790 ..	268.1	280.9	293.7	306.4	319.1	331.8	344.6	357.4
of which: Short-term.............................	8 792 ..	*268.1*	*280.9*	*293.7*	*306.4*	*319.1*	*331.8*	*344.6*	*357.4*
Banks..	8 793 ..	....	....	....	....	....	....	....	....
of which: Short-term.............................	8 795 ..	....	....	....	....	....	....	....	....
Other sectors...	8 796 ..	....	....	....	....	....	....	....	....
of which: Short-term.............................	8 798 ..	....	....	....	....	....	....	....	....
NET INTERNATIONAL INVESTMENT POSITION........	8 995 ..	**−774.6**	**−899.4**	**−1,072.2**	**−1,118.1**	**−1,695.4**	**−2,305.0**	**−2,233.0**	**−2,721.7**
Conversion rates: riels per U.S. dollar (end of period)..	0 102 ..	**3,984.0**	**4,027.0**	**4,112.0**	**4,057.0**	**3,999.0**	**4,077.0**	**4,165.0**	**4,051.0**

Table 1. ANALYTIC PRESENTATION, 2003–2010

(Millions of U.S. dollars)

	Code	2003	2004	2005	2006	2007	2008	2009	2010
A. Current Account[1]	4 993 Z.	**−596.5**	**−415.4**	**−493.5**	**193.3**	**285.7**	**−449.7**	**−1,118.7**	**−856.3**
Goods: exports f.o.b.	2 100 ..	2,483.4	2,708.3	3,265.2	3,848.6	4,956.0	5,890.0	4,169.9	4,485.2
Goods: imports f.o.b.	3 100 ..	−2,214.1	−2,473.7	−2,889.8	−3,178.5	−4,221.3	−5,424.0	−4,559.0	−4,662.6
Balance on Goods	4 100 ..	*269.3*	*234.7*	*375.4*	*670.1*	*734.8*	*466.0*	*−389.2*	*−177.4*
Services: credit	2 200 ..	644.6	1,108.7	969.9	1,016.5	1,370.0	1,483.7	1,248.9	1,159.3
Services: debit	3 200 ..	−1,222.5	−1,491.0	−1,454.8	−1,474.9	−1,764.3	−2,668.3	−1,779.9	−1,745.6
Balance on Goods and Services	4 991 ..	*−308.6*	*−147.7*	*−109.5*	*211.7*	*340.4*	*−718.6*	*−920.2*	*−763.7*
Income: credit	2 300 ..	108.5	105.1	44.9	46.3	66.9	65.8	131.4	93.1
Income: debit	3 300 ..	−518.2	−548.5	−665.3	−377.5	−566.0	−394.5	−608.5	−331.7
Balance on Goods, Services, and Income	4 992 ..	*−718.3*	*−591.2*	*−729.9*	*−119.5*	*−158.7*	*−1,047.3*	*−1,397.2*	*−1,002.3*
Current transfers: credit	2 379 Z.	205.0	225.1	331.7	526.8	619.8	774.6	532.0	334.3
Current transfers: debit	3 379 ..	−83.2	−49.4	−95.3	−214.0	−175.4	−177.0	−253.5	−188.3
B. Capital Account[1]	4 994 Z.	**111.8**	**42.3**	**203.8**	**1,585.5**	**197.2**	**146.5**	**184.1**	**147.0**
Capital account: credit	2 994 Z.	123.0	42.8	204.1	1,586.0	197.7	152.4	192.2	148.3
Capital account: debit	3 994 ..	−11.1	−.5	−.3	−.5	−.5	−6.0	−8.0	−1.3
Total, Groups A Plus B	4 981 ..	*−484.7*	*−373.1*	*−289.7*	*1,778.9*	*482.9*	*−303.3*	*−934.6*	*−709.3*
C. Financial Account[1]	4 995 W.	**129.8**	**−115.2**	**−77.6**	**−332.2**	**156.6**	**365.2**	**1,004.7**	**527.4**
Direct investment abroad	4 505 ..	−8.5	−9.5	23.2	48.0	6.0	47.3	140.8	35.8
Direct investment in Cameroon	4 555 Z.	336.3	86.1	234.0	16.4	191.0	−24.2	668.3	−.6
Portfolio investment assets	4 602 ..	−2.4	38.9	−9.8	−.8	−3.4	−39.3	−97.2	−10.8
Equity securities	4 610 ..	−1.6	−.1	−10.2	−.8	−2.8	5.1	6.5	−4.4
Debt securities	4 619 ..	−.8	38.9	.4	....	−.7	−44.4	−103.7	−6.4
Portfolio investment liabilities	4 652 Z.	.2	−8.2	−3.1	−3.8	−14.5	−1.4	−.7	85.2
Equity securities	4 660 ..	.2	−8.2	−4.2	−5.6	−14.5	−1.2	−.3	....
Debt securities	4 669 Z.	....	.1	1.1	1.8	....	−.2	−.5	85.1
Financial derivatives	4 910 ..	....	....	....	....	....	....	....	....
Financial derivatives assets	4 900 ..	....	....	....	....	....	....	....	....
Financial derivatives liabilities	4 905 ..	....	....	....	....	....	....	....	....
Other investment assets	4 703 ..	79.9	72.1	67.0	−319.5	−2.1	−66.4	−100.9	550.6
Monetary authorities	4 701 ..	....	....	....	....	....	....	....	....
General government	4 704 ..	....	....	1.3	−9.5	−4.1	....	....	....
Banks	4 705 ..	−15.7	−44.9	−76.1	−81.9	−136.3	−143.4	−51.6	59.9
Other sectors	4 728 ..	95.6	117.0	141.8	−228.2	138.2	77.0	−49.3	490.7
Other investment liabilities	4 753 W.	−275.7	−294.6	−388.9	−72.6	−20.4	449.2	394.4	−132.8
Monetary authorities	4 753 WA	−4.1	−2.4	3.7	−3.3	−10.9	2.0	277.2	21.1
General government	4 753 ZB	9.6	−481.6	−465.4	−483.3	−141.0	−178.2	−143.8	−120.7
Banks	4 753 ZC	−4.8	26.2	78.5	−31.0	54.4	−53.1	37.3	24.3
Other sectors	4 753 ZD	−276.4	163.2	−5.8	445.0	77.1	678.5	223.6	−57.4
Total, Groups A Through C	4 983 ..	*−354.9*	*−488.3*	*−367.3*	*1,446.6*	*639.4*	*61.9*	*70.1*	*−181.9*
D. Net Errors and Omissions	4 998 ..	**84.4**	**54.0**	**−29.4**	**170.0**	**179.9**	**205.1**	**159.7**	**188.8**
Total, Groups A Through D	4 984 ..	*−270.5*	*−434.3*	*−396.7*	*1,616.6*	*819.4*	*267.0*	*229.8*	*6.8*
E. Reserves and Related Items	4 802 A.	**270.5**	**434.3**	**396.7**	**−1,616.6**	**−819.4**	**−267.0**	**−229.8**	**−6.8**
Reserve assets	4 802 ..	105.9	−127.2	−243.4	−627.0	−919.3	−354.8	−472.4	−226.1
Use of Fund credit and loans	4 766 ..	12.0	−27.9	−36.2	−268.3	8.0	8.5	148.2	....
Exceptional financing	4 920 ..	152.6	589.3	676.3	−721.2	92.0	79.3	94.5	219.3
Conversion rates: CFA francs per U.S. dollar	0 101 ..	**581.2**	**528.3**	**527.5**	**522.9**	**479.3**	**447.8**	**472.2**	**495.3**

[1] Excludes components that have been classified in the categories of Group E.

Table 2. STANDARD PRESENTATION, 2003–2010

(Millions of U.S. dollars)

	Code	2003	2004	2005	2006	2007	2008	2009	2010
CURRENT ACCOUNT	4 993 ..	**−596.5**	**−415.4**	**−493.5**	**193.3**	**285.7**	**−449.7**	**−1,118.7**	**−856.3**
A. GOODS	4 100 ..	**269.3**	**234.7**	**375.4**	**670.1**	**734.8**	**466.0**	**−389.2**	**−177.4**
Credit	2 100 ..	**2,483.4**	**2,708.3**	**3,265.2**	**3,848.6**	**4,956.0**	**5,890.0**	**4,169.9**	**4,485.2**
General merchandise: exports f.o.b.	2 110 ..	2,473.0	2,690.5	3,222.4	3,807.4	4,891.6	5,808.2	4,042.4	4,292.3
Goods for processing: exports f.o.b.	2 150 ..	....	....	....	....	....	48.4	105.6	171.9
Repairs on goods	2 160 ..	....	.2	....	....	....	....	....	....
Goods procured in ports by carriers	2 170 ..	10.4	17.7	42.9	41.3	64.4	33.4	21.9	20.9
Nonmonetary gold	2 180 ..	....	....	....	....	....	....	....	....
Debit	3 100 ..	**−2,214.1**	**−2,473.7**	**−2,889.8**	**−3,178.5**	**−4,221.3**	**−5,424.0**	**−4,559.0**	**−4,662.6**
General merchandise: imports f.o.b.	3 110 ..	−2,205.7	−2,459.7	−2,869.1	−3,159.4	−4,215.1	−5,356.1	−4,270.5	−4,624.5
Goods for processing: imports f.o.b.	3 150 ..	....	....	....	....	....	−66.1	−287.0	−36.7
Repairs on goods	3 160 ..	....	−1.1	−6.3	−10.3	....	....	....	....
Goods procured in ports by carriers	3 170 ..	−8.4	−12.9	−14.4	−8.8	−6.2	−1.7	−1.5	−1.4
Nonmonetary gold	3 180 ..	....	....	....	....	....	....	....	....
B. SERVICES	4 200 ..	**−577.9**	**−382.4**	**−484.9**	**−458.4**	**−394.3**	**−1,184.6**	**−531.0**	**−586.2**
Total credit	2 200 ..	*644.6*	*1,108.7*	*969.9*	*1,016.5*	*1,370.0*	*1,483.7*	*1,248.9*	*1,159.3*
Total debit	3 200 ..	*−1,222.5*	*−1,491.0*	*−1,454.8*	*−1,474.9*	*−1,764.3*	*−2,668.3*	*−1,779.9*	*−1,745.6*
Transportation services, credit	2 205 ..	**235.2**	**335.2**	**424.9**	**502.6**	**618.5**	**553.2**	**490.6**	**478.2**
Passenger	2 850 ..	*84.0*	*53.5*	*53.6*	*50.4*	*27.7*	*10.7*	*1.0*	*11.8*
Freight	2 851 ..	*124.0*	*222.8*	*304.3*	*372.0*	*490.1*	*494.1*	*449.3*	*427.9*
Other	2 852 ..	*27.2*	*58.9*	*67.0*	*80.2*	*100.8*	*48.3*	*40.3*	*38.5*
Sea transport, passenger	2 207 ..	....	....	....	....	....	....	....	....
Sea transport, freight	2 208 ..	84.7	42.2	5.3	11.1	59.7	32.2	36.8	37.6
Sea transport, other	2 209 ..	8.7	24.7	28.2	19.7	33.1	29.6	9.8	13.8
Air transport, passenger	2 211 ..	84.0	53.5	53.6	50.4	27.7	10.7	1.0	11.8
Air transport, freight	2 212 ..	10.2	6.8	9.6	10.3	9.8	11.9	.4	1.0
Air transport, other	2 213 ..	14.1	30.5	11.4	36.6	46.0	15.6	29.4	22.9
Other transport, passenger	2 215 ..	....	....	....	....	....	....	....	....
Other transport, freight	2 216 ..	29.2	173.8	289.4	350.7	420.6	450.0	412.2	389.3
Other transport, other	2 217 ..	4.4	3.7	27.4	23.8	21.7	3.2	1.1	1.8
Transportation services, debit	3 205 ..	**−353.1**	**−383.5**	**−467.4**	**−452.9**	**−657.1**	**−804.3**	**−555.6**	**−616.7**
Passenger	3 850 ..	*−101.4*	*−71.4*	*−124.6*	*−109.2*	*−98.1*	*−152.7*	*−86.7*	*−79.4*
Freight	3 851 ..	*−236.0*	*−297.0*	*−314.4*	*−309.6*	*−531.2*	*−643.2*	*−463.8*	*−532.0*
Other	3 852 ..	*−15.8*	*−15.1*	*−28.4*	*−34.1*	*−27.8*	*−8.4*	*−5.1*	*−5.2*
Sea transport, passenger	3 207 ..	....	....	....	....	....	....	....	....
Sea transport, freight	3 208 ..	−224.6	−284.8	−301.4	−272.8	−461.9	−596.5	−441.2	−510.1
Sea transport, other	3 209 ..	−3.4	−3.3	−3.0	−7.4	−8.1	−3.1	−1.0	−4.1
Air transport, passenger	3 211 ..	−101.4	−71.4	−124.6	−109.2	−98.1	−152.7	−86.7	−79.4
Air transport, freight	3 212 ..	−10.7	−10.8	−11.5	−33.2	−55.4	−30.6	−20.6	−19.9
Air transport, other	3 213 ..	−11.4	−11.5	−24.3	−24.5	−13.4	−3.8	−3.3	−.3
Other transport, passenger	3 215 ..	....	....	....	....	....	....	....	....
Other transport, freight	3 216 ..	−.7	−1.4	−1.6	−3.6	−14.0	−16.1	−2.0	−2.1
Other transport, other	3 217 ..	−.9	−.3	−1.0	−2.1	−6.4	−1.6	−.8	−.8
Travel, credit	2 236 ..	**182.3**	**157.7**	**175.1**	**181.1**	**226.1**	**155.8**	**269.8**	**159.3**
Business travel	2 237 ..	12.4	9.5	16.2	22.9	56.4	28.4	12.9	15.7
Personal travel	2 240 ..	169.9	148.2	158.8	158.2	169.7	127.4	256.9	143.6
Travel, debit	3 236 ..	**−171.2**	**−323.1**	**−355.1**	**−412.5**	**−368.1**	**−410.3**	**−388.7**	**−186.0**
Business travel	3 237 ..	−88.3	−92.8	−152.8	−176.4	−199.2	−197.2	−134.5	−67.1
Personal travel	3 240 ..	−82.8	−230.3	−202.2	−236.1	−168.9	−213.1	−254.2	−118.9
Other services, credit	2 200 BA ..	**227.1**	**615.7**	**370.0**	**332.8**	**525.3**	**774.7**	**488.5**	**521.8**
Communications	2 245 ..	19.2	52.2	56.0	42.2	45.0	96.9	59.8	40.9
Construction	2 249 ..	1.4	2.5	2.2	1.4	2.0	5.4	2.9	4.2
Insurance	2 253 ..	35.6	43.8	46.4	12.7	39.9	46.2	54.4	40.5
Financial	2 260 ..	1.8	6.0	4.4	2.9	3.1	11.5	6.2	8.8
Computer and information	2 262 ..	2.4	1.2	.2	.1	.2	1.3	.7	1.0
Royalties and licence fees	2 266 ..	.2	.1	.3	.2	.3	.4	.2	.3
Other business services	2 268 ..	104.0	440.5	129.3	143.9	289.9	457.7	239.5	354.0
Personal, cultural, and recreational	2 287 ..	10.6	16.8	17.9	12.8	13.9	26.2	17.2	17.5
Government, n.i.e.	2 291 ..	51.9	52.6	113.2	116.5	130.9	129.0	107.7	54.7
Other services, debit	3 200 BA ..	**−698.2**	**−784.4**	**−632.3**	**−609.5**	**−739.1**	**−1,453.7**	**−835.7**	**−942.8**
Communications	3 245 ..	−57.7	−28.8	−46.8	−21.3	−9.2	−123.6	−86.5	−11.1
Construction	3 249 ..	−11.2	−4.1	−16.4	−10.4	−11.3	−16.3	−8.1	−11.7
Insurance	3 253 ..	−81.1	−95.6	−100.7	−78.8	−95.7	−137.6	−134.4	−100.6
Financial	3 260 ..	−11.7	−9.9	−13.7	−8.7	−9.5	−29.5	−14.6	−21.2
Computer and information	3 262 ..	−22.3	−9.1	−2.7	−1.8	−2.0	−8.8	−4.3	−6.3
Royalties and licence fees	3 266 ..	−1.7	−1.9	−8.2	−5.2	−5.7	−16.1	−8.0	−11.6
Other business services	3 268 ..	−463.1	−588.3	−414.7	−415.5	−550.9	−1,029.1	−515.8	−750.5
Personal, cultural, and recreational	3 287 ..	−4.2	−3.9	−2.4	−8.9	−9.7	−2.4	−4.5	−.9
Government, n.i.e.	3 291 ..	−45.1	−42.9	−26.7	−58.9	−45.1	−90.3	−59.5	−28.9

Table 2 (Continued). STANDARD PRESENTATION, 2003–2010

(Millions of U.S. dollars)

	Code	2003	2004	2005	2006	2007	2008	2009	2010
C. INCOME...	4 300 ..	**−409.7**	**−443.5**	**−620.4**	**−331.2**	**−499.1**	**−328.7**	**−477.1**	**−238.6**
Total credit..	2 300 ..	*108.5*	*105.1*	*44.9*	*46.3*	*66.9*	*65.8*	*131.4*	*93.1*
Total debit...	3 300 ..	*−518.2*	*−548.5*	*−665.3*	*−377.5*	*−566.0*	*−394.5*	*−608.5*	*−331.7*
Compensation of employees, credit..................	2 310 ..	**14.9**	**5.0**	**9.9**	**12.3**	**15.0**	**25.4**	**35.9**	**21.2**
Compensation of employees, debit...................	3 310 ..	**−27.7**	**−19.6**	**−36.0**	**−43.6**	**−47.6**	**−36.1**	**−71.1**	**−26.4**
Investment income, credit................................	2 320 ..	**93.6**	**100.1**	**35.1**	**34.0**	**51.9**	**40.5**	**95.6**	**71.8**
Direct investment income.................................	2 330 ..	74.3	77.9	10.1	17.6	29.5	10.0	−.1	32.9
Dividends and distributed branch profits......................	2 332 ..	55.4	70.8	10.5	20.4	26.1	10.9	.7	33.0
Reinvested earnings and undistributed branch profits.....	2 333 ..	18.9	7.1	−.4	−2.8	3.4	−.9	−.8	−.1
Income on debt (interest).................................	2 334 ..	....	....	....	....	....	....	....	....
Portfolio investment income.............................	2 339 ..	5.9	5.2	.3	1.0	1.6	1.7	1.0	29.7
Income on equity..	2 340 ..	4.1	5.1	.2	....	.3	.2	.2	6.0
Income on bonds and notes..........................	2 350 ..	....	....	....	....	....	....	....	....
Income on money market instruments..............	2 360 ..	....	....	....	....	....	....	....	....
Other investment income..............................	2 370 ..	13.5	17.0	24.7	15.4	20.8	28.8	94.6	9.2
Investment income, debit................................	3 320 ..	**−490.5**	**−528.9**	**−629.3**	**−333.9**	**−518.5**	**−358.4**	**−537.4**	**−305.2**
Direct investment income.................................	3 330 ..	−123.9	−186.1	−288.6	−9.8	−385.2	−164.6	−435.8	−165.5
Dividends and distributed branch profits......................	3 332 ..	−62.7	−121.8	−168.8	−92.5	−212.3	−227.9	−139.7	−54.9
Reinvested earnings and undistributed branch profits.....	3 333 ..	−61.2	−64.3	−119.7	82.6	−172.9	68.7	−296.1	−110.6
Income on debt (interest).................................	3 334 ..	....	....	....	....	....	−5.4	....	....
Portfolio investment income.............................	3 339 ..	−44.1	−15.3	−.2	−2.7	−1.1	−28.3	5.5	−69.0
Income on equity..	3 340 ..	−38.1	−15.0	−.1	....	−.3	−26.2	13.3	−47.4
Income on bonds and notes..........................	3 350 ..	....	....	....	....	....	....	....	....
Income on money market instruments..............	3 360 ..	....	....	....	....	....	....	....	....
Other investment income..............................	3 370 ..	−322.4	−327.5	−340.5	−321.3	−132.2	−165.6	−107.1	−70.8
D. CURRENT TRANSFERS...................................	4 379 ..	**121.7**	**175.7**	**236.4**	**312.8**	**444.4**	**597.6**	**278.6**	**146.0**
Credit..	2 379 ..	**205.0**	**225.1**	**331.7**	**526.8**	**619.8**	**774.6**	**532.0**	**334.3**
General government....................................	2 380 ..	91.5	70.0	50.2	123.6	145.6	143.4	148.4	154.1
Other sectors..	2 390 ..	113.5	155.1	281.5	403.1	474.2	631.1	383.6	180.3
Workers' remittances.................................	2 391 ..	60.6	98.4	67.1	117.6	152.3	136.7	148.5	93.6
Other current transfers..............................	2 392 ..	52.9	56.7	214.3	285.5	321.9	494.5	235.1	86.6
Debit..	3 379 ..	**−83.2**	**−49.4**	**−95.3**	**−214.0**	**−175.4**	**−177.0**	**−253.5**	**−188.3**
General government....................................	3 380 ..	−8.5	−9.7	−7.4	−9.5	−13.4	−1.6	−18.3	−48.8
Other sectors..	3 390 ..	−74.8	−39.6	−87.9	−204.5	−162.0	−175.4	−235.1	−139.5
Workers' remittances.................................	3 391 ..	−29.0	−22.5	−20.2	−48.1	−42.0	−20.3	−58.8	−27.8
Other current transfers..............................	3 392 ..	−45.8	−17.1	−67.7	−156.4	−120.0	−155.1	−176.3	−111.8
CAPITAL AND FINANCIAL ACCOUNT......................	4 996 ..	**512.1**	**361.4**	**522.8**	**−363.3**	**−465.6**	**244.6**	**959.0**	**667.5**
CAPITAL ACCOUNT.......................................	4 994 ..	**111.8**	**42.3**	**203.8**	**1,585.5**	**197.2**	**146.5**	**184.1**	**147.0**
Total credit..	2 994 ..	*123.0*	*42.8*	*204.1*	*1,586.0*	*197.7*	*152.4*	*192.2*	*148.3*
Total debit...	3 994 ..	*−11.1*	*−.5*	*−.3*	*−.5*	*−.5*	*−6.0*	*−8.0*	*−1.3*
Capital transfers, credit..........................	2 400 ..	**123.0**	**42.8**	**204.1**	**1,586.0**	**197.7**	**152.4**	**192.2**	**148.3**
General government....................................	2 401 ..	96.7	37.7	174.5	1,537.9	155.7	147.4	184.0	144.0
Debt forgiveness.......................................	2 402 ..	96.7	37.7	101.5	1,249.6	....	147.4	124.3	124.2
Other capital transfers...............................	2 410 ..	....	....	73.0	288.3	155.7	....	59.7	19.8
Other sectors..	2 430 ..	26.3	5.1	29.6	48.2	42.0	5.0	8.1	4.4
Migrants' transfers....................................	2 431 ..	.1	....	.3	....	....	4.8	8.1	....
Debt forgiveness.......................................	2 432 ..	....	....	....	....	....	....	....	....
Other capital transfers...............................	2 440 ..	26.2	5.1	29.3	48.2	42.0	.2	....	4.4
Capital transfers, debit...........................	3 400 ..	....	....	**−.3**	....	....	**−5.3**	**−7.5**	....
General government....................................	3 401 ..	....	....	....	....	....	....	....	....
Debt forgiveness.......................................	3 402 ..	....	....	....	....	....	....	....	....
Other capital transfers...............................	3 410 ..	....	....	....	....	....	....	....	....
Other sectors..	3 430 ..	....	....	−.3	....	....	−5.3	−7.5	....
Migrants' transfers....................................	3 431 ..	....	....	−.2	....	....	−5.3	−7.5	....
Debt forgiveness.......................................	3 432 ..	....	....	....	....	....	....	....	....
Other capital transfers...............................	3 440 ..	....	....	−.1	....	....	....	....	....
Nonproduced nonfinancial assets, credit............	2 480 ..	....	....	....	....	....	....	....	....
Nonproduced nonfinancial assets, debit..............	3 480 ..	**−11.1**	**−.5**	....	**−.5**	**−.5**	**−.7**	**−.5**	**−1.3**

Table 2 (Continued). STANDARD PRESENTATION, 2003–2010

(Millions of U.S. dollars)

	Code	2003	2004	2005	2006	2007	2008	2009	2010
FINANCIAL ACCOUNT	4 995 ..	**400.2**	**319.1**	**319.0**	**−1,948.8**	**−662.8**	**98.2**	**774.9**	**520.5**
A. DIRECT INVESTMENT	4 500 ..	**327.8**	**76.6**	**257.2**	**64.4**	**197.0**	**23.1**	**809.1**	**35.3**
Direct investment abroad	4 505 ..	**−8.5**	**−9.5**	**23.2**	**48.0**	**6.0**	**47.3**	**140.8**	**35.8**
Equity capital	4 510 ..	3.3	−3.3	−6.5	−3.5	1.7	−23.7	29.2	−45.6
Claims on affiliated enterprises	4 515 ..	−1.8	−3.9	−7.1	−3.7	−6.7	−37.4	32.2	−47.7
Liabilities to affiliated enterprises	4 520 ..	5.1	.6	.6	.2	8.4	13.7	−3.0	2.0
Reinvested earnings	4 525 ..	−18.9	−7.1	.4	2.8	−3.4	.9	.8	.1
Other capital	4 530 ..	7.1	.8	29.3	48.7	7.8	70.1	110.8	81.3
Claims on affiliated enterprises	4 535 ..	−1.0	....	−.8	25.0	−.1	92.1	82.8	72.4
Liabilities to affiliated enterprises	4 540 ..	8.1	.8	30.1	23.7	7.9	−21.9	28.0	8.9
Direct investment in Cameroon	4 555 ..	**336.3**	**86.1**	**234.0**	**16.4**	**191.0**	**−24.2**	**668.3**	**−.6**
Equity capital	4 560 ..	5.1	42.2	1.9	15.2	36.0	90.3	510.3	−224.5
Claims on direct investors	4 565 ..	−12.4	−21.6	2.1	....	−4.1	−20.8	−7.5	−639.4
Liabilities to direct investors	4 570 ..	17.6	63.8	−.2	15.2	40.2	111.1	517.8	414.8
Reinvested earnings	4 575 ..	61.2	64.3	119.7	−82.6	172.9	−68.7	296.1	110.6
Other capital	4 580 ..	269.9	−20.4	112.4	83.8	−17.9	−45.8	−138.1	113.4
Claims on direct investors	4 585 ..	27.8	41.2	19.2	−18.8	22.1	−32.5	−39.5	112.0
Liabilities to direct investors	4 590 ..	242.1	−61.7	93.2	102.5	−40.0	−13.3	−98.6	1.4
B. PORTFOLIO INVESTMENT	4 600 ..	**−2.2**	**30.7**	**−12.9**	**−4.6**	**−17.9**	**−40.7**	**−97.9**	**74.3**
Assets	4 602 ..	**−2.4**	**38.9**	**−9.8**	**−.8**	**−3.4**	**−39.3**	**−97.2**	**−10.8**
Equity securities	4 610 ..	−1.6	−.1	−10.2	−.8	−2.8	5.1	6.5	−4.4
Monetary authorities	4 611 ..	....	....	....	....	....	....	....	....
General government	4 612 ..	....	....	....	....	....	....	....	....
Banks	4 613 ..	−.2	....	−7.7	−.9	−5.9	5.9	6.5	−2.9
Other sectors	4 614 ..	−1.4	....	−2.6	.1	3.2	−.8	....	−1.6
Debt securities	4 619 ..	−.8	38.9	.4	....	−.7	−44.4	−103.7	−6.4
Bonds and notes	4 620 ..	−.8	38.9	.4	....	−.7	−44.4	−103.7	−6.4
Monetary authorities	4 621 ..	....	....	....	....	....	....	....	....
General government	4 622 ..	....	....	....	....	....	....	....	....
Banks	4 623 ..	....	.3	−.4	....	−.7	−6.7	−6.5	−6.7
Other sectors	4 624 ..	−.8	38.7	.8	....	....	−37.7	−97.2	.3
Money market instruments	4 630 ..	....	....	....	....	....	....	....	....
Monetary authorities	4 631 ..	....	....	....	....	....	....	....	....
General government	4 632 ..	....	....	....	....	....	....	....	....
Banks	4 633 ..	....	....	....	....	....	....	....	....
Other sectors	4 634 ..	....	....	....	....	....	....	....	....
Liabilities	4 652 ..	**.2**	**−8.2**	**−3.1**	**−3.8**	**−14.5**	**−1.4**	**−.7**	**85.2**
Equity securities	4 660 ..	.2	−8.2	−4.2	−5.6	−14.5	−1.2	−.3	....
Banks	4 663 ..	.1	....	−.9	....	−.2	−1.4	....	....
Other sectors	4 664 ..	.1	−8.2	−3.3	−5.6	−14.3	.1	−.3	....
Debt securities	4 669 ..	....	.1	1.1	1.8	....	−.2	−.5	85.1
Bonds and notes	4 670 ..	....	.1	1.1	1.8	....	−.2	−.5	85.1
Monetary authorities	4 671 ..	....	....	....	....	....	....	....	....
General government	4 672 ..	....	....	....	....	....	....	....	85.0
Banks	4 673 ..	....	....	....	....	....	....	....	....
Other sectors	4 674 ..	....	.1	1.1	1.8	....	−.2	−.5	.1
Money market instruments	4 680 ..	....	....	....	....	....	....	....	....
Monetary authorities	4 681 ..	....	....	....	....	....	....	....	....
General government	4 682 ..	....	....	....	....	....	....	....	....
Banks	4 683 ..	....	....	....	....	....	....	....	....
Other sectors	4 684 ..	....	....	....	....	....	....	....	....
C. FINANCIAL DERIVATIVES	4 910 ..	....	....	....	....	....	....	....	....
Monetary authorities	4 911 ..	....	....	....	....	....	....	....	....
General government	4 912 ..	....	....	....	....	....	....	....	....
Banks	4 913 ..	....	....	....	....	....	....	....	....
Other sectors	4 914 ..	....	....	....	....	....	....	....	....
Assets	4 900 ..	....	....	....	....	....	....	....	....
Monetary authorities	4 901 ..	....	....	....	....	....	....	....	....
General government	4 902 ..	....	....	....	....	....	....	....	....
Banks	4 903 ..	....	....	....	....	....	....	....	....
Other sectors	4 904 ..	....	....	....	....	....	....	....	....
Liabilities	4 905 ..	....	....	....	....	....	....	....	....
Monetary authorities	4 906 ..	....	....	....	....	....	....	....	....
General government	4 907 ..	....	....	....	....	....	....	....	....
Banks	4 908 ..	....	....	....	....	....	....	....	....
Other sectors	4 909 ..	....	....	....	....	....	....	....	....

Table 2 (Concluded). STANDARD PRESENTATION, 2003–2010

(Millions of U.S. dollars)

	Code	2003	2004	2005	2006	2007	2008	2009	2010
D. OTHER INVESTMENT	4 700	**−31.2**	**339.0**	**318.2**	**−1,381.6**	**77.4**	**470.6**	**536.1**	**637.1**
Assets	4 703	**79.9**	**72.1**	**67.0**	**−319.5**	**−2.1**	**−66.4**	**−100.9**	**550.6**
Trade credits	4 706	1.8	80.5	11.0	−316.3	52.7	−196.2	13.3	100.1
General government	4 707	....	....	....	....	....	....	....	....
of which: Short-term	4 709	....	....	....	....	....	....	....	....
Other sectors	4 710	1.8	80.5	11.0	−316.3	52.7	−196.2	13.3	100.1
of which: Short-term	4 712	1.8	80.7	11.0	−319.5	54.6	−179.2	14.3	93.7
Loans	4 714	−25.6	−4.6	−15.2	−30.8	−39.5	−75.3	−22.5	−139.6
Monetary authorities	4 715	....	....	....	....	....	....	....	....
of which: Short-term	4 718	....	....	....	....	....	....	....	....
General government	4 719	....	....	....	....	....	....	....	....
of which: Short-term	4 721	....	....	....	....	....	....	....	....
Banks	4 722	−26.6	.1	−22.3	−27.6	−30.9	−77.5	−21.4	−121.0
of which: Short-term	4 724	....	....	....	....	....	.5	....	....
Other sectors	4 725	1.0	−4.7	7.0	−3.2	−8.6	2.3	−1.1	−18.6
of which: Short-term	4 727	.3	.6	2.1	−.4	−8.5	1.5	−1.1	−18.6
Currency and deposits	4 730	55.6	−1.7	29.1	13.6	−7.4	−213.2	−515.4	297.6
Monetary authorities	4 731	....	....	....	....	....	....	....	....
General government	4 732	....	....	1.3	−9.5	−4.1	....	....	....
Banks	4 733	10.5	−46.1	−52.5	−52.3	−104.1	−54.6	−29.1	216.3
Other sectors	4 734	45.1	44.4	80.3	75.4	100.7	−158.6	−486.2	81.3
Other assets	4 736	48.1	−2.1	42.1	14.0	−7.9	418.2	423.6	292.4
Monetary authorities	4 737	....	....	....	....	....	....	....	....
of which: Short-term	4 739	....	....	....	....	....	....	....	....
General government	4 740	....	....	....	....	....	....	....	....
of which: Short-term	4 742	....	....	....	....	....	....	....	....
Banks	4 743	.4	1.2	−1.3	−1.9	−1.3	−11.2	−1.1	−35.5
of which: Short-term	4 745	.4	1.2	−1.3	−1.9	−1.3	−11.2	−1.1	−35.5
Other sectors	4 746	47.7	−3.3	43.4	15.9	−6.6	429.4	424.7	327.9
of which: Short-term	4 748	47.7	−3.3	43.4	15.9	−6.6	429.4	424.7	327.9
Liabilities	4 753	**−111.1**	**266.8**	**251.2**	**−1,062.1**	**79.6**	**537.0**	**637.0**	**86.5**
Trade credits	4 756	4.8	49.5	49.1	379.9	192.5	520.4	−201.7	132.5
General government	4 757	....	....	....	....	....	....	....	....
of which: Short-term	4 759	....	....	....	....	....	....	....	....
Other sectors	4 760	4.8	49.5	49.1	379.9	192.5	520.4	−201.7	132.5
of which: Short-term	4 762	−61.7	42.8	61.2	142.4	65.5	301.2	−443.9	−251.0
Loans	4 764	−369.1	−380.2	−414.1	−1,927.2	−131.2	−96.2	−43.7	358.4
Monetary authorities	4 765	12.0	−27.9	−36.2	−268.3	8.0	8.5	148.2	....
of which: Use of Fund credit and loans from the Fund	4 766	12.0	−27.9	−36.2	−268.3	8.0	8.5	148.2	....
of which: Short-term	4 768	....	....	....	....	....	....	....	....
General government	4 769	−337.3	−365.6	−361.0	−1,608.5	−43.3	−4.2	−49.3	98.5
of which: Short-term	4 771	....	....	....	....	....	....	....	....
Banks	4 772	15.9	10.8	−9.9	−11.4	−9.9	−3.3	8.0	−1.2
of which: Short-term	4 774	−.7	12.6	−5.6	−11.4	−6.3	−4.7	−1.7	−1.2
Other sectors	4 775	−59.8	2.4	−7.0	−38.9	−86.0	−97.1	−150.5	261.1
of which: Short-term	4 777	−6.8	−13.2	33.6	59.4	.1	.3	1.0	11.3
Currency and deposits	4 780	−24.9	12.9	79.3	−38.2	36.0	−54.3	29.3	24.0
Monetary authorities	4 781	−4.1	−2.4	3.7	−3.3	−10.9	1.0	....	4.3
General government	4 782	....	....	....	....	....	....	....	....
Banks	4 783	−20.8	15.3	75.5	−34.9	46.9	−55.3	29.3	19.7
Other sectors	4 784	....	....	....	....	....	....	....	....
Other liabilities	4 786	278.1	584.6	537.0	523.3	−17.7	167.1	853.2	−428.5
Monetary authorities	4 787	....	....	....	....	....	1.0	277.2	16.8
of which: Short-term	4 789	....	....	....	....	....	1.0	38.5	16.8
General government	4 790	499.5	473.3	491.1	344.0	−7.6	−95.7	....	....
of which: Short-term	4 792	404.3	395.4	415.6	344.0	−7.6	−95.7	....	....
Banks	4 793	....	....	12.8	15.3	17.3	5.5	.1	5.7
of which: Short-term	4 795	....	....	12.8	15.3	17.3	5.5	.1	5.7
Other sectors	4 796	−221.3	111.3	33.0	164.0	−27.5	256.2	575.9	−451.0
of which: Short-term	4 798	−221.3	111.3	33.0	164.0	−27.5	256.2	575.9	−451.0
E. RESERVE ASSETS	4 802	**105.9**	**−127.2**	**−243.4**	**−627.0**	**−919.3**	**−354.8**	**−472.4**	**−226.1**
Monetary gold	4 812	....	....	....	....	....	....	....	....
Special drawing rights	4 811	−.2	.8	−1.5	−2.4	.1	.1	−238.2	202.4
Reserve position in the Fund	4 810	−.1	....	−.1	−.1	....	−.1	....	....
Foreign exchange	4 803	106.9	−126.6	−243.3	−623.1	−918.1	−309.4	127.3	116.7
Other claims	4 813	−.8	−1.4	1.5	−1.5	−1.2	−45.5	−361.5	−545.1
NET ERRORS AND OMISSIONS	4 998	**84.4**	**54.0**	**−29.4**	**170.0**	**179.9**	**205.1**	**159.7**	**188.8**

Canada   156

Table 1. ANALYTIC PRESENTATION, 2003–2010

(Millions of U.S. dollars)

	Code	2003	2004	2005	2006	2007	2008	2009	2010
A. Current Account[1]	4 993 Z.	**10,696**	**22,946**	**21,714**	**18,084**	**12,003**	**6,376**	**−40,024**	**−49,307**
Goods: exports f.o.b.	2 100 ..	285,186	330,011	371,945	400,249	432,083	461,651	324,521	393,183
Goods: imports f.o.b.	3 100 ..	−244,904	−279,508	−320,209	−356,595	−388,313	−417,849	−328,915	−401,865
Balance on Goods	4 100 ..	*40,283*	*50,503*	*51,736*	*43,655*	*43,770*	*43,803*	*−4,394*	*−8,682*
Services: credit	2 200 ..	44,242	50,286	55,829	60,353	65,338	68,359	60,089	69,166
Services: debit	3 200 ..	−52,454	−58,776	−65,749	−72,760	−82,788	−88,791	−79,268	−91,255
Balance on Goods and Services	4 991 ..	*32,070*	*42,013*	*41,816*	*31,248*	*26,320*	*23,371*	*−23,572*	*−30,770*
Income: credit	2 300 ..	21,050	29,374	41,143	58,675	72,121	66,799	48,754	60,021
Income: debit	3 300 ..	−42,295	−47,926	−60,018	−70,564	−84,663	−82,802	−62,813	−75,988
Balance on Goods, Services, and Income	4 992 ..	*10,825*	*23,461*	*22,941*	*19,359*	*13,778*	*7,368*	*−37,631*	*−46,738*
Current transfers: credit	2 379 Z.	4,814	5,518	6,637	8,411	8,896	9,882	7,591	8,999
Current transfers: debit	3 379 ..	−4,943	−6,033	−7,864	−9,686	−10,671	−10,873	−9,984	−11,569
B. Capital Account[1]	4 994 Z.	**3,020**	**3,416**	**4,858**	**3,705**	**3,934**	**4,324**	**3,344**	**4,620**
Capital account: credit	2 994 Z.	3,431	3,949	5,444	4,322	4,652	5,100	4,610	5,293
Capital account: debit	3 994 ..	−410	−533	−586	−617	−718	−776	−1,266	−673
Total, Groups A Plus B	4 981 ..	*13,717*	*26,361*	*26,572*	*21,789*	*15,937*	*10,701*	*−36,681*	*−44,687*
C. Financial Account[1]	4 995 W.	**−18,070**	**−31,510**	**−22,950**	**−22,961**	**−13,145**	**−6,001**	**47,369**	**47,357**
Direct investment abroad	4 505 ..	−23,623	−42,639	−27,626	−46,352	−57,738	−81,163	−42,899	−39,130
Direct investment in Canada	4 555 Z.	7,206	−741	25,901	60,294	117,654	57,877	22,465	23,587
Portfolio investment assets	4 602 ..	−13,829	−18,924	−44,222	−69,392	−42,775	8,390	−6,282	−14,017
Equity securities	4 610 ..	−5,816	−6,197	−18,104	−24,776	−28,892	−8,594	−13,023	−12,938
Debt securities	4 619 ..	−8,013	−12,727	−26,118	−44,617	−13,883	16,985	6,741	−1,079
Portfolio investment liabilities	4 652 Z.	14,127	41,807	10,884	27,374	−32,014	31,582	97,720	114,112
Equity securities	4 660 ..	9,947	27,145	7,565	9,501	−42,041	3,109	23,349	17,775
Debt securities	4 669 Z.	4,180	14,662	3,319	17,873	10,027	28,472	74,370	96,337
Financial derivatives	4 910 ..	....	....	....	....	....	....	....	....
Financial derivatives assets	4 900 ..	....	....	....	....	....	....	....	....
Financial derivatives liabilities	4 905 ..	....	....	....	....	....	....	....	....
Other investment assets	4 703 ..	−14,209	−7,065	−17,846	−30,834	−57,688	−35,619	−35,740	−46,845
Monetary authorities	4 701 ..	....	....	....	....	....	....	....	....
General government	4 704 ..	339	−210	−395	−281	−477	−880	−408	−651
Banks	4 705 ..	−15,172	−983	−16,291	−9,474	−43,745	−20,941	−20,615	−25,683
Other sectors	4 728 ..	624	−5,872	−1,160	−21,079	−13,467	−13,798	−14,717	−20,511
Other investment liabilities	4 753 W.	12,257	−3,948	29,959	35,950	59,417	12,931	12,106	9,650
Monetary authorities	4 753 WA	....	....	....	....	....	....	8,135	....
General government	4 753 ZB	−527	−754	−138	−109	−132	−48	−376	−191
Banks	4 753 ZC	12,557	−1,000	40,912	18,134	45,447	23,838	20,592	10,783
Other sectors	4 753 ZD	227	−2,194	−10,815	17,925	14,102	−10,859	−16,246	−942
Total, Groups A Through C	4 983 ..	*−4,353*	*−5,149*	*3,622*	*−1,172*	*2,792*	*4,699*	*10,688*	*2,670*
D. Net Errors and Omissions	4 998 ..	**1,098**	**2,313**	**−2,287**	**1,998**	**1,114**	**−2,930**	**−218**	**1,145**
Total, Groups A Through D	4 984 ..	*−3,255*	*−2,836*	*1,335*	*826*	*3,906*	*1,769*	*10,470*	*3,815*
E. Reserves and Related Items	4 802 A.	**3,255**	**2,836**	**−1,335**	**−826**	**−3,906**	**−1,769**	**−10,470**	**−3,815**
Reserve assets	4 802 ..	3,255	2,836	−1,335	−826	−3,906	−1,769	−10,470	−3,815
Use of Fund credit and loans	4 766 ..	....	....	....	....	....	....	....	....
Exceptional financing	4 920 ..	....	....	....	....	....	....	....	....
Conversion rates: Canadian dollars per U.S. dollar	0 101 ..	**1.4011**	**1.3010**	**1.2118**	**1.1344**	**1.0741**	**1.0670**	**1.1431**	**1.0302**

[1] Excludes components that have been classified in the categories of Group E.

Table 2. STANDARD PRESENTATION, 2003–2010

(Millions of U.S. dollars)

	Code	2003	2004	2005	2006	2007	2008	2009	2010
CURRENT ACCOUNT.................................	4 993 ..	**10,696**	**22,946**	**21,714**	**18,084**	**12,003**	**6,376**	**–40,024**	**–49,307**
A. GOODS..	4 100 ..	**40,283**	**50,503**	**51,736**	**43,655**	**43,770**	**43,803**	**–4,394**	**–8,682**
Credit..	2 100 ..	**285,186**	**330,011**	**371,945**	**400,249**	**432,083**	**461,651**	**324,521**	**393,183**
General merchandise: exports f.o.b...........	2 110 ..	283,351	327,427	368,558	395,371	426,373	453,156	316,016	378,355
Goods for processing: exports f.o.b.........	2 150 ..	....	....	....	....	....	....	....	....
Repairs on goods................................	2 160 ..	....	....	....	....	....	....	....	....
Goods procured in ports by carriers.........	2 170 ..	....	....	....	....	....	....	....	....
Nonmonetary gold..............................	2 180 ..	1,835	2,585	3,387	4,879	5,710	8,495	8,505	14,828
Debit..	3 100 ..	**–244,904**	**–279,508**	**–320,209**	**–356,595**	**–388,313**	**–417,849**	**–328,915**	**–401,865**
General merchandise: imports f.o.b..........	3 110 ..	–244,533	–278,006	–317,917	–353,235	–384,180	–412,199	–323,165	–393,472
Goods for processing: imports f.o.b.........	3 150 ..	....	....	....	....	....	....	....	....
Repairs on goods................................	3 160 ..	....	....	....	....	....	....	....	....
Goods procured in ports by carriers.........	3 170 ..	....	....	....	....	....	....	....	....
Nonmonetary gold..............................	3 180 ..	–371	–1,502	–2,292	–3,360	–4,134	–5,649	–5,750	–8,393
B. SERVICES....................................	4 200 ..	**–8,212**	**–8,490**	**–9,920**	**–12,407**	**–17,450**	**–20,432**	**–19,179**	**–22,089**
Total credit....................................	2 200 ..	*44,242*	*50,286*	*55,829*	*60,353*	*65,338*	*68,359*	*60,089*	*69,166*
Total debit.....................................	3 200 ..	*–52,454*	*–58,776*	*–65,749*	*–72,760*	*–82,788*	*–88,791*	*–79,268*	*–91,255*
Transportation services, credit...........	2 205 ..	**7,125**	**8,486**	**9,728**	**10,470**	**11,118**	**11,500**	**9,293**	**11,656**
Passenger.......................................	2 850 ..	*1,634*	*2,106*	*2,238*	*2,289*	*2,381*	*2,560*	*1,852*	*2,616*
Freight..	2 851 ..	*3,098*	*3,462*	*3,810*	*4,090*	*4,336*	*4,328*	*3,541*	*4,291*
Other..	2 852 ..	*2,393*	*2,917*	*3,680*	*4,091*	*4,400*	*4,612*	*3,900*	*4,749*
Sea transport, passenger......................	2 207 ..	13	14	19	20	29	47	23	24
Sea transport, freight..........................	2 208 ..	664	820	930	1,061	1,232	1,186	917	1,139
Sea transport, other...........................	2 209 ..	1,088	1,419	1,877	2,069	2,273	1,918	1,498	1,853
Air transport, passenger.......................	2 211 ..	1,602	2,073	2,200	2,254	2,335	2,491	1,814	2,578
Air transport, freight..........................	2 212 ..	....	....	....	....	....	....	....	....
Air transport, other............................	2 213 ..	1,306	1,498	1,802	2,022	2,128	2,694	2,402	2,896
Other transport, passenger...................	2 215 ..	20	19	19	15	17	21	16	15
Other transport, freight.......................	2 216 ..	2,433	2,643	2,880	3,029	3,104	3,142	2,624	3,152
Other transport, other.........................	2 217 ..	....	....	....	....	....	....	....	....
Transportation services, debit............	3 205 ..	**–10,390**	**–12,248**	**–14,484**	**–16,329**	**–18,576**	**–20,538**	**–16,910**	**–20,422**
Passenger.......................................	3 850 ..	*–2,972*	*–3,743*	*–4,717*	*–5,455*	*–6,483*	*–6,698*	*–6,046*	*–7,242*
Freight..	3 851 ..	*–7,012*	*–8,019*	*–9,140*	*–10,286*	*–11,217*	*–12,621*	*–10,204*	*–12,413*
Other..	3 852 ..	*–406*	*–486*	*–627*	*–588*	*–876*	*–1,218*	*–659*	*–767*
Sea transport, passenger......................	3 207 ..	–90	–111	–107	–133	–181	–150	–104	–156
Sea transport, freight..........................	3 208 ..	–3,862	–4,619	–5,387	–6,244	–6,956	–7,762	–6,452	–7,891
Sea transport, other...........................	3 209 ..	–406	–486	–627	–588	–876	–1,218	–659	–767
Air transport, passenger.......................	3 211 ..	–2,775	–3,554	–4,506	–5,205	–6,126	–6,347	–5,696	–6,776
Air transport, freight..........................	3 212 ..	–1,475	–1,608	–1,872	–2,058	–2,273	–2,834	–2,001	–2,478
Air transport, other............................	3 213 ..	....	....	....	....	....	....	....	....
Other transport, passenger...................	3 215 ..	–107	–78	–104	–117	–176	–201	–247	–310
Other transport, freight.......................	3 216 ..	–1,674	–1,792	–1,882	–1,985	–1,989	–2,025	–1,751	–2,045
Other transport, other.........................	3 217 ..	....	....	....	....	....	....	....	....
Travel, credit.................................	2 236 ..	**10,601**	**13,029**	**13,768**	**14,555**	**15,568**	**15,668**	**13,733**	**15,711**
Business travel..................................	2 237 ..	1,703	2,043	2,301	2,552	2,704	2,866	2,223	2,640
Personal travel..................................	2 240 ..	8,899	10,986	11,467	12,003	12,864	12,802	11,510	13,070
Travel, debit..................................	3 236 ..	**–13,337**	**–15,524**	**–18,017**	**–20,542**	**–24,716**	**–27,210**	**–24,170**	**–29,558**
Business travel..................................	3 237 ..	–2,423	–2,408	–2,941	–3,302	–3,974	–3,844	–3,103	–3,781
Personal travel..................................	3 240 ..	–10,914	–13,115	–15,076	–17,240	–20,742	–23,366	–21,066	–25,777
Other services, credit........................	2 200 BA	**26,516**	**28,771**	**32,333**	**35,327**	**38,652**	**41,191**	**37,064**	**41,799**
Communications................................	2 245 ..	1,697	1,881	1,958	2,122	2,231	2,489	2,605	2,959
Construction....................................	2 249 ..	95	128	181	249	313	231	198	259
Insurance.......................................	2 253 ..	3,433	3,188	3,212	3,373	3,785	4,179	3,983	4,392
Financial..	2 260 ..	1,149	1,132	1,954	2,581	3,218	3,076	2,530	3,312
Computer and information.....................	2 262 ..	2,796	3,014	3,600	4,296	4,597	5,007	4,216	4,893
Royalties and licence fees.....................	2 266 ..	2,810	3,008	2,765	3,173	3,505	3,599	3,420	3,813
Other business services........................	2 268 ..	12,011	13,354	15,183	15,773	17,159	18,792	16,396	18,236
Personal, cultural, and recreational...........	2 287 ..	1,414	1,838	2,070	2,286	2,291	2,184	2,079	2,198
Government, n.i.e...............................	2 291 ..	1,111	1,228	1,411	1,472	1,553	1,633	1,637	1,734
Other services, debit.........................	3 200 BA	**–28,727**	**–31,004**	**–33,248**	**–35,888**	**–39,496**	**–41,043**	**–38,188**	**–41,274**
Communications................................	3 245 ..	–1,468	–1,651	–1,489	–1,606	–1,908	–1,910	–1,968	–2,287
Construction....................................	3 249 ..	–86	–147	–175	–103	–215	–311	–292	–227
Insurance.......................................	3 253 ..	–4,931	–4,715	–5,008	–5,452	–6,123	–6,134	–5,758	–6,240
Financial..	3 260 ..	–1,958	–2,158	–2,732	–3,697	–4,070	–3,944	–3,718	–3,658
Computer and information.....................	3 262 ..	–1,636	–1,705	–1,802	–2,033	–2,502	–2,662	–2,688	–2,904
Royalties and licence fees.....................	3 266 ..	–5,622	–6,574	–6,902	–6,978	–8,200	–8,648	–8,126	–8,665
Other business services........................	3 268 ..	–10,624	–11,457	–12,459	–13,036	–13,238	–14,087	–12,437	–13,392
Personal, cultural, and recreational...........	3 287 ..	–1,720	–1,844	–1,838	–2,065	–2,176	–2,160	–2,039	–2,608
Government, n.i.e...............................	3 291 ..	–683	–753	–843	–918	–1,065	–1,186	–1,162	–1,292

2011, International Monetary Fund: *Balance of Payments Statistics Yearbook*

Table 2 (Continued). STANDARD PRESENTATION, 2003–2010

(Millions of U.S. dollars)

	Code	2003	2004	2005	2006	2007	2008	2009	2010
C. INCOME	4 300	**−21,245**	**−18,552**	**−18,875**	**−11,889**	**−12,541**	**−16,003**	**−14,059**	**−15,968**
Total credit	2 300	*21,050*	*29,374*	*41,143*	*58,675*	*72,121*	*66,799*	*48,754*	*60,021*
Total debit	3 300	*−42,295*	*−47,926*	*−60,018*	*−70,564*	*−84,663*	*−82,802*	*−62,813*	*−75,988*
Compensation of employees, credit	2 310	....	....	....	....	....	....	....	....
Compensation of employees, debit	3 310	....	....	....	....	....	....	....	....
Investment income, credit	2 320	**21,050**	**29,374**	**41,143**	**58,675**	**72,121**	**66,799**	**48,754**	**60,021**
Direct investment income	2 330	9,950	16,331	22,805	32,688	39,615	34,471	24,782	36,763
Dividends and distributed branch profits	2 332	3,533	4,662	8,527	14,557	15,785	16,072	9,885	14,081
Reinvested earnings and undistributed branch profits	2 333	6,179	11,089	13,414	16,663	22,020	17,074	13,224	20,435
Income on debt (interest)	2 334	238	581	864	1,469	1,810	1,325	1,673	2,247
Portfolio investment income	2 339	6,183	7,764	10,230	15,281	20,644	21,010	17,343	16,869
Income on equity	2 340	4,778	5,901	7,209	9,878	13,100	14,693	12,323	12,017
Income on bonds and notes	2 350	1,312	1,708	2,744	4,817	6,896	6,131	4,996	4,837
Income on money market instruments	2 360	93	155	277	587	648	187	24	15
Other investment income	2 370	4,916	5,278	8,108	10,705	11,862	11,317	6,629	6,389
Investment income, debit	3 320	**−42,295**	**−47,926**	**−60,018**	**−70,564**	**−84,663**	**−82,802**	**−62,813**	**−75,988**
Direct investment income	3 330	−16,931	−21,188	−29,775	−32,492	−40,004	−38,470	−26,645	−35,671
Dividends and distributed branch profits	3 332	−8,055	−9,603	−15,679	−18,160	−18,814	−19,157	−16,305	−22,310
Reinvested earnings and undistributed branch profits	3 333	−7,491	−9,987	−11,684	−11,304	−17,510	−15,470	−7,202	−10,196
Income on debt (interest)	3 334	−1,385	−1,597	−2,411	−3,028	−3,679	−3,843	−3,138	−3,166
Portfolio investment income	3 339	−20,590	−21,518	−23,256	−25,384	−28,762	−30,746	−29,432	−34,509
Income on equity	3 340	−2,354	−2,874	−3,951	−5,637	−7,439	−8,586	−7,243	−8,793
Income on bonds and notes	3 350	−17,871	−18,353	−18,852	−18,876	−20,355	−21,602	−21,922	−25,541
Income on money market instruments	3 360	−365	−291	−452	−871	−968	−558	−267	−175
Other investment income	3 370	−4,774	−5,220	−6,987	−12,689	−15,896	−13,587	−6,736	−5,809
D. CURRENT TRANSFERS	4 379	**−129**	**−515**	**−1,228**	**−1,275**	**−1,775**	**−991**	**−2,393**	**−2,569**
Credit	2 379	**4,814**	**5,518**	**6,637**	**8,411**	**8,896**	**9,882**	**7,591**	**8,999**
General government	2 380	2,969	3,585	4,527	6,155	6,465	7,272	5,090	5,799
Other sectors	2 390	1,846	1,933	2,109	2,257	2,430	2,610	2,501	3,201
Workers' remittances	2 391	....	....	....	....	....	....	....	....
Other current transfers	2 392	1,846	1,933	2,109	2,257	2,430	2,610	2,501	3,201
Debit	3 379	**−4,943**	**−6,033**	**−7,864**	**−9,686**	**−10,671**	**−10,873**	**−9,984**	**−11,569**
General government	3 380	−2,059	−2,351	−3,201	−3,111	−3,413	−3,940	−3,682	−4,456
Other sectors	3 390	−2,883	−3,682	−4,663	−6,575	−7,257	−6,934	−6,302	−7,113
Workers' remittances	3 391	....	....	....	....	....	....	....	....
Other current transfers	3 392	−2,883	−3,682	−4,663	−6,575	−7,257	−6,934	−6,302	−7,113
CAPITAL AND FINANCIAL ACCOUNT	4 996	**−11,795**	**−25,259**	**−19,427**	**−20,082**	**−13,117**	**−3,446**	**40,243**	**48,163**
CAPITAL ACCOUNT	4 994	**3,020**	**3,416**	**4,858**	**3,705**	**3,934**	**4,324**	**3,344**	**4,620**
Total credit	2 994	*3,431*	*3,949*	*5,444*	*4,322*	*4,652*	*5,100*	*4,610*	*5,293*
Total debit	3 994	*−410*	*−533*	*−586*	*−617*	*−718*	*−776*	*−1,266*	*−673*
Capital transfers, credit	2 400	**3,431**	**3,949**	**5,444**	**4,322**	**4,652**	**5,100**	**4,610**	**5,293**
General government	2 401	....	....	....	....	....	....	....	....
Debt forgiveness	2 402	....	....	....	....	....	....	....	....
Other capital transfers	2 410	....	....	....	....	....	....	....	....
Other sectors	2 430	....	....	....	....	....	....	....	....
Migrants' transfers	2 431	....	....	....	....	....	....	....	....
Debt forgiveness	2 432	....	....	....	....	....	....	....	....
Other capital transfers	2 440	....	....	....	....	....	....	....	....
Capital transfers, debit	3 400	**−406**	**−533**	**−584**	**−617**	**−718**	**−776**	**−817**	**−673**
General government	3 401	....	....	....	....	....	....	....	....
Debt forgiveness	3 402	....	....	....	....	....	....	....	....
Other capital transfers	3 410	....	....	....	....	....	....	....	....
Other sectors	3 430	....	....	....	....	....	....	....	....
Migrants' transfers	3 431	....	....	....	....	....	....	....	....
Debt forgiveness	3 432	....	....	....	....	....	....	....	....
Other capital transfers	3 440	....	....	....	....	....	....	....	....
Nonproduced nonfinancial assets, credit	2 480	....	....	....	....	....	....	....	....
Nonproduced nonfinancial assets, debit	3 480	**−4**	....	**−2**	....	....	....	**−450**	....

Table 2 (Continued). STANDARD PRESENTATION, 2003–2010

(Millions of U.S. dollars)

	Code	2003	2004	2005	2006	2007	2008	2009	2010
FINANCIAL ACCOUNT	4 995	**−14,815**	**−28,675**	**−24,285**	**−23,787**	**−17,051**	**−7,771**	**36,899**	**43,542**
A. DIRECT INVESTMENT	4 500	**−16,417**	**−43,380**	**−1,725**	**13,942**	**59,916**	**−23,286**	**−20,434**	**−15,544**
Direct investment abroad	4 505	**−23,623**	**−42,639**	**−27,626**	**−46,352**	**−57,738**	**−81,163**	**−42,899**	**−39,130**
Equity capital	4 510	....	....	....	....	....	....	....	....
Claims on affiliated enterprises	4 515	....	....	....	....	....	....	....	....
Liabilities to affiliated enterprises	4 520	....	....	....	....	....	....	....	....
Reinvested earnings	4 525	−6,179	−11,089	−13,414	−16,663	−22,020	−17,074	−13,224	−20,435
Other capital	4 530	−17,444	−31,550	−14,211	−29,689	−35,719	−64,089	−29,674	−18,696
Claims on affiliated enterprises	4 535	−16,575	−32,130	−13,808	−30,465	−36,594	−72,419	−22,842	−19,332
Liabilities to affiliated enterprises	4 540	−869	580	−404	776	875	8,331	−6,832	636
Direct investment in Canada	4 555	**7,206**	**−741**	**25,901**	**60,294**	**117,654**	**57,877**	**22,465**	**23,587**
Equity capital	4 560	....	....	....	....	....	....	....	....
Claims on direct investors	4 565	....	....	....	....	....	....	....	....
Liabilities to direct investors	4 570	....	....	....	....	....	....	....	....
Reinvested earnings	4 575	7,491	9,987	11,684	11,304	17,510	15,470	7,202	10,196
Other capital	4 580	−285	−10,729	14,217	48,990	100,144	42,407	15,263	13,391
Claims on direct investors	4 585	−675	−1,603	−48	−3,232	117	637	−163	3,590
Liabilities to direct investors	4 590	390	−9,126	14,265	52,222	100,027	41,770	15,426	9,801
B. PORTFOLIO INVESTMENT	4 600	**298**	**22,883**	**−33,338**	**−42,018**	**−74,789**	**39,972**	**91,437**	**100,096**
Assets	4 602	**−13,829**	**−18,924**	**−44,222**	**−69,392**	**−42,775**	**8,390**	**−6,282**	**−14,017**
Equity securities	4 610	−5,816	−6,197	−18,104	−24,776	−28,892	−8,594	−13,023	−12,938
Monetary authorities	4 611	....	....	....	....	....	....	....	....
General government	4 612	....	....	....	....	....	....	....	....
Banks	4 613	....	....	....	....	....	....	....	....
Other sectors	4 614	−5,816	−6,197	−18,104	−24,776	−28,892	−8,594	−13,023	−12,938
Debt securities	4 619	−8,013	−12,727	−26,118	−44,617	−13,883	16,985	6,741	−1,079
Bonds and notes	4 620	−5,603	−11,956	−24,393	−38,604	−24,946	12,492	8,214	1,253
Monetary authorities	4 621	....	....	....	....	....	....	....	....
General government	4 622	....	....	....	....	....	....	....	....
Banks	4 623	....	....	....	....	....	....	....	....
Other sectors	4 624	−5,603	−11,956	−24,393	−38,604	−24,946	12,492	8,214	1,253
Money market instruments	4 630	−2,410	−771	−1,725	−6,013	11,064	4,493	−1,473	−2,332
Monetary authorities	4 631	....	....	....	....	....	....	....	....
General government	4 632	....	....	....	....	....	....	....	....
Banks	4 633	....	....	....	....	....	....	....	....
Other sectors	4 634	−2,410	−771	−1,725	−6,013	11,064	4,493	−1,473	−2,332
Liabilities	4 652	**14,127**	**41,807**	**10,884**	**27,374**	**−32,014**	**31,582**	**97,720**	**114,112**
Equity securities	4 660	9,947	27,145	7,565	9,501	−42,041	3,109	23,349	17,775
Banks	4 663	....	....	....	....	....	....	....	....
Other sectors	4 664	9,947	27,145	7,565	9,501	−42,041	3,109	23,349	17,775
Debt securities	4 669	4,180	14,662	3,319	17,873	10,027	28,472	74,370	96,337
Bonds and notes	4 670	5,285	14,938	2,815	14,595	11,113	19,171	75,020	93,255
Monetary authorities	4 671	....	....	....	....	....	....	....	....
General government	4 672	−14,260	−2,967	−1,145	529	−9,315	2,149	37,496	58,774
Banks	4 673	−423	−65	−37	−402	−39	169	−174	2,245
Other sectors	4 674	19,968	17,970	3,997	14,468	20,467	16,853	37,698	32,236
Money market instruments	4 680	−1,105	−277	505	3,278	−1,086	9,301	−649	3,082
Monetary authorities	4 681	....	....	....	....	....	....	....	....
General government	4 682	−219	−2,033	970	2,895	−1,953	8,874	1,800	2,418
Banks	4 683	....	....	....	....	....	....	....	....
Other sectors	4 684	−886	1,756	−465	384	867	427	−2,450	664
C. FINANCIAL DERIVATIVES	4 910	....	....	....	....	....	....	....	....
Monetary authorities	4 911	....	....	....	....	....	....	....	....
General government	4 912	....	....	....	....	....	....	....	....
Banks	4 913	....	....	....	....	....	....	....	....
Other sectors	4 914	....	....	....	....	....	....	....	....
Assets	4 900	....	....	....	....	....	....	....	....
Monetary authorities	4 901	....	....	....	....	....	....	....	....
General government	4 902	....	....	....	....	....	....	....	....
Banks	4 903	....	....	....	....	....	....	....	....
Other sectors	4 904	....	....	....	....	....	....	....	....
Liabilities	4 905	....	....	....	....	....	....	....	....
Monetary authorities	4 906	....	....	....	....	....	....	....	....
General government	4 907	....	....	....	....	....	....	....	....
Banks	4 908	....	....	....	....	....	....	....	....
Other sectors	4 909	....	....	....	....	....	....	....	....

Table 2 (Concluded). STANDARD PRESENTATION, 2003–2010

(Millions of U.S. dollars)

	Code	2003	2004	2005	2006	2007	2008	2009	2010
D. OTHER INVESTMENT	4 700 ..	**−1,951**	**−11,013**	**12,113**	**5,116**	**1,728**	**−22,687**	**−23,635**	**−37,195**
Assets	4 703 ..	**−14,209**	**−7,065**	**−17,846**	**−30,834**	**−57,688**	**−35,619**	**−35,740**	**−46,845**
Trade credits	4 706 ..	666	−75	287	−1,478	857	−47	111	201
General government	4 707 ..	....	....	....	....	....	....	....	....
of which: Short-term	4 709 ..	....	....	....	....	....	....	....	....
Other sectors	4 710 ..	666	−75	287	−1,478	857	−47	111	201
of which: Short-term	4 712 ..	....	....	....	....	....	....	....	....
Loans	4 714 ..	5,909	2,971	6,091	−10,488	−9,871	−64	−15,778	−15,905
Monetary authorities	4 715 ..	....	....	....	....	....	....	....	....
of which: Short-term	4 718 ..	....	....	....	....	....	....	....	....
General government	4 719 ..	507	−22	−165	9	−193	−205	−115	−652
of which: Short-term	4 721 ..	....	....	....	....	....	....	....	....
Banks	4 722 ..	3,221	−1,545	−1,987	−5,642	−2,026	4,340	−15,546	−10,505
of which: Short-term	4 724 ..	....	....	....	....	....	....	....	....
Other sectors	4 725 ..	2,181	4,539	8,244	−4,855	−7,652	−4,199	−116	−4,748
of which: Short-term	4 727 ..	....	....	....	....	....	....	....	....
Currency and deposits	4 730 ..	−13,237	−8,351	−12,645	−8,015	−39,609	−36,983	−18,218	−11,331
Monetary authorities	4 731 ..	....	....	....	....	....	....	....	....
General government	4 732 ..	....	....	....	....	....	....	....	....
Banks	4 733 ..	−11,699	−1,978	−7,786	7,070	−28,729	−31,442	−3,212	4,588
Other sectors	4 734 ..	−1,537	−6,373	−4,859	−15,084	−10,879	−5,540	−15,006	−15,919
Other assets	4 736 ..	−7,548	−1,610	−11,579	−10,853	−9,065	1,475	−1,855	−19,810
Monetary authorities	4 737 ..	....	....	....	....	....	....	....	....
of which: Short-term	4 739 ..	....	....	....	....	....	....	....	....
General government	4 740 ..	−168	−188	−230	−290	−284	−675	−293	1
of which: Short-term	4 742 ..	....	....	....	....	....	....	....	....
Banks	4 743 ..	−6,693	2,540	−6,517	−10,902	−12,989	6,161	−1,857	−19,766
of which: Short-term	4 745 ..	....	....	....	....	....	....	....	....
Other sectors	4 746 ..	−686	−3,963	−4,832	338	4,208	−4,011	295	−45
of which: Short-term	4 748 ..	....	....	....	....	....	....	....	....
Liabilities	4 753 ..	**12,257**	**−3,948**	**29,959**	**35,950**	**59,417**	**12,931**	**12,106**	**9,650**
Trade credits	4 756 ..	−645	158	492	143	341	729	−480	−337
General government	4 757 ..	....	....	....	....	....	....	....	....
of which: Short-term	4 759 ..	....	....	....	....	....	....	....	....
Other sectors	4 760 ..	−645	158	492	143	341	729	−480	−337
of which: Short-term	4 762 ..	....	....	....	....	....	....	....	....
Loans	4 764 ..	1,724	−1,744	4,573	17,399	11,893	4,692	−8,514	8,471
Monetary authorities	4 765 ..	....	....	....	....	....	....	....	....
of which: Use of Fund credit and loans from the Fund..	4 766 ..	....	....	....	....	....	....	....	....
of which: Short-term	4 768 ..	....	....	....	....	....	....	....	....
General government	4 769 ..	−315	−639	....	....	....	−297	....	−144
of which: Short-term	4 771 ..	....	....	....	....	....	....	....	....
Banks	4 772 ..	....	....	....	....	....	....	....	....
of which: Short-term	4 774 ..	....	....	....	....	....	....	....	....
Other sectors	4 775 ..	2,039	−1,104	4,573	17,399	11,893	4,989	−8,514	8,616
of which: Short-term	4 777 ..	....	....	....	....	....	....	....	....
Currency and deposits	4 780 ..	12,494	−985	23,971	18,131	43,452	9,000	12,635	75
Monetary authorities	4 781 ..	....	....	....	....	....	....	....	....
General government	4 782 ..	....	....	....	....	....	....	....	....
Banks	4 783 ..	12,557	−1,000	40,912	18,134	45,447	23,838	20,592	10,783
Other sectors	4 784 ..	−64	15	−16,942	−2	−1,995	−14,838	−7,957	−10,709
Other liabilities	4 786 ..	−1,316	−1,377	923	277	3,730	−1,490	8,465	1,441
Monetary authorities	4 787 ..	....	....	....	....	....	....	8,135	....
of which: Short-term	4 789 ..	....	....	....	....	....	....	....	....
General government	4 790 ..	−212	−115	−138	−109	−132	249	−376	−47
of which: Short-term	4 792 ..	....	....	....	....	....	....	....	....
Banks	4 793 ..	....	....	....	....	....	....	....	....
of which: Short-term	4 795 ..	....	....	....	....	....	....	....	....
Other sectors	4 796 ..	−1,104	−1,262	1,061	386	3,863	−1,739	705	1,487
of which: Short-term	4 798 ..	....	....	....	....	....	....	....	....
E. RESERVE ASSETS	4 802 ..	**3,255**	**2,836**	**−1,335**	**−826**	**−3,906**	**−1,769**	**−10,470**	**−3,815**
Monetary gold	4 812 ..	....	....	....	....	....	....	....	....
Special drawing rights	4 811 ..	−49	−46	−48	−19	−4	−1	−8,173	−5
Reserve position in the Fund	4 810 ..	69	648	1,702	624	204	−591	−1,133	−666
Foreign exchange	4 803 ..	3,235	2,233	−2,989	−1,431	−4,106	−1,177	−1,164	−3,144
Other claims	4 813 ..	....	....	....	....	....	....	....	....
NET ERRORS AND OMISSIONS	4 998 ..	**1,098**	**2,313**	**−2,287**	**1,998**	**1,114**	**−2,930**	**−218**	**1,145**

Table 3. INTERNATIONAL INVESTMENT POSITION (End-period stocks), 2003–2010

(Millions of U.S. dollars)

	Code	2003	2004	2005	2006	2007	2008	2009	2010
ASSETS	8 995 C.	**710,478**	**791,633**	**855,659**	**1,019,569**	**1,213,076**	**1,220,526**	**1,396,016**	**1,473,390**
Direct investment abroad	8 505 ..	**312,167**	**372,671**	**388,317**	**450,313**	**521,653**	**524,274**	**593,523**	**616,134**
Equity capital and reinvested earnings	8 506 ..	288,234	340,948	364,027	417,332	498,816	506,375	565,145	586,676
Claims on affiliated enterprises	8 507 ..	....	....	....	....	....	....	....	....
Liabilities to affiliated enterprises	8 508 ..	....	....	....	....	....	....	....	....
Other capital	8 530 ..	23,933	31,723	24,290	32,981	22,836	17,899	28,377	29,458
Claims on affiliated enterprises	8 535 ..	....	....	....	....	....	....	....	....
Liabilities to affiliated enterprises	8 540 ..	....	....	....	....	....	....	....	....
Portfolio investment	8 602 ..	**194,196**	**220,515**	**250,934**	**318,639**	**373,959**	**348,119**	**382,956**	**393,918**
Equity securities	8 610 ..	150,797	162,656	169,021	195,072	229,356	226,880	249,584	258,533
Monetary authorities	8 611 ..	....	....	....	....	....	....	....	....
General government	8 612 ..	....	....	....	....	....	....	....	....
Banks	8 613 ..	....	....	....	....	....	....	....	....
Other sectors	8 614 ..	150,797	162,656	169,021	195,072	229,356	226,880	249,584	258,533
Debt securities	8 619 ..	43,400	57,859	81,913	123,567	144,603	121,239	133,372	135,385
Bonds and notes	8 620 ..	34,925	48,654	70,702	106,434	137,001	118,391	128,949	128,666
Monetary authorities	8 621 ..	....	....	....	....	....	....	....	....
General government	8 622 ..	....	....	....	....	....	....	....	....
Banks	8 623 ..	....	....	....	....	....	....	....	....
Other sectors	8 624 ..	34,925	48,654	70,702	106,434	137,001	118,391	128,949	128,666
Money market instruments	8 630 ..	8,475	9,205	11,211	17,133	7,602	2,848	4,423	6,719
Monetary authorities	8 631 ..	....	....	....	....	....	....	....	....
General government	8 632 ..	....	....	....	....	....	....	....	....
Banks	8 633 ..	....	....	....	....	....	....	....	....
Other sectors	8 634 ..	8,475	9,205	11,211	17,133	7,602	2,848	4,423	6,719
Financial derivatives	8 900 ..	....	....	....	....	....	....	....	....
Monetary authorities	8 901 ..	....	....	....	....	....	....	....	....
General government	8 902 ..	....	....	....	....	....	....	....	....
Banks	8 903 ..	....	....	....	....	....	....	....	....
Other sectors	8 904 ..	....	....	....	....	....	....	....	....
Other investment	8 703 ..	**168,777**	**164,936**	**183,746**	**215,469**	**276,386**	**306,178**	**366,068**	**408,063**
Trade credits	8 706 ..	6,151	6,359	6,277	7,671	7,491	5,893	6,775	6,877
General government	8 707 ..	....	....	....	....	....	....	....	....
of which: Short-term	8 709 ..	....	....	....	....	....	....	....	....
Other sectors	8 710 ..	6,151	6,359	6,277	7,671	7,491	5,893	6,775	6,877
of which: Short-term	8 712 ..	....	....	....	....	....	....	....	....
Loans	8 714 ..	45,208	41,100	39,437	62,593	78,205	76,359	98,872	109,462
Monetary authorities	8 715 ..	....	....	....	....	....	....	....	....
of which: Short-term	8 718 ..	....	....	....	....	....	....	....	....
General government	8 719 ..	23,525	17,862	16,826	19,269	20,816	24,811	25,139	24,175
of which: Short-term	8 721 ..	....	....	....	....	....	....	....	....
Banks	8 722 ..	11,118	13,397	15,690	30,480	36,071	30,646	49,623	57,294
of which: Short-term	8 724 ..	....	....	....	....	....	....	....	....
Other sectors	8 725 ..	10,565	9,840	6,920	12,844	21,319	20,902	24,111	27,993
of which: Short-term	8 727 ..	....	....	....	....	....	....	....	....
Currency and deposits	8 730 ..	85,018	90,929	103,746	113,465	159,799	185,181	215,001	225,561
Monetary authorities	8 731 ..	....	....	....	....	....	....	....	....
General government	8 732 ..	....	....	....	....	....	....	....	....
Banks	8 733 ..	55,934	59,401	67,492	61,959	93,930	119,575	126,717	120,573
Other sectors	8 734 ..	29,084	31,528	36,254	51,506	65,869	65,607	88,284	104,988
Other assets	8 736 ..	32,401	26,548	34,286	31,740	30,890	38,745	45,420	66,163
Monetary authorities	8 737 ..	....	....	....	....	....	....	....	....
of which: Short-term	8 739 ..	....	....	....	....	....	....	....	....
General government	8 740 ..	....	....	....	....	....	....	....	....
of which: Short-term	8 742 ..	....	....	....	....	....	....	....	....
Banks	8 743 ..	10,562	274	2,579	....	....	....	....	9,722
of which: Short-term	8 745 ..	....	....	....	....	....	....	....	....
Other sectors	8 746 ..	21,838	26,274	31,708	31,740	30,890	38,745	45,420	56,441
of which: Short-term	8 748 ..	....	....	....	....	....	....	....	....
Reserve assets	8 802 ..	**35,338**	**33,512**	**32,661**	**35,149**	**41,078**	**41,956**	**53,469**	**55,275**
Monetary gold	8 812 ..	6	6	5	6	6	6	6	6
Special drawing rights	8 811 ..	838	924	897	963	1,016	991	9,212	9,054
Reserve position in the Fund	8 810 ..	3,847	3,338	1,401	833	661	1,249	2,424	3,056
Foreign exchange	8 803 ..	30,647	29,243	30,358	33,347	39,395	39,709	41,827	43,159
Other claims	8 813 ..	....	....	....	....	....	....	....	....

Table 3 (Concluded). INTERNATIONAL INVESTMENT POSITION (End-period stocks), 2003–2010

(Millions of U.S. dollars)

	Code	2003	2004	2005	2006	2007	2008	2009	2010
LIABILITIES..	8 995 D.	**870,018**	**949,830**	**997,283**	**1,092,188**	**1,340,309**	**1,259,943**	**1,492,190**	**1,660,127**
Direct investment in Canada.............................	8 555 ..	**274,269**	**315,262**	**341,630**	**376,425**	**497,204**	**443,191**	**523,197**	**561,111**
Equity capital and reinvested earnings..................	8 556 ..	225,080	261,179	283,321	315,884	421,178	339,670	398,169	448,847
Claims on direct investors..................	8 557 ..	....	....	....	....	....	....	....	....
Liabilities to direct investors..................	8 558 ..	....	....	....	....	....	....	....	....
Other capital..................	8 580 ..	49,189	54,083	58,309	60,541	76,026	103,521	125,029	112,264
Claims on direct investors..................	8 585 ..	....	....	....	....	....	....	....	....
Liabilities to direct investors..................	8 590 ..	....	....	....	....	....	....	....	....
Portfolio investment.............................	8 652 ..	**394,960**	**433,614**	**431,295**	**457,163**	**508,469**	**483,876**	**613,016**	**730,257**
Equity securities..................	8 660 ..	64,466	83,119	80,319	84,999	96,921	80,665	105,935	120,125
Banks..................	8 663 ..	....	....	....	....	....	....	....	....
Other sectors..................	8 664 ..	64,466	83,119	80,319	84,999	96,921	80,665	105,935	120,125
Debt securities..................	8 669 ..	330,494	350,496	350,976	372,164	411,548	403,211	507,081	610,132
Bonds and notes..................	8 670 ..	313,945	334,194	333,129	351,127	389,284	374,713	475,658	574,605
Monetary authorities..................	8 671 ..	....	....	....	....	....	....	....	....
General government..................	8 672 ..	127,214	130,862	127,809	130,614	133,802	121,812	172,550	234,902
Banks..................	8 673 ..	1,536	1,881	1,973	1,746	1,765	1,799	3,623	14,392
Other sectors..................	8 674 ..	185,195	201,451	203,346	218,766	253,718	251,102	299,485	325,311
Money market instruments..................	8 680 ..	16,549	16,302	17,847	21,037	22,264	28,498	31,423	35,528
Monetary authorities..................	8 681 ..	....	....	....	....	....	....	....	....
General government..................	8 682 ..	9,281	7,577	8,917	11,751	11,482	18,232	23,358	26,652
Banks..................	8 683 ..	....	....	....	....	....	....	....	....
Other sectors..................	8 684 ..	7,268	8,725	8,930	9,287	10,783	10,266	8,065	8,875
Financial derivatives.............................	8 905 ..	....	....	....	....	....	....	....	....
Monetary authorities..................	8 906 ..	....	....	....	....	....	....	....	....
General government..................	8 907 ..	....	....	....	....	....	....	....	....
Banks..................	8 908 ..	....	....	....	....	....	....	....	....
Other sectors..................	8 909 ..	....	....	....	....	....	....	....	....
Other investment.............................	8 753 ..	**200,789**	**200,953**	**224,358**	**258,601**	**334,636**	**332,876**	**355,977**	**368,759**
Trade credits..................	8 756 ..	4,873	5,142	5,831	5,991	6,470	5,825	6,332	6,220
General government..................	8 757 ..	....	....	....	....	....	....	....	....
of which: Short-term..................	8 759 ..	....	....	....	....	....	....	....	....
Other sectors..................	8 760 ..	4,873	5,142	5,831	5,991	6,470	5,825	6,332	6,220
of which: Short-term..................	8 762 ..	....	....	....	....	....	....	....	....
Loans..................	8 764 ..	42,173	36,681	32,820	45,480	61,921	66,706	64,812	78,515
Monetary authorities..................	8 765 ..	....	....	....	....	....	....	....	....
of which: Use of Fund credit and loans from the Fund....	8 766 ..	....	....	....	....	....	....	....	....
of which: Short-term..................	8 768 ..	....	....	....	....	....	....	....	....
General government..................	8 769 ..	924	292	383	381	421	122	143	....
of which: Short-term..................	8 771 ..	....	....	....	....	....	....	....	....
Banks..................	8 772 ..	....	....	....	....	....	....	....	....
of which: Short-term..................	8 774 ..	....	....	....	....	....	....	....	....
Other sectors..................	8 775 ..	41,248	36,388	32,438	45,099	61,500	66,583	64,668	78,515
of which: Short-term..................	8 777 ..	....	....	....	....	....	....	....	....
Currency and deposits..................	8 780 ..	141,704	146,210	172,627	194,612	246,450	246,298	269,874	268,151
Monetary authorities..................	8 781 ..	....	....	....	....	....	....	....	....
General government..................	8 782 ..	....	....	....	....	....	....	....	....
Banks..................	8 783 ..	141,643	146,127	172,526	194,515	246,295	246,055	269,616	267,982
Other sectors..................	8 784 ..	62	83	102	97	156	243	258	169
Other liabilities..................	8 786 ..	12,039	12,920	13,079	12,518	19,795	14,048	14,959	15,874
Monetary authorities..................	8 787 ..	....	....	....	....	....	....	....	....
of which: Short-term..................	8 789 ..	....	....	....	....	....	....	....	....
General government..................	8 790 ..	375	316	217	158	111	387	83	98
of which: Short-term..................	8 792 ..	....	....	....	....	....	....	....	....
Banks..................	8 793 ..	....	....	....	....	....	....	....	....
of which: Short-term..................	8 795 ..	....	....	....	....	....	....	....	....
Other sectors..................	8 796 ..	11,664	12,604	12,862	12,361	19,683	13,660	14,876	15,775
of which: Short-term..................	8 798 ..	....	....	....	....	....	....	....	....
NET INTERNATIONAL INVESTMENT POSITION........	8 995 ..	**−159,541**	**−158,197**	**−141,624**	**−72,619**	**−127,233**	**−39,417**	**−96,174**	**−186,738**
Conversion rates: Canadian dollars per U.S. dollar (end of period)............................	0 102 ..	**1.2924**	**1.2036**	**1.1645**	**1.1653**	**.9881**	**1.2246**	**1.0466**	**1.0009**

Table 1. ANALYTIC PRESENTATION, 2003–2010

(Millions of U.S. dollars)

	Code	2003	2004	2005	2006	2007	2008	2009	2010
A. Current Account[1]	4 993 Z.	**−90.63**	**−130.01**	**−40.67**	**−82.73**	**−198.26**	**−205.48**	**−239.29**	**−184.29**
Goods: exports f.o.b.	2 100 ..	52.80	57.45	88.85	95.70	81.80	115.72	93.96	135.34
Goods: imports f.o.b.	3 100 ..	−361.37	−435.40	−437.67	−559.55	−745.67	−830.71	−770.78	−814.16
Balance on Goods	4 100 ..	*−308.57*	*−377.95*	*−348.83*	*−463.85*	*−663.86*	*−714.98*	*−676.83*	*−678.83*
Services: credit	2 200 ..	202.46	238.79	269.42	382.26	490.85	601.17	486.19	518.25
Services: debit	3 200 ..	−188.51	−206.67	−208.61	−249.91	−294.40	−358.75	−318.30	−296.10
Balance on Goods and Services	4 991 ..	*−294.61*	*−345.83*	*−288.02*	*−331.50*	*−467.41*	*−472.57*	*−508.93*	*−456.68*
Income: credit	2 300 ..	16.20	17.76	19.23	19.07	26.73	27.69	22.89	13.99
Income: debit	3 300 ..	−29.38	−36.25	−52.70	−59.39	−58.90	−75.73	−66.29	−82.11
Balance on Goods, Services, and Income	4 992 ..	*−307.80*	*−364.31*	*−321.49*	*−371.81*	*−499.59*	*−520.61*	*−552.34*	*−524.80*
Current transfers: credit	2 379 Z.	235.42	277.63	311.99	333.99	405.52	422.28	391.45	409.65
Current transfers: debit	3 379 ..	−18.24	−43.33	−31.17	−44.91	−104.20	−107.15	−78.40	−69.14
B. Capital Account[1]	4 994 Z.	**25.15**	**23.57**	**20.71**	**17.47**	**27.03**	**26.75**	**45.89**	**39.85**
Capital account: credit	2 994 Z.	25.15	23.57	21.07	17.47	27.03	26.75	45.89	39.85
Capital account: debit	3 994 ..	....	....	−.36	....	....	....	....	....
Total, Groups A Plus B	4 981 ..	*−65.47*	*−106.44*	*−19.96*	*−65.26*	*−171.23*	*−178.73*	*−193.41*	*−144.44*
C. Financial Account[1]	4 995 W.	**81.55**	**124.48**	**83.15**	**151.19**	**278.47**	**315.54**	**228.29**	**243.86**
Direct investment abroad	4 505 ..	−.86	....	....	....	−.35	2.51	.17	.15
Direct investment in Cape Verde	4 555 Z.	39.26	67.59	80.44	131.82	191.87	211.32	119.78	111.70
Portfolio investment assets	4 602 ..	....	....	....	−.13	−.40	....	....	....
Equity securities	4 610 ..	....	....	....	−.13	−.40	....	....	....
Debt securities	4 619 ..	....	....	....	....	....	....	....	....
Portfolio investment liabilities	4 652 Z.	....	....	....	.29	4.13	.14	5.64	.01
Equity securities	4 660 ..	....	....	....	.29	2.22	....	1.84	....
Debt securities	4 669 Z.	....	....	....	....	1.91	.14	3.80	.01
Financial derivatives	4 910 ..	....	....	....	....	....	....	....	....
Financial derivatives assets	4 900 ..	....	....	....	....	....	....	....	....
Financial derivatives liabilities	4 905 ..	....	....	....	....	....	....	....	....
Other investment assets	4 703 ..	−7.54	−7.54	−76.28	14.56	−9.18	40.87	16.93	−6.20
Monetary authorities	4 701 ..	2.00	4.78	−.37	.30	.30	−2.61	.18	1.55
General government	4 704 ..	−5.22	....	−2.21	....	....	....	....	....
Banks	4 705 ..	−4.32	−12.32	−64.16	14.54	−7.10	43.31	16.74	−8.29
Other sectors	4 728 ..	....	.01	−9.54	−.28	−2.38	.17	....	.55
Other investment liabilities	4 753 W.	50.70	64.42	78.99	4.66	92.40	60.71	85.77	138.20
Monetary authorities	4 753 WA	−.66	−.28	.08	−.07	−.07	1.85	17.40	.71
General government	4 753 ZB	14.30	6.62	26.72	25.48	28.81	42.52	81.44	177.27
Banks	4 753 ZC	33.86	7.79	31.20	−42.44	12.89	7.13	−13.22	7.20
Other sectors	4 753 ZD	3.20	50.30	20.98	21.69	50.76	9.21	.15	−46.98
Total, Groups A Through C	4 983 ..	*16.08*	*18.04*	*63.18*	*85.93*	*107.24*	*136.81*	*34.89*	*99.42*
D. Net Errors and Omissions	4 998 ..	**−12.40**	**9.74**	**1.73**	**−9.98**	**−.12**	**−107.75**	**−45.69**	**−70.30**
Total, Groups A Through D	4 984 ..	*3.68*	*27.78*	*64.92*	*75.96*	*107.11*	*29.06*	*−10.80*	*29.12*
E. Reserves and Related Items	4 802 A.	**−3.68**	**−27.78**	**−64.92**	**−75.96**	**−107.11**	**−29.06**	**10.80**	**−29.12**
Reserve assets	4 802 ..	1.46	−37.40	−56.07	−57.99	−86.86	−28.10	5.71	−27.20
Use of Fund credit and loans	4 766 ..	3.52	1.80	3.72	....	−.19	−.77	−1.53	−2.25
Exceptional financing	4 920 ..	−8.67	7.83	−12.56	−17.97	−20.07	−.19	6.62	.34
Conversion rates: Cape Verde escudos per U.S. dollar	0 101 ..	**97.703**	**88.808**	**88.670**	**87.901**	**80.567**	**75.279**	**79.377**	**83.259**

[1] Excludes components that have been classified in the categories of Group E.

Table 2. STANDARD PRESENTATION, 2003–2010

(Millions of U.S. dollars)

	Code	2003	2004	2005	2006	2007	2008	2009	2010
CURRENT ACCOUNT	4 993	−90.63	−130.01	−40.67	−82.73	−198.26	−205.48	−239.29	−184.29
A. GOODS	4 100	−308.57	−377.95	−348.83	−463.85	−663.86	−714.98	−676.83	−678.83
Credit	2 100	52.80	57.45	88.85	95.70	81.80	115.72	93.96	135.34
General merchandise: exports f.o.b.	2 110	3.00	2.65	9.09	12.88	9.71	21.92	26.23	36.38
Goods for processing: exports f.o.b.	2 150	11.09	13.47	9.75	8.85	11.33	11.72	10.38	10.13
Repairs on goods	2 160	1.69	1.66	1.96	1.02	.80	1.12	3.06	2.47
Goods procured in ports by carriers	2 170	37.02	39.66	68.05	72.94	59.97	80.96	54.28	86.37
Nonmonetary gold	2 180	....	....	....	....	....	....	....	....
Debit	3 100	−361.37	−435.40	−437.67	−559.55	−745.67	−830.71	−770.78	−814.16
General merchandise: imports f.o.b.	3 110	−339.53	−415.25	−413.82	−524.33	−719.98	−792.27	−737.07	−791.52
Goods for processing: imports f.o.b.	3 150	−7.28	−8.43	−4.49	−5.66	−6.63	−6.40	−6.41	−6.63
Repairs on goods	3 160	−7.27	−5.10	−6.00	−9.15	−7.15	−7.91	−7.68	−5.56
Goods procured in ports by carriers	3 170	−7.28	−6.61	−13.36	−20.40	−11.91	−24.13	−19.63	−10.46
Nonmonetary gold	3 180	....	....	....	....	....	....	....	....
B. SERVICES	4 200	13.95	32.12	60.81	132.35	196.45	242.42	167.89	222.15
Total credit	2 200	*202.46*	*238.79*	*269.42*	*382.26*	*490.85*	*601.17*	*486.19*	*518.25*
Total debit	3 200	*−188.51*	*−206.67*	*−208.61*	*−249.91*	*−294.40*	*−358.75*	*−318.30*	*−296.10*
Transportation services, credit	2 205	83.15	99.05	105.86	123.54	126.69	179.61	139.77	178.46
Passenger	2 850	*47.81*	*53.57*	*55.27*	*71.12*	*71.12*	*79.81*	*63.35*	*108.81*
Freight	2 851	*.01*	*....*	*.59*	*.53*	*.03*	*....*	*.03*	*....*
Other	2 852	*35.34*	*45.48*	*50.01*	*51.90*	*55.54*	*99.80*	*76.39*	*69.65*
Sea transport, passenger	2 207	....	....	....	....	....	....	.09	
Sea transport, freight	2 208	.01	....	.59	.53	.03	....	.03	....
Sea transport, other	2 209	1.96	3.71	6.39	5.31	5.99	3.31	2.91	5.21
Air transport, passenger	2 211	47.81	53.57	55.27	71.12	71.12	79.81	63.27	108.81
Air transport, freight	2 212	....	....	....	....	....	....	....	....
Air transport, other	2 213	33.37	41.77	43.62	46.58	49.56	96.49	73.48	64.44
Other transport, passenger	2 215	....	....	....	....	....	....	....	....
Other transport, freight	2 216	....	....	....	....	....	....	....	....
Other transport, other	2 217	....	....	....	....	....	....	....	....
Transportation services, debit	3 205	−90.00	−91.13	−97.94	−127.25	−131.34	−161.43	−126.25	−102.12
Passenger	3 850	*−15.64*	*−14.60*	*−15.43*	*−24.02*	*−16.06*	*−10.36*	*−8.75*	*−9.33*
Freight	3 851	*−31.49*	*−33.23*	*−39.17*	*−51.02*	*−63.21*	*−79.47*	*−63.30*	*−56.58*
Other	3 852	*−42.87*	*−43.30*	*−43.34*	*−52.20*	*−52.07*	*−71.60*	*−54.20*	*−36.21*
Sea transport, passenger	3 207	....	....	....	....	....	....	−.03	
Sea transport, freight	3 208	−31.48	−33.18	−39.16	−50.26	−63.21	−79.38	−63.30	−56.54
Sea transport, other	3 209	−.22	....	−.01	−2.92	−4.56	−.02	−.02	−.27
Air transport, passenger	3 211	−15.64	−14.60	−15.43	−24.02	−16.06	−10.36	−8.72	−9.33
Air transport, freight	3 212	−.01	−.05	−.02	−.77	−.01	−.10	....	−.03
Air transport, other	3 213	−42.65	−43.29	−43.32	−49.28	−47.51	−71.58	−54.18	−35.94
Other transport, passenger	3 215	....	....	....	....	....	....	....	....
Other transport, freight	3 216	....	....	....	....	....	....	....	....
Other transport, other	3 217	....	....	....	....	....	....	....	....
Travel, credit	2 236	86.80	99.41	122.01	208.85	303.93	351.79	293.30	289.41
Business travel	2 237	1.52	2.58	5.95	9.40	11.17	13.53	23.73	16.48
Personal travel	2 240	85.28	96.83	116.06	199.46	292.76	338.27	269.56	272.94
Travel, debit	3 236	−72.70	−77.74	−67.23	−82.38	−106.94	−132.78	−135.58	−127.34
Business travel	3 237	−9.39	−7.28	−11.68	−19.43	−29.04	−34.91	−52.75	−56.14
Personal travel	3 240	−63.31	−70.46	−55.55	−62.96	−77.90	−97.87	−82.83	−71.20
Other services, credit	2 200 BA	32.51	40.33	41.55	49.87	60.23	69.77	53.12	50.37
Communications	2 245	14.59	17.05	18.77	22.72	25.91	30.35	27.95	23.24
Construction	2 249	....	....	....	....	.11	.01	.14	.01
Insurance	2 253	1.17	1.73	3.26	4.17	5.03	7.81	7.46	5.58
Financial	2 260	.15	.06	.64	1.16	1.02	1.21	1.37	.89
Computer and information	2 262	.04	.10	.02	.02	.01	.49	.08	.01
Royalties and licence fees	2 266	.07	....	....	....	....	....	....	....
Other business services	2 268	3.52	3.00	2.69	.87	3.58	3.19	1.24	.94
Personal, cultural, and recreational	2 287	.05	.04	.01	.01	1.93	.13	.21	.01
Government, n.i.e.	2 291	12.92	18.35	16.15	20.90	22.65	26.58	14.66	19.70
Other services, debit	3 200 BA	−25.80	−37.80	−43.44	−40.28	−56.12	−64.54	−56.46	−66.65
Communications	3 245	−3.43	−2.88	−3.34	−3.27	−4.12	−6.63	−7.50	−4.01
Construction	3 249	....	....	....	....	....	....	−.84	−2.11
Insurance	3 253	−5.23	−7.24	−7.51	−9.73	−13.30	−17.02	−15.17	−16.05
Financial	3 260	−1.91	−2.55	−3.85	−2.68	−1.32	−1.81	−2.29	−2.30
Computer and information	3 262	−2.94	−3.80	−4.69	−3.57	−8.81	−5.36	−4.91	−4.84
Royalties and licence fees	3 266	−.05	−.26	−.07	....	−1.29	−.03	....	−.34
Other business services	3 268	−6.34	−8.28	−15.74	−12.23	−16.07	−23.20	−13.84	−24.80
Personal, cultural, and recreational	3 287	−.31	−.30	−.64	−.72	−1.81	−.65	−.80	−1.74
Government, n.i.e.	3 291	−5.60	−12.49	−7.60	−8.07	−9.40	−9.85	−11.10	−10.46

Table 2 (Continued). STANDARD PRESENTATION, 2003–2010

(Millions of U.S. dollars)

	Code	2003	2004	2005	2006	2007	2008	2009	2010
C. INCOME	4 300	**−13.19**	**−18.49**	**−33.47**	**−40.32**	**−32.17**	**−48.05**	**−43.41**	**−68.11**
Total credit	2 300	*16.20*	*17.76*	*19.23*	*19.07*	*26.73*	*27.69*	*22.89*	*13.99*
Total debit	3 300	*−29.38*	*−36.25*	*−52.70*	*−59.39*	*−58.90*	*−75.73*	*−66.29*	*−82.11*
Compensation of employees, credit	2 310	.17	.39	.15	.78	.41	.90	.37	.53
Compensation of employees, debit	3 310	−.54	−.62	−1.27	−.65	−1.47	−2.42	−4.70	−1.52
Investment income, credit	2 320	16.03	17.37	19.08	18.29	26.32	26.79	22.51	13.46
Direct investment income	2 330	.96	....	....	.03	....	.03	....	.17
Dividends and distributed branch profits	2 332	.11	....	....	.03	....	.03	....	....
Reinvested earnings and undistributed branch profits	2 333	.86	....	....	....	....	....	....	....
Income on debt (interest)	2 334	....	....	....	....	....	....	....	.17
Portfolio investment income	2 339	5.91	8.58	7.41	4.11	4.69	5.75	6.06	6.07
Income on equity	2 340	4.95	6.97	7.41	4.11	4.69	5.75	6.06	6.07
Income on bonds and notes	2 350	.97	1.61	....	....	....	....	....	....
Income on money market instruments	2 360	....	....	....	....	....	....	....	....
Other investment income	2 370	9.15	8.79	11.66	14.16	21.62	21.00	16.45	7.23
Investment income, debit	3 320	**−28.84**	**−35.62**	**−51.43**	**−58.74**	**−57.43**	**−73.31**	**−61.60**	**−80.58**
Direct investment income	3 330	−2.78	−3.75	−10.85	−24.08	−28.20	−38.21	−26.33	−49.67
Dividends and distributed branch profits	3 332	−1.82	−3.49	−10.38	−18.20	−17.15	−34.99	−22.96	−47.25
Reinvested earnings and undistributed branch profits	3 333	−.96	−.26	−.20	−5.57	−10.48	−2.69	−2.09	−.02
Income on debt (interest)	3 334	....	....	−.27	−.31	−.57	−.53	−1.28	−2.40
Portfolio investment income	3 339	....	....	....	−.03	−.76	−.41	−6.47	−.11
Income on equity	3 340	....	....	....	−.03	−.76	−.34	−1.50	....
Income on bonds and notes	3 350	....	....	....	....	....	−.07	−4.96	−.11
Income on money market instruments	3 360	....	....	....	....	....	....	....	....
Other investment income	3 370	−26.06	−31.87	−40.58	−34.63	−28.46	−34.69	−28.79	−30.80
D. CURRENT TRANSFERS	4 379	**217.17**	**234.30**	**280.82**	**289.08**	**301.32**	**315.13**	**313.05**	**340.51**
Credit	2 379	**235.42**	**277.63**	**311.99**	**333.99**	**405.52**	**422.28**	**391.45**	**409.65**
General government	2 380	50.21	54.85	50.11	51.78	74.24	106.22	90.48	109.32
Other sectors	2 390	185.21	222.78	261.88	282.22	331.29	316.06	300.97	300.33
Workers' remittances	2 391	108.37	112.97	136.50	135.83	138.46	154.21	136.38	130.39
Other current transfers	2 392	76.84	109.82	125.38	146.38	192.83	161.85	164.59	169.94
Debit	3 379	**−18.24**	**−43.33**	**−31.17**	**−44.91**	**−104.20**	**−107.15**	**−78.40**	**−69.14**
General government	3 380	−1.06	−1.20	−1.99	−4.04	−5.67	−2.66	−1.98	−3.33
Other sectors	3 390	−17.18	−42.13	−29.18	−40.87	−98.53	−104.49	−76.42	−65.82
Workers' remittances	3 391	−6.65	−11.35	−3.90	−5.07	−4.55	−7.59	−7.14	−6.22
Other current transfers	3 392	−10.53	−30.78	−25.28	−35.80	−93.98	−96.90	−69.29	−59.60
CAPITAL AND FINANCIAL ACCOUNT	4 996	**103.02**	**120.27**	**38.94**	**92.71**	**198.39**	**313.23**	**284.98**	**254.59**
CAPITAL ACCOUNT	4 994	**25.15**	**23.57**	**20.71**	**17.47**	**27.03**	**26.75**	**45.89**	**39.85**
Total credit	2 994	*25.15*	*23.57*	*21.07*	*17.47*	*27.03*	*26.75*	*45.89*	*39.85*
Total debit	3 994	....	....	*−.36*	....	....	....	....	....
Capital transfers, credit	2 400	**25.15**	**23.57**	**21.07**	**17.47**	**27.03**	**26.75**	**45.89**	**39.85**
General government	2 401	25.15	23.57	20.94	17.47	26.92	26.24	44.49	38.26
Debt forgiveness	2 402	....	....	....	....	.33	....	....	....
Other capital transfers	2 410	25.15	23.57	20.94	17.47	26.59	26.24	44.49	38.26
Other sectors	2 430	....	....	.13	....	.11	.51	1.39	1.59
Migrants' transfers	2 431	....	....	....	....	....	....	1.39	1.59
Debt forgiveness	2 432	....	....	....	....	....	....	....	....
Other capital transfers	2 440	....	....	.13	....	.11	.51	....	....
Capital transfers, debit	3 400	....	....	**−.36**	....	....	....	....	....
General government	3 401	....	....	−.12	....	....	....	....	....
Debt forgiveness	3 402	....	....	....	....	....	....	....	....
Other capital transfers	3 410	....	....	....	....	....	....	....	....
Other sectors	3 430	....	....	−.24	....	....	....	....	....
Migrants' transfers	3 431	....	....	....	....	....	....	....	....
Debt forgiveness	3 432	....	....	....	....	....	....	....	....
Other capital transfers	3 440	....	....	−.24	....	....	....	....	....
Nonproduced nonfinancial assets, credit	2 480	....	....	....	....	....	....	....	....
Nonproduced nonfinancial assets, debit	3 480	....	....	....	....	....	....	....	....

Cape Verde 624

Table 2 (Continued). STANDARD PRESENTATION, 2003–2010

(Millions of U.S. dollars)

	Code	2003	2004	2005	2006	2007	2008	2009	2010
FINANCIAL ACCOUNT	4 995	**77.87**	**96.71**	**18.23**	**75.24**	**171.36**	**286.48**	**239.09**	**214.74**
A. DIRECT INVESTMENT	4 500	**38.40**	**67.59**	**80.44**	**131.82**	**191.52**	**213.83**	**119.95**	**111.85**
Direct investment abroad	4 505	−.86	....	....	....	−.35	2.51	.17	.15
Equity capital	4 510	....	....	....	....	−.35	−.03	−.09	.17
Claims on affiliated enterprises	4 515	....	....	....	....	....	....	....	....
Liabilities to affiliated enterprises	4 520	....	....	....	....	....	....	....	....
Reinvested earnings	4 525	−.86	....	....	....	....	....	....	....
Other capital	4 530	....	....	....	....	....	2.55	.26	−.02
Claims on affiliated enterprises	4 535	....	....	....	....	....	....	.26	.02
Liabilities to affiliated enterprises	4 540	....	....	....	....	....	....	....	−.04
Direct investment in Cape Verde	4 555	**39.26**	**67.59**	**80.44**	**131.82**	**191.87**	**211.32**	**119.78**	**111.70**
Equity capital	4 560	38.29	54.12	63.20	143.26	182.27	207.75	114.50	90.81
Claims on direct investors	4 565	....	....	....	....	....	....	....	....
Liabilities to direct investors	4 570	....	....	....	....	....	....	....	....
Reinvested earnings	4 575	.96	.26	.20	5.57	10.48	2.69	2.09	.02
Other capital	4 580	.01	13.22	17.04	−17.01	−.89	.88	3.19	20.88
Claims on direct investors	4 585	.01	....	−.01	.25	....	.31	1.32	....
Liabilities to direct investors	4 590	....	13.22	17.04	−17.26	−.89	.56	1.87	20.88
B. PORTFOLIO INVESTMENT	4 600	....	....	....	**.16**	**3.74**	**.14**	**5.64**	**.01**
Assets	4 602	....	....	....	**−.13**	**−.40**	....	....	....
Equity securities	4 610	....	....	....	−.13	−.40	....	....	....
Monetary authorities	4 611	....	....	....	....	....	....	....	....
General government	4 612	....	....	....	....	....	....	....	....
Banks	4 613	....	....	....	....	....	....	....	....
Other sectors	4 614	....	....	....	−.13	−.40	....	....	....
Debt securities	4 619	....	....	....	....	....	....	....	....
Bonds and notes	4 620	....	....	....	....	....	....	....	....
Monetary authorities	4 621	....	....	....	....	....	....	....	....
General government	4 622	....	....	....	....	....	....	....	....
Banks	4 623	....	....	....	....	....	....	....	....
Other sectors	4 624	....	....	....	....	....	....	....	....
Money market instruments	4 630	....	....	....	....	....	....	....	....
Monetary authorities	4 631	....	....	....	....	....	....	....	....
General government	4 632	....	....	....	....	....	....	....	....
Banks	4 633	....	....	....	....	....	....	....	....
Other sectors	4 634	....	....	....	....	....	....	....	....
Liabilities	4 652	....	....	....	**.29**	**4.13**	**.14**	**5.64**	**.01**
Equity securities	4 660	....	....	....	.29	2.22	....	1.84	....
Banks	4 663	....	....	....	....	....	....	....	....
Other sectors	4 664	....	....	....	.29	2.22	....	1.84	....
Debt securities	4 669	....	....	....	....	1.91	.14	3.80	.01
Bonds and notes	4 670	....	....	....	....	1.91	.14	3.80	.01
Monetary authorities	4 671	....	....	....	....	....	....	....	....
General government	4 672	....	....	....	....	....	....	....	....
Banks	4 673	....	....	....	....	....	....	....	....
Other sectors	4 674	....	....	....	....	1.91	.14	3.80	.01
Money market instruments	4 680	....	....	....	....	....	....	....	....
Monetary authorities	4 681	....	....	....	....	....	....	....	....
General government	4 682	....	....	....	....	....	....	....	....
Banks	4 683	....	....	....	....	....	....	....	....
Other sectors	4 684	....	....	....	....	....	....	....	....
C. FINANCIAL DERIVATIVES	4 910	....	....	....	....	....	....	....	....
Monetary authorities	4 911	....	....	....	....	....	....	....	....
General government	4 912	....	....	....	....	....	....	....	....
Banks	4 913	....	....	....	....	....	....	....	....
Other sectors	4 914	....	....	....	....	....	....	....	....
Assets	4 900	....	....	....	....	....	....	....	....
Monetary authorities	4 901	....	....	....	....	....	....	....	....
General government	4 902	....	....	....	....	....	....	....	....
Banks	4 903	....	....	....	....	....	....	....	....
Other sectors	4 904	....	....	....	....	....	....	....	....
Liabilities	4 905	....	....	....	....	....	....	....	....
Monetary authorities	4 906	....	....	....	....	....	....	....	....
General government	4 907	....	....	....	....	....	....	....	....
Banks	4 908	....	....	....	....	....	....	....	....
Other sectors	4 909	....	....	....	....	....	....	....	....

Table 2 (Concluded). STANDARD PRESENTATION, 2003–2010

(Millions of U.S. dollars)

	Code	2003	2004	2005	2006	2007	2008	2009	2010
D. OTHER INVESTMENT	4 700	**38.01**	**66.52**	**−6.14**	**1.25**	**62.96**	**100.61**	**107.79**	**130.08**
Assets	4 703	**−7.54**	**−7.54**	**−76.28**	**14.56**	**−9.18**	**40.87**	**16.93**	**−6.20**
Trade credits	4 706	....	.01	.03	−.27	....	.09	....	....
General government	4 707	....	....	....	....	....	....	....	....
of which: Short-term	4 709	....	....	....	....	....	....	....	....
Other sectors	4 710	....	.01	.03	−.27	....	.09	....	....
of which: Short-term	4 712	....	.01	.03	....	....	....	....	....
Loans	4 714	.61	.66	−3.28	−3.75	−6.54	−11.09	−8.11	−11.73
Monetary authorities	4 715	....	....	....	....	....	....	....	....
of which: Short-term	4 718	....	....	....	....	....	....	....	....
General government	4 719	....	....	....	....	....	....	....	....
of which: Short-term	4 721	....	....	....	....	....	....	....	....
Banks	4 722	.61	.66	−3.28	−3.75	−6.54	−11.17	−8.11	−11.73
of which: Short-term	4 724	*.53*	*.84*	....	....	....	....	*−2.82*	*3.52*
Other sectors	4 725	....	....	....	....	....	.08	....	....
of which: Short-term	4 727	....	....	....	....	....	....	....	....
Currency and deposits	4 730	....	....	−4.79	−.01	−2.38	....	....	.55
Monetary authorities	4 731	....	....	....	....	....	....	....	....
General government	4 732	....	....	....	....	....	....	....	....
Banks	4 733	....	....	....	....	....	....	....	....
Other sectors	4 734	....	....	−4.79	−.01	−2.38	....	....	.55
Other assets	4 736	−8.15	−8.20	−68.25	18.59	−.25	51.87	25.03	4.99
Monetary authorities	4 737	2.00	4.78	−.37	.30	.30	−2.61	.18	1.55
of which: Short-term	4 739	*−1.01*	*3.29*	*−.23*	*.19*	*.19*	*−.07*	*.03*	*1.68*
General government	4 740	−5.22	....	−2.21	....	....	....	....	....
of which: Short-term	4 742	*−5.22*	....	*−2.21*	....	....	....	....	....
Banks	4 743	−4.93	−12.98	−60.88	18.29	−.55	54.48	24.85	3.44
of which: Short-term	4 745	*−4.78*	*−2.31*	*−30.67*	*22.17*	*−11.31*	*26.78*	*23.83*	*2.87*
Other sectors	4 746	....	....	−4.79	....	....	....	....	....
of which: Short-term	4 748	....	....	*−4.79*	....	....	....	....	....
Liabilities	4 753	**45.56**	**74.05**	**70.14**	**−13.31**	**72.14**	**59.74**	**90.86**	**136.28**
Trade credits	4 756	−1.82	1.66	6.15	3.13	4.90	13.99	16.71	5.20
General government	4 757	....	....	....	....	....	....	....	....
of which: Short-term	4 759	....	....	....	....	....	....	....	....
Other sectors	4 760	−1.82	1.66	6.15	3.13	4.90	13.99	16.71	5.20
of which: Short-term	4 762	*−1.82*	*1.66*	*6.15*	*3.14*	*5.01*	*15.66*	*18.11*	*11.18*
Loans	4 764	13.84	71.18	51.68	−23.05	47.25	40.47	69.51	142.92
Monetary authorities	4 765	2.86	1.52	3.80	−.07	−.26	1.07	2.51	−1.54
of which: Use of Fund credit and loans from the Fund	4 766	*3.52*	*1.80*	*3.72*	....	*−.19*	*−.77*	*−1.53*	*−2.25*
of which: Short-term	4 768	*−.11*	....	....	....	....	*1.82*	*4.04*	*.67*
General government	4 769	14.41	5.21	26.72	25.48	28.81	42.52	81.44	177.27
of which: Short-term	4 771	*.11*	*−.17*	....	....	....	....	....	....
Banks	4 772	−2.91	7.80	17.58	−49.05	−7.10	1.86	2.12	−5.02
of which: Short-term	4 774	....	....	*1.51*	*−51.47*	*−3.51*	*−.13*	*4.03*	*.08*
Other sectors	4 775	−.53	56.65	3.58	.59	25.79	−4.98	−16.56	−27.78
of which: Short-term	4 777	*−5.55*	*8.00*	*−11.25*	*−17.97*	*−20.07*	*−.19*	....	*−.04*
Currency and deposits	4 780	33.27	....	13.63	6.61	19.99	5.28	−8.72	−11.84
Monetary authorities	4 781	....	....	....	....	....	....	....	....
General government	4 782	....	....	....	....	....	....	....	....
Banks	4 783	33.27	....	13.63	6.61	19.99	5.28	−8.72	12.60
Other sectors	4 784	....	....	....	....	....	....	....	−24.44
Other liabilities	4 786	.27	1.22	−1.31	....	....	....	13.36	....
Monetary authorities	4 787	....	....	....	....	....	....	13.36	....
of which: Short-term	4 789	....	....	....	....	....	....	....	....
General government	4 790	....	1.23	−1.31	....	....	....	....	....
of which: Short-term	4 792	....	....	*−1.31*	....	....	....	....	....
Banks	4 793	.27	−.02	....	....	....	....	....	....
of which: Short-term	4 795	*.27*	*−.02*	....	....	....	....	....	....
Other sectors	4 796	....	....	....	....	....	....	....	....
of which: Short-term	4 798	....	....	....	....	....	....	....	....
E. RESERVE ASSETS	4 802	**1.46**	**−37.40**	**−56.07**	**−57.99**	**−86.86**	**−28.10**	**5.71**	**−27.20**
Monetary gold	4 812	....	....	....	....	....	....	....	....
Special drawing rights	4 811	....	−.03	.01	.02	−.11	−.12	−12.60	2.26
Reserve position in the Fund	4 810	....	....	−.02	....	....	....	....	....
Foreign exchange	4 803	1.46	−37.37	−56.06	−58.01	−86.75	−27.98	18.31	−29.46
Other claims	4 813	....	....	....	....	....	....	....	....
NET ERRORS AND OMISSIONS	4 998	**−12.40**	**9.74**	**1.73**	**−9.98**	**−.12**	**−107.75**	**−45.69**	**−70.30**

Table 3. INTERNATIONAL INVESTMENT POSITION (End-period stocks), 2003–2010

(Millions of U.S. dollars)

	Code	2003	2004	2005	2006	2007	2008	2009	2010
ASSETS	8 995 C.	....	**354.61**	**427.85**	**525.49**	**693.06**	**638.32**	....	....
Direct investment abroad	8 505 ..	....	....	....	....	**.39**	**.35**	....	....
Equity capital and reinvested earnings	8 506 ..	....	....	....	....	.39	.41	....	....
Claims on affiliated enterprises	8 507 ..	....	....	....	....	.39	.41	....	....
Liabilities to affiliated enterprises	8 508 ..	....	....	....	....	....	....	....	....
Other capital	8 530 ..	....	....	....	....	....	−.06	....	....
Claims on affiliated enterprises	8 535 ..	....	....	....	....	....	....	....	....
Liabilities to affiliated enterprises	8 540 ..	....	....	....	....	....	....	....	....
Portfolio investment	8 602 ..	....	....	....	**.13**	**.59**	**.55**	....	....
Equity securities	8 610 ..	....	....	....	.13	.59	.55	....	....
Monetary authorities	8 611 ..	....	....	....	....	....	....	....	....
General government	8 612 ..	....	....	....	....	....	....	....	....
Banks	8 613 ..	....	....	....	....	....	....	....	....
Other sectors	8 614 ..	....	....	....	.13	.59	.55	....	....
Debt securities	8 619 ..	....	....	....	....	....	....	....	....
Bonds and notes	8 620 ..	....	....	....	....	....	....	....	....
Monetary authorities	8 621 ..	....	....	....	....	....	....	....	....
General government	8 622 ..	....	....	....	....	....	....	....	....
Banks	8 623 ..	....	....	....	....	....	....	....	....
Other sectors	8 624 ..	....	....	....	....	....	....	....	....
Money market instruments	8 630 ..	....	....	....	....	....	....	....	....
Monetary authorities	8 631 ..	....	....	....	....	....	....	....	....
General government	8 632 ..	....	....	....	....	....	....	....	....
Banks	8 633 ..	....	....	....	....	....	....	....	....
Other sectors	8 634 ..	....	....	....	....	....	....	....	....
Financial derivatives	8 900 ..	....	....	....	....	....	....	....	....
Monetary authorities	8 901 ..	....	....	....	....	....	....	....	....
General government	8 902 ..	....	....	....	....	....	....	....	....
Banks	8 903 ..	....	....	....	....	....	....	....	....
Other sectors	8 904 ..	....	....	....	....	....	....	....	....
Other investment	8 703 ..	....	**215.08**	**253.88**	**270.90**	**312.61**	**250.10**	....	....
Trade credits	8 706 ..	....	−.01	−.04	.23	.26	.15	....	....
General government	8 707 ..	....	....	....	....	....	....	....	....
of which: Short-term	8 709 ..	....	....	....	....	....	....	....	....
Other sectors	8 710 ..	....	−.01	−.04	.23	.26	.15	....	....
of which: Short-term	8 712 ..	....	*−.01*	*−.04*	*−.05*	*−.05*	*−.15*	....	....
Loans	8 714 ..	....	8.75	10.68	15.87	24.89	33.95	....	....
Monetary authorities	8 715 ..	....	....	....	....	....	....	....	....
of which: Short-term	8 718 ..	....	....	....	....	....	....	....	....
General government	8 719 ..	....	....	....	....	....	....	....	....
of which: Short-term	8 721 ..	....	....	....	....	....	....	....	....
Banks	8 722 ..	....	8.75	10.68	15.87	24.89	34.03	....	....
of which: Short-term	8 724 ..	....	....	....	....	....	....	....	....
Other sectors	8 725 ..	....	....	....	....	....	−.08	....	....
of which: Short-term	8 727 ..	....	....	....	....	....	....	....	....
Currency and deposits	8 730 ..	....	3.06	7.40	8.28	11.67	11.04	....	....
Monetary authorities	8 731 ..	....	....	....	....	....	....	....	....
General government	8 732 ..	....	....	....	....	....	....	....	....
Banks	8 733 ..	....	....	....	....	....	....	....	....
Other sectors	8 734 ..	....	3.06	7.40	8.28	11.67	11.04	....	....
Other assets	8 736 ..	....	203.28	235.83	246.52	275.78	204.96	....	....
Monetary authorities	8 737 ..	....	2.80	2.76	2.77	2.78	2.73	....	....
of which: Short-term	8 739 ..	....	*1.80*	*1.77*	*1.77*	*1.77*	*1.75*	....	....
General government	8 740 ..	....	148.67	130.90	146.13	163.34	154.42	....	....
of which: Short-term	8 742 ..	....	....	....	....	....	....	....	....
Banks	8 743 ..	....	51.82	102.17	97.62	109.66	47.81	....	....
of which: Short-term	8 745 ..	....	*34.62*	*57.92*	*44.26*	*61.88*	*32.90*	....	....
Other sectors	8 746 ..	....	....	....	....	....	....	....	....
of which: Short-term	8 748 ..	....	....	....	....	....	....	....	....
Reserve assets	8 802 ..	....	**139.53**	**173.97**	**254.46**	**379.48**	**387.32**	....	....
Monetary gold	8 812 ..	....	....	....	....	....	....	....	....
Special drawing rights	8 811 ..	....	.04	.02	....	.12	.24	12.88	10.37
Reserve position in the Fund	8 810 ..	.01	.01	.02	.02	.03	.02	.03	.02
Foreign exchange	8 803 ..	....	139.49	173.92	254.43	379.33	387.05	....	....
Other claims	8 813 ..	....	....	....	....	....	....	....	....

Table 3 (Concluded). INTERNATIONAL INVESTMENT POSITION (End-period stocks), 2003–2010

(Millions of U.S. dollars)

	Code	2003	2004	2005	2006	2007	2008	2009	2010
LIABILITIES	8 995 D.	....	**1,066.66**	**1,070.87**	**1,299.39**	**1,758.99**	**1,918.66**	....	....
Direct investment in Cape Verde	8 555 ..	....	**326.40**	**360.06**	**539.12**	**807.39**	**961.13**	....	....
Equity capital and reinvested earnings	8 556 ..	....	314.41	333.18	526.26	794.01	948.48	....	....
Claims on direct investors	8 557 ..	....	....	....	....	....	....		
Liabilities to direct investors	8 558 ..	....	314.41	333.18	526.26	794.01	948.48		
Other capital	8 580 ..	....	11.99	26.88	12.87	13.39	12.65		
Claims on direct investors	8 585 ..	....	−.30	−.27	−.04	−.05	.30		
Liabilities to direct investors	8 590 ..	....	12.29	27.14	12.91	13.43	12.35		
Portfolio investment	8 652 ..	....	**.07**	**.06**	**.36**	**4.72**	**4.59**	....	....
Equity securities	8 660 ..	....	.07	.06	.36	2.67	2.53		
Banks	8 663 ..	....	....	....	....	....	....		
Other sectors	8 664 ..	....	.07	.06	.36	2.67	2.53		
Debt securities	8 669 ..	....	....	....	....	2.04	2.06		
Bonds and notes	8 670 ..	....	....	....	....	2.04	2.06		
Monetary authorities	8 671 ..	....	....	....	....	....	....		
General government	8 672 ..	....	....	....	....	....	....		
Banks	8 673 ..	....	....	....	....	....	....		
Other sectors	8 674 ..	....	....	....	....	....	....		
Money market instruments	8 680 ..	....	....	....	....	....	....		
Monetary authorities	8 681 ..	....	....	....	....	....	....		
General government	8 682 ..	....	....	....	....	....	....		
Banks	8 683 ..	....	....	....	....	....	....		
Other sectors	8 684 ..	....	....	....	....	....	....		
Financial derivatives	8 905 ..	....	....	....	....	....	....	....	....
Monetary authorities	8 906 ..	....	....	....	....	....	....		
General government	8 907 ..	....	....	....	....	....	....		
Banks	8 908 ..	....	....	....	....	....	....		
Other sectors	8 909 ..	....	....	....	....	....	....		
Other investment	8 753 ..	....	**740.18**	**710.75**	**759.91**	**946.88**	**952.95**	....	....
Trade credits	8 756 ..	....	8.45	13.24	17.74	25.58	38.16		
General government	8 757 ..	....	....	....	....	....	....		
of which: Short-term	8 759 ..	....	....	....	....	....	....		
Other sectors	8 760 ..	....	8.45	13.24	17.74	25.58	38.16		
of which: Short-term	8 762 ..	....	*8.45*	*13.24*	*17.75*	*25.70*	*39.82*		
Loans	8 764 ..	....	708.41	665.51	699.42	851.90	843.61		
Monetary authorities	8 765 ..	....	10.25	13.03	13.69	14.16	14.71		
of which: Use of Fund credit and loans from the Fund	8 766 ..	*7.31*	*9.55*	*12.35*	*13.00*	*13.46*	*12.36*	*11.04*	*8.57*
of which: Short-term	8 768 ..	....	*.10*	*.08*	*.09*	*.10*	*1.75*		
General government	8 769 ..	....	542.82	487.29	572.20	670.58	674.50		
of which: Short-term	8 771 ..	....	*10.90*	....	....	....	....		
Banks	8 772 ..	....	6.40	21.46	27.80	23.23	23.64		
of which: Short-term	8 774 ..	....	*3.83*	*4.61*	*6.46*	*3.32*	*2.98*		
Other sectors	8 775 ..	....	148.94	143.74	85.73	143.93	130.76		
of which: Short-term	8 777 ..	....	....	....	....	....	*−.17*		
Currency and deposits	8 780 ..	....	21.97	32.00	42.75	69.40	71.17		
Monetary authorities	8 781 ..	....	....	....	....	....	....		
General government	8 782 ..	....	....	....	....	....	....		
Banks	8 783 ..	....	21.97	32.00	42.75	69.40	71.17		
Other sectors	8 784 ..	....	....	....	....	....	....		
Other liabilities	8 786 ..	....	1.36	....	....	.01	.01		
Monetary authorities	8 787 ..	....	....	....	....	....	....		
of which: Short-term	8 789 ..	....	....	....	....	....	....		
General government	8 790 ..	....	1.36	....	....	.01	.01		
of which: Short-term	8 792 ..	....	*1.36*	....	....	....	....		
Banks	8 793 ..	....	....	....	....	....	....		
of which: Short-term	8 795 ..	....	....	....	....	....	....		
Other sectors	8 796 ..	....	....	....	....	....	....		
of which: Short-term	8 798 ..	....	....	....	....	....	....		
NET INTERNATIONAL INVESTMENT POSITION	8 995 ..	....	**−712.05**	**−643.02**	**−773.90**	**−1,065.92**	**−1,280.34**	....	....
Conversion rates: Cape Verde escudos per U.S. dollar (end of period)	0 102 ..	87.308	80.956	93.473	83.728	74.907	79.234	76.544	82.525

Table 1. ANALYTIC PRESENTATION, 2003–2010

(Millions of U.S. dollars)

	Code	2003	2004	2005	2006	2007	2008	2009	2010
A. Current Account[1]	4 993 Z.	**−779**	**2,074**	**1,449**	**7,154**	**7,458**	**−3,307**	**2,570**	**3,802**
Goods: exports f.o.b.	2 100 ..	21,664	32,520	41,267	58,680	67,972	66,259	54,004	71,028
Goods: imports f.o.b.	3 100 ..	−17,941	−22,935	−30,492	−35,900	−44,031	−57,730	−39,888	−55,174
Balance on Goods	4 100 ..	*3,723*	*9,585*	*10,775*	*22,780*	*23,941*	*8,529*	*14,117*	*15,855*
Services: credit	2 200 ..	5,070	6,034	7,134	7,830	8,962	10,823	8,634	10,797
Services: debit	3 200 ..	−5,688	−6,780	−7,756	−8,462	−9,950	−11,787	−10,078	−11,816
Balance on Goods and Services	4 991 ..	*3,105*	*8,839*	*10,153*	*22,149*	*22,954*	*7,565*	*12,673*	*14,836*
Income: credit	2 300 ..	1,552	1,983	2,452	3,374	6,325	5,928	5,345	5,995
Income: debit	3 300 ..	−6,041	−9,820	−12,939	−21,775	−24,950	−19,730	−17,011	−21,419
Balance on Goods, Services, and Income	4 992 ..	*−1,384*	*1,003*	*−334*	*3,748*	*4,329*	*−6,237*	*1,007*	*−588*
Current transfers: credit	2 379 Z.	901	1,411	2,199	4,003	3,857	3,875	2,512	5,481
Current transfers: debit	3 379 ..	−296	−339	−416	−596	−728	−945	−949	−1,091
B. Capital Account[1]	4 994 Z.	**....**	**5**	**41**	**13**	**16**	**3**	**15**	**5,641**
Capital account: credit	2 994 Z.	....	5	41	13	16	3	15	5,641
Capital account: debit	3 994 ..	....	....	....	....	....	....	....	....
Total, Groups A Plus B	4 981 ..	*−779*	*2,080*	*1,490*	*7,168*	*7,474*	*−3,304*	*2,585*	*9,442*
C. Financial Account[1]	4 995 W.	**1,145**	**−2,001**	**1,550**	**−3,644**	**−10,238**	**8,598**	**−1,709**	**−5,884**
Direct investment abroad	4 505 ..	−1,606	−1,563	−2,183	−2,171	−2,573	−8,041	−8,061	−8,744
Direct investment in Chile	4 555 Z.	4,307	7,173	6,984	7,298	12,534	15,150	12,874	15,095
Portfolio investment assets	4 602 ..	−4,699	−4,430	−4,227	−10,085	−15,953	−10,252	−13,691	−16,503
Equity securities	4 610 ..	−4,853	−3,205	−4,025	−2,264	−10,150	−5,162	−20,172	−11,674
Debt securities	4 619 ..	154	−1,225	−203	−7,820	−5,803	−5,090	6,481	−4,829
Portfolio investment liabilities	4 652 Z.	2,054	1,122	1,394	846	−508	2,633	1,922	9,432
Equity securities	4 660 ..	318	8	1,571	−124	388	1,948	328	1,748
Debt securities	4 669 Z.	1,736	1,114	−176	970	−896	685	1,594	7,684
Financial derivatives	4 910 ..	118	−84	−63	301	454	−952	−295	−922
Financial derivatives assets	4 900 ..	1,840	639	1,244	1,552	2,608	11,708	8,650	8,836
Financial derivatives liabilities	4 905 ..	−1,722	−723	−1,307	−1,251	−2,154	−12,660	−8,945	−9,759
Other investment assets	4 703 ..	−571	−3,389	−2,384	−3,927	−11,098	3,715	−1,412	−7,394
Monetary authorities	4 701 ..	−60	....	....	....	....	....	....	....
General government	4 704 ..	1	....	....	−591	−5,831	902	766	−388
Banks	4 705 ..	299	−166	−557	−1,042	−1,838	−136	−952	99
Other sectors	4 728 ..	−811	−3,223	−1,827	−2,294	−3,429	2,949	−1,226	−7,105
Other investment liabilities	4 753 W.	1,543	−829	2,028	4,094	6,906	6,346	6,955	3,152
Monetary authorities	4 753 WA	−3	6	....	−12	−3	−11	1,063	−8
General government	4 753 ZB	−117	−115	−443	−17	−12	−123	24	−13
Banks	4 753 ZC	1,606	170	1,276	15	2,768	1,648	2,771	181
Other sectors	4 753 ZD	57	−890	1,195	4,108	4,153	4,832	3,096	2,992
Total, Groups A Through C	4 983 ..	*367*	*79*	*3,040*	*3,524*	*−2,764*	*5,294*	*875*	*3,559*
D. Net Errors and Omissions	4 998 ..	**−724**	**−270**	**−1,329**	**−1,525**	**−449**	**1,167**	**773**	**−536**
Total, Groups A Through D	4 984 ..	*−357*	*−191*	*1,711*	*1,998*	*−3,214*	*6,461*	*1,648*	*3,023*
E. Reserves and Related Items	4 802 A.	**357**	**191**	**−1,711**	**−1,998**	**3,214**	**−6,461**	**−1,648**	**−3,023**
Reserve assets	4 802 ..	357	191	−1,711	−1,998	3,214	−6,461	−1,648	−3,023
Use of Fund credit and loans	4 766 ..	....	....	....	....	....	....	....	....
Exceptional financing	4 920 ..	....	....	....	....	....	....	....	....
Conversion rates: Chilean pesos per U.S. dollar	0 101 ..	**691.40**	**609.53**	**559.77**	**530.28**	**522.46**	**522.46**	**560.86**	**510.25**

[1] Excludes components that have been classified in the categories of Group E.

Table 2. STANDARD PRESENTATION, 2003–2010

(Millions of U.S. dollars)

	Code	2003	2004	2005	2006	2007	2008	2009	2010
CURRENT ACCOUNT	4 993	**−779**	**2,074**	**1,449**	**7,154**	**7,458**	**−3,307**	**2,570**	**3,802**
A. GOODS	4 100	**3,723**	**9,585**	**10,775**	**22,780**	**23,941**	**8,529**	**14,117**	**15,855**
Credit	2 100	**21,664**	**32,520**	**41,267**	**58,680**	**67,972**	**66,259**	**54,004**	**71,028**
General merchandise: exports f.o.b.	2 110	21,128	31,959	40,557	57,727	66,948	64,903	52,689	69,589
Goods for processing: exports f.o.b.	2 150	....	....	....	....	....	....	....	....
Repairs on goods	2 160	1	1	1	2	1	....	....	1
Goods procured in ports by carriers	2 170	187	243	358	420	445	592	409	394
Nonmonetary gold	2 180	348	318	351	531	577	763	907	1,045
Debit	3 100	**−17,941**	**−22,935**	**−30,492**	**−35,900**	**−44,031**	**−57,730**	**−39,888**	**−55,174**
General merchandise: imports f.o.b.	3 110	−17,554	−22,468	−29,809	−35,050	−43,069	−56,133	−38,994	−53,791
Goods for processing: imports f.o.b.	3 150	....	....	....	....	....	....	....	....
Repairs on goods	3 160	−56	−66	−63	−37	−63	−67	−11	−7
Goods procured in ports by carriers	3 170	−332	−401	−621	−813	−899	−1,530	−883	−1,375
Nonmonetary gold	3 180	....	....	....	....	....	....	....	....
B. SERVICES	4 200	**−618**	**−746**	**−622**	**−631**	**−987**	**−964**	**−1,444**	**−1,019**
Total credit	2 200	*5,070*	*6,034*	*7,134*	*7,830*	*8,962*	*10,823*	*8,634*	*10,797*
Total debit	3 200	*−5,688*	*−6,780*	*−7,756*	*−8,462*	*−9,950*	*−11,787*	*−10,078*	*−11,816*
Transportation services, credit	2 205	**2,771**	**3,457**	**4,301**	**4,695**	**5,213**	**6,503**	**4,774**	**6,466**
Passenger	2 850	*426*	*476*	*573*	*678*	*749*	*863*	*746*	*777*
Freight	2 851	*1,537*	*1,964*	*2,498*	*2,589*	*2,872*	*3,674*	*2,634*	*4,103*
Other	2 852	*807*	*1,017*	*1,230*	*1,428*	*1,593*	*1,967*	*1,393*	*1,586*
Sea transport, passenger	2 207	7	9	9	16	20	22	19	16
Sea transport, freight	2 208	1,016	1,300	1,745	1,729	1,959	2,543	1,849	3,152
Sea transport, other	2 209	602	792	998	1,159	1,290	1,659	1,113	1,292
Air transport, passenger	2 211	410	458	551	644	708	820	709	737
Air transport, freight	2 212	397	541	605	692	711	898	581	738
Air transport, other	2 213	167	178	181	213	240	238	210	217
Other transport, passenger	2 215	9	10	14	19	22	21	18	24
Other transport, freight	2 216	125	123	149	168	201	233	204	213
Other transport, other	2 217	39	47	50	56	63	70	70	76
Transportation services, debit	3 205	**−2,585**	**−3,354**	**−4,135**	**−4,571**	**−5,274**	**−6,765**	**−4,892**	**−6,661**
Passenger	3 850	*−259*	*−274*	*−304*	*−334*	*−382*	*−392*	*−337*	*−425*
Freight	3 851	*−960*	*−1,347*	*−1,571*	*−1,779*	*−2,302*	*−3,234*	*−2,032*	*−2,792*
Other	3 852	*−1,366*	*−1,733*	*−2,260*	*−2,458*	*−2,591*	*−3,140*	*−2,522*	*−3,445*
Sea transport, passenger	3 207	....	....	....	....	....	....	....	−1
Sea transport, freight	3 208	−576	−808	−1,021	−1,163	−1,630	−2,476	−1,408	−1,993
Sea transport, other	3 209	−1,027	−1,405	−1,893	−2,040	−2,154	−2,672	−2,099	−2,995
Air transport, passenger	3 211	−235	−247	−272	−295	−339	−343	−290	−375
Air transport, freight	3 212	−202	−283	−236	−283	−347	−356	−266	−410
Air transport, other	3 213	−211	−227	−251	−288	−290	−305	−256	−273
Other transport, passenger	3 215	−24	−27	−31	−39	−42	−49	−47	−48
Other transport, freight	3 216	−182	−256	−314	−334	−324	−401	−358	−389
Other transport, other	3 217	−128	−101	−116	−130	−147	−163	−168	−177
Travel, credit	2 236	**883**	**1,095**	**1,109**	**1,213**	**1,477**	**1,674**	**1,604**	**1,636**
Business travel	2 237	678	167	151	172	261	551	513	638
Personal travel	2 240	206	928	958	1,042	1,217	1,123	1,091	998
Travel, debit	3 236	**−850**	**−977**	**−1,051**	**−1,239**	**−1,660**	**−1,397**	**−1,628**	**−1,914**
Business travel	3 237	−541	−359	−379	−445	−494	−597	−516	−756
Personal travel	3 240	−309	−618	−671	−795	−1,167	−801	−1,111	−1,158
Other services, credit	2 200 BA	**1,415**	**1,482**	**1,724**	**1,922**	**2,271**	**2,646**	**2,257**	**2,696**
Communications	2 245	158	163	148	143	151	204	153	146
Construction	2 249	....	....	....	....	....	....	....	....
Insurance	2 253	124	136	163	189	224	258	233	286
Financial	2 260	30	31	34	37	40	47	42	45
Computer and information	2 262	81	71	74	78	82	96	84	91
Royalties and licence fees	2 266	45	48	54	55	61	64	59	64
Other business services	2 268	830	890	1,087	1,236	1,518	1,759	1,499	1,865
Personal, cultural, and recreational	2 287	68	58	69	78	84	111	82	87
Government, n.i.e.	2 291	79	84	94	104	111	108	106	112
Other services, debit	3 200 BA	**−2,252**	**−2,449**	**−2,570**	**−2,651**	**−3,015**	**−3,625**	**−3,558**	**−3,241**
Communications	3 245	−156	−160	−158	−137	−164	−217	−161	−173
Construction	3 249	....	....	....	....	....	....	....	....
Insurance	3 253	−435	−451	−463	−431	−506	−646	−886	−510
Financial	3 260	−214	−283	−256	−319	−368	−536	−531	−459
Computer and information	3 262	−75	−74	−71	−73	−58	−71	−65	−70
Royalties and licence fees	3 266	−257	−307	−348	−384	−448	−513	−461	−496
Other business services	3 268	−935	−999	−1,037	−1,040	−1,215	−1,325	−1,173	−1,229
Personal, cultural, and recreational	3 287	−47	−48	−53	−55	−42	−47	−51	−55
Government, n.i.e.	3 291	−132	−127	−184	−212	−216	−270	−231	−248

Table 2 (Continued). STANDARD PRESENTATION, 2003–2010

(Millions of U.S. dollars)

	Code	2003	2004	2005	2006	2007	2008	2009	2010
C. INCOME	4 300	**−4,489**	**−7,837**	**−10,487**	**−18,401**	**−18,625**	**−13,802**	**−11,666**	**−15,424**
Total credit	2 300	*1,552*	*1,983*	*2,452*	*3,374*	*6,325*	*5,928*	*5,345*	*5,995*
Total debit	3 300	*−6,041*	*−9,820*	*−12,939*	*−21,775*	*−24,950*	*−19,730*	*−17,011*	*−21,419*
Compensation of employees, credit	2 310	**12**	**12**	**13**	**3**	**3**	**3**	**4**	**3**
Compensation of employees, debit	3 310	**−15**	**−15**	**−16**	**−6**	**−6**	**−6**	**−6**	**−5**
Investment income, credit	2 320	**1,541**	**1,972**	**2,439**	**3,372**	**6,322**	**5,926**	**5,341**	**5,991**
Direct investment income	2 330	652	951	1,063	1,141	2,761	2,859	2,820	3,662
Dividends and distributed branch profits	2 332	103	115	87	117	333	503	231	474
Reinvested earnings and undistributed branch profits	2 333	547	824	946	998	2,394	2,306	2,571	3,174
Income on debt (interest)	2 334	2	12	30	25	33	50	18	14
Portfolio investment income	2 339	449	591	761	1,157	2,298	1,967	1,888	1,940
Income on equity	2 340	341	351	545	835	1,375	1,121	1,141	1,340
Income on bonds and notes	2 350	101	231	202	152	639	756	706	522
Income on money market instruments	2 360	6	9	13	170	284	90	41	78
Other investment income	2 370	439	429	615	1,075	1,263	1,100	633	389
Investment income, debit	3 320	**−6,026**	**−9,805**	**−12,923**	**−21,770**	**−24,944**	**−19,724**	**−17,006**	**−21,414**
Direct investment income	3 330	−4,611	−8,231	−11,416	−19,913	−22,832	−17,430	−14,801	−18,956
Dividends and distributed branch profits	3 332	−1,154	−2,076	−4,729	−12,716	−12,554	−10,713	−4,164	−11,011
Reinvested earnings and undistributed branch profits	3 333	−3,335	−5,952	−6,539	−7,143	−10,182	−6,597	−10,519	−7,839
Income on debt (interest)	3 334	−123	−203	−148	−54	−97	−121	−118	−106
Portfolio investment income	3 339	−817	−1,137	−928	−927	−1,156	−1,198	−1,203	−1,275
Income on equity	3 340	−193	−424	−224	−217	−317	−440	−349	−337
Income on bonds and notes	3 350	−624	−713	−704	−711	−839	−759	−854	−938
Income on money market instruments	3 360	....	....	....	....	....	....	....	....
Other investment income	3 370	−598	−437	−579	−929	−956	−1,096	−1,001	−1,183
D. CURRENT TRANSFERS	4 379	**605**	**1,072**	**1,783**	**3,406**	**3,129**	**2,930**	**1,563**	**4,390**
Credit	2 379	**901**	**1,411**	**2,199**	**4,003**	**3,857**	**3,875**	**2,512**	**5,481**
General government	2 380	519	878	1,352	2,924	2,556	2,409	1,242	2,817
Other sectors	2 390	382	533	847	1,078	1,301	1,466	1,270	2,664
Workers' remittances	2 391	....	....	....	....	....	....	....	....
Other current transfers	2 392	382	533	847	1,078	1,301	1,466	1,270	2,664
Debit	3 379	**−296**	**−339**	**−416**	**−596**	**−728**	**−945**	**−949**	**−1,091**
General government	3 380	−52	−37	−35	−21	−34	−30	−29	−59
Other sectors	3 390	−244	−302	−381	−575	−694	−915	−920	−1,032
Workers' remittances	3 391	....	....	....	....	....	....	....	....
Other current transfers	3 392	−244	−302	−381	−575	−694	−915	−920	−1,032
CAPITAL AND FINANCIAL ACCOUNT	4 996	**1,503**	**−1,804**	**−120**	**−5,629**	**−7,009**	**2,140**	**−3,343**	**−3,266**
CAPITAL ACCOUNT	4 994	....	**5**	**41**	**13**	**16**	**3**	**15**	**5,641**
Total credit	2 994	....	*5*	*41*	*13*	*16*	*3*	*15*	*5,641*
Total debit	3 994	....	....	....	....	....	....	....	....
Capital transfers, credit	2 400	....	**5**	**11**	**13**	**16**	**3**	**15**	**5,641**
General government	2 401	....	....	....	....	....	....	....	....
Debt forgiveness	2 402	....	....	....	....	....	....	....	....
Other capital transfers	2 410	....	....	....	....	....	....	....	....
Other sectors	2 430	....	5	11	13	16	3	15	5,641
Migrants' transfers	2 431	....	....	....	....	....	....	....	....
Debt forgiveness	2 432	....	5	11					
Other capital transfers	2 440	....	....		13	16	3	15	5,641
Capital transfers, debit	3 400	....	....	....	....	....	....	....	....
General government	3 401	....	....	....	....	....	....	....	....
Debt forgiveness	3 402	....	....	....	....	....	....	....	....
Other capital transfers	3 410	....	....	....	....	....	....	....	....
Other sectors	3 430	....	....	....	....	....	....	....	....
Migrants' transfers	3 431	....	....	....	....	....	....	....	....
Debt forgiveness	3 432	....	....	....	....	....	....	....	....
Other capital transfers	3 440	....	....	....	....	....	....	....	....
Nonproduced nonfinancial assets, credit	2 480	....	....	**30**	....	....	....	....	....
Nonproduced nonfinancial assets, debit	3 480	....	....	....	....	....	....	....	....

Table 2 (Continued). STANDARD PRESENTATION, 2003–2010

(Millions of U.S. dollars)

	Code	2003	2004	2005	2006	2007	2008	2009	2010
FINANCIAL ACCOUNT	4 995	**1,503**	**−1,809**	**−161**	**−5,642**	**−7,025**	**2,137**	**−3,357**	**−8,907**
A. DIRECT INVESTMENT	4 500	**2,701**	**5,610**	**4,801**	**5,127**	**9,961**	**7,109**	**4,813**	**6,351**
Direct investment abroad	4 505	**−1,606**	**−1,563**	**−2,183**	**−2,171**	**−2,573**	**−8,041**	**−8,061**	**−8,744**
Equity capital	4 510	−588	−507	−763	−896	462	−5,102	−4,497	−4,568
Claims on affiliated enterprises	4 515	−588	−507	−763	−896	462	−5,102	−4,497	−4,568
Liabilities to affiliated enterprises	4 520	....	....	....	....	....	....	....	....
Reinvested earnings	4 525	−547	−824	−946	−998	−2,394	−2,306	−2,571	−3,174
Other capital	4 530	−472	−232	−475	−277	−641	−633	−993	−1,002
Claims on affiliated enterprises	4 535	−472	−232	−475	−277	−641	−633	−993	−1,002
Liabilities to affiliated enterprises	4 540	....	....	....	....	....	....	....	....
Direct investment in Chile	4 555	**4,307**	**7,173**	**6,984**	**7,298**	**12,534**	**15,150**	**12,874**	**15,095**
Equity capital	4 560	1,546	1,243	781	1,980	2,622	7,775	1,822	4,844
Claims on direct investors	4 565	....	....	....	....	....	....	....	....
Liabilities to direct investors	4 570	1,546	1,243	781	1,980	2,622	7,775	1,822	4,844
Reinvested earnings	4 575	3,335	5,952	6,539	7,143	10,182	6,597	10,519	7,839
Other capital	4 580	−574	−22	−336	−1,824	−270	778	532	2,411
Claims on direct investors	4 585	....	....	....	....	....	....	....	....
Liabilities to direct investors	4 590	−574	−22	−336	−1,824	−270	778	532	2,411
B. PORTFOLIO INVESTMENT	4 600	**−2,645**	**−3,308**	**−2,833**	**−9,238**	**−16,461**	**−7,619**	**−11,769**	**−7,071**
Assets	4 602	**−4,699**	**−4,430**	**−4,227**	**−10,085**	**−15,953**	**−10,252**	**−13,691**	**−16,503**
Equity securities	4 610	−4,853	−3,205	−4,025	−2,264	−10,150	−5,162	−20,172	−11,674
Monetary authorities	4 611	....	....	....	....	....	....	....	....
General government	4 612	....	....	....	....	....	....	−1	....
Banks	4 613	....	−3	−17	−17	....	3	−13	23
Other sectors	4 614	−4,853	−3,202	−4,008	−2,247	−10,150	−5,165	−20,158	−11,697
Debt securities	4 619	154	−1,225	−203	−7,820	−5,803	−5,090	6,481	−4,829
Bonds and notes	4 620	−9	−131	−139	−914	−10,718	−3,486	3,872	−2,312
Monetary authorities	4 621	....	....	....	....	....	....	....	....
General government	4 622	....	....	....	−418	−10,041	−4,008	4,897	−627
Banks	4 623	−96	−72	−26	92	−61	195	41	−8
Other sectors	4 624	87	−59	−114	−588	−617	328	−1,066	−1,677
Money market instruments	4 630	163	−1,095	−63	−6,906	4,915	−1,604	2,608	−2,517
Monetary authorities	4 631	....	....	....	....	....	....	....	....
General government	4 632	....	....	....	−6,756	4,912	−942	2,291	−1,975
Banks	4 633	6	....	−3	3	....	....	−4	−7
Other sectors	4 634	157	−1,095	−60	−154	3	−662	321	−535
Liabilities	4 652	**2,054**	**1,122**	**1,394**	**846**	**−508**	**2,633**	**1,922**	**9,432**
Equity securities	4 660	318	8	1,571	−124	388	1,948	328	1,748
Banks	4 663	74	−58	85	−209	−39	119	198	−111
Other sectors	4 664	244	66	1,485	85	428	1,830	130	1,859
Debt securities	4 669	1,736	1,114	−176	970	−896	685	1,594	7,684
Bonds and notes	4 670	1,736	1,114	−176	932	−992	....	1,665	7,465
Monetary authorities	4 671	....	....	....	....	....	....	....	....
General government	4 672	999	242	−461	43	−584	−587	−409	1,585
Banks	4 673	−8	700	−207	197	−151	−32	442	2,534
Other sectors	4 674	745	172	492	691	−257	619	1,632	3,346
Money market instruments	4 680	....	....	....	39	96	685	−71	219
Monetary authorities	4 681	....	....	....	3	....	....	....	....
General government	4 682	....	....	....	....	....	....	....	....
Banks	4 683	....	....	....	36	96	685	−71	219
Other sectors	4 684	....	....	....	....	....	....	....	....
C. FINANCIAL DERIVATIVES	4 910	**118**	**−84**	**−63**	**301**	**454**	**−952**	**−295**	**−922**
Monetary authorities	4 911	....	....	....	....	....	....	....	....
General government	4 912	....	....	....	....	....	....	....	....
Banks	4 913	48	12	239	118	211	−228	451	567
Other sectors	4 914	70	−96	−301	183	243	−725	−747	−1,490
Assets	4 900	**1,840**	**639**	**1,244**	**1,552**	**2,608**	**11,708**	**8,650**	**8,836**
Monetary authorities	4 901	....	....	....	....	....	....	....	....
General government	4 902	....	....	....	....	....	....	....	....
Banks	4 903	1,614	257	733	1,117	2,033	6,282	4,110	4,511
Other sectors	4 904	227	382	512	435	575	5,426	4,540	4,325
Liabilities	4 905	**−1,722**	**−723**	**−1,307**	**−1,251**	**−2,154**	**−12,660**	**−8,945**	**−9,759**
Monetary authorities	4 906	....	....	....	....	....	....	....	....
General government	4 907	....	....	....	....	....	....	....	....
Banks	4 908	−1,566	−246	−494	−999	−1,822	−6,510	−3,659	−3,944
Other sectors	4 909	−156	−477	−813	−252	−333	−6,150	−5,287	−5,815

Table 2 (Concluded). STANDARD PRESENTATION, 2003–2010

(Millions of U.S. dollars)

	Code	2003	2004	2005	2006	2007	2008	2009	2010
D. OTHER INVESTMENT	4 700 ..	**972**	**−4,218**	**−356**	**167**	**−4,191**	**10,062**	**5,542**	**−4,241**
Assets	4 703 ..	**−571**	**−3,389**	**−2,384**	**−3,927**	**−11,098**	**3,715**	**−1,412**	**−7,394**
Trade credits	4 706 ..	−996	−1,601	−1,584	−1,386	−3,041	2,539	−3,071	−3,241
General government	4 707 ..	....	....	....	....	....	....	....	....
of which: Short-term	4 709 ..	....	....	....	....	....	....	....	....
Other sectors	4 710 ..	−996	−1,601	−1,584	−1,386	−3,041	2,539	−3,071	−3,241
of which: Short-term	4 712 ..	−996	−1,601	−1,584	−1,386	−3,041	2,539	−3,071	−3,241
Loans	4 714 ..	44	....	−5	−242	−729	−848	−290	−806
Monetary authorities	4 715 ..	....	....	....	....	....	....	....	....
of which: Short-term	4 718 ..	....	....	....	....	....	....	....	....
General government	4 719 ..	....	....	....	....	....	....	....	....
of which: Short-term	4 721 ..	....	....	....	....	....	....	....	....
Banks	4 722 ..	44	....	−3	−223	−726	−690	442	−734
of which: Short-term	4 724 ..	112	−111	37	−147	−504	50	82	−689
Other sectors	4 725 ..	....	....	−2	−19	−3	−157	−732	−72
of which: Short-term	4 727 ..	....	....	−2	−19	−3	−157	−732	−72
Currency and deposits	4 730 ..	441	−1,788	−795	−2,299	−7,328	2,024	1,949	−585
Monetary authorities	4 731 ..	....	....	....	....	....	....	....	....
General government	4 732 ..	1	....	....	−591	−5,831	902	766	−388
Banks	4 733 ..	255	−166	−554	−819	−1,113	555	−1,394	833
Other sectors	4 734 ..	185	−1,622	−241	−889	−384	567	2,577	−1,030
Other assets	4 736 ..	−60	....	....	....	....	....	....	−2,762
Monetary authorities	4 737 ..	−60	....	....	....	....	....	....	....
of which: Short-term	4 739 ..	....	....	....	....	....	....	....	....
General government	4 740 ..	....	....	....	....	....	....	....	....
of which: Short-term	4 742 ..	....	....	....	....	....	....	....	....
Banks	4 743 ..	....	....	....	....	....	....	....	....
of which: Short-term	4 745 ..	....	....	....	....	....	....	....	....
Other sectors	4 746 ..	....	....	....	....	....	....	....	−2,762
of which: Short-term	4 748 ..	....	....	....	....	....	....	....	−2,762
Liabilities	4 753 ..	**1,543**	**−829**	**2,028**	**4,094**	**6,906**	**6,346**	**6,955**	**3,152**
Trade credits	4 756 ..	−35	831	437	1,749	1,508	−580	−445	2,951
General government	4 757 ..	....	....	−229	−65	−23	−24	−11	−7
of which: Short-term	4 759 ..	....	....	....	....	....	....	....	....
Other sectors	4 760 ..	−35	831	665	1,814	1,532	−556	−434	2,957
of which: Short-term	4 762 ..	102	929	795	1,420	1,971	88	−277	2,994
Loans	4 764 ..	1,459	−1,576	1,617	2,330	5,409	6,801	6,092	−116
Monetary authorities	4 765 ..	....	....	....	....	....	....	....	....
of which: Use of Fund credit and loans from the Fund..	4 766 ..	....	....	....	....	....	....	....	....
of which: Short-term	4 768 ..	....	....	....	....	....	....	....	....
General government	4 769 ..	−117	−115	−215	48	11	−99	35	−6
of which: Short-term	4 771 ..	....	....	....	....	....	1	−1	....
Banks	4 772 ..	1,485	260	1,302	−12	2,776	1,513	2,528	−144
of which: Short-term	4 774 ..	1,016	−15	−1,133	647	−987	1,261	4,686	−1,696
Other sectors	4 775 ..	92	−1,721	530	2,294	2,622	5,388	3,530	34
of which: Short-term	4 777 ..	765	−290	−214	74	599	1,526	−1,456	−170
Currency and deposits	4 780 ..	121	−91	−26	18	−10	125	230	319
Monetary authorities	4 781 ..	....	....	....	−8	−2	−10	−14	−5
General government	4 782 ..	....	....	....	....	....	....	....	....
Banks	4 783 ..	121	−91	−26	27	−8	135	244	325
Other sectors	4 784 ..	....	....	....	....	....	....	....	....
Other liabilities	4 786 ..	−2	7	1	−3	−1	−1	1,077	−2
Monetary authorities	4 787 ..	−2	7	1	−3	−1	−1	1,077	−2
of which: Short-term	4 789 ..	−2	7	1	−3	−1	−1	−8	−2
General government	4 790 ..	....	....	....	....	....	....	....	....
of which: Short-term	4 792 ..	....	....	....	....	....	....	....	....
Banks	4 793 ..	....	....	....	....	....	....	....	....
of which: Short-term	4 795 ..	....	....	....	....	....	....	....	....
Other sectors	4 796 ..	....	....	....	....	....	....	....	....
of which: Short-term	4 798 ..	....	....	....	....	....	....	....	....
E. RESERVE ASSETS	4 802 ..	**357**	**191**	**−1,711**	**−1,998**	**3,214**	**−6,461**	**−1,648**	**−3,023**
Monetary gold	4 812 ..	....	....	....	....	....	....	....	....
Special drawing rights	4 811 ..	−5	−5	−4	1	4	−5	−1,085	−88
Reserve position in the Fund	4 810 ..	−40	156	228	82	29	−79	−117	....
Foreign exchange	4 803 ..	404	50	−1,924	−2,079	3,217	−6,362	−444	−2,984
Other claims	4 813 ..	−1	−10	−10	−2	−36	−15	−2	50
NET ERRORS AND OMISSIONS	4 998 ..	**−724**	**−270**	**−1,329**	**−1,525**	**−449**	**1,167**	**773**	**−536**

Table 3. INTERNATIONAL INVESTMENT POSITION (End-period stocks), 2003–2010

(Millions of U.S. dollars)

	Code	2003	2004	2005	2006	2007	2008	2009	2010
ASSETS	8 995 C.	**60,998**	**75,975**	**91,898**	**120,957**	**164,585**	**142,711**	**188,707**	**235,916**
Direct investment abroad	8 505 ..	**13,681**	**17,413**	**21,359**	**26,025**	**31,688**	**31,820**	**41,339**	**49,838**
Equity capital and reinvested earnings	8 506 ..	11,790	15,290	18,761	23,150	28,173	27,672	36,197	43,694
Claims on affiliated enterprises	8 507 ..	11,790	15,290	18,761	23,150	28,173	27,672	36,197	43,694
Liabilities to affiliated enterprises	8 508 ..	....	....	....	....	....	....	....	....
Other capital	8 530 ..	1,891	2,123	2,597	2,875	3,516	4,149	5,142	6,144
Claims on affiliated enterprises	8 535 ..	1,891	2,123	2,597	2,875	3,516	4,149	5,142	6,144
Liabilities to affiliated enterprises	8 540 ..	....	....	....	....	....	....	....	....
Portfolio investment	8 602 ..	**21,374**	**28,551**	**37,041**	**55,329**	**83,449**	**57,299**	**90,243**	**119,325**
Equity securities	8 610 ..	18,753	24,321	32,741	43,021	64,176	33,250	71,179	94,546
Monetary authorities	8 611 ..	....	....	....	....	....	....		
General government	8 612 ..	....	....	....	....	....	....	1	1
Banks	8 613 ..	....	3	18	36	62	60	72	49
Other sectors	8 614 ..	18,753	24,319	32,724	42,985	64,114	33,191	71,105	94,496
Debt securities	8 619 ..	2,621	4,229	4,300	12,308	19,273	24,049	19,065	24,779
Bonds and notes	8 620 ..	2,559	3,006	3,039	3,785	15,275	18,459	15,958	19,002
Monetary authorities	8 621 ..	....	....	....	....	....	....	....	....
General government	8 622 ..	....	....	....	418	11,070	15,779	11,287	11,911
Banks	8 623 ..	206	279	305	237	366	171	130	138
Other sectors	8 624 ..	2,353	2,727	2,734	3,129	3,839	2,509	4,540	6,953
Money market instruments	8 630 ..	62	1,223	1,261	8,523	3,998	5,589	3,107	5,778
Monetary authorities	8 631 ..	....	....	....					
General government	8 632 ..	....	....	....	6,756	2,148	3,441	1,106	3,024
Banks	8 633 ..	....	....	3	....	....	....	4	11
Other sectors	8 634 ..	61	1,222	1,258	1,767	1,849	2,148	1,997	2,743
Financial derivatives	8 900 ..	**535**	**995**	**1,023**	**827**	**1,718**	**3,027**	**3,577**	**3,470**
Monetary authorities	8 901 ..	....	....	....	....	....	....		....
General government	8 902 ..	....	....	....	....	....	....		
Banks	8 903 ..	309	579	782	710	1,501	2,429	3,174	2,522
Other sectors	8 904 ..	225	416	241	117	217	598	403	948
Other investment	8 703 ..	**9,557**	**13,001**	**15,513**	**19,348**	**30,820**	**27,404**	**28,170**	**35,420**
Trade credits	8 706 ..	3,471	5,072	6,656	8,042	11,084	8,544	11,615	14,856
General government	8 707 ..	....	....	....	....	....	....	....	....
of which: Short-term	8 709 ..	....	....	....	....	....	....	....	....
Other sectors	8 710 ..	3,471	5,072	6,656	8,042	11,084	8,544	11,615	14,856
of which: Short-term	8 712 ..	*3,471*	*5,072*	*6,656*	*8,042*	*11,084*	*8,544*	*11,615*	*14,856*
Loans	8 714 ..	679	676	681	1,004	1,731	2,578	2,868	3,674
Monetary authorities	8 715 ..	....	....	....	....	....	....	....	....
of which: Short-term	8 718 ..	....	....	....	....	....	....	....	....
General government	8 719 ..	....	....	....	....	....	....	....	....
of which: Short-term	8 721 ..	....	....	....	....	....	....	....	....
Banks	8 722 ..	679	676	679	983	1,707	2,397	1,955	2,688
of which: Short-term	8 724 ..	*392*	*501*	*464*	*684*	*1,188*	*1,469*	*1,387*	*2,076*
Other sectors	8 725 ..	....	....	2	21	24	181	913	986
of which: Short-term	8 727 ..	....	....	*2*	*21*	*24*	*181*	*913*	*986*
Currency and deposits	8 730 ..	5,345	7,188	7,824	9,947	17,647	15,925	13,329	13,772
Monetary authorities	8 731 ..	....	....	....	....	....	....	....	....
General government	8 732 ..	....	....	....	591	6,651	5,693	4,268	4,547
Banks	8 733 ..	725	897	1,451	2,031	3,182	2,627	4,021	3,188
Other sectors	8 734 ..	4,620	6,291	6,373	7,325	7,814	7,604	5,040	6,036
Other assets	8 736 ..	62	65	352	355	358	357	358	3,119
Monetary authorities	8 737 ..	62	65	244	248	251	249	250	249
of which: Short-term	8 739 ..	....	....	....	....	....	....	....	....
General government	8 740 ..	....	....	108	108	108	108	108	108
of which: Short-term	8 742 ..	....	....	....	....	....	....	....	....
Banks	8 743 ..	....	....	....	....	....	....	....	....
of which: Short-term	8 745 ..	....	....	....	....	....	....	....	....
Other sectors	8 746 ..	....	....	....	....	....	....	....	2,762
of which: Short-term	8 748 ..	....	....	....	....	....	....	....	*2,762*
Reserve assets	8 802 ..	**15,852**	**16,016**	**16,962**	**19,428**	**16,910**	**23,161**	**25,377**	**27,863**
Monetary gold	8 812 ..	3	3	3	4	5	6	9	11
Special drawing rights	8 811 ..	46	53	52	54	53	57	1,147	1,217
Reserve position in the Fund	8 810 ..	583	446	188	113	88	167	287	282
Foreign exchange	8 803 ..	15,211	15,495	16,689	19,225	16,695	22,849	23,849	26,318
Other claims	8 813 ..	10	19	30	32	68	83	85	35

Table 3 (Concluded). INTERNATIONAL INVESTMENT POSITION (End-period stocks), 2003–2010

(Millions of U.S. dollars)

	Code	2003	2004	2005	2006	2007	2008	2009	2010
LIABILITIES	8 995 D.	**98,494**	**106,169**	**124,564**	**136,685**	**163,858**	**172,546**	**207,660**	**245,942**
Direct investment in Chile	8 555 ..	**54,082**	**60,540**	**74,196**	**80,297**	**99,413**	**99,359**	**121,395**	**139,538**
Equity capital and reinvested earnings	8 556 ..	49,841	56,319	69,932	77,907	96,597	95,955	117,320	132,902
Claims on direct investors	8 557 ..	....	....	....	....	....	....	....	....
Liabilities to direct investors	8 558 ..	49,841	56,319	69,932	77,907	96,597	95,955	117,320	132,902
Other capital	8 580 ..	4,240	4,221	4,264	2,390	2,816	3,404	4,075	6,636
Claims on direct investors	8 585 ..	....	....	....	....	....	....	....	....
Liabilities to direct investors	8 590 ..	4,240	4,221	4,264	2,390	2,816	3,404	4,075	6,636
Portfolio investment	8 652 ..	**14,632**	**16,192**	**17,985**	**19,822**	**19,962**	**20,014**	**27,594**	**42,924**
Equity securities	8 660 ..	3,974	4,622	6,832	8,051	9,191	8,959	14,115	21,754
Banks	8 663 ..	815	1,057	1,420	1,329	1,326	993	2,024	3,763
Other sectors	8 664 ..	3,158	3,565	5,412	6,722	7,865	7,966	12,092	17,991
Debt securities	8 669 ..	10,658	11,571	11,153	11,771	10,771	11,055	13,479	21,169
Bonds and notes	8 670 ..	10,658	11,571	11,153	11,733	10,637	10,236	12,730	20,200
Monetary authorities	8 671 ..	....	....	....	....	....	....	....	....
General government	8 672 ..	3,520	3,667	3,206	3,078	2,486	1,987	1,588	3,138
Banks	8 673 ..	650	1,335	1,108	1,315	1,154	1,071	1,597	4,070
Other sectors	8 674 ..	6,489	6,569	6,840	7,339	6,997	7,177	9,545	12,992
Money market instruments	8 680 ..	....	....	....	39	134	819	749	969
Monetary authorities	8 681 ..	....	....	....	3	3	3	3	3
General government	8 682 ..	....	....	....	....	....	....	....	....
Banks	8 683 ..	....	....	....	36	132	817	746	966
Other sectors	8 684 ..	....	....	....	....	....	....	....	....
Financial derivatives	8 905 ..	**222**	**695**	**954**	**931**	**2,129**	**4,088**	**2,547**	**4,012**
Monetary authorities	8 906 ..	....	....	....	....	....	....	....	....
General government	8 907 ..	....	....	....	....	....	....	....	....
Banks	8 908 ..	....	....	....	....	1,278	3,279	1,614	2,466
Other sectors	8 909 ..	....	....	....	....	851	809	933	1,546
Other investment	8 753 ..	**29,558**	**28,741**	**31,429**	**35,635**	**42,353**	**49,084**	**56,124**	**59,468**
Trade credits	8 756 ..	5,275	6,108	6,774	8,589	10,121	9,564	9,131	12,088
General government	8 757 ..	....	....	....	....	....	....	....	....
of which: Short-term	8 759 ..	....	....	....	....	....	....	....	....
Other sectors	8 760 ..	5,275	6,108	6,774	8,589	10,121	9,564	9,131	12,088
of which: Short-term	8 762 ..	*3,364*	*4,293*	*5,088*	*6,508*	*8,479*	*8,566*	*8,290*	*11,283*
Loans	8 764 ..	24,100	22,533	24,415	26,793	31,796	38,965	45,108	45,194
Monetary authorities	8 765 ..	1	1	....	....	....	....	....	....
of which: Use of Fund credit and loans from the Fund....	8 766 ..	....	....	....	....	....	....	....	....
of which: Short-term	8 768 ..	....	....	....	....	....	....	....	....
General government	8 769 ..	1,392	1,287	1,068	1,127	1,152	1,041	1,082	1,077
of which: Short-term	8 771 ..	....	....	....	....	....	*1*	....	....
Banks	8 772 ..	4,660	4,915	6,230	6,220	9,069	11,008	13,440	13,309
of which: Short-term	8 774 ..	*2,250*	*2,236*	*1,104*	*1,752*	*765*	*2,026*	*6,712*	*5,021*
Other sectors	8 775 ..	18,047	16,330	17,117	19,446	21,575	26,916	30,587	30,808
of which: Short-term	8 777 ..	*1,219*	*823*	*612*	*682*	*1,281*	*2,807*	*1,351*	*1,189*
Currency and deposits	8 780 ..	175	85	223	239	232	355	600	926
Monetary authorities	8 781 ..	....	....	165	154	155	142	144	145
General government	8 782 ..	....	....	....	....	....	....	....	....
Banks	8 783 ..	175	85	58	85	77	212	456	781
Other sectors	8 784 ..	....	....	....	....	....	....	....	....
Other liabilities	8 786 ..	9	16	16	14	205	201	1,284	1,260
Monetary authorities	8 787 ..	9	16	16	14	205	201	1,284	1,260
of which: Short-term	8 789 ..	*9*	*16*	*16*	*14*	*13*	*12*	*4*	*2*
General government	8 790 ..	....	....	....	....	....	....	....	....
of which: Short-term	8 792 ..	....	....	....	....	....	....	....	....
Banks	8 793 ..	....	....	....	....	....	....	....	....
of which: Short-term	8 795 ..	....	....	....	....	....	....	....	....
Other sectors	8 796 ..	....	....	....	....	....	....	....	....
of which: Short-term	8 798 ..	....	....	....	....	....	....	....	....
NET INTERNATIONAL INVESTMENT POSITION	8 995 ..	**−37,496**	**−30,194**	**−32,665**	**−15,728**	**728**	**−29,835**	**−18,953**	**−10,026**
Conversion rates: Chilean pesos per U.S. dollar (end of period)	0 102 ..	**599.42**	**559.83**	**514.21**	**534.43**	**495.82**	**629.11**	**506.43**	**468.37**

Table 1. ANALYTIC PRESENTATION, 2003–2010

(Millions of U.S. dollars)

	Code	2003	2004	2005	2006	2007	2008	2009	2010
A. Current Account[1]	4 993 Z.	**45,875**	**68,659**	**134,082**	**232,746**	**353,996**	**412,364**	**261,120**	**305,374**
Goods: exports f.o.b.	2 100 ..	438,270	593,393	762,484	969,682	1,220,000	1,434,601	1,203,797	1,581,417
Goods: imports f.o.b.	3 100 ..	−393,618	−534,410	−628,295	−751,936	−904,618	−1,073,919	−954,287	−1,327,238
Balance on Goods	4 100 ..	*44,652*	*58,982*	*134,189*	*217,746*	*315,381*	*360,682*	*249,509*	*254,180*
Services: credit	2 200 ..	46,734	62,434	74,404	91,999	122,206	147,112	129,549	171,203
Services: debit	3 200 ..	−55,306	−72,133	−83,795	−100,833	−130,111	−158,924	−158,947	−193,321
Balance on Goods and Services	4 991 ..	*36,079*	*49,284*	*124,798*	*208,912*	*307,477*	*348,870*	*220,112*	*232,062*
Income: credit	2 300 ..	16,095	20,544	38,959	54,642	83,030	101,615	108,582	144,622
Income: debit	3 300 ..	−23,933	−24,067	−55,060	−60,007	−75,178	−83,920	−101,321	−114,242
Balance on Goods, Services, and Income	4 992 ..	*28,241*	*45,761*	*108,697*	*203,547*	*315,329*	*366,565*	*227,372*	*262,442*
Current transfers: credit	2 379 Z.	18,482	24,326	27,735	31,578	42,646	52,565	42,645	49,521
Current transfers: debit	3 379 ..	−848	−1,428	−2,349	−2,378	−3,978	−6,766	−8,897	−6,588
B. Capital Account[1]	4 994 Z.	**−48**	**−69**	**4,102**	**4,020**	**3,099**	**3,051**	**3,958**	**4,630**
Capital account: credit	2 994 Z.	....	....	4,155	4,102	3,315	3,320	4,204	4,815
Capital account: debit	3 994 ..	−48	−69	−53	−82	−216	−268	−247	−185
Total, Groups A Plus B	4 981 ..	*45,827*	*68,590*	*138,184*	*236,766*	*357,096*	*415,415*	*265,078*	*310,004*
C. Financial Account[1]	4 995 W.	**52,774**	**110,729**	**96,944**	**48,629**	**92,049**	**43,270**	**176,855**	**221,414**
Direct investment abroad	4 505 ..	152	−1,805	−11,306	−21,160	−16,995	−53,471	−43,898	−60,151
Direct investment in China, P.R.: Mainland	4 555 Z.	47,077	54,936	117,208	124,082	160,052	175,148	114,215	185,081
Portfolio investment assets	4 602 ..	2,983	6,486	−26,157	−110,419	−2,324	32,750	9,888	−7,643
Equity securities	4 610 ..	....	....	....	−1,454	−15,189	−1,117	−33,815	−8,429
Debt securities	4 619 ..	2,983	6,486	−26,157	−108,965	12,865	33,867	43,703	787
Portfolio investment liabilities	4 652 Z.	8,444	13,203	21,224	42,861	20,996	9,910	28,804	31,681
Equity securities	4 660 ..	7,729	10,923	20,346	42,861	18,510	8,721	28,161	31,357
Debt securities	4 669 Z.	715	2,280	878	....	2,486	1,189	643	324
Financial derivatives	4 910 ..	....	....	....	....	....	....	....	....
Financial derivatives assets	4 900 ..	....	....	....	....	....	....	....	....
Financial derivatives liabilities	4 905 ..	....	....	....	....	....	....	....	....
Other investment assets	4 703 ..	−17,922	1,980	−48,947	−31,853	−151,486	−106,074	9,365	−116,262
Monetary authorities	4 701 ..	....	....	−4,354	−3,572	−113,980	−55,105	45,617	24,453
General government	4 704 ..	....	....	....	....	....	....	−54	6
Banks	4 705 ..	−15,733	2,959	−23,656	3,049	−23,360	−49,405	22,106	−24,003
Other sectors	4 728 ..	−2,189	−979	−20,938	−31,331	−14,146	−1,564	−58,303	−116,718
Other investment liabilities	4 753 W.	12,040	35,928	44,921	45,118	81,806	−14,992	58,483	188,708
Monetary authorities	4 753 WA	....	....	1,778	4,101	1,795	709	11,568	34,124
General government	4 753 ZB	−2,758	999	−360	483	−550	−256	760	434
Banks	4 753 ZC	10,269	13,375	9,186	25,279	6,853	−13,618	3,117	91,503
Other sectors	4 753 ZD	4,529	21,554	34,318	15,255	73,709	−1,828	43,038	62,648
Total, Groups A Through C	4 983 ..	*98,601*	*179,319*	*235,127*	*285,395*	*449,144*	*458,685*	*441,933*	*531,419*
D. Net Errors and Omissions	4 998 ..	**38,854**	**10,531**	**15,847**	**−745**	**11,507**	**20,868**	**−41,425**	**−59,760**
Total, Groups A Through D	4 984 ..	*137,455*	*189,849*	*250,975*	*284,651*	*460,651*	*479,553*	*400,508*	*471,659*
E. Reserves and Related Items	4 802 A.	**−137,455**	**−189,849**	**−250,975**	**−284,651**	**−460,651**	**−479,553**	**−400,508**	**−471,659**
Reserve assets	4 802 ..	−137,455	−189,849	−250,975	−284,651	−460,651	−479,553	−400,508	−471,659
Use of Fund credit and loans	4 766 ..	....	....	....	....	....	....	....	....
Exceptional financing	4 920 ..	....	....	....	....	....	....	....	....
Conversion rates: yuan per U.S. dollar	0 101 ..	**8.2770**	**8.2768**	**8.1943**	**7.9734**	**7.6075**	**6.9487**	**6.8314**	**6.7703**

[1] Excludes components that have been classified in the categories of Group E.

Table 2. STANDARD PRESENTATION, 2003–2010

(Millions of U.S. dollars)

	Code	2003	2004	2005	2006	2007	2008	2009	2010
CURRENT ACCOUNT	4 993	**45,875**	**68,659**	**134,082**	**232,746**	**353,996**	**412,364**	**261,120**	**305,374**
A. GOODS	4 100	**44,652**	**58,982**	**134,189**	**217,746**	**315,381**	**360,682**	**249,509**	**254,180**
Credit	2 100	**438,270**	**593,393**	**762,484**	**969,682**	**1,220,000**	**1,434,601**	**1,203,797**	**1,581,417**
General merchandise: exports f.o.b.	2 110	195,810	264,314	344,229	456,878	597,127	751,109	612,885	836,155
Goods for processing: exports f.o.b.	2 150	241,869	328,015	416,509	510,399	617,700	675,301	587,027	740,519
Repairs on goods	2 160	271	432	584	788	2,943	3,621	1,647	1,728
Goods procured in ports by carriers	2 170	318	632	1,162	1,618	2,229	4,570	2,238	3,015
Nonmonetary gold	2 180	....	....	....	....	....	....	....	....
Debit	3 100	**−393,618**	**−534,410**	**−628,295**	**−751,936**	**−904,618**	**−1,073,919**	**−954,287**	**−1,327,238**
General merchandise: imports f.o.b.	3 110	−235,619	−319,651	−363,093	−441,216	−549,026	−707,896	−644,498	−924,148
Goods for processing: imports f.o.b.	3 150	−156,673	−213,149	−263,078	−308,129	−352,009	−361,208	−306,231	−398,087
Repairs on goods	3 160	−240	−160	−216	−203	−171	−94	−377	−684
Goods procured in ports by carriers	3 170	−1,085	−1,450	−1,908	−2,388	−3,412	−4,721	−3,181	−4,319
Nonmonetary gold	3 180	....	....	....	....	....	....	....	....
B. SERVICES	4 200	**−8,573**	**−9,699**	**−9,391**	**−8,834**	**−7,905**	**−11,812**	**−29,398**	**−22,118**
Total credit	2 200	*46,734*	*62,434*	*74,404*	*91,999*	*122,206*	*147,112*	*129,549*	*171,203*
Total debit	3 200	*−55,306*	*−72,133*	*−83,795*	*−100,833*	*−130,111*	*−158,924*	*−158,947*	*−193,321*
Transportation services, credit	2 205	**7,906**	**12,067**	**15,427**	**21,015**	**31,324**	**38,418**	**23,569**	**34,211**
Passenger	2 850	*1,301*	*2,016*	*2,546*	*3,183*	*3,893*	*3,287*	*2,957*	*4,340*
Freight	2 851	*4,952*	*8,118*	*10,680*	*15,098*	*24,085*	*30,924*	*15,910*	*24,379*
Other	2 852	*1,653*	*1,933*	*2,200*	*2,734*	*3,346*	*4,207*	*4,702*	*5,492*
Sea transport, passenger	2 207	47	39	41	24	26	37	30	30
Sea transport, freight	2 208	3,973	6,582	8,819	12,502	19,836	25,415	12,602	19,001
Sea transport, other	2 209	....	....	....	....	....	....	2,175	3,897
Air transport, passenger	2 211	1,078	1,760	2,230	2,796	3,449	3,106	2,860	4,263
Air transport, freight	2 212	871	1,322	1,651	2,321	3,832	4,959	2,955	5,014
Air transport, other	2 213	....	....	....	....	....	....	468	613
Other transport, passenger	2 215	177	218	274	363	417	144	67	48
Other transport, freight	2 216	108	213	210	276	417	551	353	364
Other transport, other	2 217	1,653	1,933	2,200	2,734	3,346	4,207	2,059	981
Transportation services, debit	3 205	**−18,233**	**−24,544**	**−28,448**	**−34,369**	**−43,271**	**−50,329**	**−46,574**	**−63,257**
Passenger	3 850	*−1,529*	*−2,211*	*−2,956*	*−3,920*	*−3,478*	*−4,830*	*−3,406*	*−4,960*
Freight	3 851	*−15,938*	*−21,270*	*−24,436*	*−29,382*	*−38,202*	*−43,571*	*−40,198*	*−55,383*
Other	3 852	*−765*	*−1,063*	*−1,056*	*−1,066*	*−1,591*	*−1,927*	*−2,970*	*−2,914*
Sea transport, passenger	3 207	−11	−13	−8	−11	−9	−16	−15	−15
Sea transport, freight	3 208	−13,121	−18,561	−21,745	−25,853	−35,132	−40,583	−35,164	−47,691
Sea transport, other	3 209	....	....	....	....	....	....	−1,037	−1,582
Air transport, passenger	3 211	−1,490	−2,165	−2,909	−3,877	−3,421	−4,764	−3,367	−4,932
Air transport, freight	3 212	−2,167	−2,100	−1,865	−2,250	−2,403	−2,302	−3,264	−6,016
Air transport, other	3 213	....	....	....	....	....	....	−452	−790
Other transport, passenger	3 215	−28	−34	−39	−32	−48	−50	−24	−12
Other transport, freight	3 216	−651	−609	−826	−1,279	−667	−685	−1,770	−1,676
Other transport, other	3 217	−765	−1,063	−1,056	−1,066	−1,591	−1,927	−1,481	−542
Travel, credit	2 236	**17,406**	**25,739**	**29,296**	**33,949**	**37,233**	**40,843**	**39,675**	**45,814**
Business travel	2 237	....	....	....	....	....	....	....	....
Personal travel	2 240	....	....	....	....	....	....	....	....
Travel, debit	3 236	**−15,187**	**−19,149**	**−21,759**	**−24,322**	**−29,786**	**−36,157**	**−43,702**	**−54,880**
Business travel	3 237	....	....	....	....	....	....	....	....
Personal travel	3 240	....	....	....	....	....	....	....	....
Other services, credit	2 200 BA	**21,421**	**24,628**	**29,682**	**37,035**	**53,650**	**67,851**	**66,305**	**91,179**
Communications	2 245	638	440	485	738	1,175	1,570	1,198	1,220
Construction	2 249	1,290	1,467	2,593	2,753	5,377	10,329	9,463	14,495
Insurance	2 253	313	381	549	548	904	1,383	1,596	1,727
Financial	2 260	152	94	145	145	230	315	437	1,331
Computer and information	2 262	1,102	1,637	1,840	2,958	4,345	6,252	6,512	9,256
Royalties and licence fees	2 266	107	236	157	205	343	571	429	830
Other business services	2 268	17,427	19,952	23,283	28,973	40,408	46,349	45,623	61,242
Personal, cultural, and recreational	2 287	33	41	134	137	316	418	97	123
Government, n.i.e.	2 291	359	378	495	579	552	666	950	955
Other services, debit	3 200 BA	**−21,886**	**−28,440**	**−33,589**	**−42,142**	**−57,054**	**−72,438**	**−68,671**	**−75,184**
Communications	3 245	−427	−472	−603	−764	−1,082	−1,510	−1,210	−1,137
Construction	3 249	−1,183	−1,339	−1,619	−2,050	−2,910	−4,363	−5,868	−5,072
Insurance	3 253	−4,564	−6,124	−7,200	−8,831	−10,664	−12,743	−11,309	−15,755
Financial	3 260	−233	−138	−159	−891	−557	−566	−726	−1,387
Computer and information	3 262	−1,036	−1,253	−1,623	−1,739	−2,208	−3,165	−3,233	−2,965
Royalties and licence fees	3 266	−3,548	−4,497	−5,321	−6,634	−8,192	−10,319	−11,065	−13,040
Other business services	3 268	−10,371	−13,911	−16,286	−20,605	−30,431	−38,597	−34,143	−34,310
Personal, cultural, and recreational	3 287	−70	−176	−154	−121	−154	−255	−278	−371
Government, n.i.e.	3 291	−454	−531	−623	−506	−857	−920	−840	−1,147

Table 2 (Continued). STANDARD PRESENTATION, 2003–2010

(Millions of U.S. dollars)

	Code	2003	2004	2005	2006	2007	2008	2009	2010
C. INCOME	4 300	**−7,838**	**−3,523**	**−16,101**	**−5,365**	**7,852**	**17,694**	**7,260**	**30,380**
Total credit	2 300	*16,095*	*20,544*	*38,959*	*54,642*	*83,030*	*101,615*	*108,582*	*144,622*
Total debit	3 300	*−23,933*	*−24,067*	*−55,060*	*−60,007*	*−75,178*	*−83,920*	*−101,321*	*−114,242*
Compensation of employees, credit	2 310	**1,283**	**2,014**	**3,337**	**4,319**	**6,833**	**9,137**	**9,209**	**13,636**
Compensation of employees, debit	3 310	**−1,120**	**−1,382**	**−1,817**	**−2,330**	**−2,493**	**−2,736**	**−2,052**	**−1,455**
Investment income, credit	2 320	**14,812**	**18,530**	**35,622**	**50,322**	**76,197**	**92,478**	**99,372**	**130,986**
Direct investment income	2 330	100	218	3,385	7,831	9,663	14,448	11,072	19,117
Dividends and distributed branch profits	2 332	100	218	462	1,181	3,591	5,116	2,481	2,738
Reinvested earnings and undistributed branch profits	2 333	....	....	2,924	6,650	6,072	9,331	8,547	16,314
Income on debt (interest)	2 334	....	....	....	....	....	....	44	66
Portfolio investment income	2 339	369	831	2,758	2,849	4,457	5,616	4,468	7,866
Income on equity	2 340	349	749	1,341	1,763	903	1,821	729	3,796
Income on bonds and notes	2 350	....	....	....	....	....	....	....	....
Income on money market instruments	2 360	....	....	....	....	....	....	....	....
Other investment income	2 370	14,342	17,480	29,479	39,642	62,077	72,415	83,832	104,002
Investment income, debit	3 320	**−22,813**	**−22,685**	**−53,243**	**−57,677**	**−72,685**	**−81,184**	**−99,269**	**−112,787**
Direct investment income	3 330	−17,353	−17,415	−47,776	−49,758	−61,547	−72,609	−90,805	−103,476
Dividends and distributed branch profits	3 332	−10,158	−14,031	−18,928	−24,411	−39,514	−42,211	−50,256	−52,477
Reinvested earnings and undistributed branch profits	3 333	−7,195	−3,000	−28,345	−24,713	−21,136	−29,594	−39,502	−49,944
Income on debt (interest)	3 334	....	−383	−503	−634	−897	−805	−1,047	−1,055
Portfolio investment income	3 339	....	−225	−424	−162	−528	−3,896	−5,314	−4,776
Income on equity	3 340	....	....	....	....	....	−3,420	−4,878	−4,565
Income on bonds and notes	3 350	....	....	....	....	....	....	....	....
Income on money market instruments	3 360	....	....	....	....	....	....	....	....
Other investment income	3 370	−5,460	−5,045	−5,042	−7,757	−10,610	−4,679	−3,150	−4,535
D. CURRENT TRANSFERS	4 379	**17,634**	**22,898**	**25,385**	**29,199**	**38,668**	**45,799**	**33,748**	**42,932**
Credit	2 379	**18,482**	**24,326**	**27,735**	**31,578**	**42,646**	**52,565**	**42,645**	**49,521**
General government	2 380	114	98	49	65	35	49	43	22
Other sectors	2 390	18,369	24,229	27,686	31,513	42,611	52,516	42,602	49,499
Workers' remittances	2 391	3,343	4,627	5,495	6,830	10,679	13,557	13,693	19,804
Other current transfers	2 392	15,026	19,602	22,191	24,682	31,931	38,959	28,909	29,695
Debit	3 379	**−848**	**−1,428**	**−2,349**	**−2,378**	**−3,978**	**−6,766**	**−8,897**	**−6,588**
General government	3 380	−106	−187	−225	−211	−201	−231	−291	−294
Other sectors	3 390	−743	−1,242	−2,124	−2,167	−3,777	−6,535	−8,606	−6,295
Workers' remittances	3 391	−477	−616	−732	−695	−1,879	−3,000	−2,393	−299
Other current transfers	3 392	−266	−626	−1,392	−1,472	−1,898	−3,535	−6,214	−5,996
CAPITAL AND FINANCIAL ACCOUNT	4 996	**−84,729**	**−79,190**	**−149,929**	**−232,001**	**−365,503**	**−433,232**	**−219,696**	**−245,614**
CAPITAL ACCOUNT	4 994	**−48**	**−69**	**4,102**	**4,020**	**3,099**	**3,051**	**3,958**	**4,630**
Total credit	2 994	....	....	*4,155*	*4,102*	*3,315*	*3,320*	*4,204*	*4,815*
Total debit	3 994	*−48*	*−69*	*−53*	*−82*	*−216*	*−268*	*−247*	*−185*
Capital transfers, credit	2 400	....	....	**4,155**	**4,102**	**3,315**	**3,320**	**3,510**	**4,185**
General government	2 401	....	....	....	....	....	....	....	....
Debt forgiveness	2 402	....	....	....	....	....	....	....	....
Other capital transfers	2 410	....	....	....	....	....	....	....	....
Other sectors	2 430	....	....	4,155	4,102	3,315	3,320	3,510	4,185
Migrants' transfers	2 431	....	....	....	....	....	....	....	....
Debt forgiveness	2 432	....	....	....	....	....	....	....	....
Other capital transfers	2 440	....	....	....	....	....	....	....	....
Capital transfers, debit	3 400	**−48**	**−69**	**−53**	**−82**	**−216**	**−268**	**−198**	**−132**
General government	3 401	....	....	....	....	....	....	....	....
Debt forgiveness	3 402	....	....	....	....	....	....	....	....
Other capital transfers	3 410	....	....	....	....	....	....	....	....
Other sectors	3 430	−48	−69	−53	−82	−216	−268	−198	−132
Migrants' transfers	3 431	....	....	....	....	....	....	....	....
Debt forgiveness	3 432	....	....	....	....	....	....	....	....
Other capital transfers	3 440	....	....	....	....	....	....	....	....
Nonproduced nonfinancial assets, credit	2 480	....	....	....	....	....	....	**695**	**630**
Nonproduced nonfinancial assets, debit	3 480	....	....	....	....	....	....	**−48**	**−53**

Table 2 (Continued). STANDARD PRESENTATION, 2003–2010

(Millions of U.S. dollars)

	Code	2003	2004	2005	2006	2007	2008	2009	2010
FINANCIAL ACCOUNT	4 995	−84,681	−79,120	−154,031	−236,021	−368,602	−436,283	−223,653	−250,244
A. DIRECT INVESTMENT	4 500	47,229	53,131	105,903	102,922	143,057	121,677	70,316	124,930
Direct investment abroad	4 505	152	−1,805	−11,306	−21,160	−16,995	−53,471	−43,898	−60,151
Equity capital	4 510	−817	−1,540	−4,238	−5,170	−6,748	−23,769	−20,052	−48,107
Claims on affiliated enterprises	4 515	−924	−1,659	−4,553	−5,424	−7,652	−24,365	−21,714	−51,444
Liabilities to affiliated enterprises	4 520	106	119	315	254	904	597	1,662	3,337
Reinvested earnings	4 525	....	....	−2,924	−6,650	−6,072	−9,331	−8,547	−16,314
Other capital	4 530	970	−265	−4,144	−9,340	−4,174	−20,371	−15,299	4,270
Claims on affiliated enterprises	4 535	−926	−422	−4,394	−9,803	−5,200	−21,950	−17,800	....
Liabilities to affiliated enterprises	4 540	1,896	157	250	463	1,026	1,579	2,501	4,270
Direct investment in China, P.R.: Mainland	4 555	47,077	54,936	117,208	124,082	160,052	175,148	114,215	185,081
Equity capital	4 560	37,397	51,764	78,917	87,707	126,931	126,291	72,893	121,782
Claims on direct investors	4 565	−3,055	−2,267	−2,831	−3,035	−4,248	−5,808	−18,730	−11,607
Liabilities to direct investors	4 570	40,452	54,032	81,748	90,742	131,179	132,099	91,624	133,388
Reinvested earnings	4 575	7,195	3,000	28,345	24,713	21,136	29,594	39,502	49,944
Other capital	4 580	2,485	172	9,946	11,662	11,985	19,263	1,819	13,355
Claims on direct investors	4 585	−3,373	−3,426	−3,548	−5,437	−6,963	−7,280	−13,113	−10,070
Liabilities to direct investors	4 590	5,858	3,598	13,494	17,099	18,947	26,542	14,932	23,424
B. PORTFOLIO INVESTMENT	4 600	11,427	19,690	−4,933	−67,558	18,672	42,660	38,691	24,038
Assets	4 602	2,983	6,486	−26,157	−110,419	−2,324	32,750	9,888	−7,643
Equity securities	4 610	....	....	....	−1,454	−15,189	−1,117	−33,815	−8,429
Monetary authorities	4 611	....	....	....	....	....	....	....	....
General government	4 612	....	....	....	....	....	....	....	....
Banks	4 613	....	....	....	....	....	....	....	....
Other sectors	4 614	....	....	....	−1,454	−15,189	−1,117	−33,815	−8,429
Debt securities	4 619	2,983	6,486	−26,157	−108,965	12,865	33,867	43,703	787
Bonds and notes	4 620	2,983	6,486	−25,482	−106,737	10,591	37,563	36,956	1,852
Monetary authorities	4 621	....	....	....	....	....	....	....	....
General government	4 622	....	....	....	....	....	....	....	....
Banks	4 623	2,973	6,528	−25,032	−53,234	21,543	34,336	44,190	5,060
Other sectors	4 624	10	−41	−450	−53,503	−10,952	3,227	−7,234	−3,208
Money market instruments	4 630	....	....	−675	−2,228	2,274	−3,696	6,747	−1,065
Monetary authorities	4 631	....	....	....	....	....	....	....	....
General government	4 632	....	....	....	....	....	....	....	....
Banks	4 633	....	....	−675	−2,228	2,274	−3,696	−13	229
Other sectors	4 634	....	....	....	....	....	....	6,760	−1,294
Liabilities	4 652	8,444	13,203	21,224	42,861	20,996	9,910	28,804	31,681
Equity securities	4 660	7,729	10,923	20,346	42,861	18,510	8,721	28,161	31,357
Banks	4 663	....	....	....	....	....	....	....	....
Other sectors	4 664	....	....	....	....	....	....	....	....
Debt securities	4 669	715	2,280	878	....	2,486	1,189	643	324
Bonds and notes	4 670	717	2,283	567	....	2,486	1,189	643	324
Monetary authorities	4 671	....	....	....	....	....	....	....	....
General government	4 672	1,450	1,732	....	....	....	....	379	....
Banks	4 673	−506	519	548	....	989	1,315	293	324
Other sectors	4 674	−227	33	19	....	1,497	−126	−28	....
Money market instruments	4 680	−2	−3	311	....	....	....	....	....
Monetary authorities	4 681	....	....	....	....	....	....	....	....
General government	4 682	....	....	....	....	....	....	....	....
Banks	4 683	....	....	−3	....	....	....	....	....
Other sectors	4 684	−2	−3	314	....	....	....	....	....
C. FINANCIAL DERIVATIVES	4 910	....	....	....	....	....	....	....	....
Monetary authorities	4 911	....	....	....	....	....	....	....	....
General government	4 912	....	....	....	....	....	....	....	....
Banks	4 913	....	....	....	....	....	....	....	....
Other sectors	4 914	....	....	....	....	....	....	....	....
Assets	4 900	....	....	....	....	....	....	....	....
Monetary authorities	4 901	....	....	....	....	....	....	....	....
General government	4 902	....	....	....	....	....	....	....	....
Banks	4 903	....	....	....	....	....	....	....	....
Other sectors	4 904	....	....	....	....	....	....	....	....
Liabilities	4 905	....	....	....	....	....	....	....	....
Monetary authorities	4 906	....	....	....	....	....	....	....	....
General government	4 907	....	....	....	....	....	....	....	....
Banks	4 908	....	....	....	....	....	....	....	....
Other sectors	4 909	....	....	....	....	....	....	....	....

Table 2 (Concluded). STANDARD PRESENTATION, 2003–2010

(Millions of U.S. dollars)

	Code	2003	2004	2005	2006	2007	2008	2009	2010
D. OTHER INVESTMENT	4 700	**−5,882**	**37,908**	**−4,026**	**13,265**	**−69,680**	**−121,067**	**67,848**	**72,446**
Assets	4 703	**−17,922**	**1,980**	**−48,947**	**−31,853**	**−151,486**	**−106,074**	**9,365**	**−116,262**
Trade credits	4 706	−1,465	−15,897	−22,905	−26,148	−23,800	5,867	−54,435	−61,635
General government	4 707	....	....	....	....	....	....	....	....
of which: Short-term	4 709	....	....	....	....	....	....	....	....
Other sectors	4 710	−1,465	−15,897	−22,905	−26,148	−23,800	5,867	−54,435	−61,635
of which: Short-term	4 712	−1,465	−14,561	−21,989	−24,318	−22,134	5,456	−50,625	−57,321
Loans	4 714	13,927	−9,658	−12,993	4,928	−20,806	−18,501	12,996	−21,041
Monetary authorities	4 715	....	....	....	....	....	....	....	....
of which: Short-term	4 718	....	....	....	....	....	....	....	....
General government	4 719	....	....	....	....	....	....	−54	6
of which: Short-term	4 721	....	....	....	....	....	....	−54	6
Banks	4 722	20,822	−9,070	−13,464	5,148	−20,412	−18,962	12,881	−21,513
of which: Short-term	4 724	21,515	−8,013	−11,959	8,095	−16,293	−12,393	44,385	6,154
Other sectors	4 725	−6,895	−588	471	−220	−394	461	170	466
of which: Short-term	4 727	−6,895	−588	471	−220	−394	461	170	466
Currency and deposits	4 730	−6,552	20,207	−10,317	−9,904	−2,382	−33,528	5,171	−58,013
Monetary authorities	4 731	....	....	....	....	....	....	....	....
General government	4 732	....	....	....	....	....	....	....	....
Banks	4 733	−6,125	20,182	−10,192	−2,099	−2,948	−30,443	9,225	−2,490
Other sectors	4 734	−427	25	−126	−7,806	566	−3,085	−4,054	−55,523
Other assets	4 736	−23,832	7,328	−2,732	−728	−104,499	−59,912	45,633	24,428
Monetary authorities	4 737	....	....	−4,354	−3,572	−113,980	−55,105	45,617	24,453
of which: Short-term	4 739	....	....	−4,354	−3,572	−113,980	−55,105	45,617	24,453
General government	4 740	....	....	....	....	....	....	....	....
of which: Short-term	4 742	....	....	....	....	....	....	....	....
Banks	4 743	−30,430	−8,153	....	....	....	....	....	....
of which: Short-term	4 745	14,570	−8,153	....	....	....	....	....	....
Other sectors	4 746	6,598	15,481	1,622	2,844	9,481	−4,807	16	−25
of which: Short-term	4 748	6,598	15,481	1,622	2,844	9,481	−4,807	16	−25
Liabilities	4 753	**12,040**	**35,928**	**44,921**	**45,118**	**81,806**	**−14,992**	**58,483**	**188,708**
Trade credits	4 756	4,720	18,595	25,412	13,227	29,100	−19,049	32,058	49,515
General government	4 757	....	....	....	....	....	....	....	....
of which: Short-term	4 759	....	....	....	....	....	....	....	....
Other sectors	4 760	4,720	18,595	25,412	13,227	29,100	−19,049	32,058	49,515
of which: Short-term	4 762	4,720	15,733	24,243	12,301	27,063	−17,716	29,814	46,049
Loans	4 764	6,614	13,753	2,924	11,038	17,296	3,621	3,749	79,105
Monetary authorities	4 765	....	....	....	....	....	....	....	....
of which: Use of Fund credit and loans from the Fund	4 766	....	....	....	....	....	....	....	....
of which: Short-term	4 768	....	....	....	....	....	....	....	....
General government	4 769	−2,758	986	−360	483	−550	−256	760	434
of which: Short-term	4 771	10	....	....	....	17	2	1	....
Banks	4 772	9,684	9,828	2,353	8,429	14,975	−4,101	6,462	69,756
of which: Short-term	4 774	11,965	6,862	809	5,954	8,927	−7,277	14,673	64,075
Other sectors	4 775	−312	2,939	931	2,126	2,871	7,978	−3,473	8,916
of which: Short-term	4 777	−5	2,076	670	990	1,364	4,172	−1,237	4,980
Currency and deposits	4 780	742	1,561	13,366	10,710	34,317	2,702	11,575	60,347
Monetary authorities	4 781	....	....	1,371	188	689	2,971	576	34,513
General government	4 782	....	12	....	....	....	....	....	....
Banks	4 783	738	1,547	3,999	10,522	−8,137	−9,490	−3,451	21,654
Other sectors	4 784	4	1	7,995	....	41,765	9,221	14,450	4,180
Other liabilities	4 786	−37	2,019	3,220	10,143	1,093	−2,267	11,101	−259
Monetary authorities	4 787	....	....	407	3,913	1,105	−2,262	10,992	−389
of which: Short-term	4 789	....	....	....	....	....	....	....	....
General government	4 790	....	....	....	....	....	....	....	....
of which: Short-term	4 792	....	....	....	....	....	....	....	....
Banks	4 793	−153	2,000	2,834	6,328	15	−27	105	93
of which: Short-term	4 795	−148	2,018	2,745	6,260	−8	−39	105	93
Other sectors	4 796	116	19	−20	−98	−27	22	4	37
of which: Short-term	4 798	1,127	−32	14	20	−32	9	4	32
E. RESERVE ASSETS	4 802	**−137,455**	**−189,849**	**−250,975**	**−284,651**	**−460,651**	**−479,553**	**−400,508**	**−471,659**
Monetary gold	4 812	....	....	....	....	....	....	−4,876	....
Special drawing rights	4 811	−11	−92	−107	245	−68	−38	−11,257	−54
Reserve position in the Fund	4 810	269	619	1,705	371	282	−1,173	−2,324	−2,048
Foreign exchange	4 803	−137,713	−190,377	−252,573	−285,267	−460,865	−478,342	−382,051	−469,556
Other claims	4 813	....	....	....	....	....	....	....	....
NET ERRORS AND OMISSIONS	4 998	**38,854**	**10,531**	**15,847**	**−745**	**11,507**	**20,868**	**−41,425**	**−59,760**

Table 3. INTERNATIONAL INVESTMENT POSITION (End-period stocks), 2003–2010

(Millions of U.S. dollars)

	Code	2003	2004	2005	2006	2007	2008	2009	2010
ASSETS	8 995 C.	....	933,439	1,229,107	1,690,430	2,416,204	2,956,691	3,457,066	4,126,043
Direct investment abroad	8 505 ..	....	52,704	64,493	90,630	115,960	185,694	245,750	310,836
Equity capital and reinvested earnings	8 506 ..	....	....	....	....	....	....	....	....
Claims on affiliated enterprises	8 507 ..	....	....	....	....	....	....	....	....
Liabilities to affiliated enterprises	8 508 ..	....	....	....	....	....	....	....	....
Other capital	8 530 ..	....	....	....	....	....	....	....	....
Claims on affiliated enterprises	8 535 ..	....	....	....	....	....	....	....	....
Liabilities to affiliated enterprises	8 540 ..	....	....	....	....	....	....	....	....
Portfolio investment	8 602 ..	....	92,028	116,739	265,179	284,620	252,509	242,774	257,112
Equity securities	8 610 ..	....	....	....	1,454	19,643	21,389	54,575	63,004
Monetary authorities	8 611 ..	....	....	....	....	....	....	....	....
General government	8 612 ..	....	....	....	....	....	....	....	....
Banks	8 613 ..	....	....	....	....	....	....	....	....
Other sectors	8 614 ..	....	....	....	....	....	....	....	....
Debt securities	8 619 ..	....	92,028	116,739	263,725	264,978	231,120	188,199	194,108
Bonds and notes	8 620 ..	....	....	....	....	....	....	....	....
Monetary authorities	8 621 ..	....	....	....	....	....	....	....	....
General government	8 622 ..	....	....	....	....	....	....	....	....
Banks	8 623 ..	....	....	....	....	....	....	....	....
Other sectors	8 624 ..	....	....	....	....	....	....	....	....
Money market instruments	8 630 ..	....	....	....	....	....	....	....	....
Monetary authorities	8 631 ..	....	....	....	....	....	....	....	....
General government	8 632 ..	....	....	....	....	....	....	....	....
Banks	8 633 ..	....	....	....	....	....	....	....	....
Other sectors	8 634 ..	....	....	....	....	....	....	....	....
Financial derivatives	8 900 ..	....	....	....	....	....	....	....	....
Monetary authorities	8 901 ..	....	....	....	....	....	....	....	....
General government	8 902 ..	....	....	....	....	....	....	....	....
Banks	8 903 ..	....	....	....	....	....	....	....	....
Other sectors	8 904 ..	....	....	....	....	....	....	....	....
Other investment	8 703 ..	....	165,756	216,384	253,854	468,305	552,287	515,365	643,910
Trade credits	8 706 ..	....	43,179	66,084	92,233	116,033	110,166	164,601	226,136
General government	8 707 ..	....	....	....	....	....	....	....	....
of which: Short-term	8 709 ..	....	....	....	....	....	....	....	....
Other sectors	8 710 ..	....	....	....	....	....	....	....	....
of which: Short-term	8 712 ..	....	....	....	....	....	....	....	....
Loans	8 714 ..	....	58,960	71,935	67,019	88,755	107,130	97,388	117,440
Monetary authorities	8 715 ..	....	....	....	....	....	....	....	....
of which: Short-term	8 718 ..	....	....	....	....	....	....	....	....
General government	8 719 ..	....	....	....	....	....	....	....	....
of which: Short-term	8 721 ..	....	....	....	....	....	....	....	....
Banks	8 722 ..	....	....	....	....	....	....	....	....
of which: Short-term	8 724 ..	....	....	....	....	....	....	....	....
Other sectors	8 725 ..	....	....	....	....	....	....	....	....
of which: Short-term	8 727 ..	....	....	....	....	....	....	....	....
Currency and deposits	8 730 ..	....	55,320	67,481	73,552	137,970	152,913	131,004	198,510
Monetary authorities	8 731 ..	....	....	....	....	....	....	....	....
General government	8 732 ..	....	....	....	....	....	....	....	....
Banks	8 733 ..	....	....	....	....	....	....	....	....
Other sectors	8 734 ..	....	....	....	....	....	....	....	....
Other assets	8 736 ..	....	8,298	10,884	21,050	125,548	182,078	122,372	101,825
Monetary authorities	8 737 ..	....	....	....	....	....	....	....	....
of which: Short-term	8 739 ..	....	....	....	....	....	....	....	....
General government	8 740 ..	....	....	....	....	....	....	....	....
of which: Short-term	8 742 ..	....	....	....	....	....	....	....	....
Banks	8 743 ..	....	....	....	....	....	....	....	....
of which: Short-term	8 745 ..	....	....	....	....	....	....	....	....
Other sectors	8 746 ..	....	....	....	....	....	....	....	....
of which: Short-term	8 748 ..	....	....	....	....	....	....	....	....
Reserve assets	8 802 ..	....	622,950	831,491	1,080,767	1,547,318	1,966,200	2,453,177	2,914,184
Monetary gold	8 812 ..	....	8,451	9,977	12,274	17,037	16,940	37,133	48,105
Special drawing rights	8 811 ..	1,102	1,247	1,251	1,068	1,192	1,199	12,510	12,344
Reserve position in the Fund	8 810 ..	3,798	3,320	1,391	1,081	840	2,031	4,382	6,397
Foreign exchange	8 803 ..	....	609,932	818,872	1,066,344	1,528,249	1,946,030	2,399,152	2,847,338
Other claims	8 813 ..	....	....	....	....	....	....	....	....

Table 3 (Concluded). INTERNATIONAL INVESTMENT POSITION (End-period stocks), 2003–2010

(Millions of U.S. dollars)

	Code	2003	2004	2005	2006	2007	2008	2009	2010
LIABILITIES	8 995 D.	....	652,677	815,633	1,050,266	1,228,089	1,462,875	1,946,385	2,335,391
Direct investment in China, P.R.: Mainland	8 555	....	368,970	471,549	614,383	703,667	915,524	1,314,771	1,476,441
Equity capital and reinvested earnings	8 556	....	....	....	....	....	....	....	....
Claims on direct investors	8 557	....	....	....	....	....	....	....	....
Liabilities to direct investors	8 558	....	....	....	....	....	....	....	....
Other capital	8 580	....	....	....	....	....	....	....	....
Claims on direct investors	8 585	....	....	....	....	....	....	....	....
Liabilities to direct investors	8 590	....	....	....	....	....	....	....	....
Portfolio investment	8 652	....	56,623	76,617	120,715	146,648	167,750	189,985	221,605
Equity securities	8 660	....	43,290	63,636	106,497	129,013	150,530	174,765	206,123
Banks	8 663	....	....	....	....	....	....	....	....
Other sectors	8 664	....	....	....	....	....	....	....	....
Debt securities	8 669	....	13,332	12,981	14,217	17,635	17,220	15,219	15,483
Bonds and notes	8 670	....	....	....	....	....	....	....	....
Monetary authorities	8 671	....	....	....	....	....	....	....	....
General government	8 672	....	....	....	....	....	....	....	....
Banks	8 673	....	....	....	....	....	....	....	....
Other sectors	8 674	....	....	....	....	....	....	....	....
Money market instruments	8 680	....	....	....	....	....	....	....	....
Monetary authorities	8 681	....	....	....	....	....	....	....	....
General government	8 682	....	....	....	....	....	....	....	....
Banks	8 683	....	....	....	....	....	....	....	....
Other sectors	8 684	....	....	....	....	....	....	....	....
Financial derivatives	8 905	....	....	....	....	....	....	....	....
Monetary authorities	8 906	....	....	....	....	....	....	....	....
General government	8 907	....	....	....	....	....	....	....	....
Banks	8 908	....	....	....	....	....	....	....	....
Other sectors	8 909	....	....	....	....	....	....	....	....
Other investment	8 753	....	227,084	267,466	315,167	377,774	379,601	441,630	637,345
Trade credits	8 756	....	80,917	106,328	119,555	148,655	129,606	161,664	211,180
General government	8 757	....	....	....	....	....	....	....	....
of which: Short-term	8 759	....	....	....	....	....	....	....	....
Other sectors	8 760	....	....	....	....	....	....	....	....
of which: Short-term	8 762	....	....	....	....	....	....	....	....
Loans	8 764	....	88,048	86,988	98,480	103,349	102,995	163,594	238,890
Monetary authorities	8 765	....	....	....	....	....	....	....	....
of which: Use of Fund credit and loans from the Fund	8 766	....	....	....	....	....	....	....	....
of which: Short-term	8 768	....	....	....	....	....	....	....	....
General government	8 769	....	....	....	....	....	....	....	....
of which: Short-term	8 771	....	....	....	....	....	....	....	....
Banks	8 772	....	....	....	....	....	....	....	....
of which: Short-term	8 774	....	....	....	....	....	....	....	....
Other sectors	8 775	....	....	....	....	....	....	....	....
of which: Short-term	8 777	....	....	....	....	....	....	....	....
Currency and deposits	8 780	....	38,125	48,430	59,468	79,083	91,828	93,685	165,025
Monetary authorities	8 781	....	....	....	....	....	....	....	....
General government	8 782	....	....	....	....	....	....	....	....
Banks	8 783	....	....	....	....	....	....	....	....
Other sectors	8 784	....	....	....	....	....	....	....	....
Other liabilities	8 786	....	19,994	25,720	37,664	46,686	55,172	22,687	22,249
Monetary authorities	8 787	....	....	....	....	....	....	....	....
of which: Short-term	8 789	....	....	....	....	....	....	....	....
General government	8 790	....	....	....	....	....	....	....	....
of which: Short-term	8 792	....	....	....	....	....	....	....	....
Banks	8 793	....	....	....	....	....	....	....	....
of which: Short-term	8 795	....	....	....	....	....	....	....	....
Other sectors	8 796	....	....	....	....	....	....	....	....
of which: Short-term	8 798	....	....	....	....	....	....	....	....
NET INTERNATIONAL INVESTMENT POSITION	8 995	....	280,762	413,474	640,164	1,188,115	1,493,816	1,510,681	1,790,652
Conversion rates: yuan per U.S. dollar (end of period)	0 102	8.2767	8.2765	8.0702	7.8087	7.3046	6.8346	6.8282	6.6229

Table 1. ANALYTIC PRESENTATION, 2003–2010

(Millions of U.S. dollars)

	Code	2003	2004	2005	2006	2007	2008	2009	2010
A. Current Account[1]	4 993 Z.	**16,470**	**15,731**	**20,181**	**22,928**	**25,547**	**29,494**	**17,963**	**13,936**
Goods: exports f.o.b.	2 100 ..	224,656	260,263	289,579	317,600	345,979	365,236	321,836	394,015
Goods: imports f.o.b.	3 100 ..	−230,435	−269,575	−297,206	−331,634	−365,679	−388,353	−348,698	−436,980
Balance on Goods	4 100 ..	*−5,779*	*−9,312*	*−7,627*	*−14,033*	*−19,701*	*−23,117*	*−26,862*	*−42,965*
Services: credit	2 200 ..	46,555	55,160	63,709	72,735	84,722	92,292	86,411	106,432
Services: debit	3 200 ..	−26,126	−31,138	−33,979	−37,060	−42,591	−47,062	−43,939	−50,869
Balance on Goods and Services	4 991 ..	*14,651*	*14,710*	*22,104*	*21,642*	*22,430*	*22,113*	*15,610*	*12,598*
Income: credit	2 300 ..	43,181	52,003	64,806	83,865	114,720	118,546	100,773	116,536
Income: debit	3 300 ..	−39,525	−48,997	−64,604	−80,346	−109,027	−107,845	−95,243	−111,829
Balance on Goods, Services, and Income	4 992 ..	*18,307*	*17,716*	*22,305*	*25,161*	*28,123*	*32,814*	*21,139*	*17,305*
Current transfers: credit	2 379 Z.	529	626	943	960	938	611	469	614
Current transfers: debit	3 379 ..	−2,366	−2,611	−3,067	−3,194	−3,513	−3,931	−3,646	−3,983
B. Capital Account[1]	4 994 Z.	**−1,065**	**−329**	**−634**	**−373**	**1,324**	**2,105**	**4,671**	**5,233**
Capital account: credit	2 994 Z.	132	1,152	1,001	1,415	3,479	4,522	6,816	7,819
Capital account: debit	3 994 ..	−1,197	−1,480	−1,636	−1,788	−2,155	−2,417	−2,144	−2,586
Total, Groups A Plus B	4 981 ..	*15,405*	*15,402*	*19,546*	*22,555*	*26,871*	*31,599*	*22,634*	*19,168*
C. Financial Account[1]	4 995 W.	**−20,953**	**−20,094**	**−21,448**	**−20,621**	**−19,855**	**2,139**	**46,147**	**−13,774**
Direct investment abroad	4 505 ..	−5,492	−45,715	−27,201	−44,978	−61,119	−50,549	−63,994	−76,093
Direct investment in China, P.R.: Hong Kong	4 555 Z.	13,624	34,032	33,618	45,054	54,365	59,614	52,395	68,915
Portfolio investment assets	4 602 ..	−35,386	−43,214	−40,723	−41,751	−77,899	−25,353	−52,086	−66,663
Equity securities	4 610 ..	−9,951	−30,486	−27,954	−15,601	−69,337	−18,290	−25,695	−46,503
Debt securities	4 619 ..	−25,435	−12,728	−12,768	−26,149	−8,562	−7,062	−26,391	−20,160
Portfolio investment liabilities	4 652 Z.	1,386	3,882	9,256	15,038	75,166	−12,799	9,197	5,791
Equity securities	4 660 ..	5,771	1,979	9,961	14,480	43,625	17,423	9,492	2,810
Debt securities	4 669 Z.	−4,385	1,902	−705	558	31,540	−30,222	−295	2,980
Financial derivatives	4 910 ..	10,047	5,693	3,920	3,338	5,574	8,126	3,169	3,752
Financial derivatives assets	4 900 ..	30,005	20,605	20,797	19,437	29,818	68,601	48,542	35,215
Financial derivatives liabilities	4 905 ..	−19,958	−14,912	−16,877	−16,099	−24,244	−60,474	−45,373	−31,462
Other investment assets	4 703 ..	−28,671	−32,609	−18,750	−58,465	−163,084	46,105	97,012	−63,297
Monetary authorities	4 701 ..	....	....	....	....	....	....	....	....
General government	4 704 ..	....	....	....	....	....	....	....	....
Banks	4 705 ..	−18,154	−37,563	−4,062	−57,693	−124,293	27,388	76,528	−63,285
Other sectors	4 728 ..	−10,517	4,954	−14,688	−772	−38,790	18,717	20,484	−13
Other investment liabilities	4 753 W.	23,539	57,838	18,432	61,143	147,141	−23,006	454	113,823
Monetary authorities	4 753 WA	....	....	....	....	....	....	....	....
General government	4 753 ZB	....	....	....	....	....	....	....	....
Banks	4 753 ZC	20,199	56,992	5,623	52,411	132,503	382	6,606	111,257
Other sectors	4 753 ZD	3,340	845	12,809	8,732	14,638	−23,388	−6,152	2,565
Total, Groups A Through C	4 983 ..	*−5,548*	*−4,691*	*−1,901*	*1,934*	*7,016*	*33,739*	*68,781*	*5,395*
D. Net Errors and Omissions	4 998 ..	**6,542**	**7,977**	**3,279**	**4,082**	**7,688**	**209**	**2,080**	**3,759**
Total, Groups A Through D	4 984 ..	*994*	*3,286*	*1,378*	*6,016*	*14,704*	*33,948*	*70,860*	*9,153*
E. Reserves and Related Items	4 802 A.	**−994**	**−3,286**	**−1,378**	**−6,016**	**−14,704**	**−33,948**	**−70,860**	**−9,153**
Reserve assets	4 802 ..	−994	−3,286	−1,378	−6,016	−14,704	−33,948	−70,860	−9,153
Use of Fund credit and loans	4 766 ..	....	....	....	....	....	....	....	....
Exceptional financing	4 920 ..	....	....	....	....	....	....	....	....
Conversion rates: Hong Kong dollars per U.S. dollar	0 101 ..	**7.7868**	**7.7880**	**7.7773**	**7.7678**	**7.8014**	**7.7868**	**7.7518**	**7.7692**

[1] Excludes components that have been classified in the categories of Group E.

Table 2. STANDARD PRESENTATION, 2003–2010

(Millions of U.S. dollars)

	Code	2003	2004	2005	2006	2007	2008	2009	2010
CURRENT ACCOUNT	4 993	**16,470**	**15,731**	**20,181**	**22,928**	**25,547**	**29,494**	**17,963**	**13,936**
A. GOODS	4 100	−5,779	−9,312	−7,627	−14,033	−19,701	−23,117	−26,862	−42,965
Credit	2 100	224,656	260,263	289,579	317,600	345,979	365,236	321,836	394,015
General merchandise: exports f.o.b.	2 110	....	....	....	....	....	....	....	....
Goods for processing: exports f.o.b.	2 150	....	....	....	....	....	....	....	....
Repairs on goods	2 160	....	....	....	....	....	....	....	....
Goods procured in ports by carriers	2 170	....	....	....	....	....	....	....	....
Nonmonetary gold	2 180	....	....	....	....	....	....	....	....
Debit	3 100	−230,435	−269,575	−297,206	−331,634	−365,679	−388,353	−348,698	−436,980
General merchandise: imports f.o.b.	3 110	....	....	....	....	....	....	....	....
Goods for processing: imports f.o.b.	3 150	....	....	....	....	....	....	....	....
Repairs on goods	3 160	....	....	....	....	....	....	....	....
Goods procured in ports by carriers	3 170	....	....	....	....	....	....	....	....
Nonmonetary gold	3 180	....	....	....	....	....	....	....	....
B. SERVICES	4 200	**20,430**	**24,022**	**29,730**	**35,675**	**42,131**	**45,230**	**42,472**	**55,563**
Total credit	2 200	*46,555*	*55,160*	*63,709*	*72,735*	*84,722*	*92,292*	*86,411*	*106,432*
Total debit	3 200	*−26,126*	*−31,138*	*−33,979*	*−37,060*	*−42,591*	*−47,062*	*−43,939*	*−50,869*
Transportation services, credit	2 205	**13,832**	**17,358**	**20,318**	**22,423**	**25,581**	**28,886**	**23,688**	....
Passenger	2 850	....	....	....	....	....	....	....	....
Freight	2 851	....	....	....	....	....	....	....	....
Other	2 852	....	....	....	....	....	....	....	....
Sea transport, passenger	2 207	....	....	....	....	....	....	....	....
Sea transport, freight	2 208	....	....	....	....	....	....	....	....
Sea transport, other	2 209	....	....	....	....	....	....	....	....
Air transport, passenger	2 211	....	....	....	....	....	....	....	....
Air transport, freight	2 212	....	....	....	....	....	....	....	....
Air transport, other	2 213	....	....	....	....	....	....	....	....
Other transport, passenger	2 215	....	....	....	....	....	....	....	....
Other transport, freight	2 216	....	....	....	....	....	....	....	....
Other transport, other	2 217	....	....	....	....	....	....	....	....
Transportation services, debit	3 205	**−6,719**	**−8,687**	**−10,462**	**−11,616**	**−13,925**	**−15,831**	**−12,246**	....
Passenger	3 850	....	....	....	....	....	....	....	....
Freight	3 851	....	....	....	....	....	....	....	....
Other	3 852	....	....	....	....	....	....	....	....
Sea transport, passenger	3 207	....	....	....	....	....	....	....	....
Sea transport, freight	3 208	....	....	....	....	....	....	....	....
Sea transport, other	3 209	....	....	....	....	....	....	....	....
Air transport, passenger	3 211	....	....	....	....	....	....	....	....
Air transport, freight	3 212	....	....	....	....	....	....	....	....
Air transport, other	3 213	....	....	....	....	....	....	....	....
Other transport, passenger	3 215	....	....	....	....	....	....	....	....
Other transport, freight	3 216	....	....	....	....	....	....	....	....
Other transport, other	3 217	....	....	....	....	....	....	....	....
Travel, credit	2 236	**7,141**	**8,999**	**10,296**	**11,637**	**13,758**	**15,307**	**16,408**	....
Business travel	2 237	....	....	....	....	....	....	....	....
Personal travel	2 240	....	....	....	....	....	....	....	....
Travel, debit	3 236	**−11,448**	**−13,269**	**−13,305**	**−14,043**	**−15,042**	**−16,093**	**−15,669**	....
Business travel	3 237	....	....	....	....	....	....	....	....
Personal travel	3 240	....	....	....	....	....	....	....	....
Other services, credit	2 200 BA	**25,582**	**28,803**	**33,095**	**38,676**	**45,383**	**48,099**	**46,315**	....
Communications	2 245	756	852	942	834	866	882	894	....
Construction	2 249	510	378	313	268	346	203	139	....
Insurance	2 253	394	411	414	417	468	547	496	....
Financial	2 260	3,763	4,556	6,270	9,268	12,441	11,995	11,286	....
Computer and information	2 262	245	245	265	358	277	681	683	....
Royalties and licence fees	2 266	341	218	245	259	358	380	383	....
Other business services	2 268	19,382	21,798	24,318	26,930	30,293	33,079	32,230	....
Personal, cultural, and recreational	2 287	137	290	270	280	272	265	135	....
Government, n.i.e.	2 291	55	56	58	61	63	66	68	....
Other services, debit	3 200 BA	**−7,959**	**−9,181**	**−10,211**	**−11,402**	**−13,624**	**−15,139**	**−16,024**	....
Communications	3 245	−941	−1,124	−1,141	−1,072	−1,080	−1,188	−1,152	....
Construction	3 249	−399	−346	−273	−241	−295	−165	−119	....
Insurance	3 253	−622	−611	−606	−613	−711	−726	−680	....
Financial	3 260	−878	−1,165	−1,406	−2,017	−2,807	−3,137	−3,305	....
Computer and information	3 262	−282	−395	−427	−371	−423	−512	−553	....
Royalties and licence fees	3 266	−864	−1,111	−1,289	−1,357	−1,504	−1,610	−1,700	....
Other business services	3 268	−3,772	−4,223	−4,878	−5,519	−6,596	−7,517	−8,293	....
Personal, cultural, and recreational	3 287	−68	−52	−52	−56	−67	−140	−92	....
Government, n.i.e.	3 291	−132	−154	−141	−155	−141	−143	−130	....

Table 2 (Continued). STANDARD PRESENTATION, 2003–2010

(Millions of U.S. dollars)

	Code	2003	2004	2005	2006	2007	2008	2009	2010
C. INCOME	4 300	**3,656**	**3,006**	**201**	**3,520**	**5,693**	**10,701**	**5,530**	**4,707**
Total credit	2 300	*43,181*	*52,003*	*64,806*	*83,865*	*114,720*	*118,546*	*100,773*	*116,536*
Total debit	3 300	*–39,525*	*–48,997*	*–64,604*	*–80,346*	*–109,027*	*–107,845*	*–95,243*	*–111,829*
Compensation of employees, credit	2 310	**120**	**240**	**297**	**294**	**317**	**355**	**348**	**347**
Compensation of employees, debit	3 310	**–317**	**–321**	**–348**	**–377**	**–388**	**–393**	**–413**	**–433**
Investment income, credit	2 320	**43,061**	**51,763**	**64,509**	**83,571**	**114,403**	**118,190**	**100,425**	**116,189**
Direct investment income	2 330	25,143	29,543	35,046	44,593	63,399	73,944	73,518	87,674
Dividends and distributed branch profits	2 332	15,764	19,781	14,472	17,446	25,573	26,762	23,981	23,620
Reinvested earnings and undistributed branch profits	2 333	8,931	9,084	19,975	26,246	36,884	46,541	49,131	63,672
Income on debt (interest)	2 334	448	678	599	901	942	641	406	382
Portfolio investment income	2 339	13,586	16,041	18,077	22,022	27,043	27,537	20,835	24,036
Income on equity	2 340	4,690	6,435	6,764	7,674	10,580	12,716	8,160	11,734
Income on bonds and notes	2 350	8,329	8,958	10,510	13,018	14,716	13,599	11,841	11,670
Income on money market instruments	2 360	566	648	803	1,330	1,746	1,222	834	632
Other investment income	2 370	4,332	6,179	11,386	16,957	23,961	16,710	6,072	4,479
Investment income, debit	3 320	**–39,208**	**–48,677**	**–64,256**	**–79,969**	**–108,640**	**–107,452**	**–94,830**	**–111,396**
Direct investment income	3 330	–32,700	–40,269	–50,800	–60,643	–83,218	–83,504	–80,456	–98,041
Dividends and distributed branch profits	3 332	–15,981	–17,219	–24,668	–24,254	–30,082	–35,122	–32,815	–31,982
Reinvested earnings and undistributed branch profits	3 333	–16,027	–22,443	–25,508	–35,736	–51,865	–47,243	–46,951	–65,273
Income on debt (interest)	3 334	–691	–607	–624	–653	–1,271	–1,139	–690	–787
Portfolio investment income	3 339	–3,597	–4,032	–4,927	–6,663	–8,437	–10,262	–8,781	–9,302
Income on equity	3 340	–3,172	–3,685	–4,523	–6,254	–7,831	–9,611	–8,286	–8,755
Income on bonds and notes	3 350	–404	–339	–393	–367	–521	–578	–481	–543
Income on money market instruments	3 360	–21	–7	–11	–42	–86	–73	–14	–3
Other investment income	3 370	–2,911	–4,376	–8,530	–12,663	–16,984	–13,686	–5,594	–4,053
D. CURRENT TRANSFERS	4 379	**–1,837**	**–1,985**	**–2,124**	**–2,234**	**–2,576**	**–3,320**	**–3,177**	**–3,369**
Credit	2 379	**529**	**626**	**943**	**960**	**938**	**611**	**469**	**614**
General government	2 380	....	....	....	....	....	....	....	....
Other sectors	2 390	529	626	943	960	938	611	469	614
Workers' remittances	2 391	....	....	....	....	....	....	....	....
Other current transfers	2 392	....	....	....	....	....	....	....	....
Debit	3 379	**–2,366**	**–2,611**	**–3,067**	**–3,194**	**–3,513**	**–3,931**	**–3,646**	**–3,983**
General government	3 380	–171	–171	–181	–196	–224	–290	–232	–234
Other sectors	3 390	–2,194	–2,440	–2,886	–2,998	–3,289	–3,641	–3,414	–3,749
Workers' remittances	3 391	....	....	....	....	....	....	....	....
Other current transfers	3 392	....	....	....	....	....	....	....	....
CAPITAL AND FINANCIAL ACCOUNT	4 996	**–23,011**	**–23,708**	**–23,460**	**–27,010**	**–33,235**	**–29,703**	**–20,042**	**–17,694**
CAPITAL ACCOUNT	4 994	**–1,065**	**–329**	**–634**	**–373**	**1,324**	**2,105**	**4,671**	**5,233**
Total credit	2 994	*132*	*1,152*	*1,001*	*1,415*	*3,479*	*4,522*	*6,816*	*7,819*
Total debit	3 994	*–1,197*	*–1,480*	*–1,636*	*–1,788*	*–2,155*	*–2,417*	*–2,144*	*–2,586*
Capital transfers, credit	2 400	**132**	**1,152**	**1,001**	**1,415**	**3,479**	**4,522**	**6,816**	**7,819**
General government	2 401	....	....	....	....	....	....	....	....
Debt forgiveness	2 402	....	....	....	....	....	....	....	....
Other capital transfers	2 410	....	....	....	....	....	....	....	....
Other sectors	2 430	132	1,152	1,001	1,415	3,479	4,522	6,816	7,819
Migrants' transfers	2 431	....	....	....	....	....	....	....	....
Debt forgiveness	2 432	....	....	....	....	....	....	....	....
Other capital transfers	2 440	....	....	....	....	....	....	....	....
Capital transfers, debit	3 400	**–1,197**	**–1,480**	**–1,636**	**–1,788**	**–2,155**	**–2,417**	**–2,144**	**–2,586**
General government	3 401	....	....	....	....	....	....	–252	–398
Debt forgiveness	3 402	....	....	....	....	....	....	....	....
Other capital transfers	3 410	....	....	....	....	....	....	....	....
Other sectors	3 430	–1,197	–1,480	–1,636	–1,788	–2,155	–2,417	–1,893	–2,188
Migrants' transfers	3 431	....	....	....	....	....	....	....	....
Debt forgiveness	3 432	....	....	....	....	....	....	....	....
Other capital transfers	3 440	....	....	....	....	....	....	....	....
Nonproduced nonfinancial assets, credit	2 480	....	....	....	....	....	....	....	....
Nonproduced nonfinancial assets, debit	3 480	....	....	....	....	....	....	....	....

Table 2 (Continued). STANDARD PRESENTATION, 2003–2010

(Millions of U.S. dollars)

	Code	2003	2004	2005	2006	2007	2008	2009	2010
FINANCIAL ACCOUNT	4 995	−21,946	−23,380	−22,825	−26,637	−34,559	−31,808	−24,714	−22,927
A. DIRECT INVESTMENT	4 500	8,132	−11,683	6,417	75	−6,754	9,065	−11,599	−7,178
Direct investment abroad	4 505	−5,492	−45,715	−27,201	−44,978	−61,119	−50,549	−63,994	−76,093
Equity capital	4 510	−3,097	−11,401	−8,207	−5,917	−11,100	−4,743	−16,801	−8,190
Claims on affiliated enterprises	4 515	−3,097	−11,401	−8,207	−5,917	−11,100	−4,743	−16,801	−8,190
Liabilities to affiliated enterprises	4 520	....	....	....	....	....	....	....	....
Reinvested earnings	4 525	−8,931	−9,084	−19,975	−26,246	−36,884	−46,541	−49,131	−63,672
Other capital	4 530	6,536	−25,230	981	−12,815	−13,135	735	1,937	−4,230
Claims on affiliated enterprises	4 535	4,307	−13,337	−3,247	−12,905	−14,383	−804	−1,679	−6,554
Liabilities to affiliated enterprises	4 540	2,229	−11,892	4,228	89	1,248	1,539	3,616	2,324
Direct investment in China, P.R.: Hong Kong	4 555	13,624	34,032	33,618	45,054	54,365	59,614	52,395	68,915
Equity capital	4 560	590	3,793	3,665	1,999	4,782	9,644	5,102	1,210
Claims on direct investors	4 565	....	....	....	....	....	....	....	....
Liabilities to direct investors	4 570	590	3,793	3,665	1,999	4,782	9,644	5,102	1,210
Reinvested earnings	4 575	16,027	22,443	25,508	35,736	51,865	47,243	46,951	65,273
Other capital	4 580	−2,993	7,796	4,445	7,318	−2,282	2,728	343	2,432
Claims on direct investors	4 585	−3,061	−563	−915	604	−2,632	−6,503	2,484	1,717
Liabilities to direct investors	4 590	68	8,360	5,359	6,714	350	9,231	−2,141	716
B. PORTFOLIO INVESTMENT	4 600	−34,000	−39,332	−31,467	−26,712	−2,733	−38,151	−42,889	−60,873
Assets	4 602	−35,386	−43,214	−40,723	−41,751	−77,899	−25,353	−52,086	−66,663
Equity securities	4 610	−9,951	−30,486	−27,954	−15,601	−69,337	−18,290	−25,695	−46,503
Monetary authorities	4 611	....	....	....	....	....	....	....	....
General government	4 612	....	....	....	....	....	....	....	....
Banks	4 613	−139	−765	−1,548	−96	−233	1,547	49	−42
Other sectors	4 614	−9,811	−29,721	−26,406	−15,505	−69,104	−19,837	−25,744	−46,461
Debt securities	4 619	−25,435	−12,728	−12,768	−26,149	−8,562	−7,062	−26,391	−20,160
Bonds and notes	4 620	−23,791	−9,083	−11,045	−7,579	−2,353	17,908	−42,094	−2,343
Monetary authorities	4 621	....	....	....	....	....	....	....	....
General government	4 622	....	....	....	....	....	....	....	....
Banks	4 623	−10,340	−1,381	−8,320	−7,722	2,684	6,610	−27,108	5,382
Other sectors	4 624	−13,450	−7,701	−2,725	143	−5,037	11,298	−14,986	−7,725
Money market instruments	4 630	−1,644	−3,646	−1,723	−18,571	−6,209	−24,970	15,703	−17,817
Monetary authorities	4 631	....	....	....	....	....	....	....	....
General government	4 632	....	....	....	....	....	....	....	....
Banks	4 633	−991	−3,524	300	−18,132	−7,572	−20,251	23,135	−19,492
Other sectors	4 634	−653	−122	−2,024	−439	1,363	−4,719	−7,432	1,675
Liabilities	4 652	1,386	3,882	9,256	15,038	75,166	−12,799	9,197	5,791
Equity securities	4 660	5,771	1,979	9,961	14,480	43,625	17,423	9,492	2,810
Banks	4 663	349	−397	−718	1,076	2,130	−1,413	−422	−967
Other sectors	4 664	5,422	2,377	10,678	13,404	41,495	18,836	9,915	3,777
Debt securities	4 669	−4,385	1,902	−705	558	31,540	−30,222	−295	2,980
Bonds and notes	4 670	−3,825	1,774	−856	517	10,148	−9,124	57	2,002
Monetary authorities	4 671	....	....	....	....	....	....	....	....
General government	4 672	....	....	....	....	....	....	....	....
Banks	4 673	−2,056	973	888	−335	1,231	−574	185	455
Other sectors	4 674	−1,769	801	−1,744	852	8,917	−8,551	−129	1,548
Money market instruments	4 680	−560	129	151	42	21,393	−21,098	−352	978
Monetary authorities	4 681	....	....	....	....	....	....	....	....
General government	4 682	....	....	....	....	....	....	....	....
Banks	4 683	−265	181	135	−42	21,356	−20,944	−462	949
Other sectors	4 684	−295	−52	16	84	37	−155	110	29
C. FINANCIAL DERIVATIVES	4 910	10,047	5,693	3,920	3,338	5,574	8,126	3,169	3,752
Monetary authorities	4 911	....	....	....	....	....	....	....	....
General government	4 912	....	....	....	....	....	....	....	....
Banks	4 913	9,505	5,787	2,788	1,993	5,181	3,621	743	1,659
Other sectors	4 914	542	−94	1,132	1,345	393	4,505	2,426	2,094
Assets	4 900	30,005	20,605	20,797	19,437	29,818	68,601	48,542	35,215
Monetary authorities	4 901	....	....	....	....	....	....	....	....
General government	4 902	....	....	....	....	....	....	....	....
Banks	4 903	27,666	19,041	18,086	16,262	24,748	62,187	45,674	32,679
Other sectors	4 904	2,339	1,564	2,711	3,175	5,069	6,414	2,868	2,536
Liabilities	4 905	−19,958	−14,912	−16,877	−16,099	−24,244	−60,474	−45,373	−31,462
Monetary authorities	4 906	....	....	....	....	....	....	....	....
General government	4 907	....	....	....	....	....	....	....	....
Banks	4 908	−18,162	−13,254	−15,298	−14,269	−19,567	−58,566	−44,931	−31,020
Other sectors	4 909	−1,796	−1,658	−1,579	−1,831	−4,677	−1,908	−442	−442

Table 2 (Concluded). STANDARD PRESENTATION, 2003–2010

(Millions of U.S. dollars)

	Code	2003	2004	2005	2006	2007	2008	2009	2010
D. OTHER INVESTMENT	4 700	**−5,132**	**25,229**	**−318**	**2,678**	**−15,942**	**23,099**	**97,466**	**50,525**
Assets	4 703	**−28,671**	**−32,609**	**−18,750**	**−58,465**	**−163,084**	**46,105**	**97,012**	**−63,297**
Trade credits	4 706	−7,049	−9,251	−3,617	373	−6,767	−7,263	−1,416	−4,694
General government	4 707	....	....	....	....	....	....	....	....
of which: Short-term	4 709	....	....	....	....	....	....	....	....
Other sectors	4 710	−7,049	−9,251	−3,617	373	−6,767	−7,263	−1,416	−4,694
of which: Short-term	4 712	....	....	....	....	....	....	....	....
Loans	4 714	3,957	−5,776	−128	−2,830	−42,960	10,403	27,497	−25,737
Monetary authorities	4 715	....	....	....	....	....	....	....	....
of which: Short-term	4 718	....	....	....	....	....	....	....	....
General government	4 719	....	....	....	....	....	....	....	....
of which: Short-term	4 721	....	....	....	....	....	....	....	....
Banks	4 722	3,667	−4,163	−700	−3,172	−31,056	−10,991	24,372	−26,972
of which: Short-term	4 724	....	....	....	....	....	....	....	....
Other sectors	4 725	290	−1,613	572	343	−11,904	21,395	3,125	1,235
of which: Short-term	4 727	....	....	....	....	....	....	....	....
Currency and deposits	4 730	−25,276	−17,990	−14,663	−53,667	−105,051	39,935	69,928	−29,286
Monetary authorities	4 731	....	....	....	....	....	....	....	....
General government	4 732	....	....	....	....	....	....	....	....
Banks	4 733	−21,908	−33,672	−2,774	−52,415	−92,020	38,560	51,021	−32,682
Other sectors	4 734	−3,368	15,682	−11,888	−1,252	−13,031	1,375	18,907	3,396
Other assets	4 736	−303	409	−343	−2,340	−8,305	3,030	1,003	−3,580
Monetary authorities	4 737	....	....	....	....	....	....	....	....
of which: Short-term	4 739	....	....	....	....	....	....	....	....
General government	4 740	....	....	....	....	....	....	....	....
of which: Short-term	4 742	....	....	....	....	....	....	....	....
Banks	4 743	87	273	−588	−2,105	−1,217	−181	1,136	−3,631
of which: Short-term	4 745	....	....	....	....	....	....	....	....
Other sectors	4 746	−390	136	246	−235	−7,089	3,210	−132	51
of which: Short-term	4 748	....	....	....	....	....	....	....	....
Liabilities	4 753	**23,539**	**57,838**	**18,432**	**61,143**	**147,141**	**−23,006**	**454**	**113,823**
Trade credits	4 756	1,847	1,453	647	−1,936	720	422	214	1,062
General government	4 757	....	....	....	....	....	....	....	....
of which: Short-term	4 759	....	....	....	....	....	....	....	....
Other sectors	4 760	1,847	1,453	647	−1,936	720	422	214	1,062
of which: Short-term	4 762	....	....	....	....	....	....	....	....
Loans	4 764	784	128	8,881	10,298	2,236	−15,940	−6,634	3,311
Monetary authorities	4 765	....	....	....	....	....	....	....	....
of which: Use of Fund credit and loans from the Fund	4 766	....	....	....	....	....	....	....	....
of which: Short-term	4 768	....	....	....	....	....	....	....	....
General government	4 769	....	....	....	....	....	....	....	....
of which: Short-term	4 771	....	....	....	....	....	....	....	....
Banks	4 772	−931	1,477	−673	−897	1,087	2,399	−1,215	1,642
of which: Short-term	4 774	....	....	....	....	....	....	....	....
Other sectors	4 775	1,715	−1,349	9,554	11,195	1,149	−18,339	−5,419	1,669
of which: Short-term	4 777	....	....	....	....	....	....	....	....
Currency and deposits	4 780	20,914	56,562	6,069	52,612	130,147	−3,431	9,424	108,358
Monetary authorities	4 781	....	....	....	....	....	....	....	....
General government	4 782	....	....	....	....	....	....	....	....
Banks	4 783	20,932	56,484	5,964	52,242	129,483	−2,680	9,919	108,358
Other sectors	4 784	−18	79	105	370	664	−751	−495	....
Other liabilities	4 786	−6	−305	2,834	169	14,037	−4,057	−2,549	1,092
Monetary authorities	4 787	....	....	....	....	....	....	....	....
of which: Short-term	4 789	....	....	....	....	....	....	....	....
General government	4 790	....	....	....	....	....	....	....	....
of which: Short-term	4 792	....	....	....	....	....	....	....	....
Banks	4 793	199	−968	331	1,066	1,933	663	−2,097	1,258
of which: Short-term	4 795	....	....	....	....	....	....	....	....
Other sectors	4 796	−204	663	2,504	−897	12,104	−4,720	−452	−166
of which: Short-term	4 798	....	....	....	....	....	....	....	....
E. RESERVE ASSETS	4 802	**−994**	**−3,286**	**−1,378**	**−6,016**	**−14,704**	**−33,948**	**−70,860**	**−9,153**
Monetary gold	4 812	....	....	....	....	....	....	....	....
Special drawing rights	4 811	....	....	....	....	....	....	....	....
Reserve position in the Fund	4 810	....	....	....	....	....	....	....	....
Foreign exchange	4 803	−994	−3,286	−1,378	−6,016	−14,704	−33,948	−70,860	−9,153
Other claims	4 813	....	....	....	....	....	....	....	....
NET ERRORS AND OMISSIONS	4 998	**6,542**	**7,977**	**3,279**	**4,082**	**7,688**	**209**	**2,080**	**3,759**

Table 3. INTERNATIONAL INVESTMENT POSITION (End-period stocks), 2003–2010

(Billions of U.S. dollars)

	Code	2003	2004	2005	2006	2007	2008	2009	2010
ASSETS	8 995 C.	**1,185.41**	**1,376.31**	**1,494.78**	**1,929.22**	**2,716.67**	**2,260.66**	**2,554.51**	**2,885.26**
Direct investment abroad	8 505 ..	**339.65**	**403.12**	**471.32**	**677.15**	**1,011.21**	**762.04**	**832.15**	**948.49**
Equity capital and reinvested earnings	8 506 ..	276.42	310.18	375.76	561.29	890.22	635.75	706.56	810.90
Claims on affiliated enterprises	8 507 ..	276.42	310.18	375.76	561.29	890.22	635.75	706.56	810.90
Liabilities to affiliated enterprises	8 508 ..	....	....	....	....	....	....	....	....
Other capital	8 530 ..	63.23	92.94	95.56	115.87	120.99	126.29	125.59	137.59
Claims on affiliated enterprises	8 535 ..	95.41	113.88	121.92	139.42	146.05	152.14	153.35	171.93
Liabilities to affiliated enterprises	8 540 ..	−32.18	−20.93	−26.36	−23.56	−25.06	−25.85	−27.77	−34.34
Portfolio investment	8 602 ..	**334.91**	**400.89**	**436.60**	**580.55**	**778.58**	**557.16**	**811.48**	**929.00**
Equity securities	8 610 ..	152.83	199.68	227.85	338.90	514.54	275.18	498.74	584.12
Monetary authorities	8 611 .	....	....	....	....	....	....	....	....
General government	8 612 .	....	....	....	....	....	....	....	....
Banks	8 613 ..	.27	1.16	2.88	3.20	5.15	2.07	2.44	3.13
Other sectors	8 614 ..	152.56	198.52	224.97	335.70	509.39	273.10	496.30	580.99
Debt securities	8 619 ..	182.08	201.20	208.75	241.65	264.04	281.98	312.74	344.88
Bonds and notes	8 620 ..	154.10	169.49	175.11	189.32	205.33	197.56	244.92	254.22
Monetary authorities	8 621 ..	....	....	....	....	....	....	....	....
General government	8 622 ..	....	....	....	....	....	....	....	....
Banks	8 623 ..	98.19	101.44	107.59	118.55	123.32	123.74	153.73	149.98
Other sectors	8 624 ..	55.90	68.05	67.52	70.77	82.01	73.82	91.19	104.24
Money market instruments	8 630 ..	27.98	31.72	33.64	52.34	58.70	84.42	67.82	90.66
Monetary authorities	8 631 ..	....	....	....	....	....	....	....	....
General government	8 632 ..	....	....	....	....	....	....	....	....
Banks	8 633 ..	23.91	27.34	27.18	45.42	53.09	73.91	49.96	76.25
Other sectors	8 634 ..	4.08	4.38	6.45	6.91	5.61	10.51	17.86	14.41
Financial derivatives	8 900 ..	**19.85**	**22.44**	**17.19**	**22.54**	**47.89**	**87.13**	**48.90**	**58.92**
Monetary authorities	8 901 ..	....	....	....	....	....	....	....	....
General government	8 902 ..	....	....	....	....	....	....	....	....
Banks	8 903 ..	16.62	17.60	12.93	16.96	33.81	78.93	34.49	43.78
Other sectors	8 904 ..	3.23	4.84	4.26	5.58	14.08	8.21	14.41	15.14
Other investment	8 703 ..	**372.60**	**426.30**	**445.38**	**515.72**	**726.36**	**671.80**	**606.21**	**680.14**
Trade credits	8 706 ..	8.86	8.84	9.80	11.21	15.04	13.20	12.88	18.28
General government	8 707 ..	....	....	....	....	....	....	....	....
of which: Short-term	8 709 ..	....	....	....	....	....	....	....	....
Other sectors	8 710 ..	8.86	8.84	9.80	11.21	15.04	13.20	12.88	18.28
of which: Short-term	8 712 ..	....	....	....	....	....	....	....	....
Loans	8 714 ..	49.55	54.14	55.17	59.46	108.40	110.82	93.59	133.51
Monetary authorities	8 715 ..	....	....	....	....	....	....	....	....
of which: Short-term	8 718 ..	....	....	....	....	....	....	....	....
General government	8 719 ..	....	....	....	....	....	....	....	....
of which: Short-term	8 721 ..	....	....	....	....	....	....	....	....
Banks	8 722 ..	43.02	46.15	46.62	51.57	86.41	97.98	84.90	125.84
of which: Short-term	8 724 ..	....	....	....	....	....	....	....	....
Other sectors	8 725 ..	6.53	7.99	8.55	7.90	21.99	12.84	8.68	7.66
of which: Short-term	8 727 ..	....	....	....	....	....	....	....	....
Currency and deposits	8 730 ..	308.06	357.14	371.72	434.14	576.02	533.08	486.56	509.64
Monetary authorities	8 731 ..	....	....	....	....	....	....	....	....
General government	8 732 ..	....	....	....	....	....	....	....	....
Banks	8 733 ..	255.50	292.28	301.47	357.95	474.01	433.63	404.88	426.29
Other sectors	8 734 ..	52.56	64.86	70.25	76.20	102.01	99.46	81.68	83.35
Other assets	8 736 ..	6.14	6.17	8.69	10.90	26.90	14.70	13.19	18.72
Monetary authorities	8 737 ..	....	....	....	....	....	....	....	....
of which: Short-term	8 739 ..	....	....	....	....	....	....	....	....
General government	8 740 ..	....	....	....	....	....	....	....	....
of which: Short-term	8 742 ..	....	....	....	....	....	....	....	....
Banks	8 743 ..	1.12	2.16	2.66	4.85	5.55	5.65	4.56	9.81
of which: Short-term	8 745 ..	....	....	....	....	....	....	....	....
Other sectors	8 746 ..	5.02	4.01	6.02	6.05	21.36	9.05	8.63	8.91
of which: Short-term	8 748 ..	....	....	....	....	....	....	....	....
Reserve assets	8 802 ..	**118.40**	**123.56**	**124.30**	**133.26**	**152.62**	**182.53**	**255.77**	**268.70**
Monetary gold	8 812 ..	....	....	....	....	....	....	....	....
Special drawing rights	8 811 ..	....	....	....	....	....	....	....	....
Reserve position in the Fund	8 810 ..	....	....	....	....	....	....	....	....
Foreign exchange	8 803 ..	....	....	....	....	....	....	....	....
Other claims	8 813 ..	....	....	....	....	....	....	....	....

Table 3 (Concluded). INTERNATIONAL INVESTMENT POSITION (End-period stocks), 2003–2010

(Billions of U.S. dollars)

	Code	2003	2004	2005	2006	2007	2008	2009	2010
LIABILITIES..	8 995 D.	**791.25**	**951.56**	**1,055.42**	**1,410.89**	**2,232.97**	**1,637.91**	**1,834.45**	**2,191.46**
Direct investment in China: P.R.: Hong Kong.......	8 555 ..	**381.34**	**453.06**	**523.22**	**742.42**	**1,177.54**	**816.18**	**936.37**	**1,097.62**
Equity capital and reinvested earnings....................	8 556 ..	330.62	392.61	457.19	662.30	1,096.81	734.82	847.89	1,005.99
Claims on direct investors................................	8 557 ..	....	....	....	....	....	....	....	....
Liabilities to direct investors..........................	8 558 ..	330.62	392.61	457.19	662.30	1,096.81	734.82	847.89	1,005.99
Other capital..	8 580 ..	50.72	60.45	66.03	80.12	80.73	81.36	88.49	91.63
Claims on direct investors................................	8 585 ..	−15.19	−14.81	−14.69	−12.50	−16.04	−22.85	−20.37	−16.22
Liabilities to direct investors..........................	8 590 ..	65.91	75.26	80.73	92.62	96.77	104.21	108.86	107.86
Portfolio investment..................................	8 652 ..	**125.31**	**155.26**	**178.44**	**259.66**	**477.60**	**229.91**	**340.81**	**402.68**
Equity securities..	8 660 ..	115.69	143.41	167.57	247.87	433.62	214.49	326.14	383.87
Banks..	8 663 ..	8.33	8.48	6.71	11.08	16.77	7.27	9.81	10.88
Other sectors..	8 664 ..	107.36	134.93	160.86	236.79	416.85	207.22	316.33	373.00
Debt securities..	8 669 ..	9.62	11.86	10.87	11.79	43.98	15.42	14.67	18.80
Bonds and notes..	8 670 ..	6.44	8.50	7.52	7.84	18.72	11.15	11.16	14.05
Monetary authorities.....................................	8 671 ..	....	....	....	....	....	....	....	....
General government.......................................	8 672 ..	....	....	....	....	....	....	....	....
Banks..	8 673 ..	2.60	3.77	4.46	3.59	4.88	4.57	4.70	5.13
Other sectors..	8 674 ..	3.84	4.73	3.05	4.24	13.85	6.58	6.47	8.91
Money market instruments.................................	8 680 ..	3.18	3.36	3.35	3.96	25.26	4.27	3.51	4.76
Monetary authorities.....................................	8 681 ..	....	....	....	....	....	....	....	....
General government.......................................	8 682 ..	....	....	....	....	....	....	....	....
Banks..	8 683 ..	2.88	3.12	3.10	3.63	24.89	4.04	3.17	4.22
Other sectors..	8 684 ..	.30	.24	.25	.33	.37	.23	.34	.54
Financial derivatives................................	8 905 ..	**19.60**	**21.14**	**17.10**	**20.37**	**32.54**	**73.89**	**40.03**	**48.69**
Monetary authorities.....................................	8 906 ..	....	....	....	....	....	....	....	....
General government.......................................	8 907 ..	....	....	....	....	....	....	....	....
Banks..	8 908 ..	17.01	18.25	14.18	16.47	28.78	70.08	34.43	42.38
Other sectors..	8 909 ..	2.59	2.89	2.92	3.90	3.76	3.80	5.60	6.31
Other investment.....................................	8 753 ..	**265.00**	**322.10**	**336.67**	**388.45**	**545.29**	**517.93**	**517.23**	**642.47**
Trade credits..	8 756 ..	5.82	5.95	6.58	6.02	7.69	6.69	6.54	10.31
General government.......................................	8 757 ..	....	....	....	....	....	....	....	....
of which: Short-term.....................................	8 759 ..	....	....	....	....	....	....	....	....
Other sectors..	8 760 ..	5.82	5.95	6.58	6.02	7.69	6.69	6.54	10.31
of which: Short-term.....................................	8 762 ..	....	....	....	....	....	....	....	....
Loans..	8 764 ..	21.84	20.78	29.99	38.86	41.85	32.89	24.29	27.93
Monetary authorities.....................................	8 765 ..	....	....	....	....	....	....	....	....
of which: Use of Fund credit and loans from the Fund....	8 766 ..	....	....	....	....	....	....	....	....
of which: Short-term.....................................	8 768 ..	....	....	....	....	....	....	....	....
General government.......................................	8 769 ..	....	....	....	....	....	....	....	....
of which: Short-term.....................................	8 771 ..	....	....	....	....	....	....	....	....
Banks..	8 772 ..	5.61	6.39	4.70	3.80	5.09	8.25	5.83	8.19
of which: Short-term.....................................	8 774 ..	....	....	....	....	....	....	....	....
Other sectors..	8 775 ..	16.22	14.40	25.29	35.06	36.76	24.64	18.46	19.74
of which: Short-term.....................................	8 777 ..	....	....	....	....	....	....	....	....
Currency and deposits....................................	8 780 ..	230.55	288.86	288.85	333.18	465.03	462.85	475.30	588.76
Monetary authorities.....................................	8 781 ..	....	....	....	....	....	....	....	....
General government.......................................	8 782 ..	....	....	....	....	....	....	....	....
Banks..	8 783 ..	230.44	288.70	288.63	332.45	463.87	462.15	474.58	588.10
Other sectors..	8 784 ..	.10	.16	.22	.73	1.16	.70	.72	.67
Other liabilities..	8 786 ..	6.80	6.50	11.25	10.39	30.72	15.50	11.11	15.46
Monetary authorities.....................................	8 787 ..	....	....	....	....	....	....	....	....
of which: Short-term.....................................	8 789 ..	....	....	....	....	....	....	....	....
General government.......................................	8 790 ..	....	....	....	....	....	....	....	....
of which: Short-term.....................................	8 792 ..	....	....	....	....	....	....	....	....
Banks..	8 793 ..	.91	1.43	1.76	2.81	4.99	5.47	3.43	6.81
of which: Short-term.....................................	8 795 ..	....	....	....	....	....	....	....	....
Other sectors..	8 796 ..	5.88	5.07	9.49	7.57	25.73	10.03	7.68	8.65
of which: Short-term.....................................	8 798 ..	....	....	....	....	....	....	....	....
NET INTERNATIONAL INVESTMENT POSITION........	8 995 ..	**394.16**	**424.75**	**439.36**	**518.33**	**483.70**	**622.76**	**720.06**	**693.81**
Conversion rates: Hong Kong dollars per U.S. dollar (end of period)...........................	0 102 ..	**7.7630**	**7.7735**	**7.7525**	**7.7745**	**7.8015**	**7.7505**	**7.7555**	**7.7745**

Table 1. ANALYTIC PRESENTATION, 2003–2010

(Millions of U.S. dollars)

	Code	2003	2004	2005	2006	2007	2008	2009	2010
A. Current Account[1]	4 993 Z.	**2,596**	**3,558**	**2,942**	**2,437**	**4,300**	**4,035**	**6,777**	**12,233**
Goods: exports f.o.b.	2 100 ..	2,585	2,816	2,478	2,559	2,544	2,098	1,098	1,045
Goods: imports f.o.b.	3 100 ..	−3,675	−4,541	−4,844	−5,815	−7,240	−7,224	−5,516	−6,312
Balance on Goods	4 100 ..	*−1,091*	*−1,726*	*−2,366*	*−3,256*	*−4,695*	*−5,126*	*−4,418*	*−5,267*
Services: credit	2 200 ..	5,711	8,102	8,567	10,459	14,202	17,760	18,821	28,682
Services: debit	3 200 ..	−1,847	−2,200	−2,384	−2,974	−4,485	−5,687	−4,931	−7,544
Balance on Goods and Services	4 991 ..	*2,773*	*4,176*	*3,817*	*4,229*	*5,022*	*6,947*	*9,472*	*15,870*
Income: credit	2 300 ..	395	387	806	1,426	1,945	1,658	1,132	1,106
Income: debit	3 300 ..	−547	−960	−1,580	−2,983	−2,100	−3,766	−2,993	−4,019
Balance on Goods, Services, and Income	4 992 ..	*2,621*	*3,604*	*3,043*	*2,672*	*4,867*	*4,839*	*7,611*	*12,957*
Current transfers: credit	2 379 Z.	83	79	83	108	101	91	104	97
Current transfers: debit	3 379 ..	−108	−124	−184	−343	−668	−895	−937	−821
B. Capital Account[1]	4 994 Z.	**88**	**274**	**515**	**438**	**319**	**393**	**634**	**20**
Capital account: credit	2 994 Z.	113	302	534	456	339	444	660	46
Capital account: debit	3 994 ..	−25	−28	−20	−18	−20	−51	−26	−26
Total, Groups A Plus B	4 981 ..	*2,684*	*3,832*	*3,457*	*2,875*	*4,618*	*4,428*	*7,411*	*12,253*
C. Financial Account[1]	4 995 W.	**−1,679**	**−1,558**	**−262**	**−814**	**6,979**	**3,345**	**−2,601**	**−1,232**
Direct investment abroad	4 505 ..	2	81	−60	−512	−3	92	708	499
Direct investment in China, P.R.: Macao	4 555 Z.	517	768	1,767	2,643	5,036	3,064	1,797	3,530
Portfolio investment assets	4 602 ..	−1,191	−2,181	−617	−1,435	−1,251	−1,391	−1,674	−1,007
Equity securities	4 610 ..	−358	−487	−356	−213	−1,476	−796	−1,036	−660
Debt securities	4 619 ..	−834	−1,694	−261	−1,221	225	−595	−638	−347
Portfolio investment liabilities	4 652 Z.	....	....	....	....	....	3	−1	164
Equity securities	4 660 ..	....	....	....	....	....	3	−1	1
Debt securities	4 669 Z.	....	....	....	....	....	....	....	163
Financial derivatives	4 910 ..	−114	−584	−522	−212	48	−29	−15	−8
Financial derivatives assets	4 900 ..	−114	−584	−522	−212	48	−29	−15	−8
Financial derivatives liabilities	4 905 ..	....	....	....	....	....	....	....	....
Other investment assets	4 703 ..	−816	−179	−4,428	−5,525	−3,249	−2,704	−7,608	−9,600
Monetary authorities	4 701 ..	....	....	....	....	....	....	....	....
General government	4 704 ..	−12	−107	−173	−26	38	69	−7	....
Banks	4 705 ..	−760	−58	−4,158	−4,781	−3,187	−2,731	−7,713	....
Other sectors	4 728 ..	−44	−14	−97	−718	−99	−42	112	....
Other investment liabilities	4 753 W.	−77	538	3,599	4,227	6,398	4,310	4,193	5,189
Monetary authorities	4 753 WA	....	....	....	....	....	....	....	....
General government	4 753 ZB	....	....	....	....	....	....	....	....
Banks	4 753 ZC	−119	414	3,441	2,670	3,825	2,731	4,968	....
Other sectors	4 753 ZD	41	124	159	1,557	2,573	1,579	−775	....
Total, Groups A Through C	4 983 ..	*1,005*	*2,275*	*3,194*	*2,062*	*11,597*	*7,773*	*4,810*	*11,021*
D. Net Errors and Omissions	4 998 ..	**−514**	**−1,250**	**−2,068**	**−4**	**−8,090**	**−5,499**	**−2,695**	**−5,864**
Total, Groups A Through D	4 984 ..	*491*	*1,024*	*1,126*	*2,058*	*3,507*	*2,274*	*2,115*	*5,158*
E. Reserves and Related Items	4 802 A.	**−491**	**−1,024**	**−1,126**	**−2,058**	**−3,507**	**−2,274**	**−2,115**	**−5,158**
Reserve assets	4 802 ..	−491	−1,024	−1,126	−2,058	−3,507	−2,274	−2,115	−5,158
Use of Fund credit and loans	4 766 ..	....	....	....	....	....	....	....	....
Exceptional financing	4 920 ..	....	....	....	....	....	....	....	....
Conversion rates: patacas per U.S. dollar	0 101 ..	**8.0212**	**8.0222**	**8.0111**	**8.0014**	**8.0359**	**8.0201**	**7.9843**	**8.0022**

[1] Excludes components that have been classified in the categories of Group E.

Table 2. STANDARD PRESENTATION, 2003–2010

(Millions of U.S. dollars)

	Code	2003	2004	2005	2006	2007	2008	2009	2010
CURRENT ACCOUNT...........................	4 993 ..	**2,596**	**3,558**	**2,942**	**2,437**	**4,300**	**4,035**	**6,777**	**12,233**
A. GOODS...	4 100 ..	**−1,091**	**−1,726**	**−2,366**	**−3,256**	**−4,695**	**−5,126**	**−4,418**	**−5,267**
Credit..	2 100 ..	**2,585**	**2,816**	**2,478**	**2,559**	**2,544**	**2,098**	**1,098**	**1,045**
General merchandise: exports f.o.b............	2 110 ..	2,581	2,812	2,474	2,557	2,542	2,093	1,086	1,038
Goods for processing: exports f.o.b...........	2 150 ..	....	....	....	....	....	....	....	....
Repairs on goods....................................	2 160 ..	4	3	4	2	2	5	12	6
Goods procured in ports by carriers...........	2 170 ..	....	....	....	....	....	....	....	....
Nonmonetary gold..................................	2 180 ..	....	....	....	....	....	....	....	1
Debit...	3 100 ..	**−3,675**	**−4,541**	**−4,844**	**−5,815**	**−7,240**	**−7,224**	**−5,516**	**−6,312**
General merchandise: imports f.o.b............	3 110 ..	−3,608	−4,467	−4,738	−5,698	−7,109	−7,024	−5,368	−6,145
Goods for processing: imports f.o.b...........	3 150 ..	....	....	....	....	....	....	....	....
Repairs on goods....................................	3 160 ..	−42	−34	−44	−46	−55	−69	−80	−63
Goods procured in ports by carriers...........	3 170 ..	−26	−40	−61	−71	−75	−129	−68	−96
Nonmonetary gold..................................	3 180 ..	....	....	−2	....	−1	−2	....	−8
B. SERVICES.....................................	4 200 ..	**3,864**	**5,902**	**6,183**	**7,485**	**9,717**	**12,072**	**13,890**	**21,137**
Total credit...	2 200 ..	*5,711*	*8,102*	*8,567*	*10,459*	*14,202*	*17,760*	*18,821*	*28,682*
Total debit...	3 200 ..	*−1,847*	*−2,200*	*−2,384*	*−2,974*	*−4,485*	*−5,687*	*−4,931*	*−7,544*
Transportation services, credit...........	2 205 ..	**241**	**346**	**399**	**457**	**473**	**446**	**351**	**452**
Passenger...	2 850 ..	*164*	*225*	*257*	*306*	*328*	*349*	*303*	....
Freight...	2 851 ..	*46*	*83*	*107*	*116*	*113*	*67*	*27*	....
Other...	2 852 ..	*31*	*37*	*34*	*35*	*33*	*30*	*22*	....
Sea transport, passenger..........................	2 207 ..	....	....	....	....	....	....		
Sea transport, freight..............................	2 208 ..	....	....	....	....	....	....		
Sea transport, other................................	2 209 ..	....	....	....	....	....	....		
Air transport, passenger...........................	2 211 ..	....	....	....	....	....	....		
Air transport, freight...............................	2 212 ..	....	....	....	....	....	....		
Air transport, other.................................	2 213 ..	....	....	....	....	....	....		
Other transport, passenger.......................	2 215 ..	....	....	....	....	....	....		
Other transport, freight...........................	2 216 ..	....	....	....	....	....	....		
Other transport, other.............................	2 217 ..	....	....	....	....	....	....		
Transportation services, debit............	3 205 ..	**−120**	**−153**	**−216**	**−254**	**−307**	**−281**	**−237**	**−246**
Passenger...	3 850 ..	*−16*	*−17*	*−63*	*−73*	*−82*	*−74*	*−68*	....
Freight...	3 851 ..	*−79*	*−102*	*−112*	*−134*	*−177*	*−154*	*−117*	....
Other...	3 852 ..	*−25*	*−34*	*−42*	*−47*	*−48*	*−53*	*−52*	....
Sea transport, passenger..........................	3 207 ..	....	....	....	....	....	....		
Sea transport, freight..............................	3 208 ..	....	....	....	....	....	....		
Sea transport, other................................	3 209 ..	....	....	....	....	....	....		
Air transport, passenger...........................	3 211 ..	....	....	....	....	....	....		
Air transport, freight...............................	3 212 ..	....	....	....	....	....	....		
Air transport, other.................................	3 213 ..	....	....	....	....	....	....		
Other transport, passenger.......................	3 215 ..	....	....	....	....	....	....		
Other transport, freight...........................	3 216 ..	....	....	....	....	....	....		
Other transport, other.............................	3 217 ..	....	....	....	....	....	....		
Travel, credit....................................	2 236 ..	**5,260**	**7,518**	**7,933**	**9,749**	**13,405**	**16,948**	**18,142**	**27,790**
Business travel..	2 237 ..	628	899	1,264	1,261	1,468	1,856	1,804	1,387
Personal travel..	2 240 ..	4,632	6,619	6,669	8,488	11,937	15,092	16,338	26,403
Travel, debit.....................................	3 236 ..	**−455**	**−512**	**−552**	**−575**	**−698**	**−834**	**−901**	**−1,035**
Business travel..	3 237 ..	−4	−9	−7	−12	−17	−19	−14	−20
Personal travel..	3 240 ..	−451	−503	−545	−563	−681	−815	−886	−1,015
Other services, credit........................	2 200 BA	**210**	**238**	**235**	**252**	**324**	**365**	**328**	**440**
Communications......................................	2 245 ..	45	48	56	57	89	98	73	83
Construction...	2 249 ..	....	....	....	....	....	....	....	....
Insurance...	2 253 ..	19	19	15	19	23	20	18	31
Financial..	2 260 ..	23	32	32	46	83	66	82	108
Computer and information........................	2 262 ..	....	....	....	....	....	....	....	....
Royalties and licence fees........................	2 266 ..	....	....	....	....	....	....	....	....
Other business services............................	2 268 ..	122	139	132	131	129	182	155	218
Personal, cultural, and recreational...........	2 287 ..	....	....	....	....	....	....	....	....
Government, n.i.e.....................................	2 291 ..	....	....	....	....	....	....	....	....
Other services, debit.........................	3 200 BA	**−1,272**	**−1,535**	**−1,616**	**−2,144**	**−3,480**	**−4,572**	**−3,793**	**−6,263**
Communications......................................	3 245 ..	−38	−39	−41	−43	−57	−65	−63	−67
Construction...	3 249 ..	....	....	....	....	....	....	....	....
Insurance...	3 253 ..	−73	−77	−93	−102	−129	−101	−78	−96
Financial..	3 260 ..	−10	−12	−12	−14	−26	−26	−33	−48
Computer and information........................	3 262 ..	−17	−24	−25	−33	−46	−42	−39	−15
Royalties and licence fees........................	3 266 ..	−2	−3	−5	−6	−45	−102	−122	....
Other business services............................	3 268 ..	−1,105	−1,351	−1,400	−1,899	−3,119	−4,159	−3,365	−5,742
Personal, cultural, and recreational...........	3 287 ..	....	....	....	....	....	....	....	....
Government, n.i.e.....................................	3 291 ..	−28	−30	−39	−47	−58	−77	−94	−296

Table 2 (Continued). STANDARD PRESENTATION, 2003–2010

(Millions of U.S. dollars)

	Code	2003	2004	2005	2006	2007	2008	2009	2010
C. INCOME......................................	4 300	**−152**	**−573**	**−774**	**−1,557**	**−155**	**−2,108**	**−1,861**	**−2,913**
Total credit...	2 300	*395*	*387*	*806*	*1,426*	*1,945*	*1,658*	*1,132*	*1,106*
Total debit..	3 300	*−547*	*−960*	*−1,580*	*−2,983*	*−2,100*	*−3,766*	*−2,993*	*−4,019*
Compensation of employees, credit..................	2 310	....	....	....	....	....	....	....	....
Compensation of employees, debit..................	3 310	**−11**	**−26**	**−52**	**−151**	**−168**	**−196**	**−121**	**−97**
Investment income, credit.........................	2 320	**395**	**387**	**806**	**1,426**	**1,945**	**1,658**	**1,132**	**1,106**
Direct investment income..........................	2 330	−5	−2	35	56	70	−31	42	33
Dividends and distributed branch profits...........	2 332	8	12	4	16	9	2	16	....
Reinvested earnings and undistributed branch profits.....	2 333	−13	−15	31	40	61	−31	46	....
Income on debt (interest).........................	2 334	....	....	1	1	....	−2	−20	....
Portfolio investment income.......................	2 339	194	213	271	333	497	531	444	452
Income on equity................................	2 340	36	44	51	59	62	106	94	129
Income on bonds and notes.......................	2 350	143	155	200	252	386	395	343	303
Income on money market instruments..........	2 360	15	14	21	23	49	31	7	20
Other investment income..........................	2 370	206	176	501	1,036	1,378	1,158	645	621
Investment income, debit..........................	3 320	**−537**	**−933**	**−1,529**	**−2,832**	**−1,931**	**−3,571**	**−2,872**	**−3,922**
Direct investment income..........................	3 330	−494	−899	−1,408	−2,469	−1,378	−2,710	−2,460	−3,532
Dividends and distributed branch profits...........	3 332	−226	−609	−707	−800	−565	−1,264	−1,549	....
Reinvested earnings and undistributed branch profits.....	3 333	−263	−285	−695	−1,664	−808	−1,438	−894	....
Income on debt (interest).........................	3 334	−5	−5	−6	−4	−5	−8	−17	....
Portfolio investment income.......................	3 339	−6	−7	−8	−12	−42	−90	−47	−31
Income on equity................................	3 340	−2	−3	−5	−8	−17	−53	−35	−21
Income on bonds and notes.......................	3 350	....	....	....	....	....	....	....	....
Income on money market instruments..........	3 360	−4	−5	−3	−4	−25	−37	−13	−10
Other investment income..........................	3 370	−36	−27	−113	−351	−512	−771	−364	−360
D. CURRENT TRANSFERS..................................	4 379	**−25**	**−45**	**−101**	**−235**	**−568**	**−804**	**−834**	**−724**
Credit..	2 379	**83**	**79**	**83**	**108**	**101**	**91**	**104**	**97**
General government................................	2 380	....	....	....	....	....	....	....	....
Other sectors.....................................	2 390	83	79	83	108	101	91	104	97
Workers' remittances............................	2 391	48	53	53	55	60	63	65	69
Other current transfers..........................	2 392	35	26	30	53	40	28	39	28
Debit..	3 379	**−108**	**−124**	**−184**	**−343**	**−668**	**−895**	**−937**	**−821**
General government................................	3 380	−2	−2	−11	−3	−3	−92	−368	−332
Other sectors.....................................	3 390	−105	−122	−173	−340	−665	−803	−569	−489
Workers' remittances............................	3 391	−83	−106	−156	−326	−655	−741	−545	−446
Other current transfers..........................	3 392	−22	−16	−17	−14	−10	−62	−24	−43
CAPITAL AND FINANCIAL ACCOUNT.....................	4 996	**−2,082**	**−2,308**	**−874**	**−2,433**	**3,791**	**1,464**	**−4,082**	**−6,370**
CAPITAL ACCOUNT...................................	4 994	**88**	**274**	**515**	**438**	**319**	**393**	**634**	**20**
Total credit...	2 994	*113*	*302*	*534*	*456*	*339*	*444*	*660*	*46*
Total debit..	3 994	*−25*	*−28*	*−20*	*−18*	*−20*	*−51*	*−26*	*−26*
Capital transfers, credit............................	2 400	**113**	**302**	**534**	**456**	**339**	**444**	**660**	**46**
General government................................	2 401	....	....	....	....	....	....	....	....
Debt forgiveness.................................	2 402	....	....	....	....	....	....	....	....
Other capital transfers...........................	2 410	....	....	....	....	....	....	....	....
Other sectors.....................................	2 430	113	302	534	456	339	444	660	46
Migrants' transfers..............................	2 431	113	302	534	456	339	444	660	46
Debt forgiveness.................................	2 432	....	....	....	....	....	....	....	....
Other capital transfers...........................	2 440	....	....	....	....	....	....	....	....
Capital transfers, debit............................	3 400	**−25**	**−28**	**−20**	**−17**	**−15**	**−31**	**−26**	**−26**
General government................................	3 401	....	....	....	....	....	−7	....	....
Debt forgiveness.................................	3 402	....	....	....	....	....	....	....	....
Other capital transfers...........................	3 410	....	....	....	....	....	−7	....	....
Other sectors.....................................	3 430	−25	−28	−20	−17	−15	−23	−26	−26
Migrants' transfers..............................	3 431	−25	−28	−20	−17	−15	−23	−26	−26
Debt forgiveness.................................	3 432	....	....	....	....	....	....	....	....
Other capital transfers...........................	3 440	....	....	....	....	....	....	....	....
Nonproduced nonfinancial assets, credit............	2 480	....	....	....	....	....	....	....	....
Nonproduced nonfinancial assets, debit.............	3 480	**−1**	....	....	....	**−5**	**−20**	....	....

Table 2 (Continued). STANDARD PRESENTATION, 2003–2010

(Millions of U.S. dollars)

	Code	2003	2004	2005	2006	2007	2008	2009	2010
FINANCIAL ACCOUNT	4 995	−2,170	−2,582	−1,388	−2,872	3,472	1,071	−4,715	−6,389
A. DIRECT INVESTMENT	4 500	519	849	1,706	2,131	5,033	3,156	2,505	4,029
Direct investment abroad	4 505	2	81	−60	−512	−3	92	708	499
Equity capital	4 510	3	86	−1	106	−4	1	−64	....
Claims on affiliated enterprises	4 515	3	86	−1	106	−4	1	−64	....
Liabilities to affiliated enterprises	4 520	....	....	....	....	....	....	....	....
Reinvested earnings	4 525	13	15	−31	−40	−61	31	−46	....
Other capital	4 530	−14	−20	−29	−579	62	61	819	....
Claims on affiliated enterprises	4 535	2	−20	−36	−578	−5	23	106	....
Liabilities to affiliated enterprises	4 540	−16	....	8	−1	67	38	713	....
Direct investment in China, P.R.: Macao	4 555	517	768	1,767	2,643	5,036	3,064	1,797	3,530
Equity capital	4 560	76	2	132	173	412	679	43	....
Claims on direct investors	4 565	....	....	....	....	....	....	....	
Liabilities to direct investors	4 570	76	2	132	173	412	679	43	
Reinvested earnings	4 575	263	285	695	1,664	808	1,438	894	
Other capital	4 580	177	481	940	806	3,816	947	860	
Claims on direct investors	4 585	−5	−4	3	−147	−224	−899	833	
Liabilities to direct investors	4 590	182	485	937	953	4,040	1,846	27	
B. PORTFOLIO INVESTMENT	4 600	−1,192	−2,181	−617	−1,435	−1,251	−1,388	−1,675	−843
Assets	4 602	−1,191	−2,181	−617	−1,435	−1,251	−1,391	−1,674	−1,007
Equity securities	4 610	−358	−487	−356	−213	−1,476	−796	−1,036	−660
Monetary authorities	4 611	....	....						
General government	4 612	−76	−172	2	....	−59	−89	−14	−9
Banks	4 613	6	−2	17	20	11	−8	5	....
Other sectors	4 614	−287	−313	−376	−234	−1,429	−698	−1,027	−651
Debt securities	4 619	−834	−1,694	−261	−1,221	225	−595	−638	−347
Bonds and notes	4 620	−777	−824	−199	−1,313	364	393	−1,045	−285
Monetary authorities	4 621	....	....						
General government	4 622	−161	151	−107	−137	−118	−60	−50	137
Banks	4 623	−504	−671	−13	−629	719	923	−847	172
Other sectors	4 624	−113	−303	−79	−548	−238	−470	−148	−594
Money market instruments	4 630	−56	−870	−62	92	−140	−988	407	−62
Monetary authorities	4 631	....	....						
General government	4 632	....	1	−1					
Banks	4 633	47	−327	−78	−23	−113	−205	399	186
Other sectors	4 634	−103	−544	17	115	−26	−783	8	−248
Liabilities	4 652	....	....	....	....	....	3	−1	164
Equity securities	4 660	....	....	....	....	....	3	−1	1
Banks	4 663	....	....	....	....	....		−1	....
Other sectors	4 664	....	....	....	....	....	3	....	1
Debt securities	4 669	....	....	....	....	....			163
Bonds and notes	4 670	....	....	....	....	....			163
Monetary authorities	4 671								
General government	4 672								
Banks	4 673								163
Other sectors	4 674								
Money market instruments	4 680	....	....	....	....	....			
Monetary authorities	4 681								
General government	4 682								
Banks	4 683	....	....						
Other sectors	4 684	....							
C. FINANCIAL DERIVATIVES	4 910	−114	−584	−522	−212	48	−29	−15	−8
Monetary authorities	4 911	....	....						
General government	4 912	....	....	....	....	....	....	2	1
Banks	4 913	−144	−348	−632	−211	47	−32	1	−37
Other sectors	4 914	30	−236	109	−1	1	3	−18	28
Assets	4 900	−114	−584	−522	−212	48	−29	−15	−8
Monetary authorities	4 901	....	....						
General government	4 902	....	....	....	....	....	....	2	1
Banks	4 903	−144	−348	−632	−211	47	−32	1	−37
Other sectors	4 904	30	−236	109	−1	1	3	−18	28
Liabilities	4 905	....	....	....	....	....	....	....	....
Monetary authorities	4 906	....	....						
General government	4 907	....	....						
Banks	4 908	....	....						
Other sectors	4 909	....	....						

Table 2 (Concluded). STANDARD PRESENTATION, 2003–2010

(Millions of U.S. dollars)

	Code	2003	2004	2005	2006	2007	2008	2009	2010
D. OTHER INVESTMENT	4 700	**−893**	**359**	**−829**	**−1,298**	**3,150**	**1,606**	**−3,415**	**−4,410**
Assets	4 703	**−816**	**−179**	**−4,428**	**−5,525**	**−3,249**	**−2,704**	**−7,608**	**−9,600**
Trade credits	4 706	−17	10	−35	−14	−77	13	−37	....
General government	4 707	....	....	....	....	....	....	....	....
of which: Short-term	4 709	....	....	....	....	....	....	....	....
Other sectors	4 710	−17	10	−35	−14	−77	13	−37	....
of which: Short-term	4 712	....	....	....	....	....	....	....	....
Loans	4 714	43	−167	−764	−971	−1,298	−1,559	−3,412	....
Monetary authorities	4 715	....	....	....	....	....	....	....	....
of which: Short-term	4 718	....	....	....	....	....	....	....	....
General government	4 719	....	....	....	....	....	....	....	....
of which: Short-term	4 721	....	....	....	....	....	....	....	....
Banks	4 722	49	−180	−764	−968	−1,298	−1,583	−3,381	....
of which: Short-term	4 724	....	....	....	....	....	....	....	....
Other sectors	4 725	−6	13	....	−3	....	24	−32	....
of which: Short-term	4 727	....	....	....	....	....	....	....	....
Currency and deposits	4 730	−446	56	127	−1,730	−2,049	−568	−3,477	....
Monetary authorities	4 731	....	....	....	....	....	....	....	....
General government	4 732	−12	−107	−173	−26	38	69	−7	....
Banks	4 733	−416	202	342	−1,012	−2,076	−614	−3,652	....
Other sectors	4 734	−18	−39	−42	−692	−10	−23	182	....
Other assets	4 736	−396	−78	−3,757	−2,810	176	−590	−681	....
Monetary authorities	4 737	....	....	....	....	....	....	....	....
of which: Short-term	4 739	....	....	....	....	....	....	....	....
General government	4 740	....	....	....	....	....	....	....	....
of which: Short-term	4 742	....	....	....	....	....	....	....	....
Banks	4 743	−393	−80	−3,737	−2,801	187	−534	−680	....
of which: Short-term	4 745	....	....	....	....	....	....	....	....
Other sectors	4 746	−3	1	−20	−8	−11	−56	−2	....
of which: Short-term	4 748	....	....	....	....	....	....	....	....
Liabilities	4 753	**−77**	**538**	**3,599**	**4,227**	**6,398**	**4,310**	**4,193**	**5,189**
Trade credits	4 756	16	−4	30	142	224	−53	−16	....
General government	4 757	....	....	....	....	....	....	....	....
of which: Short-term	4 759	....	....	....	....	....	....	....	....
Other sectors	4 760	16	−4	30	142	224	−53	−16	....
of which: Short-term	4 762	....	....	....	....	....	....	....	....
Loans	4 764	27	149	37	1,399	2,235	1,255	−874	....
Monetary authorities	4 765	....	....	....	....	....	....	....	....
of which: Use of Fund credit and loans from the Fund..	4 766	....	....	....	....	....	....	....	....
of which: Short-term	4 768	....	....	....	....	....	....	....	....
General government	4 769	....	....	....	....	....	....	....	....
of which: Short-term	4 771	....	....	....	....	....	....	....	....
Banks	4 772	4	22	−56	144	−67	−141	−35	....
of which: Short-term	4 774	....	....	....	....	....	....	....	....
Other sectors	4 775	22	127	93	1,255	2,301	1,396	−839	....
of which: Short-term	4 777	....	....	....	....	....	....	....	....
Currency and deposits	4 780	42	390	2,887	1,667	3,398	2,663	5,082	....
Monetary authorities	4 781	....	....	....	....	....	....	....	....
General government	4 782	....	....	....	....	....	....	....	....
Banks	4 783	42	390	2,887	1,667	3,398	2,663	5,082	....
Other sectors	4 784	....	....	....	....	....	....	....	....
Other liabilities	4 786	−163	3	645	1,019	542	444	....	....
Monetary authorities	4 787	....	....	....	....	....	....	....	....
of which: Short-term	4 789	....	....	....	....	....	....	....	....
General government	4 790	....	....	....	....	....	....	....	....
of which: Short-term	4 792	....	....	....	....	....	....	....	....
Banks	4 793	−165	2	609	859	494	209	−80	....
of which: Short-term	4 795	....	....	....	....	....	....	....	....
Other sectors	4 796	3	1	36	160	48	235	79	....
of which: Short-term	4 798	....	....	....	....	....	....	....	....
E. RESERVE ASSETS	4 802	**−491**	**−1,024**	**−1,126**	**−2,058**	**−3,507**	**−2,274**	**−2,115**	**−5,158**
Monetary gold	4 812	....	....	....	....	....	....	....	....
Special drawing rights	4 811	....	....	....	....	....	....	....	....
Reserve position in the Fund	4 810	....	....	....	....	....	....	....	....
Foreign exchange	4 803	−491	−1,024	−1,127	−2,059	−3,507	−2,265	−2,120	−5,157
Other claims	4 813	....	−1	1	1	....	−10	5	....
NET ERRORS AND OMISSIONS	4 998	**−514**	**−1,250**	**−2,068**	**−4**	**−8,090**	**−5,499**	**−2,695**	**−5,864**

Table 1. ANALYTIC PRESENTATION, 2003–2010

(Millions of U.S. dollars)

	Code	2003	2004	2005	2006	2007	2008	2009	2010
A. Current Account[1]	4 993 Z.	**−979**	**−910**	**−1,886**	**−2,989**	**−5,977**	**−6,923**	**−5,157**	**−9,032**
Goods: exports f.o.b.	2 100 ..	13,813	17,224	21,729	25,181	30,577	38,534	34,026	40,777
Goods: imports f.o.b.	3 100 ..	−13,258	−15,878	−20,134	−24,859	−31,173	−37,563	−31,479	−38,628
Balance on Goods	4 100 ..	*556*	*1,346*	*1,595*	*322*	*−596*	*971*	*2,546*	*2,150*
Services: credit	2 200 ..	1,921	2,258	2,668	3,377	3,636	4,137	4,202	4,446
Services: debit	3 200 ..	−3,360	−3,938	−4,770	−5,496	−6,243	−7,210	−7,030	−7,986
Balance on Goods and Services	4 991 ..	*−883*	*−334*	*−507*	*−1,797*	*−3,203*	*−2,101*	*−281*	*−1,390*
Income: credit	2 300 ..	547	666	1,070	1,519	1,855	1,745	1,289	1,370
Income: debit	3 300 ..	−3,951	−4,967	−6,531	−7,454	−9,857	−12,078	−10,777	−13,487
Balance on Goods, Services, and Income	4 992 ..	*−4,287*	*−4,635*	*−5,968*	*−7,732*	*−11,205*	*−12,435*	*−9,770*	*−13,507*
Current transfers: credit	2 379 Z.	3,565	3,994	4,342	5,037	5,642	5,898	5,253	5,343
Current transfers: debit	3 379 ..	−256	−270	−260	−294	−413	−386	−640	−868
B. Capital Account[1]	4 994 Z.	….	….	….	….	….	….	….	….
Capital account: credit	2 994 Z.	….	….	….	….	….	….	….	….
Capital account: debit	3 994 ..	….	….	….	….	….	….	….	….
Total, Groups A Plus B	4 981 ..	*−979*	*−910*	*−1,886*	*−2,989*	*−5,977*	*−6,923*	*−5,157*	*−9,032*
C. Financial Account[1]	4 995 W.	**643**	**3,127**	**3,232**	**2,892**	**10,321**	**9,424**	**6,353**	**11,942**
Direct investment abroad	4 505 ..	−938	−142	−4,662	−1,098	−913	−2,254	−3,088	−6,562
Direct investment in Colombia	4 555 Z.	1,720	3,016	10,252	6,656	9,049	10,596	7,137	6,765
Portfolio investment assets	4 602 ..	−1,753	−1,565	−1,689	−3,333	−993	188	−2,802	−1,768
Equity securities	4 610 ..	….	….	….	….	….	….	….	….
Debt securities	4 619 ..	−1,753	−1,565	−1,689	−3,333	−993	188	−2,802	−1,768
Portfolio investment liabilities	4 652 Z.	130	1,306	−53	902	1,884	−1,195	4,668	3,263
Equity securities	4 660 ..	−52	130	86	−30	790	−86	67	1,351
Debt securities	4 669 Z.	181	1,176	−138	932	1,094	−1,109	4,601	1,912
Financial derivatives	4 910 ..	−101	−190	−62	−9	….	….	….	….
Financial derivatives assets	4 900 ..	….	….	….	….	….	….	….	….
Financial derivatives liabilities	4 905 ..	−101	−190	−62	−9	….	….	….	….
Other investment assets	4 703 ..	1,633	425	−183	−732	−2,237	−173	−1,615	486
Monetary authorities	4 701 ..	−13	−77	−4	10	−9	−67	110	−4
General government	4 704 ..	−30	−51	−48	−47	−20	−1	−8	−8
Banks	4 705 ..	−149	59	−474	223	−971	880	−218	191
Other sectors	4 728 ..	1,824	495	343	−917	−1,237	−985	−1,498	308
Other investment liabilities	4 753 W.	−48	278	−371	505	3,532	2,262	2,052	9,759
Monetary authorities	4 753 WA	−12	−68	5	−5	50	−37	966	3
General government	4 753 ZB	2,180	598	−1,063	852	130	1,263	1,491	1,219
Banks	4 753 ZC	−577	619	690	−542	1,154	164	−1,231	3,449
Other sectors	4 753 ZD	−1,639	−871	−3	200	2,197	872	826	5,089
Total, Groups A Through C	4 983 ..	*−336*	*2,217*	*1,346*	*−97*	*4,344*	*2,501*	*1,197*	*2,910*
D. Net Errors and Omissions	4 998 ..	**139**	**246**	**378**	**120**	**344**	**70**	**245**	**207**
Total, Groups A Through D	4 984 ..	*−197*	*2,463*	*1,724*	*23*	*4,688*	*2,571*	*1,441*	*3,117*
E. Reserves and Related Items	4 802 A.	**197**	**−2,463**	**−1,724**	**−23**	**−4,688**	**−2,571**	**−1,441**	**−3,117**
Reserve assets	4 802 ..	197	−2,463	−1,724	−23	−4,688	−2,571	−1,441	−3,117
Use of Fund credit and loans	4 766 ..	….	….	….	….	….	….	….	….
Exceptional financing	4 920 ..	….	….	….	….	….	….	….	….
Conversion rates: Colombian pesos per U.S. dollar	0 101 ..	2,877.65	2,628.61	2,320.83	2,361.14	2,078.29	1,967.71	2,158.26	1,898.57

[1] Excludes components that have been classified in the categories of Group E.

Table 2. STANDARD PRESENTATION, 2003–2010

(Millions of U.S. dollars)

	Code	2003	2004	2005	2006	2007	2008	2009	2010
CURRENT ACCOUNT	4 993	**−979**	**−910**	**−1,886**	**−2,989**	**−5,977**	**−6,923**	**−5,157**	**−9,032**
A. GOODS	4 100	**556**	**1,346**	**1,595**	**322**	**−596**	**971**	**2,546**	**2,150**
Credit	2 100	**13,813**	**17,224**	**21,729**	**25,181**	**30,577**	**38,534**	**34,026**	**40,777**
General merchandise: exports f.o.b.	2 110	13,153	16,550	21,053	24,710	30,048	37,334	32,327	38,455
Goods for processing: exports f.o.b.	2 150	5	6	9	12	15	38	22	40
Repairs on goods	2 160	10	23	9	3	5	5	2	11
Goods procured in ports by carriers	2 170	57	84	141	175	177	267	137	176
Nonmonetary gold	2 180	588	561	517	281	332	891	1,537	2,095
Debit	3 100	**−13,258**	**−15,878**	**−20,134**	**−24,859**	**−31,173**	**−37,563**	**−31,479**	**−38,628**
General merchandise: imports f.o.b.	3 110	−13,149	−15,750	−19,972	−24,646	−30,941	−37,229	−31,273	−38,353
Goods for processing: imports f.o.b.	3 150	....	....	....	....	....	....	....	....
Repairs on goods	3 160	−50	−40	−39	−48	−44	−52	−45	−69
Goods procured in ports by carriers	3 170	−60	−88	−124	−166	−187	−282	−161	−205
Nonmonetary gold	3 180	....	....	....	....	....	....	....	....
B. SERVICES	4 200	**−1,439**	**−1,680**	**−2,102**	**−2,119**	**−2,607**	**−3,072**	**−2,827**	**−3,539**
Total credit	2 200	*1,921*	*2,258*	*2,668*	*3,377*	*3,636*	*4,137*	*4,202*	*4,446*
Total debit	3 200	*−3,360*	*−3,938*	*−4,770*	*−5,496*	*−6,243*	*−7,210*	*−7,030*	*−7,986*
Transportation services, credit	2 205	**623**	**679**	**780**	**899**	**1,104**	**1,239**	**1,136**	**1,207**
Passenger	2 850	*298*	*308*	*352*	*455*	*593*	*655*	*672*	*714*
Freight	2 851	*152*	*177*	*200*	*215*	*269*	*316*	*252*	*259*
Other	2 852	*172*	*195*	*227*	*229*	*242*	*268*	*212*	*234*
Sea transport, passenger	2 207	....	....	....	....	....	....	....	....
Sea transport, freight	2 208	18	36	42	40	64	83	40	49
Sea transport, other	2 209	95	101	118	115	142	155	113	144
Air transport, passenger	2 211	298	308	352	455	593	655	672	714
Air transport, freight	2 212	105	103	105	108	105	138	118	154
Air transport, other	2 213	77	94	109	114	100	112	99	90
Other transport, passenger	2 215	....	....	....	....	....	....	....	....
Other transport, freight	2 216	30	38	53	67	99	95	95	56
Other transport, other	2 217	....	....	....	....	....	....	....	....
Transportation services, debit	3 205	**−1,260**	**−1,613**	**−2,107**	**−2,253**	**−2,623**	**−3,008**	**−2,329**	**−2,823**
Passenger	3 850	*−287*	*−358*	*−435*	*−467*	*−556*	*−598*	*−549*	*−547*
Freight	3 851	*−789*	*−1,002*	*−1,366*	*−1,399*	*−1,686*	*−2,094*	*−1,466*	*−1,924*
Other	3 852	*−184*	*−253*	*−306*	*−387*	*−381*	*−316*	*−314*	*−353*
Sea transport, passenger	3 207	....	....	....	....	....	....	....	....
Sea transport, freight	3 208	−654	−831	−1,147	−1,157	−1,450	−1,839	−1,257	−1,593
Sea transport, other	3 209	−22	−48	−59	−73	−79	−79	−51	−82
Air transport, passenger	3 211	−287	−358	−435	−467	−556	−598	−549	−547
Air transport, freight	3 212	−112	−143	−188	−209	−199	−221	−179	−304
Air transport, other	3 213	−162	−206	−247	−314	−302	−237	−262	−270
Other transport, passenger	3 215	....	....	....	....	....	....	....	....
Other transport, freight	3 216	−23	−27	−31	−32	−37	−34	−30	−26
Other transport, other	3 217	....	....	....	....	....	....	....	....
Travel, credit	2 236	**893**	**1,061**	**1,222**	**1,554**	**1,669**	**1,844**	**1,999**	**2,083**
Business travel	2 237	....	....	....	....	....	....	....	....
Personal travel	2 240	893	1,061	1,222	1,554	1,669	1,844	1,999	2,083
Travel, debit	3 236	**−1,062**	**−1,111**	**−1,130**	**−1,332**	**−1,537**	**−1,739**	**−1,752**	**−1,826**
Business travel	3 237	....	....	....	....	....	....	....	....
Personal travel	3 240	−1,062	−1,111	−1,130	−1,332	−1,537	−1,739	−1,752	−1,826
Other services, credit	2 200 BA	**405**	**518**	**666**	**924**	**863**	**1,055**	**1,068**	**1,156**
Communications	2 245	133	183	217	252	256	249	280	222
Construction	2 249	....	....	....	....	....	....	....	....
Insurance	2 253	....	....	....	....	....	....	....	....
Financial	2 260	36	31	31	59	68	70	48	45
Computer and information	2 262	16	17	21	35	30	47	29	46
Royalties and licence fees	2 266	6	8	10	11	17	30	39	56
Other business services	2 268	113	171	272	445	376	535	554	612
Personal, cultural, and recreational	2 287	31	39	41	46	38	45	30	84
Government, n.i.e.	2 291	69	70	74	76	77	80	87	90
Other services, debit	3 200 BA	**−1,039**	**−1,214**	**−1,532**	**−1,911**	**−2,082**	**−2,462**	**−2,949**	**−3,337**
Communications	3 245	−108	−144	−152	−199	−201	−202	−279	−210
Construction	3 249	....	....	....	....	....	−7	−3	−1
Insurance	3 253	−238	−249	−290	−317	−375	−436	−440	−576
Financial	3 260	−101	−95	−145	−162	−125	−144	−124	−132
Computer and information	3 262	−72	−66	−119	−143	−72	−118	−109	−152
Royalties and licence fees	3 266	−76	−82	−118	−127	−188	−263	−299	−362
Other business services	3 268	−354	−481	−600	−837	−994	−1,171	−1,596	−1,706
Personal, cultural, and recreational	3 287	−29	−31	−44	−58	−54	−41	−35	−111
Government, n.i.e.	3 291	−62	−65	−66	−68	−73	−79	−64	−87

Table 2 (Continued). STANDARD PRESENTATION, 2003–2010

(Millions of U.S. dollars)

	Code	2003	2004	2005	2006	2007	2008	2009	2010
C. INCOME	4 300	**−3,404**	**−4,301**	**−5,461**	**−5,935**	**−8,002**	**−10,333**	**−9,488**	**−12,117**
Total credit	2 300	*547*	*666*	*1,070*	*1,519*	*1,855*	*1,745*	*1,289*	*1,370*
Total debit	3 300	*−3,951*	*−4,967*	*−6,531*	*−7,454*	*−9,857*	*−12,078*	*−10,777*	*−13,487*
Compensation of employees, credit	2 310	**16**	**20**	**32**	**38**	**30**	**42**	**35**	**34**
Compensation of employees, debit	3 310	**−12**	**−19**	**−19**	**−19**	**−29**	**−29**	**−33**	**−40**
Investment income, credit	2 320	**531**	**646**	**1,038**	**1,480**	**1,824**	**1,703**	**1,254**	**1,335**
Direct investment income	2 330	120	152	166	359	401	486	686	890
Dividends and distributed branch profits	2 332	120	152	166	359	401	486	686	890
Reinvested earnings and undistributed branch profits	2 333	....	....	....	....	....	....	....	....
Income on debt (interest)	2 334	....	....	....	....	....	....	....	....
Portfolio investment income	2 339	319	436	780	708	905	1,060	500	261
Income on equity	2 340	66	113	224	....	....	213	85	61
Income on bonds and notes	2 350	....	....	....	....	....	....	....	....
Income on money market instruments	2 360	254	322	556	708	905	847	415	200
Other investment income	2 370	91	59	91	413	518	157	68	184
Investment income, debit	3 320	**−3,938**	**−4,948**	**−6,512**	**−7,435**	**−9,827**	**−12,049**	**−10,744**	**−13,446**
Direct investment income	3 330	−1,515	−2,433	−3,565	−4,591	−6,598	−8,706	−7,628	−9,983
Dividends and distributed branch profits	3 332	−1,193	−1,838	−2,568	−3,096	−4,616	−6,374	−5,484	−7,208
Reinvested earnings and undistributed branch profits	3 333	−322	−595	−996	−1,495	−1,983	−2,332	−2,143	−2,775
Income on debt (interest)	3 334	....	....	....	....	....	....	....	....
Portfolio investment income	3 339	−1,219	−1,340	−1,630	−1,381	−1,523	−1,610	−1,472	−1,872
Income on equity	3 340	−10	−20	−20	−24	−69	−58	−38	−87
Income on bonds and notes	3 350	−1,209	−1,320	−1,610	−1,356	−1,454	−1,552	−1,434	−1,785
Income on money market instruments	3 360	....	....	....	....	....	....	....	....
Other investment income	3 370	−1,204	−1,175	−1,317	−1,464	−1,706	−1,733	−1,645	−1,591
D. CURRENT TRANSFERS	4 379	**3,309**	**3,724**	**4,082**	**4,743**	**5,228**	**5,512**	**4,613**	**4,475**
Credit	2 379	**3,565**	**3,994**	**4,342**	**5,037**	**5,642**	**5,898**	**5,253**	**5,343**
General government	2 380	340	397	501	531	267	192	220	171
Other sectors	2 390	3,225	3,597	3,841	4,505	5,374	5,706	5,033	5,171
Workers' remittances	2 391	3,060	3,170	3,314	3,890	4,493	4,842	4,145	4,023
Other current transfers	2 392	165	427	527	616	882	864	888	1,148
Debit	3 379	**−256**	**−270**	**−260**	**−294**	**−413**	**−386**	**−640**	**−868**
General government	3 380	−7	−6	−34	−27	−19	−24	−62	−97
Other sectors	3 390	−249	−264	−227	−266	−394	−362	−577	−771
Workers' remittances	3 391	−52	−31	−37	−47	−66	−59	−60	−72
Other current transfers	3 392	−196	−232	−189	−220	−328	−303	−518	−699
CAPITAL AND FINANCIAL ACCOUNT	4 996	**840**	**665**	**1,508**	**2,869**	**5,633**	**6,852**	**4,912**	**8,825**
CAPITAL ACCOUNT	4 994	....	....	....	....	....	....	....	....
Total credit	2 994	....	....	....	....	....	....	....	....
Total debit	3 994	....	....	....	....	....	....	....	....
Capital transfers, credit	2 400	....	....	....	....	....	....	....	....
General government	2 401	....	....	....	....	....	....	....	....
Debt forgiveness	2 402	....	....	....	....	....	....	....	....
Other capital transfers	2 410	....	....	....	....	....	....	....	....
Other sectors	2 430	....	....	....	....	....	....	....	....
Migrants' transfers	2 431	....	....	....	....	....	....	....	....
Debt forgiveness	2 432	....	....	....	....	....	....	....	....
Other capital transfers	2 440	....	....	....	....	....	....	....	....
Capital transfers, debit	3 400	....	....	....	....	....	....	....	....
General government	3 401	....	....	....	....	....	....	....	....
Debt forgiveness	3 402	....	....	....	....	....	....	....	....
Other capital transfers	3 410	....	....	....	....	....	....	....	....
Other sectors	3 430	....	....	....	....	....	....	....	....
Migrants' transfers	3 431	....	....	....	....	....	....	....	....
Debt forgiveness	3 432	....	....	....	....	....	....	....	....
Other capital transfers	3 440	....	....	....	....	....	....	....	....
Nonproduced nonfinancial assets, credit	2 480	....	....	....	....	....	....	....	....
Nonproduced nonfinancial assets, debit	3 480	....	....	....	....	....	....	....	....

Table 2 (Continued). STANDARD PRESENTATION, 2003–2010

(Millions of U.S. dollars)

	Code	2003	2004	2005	2006	2007	2008	2009	2010
FINANCIAL ACCOUNT	4 995	**840**	**665**	**1,508**	**2,869**	**5,633**	**6,852**	**4,912**	**8,825**
A. DIRECT INVESTMENT	4 500	**783**	**2,873**	**5,590**	**5,558**	**8,136**	**8,342**	**4,049**	**203**
Direct investment abroad	4 505	−938	−142	−4,662	−1,098	−913	−2,254	−3,088	−6,562
Equity capital	4 510	−938	−142	−4,662	−1,098	−913	−2,254	−3,088	−6,562
Claims on affiliated enterprises	4 515	−938	−142	−4,662	−1,098	−913	−2,254	−3,088	−6,562
Liabilities to affiliated enterprises	4 520	....	....	....	....	....	....	....	....
Reinvested earnings	4 525	....	....	....	....	....	....	....	....
Other capital	4 530	....	....	....	....	....	....	....	....
Claims on affiliated enterprises	4 535	....	....	....	....	....	....	....	....
Liabilities to affiliated enterprises	4 540	....	....	....	....	....	....	....	....
Direct investment in Colombia	4 555	**1,720**	**3,016**	**10,252**	**6,656**	**9,049**	**10,596**	**7,137**	**6,765**
Equity capital	4 560	1,436	2,489	9,270	5,193	7,462	7,803	4,951	4,015
Claims on direct investors	4 565	....	....	....	....	....	....	....	....
Liabilities to direct investors	4 570	1,436	2,489	9,270	5,193	7,462	7,803	4,951	4,015
Reinvested earnings	4 575	322	595	996	1,495	1,983	2,332	2,143	2,775
Other capital	4 580	−37	−68	−15	−31	−396	461	42	−25
Claims on direct investors	4 585	....	....	....	....	−438	438	....	....
Liabilities to direct investors	4 590	−37	−68	−15	−31	42	23	42	−25
B. PORTFOLIO INVESTMENT	4 600	**−1,624**	**−259**	**−1,742**	**−2,431**	**891**	**−1,007**	**1,867**	**1,495**
Assets	4 602	**−1,753**	**−1,565**	**−1,689**	**−3,333**	**−993**	**188**	**−2,802**	**−1,768**
Equity securities	4 610	....	....	....	....	....	....	....	....
Monetary authorities	4 611	....	....	....	....	....	....	....	....
General government	4 612	....	....	....	....	....	....	....	....
Banks	4 613	....	....	....	....	....	....	....	....
Other sectors	4 614	....	....	....	....	....	....	....	....
Debt securities	4 619	−1,753	−1,565	−1,689	−3,333	−993	188	−2,802	−1,768
Bonds and notes	4 620	−1,135	−391	98	−953	−384	515	−3,101	−2,368
Monetary authorities	4 621	....	....	....	....	....	....	....	....
General government	4 622	....	....	....	....	....	....	....	....
Banks	4 623	....	....	....	....	....	....	....	....
Other sectors	4 624	−1,135	−391	98	−953	−384	515	−3,101	−2,368
Money market instruments	4 630	−618	−1,174	−1,787	−2,379	−610	−327	299	600
Monetary authorities	4 631	....	....	....	....	....	....	....	....
General government	4 632	−260	−488	−264	−593	1,505	−116	−1,834	1,060
Banks	4 633	−36	−446	−938	−782	53	−277	12	−1,822
Other sectors	4 634	−322	−240	−585	−1,005	−2,168	66	2,121	1,362
Liabilities	4 652	**130**	**1,306**	**−53**	**902**	**1,884**	**−1,195**	**4,668**	**3,263**
Equity securities	4 660	−52	130	86	−30	790	−86	67	1,351
Banks	4 663	....	....	....	....	....	....	....	....
Other sectors	4 664	−52	130	86	−30	790	−86	67	1,351
Debt securities	4 669	181	1,176	−138	932	1,094	−1,109	4,601	1,912
Bonds and notes	4 670	181	1,176	−138	932	1,094	−1,109	4,601	1,912
Monetary authorities	4 671	....	....	....	....	....	....	....	....
General government	4 672	−186	1,080	−61	1,817	300	−1,090	2,659	1,328
Banks	4 673	....	....	....	−250	565	....	....	620
Other sectors	4 674	367	96	−77	−635	228	−19	1,942	−36
Money market instruments	4 680	....	....	....	....	....	....	....	....
Monetary authorities	4 681	....	....	....	....	....	....	....	....
General government	4 682	....	....	....	....	....	....	....	....
Banks	4 683	....	....	....	....	....	....	....	....
Other sectors	4 684	....	....	....	....	....	....	....	....
C. FINANCIAL DERIVATIVES	4 910	**−101**	**−190**	**−62**	**−9**	....	....	....	....
Monetary authorities	4 911	....	....	....	....	....	....	....	....
General government	4 912	....	....	....	....	....	....	....	....
Banks	4 913	....	....	....	....	....	....	....	....
Other sectors	4 914	−101	−190	−62	−9	....	....	....	....
Assets	4 900	....	....	....	....	....	....	....	....
Monetary authorities	4 901	....	....	....	....	....	....	....	....
General government	4 902	....	....	....	....	....	....	....	....
Banks	4 903	....	....	....	....	....	....	....	....
Other sectors	4 904	....	....	....	....	....	....	....	....
Liabilities	4 905	**−101**	**−190**	**−62**	**−9**	....	....	....	....
Monetary authorities	4 906	....	....	....	....	....	....	....	....
General government	4 907	....	....	....	....	....	....	....	....
Banks	4 908	....	....	....	....	....	....	....	....
Other sectors	4 909	−101	−190	−62	−9	....	....	....	....

Table 2 (Concluded). STANDARD PRESENTATION, 2003–2010
(Millions of U.S. dollars)

	Code	2003	2004	2005	2006	2007	2008	2009	2010
D. OTHER INVESTMENT	4 700	**1,585**	**703**	**−555**	**−227**	**1,294**	**2,088**	**437**	**10,245**
Assets	4 703	**1,633**	**425**	**−183**	**−732**	**−2,237**	**−173**	**−1,615**	**486**
Trade credits	4 706	394	15	−219	−402	−308	−173	−80	−5
General government	4 707	....	....	....	....	....	....	....	....
of which: Short-term	4 709	....	....	....	....	....	....	....	....
Other sectors	4 710	394	15	−219	−402	−308	−173	−80	−5
of which: Short-term	4 712	394	15	−219	−402	−308	−173	−80	−5
Loans	4 714	227	66	−629	−313	−1,510	−45	−632	20
Monetary authorities	4 715	....	....	....	....	....	....	....	....
of which: Short-term	4 718	....	....	....	....	....	....	....	....
General government	4 719	....	....	....	....	....	....	....	....
of which: Short-term	4 721	....	....	....	....	....	....	....	....
Banks	4 722	−25	44	−447	228	−872	874	−116	168
of which: Short-term	4 724	−30	39	−450	228	−872	874	−116	168
Other sectors	4 725	252	21	−181	−541	−639	−919	−516	−148
of which: Short-term	4 727	252	21	−181	−541	−639	−919	−516	−148
Currency and deposits	4 730	1,055	472	716	28	−354	101	−994	510
Monetary authorities	4 731	....	....	....	....	....	....	....	....
General government	4 732	....	....	....	....	....	....	....	....
Banks	4 733	−124	14	−27	−6	−100	6	−102	24
Other sectors	4 734	1,178	458	743	34	−255	95	−892	486
Other assets	4 736	−43	−128	−52	−45	−65	−56	92	−39
Monetary authorities	4 737	−13	−77	−4	10	−9	−67	110	−4
of which: Short-term	4 739	−4	−71	−3	10	−9	−47	104	7
General government	4 740	−30	−51	−48	−47	−20	−1	−8	−8
of which: Short-term	4 742	....	....	....	....	....	....	....	....
Banks	4 743	....	....	....	....	....	....	....	....
of which: Short-term	4 745	....	....	....	....	....	....	....	....
Other sectors	4 746	....	....	....	−8	−35	12	−9	−26
of which: Short-term	4 748	....	....	....	....	−19	12	−9	−26
Liabilities	4 753	**−48**	**278**	**−371**	**505**	**3,532**	**2,262**	**2,052**	**9,759**
Trade credits	4 756	319	265	288	−90	188	474	−468	296
General government	4 757	−24	−7	12	−27	−10	−3	−3	−2
of which: Short-term	4 759	....	....	....	....	....	....	....	....
Other sectors	4 760	342	272	276	−63	197	477	−465	298
of which: Short-term	4 762	320	317	238	−2	72	292	−711	301
Loans	4 764	−390	21	−666	587	3,288	1,779	1,506	9,355
Monetary authorities	4 765	−12	−68	5	−5	50	−37	−8	3
of which: Use of Fund credit and loans from the Fund	4 766	....	....	....	....	....	....	....	....
of which: Short-term	4 768	2	−2	5	−5	50	−37	−8	3
General government	4 769	2,204	605	−1,075	878	140	1,266	1,494	1,221
of which: Short-term	4 771	....	24	−24	....	....	....	....	....
Banks	4 772	−577	619	690	−542	1,154	164	−1,231	3,449
of which: Short-term	4 774	−349	698	358	−396	735	253	−1,045	2,361
Other sectors	4 775	−2,004	−1,134	−286	255	1,944	386	1,251	4,682
of which: Short-term	4 777	−147	366	55	−316	−344	−45	51	1,480
Currency and deposits	4 780	....	....	....	....	....	....	....	....
Monetary authorities	4 781	....	....	....	....	....	....	....	....
General government	4 782	....	....	....	....	....	....	....	....
Banks	4 783	....	....	....	....	....	....	....	....
Other sectors	4 784	....	....	....	....	....	....	....	....
Other liabilities	4 786	23	−8	7	7	56	9	1,015	108
Monetary authorities	4 787	....	....	....	....	....	....	975	....
of which: Short-term	4 789	....	....	....	....	....	....	....	....
General government	4 790	....	....	....	....	....	....	....	....
of which: Short-term	4 792	....	....	....	....	....	....	....	....
Banks	4 793	....	....	....	....	....	....	....	....
of which: Short-term	4 795	....	....	....	....	....	....	....	....
Other sectors	4 796	23	−8	7	7	56	9	41	108
of which: Short-term	4 798	23	−8	7	7	56	9	41	108
E. RESERVE ASSETS	4 802	**197**	**−2,463**	**−1,724**	**−23**	**−4,688**	**−2,571**	**−1,441**	**−3,117**
Monetary gold	4 812	−10	−8	−19	3	−20	−31	−12	....
Special drawing rights	4 811	−3	−2	−6	−11	−16	−15	−949	6
Reserve position in the Fund	4 810	....	....	....	....	....	....	43	137
Foreign exchange	4 803	210	−2,453	−1,698	−14	−4,651	−2,526	−523	−3,260
Other claims	4 813	....	....	....	....	....	....	....	....
NET ERRORS AND OMISSIONS	4 998	**139**	**246**	**378**	**120**	**344**	**70**	**245**	**207**

Table 3. INTERNATIONAL INVESTMENT POSITION (End-period stocks), 2003–2010

(Millions of U.S. dollars)

	Code	2003	2004	2005	2006	2007	2008	2009	2010
ASSETS	8 995 C.	**29,786**	**33,444**	**41,294**	**46,997**	**56,646**	**61,899**	**70,844**	**81,739**
Direct investment abroad	8 505	**4,390**	**4,357**	**8,915**	**10,013**	**10,926**	**13,180**	**16,268**	**22,830**
Equity capital and reinvested earnings	8 506	4,390	4,357	8,915	10,013	10,926	13,180	16,268	22,830
Claims on affiliated enterprises	8 507	4,390	4,357	8,915	10,013	10,926	13,180	16,268	22,830
Liabilities to affiliated enterprises	8 508	....	....	....	....	....	....	....	....
Other capital	8 530	....	....	....	....	....	....	....	....
Claims on affiliated enterprises	8 535	....	....	....	....	....	....	....	....
Liabilities to affiliated enterprises	8 540	....	....	....	....	....	....	....	....
Portfolio investment	8 602	**8,637**	**10,201**	**11,891**	**15,223**	**16,217**	**16,028**	**18,830**	**20,598**
Equity securities	8 610	....	....	....	....	....	....	....	....
Monetary authorities	8 611	....	....	....	....	....	....	....	....
General government	8 612	....	....	....	....	....	....	....	....
Banks	8 613	....	....	....	....	....	....	....	....
Other sectors	8 614	....	....	....	....	....	....	....	....
Debt securities	8 619	8,637	10,201	11,891	15,223	16,217	16,028	18,830	20,598
Bonds and notes	8 620	5,363	5,754	5,655	6,609	6,992	6,477	9,578	11,946
Monetary authorities	8 621	....	....	....	....	....	....	....	....
General government	8 622	....	....	....	....	....	....	....	....
Banks	8 623	....	....	....	....	....	....	....	....
Other sectors	8 624	5,363	5,754	5,655	6,609	6,992	6,477	9,578	11,946
Money market instruments	8 630	3,274	4,448	6,235	8,615	9,224	9,551	9,252	8,652
Monetary authorities	8 631	....	....	....	....	....	....	....	....
General government	8 632	626	1,113	1,377	1,970	465	581	2,416	1,355
Banks	8 633	278	725	1,663	2,445	2,392	2,669	2,657	4,478
Other sectors	8 634	2,370	2,610	3,195	4,200	6,367	6,301	4,180	2,818
Financial derivatives	8 900	....	....	....	....	....	....	....	....
Monetary authorities	8 901	....	....	....	....	....	....	....	....
General government	8 902	....	....	....	....	....	....	....	....
Banks	8 903	....	....	....	....	....	....	....	....
Other sectors	8 904	....	....	....	....	....	....	....	....
Other investment	8 703	**6,158**	**5,745**	**5,936**	**6,725**	**8,978**	**9,146**	**10,776**	**10,249**
Trade credits	8 706	1,355	1,339	1,558	1,960	2,268	2,441	2,521	2,526
General government	8 707	....	....	....	....	....	....	....	....
of which: Short-term	8 709	....	....	....	....	....	....	....	....
Other sectors	8 710	1,355	1,339	1,558	1,960	2,268	2,441	2,521	2,526
of which: Short-term	8 712	*1,355*	*1,339*	*1,558*	*1,960*	*2,268*	*2,441*	*2,521*	*2,526*
Loans	8 714	1,053	987	1,616	1,929	3,439	3,485	4,117	4,097
Monetary authorities	8 715	....	....	....	....	....	....	....	....
of which: Short-term	8 718	....	....	....	....	....	....	....	....
General government	8 719	....	....	....	....	....	....	....	....
of which: Short-term	8 721	....	....	....	....	....	....	....	....
Banks	8 722	162	117	565	337	1,208	334	451	283
of which: Short-term	8 724	*154*	*115*	*565*	*337*	*1,208*	*334*	*451*	*283*
Other sectors	8 725	891	870	1,051	1,592	2,231	3,150	3,666	3,814
of which: Short-term	8 727	*891*	*869*	*1,051*	*1,592*	*2,230*	*3,150*	*3,665*	*3,813*
Currency and deposits	8 730	2,612	2,140	1,424	1,396	1,750	1,649	2,643	2,133
Monetary authorities	8 731	....	....	....	....	....	....	....	....
General government	8 732	....	....	....	....	....	....	....	....
Banks	8 733	234	220	247	252	352	346	448	424
Other sectors	8 734	2,378	1,920	1,177	1,143	1,398	1,303	2,196	1,709
Other assets	8 736	1,138	1,278	1,338	1,441	1,520	1,572	1,495	1,493
Monetary authorities	8 737	838	927	939	954	994	1,056	962	925
of which: Short-term	8 739	*6*	*77*	*80*	*69*	*78*	*125*	*21*	*15*
General government	8 740	300	351	399	446	467	468	476	485
of which: Short-term	8 742	....	....	....	....	....	....	....	....
Banks	8 743	....	....	....	....	....	....	....	....
of which: Short-term	8 745	....	....	....	....	....	....	....	....
Other sectors	8 746	....	....	....	40	60	48	57	83
of which: Short-term	8 748	....	....	....	*40*	*60*	*48*	*57*	*83*
Reserve assets	8 802	**10,601**	**13,141**	**14,552**	**15,036**	**20,526**	**23,545**	**24,970**	**28,063**
Monetary gold	8 812	136	143	168	141	185	191	243	311
Special drawing rights	8 811	171	181	173	193	220	229	1,184	1,157
Reserve position in the Fund	8 810	425	444	408	430	452	440	406	260
Foreign exchange	8 803	9,848	12,353	13,784	14,252	19,650	22,665	23,117	26,315
Other claims	8 813	20	20	20	20	20	20	20	20

Table 3 (Concluded). INTERNATIONAL INVESTMENT POSITION (End-period stocks), 2003–2010

(Millions of U.S. dollars)

	Code	2003	2004	2005	2006	2007	2008	2009	2010
LIABILITIES	8 995 D.	**59,097**	**65,525**	**76,905**	**87,108**	**104,536**	**115,737**	**130,828**	**151,685**
Direct investment in Colombia	8 555	**20,540**	**24,783**	**36,903**	**45,228**	**56,448**	**67,287**	**75,087**	**82,425**
Equity capital and reinvested earnings	8 556	20,400	24,712	36,846	45,202	56,819	67,196	74,954	82,316
Claims on direct investors	8 557	....	....	....	....	....	....	....	....
Liabilities to direct investors	8 558	20,400	24,712	36,846	45,202	56,819	67,196	74,954	82,316
Other capital	8 580	140	72	57	26	−370	91	133	108
Claims on direct investors	8 585	....	....	....	....	−438	....	....	....
Liabilities to direct investors	8 590	140	72	57	26	68	91	133	108
Portfolio investment	8 652	**12,952**	**14,750**	**14,632**	**15,880**	**18,406**	**16,493**	**21,536**	**25,197**
Equity securities	8 660	405	719	899	874	1,901	1,352	1,573	3,004
Banks	8 663	....	....	....	....	....	....	....	....
Other sectors	8 664	405	719	899	874	1,901	1,352	1,573	3,004
Debt securities	8 669	12,546	14,031	13,733	15,007	16,505	15,141	19,962	22,193
Bonds and notes	8 670	12,546	14,031	13,733	15,007	16,505	15,141	19,962	22,193
Monetary authorities	8 671	....	....	....	....	....	....	....	....
General government	8 672	11,342	12,731	12,510	14,669	15,383	14,067	16,935	18,562
Banks	8 673	250	250	250	....	565	565	565	1,185
Other sectors	8 674	955	1,050	973	338	557	509	2,463	2,446
Money market instruments	8 680	....	....	....	....	....	....	....	....
Monetary authorities	8 681	....	....	....	....	....	....	....	....
General government	8 682	....	....	....	....	....	....	....	....
Banks	8 683	....	....	....	....	....	....	....	....
Other sectors	8 684	....	....	....	....	....	....	....	....
Financial derivatives	8 905	**12**	....	....	....	....	....	....	....
Monetary authorities	8 906	....	....	....	....	....	....	....	....
General government	8 907	....	....	....	....	....	....	....	....
Banks	8 908	....	....	....	....	....	....	....	....
Other sectors	8 909	12	....	....	....	....	....	....	....
Other investment	8 753	**25,593**	**25,991**	**25,371**	**26,000**	**29,682**	**31,957**	**34,205**	**44,064**
Trade credits	8 756	1,748	2,012	2,291	2,202	2,383	2,856	2,388	2,686
General government	8 757	56	49	60	34	24	21	17	15
of which: Short-term	8 759	....	....	....	....	....	....	....	....
Other sectors	8 760	1,691	1,963	2,232	2,169	2,358	2,836	2,371	2,671
of which: Short-term	8 762	*776*	*1,094*	*1,332*	*1,330*	*1,402*	*1,695*	*984*	*1,285*
Loans	8 764	23,597	23,739	22,832	23,513	26,967	28,758	30,271	39,737
Monetary authorities	8 765	73	7	9	4	54	17	9	12
of which: Use of Fund credit and loans from the Fund	8 766	....	....	....	....	....	....	....	....
of which: Short-term	8 768	*6*	*4*	*9*	*4*	*54*	*17*	*9*	*12*
General government	8 769	9,301	9,978	8,747	9,694	9,916	11,205	12,661	13,888
of which: Short-term	8 771	....	*24*	....	....	....	....	....	....
Banks	8 772	1,326	1,944	2,630	2,093	3,256	3,420	2,200	5,717
of which: Short-term	8 774	*884*	*1,581*	*1,940*	*1,544*	*2,280*	*2,532*	*1,487*	*3,848*
Other sectors	8 775	12,897	11,810	11,446	11,721	13,741	14,116	15,401	20,120
of which: Short-term	8 777	*1,653*	*2,019*	*2,074*	*1,458*	*1,114*	*1,070*	*1,121*	*2,579*
Currency and deposits	8 780	....	....	....	....	....	....	....	....
Monetary authorities	8 781	....	....	....	....	....	....	....	....
General government	8 782	....	....	....	....	....	....	....	....
Banks	8 783	....	....	....	....	....	....	....	....
Other sectors	8 784	....	....	....	....	....	....	....	....
Other liabilities	8 786	248	239	247	286	332	342	1,546	1,641
Monetary authorities	8 787	57	56	57	48	38	40	1,202	1,190
of which: Short-term	8 789	....	....	....	....	....	....	....	....
General government	8 790	....	....	....	....	....	....	....	....
of which: Short-term	8 792	....	....	....	....	....	....	....	....
Banks	8 793	....	....	....	....	....	....	....	....
of which: Short-term	8 795	....	....	....	....	....	....	....	....
Other sectors	8 796	191	183	190	238	294	303	343	451
of which: Short-term	8 798	*191*	*183*	*190*	*238*	*294*	*303*	*343*	*451*
NET INTERNATIONAL INVESTMENT POSITION	8 995	−29,311	−32,081	−35,611	−40,111	−47,890	−53,838	−59,985	−69,946
Conversion rates: Colombian pesos per U.S. dollar (end of period)	0 102	2,780.82	2,412.10	2,284.22	2,225.44	1,987.81	2,198.09	2,044.23	1,989.88

Table 1. ANALYTIC PRESENTATION, 2003–2010

(Millions of U.S. dollars)

	Code	2003	2004	2005	2006	2007	2008	2009	2010
A. Current Account[1]	4 993 Z.	**520.5**	**674.4**	**695.6**	**124.1**	**−2,181.0**	....	....	....
Goods: exports f.o.b.	2 100 ..	2,636.6	3,433.2	4,745.3	6,065.7	5,808.0	....	....	....
Goods: imports f.o.b.	3 100 ..	−831.2	−969.0	−1,305.5	−2,003.5	−2,858.1	....	....	....
Balance on Goods	4 100 ..	*1,805.4*	*2,464.2*	*3,439.8*	*4,062.2*	*2,949.9*	....	....	....
Services: credit	2 200 ..	194.1	196.7	220.5	266.0	319.4	....	....	....
Services: debit	3 200 ..	−875.4	−1,016.3	−1,417.1	−2,425.9	−3,527.7	....	....	....
Balance on Goods and Services	4 991 ..	*1,124.1*	*1,644.6*	*2,243.2*	*1,902.3*	*−258.3*	....	....	....
Income: credit	2 300 ..	10.3	13.3	17.6	20.1	23.4	....	....	....
Income: debit	3 300 ..	−596.4	−961.8	−1,595.5	−1,772.6	−1,908.1	....	....	....
Balance on Goods, Services, and Income	4 992 ..	*538.0*	*696.0*	*665.3*	*149.7*	*−2,143.1*	....	....	....
Current transfers: credit	2 379 Z.	26.5	34.5	87.2	37.9	43.0	....	....	....
Current transfers: debit	3 379 ..	−44.0	−56.0	−56.9	−63.5	−81.0	....	....	....
B. Capital Account[1]	4 994 Z.	**16.9**	**12.7**	**11.2**	**9.6**	**31.7**	....	....	....
Capital account: credit	2 994 Z.	17.7	15.1	11.2	9.6	31.7	....	....	....
Capital account: debit	3 994 ..	−.9	−2.5	....	....	....	....	....	....
Total, Groups A Plus B	4 981 ..	*537.3*	*687.1*	*706.8*	*133.7*	*−2,149.3*	....	....	....
C. Financial Account[1]	4 995 W.	**−701.5**	**−775.0**	**−226.7**	**425.9**	**2,546.8**	....	....	....
Direct investment abroad	4 505 ..	−1.7	−4.5	....	....	....	....	....	....
Direct investment in the Republic of Congo	4 555 Z.	323.1	−8.5	513.6	1,487.7	2,638.4	....	....	....
Portfolio investment assets	4 602 ..	....	....	−1.1	−1.3	−1.5	....	....	....
Equity securities	4 610 ..	....	....	−1.1	−1.3	−1.5	....	....	....
Debt securities	4 619 ..	....	....	....	....	....	....	....	....
Portfolio investment liabilities	4 652 Z.	−.2	2.1	....	....	....	....	....	....
Equity securities	4 660 ..	....	....	....	....	....	....	....	....
Debt securities	4 669 Z.	−.2	2.1	....	....	....	....	....	....
Financial derivatives	4 910 ..	....	....	....	....	....	....	....	....
Financial derivatives assets	4 900 ..	....	....	....	....	....	....	....	....
Financial derivatives liabilities	4 905 ..	....	....	....	....	....	....	....	....
Other investment assets	4 703 ..	−180.3	−440.7	−246.5	−228.9	266.2	....	....	....
Monetary authorities	4 701 ..	....	....	....	....	....	....	....	....
General government	4 704 ..	....	....	....	....	....	....	....	....
Banks	4 705 ..	125.3	−35.8	....	....	....	....	....	....
Other sectors	4 728 ..	−305.6	−404.9	−246.5	−228.9	266.2	....	....	....
Other investment liabilities	4 753 W.	−842.4	−323.3	−492.7	−831.5	−356.4	....	....	....
Monetary authorities	4 753 WA	−4.1	.9	....	....	....	....	....	....
General government	4 753 ZB	−283.7	−267.1	−519.8	−562.1	−494.9	....	....	....
Banks	4 753 ZC	−38.9	12.9	−110.5	−130.6	−49.2	....	....	....
Other sectors	4 753 ZD	−515.6	−70.0	137.6	−138.8	187.8	....	....	....
Total, Groups A Through C	4 983 ..	*−164.1*	*−87.8*	*480.0*	*559.6*	*397.5*	....	....	....
D. Net Errors and Omissions	4 998 ..	**−116.0**	**−92.8**	**30.5**	**142.5**	**−201.1**	....	....	....
Total, Groups A Through D	4 984 ..	*−280.1*	*−180.7*	*510.5*	*702.1*	*196.4*	....	....	....
E. Reserves and Related Items	4 802 A.	**280.1**	**180.7**	**−510.5**	**−702.1**	**−196.4**	....	....	....
Reserve assets	4 802 ..	2.6	−75.4	−659.5	−975.2	−88.1	....	....	....
Use of Fund credit and loans	4 766 ..	−7.6	.2	−.4	7.6	....	....	....	....
Exceptional financing	4 920 ..	285.0	255.9	149.4	265.4	−108.3	....	....	....
Conversion rates: CFA francs per U.S. dollar	0 101 ..	**581.20**	**528.28**	**527.47**	**522.89**	**479.27**	**447.81**	**472.19**	**495.28**

[1] Excludes components that have been classified in the categories of Group E.

Table 2. STANDARD PRESENTATION, 2003–2010

(Millions of U.S. dollars)

	Code	2003	2004	2005	2006	2007	2008	2009	2010
CURRENT ACCOUNT	4 993 ..	**520.5**	**674.4**	**695.6**	**124.1**	**−2,181.0**	....	....	....
A. GOODS	4 100 ..	**1,805.4**	**2,464.2**	**3,439.8**	**4,062.2**	**2,949.9**	....	....	....
Credit	2 100 ..	**2,636.6**	**3,433.2**	**4,745.3**	**6,065.7**	**5,808.0**	....	....	....
General merchandise: exports f.o.b.	2 110 ..	2,636.6	3,433.2	4,745.3	6,065.7	5,808.0	....	....	....
Goods for processing: exports f.o.b.	2 150 ..	....	....	....	....	....	....	....	....
Repairs on goods	2 160 ..	....	....	....	....	....	....	....	....
Goods procured in ports by carriers	2 170 ..	....	....	....	....	....	....	....	....
Nonmonetary gold	2 180 ..	....	....	....	....	....	....	....	....
Debit	3 100 ..	**−831.2**	**−969.0**	**−1,305.5**	**−2,003.5**	**−2,858.1**	....	....	....
General merchandise: imports f.o.b.	3 110 ..	−831.2	−969.0	−1,305.5	−2,003.5	−2,858.1	....	....	....
Goods for processing: imports f.o.b.	3 150 ..	....	....	....	....	....	....	....	....
Repairs on goods	3 160 ..	....	....	....	....	....	....	....	....
Goods procured in ports by carriers	3 170 ..	....	....	....	....	....	....	....	....
Nonmonetary gold	3 180 ..	....	....	....	....	....	....	....	....
B. SERVICES	4 200 ..	**−681.3**	**−819.6**	**−1,196.7**	**−2,159.9**	**−3,208.2**	....	....	....
Total credit	2 200 ..	*194.1*	*196.7*	*220.5*	*266.0*	*319.4*	....	....	....
Total debit	3 200 ..	*−875.4*	*−1,016.3*	*−1,417.1*	*−2,425.9*	*−3,527.7*	....	....	....
Transportation services, credit	2 205 ..	**31.5**	**31.6**	**9.9**	**12.6**	**12.1**	....	....	....
Passenger	2 850 ..	*1.0*	*1.1*	....	....	....	....	....	....
Freight	2 851 ..	*7.2*	*6.1*	*9.9*	*12.6*	*12.1*	....	....	....
Other	2 852 ..	*23.2*	*24.4*	....	....	....	....	....	....
Sea transport, passenger	2 207 ..	....	....	....	....	....	....	....	....
Sea transport, freight	2 208 ..	....	....	9.9	12.6	12.1	....	....	....
Sea transport, other	2 209 ..	....	....	....	....	....	....	....	....
Air transport, passenger	2 211 ..	....	....	....	....	....	....	....	....
Air transport, freight	2 212 ..	....	....	....	....	....	....	....	....
Air transport, other	2 213 ..	....	....	....	....	....	....	....	....
Other transport, passenger	2 215 ..	....	....	....	....	....	....	....	....
Other transport, freight	2 216 ..	....	....	....	....	....	....	....	....
Other transport, other	2 217 ..	....	....	....	....	....	....	....	....
Transportation services, debit	3 205 ..	**−164.0**	**−220.7**	**−235.1**	**−360.7**	**−529.1**	....	....	....
Passenger	3 850 ..	*−40.1*	*−72.7*	....	....	....	....	....	....
Freight	3 851 ..	*−122.5*	*−146.9*	*−235.1*	*−360.7*	*−529.1*	....	....	....
Other	3 852 ..	*−1.4*	*−1.1*	....	....	....	....	....	....
Sea transport, passenger	3 207 ..	....	....	....	....	....	....	....	....
Sea transport, freight	3 208 ..	....	....	−235.1	−360.7	−529.1	....	....	....
Sea transport, other	3 209 ..	....	....	....	....	....	....	....	....
Air transport, passenger	3 211 ..	....	....	....	....	....	....	....	....
Air transport, freight	3 212 ..	....	....	....	....	....	....	....	....
Air transport, other	3 213 ..	....	....	....	....	....	....	....	....
Other transport, passenger	3 215 ..	....	....	....	....	....	....	....	....
Other transport, freight	3 216 ..	....	....	....	....	....	....	....	....
Other transport, other	3 217 ..	....	....	....	....	....	....	....	....
Travel, credit	2 236 ..	**28.7**	**22.1**	**40.4**	**45.3**	**54.5**	....	....	....
Business travel	2 237 ..	.7	2.3	....	....	....	....	....	....
Personal travel	2 240 ..	28.0	19.9	40.4	45.3	54.5	....	....	....
Travel, debit	3 236 ..	**−77.9**	**−103.2**	**−111.9**	**−132.3**	**−167.5**	....	....	....
Business travel	3 237 ..	−38.9	−49.6	....	....	....	....	....	....
Personal travel	3 240 ..	−39.1	−53.6	−111.9	−132.3	−167.5	....	....	....
Other services, credit	2 200 BA	**133.9**	**142.9**	**170.2**	**208.1**	**252.9**	....	....	....
Communications	2 245 ..	5.3	9.5	....	....	....	....	....	....
Construction	2 249 ..	....	....	....	....	....	....	....	....
Insurance	2 253 ..	29.4	29.2	58.2	77.5	95.1	....	....	....
Financial	2 260 ..	....	....	....	....	....	....	....	....
Computer and information	2 262 ..	....	....	....	....	....	....	....	....
Royalties and licence fees	2 266 ..	....	....	....	....	....	....	....	....
Other business services	2 268 ..	80.4	80.1	98.0	115.9	141.0	....	....	....
Personal, cultural, and recreational	2 287 ..	9.3	10.8	....	....	....	....	....	....
Government, n.i.e.	2 291 ..	9.5	13.4	14.0	14.7	16.7	....	....	....
Other services, debit	3 200 BA	**−633.5**	**−692.4**	**−1,070.2**	**−1,932.9**	**−2,831.0**	....	....	....
Communications	3 245 ..	−13.4	−13.8	....	....	....	....	....	....
Construction	3 249 ..	....	....	....	....	....	....	....	....
Insurance	3 253 ..	−69.0	−63.6	−127.0	−150.3	−182.8	....	....	....
Financial	3 260 ..	....	....	....	....	....	....	....	....
Computer and information	3 262 ..	....	....	....	....	....	....	....	....
Royalties and licence fees	3 266 ..	....	....	....	....	....	....	....	....
Other business services	3 268 ..	−538.4	−607.2	−938.8	−1,778.2	−2,643.2	....	....	....
Personal, cultural, and recreational	3 287 ..	−3.4	−3.6	....	....	....	....	....	....
Government, n.i.e.	3 291 ..	−9.3	−4.2	−4.4	−4.4	−5.0	....	....	....

Table 2 (Continued). STANDARD PRESENTATION, 2003–2010

(Millions of U.S. dollars)

	Code	2003	2004	2005	2006	2007	2008	2009	2010
C. INCOME	4 300	**−586.0**	**−948.5**	**−1,577.9**	**−1,752.6**	**−1,884.8**	....	....	....
Total credit	2 300	*10.3*	*13.3*	*17.6*	*20.1*	*23.4*	....	....	....
Total debit	3 300	*−596.4*	*−961.8*	*−1,595.5*	*−1,772.6*	*−1,908.1*	....	....	....
Compensation of employees, credit	2 310	**7.7**	**9.3**	**11.4**	**13.2**	**14.8**	....	....	....
Compensation of employees, debit	3 310	**−33.6**	**−42.6**	**−58.8**	**−73.1**	**−93.3**	....	....	....
Investment income, credit	2 320	**2.6**	**4.0**	**6.3**	**6.9**	**8.6**	....	....	....
Direct investment income	2 330	1.2	1.1	....	....	....	....	....	....
Dividends and distributed branch profits	2 332	1.2	1.1	....	....	....	....	....	....
Reinvested earnings and undistributed branch profits	2 333	....	....	....	....	....	....	....	....
Income on debt (interest)	2 334	....	....	....	....	....	....	....	....
Portfolio investment income	2 339	.9	1.1	....	....	....	....	....	....
Income on equity	2 340	.2	.2	....	....	....	....	....	....
Income on bonds and notes	2 350	.7	.9	....	....	....	....	....	....
Income on money market instruments	2 360	....	....	....	....	....	....	....	....
Other investment income	2 370	.5	1.7	6.3	6.9	8.6	....	....	....
Investment income, debit	3 320	**−562.8**	**−919.2**	**−1,536.8**	**−1,699.6**	**−1,814.9**	....	....	....
Direct investment income	3 330	−387.8	−647.0	−1,296.4	−1,402.6	−1,651.1	....	....	....
Dividends and distributed branch profits	3 332	−26.8	−341.7	−495.4	−538.2	−469.9	....	....	....
Reinvested earnings and undistributed branch profits	3 333	−361.0	−305.3	−801.0	−864.4	−1,181.2	....	....	....
Income on debt (interest)	3 334	....	....	....	....	....	....	....	....
Portfolio investment income	3 339	−.3	....	....	....	....	....	....	....
Income on equity	3 340	−.3	....	....	....	....	....	....	....
Income on bonds and notes	3 350	....	....	....	....	....	....	....	....
Income on money market instruments	3 360	....	....	....	....	....	....	....	....
Other investment income	3 370	−174.6	−272.2	−240.4	−297.0	−163.8	....	....	....
D. CURRENT TRANSFERS	4 379	**−17.5**	**−21.6**	**30.3**	**−25.6**	**−38.0**	....	....	....
Credit	2 379	**26.5**	**34.5**	**87.2**	**37.9**	**43.0**	....	....	....
General government	2 380	10.3	11.2	63.5	13.2	16.1	....	....	....
Other sectors	2 390	16.2	23.3	23.7	24.7	26.9	....	....	....
Workers' remittances	2 391	4.6	5.7	....	....	....	....	....	....
Other current transfers	2 392	11.5	17.6	23.7	24.7	26.9	....	....	....
Debit	3 379	**−44.0**	**−56.0**	**−56.9**	**−63.5**	**−81.0**	....	....	....
General government	3 380	−1.0	−.2	−.2	−.2	−1.3	....	....	....
Other sectors	3 390	−43.0	−55.8	−56.7	−63.3	−79.7	....	....	....
Workers' remittances	3 391	−5.7	−6.8	−7.4	−7.6	−9.0	....	....	....
Other current transfers	3 392	−37.3	−49.0	−49.3	−55.7	−70.7	....	....	....
CAPITAL AND FINANCIAL ACCOUNT	4 996	**−404.5**	**−581.6**	**−726.0**	**−266.6**	**2,382.1**	....	....	....
CAPITAL ACCOUNT	4 994	**17.0**	**201.0**	**11.2**	**9.6**	**31.7**	....	....	....
Total credit	2 994	*17.8*	*203.5*	*11.2*	*9.6*	*31.7*	....	....	....
Total debit	3 994	*−.9*	*−2.5*	....	....	....	....	....	....
Capital transfers, credit	2 400	**17.8**	**203.5**	**11.2**	**9.6**	**31.7**	....	....	....
General government	2 401	17.0	203.3	11.2	9.6	31.7	....	....	....
Debt forgiveness	2 402	.1	188.3	....	....	....	....	....	....
Other capital transfers	2 410	16.9	15.0	....	....	....	....	....	....
Other sectors	2 430	.9	.2	....	....	....	....	....	....
Migrants' transfers	2 431	....	....	....	....	....	....	....	....
Debt forgiveness	2 432	....	....	....	....	....	....	....	....
Other capital transfers	2 440	.9	.2	....	....	....	....	....	....
Capital transfers, debit	3 400	....	....	....	....	....	....	....	....
General government	3 401	....	....	....	....	....	....	....	....
Debt forgiveness	3 402	....	....	....	....	....	....	....	....
Other capital transfers	3 410	....	....	....	....	....	....	....	....
Other sectors	3 430	....	....	....	....	....	....	....	....
Migrants' transfers	3 431	....	....	....	....	....	....	....	....
Debt forgiveness	3 432	....	....	....	....	....	....	....	....
Other capital transfers	3 440	....	....	....	....	....	....	....	....
Nonproduced nonfinancial assets, credit	2 480	....	....	....	....	....	....	....	....
Nonproduced nonfinancial assets, debit	3 480	**−.9**	**−2.5**	....	....	....	....	....	....

Table 2 (Continued). STANDARD PRESENTATION, 2003–2010

(Millions of U.S. dollars)

	Code	2003	2004	2005	2006	2007	2008	2009	2010
FINANCIAL ACCOUNT	4 995	**−421.5**	**−782.6**	**−737.2**	**−276.2**	**2,350.4**	....	....	....
A. DIRECT INVESTMENT	4 500	**321.4**	**−13.1**	**513.6**	**1,487.7**	**2,638.4**	....	....	....
Direct investment abroad	4 505	**−1.7**	**−4.5**	....	....	....	....	....	....
Equity capital	4 510	....	....	....	....	....	....	....	....
Claims on affiliated enterprises	4 515	....	....	....	....	....	....	....	....
Liabilities to affiliated enterprises	4 520	....	....	....	....	....	....	....	....
Reinvested earnings	4 525	....	....	....	....	....	....	....	....
Other capital	4 530	−1.7	−4.5	....	....	....	....	....	....
Claims on affiliated enterprises	4 535	....	....	....	....	....	....	....	....
Liabilities to affiliated enterprises	4 540	−1.7	−4.5	....	....	....	....	....	....
Direct investment in the Republic of Congo	4 555	**323.1**	**−8.5**	**513.6**	**1,487.7**	**2,638.4**	....	....	....
Equity capital	4 560	.5	4.5	....	....	....	....	....	....
Claims on direct investors	4 565	....	....	....	....	....	....	....	....
Liabilities to direct investors	4 570	.5	4.5	....	....	....	....	....	....
Reinvested earnings	4 575	361.0	305.3	801.0	864.4	1,181.2	....	....	....
Other capital	4 580	−38.4	−318.4	−287.4	623.3	1,457.2	....	....	....
Claims on direct investors	4 585	101.9	−101.5	−287.4	....	....	....	....	....
Liabilities to direct investors	4 590	−140.2	−216.9	....	623.3	1,457.2	....	....	....
B. PORTFOLIO INVESTMENT	4 600	**−.2**	**2.1**	**−1.1**	**−1.3**	**−1.5**	....	....	....
Assets	4 602	....	....	**−1.1**	**−1.3**	**−1.5**	....	....	....
Equity securities	4 610	....	....	−1.1	−1.3	−1.5	....	....	....
Monetary authorities	4 611	....	....	....	....	....	....	....	....
General government	4 612	....	....	....	....	....	....	....	....
Banks	4 613	....	....	....	....	....	....	....	....
Other sectors	4 614	....	....	−1.1	−1.3	−1.5	....	....	....
Debt securities	4 619	....	....	....	....	....	....	....	....
Bonds and notes	4 620	....	....	....	....	....	....	....	....
Monetary authorities	4 621	....	....	....	....	....	....	....	....
General government	4 622	....	....	....	....	....	....	....	....
Banks	4 623	....	....	....	....	....	....	....	....
Other sectors	4 624	....	....	....	....	....	....	....	....
Money market instruments	4 630	....	....	....	....	....	....	....	....
Monetary authorities	4 631	....	....	....	....	....	....	....	....
General government	4 632	....	....	....	....	....	....	....	....
Banks	4 633	....	....	....	....	....	....	....	....
Other sectors	4 634	....	....	....	....	....	....	....	....
Liabilities	4 652	**−.2**	**2.1**	....	....	....	....	....	....
Equity securities	4 660	....	....	....	....	....	....	....	....
Banks	4 663	....	....	....	....	....	....	....	....
Other sectors	4 664	....	....	....	....	....	....	....	....
Debt securities	4 669	−.2	2.1	....	....	....	....	....	....
Bonds and notes	4 670	−.2	2.1	....	....	....	....	....	....
Monetary authorities	4 671	....	....	....	....	....	....	....	....
General government	4 672	....	....	....	....	....	....	....	....
Banks	4 673	....	....	....	....	....	....	....	....
Other sectors	4 674	−.2	2.1	....	....	....	....	....	....
Money market instruments	4 680	....	....	....	....	....	....	....	....
Monetary authorities	4 681	....	....	....	....	....	....	....	....
General government	4 682	....	....	....	....	....	....	....	....
Banks	4 683	....	....	....	....	....	....	....	....
Other sectors	4 684	....	....	....	....	....	....	....	....
C. FINANCIAL DERIVATIVES	4 910	....	....	....	....	....	....	....	....
Monetary authorities	4 911	....	....	....	....	....	....	....	....
General government	4 912	....	....	....	....	....	....	....	....
Banks	4 913	....	....	....	....	....	....	....	....
Other sectors	4 914	....	....	....	....	....	....	....	....
Assets	4 900	....	....	513.6	1,487.7	....	....	....	....
Monetary authorities	4 901	....	....	....	....	....	....	....	....
General government	4 902	....	....	....	....	....	....	....	....
Banks	4 903	....	....	....	....	....	....	....	....
Other sectors	4 904	....	....	....	....	....	....	....	....
Liabilities	4 905	−38.4	....	....	....	....	....	....	....
Monetary authorities	4 906	....	....	....	....	....	....	....	....
General government	4 907	....	....	....	....	....	....	....	....
Banks	4 908	....	....	....	....	....	....	....	....
Other sectors	4 909	....	....	....	....	....	....	....	....

Table 2 (Concluded). STANDARD PRESENTATION, 2003–2010

(Millions of U.S. dollars)

	Code	2003	2004	2005	2006	2007	2008	2009	2010
D. OTHER INVESTMENT................................	4 700 ..	**−745.3**	**−696.2**	**−590.2**	**−787.4**	**−198.4**	....	....	....
Assets..	4 703 ..	**−180.3**	**−440.7**	**−246.5**	**−228.9**	**266.2**	....	....	....
Trade credits...................................	4 706 ..	−173.6	−279.0	−246.5	−228.9	266.2	....	....	....
General government......................	4 707 ..	....	....	....	....	....	....	....	....
of which: Short-term....................	4 709 ..	....	....	....	....	....			
Other sectors..............................	4 710 ..	−173.6	−279.0	−246.5	−228.9	266.2	....		
of which: Short-term....................	4 712 ..	*−173.6*	*−279.0*	*−246.5*	*−228.9*	*266.2*			
Loans..	4 714 ..	.3	....						
Monetary authorities......................	4 715 ..	....	....	....	....	....			
of which: Short-term....................	4 718 ..	....	....	....	....	....			
General government......................	4 719 ..	....	....	....	....	....			
of which: Short-term....................	4 721 ..	....	....	....	....	....			
Banks...	4 722 ..	.3	....	....	....	....			
of which: Short-term....................	4 724 ..	*.3*	....	....	....	....			
Other sectors..............................	4 725 ..	....	....	....	....	....			
of which: Short-term....................	4 727 ..	....	....	....	....	....			
Currency and deposits.....................	4 730 ..	−4.3	−171.9	....	....	....			
Monetary authorities......................	4 731 ..	....	....	....	....	....			
General government......................	4 732 ..	....	....	....	....	....			
Banks...	4 733 ..	124.9	−35.8	....	....	....			
Other sectors..............................	4 734 ..	−129.2	−136.1	....	....	....			
Other assets....................................	4 736 ..	−2.8	10.2	....	....	....			
Monetary authorities......................	4 737 ..	....	....	....	....	....			
of which: Short-term....................	4 739 ..	....	....	....	....	....			
General government......................	4 740 ..	....	....	....	....	....			
of which: Short-term....................	4 742 ..	....	....	....	....	....			
Banks...	4 743 ..	....	....	....	....	....			
of which: Short-term....................	4 745 ..	....	....	....	....	....			
Other sectors..............................	4 746 ..	−2.8	10.2	....	....	....			
of which: Short-term....................	4 748 ..	*−2.8*	*10.2*	....	....	....			
Liabilities..	4 753 ..	**−565.0**	**−255.6**	**−343.8**	**−558.5**	**−464.7**	....		....
Trade credits...................................	4 756 ..	−193.4	23.7	....	....	....			
General government......................	4 757 ..	....	....	....	....	....			
of which: Short-term....................	4 759 ..	....	....	....	....	....			
Other sectors..............................	4 760 ..	−193.4	23.7	....	....	....			
of which: Short-term....................	4 762 ..	*−193.4*	*23.7*	....	....	....			
Loans..	4 764 ..	−615.3	−242.7	−493.2	−823.9	−356.4			
Monetary authorities......................	4 765 ..	−9.3	138.0	−.4	7.6	....			
of which: Use of Fund credit and loans from the Fund..	4 766 ..	*−7.6*	*.2*	*−.4*	*7.6*	....			
of which: Short-term....................	4 768 ..	*−4.1*	*.9*	....	....	....			
General government......................	4 769 ..	−283.7	−267.1	−519.8	−562.1	−494.9			
of which: Short-term....................	4 771 ..	....	....	....	....	....			
Banks...	4 772 ..	....	....	−110.5	−130.6	−49.2			
of which: Short-term....................	4 774 ..	....	....	*−110.5*	*−130.6*	*−49.2*			
Other sectors..............................	4 775 ..	−322.3	−113.6	137.6	−138.8	187.8			
of which: Short-term....................	4 777 ..	....	....	....	....	....			
Currency and deposits.....................	4 780 ..	−38.9	13.3	....	....	....			
Monetary authorities......................	4 781 ..	....	....	....	....	....			
General government......................	4 782 ..	....	....	....	....	....			
Banks...	4 783 ..	−38.9	12.9	....	....	....			
Other sectors..............................	4 784 ..	....	.4	....	....	....			
Other liabilities...............................	4 786 ..	282.5	−49.8	149.4	265.4	−108.3			
Monetary authorities......................	4 787 ..	282.5	−69.3	149.4	265.4	−108.3			
of which: Short-term....................	4 789 ..	*282.5*	*−69.3*	*149.4*	*265.4*	*−108.3*			
General government......................	4 790 ..	....	....	....	....	....			
of which: Short-term....................	4 792 ..	....	....	....	....	....			
Banks...	4 793 ..	....	....	....	....	....			
of which: Short-term....................	4 795 ..	....	....	....	....	....			
Other sectors..............................	4 796 ..	....	19.5	....	....	....			
of which: Short-term....................	4 798 ..	....	*19.5*	....	....	....			
E. RESERVE ASSETS.............................	4 802 ..	**2.6**	**−75.4**	**−659.5**	**−975.2**	**−88.1**	....	....	....
Monetary gold.................................	4 812 ..	....	....	....	....	....			
Special drawing rights......................	4 811 ..	2.7	−6.5	4.5	2.3	....			
Reserve position in the Fund..............	4 810 ..	....	....	....	....	−.1			
Foreign exchange.............................	4 803 ..	....	−68.9	−663.9	−977.5	−88.1			
Other claims...................................	4 813 ..	....	....	....	....	....			
NET ERRORS AND OMISSIONS.............................	4 998 ..	**−116.0**	**−92.8**	**30.5**	**142.5**	**−201.1**	....	....	....

Table 1. ANALYTIC PRESENTATION, 2003–2010

(Millions of U.S. dollars)

	Code	2003	2004	2005	2006	2007	2008	2009	2010
A. Current Account[1]	4 993 Z.	**−880.1**	**−795.8**	**−981.0**	**−1,022.6**	**−1,646.4**	**−2,787.3**	**−576.0**	**−1,438.7**
Goods: exports f.o.b.	2 100 ..	6,163.0	6,369.7	7,099.4	8,101.7	9,299.5	9,555.4	8,838.2	9,481.5
Goods: imports f.o.b.	3 100 ..	−7,252.3	−7,791.0	−9,258.3	−10,828.9	−12,284.9	−14,568.7	−10,877.3	−12,949.4
Balance on Goods	4 100 ..	*−1,089.4*	*−1,421.3*	*−2,158.9*	*−2,727.1*	*−2,985.5*	*−5,013.3*	*−2,039.1*	*−3,467.9*
Services: credit	2 200 ..	2,021.0	2,241.8	2,621.6	2,971.7	3,552.2	4,083.3	3,592.9	4,180.2
Services: debit	3 200 ..	−1,244.6	−1,384.5	−1,505.6	−1,620.6	−1,818.1	−1,882.4	−1,404.8	−1,773.3
Balance on Goods and Services	4 991 ..	*−313.0*	*−563.9*	*−1,042.9*	*−1,376.1*	*−1,251.4*	*−2,812.4*	*149.0*	*−1,061.0*
Income: credit	2 300 ..	146.5	144.5	806.9	1,135.1	707.7	696.8	219.3	199.3
Income: debit	3 300 ..	−922.3	−588.8	−1,015.4	−1,130.8	−1,572.4	−1,113.9	−1,303.0	−947.5
Balance on Goods, Services, and Income	4 992 ..	*−1,088.8*	*−1,008.2*	*−1,251.4*	*−1,371.8*	*−2,116.1*	*−3,229.5*	*−934.7*	*−1,809.2*
Current transfers: credit	2 379 Z.	368.8	371.2	470.6	586.1	734.6	706.6	593.3	609.7
Current transfers: debit	3 379 ..	−160.0	−158.7	−200.1	−237.0	−264.8	−264.4	−234.6	−239.3
B. Capital Account[1]	4 994 Z.	**23.7**	**11.5**	**15.9**	**1.1**	**21.2**	**7.4**	**58.3**	**54.7**
Capital account: credit	2 994 Z.	23.8	11.5	15.9	1.1	21.2	7.4	58.3	81.7
Capital account: debit	3 994 ..	−.1	....	....	....	....	....	....	−26.9
Total, Groups A Plus B	4 981 ..	*−856.4*	*−784.3*	*−965.1*	*−1,021.5*	*−1,625.2*	*−2,779.9*	*−517.7*	*−1,384.0*
C. Financial Account[1]	4 995 W.	**595.2**	**471.8**	**877.9**	**1,886.7**	**2,432.0**	**2,521.5**	**504.7**	**1,832.0**
Direct investment abroad	4 505 ..	−26.9	−60.6	43.0	−98.1	−262.4	−5.9	−7.5	−24.8
Direct investment in Costa Rica	4 555 Z.	575.1	793.8	861.0	1,469.1	1,896.1	2,078.2	1,346.5	1,465.6
Portfolio investment assets	4 602 ..	−91.6	53.1	−680.7	−509.3	−170.4	537.3	−321.7	218.6
Equity securities	4 610 ..	−1.5	−6.6	−6.1	3.9	−42.2	−11.5	−2.7	2.3
Debt securities	4 619 ..	−90.1	59.8	−674.6	−513.2	−128.2	548.8	−319.0	216.3
Portfolio investment liabilities	4 652 Z.	−304.5	−239.5	....	....	....	−93.7	−105.7	....
Equity securities	4 660 ..	....	....	....	....	....	....	....	....
Debt securities	4 669 Z.	−304.5	−239.5	....	....	....	−93.7	−105.7	....
Financial derivatives	4 910 ..	....	....	....	....	....	....	....	....
Financial derivatives assets	4 900 ..	....	....	....	....	....	....	....	....
Financial derivatives liabilities	4 905 ..	....	....	....	....	....	....	....	....
Other investment assets	4 703 ..	162.4	−308.7	154.5	654.6	−155.8	−684.6	332.2	−376.5
Monetary authorities	4 701 ..	−27.6	−4.1	−4.0	−3.7	−2.9	−.7	−34.2	−6.2
General government	4 704 ..	....	....	....	....	....	....	....	....
Banks	4 705 ..	−35.2	−318.4	−163.3	81.9	119.8	−566.7	418.2	−66.8
Other sectors	4 728 ..	225.2	13.9	321.8	576.3	−272.7	−117.2	−51.8	−303.5
Other investment liabilities	4 753 W.	280.8	233.5	500.2	370.4	1,124.4	690.2	−739.2	549.0
Monetary authorities	4 753 WA	−47.4	−77.0	−66.6	−85.8	−5.9	−7.8	193.9	−3.6
General government	4 753 ZB	−86.5	−69.9	−2.0	−52.9	−55.3	−43.2	−22.3	487.6
Banks	4 753 ZC	173.2	106.8	32.4	124.0	608.8	248.6	−799.9	119.0
Other sectors	4 753 ZD	241.5	273.7	536.4	385.0	576.8	492.5	−111.0	−53.9
Total, Groups A Through C	4 983 ..	*−261.2*	*−312.6*	*−87.2*	*865.1*	*806.8*	*−258.3*	*−13.0*	*447.9*
D. Net Errors and Omissions	4 998 ..	**35.1**	**63.7**	**144.5**	**149.5**	**171.0**	**−47.6**	**131.6**	**−41.2**
Total, Groups A Through D	4 984 ..	*−226.1*	*−248.8*	*57.2*	*1,014.7*	*977.7*	*−305.9*	*118.6*	*406.7*
E. Reserves and Related Items	4 802 A.	**226.1**	**248.8**	**−57.2**	**−1,014.7**	**−977.7**	**305.9**	**−118.6**	**−406.7**
Reserve assets	4 802 ..	−338.9	−80.3	−393.5	−1,030.8	−1,147.7	348.0	−259.9	−561.1
Use of Fund credit and loans	4 766 ..	....	....	....	....	....	....	....	....
Exceptional financing	4 920 ..	564.9	329.1	336.2	16.2	170.0	−42.0	141.3	154.5
Conversion rates: Costa Rican colones per U.S. dollar	0 101 ..	**398.66**	**437.94**	**477.79**	**511.30**	**516.62**	**526.24**	**573.29**	**525.83**

[1] Excludes components that have been classified in the categories of Group E.

Table 2. STANDARD PRESENTATION, 2003–2010

(Millions of U.S. dollars)

	Code	2003	2004	2005	2006	2007	2008	2009	2010
CURRENT ACCOUNT...............................	4 993 ..	**−880.1**	**−795.8**	**−981.0**	**−1,022.6**	**−1,646.4**	**−2,787.3**	**−576.0**	**−1,438.7**
A. GOODS.........................	4 100 ..	**−1,089.4**	**−1,421.3**	**−2,158.9**	**−2,727.1**	**−2,985.5**	**−5,013.3**	**−2,039.1**	**−3,467.9**
Credit................................	2 100 ..	**6,163.0**	**6,369.7**	**7,099.4**	**8,101.7**	**9,299.5**	**9,555.4**	**8,838.2**	**9,481.5**
General merchandise: exports f.o.b.	2 110 ..	2,467.6	2,671.3	2,906.9	3,225.6	3,623.4	4,032.2	3,787.6	4,248.3
Goods for processing: exports f.o.b.	2 150 ..	3,635.0	3,621.1	4,072.3	4,537.7	5,431.1	5,170.9	4,891.4	5,103.8
Repairs on goods	2 160 ..	....	....	.3	236.2	114.2	159.3	61.6	49.7
Goods procured in ports by carriers	2 170 ..	60.4	77.3	119.9	102.3	130.8	193.0	97.6	79.7
Nonmonetary gold	2 180 ..	....	....	....	....	....	....	....	....
Debit................................	3 100 ..	**−7,252.3**	**−7,791.0**	**−9,258.3**	**−10,828.9**	**−12,284.9**	**−14,568.7**	**−10,877.3**	**−12,949.4**
General merchandise: imports f.o.b.	3 110 ..	−5,014.8	−5,350.3	−6,303.8	−7,275.0	−8,963.1	−11,151.7	−8,186.5	−9,765.3
Goods for processing: imports f.o.b.	3 150 ..	−2,206.5	−2,393.4	−2,920.7	−3,522.4	−3,284.1	−3,370.0	−2,669.6	−3,141.9
Repairs on goods	3 160 ..	−9.4	−18.0	....	....	−.1	....	....	−.2
Goods procured in ports by carriers	3 170 ..	−21.6	−29.2	−33.8	−31.5	−37.6	−46.9	−21.2	−41.9
Nonmonetary gold	3 180 ..	....	....	....	....	....	....	....	....
B. SERVICES.......................	4 200 ..	**776.4**	**857.4**	**1,116.0**	**1,351.1**	**1,734.0**	**2,200.9**	**2,188.1**	**2,406.9**
Total credit...............	2 200 ..	*2,021.0*	*2,241.8*	*2,621.6*	*2,971.7*	*3,552.2*	*4,083.3*	*3,592.9*	*4,180.2*
Total debit...............	3 200 ..	*−1,244.6*	*−1,384.5*	*−1,505.6*	*−1,620.6*	*−1,818.1*	*−1,882.4*	*−1,404.8*	*−1,773.3*
Transportation services, credit..........	2 205 ..	**240.4**	**245.7**	**282.4**	**259.4**	**317.0**	**371.0**	**289.3**	**307.9**
Passenger...............	2 850 ..	*131.2*	*126.6*	*138.5*	*157.6*	*195.2*	*250.4*	*186.3*	*180.3*
Freight...............	2 851 ..	*15.1*	*17.6*	*17.5*	*22.8*	*35.4*	*39.1*	*27.0*	*23.4*
Other...............	2 852 ..	*94.1*	*101.5*	*126.3*	*79.0*	*86.3*	*81.5*	*75.9*	*104.1*
Sea transport, passenger	2 207 ..	....	....	....	....	....	....	....	....
Sea transport, freight	2 208 ..	....	....	....	....	....	....	....	....
Sea transport, other	2 209 ..	43.4	40.3	52.6	46.7	50.4	46.9	43.3	46.7
Air transport, passenger	2 211 ..	128.9	123.9	135.6	155.3	192.6	247.3	183.5	177.2
Air transport, freight	2 212 ..	.5	.4	.1	.1	.1	.2	.2	.6
Air transport, other	2 213 ..	50.6	61.1	73.6	32.3	35.9	34.6	32.6	56.2
Other transport, passenger	2 215 ..	2.3	2.7	2.9	2.3	2.7	3.1	2.8	3.1
Other transport, freight	2 216 ..	14.7	17.2	17.4	22.7	35.3	38.9	26.9	22.9
Other transport, other	2 217 ..	....	....	.1	....	....	....	....	1.3
Transportation services, debit..........	3 205 ..	**−508.3**	**−581.8**	**−632.5**	**−630.0**	**−642.4**	**−683.2**	**−504.0**	**−666.5**
Passenger...............	3 850 ..	*−81.0*	*−74.5*	*−86.3*	*−91.7*	*−116.6*	*−124.6*	*−94.6*	*−109.2*
Freight...............	3 851 ..	*−395.5*	*−473.5*	*−516.7*	*−508.8*	*−489.2*	*−527.4*	*−384.0*	*−525.6*
Other...............	3 852 ..	*−31.7*	*−33.8*	*−29.5*	*−29.5*	*−36.6*	*−31.2*	*−25.4*	*−31.7*
Sea transport, passenger	3 207 ..	....	....	....	....	....	....	....	....
Sea transport, freight	3 208 ..	−395.5	−473.5	−516.7	−508.8	−489.2	−527.4	−384.0	−356.9
Sea transport, other	3 209 ..	....	....	....	....	....	....	....	....
Air transport, passenger	3 211 ..	−81.0	−74.5	−86.3	−91.7	−116.6	−124.6	−94.6	−109.2
Air transport, freight	3 212 ..	....	....	....	....	....	....	....	−98.8
Air transport, other	3 213 ..	−29.6	−31.6	−27.1	−27.1	−33.7	−28.5	−22.7	−29.0
Other transport, passenger	3 215 ..	....	....	....	....	....	....	....	....
Other transport, freight	3 216 ..	....	....	....	....	....	....	....	−69.9
Other transport, other	3 217 ..	−2.2	−2.2	−2.4	−2.4	−2.8	−2.7	−2.7	−2.7
Travel, credit........................	2 236 ..	**1,293.1**	**1,458.5**	**1,670.8**	**1,707.1**	**2,026.2**	**2,282.9**	**1,815.0**	**2,008.6**
Business travel	2 237 ..	1.4	1.1	2.1	1.5	1.6	1.9	1.8	1.8
Personal travel	2 240 ..	1,291.7	1,457.4	1,668.7	1,705.6	2,024.7	2,281.0	1,813.2	2,006.9
Travel, debit........................	3 236 ..	**−353.2**	**−405.7**	**−469.5**	**−485.3**	**−633.5**	**−593.5**	**−367.7**	**−425.1**
Business travel	3 237 ..	−1.0	−1.3	−1.1	−1.2	−1.2	−1.5	−1.1	−1.1
Personal travel	3 240 ..	−352.2	−404.4	−468.5	−484.0	−632.3	−591.9	−366.6	−424.0
Other services, credit................	2 200 BA	**487.5**	**537.6**	**668.4**	**1,005.1**	**1,208.9**	**1,429.5**	**1,488.7**	**1,863.7**
Communications	2 245 ..	23.5	25.6	34.9	39.4	46.5	39.2	45.2	39.5
Construction	2 249 ..	....	....	....	....	....	....	....	....
Insurance	2 253 ..	....	....	....	....	....	....	....	....
Financial	2 260 ..	4.7	9.7	9.0	11.7	11.5	13.9	16.4	25.7
Computer and information	2 262 ..	166.8	200.3	254.8	417.5	499.6	683.5	758.2	1,070.7
Royalties and licence fees	2 266 ..	.5	.5	.1	....	....	.6	.6	7.5
Other business services	2 268 ..	260.6	266.7	332.4	497.4	619.7	662.0	642.3	688.5
Personal, cultural, and recreational	2 287 ..	.1	.1	.1	.1	.1	.1	.1	.1
Government, n.i.e.	2 291 ..	31.4	34.6	37.0	38.9	31.5	30.2	26.0	31.7
Other services, debit................	3 200 BA	**−383.2**	**−397.0**	**−403.6**	**−505.3**	**−542.2**	**−605.7**	**−533.1**	**−681.8**
Communications	3 245 ..	−51.4	−55.1	−60.8	−94.3	−91.9	−109.7	−100.0	−99.3
Construction	3 249 ..	....	....	....	....	....	....	....	....
Insurance	3 253 ..	−64.1	−85.2	−90.0	−86.4	−116.7	−148.7	−119.1	−126.9
Financial	3 260 ..	−1.9	−3.8	−6.4	−14.0	−14.2	−11.7	−9.6	−18.0
Computer and information	3 262 ..	−10.2	−16.4	−11.0	−13.6	−15.0	−6.1	−11.6	−21.6
Royalties and licence fees	3 266 ..	−63.9	−51.4	−56.9	−87.5	−52.7	−62.2	−64.6	−63.6
Other business services	3 268 ..	−178.2	−171.0	−174.6	−205.5	−247.5	−263.1	−223.7	−347.9
Personal, cultural, and recreational	3 287 ..	−.1	−.1	−.1	−.1	−.1	−.1	−.1	−.1
Government, n.i.e.	3 291 ..	−13.4	−14.1	−3.8	−3.9	−4.0	−4.1	−4.2	−4.4

Table 2 (Continued). STANDARD PRESENTATION, 2003–2010

(Millions of U.S. dollars)

	Code	2003	2004	2005	2006	2007	2008	2009	2010
C. INCOME	4 300	**−775.9**	**−444.3**	**−208.5**	**4.3**	**−864.7**	**−417.1**	**−1,083.7**	**−748.2**
Total credit	2 300	*146.5*	*144.5*	*806.9*	*1,135.1*	*707.7*	*696.8*	*219.3*	*199.3*
Total debit	3 300	*−922.3*	*−588.8*	*−1,015.4*	*−1,130.8*	*−1,572.4*	*−1,113.9*	*−1,303.0*	*−947.5*
Compensation of employees, credit	2 310	**14.9**	**17.3**	**20.6**	**23.3**	**22.3**	**20.9**	**24.5**	**25.2**
Compensation of employees, debit	3 310	**−36.3**	**−36.6**	**−13.1**	**−13.5**	**−13.9**	**−14.3**	**−14.8**	**−32.4**
Investment income, credit	2 320	**131.6**	**127.1**	**786.3**	**1,111.8**	**685.4**	**676.0**	**194.8**	**174.1**
Direct investment income	2 330	18.2	5.0	594.6	739.9	133.3	280.7	16.5	21.9
Dividends and distributed branch profits	2 332	24.0	....	578.2	728.5	105.9	277.1	....	5.5
Reinvested earnings and undistributed branch profits	2 333	−6.0	1.3	9.3	3.7	19.6	−3.4	1.2	12.4
Income on debt (interest)	2 334	.1	3.7	7.0	7.7	7.7	6.9	15.3	4.0
Portfolio investment income	2 339	3.1	8.6	72.1	106.4	144.4	130.2	100.6	90.9
Income on equity	2 340	....	....	....	....	....	....	....	....
Income on bonds and notes	2 350	3.1	8.6	72.1	106.4	144.4	130.2	100.6	90.9
Income on money market instruments	2 360	....	....	....	....	....	....	....	....
Other investment income	2 370	110.3	113.6	119.6	265.6	407.7	265.1	77.7	61.3
Investment income, debit	3 320	**−886.1**	**−552.1**	**−1,002.3**	**−1,117.3**	**−1,558.5**	**−1,099.6**	**−1,288.2**	**−915.2**
Direct investment income	3 330	−643.5	−329.6	−742.8	−852.8	−1,131.1	−749.4	−985.9	−606.0
Dividends and distributed branch profits	3 332	−252.6	30.2	−647.2	−440.2	−599.4	−301.0	−509.1	−156.9
Reinvested earnings and undistributed branch profits	3 333	−389.9	−356.9	−91.5	−410.2	−521.0	−446.0	−471.2	−448.6
Income on debt (interest)	3 334	−1.0	−2.9	−4.2	−2.4	−10.8	−2.4	−5.6	−.5
Portfolio investment income	3 339	−65.2	−61.9	−49.2	−74.5	−79.8	−82.4	−62.6	−62.9
Income on equity	3 340	....	....	....	....	....	....	....	....
Income on bonds and notes	3 350	−65.2	−61.9	−49.2	−74.5	−79.8	−82.4	−62.6	−62.9
Income on money market instruments	3 360	....	....	....	....	....	....	....	....
Other investment income	3 370	−177.3	−160.6	−210.3	−190.0	−347.6	−267.8	−239.8	−246.2
D. CURRENT TRANSFERS	4 379	**208.8**	**212.4**	**270.4**	**349.2**	**469.8**	**442.2**	**358.7**	**370.4**
Credit	2 379	**368.8**	**371.2**	**470.6**	**586.1**	**734.6**	**706.6**	**593.3**	**609.7**
General government	2 380	7.6	9.8	8.2	22.1	19.1	41.0	34.2	22.3
Other sectors	2 390	361.2	361.3	462.3	564.0	715.5	665.6	559.1	587.4
Workers' remittances	2 391	306.0	302.2	399.8	489.8	595.6	583.9	488.6	505.5
Other current transfers	2 392	55.2	59.1	62.6	74.2	119.9	81.8	70.6	82.0
Debit	3 379	**−160.0**	**−158.7**	**−200.1**	**−237.0**	**−264.8**	**−264.4**	**−234.6**	**−239.3**
General government	3 380	−4.0	−3.6	−3.9	−3.8	−7.1	−9.8	−10.5	−12.0
Other sectors	3 390	−156.0	−155.2	−196.2	−233.1	−257.8	−254.6	−224.1	−227.3
Workers' remittances	3 391	−155.7	−154.9	−195.9	−232.9	−257.5	−254.3	−223.8	−227.0
Other current transfers	3 392	−.2	−.2	−.2	−.3	−.3	−.3	−.3	−.3
CAPITAL AND FINANCIAL ACCOUNT	4 996	**844.9**	**732.1**	**836.5**	**873.1**	**1,475.4**	**2,834.9**	**444.5**	**1,480.0**
CAPITAL ACCOUNT	4 994	**25.3**	**12.7**	**15.9**	**1.1**	**21.2**	**7.4**	**58.3**	**54.7**
Total credit	2 994	*25.4*	*12.7*	*15.9*	*1.1*	*21.2*	*7.4*	*58.3*	*81.7*
Total debit	3 994	*−.1*	....	....	....	....	....	....	*−26.9*
Capital transfers, credit	2 400	**25.4**	**12.7**	**15.9**	**1.1**	**21.2**	**7.4**	**58.3**	**81.7**
General government	2 401	4.7	3.3	....	.4	21.2	7.4	32.8	49.7
Debt forgiveness	2 402	1.6	1.2	....	.4	1.2	2.4	2.3	2.2
Other capital transfers	2 410	3.0	2.1	....	....	20.0	5.0	30.5	47.5
Other sectors	2 430	20.8	9.4	15.9	.7	....	....	25.5	32.0
Migrants' transfers	2 431	....	....	....	....	....	....	....	21.1
Debt forgiveness	2 432	....	8.6	....	....	....	....	....	....
Other capital transfers	2 440	20.8	.8	15.9	.7	....	....	25.5	10.9
Capital transfers, debit	3 400	**−.1**	....	....	....	....	....	....	**−26.9**
General government	3 401	−.1	....	....	....	....	....	....	−15.0
Debt forgiveness	3 402	....	....	....	....	....	....	....	....
Other capital transfers	3 410	−.1	....	....	....	....	....	....	−15.0
Other sectors	3 430	....	....	....	....	....	....	....	−11.9
Migrants' transfers	3 431	....	....	....	....	....	....	....	−11.9
Debt forgiveness	3 432	....	....	....	....	....	....	....	....
Other capital transfers	3 440	....	....	....	....	....	....	....	....
Nonproduced nonfinancial assets, credit	2 480	....	....	....	....	....	....	....	....
Nonproduced nonfinancial assets, debit	3 480	....	....	....	....	....	....	....	....

Table 2 (Continued). STANDARD PRESENTATION, 2003–2010

(Millions of U.S. dollars)

	Code	2003	2004	2005	2006	2007	2008	2009	2010
FINANCIAL ACCOUNT	4 995	819.6	719.4	820.7	872.0	1,454.2	2,827.5	386.1	1,425.3
A. DIRECT INVESTMENT	4 500	548.1	733.3	904.0	1,371.0	1,633.7	2,072.3	1,339.0	1,440.9
Direct investment abroad	4 505	−26.9	−60.6	43.0	−98.1	−262.4	−5.9	−7.5	−24.8
Equity capital	4 510	−35.3	−63.3	51.6	−109.8	−236.5	−4.9	−.5	−3.9
Claims on affiliated enterprises	4 515	−35.3	−63.3	51.6	−109.8	−236.5	−4.9	−.5	−3.9
Liabilities to affiliated enterprises	4 520	....	....	....	....	....	....	....	....
Reinvested earnings	4 525	6.0	−1.3	−9.3	−3.7	−19.6	3.4	−1.2	−12.4
Other capital	4 530	2.4	4.0	.7	15.4	−6.3	−4.4	−5.7	−8.5
Claims on affiliated enterprises	4 535	2.4	4.0	.7	15.4	−6.3	−4.4	−5.7	−8.5
Liabilities to affiliated enterprises	4 540	....	....	....	....	....	....	....	....
Direct investment in Costa Rica	4 555	575.1	793.8	861.0	1,469.1	1,896.1	2,078.2	1,346.5	1,465.6
Equity capital	4 560	255.9	312.8	483.1	1,034.2	1,377.3	1,593.6	1,049.9	867.3
Claims on direct investors	4 565	....	....	....	....	....	....	....	....
Liabilities to direct investors	4 570	255.9	312.8	483.1	1,034.2	1,377.3	1,593.6	1,049.9	867.3
Reinvested earnings	4 575	389.9	356.9	91.5	410.2	521.0	446.0	471.2	448.6
Other capital	4 580	−70.8	124.1	286.4	24.7	−2.2	38.6	−174.5	149.7
Claims on direct investors	4 585	....	....	....	....	....	....	....	....
Liabilities to direct investors	4 590	−70.8	124.1	286.4	24.7	−2.2	38.6	−174.5	149.7
B. PORTFOLIO INVESTMENT	4 600	11.2	141.6	−344.5	−493.1	−.4	401.6	−286.1	373.1
Assets	4 602	−91.6	53.1	−680.7	−509.3	−170.4	537.3	−321.7	218.6
Equity securities	4 610	−1.5	−6.6	−6.1	3.9	−42.2	−11.5	−2.7	2.3
Monetary authorities	4 611	....	....	....	....	....	....	....	....
General government	4 612	....	....	....	....	....	....	....	....
Banks	4 613	....	....	....	....	....	....	....	−.6
Other sectors	4 614	−1.5	−6.6	−6.1	3.9	−42.2	−11.5	−2.7	2.9
Debt securities	4 619	−90.1	59.8	−674.6	−513.2	−128.2	548.8	−319.0	216.3
Bonds and notes	4 620	−90.1	59.8	−674.6	−513.2	−128.2	548.8	−319.0	216.3
Monetary authorities	4 621	....	....	....	....	....	....	....	....
General government	4 622	....	....	....	....	....	....	....	....
Banks	4 623	....	....	....	....	....	....	−267.2	119.3
Other sectors	4 624	−90.1	59.8	−674.6	−513.2	−128.2	548.8	−51.7	97.0
Money market instruments	4 630	....	....	....	....	....	....	....	....
Monetary authorities	4 631	....	....	....	....	....	....	....	....
General government	4 632	....	....	....	....	....	....	....	....
Banks	4 633	....	....	....	....	....	....	....	....
Other sectors	4 634	....	....	....	....	....	....	....	....
Liabilities	4 652	102.8	88.4	336.2	16.2	170.0	−135.7	35.6	154.5
Equity securities	4 660	....	....	....	....	....	....	....	....
Banks	4 663	....	....	....	....	....	....	....	....
Other sectors	4 664	....	....	....	....	....	....	....	....
Debt securities	4 669	102.8	88.4	336.2	16.2	170.0	−135.7	35.6	154.5
Bonds and notes	4 670	102.8	88.4	336.2	16.2	170.0	−135.7	35.6	154.5
Monetary authorities	4 671	−46.1	−184.4	....	....	....	....	....	....
General government	4 672	29.5	242.1	332.6	23.5	136.9	−142.3	50.1	142.6
Banks	4 673	6.6	....	....	....	....	....	....	....
Other sectors	4 674	112.8	30.7	3.6	−7.4	33.1	6.6	−14.4	11.9
Money market instruments	4 680	....	....	....	....	....	....	....	....
Monetary authorities	4 681	....	....	....	....	....	....	....	....
General government	4 682	....	....	....	....	....	....	....	....
Banks	4 683	....	....	....	....	....	....	....	....
Other sectors	4 684	....	....	....	....	....	....	....	....
C. FINANCIAL DERIVATIVES	4 910	....	....	....	....	....	....	....	....
Monetary authorities	4 911	....	....	....	....	....	....	....	....
General government	4 912	....	....	....	....	....	....	....	....
Banks	4 913	....	....	....	....	....	....	....	....
Other sectors	4 914	....	....	....	....	....	....	....	....
Assets	4 900	....	....	....	....	....	....	....	....
Monetary authorities	4 901	....	....	....	....	....	....	....	....
General government	4 902	....	....	....	....	....	....	....	....
Banks	4 903	....	....	....	....	....	....	....	....
Other sectors	4 904	....	....	....	....	....	....	....	....
Liabilities	4 905	....	....	....	....	....	....	....	....
Monetary authorities	4 906	....	....	....	....	....	....	....	....
General government	4 907	....	....	....	....	....	....	....	....
Banks	4 908	....	....	....	....	....	....	....	....
Other sectors	4 909	....	....	....	....	....	....	....	....

Table 2 (Concluded). STANDARD PRESENTATION, 2003–2010

(Millions of U.S. dollars)

	Code	2003	2004	2005	2006	2007	2008	2009	2010
D. OTHER INVESTMENT	4 700 ..	**599.2**	**−75.2**	**654.6**	**1,025.0**	**968.6**	**5.6**	**−406.9**	**172.5**
Assets	4 703 ..	**162.4**	**−308.7**	**154.5**	**654.6**	**−155.8**	**−684.6**	**332.2**	**−376.5**
Trade credits	4 706 ..	−18.8	−28.8	−52.6	−58.2	−52.3	−95.2	46.4	−182.4
General government	4 707 ..	....	....	....	....	....	....	....	....
of which: Short-term	4 709 ..	....	....	....	....	....	....	....	....
Other sectors	4 710 ..	−18.8	−28.8	−52.6	−58.2	−52.3	−95.2	46.4	−182.4
of which: Short-term	4 712 ..	*−25.1*	*−9.2*	*−46.3*	*−64.7*	*−28.1*	*−85.3*	*33.8*	*−102.5*
Loans	4 714 ..	1.7	4.1	10.6	−28.6	−15.3	56.6	7.5	−56.4
Monetary authorities	4 715 ..	....	....	....	....	....	....	....	....
of which: Short-term	4 718 ..	....	....	....	....	....	....	....	....
General government	4 719 ..	....	....	....	....	....	....	....	....
of which: Short-term	4 721 ..	....	....	....	....	....	....	....	....
Banks	4 722 ..	....	.8	−8.7	−2.9	−3.4	56.7	8.7	....
of which: Short-term	4 724 ..	....	*.1*	*.2*	....	....	....	....	....
Other sectors	4 725 ..	1.7	3.3	19.3	−25.8	−11.9	−.2	−1.1	−56.4
of which: Short-term	4 727 ..	*1.9*	*2.0*	*9.7*	*−3.0*	*3.5*	*2.3*	*−4.6*	*−31.1*
Currency and deposits	4 730 ..	207.2	−278.9	208.7	744.9	−76.5	−649.4	307.5	−112.0
Monetary authorities	4 731 ..	....	....	....	....	....	....	....	....
General government	4 732 ..	....	....	....	....	....	....	....	....
Banks	4 733 ..	−35.2	−316.8	−149.0	90.1	126.5	−629.9	410.3	−66.8
Other sectors	4 734 ..	242.4	37.9	357.7	654.8	−203.0	−19.5	−102.8	−45.3
Other assets	4 736 ..	−27.7	−5.0	−12.1	−3.5	−11.5	3.5	−29.2	−25.7
Monetary authorities	4 737 ..	−27.6	−4.1	−4.0	−3.7	−2.9	−.7	−34.2	−6.2
of which: Short-term	4 739 ..	....	....	....	....	....	....	....	....
General government	4 740 ..	....	....	....	....	....	....	....	....
of which: Short-term	4 742 ..	....	....	....	....	....	....	....	....
Banks	4 743 ..	....	−2.5	−5.6	−5.3	−3.2	6.5	−.7	....
of which: Short-term	4 745 ..	....	*−2.5*	*−5.6*	*−5.3*	*−3.2*	*6.5*	*−.7*	....
Other sectors	4 746 ..	−.1	1.5	−2.6	5.4	−5.4	−2.3	5.7	−19.4
of which: Short-term	4 748 ..	*−1.1*	*2.7*	*−.8*	*2.5*	*−4.5*	*.7*	*−4.5*	*−6.0*
Liabilities	4 753 ..	**436.8**	**233.5**	**500.2**	**370.4**	**1,124.4**	**690.2**	**−739.2**	**549.0**
Trade credits	4 756 ..	21.8	236.0	443.7	109.8	146.5	107.0	−269.1	44.8
General government	4 757 ..	....	....	....	....	....	....	....	....
of which: Short-term	4 759 ..	....	....	....	....	....	....	....	....
Other sectors	4 760 ..	21.8	236.0	443.7	109.8	146.5	107.0	−269.1	44.8
of which: Short-term	4 762 ..	*28.5*	*208.8*	*298.4*	*61.3*	*108.5*	*243.8*	*−357.1*	*86.2*
Loans	4 764 ..	427.7	15.2	52.7	262.2	977.9	422.5	−783.7	562.6
Monetary authorities	4 765 ..	104.3	−75.1	−64.5	−85.3	−7.2	−7.4	−11.9	−7.3
of which: Use of Fund credit and loans from the Fund	4 766 ..	....	....	....	....	....	....	....	....
of which: Short-term	4 768 ..	....	....	....	....	....	....	....	....
General government	4 769 ..	−86.5	−69.9	−2.0	−52.9	−55.3	−43.2	−22.3	487.6
of which: Short-term	4 771 ..	....	....	....	....	....	....	....	....
Banks	4 772 ..	197.1	127.4	28.7	119.1	613.8	206.3	−888.9	131.0
of which: Short-term	4 774 ..	*207.2*	*82.4*	*−124.5*	*94.9*	*643.4*	*−14.3*	*−1,018.1*	*58.6*
Other sectors	4 775 ..	212.8	32.9	90.5	281.3	426.6	266.9	139.4	−48.7
of which: Short-term	4 777 ..	*41.8*	*−24.9*	*83.0*	*131.3*	*64.8*	*113.4*	*−77.0*	*20.4*
Currency and deposits	4 780 ..	−23.9	−18.4	3.2	.2	−2.7	42.6	72.8	−12.0
Monetary authorities	4 781 ..	....	....	....	....	....	....	....	....
General government	4 782 ..	....	....	....	....	....	....	....	....
Banks	4 783 ..	−23.9	−18.4	3.2	.2	−2.7	42.6	72.8	−12.0
Other sectors	4 784 ..	....	....	....	....	....	....	....	....
Other liabilities	4 786 ..	11.2	.6	.6	−1.9	2.8	118.1	240.9	−46.4
Monetary authorities	4 787 ..	4.3	−1.9	−2.1	−.5	1.3	−.3	205.9	3.7
of which: Short-term	4 789 ..	....	....	....	....	....	....	....	....
General government	4 790 ..	....	....	....	....	....	....	....	....
of which: Short-term	4 792 ..	....	....	....	....	....	....	....	....
Banks	4 793 ..	....	−2.3	.5	4.6	−2.2	−.3	16.3	....
of which: Short-term	4 795 ..	....	*.3*	*.5*	*4.6*	*−2.2*	*−.3*	*16.3*	....
Other sectors	4 796 ..	6.9	4.7	2.2	−6.1	3.7	118.7	18.8	−50.0
of which: Short-term	4 798 ..	*5.2*	*3.9*	*1.4*	*−4.6*	*3.8*	*118.9*	*16.9*	*−44.3*
E. RESERVE ASSETS	4 802 ..	**−338.9**	**−80.3**	**−393.5**	**−1,030.8**	**−1,147.7**	**348.0**	**−259.9**	**−561.1**
Monetary gold	4 812 ..	....	....	....	....	....	....	....	....
Special drawing rights	4 811 ..	....	−.1	.1	....	−.1	−.2	−207.2	.4
Reserve position in the Fund	4 810 ..	....	....	....	....	....	....	....	....
Foreign exchange	4 803 ..	−352.9	−77.0	−387.9	−1,015.5	−1,125.1	330.6	−60.4	−560.9
Other claims	4 813 ..	14.0	−3.2	−5.7	−15.3	−22.6	17.6	7.7	−.6
NET ERRORS AND OMISSIONS	4 998 ..	**35.1**	**63.7**	**144.5**	**149.5**	**171.0**	**−47.6**	**131.6**	**−41.2**

Table 3. INTERNATIONAL INVESTMENT POSITION (End-period stocks), 2003–2010

(Millions of U.S. dollars)

	Code	2003	2004	2005	2006	2007	2008	2009	2010
ASSETS	8 995 C.	**4,430.7**	**6,792.0**	**7,847.3**	**9,780.2**	**12,029.5**	**12,301.2**	**12,179.2**	**12,395.7**
Direct investment abroad	8 505 ..	**152.4**	**196.9**	**153.6**	**262.9**	**525.3**	**531.2**	**544.6**	**88.3**
Equity capital and reinvested earnings	8 506 ..	141.4	189.9	147.3	260.6	516.8	518.3	525.9	73.6
Claims on affiliated enterprises	8 507 ..	157.6	206.1	163.5	276.9	533.0	534.5	542.2	89.8
Liabilities to affiliated enterprises	8 508 ..	−16.3	−16.3	−16.3	−16.3	−16.3	−16.3	−16.3	−16.3
Other capital	8 530 ..	11.0	7.0	6.3	2.2	8.5	12.9	18.7	14.7
Claims on affiliated enterprises	8 535 ..	11.0	7.0	6.3	2.2	8.5	12.9	18.7	14.7
Liabilities to affiliated enterprises	8 540 ..	....	....	....	....	....	....	....	....
Portfolio investment	8 602 ..	**222.7**	**169.5**	**807.1**	**1,317.9**	**1,488.2**	**950.9**	**1,496.1**	**1,373.8**
Equity securities	8 610 ..	4.3	10.9	17.0	13.1	55.3	66.8	263.4	402.5
Monetary authorities	8 611 ..	....	....	....	....	....	....	....	....
General government	8 612 ..	....	....	....	....	....	....	....	....
Banks	8 613 ..	....	....	....	....	....	....	.1	31.1
Other sectors	8 614 ..	4.3	10.9	17.0	13.1	55.3	66.8	263.3	371.5
Debt securities	8 619 ..	218.4	158.6	790.0	1,304.7	1,432.9	884.1	1,232.7	971.3
Bonds and notes	8 620 ..	218.4	158.6	790.0	1,304.7	1,432.9	884.1	1,232.7	971.3
Monetary authorities	8 621 ..	....	....	....	....	....	....	....	....
General government	8 622 ..	....	....	....	....	....	....	....	....
Banks	8 623 ..	....	....	....	....	....	....	707.7	554.9
Other sectors	8 624 ..	218.4	158.6	790.0	1,304.7	1,432.9	884.1	525.0	416.3
Money market instruments	8 630 ..	....	....	....	....	....	....	....	....
Monetary authorities	8 631 ..	....	....	....	....	....	....	....	....
General government	8 632 ..	....	....	....	....	....	....	....	....
Banks	8 633 ..	....	....	....	....	....	....	....	....
Other sectors	8 634 ..	....	....	....	....	....	....	....	....
Financial derivatives	8 900 ..	....	....	....	....	....	....	....	....
Monetary authorities	8 901 ..	....	....	....	....	....	....	....	....
General government	8 902 ..	....	....	....	....	....	....	....	....
Banks	8 903 ..	....	....	....	....	....	....	....	....
Other sectors	8 904 ..	....	....	....	....	....	....	....	....
Other investment	8 703 ..	**2,136.0**	**4,503.8**	**4,574.0**	**5,084.9**	**5,902.4**	**7,020.0**	**6,072.4**	**6,303.8**
Trade credits	8 706 ..	601.6	566.5	593.3	637.4	705.4	743.1	737.1	939.1
General government	8 707 ..	....	....	....	....	....	....	....	....
of which: Short-term	8 709 ..	....	....	....	....	....	....	....	....
Other sectors	8 710 ..	601.6	566.5	593.3	637.4	705.4	743.1	737.1	939.1
of which: Short-term	8 712 ..	*560.7*	*519.1*	*545.1*	*599.0*	*638.0*	*663.7*	*619.7*	*731.6*
Loans	8 714 ..	96.0	81.7	68.4	94.7	119.2	125.3	93.1	209.0
Monetary authorities	8 715 ..	....	....	....	....	....	....	....	....
of which: Short-term	8 718 ..	....	....	....	....	....	....	....	....
General government	8 719 ..	....	....	....	....	....	....	....	....
of which: Short-term	8 721 ..	....	....	....	....	....	....	....	....
Banks	8 722 ..	....	.1	9.5	12.4	15.8	5.7	−.5	57.5
of which: Short-term	8 724 ..	....	....	....	....	....	....	....	....
Other sectors	8 725 ..	96.0	81.6	58.9	82.3	103.4	119.6	93.6	151.5
of which: Short-term	8 727 ..	*38.7*	*32.2*	*21.1*	*23.3*	*24.0*	*20.4*	*27.8*	*56.4*
Currency and deposits	8 730 ..	1,269.3	3,683.2	3,734.3	3,563.4	4,115.8	5,193.3	4,253.1	4,152.1
Monetary authorities	8 731 ..	35.7	35.7	35.7	35.7	35.7	35.7	35.7	35.7
General government	8 732 ..	....	....	....	....	....	....	....	....
Banks	8 733 ..	244.2	561.0	746.8	656.7	523.1	1,153.0	742.8	778.4
Other sectors	8 734 ..	989.4	3,086.5	2,951.8	2,871.0	3,557.0	4,004.5	3,474.6	3,338.0
Other assets	8 736 ..	169.1	172.5	178.0	789.4	961.9	958.9	989.1	1,003.6
Monetary authorities	8 737 ..	125.2	129.3	127.2	739.5	902.1	902.8	936.9	943.2
of which: Short-term	8 739 ..	....	....	....	....	....	....	....	....
General government	8 740 ..	....	....	....	....	....	....	....	....
of which: Short-term	8 742 ..	....	....	....	....	....	....	....	....
Banks	8 743 ..	....	2.5	8.0	13.3	16.5	10.1	10.8	8.4
of which: Short-term	8 745 ..	....	*2.5*	*8.0*	*13.3*	*16.5*	*10.1*	*10.8*	*8.4*
Other sectors	8 746 ..	43.9	40.7	42.8	36.6	43.3	46.0	41.4	52.1
of which: Short-term	8 748 ..	*21.7*	*17.3*	*17.3*	*14.0*	*19.8*	*19.6*	*33.5*	*26.7*
Reserve assets	8 802 ..	**1,919.6**	**1,921.8**	**2,312.6**	**3,114.6**	**4,113.6**	**3,798.7**	**4,066.2**	**4,629.7**
Monetary gold	8 812 ..	....	....	....	....	....	....	....	....
Special drawing rights	8 811 ..	.1	.1	....	....	.1	.3	208.3	204.2
Reserve position in the Fund	8 810 ..	29.7	31.1	28.6	30.1	31.6	30.8	31.4	30.8
Foreign exchange	8 803 ..	1,740.2	1,733.8	2,121.5	2,906.6	4,041.2	3,744.5	3,811.2	4,377.4
Other claims	8 813 ..	149.7	156.8	162.5	177.8	40.6	23.0	15.3	17.3

Table 3 (Concluded). INTERNATIONAL INVESTMENT POSITION (End-period stocks), 2003–2010

(Millions of U.S. dollars)

	Code	2003	2004	2005	2006	2007	2008	2009	2010
LIABILITIES..	8 995 D.	**9,553.2**	**9,854.2**	**11,519.9**	**13,253.9**	**16,563.3**	**19,063.8**	**20,075.0**	**21,931.0**
Direct investment in Costa Rica.........................	8 555 ..	**4,261.9**	**4,632.1**	**5,416.9**	**6,780.4**	**8,802.8**	**10,877.8**	**12,385.8**	**13,500.1**
Equity capital and reinvested earnings...........................	8 556 ..	3,952.8	4,193.9	4,684.2	5,975.0	8,020.7	9,972.1	11,668.2	13,250.7
Claims on direct investors.....................................	8 557 ..	....	....	....	....	....	....	....	....
Liabilities to direct investors.................................	8 558 ..	3,952.8	4,193.9	4,684.2	5,975.0	8,020.7	9,972.1	11,668.2	13,250.7
Other capital...	8 580 ..	309.2	438.2	732.7	805.5	782.0	905.7	717.7	249.3
Claims on direct investors.....................................	8 585 ..	....	....	....	....	....	....	....	....
Liabilities to direct investors.................................	8 590 ..	309.2	438.2	732.7	805.5	782.0	905.7	717.7	249.3
Portfolio investment..................................	8 652 ..	**863.6**	**632.7**	**961.2**	**1,004.3**	**1,157.2**	**921.7**	**1,010.2**	**1,187.1**
Equity securities...	8 660 ..	....	....	....	....	....	....	....	....
Banks..	8 663 ..	....	....	....	....	....	....	....	....
Other sectors...	8 664 ..	....	....	....	....	....	....	....	....
Debt securities..	8 669 ..	863.6	632.7	961.2	1,004.3	1,157.2	921.7	1,010.2	1,187.1
Bonds and notes..	8 670 ..	863.6	632.7	961.2	1,004.3	1,157.2	921.7	1,010.2	1,187.1
Monetary authorities....................................	8 671 ..	181.9	....	....	....	....	....	....	....
General government....................................	8 672 ..	538.8	481.7	955.6	1,001.0	1,122.1	883.5	985.2	1,148.0
Banks...	8 673 ..	17.6	17.6	....	....	....	....	....	....
Other sectors..	8 674 ..	125.3	133.3	5.6	3.3	35.1	38.2	25.1	39.1
Money market instruments.................................	8 680 ..	....	....	....	....	....	....	....	....
Monetary authorities....................................	8 681 ..	....	....	....	....	....	....	....	....
General government....................................	8 682 ..	....	....	....	....	....	....	....	....
Banks...	8 683 ..	....	....	....	....	....	....	....	....
Other sectors..	8 684 ..	....	....	....	....	....	....	....	....
Financial derivatives...............................	8 905 ..	....	....	....	....	....	....	....	....
Monetary authorities..	8 906 ..	....	....	....	....	....	....	....	....
General government...	8 907 ..	....	....	....	....	....	....	....	....
Banks..	8 908 ..	....	....	....	....	....	....	....	....
Other sectors...	8 909 ..	....	....	....	....	....	....	....	....
Other investment....................................	8 753 ..	**4,427.6**	**4,589.5**	**5,141.8**	**5,469.1**	**6,603.3**	**7,264.2**	**6,678.9**	**7,243.8**
Trade credits..	8 756 ..	990.2	1,151.0	1,517.2	1,551.5	1,721.5	1,548.9	1,257.9	1,302.2
General government...	8 757 ..	....	....	....	....	....	....	....	....
of which: Short-term....................................	8 759 ..								
Other sectors...	8 760 ..	990.2	1,151.0	1,517.2	1,551.5	1,721.5	1,548.9	1,257.9	1,302.2
of which: Short-term....................................	8 762 ..	*824.0*	*974.1*	*1,211.1*	*1,257.5*	*1,386.3*	*1,318.8*	*931.2*	*966.9*
Loans..	8 764 ..	3,361.5	3,375.2	3,566.0	3,861.6	4,825.3	5,502.5	4,881.9	5,471.7
Monetary authorities..	8 765 ..	308.8	234.3	168.5	84.1	77.7	69.8	58.0	50.7
of which: Use of Fund credit and loans from the Fund....	8 766 ..	....	....	....	....	....	....	....	....
of which: Short-term....................................	8 768 ..	....	....	....	....	....	....	....	....
General government...	8 769 ..	703.1	651.2	617.4	570.6	528.3	499.7	476.9	976.8
of which: Short-term....................................	8 771 ..	....	....	....	....	....	....	....	....
Banks..	8 772 ..	877.3	1,004.6	1,031.1	1,145.5	1,684.2	2,348.1	1,442.9	1,566.8
of which: Short-term....................................	8 774 ..	*588.6*	*671.0*	*551.5*	*641.7*	*1,309.0*	*1,649.5*	*651.1*	*709.7*
Other sectors...	8 775 ..	1,472.2	1,485.0	1,749.0	2,061.4	2,535.1	2,584.9	2,904.1	2,877.4
of which: Short-term....................................	8 777 ..	*252.5*	*221.4*	*289.7*	*413.7*	*486.0*	*440.9*	*481.6*	*539.6*
Currency and deposits..	8 780 ..	1.2	....	7.4	7.6	4.9	47.5	120.3	108.2
Monetary authorities..	8 781 ..	....	....	....	....	....	....	....	....
General government...	8 782 ..	....	....	....	....	....	....	....	....
Banks..	8 783 ..	1.2	....	7.4	7.6	4.9	47.5	120.3	108.2
Other sectors...	8 784 ..	....	....	....	....	....	....	....	....
Other liabilities...	8 786 ..	74.7	63.2	51.2	48.4	51.6	165.4	418.8	361.7
Monetary authorities..	8 787 ..	26.8	24.9	10.4	9.9	11.2	10.9	245.4	241.1
of which: Short-term....................................	8 789 ..	....	....	....	....	....	....	....	....
General government...	8 790 ..	....	....	....	....	....	....	....	....
of which: Short-term....................................	8 792 ..	....	....	....	....	....	....	....	....
Banks..	8 793 ..	....	.3	2.3	7.0	4.7	4.5	20.7	27.8
of which: Short-term....................................	8 795 ..	....	*.3*	*2.3*	*6.9*	*4.7*	*4.4*	*20.7*	*27.7*
Other sectors...	8 796 ..	47.8	38.0	38.5	31.6	35.6	150.0	152.7	92.8
of which: Short-term....................................	8 798 ..	*38.2*	*33.7*	*33.5*	*28.0*	*32.8*	*147.1*	*136.4*	*78.7*
NET INTERNATIONAL INVESTMENT POSITION........	8 995 ..	**−5,122.5**	**−3,062.2**	**−3,672.6**	**−3,473.7**	**−4,533.8**	**−6,762.5**	**−7,895.7**	**−9,535.3**
Conversion rates: Costa Rican colones per U.S. dollar (end of period)...	0 102 ..	**418.53**	**458.61**	**496.68**	**517.90**	**498.10**	**555.47**	**565.24**	**512.97**

Table 1. ANALYTIC PRESENTATION, 2003–2010

(Millions of U.S. dollars)

	Code	2003	2004	2005	2006	2007	2008	2009	2010
A. Current Account[1]	4 993 Z.	**294.2**	**240.9**	**39.7**	**479.0**	**−139.0**	**451.6**	**1,670.2**	....
Goods: exports f.o.b.	2 100 ..	5,787.7	6,919.3	7,697.4	8,477.3	8,668.8	10,390.1	10,503.3	....
Goods: imports f.o.b.	3 100 ..	−3,230.9	−4,291.4	−5,251.1	−5,368.3	−6,104.4	−7,068.6	−6,318.1	....
Balance on Goods	4 100 ..	*2,556.8*	*2,627.9*	*2,446.3*	*3,109.0*	*2,564.4*	*3,321.5*	*4,185.2*	
Services: credit	2 200 ..	664.0	762.7	832.5	844.6	933.0	1,024.5	975.0	
Services: debit	3 200 ..	−1,780.2	−2,032.6	−2,123.5	−2,233.1	−2,483.7	−2,659.9	−2,485.0	
Balance on Goods and Services	4 991 ..	*1,440.6*	*1,358.0*	*1,155.3*	*1,720.5*	*1,013.7*	*1,686.1*	*2,675.2*	
Income: credit	2 300 ..	170.6	189.7	193.9	196.2	218.1	236.6	223.9	
Income: debit	3 300 ..	−830.1	−841.3	−847.1	−906.4	−1,027.5	−1,138.7	−1,114.0	
Balance on Goods, Services, and Income	4 992 ..	*781.1*	*706.3*	*502.0*	*1,010.3*	*204.3*	*784.0*	*1,785.1*	
Current transfers: credit	2 379 Z.	196.4	187.4	194.8	217.7	476.6	582.3	760.9	
Current transfers: debit	3 379 ..	−683.3	−652.8	−657.2	−749.0	−819.9	−914.8	−875.8	....
B. Capital Account[1]	4 994 Z.	**13.7**	**145.9**	**185.2**	**33.0**	**92.9**	**89.3**	**103.8**	....
Capital account: credit	2 994 Z.	14.1	146.4	185.8	33.6	93.5	89.9	104.8	
Capital account: debit	3 994 ..	−.4	−.5	−.6	−.6	−.6	−.5	−1.1	
Total, Groups A Plus B	4 981 ..	*307.9*	*386.7*	*224.9*	*512.0*	*−46.2*	*540.9*	*1,774.0*	
C. Financial Account[1]	4 995 W.	**−1,035.3**	**−263.4**	**−482.5**	**−278.5**	**326.9**	**−203.9**	**−807.0**	....
Direct investment abroad	4 505 ..	....	....	....	....	....	....	....	
Direct investment in Côte d'Ivoire	4 555 Z.	165.3	283.0	311.9	318.9	426.8	446.1	380.9	
Portfolio investment assets	4 602 ..	−33.8	−37.5	−49.9	−24.2	−42.9	−28.6	−42.1	....
Equity securities	4 610 ..	−14.1	−6.6	26.9	−6.0	−7.7	−8.3	−42.1	
Debt securities	4 619 ..	−19.7	−30.9	−76.8	−18.2	−35.2	−20.3	....	
Portfolio investment liabilities	4 652 Z.	67.0	8.9	48.1	45.3	145.6	76.6	−8.8	....
Equity securities	4 660 ..	15.8	−4.9	13.9	1.6	1.6	1.9	−8.8	
Debt securities	4 669 Z.	51.3	13.8	34.2	43.7	143.9	74.6	....	
Financial derivatives	4 910 ..	−5.3	4.3	−4.3	−6.3	−7.0	−6.2	....	
Financial derivatives assets	4 900 ..	−7.9	−6.0	−5.2	−6.3	−7.0	−6.2	....	
Financial derivatives liabilities	4 905 ..	2.6	10.2	.9	....	....	....	....	
Other investment assets	4 703 ..	−341.7	−402.5	−497.9	−501.1	−377.1	−369.9	−1,432.0	
Monetary authorities	4 701 ..	....	....	....	....	....	....	....	
General government	4 704 ..	−4.0	−6.6	−3.2	−5.4	−1.3	....	−2.3	
Banks	4 705 ..	62.6	−32.9	−66.8	26.1	1.4	55.1	−60.0	
Other sectors	4 728 ..	−400.3	−363.0	−427.9	−521.8	−377.3	−425.0	−1,369.7	
Other investment liabilities	4 753 W.	−886.9	−119.6	−290.3	−111.1	181.6	−322.0	295.1	....
Monetary authorities	4 753 WA	−8.4	−5.6	−38.7	55.1	9.3	−5.4	479.6	
General government	4 753 ZB	−678.8	....	....	....	....	....	....	
Banks	4 753 ZC	−9.6	39.4	−42.8	47.9	−.2	−114.9	69.1	
Other sectors	4 753 ZD	−190.1	−153.5	−208.8	−214.2	172.4	−201.7	−253.6	....
Total, Groups A Through C	4 983 ..	*−727.3*	*123.3*	*−257.6*	*233.4*	*280.8*	*337.0*	*967.0*	....
D. Net Errors and Omissions	4 998 ..	**−887.9**	**26.6**	**−57.5**	**−10.1**	**39.9**	**−106.5**	**.8**	....
Total, Groups A Through D	4 984 ..	*−1,615.3*	*149.9*	*−315.1*	*223.3*	*320.7*	*230.5*	*967.8*	....
E. Reserves and Related Items	4 802 A.	**1,615.3**	**−149.9**	**315.1**	**−223.3**	**−320.7**	**−230.5**	**−967.8**	....
Reserve assets	4 802 ..	840.1	−249.7	148.4	−314.8	−473.9	135.5	−915.4	....
Use of Fund credit and loans	4 766 ..	−106.4	−127.1	−90.6	−57.7	15.1	21.7	155.2	....
Exceptional financing	4 920 ..	881.6	226.9	257.3	149.2	138.1	−387.7	−207.5	....
Conversion rates: CFA francs per U.S. dollar	0 101 ..	**581.20**	**528.28**	**527.47**	**522.89**	**479.27**	**447.81**	**472.19**	**495.28**

[1] Excludes components that have been classified in the categories of Group E.

Table 2. STANDARD PRESENTATION, 2003–2010

(Millions of U.S. dollars)

	Code	2003	2004	2005	2006	2007	2008	2009	2010
CURRENT ACCOUNT	4 993 ..	**294.2**	**240.9**	**39.7**	**479.0**	**−139.0**	**451.6**	**1,670.2**	....
A. GOODS	4 100 ..	**2,556.8**	**2,627.9**	**2,446.3**	**3,109.0**	**2,564.4**	**3,321.5**	**4,185.2**	....
Credit	2 100 ..	**5,787.7**	**6,919.3**	**7,697.4**	**8,477.3**	**8,668.8**	**10,390.1**	**10,503.3**	....
General merchandise: exports f.o.b.	2 110 ..	5,616.3	6,700.7	7,469.0	8,237.3	8,417.1	10,079.6	10,503.3	....
Goods for processing: exports f.o.b.	2 150 ..	72.1	85.3	94.5	96.7	95.8	116.7	....	
Repairs on goods	2 160 ..	17.4	17.1	14.0	18.4	24.6	21.7	....	
Goods procured in ports by carriers	2 170 ..	81.9	100.7	100.2	99.3	98.6	115.2		
Nonmonetary gold	2 180 ..	....	15.5	19.8	25.7	32.6	56.8		
Debit	3 100 ..	**−3,230.9**	**−4,291.4**	**−5,251.1**	**−5,368.3**	**−6,104.4**	**−7,068.6**	**−6,318.1**	....
General merchandise: imports f.o.b.	3 110 ..	−3,076.2	−4,126.2	−5,080.0	−5,190.3	−5,915.0	−6,858.2	−6,318.1	....
Goods for processing: imports f.o.b.	3 150 ..	−142.6	−149.2	−153.9	−158.9	−167.4	−186.4	....	
Repairs on goods	3 160 ..	....	−.1	−.4	....	....	....		
Goods procured in ports by carriers	3 170 ..	−12.0	−16.0	−16.8	−19.1	−22.0	−24.0		
Nonmonetary gold	3 180 ..	....	....	....	....	....	....		
B. SERVICES	4 200 ..	**−1,116.2**	**−1,269.9**	**−1,291.1**	**−1,388.5**	**−1,550.6**	**−1,635.4**	**−1,510.0**	....
Total credit	2 200 ..	*664.0*	*762.7*	*832.5*	*844.6*	*933.0*	*1,024.5*	*975.0*	....
Total debit	3 200 ..	*−1,780.2*	*−2,032.6*	*−2,123.5*	*−2,233.1*	*−2,483.7*	*−2,659.9*	*−2,485.0*	....
Transportation services, credit	2 205 ..	**114.1**	**138.3**	**188.6**	**202.2**	**210.6**	**235.3**	**234.1**	....
Passenger	2 850 ..	*7.4*	*8.9*	*9.6*	*10.7*	*11.8*	*13.2*	....	
Freight	2 851 ..	*31.3*	*40.5*	*50.9*	*42.0*	*46.2*	*48.5*	*47.1*	....
Other	2 852 ..	*75.4*	*88.9*	*128.1*	*149.5*	*152.6*	*173.7*	*187.0*	....
Sea transport, passenger	2 207 ..	....	....	....	....	....	....		
Sea transport, freight	2 208 ..	....	....	....	....	....	....	47.1	
Sea transport, other	2 209 ..	62.1	74.1	82.0	92.3	99.5	113.1	....	
Air transport, passenger	2 211 ..	3.6	4.2	4.4	4.7	5.1	5.9	....	
Air transport, freight	2 212 ..	....	....	....	....	....	....		
Air transport, other	2 213 ..	13.2	14.8	46.1	57.2	53.2	60.5	....	
Other transport, passenger	2 215 ..	3.8	4.7	5.2	6.0	6.7	7.3	....	
Other transport, freight	2 216 ..	31.3	40.5	50.9	42.0	46.2	48.5	....	
Other transport, other	2 217 ..	....	....	....	....	....	....	187.0	
Transportation services, debit	3 205 ..	**−702.7**	**−914.7**	**−1,092.4**	**−1,141.3**	**−1,303.7**	**−1,512.6**	**−1,347.1**	....
Passenger	3 850 ..	*−164.0*	*−190.1*	*−194.6*	*−210.2*	*−234.1*	*−255.8*	....	
Freight	3 851 ..	*−477.3*	*−647.5*	*−845.4*	*−877.5*	*−1,009.8*	*−1,191.5*	*−1,053.9*	....
Other	3 852 ..	*−61.4*	*−77.1*	*−52.4*	*−53.7*	*−59.8*	*−65.3*	*−293.2*	....
Sea transport, passenger	3 207 ..	....	....	....	....	....	....		
Sea transport, freight	3 208 ..	−437.2	−588.0	−771.2	−803.8	−925.0	−1,089.8	−1,053.9	
Sea transport, other	3 209 ..	−38.5	−51.3	−26.2	−27.0	−30.0	−32.8	....	
Air transport, passenger	3 211 ..	−164.0	−190.1	−194.6	−210.2	−234.1	−255.8		
Air transport, freight	3 212 ..	−22.0	−32.6	−40.6	−40.4	−46.5	−55.7	....	
Air transport, other	3 213 ..	−22.5	−25.3	−25.9	−26.7	−29.7	−32.5		
Other transport, passenger	3 215 ..	....	....	....	....	....	....		
Other transport, freight	3 216 ..	−18.1	−26.9	−33.6	−33.3	−38.4	−46.0	....	
Other transport, other	3 217 ..	−.3	−.4	−.4	....	....	....	−293.2	....
Travel, credit	2 236 ..	**69.0**	**81.6**	**83.3**	**93.1**	**102.9**	**115.6**	**113.4**	....
Business travel	2 237 ..	42.3	53.5	56.2	65.2	72.2	82.2	....	
Personal travel	2 240 ..	26.7	28.1	27.0	27.8	30.7	33.4	113.4	
Travel, debit	3 236 ..	**−387.3**	**−381.5**	**−353.9**	**−372.6**	**−371.6**	**−356.4**	**−344.5**	....
Business travel	3 237 ..	−17.7	−20.1	−21.1	−25.5	−28.3	−30.9	....	
Personal travel	3 240 ..	−369.6	−361.4	−332.8	−347.1	−343.3	−325.5	−344.5	
Other services, credit	2 200 BA ..	**480.9**	**542.8**	**560.5**	**549.3**	**619.5**	**673.6**	**627.6**	....
Communications	2 245 ..	70.9	81.8	86.0	87.8	97.3	106.5	....	
Construction	2 249 ..	10.7	17.6	16.8	21.7	29.6	30.8	....	
Insurance	2 253 ..	38.2	42.3	33.5	35.4	38.3	41.9	....	
Financial	2 260 ..	47.5	53.0	54.0	55.2	61.1	66.9	....	
Computer and information	2 262 ..	1.6	4.4	4.9	4.9	5.4	5.9	....	
Royalties and licence fees	2 266 ..	....	.2	....	....	....	.3	....	
Other business services	2 268 ..	207.9	221.5	230.1	205.9	229.9	252.7	468.1	
Personal, cultural, and recreational	2 287 ..	....	....	....	....	....	....		
Government, n.i.e.	2 291 ..	104.1	122.1	135.2	138.3	157.9	168.5	159.4	
Other services, debit	3 200 BA ..	**−690.2**	**−736.5**	**−677.2**	**−719.1**	**−808.3**	**−790.9**	**−793.4**	....
Communications	3 245 ..	−66.8	−61.0	−65.4	−66.7	−73.9	−79.9	....	
Construction	3 249 ..	−1.6	−4.1	−2.4	−4.1	−5.3	−8.0	....	
Insurance	3 253 ..	−45.6	−64.4	−63.6	−65.5	−73.0	−77.2	....	
Financial	3 260 ..	−110.5	−124.5	−119.6	−129.1	−143.8	−138.5	....	
Computer and information	3 262 ..	−11.0	−8.3	−6.1	−6.2	−6.9	−6.6	....	
Royalties and licence fees	3 266 ..	−10.7	−21.9	−10.3	−9.6	−22.0	−21.2	....	
Other business services	3 268 ..	−320.0	−314.7	−267.2	−290.6	−261.9	−285.9	−632.3	
Personal, cultural, and recreational	3 287 ..	−.7	−.8	−.8	−.8	−.9	−1.0	....	
Government, n.i.e.	3 291 ..	−123.4	−136.9	−141.8	−146.4	−220.7	−172.5	−161.1	....

Côte d'Ivoire 662

Table 2 (Continued). STANDARD PRESENTATION, 2003–2010

(Millions of U.S. dollars)

	Code	2003	2004	2005	2006	2007	2008	2009	2010
C. INCOME	4 300	**−659.5**	**−651.7**	**−653.2**	**−710.3**	**−809.4**	**−902.1**	**−890.0**	....
Total credit	2 300	*170.6*	*189.7*	*193.9*	*196.2*	*218.1*	*236.6*	*223.9*	....
Total debit	3 300	*−830.1*	*−841.3*	*−847.1*	*−906.4*	*−1,027.5*	*−1,138.7*	*−1,114.0*	....
Compensation of employees, credit	2 310	**141.6**	**158.2**	**161.3**	**164.7**	**182.3**	**196.4**	**185.5**	....
Compensation of employees, debit	3 310	**−14.6**	**−16.4**	**−16.8**	**−17.3**	**−19.2**	**−21.0**	**−19.5**	....
Investment income, credit	2 320	**29.0**	**31.5**	**32.6**	**31.5**	**35.7**	**40.2**	**38.5**	....
Direct investment income	2 330	3.0	3.2	4.6	4.7	5.3	5.8	....	....
Dividends and distributed branch profits	2 332	2.2	2.6	2.7	2.9	3.3	3.7	....	....
Reinvested earnings and undistributed branch profits	2 333	....	....	....	....	....	....	....	....
Income on debt (interest)	2 334	.8	.6	1.8	1.9	2.0	2.1	....	....
Portfolio investment income	2 339	4.4	4.4	5.3	4.6	5.2	5.8	....	....
Income on equity	2 340	.3	....	.2	....	....	.2	....	....
Income on bonds and notes	2 350	2.0	2.1	2.7	2.2	2.5	2.7	....	....
Income on money market instruments	2 360	2.1	2.3	2.3	2.4	2.7	2.9	....	....
Other investment income	2 370	21.6	23.9	22.8	22.2	25.2	28.6	38.5	....
Investment income, debit	3 320	**−815.4**	**−824.9**	**−830.4**	**−889.2**	**−1,008.2**	**−1,117.6**	**−1,094.4**	....
Direct investment income	3 330	−334.7	−363.7	−370.1	−477.9	−530.8	−581.2	....	....
Dividends and distributed branch profits	3 332	−171.0	−185.0	−188.3	−243.1	−270.0	−295.6	....	....
Reinvested earnings and undistributed branch profits	3 333	−99.3	−105.4	−107.2	−138.4	−153.7	−168.3	....	....
Income on debt (interest)	3 334	−64.4	−73.4	−74.7	−96.4	−107.1	−117.3	....	....
Portfolio investment income	3 339	−40.1	−42.3	−48.2	−57.2	−63.5	−70.5	....	....
Income on equity	3 340	−33.7	−36.5	−37.3	−45.8	−50.9	−56.7	....	....
Income on bonds and notes	3 350	−6.4	−5.8	−10.9	−11.4	−12.6	−13.8	....	....
Income on money market instruments	3 360	−.1	....	....	....	....	....	....	....
Other investment income	3 370	−440.6	−418.9	−412.0	−354.0	−413.9	−466.0	−1,094.4	....
D. CURRENT TRANSFERS	4 379	**−486.9**	**−465.5**	**−462.4**	**−531.3**	**−343.3**	**−332.5**	**−114.9**	....
Credit	2 379	**196.4**	**187.4**	**194.8**	**217.7**	**476.6**	**582.3**	**760.9**	....
General government	2 380	55.4	4.0	....	....	219.1	323.2	553.8	....
Other sectors	2 390	141.0	183.4	194.8	217.7	257.5	259.1	207.1	....
Workers' remittances	2 391	....	1.0	1.9	2.1	2.4	2.5	....	....
Other current transfers	2 392	141.0	182.4	192.9	215.6	255.1	256.5	207.1	....
Debit	3 379	**−683.3**	**−652.8**	**−657.2**	**−749.0**	**−819.9**	**−914.8**	**−875.8**	....
General government	3 380	−19.1	−21.4	−21.8	−36.2	−55.7	−71.4	−58.5	....
Other sectors	3 390	−664.2	−631.5	−635.4	−712.8	−764.2	−843.4	−817.4	....
Workers' remittances	3 391	−613.2	−575.0	−580.2	−643.2	−679.1	−734.6	....	....
Other current transfers	3 392	−50.9	−56.5	−55.2	−69.6	−85.1	−108.8	−817.4	....
CAPITAL AND FINANCIAL ACCOUNT	4 996	**593.7**	**−267.4**	**17.8**	**−468.9**	**99.1**	**−345.1**	**−1,671.0**	....
CAPITAL ACCOUNT	4 994	**13.7**	**145.9**	**185.2**	**33.0**	**92.9**	**89.3**	**222.6**	....
Total credit	2 994	*14.1*	*146.4*	*185.8*	*33.6*	*93.5*	*89.9*	*223.6*	....
Total debit	3 994	*−.4*	*−.5*	*−.6*	*−.6*	*−.6*	*−.5*	*−1.1*	....
Capital transfers, credit	2 400	**14.1**	**143.7**	**181.3**	**28.9**	**91.0**	**87.0**	**223.6**	....
General government	2 401	14.1	143.7	179.3	28.9	91.0	86.6	223.6	....
Debt forgiveness	2 402	....	....	....	....	....	....	118.8	....
Other capital transfers	2 410	14.1	143.7	179.3	28.9	91.0	86.6	104.8	....
Other sectors	2 430	....	....	1.9	....	....	.3	....	....
Migrants' transfers	2 431	....	....	....	....	....	....	....	....
Debt forgiveness	2 432	....	....	....	....	....	....	....	....
Other capital transfers	2 440	....	....	1.9	....	....	.3	....	....
Capital transfers, debit	3 400	....	....	....	....	....	....	....	....
General government	3 401	....	....	....	....	....	....	....	....
Debt forgiveness	3 402	....	....	....	....	....	....	....	....
Other capital transfers	3 410	....	....	....	....	....	....	....	....
Other sectors	3 430	....	....	....	....	....	....	....	....
Migrants' transfers	3 431	....	....	....	....	....	....	....	....
Debt forgiveness	3 432	....	....	....	....	....	....	....	....
Other capital transfers	3 440	....	....	....	....	....	....	....	....
Nonproduced nonfinancial assets, credit	2 480	....	**2.7**	**4.6**	**4.7**	**2.5**	**2.9**	....	....
Nonproduced nonfinancial assets, debit	3 480	**−.4**	**−.5**	**−.6**	**−.6**	**−.6**	**−.5**	**−1.1**	....

Table 2 (Continued). STANDARD PRESENTATION, 2003–2010

(Millions of U.S. dollars)

	Code	2003	2004	2005	2006	2007	2008	2009	2010
FINANCIAL ACCOUNT	4 995 ..	**580.0**	**−413.3**	**−167.4**	**−501.8**	**6.3**	**−434.4**	**−1,893.6**	....
A. DIRECT INVESTMENT	4 500 ..	**165.3**	**283.0**	**311.9**	**318.9**	**426.8**	**446.1**	**380.9**	....
Direct investment abroad	4 505 ..	....	....	....	....	....	....	....	....
Equity capital	4 510 ..	....	....	....	....	....	....	....	
Claims on affiliated enterprises	4 515 ..	....	....	....	....	....	....	....	
Liabilities to affiliated enterprises	4 520 ..	....	....	....	....	....	....	....	
Reinvested earnings	4 525 ..	....	....	....	....	....	....	....	
Other capital	4 530 ..	....	....	....	....	....	....	....	
Claims on affiliated enterprises	4 535 ..	....	....	....	....	....	....	....	
Liabilities to affiliated enterprises	4 540 ..	....	....	....	....	....	....	....	
Direct investment in Côte d'Ivoire	4 555 ..	**165.3**	**283.0**	**311.9**	**318.9**	**426.8**	**446.1**	**380.9**	....
Equity capital	4 560 ..	119.7	221.4	195.1	165.2	250.5	263.0	....	
Claims on direct investors	4 565 ..	....	....	....	....	....	....	....	
Liabilities to direct investors	4 570 ..	119.7	221.4	195.1	165.2	250.5	263.0	....	
Reinvested earnings	4 575 ..	99.3	105.4	107.2	138.4	153.7	168.3	....	
Other capital	4 580 ..	−53.6	−43.8	9.6	15.2	22.5	14.8	380.9	....
Claims on direct investors	4 585 ..	−45.1	−47.1	−37.0	−31.8	−16.4	−20.3	−37.6	
Liabilities to direct investors	4 590 ..	−8.5	3.3	46.6	47.0	38.9	35.2	418.5	....
B. PORTFOLIO INVESTMENT	4 600 ..	**33.2**	**−28.6**	**−1.8**	**21.1**	**102.7**	**48.0**	**−50.9**	....
Assets	4 602 ..	**−33.8**	**−37.5**	**−49.9**	**−24.2**	**−42.9**	**−28.6**	**−42.1**	....
Equity securities	4 610 ..	−14.1	−6.6	26.9	−6.0	−7.7	−8.3	−42.1	....
Monetary authorities	4 611 ..	....	....	....	....	....	....		
General government	4 612 ..	....	....	....	....	....	....		
Banks	4 613 ..	....	....	15.6	....	....	....		
Other sectors	4 614 ..	−14.1	−6.6	11.3	−6.0	−7.7	−8.3	−42.1	
Debt securities	4 619 ..	−19.7	−30.9	−76.8	−18.2	−35.2	−20.3		
Bonds and notes	4 620 ..	−11.5	−19.6	−29.5	−20.3	−33.8	−20.3		
Monetary authorities	4 621 ..	....	....	....	....	....	....		
General government	4 622 ..	....	....	....	....	−11.3	....		
Banks	4 623 ..	....	....	−9.5	....	....	....		
Other sectors	4 624 ..	−11.5	−19.6	−20.0	−20.3	−22.5	−20.3		
Money market instruments	4 630 ..	−8.2	−11.2	−47.3	2.1	−1.4	....		
Monetary authorities	4 631 ..	....	....	....	....	....	....		
General government	4 632 ..	....	....	....	....	....	....		
Banks	4 633 ..	....	....	−26.5	....	....	....		
Other sectors	4 634 ..	−8.2	−11.2	−20.8	2.1	−1.4	....		
Liabilities	4 652 ..	**67.0**	**8.9**	**48.1**	**45.3**	**145.6**	**76.6**	**−8.8**	....
Equity securities	4 660 ..	15.8	−4.9	13.9	1.6	1.6	1.9	−8.8	
Banks	4 663 ..	....	−4.3	12.1	....	....	....		
Other sectors	4 664 ..	15.8	−.6	1.8	1.6	1.6	1.9	−8.8	
Debt securities	4 669 ..	51.3	13.8	34.2	43.7	143.9	74.6		
Bonds and notes	4 670 ..	51.3	12.3	29.5	42.4	58.6	52.3		
Monetary authorities	4 671 ..	....	....	....	....	....	....		
General government	4 672 ..	51.1	2.3	28.2	43.2	59.0	51.1		
Banks	4 673 ..	....	....	....	....	....	....		
Other sectors	4 674 ..	.1	10.0	1.2	−.8	−.5	1.2		
Money market instruments	4 680 ..	....	1.5	4.7	1.3	85.3	22.3		
Monetary authorities	4 681 ..	....	....	....	....	....	....		
General government	4 682 ..	....	....	4.7	1.3	85.3	22.3		
Banks	4 683 ..	....	....	....	....	....	....		
Other sectors	4 684 ..	....	1.5	....	....	....	....		
C. FINANCIAL DERIVATIVES	4 910 ..	**−5.3**	**4.3**	**−4.3**	**−6.3**	**−7.0**	**−6.2**	....	....
Monetary authorities	4 911 ..	....	....	....	....	....	....		
General government	4 912 ..	....	....	....	....	....	....		
Banks	4 913 ..	....	....	....	....	....	....		
Other sectors	4 914 ..	−5.3	4.3	−4.3	−6.3	−7.0	−6.2		
Assets	4 900 ..	**−7.9**	**−6.0**	**−5.2**	**−6.3**	**−7.0**	**−6.2**	....	....
Monetary authorities	4 901 ..	....	....	....	....	....	....		
General government	4 902 ..	....	....	....	....	....	....		
Banks	4 903 ..	....	....	....	....	....	....		
Other sectors	4 904 ..	−7.9	−6.0	−5.2	−6.3	−7.0	−6.2		
Liabilities	4 905 ..	**2.6**	**10.2**	**.9**	....	....	....	....	....
Monetary authorities	4 906 ..	....	....	....	....	....	....		
General government	4 907 ..	....	....	....	....	....	....		
Banks	4 908 ..	....	....	....	....	....	....		
Other sectors	4 909 ..	2.6	10.2	.9	....	....	....		

Table 2 (Concluded). STANDARD PRESENTATION, 2003–2010

(Millions of U.S. dollars)

	Code	2003	2004	2005	2006	2007	2008	2009	2010
D. OTHER INVESTMENT	4 700	**−453.3**	**−422.3**	**−621.6**	**−520.7**	**−42.3**	**−1,057.8**	**−1,308.1**	....
Assets	4 703	**−341.7**	**−402.5**	**−497.9**	**−501.1**	**−377.1**	**−369.9**	**−1,432.0**	....
Trade credits	4 706	−74.1	−116.5	−118.9	−134.7	−90.7	−111.7	....	
General government	4 707	....	....	....	....	....	....	....	
of which: Short-term	4 709	....	....	....	....	....	....	....	
Other sectors	4 710	−74.1	−116.5	−118.9	−134.7	−90.7	−111.7	....	
of which: Short-term	4 712	*−74.1*	*−116.5*	*−118.9*	*−134.7*	*−90.7*	*−111.7*	....	
Loans	4 714	38.7	−74.1	−.3	−3.6	−25.4	31.5	....	
Monetary authorities	4 715	....	....	....	....	....	....	....	
of which: Short-term	4 718	....	....	....	....	....	....	....	
General government	4 719	....	....	....	....	....	....	....	
of which: Short-term	4 721	....	....	....	....	....	....	....	
Banks	4 722	48.5	−63.3	8.4	7.9	−18.4	35.7	....	
of which: Short-term	4 724	*44.7*	*−57.8*	*5.7*	*12.4*	*3.9*	*34.0*	....	
Other sectors	4 725	−9.8	−10.8	−8.7	−11.6	−7.0	−4.3		
of which: Short-term	4 727	....	....	....	....	....	....		
Currency and deposits	4 730	−236.9	−141.4	−315.5	−263.2	−155.9	−163.9		
Monetary authorities	4 731	....	....	....	....	....	....		
General government	4 732	....	....	....	....	....	....		
Banks	4 733	11.0	32.1	−78.0	18.1	20.8	18.2		
Other sectors	4 734	−247.9	−173.5	−237.5	−281.3	−176.6	−182.1	....	
Other assets	4 736	−69.4	−70.4	−63.2	−99.6	−105.2	−125.7	−1,432.0	....
Monetary authorities	4 737	....	....	....	....	....	....		
of which: Short-term	4 739	....	....	....	....	....	....		
General government	4 740	−4.0	−6.6	−3.2	−5.4	−1.3	....	−2.3	
of which: Short-term	4 742	*.2*	*.2*	*−3.2*	....	....	....		
Banks	4 743	3.1	−1.6	2.8	....	−1.0	1.2	−60.0	
of which: Short-term	4 745	*3.1*	*−1.6*	*2.8*	....	*−1.0*	*1.2*	*−60.0*	
Other sectors	4 746	−68.5	−62.1	−62.8	−94.2	−103.0	−126.9	−1,369.7	
of which: Short-term	4 748	*−68.5*	*−62.1*	*−62.8*	*−94.2*	*−103.0*	*−126.9*	*−1,369.7*	
Liabilities	4 753	**−111.7**	**−19.8**	**−123.7**	**−19.6**	**334.8**	**−687.9**	**123.9**	....
Trade credits	4 756	−186.6	−168.3	−211.4	−217.4	169.0	−209.8	....	
General government	4 757	....	....	....	....	....	....	....	
of which: Short-term	4 759	....	....	....	....	....	....	....	
Other sectors	4 760	−186.6	−168.3	−211.4	−217.4	169.0	−209.8	....	
of which: Short-term	4 762	*−186.6*	*−168.3*	*−211.4*	*−217.4*	*169.0*	*−209.8*	....	
Loans	4 764	−588.1	−714.9	−642.5	−592.9	−292.6	−550.0	184.2	
Monetary authorities	4 765	−106.4	−127.1	−90.6	−57.7	15.1	21.7	208.1	
of which: Use of Fund credit and loans from the Fund	4 766	*−106.4*	*−127.1*	*−90.6*	*−57.7*	*15.1*	*21.7*	*155.2*	
of which: Short-term	4 768	....	....	....	....	....	....	....	
General government	4 769	−454.9	−584.5	−534.4	−511.2	−418.1	−444.2	−23.9	
of which: Short-term	4 771	....	....	....	....	....	....	*233.0*	
Banks	4 772	−18.8	23.4	−11.0	−18.2	109.0	−130.0	....	
of which: Short-term	4 774	....	....	*−14.8*	*−19.5*	*86.4*	*−102.0*	....	
Other sectors	4 775	−7.9	−26.7	−6.4	−5.8	1.5	2.4	....	
of which: Short-term	4 777	*23.5*	*12.7*	*5.0*	*5.8*	*5.4*	*5.7*	....	
Currency and deposits	4 780	9.4	19.1	−33.6	76.5	−106.4	4.4	....	
Monetary authorities	4 781	−1.2	2.5	−1.8	10.9	2.6	−11.2	....	
General government	4 782	....	....	....	....	....	....		
Banks	4 783	10.6	16.6	−31.7	65.6	−109.0	15.6	....	
Other sectors	4 784	....	....	....	....	....	....		
Other liabilities	4 786	653.7	844.4	763.8	714.1	564.7	67.5	−60.3	....
Monetary authorities	4 787	−7.2	−8.1	−36.9	44.2	6.7	5.8	426.6	
of which: Short-term	4 789	....	....	....	....	....	....	....	
General government	4 790	657.8	811.4	791.7	660.4	556.3	56.5	−302.4	
of which: Short-term	4 792	*657.8*	*811.4*	*791.7*	*660.4*	*556.3*	*56.5*	*−302.4*	
Banks	4 793	−1.4	−.5	−.1	.5	−.2	−.5	69.1	
of which: Short-term	4 795	*−1.4*	*−.5*	*−.1*	*.5*	*−.2*	*−.5*	*69.1*	
Other sectors	4 796	4.5	41.6	9.1	9.0	1.9	5.7	−253.6	
of which: Short-term	4 798	*4.5*	*41.6*	*9.1*	*9.0*	*1.9*	*5.7*	*−253.6*	
E. RESERVE ASSETS	4 802	**840.1**	**−249.7**	**148.4**	**−314.8**	**−473.9**	**135.5**	**−915.4**	....
Monetary gold	4 812	....	....	....	....	....	....	....	
Special drawing rights	4 811	1.0	.1	−.5	−.3	.5	−.7	−424.8	
Reserve position in the Fund	4 810	−.2	....	−.1	−.1	−.1	−.1	−.1	
Foreign exchange	4 803	839.3	−249.7	148.9	−314.4	−474.3	136.3	−490.5	
Other claims	4 813	....	....	....	....	....	....	....	
NET ERRORS AND OMISSIONS	4 998	**−887.9**	**26.6**	**−57.5**	**−10.1**	**39.9**	**−106.5**	**.8**	....

Table 3. INTERNATIONAL INVESTMENT POSITION (End-period stocks), 2003–2010

(Millions of U.S. dollars)

	Code	2003	2004	2005	2006	2007	2008	2009	2010
ASSETS	8 995 C.	**5,361.5**	**6,545.2**	**6,052.7**	**7,645.5**	**9,514.7**	**9,252.6**	**12,041.4**	....
Direct investment abroad	8 505 ..	....	....	....	....	....	....	....	....
Equity capital and reinvested earnings	8 506 ..	....	....	....	....	....	....	....	....
Claims on affiliated enterprises	8 507 ..	....	....	....	....	....	....	....	....
Liabilities to affiliated enterprises	8 508 ..	....	....	....	....	....	....	....	....
Other capital	8 530 ..	....	....	....	....	....	....	....	....
Claims on affiliated enterprises	8 535 ..	....	....	....	....	....	....	....	....
Liabilities to affiliated enterprises	8 540 ..	....	....	....	....	....	....	....	....
Portfolio investment	8 602 ..	**335.9**	**409.9**	**407.3**	**486.7**	**597.7**	**598.1**	**662.9**	....
Equity securities	8 610 ..	35.4	45.4	13.8	21.7	32.6	38.7	83.8	....
Monetary authorities	8 611 ..	....	....	....	....	....	....	....	....
General government	8 612 ..	....	....	....	....	....	....	....	....
Banks	8 613 ..	....	....	....	....	....	....	....	....
Other sectors	8 614 ..	35.4	....	....	....	....	....	....	....
Debt securities	8 619 ..	300.5	364.5	393.5	465.0	565.1	559.4	579.1	....
Bonds and notes	8 620 ..	....	....	....	....	....	....	....	....
Monetary authorities	8 621 ..	....	....	....	....	....	....	....	....
General government	8 622 ..	....	....	....	....	....	....	....	....
Banks	8 623 ..	....	....	....	....	....	....	....	....
Other sectors	8 624 ..	....	....	....	....	....	....	....	....
Money market instruments	8 630 ..	300.5	364.5	393.5	465.0	565.1	559.4	579.1	....
Monetary authorities	8 631 ..	....	....	....	....	....	....	....	....
General government	8 632 ..	....	....	....	....	....	....	....	....
Banks	8 633 ..	....	....	....	....	....	....	....	....
Other sectors	8 634 ..	300.5	364.5	393.5	465.0	565.1	559.4	579.1	....
Financial derivatives	8 900 ..	....	....	....	....	....	....	....	....
Monetary authorities	8 901 ..	....	....	....	....	....	....	....	....
General government	8 902 ..	....	....	....	....	....	....	....	....
Banks	8 903 ..	....	....	....	....	....	....	....	....
Other sectors	8 904 ..	....	....	....	....	....	....	....	....
Other investment	8 703 ..	**3,721.7**	**4,455.3**	**4,331.0**	**5,361.1**	**6,398.0**	**6,401.8**	**8,111.7**	....
Trade credits	8 706 ..	1,043.9	1,253.6	1,198.6	1,479.4	1,751.3	1,761.7	1,823.6	....
General government	8 707 ..	....	....	....	....	....	....	....	....
of which: Short-term	8 709 ..	....	....	....	....	....	....	....	....
Other sectors	8 710 ..	1,043.9	1,253.6	1,198.6	1,479.4	1,751.3	1,761.7	1,823.6	....
of which: Short-term	8 712 ..	....	....	....	....	....	....	....	....
Loans	8 714 ..	76.7	163.9	142.3	162.6	209.1	169.5	175.5	....
Monetary authorities	8 715 ..	....	....	....	....	....	....	....	....
of which: Short-term	8 718 ..	....	....	....	....	....	....	....	....
General government	8 719 ..	....	....	....	....	....	....	....	....
of which: Short-term	8 721 ..	....	....	....	....	....	....	....	....
Banks	8 722 ..	....	....	....	....	....	....	....	....
of which: Short-term	8 724 ..	....	....	....	....	....	....	....	....
Other sectors	8 725 ..	76.7	163.9	142.3	162.6	209.1	169.5	175.5	....
of which: Short-term	8 727 ..	....	....	....	....	....	....	....	....
Currency and deposits	8 730 ..	2,214.1	2,543.0	2,501.7	3,069.1	3,598.2	3,557.4	3,682.3	....
Monetary authorities	8 731 ..	....	....	....	....	....	....	....	....
General government	8 732 ..	....	....	....	....	....	....	....	....
Banks	8 733 ..	....	351.2	412.9	470.4	544.1	570.4	652.5	....
Other sectors	8 734 ..	2,214.1	2,191.8	2,088.8	2,598.7	3,054.0	2,986.9	3,029.9	....
Other assets	8 736 ..	387.1	494.7	488.5	649.9	839.6	913.2	2,430.2	....
Monetary authorities	8 737 ..	....	....	....	....	....	....	....	....
of which: Short-term	8 739 ..	....	....	....	....	....	....	....	....
General government	8 740 ..	....	....	....	....	....	....	....	....
of which: Short-term	8 742 ..	....	....	....	....	....	....	....	....
Banks	8 743 ..	....	....	....	....	....	....	....	....
of which: Short-term	8 745 ..	....	....	....	....	....	....	....	....
Other sectors	8 746 ..	387.1	494.7	488.5	649.9	839.6	913.2	2,430.2	....
of which: Short-term	8 748 ..	....	....	....	....	....	....	....	....
Reserve assets	8 802 ..	**1,303.8**	**1,680.0**	**1,314.4**	**1,797.7**	**2,519.0**	**2,252.7**	**3,266.8**	....
Monetary gold	8 812 ..	....	....	....	....	....	....	....	....
Special drawing rights	8 811 ..	.3	.2	.6	1.0	.6	1.2	427.5	420.5
Reserve position in the Fund	8 810 ..	.8	.9	.9	1.0	1.1	1.2	1.3	1.3
Foreign exchange	8 803 ..	1,302.7	1,678.9	1,312.8	1,795.7	2,517.3	2,250.3	2,838.1	....
Other claims	8 813 ..	....	....	....	....	....	....	....	....

Table 3 (Concluded). INTERNATIONAL INVESTMENT POSITION (End-period stocks), 2003–2010

(Millions of U.S. dollars)

	Code	2003	2004	2005	2006	2007	2008	2009	2010
LIABILITIES...	8 995 D.	**17,844.4**	**18,863.8**	**16,838.2**	**19,265.3**	**22,465.2**	**21,542.2**	**21,639.4**	....
Direct investment in Côte d'Ivoire.......................	8 555 ..	**3,572.1**	**4,162.8**	**3,901.3**	**4,690.1**	**5,701.5**	**5,814.0**	**6,413.2**	....
Equity capital and reinvested earnings...................	8 556 ..	3,572.1	4,162.8	3,901.3	4,690.1	5,701.5	5,814.0	6,413.2	....
Claims on direct investors.........................	8 557 ..	....	....	....	....	....	....	....	....
Liabilities to direct investors....................	8 558 ..	....	....	....	....	....	....	....	....
Other capital..	8 580 ..	....	....	....	....	....	....	....	....
Claims on direct investors.........................	8 585 ..	....	....	....	....	....	....	....	....
Liabilities to direct investors....................	8 590 ..	....	....	....	....	....	....	....	....
Portfolio investment.......................................	8 652 ..	**435.2**	**490.4**	**471.2**	**573.6**	**797.7**	**826.9**	**846.8**	....
Equity securities.......................................	8 660 ..	....	....	....	....	....	....	....	....
Banks..	8 663 ..	....	....	....	....	....	....	....	....
Other sectors.......................................	8 664 ..	....	....	....	....	....	....	....	....
Debt securities...	8 669 ..	435.2	490.4	471.2	573.6	797.7	826.9	846.8	....
Bonds and notes...................................	8 670 ..	....	....	....	....	....	....	....	....
Monetary authorities...........................	8 671 ..	....	....	....	....	....	....	....	....
General government...........................	8 672 ..	....	....	....	....	....	....	....	....
Banks..	8 673 ..	....	....	....	....	....	....	....	....
Other sectors.......................................	8 674 ..	....	....	....	....	....	....	....	....
Money market instruments...........................	8 680 ..	435.2	490.4	471.2	573.6	797.7	826.9	846.8	....
Monetary authorities...........................	8 681 ..	....	....	....	....	....	....	....	....
General government...........................	8 682 ..	....	....	....	....	....	....	....	....
Banks..	8 683 ..	....	....	....	....	....	....	....	....
Other sectors.......................................	8 684 ..	435.2	490.4	471.2	573.6	797.7	826.9	846.8	....
Financial derivatives.....................................	8 905 ..	....	....	....	....	....	....	....	....
Monetary authorities...................................	8 906 ..	....	....	....	....	....	....	....	....
General government...................................	8 907 ..	....	....	....	....	....	....	....	....
Banks..	8 908 ..	....	....	....	....	....	....	....	....
Other sectors...	8 909 ..	....	....	....	....	....	....	....	....
Other investment...	8 753 ..	**13,837.0**	**14,210.6**	**12,465.8**	**14,001.7**	**15,966.1**	**14,901.4**	**14,379.4**	....
Trade credits...	8 756 ..	932.9	821.5	511.0	342.2	564.3	334.2	345.9	....
General government................................	8 757 ..	....	....	....	....	....	....	....	....
of which: Short-term...........................	8 759 ..	....	....	....	....	....	....	....	....
Other sectors.......................................	8 760 ..	932.9	821.5	511.0	342.2	564.3	334.2	345.9	....
of which: Short-term...........................	8 762 ..	....	....	....	....	....	....	....	....
Loans..	8 764 ..	12,436.4	12,827.7	11,526.9	13,044.9	14,820.2	14,000.4	13,464.3	....
Monetary authorities...............................	8 765 ..	425.0	311.4	198.4	150.1	173.5	188.3	351.8	....
of which: Use of Fund credit and loans from the Fund....	8 766 ..	*425.0*	*311.4*	*198.4*	*150.1*	*173.5*	*188.3*	*351.8*	*382.6*
of which: Short-term...........................	8 768 ..	....	....	....	....	....	....	....	....
General government...........................	8 769 ..	11,841.9	12,337.1	11,189.9	12,765.4	14,383.2	13,684.1	12,980.1	....
of which: Short-term...........................	8 771 ..	*1,233.8*	*2,263.5*	*2,795.9*	*3,774.0*	*5,183.4*	*5,245.5*	*1,270.9*	....
Banks..	8 772 ..	127.9	163.6	131.2	127.4	259.6	121.9	126.2	....
of which: Short-term...........................	8 774 ..	*127.9*	*163.6*	*131.2*	*127.4*	*259.6*	*121.9*	*126.2*	....
Other sectors.......................................	8 775 ..	41.6	15.6	7.4	2.1	4.0	6.1	6.3	....
of which: Short-term...........................	8 777 ..	....	....	....	....	....	....	....	....
Currency and deposits................................	8 780 ..	194.9	231.1	168.3	268.3	185.4	181.9	188.3	....
Monetary authorities...............................	8 781 ..	....	....	....	....	....	....	....	....
General government...........................	8 782 ..	....	....	....	....	....	....	....	....
Banks..	8 783 ..	194.9	231.1	168.3	268.3	185.4	181.9	188.3	....
Other sectors.......................................	8 784 ..	....	....	....	....	....	....	....	....
Other liabilities.......................................	8 786 ..	272.7	330.3	259.6	346.2	396.1	384.9	380.9	....
Monetary authorities...............................	8 787 ..	....	....	....	....	....	....	487.4	....
of which: Short-term...........................	8 789 ..	....	....	....	....	....	....	....	....
General government...........................	8 790 ..	....	....	....	....	....	....	....	....
of which: Short-term...........................	8 792 ..	....	....	....	....	....	....	....	....
Banks..	8 793 ..	272.7	330.3	259.6	346.2	396.1	384.9	−106.5	....
of which: Short-term...........................	8 795 ..	*272.7*	*330.3*	*259.6*	*346.2*	*396.1*	*384.9*	*−106.5*	....
Other sectors.......................................	8 796 ..	....	....	....	....	....	....	....	....
of which: Short-term...........................	8 798 ..	....	....	....	....	....	....	....	....
NET INTERNATIONAL INVESTMENT POSITION........	8 995 ..	**−12,482.9**	**−12,318.6**	**−10,785.5**	**−11,619.8**	**−12,950.5**	**−12,289.6**	**−9,598.0**	....
Conversion rates: CFA francs per U.S. dollar (end of period)..	0 102 ..	**519.36**	**481.58**	**556.04**	**498.07**	**445.59**	**471.34**	**455.34**	**490.91**

Table 1. ANALYTIC PRESENTATION, 2003–2010

(Millions of U.S. dollars)

	Code	2003	2004	2005	2006	2007	2008	2009	2010
A. Current Account[1]	4 993 Z.	**−2,082.4**	**−1,779.4**	**−2,455.5**	**−3,213.5**	**−4,295.6**	**−6,028.3**	**−3,167.6**	**−900.7**
Goods: exports f.o.b.	2 100 ..	6,311.4	8,214.5	8,959.8	10,644.4	12,622.7	14,460.4	10,735.8	12,066.6
Goods: imports f.o.b.	3 100 ..	−14,216.0	−16,560.3	−18,301.3	−21,130.9	−25,556.1	−30,416.0	−21,025.5	−19,943.8
Balance on Goods	4 100 ..	*−7,904.6*	*−8,345.8*	*−9,341.5*	*−10,486.5*	*−12,933.4*	*−15,955.6*	*−10,289.7*	*−7,877.2*
Services: credit	2 200 ..	8,568.8	9,373.2	9,921.0	10,800.3	12,471.1	15,162.2	11,890.0	11,020.6
Services: debit	3 200 ..	−2,919.5	−3,487.9	−3,320.7	−3,455.4	−3,772.4	−4,419.8	−3,743.0	−3,452.1
Balance on Goods and Services	4 991 ..	*−2,255.3*	*−2,460.5*	*−2,741.3*	*−3,141.6*	*−4,234.6*	*−5,213.2*	*−2,142.7*	*−308.7*
Income: credit	2 300 ..	525.9	896.5	909.2	1,167.6	1,840.5	2,060.8	1,116.2	1,203.2
Income: debit	3 300 ..	−1,760.0	−1,701.1	−2,098.8	−2,629.7	−3,332.1	−4,452.2	−3,591.4	−3,249.1
Balance on Goods, Services, and Income	4 992 ..	*−3,489.4*	*−3,265.1*	*−3,930.8*	*−4,603.7*	*−5,726.2*	*−7,604.5*	*−4,617.9*	*−2,354.6*
Current transfers: credit	2 379 Z.	1,741.4	1,974.0	2,027.2	2,060.5	2,164.4	2,468.2	2,247.9	2,246.4
Current transfers: debit	3 379 ..	−334.4	−488.2	−551.9	−670.4	−733.9	−892.0	−797.6	−792.5
B. Capital Account[1]	4 994 Z.	**118.5**	**39.4**	**64.2**	**−158.6**	**38.3**	**23.3**	**61.1**	**45.5**
Capital account: credit	2 994 Z.	132.6	48.8	70.5	54.4	72.2	76.8	97.3	76.4
Capital account: debit	3 994 ..	−14.1	−9.4	−6.2	−213.0	−33.9	−53.4	−36.2	−30.9
Total, Groups A Plus B	4 981 ..	*−1,963.8*	*−1,740.0*	*−2,391.2*	*−3,372.1*	*−4,257.3*	*−6,005.0*	*−3,106.5*	*−855.2*
C. Financial Account[1]	4 995 W.	**4,719.8**	**3,113.0**	**4,706.7**	**6,883.2**	**7,046.5**	**7,937.7**	**6,482.8**	**1,679.8**
Direct investment abroad	4 505 ..	−121.5	−346.3	−237.1	−261.2	−283.2	−1,317.2	−1,244.5	147.1
Direct investment in Croatia	4 555 Z.	2,048.8	1,078.6	1,788.1	3,461.7	4,996.1	6,023.3	2,861.5	334.2
Portfolio investment assets	4 602 ..	144.2	−952.0	−711.9	−586.8	−519.0	−306.7	−891.8	−437.4
Equity securities	4 610 ..	−65.7	−47.6	−238.7	−405.1	−1,116.5	219.5	−160.7	−637.4
Debt securities	4 619 ..	210.0	−904.3	−473.2	−181.7	597.5	−526.2	−731.0	200.0
Portfolio investment liabilities	4 652 Z.	830.8	1,237.5	−796.5	376.5	1,037.9	−707.8	1,579.8	907.3
Equity securities	4 660 ..	15.7	177.6	112.9	417.7	436.7	−111.4	24.5	111.6
Debt securities	4 669 Z.	815.0	1,059.9	−909.4	−41.1	601.2	−596.4	1,555.3	795.7
Financial derivatives	4 910 ..	....	....	−118.3	....	....	....	....	−333.6
Financial derivatives assets	4 900 ..	....	....	....	....	....	....	....	214.1
Financial derivatives liabilities	4 905 ..	....	....	−118.3	....	....	....	....	−547.7
Other investment assets	4 703 ..	−2,443.0	−618.1	1,318.1	−966.1	−2,332.2	−2,250.4	901.1	965.1
Monetary authorities	4 701 ..	....	....	....	....	....	....	....	....
General government	4 704 ..	....	....	....	....	....	....	....	....
Banks	4 705 ..	−2,304.4	−553.2	1,685.6	−781.1	−1,923.1	−263.2	449.6	610.8
Other sectors	4 728 ..	−138.6	−64.9	−367.5	−185.0	−409.1	−1,987.2	451.5	354.3
Other investment liabilities	4 753 W.	4,260.5	2,713.4	3,464.3	4,859.1	4,146.8	6,496.4	3,276.7	97.2
Monetary authorities	4 753 WA	378.8	−440.4	.1	.1	−.1	−.3	471.9	....
General government	4 753 ZB	407.2	704.7	123.9	196.4	226.5	136.1	−18.2	187.1
Banks	4 753 ZC	2,184.1	1,504.4	1,483.4	1,679.2	−1,687.5	981.4	1,462.0	−334.3
Other sectors	4 753 ZD	1,290.4	944.6	1,856.9	2,983.3	5,607.8	5,379.2	1,360.9	244.3
Total, Groups A Through C	4 983 ..	*2,756.0*	*1,373.0*	*2,315.5*	*3,511.1*	*2,789.2*	*1,932.7*	*3,376.3*	*824.5*
D. Net Errors and Omissions	4 998 ..	**−1,355.2**	**−1,304.8**	**−1,293.2**	**−1,783.8**	**−1,807.3**	**−2,323.9**	**−1,540.0**	**−816.9**
Total, Groups A Through D	4 984 ..	*1,400.8*	*68.2*	*1,022.3*	*1,727.2*	*981.9*	*−391.3*	*1,836.3*	*7.7*
E. Reserves and Related Items	4 802 A.	**−1,400.8**	**−68.2**	**−1,022.3**	**−1,727.2**	**−981.9**	**391.3**	**−1,836.3**	**−7.7**
Reserve assets	4 802 ..	−1,400.8	−68.2	−1,022.3	−1,727.2	−981.9	391.3	−1,836.3	−7.7
Use of Fund credit and loans	4 766 ..	....	....	....	....	....	....	....	....
Exceptional financing	4 920 ..	....	....	....	....	....	....	....	....
Conversion rates: kunas per U.S. dollar	0 101 ..	**6.7050**	**6.0343**	**5.9492**	**5.8378**	**5.3645**	**4.9350**	**5.2839**	**5.4980**

[1] Excludes components that have been classified in the categories of Group E.

Table 2. STANDARD PRESENTATION, 2003–2010

(Millions of U.S. dollars)

	Code	2003	2004	2005	2006	2007	2008	2009	2010
CURRENT ACCOUNT.....................................	4 993 ..	**−2,082.4**	**−1,779.4**	**−2,455.5**	**−3,213.5**	**−4,295.6**	**−6,028.3**	**−3,167.6**	**−900.7**
A. GOODS...	4 100 ..	**−7,904.6**	**−8,345.8**	**−9,341.5**	**−10,486.5**	**−12,933.4**	**−15,955.6**	**−10,289.7**	**−7,877.2**
Credit..	2 100 ..	**6,311.4**	**8,214.5**	**8,959.8**	**10,644.4**	**12,622.7**	**14,460.4**	**10,735.8**	**12,066.6**
General merchandise: exports f.o.b............	2 110 ..	6,241.4	8,130.1	8,868.6	10,507.4	12,457.8	14,222.4	10,580.2	11,910.3
Goods for processing: exports f.o.b..........	2 150 ..	....	....	....	....	....	....	....	....
Repairs on goods....................................	2 160 ..	66.6	79.8	86.6	99.5	115.3	148.0	115.1	105.6
Goods procured in ports by carriers...........	2 170 ..	3.4	4.6	4.6	37.5	49.6	90.0	40.4	50.6
Nonmonetary gold..................................	2 180 ..	....	....	....	....	....	....	....	....
Debit...	3 100 ..	**−14,216.0**	**−16,560.3**	**−18,301.3**	**−21,130.9**	**−25,556.1**	**−30,416.0**	**−21,025.5**	**−19,943.8**
General merchandise: imports f.o.b............	3 110 ..	−14,149.7	−16,482.2	−18,191.7	−21,016.9	−25,403.0	−30,196.3	−20,873.7	−19,813.1
Goods for processing: imports f.o.b..........	3 150 ..	....	....	....	....	....	....	....	....
Repairs on goods....................................	3 160 ..	−34.2	−39.0	−47.4	−50.7	−71.8	−84.9	−69.3	−47.7
Goods procured in ports by carriers...........	3 170 ..	−32.1	−39.1	−62.2	−63.2	−81.4	−134.8	−82.5	−83.1
Nonmonetary gold..................................	3 180 ..	....	....	....	....	....	....	....	....
B. SERVICES...	4 200 ..	**5,649.3**	**5,885.3**	**6,600.2**	**7,344.9**	**8,698.8**	**10,742.4**	**8,147.0**	**7,568.6**
Total credit...	2 200 ..	*8,568.8*	*9,373.2*	*9,921.0*	*10,800.3*	*12,471.1*	*15,162.2*	*11,890.0*	*11,020.6*
Total debit..	3 200 ..	*−2,919.5*	*−3,487.9*	*−3,320.7*	*−3,455.4*	*−3,772.4*	*−4,419.8*	*−3,743.0*	*−3,452.1*
Transportation services, credit..............	2 205 ..	**788.4**	**982.4**	**1,093.2**	**1,306.9**	**1,596.1**	**1,787.6**	**1,047.1**	**1,071.3**
Passenger..	2 850 ..	*203.5*	*217.6*	*255.1*	*306.0*	*367.6*	*401.5*	*223.7*	*158.5*
Freight...	2 851 ..	*429.8*	*564.2*	*582.4*	*694.2*	*857.4*	*960.2*	*504.1*	*577.8*
Other...	2 852 ..	*155.1*	*200.6*	*255.7*	*306.7*	*371.1*	*425.9*	*319.3*	*335.0*
Sea transport, passenger.........................	2 207 ..	14.0	16.0	15.7	19.9	22.2	26.4	14.3	14.3
Sea transport, freight..............................	2 208 ..	268.8	363.2	368.0	448.5	551.7	594.3	235.0	283.0
Sea transport, other................................	2 209 ..	31.8	40.8	67.5	73.9	90.0	106.7	62.9	74.7
Air transport, passenger..........................	2 211 ..	171.5	181.4	219.9	269.0	326.7	354.3	193.7	129.3
Air transport, freight...............................	2 212 ..	1.2	1.6	1.7	1.8	3.0	4.3	1.8	1.3
Air transport, other.................................	2 213 ..	74.7	93.2	103.2	114.1	138.3	147.5	105.2	110.7
Other transport, passenger......................	2 215 ..	18.0	20.1	19.5	17.1	18.8	20.8	15.7	15.0
Other transport, freight...........................	2 216 ..	159.9	199.4	212.7	243.9	302.7	361.6	267.2	293.5
Other transport, other.............................	2 217 ..	48.6	66.6	85.0	118.7	142.8	171.8	151.1	149.6
Transportation services, debit...............	3 205 ..	**−441.2**	**−533.1**	**−546.0**	**−616.3**	**−718.8**	**−860.8**	**−560.7**	**−547.5**
Passenger..	3 850 ..	*−37.0*	*−33.0*	*−32.0*	*−33.4*	*−39.7*	*−43.3*	*−21.0*	*−20.5*
Freight...	3 851 ..	*−227.8*	*−298.4*	*−301.5*	*−348.6*	*−423.9*	*−499.6*	*−344.2*	*−333.4*
Other...	3 852 ..	*−176.4*	*−201.6*	*−212.5*	*−234.3*	*−255.2*	*−317.9*	*−195.5*	*−193.6*
Sea transport, passenger.........................	3 207 ..	−.2	−.3	−.3	−.2	−.8	−3.8	....	....
Sea transport, freight..............................	3 208 ..	−25.8	−63.3	−36.7	−41.2	−49.2	−58.5	−41.2	−46.3
Sea transport, other................................	3 209 ..	−83.7	−86.0	−94.3	−92.3	−99.6	−124.5	−65.2	−69.1
Air transport, passenger..........................	3 211 ..	−27.9	−23.2	−21.3	−22.3	−27.9	−27.3	−10.6	−13.7
Air transport, freight...............................	3 212 ..	−24.3	−28.3	−32.3	−36.6	−45.4	−55.0	−36.6	−34.2
Air transport, other.................................	3 213 ..	−63.2	−81.9	−81.0	−98.9	−121.2	−149.5	−92.5	−84.1
Other transport, passenger......................	3 215 ..	−8.9	−9.6	−10.5	−10.9	−11.0	−12.2	−10.3	−6.8
Other transport, freight...........................	3 216 ..	−177.7	−206.8	−232.5	−270.8	−329.4	−386.1	−266.5	−252.9
Other transport, other.............................	3 217 ..	−29.5	−33.6	−37.2	−43.0	−34.4	−43.8	−37.7	−40.4
Travel, credit......................................	2 236 ..	**6,310.5**	**6,726.7**	**7,370.1**	**7,990.1**	**9,233.2**	**11,280.1**	**9,000.0**	**8,050.3**
Business travel.......................................	2 237 ..	297.1	403.0	623.3	489.1	533.5	572.6	356.1	310.6
Personal travel.......................................	2 240 ..	6,013.3	6,323.7	6,746.8	7,501.0	8,699.7	10,707.5	8,644.0	7,739.7
Travel, debit..	3 236 ..	**−672.4**	**−847.9**	**−753.9**	**−736.6**	**−985.2**	**−1,112.6**	**−1,013.1**	**−833.2**
Business travel.......................................	3 237 ..	−330.1	−370.1	−333.7	−288.8	−369.1	−381.4	−337.3	−238.4
Personal travel.......................................	3 240 ..	−342.3	−477.9	−420.2	−447.7	−616.1	−731.3	−675.7	−594.8
Other services, credit..........................	2 200 BA ..	**1,469.9**	**1,664.2**	**1,457.7**	**1,503.4**	**1,641.9**	**2,094.5**	**1,842.9**	**1,899.0**
Communications.....................................	2 245 ..	212.8	190.2	238.3	255.6	292.7	317.8	260.7	227.4
Construction...	2 249 ..	444.3	467.4	42.9	78.3	85.1	155.2	152.8	155.1
Insurance...	2 253 ..	19.7	19.3	21.8	25.5	31.2	33.5	29.2	31.3
Financial..	2 260 ..	48.2	33.8	34.2	47.5	50.7	48.9	59.5	69.1
Computer and information.......................	2 262 ..	62.2	65.0	84.7	84.4	116.3	152.4	163.1	170.6
Royalties and licence fees........................	2 266 ..	34.6	40.5	73.1	47.2	39.6	43.7	32.3	31.8
Other business services...........................	2 268 ..	614.5	817.7	933.2	915.2	959.9	1,210.7	1,047.5	1,137.0
Personal, cultural, and recreational...........	2 287 ..	33.3	29.6	28.7	49.0	65.8	130.3	97.0	76.1
Government, n.i.e....................................	2 291 ..	.3	.8	.8	.7	.7	1.9	.7	.6
Other services, debit...........................	3 200 BA ..	**−1,805.9**	**−2,106.9**	**−2,020.8**	**−2,102.6**	**−2,068.4**	**−2,446.4**	**−2,169.3**	**−2,071.3**
Communications.....................................	3 245 ..	−73.5	−104.1	−124.8	−118.9	−158.6	−179.7	−143.2	−136.0
Construction...	3 249 ..	−279.0	−335.4	−4.9	−4.0	−11.7	−13.8	−6.7	−5.5
Insurance...	3 253 ..	−45.3	−42.6	−47.4	−59.3	−70.6	−65.9	−66.5	−69.0
Financial..	3 260 ..	−142.2	−84.8	−88.3	−126.3	−83.7	−100.3	−112.6	−139.3
Computer and information.......................	3 262 ..	−108.2	−124.6	−148.1	−178.5	−216.2	−268.3	−243.2	−231.6
Royalties and licence fees........................	3 266 ..	−131.1	−146.0	−192.5	−174.8	−213.6	−257.5	−212.6	−225.2
Other business services...........................	3 268 ..	−953.2	−1,173.3	−1,307.8	−1,312.6	−1,154.2	−1,353.2	−1,194.9	−1,091.1
Personal, cultural, and recreational...........	3 287 ..	−41.5	−53.1	−56.2	−71.2	−93.5	−133.1	−126.9	−110.6
Government, n.i.e....................................	3 291 ..	−31.9	−42.8	−51.0	−56.9	−66.2	−74.7	−62.7	−63.1

Table 2 (Continued). STANDARD PRESENTATION, 2003–2010

(Millions of U.S. dollars)

	Code	2003	2004	2005	2006	2007	2008	2009	2010
C. INCOME..........	4 300 ..	**−1,234.1**	**−804.6**	**−1,189.5**	**−1,462.1**	**−1,491.5**	**−2,391.3**	**−2,475.2**	**−2,045.9**
Total credit..........	2 300 ..	*525.9*	*896.5*	*909.2*	*1,167.6*	*1,840.5*	*2,060.8*	*1,116.2*	*1,203.2*
Total debit..........	3 300 ..	*−1,760.0*	*−1,701.1*	*−2,098.8*	*−2,629.7*	*−3,332.1*	*−4,452.2*	*−3,591.4*	*−3,249.1*
Compensation of employees, credit..........	2 310 ..	**246.8**	**333.5**	**359.2**	**510.5**	**724.4**	**880.5**	**870.5**	**862.8**
Compensation of employees, debit..........	3 310 ..	**−38.4**	**−42.6**	**−36.3**	**−39.0**	**−46.1**	**−52.0**	**−52.4**	**−47.7**
Investment income, credit..........	2 320 ..	**279.1**	**563.0**	**550.0**	**657.2**	**1,116.1**	**1,180.4**	**245.7**	**340.4**
Direct investment income..........	2 330 ..	39.2	215.2	138.3	102.2	236.5	293.1	−93.0	109.7
Dividends and distributed branch profits..........	2 332 ..	2.2	8.4	53.0	14.1	58.9	98.1	56.7	83.4
Reinvested earnings and undistributed branch profits.....	2 333 ..	35.3	203.2	78.4	81.3	165.5	180.6	−163.8	9.1
Income on debt (interest)..........	2 334 ..	1.7	3.6	7.0	6.8	12.1	14.3	14.1	17.3
Portfolio investment income..........	2 339 ..	....	40.4	57.3	79.9	122.1	121.8	111.5	77.2
Income on equity..........	2 340 ..	....	....	....	....	....	....	1.5	1.3
Income on bonds and notes..........	2 350 ..	....	36.4	52.3	67.9	99.9	101.9	85.5	61.0
Income on money market instruments..........	2 360 ..	....	4.0	4.9	12.1	22.2	19.9	24.5	14.9
Other investment income..........	2 370 ..	239.9	307.4	354.4	475.0	757.5	765.6	227.2	153.5
Investment income, debit..........	3 320 ..	**−1,721.7**	**−1,658.5**	**−2,062.5**	**−2,590.7**	**−3,285.9**	**−4,400.1**	**−3,539.0**	**−3,201.4**
Direct investment income..........	3 330 ..	−1,018.5	−753.1	−1,072.9	−1,357.4	−1,477.8	−2,056.7	−1,489.5	−1,507.9
Dividends and distributed branch profits..........	3 332 ..	−296.4	−338.9	−275.5	−358.7	−670.5	−996.4	−762.0	−584.3
Reinvested earnings and undistributed branch profits.....	3 333 ..	−673.9	−351.3	−720.4	−900.0	−653.0	−800.8	−456.1	−635.3
Income on debt (interest)..........	3 334 ..	−48.2	−62.8	−77.0	−98.7	−154.4	−259.6	−271.5	−288.2
Portfolio investment income..........	3 339 ..	−270.2	−351.2	−329.2	−315.4	−379.7	−390.6	−346.2	−458.4
Income on equity..........	3 340 ..	−5.8	−4.8	−2.7	−5.1	−9.4	−3.1	−7.1	−9.3
Income on bonds and notes..........	3 350 ..	−264.1	−345.7	−326.5	−310.3	−370.3	−387.5	−336.1	−434.2
Income on money market instruments..........	3 360 ..	−.3	−.7	....	....	....	....	−3.0	−14.9
Other investment income..........	3 370 ..	−433.0	−554.2	−660.4	−917.9	−1,428.4	−1,952.8	−1,703.2	−1,235.2
D. CURRENT TRANSFERS..........	4 379 ..	**1,407.0**	**1,485.7**	**1,475.3**	**1,390.1**	**1,430.5**	**1,576.2**	**1,450.3**	**1,453.9**
Credit..........	2 379 ..	**1,741.4**	**1,974.0**	**2,027.2**	**2,060.5**	**2,164.4**	**2,468.2**	**2,247.9**	**2,246.4**
General government..........	2 380 ..	240.3	223.3	276.0	322.8	358.7	492.4	432.7	419.6
Other sectors..........	2 390 ..	1,501.2	1,750.7	1,751.3	1,737.8	1,805.8	1,975.8	1,815.2	1,826.8
Workers' remittances..........	2 391 ..	228.8	293.9	333.6	314.3	410.9	422.7	403.9	377.2
Other current transfers..........	2 392 ..	1,272.3	1,456.8	1,417.7	1,423.5	1,394.8	1,553.1	1,411.3	1,449.6
Debit..........	3 379 ..	**−334.4**	**−488.2**	**−551.9**	**−670.4**	**−733.9**	**−892.0**	**−797.6**	**−792.5**
General government..........	3 380 ..	−161.7	−220.0	−260.2	−332.4	−379.9	−525.6	−472.7	−459.1
Other sectors..........	3 390 ..	−172.7	−268.2	−291.7	−338.0	−354.0	−366.4	−324.8	−333.4
Workers' remittances..........	3 391 ..	−48.4	−48.4	−59.6	−78.7	−108.2	−125.5	−115.0	−95.6
Other current transfers..........	3 392 ..	−124.3	−219.8	−232.1	−259.3	−245.8	−241.0	−209.8	−237.8
CAPITAL AND FINANCIAL ACCOUNT..........	4 996 ..	**3,437.6**	**3,084.2**	**3,748.6**	**4,997.4**	**6,102.9**	**8,352.3**	**4,707.6**	**1,717.6**
CAPITAL ACCOUNT..........	4 994 ..	**118.5**	**39.4**	**64.2**	**−158.6**	**38.3**	**23.3**	**61.1**	**45.5**
Total credit..........	2 994 ..	*132.6*	*48.8*	*70.5*	*54.4*	*72.2*	*76.8*	*97.3*	*76.4*
Total debit..........	3 994 ..	*−14.1*	*−9.4*	*−6.2*	*−213.0*	*−33.9*	*−53.4*	*−36.2*	*−30.9*
Capital transfers, credit..........	2 400 ..	**77.9**	**48.8**	**70.5**	**51.6**	**62.8**	**64.5**	**68.6**	**74.6**
General government..........	2 401 ..	37.0	11.4	52.0	17.5	3.9	6.7	6.1	....
Debt forgiveness..........	2 402 ..	37.0	11.4	5.1	17.5	3.9	6.7	6.1	....
Other capital transfers..........	2 410 ..	....	....	46.9	....	....	....	....	....
Other sectors..........	2 430 ..	40.9	37.3	18.4	34.1	58.9	57.8	62.5	74.6
Migrants' transfers..........	2 431 ..	40.9	37.3	18.4	34.1	58.9	57.8	62.5	74.6
Debt forgiveness..........	2 432 ..	....	....	....	....	....	....	....	....
Other capital transfers..........	2 440 ..	....	....	....	....	....	....	....	....
Capital transfers, debit..........	3 400 ..	**−14.1**	**−9.4**	**−6.2**	**−208.7**	**−15.6**	**−16.6**	**−6.9**	**−20.4**
General government..........	3 401 ..	−2.4	−.5	−1.7	−.4	−7.2	....	....	.4
Debt forgiveness..........	3 402 ..	−2.4	−.5	−1.7	−.4	−7.2	....	....	.4
Other capital transfers..........	3 410 ..	....	....	....	....	....	....	....	....
Other sectors..........	3 430 ..	−11.7	−8.9	−4.6	−208.3	−8.4	−16.6	−6.9	−20.8
Migrants' transfers..........	3 431 ..	−11.7	−8.9	−4.6	−208.3	−8.4	−16.6	−6.9	−20.8
Debt forgiveness..........	3 432 ..	....	....	....	....	....	....	....	....
Other capital transfers..........	3 440 ..	....	....	....	....	....	....	....	....
Nonproduced nonfinancial assets, credit..........	2 480 ..	**54.7**	....	....	**2.8**	**9.4**	**12.3**	**28.7**	**1.8**
Nonproduced nonfinancial assets, debit..........	3 480 ..	....	....	....	**−4.3**	**−18.2**	**−36.8**	**−29.3**	**−10.5**

Croatia 960

Table 2 (Continued). STANDARD PRESENTATION, 2003–2010

(Millions of U.S. dollars)

	Code	2003	2004	2005	2006	2007	2008	2009	2010
FINANCIAL ACCOUNT	4 995	**3,319.0**	**3,044.8**	**3,684.4**	**5,155.9**	**6,064.6**	**8,328.9**	**4,646.5**	**1,672.1**
A. DIRECT INVESTMENT	4 500	**1,927.3**	**732.3**	**1,551.0**	**3,200.5**	**4,712.9**	**4,706.1**	**1,617.0**	**481.3**
Direct investment abroad	4 505	**−121.5**	**−346.3**	**−237.1**	**−261.2**	**−283.2**	**−1,317.2**	**−1,244.5**	**147.1**
Equity capital	4 510	−80.2	−117.9	−70.1	−183.2	−193.6	−1,288.9	−1,426.3	350.4
Claims on affiliated enterprises	4 515	−80.2	−118.4	−70.4	−183.2	−193.6	−1,288.9	−1,426.3	350.4
Liabilities to affiliated enterprises	4 520	....	.4	.3	....	....	....	....	....
Reinvested earnings	4 525	−35.3	−203.2	−78.4	−81.3	−165.5	−180.6	163.8	−9.1
Other capital	4 530	−6.1	−25.2	−88.7	3.3	75.9	152.3	18.0	−194.2
Claims on affiliated enterprises	4 535	−18.1	−30.8	−74.2	−18.3	27.9	154.3	−27.8	−500.7
Liabilities to affiliated enterprises	4 540	12.0	5.6	−14.4	21.6	48.0	−2.1	45.8	306.5
Direct investment in Croatia	4 555	**2,048.8**	**1,078.6**	**1,788.1**	**3,461.7**	**4,996.1**	**6,023.3**	**2,861.5**	**334.2**
Equity capital	4 560	894.2	381.1	1,001.8	2,192.0	2,985.3	3,146.4	979.2	551.6
Claims on direct investors	4 565	....	−.3	....	−.1	....	....	....	....
Liabilities to direct investors	4 570	894.2	381.4	1,001.9	2,192.1	2,985.3	3,146.4	979.2	551.6
Reinvested earnings	4 575	673.9	351.3	720.4	900.0	653.0	800.8	456.1	635.3
Other capital	4 580	480.7	346.1	65.8	369.6	1,357.9	2,076.1	1,426.2	−852.8
Claims on direct investors	4 585	−1.8	−21.5	−3.2	15.6	25.3	−31.6	−43.2	−25.9
Liabilities to direct investors	4 590	482.6	367.6	69.0	354.1	1,332.6	2,107.7	1,469.4	−826.9
B. PORTFOLIO INVESTMENT	4 600	**975.0**	**285.6**	**−1,508.4**	**−210.3**	**519.0**	**−1,014.4**	**688.0**	**469.9**
Assets	4 602	**144.2**	**−952.0**	**−711.9**	**−586.8**	**−519.0**	**−306.7**	**−891.8**	**−437.4**
Equity securities	4 610	−65.7	−47.6	−238.7	−405.1	−1,116.5	219.5	−160.7	−637.4
Monetary authorities	4 611	....	....	....	....	....	....	....	....
General government	4 612	....	....	....	....	....	....	....	....
Banks	4 613	.4	....	....	3.3	....	....	....	....
Other sectors	4 614	−66.1	−47.6	−238.7	−408.3	−1,116.5	219.5	−160.7	−637.4
Debt securities	4 619	210.0	−904.3	−473.2	−181.7	597.5	−526.2	−731.0	200.0
Bonds and notes	4 620	194.8	−735.0	−497.8	145.3	446.4	−404.0	−223.7	336.6
Monetary authorities	4 621	....	....	....	....	....	....	....	....
General government	4 622	....	....	....	....	....	....	....	....
Banks	4 623	211.8	−744.7	−453.4	202.0	363.1	−257.8	−109.0	245.7
Other sectors	4 624	−16.9	9.7	−44.4	−56.6	83.3	−146.2	−114.7	90.9
Money market instruments	4 630	15.1	−169.3	24.6	−327.1	151.1	−122.1	−507.4	−136.6
Monetary authorities	4 631	....	....	....	....	....	....	....	....
General government	4 632	....	....	....	....	....	....	....	....
Banks	4 633	7.8	−169.3	24.6	−327.1	151.1	−121.9	−507.4	−136.6
Other sectors	4 634	7.3	....	....	....	....	−.3	....	....
Liabilities	4 652	**830.8**	**1,237.5**	**−796.5**	**376.5**	**1,037.9**	**−707.8**	**1,579.8**	**907.3**
Equity securities	4 660	15.7	177.6	112.9	417.7	436.7	−111.4	24.5	111.6
Banks	4 663	−2.8	.9	−16.9	35.6	....	....	....	....
Other sectors	4 664	18.5	176.8	129.7	382.1	436.7	−111.4	24.5	111.6
Debt securities	4 669	815.0	1,059.9	−909.4	−41.1	601.2	−596.4	1,555.3	795.7
Bonds and notes	4 670	775.9	1,099.9	−909.4	−41.1	601.2	−596.3	1,338.9	422.9
Monetary authorities	4 671	....	....	....	....	....	....	....	....
General government	4 672	568.0	172.7	−925.3	−131.1	114.9	−517.9	1,382.6	428.9
Banks	4 673	....	556.1	5.1	1.2	1.3	−4.2	−630.2	−.3
Other sectors	4 674	208.0	371.1	10.9	88.7	485.0	−74.1	586.6	−5.7
Money market instruments	4 680	39.1	−39.9	....	....	....	−.1	216.4	372.7
Monetary authorities	4 681	....	....	....	....	....	....	....	....
General government	4 682	....	....	....	....	....	....	216.2	372.7
Banks	4 683	....	....	....	....	....	....	....	....
Other sectors	4 684	39.1	−39.9	....	....	....	−.1	.1	....
C. FINANCIAL DERIVATIVES	4 910	....	....	**−118.3**	....	....	....	....	**−333.6**
Monetary authorities	4 911	....	....	....	....	....	....	....	....
General government	4 912	....	....	....	....	....	....	....	....
Banks	4 913	....	....	....	....	....	....	....	−333.6
Other sectors	4 914	....	....	−118.3	....	....	....	....	....
Assets	4 900	....	....	....	....	....	....	....	**214.1**
Monetary authorities	4 901	....	....	....	....	....	....	....	....
General government	4 902	....	....	....	....	....	....	....	....
Banks	4 903	....	....	....	....	....	....	....	214.1
Other sectors	4 904	....	....	....	....	....	....	....	....
Liabilities	4 905	....	....	**−118.3**	....	....	....	....	**−547.7**
Monetary authorities	4 906	....	....	....	....	....	....	....	....
General government	4 907	....	....	....	....	....	....	....	....
Banks	4 908	....	....	....	....	....	....	....	−547.7
Other sectors	4 909	....	....	−118.3	....	....	....	....	....

Table 2 (Concluded). STANDARD PRESENTATION, 2003–2010

(Millions of U.S. dollars)

	Code	2003	2004	2005	2006	2007	2008	2009	2010
D. OTHER INVESTMENT	4 700 ..	**1,817.5**	**2,095.2**	**4,782.4**	**3,893.0**	**1,814.6**	**4,246.0**	**4,177.8**	**1,062.2**
Assets	4 703 ..	**−2,443.0**	**−618.1**	**1,318.1**	**−966.1**	**−2,332.2**	**−2,250.4**	**901.1**	**965.1**
Trade credits	4 706 ..	−28.3	−234.5	−160.8	−38.0	−129.8	−233.0	212.9	94.1
General government	4 707 ..	....	....	....	....	....	....	....	....
of which: Short-term	4 709 ..	....	....	....	....	....	....	....	....
Other sectors	4 710 ..	−28.3	−234.5	−160.8	−38.0	−129.8	−233.0	212.9	94.1
of which: Short-term	4 712 ..	....	*−256.5*	*−175.0*	*−32.2*	*−40.8*	*−271.3*	*133.6*	*64.9*
Loans	4 714 ..	−102.2	53.6	−140.8	−189.9	−1.4	−158.1	49.3	−104.3
Monetary authorities	4 715 ..	....	....	....	....	....	....	....	....
of which: Short-term	4 718 ..	....	....	....	....	....	....	....	....
General government	4 719 ..	....	....	....	....	....	....	....	....
of which: Short-term	4 721 ..	....	....	....	....	....	....	....	....
Banks	4 722 ..	4.3	4.1	−34.9	−98.4	−45.4	−95.3	23.7	−78.9
of which: Short-term	4 724 ..	*−1.3*	*5.1*	*−10.0*	*−24.3*	*−11.4*	*−56.4*	*68.8*	*−11.6*
Other sectors	4 725 ..	−106.5	49.6	−106.0	−91.5	43.9	−62.8	25.5	−25.3
of which: Short-term	4 727 ..	*.1*	*−1.7*	*1.2*	*.3*	*.6*	*−5.3*	*.3*	*−47.3*
Currency and deposits	4 730 ..	−2,312.5	−437.3	1,619.7	−738.3	−2,201.0	−1,859.4	639.0	975.3
Monetary authorities	4 731 ..	....	....	....	....	....	....	....	....
General government	4 732 ..	....	....	....	....	....	....	....	....
Banks	4 733 ..	−2,308.8	−557.3	1,720.4	−682.7	−1,877.8	−167.9	425.9	689.7
Other sectors	4 734 ..	−3.7	120.0	−100.7	−55.6	−323.3	−1,691.5	213.1	285.6
Other assets	4 736 ..	....	....	....	....	....	....	....	....
Monetary authorities	4 737 ..	....	....	....	....	....	....	....	....
of which: Short-term	4 739 ..	....	....	....	....	....	....	....	....
General government	4 740 ..	....	....	....	....	....	....	....	....
of which: Short-term	4 742 ..	....	....	....	....	....	....	....	....
Banks	4 743 ..	....	....	....	....	....	....	....	....
of which: Short-term	4 745 ..	....	....	....	....	....	....	....	....
Other sectors	4 746 ..	....	....	....	....	....	....	....	....
of which: Short-term	4 748 ..	....	....	....	....	....	....	....	....
Liabilities	4 753 ..	**4,260.5**	**2,713.4**	**3,464.3**	**4,859.1**	**4,146.8**	**6,496.4**	**3,276.7**	**97.2**
Trade credits	4 756 ..	−51.0	−76.7	25.7	7.0	407.8	113.0	−187.5	39.2
General government	4 757 ..	1.8	−.4	.6	−.9	−.9	−.8	−.1	....
of which: Short-term	4 759 ..	....	....	....	....	....	....	....	....
Other sectors	4 760 ..	−52.8	−76.4	25.1	7.9	408.7	113.8	−187.5	39.2
of which: Short-term	4 762 ..	....	*−55.5*	*−8.8*	*13.2*	*180.7*	*55.4*	*−108.0*	*76.1*
Loans	4 764 ..	3,282.3	2,109.6	2,994.2	3,835.5	4,040.3	5,427.6	1,390.2	112.4
Monetary authorities	4 765 ..	378.7	−440.4	....	....	....	....	....	....
of which: Use of Fund credit and loans from the Fund	4 766 ..	....	....	....	....	....	....	....	....
of which: Short-term	4 768 ..	*379.1*	*−440.4*	....	....	....	....	....	....
General government	4 769 ..	405.4	705.1	123.4	197.3	227.4	136.9	−18.1	187.1
of which: Short-term	4 771 ..	....	....	....	....	....	*42.4*	*−44.0*	....
Banks	4 772 ..	1,154.1	827.7	1,043.4	666.0	−1,384.0	41.9	−166.0	−278.4
of which: Short-term	4 774 ..	*86.5*	*−101.8*	*699.4*	*168.1*	*−563.6*	*499.1*	*−415.2*	*133.7*
Other sectors	4 775 ..	1,344.0	1,017.2	1,827.4	2,972.2	5,196.9	5,248.8	1,574.3	203.7
of which: Short-term	4 777 ..	*53.2*	*43.0*	*69.1*	*106.2*	*825.0*	*487.1*	*385.8*	*257.8*
Currency and deposits	4 780 ..	1,030.1	676.7	441.0	1,013.2	−305.0	954.0	1,597.7	−55.9
Monetary authorities	4 781 ..	.1	....	.1	.1	−.1	−.3	−1.6	....
General government	4 782 ..	....	....	....	....	....	....	....	....
Banks	4 783 ..	1,030.0	676.7	440.0	1,013.2	−303.5	939.5	1,628.0	−55.9
Other sectors	4 784 ..	....	....	.9	−.1	−1.4	14.7	−28.8	....
Other liabilities	4 786 ..	−.8	3.8	3.5	3.3	3.7	1.9	476.4	1.4
Monetary authorities	4 787 ..	....	....	....	....	....	....	473.5	....
of which: Short-term	4 789 ..	....	....	....	....	....	....	....	....
General government	4 790 ..	....	....	....	....	....	....	....	....
of which: Short-term	4 792 ..	....	....	....	....	....	....	....	....
Banks	4 793 ..	....	....	....	....	....	....	....	....
of which: Short-term	4 795 ..	....	....	....	....	....	....	....	....
Other sectors	4 796 ..	−.8	3.8	3.5	3.3	3.7	1.9	2.8	1.4
of which: Short-term	4 798 ..	....	....	....	....	....	....	....	....
E. RESERVE ASSETS	4 802 ..	**−1,400.8**	**−68.2**	**−1,022.3**	**−1,727.2**	**−981.9**	**391.3**	**−1,836.3**	**−7.7**
Monetary gold	4 812 ..	....	....	....	....	....	....	....	....
Special drawing rights	4 811 ..	1.5	....	−.2	.1	−.1	....	−473.3	....
Reserve position in the Fund	4 810 ..	....	....	....	....	....	....	....	....
Foreign exchange	4 803 ..	−1,402.3	−68.2	−1,022.1	−1,727.4	−981.8	391.2	−1,363.0	−7.6
Other claims	4 813 ..	....	....	....	....	....	....	....	....
NET ERRORS AND OMISSIONS	4 998 ..	**−1,355.2**	**−1,304.8**	**−1,293.2**	**−1,783.8**	**−1,807.3**	**−2,323.9**	**−1,540.0**	**−816.9**

Table 3. INTERNATIONAL INVESTMENT POSITION (End-period stocks), 2003–2010

(Millions of U.S. dollars)

	Code	2003	2004	2005	2006	2007	2008	2009	2010
ASSETS	8 995 C.	17,930.8	20,573.6	19,003.1	23,902.7	31,799.0	31,969.3	35,365.6	30,712.6
Direct investment abroad	8 505	2,033.0	2,127.6	2,046.7	2,413.9	3,791.3	5,328.1	6,541.4	4,121.2
Equity capital and reinvested earnings	8 506	1,983.4	2,044.4	1,905.5	2,271.5	3,642.9	5,058.6	6,407.6	3,800.9
Claims on affiliated enterprises	8 507	1,983.4	2,044.4	1,905.5	2,271.5	3,642.9	5,058.6	6,407.6	3,800.9
Liabilities to affiliated enterprises	8 508	....	....	....	....	....	....	....	....
Other capital	8 530	49.6	83.2	141.2	142.4	148.4	269.6	133.8	320.3
Claims on affiliated enterprises	8 535	....	....	....	....	....	....	....	....
Liabilities to affiliated enterprises	8 540	....	....	....	....	....	....	....	....
Portfolio investment	8 602	921.6	2,049.5	2,550.6	3,274.5	4,776.5	3,752.4	4,904.6	4,750.9
Equity securities	8 610	176.6	240.7	449.1	736.4	2,564.7	932.9	1,149.0	1,665.2
Monetary authorities	8 611	....	....	....	....	....	....	....	....
General government	8 612	2.9	....	....	....	....	....	....	....
Banks	8 613	5.9	6.9	7.0	8.8	12.2	16.5	18.4	14.7
Other sectors	8 614	167.8	233.8	442.1	727.6	2,552.5	916.5	1,130.5	1,650.5
Debt securities	8 619	745.1	1,808.8	2,101.5	2,538.1	2,211.8	2,819.5	3,755.7	3,085.7
Bonds and notes	8 620	742.0	1,590.5	1,927.4	2,022.7	1,799.8	2,276.2	2,738.4	1,981.0
Monetary authorities	8 621	....	....	....	....	....	....	....	....
General government	8 622	....	....	....	....	....	....	....	....
Banks	8 623	699.9	1,555.0	1,784.8	1,786.0	1,605.9	1,873.2	1,993.9	1,620.2
Other sectors	8 624	42.1	35.5	142.6	236.7	193.9	403.0	744.5	360.8
Money market instruments	8 630	3.0	218.3	174.1	515.4	412.0	543.3	1,017.2	1,104.7
Monetary authorities	8 631	....	....	....	....	....	....	....	....
General government	8 632	....	....	....	....	....	....	....	....
Banks	8 633	3.0	218.3	174.1	515.4	412.0	543.3	1,017.2	1,104.7
Other sectors	8 634	....	....	....	....	....	....	....	....
Financial derivatives	8 900	....	....	....	....	....	....	34.6	21.9
Monetary authorities	8 901	....	....	....	....	....	....	....	....
General government	8 902	....	....	....	....	....	....	....	....
Banks	8 903	....	....	....	....	....	....	34.6	21.9
Other sectors	8 904	....	....	....	....	....	....	....	....
Other investment	8 703	6,785.6	7,638.3	5,605.5	6,726.4	9,556.7	9,931.3	8,990.5	7,686.1
Trade credits	8 706	316.6	302.4	311.1	303.5	365.7	319.3	177.1	106.8
General government	8 707	....	....	....	....	....	....	....	....
of which: Short-term	8 709	....	....	....	....	....	....	....	....
Other sectors	8 710	316.6	302.4	311.1	303.5	365.7	319.3	177.1	106.8
of which: Short-term	8 712	52.2	55.5	85.2	69.7	29.6	31.4	38.8	25.4
Loans	8 714	127.6	139.1	172.9	315.3	435.5	619.3	552.1	613.9
Monetary authorities	8 715	.8	.8	.7	.8	.8	.8	.8	.8
of which: Short-term	8 718	....	....	....	....	....	....	....	....
General government	8 719	....	....	....	....	....	....	....	....
of which: Short-term	8 721	....	....	....	....	....	....	....	....
Banks	8 722	108.8	111.1	133.9	248.2	315.6	405.4	387.8	438.6
of which: Short-term	8 724	29.9	25.9	33.0	63.8	80.5	130.3	52.4	59.8
Other sectors	8 725	18.0	27.2	38.3	66.3	119.1	213.1	163.4	174.5
of which: Short-term	8 727	....	1.8	.4	.3	.1	4.6	.4	50.0
Currency and deposits	8 730	6,341.5	7,196.8	5,121.5	6,107.2	8,755.4	8,992.8	8,261.3	6,965.3
Monetary authorities	8 731	....	....	....	....	....	....	....	....
General government	8 732	102.3	12.1	64.1	34.8	102.5	129.0	27.1	35.4
Banks	8 733	4,895.2	5,878.7	3,682.4	4,608.4	6,927.9	6,909.8	6,378.2	5,385.0
Other sectors	8 734	1,344.0	1,306.0	1,375.0	1,464.0	1,725.0	1,954.0	1,856.0	1,545.0
Other assets	8 736	....	....	....	.5	....	....	....	....
Monetary authorities	8 737	....	....	....	....	....	....	....	....
of which: Short-term	8 739	....	....	....	....	....	....	....	....
General government	8 740	....	....	....	....	....	....	....	....
of which: Short-term	8 742	....	....	....	....	....	....	....	....
Banks	8 743	....	....	....	.5	....	....	....	....
of which: Short-term	8 745	....	....	....	.5	....	....	....	....
Other sectors	8 746	....	....	....	....	....	....	....	....
of which: Short-term	8 748	....	....	....	....	....	....	....	....
Reserve assets	8 802	8,190.5	8,758.2	8,800.3	11,487.8	13,674.5	12,957.4	14,894.5	14,132.5
Monetary gold	8 812	....	....	....	....	....	....	....	....
Special drawing rights	8 811	....	.1	.3	.2	.3	.2	475.2	466.9
Reserve position in the Fund	8 810	.2	.2	.2	.2	.3	.2	.2	.2
Foreign exchange	8 803	8,190.2	8,757.9	8,799.8	11,487.4	13,674.0	12,956.9	14,419.0	13,665.4
Other claims	8 813	....	....	....	....	....	....	....	....

Table 3 (Concluded). INTERNATIONAL INVESTMENT POSITION (End-period stocks), 2003–2010

(Millions of U.S. dollars)

	Code	2003	2004	2005	2006	2007	2008	2009	2010
LIABILITIES	8 995 D.	31,325.6	41,493.2	42,937.1	64,001.1	90,836.6	81,667.3	91,664.7	87,358.7
Direct investment in Croatia	8 555	8,509.4	12,403.4	14,591.2	27,363.6	44,977.5	31,526.7	35,829.8	34,018.4
Equity capital and reinvested earnings	8 556	6,214.8	9,684.6	11,737.6	23,649.6	39,343.7	23,313.4	25,402.3	24,602.5
Claims on direct investors	8 557	....	....	....	....	....	....	....	....
Liabilities to direct investors	8 558	6,214.8	9,684.6	11,737.6	23,649.6	39,343.7	23,313.4	25,402.3	24,602.5
Other capital	8 580	2,294.5	2,718.8	2,853.7	3,714.1	5,633.8	8,213.3	10,427.5	9,415.9
Claims on direct investors	8 585	....	....	....	....	....	....	....	....
Liabilities to direct investors	8 590	....	....	....	....	....	....	....	....
Portfolio investment	8 652	6,146.9	8,140.2	6,543.6	7,682.4	9,755.4	7,733.9	9,301.4	9,428.9
Equity securities	8 660	291.7	664.2	765.0	1,333.5	2,236.7	872.0	944.0	978.9
Banks	8 663	57.9	88.0	99.3	188.6	242.0	94.5	89.5	75.4
Other sectors	8 664	233.8	576.2	665.7	1,144.9	1,994.7	777.5	854.5	903.5
Debt securities	8 669	5,855.2	7,476.0	5,778.6	6,348.9	7,518.6	6,861.9	8,357.3	8,450.0
Bonds and notes	8 670	5,813.1	7,476.0	5,778.6	6,185.8	7,454.4	6,826.9	8,112.8	7,828.9
Monetary authorities	8 671	....	....	....					
General government	8 672	5,248.7	5,839.9	4,334.5	4,479.8	5,004.7	4,492.3	5,708.5	5,713.7
Banks	8 673	....	616.8	540.2	602.9	674.3	649.0	12.9	11.8
Other sectors	8 674	564.5	1,019.3	903.9	1,103.1	1,775.3	1,685.5	2,391.4	2,103.4
Money market instruments	8 680	42.1	....	....	163.1	64.2	35.0	244.5	621.1
Monetary authorities	8 681	....	....	....					
General government	8 682		....	....	163.1	64.2	35.0	244.5	621.1
Banks	8 683	....	....	....					
Other sectors	8 684	42.1	....						
Financial derivatives	8 905	....	....	....	....	....	....	74.9	261.9
Monetary authorities	8 906	....	....	....	....	....	....		
General government	8 907	....	....	....	....	....	....	....	....
Banks	8 908	....	....	....	....	....	....	74.9	261.9
Other sectors	8 909	....	....	....	....	....	....	....	....
Other investment	8 753	16,669.3	20,949.5	21,802.3	28,955.1	36,103.8	42,406.7	46,458.7	43,649.6
Trade credits	8 756	287.6	285.0	295.3	322.4	496.3	522.0	494.4	459.3
General government	8 757	3.1	3.0	3.1	2.5	1.7	1.0	....	....
of which: Short-term	8 759								
Other sectors	8 760	284.5	282.0	292.2	319.9	494.6	521.0	494.4	459.3
of which: Short-term	8 762	28.1	32.2	32.9	47.3	45.7	56.1	40.5	40.9
Loans	8 764	12,958.8	16,251.5	17,205.4	22,841.3	29,516.4	34,584.6	36,335.2	34,088.0
Monetary authorities	8 765	454.1	....	....	....	....	....	....	....
of which: Use of Fund credit and loans from the Fund	8 766	....	....	....	....	....	....	....	....
of which: Short-term	8 768	454.1	....	....	....	....	....	....	....
General government	8 769	2,208.7	3,066.2	2,942.3	3,369.5	3,840.3	2,237.0	2,286.5	2,385.6
of which: Short-term	8 771	....	....	....	....	....	45.0		
Banks	8 772	4,254.2	5,495.5	5,784.9	7,069.3	6,283.9	6,388.5	6,248.9	5,693.9
of which: Short-term	8 774	755.6	708.6	1,261.7	1,516.3	1,045.6	1,594.1	1,159.3	1,240.2
Other sectors	8 775	6,041.8	7,689.8	8,478.2	12,402.5	19,392.2	25,959.1	27,799.8	26,008.5
of which: Short-term	8 777	146.0	205.0	237.5	305.7	1,215.2	969.6	1,060.4	823.8
Currency and deposits	8 780	3,422.9	4,413.0	4,301.7	5,791.3	6,091.0	7,300.1	9,084.6	8,567.3
Monetary authorities	8 781	3.2	3.2	3.1	3.4	3.5	3.2	1.6	1.6
General government	8 782	....	....	....	....	....	....	....	....
Banks	8 783	3,419.7	4,409.8	4,298.5	5,788.0	6,087.6	7,281.8	9,083.0	8,565.7
Other sectors	8 784	....	....	....	....	....	15.0	....	....
Other liabilities	8 786	....	....	....	....	....	....	544.5	534.9
Monetary authorities	8 787	....	....	....	....	....	....	544.5	534.9
of which: Short-term	8 789	....	....	....	....	....	....	....	....
General government	8 790	....	....	....	....	....	....	....	....
of which: Short-term	8 792	....	....	....	....	....	....	....	....
Banks	8 793	....	....	....	....	....	....	....	....
of which: Short-term	8 795	....	....	....	....	....	....	....	....
Other sectors	8 796	....	....	....	....	....	....	....	....
of which: Short-term	8 798	....	....	....	....	....	....	....	....
NET INTERNATIONAL INVESTMENT POSITION	8 995	−13,394.8	−20,919.6	−23,934.0	−40,098.5	−59,037.6	−49,698.0	−56,299.1	−56,646.2
Conversion rates: kunas per U.S. dollar (end of period)	0 102	6.1185	5.6369	6.2336	5.5784	4.9855	5.1555	5.0893	5.5683

Table 1. ANALYTIC PRESENTATION, 2003–2010

(Millions of U.S. dollars)

	Code	2003	2004	2005	2006	2007	2008	2009	2010
A. Current Account[1]	4 993 Z.	−292.1	−826.8	−970.9	−1,279.4	−1,830.9	−3,287.4	−2,075.8	−2,802.7
Goods: exports f.o.b.	2 100 ..	925.0	1,173.5	1,544.7	1,393.0	1,482.9	1,753.4	1,387.8	1,518.4
Goods: imports f.o.b.	3 100 ..	−4,107.8	−5,222.1	−5,791.8	−6,334.9	−7,957.0	−10,000.9	−7,539.4	−8,032.4
Balance on Goods	4 100 ..	*−3,182.8*	*−4,048.7*	*−4,247.1*	*−4,941.9*	*−6,474.1*	*−8,247.5*	*−6,151.6*	*−6,514.1*
Services: credit	2 200 ..	5,371.8	6,235.0	6,502.0	7,159.6	8,803.0	9,622.0	7,997.0	8,226.2
Services: debit	3 200 ..	−2,236.7	−2,644.1	−2,706.0	−2,938.7	−3,763.8	−4,290.9	−3,288.1	−3,202.8
Balance on Goods and Services	4 991 ..	*−47.7*	*−457.8*	*−451.2*	*−720.9*	*−1,434.9*	*−2,916.5*	*−1,442.7*	*−1,490.7*
Income: credit	2 300 ..	905.5	1,160.1	1,634.8	2,139.1	4,163.5	3,964.8	5,101.0	3,234.5
Income: debit	3 300 ..	−1,294.5	−1,697.3	−2,246.6	−2,903.6	−4,546.2	−4,236.8	−5,450.8	−4,501.6
Balance on Goods, Services, and Income	4 992 ..	*−436.8*	*−995.0*	*−1,063.0*	*−1,485.4*	*−1,817.6*	*−3,188.5*	*−1,792.4*	*−2,757.7*
Current transfers: credit	2 379 Z.	386.3	585.1	631.2	822.3	822.3	953.2	632.5	1,133.9
Current transfers: debit	3 379 ..	−241.6	−416.9	−539.1	−616.2	−835.6	−1,052.1	−915.9	−1,178.9
B. Capital Account[1]	4 994 Z.	**37.9**	**133.9**	**86.9**	**33.2**	**8.1**	**9.8**	**87.2**	**38.4**
Capital account: credit	2 994 Z.	59.0	191.7	131.1	97.8	87.8	80.8	144.1	79.1
Capital account: debit	3 994 ..	−21.0	−57.8	−44.2	−64.6	−79.6	−71.1	−56.9	−40.8
Total, Groups A Plus B	4 981 ..	*−254.1*	*−692.9*	*−884.0*	*−1,246.1*	*−1,822.8*	*−3,277.7*	*−1,988.6*	*−2,764.3*
C. Financial Account[1]	4 995 W.	**46.0**	**912.2**	**1,421.5**	**2,270.2**	**2,335.0**	**3,040.7**	**2,026.2**	**2,659.0**
Direct investment abroad	4 505 ..	−589.7	−711.7	−547.6	−896.3	−1,263.0	−3,382.4	−910.3	−1,003.9
Direct investment in Cyprus	4 555 Z.	908.1	1,118.8	1,162.0	1,870.9	2,295.5	953.3	3,505.1	1,885.9
Portfolio investment assets	4 602 ..	−521.2	−1,812.6	−1,620.3	−3,158.4	593.8	−16,996.3	−19,210.6	−3,115.3
Equity securities	4 610 ..	161.9	−74.4	−18.4	31.9	−93.6	−70.1	−1,662.3	−2,475.7
Debt securities	4 619 ..	−683.1	−1,738.1	−1,601.9	−3,190.2	687.4	−16,926.2	−17,548.3	−639.7
Portfolio investment liabilities	4 652 Z.	802.5	2,979.0	1,566.5	3,010.0	−1,089.4	−772.7	1,308.9	162.3
Equity securities	4 660 ..	−.1	−13.9	13.2	45.9	1.5	−70.5	24.4	439.9
Debt securities	4 669 Z.	802.6	2,992.9	1,553.3	2,964.1	−1,090.8	−702.2	1,284.4	−277.6
Financial derivatives	4 910 ..	16.6	−44.7	−15.2	−160.4	136.8	−146.2	401.8	−176.7
Financial derivatives assets	4 900 ..	16.6	−23.6	−16.5	−151.9	134.3	126.6	451.6	301.8
Financial derivatives liabilities	4 905 ..	....	−21.1	1.3	−8.5	2.5	−272.8	−49.7	−478.5
Other investment assets	4 703 ..	−2,357.0	−3,133.5	−7,154.0	−3,559.6	−13,964.1	−17,026.4	−3,340.2	20,884.8
Monetary authorities	4 701 ..	....	35.9	....	....	....	2,705.8	21.1	954.7
General government	4 704 ..	−20.8	−17.6	11.2	18.6	−38.1	−1.8	....	−1.4
Banks	4 705 ..	−2,482.3	−3,078.9	−7,807.0	−3,857.0	−13,601.7	−17,286.3	−2,173.8	18,252.8
Other sectors	4 728 ..	146.1	−72.8	641.7	278.8	−324.4	−2,444.1	−1,187.6	1,678.7
Other investment liabilities	4 753 W.	1,786.6	2,516.8	8,030.1	5,163.9	15,625.5	40,411.3	20,271.5	−15,978.0
Monetary authorities	4 753 WA	−2.5	−1.8	1.1	6.6	170.6	9,864.3	301.0	−908.6
General government	4 753 ZB	244.6	162.9	135.2	28.9	106.2	102.2	−33.7	−24.0
Banks	4 753 ZC	1,590.5	2,425.2	7,613.5	5,237.1	15,244.8	32,489.7	23,204.9	−15,709.9
Other sectors	4 753 ZD	−46.0	−69.5	280.4	−108.7	103.9	−2,044.9	−3,200.7	664.4
Total, Groups A Through C	4 983 ..	*−208.2*	*219.3*	*537.5*	*1,024.0*	*512.3*	*−237.0*	*37.6*	*−105.3*
D. Net Errors and Omissions	4 998 ..	**20.6**	**152.1**	**165.2**	**−11.8**	**−762.1**	**−183.2**	**42.9**	**−152.4**
Total, Groups A Through D	4 984 ..	*−187.6*	*371.4*	*702.7*	*1,012.2*	*−249.8*	*−420.2*	*80.5*	*−257.7*
E. Reserves and Related Items	4 802 A.	**187.6**	**−371.4**	**−702.7**	**−1,012.2**	**249.8**	**420.2**	**−80.5**	**257.7**
Reserve assets	4 802 ..	187.6	−371.4	−702.7	−1,012.2	249.8	420.2	−80.5	257.7
Use of Fund credit and loans	4 766 ..	....	....	....	....	....	....	....	....
Exceptional financing	4 920 ..	....	....	....	....	....	....	....	....
Conversion rates: Cyprus pounds per U.S. dollar	0 101 ..	**.5174**	**.4686**	**.4641**	**.4589**	**.4261**	....	....	....
Conversion rates: euros per U.S. dollar	0 103 ..	**.8860**	**.8054**	**.8041**	**.7971**	**.7306**	**.6827**	**.7198**	**.7550**

[1] Excludes components that have been classified in the categories of Group E.

Table 2. STANDARD PRESENTATION, 2003–2010

(Millions of U.S. dollars)

	Code	2003	2004	2005	2006	2007	2008	2009	2010
CURRENT ACCOUNT	4 993 ..	−292.1	−826.8	−970.9	−1,279.4	−1,830.9	−3,287.4	−2,075.8	−2,802.7
A. GOODS	4 100 ..	−3,182.8	−4,048.7	−4,247.1	−4,941.9	−6,474.1	−8,247.5	−6,151.6	−6,514.1
Credit	2 100 ..	925.0	1,173.5	1,544.7	1,393.0	1,482.9	1,753.4	1,387.8	1,518.4
General merchandise: exports f.o.b.	2 110 ..	834.5	1,082.8	1,302.8	1,133.4	1,248.7	1,409.1	1,160.7	1,288.9
Goods for processing: exports f.o.b.	2 150 ..	....	....	....	....	....	....	....	....
Repairs on goods	2 160 ..	.7	.4	.2	....	.8	....	35.4	....
Goods procured in ports by carriers	2 170 ..	89.6	90.1	241.5	259.7	233.3	344.3	191.4	229.2
Nonmonetary gold	2 180 ..	.1	.1	.2	....	.1	....	.2	.3
Debit	3 100 ..	−4,107.8	−5,222.1	−5,791.8	−6,334.9	−7,957.0	−10,000.9	−7,539.4	−8,032.4
General merchandise: imports f.o.b.	3 110 ..	−3,981.4	−5,154.4	−5,698.1	−6,207.1	−7,852.9	−9,880.9	−7,300.0	−7,870.6
Goods for processing: imports f.o.b.	3 150 ..	....	....	....	....	....	....	....	....
Repairs on goods	3 160 ..	−44.2	−6.0	−5.9	−38.3	−9.6	−8.1	−76.9	−1.9
Goods procured in ports by carriers	3 170 ..	−81.3	−59.3	−86.8	−88.2	−91.9	−110.2	−161.1	−159.2
Nonmonetary gold	3 180 ..	−1.0	−2.4	−1.0	−1.3	−2.5	−1.8	−1.4	−.7
B. SERVICES	4 200 ..	3,135.1	3,590.9	3,796.0	4,221.0	5,039.2	5,331.1	4,708.9	5,023.4
Total credit	2 200 ..	*5,371.8*	*6,235.0*	*6,502.0*	*7,159.6*	*8,803.0*	*9,622.0*	*7,997.0*	*8,226.2*
Total debit	3 200 ..	*−2,236.7*	*−2,644.1*	*−2,706.0*	*−2,938.7*	*−3,763.8*	*−4,290.9*	*−3,288.1*	*−3,202.8*
Transportation services, credit	2 205 ..	1,239.6	1,436.2	1,543.4	1,657.4	2,119.0	2,605.4	2,154.6	1,930.0
Passenger	2 850 ..	*227.8*	*311.4*	*325.6*	*309.7*	*422.4*	*406.7*	*278.7*	*262.9*
Freight	2 851 ..	*264.6*	*309.0*	*317.7*	*443.4*	*644.3*	*890.7*	*858.7*	*738.5*
Other	2 852 ..	*747.2*	*815.8*	*900.1*	*904.3*	*1,052.4*	*1,308.0*	*1,017.2*	*928.6*
Sea transport, passenger	2 207 ..	1.8	75.8	75.9	81.5	85.7	44.8	18.6	8.8
Sea transport, freight	2 208 ..	246.9	285.1	295.3	309.6	418.7	749.5	770.6	672.7
Sea transport, other	2 209 ..	537.3	697.0	744.7	755.8	893.2	1,203.0	956.9	870.1
Air transport, passenger	2 211 ..	226.0	235.6	249.7	228.2	336.7	361.9	260.1	254.1
Air transport, freight	2 212 ..	17.4	23.1	21.9	116.0	190.2	109.7	64.5	42.0
Air transport, other	2 213 ..	205.0	100.8	106.9	136.9	155.1	104.8	59.6	57.5
Other transport, passenger	2 215 ..	....	....	....	....	....	....	....	....
Other transport, freight	2 216 ..	.4	.8	.5	17.8	35.3	31.6	23.5	23.8
Other transport, other	2 217 ..	4.9	18.0	48.4	11.5	4.1	.2	.7	.9
Transportation services, debit	3 205 ..	−1,077.3	−1,116.4	−1,079.7	−1,075.3	−1,208.1	−1,622.0	−1,247.4	−1,287.3
Passenger	3 850 ..	*−89.4*	*−96.0*	*−69.0*	*−64.2*	*−75.2*	*−302.4*	*−338.3*	*−290.8*
Freight	3 851 ..	*−449.3*	*−574.1*	*−511.4*	*−555.8*	*−701.8*	*−868.6*	*−649.2*	*−745.0*
Other	3 852 ..	*−538.6*	*−446.3*	*−499.2*	*−455.3*	*−431.1*	*−451.0*	*−259.9*	*−251.5*
Sea transport, passenger	3 207 ..	−8.2	−2.5	−2.8	−1.4	−3.2	−19.1	−9.5	−7.0
Sea transport, freight	3 208 ..	−297.2	−380.7	−339.4	−369.2	−465.3	−577.9	−419.7	−477.4
Sea transport, other	3 209 ..	−396.8	−273.8	−335.7	−368.3	−294.1	−326.7	−181.0	−171.8
Air transport, passenger	3 211 ..	−81.2	−93.5	−66.2	−62.7	−72.0	−283.3	−328.9	−283.8
Air transport, freight	3 212 ..	−148.6	−190.4	−169.7	−184.6	−232.7	−288.8	−209.8	−217.0
Air transport, other	3 213 ..	−117.2	−154.7	−159.0	−79.6	−133.0	−118.4	−76.0	−76.7
Other transport, passenger	3 215 ..	....	....	....	....	....	....	....	....
Other transport, freight	3 216 ..	−3.5	−3.0	−2.3	−2.0	−3.8	−1.9	−19.7	−50.6
Other transport, other	3 217 ..	−24.5	−17.9	−4.5	−7.4	−4.0	−5.9	−2.9	−3.0
Travel, credit	2 236 ..	2,097.1	2,241.3	2,317.8	2,380.9	2,686.0	2,768.3	2,180.3	2,153.4
Business travel	2 237 ..	104.6	119.5	120.1	134.2	198.7	174.2	146.9	127.4
Personal travel	2 240 ..	1,992.5	2,121.7	2,197.7	2,246.7	2,487.4	2,594.0	2,033.4	2,026.0
Travel, debit	3 236 ..	−611.2	−811.1	−931.8	−966.5	−1,479.3	−1,547.1	−1,265.6	−1,144.9
Business travel	3 237 ..	−15.4	−28.4	−17.5	−21.9	−31.5	−328.2	−274.6	−197.6
Personal travel	3 240 ..	−595.8	−782.7	−914.3	−944.6	−1,447.8	−1,218.9	−991.0	−947.2
Other services, credit	2 200 BA	2,035.1	2,557.6	2,640.8	3,121.4	3,998.0	4,248.3	3,662.1	4,142.7
Communications	2 245 ..	50.7	35.2	35.6	92.4	117.4	104.5	107.8	93.1
Construction	2 249 ..	153.2	145.6	165.7	199.2	202.3	154.0	53.5	51.2
Insurance	2 253 ..	34.3	44.7	56.4	113.8	117.6	181.6	98.5	46.5
Financial	2 260 ..	147.2	220.2	264.4	313.8	735.2	1,223.3	1,122.8	1,153.8
Computer and information	2 262 ..	91.9	250.3	229.2	202.1	274.7	211.9	97.6	98.2
Royalties and licence fees	2 266 ..	15.0	17.7	15.1	16.0	21.1	12.1	12.0	8.5
Other business services	2 268 ..	1,169.9	1,461.4	1,508.5	1,743.4	1,954.2	2,053.5	1,926.5	2,467.0
Personal, cultural, and recreational	2 287 ..	9.7	24.8	41.1	52.9	77.0	52.9	36.4	41.8
Government, n.i.e.	2 291 ..	363.3	357.7	324.8	387.8	498.4	254.4	206.9	182.6
Other services, debit	3 200 BA	−548.2	−716.6	−694.6	−896.9	−1,076.4	−1,121.8	−775.1	−770.6
Communications	3 245 ..	−66.1	−78.3	−94.5	−125.9	−142.0	−149.3	−94.0	−75.9
Construction	3 249 ..	−14.4	−15.1	−10.9	−23.3	−28.5	−21.8	−12.9	−14.5
Insurance	3 253 ..	−46.4	−71.2	−65.1	−75.6	−84.8	−67.4	−45.8	−41.4
Financial	3 260 ..	−45.5	−100.1	−92.8	−131.8	−161.6	−222.7	−109.5	−211.3
Computer and information	3 262 ..	−36.8	−32.8	−34.8	−34.0	−38.2	−28.7	−24.7	−39.2
Royalties and licence fees	3 266 ..	−38.6	−53.4	−44.7	−60.5	−55.6	−44.9	−41.0	−30.9
Other business services	3 268 ..	−130.4	−225.3	−203.4	−291.8	−355.5	−396.2	−327.1	−223.0
Personal, cultural, and recreational	3 287 ..	−22.3	−48.6	−56.0	−64.9	−81.3	−76.0	−44.2	−45.9
Government, n.i.e.	3 291 ..	−147.6	−91.9	−92.3	−89.0	−129.1	−114.7	−75.9	−88.4

Table 2 (Continued). STANDARD PRESENTATION, 2003–2010

(Millions of U.S. dollars)

	Code	2003	2004	2005	2006	2007	2008	2009	2010
C. INCOME..	4 300 ..	**−389.0**	**−537.2**	**−611.8**	**−764.5**	**−382.7**	**−272.1**	**−349.7**	**−1,267.1**
Total credit..	2 300 ..	*905.5*	*1,160.1*	*1,634.8*	*2,139.1*	*4,163.5*	*3,964.8*	*5,101.0*	*3,234.5*
Total debit...	3 300 ..	*−1,294.5*	*−1,697.3*	*−2,246.6*	*−2,903.6*	*−4,546.2*	*−4,236.8*	*−5,450.8*	*−4,501.6*
Compensation of employees, credit..................	2 310 ..	**25.4**	**33.1**	**53.9**	**34.5**	**43.5**	**88.1**	**39.0**	**41.3**
Compensation of employees, debit....................	3 310 ..	**−137.2**	**−159.2**	**−185.3**	**−184.3**	**−223.4**	**−408.4**	**−241.2**	**−221.8**
Investment income, credit...............................	2 320 ..	**880.1**	**1,127.0**	**1,580.8**	**2,104.6**	**4,120.0**	**3,876.7**	**5,062.1**	**3,193.2**
Direct investment income..............................	2 330 ..	306.8	390.3	518.8	607.3	849.4	673.4	2,259.9	397.4
Dividends and distributed branch profits..........	2 332 ..	10.8	14.2	120.6	113.1	176.2	101.1	1,238.2	253.0
Reinvested earnings and undistributed branch profits.....	2 333 ..	246.8	290.2	238.9	317.3	422.9	365.4	255.5	43.6
Income on debt (interest)............................	2 334 ..	49.2	85.9	159.4	176.9	250.3	206.9	766.2	100.8
Portfolio investment income..........................	2 339 ..	126.3	190.1	228.0	488.9	1,679.2	1,540.6	1,264.6	1,243.1
Income on equity.....................................	2 340 ..	28.9	36.9	37.8	76.8	144.5	224.1	47.1	45.1
Income on bonds and notes.........................	2 350 ..	81.1	142.2	182.5	408.6	1,459.2	1,208.3	1,196.2	1,173.9
Income on money market instruments.............	2 360 ..	16.4	11.1	7.6	3.4	75.6	108.2	21.3	24.0
Other investment income.............................	2 370 ..	447.0	546.6	834.1	1,008.4	1,591.4	1,662.7	1,537.6	1,552.7
Investment income, debit................................	3 320 ..	**−1,157.3**	**−1,538.1**	**−2,061.3**	**−2,719.3**	**−4,322.8**	**−3,828.4**	**−5,209.6**	**−4,279.8**
Direct investment income..............................	3 330 ..	−727.4	−961.7	−1,222.9	−1,646.0	−2,406.4	−1,301.9	−3,143.9	−2,240.4
Dividends and distributed branch profits..........	3 332 ..	−329.1	−409.3	−535.1	−602.3	−1,109.8	−838.6	−983.9	−1,069.3
Reinvested earnings and undistributed branch profits.....	3 333 ..	−262.0	−482.4	−538.1	−823.6	−973.0	52.0	−1,473.0	−1,133.6
Income on debt (interest)............................	3 334 ..	−136.3	−70.1	−149.8	−220.1	−323.6	−515.2	−687.0	−37.5
Portfolio investment income..........................	3 339 ..	−105.1	−228.0	−249.4	−387.2	−880.3	−1,212.0	−819.9	−912.7
Income on equity.....................................	3 340 ..	−10.2	−44.6	−12.3	−60.3	−351.1	−436.5	−176.3	−225.1
Income on bonds and notes.........................	3 350 ..	−93.4	−142.8	−187.5	−280.7	−443.3	−649.5	−575.8	−662.2
Income on money market instruments.............	3 360 ..	−1.5	−40.6	−49.6	−46.2	−85.9	−126.0	−67.9	−25.4
Other investment income.............................	3 370 ..	−324.8	−348.3	−589.0	−686.1	−1,036.1	−1,314.5	−1,245.8	−1,126.7
D. CURRENT TRANSFERS.................................	4 379 ..	**144.7**	**168.2**	**92.1**	**206.0**	**−13.3**	**−98.9**	**−283.4**	**−44.9**
Credit..	2 379 ..	**386.3**	**585.1**	**631.2**	**822.3**	**822.3**	**953.2**	**632.5**	**1,133.9**
General government.....................................	2 380 ..	48.9	173.7	234.5	308.3	241.4	165.8	154.4	164.4
Other sectors..	2 390 ..	337.3	411.4	396.7	514.0	580.9	787.4	478.1	969.6
Workers' remittances.................................	2 391 ..	6.4	44.3	50.9	69.9	98.7	169.7	91.2	97.4
Other current transfers..............................	2 392 ..	330.9	367.1	345.8	444.1	482.2	617.7	386.9	872.2
Debit..	3 379 ..	**−241.6**	**−416.9**	**−539.1**	**−616.2**	**−835.6**	**−1,052.1**	**−915.9**	**−1,178.9**
General government.....................................	3 380 ..	−2.7	−132.3	−210.9	−203.6	−272.9	−303.2	−313.2	−314.8
Other sectors..	3 390 ..	−238.9	−284.5	−328.2	−412.7	−562.7	−748.9	−602.7	−864.1
Workers' remittances.................................	3 391 ..	−46.7	−54.2	−55.4	−55.2	−81.3	−115.0	−120.1	−153.6
Other current transfers..............................	3 392 ..	−192.2	−230.3	−272.8	−357.5	−481.4	−633.9	−482.6	−710.5
CAPITAL AND FINANCIAL ACCOUNT......................	4 996 ..	**271.5**	**674.7**	**805.7**	**1,291.2**	**2,593.0**	**3,470.7**	**2,032.9**	**2,955.0**
CAPITAL ACCOUNT...	4 994 ..	**37.9**	**133.9**	**86.9**	**33.2**	**8.1**	**9.8**	**87.2**	**38.4**
Total credit..	2 994 ..	*59.0*	*191.7*	*131.1*	*97.8*	*87.8*	*80.8*	*144.1*	*79.1*
Total debit...	3 994 ..	*−21.0*	*−57.8*	*−44.2*	*−64.6*	*−79.6*	*−71.1*	*−56.9*	*−40.8*
Capital transfers, credit.................................	2 400 ..	**59.0**	**191.7**	**131.1**	**97.8**	**87.8**	**80.8**	**144.1**	**79.1**
General government.....................................	2 401 ..	6.5	24.1	46.5	33.2	57.8	59.7	120.8	72.0
Debt forgiveness.....................................	2 402 ..	. . . .	. . . .	. . . .	. . . .	. . . .	. . . .	. . . .	. . . .
Other capital transfers..............................	2 410 ..	6.5	24.1	46.5	33.2	57.8	59.7	120.8	72.0
Other sectors..	2 430 ..	52.5	167.5	84.7	64.7	29.9	21.1	23.3	7.1
Migrants' transfers..................................	2 431 ..	52.5	167.5	84.7	64.7	29.9	21.1	23.3	7.1
Debt forgiveness.....................................	2 432 ..	. . . .	. . . .	. . . .	. . . .	. . . .	. . . .	. . . .	. . . .
Other capital transfers..............................	2 440 ..	. . . .	. . . .	. . . .	. . . .	. . . .	. . . .	. . . .	. . . .
Capital transfers, debit..................................	3 400 ..	**−21.0**	**−57.8**	**−44.2**	**−64.6**	**−79.6**	**−71.1**	**−56.9**	**−40.8**
General government.....................................	3 401 ..	−2.8	−15.8	−11.6	−25.3	−14.0	−10.1	−9.2	−12.4
Debt forgiveness.....................................	3 402 ..	. . . .	. . . .	. . . .	. . . .	. . . .	. . . .	. . . .	. . . .
Other capital transfers..............................	3 410 ..	−2.8	−15.8	−11.6	−25.3	−14.0	−10.1	−9.2	−12.4
Other sectors..	3 430 ..	−18.2	−41.9	−32.6	−39.3	−65.6	−61.0	−47.7	−28.4
Migrants' transfers..................................	3 431 ..	−18.2	−41.9	−32.6	−39.3	−65.6	−61.0	−47.7	−28.4
Debt forgiveness.....................................	3 432 ..	. . . .	. . . .	. . . .	. . . .	. . . .	. . . .	. . . .	. . . .
Other capital transfers..............................	3 440 ..	. . . .	. . . .	. . . .	. . . .	. . . .	. . . .	. . . .	. . . .
Nonproduced nonfinancial assets, credit.............	2 480 ..	. . . .	. . . .	. . . .	. . . .	. . . .	. . . .	. . . .	. . . .
Nonproduced nonfinancial assets, debit.............	3 480 ..	. . . .	. . . .	. . . .	. . . .	. . . .	. . . .	. . . .	. . . .

2011, International Monetary Fund: *Balance of Payments Statistics Yearbook*

Table 2 (Continued). STANDARD PRESENTATION, 2003–2010

(Millions of U.S. dollars)

	Code	2003	2004	2005	2006	2007	2008	2009	2010
FINANCIAL ACCOUNT	4 995 ..	**233.6**	**540.8**	**718.8**	**1,258.0**	**2,584.8**	**3,460.9**	**1,945.7**	**2,916.6**
A. DIRECT INVESTMENT	4 500 ..	**318.5**	**407.1**	**614.4**	**974.6**	**1,032.5**	**−2,429.0**	**2,594.8**	**881.9**
Direct investment abroad	4 505 ..	**−589.7**	**−711.7**	**−547.6**	**−896.3**	**−1,263.0**	**−3,382.4**	**−910.3**	**−1,003.9**
Equity capital	4 510 ..	−137.6	−253.8	−122.3	−2,386.9	−784.1	−1,830.3	−395.4	−395.2
Claims on affiliated enterprises	4 515 ..	−137.6	−253.8	−122.3	−2,386.9	−784.1	−1,830.3	−395.4	−395.2
Liabilities to affiliated enterprises	4 520 ..	....	....	....	....	....	....	....	....
Reinvested earnings	4 525 ..	−246.8	−290.2	−238.9	−317.3	−422.9	−365.4	−255.5	−43.6
Other capital	4 530 ..	−205.3	−167.7	−186.5	1,807.9	−56.0	−1,186.6	−259.4	−565.1
Claims on affiliated enterprises	4 535 ..	−205.3	−167.7	−186.5	1,807.9	−56.0	−1,179.2	−180.2	−565.1
Liabilities to affiliated enterprises	4 540 ..	....	....	....	....	....	−7.4	−79.2	....
Direct investment in Cyprus	4 555 ..	**908.1**	**1,118.8**	**1,162.0**	**1,870.9**	**2,295.5**	**953.3**	**3,505.1**	**1,885.9**
Equity capital	4 560 ..	254.3	386.1	503.8	629.2	952.9	572.0	875.1	373.5
Claims on direct investors	4 565 ..	....	....	....	....	....	....	....	....
Liabilities to direct investors	4 570 ..	254.3	386.1	503.8	629.2	952.9	572.0	875.1	373.5
Reinvested earnings	4 575 ..	262.0	482.4	538.1	823.6	973.0	−52.0	1,473.0	1,133.6
Other capital	4 580 ..	391.8	250.3	120.1	418.1	369.6	433.3	1,157.0	378.8
Claims on direct investors	4 585 ..	....	....	....	−1.5	....	47.8	152.9	....
Liabilities to direct investors	4 590 ..	391.8	250.3	120.1	419.6	369.6	385.6	1,004.0	378.8
B. PORTFOLIO INVESTMENT	4 600 ..	**281.3**	**1,166.5**	**−53.7**	**−148.3**	**−495.6**	**−17,769.0**	**−17,901.8**	**−2,953.1**
Assets	4 602 ..	**−521.2**	**−1,812.6**	**−1,620.3**	**−3,158.4**	**593.8**	**−16,996.3**	**−19,210.6**	**−3,115.3**
Equity securities	4 610 ..	161.9	−74.4	−18.4	31.9	−93.6	−70.1	−1,662.3	−2,475.7
Monetary authorities	4 611 ..	....	....	....	....	....	....	....	....
General government	4 612 ..	....	....	....	....	....	....	....	....
Banks	4 613 ..	158.5	−58.5	−31.3	−181.8	175.2	11.1	10.3	−16.6
Other sectors	4 614 ..	3.4	−16.0	12.9	213.6	−268.8	−81.2	−1,672.7	−2,459.1
Debt securities	4 619 ..	−683.1	−1,738.1	−1,601.9	−3,190.2	687.4	−16,926.2	−17,548.3	−639.7
Bonds and notes	4 620 ..	−644.5	−1,724.3	−1,783.0	−3,317.6	858.2	−12,969.2	−17,767.8	697.4
Monetary authorities	4 621 ..	....	....	....	....	....	−1,924.9	268.5	−785.3
General government	4 622 ..	....	....	....	....	....	....	....	....
Banks	4 623 ..	−644.5	−1,730.9	−1,782.4	−3,316.8	803.3	−10,985.5	−16,011.4	3,871.8
Other sectors	4 624 ..	....	6.6	−.5	−.7	54.9	−58.8	−2,024.8	−2,389.0
Money market instruments	4 630 ..	−38.6	−13.8	181.1	127.4	−170.8	−3,957.0	219.5	−1,337.1
Monetary authorities	4 631 ..	....	....	....	....	....	....	....	....
General government	4 632 ..	....	....	....	....	....	....	....	....
Banks	4 633 ..	−38.6	−13.8	181.1	127.6	−170.8	−3,957.3	448.1	−1,269.0
Other sectors	4 634 ..	....	....	....	−.2	....	.3	−228.7	−68.1
Liabilities	4 652 ..	**802.5**	**2,979.0**	**1,566.5**	**3,010.0**	**−1,089.4**	**−772.7**	**1,308.9**	**162.3**
Equity securities	4 660 ..	−.1	−13.9	13.2	45.9	1.5	−70.5	24.4	439.9
Banks	4 663 ..	−3.5	−21.4	−3.4	−21.9	10.4	−102.7	26.4	374.8
Other sectors	4 664 ..	3.5	7.5	16.6	67.8	−8.9	32.2	−2.0	65.0
Debt securities	4 669 ..	802.6	2,992.9	1,553.3	2,964.1	−1,090.8	−702.2	1,284.4	−277.6
Bonds and notes	4 670 ..	618.8	1,409.0	1,215.2	513.3	1,578.5	−191.7	1,953.2	641.5
Monetary authorities	4 671 ..	....	....	....	....	....	....	....	....
General government	4 672 ..	....	608.5	....	....	....	−525.4	2,030.9	862.4
Banks	4 673 ..	618.8	800.5	1,215.2	858.8	1,752.2	381.0	−128.3	−271.2
Other sectors	4 674 ..	....	....	....	−345.5	−173.7	−47.2	50.5	50.2
Money market instruments	4 680 ..	183.8	1,583.9	338.1	2,450.8	−2,669.4	−510.5	−668.7	−919.1
Monetary authorities	4 681 ..	....	....	....	....	....	....	....	....
General government	4 682 ..	183.1	10.8	−244.6	....	....	709.5	160.2	−936.6
Banks	4 683 ..	.6	1,573.1	582.7	2,450.8	−2,637.2	−1,283.6	−769.8	.2
Other sectors	4 684 ..	....	....	....	....	−32.2	63.5	−59.1	17.2
C. FINANCIAL DERIVATIVES	4 910 ..	**16.6**	**−44.7**	**−15.2**	**−160.4**	**136.8**	**−146.2**	**401.8**	**−176.7**
Monetary authorities	4 911 ..	....	....	....	....	....	121.8	368.6	....
General government	4 912 ..	....	....	....	....	....	....	....	....
Banks	4 913 ..	16.4	−40.3	−13.9	−164.7	142.2	−293.7	39.8	−175.4
Other sectors	4 914 ..	.2	−4.4	−1.3	4.3	−5.4	25.7	−6.5	−1.3
Assets	4 900 ..	**16.6**	**−23.6**	**−16.5**	**−151.9**	**134.3**	**126.6**	**451.6**	**301.8**
Monetary authorities	4 901 ..	....	....	....	....	....	121.8	368.6	....
General government	4 902 ..	....	....	....	....	....	....	....	....
Banks	4 903 ..	16.4	−19.2	−13.9	−151.9	134.3	−7.3	71.5	301.8
Other sectors	4 904 ..	.2	−4.4	−2.6	....	....	12.1	11.5	....
Liabilities	4 905 ..	**....**	**−21.1**	**1.3**	**−8.5**	**2.5**	**−272.8**	**−49.7**	**−478.5**
Monetary authorities	4 906 ..	....	....	....	....	....	....	....	....
General government	4 907 ..	....	....	....	....	....	....	....	....
Banks	4 908 ..	....	−21.1	....	−12.8	7.9	−286.4	−31.8	−477.2
Other sectors	4 909 ..	....	....	1.3	4.3	−5.4	13.6	−18.0	−1.3

Table 2 (Concluded). STANDARD PRESENTATION, 2003–2010

(Millions of U.S. dollars)

	Code	2003	2004	2005	2006	2007	2008	2009	2010
D. OTHER INVESTMENT	4 700	−570.4	−616.7	876.1	1,604.3	1,661.4	23,384.9	16,931.3	4,906.8
Assets	4 703	−2,357.0	−3,133.5	−7,154.0	−3,559.6	−13,964.1	−17,026.4	−3,340.2	20,884.8
Trade credits	4 706	−17.7	−15.9	13.8	21.2	−33.3	11.2	20.4	8.8
General government	4 707	−17.7	−15.9	13.8	21.2	−36.0	−1.8	....	−1.4
of which: Short-term	4 709	....	....	....	....	−22.3	....	....	....
Other sectors	4 710	....	....	....	....	2.8	13.0	20.4	10.2
of which: Short-term	4 712	....	....	....	....	2.8	....	....	....
Loans	4 714	−651.8	−2,417.4	−1,122.2	−782.6	−6,076.4	607.1	−4,198.4	−414.7
Monetary authorities	4 715	....	....	....	....	....	....	....	....
of which: Short-term	4 718	....	....	....	....	....	....	....	....
General government	4 719	....	....	....	....	....	....	....	....
of which: Short-term	4 721	....	....	....	....	....	....	....	....
Banks	4 722	−651.8	−2,417.4	−1,122.2	−782.6	−6,018.1	595.4	−4,198.4	−414.7
of which: Short-term	4 724	−1.2	3.0	.8	−52.5	−416.4	670.9	−1,662.2	−257.4
Other sectors	4 725	....	....	....	....	−58.3	11.7	....	....
of which: Short-term	4 727	....	....	....	....	....	....	....	....
Currency and deposits	4 730	−1,700.9	−694.1	−6,049.4	−2,795.6	−7,852.4	−17,644.7	837.7	21,290.8
Monetary authorities	4 731	....	35.9	....	....	....	2,705.8	21.1	954.7
General government	4 732	....	....	....	....	....	....	....	....
Banks	4 733	−1,847.0	−657.1	−6,691.1	−3,074.4	−7,583.5	−17,881.6	2,024.6	18,667.5
Other sectors	4 734	146.1	−72.8	641.7	278.8	−268.9	−2,468.8	−1,208.0	1,668.5
Other assets	4 736	13.4	−6.2	3.7	−2.6	−2.1	....	....	....
Monetary authorities	4 737	....	....	....	....	....	....	....	....
of which: Short-term	4 739	....	....	....	....	....	....	....	....
General government	4 740	−3.1	−1.7	−2.6	−2.6	−2.1	....	....	....
of which: Short-term	4 742	....	....	....	....	....	....	....	....
Banks	4 743	16.5	−4.5	6.3	....	....	....	....	....
of which: Short-term	4 745	....	....	....	....	....	....	....	....
Other sectors	4 746	....	....	....	....	....	....	....	....
of which: Short-term	4 748	....	....	....	....	....	....	....	....
Liabilities	4 753	1,786.6	2,516.8	8,030.1	5,163.9	15,625.5	40,411.3	20,271.5	−15,978.0
Trade credits	4 756	11.7	68.7	91.8	−32.6	228.6	36.2	−158.2	181.5
General government	4 757	....	....	....	....	....	....	....	....
of which: Short-term	4 759	....	....	....	....	....	....	....	....
Other sectors	4 760	11.7	68.7	91.8	−32.6	228.6	36.2	−158.2	181.5
of which: Short-term	4 762	13.2	71.3	94.4	−31.9	147.8	36.7	−158.2	181.5
Loans	4 764	636.5	905.1	1,099.4	1,008.8	3,330.1	10,440.1	−2,039.5	2,081.8
Monetary authorities	4 765	....	....	....	....	....	9,861.9	123.9	−908.6
of which: Use of Fund credit and loans from the Fund	4 766	....	....	....	....	....	....	....	....
of which: Short-term	4 768	....	....	....	....	....	9,861.9	123.9	−908.6
General government	4 769	244.6	162.9	135.2	28.9	101.0	102.2	−33.7	−24.0
of which: Short-term	4 771	....	....	....	....	....	....	−33.7	−49.7
Banks	4 772	449.6	880.5	775.7	1,056.1	3,353.7	2,557.2	912.6	2,531.4
of which: Short-term	4 774	....	....	....	252.3	1,116.7	1,905.0	755.5	1,370.7
Other sectors	4 775	−57.7	−138.2	188.6	−76.2	−124.6	−2,081.1	−3,042.4	482.9
of which: Short-term	4 777	11.2	−.6	233.9	12.7	−108.5	−2,249.5	−3,019.9	776.5
Currency and deposits	4 780	1,138.4	1,543.0	6,838.9	4,187.7	12,066.8	29,932.6	22,292.2	−18,241.3
Monetary authorities	4 781	−2.5	−1.8	1.1	6.6	170.6	....	....	....
General government	4 782	....	....	....	....	5.2	....	....	....
Banks	4 783	1,140.9	1,544.7	6,837.8	4,181.1	11,891.0	29,932.6	22,292.2	−18,241.3
Other sectors	4 784	....	....	....	....	....	....	....	....
Other liabilities	4 786	....	....	....	....	....	2.4	177.0	....
Monetary authorities	4 787	....	....	....	....	....	2.4	177.0	....
of which: Short-term	4 789	....	....	....	....	....	2.4	....	....
General government	4 790	....	....	....	....	....	....	....	....
of which: Short-term	4 792	....	....	....	....	....	....	....	....
Banks	4 793	....	....	....	....	....	....	....	....
of which: Short-term	4 795	....	....	....	....	....	....	....	....
Other sectors	4 796	....	....	....	....	....	....	....	....
of which: Short-term	4 798	....	....	....	....	....	....	....	....
E. RESERVE ASSETS	4 802	187.6	−371.4	−702.7	−1,012.2	249.8	420.2	−80.5	257.7
Monetary gold	4 812	....	....	....	....	....	....	....	....
Special drawing rights	4 811	−.6	−.8	−.6	.3	.8	.7	−183.7	−4.1
Reserve position in the Fund	4 810	−25.3	29.0	37.3	11.1	6.9	−11.9	−17.1	−5.4
Foreign exchange	4 803	213.5	−399.7	−739.4	−1,023.7	242.2	431.4	120.4	267.2
Other claims	4 813	....	....	....	....	....	....	....	....
NET ERRORS AND OMISSIONS	4 998	20.6	152.1	165.2	−11.8	−762.1	−183.2	42.9	−152.4

Table 3. INTERNATIONAL INVESTMENT POSITION (End-period stocks), 2003–2010

(Millions of U.S. dollars)

	Code	2003	2004	2005	2006	2007	2008	2009	2010
ASSETS.................................	8 995 C.	**29,276.2**	**40,613.7**	**47,756.8**	**71,366.8**	**91,976.0**	**118,860.0**	**146,060.0**	**119,844.1**
Direct investment abroad................	8 505 ..	**2,058.3**	**3,155.4**	**3,587.2**	**6,833.9**	**8,930.8**	**10,777.6**	**10,663.9**	**8,602.7**
Equity capital and reinvested earnings......	8 506 ..	1,553.6	2,431.3	2,778.0	5,882.2	7,807.3	9,171.4	10,446.8	8,081.8
Claims on affiliated enterprises.........	8 507 ..	1,553.6	2,431.3	2,778.0	5,882.2	7,807.3	9,171.4	10,446.8	8,081.8
Liabilities to affiliated enterprises.......	8 508 ..	....	....	....	....	....	....	....	....
Other capital............................	8 530 ..	504.7	724.1	809.2	951.7	1,123.5	1,606.3	217.1	521.0
Claims on affiliated enterprises.........	8 535 ..	515.2	734.5	809.2	951.7	1,123.5	1,606.3	217.1	521.0
Liabilities to affiliated enterprises.......	8 540 ..	−10.5	−10.4	....	....	....	....	....	....
Portfolio investment......................	8 602 ..	**6,581.0**	**10,378.8**	**13,378.5**	**26,437.3**	**26,033.1**	**39,562.5**	**61,937.1**	**49,674.3**
Equity securities.......................	8 610 ..	1,211.0	1,909.1	2,373.4	4,432.4	5,012.2	1,406.8	3,038.4	3,009.3
Monetary authorities.................	8 611 ..	....	....	....	....	....	....	....	....
General government..................	8 612 ..	....	....	....	....	....	....	....	....
Banks................................	8 613 ..	202.4	147.3	125.6	237.5	49.3	4.5	2.2	2.1
Other sectors.........................	8 614 ..	1,008.5	1,761.8	2,247.8	4,195.0	4,962.9	1,402.2	3,036.1	3,007.3
Debt securities.........................	8 619 ..	5,370.0	8,469.7	11,005.1	22,004.8	21,020.9	38,155.7	58,898.7	46,664.9
Bonds and notes......................	8 620 ..	4,662.7	7,773.1	10,682.4	21,403.6	20,417.8	37,600.0	58,708.8	45,231.4
Monetary authorities...............	8 621 ..	....	....	....	....	....	3,743.5	3,951.9	4,361.4
General government................	8 622 ..	....	....	....	....	....	....	....	....
Banks...............................	8 623 ..	4,155.0	7,382.1	10,034.0	20,377.3	19,328.4	33,186.8	52,631.3	37,890.1
Other sectors........................	8 624 ..	507.7	391.0	648.4	1,026.2	1,089.4	669.7	2,125.6	2,979.9
Money market instruments.............	8 630 ..	707.3	696.7	322.6	601.3	603.1	555.7	190.0	1,433.6
Monetary authorities...............	8 631 ..	....	....	....	....	....	....	....	....
General government................	8 632 ..	....	....	....	....	....	....	....	....
Banks...............................	8 633 ..	368.0	600.4	176.8	287.8	252.7	475.9	143.2	1,400.2
Other sectors........................	8 634 ..	339.4	96.2	145.8	313.4	350.4	79.7	46.8	33.4
Financial derivatives.....................	8 900 ..	**5.0**	**42.6**	**51.8**	**506.8**	**331.9**	**606.2**	**514.0**	**165.8**
Monetary authorities....................	8 901 ..	....	....	....	....	....	....	....	....
General government.....................	8 902 ..	....	....	....	....	....	....	....	....
Banks..................................	8 903 ..	2.8	37.7	45.2	498.0	317.9	599.1	508.2	162.9
Other sectors...........................	8 904 ..	2.2	4.9	6.7	8.8	14.0	7.1	5.8	2.9
Other investment.........................	8 703 ..	**17,142.5**	**22,962.2**	**26,410.7**	**31,724.4**	**50,168.5**	**66,910.3**	**71,654.9**	**60,256.0**
Trade credits...........................	8 706 ..	122.6	179.2	209.8	170.3	214.3	177.8	143.5	195.4
General government..................	8 707 ..	45.3	58.2	63.5	51.8	75.2	....	....	....
of which: Short-term...............	8 709 ..	....	....	....	....	....	....	....	....
Other sectors.........................	8 710 ..	77.3	121.0	146.3	118.6	139.1	177.8	143.5	195.4
of which: Short-term...............	8 712 ..	*77.3*	*121.0*	*146.3*	*118.6*	*139.1*	*177.8*	*143.5*	*195.4*
Loans..................................	8 714 ..	3,718.0	6,592.8	6,026.4	11,933.6	19,181.7	25,638.0	22,816.9	19,319.0
Monetary authorities.................	8 715 ..	....	....	....	....	....	....	....	....
of which: Short-term...............	8 718 ..	....	....	....	....	....	....	....	....
General government..................	8 719 ..	....	....	....	....	....	....	....	57.5
of which: Short-term...............	8 721 ..	....	....	....	....	....	....	....	....
Banks................................	8 722 ..	3,690.6	6,567.7	6,001.2	11,911.1	19,181.7	25,638.0	22,816.9	19,261.6
of which: Short-term...............	8 724 ..	*6.9*	*4.7*	*3.2*	*7,749.1*	*10,664.3*	*11,106.7*	*13,409.0*	*10,308.2*
Other sectors.........................	8 725 ..	27.4	25.1	25.2	22.5	....	....	....	....
of which: Short-term...............	8 727 ..	....	....	....	....	....	....	....	....
Currency and deposits..................	8 730 ..	13,265.2	16,162.5	20,154.6	19,611.4	30,759.5	41,083.4	48,685.8	40,735.6
Monetary authorities.................	8 731 ..	....	....	....	....	....	361.7	353.4	395.9
General government..................	8 732 ..	....	....	....	....	....	....	....	....
Banks................................	8 733 ..	8,171.3	9,701.8	14,761.5	13,648.3	23,598.9	33,383.5	40,089.4	34,242.9
Other sectors.........................	8 734 ..	5,093.9	6,460.8	5,393.0	5,963.1	7,160.6	7,338.2	8,243.0	6,096.7
Other assets...........................	8 736 ..	36.7	27.6	20.0	9.0	13.1	11.1	8.6	6.0
Monetary authorities.................	8 737 ..	....	....	....	....	....	....	....	....
of which: Short-term...............	8 739 ..	....	....	....	....	....	....	....	....
General government..................	8 740 ..	3.5	1.9	4.0	9.0	13.1	11.1	8.6	6.0
of which: Short-term...............	8 742 ..	....	....	....	....	....	....	....	....
Banks................................	8 743 ..	33.3	25.8	15.9	....	....	....	....	....
of which: Short-term...............	8 745 ..	....	....	....	....	....	....	....	....
Other sectors.........................	8 746 ..	....	....	....	....	....	....	....	....
of which: Short-term...............	8 748 ..	....	....	....	....	....	....	....	....
Reserve assets...........................	8 802 ..	**3,489.4**	**4,074.7**	**4,328.7**	**5,864.6**	**6,511.7**	**1,003.4**	**1,290.1**	**1,145.3**
Monetary gold..........................	8 812 ..	197.0	201.9	232.4	292.2	388.7	386.5	493.2	630.4
Special drawing rights...................	8 811 ..	3.0	3.9	4.2	4.1	3.5	2.7	187.1	188.0
Reserve position in the Fund.............	8 810 ..	99.3	73.4	31.1	21.2	15.0	26.9	44.4	49.1
Foreign exchange.......................	8 803 ..	3,188.6	3,793.8	4,059.6	5,545.5	6,102.7	585.7	563.6	276.2
Other claims...........................	8 813 ..	1.5	1.6	1.4	1.6	1.8	1.7	1.7	1.6

Table 3 (Concluded). INTERNATIONAL INVESTMENT POSITION (End-period stocks), 2003–2010

(Millions of U.S. dollars)

	Code	2003	2004	2005	2006	2007	2008	2009	2010
LIABILITIES	8 995 D.	**28,648.7**	**38,200.5**	**44,546.2**	**64,088.1**	**89,083.7**	**124,334.6**	**152,556.9**	**123,891.4**
Direct investment in Cyprus	8 555	**6,754.8**	**8,500.0**	**8,482.8**	**13,754.0**	**17,711.4**	**16,328.1**	**19,605.5**	**11,627.8**
Equity capital and reinvested earnings	8 556	4,591.7	5,879.3	6,092.1	10,654.9	13,881.8	12,458.4	18,793.3	11,178.6
Claims on direct investors	8 557	–.6	–.6	....	....	....	....	....	....
Liabilities to direct investors	8 558	4,592.2	5,879.9	6,092.1	10,654.9	13,881.8	12,458.4	18,793.3	11,178.6
Other capital	8 580	2,163.2	2,620.8	2,390.8	3,099.0	3,829.5	3,869.7	812.2	449.2
Claims on direct investors	8 585	....	....	....	....	....	....	....	....
Liabilities to direct investors	8 590	2,163.2	2,620.8	2,390.8	3,099.0	3,829.5	3,869.7	812.2	449.2
Portfolio investment	8 652	**3,158.0**	**7,272.5**	**8,692.9**	**13,444.3**	**14,380.7**	**11,330.1**	**13,899.6**	**4,847.6**
Equity securities	8 660	151.1	176.4	313.2	1,077.8	1,003.9	1,213.7	1,973.1	1,364.0
Banks	8 663	107.9	121.5	203.0	807.7	830.7	855.9	335.7	404.1
Other sectors	8 664	43.2	54.9	110.3	270.0	173.3	357.8	1,637.5	959.9
Debt securities	8 669	3,006.9	7,096.1	8,379.7	12,366.6	13,376.7	10,116.4	11,926.4	3,483.6
Bonds and notes	8 670	2,765.9	5,047.9	5,682.8	6,245.1	8,720.0	8,212.8	10,770.1	3,239.0
Monetary authorities	8 671	....	....	....	....	....	....	....	....
General government	8 672	1,491.6	2,264.2	1,942.1	1,821.1	2,060.9	1,461.3	3,673.5	42.8
Banks	8 673	1,273.8	2,783.7	3,740.7	4,423.9	6,659.1	6,533.9	6,557.5	2,654.0
Other sectors	8 674	.4	....	....	....	....	217.7	539.1	542.2
Money market instruments	8 680	241.0	2,048.2	2,696.9	6,121.5	4,656.7	1,903.6	1,156.4	244.7
Monetary authorities	8 681	....	....	....	....	....	....	....	....
General government	8 682	241.0	266.0	....	....	....	668.0	901.2	....
Banks	8 683	....	1,782.2	2,696.9	6,121.5	4,656.7	1,131.2	195.8	175.6
Other sectors	8 684	....	....	....	....	....	104.4	59.4	69.1
Financial derivatives	8 905	**23.3**	**27.9**	**23.0**	**421.5**	**481.5**	**1,178.8**	**1,066.6**	**578.0**
Monetary authorities	8 906	....	....	....	....	....	....	....	....
General government	8 907	....	....	....	....	....	....	....	....
Banks	8 908	22.5	27.9	21.8	409.5	474.1	1,174.7	1,063.7	576.8
Other sectors	8 909	.9	....	1.2	11.9	7.3	4.0	2.9	1.2
Other investment	8 753	**18,712.6**	**22,400.0**	**27,347.4**	**36,468.3**	**56,510.2**	**95,497.7**	**117,985.2**	**106,837.9**
Trade credits	8 756	596.0	698.4	659.2	761.8	903.3	1,115.2	46.0	1,028.2
General government	8 757	....	....	....	....	....	....	....	....
of which: Short-term	8 759	....	....	....	....	....	....	....	....
Other sectors	8 760	596.0	698.4	659.2	761.8	903.3	1,115.2	46.0	1,028.2
of which: Short-term	8 762	528.5	634.0	598.4	696.4	820.3	1,003.7	41.4	925.4
Loans	8 764	4,068.5	5,049.1	5,601.4	11,215.8	14,331.5	46,208.8	54,771.8	50,319.0
Monetary authorities	8 765	29.1	30.1	27.2	28.9	39.7	9,063.7	9,382.1	8,612.2
of which: Use of Fund credit and loans from the Fund	8 766	....	....	....	....	....	....	....	....
of which: Short-term	8 768	....	....	....	....	....	9,063.7	9,382.1	8,612.2
General government	8 769	591.7	753.6	754.3	864.5	1,077.6	1,162.1	1,163.4	1,187.9
of which: Short-term	8 771	....	....	....	....	....	....	....	....
Banks	8 772	2,100.6	3,017.1	3,601.4	8,999.6	11,760.0	32,115.8	41,972.9	36,857.5
of which: Short-term	8 774	....	....	....	5,989.4	7,466.2	24,086.8	31,479.6	27,643.1
Other sectors	8 775	1,347.0	1,248.4	1,218.5	1,322.8	1,454.2	3,867.3	2,253.4	3,661.3
of which: Short-term	8 777	63.2	22.6	63.5	81.5	96.2	309.4	180.3	292.9
Currency and deposits	8 780	14,047.9	16,652.2	21,086.6	24,490.7	41,275.5	48,173.7	62,959.3	55,286.2
Monetary authorities	8 781	15.9	15.3	14.3	22.4	....	....	....	....
General government	8 782	....	....	....	....	....	....	....	....
Banks	8 783	14,032.0	16,637.0	21,072.3	24,468.3	41,275.5	48,173.7	62,959.3	55,286.2
Other sectors	8 784	....	....	....	....	....	....	....	....
Other liabilities	8 786	.2	.2	.2	....	....	....	208.2	204.5
Monetary authorities	8 787	.2	.2	.2	....	....	....	208.2	204.5
of which: Short-term	8 789	....	....	....	....	....	....	....	....
General government	8 790	....	....	....	....	....	....	....	....
of which: Short-term	8 792	....	....	....	....	....	....	....	....
Banks	8 793	....	....	....	....	....	....	....	....
of which: Short-term	8 795	....	....	....	....	....	....	....	....
Other sectors	8 796	....	....	....	....	....	....	....	....
of which: Short-term	8 798	....	....	....	....	....	....	....	....
NET INTERNATIONAL INVESTMENT POSITION	8 995	**627**	**2,413**	**3,211**	**7,279**	**2,892**	**–5,475**	**–6,497**	**–4,047**
Conversion rates: Cyprus pounds per U.S. dollar (end of period)	0 102	.4652	.4250	.4844	.4391	.3978	....	....	....
Conversion rates: euros per U.S. dollar (end of period)	0 104	.7918	.7342	.8477	.7593	.6793	.7185	.6942	.7484

Table 1. ANALYTIC PRESENTATION, 2003–2010

(Millions of U.S. dollars)

	Code	2003	2004	2005	2006	2007	2008	2009	2010
A. Current Account[1]................................	4 993 Z.	**−5,785**	**−5,749**	**−1,577**	**−3,559**	**−5,754**	**−1,247**	**−6,201**	**−7,188**
Goods: exports f.o.b...............................	2 100 ..	48,705	67,220	77,951	95,151	122,791	146,180	107,514	126,414
Goods: imports f.o.b...............................	3 100 ..	−51,224	−67,748	−75,430	−92,308	−116,878	−139,846	−103,283	−123,600
Balance on Goods...............................	4 100 ..	*−2,519*	*−529*	*2,522*	*2,843*	*5,913*	*6,334*	*4,231*	*2,814*
Services: credit.....................................	2 200 ..	7,789	9,643	11,765	13,941	16,930	21,802	20,378	21,656
Services: debit.....................................	3 200 ..	−7,320	−9,008	−10,217	−11,942	−14,490	−17,890	−16,931	−18,212
Balance on Goods and Services.............	4 991 ..	*−2,049*	*107*	*4,070*	*4,842*	*8,353*	*10,246*	*7,678*	*6,259*
Income: credit.....................................	2 300 ..	2,681	3,405	4,390	5,674	7,492	10,126	4,917	4,543
Income: debit.....................................	3 300 ..	−6,966	−9,497	−10,364	−13,160	−20,239	−20,635	−18,212	−17,899
Balance on Goods, Services, and Income....	4 992 ..	*−6,334*	*−5,985*	*−1,904*	*−2,644*	*−4,393*	*−263*	*−5,617*	*−7,098*
Current transfers: credit.......................	2 379 Z.	1,663	2,081	3,219	2,215	3,153	3,974	3,337	3,921
Current transfers: debit.......................	3 379 ..	−1,114	−1,845	−2,892	−3,130	−4,514	−4,957	−3,921	−4,011
B. Capital Account[1]................................	4 994 Z.	**−3**	**−602**	**196**	**380**	**1,022**	**1,779**	**2,195**	**1,768**
Capital account: credit.........................	2 994 Z.	7	218	230	636	1,109	2,573	4,038	2,076
Capital account: debit.........................	3 994 ..	−10	−820	−35	−257	−87	−795	−1,843	−308
Total, Groups A Plus B.......................	4 981 ..	*−5,788*	*−6,351*	*−1,382*	*−3,179*	*−4,732*	*532*	*−4,006*	*−5,420*
C. Financial Account[1].............................	4 995 W.	**5,620**	**7,036**	**6,379**	**4,205**	**6,389**	**3,584**	**9,725**	**9,431**
Direct investment abroad......................	4 505 ..	−208	−1,037	27	−1,479	−1,642	−4,315	−917	−1,758
Direct investment in Czech Republic.......	4 555 Z.	2,021	4,978	11,602	5,522	10,606	6,573	2,869	6,720
Portfolio investment assets...................	4 602 ..	−2,934	−2,806	−3,467	−3,004	−4,849	−498	3,419	705
Equity securities..............................	4 610 ..	188	−1,448	−1,472	−1,938	−3,213	−794	1,091	−28
Debt securities................................	4 619 ..	−3,122	−1,359	−1,994	−1,066	−1,635	296	2,328	734
Portfolio investment liabilities..............	4 652 Z.	1,753	4,795	79	1,877	2,161	458	5,169	7,371
Equity securities..............................	4 660 ..	1,104	738	−1,540	268	−268	−1,124	−311	287
Debt securities................................	4 669 Z.	649	4,057	1,619	1,608	2,430	1,582	5,480	7,084
Financial derivatives............................	4 910 ..	143	−146	−112	−282	27	−803	−381	−219
Financial derivatives assets...................	4 900 ..	257	−660	−130	−504	−871	2,121	2,578	3,443
Financial derivatives liabilities...............	4 905 ..	−114	514	18	222	898	−2,924	−2,959	−3,663
Other investment assets.......................	4 703 ..	2,279	−1,072	−4,728	−1,480	−7,105	−5,359	777	−4,512
Monetary authorities........................	4 701 ..	....	−7	−7	....	....	....	....	....
General government.........................	4 704 ..	278	941	583	217	−33	8	5	9
Banks..	4 705 ..	1,469	−1,252	−4,599	527	−6,672	−3,532	2,207	−2,571
Other sectors..................................	4 728 ..	533	−754	−705	−2,224	−401	−1,835	−1,435	−1,950
Other investment liabilities..................	4 753 W.	2,565	2,325	2,978	3,052	7,191	7,529	−1,210	1,124
Monetary authorities........................	4 753 WA	−2	27	204	−172	−28	26	1,319	−20
General government.........................	4 753 ZB	372	411	862	442	145	479	690	816
Banks..	4 753 ZC	1,214	−477	536	792	5,826	4,552	−3,626	1,924
Other sectors..................................	4 753 ZD	981	2,365	1,376	1,989	1,248	2,472	406	−1,596
Total, Groups A Through C..................	4 983 ..	*−168*	*685*	*4,997*	*1,026*	*1,658*	*4,116*	*5,719*	*4,011*
D. Net Errors and Omissions..................	4 998 ..	**611**	**−422**	**−1,118**	**−934**	**−786**	**−1,696**	**−1,434**	**−1,935**
Total, Groups A Through D..................	4 984 ..	*442*	*263*	*3,879*	*92*	*872*	*2,420*	*4,285*	*2,076*
E. Reserves and Related Items...............	4 802 A.	**−442**	**−263**	**−3,879**	**−92**	**−872**	**−2,420**	**−4,285**	**−2,076**
Reserve assets.....................................	4 802 ..	−442	−263	−3,879	−92	−872	−2,420	−4,285	−2,076
Use of Fund credit and loans................	4 766 ..	....	....	....	....	....	....	....	....
Exceptional financing...........................	4 920 ..	....	....	....	....	....	....	....	....
Conversion rates: Czech koruny per U.S. dollar.....	0 101 ..	**28.209**	**25.700**	**23.957**	**22.596**	**20.294**	**17.072**	**19.063**	**19.098**

[1] Excludes components that have been classified in the categories of Group E.

Table 2. STANDARD PRESENTATION, 2003–2010

(Millions of U.S. dollars)

	Code	2003	2004	2005	2006	2007	2008	2009	2010
CURRENT ACCOUNT	4 993	**−5,785**	**−5,749**	**−1,577**	**−3,559**	**−5,754**	**−1,247**	**−6,201**	**−7,188**
A. GOODS	4 100	−2,519	−529	2,522	2,843	5,913	6,334	4,231	2,814
Credit	2 100	48,705	67,220	77,951	95,151	122,791	146,180	107,514	126,414
General merchandise: exports f.o.b.	2 110	35,277	55,902	70,737	87,978	115,146	137,221	101,294	120,123
Goods for processing: exports f.o.b.	2 150	13,172	10,958	7,203	7,159	7,624	8,926	6,180	6,211
Repairs on goods	2 160	196	333	....	....	....	....	....	....
Goods procured in ports by carriers	2 170	....	....	....	....	....	....	....	....
Nonmonetary gold	2 180	60	26	12	14	21	33	41	81
Debit	3 100	−51,224	−67,748	−75,430	−92,308	−116,878	−139,846	−103,283	−123,600
General merchandise: imports f.o.b.	3 110	−41,278	−59,148	−69,270	−86,164	−110,288	−132,360	−98,104	−118,039
Goods for processing: imports f.o.b.	3 150	−9,716	−8,252	−5,963	−5,960	−6,381	−7,196	−4,914	−5,277
Repairs on goods	3 160	−219	−254	....	....	....	....	....	....
Goods procured in ports by carriers	3 170	....	−89	−189	−160	−176	−233	−197	−170
Nonmonetary gold	3 180	−11	−6	−8	−24	−33	−57	−68	−113
B. SERVICES	4 200	**470**	**636**	**1,548**	**1,999**	**2,441**	**3,912**	**3,447**	**3,444**
Total credit	2 200	*7,789*	*9,643*	*11,765*	*13,941*	*16,930*	*21,802*	*20,378*	*21,656*
Total debit	3 200	*−7,320*	*−9,008*	*−10,217*	*−11,942*	*−14,490*	*−17,890*	*−16,931*	*−18,212*
Transportation services, credit	2 205	**2,154**	**2,724**	**3,197**	**3,800**	**5,040**	**6,264**	**4,677**	**5,097**
Passenger	2 850	*503*	*744*	*959*	*818*	*859*	*1,009*	*921*	*896*
Freight	2 851	*1,463*	*1,785*	*1,974*	*2,603*	*3,446*	*4,293*	*2,888*	*3,294*
Other	2 852	*187*	*195*	*263*	*378*	*735*	*962*	*869*	*907*
Sea transport, passenger	2 207	3	3	....	....	....	....	....	....
Sea transport, freight	2 208	16	27	25	53	47	72	33	40
Sea transport, other	2 209	24	12	10	15	7	16	8	9
Air transport, passenger	2 211	494	731	952	802	834	987	889	856
Air transport, freight	2 212	26	46	74	55	223	286	172	212
Air transport, other	2 213	49	80	111	157	202	265	219	185
Other transport, passenger	2 215	7	10	7	16	25	22	32	39
Other transport, freight	2 216	1,421	1,711	1,875	2,495	3,176	3,935	2,683	3,043
Other transport, other	2 217	114	103	143	207	525	681	642	712
Transportation services, debit	3 205	**−1,200**	**−1,862**	**−2,342**	**−2,754**	**−3,624**	**−4,457**	**−3,317**	**−4,125**
Passenger	3 850	*−243*	*−402*	*−198*	*−109*	*−124*	*−144*	*−81*	*−101*
Freight	3 851	*−660*	*−1,225*	*−1,634*	*−2,130*	*−2,774*	*−3,518*	*−2,377*	*−3,125*
Other	3 852	*−297*	*−235*	*−510*	*−515*	*−727*	*−795*	*−859*	*−899*
Sea transport, passenger	3 207	−3	−4	....	....	....	....	....	....
Sea transport, freight	3 208	−23	−44	−68	−79	−133	−184	−105	−157
Sea transport, other	3 209	−123	−96	−41	−80	−50	−124	−86	−131
Air transport, passenger	3 211	−232	−387	−195	−95	−105	−126	−60	−84
Air transport, freight	3 212	−55	−105	−126	−147	−246	−303	−200	−246
Air transport, other	3 213	−50	−53	−358	−299	−450	−378	−503	−475
Other transport, passenger	3 215	−9	−11	−3	−13	−18	−18	−20	−17
Other transport, freight	3 216	−582	−1,075	−1,440	−1,905	−2,395	−3,031	−2,073	−2,722
Other transport, other	3 217	−124	−86	−110	−136	−227	−293	−269	−292
Travel, credit	2 236	**3,566**	**4,187**	**4,676**	**5,541**	**6,388**	**7,204**	**6,477**	**6,674**
Business travel	2 237	831	967	1,088	1,179	1,332	1,967	1,692	1,605
Personal travel	2 240	2,735	3,220	3,588	4,362	5,055	5,237	4,785	5,069
Travel, debit	3 236	**−1,934**	**−2,280**	**−2,405**	**−2,765**	**−3,648**	**−4,585**	**−4,077**	**−4,064**
Business travel	3 237	−333	−441	−465	−490	−591	−784	−677	−608
Personal travel	3 240	−1,602	−1,840	−1,939	−2,276	−3,057	−3,801	−3,400	−3,455
Other services, credit	2 200 BA	**2,070**	**2,732**	**3,893**	**4,600**	**5,502**	**8,333**	**9,224**	**9,886**
Communications	2 245	104	219	381	433	573	588	551	537
Construction	2 249	112	117	230	215	312	469	490	976
Insurance	2 253	1	8	10	9	12	109	238	274
Financial	2 260	174	421	424	391	299	181	66	66
Computer and information	2 262	77	141	587	885	803	1,344	1,330	1,257
Royalties and licence fees	2 266	50	38	39	31	35	55	99	105
Other business services	2 268	1,406	1,553	2,097	2,486	3,243	5,414	6,278	6,442
Personal, cultural, and recreational	2 287	111	199	90	116	190	122	135	197
Government, n.i.e.	2 291	35	36	35	35	36	51	37	32
Other services, debit	3 200 BA	**−4,185**	**−4,865**	**−5,470**	**−6,422**	**−7,217**	**−8,848**	**−9,537**	**−10,023**
Communications	3 245	−302	−493	−372	−439	−523	−620	−753	−836
Construction	3 249	−275	−203	−184	−175	−184	−391	−276	−619
Insurance	3 253	−147	−195	−269	−241	−247	−367	−377	−405
Financial	3 260	−555	−948	−906	−1,090	−744	−602	−331	−60
Computer and information	3 262	−150	−220	−457	−538	−759	−910	−1,013	−1,244
Royalties and licence fees	3 266	−176	−174	−484	−528	−653	−747	−742	−774
Other business services	3 268	−2,347	−2,439	−2,601	−3,207	−3,859	−4,916	−5,802	−5,764
Personal, cultural, and recreational	3 287	−155	−118	−89	−129	−160	−170	−144	−233
Government, n.i.e.	3 291	−80	−75	−108	−75	−88	−123	−98	−88

Czech Republic 935

Table 2 (Continued). STANDARD PRESENTATION, 2003–2010

(Millions of U.S. dollars)

	Code	2003	2004	2005	2006	2007	2008	2009	2010
C. INCOME	4 300	**−4,285**	**−6,092**	**−5,973**	**−7,486**	**−12,747**	**−10,509**	**−13,295**	**−13,357**
Total credit	2 300	*2,681*	*3,405*	*4,390*	*5,674*	*7,492*	*10,126*	*4,917*	*4,543*
Total debit	3 300	*−6,966*	*−9,497*	*−10,364*	*−13,160*	*−20,239*	*−20,635*	*−18,212*	*−17,899*
Compensation of employees, credit	2 310	**494**	**805**	**917**	**1,054**	**1,174**	**1,234**	**1,094**	**979**
Compensation of employees, debit	3 310	**−1,100**	**−1,426**	**−1,384**	**−1,016**	**−1,437**	**−2,355**	**−1,799**	**−1,167**
Investment income, credit	2 320	**2,188**	**2,599**	**3,474**	**4,620**	**6,319**	**8,892**	**3,823**	**3,564**
Direct investment income	2 330	129	387	489	685	1,359	3,973	825	1,185
Dividends and distributed branch profits	2 332	2	48	634	167	341	549	349	445
Reinvested earnings and undistributed branch profits	2 333	123	337	−155	511	1,015	3,418	472	736
Income on debt (interest)	2 334	5	2	10	6	3	6	4	4
Portfolio investment income	2 339	456	565	748	1,032	1,362	742	666	485
Income on equity	2 340	22	66	133	242	423	139	141	52
Income on bonds and notes	2 350	424	492	602	788	937	602	518	432
Income on money market instruments	2 360	10	7	13	2	1	1	7	1
Other investment income	2 370	1,602	1,648	2,236	2,903	3,599	4,177	2,331	1,894
Investment income, debit	3 320	**−5,866**	**−8,070**	**−8,979**	**−12,144**	**−18,802**	**−18,280**	**−16,413**	**−16,732**
Direct investment income	3 330	−4,222	−6,089	−6,641	−9,219	−15,347	−14,040	−13,586	−13,747
Dividends and distributed branch profits	3 332	−1,874	−2,851	−3,009	−4,997	−7,940	−11,038	−9,378	−8,796
Reinvested earnings and undistributed branch profits	3 333	−2,161	−2,952	−3,265	−3,863	−6,947	−2,429	−3,572	−4,320
Income on debt (interest)	3 334	−187	−286	−367	−359	−460	−573	−635	−631
Portfolio investment income	3 339	−417	−454	−483	−847	−926	−1,263	−1,125	−1,399
Income on equity	3 340	−148	−237	−178	−442	−246	−566	−348	−427
Income on bonds and notes	3 350	−269	−217	−304	−405	−680	−687	−776	−972
Income on money market instruments	3 360	....	....	−2	....	−1	−11	....	....
Other investment income	3 370	−1,227	−1,527	−1,856	−2,078	−2,529	−2,977	−1,703	−1,586
D. CURRENT TRANSFERS	4 379	**548**	**236**	**327**	**−915**	**−1,361**	**−984**	**−584**	**−90**
Credit	2 379	**1,663**	**2,081**	**3,219**	**2,215**	**3,153**	**3,974**	**3,337**	**3,921**
General government	2 380	851	1,524	1,681	1,507	2,013	3,057	2,897	3,595
Other sectors	2 390	812	557	1,538	708	1,140	916	440	326
Workers' remittances	2 391	....	....	100	128	150	113	96	97
Other current transfers	2 392	812	557	1,437	581	991	803	344	228
Debit	3 379	**−1,114**	**−1,845**	**−2,892**	**−3,130**	**−4,514**	**−4,957**	**−3,921**	**−4,011**
General government	3 380	−582	−958	−1,846	−1,776	−2,135	−3,015	−2,189	−2,244
Other sectors	3 390	−532	−888	−1,046	−1,354	−2,379	−1,942	−1,733	−1,768
Workers' remittances	3 391	....	....	−291	−462	−630	−590	−747	−614
Other current transfers	3 392	−532	−888	−755	−892	−1,749	−1,352	−985	−1,154
CAPITAL AND FINANCIAL ACCOUNT	4 996	**5,175**	**6,172**	**2,696**	**4,493**	**6,540**	**2,943**	**7,636**	**9,123**
CAPITAL ACCOUNT	4 994	**−3**	**−602**	**196**	**380**	**1,022**	**1,779**	**2,195**	**1,768**
Total credit	2 994	*7*	*218*	*230*	*636*	*1,109*	*2,573*	*4,038*	*2,076*
Total debit	3 994	*−10*	*−820*	*−35*	*−257*	*−87*	*−795*	*−1,843*	*−308*
Capital transfers, credit	2 400	**5**	**211**	**225**	**545**	**1,032**	**1,473**	**1,930**	**1,319**
General government	2 401	....	201	216	537	1,023	1,460	1,870	1,274
Debt forgiveness	2 402	....	....	....	....	....	....	....	....
Other capital transfers	2 410	....	201	216	537	1,023	1,460	1,870	1,274
Other sectors	2 430	5	9	9	8	9	13	61	46
Migrants' transfers	2 431	5	9	9	8	9	13	61	46
Debt forgiveness	2 432	....	....	....	....	....	....	....	....
Other capital transfers	2 440	....	....	....	....	....	....	....	....
Capital transfers, debit	3 400	**−3**	**−801**	**−20**	**−209**	**−25**	**−99**	**−48**	**−46**
General government	3 401	....	−795	−18	−206	−22	−97	−26	−16
Debt forgiveness	3 402	....	−789	−11	−196	−10	−80	−13	....
Other capital transfers	3 410	....	−7	−7	−10	−12	−17	−13	−16
Other sectors	3 430	−3	−5	−2	−3	−2	−3	−22	−30
Migrants' transfers	3 431	−3	−5	−2	−3	−2	−3	−22	−30
Debt forgiveness	3 432	....	....	....	....	....	....	....	....
Other capital transfers	3 440	....	....	....	....	....	....	....	....
Nonproduced nonfinancial assets, credit	2 480	**2**	**7**	**5**	**91**	**77**	**1,101**	**2,107**	**757**
Nonproduced nonfinancial assets, debit	3 480	**−7**	**−19**	**−15**	**−47**	**−62**	**−695**	**−1,794**	**−262**

Table 2 (Continued). STANDARD PRESENTATION, 2003–2010

(Millions of U.S. dollars)

	Code	2003	2004	2005	2006	2007	2008	2009	2010
FINANCIAL ACCOUNT	4 995	**5,178**	**6,773**	**2,500**	**4,113**	**5,518**	**1,164**	**5,440**	**7,355**
A. DIRECT INVESTMENT	4 500	**1,813**	**3,940**	**11,629**	**4,043**	**8,964**	**2,258**	**1,952**	**4,962**
Direct investment abroad	4 505	**−208**	**−1,037**	**27**	**−1,479**	**−1,642**	**−4,315**	**−917**	**−1,758**
Equity capital	4 510	12	−476	−321	−1,003	−284	−1,012	−334	−313
Claims on affiliated enterprises	4 515	12	−476	−321	−1,003	−284	−1,012	−334	−313
Liabilities to affiliated enterprises	4 520	....	....	....	....	....	....	....	....
Reinvested earnings	4 525	−123	−337	155	−511	−1,015	−3,418	−472	−736
Other capital	4 530	−97	−225	193	35	−344	115	−111	−709
Claims on affiliated enterprises	4 535	−97	−225	193	35	−344	115	−111	−709
Liabilities to affiliated enterprises	4 540	....	....						
Direct investment in Czech Republic	4 555	**2,021**	**4,978**	**11,602**	**5,522**	**10,606**	**6,573**	**2,869**	**6,720**
Equity capital	4 560	−130	1,777	7,629	1,941	2,523	1,077	1,014	1,441
Claims on direct investors	4 565	....	....						
Liabilities to direct investors	4 570	−130	1,777	7,629	1,941	2,523	1,077	1,014	1,441
Reinvested earnings	4 575	2,161	2,952	3,265	3,863	6,947	2,429	3,572	4,320
Other capital	4 580	−9	249	708	−282	1,136	3,067	−1,717	959
Claims on direct investors	4 585	....	....						
Liabilities to direct investors	4 590	−9	249	708	−282	1,136	3,067	−1,717	959
B. PORTFOLIO INVESTMENT	4 600	**−1,181**	**1,988**	**−3,388**	**−1,127**	**−2,687**	**−40**	**8,588**	**8,076**
Assets	4 602	**−2,934**	**−2,806**	**−3,467**	**−3,004**	**−4,849**	**−498**	**3,419**	**705**
Equity securities	4 610	188	−1,448	−1,472	−1,938	−3,213	−794	1,091	−28
Monetary authorities	4 611	....	....	....	....				
General government	4 612	565	−125	−5	1	−4	12	−3	−1
Banks	4 613	−138	−58	−10	−174	−277	−330	131	−125
Other sectors	4 614	−239	−1,264	−1,458	−1,764	−2,932	−476	963	97
Debt securities	4 619	−3,122	−1,359	−1,994	−1,066	−1,635	296	2,328	734
Bonds and notes	4 620	−3,002	−1,717	−1,992	−960	−1,823	560	2,071	740
Monetary authorities	4 621								
General government	4 622	−42	−241	−122	140	37	62	33	39
Banks	4 623	−1,640	−861	−882	−742	−691	728	2,058	1,091
Other sectors	4 624	−1,320	−614	−988	−358	−1,170	−229	−21	−390
Money market instruments	4 630	−120	358	−2	−107	188	−264	257	−6
Monetary authorities	4 631	....	....	....	....				
General government	4 632	−34	247	−2	18	−3	−4		....
Banks	4 633	−3	36	4	−15	26	−56	77	−62
Other sectors	4 634	−82	75	−4	−110	165	−204	180	56
Liabilities	4 652	**1,753**	**4,795**	**79**	**1,877**	**2,161**	**458**	**5,169**	**7,371**
Equity securities	4 660	1,104	738	−1,540	268	−268	−1,124	−311	287
Banks	4 663	97	−14	54	−102	245	−775	−34	3
Other sectors	4 664	1,008	751	−1,595	371	−513	−350	−277	284
Debt securities	4 669	649	4,057	1,619	1,608	2,430	1,582	5,480	7,084
Bonds and notes	4 670	644	3,759	1,920	1,619	2,196	1,796	5,577	6,907
Monetary authorities	4 671	....	....	....	....				
General government	4 672	97	2,709	2,267	409	790	424	2,343	3,853
Banks	4 673	221	196	−3	236	391	293	729	308
Other sectors	4 674	326	854	−344	974	1,015	1,078	2,505	2,745
Money market instruments	4 680	5	298	−301	−10	234	−214	−97	177
Monetary authorities	4 681	....	....	....	....				
General government	4 682	−2	106	−167	−33	285	−182	−8	211
Banks	4 683	7	85	−92	64	−72	73	−103	−16
Other sectors	4 684	....	107	−42	−42	22	−105	13	−18
C. FINANCIAL DERIVATIVES	4 910	**143**	**−146**	**−112**	**−282**	**27**	**−803**	**−381**	**−219**
Monetary authorities	4 911						−44		
General government	4 912	....	....	....	....	....			
Banks	4 913	143	−146	−112	−282	27	−733		
Other sectors	4 914	....	....	....	....	....	−27		
Assets	4 900	**257**	**−660**	**−130**	**−504**	**−871**	**2,121**	**2,578**	**3,443**
Monetary authorities	4 901	....	....	....	....	....	152		
General government	4 902	....	....	....	....	....			
Banks	4 903	257	−660	−130	−504	−871	1,913		
Other sectors	4 904	....	....	....	....	....	56		
Liabilities	4 905	**−114**	**514**	**18**	**222**	**898**	**−2,924**	**−2,959**	**−3,663**
Monetary authorities	4 906	....	....	....	....	....	−196		
General government	4 907	....	....	....	....	....			
Banks	4 908	−114	514	18	222	898	−2,646		
Other sectors	4 909	....	....	....	....	....	−82		

2011, International Monetary Fund: *Balance of Payments Statistics Yearbook*

Table 2 (Concluded). STANDARD PRESENTATION, 2003–2010

(Millions of U.S. dollars)

	Code	2003	2004	2005	2006	2007	2008	2009	2010
D. OTHER INVESTMENT...............	4 700 ..	**4,845**	**1,253**	**−1,750**	**1,572**	**86**	**2,170**	**−434**	**−3,387**
Assets...............	4 703 ..	**2,279**	**−1,072**	**−4,728**	**−1,480**	**−7,105**	**−5,359**	**777**	**−4,512**
Trade credits...............	4 706 ..	809	−659	−614	−429	−947	−1,012	−265	−1,334
General government...............	4 707 ..	....	....	....	....	....	....	....	....
of which: Short-term...............	4 709 ..	....	....	....	....	....	....	....	....
Other sectors...............	4 710 ..	809	−659	−614	−429	−947	−1,012	−265	−1,334
of which: Short-term...............	4 712 ..	*816*	*−655*	*−618*	*−413*	*−943*	*−1,003*	*−270*	*−1,342*
Loans...............	4 714 ..	−1,365	1,086	−1,335	−553	−2,419	−2,763	789	−1,470
Monetary authorities...............	4 715 ..	....	....	....	....	....	....	....	....
of which: Short-term...............	4 718 ..	....	....	....	....	....	....	....	....
General government...............	4 719 ..	9	3	....	....	....	....	....	....
of which: Short-term...............	4 721 ..	*−3*	*3*	....	....	....	....	....	....
Banks...............	4 722 ..	−1,375	1,083	−1,335	−555	−2,363	−2,813	720	−1,458
of which: Short-term...............	4 724 ..	*−819*	*950*	*−260*	*−44*	*−574*	*−1,678*	*483*	*−349*
Other sectors...............	4 725 ..	....	....	....	2	−56	50	69	−12
of which: Short-term...............	4 727 ..	....	....	....	*2*	*−56*	*50*	*69*	*−12*
Currency and deposits...............	4 730 ..	2,736	−2,329	−3,119	−691	−3,678	−1,617	315	−1,708
Monetary authorities...............	4 731 ..	....	....	....	....	....	....	....	....
General government...............	4 732 ..	78	....	....	....	....	....	....	....
Banks...............	4 733 ..	2,815	−2,332	−3,267	1,105	−4,281	−730	1,550	−1,104
Other sectors...............	4 734 ..	−156	3	148	−1,796	603	−887	−1,235	−604
Other assets...............	4 736 ..	99	830	341	193	−60	32	−62	....
Monetary authorities...............	4 737 ..	....	−7	−7	....	....	....	....	....
of which: Short-term...............	4 739 ..	....	....	....	....	....	....	....	....
General government...............	4 740 ..	191	938	583	217	−33	8	5	9
of which: Short-term...............	4 742 ..	....	....	....	....	....	....	....	....
Banks...............	4 743 ..	28	−4	4	−23	−28	12	−63	−8
of which: Short-term...............	4 745 ..	*35*	*3*	*1*	*−12*	*−22*	*−91*	*−63*	*−8*
Other sectors...............	4 746 ..	−120	−98	−238	−1	....	13	−3	....
of which: Short-term...............	4 748 ..	....	....	....	....	....	....	....	....
Liabilities...............	4 753 ..	**2,565**	**2,325**	**2,978**	**3,052**	**7,191**	**7,529**	**−1,210**	**1,124**
Trade credits...............	4 756 ..	−500	846	1,034	−37	1,026	243	476	−693
General government...............	4 757 ..	....	....	397	−3	−41	−84	−71	−84
of which: Short-term...............	4 759 ..	....	....	....	....	....	....	....	....
Other sectors...............	4 760 ..	−500	846	637	−34	1,067	327	546	−609
of which: Short-term...............	4 762 ..	*−482*	*891*	*417*	*−64*	*864*	*212*	*677*	*−497*
Loans...............	4 764 ..	1,707	2,128	1,332	3,230	1,819	4,482	−1,111	83
Monetary authorities...............	4 765 ..	−1	−1	−1	−1	−1	−1	....	....
of which: Use of Fund credit and loans from the Fund..	4 766 ..	....	....	....	....	....	....	....	....
of which: Short-term...............	4 768 ..	....	....	....	....	....	....	....	....
General government...............	4 769 ..	372	411	465	446	186	563	761	900
of which: Short-term...............	4 771 ..	....	....	....	....	....	....	....	....
Banks...............	4 772 ..	−146	199	129	763	1,453	1,774	−1,731	170
of which: Short-term...............	4 774 ..	*−27*	*231*	*212*	*271*	*641*	*822*	*−1,386*	*−24*
Other sectors...............	4 775 ..	1,482	1,519	739	2,022	181	2,145	−141	−987
of which: Short-term...............	4 777 ..	*697*	*408*	*−193*	*13*	*470*	*1,318*	*−473*	*−19*
Currency and deposits...............	4 780 ..	1,385	−738	492	−165	4,274	2,613	−1,879	1,489
Monetary authorities...............	4 781 ..	−1	28	205	−171	−27	26	99	−20
General government...............	4 782 ..	....	....	....	....	....	....	....	....
Banks...............	4 783 ..	1,386	−766	287	5	4,301	2,587	−1,978	1,508
Other sectors...............	4 784 ..	....	....	....	....	....	....	....	....
Other liabilities...............	4 786 ..	−26	90	120	24	71	191	1,305	246
Monetary authorities...............	4 787 ..	....	....	....	....	....	....	1,220	....
of which: Short-term...............	4 789 ..	....	....	....	....	....	....	....	....
General government...............	4 790 ..	....	....	....	....	....	....	....	....
of which: Short-term...............	4 792 ..	....	....	....	....	....	....	....	....
Banks...............	4 793 ..	−26	90	120	24	71	191	84	246
of which: Short-term...............	4 795 ..	*−34*	*90*	*118*	*26*	*67*	*194*	*61*	*256*
Other sectors...............	4 796 ..	....	....	....	....	....	....	....	....
of which: Short-term...............	4 798 ..	....	....	....	....	....	....	....	....
E. RESERVE ASSETS...............	4 802 ..	**−442**	**−263**	**−3,879**	**−92**	**−872**	**−2,420**	**−4,285**	**−2,076**
Monetary gold...............	4 812 ..	....	....	....	....	....	....	....	....
Special drawing rights...............	4 811 ..	−4	4	−7	−4	−3	−2	−1,221	−1
Reserve position in the Fund...............	4 810 ..	−200	75	201	76	31	−77	−75	−108
Foreign exchange...............	4 803 ..	−918	−315	−4,064	−160	−631	−2,099	−1,678	−1,623
Other claims...............	4 813 ..	679	−28	−8	−5	−270	−241	−1,311	−344
NET ERRORS AND OMISSIONS...............	4 998 ..	**611**	**−422**	**−1,118**	**−934**	**−786**	**−1,696**	**−1,434**	**−1,935**

Table 3. INTERNATIONAL INVESTMENT POSITION (End-period stocks), 2003–2010

(Millions of U.S. dollars)

	Code	2003	2004	2005	2006	2007	2008	2009	2010
ASSETS	8 995 C.	**59,926**	**69,276**	**76,273**	**90,451**	**117,195**	**122,751**	**126,273**	**130,010**
Direct investment abroad	8 505 ..	**2,284**	**3,760**	**3,610**	**5,017**	**8,557**	**12,531**	**14,805**	**15,523**
Equity capital and reinvested earnings	8 506 ..	1,987	3,160	3,256	4,634	7,757	11,851	13,975	14,059
Claims on affiliated enterprises	8 507 ..	1,987	3,160	3,256	4,634	7,757	11,851	13,975	14,059
Liabilities to affiliated enterprises	8 508 ..	....	....	....	....	....	....	....	....
Other capital	8 530 ..	297	600	354	383	800	680	829	1,464
Claims on affiliated enterprises	8 535 ..	297	600	354	383	800	680	829	1,464
Liabilities to affiliated enterprises	8 540 ..	....	....	....	....	....	....	....	....
Portfolio investment	8 602 ..	**13,408**	**16,644**	**19,026**	**25,492**	**34,220**	**26,111**	**24,847**	**24,171**
Equity securities	8 610 ..	1,845	3,404	5,977	9,692	14,204	9,806	10,148	11,050
Monetary authorities	8 611 ..	....	....	....	....	....	....	....	....
General government	8 612 ..	31	179	160	194	196	126	159	142
Banks	8 613 ..	258	379	300	582	1,053	656	173	162
Other sectors	8 614 ..	1,557	2,846	5,517	8,916	12,955	9,024	9,815	10,745
Debt securities	8 619 ..	11,563	13,240	13,049	15,800	20,016	16,305	14,699	13,122
Bonds and notes	8 620 ..	11,183	13,098	12,980	15,601	19,969	15,982	14,597	13,032
Monetary authorities	8 621 ..	....	....	....	....	....	....	....	....
General government	8 622 ..	211	145	215	118	215	153	100	58
Banks	8 623 ..	6,348	8,055	7,744	9,280	11,121	9,528	7,613	5,811
Other sectors	8 624 ..	4,623	4,898	5,022	6,203	8,633	6,302	6,884	7,162
Money market instruments	8 630 ..	380	142	69	199	47	323	102	90
Monetary authorities	8 631 ..	....	....	....	....	....	....	....	....
General government	8 632 ..	254	....	35	....	1	4	....	....
Banks	8 633 ..	39	98	11	26	....	86	5	68
Other sectors	8 634 ..	87	44	23	173	46	232	98	22
Financial derivatives	8 900 ..	**941**	**1,775**	**1,731**	**2,558**	**3,846**	**8,187**	**6,501**	**6,076**
Monetary authorities	8 901 ..	....	....	....	....	23	86	....	....
General government	8 902 ..	....	....	....	....	....	....	....	....
Banks	8 903 ..	941	1,775	1,731	2,558	3,823	6,357	....	....
Other sectors	8 904 ..	....	....	....	....	....	1,744	....	....
Other investment	8 703 ..	**16,336**	**18,648**	**22,351**	**25,929**	**35,666**	**38,910**	**38,510**	**41,748**
Trade credits	8 706 ..	4,271	5,492	6,050	8,891	9,772	4,762	4,706	6,023
General government	8 707 ..	....	....	....	....	....	....	....	....
of which: Short-term	8 709 ..	....	....	....	....	....	....	....	....
Other sectors	8 710 ..	4,271	5,492	6,050	8,891	9,772	4,762	4,706	6,023
of which: Short-term	8 712 ..	*3,903*	*5,096*	*5,665*	*8,574*	*9,487*	*4,569*	*4,518*	*5,847*
Loans	8 714 ..	4,048	3,044	4,098	5,070	8,046	10,222	9,849	11,014
Monetary authorities	8 715 ..	8	9	8	9	9	9	9	9
of which: Short-term	8 718 ..	....	....	....	....	....	....	....	....
General government	8 719 ..	3	....	....	....	....	....	....	....
of which: Short-term	8 721 ..	*3*	....	....	....	....	....	....	....
Banks	8 722 ..	4,036	3,035	4,089	5,061	8,037	10,166	9,823	10,987
of which: Short-term	8 724 ..	*1,841*	*988*	*1,139*	*1,305*	*2,042*	*3,357*	*2,964*	*3,325*
Other sectors	8 725 ..	....	....	....	....	....	47	18	18
of which: Short-term	8 727 ..	....	....	....	....	....	*45*	*12*	*17*
Currency and deposits	8 730 ..	4,715	7,700	10,331	10,204	15,957	21,956	21,861	22,607
Monetary authorities	8 731 ..	....	....	....	....	....	....	....	....
General government	8 732 ..	1	....	....	....	....	....	....	....
Banks	8 733 ..	4,714	7,699	10,331	10,204	15,957	15,319	14,263	14,851
Other sectors	8 734 ..	....	....	....	....	....	6,637	7,598	7,756
Other assets	8 736 ..	3,303	2,413	1,872	1,765	1,891	1,970	2,094	2,104
Monetary authorities	8 737 ..	14	21	124	141	154	160	171	193
of which: Short-term	8 739 ..	*4*	*3*	*3*	*6*	*6*	*4*	*6*	*7*
General government	8 740 ..	3,098	2,171	1,562	1,432	1,513	1,627	1,675	1,655
of which: Short-term	8 742 ..	....	....	....	....	....	....	....	....
Banks	8 743 ..	109	119	103	136	176	164	229	237
of which: Short-term	8 745 ..	*40*	*40*	*33*	*50*	*77*	*164*	*229*	*237*
Other sectors	8 746 ..	82	101	82	56	47	19	19	19
of which: Short-term	8 748 ..	....	....	....	....	....	....	....	....
Reserve assets	8 802 ..	**26,957**	**28,450**	**29,555**	**31,454**	**34,905**	**37,013**	**41,611**	**42,493**
Monetary gold	8 812 ..	186	190	225	273	356	358	454	584
Special drawing rights	8 811 ..	9	5	12	17	20	21	1,245	1,224
Reserve position in the Fund	8 810 ..	468	410	181	111	84	162	241	349
Foreign exchange	8 803 ..	26,290	27,304	29,133	31,050	34,188	35,973	37,736	37,998
Other claims	8 813 ..	4	540	5	4	257	499	1,934	2,337

Table 3 (Concluded). INTERNATIONAL INVESTMENT POSITION (End-period stocks), 2003–2010

(Millions of U.S. dollars)

	Code	2003	2004	2005	2006	2007	2008	2009	2010
LIABILITIES	8 995 D.	**80,485**	**106,163**	**110,243**	**142,232**	**195,478**	**201,470**	**221,517**	**229,751**
Direct investment in Czech Republic	8 555 ..	**45,287**	**57,259**	**60,662**	**79,841**	**112,408**	**113,174**	**125,827**	**129,893**
Equity capital and reinvested earnings	8 556 ..	39,346	50,161	53,526	71,731	101,914	100,821	113,464	117,030
Claims on direct investors	8 557 ..	....	....	....	....	....	....	....	....
Liabilities to direct investors	8 558 ..	39,346	50,161	53,526	71,731	101,914	100,821	113,464	117,030
Other capital	8 580 ..	5,940	7,098	7,136	8,110	10,494	12,352	12,364	12,863
Claims on direct investors	8 585 ..	....	....	....	....	....	....	....	....
Liabilities to direct investors	8 590 ..	5,940	7,098	7,136	8,110	10,494	12,352	12,364	12,863
Portfolio investment	8 652 ..	**8,717**	**17,036**	**17,806**	**23,376**	**30,775**	**26,264**	**35,575**	**41,851**
Equity securities	8 660 ..	5,488	9,339	8,968	11,573	14,521	9,293	11,411	10,837
Banks	8 663 ..	1,168	2,598	2,507	2,407	3,153	2,069	2,965	3,288
Other sectors	8 664 ..	4,320	6,741	6,461	9,166	11,369	7,223	8,446	7,549
Debt securities	8 669 ..	3,229	7,697	8,838	11,803	16,253	16,971	24,164	31,014
Bonds and notes	8 670 ..	3,143	7,309	8,702	11,656	15,708	16,690	23,857	30,251
Monetary authorities	8 671 ..	....	....	....	....	....	....	....	....
General government	8 672 ..	1,815	5,172	6,860	8,878	11,218	11,309	14,946	18,425
Banks	8 673 ..	593	551	560	678	1,129	1,356	2,122	2,550
Other sectors	8 674 ..	735	1,586	1,281	2,100	3,362	4,025	6,790	9,276
Money market instruments	8 680 ..	85	388	136	147	545	281	307	763
Monetary authorities	8 681 ..	....	....	....	....	....	....	....	....
General government	8 682 ..	28	149	45	17	317	143	261	751
Banks	8 683 ..	58	155	53	130	111	132	27	11
Other sectors	8 684 ..	....	84	38	....	117	6	19	1
Financial derivatives	8 905 ..	**758**	**1,422**	**1,296**	**1,748**	**2,999**	**8,268**	**6,174**	**5,286**
Monetary authorities	8 906 ..	....	....	....	....	41	130	....	....
General government	8 907 ..	....	....	....	....	....	....	....	....
Banks	8 908 ..	758	1,422	1,296	1,748	2,958	7,125	....	....
Other sectors	8 909 ..	....	....	....	....	....	1,013	....	....
Other investment	8 753 ..	**25,724**	**30,445**	**30,479**	**37,267**	**49,296**	**53,765**	**53,940**	**52,720**
Trade credits	8 756 ..	2,435	3,718	4,352	4,721	6,172	5,926	6,501	5,464
General government	8 757 ..	....	....	392	458	480	375	313	223
of which: Short-term	8 759 ..	....	....	....	....	....	....	....	....
Other sectors	8 760 ..	2,435	3,718	3,960	4,263	5,692	5,551	6,188	5,241
of which: Short-term	8 762 ..	*1,881*	*3,142*	*3,201*	*3,535*	*4,796*	*4,745*	*5,552*	*4,760*
Loans	8 764 ..	14,634	18,279	17,645	23,301	28,180	31,372	31,485	30,169
Monetary authorities	8 765 ..	4	3	2	1	....	....	....	....
of which: Use of Fund credit and loans from the Fund....	8 766 ..	....	....	....	....	....	....	....	....
of which: Short-term	8 768 ..	....	....	....	....	....	....	....	....
General government	8 769 ..	875	1,434	1,736	2,497	3,163	3,444	4,556	5,372
of which: Short-term	8 771 ..	....	....	....	....	....	....	....	....
Banks	8 772 ..	2,125	2,454	2,323	3,432	5,403	7,406	5,798	5,690
of which: Short-term	8 774 ..	*202*	*474*	*629*	*989*	*1,793*	*2,515*	*1,115*	*1,048*
Other sectors	8 775 ..	11,630	14,388	13,584	17,370	19,613	20,522	21,132	19,107
of which: Short-term	8 777 ..	*1,670*	*2,294*	*1,864*	*2,133*	*2,897*	*4,015*	*3,672*	*3,481*
Currency and deposits	8 780 ..	7,927	7,721	7,674	8,286	13,786	15,290	13,647	14,678
Monetary authorities	8 781 ..	1	39	241	85	68	92	204	201
General government	8 782 ..	....	....	....	....	....	....	....	....
Banks	8 783 ..	7,926	7,683	7,433	8,201	13,718	15,198	13,442	14,477
Other sectors	8 784 ..	....	....	....	....	....	....	....	....
Other liabilities	8 786 ..	729	726	809	959	1,158	1,178	2,308	2,409
Monetary authorities	8 787 ..	....	....	....	....	....	....	1,223	1,202
of which: Short-term	8 789 ..	....	....	....	....	....	....	....	....
General government	8 790 ..	....	....	....	....	....	....	....	....
of which: Short-term	8 792 ..	....	....	....	....	....	....	....	....
Banks	8 793 ..	341	462	532	634	772	843	950	1,183
of which: Short-term	8 795 ..	*325*	*444*	*513*	*614*	*747*	*822*	*906*	*1,148*
Other sectors	8 796 ..	387	264	276	326	385	334	134	25
of which: Short-term	8 798 ..	....	....	....	....	....	....	....	....
NET INTERNATIONAL INVESTMENT POSITION	8 995 ..	**−20,560**	**−36,886**	**−33,970**	**−51,781**	**−78,284**	**−78,719**	**−95,243**	**−99,740**
Conversion rates: Czech koruny per U.S. dollar (end of period)	0 102 ..	**25.654**	**22.365**	**24.588**	**20.876**	**18.078**	**19.346**	**18.368**	**18.751**

Table 1. ANALYTIC PRESENTATION, 2003–2010

(Millions of U.S. dollars)

	Code	2003	2004	2005	2006	2007	2008	2009	2010
A. Current Account[1]	4 993 Z.	**6,963**	**5,941**	**11,104**	**8,218**	**4,769**	**9,095**	**11,222**	**16,210**
Goods: exports f.o.b.	2 100 ..	64,537	75,050	82,486	90,732	100,720	115,135	91,930	96,044
Goods: imports f.o.b.	3 100 ..	−54,840	−65,524	−75,153	−87,684	−100,329	−114,216	−83,826	−87,348
Balance on Goods	4 100 ..	*9,697*	*9,527*	*7,333*	*3,048*	*391*	*919*	*8,103*	*8,696*
Services: credit	2 200 ..	31,672	36,304	43,371	52,308	61,965	72,661	55,346	60,388
Services: debit	3 200 ..	−28,254	−33,401	−37,002	−45,232	−53,998	−62,561	−50,912	−52,086
Balance on Goods and Services	4 991 ..	*13,116*	*12,430*	*13,702*	*10,124*	*8,359*	*11,020*	*12,538*	*16,998*
Income: credit	2 300 ..	11,180	12,784	24,929	27,764	34,639	37,395	26,102	27,527
Income: debit	3 300 ..	−13,796	−15,114	−23,331	−24,910	−32,901	−33,823	−22,170	−22,549
Balance on Goods, Services, and Income	4 992 ..	*10,499*	*10,100*	*15,300*	*12,978*	*10,098*	*14,592*	*16,470*	*21,976*
Current transfers: credit	2 379 Z.	4,615	5,120	3,562	3,577	3,928	4,650	4,622	4,070
Current transfers: debit	3 379 ..	−8,151	−9,279	−7,758	−8,336	−9,257	−10,147	−9,871	−9,836
B. Capital Account[1]	4 994 Z.	**−7**	**13**	**518**	**6**	**50**	**75**	**−45**	**116**
Capital account: credit	2 994 Z.	344	511	1,032	458	435	493	483	484
Capital account: debit	3 994 ..	−351	−498	−514	−452	−385	−418	−528	−368
Total, Groups A Plus B	4 981 ..	*6,957*	*5,954*	*11,622*	*8,225*	*4,819*	*9,170*	*11,177*	*16,326*
C. Financial Account[1]	4 995 W.	**−5,129**	**−19,023**	**−10,579**	**−8,609**	**−4,125**	**6,964**	**25,930**	**8,088**
Direct investment abroad	4 505 ..	−856	9,930	−16,206	−8,146	−19,995	−15,241	−6,436	−2,971
Direct investment in Denmark	4 555 Z.	1,185	−8,804	12,834	2,420	11,809	2,606	2,905	−680
Portfolio investment assets	4 602 ..	−21,930	−24,768	−33,037	−26,086	−27,522	−8,634	−23,339	−17,186
Equity securities	4 610 ..	−3,467	−7,299	−14,239	−22,032	−8,851	9,274	−8,205	−6,187
Debt securities	4 619 ..	−18,463	−17,469	−18,798	−4,054	−18,671	−17,908	−15,134	−10,999
Portfolio investment liabilities	4 652 Z.	6,010	10,055	21,081	9,240	20,048	17,900	35,655	15,907
Equity securities	4 660 ..	1,389	1,562	−3,005	−5,453	2,607	2,793	8,152	7,414
Debt securities	4 669 Z.	4,621	8,493	24,086	14,694	17,441	15,107	27,503	8,493
Financial derivatives	4 910 ..	−12	3,206	2,161	2,636	136	2,843	2,985	4,805
Financial derivatives assets	4 900 ..	−12	3,206	2,161	2,636	136	2,843	2,985	4,805
Financial derivatives liabilities	4 905 ..	....	....	....	....	....	....	....	....
Other investment assets	4 703 ..	−9,314	−9,021	−19,973	−24,098	−45,484	−22,412	35,942	−7,698
Monetary authorities	4 701 ..	56	−13	....	....	....	....	....	....
General government	4 704 ..	365	31	473	−147	195	78	−111	−96
Banks	4 705 ..	−12,623	−14,576	−20,658	−23,687	−43,016	−21,953	33,936	−4,691
Other sectors	4 728 ..	2,888	5,537	212	−264	−2,662	−537	2,117	−2,911
Other investment liabilities	4 753 W.	19,789	378	22,561	35,425	56,882	29,902	−21,784	15,912
Monetary authorities	4 753 WA	−27	−230	116	280	246	20,935	−18,798	−494
General government	4 753 ZB	−438	−177	7	−14	2	−55	−20	43
Banks	4 753 ZC	24,714	9,567	14,496	25,764	57,260	−9,144	−6,468	5,513
Other sectors	4 753 ZD	−4,461	−8,782	7,942	9,396	−625	18,165	3,501	10,849
Total, Groups A Through C	4 983 ..	*1,828*	*−13,069*	*1,043*	*−384*	*694*	*16,134*	*37,107*	*24,415*
D. Net Errors and Omissions	4 998 ..	**2,846**	**11,644**	**−2,549**	**−5,604**	**−905**	**−8,711**	**−3,436**	**−20,136**
Total, Groups A Through D	4 984 ..	*4,674*	*−1,426*	*−1,506*	*−5,988*	*−211*	*7,423*	*33,670*	*4,279*
E. Reserves and Related Items	4 802 A.	**−4,674**	**1,426**	**1,506**	**5,988**	**211**	**−7,423**	**−33,670**	**−4,279**
Reserve assets	4 802 ..	−4,674	1,426	1,506	5,988	211	−7,423	−33,670	−4,279
Use of Fund credit and loans	4 766 ..	....	....	....	....	....	....	....	....
Exceptional financing	4 920 ..	....	....	....	....	....	....	....	....
Conversion rates: Danish kroner per U.S. dollar	0 101 ..	**6.5877**	**5.9911**	**5.9969**	**5.9468**	**5.4437**	**5.0981**	**5.3609**	**5.6241**

[1] Excludes components that have been classified in the categories of Group E.

Table 2. STANDARD PRESENTATION, 2003–2010

(Millions of U.S. dollars)

	Code	2003	2004	2005	2006	2007	2008	2009	2010
CURRENT ACCOUNT..	4 993 ..	**6,963**	**5,941**	**11,104**	**8,218**	**4,769**	**9,095**	**11,222**	**16,210**
A. GOODS..	4 100 ..	**9,697**	**9,527**	**7,333**	**3,048**	**391**	**919**	**8,103**	**8,696**
Credit..	2 100 ..	**64,537**	**75,050**	**82,486**	**90,732**	**100,720**	**115,135**	**91,930**	**96,044**
General merchandise: exports f.o.b..............................	2 110 ..	64,537	75,050	82,486	90,732	100,720	115,135	91,930	96,044
Goods for processing: exports f.o.b..........................	2 150 ..	....	....	....	....	....	....	....	....
Repairs on goods..	2 160 ..	....	....	....	....	....	....	....	....
Goods procured in ports by carriers.........................	2 170 ..	....	....	....	....	....	....	....	....
Nonmonetary gold..	2 180 ..	....	....	....	....	....	....	....	....
Debit..	3 100 ..	**−54,840**	**−65,524**	**−75,153**	**−87,684**	**−100,329**	**−114,216**	**−83,826**	**−87,348**
General merchandise: imports f.o.b..............................	3 110 ..	−54,840	−65,524	−75,153	−87,684	−100,329	−114,216	−83,826	−87,348
Goods for processing: imports f.o.b..........................	3 150 ..	....	....	....	....	....	....	....	....
Repairs on goods..	3 160 ..	....	....	....	....	....	....	....	....
Goods procured in ports by carriers.........................	3 170 ..	....	....	....	....	....	....	....	....
Nonmonetary gold..	3 180 ..	....	....	....	....	....	....	....	....
B. SERVICES..	4 200 ..	**3,418**	**2,903**	**6,369**	**7,076**	**7,968**	**10,100**	**4,434**	**8,302**
Total credit..	2 200 ..	*31,672*	*36,304*	*43,371*	*52,308*	*61,965*	*72,661*	*55,346*	*60,388*
Total debit..	3 200 ..	*−28,254*	*−33,401*	*−37,002*	*−45,232*	*−53,998*	*−62,561*	*−50,912*	*−52,086*
Transportation services, credit...................	2 205 ..	**14,023**	**17,089**	....	....	....	....	....	....
Passenger..	2 850 ..	....	....	....	....	....	....	....	....
Freight..	2 851 ..	....	....	....	....	....	....	....	....
Other..	2 852 ..	*14,023*	*17,089*	....	....	....	....	....	....
Sea transport, passenger..............................	2 207 ..	....	....	....	....	....	....	....	....
Sea transport, freight..............................	2 208 ..	....	....	....	....	....	....	....	....
Sea transport, other..............................	2 209 ..	14,023	17,089	....	....	....	....	....	....
Air transport, passenger..............................	2 211 ..	....	....	....	....	....	....	....	....
Air transport, freight..............................	2 212 ..	....	....	....	....	....	....	....	....
Air transport, other..............................	2 213 ..	....	....	....	....	....	....	....	....
Other transport, passenger..............................	2 215 ..	....	....	....	....	....	....	....	....
Other transport, freight..............................	2 216 ..	....	....	....	....	....	....	....	....
Other transport, other..............................	2 217 ..	....	....	....	....	....	....	....	....
Transportation services, debit...................	3 205 ..	**−12,027**	**−14,484**	....	....	....	....	....	....
Passenger..	3 850 ..	....	....	....	....	....	....	....	....
Freight..	3 851 ..	....	....	....	....	....	....	....	....
Other..	3 852 ..	*−12,027*	*−14,484*	....	....	....	....	....	....
Sea transport, passenger..............................	3 207 ..	....	....	....	....	....	....	....	....
Sea transport, freight..............................	3 208 ..	....	....	....	....	....	....	....	....
Sea transport, other..............................	3 209 ..	−12,027	−14,484	....	....	....	....	....	....
Air transport, passenger..............................	3 211 ..	....	....	....	....	....	....	....	....
Air transport, freight..............................	3 212 ..	....	....	....	....	....	....	....	....
Air transport, other..............................	3 213 ..	....	....	....	....	....	....	....	....
Other transport, passenger..............................	3 215 ..	....	....	....	....	....	....	....	....
Other transport, freight..............................	3 216 ..	....	....	....	....	....	....	....	....
Other transport, other..............................	3 217 ..	....	....	....	....	....	....	....	....
Travel, credit..	2 236 ..	**5,271**	**5,652**	....	....	....	....	....	....
Business travel..	2 237 ..	....	....	....	....	....	....	....	....
Personal travel..	2 240 ..	5,271	5,652	....	....	....	....	....	....
Travel, debit..	3 236 ..	**−6,659**	**−7,279**	....	....	....	....	....	....
Business travel..	3 237 ..	....	....	....	....	....	....	....	....
Personal travel..	3 240 ..	−6,659	−7,279	....	....	....	....	....	....
Other services, credit..............................	2 200 BA ..	**12,378**	**13,563**	....	....	....	....	....	....
Communications..	2 245 ..	....	....	....	....	....	....	....	....
Construction..	2 249 ..	....	....	....	....	....	....	....	....
Insurance..	2 253 ..	....	....	....	....	....	....	....	....
Financial..	2 260 ..	....	....	....	....	....	....	....	....
Computer and information..............................	2 262 ..	....	....	....	....	....	....	....	....
Royalties and licence fees..............................	2 266 ..	....	....	....	....	....	....	....	....
Other business services..............................	2 268 ..	12,378	13,563	....	....	....	....	....	....
Personal, cultural, and recreational..................	2 287 ..	....	....	....	....	....	....	....	....
Government, n.i.e..	2 291 ..	....	....	....	....	....	....	....	....
Other services, debit..............................	3 200 BA ..	**−9,568**	**−11,638**	....	....	....	....	....	....
Communications..	3 245 ..	....	....	....	....	....	....	....	....
Construction..	3 249 ..	....	....	....	....	....	....	....	....
Insurance..	3 253 ..	....	....	....	....	....	....	....	....
Financial..	3 260 ..	....	....	....	....	....	....	....	....
Computer and information..............................	3 262 ..	....	....	....	....	....	....	....	....
Royalties and licence fees..............................	3 266 ..	....	....	....	....	....	....	....	....
Other business services..............................	3 268 ..	−9,568	−11,638	....	....	....	....	....	....
Personal, cultural, and recreational..................	3 287 ..	....	....	....	....	....	....	....	....
Government, n.i.e..	3 291 ..	....	....	....	....	....	....	....	....

Table 2 (Continued). STANDARD PRESENTATION, 2003–2010

(Millions of U.S. dollars)

	Code	2003	2004	2005	2006	2007	2008	2009	2010
C. INCOME	4 300	**−2,616**	**−2,330**	**1,598**	**2,854**	**1,738**	**3,572**	**3,933**	**4,978**
Total credit	2 300	*11,180*	*12,784*	*24,929*	*27,764*	*34,639*	*37,395*	*26,102*	*27,527*
Total debit	3 300	*−13,796*	*−15,114*	*−23,331*	*−24,910*	*−32,901*	*−33,823*	*−22,170*	*−22,549*
Compensation of employees, credit	2 310	**941**	**1,075**	**867**	**982**	**819**	**905**	**894**	**1,185**
Compensation of employees, debit	3 310	**−1,029**	**−1,226**	**−1,488**	**−1,766**	**−3,019**	**−3,994**	**−3,413**	**−2,888**
Investment income, credit	2 320	**10,239**	**11,709**	**24,062**	**26,782**	**33,820**	**36,490**	**25,208**	**26,342**
Direct investment income	2 330	4,534	4,163	13,592	12,601	14,881	14,327	12,485	14,740
Dividends and distributed branch profits	2 332	4,195	2,730	6,873	8,244	7,682	12,316	10,794	8,484
Reinvested earnings and undistributed branch profits	2 333	−296	931	5,037	2,523	5,150	−988	−540	4,632
Income on debt (interest)	2 334	635	501	1,682	1,833	2,049	3,000	2,231	1,624
Portfolio investment income	2 339	3,206	5,152	6,654	9,015	10,489	11,921	8,966	8,971
Income on equity	2 340	628	1,226	1,729	4,093	5,069	5,148	2,581	3,028
Income on bonds and notes	2 350	2,567	3,839	4,531	4,528	4,987	6,231	5,875	5,468
Income on money market instruments	2 360	11	87	394	394	434	542	511	475
Other investment income	2 370	2,499	2,394	3,817	5,166	8,450	10,242	3,758	2,631
Investment income, debit	3 320	**−12,767**	**−13,888**	**−21,844**	**−23,144**	**−29,882**	**−29,829**	**−18,757**	**−19,661**
Direct investment income	3 330	−4,413	−4,715	−10,918	−8,671	−11,238	−8,584	−6,629	−9,723
Dividends and distributed branch profits	3 332	−5,240	−2,893	−7,818	−7,049	−8,572	−9,487	−7,841	−4,469
Reinvested earnings and undistributed branch profits	3 333	1,516	−1,174	−1,759	142	−372	3,550	3,218	−3,739
Income on debt (interest)	3 334	−689	−648	−1,341	−1,764	−2,294	−2,647	−2,006	−1,515
Portfolio investment income	3 339	−4,486	−4,928	−6,907	−7,921	−8,435	−9,404	−7,983	−7,501
Income on equity	3 340	−482	−633	−1,201	−1,656	−1,106	−1,598	−861	−848
Income on bonds and notes	3 350	−3,985	−4,272	−5,592	−6,140	−7,181	−7,649	−6,979	−6,519
Income on money market instruments	3 360	−19	−23	−114	−125	−147	−156	−143	−133
Other investment income	3 370	−3,867	−4,245	−4,019	−6,552	−10,209	−11,841	−4,145	−2,438
D. CURRENT TRANSFERS	4 379	**−3,536**	**−4,159**	**−4,196**	**−4,760**	**−5,329**	**−5,497**	**−5,248**	**−5,766**
Credit	2 379	**4,615**	**5,120**	**3,562**	**3,577**	**3,928**	**4,650**	**4,622**	**4,070**
General government	2 380	600	666	....	....	....	....	....	....
Other sectors	2 390	4,015	4,454	....	....	....	....	....	....
Workers' remittances	2 391	....	....	....	....	....	....	....	....
Other current transfers	2 392	....	....	....	....	....	....	....	....
Debit	3 379	**−8,151**	**−9,279**	**−7,758**	**−8,336**	**−9,257**	**−10,147**	**−9,871**	**−9,836**
General government	3 380	−4,890	−5,567	....	....	....	....	....	....
Other sectors	3 390	−3,260	−3,712	....	....	....	....	....	....
Workers' remittances	3 391	....	....	....	....	....	....	....	....
Other current transfers	3 392	....	....	....	....	....	....	....	....
CAPITAL AND FINANCIAL ACCOUNT	4 996	**−9,809**	**−17,585**	**−8,555**	**−2,615**	**−3,864**	**−384**	**−7,786**	**3,925**
CAPITAL ACCOUNT	4 994	**−7**	**13**	**518**	**6**	**50**	**75**	**−45**	**116**
Total credit	2 994	*344*	*511*	*1,032*	*458*	*435*	*493*	*483*	*484*
Total debit	3 994	*−351*	*−498*	*−514*	*−452*	*−385*	*−418*	*−528*	*−368*
Capital transfers, credit	2 400	**344**	**511**	....	....	....	....	....	....
General government	2 401	....	....	....	....	....	....	....	....
Debt forgiveness	2 402	....	....	....	....	....	....	....	....
Other capital transfers	2 410	....	....	....	....	....	....	....	....
Other sectors	2 430	....	....	....	....	....	....	....	....
Migrants' transfers	2 431	....	....	....	....	....	....	....	....
Debt forgiveness	2 432	....	....	....	....	....	....	....	....
Other capital transfers	2 440	....	....	....	....	....	....	....	....
Capital transfers, debit	3 400	**−351**	**−498**	....	....	....	....	....	....
General government	3 401	....	....	....	....	....	....	....	....
Debt forgiveness	3 402	....	....	....	....	....	....	....	....
Other capital transfers	3 410	....	....	....	....	....	....	....	....
Other sectors	3 430	....	....	....	....	....	....	....	....
Migrants' transfers	3 431	....	....	....	....	....	....	....	....
Debt forgiveness	3 432	....	....	....	....	....	....	....	....
Other capital transfers	3 440	....	....	....	....	....	....	....	....
Nonproduced nonfinancial assets, credit	2 480	....	....	....	....	....	....	....	....
Nonproduced nonfinancial assets, debit	3 480	....	....	....	....	....	....	....	....

Table 2 (Continued). STANDARD PRESENTATION, 2003–2010

(Millions of U.S. dollars)

	Code	2003	2004	2005	2006	2007	2008	2009	2010
FINANCIAL ACCOUNT	4 995	**−9,803**	**−17,598**	**−9,073**	**−2,621**	**−3,914**	**−459**	**−7,741**	**3,809**
A. DIRECT INVESTMENT	4 500	**329**	**1,126**	**−3,372**	**−5,726**	**−8,186**	**−12,635**	**−3,531**	**−3,651**
Direct investment abroad	4 505	**−856**	**9,930**	**−16,206**	**−8,146**	**−19,995**	**−15,241**	**−6,436**	**−2,971**
Equity capital	4 510	6,995	−1,882	−6,716	−5,644	−8,987	3,043	−7,784	2,475
Claims on affiliated enterprises	4 515	....	....	....	....	....	....	....	....
Liabilities to affiliated enterprises	4 520	....	....	....	....	....	....	....	....
Reinvested earnings	4 525	296	−931	−5,037	−2,523	−5,150	988	540	−4,632
Other capital	4 530	−8,148	12,743	−4,453	21	−5,858	−19,272	808	−813
Claims on affiliated enterprises	4 535	....	....	....	....	....	....	....	....
Liabilities to affiliated enterprises	4 540	....	....	....	....	....	....	....	....
Direct investment in Denmark	4 555	**1,185**	**−8,804**	**12,834**	**2,420**	**11,809**	**2,606**	**2,905**	**−680**
Equity capital	4 560	2,413	−8,324	8,682	−3,482	9,503	2,817	3,765	−1,631
Claims on direct investors	4 565	....	....	....	....	....	....	....	....
Liabilities to direct investors	4 570	....	....	....	....	....	....	....	....
Reinvested earnings	4 575	−1,516	1,174	1,759	−142	372	−3,550	−3,218	3,739
Other capital	4 580	287	−1,655	2,393	6,044	1,934	3,339	2,358	−2,789
Claims on direct investors	4 585	....	....	....	....	....	....	....	....
Liabilities to direct investors	4 590	....	....	....	....	....	....	....	....
B. PORTFOLIO INVESTMENT	4 600	**−15,920**	**−14,713**	**−11,956**	**−16,846**	**−7,474**	**9,266**	**12,317**	**−1,279**
Assets	4 602	**−21,930**	**−24,768**	**−33,037**	**−26,086**	**−27,522**	**−8,634**	**−23,339**	**−17,186**
Equity securities	4 610	−3,467	−7,299	−14,239	−22,032	−8,851	9,274	−8,205	−6,187
Monetary authorities	4 611	....	....	5	....	....	....	−11	−9
General government	4 612	322	34	−8	−4	−9	−274	129	47
Banks	4 613	−298	−432	−2,595	−2,015	1,696	1,033	858	−663
Other sectors	4 614	−3,491	−6,900	−11,641	−20,013	−10,538	8,515	−9,181	−5,562
Debt securities	4 619	−18,463	−17,469	−18,798	−4,054	−18,671	−17,908	−15,134	−10,999
Bonds and notes	4 620	−16,603	−17,542	−18,563	−2,461	−7,508	−21,328	−8,874	−11,797
Monetary authorities	4 621	....	....	....	....	....	....	....	....
General government	4 622	−5,331	−1,525	−42	15	−35	24	−280	−68
Banks	4 623	−4,729	−1,730	919	−6,423	−5,041	−7,216	5,893	4,768
Other sectors	4 624	−6,543	−14,286	−19,439	3,947	−2,433	−14,137	−14,486	−16,498
Money market instruments	4 630	−1,859	73	−235	−1,594	−11,163	3,420	−6,260	798
Monetary authorities	4 631	....	....	....	....	....	....	....	....
General government	4 632	....	....	−5	2	2	....	−1	....
Banks	4 633	−1,346	894	−110	330	−1,864	1,513	−2,024	845
Other sectors	4 634	−514	−821	−121	−1,926	−9,301	1,907	−4,235	−46
Liabilities	4 652	**6,010**	**10,055**	**21,081**	**9,240**	**20,048**	**17,900**	**35,655**	**15,907**
Equity securities	4 660	1,389	1,562	−3,005	−5,453	2,607	2,793	8,152	7,414
Banks	4 663	−616	−674	−211	1,322	−1,694	−1,035	1,619	813
Other sectors	4 664	2,005	2,235	−2,794	−6,776	4,302	3,828	6,534	6,600
Debt securities	4 669	4,621	8,493	24,086	14,694	17,441	15,107	27,503	8,493
Bonds and notes	4 670	2,951	3,864	20,416	15,355	18,170	−12,721	43,412	10,460
Monetary authorities	4 671	....	....	....	....	....	....	....	....
General government	4 672	−6,802	−6,080	−2,320	−4,069	2,303	111	14,332	−1,176
Banks	4 673	6,448	7,962	21,662	19,201	19,453	−11,882	25,750	11,130
Other sectors	4 674	3,305	1,983	1,073	223	−3,586	−950	3,329	506
Money market instruments	4 680	1,671	4,629	3,671	−661	−729	27,828	−15,910	−1,967
Monetary authorities	4 681	....	....	....	....	....	....	....	....
General government	4 682	−1,070	991	−75	−1,614	−1,470	8,957	−9,317	2,671
Banks	4 683	2,710	3,587	3,632	1,028	493	19,548	−6,581	−4,621
Other sectors	4 684	31	51	114	−75	248	−677	−12	−17
C. FINANCIAL DERIVATIVES	4 910	**−12**	**3,206**	**2,161**	**2,636**	**136**	**2,843**	**2,985**	**4,805**
Monetary authorities	4 911	....	....	....	....	....	....	....	....
General government	4 912	....	....	278	−147	160	−22	78	511
Banks	4 913	37	−32	−367	−75	836	−743	−694	681
Other sectors	4 914	−50	3,239	2,251	2,858	−859	3,608	3,602	3,614
Assets	4 900	**−12**	**3,206**	**2,161**	**2,636**	**136**	**2,843**	**2,985**	**4,805**
Monetary authorities	4 901	....	....	....	....	....	....	....	....
General government	4 902	....	....	278	−147	160	−22	78	511
Banks	4 903	37	−32	−367	−75	836	−743	−694	681
Other sectors	4 904	−50	3,239	2,251	2,858	−859	3,608	3,602	3,614
Liabilities	4 905	....	....	....	....	....	....	....	....
Monetary authorities	4 906	....	....	....	....	....	....	....	....
General government	4 907	....	....	....	....	....	....	....	....
Banks	4 908	....	....	....	....	....	....	....	....
Other sectors	4 909	....	....	....	....	....	....	....	....

Table 2 (Concluded). STANDARD PRESENTATION, 2003–2010
(Millions of U.S. dollars)

	Code	2003	2004	2005	2006	2007	2008	2009	2010
D. OTHER INVESTMENT	4 700	**10,475**	**−8,642**	**2,588**	**11,328**	**11,399**	**7,490**	**14,158**	**8,214**
Assets	4 703	**−9,314**	**−9,021**	**−19,973**	**−24,098**	**−45,484**	**−22,412**	**35,942**	**−7,698**
Trade credits	4 706	2,663	5,716	−318	−760	−1,239	446	1,073	−859
General government	4 707	....	....	−11	11	1	−10	15	−24
of which: Short-term	4 709	....	....	....	....	....	....	....	....
Other sectors	4 710	2,663	5,716	−306	−771	−1,240	456	1,058	−835
of which: Short-term	4 712	....	....	....	....	....	....	....	....
Loans	4 714	....	....	....	....	....	....	....	....
Monetary authorities	4 715	....	....	....	....	....	....	....	....
of which: Short-term	4 718	....	....	....	....	....	....	....	....
General government	4 719	....	....	....	....	....	....	....	....
of which: Short-term	4 721	....	....	....	....	....	....	....	....
Banks	4 722	....	....	....	....	....	....	....	....
of which: Short-term	4 724	....	....	....	....	....	....	....	....
Other sectors	4 725	....	....	....	....	....	....	....	....
of which: Short-term	4 727	....	....	....	....	....	....	....	....
Currency and deposits	4 730	−11,959	−14,742	−19,821	−21,491	−43,819	−21,928	33,881	−6,770
Monetary authorities	4 731	56	−13	....	....	....	....	....	....
General government	4 732	365	31	280	−8	171	41	14	13
Banks	4 733	−12,623	−14,576	−20,573	−21,975	−42,658	−21,190	32,893	−4,724
Other sectors	4 734	243	−183	472	492	−1,332	−778	974	−2,059
Other assets	4 736	−19	5	166	−1,847	−425	−930	989	−69
Monetary authorities	4 737	....	....	....	....	....	....	....	....
of which: Short-term	4 739	....	....	....	....	....	....	....	....
General government	4 740	....	....	205	−150	22	47	−139	−85
of which: Short-term	4 742	....	....	....	....	....	....	....	....
Banks	4 743	....	....	−85	−1,712	−358	−762	1,043	33
of which: Short-term	4 745	....	....	....	....	....	....	....	....
Other sectors	4 746	−19	5	46	15	−90	−214	85	−18
of which: Short-term	4 748	....	....	....	....	....	....	....	....
Liabilities	4 753	**19,789**	**378**	**22,561**	**35,425**	**56,882**	**29,902**	**−21,784**	**15,912**
Trade credits	4 756	−3,838	−7,134	1,011	949	1,053	1,164	−1,274	682
General government	4 757	....	....	7	49	−26	−1	5	43
of which: Short-term	4 759	....	....	....	....	....	....	....	....
Other sectors	4 760	−3,838	−7,134	1,004	900	1,079	1,165	−1,279	639
of which: Short-term	4 762	....	....	....	....	....	....	....	....
Loans	4 764	23,652	7,536	7,129	8,026	−1,816	17,258	4,550	10,135
Monetary authorities	4 765	−27	−230	....	....	....	....	....	....
of which: Use of Fund credit and loans from the Fund	4 766	....	....	....	....	....	....	....	....
of which: Short-term	4 768	....	....	....	....	....	....	....	....
General government	4 769	−438	−177	....	−63	28	−53	−25	....
of which: Short-term	4 771	....	....	....	....	....	....	....	....
Banks	4 772	24,714	9,567	....	....	....	....	....	....
of which: Short-term	4 774	....	....	....	....	....	....	....	....
Other sectors	4 775	−598	−1,624	7,130	8,089	−1,844	17,312	4,575	10,136
of which: Short-term	4 777	....	....	....	....	....	....	....	....
Currency and deposits	4 780	....	....	14,450	24,764	56,764	10,941	−26,755	5,084
Monetary authorities	4 781	....	....	116	280	246	20,935	−20,910	−494
General government	4 782	....	....	....	....	....	....	....	....
Banks	4 783	....	....	14,333	24,484	56,518	−9,995	−5,844	5,578
Other sectors	4 784	....	....	....	....	....	....	....	....
Other liabilities	4 786	−25	−24	−29	1,686	882	539	1,695	10
Monetary authorities	4 787	....	....	....	....	....	....	2,113	....
of which: Short-term	4 789	....	....	....	....	....	....	....	....
General government	4 790	....	....	....	....	....	....	....	....
of which: Short-term	4 792	....	....	....	....	....	....	....	....
Banks	4 793	....	....	162	1,279	742	851	−623	−65
of which: Short-term	4 795	....	....	....	....	....	....	....	....
Other sectors	4 796	−25	−24	−192	407	140	−312	205	75
of which: Short-term	4 798	....	....	....	....	....	....	....	....
E. RESERVE ASSETS	4 802	**−4,674**	**1,426**	**1,506**	**5,988**	**211**	**−7,423**	**−33,670**	**−4,279**
Monetary gold	4 812	....	−1	....	....	....	....	....	....
Special drawing rights	4 811	31	38	−71	−225	23	5	−2,052	−1
Reserve position in the Fund	4 810	49	214	474	98	60	−152	−316	−186
Foreign exchange	4 803	−4,713	1,175	1,107	6,169	205	−7,330	−28,468	−6,719
Other claims	4 813	−42	....	−4	−54	−77	54	−2,834	2,628
NET ERRORS AND OMISSIONS	4 998	**2,846**	**11,644**	**−2,549**	**−5,604**	**−905**	**−8,711**	**−3,436**	**−20,136**

Table 3. INTERNATIONAL INVESTMENT POSITION (End-period stocks), 2003–2010

(Millions of U.S. dollars)

	Code	2003	2004	2005	2006	2007	2008	2009	2010
ASSETS	8 995 C.	**380,902**	**471,710**	**478,531**	**574,355**	**713,467**	**679,756**	**747,669**	**775,835**
Direct investment abroad	8 505	**90,292**	**109,024**	**111,442**	**124,932**	**158,387**	**164,390**	**178,190**	**187,287**
Equity capital and reinvested earnings	8 506	69,342	86,162	89,502	102,285	128,157	122,943	140,581	148,400
Claims on affiliated enterprises	8 507	....	....	....	....	....	....	....	....
Liabilities to affiliated enterprises	8 508	....	....	....	....	....	....	....	....
Other capital	8 530	20,951	22,862	21,940	22,647	30,231	41,447	37,609	38,886
Claims on affiliated enterprises	8 535	27,935	32,373	33,054	34,752	46,354	61,016	59,203	60,076
Liabilities to affiliated enterprises	8 540	−6,984	−9,511	−11,114	−12,104	−16,124	−19,569	−21,594	−21,190
Portfolio investment	8 602	**127,033**	**160,851**	**196,731**	**251,885**	**301,287**	**233,423**	**296,602**	**314,631**
Equity securities	8 610	52,118	65,428	88,374	132,047	156,798	85,172	118,116	131,114
Monetary authorities	8 611	171	258	209	239	268	255	275	288
General government	8 612	3,457	4,448	208	186	64	227	285	271
Banks	8 613	3,338	4,363	6,104	9,090	10,401	5,473	6,472	5,645
Other sectors	8 614	45,152	56,359	81,853	122,531	146,064	79,216	111,084	124,909
Debt securities	8 619	74,915	95,423	108,357	119,838	144,489	148,251	178,486	183,517
Bonds and notes	8 620	73,561	94,233	106,572	118,570	138,097	146,229	171,167	177,415
Monetary authorities	8 621	....	....	....	....	....	....	....	....
General government	8 622	14,946	17,930	101	85	110	56	379	439
Banks	8 623	15,811	18,887	15,387	23,988	30,310	34,094	31,449	25,576
Other sectors	8 624	42,803	57,416	91,084	94,497	107,676	112,079	139,339	151,400
Money market instruments	8 630	1,354	1,190	1,785	1,268	6,393	2,023	7,319	6,102
Monetary authorities	8 631	....	....	....	....	....	....	....	....
General government	8 632	246	....	5	3	....	....	....	....
Banks	8 633	674	487	418	171	2,133	629	2,714	1,842
Other sectors	8 634	435	703	1,362	1,094	4,259	1,393	4,604	4,260
Financial derivatives	8 900	**23,566**	**36,560**	**13,497**	**8,350**	**−8**	**15,731**	**4,117**	**6,988**
Monetary authorities	8 901	249	218	....	....	....	....	....	....
General government	8 902	1,446	1,579	1,067	591	103	549	361	1,077
Banks	8 903	17,893	30,428	275	2,276	1,992	−1,223	−1,592	1,838
Other sectors	8 904	3,978	4,334	12,155	5,483	−2,103	16,404	5,349	4,073
Other investment	8 703	**101,816**	**125,174**	**122,803**	**157,970**	**219,409**	**223,784**	**191,977**	**190,221**
Trade credits	8 706	9,538	10,393	5,918	7,284	9,305	8,500	7,291	7,964
General government	8 707	1,222	1,331	16	5	5	16	1	26
of which: Short-term	8 709	....	....	....	....	....	....	....	....
Other sectors	8 710	8,316	9,062	5,902	7,278	9,299	8,484	7,290	7,938
of which: Short-term	8 712	....	....	....	....	....	....	....	....
Loans	8 714	26,960	33,100	....	....	....	....	....	....
Monetary authorities	8 715	....	....	....	....	....	....	....	....
of which: Short-term	8 718	....	....	....	....	....	....	....	....
General government	8 719	....	....	....	....	....	....	....	....
of which: Short-term	8 721	....	....	....	....	....	....	....	....
Banks	8 722	24,864	30,816	....	....	....	....	....	....
of which: Short-term	8 724	....	....	....	....	....	....	....	....
Other sectors	8 725	2,096	2,284	....	....	....	....	....	....
of which: Short-term	8 727	....	....	....	....	....	....	....	....
Currency and deposits	8 730	60,060	75,804	113,850	145,425	203,848	208,277	178,547	176,395
Monetary authorities	8 731	....	....	....	....	....	....	....	....
General government	8 732	1	2	766	864	787	713	712	645
Banks	8 733	57,038	72,417	108,894	140,800	197,449	201,201	172,617	168,544
Other sectors	8 734	3,021	3,385	4,190	3,761	5,612	6,363	5,218	7,206
Other assets	8 736	5,257	5,876	3,035	5,261	6,256	7,007	6,139	5,863
Monetary authorities	8 737	....	....	....	....	....	....	....	....
of which: Short-term	8 739	....	....	....	....	....	....	....	....
General government	8 740	3,745	4,081	2,270	2,700	2,992	2,827	3,036	2,888
of which: Short-term	8 742	....	....	....	....	....	....	....	....
Banks	8 743	318	496	442	2,303	2,959	3,634	2,624	2,469
of which: Short-term	8 745	....	....	....	....	....	....	....	....
Other sectors	8 746	1,193	1,300	323	259	305	546	479	505
of which: Short-term	8 748	....	....	....	....	....	....	....	....
Reserve assets	8 802	**38,194**	**40,102**	**34,057**	**31,218**	**34,392**	**42,428**	**76,783**	**76,709**
Monetary gold	8 812	889	931	1,098	1,360	1,790	1,851	2,362	3,017
Special drawing rights	8 811	81	45	112	342	335	320	2,384	2,343
Reserve position in the Fund	8 810	1,020	843	309	222	171	323	648	826
Foreign exchange	8 803	36,204	38,283	26,334	23,811	27,647	33,036	62,371	62,640
Other claims	8 813	....	....	6,205	5,483	4,450	6,899	9,018	7,883

Table 3 (Concluded). INTERNATIONAL INVESTMENT POSITION (End-period stocks), 2003–2010

(Millions of U.S. dollars)

	Code	2003	2004	2005	2006	2007	2008	2009	2010
LIABILITIES...............	8 995 D.	**409,410**	**493,679**	**468,939**	**574,868**	**732,721**	**697,067**	**735,993**	**745,956**
Direct investment in Denmark...............	8 555 ..	**87,888**	**99,349**	**97,932**	**109,559**	**134,995**	**121,709**	**119,151**	**106,350**
Equity capital and reinvested earnings...............	8 556 ..	72,924	78,499	79,747	85,056	106,919	96,701	95,670	87,245
Claims on direct investors...............	8 557 ..	....	....	....	....	....	....	....	....
Liabilities to direct investors...............	8 558 ..	....	....	....	....	....	....	....	....
Other capital...............	8 580 ..	14,964	20,850	18,186	24,503	28,076	25,009	23,481	19,105
Claims on direct investors...............	8 585 ..	−5,319	−7,682	−7,077	−11,095	−10,359	−10,759	−13,286	−11,293
Liabilities to direct investors...............	8 590 ..	20,283	28,532	25,263	35,599	38,435	35,767	36,767	30,398
Portfolio investment...............	8 652 ..	**159,180**	**197,683**	**210,159**	**251,128**	**304,533**	**272,477**	**329,374**	**347,993**
Equity securities...............	8 660 ..	31,258	44,459	49,097	62,886	83,207	45,702	66,976	92,636
Banks...............	8 663 ..	6,557	7,874	8,574	12,691	9,788	2,026	5,863	7,367
Other sectors...............	8 664 ..	24,700	36,585	40,522	50,196	73,419	43,676	61,113	85,268
Debt securities...............	8 669 ..	127,923	153,225	161,062	188,241	221,326	226,776	262,397	255,358
Bonds and notes...............	8 670 ..	109,645	127,090	134,545	161,824	195,387	172,950	224,719	221,400
Monetary authorities...............	8 671 ..	....	....	....	....	....	....	....	....
General government...............	8 672 ..	36,198	37,772	30,954	29,033	34,290	34,488	50,317	47,045
Banks...............	8 673 ..	58,212	69,817	84,062	111,561	141,652	121,950	152,857	153,236
Other sectors...............	8 674 ..	15,234	19,501	19,529	21,229	19,446	16,512	21,545	21,119
Money market instruments...............	8 680 ..	18,278	26,134	26,517	26,417	25,939	53,826	37,679	33,957
Monetary authorities...............	8 681 ..	93	131	....	....	....	....	....	....
General government...............	8 682 ..	2,218	5,705	4,035	2,802	1,487	10,598	1,020	3,718
Banks...............	8 683 ..	15,498	19,651	21,619	22,793	23,365	42,923	36,366	29,965
Other sectors...............	8 684 ..	469	647	863	822	1,087	304	293	274
Financial derivatives...............	8 905 ..	**20,442**	**32,582**	....	....	....	....	....	....
Monetary authorities...............	8 906 ..	....	2	....	....	....	....	....	....
General government...............	8 907 ..	199	217	....	....	....	....	....	....
Banks...............	8 908 ..	17,978	29,895	....	....	....	....	....	....
Other sectors...............	8 909 ..	2,265	2,467	....	....	....	....	....	....
Other investment...............	8 753 ..	**141,900**	**164,064**	**160,849**	**214,181**	**293,193**	**302,880**	**287,468**	**291,613**
Trade credits...............	8 756 ..	4,707	5,129	4,257	5,589	7,061	7,825	6,646	7,182
General government...............	8 758 ..	....	....	....	....	....	....	....	....
of which: Short-term...............	8 759 ..	....	....	....	....	....	....	....	....
Other sectors...............	8 760 ..	4,650	5,066	4,244	5,527	7,022	7,786	6,602	7,100
of which: Short-term...............	8 762 ..	....	....	....	....	....	....	....	....
Loans...............	8 764 ..	120,410	134,348	24,602	35,941	39,098	52,449	59,555	63,997
Monetary authorities...............	8 765 ..	....	....	....	....	....	....	....	....
of which: Use of Fund credit and loans from the Fund....	8 766 ..	....	....	....	....	....	....	....	....
of which: Short-term...............	8 768 ..	....	....	....	....	....	....	....	....
General government...............	8 769 ..	32	21	284	132	82	28	1	1
of which: Short-term...............	8 771 ..	....	....	....	....	....	....	....	....
Banks...............	8 772 ..	96,514	107,647	....	....	....	....	....	....
of which: Short-term...............	8 774 ..	....	....	....	....	....	....	....	....
Other sectors...............	8 775 ..	23,863	26,680	24,318	35,809	39,016	52,421	59,554	63,997
of which: Short-term...............	8 777 ..	....	....	....	....	....	....	....	....
Currency and deposits...............	8 780 ..	14,633	22,219	128,689	166,538	239,569	234,967	211,487	210,844
Monetary authorities...............	8 781 ..	519	321	405	723	1,016	22,866	966	819
General government...............	8 782 ..	....	....	....	....	....	....	....	....
Banks...............	8 783 ..	14,114	21,898	128,284	165,816	238,552	212,101	210,520	210,025
Other sectors...............	8 784 ..	....	....	....	....	....	....	....	....
Other liabilities...............	8 786 ..	2,151	2,369	3,301	6,112	7,465	7,640	9,781	9,590
Monetary authorities...............	8 787 ..	....	....	....	....	....	....	2,401	2,359
of which: Short-term...............	8 789 ..	....	....	....	....	....	....	....	....
General government...............	8 790 ..	....	....	....	....	....	....	....	....
of which: Short-term...............	8 792 ..	....	....	....	....	....	....	....	....
Banks...............	8 793 ..	275	324	447	1,869	2,897	3,680	3,073	2,799
of which: Short-term...............	8 795 ..	....	....	....	....	....	....	....	....
Other sectors...............	8 796 ..	1,877	2,045	2,854	4,244	4,568	3,959	4,307	4,432
of which: Short-term...............	8 798 ..	....	....	....	....	....	....	....	....
NET INTERNATIONAL INVESTMENT POSITION.........	8 995 ..	**−28,509**	**−21,969**	**9,592**	**−513**	**−19,254**	**−17,311**	**11,677**	**29,879**
Conversion rates: Danish kroner per U.S. dollar (end of period)...............	0 102 ..	**5.9576**	**5.4676**	**6.3241**	**5.6614**	**5.0753**	**5.2849**	**5.1901**	**5.6133**

Table 1. ANALYTIC PRESENTATION, 2003–2010

(Millions of U.S. dollars)

	Code	2003	2004	2005	2006	2007	2008	2009	2010
A. Current Account¹....................	4 993 Z.	**38.1**	**3.2**	**20.1**	**−16.6**	**−171.4**	**−225.4**	**−71.1**	**50.5**
Goods: exports f.o.b...............	2 100 ..	37.2	38.0	39.5	55.2	58.1	68.8	77.4	85.1
Goods: imports f.o.b...............	3 100 ..	−238.2	−261.4	−277.3	−335.7	−473.2	−574.1	−450.7	−363.8
Balance on Goods...............	4 100 ..	*−201.0*	*−223.4*	*−237.8*	*−280.5*	*−415.2*	*−505.3*	*−373.3*	*−278.6*
Services: credit....................	2 200 ..	215.7	212.7	248.4	251.5	248.5	296.9	322.0	335.7
Services: debit.....................	3 200 ..	−67.0	−77.2	−83.8	−89.3	−107.7	−129.5	−127.6	−119.1
Balance on Goods and Services............	4 991 ..	*−52.2*	*−87.9*	*−73.2*	*−118.4*	*−274.4*	*−337.9*	*−178.9*	*−62.0*
Income: credit....................	2 300 ..	31.2	33.3	32.0	34.9	35.2	45.6	37.0	32.8
Income: debit.....................	3 300 ..	−10.3	−10.7	−11.2	−11.8	−11.3	−12.9	−15.3	−15.4
Balance on Goods, Services, and Income..........	4 992 ..	*−31.3*	*−65.3*	*−52.4*	*−95.3*	*−250.6*	*−305.2*	*−157.2*	*−44.7*
Current transfers: credit...........	2 379 Z.	75.3	74.1	78.3	85.5	85.9	87.2	92.2	108.7
Current transfers: debit...........	3 379 ..	−5.8	−5.6	−5.8	−6.8	−6.7	−7.3	−6.1	−13.5
B. Capital Account¹....................	4 994 Z.	**−7.2**	**19.7**	**26.8**	**9.3**	**35.3**	**53.7**	**55.1**	**55.3**
Capital account: credit...........	2 994 Z.	4.8	19.7	26.8	9.3	35.3	53.7	55.1	55.3
Capital account: debit............	3 994 ..	−12.0	....	....	....	....	....	....	....
Total, Groups A Plus B...........	4 981 ..	*30.9*	*22.8*	*46.9*	*−7.3*	*−136.1*	*−171.6*	*−16.0*	*105.8*
C. Financial Account¹....................	4 995 W.	**−37.1**	**−35.7**	**−32.8**	**63.7**	**73.4**	**219.9**	**−59.6**	**4.2**
Direct investment abroad............	4 505 ..	....	....	....	....	....	....	....	....
Direct investment in Djibouti........	4 555 Z.	14.2	38.5	22.2	108.3	195.4	227.7	96.9	36.5
Portfolio investment assets.........	4 602 ..	....	....	....	....	....	....	....	....
Equity securities................	4 610 ..	....	....	....	....	....	....	....	....
Debt securities.................	4 619 ..	....	....	....	....	....	....	....	....
Portfolio investment liabilities......	4 652 Z.	....	....	....	....	....	....	....	....
Equity securities................	4 660 ..	....	....	....	....	....	....	....	....
Debt securities.................	4 669 Z.	....	....	....	....	....	....	....	....
Financial derivatives.............	4 910 ..	....	....	....	....	....	....	....	....
Financial derivatives assets........	4 900 ..	....	....	....	....	....	....	....	....
Financial derivatives liabilities.....	4 905 ..	....	....	....	....	....	....	....	....
Other investment assets..........	4 703 ..	−53.9	−84.0	−65.1	−62.0	−148.3	18.5	−205.5	−87.8
Monetary authorities............	4 701 ..	....	....	....	....	....	....	....	....
General government............	4 704 ..	....	....	....	....	....	....	....	....
Banks........................	4 705 ..	−44.8	−76.7	−57.8	−54.8	−38.1	−65.4	−192.6	−57.8
Other sectors.................	4 728 ..	−9.2	−7.3	−7.3	−7.2	−110.2	83.9	−12.9	−30.0
Other investment liabilities........	4 753 W.	2.6	9.8	10.2	17.5	26.3	−26.2	49.0	55.5
Monetary authorities............	4 753 WA	....	....	....	....	....	....	21.9	....
General government............	4 753 ZB	−3.6	−4.1	−5.7	−6.5	−6.7	−6.5	−7.5	−6.3
Banks........................	4 753 ZC	−6.7	5.5	4.1	13.8	21.5	−14.3	38.7	53.4
Other sectors.................	4 753 ZD	12.9	8.3	11.8	10.2	11.5	−5.5	−4.0	8.4
Total, Groups A Through C........	4 983 ..	*−6.2*	*−12.8*	*14.1*	*56.5*	*−62.7*	*48.3*	*−75.6*	*110.0*
D. Net Errors and Omissions..............	4 998 ..	**1.5**	**−15.7**	**−45.4**	**−51.8**	**37.6**	**−57.2**	**50.2**	**−112.9**
Total, Groups A Through D........	4 984 ..	*−4.7*	*−28.5*	*−31.3*	*4.7*	*−25.1*	*−9.0*	*−25.4*	*−2.8*
E. Reserves and Related Items............	4 802 A.	**4.7**	**28.5**	**31.3**	**−4.7**	**25.1**	**9.0**	**25.4**	**2.8**
Reserve assets..................	4 802 ..	−25.5	5.9	7.4	−30.4	−13.5	−43.7	−44.3	−13.6
Use of Fund credit and loans........	4 766 ..	−1.8	−.2	−.8	−1.6	−2.8	1.7	−1.9	−3.3
Exceptional financing............	4 920 ..	32.1	22.8	24.7	27.3	41.4	51.0	71.6	19.8
Conversion rates: Djibouti francs per U.S. dollar............	0 101 ..	**177.72**	**177.72**	**177.72**	**177.72**	**177.72**	**177.72**	**177.72**	**177.72**

¹ Excludes components that have been classified in the categories of Group E.

Table 2. STANDARD PRESENTATION, 2003–2010

(Millions of U.S. dollars)

	Code	2003	2004	2005	2006	2007	2008	2009	2010
CURRENT ACCOUNT	4 993	**38.1**	**3.2**	**20.1**	**−16.6**	**−171.4**	**−225.4**	**−71.1**	**50.5**
A. GOODS	4 100	**−201.0**	**−223.4**	**−237.8**	**−280.5**	**−415.2**	**−505.3**	**−373.3**	**−278.6**
Credit	2 100	**37.2**	**38.0**	**39.5**	**55.2**	**58.1**	**68.8**	**77.4**	**85.1**
General merchandise: exports f.o.b.	2 110	37.2	38.0	39.5	55.2	58.1	68.8	77.4	85.1
Goods for processing: exports f.o.b.	2 150	....	....	....	....	....	....	....	....
Repairs on goods	2 160	....	....	....	....	....	....	....	....
Goods procured in ports by carriers	2 170	....	....	....	....	....	....	....	....
Nonmonetary gold	2 180	....	....	....	....	....	....	....	....
Debit	3 100	**−238.2**	**−261.4**	**−277.3**	**−335.7**	**−473.2**	**−574.1**	**−450.7**	**−363.8**
General merchandise: imports f.o.b.	3 110	−238.2	−261.4	−277.3	−335.7	−473.2	−574.1	−450.7	−363.8
Goods for processing: imports f.o.b.	3 150	....	....	....	....	....	....	....	....
Repairs on goods	3 160	....	....	....	....	....	....	....	....
Goods procured in ports by carriers	3 170	....	....	....	....	....	....	....	....
Nonmonetary gold	3 180	....	....	....	....	....	....	....	....
B. SERVICES	4 200	**148.7**	**135.5**	**164.6**	**162.2**	**140.7**	**167.4**	**194.5**	**216.6**
Total credit	2 200	*215.7*	*212.7*	*248.4*	*251.5*	*248.5*	*296.9*	*322.0*	*335.7*
Total debit	3 200	*−67.0*	*−77.2*	*−83.8*	*−89.3*	*−107.7*	*−129.5*	*−127.6*	*−119.1*
Transportation services, credit	2 205	**68.2**	**67.8**	**74.9**	**73.5**	**71.6**	**108.4**	**110.4**	**114.9**
Passenger	2 850	....	....	....	....	....	....	....	....
Freight	2 851	....	....	....	....	....	....	....	....
Other	2 852	*68.2*	*67.8*	*74.9*	*73.5*	*71.6*	*108.4*	*110.4*	*114.9*
Sea transport, passenger	2 207	....	....	....	....	....	....	....	....
Sea transport, freight	2 208	....	....	....	....	....	....	....	....
Sea transport, other	2 209	38.6	38.2	42.8	41.7	38.0	57.5	58.5	60.9
Air transport, passenger	2 211	....	....	....	....	....	....	....	....
Air transport, freight	2 212	....	....	....	....	....	....	....	....
Air transport, other	2 213	10.0	10.0	10.1	10.3	11.0	16.6	16.9	17.6
Other transport, passenger	2 215	....	....	....	....	....	....	....	....
Other transport, freight	2 216	....	....	....	....	....	....	....	....
Other transport, other	2 217	19.6	19.7	22.0	21.6	22.7	34.3	35.0	36.4
Transportation services, debit	3 205	**−39.2**	**−47.7**	**−53.0**	**−56.8**	**−75.5**	**−89.4**	**−83.3**	**−69.6**
Passenger	3 850	*−7.1*	*−11.2*	*−11.5*	*−11.5*	*−11.6*	*−11.8*	*−11.7*	*−11.9*
Freight	3 851	*−32.2*	*−36.5*	*−41.6*	*−45.3*	*−63.9*	*−77.5*	*−71.6*	*−57.8*
Other	3 852	....	....	....	....	....	....	....	....
Sea transport, passenger	3 207	....	....	....	....	....	....	....	....
Sea transport, freight	3 208	−32.2	−36.5	−41.6	−45.3	−63.9	−77.5	−71.6	−57.8
Sea transport, other	3 209	....	....	....	....	....	....	....	....
Air transport, passenger	3 211	−7.1	−11.2	−11.5	−11.5	−11.6	−11.8	−11.7	−11.9
Air transport, freight	3 212	....	....	....	....	....	....	....	....
Air transport, other	3 213	....	....	....	....	....	....	....	....
Other transport, passenger	3 215	....	....	....	....	....	....	....	....
Other transport, freight	3 216	....	....	....	....	....	....	....	....
Other transport, other	3 217	....	....	....	....	....	....	....	....
Travel, credit	2 236	**6.9**	**6.8**	**7.1**	**9.8**	**6.8**	**7.8**	**16.0**	**18.0**
Business travel	2 237	6.9	6.8	7.1	9.8	6.8	7.8	16.0	18.0
Personal travel	2 240	....	....	....	....	....	....	....	....
Travel, debit	3 236	**−2.8**	**−2.8**	**−2.8**	**−3.4**	**−2.6**	**−3.7**	**−5.8**	**−8.6**
Business travel	3 237	....	....	....	....	....	....	....	....
Personal travel	3 240	−2.8	−2.8	−2.8	−3.4	−2.6	−3.7	−5.8	−8.6
Other services, credit	2 200 BA	**140.6**	**138.1**	**166.3**	**168.1**	**170.0**	**180.6**	**195.7**	**202.8**
Communications	2 245	5.6	5.6	5.8	6.1	6.5	6.7	7.5	7.8
Construction	2 249	....	....	....	....	....	....	....	....
Insurance	2 253	....	....	....	....	....	....	....	....
Financial	2 260	....	....	....	....	....	....	....	....
Computer and information	2 262	....	....	....	....	....	....	....	....
Royalties and licence fees	2 266	....	....	....	....	....	....	....	....
Other business services	2 268	6.5	6.7	6.9	7.3	7.4	7.9	8.0	8.1
Personal, cultural, and recreational	2 287	....	....	....	....	....	....	....	....
Government, n.i.e.	2 291	128.5	125.8	153.6	154.6	156.1	166.0	180.1	186.9
Other services, debit	3 200 BA	**−25.0**	**−26.7**	**−27.9**	**−29.0**	**−29.7**	**−36.5**	**−38.5**	**−40.9**
Communications	3 245	....	....	....	....	....	....	....	....
Construction	3 249	....	....	....	....	....	....	....	....
Insurance	3 253	−7.4	−8.6	−8.6	−8.5	−8.7	−14.5	−11.4	−11.0
Financial	3 260	....	....	....	....	....	....	....	....
Computer and information	3 262	....	....	....	....	....	....	....	....
Royalties and licence fees	3 266	....	....	....	....	....	....	....	....
Other business services	3 268	−10.9	−11.2	−11.6	−11.9	−12.4	−13.0	−13.6	−14.6
Personal, cultural, and recreational	3 287	....	....	....	....	....	....	....	....
Government, n.i.e.	3 291	−6.7	−6.9	−7.7	−8.6	−8.7	−9.0	−13.5	−15.3

Table 2 (Continued). STANDARD PRESENTATION, 2003–2010

(Millions of U.S. dollars)

	Code	2003	2004	2005	2006	2007	2008	2009	2010
C. INCOME	4 300	**20.9**	**22.5**	**20.8**	**23.0**	**23.9**	**32.7**	**21.7**	**17.4**
Total credit	2 300	*31.2*	*33.3*	*32.0*	*34.9*	*35.2*	*45.6*	*37.0*	*32.8*
Total debit	3 300	*−10.3*	*−10.7*	*−11.2*	*−11.8*	*−11.3*	*−12.9*	*−15.3*	*−15.4*
Compensation of employees, credit	2 310	**21.8**	**21.8**	**22.9**	**24.8**	**25.1**	**26.1**	**26.5**	**26.1**
Compensation of employees, debit	3 310	....	....	....	....	....	....	....	....
Investment income, credit	2 320	**9.5**	**11.5**	**9.1**	**10.0**	**10.1**	**19.5**	**10.5**	**6.7**
Direct investment income	2 330	....	....	....	....	....	....	....	....
Dividends and distributed branch profits	2 332	....	....	....	....	....	....	....	....
Reinvested earnings and undistributed branch profits	2 333	....	....	....	....	....	....	....	....
Income on debt (interest)	2 334	....	....	....	....	....	....	....	....
Portfolio investment income	2 339	....	....	....	....	....	....	....	....
Income on equity	2 340	....	....	....	....	....	....	....	....
Income on bonds and notes	2 350	....	....	....	....	....	....	....	....
Income on money market instruments	2 360	....	....	....	....	....	....	....	....
Other investment income	2 370	9.5	11.5	9.1	10.0	10.1	19.5	10.5	6.7
Investment income, debit	3 320	**−10.3**	**−10.7**	**−11.2**	**−11.8**	**−11.3**	**−12.9**	**−15.3**	**−15.4**
Direct investment income	3 330	−6.0	−6.0	−5.9	−5.9	−4.2	−5.0	−6.5	−6.8
Dividends and distributed branch profits	3 332	−2.4	−2.4	−2.3	−2.3	−.7	−1.3	−2.8	−1.3
Reinvested earnings and undistributed branch profits	3 333	−3.5	−3.5	−3.6	−3.6	−3.6	−3.8	−3.8	−5.5
Income on debt (interest)	3 334	....	....	....	....	....	....	....	....
Portfolio investment income	3 339	....	....	....	....	....	....	....	....
Income on equity	3 340	....	....	....	....	....	....	....	....
Income on bonds and notes	3 350	....	....	....	....	....	....	....	....
Income on money market instruments	3 360	....	....	....	....	....	....	....	....
Other investment income	3 370	−4.3	−4.8	−5.3	−6.0	−7.1	−7.8	−8.7	−8.6
D. CURRENT TRANSFERS	4 379	**69.4**	**68.5**	**72.6**	**78.8**	**79.2**	**79.8**	**86.1**	**95.2**
Credit	2 379	**75.3**	**74.1**	**78.3**	**85.5**	**85.9**	**87.2**	**92.2**	**108.7**
General government	2 380	31.4	28.9	28.9	28.9	28.9	28.9	28.9	28.9
Other sectors	2 390	43.8	45.2	49.4	56.6	56.9	58.2	63.3	79.8
Workers' remittances	2 391	2.9	3.0	3.0	3.7	3.5	4.3	6.0	6.6
Other current transfers	2 392	40.9	42.2	46.4	52.9	53.4	53.9	57.3	73.2
Debit	3 379	**−5.8**	**−5.6**	**−5.8**	**−6.8**	**−6.7**	**−7.3**	**−6.1**	**−13.5**
General government	3 380	−1.0	−1.0	−1.1	−2.0	−2.0	−2.2	−.3	−1.9
Other sectors	3 390	−4.8	−4.7	−4.7	−4.7	−4.7	−5.1	−5.8	−11.6
Workers' remittances	3 391	−4.8	−4.7	−4.7	−4.7	−4.7	−5.1	−5.8	−11.6
Other current transfers	3 392	....	....	....	....	....	....	....	....
CAPITAL AND FINANCIAL ACCOUNT	4 996	**−39.6**	**12.5**	**25.3**	**68.4**	**133.7**	**282.6**	**20.9**	**62.4**
CAPITAL ACCOUNT	4 994	**−7.2**	**19.7**	**26.8**	**9.3**	**35.3**	**53.7**	**55.1**	**55.3**
Total credit	2 994	*4.8*	*19.7*	*26.8*	*9.3*	*35.3*	*53.7*	*55.1*	*55.3*
Total debit	3 994	*−12.0*	....	....	....	....	....	....	....
Capital transfers, credit	2 400	**4.8**	**19.7**	**26.8**	**9.3**	**35.3**	**53.7**	**55.1**	**55.3**
General government	2 401	4.8	19.7	26.8	9.3	35.3	53.7	55.1	55.3
Debt forgiveness	2 402	....	....	....	....	....	....	....	....
Other capital transfers	2 410	4.8	19.7	26.8	9.3	35.3	53.7	55.1	55.3
Other sectors	2 430	....	....	....	....	....	....	....	....
Migrants' transfers	2 431	....	....	....	....	....	....	....	....
Debt forgiveness	2 432	....	....	....	....	....	....	....	....
Other capital transfers	2 440	....	....	....	....	....	....	....	....
Capital transfers, debit	3 400	**−12.0**	....	....	....	....	....	....	....
General government	3 401	....	....	....	....	....	....	....	....
Debt forgiveness	3 402	....	....	....	....	....	....	....	....
Other capital transfers	3 410	....	....	....	....	....	....	....	....
Other sectors	3 430	−12.0	....	....	....	....	....	....	....
Migrants' transfers	3 431	....	....	....	....	....	....	....	....
Debt forgiveness	3 432	....	....	....	....	....	....	....	....
Other capital transfers	3 440	−12.0	....	....	....	....	....	....	....
Nonproduced nonfinancial assets, credit	2 480	....	....	....	....	....	....	....	....
Nonproduced nonfinancial assets, debit	3 480	....	....	....	....	....	....	....	....

Table 2 (Continued). STANDARD PRESENTATION, 2003–2010

(Millions of U.S. dollars)

	Code	2003	2004	2005	2006	2007	2008	2009	2010
FINANCIAL ACCOUNT........................	4 995 ..	**−32.4**	**−7.2**	**−1.5**	**59.1**	**98.5**	**228.9**	**−34.3**	**7.1**
A. DIRECT INVESTMENT.......................	4 500 ..	**14.2**	**38.5**	**22.2**	**108.3**	**195.4**	**227.7**	**96.9**	**36.5**
Direct investment abroad................	4 505 ..	....	....	....	....	....	....	....	....
Equity capital................................	4 510 ..	....	....	....	....	....	....	....	....
Claims on affiliated enterprises........	4 515 ..	....	....	....	....	....	....	....	....
Liabilities to affiliated enterprises.....	4 520 ..	....	....	....	....	....	....	....	....
Reinvested earnings........................	4 525 ..	....	....	....	....	....	....	....	....
Other capital.................................	4 530 ..	....	....	....	....	....	....	....	....
Claims on affiliated enterprises........	4 535 ..	....	....	....	....	....	....	....	....
Liabilities to affiliated enterprises.....	4 540 ..	....	....	....	....	....	....	....	....
Direct investment in Djibouti...........	4 555 ..	**14.2**	**38.5**	**22.2**	**108.3**	**195.4**	**227.7**	**96.9**	**36.5**
Equity capital................................	4 560 ..	10.7	35.0	18.7	104.7	191.8	223.9	93.1	31.0
Claims on direct investors..............	4 565 ..	....	....	....	....	....	....	....	....
Liabilities to direct investors..........	4 570 ..	10.7	35.0	18.7	104.7	191.8	223.9	93.1	31.0
Reinvested earnings........................	4 575 ..	3.5	3.5	3.6	3.6	3.6	3.8	3.8	5.5
Other capital.................................	4 580 ..	....	....	....	....	....	....	....	....
Claims on direct investors..............	4 585 ..	....	....	....	....	....	....	....	....
Liabilities to direct investors..........	4 590 ..	....	....	....	....	....	....	....	....
B. PORTFOLIO INVESTMENT..................	4 600 ..	....	....	....	....	....	....	....	....
Assets......................................	4 602 ..	....	....	....	....	....	....	....	....
Equity securities...........................	4 610 ..	....	....	....	....	....	....	....	....
Monetary authorities.....................	4 611 ..	....	....	....	....	....	....	....	....
General government......................	4 612 ..	....	....	....	....	....	....	....	....
Banks..	4 613 ..	....	....	....	....	....	....	....	....
Other sectors..............................	4 614 ..	....	....	....	....	....	....	....	....
Debt securities..............................	4 619 ..	....	....	....	....	....	....	....	....
Bonds and notes..........................	4 620 ..	....	....	....	....	....	....	....	....
Monetary authorities...................	4 621 ..	....	....	....	....	....	....	....	....
General government....................	4 622 ..	....	....	....	....	....	....	....	....
Banks......................................	4 623 ..	....	....	....	....	....	....	....	....
Other sectors............................	4 624 ..	....	....	....	....	....	....	....	....
Money market instruments.............	4 630 ..	....	....	....	....	....	....	....	....
Monetary authorities...................	4 631 ..	....	....	....	....	....	....	....	....
General government....................	4 632 ..	....	....	....	....	....	....	....	....
Banks......................................	4 633 ..	....	....	....	....	....	....	....	....
Other sectors............................	4 634 ..	....	....	....	....	....	....	....	....
Liabilities.................................	4 652 ..	....	....	....	....	....	....	....	....
Equity securities...........................	4 660 ..	....	....	....	....	....	....	....	....
Banks..	4 663 ..	....	....	....	....	....	....	....	....
Other sectors..............................	4 664 ..	....	....	....	....	....	....	....	....
Debt securities..............................	4 669 ..	....	....	....	....	....	....	....	....
Bonds and notes..........................	4 670 ..	....	....	....	....	....	....	....	....
Monetary authorities...................	4 671 ..	....	....	....	....	....	....	....	....
General government....................	4 672 ..	....	....	....	....	....	....	....	....
Banks......................................	4 673 ..	....	....	....	....	....	....	....	....
Other sectors............................	4 674 ..	....	....	....	....	....	....	....	....
Money market instruments.............	4 680 ..	....	....	....	....	....	....	....	....
Monetary authorities...................	4 681 ..	....	....	....	....	....	....	....	....
General government....................	4 682 ..	....	....	....	....	....	....	....	....
Banks......................................	4 683 ..	....	....	....	....	....	....	....	....
Other sectors............................	4 684 ..	....	....	....	....	....	....	....	....
C. FINANCIAL DERIVATIVES..................	4 910 ..	....	....	....	....	....	....	....	....
Monetary authorities.....................	4 911 ..	....	....	....	....	....	....	....	....
General government......................	4 912 ..	....	....	....	....	....	....	....	....
Banks..	4 913 ..	....	....	....	....	....	....	....	....
Other sectors..............................	4 914 ..	....	....	....	....	....	....	....	....
Assets......................................	4 900 ..	....	....	....	....	....	....	....	....
Monetary authorities.....................	4 901 ..	....	....	....	....	....	....	....	....
General government......................	4 902 ..	....	....	....	....	....	....	....	....
Banks..	4 903 ..	....	....	....	....	....	....	....	....
Other sectors..............................	4 904 ..	....	....	....	....	....	....	....	....
Liabilities.................................	4 905 ..	....	....	....	....	....	....	....	....
Monetary authorities.....................	4 906 ..	....	....	....	....	....	....	....	....
General government......................	4 907 ..	....	....	....	....	....	....	....	....
Banks..	4 908 ..	....	....	....	....	....	....	....	....
Other sectors..............................	4 909 ..	....	....	....	....	....	....	....	....

Table 2 (Concluded). STANDARD PRESENTATION, 2003–2010

(Millions of U.S. dollars)

	Code	2003	2004	2005	2006	2007	2008	2009	2010
D. OTHER INVESTMENT.........	4 700 ..	**−21.1**	**−51.6**	**−31.1**	**−18.8**	**−83.4**	**44.9**	**−86.8**	**−15.8**
Assets..............	4 703 ..	**−53.9**	**−84.0**	**−65.1**	**−62.0**	**−148.3**	**18.5**	**−205.5**	**−87.8**
Trade credits............	4 706 ..	....	....	....	....	....	....	....	....
General government..........	4 707 ..	....	....	....	....	....	....	....	....
of which: Short-term..	4 709 ..	....	....	....	....	....	....	....	....
Other sectors............	4 710 ..	....	....	....	....	....	....	....	....
of which: Short-term..	4 712 ..	....	....	....	....	....	....	....	....
Loans...............	4 714 ..	....	....	....	....	−14.0	2.3	−97.7	16.5
Monetary authorities...........	4 715 ..	....	....	....	....	....	....	....	....
of which: Short-term..	4 718 ..	....	....	....	....	....	....	....	....
General government..........	4 719 ..	....	....	....	....	....	....	....	....
of which: Short-term..	4 721 ..	....	....	....	....	....	....	....	....
Banks...............	4 722 ..	....	....	....	....	−14.0	2.3	−97.7	16.5
of which: Short-term..	4 724 ..	....	....	....	....	*−14.0*	*2.3*	*−97.7*	*16.5*
Other sectors............	4 725 ..	....	....	....	....	....	....	....	....
of which: Short-term..	4 727 ..	....	....	....	....	....	....	....	....
Currency and deposits.........	4 730 ..	−53.9	−84.0	−65.1	−62.0	−134.2	16.2	−107.8	−104.3
Monetary authorities...........	4 731 ..	....	....	....	....	....	....	....	....
General government..........	4 732 ..	....	....	....	....	....	....	....	....
Banks...............	4 733 ..	−44.8	−76.7	−57.8	−54.8	−24.1	−67.7	−94.9	−74.3
Other sectors............	4 734 ..	−9.2	−7.3	−7.3	−7.2	−110.2	83.9	−12.9	−30.0
Other assets............	4 736 ..	....	....	....	....	....	....	....	....
Monetary authorities...........	4 737 ..	....	....	....	....	....	....	....	....
of which: Short-term..	4 739 ..	....	....	....	....	....	....	....	....
General government..........	4 740 ..	....	....	....	....	....	....	....	....
of which: Short-term..	4 742 ..	....	....	....	....	....	....	....	....
Banks...............	4 743 ..	....	....	....	....	....	....	....	....
of which: Short-term..	4 745 ..	....	....	....	....	....	....	....	....
Other sectors............	4 746 ..	....	....	....	....	....	....	....	....
of which: Short-term..	4 748 ..	....	....	....	....	....	....	....	....
Liabilities............	4 753 ..	**32.8**	**32.4**	**34.0**	**43.2**	**64.9**	**26.4**	**118.7**	**72.0**
Trade credits............	4 756 ..	....	....	....	....	....	....	....	....
General government..........	4 757 ..	....	....	....	....	....	....	....	....
of which: Short-term..	4 759 ..	....	....	....	....	....	....	....	....
Other sectors............	4 760 ..	....	....	....	....	....	....	....	....
of which: Short-term..	4 762 ..	....	....	....	....	....	....	....	....
Loans...............	4 764 ..	39.5	26.8	30.0	29.4	43.4	40.7	58.1	18.6
Monetary authorities...........	4 765 ..	−1.8	.8	−.8	−1.7	−2.9	1.6	1.3	−3.8
of which: Use of Fund credit and loans from the Fund..	4 766 ..	*−1.8*	*−.2*	*−.8*	*−1.6*	*−2.8*	*1.7*	*−1.9*	*−3.3*
of which: Short-term..	4 768 ..	....	*1.0*	....	....	....	....	....	....
General government..........	4 769 ..	28.4	17.7	19.0	20.9	34.8	44.6	60.8	14.0
of which: Short-term..	4 771 ..	....	....	....	....	....	....	....	....
Banks...............	4 772 ..	....	....	....	....	....	....	....	....
of which: Short-term..	4 774 ..	....	....	....	....	....	....	....	....
Other sectors............	4 775 ..	12.9	8.3	11.8	10.2	11.5	−5.5	−4.0	8.4
of which: Short-term..	4 777 ..	....	....	....	....	....	....	....	....
Currency and deposits.........	4 780 ..	−6.7	5.5	4.1	13.8	21.5	−14.3	38.7	53.4
Monetary authorities...........	4 781 ..	....	....	....	....	....	....	....	....
General government..........	4 782 ..	....	....	....	....	....	....	....	....
Banks...............	4 783 ..	−6.7	5.5	4.1	13.8	21.5	−14.3	38.7	53.4
Other sectors............	4 784 ..	....	....	....	....	....	....	....	....
Other liabilities..........	4 786 ..	....	....	....	....	....	....	21.9	....
Monetary authorities...........	4 787 ..	....	....	....	....	....	....	21.9	....
of which: Short-term..	4 789 ..	....	....	....	....	....	....	....	....
General government..........	4 790 ..	....	....	....	....	....	....	....	....
of which: Short-term..	4 792 ..	....	....	....	....	....	....	....	....
Banks...............	4 793 ..	....	....	....	....	....	....	....	....
of which: Short-term..	4 795 ..	....	....	....	....	....	....	....	....
Other sectors............	4 796 ..	....	....	....	....	....	....	....	....
of which: Short-term..	4 798 ..	....	....	....	....	....	....	....	....
E. RESERVE ASSETS................	4 802 ..	**−25.5**	**5.9**	**7.4**	**−30.4**	**−13.5**	**−43.7**	**−44.3**	**−13.6**
Monetary gold............	4 812 ..	....	....	....	....	....	....	....	....
Special drawing rights..........	4 811 ..	.9	−.8	.9	−.8	.8	....	−20.3	3.3
Reserve position in the Fund..........	4 810 ..	....	....	....	....	....	....	....	....
Foreign exchange...........	4 803 ..	−26.4	6.8	6.5	−29.6	−14.3	−43.7	−24.0	−16.9
Other claims............	4 813 ..	....	....	....	....	....	....	....	....
NET ERRORS AND OMISSIONS..............	4 998 ..	**1.5**	**−15.7**	**−45.4**	**−51.8**	**37.6**	**−57.2**	**50.2**	**−112.9**

Table 3. INTERNATIONAL INVESTMENT POSITION (End-period stocks), 2003–2010

(Millions of U.S. dollars)

	Code	2003	2004	2005	2006	2007	2008	2009	2010
ASSETS	8 995 C.	**560.8**	**634.7**	**662.3**	**755.3**	**895.9**	**922.3**	**1,066.3**	**1,098.2**
Direct investment abroad	8 505	....	....	....	....	....	....	....	....
Equity capital and reinvested earnings	8 506	....	....	....	....	....	....	....	....
Claims on affiliated enterprises	8 507	....	....	....	....	....	....	....	....
Liabilities to affiliated enterprises	8 508	....	....	....	....	....	....	....	....
Other capital	8 530	....	....	....	....	....	....	....	....
Claims on affiliated enterprises	8 535	....	....	....	....	....	....	....	....
Liabilities to affiliated enterprises	8 540	....	....	....	....	....	....	....	....
Portfolio investment	8 602	....	....	....	....	....	....	....	....
Equity securities	8 610	....	....	....	....	....	....	....	....
Monetary authorities	8 611	....	....	....	....	....	....	....	....
General government	8 612	....	....	....	....	....	....	....	....
Banks	8 613	....	....	....	....	....	....	....	....
Other sectors	8 614	....	....	....	....	....	....	....	....
Debt securities	8 619	....	....	....	....	....	....	....	....
Bonds and notes	8 620	....	....	....	....	....	....	....	....
Monetary authorities	8 621	....	....	....	....	....	....	....	....
General government	8 622	....	....	....	....	....	....	....	....
Banks	8 623	....	....	....	....	....	....	....	....
Other sectors	8 624	....	....	....	....	....	....	....	....
Money market instruments	8 630	....	....	....	....	....	....	....	....
Monetary authorities	8 631	....	....	....	....	....	....	....	....
General government	8 632	....	....	....	....	....	....	....	....
Banks	8 633	....	....	....	....	....	....	....	....
Other sectors	8 634	....	....	....	....	....	....	....	....
Financial derivatives	8 900	....	....	....	....	....	....	....	....
Monetary authorities	8 901	....	....	....	....	....	....	....	....
General government	8 902	....	....	....	....	....	....	....	....
Banks	8 903	....	....	....	....	....	....	....	....
Other sectors	8 904	....	....	....	....	....	....	....	....
Other investment	8 703	**459.7**	**540.6**	**576.0**	**638.6**	**765.5**	**748.3**	**847.9**	**866.6**
Trade credits	8 706	....	....	....	....	....	....	....	....
General government	8 707	....	....	....	....	....	....	....	....
of which: Short-term	8 709	....	....	....	....	....	....	....	....
Other sectors	8 710	....	....	....	....	....	....	....	....
of which: Short-term	8 712	....	....	....	....	....	....	....	....
Loans	8 714	281.4	351.1	419.4	457.7	471.7	469.4	567.1	550.6
Monetary authorities	8 715	....	....	....	....	....	....	....	....
of which: Short-term	8 718	....	....	....	....	....	....	....	....
General government	8 719	....	....	....	....	....	....	....	....
of which: Short-term	8 721	....	....	....	....	....	....	....	....
Banks	8 722	281.4	351.1	419.4	457.7	471.7	469.4	567.1	550.6
of which: Short-term	8 724	*281.4*	*351.1*	*419.4*	*457.7*	*471.7*	*469.4*	*567.1*	*550.6*
Other sectors	8 725	....	....	....	....	....	....	....	....
of which: Short-term	8 727	....	....	....	....	....	....	....	....
Currency and deposits	8 730	178.4	189.5	156.6	180.9	293.8	278.9	280.8	316.0
Monetary authorities	8 731	....	....	....	....	....	....	....	....
General government	8 732	....	....	....	....	....	....	....	....
Banks	8 733	10.4	15.5	16.6	18.9	28.8	104.9	100.8	113.0
Other sectors	8 734	168.0	174.0	140.0	162.0	265.0	174.0	180.0	203.0
Other assets	8 736	....	....	....	....	....	....	....	....
Monetary authorities	8 737	....	....	....	....	....	....	....	....
of which: Short-term	8 739	....	....	....	....	....	....	....	....
General government	8 740	....	....	....	....	....	....	....	....
of which: Short-term	8 742	....	....	....	....	....	....	....	....
Banks	8 743	....	....	....	....	....	....	....	....
of which: Short-term	8 745	....	....	....	....	....	....	....	....
Other sectors	8 746	....	....	....	....	....	....	....	....
of which: Short-term	8 748	....	....	....	....	....	....	....	....
Reserve assets	8 802	**101.1**	**94.1**	**86.3**	**116.7**	**130.3**	**174.0**	**218.4**	**231.6**
Monetary gold	8 812	....	....	....	....	....	....	....	....
Special drawing rights	8 811	.1	1.0	....	.8	.1	.1	20.5	16.7
Reserve position in the Fund	8 810	1.6	1.7	1.6	1.7	1.7	1.7	1.7	1.7
Foreign exchange	8 803	99.4	91.4	84.7	114.2	128.5	172.2	196.2	213.2
Other claims	8 813	....	....	....	....	....	....	....	....

Table 3 (Concluded). INTERNATIONAL INVESTMENT POSITION (End-period stocks), 2003–2010

(Millions of U.S. dollars)

	Code	2003	2004	2005	2006	2007	2008	2009	2010
LIABILITIES	8 995 D.	**463.5**	**524.6**	**535.8**	**586.3**	**685.0**	**879.0**	**1,058.8**	**1,121.8**
Direct investment in Djibouti	8 555 ..	**61.2**	**85.5**	**104.4**	**130.3**	**180.9**	**235.3**	**295.1**	**331.6**
Equity capital and reinvested earnings	8 556 ..	61.2	85.5	104.4	130.3	180.9	235.3	295.1	331.6
Claims on direct investors	8 557 ..	....	....	....	....	....	....	....	....
Liabilities to direct investors	8 558 ..	61.2	85.5	104.4	130.3	180.9	235.3	295.1	331.6
Other capital	8 580 ..	....	....	....	....	....	....	....	....
Claims on direct investors	8 585 ..	....	....	....	....	....	....	....	....
Liabilities to direct investors	8 590 ..	....	....	....	....	....	....	....	....
Portfolio investment	8 652 ..	....	....	....	....	....	....	....	....
Equity securities	8 660 ..	....	....	....	....	....	....	....	....
Banks	8 663 ..	....	....	....	....	....	....	....	....
Other sectors	8 664 ..	....	....	....	....	....	....	....	....
Debt securities	8 669 ..	....	....	....	....	....	....	....	....
Bonds and notes	8 670 ..	....	....	....	....	....	....	....	....
Monetary authorities	8 671 ..	....	....	....	....	....	....	....	....
General government	8 672 ..	....	....	....	....	....	....	....	....
Banks	8 673 ..	....	....	....	....	....	....	....	....
Other sectors	8 674 ..	....	....	....	....	....	....	....	....
Money market instruments	8 680 ..	....	....	....	....	....	....	....	....
Monetary authorities	8 681 ..	....	....	....	....	....	....	....	....
General government	8 682 ..	....	....	....	....	....	....	....	....
Banks	8 683 ..	....	....	....	....	....	....	....	....
Other sectors	8 684 ..	....	....	....	....	....	....	....	....
Financial derivatives	8 905 ..	....	....	....	....	....	....	....	....
Monetary authorities	8 906 ..	....	....	....	....	....	....	....	....
General government	8 907 ..	....	....	....	....	....	....	....	....
Banks	8 908 ..	....	....	....	....	....	....	....	....
Other sectors	8 909 ..	....	....	....	....	....	....	....	....
Other investment	8 753 ..	**402.3**	**439.2**	**431.4**	**456.0**	**504.2**	**643.7**	**763.8**	**790.3**
Trade credits	8 756 ..	....	....	....	....	....	....	....	....
General government	8 757 ..	....	....	....	....	....	....	....	....
of which: Short-term	8 759 ..	....	....	....	....	....	....	....	....
Other sectors	8 760 ..	....	....	....	....	....	....	....	....
of which: Short-term	8 762 ..	....	....	....	....	....	....	....	....
Loans	8 764 ..	387.4	413.9	393.4	420.0	449.5	588.0	659.4	657.7
Monetary authorities	8 765 ..	20.4	21.2	18.7	18.0	16.1	17.4	15.8	12.1
of which: Use of Fund credit and loans from the Fund	8 766 ..	*20.4*	*21.2*	*18.7*	*18.0*	*16.1*	*17.4*	*15.8*	*12.1*
of which: Short-term	8 768 ..	....	....	....	....	....	....	....	....
General government	8 769 ..	233.6	253.4	241.8	271.4	289.4	366.3	459.9	469.7
of which: Short-term	8 771 ..	....	....	....	....	....	....	....	....
Banks	8 772 ..	3.6	.2	4.9	....	1.4	2.6	17.5	11.9
of which: Short-term	8 774 ..	*3.6*	*.2*	*4.9*	....	*1.4*	*2.6*	*17.5*	*11.9*
Other sectors	8 775 ..	129.7	139.1	128.1	130.6	142.6	201.6	166.2	164.0
of which: Short-term	8 777 ..	....	....	....	....	....	....	....	....
Currency and deposits	8 780 ..	14.9	25.3	38.0	36.0	54.7	55.8	80.6	109.2
Monetary authorities	8 781 ..	1.0	.3	.3	.3	.2	.6	.2	.2
General government	8 782 ..	....	....	....	....	....	....	....	....
Banks	8 783 ..	13.9	25.0	37.6	35.7	54.5	55.2	80.4	109.1
Other sectors	8 784 ..	....	....	....	....	....	....	....	....
Other liabilities	8 786 ..	....	....	....	....	....	....	23.8	23.3
Monetary authorities	8 787 ..	....	....	....	....	....	....	23.8	23.3
of which: Short-term	8 789 ..	....	....	....	....	....	....	....	....
General government	8 790 ..	....	....	....	....	....	....	....	....
of which: Short-term	8 792 ..	....	....	....	....	....	....	....	....
Banks	8 793 ..	....	....	....	....	....	....	....	....
of which: Short-term	8 795 ..	....	....	....	....	....	....	....	....
Other sectors	8 796 ..	....	....	....	....	....	....	....	....
of which: Short-term	8 798 ..	....	....	....	....	....	....	....	....
NET INTERNATIONAL INVESTMENT POSITION	8 995 ..	**97.4**	**110.1**	**126.5**	**169.0**	**210.8**	**43.3**	**7.4**	**−23.6**
Conversion rates: Djibouti francs per U.S. dollar (end of period)	0 102 ..	**177.72**	**177.72**	**177.72**	**177.72**	**177.72**	**177.72**	**177.72**	**177.72**

Table 1. ANALYTIC PRESENTATION, 2003–2010

(Millions of U.S. dollars)

	Code	2003	2004	2005	2006	2007	2008	2009	2010
A. Current Account[1]	4 993 Z.	**−53.18**	**−58.86**	**−76.08**	**−49.85**	**−86.95**	**−124.29**	**−101.92**	**−96.83**
Goods: exports f.o.b.	2 100 ..	41.01	42.92	42.91	44.26	39.02	43.89	36.82	34.35
Goods: imports f.o.b.	3 100 ..	−112.59	−127.76	−145.93	−146.87	−172.34	−217.38	−198.23	−193.65
Balance on Goods	4 100 ..	*−71.58*	*−84.84*	*−103.02*	*−102.61*	*−133.32*	*−173.49*	*−161.41*	*−159.31*
Services: credit	2 200 ..	77.40	87.56	86.45	100.17	108.82	118.44	117.86	117.79
Services: debit	3 200 ..	−44.75	−46.35	−50.19	−51.98	−63.99	−69.95	−63.81	−62.96
Balance on Goods and Services	4 991 ..	*−38.93*	*−43.63*	*−66.77*	*−54.42*	*−88.49*	*−125.00*	*−107.37*	*−104.48*
Income: credit	2 300 ..	2.23	3.81	5.93	6.17	8.54	8.42	6.57	6.56
Income: debit	3 300 ..	−29.24	−37.14	−34.91	−21.17	−28.15	−26.75	−20.22	−18.80
Balance on Goods, Services, and Income	4 992 ..	*−65.94*	*−76.97*	*−95.75*	*−69.43*	*−108.10*	*−143.33*	*−121.02*	*−116.73*
Current transfers: credit	2 379 Z.	20.61	24.44	28.40	25.52	28.53	26.54	25.51	26.27
Current transfers: debit	3 379 ..	−7.85	−6.33	−8.74	−5.95	−7.38	−7.50	−6.41	−6.37
B. Capital Account[1]	4 994 Z.	**18.78**	**23.78**	**18.28**	**27.96**	**57.97**	**57.56**	**43.98**	**29.11**
Capital account: credit	2 994 Z.	18.91	23.91	18.43	28.11	58.13	57.72	44.15	29.28
Capital account: debit	3 994 ..	−.13	−.13	−.14	−.15	−.16	−.16	−.16	−.17
Total, Groups A Plus B	4 981 ..	*−34.39*	*−35.08*	*−57.80*	*−21.90*	*−28.97*	*−66.74*	*−57.94*	*−67.72*
C. Financial Account[1]	4 995 W.	**12.23**	**1.30**	**55.49**	**30.46**	**31.59**	**55.30**	**63.79**	**74.38**
Direct investment abroad	4 505 ..	....	....	....	....	....	....	....	....
Direct investment in Dominica	4 555 Z.	31.47	26.17	19.24	25.91	40.49	56.55	41.31	30.82
Portfolio investment assets	4 602 ..	−.17	−2.30	−.46	−.73	1.08	−2.61	−.46	2.20
Equity securities	4 610 ..	....	....	....	....	....	....	....	....
Debt securities	4 619 ..	....	....	....	....	....	....	....	....
Portfolio investment liabilities	4 652 Z.	3.64	−.17	4.24	.62	.63	−.68	.64	.64
Equity securities	4 660 ..	....	....	....	....	....	....	....	....
Debt securities	4 669 Z.	....	....	....	....	....	....	....	....
Financial derivatives	4 910 ..	....	....	....	....	....	....	....	....
Financial derivatives assets	4 900 ..	....	....	....	....	....	....	....	....
Financial derivatives liabilities	4 905 ..	....	....	....	....	....	....	....	....
Other investment assets	4 703 ..	−38.73	−33.77	−7.27	−29.13	−36.10	−31.08	−42.87	−19.44
Monetary authorities	4 701 ..	....	....	....	....	....	....	....	....
General government	4 704 ..	....	....	....	....	....	....	....	....
Banks	4 705 ..	−34.13	−28.50	....	−12.44	−18.85	−17.56	−10.34	....
Other sectors	4 728 ..	−4.60	−5.27	−7.27	−16.69	−17.26	−13.53	−32.53	−19.44
Other investment liabilities	4 753 W.	16.01	11.36	39.74	33.78	25.50	33.13	65.18	60.16
Monetary authorities	4 753 WA	....	....	....	....	....	....	11.32	....
General government	4 753 ZB	....	....	....	....	....	....	....	....
Banks	4 753 ZC	....	....	8.83	....	....	....	....	10.22
Other sectors	4 753 ZD	16.01	11.36	30.91	33.78	25.50	33.13	53.85	49.94
Total, Groups A Through C	4 983 ..	*−22.17*	*−33.78*	*−2.31*	*8.56*	*2.62*	*−11.44*	*5.85*	*6.67*
D. Net Errors and Omissions	4 998 ..	**20.11**	**27.06**	**13.54**	**3.01**	**−1.45**	**4.81**	**8.99**	**−1.91**
Total, Groups A Through D	4 984 ..	*−2.05*	*−6.72*	*11.23*	*11.57*	*1.16*	*−6.63*	*14.84*	*4.76*
E. Reserves and Related Items	4 802 A.	**2.05**	**6.72**	**−11.23**	**−11.57**	**−1.16**	**6.63**	**−14.84**	**−4.76**
Reserve assets	4 802 ..	−2.72	5.82	−14.40	−13.42	1.29	3.38	−19.15	−3.67
Use of Fund credit and loans	4 766 ..	4.77	.90	3.17	1.85	−2.46	3.25	4.30	−1.08
Exceptional financing	4 920 ..	....	....	....	....	....	....	....	....
Conversion rates: Eastern Caribbean dollars per U.S. dollar	0 101 ..	**2.7000**	**2.7000**	**2.7000**	**2.7000**	**2.7000**	**2.7000**	**2.7000**	**2.7000**

[1] Excludes components that have been classified in the categories of Group E.

Table 2. STANDARD PRESENTATION, 2003–2010

(Millions of U.S. dollars)

	Code	2003	2004	2005	2006	2007	2008	2009	2010
CURRENT ACCOUNT	4 993	−53.18	−58.86	−76.08	−49.85	−86.95	−124.29	−101.92	−96.83
A. GOODS	4 100	−71.58	−84.84	−103.02	−102.61	−133.32	−173.49	−161.41	−159.31
Credit	2 100	41.01	42.92	42.91	44.26	39.02	43.89	36.82	34.35
General merchandise: exports f.o.b.	2 110	40.00	41.39	41.43	41.47	36.35	39.99	34.01	31.72
Goods for processing: exports f.o.b.	2 150	....	....	....	....	....	....	....	....
Repairs on goods	2 160	....	....	....	....	....	....	....	....
Goods procured in ports by carriers	2 170	1.01	1.53	1.48	2.79	2.67	3.89	2.81	2.62
Nonmonetary gold	2 180	....	....	....	....	....	....	....	....
Debit	3 100	−112.59	−127.76	−145.93	−146.87	−172.34	−217.38	−198.23	−193.65
General merchandise: imports f.o.b.	3 110	−112.59	−127.76	−145.93	−146.87	−172.34	−217.38	−198.23	−193.65
Goods for processing: imports f.o.b.	3 150	....	....	....	....	....	....	....	....
Repairs on goods	3 160	....	....	....	....	....	....	....	....
Goods procured in ports by carriers	3 170	....	....	....	....	....	....	....	....
Nonmonetary gold	3 180	....	....	....	....	....	....	....	....
B. SERVICES	4 200	32.66	41.21	36.26	48.19	44.84	48.49	54.04	54.83
Total credit	2 200	*77.40*	*87.56*	*86.45*	*100.17*	*108.82*	*118.44*	*117.86*	*117.79*
Total debit	3 200	*−44.75*	*−46.35*	*−50.19*	*−51.98*	*−63.99*	*−69.95*	*−63.81*	*−62.96*
Transportation services, credit	2 205	4.94	6.08	4.02	3.70	3.72	4.85	4.61	4.73
Passenger	2 850	....	....	....	....	....	....	....	....
Freight	2 851	....	....	....	....	....	....	....	....
Other	2 852	....	....	....	....	....	....	....	....
Sea transport, passenger	2 207	....	....	....	....	....	....	....	....
Sea transport, freight	2 208	....	....	....	....	....	....	....	....
Sea transport, other	2 209	....	....	....	....	....	....	....	....
Air transport, passenger	2 211	....	....	....	....	....	....	....	....
Air transport, freight	2 212	....	....	....	....	....	....	....	....
Air transport, other	2 213	....	....	....	....	....	....	....	....
Other transport, passenger	2 215	....	....	....	....	....	....	....	....
Other transport, freight	2 216	....	....	....	....	....	....	....	....
Other transport, other	2 217	....	....	....	....	....	....	....	....
Transportation services, debit	3 205	−19.85	−21.94	−26.90	−24.88	−31.05	−34.85	−32.57	−32.21
Passenger	3 850	....	....	....	....	....	....	....	....
Freight	3 851	....	....	....	....	....	....	....	....
Other	3 852	....	....	....	....	....	....	....	....
Sea transport, passenger	3 207	....	....	....	....	....	....	....	....
Sea transport, freight	3 208	....	....	....	....	....	....	....	....
Sea transport, other	3 209	....	....	....	....	....	....	....	....
Air transport, passenger	3 211	....	....	....	....	....	....	....	....
Air transport, freight	3 212	....	....	....	....	....	....	....	....
Air transport, other	3 213	....	....	....	....	....	....	....	....
Other transport, passenger	3 215	....	....	....	....	....	....	....	....
Other transport, freight	3 216	....	....	....	....	....	....	....	....
Other transport, other	3 217	....	....	....	....	....	....	....	....
Travel, credit	2 236	52.35	60.63	57.03	71.69	74.47	81.77	84.22	86.50
Business travel	2 237	....	....	....	....	....	....	....	....
Personal travel	2 240	....	....	....	....	....	....	....	....
Travel, debit	3 236	−8.92	−9.17	−9.74	−9.79	−10.57	−11.14	−12.77	−12.97
Business travel	3 237	....	....	....	....	....	....	....	....
Personal travel	3 240	....	....	....	....	....	....	....	....
Other services, credit	2 200 BA	20.11	20.84	25.40	24.79	30.64	31.82	29.03	26.56
Communications	2 245	7.15	8.25	8.12	9.14	12.21	11.70	9.75	9.90
Construction	2 249	....	....	....	....	....	....	....	....
Insurance	2 253	1.99	1.30	1.76	2.23	2.23	2.58	2.11	2.14
Financial	2 260	....	....	....	....	....	....	....	....
Computer and information	2 262	....	....	....	....	....	....	....	....
Royalties and licence fees	2 266	....	....	....	....	....	....	....	....
Other business services	2 268	10.00	9.96	14.31	11.84	14.92	15.61	12.26	12.45
Personal, cultural, and recreational	2 287	....	....	....	....	....	....	....	....
Government, n.i.e.	2 291	.97	1.34	1.22	1.57	1.28	1.93	4.92	2.07
Other services, debit	3 200 BA	−15.97	−15.23	−13.56	−17.32	−22.37	−23.95	−18.48	−17.78
Communications	3 245	−1.83	−1.61	−1.31	−3.11	−2.85	−2.91	−2.70	−2.87
Construction	3 249	−.86	−.33	−.48	−.42	−3.34	−3.27	−1.80	−.95
Insurance	3 253	−4.43	−5.17	−5.74	−6.96	−8.23	−8.29	−7.58	−7.52
Financial	3 260	....	....	....	....	....	....	....	....
Computer and information	3 262	....	....	−.02	−.02	−.25	−.35	−.18	−.18
Royalties and licence fees	3 266	−.06	−.08	−.11	−.24	−.61	−.62	−.44	−.44
Other business services	3 268	−4.90	−6.47	−3.80	−4.92	−5.74	−7.42	−4.81	−4.83
Personal, cultural, and recreational	3 287	....	....	....	....	....	....	....	....
Government, n.i.e.	3 291	−3.88	−1.57	−2.10	−1.65	−1.34	−1.09	−.98	−.99

Table 2 (Continued). STANDARD PRESENTATION, 2003–2010

(Millions of U.S. dollars)

	Code	2003	2004	2005	2006	2007	2008	2009	2010
C. INCOME	4 300	−27.02	−33.33	−28.98	−15.00	−19.61	−18.34	−13.65	−12.25
Total credit	2 300	*2.23*	*3.81*	*5.93*	*6.17*	*8.54*	*8.42*	*6.57*	*6.56*
Total debit	3 300	*−29.24*	*−37.14*	*−34.91*	*−21.17*	*−28.15*	*−26.75*	*−20.22*	*−18.80*
Compensation of employees, credit	2 310	.62	1.57	1.38	1.09	.93	.92	1.06	1.09
Compensation of employees, debit	3 310	....	....	....	....	....	....	....	....
Investment income, credit	2 320	1.61	2.24	4.55	5.08	7.61	7.50	5.51	5.46
Direct investment income	2 330	.04	....	....	....	....	1.62	.04	....
Dividends and distributed branch profits	2 332	....	....	....	....	....	1.62	....	....
Reinvested earnings and undistributed branch profits	2 333	....	....	....	....	....	....	....	....
Income on debt (interest)	2 334	.04	....	....	....	....	....	.04	....
Portfolio investment income	2 339	.43	.06	.08	.70	1.24	2.11	1.16	1.13
Income on equity	2 340	.43	.06	.08	.70	1.24	2.11	1.16	1.13
Income on bonds and notes	2 350	....	....	....	....	....	....	....	....
Income on money market instruments	2 360	....	....	....	....	....	....	....	....
Other investment income	2 370	1.14	2.17	4.46	4.38	6.36	3.76	4.30	4.33
Investment income, debit	3 320	−29.24	−37.14	−34.91	−21.17	−28.15	−26.75	−20.22	−18.80
Direct investment income	3 330	−15.82	−21.79	−22.68	−7.38	−12.99	−12.51	−13.35	−11.45
Dividends and distributed branch profits	3 332	−2.85	−4.96	−6.04	−2.22	−2.60	−3.58	−6.71	−4.70
Reinvested earnings and undistributed branch profits	3 333	−12.63	−16.60	−16.40	−4.99	−10.25	−8.83	−6.24	−6.33
Income on debt (interest)	3 334	−.34	−.22	−.24	−.17	−.14	−.10	−.41	−.41
Portfolio investment income	3 339	−4.74	−4.60	−3.20	−3.27	−.42	−.73	−1.66	−.03
Income on equity	3 340	−4.74	−4.60	−3.20	−3.27	−.42	−.73	−1.66	−.03
Income on bonds and notes	3 350	....	....	....	....	....	....	....	....
Income on money market instruments	3 360	....	....	....	....	....	....	....	....
Other investment income	3 370	−8.68	−10.75	−9.02	−10.52	−14.74	−13.52	−5.20	−7.33
D. CURRENT TRANSFERS	4 379	12.77	18.11	19.67	19.57	21.15	19.04	19.10	19.90
Credit	2 379	20.61	24.44	28.40	25.52	28.53	26.54	25.51	26.27
General government	2 380	3.19	2.84	4.61	2.76	2.65	2.48	1.94	2.00
Other sectors	2 390	17.43	21.61	23.79	22.77	25.88	24.06	23.56	24.27
Workers' remittances	2 391	14.18	18.46	20.39	20.98	21.55	21.77	21.08	21.71
Other current transfers	2 392	3.24	3.15	3.40	1.78	4.33	2.29	2.49	2.56
Debit	3 379	−7.85	−6.33	−8.74	−5.95	−7.38	−7.50	−6.41	−6.37
General government	3 380	−2.81	−3.09	−4.38	−2.47	−2.98	−2.54	−1.93	−1.96
Other sectors	3 390	−5.04	−3.24	−4.36	−3.47	−4.39	−4.96	−4.48	−4.41
Workers' remittances	3 391	−.01	−.01	−.01	−.01	−.01	−.01	−.01	−.01
Other current transfers	3 392	−5.03	−3.24	−4.35	−3.47	−4.38	−4.95	−4.47	−4.40
CAPITAL AND FINANCIAL ACCOUNT	4 996	33.06	31.80	62.54	46.85	88.40	119.49	92.93	98.74
CAPITAL ACCOUNT	4 994	18.78	23.78	18.28	27.96	57.97	57.56	43.98	29.11
Total credit	2 994	*18.91*	*23.91*	*18.43*	*28.11*	*58.13*	*57.72*	*44.15*	*29.28*
Total debit	3 994	*−.13*	*−.13*	*−.14*	*−.15*	*−.16*	*−.16*	*−.16*	*−.17*
Capital transfers, credit	2 400	18.91	23.91	18.43	28.10	58.13	57.72	44.15	29.28
General government	2 401	15.90	20.79	15.22	24.80	54.75	54.30	40.83	25.87
Debt forgiveness	2 402	....	....	....	....	....	....	....	....
Other capital transfers	2 410	15.90	20.79	15.22	24.80	54.75	54.30	40.83	25.87
Other sectors	2 430	3.01	3.12	3.20	3.30	3.39	3.42	3.31	3.41
Migrants' transfers	2 431	3.01	3.12	3.20	3.30	3.39	3.42	3.31	3.41
Debt forgiveness	2 432	....	....	....	....	....	....	....	....
Other capital transfers	2 440	....	....	....	....	....	....	....	....
Capital transfers, debit	3 400	−.13	−.13	−.14	−.15	−.16	−.16	−.16	−.17
General government	3 401	....	....	....	....	....	....	....	....
Debt forgiveness	3 402	....	....	....	....	....	....	....	....
Other capital transfers	3 410	....	....	....	....	....	....	....	....
Other sectors	3 430	−.13	−.13	−.14	−.15	−.16	−.16	−.16	−.17
Migrants' transfers	3 431	−.13	−.13	−.14	−.15	−.16	−.16	−.16	−.17
Debt forgiveness	3 432	....	....	....	....	....	....	....	....
Other capital transfers	3 440	....	....	....	....	....	....	....	....
Nonproduced nonfinancial assets, credit	2 480	....	....	....	.01	....	....	....	....
Nonproduced nonfinancial assets, debit	3 480	....	....	....	....	....	....	....	....

Table 2 (Continued). STANDARD PRESENTATION, 2003–2010

(Millions of U.S. dollars)

	Code	2003	2004	2005	2006	2007	2008	2009	2010
FINANCIAL ACCOUNT..	4 995 ..	**14.28**	**8.02**	**44.26**	**18.89**	**30.43**	**61.93**	**48.95**	**69.63**
A. DIRECT INVESTMENT.....................................	4 500 ..	**31.47**	**26.17**	**19.24**	**25.91**	**40.49**	**56.55**	**41.31**	**30.82**
Direct investment abroad..........................	4 505 ..	....	....	....	....	....	....	....	....
Equity capital...	4 510 ..	....	....	....	....	....	....	....	....
Claims on affiliated enterprises....................	4 515 ..	....	....	....	....	....	....	....	....
Liabilities to affiliated enterprises.................	4 520 ..	....	....	....	....	....	....	....	....
Reinvested earnings.....................................	4 525 ..	....	....	....	....	....	....	....	....
Other capital..	4 530 ..	....	....	....	....	....	....	....	....
Claims on affiliated enterprises....................	4 535 ..	....	....	....	....	....	....	....	....
Liabilities to affiliated enterprises.................	4 540 ..	....	....	....	....	....	....	....	....
Direct investment in Dominica....................	4 555 ..	**31.47**	**26.17**	**19.24**	**25.91**	**40.49**	**56.55**	**41.31**	**30.82**
Equity capital...	4 560 ..	11.72	3.33	5.28	4.78	27.32	36.31	18.97	9.48
Claims on direct investors...........................	4 565 ..	....	....	....	....	....	....	....	....
Liabilities to direct investors.......................	4 570 ..	11.72	3.33	5.28	4.78	27.32	36.31	18.97	9.48
Reinvested earnings.....................................	4 575 ..	12.63	16.60	16.40	4.99	10.25	8.83	6.24	6.33
Other capital..	4 580 ..	7.12	6.24	−2.45	16.14	2.91	11.41	16.11	15.00
Claims on direct investors...........................	4 585 ..	....	....	....	....	....	....	....	....
Liabilities to direct investors.......................	4 590 ..	7.12	6.24	−2.45	16.14	2.91	11.41	16.11	15.00
B. PORTFOLIO INVESTMENT............................	4 600 ..	**3.47**	**−2.47**	**3.78**	**−.10**	**1.71**	**−3.29**	**.18**	**2.84**
Assets...	4 602 ..	**−.17**	**−2.30**	**−.46**	**−.73**	**1.08**	**−2.61**	**−.46**	**2.20**
Equity securities...	4 610 ..	....	....	....	....	....	....	....	....
Monetary authorities................................	4 611 ..	....	....	....	....	....	....	....	....
General government.................................	4 612 ..	....	....	....	....	....	....	....	....
Banks..	4 613 ..	....	....	....	....	....	....	....	....
Other sectors...	4 614 ..	....	....	....	....	....	....	....	....
Debt securities...	4 619 ..	....	....	....	....	....	....	....	....
Bonds and notes......................................	4 620 ..	....	....	....	....	....	....	....	....
Monetary authorities..............................	4 621 ..	....	....	....	....	....	....	....	....
General government...............................	4 622 ..	....	....	....	....	....	....	....	....
Banks..	4 623 ..	....	....	....	....	....	....	....	....
Other sectors...	4 624 ..	....	....	....	....	....	....	....	....
Money market instruments.........................	4 630 ..	....	....	....	....	....	....	....	....
Monetary authorities..............................	4 631 ..	....	....	....	....	....	....	....	....
General government...............................	4 632 ..	....	....	....	....	....	....	....	....
Banks..	4 633 ..	....	....	....	....	....	....	....	....
Other sectors...	4 634 ..	....	....	....	....	....	....	....	....
Liabilities...	4 652 ..	**3.64**	**−.17**	**4.24**	**.62**	**.63**	**−.68**	**.64**	**.64**
Equity securities...	4 660 ..	....	....	....	....	....	....	....	....
Banks..	4 663 ..	....	....	....	....	....	....	....	....
Other sectors...	4 664 ..	....	....	....	....	....	....	....	....
Debt securities...	4 669 ..	....	....	....	....	....	....	....	....
Bonds and notes......................................	4 670 ..	....	....	....	....	....	....	....	....
Monetary authorities..............................	4 671 ..	....	....	....	....	....	....	....	....
General government...............................	4 672 ..	....	....	....	....	....	....	....	....
Banks..	4 673 ..	....	....	....	....	....	....	....	....
Other sectors...	4 674 ..	....	....	....	....	....	....	....	....
Money market instruments.........................	4 680 ..	....	....	....	....	....	....	....	....
Monetary authorities..............................	4 681 ..	....	....	....	....	....	....	....	....
General government...............................	4 682 ..	....	....	....	....	....	....	....	....
Banks..	4 683 ..	....	....	....	....	....	....	....	....
Other sectors...	4 684 ..	....	....	....	....	....	....	....	....
C. FINANCIAL DERIVATIVES..............................	4 910 ..	....	....	....	....	....	....	....	....
Monetary authorities....................................	4 911 ..	....	....	....	....	....	....	....	....
General government....................................	4 912 ..	....	....	....	....	....	....	....	....
Banks...	4 913 ..	....	....	....	....	....	....	....	....
Other sectors..	4 914 ..	....	....	....	....	....	....	....	....
Assets...	4 900 ..	....	....	....	....	....	....	....	....
Monetary authorities................................	4 901 ..	....	....	....	....	....	....	....	....
General government.................................	4 902 ..	....	....	....	....	....	....	....	....
Banks..	4 903 ..	....	....	....	....	....	....	....	....
Other sectors...	4 904 ..	....	....	....	....	....	....	....	....
Liabilities...	4 905 ..	....	....	....	....	....	....	....	....
Monetary authorities................................	4 906 ..	....	....	....	....	....	....	....	....
General government.................................	4 907 ..	....	....	....	....	....	....	....	....
Banks..	4 908 ..	....	....	....	....	....	....	....	....
Other sectors...	4 909 ..	....	....	....	....	....	....	....	....

Table 2 (Concluded). STANDARD PRESENTATION, 2003–2010

(Millions of U.S. dollars)

	Code	2003	2004	2005	2006	2007	2008	2009	2010
D. OTHER INVESTMENT	4 700 ..	−17.95	−21.50	35.64	6.50	−13.06	5.29	26.61	39.64
Assets	4 703 ..	−38.73	−33.77	−7.27	−29.13	−36.10	−31.08	−42.87	−19.44
Trade credits	4 706 ..	....	....	....	....	....	....	....	....
General government	4 707 ..	....	....	....	....	....	....	....	....
of which: Short-term	4 709 ..	....	....	....	....	....	....	....	....
Other sectors	4 710 ..	....	....	....	....	....	....	....	....
of which: Short-term	4 712 ..	....	....	....	....	....	....	....	....
Loans	4 714 ..	−34.13	−28.50	....	−12.44	−18.85	−17.56	−10.34	....
Monetary authorities	4 715 ..	....	....	....	....	....	....	....	....
of which: Short-term	4 718 ..	....	....	....	....	....	....	....	....
General government	4 719 ..	....	....	....	....	....	....	....	....
of which: Short-term	4 721 ..	....	....	....	....	....	....	....	....
Banks	4 722 ..	−34.13	−28.50	....	−12.44	−18.85	−17.56	−10.34	....
of which: Short-term	4 724 ..	....	....	....	....	....	....	....	....
Other sectors	4 725 ..	....	....	....	....	....	....	....	....
of which: Short-term	4 727 ..	....	....	....	....	....	....	....	....
Currency and deposits	4 730 ..	....	....	....	....	....	....	....	....
Monetary authorities	4 731 ..	....	....	....	....	....	....	....	....
General government	4 732 ..	....	....	....	....	....	....	....	....
Banks	4 733 ..	....	....	....	....	....	....	....	....
Other sectors	4 734 ..	....	....	....	....	....	....	....	....
Other assets	4 736 ..	−4.60	−5.27	−7.27	−16.69	−17.26	−13.53	−32.53	−19.44
Monetary authorities	4 737 ..	....	....	....	....	....	....	....	....
of which: Short-term	4 739 ..	....	....	....	....	....	....	....	....
General government	4 740 ..	....	....	....	....	....	....	....	....
of which: Short-term	4 742 ..	....	....	....	....	....	....	....	....
Banks	4 743 ..	....	....	....	....	....	....	....	....
of which: Short-term	4 745 ..	....	....	....	....	....	....	....	....
Other sectors	4 746 ..	−4.60	−5.27	−7.27	−16.69	−17.26	−13.53	−32.53	−19.44
of which: Short-term	4 748 ..	....	....	....	....	....	....	....	....
Liabilities	4 753 ..	20.78	12.26	42.90	35.63	23.04	36.38	69.48	59.08
Trade credits	4 756 ..	....	....	....	....	....	....	....	....
General government	4 757 ..	....	....	....	....	....	....	....	....
of which: Short-term	4 759 ..	....	....	....	....	....	....	....	....
Other sectors	4 760 ..	....	....	....	....	....	....	....	....
of which: Short-term	4 762 ..	....	....	....	....	....	....	....	....
Loans	4 764 ..	4.77	.90	3.17	1.85	−2.46	3.25	4.30	−1.08
Monetary authorities	4 765 ..	4.77	.90	3.17	1.85	−2.46	3.25	4.30	−1.08
of which: Use of Fund credit and loans from the Fund..	4 766 ..	4.77	.90	3.17	1.85	−2.46	3.25	4.30	−1.08
of which: Short-term	4 768 ..	....	....	....	....	....	....	....	....
General government	4 769 ..	....	....	....	....	....	....	....	....
of which: Short-term	4 771 ..	....	....	....	....	....	....	....	....
Banks	4 772 ..	....	....	....	....	....	....	....	....
of which: Short-term	4 774 ..	....	....	....	....	....	....	....	....
Other sectors	4 775 ..	....	....	....	....	....	....	....	....
of which: Short-term	4 777 ..	....	....	....	....	....	....	....	....
Currency and deposits	4 780 ..	....	....	....	....	....	....	....	....
Monetary authorities	4 781 ..	....	....	....	....	....	....	....	....
General government	4 782 ..	....	....	....	....	....	....	....	....
Banks	4 783 ..	....	....	....	....	....	....	....	....
Other sectors	4 784 ..	....	....	....	....	....	....	....	....
Other liabilities	4 786 ..	16.01	11.36	39.74	33.78	25.50	33.13	65.18	60.16
Monetary authorities	4 787 ..	....	....	....	....	....	....	11.32	....
of which: Short-term	4 789 ..	....	....	....	....	....	....	....	....
General government	4 790 ..	....	....	....	....	....	....	....	....
of which: Short-term	4 792 ..	....	....	....	....	....	....	....	....
Banks	4 793 ..	....	....	8.83	....	....	....	....	10.22
of which: Short-term	4 795 ..	....	....	....	....	....	....	....	....
Other sectors	4 796 ..	16.01	11.36	30.91	33.78	25.50	33.13	53.85	49.94
of which: Short-term	4 798 ..	....	....	....	....	....	....	....	....
E. RESERVE ASSETS	4 802 ..	−2.72	5.82	−14.40	−13.42	1.29	3.38	−19.15	−3.67
Monetary gold	4 812 ..	....	....	....	....	....	....	....	....
Special drawing rights	4 811 ..	....	−.05	.04	....	−.03	.02	−10.91	1.09
Reserve position in the Fund	4 810 ..	....	....	....	....	....	....	....	....
Foreign exchange	4 803 ..	−.48	.40	−7.54	.46	−1.25	−1.99	1.13	−2.82
Other claims	4 813 ..	−2.24	5.46	−6.89	−13.87	2.57	5.35	−9.36	−1.94
NET ERRORS AND OMISSIONS	4 998 ..	20.11	27.06	13.54	3.01	−1.45	4.81	8.99	−1.91

Table 1. ANALYTIC PRESENTATION, 2003–2010

(Millions of U.S. dollars)

	Code	2003	2004	2005	2006	2007	2008	2009	2010
A. Current Account[1]..............	4 993 Z.	**1,036.2**	**1,041.5**	**–473.0**	**–1,287.4**	**–2,166.3**	**–4,518.6**	**–2,330.9**	**–4,434.9**
Goods: exports f.o.b.	2 100 ..	5,470.8	5,935.9	6,144.7	6,610.2	7,160.2	6,747.5	5,482.9	6,598.1
Goods: imports f.o.b.	3 100 ..	–7,626.8	–7,888.0	–9,869.4	–12,173.9	–13,597.0	–15,992.9	–12,295.9	–15,298.9
Balance on Goods	4 100 ..	*–2,156.0*	*–1,952.1*	*–3,724.7*	*–5,563.7*	*–6,436.8*	*–9,245.4*	*–6,813.0*	*–8,700.8*
Services: credit	2 200 ..	3,468.8	3,503.9	3,935.0	4,567.2	4,824.9	4,951.2	4,835.9	5,098.7
Services: debit	3 200 ..	–1,219.4	–1,213.2	–1,478.2	–1,582.0	–1,772.4	–1,989.4	–1,848.6	–2,162.8
Balance on Goods and Services	4 991 ..	*93.4*	*338.6*	*–1,267.9*	*–2,578.5*	*–3,384.3*	*–6,283.6*	*–3,825.7*	*–5,764.9*
Income: credit	2 300 ..	340.7	321.8	418.1	699.7	828.6	728.7	461.1	499.6
Income: debit	3 300 ..	–1,733.8	–2,146.4	–2,320.4	–2,552.7	–3,011.8	–2,476.6	–2,181.9	–2,287.8
Balance on Goods, Services, and Income	4 992 ..	*–1,299.7*	*–1,486.0*	*–3,170.1*	*–4,431.5*	*–5,567.5*	*–8,031.5*	*–5,546.5*	*–7,553.1*
Current transfers: credit	2 379 Z.	2,512.2	2,701.4	2,907.7	3,365.6	3,654.8	3,789.1	3,499.4	3,473.3
Current transfers: debit	3 379 ..	–176.3	–173.9	–210.6	–221.5	–253.6	–276.2	–283.8	–355.1
B. Capital Account[1]..............	4 994 Z.	....	....	....	254.2	195.1	135.0	106.5	81.9
Capital account: credit	2 994 Z.	....	....	....	254.2	195.1	135.0	106.5	81.9
Capital account: debit	3 994 ..	....	....	....	....	....	....	....	....
Total, Groups A Plus B	4 981 ..	*1,036.2*	*1,041.5*	*–473.0*	*–1,033.2*	*–1,971.2*	*–4,383.6*	*–2,224.4*	*–4,353.0*
C. Financial Account[1]..............	4 995 W.	**–15.9**	**117.6**	**1,635.9**	**1,350.6**	**2,185.8**	**4,073.5**	**2,760.9**	**4,406.8**
Direct investment abroad	4 505 ..	....	....	....	....	....	....	....	....
Direct investment in Dominican Republic	4 555 Z.	613.0	909.0	1,122.7	1,084.6	1,667.4	2,870.0	2,165.4	1,625.8
Portfolio investment assets	4 602 ..	–19.7	–7.6	–82.2	–328.7	172.8	107.7	46.8	–10.3
Equity securities	4 610 ..	–6.5	–2.2	.9	17.7	....	–10.3	2.3	–1.0
Debt securities	4 619 ..	–13.2	–5.4	–83.1	–346.4	172.8	118.0	44.5	–9.3
Portfolio investment liabilities	4 652 Z.	563.5	–16.7	326.4	1,102.5	776.3	–483.5	–496.3	535.2
Equity securities	4 660 ..	....	....	....	....	....	....	....	....
Debt securities	4 669 Z.	563.5	–16.7	326.4	1,102.5	776.3	–483.5	–496.3	535.2
Financial derivatives	4 910 ..	....	....	....	....	....	....	....	....
Financial derivatives assets	4 900 ..	....	....	....	....	....	....	....	....
Financial derivatives liabilities	4 905 ..	....	....	....	....	....	....	....	....
Other investment assets	4 703 ..	–1,159.1	–428.7	62.4	–1,367.8	–782.8	541.3	255.4	352.3
Monetary authorities	4 701 ..	1.8	–1.9	–44.5	–11.5	–24.6	–23.5	4.7	19.4
General government	4 704 ..	....	....	....	....	....	....	....	....
Banks	4 705 ..	–136.6	–377.7	21.7	105.6	–345.8	234.2	22.9	221.0
Other sectors	4 728 ..	–1,024.3	–49.1	85.2	–1,461.9	–412.4	330.6	227.8	111.9
Other investment liabilities	4 753 W.	–13.6	–338.4	206.7	860.0	352.1	1,038.0	789.6	1,903.8
Monetary authorities	4 753 WA	–223.3	–38.6	–38.0	–30.2	–24.8	–13.9	264.2	–11.8
General government	4 753 ZB	445.8	305.8	94.4	366.6	332.3	784.9	810.9	711.7
Banks	4 753 ZC	–100.5	–254.5	–72.1	24.0	10.8	413.5	–108.7	431.5
Other sectors	4 753 ZD	–135.6	–351.1	222.4	499.6	33.8	–146.5	–176.8	772.4
Total, Groups A Through C	4 983 ..	*1,020.3*	*1,159.1*	*1,162.9*	*317.4*	*214.6*	*–310.1*	*536.5*	*53.8*
D. Net Errors and Omissions..............	4 998 ..	**–1,568.2**	**–981.2**	**–456.3**	**–123.0**	**411.7**	**–14.6**	**–125.3**	**10.9**
Total, Groups A Through D	4 984 ..	*–548.0*	*177.9*	*706.6*	*194.3*	*626.3*	*–324.7*	*411.2*	*64.7*
E. Reserves and Related Items..............	4 802 A.	**548.0**	**–177.9**	**–706.6**	**–194.3**	**–626.3**	**324.7**	**–411.2**	**–64.7**
Reserve assets	4 802 ..	357.8	–540.2	–1,110.3	–344.7	–682.3	308.0	–642.3	–458.9
Use of Fund credit and loans	4 766 ..	94.5	65.5	219.0	37.8	62.9	–41.7	274.0	390.3
Exceptional financing	4 920 ..	95.7	296.9	184.7	112.6	–6.8	58.3	–42.9	3.9
Conversion rates: Dominican pesos per U.S. dollar..............	0 101 ..	**30.831**	**42.120**	**30.409**	**33.365**	**33.263**	**34.624**	**36.027**	**36.875**

[1] Excludes components that have been classified in the categories of Group E.

Table 2. STANDARD PRESENTATION, 2003–2010

(Millions of U.S. dollars)

	Code	2003	2004	2005	2006	2007	2008	2009	2010
CURRENT ACCOUNT....................................	4 993 ..	**1,036.2**	**1,041.5**	**−473.0**	**−1,287.4**	**−2,166.3**	**−4,518.6**	**−2,330.9**	**−4,434.9**
A. GOODS....................................	4 100 ..	**−2,156.0**	**−1,952.1**	**−3,724.7**	**−5,563.7**	**−6,436.8**	**−9,245.4**	**−6,813.0**	**−8,700.8**
Credit....................................	2 100 ..	**5,470.8**	**5,935.9**	**6,144.7**	**6,610.2**	**7,160.2**	**6,747.5**	**5,482.9**	**6,598.1**
General merchandise: exports f.o.b....................	2 110 ..	912.2	1,016.8	1,058.3	1,556.3	2,220.5	1,850.9	1,353.5	2,097.5
Goods for processing: exports f.o.b..................	2 150 ..	4,406.8	4,685.2	4,749.6	4,678.8	4,525.1	4,354.1	3,793.6	4,080.0
Repairs on goods....................................	2 160 ..	....	....	....	....	....	....	....	....
Goods procured in ports by carriers.................	2 170 ..	151.8	233.9	336.8	375.1	414.6	542.5	335.8	420.6
Nonmonetary gold....................................	2 180 ..	....	....	....	....	....	....	....	....
Debit....................................	3 100 ..	**−7,626.8**	**−7,888.0**	**−9,869.4**	**−12,173.9**	**−13,597.0**	**−15,992.9**	**−12,295.9**	**−15,298.9**
General merchandise: imports f.o.b..................	3 110 ..	−5,095.9	−5,368.1	−7,366.3	−9,558.8	−11,097.3	−13,564.0	−9,946.1	−12,885.2
Goods for processing: imports f.o.b..................	3 150 ..	−2,530.9	−2,519.9	−2,503.1	−2,615.1	−2,499.7	−2,428.9	−2,349.8	−2,413.7
Repairs on goods....................................	3 160 ..	....	....	....	....	....	....	....	....
Goods procured in ports by carriers.................	3 170 ..	....	....	....	....	....	....	....	....
Nonmonetary gold....................................	3 180 ..	....	....	....	....	....	....	....	....
B. SERVICES....................................	4 200 ..	**2,249.4**	**2,290.7**	**2,456.8**	**2,985.2**	**3,052.5**	**2,961.8**	**2,987.3**	**2,935.9**
Total credit....................................	2 200 ..	*3,468.8*	*3,503.9*	*3,935.0*	*4,567.2*	*4,824.9*	*4,951.2*	*4,835.9*	*5,098.7*
Total debit....................................	3 200 ..	*−1,219.4*	*−1,213.2*	*−1,478.2*	*−1,582.0*	*−1,772.4*	*−1,989.4*	*−1,848.6*	*−2,162.8*
Transportation services, credit..............	2 205 ..	**98.1**	**100.3**	**128.4**	**297.5**	**351.6**	**363.1**	**351.8**	**385.7**
Passenger....................................	2 850 ..								
Freight....................................	2 851 ..	*63.3*	*63.0*	*89.6*	*98.9*	*113.9*	*121.3*	*97.5*	*120.1*
Other....................................	2 852 ..	*34.8*	*37.3*	*38.8*	*198.6*	*237.7*	*241.8*	*254.3*	*265.6*
Sea transport, passenger..........................	2 207 ..	....	....	....	....	....	....	....	....
Sea transport, freight............................	2 208 ..	59.8	59.7	85.1	94.0	108.8	115.8	93.1	114.3
Sea transport, other..............................	2 209 ..	....	....	....	....	....	....	....	....
Air transport, passenger..........................	2 211 ..	....	....	....	....	....	....	....	....
Air transport, freight............................	2 212 ..	3.5	3.3	4.5	4.9	5.1	5.5	4.4	5.8
Air transport, other..............................	2 213 ..	3.6	3.8	3.9	4.1	4.3	4.9	3.0	3.0
Other transport, passenger........................	2 215 ..	....	....	....	....	....	....	....	....
Other transport, freight..........................	2 216 ..	....	....	....	....	....	....	....	....
Other transport, other............................	2 217 ..	31.2	33.5	34.9	194.5	233.4	236.9	251.3	262.6
Transportation services, debit...............	3 205 ..	**−689.1**	**−650.3**	**−865.8**	**−938.6**	**−1,109.2**	**−1,162.3**	**−1,006.0**	**−1,200.7**
Passenger....................................	3 850 ..	*−136.2*	*−137.5*	*−159.1*	*−161.7*	*−205.3*	*−205.1*	*−163.9*	*−158.7*
Freight....................................	3 851 ..	*−550.2*	*−509.8*	*−706.7*	*−776.9*	*−903.9*	*−957.2*	*−842.1*	*−1,042.0*
Other....................................	3 852 ..	*−2.7*	*−3.0*						
Sea transport, passenger..........................	3 207 ..	....	....	....	....	....	....	....	....
Sea transport, freight............................	3 208 ..	−515.2	−476.3	−661.9	−726.8	−852.9	−901.4	−796.9	−985.0
Sea transport, other..............................	3 209 ..	....	....	....	....	....	....	....	....
Air transport, passenger..........................	3 211 ..	−136.2	−137.5	−159.1	−161.7	−205.3	−205.1	−163.9	−158.7
Air transport, freight............................	3 212 ..	−35.0	−33.5	−44.8	−50.1	−51.0	−55.8	−45.2	−57.0
Air transport, other..............................	3 213 ..	−2.7	−3.0	....	....	....	....	....	....
Other transport, passenger........................	3 215 ..	....	....	....	....	....	....	....	....
Other transport, freight..........................	3 216 ..	....	....	....	....	....	....	....	....
Other transport, other............................	3 217 ..	....	....	....	....	....	....	....	....
Travel, credit..................................	2 236 ..	**3,127.8**	**3,151.6**	**3,518.3**	**3,916.8**	**4,064.2**	**4,165.9**	**4,048.8**	**4,209.1**
Business travel....................................	2 237 ..	20.6	18.0	21.3	22.4	23.4	16.7	14.6	18.5
Personal travel....................................	2 240 ..	3,107.2	3,133.6	3,497.0	3,894.4	4,040.8	4,149.2	4,034.2	4,190.6
Travel, debit...................................	3 236 ..	**−271.6**	**−309.8**	**−352.2**	**−333.0**	**−325.9**	**−327.0**	**−340.6**	**−382.5**
Business travel....................................	3 237 ..								
Personal travel....................................	3 240 ..	−271.6	−309.8	−352.2	−333.0	−325.9	−327.0	−340.6	−382.5
Other services, credit........................	2 200 BA	**242.9**	**252.0**	**288.3**	**352.9**	**409.1**	**422.2**	**435.3**	**503.9**
Communications....................................	2 245 ..	113.5	118.2	117.9	157.3	162.8	189.2	190.8	213.4
Construction......................................	2 249 ..	....	....	....	....	....	....	....	....
Insurance...	2 253 ..	....	....	21.8	24.7	27.4	29.1	24.2	25.7
Financial...	2 260 ..	3.0	3.2	18.4	29.0	17.1	16.1	20.5	21.4
Computer and information..........................	2 262 ..	17.6	18.2	15.4	12.8	13.2	8.0	10.5	17.0
Royalties and licence fees........................	2 266 ..	....	....	....	....	....	....	....	....
Other business services...........................	2 268 ..	41.1	43.1	44.7	58.2	116.8	116.1	106.4	125.2
Personal, cultural, and recreational...............	2 287 ..	....	....	....	....	....	....	....	....
Government, n.i.e..................................	2 291 ..	67.7	69.3	70.1	70.9	71.8	63.7	82.9	101.2
Other services, debit.........................	3 200 BA	**−258.7**	**−253.1**	**−260.2**	**−310.4**	**−337.3**	**−500.1**	**−502.0**	**−579.6**
Communications....................................	3 245 ..	−20.1	−23.7	−20.6	−28.6	−41.4	−48.9	−37.3	−45.2
Construction......................................	3 249 ..	....	....	....	....	....	....	....	....
Insurance...	3 253 ..	−89.7	−87.0	−101.9	−98.9	−108.4	−112.3	−110.8	−118.4
Financial...	3 260 ..	−38.2	−25.7	−18.1	−31.8	−25.9	−28.0	−50.0	−67.8
Computer and information..........................	3 262 ..	−6.5	−6.7	−7.6	−10.7	−11.6	−15.3	−13.2	−24.2
Royalties and licence fees........................	3 266 ..	−30.1	−30.1	−30.8	−31.5	−31.9	−50.7	−53.4	−62.8
Other business services...........................	3 268 ..	−33.5	−34.3	−33.8	−36.4	−36.7	−149.8	−120.3	−140.7
Personal, cultural, and recreational...............	3 287 ..	....	....	....	−.8	−.4	−.5	−1.0	−1.5
Government, n.i.e..................................	3 291 ..	−40.6	−45.6	−47.4	−71.7	−81.0	−94.6	−116.0	−119.0

Table 2 (Continued). STANDARD PRESENTATION, 2003–2010

(Millions of U.S. dollars)

	Code	2003	2004	2005	2006	2007	2008	2009	2010
C. INCOME	4 300	**−1,393.1**	**−1,824.6**	**−1,902.2**	**−1,853.0**	**−2,183.2**	**−1,747.9**	**−1,720.8**	**−1,788.2**
Total credit	2 300	*340.7*	*321.8*	*418.1*	*699.7*	*828.6*	*728.7*	*461.1*	*499.6*
Total debit	3 300	*−1,733.8*	*−2,146.4*	*−2,320.4*	*−2,552.7*	*−3,011.8*	*−2,476.6*	*−2,181.9*	*−2,287.8*
Compensation of employees, credit	2 310	**264.9**	**271.0**	**289.4**	**316.0**	**351.3**	**384.0**	**373.2**	**435.0**
Compensation of employees, debit	3 310	**−22.9**	**−23.9**	**−24.7**	**−26.6**	**−28.2**	**−34.5**	**−26.9**	**−32.6**
Investment income, credit	2 320	**75.8**	**50.8**	**128.7**	**383.7**	**477.3**	**344.7**	**87.9**	**64.6**
Direct investment income	2 330	....	....	....	....	....	....	....	....
Dividends and distributed branch profits	2 332	....	....	....	....	....	....	....	....
Reinvested earnings and undistributed branch profits	2 333	....	....	....	....	....	....	....	....
Income on debt (interest)	2 334	....	....	....	....	....	....	....	....
Portfolio investment income	2 339	7.6	11.2	10.6	66.3	56.4	62.2	13.7	11.8
Income on equity	2 340	....	....	....	....	....	....	....	....
Income on bonds and notes	2 350	7.6	11.2	10.6	66.3	56.4	62.2	13.7	11.8
Income on money market instruments	2 360	....	....	....	....	....	....	....	....
Other investment income	2 370	68.2	39.6	118.1	317.4	420.9	282.5	74.2	52.8
Investment income, debit	3 320	**−1,710.9**	**−2,122.5**	**−2,295.7**	**−2,526.1**	**−2,983.6**	**−2,442.1**	**−2,155.0**	**−2,255.2**
Direct investment income	3 330	−1,390.5	−1,651.8	−1,765.0	−1,931.7	−2,194.4	−1,668.5	−1,518.1	−1,639.3
Dividends and distributed branch profits	3 332	−1,401.8	−1,118.7	−1,269.7	−1,209.1	−1,691.7	−1,273.1	−1,135.1	−1,205.2
Reinvested earnings and undistributed branch profits	3 333	118.8	−506.0	−483.8	−714.4	−498.1	−393.9	−365.4	−396.0
Income on debt (interest)	3 334	−107.5	−27.1	−11.5	−8.2	−4.6	−1.5	−17.6	−38.1
Portfolio investment income	3 339	−85.2	−137.1	−154.6	−223.5	−373.0	−393.3	−323.8	−307.2
Income on equity	3 340	....	−5.0	−3.9	−1.1	−2.5	−3.1	−2.9	−3.0
Income on bonds and notes	3 350	−85.2	−111.6	−118.0	−157.7	−239.4	−237.6	−218.5	−228.8
Income on money market instruments	3 360	....	−20.5	−32.7	−64.7	−131.1	−152.6	−102.4	−75.4
Other investment income	3 370	−235.2	−333.6	−376.1	−370.9	−416.2	−380.3	−313.1	−308.7
D. CURRENT TRANSFERS	4 379	**2,335.9**	**2,527.5**	**2,697.1**	**3,144.1**	**3,401.2**	**3,512.9**	**3,215.6**	**3,118.2**
Credit	2 379	**2,512.2**	**2,701.4**	**2,907.7**	**3,365.6**	**3,654.8**	**3,789.1**	**3,499.4**	**3,473.3**
General government	2 380	125.5	140.6	176.5	232.5	279.8	232.3	218.4	237.4
Other sectors	2 390	2,386.7	2,560.8	2,731.2	3,133.1	3,375.0	3,556.8	3,281.0	3,235.9
Workers' remittances	2 391	2,060.5	2,230.2	2,429.8	2,737.8	3,045.7	3,221.5	3,041.5	2,994.2
Other current transfers	2 392	326.2	330.6	301.4	395.3	329.3	335.3	239.5	241.7
Debit	3 379	**−176.3**	**−173.9**	**−210.6**	**−221.5**	**−253.6**	**−276.2**	**−283.8**	**−355.1**
General government	3 380	−2.4	−2.5	−2.7	−2.5	−2.5	−6.2	−6.6	−48.0
Other sectors	3 390	−173.9	−171.4	−207.9	−219.0	−251.1	−270.0	−277.2	−307.1
Workers' remittances	3 391	....	....	....	....	....	....	....	....
Other current transfers	3 392	−173.9	−171.4	−207.9	−219.0	−251.1	−270.0	−277.2	−307.1
CAPITAL AND FINANCIAL ACCOUNT	4 996	**532.1**	**−60.2**	**929.3**	**1,410.4**	**1,754.6**	**4,533.2**	**2,456.2**	**4,424.0**
CAPITAL ACCOUNT	4 994	**6.0**	**4.3**	**....**	**290.1**	**205.9**	**144.4**	**407.2**	**86.7**
Total credit	2 994	*6.0*	*4.3*	*....*	*290.1*	*205.9*	*144.4*	*407.2*	*86.7*
Total debit	3 994	....	....	....	....	....	....	....	....
Capital transfers, credit	2 400	**6.0**	**4.3**	**....**	**290.1**	**205.9**	**144.4**	**407.2**	**86.7**
General government	2 401	6.0	4.3	....	42.3	21.3	10.3	300.7	4.8
Debt forgiveness	2 402	6.0	4.3	....	35.9	10.8	9.4	300.7	4.8
Other capital transfers	2 410	....	....	....	6.4	10.5	.9	....	....
Other sectors	2 430	....	....	....	247.8	184.6	134.1	106.5	81.9
Migrants' transfers	2 431	....	....	....	30.5	29.9	61.5	52.4	43.9
Debt forgiveness	2 432	....	....	....	....	....	....	....	....
Other capital transfers	2 440	....	....	....	217.3	154.7	72.6	54.1	38.0
Capital transfers, debit	3 400	**....**	**....**	**....**	**....**	**....**	**....**	**....**	**....**
General government	3 401	....	....	....	....	....	....	....	....
Debt forgiveness	3 402	....	....	....	....	....	....	....	....
Other capital transfers	3 410	....	....	....	....	....	....	....	....
Other sectors	3 430	....	....	....	....	....	....	....	....
Migrants' transfers	3 431	....	....	....	....	....	....	....	....
Debt forgiveness	3 432	....	....	....	....	....	....	....	....
Other capital transfers	3 440	....	....	....	....	....	....	....	....
Nonproduced nonfinancial assets, credit	2 480	....	....	....	....	....	....	....	....
Nonproduced nonfinancial assets, debit	3 480	....	....	....	....	....	....	....	....

Table 2 (Continued). STANDARD PRESENTATION, 2003–2010

(Millions of U.S. dollars)

	Code	2003	2004	2005	2006	2007	2008	2009	2010
FINANCIAL ACCOUNT	4 995	**526.1**	**−64.6**	**929.3**	**1,120.3**	**1,548.7**	**4,388.8**	**2,049.0**	**4,337.3**
A. DIRECT INVESTMENT	4 500	**613.0**	**909.0**	**1,122.7**	**1,084.6**	**1,667.4**	**2,870.0**	**2,165.4**	**2,027.3**
Direct investment abroad	4 505	....	....	....	....	....	....	....	....
Equity capital	4 510	....	....	....	....	....	....	....	....
Claims on affiliated enterprises	4 515	....	....	....	....	....	....	....	....
Liabilities to affiliated enterprises	4 520	....	....	....	....	....	....	....	....
Reinvested earnings	4 525	....	....	....	....	....	....	....	....
Other capital	4 530	....	....	....	....	....	....	....	....
Claims on affiliated enterprises	4 535	....	....	....	....	....	....	....	....
Liabilities to affiliated enterprises	4 540	....	....	....	....	....	....	....	....
Direct investment in Dominican Republic	4 555	**613.0**	**909.0**	**1,122.7**	**1,084.6**	**1,667.4**	**2,870.0**	**2,165.4**	**2,027.3**
Equity capital	4 560	583.1	482.2	687.8	764.6	1,615.6	2,198.6	704.3	934.1
Claims on direct investors	4 565	....	....	....	....	....	....	....	....
Liabilities to direct investors	4 570	583.1	482.2	687.8	764.6	1,615.6	2,198.6	704.3	934.1
Reinvested earnings	4 575	−118.8	506.0	483.8	714.4	498.1	393.9	365.4	396.0
Other capital	4 580	148.7	−79.2	−48.9	−394.4	−446.3	277.5	1,095.7	697.2
Claims on direct investors	4 585	−3.5	−25.4	4.3	−444.1	−585.5	141.6	470.1	203.0
Liabilities to direct investors	4 590	152.2	−53.7	−53.2	49.7	139.2	135.9	625.6	494.2
B. PORTFOLIO INVESTMENT	4 600	**543.8**	**−24.3**	**244.2**	**773.8**	**949.1**	**−375.8**	**−449.5**	**524.9**
Assets	4 602	**−19.7**	**−7.6**	**−82.2**	**−328.7**	**172.8**	**107.7**	**46.8**	**−10.3**
Equity securities	4 610	−6.5	−2.2	.9	17.7	....	−10.3	2.3	−1.0
Monetary authorities	4 611	....	....	....	....	....	....	....	....
General government	4 612	....	....	....	....	....	....	....	....
Banks	4 613	−6.5	−2.2	.9	17.7	....	−10.3	2.3	−1.0
Other sectors	4 614	....	....	....	....	....	....	....	....
Debt securities	4 619	−13.2	−5.4	−83.1	−346.4	172.8	118.0	44.5	−9.3
Bonds and notes	4 620	−5.7	−6.1	−6.5	−7.1	−7.6	−8.2	−8.6	−9.3
Monetary authorities	4 621	−5.7	−6.1	−6.5	−7.1	−7.6	−8.2	−8.6	−9.3
General government	4 622	....	....	....	....	....	....	....	....
Banks	4 623	....	....	....	....	....	....	....	....
Other sectors	4 624	....	....	....	....	....	....	....	....
Money market instruments	4 630	−7.5	.7	−76.6	−339.3	180.4	126.2	53.1	....
Monetary authorities	4 631	....	....	....	....	....	....	....	....
General government	4 632	....	....	....	....	....	....	....	....
Banks	4 633	−7.5	.7	−76.6	−339.3	180.4	126.2	53.1	....
Other sectors	4 634	....	....	....	....	....	....	....	....
Liabilities	4 652	**563.5**	**−16.7**	**326.4**	**1,102.5**	**776.3**	**−483.5**	**−496.3**	**535.2**
Equity securities	4 660	....	....	....	....	....	....	....	....
Banks	4 663	....	....	....	....	....	....	....	....
Other sectors	4 664	....	....	....	....	....	....	....	....
Debt securities	4 669	563.5	−16.7	326.4	1,102.5	776.3	−483.5	−496.3	535.2
Bonds and notes	4 670	579.8	−19.8	29.6	736.0	287.1	−260.3	−127.9	629.6
Monetary authorities	4 671	−19.0	−19.0	−19.0	−19.0	−19.0	−19.0	−19.0	....
General government	4 672	599.6	....	49.3	333.8	−105.4	−105.4	−106.2	642.4
Banks	4 673	−.1	−.1	−.1	−.1	−.1	....	....	....
Other sectors	4 674	−.7	−.7	−.7	421.2	411.6	−135.9	−2.7	−12.8
Money market instruments	4 680	−16.3	3.1	296.8	366.5	489.2	−223.2	−368.4	−94.4
Monetary authorities	4 681	11.3	3.1	281.0	381.8	488.6	−223.5	−368.5	−100.1
General government	4 682	....	....	....	....	....	....	....	....
Banks	4 683	−27.6	....	15.8	−15.3	.6	.3	.1	5.7
Other sectors	4 684	....	....	....	....	....	....	....	....
C. FINANCIAL DERIVATIVES	4 910	....	....	....	....	....	....	....	....
Monetary authorities	4 911	....	....	....	....	....	....	....	....
General government	4 912	....	....	....	....	....	....	....	....
Banks	4 913	....	....	....	....	....	....	....	....
Other sectors	4 914	....	....	....	....	....	....	....	....
Assets	4 900	....	....	....	....	....	....	....	....
Monetary authorities	4 901	....	....	....	....	....	....	....	....
General government	4 902	....	....	....	....	....	....	....	....
Banks	4 903	....	....	....	....	....	....	....	....
Other sectors	4 904	....	....	....	....	....	....	....	....
Liabilities	4 905	....	....	....	....	....	....	....	....
Monetary authorities	4 906	....	....	....	....	....	....	....	....
General government	4 907	....	....	....	....	....	....	....	....
Banks	4 908	....	....	....	....	....	....	....	....
Other sectors	4 909	....	....	....	....	....	....	....	....

Table 2 (Concluded). STANDARD PRESENTATION, 2003–2010

(Millions of U.S. dollars)

	Code	2003	2004	2005	2006	2007	2008	2009	2010
D. OTHER INVESTMENT	4 700	−988.5	−409.1	672.7	−393.3	−385.4	1,586.6	975.4	2,244.0
Assets	4 703	−1,159.1	−428.7	62.4	−1,367.8	−782.8	541.3	255.4	352.3
Trade credits	4 706	23.8	....	....	....	....	....	....	....
General government	4 707	....	....	....	....	....	....	....	....
of which: Short-term	4 709	....	....	....	....	....	....	....	....
Other sectors	4 710	23.8	....	....	....	....	....	....	....
of which: Short-term	4 712	23.8	....	....	....	....	....	....	....
Loans	4 714	....	30.3	2.9	3.5	.2	.5	−2.5	−.9
Monetary authorities	4 715	....	....	....	....	....	....	....	....
of which: Short-term	4 718	....	....	....	....	....	....	....	....
General government	4 719	....	....	....	....	....	....	....	....
of which: Short-term	4 721	....	....	....	....	....	....	....	....
Banks	4 722	....	30.3	2.9	3.5	.2	.5	−2.5	−.9
of which: Short-term	4 724	....	30.3	2.9	3.5	.2	.5	−2.5	−.9
Other sectors	4 725	....	....	....	....	....	....	....	....
of which: Short-term	4 727	....	....	....	....	....	....	....	....
Currency and deposits	4 730	−1,102.5	−562.6	242.5	−796.6	−426.6	275.8	250.7	371.5
Monetary authorities	4 731	−.2	−.3	−.7	−1.2	−1.2	−.4	....	....
General government	4 732	....	....	....	....	....	....	....	....
Banks	4 733	−61.8	−453.5	21.1	260.2	−231.1	−4.7	−1.3	204.4
Other sectors	4 734	−1,040.5	−108.8	222.1	−1,055.6	−194.3	280.9	252.0	167.1
Other assets	4 736	−80.4	103.6	−183.0	−574.7	−356.4	265.0	7.2	−18.3
Monetary authorities	4 737	2.0	−1.6	−43.8	−10.3	−23.4	−23.1	4.7	19.4
of which: Short-term	4 739	2.4	−1.1	−43.2	−9.4	2.0	−31.4	10.6	13.7
General government	4 740	....	....	....	....	....	....	....	....
of which: Short-term	4 742	....	....	....	....	....	....	....	....
Banks	4 743	−74.8	45.5	−2.3	−158.1	−114.9	238.4	26.7	17.5
of which: Short-term	4 745	−74.8	45.5	−2.3	−158.1	−114.9	238.4	26.7	17.5
Other sectors	4 746	−7.6	59.7	−136.9	−406.3	−218.1	49.7	−24.2	−55.2
of which: Short-term	4 748	−7.6	59.7	−136.9	−406.3	−218.1	49.9	−24.3	−55.2
Liabilities	4 753	170.6	19.6	610.4	974.5	397.4	1,045.3	720.0	1,891.7
Trade credits	4 756	−141.0	27.3	190.1	146.1	291.5	137.4	−81.6	171.2
General government	4 757	....	....	....	....	....	....	....	....
of which: Short-term	4 759	....	....	....	....	....	....	....	....
Other sectors	4 760	−141.0	27.3	190.1	146.1	291.5	137.4	−81.6	171.2
of which: Short-term	4 762	−130.2	27.3	190.1	146.1	291.5	137.4	−81.6	171.2
Loans	4 764	317.6	−304.7	681.6	791.0	160.3	867.9	854.2	2,116.0
Monetary authorities	4 765	−61.5	33.2	191.3	15.4	38.1	−55.6	261.4	378.5
of which: Use of Fund credit and loans from the Fund	4 766	94.5	65.5	219.0	37.8	62.9	−41.7	274.0	390.3
of which: Short-term	4 768	−129.4	−4.9	−3.2	−.1	....	−.6	−.3	....
General government	4 769	445.8	305.8	510.6	444.3	366.0	784.9	810.9	711.7
of which: Short-term	4 771	9.6	4.7	−14.2	....	....	....	....	....
Banks	4 772	−55.6	−250.4	−72.0	−6.4	19.3	415.1	−109.7	424.6
of which: Short-term	4 774	−58.8	−180.9	−21.6	−4.8	24.7	439.8	−130.8	391.9
Other sectors	4 775	−11.1	−393.3	51.7	337.7	−263.1	−276.5	−108.4	601.2
of which: Short-term	4 777	−107.9	−46.4	−10.2	272.6	−140.5	−25.3	−47.3	−5.7
Currency and deposits	4 780	−109.3	−7.0	−9.7	23.1	−9.8	−1.7	2.0	6.8
Monetary authorities	4 781	−67.3	−6.3	−10.3	−5.4	....	....	....	....
General government	4 782	....	....	....	....	....	....	....	....
Banks	4 783	−42.0	−.7	.6	28.5	−9.8	−1.7	2.0	6.8
Other sectors	4 784	....	....	....	....	....	....	....	....
Other liabilities	4 786	103.3	304.0	−251.6	14.3	−44.6	41.6	−54.6	−402.3
Monetary authorities	4 787	.1	1.1	1.3	−2.5	....	....	276.8	....
of which: Short-term	4 789	.1	1.1	1.3	−2.5	....	....	....	....
General government	4 790	59.7	58.7	−259.5	−25.5	−70.5	6.7	−54.5	−.9
of which: Short-term	4 792	59.7	58.7	−259.5	−25.5	−70.5	6.7	−54.5	−.9
Banks	4 793	−3.0	−3.4	−.7	2.0	−2.3	.1	−1.0	.1
of which: Short-term	4 795	−3.0	−3.4	−.7	2.0	−2.3	.1	−1.0	.1
Other sectors	4 796	46.5	247.6	7.3	40.3	28.2	34.8	−275.9	−401.5
of which: Short-term	4 798	46.5	247.6	7.3	40.3	28.2	34.8	−275.9	−401.5
E. RESERVE ASSETS	4 802	357.8	−540.2	−1,110.3	−344.7	−682.3	308.0	−642.3	−458.9
Monetary gold	4 812	....	....	....	....	....	....	....	....
Special drawing rights	4 811	.2	−1.3	.9	−23.7	−70.4	60.4	−239.3	151.5
Reserve position in the Fund	4 810	....	....	....	....	....	....	....	....
Foreign exchange	4 803	357.6	−538.9	−1,111.2	−191.6	−571.6	251.6	−343.0	−581.1
Other claims	4 813	....	....	....	−129.4	−40.3	−4.0	−60.0	−29.3
NET ERRORS AND OMISSIONS	4 998	−1,568.2	−981.2	−456.3	−123.0	411.7	−14.6	−125.3	10.9

Table 3. INTERNATIONAL INVESTMENT POSITION (End-period stocks), 2003–2010

(Millions of U.S. dollars)

	Code	2003	2004	2005	2006	2007	2008	2009	2010
ASSETS	8 995 C.	**3,069.4**	**3,964.8**	**5,148.1**	**9,800.7**	**11,144.2**	**10,306.7**	**10,664.2**	**10,180.3**
Direct investment abroad	8 505 ..	....	....	....	....	....	....	....	....
Equity capital and reinvested earnings	8 506 ..	....	....	....	....	....	....	....	....
Claims on affiliated enterprises	8 507 ..	....	....	....	....	....	....	....	....
Liabilities to affiliated enterprises	8 508 ..	....	....	....	....	....	....	....	....
Other capital	8 530 ..	....	....	....	....	....	....	....	....
Claims on affiliated enterprises	8 535 ..	....	....	....	....	....	....	....	....
Liabilities to affiliated enterprises	8 540 ..	....	....	....	....	....	....	....	....
Portfolio investment	8 602 ..	**114.7**	**122.3**	**204.6**	**533.3**	**360.5**	**252.8**	**206.3**	**216.9**
Equity securities	8 610 ..	18.0	20.2	19.3	1.6	1.6	11.9	9.6	10.6
Monetary authorities	8 611 ..	....	....	....	....	....	....	....	....
General government	8 612 ..	....	....	....	....	....	....	....	....
Banks	8 613 ..	18.0	20.2	19.3	1.6	1.6	11.9	9.6	10.6
Other sectors	8 614 ..	....	....	....	....	....	....	....	....
Debt securities	8 619 ..	96.7	102.1	185.3	531.7	358.9	240.9	196.7	206.3
Bonds and notes	8 620 ..	78.3	84.4	91.0	98.1	105.7	113.9	122.8	132.4
Monetary authorities	8 621 ..	78.3	84.4	91.0	98.1	105.7	113.9	122.8	132.4
General government	8 622 ..	....	....	....	....	....	....	....	....
Banks	8 623 ..	....	....	....	....	....	....	....	....
Other sectors	8 624 ..	....	....	....	....	....	....	....	....
Money market instruments	8 630 ..	18.4	17.7	94.3	433.6	253.2	127.0	73.9	73.9
Monetary authorities	8 631 ..	....	....	....	....	....	....	....	....
General government	8 632 ..	....	....	....	....	....	....	....	....
Banks	8 633 ..	18.4	17.7	94.3	433.6	253.2	127.0	73.9	73.9
Other sectors	8 634 ..	....	....	....	....	....	....	....	....
Financial derivatives	8 900 ..	....	....	....	....	....	....	....	....
Monetary authorities	8 901 ..	....	....	....	....	....	....	....	....
General government	8 902 ..	....	....	....	....	....	....	....	....
Banks	8 903 ..	....	....	....	....	....	....	....	....
Other sectors	8 904 ..	....	....	....	....	....	....	....	....
Other investment	8 703 ..	**2,675.4**	**3,019.3**	**3,014.3**	**6,986.6**	**7,803.9**	**7,391.9**	**7,150.7**	**6,197.9**
Trade credits	8 706 ..	....	....	....	....	....	....	....	....
General government	8 707 ..	....	....	....	....	....	....	....	....
of which: Short-term	8 709 ..	....	....	....	....	....	....	....	....
Other sectors	8 710 ..	....	....	....	....	....	....	....	....
of which: Short-term	8 712 ..	....	....	....	....	....	....	....	....
Loans	8 714 ..	41.0	10.7	7.8	5.1	4.9	4.4	6.9	7.8
Monetary authorities	8 715 ..	....	....	....	....	....	....	....	....
of which: Short-term	8 718 ..	....	....	....	....	....	....	....	....
General government	8 719 ..	....	....	....	....	....	....	....	....
of which: Short-term	8 721 ..	....	....	....	....	....	....	....	....
Banks	8 722 ..	41.0	10.7	7.8	5.1	4.9	4.4	6.9	7.8
of which: Short-term	8 724 ..	*41.0*	*10.7*	*7.8*	*5.1*	*4.9*	*4.4*	*6.9*	*7.8*
Other sectors	8 725 ..	....	....	....	....	....	....	....	....
of which: Short-term	8 727 ..	....	....	....	....	....	....	....	....
Currency and deposits	8 730 ..	2,352.6	2,850.7	2,592.7	5,668.3	6,129.6	5,982.0	5,743.5	4,921.2
Monetary authorities	8 731 ..	22.2	22.5	23.2	24.4	25.6	26.0	26.0	26.1
General government	8 732 ..	....	....	....	....	....	....	....	....
Banks	8 733 ..	505.6	959.1	938.0	677.8	908.9	913.6	914.9	713.7
Other sectors	8 734 ..	1,824.8	1,869.1	1,631.5	4,966.1	5,195.1	5,042.4	4,802.6	4,181.4
Other assets	8 736 ..	281.8	157.9	413.7	1,313.2	1,669.4	1,405.5	1,400.3	1,268.9
Monetary authorities	8 737 ..	32.5	34.1	77.9	433.8	457.3	480.4	475.7	456.5
of which: Short-term	8 739 ..	*.6*	*1.7*	*44.9*	*28.0*	*26.0*	*57.4*	*46.8*	*33.1*
General government	8 740 ..	....	....	....	....	....	....	....	....
of which: Short-term	8 742 ..	....	....	....	....	....	....	....	....
Banks	8 743 ..	79.0	33.5	35.8	193.9	308.8	70.4	43.7	26.2
of which: Short-term	8 745 ..	*79.0*	*33.5*	*35.8*	*193.9*	*308.8*	*70.4*	*43.7*	*26.2*
Other sectors	8 746 ..	170.3	90.3	300.0	685.5	903.3	854.7	880.9	786.2
of which: Short-term	8 748 ..	*170.3*	*90.3*	*300.0*	*685.5*	*903.3*	*854.7*	*880.9*	*786.2*
Reserve assets	8 802 ..	**279.3**	**823.2**	**1,929.3**	**2,280.9**	**2,979.8**	**2,662.0**	**3,307.1**	**3,765.5**
Monetary gold	8 812 ..	7.6	8.0	9.4	11.6	15.3	15.9	19.9	25.7
Special drawing rights	8 811 ..	.1	1.6	.6	24.5	98.6	36.0	275.6	117.7
Reserve position in the Fund	8 810 ..	....	....	....	....	....	....	....	....
Foreign exchange	8 803 ..	271.6	813.6	1,919.3	2,115.4	2,696.2	2,437.0	2,783.7	3,364.8
Other claims	8 813 ..	....	....	....	129.4	169.7	173.1	227.9	257.2

Table 3 (Concluded). INTERNATIONAL INVESTMENT POSITION (End-period stocks), 2003–2010

(Millions of U.S. dollars)

	Code	2003	2004	2005	2006	2007	2008	2009	2010
LIABILITIES	8 995 D.	**11,959.2**	**12,900.1**	**14,985.9**	**18,375.4**	**21,190.2**	**24,070.7**	**26,991.1**	**31,215.7**
Direct investment in Dominican Republic	8 555 ..	**3,598.4**	**3,955.7**	**5,276.0**	**6,373.8**	**8,081.4**	**10,960.9**	**13,105.5**	**15,075.1**
Equity capital and reinvested earnings	8 556 ..	3,127.9	3,597.3	4,923.1	6,389.9	8,573.7	11,194.6	12,226.6	13,502.6
Claims on direct investors	8 557 ..	....	....	....	....	....	....	....	....
Liabilities to direct investors	8 558 ..	3,127.9	3,597.3	4,923.1	6,389.9	8,573.7	11,194.6	12,226.6	13,502.6
Other capital	8 580 ..	470.5	358.5	352.9	−16.1	−492.3	−233.7	878.9	1,572.5
Claims on direct investors	8 585 ..	−155.1	−119.2	−43.7	−472.0	−1,082.7	−939.2	−454.7	−251.7
Liabilities to direct investors	8 590 ..	625.6	477.7	396.7	456.0	590.5	705.6	1,333.7	1,824.3
Portfolio investment	8 652 ..	**1,401.9**	**1,600.4**	**2,038.0**	**3,264.6**	**3,937.7**	**2,827.8**	**2,877.2**	**3,525.6**
Equity securities	8 660 ..	....	....	....	....	....	....	....	....
Banks	8 663 ..	....	....	....	....	....	....	....	....
Other sectors	8 664 ..	....	....	....	....	....	....	....	....
Debt securities	8 669 ..	1,401.9	1,600.4	2,038.0	3,264.6	3,937.7	2,827.8	2,877.2	3,525.6
Bonds and notes	8 670 ..	1,319.6	1,428.2	1,620.1	2,474.7	2,678.1	1,837.6	2,274.8	3,037.3
Monetary authorities	8 671 ..	431.1	412.5	394.4	375.6	356.0	335.8	316.0	316.0
General government	8 672 ..	871.0	999.0	1,209.7	1,662.0	1,473.5	789.0	1,249.5	2,012.3
Banks	8 673 ..	1.1	1.1	1.0	1.0	.9	.9	.8	−.1
Other sectors	8 674 ..	16.4	15.7	15.0	436.2	847.7	711.9	708.5	709.1
Money market instruments	8 680 ..	82.3	172.2	417.9	789.9	1,259.6	990.2	602.4	488.3
Monetary authorities	8 681 ..	82.1	172.2	402.1	789.4	1,258.5	988.8	600.9	481.1
General government	8 682 ..	....	....	....	....	....	....	....	....
Banks	8 683 ..	.2	....	15.8	.5	1.1	1.4	1.5	7.2
Other sectors	8 684 ..	....	....	....	....	....	....	....	....
Financial derivatives	8 905 ..	....	....	....	....	....	....	....	....
Monetary authorities	8 906 ..	....	....	....	....	....	....	....	....
General government	8 907 ..	....	....	....	....	....	....	....	....
Banks	8 908 ..	....	....	....	....	....	....	....	....
Other sectors	8 909 ..	....	....	....	....	....	....	....	....
Other investment	8 753 ..	**6,958.9**	**7,343.9**	**7,671.9**	**8,737.0**	**9,171.2**	**10,282.1**	**11,008.4**	**12,615.0**
Trade credits	8 756 ..	199.9	227.3	464.0	610.1	907.9	1,044.4	954.5	1,072.2
General government	8 757 ..	....	....	....	....	....	....	....	....
of which: Short-term	8 759 ..	....	....	....	....	....	....	....	....
Other sectors	8 760 ..	199.9	227.3	464.0	610.1	907.9	1,044.4	954.5	1,072.2
of which: Short-term	8 762 ..	*199.9*	*227.3*	*464.0*	*610.1*	*907.9*	*1,044.4*	*954.5*	*1,072.2*
Loans	8 764 ..	6,430.8	6,474.8	6,831.9	7,715.9	7,908.5	8,797.0	9,617.2	11,514.2
Monetary authorities	8 765 ..	329.2	374.8	536.8	570.2	636.0	569.9	831.0	1,192.1
of which: Use of Fund credit and loans from the Fund	8 766 ..	*130.1*	*204.0*	*400.5*	*459.4*	*547.6*	*492.3*	*766.5*	*1,139.4*
of which: Short-term	8 768 ..	*10.0*	*4.6*	*1.5*	*1.5*	*1.5*	*.7*	*.4*	*.2*
General government	8 769 ..	3,971.8	4,404.3	4,298.5	4,835.0	5,192.8	5,999.3	6,778.6	7,490.5
of which: Short-term	8 771 ..	*9.6*	*15.4*	*10.0*	*10.0*	*10.0*	*10.0*	*10.0*	*10.0*
Banks	8 772 ..	481.9	231.8	162.6	156.1	175.4	590.5	480.8	729.5
of which: Short-term	8 774 ..	*289.4*	*111.7*	*90.9*	*86.0*	*107.4*	*547.2*	*416.4*	*610.0*
Other sectors	8 775 ..	1,647.9	1,463.9	1,834.0	2,154.6	1,904.3	1,637.3	1,526.8	2,102.0
of which: Short-term	8 777 ..	*81.3*	*20.7*	*10.5*	*283.1*	*142.4*	*117.1*	*69.8*	*71.2*
Currency and deposits	8 780 ..	26.8	19.8	10.2	33.3	23.5	21.8	23.8	30.6
Monetary authorities	8 781 ..	25.6	19.3	9.1	3.7	3.7	3.7	3.7	3.7
General government	8 782 ..	....	....	....	....	....	....	....	....
Banks	8 783 ..	1.2	.5	1.1	29.6	19.8	18.1	20.1	26.9
Other sectors	8 784 ..	....	....	....	....	....	....	....	....
Other liabilities	8 786 ..	301.4	622.1	365.8	377.6	331.3	418.9	412.9	−2.0
Monetary authorities	8 787 ..	.4	1.2	2.4	−.1	−.1	48.6	376.0	367.8
of which: Short-term	8 789 ..	*.4*	*1.2*	*2.4*	*−.1*	*−.1*	*−.1*	*−.1*	*−.1*
General government	8 790 ..	173.5	234.0	−25.5	−51.0	−121.5	−114.8	−169.3	−170.2
of which: Short-term	8 792 ..	*173.5*	*234.0*	*−25.5*	*−51.0*	*−121.5*	*−114.8*	*−169.3*	*−170.2*
Banks	8 793 ..	8.2	4.8	6.5	4.9	1.3	.1	−2.2	−3.4
of which: Short-term	8 795 ..	*2.9*	*1.9*	*4.2*	*1.5*	*−1.9*	*−2.6*	*−4.7*	*−5.9*
Other sectors	8 796 ..	119.3	382.1	382.4	423.8	451.6	485.0	208.4	−196.2
of which: Short-term	8 798 ..	*119.3*	*382.1*	*382.4*	*423.8*	*451.6*	*484.0*	*207.4*	*−197.2*
NET INTERNATIONAL INVESTMENT POSITION	8 995 ..	**−8,889.8**	**−8,935.3**	**−9,837.7**	**−8,574.6**	**−10,046.0**	**−13,764.0**	**−16,326.9**	**−21,035.4**
Conversion rates: Dominican pesos per U.S. dollar (end of period)	0 102 ..	**37.250**	**31.109**	**34.879**	**33.797**	**34.342**	**35.458**	**36.210**	**37.541**

Table 1. ANALYTIC PRESENTATION, 2003–2010

(Millions of U.S. dollars)

	Code	2003	2004	2005	2006	2007	2008	2009	2010
A. Current Account[1]	4 993 Z.	**−668.34**	**−538.15**	**−803.89**	**−1,234.04**	**−1,578.92**	**−1,739.59**	**−1,150.03**	**−959.52**
Goods: exports f.o.b.	2 100 ..	334.02	343.34	370.27	360.75	361.67	449.41	432.24	421.81
Goods: imports f.o.b.	3 100 ..	−1,500.83	−1,580.14	−1,857.47	−2,205.58	−2,462.56	−2,718.09	−2,159.93	−2,095.98
Balance on Goods	4 100 ..	*−1,166.81*	*−1,236.80*	*−1,487.20*	*−1,844.83*	*−2,100.89*	*−2,268.68*	*−1,727.69*	*−1,674.17*
Services: credit	2 200 ..	1,272.93	1,465.68	1,535.60	1,538.02	1,620.66	1,640.11	1,517.04	1,557.57
Services: debit	3 200 ..	−662.20	−706.87	−806.21	−899.86	−999.43	−1,004.32	−869.06	−852.62
Balance on Goods and Services	4 991 ..	*−556.08*	*−477.99*	*−757.80*	*−1,206.66*	*−1,479.66*	*−1,632.89*	*−1,079.71*	*−969.22*
Income: credit	2 300 ..	31.50	48.27	75.64	101.65	102.98	68.91	72.90	74.30
Income: debit	3 300 ..	−272.90	−329.88	−309.82	−299.04	−340.40	−336.87	−310.85	−255.20
Balance on Goods, Services, and Income	4 992 ..	*−797.48*	*−759.59*	*−991.99*	*−1,404.05*	*−1,717.07*	*−1,900.85*	*−1,317.66*	*−1,150.12*
Current transfers: credit	2 379 Z.	218.80	304.22	273.81	269.80	263.75	274.80	271.56	293.90
Current transfers: debit	3 379 ..	−89.66	−82.78	−85.71	−99.80	−125.60	−113.54	−103.92	−103.30
B. Capital Account[1]	4 994 Z.	**131.18**	**132.07**	**332.11**	**175.64**	**223.21**	**219.39**	**205.95**	**181.61**
Capital account: credit	2 994 Z.	139.45	140.57	340.85	184.70	232.55	229.31	215.71	191.35
Capital account: debit	3 994 ..	−8.27	−8.50	−8.74	−9.06	−9.34	−9.92	−9.76	−9.73
Total, Groups A Plus B	4 981 ..	*−537.16*	*−406.08*	*−471.79*	*−1,058.41*	*−1,355.71*	*−1,520.19*	*−944.08*	*−777.91*
C. Financial Account[1]	4 995 W.	**628.93**	**439.45**	**535.45**	**1,105.80**	**1,313.19**	**1,382.08**	**1,100.25**	**649.42**
Direct investment abroad	4 505 ..	....	....	....	....	....	....	....	....
Direct investment in Eastern Caribbean Currency Union	4 555 Z.	555.64	458.60	644.42	1,073.97	1,197.83	982.73	694.01	576.40
Portfolio investment assets	4 602 ..	−2.75	−20.85	−1.43	−17.42	−7.56	−2.01	−21.65	.91
Equity securities	4 610 ..	....	....	....	....	....	....	....	....
Debt securities	4 619 ..	....	....	....	....	....	....	....	....
Portfolio investment liabilities	4 652 Z.	169.30	101.36	34.28	26.91	−22.16	11.95	5.19	−13.00
Equity securities	4 660 ..	....	....	....	....	....	....	....	....
Debt securities	4 669 Z.	....	....	....	....	....	....	....	....
Financial derivatives	4 910 ..	....	....	....	....	....	....	....	....
Financial derivatives assets	4 900 ..	....	....	....	....	....	....	....	....
Financial derivatives liabilities	4 905 ..	....	....	....	....	....	....	....	....
Other investment assets	4 703 ..	−284.44	−282.37	−555.72	−203.05	−277.37	−224.51	−242.20	−246.10
Monetary authorities	4 701 ..	....	....	....	....	....	....	....	....
General government	4 704 ..	....	....	....	....	....	....	....	....
Banks	4 705 ..	−168.20	−98.81	−77.41	....	....	....	....	....
Other sectors	4 728 ..	−116.24	−183.55	−478.30	−203.05	−277.37	−224.51	−242.20	−246.10
Other investment liabilities	4 753 W.	191.18	182.72	413.90	225.40	422.45	613.92	664.90	331.21
Monetary authorities	4 753 WA	....	....	....	....	....	....	93.59	....
General government	4 753 ZB	....	....	....	....	....	....	....	....
Banks	4 753 ZC	....	....	....	30.72	122.66	275.11	182.84	14.46
Other sectors	4 753 ZD	191.18	182.72	413.90	194.68	299.79	338.82	388.47	316.75
Total, Groups A Through C	4 983 ..	*91.77*	*33.37*	*63.66*	*47.39*	*−42.52*	*−138.11*	*156.17*	*−128.48*
D. Net Errors and Omissions	4 998 ..	**−53.48**	**63.21**	**−85.23**	**35.59**	**81.93**	**104.69**	**−28.51**	**191.81**
Total, Groups A Through D	4 984 ..	*38.29*	*96.58*	*−21.57*	*82.99*	*39.41*	*−33.42*	*127.66*	*63.33*
E. Reserves and Related Items	4 802 A.	**−38.29**	**−96.58**	**21.03**	**−89.58**	**−50.95**	**33.42**	**−127.66**	**−63.33**
Reserve assets	4 802 ..	−45.87	−101.91	17.85	−92.08	−46.25	18.59	−150.86	−103.81
Use of Fund credit and loans	4 766 ..	7.58	5.33	3.17	2.50	−4.70	14.83	23.20	40.48
Exceptional financing	4 920 ..	....	....	....	....	....	....	....	....
Conversion rates: Eastern Caribbean dollars per U.S. dollar	0 101 ..	**2.7000**	**2.7000**	**2.7000**	**2.7000**	**2.7000**	**2.7000**	**2.7000**	**2.7000**

[1] Excludes components that have been classified in the categories of Group E.

2011, International Monetary Fund: *Balance of Payments Statistics Yearbook*

Table 2. STANDARD PRESENTATION, 2003–2010

(Millions of U.S. dollars)

	Code	2003	2004	2005	2006	2007	2008	2009	2010
CURRENT ACCOUNT..	4 993 ..	**−668.34**	**−538.15**	**−803.89**	**−1,234.04**	**−1,578.92**	**−1,739.59**	**−1,150.03**	**−959.52**
A. GOODS..	4 100 ..	**−1,166.81**	**−1,236.80**	**−1,487.20**	**−1,844.83**	**−2,100.89**	**−2,268.68**	**−1,727.69**	**−1,674.17**
Credit..	2 100 ..	**334.02**	**343.34**	**370.27**	**360.75**	**361.67**	**449.41**	**432.24**	**421.81**
General merchandise: exports f.o.b........	2 110 ..	288.07	276.43	282.91	267.26	282.26	366.01	376.61	363.09
Goods for processing: exports f.o.b........	2 150 ..	....	....	....	....	....	....	....	....
Repairs on goods.....................................	2 160 ..	.03	.14	.15	.14	.16	.19	.28	.29
Goods procured in ports by carriers........	2 170 ..	45.91	66.77	87.20	93.36	79.25	83.21	55.35	58.42
Nonmonetary gold..................................	2 180 ..	....	....	....	....	....	....	....	....
Debit...	3 100 ..	**−1,500.83**	**−1,580.14**	**−1,857.47**	**−2,205.58**	**−2,462.56**	**−2,718.09**	**−2,159.93**	**−2,095.98**
General merchandise: imports f.o.b........	3 110 ..	−1,492.24	−1,570.66	−1,845.71	−2,192.96	−2,453.05	−2,699.20	−2,149.28	−2,085.65
Goods for processing: imports f.o.b........	3 150 ..	....	....	....	....	....	....	....	....
Repairs on goods.....................................	3 160 ..	....	....	....	....	....	....	....	....
Goods procured in ports by carriers........	3 170 ..	−8.59	−9.48	−11.76	−12.63	−9.51	−18.90	−10.65	−10.33
Nonmonetary gold..................................	3 180 ..	....	....	....	....	....	....	....	....
B. SERVICES...	4 200 ..	**610.73**	**758.81**	**729.40**	**638.17**	**621.24**	**635.79**	**647.98**	**704.95**
Total credit..	2 200 ..	*1,272.93*	*1,465.68*	*1,535.60*	*1,538.02*	*1,620.66*	*1,640.11*	*1,517.04*	*1,557.57*
Total debit..	3 200 ..	*−662.20*	*−706.87*	*−806.21*	*−899.86*	*−999.43*	*−1,004.32*	*−869.06*	*−852.62*
Transportation services, credit............	2 205 ..	**123.01**	**134.25**	**146.55**	**144.69**	**158.67**	**198.21**	**200.19**	**199.28**
Passenger..	2 850 ..	....	....	....	....	....	....	....	....
Freight..	2 851 ..	....	....	....	....	....	....	....	....
Other..	2 852 ..	....	....	....	....	....	....	....	....
Sea transport, passenger........................	2 207 ..	....	....	....	....	....	....	....	....
Sea transport, freight.............................	2 208 ..	....	....	....	....	....	....	....	....
Sea transport, other...............................	2 209 ..	....	....	....	....	....	....	....	....
Air transport, passenger.........................	2 211 ..	....	....	....	....	....	....	....	....
Air transport, freight..............................	2 212 ..	....	....	....	....	....	....	....	....
Air transport, other................................	2 213 ..	....	....	....	....	....	....	....	....
Other transport, passenger....................	2 215 ..	....	....	....	....	....	....	....	....
Other transport, freight..........................	2 216 ..	....	....	....	....	....	....	....	....
Other transport, other............................	2 217 ..	....	....	....	....	....	....	....	....
Transportation services, debit............	3 205 ..	**−261.66**	**−275.66**	**−320.75**	**−357.13**	**−395.13**	**−427.02**	**−348.58**	**−346.93**
Passenger..	3 850 ..	....	....	....	....	....	....	....	....
Freight..	3 851 ..	....	....	....	....	....	....	....	....
Other..	3 852 ..	....	....	....	....	....	....	....	....
Sea transport, passenger........................	3 207 ..	....	....	....	....	....	....	....	....
Sea transport, freight.............................	3 208 ..	....	....	....	....	....	....	....	....
Sea transport, other...............................	3 209 ..	....	....	....	....	....	....	....	....
Air transport, passenger.........................	3 211 ..	....	....	....	....	....	....	....	....
Air transport, freight..............................	3 212 ..	....	....	....	....	....	....	....	....
Air transport, other................................	3 213 ..	....	....	....	....	....	....	....	....
Other transport, passenger....................	3 215 ..	....	....	....	....	....	....	....	....
Other transport, freight..........................	3 216 ..	....	....	....	....	....	....	....	....
Other transport, other............................	3 217 ..	....	....	....	....	....	....	....	....
Travel, credit.......................................	2 236 ..	**976.28**	**1,087.45**	**1,139.48**	**1,146.21**	**1,179.49**	**1,150.54**	**1,054.36**	**1,098.31**
Business travel..	2 237 ..	....	....	....	....	....	....	....	....
Personal travel..	2 240 ..	....	....	....	....	....	....	....	....
Travel, debit..	3 236 ..	**−119.45**	**−127.13**	**−137.02**	**−154.64**	**−171.35**	**−178.57**	**−168.42**	**−164.74**
Business travel..	3 237 ..	....	....	....	....	....	....	....	....
Personal travel..	3 240 ..	....	....	....	....	....	....	....	....
Other services, credit...........................	2 200 BA	**173.64**	**243.98**	**249.57**	**247.13**	**282.51**	**291.36**	**262.48**	**259.98**
Communications......................................	2 245 ..	50.45	54.21	58.00	54.39	65.35	70.74	62.95	63.48
Construction..	2 249 ..	.06	.25	.38	.19	.31	.41	.49	.47
Insurance...	2 253 ..	21.07	69.53	43.16	30.42	36.42	40.22	33.15	32.83
Financial..	2 260 ..	....	....	....	....	....	....	....	....
Computer and information......................	2 262 ..	2.43	2.43	3.33	....	....	....	.01	.01
Royalties and licence fees.......................	2 266 ..	.11	....	....	.06	.06	.07	.43	.44
Other business services..........................	2 268 ..	82.93	99.35	123.53	135.66	154.50	152.15	134.84	134.49
Personal, cultural, and recreational........	2 287 ..	....	....	....	....	....	....	....	....
Government, n.i.e....................................	2 291 ..	16.59	18.21	21.16	26.40	25.86	27.76	30.61	28.27
Other services, debit............................	3 200 BA	**−281.09**	**−304.08**	**−348.43**	**−388.09**	**−432.94**	**−398.72**	**−352.06**	**−340.96**
Communications......................................	3 245 ..	−21.52	−24.13	−31.36	−24.12	−27.51	−27.68	−24.42	−24.84
Construction..	3 249 ..	−19.00	−21.98	−38.41	−70.93	−75.17	−38.29	−26.85	−21.68
Insurance...	3 253 ..	−74.67	−76.66	−91.17	−107.26	−116.70	−130.18	−113.62	−111.06
Financial..	3 260 ..	....	....	....	....	....	....	....	....
Computer and information......................	3 262 ..	−.75	−.53	−.13	−.26	−.38	−.50	−.34	−.34
Royalties and licence fees.......................	3 266 ..	−5.41	−6.28	−6.86	−8.56	−9.60	−14.47	−13.73	−13.77
Other business services..........................	3 268 ..	−120.48	−130.99	−138.36	−142.30	−161.79	−147.04	−137.98	−136.73
Personal, cultural, and recreational........	3 287 ..	....	....	....	....	....	....	....	....
Government, n.i.e....................................	3 291 ..	−39.26	−43.51	−42.15	−34.65	−41.80	−40.56	−35.12	−32.54

Table 2 (Continued). STANDARD PRESENTATION, 2003–2010

(Millions of U.S. dollars)

	Code	2003	2004	2005	2006	2007	2008	2009	2010
C. INCOME	4 300	**−241.40**	**−281.60**	**−234.18**	**−197.39**	**−237.41**	**−267.96**	**−237.95**	**−180.90**
Total credit	2 300	*31.50*	*48.27*	*75.64*	*101.65*	*102.98*	*68.91*	*72.90*	*74.30*
Total debit	3 300	*−272.90*	*−329.88*	*−309.82*	*−299.04*	*−340.40*	*−336.87*	*−310.85*	*−255.20*
Compensation of employees, credit	2 310	**7.34**	**12.63**	**12.48**	**16.87**	**20.25**	**19.01**	**18.20**	**18.69**
Compensation of employees, debit	3 310	**−3.81**	**−3.96**	**−3.96**	**−1.59**	**−5.82**	**−3.26**	**−2.16**	**−2.02**
Investment income, credit	2 320	**24.16**	**35.64**	**63.16**	**84.78**	**82.73**	**49.90**	**54.69**	**55.61**
Direct investment income	2 330	.22	.15	.10	.15	.12	2.05	.57	.37
Dividends and distributed branch profits	2 332	.16	.15	.09	.10	.08	1.65	.02	.02
Reinvested earnings and undistributed branch profits	2 333	....	....	....	....	....	....	....	....
Income on debt (interest)	2 334	.06	....	....	.04	.03	.40	.54	.34
Portfolio investment income	2 339	7.43	7.56	8.36	19.36	19.31	13.62	22.68	24.19
Income on equity	2 340	7.43	7.56	8.36	19.36	19.31	13.62	22.68	24.19
Income on bonds and notes	2 350	....	....	....	....	....	....	....	....
Income on money market instruments	2 360	....	....	....	....	....	....	....	....
Other investment income	2 370	16.51	27.93	54.70	65.27	63.31	34.23	31.45	31.06
Investment income, debit	3 320	**−269.10**	**−325.92**	**−305.86**	**−297.45**	**−334.58**	**−333.61**	**−308.68**	**−253.19**
Direct investment income	3 330	−149.15	−171.56	−176.50	−154.80	−188.08	−196.75	−185.08	−144.05
Dividends and distributed branch profits	3 332	−63.39	−73.02	−80.58	−84.98	−102.21	−119.03	−139.11	−98.00
Reinvested earnings and undistributed branch profits	3 333	−71.35	−85.70	−82.27	−56.62	−70.51	−63.95	−32.63	−32.89
Income on debt (interest)	3 334	−14.41	−12.84	−13.65	−13.19	−15.36	−13.77	−13.33	−13.15
Portfolio investment income	3 339	−35.89	−43.09	−26.04	−27.72	−18.52	−20.93	−18.82	−12.88
Income on equity	3 340	−35.89	−43.09	−26.04	−27.72	−18.52	−20.93	−18.82	−12.88
Income on bonds and notes	3 350	....	....	....	....	....	....	....	....
Income on money market instruments	3 360	....	....	....	....	....	....	....	....
Other investment income	3 370	−84.05	−111.27	−103.32	−114.93	−127.97	−115.93	−104.79	−96.25
D. CURRENT TRANSFERS	4 379	**129.14**	**221.44**	**188.09**	**170.01**	**138.15**	**161.27**	**167.64**	**190.60**
Credit	2 379	**218.80**	**304.22**	**273.81**	**269.80**	**263.75**	**274.80**	**271.56**	**293.90**
General government	2 380	68.87	94.93	87.86	87.92	73.43	81.19	86.10	102.75
Other sectors	2 390	149.94	209.29	185.95	181.88	190.32	193.62	185.45	191.15
Workers' remittances	2 391	128.72	159.87	144.06	150.02	156.37	161.60	156.19	159.13
Other current transfers	2 392	21.22	49.42	41.90	31.87	33.95	32.02	29.27	32.02
Debit	3 379	**−89.66**	**−82.78**	**−85.71**	**−99.80**	**−125.60**	**−113.54**	**−103.92**	**−103.30**
General government	3 380	−23.31	−24.27	−25.94	−23.86	−31.65	−26.18	−20.65	−20.57
Other sectors	3 390	−66.35	−58.50	−59.77	−75.94	−93.96	−87.36	−83.27	−82.73
Workers' remittances	3 391	−21.02	−22.64	−24.04	−27.87	−32.51	−31.88	−27.50	−27.00
Other current transfers	3 392	−45.33	−35.86	−35.73	−48.07	−61.45	−55.48	−55.78	−55.73
CAPITAL AND FINANCIAL ACCOUNT	4 996	**721.82**	**474.94**	**889.12**	**1,198.45**	**1,496.99**	**1,634.90**	**1,178.54**	**767.71**
CAPITAL ACCOUNT	4 994	**131.18**	**132.07**	**332.11**	**175.64**	**223.21**	**219.39**	**205.95**	**181.61**
Total credit	2 994	*139.45*	*140.57*	*340.85*	*184.70*	*232.55*	*229.31*	*215.71*	*191.35*
Total debit	3 994	*−8.27*	*−8.50*	*−8.74*	*−9.06*	*−9.34*	*−9.92*	*−9.76*	*−9.73*
Capital transfers, credit	2 400	**139.27**	**140.57**	**340.85**	**184.61**	**232.55**	**229.31**	**215.71**	**191.35**
General government	2 401	92.88	91.82	286.33	127.48	172.52	169.33	158.00	132.21
Debt forgiveness	2 402	....	15.65	202.69	....	55.56	....	....	....
Other capital transfers	2 410	92.88	76.17	83.64	127.48	116.96	169.33	158.00	132.21
Other sectors	2 430	46.38	48.76	54.52	57.13	60.03	59.98	57.71	59.13
Migrants' transfers	2 431	46.38	48.76	54.52	57.13	60.03	59.98	57.71	59.13
Debt forgiveness	2 432	....	....	....	....	....	....	....	....
Other capital transfers	2 440	....	....	....	....	....	....	....	....
Capital transfers, debit	3 400	**−8.27**	**−8.50**	**−8.74**	**−9.06**	**−9.34**	**−9.92**	**−9.76**	**−9.73**
General government	3 401	....	....	....	....	....	....	....	....
Debt forgiveness	3 402	....	....	....	....	....	....	....	....
Other capital transfers	3 410	....	....	....	....	....	....	....	....
Other sectors	3 430	−8.27	−8.50	−8.74	−9.06	−9.34	−9.92	−9.76	−9.73
Migrants' transfers	3 431	−8.27	−8.50	−8.74	−9.06	−9.34	−9.92	−9.76	−9.73
Debt forgiveness	3 432	....	....	....	....	....	....	....	....
Other capital transfers	3 440	....	....	....	....	....	....	....	....
Nonproduced nonfinancial assets, credit	2 480	**.19**	**....**	**....**	**.09**	**....**	**....**	**....**	**....**
Nonproduced nonfinancial assets, debit	3 480	**....**	**....**	**....**	**....**	**....**	**....**	**....**	**....**

Table 2 (Continued). STANDARD PRESENTATION, 2003–2010

(Millions of U.S. dollars)

	Code	2003	2004	2005	2006	2007	2008	2009	2010
FINANCIAL ACCOUNT	4 995 ..	**590.63**	**342.87**	**557.02**	**1,022.81**	**1,273.78**	**1,415.50**	**972.59**	**586.10**
A. DIRECT INVESTMENT	4 500 ..	**555.64**	**458.60**	**644.42**	**1,073.97**	**1,197.83**	**982.73**	**694.01**	**576.40**
Direct investment abroad	4 505 ..	....	....	....	....	....	....	....	....
Equity capital	4 510 ..	....	....	....	....	....	....	....	....
Claims on affiliated enterprises	4 515 ..	....	....	....	....	....	....	....	....
Liabilities to affiliated enterprises	4 520 ..	....	....	....	....	....	....	....	....
Reinvested earnings	4 525 ..	....	....	....	....	....	....	....	....
Other capital	4 530 ..	....	....	....	....	....	....	....	....
Claims on affiliated enterprises	4 535 ..	....	....	....	....	....	....	....	....
Liabilities to affiliated enterprises	4 540 ..	....	....	....	....	....	....	....	....
Direct investment in ECCU	4 555 ..	**555.64**	**458.60**	**644.42**	**1,073.97**	**1,197.83**	**982.73**	**694.01**	**576.40**
Equity capital	4 560 ..	171.14	167.14	412.77	640.66	755.58	535.36	365.41	265.06
Claims on direct investors	4 565 ..	....	....	....	....	....	....	....	....
Liabilities to direct investors	4 570 ..	171.14	167.14	412.77	640.66	755.58	535.36	365.41	265.06
Reinvested earnings	4 575 ..	71.35	85.70	82.27	56.62	70.51	63.95	32.63	32.89
Other capital	4 580 ..	313.15	205.76	149.38	376.68	371.73	383.42	295.96	278.45
Claims on direct investors	4 585 ..	....	....	....	....	....	....	....	....
Liabilities to direct investors	4 590 ..	313.15	205.76	149.38	376.68	371.73	383.42	295.96	278.45
B. PORTFOLIO INVESTMENT	4 600 ..	**166.55**	**80.50**	**33.40**	**16.08**	**−18.17**	**9.94**	**−16.46**	**−12.09**
Assets	4 602 ..	**−2.75**	**−20.85**	**−1.43**	**−17.42**	**−7.56**	**−2.01**	**−21.65**	**.91**
Equity securities	4 610 ..	....	....	....	....	....	....	....	....
Monetary authorities	4 611 ..	....	....	....	....	....	....	....	....
General government	4 612 ..	....	....	....	....	....	....	....	....
Banks	4 613 ..	....	....	....	....	....	....	....	....
Other sectors	4 614 ..	....	....	....	....	....	....	....	....
Debt securities	4 619 ..	....	....	....	....	....	....	....	....
Bonds and notes	4 620 ..	....	....	....	....	....	....	....	....
Monetary authorities	4 621 ..	....	....	....	....	....	....	....	....
General government	4 622 ..	....	....	....	....	....	....	....	....
Banks	4 623 ..	....	....	....	....	....	....	....	....
Other sectors	4 624 ..	....	....	....	....	....	....	....	....
Money market instruments	4 630 ..	....	....	....	....	....	....	....	....
Monetary authorities	4 631 ..	....	....	....	....	....	....	....	....
General government	4 632 ..	....	....	....	....	....	....	....	....
Banks	4 633 ..	....	....	....	....	....	....	....	....
Other sectors	4 634 ..	....	....	....	....	....	....	....	....
Liabilities	4 652 ..	**169.30**	**101.36**	**34.82**	**33.50**	**−10.61**	**11.95**	**5.19**	**−13.00**
Equity securities	4 660 ..	....	....	....	....	....	....	....	....
Banks	4 663 ..	....	....	....	....	....	....	....	....
Other sectors	4 664 ..	....	....	....	....	....	....	....	....
Debt securities	4 669 ..	....	....	....	....	....	....	....	....
Bonds and notes	4 670 ..	....	....	....	....	....	....	....	....
Monetary authorities	4 671 ..	....	....	....	....	....	....	....	....
General government	4 672 ..	....	....	....	....	....	....	....	....
Banks	4 673 ..	....	....	....	....	....	....	....	....
Other sectors	4 674 ..	....	....	....	....	....	....	....	....
Money market instruments	4 680 ..	....	....	....	....	....	....	....	....
Monetary authorities	4 681 ..	....	....	....	....	....	....	....	....
General government	4 682 ..	....	....	....	....	....	....	....	....
Banks	4 683 ..	....	....	....	....	....	....	....	....
Other sectors	4 684 ..	....	....	....	....	....	....	....	....
C. FINANCIAL DERIVATIVES	4 910 ..	....	....	....	....	....	....	....	....
Monetary authorities	4 911 ..	....	....	....	....	....	....	....	....
General government	4 912 ..	....	....	....	....	....	....	....	....
Banks	4 913 ..	....	....	....	....	....	....	....	....
Other sectors	4 914 ..	....	....	....	....	....	....	....	....
Assets	4 900 ..	....	....	....	....	....	....	....	....
Monetary authorities	4 901 ..	....	....	....	....	....	....	....	....
General government	4 902 ..	....	....	....	....	....	....	....	....
Banks	4 903 ..	....	....	....	....	....	....	....	....
Other sectors	4 904 ..	....	....	....	....	....	....	....	....
Liabilities	4 905 ..	....	....	....	....	....	....	....	....
Monetary authorities	4 906 ..	....	....	....	....	....	....	....	....
General government	4 907 ..	....	....	....	....	....	....	....	....
Banks	4 908 ..	....	....	....	....	....	....	....	....
Other sectors	4 909 ..	....	....	....	....	....	....	....	....

Table 2 (Concluded). STANDARD PRESENTATION, 2003–2010

(Millions of U.S. dollars)

	Code	2003	2004	2005	2006	2007	2008	2009	2010
D. OTHER INVESTMENT	4 700	**−85.68**	**−94.32**	**−138.65**	**24.84**	**140.38**	**404.23**	**445.90**	**125.60**
Assets	4 703	**−284.44**	**−282.37**	**−555.72**	**−203.05**	**−277.37**	**−224.51**	**−242.20**	**−246.10**
Trade credits	4 706	....	....	....	....	....	....	....	....
General government	4 707	....	....	....	....	....	....	....	....
of which: Short-term	4 709	....	....	....	....	....	....	....	....
Other sectors	4 710	....	....	....	....	....	....	....	....
of which: Short-term	4 712	....	....	....	....	....	....	....	....
Loans	4 714	−168.20	−98.81	−77.41	....	....	....	....	....
Monetary authorities	4 715	....	....	....	....	....	....	....	....
of which: Short-term	4 718	....	....	....	....	....	....	....	....
General government	4 719	....	....	....	....	....	....	....	....
of which: Short-term	4 721	....	....	....	....	....	....	....	....
Banks	4 722	−168.20	−98.81	−77.41	....	....	....	....	....
of which: Short-term	4 724	....	....	....	....	....	....	....	....
Other sectors	4 725	....	....	....	....	....	....	....	....
of which: Short-term	4 727	....	....	....	....	....	....	....	....
Currency and deposits	4 730	....	....	....	....	....	....	....	....
Monetary authorities	4 731	....	....	....	....	....	....	....	....
General government	4 732	....	....	....	....	....	....	....	....
Banks	4 733	....	....	....	....	....	....	....	....
Other sectors	4 734	....	....	....	....	....	....	....	....
Other assets	4 736	−116.24	−183.55	−478.30	−203.05	−277.37	−224.51	−242.20	−246.10
Monetary authorities	4 737	....	....	....	....	....	....	....	....
of which: Short-term	4 739	....	....	....	....	....	....	....	....
General government	4 740	....	....	....	....	....	....	....	....
of which: Short-term	4 742	....	....	....	....	....	....	....	....
Banks	4 743	....	....	....	....	....	....	....	....
of which: Short-term	4 745	....	....	....	....	....	....	....	....
Other sectors	4 746	−116.24	−183.55	−478.30	−203.05	−277.37	−224.51	−242.20	−246.10
of which: Short-term	4 748	....	....	....	....	....	....	....	....
Liabilities	4 753	**198.76**	**188.05**	**417.07**	**227.89**	**417.75**	**628.75**	**688.10**	**371.69**
Trade credits	4 756	....	....	....	....	....	....	....	....
General government	4 757	....	....	....	....	....	....	....	....
of which: Short-term	4 759	....	....	....	....	....	....	....	....
Other sectors	4 760	....	....	....	....	....	....	....	....
of which: Short-term	4 762	....	....	....	....	....	....	....	....
Loans	4 764	7.58	5.33	3.17	2.50	−4.70	14.83	23.20	40.48
Monetary authorities	4 765	7.58	5.33	3.17	2.50	−4.70	14.83	23.20	40.48
of which: Use of Fund credit and loans from the Fund	4 766	*7.58*	*5.33*	*3.17*	*2.50*	*−4.70*	*14.83*	*23.20*	*40.48*
of which: Short-term	4 768	....	....	....	....	....	....	....	....
General government	4 769	....	....	....	....	....	....	....	....
of which: Short-term	4 771	....	....	....	....	....	....	....	....
Banks	4 772	....	....	....	....	....	....	....	....
of which: Short-term	4 774	....	....	....	....	....	....	....	....
Other sectors	4 775	....	....	....	....	....	....	....	....
of which: Short-term	4 777	....	....	....	....	....	....	....	....
Currency and deposits	4 780	....	....	....	....	....	....	....	....
Monetary authorities	4 781	....	....	....	....	....	....	....	....
General government	4 782	....	....	....	....	....	....	....	....
Banks	4 783	....	....	....	....	....	....	....	....
Other sectors	4 784	....	....	....	....	....	....	....	....
Other liabilities	4 786	191.18	182.72	413.90	225.40	422.45	613.92	664.90	331.21
Monetary authorities	4 787	....	....	....	....	....	....	93.59	....
of which: Short-term	4 789	....	....	....	....	....	....	....	....
General government	4 790	....	....	....	....	....	....	....	....
of which: Short-term	4 792	....	....	....	....	....	....	....	....
Banks	4 793	....	....	....	30.72	122.66	275.11	182.84	14.46
of which: Short-term	4 795	....	....	....	....	....	....	....	....
Other sectors	4 796	191.18	182.72	413.90	194.68	299.79	338.82	388.47	316.75
of which: Short-term	4 798	....	....	....	....	....	....	....	....
E. RESERVE ASSETS	4 802	**−45.87**	**−101.91**	**17.85**	**−92.08**	**−46.25**	**18.59**	**−150.86**	**−103.81**
Monetary gold	4 812								
Special drawing rights	4 811	−.06	3.73	....	−.19	−.03	−1.15	−92.52	30.10
Reserve position in the Fund	4 810	−.01	....	....	....	....	....	....	−.04
Foreign exchange	4 803	.46	−8.24	−9.77	1.91	10.07	−.61	1.13	−5.98
Other claims	4 813	−46.26	−97.40	27.62	−93.79	−56.29	20.35	−59.47	−127.89
NET ERRORS AND OMISSIONS	4 998	**−53.48**	**63.21**	**−85.23**	**35.59**	**81.93**	**104.69**	**−28.51**	**191.81**

Table 1. ANALYTIC PRESENTATION, 2003–2010

(Millions of U.S. dollars)

	Code	2003	2004	2005	2006	2007	2008	2009	2010
A. Current Account[1]	4 993 Z.	**−422**	**−542**	**347**	**1,618**	**1,588**	**1,467**	**−90**	**−1,785**
Goods: exports f.o.b.	2 100 ..	6,446	7,968	10,468	13,176	14,870	19,461	14,412	18,137
Goods: imports f.o.b.	3 100 ..	−6,366	−7,684	−9,709	−11,408	−13,047	−17,912	−14,268	−19,641
Balance on Goods	4 100 ..	*80*	*284*	*758*	*1,768*	*1,823*	*1,549*	*144*	*−1,504*
Services: credit	2 200 ..	881	1,014	1,012	1,037	1,200	1,442	1,337	1,473
Services: debit	3 200 ..	−1,624	−1,968	−2,142	−2,341	−2,572	−3,013	−2,618	−3,010
Balance on Goods and Services	4 991 ..	*−664*	*−670*	*−371*	*464*	*452*	*−23*	*−1,138*	*−3,040*
Income: credit	2 300 ..	27	37	86	165	259	315	106	76
Income: debit	3 300 ..	−1,555	−1,940	−2,029	−2,114	−2,306	−1,771	−1,490	−1,130
Balance on Goods, Services, and Income	4 992 ..	*−2,192*	*−2,572*	*−2,314*	*−1,485*	*−1,595*	*−1,479*	*−2,522*	*−4,095*
Current transfers: credit	2 379 Z.	1,791	2,049	2,781	3,234	3,333	3,107	2,719	2,654
Current transfers: debit	3 379 ..	−22	−18	−120	−130	−149	−162	−287	−345
B. Capital Account[1]	4 994 Z.	**8**	**8**	**16**	**19**	**15**	**20**	**18**	**23**
Capital account: credit	2 994 Z.	17	18	26	29	25	30	29	33
Capital account: debit	3 994 ..	−9	−10	−10	−10	−10	−10	−11	−11
Total, Groups A Plus B	4 981 ..	*−415*	*−534*	*363*	*1,637*	*1,603*	*1,487*	*−73*	*−1,762*
C. Financial Account[1]	4 995 W.	**383**	**239**	**1**	**−1,982**	**−157**	**−368**	**−2,050**	**670**
Direct investment abroad	4 505 ..	....	....	....	....	....	....	....	....
Direct investment in Ecuador	4 555 Z.	872	837	493	271	194	1,006	319	167
Portfolio investment assets	4 602 ..	−312	−191	−228	−641	−116	217	−152	−721
Equity securities	4 610 ..	1	−24	−22	−61	−40	5	−110	−534
Debt securities	4 619 ..	−313	−167	−206	−580	−76	212	−42	−187
Portfolio investment liabilities	4 652 Z.	8	....	594	−743	−3	−4	−2,989	−10
Equity securities	4 660 ..	9	1	2	....	....	1	2	....
Debt securities	4 669 Z.	−1	−1	593	−743	−3	−5	−2,992	−11
Financial derivatives	4 910 ..	....	....	....	....	....	....	....	....
Financial derivatives assets	4 900 ..	....	....	....	....	....	....	....	....
Financial derivatives liabilities	4 905 ..	....	....	....	....	....	....	....	....
Other investment assets	4 703 ..	−190	−893	−729	−1,957	−1,485	−1,398	−1,095	582
Monetary authorities	4 701 ..	298	227	403	−780	−141	−2,739	−2,523	−4,375
General government	4 704 ..	....	....	....	....	−163	−34	−283	−203
Banks	4 705 ..	311	158	238	579	90	−265	241	727
Other sectors	4 728 ..	−799	−1,277	−1,369	−1,756	−1,270	1,640	1,471	4,432
Other investment liabilities	4 753 W.	5	486	−129	1,088	1,252	−189	1,867	652
Monetary authorities	4 753 WA	−2	−40	−83	17	23	17	420	−18
General government	4 753 ZB	−10	−423	−581	4	234	−591	1,482	677
Banks	4 753 ZC	−20	13	−34	49	19	46	−91	82
Other sectors	4 753 ZD	37	935	570	1,018	976	339	55	−88
Total, Groups A Through C	4 983 ..	*−32*	*−295*	*365*	*−345*	*1,446*	*1,118*	*−2,123*	*−1,092*
D. Net Errors and Omissions	4 998 ..	**102**	**687**	**501**	**271**	**−39**	**−183**	**−660**	**−119**
Total, Groups A Through D	4 984 ..	*70*	*392*	*865*	*−74*	*1,407*	*935*	*−2,783*	*−1,211*
E. Reserves and Related Items	4 802 A.	**−70**	**−392**	**−865**	**74**	**−1,407**	**−935**	**2,783**	**1,211**
Reserve assets	4 802 ..	−150	−275	−714	125	−1,495	−954	686	1,169
Use of Fund credit and loans	4 766 ..	48	−112	−196	−58	−23	....	....	....
Exceptional financing	4 920 ..	32	−5	44	7	111	18	2,097	42

[1] Excludes components that have been classified in the categories of Group E.

Table 2. STANDARD PRESENTATION, 2003–2010

(Millions of U.S. dollars)

	Code	2003	2004	2005	2006	2007	2008	2009	2010
CURRENT ACCOUNT.....................	4 993 ..	**−422**	**−542**	**347**	**1,618**	**1,588**	**1,467**	**−90**	**−1,785**
A. GOODS....................................	4 100 ..	**80**	**284**	**758**	**1,768**	**1,823**	**1,549**	**144**	**−1,504**
Credit....................................	2 100 ..	**6,446**	**7,968**	**10,468**	**13,176**	**14,870**	**19,461**	**14,412**	**18,137**
General merchandise: exports f.o.b.	2 110 ..	6,306	7,832	10,247	12,904	14,556	19,070	14,127	17,766
Goods for processing: exports f.o.b.	2 150 ..	....	....	....	....	....	....	....	....
Repairs on goods............................	2 160 ..	5	6	6	6	6	6	6	6
Goods procured in ports by carriers..	2 170 ..	135	130	214	266	308	385	279	365
Nonmonetary gold.........................	2 180 ..	....	....	....	....	....	....	....	....
Debit.....................................	3 100 ..	**−6,366**	**−7,684**	**−9,709**	**−11,408**	**−13,047**	**−17,912**	**−14,268**	**−19,641**
General merchandise: imports f.o.b.	3 110 ..	−6,344	−7,657	−9,687	−11,385	−13,024	−17,889	−14,246	−19,618
Goods for processing: imports f.o.b.	3 150 ..	....	....	....	....	....	....	....	....
Repairs on goods............................	3 160 ..	−5	−10	−6	−6	−6	−6	−6	−6
Goods procured in ports by carriers..	3 170 ..	−17	−17	−17	−17	−17	−17	−17	−17
Nonmonetary gold.........................	3 180 ..	....	....	....	....	....	....	....	....
B. SERVICES...............................	4 200 ..	**−743**	**−954**	**−1,130**	**−1,305**	**−1,371**	**−1,571**	**−1,282**	**−1,536**
Total credit.................................	2 200 ..	*881*	*1,014*	*1,012*	*1,037*	*1,200*	*1,442*	*1,337*	*1,473*
Total debit..................................	3 200 ..	*−1,624*	*−1,968*	*−2,142*	*−2,341*	*−2,572*	*−3,013*	*−2,618*	*−3,010*
Transportation services, credit.........	2 205 ..	**269**	**340**	**335**	**352**	**348**	**367**	**345**	**361**
Passenger...................................	2 850 ..	*2*	*2*	*2*	*2*	*3*	*3*	*4*	*5*
Freight......................................	2 851 ..	*236*	*302*	*292*	*300*	*293*	*298*	*292*	*296*
Other..	2 852 ..	*30*	*36*	*41*	*50*	*51*	*65*	*49*	*60*
Sea transport, passenger.................	2 207 ..	....	....	....	....	....	....	....	....
Sea transport, freight.....................	2 208 ..	220	275	271	276	269	277	268	269
Sea transport, other.......................	2 209 ..	17	24	31	40	43	58	43	54
Air transport, passenger..................	2 211 ..	2	2	2	2	3	3	4	5
Air transport, freight......................	2 212 ..	17	28	21	25	24	22	25	27
Air transport, other........................	2 213 ..	13	12	10	9	8	7	6	6
Other transport, passenger..............	2 215 ..	....	....	....	....	....	....	....	....
Other transport, freight...................	2 216 ..	....	....	....	....	....	....	....	....
Other transport, other....................	2 217 ..	....	....	....	....	....	....	....	....
Transportation services, debit.........	3 205 ..	**−668**	**−911**	**−1,043**	**−1,171**	**−1,327**	**−1,669**	**−1,369**	**−1,731**
Passenger...................................	3 850 ..	*−146*	*−186*	*−215*	*−240*	*−229*	*−248*	*−257*	*−294*
Freight......................................	3 851 ..	*−460*	*−654*	*−722*	*−830*	*−981*	*−1,278*	*−991*	*−1,283*
Other..	3 852 ..	*−62*	*−71*	*−105*	*−101*	*−118*	*−143*	*−121*	*−154*
Sea transport, passenger.................	3 207 ..	....	....	....	....	....	....	....	....
Sea transport, freight.....................	3 208 ..	−358	−530	−573	−677	−829	−1,095	−835	−1,090
Sea transport, other.......................	3 209 ..	−25	−32	−38	−47	−58	−77	−59	−77
Air transport, passenger..................	3 211 ..	−146	−186	−215	−240	−229	−248	−257	−294
Air transport, freight......................	3 212 ..	−62	−80	−98	−100	−94	−117	−93	−118
Air transport, other........................	3 213 ..	−37	−39	−67	−54	−59	−66	−62	−78
Other transport, passenger..............	3 215 ..	....	....	....	....	....	....	....	....
Other transport, freight...................	3 216 ..	−39	−44	−51	−53	−58	−67	−63	−75
Other transport, other....................	3 217 ..	....	....	....	....	....	....	....	....
Travel, credit..............................	2 236 ..	**406**	**462**	**486**	**490**	**623**	**742**	**670**	**781**
Business travel..............................	2 237 ..	96	112	123	126	161	192	173	202
Personal travel..............................	2 240 ..	311	351	363	364	462	550	497	580
Travel, debit...............................	3 236 ..	**−354**	**−391**	**−429**	**−466**	**−504**	**−542**	**−549**	**−568**
Business travel..............................	3 237 ..	−96	−106	−116	−127	−137	−147	−149	−154
Personal travel..............................	3 240 ..	−258	−285	−312	−340	−367	−395	−400	−414
Other services, credit....................	2 200 BA	**206**	**211**	**191**	**194**	**229**	**333**	**321**	**331**
Communications............................	2 245 ..	103	100	80	76	97	196	169	162
Construction................................	2 249 ..	....	....	....	....	....	....	....	....
Insurance....................................	2 253 ..	1	....	1	....	....	....	....	....
Financial.....................................	2 260 ..	....	....	....	....	....	....	....	....
Computer and information...............	2 262 ..	....	....	....	....	....	....	....	....
Royalties and licence fees................	2 266 ..	....	....	....	....	....	....	....	....
Other business services...................	2 268 ..	....	....	....	....	....	....	....	....
Personal, cultural, and recreational.....	2 287 ..	34	36	39	41	44	47	54	66
Government, n.i.e...........................	2 291 ..	69	74	72	78	88	90	98	103
Other services, debit.....................	3 200 BA	**−602**	**−666**	**−671**	**−704**	**−741**	**−802**	**−700**	**−710**
Communications............................	3 245 ..	−5	−6	−6	−7	−7	−28	−26	−24
Construction................................	3 249 ..	....	....	....	....	....	....	....	....
Insurance....................................	3 253 ..	−117	−137	−140	−139	−140	−179	−158	−214
Financial.....................................	3 260 ..	−6	−4	−5	−5	−5	−5	−3	−19
Computer and information...............	3 262 ..	....	....	....	....	....	....	....	....
Royalties and licence fees................	3 266 ..	−43	−43	−43	−44	−45	−47	−47	−54
Other business services...................	3 268 ..	−289	−298	−308	−318	−327	−338	−265	−172
Personal, cultural, and recreational.....	3 287 ..	−92	−98	−106	−116	−126	−137	−151	−168
Government, n.i.e...........................	3 291 ..	−50	−79	−63	−77	−91	−69	−51	−60

Table 2 (Continued). STANDARD PRESENTATION, 2003–2010

(Millions of U.S. dollars)

	Code	2003	2004	2005	2006	2007	2008	2009	2010
C. INCOME	4 300	**−1,528**	**−1,903**	**−1,942**	**−1,949**	**−2,047**	**−1,456**	**−1,384**	**−1,054**
Total credit	2 300	*27*	*37*	*86*	*165*	*259*	*315*	*106*	*76*
Total debit	3 300	*−1,555*	*−1,940*	*−2,029*	*−2,114*	*−2,306*	*−1,771*	*−1,490*	*−1,130*
Compensation of employees, credit	2 310	**6**	**6**	**7**	**6**	**6**	**6**	**7**	**8**
Compensation of employees, debit	3 310	**−7**	**−7**	**−6**	**−5**	**−5**	**−6**	**−6**	**−7**
Investment income, credit	2 320	**21**	**31**	**80**	**159**	**253**	**309**	**99**	**68**
Direct investment income	2 330	....	....	....	....	....	....	....	....
Dividends and distributed branch profits	2 332	....	....	....	....	....	....	....	....
Reinvested earnings and undistributed branch profits	2 333	....	....	....	....	....	....	....	....
Income on debt (interest)	2 334	....	....	....	....	....	....	....	....
Portfolio investment income	2 339	....	....	....	....	....	....	....	....
Income on equity	2 340	....	....	....	....	....	....	....	....
Income on bonds and notes	2 350	....	....	....	....	....	....	....	....
Income on money market instruments	2 360	....	....	....	....	....	....	....	....
Other investment income	2 370	21	31	80	159	253	309	99	68
Investment income, debit	3 320	**−1,548**	**−1,934**	**−2,023**	**−2,109**	**−2,300**	**−1,766**	**−1,483**	**−1,123**
Direct investment income	3 330	−595	−964	−1,004	−977	−1,160	−785	−822	−538
Dividends and distributed branch profits	3 332	−289	−278	−369	−389	−508	−331	−415	−220
Reinvested earnings and undistributed branch profits	3 333	−141	−422	−400	−395	−411	−298	−256	−213
Income on debt (interest)	3 334	−165	−264	−235	−193	−241	−156	−151	−105
Portfolio investment income	3 339	−317	−344	−372	−416	−399	−337	−65	−64
Income on equity	3 340	....	....	....	....	....	....	....	....
Income on bonds and notes	3 350	−317	−344	−372	−416	−399	−337	−65	−64
Income on money market instruments	3 360	....	....	....	....	....	....	....	....
Other investment income	3 370	−636	−626	−647	−715	−741	−643	−596	−521
D. CURRENT TRANSFERS	4 379	**1,769**	**2,030**	**2,661**	**3,104**	**3,184**	**2,946**	**2,432**	**2,310**
Credit	2 379	**1,791**	**2,049**	**2,781**	**3,234**	**3,333**	**3,107**	**2,719**	**2,654**
General government	2 380	130	135	194	221	171	200	206	217
Other sectors	2 390	1,662	1,914	2,587	3,013	3,161	2,907	2,513	2,437
Workers' remittances	2 391	1,627	1,832	2,454	2,928	3,088	2,822	2,495	2,324
Other current transfers	2 392	34	82	133	85	73	85	18	113
Debit	3 379	**−22**	**−18**	**−120**	**−130**	**−149**	**−162**	**−287**	**−345**
General government	3 380	−21	−18	−32	−22	−13	−10	−8	−36
Other sectors	3 390	−1	−1	−88	−108	−136	−152	−279	−308
Workers' remittances	3 391	....	....	−48	−57	−78	−60	−75	−72
Other current transfers	3 392	−1	−1	−40	−51	−58	−92	−204	−236
CAPITAL AND FINANCIAL ACCOUNT	4 996	**320**	**−145**	**−848**	**−1,889**	**−1,549**	**−1,284**	**750**	**1,904**
CAPITAL ACCOUNT	4 994	**61**	**14**	**73**	**26**	**58**	**45**	**1,990**	**42**
Total credit	2 994	*70*	*24*	*83*	*37*	*68*	*56*	*2,001*	*53*
Total debit	3 994	*−9*	*−10*	*−10*	*−10*	*−10*	*−10*	*−11*	*−11*
Capital transfers, credit	2 400	**70**	**24**	**83**	**37**	**68**	**56**	**2,001**	**53**
General government	2 401	70	24	83	37	68	56	2,001	53
Debt forgiveness	2 402	66	20	77	31	60	46	1,994	43
Other capital transfers	2 410	3	4	6	6	8	9	7	10
Other sectors	2 430	....	....	....	....	....	....	....	....
Migrants' transfers	2 431	....	....	....	....	....	....	....	....
Debt forgiveness	2 432	....	....	....	....	....	....	....	....
Other capital transfers	2 440	....	....	....	....	....	....	....	....
Capital transfers, debit	3 400	....	....	....	....	....	....	....	....
General government	3 401	....	....	....	....	....	....	....	....
Debt forgiveness	3 402	....	....	....	....	....	....	....	....
Other capital transfers	3 410	....	....	....	....	....	....	....	....
Other sectors	3 430	....	....	....	....	....	....	....	....
Migrants' transfers	3 431	....	....	....	....	....	....	....	....
Debt forgiveness	3 432	....	....	....	....	....	....	....	....
Other capital transfers	3 440	....	....	....	....	....	....	....	....
Nonproduced nonfinancial assets, credit	2 480	....	....	....	....	....	....	....	....
Nonproduced nonfinancial assets, debit	3 480	**−9**	**−10**	**−10**	**−10**	**−10**	**−10**	**−11**	**−11**

Table 2 (Continued). STANDARD PRESENTATION, 2003–2010

(Millions of U.S. dollars)

	Code	2003	2004	2005	2006	2007	2008	2009	2010
FINANCIAL ACCOUNT	4 995	**260**	**−158**	**−921**	**−1,915**	**−1,607**	**−1,329**	**−1,240**	**1,862**
A. DIRECT INVESTMENT	4 500	**872**	**837**	**493**	**271**	**194**	**1,006**	**319**	**167**
Direct investment abroad	4 505	....	....	....	....	....	....	....	....
Equity capital	4 510	....	....	....	....	....	....	....	....
Claims on affiliated enterprises	4 515	....	....	....	....	....	....	....	....
Liabilities to affiliated enterprises	4 520	....	....	....	....	....	....	....	....
Reinvested earnings	4 525	....	....	....	....	....	....	....	....
Other capital	4 530	....	....	....	....	....	....	....	....
Claims on affiliated enterprises	4 535	....	....	....	....	....	....	....	....
Liabilities to affiliated enterprises	4 540	....	....	....	....	....	....	....	....
Direct investment in Ecuador	4 555	**872**	**837**	**493**	**271**	**194**	**1,006**	**319**	**167**
Equity capital	4 560	207	145	119	136	151	229	278	265
Claims on direct investors	4 565	....	....	....	....	....	....	....	....
Liabilities to direct investors	4 570	207	145	119	136	151	229	278	265
Reinvested earnings	4 575	141	422	400	395	411	298	256	213
Other capital	4 580	524	269	−26	−260	−368	478	−215	−310
Claims on direct investors	4 585	....	....	....	....	....	....	....	....
Liabilities to direct investors	4 590	524	269	−26	−260	−368	478	−215	−310
B. PORTFOLIO INVESTMENT	4 600	**−304**	**−190**	**366**	**−1,384**	**−118**	**213**	**−3,142**	**−731**
Assets	4 602	**−312**	**−191**	**−228**	**−641**	**−116**	**217**	**−152**	**−721**
Equity securities	4 610	1	−24	−22	−61	−40	5	−110	−534
Monetary authorities	4 611	....	....	....	....	....	....	....	....
General government	4 612	1	−24	−22	−61	−40	5	−110	−534
Banks	4 613	....	....	....	....	....	....	....	....
Other sectors	4 614	....	....	....	....	....	....	....	....
Debt securities	4 619	−313	−167	−206	−580	−76	212	−42	−187
Bonds and notes	4 620	−313	−167	−206	−580	−76	212	−42	−187
Monetary authorities	4 621	....	....	....	....	....	....	....	....
General government	4 622	−313	−167	−206	−580	−76	212	−42	−187
Banks	4 623	....	....	....	....	....	....	....	....
Other sectors	4 624	....	....	....	....	....	....	....	....
Money market instruments	4 630	....	....	....	....	....	....	....	....
Monetary authorities	4 631	....	....	....	....	....	....	....	....
General government	4 632	....	....	....	....	....	....	....	....
Banks	4 633	....	....	....	....	....	....	....	....
Other sectors	4 634	....	....	....	....	....	....	....	....
Liabilities	4 652	**8**	....	**594**	**−743**	**−3**	**−4**	**−2,989**	**−10**
Equity securities	4 660	9	1	2	....	....	1	2	....
Banks	4 663	....	....	....	....	....	....	....	....
Other sectors	4 664	9	1	2	....	....	1	2	....
Debt securities	4 669	−1	−1	593	−743	−3	−5	−2,992	−11
Bonds and notes	4 670	−1	−1	593	−743	−3	−5	−2,992	−11
Monetary authorities	4 671	....	....	....	....	....	....	....	....
General government	4 672	−1	−1	593	−743	−3	−5	−2,992	−11
Banks	4 673	....	....	....	....	....	....	....	....
Other sectors	4 674	....	....	....	....	....	....	....	....
Money market instruments	4 680	....	....	....	....	....	....	....	....
Monetary authorities	4 681	....	....	....	....	....	....	....	....
General government	4 682	....	....	....	....	....	....	....	....
Banks	4 683	....	....	....	....	....	....	....	....
Other sectors	4 684	....	....	....	....	....	....	....	....
C. FINANCIAL DERIVATIVES	4 910	....	....	....	....	....	....	....	....
Monetary authorities	4 911	....	....	....	....	....	....	....	....
General government	4 912	....	....	....	....	....	....	....	....
Banks	4 913	....	....	....	....	....	....	....	....
Other sectors	4 914	....	....	....	....	....	....	....	....
Assets	4 900	....	....	....	....	....	....	....	....
Monetary authorities	4 901	....	....	....	....	....	....	....	....
General government	4 902	....	....	....	....	....	....	....	....
Banks	4 903	....	....	....	....	....	....	....	....
Other sectors	4 904	....	....	....	....	....	....	....	....
Liabilities	4 905	....	....	....	....	....	....	....	....
Monetary authorities	4 906	....	....	....	....	....	....	....	....
General government	4 907	....	....	....	....	....	....	....	....
Banks	4 908	....	....	....	....	....	....	....	....
Other sectors	4 909	....	....	....	....	....	....	....	....

2011, International Monetary Fund: *Balance of Payments Statistics Yearbook*

Table 2 (Concluded). STANDARD PRESENTATION, 2003–2010

(Millions of U.S. dollars)

	Code	2003	2004	2005	2006	2007	2008	2009	2010
D. OTHER INVESTMENT	4 700 ..	**−158**	**−530**	**−1,066**	**−928**	**−188**	**−1,594**	**897**	**1,257**
Assets	4 703 ..	**−190**	**−893**	**−729**	**−1,957**	**−1,485**	**−1,398**	**−1,095**	**582**
Trade credits	4 706 ..	−277	−312	−309	−391	−541	−537	−552	−575
General government	4 707 ..	....	....	....	....	−163	−34	−283	−203
of which: Short-term	4 709 ..	....	....	....	....	....	....	....	....
Other sectors	4 710 ..	−277	−312	−309	−391	−378	−503	−269	−372
of which: Short-term	4 712 ..	−277	−312	−309	−391	−378	−503	−269	−372
Loans	4 714 ..	....	....	....	....	....	....	....	....
Monetary authorities	4 715 ..	....	....	....	....	....	....	....	....
of which: Short-term	4 718 ..	....	....	....	....	....	....	....	....
General government	4 719 ..	....	....	....	....	....	....	....	....
of which: Short-term	4 721 ..	....	....	....	....	....	....	....	....
Banks	4 722 ..	....	....	....	....	....	....	....	....
of which: Short-term	4 724 ..	....	....	....	....	....	....	....	....
Other sectors	4 725 ..	....	....	....	....	....	....	....	....
of which: Short-term	4 727 ..	....	....	....	....	....	....	....	....
Currency and deposits	4 730 ..	379	−207	−260	−390	−18	195	−18	1,065
Monetary authorities	4 731 ..	438	284	513	164	−726	−2,382	−2,718	−4,340
General government	4 732 ..	....	29	−109	409	770	−14	....	268
Banks	4 733 ..	462	446	396	403	830	−117	632	640
Other sectors	4 734 ..	−521	−965	−1,061	−1,365	−893	2,708	2,069	4,497
Other assets	4 736 ..	−291	−374	−160	−1,177	−926	−1,055	−525	91
Monetary authorities	4 737 ..	−140	−57	−111	−945	585	−356	196	−35
of which: Short-term	4 739 ..	....	....	....	....	....	....	....	....
General government	4 740 ..	....	−29	109	−409	−770	14	....	−268
of which: Short-term	4 742 ..	....	....	....	....	....	....	....	....
Banks	4 743 ..	−151	−289	−158	176	−740	−148	−391	87
of which: Short-term	4 745 ..	....	....	....	....	....	....	....	....
Other sectors	4 746 ..	....	....	....	....	....	−565	−329	307
of which: Short-term	4 748 ..	....	....	....	....	....	....	....	....
Liabilities	4 753 ..	**32**	**363**	**−337**	**1,029**	**1,297**	**−196**	**1,991**	**675**
Trade credits	4 756 ..	106	342	312	362	514	782	1,311	....
General government	4 757 ..	1	1	−10	−8	−9	−3	799	−499
of which: Short-term	4 759 ..	....	....	....	....	....	....	....	....
Other sectors	4 760 ..	106	342	322	369	524	786	512	500
of which: Short-term	4 762 ..	....	....	....	....	....	....	....	....
Loans	4 764 ..	−21	−26	−578	589	666	−1,037	224	675
Monetary authorities	4 765 ..	1	−176	−229	−59	−23	−1	−1	−1
of which: Use of Fund credit and loans from the Fund..	4 766 ..	48	−112	−196	−58	−23	....	....	....
of which: Short-term	4 768 ..	−47	−64	−34	−1	....	−1	−1	−1
General government	4 769 ..	68	−424	−571	12	243	−588	683	1,176
of which: Short-term	4 771 ..	....	....	....	....	....	....	....	....
Banks	4 772 ..	−21	−20	−25	−13	−7	−2	−2	88
of which: Short-term	4 774 ..	....	....	....	....	....	....	....	....
Other sectors	4 775 ..	−69	594	248	649	452	−446	−457	−588
of which: Short-term	4 777 ..	....	....	....	....	....	....	....	....
Currency and deposits	4 780 ..	46	58	−58	79	49	65	−67	−24
Monetary authorities	4 781 ..	45	25	−49	17	24	17	22	−18
General government	4 782 ..	....	....	....	....	....	....	....	....
Banks	4 783 ..	1	33	−9	62	25	48	−89	−6
Other sectors	4 784 ..	....	....	....	....	....	....	....	....
Other liabilities	4 786 ..	−99	−11	−13	−1	68	−7	524	23
Monetary authorities	4 787 ..	....	....	....	....	....	....	399	....
of which: Short-term	4 789 ..	....	....	....	....	....	....	....	....
General government	4 790 ..	−89	−9	−12	−1	69	−6	125	23
of which: Short-term	4 792 ..	−89	−9	−12	−1	69	−6	125	23
Banks	4 793 ..	−11	−2	−1	....	−1	....	....	....
of which: Short-term	4 795 ..	−11	−2	−1	....	−1	....	....	....
Other sectors	4 796 ..	....	....	....	....	....	−1	....	....
of which: Short-term	4 798 ..	....	....	....	....	....	−1	....	....
E. RESERVE ASSETS	4 802 ..	**−150**	**−275**	**−714**	**125**	**−1,495**	**−954**	**686**	**1,169**
Monetary gold	4 812 ..	−55	−20	−65	−101	−170	−30	−184	−269
Special drawing rights	4 811 ..	1	−55	32	15	−16	−3	4	1
Reserve position in the Fund	4 810 ..	....	....	....	....	....	....	....	....
Foreign exchange	4 803 ..	−94	−196	−684	212	−1,307	−949	865	1,459
Other claims	4 813 ..	−3	−5	3	−1	−2	28	1	−23
NET ERRORS AND OMISSIONS	4 998 ..	**102**	**687**	**501**	**271**	**−39**	**−183**	**−660**	**−119**

Table 3. INTERNATIONAL INVESTMENT POSITION (End-period stocks), 2003–2010

(Millions of U.S. dollars)

	Code	2003	2004	2005	2006	2007	2008	2009	2010
ASSETS	8 995 C.	**4,369**	**5,730**	**7,396**	**13,187**	**16,386**	**18,514**	**19,080**	**18,040**
Direct investment abroad	8 505	....	....	....	....	....	....	....	....
Equity capital and reinvested earnings	8 506	....	....	....	....	....	....	....	....
Claims on affiliated enterprises	8 507	....	....	....	....	....	....	....	....
Liabilities to affiliated enterprises	8 508	....	....	....	....	....	....	....	....
Other capital	8 530	....	....	....	....	....	....	....	....
Claims on affiliated enterprises	8 535	....	....	....	....	....	....	....	....
Liabilities to affiliated enterprises	8 540	....	....	....	....	....	....	....	....
Portfolio investment	8 602	**740**	**931**	**1,159**	**1,800**	**1,915**	**1,699**	**1,851**	**2,572**
Equity securities	8 610	135	159	182	....	....	....	....	....
Monetary authorities	8 611	....	....	....	....	....	....	....	....
General government	8 612	....	....	....	....	....	....	....	....
Banks	8 613	135	159	182	....	....	....	....	....
Other sectors	8 614	....	....	....	....	....	....	....	....
Debt securities	8 619	605	771	977	....	....	....	....	....
Bonds and notes	8 620	605	771	977	....	....	....	....	....
Monetary authorities	8 621	....	....	....	....	....	....	....	....
General government	8 622	....	....	....	....	....	....	....	....
Banks	8 623	605	771	977	....	....	....	....	....
Other sectors	8 624	....	....	....	....	....	....	....	....
Money market instruments	8 630	....	....	....	....	....	....	....	....
Monetary authorities	8 631	....	....	....	....	....	....	....	....
General government	8 632	....	....	....	....	....	....	....	....
Banks	8 633	....	....	....	....	....	....	....	....
Other sectors	8 634	....	....	....	....	....	....	....	....
Financial derivatives	8 900	....	....	....	....	....	....	....	....
Monetary authorities	8 901	....	....	....	....	....	....	....	....
General government	8 902	....	....	....	....	....	....	....	....
Banks	8 903	....	....	....	....	....	....	....	....
Other sectors	8 904	....	....	....	....	....	....	....	....
Other investment	8 703	**2,469**	**3,361**	**4,090**	**9,364**	**10,950**	**12,342**	**13,437**	**12,847**
Trade credits	8 706	....	....	....	....	....	....	....	....
General government	8 707	....	....	....	....	....	....	....	....
of which: Short-term	8 709	....	....	....	....	....	....	....	....
Other sectors	8 710	....	....	....	....	....	....	....	....
of which: Short-term	8 712	....	....	....	....	....	....	....	....
Loans	8 714	....	....	....	....	....	....	....	....
Monetary authorities	8 715	....	....	....	....	....	....	....	....
of which: Short-term	8 718	....	....	....	....	....	....	....	....
General government	8 719	....	....	....	....	....	....	....	....
of which: Short-term	8 721	....	....	....	....	....	....	....	....
Banks	8 722	....	....	....	....	....	....	....	....
of which: Short-term	8 724	....	....	....	....	....	....	....	....
Other sectors	8 725	....	....	....	....	....	....	....	....
of which: Short-term	8 727	....	....	....	....	....	....	....	....
Currency and deposits	8 730	2,469	3,361	4,090	....	....	....	....	....
Monetary authorities	8 731	....	....	....	....	....	....	....	....
General government	8 732	....	....	....	....	....	....	....	....
Banks	8 733	2,469	3,361	4,090	....	....	....	....	....
Other sectors	8 734	....	....	....	....	....	....	....	....
Other assets	8 736	....	....	....	....	....	....	....	....
Monetary authorities	8 737	....	....	....	....	....	....	....	....
of which: Short-term	8 739	....	....	....	....	....	....	....	....
General government	8 740	....	....	....	....	....	....	....	....
of which: Short-term	8 742	....	....	....	....	....	....	....	....
Banks	8 743	....	....	....	....	....	....	....	....
of which: Short-term	8 745	....	....	....	....	....	....	....	....
Other sectors	8 746	....	....	....	....	....	....	....	....
of which: Short-term	8 748	....	....	....	....	....	....	....	....
Reserve assets	8 802	**1,161**	**1,438**	**2,147**	**2,023**	**3,521**	**4,473**	**3,792**	**2,622**
Monetary gold	8 812	348	368	433	534	704	735	919	1,187
Special drawing rights	8 811	1	56	22	8	24	26	26	25
Reserve position in the Fund	8 810	25	27	25	26	27	26	27	26
Foreign exchange	8 803	789	984	1,668	1,456	2,763	3,711	2,847	1,387
Other claims	8 813	−2	3	−1	....	2	−26	−27	−4

Table 3 (Concluded). INTERNATIONAL INVESTMENT POSITION (End-period stocks), 2003–2010

(Millions of U.S. dollars)

	Code	2003	2004	2005	2006	2007	2008	2009	2010
LIABILITIES	8 995 D.	**24,121**	**25,394**	**26,215**	**26,753**	**28,261**	**29,066**	**28,309**	**29,133**
Direct investment in Ecuador	8 555	**8,530**	**9,367**	**9,861**	**10,132**	**10,326**	**11,332**	**11,651**	**11,818**
Equity capital and reinvested earnings	8 556	8,530	9,367	9,861	10,132	10,326	11,332	11,651	11,818
Claims on direct investors	8 557	....	....	....	....	....	....	....	....
Liabilities to direct investors	8 558	8,530	9,367	9,861	10,132	10,326	11,332	11,651	11,818
Other capital	8 580	....	....	....	....	....	....	....	....
Claims on direct investors	8 585	....	....	....	....	....	....	....	....
Liabilities to direct investors	8 590	....	....	....	....	....	....	....	....
Portfolio investment	8 652	**4,142**	**4,143**	**4,791**	**4,048**	**4,045**	**4,042**	**1,052**	**1,042**
Equity securities	8 660	66	67	69	69	69	70	73	73
Banks	8 663	....	....	....	....	....	....	....	....
Other sectors	8 664	66	67	69	....	....	....	....	....
Debt securities	8 669	4,077	4,076	4,723	3,980	3,976	3,971	979	969
Bonds and notes	8 670	4,077	4,076	4,723	....	....	....	....	....
Monetary authorities	8 671	....	....	....					
General government	8 672	4,077	4,076	4,723	....	....	....	....	....
Banks	8 673	....	....	....					
Other sectors	8 674	....	....	....					
Money market instruments	8 680	....	....	....					
Monetary authorities	8 681	....	....	....					
General government	8 682	....	....	....					
Banks	8 683	....	....	....					
Other sectors	8 684	....	....	....					
Financial derivatives	8 905	....	....	....	....	....	....	....	....
Monetary authorities	8 906	....	....	....	....	....	....	....	....
General government	8 907	....	....	....	....	....	....	....	....
Banks	8 908	....	....	....	....	....	....	....	....
Other sectors	8 909	....	....	....	....	....	....	....	....
Other investment	8 753	**11,449**	**11,884**	**11,563**	**12,573**	**13,889**	**13,693**	**15,606**	**16,272**
Trade credits	8 756	255	597	909	1,271	1,786	2,569	3,880	3,880
General government	8 757	....	....	....	....	....	....	....	....
of which: Short-term	8 759	....	....	....	....	....	....	....	....
Other sectors	8 760	255	597	909	....	....	....	....	....
of which: Short-term	8 762	....	....	....	....	....	....	....	....
Loans	8 764	10,403	10,449	9,889	10,457	11,141	10,104	10,327	11,002
Monetary authorities	8 765	442	278	33	....	....	....	....	....
of which: Use of Fund credit and loans from the Fund	8 766	*390*	*290*	*78*	*23*	....	....	....	....
of which: Short-term	8 768	*53*	*−12*	*−46*	....	....	....	....	....
General government	8 769	5,537	5,113	4,542	....	....	....	....	....
of which: Short-term	8 771	....	....	....	....	....	....	....	....
Banks	8 772	393	374	349	....	....	....	....	....
of which: Short-term	8 774	....	....	....	....	....	....	....	....
Other sectors	8 775	4,030	4,684	4,966	....	....	....	....	....
of which: Short-term	8 777	*1,647*	*1,707*	*1,741*	....	....	....	....	....
Currency and deposits	8 780	765	823	765	844	893	958	891	868
Monetary authorities	8 781	....	....	....	....	....	....	....	....
General government	8 782	....	....	....	....	....	....	....	....
Banks	8 783	765	823	765	....	....	....	....	....
Other sectors	8 784	....	....	....	....	....	....	....	....
Other liabilities	8 786	26	15	1	1	69	62	508	522
Monetary authorities	8 787	−4	−4	−4	....	....	....	....	....
of which: Short-term	8 789	*−4*	*−4*	*−4*	....	....	....	....	....
General government	8 790	82	73	61	....	....	....	....	....
of which: Short-term	8 792	*82*	*73*	*61*	....	....	....	....	....
Banks	8 793	−52	−54	−56	....	....	....	....	....
of which: Short-term	8 795	*−52*	*−54*	*−56*	....	....	....	....	....
Other sectors	8 796	1	....	....	....	....	....	....	....
of which: Short-term	8 798	*1*	....	....	....	....	....	....	....
NET INTERNATIONAL INVESTMENT POSITION	8 995	**−19,752**	**−19,664**	**−18,819**	**−13,566**	**−11,874**	**−10,552**	**−9,230**	**−11,092**

Table 1. ANALYTIC PRESENTATION, 2003–2010

(Millions of U.S. dollars)

	Code	2003	2004	2005	2006	2007	2008	2009	2010
A. Current Account[1]	4 993 Z.	**3,743**	**3,922**	**2,103**	**2,635**	**412**	**−1,415**	**−3,349**	**−4,504**
Goods: exports f.o.b.	2 100 ..	8,987	12,320	16,073	20,546	24,455	29,849	23,089	25,024
Goods: imports f.o.b.	3 100 ..	−13,189	−18,895	−23,818	−28,984	−39,354	−49,608	−39,907	−45,145
Balance on Goods	4 100 ..	*−4,201*	*−6,576*	*−7,745*	*−8,438*	*−14,900*	*−19,759*	*−16,818*	*−20,120*
Services: credit	2 200 ..	11,073	14,197	14,643	16,135	19,943	24,912	21,520	23,807
Services: debit	3 200 ..	−6,474	−8,020	−10,508	−11,569	−14,342	−17,615	−13,935	−14,718
Balance on Goods and Services	4 991 ..	*398*	*−399*	*−3,611*	*−3,873*	*−9,299*	*−12,462*	*−9,233*	*−11,031*
Income: credit	2 300 ..	578	572	1,425	2,560	3,309	3,065	992	534
Income: debit	3 300 ..	−832	−818	−1,460	−1,822	−1,921	−1,776	−3,068	−6,446
Balance on Goods, Services, and Income	4 992 ..	*145*	*−645*	*−3,645*	*−3,134*	*−7,911*	*−11,173*	*−11,309*	*−16,943*
Current transfers: credit	2 379 Z.	3,708	4,615	5,831	5,933	8,562	10,072	8,305	12,836
Current transfers: debit	3 379 ..	−109	−48	−82	−163	−240	−314	−345	−397
B. Capital Account[1]	4 994 Z.	....	....	**−40**	**−36**	**2**	**−1**	**−19**	**−39**
Capital account: credit	2 994 Z.	....	....	....	5	5	1	1	....
Capital account: debit	3 994 ..	....	....	−40	−41	−3	−1	−20	−40
Total, Groups A Plus B	4 981 ..	*3,743*	*3,922*	*2,063*	*2,600*	*414*	*−1,415*	*−3,368*	*−4,543*
C. Financial Account[1]	4 995 W.	**−5,725**	**−4,461**	**5,591**	**−297**	**3,023**	**5,274**	**1,336**	**6,470**
Direct investment abroad	4 505 ..	−21	−159	−92	−148	−665	−1,920	−571	−1,176
Direct investment in Egypt	4 555 Z.	237	1,253	5,376	10,043	11,578	9,495	6,712	6,386
Portfolio investment assets	4 602 ..	−25	324	−60	−703	−846	−623	−267	−445
Equity securities	4 610 ..	−25	324	−60	−703	−846	−623	−267	−445
Debt securities	4 619 ..	....	....	....	....	....	....	....	....
Portfolio investment liabilities	4 652 Z.	−18	−85	3,528	3	−2,728	−7,027	−260	10,887
Equity securities	4 660 ..	37	26	729	502	−3,199	−674	393	1,724
Debt securities	4 669 Z.	−55	−111	2,799	−499	471	−6,353	−653	9,162
Financial derivatives	4 910 ..	....	....	....	....	....	....	....	....
Financial derivatives assets	4 900 ..	....	....	....	....	....	....	....	....
Financial derivatives liabilities	4 905 ..	....	....	....	....	....	....	....	....
Other investment assets	4 703 ..	−4,651	−5,888	−3,246	−9,743	−5,498	4,633	−5,879	−11,185
Monetary authorities	4 701 ..	−38	−4	....	−100	−101	17	−71	24
General government	4 704 ..	....	....	....	....	....	....	....	....
Banks	4 705 ..	−1,682	−3,215	−2,765	−8,573	−4,585	10,123	−2,407	−6,291
Other sectors	4 728 ..	−2,931	−2,669	−481	−1,070	−812	−5,507	−3,401	−4,919
Other investment liabilities	4 753 W.	−1,248	94	85	252	1,182	717	1,601	2,003
Monetary authorities	4 753 WA	6	−16	−2	3	16	15	1,193	−14
General government	4 753 ZB	−1,673	−1,740	−1,901	−1,697	−1,792	−1,992	−2,025	−2,151
Banks	4 753 ZC	−601	−326	128	−300	930	1,107	−385	2,203
Other sectors	4 753 ZD	1,020	2,175	1,860	2,246	2,028	1,588	2,818	1,965
Total, Groups A Through C	4 983 ..	*−1,982*	*−539*	*7,653*	*2,303*	*3,436*	*3,859*	*−2,033*	*1,927*
D. Net Errors and Omissions	4 998 ..	**1,575**	**−45**	**−2,427**	**634**	**251**	**−2,928**	**398**	**−2,145**
Total, Groups A Through D	4 984 ..	*−407*	*−584*	*5,226*	*2,937*	*3,687*	*931*	*−1,635*	*−218*
E. Reserves and Related Items	4 802 A.	**407**	**584**	**−5,226**	**−2,937**	**−3,687**	**−931**	**1,635**	**218**
Reserve assets	4 802 ..	−395	−684	−6,319	−3,608	−5,475	−1,755	156	−1,276
Use of Fund credit and loans	4 766 ..	....	....	....	....	....	....	....	....
Exceptional financing	4 920 ..	801	1,269	1,093	671	1,788	824	1,478	1,495
Conversion rates: Egyptian pounds per U.S. dollar	0 101 ..	**5.8509**	**6.1962**	**5.7788**	**5.7332**	**5.6354**	**5.4325**	**5.5446**	**5.6219**

[1] Excludes components that have been classified in the categories of Group E.

Table 2. STANDARD PRESENTATION, 2003–2010

(Millions of U.S. dollars)

	Code	2003	2004	2005	2006	2007	2008	2009	2010
CURRENT ACCOUNT	4 993	**3,743**	**3,922**	**2,103**	**2,635**	**412**	**−1,415**	**−3,349**	**−4,504**
A. GOODS	4 100	**−4,201**	**−6,576**	**−7,745**	**−8,438**	**−14,900**	**−19,759**	**−16,818**	**−20,120**
Credit	2 100	**8,987**	**12,320**	**16,073**	**20,546**	**24,455**	**29,849**	**23,089**	**25,024**
General merchandise: exports f.o.b.	2 110	8,368	11,478	15,238	19,590	23,363	28,139	22,323	23,940
Goods for processing: exports f.o.b.	2 150	....	....	....	....	....	....	....	....
Repairs on goods	2 160	....	....	....	....	....	....	....	....
Goods procured in ports by carriers	2 170	620	842	836	956	1,092	1,710	766	1,084
Nonmonetary gold	2 180	....	....	....	....	....	....	....	....
Debit	3 100	**−13,189**	**−18,895**	**−23,818**	**−28,984**	**−39,354**	**−49,608**	**−39,907**	**−45,145**
General merchandise: imports f.o.b.	3 110	−13,105	−18,834	−23,676	−28,843	−39,160	−49,105	−39,602	−44,749
Goods for processing: imports f.o.b.	3 150	....	....	....	....	....	....	....	....
Repairs on goods	3 160	....	....	....	....	....	....	....	....
Goods procured in ports by carriers	3 170	−84	−61	−143	−140	−195	−503	−305	−396
Nonmonetary gold	3 180	....	....	....	....	....	....	....	....
B. SERVICES	4 200	**4,599**	**6,177**	**4,135**	**4,565**	**5,601**	**7,297**	**7,585**	**9,089**
Total credit	2 200	*11,073*	*14,197*	*14,643*	*16,135*	*19,943*	*24,912*	*21,520*	*23,807*
Total debit	3 200	*−6,474*	*−8,020*	*−10,508*	*−11,569*	*−14,342*	*−17,615*	*−13,935*	*−14,718*
Transportation services, credit	2 205	**3,299**	**4,016**	**4,746**	**5,489**	**6,949**	**8,160**	**6,698**	**7,916**
Passenger	2 850	*120*	*203*	*355*	*542*	*1,024*	*1,119*	*1,002*	*1,105*
Freight	2 851	*350*	*398*	*522*	*674*	*610*	*915*	*782*	*1,394*
Other	2 852	*2,829*	*3,415*	*3,869*	*4,273*	*5,315*	*6,126*	*4,915*	*5,416*
Sea transport, passenger	2 207	1	2	4	21	22	2	27	5
Sea transport, freight	2 208	347	393	486	651	578	774	624	1,245
Sea transport, other	2 209	....	....	....	....	....	....	....	....
Air transport, passenger	2 211	119	201	351	522	1,002	1,117	975	1,100
Air transport, freight	2 212	3	5	36	22	32	142	158	149
Air transport, other	2 213	....	....	....	....	....	....	....	....
Other transport, passenger	2 215	....	....	....	....	....	....	....	....
Other transport, freight	2 216	....	....	....	....	....	....	....	....
Other transport, other	2 217	2,829	3,415	3,869	4,273	5,315	6,126	4,915	5,416
Transportation services, debit	3 205	**−2,013**	**−2,986**	**−3,731**	**−4,525**	**−6,017**	**−7,321**	**−5,701**	**−6,575**
Passenger	3 850	*−144*	*−286*	*−303*	*−372*	*−440*	*−475*	*−403*	*−456*
Freight	3 851	*−1,783*	*−2,632*	*−3,222*	*−3,865*	*−5,129*	*−6,449*	*−5,053*	*−5,827*
Other	3 852	*−86*	*−69*	*−207*	*−288*	*−448*	*−398*	*−245*	*−293*
Sea transport, passenger	3 207	−2	−2	−2	−1	−3	−10	−5	−1
Sea transport, freight	3 208	−1,774	−2,619	−3,212	−3,843	−5,094	−6,384	−5,009	−5,804
Sea transport, other	3 209	−2	−2	−1	−2	−2	−5	−7	−17
Air transport, passenger	3 211	−143	−284	−301	−371	−437	−465	−398	−455
Air transport, freight	3 212	−3	−3	−1	−8	−22	−44	−23	−9
Air transport, other	3 213	−84	−29	−140	−72	−253	−223	−210	−232
Other transport, passenger	3 215	....	....	....	....	....	....	....	....
Other transport, freight	3 216	−6	−9	−9	−14	−13	−21	−21	−14
Other transport, other	3 217	....	−39	−66	−214	−194	−170	−29	−44
Travel, credit	2 236	**4,584**	**6,125**	**6,851**	**7,591**	**9,303**	**10,985**	**10,755**	**12,528**
Business travel	2 237	....	....	....	....	....	....	....	....
Personal travel	2 240	....	....	....	....	....	....	....	....
Travel, debit	3 236	**−1,321**	**−1,257**	**−1,629**	**−1,784**	**−2,446**	**−2,915**	**−2,538**	**−2,240**
Business travel	3 237	−89	−83	−80	−79	−102	−80	−120	−168
Personal travel	3 240	−1,232	−1,175	−1,549	−1,705	−2,344	−2,835	−2,419	−2,072
Other services, credit	2 200 BA	**3,190**	**4,055**	**3,046**	**3,055**	**3,691**	**5,767**	**4,066**	**3,363**
Communications	2 245	309	405	362	496	757	1,611	842	844
Construction	2 249	222	406	503	430	984	1,345	676	711
Insurance	2 253	37	38	58	36	82	216	75	97
Financial	2 260	80	74	137	149	86	269	196	180
Computer and information	2 262	23	33	25	52	88	219	171	152
Royalties and licence fees	2 266	121	100	136	138	122	....	....	....
Other business services	2 268	2,092	2,780	1,549	1,337	1,197	1,789	1,787	1,092
Personal, cultural, and recreational	2 287	72	69	83	116	92	74	103	99
Government, n.i.e.	2 291	236	150	194	301	284	244	218	189
Other services, debit	3 200 BA	**−3,140**	**−3,776**	**−5,148**	**−5,260**	**−5,879**	**−7,378**	**−5,696**	**−5,903**
Communications	3 245	−148	−224	−406	−309	−471	−785	−475	−338
Construction	3 249	−108	−171	−231	−166	−257	−335	−262	−386
Insurance	3 253	−423	−588	−781	−978	−1,282	−1,584	−1,355	−1,459
Financial	3 260	−26	−27	−198	−67	−85	−72	−91	−34
Computer and information	3 262	−27	−24	−27	−30	−36	−79	−134	−161
Royalties and licence fees	3 266	−165	−108	−182	−159	−241	−322	−285	−226
Other business services	3 268	−1,793	−2,069	−2,301	−2,232	−2,224	−2,843	−1,860	−1,490
Personal, cultural, and recreational	3 287	−15	−15	−22	−39	−29	−80	−66	−82
Government, n.i.e.	3 291	−436	−550	−1,001	−1,281	−1,255	−1,280	−1,170	−1,727

Table 2 (Continued). STANDARD PRESENTATION, 2003–2010

(Millions of U.S. dollars)

	Code	2003	2004	2005	2006	2007	2008	2009	2010
C. INCOME	4 300	**−253**	**−246**	**−35**	**738**	**1,388**	**1,289**	**−2,076**	**−5,912**
Total credit	2 300	*578*	*572*	*1,425*	*2,560*	*3,309*	*3,065*	*992*	*534*
Total debit	3 300	*−832*	*−818*	*−1,460*	*−1,822*	*−1,921*	*−1,776*	*−3,068*	*−6,446*
Compensation of employees, credit	2 310	....	....	....	....	....	....	....	....
Compensation of employees, debit	3 310	....	....	....	....	....	....	....	....
Investment income, credit	2 320	**578**	**572**	**1,425**	**2,560**	**3,309**	**3,065**	**992**	**534**
Direct investment income	2 330	76	16	92	110	46	61	79	169
Dividends and distributed branch profits	2 332	76	16	92	110	46	61	79	169
Reinvested earnings and undistributed branch profits	2 333	....	....	....	....	....	....	....	....
Income on debt (interest)	2 334	....	....	....	....	....	....	....	....
Portfolio investment income	2 339	91	92	132	152	679	1,118	691	199
Income on equity	2 340	....	....	....	....	....	....	....	....
Income on bonds and notes	2 350	91	92	132	152	679	1,118	691	199
Income on money market instruments	2 360	....	....	....	....	....	....	....	....
Other investment income	2 370	412	465	1,201	2,298	2,585	1,886	221	167
Investment income, debit	3 320	**−832**	**−818**	**−1,460**	**−1,822**	**−1,921**	**−1,776**	**−3,068**	**−6,446**
Direct investment income	3 330	−47	−56	−647	−915	−1,015	−680	−2,101	−5,268
Dividends and distributed branch profits	3 332	−47	−56	−647	−843	−914	−290	−1,093	−3,909
Reinvested earnings and undistributed branch profits	3 333	....	....	....	−72	−101	−390	−1,008	−1,360
Income on debt (interest)	3 334	....	....	....	....	....	....	....	....
Portfolio investment income	3 339	−65	−61	−153	−209	−180	−365	−229	−560
Income on equity	3 340	....	....	....	....	....	....	....	....
Income on bonds and notes	3 350	−65	−61	−153	−209	−180	−365	−229	−560
Income on money market instruments	3 360	....	....	....	....	....	....	....	....
Other investment income	3 370	−720	−702	−661	−699	−726	−732	−739	−617
D. CURRENT TRANSFERS	4 379	**3,599**	**4,567**	**5,748**	**5,770**	**8,322**	**9,758**	**7,960**	**12,439**
Credit	2 379	**3,708**	**4,615**	**5,831**	**5,933**	**8,562**	**10,072**	**8,305**	**12,836**
General government	2 380	696	1,218	766	541	824	1,324	1,086	298
Other sectors	2 390	3,012	3,397	5,064	5,392	7,738	8,749	7,219	12,538
Workers' remittances	2 391	2,961	3,341	5,017	5,330	7,656	8,694	7,150	12,453
Other current transfers	2 392	51	56	47	63	82	55	70	85
Debit	3 379	**−109**	**−48**	**−82**	**−163**	**−240**	**−314**	**−345**	**−397**
General government	3 380	−29	−32	−25	−28	−60	−63	−75	−79
Other sectors	3 390	−80	−16	−57	−135	−180	−250	−271	−318
Workers' remittances	3 391	−79	−13	−57	−135	−180	−241	−255	−305
Other current transfers	3 392	−1	−3	....	....	....	−9	−16	−13
CAPITAL AND FINANCIAL ACCOUNT	4 996	**−5,318**	**−3,876**	**324**	**−3,269**	**−662**	**4,342**	**2,951**	**6,649**
CAPITAL ACCOUNT	4 994	....	....	**−40**	**−36**	**2**	**−1**	**−19**	**−39**
Total credit	2 994	....	....	....	*5*	*5*	*1*	*1*	....
Total debit	3 994	....	....	*−40*	*−41*	*−3*	*−1*	*−20*	*−40*
Capital transfers, credit	2 400	....	....	....	**5**	**5**	**1**	**1**	....
General government	2 401	....	....	....	....	....	....	....	....
Debt forgiveness	2 402	....	....	....	....	....	....	....	....
Other capital transfers	2 410	....	....	....	....	....	....	....	....
Other sectors	2 430	....	....	....	5	5	1	1	....
Migrants' transfers	2 431	....	....	....	....	....	....	....	....
Debt forgiveness	2 432	....	....	....	....	....	....	....	....
Other capital transfers	2 440	....	....	....	5	5	1	1	....
Capital transfers, debit	3 400	....	....	**−40**	**−41**	**−3**	**−1**	**−20**	**−40**
General government	3 401	....	....	−40	−40	....	....	....	....
Debt forgiveness	3 402	....	....	....	....	....	....	....	....
Other capital transfers	3 410	....	....	−40	−40	....	....	....	....
Other sectors	3 430	....	....	....	−1	−3	−1	−20	−40
Migrants' transfers	3 431	....	....	....	....	....	....	....	....
Debt forgiveness	3 432	....	....	....	....	....	....	....	....
Other capital transfers	3 440	....	....	....	−1	−3	−1	−20	−40
Nonproduced nonfinancial assets, credit	2 480	....	....	....	....	....	....	....	....
Nonproduced nonfinancial assets, debit	3 480	....	....	....	....	....	....	....	....

Table 2 (Continued). STANDARD PRESENTATION, 2003–2010

(Millions of U.S. dollars)

	Code	2003	2004	2005	2006	2007	2008	2009	2010
FINANCIAL ACCOUNT............................	4 995 ..	**−5,318**	**−3,876**	**364**	**−3,234**	**−664**	**4,343**	**2,970**	**6,688**
A. DIRECT INVESTMENT...........................	4 500 ..	**217**	**1,094**	**5,284**	**9,894**	**10,913**	**7,574**	**6,140**	**5,210**
Direct investment abroad.........................	4 505 ..	**−21**	**−159**	**−92**	**−148**	**−665**	**−1,920**	**−571**	**−1,176**
Equity capital.................................	4 510 ..	....	....	....	....	....	....	....	....
Claims on affiliated enterprises.................	4 515 ..	....	....	....	....	....	....	....	....
Liabilities to affiliated enterprises.............	4 520 ..	....	....	....	....	....	....	....	....
Reinvested earnings............................	4 525 ..	....	....	....	....	....	....	....	....
Other capital.................................	4 530 ..	−21	−159	−92	−148	−665	−1,920	−571	−1,176
Claims on affiliated enterprises.................	4 535 ..	−21	−159	−92	−148	−665	−1,920	−571	−1,176
Liabilities to affiliated enterprises.............	4 540 ..	....	....	....	....	....	....	....	....
Direct investment in Egypt........................	4 555 ..	**237**	**1,253**	**5,376**	**10,043**	**11,578**	**9,495**	**6,712**	**6,386**
Equity capital.................................	4 560 ..	....	....	....	....	....	....	....	....
Claims on direct investors.....................	4 565 ..	....	....	....	....	....	....	....	....
Liabilities to direct investors..................	4 570 ..	....	....	....	....	....	....	....	....
Reinvested earnings............................	4 575 ..	....	....	....	72	101	390	1,008	1,360
Other capital.................................	4 580 ..	237	1,253	5,376	9,971	11,478	9,105	5,704	5,026
Claims on direct investors.....................	4 585 ..	....	....	....	....	....	....	....	....
Liabilities to direct investors..................	4 590 ..	237	1,253	5,376	9,971	11,478	9,105	5,704	5,026
B. PORTFOLIO INVESTMENT.........................	4 600 ..	**−43**	**239**	**3,468**	**−700**	**−3,574**	**−7,650**	**−527**	**10,442**
Assets..	4 602 ..	**−25**	**324**	**−60**	**−703**	**−846**	**−623**	**−267**	**−445**
Equity securities..............................	4 610 ..	−25	324	−60	−703	−846	−623	−267	−445
Monetary authorities..........................	4 611 ..	....	....	....	....	....	....	....	....
General government...........................	4 612 ..	....	....	....	....	....	....	....	....
Banks.....................................	4 613 ..	....	....	....	....	....	....	....	....
Other sectors...............................	4 614 ..	−25	324	−60	−703	−846	−623	−267	−445
Debt securities...............................	4 619 ..	....	....	....	....	....	....	....	....
Bonds and notes.............................	4 620 ..	....	....	....	....	....	....	....	....
Monetary authorities........................	4 621 ..	....	....	....	....	....	....	....	....
General government.........................	4 622 ..	....	....	....	....	....	....	....	....
Banks...................................	4 623 ..	....	....	....	....	....	....	....	....
Other sectors.............................	4 624 ..	....	....	....	....	....	....	....	....
Money market instruments....................	4 630 ..	....	....	....	....	....	....	....	....
Monetary authorities........................	4 631 ..	....	....	....	....	....	....	....	....
General government.........................	4 632 ..	....	....	....	....	....	....	....	....
Banks...................................	4 633 ..	....	....	....	....	....	....	....	....
Other sectors.............................	4 634 ..	....	....	....	....	....	....	....	....
Liabilities...................................	4 652 ..	**−18**	**−85**	**3,528**	**3**	**−2,728**	**−7,027**	**−260**	**10,887**
Equity securities..............................	4 660 ..	37	26	729	502	−3,199	−674	393	1,724
Banks.....................................	4 663 ..	....	....	....	....	....	....	....	....
Other sectors...............................	4 664 ..	37	26	729	502	−3,199	−674	393	1,724
Debt securities...............................	4 669 ..	−55	−111	2,799	−499	471	−6,353	−653	9,162
Bonds and notes.............................	4 670 ..	−55	−111	2,799	−499	789	−761	−590	2,174
Monetary authorities........................	4 671 ..	....	....	....	....	....	....	....	....
General government.........................	4 672 ..	−55	−111	2,799	−499	789	−761	−590	2,174
Banks...................................	4 673 ..	....	....	....	....	....	....	....	....
Other sectors.............................	4 674 ..	....	....	....	....	....	....	....	....
Money market instruments....................	4 680 ..	....	....	....	....	−317	−5,593	−63	6,989
Monetary authorities........................	4 681 ..	....	....	....	....	−660		....	....
General government.........................	4 682 ..	....	....	....	....	343	−5,593	−63	6,989
Banks...................................	4 683 ..	....	....	....	....	....	....	....	....
Other sectors.............................	4 684 ..	....	....	....	....	....	....	....	....
C. FINANCIAL DERIVATIVES........................	4 910 ..	....	....	....	....	....	....	....	....
Monetary authorities..........................	4 911 ..	....	....	....	....	....	....	....	....
General government...........................	4 912 ..	....	....	....	....	....	....	....	....
Banks.....................................	4 913 ..	....	....	....	....	....	....	....	....
Other sectors...............................	4 914 ..	....	....	....	....	....	....	....	....
Assets..	4 900 ..	....	....	....	....	....	....	....	....
Monetary authorities..........................	4 901 ..	....	....	....	....	....	....	....	....
General government...........................	4 902 ..	....	....	....	....	....	....	....	....
Banks.....................................	4 903 ..	....	....	....	....	....	....	....	....
Other sectors...............................	4 904 ..	....	....	....	....	....	....	....	....
Liabilities...................................	4 905 ..	....	....	....	....	....	....	....	....
Monetary authorities..........................	4 906 ..	....	....	....	....	....	....	....	....
General government...........................	4 907 ..	....	....	....	....	....	....	....	....
Banks.....................................	4 908 ..	....	....	....	....	....	....	....	....
Other sectors...............................	4 909 ..	....	....	....	....	....	....	....	....

Table 2 (Concluded). STANDARD PRESENTATION, 2003–2010

(Millions of U.S. dollars)

	Code	2003	2004	2005	2006	2007	2008	2009	2010
D. OTHER INVESTMENT	4 700	**−5,098**	**−4,525**	**−2,068**	**−8,820**	**−2,529**	**6,173**	**−2,799**	**−7,688**
Assets	4 703	**−4,651**	**−5,888**	**−3,246**	**−9,743**	**−5,498**	**4,633**	**−5,879**	**−11,185**
Trade credits	4 706	....	....	....	....	....	....	....	....
General government	4 707	....	....	....	....	....	....	....	....
of which: Short-term	4 709	....	....	....	....	....	....	....	....
Other sectors	4 710	....	....	....	....	....	....	....	....
of which: Short-term	4 712	....	....	....	....	....	....	....	....
Loans	4 714	....	....	....	....	....	....	....	....
Monetary authorities	4 715	....	....	....	....	....	....	....	....
of which: Short-term	4 718	....	....	....	....	....	....	....	....
General government	4 719	....	....	....	....	....	....	....	....
of which: Short-term	4 721	....	....	....	....	....	....	....	....
Banks	4 722	....	....	....	....	....	....	....	....
of which: Short-term	4 724	....	....	....	....	....	....	....	....
Other sectors	4 725	....	....	....	....	....	....	....	....
of which: Short-term	4 727	....	....	....	....	....	....	....	....
Currency and deposits	4 730	−1,682	−3,215	−2,765	−8,573	−4,585	10,123	−2,407	−6,291
Monetary authorities	4 731	....	....	....	....	....	....	....	....
General government	4 732	....	....	....	....	....	....	....	....
Banks	4 733	−1,682	−3,215	−2,765	−8,573	−4,585	10,123	−2,407	−6,291
Other sectors	4 734	....	....	....	....	....	....	....	....
Other assets	4 736	−2,969	−2,673	−481	−1,170	−913	−5,490	−3,472	−4,895
Monetary authorities	4 737	−38	−4	....	−100	−101	17	−71	24
of which: Short-term	4 739	....	....	....	....	....	....	....	....
General government	4 740	....	....	....	....	....	....	....	....
of which: Short-term	4 742	....	....	....	....	....	....	....	....
Banks	4 743	....	....	....	....	....	....	....	....
of which: Short-term	4 745	....	....	....	....	....	....	....	....
Other sectors	4 746	−2,931	−2,669	−481	−1,070	−812	−5,507	−3,401	−4,919
of which: Short-term	4 748	*−2,931*	*−2,669*	*−481*	*−1,070*	*−812*	*−5,507*	*−3,401*	*−4,919*
Liabilities	4 753	**−446**	**1,363**	**1,178**	**923**	**2,970**	**1,541**	**3,079**	**3,498**
Trade credits	4 756	1,020	2,175	1,860	2,246	2,028	1,588	2,818	1,965
General government	4 757	....	....	....	....	....	....	....	....
of which: Short-term	4 759	....	....	....	....	....	....	....	....
Other sectors	4 760	1,020	2,175	1,860	2,246	2,028	1,588	2,818	1,965
of which: Short-term	4 762	*1,280*	*2,270*	*2,033*	*2,743*	*2,199*	*2,395*	*2,830*	*2,011*
Loans	4 764	−871	−471	−808	−1,026	−4	−1,169	−547	−656
Monetary authorities	4 765	....	....	....	....	....	....	....	....
of which: Use of Fund credit and loans from the Fund	4 766	....	....	....	....	....	....	....	....
of which: Short-term	4 768	....	....	....	....	....	....	....	....
General government	4 769	−871	−471	−808	−1,026	−4	−1,169	−547	−656
of which: Short-term	4 771	....	....	....	....	....	....	....	....
Banks	4 772	....	....	....	....	....	....	....	....
of which: Short-term	4 774	....	....	....	....	....	....	....	....
Other sectors	4 775	....	....	....	....	....	....	....	....
of which: Short-term	4 777	....	....	....	....	....	....	....	....
Currency and deposits	4 780	−601	−326	128	−300	930	1,107	−385	2,203
Monetary authorities	4 781	....	....	....	....	....	....	....	....
General government	4 782	....	....	....	....	....	....	....	....
Banks	4 783	−601	−326	128	−300	930	1,107	−385	2,203
Other sectors	4 784	....	....	....	....	....	....	....	....
Other liabilities	4 786	6	−16	−2	3	16	15	1,193	−14
Monetary authorities	4 787	6	−16	−2	3	16	15	1,193	−14
of which: Short-term	4 789	*−1*	*1*	....	*−1*	*−3*	*15*	*−10*	*−3*
General government	4 790	....	....	....	....	....	....	....	....
of which: Short-term	4 792	....	....	....	....	....	....	....	....
Banks	4 793	....	....	....	....	....	....	....	....
of which: Short-term	4 795	....	....	....	....	....	....	....	....
Other sectors	4 796	....	....	....	....	....	....	....	....
of which: Short-term	4 798	....	....	....	....	....	....	....	....
E. RESERVE ASSETS	4 802	**−395**	**−684**	**−6,319**	**−3,608**	**−5,475**	**−1,755**	**156**	**−1,276**
Monetary gold	4 812	....	....	....	....	....	....	....	....
Special drawing rights	4 811	−90	29	55	−14	−7	22	−1,191	22
Reserve position in the Fund	4 810	....	....	....	....	....	....	....	....
Foreign exchange	4 803	−304	−713	−6,374	−3,594	−5,469	−1,777	1,347	−1,298
Other claims	4 813	....	....	....	....	....	....	....	....
NET ERRORS AND OMISSIONS	4 998	**1,575**	**−45**	**−2,427**	**634**	**251**	**−2,928**	**398**	**−2,145**

2011, International Monetary Fund: *Balance of Payments Statistics Yearbook*

Table 3. INTERNATIONAL INVESTMENT POSITION (End-period stocks), 2003–2010

(Millions of U.S. dollars)

	Code	2003	2004	2005	2006	2007	2008	2009	2010
ASSETS	8 995 C.	....	**36,003**	**46,723**	**61,559**	**76,365**	**67,351**	**72,700**	....
Direct investment abroad	8 505 ..	....	**875**	**967**	**1,116**	**1,781**	**3,701**	**4,273**	....
Equity capital and reinvested earnings	8 506 ..	....	....	....	....	....	....	....	....
Claims on affiliated enterprises	8 507 ..	....	....	....	....	....	....	....	....
Liabilities to affiliated enterprises	8 508 ..	....	....	....	....	....	....	....	....
Other capital	8 530 ..	....	....	....	....	....	....	....	....
Claims on affiliated enterprises	8 535 ..	....	....	....	....	....	....	....	....
Liabilities to affiliated enterprises	8 540 ..	....	....	....	....	....	....	....	....
Portfolio investment	8 602 ..	....	**1,790**	**2,150**	**2,434**	**2,779**	**1,947**	**4,120**	....
Equity securities	8 610 ..	....	782	898	886	1,098	911	966	....
Monetary authorities	8 611 ..	....	....	....	....	....	....	....	....
General government	8 612 ..	....	....	....	....	....	....	....	....
Banks	8 613 ..	....	762	879	865	1,079	892	884	....
Other sectors	8 614 ..	....	20	20	21	19	19	82	....
Debt securities	8 619 ..	....	1,008	1,252	1,548	1,681	1,036	3,155	....
Bonds and notes	8 620 ..	....	986	1,202	1,498	1,545	910	1,624	....
Monetary authorities	8 621 ..	....	....	....	....	....	....		....
General government	8 622 ..	....	....	....	....	....	....		....
Banks	8 623 ..	....	986	1,202	1,498	1,545	910	1,623	....
Other sectors	8 624 ..	....	....	....	....	....	....	1	....
Money market instruments	8 630 ..	....	22	50	50	136	127	1,530	....
Monetary authorities	8 631 ..	....	....	....	....	....	....		....
General government	8 632 ..	....	....	....	....	....	....		....
Banks	8 633 ..	....	22	50	50	136	127	231	....
Other sectors	8 634 ..	....						1,299	....
Financial derivatives	8 900 ..	....	....	....	....	....	....	....	....
Monetary authorities	8 901 ..	....	....	....	....	....	....	....	....
General government	8 902 ..	....	....	....	....	....	....	....	....
Banks	8 903 ..	....	....	....	....	....	....	....	....
Other sectors	8 904 ..	....	....	....	....	....	....	....	....
Other investment	8 703 ..	....	**18,861**	**22,374**	**32,854**	**40,628**	**28,656**	**30,839**	....
Trade credits	8 706 ..	....	....	....	....	....	....	....	....
General government	8 707 ..	....	....	....	....	....	....	....	....
of which: Short-term	8 709 ..	....	....	....	....	....	....	....	....
Other sectors	8 710 ..	....	....	....	....	....	....	....	....
of which: Short-term	8 712 ..	....	....	....	....	....	....	....	....
Loans	8 714 ..	....	271	428	476	1,486	1,777	3,178	....
Monetary authorities	8 715 ..	....	....	....	....	....	....	....	....
of which: Short-term	8 718 ..	....	....	....	....	....	....	....	....
General government	8 719 ..	....	....	....	....	....	....	....	....
of which: Short-term	8 721 ..	....	....	....	....	....	....	....	....
Banks	8 722 ..	....	271	428	476	1,486	1,777	3,178	....
of which: Short-term	8 724 ..	....	*203*	*299*	*324*	*997*	*1,183*	*2,045*	....
Other sectors	8 725 ..	....	....	....	....	....	....	....	....
of which: Short-term	8 727 ..	....	....	....	....	....	....	....	....
Currency and deposits	8 730 ..	....	17,525	21,355	31,495	36,355	25,443	25,989	....
Monetary authorities	8 731 ..	....	....	....	....	....	....	....	....
General government	8 732 ..	....	....	....	....	....	....	....	....
Banks	8 733 ..	....	8,730	11,165	19,231	22,061	11,795	12,629	....
Other sectors	8 734 ..	....	8,795	10,190	12,264	14,294	13,648	13,360	....
Other assets	8 736 ..	....	1,065	591	884	2,787	1,436	1,672	....
Monetary authorities	8 737 ..	....	1,065	591	884	2,787	1,436	1,672	....
of which: Short-term	8 739 ..	....	*1,065*	*591*	*884*	*2,787*	*1,436*	*1,672*	....
General government	8 740 ..	....	....	....	....	....	....	....	....
of which: Short-term	8 742 ..	....	....	....	....	....	....	....	....
Banks	8 743 ..	....	....	....	....	....	....	....	....
of which: Short-term	8 745 ..	....	....	....	....	....	....	....	....
Other sectors	8 746 ..	....	....	....	....	....	....	....	....
of which: Short-term	8 748 ..	....	....	....	....	....	....	....	....
Reserve assets	8 802 ..	....	**14,477**	**21,231**	**25,155**	**31,178**	**33,047**	**33,468**	....
Monetary gold	8 812 ..	....	717	1,259	1,526	2,042	2,113	2,684	....
Special drawing rights	8 811 ..	189	165	101	121	134	108	1,306	1,261
Reserve position in the Fund	8 810 ..	....	....	....	....	....	....	....	....
Foreign exchange	8 803 ..	....	13,595	19,872	23,509	29,002	30,825	29,478	....
Other claims	8 813 ..	....	....	....	....	....	....	....	....

Table 3 (Concluded). INTERNATIONAL INVESTMENT POSITION (End-period stocks), 2003–2010

(Millions of U.S. dollars)

	Code	2003	2004	2005	2006	2007	2008	2009	2010
LIABILITIES....................	8 995 D.	....	**56,552**	**62,803**	**72,369**	**84,729**	**94,379**	**102,439**	....
Direct investment in Egypt....................	8 555 ..	....	**23,506**	**28,882**	**38,925**	**50,503**	**59,997**	**66,709**	....
Equity capital and reinvested earnings............	8 556 ..	....	....	....	....	....	....	....	....
Claims on direct investors....................	8 557 ..	....	....	....	....	....	....	....	....
Liabilities to direct investors....................	8 558 ..	....	....	....	....	....	....	....	....
Other capital....................	8 580 ..	....	....	....	....	....	....	....	....
Claims on direct investors....................	8 585 ..	....	....	....	....	....	....	....	....
Liabilities to direct investors....................	8 590 ..	....	....	....	....	....	....	....	....
Portfolio investment....................	8 652 ..	....	**2,530**	**6,058**	**6,063**	**4,032**	**4,433**	**4,108**	....
Equity securities....................	8 660 ..	....	1,946	2,676	3,178	....	1,495	1,757	....
Banks....................	8 663 ..	....	....	....	....	....	....	....	....
Other sectors....................	8 664 ..	....	1,946	2,676	3,178	....	1,495	1,757	....
Debt securities....................	8 669 ..	....	584	3,382	2,885	4,032	2,938	2,351	....
Bonds and notes....................	8 670 ..	....	584	3,382	2,885	3,689	2,938	2,351	....
Monetary authorities....................	8 671 ..	....	....	....	....	....	....	....	....
General government....................	8 672 ..	....	584	3,382	2,885	3,689	2,938	2,351	....
Banks....................	8 673 ..	....	....	....	....	....	....	....	....
Other sectors....................	8 674 ..	....	....	....	....	....	....	....	....
Money market instruments....................	8 680 ..	....	....	....	....	343	....	....	....
Monetary authorities....................	8 681 ..	....	....	....	....	....	....	....	....
General government....................	8 682 ..	....	....	....	....	343	....	....	....
Banks....................	8 683 ..	....	....	....	....	....	....	....	....
Other sectors....................	8 684 ..	....	....	....	....	....	....	....	....
Financial derivatives....................	8 905 ..	....	....	....	....	....	....	....	....
Monetary authorities....................	8 906 ..	....	....	....	....	....	....	....	....
General government....................	8 907 ..	....	....	....	....	....	....	....	....
Banks....................	8 908 ..	....	....	....	....	....	....	....	....
Other sectors....................	8 909 ..	....	....	....	....	....	....	....	....
Other investment....................	8 753 ..	....	**30,516**	**27,863**	**27,382**	**30,194**	**29,949**	**31,621**	....
Trade credits....................	8 756 ..	....	694	814	973	1,005	1,460	1,291	....
General government....................	8 757 ..	....	....	....	....	....	....	....	....
of which: Short-term....................	8 759 ..	....	....	....	....	....	....	....	....
Other sectors....................	8 760 ..	....	694	814	973	1,005	1,460	1,291	....
of which: Short-term....................	8 762 ..	....	*694*	*814*	*973*	*1,005*	*1,460*	*1,291*	....
Loans....................	8 764 ..	....	28,349	25,839	25,672	27,989	27,144	27,659	....
Monetary authorities....................	8 765 ..	....	336	381	343	311	210	142	....
of which: Use of Fund credit and loans from the Fund....	8 766 ..	....	....	....	....	....	....	....	....
of which: Short-term....................	8 768 ..	....	....	....	....	....	....	....	....
General government....................	8 769 ..	....	19,163	16,917	17,051	18,605	23,638	24,000	....
of which: Short-term....................	8 771 ..	....	....	....	....	....	....	....	....
Banks....................	8 772 ..	....	1,096	1,602	1,277	1,388	678	662	....
of which: Short-term....................	8 774 ..	....	*51*	*30*	*9*	*30*	*37*	*8*	....
Other sectors....................	8 775 ..	....	7,755	6,940	7,002	7,685	2,619	2,856	....
of which: Short-term....................	8 777 ..	....	....	....	....	....	....	....	....
Currency and deposits....................	8 780 ..	....	1,208	1,090	610	1,009	1,139	1,262	....
Monetary authorities....................	8 781 ..	....	650	550	....	....	....	....	....
General government....................	8 782 ..	....	....	....	....	....	....	....	....
Banks....................	8 783 ..	....	558	540	610	1,009	1,139	1,262	....
Other sectors....................	8 784 ..	....	....	....	....	....	....	....	....
Other liabilities....................	8 786 ..	....	264	120	127	191	206	1,408	....
Monetary authorities....................	8 787 ..	....	....	....	....	....	....	1,408	....
of which: Short-term....................	8 789 ..	....	....	....	....	....	....	....	....
General government....................	8 790 ..	....	....	....	....	....	....	....	....
of which: Short-term....................	8 792 ..	....	....	....	....	....	....	....	....
Banks....................	8 793 ..	....	264	120	127	191	206	....	....
of which: Short-term....................	8 795 ..	....	*264*	*120*	*127*	*191*	*206*	....	....
Other sectors....................	8 796 ..	....	....	....	....	....	....	....	....
of which: Short-term....................	8 798 ..	....	....	....	....	....	....	....	....
NET INTERNATIONAL INVESTMENT POSITION........	8 995 ..	....	**−20,549**	**−16,080**	**−10,810**	**−8,364**	**−27,028**	**−29,738**	....
Conversion rates: Egyptian pounds per U.S. dollar (end of period)....................	0 102 ..	6.1532	6.1314	5.7322	5.7036	5.5038	5.5041	5.4754	5.7926

2011, International Monetary Fund: *Balance of Payments Statistics Yearbook*

Table 1. ANALYTIC PRESENTATION, 2003–2010

(Millions of U.S. dollars)

	Code	2003	2004	2005	2006	2007	2008	2009	2010
A. Current Account[1].....................	4 993 Z.	**−702.2**	**−627.7**	**−621.6**	**−765.6**	**−1,216.6**	**−1,532.2**	**−304.2**	**−488.3**
Goods: exports f.o.b................	2 100 ..	3,152.6	3,339.2	3,464.8	3,783.2	4,069.7	4,702.6	3,929.8	4,576.7
Goods: imports f.o.b................	3 100 ..	−5,439.2	−5,999.5	−6,502.0	−7,419.2	−8,434.5	−9,379.4	−7,037.1	−8,188.7
Balance on Goods................	4 100 ..	*−2,286.6*	*−2,660.3*	*−3,037.2*	*−3,636.0*	*−4,364.8*	*−4,676.8*	*−3,107.9*	*−3,612.0*
Services: credit......................	2 200 ..	948.3	1,089.6	945.7	1,014.9	1,134.0	1,058.1	862.9	976.0
Services: debit.......................	3 200 ..	−1,055.1	−1,154.1	−1,074.6	−1,179.0	−1,275.1	−1,271.0	−953.1	−1,069.9
Balance on Goods and Services.........	4 991 ..	*−2,393.4*	*−2,724.8*	*−3,166.1*	*−3,800.1*	*−4,505.9*	*−4,889.7*	*−3,198.0*	*−3,705.9*
Income: credit.......................	2 300 ..	140.4	143.7	174.7	234.4	308.0	179.3	76.6	119.6
Income: debit........................	3 300 ..	−563.4	−601.6	−665.0	−671.9	−764.3	−568.3	−624.5	−500.6
Balance on Goods, Services, and Income.........	4 992 ..	*−2,816.5*	*−3,182.7*	*−3,656.4*	*−4,237.6*	*−4,962.2*	*−5,278.8*	*−3,746.0*	*−4,086.9*
Current transfers: credit..........	2 379 Z.	2,200.2	2,615.1	3,106.2	3,548.8	3,841.3	3,846.7	3,558.9	3,670.2
Current transfers: debit..........	3 379 ..	−85.9	−60.1	−71.4	−76.8	−95.7	−100.1	−117.1	−71.6
B. Capital Account[1].....................	4 994 Z.	**112.9**	**100.3**	**93.6**	**96.8**	**152.8**	**79.8**	**131.2**	**232.0**
Capital account: credit...........	2 994 Z.	113.4	100.8	94.0	97.3	153.8	80.6	132.0	233.0
Capital account: debit............	3 994 ..	−.5	−.5	−.4	−.5	−1.0	−.8	−.8	−1.0
Total, Groups A Plus B............	4 981 ..	*−589.3*	*−527.4*	*−528.0*	*−668.8*	*−1,063.8*	*−1,452.4*	*−173.0*	*−256.3*
C. Financial Account[1].....................	4 995 W.	**1,048.8**	**123.0**	**−126.0**	**335.4**	**−901.1**	**1,080.7**	**−597.0**	**−185.3**
Direct investment abroad............	4 505 ..	−18.6	2.8	−112.9	26.3	−95.2	−79.4	−1.8	−61.3
Direct investment in El Salvador............	4 555 Z.	141.2	363.3	55.1	17.5	105.1	371.2	231.0	−5.6
Portfolio investment assets............	4 602 ..	−263.7	−124.8	38.7	49.7	−103.4	195.7	350.2	−117.4
Equity securities................	4 610 ..	....	....	48.6	56.3	65.9	−196.5	349.0	−115.4
Debt securities.................	4 619 ..	−263.7	−124.8	−9.9	−6.6	−169.3	392.2	1.2	−2.0
Portfolio investment liabilities............	4 652 Z.	452.8	181.9	−370.2	74.2	−78.7	−74.3	7.2	31.0
Equity securities................	4 660 ..	....	....	....	....	....	....	....	....
Debt securities.................	4 669 Z.	452.8	181.9	−370.2	74.2	−78.7	−74.3	7.2	31.0
Financial derivatives..............	4 910 ..	....	....	....	....	....	....	....	....
Financial derivatives assets......	4 900 ..	....	....	....	....	....	....	....	....
Financial derivatives liabilities......	4 905 ..	....	....	....	....	....	....	....	....
Other investment assets...........	4 703 ..	19.6	−159.8	−246.7	72.7	−472.5	25.7	−629.1	235.7
Monetary authorities............	4 701 ..	....	....	....	....	....	....	....	....
General government.............	4 704 ..	....	....	....	....	....	....	....	....
Banks...........................	4 705 ..	133.7	−19.7	−182.0	50.3	−205.6	90.8	−179.6	108.7
Other sectors..................	4 728 ..	−114.1	−140.2	−64.7	22.4	−266.9	−65.1	−449.5	127.0
Other investment liabilities...........	4 753 W.	717.5	−140.4	510.0	95.0	−256.4	641.8	−554.5	−267.7
Monetary authorities............	4 753 WA	76.7	−31.0	5.0	−67.7	−24.0	264.5	97.0	−58.8
General government.............	4 753 ZB	33.2	−76.6	41.4	−42.3	−89.9	71.8	366.1	284.6
Banks...........................	4 753 ZC	491.6	214.0	11.4	−249.9	−360.6	244.7	−653.0	−333.0
Other sectors..................	4 753 ZD	116.0	−246.8	452.2	454.9	218.0	60.9	−364.7	−160.4
Total, Groups A Through C............	4 983 ..	*459.5*	*−404.5*	*−653.9*	*−333.4*	*−1,964.8*	*−371.7*	*−769.9*	*−441.6*
D. Net Errors and Omissions...............	4 998 ..	**−143.3**	**352.0**	**−449.0**	**−484.5**	**783.1**	**164.1**	**659.5**	**−15.3**
Total, Groups A Through D............	4 984 ..	*316.2*	*−52.5*	*−1,102.9*	*−817.9*	*−1,181.7*	*−207.6*	*−110.4*	*−456.8*
E. Reserves and Related Items...............	4 802 A.	**−316.2**	**52.5**	**1,102.9**	**817.9**	**1,181.7**	**207.6**	**110.4**	**456.8**
Reserve assets....................	4 802 ..	−316.2	52.5	190.3	−46.6	−279.0	−333.5	−424.4	296.0
Use of Fund credit and loans....	4 766 ..	....	....	....	....	....	....	....	....
Exceptional financing............	4 920 ..	....	....	912.6	864.5	1,460.7	541.1	534.8	160.9

[1] Excludes components that have been classified in the categories of Group E.

Table 2. STANDARD PRESENTATION, 2003–2010

(Millions of U.S. dollars)

	Code	2003	2004	2005	2006	2007	2008	2009	2010
CURRENT ACCOUNT...	4 993 ..	**−702.2**	**−627.7**	**−621.6**	**−765.6**	**−1,216.6**	**−1,532.2**	**−304.2**	**−488.3**
A. GOODS..	4 100 ..	**−2,286.6**	**−2,660.3**	**−3,037.2**	**−3,636.0**	**−4,364.8**	**−4,676.8**	**−3,107.9**	**−3,612.0**
Credit..	2 100 ..	**3,152.6**	**3,339.2**	**3,464.8**	**3,783.2**	**4,069.7**	**4,702.6**	**3,929.8**	**4,576.7**
General merchandise: exports f.o.b....................	2 110 ..	1,250.4	1,375.6	1,847.7	2,227.8	2,763.9	3,229.9	2,898.1	3,331.3
Goods for processing: exports f.o.b..................	2 150 ..	1,873.0	1,923.2	1,575.7	1,479.3	1,224.8	1,368.5	945.3	1,134.4
Repairs on goods...	2 160 ..	21.8	31.5	25.0	49.2	51.2	58.6	60.9	74.8
Goods procured in ports by carriers.................	2 170 ..	7.4	8.6	16.1	26.9	29.8	43.8	21.8	28.2
Nonmonetary gold...	2 180 ..	....	.4	.3	....	....	1.8	3.7	8.1
Debit..	3 100 ..	**−5,439.2**	**−5,999.5**	**−6,502.0**	**−7,419.2**	**−8,434.5**	**−9,379.4**	**−7,037.7**	**−8,188.7**
General merchandise: imports f.o.b..................	3 110 ..	−3,992.0	−4,469.0	−5,335.9	−6,276.6	−7,471.0	−8,307.7	−6,374.4	−7,377.1
Goods for processing: imports f.o.b..................	3 150 ..	−1,379.3	−1,458.2	−1,068.4	−1,027.4	−854.3	−950.9	−576.8	−720.8
Repairs on goods...	3 160 ..	−35.7	−31.3	−40.1	−52.9	−46.2	−39.7	−30.9	−29.7
Goods procured in ports by carriers.................	3 170 ..	−31.8	−40.9	−57.6	−62.2	−63.0	−81.1	−55.6	−61.0
Nonmonetary gold...	3 180 ..	−.4	−.1	....	....	....	....	....	....
B. SERVICES...	4 200 ..	**−106.8**	**−64.5**	**−128.9**	**−164.1**	**−141.1**	**−212.9**	**−90.1**	**−93.9**
Total credit..	2 200 ..	*948.3*	*1,089.6*	*945.7*	*1,014.9*	*1,134.0*	*1,058.1*	*862.9*	*976.0*
Total debit...	3 200 ..	*−1,055.1*	*−1,154.1*	*−1,074.6*	*−1,179.0*	*−1,275.1*	*−1,271.0*	*−953.1*	*−1,069.9*
Transportation services, credit......................	2 205 ..	**330.8**	**342.6**	**344.6**	**352.3**	**368.4**	**351.0**	**272.4**	**300.6**
Passenger..	2 850 ..	*282.1*	*295.5*	*294.6*	*304.2*	*311.1*	*285.7*	*229.6*	*255.6*
Freight...	2 851 ..	*6.6*	*7.7*	*7.2*	*6.8*	*6.6*	*6.9*	*5.9*	*6.0*
Other...	2 852 ..	*42.1*	*39.5*	*42.9*	*41.3*	*50.7*	*58.4*	*36.9*	*39.0*
Sea transport, passenger..................................	2 207 ..	....	....	....	....	....	....	....	....
Sea transport, freight.......................................	2 208 ..	....	....	....	....	....	....	....	....
Sea transport, other...	2 209 ..	28.1	28.3	27.9	30.6	31.6	47.0	26.2	28.4
Air transport, passenger...................................	2 211 ..	280.5	293.6	292.5	302.1	309.2	282.1	227.1	252.4
Air transport, freight..	2 212 ..	6.6	7.7	7.2	6.8	6.6	6.9	5.9	6.0
Air transport, other..	2 213 ..	13.3	11.2	14.5	10.6	11.8	11.3	10.5	10.4
Other transport, passenger..............................	2 215 ..	1.6	1.9	2.1	2.1	1.9	3.6	2.5	3.2
Other transport, freight....................................	2 216 ..	....	....	....	....	....	....	....	....
Other transport, other......................................	2 217 ..	.7	....	.5	.1	7.3	.1	.2	.2
Transportation services, debit........................	3 205 ..	**−477.8**	**−504.6**	**−513.7**	**−557.0**	**−600.9**	**−646.2**	**−440.9**	**−460.6**
Passenger..	3 850 ..	*−81.9*	*−80.9*	*−82.3*	*−82.5*	*−84.8*	*−84.8*	*−66.3*	*−61.4*
Freight...	3 851 ..	*−340.5*	*−357.1*	*−353.4*	*−394.2*	*−424.7*	*−478.3*	*−312.3*	*−330.1*
Other...	3 852 ..	*−55.4*	*−66.6*	*−78.0*	*−80.3*	*−91.4*	*−83.1*	*−62.3*	*−69.0*
Sea transport, passenger..................................	3 207 ..	....	....	....	....	....	....	....	....
Sea transport, freight.......................................	3 208 ..	−148.4	−151.7	−141.7	−157.6	−173.5	−219.2	−95.9	−86.4
Sea transport, other...	3 209 ..	....	....	−.2	−.2	....	−.3	....	....
Air transport, passenger...................................	3 211 ..	−80.8	−80.3	−81.8	−82.0	−84.4	−84.4	−65.1	−61.0
Air transport, freight..	3 212 ..	−24.3	−24.8	−23.8	−28.0	−33.3	−29.8	−22.1	−26.2
Air transport, other..	3 213 ..	−54.7	−66.6	−77.6	−80.0	−91.2	−82.7	−62.2	−69.0
Other transport, passenger..............................	3 215 ..	−1.1	−.6	−.5	−.5	−.4	−.4	−1.2	−.4
Other transport, freight....................................	3 216 ..	−167.8	−180.6	−187.9	−208.6	−217.9	−229.3	−194.3	−217.5
Other transport, other......................................	3 217 ..	−.7	....	−.2	−.1	−.2	−.1	−.1	....
Travel, credit...	2 236 ..	**382.4**	**452.5**	**360.9**	**381.5**	**482.1**	**424.5**	**319.3**	**390.0**
Business travel...	2 237 ..	119.6	41.7	44.9	50.0	127.1	67.0	56.4	76.0
Personal travel...	2 240 ..	262.8	410.8	316.0	331.5	355.0	357.5	262.9	314.0
Travel, debit..	3 236 ..	**−228.9**	**−292.0**	**−206.1**	**−224.0**	**−278.5**	**−240.8**	**−186.7**	**−218.9**
Business travel...	3 237 ..	−29.1	−68.5	−38.6	−41.7	−58.1	−34.7	−29.9	−31.7
Personal travel...	3 240 ..	−199.9	−223.5	−167.5	−182.4	−220.4	−206.1	−156.8	−187.3
Other services, credit....................................	2 200 BA ..	**235.1**	**294.5**	**240.2**	**281.1**	**283.5**	**282.6**	**271.2**	**285.5**
Communications..	2 245 ..	122.9	139.3	122.7	135.7	162.1	153.7	140.9	172.0
Construction..	2 249 ..	10.0	18.6	24.1	45.4	22.9	33.1	24.9	18.4
Insurance...	2 253 ..	31.2	34.8	32.4	34.7	37.1	45.5	57.1	29.3
Financial..	2 260 ..	2.8	9.7	7.1	3.4	4.2	1.4	.9	3.0
Computer and information...............................	2 262 ..	.4	.4	....	.7	....	.9	.1	.7
Royalties and licence fees................................	2 266 ..	.2	.1	2.4	.5	.3	1.4	.4	.4
Other business services...................................	2 268 ..	25.3	40.4	21.2	21.9	17.3	18.8	17.6	29.6
Personal, cultural, and recreational..................	2 287 ..	....	.2	....	....	....	....	.1	....
Government, n.i.e..	2 291 ..	42.3	51.0	30.3	38.8	39.6	27.9	29.1	32.2
Other services, debit.....................................	3 200 BA ..	**−348.4**	**−357.5**	**−354.9**	**−398.0**	**−395.7**	**−384.0**	**−325.5**	**−390.3**
Communications..	3 245 ..	−36.9	−34.0	−25.2	−25.5	−30.8	−44.8	−32.3	−39.7
Construction..	3 249 ..	−6.3	−6.5	−12.7	−8.5	−8.0	−13.6	−10.3	−6.3
Insurance...	3 253 ..	−106.2	−108.4	−109.2	−133.4	−126.1	−140.5	−124.5	−125.5
Financial..	3 260 ..	−19.7	−28.5	−13.0	−9.3	−9.8	−11.9	−7.8	−7.8
Computer and information...............................	3 262 ..	−3.1	−6.1	−2.9	−3.9	−7.4	−4.9	−4.2	−6.9
Royalties and licence fees................................	3 266 ..	−22.2	−17.8	−30.4	−27.3	−24.1	−33.7	−26.1	−31.5
Other business services...................................	3 268 ..	−137.2	−130.8	−138.1	−162.3	−156.4	−100.3	−88.3	−126.0
Personal, cultural, and recreational..................	3 287 ..	−1.2	−1.5	−1.6	−1.3	−1.9	−1.0	−.6	−1.3
Government, n.i.e..	3 291 ..	−15.6	−24.0	−21.8	−26.4	−31.2	−33.3	−31.6	−45.4

Table 2 (Continued). STANDARD PRESENTATION, 2003–2010

(Millions of U.S. dollars)

	Code	2003	2004	2005	2006	2007	2008	2009	2010
C. INCOME	4 300	**−423.0**	**−457.9**	**−490.3**	**−437.5**	**−456.3**	**−389.1**	**−548.0**	**−381.0**
Total credit	2 300	*140.4*	*143.7*	*174.7*	*234.4*	*308.0*	*179.3*	*76.6*	*119.6*
Total debit	3 300	*−563.4*	*−601.6*	*−665.0*	*−671.9*	*−764.3*	*−568.3*	*−624.5*	*−500.6*
Compensation of employees, credit	2 310	**16.0**	**15.4**	**11.3**	**11.9**	**13.8**	**12.8**	**15.2**	**16.5**
Compensation of employees, debit	3 310	**−24.3**	**−32.3**	**−24.0**	**−28.0**	**−27.5**	**−18.5**	**−20.1**	**−22.1**
Investment income, credit	2 320	**124.4**	**128.3**	**163.4**	**222.5**	**294.2**	**166.5**	**61.4**	**103.1**
Direct investment income	2 330	7.5	5.3	14.4	19.6	26.0	14.5	7.1	61.3
Dividends and distributed branch profits	2 332	....	1.1	1.4	2.2	2.4	1.7	1.5	....
Reinvested earnings and undistributed branch profits	2 333	....	....	....	....	....	....	1.7	61.3
Income on debt (interest)	2 334	7.5	4.2	13.0	17.4	23.6	12.7	3.9	....
Portfolio investment income	2 339	13.9	39.9	36.9	40.2	35.5	21.9	4.2	1.5
Income on equity	2 340	....	....	....	....	....	....	....	....
Income on bonds and notes	2 350	....	....	....	....	....	....	....	....
Income on money market instruments	2 360	13.9	39.9	36.9	40.2	35.5	21.9	4.2	1.5
Other investment income	2 370	103.0	83.1	112.1	162.7	232.7	130.1	50.1	40.3
Investment income, debit	3 320	**−539.1**	**−569.3**	**−641.0**	**−643.9**	**−736.7**	**−549.8**	**−604.4**	**−478.5**
Direct investment income	3 330	−84.9	−80.4	−181.0	−91.1	−158.7	−39.4	−171.6	−101.8
Dividends and distributed branch profits	3 332	−41.0	−33.8	−87.7	−41.9	−119.2	−.1	−52.6	−2.7
Reinvested earnings and undistributed branch profits	3 333	−3.3	−9.3	−56.1	−3.3	−1.9	−6.2	−109.2	−95.2
Income on debt (interest)	3 334	−40.6	−37.4	−37.2	−45.9	−37.6	−33.1	−9.8	−3.9
Portfolio investment income	3 339	−163.3	−184.5	−134.4	−175.4	−182.5	−171.4	−170.6	−157.7
Income on equity	3 340	....	....	....	....	....	....	....	....
Income on bonds and notes	3 350	....	....	−130.5	−175.4	−182.5	−171.4	−170.6	−157.7
Income on money market instruments	3 360	−163.3	−184.5	−3.9	....	....	....	....	....
Other investment income	3 370	−290.9	−304.4	−325.6	−377.4	−395.6	−339.1	−262.2	−219.0
D. CURRENT TRANSFERS	4 379	**2,114.3**	**2,555.0**	**3,034.8**	**3,472.0**	**3,745.6**	**3,746.6**	**3,441.8**	**3,598.7**
Credit	2 379	**2,200.2**	**2,615.1**	**3,106.2**	**3,548.8**	**3,841.3**	**3,846.7**	**3,558.9**	**3,670.2**
General government	2 380	13.6	13.6	19.2	14.8	40.9	17.2	17.9	93.9
Other sectors	2 390	2,186.6	2,601.5	3,087.0	3,534.0	3,800.5	3,829.6	3,541.0	3,576.3
Workers' remittances	2 391	2,105.3	2,547.6	3,017.3	3,470.8	3,695.3	3,742.0	3,387.2	3,430.9
Other current transfers	2 392	81.3	53.9	69.7	63.2	105.2	87.6	153.9	145.4
Debit	3 379	**−85.9**	**−60.1**	**−71.4**	**−76.8**	**−95.7**	**−100.1**	**−117.1**	**−71.6**
General government	3 380	....	....	....	....	....	....	....	....
Other sectors	3 390	−85.9	−60.1	−71.4	−76.8	−95.7	−100.1	−117.1	−71.6
Workers' remittances	3 391	....	....	....	....	....	....	....	....
Other current transfers	3 392	−85.9	−60.1	−71.4	−76.8	−95.7	−100.1	−117.1	−71.6
CAPITAL AND FINANCIAL ACCOUNT	4 996	**845.5**	**275.8**	**1,070.6**	**1,250.1**	**433.5**	**1,368.1**	**−355.4**	**503.5**
CAPITAL ACCOUNT	4 994	**112.9**	**100.3**	**93.6**	**96.8**	**152.8**	**79.8**	**131.2**	**232.0**
Total credit	2 994	*113.4*	*100.8*	*94.0*	*97.3*	*153.8*	*80.6*	*132.0*	*233.0*
Total debit	3 994	*−.5*	*−.5*	*−.4*	*−.5*	*−1.0*	*−.8*	*−.8*	*−1.0*
Capital transfers, credit	2 400	**113.4**	**100.8**	**94.0**	**97.3**	**153.8**	**80.6**	**132.0**	**233.0**
General government	2 401	1.8	2.0	42.4	43.9	96.2	18.0	57.4	125.3
Debt forgiveness	2 402	....	....	....	....	....	....	....	....
Other capital transfers	2 410	1.8	2.0	42.4	43.9	96.2	18.0	57.4	125.3
Other sectors	2 430	111.6	98.8	51.6	53.4	57.6	62.6	74.6	107.7
Migrants' transfers	2 431	1.1	1.1	1.1	1.8	2.5	3.4	2.3	2.0
Debt forgiveness	2 432	....	....	....	....	....	....	....	....
Other capital transfers	2 440	110.5	97.7	50.5	51.6	55.1	59.2	72.3	105.7
Capital transfers, debit	3 400	**−.5**	**−.5**	**−.4**	**−.5**	**−1.0**	**−.8**	**−.8**	**−1.0**
General government	3 401	....	....	....	....	....	....	....	....
Debt forgiveness	3 402	....	....	....	....	....	....	....	....
Other capital transfers	3 410	....	....	....	....	....	....	....	....
Other sectors	3 430	−.5	−.5	−.4	−.5	−1.0	−.8	−.8	−1.0
Migrants' transfers	3 431	−.5	−.5	−.4	−.5	−1.0	−.8	−.8	−1.0
Debt forgiveness	3 432	....	....	....	....	....	....	....	....
Other capital transfers	3 440	....	....	....	....	....	....	....	....
Nonproduced nonfinancial assets, credit	2 480	....	....	....	....	....	....	....	....
Nonproduced nonfinancial assets, debit	3 480	....	....	....	....	....	....	....	....

Table 2 (Continued). STANDARD PRESENTATION, 2003–2010

(Millions of U.S. dollars)

	Code	2003	2004	2005	2006	2007	2008	2009	2010
FINANCIAL ACCOUNT	4 995	**732.6**	**175.5**	**977.0**	**1,153.3**	**280.7**	**1,288.3**	**−486.6**	**271.6**
A. DIRECT INVESTMENT	4 500	**122.6**	**366.0**	**398.2**	**267.4**	**1,455.3**	**823.6**	**364.1**	**77.7**
Direct investment abroad	4 505	**−18.6**	**2.8**	**−112.9**	**26.3**	**−95.2**	**−79.4**	**−1.8**	**−61.3**
Equity capital	4 510	−18.6	3.6	−14.3	1.1	3.5	−14.5	−.1	....
Claims on affiliated enterprises	4 515	−18.6	3.6	−14.3	1.1	3.5	−14.5	−.1	....
Liabilities to affiliated enterprises	4 520	....	....	....	....	....	....		
Reinvested earnings	4 525	....	....	....	....	....	....	−1.7	−61.3
Other capital	4 530	....	−.8	−98.6	25.2	−98.7	−65.0	....	....
Claims on affiliated enterprises	4 535	....	−.8	−98.6	25.2	−98.7	−65.0		
Liabilities to affiliated enterprises	4 540	....					....		
Direct investment in El Salvador	4 555	**141.2**	**363.3**	**511.1**	**241.1**	**1,550.5**	**903.1**	**365.8**	**139.0**
Equity capital	4 560	125.4	397.6	456.0	223.6	1,445.4	531.9	131.9	141.6
Claims on direct investors	4 565	....	....	....	....	....	....	....	−12.4
Liabilities to direct investors	4 570	125.4	397.6	456.0	223.6	1,445.4	531.9	131.9	154.0
Reinvested earnings	4 575	3.3	9.3	56.1	3.3	1.9	6.2	109.2	95.2
Other capital	4 580	12.5	−43.7	−1.0	14.2	103.2	365.0	124.7	−97.9
Claims on direct investors	4 585	....	....	....	....	....	....	−2.9	1.4
Liabilities to direct investors	4 590	12.5	−43.7	−1.0	14.2	103.2	365.0	127.6	−99.3
B. PORTFOLIO INVESTMENT	4 600	**189.1**	**57.1**	**125.1**	**764.8**	**−166.8**	**130.6**	**757.4**	**−70.1**
Assets	4 602	**−263.7**	**−124.8**	**38.7**	**49.7**	**−103.4**	**195.7**	**350.2**	**−117.4**
Equity securities	4 610	....	....	48.6	56.3	65.9	−196.5	349.0	−115.4
Monetary authorities	4 611	....	....	....	....	....	....	....	....
General government	4 612	....	....	20.6	−12.7	−10.9	1.9	−2.2	5.0
Banks	4 613	....	....	23.2	69.4	98.7	−193.0	371.5	−119.3
Other sectors	4 614	....	....	4.8	−.4	−21.9	−5.3	−20.3	−1.1
Debt securities	4 619	−263.7	−124.8	−9.9	−6.6	−169.3	392.2	1.2	−2.0
Bonds and notes	4 620	....	....	−9.9	−6.6	−169.3	392.2	1.2	−2.0
Monetary authorities	4 621	....	....						
General government	4 622	....	....						
Banks	4 623	....	....						
Other sectors	4 624	....	....	−9.9	−6.6	−169.3	392.2	1.2	−2.0
Money market instruments	4 630	−263.7	−124.8	....					
Monetary authorities	4 631	....	....						
General government	4 632	....	....						
Banks	4 633	−242.5	−106.6						
Other sectors	4 634	−21.2	−18.2	....					
Liabilities	4 652	**452.8**	**181.9**	**86.4**	**715.1**	**−63.4**	**−65.1**	**407.2**	**47.3**
Equity securities	4 660	....	....	....	....	....	....	....	....
Banks	4 663	....	....	....	....	....	....	....	....
Other sectors	4 664	....	....	....	....	....	....	....	....
Debt securities	4 669	452.8	181.9	86.4	715.1	−63.4	−65.1	407.2	47.3
Bonds and notes	4 670	394.2	133.7	179.1	711.6	−56.3	−63.2	410.3	−3.2
Monetary authorities	4 671	92.0	−34.8	−30.5	−21.7	....	....	....	....
General government	4 672	301.8	168.5	209.6	733.3	−56.3	−63.2	410.3	−3.2
Banks	4 673	....	....	....	....	....	....	....	....
Other sectors	4 674	.4	....	....	....	....	....	....	....
Money market instruments	4 680	58.6	48.2	−92.7	3.5	−7.1	−1.9	−3.1	50.5
Monetary authorities	4 681	....	....	....	....	....	....	....	....
General government	4 682	58.3	48.2	−92.7	3.5	−7.1	−1.9	−3.1	50.5
Banks	4 683	....	....	....	....	....	....	....	....
Other sectors	4 684	.3	....	....	....	....	....	....	....
C. FINANCIAL DERIVATIVES	4 910	....	....	....	....	....	....	....	....
Monetary authorities	4 911	....	....	....	....	....	....	....	....
General government	4 912	....	....	....	....	....	....	....	....
Banks	4 913	....	....	....	....	....	....	....	....
Other sectors	4 914	....	....	....	....	....	....	....	....
Assets	4 900	....	....	....	....	....	....	....	....
Monetary authorities	4 901	....	....	....	....	....	....	....	....
General government	4 902	....	....	....	....	....	....	....	....
Banks	4 903	....	....	....	....	....	....	....	....
Other sectors	4 904	....	....	....	....	....	....	....	....
Liabilities	4 905	....	....	....	....	....	....	....	....
Monetary authorities	4 906	....	....	....	....	....	....	....	....
General government	4 907	....	....	....	....	....	....	....	....
Banks	4 908	....	....	....	....	....	....	....	....
Other sectors	4 909	....	....	....	....	....	....	....	....

El Salvador 253

Table 2 (Concluded). STANDARD PRESENTATION, 2003–2010

(Millions of U.S. dollars)

	Code	2003	2004	2005	2006	2007	2008	2009	2010
D. OTHER INVESTMENT	4 700	**737.1**	**−300.2**	**263.3**	**167.7**	**−728.9**	**667.5**	**−1,183.6**	**−32.0**
Assets	4 703	**19.6**	**−159.8**	**−246.7**	**72.7**	**−472.5**	**25.7**	**−629.1**	**235.7**
Trade credits	4 706	−17.3	−72.5	−99.2	−72.8	−13.4	118.3	−371.2	87.8
General government	4 707	....	....	....	....	....	....	....	....
of which: Short-term	4 709	....	....	....	....	....	....	....	....
Other sectors	4 710	−17.3	−72.5	−99.2	−72.8	−13.4	118.3	−371.2	87.8
of which: Short-term	4 712	−17.3	−72.5	−99.2	−72.8	−13.4	118.3	−371.2	87.8
Loans	4 714	61.6	−7.0	−117.6	9.5	−51.7	59.9	78.2	253.1
Monetary authorities	4 715	....	....	....	....	....	....	....	....
of which: Short-term	4 718	....	....	....	....	....	....	....	....
General government	4 719	....	....	....	....	....	....	....	....
of which: Short-term	4 721	....	....	....	....	....	....	....	....
Banks	4 722	59.4	3.7	−119.6	9.1	−68.1	82.0	84.0	135.3
of which: Short-term	4 724	59.4	3.7	....	....	....	....	....	....
Other sectors	4 725	2.2	−10.8	2.0	.4	16.4	−22.1	−5.8	117.9
of which: Short-term	4 727	....	....	....	....	....	....	....	....
Currency and deposits	4 730	−12.3	−90.6	−36.0	134.0	−404.0	−151.8	−335.6	−104.1
Monetary authorities	4 731	....	....	....	....	....	....	....	....
General government	4 732	....	....	....	....	....	....	....	....
Banks	4 733	73.5	−23.4	−62.3	41.4	−137.3	8.6	−263.8	−26.7
Other sectors	4 734	−85.8	−67.2	26.3	92.6	−266.6	−160.4	−71.8	−77.4
Other assets	4 736	−12.4	10.3	6.2	2.0	−3.4	−.7	−.5	−1.1
Monetary authorities	4 737	....	....	....	....	....	....	....	....
of which: Short-term	4 739	....	....	....	....	....	....	....	....
General government	4 740	....	....	....	....	....	....	....	....
of which: Short-term	4 742	....	....	....	....	....	....	....	....
Banks	4 743	.8	....	....	−.2	−.2	.2	.2	.1
of which: Short-term	4 745	.8	....	....	−.2	−.2	.2	.2	
Other sectors	4 746	−13.2	10.3	6.2	2.2	−3.3	−.9	−.7	−1.2
of which: Short-term	4 748	−13.2	10.3	....	....	....	....	....	....
Liabilities	4 753	**717.5**	**−140.4**	**510.0**	**95.0**	**−256.4**	**641.8**	**−554.5**	**−267.7**
Trade credits	4 756	59.7	41.1	184.3	−154.0	7.0	48.0	−4.4	−19.8
General government	4 757	....	....	....	....	....	....	....	....
of which: Short-term	4 759	....	....	....	....	....	....	....	....
Other sectors	4 760	59.7	41.1	184.3	−154.0	7.0	48.0	−4.4	−19.8
of which: Short-term	4 762	59.7	41.1	184.3	−154.0	7.0	48.0	−4.4	−19.8
Loans	4 764	692.8	−169.8	356.8	240.2	−273.3	592.7	−768.4	−240.2
Monetary authorities	4 765	75.4	−29.6	27.9	−75.7	−35.2	264.3	−118.4	−54.3
of which: Use of Fund credit and loans from the Fund	4 766	....	....	....	....	....	....	....	....
of which: Short-term	4 768	....	....	....	....	....	....	....	....
General government	4 769	33.2	−76.6	41.4	−42.3	−89.9	71.8	366.1	284.6
of which: Short-term	4 771	....	....	....	....	....	....	....	....
Banks	4 772	491.6	214.0	11.4	−249.9	−360.4	244.7	−653.0	−333.0
of which: Short-term	4 774	284.0	30.1	−19.8	−420.3	−136.8	189.0	−430.6	−256.9
Other sectors	4 775	92.6	−277.6	276.1	608.1	212.3	12.0	−363.1	−137.5
of which: Short-term	4 777	−29.0	−112.9	−6.9	29.4	164.9	66.9	−272.2	32.7
Currency and deposits	4 780	−1.2	−1.7	−22.0	11.6	11.0	−3.2	2.0	−3.9
Monetary authorities	4 781	−1.2	−1.7	−22.0	11.6	11.0	−3.2	2.0	−3.9
General government	4 782	....	....	....	....	....	....	....	....
Banks	4 783	....	....	....	....	....	....	....	....
Other sectors	4 784	....	....	....	....	....	....	....	....
Other liabilities	4 786	−33.8	−10.0	−9.1	−2.8	−1.1	4.3	216.3	−3.8
Monetary authorities	4 787	2.5	.3	−.9	−3.6	.3	3.4	213.5	−.6
of which: Short-term	4 789	....	....	−.9	−3.6	.3	3.4	−3.5	−.6
General government	4 790	....	....	....	....	....	....	....	....
of which: Short-term	4 792	....	....	....	....	....	....	....	....
Banks	4 793	....	....	....	....	−.2	....	....	....
of which: Short-term	4 795	....	....	....	....	−.2	....	....	....
Other sectors	4 796	−36.3	−10.3	−8.2	.8	−1.2	.9	2.8	−3.1
of which: Short-term	4 798	−36.3	−10.3	−8.2	.8	−1.2	.9	2.8	−3.1
E. RESERVE ASSETS	4 802	**−316.2**	**52.5**	**190.3**	**−46.6**	**−279.0**	**−333.5**	**−424.4**	**296.0**
Monetary gold	4 812	....	....	....	....	....	....	....	....
Special drawing rights	4 811	....	....	....	....	....	−.1	−217.0	.1
Reserve position in the Fund	4 810	....	....	....	....	....	....	....	....
Foreign exchange	4 803	−316.2	52.5	190.3	−46.6	−279.0	−333.4	−207.4	295.9
Other claims	4 813	....	....	....	....	....	....	....	....
NET ERRORS AND OMISSIONS	4 998	**−143.3**	**352.0**	**−449.0**	**−484.5**	**783.1**	**164.1**	**659.5**	**−15.3**

Table 3. INTERNATIONAL INVESTMENT POSITION (End-period stocks), 2003–2010

(Millions of U.S. dollars)

	Code	2003	2004	2005	2006	2007	2008	2009	2010
ASSETS...	8 995 C.	**4,473.4**	**4,750.8**	**5,425.7**	**5,705.5**	**6,659.2**	**6,780.2**	**7,123.3**	**7,037.9**
Direct investment abroad..................................	8 505 ..	**146.3**	**93.0**	**310.1**	**283.7**	**379.1**	**458.9**	**6.6**	**6.7**
Equity capital and reinvested earnings....	8 506 ..	23.7	19.0	33.6	32.4	29.0	43.8	6.6	6.7
Claims on affiliated enterprises........	8 507 ..	23.7	19.0	33.6	32.4	29.0	43.8	6.6	6.7
Liabilities to affiliated enterprises.....	8 508 ..	....	....	....	....	....	....		
Other capital...................................	8 530 ..	122.6	73.9	276.6	251.3	350.1	415.1	....	....
Claims on affiliated enterprises........	8 535 ..	122.6	73.9	276.6	251.3	350.1	415.1		
Liabilities to affiliated enterprises.....	8 540 ..	....	....	....	....	....	....		
Portfolio investment...........................	8 602 ..	**859.6**	**1,069.2**	**753.5**	**691.2**	**783.7**	**589.8**	**237.3**	**361.1**
Equity securities...............................	8 610 ..	260.4	257.9	75.9	76.3	98.3	103.6	123.8	125.5
Monetary authorities......................	8 611 ..	....	....	....	....	....	....	....	....
General government......................	8 612 ..	....	....	72.7	72.7	72.7	72.7	72.7	72.7
Banks...	8 613 ..	....	....	....	....	....	....		
Other sectors...............................	8 614 ..	260.4	257.9	3.1	3.6	25.5	30.8	51.1	52.8
Debt securities.................................	8 619 ..	599.2	811.3	677.6	614.9	685.5	486.3	113.5	235.6
Bonds and notes............................	8 620 ..	599.2	811.3	677.6	614.9	685.5	486.3	113.5	235.6
Monetary authorities..................	8 621 ..	....	....	....	....	....	....	....	....
General government..................	8 622 ..	....	....	....	....	....	....		
Banks......................................	8 623 ..	367.4	473.9	450.7	381.3	282.6	475.6	104.2	223.4
Other sectors............................	8 624 ..	231.8	337.4	226.9	233.6	402.8	10.7	9.4	12.2
Money market instruments..............	8 630 ..	....	....	....	....	....	....	....	....
Monetary authorities..................	8 631 ..	....	....	....	....	....	....		
General government..................	8 632 ..	....	....	....	....	....	....		
Banks......................................	8 633 ..	....	....	....	....	....	....		
Other sectors............................	8 634 ..	....	....	....	....	....	....		
Financial derivatives..........................	8 900 ..	....	....	....	....	....	....	....	....
Monetary authorities........................	8 901 ..	....	....	....	....	....	....		
General government..........................	8 902 ..	....	....	....	....	....	....		
Banks..	8 903 ..	....	....	....	....	....	....		
Other sectors....................................	8 904 ..	....	....	....	....	....	....		
Other investment...............................	8 703 ..	**1,557.4**	**1,695.7**	**2,529.0**	**2,822.3**	**3,297.6**	**3,186.5**	**3,893.0**	**3,786.9**
Trade credits....................................	8 706 ..	328.2	386.9	478.5	551.3	564.7	382.2	753.3	699.1
General government........................	8 707 ..	....	....	....	....	....	....		
of which: Short-term..................	8 709 ..	....	....	....	....	....	....		
Other sectors................................	8 710 ..	328.2	386.9	478.5	551.3	564.7	382.2	753.3	699.1
of which: Short-term..................	8 712 ..	*328.2*	*386.9*	*478.5*	*551.3*	*564.7*	*382.2*	*753.3*	*699.1*
Loans...	8 714 ..	338.7	349.1	455.8	446.4	498.1	438.0	421.3	212.3
Monetary authorities......................	8 715 ..	....	....	....	....	....	....		
of which: Short-term..................	8 718 ..	....	....	....	....	....	....		
General government........................	8 719 ..	....	....	....	....	....	....		
of which: Short-term..................	8 721 ..	....	....	....	....	....	....		
Banks...	8 722 ..	313.4	309.7	429.3	420.2	488.4	406.2	322.3	186.9
of which: Short-term..................	8 724 ..	*313.4*	*309.7*	*429.3*	*420.2*	*488.4*	*406.2*	*322.3*	*186.9*
Other sectors................................	8 725 ..	25.3	39.4	26.5	26.2	9.7	31.8	99.1	25.4
of which: Short-term..................	8 727 ..	*25.3*	*39.4*	....	....	....	*11.2*	*6.0*	*16.7*
Currency and deposits.......................	8 730 ..	852.1	938.3	1,557.5	1,789.4	2,195.9	2,326.5	2,678.1	2,834.2
Monetary authorities......................	8 731 ..	....	....	....	....	....	....		
General government........................	8 732 ..	....	....	....	....	....	....		
Banks...	8 733 ..	295.0	318.4	380.8	340.3	477.6	469.0	732.8	759.5
Other sectors................................	8 734 ..	557.1	619.9	1,176.7	1,449.1	1,718.4	1,857.5	1,945.3	2,074.6
Other assets....................................	8 736 ..	38.4	21.4	37.2	35.2	38.8	39.8	40.3	41.3
Monetary authorities......................	8 737 ..	....	....	4.0	4.0	4.0	4.0	4.0	4.0
of which: Short-term..................	8 739 ..	....	....	....	....	....	....		
General government........................	8 740 ..	....	....	19.9	19.9	19.9	19.9	19.9	19.9
of which: Short-term..................	8 742 ..	....	....	....	....	....	....		
Banks...	8 743 ..	.1	.1	.1	.2	.4	.4	.1	.1
of which: Short-term..................	8 745 ..	*.1*	*.1*	*.1*	*.2*	*.4*	*.4*	*.1*	*.1*
Other sectors................................	8 746 ..	38.4	21.3	13.2	11.0	14.5	15.5	16.2	17.3
of which: Short-term..................	8 748 ..	....	....	....	....	....	....		
Reserve assets...................................	8 802 ..	**1,910.1**	**1,892.9**	**1,833.0**	**1,908.2**	**2,198.7**	**2,545.0**	**2,986.3**	**2,883.2**
Monetary gold..................................	8 812 ..	117.8	138.9	110.2	84.0	88.8	101.9	117.5	313.6
Special drawing rights........................	8 811 ..	37.1	38.8	35.7	37.6	39.5	38.5	256.8	252.3
Reserve position in the Fund................	8 810 ..	....	....	....	....	....	....		
Foreign exchange..............................	8 803 ..	1,754.4	1,714.1	1,684.9	1,782.2	2,069.5	2,404.1	2,611.8	2,317.2
Other claims....................................	8 813 ..	.8	1.1	2.2	4.4	.9	.5	.1	.1

Table 3 (Concluded). INTERNATIONAL INVESTMENT POSITION (End-period stocks), 2003–2010

(Millions of U.S. dollars)

	Code	2003	2004	2005	2006	2007	2008	2009	2010
LIABILITIES	8 995 D.	**11,192.1**	**11,866.1**	**13,177.5**	**14,461.7**	**15,682.0**	**16,258.2**	**17,213.9**	**17,735.2**
Direct investment in El Salvador	8 555 ..	**3,275.4**	**3,655.5**	**4,166.5**	**4,407.8**	**5,958.4**	**6,862.4**	**7,682.0**	**7,818.4**
Equity capital and reinvested earnings	8 556 ..	2,589.2	2,996.1	3,508.1	3,735.0	5,182.5	5,721.5	6,851.4	7,058.2
Claims on direct investors	8 557 ..	....	....	....	....	....	....	....	....
Liabilities to direct investors	8 558 ..	2,589.2	2,996.1	3,508.1	3,735.0	5,182.5	5,721.5	6,851.4	7,058.2
Other capital	8 580 ..	686.2	659.4	658.4	672.8	775.9	1,140.9	830.6	760.2
Claims on direct investors	8 585 ..	....	....	....	....	....	....	....	....
Liabilities to direct investors	8 590 ..	686.2	659.4	658.4	672.8	775.9	1,140.9	830.6	760.2
Portfolio investment	8 652 ..	**1,402.5**	**1,569.6**	**1,786.0**	**2,719.3**	**2,618.7**	**1,572.6**	**2,236.6**	**2,850.3**
Equity securities	8 660 ..	....	....	....	....	....	....	....	....
Banks	8 663 ..	....	....	....	....	....	....	....	....
Other sectors	8 664 ..	....	....	....	....	....	....	....	....
Debt securities	8 669 ..	1,402.5	1,569.6	1,786.0	2,719.3	2,618.7	1,572.6	2,236.6	2,850.3
Bonds and notes	8 670 ..	1,250.5	1,410.4	1,750.3	2,702.3	2,608.7	1,564.6	2,231.7	2,850.3
Monetary authorities	8 671 ..	....	....	....	....	....	....	....	....
General government	8 672 ..	1,250.5	1,410.4	1,750.3	2,702.3	2,608.7	1,564.6	2,231.7	2,850.3
Banks	8 673 ..	....	....	....	....	....	....	....	....
Other sectors	8 674 ..	....	....	....	....	....	....	....	....
Money market instruments	8 680 ..	152.0	159.2	35.7	17.0	10.0	8.0	4.9	....
Monetary authorities	8 681 ..	92.0	52.2	21.7	....	....	....	....	....
General government	8 682 ..	60.0	107.0	14.0	17.0	10.0	8.0	4.9	....
Banks	8 683 ..	....	....	....	....	....	....	....	....
Other sectors	8 684 ..	....	....	....	....	....	....	....	....
Financial derivatives	8 905 ..	....	....	....	....	....	....	....	....
Monetary authorities	8 906 ..	....	....	....	....	....	....	....	....
General government	8 907 ..	....	....	....	....	....	....	....	....
Banks	8 908 ..	....	....	....	....	....	....	....	....
Other sectors	8 909 ..	....	....	....	....	....	....	....	....
Other investment	8 753 ..	**6,514.3**	**6,641.0**	**7,225.0**	**7,334.7**	**7,104.9**	**7,823.2**	**7,295.3**	**7,066.5**
Trade credits	8 756 ..	308.3	408.1	592.4	438.4	445.4	493.4	489.1	469.3
General government	8 757 ..	....	....	....	....	....	....	....	....
of which: Short-term	8 759 ..	....	....	....	....	....	....	....	....
Other sectors	8 760 ..	308.3	408.1	592.4	438.4	445.4	493.4	489.1	469.3
of which: Short-term	8 762 ..	*308.3*	*408.1*	*592.4*	*438.4*	*445.4*	*493.4*	*489.1*	*469.3*
Loans	8 764 ..	6,149.6	6,186.8	6,560.4	6,825.2	6,587.5	7,255.5	6,514.2	6,312.6
Monetary authorities	8 765 ..	170.5	145.7	173.6	96.2	61.0	325.3	206.9	151.4
of which: Use of Fund credit and loans from the Fund	8 766 ..	....	....	....	....	....	....	....	....
of which: Short-term	8 768 ..	....	....	....	....	....	....	....	....
General government	8 769 ..	2,629.0	2,626.4	2,637.7	2,646.5	2,626.3	2,729.1	3,132.1	3,433.9
of which: Short-term	8 771 ..	....	....	....	....	....	....	....	....
Banks	8 772 ..	1,592.1	1,806.2	1,817.5	1,568.0	1,207.7	1,452.6	799.7	466.8
of which: Short-term	8 774 ..	*900.7*	*930.8*	*910.9*	*490.7*	*354.0*	*543.2*	*112.5*	*36.4*
Other sectors	8 775 ..	1,758.0	1,608.5	1,931.5	2,514.6	2,692.5	2,748.4	2,375.4	2,260.6
of which: Short-term	8 777 ..	*359.0*	*292.3*	*285.4*	*314.7*	*479.7*	*546.6*	*274.3*	*307.1*
Currency and deposits	8 780 ..	27.6	26.0	25.5	24.4	24.5	23.1	22.9	24.0
Monetary authorities	8 781 ..	27.6	26.0	25.5	24.4	24.5	23.1	22.9	24.0
General government	8 782 ..	....	....	....	....	....	....	....	....
Banks	8 783 ..	....	....	....	....	....	....	....	....
Other sectors	8 784 ..	....	....	....	....	....	....	....	....
Other liabilities	8 786 ..	28.7	20.1	46.8	46.6	47.5	51.2	269.1	260.5
Monetary authorities	8 787 ..	4.2	4.5	40.0	38.8	40.6	43.8	259.1	254.0
of which: Short-term	8 789 ..	*4.2*	*4.5*	*4.3*	*1.3*	*1.5*	*4.9*	*2.3*	*1.7*
General government	8 790 ..	....	....	....	....	....	....	....	....
of which: Short-term	8 792 ..	....	....	....	....	....	....	....	....
Banks	8 793 ..	4.3	4.5	3.8	4.1	4.4	4.1	4.0	3.6
of which: Short-term	8 795 ..	*4.3*	*4.5*	*3.8*	*4.1*	*4.4*	*4.1*	*4.0*	*3.6*
Other sectors	8 796 ..	20.2	11.1	3.0	3.7	2.5	3.3	6.0	2.9
of which: Short-term	8 798 ..	....	....	*3.0*	*3.7*	*2.5*	*3.3*	*6.0*	*2.9*
NET INTERNATIONAL INVESTMENT POSITION	8 995 ..	**−6,718.7**	**−7,115.3**	**−7,751.8**	**−8,756.2**	**−9,022.8**	**−9,478.0**	**−10,090.6**	**−10,697.3**

Table 1. ANALYTIC PRESENTATION, 2003–2010

(Millions of U.S. dollars)

	Code	2003	2004	2005	2006	2007	2008	2009	2010
A. Current Account[1]	4 993 Z.	−1,115.3	−1,369.2	−1,386.4	−2,585.5	−3,503.2	−2,356.3	740.8	673.2
Goods: exports f.o.b.	2 100 ..	4,597.0	5,929.1	7,876.7	9,770.5	11,153.8	12,572.4	9,145.8	11,641.3
Goods: imports f.o.b.	3 100 ..	−6,164.0	−7,876.6	−9,796.5	−12,676.8	−14,772.6	−15,696.2	−9,921.1	−11,972.0
Balance on Goods	4 100 ..	*−1,567.0*	*−1,947.6*	*−1,919.8*	*−2,906.3*	*−3,618.9*	*−3,123.8*	*−775.2*	*−330.7*
Services: credit	2 200 ..	2,223.7	2,847.9	3,239.4	3,617.7	4,517.3	5,192.1	4,434.7	4,527.9
Services: debit	3 200 ..	−1,392.9	−1,745.4	−2,197.9	−2,494.7	−3,087.0	−3,362.8	−2,535.2	−2,798.5
Balance on Goods and Services	4 991 ..	*−736.2*	*−845.1*	*−878.3*	*−1,783.3*	*−2,188.6*	*−1,294.5*	*1,124.3*	*1,398.7*
Income: credit	2 300 ..	249.3	436.2	730.7	1,091.5	1,662.3	1,700.0	917.0	907.3
Income: debit	3 300 ..	−785.3	−1,074.3	−1,300.3	−1,956.4	−3,112.6	−3,013.0	−1,614.1	−1,973.8
Balance on Goods, Services, and Income	4 992 ..	*−1,272.2*	*−1,483.1*	*−1,447.9*	*−2,648.2*	*−3,638.9*	*−2,607.6*	*427.2*	*332.2*
Current transfers: credit	2 379 Z.	266.5	416.7	465.6	528.9	652.7	726.1	709.4	788.7
Current transfers: debit	3 379 ..	−109.5	−302.7	−404.1	−466.2	−517.1	−474.8	−395.7	−447.6
B. Capital Account[1]	4 994 Z.	**49.6**	**86.4**	**103.0**	**363.0**	**241.2**	**285.1**	**690.2**	**693.8**
Capital account: credit	2 994 Z.	57.8	93.2	109.5	383.4	297.1	306.3	695.8	702.1
Capital account: debit	3 994 ..	−8.2	−6.8	−6.5	−20.4	−55.9	−21.2	−5.6	−8.3
Total, Groups A Plus B	4 981 ..	*−1,065.7*	*−1,282.8*	*−1,283.4*	*−2,222.4*	*−3,262.1*	*−2,071.1*	*1,431.0*	*1,367.0*
C. Financial Account[1]	4 995 W.	**1,274.6**	**1,717.0**	**1,520.1**	**3,028.6**	**3,321.6**	**2,551.7**	**−1,315.8**	**−2,191.4**
Direct investment abroad	4 505 ..	−156.1	−268.2	−687.5	−1,111.8	−1,742.7	−1,130.6	−1,575.2	−127.2
Direct investment in Estonia	4 555 Z.	919.0	965.8	2,941.3	1,787.4	2,720.0	1,748.5	1,908.2	1,539.1
Portfolio investment assets	4 602 ..	−394.3	−380.6	−871.6	−1,214.6	−735.5	943.9	−678.6	−364.6
Equity securities	4 610 ..	−75.5	−232.4	−387.7	−366.9	−662.6	376.5	−68.5	−396.7
Debt securities	4 619 ..	−318.8	−148.2	−483.9	−847.7	−72.9	567.4	−610.1	32.0
Portfolio investment liabilities	4 652 Z.	561.2	1,114.3	−1,382.2	−68.6	240.7	−244.6	−1,408.3	−193.0
Equity securities	4 660 ..	110.6	176.1	−1,362.8	308.6	289.4	−300.7	−133.0	15.2
Debt securities	4 669 Z.	450.5	938.1	−19.4	−377.2	−48.7	56.1	−1,275.3	−208.2
Financial derivatives	4 910 ..	−1.8	−.3	−7.5	5.8	−71.5	71.8	15.9	40.8
Financial derivatives assets	4 900 ..	−9.9	−2.9	1.3	−15.4	−77.5	62.5	22.5	−3.5
Financial derivatives liabilities	4 905 ..	8.1	2.6	−8.8	21.2	6.0	9.3	−6.6	44.3
Other investment assets	4 703 ..	−154.4	−949.1	−917.6	60.5	−2,056.8	−488.0	1,237.4	−1,736.2
Monetary authorities	4 701 ..	.1	−.8	−.1	....	.1	.3	....	....
General government	4 704 ..	39.8	−60.4	−56.8	52.4	−38.5	−120.0	−37.1	−24.8
Banks	4 705 ..	−87.0	−674.6	−1,004.2	597.7	−1,581.1	−186.4	1,310.7	−256.0
Other sectors	4 728 ..	−107.3	−213.2	143.4	−589.5	−437.2	−181.9	−36.3	−1,455.3
Other investment liabilities	4 753 W.	501.1	1,235.2	2,445.3	3,569.9	4,967.2	1,650.6	−815.1	−1,350.2
Monetary authorities	4 753 WA	43.5	17.9	−54.7	30.9	70.4	−159.0	107.3	6.7
General government	4 753 ZB	29.2	133.6	39.5	18.4	−5.9	79.1	264.6	127.8
Banks	4 753 ZC	336.3	948.0	1,960.6	2,015.3	4,535.6	1,416.9	−713.6	−1,940.2
Other sectors	4 753 ZD	92.0	135.7	499.9	1,505.3	367.1	313.5	−473.4	455.4
Total, Groups A Through C	4 983 ..	*208.9*	*434.2*	*236.7*	*806.1*	*59.5*	*480.5*	*115.2*	*−824.5*
D. Net Errors and Omissions	4 998 ..	**−39.5**	**−163.0**	**148.8**	**−185.4**	**50.7**	**239.4**	**−83.0**	**−287.7**
Total, Groups A Through D	4 984 ..	*169.4*	*271.2*	*385.5*	*620.7*	*110.3*	*719.9*	*32.2*	*−1,112.1*
E. Reserves and Related Items	4 802 A.	**−169.4**	**−271.2**	**−385.5**	**−620.7**	**−110.3**	**−719.9**	**−32.2**	**1,112.1**
Reserve assets	4 802 ..	−169.4	−271.2	−385.5	−620.7	−110.3	−719.9	−32.2	1,112.1
Use of Fund credit and loans	4 766 ..	....	....	....	....	....	....	....	....
Exceptional financing	4 920 ..	....	....	....	....	....	....	....	....
Conversion rates: krooni per U.S. dollar	0 101 ..	**13.856**	**12.596**	**12.584**	**12.465**	**11.434**	**10.694**	**11.257**	**11.807**
Conversion rates: euros per U.S. dollar	0 103 ..	**.8860**	**.8054**	**.8041**	**.7971**	**.7306**	**.6827**	**.7198**	**.7550**

[1] Excludes components that have been classified in the categories of Group E.

Table 2. STANDARD PRESENTATION, 2003–2010

(Millions of U.S. dollars)

	Code	2003	2004	2005	2006	2007	2008	2009	2010
CURRENT ACCOUNT	4 993 ..	**−1,115.3**	**−1,369.2**	**−1,386.4**	**−2,585.5**	**−3,503.2**	**−2,356.3**	**740.8**	**673.2**
A. GOODS	4 100 ..	**−1,567.0**	**−1,947.6**	**−1,919.8**	**−2,906.3**	**−3,618.9**	**−3,123.8**	**−775.2**	**−330.7**
Credit	2 100 ..	**4,597.0**	**5,929.1**	**7,876.7**	**9,770.5**	**11,153.8**	**12,572.4**	**9,145.8**	**11,641.3**
General merchandise: exports f.o.b.	2 110 ..	3,203.5	4,895.5	7,019.2	8,124.1	9,735.7	11,291.7	7,914.5	10,093.5
Goods for processing: exports f.o.b.	2 150 ..	1,365.3	1,000.7	805.4	1,606.5	1,353.6	1,208.2	1,168.3	1,455.4
Repairs on goods	2 160 ..	19.1	31.1	45.8	32.9	48.1	66.9	55.5	36.9
Goods procured in ports by carriers	2 170 ..	9.1	1.7	6.2	1.9	3.1	5.6	3.8	7.0
Nonmonetary gold	2 180 ..	....	....	.1	5.1	13.2	....	3.8	48.5
Debit	3 100 ..	**−6,164.0**	**−7,876.6**	**−9,796.5**	**−12,676.8**	**−14,772.6**	**−15,696.2**	**−9,921.1**	**−11,972.0**
General merchandise: imports f.o.b.	3 110 ..	−5,037.5	−6,984.4	−8,992.3	−11,042.5	−13,360.2	−14,109.8	−8,636.7	−10,519.4
Goods for processing: imports f.o.b.	3 150 ..	−1,090.6	−837.3	−729.7	−1,521.0	−1,258.5	−1,333.0	−1,125.9	−1,235.1
Repairs on goods	3 160 ..	−6.2	−10.4	−21.0	−22.0	−22.5	−24.5	−14.9	−15.7
Goods procured in ports by carriers	3 170 ..	−29.1	−43.7	−52.5	−84.6	−116.9	−198.5	−126.6	−151.7
Nonmonetary gold	3 180 ..	−.5	−.8	−1.1	−6.8	−14.6	−30.4	−17.0	−50.2
B. SERVICES	4 200 ..	**830.7**	**1,102.5**	**1,041.5**	**1,123.0**	**1,430.3**	**1,829.3**	**1,899.6**	**1,729.4**
Total credit	2 200 ..	*2,223.7*	*2,847.9*	*3,239.4*	*3,617.7*	*4,517.3*	*5,192.1*	*4,434.7*	*4,527.9*
Total debit	3 200 ..	*−1,392.9*	*−1,745.4*	*−2,197.9*	*−2,494.7*	*−3,087.0*	*−3,362.8*	*−2,535.2*	*−2,798.5*
Transportation services, credit	2 205 ..	**972.0**	**1,216.0**	**1,277.9**	**1,514.9**	**1,843.7**	**2,016.9**	**1,629.8**	**1,781.4**
Passenger	2 850 ..	*212.0*	*224.4*	*258.1*	*337.2*	*379.8*	*449.6*	*354.9*	*347.0*
Freight	2 851 ..	*506.8*	*695.4*	*663.8*	*759.2*	*938.6*	*959.0*	*708.3*	*847.9*
Other	2 852 ..	*253.3*	*296.2*	*356.1*	*418.5*	*525.3*	*608.2*	*566.6*	*586.5*
Sea transport, passenger	2 207 ..	152.6	124.8	140.4	184.8	244.2	316.3	283.6	278.6
Sea transport, freight	2 208 ..	165.8	234.5	228.8	279.5	409.7	390.1	253.4	313.5
Sea transport, other	2 209 ..	139.6	132.3	162.0	268.9	243.7	181.7	150.6	145.6
Air transport, passenger	2 211 ..	54.0	93.0	110.1	143.1	126.7	126.5	63.6	57.8
Air transport, freight	2 212 ..	13.9	16.1	39.2	30.6	40.2	26.8	23.7	21.9
Air transport, other	2 213 ..	16.1	25.8	28.7	22.5	30.2	52.5	33.8	32.5
Other transport, passenger	2 215 ..	5.4	6.7	7.6	9.3	8.9	6.8	7.8	10.7
Other transport, freight	2 216 ..	327.1	444.7	395.8	449.1	488.7	542.2	431.2	512.5
Other transport, other	2 217 ..	97.5	138.1	165.3	127.1	251.4	374.1	382.1	408.5
Transportation services, debit	3 205 ..	**−515.7**	**−724.3**	**−950.3**	**−1,037.3**	**−1,278.2**	**−1,252.6**	**−819.2**	**−969.7**
Passenger	3 850 ..	*−85.0*	*−86.7*	*−90.9*	*−120.0*	*−134.1*	*−129.7*	*−90.6*	*−88.8*
Freight	3 851 ..	*−316.2*	*−462.8*	*−631.8*	*−706.6*	*−838.2*	*−812.4*	*−495.2*	*−609.3*
Other	3 852 ..	*−114.5*	*−174.7*	*−227.6*	*−210.7*	*−305.9*	*−310.5*	*−233.4*	*−271.6*
Sea transport, passenger	3 207 ..	−26.3	−26.7	−27.5	−34.2	−33.1	−31.7	−17.5	−20.7
Sea transport, freight	3 208 ..	−132.3	−174.2	−255.9	−293.4	−357.1	−329.9	−178.9	−231.8
Sea transport, other	3 209 ..	−48.7	−71.9	−96.7	−92.2	−144.4	−161.6	−112.9	−117.8
Air transport, passenger	3 211 ..	−49.7	−51.1	−54.2	−74.8	−88.3	−86.7	−63.1	−50.8
Air transport, freight	3 212 ..	−47.7	−72.2	−103.9	−114.8	−129.8	−134.1	−82.2	−112.3
Air transport, other	3 213 ..	−13.8	−33.0	−50.5	−41.9	−28.5	−12.5	−22.7	−18.4
Other transport, passenger	3 215 ..	−9.0	−8.9	−9.2	−11.0	−12.7	−11.3	−9.9	−17.2
Other transport, freight	3 216 ..	−136.2	−216.4	−272.0	−298.3	−351.3	−348.4	−234.2	−265.2
Other transport, other	3 217 ..	−52.0	−69.8	−80.4	−76.7	−132.9	−136.4	−97.9	−135.5
Travel, credit	2 236 ..	**671.0**	**886.6**	**971.2**	**1,023.9**	**1,035.5**	**1,191.9**	**1,090.2**	**1,065.1**
Business travel	2 237 ..	180.4	229.5	229.9	228.2	249.5	246.8	227.6	228.4
Personal travel	2 240 ..	490.5	657.1	741.4	795.6	786.0	945.2	862.6	836.7
Travel, debit	3 236 ..	**−319.0**	**−398.8**	**−438.7**	**−585.9**	**−670.0**	**−807.8**	**−605.6**	**−630.1**
Business travel	3 237 ..	−105.6	−146.6	−173.7	−223.4	−245.7	−248.7	−161.3	−170.4
Personal travel	3 240 ..	−213.4	−252.2	−264.9	−362.5	−424.4	−559.1	−444.3	−459.6
Other services, credit	2 200 BA ..	**580.7**	**745.2**	**990.3**	**1,079.0**	**1,638.0**	**1,983.2**	**1,714.8**	**1,681.4**
Communications	2 245 ..	38.7	63.6	78.0	80.1	125.5	195.8	193.8	199.7
Construction	2 249 ..	85.6	88.6	187.3	87.3	201.0	362.1	213.3	213.9
Insurance	2 253 ..	15.1	14.5	10.4	11.4	14.2	15.1	11.0	9.6
Financial	2 260 ..	16.0	22.9	45.8	71.4	128.7	89.3	70.2	92.7
Computer and information	2 262 ..	31.1	38.8	53.6	92.4	163.9	175.7	185.6	204.4
Royalties and licence fees	2 266 ..	5.2	4.0	5.4	6.6	10.7	26.9	24.6	20.4
Other business services	2 268 ..	352.1	467.2	556.3	676.3	932.4	1,050.7	956.4	883.6
Personal, cultural, and recreational	2 287 ..	1.8	3.5	5.2	7.7	11.8	16.6	14.4	14.5
Government, n.i.e.	2 291 ..	35.1	42.2	48.2	45.7	49.8	51.1	45.5	42.7
Other services, debit	3 200 BA ..	**−558.2**	**−622.3**	**−809.0**	**−871.6**	**−1,138.8**	**−1,302.4**	**−1,110.4**	**−1,198.8**
Communications	3 245 ..	−45.5	−72.4	−90.9	−90.7	−116.1	−204.1	−171.1	−200.2
Construction	3 249 ..	−92.9	−91.7	−184.5	−135.8	−95.3	−109.6	−106.2	−108.7
Insurance	3 253 ..	−1.9	−1.3	−1.2	−1.7	−1.0	−1.1	−1.2	−3.4
Financial	3 260 ..	−20.4	−23.5	−39.0	−52.0	−86.2	−51.2	−36.5	−49.2
Computer and information	3 262 ..	−21.5	−28.6	−32.7	−47.1	−70.9	−96.9	−89.8	−95.4
Royalties and licence fees	3 266 ..	−14.2	−18.0	−24.9	−29.4	−40.3	−49.8	−45.8	−60.0
Other business services	3 268 ..	−336.7	−353.7	−406.6	−475.0	−669.5	−726.0	−612.2	−643.2
Personal, cultural, and recreational	3 287 ..	−1.7	−2.5	−4.6	−6.8	−9.0	−15.0	−12.0	−10.1
Government, n.i.e.	3 291 ..	−23.4	−30.7	−24.4	−33.0	−50.5	−47.8	−35.6	−28.7

Table 2 (Continued). STANDARD PRESENTATION, 2003–2010

(Millions of U.S. dollars)

	Code	2003	2004	2005	2006	2007	2008	2009	2010
C. INCOME	4 300	**−536.0**	**−638.1**	**−569.6**	**−864.9**	**−1,450.3**	**−1,313.0**	**−697.1**	**−1,066.5**
Total credit	2 300	*249.3*	*436.2*	*730.7*	*1,091.5*	*1,662.3*	*1,700.0*	*917.0*	*907.3*
Total debit	3 300	*−785.3*	*−1,074.3*	*−1,300.3*	*−1,956.4*	*−3,112.6*	*−3,013.0*	*−1,614.1*	*−1,973.8*
Compensation of employees, credit	2 310	**42.0**	**155.0**	**254.5**	**392.2**	**381.2**	**309.3**	**252.3**	**267.2**
Compensation of employees, debit	3 310	**−16.4**	**−25.2**	**−49.2**	**−73.9**	**−90.7**	**−96.2**	**−75.7**	**−90.8**
Investment income, credit	2 320	**207.2**	**281.2**	**476.2**	**699.2**	**1,281.1**	**1,390.7**	**664.6**	**640.0**
Direct investment income	2 330	91.9	152.4	314.7	456.5	806.9	835.2	411.2	405.8
Dividends and distributed branch profits	2 332	30.6	64.1	83.2	37.7	291.4	512.3	136.9	82.0
Reinvested earnings and undistributed branch profits	2 333	53.2	74.6	212.0	390.6	451.0	198.7	141.1	237.5
Income on debt (interest)	2 334	8.2	13.7	19.5	28.2	64.5	124.2	133.2	86.3
Portfolio investment income	2 339	58.1	69.0	82.6	155.0	262.8	297.0	159.0	136.3
Income on equity	2 340	6.5	9.8	10.8	15.8	28.8	32.0	21.0	35.3
Income on bonds and notes	2 350	33.3	44.4	58.7	93.5	157.1	165.2	99.1	79.8
Income on money market instruments	2 360	18.3	14.8	13.1	45.6	76.9	99.8	39.0	21.1
Other investment income	2 370	57.2	59.8	78.9	87.8	211.4	258.5	94.5	98.0
Investment income, debit	3 320	**−768.9**	**−1,049.1**	**−1,251.1**	**−1,882.5**	**−3,021.8**	**−2,916.8**	**−1,538.4**	**−1,883.0**
Direct investment income	3 330	−628.5	−861.1	−1,006.8	−1,550.9	−2,318.3	−1,903.9	−1,023.9	−1,549.0
Dividends and distributed branch profits	3 332	−133.2	−177.1	−250.4	−212.7	−278.7	−435.1	−312.2	−219.5
Reinvested earnings and undistributed branch profits	3 333	−465.6	−643.0	−704.7	−1,259.3	−1,878.6	−1,303.8	−568.1	−1,230.6
Income on debt (interest)	3 334	−29.7	−41.0	−51.7	−78.8	−161.0	−165.0	−143.6	−98.9
Portfolio investment income	3 339	−57.9	−84.5	−112.9	−88.3	−217.5	−159.5	−94.1	−49.1
Income on equity	3 340	−15.6	−26.7	−35.1	−21.9	−127.7	−36.6	−35.7	−17.4
Income on bonds and notes	3 350	−38.8	−49.0	−66.3	−64.8	−88.0	−122.4	−56.7	−31.0
Income on money market instruments	3 360	−3.6	−8.8	−11.5	−1.7	−1.8	−.6	−1.7	−.8
Other investment income	3 370	−82.5	−103.6	−131.3	−243.3	−486.0	−853.4	−420.4	−284.9
D. CURRENT TRANSFERS	4 379	**157.0**	**113.9**	**61.5**	**62.7**	**135.6**	**251.3**	**313.6**	**341.1**
Credit	2 379	**266.5**	**416.7**	**465.6**	**528.9**	**652.7**	**726.1**	**709.4**	**788.7**
General government	2 380	147.4	186.8	225.7	251.0	276.7	266.2	281.2	318.8
Other sectors	2 390	119.0	229.8	239.9	278.0	376.0	459.8	428.1	469.9
Workers' remittances	2 391	9.2	11.9	9.5	9.6	29.7	60.3	57.0	54.9
Other current transfers	2 392	109.8	217.9	230.4	268.3	346.3	399.5	371.1	414.9
Debit	3 379	**−109.5**	**−302.7**	**−404.1**	**−466.2**	**−517.1**	**−474.8**	**−395.7**	**−447.6**
General government	3 380	−17.7	−153.0	−258.6	−258.5	−290.2	−285.2	−244.7	−236.9
Other sectors	3 390	−91.8	−149.7	−145.6	−207.7	−226.9	−189.5	−151.0	−210.7
Workers' remittances	3 391	−2.2	−1.3	−1.2	−1.5	−1.9	−1.6	−2.4	−3.5
Other current transfers	3 392	−89.6	−148.4	−144.3	−206.2	−225.0	−187.9	−148.7	−207.2
CAPITAL AND FINANCIAL ACCOUNT	4 996	**1,154.8**	**1,532.2**	**1,237.6**	**2,770.9**	**3,452.5**	**2,116.9**	**−657.8**	**−385.6**
CAPITAL ACCOUNT	4 994	**49.6**	**86.4**	**103.0**	**363.0**	**241.2**	**285.1**	**690.2**	**693.8**
Total credit	2 994	*57.8*	*93.2*	*109.5*	*383.4*	*297.1*	*306.3*	*695.8*	*702.1*
Total debit	3 994	*−8.2*	*−6.8*	*−6.5*	*−20.4*	*−55.9*	*−21.2*	*−5.6*	*−8.3*
Capital transfers, credit	2 400	**55.6**	**90.8**	**94.2**	**194.8**	**282.7**	**304.9**	**690.7**	**521.0**
General government	2 401	40.9	40.9	35.6	133.8	169.1	99.8	336.4	265.1
Debt forgiveness	2 402	....	....	....	....	....	....	....	....
Other capital transfers	2 410	40.9	40.9	35.6	133.8	169.1	99.8	336.4	265.1
Other sectors	2 430	14.7	50.0	58.6	61.0	113.6	205.1	354.3	255.8
Migrants' transfers	2 431	....	....	....	....	....	....	....	....
Debt forgiveness	2 432	14.3	1.7	3.3	10.9	5.3	20.8	....	1.9
Other capital transfers	2 440	.3	48.3	55.3	50.2	108.3	184.4	354.3	253.9
Capital transfers, debit	3 400	**−2.1**	**−2.1**	**−3.8**	**−13.5**	**−48.9**	**−13.7**	**−1.4**	**−8.1**
General government	3 401	....	....	....	−.1	−22.8	....	−.1	−.2
Debt forgiveness	3 402	....	....	....	....	....	....	....	....
Other capital transfers	3 410	....	....	....	−.1	−22.8	....	−.1	−.2
Other sectors	3 430	−2.1	−2.1	−3.8	−13.5	−26.1	−13.7	−1.3	−7.9
Migrants' transfers	3 431	....	....	....	....	....	....	....	....
Debt forgiveness	3 432	−1.8	−2.1	−3.8	−11.9	−23.6	−9.8	....	−7.9
Other capital transfers	3 440	−.4	....	....	−1.6	−2.5	−3.8	−1.3	....
Nonproduced nonfinancial assets, credit	2 480	**2.2**	**2.4**	**15.2**	**188.6**	**14.4**	**1.4**	**5.0**	**181.1**
Nonproduced nonfinancial assets, debit	3 480	**−6.0**	**−4.7**	**−2.6**	**−6.8**	**−7.0**	**−7.5**	**−4.2**	**−.2**

Table 2 (Continued). STANDARD PRESENTATION, 2003–2010

(Millions of U.S. dollars)

	Code	2003	2004	2005	2006	2007	2008	2009	2010
FINANCIAL ACCOUNT	4 995	**1,105.2**	**1,445.8**	**1,134.6**	**2,407.9**	**3,211.3**	**1,831.8**	**−1,348.0**	**−1,079.3**
A. DIRECT INVESTMENT	4 500	**762.9**	**697.6**	**2,253.8**	**675.6**	**977.4**	**617.9**	**333.0**	**1,411.9**
Direct investment abroad	4 505	−156.1	−268.2	−687.5	−1,111.8	−1,742.7	−1,130.6	−1,575.2	−127.2
Equity capital	4 510	−79.2	−169.0	−407.6	−476.8	−896.9	−227.5	−1,113.5	−106.9
Claims on affiliated enterprises	4 515	−79.2	−169.0	−407.6	−476.8	−896.9	−227.5	−1,113.5	−106.9
Liabilities to affiliated enterprises	4 520	....	....	....	....	....	....	....	....
Reinvested earnings	4 525	−53.2	−74.6	−212.0	−390.6	−451.0	−198.7	−141.1	−237.5
Other capital	4 530	−23.8	−24.6	−67.8	−244.4	−394.8	−704.3	−320.6	217.1
Claims on affiliated enterprises	4 535	−45.6	−34.7	−90.6	−306.1	−524.1	−618.8	−214.9	89.8
Liabilities to affiliated enterprises	4 540	21.8	10.1	22.8	61.7	129.3	−85.6	−105.7	127.4
Direct investment in Estonia	4 555	**919.0**	**965.8**	**2,941.3**	**1,787.4**	**2,720.0**	**1,748.5**	**1,908.2**	**1,539.1**
Equity capital	4 560	378.4	368.0	2,293.7	176.7	374.4	282.0	1,764.3	478.6
Claims on direct investors	4 565	....	....	....	....	....	....	....	....
Liabilities to direct investors	4 570	378.4	368.0	2,293.7	176.7	374.4	282.0	1,764.3	478.6
Reinvested earnings	4 575	465.6	643.0	704.7	1,259.3	1,878.6	1,303.8	568.1	1,230.6
Other capital	4 580	75.0	−45.2	−57.2	351.4	467.0	162.7	−424.2	−170.1
Claims on direct investors	4 585	−96.9	−110.5	−163.2	−363.1	−579.7	−209.6	−63.4	−292.8
Liabilities to direct investors	4 590	171.9	65.4	106.1	714.5	1,046.7	372.3	−360.8	122.7
B. PORTFOLIO INVESTMENT	4 600	**166.8**	**733.7**	**−2,253.9**	**−1,283.3**	**−494.8**	**699.3**	**−2,086.9**	**−557.7**
Assets	4 602	**−394.3**	**−380.6**	**−871.6**	**−1,214.6**	**−735.5**	**943.9**	**−678.6**	**−364.6**
Equity securities	4 610	−75.5	−232.4	−387.7	−366.9	−662.6	376.5	−68.5	−396.7
Monetary authorities	4 611	....	....	−.3	....	....	....	....	....
General government	4 612	−4.1	−3.3	−.7	−13.6	−9.9	.8	25.6	11.7
Banks	4 613	−.4	−1.9	−10.1	−.6	5.5	12.6	.9	−.4
Other sectors	4 614	−71.0	−227.2	−376.7	−352.8	−658.2	363.2	−95.0	−408.0
Debt securities	4 619	−318.8	−148.2	−483.9	−847.7	−72.9	567.4	−610.1	32.0
Bonds and notes	4 620	−84.4	−290.5	−217.3	−909.2	195.5	193.6	−64.6	−50.9
Monetary authorities	4 621	....	....	....	....	....	....	....	....
General government	4 622	38.3	−106.1	51.2	−716.3	−59.6	173.8	355.7	−20.3
Banks	4 623	.1	−117.5	−13.7	−23.8	56.1	85.6	−217.9	−132.6
Other sectors	4 624	−122.8	−67.0	−254.8	−169.1	198.9	−65.8	−202.4	101.9
Money market instruments	4 630	−234.4	142.3	−266.6	61.5	−268.4	373.9	−545.5	83.0
Monetary authorities	4 631	....	....	....	....	....	....	....	....
General government	4 632	−343.3	57.9	−166.5	264.7	−270.7	225.2	−186.8	46.4
Banks	4 633	77.1	79.8	−46.0	−189.1	129.4	153.0	−422.2	37.9
Other sectors	4 634	31.9	4.7	−54.1	−14.2	−127.1	−4.3	63.5	−1.3
Liabilities	4 652	**561.2**	**1,114.3**	**−1,382.2**	**−68.6**	**240.7**	**−244.6**	**−1,408.3**	**−193.0**
Equity securities	4 660	110.6	176.1	−1,362.8	308.6	289.4	−300.7	−133.0	15.2
Banks	4 663	16.8	11.5	−1,807.9	2.1	1.8	−3.9	.3	3.0
Other sectors	4 664	93.8	164.7	445.1	306.5	287.6	−296.8	−133.3	12.2
Debt securities	4 669	450.5	938.1	−19.4	−377.2	−48.7	56.1	−1,275.3	−208.2
Bonds and notes	4 670	99.5	1,118.4	142.1	−349.4	−40.9	56.1	−1,277.6	−204.4
Monetary authorities	4 671	....	....	....	....	....	....	....	....
General government	4 672	−6.6	26.6	10.5	70.6	−85.8	56.3	33.2	−115.5
Banks	4 673	125.9	1,053.9	−62.7	−394.6	−45.7	−29.6	−1,239.5	−55.4
Other sectors	4 674	−19.7	37.9	194.3	−25.4	90.6	29.4	−71.2	−33.6
Money market instruments	4 680	351.0	−180.3	−161.5	−27.8	−7.8	....	2.3	−3.8
Monetary authorities	4 681	....	....	....	....	....	....	....	....
General government	4 682	....	....	....	....	....	....	....	....
Banks	4 683	353.0	−177.3	−162.0	−27.8	−7.4	−2.7	−.8	....
Other sectors	4 684	−2.0	−3.0	.5	....	−.4	2.7	3.1	−3.8
C. FINANCIAL DERIVATIVES	4 910	**−1.8**	**−.3**	**−7.5**	**5.8**	**−71.5**	**71.8**	**15.9**	**40.8**
Monetary authorities	4 911	....	....	....	....	....	....	....	....
General government	4 912	....	....	−.2	.8	1.6	−1.5	2.7	−.2
Banks	4 913	−1.8	−.3	−5.5	15.3	−72.4	68.8	.6	13.3
Other sectors	4 914	....	....	−1.8	−10.2	−.7	4.5	12.6	27.8
Assets	4 900	**−9.9**	**−2.9**	**1.3**	**−15.4**	**−77.5**	**62.5**	**22.5**	**−3.5**
Monetary authorities	4 901	....	....	....	....	....	....	....	....
General government	4 902	....	....	.1	1.5	3.0	1.6	2.2	1.9
Banks	4 903	−9.9	−2.9	3.0	−5.6	−72.1	42.3	20.3	8.0
Other sectors	4 904	....	....	−1.8	−11.3	−8.4	18.7	.1	−13.3
Liabilities	4 905	**8.1**	**2.6**	**−8.8**	**21.2**	**6.0**	**9.3**	**−6.6**	**44.3**
Monetary authorities	4 906	....	....	....	....	....	....	....	....
General government	4 907	....	....	−.3	−.7	−1.4	−3.1	.5	−2.1
Banks	4 908	8.1	2.6	−8.5	20.8	−.3	26.5	−19.7	5.3
Other sectors	4 909	....	....	.1	1.1	7.7	−14.1	12.6	41.1

Table 2 (Concluded). STANDARD PRESENTATION, 2003–2010
(Millions of U.S. dollars)

	Code	2003	2004	2005	2006	2007	2008	2009	2010
D. OTHER INVESTMENT	4 700	346.7	286.1	1,527.7	3,630.4	2,910.5	1,162.6	422.2	−3,086.4
Assets	4 703	−154.4	−949.1	−917.6	60.5	−2,056.8	−488.0	1,237.4	−1,736.2
Trade credits	4 706	−68.8	−81.2	−161.6	−284.6	−50.1	−187.7	242.7	−506.6
General government	4 707	−2.8	5.9	.1	−1.5	5.2	−31.3	6.6	10.1
of which: Short-term	4 709	−2.8	5.9	.1	−1.5	5.2	−31.3	6.6	10.1
Other sectors	4 710	−65.9	−87.2	−161.7	−283.1	−55.3	−156.4	236.1	−516.7
of which: Short-term	4 712	−65.9	−87.2	−161.7	−283.1	−55.3	−156.4	236.1	−516.7
Loans	4 714	−236.7	−676.9	280.5	−198.9	−898.2	−160.1	155.1	−371.2
Monetary authorities	4 715	....	....	....	....	....	....	....	....
of which: Short-term	4 718	....	....	....	....	....	....	....	....
General government	4 719	....	....	....	....	....	....	....	....
of which: Short-term	4 721	....	....	....	....	....	....	....	....
Banks	4 722	−171.3	−509.0	−104.1	−74.9	−807.4	−192.1	302.2	201.2
of which: Short-term	4 724	−150.0	−106.7	−316.9	113.0	−694.9	−169.1	273.5	174.3
Other sectors	4 725	−65.3	−167.8	384.6	−124.0	−90.8	32.0	−147.1	−572.4
of which: Short-term	4 727	−43.2	−86.5	188.5	−72.6	9.5	117.7	−54.8	−128.3
Currency and deposits	4 730	140.9	−135.8	−945.6	516.7	−1,028.7	−35.8	910.4	−635.6
Monetary authorities	4 731	....	....	....	....	....	....	....	....
General government	4 732	43.2	−15.1	−1.3	34.8	−1.9	−.7	−6.9	2.5
Banks	4 733	66.9	−164.3	−866.1	665.2	−744.7	1.7	964.0	−385.3
Other sectors	4 734	30.9	43.6	−78.2	−183.3	−282.2	−36.8	−46.8	−252.7
Other assets	4 736	10.1	−55.2	−91.0	27.3	−79.7	−104.3	−70.9	−222.8
Monetary authorities	4 737	.1	−.8	−.1	....	.1	.3	....	....
of which: Short-term	4 739	....	....	....	....	....	....	....	....
General government	4 740	−.5	−51.3	−55.6	19.1	−41.9	−88.0	−36.8	−37.4
of which: Short-term	4 742	−.2	−47.8	−50.8	23.6	−33.4	−75.7	−29.3	−33.4
Banks	4 743	17.5	−1.2	−34.0	7.3	−29.0	4.1	44.5	−71.9
of which: Short-term	4 745	17.5	−1.2	−34.0	7.3	−29.0	4.1	44.5	−71.9
Other sectors	4 746	−6.9	−1.8	−1.3	.9	−8.9	−20.7	−78.5	−113.5
of which: Short-term	4 748	−6.9	−1.8	−1.3	.9	−8.9	−20.7	−78.5	−113.6
Liabilities	4 753	501.1	1,235.2	2,445.3	3,569.9	4,967.2	1,650.6	−815.1	−1,350.2
Trade credits	4 756	−8.0	46.2	135.4	260.4	−31.3	62.4	−450.1	490.7
General government	4 757	....	....	....	....	....	−.1	.1	.1
of which: Short-term	4 759	....	....	....	....	....	−.1	.1	.1
Other sectors	4 760	−8.0	46.2	135.4	260.4	−31.3	62.5	−450.2	490.6
of which: Short-term	4 762	−8.0	46.2	135.4	260.4	−31.3	62.5	−450.2	490.6
Loans	4 764	234.5	366.8	1,949.3	1,528.8	3,322.5	118.8	214.0	47.3
Monetary authorities	4 765	43.5	17.9	−54.7	30.9	70.4	−159.0	10.1	−13.4
of which: Use of Fund credit and loans from the Fund	4 766	....	....	....	....	....	....	....	....
of which: Short-term	4 768	43.5	17.9	−54.7	30.9	70.4	−159.0	10.1	−13.4
General government	4 769	29.2	−15.5	−13.6	−2.5	−20.7	19.0	234.3	−14.6
of which: Short-term	4 771	....	....	....	....	....	....	....	....
Banks	4 772	57.5	262.4	1,663.1	255.9	2,864.8	−4.5	−3.0	133.5
of which: Short-term	4 774	−150.8	60.6	795.2	−442.6	157.1	....	....	.3
Other sectors	4 775	104.2	102.0	354.5	1,244.5	407.9	263.3	−27.5	−58.2
of which: Short-term	4 777	31.1	−15.9	−1.1	509.2	241.6	75.1	79.3	319.4
Currency and deposits	4 780	341.7	697.8	235.7	1,690.9	1,663.3	1,351.8	−573.6	−2,134.8
Monetary authorities	4 781	....	....	....	....	....	....	....	....
General government	4 782	....	....	....	....	....	....	....	....
Banks	4 783	341.6	697.8	235.7	1,690.9	1,663.3	1,351.8	−573.6	−2,134.7
Other sectors	4 784	....	....	....	....	....	....	....	....
Other liabilities	4 786	−67.1	124.3	124.9	89.7	12.8	117.6	−5.3	246.6
Monetary authorities	4 787	....	....	....	....	....	.1	97.1	20.2
of which: Short-term	4 789	....	....	....	....	....	.1	.2	20.2
General government	4 790	....	149.1	53.2	20.9	14.8	60.2	30.3	142.4
of which: Short-term	4 792	....	....	....	....	....	....	....	....
Banks	4 793	−62.8	−12.2	61.8	68.4	7.5	69.6	−137.0	61.0
of which: Short-term	4 795	−62.8	−12.2	61.8	68.4	7.5	69.6	−137.0	61.0
Other sectors	4 796	−4.2	−12.5	10.0	.4	−9.5	−12.3	4.3	23.0
of which: Short-term	4 798	−4.2	−12.5	9.3	−3.1	−4.4	−12.3	4.3	23.0
E. RESERVE ASSETS	4 802	−169.4	−271.2	−385.5	−620.7	−110.3	−719.9	−32.2	1,112.1
Monetary gold	4 812	....	....	....	....	....	....	....	....
Special drawing rights	4 811	....	....	....	....	....	....	−96.9	....
Reserve position in the Fund	4 810	....	....	....	....	....	....	....	....
Foreign exchange	4 803	−167.5	−269.0	−383.5	−620.5	−109.5	−779.9	66.5	1,171.3
Other claims	4 813	−1.8	−2.2	−2.0	−.2	−.8	60.0	−1.7	−59.2
NET ERRORS AND OMISSIONS	4 998	−39.5	−163.0	148.8	−185.4	50.7	239.4	−83.0	−287.7

Table 3. INTERNATIONAL INVESTMENT POSITION (End-period stocks), 2003–2010

(Millions of U.S. dollars)

	Code	2003	2004	2005	2006	2007	2008	2009	2010
ASSETS	8 995 C.	**6,137.7**	**8,834.4**	**10,801.7**	**15,558.6**	**23,065.1**	**21,880.0**	**21,710.7**	**21,748.7**
Direct investment abroad	8 505	**1,028.3**	**1,418.8**	**1,939.5**	**3,597.4**	**6,166.6**	**6,712.5**	**6,630.8**	**5,778.3**
Equity capital and reinvested earnings	8 506	721.6	1,057.3	1,524.2	2,838.2	4,898.8	4,791.3	4,423.6	3,967.7
Claims on affiliated enterprises	8 507	721.6	1,057.3	1,524.2	2,838.2	4,898.8	4,791.3	4,423.6	3,967.7
Liabilities to affiliated enterprises	8 508	....	....	....	....	....	....	....	....
Other capital	8 530	306.7	361.5	415.3	759.2	1,267.7	1,921.2	2,207.2	1,810.6
Claims on affiliated enterprises	8 535	364.1	443.0	531.4	944.3	1,618.9	2,187.8	2,381.0	2,109.5
Liabilities to affiliated enterprises	8 540	−57.4	−81.5	−116.1	−185.1	−351.1	−266.6	−173.8	−298.9
Portfolio investment	8 602	**1,560.5**	**2,244.0**	**2,962.9**	**4,821.6**	**6,414.0**	**3,807.8**	**4,978.7**	**5,274.3**
Equity securities	8 610	210.3	534.9	1,014.8	1,786.5	2,940.7	1,136.9	1,590.4	2,130.1
Monetary authorities	8 611	....	....	.3	.3	.3	.3	.3	.3
General government	8 612	4.7	9.5	9.3	24.2	39.4	38.1	12.6	....
Banks	8 613	2.6	4.9	14.7	21.3	17.3	3.0	3.3	3.6
Other sectors	8 614	203.0	520.5	990.6	1,740.7	2,883.8	1,095.5	1,574.1	2,126.2
Debt securities	8 619	1,350.2	1,709.1	1,948.1	3,035.0	3,473.3	2,670.9	3,388.4	3,144.1
Bonds and notes	8 620	690.0	1,078.9	1,139.3	2,180.2	2,246.1	1,858.1	1,983.4	1,947.3
Monetary authorities	8 621	....	....	....	....	....	....	....	....
General government	8 622	345.7	490.2	370.5	1,144.6	1,328.4	1,093.4	755.7	701.9
Banks	8 623	3.7	130.0	124.6	159.6	116.0	31.0	257.4	380.6
Other sectors	8 624	340.7	458.7	644.2	875.9	801.8	733.7	970.4	864.8
Money market instruments	8 630	660.2	630.1	808.8	854.9	1,227.2	812.8	1,404.9	1,196.9
Monetary authorities	8 631	....	....	....	....	....	....	....	....
General government	8 632	485.5	464.5	556.1	355.0	676.7	413.5	581.3	507.9
Banks	8 633	98.7	19.8	62.1	271.2	184.6	39.2	517.8	448.2
Other sectors	8 634	76.0	145.8	190.5	228.7	365.9	360.1	305.9	240.8
Financial derivatives	8 900	**26.9**	**32.1**	**27.2**	**46.0**	**137.9**	**75.4**	**44.1**	**45.0**
Monetary authorities	8 901	....	....	....	....	....	....	....	....
General government	8 902	....	....	....	1.6	2.3	3.5	.6	.1
Banks	8 903	26.9	32.1	25.2	29.3	109.6	62.6	41.3	30.1
Other sectors	8 904	....	....	2.1	15.1	26.0	9.3	2.2	14.9
Other investment	8 703	**2,137.4**	**3,343.2**	**3,922.6**	**4,302.9**	**7,051.7**	**7,312.3**	**6,076.6**	**8,101.7**
Trade credits	8 706	459.1	609.1	678.9	1,080.5	1,376.9	1,535.6	1,357.0	2,090.5
General government	8 707	11.6	5.9	5.4	7.6	2.8	33.9	26.6	15.5
of which: Short-term	8 709	*11.6*	*5.9*	*5.4*	*7.6*	*2.8*	*33.9*	*26.6*	*15.5*
Other sectors	8 710	447.5	603.1	673.5	1,072.8	1,374.1	1,501.8	1,330.4	2,075.0
of which: Short-term	8 712	*447.5*	*603.1*	*673.5*	*1,072.8*	*1,374.1*	*1,501.8*	*1,330.4*	*2,075.0*
Loans	8 714	1,146.2	1,949.2	1,552.5	1,862.9	2,976.9	1,633.8	1,449.8	2,116.6
Monetary authorities	8 715	....	....	....	....	....	....	....	....
of which: Short-term	8 718	....	....	....	....	....	....	....	....
General government	8 719	....	....	....	....	....	....	....	....
of which: Short-term	8 721	....	....	....	....	....	....	....	....
Banks	8 722	642.5	1,251.0	1,156.9	1,323.1	2,302.7	1,046.2	739.0	470.1
of which: Short-term	8 724	*521.0*	*682.4*	*899.4*	*869.8*	*1,701.6*	*519.1*	*228.3*	*25.0*
Other sectors	8 725	503.8	698.2	395.5	539.8	674.2	587.6	710.7	1,646.6
of which: Short-term	8 727	*172.2*	*272.3*	*211.3*	*330.3*	*361.2*	*218.6*	*225.0*	*635.5*
Currency and deposits	8 730	479.4	668.2	1,521.8	1,183.0	2,412.0	3,760.2	2,864.7	3,314.1
Monetary authorities	8 731	....	....	....	....	....	....	....	....
General government	8 732	18.2	36.8	36.2	2.3	4.7	4.5	11.8	8.6
Banks	8 733	376.3	574.9	1,353.2	822.4	1,691.8	2,987.4	2,017.8	2,293.8
Other sectors	8 734	84.9	56.5	132.4	358.2	715.5	768.2	835.1	1,011.6
Other assets	8 736	52.7	116.8	169.4	176.6	286.0	382.7	405.1	580.5
Monetary authorities	8 737	.9	1.9	1.7	1.8	2.0	1.6	1.7	1.6
of which: Short-term	8 739	....	....	....	....	....	....	....	....
General government	8 740	7.5	62.3	110.8	101.4	157.0	251.5	286.9	301.2
of which: Short-term	8 742	*.3*	*50.6*	*96.1*	*80.3*	*124.3*	*208.5*	*234.9*	*248.9*
Banks	8 743	24.6	31.9	45.4	45.2	75.7	66.9	23.8	95.7
of which: Short-term	8 745	*24.6*	*31.9*	*45.4*	*45.2*	*75.7*	*66.9*	*23.8*	*95.7*
Other sectors	8 746	19.7	20.7	11.5	28.2	51.3	62.6	92.7	182.0
of which: Short-term	8 748	*19.6*	*20.6*	*11.4*	*28.1*	*51.2*	*62.5*	*92.6*	*181.9*
Reserve assets	8 802	**1,384.7**	**1,796.2**	**1,949.5**	**2,790.7**	**3,295.0**	**3,972.0**	**3,980.5**	**2,549.4**
Monetary gold	8 812	3.4	3.6	4.2	5.2	6.9	7.2	9.1	11.6
Special drawing rights	8 811	.1	.1	.1	.1	.1	.1	97.2	95.5
Reserve position in the Fund	8 810	....	....	....	....	....	....	....	....
Foreign exchange	8 803	1,373.3	1,788.1	1,943.1	2,783.3	3,281.6	3,920.8	3,871.7	1,919.3
Other claims	8 813	7.9	4.4	2.0	2.1	6.4	44.0	2.5	522.9

Table 3 (Concluded). INTERNATIONAL INVESTMENT POSITION (End-period stocks), 2003–2010

(Millions of U.S. dollars)

	Code	2003	2004	2005	2006	2007	2008	2009	2010
LIABILITIES	8 995 D.	**13,378.7**	**20,094.2**	**21,915.1**	**28,585.0**	**40,094.1**	**39,452.8**	**38,052.3**	**35,665.5**
Direct investment in Estonia	8 555 ..	**7,001.8**	**10,058.6**	**11,289.6**	**12,699.5**	**16,747.1**	**16,589.8**	**16,782.1**	**16,436.7**
Equity capital and reinvested earnings	8 556 ..	5,808.5	8,766.1	10,187.8	10,940.1	14,262.9	14,129.3	14,569.9	14,241.0
Claims on direct investors	8 557 ..	....	....	....	....	....	....	....	....
Liabilities to direct investors	8 558 ..	5,808.5	8,766.1	10,187.8	10,940.1	14,262.9	14,129.3	14,569.9	14,241.0
Other capital	8 580 ..	1,193.3	1,292.5	1,101.8	1,759.4	2,484.2	2,460.5	2,212.2	2,195.6
Claims on direct investors	8 585 ..	–403.6	–564.4	–668.7	–1,133.6	–1,908.3	–2,043.8	–2,139.7	–1,609.5
Liabilities to direct investors	8 590 ..	1,596.9	1,856.9	1,770.5	2,893.0	4,392.5	4,504.2	4,351.9	3,805.2
Portfolio investment	8 652 ..	**2,383.4**	**4,504.7**	**3,380.6**	**3,898.3**	**4,594.5**	**2,941.9**	**1,872.4**	**1,914.5**
Equity securities	8 660 ..	949.6	1,942.0	1,195.7	1,884.6	2,442.7	739.8	877.8	1,192.7
Banks	8 663 ..	712.0	1,403.7	.6	3.6	6.1	4.2	4.6	9.9
Other sectors	8 664 ..	237.6	538.3	1,195.1	1,881.0	2,436.6	735.6	873.2	1,182.8
Debt securities	8 669 ..	1,433.9	2,562.7	2,184.9	2,013.7	2,151.8	2,202.2	994.6	721.8
Bonds and notes	8 670 ..	1,055.3	2,321.0	2,147.8	2,003.2	2,145.7	2,194.7	984.8	716.6
Monetary authorities	8 671 ..	....	....	....	....	....	....	....	....
General government	8 672 ..	138.6	179.9	161.8	248.9	181.1	225.1	268.6	131.6
Banks	8 673 ..	640.7	1,809.4	1,505.1	1,243.1	1,343.5	1,259.8	67.1	6.0
Other sectors	8 674 ..	276.1	331.7	480.9	511.2	621.1	709.9	649.1	578.9
Money market instruments	8 680 ..	378.6	241.8	37.2	10.5	6.1	7.4	9.9	5.2
Monetary authorities	8 681 ..	....	....	....	....	....	....	....	....
General government	8 682 ..	....	....	....	....	....	....	....	....
Banks	8 683 ..	375.9	241.1	36.0	9.1	3.5	.8	....	....
Other sectors	8 684 ..	2.7	.6	1.1	1.3	2.6	6.6	9.9	5.2
Financial derivatives	8 905 ..	**16.8**	**20.7**	**10.0**	**33.2**	**47.3**	**69.2**	**68.7**	**120.9**
Monetary authorities	8 906 ..	....	....	....	....	....	....	....	....
General government	8 907 ..	....	....	....	.4	.1	1.1	2.3	.9
Banks	8 908 ..	16.8	20.5	9.7	31.3	36.8	66.5	50.0	52.3
Other sectors	8 909 ..	....	.2	.4	1.5	10.3	1.6	16.3	67.7
Other investment	8 753 ..	**3,976.6**	**5,510.1**	**7,234.8**	**11,954.0**	**18,705.3**	**19,851.9**	**19,329.2**	**17,193.4**
Trade credits	8 756 ..	583.8	721.2	802.4	1,159.2	1,267.3	1,267.1	892.5	1,514.6
General government	8 757 ..	....	....	....	....	....	.1	.2	.3
of which: Short-term	8 759 ..	....	....	....	....	....	.1	.2	.3
Other sectors	8 760 ..	583.8	721.2	802.4	1,159.2	1,267.3	1,267.0	892.4	1,514.3
of which: Short-term	8 762 ..	583.8	721.2	802.4	1,159.2	1,267.3	1,267.0	892.4	1,514.3
Loans	8 764 ..	1,965.0	2,498.7	4,101.1	6,164.2	10,459.9	4,215.4	4,426.1	4,495.5
Monetary authorities	8 765 ..	38.7	43.9	3.4	37.2	124.2	9.7	16.0	....
of which: Use of Fund credit and loans from the Fund	8 766 ..	....	....	....	....	....	....	....	....
of which: Short-term	8 768 ..	38.7	43.9	3.4	37.2	124.2	9.7	16.0	....
General government	8 769 ..	174.2	171.5	135.3	147.8	143.1	161.0	392.4	349.3
of which: Short-term	8 771 ..	....	....	....	....	....	....	....	....
Banks	8 772 ..	560.7	892.2	2,369.0	2,933.2	6,394.7	22.3	19.5	188.6
of which: Short-term	8 774 ..	6.8	77.3	826.3	461.2	810.9	....	....	3.0
Other sectors	8 775 ..	1,191.3	1,391.1	1,593.4	3,046.0	3,797.9	4,022.4	3,998.2	3,957.7
of which: Short-term	8 777 ..	198.0	189.8	145.0	713.0	1,042.8	808.0	883.7	1,295.9
Currency and deposits	8 780 ..	1,325.4	2,201.4	2,133.5	4,148.1	6,425.7	13,744.7	13,342.6	10,339.6
Monetary authorities	8 781 ..	.3	.4	.3	.3	.4	.3	.3	.3
General government	8 782 ..	....	....	....	....	....	....	....	....
Banks	8 783 ..	1,325.0	2,201.0	2,133.2	4,147.7	6,425.4	13,744.4	13,342.2	10,339.3
Other sectors	8 784 ..	....	....	....	....	....	....	....	....
Other liabilities	8 786 ..	102.5	88.9	197.9	482.6	552.3	624.7	668.0	843.7
Monetary authorities	8 787 ..	....	....	....	1.1	1.2	.1	97.4	106.2
of which: Short-term	8 789 ..	....	....	....	1.1	1.2	.1	.3	10.8
General government	8 790 ..	....	....	57.1	233.4	322.0	356.7	414.1	526.4
of which: Short-term	8 792 ..	....	....	57.1	....	....	....	....	....
Banks	8 793 ..	85.4	81.0	120.0	211.1	197.5	255.2	114.7	159.8
of which: Short-term	8 795 ..	85.4	81.0	120.0	211.1	197.5	255.2	114.7	159.8
Other sectors	8 796 ..	17.1	7.9	20.9	37.0	31.6	12.7	41.8	51.3
of which: Short-term	8 798 ..	17.1	7.9	20.2	32.6	31.6	12.7	41.8	51.3
NET INTERNATIONAL INVESTMENT POSITION	8 995 ..	**–7,240.9**	**–11,259.8**	**–11,113.3**	**–13,026.5**	**–17,029.1**	**–17,572.8**	**–16,341.6**	**–13,916.8**
Conversion rates: krooni per U.S. dollar (end of period)	0 102 ..	**12.410**	**11.471**	**13.221**	**11.882**	**10.638**	**11.105**	**10.865**	**11.711**
Conversion rates: euros per U.S. dollar (end of period)	0 104 ..	**.7918**	**.7342**	**.8477**	**.7593**	**.6793**	**.7185**	**.6942**	**.7484**

Table 1. ANALYTIC PRESENTATION, 2003–2010

(Millions of U.S. dollars)

	Code	2003	2004	2005	2006	2007	2008	2009	2010
A. Current Account[1]	4 993 Z.	−136.4	−667.8	−1,567.8	−1,785.9	−828.0	−1,805.7	−2,190.7	−425.4
Goods: exports f.o.b.	2 100 ..	496.4	678.3	917.3	1,024.7	1,284.9	1,554.7	1,538.1	2,400.0
Goods: imports f.o.b.	3 100 ..	−1,895.0	−2,768.5	−3,700.9	−4,105.6	−5,155.6	−7,206.3	−6,819.0	−7,364.5
Balance on Goods	4 100 ..	*−1,398.6*	*−2,090.2*	*−2,783.5*	*−3,080.9*	*−3,870.8*	*−5,651.6*	*−5,280.9*	*−4,964.6*
Services: credit	2 200 ..	761.7	1,005.5	1,012.1	1,174.0	1,368.0	1,959.3	1,894.9	2,244.5
Services: debit	3 200 ..	−708.7	−958.3	−1,193.8	−1,170.7	−1,752.1	−2,410.3	−2,226.9	−2,546.5
Balance on Goods and Services	4 991 ..	*−1,345.6*	*−2,043.0*	*−2,965.2*	*−3,077.6*	*−4,254.9*	*−6,102.6*	*−5,612.9*	*−5,266.6*
Income: credit	2 300 ..	18.9	31.7	43.4	55.8	76.5	37.5	6.5	8.1
Income: debit	3 300 ..	−43.1	−60.3	−48.0	−37.8	−36.9	−35.9	−43.3	−71.7
Balance on Goods, Services, and Income	4 992 ..	*−1,369.8*	*−2,071.6*	*−2,969.8*	*−3,059.7*	*−4,215.3*	*−6,101.0*	*−5,649.7*	*−5,330.1*
Current transfers: credit	2 379 Z.	1,266.5	1,420.6	1,426.0	1,297.2	3,414.9	4,343.8	3,499.7	4,987.9
Current transfers: debit	3 379 ..	−33.1	−16.8	−23.9	−23.4	−27.5	−48.5	−40.7	−83.2
B. Capital Account[1]	4 994 Z.	....	....	....	....	....	....	....	....
Capital account: credit	2 994 Z.	....	....	....	....	....	....	....	....
Capital account: debit	3 994 ..	....	....	....	....	....	....	....	....
Total, Groups A Plus B	4 981 ..	*−136.4*	*−667.8*	*−1,567.8*	*−1,785.9*	*−828.0*	*−1,805.7*	*−2,190.7*	*−425.4*
C. Financial Account[1]	4 995 W.	**246.9**	**73.2**	**758.6**	**976.3**	**447.7**	**736.7**	**1,654.3**	**2,368.5**
Direct investment abroad	4 505 ..	....	....	....	....	....	....	....	....
Direct investment in Ethiopia	4 555 Z.	....	....	265.1	545.3	222.0	108.5	221.5	288.3
Portfolio investment assets	4 602 ..	....	....	....	....	....	....	....	....
Equity securities	4 610 ..	....	....	....	....	....	....	....	....
Debt securities	4 619 ..	....	....	....	....	....	....	....	....
Portfolio investment liabilities	4 652 Z.	....	....	....	....	....	....	....	....
Equity securities	4 660 ..	....	....	....	....	....	....	....	....
Debt securities	4 669 Z.	....	....	....	....	....	....	....	....
Financial derivatives	4 910 ..	....	....	....	....	....	....	....	....
Financial derivatives assets	4 900 ..	....	....	....	....	....	....	....	....
Financial derivatives liabilities	4 905 ..	....	....	....	....	....	....	....	....
Other investment assets	4 703 ..	68.8	−261.8	302.2	73.3	−108.1	113.0	420.3	1,084.6
Monetary authorities	4 701 ..	....	....	....	....	....	....	....	....
General government	4 704 ..	....	....	....	....	....	....	....	....
Banks	4 705 ..	95.0	−251.0	245.8	60.0	−171.8	68.9	245.5	1,118.7
Other sectors	4 728 ..	−26.2	−10.7	56.5	13.3	63.6	44.1	174.8	−34.1
Other investment liabilities	4 753 W.	178.1	335.0	191.2	357.7	333.8	515.2	1,012.6	995.6
Monetary authorities	4 753 WA	11.0	9.2	−17.0	−4.4	1.8	26.3	197.3	36.0
General government	4 753 ZB	147.7	386.2	224.9	332.8	302.6	455.2	742.8	841.3
Banks	4 753 ZC	24.0	−18.6	1.0	13.6	49.1	64.8	69.1	78.8
Other sectors	4 753 ZD	−4.5	−41.7	−17.6	15.8	−19.7	−31.1	3.3	39.6
Total, Groups A Through C	4 983 ..	*110.5*	*−594.7*	*−809.2*	*−809.6*	*−380.3*	*−1,069.1*	*−536.4*	*1,943.1*
D. Net Errors and Omissions	4 998 ..	**−390.1**	**−354.1**	**486.3**	**1,161.3**	**−156.5**	**1,450.7**	**−793.1**	**−2,929.9**
Total, Groups A Through D	4 984 ..	*−279.6*	*−948.8*	*−322.9*	*351.7*	*−536.8*	*381.6*	*−1,329.5*	*−986.8*
E. Reserves and Related Items	4 802 A.	**279.6**	**948.8**	**322.9**	**−351.7**	**536.8**	**−381.6**	**1,329.5**	**986.8**
Reserve assets	4 802 ..	76.9	544.3	330.3	−189.6	536.8	−381.6	1,163.8	865.3
Use of Fund credit and loans	4 766 ..	.6	17.8	−8.7	−162.2	....	....	165.7	121.5
Exceptional financing	4 920 ..	202.1	386.8	1.2	....	....	....	....	....
Conversion rates: birr per U.S. dollar	0 101 ..	**8.600**	**8.636**	**8.666**	**8.699**	**8.966**	**9.600**	**11.778**	**14.410**

[1] Excludes components that have been classified in the categories of Group E.

Table 2. STANDARD PRESENTATION, 2003–2010

(Millions of U.S. dollars)

	Code	2003	2004	2005	2006	2007	2008	2009	2010
CURRENT ACCOUNT	4 993	**−136.4**	**−667.8**	**−1,567.8**	**−1,785.9**	**−828.0**	**−1,805.7**	**−2,190.7**	**−425.4**
A. GOODS	4 100	**−1,398.6**	**−2,090.2**	**−2,783.5**	**−3,080.9**	**−3,870.8**	**−5,651.6**	**−5,280.9**	**−4,964.6**
Credit	2 100	**496.4**	**678.3**	**917.3**	**1,024.7**	**1,284.9**	**1,554.7**	**1,538.1**	**2,400.0**
General merchandise: exports f.o.b.	2 110	496.4	678.3	917.3	1,024.7	1,284.9	1,554.7	1,538.1	2,400.0
Goods for processing: exports f.o.b.	2 150	....	....	....	....	....	....	....	....
Repairs on goods	2 160	....	....	....	....	....	....	....	....
Goods procured in ports by carriers	2 170	....	....	....	....	....	....	....	....
Nonmonetary gold	2 180	....	....	....	....	....	....	....	....
Debit	3 100	**−1,895.0**	**−2,768.5**	**−3,700.9**	**−4,105.6**	**−5,155.6**	**−7,206.3**	**−6,819.0**	**−7,364.5**
General merchandise: imports f.o.b.	3 110	−1,895.0	−2,768.5	−3,700.9	−4,105.6	−5,155.6	−7,206.3	−6,819.0	−7,364.5
Goods for processing: imports f.o.b.	3 150	....	....	....	....	....	....	....	....
Repairs on goods	3 160	....	....	....	....	....	....	....	....
Goods procured in ports by carriers	3 170	....	....	....	....	....	....	....	....
Nonmonetary gold	3 180	....	....	....	....	....	....	....	....
B. SERVICES	4 200	**53.1**	**47.2**	**−181.7**	**3.3**	**−384.1**	**−451.0**	**−332.0**	**−302.0**
Total credit	2 200	*761.7*	*1,005.5*	*1,012.1*	*1,174.0*	*1,368.0*	*1,959.3*	*1,894.9*	*2,244.5*
Total debit	3 200	*−708.7*	*−958.3*	*−1,193.8*	*−1,170.7*	*−1,752.1*	*−2,410.3*	*−2,226.9*	*−2,546.5*
Transportation services, credit	2 205	**298.5**	**369.7**	**465.6**	**584.0**	**732.3**	**1,048.1**	**992.1**	**1,177.1**
Passenger	2 850	*221.7*	*284.4*	*365.3*	*477.2*	*614.4*	*806.9*	*790.0*	*912.2*
Freight	2 851	*43.6*	*54.7*	*63.3*	*81.9*	*88.0*	*141.8*	*113.6*	*178.0*
Other	2 852	*33.2*	*30.5*	*37.0*	*24.9*	*30.0*	*99.4*	*88.4*	*87.0*
Sea transport, passenger	2 207	....	....	....	....	....	....	....	....
Sea transport, freight	2 208	9.9	14.0	18.3	12.4	19.6	37.7	19.4	36.0
Sea transport, other	2 209	....	....	....	....	....	....	....	....
Air transport, passenger	2 211	221.7	284.4	365.3	477.2	614.4	806.9	790.0	912.2
Air transport, freight	2 212	33.6	40.7	45.0	69.5	68.4	104.1	94.2	142.0
Air transport, other	2 213	19.3	24.6	30.8	16.9	19.9	84.4	73.1	71.9
Other transport, passenger	2 215	....	....	....	....	....	....	....	....
Other transport, freight	2 216	....	....	....	....	....	....	....	....
Other transport, other	2 217	13.9	5.9	6.2	7.9	10.1	15.0	15.4	15.1
Transportation services, debit	3 205	**−410.5**	**−580.5**	**−764.5**	**−634.1**	**−1,122.8**	**−1,612.1**	**−1,477.0**	**−1,654.6**
Passenger	3 850	*−13.1*	*−1.1*	....	....	....	....	*−.9*	....
Freight	3 851	*−189.1*	*−276.3*	*−369.4*	*−97.1*	*−514.6*	*−719.3*	*−680.6*	*−735.1*
Other	3 852	*−208.3*	*−303.0*	*−395.1*	*−537.0*	*−608.2*	*−892.8*	*−795.4*	*−919.5*
Sea transport, passenger	3 207	....	....	....	....	....	....	....	....
Sea transport, freight	3 208	....	....	....	....	....	....	....	....
Sea transport, other	3 209	−30.1	−80.7	−127.7	−160.2	−169.0	−215.7	−193.4	−207.5
Air transport, passenger	3 211	−13.1	−1.1	....	....	....	....	−.9	....
Air transport, freight	3 212	....	....	....	....	....	....	....	....
Air transport, other	3 213	−172.1	−213.3	−255.2	−366.7	−422.4	−653.7	−579.4	−688.2
Other transport, passenger	3 215	....	....	....	....	....	....	....	....
Other transport, freight	3 216	....	....	....	....	....	....	....	....
Other transport, other	3 217	−6.1	−9.0	−12.1	−10.2	−16.8	−23.4	−22.6	−23.9
Travel, credit	2 236	**114.3**	**173.6**	**168.3**	**162.0**	**176.4**	**377.0**	**329.1**	**522.0**
Business travel	2 237	1.6	6.3	35.1	29.6	9.2	7.5	4.3	.3
Personal travel	2 240	112.6	167.2	133.1	132.4	167.2	369.5	324.8	521.7
Travel, debit	3 236	**−49.6**	**−58.3**	**−76.7**	**−96.8**	**−106.9**	**−155.8**	**−138.2**	**−142.9**
Business travel	3 237	−33.8	−39.5	−48.9	−65.1	−74.6	−85.6	−80.6	−93.0
Personal travel	3 240	−15.8	−18.8	−27.8	−31.7	−32.3	−70.2	−57.6	−49.9
Other services, credit	2 200 BA	**349.0**	**462.2**	**378.2**	**428.0**	**459.2**	**534.3**	**573.8**	**545.3**
Communications	2 245	21.4	41.6	41.2	55.7	85.5	75.0	99.3	101.1
Construction	2 249	....	....	12.6	11.1	18.4	25.3	24.0	13.9
Insurance	2 253	.8	1.1	5.5	9.3	4.1	.8	.1	3.7
Financial	2 260	5.0	2.9	25.7	10.9	53.9	22.2	22.0	.2
Computer and information	2 262	.3	....	.1	.5	.6	1.8	.9	.6
Royalties and licence fees	2 266	....	....	....	....	.1	.1	2.2	.2
Other business services	2 268	147.5	211.4	70.0	56.0	111.1	224.5	205.2	172.1
Personal, cultural, and recreational	2 287	.6	....	....	.5	.4	.2	.8	....
Government, n.i.e.	2 291	173.4	205.2	223.0	284.0	185.1	184.3	219.2	253.4
Other services, debit	3 200 BA	**−248.5**	**−319.5**	**−352.6**	**−439.8**	**−522.4**	**−642.4**	**−611.7**	**−749.0**
Communications	3 245	−10.1	−14.2	−17.9	−32.0	−16.7	−19.4	−51.1	−25.8
Construction	3 249	−67.3	−77.6	−120.9	−178.7	−261.8	−290.7	−288.4	−361.0
Insurance	3 253	−37.8	−45.9	−56.3	−64.6	−69.6	−97.2	−90.9	−104.1
Financial	3 260	−5.0	−.7	−3.3	−1.3	−1.9	−.5	−6.5	−1.3
Computer and information	3 262	−1.6	−3.2	−4.3	−3.5	−5.1	−3.8	−6.8	−4.1
Royalties and licence fees	3 266	−.1	−.5	−.6	−.8	−2.1	−1.7	−2.8	−1.0
Other business services	3 268	−106.6	−150.8	−133.7	−142.5	−149.8	−198.1	−128.1	−239.2
Personal, cultural, and recreational	3 287	−.1	−.2	....	....	....	....	....	....
Government, n.i.e.	3 291	−19.9	−26.5	−15.8	−16.3	−15.4	−31.0	−37.1	−12.4

Table 2 (Continued). STANDARD PRESENTATION, 2003–2010

(Millions of U.S. dollars)

	Code	2003	2004	2005	2006	2007	2008	2009	2010
C. INCOME	4 300	**−24.2**	**−28.6**	**−4.6**	**17.9**	**39.5**	**1.6**	**−36.8**	**−63.5**
Total credit	2 300	*18.9*	*31.7*	*43.4*	*55.8*	*76.5*	*37.5*	*6.5*	*8.1*
Total debit	3 300	*−43.1*	*−60.3*	*−48.0*	*−37.8*	*−36.9*	*−35.9*	*−43.3*	*−71.7*
Compensation of employees, credit	2 310	....	....	....	3.0	1.9	....	....	....
Compensation of employees, debit	3 310	−.7	....	....	....	....	−.1	....	−1.9
Investment income, credit	2 320	**18.9**	**31.7**	**43.4**	**52.8**	**74.6**	**37.5**	**6.5**	**8.1**
Direct investment income	2 330	....	.6	.1	.1	.4	.1	.1	....
Dividends and distributed branch profits	2 332	....	.6	.1	.1	.4	.1	.1	....
Reinvested earnings and undistributed branch profits	2 333	....	....	....	....	....	....	....	....
Income on debt (interest)	2 334	....	....	....	....	....	....	....	....
Portfolio investment income	2 339	....	....	....	....	....	....	....	....
Income on equity	2 340	....	....	....	....	....	....	....	....
Income on bonds and notes	2 350	....	....	....	....	....	....	....	....
Income on money market instruments	2 360	....	....	....	....	....	....	....	....
Other investment income	2 370	18.9	31.1	43.3	52.7	74.2	37.4	6.4	8.1
Investment income, debit	3 320	**−42.3**	**−60.3**	**−48.0**	**−37.8**	**−36.9**	**−35.8**	**−43.3**	**−69.8**
Direct investment income	3 330	−16.9	−27.9	−21.5	−23.7	−18.1	−16.7	−17.7	−35.1
Dividends and distributed branch profits	3 332	−16.9	−27.9	−21.5	−23.7	−18.1	−16.7	−17.7	−35.1
Reinvested earnings and undistributed branch profits	3 333	....	....	....	....	....	....	....	....
Income on debt (interest)	3 334	....	....	....	....	....	....	....	....
Portfolio investment income	3 339	....	....	....	....	....	....	....	....
Income on equity	3 340	....	....	....	....	....	....	....	....
Income on bonds and notes	3 350	....	....	....	....	....	....	....	....
Income on money market instruments	3 360	....	....	....	....	....	....	....	....
Other investment income	3 370	−25.4	−32.4	−26.6	−14.2	−18.8	−19.0	−25.6	−34.7
D. CURRENT TRANSFERS	4 379	**1,233.4**	**1,403.8**	**1,402.1**	**1,273.8**	**3,387.3**	**4,295.3**	**3,459.1**	**4,904.7**
Credit	2 379	**1,266.5**	**1,420.6**	**1,426.0**	**1,297.2**	**3,414.9**	**4,343.8**	**3,499.7**	**4,987.9**
General government	2 380	660.5	664.9	562.8	381.1	1,338.3	1,633.0	889.1	2,131.2
Other sectors	2 390	606.0	755.7	863.2	916.1	2,076.5	2,710.9	2,610.7	2,856.7
Workers' remittances	2 391	46.5	133.7	173.5	169.2	355.9	386.7	261.6	345.2
Other current transfers	2 392	559.6	621.9	689.7	746.9	1,720.6	2,324.2	2,349.1	2,511.5
Debit	3 379	**−33.1**	**−16.8**	**−23.9**	**−23.4**	**−27.5**	**−48.5**	**−40.7**	**−83.2**
General government	3 380	−4.9	−6.2	−5.9	−8.6	−11.5	−21.4	−10.5	−35.3
Other sectors	3 390	−28.2	−10.6	−18.0	−14.8	−16.0	−27.2	−30.2	−48.0
Workers' remittances	3 391	−16.5	−9.2	−16.4	−14.1	−14.6	−21.2	−26.5	−64.4
Other current transfers	3 392	−11.7	−1.4	−1.6	−.7	−1.4	−6.0	−3.6	16.4
CAPITAL AND FINANCIAL ACCOUNT	4 996	**526.5**	**1,022.0**	**1,081.4**	**624.6**	**984.5**	**355.0**	**2,983.8**	**3,355.3**
CAPITAL ACCOUNT	4 994	**13.8**	....	....	....	....	....	....	....
Total credit	2 994	*13.8*	....	....	....	....	....	....	....
Total debit	3 994	....	....	....	....	....	....	....	....
Capital transfers, credit	2 400	**13.8**	....	....	....	....	....	....	....
General government	2 401	13.8	....	....	....	....	....	....	....
Debt forgiveness	2 402	13.8	....	....	....	....	....	....	....
Other capital transfers	2 410	....	....	....	....	....	....	....	....
Other sectors	2 430	....	....	....	....	....	....	....	....
Migrants' transfers	2 431	....	....	....	....	....	....	....	....
Debt forgiveness	2 432	....	....	....	....	....	....	....	....
Other capital transfers	2 440	....	....	....	....	....	....	....	....
Capital transfers, debit	3 400	....	....	....	....	....	....	....	....
General government	3 401	....	....	....	....	....	....	....	....
Debt forgiveness	3 402	....	....	....	....	....	....	....	....
Other capital transfers	3 410	....	....	....	....	....	....	....	....
Other sectors	3 430	....	....	....	....	....	....	....	....
Migrants' transfers	3 431	....	....	....	....	....	....	....	....
Debt forgiveness	3 432	....	....	....	....	....	....	....	....
Other capital transfers	3 440	....	....	....	....	....	....	....	....
Nonproduced nonfinancial assets, credit	2 480	....	....	....	....	....	....	....	....
Nonproduced nonfinancial assets, debit	3 480	....	....	....	....	....	....	....	....

Table 2 (Continued). STANDARD PRESENTATION, 2003–2010

(Millions of U.S. dollars)

	Code	2003	2004	2005	2006	2007	2008	2009	2010
FINANCIAL ACCOUNT............................	4 995 ..	**512.7**	**1,022.0**	**1,081.4**	**624.6**	**984.5**	**355.0**	**2,983.8**	**3,355.3**
A. DIRECT INVESTMENT.........................	4 500 ..	....	....	**265.1**	**545.3**	**222.0**	**108.5**	**221.5**	**288.3**
Direct investment abroad.......................	4 505 ..	....	....	....	....	....	....	....	....
Equity capital..	4 510 ..	....	....	....	....	....	....	....	....
Claims on affiliated enterprises...............	4 515 ..	....	....	....	....	....	....	....	....
Liabilities to affiliated enterprises...........	4 520 ..	....	....	....	....	....	....	....	....
Reinvested earnings.................................	4 525 ..	....	....	....	....	....	....	....	....
Other capital...	4 530 ..	....	....	....	....	....	....	....	....
Claims on affiliated enterprises...............	4 535 ..	....	....	....	....	....	....	....	....
Liabilities to affiliated enterprises...........	4 540 ..	....	....	....	....	....	....	....	....
Direct investment in Ethiopia..............	4 555 ..	....	....	**265.1**	**545.3**	**222.0**	**108.5**	**221.5**	**288.3**
Equity capital..	4 560 ..	....	....	....	....	....	....	....	....
Claims on direct investors.......................	4 565 ..	....	....	....	....	....	....	....	....
Liabilities to direct investors...................	4 570 ..	....	....	....	....	....	....	....	....
Reinvested earnings.................................	4 575 ..	....	....	....	....	....	....	....	....
Other capital...	4 580 ..	....	....	265.1	545.3	222.0	108.5	221.5	288.3
Claims on direct investors.......................	4 585 ..	....	....	265.1	545.3	222.0	108.5	221.5	288.3
Liabilities to direct investors...................	4 590 ..	....	....	....	....	....	....	....	....
B. PORTFOLIO INVESTMENT....................	4 600 ..	....	....	....	....	....	....	....	....
Assets...	4 602 ..	....	....	....	....	....	....	....	....
Equity securities.....................................	4 610 ..	....	....	....	....	....	....	....	....
Monetary authorities..............................	4 611 ..	....	....	....	....	....	....	....	....
General government...............................	4 612 ..	....	....	....	....	....	....	....	....
Banks...	4 613 ..	....	....	....	....	....	....	....	....
Other sectors...	4 614 ..	....	....	....	....	....	....	....	....
Debt securities.......................................	4 619 ..	....	....	....	....	....	....	....	....
Bonds and notes....................................	4 620 ..	....	....	....	....	....	....	....	....
Monetary authorities..............................	4 621 ..	....	....	....	....	....	....	....	....
General government...............................	4 622 ..	....	....	....	....	....	....	....	....
Banks...	4 623 ..	....	....	....	....	....	....	....	....
Other sectors...	4 624 ..	....	....	....	....	....	....	....	....
Money market instruments.....................	4 630 ..	....	....	....	....	....	....	....	....
Monetary authorities..............................	4 631 ..	....	....	....	....	....	....	....	....
General government...............................	4 632 ..	....	....	....	....	....	....	....	....
Banks...	4 633 ..	....	....	....	....	....	....	....	....
Other sectors...	4 634 ..	....	....	....	....	....	....	....	....
Liabilities...	4 652 ..	....	....	....	....	....	....	....	....
Equity securities.....................................	4 660 ..	....	....	....	....	....	....	....	....
Banks...	4 663 ..	....	....	....	....	....	....	....	....
Other sectors...	4 664 ..	....	....	....	....	....	....	....	....
Debt securities.......................................	4 669 ..	....	....	....	....	....	....	....	....
Bonds and notes....................................	4 670 ..	....	....	....	....	....	....	....	....
Monetary authorities..............................	4 671 ..								
General government...............................	4 672 ..								
Banks...	4 673 ..								
Other sectors...	4 674 ..								
Money market instruments.....................	4 680 ..								
Monetary authorities..............................	4 681 ..								
General government...............................	4 682 ..								
Banks...	4 683 ..								
Other sectors...	4 684 ..								
C. FINANCIAL DERIVATIVES....................	4 910 ..	....	....	....	....	....	....	....	....
Monetary authorities..............................	4 911 ..	....	....	....	....	....	....	....	....
General government...............................	4 912 ..	....	....	....	....	....	....	....	....
Banks...	4 913 ..	....	....	....	....	....	....	....	....
Other sectors...	4 914 ..	....	....	....	....	....	....	....	....
Assets...	4 900 ..	....	....	....	....	....	....	....	....
Monetary authorities..............................	4 901 ..	....	....	....	....	....	....	....	....
General government...............................	4 902 ..	....	....	....	....	....	....	....	....
Banks...	4 903 ..	....	....	....	....	....	....	....	....
Other sectors...	4 904 ..	....	....	....	....	....	....	....	....
Liabilities...	4 905 ..	....	....	....	....	....	....	....	....
Monetary authorities..............................	4 906 ..	....	....	....	....	....	....	....	....
General government...............................	4 907 ..	....	....	....	....	....	....	....	....
Banks...	4 908 ..	....	....	....	....	....	....	....	....
Other sectors...	4 909 ..	....	....	....	....	....	....	....	....

Table 2 (Concluded). STANDARD PRESENTATION, 2003–2010

(Millions of U.S. dollars)

	Code	2003	2004	2005	2006	2007	2008	2009	2010
D. OTHER INVESTMENT............................	4 700 ..	**435.8**	**477.7**	**486.0**	**268.9**	**225.7**	**628.1**	**1,598.5**	**2,201.8**
Assets..	4 703 ..	**68.8**	**−261.8**	**302.2**	**73.3**	**−108.1**	**113.0**	**420.3**	**1,084.6**
Trade credits...............................	4 706 ..	21.9	−24.7	....	....	....	....	....	....
General government..................	4 707 ..	....	....	....	....	....	....	....	....
of which: Short-term...........	4 709 ..	....	....	....	....	....	....	....	....
Other sectors..........................	4 710 ..	21.9	−24.7	....	....	....	....	....	....
of which: Short-term...........	4 712 ..	*21.9*	*−24.7*	....	....	....	....	....	....
Loans..	4 714 ..	....	....	....	....	....	....	....	....
Monetary authorities..............	4 715 ..	....	....	....	....	....	....	....	....
of which: Short-term...........	4 718 ..	....	....	....	....	....	....	....	....
General government..................	4 719 ..	....	....	....	....	....	....	....	....
of which: Short-term...........	4 721 ..	....	....	....	....	....	....	....	....
Banks.......................................	4 722 ..	....	....	....	....	....	....	....	....
of which: Short-term...........	4 724 ..	....	....	....	....	....	....	....	....
Other sectors..........................	4 725 ..	....	....	....	....	....	....	....	....
of which: Short-term...........	4 727 ..	....	....	....	....	....	....	....	....
Currency and deposits..................	4 730 ..	46.9	−237.1	302.2	73.3	−108.1	113.0	420.3	1,084.6
Monetary authorities..............	4 731 ..	....	....	....	....	....	....	....	....
General government..................	4 732 ..	....	....	....	....	....	....	....	....
Banks.......................................	4 733 ..	95.0	−251.0	245.8	60.0	−171.8	68.9	245.5	1,118.7
Other sectors..........................	4 734 ..	−48.1	14.0	56.5	13.3	63.6	44.1	174.8	−34.1
Other assets................................	4 736 ..	....	....	....	....	....	....	....	....
Monetary authorities..............	4 737 ..	....	....	....	....	....	....	....	....
of which: Short-term...........	4 739 ..	....	....	....	....	....	....	....	....
General government..................	4 740 ..	....	....	....	....	....	....	....	....
of which: Short-term...........	4 742 ..	....	....	....	....	....	....	....	....
Banks.......................................	4 743 ..	....	....	....	....	....	....	....	....
of which: Short-term...........	4 745 ..	....	....	....	....	....	....	....	....
Other sectors..........................	4 746 ..	....	....	....	....	....	....	....	....
of which: Short-term...........	4 748 ..	....	....	....	....	....	....	....	....
Liabilities......................................	4 753 ..	**367.0**	**739.5**	**183.7**	**195.6**	**333.8**	**515.2**	**1,178.2**	**1,117.2**
Trade credits...............................	4 756 ..	7.7	−10.0	....	....	....	....	....	....
General government..................	4 757 ..	....	....	....	....	....	....	....	....
of which: Short-term...........	4 759 ..	....	....	....	....	....	....	....	....
Other sectors..........................	4 760 ..	7.7	−10.0	....	....	....	....	....	....
of which: Short-term...........	4 762 ..	*7.7*	*−10.0*	....	....	....	....	....	....
Loans..	4 764 ..	242.3	704.3	199.8	186.3	282.9	424.1	911.8	1,002.4
Monetary authorities..............	4 765 ..	.6	17.8	−8.7	−162.2	....	....	165.7	121.5
of which: Use of Fund credit and loans from the Fund..	4 766 ..	*.6*	*17.8*	*−8.7*	*−162.2*	....	....	*165.7*	*121.5*
of which: Short-term...........	4 768 ..	....	....	....	....	....	....	....	....
General government..................	4 769 ..	147.7	386.2	224.9	332.8	302.6	455.2	742.8	841.3
of which: Short-term...........	4 771 ..	....	....	....	....	....	....	....	....
Banks.......................................	4 772 ..	....	....	....	....	....	....	....	....
of which: Short-term...........	4 774 ..	....	....	....	....	....	....	....	....
Other sectors..........................	4 775 ..	94.0	300.4	−16.4	15.8	−19.7	−31.1	3.3	39.6
of which: Short-term...........	4 777 ..	*6.4*	*−1.3*	*6.7*	*15.8*	*−10.2*	*−11.5*	*3.3*	*39.6*
Currency and deposits..................	4 780 ..	35.0	−9.5	−16.0	9.2	50.9	91.0	84.0	114.8
Monetary authorities..............	4 781 ..	11.0	9.2	−17.0	−4.4	1.8	26.3	14.8	36.0
General government..................	4 782 ..	....	....	....	....	....	....	....	....
Banks.......................................	4 783 ..	24.0	−18.6	1.0	13.6	49.1	64.8	69.1	78.8
Other sectors..........................	4 784 ..	....	....	....	....	....	....	....	....
Other liabilities..........................	4 786 ..	82.1	54.6	....	....	....	....	182.5	....
Monetary authorities..............	4 787 ..	....	....	....	....	....	....	182.5	....
of which: Short-term...........	4 789 ..	....	....	....	....	....	....	....	....
General government..................	4 790 ..	82.1	54.6	....	....	....	....	....	....
of which: Short-term...........	4 792 ..	*82.1*	*54.6*	....	....	....	....	....	....
Banks.......................................	4 793 ..	....	....	....	....	....	....	....	....
of which: Short-term...........	4 795 ..	....	....	....	....	....	....	....	....
Other sectors..........................	4 796 ..	....	....	....	....	....	....	....	....
of which: Short-term...........	4 798 ..	....	....	....	....	....	....	....	....
E. RESERVE ASSETS..............................	4 802 ..	**76.9**	**544.3**	**330.3**	**−189.6**	**536.8**	**−381.6**	**1,163.8**	**865.3**
Monetary gold.............................	4 812 ..	....	....	−11.2	8.6	26.4	−43.1	15.7	12.1
Special drawing rights..................	4 811 ..	.1	−.4	.3	.1	....	....	−25.8	−121.1
Reserve position in the Fund.........	4 810 ..	....	....	....	−.2	−.1	−.1	−.1	....
Foreign exchange........................	4 803 ..	76.9	544.6	341.2	−198.1	510.5	−338.4	1,174.0	974.3
Other claims...............................	4 813 ..	....	....	....	....	....	....	....	....
NET ERRORS AND OMISSIONS..............	4 998 ..	**−390.1**	**−354.1**	**486.3**	**1,161.3**	**−156.5**	**1,450.7**	**−793.1**	**−2,929.9**

Table 1. ANALYTIC PRESENTATION, 2003–2010

(Billions of U.S. dollars)

	Code	2003	2004	2005	2006	2007	2008	2009	2010
A. Current Account[1]	4 993 Z.	**24.90**	**81.19**	**19.18**	**−.33**	**24.86**	**−198.22**	**−31.33**	**−53.55**
Goods: exports f.o.b.	2 100 ..	1,175.05	1,412.84	1,529.17	1,760.24	2,086.30	2,331.50	1,817.00	2,069.19
Goods: imports f.o.b.	3 100 ..	−1,062.11	−1,287.46	−1,463.75	−1,730.92	−2,010.54	−2,352.87	−1,761.29	−2,042.56
Balance on Goods	4 100 ..	*112.94*	*125.38*	*65.42*	*29.32*	*75.76*	*−21.37*	*55.70*	*26.63*
Services: credit	2 200 ..	373.13	447.28	497.46	548.72	671.64	752.42	659.97	681.70
Services: debit	3 200 ..	−348.07	−413.04	−456.44	−502.70	−613.71	−694.05	−613.86	−629.40
Balance on Goods and Services	4 991 ..	*138.00*	*159.62*	*106.44*	*75.33*	*133.69*	*37.00*	*101.82*	*78.93*
Income: credit	2 300 ..	283.92	374.66	482.06	630.31	828.84	772.52	585.77	570.12
Income: debit	3 300 ..	−333.97	−379.39	−477.22	−605.74	−817.52	−865.07	−593.24	−568.39
Balance on Goods, Services, and Income	4 992 ..	*87.95*	*154.89*	*111.28*	*99.91*	*145.01*	*−55.54*	*94.34*	*80.67*
Current transfers: credit	2 379 Z.	92.65	100.49	103.96	110.15	119.86	131.39	130.53	115.90
Current transfers: debit	3 379 ..	−155.70	−174.19	−196.06	−210.38	−240.02	−274.07	−256.20	−250.11
B. Capital Account[1]	4 994 Z.	**14.34**	**20.46**	**14.24**	**11.74**	**5.41**	**13.21**	**8.49**	**8.15**
Capital account: credit	2 994 Z.	27.32	30.39	30.30	29.81	35.02	35.61	28.19	28.96
Capital account: debit	3 994 ..	−12.98	−9.93	−16.06	−18.07	−29.61	−22.40	−19.69	−20.81
Total, Groups A Plus B	4 981 ..	*39.24*	*101.65*	*33.42*	*11.41*	*30.27*	*−185.01*	*−22.83*	*−45.40*
C. Financial Account[1]	4 995 W.	**−47.57**	**−122.89**	**−71.35**	**−27.85**	**−1.88**	**204.35**	**70.25**	**77.25**
Direct investment abroad	4 505 ..	−164.69	−215.29	−453.55	−542.69	−706.04	−491.78	−448.47	−183.46
Direct investment in the Euro Area	4 555 Z.	153.28	114.82	194.10	328.56	581.87	141.48	301.56	123.08
Portfolio investment assets	4 602 ..	−318.08	−428.80	−514.64	−650.47	−601.34	−28.96	−124.77	−186.97
Equity securities	4 610 ..	−90.34	−132.42	−165.99	−193.24	−86.86	135.31	−72.79	−105.30
Debt securities	4 619 ..	−227.74	−296.38	−348.66	−457.23	−514.48	−164.28	−51.98	−81.67
Portfolio investment liabilities	4 652 Z.	381.38	486.07	660.22	889.12	770.03	432.55	499.22	363.54
Equity securities	4 660 ..	127.39	131.98	291.94	309.73	223.63	−115.34	165.63	165.40
Debt securities	4 669 Z.	253.99	354.09	368.28	579.39	546.40	547.89	333.59	198.14
Financial derivatives	4 910 ..	−15.57	−10.53	−21.59	.22	−92.90	−119.09	50.33	11.54
Financial derivatives assets	4 900 ..	....	....	....	....	....	....	....	....
Financial derivatives liabilities	4 905 ..	−15.57	−10.53	−21.59	.22	−92.90	−119.09	50.33	11.54
Other investment assets	4 703 ..	−282.26	−425.21	−737.66	−998.55	−1,236.85	−42.38	726.55	−198.11
Monetary authorities	4 701 ..	−.92	−.15	−.69	11.05	−30.03	13.22	−.16	3.95
General government	4 704 ..	−.41	−1.84	9.57	8.63	10.62	8.53	−15.03	−52.50
Banks	4 705 ..	−171.68	−329.62	−502.34	−688.90	−724.02	23.84	565.57	−12.14
Other sectors	4 728 ..	−109.25	−93.60	−244.19	−329.34	−493.41	−87.97	176.17	−137.41
Other investment liabilities	4 753 W.	198.38	356.04	801.78	945.97	1,283.34	312.53	−934.16	147.63
Monetary authorities	4 753 WA	12.32	9.70	8.65	25.85	126.76	404.04	−251.20	12.19
General government	4 753 ZB	−3.62	−5.28	−2.54	2.56	−1.87	12.12	14.93	88.14
Banks	4 753 ZC	151.36	307.46	605.31	631.14	827.68	−191.74	−489.23	7.35
Other sectors	4 753 ZD	38.32	44.16	190.36	286.41	330.77	88.11	−208.66	39.94
Total, Groups A Through C	4 983 ..	*−8.33*	*−21.24*	*−37.93*	*−16.44*	*28.38*	*19.34*	*47.42*	*31.85*
D. Net Errors and Omissions	4 998 ..	**−24.48**	**5.68**	**15.02**	**19.00**	**−22.69**	**−14.48**	**12.38**	**−18.27**
Total, Groups A Through D	4 984 ..	*−32.80*	*−15.56*	*−22.91*	*2.57*	*5.69*	*4.86*	*59.80*	*13.58*
E. Reserves and Related Items	4 802 A.	**32.80**	**15.56**	**22.91**	**−2.57**	**−5.69**	**−4.86**	**−59.80**	**−13.58**
Reserve assets	4 802 ..	32.80	15.56	22.91	−2.57	−5.69	−4.86	−59.80	−13.58
Use of Fund credit and loans	4 766 ..	....	....	....	....	....	....	....	....
Exceptional financing	4 920 ..	....	....	....	....	....	....	....	....
Conversion rates: euros per U.S. dollar	0 103 ..	**.8860**	**.8054**	**.8041**	**.7971**	**.7306**	**.6827**	**.7198**	**.7550**

[1] Excludes components that have been classified in the categories of Group E.

Table 2. STANDARD PRESENTATION, 2003–2010

(Billions of U.S. dollars)

	Code	2003	2004	2005	2006	2007	2008	2009	2010
CURRENT ACCOUNT	4 993 ..	24.90	81.19	19.18	−.33	24.86	−198.22	−31.33	−53.55
A. GOODS	4 100 ..	112.94	125.38	65.42	29.32	75.76	−21.37	55.70	26.63
Credit	2 100 ..	1,175.05	1,412.84	1,529.17	1,760.24	2,086.30	2,331.50	1,817.00	2,069.19
General merchandise: exports f.o.b	2 110 ..	....	....	....	....	....	....	....	....
Goods for processing: exports f.o.b	2 150 ..	....	....	....	....	....	....	....	....
Repairs on goods	2 160 ..	....	....	....	....	....	....	....	....
Goods procured in ports by carriers	2 170 ..	....	....	....	....	....	....	....	....
Nonmonetary gold	2 180 ..	....	....	....	....	....	....	....	....
Debit	3 100 ..	−1,062.11	−1,287.46	−1,463.75	−1,730.92	−2,010.54	−2,352.87	−1,761.29	−2,042.56
General merchandise: imports f.o.b	3 110 ..	....	....	....	....	....	....	....	....
Goods for processing: imports f.o.b	3 150 ..	....	....	....	....	....	....	....	....
Repairs on goods	3 160 ..	....	....	....	....	....	....	....	....
Goods procured in ports by carriers	3 170 ..	....	....	....	....	....	....	....	....
Nonmonetary gold	3 180 ..	....	....	....	....	....	....	....	....
B. SERVICES	4 200 ..	25.07	34.24	41.02	46.01	57.93	58.36	46.11	52.30
Total credit	2 200 ..	*373.13*	*447.28*	*497.46*	*548.72*	*671.64*	*752.42*	*659.97*	*681.70*
Total debit	3 200 ..	*−348.07*	*−413.04*	*−456.44*	*−502.70*	*−613.71*	*−694.05*	*−613.86*	*−629.40*
Transportation services, credit	2 205 ..	....	....	....	....	....	....	....	....
Passenger	2 850 ..	....	....	....	....	....	....	....	....
Freight	2 851 ..	....	....	....	....	....	....	....	....
Other	2 852 ..	....	....	....	....	....	....	....	....
Sea transport, passenger	2 207 ..	....	....	....	....	....	....	....	....
Sea transport, freight	2 208 ..	....	....	....	....	....	....	....	....
Sea transport, other	2 209 ..	....	....	....	....	....	....	....	....
Air transport, passenger	2 211 ..	....	....	....	....	....	....	....	....
Air transport, freight	2 212 ..	....	....	....	....	....	....	....	....
Air transport, other	2 213 ..	....	....	....	....	....	....	....	....
Other transport, passenger	2 215 ..	....	....	....	....	....	....	....	....
Other transport, freight	2 216 ..	....	....	....	....	....	....	....	....
Other transport, other	2 217 ..	....	....	....	....	....	....	....	....
Transportation services, debit	3 205 ..	....	....	....	....	....	....	....	....
Passenger	3 850 ..	....	....	....	....	....	....	....	....
Freight	3 851 ..	....	....	....	....	....	....	....	....
Other	3 852 ..	....	....	....	....	....	....	....	....
Sea transport, passenger	3 207 ..	....	....	....	....	....	....	....	....
Sea transport, freight	3 208 ..	....	....	....	....	....	....	....	....
Sea transport, other	3 209 ..	....	....	....	....	....	....	....	....
Air transport, passenger	3 211 ..	....	....	....	....	....	....	....	....
Air transport, freight	3 212 ..	....	....	....	....	....	....	....	....
Air transport, other	3 213 ..	....	....	....	....	....	....	....	....
Other transport, passenger	3 215 ..	....	....	....	....	....	....	....	....
Other transport, freight	3 216 ..	....	....	....	....	....	....	....	....
Other transport, other	3 217 ..	....	....	....	....	....	....	....	....
Travel, credit	2 236 ..	....	....	....	....	....	....	....	....
Business travel	2 237 ..	....	....	....	....	....	....	....	....
Personal travel	2 240 ..	....	....	....	....	....	....	....	....
Travel, debit	3 236 ..	....	....	....	....	....	....	....	....
Business travel	3 237 ..	....	....	....	....	....	....	....	....
Personal travel	3 240 ..	....	....	....	....	....	....	....	....
Other services, credit	2 200 BA	....	....	....	....	....	....	....	....
Communications	2 245 ..	....	....	....	....	....	....	....	....
Construction	2 249 ..	....	....	....	....	....	....	....	....
Insurance	2 253 ..	....	....	....	....	....	....	....	....
Financial	2 260 ..	....	....	....	....	....	....	....	....
Computer and information	2 262 ..	....	....	....	....	....	....	....	....
Royalties and licence fees	2 266 ..	....	....	....	....	....	....	....	....
Other business services	2 268 ..	....	....	....	....	....	....	....	....
Personal, cultural, and recreational	2 287 ..	....	....	....	....	....	....	....	....
Government, n.i.e	2 291 ..	....	....	....	....	....	....	....	....
Other services, debit	3 200 BA	....	....	....	....	....	....	....	....
Communications	3 245 ..	....	....	....	....	....	....	....	....
Construction	3 249 ..	....	....	....	....	....	....	....	....
Insurance	3 253 ..	....	....	....	....	....	....	....	....
Financial	3 260 ..	....	....	....	....	....	....	....	....
Computer and information	3 262 ..	....	....	....	....	....	....	....	....
Royalties and licence fees	3 266 ..	....	....	....	....	....	....	....	....
Other business services	3 268 ..	....	....	....	....	....	....	....	....
Personal, cultural, and recreational	3 287 ..	....	....	....	....	....	....	....	....
Government, n.i.e	3 291 ..	....	....	....	....	....	....	....	....

Table 2 (Continued). STANDARD PRESENTATION, 2003–2010

(Billions of U.S. dollars)

	Code	2003	2004	2005	2006	2007	2008	2009	2010
C. INCOME	4 300	**−50.05**	**−4.73**	**4.83**	**24.57**	**11.33**	**−92.54**	**−7.47**	**1.74**
Total credit	2 300	*283.92*	*374.66*	*482.06*	*630.31*	*828.84*	*772.52*	*585.77*	*570.12*
Total debit	3 300	*−333.97*	*−379.39*	*−477.22*	*−605.74*	*−817.52*	*−865.07*	*−593.24*	*−568.39*
Compensation of employees, credit	2 310	**17.52**	**19.48**	**20.16**	**21.07**	**24.87**	**29.76**	**30.45**	**30.68**
Compensation of employees, debit	3 310	**−8.64**	**−9.65**	**−11.65**	**−12.38**	**−15.49**	**−19.27**	**−19.43**	**−18.54**
Investment income, credit	2 320	**266.39**	**355.18**	**461.90**	**609.24**	**803.97**	**742.76**	**555.32**	**539.44**
Direct investment income	2 330	93.22	152.13	203.28	260.56	332.56	254.90	237.77	260.58
Dividends and distributed branch profits	2 332	63.61	84.88	132.32	182.69	195.18	215.75	180.49	234.33
Reinvested earnings and undistributed branch profits	2 333	16.23	49.85	51.20	52.09	98.28	−6.68	22.62	−3.92
Income on debt (interest)	2 334	13.37	17.41	19.76	25.78	39.10	45.84	34.65	30.17
Portfolio investment income	2 339	95.42	119.06	140.91	178.61	224.17	233.48	175.19	168.92
Income on equity	2 340	21.24	29.10	39.14	49.10	61.87	58.37	38.02	39.45
Income on bonds and notes	2 350	....	....	....	....	....	....	....	....
Income on money market instruments	2 360	....	....	....	....	....	....	....	....
Other investment income	2 370	77.76	84.00	117.70	170.07	247.24	254.38	142.36	109.94
Investment income, debit	3 320	**−325.33**	**−369.74**	**−465.57**	**−593.36**	**−802.03**	**−845.80**	**−573.81**	**−549.85**
Direct investment income	3 330	−93.32	−117.57	−152.53	−168.00	−223.19	−207.67	−170.55	−181.01
Dividends and distributed branch profits	3 332	−58.54	−69.82	−146.70	−96.18	−128.04	−143.60	−121.30	−131.41
Reinvested earnings and undistributed branch profits	3 333	−20.44	−31.09	14.93	−46.48	−58.44	−24.89	−15.82	−23.05
Income on debt (interest)	3 334	−14.35	−16.66	−20.76	−25.34	−36.71	−39.19	−33.43	−26.55
Portfolio investment income	3 339	−149.57	−161.83	−186.95	−236.70	−308.30	−355.55	−274.76	−275.38
Income on equity	3 340	−59.87	−67.23	−85.90	−121.02	−155.16	−166.46	−106.78	−112.64
Income on bonds and notes	3 350	....	....	....	....	....	....	....	....
Income on money market instruments	3 360	....	....	....	....	....	....	....	....
Other investment income	3 370	−82.43	−90.34	−126.09	−188.66	−270.54	−282.58	−128.49	−93.46
D. CURRENT TRANSFERS	4 379	**−63.05**	**−73.70**	**−92.09**	**−100.23**	**−120.15**	**−142.68**	**−125.67**	**−134.22**
Credit	2 379	**92.65**	**100.49**	**103.96**	**110.15**	**119.86**	**131.39**	**130.53**	**115.90**
General government	2 380	50.98	55.72	58.46	63.29	68.71	70.79	70.63	57.23
Other sectors	2 390	41.68	44.77	45.51	46.86	51.16	60.60	59.90	58.67
Workers' remittances	2 391	6.10	6.47	6.20	6.72	8.64	9.88	8.89	8.35
Other current transfers	2 392	35.58	38.31	39.31	40.14	42.51	50.73	51.01	50.32
Debit	3 379	**−155.70**	**−174.19**	**−196.06**	**−210.38**	**−240.02**	**−274.07**	**−256.20**	**−250.11**
General government	3 380	−108.82	−120.99	−136.06	−141.37	−159.04	−175.75	−164.03	−158.35
Other sectors	3 390	−46.89	−53.20	−60.00	−69.01	−80.98	−98.32	−92.17	−91.76
Workers' remittances	3 391	−10.91	−14.44	−18.02	−21.82	−28.22	−31.51	−31.33	−29.17
Other current transfers	3 392	−35.97	−38.76	−41.99	−47.18	−52.76	−66.81	−60.84	−62.59
CAPITAL AND FINANCIAL ACCOUNT	4 996	**−.43**	**−86.87**	**−34.20**	**−18.68**	**−2.17**	**212.70**	**18.95**	**71.82**
CAPITAL ACCOUNT	4 994	**14.34**	**20.46**	**14.24**	**11.74**	**5.41**	**13.21**	**8.49**	**8.15**
Total credit	2 994	*27.32*	*30.39*	*30.30*	*29.81*	*35.02*	*35.61*	*28.19*	*28.96*
Total debit	3 994	*−12.98*	*−9.93*	*−16.06*	*−18.07*	*−29.61*	*−22.40*	*−19.69*	*−20.81*
Capital transfers, credit	2 400	....	....	....	....	....	....	....	....
General government	2 401	....	....	....	....	....	....	....	....
Debt forgiveness	2 402	....	....	....	....	....	....	....	....
Other capital transfers	2 410	....	....	....	....	....	....	....	....
Other sectors	2 430	....	....	....	....	....	....	....	....
Migrants' transfers	2 431	....	....	....	....	....	....	....	....
Debt forgiveness	2 432	....	....	....	....	....	....	....	....
Other capital transfers	2 440	....	....	....	....	....	....	....	....
Capital transfers, debit	3 400	....	....	....	....	....	....	....	....
General government	3 401	....	....	....	....	....	....	....	....
Debt forgiveness	3 402	....	....	....	....	....	....	....	....
Other capital transfers	3 410	....	....	....	....	....	....	....	....
Other sectors	3 430	....	....	....	....	....	....	....	....
Migrants' transfers	3 431	....	....	....	....	....	....	....	....
Debt forgiveness	3 432	....	....	....	....	....	....	....	....
Other capital transfers	3 440	....	....	....	....	....	....	....	....
Nonproduced nonfinancial assets, credit	2 480	....	....	....	....	....	....	....	....
Nonproduced nonfinancial assets, debit	3 480	....	....	....	....	....	....	....	....

Table 2 (Continued). STANDARD PRESENTATION, 2003–2010

(Billions of U.S. dollars)

	Code	2003	2004	2005	2006	2007	2008	2009	2010
FINANCIAL ACCOUNT	4 995	−14.77	−107.33	−48.43	−30.42	−7.58	199.49	10.46	63.67
A. DIRECT INVESTMENT	4 500	−11.41	−100.48	−259.45	−214.13	−124.17	−350.30	−146.91	−60.38
Direct investment abroad	4 505	−164.69	−215.29	−453.55	−542.69	−706.04	−491.78	−448.47	−183.46
Equity capital	4 510	−130.77	−175.16	−331.53	−383.41	−439.77	−296.54	−302.95	−46.32
Claims on affiliated enterprises	4 515	....	....	....	....	....	....	....	....
Liabilities to affiliated enterprises	4 520	....	....	....	....	....	....	....	....
Reinvested earnings	4 525	−16.23	−49.85	−51.20	−52.09	−98.28	6.68	−22.62	3.92
Other capital	4 530	−17.69	9.72	−70.83	−107.19	−167.99	−201.92	−122.90	−141.06
Claims on affiliated enterprises	4 535	....	....	....	....	....	....	....	....
Liabilities to affiliated enterprises	4 540	....	....	....	....	....	....	....	....
Direct investment in the Euro Area	4 555	153.28	114.82	194.10	328.56	581.87	141.48	301.56	123.08
Equity capital	4 560	123.70	84.13	169.09	240.52	375.18	56.57	286.61	161.89
Claims on direct investors	4 565	....	....	....	....	....	....	....	....
Liabilities to direct investors	4 570	....	....	....	....	....	....	....	....
Reinvested earnings	4 575	20.44	31.09	−14.93	46.48	58.44	24.89	15.82	23.05
Other capital	4 580	9.15	−.40	39.95	41.56	148.25	60.02	−.88	−61.86
Claims on direct investors	4 585	....	....	....	....	....	....	....	....
Liabilities to direct investors	4 590	....	....	....	....	....	....	....	....
B. PORTFOLIO INVESTMENT	4 600	63.30	57.28	145.58	238.65	168.69	403.58	374.45	176.57
Assets	4 602	−318.08	−428.80	−514.64	−650.47	−601.34	−28.96	−124.77	−186.97
Equity securities	4 610	−90.34	−132.42	−165.99	−193.24	−86.86	135.31	−72.79	−105.30
Monetary authorities	4 611	−.39	−.02	−.17	−.05	.02	−.89	.03	.24
General government	4 612	−2.95	−4.51	−4.29	−9.94	−11.43	−.18	−2.12	−1.50
Banks	4 613	−15.69	−27.32	−18.15	−25.56	−37.05	53.69	3.58	−12.69
Other sectors	4 614	−71.31	−100.57	−143.37	−157.69	−38.40	82.69	−74.29	−91.35
Debt securities	4 619	−227.74	−296.38	−348.66	−457.23	−514.48	−164.28	−51.98	−81.67
Bonds and notes	4 620	−200.28	−224.62	−327.43	−375.73	−401.76	−139.18	−47.08	−140.00
Monetary authorities	4 621	−2.66	1.23	−.90	−3.27	−6.22	−5.15	4.88	1.52
General government	4 622	−.26	−2.62	−.96	−3.77	−4.51	−4.18	−22.53	−69.88
Banks	4 623	−51.27	−102.14	−142.90	−216.23	−196.54	−62.68	129.10	161.86
Other sectors	4 624	−146.09	−121.09	−182.67	−152.47	−194.50	−67.18	−158.54	−233.50
Money market instruments	4 630	−27.46	−71.76	−21.23	−81.50	−112.71	−25.09	−4.90	58.33
Monetary authorities	4 631	.24	−.06	.13	−11.31	−36.44	−26.34	17.91	15.09
General government	4 632	.81	.48	−.56	.49	.07	−.52	−1.35	2.54
Banks	4 633	−51.04	−53.89	−21.44	−56.81	−51.31	−32.64	−29.89	59.93
Other sectors	4 634	22.53	−18.29	.64	−13.86	−25.04	34.41	8.43	−19.24
Liabilities	4 652	381.38	486.07	660.22	889.12	770.03	432.55	499.22	363.54
Equity securities	4 660	127.39	131.98	291.94	309.73	223.63	−115.34	165.63	165.40
Banks	4 663	....	....	....	121.24	39.61	125.18	2.52	−6.33
Other sectors	4 664	....	....	....	188.49	184.02	−240.52	163.11	171.74
Debt securities	4 669	253.99	354.09	368.28	579.39	546.40	547.89	333.59	198.14
Bonds and notes	4 670	220.29	334.19	318.63	605.76	463.93	293.89	166.06	195.52
Monetary authorities	4 671	....	....	....	....	....	....	....	....
General government	4 672	....	....	....	159.16	173.16	236.38	124.56	245.28
Banks	4 673	....	....	....	243.05	208.76	26.99	13.05	60.40
Other sectors	4 674	....	....	....	203.55	82.02	30.52	28.44	−110.16
Money market instruments	4 680	33.70	19.90	49.65	−26.37	82.46	254.00	167.54	2.62
Monetary authorities	4 681	....	....	....	....	....	....	....	....
General government	4 682	....	....	....	−49.06	23.77	265.51	212.97	−46.99
Banks	4 683	....	....	....	31.93	75.41	−46.61	−15.14	63.92
Other sectors	4 684	....	....	....	−9.24	−16.72	35.10	−30.29	−14.31
C. FINANCIAL DERIVATIVES	4 910	−15.57	−10.53	−21.59	.22	−92.90	−119.09	50.33	11.54
Monetary authorities	4 911	....	....	....	....	....	....	....	....
General government	4 912	....	....	....	....	....	....	....	....
Banks	4 913	....	....	....	....	....	....	....	....
Other sectors	4 914	....	....	....	....	....	....	....	....
Assets	4 900	....	....	....	....	....	....	....	....
Monetary authorities	4 901	....	....	....	....	....	....	....	....
General government	4 902	....	....	....	....	....	....	....	....
Banks	4 903	....	....	....	....	....	....	....	....
Other sectors	4 904	....	....	....	....	....	....	....	....
Liabilities	4 905	−15.57	−10.53	−21.59	.22	−92.90	−119.09	50.33	11.54
Monetary authorities	4 906	....	....	....	....	....	....	....	....
General government	4 907	....	....	....	....	....	....	....	....
Banks	4 908	....	....	....	....	....	....	....	....
Other sectors	4 909	....	....	....	....	....	....	....	....

Table 2 (Concluded). STANDARD PRESENTATION, 2003–2010

(Billions of U.S. dollars)

	Code	2003	2004	2005	2006	2007	2008	2009	2010
D. OTHER INVESTMENT	4 700	**−83.88**	**−69.16**	**64.12**	**−52.59**	**46.49**	**270.15**	**−207.61**	**−50.48**
Assets	4 703	**−282.26**	**−425.21**	**−737.66**	**−998.55**	**−1,236.85**	**−42.38**	**726.55**	**−198.11**
Trade credits	4 706	−1.36	−7.38	−7.73	−1.11	−17.35	−.12	−.85	−15.53
General government	4 707	−.07	−.01	3.40	6.53	1.92	1.68	.59	.29
of which: Short-term	4 709	....	....	....	....	....	....	....	....
Other sectors	4 710	−1.29	−7.37	−11.14	−7.65	−19.28	−1.79	−1.44	−15.82
of which: Short-term	4 712	....	....	....	....	....	....	....	....
Loans	4 714	−184.08	−387.09	−686.56	−930.14	−1,112.81	−45.17	633.76	−111.50
Monetary authorities	4 715	−.92	.19	−.56	11.05	−30.03	13.23	−.16	3.85
of which: Short-term	4 718	....	....	....	....	....	....	....	....
General government	4 719	−.57	1.84	10.63	11.52	2.32	2.43	−12.26	−45.49
of which: Short-term	4 721	....	....	....	....	....	....	....	....
Banks	4 722	−171.19	−324.84	−496.16	−681.56	−713.88	46.43	537.43	−.73
of which: Short-term	4 724	....	....	....	....	....	....	....	....
Other sectors	4 725	−11.40	−64.29	−200.47	−271.15	−371.23	−107.26	108.75	−69.12
of which: Short-term	4 727	....	....	....	....	....	....	....	....
Currency and deposits	4 730	−92.55	−18.74	−13.72	−41.04	−77.58	40.75	73.85	−44.29
Monetary authorities	4 731	....	....	....	....	....	....	....	....
General government	4 732	1.28	−2.14	−3.01	−8.51	7.63	6.59	−.89	−6.09
Banks	4 733	....	....	....	....	....	....	....	....
Other sectors	4 734	−93.83	−16.61	−10.71	−32.53	−85.22	34.16	74.74	−38.20
Other assets	4 736	−4.27	−11.99	−29.64	−26.26	−29.09	−37.84	19.79	−26.79
Monetary authorities	4 737	....	−.34	−.13	....	....	−.02	....	.10
of which: Short-term	4 739	....	....	....	....	....	....	....	....
General government	4 740	−1.04	−1.54	−1.45	−.91	−1.26	−2.17	−2.47	−1.22
of which: Short-term	4 742	....	....	....	....	....	....	....	....
Banks	4 743	−.50	−4.78	−6.18	−7.34	−10.15	−22.59	28.14	−11.41
of which: Short-term	4 745	....	....	....	....	....	....	....	....
Other sectors	4 746	−2.74	−5.33	−21.88	−18.01	−17.69	−13.08	−5.88	−14.26
of which: Short-term	4 748	....	....	....	....	....	....	....	....
Liabilities	4 753	**198.38**	**356.04**	**801.78**	**945.97**	**1,283.34**	**312.53**	**−934.16**	**147.63**
Trade credits	4 756	4.83	11.74	16.50	15.78	13.77	15.12	−8.25	14.50
General government	4 757	....	.01	....	−.01	.01	....	.04	.03
of which: Short-term	4 759	....	....	....	....	....	....	....	....
Other sectors	4 760	4.83	11.73	16.50	15.79	13.76	15.12	−8.30	14.48
of which: Short-term	4 762	....	....	....	....	....	....	....	....
Loans	4 764	193.02	338.85	775.43	907.04	1,265.27	273.31	−944.77	97.88
Monetary authorities	4 765	12.37	9.61	8.66	25.84	126.79	403.96	−317.21	8.67
of which: Use of Fund credit and loans from the Fund	4 766	....	....	....	....	....	....	....	....
of which: Short-term	4 768	....	....	....	....	....	....	....	....
General government	4 769	−3.94	−5.08	−2.21	2.69	−3.27	14.24	14.84	87.37
of which: Short-term	4 771	....	....	....	....	....	....	....	....
Banks	4 772	151.53	303.90	603.74	622.88	821.71	−207.32	−474.11	−.95
of which: Short-term	4 774	....	....	....	....	....	....	....	....
Other sectors	4 775	33.06	30.41	165.24	255.63	320.03	62.43	−168.29	2.79
of which: Short-term	4 777	....	....	....	....	....	....	....	....
Currency and deposits	4 780	....	....	....	....	....	....	....	....
Monetary authorities	4 781	....	....	....	....	....	....	....	....
General government	4 782	....	....	....	....	....	....	....	....
Banks	4 783	....	....	....	....	....	....	....	....
Other sectors	4 784	....	....	....	....	....	....	....	....
Other liabilities	4 786	.53	5.45	9.85	23.14	4.30	24.11	18.87	35.25
Monetary authorities	4 787	−.04	.08	−.01	.01	−.04	.08	66.01	3.52
of which: Short-term	4 789	....	....	....	....	....	....	.19	3.52
General government	4 790	.32	−.21	−.33	−.12	1.39	−2.12	.05	.75
of which: Short-term	4 792	....	....	....	....	....	....	....	....
Banks	4 793	−.17	3.56	1.57	8.25	5.97	15.59	−15.12	8.30
of which: Short-term	4 795	....	....	....	....	....	....	....	....
Other sectors	4 796	.42	2.02	8.62	14.99	−3.03	10.56	−32.07	22.68
of which: Short-term	4 798	....	....	....	....	....	....	....	....
E. RESERVE ASSETS	4 802	**32.80**	**15.56**	**22.91**	**−2.57**	**−5.69**	**−4.86**	**−59.80**	**−13.58**
Monetary gold	4 812	1.95	1.46	4.81	5.28	4.42	3.87	2.74	.01
Special drawing rights	4 811	−.03	.46	−.21	−.70	−.47	.14	−66.34	−.15
Reserve position in the Fund	4 810	−.51	5.07	11.24	6.02	1.92	−4.97	−4.58	−5.95
Foreign exchange	4 803	31.40	8.58	7.07	−13.17	−11.57	−3.91	8.38	−7.49
Other claims	4 813	....	....	....	....	....	....	....	....
NET ERRORS AND OMISSIONS	4 998	**−24.48**	**5.68**	**15.02**	**19.00**	**−22.69**	**−14.48**	**12.38**	**−18.27**

Table 3. INTERNATIONAL INVESTMENT POSITION (End-period stocks), 2003–2010

(Billions of U.S. dollars)

	Code	2003	2004	2005	2006	2007	2008	2009	2010
ASSETS	8 995 C.	**10,133.76**	**12,030.54**	**13,048.27**	**16,653.13**	**21,200.29**	**19,510.42**	**20,583.88**	**21,970.97**
Direct investment abroad	8 505	**2,742.29**	**3,111.12**	**3,322.06**	**4,204.58**	**5,548.03**	**5,435.71**	**6,138.36**	**6,276.57**
Equity capital and reinvested earnings	8 506	2,183.54	2,528.37	2,701.33	3,432.34	4,432.42	4,218.97	4,740.75	4,842.56
Claims on affiliated enterprises	8 507	....	....	....	....	....	....	....	....
Liabilities to affiliated enterprises	8 508	....	....	....	....	....	....	....	....
Other capital	8 530	558.75	582.75	620.74	772.24	1,115.61	1,216.74	1,397.61	1,434.01
Claims on affiliated enterprises	8 535	....	....	....	....	....	....	....	....
Liabilities to affiliated enterprises	8 540	....	....	....	....	....	....	....	....
Portfolio investment	8 602	**3,355.18**	**4,136.43**	**4,567.32**	**5,730.56**	**6,802.35**	**5,189.48**	**6,087.66**	**6,466.24**
Equity securities	8 610	1,377.84	1,702.54	2,035.48	2,549.21	2,888.89	1,570.36	2,144.30	2,550.42
Monetary authorities	8 611	2.19	2.85	3.49	3.70	4.12	4.13	4.92	4.78
General government	8 612	14.46	22.24	32.01	48.77	65.63	37.75	49.58	63.66
Banks	8 613	67.70	100.76	117.34	161.28	199.90	91.10	104.83	119.93
Other sectors	8 614	1,293.49	1,576.69	1,882.64	2,335.46	2,619.24	1,437.39	1,984.97	2,362.05
Debt securities	8 619	1,977.34	2,433.89	2,531.83	3,181.35	3,913.46	3,619.11	3,943.36	3,915.82
Bonds and notes	8 620	1,672.52	2,042.83	2,155.39	2,680.87	3,338.74	3,014.43	3,369.95	3,379.85
Monetary authorities	8 621	10.43	8.81	8.10	11.99	20.99	25.92	24.50	20.75
General government	8 622	10.12	13.16	13.90	18.42	25.28	25.66	52.48	102.81
Banks	8 623	582.52	739.17	815.12	1,114.47	1,421.70	1,319.14	1,297.22	1,057.16
Other sectors	8 624	1,069.45	1,281.69	1,318.26	1,536.00	1,870.76	1,643.70	1,995.75	2,199.13
Money market instruments	8 630	304.83	391.06	376.44	500.48	574.72	604.69	573.41	535.98
Monetary authorities	8 631	1.39	1.24	.89	12.14	48.93	85.63	64.65	55.68
General government	8 632	.70	.53	.33	.23	.73	1.77	2.89	.26
Banks	8 633	241.88	315.32	313.21	398.15	388.72	412.49	406.79	364.97
Other sectors	8 634	60.86	73.97	62.01	89.96	136.34	104.80	99.08	115.07
Financial derivatives	8 900	**171.65**	**215.05**	**226.93**	**286.00**	**515.09**	**875.32**	**732.58**	**1,647.94**
Monetary authorities	8 901	....	....	....	....	....	....	....	....
General government	8 902	....	....	....	....	....	....	....	....
Banks	8 903	....	....	....	....	....	....	....	....
Other sectors	8 904	....	....	....	....	....	....	....	....
Other investment	8 703	**3,477.27**	**4,185.14**	**4,554.41**	**6,002.82**	**7,823.66**	**7,489.12**	**6,959.22**	**6,790.67**
Trade credits	8 706	238.67	263.78	244.07	263.94	305.37	279.26	288.69	300.71
General government	8 707	30.25	31.99	23.20	18.61	18.65	17.13	12.08	10.18
of which: Short-term	8 709	....	....	....	....	....	....	....	....
Other sectors	8 710	208.41	231.78	220.86	245.33	286.72	262.14	276.60	290.52
of which: Short-term	8 712	....	....	....	....	....	....	....	....
Loans	8 714	2,608.87	3,214.14	3,605.60	4,882.69	6,447.95	6,194.53	5,717.85	5,552.08
Monetary authorities	8 715	5.59	6.12	5.71	13.49	48.80	38.50	42.36	42.63
of which: Short-term	8 718	....	....	....	....	....	....	....	....
General government	8 719	70.39	77.05	58.35	52.16	51.34	46.49	75.22	129.20
of which: Short-term	8 721	....	....	....	....	....	....	....	....
Banks	8 722	2,197.80	2,667.58	2,906.45	3,822.23	4,823.62	4,488.16	4,043.48	3,929.86
of which: Short-term	8 724	....	....	....	....	....	....	....	....
Other sectors	8 725	335.09	463.39	635.09	994.82	1,524.19	1,621.39	1,556.79	1,450.39
of which: Short-term	8 727	....	....	....	....	....	....	....	....
Currency and deposits	8 730	421.52	466.57	442.43	543.46	709.32	612.74	589.44	634.76
Monetary authorities	8 731	....	....	....	....	....	....	....	....
General government	8 732	7.31	11.26	13.94	24.93	20.17	12.30	16.34	28.02
Banks	8 733	....	....	....	....	....	....	....	....
Other sectors	8 734	414.20	455.30	428.48	518.53	689.15	600.44	573.10	606.74
Other assets	8 736	208.22	240.66	262.32	312.72	361.02	402.59	363.24	303.13
Monetary authorities	8 737	.73	.13	.20	.22	.40	.39	.40	.26
of which: Short-term	8 739	....	....	....	....	....	....	....	....
General government	8 740	53.96	58.27	57.47	62.49	50.05	49.82	53.38	54.37
of which: Short-term	8 742	....	....	....	....	....	....	....	....
Banks	8 743	48.46	61.58	68.75	82.93	105.54	82.26	43.93	43.22
of which: Short-term	8 745	....	....	....	....	....	....	....	....
Other sectors	8 746	105.07	120.69	135.92	167.09	205.02	270.12	265.53	205.28
of which: Short-term	8 748	....	....	....	....	....	....	....	....
Reserve assets	8 802	**387.35**	**382.79**	**377.55**	**429.18**	**511.16**	**520.78**	**666.06**	**789.55**
Monetary gold	8 812	164.21	170.82	192.82	232.17	295.86	302.06	383.29	489.30
Special drawing rights	8 811	5.54	5.32	5.11	6.08	6.87	6.56	73.22	72.08
Reserve position in the Fund	8 810	29.43	25.45	12.46	6.89	5.24	10.18	15.19	21.04
Foreign exchange	8 803	188.18	181.20	167.17	184.04	203.19	201.97	194.36	207.13
Other claims	8 813	....	....	....	....	....	....	....	....

Table 3 (Concluded). INTERNATIONAL INVESTMENT POSITION (End-period stocks), 2003–2010

(Billions of U.S. dollars)

	Code	2003	2004	2005	2006	2007	2008	2009	2010
LIABILITIES	8 995 D.	**11,099.26**	**13,174.92**	**13,870.72**	**17,941.15**	**22,989.60**	**21,749.89**	**22,758.12**	**23,620.15**
Direct investment in the Euro Area	8 555	**2,630.29**	**3,036.43**	**2,878.70**	**3,588.58**	**4,731.36**	**4,600.19**	**5,002.55**	**4,966.54**
Equity capital and reinvested earnings	8 556	1,905.29	2,241.17	2,156.96	2,748.46	3,508.82	3,267.48	3,638.90	3,757.18
Claims on direct investors	8 557	....	....	....	....	....	....	....	....
Liabilities to direct investors	8 558	....	....	....	....	....	....	....	....
Other capital	8 580	725.00	795.26	721.74	840.12	1,222.55	1,332.71	1,363.65	1,209.36
Claims on direct investors	8 585	....	....	....	....	....	....	....	....
Liabilities to direct investors	8 590	....	....	....	....	....	....	....	....
Portfolio investment	8 652	**4,534.51**	**5,531.70**	**5,986.67**	**7,853.93**	**9,644.41**	**8,281.26**	**9,711.14**	**9,851.61**
Equity securities	8 660	1,985.05	2,372.86	2,825.80	3,997.12	4,860.92	3,041.24	3,964.67	4,243.14
Banks	8 663	....	....	644.52	745.91	842.37	858.54	989.17	878.53
Other sectors	8 664	....	....	2,181.28	3,251.21	4,018.55	2,182.71	2,975.49	3,364.61
Debt securities	8 669	2,549.46	3,158.83	3,160.87	3,856.81	4,783.49	5,240.02	5,746.48	5,608.47
Bonds and notes	8 670	2,246.30	2,850.81	2,801.66	3,571.01	4,425.23	4,707.18	4,986.80	4,969.19
Monetary authorities	8 671	....	....	....	....	....	....	....	....
General government	8 672	....	....	1,121.65	1,324.92	1,637.15	1,996.21	2,129.28	2,240.92
Banks	8 673	....	....	996.39	1,279.96	1,683.08	1,669.18	1,630.94	1,534.52
Other sectors	8 674	....	....	683.62	966.13	1,105.00	1,041.79	1,226.58	1,193.75
Money market instruments	8 680	303.16	308.03	359.21	285.80	358.26	532.84	759.68	639.28
Monetary authorities	8 681	....	....	....	....	....	....	....	....
General government	8 682	....	....	183.02	83.62	118.44	378.87	612.26	476.62
Banks	8 683	....	....	125.51	161.81	204.42	86.32	97.68	109.00
Other sectors	8 684	....	....	50.68	40.37	35.40	67.65	49.74	53.65
Financial derivatives	8 905	**196.93**	**265.81**	**252.16**	**313.44**	**557.53**	**917.09**	**797.95**	**1,708.07**
Monetary authorities	8 906	....	....	....	....	....	....	....	....
General government	8 907	....	....	....	....	....	....	....	....
Banks	8 908	....	....	....	....	....	....	....	....
Other sectors	8 909	....	....	....	....	....	....	....	....
Other investment	8 753	**3,737.53**	**4,340.98**	**4,753.20**	**6,185.20**	**8,056.30**	**7,951.34**	**7,246.48**	**7,093.93**
Trade credits	8 756	142.47	159.73	158.87	187.95	251.98	247.23	252.08	256.85
General government	8 757	.04	.01	.01	.01	.02	.02	.02	.06
of which: Short-term	8 759	....	....	....	....	....	....	....	....
Other sectors	8 760	142.43	159.72	158.86	187.94	251.96	247.21	252.07	256.79
of which: Short-term	8 762	....	....	....	....	....	....	....	....
Loans	8 764	3,492.98	4,053.53	4,452.28	5,798.68	7,519.70	7,374.68	6,601.74	6,503.08
Monetary authorities	8 765	83.63	101.65	97.42	153.09	297.13	671.66	362.41	355.21
of which: Use of Fund credit and loans from the Fund	8 766	....	....	....	....	....	....	....	....
of which: Short-term	8 768	....	....	....	....	....	....	....	....
General government	8 769	53.25	57.40	50.31	60.30	67.06	79.53	96.61	194.71
of which: Short-term	8 771	....	....	....	....	....	....	....	....
Banks	8 772	2,833.12	3,301.49	3,591.37	4,506.29	5,665.28	5,152.04	4,831.98	4,617.71
of which: Short-term	8 774	....	....	....	....	....	....	....	....
Other sectors	8 775	522.98	592.99	713.17	1,079.01	1,490.23	1,471.45	1,310.75	1,335.45
of which: Short-term	8 777	....	....	....	....	....	....	....	....
Currency and deposits	8 780	....	....	....	....	....	....	....	....
Monetary authorities	8 781	....	....	....	....	....	....	....	....
General government	8 782	....	....	....	....	....	....	....	....
Banks	8 783	....	....	....	....	....	....	....	....
Other sectors	8 784	....	....	....	....	....	....	....	....
Other liabilities	8 786	102.08	127.72	142.05	198.56	284.62	329.44	392.65	333.99
Monetary authorities	8 787	.21	.30	.27	.32	.35	.38	74.30	76.46
of which: Short-term	8 789	....	....	....	....	....	....	.50	3.96
General government	8 790	4.84	4.86	4.49	5.44	7.99	5.60	5.75	8.35
of which: Short-term	8 792	....	....	....	....	....	....	....	....
Banks	8 793	39.51	57.26	60.39	71.42	97.59	75.02	55.44	60.70
of which: Short-term	8 795	....	....	....	....	....	....	....	....
Other sectors	8 796	57.52	65.30	76.90	121.38	178.70	248.44	257.16	188.49
of which: Short-term	8 798	....	....	....	....	....	....	....	....
NET INTERNATIONAL INVESTMENT POSITION	8 995	**−965.50**	**−1,144.38**	**−822.45**	**−1,288.02**	**−1,789.31**	**−2,239.48**	**−2,174.24**	**−1,649.18**
Conversion rates: euros per U.S. dollar (end of period)	0 104	**.7918**	**.7342**	**.8477**	**.7593**	**.6793**	**.7185**	**.6942**	**.7484**

Table 1. ANALYTIC PRESENTATION, 2003–2010
(Millions of U.S. dollars)

	Code	2003	2004	2005	2006	2007	2008	2009	2010
A. Current Account[1]	4 993 Z.	**−6.6**	....	....	....	....	....	....	....
Goods: exports f.o.b.	2 100 ..	593.7	....	....	....	....	....	....	....
Goods: imports f.o.b.	3 100 ..	−683.5	....	....	....	....	....	....	....
Balance on Goods	4 100 ..	*−89.8*	....	....	....	....	....	....	....
Services: credit	2 200 ..	77.5	....	....	....	....	....	....	....
Services: debit	3 200 ..	−146.9	....	....	....	....	....	....	....
Balance on Goods and Services	4 991 ..	*−159.2*	....	....	....	....	....	....	....
Income: credit	2 300 ..	106.3	....	....	....	....	....	....	....
Income: debit	3 300 ..	−76.3	....	....	....	....	....	....	....
Balance on Goods, Services, and Income	4 992 ..	*−129.2*	....	....	....	....	....	....	....
Current transfers: credit	2 379 Z.	128.2	....	....	....	....	....	....	....
Current transfers: debit	3 379 ..	−5.6	....	....	....	....	....	....	....
B. Capital Account[1]	4 994 Z.	....	....	....	....	....	....	....	....
Capital account: credit	2 994 Z.	....							
Capital account: debit	3 994 ..	....							
Total, Groups A Plus B	4 981 ..	*−6.6*	....						
C. Financial Account[1]	4 995 W.	....	....	....	....	....	....	....	....
Direct investment abroad	4 505 ..	....	....	....	....	....	....	....	....
Direct investment in Faroe Islands	4 555 Z.	....	....	....	....	....	....	....	....
Portfolio investment assets	4 602 ..	....	....	....	....	....	....	....	....
Equity securities	4 610 ..	....	....	....	....	....	....	....	....
Debt securities	4 619 ..	....	....	....	....	....	....	....	....
Portfolio investment liabilities	4 652 Z.	....	....	....	....	....	....	....	....
Equity securities	4 660 ..	....	....	....	....	....	....	....	....
Debt securities	4 669 Z.	....	....	....	....	....	....	....	....
Financial derivatives	4 910 ..	....	....	....	....	....	....	....	....
Financial derivatives assets	4 900 ..	....	....	....	....	....	....	....	....
Financial derivatives liabilities	4 905 ..	....	....	....	....	....	....	....	....
Other investment assets	4 703 ..	....	....	....	....	....	....	....	....
Monetary authorities	4 701 ..	....	....	....	....	....	....	....	....
General government	4 704 ..	....	....	....	....	....	....	....	....
Banks	4 705 ..	....	....	....	....	....	....	....	....
Other sectors	4 728 ..	....	....	....	....	....	....	....	....
Other investment liabilities	4 753 W.	....	....	....	....	....	....	....	....
Monetary authorities	4 753 WA	....	....	....	....	....	....	....	....
General government	4 753 ZB	....	....	....	....	....	....	....	....
Banks	4 753 ZC	....	....	....	....	....	....	....	....
Other sectors	4 753 ZD	....	....	....	....	....	....	....	....
Total, Groups A Through C	4 983 ..	*−6.6*	....	....	....	....	....	....	....
D. Net Errors and Omissions	4 998 ..	....	....	....	....	....	....	....	....
Total, Groups A Through D	4 984 ..	....	....	....	....	....	....	....	....
E. Reserves and Related Items	4 802 A.	....	....	....	....	....	....	....	....
Reserve assets	4 802 ..	....	....	....	....	....	....	....	....
Use of Fund credit and loans	4 766 ..	....	....	....	....	....	....	....	....
Exceptional financing	4 920 ..	....	....	....	....	....	....	....	....
Conversion rates: Danish kroner per U.S. dollar	0 101 ..	**6.5877**	**5.9911**	**5.9969**	**5.9468**	**5.4437**	**5.0981**	**5.3609**	**5.6241**

[1] Excludes components that have been classified in the categories of Group E.

Table 2. STANDARD PRESENTATION, 2003–2010

(Millions of U.S. dollars)

	Code	2003	2004	2005	2006	2007	2008	2009	2010
CURRENT ACCOUNT	4 993	**−6.6**	....	....	....	....	....	....	....
A. GOODS	4 100	**−89.8**	....	....	....	....	....	....	....
Credit	2 100	**593.7**	....	....	....	....	....	....	....
General merchandise: exports f.o.b.	2 110	....	....	....	....	....	....	....	....
Goods for processing: exports f.o.b.	2 150	....	....	....	....	....	....	....	....
Repairs on goods	2 160	....	....	....	....	....	....	....	....
Goods procured in ports by carriers	2 170	....	....	....	....	....	....	....	....
Nonmonetary gold	2 180	....	....	....	....	....	....	....	....
Debit	3 100	**−683.5**	....	....	....	....	....	....	....
General merchandise: imports f.o.b.	3 110	....	....	....	....	....	....	....	....
Goods for processing: imports f.o.b.	3 150	....	....	....	....	....	....	....	....
Repairs on goods	3 160	....	....	....	....	....	....	....	....
Goods procured in ports by carriers	3 170	....	....	....	....	....	....	....	....
Nonmonetary gold	3 180	....	....	....	....	....	....	....	....
B. SERVICES	4 200	**−69.4**	....	....	....	....	....	....	....
Total credit	2 200	*77.5*	....	....	....	....	....	....	....
Total debit	3 200	*−146.9*	....	....	....	....	....	....	....
Transportation services, credit	2 205	**34.3**	....	....	....	....	....	....	....
Passenger	2 850	....	....	....	....	....	....	....	....
Freight	2 851	....	....	....	....	....	....	....	....
Other	2 852	....	....	....	....	....	....	....	....
Sea transport, passenger	2 207	....	....	....	....	....	....	....	....
Sea transport, freight	2 208	....	....	....	....	....	....	....	....
Sea transport, other	2 209	....	....	....	....	....	....	....	....
Air transport, passenger	2 211	....	....	....	....	....	....	....	....
Air transport, freight	2 212	....	....	....	....	....	....	....	....
Air transport, other	2 213	....	....	....	....	....	....	....	....
Other transport, passenger	2 215	....	....	....	....	....	....	....	....
Other transport, freight	2 216	....	....	....	....	....	....	....	....
Other transport, other	2 217	....	....	....	....	....	....	....	....
Transportation services, debit	3 205	**−39.2**	....	....	....	....	....	....	....
Passenger	3 850	....	....	....	....	....	....	....	....
Freight	3 851	....	....	....	....	....	....	....	....
Other	3 852	....	....	....	....	....	....	....	....
Sea transport, passenger	3 207	....	....	....	....	....	....	....	....
Sea transport, freight	3 208	....	....	....	....	....	....	....	....
Sea transport, other	3 209	....	....	....	....	....	....	....	....
Air transport, passenger	3 211	....	....	....	....	....	....	....	....
Air transport, freight	3 212	....	....	....	....	....	....	....	....
Air transport, other	3 213	....	....	....	....	....	....	....	....
Other transport, passenger	3 215	....	....	....	....	....	....	....	....
Other transport, freight	3 216	....	....	....	....	....	....	....	....
Other transport, other	3 217	....	....	....	....	....	....	....	....
Travel, credit	2 236	**31.0**	....	....	....	....	....	....	....
Business travel	2 237	21.8	....	....	....	....	....	....	....
Personal travel	2 240	9.2	....	....	....	....	....	....	....
Travel, debit	3 236	**−56.9**	....	....	....	....	....	....	....
Business travel	3 237	−39.1	....	....	....	....	....	....	....
Personal travel	3 240	−17.8	....	....	....	....	....	....	....
Other services, credit	2 200 BA	**12.3**	....	....	....	....	....	....	....
Communications	2 245	1.9	....	....	....	....	....	....	....
Construction	2 249	4.6	....	....	....	....	....	....	....
Insurance	2 253	2.6	....	....	....	....	....	....	....
Financial	2 260	.5	....	....	....	....	....	....	....
Computer and information	2 262	.2	....	....	....	....	....	....	....
Royalties and licence fees	2 266	....	....	....	....	....	....	....	....
Other business services	2 268	1.4	....	....	....	....	....	....	....
Personal, cultural, and recreational	2 287	.9	....	....	....	....	....	....	....
Government, n.i.e.	2 291	.1	....	....	....	....	....	....	....
Other services, debit	3 200 BA	**−50.8**	....	....	....	....	....	....	....
Communications	3 245	−3.3	....	....	....	....	....	....	....
Construction	3 249	−19.0	....	....	....	....	....	....	....
Insurance	3 253	−7.2	....	....	....	....	....	....	....
Financial	3 260	−.3	....	....	....	....	....	....	....
Computer and information	3 262	−4.6	....	....	....	....	....	....	....
Royalties and licence fees	3 266	−3.2	....	....	....	....	....	....	....
Other business services	3 268	−10.2	....	....	....	....	....	....	....
Personal, cultural, and recreational	3 287	−1.5	....	....	....	....	....	....	....
Government, n.i.e.	3 291	−1.4	....	....	....	....	....	....	....

Table 2 (Continued). STANDARD PRESENTATION, 2003–2010

(Millions of U.S. dollars)

	Code	2003	2004	2005	2006	2007	2008	2009	2010
C. INCOME	4 300	**30.0**	....	....	....	....	....	....	....
Total credit	2 300	*106.3*	....	....	....	....	....	....	....
Total debit	3 300	*−76.3*	....	....	....	....	....	....	....
Compensation of employees, credit	2 310	**44.4**	....	....	....	....	....	....	....
Compensation of employees, debit	3 310	**−5.1**	....	....	....	....	....	....	....
Investment income, credit	2 320	**61.9**	....	....	....	....	....	....	....
Direct investment income	2 330	1.6	....	....	....	....	....	....	....
Dividends and distributed branch profits	2 332	....	....	....	....	....	....	....	....
Reinvested earnings and undistributed branch profits	2 333	....	....	....	....	....	....	....	....
Income on debt (interest)	2 334	....	....	....	....	....	....	....	....
Portfolio investment income	2 339	2.3	....	....	....	....	....	....	....
Income on equity	2 340	....	....	....	....	....	....	....	....
Income on bonds and notes	2 350	....	....	....	....	....	....	....	....
Income on money market instruments	2 360	....	....	....	....	....	....	....	....
Other investment income	2 370	58.1	....	....	....	....	....	....	....
Investment income, debit	3 320	**−71.2**	....	....	....	....	....	....	....
Direct investment income	3 330	−6.2	....	....	....	....	....	....	....
Dividends and distributed branch profits	3 332	....	....	....	....	....	....	....	....
Reinvested earnings and undistributed branch profits	3 333	....	....	....	....	....	....	....	....
Income on debt (interest)	3 334	....	....	....	....	....	....	....	....
Portfolio investment income	3 339	−2.0	....	....	....	....	....	....	....
Income on equity	3 340	....	....	....	....	....	....	....	....
Income on bonds and notes	3 350	....	....	....	....	....	....	....	....
Income on money market instruments	3 360	....	....	....	....	....	....	....	....
Other investment income	3 370	−63.0	....	....	....	....	....	....	....
D. CURRENT TRANSFERS	4 379	**122.6**	....	....	....	....	....	....	....
Credit	2 379	**128.2**	....	....	....	....	....	....	....
General government	2 380	111.7	....	....	....	....	....	....	....
Other sectors	2 390	16.5	....	....	....	....	....	....	....
Workers' remittances	2 391	....	....	....	....	....	....	....	....
Other current transfers	2 392	....	....	....	....	....	....	....	....
Debit	3 379	**−5.6**	....	....	....	....	....	....	....
General government	3 380	−.8	....	....	....	....	....	....	....
Other sectors	3 390	−4.8	....	....	....	....	....	....	....
Workers' remittances	3 391	....	....	....	....	....	....	....	....
Other current transfers	3 392	....	....	....	....	....	....	....	....
CAPITAL AND FINANCIAL ACCOUNT	4 996	....	....	....	....	....	....	....	....
CAPITAL ACCOUNT	4 994	....	....	....	....	....	....	....	....
Total credit	2 994	....	....	....	....	....	....	....	....
Total debit	3 994	....	....	....	....	....	....	....	....
Capital transfers, credit	2 400	....	....	....	....	....	....	....	....
General government	2 401	....	....	....	....	....	....	....	....
Debt forgiveness	2 402	....	....	....	....	....	....	....	....
Other capital transfers	2 410	....	....	....	....	....	....	....	....
Other sectors	2 430	....	....	....	....	....	....	....	....
Migrants' transfers	2 431	....	....	....	....	....	....	....	....
Debt forgiveness	2 432	....	....	....	....	....	....	....	....
Other capital transfers	2 440	....	....	....	....	....	....	....	....
Capital transfers, debit	3 400	....	....	....	....	....	....	....	....
General government	3 401	....	....	....	....	....	....	....	....
Debt forgiveness	3 402	....	....	....	....	....	....	....	....
Other capital transfers	3 410	....	....	....	....	....	....	....	....
Other sectors	3 430	....	....	....	....	....	....	....	....
Migrants' transfers	3 431	....	....	....	....	....	....	....	....
Debt forgiveness	3 432	....	....	....	....	....	....	....	....
Other capital transfers	3 440	....	....	....	....	....	....	....	....
Nonproduced nonfinancial assets, credit	2 480	....	....	....	....	....	....	....	....
Nonproduced nonfinancial assets, debit	3 480	....	....	....	....	....	....	....	....

Table 2 (Continued). STANDARD PRESENTATION, 2003–2010

(Millions of U.S. dollars)

	Code	2003	2004	2005	2006	2007	2008	2009	2010
FINANCIAL ACCOUNT	4 995	....	....	....	....	....	....	....	....
A. DIRECT INVESTMENT	4 500	....	....	....	....	....	....	....	....
Direct investment abroad	4 505	....	....	....	....	....	....	....	....
Equity capital	4 510	....	....	....	....	....	....	....	....
Claims on affiliated enterprises	4 515	....	....	....	....	....	....	....	....
Liabilities to affiliated enterprises	4 520	....	....	....	....	....	....	....	....
Reinvested earnings	4 525	....	....	....	....	....	....	....	....
Other capital	4 530	....	....	....	....	....	....	....	....
Claims on affiliated enterprises	4 535	....	....	....	....	....	....	....	....
Liabilities to affiliated enterprises	4 540	....	....	....	....	....	....	....	....
Direct investment in Faroe Islands	4 555	....	....	....	....	....	....	....	....
Equity capital	4 560	....	....	....	....	....	....	....	....
Claims on direct investors	4 565	....	....	....	....	....	....	....	....
Liabilities to direct investors	4 570	....	....	....	....	....	....	....	....
Reinvested earnings	4 575	....	....	....	....	....	....	....	....
Other capital	4 580	....	....	....	....	....	....	....	....
Claims on direct investors	4 585	....	....	....	....	....	....	....	....
Liabilities to direct investors	4 590	....	....	....	....	....	....	....	....
B. PORTFOLIO INVESTMENT	4 600	....	....	....	....	....	....	....	....
Assets	4 602	....	....	....	....	....	....	....	....
Equity securities	4 610	....	....	....	....	....	....	....	....
Monetary authorities	4 611	....	....	....	....	....	....	....	....
General government	4 612	....	....	....	....	....	....	....	....
Banks	4 613	....	....	....	....	....	....	....	....
Other sectors	4 614	....	....	....	....	....	....	....	....
Debt securities	4 619	....	....	....	....	....	....	....	....
Bonds and notes	4 620	....	....	....	....	....	....	....	....
Monetary authorities	4 621	....	....	....	....	....	....	....	....
General government	4 622	....	....	....	....	....	....	....	....
Banks	4 623	....	....	....	....	....	....	....	....
Other sectors	4 624	....	....	....	....	....	....	....	....
Money market instruments	4 630	....	....	....	....	....	....	....	....
Monetary authorities	4 631	....	....	....	....	....	....	....	....
General government	4 632	....	....	....	....	....	....	....	....
Banks	4 633	....	....	....	....	....	....	....	....
Other sectors	4 634	....	....	....	....	....	....	....	....
Liabilities	4 652	....	....	....	....	....	....	....	....
Equity securities	4 660	....	....	....	....	....	....	....	....
Banks	4 663	....	....	....	....	....	....	....	....
Other sectors	4 664	....	....	....	....	....	....	....	....
Debt securities	4 669	....	....	....	....	....	....	....	....
Bonds and notes	4 670	....	....	....	....	....	....	....	....
Monetary authorities	4 671	....	....	....	....	....	....	....	....
General government	4 672	....	....	....	....	....	....	....	....
Banks	4 673	....	....	....	....	....	....	....	....
Other sectors	4 674	....	....	....	....	....	....	....	....
Money market instruments	4 680	....	....	....	....	....	....	....	....
Monetary authorities	4 681	....	....	....	....	....	....	....	....
General government	4 682	....	....	....	....	....	....	....	....
Banks	4 683	....	....	....	....	....	....	....	....
Other sectors	4 684	....	....	....	....	....	....	....	....
C. FINANCIAL DERIVATIVES	4 910	....	....	....	....	....	....	....	....
Monetary authorities	4 911	....	....	....	....	....	....	....	....
General government	4 912	....	....	....	....	....	....	....	....
Banks	4 913	....	....	....	....	....	....	....	....
Other sectors	4 914	....	....	....	....	....	....	....	....
Assets	4 900	....	....	....	....	....	....	....	....
Monetary authorities	4 901	....	....	....	....	....	....	....	....
General government	4 902	....	....	....	....	....	....	....	....
Banks	4 903	....	....	....	....	....	....	....	....
Other sectors	4 904	....	....	....	....	....	....	....	....
Liabilities	4 905	....	....	....	....	....	....	....	....
Monetary authorities	4 906	....	....	....	....	....	....	....	....
General government	4 907	....	....	....	....	....	....	....	....
Banks	4 908	....	....	....	....	....	....	....	....
Other sectors	4 909	....	....	....	....	....	....	....	....

Table 2 (Concluded). STANDARD PRESENTATION, 2003–2010

(Millions of U.S. dollars)

	Code	2003	2004	2005	2006	2007	2008	2009	2010
D. OTHER INVESTMENT	4 700 ..	....	....	....	....	....	....	....	....
Assets	4 703 ..	....	....	....	....	....	....	....	....
Trade credits	4 706 ..	....	....	....	....	....	....	....	....
General government	4 707 ..	....	....	....	....	....	....	....	....
of which: Short-term	4 709 ..	....	....	....	....	....	....	....	....
Other sectors	4 710 ..	....	....	....	....	....	....	....	....
of which: Short-term	4 712 ..	....	....	....	....	....	....	....	....
Loans	4 714 ..	....	....	....	....	....	....	....	....
Monetary authorities	4 715 ..	....	....	....	....	....	....	....	....
of which: Short-term	4 718 ..	....	....	....	....	....	....	....	....
General government	4 719 ..	....	....	....	....	....	....	....	....
of which: Short-term	4 721 ..	....	....	....	....	....	....	....	....
Banks	4 722 ..	....	....	....	....	....	....	....	....
of which: Short-term	4 724 ..	....	....	....	....	....	....	....	....
Other sectors	4 725 ..	....	....	....	....	....	....	....	....
of which: Short-term	4 727 ..	....	....	....	....	....	....	....	....
Currency and deposits	4 730 ..	....	....	....	....	....	....	....	....
Monetary authorities	4 731 ..	....	....	....	....	....	....	....	....
General government	4 732 ..	....	....	....	....	....	....	....	....
Banks	4 733 ..	....	....	....	....	....	....	....	....
Other sectors	4 734 ..	....	....	....	....	....	....	....	....
Other assets	4 736 ..	....	....	....	....	....	....	....	....
Monetary authorities	4 737 ..	....	....	....	....	....	....	....	....
of which: Short-term	4 739 ..	....	....	....	....	....	....	....	....
General government	4 740 ..	....	....	....	....	....	....	....	....
of which: Short-term	4 742 ..	....	....	....	....	....	....	....	....
Banks	4 743 ..	....	....	....	....	....	....	....	....
of which: Short-term	4 745 ..	....	....	....	....	....	....	....	....
Other sectors	4 746 ..	....	....	....	....	....	....	....	....
of which: Short-term	4 748 ..	....	....	....	....	....	....	....	....
Liabilities	4 753 ..	....	....	....	....	....	....	....	....
Trade credits	4 756 ..	....	....	....	....	....	....	....	....
General government	4 757 ..	....	....	....	....	....	....	....	....
of which: Short-term	4 759 ..	....	....	....	....	....	....	....	....
Other sectors	4 760 ..	....	....	....	....	....	....	....	....
of which: Short-term	4 762 ..	....	....	....	....	....	....	....	....
Loans	4 764 ..	....	....	....	....	....	....	....	....
Monetary authorities	4 765 ..	....	....	....	....	....	....	....	....
of which: Use of Fund credit and loans from the Fund	4 766 ..	....	....	....	....	....	....	....	....
of which: Short-term	4 768 ..	....	....	....	....	....	....	....	....
General government	4 769 ..	....	....	....	....	....	....	....	....
of which: Short-term	4 771 ..	....	....	....	....	....	....	....	....
Banks	4 772 ..	....	....	....	....	....	....	....	....
of which: Short-term	4 774 ..	....	....	....	....	....	....	....	....
Other sectors	4 775 ..	....	....	....	....	....	....	....	....
of which: Short-term	4 777 ..	....	....	....	....	....	....	....	....
Currency and deposits	4 780 ..	....	....	....	....	....	....	....	....
Monetary authorities	4 781 ..	....	....	....	....	....	....	....	....
General government	4 782 ..	....	....	....	....	....	....	....	....
Banks	4 783 ..	....	....	....	....	....	....	....	....
Other sectors	4 784 ..	....	....	....	....	....	....	....	....
Other liabilities	4 786 ..	....	....	....	....	....	....	....	....
Monetary authorities	4 787 ..	....	....	....	....	....	....	....	....
of which: Short-term	4 789 ..	....	....	....	....	....	....	....	....
General government	4 790 ..	....	....	....	....	....	....	....	....
of which: Short-term	4 792 ..	....	....	....	....	....	....	....	....
Banks	4 793 ..	....	....	....	....	....	....	....	....
of which: Short-term	4 795 ..	....	....	....	....	....	....	....	....
Other sectors	4 796 ..	....	....	....	....	....	....	....	....
of which: Short-term	4 798 ..	....	....	....	....	....	....	....	....
E. RESERVE ASSETS	4 802 ..	....	....	....	....	....	....	....	....
Monetary gold	4 812 ..	....	....	....	....	....	....	....	....
Special drawing rights	4 811 ..	....	....	....	....	....	....	....	....
Reserve position in the Fund	4 810 ..	....	....	....	....	....	....	....	....
Foreign exchange	4 803 ..	....	....	....	....	....	....	....	....
Other claims	4 813 ..	....	....	....	....	....	....	....	....
NET ERRORS AND OMISSIONS	4 998 ..	....	....	....	....	....	....	....	....

Table 1. ANALYTIC PRESENTATION, 2003–2010

(Millions of U.S. dollars)

	Code	2003	2004	2005	2006	2007	2008	2009	2010
A. Current Account[1]	4 993 Z.	**−53.6**	**−253.2**	**−302.4**	**−602.7**	**−484.2**	**−652.8**	**−238.2**	**−416.0**
Goods: exports f.o.b.	2 100 ..	673.7	712.7	682.9	666.7	731.0	871.9	625.9	819.5
Goods: imports f.o.b.	3 100 ..	−1,066.2	−1,286.5	−1,454.8	−1,635.0	−1,644.4	−2,056.1	−1,300.9	−1,601.4
Balance on Goods	4 100 ..	*−392.5*	*−573.8*	*−771.9*	*−968.3*	*−913.4*	*−1,184.3*	*−674.9*	*−782.0*
Services: credit	2 200 ..	619.3	691.8	850.6	813.9	854.9	978.1	706.3	861.2
Services: debit	3 200 ..	−386.2	−465.7	−505.9	−521.4	−520.1	−597.3	−451.1	−509.5
Balance on Goods and Services	4 991 ..	*−159.4*	*−347.6*	*−427.2*	*−675.8*	*−578.6*	*−803.4*	*−419.8*	*−430.3*
Income: credit	2 300 ..	93.0	146.7	81.8	66.0	67.0	72.3	61.3	78.3
Income: debit	3 300 ..	−104.4	−157.2	−127.6	−186.7	−152.1	−96.2	−57.8	−179.9
Balance on Goods, Services, and Income	4 992 ..	*−170.8*	*−358.2*	*−472.9*	*−796.4*	*−663.6*	*−827.4*	*−416.3*	*−531.9*
Current transfers: credit	2 379 Z.	187.8	188.2	259.9	291.6	241.1	247.8	227.3	168.7
Current transfers: debit	3 379 ..	−70.5	−83.2	−89.3	−97.8	−61.7	−73.2	−49.1	−52.7
B. Capital Account[1]	4 994 Z.	**5.1**	**3.0**	**7.9**	**−.4**	**13.3**	**16.3**	**27.0**	**27.1**
Capital account: credit	2 994 Z.	27.5	28.8	34.2	22.1	35.0	47.7	42.1	40.1
Capital account: debit	3 994 ..	−22.4	−25.8	−26.3	−22.5	−21.7	−31.4	−15.1	−13.0
Total, Groups A Plus B	4 981 ..	*−48.5*	*−250.2*	*−294.5*	*−603.1*	*−470.9*	*−636.5*	*−211.2*	*−388.9*
C. Financial Account[1]	4 995 W.	**31.3**	**297.0**	**105.9**	**310.9**	**453.6**	**235.0**	**225.9**	**265.6**
Direct investment abroad	4 505 ..	−3.9	−3.2	−10.3	−.6	6.4	8.8	−3.0	−5.8
Direct investment in Fiji	4 555 Z.	40.3	250.6	155.7	412.4	337.8	309.4	56.1	196.2
Portfolio investment assets	4 602 ..	.1	....	....	−.1	.1	....	....	....
Equity securities	4 610 ..	.1	....	....	−.1	.1	....	....	....
Debt securities	4 619 ..	....	....	....	....	....	....	....	....
Portfolio investment liabilities	4 652 Z.	.3	−.3	1.7	−3.0	4.2	1.4	−1.1	.1
Equity securities	4 660 ..	.3	−.3	1.7	−3.0	4.2	1.4	−1.1	.1
Debt securities	4 669 Z.	....	....	....	....	....	....	....	....
Financial derivatives	4 910 ..	....	....	....	....	....	....	....	....
Financial derivatives assets	4 900 ..	....	....	....	....	....	....	....	....
Financial derivatives liabilities	4 905 ..	....	....	....	....	....	....	....	....
Other investment assets	4 703 ..	−56.2	68.5	−46.9	−131.9	97.6	−179.6	10.8	38.7
Monetary authorities	4 701 ..	....	....	....	....	....	....	....	....
General government	4 704 ..	−2.0	−.9	−.3	−144.5	123.2	−70.5	43.1	−3.2
Banks	4 705 ..	−29.3	105.8	−22.3	46.5	−4.0	−69.9	−39.3	47.6
Other sectors	4 728 ..	−24.9	−36.4	−24.3	−34.0	−21.7	−39.2	7.0	−5.6
Other investment liabilities	4 753 W.	50.7	−18.5	5.7	34.1	7.5	94.9	163.2	36.5
Monetary authorities	4 753 WA	−.2	−.2	....	−1.1	4.3	−2.5	91.2	1.0
General government	4 753 ZB	....	....	....	....	....	....	....	−11.0
Banks	4 753 ZC	−8.2	−41.9	35.6	−29.0	.4	77.9	54.8	−56.3
Other sectors	4 753 ZD	59.1	23.6	−29.8	64.2	2.8	19.5	17.3	102.8
Total, Groups A Through C	4 983 ..	*−17.2*	*46.8*	*−188.6*	*−292.2*	*−17.3*	*−401.5*	*14.8*	*−123.3*
D. Net Errors and Omissions	4 998 ..	**−47.2**	**53.8**	**64.4**	**−55.3**	**169.1**	**200.9**	**54.0**	**257.1**
Total, Groups A Through D	4 984 ..	*−64.4*	*100.6*	*−124.1*	*−347.5*	*151.9*	*−200.6*	*68.8*	*133.8*
E. Reserves and Related Items	4 802 A.	**64.4**	**−100.6**	**124.1**	**347.5**	**−151.9**	**200.6**	**−68.8**	**−133.8**
Reserve assets	4 802 ..	−23.9	−75.6	104.8	165.8	−192.6	167.2	−188.4	−138.3
Use of Fund credit and loans	4 766 ..	....	....	....	....	....	....	....	....
Exceptional financing	4 920 ..	88.3	−25.0	19.3	181.7	40.7	33.4	119.7	4.5
Conversion rates: Fiji dollars per U.S. dollar	0 101 ..	**1.8956**	**1.7330**	**1.6910**	**1.7312**	**1.6103**	**1.5937**	**1.9557**	**1.9183**

---

[1] Excludes components that have been classified in the categories of Group E.

Table 2. STANDARD PRESENTATION, 2003–2010

(Millions of U.S. dollars)

	Code	2003	2004	2005	2006	2007	2008	2009	2010
CURRENT ACCOUNT........................	4 993 ..	**−52.5**	**−251.2**	**−299.8**	**−599.0**	**−482.0**	**−644.8**	**−236.0**	**−411.5**
A. GOODS............................	4 100 ..	**−392.5**	**−573.8**	**−771.9**	**−968.3**	**−913.4**	**−1,184.3**	**−674.9**	**−782.0**
Credit............................	2 100 ..	**673.7**	**712.7**	**682.9**	**666.7**	**731.0**	**871.9**	**625.9**	**819.5**
General merchandise: exports f.o.b....................	2 110 ..	589.8	559.2	558.3	579.5	663.5	788.6	573.2	695.0
Goods for processing: exports f.o.b...................	2 150 ..	....	....	....	....	....	....	....	....
Repairs on goods.......................	2 160 ..	24.0	77.3	26.4	26.4	31.7	17.3	7.6	6.2
Goods procured in ports by carriers................	2 170 ..	19.4	25.4	63.1	35.9	34.3	50.0	24.0	71.3
Nonmonetary gold.......................	2 180 ..	40.5	50.9	35.1	24.9	1.6	15.9	21.1	47.0
Debit............................	3 100 ..	**−1,066.2**	**−1,286.5**	**−1,454.8**	**−1,635.0**	**−1,644.4**	**−2,056.1**	**−1,300.9**	**−1,601.4**
General merchandise: imports f.o.b....................	3 110 ..	−1,025.1	−1,234.9	−1,377.0	−1,554.9	−1,558.2	−1,948.4	−1,238.4	−1,541.2
Goods for processing: imports f.o.b...................	3 150 ..	....	....	....	....	....	....	....	....
Repairs on goods.......................	3 160 ..	−15.2	−12.4	−22.3	−27.8	−15.0	−17.7	−16.1	−4.0
Goods procured in ports by carriers................	3 170 ..	−25.6	−39.0	−55.4	−52.1	−71.2	−90.0	−46.5	−56.2
Nonmonetary gold.......................	3 180 ..	−.2	−.2	−.1	−.1	....	....	....	....
B. SERVICES..........................	4 200 ..	**233.1**	**226.2**	**344.7**	**292.6**	**334.7**	**380.8**	**255.1**	**351.7**
Total credit...........................	2 200 ..	*619.3*	*691.8*	*850.6*	*813.9*	*854.9*	*978.1*	*706.3*	*861.2*
Total debit...........................	3 200 ..	*−386.2*	*−465.7*	*−505.9*	*−521.4*	*−520.1*	*−597.3*	*−451.1*	*−509.5*
Transportation services, credit............	2 205 ..	**184.4**	**194.1**	**290.8**	**249.0**	**290.6**	**368.7**	**235.9**	**244.9**
Passenger...........................	2 850 ..	*151.1*	*164.5*	*236.9*	*203.5*	*225.7*	*293.6*	*184.6*	*189.7*
Freight............................	2 851 ..	*12.0*	*12.2*	*26.0*	*21.6*	*20.6*	*25.4*	*16.5*	*22.4*
Other.............................	2 852 ..	*21.3*	*17.5*	*27.9*	*23.9*	*44.3*	*49.7*	*34.9*	*32.8*
Sea transport, passenger.................	2 207 ..	....	....	....	....	....	....	....	....
Sea transport, freight..................	2 208 ..	2.9	2.5	4.7	6.9	3.6	6.4	4.1	7.5
Sea transport, other...................	2 209 ..	8.2	9.2	8.8	10.3	26.9	31.9	17.9	14.1
Air transport, passenger.................	2 211 ..	151.1	164.5	236.9	203.5	225.7	293.6	184.6	189.7
Air transport, freight..................	2 212 ..	9.2	9.6	21.3	14.8	16.9	19.0	12.4	14.9
Air transport, other...................	2 213 ..	13.0	8.2	19.0	13.6	17.4	17.8	17.0	18.6
Other transport, passenger...............	2 215 ..	....	....	....	....	....	....	....	....
Other transport, freight................	2 216 ..	....	....	....	....	....	....	....	....
Other transport, other.................	2 217 ..	....	....	....	....	....	....	....	....
Transportation services, debit............	3 205 ..	**−232.9**	**−278.9**	**−287.4**	**−297.6**	**−315.8**	**−381.2**	**−248.5**	**−265.9**
Passenger...........................	3 850 ..	*−18.5*	*−24.4*	*−26.2*	*−22.4*	*−37.6*	*−43.1*	*−34.0*	*−13.7*
Freight............................	3 851 ..	*−121.7*	*−142.6*	*−155.7*	*−184.8*	*−185.1*	*−233.5*	*−150.9*	*−184.8*
Other.............................	3 852 ..	*−92.7*	*−111.8*	*−105.6*	*−90.3*	*−93.1*	*−104.6*	*−63.6*	*−67.4*
Sea transport, passenger.................	3 207 ..	....	....	....	....	....	....	....	....
Sea transport, freight..................	3 208 ..	−111.6	−133.5	−148.5	−166.9	−166.4	−209.1	−133.1	−166.5
Sea transport, other...................	3 209 ..	....	....	....	....	−.1	....	−.5	....
Air transport, passenger.................	3 211 ..	−18.5	−24.4	−26.2	−22.4	−37.6	−43.1	−34.0	−13.7
Air transport, freight..................	3 212 ..	−10.0	−9.1	−7.2	−17.9	−18.7	−24.5	−17.8	−18.4
Air transport, other...................	3 213 ..	−92.7	−111.8	−105.6	−90.3	−93.0	−104.6	−63.0	−67.4
Other transport, passenger...............	3 215 ..	....	....	....	....	....	....	....	....
Other transport, freight................	3 216 ..	....	....	....	....	....	....	....	....
Other transport, other.................	3 217 ..	....	....	....	....	....	....	....	....
Travel, credit........................	2 236 ..	**345.1**	**423.3**	**485.3**	**480.2**	**498.7**	**546.9**	**422.0**	**522.6**
Business travel........................	2 237 ..	17.7	22.7	27.8	31.5	27.7	33.8	28.6	33.3
Personal travel.......................	2 240 ..	327.5	400.6	457.6	448.7	471.0	513.1	393.4	489.2
Travel, debit........................	3 236 ..	**−69.6**	**−93.7**	**−106.0**	**−101.4**	**−92.4**	**−95.8**	**−94.5**	**−87.6**
Business travel........................	3 237 ..	−1.8	−5.5	−6.3	−6.5	−6.0	−5.5	−4.9	−3.7
Personal travel.......................	3 240 ..	−67.8	−88.2	−99.7	−94.9	−86.4	−90.3	−89.6	−84.0
Other services, credit..................	2 200 BA	**89.8**	**74.4**	**74.4**	**84.7**	**65.5**	**62.5**	**48.4**	**93.8**
Communications.......................	2 245 ..	26.3	29.4	28.7	21.6	18.5	25.4	12.2	10.0
Construction.........................	2 249 ..	.2	....	....	....	.4	....	....	....
Insurance...........................	2 253 ..	.8	.5	.5	.6	.6	.6	.5	....
Financial............................	2 260 ..	1.1	1.4	1.5	1.5	.9	.4	.4	.5
Computer and information................	2 262 ..	.4	2.5	2.5	2.4	3.6	1.7	1.9	1.1
Royalties and licence fees................	2 266 ..	1.1	.1	.1	.2	.1	....	.6	.5
Other business services..................	2 268 ..	31.1	20.0	21.5	23.8	15.9	15.2	14.5	21.0
Personal, cultural, and recreational.........	2 287 ..	....	.3	.6	.8	.6	.6	.6	1.2
Government, n.i.e......................	2 291 ..	28.8	20.2	19.0	33.7	25.0	18.4	17.7	59.3
Other services, debit..................	3 200 BA	**−83.7**	**−93.1**	**−112.4**	**−122.5**	**−111.9**	**−120.2**	**−108.1**	**−155.9**
Communications.......................	3 245 ..	−12.8	−16.0	−19.1	−16.1	−9.6	−14.6	−35.4	−70.8
Construction.........................	3 249 ..	−1.9	....	−.1	−.3	−.6	−.3	−.1	....
Insurance...........................	3 253 ..	−23.6	−25.7	−29.6	−29.8	−30.8	−35.3	−25.6	−28.4
Financial............................	3 260 ..	−1.1	−1.2	−.9	−.9	−.1	−.6	−.7	−.7
Computer and information................	3 262 ..	−5.0	−10.8	−12.4	−7.9	−16.7	−16.2	−10.9	−11.3
Royalties and licence fees................	3 266 ..	−1.0	−.8	−1.2	−1.0	−1.6	−2.4	−1.3	−.9
Other business services..................	3 268 ..	−33.3	−33.6	−43.6	−55.1	−45.4	−43.2	−29.1	−36.5
Personal, cultural, and recreational.........	3 287 ..	−2.4	−2.4	−2.4	−4.4	−2.3	−3.1	−.8	−2.1
Government, n.i.e......................	3 291 ..	−2.6	−2.6	−3.1	−7.0	−4.9	−4.5	−4.2	−5.4

Table 2 (Continued). STANDARD PRESENTATION, 2003–2010

(Millions of U.S. dollars)

	Code	2003	2004	2005	2006	2007	2008	2009	2010
C. INCOME	4 300	**−11.4**	**−10.6**	**−45.7**	**−120.6**	**−85.0**	**−23.9**	**3.5**	**−101.6**
Total credit	2 300	*93.0*	*146.7*	*81.8*	*66.0*	*67.0*	*72.3*	*61.3*	*78.3*
Total debit	3 300	*−104.4*	*−157.2*	*−127.6*	*−186.7*	*−152.1*	*−96.2*	*−57.8*	*−179.9*
Compensation of employees, credit	2 310	**70.0**	**117.4**	**49.0**	**38.9**	**45.3**	**50.0**	**48.2**	**62.0**
Compensation of employees, debit	3 310	**−1.8**	**−2.5**	**−3.3**	**−5.2**	**−5.3**	**−8.2**	**−4.4**	**−5.4**
Investment income, credit	2 320	**23.0**	**29.3**	**32.9**	**27.2**	**21.8**	**22.4**	**13.0**	**16.2**
Direct investment income	2 330	3.9	3.8	5.8	2.2	1.2	1.2	3.0	5.3
Dividends and distributed branch profits	2 332	.1	.6	....	.5	1.2	1.2	.5	.7
Reinvested earnings and undistributed branch profits	2 333	3.9	3.1	5.8	.6	....	....	2.5	4.5
Income on debt (interest)	2 334	....	.1	....	1.2	....	....	....	.1
Portfolio investment income	2 339	5.1	8.2	9.8	15.0	7.5	7.7	3.2	1.0
Income on equity	2 340	4.4	6.3	8.2	10.8	.1	2.9	2.1	.2
Income on bonds and notes	2 350	....	....	....	4.2	7.3	4.8	1.1	.1
Income on money market instruments	2 360	....	....	....	....	....	....	....	.8
Other investment income	2 370	14.0	17.3	17.3	10.0	13.1	13.5	6.8	9.9
Investment income, debit	3 320	**−102.6**	**−154.8**	**−124.3**	**−181.5**	**−146.8**	**−88.0**	**−53.4**	**−174.5**
Direct investment income	3 330	−85.2	−140.9	−114.7	−162.5	−116.9	−56.9	−30.3	−143.4
Dividends and distributed branch profits	3 332	−38.5	−45.5	−25.2	−30.9	−36.4	−19.6	−21.4	−21.1
Reinvested earnings and undistributed branch profits	3 333	−42.3	−89.8	−78.1	−127.6	−80.1	−37.2	−8.8	−122.3
Income on debt (interest)	3 334	−4.3	−5.6	−11.4	−4.0	−.4	−.1	....	....
Portfolio investment income	3 339	−7.6	−4.9	−2.9	−12.4	−13.1	−15.8	−12.9	−10.5
Income on equity	3 340	−7.6	−4.9	−2.9	−12.4	−2.8	−5.3	−2.7	−.2
Income on bonds and notes	3 350	....	....	....	....	−10.3	−10.5	−10.2	−10.3
Income on money market instruments	3 360	....	....	....	....	....	....	....	....
Other investment income	3 370	−9.8	−9.1	−6.7	−6.6	−16.8	−15.3	−10.3	−20.7
D. CURRENT TRANSFERS	4 379	**118.3**	**106.9**	**173.1**	**197.4**	**181.6**	**182.5**	**180.4**	**120.4**
Credit	2 379	**188.8**	**190.1**	**262.5**	**295.3**	**243.3**	**255.7**	**229.5**	**173.2**
General government	2 380	1.1	2.0	2.6	3.7	2.2	7.9	2.2	4.5
Other sectors	2 390	187.8	188.2	259.9	291.6	241.1	247.8	227.3	168.7
Workers' remittances	2 391	53.7	55.3	133.9	144.5	115.1	72.8	104.6	94.8
Other current transfers	2 392	134.1	132.9	126.0	147.1	126.0	175.0	122.7	73.8
Debit	3 379	**−70.5**	**−83.2**	**−89.3**	**−97.8**	**−61.7**	**−73.2**	**−49.1**	**−52.7**
General government	3 380	....	....	−1.7	−1.6	−1.6	−1.6	−1.7	−1.9
Other sectors	3 390	−70.5	−83.2	−87.7	−96.2	−60.1	−71.6	−47.4	−50.8
Workers' remittances	3 391	−2.1	−13.7	−4.6	−4.6	−3.9	−4.7	−2.8	−4.3
Other current transfers	3 392	−68.5	−69.5	−83.1	−91.7	−56.3	−66.9	−44.6	−46.6
CAPITAL AND FINANCIAL ACCOUNT	4 996	**99.7**	**197.5**	**235.4**	**654.3**	**312.9**	**444.0**	**182.0**	**154.4**
CAPITAL ACCOUNT	4 994	**5.1**	**3.0**	**7.9**	**−.4**	**13.3**	**16.3**	**27.0**	**27.1**
Total credit	2 994	*27.5*	*28.8*	*34.2*	*22.1*	*35.0*	*47.7*	*42.1*	*40.1*
Total debit	3 994	*−22.4*	*−25.8*	*−26.3*	*−22.5*	*−21.7*	*−31.4*	*−15.1*	*−13.0*
Capital transfers, credit	2 400	**27.5**	**28.8**	**34.2**	**22.1**	**35.0**	**47.7**	**42.1**	**40.1**
General government	2 401	23.3	24.5	27.3	17.4	30.1	39.1	36.9	32.1
Debt forgiveness	2 402	....	....	....	....	....	....	....	....
Other capital transfers	2 410	23.3	24.5	27.3	17.4	30.1	39.1	36.9	32.1
Other sectors	2 430	4.3	4.3	7.0	4.6	4.9	8.5	5.2	8.0
Migrants' transfers	2 431	.5	.6	2.2	1.4	.1	.7	1.0	1.1
Debt forgiveness	2 432	....	....	....	....	....	....	....	....
Other capital transfers	2 440	3.7	3.7	4.8	3.2	4.8	7.8	4.1	6.9
Capital transfers, debit	3 400	**−22.4**	**−25.8**	**−26.3**	**−22.5**	**−21.7**	**−31.4**	**−15.1**	**−13.0**
General government	3 401	....	....	....	....	....	....	....	....
Debt forgiveness	3 402	....	....	....	....	....	....	....	....
Other capital transfers	3 410	....	....	....	....	....	....	....	....
Other sectors	3 430	−22.4	−25.8	−26.3	−22.5	−21.7	−31.4	−15.1	−13.0
Migrants' transfers	3 431	−22.4	−25.8	−26.3	−22.5	−21.7	−31.4	−15.1	−13.0
Debt forgiveness	3 432	....	....	....	....	....	....	....	....
Other capital transfers	3 440	....	....	....	....	....	....	....	....
Nonproduced nonfinancial assets, credit	2 480	....	....	....	....	....	....	....	....
Nonproduced nonfinancial assets, debit	3 480	....	....	....	....	....	....	....	....

Table 2 (Continued). STANDARD PRESENTATION, 2003–2010

(Millions of U.S. dollars)

	Code	2003	2004	2005	2006	2007	2008	2009	2010
FINANCIAL ACCOUNT..	4 995 ..	**94.6**	**194.4**	**227.4**	**654.7**	**299.6**	**427.7**	**155.0**	**127.3**
A. DIRECT INVESTMENT..	4 500 ..	**36.5**	**247.4**	**145.4**	**411.8**	**344.2**	**318.2**	**53.0**	**190.4**
Direct investment abroad..................................	4 505 ..	**−3.9**	**−3.2**	**−10.3**	**−.6**	**6.4**	**8.8**	**−3.0**	**−5.8**
Equity capital...	4 510 ..	....	−.2	−4.5	....	6.4	8.8	−.5	−.9
Claims on affiliated enterprises............................	4 515 ..	....	−.2	−4.5	....	6.4	8.8	−.5	−.9
Liabilities to affiliated enterprises........................	4 520 ..	....	....	....	....	....	....	....	....
Reinvested earnings...	4 525 ..	−3.9	−3.1	−5.8	−.6	....	....	−2.5	−4.9
Other capital..	4 530 ..	....	....	....	....	....	....	....	....
Claims on affiliated enterprises............................	4 535 ..	....	....	....	....	....	....	....	....
Liabilities to affiliated enterprises........................	4 540 ..	....	....	....	....	....	....	....	....
Direct investment in Fiji..................................	4 555 ..	**40.3**	**250.6**	**155.7**	**412.4**	**337.8**	**309.4**	**56.1**	**196.2**
Equity capital..	4 560 ..	.7	167.1	73.0	282.6	256.6	272.3	50.5	67.4
Claims on direct investors....................................	4 565 ..	....	....	....	....	....	....	....	....
Liabilities to direct investors................................	4 570 ..	.7	167.1	73.0	282.6	256.6	272.3	50.5	67.4
Reinvested earnings...	4 575 ..	42.3	89.8	78.1	127.6	80.1	37.2	8.8	122.3
Other capital..	4 580 ..	−2.7	−6.2	4.6	2.2	1.1	−.1	−3.2	6.4
Claims on direct investors....................................	4 585 ..	....	....	....	....	....	....	....	....
Liabilities to direct investors................................	4 590 ..	−2.7	−6.2	4.6	2.2	1.1	−.1	−3.2	6.4
B. PORTFOLIO INVESTMENT................................	4 600 ..	**.3**	**−.3**	**1.7**	**144.0**	**4.3**	**1.4**	**−1.1**	**.1**
Assets...	4 602 ..	**.1**	**....**	**....**	**−.1**	**.1**	**....**	**....**	**....**
Equity securities...	4 610 ..	.1	....	....	−.1	.1	....	....	....
Monetary authorities..	4 611 ..	....	....	....	....	....	....	....	....
General government...	4 612 ..	....	....	....	....	....	....	....	....
Banks..	4 613 ..	.1	....	....	−.1	.1	....	....	....
Other sectors..	4 614 ..	....	....	....	....	....	....	....	....
Debt securities...	4 619 ..	....	....	....	....	....	....	....	....
Bonds and notes..	4 620 ..	....	....	....	....	....	....	....	....
Monetary authorities..	4 621 ..	....	....	....	....	....	....	....	....
General government...	4 622 ..	....	....	....	....	....	....	....	....
Banks..	4 623 ..	....	....	....	....	....	....	....	....
Other sectors..	4 624 ..	....	....	....	....	....	....	....	....
Money market instruments...................................	4 630 ..	....	....	....	....	....	....	....	....
Monetary authorities..	4 631 ..	....	....	....	....	....	....	....	....
General government...	4 632 ..	....	....	....	....	....	....	....	....
Banks..	4 633 ..	....	....	....	....	....	....	....	....
Other sectors..	4 634 ..	....	....	....	....	....	....	....	....
Liabilities..	4 652 ..	**.3**	**−.3**	**1.7**	**144.1**	**4.2**	**1.4**	**−1.1**	**.1**
Equity securities...	4 660 ..	.3	−.3	1.7	−3.0	4.2	1.4	−1.1	.1
Banks..	4 663 ..	....	....	....	....	....	....	....	....
Other sectors..	4 664 ..	....	−.3	1.7	−3.0	4.2	1.4	−1.1	.1
Debt securities...	4 669 ..	....	....	....	147.1	....	....	....	....
Bonds and notes..	4 670 ..	....	....	....	147.1	....	....	....	....
Monetary authorities..	4 671 ..	....	....	....	147.1	....	....	....	....
General government...	4 672 ..	....	....	....	....	....	....	....	....
Banks..	4 673 ..	....	....	....	....	....	....	....	....
Other sectors..	4 674 ..	....	....	....	....	....	....	....	....
Money market instruments...................................	4 680 ..	....	....	....	....	....	....	....	....
Monetary authorities..	4 681 ..	....	....	....	....	....	....	....	....
General government...	4 682 ..	....	....	....	....	....	....	....	....
Banks..	4 683 ..	....	....	....	....	....	....	....	....
Other sectors..	4 684 ..	....	....	....	....	....	....	....	....
C. FINANCIAL DERIVATIVES................................	4 910 ..	**....**	**....**	**....**	**....**	**....**	**....**	**....**	**....**
Monetary authorities..	4 911 ..	....	....	....	....	....	....	....	....
General government...	4 912 ..	....	....	....	....	....	....	....	....
Banks..	4 913 ..	....	....	....	....	....	....	....	....
Other sectors..	4 914 ..	....	....	....	....	....	....	....	....
Assets...	4 900 ..	**....**	**....**	**....**	**....**	**....**	**....**	**....**	**....**
Monetary authorities..	4 901 ..	....	....	....	....	....	....	....	....
General government...	4 902 ..	....	....	....	....	....	....	....	....
Banks..	4 903 ..	....	....	....	....	....	....	....	....
Other sectors..	4 904 ..	....	....	....	....	....	....	....	....
Liabilities..	4 905 ..	**....**	**....**	**....**	**....**	**....**	**....**	**....**	**....**
Monetary authorities..	4 906 ..	....	....	....	....	....	....	....	....
General government...	4 907 ..	....	....	....	....	....	....	....	....
Banks..	4 908 ..	....	....	....	....	....	....	....	....
Other sectors..	4 909 ..	....	....	....	....	....	....	....	....

Table 2 (Concluded). STANDARD PRESENTATION, 2003–2010

(Millions of U.S. dollars)

	Code	2003	2004	2005	2006	2007	2008	2009	2010
D. OTHER INVESTMENT	4 700	**81.7**	**23.0**	**−24.4**	**−66.9**	**143.6**	**−59.1**	**291.4**	**75.2**
Assets	4 703	**−56.2**	**68.5**	**−46.9**	**−131.9**	**97.6**	**−179.6**	**10.8**	**38.7**
Trade credits	4 706	−71.7	−30.2	−26.2	−25.7	−12.8	−27.0	7.1	−2.0
General government	4 707	....	....	....	....	....	....	....	....
of which: Short-term	4 709	....	....	....	....	....	....	....	....
Other sectors	4 710	−71.7	−30.2	−26.2	−25.7	−12.8	−27.0	7.1	−2.0
of which: Short-term	4 712	−71.7	−30.2	−26.2	−25.7	−12.8	−27.0	7.1	−2.0
Loans	4 714	37.4	62.3	−8.2	10.7	−.1	−56.2	−31.4	−.9
Monetary authorities	4 715	....	....	....	....	....	....	....	....
of which: Short-term	4 718	....	....	....	....	....	....	....	....
General government	4 719	....	....	....	....	....	....	....	....
of which: Short-term	4 721	....	....	....	....	....	....	....	....
Banks	4 722	−9.5	68.5	−10.1	19.0	8.8	−44.0	−31.3	2.7
of which: Short-term	4 724	....	....	....	....	....	....	....	....
Other sectors	4 725	46.9	−6.2	1.9	−8.3	−8.9	−12.2	−.1	−3.7
of which: Short-term	4 727	....	....	....	....	....	....	....	....
Currency and deposits	4 730	−.8	1.3	−1.1	−143.2	121.9	−70.2	41.6	−3.8
Monetary authorities	4 731	....	....	....	....	....	....	....	....
General government	4 732	−.1	.6	−.3	−144.5	123.2	−70.5	43.1	−3.2
Banks	4 733	−.7	.7	−.8	1.3	−1.3	.3	−1.5	−.6
Other sectors	4 734	....	....	....	....	....	....	....	....
Other assets	4 736	−21.1	35.1	−11.4	26.2	−11.5	−26.2	−6.5	45.4
Monetary authorities	4 737	....	....	....	....	....	....	....	....
of which: Short-term	4 739	....	....	....	....	....	....	....	....
General government	4 740	−2.0	−1.5	....	....	....	....	....	....
of which: Short-term	4 742	−2.0	−1.5	....	....	....	....	....	....
Banks	4 743	−19.1	36.6	−11.4	26.2	−11.5	−26.2	−6.5	45.4
of which: Short-term	4 745	−13.4	53.2	−12.9	49.8	−11.7	−34.1	−6.7	38.1
Other sectors	4 746	....	....	....	....	....	....	....	....
of which: Short-term	4 748	....	....	....	....	....	....	....	....
Liabilities	4 753	**138.0**	**−45.4**	**22.4**	**65.0**	**46.0**	**120.4**	**280.6**	**36.5**
Trade credits	4 756	59.1	23.6	−29.8	64.2	2.8	19.5	17.3	20.0
General government	4 757	....	....	....	....	....	....	....	....
of which: Short-term	4 759	....	....	....	....	....	....	....	....
Other sectors	4 760	59.1	23.6	−29.8	64.2	2.8	19.5	17.3	20.0
of which: Short-term	4 762	59.1	23.6	−29.8	64.2	2.8	19.5	17.3	20.0
Loans	4 764	87.3	−26.9	16.7	30.9	38.5	25.5	117.4	71.7
Monetary authorities	4 765	....	....	....	....	....	....	....	....
of which: Use of Fund credit and loans from the Fund..	4 766	....	....	....	....	....	....	....	....
of which: Short-term	4 768	....	....	....	....	....	....	....	....
General government	4 769	6.6	−1.1	−2.4	1.9	.7	−4.9	−8.9	−11.0
of which: Short-term	4 771	....	....	....	....	....	....	....	....
Banks	4 772	....	....	....	....	....	....	....	....
of which: Short-term	4 774	....	....	....	....	....	....	....	....
Other sectors	4 775	80.7	−25.8	19.1	29.0	37.8	30.4	126.3	82.7
of which: Short-term	4 777	....	....	....	....	....	....	....	....
Currency and deposits	4 780	.6	−47.2	25.5	−55.9	−1.6	53.8	14.8	−8.4
Monetary authorities	4 781	....	....	....	....	....	....	....	....
General government	4 782	....	....	....	....	....	....	....	....
Banks	4 783	.6	−47.2	25.5	−55.9	−1.6	53.8	14.8	−8.4
Other sectors	4 784	....	....	....	....	....	....	....	....
Other liabilities	4 786	−9.0	5.1	10.1	25.8	6.3	21.6	131.1	−46.9
Monetary authorities	4 787	−.2	−.2	....	−1.1	4.3	−2.5	91.2	1.0
of which: Short-term	4 789	−.2	−.2	....	−1.1	4.3	−2.5	−2.8	1.0
General government	4 790	....	....	....	....	....	....	....	....
of which: Short-term	4 792	....	....	....	....	....	....	....	....
Banks	4 793	−8.8	5.3	10.1	26.9	2.0	24.1	40.0	−47.9
of which: Short-term	4 795	3.4	−3.4	9.8	4.3	−6.9	44.9	39.1	−39.8
Other sectors	4 796	....	....	....	....	....	....	....	....
of which: Short-term	4 798	....	....	....	....	....	....	....	....
E. RESERVE ASSETS	4 802	**−23.9**	**−75.6**	**104.8**	**165.8**	**−192.6**	**167.2**	**−188.4**	**−138.3**
Monetary gold	4 812	....	....	....	....	....	....	....	....
Special drawing rights	4 811	−.2	−.2	−.4	−.5	−.7	−.7	−94.1	24.5
Reserve position in the Fund	4 810	−.2	−.1	−.1	−.3	−.3	−.2	−.3	−.4
Foreign exchange	4 803	−6.7	−34.2	133.9	16.8	−186.9	155.8	−116.1	−160.5
Other claims	4 813	−16.9	−41.0	−28.7	149.7	−4.7	12.4	22.0	−2.0
NET ERRORS AND OMISSIONS	4 998	**−47.2**	**53.8**	**64.4**	**−55.3**	**169.1**	**200.9**	**54.0**	**257.1**

Table 1. ANALYTIC PRESENTATION, 2003–2010

(Millions of U.S. dollars)

	Code	2003	2004	2005	2006	2007	2008	2009	2010
A. Current Account[1]	4 993 Z.	**8,534**	**12,542**	**6,993**	**9,497**	**10,610**	**6,699**	**4,976**	**4,459**
Goods: exports f.o.b.	2 100 ..	52,740	61,139	65,451	77,552	90,147	96,918	62,910	70,132
Goods: imports f.o.b.	3 100 ..	−39,790	−48,368	−55,887	−66,046	−77,645	−87,215	−58,648	−66,186
Balance on Goods	4 100 ..	*12,950*	*12,770*	*9,564*	*11,505*	*12,503*	*9,703*	*4,262*	*3,947*
Services: credit	2 200 ..	11,470	15,168	17,010	17,520	23,394	31,879	28,045	27,847
Services: debit	3 200 ..	−12,149	−14,563	−17,732	−18,641	−22,715	−30,671	−27,101	−27,650
Balance on Goods and Services	4 991 ..	*12,271*	*13,375*	*8,841*	*10,385*	*13,182*	*10,911*	*5,207*	*4,144*
Income: credit	2 300 ..	9,349	13,129	14,406	18,356	23,747	23,174	15,279	18,327
Income: debit	3 300 ..	−11,980	−12,884	−14,754	−17,547	−24,389	−25,011	−13,166	−15,805
Balance on Goods, Services, and Income	4 992 ..	*9,639*	*13,620*	*8,494*	*11,193*	*12,541*	*9,074*	*7,320*	*6,666*
Current transfers: credit	2 379 Z.	1,911	2,040	1,953	1,942	2,296	2,386	2,262	2,243
Current transfers: debit	3 379 ..	−3,016	−3,118	−3,453	−3,638	−4,227	−4,761	−4,606	−4,450
B. Capital Account[1]	4 994 Z.	**149**	**188**	**336**	**212**	**210**	**246**	**202**	**212**
Capital account: credit	2 994 Z.	154	189	337	225	237	274	224	221
Capital account: debit	3 994 ..	−5	−1	−1	−13	−27	−28	−22	−10
Total, Groups A Plus B	4 981 ..	*8,683*	*12,730*	*7,329*	*9,709*	*10,820*	*6,944*	*5,178*	*4,671*
C. Financial Account[1]	4 995 W.	**−9,217**	**−9,475**	**−3,610**	**−12,235**	**526**	**11,602**	**7,415**	**−3,997**
Direct investment abroad	4 505 ..	2,272	1,146	−4,415	−4,885	−7,220	−8,442	−4,944	−10,647
Direct investment in Finland	4 555 Z.	3,472	2,871	4,806	7,723	12,682	−2,286	456	7,072
Portfolio investment assets	4 602 ..	−9,803	−24,503	−17,917	−33,109	−16,102	−1,299	−39,382	−29,520
Equity securities	4 610 ..	−5,532	−10,219	−9,412	−14,790	−13,530	5,213	−19,137	−16,401
Debt securities	4 619 ..	−4,271	−14,284	−8,505	−18,320	−2,571	−6,511	−20,244	−13,119
Portfolio investment liabilities	4 652 Z.	7,901	13,110	10,456	21,871	11,121	7,157	29,106	20,967
Equity securities	4 660 ..	−597	103	4,989	5,366	5,279	−1,782	−273	1,980
Debt securities	4 669 Z.	8,498	13,007	5,467	16,505	5,842	8,939	29,378	18,987
Financial derivatives	4 910 ..	1,715	522	2,168	146	−907	1,670	3,020	−430
Financial derivatives assets	4 900 ..	....	....	....	....	....	....	....	....
Financial derivatives liabilities	4 905 ..	1,715	522	2,168	146	−907	1,670	3,020	−430
Other investment assets	4 703 ..	−12,644	−11,851	−1,776	−15,801	−11,069	−13,544	−6,282	−25,284
Monetary authorities	4 701 ..	−54	157	9	−287	144	−143	−480	−564
General government	4 704 ..	−3,049	−968	1,415	−2,811	−802	....	−1,067	....
Banks	4 705 ..	−10,282	−11,185	−2,272	−11,203	−9,215	−17,911	−5,380	−10,218
Other sectors	4 728 ..	740	146	−928	−1,501	−1,167	−804	645	−502
Other investment liabilities	4 753 W.	−2,129	9,230	3,068	11,820	12,021	28,346	25,441	33,845
Monetary authorities	4 753 WA	696	−2,132	−3,393	193	−2,706	−2,573	−4,127	−12,530
General government	4 753 ZB	2,396	122	−864	−1,853	213	688	977	−549
Banks	4 753 ZC	−3,459	13,197	6,084	12,780	10,865	19,722	31,450	47,234
Other sectors	4 753 ZD	−1,762	−1,958	1,241	700	3,649	10,508	−2,865	−327
Total, Groups A Through C	4 983 ..	*−533*	*3,255*	*3,719*	*−2,526*	*11,346*	*18,547*	*12,593*	*674*
D. Net Errors and Omissions	4 998 ..	**26**	**−2,441**	**−3,898**	**−1,794**	**−11,026**	**−18,308**	**−10,076**	**−2,847**
Total, Groups A Through D	4 984 ..	*−508*	*814*	*−180*	*−4,321*	*320*	*238*	*2,516*	*−2,173*
E. Reserves and Related Items	4 802 A.	**508**	**−814**	**180**	**4,321**	**−320**	**−238**	**−2,516**	**2,173**
Reserve assets	4 802 ..	508	−814	180	4,321	−320	−238	−2,516	2,173
Use of Fund credit and loans	4 766 ..	....	....	....	....	....	....	....	....
Exceptional financing	4 920 ..	....	....	....	....	....	....	....	....
Conversion rates: euros per U.S. dollar	0 103 ..	**.8860**	**.8054**	**.8041**	**.7971**	**.7306**	**.6827**	**.7198**	**.7550**

[1] Excludes components that have been classified in the categories of Group E.

Table 2. STANDARD PRESENTATION, 2003–2010

(Millions of U.S. dollars)

	Code	2003	2004	2005	2006	2007	2008	2009	2010
CURRENT ACCOUNT	4 993	**8,534**	**12,542**	**6,993**	**9,497**	**10,610**	**6,699**	**4,976**	**4,459**
A. GOODS	4 100	**12,950**	**12,770**	**9,564**	**11,505**	**12,503**	**9,703**	**4,262**	**3,947**
Credit	2 100	**52,740**	**61,139**	**65,451**	**77,552**	**90,147**	**96,918**	**62,910**	**70,132**
General merchandise: exports f.o.b.	2 110	51,812	60,124	64,452	75,816	88,504	95,458	61,833	68,644
Goods for processing: exports f.o.b.	2 150	798	877	879	1,587	1,506	1,319	897	1,200
Repairs on goods	2 160	....	....	....	....	....	....	....	....
Goods procured in ports by carriers	2 170	64	70	70	71	77	83	56	53
Nonmonetary gold	2 180	67	68	50	....	....	....	....	....
Debit	3 100	**–39,790**	**–48,368**	**–55,887**	**–66,046**	**–77,645**	**–87,215**	**–58,648**	**–66,186**
General merchandise: imports f.o.b.	3 110	–38,552	–47,093	–54,480	–63,639	–75,185	–84,717	–56,636	–63,951
Goods for processing: imports f.o.b.	3 150	–844	–928	–930	–1,862	–1,828	–1,622	–1,413	–1,465
Repairs on goods	3 160	....	....	....	....	....	....	....	....
Goods procured in ports by carriers	3 170	–381	–333	–464	–527	–606	–429	–384	–505
Nonmonetary gold	3 180	–13	–15	–13	....	....	....	....	....
B. SERVICES	4 200	**–679**	**605**	**–723**	**–1,121**	**679**	**1,208**	**944**	**197**
Total credit	2 200	*11,470*	*15,168*	*17,010*	*17,520*	*23,394*	*31,879*	*28,045*	*27,847*
Total debit	3 200	*–12,149*	*–14,563*	*–17,732*	*–18,641*	*–22,715*	*–30,671*	*–27,101*	*–27,650*
Transportation services, credit	2 205	**2,000**	**2,400**	**2,440**	**2,757**	**3,263**	**3,652**	**2,825**	**3,113**
Passenger	2 850	*807*	*908*	*890*	*1,129*	*1,450*	*1,641*	*1,327*	*1,470*
Freight	2 851	*830*	*1,073*	*1,112*	*1,185*	*1,349*	*1,528*	*1,093*	*1,354*
Other	2 852	*363*	*419*	*438*	*444*	*464*	*482*	*404*	*288*
Sea transport, passenger	2 207	316	330	326	....	....	551	471	472
Sea transport, freight	2 208	589	782	799	....	....	1,108	772	908
Sea transport, other	2 209	261	286	285	....	....	336	276	287
Air transport, passenger	2 211	492	578	564	....	....	....	....	....
Air transport, freight	2 212	90	125	146	....	....	....	....	....
Air transport, other	2 213	102	132	152	....	....	147	128	....
Other transport, passenger	2 215	....	....	....	....	....	....	....	....
Other transport, freight	2 216	151	166	167	....	....	198	186	177
Other transport, other	2 217	....	1	1	....	....	....	....	1
Transportation services, debit	3 205	**–2,897**	**–3,606**	**–4,248**	**–4,822**	**–5,744**	**–7,334**	**–4,550**	**–5,521**
Passenger	3 850	*–521*	*–562*	*–565*	*–670*	*–829*	*–1,033*	*–832*	*–963*
Freight	3 851	*–1,982*	*–2,571*	*–3,125*	*–3,768*	*–4,516*	*–5,935*	*–3,407*	*–4,230*
Other	3 852	*–394*	*–472*	*–559*	*–383*	*–399*	*–366*	*–310*	*–328*
Sea transport, passenger	3 207	–215	–209	–211	....	....	–399	–344	–341
Sea transport, freight	3 208	–1,678	–2,050	–2,431	....	....	–4,152	–2,331	–2,784
Sea transport, other	3 209	–311	–377	–462	....	....	–366	–310	–318
Air transport, passenger	3 211	–306	–353	–354	....	....	....	....	....
Air transport, freight	3 212	–92	–112	–128	....	....	–432	–217	–258
Air transport, other	3 213	–80	–92	–94	....	....	....	....	....
Other transport, passenger	3 215	....	....	....	....	....	....	....	....
Other transport, freight	3 216	–212	–409	–565	....	....	–1,351	–860	–1,187
Other transport, other	3 217	–3	–4	–4	....	....	....	....	–9
Travel, credit	2 236	**1,869**	**2,067**	**2,180**	**2,380**	**2,837**	**3,220**	**2,814**	**2,892**
Business travel	2 237	740	904	882	1,029	1,148	1,171	1,020	1,051
Personal travel	2 240	1,129	1,162	1,299	1,351	1,689	2,049	1,795	1,841
Travel, debit	3 236	**–2,433**	**–2,821**	**–3,057**	**–3,424**	**–3,983**	**–4,501**	**–4,373**	**–4,239**
Business travel	3 237	–732	–842	–1,009	–1,204	–1,161	–1,321	–1,003	–936
Personal travel	3 240	–1,701	–1,979	–2,047	–2,220	–2,822	–3,180	–3,370	–3,303
Other services, credit	2 200 BA	**7,600**	**10,701**	**12,389**	**12,383**	**17,294**	**24,955**	**22,406**	**21,730**
Communications	2 245	229	312	393	429	431	494	329	296
Construction	2 249	410	746	573	351	424	1,317	1,303	1,109
Insurance	2 253	47	62	62	67	139	174	170	111
Financial	2 260	....	124	81	74	424	635	522	566
Computer and information	2 262	566	755	1,511	1,475	1,846	8,190	7,048	6,515
Royalties and licence fees	2 266	501	839	1,206	1,070	1,281	1,488	1,754	2,340
Other business services	2 268	5,732	7,744	8,439	8,787	12,661	12,506	11,149	10,667
Personal, cultural, and recreational	2 287	30	16	13	24	19	....	7	9
Government, n.i.e.	2 291	86	103	112	106	68	150	125	118
Other services, debit	3 200 BA	**–6,820**	**–8,136**	**–10,427**	**–10,396**	**–12,974**	**–18,484**	**–17,867**	**–16,940**
Communications	3 245	–281	–283	–590	–538	–437	–551	–559	–527
Construction	3 249	–295	–617	–483	–329	–340	–604	–520	–539
Insurance	3 253	–70	–145	–145	–192	–351	–366	–312	–408
Financial	3 260	....	–65	–95	–173	–215	–202	–204	–556
Computer and information	3 262	–482	–735	–1,157	–1,126	–1,501	–1,920	–3,342	–2,149
Royalties and licence fees	3 266	–616	–800	–1,123	–1,299	–1,441	–2,036	–1,267	–1,236
Other business services	3 268	–4,923	–5,321	–6,669	–6,689	–8,614	–12,552	–11,396	–11,249
Personal, cultural, and recreational	3 287	–25	–29	–23	–27	–77	–253	–268	–276
Government, n.i.e.	3 291	–128	–141	–141	–23	....	....	....	....

Table 2 (Continued). STANDARD PRESENTATION, 2003–2010

(Millions of U.S. dollars)

	Code	2003	2004	2005	2006	2007	2008	2009	2010
C. INCOME	4 300	**−2,632**	**245**	**−348**	**808**	**−641**	**−1,837**	**2,113**	**2,523**
Total credit	2 300	*9,349*	*13,129*	*14,406*	*18,356*	*23,747*	*23,174*	*15,279*	*18,327*
Total debit	3 300	*−11,980*	*−12,884*	*−14,754*	*−17,547*	*−24,389*	*−25,011*	*−13,166*	*−15,805*
Compensation of employees, credit	2 310	**526**	**666**	**693**	**698**	**762**	**818**	**859**	**848**
Compensation of employees, debit	3 310	**−149**	**−225**	**−249**	**−309**	**−367**	**−428**	**−429**	**−428**
Investment income, credit	2 320	**8,823**	**12,462**	**13,714**	**17,657**	**22,985**	**22,356**	**14,420**	**17,479**
Direct investment income	2 330	4,581	6,471	7,030	9,298	11,641	10,684	8,595	11,068
Dividends and distributed branch profits	2 332	3,645	2,693	4,552	8,644	4,228	....	....	....
Reinvested earnings and undistributed branch profits	2 333	515	3,189	1,906	−1,080	1,666	2,514	2,733	3,470
Income on debt (interest)	2 334	420	589	572	545	818	929	624	439
Portfolio investment income	2 339	2,927	4,272	4,708	5,744	7,568	7,260	4,282	5,627
Income on equity	2 340	420	885	1,151	1,579	1,820	....	998	1,347
Income on bonds and notes	2 350	2,425	3,308	3,472	4,041	5,020	5,247	3,161	4,218
Income on money market instruments	2 360	82	79	85	124	249	192	123	61
Other investment income	2 370	1,315	1,719	1,976	2,615	3,776	4,412	1,543	785
Investment income, debit	3 320	**−11,831**	**−12,659**	**−14,505**	**−17,239**	**−24,022**	**−24,584**	**−12,737**	**−15,376**
Direct investment income	3 330	−4,314	−4,918	−4,829	−6,310	−9,895	−7,832	−2,565	−5,467
Dividends and distributed branch profits	3 332	−2,022	−3,194	−3,296	−2,755	−3,243	....	....	....
Reinvested earnings and undistributed branch profits	3 333	−1,822	−1,257	−1,234	−3,127	70	−1,591	2,780	−1,022
Income on debt (interest)	3 334	−470	−467	−299	−419	−638	−826	−941	−998
Portfolio investment income	3 339	−5,924	−6,318	−7,733	−8,596	−10,785	−12,453	−8,521	−8,751
Income on equity	3 340	−2,046	−2,524	−3,572	−3,843	−4,885	....	−3,443	−3,292
Income on bonds and notes	3 350	−3,818	−3,582	−3,667	−3,799	−5,001	−5,602	−4,713	−5,181
Income on money market instruments	3 360	−60	−212	−494	−954	−818	−722	−365	−278
Other investment income	3 370	−1,593	−1,424	−1,944	−2,332	−3,342	−4,299	−1,652	−1,158
D. CURRENT TRANSFERS	4 379	**−1,105**	**−1,078**	**−1,501**	**−1,696**	**−1,931**	**−2,376**	**−2,344**	**−2,207**
Credit	2 379	**1,911**	**2,040**	**1,953**	**1,942**	**2,296**	**2,386**	**2,262**	**2,243**
General government	2 380	315	339	357	373	475	466	440	477
Other sectors	2 390	1,596	1,701	1,595	1,569	1,821	1,919	1,822	1,766
Workers' remittances	2 391	....	....	....	....	....	....	....	....
Other current transfers	2 392	1,596	1,701	1,595	1,569	1,821	1,919	1,822	1,766
Debit	3 379	**−3,016**	**−3,118**	**−3,453**	**−3,638**	**−4,227**	**−4,761**	**−4,606**	**−4,450**
General government	3 380	−2,401	−2,629	−2,960	−2,590	−2,825	−3,245	−3,334	−3,157
Other sectors	3 390	−615	−489	−494	−1,048	−1,401	−1,516	−1,273	−1,293
Workers' remittances	3 391	....	....	−17	−22	−24	−30	−25	−24
Other current transfers	3 392	−615	−489	−477	−1,026	−1,377	−1,487	−1,248	−1,269
CAPITAL AND FINANCIAL ACCOUNT	4 996	**−8,560**	**−10,102**	**−3,095**	**−7,703**	**416**	**11,610**	**5,101**	**−1,612**
CAPITAL ACCOUNT	4 994	**149**	**188**	**336**	**212**	**210**	**246**	**202**	**212**
Total credit	2 994	*154*	*189*	*337*	*225*	*237*	*274*	*224*	*221*
Total debit	3 994	*−5*	*−1*	*−1*	*−13*	*−27*	*−28*	*−22*	*−10*
Capital transfers, credit	2 400	**154**	**189**	**181**	**211**	**222**	**257**	**224**	**221**
General government	2 401	128	152	148	166	180	215	192	166
Debt forgiveness	2 402	....	....	....	....	....	....	....	....
Other capital transfers	2 410	128	152	148	166	180	215	192	166
Other sectors	2 430	26	37	32	45	42	43	32	56
Migrants' transfers	2 431	....	....	....	....	....	....	....	....
Debt forgiveness	2 432	....	....	....	....	....	....	....	....
Other capital transfers	2 440	26	37	32	45	42	43	32	56
Capital transfers, debit	3 400	**−5**	**−1**	**−1**	**−13**	**−27**	**−28**	**−22**	**−10**
General government	3 401	−5	−1	−1	−13	−27	−28	−22	−10
Debt forgiveness	3 402	....	....	....	....	....	....	....	....
Other capital transfers	3 410	−5	−1	−1	−13	−27	−28	−22	−10
Other sectors	3 430	....	....	....	....	....	....	....	....
Migrants' transfers	3 431	....	....	....	....	....	....	....	....
Debt forgiveness	3 432	....	....	....	....	....	....	....	....
Other capital transfers	3 440	....	....	....	....	....	....	....	....
Nonproduced nonfinancial assets, credit	2 480	....	....	**157**	**14**	**15**	**16**	....	....
Nonproduced nonfinancial assets, debit	3 480	....	....	....	....	....	....	....	....

Table 2 (Continued). STANDARD PRESENTATION, 2003–2010

(Millions of U.S. dollars)

	Code	2003	2004	2005	2006	2007	2008	2009	2010
FINANCIAL ACCOUNT	4 995	−8,709	−10,289	−3,431	−7,915	207	11,364	4,899	−1,824
A. DIRECT INVESTMENT	4 500	5,744	4,017	390	2,839	5,462	−10,727	−4,488	−3,575
Direct investment abroad	4 505	2,272	1,146	−4,415	−4,885	−7,220	−8,442	−4,944	−10,647
Equity capital	4 510	7,963	−1,780	−2,307	−10,245	−9,089	−19,965	−4,368	−3,530
Claims on affiliated enterprises	4 515	7,899	−1,712	−2,307	−10,245	−9,089	−19,965	−4,368	−3,530
Liabilities to affiliated enterprises	4 520	64	−68	....	....	....	....		
Reinvested earnings	4 525	−515	−3,189	−1,906	1,080	−1,666	−2,514	−2,733	−3,470
Other capital	4 530	−5,176	6,115	−202	4,281	3,535	14,037	2,158	−3,647
Claims on affiliated enterprises	4 535	−6,337	2,253	−6,419	9,847	−3,368	−613	12,219	−5,692
Liabilities to affiliated enterprises	4 540	1,161	3,862	6,217	−5,566	6,903	14,650	−10,061	2,045
Direct investment in Finland	4 555	3,472	2,871	4,806	7,723	12,682	−2,286	456	7,072
Equity capital	4 560	1,080	739	1,233	2,819	9,381	918	....	....
Claims on direct investors	4 565	....	....	....	....	....	....		
Liabilities to direct investors	4 570	1,080	739	1,233	2,819	9,381	918		
Reinvested earnings	4 575	1,822	1,257	1,234	3,127	−70	1,591	−2,780	1,022
Other capital	4 580	570	876	2,339	1,777	3,371	−4,794	−768	−1,100
Claims on direct investors	4 585	−1,266	−107	147	−2,475	−2,400	−7,047	−737	−2,343
Liabilities to direct investors	4 590	1,836	982	2,192	4,252	5,771	2,252	−31	1,243
B. PORTFOLIO INVESTMENT	4 600	−1,902	−11,393	−7,461	−11,238	−4,981	5,858	−10,276	−8,553
Assets	4 602	−9,803	−24,503	−17,917	−33,109	−16,102	−1,299	−39,382	−29,520
Equity securities	4 610	−5,532	−10,219	−9,412	−14,790	−13,530	5,213	−19,137	−16,401
Monetary authorities	4 611	−65	−20	−54	−44	−15	−9	−30	−12
General government	4 612	−3,428	−6,239	−3,879	−8,321	−8,663	2,645	−8,499	−10,915
Banks	4 613	−23	−104	−146	−359	175	−821	....	−123
Other sectors	4 614	−2,016	−3,857	−5,333	−6,066	−5,027	3,397	−10,285	−5,351
Debt securities	4 619	−4,271	−14,284	−8,505	−18,320	−2,571	−6,511	−20,244	−13,119
Bonds and notes	4 620	−3,632	−13,627	−9,822	−16,290	−1,383	−9,514	−17,759	−14,410
Monetary authorities	4 621	−27	−88	−46	−5,800	−3,144	−520	−380	−4,981
General government	4 622	−1,049	−6,256	−4,083	−2,367	4,668	−3,013	113	8,274
Banks	4 623	−410	−2,385	−1,354	−5,456	−2,589	−2,765	−15,367	−16,381
Other sectors	4 624	−2,146	−4,898	−4,338	−2,666	−318	−3,216	−2,125	−1,322
Money market instruments	4 630	−639	−657	1,317	−2,030	−1,188	3,002	−2,485	1,290
Monetary authorities	4 631	....	−27	−56	−617	640	10	−38	62
General government	4 632	−264	−8	29	173	−175	−219	−4,238	2,215
Banks	4 633	−321	−274	410	−417	−699	708	950	−928
Other sectors	4 634	−53	−348	934	−1,169	−912	2,503	841	−59
Liabilities	4 652	7,901	13,110	10,456	21,871	11,121	7,157	29,106	20,967
Equity securities	4 660	−597	103	4,989	5,366	5,279	−1,782	−273	1,980
Banks	4 663	295	261	927	1,093	616	−648	−452	−129
Other sectors	4 664	−892	−158	4,061	4,273	4,663	−1,134	179	2,109
Debt securities	4 669	8,498	13,007	5,467	16,505	5,842	8,939	29,378	18,987
Bonds and notes	4 670	8,354	5,356	6,367	12,168	3,289	2,226	20,810	21,076
Monetary authorities	4 671	....	−1	....	....	....	....	....	....
General government	4 672	6,442	1,274	2,646	1,610	−186	74	8,808	15,536
Banks	4 673	1,257	3,860	4,756	9,491	3,880	4,654	5,189	5,540
Other sectors	4 674	655	222	−1,035	1,068	−405	−2,503	6,813	....
Money market instruments	4 680	144	7,652	−899	4,337	2,553	6,713	8,568	−2,089
Monetary authorities	4 681	....	....	....	....	....	....	....	
General government	4 682	−1,383	3,111	−4,651	3,796	−149	765	5,850	1,062
Banks	4 683	1,248	5,327	3,373	1,139	3,319	2,719	5,283	−3,076
Other sectors	4 684	279	−786	379	−598	−617	....	−2,565	−75
C. FINANCIAL DERIVATIVES	4 910	1,715	522	2,168	146	−907	1,670	3,020	−430
Monetary authorities	4 911	....	....	....	....	....	....	....	2
General government	4 912	575	−184	330	−7	−1,387	2,691	−532	−879
Banks	4 913	234	−156	966	−301	−130	−3,400	468	....
Other sectors	4 914	905	862	872	453	609	2,379	3,084	−276
Assets	4 900	....	....	....	....	....	....	....	....
Monetary authorities	4 901	....	....	....	....	....	....	....	....
General government	4 902	....	....	....	....	....	....	....	....
Banks	4 903	....	....	....	....	....	....	....	....
Other sectors	4 904	....	....	....	....	....	....	....	....
Liabilities	4 905	1,715	522	2,168	146	−907	1,670	3,020	−430
Monetary authorities	4 906	....	....	....	....	....	....	....	2
General government	4 907	575	−184	330	−7	−1,387	2,691	−532	−879
Banks	4 908	234	−156	966	−301	−130	−3,400	468	....
Other sectors	4 909	905	862	872	453	609	2,379	3,084	−276

2011, International Monetary Fund: *Balance of Payments Statistics Yearbook*

Table 2 (Concluded). STANDARD PRESENTATION, 2003–2010

(Millions of U.S. dollars)

	Code	2003	2004	2005	2006	2007	2008	2009	2010
D. OTHER INVESTMENT	4 700	**−14,774**	**−2,621**	**1,293**	**−3,981**	**952**	**14,802**	**19,159**	**8,561**
Assets	4 703	**−12,644**	**−11,851**	**−1,776**	**−15,801**	**−11,069**	**−13,544**	**−6,282**	**−25,284**
Trade credits	4 706	370	450	125	−251	−858	532	523	522
General government	4 707	−121	−11	−35	122	26	202	−150	−181
of which: Short-term	4 709	....	....	....	−1	−7	....	....	....
Other sectors	4 710	491	461	160	−373	−884	329	672	703
of which: Short-term	4 712	*290*	*465*	*167*	....	....	*389*	*591*	*642*
Loans	4 714	1,465	−860	−1,987	−2,961	−1,636	−4,451	3,174	−28,147
Monetary authorities	4 715	....	....	....	5	−244	−60	−503	−555
of which: Short-term	4 718	....	....	....	*5*	*−244*	*−60*	*−503*	*−555*
General government	4 719	....	....	....	....	....	....	−96	....
of which: Short-term	4 721	....	....	....	....	....	....	....	....
Banks	4 722	711	−1,022	−2,166	−2,583	−1,475	−3,383	4,118	−26,288
of which: Short-term	4 724	*320*	*−1,042*	*−1,190*	*−906*	*−1,833*	*−1,511*	*3,739*	....
Other sectors	4 725	754	163	179	−383	112	−1,038	−345	−577
of which: Short-term	4 727	*234*	*−3*	....	....	....	....	....	....
Currency and deposits	4 730	−14,571	−10,082	183	−12,961	−8,279	1,930	−18,802	10,526
Monetary authorities	4 731	−54	161	9	−291	389	−83	32	23
General government	4 732	−2,970	−1,132	1,233	−3,234	−840	5,196	−613	−4,781
Banks	4 733	−11,151	−8,894	−123	−9,074	−7,187	−3,082	−18,579	16,069
Other sectors	4 734	−397	−217	−936	−361	−640	−100	358	−785
Other assets	4 736	93	−1,359	−96	372	−297	−11,555	8,823	−8,186
Monetary authorities	4 737	....	−5	....	−1	....	....	−8	−32
of which: Short-term	4 739	....	....	....	*−1*	*−1*	....	*−2*	*−32*
General government	4 740	43	175	217	302	12	−114	−209	....
of which: Short-term	4 742	....	*−1*	*1*	....	*1*	*−115*	*−209*	....
Banks	4 743	157	−1,270	17	454	−553	−11,446	9,081	....
of which: Short-term	4 745	*141*	*−1,270*	*18*	....	....	....	....	....
Other sectors	4 746	−108	−261	−331	−383	245	5	−41	157
of which: Short-term	4 748	*−94*	*−274*	*−347*	*−383*	*242*	*6*	*−40*	*98*
Liabilities	4 753	**−2,129**	**9,230**	**3,068**	**11,820**	**12,021**	**28,346**	**25,441**	**33,845**
Trade credits	4 756	171	243	650	−16	454	252	−806	770
General government	4 757	....	....	....	....	....	....	....	....
of which: Short-term	4 759	....	....	....	....	....	....	....	....
Other sectors	4 760	171	243	650	−16	454	252	−806	770
of which: Short-term	4 762	*413*	*164*	*616*	....	....	*115*	*−560*	*458*
Loans	4 764	513	−1,113	−23	−1,547	4,122	11,461	3,510	26,233
Monetary authorities	4 765	....	831	−685	−515	118	−99	1,151	281
of which: Use of Fund credit and loans from the Fund	4 766	....	....	....	....	....	....	....	....
of which: Short-term	4 768	....	*831*	*−685*	*−515*	*118*	*−99*	*1,151*	*281*
General government	4 769	2,404	104	−829	−1,846	218	687	977	−549
of which: Short-term	4 771	*2,036*	*311*	*−710*	*−1,872*	*431*	....	*1,112*	*−606*
Banks	4 772	63	373	569	315	606	1,707	2,652	28,361
of which: Short-term	4 774	*−15*	*89*	*461*	*64*	*334*	*1,808*	*167*	*27,258*
Other sectors	4 775	−1,954	−2,421	923	499	3,180	9,167	−1,270	−1,860
of which: Short-term	4 777	*−241*	*−392*	*119*	*41*	*−95*	*730*	*−895*	*−517*
Currency and deposits	4 780	−2,873	8,569	2,646	11,986	8,127	14,642	15,895	−1,726
Monetary authorities	4 781	696	−2,963	−2,708	708	−2,824	−2,474	−6,913	−12,811
General government	4 782	....	....	....	....	....	....	....	....
Banks	4 783	−3,569	11,532	5,354	11,278	10,951	17,116	22,808	11,084
Other sectors	4 784	....	....	....	....	....	....	....	....
Other liabilities	4 786	60	1,531	−205	1,397	−682	1,990	6,843	8,568
Monetary authorities	4 787	....	....	1	....	....	....	1,635	....
of which: Short-term	4 789	....	....	*1*	....	....	....	....	....
General government	4 790	−8	19	−34	−7	−5	1	....	....
of which: Short-term	4 792	....	*28*	*−25*	....	....	*1*	....	....
Banks	4 793	47	1,292	161	1,188	−692	899	5,989	7,789
of which: Short-term	4 795	*28*	*1,218*	*251*	*1,182*	....	*915*	*6,018*	*7,753*
Other sectors	4 796	21	220	−332	217	15	1,089	−788	762
of which: Short-term	4 798	*136*	*214*	*216*	*259*	....	*1,400*	*−859*	*727*
E. RESERVE ASSETS	4 802	**508**	**−814**	**180**	**4,321**	**−320**	**−238**	**−2,516**	**2,173**
Monetary gold	4 812	....	....	....	....	....	....	....	....
Special drawing rights	4 811	24	39	−8	−23	−38	−2	−1,635	10
Reserve position in the Fund	4 810	−61	173	301	128	42	−117	−168	−144
Foreign exchange	4 803	545	−1,026	−113	4,216	−323	−119	−713	2,308
Other claims	4 813	....	....	....	....	....	....	....	....
NET ERRORS AND OMISSIONS	4 998	**26**	**−2,441**	**−3,898**	**−1,794**	**−11,026**	**−18,308**	**−10,076**	**−2,847**

Table 3. INTERNATIONAL INVESTMENT POSITION (End-period stocks), 2003–2010

(Millions of U.S. dollars)

	Code	2003	2004	2005	2006	2007	2008	2009	2010
ASSETS..	8 995 C.	**287,064**	**369,355**	**361,016**	**456,591**	**559,361**	**564,475**	**649,263**	**731,962**
Direct investment abroad......................	8 505 ..	**76,050**	**85,022**	**81,860**	**96,208**	**116,531**	**114,139**	**129,184**	**136,810**
Equity capital and reinvested earnings........	8 506 ..	43,706	57,195	57,075	74,062	95,895	108,553	124,938	130,637
Claims on affiliated enterprises............	8 507 ..	43,801	57,311	57,075	....	....	108,553	124,938	130,637
Liabilities to affiliated enterprises.........	8 508 ..	−95	−116	....	....	....	....	....	....
Other capital..................................	8 530 ..	32,344	27,828	24,786	22,146	20,636	5,585	4,246	6,173
Claims on affiliated enterprises............	8 535 ..	44,691	44,801	45,467	39,703	47,066	45,079	36,900	40,318
Liabilities to affiliated enterprises.........	8 540 ..	−12,347	−16,973	−20,681	−17,557	−26,430	−39,494	−32,654	−34,145
Portfolio investment...........................	8 602 ..	**106,974**	**146,344**	**154,339**	**213,938**	**256,021**	**179,868**	**251,631**	**283,389**
Equity securities.............................	8 610 ..	36,082	53,282	64,511	96,258	122,330	61,676	101,302	129,346
Monetary authorities.......................	8 611 ..	401	463	465	540	616	526	627	616
General government........................	8 612 ..	16,715	27,211	32,827	49,628	66,124	35,145	55,602	74,032
Banks....................................	8 613 ..	64	186	328	755	693	1,226	1,566	1,615
Other sectors.............................	8 614 ..	18,903	25,422	30,891	45,336	54,897	24,779	43,506	53,083
Debt securities..............................	8 619 ..	70,892	93,062	89,828	117,679	133,691	118,193	150,329	154,042
Bonds and notes...........................	8 620 ..	66,252	87,335	86,037	111,179	125,619	111,998	142,406	147,496
Monetary authorities....................	8 621 ..	690	798	769	6,906	10,986	11,105	11,868	15,715
General government.....................	8 622 ..	37,493	47,477	45,083	50,534	50,204	44,056	51,359	39,885
Banks.................................	8 623 ..	9,547	13,083	12,708	19,739	25,826	22,193	38,569	51,991
Other sectors..........................	8 624 ..	18,521	25,977	27,477	34,000	38,604	34,645	40,611	39,905
Money market instruments.................	8 630 ..	4,641	5,727	3,791	6,500	8,072	6,194	7,923	6,547
Monetary authorities....................	8 631 ..	....	30	74	767	163	152	194	110
General government.....................	8 632 ..	405	454	351	299	534	1,434	5,269	3,047
Banks.................................	8 633 ..	2,489	2,966	2,257	2,957	3,469	2,940	2,057	2,930
Other sectors..........................	8 634 ..	1,746	2,278	1,109	2,477	3,906	1,668	403	459
Financial derivatives..........................	8 900 ..	**26,131**	**38,806**	**34,927**	**36,687**	**53,394**	**129,755**	**116,824**	**144,757**
Monetary authorities.........................	8 901 ..	47	....	....	....	6	51	439	....
General government..........................	8 902 ..	1,588	2,100	1,869	3,755	5,678	5,258	5,709	8,152
Banks.......................................	8 903 ..	23,213	35,644	32,216	32,064	46,650	....	....	....
Other sectors...............................	8 904 ..	1,283	1,062	842	868	1,061	4,074	2,553	3,158
Other investment..............................	8 703 ..	**66,736**	**86,270**	**78,559**	**102,260**	**125,030**	**132,371**	**140,174**	**157,456**
Trade credits................................	8 706 ..	6,444	8,903	7,076	7,730	10,788	8,619	8,018	7,749
General government........................	8 707 ..	1,380	1,434	1,149	1,137	1,253	964	1,142	1,244
of which: Short-term...................	8 709 ..	....	....	....	*1*	*8*	....	....	....
Other sectors.............................	8 710 ..	5,064	7,468	5,926	6,593	9,535	7,656	6,877	6,504
of which: Short-term...................	8 712 ..	*4,737*	*7,433*	*5,885*	*6,499*	....	*7,430*	*6,729*	*6,447*
Loans.......................................	8 714 ..	3,823	4,624	5,996	9,699	12,945	17,344	14,443	41,203
Monetary authorities......................	8 715 ..	....	....	....	....	293	343	824	1,398
of which: Short-term...................	8 718 ..	....	....	....	....	*293*	*343*	*824*	*1,398*
General government........................	8 719 ..	....	69	60	66	105	71	167	911
of which: Short-term...................	8 721 ..	....	....	....	....	....	....	....	....
Banks....................................	8 722 ..	2,231	3,551	5,229	8,441	10,715	15,007	11,107	36,654
of which: Short-term...................	8 724 ..	*800*	*1,901*	*2,839*	*4,074*	*6,340*	*7,967*	*4,292*	*32,559*
Other sectors.............................	8 725 ..	1,592	1,004	707	1,191	1,832	1,923	2,345	2,240
of which: Short-term...................	8 727 ..	*194*	*10*	*8*	....	*8*	*52*	....	*7*
Currency and deposits.......................	8 730 ..	53,453	68,036	61,205	14,591	96,344	89,791	110,000	94,375
Monetary authorities......................	8 731 ..	1,173	1,094	929	1,347	1,091	1,108	1,114	1,013
General government........................	8 732 ..	5,775	7,544	5,708	9,639	11,224	5,643	7,185	11,972
Banks....................................	8 733 ..	44,960	57,424	51,759	....	79,259	78,761	99,369	78,483
Other sectors.............................	8 734 ..	1,546	1,974	2,809	3,605	4,771	4,279	2,332	2,907
Other assets................................	8 736 ..	3,017	4,708	4,282	4,307	4,953	16,617	7,713	14,129
Monetary authorities......................	8 737 ..	88	100	87	97	108	102	113	135
of which: Short-term...................	8 739 ..	....	....	....	....	....	....	....	*135*
General government........................	8 740 ..	2,043	2,094	1,759	1,613	1,688	1,751	1,961	2,144
of which: Short-term...................	8 742 ..	*1*	*1*	....	....	*1*	*110*	*330*	*553*
Banks....................................	8 743 ..	603	2,089	1,775	1,496	2,299	13,965	4,805	10,791
of which: Short-term...................	8 745 ..	*603*	*2,069*	*1,775*	*1,476*	*2,210*	....	....	*10,791*
Other sectors.............................	8 746 ..	283	425	661	1,101	858	799	834	1,060
of which: Short-term...................	8 748 ..	*219*	*399*	*648*	*1,096*	....	*795*	*831*	*689*
Reserve assets................................	8 802 ..	**11,174**	**12,912**	**11,330**	**7,498**	**8,383**	**8,342**	**11,451**	**9,551**
Monetary gold...............................	8 812 ..	658	691	809	1,002	1,319	1,364	1,740	2,223
Special drawing rights.......................	8 811 ..	195	166	162	193	243	239	1,884	1,841
Reserve position in the Fund.................	8 810 ..	776	631	283	166	131	248	423	566
Foreign exchange............................	8 803 ..	9,545	11,425	10,076	6,136	6,691	6,491	7,403	4,921
Other claims................................	8 813 ..	....	....	....	....	....	....	....	....

Table 3 (Concluded). INTERNATIONAL INVESTMENT POSITION (End-period stocks), 2003–2010

(Millions of U.S. dollars)

	Code	2003	2004	2005	2006	2007	2008	2009	2010
LIABILITIES..	8 995 D.	**335,465**	**390,093**	**389,803**	**485,672**	**633,243**	**589,611**	**651,623**	**709,959**
Direct investment in Finland.............................	8 555 ..	**50,257**	**57,379**	**54,802**	**70,569**	**91,703**	**83,525**	**84,662**	**85,801**
Equity capital and reinvested earnings..........................	8 556 ..	37,403	43,708	41,225	54,986	71,522	67,042	68,458	72,642
Claims on direct investors..................................	8 557 ..	−4	−20	−6	....	....	−5	....	....
Liabilities to direct investors.............................	8 558 ..	37,408	43,729	41,231	....	....	67,047	....	....
Other capital..	8 580 ..	12,853	13,671	13,576	15,583	20,181	16,483	16,203	13,159
Claims on direct investors..................................	8 585 ..	−4,635	−4,680	−3,436	−6,233	−9,109	−13,746	−14,311	−15,368
Liabilities to direct investors.............................	8 590 ..	17,489	18,351	17,012	21,816	29,290	30,229	30,514	28,527
Portfolio investment....................................	8 652 ..	**198,870**	**221,820**	**230,331**	**289,490**	**379,635**	**246,974**	**293,218**	**301,995**
Equity securities...	8 660 ..	103,315	102,974	119,952	154,813	229,908	99,159	107,778	105,624
Banks...	8 663 ..	1,703	2,563	3,022	3,945	4,200	4,704	4,285	3,879
Other sectors...	8 664 ..	101,612	100,411	116,930	150,867	225,708	94,455	103,492	101,745
Debt securities..	8 669 ..	95,555	118,846	110,379	134,677	149,727	147,815	185,440	196,371
Bonds and notes..	8 670 ..	81,155	96,197	90,451	110,033	122,983	117,409	145,566	157,849
Monetary authorities....................................	8 671 ..	....	....	....	....	....	....	....	....
General government....................................	8 672 ..	55,207	63,845	56,237	58,764	62,781	58,738	70,952	82,668
Banks..	8 673 ..	11,012	15,249	19,340	31,754	38,713	40,318	48,696	50,145
Other sectors..	8 674 ..	14,936	17,103	14,874	19,515	21,489	18,353	25,918	25,036
Money market instruments..............................	8 680 ..	14,400	22,648	19,928	24,645	26,744	30,406	39,874	38,522
Monetary authorities....................................	8 681 ..	....	....	....	....	....	....	....	....
General government....................................	8 682 ..	5,082	9,604	4,476	8,926	9,832	9,830	15,641	15,141
Banks..	8 683 ..	8,693	12,635	14,742	15,332	16,033	16,758	....	22,203
Other sectors..	8 684 ..	624	409	710	386	878	3,818	1,318	1,178
Financial derivatives...................................	8 905 ..	**26,021**	**37,544**	**34,019**	**35,644**	**51,096**	**129,390**	**113,675**	**138,005**
Monetary authorities..	8 906 ..	45	....	1	....	4	52	435	....
General government..	8 907 ..	1,878	2,058	1,365	2,862	3,564	4,076	4,796	6,492
Banks...	8 908 ..	23,179	34,649	32,048	31,747	46,429	....	....	....
Other sectors...	8 909 ..	919	838	605	1,034	1,099	2,720	2,205	2,741
Other investment.......................................	8 753 ..	**60,318**	**73,349**	**70,651**	**89,969**	**110,809**	**129,722**	**160,068**	**184,158**
Trade credits...	8 756 ..	4,384	5,246	5,758	6,117	7,719	8,471	7,490	8,250
General government.......................................	8 757 ..	....	....	....	....	....	....	....	....
of which: Short-term.................................	8 759 ..	....	....	....	....	....	....	....	....
Other sectors...	8 760 ..	4,384	5,246	5,758	6,117	7,719	8,471	7,490	8,250
of which: Short-term.................................	8 762 ..	*4,230*	*5,034*	*5,520*	*5,881*	....	*8,125*	*7,363*	*7,817*
Loans...	8 764 ..	24,690	24,871	22,182	24,827	32,164	39,407	43,690	65,777
Monetary authorities.....................................	8 765 ..	314	1,266	503	....	129	47	1,216	1,394
of which: Use of Fund credit and loans from the Fund....	8 766 ..	....	....	....	....	....	....	....	....
of which: Short-term.................................	8 768 ..	*314*	*1,266*	*503*	....	*129*	*47*	*1,216*	*1,394*
General government.......................................	8 769 ..	6,744	7,788	6,277	4,983	5,730	5,889	7,102	6,118
of which: Short-term.................................	8 771 ..	*2,451*	*2,922*	*2,000*	*211*	*700*	*1,401*	*2,576*	*1,860*
Banks..	8 772 ..	1,798	2,214	2,609	3,082	3,895	4,281	7,061	34,744
of which: Short-term.................................	8 774 ..	*97*	*130*	*572*	*665*	*1,039*	*1,631*	*1,818*	*28,704*
Other sectors..	8 775 ..	15,834	13,604	12,793	16,762	22,411	29,191	28,312	23,521
of which: Short-term.................................	8 777 ..	*2,446*	*380*	*444*	*472*	*419*	*1,109*	*294*	*112*
Currency and deposits......................................	8 780 ..	29,033	39,115	38,984	53,288	64,562	74,518	93,982	88,618
Monetary authorities.....................................	8 781 ..	3,502	711	−1,981	−1,521	−4,341	−7,215	−13,724	−25,954
General government.......................................	8 782 ..	....	....	....	....	....	....	....	....
Banks..	8 783 ..	25,531	38,404	40,964	54,809	68,903	81,733	107,706	114,572
Other sectors..	8 784 ..	....	....	....	....	....	....	....	....
Other liabilities...	8 786 ..	2,210	4,117	3,727	2,222	6,364	7,326	14,907	21,514
Monetary authorities.....................................	8 787 ..	....	....	....	....	....	....	1,865	1,832
of which: Short-term.................................	8 789 ..	....	....	....	....	....	....	....	....
General government.......................................	8 790 ..	31	54	14	4	....	1	11	....
of which: Short-term.................................	8 792 ..	....	*31*	*4*	....	....	*1*	*11*	....
Banks..	8 793 ..	633	2,150	2,135	....	3,264	3,698	....	15,926
of which: Short-term.................................	8 795 ..	*613*	*2,040*	*2,134*	....	....	*3,600*	....	*15,926*
Other sectors..	8 796 ..	1,546	1,913	1,578	2,218	3,100	3,626	3,248	3,708
of which: Short-term.................................	8 798 ..	*295*	*492*	*591*	....	*1,652*	*2,088*	*1,266*	*1,440*
NET INTERNATIONAL INVESTMENT POSITION........	8 995 ..	**−48,401**	**−20,738**	**−28,787**	**−29,081**	**−73,882**	**−25,136**	**−2,360**	**22,003**
Conversion rates: euros per U.S. dollar (end of period)...	0 104 ..	**.7918**	**.7342**	**.8477**	**.7593**	**.6793**	**.7185**	**.6942**	**.7484**

Table 1. ANALYTIC PRESENTATION, 2003–2010

(Billions of U.S. dollars)

	Code	2003	2004	2005	2006	2007	2008	2009	2010
A. Current Account[1]	4 993 Z.	**12.86**	**11.03**	**−10.26**	**−12.99**	**−26.61**	**−49.88**	**−39.87**	**−44.50**
Goods: exports f.o.b.	2 100 ..	361.93	421.11	439.45	484.77	548.53	605.33	475.87	517.15
Goods: imports f.o.b.	3 100 ..	−358.50	−425.95	−467.29	−522.89	−605.34	−692.60	−535.82	−588.36
Balance on Goods	4 100 ..	*3.43*	*−4.85*	*−27.84*	*−38.12*	*−56.81*	*−87.28*	*−59.94*	*−71.21*
Services: credit	2 200 ..	101.58	114.63	122.22	128.94	149.60	166.33	144.64	144.97
Services: debit	3 200 ..	−87.56	−99.69	−106.96	−113.41	−129.87	−141.87	−130.33	−132.21
Balance on Goods and Services	4 991 ..	*17.45*	*10.10*	*−12.58*	*−22.59*	*−37.08*	*−62.82*	*−45.63*	*−58.45*
Income: credit	2 300 ..	89.36	119.72	156.13	200.22	253.89	269.07	210.54	208.46
Income: debit	3 300 ..	−74.49	−97.10	−126.72	−162.85	−211.01	−221.06	−166.70	−159.57
Balance on Goods, Services, and Income	4 992 ..	*32.32*	*32.72*	*16.82*	*14.78*	*5.80*	*−14.80*	*−1.78*	*−9.56*
Current transfers: credit	2 379 Z.	24.05	25.44	25.41	27.11	28.93	29.13	26.07	24.06
Current transfers: debit	3 379 ..	−43.51	−47.14	−52.49	−54.88	−61.33	−64.21	−64.15	−59.01
B. Capital Account[1]	4 994 Z.	**−8.26**	**1.81**	**.66**	**−.27**	**2.47**	**1.04**	**.46**	**.07**
Capital account: credit	2 994 Z.	1.94	3.35	2.57	1.90	3.42	2.13	1.39	1.32
Capital account: debit	3 994 ..	−10.20	−1.54	−1.91	−2.17	−.95	−1.09	−.93	−1.24
Total, Groups A Plus B	4 981 ..	*4.60*	*12.84*	*−9.60*	*−13.26*	*−24.14*	*−48.83*	*−39.41*	*−44.43*
C. Financial Account[1]	4 995 W.	**13.53**	**−6.26**	**−9.48**	**40.61**	**40.36**	**13.79**	**67.58**	**31.76**
Direct investment abroad	4 505 ..	−53.38	−56.90	−113.83	−111.41	−167.09	−159.94	−103.08	−84.39
Direct investment in France	4 555 Z.	43.06	32.83	85.00	71.83	98.31	66.54	35.12	33.67
Portfolio investment assets	4 602 ..	−192.71	−232.48	−243.64	−325.36	−281.84	−158.60	−106.29	28.60
Equity securities	4 610 ..	−48.09	−60.85	−53.98	−72.19	−40.13	−56.98	−41.36	−23.48
Debt securities	4 619 ..	−144.62	−171.63	−189.67	−253.18	−241.71	−101.62	−64.93	52.08
Portfolio investment liabilities	4 652 Z.	198.84	166.34	225.25	191.27	113.35	184.78	452.95	128.93
Equity securities	4 660 ..	20.71	31.77	64.15	94.05	−10.37	−18.10	75.14	−8.44
Debt securities	4 669 Z.	178.13	134.57	161.10	97.22	123.72	202.88	377.82	137.37
Financial derivatives	4 910 ..	−7.05	6.21	6.36	4.19	58.96	−16.64	−22.88	45.17
Financial derivatives assets	4 900 ..	....	....	....	....	....	....	....	....
Financial derivatives liabilities	4 905 ..	−7.05	6.21	6.36	4.19	58.96	−16.64	−22.88	45.17
Other investment assets	4 703 ..	−14.84	−116.15	−276.85	−153.21	−264.60	70.04	73.70	−159.72
Monetary authorities	4 701 ..	.01	11.42	4.34	14.47	−20.16	15.17	−4.44	−14.36
General government	4 704 ..	−.76	3.74	4.55	2.03	10.33	3.17	−.90	−4.38
Banks	4 705 ..	−3.91	−121.43	−287.82	−161.98	−249.80	44.40	86.60	−140.16
Other sectors	4 728 ..	−10.18	−9.87	2.08	−7.71	−4.97	7.30	−7.55	−.83
Other investment liabilities	4 753 W.	39.60	193.90	308.24	363.31	483.27	27.62	−261.95	39.50
Monetary authorities	4 753 WA	2.11	1.82	−3.40	10.42	94.76	188.42	−42.53	−39.70
General government	4 753 ZB	−.45	2.41	−6.19	3.74	.90	7.17	−5.87	.30
Banks	4 753 ZC	39.26	169.34	285.22	328.50	378.21	−181.99	−194.60	78.52
Other sectors	4 753 ZD	−1.32	20.33	32.60	20.64	9.40	14.02	−18.96	.38
Total, Groups A Through C	4 983 ..	*18.13*	*6.59*	*−19.08*	*27.35*	*16.22*	*−35.04*	*28.17*	*−12.67*
D. Net Errors and Omissions	4 998 ..	**−16.84**	**−2.48**	**10.03**	**−15.57**	**−16.55**	**23.02**	**−18.82**	**20.45**
Total, Groups A Through D	4 984 ..	*1.29*	*4.11*	*−9.05*	*11.78*	*−.33*	*−12.02*	*9.35*	*7.79*
E. Reserves and Related Items	4 802 A.	**−1.29**	**−4.11**	**9.05**	**−11.78**	**.33**	**12.02**	**−9.35**	**−7.79**
Reserve assets	4 802 ..	−1.29	−4.11	9.05	−11.78	.33	12.02	−9.35	−7.79
Use of Fund credit and loans	4 766 ..	....	....	....	....	....	....	....	....
Exceptional financing	4 920 ..	....	....	....	....	....	....	....	....
Conversion rates: euros per U.S. dollar	0 103 ..	**.8860**	**.8054**	**.8041**	**.7971**	**.7306**	**.6827**	**.7198**	**.7550**

[1] Excludes components that have been classified in the categories of Group E.

Table 2. STANDARD PRESENTATION, 2003–2010

(Billions of U.S. dollars)

	Code	2003	2004	2005	2006	2007	2008	2009	2010
CURRENT ACCOUNT	4 993 ..	**12.86**	**11.03**	**−10.26**	**−12.99**	**−26.61**	**−49.88**	**−39.87**	**−44.50**
A. GOODS	4 100 ..	**3.43**	**−4.85**	**−27.84**	**−38.12**	**−56.81**	**−87.28**	**−59.94**	**−71.21**
Credit	2 100 ..	**361.93**	**421.11**	**439.45**	**484.77**	**548.53**	**605.33**	**475.87**	**517.15**
General merchandise: exports f.o.b.	2 110 ..	351.87	409.29	428.04	472.42	532.42	584.68	456.20	499.87
Goods for processing: exports f.o.b.	2 150 ..	9.25	10.60	9.90	10.46	13.93	17.56	17.62	14.89
Repairs on goods	2 160 ..	....	....	....	....	....	....	....	....
Goods procured in ports by carriers	2 170 ..	.81	1.22	1.51	1.89	2.18	3.09	2.05	2.38
Nonmonetary gold	2 180 ..	....	....	....	....	....	....	....	....
Debit	3 100 ..	**−358.50**	**−425.95**	**−467.29**	**−522.89**	**−605.34**	**−692.60**	**−535.82**	**−588.36**
General merchandise: imports f.o.b.	3 110 ..	−347.74	−413.49	−453.78	−507.80	−586.45	−668.23	−516.79	−570.88
Goods for processing: imports f.o.b.	3 150 ..	−9.07	−10.65	−10.79	−11.29	−14.89	−17.30	−15.03	−12.32
Repairs on goods	3 160 ..	....	....	....	....	....	....	....	....
Goods procured in ports by carriers	3 170 ..	−1.69	−1.81	−2.73	−3.79	−4.00	−7.08	−4.00	−5.15
Nonmonetary gold	3 180 ..	....	....	....	....	....	....	....	....
B. SERVICES	4 200 ..	**14.02**	**14.94**	**15.26**	**15.53**	**19.72**	**24.46**	**14.31**	**12.76**
Total credit	2 200 ..	*101.58*	*114.63*	*122.22*	*128.94*	*149.60*	*166.33*	*144.64*	*144.97*
Total debit	3 200 ..	*−87.56*	*−99.69*	*−106.96*	*−113.41*	*−129.87*	*−141.87*	*−130.33*	*−132.21*
Transportation services, credit	2 205 ..	**21.60**	**26.41**	**28.20**	**31.90**	**37.85**	**40.69**	**31.95**	**35.92**
Passenger	2 850 ..	....	....	....	....	....	....	....	....
Freight	2 851 ..	....	....	....	....	....	....	....	....
Other	2 852 ..	....	....	....	....	....	....	....	....
Sea transport, passenger	2 207 ..	....	....	....	....	....	....	....	....
Sea transport, freight	2 208 ..	....	....	....	....	....	....	....	....
Sea transport, other	2 209 ..	....	....	....	....	....	....	....	....
Air transport, passenger	2 211 ..	....	....	....	....	....	....	....	....
Air transport, freight	2 212 ..	....	....	....	....	....	....	....	....
Air transport, other	2 213 ..	....	....	....	....	....	....	....	....
Other transport, passenger	2 215 ..	....	....	....	....	....	....	....	....
Other transport, freight	2 216 ..	....	....	....	....	....	....	....	....
Other transport, other	2 217 ..	....	....	....	....	....	....	....	....
Transportation services, debit	3 205 ..	**−21.28**	**−30.12**	**−32.46**	**−34.24**	**−38.18**	**−42.32**	**−32.91**	**−35.88**
Passenger	3 850 ..	....	....	....	....	....	....	....	....
Freight	3 851 ..	....	....	....	....	....	....	....	....
Other	3 852 ..	....	....	....	....	....	....	....	....
Sea transport, passenger	3 207 ..	....	....	....	....	....	....	....	....
Sea transport, freight	3 208 ..	....	....	....	....	....	....	....	....
Sea transport, other	3 209 ..	....	....	....	....	....	....	....	....
Air transport, passenger	3 211 ..	....	....	....	....	....	....	....	....
Air transport, freight	3 212 ..	....	....	....	....	....	....	....	....
Air transport, other	3 213 ..	....	....	....	....	....	....	....	....
Other transport, passenger	3 215 ..	....	....	....	....	....	....	....	....
Other transport, freight	3 216 ..	....	....	....	....	....	....	....	....
Other transport, other	3 217 ..	....	....	....	....	....	....	....	....
Travel, credit	2 236 ..	**39.39**	**44.90**	**43.95**	**46.51**	**54.21**	**57.23**	**49.58**	**46.02**
Business travel	2 237 ..	....	....	....	....	....	....	....	....
Personal travel	2 240 ..	....	....	....	....	....	....	....	....
Travel, debit	3 236 ..	**−28.06**	**−30.02**	**−31.73**	**−32.69**	**−38.26**	**−41.28**	**−38.42**	**−38.35**
Business travel	3 237 ..	....	....	....	....	....	....	....	....
Personal travel	3 240 ..	....	....	....	....	....	....	....	....
Other services, credit	2 200 BA	**40.59**	**43.32**	**50.07**	**50.54**	**57.54**	**68.42**	**63.11**	**63.03**
Communications	2 245 ..	2.51	3.06	3.53	3.81	4.44	4.53	4.63	4.46
Construction	2 249 ..	2.80	3.19	3.63	4.15	5.30	6.60	6.97	6.31
Insurance	2 253 ..	2.07	.87	1.13	.82	1.04	.83	1.35	1.24
Financial	2 260 ..	1.08	1.46	1.43	1.34	1.82	1.96	2.18	2.57
Computer and information	2 262 ..	1.26	1.49	1.71	1.97	1.90	1.86	1.64	1.63
Royalties and licence fees	2 266 ..	4.07	5.17	6.22	6.23	8.84	11.04	9.77	10.41
Other business services	2 268 ..	24.13	24.93	29.41	29.57	31.18	38.18	33.71	33.32
Personal, cultural, and recreational	2 287 ..	1.86	2.30	2.16	1.74	1.96	2.23	1.90	2.02
Government, n.i.e.	2 291 ..	.79	.86	.86	.89	1.06	1.20	.96	1.08
Other services, debit	3 200 BA	**−38.23**	**−39.55**	**−42.78**	**−46.48**	**−53.43**	**−58.27**	**−59.00**	**−57.99**
Communications	3 245 ..	−1.98	−1.94	−2.17	−2.16	−2.72	−3.14	−3.77	−3.84
Construction	3 249 ..	−1.36	−1.75	−1.62	−1.77	−2.11	−2.55	−3.34	−2.98
Insurance	3 253 ..	−2.39	−1.41	−2.27	−2.33	−2.08	−2.05	−2.42	−2.96
Financial	3 260 ..	−1.93	−2.50	−2.38	−2.08	−1.95	−1.92	−1.37	−2.06
Computer and information	3 262 ..	−1.24	−1.44	−1.79	−1.99	−2.29	−2.26	−2.16	−1.92
Royalties and licence fees	3 266 ..	−2.43	−3.06	−3.09	−3.31	−4.73	−5.46	−5.30	−5.56
Other business services	3 268 ..	−23.47	−23.70	−25.65	−29.10	−33.14	−36.18	−36.13	−34.12
Personal, cultural, and recreational	3 287 ..	−2.34	−2.62	−2.82	−2.69	−3.16	−3.68	−3.66	−3.73
Government, n.i.e.	3 291 ..	−1.09	−1.13	−.98	−1.05	−1.24	−1.04	−.86	−.82

Table 2 (Continued). STANDARD PRESENTATION, 2003–2010

(Billions of U.S. dollars)

	Code	2003	2004	2005	2006	2007	2008	2009	2010
C. INCOME.....................................	4 300 ..	**14.87**	**22.63**	**29.40**	**37.37**	**42.88**	**48.01**	**43.85**	**48.89**
Total credit.....................................	2 300 ..	*89.36*	*119.72*	*156.13*	*200.22*	*253.89*	*269.07*	*210.54*	*208.46*
Total debit......................................	3 300 ..	*−74.49*	*−97.10*	*−126.72*	*−162.85*	*−211.01*	*−221.06*	*−166.70*	*−159.57*
Compensation of employees, credit..................	2 310 ..	**10.86**	**11.82**	**11.43**	**11.89**	**13.22**	**15.11**	**14.65**	**14.44**
Compensation of employees, debit...................	3 310 ..	**−1.54**	**−1.17**	**−1.07**	**−1.13**	**−1.29**	**−1.25**	**−1.27**	**−1.29**
Investment income, credit........................	2 320 ..	**78.50**	**107.90**	**144.70**	**188.33**	**240.66**	**253.96**	**195.89**	**194.03**
Direct investment income................................	2 330 ..	16.33	32.52	53.29	64.11	69.29	63.07	56.62	73.27
Dividends and distributed branch profits................	2 332 ..	14.34	19.45	26.29	32.57	34.54	51.73	44.65	41.31
Reinvested earnings and undistributed branch profits.....	2 333 ..	1.99	13.07	27.00	31.53	34.76	11.34	11.97	31.95
Income on debt (interest).............................	2 334 ..	....	....	....	....	....	....	....	....
Portfolio investment income............................	2 339 ..	39.73	54.75	62.64	79.32	103.72	118.07	107.29	100.99
Income on equity....................................	2 340 ..	1.95	4.66	7.01	9.11	12.28	12.04	7.46	6.11
Income on bonds and notes............................	2 350 ..	....	46.47	50.95	63.78	80.24	93.06	93.60	91.42
Income on money market instruments....................	2 360 ..	....	3.61	4.68	6.42	11.21	12.97	6.22	3.46
Other investment income...............................	2 370 ..	22.44	20.64	28.76	44.91	67.65	72.82	31.99	19.77
Investment income, debit.........................	3 320 ..	**−72.95**	**−95.93**	**−125.65**	**−161.72**	**−209.72**	**−219.81**	**−165.43**	**−158.29**
Direct investment income................................	3 330 ..	−4.80	−13.11	−27.17	−30.00	−35.22	−25.32	−21.04	−28.00
Dividends and distributed branch profits................	3 332 ..	−6.97	−7.10	−9.48	−18.15	−20.53	−22.64	−19.26	−11.01
Reinvested earnings and undistributed branch profits.....	3 333 ..	2.17	−6.01	−17.68	−11.85	−14.69	−2.68	−1.79	−16.99
Income on debt (interest).............................	3 334 ..	....	....	....	....	....	....	....	....
Portfolio investment income............................	3 339 ..	−45.23	−59.26	−65.30	−80.46	−94.56	−108.50	−107.26	−107.30
Income on equity....................................	3 340 ..	−6.29	−8.21	−9.67	−13.27	−16.35	−22.12	−18.19	−17.32
Income on bonds and notes............................	3 350 ..	....	−48.16	−51.85	−61.89	−69.79	−76.93	−84.78	−87.40
Income on money market instruments....................	3 360 ..	....	−2.89	−3.79	−5.30	−8.42	−9.46	−4.29	−2.57
Other investment income...............................	3 370 ..	−22.93	−23.55	−33.19	−51.26	−79.94	−85.98	−37.12	−22.99
D. CURRENT TRANSFERS............................	4 379 ..	**−19.46**	**−21.69**	**−27.08**	**−27.77**	**−32.41**	**−35.07**	**−38.08**	**−34.94**
Credit...	2 379 ..	**24.05**	**25.44**	**25.41**	**27.11**	**28.93**	**29.13**	**26.07**	**24.06**
General government...................................	2 380 ..	14.69	16.48	16.96	17.95	18.54	18.48	16.82	15.29
Other sectors.......................................	2 390 ..	9.36	8.96	8.45	9.16	10.39	10.65	9.24	8.77
Workers' remittances...............................	2 391 ..	.45	.46	.51	1.14	1.22	1.17	1.07	1.00
Other current transfers.............................	2 392 ..	8.91	8.50	7.93	8.02	9.17	9.48	8.17	7.77
Debit...	3 379 ..	**−43.51**	**−47.14**	**−52.49**	**−54.88**	**−61.33**	**−64.21**	**−64.15**	**−59.01**
General government...................................	3 380 ..	−27.54	−30.12	−35.26	−35.37	−37.78	−41.41	−42.40	−39.02
Other sectors.......................................	3 390 ..	−15.97	−17.01	−17.23	−19.51	−23.56	−22.79	−21.75	−19.99
Workers' remittances...............................	3 391 ..	−2.85	−3.09	−3.11	−4.38	−4.71	−5.00	−3.97	−3.80
Other current transfers.............................	3 392 ..	−13.12	−13.92	−14.12	−15.12	−18.84	−17.79	−17.78	−16.18
CAPITAL AND FINANCIAL ACCOUNT.....................	4 996 ..	**3.97**	**−8.55**	**.23**	**28.56**	**43.16**	**26.86**	**58.69**	**24.04**
CAPITAL ACCOUNT.................................	4 994 ..	**−8.26**	**1.81**	**.66**	**−.27**	**2.47**	**1.04**	**.46**	**.07**
Total credit.....................................	2 994 ..	*1.94*	*3.35*	*2.57*	*1.90*	*3.42*	*2.13*	*1.39*	*1.32*
Total debit......................................	3 994 ..	*−10.20*	*−1.54*	*−1.91*	*−2.17*	*−.95*	*−1.09*	*−.93*	*−1.24*
Capital transfers, credit.........................	2 400 ..	**1.91**	**2.30**	**2.37**	**1.71**	**2.03**	**2.12**	**1.37**	**1.29**
General government...................................	2 401 ..	1.58	1.87	1.83	1.33	1.72	1.80	1.22	1.10
Debt forgiveness....................................	2 402 ..	....	....	....	....	....	....	....	....
Other capital transfers..............................	2 410 ..	1.58	1.87	1.83	1.33	1.72	1.80	1.22	1.10
Other sectors.......................................	2 430 ..	.34	.43	.54	.38	.32	.31	.15	.19
Migrants' transfers.................................	2 431 ..	....	....	....	....	....	.31	.15	.19
Debt forgiveness....................................	2 432 ..	....	.09	.10	....	.01	....	....	....
Other capital transfers..............................	2 440 ..	.34	.35	.45	.38	.30	....	....	....
Capital transfers, debit..........................	3 400 ..	**−10.12**	**−1.44**	**−1.79**	**−1.52**	**−.79**	**−.85**	**−.89**	**−1.21**
General government...................................	3 401 ..	−1.73	−1.06	−1.12	−1.20	−.42	−.65	−.71	−1.01
Debt forgiveness....................................	3 402 ..	−1.50	−.75	−.87	−.95	−.14	−.38	−.42	−.76
Other capital transfers..............................	3 410 ..	−.23	−.31	−.25	−.25	−.27	−.27	−.29	−.25
Other sectors.......................................	3 430 ..	−8.39	−.38	−.67	−.32	−.37	−.20	−.18	−.20
Migrants' transfers.................................	3 431 ..	....	....	....	....	....	−.20	−.17	−.17
Debt forgiveness....................................	3 432 ..	−8.18	−.20	−.45	−.10	−.11	....	....	−.02
Other capital transfers..............................	3 440 ..	−.20	−.19	−.22	−.21	−.26	....	....	....
Nonproduced nonfinancial assets, credit............	2 480 ..	**.02**	**1.05**	**.20**	**.19**	**1.39**	**.01**	**.02**	**.03**
Nonproduced nonfinancial assets, debit.............	3 480 ..	**−.08**	**−.10**	**−.11**	**−.65**	**−.16**	**−.24**	**−.05**	**−.03**

Table 2 (Continued). STANDARD PRESENTATION, 2003–2010

(Billions of U.S. dollars)

	Code	2003	2004	2005	2006	2007	2008	2009	2010
FINANCIAL ACCOUNT	4 995	12.23	−10.36	−.43	28.83	40.69	25.81	58.23	23.97
A. DIRECT INVESTMENT	4 500	−10.32	−24.07	−28.83	−39.58	−68.78	−93.41	−67.96	−50.72
Direct investment abroad	4 505	−53.38	−56.90	−113.83	−111.41	−167.09	−159.94	−103.08	−84.39
Equity capital	4 510	−13.82	−32.00	−33.78	−73.29	−78.43	−87.02	−54.43	−27.05
Claims on affiliated enterprises	4 515	−13.82	−32.00	−33.78	−73.29	−78.43	−87.02	−54.43	−27.05
Liabilities to affiliated enterprises	4 520	....	....	....	....	....	....	....	....
Reinvested earnings	4 525	−1.99	−13.07	−27.00	−31.53	−34.76	−11.34	−11.97	−31.95
Other capital	4 530	−37.57	−11.83	−53.04	−6.59	−53.90	−61.58	−36.68	−25.39
Claims on affiliated enterprises	4 535	−35.73	−14.47	−57.08	−22.53	−47.68	−59.15	−37.46	−35.63
Liabilities to affiliated enterprises	4 540	−1.84	2.64	4.04	15.95	−6.23	−2.43	.78	10.24
Direct investment in France	4 555	43.06	32.83	85.00	71.83	98.31	66.54	35.12	33.67
Equity capital	4 560	17.61	5.23	22.94	27.38	30.75	20.91	21.22	14.48
Claims on direct investors	4 565	....	....	....	....	....	....	....	....
Liabilities to direct investors	4 570	17.61	5.23	22.94	27.38	30.75	20.91	21.22	14.48
Reinvested earnings	4 575	−2.17	6.01	17.68	11.85	14.69	2.68	1.79	16.99
Other capital	4 580	27.62	21.59	44.37	32.60	52.87	42.95	12.12	2.20
Claims on direct investors	4 585	−1.57	−1.26	.25	−.88	−.98	....	−1.11	−6.60
Liabilities to direct investors	4 590	29.19	22.85	44.12	33.48	53.85	42.95	13.22	8.80
B. PORTFOLIO INVESTMENT	4 600	6.13	−66.14	−18.40	−134.10	−168.49	26.17	346.67	157.53
Assets	4 602	−192.71	−232.48	−243.64	−325.36	−281.84	−158.60	−106.29	28.60
Equity securities	4 610	−48.09	−60.85	−53.98	−72.19	−40.13	−56.98	−41.36	−23.48
Monetary authorities	4 611	....	....	....	....	.03	....	....	....
General government	4 612	....	....	....	−3.31	−4.44	−4.06	−1.02	2.93
Banks	4 613	−16.27	−24.60	9.66	−.08	−21.76	−1.25	−3.44	−17.85
Other sectors	4 614	−31.81	−36.25	−63.63	−68.80	−13.96	−51.67	−36.91	−8.56
Debt securities	4 619	−144.62	−171.63	−189.67	−253.18	−241.71	−101.62	−64.93	52.08
Bonds and notes	4 620	−115.14	−156.05	−176.21	−251.63	−250.06	−2.70	−16.97	−.59
Monetary authorities	4 621	....	−6.72	−7.72	−6.20	−19.48	−38.28	−9.23	−10.17
General government	4 622	....	....	....	−6.13	−8.55	−1.94	−2.41	−3.13
Banks	4 623	−35.75	−74.56	−95.30	−161.11	−11.28	−.64	98.07	111.74
Other sectors	4 624	−79.38	−74.78	−73.19	−78.20	−210.75	38.16	−103.40	−99.03
Money market instruments	4 630	−29.49	−15.58	−13.45	−1.54	8.36	−98.93	−47.96	52.67
Monetary authorities	4 631	....	−.25	−.55	−13.61	−35.10	−21.83	7.10	14.42
General government	4 632	....	....	....	−.20	−.05	−.01	−2.62	.07
Banks	4 633	−28.24	−5.24	−7.84	37.73	27.67	−76.42	−58.72	40.83
Other sectors	4 634	−1.25	−10.09	−5.07	−25.46	15.84	−.66	6.28	−2.65
Liabilities	4 652	198.84	166.34	225.25	191.27	113.35	184.78	452.95	128.93
Equity securities	4 660	20.71	31.77	64.15	94.05	−10.37	−18.10	75.14	−8.44
Banks	4 663	−2.53	−3.02	8.09	33.17	−12.71	12.62	11.25	−17.88
Other sectors	4 664	23.24	34.79	56.06	60.88	2.34	−30.72	63.89	9.43
Debt securities	4 669	178.13	134.57	161.10	97.22	123.72	202.88	377.82	137.37
Bonds and notes	4 670	161.87	118.27	136.60	114.75	109.77	123.59	272.77	133.73
Monetary authorities	4 671	....	....	....	....	....	....	....	....
General government	4 672	66.84	95.73	90.42	57.60	24.83	66.01	109.82	69.08
Banks	4 673	53.05	43.35	48.56	44.51	66.68	24.23	25.59	52.21
Other sectors	4 674	41.98	−20.80	−2.39	12.64	18.26	33.35	137.35	12.44
Money market instruments	4 680	16.27	16.29	24.50	−17.53	13.94	79.29	105.05	3.64
Monetary authorities	4 681	....	....	....	....	....	....	....	....
General government	4 682	17.99	14.07	2.00	−35.42	5.44	76.35	97.55	−6.54
Banks	4 683	−5.31	3.18	18.94	14.92	14.26	−4.43	6.82	9.64
Other sectors	4 684	3.59	−.95	3.57	2.97	−5.76	7.37	.68	.54
C. FINANCIAL DERIVATIVES	4 910	−7.05	6.21	6.36	4.19	58.96	−16.64	−22.88	45.17
Monetary authorities	4 911	....	....	....	....	....	....	....	....
General government	4 912	....	....	....	....	....	....	....	....
Banks	4 913	−7.05	6.21	6.36	4.19	58.96	−16.64	−22.88	45.17
Other sectors	4 914	....	....	....	....	....	....	....	....
Assets	4 900	....	....	....	....	....	....	....	....
Monetary authorities	4 901	....	....	....	....	....	....	....	....
General government	4 902	....	....	....	....	....	....	....	....
Banks	4 903	....	....	....	....	....	....	....	....
Other sectors	4 904	....	....	....	....	....	....	....	....
Liabilities	4 905	−7.05	6.21	6.36	4.19	58.96	−16.64	−22.88	45.17
Monetary authorities	4 906	....	....	....	....	....	....	....	....
General government	4 907	....	....	....	....	....	....	....	....
Banks	4 908	−7.05	6.21	6.36	4.19	58.96	−16.64	−22.88	45.17
Other sectors	4 909	....	....	....	....	....	....	....	....

Table 2 (Concluded). STANDARD PRESENTATION, 2003–2010

(Billions of U.S. dollars)

	Code	2003	2004	2005	2006	2007	2008	2009	2010
D. OTHER INVESTMENT	4 700	**24.76**	**77.75**	**31.39**	**210.10**	**218.67**	**97.66**	**−188.25**	**−120.22**
Assets	4 703	**−14.84**	**−116.15**	**−276.85**	**−153.21**	**−264.60**	**70.04**	**73.70**	**−159.72**
Trade credits	4 706	.87	−3.10	5.70	4.11	2.31	5.44	−2.07	−.83
General government	4 707	1.67	1.73	3.45	6.67	2.11	1.72	.72	.38
of which: Short-term	4 709	....	....	....	....	....	....	....	....
Other sectors	4 710	−.80	−4.84	2.25	−2.55	.19	3.72	−2.79	−1.20
of which: Short-term	4 712	−.80	−4.84	2.25	−2.55	.19	3.72	−2.79	−1.20
Loans	4 714	−6.70	−108.79	167.93	94.94	−98.23	−11.19	−32.11	−123.06
Monetary authorities	4 715	.01	11.42	5.13	14.28	−19.23	12.60	−4.84	−14.02
of which: Short-term	4 718	.01	11.42	5.13	14.28	−19.23	12.60	−4.84	−14.02
General government	4 719	−2.40	2.05	.26	.49	1.06	1.43	−1.66	−4.74
of which: Short-term	4 721	....	.89	....	....	....	....	....	....
Banks	4 722	−3.91	−121.43	164.02	82.68	−81.20	−24.25	−26.55	−104.91
of which: Short-term	4 724	24.58	−103.24	162.92	40.62	−34.93	5.14	−35.83	−114.50
Other sectors	4 725	−.40	−.82	−1.48	−2.51	1.13	−.97	.94	.60
of which: Short-term	4 727	−.40	−.82	−1.19	−2.55	1.13	−.97	.94	.61
Currency and deposits	4 730	−8.97	−4.24	−450.44	−252.26	−168.67	75.79	107.86	−35.51
Monetary authorities	4 731	....	....	−.79	.19	−.93	2.57	.38	−.02
General government	4 732	.01	−.02	.87	−5.13	7.15	.02	.04	−.01
Banks	4 733	....	....	−451.84	−244.66	−168.60	68.65	113.14	−35.25
Other sectors	4 734	−8.98	−4.21	1.31	−2.65	−6.29	4.55	−5.70	−.23
Other assets	4 736	−.03	−.02	−.04	....	....	....	.02	−.32
Monetary authorities	4 737	....	....	....	....	....	....	.02	−.32
of which: Short-term	4 739	....	....	....	....	....	....	....	....
General government	4 740	−.03	−.02	−.04	....	....	....	....	....
of which: Short-term	4 742	....	....	....	....	....	....	....	....
Banks	4 743	....	....	....	....	....	....	....	....
of which: Short-term	4 745	....	....	....	....	....	....	....	....
Other sectors	4 746	....	....	....	....	....	....	....	....
of which: Short-term	4 748	....	....	....	....	....	....	....	....
Liabilities	4 753	**39.60**	**193.90**	**308.24**	**363.31**	**483.27**	**27.62**	**−261.95**	**39.50**
Trade credits	4 756	−3.32	9.16	5.45	2.49	−4.18	2.31	8.91	5.00
General government	4 757	....	....	....	....	....	....	....	....
of which: Short-term	4 759	....	....	....	....	....	....	....	....
Other sectors	4 760	−3.32	9.16	5.45	2.49	−4.18	2.31	8.91	5.00
of which: Short-term	4 762	....	....	5.45	2.49	−4.18	2.31	8.91	5.00
Loans	4 764	42.92	184.75	306.41	346.68	408.49	−21.67	−298.35	31.35
Monetary authorities	4 765	2.11	1.82	....	....	16.49	148.61	−74.22	−43.27
of which: Use of Fund credit and loans from the Fund	4 766	....	....	....	....	....	....	....	....
of which: Short-term	4 768	2.11	1.82	....	....	16.49	148.61	−74.22	−43.27
General government	4 769	−.45	2.41	−5.97	.03	.21	....	−1.66	.72
of which: Short-term	4 771	....	2.88	−5.00	....	....	....	....	....
Banks	4 772	39.26	169.34	285.22	328.50	378.21	−181.99	−194.60	78.52
of which: Short-term	4 774	−3.05	144.46	199.47	238.20	238.67	−122.41	−130.37	62.36
Other sectors	4 775	1.99	11.18	27.15	18.15	13.58	11.71	−27.87	−4.62
of which: Short-term	4 777	....	11.65	18.16	6.79	5.83	−1.03	−24.40	−1.66
Currency and deposits	4 780	....	....	−3.62	14.13	78.97	46.98	13.34	3.15
Monetary authorities	4 781	....	....	−3.40	10.42	78.28	39.81	17.54	3.57
General government	4 782	....	....	−.22	3.71	.69	7.17	−4.21	−.42
Banks	4 783	....	....	....	....	....	....	....	....
Other sectors	4 784	....	....	....	....	....	....	....	....
Other liabilities	4 786	....	....	....	....	....	....	14.15	....
Monetary authorities	4 787	....	....	....	....	....	....	14.15	....
of which: Short-term	4 789	....	....	....	....	....	....	....	....
General government	4 790	....	....	....	....	....	....	....	....
of which: Short-term	4 792	....	....	....	....	....	....	....	....
Banks	4 793	....	....	....	....	....	....	....	....
of which: Short-term	4 795	....	....	....	....	....	....	....	....
Other sectors	4 796	....	....	....	....	....	....	....	....
of which: Short-term	4 798	....	....	....	....	....	....	....	....
E. RESERVE ASSETS	4 802	**−1.29**	**−4.11**	**9.05**	**−11.78**	**.33**	**12.02**	**−9.35**	**−7.79**
Monetary gold	4 812	....	.56	2.35	2.09	2.32	3.11	1.73	....
Special drawing rights	4 811	−.08	−.08	−.08	−.02	....	....	−14.20	−.03
Reserve position in the Fund	4 810	.04	1.17	2.11	1.55	.35	−1.15	−1.31	−.94
Foreign exchange	4 803	−1.25	−5.76	4.67	−15.41	−2.34	10.06	4.44	−6.81
Other claims	4 813	....	....	....	....	....	....	....	....
NET ERRORS AND OMISSIONS	4 998	**−16.84**	**−2.48**	**10.03**	**−15.57**	**−16.55**	**23.02**	**−18.82**	**20.45**

Table 3. INTERNATIONAL INVESTMENT POSITION (End-period stocks), 2003–2010

(Billions of U.S. dollars)

	Code	2003	2004	2005	2006	2007	2008	2009	2010
ASSETS..	8 995 C.	**3,415.78**	**4,236.02**	**4,579.33**	**5,887.59**	**7,181.79**	**6,053.71**	**6,892.76**	**6,756.70**
Direct investment abroad.................	8 505 ..	**946.73**	**1,153.83**	**1,232.23**	**1,609.82**	**1,794.80**	**1,267.87**	**1,661.60**	**1,523.04**
Equity capital and reinvested earnings....	8 506 ..	702.35	877.87	943.41	1,288.09	1,388.54	827.06	1,169.00	1,030.02
Claims on affiliated enterprises.............	8 507 ..	....	....	....	....	....	....	....	....
Liabilities to affiliated enterprises.........	8 508 ..	....	....	....	....	....	....	....	....
Other capital.......................................	8 530 ..	244.38	275.96	288.83	321.73	406.26	440.81	492.60	493.02
Claims on affiliated enterprises.............	8 535 ..	....	....	....	....	414.43	446.03	499.41	510.01
Liabilities to affiliated enterprises.........	8 540 ..	....	....	....	....	−8.17	−5.22	−6.81	−17.00
Portfolio investment..........................	8 602 ..	**1,369.56**	**1,750.72**	**1,873.26**	**2,437.74**	**2,965.00**	**2,584.90**	**2,962.29**	**2,805.65**
Equity securities...................................	8 610 ..	340.24	442.66	524.88	716.80	826.85	474.75	647.10	682.10
Monetary authorities.........................	8 611 ..	.01	.53	.63	.71	.75	.72	.75	.69
General government..........................	8 612 ..	.54	3.42	11.90	18.44	24.51	15.32	20.53	17.97
Banks..	8 613 ..	75.86	106.60	107.25	128.29	162.48	88.94	110.21	131.27
Other sectors....................................	8 614 ..	263.83	332.11	405.11	569.37	639.11	369.76	515.62	532.17
Debt securities.....................................	8 619 ..	1,029.32	1,308.07	1,348.37	1,720.94	2,138.15	2,110.15	2,315.19	2,123.54
Bonds and notes...............................	8 620 ..	909.76	1,163.83	1,199.73	1,541.75	1,951.65	1,819.65	1,960.41	1,832.77
Monetary authorities.....................	8 621 ..	.80	8.20	14.26	21.56	44.13	78.90	92.59	93.59
General government.......................	8 622 ..	1.16	.93	3.16	9.56	19.20	20.53	24.16	25.52
Banks..	8 623 ..	424.97	531.78	547.72	748.73	831.38	758.41	699.76	557.53
Other sectors................................	8 624 ..	482.83	622.93	634.58	761.90	1,056.94	961.82	1,143.91	1,156.13
Money market instruments.................	8 630 ..	119.56	144.23	148.64	179.19	186.50	290.50	354.78	290.77
Monetary authorities.....................	8 631 ..	....	.27	1.50	16.05	52.08	86.95	78.07	69.79
General government.......................	8 632 ..	....	....	.05	.30	.40	.46	3.13	2.90
Banks..	8 633 ..	105.74	127.64	130.64	117.36	100.26	169.58	243.52	187.23
Other sectors................................	8 634 ..	13.82	16.32	16.46	45.48	33.76	33.51	30.07	30.85
Financial derivatives..........................	8 900 ..	**117.55**	**159.19**	**146.88**	**209.68**	**354.75**	**325.71**	**393.96**	**433.62**
Monetary authorities............................	8 901 ..	....	....	....	....	....	....	....	....
General government..............................	8 902 ..	....	....	....	....	....	....	....	....
Banks..	8 903 ..	....	....	....	....	....	....	....	....
Other sectors.......................................	8 904 ..	117.55	159.19	146.88	209.68	354.75	325.71	393.96	433.62
Other investment...............................	8 703 ..	**911.19**	**1,094.94**	**1,252.59**	**1,532.11**	**1,951.52**	**1,772.30**	**1,741.82**	**1,828.15**
Trade credits..	8 706 ..	111.88	124.32	104.91	110.33	126.16	118.14	112.81	106.40
General government..........................	8 707 ..	30.44	32.31	23.56	18.96	18.78	17.08	12.00	10.06
of which: Short-term.....................	8 709 ..	....	....	....	....	....	....	....	....
Other sectors....................................	8 710 ..	81.44	92.01	81.35	91.36	107.37	101.07	100.81	96.34
of which: Short-term.....................	8 712 ..	*81.44*	*92.01*	*81.35*	*91.36*	*107.37*	*101.07*	*100.81*	*96.34*
Loans...	8 714 ..	782.44	953.06	238.78	307.78	436.42	427.79	477.67	584.72
Monetary authorities.........................	8 715 ..	42.64	33.58	14.11	18.78	41.95	28.63	38.23	56.90
of which: Short-term.....................	8 718 ..	*42.64*	*33.58*	*14.11*	*18.78*	*41.95*	*28.63*	*38.23*	*56.90*
General government..........................	8 719 ..	20.07	20.62	15.83	15.71	16.41	13.72	16.08	20.11
of which: Short-term.....................	8 721 ..	*3.07*	*3.58*	*1.30*	....	....	....	....	....
Banks..	8 722 ..	621.45	788.51	206.64	269.76	375.43	381.98	420.50	506.09
of which: Short-term.....................	8 724 ..	*439.08*	*574.93*	*85.78*	*121.36*	*167.94*	*154.97*	*197.15*	*305.59*
Other sectors....................................	8 725 ..	98.29	110.36	2.21	3.53	2.62	3.47	2.87	1.63
of which: Short-term.....................	8 727 ..	*97.28*	*108.36*	*2.17*	*3.53*	*2.62*	*3.47*	*2.87*	*1.63*
Currency and deposits...........................	8 730 ..	....	....	890.54	1,094.73	1,365.80	1,202.54	1,126.19	1,112.24
Monetary authorities.........................	8 731 ..	....	....	11.95	12.95	15.16	11.84	11.81	10.96
General government..........................	8 732 ..	....	....	1.00	8.09	.99	.77	.55	1.14
Banks..	8 733 ..	....	....	785.13	975.55	1,236.06	1,091.29	1,006.16	994.72
Other sectors....................................	8 734 ..	....	....	92.46	98.14	113.59	98.64	107.67	105.43
Other assets..	8 736 ..	16.87	17.56	18.36	19.27	23.14	23.83	25.14	24.79
Monetary authorities.........................	8 737 ..	1.06	1.13	.98	1.09	1.22	1.16	1.18	1.42
of which: Short-term.....................	8 739 ..	....	....	....	....	....	....	....	....
General government..........................	8 740 ..	15.81	16.43	17.38	18.17	21.92	22.67	23.96	23.37
of which: Short-term.....................	8 742 ..	....	....	....	....	....	....	....	....
Banks..	8 743 ..	....	....	....	....	....	....	....	....
of which: Short-term.....................	8 745 ..	....	....	....	....	....	....	....	....
Other sectors....................................	8 746 ..	....	....	....	....	....	....	....	....
of which: Short-term.....................	8 748 ..	....	....	....	....	....	....	....	....
Reserve assets...................................	8 802 ..	**70.75**	**77.34**	**74.36**	**98.24**	**115.72**	**102.92**	**133.09**	**166.24**
Monetary gold......................................	8 812 ..	40.58	42.03	46.61	55.59	70.01	69.31	86.45	110.42
Special drawing rights...........................	8 811 ..	.76	.87	.88	.95	.99	.97	15.23	15.00
Reserve position in the Fund..................	8 810 ..	6.30	5.36	2.88	1.42	1.13	2.27	3.67	4.59
Foreign exchange..................................	8 803 ..	23.10	29.07	24.00	40.29	43.59	30.38	27.73	36.22
Other claims..	8 813 ..	....	....	....	....	....	....	....	....

Table 3 (Concluded). INTERNATIONAL INVESTMENT POSITION (End-period stocks), 2003–2010

(Billions of U.S. dollars)

	Code	2003	2004	2005	2006	2007	2008	2009	2010
LIABILITIES...	8 995 D.	**3,402.75**	**4,259.22**	**4,556.58**	**5,861.16**	**7,222.93**	**6,400.18**	**7,141.60**	**7,029.63**
Direct investment in France................................	8 555 ..	**653.11**	**867.48**	**888.94**	**1,107.29**	**1,247.38**	**904.65**	**1,083.60**	**1,008.38**
Equity capital and reinvested earnings.....................	8 556 ..	463.22	627.75	644.33	804.37	860.40	502.19	656.50	601.90
Claims on direct investors................................	8 557 ..	....	....	....	....	....	....	....	....
Liabilities to direct investors...........................	8 558 ..	....	....	....	....	....	....	....	....
Other capital..	8 580 ..	189.89	239.73	244.61	302.92	386.99	402.45	427.11	406.47
Claims on direct investors................................	8 585 ..	....	....	....	....	−2.75	−3.73	−4.81	−11.05
Liabilities to direct investors...........................	8 590 ..	....	....	....	....	389.74	406.18	431.92	417.52
Portfolio investment..........................	8 652 ..	**1,626.50**	**1,988.41**	**2,081.90**	**2,585.26**	**2,926.40**	**2,605.97**	**3,335.41**	**3,273.85**
Equity securities..	8 660 ..	490.90	593.86	690.45	990.33	1,060.38	624.82	852.55	790.11
Banks..	8 663 ..	69.33	76.75	90.57	152.42	134.37	76.21	118.50	79.12
Other sectors..	8 664 ..	421.58	517.11	599.89	837.91	926.01	548.61	734.04	710.99
Debt securities...	8 669 ..	1,135.60	1,394.55	1,391.44	1,594.93	1,866.02	1,981.15	2,482.86	2,483.74
Bonds and notes..	8 670 ..	1,025.27	1,257.38	1,246.64	1,454.47	1,696.27	1,742.45	2,125.27	2,153.09
Monetary authorities...............................	8 671 ..	....	....	....	....	....	....	....	....
General government................................	8 672 ..	464.24	626.92	635.59	743.34	840.48	900.82	1,045.73	1,054.76
Banks..	8 673 ..	267.78	336.36	353.30	421.91	525.95	537.38	597.52	621.51
Other sectors....................................	8 674 ..	293.24	294.10	257.75	289.21	329.84	304.25	482.02	476.82
Money market instruments..........................	8 680 ..	110.34	137.16	144.81	140.46	169.75	238.70	357.59	330.66
Monetary authorities...............................	8 681 ..	....	....	....	....	....	....	....	....
General government................................	8 682 ..	77.78	101.00	91.21	64.14	78.36	151.29	259.34	237.35
Banks..	8 683 ..	26.18	30.27	45.11	63.57	83.63	72.91	82.78	78.69
Other sectors....................................	8 684 ..	6.38	5.90	8.48	12.75	7.76	14.50	15.47	14.62
Financial derivatives..............................	8 905 ..	**147.80**	**186.04**	**173.89**	**248.83**	**460.18**	**402.62**	**449.22**	**530.71**
Monetary authorities.....................................	8 906 ..	....	....	....	....	....	....	....	....
General government......................................	8 907 ..	....	....	....	....	....	....	....	....
Banks..	8 908 ..	....	....	....	....	....	....	....	....
Other sectors..	8 909 ..	147.80	186.04	173.89	248.83	460.18	402.62	449.22	530.71
Other investment...................................	8 753 ..	**975.34**	**1,217.30**	**1,411.85**	**1,919.78**	**2,588.97**	**2,486.94**	**2,273.37**	**2,216.69**
Trade credits...	8 756 ..	81.78	89.01	87.81	96.63	123.17	122.93	122.41	121.19
General government...................................	8 757 ..	....	....	....	....	....	....	....	....
of which: Short-term...............................	8 759 ..	....	....	....	....	....	....	....	....
Other sectors...	8 760 ..	81.78	89.01	87.81	96.63	123.17	122.93	122.41	121.19
of which: Short-term...............................	8 762 ..	*81.78*	*89.01*	*87.81*	*96.63*	*123.17*	*122.93*	*122.41*	*121.19*
Loans..	8 764 ..	893.56	1,128.28	1,321.18	1,791.63	2,354.11	2,225.62	1,972.73	1,915.60
Monetary authorities.................................	8 765 ..	4.40	6.17	....	....	17.58	163.78	89.33	37.88
of which: Use of Fund credit and loans from the Fund....	8 766 ..	....	....	....	....	....	....	....	....
of which: Short-term...............................	8 768 ..	*4.40*	*6.17*	....	....	*17.58*	*163.78*	*89.33*	*37.88*
General government...................................	8 769 ..	23.74	28.25	19.00	24.68	28.06	34.37	29.16	27.41
of which: Short-term...............................	8 771 ..	*13.29*	*17.61*	*10.64*	*15.62*	*18.02*	*24.88*	*21.09*	*19.21*
Banks..	8 772 ..	788.33	1,008.49	1,198.75	1,639.65	2,157.55	1,872.17	1,724.76	1,735.23
of which: Short-term...............................	8 774 ..	*619.07*	*786.95*	*909.86*	*1,222.91*	*1,559.28*	*1,366.00*	*1,270.41*	*1,288.50*
Other sectors..	8 775 ..	77.09	85.38	103.42	127.30	150.92	155.30	129.48	115.09
of which: Short-term...............................	8 777 ..	*64.70*	*73.49*	*92.41*	*102.73*	*113.94*	*107.02*	*78.57*	*69.51*
Currency and deposits...................................	8 780 ..	....	....	2.87	31.52	111.69	138.39	162.34	164.29
Monetary authorities.................................	8 781 ..	....	....	2.87	31.52	111.69	138.39	162.34	164.29
General government...................................	8 782 ..	....	....	....	....	....	....	....	....
Banks..	8 783 ..	....	....	....	....	....	....	....	....
Other sectors..	8 784 ..	....	....	....	....	....	....	....	....
Other liabilities...	8 786 ..	....	....	....	....	....	....	15.89	15.61
Monetary authorities.................................	8 787 ..	....	....	....	....	....	....	15.89	15.61
of which: Short-term...............................	8 789 ..	....	....	....	....	....	....	....	....
General government...................................	8 790 ..	....	....	....	....	....	....	....	....
of which: Short-term...............................	8 792 ..	....	....	....	....	....	....	....	....
Banks..	8 793 ..	....	....	....	....	....	....	....	....
of which: Short-term...............................	8 795 ..	....	....	....	....	....	....	....	....
Other sectors..	8 796 ..	....	....	....	....	....	....	....	....
of which: Short-term...............................	8 798 ..	....	....	....	....	....	....	....	....
NET INTERNATIONAL INVESTMENT POSITION........	8 995 ..	**13.03**	**−23.20**	**22.75**	**26.43**	**−41.14**	**−346.47**	**−248.84**	**−272.93**
Conversion rates: euros per U.S. dollar (end of period)...	0 104 ..	.7918	.7342	.8477	.7593	.6793	.7185	.6942	.7484

Table 1. ANALYTIC PRESENTATION, 2003–2010

(Millions of U.S. dollars)

	Code	2003	2004	2005	2006	2007	2008	2009	2010
A. Current Account[1]....................	4 993 Z.	**−119**	**186**	**9**	**160**	**271**	**−91**	**154**	**2**
Goods: exports f.o.b..........................	2 100 ..	149	179	212	197	193	201	150	160
Goods: imports f.o.b..........................	3 100 ..	−1,530	−1,440	−1,593	−1,612	−1,829	−2,158	−1,698	−1,802
Balance on Goods..........................	4 100 ..	*−1,381*	*−1,260*	*−1,381*	*−1,415*	*−1,636*	*−1,956*	*−1,548*	*−1,642*
Services: credit..............................	2 200 ..	954	1,028	1,081	1,033	1,201	1,192	1,030	955
Services: debit..............................	3 200 ..	−599	−666	−737	−546	−617	−719	−713	−637
Balance on Goods and Services..........	4 991 ..	*−1,025*	*−899*	*−1,037*	*−929*	*−1,052*	*−1,483*	*−1,230*	*−1,324*
Income: credit..............................	2 300 ..	567	658	588	668	731	822	774	742
Income: debit..............................	3 300 ..	−102	−98	−67	−75	−137	−150	−152	−136
Balance on Goods, Services, and Income......	4 992 ..	*−560*	*−339*	*−515*	*−336*	*−458*	*−812*	*−608*	*−718*
Current transfers: credit......................	2 379 Z.	638	754	751	786	1,079	1,092	1,104	1,135
Current transfers: debit......................	3 379 ..	−197	−229	−227	−290	−349	−370	−342	−415
B. Capital Account[1]....................	4 994 Z.	**−1**	**−1**	**−1**	....	....	....	....	**−1**
Capital account: credit......................	2 994 Z.	....	....	....	....	....	....	....	....
Capital account: debit......................	3 994 ..	−1	−1	−1	....	....	....	....	−1
Total, Groups A Plus B....................	4 981 ..	*−120*	*185*	*8*	*159*	*271*	*−91*	*154*	*1*
C. Financial Account[1]....................	4 995 W.	**104**	**−125**	**−32**	**4**	**−334**	**−124**	**−251**	**112**
Direct investment abroad....................	4 505 ..	−6	−9	−16	−10	−14	−30	−8	−89
Direct investment in French Polynesia......	4 555 Z.	58	6	8	31	58	14	10	95
Portfolio investment assets..................	4 602 ..	−75	−20	−66	17	20	−116	−127	−2
Equity securities..........................	4 610 ..	....	....	....	....	....	....	....	....
Debt securities..........................	4 619 ..	−75	−20	−66	17	20	−116	−127	−2
Portfolio investment liabilities..............	4 652 Z.	....	....	....	....	....	....	....	....
Equity securities..........................	4 660 ..	....	....	....	....	....	....	....	....
Debt securities..........................	4 669 Z.	....	....	....	....	....	....	....	....
Financial derivatives........................	4 910 ..	....	....	....	....	....	....	....	....
Financial derivatives assets..................	4 900 ..	....	....	....	....	....	....	....	....
Financial derivatives liabilities..............	4 905 ..	....	....	....	....	....	....	....	....
Other investment assets....................	4 703 ..	64	−227	−235	96	529	625	896	688
Monetary authorities......................	4 701 ..	15	54	76	338	733	1,094	964	986
General government......................	4 704 ..	....	....	....	....	....	....	....	....
Banks....................................	4 705 ..	141	−55	−212	−175	−74	−318	101	−176
Other sectors............................	4 728 ..	−93	−227	−99	−67	−129	−151	−168	−122
Other investment liabilities..................	4 753 W.	63	125	276	−129	−927	−617	−1,023	−580
Monetary authorities......................	4 753 WA	....	....	....	....	....	....	....	....
General government......................	4 753 ZB	−4	−42	67	−387	−784	−915	−1,001	−890
Banks....................................	4 753 ZC	−19	180	224	235	−91	307	81	386
Other sectors............................	4 753 ZD	85	−14	−14	22	−52	−9	−103	−75
Total, Groups A Through C..................	4 983 ..	*−16*	*60*	*−25*	*164*	*−62*	*−215*	*−98*	*113*
D. Net Errors and Omissions..................	4 998 ..	**16**	**−60**	**25**	**−164**	**62**	**215**	**98**	**−113**
Total, Groups A Through D..................	4 984 ..	....	....	....	....	....	....	....	....
E. Reserves and Related Items..................	4 802 A.	....	....	....	....	....	....	....	....
Reserve assets..............................	4 802 ..	....	....	....	....	....	....	....	....
Use of Fund credit and loans..............	4 766 ..	....	....	....	....	....	....	....	....
Exceptional financing......................	4 920 ..	....	....	....	....	....	....	....	....
Conversion rates: CFP francs per U.S. dollar..........	0 101 ..	**105.7320**	**96.1056**	**95.9570**	**95.1242**	**87.1882**	**81.4642**	**85.9001**	**90.1008**

[1] Excludes components that have been classified in the categories of Group E.

Table 2. STANDARD PRESENTATION, 2003–2010

(Millions of U.S. dollars)

	Code	2003	2004	2005	2006	2007	2008	2009	2010
CURRENT ACCOUNT	4 993	−119	186	9	160	271	−91	154	2
A. GOODS	4 100	−1,381	−1,260	−1,381	−1,415	−1,636	−1,956	−1,548	−1,642
Credit	2 100	149	179	212	197	193	201	150	160
General merchandise: exports f.o.b.	2 110	148	179	211	196	191	198	146	151
Goods for processing: exports f.o.b.	2 150	....	....	....	....	....	....	....	....
Repairs on goods	2 160	....	....	....	....	....	....	....	....
Goods procured in ports by carriers	2 170	1	1	1	1	1	3	5	9
Nonmonetary gold	2 180	....	....	....	....	....	....	....	....
Debit	3 100	−1,530	−1,440	−1,593	−1,612	−1,829	−2,158	−1,698	−1,802
General merchandise: imports f.o.b.	3 110	−1,513	−1,423	−1,555	−1,549	−1,746	−2,046	−1,622	−1,633
Goods for processing: imports f.o.b.	3 150	....	....	....	....	....	....	....	....
Repairs on goods	3 160	−2	....	....	....	....	....	....	....
Goods procured in ports by carriers	3 170	−15	−17	−38	−63	−83	−111	−75	−169
Nonmonetary gold	3 180	....	....	....	....	....	....	....	....
B. SERVICES	4 200	355	362	344	486	584	473	317	318
Total credit	2 200	*954*	*1,028*	*1,081*	*1,033*	*1,201*	*1,192*	*1,030*	*955*
Total debit	3 200	*−599*	*−666*	*−737*	*−546*	*−617*	*−719*	*−713*	*−637*
Transportation services, credit	2 205	186	226	246	245	292	246	202	227
Passenger	2 850	*171*	*214*	*229*	....	....	....	....	....
Freight	2 851	*16*	*12*	*17*	*245*	*292*	*246*	*202*	*227*
Other	2 852	....	....	....	....	....	....	....	....
Sea transport, passenger	2 207	....	....	....	....	....	....	....	....
Sea transport, freight	2 208	16	12	17	17	24	31	24	29
Sea transport, other	2 209	....	....	....	....	....	....	....	....
Air transport, passenger	2 211	171	214	229	....	....	....	....	....
Air transport, freight	2 212				228	268	215	178	198
Air transport, other	2 213	....	....	....	....	....	....	....	....
Other transport, passenger	2 215	....	....	....	....	....	....	....	....
Other transport, freight	2 216	....	....	....	....	....	....	....	....
Other transport, other	2 217	....	....	....	....	....	....	....	....
Transportation services, debit	3 205	−180	−198	−203	−205	−318	−318	−246	−239
Passenger	3 850	*−99*	*−114*	*−118*	....	....	....	....	....
Freight	3 851	*−81*	*−84*	*−86*	*−205*	*−318*	*−318*	*−246*	*−239*
Other	3 852	....	....	....	....	....	....	....	....
Sea transport, passenger	3 207	....	....	....	....	....	....	....	....
Sea transport, freight	3 208	−81	−84	−86	−71	−69	−89	−71	−72
Sea transport, other	3 209	....	....	....	....	....	....	....	....
Air transport, passenger	3 211	−99	−114	−118	....	....	....	....	....
Air transport, freight	3 212				−134	−249	−229	−175	−167
Air transport, other	3 213	....	....	....	....	....	....	....	....
Other transport, passenger	3 215	....	....	....	....	....	....	....	....
Other transport, freight	3 216	....	....	....	....	....	....	....	....
Other transport, other	3 217	....	....	....	....	....	....	....	....
Travel, credit	2 236	480	523	530	463	537	522	440	403
Business travel	2 237	....	....	....	....	....	....	....	....
Personal travel	2 240	480	523	530	463	537	522	440	403
Travel, debit	3 236	−236	−311	−312	−122	−153	−159	−164	−159
Business travel	3 237	....	....	....	....	....	....	....	....
Personal travel	3 240	−236	−311	−312	−122	−153	−159	−164	−159
Other services, credit	2 200 BA	288	279	304	325	372	424	388	326
Communications	2 245	4	16	19	19	11	40	42	24
Construction	2 249	2	4	3	....	....	....	....	2
Insurance	2 253	2	4	4	9	12	5	2	2
Financial	2 260	1	6	15	4	6	4	5	6
Computer and information	2 262	....	....	....	....	....	....	....	....
Royalties and licence fees	2 266	1	1	1	....	....	....	....	....
Other business services	2 268	125	104	134	137	167	174	164	135
Personal, cultural, and recreational	2 287	8	5	4	4	9	18	6	7
Government, n.i.e.	2 291	146	139	124	152	167	183	168	150
Other services, debit	3 200 BA	−184	−158	−222	−220	−146	−243	−303	−238
Communications	3 245	−4	−7	−9	−8	−6	−19	−71	−68
Construction	3 249	−10	−8	−6	....	−3	−1	−1	−17
Insurance	3 253	−20	−17	−22	−26	−16	−17	−22	−23
Financial	3 260	−1	−6	−5	−5	−4	−21	−34	−4
Computer and information	3 262	....	−2	−1	....	....	....	....	....
Royalties and licence fees	3 266	−2	−2	−1	−2	−1	−2	−3	−3
Other business services	3 268	−138	−106	−166	−168	−109	−172	−158	−112
Personal, cultural, and recreational	3 287	−7	−10	−10	−9	−6	−11	−5	−7
Government, n.i.e.	3 291	−1	−1	−1	−1	−1	−1	−8	−4

Table 2 (Continued). STANDARD PRESENTATION, 2003–2010

(Millions of U.S. dollars)

	Code	2003	2004	2005	2006	2007	2008	2009	2010
C. INCOME..	4 300 ..	**465**	**560**	**521**	**593**	**594**	**671**	**622**	**606**
Total credit...	2 300 ..	*567*	*658*	*588*	*668*	*731*	*822*	*774*	*742*
Total debit..	3 300 ..	*−102*	*−98*	*−67*	*−75*	*−137*	*−150*	*−152*	*−136*
Compensation of employees, credit..................	2 310 ..	**496**	**583**	**546**	**607**	**675**	**752**	**712**	**687**
Compensation of employees, debit...................	3 310 ..	**−25**	**−14**	**−14**	**−15**	**−16**	**−28**	**−30**	**−24**
Investment income, credit..............................	2 320 ..	**71**	**74**	**42**	**60**	**56**	**70**	**62**	**54**
Direct investment income.............................	2 330 ..	....	....	1	....	2	1	....	1
Dividends and distributed branch profits........................	2 332 ..	....	....	1	....	2	1	....	1
Reinvested earnings and undistributed branch profits.....	2 333 ..	....	....	....	....	....	....	....	....
Income on debt (interest)........................	2 334 ..	....	....	....	....	....	....	....	....
Portfolio investment income..........................	2 339 ..	37	44	23	22	15	22	21	15
Income on equity..............................	2 340 ..	....	....	....	....	....	....	....	....
Income on bonds and notes...........................	2 350 ..	37	44	23	22	15	22	21	15
Income on money market instruments........................	2 360 ..	....	....	....	....	....	....	....	....
Other investment income..............................	2 370 ..	34	30	19	38	39	47	42	38
Investment income, debit..............................	3 320 ..	**−78**	**−84**	**−52**	**−60**	**−121**	**−123**	**−122**	**−112**
Direct investment income.............................	3 330 ..	−2	−2	−2	−5	−8	−6	−6	−11
Dividends and distributed branch profits........................	3 332 ..	−2	−2	−2	−5	−8	−6	−6	−11
Reinvested earnings and undistributed branch profits.....	3 333 ..	....	....	....	....	....	....	....	....
Income on debt (interest)........................	3 334 ..	....	....	....	....	....	....	....	....
Portfolio investment income..........................	3 339 ..	−3	−21	−2	−1	−26	−16	−24	−16
Income on equity..............................	3 340 ..	....	....	....	....	....	....	....	....
Income on bonds and notes...........................	3 350 ..	−3	−21	−2	−1	−26	−16	−24	−16
Income on money market instruments........................	3 360 ..	....	....	....	....	....	....	....	....
Other investment income..............................	3 370 ..	−73	−61	−49	−54	−88	−100	−92	−85
D. CURRENT TRANSFERS..............................	4 379 ..	**441**	**524**	**524**	**496**	**730**	**722**	**762**	**719**
Credit...	2 379 ..	**638**	**754**	**751**	**786**	**1,079**	**1,092**	**1,104**	**1,135**
General government...................................	2 380 ..	586	670	669	712	879	894	904	908
Other sectors...	2 390 ..	52	84	83	73	200	198	199	227
Workers' remittances.............................	2 391 ..	12	15	11	14	14	11	16	13
Other current transfers............................	2 392 ..	40	69	71	59	186	187	184	214
Debit...	3 379 ..	**−197**	**−229**	**−227**	**−290**	**−349**	**−370**	**−342**	**−415**
General government...................................	3 380 ..	−40	−50	−64	−136	−158	−170	−159	−172
Other sectors...	3 390 ..	−156	−179	−163	−154	−191	−200	−183	−243
Workers' remittances.............................	3 391 ..	−27	−32	−33	−36	−40	−42	−34	−47
Other current transfers............................	3 392 ..	−130	−147	−130	−118	−152	−158	−149	−196
CAPITAL AND FINANCIAL ACCOUNT....................	4 996 ..	**103**	**−126**	**−33**	**4**	**−334**	**−124**	**−251**	**111**
CAPITAL ACCOUNT...............................	4 994 ..	**−1**	**−1**	**−1**	....	....	....	....	**−1**
Total credit..	2 994 ..	....	....	....	....	....	....	....	....
Total debit...	3 994 ..	*−1*	*−1*	*−1*	....	....	....	....	*−1*
Capital transfers, credit............................	2 400 ..	....	....	....	....	....	....	....	....
General government...................................	2 401 ..	....	....	....	....	....	....	....	....
Debt forgiveness..................................	2 402 ..	....	....	....	....	....	....	....	....
Other capital transfers............................	2 410 ..	....	....	....	....	....	....	....	....
Other sectors...	2 430 ..	....	....	....	....	....	....	....	....
Migrants' transfers...............................	2 431 ..	....	....	....	....	....	....	....	....
Debt forgiveness..................................	2 432 ..	....	....	....	....	....	....	....	....
Other capital transfers............................	2 440 ..	....	....	....	....	....	....	....	....
Capital transfers, debit............................	3 400 ..	**−1**	**−1**	**−1**	....	....	....	....	**−1**
General government...................................	3 401 ..	....	....	....	....	....	....	....	....
Debt forgiveness..................................	3 402 ..	....	....	....	....	....	....	....	....
Other capital transfers............................	3 410 ..	....	....	....	....	....	....	....	....
Other sectors...	3 430 ..	−1	−1	−1	....	....	....	....	−1
Migrants' transfers...............................	3 431 ..	....	....	....	....	....	....	....	....
Debt forgiveness..................................	3 432 ..	....	....	....	....	....	....	....	....
Other capital transfers............................	3 440 ..	−1	−1	−1	....	....	....	....	−1
Nonproduced nonfinancial assets, credit............	2 480 ..	....	....	....	....	....	....	....	....
Nonproduced nonfinancial assets, debit.............	3 480 ..	....	....	....	....	....	....	....	....

Table 2 (Continued). STANDARD PRESENTATION, 2003–2010

(Millions of U.S. dollars)

	Code	2003	2004	2005	2006	2007	2008	2009	2010
FINANCIAL ACCOUNT................................	4 995 ..	**104**	**−125**	**−32**	**4**	**−334**	**−124**	**−251**	**112**
A. DIRECT INVESTMENT............................	4 500 ..	**53**	**−3**	**−8**	**20**	**45**	**−16**	**2**	**6**
Direct investment abroad....................	4 505 ..	**−6**	**−9**	**−16**	**−10**	**−14**	**−30**	**−8**	**−89**
Equity capital..	4 510 ..	−7	−13	−16	−10	−14	−26	−8	−86
Claims on affiliated enterprises...............	4 515 ..	−7	−13	−16	−10	−14	−26	−8	−86
Liabilities to affiliated enterprises...........	4 520 ..	....	....	....	....	....	....	....	....
Reinvested earnings..............................	4 525 ..	....	....						
Other capital..	4 530 ..	2	3	....	....	1	−4	....	−3
Claims on affiliated enterprises...............	4 535 ..	2	3	....	....	1	−4		−3
Liabilities to affiliated enterprises...........	4 540 ..	....	....	....	....				
Direct investment in French Polynesia.............	4 555 ..	**58**	**6**	**8**	**31**	**58**	**14**	**10**	**95**
Equity capital..	4 560 ..	58	8	9	31	55	14	....	90
Claims on direct investors......................	4 565 ..	....	....				....		
Liabilities to direct investors..................	4 570 ..	58	8	9	31	55	14	....	90
Reinvested earnings..............................	4 575 ..							....	....
Other capital..	4 580 ..	....	−2	−1	....	3	....	10	5
Claims on direct investors......................	4 585 ..	....							
Liabilities to direct investors..................	4 590 ..	....	−2	−1		3		10	5
B. PORTFOLIO INVESTMENT........................	4 600 ..	**−75**	**−20**	**−66**	**17**	**20**	**−116**	**−127**	**−2**
Assets..	4 602 ..	**−75**	**−20**	**−66**	**17**	**20**	**−116**	**−127**	**−2**
Equity securities....................................	4 610 ..	....	....	....	....	....	....	....	....
Monetary authorities............................	4 611 ..	....	....	....	....	....	....	....	....
General government..............................	4 612 ..	....	....	....	....	....	....	....	....
Banks..	4 613 ..	....	....	....	....	....	....	....	....
Other sectors..	4 614 ..	....	....	....	....	....	....	....	....
Debt securities......................................	4 619 ..	−75	−20	−66	17	20	−116	−127	−2
Bonds and notes..................................	4 620 ..	−75	−20	−66	17	20	−116	−127	−2
Monetary authorities............................	4 621 ..	....	....	....	....	....	....	....	....
General government..............................	4 622 ..	....	....	....	....	....	....	....	....
Banks..	4 623 ..	....	....	....	....	....	....	....	....
Other sectors..	4 624 ..	−75	−20	−66	17	20	−116	−127	−2
Money market instruments.....................	4 630 ..	....	....	....	....	....	....	....	....
Monetary authorities............................	4 631 ..	....	....	....	....	....	....	....	....
General government..............................	4 632 ..	....	....	....	....	....	....	....	....
Banks..	4 633 ..	....	....	....	....	....	....	....	....
Other sectors..	4 634 ..	....	....	....	....	....	....	....	....
Liabilities..	4 652 ..	....	....	....	....	....	....	....	....
Equity securities....................................	4 660 ..	....	....	....	....	....	....	....	....
Banks..	4 663 ..	....	....	....	....	....	....	....	....
Other sectors..	4 664 ..	....	....	....	....	....	....	....	....
Debt securities......................................	4 669 ..	....	....	....	....	....	....	....	....
Bonds and notes..................................	4 670 ..	....	....	....	....	....	....	....	....
Monetary authorities............................	4 671 ..	....	....	....	....	....	....	....	....
General government..............................	4 672 ..	....	....	....	....	....	....	....	....
Banks..	4 673 ..	....	....	....	....	....	....	....	....
Other sectors..	4 674 ..	....	....	....	....	....	....	....	....
Money market instruments.....................	4 680 ..	....	....	....	....	....	....	....	....
Monetary authorities............................	4 681 ..	....	....	....	....	....	....	....	....
General government..............................	4 682 ..	....	....	....	....	....	....	....	....
Banks..	4 683 ..	....	....	....	....	....	....	....	....
Other sectors..	4 684 ..	....	....	....	....	....	....	....	....
C. FINANCIAL DERIVATIVES........................	4 910 ..	....	....	....	....	....	....	....	....
Monetary authorities............................	4 911 ..	....	....	....	....	....	....	....	....
General government..............................	4 912 ..	....	....	....	....	....	....	....	....
Banks..	4 913 ..	....	....	....	....	....	....	....	....
Other sectors..	4 914 ..	....	....	....	....	....	....	....	....
Assets..	4 900 ..	....	....	....	....	....	....	....	....
Monetary authorities............................	4 901 ..	....	....	....	....	....	....	....	....
General government..............................	4 902 ..	....	....	....	....	....	....	....	....
Banks..	4 903 ..	....	....	....	....	....	....	....	....
Other sectors..	4 904 ..	....	....	....	....	....	....	....	....
Liabilities..	4 905 ..	....	....	....	....	....	....	....	....
Monetary authorities............................	4 906 ..	....	....	....	....	....	....	....	....
General government..............................	4 907 ..	....	....	....	....	....	....	....	....
Banks..	4 908 ..	....	....	....	....	....	....	....	....
Other sectors..	4 909 ..	....	....	....	....	....	....	....	....

Table 2 (Concluded). STANDARD PRESENTATION, 2003–2010

(Millions of U.S. dollars)

	Code	2003	2004	2005	2006	2007	2008	2009	2010
D. OTHER INVESTMENT.....................................	4 700 ..	**127**	**−103**	**41**	**−33**	**−398**	**9**	**−127**	**109**
Assets..	4 703 ..	**64**	**−227**	**−235**	**96**	**529**	**625**	**896**	**688**
Trade credits..	4 706 ..	....	....	....	....	....	....	....	....
General government.............................	4 707 ..	....	....	....	....	....	....	....	....
of which: Short-term........................	4 709 ..	....	....	....	....	....	....	....	....
Other sectors......................................	4 710 ..	....	....	....	....	....	....	....	....
of which: Short-term........................	4 712 ..	....	....	....	....	....	....	....	....
Loans..	4 714 ..	64	−227	−235	96	529	625	896	688
Monetary authorities.............................	4 715 ..	15	54	76	338	733	1,094	964	986
of which: Short-term........................	4 718 ..	*15*	*54*	*76*	*338*	*733*	*1,094*	*964*	*986*
General government.............................	4 719 ..	....	....	....	....	....	....	....	....
of which: Short-term........................	4 721 ..	....	....	....	....	....	....	....	....
Banks...	4 722 ..	141	−55	−212	−175	−74	−318	101	−176
of which: Short-term........................	4 724 ..	*141*	*−55*	*−212*	*−175*	*−74*	*−318*	*101*	*−176*
Other sectors......................................	4 725 ..	−93	−227	−99	−67	−129	−151	−168	−122
of which: Short-term........................	4 727 ..	*−93*	*−227*	*−99*	*−67*	*−129*	*−151*	*−168*	*−122*
Currency and deposits...............................	4 730 ..	....	....	....	....	....	....	....	....
Monetary authorities.............................	4 731 ..	....	....	....	....	....	....	....	....
General government.............................	4 732 ..	....	....	....	....	....	....	....	....
Banks...	4 733 ..	....	....	....	....	....	....	....	....
Other sectors......................................	4 734 ..	....	....	....	....	....	....	....	....
Other assets..	4 736 ..	....	....	....	....	....	....	....	....
Monetary authorities.............................	4 737 ..	....	....	....	....	....	....	....	....
of which: Short-term........................	4 739 ..	....	....	....	....	....	....	....	....
General government.............................	4 740 ..	....	....	....	....	....	....	....	....
of which: Short-term........................	4 742 ..	....	....	....	....	....	....	....	....
Banks...	4 743 ..	....	....	....	....	....	....	....	....
of which: Short-term........................	4 745 ..	....	....	....	....	....	....	....	....
Other sectors......................................	4 746 ..	....	....	....	....	....	....	....	....
of which: Short-term........................	4 748 ..	....	....	....	....	....	....	....	....
Liabilities..	4 753 ..	**63**	**125**	**276**	**−129**	**−927**	**−617**	**−1,023**	**−580**
Trade credits..	4 756 ..	....	....	....	....	....	....	....	....
General government.............................	4 757 ..	....	....	....	....	....	....	....	....
of which: Short-term........................	4 759 ..	....	....	....	....	....	....	....	....
Other sectors......................................	4 760 ..	....	....	....	....	....	....	....	....
of which: Short-term........................	4 762 ..	....	....	....	....	....	....	....	....
Loans..	4 764 ..	63	125	276	−129	−927	−617	−1,023	−580
Monetary authorities.............................	4 765 ..	....	....	....	....	....	....	....	....
of which: Use of Fund credit and loans from the Fund ..	4 766 ..	....	....	....	....	....	....	....	....
of which: Short-term........................	4 768 ..	....	....	....	....	....	....	....	....
General government.............................	4 769 ..	−4	−42	67	−387	−784	−915	−1,001	−890
of which: Short-term........................	4 771 ..	*−4*	*−42*	*67*	*−387*	*−784*	*−915*	*−1,001*	*−890*
Banks...	4 772 ..	−19	180	224	235	−91	307	81	386
of which: Short-term........................	4 774 ..	*−19*	*180*	*224*	*235*	*−91*	*307*	*81*	*386*
Other sectors......................................	4 775 ..	85	−14	−14	22	−52	−9	−103	−75
of which: Short-term........................	4 777 ..	*85*	*−14*	*−14*	*22*	*−52*	*−9*	*−103*	*−75*
Currency and deposits...............................	4 780 ..	....	....	....	....	....	....	....	....
Monetary authorities.............................	4 781 ..	....	....	....	....	....	....	....	....
General government.............................	4 782 ..	....	....	....	....	....	....	....	....
Banks...	4 783 ..	....	....	....	....	....	....	....	....
Other sectors......................................	4 784 ..	....	....	....	....	....	....	....	....
Other liabilities.......................................	4 786 ..	....	....	....	....	....	....	....	....
Monetary authorities.............................	4 787 ..	....	....	....	....	....	....	....	....
of which: Short-term........................	4 789 ..	....	....	....	....	....	....	....	....
General government.............................	4 790 ..	....	....	....	....	....	....	....	....
of which: Short-term........................	4 792 ..	....	....	....	....	....	....	....	....
Banks...	4 793 ..	....	....	....	....	....	....	....	....
of which: Short-term........................	4 795 ..	....	....	....	....	....	....	....	....
Other sectors......................................	4 796 ..	....	....	....	....	....	....	....	....
of which: Short-term........................	4 798 ..	....	....	....	....	....	....	....	....
E. RESERVE ASSETS......................................	4 802 ..	....	....	....	....	....	....	....	....
Monetary gold..	4 812 ..	....	....	....	....	....	....	....	....
Special drawing rights...............................	4 811 ..	....	....	....	....	....	....	....	....
Reserve position in the Fund.......................	4 810 ..	....	....	....	....	....	....	....	....
Foreign exchange......................................	4 803 ..	....	....	....	....	....	....	....	....
Other claims..	4 813 ..	....	....	....	....	....	....	....	....
NET ERRORS AND OMISSIONS............................	4 998 ..	**16**	**−60**	**25**	**−164**	**62**	**215**	**98**	**−113**

Table 1. ANALYTIC PRESENTATION, 2003–2010

(Millions of U.S. dollars)

	Code	2003	2004	2005	2006	2007	2008	2009	2010
A. Current Account[1]	4 993 Z.	**−37**	**257**	**−112**	**−414**	**−294**	**−1,419**	**−824**	**−1,463**
Goods: exports f.o.b.	2 100 ..	783	1,009	1,090	1,345	2,104	1,280	1,018	1,294
Goods: imports f.o.b.	3 100 ..	−1,408	−1,473	−1,641	−1,933	−2,590	−3,036	−2,347	−3,050
Balance on Goods	4 100 ..	*−625*	*−464*	*−551*	*−588*	*−486*	*−1,756*	*−1,329*	*−1,756*
Services: credit	2 200 ..	429	487	380	453	543	583	499	547
Services: debit	3 200 ..	−538	−599	−841	−1,130	−1,320	−1,390	−1,102	−1,384
Balance on Goods and Services	4 991 ..	*−735*	*−576*	*−1,012*	*−1,264*	*−1,263*	*−2,563*	*−1,933*	*−2,593*
Income: credit	2 300 ..	478	529	596	600	597	705	626	659
Income: debit	3 300 ..	−140	−116	−114	−178	−198	−238	−188	−178
Balance on Goods, Services, and Income	4 992 ..	*−396*	*−163*	*−530*	*−842*	*−864*	*−2,096*	*−1,494*	*−2,112*
Current transfers: credit	2 379 Z.	543	609	626	648	878	1,039	986	968
Current transfers: debit	3 379 ..	−183	−189	−209	−220	−308	−362	−315	−319
B. Capital Account[1]	4 994 Z.	**1**	**6**	**9**	**4**	**4**	**1**	**6**	**2**
Capital account: credit	2 994 Z.	7	9	11	11	14	20	12	5
Capital account: debit	3 994 ..	−5	−3	−2	−7	−10	−18	−6	−3
Total, Groups A Plus B	4 981 ..	*−36*	*262*	*−103*	*−410*	*−290*	*−1,418*	*−818*	*−1,460*
C. Financial Account[1]	4 995 W.	**124**	**−196**	**19**	**480**	**22**	**1,286**	**728**	**1,398**
Direct investment abroad	4 505 ..	−14	−11	−31	−31	−7	−64	−58	−76
Direct investment in New Caledonia	4 555 Z.	116	27	−7	749	417	1,746	1,182	1,439
Portfolio investment assets	4 602 ..	8	135	241	−34	−134	218	169	130
Equity securities	4 610 ..	....	....	....	....	....	....	....	....
Debt securities	4 619 ..	8	135	241	−34	−134	218	169	130
Portfolio investment liabilities	4 652 Z.	....	....	....	....	....	....	....	....
Equity securities	4 660 ..	....	....	....	....	....	....	....	....
Debt securities	4 669 Z.	....	....	....	....	....	....	....	....
Financial derivatives	4 910 ..	....	....	....	....	....	....	....	....
Financial derivatives assets	4 900 ..	....	....	....	....	....	....	....	....
Financial derivatives liabilities	4 905 ..	....	....	....	....	....	....	....	....
Other investment assets	4 703 ..	8	−549	−379	−201	−225	−526	−543	−75
Monetary authorities	4 701 ..	....	−42	−41	−70	−74	−298	−263	−119
General government	4 704 ..	....	....	....	....	....	....	....	....
Banks	4 705 ..	−15	−328	−230	1	−26	−92	−64	−93
Other sectors	4 728 ..	22	−179	−109	−132	−125	−136	−215	137
Other investment liabilities	4 753 W.	6	201	194	−3	−29	−88	−22	−21
Monetary authorities	4 753 WA	....	....	....	....	....	....	....	....
General government	4 753 ZB	6	−49	−33	−31	−42	−38	−57	−30
Banks	4 753 ZC	−27	186	213	28	211	−9	45	−51
Other sectors	4 753 ZD	27	64	14	....	−199	−42	−11	60
Total, Groups A Through C	4 983 ..	*89*	*67*	*−85*	*70*	*−268*	*−131*	*−90*	*−62*
D. Net Errors and Omissions	4 998 ..	**−89**	**−67**	**85**	**−70**	**268**	**131**	**90**	**62**
Total, Groups A Through D	4 984 ..	....	....	....	....	....	....	....	....
E. Reserves and Related Items	4 802 A.	....	....	....	....	....	....	....	....
Reserve assets	4 802 ..	....	....	....	....	....	....	....	....
Use of Fund credit and loans	4 766 ..	....	....	....	....	....	....	....	....
Exceptional financing	4 920 ..	....	....	....	....	....	....	....	....
Conversion rates: CFP francs per U.S.dollar	0 101 ..	**105.7320**	**96.1056**	**95.9570**	**95.1242**	**87.1882**	**81.4642**	**85.9001**	**90.1008**

[1] Excludes components that have been classified in the categories of Group E.

Table 2. STANDARD PRESENTATION, 2003–2010

(Millions of U.S. dollars)

	Code	2003	2004	2005	2006	2007	2008	2009	2010
CURRENT ACCOUNT........................	4 993 ..	−37	257	−112	−414	−294	−1,419	−824	−1,463
A. GOODS............................	4 100 ..	−625	−464	−551	−588	−486	−1,756	−1,329	−1,756
Credit............................	2 100 ..	783	1,009	1,090	1,345	2,104	1,280	1,018	1,294
General merchandise: exports f.o.b.	2 110 ..	780	1,008	1,088	1,342	2,094	1,255	1,003	1,270
Goods for processing: exports f.o.b.	2 150 ..	....	....	....	....	....	....	....	....
Repairs on goods	2 160 ..	....	....	....	....	....	....	....	....
Goods procured in ports by carriers	2 170 ..	2	1	1	2	10	25	15	23
Nonmonetary gold	2 180 ..	....	....	....	....	....	....	....	....
Debit............................	3 100 ..	−1,408	−1,473	−1,641	−1,933	−2,590	−3,036	−2,347	−3,050
General merchandise: imports f.o.b.	3 110 ..	−1,401	−1,465	−1,625	−1,910	−2,568	−2,957	−2,321	−3,027
Goods for processing: imports f.o.b.	3 150 ..	....	....	....	....	....	....	....	....
Repairs on goods	3 160 ..	....	....	−2	....	....	....	....	....
Goods procured in ports by carriers	3 170 ..	−6	−8	−14	−22	−22	−79	−26	−22
Nonmonetary gold	3 180 ..	....	....	....	....	....	....	....	....
B. SERVICES........................	4 200 ..	−110	−112	−461	−676	−777	−807	−603	−837
Total credit	2 200 ..	*429*	*487*	*380*	*453*	*543*	*583*	*499*	*547*
Total debit	3 200 ..	*−538*	*−599*	*−841*	*−1,130*	*−1,320*	*−1,390*	*−1,102*	*−1,384*
Transportation services, credit	2 205 ..	66	65	66	78	138	140	117	119
Passenger	2 850 ..	....	....	....	....	....	....	....	....
Freight	2 851 ..	*66*	*65*	*66*	*78*	*138*	*140*	*117*	*119*
Other	2 852 ..	....	....	....	....	....	....	....	....
Sea transport, passenger	2 207 ..	....	....	....	....	....	....	....	....
Sea transport, freight	2 208 ..	21	28	17	26	40	25	22	28
Sea transport, other	2 209 ..	....	....	....	....	....	....	....	....
Air transport, passenger	2 211 ..	....	....	....	....	....	....	....	....
Air transport, freight	2 212 ..	45	37	49	52	99	115	95	91
Air transport, other	2 213 ..	....	....	....	....	....	....	....	....
Other transport, passenger	2 215 ..	....	....	....	....	....	....	....	....
Other transport, freight	2 216 ..	....	....	....	....	....	....	....	....
Other transport, other	2 217 ..	....	....	....	....	....	....	....	....
Transportation services, debit	3 205 ..	−151	−167	−212	−251	−323	−392	−315	−353
Passenger	3 850 ..	....	....	....	....	....	....	....	....
Freight	3 851 ..	*−151*	*−167*	*−212*	*−251*	*−323*	*−392*	*−315*	*−353*
Other	3 852 ..	....	....	....	....	....	....	....	....
Sea transport, passenger	3 207 ..	....	....	....	....	....	....	....	....
Sea transport, freight	3 208 ..	−62	−72	−106	−132	−176	−206	−155	−189
Sea transport, other	3 209 ..	....	....	....	....	....	....	....	....
Air transport, passenger	3 211 ..	....	....	....	....	....	....	....	....
Air transport, freight	3 212 ..	−89	−94	−105	−120	−147	−186	−160	−164
Air transport, other	3 213 ..	....	....	....	....	....	....	....	....
Other transport, passenger	3 215 ..	....	....	....	....	....	....	....	....
Other transport, freight	3 216 ..	....	....	....	....	....	....	....	....
Other transport, other	3 217 ..	....	....	....	....	....	....	....	....
Travel, credit........................	2 236 ..	196	241	149	122	142	152	141	132
Business travel	2 237 ..	....	....	....	....	....	....	....	....
Personal travel	2 240 ..	196	241	149	122	142	152	141	132
Travel, debit........................	3 236 ..	−128	−167	−122	−129	−149	−168	−169	−179
Business travel	3 237 ..	....	....	....	....	....	....	....	....
Personal travel	3 240 ..	−128	−167	−122	−129	−149	−168	−169	−179
Other services, credit	2 200 BA ..	166	181	166	253	263	291	241	296
Communications	2 245 ..	5	6	1	5	2	2	....	2
Construction	2 249 ..	27	29	5	25	16	28	35	37
Insurance	2 253 ..	1	2	1	1	2	1	2	5
Financial	2 260 ..	....	2	1	....	4	10	....	5
Computer and information	2 262 ..	....	....	....	....	....	1	1	1
Royalties and licence fees	2 266 ..	....	....	....	1	....	1	1	1
Other business services	2 268 ..	35	40	40	66	60	73	65	122
Personal, cultural, and recreational	2 287 ..	2	2	1	5	15	6	1	7
Government, n.i.e.	2 291 ..	95	100	117	149	163	170	136	115
Other services, debit	3 200 BA ..	−259	−265	−507	−749	−848	−830	−617	−852
Communications	3 245 ..	−8	−9	−12	−22	−9	−12	−5	−5
Construction	3 249 ..	−33	−11	−93	−118	−322	−80	−15	−32
Insurance	3 253 ..	−22	−26	−20	−21	−29	−32	−34	−32
Financial	3 260 ..	−2	−3	−1	....	−2	−2	−1	−2
Computer and information	3 262 ..	−6	−5	−4	−4	−7	−26	−14	−11
Royalties and licence fees	3 266 ..	−3	−3	−2	−2	−3	−5	−2	−2
Other business services	3 268 ..	−177	−198	−336	−540	−420	−601	−509	−738
Personal, cultural, and recreational	3 287 ..	−8	−11	−38	−41	−56	−72	−38	−29
Government, n.i.e.	3 291 ..	....	−1	−1	−1	−1	−1	−1	−1

Table 2 (Continued). STANDARD PRESENTATION, 2003–2010

(Millions of U.S. dollars)

	Code	2003	2004	2005	2006	2007	2008	2009	2010
C. INCOME	4 300	**338**	**413**	**482**	**422**	**399**	**467**	**438**	**481**
Total credit	2 300	*478*	*529*	*596*	*600*	*597*	*705*	*626*	*659*
Total debit	3 300	*–140*	*–116*	*–114*	*–178*	*–198*	*–238*	*–188*	*–178*
Compensation of employees, credit	2 310	**444**	**485**	**507**	**533**	**488**	**538**	**504**	**547**
Compensation of employees, debit	3 310	**–15**	**–15**	**–17**	**–32**	**–37**	**–50**	**–78**	**–56**
Investment income, credit	2 320	**34**	**44**	**89**	**67**	**109**	**167**	**122**	**112**
Direct investment income	2 330	....	1	3	6	31	65	34	....
Dividends and distributed branch profits	2 332	....	1	3	6	31	65	34	....
Reinvested earnings and undistributed branch profits	2 333	....	....	....	....	....	....	....	....
Income on debt (interest)	2 334	....	....	....	....	....	....	....	....
Portfolio investment income	2 339	17	24	61	33	41	60	42	62
Income on equity	2 340	....	....	....	....	....	....	....	....
Income on bonds and notes	2 350	17	24	61	33	41	60	42	62
Income on money market instruments	2 360	....	....	....	....	....	....	....	....
Other investment income	2 370	18	19	25	27	37	43	47	49
Investment income, debit	3 320	**–125**	**–102**	**–96**	**–146**	**–161**	**–189**	**–110**	**–122**
Direct investment income	3 330	–7	–3	–42	–85	–66	–92	–23	–39
Dividends and distributed branch profits	3 332	–7	–3	–42	–85	–66	–92	–23	–39
Reinvested earnings and undistributed branch profits	3 333	....	....	....	....	....	....	....	....
Income on debt (interest)	3 334	....	....	....	....	....	....	....	....
Portfolio investment income	3 339	–34	–43	–3	–2	–8	–12	–6	–21
Income on equity	3 340	....	....	....	....	....	....	....	....
Income on bonds and notes	3 350	–34	–43	–3	–2	–8	–12	–6	–21
Income on money market instruments	3 360	....	....	....	....	....	....	....	....
Other investment income	3 370	–85	–56	–52	–59	–87	–84	–81	–61
D. CURRENT TRANSFERS	4 379	**359**	**420**	**417**	**428**	**570**	**677**	**671**	**649**
Credit	2 379	**543**	**609**	**626**	**648**	**878**	**1,039**	**986**	**968**
General government	2 380	483	570	585	596	677	807	762	717
Other sectors	2 390	60	39	41	52	201	231	224	251
Workers' remittances	2 391	5	8	5	4	3	6	6	5
Other current transfers	2 392	55	31	36	48	198	225	218	246
Debit	3 379	**–183**	**–189**	**–209**	**–220**	**–308**	**–362**	**–315**	**–319**
General government	3 380	–130	–152	–155	–150	–232	–257	–200	–182
Other sectors	3 390	–54	–37	–55	–70	–76	–104	–116	–137
Workers' remittances	3 391	–6	–7	–10	–18	–18	–18	–15	–10
Other current transfers	3 392	–48	–30	–44	–51	–57	–86	–101	–126
CAPITAL AND FINANCIAL ACCOUNT	4 996	**126**	**–190**	**28**	**484**	**26**	**1,288**	**734**	**1,400**
CAPITAL ACCOUNT	4 994	**1**	**6**	**9**	**4**	**4**	**1**	**6**	**2**
Total credit	2 994	*7*	*9*	*11*	*11*	*14*	*20*	*12*	*5*
Total debit	3 994	*–5*	*–3*	*–2*	*–7*	*–10*	*–18*	*–6*	*–3*
Capital transfers, credit	2 400	**7**	**9**	**11**	**11**	**14**	**20**	**12**	**5**
General government	2 401	....	....	....	....	....	....	....	....
Debt forgiveness	2 402	....	....	....	....	....	....	....	....
Other capital transfers	2 410	....	....	....	....	....	....	....	....
Other sectors	2 430	7	9	11	11	14	20	12	5
Migrants' transfers	2 431	....	....	....	....	....	....	....	....
Debt forgiveness	2 432	....	....	....	....	....	....	....	....
Other capital transfers	2 440	7	9	11	11	14	20	12	5
Capital transfers, debit	3 400	**–5**	**–3**	**–2**	**–7**	**–10**	**–18**	**–6**	**–3**
General government	3 401	....	....	....	....	....	....	....	....
Debt forgiveness	3 402	....	....	....	....	....	....	....	....
Other capital transfers	3 410	....	....	....	....	....	....	....	....
Other sectors	3 430	–5	–3	–2	–7	–10	–18	–6	–3
Migrants' transfers	3 431	....	....	....	....	....	....	....	....
Debt forgiveness	3 432	....	....	....	....	....	....	....	....
Other capital transfers	3 440	–5	–3	–2	–7	–10	–18	–6	–3
Nonproduced nonfinancial assets, credit	2 480	....	....	....	....	....	....	....	....
Nonproduced nonfinancial assets, debit	3 480	....	....	....	....	....	....	....	....

Table 2 (Continued). STANDARD PRESENTATION, 2003–2010

(Millions of U.S. dollars)

	Code	2003	2004	2005	2006	2007	2008	2009	2010
FINANCIAL ACCOUNT	4 995	124	−196	19	480	22	1,286	728	1,398
A. DIRECT INVESTMENT	4 500	102	16	−37	719	411	1,683	1,124	1,363
Direct investment abroad	4 505	−14	−11	−31	−31	−7	−64	−58	−76
Equity capital	4 510	−1	−11	−29	−33	−3	−65	−73	−82
Claims on affiliated enterprises	4 515	−1	−11	−29	−33	−3	−65	−73	−82
Liabilities to affiliated enterprises	4 520	....	....	....	....	....	....	....	....
Reinvested earnings	4 525	....	....	....	....	....	....	....	....
Other capital	4 530	−13	....	−1	3	−4	2	15	6
Claims on affiliated enterprises	4 535	−13	....	−1	3	−4	2	15	6
Liabilities to affiliated enterprises	4 540	....	....	....	....	....	....	....	....
Direct investment in New Caledonia	4 555	116	27	−7	749	417	1,746	1,182	1,439
Equity capital	4 560	1	36	14	80	−2	52	77	95
Claims on direct investors	4 565	....	....	....	....	....	....	....	....
Liabilities to direct investors	4 570	1	36	14	80	−2	52	77	95
Reinvested earnings	4 575	....	....	....	....	....	....	....	....
Other capital	4 580	115	−8	−20	669	419	1,695	1,106	1,344
Claims on direct investors	4 585	....	....	....	....	....	....	....	....
Liabilities to direct investors	4 590	115	−8	−20	669	419	1,695	1,106	1,344
B. PORTFOLIO INVESTMENT	4 600	8	135	241	−34	−134	218	169	130
Assets	4 602	8	135	241	−34	−134	218	169	130
Equity securities	4 610	....	....	....	....	....	....	....	....
Monetary authorities	4 611	....	....	....	....	....	....	....	....
General government	4 612	....	....	....	....	....	....	....	....
Banks	4 613	....	....	....	....	....	....	....	....
Other sectors	4 614	....	....	....	....	....	....	....	....
Debt securities	4 619	8	135	241	−34	−134	218	169	130
Bonds and notes	4 620	8	135	241	−34	−134	218	169	130
Monetary authorities	4 621	....	....	....	....	....	....	....	....
General government	4 622	....	....	....	....	....	....	....	....
Banks	4 623	....	....	....	....	....	....	....	....
Other sectors	4 624	8	135	241	−34	−134	218	169	130
Money market instruments	4 630	....	....	....	....	....	....	....	....
Monetary authorities	4 631	....	....	....	....	....	....	....	....
General government	4 632	....	....	....	....	....	....	....	....
Banks	4 633	....	....	....	....	....	....	....	....
Other sectors	4 634	....	....	....	....	....	....	....	....
Liabilities	4 652	....	....	....	....	....	....	....	....
Equity securities	4 660	....	....	....	....	....	....	....	....
Banks	4 663	....	....	....	....	....	....	....	....
Other sectors	4 664	....	....	....	....	....	....	....	....
Debt securities	4 669	....	....	....	....	....	....	....	....
Bonds and notes	4 670	....	....	....	....	....	....	....	....
Monetary authorities	4 671	....	....	....	....	....	....	....	....
General government	4 672	....	....	....	....	....	....	....	....
Banks	4 673	....	....	....	....	....	....	....	....
Other sectors	4 674	....	....	....	....	....	....	....	....
Money market instruments	4 680	....	....	....	....	....	....	....	....
Monetary authorities	4 681	....	....	....	....	....	....	....	....
General government	4 682	....	....	....	....	....	....	....	....
Banks	4 683	....	....	....	....	....	....	....	....
Other sectors	4 684	....	....	....	....	....	....	....	....
C. FINANCIAL DERIVATIVES	4 910	....	....	....	....	....	....	....	....
Monetary authorities	4 911	....	....	....	....	....	....	....	....
General government	4 912	....	....	....	....	....	....	....	....
Banks	4 913	....	....	....	....	....	....	....	....
Other sectors	4 914	....	....	....	....	....	....	....	....
Assets	4 900	....	....	....	....	....	....	....	....
Monetary authorities	4 901	....	....	....	....	....	....	....	....
General government	4 902	....	....	....	....	....	....	....	....
Banks	4 903	....	....	....	....	....	....	....	....
Other sectors	4 904	....	....	....	....	....	....	....	....
Liabilities	4 905	....	....	....	....	....	....	....	....
Monetary authorities	4 906	....	....	....	....	....	....	....	....
General government	4 907	....	....	....	....	....	....	....	....
Banks	4 908	....	....	....	....	....	....	....	....
Other sectors	4 909	....	....	....	....	....	....	....	....

Table 2 (Concluded). STANDARD PRESENTATION, 2003–2010

(Millions of U.S. dollars)

	Code	2003	2004	2005	2006	2007	2008	2009	2010
D. OTHER INVESTMENT	4 700	14	−347	−185	−205	−254	−614	−565	−96
Assets	4 703	8	−549	−379	−201	−225	−526	−543	−75
Trade credits	4 706	....	....	....	....	....	....	....	....
General government	4 707	....	....	....	....	....	....	....	....
of which: Short-term	4 709	....	....	....	....	....	....	....	....
Other sectors	4 710	....	....	....	....	....	....	....	....
of which: Short-term	4 712	....	....	....	....	....	....	....	....
Loans	4 714	8	−549	−379	−201	−225	−527	−543	−75
Monetary authorities	4 715	....	−42	−41	−70	−74	−298	−263	−119
of which: Short-term	4 718	....	−42	−41	−70	−74	−298	−263	−119
General government	4 719	....	....	....	....	....	....	....	....
of which: Short-term	4 721	....	....	....	....	....	....	....	....
Banks	4 722	−15	−328	−230	1	−26	−92	−64	−93
of which: Short-term	4 724	−15	−328	−230	1	−26	−92	−64	−93
Other sectors	4 725	22	−179	−109	−132	−125	−136	−215	137
of which: Short-term	4 727	22	−179	−109	−132	−125	−136	−215	137
Currency and deposits	4 730	....	....	....	....	....	....	....	....
Monetary authorities	4 731	....	....	....	....	....	....	....	....
General government	4 732	....	....	....	....	....	....	....	....
Banks	4 733	....	....	....	....	....	....	....	....
Other sectors	4 734	....	....	....	....	....	....	....	....
Other assets	4 736	....	....	....	....	....	....	....	....
Monetary authorities	4 737	....	....	....	....	....	....	....	....
of which: Short-term	4 739	....	....	....	....	....	....	....	....
General government	4 740	....	....	....	....	....	....	....	....
of which: Short-term	4 742	....	....	....	....	....	....	....	....
Banks	4 743	....	....	....	....	....	....	....	....
of which: Short-term	4 745	....	....	....	....	....	....	....	....
Other sectors	4 746	....	....	....	....	....	....	....	....
of which: Short-term	4 748	....	....	....	....	....	....	....	....
Liabilities	4 753	6	201	194	−3	−29	−88	−22	−21
Trade credits	4 756	....	....	....	....	....	....	....	....
General government	4 757	....	....	....	....	....	....	....	....
of which: Short-term	4 759	....	....	....	....	....	....	....	....
Other sectors	4 760	....	....	....	....	....	....	....	....
of which: Short-term	4 762	....	....	....	....	....	....	....	....
Loans	4 764	6	201	194	−3	−29	−88	−22	−21
Monetary authorities	4 765	....	....	....	....	....	....	....	....
of which: Use of Fund credit and loans from the Fund	4 766	....	....	....	....	....	....	....	....
of which: Short-term	4 768	....	....	....	....	....	....	....	....
General government	4 769	6	−49	−33	−31	−42	−38	−57	−30
of which: Short-term	4 771	6	−49	−33	−31	−42	−38	−57	−30
Banks	4 772	−27	186	213	28	211	−9	45	−51
of which: Short-term	4 774	−27	186	213	28	211	−9	45	−51
Other sectors	4 775	27	64	14	....	−199	−42	−11	60
of which: Short-term	4 777	27	64	14	....	−199	−42	−11	60
Currency and deposits	4 780	....	....	....	....	....	....	....	....
Monetary authorities	4 781	....	....	....	....	....	....	....	....
General government	4 782	....	....	....	....	....	....	....	....
Banks	4 783	....	....	....	....	....	....	....	....
Other sectors	4 784	....	....	....	....	....	....	....	....
Other liabilities	4 786	....	....	....	....	....	....	....	....
Monetary authorities	4 787	....	....	....	....	....	....	....	....
of which: Short-term	4 789	....	....	....	....	....	....	....	....
General government	4 790	....	....	....	....	....	....	....	....
of which: Short-term	4 792	....	....	....	....	....	....	....	....
Banks	4 793	....	....	....	....	....	....	....	....
of which: Short-term	4 795	....	....	....	....	....	....	....	....
Other sectors	4 796	....	....	....	....	....	....	....	....
of which: Short-term	4 798	....	....	....	....	....	....	....	....
E. RESERVE ASSETS	4 802	....	....	....	....	....	....	....	....
Monetary gold	4 812	....	....	....	....	....	....	....	....
Special drawing rights	4 811	....	....	....	....	....	....	....	....
Reserve position in the Fund	4 810	....	....	....	....	....	....	....	....
Foreign exchange	4 803	....	....	....	....	....	....	....	....
Other claims	4 813	....	....	....	....	....	....	....	....
NET ERRORS AND OMISSIONS	4 998	−89	−67	85	−70	268	131	90	62

Table 1. ANALYTIC PRESENTATION, 2003–2010

(Millions of U.S. dollars)

	Code	2003	2004	2005	2006	2007	2008	2009	2010
A. Current Account[1]	4 993 Z.	**765.9**	**924.5**	**1,983.0**	....	....	....	....	....
Goods: exports f.o.b.	2 100 ..	3,178.5	4,071.6	5,463.9	....	....	....	....	....
Goods: imports f.o.b.	3 100 ..	−1,042.9	−1,215.6	−1,358.8	....	....	....	....	....
Balance on Goods	4 100 ..	*2,135.6*	*2,855.9*	*4,105.0*	....	....	....	....	....
Services: credit	2 200 ..	172.5	156.3	146.2	....	....	....	....	....
Services: debit	3 200 ..	−839.6	−939.1	−1,041.6	....	....	....	....	....
Balance on Goods and Services	4 991 ..	*1,468.5*	*2,073.1*	*3,209.6*	....	....	....	....	....
Income: credit	2 300 ..	48.3	13.3	36.5	....	....	....	....	....
Income: debit	3 300 ..	−569.9	−978.1	−994.1	....	....	....	....	....
Balance on Goods, Services, and Income	4 992 ..	*946.9*	*1,108.3*	*2,252.0*	....	....	....	....	....
Current transfers: credit	2 379 Z.	7.2	9.9	17.7	....	....	....	....	....
Current transfers: debit	3 379 ..	−188.2	−193.7	−286.7	....	....	....	....	....
B. Capital Account[1]	4 994 Z.	**43.1**	....	....	....	....	....	....	....
Capital account: credit	2 994 Z.	43.1	....	....	....	....	....	....	....
Capital account: debit	3 994 ..	....	....	....	....	....	....	....	....
Total, Groups A Plus B.	4 981 ..	*809.0*	*924.5*	*1,983.0*	....	....	....	....	....
C. Financial Account[1]	4 995 W.	**−650.1**	**−499.2**	**−1,342.0**	....	....	....	....	....
Direct investment abroad	4 505 ..	20.9	24.8	−75.4	....	....	....	....	....
Direct investment in Gabon	4 555 Z.	158.0	319.5	242.3	....	....	....	....	....
Portfolio investment assets	4 602 ..	2.5	−9.4	7.6	....	....	....	....	....
Equity securities	4 610 ..	−.1	−7.6	8.3	....	....	....	....	....
Debt securities	4 619 ..	2.6	−1.9	−.7	....	....	....	....	....
Portfolio investment liabilities	4 652 Z.	3.7	−1.4	.7	....	....	....	....	....
Equity securities	4 660 ..	....	....	....	....	....	....	....	....
Debt securities	4 669 Z.	3.7	−1.4	.7	....	....	....	....	....
Financial derivatives	4 910 ..	....	....	....	....	....	....	....	....
Financial derivatives assets	4 900 ..	....	....	....	....	....	....	....	....
Financial derivatives liabilities	4 905 ..	....	....	....	....	....	....	....	....
Other investment assets	4 703 ..	−355.7	−511.8	−1,079.1	....	....	....	....	....
Monetary authorities	4 701 ..	....	....	....	....	....	....	....	....
General government	4 704 ..	....	....	....	....	....	....	....	....
Banks	4 705 ..	−24.2	−196.6	−141.5	....	....	....	....	....
Other sectors	4 728 ..	−331.4	−315.2	−937.6	....	....	....	....	....
Other investment liabilities	4 753 W.	−479.5	−320.9	−438.1	....	....	....	....	....
Monetary authorities	4 753 WA	−10.5	24.7	−18.2	....	....	....	....	....
General government	4 753 ZB	−340.1	−273.6	−262.1	....	....	....	....	....
Banks	4 753 ZC	−18.1	−7.4	−19.8	....	....	....	....	....
Other sectors	4 753 ZD	−110.8	−64.6	−138.0	....	....	....	....	....
Total, Groups A Through C.	4 983 ..	*158.9*	*425.2*	*641.0*	....	....	....	....	....
D. Net Errors and Omissions	4 998 ..	**−259.8**	**−357.0**	**−415.1**	....	....	....	....	....
Total, Groups A Through D.	4 984 ..	*−100.9*	*68.2*	*225.9*	....	....	....	....	....
E. Reserves and Related Items	4 802 A.	**100.9**	**−68.2**	**−225.9**	....	....	....	....	....
Reserve assets	4 802 ..	−25.4	−210.9	−299.5	....	....	....	....	....
Use of Fund credit and loans	4 766 ..	−14.6	37.2	−24.5	....	....	....	....	....
Exceptional financing	4 920 ..	140.8	105.5	98.1	....	....	....	....	....
Conversion rates: CFA francs per U.S. dollar	0 101 ..	**581.20**	**528.28**	**527.47**	**522.89**	**479.27**	**447.81**	**472.19**	**495.28**

[1] Excludes components that have been classified in the categories of Group E.

Table 2. STANDARD PRESENTATION, 2003–2010

(Millions of U.S. dollars)

	Code	2003	2004	2005	2006	2007	2008	2009	2010
CURRENT ACCOUNT	4 993	765.9	924.5	1,983.0	....	....	....	....	....
A. GOODS	4 100	2,135.6	2,855.9	4,105.0	....	....	....	....	....
Credit	2 100	3,178.5	4,071.6	5,463.9	....	....	....	....	....
General merchandise: exports f.o.b.	2 110	3,176.4	4,070.8	5,458.2	....	....	....	....	....
Goods for processing: exports f.o.b.	2 150	....	....	....		....	....		
Repairs on goods	2 160	....	....	....	....	....	....	....	
Goods procured in ports by carriers	2 170	2.1	.7	5.7	....	....	....	....	....
Nonmonetary gold	2 180	....	....	....		....			
Debit	3 100	–1,042.9	–1,215.6	–1,358.8	....	....	....	....	....
General merchandise: imports f.o.b.	3 110	–1,040.9	–1,207.0	–1,358.7	....	....	....	....	
Goods for processing: imports f.o.b.	3 150	....	....	....		....	....		
Repairs on goods	3 160	....	....	....	....	....	....	....	
Goods procured in ports by carriers	3 170	–2.0	–8.7	–.2	....	....	....	....	....
Nonmonetary gold	3 180	....	....						
B. SERVICES	4 200	–667.1	–782.8	–895.4	....	....	....	....	....
Total credit	2 200	*172.5*	*156.3*	*146.2*	....	....	....		
Total debit	3 200	*–839.6*	*–939.1*	*–1,041.6*	....	....	....		
Transportation services, credit	2 205	84.6	81.3	26.4	....	....	....	....	....
Passenger	2 850	*69.4*	*63.7*	*3.9*	....	....	....	....	
Freight	2 851	*15.1*	*17.3*	*19.9*	....	....	....	....	
Other	2 852	*.1*	*.2*	*2.6*	....	....	....	....	....
Sea transport, passenger	2 207	....	....	....		....			
Sea transport, freight	2 208	15.1	17.3	19.9	....	....	....		
Sea transport, other	2 209	....	....	....		....			
Air transport, passenger	2 211	69.4	63.7	3.9	....	....	....		
Air transport, freight	2 212	....	....	....		....			
Air transport, other	2 213	.1	.2	2.6	....	....	....		....
Other transport, passenger	2 215	....	....	....		....			
Other transport, freight	2 216	....	....	....		....			
Other transport, other	2 217	....	....	....		....			
Transportation services, debit	3 205	–265.0	–308.8	–320.2	....	....	....	....	....
Passenger	3 850	*–45.0*	*–60.8*	*–71.9*	....	....	....	....	
Freight	3 851	*–186.6*	*–222.1*	*–247.1*	....	....	....	....	
Other	3 852	*–33.4*	*–26.0*	*–1.2*	....	....	....	....	
Sea transport, passenger	3 207	....	....	....		....			
Sea transport, freight	3 208	–124.4	–148.1	–164.7	....	....	....		
Sea transport, other	3 209	....	....	....		....			
Air transport, passenger	3 211	–45.0	–60.8	–71.9	....	....	....		
Air transport, freight	3 212	–62.2	–74.0	–82.4	....	....	....		
Air transport, other	3 213	–33.4	–26.0	–1.2	....	....	....		
Other transport, passenger	3 215	....	....	....		....			
Other transport, freight	3 216	....	....	....		....			
Other transport, other	3 217	....	....	....		....			
Travel, credit	2 236	14.5	9.8	9.3	....	....	....	....	....
Business travel	2 237	2.2	2.0	1.8	....	....	....	....	
Personal travel	2 240	12.3	7.8	7.4	....	....	....	....	
Travel, debit	3 236	–193.9	–213.9	–274.3	....	....	....	....	....
Business travel	3 237	–122.9	–108.4	–97.3	....	....	....	....	
Personal travel	3 240	–70.9	–105.5	–177.0	....	....	....	....	
Other services, credit	2 200 BA	73.4	65.3	110.5	....	....	....	....	....
Communications	2 245	....	....	....		....	....		
Construction	2 249	....	....	....		....	....		
Insurance	2 253	51.3	23.2	29.0	....	....	....		
Financial	2 260	....	....	....		....			
Computer and information	2 262	2.1	1.5	6.1	....	....	....		
Royalties and licence fees	2 266	....	....	....	....	....	....		
Other business services	2 268	14.3	20.1	49.5	....	....	....		
Personal, cultural, and recreational	2 287	....	....	....		....	....		
Government, n.i.e.	2 291	5.7	20.5	26.0	....	....	....		
Other services, debit	3 200 BA	–380.7	–416.4	–447.1	....	....	....	....	....
Communications	3 245	....	....	....		....	....		
Construction	3 249	....	....	....		....	....		....
Insurance	3 253	–46.9	–53.2	–66.3	....	....	....		
Financial	3 260	....	....	....		....			
Computer and information	3 262	–11.1	–8.5	–10.6	....	....	....		
Royalties and licence fees	3 266	....	....	....		....	....		
Other business services	3 268	–304.5	–336.4	–348.9	....	....	....		
Personal, cultural, and recreational	3 287	....	....	....		....	....		
Government, n.i.e.	3 291	–18.2	–18.3	–21.3	....	....	....		

Table 2 (Continued). STANDARD PRESENTATION, 2003–2010

(Millions of U.S. dollars)

	Code	2003	2004	2005	2006	2007	2008	2009	2010
C. INCOME	4 300	**−521.6**	**−964.8**	**−957.6**	....	....	....	....	....
Total credit	2 300	*48.3*	*13.3*	*36.5*	....	....	....	....	....
Total debit	3 300	*−569.9*	*−978.1*	*−994.1*	....	....	....	....	....
Compensation of employees, credit	2 310	**2.2**	**5.4**	**9.5**	....	....	....	....	....
Compensation of employees, debit	3 310	**−5.7**	**−19.1**	**−22.2**	....	....	....	....	....
Investment income, credit	2 320	**46.1**	**7.9**	**26.9**	....	....	....	....	....
Direct investment income	2 330	41.3	1.9	13.7	....	....	....	....	....
Dividends and distributed branch profits	2 332	4.6	1.4	3.0	....	....	....	....	....
Reinvested earnings and undistributed branch profits	2 333	36.6	.5	10.7	....	....	....	....	....
Income on debt (interest)	2 334	....	....	....	....	....	....	....	....
Portfolio investment income	2 339	.6	.6	.5	....	....	....	....	....
Income on equity	2 340	.1	.4	....	....	....	....	....	....
Income on bonds and notes	2 350	.5	.2	.5	....	....	....	....	....
Income on money market instruments	2 360	....	....	....	....	....	....	....	....
Other investment income	2 370	4.3	5.3	12.7	....	....	....	....	....
Investment income, debit	3 320	**−564.2**	**−959.0**	**−971.9**	....	....	....	....	....
Direct investment income	3 330	−358.7	−722.5	−764.7	....	....	....	....	....
Dividends and distributed branch profits	3 332	−246.4	−376.9	−435.1	....	....	....	....	....
Reinvested earnings and undistributed branch profits	3 333	−112.2	−345.6	−329.6	....	....	....	....	....
Income on debt (interest)	3 334	....	....	....	....	....	....	....	....
Portfolio investment income	3 339	−.7	−.6	−1.6	....	....	....	....	....
Income on equity	3 340	....	−.5	−1.3	....	....	....	....	....
Income on bonds and notes	3 350	−.7	....	−.3	....	....	....	....	....
Income on money market instruments	3 360	....	....	....	....	....	....	....	....
Other investment income	3 370	−204.9	−236.0	−205.6	....	....	....	....	....
D. CURRENT TRANSFERS	4 379	**−181.0**	**−183.9**	**−269.0**	....	....	....	....	....
Credit	2 379	**7.2**	**9.9**	**17.7**	....	....	....	....	....
General government	2 380	.8	2.1	3.0	....	....	....	....	....
Other sectors	2 390	6.4	7.8	14.7	....	....	....	....	....
Workers' remittances	2 391	3.8	1.4	1.5	....	....	....	....	....
Other current transfers	2 392	2.6	6.4	13.2	....	....	....	....	....
Debit	3 379	**−188.2**	**−193.7**	**−286.7**	....	....	....	....	....
General government	3 380	−46.3	−65.0	−56.0	....	....	....	....	....
Other sectors	3 390	−142.0	−128.8	−230.7	....	....	....	....	....
Workers' remittances	3 391	−109.5	−91.2	−163.4	....	....	....	....	....
Other current transfers	3 392	−32.5	−37.5	−67.3	....	....	....	....	....
CAPITAL AND FINANCIAL ACCOUNT	4 996	**−506.1**	**−567.5**	**−1,567.9**	....	....	....	....	....
CAPITAL ACCOUNT	4 994	**43.1**	....	....	....	....	....	....	....
Total credit	2 994	*43.1*	....	....	....	....	....	....	....
Total debit	3 994	....	....	....	....	....	....	....	....
Capital transfers, credit	2 400	**43.1**	....	....	....	....	....	....	....
General government	2 401	43.1	....	....	....	....	....	....	....
Debt forgiveness	2 402	42.6	....	....	....	....	....	....	....
Other capital transfers	2 410	.6	....	....	....	....	....	....	....
Other sectors	2 430	....	....	....	....	....	....	....	....
Migrants' transfers	2 431	....	....	....	....	....	....	....	....
Debt forgiveness	2 432	....	....	....	....	....	....	....	....
Other capital transfers	2 440	....	....	....	....	....	....	....	....
Capital transfers, debit	3 400	....	....	....	....	....	....	....	....
General government	3 401	....	....	....	....	....	....	....	....
Debt forgiveness	3 402	....	....	....	....	....	....	....	....
Other capital transfers	3 410	....	....	....	....	....	....	....	....
Other sectors	3 430	....	....	....	....	....	....	....	....
Migrants' transfers	3 431	....	....	....	....	....	....	....	....
Debt forgiveness	3 432	....	....	....	....	....	....	....	....
Other capital transfers	3 440	....	....	....	....	....	....	....	....
Nonproduced nonfinancial assets, credit	2 480	....	....	....	....	....	....	....	....
Nonproduced nonfinancial assets, debit	3 480	....	....	....	....	....	....	....	....

Table 2 (Continued). STANDARD PRESENTATION, 2003–2010

(Millions of U.S. dollars)

	Code	2003	2004	2005	2006	2007	2008	2009	2010
FINANCIAL ACCOUNT	4 995	**−549.2**	**−567.5**	**−1,567.9**	....	....	....	....	....
A. DIRECT INVESTMENT	4 500	**178.9**	**344.3**	**166.9**	....	....	....	....	....
Direct investment abroad	4 505	**20.9**	**24.8**	**−75.4**	....	....	....	....	....
Equity capital	4 510	2.0	1.3	−9.0	....	....	....	....	....
Claims on affiliated enterprises	4 515	3.6	3.1	....	....	....	....	....	....
Liabilities to affiliated enterprises	4 520	−1.7	−1.9	−9.0	....	....	....	....	....
Reinvested earnings	4 525	−36.6	−.5	−10.7	....	....	....	....	....
Other capital	4 530	55.5	24.0	−55.7	....	....	....	....	....
Claims on affiliated enterprises	4 535	52.1	30.6	−53.1	....	....	....	....	....
Liabilities to affiliated enterprises	4 540	3.4	−6.6	−2.7	....	....	....	....	....
Direct investment in Gabon	4 555	**158.0**	**319.5**	**242.3**	....	....	....	....	....
Equity capital	4 560	6.1	−25.2	26.3	....	....	....	....	....
Claims on direct investors	4 565	6.1	.3	26.3	....	....	....	....	....
Liabilities to direct investors	4 570	....	−25.5	....	....	....	....	....	....
Reinvested earnings	4 575	112.2	345.6	329.6	....	....	....	....	....
Other capital	4 580	39.7	−.8	−113.5	....	....	....	....	....
Claims on direct investors	4 585	54.0	−3.2	−121.8	....	....	....	....	....
Liabilities to direct investors	4 590	−14.4	2.4	8.2	....	....	....	....	....
B. PORTFOLIO INVESTMENT	4 600	**6.2**	**−10.8**	**8.7**	....	....	....	....	....
Assets	4 602	**2.5**	**−9.4**	**7.6**	....	....	....	....	....
Equity securities	4 610	−.1	−7.6	8.3	....	....	....	....	....
Monetary authorities	4 611	....	....	....	....	....	....	....	....
General government	4 612	....	....	....	....	....	....	....	....
Banks	4 613	....	−7.5	7.2	....	....	....	....	....
Other sectors	4 614	−.1	−.1	1.0	....	....	....	....	....
Debt securities	4 619	2.6	−1.9	−.7	....	....	....	....	....
Bonds and notes	4 620	2.6	−1.9	−.7	....	....	....	....	....
Monetary authorities	4 621	....	....	....	....	....	....	....	....
General government	4 622	....	....	....	....	....	....	....	....
Banks	4 623	....	....	....	....	....	....	....	....
Other sectors	4 624	2.6	−1.9	−.7	....	....	....	....	....
Money market instruments	4 630	....	....	....	....	....	....	....	....
Monetary authorities	4 631	....	....	....	....	....	....	....	....
General government	4 632	....	....	....	....	....	....	....	....
Banks	4 633	....	....	....	....	....	....	....	....
Other sectors	4 634	....	....	....	....	....	....	....	....
Liabilities	4 652	**3.7**	**−1.4**	**1.1**	....	....	....	....	....
Equity securities	4 660	....	....	....	....	....	....	....	....
Banks	4 663	....	....	....	....	....	....	....	....
Other sectors	4 664	....	....	....	....	....	....	....	....
Debt securities	4 669	3.7	−1.4	1.1	....	....	....	....	....
Bonds and notes	4 670	−.1	....	1.1	....	....	....	....	....
Monetary authorities	4 671	....	....	....	....	....	....	....	....
General government	4 672	....	....	....	....	....	....	....	....
Banks	4 673	....	....	....	....	....	....	....	....
Other sectors	4 674	−.1	....	1.1	....	....	....	....	....
Money market instruments	4 680	3.8	−1.4	....	....	....	....	....	....
Monetary authorities	4 681	....	....	....	....	....	....	....	....
General government	4 682	....	....	....	....	....	....	....	....
Banks	4 683	....	−.2	....	....	....	....	....	....
Other sectors	4 684	3.8	−1.2	....	....	....	....	....	....
C. FINANCIAL DERIVATIVES	4 910	....	....	....	....	....	....	....	....
Monetary authorities	4 911	....	....	....	....	....	....	....	....
General government	4 912	....	....	....	....	....	....	....	....
Banks	4 913	....	....	....	....	....	....	....	....
Other sectors	4 914	....	....	....	....	....	....	....	....
Assets	4 900	....	....	....	....	....	....	....	....
Monetary authorities	4 901	....	....	....	....	....	....	....	....
General government	4 902	....	....	....	....	....	....	....	....
Banks	4 903	....	....	....	....	....	....	....	....
Other sectors	4 904	....	....	....	....	....	....	....	....
Liabilities	4 905	....	....	....	....	....	....	....	....
Monetary authorities	4 906	....	....	....	....	....	....	....	....
General government	4 907	....	....	....	....	....	....	....	....
Banks	4 908	....	....	....	....	....	....	....	....
Other sectors	4 909	....	....	....	....	....	....	....	....

Table 2 (Concluded). STANDARD PRESENTATION, 2003–2010

(Millions of U.S. dollars)

	Code	2003	2004	2005	2006	2007	2008	2009	2010
D. OTHER INVESTMENT	4 700 ..	**−708.9**	**−690.0**	**−1,444.0**	....	....	....	....	....
Assets	4 703 ..	**−355.7**	**−511.8**	**−1,079.1**	....	....	....	....	....
Trade credits	4 706 ..	80.3	−171.9	−350.8	....	....	....	....	....
General government	4 707 ..	....	....	....	....	....	....	....	....
of which: Short-term	4 709 ..	....	....	....	....	....	....	....	....
Other sectors	4 710 ..	80.3	−171.9	−350.8	....	....	....	....	....
of which: Short-term	4 712 ..	....	....	....	....	....	....	....	....
Loans	4 714 ..	1.5	−17.5	19.3	....	....	....	....	....
Monetary authorities	4 715 ..	....	....	....	....	....	....	....	....
of which: Short-term	4 718 ..	....	....	....	....	....	....	....	....
General government	4 719 ..	....	....	....	....	....	....	....	....
of which: Short-term	4 721 ..	....	....	....	....	....	....	....	....
Banks	4 722 ..	−5.6	−22.3	27.0	....	....	....	....	....
of which: Short-term	4 724 ..	....	....	....	....	....	....	....	....
Other sectors	4 725 ..	7.0	4.8	−7.8	....	....	....	....	....
of which: Short-term	4 727 ..	....	....	....	....	....	....	....	....
Currency and deposits	4 730 ..	−436.9	−303.7	−740.6	....	....	....	....	....
Monetary authorities	4 731 ..	....	....	....	....	....	....	....	....
General government	4 732 ..	....	....	....	....	....	....	....	....
Banks	4 733 ..	−19.8	−159.7	−183.8	....	....	....	....	....
Other sectors	4 734 ..	−417.1	−144.0	−556.8	....	....	....	....	....
Other assets	4 736 ..	−.5	−18.6	−7.0	....	....	....	....	....
Monetary authorities	4 737 ..	....	....	....	....	....	....	....	....
of which: Short-term	4 739 ..	....	....	....	....	....	....	....	....
General government	4 740 ..	....	....	....	....	....	....	....	....
of which: Short-term	4 742 ..	....	....	....	....	....	....	....	....
Banks	4 743 ..	1.1	−14.6	15.2	....	....	....	....	....
of which: Short-term	4 745 ..	*1.1*	*−14.6*	*15.2*	....	....	....	....	....
Other sectors	4 746 ..	−1.6	−4.0	−22.2	....	....	....	....	....
of which: Short-term	4 748 ..	*−1.6*	*−4.0*	*−22.2*	....	....	....	....	....
Liabilities	4 753 ..	**−353.2**	**−178.2**	**−364.9**	....	....	....	....	....
Trade credits	4 756 ..	−81.4	−55.6	11.1	....	....	....	....	....
General government	4 757 ..	....	....	....	....	....	....	....	....
of which: Short-term	4 759 ..	....	....	....	....	....	....	....	....
Other sectors	4 760 ..	−81.4	−55.6	11.1	....	....	....	....	....
of which: Short-term	4 762 ..	*−77.1*	*−55.6*	*11.1*	....	....	....	....	....
Loans	4 764 ..	−359.4	−393.3	−321.1	....	....	....	....	....
Monetary authorities	4 765 ..	−14.6	37.2	−24.5	....	....	....	....	....
of which: Use of Fund credit and loans from the Fund	4 766 ..	*−14.6*	*37.2*	*−24.5*	....	....	....	....	....
of which: Short-term	4 768 ..	....	....	....	....	....	....	....	....
General government	4 769 ..	−327.5	−411.1	−295.1	....	....	....	....	....
of which: Short-term	4 771 ..	....	....	....	....	....	....	....	....
Banks	4 772 ..	−7.6	−.1	3.3	....	....	....	....	....
of which: Short-term	4 774 ..	*−7.6*	*−1.8*	*1.9*	....	....	....	....	....
Other sectors	4 775 ..	−9.7	−19.3	−4.8	....	....	....	....	....
of which: Short-term	4 777 ..	*−4.0*	*−22.5*	*−10.2*	....	....	....	....	....
Currency and deposits	4 780 ..	.2	−2.0	−13.4	....	....	....	....	....
Monetary authorities	4 781 ..	....	....	....	....	....	....	....	....
General government	4 782 ..	....	....	....	....	....	....	....	....
Banks	4 783 ..	−10.7	−7.2	−21.1	....	....	....	....	....
Other sectors	4 784 ..	10.9	5.2	7.7	....	....	....	....	....
Other liabilities	4 786 ..	87.3	272.7	−41.5	....	....	....	....	....
Monetary authorities	4 787 ..	−10.5	24.7	−18.2	....	....	....	....	....
of which: Short-term	4 789 ..	*−10.5*	*24.7*	*−18.2*	....	....	....	....	....
General government	4 790 ..	128.3	243.1	128.7	....	....	....	....	....
of which: Short-term	4 792 ..	*114.4*	*−8.7*	*−8.4*	....	....	....	....	....
Banks	4 793 ..	.2	−.1	....	....	....	....	....	....
of which: Short-term	4 795 ..	*.2*	*−.1*	....	....	....	....	....	....
Other sectors	4 796 ..	−30.6	5.1	−152.0	....	....	....	....	....
of which: Short-term	4 798 ..	*−30.6*	*5.1*	*−152.0*	....	....	....	....	....
E. RESERVE ASSETS	4 802 ..	**−25.4**	**−210.9**	**−299.5**	....	....	....	....	....
Monetary gold	4 812 ..	....	....	....	....	....	....	....	....
Special drawing rights	4 811 ..	....	−5.7	6.0	....	....	....	....	....
Reserve position in the Fund	4 810 ..	....	....	−.1	....	....	....	....	....
Foreign exchange	4 803 ..	−25.4	−205.3	−305.4	....	....	....	....	....
Other claims	4 813 ..	....	....	....	....	....	....	....	....
NET ERRORS AND OMISSIONS	4 998 ..	**−259.8**	**−357.0**	**−415.1**	....	....	....	....	....

Table 1. ANALYTIC PRESENTATION, FISCAL YEARS 2003–2010 ENDING JUNE 30

(Millions of U.S. dollars)

	Code	2003	2004	2005	2006	2007	2008	2009	2010
A. Current Account[1]............	4 993 Z.	**−2.08**	**−43.50**	**−50.50**	**−72.34**	**−65.74**	**2.93**	**29.16**	**17.16**
Goods: exports f.o.b.....................	2 100 ..	67.67	106.80	104.32	108.86	134.32	205.50	174.17	167.38
Goods: imports f.o.b.....................	3 100 ..	−136.31	−202.77	−222.61	−222.21	−279.55	−274.55	−259.96	−236.31
Balance on Goods....................	4 100 ..	*−68.64*	*−95.97*	*−118.28*	*−113.35*	*−145.23*	*−69.05*	*−85.79*	*−68.93*
Services: credit............................	2 200 ..	73.08	71.56	82.21	92.08	127.94	117.58	104.19	88.26
Services: debit.............................	3 200 ..	−31.61	−44.73	−46.88	−94.08	−86.75	−85.65	−82.57	−71.60
Balance on Goods and Services....	4 991 ..	*−27.17*	*−69.14*	*−82.95*	*−115.35*	*−104.04*	*−37.12*	*−64.16*	*−52.27*
Income: credit.............................	2 300 ..	4.10	1.75	3.23	4.53	8.99	12.72	11.68	14.35
Income: debit..............................	3 300 ..	−27.84	−28.93	−35.56	−42.39	−53.52	−47.15	−19.78	−22.40
Balance on Goods, Services, and Income....	4 992 ..	*−50.90*	*−96.33*	*−115.28*	*−153.21*	*−148.57*	*−71.56*	*−72.26*	*−60.31*
Current transfers: credit...............	2 379 Z.	77.51	76.54	90.92	107.60	105.80	96.48	160.21	212.75
Current transfers: debit................	3 379 ..	−28.69	−23.71	−26.14	−26.74	−22.97	−21.99	−58.79	−135.28
B. Capital Account[1]..............	4 994 Z.	....	....	....	....	**.49**	....	....	....
Capital account: credit.................	2 994 Z.	....	....	....	....	.49	....	....	....
Capital account: debit..................	3 994 ..	....	....	....	....	....	....	....	....
Total, Groups A Plus B...............	4 981 ..	*−2.08*	*−43.50*	*−50.50*	*−72.34*	*−65.26*	*2.93*	*29.16*	*17.16*
C. Financial Account[1]...........	4 995 W.	**−8.58**	**45.93**	**42.63**	**78.57**	**92.97**	**11.92**	**18.93**	**−15.73**
Direct investment abroad.............	4 505 ..	....	....	....	....	....	....	....	....
Direct investment in The Gambia...	4 555 Z.	19.09	55.53	53.65	82.21	78.10	78.61	39.45	37.37
Portfolio investment assets...........	4 602 ..	....	....	....	....	....	....	....	....
Equity securities......................	4 610 ..	....	....	....	....	....	....	....	....
Debt securities........................	4 619 ..	....	....	....	....	....	....	....	....
Portfolio investment liabilities.......	4 652 Z.	....	....	....	....	....	....	....	....
Equity securities......................	4 660 ..	....	....	....	....	....	....	....	....
Debt securities........................	4 669 Z.	....	....	....	....	....	....	....	....
Financial derivatives....................	4 910 ..	....	....	....	....	....	....	....	....
Financial derivatives assets..........	4 900 ..	....	....	....	....	....	....	....	....
Financial derivatives liabilities......	4 905 ..	....	....	....	....	....	....	....	....
Other investment assets..............	4 703 ..	−17.12	−15.04	−14.05	−14.10	34.18	1.30	20.06	20.30
Monetary authorities................	4 701 ..	....	....	....	....	....	....	....	....
General government................	4 704 ..	....	....	....	....	....	....	....	....
Banks....................................	4 705 ..	−17.12	−15.04	−14.05	−14.10	20.53	−10.11	5.88	12.87
Other sectors..........................	4 728 ..	....	....	....	....	13.66	11.41	14.18	7.43
Other investment liabilities..........	4 753 W.	−10.55	5.44	3.02	10.46	−19.31	−67.99	−40.58	−73.40
Monetary authorities................	4 753 WA	....	....	....	....	....	....	38.53	....
General government................	4 753 ZB	....	....	....	....	....	....	....	....
Banks....................................	4 753 ZC	−14.06	1.29	−1.51	.68	19.64	1.46	9.34	−10.81
Other sectors..........................	4 753 ZD	3.51	4.15	4.53	9.79	−38.95	−69.45	−88.45	−62.58
Total, Groups A Through C........	4 983 ..	*−10.66*	*2.43*	*−7.87*	*6.22*	*27.71*	*14.85*	*48.08*	*1.42*
D. Net Errors and Omissions.....	4 998 ..	**5.55**	**−3.30**	**−34.08**	**−5.13**	**−33.66**	**−37.53**	**−27.82**	**−94.71**
Total, Groups A Through D........	4 984 ..	*−5.10*	*−.87*	*−41.95*	*1.09*	*−5.95*	*−22.68*	*20.26*	*−93.28*
E. Reserves and Related Items....	4 802 A.	**5.10**	**.87**	**41.95**	**−1.09**	**5.95**	**22.68**	**−20.26**	**93.28**
Reserve assets............................	4 802 ..	−9.63	−30.32	−10.12	−20.57	12.77	6.30	−69.69	9.79
Use of Fund credit and loans.........	4 766 ..	....	−11.14	−2.03	−4.04	−12.42	6.38	15.63	3.08
Exceptional financing..................	4 920 ..	14.73	42.33	54.10	23.52	5.60	10.00	33.79	80.42
Conversion rates: dalasis per U.S. dollar....	0 101 ..	**27.306**	**30.030**	**28.575**	**28.066**	**24.875**	**22.192**	**26.644**	**28.012**

[1] Excludes components that have been classified in the categories of Group E.

Table 2. STANDARD PRESENTATION, FISCAL YEARS 2003–2010 ENDING JUNE 30

(Millions of U.S. dollars)

	Code	2003	2004	2005	2006	2007	2008	2009	2010
CURRENT ACCOUNT	4 993 ..	**2.75**	**−30.32**	**−43.39**	**−65.60**	**−58.41**	**10.85**	**62.95**	**52.36**
A. GOODS	4 100 ..	**−68.64**	**−95.97**	**−118.28**	**−113.35**	**−145.23**	**−69.05**	**−85.79**	**−68.93**
Credit	2 100 ..	**67.67**	**106.80**	**104.32**	**108.86**	**134.32**	**205.50**	**174.17**	**167.38**
General merchandise: exports f.o.b.	2 110 ..	60.59	100.85	96.08	102.22	125.05	189.01	170.02	161.85
Goods for processing: exports f.o.b.	2 150 ..	....	....	....	....	....	....	....	....
Repairs on goods	2 160 ..	....	....	....	....	....	....	....	....
Goods procured in ports by carriers	2 170 ..	7.08	5.95	8.25	6.65	9.27	16.49	4.15	5.53
Nonmonetary gold	2 180 ..	....	....	....	....	....	....	....	....
Debit	3 100 ..	**−136.31**	**−202.77**	**−222.61**	**−222.21**	**−279.55**	**−274.55**	**−259.96**	**−236.31**
General merchandise: imports f.o.b.	3 110 ..	−136.31	−202.77	−222.61	−222.21	−279.55	−274.21	−259.96	−236.31
Goods for processing: imports f.o.b.	3 150 ..	....	....	....	....	....	....	....	....
Repairs on goods	3 160 ..	....	....	....	....	....	....	....	....
Goods procured in ports by carriers	3 170 ..	....	....	....	....	....	−.34	....	....
Nonmonetary gold	3 180 ..	....	....	....	....	....	....	....	....
B. SERVICES	4 200 ..	**41.47**	**26.83**	**35.33**	**−2.00**	**41.19**	**31.93**	**21.63**	**16.67**
Total credit	2 200 ..	*73.08*	*71.56*	*82.21*	*92.08*	*127.94*	*117.58*	*104.19*	*88.26*
Total debit	3 200 ..	*−31.61*	*−44.73*	*−46.88*	*−94.08*	*−86.75*	*−85.65*	*−82.57*	*−71.60*
Transportation services, credit	2 205 ..	**19.47**	**17.95**	**15.91**	**16.09**	**21.95**	**20.16**	**19.59**	**36.81**
Passenger	2 850 ..	*2.07*	*3.44*	*.66*	*3.41*	*2.24*	*.23*	*.96*	*5.61*
Freight	2 851 ..	*14.64*	*12.43*	*13.23*	*10.87*	*9.75*	*10.94*	*12.87*	*14.15*
Other	2 852 ..	*2.76*	*2.08*	*2.02*	*1.80*	*9.96*	*8.99*	*5.76*	*17.05*
Sea transport, passenger	2 207 ..	....	....	....	....	....	....	....	.47
Sea transport, freight	2 208 ..	14.61	12.43	13.23	10.85	9.66	10.54	11.06	11.56
Sea transport, other	2 209 ..	....	....	....	....	....	....	....	....
Air transport, passenger	2 211 ..	2.07	3.44	.66	3.41	2.24	.23	.96	5.15
Air transport, freight	2 212 ..	.02	....	....	.02	.10	.41	1.81	2.59
Air transport, other	2 213 ..	2.76	2.08	2.02	1.80	9.96	8.99	5.76	17.05
Other transport, passenger	2 215 ..	....	....	....	....	....	....	....	....
Other transport, freight	2 216 ..	....	....	....	....	....	....	....	....
Other transport, other	2 217 ..	....	....	....	....	....	....	....	....
Transportation services, debit	3 205 ..	**−24.76**	**−35.67**	**−35.33**	**−33.95**	**−41.23**	**−39.68**	**−37.61**	**−34.19**
Passenger	3 850 ..	*−3.55*	*−1.77*	*−1.92*	*−1.55*				
Freight	3 851 ..	*−19.72*	*−29.34*	*−32.21*	*−32.15*	*−40.45*	*−39.68*	*−37.61*	*−34.19*
Other	3 852 ..	*−1.48*	*−4.56*	*−1.20*	*−.24*	*−.78*			
Sea transport, passenger	3 207 ..	....	....	....	....	....	....	....	....
Sea transport, freight	3 208 ..	−19.72	−29.34	−32.21	−32.15	−40.45	−39.68	−37.61	−34.19
Sea transport, other	3 209 ..	....	....	....	....	....	....	....	....
Air transport, passenger	3 211 ..	−3.55	−1.77	−1.92	−1.55				
Air transport, freight	3 212 ..	....	....	....	....	....	....	....	....
Air transport, other	3 213 ..	−1.48	−4.56	−1.20	−.24	−.78			
Other transport, passenger	3 215 ..	....	....	....	....	....	....	....	....
Other transport, freight	3 216 ..	....	....	....	....	....	....	....	....
Other transport, other	3 217 ..	....	....	....	....	....	....	....	....
Travel, credit	2 236 ..	**48.99**	**46.31**	**58.18**	**66.17**	**84.55**	**80.34**	**62.51**	**31.60**
Business travel	2 237 ..	....	....	....	....	....	....	....	....
Personal travel	2 240 ..	48.99	46.31	58.18	66.17	84.55	80.34	62.51	31.60
Travel, debit	3 236 ..	**−3.49**	**−3.98**	**−5.47**	**−6.40**	**−8.37**	**−7.86**	**−8.93**	**−10.57**
Business travel	3 237 ..	−2.37	−2.72	−3.66	−3.55	−5.75	−4.14	−6.01	−7.49
Personal travel	3 240 ..	−1.13	−1.26	−1.81	−2.86	−2.62	−3.72	−2.92	−3.08
Other services, credit	2 200 BA	**4.62**	**7.30**	**8.11**	**9.82**	**21.43**	**17.07**	**22.10**	**19.85**
Communications	2 245 ..	4.18	6.85	7.74	9.45	11.98	11.40	17.64	13.55
Construction	2 249 ..	....	....	....	....	9.06	3.81	3.44	5.92
Insurance	2 253 ..	.44	.45	.37	.36	.39	.57	.08	.38
Financial	2 260 ..	....	....	....	....	....	....	....	....
Computer and information	2 262 ..	....	....	....	....	....	1.29	.95	....
Royalties and licence fees	2 266 ..	....	....	....	....	....	....	....	....
Other business services	2 268 ..	....	....	....	....	....	....	....	....
Personal, cultural, and recreational	2 287 ..	....	....	....	....	....	....	....	....
Government, n.i.e.	2 291 ..	....	....	....	....	....	....	....	....
Other services, debit	3 200 BA	**−3.36**	**−5.08**	**−6.08**	**−53.73**	**−37.15**	**−38.11**	**−36.03**	**−26.83**
Communications	3 245 ..	−.06	−.26	−.36	−2.98	−7.88	−1.51	−7.74	−5.45
Construction	3 249 ..	....	....	....	....	−.49	−.22	−.95	−1.97
Insurance	3 253 ..	−3.12	−4.63	−5.04	−5.05	−7.00	−7.17	−6.30	−5.31
Financial	3 260 ..	....	....	....	....	....	....	....	....
Computer and information	3 262 ..	−.17	−.20	−.68	−.79	−1.39	−4.26	−2.31	....
Royalties and licence fees	3 266 ..	....	....	....	....	....	....	....	....
Other business services	3 268 ..	....	....	....	−44.91	−20.38	−24.95	−18.73	−14.10
Personal, cultural, and recreational	3 287 ..	....	....	....	....	....	....	....	....
Government, n.i.e.	3 291 ..	....	....	....	....	....	....	....	....

Table 2 (Continued). STANDARD PRESENTATION, FISCAL YEARS 2003–2010 ENDING JUNE 30

(Millions of U.S. dollars)

	Code	2003	2004	2005	2006	2007	2008	2009	2010
C. INCOME	4 300	**−23.74**	**−27.19**	**−32.33**	**−37.86**	**−44.53**	**−34.44**	**−8.09**	**−8.05**
Total credit	2 300	*4.10*	*1.75*	*3.23*	*4.53*	*8.99*	*12.72*	*11.68*	*14.35*
Total debit	3 300	*−27.84*	*−28.93*	*−35.56*	*−42.39*	*−53.52*	*−47.15*	*−19.78*	*−22.40*
Compensation of employees, credit	2 310	**.62**	**.61**	**.73**	**.80**	**2.11**	**9.29**	**7.56**	**8.38**
Compensation of employees, debit	3 310	**−.55**	**−.52**	**−.74**	**−.95**	**−1.15**	**−1.38**	**−1.56**	**−4.20**
Investment income, credit	2 320	**3.48**	**1.13**	**2.50**	**3.73**	**6.88**	**3.42**	**4.12**	**5.96**
Direct investment income	2 330	....	....	....	....	....	....	....	....
Dividends and distributed branch profits	2 332	....	....	....	....	....	....	....	....
Reinvested earnings and undistributed branch profits	2 333	....	....	....	....	....	....	....	....
Income on debt (interest)	2 334	....	....	....	....	....	....	....	....
Portfolio investment income	2 339	.66	.71	2.35	3.69	6.83	3.42	4.12	5.96
Income on equity	2 340	....	....	....	....	....	....	....	....
Income on bonds and notes	2 350	.66	.71	2.35	3.69	6.83	3.42	4.12	5.96
Income on money market instruments	2 360	....	....	....	....	....	....	....	....
Other investment income	2 370	2.82	.43	.15	.04	.04	....	....	....
Investment income, debit	3 320	**−27.29**	**−28.41**	**−34.81**	**−41.44**	**−52.37**	**−45.77**	**−18.22**	**−18.20**
Direct investment income	3 330	−21.08	−21.44	−26.87	−32.87	−38.44	−42.78	−11.72	−11.47
Dividends and distributed branch profits	3 332	−16.89	−15.02	−17.92	−21.88	−20.77	−23.12	−6.81	−6.65
Reinvested earnings and undistributed branch profits	3 333	−4.19	−6.42	−8.96	−10.99	−17.67	−19.66	−4.91	−4.82
Income on debt (interest)	3 334	....	....	....	....	....	....	....	....
Portfolio investment income	3 339	−6.21	−6.97	−7.94	−8.57	−13.93	−2.99	−6.50	−6.73
Income on equity	3 340	....	....	....	....	....	....	....	....
Income on bonds and notes	3 350	−.22	−.24	−.27	−.30	−4.94	−.72	−.39	−.44
Income on money market instruments	3 360	−5.98	−6.72	−7.67	−8.27	−8.98	−2.27	−6.11	−6.29
Other investment income	3 370	....	....	....	....	....	....	....	....
D. CURRENT TRANSFERS	4 379	**53.66**	**66.00**	**71.89**	**87.61**	**90.17**	**82.41**	**135.21**	**112.68**
Credit	2 379	**82.34**	**89.72**	**98.03**	**114.35**	**113.14**	**104.40**	**194.00**	**247.96**
General government	2 380	4.83	13.18	7.10	6.74	7.34	7.92	33.79	35.21
Other sectors	2 390	77.51	76.54	90.92	107.60	105.80	96.48	160.21	212.75
Workers' remittances	2 391	55.87	60.14	58.57	62.97	53.55	55.52	72.24	107.31
Other current transfers	2 392	21.64	16.40	32.35	44.63	52.25	40.96	87.97	105.43
Debit	3 379	**−28.69**	**−23.71**	**−26.14**	**−26.74**	**−22.97**	**−21.99**	**−58.79**	**−135.28**
General government	3 380	−1.11	−1.49	−1.14	−.73	−1.51	−1.62	−3.92	−.54
Other sectors	3 390	−27.58	−22.23	−25.00	−26.01	−21.47	−20.37	−54.87	−134.74
Workers' remittances	3 391	....	....	....	....	−13.49	−1.81	−6.85	−53.92
Other current transfers	3 392	−27.58	−22.23	−25.00	−26.01	−7.98	−18.56	−48.02	−80.82
CAPITAL AND FINANCIAL ACCOUNT	4 996	**−8.31**	**33.62**	**77.47**	**70.73**	**92.07**	**26.67**	**−35.13**	**42.34**
CAPITAL ACCOUNT	4 994	**4.18**	**5.04**	**.60**	....	**2.07**	**1.17**	....	....
Total credit	2 994	*4.18*	*5.04*	*.60*	....	*2.07*	*1.17*	....	....
Total debit	3 994	....	....	....	....	....	....	....	....
Capital transfers, credit	2 400	**4.18**	**5.04**	**.60**	....	**2.07**	**1.17**	....	....
General government	2 401	4.18	5.04	.60	....	2.07	1.17	....	....
Debt forgiveness	2 402	4.18	5.04	.60	....	2.07	1.17	....	....
Other capital transfers	2 410	....	....	....	....	....	....	....	....
Other sectors	2 430	....	....	....	....	....	....	....	....
Migrants' transfers	2 431	....	....	....	....	....	....	....	....
Debt forgiveness	2 432	....	....	....	....	....	....	....	....
Other capital transfers	2 440	....	....	....	....	....	....	....	....
Capital transfers, debit	3 400	....	....	....	....	....	....	....	....
General government	3 401	....	....	....	....	....	....	....	....
Debt forgiveness	3 402	....	....	....	....	....	....	....	....
Other capital transfers	3 410	....	....	....	....	....	....	....	....
Other sectors	3 430	....	....	....	....	....	....	....	....
Migrants' transfers	3 431	....	....	....	....	....	....	....	....
Debt forgiveness	3 432	....	....	....	....	....	....	....	....
Other capital transfers	3 440	....	....	....	....	....	....	....	....
Nonproduced nonfinancial assets, credit	2 480	....	....	....	....	....	....	....	....
Nonproduced nonfinancial assets, debit	3 480	....	....	....	....	....	....	....	....

Table 2 (Continued). STANDARD PRESENTATION, FISCAL YEARS 2003–2010 ENDING JUNE 30
(Millions of U.S. dollars)

	Code	2003	2004	2005	2006	2007	2008	2009	2010
FINANCIAL ACCOUNT	4 995	−12.49	28.58	76.88	70.73	90.00	25.50	−35.13	42.34
A. DIRECT INVESTMENT	4 500	19.09	55.53	53.65	82.21	78.10	78.61	39.45	37.37
Direct investment abroad	4 505	....	....	....	....	....	....	....	....
Equity capital	4 510	....	....	....	....	....	....	....	....
Claims on affiliated enterprises	4 515	....	....	....	....	....	....	....	....
Liabilities to affiliated enterprises	4 520	....	....	....	....	....	....	....	....
Reinvested earnings	4 525	....	....	....	....	....	....	....	....
Other capital	4 530	....	....	....	....	....	....	....	....
Claims on affiliated enterprises	4 535	....	....	....	....	....	....	....	....
Liabilities to affiliated enterprises	4 540	....	....	....	....	....	....	....	....
Direct investment in The Gambia	4 555	19.09	55.53	53.65	82.21	78.10	78.61	39.45	37.37
Equity capital	4 560	14.90	49.10	44.69	71.22	60.43	58.95	34.54	32.55
Claims on direct investors	4 565	....	....	....	....	....	....	....	....
Liabilities to direct investors	4 570	14.90	49.10	44.69	71.22	60.43	58.95	34.54	32.55
Reinvested earnings	4 575	4.19	6.42	8.96	10.99	17.67	19.66	4.91	4.82
Other capital	4 580	....	....	....	....	....	....	....	....
Claims on direct investors	4 585	....	....	....	....	....	....	....	....
Liabilities to direct investors	4 590	....	....	....	....	....	....	....	....
B. PORTFOLIO INVESTMENT	4 600	....	....	....	....	....	....	....	....
Assets	4 602	....	....	....	....	....	....	....	....
Equity securities	4 610	....	....	....	....	....	....	....	....
Monetary authorities	4 611	....	....	....	....	....	....	....	....
General government	4 612	....	....	....	....	....	....	....	....
Banks	4 613	....	....	....	....	....	....	....	....
Other sectors	4 614	....	....	....	....	....	....	....	....
Debt securities	4 619	....	....	....	....	....	....	....	....
Bonds and notes	4 620	....	....	....	....	....	....	....	....
Monetary authorities	4 621	....	....	....	....	....	....	....	....
General government	4 622	....	....	....	....	....	....	....	....
Banks	4 623	....	....	....	....	....	....	....	....
Other sectors	4 624	....	....	....	....	....	....	....	....
Money market instruments	4 630	....	....	....	....	....	....	....	....
Monetary authorities	4 631	....	....	....	....	....	....	....	....
General government	4 632	....	....	....	....	....	....	....	....
Banks	4 633	....	....	....	....	....	....	....	....
Other sectors	4 634	....	....	....	....	....	....	....	....
Liabilities	4 652	....	....	....	....	....	....	....	....
Equity securities	4 660	....	....	....	....	....	....	....	....
Banks	4 663	....	....	....	....	....	....	....	....
Other sectors	4 664	....	....	....	....	....	....	....	....
Debt securities	4 669	....	....	....	....	....	....	....	....
Bonds and notes	4 670	....	....	....	....	....	....	....	....
Monetary authorities	4 671	....	....	....	....	....	....	....	....
General government	4 672	....	....	....	....	....	....	....	....
Banks	4 673	....	....	....	....	....	....	....	....
Other sectors	4 674	....	....	....	....	....	....	....	....
Money market instruments	4 680	....	....	....	....	....	....	....	....
Monetary authorities	4 681	....	....	....	....	....	....	....	....
General government	4 682	....	....	....	....	....	....	....	....
Banks	4 683	....	....	....	....	....	....	....	....
Other sectors	4 684	....	....	....	....	....	....	....	....
C. FINANCIAL DERIVATIVES	4 910	....	....	....	....	....	....	....	....
Monetary authorities	4 911	....	....	....	....	....	....	....	....
General government	4 912	....	....	....	....	....	....	....	....
Banks	4 913	....	....	....	....	....	....	....	....
Other sectors	4 914	....	....	....	....	....	....	....	....
Assets	4 900	....	....	....	82.21	....	....	....	....
Monetary authorities	4 901	....	....	....	....	....	....	....	....
General government	4 902	....	....	....	71.22	....	....	....	....
Banks	4 903	....	....	....	....	....	....	....	....
Other sectors	4 904	....	....	....	....	....	....	....	....
Liabilities	4 905	....	....	....	....	....	....	....	....
Monetary authorities	4 906	....	....	....	....	....	....	....	....
General government	4 907	....	....	....	....	....	....	....	....
Banks	4 908	....	....	....	....	....	....	....	....
Other sectors	4 909	....	....	....	....	....	....	....	....

Table 2 (Concluded). STANDARD PRESENTATION, FISCAL YEARS 2003–2010 ENDING JUNE 30

(Millions of U.S. dollars)

	Code	2003	2004	2005	2006	2007	2008	2009	2010
D. OTHER INVESTMENT	4 700	−21.95	3.38	33.34	9.10	−.86	−59.41	−4.89	−4.81
Assets	4 703	−17.12	−15.04	−14.05	−14.10	34.18	1.30	20.06	20.30
Trade credits	4 706	....	....	....	....	....	....	....	....
General government	4 707	....	....	....	....	....	....	....	....
of which: Short-term	4 709	....	....	....	....	....	....	....	....
Other sectors	4 710	....	....	....	....	....	....	....	....
of which: Short-term	4 712	....	....	....	....	....	....	....	....
Loans	4 714	....		....	....	13.66	11.41	14.18	7.43
Monetary authorities	4 715	....	....	....	....	....	....	....	....
of which: Short-term	4 718	....	....	....	....	....	....	....	....
General government	4 719	....	....	....	....	....	....	....	....
of which: Short-term	4 721	....	....	....	....	....	....	....	....
Banks	4 722	....	....	....	....	....	....	....	....
of which: Short-term	4 724	....	....	....	....	....	....	....	....
Other sectors	4 725	....	....	....	....	13.66	11.41	14.18	7.43
of which: Short-term	4 727	....	....	....	....	13.66	11.41	14.18	7.43
Currency and deposits	4 730	−17.12	−15.04	−14.05	−14.10	20.53	−10.11	5.88	12.87
Monetary authorities	4 731	....	....	....	....	....	....	....	....
General government	4 732	....	....	....	....	....	....	....	....
Banks	4 733	−17.12	−15.04	−14.05	−14.10	20.53	−10.11	5.88	12.87
Other sectors	4 734	....	....	....	....	....	....	....	....
Other assets	4 736	....	....	....	....	....	....	....	....
Monetary authorities	4 737	....	....	....	....	....	....	....	....
of which: Short-term	4 739	....	....	....	....	....	....	....	....
General government	4 740	....	....	....	....	....	....	....	....
of which: Short-term	4 742	....	....	....	....	....	....	....	....
Banks	4 743	....	....	....	....	....	....	....	....
of which: Short-term	4 745	....	....	....	....	....	....	....	....
Other sectors	4 746	....	....	....	....	....	....	....	....
of which: Short-term	4 748	....	....	....	....	....	....	....	....
Liabilities	4 753	−4.83	18.42	47.39	23.20	−35.04	−60.71	−24.95	−25.11
Trade credits	4 756	3.51	4.15	4.53	9.79	−38.95	−69.45	−88.45	−62.58
General government	4 757	....	....	....	....	....	....	....	....
of which: Short-term	4 759	....	....	....	....	....	....	....	....
Other sectors	4 760	3.51	4.15	4.53	9.79	−38.95	−69.45	−88.45	−62.58
of which: Short-term	4 762	3.51	4.15	4.53	9.79	−38.95	−69.45	−88.45	−62.58
Loans	4 764	5.72	12.97	44.37	12.74	−15.73	7.28	15.63	48.29
Monetary authorities	4 765	....	−11.14	−2.03	−4.04	−12.42	6.38	15.63	3.08
of which: Use of Fund credit and loans from the Fund	4 766	....	−11.14	−2.03	−4.04	−12.42	6.38	15.63	3.08
of which: Short-term	4 768	....	....	....	....	....	....	....	....
General government	4 769	5.72	24.12	46.40	16.78	−3.32	.90	....	45.21
of which: Short-term	4 771	....	....	....	....	....	....	....	....
Banks	4 772	....	....	....	....	....	....	....	....
of which: Short-term	4 774	....	....	....	....	....	....	....	....
Other sectors	4 775	....	....	....	....	....	....	....	....
of which: Short-term	4 777	....	....	....	....	....	....	....	....
Currency and deposits	4 780	−14.06	1.29	−1.51	.68	19.64	1.46	9.34	−10.81
Monetary authorities	4 781	....	....	....	....	....	....	....	....
General government	4 782	....	....	....	....	....	....	....	....
Banks	4 783	−14.06	1.29	−1.51	.68	19.64	1.46	9.34	−10.81
Other sectors	4 784	....	....	....	....	....	....	....	....
Other liabilities	4 786	....	....	....	....	....	....	38.53	....
Monetary authorities	4 787	....	....	....	....	....	....	38.53	....
of which: Short-term	4 789	....	....	....	....	....	....	....	....
General government	4 790	....	....	....	....	....	....	....	....
of which: Short-term	4 792	....	....	....	....	....	....	....	....
Banks	4 793	....	....	....	....	....	....	....	....
of which: Short-term	4 795	....	....	....	....	....	....	....	....
Other sectors	4 796	....	....	....	....	....	....	....	....
of which: Short-term	4 798	....	....	....	....	....	....	....	....
E. RESERVE ASSETS	4 802	−9.63	−30.32	−10.12	−20.57	12.77	6.30	−69.69	9.79
Monetary gold	4 812	....	....	....	....	....	....	....	....
Special drawing rights	4 811	−.01	−.73	.57	−1.28	1.25	.14	−38.38	.02
Reserve position in the Fund	4 810	....	....	....	....	....	....	....	−.09
Foreign exchange	4 803	−7.17	−24.35	−10.80	−19.29	11.52	6.16	−31.32	9.85
Other claims	4 813	−2.45	−5.24	.12	....	....	....	....	....
NET ERRORS AND OMISSIONS	4 998	5.55	−3.30	−34.08	−5.13	−33.66	−37.53	−27.82	−94.71

Table 1. ANALYTIC PRESENTATION, 2003–2010

(Millions of U.S. dollars)

	Code	2003	2004	2005	2006	2007	2008	2009	2010
A. Current Account¹	4 993 Z.	**−391.8**	**−430.7**	**−771.6**	**−1,256.9**	**−2,122.3**	**−3,237.9**	**−1,319.0**	**−1,464.8**
Goods: exports f.o.b.	2 100 ..	830.6	1,092.1	1,472.4	1,666.5	2,088.3	2,428.0	1,893.6	2,462.2
Goods: imports f.o.b.	3 100 ..	−1,469.2	−2,007.7	−2,686.3	−3,685.9	−4,984.1	−6,264.2	−4,293.5	−5,048.5
Balance on Goods	4 100 ..	*−638.6*	*−915.6*	*−1,213.9*	*−2,019.4*	*−2,895.8*	*−3,836.2*	*−2,399.9*	*−2,586.3*
Services: credit	2 200 ..	458.8	554.8	715.0	885.1	1,094.1	1,260.5	1,313.6	1,599.3
Services: debit	3 200 ..	−397.3	−485.4	−631.5	−727.3	−932.9	−1,239.4	−973.9	−1,084.5
Balance on Goods and Services	4 991 ..	*−577.1*	*−846.3*	*−1,130.3*	*−1,861.5*	*−2,734.7*	*−3,815.2*	*−2,060.1*	*−2,071.5*
Income: credit	2 300 ..	177.4	251.7	263.3	341.2	482.5	494.2	422.9	416.3
Income: debit	3 300 ..	−164.0	−173.7	−201.7	−179.2	−445.7	−655.1	−540.7	−776.3
Balance on Goods, Services, and Income	4 992 ..	*−563.7*	*−768.3*	*−1,068.7*	*−1,699.5*	*−2,697.9*	*−3,976.1*	*−2,178.0*	*−2,431.5*
Current transfers: credit	2 379 Z.	208.3	389.0	351.5	505.6	655.6	819.8	930.0	1,051.7
Current transfers: debit	3 379 ..	−36.3	−51.5	−54.4	−63.0	−80.0	−81.7	−71.0	−85.0
B. Capital Account¹	4 994 Z.	**19.9**	**40.7**	**58.6**	**169.0**	**127.9**	**112.3**	**182.5**	**206.1**
Capital account: credit	2 994 Z.	27.9	44.1	61.6	170.0	128.2	112.4	182.6	206.2
Capital account: debit	3 994 ..	−8.0	−3.4	−2.9	−1.0	−.3	−.1	−.1	−.2
Total, Groups A Plus B	4 981 ..	*−371.9*	*−390.0*	*−713.0*	*−1,087.9*	*−1,994.4*	*−3,125.6*	*−1,136.5*	*−1,258.7*
C. Financial Account¹	4 995 W.	**385.6**	**545.5**	**742.7**	**1,588.6**	**2,307.4**	**2,286.7**	**1,427.8**	**1,112.7**
Direct investment abroad	4 505 ..	−3.8	−9.6	89.5	15.8	−76.3	−70.0	1.1	−5.9
Direct investment in Georgia	4 555 Z.	334.6	492.3	452.8	1,170.1	1,750.2	1,564.0	658.4	814.5
Portfolio investment assets	4 602 ..	....	−13.1	13.1	−2.2	−12.7	.7	−1.1	−.6
Equity securities	4 610 ..	....	....	....	−2.2	−5.1	....	−1.1	−.6
Debt securities	4 619 ..	....	−13.1	13.1	....	−7.6	.7	....	....
Portfolio investment liabilities	4 652 Z.	.6	−.6	2.4	142.4	33.6	125.9	13.2	252.7
Equity securities	4 660 ..	....	....	2.5	142.5	33.6	118.1	13.2	−20.5
Debt securities	4 669 Z.	.6	−.6	−.1	−.1	....	7.8	....	273.1
Financial derivatives	4 910 ..	....	....	....	....	1.1	7.8	.6	.8
Financial derivatives assets	4 900 ..	....	....	....	....	1.2	11.1	1.1	1.7
Financial derivatives liabilities	4 905 ..	....	....	....	....	−.2	−3.3	−.5	−1.0
Other investment assets	4 703 ..	−15.6	−27.4	−16.3	−56.5	−202.1	−264.1	191.5	−408.0
Monetary authorities	4 701 ..	.1	....	−.7	−1.9	−44.8	23.5	21.3	−1.1
General government	4 704 ..	−4.9	−4.6	−6.9	7.5	5.0	−41.6	26.3	−.3
Banks	4 705 ..	.5	−21.4	−3.7	−32.6	−200.5	−285.3	130.4	−308.1
Other sectors	4 728 ..	−11.3	−1.4	−5.0	−29.5	38.2	39.2	13.5	−98.6
Other investment liabilities	4 753 W.	69.6	103.8	201.3	318.9	813.5	922.4	564.3	459.3
Monetary authorities	4 753 WA	−.5	−.3	−.5	−.6	−56.6	−1.9	225.4	.3
General government	4 753 ZB	14.7	28.3	2.8	−14.2	94.4	191.9	359.2	336.7
Banks	4 753 ZC	4.1	26.2	164.1	243.9	747.7	571.5	−203.7	97.3
Other sectors	4 753 ZD	51.4	49.7	34.9	89.7	28.0	160.8	183.4	25.0
Total, Groups A Through C	4 983 ..	*13.6*	*155.5*	*29.8*	*500.6*	*313.0*	*−838.9*	*291.3*	*−146.0*
D. Net Errors and Omissions	4 998 ..	**−5.9**	**13.3**	**26.2**	**−61.9**	**−35.9**	**−30.7**	**54.7**	**−15.8**
Total, Groups A Through D	4 984 ..	*7.7*	*168.8*	*56.0*	*438.7*	*277.1*	*−869.6*	*346.1*	*−161.8*
E. Reserves and Related Items	4 802 A.	**−7.7**	**−168.8**	**−56.0**	**−438.7**	**−277.1**	**869.6**	**−346.1**	**161.8**
Reserve assets	4 802 ..	18.5	−177.9	−110.6	−438.6	−377.1	−130.6	−616.2	−208.2
Use of Fund credit and loans	4 766 ..	−47.4	−34.2	−12.5	−7.9	3.2	216.4	308.8	276.4
Exceptional financing	4 920 ..	21.2	43.3	67.1	7.8	96.8	783.8	−38.7	93.7
Conversion rates: lari per U.S. dollar	0 101 ..	**2.1457**	**1.9167**	**1.8127**	**1.7804**	**1.6705**	**1.4908**	**1.6705**	**1.7823**

¹ Excludes components that have been classified in the categories of Group E.

Table 2. STANDARD PRESENTATION, 2003–2010
(Millions of U.S. dollars)

	Code	2003	2004	2005	2006	2007	2008	2009	2010
CURRENT ACCOUNT	4 993	−383.7	−354.4	−709.7	−1,175.5	−2,009.4	−2,915.7	−1,210.5	−1,333.0
A. GOODS	4 100	−638.6	−915.6	−1,213.9	−2,019.4	−2,895.8	−3,836.2	−2,399.9	−2,586.3
Credit	2 100	830.6	1,092.1	1,472.4	1,666.5	2,088.3	2,428.0	1,893.6	2,462.2
General merchandise: exports f.o.b.	2 110	743.3	1,024.7	1,361.3	1,517.4	1,963.1	2,257.1	1,693.2	2,237.1
Goods for processing: exports f.o.b.	2 150	39.9	23.6	50.2	76.2	31.8	39.4	35.9	45.6
Repairs on goods	2 160	20.6	12.4	7.9	3.5	.7	.9	3.9	23.4
Goods procured in ports by carriers	2 170	8.2	12.6	18.3	20.1	23.2	30.5	44.3	70.4
Nonmonetary gold	2 180	18.6	18.8	34.7	49.4	69.4	100.1	116.2	85.8
Debit	3 100	−1,469.2	−2,007.7	−2,686.3	−3,685.9	−4,984.1	−6,264.2	−4,293.5	−5,048.5
General merchandise: imports f.o.b.	3 110	−1,420.0	−1,976.4	−2,617.8	−3,630.2	−4,941.6	−6,212.2	−4,256.4	−4,999.9
Goods for processing: imports f.o.b.	3 150	−39.0	−20.4	−49.9	−35.6	−27.3	−29.7	−19.1	−25.9
Repairs on goods	3 160	−.6	−.1	−4.1	−5.8	−1.4	−5.6	−3.6	−4.7
Goods procured in ports by carriers	3 170	−9.5	−10.8	−14.4	−14.1	−13.8	−16.7	−14.4	−17.5
Nonmonetary gold	3 180	....	....	....	−.1	−.1	....	....	−.4
B. SERVICES	4 200	61.5	69.3	83.6	157.8	161.2	21.0	339.7	514.8
Total credit	2 200	*458.8*	*554.8*	*715.0*	*885.1*	*1,094.1*	*1,260.5*	*1,313.6*	*1,599.3*
Total debit	3 200	*−397.3*	*−485.4*	*−631.5*	*−727.3*	*−932.9*	*−1,239.4*	*−973.9*	*−1,084.5*
Transportation services, credit	2 205	213.4	266.0	331.8	410.9	511.4	613.6	621.9	695.7
Passenger	2 850	*24.7*	*32.1*	*45.5*	*48.0*	*56.0*	*57.9*	*61.4*	*78.6*
Freight	2 851	*139.9*	*150.0*	*174.1*	*227.0*	*307.5*	*430.1*	*437.5*	*458.3*
Other	2 852	*48.8*	*83.9*	*112.1*	*135.9*	*147.9*	*125.7*	*123.0*	*158.8*
Sea transport, passenger	2 207	.6	.8	1.3	1.9	1.8	1.1	1.3	1.6
Sea transport, freight	2 208	1.1	2.1	3.9	5.3	5.5	5.9	5.8	8.3
Sea transport, other	2 209	39.8	58.4	70.0	87.6	102.4	77.5	76.7	101.9
Air transport, passenger	2 211	21.6	28.8	40.0	39.6	43.7	43.6	45.3	57.8
Air transport, freight	2 212	....	....	.6	.9	1.7	1.4	1.1	1.3
Air transport, other	2 213	6.6	22.2	35.9	43.0	38.1	38.0	35.2	42.4
Other transport, passenger	2 215	2.5	2.5	4.2	6.4	10.5	13.3	14.8	19.2
Other transport, freight	2 216	138.8	148.0	169.7	220.8	300.4	422.8	430.5	448.7
Other transport, other	2 217	2.3	3.3	6.1	5.3	7.4	10.2	11.1	14.5
Transportation services, debit	3 205	−137.2	−205.5	−288.0	−387.8	−507.3	−642.0	−490.9	−554.1
Passenger	3 850	*−40.3*	*−48.9*	*−68.5*	*−90.2*	*−101.1*	*−134.3*	*−130.3*	*−129.5*
Freight	3 851	*−83.5*	*−139.7*	*−192.0*	*−272.1*	*−381.3*	*−480.6*	*−336.9*	*−393.6*
Other	3 852	*−13.3*	*−16.9*	*−27.6*	*−25.4*	*−24.9*	*−27.1*	*−23.7*	*−31.0*
Sea transport, passenger	3 207	−.8	−.7	−.8	−.9	−.5	−.7	−.7	−.8
Sea transport, freight	3 208	−34.2	−62.1	−75.9	−97.6	−140.6	−175.6	−125.3	−149.3
Sea transport, other	3 209	−2.5	−3.1	−4.5	−6.2	−5.5	−5.1	−3.5	−5.0
Air transport, passenger	3 211	−31.4	−38.1	−51.5	−60.0	−65.6	−90.1	−81.7	−83.2
Air transport, freight	3 212	−10.2	−15.0	−22.7	−30.1	−52.4	−55.4	−35.6	−34.4
Air transport, other	3 213	−8.9	−11.1	−18.0	−14.9	−13.2	−13.3	−11.4	−14.2
Other transport, passenger	3 215	−8.2	−10.2	−16.1	−29.3	−35.1	−43.6	−47.9	−45.5
Other transport, freight	3 216	−39.2	−62.6	−93.4	−144.5	−188.2	−249.7	−176.1	−210.0
Other transport, other	3 217	−2.0	−2.6	−5.1	−4.4	−6.3	−8.6	−8.9	−11.7
Travel, credit	2 236	147.1	176.6	241.4	312.6	383.7	446.6	475.9	659.2
Business travel	2 237	87.3	105.4	143.3	167.7	210.2	257.8	259.2	316.5
Personal travel	2 240	59.8	71.2	98.1	144.9	173.5	188.9	216.7	342.8
Travel, debit	3 236	−130.2	−147.4	−168.8	−166.6	−175.8	−203.5	−181.5	−199.1
Business travel	3 237	−69.7	−101.7	−111.0	−112.6	−115.9	−147.5	−128.9	−129.9
Personal travel	3 240	−60.5	−45.6	−57.8	−54.1	−59.9	−55.9	−52.6	−69.2
Other services, credit	2 200 BA	98.3	112.2	141.8	161.7	198.9	200.2	215.8	244.4
Communications	2 245	24.2	17.7	19.8	17.5	14.5	23.6	28.2	27.5
Construction	2 249	....	....	....	....	2.8	2.2	6.3	9.6
Insurance	2 253	9.5	10.0	11.0	13.4	13.0	15.1	15.4	38.4
Financial	2 260	10.3	17.4	20.3	18.9	9.1	9.7	13.3	16.9
Computer and information	2 262	....	....	.1	.5	1.9	3.5	6.1	7.4
Royalties and licence fees	2 266	6.3	7.7	9.3	12.9	10.6	6.2	7.5	4.7
Other business services	2 268	7.4	10.6	10.8	8.8	20.3	27.1	36.5	41.6
Personal, cultural, and recreational	2 287	.2	2.1	3.2	5.5	8.7	8.9	14.1	13.7
Government, n.i.e.	2 291	40.4	46.6	67.4	84.1	118.0	103.8	88.6	84.6
Other services, debit	3 200 BA	−130.0	−132.6	−174.6	−172.8	−249.8	−394.0	−301.5	−331.3
Communications	3 245	−15.8	−13.3	−17.3	−14.4	−11.4	−13.1	−13.7	−12.1
Construction	3 249	−14.9	−7.1	−16.0	−4.3	−6.2	−17.8	−20.9	−9.7
Insurance	3 253	−27.9	−42.3	−58.9	−80.4	−110.8	−150.7	−108.0	−120.1
Financial	3 260	−2.0	−2.6	−2.2	−4.2	−12.2	−17.4	−17.2	−13.8
Computer and information	3 262	−.7	−.7	−1.1	−.8	−2.3	−10.6	−7.6	−6.6
Royalties and licence fees	3 266	−10.6	−5.7	−5.3	−5.0	−4.9	−8.4	−8.6	−7.4
Other business services	3 268	−15.8	−15.1	−26.1	−23.7	−34.9	−74.2	−50.8	−60.7
Personal, cultural, and recreational	3 287	....	....	....	....	−6.7	−17.9	−10.5	−11.8
Government, n.i.e.	3 291	−42.3	−45.8	−47.5	−40.1	−60.6	−83.8	−64.2	−89.2

Table 2 (Continued). STANDARD PRESENTATION, 2003–2010

(Millions of U.S. dollars)

	Code	2003	2004	2005	2006	2007	2008	2009	2010
C. INCOME	4 300	**13.3**	**78.0**	**61.6**	**162.1**	**36.8**	**−160.9**	**−117.8**	**−360.0**
Total credit	2 300	*177.4*	*251.7*	*263.3*	*341.2*	*482.5*	*494.2*	*422.9*	*416.3*
Total debit	3 300	*−164.0*	*−173.7*	*−201.7*	*−179.2*	*−445.7*	*−655.1*	*−540.7*	*−776.3*
Compensation of employees, credit	2 310	**168.0**	**236.3**	**247.2**	**315.3**	**405.6**	**419.2**	**391.5**	**381.2**
Compensation of employees, debit	3 310	**−15.6**	**−15.0**	**−18.0**	**−20.2**	**−26.4**	**−44.2**	**−30.1**	**−48.7**
Investment income, credit	2 320	**9.3**	**15.4**	**16.1**	**25.9**	**76.9**	**75.1**	**31.3**	**35.2**
Direct investment income	2 330	3.8	9.6	3.5	.1	....	5.6	.3	10.1
Dividends and distributed branch profits	2 332	....	....	....	....	....	2.4	.5	8.6
Reinvested earnings and undistributed branch profits	2 333	3.8	9.6	3.5	....	....	2.3	−1.5	.7
Income on debt (interest)	2 334	....	....	....	.1	....	1.0	1.3	.8
Portfolio investment income	2 339	2.3	2.0	5.4	9.0	24.1	28.4	16.9	9.7
Income on equity	2 340	....	....	....	....	.9	....	.2	.3
Income on bonds and notes	2 350	....	....	....	....	.6	.9	....	....
Income on money market instruments	2 360	2.3	2.0	5.4	9.0	22.6	27.4	16.7	9.5
Other investment income	2 370	3.3	3.8	7.2	16.9	52.7	41.0	14.1	15.3
Investment income, debit	3 320	**−148.4**	**−158.7**	**−183.7**	**−159.0**	**−419.3**	**−611.0**	**−510.7**	**−727.6**
Direct investment income	3 330	−88.7	−100.2	−116.2	−94.4	−297.6	−361.3	−262.8	−470.8
Dividends and distributed branch profits	3 332	−32.0	−50.3	−60.6	−27.5	−173.3	−185.3	−233.8	−153.0
Reinvested earnings and undistributed branch profits	3 333	−52.0	−45.7	−48.5	−64.5	−49.0	−76.3	50.8	−227.8
Income on debt (interest)	3 334	−4.7	−4.2	−7.2	−2.4	−75.3	−99.6	−79.9	−90.0
Portfolio investment income	3 339	−.2	−.2	−.1	−.4	−1.2	−37.4	−47.3	−59.5
Income on equity	3 340	−.1	−.1	−.1	−.4	−1.2	−10.8	−9.8	−10.9
Income on bonds and notes	3 350	....	....	....	....	....	−26.6	−37.5	−48.4
Income on money market instruments	3 360	−.1	−.2	....	....	....	....	....	−.2
Other investment income	3 370	−59.6	−58.3	−67.4	−64.1	−120.5	−212.3	−200.5	−197.3
D. CURRENT TRANSFERS	4 379	**180.0**	**413.9**	**359.0**	**523.9**	**688.5**	**1,060.4**	**967.5**	**1,098.5**
Credit	2 379	**216.3**	**465.4**	**413.4**	**587.0**	**768.5**	**1,142.0**	**1,038.5**	**1,183.4**
General government	2 380	50.0	231.6	141.4	191.4	207.0	429.3	200.2	232.4
Other sectors	2 390	166.3	233.7	272.0	395.5	561.4	712.8	838.3	951.1
Workers' remittances	2 391	64.5	64.0	93.8	153.0	245.0	305.1	317.4	416.6
Other current transfers	2 392	101.9	169.7	178.2	242.6	316.4	407.6	520.9	534.5
Debit	3 379	**−36.3**	**−51.5**	**−54.4**	**−63.0**	**−80.0**	**−81.7**	**−71.0**	**−85.0**
General government	3 380	−26.8	−39.6	−41.1	−51.6	−68.5	−64.3	−59.3	−58.0
Other sectors	3 390	−9.5	−11.9	−13.3	−11.4	−11.5	−17.4	−11.7	−26.9
Workers' remittances	3 391	−5.7	−7.4	−7.6	−3.8	−1.7	−2.4	−1.5	−1.3
Other current transfers	3 392	−3.8	−4.5	−5.7	−7.6	−9.8	−15.0	−10.2	−25.6
CAPITAL AND FINANCIAL ACCOUNT	4 996	**389.7**	**341.1**	**683.4**	**1,237.5**	**2,045.3**	**2,946.4**	**1,155.7**	**1,348.8**
CAPITAL ACCOUNT	4 994	**19.9**	**40.7**	**58.6**	**171.2**	**127.9**	**112.3**	**182.5**	**206.1**
Total credit	2 994	*27.9*	*44.1*	*61.6*	*172.2*	*128.3*	*112.4*	*182.6*	*206.2*
Total debit	3 994	*−8.0*	*−3.4*	*−2.9*	*−1.0*	*−.3*	*−.1*	*−.1*	*−.2*
Capital transfers, credit	2 400	**27.9**	**44.1**	**61.6**	**172.2**	**128.3**	**112.4**	**182.6**	**206.2**
General government	2 401	21.1	35.1	48.3	145.4	67.9	86.8	170.0	189.4
Debt forgiveness	2 402	....	....	....	54.4	....	2.3	....	....
Other capital transfers	2 410	21.1	35.1	48.3	91.0	67.9	84.5	170.0	189.4
Other sectors	2 430	6.8	9.0	13.3	26.8	60.3	25.6	12.7	16.8
Migrants' transfers	2 431	3.5	2.9	5.1	17.1	44.9	7.8	5.4	8.3
Debt forgiveness	2 432	....	....	....	....	.4	7.5	.2	1.4
Other capital transfers	2 440	3.3	6.1	8.2	9.7	15.1	10.3	7.1	7.1
Capital transfers, debit	3 400	**−8.0**	**−3.4**	**−2.9**	**−1.0**	**−.3**	**−.1**	**−.1**	**−.2**
General government	3 401	....	....	....	....	....	....	....	....
Debt forgiveness	3 402	....	....	....	....	....	....	....	....
Other capital transfers	3 410	....	....	....	....	....	....	....	....
Other sectors	3 430	−8.0	−3.4	−2.9	−1.0	−.3	−.1	−.1	−.2
Migrants' transfers	3 431	−8.0	−3.4	−2.9	−1.0	−.3	−.1	−.1	−.2
Debt forgiveness	3 432	....	....	....	....	....	....	....	....
Other capital transfers	3 440	....	....	....	....	....	....	....	....
Nonproduced nonfinancial assets, credit	2 480	....	....	....	....	....	....	....	....
Nonproduced nonfinancial assets, debit	3 480	....	....	....	....	....	....	....	....

Table 2 (Continued). STANDARD PRESENTATION, 2003–2010
(Millions of U.S. dollars)

	Code	2003	2004	2005	2006	2007	2008	2009	2010
FINANCIAL ACCOUNT	4 995	**369.8**	**300.4**	**624.8**	**1,066.3**	**1,917.4**	**2,834.1**	**973.2**	**1,142.7**
A. DIRECT INVESTMENT	4 500	**330.9**	**482.8**	**542.2**	**1,185.9**	**1,673.9**	**1,494.1**	**659.5**	**808.6**
Direct investment abroad	4 505	−3.8	−9.6	89.5	15.8	−76.3	−70.0	1.1	−5.9
Equity capital	4 510	....	....	93.0	18.0	−78.6	−67.7	.9	−4.5
Claims on affiliated enterprises	4 515	....	....	93.0	18.0	−78.6	−67.7	.9	−4.5
Liabilities to affiliated enterprises	4 520	....	....	....	....	....	....	....	....
Reinvested earnings	4 525	−3.8	−9.6	−3.5	....	....	−2.3	1.5	−.7
Other capital	4 530	....	....	....	−2.2	2.3	....	−1.3	−.7
Claims on affiliated enterprises	4 535	....	....	....	−2.2	2.3	....	−1.3	−.7
Liabilities to affiliated enterprises	4 540	....	....	....	....	....	....	....	....
Direct investment in Georgia	4 555	**334.6**	**492.3**	**452.8**	**1,170.1**	**1,750.2**	**1,564.0**	**658.4**	**814.5**
Equity capital	4 560	255.6	394.6	334.9	858.1	861.0	1,098.0	615.5	470.8
Claims on direct investors	4 565	....	....	....	....	....	....	....	....
Liabilities to direct investors	4 570	255.6	394.6	334.9	858.1	861.0	1,098.0	615.5	470.8
Reinvested earnings	4 575	52.0	45.7	48.5	64.5	49.0	76.3	−50.8	227.8
Other capital	4 580	27.1	52.0	69.4	247.5	840.3	389.7	93.7	115.9
Claims on direct investors	4 585	−.3	−.4	−.4	−.2	−127.4	−27.0	6.0	−55.3
Liabilities to direct investors	4 590	27.4	52.4	69.8	247.7	967.7	416.7	87.7	171.2
B. PORTFOLIO INVESTMENT	4 600	**.6**	**−13.6**	**15.5**	**140.3**	**21.0**	**626.6**	**12.1**	**252.0**
Assets	4 602	**....**	**−13.1**	**13.1**	**−2.2**	**−12.7**	**.7**	**−1.1**	**−.6**
Equity securities	4 610	....	....	....	−2.2	−5.1	....	−1.1	−.6
Monetary authorities	4 611	....	....	....	....	....	....	....	....
General government	4 612	....	....	....	....	....	....	....	....
Banks	4 613	....	....	....	−2.2	−5.1	....	....	....
Other sectors	4 614	....	....	....	....	....	....	−1.1	−.6
Debt securities	4 619	....	−13.1	13.1	....	−7.6	.7	....	....
Bonds and notes	4 620	....	....	....	....	−5.2	−1.7	....	....
Monetary authorities	4 621	....	....	....	....	....	....	....	....
General government	4 622	....	....	....	....	....	−6.8	....	....
Banks	4 623	....	....	....	....	−5.1	5.1	....	....
Other sectors	4 624	....	....	....	....	−.1	....	....	....
Money market instruments	4 630	....	−13.1	13.1	....	−2.4	2.4	....	....
Monetary authorities	4 631	....	....	....	....	....	....	....	....
General government	4 632	....	....	....	....	....	....	....	....
Banks	4 633	....	−13.1	13.1	....	−2.4	2.4	....	....
Other sectors	4 634	....	....	....	....	....	....	....	....
Liabilities	4 652	**.6**	**−.6**	**2.4**	**142.4**	**33.6**	**625.9**	**13.2**	**252.7**
Equity securities	4 660	....	....	2.5	142.5	33.6	118.1	13.2	−20.5
Banks	4 663	....	....	2.5	142.5	33.7	101.4	8.2	−22.3
Other sectors	4 664	....	....	....	....	....	16.7	5.0	1.8
Debt securities	4 669	.6	−.6	−.1	−.1	....	507.8	....	273.1
Bonds and notes	4 670	....	....	....	....	....	507.8	....	260.9
Monetary authorities	4 671	....	....	....	....	....	....	....	....
General government	4 672	....	....	....	....	....	507.8	....	....
Banks	4 673	....	....	....	....	....	....	....	....
Other sectors	4 674	....	....	....	....	....	....	....	260.9
Money market instruments	4 680	.6	−.6	−.1	−.1	....	....	....	12.2
Monetary authorities	4 681	....	....	....	....	....	....	....	....
General government	4 682	.6	−.6	−.1	−.1	....	....	....	....
Banks	4 683	....	....	....	....	....	....	....	12.1
Other sectors	4 684	....	....	....	....	....	....	....	.1
C. FINANCIAL DERIVATIVES	4 910	**....**	**....**	**....**	**....**	**1.1**	**7.8**	**.6**	**.8**
Monetary authorities	4 911	....	....	....	....	....	....	....	....
General government	4 912	....	....	....	....	....	....	....	....
Banks	4 913	....	....	....	....	1.1	7.8	.6	.8
Other sectors	4 914	....	....	....	....	....	....	....	....
Assets	4 900	**....**	**....**	**....**	**....**	**1.2**	**11.1**	**1.1**	**1.7**
Monetary authorities	4 901	....	....	....	....	....	....	....	....
General government	4 902	....	....	....	....	....	....	....	....
Banks	4 903	....	....	....	....	1.2	11.1	1.1	1.7
Other sectors	4 904	....	....	....	....	....	....	....	....
Liabilities	4 905	**....**	**....**	**....**	**....**	**−.2**	**−3.3**	**−.5**	**−1.0**
Monetary authorities	4 906	....	....	....	....	....	....	....	....
General government	4 907	....	....	....	....	....	....	....	....
Banks	4 908	....	....	....	....	−.2	−3.3	−.5	−1.0
Other sectors	4 909	....	....	....	....	....	....	....	....

Table 2 (Concluded). STANDARD PRESENTATION, 2003–2010

(Millions of U.S. dollars)

	Code	2003	2004	2005	2006	2007	2008	2009	2010
D. OTHER INVESTMENT	4 700 ..	**19.8**	**9.2**	**177.6**	**178.7**	**598.6**	**836.3**	**917.4**	**289.5**
Assets	4 703 ..	**−15.6**	**−27.4**	**−16.3**	**−56.5**	**−202.1**	**−264.1**	**191.5**	**−408.0**
Trade credits	4 706 ..	−15.7	−4.6	−10.5	−1.6	−5.8	39.2	−20.2	−68.3
General government	4 707 ..	−5.0	−4.7	−3.7	−2.3	−.8	....	....	....
of which: Short-term	4 709 ..	....	....	....	....	....	....	....	....
Other sectors	4 710 ..	−10.7	.1	−6.8	.7	−5.1	39.2	−20.2	−68.3
of which: Short-term	4 712 ..	−10.7	.1	−6.8	.7	−5.1	39.2	−20.2	−68.3
Loans	4 714 ..	5.0	4.1	−1.0	−28.5	−107.5	56.3	12.9	−41.3
Monetary authorities	4 715 ..	.1	....	−.7	−1.9	−44.8	23.8	21.7	−1.2
of which: Short-term	4 718 ..	.1	....	−.7	−1.9	−44.8	23.8	21.7	−1.2
General government	4 719 ..	....	....	....	....	....	....	....	....
of which: Short-term	4 721 ..	....	....	....	....	....	....	....	....
Banks	4 722 ..	5.5	4.2	−.8	4.0	−51.0	35.3	−14.7	−39.5
of which: Short-term	4 724 ..	7.0	2.2	−2.3	4.2	−38.2	37.3	−18.4	−1.3
Other sectors	4 725 ..	−.5	−.1	.4	−30.6	−11.8	−2.9	5.8	−.7
of which: Short-term	4 727 ..	−.5	−.1	.4	−30.6	30.3	−.5	−2.0	−.3
Currency and deposits	4 730 ..	−1.4	−29.1	−3.7	−24.5	−88.9	−360.9	199.2	−295.9
Monetary authorities	4 731 ..	....	....	....	.1	....	....	....	....
General government	4 732 ..	.1	.1	−1.2	9.9	4.0	−41.6	26.3	−.3
Banks	4 733 ..	−1.5	−29.2	−2.5	−35.3	−147.9	−322.2	145.0	−266.5
Other sectors	4 734 ..	....	....	....	.9	55.0	2.9	27.9	−29.1
Other assets	4 736 ..	−3.5	2.2	−1.0	−1.8	.2	1.3	−.4	−2.5
Monetary authorities	4 737 ..	....	....	....	....	....	−.3	−.5	.1
of which: Short-term	4 739 ..	....	....	....	....	....	−.3	−.5	.1
General government	4 740 ..	....	....	−2.0	−.1	1.8	....	....	....
of which: Short-term	4 742 ..	....	....	−2.0	−.1	1.8	....	....	....
Banks	4 743 ..	−3.5	3.6	−.4	−1.3	−1.6	1.6	....	−2.1
of which: Short-term	4 745 ..	−3.5	3.6	−.4	−1.3	−1.6	1.6	....	−2.1
Other sectors	4 746 ..	....	−1.4	1.4	−.5	....	....	....	−.5
of which: Short-term	4 748 ..	....	−1.4	1.4	−.5	....	....	....	−.5
Liabilities	4 753 ..	**35.4**	**36.6**	**193.9**	**235.2**	**800.6**	**1,100.4**	**725.9**	**697.6**
Trade credits	4 756 ..	3.0	14.9	26.0	34.3	−53.1	94.3	19.3	−20.0
General government	4 757 ..	....	....	....	....	....	....	....	....
of which: Short-term	4 759 ..	....	....	....	....	....	....	....	....
Other sectors	4 760 ..	3.0	14.9	26.0	34.3	−53.1	94.3	19.3	−20.0
of which: Short-term	4 762 ..	3.0	14.9	26.0	34.3	−53.1	94.3	19.3	−20.0
Loans	4 764 ..	26.0	137.2	101.4	246.6	787.2	1,039.6	413.8	626.6
Monetary authorities	4 765 ..	−48.0	−33.8	−12.7	−8.1	−53.4	214.5	309.1	276.7
of which: Use of Fund credit and loans from the Fund.	4 766 ..	−47.4	−34.2	−12.5	−7.9	3.2	216.4	308.8	276.4
of which: Short-term	4 768 ..	....	....	....	....	....	.8	.2	.3
General government	4 769 ..	14.7	111.2	48.8	−21.4	111.3	191.9	359.2	336.7
of which: Short-term	4 771 ..	−.1	.6	.4	.5	.2	.6	.5	1.7
Banks	4 772 ..	11.0	24.9	56.4	220.7	647.1	572.8	−415.3	9.6
of which: Short-term	4 774 ..	2.5	3.7	9.8	33.7	81.4	189.7	−251.1	11.3
Other sectors	4 775 ..	48.4	34.8	8.9	55.4	82.2	60.4	160.8	3.6
of which: Short-term	4 777 ..	.4	.5	.8	7.9	−15.3	5.7	14.5	11.9
Currency and deposits	4 780 ..	−4.3	−1.4	94.7	17.8	92.1	−23.9	41.4	78.9
Monetary authorities	4 781 ..	....	....	....	....	....	....	....	....
General government	4 782 ..	....	....	....	....	....	....	....	....
Banks	4 783 ..	−4.3	−1.4	94.7	17.8	92.1	−23.9	41.4	78.9
Other sectors	4 784 ..	....	....	....	....	....	....	....	....
Other liabilities	4 786 ..	10.6	−114.0	−28.2	−63.5	−25.6	−9.6	251.3	12.1
Monetary authorities	4 787 ..	.5	−.6	....	....	....	....	225.2	....
of which: Short-term	4 789 ..	.5	−.6	....	....	....	....	....	....
General government	4 790 ..	10.1	−118.8	−35.5	−86.2	−34.6	−3.9	−3.0	−10.8
of which: Short-term	4 792 ..	10.1	−118.8	−35.5	−86.2	−34.6	−3.9	−3.0	−10.8
Banks	4 793 ..	−3.4	1.3	12.0	5.1	2.6	−.7	−1.7	.4
of which: Short-term	4 795 ..	−3.4	1.3	12.0	5.1	2.6	−.7	−1.7	.4
Other sectors	4 796 ..	3.4	4.0	−4.7	17.6	6.4	−5.0	30.9	22.6
of which: Short-term	4 798 ..	3.4	4.0	−4.7	17.6	6.4	−5.0	30.9	22.6
E. RESERVE ASSETS	4 802 ..	**18.5**	**−177.9**	**−110.6**	**−438.6**	**−377.1**	**−130.6**	**−616.2**	**−208.2**
Monetary gold	4 812 ..	....	....	....	....	....	....	....	....
Special drawing rights	4 811 ..	−2.0	−6.1	9.5	.2	−13.7	2.3	−206.0	−7.9
Reserve position in the Fund	4 810 ..	....	....	....	....	....	....	....	....
Foreign exchange	4 803 ..	20.5	−171.8	−120.1	−438.8	−363.4	−133.0	−410.3	−200.4
Other claims	4 813 ..	....	....	....	....	....	....	....	....
NET ERRORS AND OMISSIONS	4 998 ..	**−5.9**	**13.3**	**26.2**	**−61.9**	**−35.9**	**−30.7**	**54.7**	**−15.8**

Table 3. INTERNATIONAL INVESTMENT POSITION (End-period stocks), 2003–2010

(Millions of U.S. dollars)

	Code	2003	2004	2005	2006	2007	2008	2009	2010
ASSETS	8 995 C.	**721.0**	**977.7**	**1,017.4**	**1,535.7**	**2,291.8**	**2,728.1**	**3,180.7**	**3,773.2**
Direct investment abroad	8 505	**101.1**	**110.6**	**21.2**	**5.4**	**89.1**	**152.7**	**149.4**	**153.5**
Equity capital and reinvested earnings	8 506	101.1	110.6	21.2	3.2	89.1	152.7	148.1	151.5
Claims on affiliated enterprises	8 507	101.1	110.6	21.2	3.2	89.1	152.7	148.1	151.5
Liabilities to affiliated enterprises	8 508	....	....	....	....	....	....	....	....
Other capital	8 530	....	....	....	2.3	....	....	1.3	2.0
Claims on affiliated enterprises	8 535	....	....	....	2.3	....	....	1.3	2.0
Liabilities to affiliated enterprises	8 540	....	....	....	....	....	....	....	....
Portfolio investment	8 602	**.1**	**13.1**	**....**	**2.2**	**7.7**	**.2**	**1.4**	**2.0**
Equity securities	8 610	.1	....	....	2.2	.2	.2	1.3	1.9
Monetary authorities	8 611	....	....	....	....	....	....	....	....
General government	8 612	....	....	....	....	....	....	....	....
Banks	8 613	.1	....	....	2.2	.1	.1	.1	.1
Other sectors	8 614	....	....	....	....	....	....	1.2	1.8
Debt securities	8 619	....	13.1	....	....	7.6	.1	.1	.1
Bonds and notes	8 620	....	....	....	....	5.2	.1	.1	.1
Monetary authorities	8 621	....	....	....	....	....	....	....	....
General government	8 622	....	....	....	....	....	....	....	....
Banks	8 623	....	....	....	....	5.1	....	....	....
Other sectors	8 624	....	....	....	....	.1	.1	.1	.1
Money market instruments	8 630	....	13.1	....	....	2.4	....	....	....
Monetary authorities	8 631	....	....	....	....	....	....	....	....
General government	8 632	....	....	....	....	....	....	....	....
Banks	8 633	....	13.1	....	....	2.4	....	....	....
Other sectors	8 634	....	....	....	....	....	....	....	....
Financial derivatives	8 900	**....**	**....**	**....**	**....**	**.1**	**.2**	**.7**	**1.3**
Monetary authorities	8 901	....	....	....	....	....	....	....	....
General government	8 902	....	....	....	....	....	....	....	....
Banks	8 903	....	....	....	....	.1	.2	.7	1.3
Other sectors	8 904	....	....	....	....	....	....	....	....
Other investment	8 703	**423.6**	**467.3**	**517.7**	**597.2**	**833.8**	**1,094.8**	**918.8**	**1,352.5**
Trade credits	8 706	127.3	138.2	144.5	152.8	177.5	164.6	207.4	288.5
General government	8 707	21.0	25.6	29.3	31.6	32.4	32.4	32.4	32.4
of which: Short-term	8 709	....	....	....	....	....	....	....	....
Other sectors	8 710	106.3	112.6	115.2	121.2	145.1	132.2	175.1	256.2
of which: Short-term	8 712	*106.3*	*112.6*	*115.2*	*121.2*	*145.1*	*132.2*	*175.1*	*256.2*
Loans	8 714	10.8	6.6	14.5	43.7	153.3	89.9	76.9	117.4
Monetary authorities	8 715	....	....	.6	2.8	51.5	24.5	3.2	4.3
of which: Short-term	8 718	....	....	*.6*	*2.8*	*51.5*	*24.5*	*3.2*	*4.3*
General government	8 719	....	....	....	....	....	....	....	....
of which: Short-term	8 721	....	....	....	....	....	....	....	....
Banks	8 722	10.3	6.0	13.7	10.1	62.3	27.6	41.8	80.6
of which: Short-term	8 724	*5.7*	*3.5*	*11.8*	*8.0*	*47.4*	*10.8*	*28.8*	*29.5*
Other sectors	8 725	.5	.6	.2	30.8	39.5	37.7	31.8	32.5
of which: Short-term	8 727	*.5*	*.6*	*.2*	*30.8*	*.5*	*9.7*	*11.7*	*11.7*
Currency and deposits	8 730	280.6	319.7	354.9	394.9	497.4	835.7	629.5	939.2
Monetary authorities	8 731	....	....	....	....	....	....	....	....
General government	8 732	16.7	16.7	15.6	7.5	3.8	25.7	.2	.5
Banks	8 733	99.9	134.5	168.8	211.3	371.5	689.8	535.0	803.8
Other sectors	8 734	164.0	168.5	170.5	176.1	122.1	120.2	94.3	134.9
Other assets	8 736	5.0	2.8	3.9	5.7	5.6	4.6	5.0	7.5
Monetary authorities	8 737	....	....	....	....	....	.3	.8	.7
of which: Short-term	8 739	....	....	....	....	....	*.3*	*.8*	*.7*
General government	8 740	.5	.5	2.5	2.6	.8	.8	.7	.7
of which: Short-term	8 742	*.5*	*.5*	*2.5*	*2.6*	*.8*	*.8*	*.7*	*.7*
Banks	8 743	4.5	.9	1.4	2.6	4.3	2.9	3.0	5.0
of which: Short-term	8 745	*4.5*	*.9*	*1.4*	*2.6*	*4.3*	*2.9*	*3.0*	*5.0*
Other sectors	8 746	....	1.4	....	.5	.5	.5	.5	1.0
of which: Short-term	8 748	....	*1.4*	....	*.5*	*.5*	*.5*	*.5*	*1.0*
Reserve assets	8 802	**196.2**	**386.7**	**478.5**	**930.8**	**1,361.2**	**1,480.2**	**2,110.3**	**2,263.8**
Monetary gold	8 812	....	....	....	....	....	....	....	....
Special drawing rights	8 811	4.9	11.2	1.0	.9	14.8	12.3	218.7	222.4
Reserve position in the Fund	8 810	....	....	....	....	....	....	....	....
Foreign exchange	8 803	191.2	375.4	477.4	929.9	1,346.3	1,467.8	1,891.6	2,041.4
Other claims	8 813	....	....	....	....	....	....	....	....

Table 3 (Concluded). INTERNATIONAL INVESTMENT POSITION (End-period stocks), 2003–2010

(Millions of U.S. dollars)

	Code	2003	2004	2005	2006	2007	2008	2009	2010
LIABILITIES	8 995 D.	**3,841.8**	**4,483.0**	**5,040.8**	**6,714.2**	**9,619.1**	**12,670.6**	**14,276.1**	**15,954.0**
Direct investment in Georgia	8 555	**1,395.3**	**1,908.2**	**2,373.6**	**3,559.2**	**5,356.1**	**6,762.5**	**7,359.5**	**8,142.2**
Equity capital and reinvested earnings	8 556	978.1	1,428.0	1,822.4	2,738.8	3,691.1	4,821.0	5,377.6	6,070.4
Claims on direct investors	8 557	....	....	....	....	....	....	....	....
Liabilities to direct investors	8 558	978.1	1,428.0	1,822.4	2,738.8	3,691.1	4,821.0	5,377.6	6,070.4
Other capital	8 580	417.2	480.3	551.2	820.4	1,665.0	1,941.5	1,981.9	2,071.8
Claims on direct investors	8 585	−5.4	−5.8	−6.1	−6.4	−133.7	−160.7	−164.0	−234.8
Liabilities to direct investors	8 590	422.6	486.1	557.4	826.7	1,798.7	2,102.2	2,146.0	2,306.6
Portfolio investment	8 652	**8.7**	**10.0**	**15.1**	**181.2**	**277.9**	**718.4**	**903.2**	**1,158.9**
Equity securities	8 660	8.1	9.9	15.0	181.2	277.9	385.9	393.7	341.9
Banks	8 663	7.9	9.7	14.9	181.1	262.1	345.8	347.0	293.4
Other sectors	8 664	.1	.1	.1	.2	15.8	40.0	46.7	48.5
Debt securities	8 669	.6	.2	.1	....	....	332.5	509.5	817.0
Bonds and notes	8 670	....	....	....	....	....	332.5	509.5	804.7
Monetary authorities	8 671	....	....	....	....	....	....	....	....
General government	8 672	....	....	....	....	....	332.5	509.5	524.2
Banks	8 673	....	....	....	....	....	....	....	....
Other sectors	8 674	....	....	....	....	....	....	....	280.6
Money market instruments	8 680	.6	.2	.1	....	....	....	....	12.3
Monetary authorities	8 681	....	....	....	....	....	....	....	....
General government	8 682	.6	.2	.1	....	....	....	....	....
Banks	8 683	....	....	....	....	....	....	....	12.2
Other sectors	8 684	....	....	....	....	....	....	....	.1
Financial derivatives	8 905	....	....	....	....	....	**.1**	**.3**	**.2**
Monetary authorities	8 906	....	....	....	....	....	....	....	....
General government	8 907	....	....	....	....	....	....	....	....
Banks	8 908	....	....	....	....	....	.1	.3	.2
Other sectors	8 909	....	....	....	....	....	....	....	....
Other investment	8 753	**2,437.8**	**2,564.7**	**2,652.1**	**2,973.8**	**3,985.1**	**5,189.7**	**6,013.1**	**6,652.7**
Trade credits	8 756	83.3	103.2	128.3	164.6	158.4	324.1	400.4	421.7
General government	8 757	....	....	....	....	....	....	....	....
of which: Short-term	8 759	....	....	....	....	....	....	....	....
Other sectors	8 760	83.3	103.2	128.3	164.6	158.4	324.1	400.4	421.7
of which: Short-term	8 762	*83.3*	*103.2*	*128.3*	*164.6*	*158.4*	*324.1*	*400.4*	*421.7*
Loans	8 764	1,985.9	2,206.9	2,208.3	2,544.3	3,491.2	4,563.8	5,018.1	5,554.6
Monetary authorities	8 765	343.8	326.6	284.9	294.7	254.2	460.9	787.4	1,051.8
of which: Use of Fund credit and loans from the Fund	8 766	*288.7*	*266.0*	*232.3*	*236.3*	*251.5*	*460.2*	*786.4*	*1,050.5*
of which: Short-term	8 768	....	....	....	....	....	*.8*	*1.0*	*1.3*
General government	8 769	1,170.7	1,335.9	1,292.0	1,330.6	1,509.4	1,683.5	2,066.4	2,363.7
of which: Short-term	8 771	*1.9*	*2.6*	*2.9*	*3.4*	*3.7*	*4.3*	*4.7*	*6.4*
Banks	8 772	89.0	114.3	187.4	409.9	1,059.1	1,664.2	1,248.9	1,257.7
of which: Short-term	8 774	*16.9*	*21.4*	*48.4*	*82.6*	*164.1*	*355.0*	*104.0*	*115.2*
Other sectors	8 775	382.4	430.1	444.0	509.1	668.5	755.1	915.4	881.4
of which: Short-term	8 777	*23.0*	*26.8*	*28.2*	*39.0*	*42.2*	*46.5*	*66.8*	*75.8*
Currency and deposits	8 780	15.9	16.4	120.2	138.5	233.1	209.0	249.6	323.6
Monetary authorities	8 781	....	....	....	....	....	....	....	....
General government	8 782	....	....	....	....	....	....	....	....
Banks	8 783	15.9	16.4	120.1	138.5	233.1	209.0	249.6	323.6
Other sectors	8 784	....	....	....	....	....	....	....	....
Other liabilities	8 786	352.7	238.2	195.3	126.4	102.4	92.8	345.1	352.8
Monetary authorities	8 787	.6	....	....	....	....	....	225.7	221.7
of which: Short-term	8 789	*.6*	....	....	....	....	....	....	....
General government	8 790	349.1	231.2	193.8	109.9	75.4	71.5	68.6	57.7
of which: Short-term	8 792	*349.1*	*231.2*	*193.8*	*109.9*	*75.4*	*71.5*	*68.6*	*57.7*
Banks	8 793	1.3	1.3	.7	.2	2.8	1.6	.2	.6
of which: Short-term	8 795	*1.3*	*1.3*	*.7*	*.2*	*2.8*	*1.6*	*.2*	*.6*
Other sectors	8 796	1.7	5.7	.8	16.3	24.1	19.7	50.6	72.8
of which: Short-term	8 798	*1.7*	*5.7*	*.8*	*16.3*	*24.1*	*19.7*	*50.6*	*72.8*
NET INTERNATIONAL INVESTMENT POSITION	8 995	−3,120.8	−3,505.3	−4,023.4	−5,178.6	−7,327.2	−9,942.6	−11,095.4	−12,180.8
Conversion rates: lari per U.S. dollar (end of period)	0 102	2.0750	1.8250	1.7925	1.7135	1.5916	1.6670	1.6858	1.7728

Table 1. ANALYTIC PRESENTATION, 2003–2010

(Billions of U.S. dollars)

	Code	2003	2004	2005	2006	2007	2008	2009	2010
A. Current Account[1]	4 993 Z.	**46.93**	**128.00**	**140.61**	**182.67**	**249.10**	**228.12**	**188.63**	**187.94**
Goods: exports f.o.b.	2 100 ..	747.37	907.79	983.14	1,136.16	1,354.26	1,501.80	1,160.99	1,303.33
Goods: imports f.o.b.	3 100 ..	−602.63	−721.75	−790.00	−938.11	−1,083.52	−1,238.77	−972.49	−1,098.61
Balance on Goods	4 100 ..	*144.74*	*186.04*	*193.14*	*198.05*	*270.75*	*263.03*	*188.50*	*204.72*
Services: credit	2 200 ..	123.87	147.50	163.87	188.12	223.51	254.68	232.59	237.81
Services: debit	3 200 ..	−173.06	−196.76	−210.99	−224.15	−260.07	−291.52	−257.12	−263.44
Balance on Goods and Services	4 991 ..	*95.55*	*136.78*	*146.02*	*162.02*	*234.18*	*226.19*	*163.97*	*179.09*
Income: credit	2 300 ..	118.53	170.23	200.02	251.69	328.31	288.35	248.68	230.54
Income: debit	3 300 ..	−135.52	−144.63	−169.18	−195.26	−268.73	−237.28	−178.37	−170.89
Balance on Goods, Services, and Income	4 992 ..	*78.57*	*162.38*	*176.86*	*218.45*	*293.76*	*277.26*	*234.28*	*238.73*
Current transfers: credit	2 379 Z.	17.50	19.04	20.77	24.55	25.03	27.20	24.25	22.73
Current transfers: debit	3 379 ..	−49.14	−53.42	−57.01	−60.32	−69.69	−76.34	−69.90	−73.52
B. Capital Account[1]	4 994 Z.	**.35**	**.52**	**−1.82**	**−.34**	**.07**	**−.19**	**.07**	**−.82**
Capital account: credit	2 994 Z.	3.23	3.30	4.31	3.97	4.75	4.90	4.99	4.24
Capital account: debit	3 994 ..	−2.87	−2.78	−6.13	−4.31	−4.67	−5.09	−4.92	−5.07
Total, Groups A Plus B	4 981 ..	*47.28*	*128.52*	*138.80*	*182.33*	*249.17*	*227.93*	*188.70*	*187.12*
C. Financial Account[1]	4 995 W.	**−71.61**	**−152.98**	**−164.42**	**−223.36**	**−289.50**	**−232.52**	**−194.97**	**−184.75**
Direct investment abroad	4 505 ..	−5.15	−19.96	−76.96	−119.22	−171.73	−81.23	−77.97	−108.36
Direct investment in Germany	4 555 Z.	30.93	−9.80	46.47	56.64	80.59	4.79	38.92	46.13
Portfolio investment assets	4 602 ..	−52.51	−128.60	−257.33	−203.39	−198.95	23.42	−96.13	−231.13
Equity securities	4 610 ..	3.89	−4.83	−78.46	−28.63	−27.93	42.88	−.61	−28.51
Debt securities	4 619 ..	−56.40	−123.77	−178.87	−174.77	−171.02	−19.46	−95.52	−202.62
Portfolio investment liabilities	4 652 Z.	113.10	147.85	221.66	181.03	414.32	50.01	−19.99	61.37
Equity securities	4 660 ..	25.23	−7.88	22.06	35.66	76.96	−65.48	11.99	−1.99
Debt securities	4 669 Z.	87.87	155.73	199.60	145.37	337.36	115.48	−31.98	63.36
Financial derivatives	4 910 ..	−2.38	−9.37	−12.02	−7.77	−119.86	−47.72	15.16	−22.92
Financial derivatives assets	4 900 ..	....	....	....	....	....	....	....	....
Financial derivatives liabilities	4 905 ..	−2.38	−9.37	−12.02	−7.77	−119.86	−47.72	15.16	−22.92
Other investment assets	4 703 ..	−170.90	−179.47	−161.90	−261.15	−455.26	−221.77	136.14	−163.59
Monetary authorities	4 701 ..	−.21	−4.03	−26.05	29.12	−91.18	−64.60	−81.72	−193.54
General government	4 704 ..	.83	2.67	4.83	1.15	11.23	4.19	3.34	−82.50
Banks	4 705 ..	−135.18	−152.35	−113.15	−256.52	−307.32	−120.09	238.91	188.02
Other sectors	4 728 ..	−36.35	−25.76	−27.52	−34.91	−68.00	−41.27	−24.38	−75.58
Other investment liabilities	4 753 W.	15.30	46.37	75.64	130.50	161.40	40.00	−191.10	233.76
Monetary authorities	4 753 WA	2.13	−2.98	−2.72	−1.64	16.15	20.78	−11.36	7.36
General government	4 753 ZB	4.03	−5.65	4.83	−.19	−5.57	10.96	−9.47	126.24
Banks	4 753 ZC	8.59	42.05	33.67	69.16	94.92	−60.16	−162.54	98.39
Other sectors	4 753 ZD	.55	12.96	39.87	63.18	55.90	68.41	−7.74	1.77
Total, Groups A Through C	4 983 ..	*−24.33*	*−24.46*	*−25.62*	*−41.02*	*−40.33*	*−4.59*	*−6.27*	*2.37*
D. Net Errors and Omissions	4 998 ..	**23.64**	**22.65**	**23.02**	**37.37**	**41.56**	**7.33**	**18.62**	**−.24**
Total, Groups A Through D	4 984 ..	*−.68*	*−1.81*	*−2.60*	*−3.65*	*1.23*	*2.74*	*12.36*	*2.13*
E. Reserves and Related Items	4 802 A.	**.68**	**1.81**	**2.60**	**3.65**	**−1.23**	**−2.74**	**−12.36**	**−2.13**
Reserve assets	4 802 ..	.68	1.81	2.60	3.65	−1.23	−2.74	−12.36	−2.13
Use of Fund credit and loans	4 766 ..	....	....	....	....	....	....	....	....
Exceptional financing	4 920 ..	....	....	....	....	....	....	....	....
Conversion rates: euros per U.S. dollar	0 103 ..	**.8860**	**.8054**	**.8041**	**.7971**	**.7306**	**.6827**	**.7198**	**.7550**

[1] Excludes components that have been classified in the categories of Group E.

Table 2. STANDARD PRESENTATION, 2003–2010

(Billions of U.S. dollars)

	Code	2003	2004	2005	2006	2007	2008	2009	2010
CURRENT ACCOUNT	4 993 ..	**46.93**	**128.00**	**140.61**	**182.67**	**249.10**	**228.12**	**188.63**	**187.94**
A. GOODS	4 100 ..	**144.74**	**186.04**	**193.14**	**198.05**	**270.75**	**263.03**	**188.50**	**204.72**
Credit	2 100 ..	**747.37**	**907.79**	**983.14**	**1,136.16**	**1,354.26**	**1,501.80**	**1,160.99**	**1,303.33**
General merchandise: exports f.o.b.	2 110 ..	702.35	852.97	924.01	1,068.95	1,284.83	1,426.09	1,093.24	1,228.52
Goods for processing: exports f.o.b.	2 150 ..	42.30	52.08	55.76	62.87	63.89	68.76	60.64	64.28
Repairs on goods	2 160 ..	1.64	1.77	2.34	2.59	2.90	3.02	3.39	3.02
Goods procured in ports by carriers	2 170 ..	.48	.48	.48	.58	.85	.97	.53	.63
Nonmonetary gold	2 180 ..	.60	.51	.56	1.17	1.79	2.97	3.20	6.88
Debit	3 100 ..	**−602.63**	**−721.75**	**−790.00**	**−938.11**	**−1,083.52**	**−1,238.77**	**−972.49**	**−1,098.61**
General merchandise: imports f.o.b.	3 110 ..	−560.48	−672.71	−737.93	−878.10	−1,020.47	−1,167.32	−913.05	−1,033.82
Goods for processing: imports f.o.b.	3 150 ..	−38.56	−44.44	−45.93	−52.13	−53.22	−56.43	−46.87	−49.24
Repairs on goods	3 160 ..	−.06	−.07	−.10	−.11	−.15	−.29	−.89	−.80
Goods procured in ports by carriers	3 170 ..	−2.87	−3.80	−4.98	−6.26	−7.76	−11.14	−7.01	−8.28
Nonmonetary gold	3 180 ..	−.66	−.73	−1.07	−1.51	−1.90	−3.59	−4.67	−6.47
B. SERVICES	4 200 ..	**−49.19**	**−49.26**	**−47.12**	**−36.03**	**−36.57**	**−36.84**	**−24.54**	**−25.63**
Total credit	2 200 ..	*123.87*	*147.50*	*163.87*	*188.12*	*223.51*	*254.68*	*232.59*	*237.81*
Total debit	3 200 ..	*−173.06*	*−196.76*	*−210.99*	*−224.15*	*−260.07*	*−291.52*	*−257.12*	*−263.44*
Transportation services, credit	2 205 ..	**27.28**	**34.81**	**41.14**	**45.49**	**54.34**	**64.50**	**52.09**	**57.51**
Passenger	2 850 ..	*6.98*	*8.78*	*11.41*	*12.65*	*13.23*	*13.48*	*12.73*	*14.57*
Freight	2 851 ..	*14.81*	*19.99*	*22.72*	*25.34*	*33.19*	*42.33*	*31.69*	*35.58*
Other	2 852 ..	*5.50*	*6.04*	*7.01*	*7.50*	*7.92*	*8.69*	*7.68*	*7.35*
Sea transport, passenger	2 207 ..	.16	.24	.27	.29	.27	.38	.27	.24
Sea transport, freight	2 208 ..	9.57	13.87	17.14	19.61	26.62	34.47	25.27	28.05
Sea transport, other	2 209 ..	1.21	1.08	1.21	1.36	1.68	2.05	1.50	1.51
Air transport, passenger	2 211 ..	6.55	8.27	10.74	11.90	12.46	12.61	11.98	13.87
Air transport, freight	2 212 ..	1.79	2.07	3.02	3.03	3.45	4.36	3.18	4.32
Air transport, other	2 213 ..	3.10	3.66	4.18	4.44	4.95	5.87	5.78	5.48
Other transport, passenger	2 215 ..	.27	.27	.40	.46	.50	.48	.48	.46
Other transport, freight	2 216 ..	3.45	4.05	2.55	2.70	3.12	3.51	3.23	3.22
Other transport, other	2 217 ..	1.18	1.30	1.61	1.70	1.29	.77	.40	.36
Transportation services, debit	3 205 ..	**−35.37**	**−42.54**	**−46.07**	**−52.33**	**−61.13**	**−70.92**	**−52.52**	**−62.83**
Passenger	3 850 ..	*−7.97*	*−9.44*	*−10.65*	*−11.85*	*−13.39*	*−14.44*	*−11.71*	*−13.63*
Freight	3 851 ..	*−16.52*	*−20.20*	*−20.70*	*−22.43*	*−25.98*	*−29.76*	*−19.94*	*−25.85*
Other	3 852 ..	*−10.88*	*−12.91*	*−14.72*	*−18.04*	*−21.75*	*−26.72*	*−20.88*	*−23.35*
Sea transport, passenger	3 207 ..	....	....	....	....	....	....	....	....
Sea transport, freight	3 208 ..	−5.98	−7.39	−6.01	−6.57	−7.48	−7.91	−3.61	−5.96
Sea transport, other	3 209 ..	−4.01	−4.97	−5.94	−8.07	−10.69	−14.27	−11.90	−13.64
Air transport, passenger	3 211 ..	−7.29	−8.89	−10.13	−11.29	−12.68	−13.68	−11.09	−13.09
Air transport, freight	3 212 ..	−.56	−.65	−2.66	−2.88	−3.33	−5.02	−2.76	−4.04
Air transport, other	3 213 ..	−2.87	−2.93	−3.11	−3.83	−3.83	−4.51	−4.67	−4.38
Other transport, passenger	3 215 ..	−.68	−.55	−.52	−.56	−.71	−.75	−.61	−.54
Other transport, freight	3 216 ..	−9.98	−12.16	−12.03	−12.98	−15.16	−16.83	−13.57	−15.85
Other transport, other	3 217 ..	−4.00	−5.00	−5.67	−6.14	−7.24	−7.94	−4.30	−5.33
Travel, credit	2 236 ..	**23.12**	**27.61**	**29.12**	**32.89**	**36.10**	**39.92**	**34.73**	**34.56**
Business travel	2 237 ..	....	....	....	....	....	....	....	....
Personal travel	2 240 ..	....	....	....	....	....	....	....	....
Travel, debit	3 236 ..	**−65.23**	**−71.19**	**−74.19**	**−74.12**	**−83.16**	**−91.60**	**−81.40**	**−77.58**
Business travel	3 237 ..	−9.20	−10.67	−11.69	−11.18	−12.96	−12.01	−10.02	−10.55
Personal travel	3 240 ..	−56.03	−60.52	−62.50	−62.94	−70.20	−79.59	−71.38	−67.03
Other services, credit	2 200 BA	**73.46**	**85.08**	**93.61**	**109.74**	**133.07**	**150.26**	**145.77**	**145.74**
Communications	2 245 ..	2.68	3.26	3.44	4.51	4.67	5.27	4.79	5.42
Construction	2 249 ..	7.11	7.10	10.41	12.38	13.60	15.96	13.60	11.64
Insurance	2 253 ..	6.76	3.63	2.16	3.79	5.86	4.65	5.25	6.08
Financial	2 260 ..	4.01	5.28	6.58	8.64	11.94	13.65	12.36	11.78
Computer and information	2 262 ..	6.70	8.09	8.39	9.99	12.75	15.40	14.82	16.33
Royalties and licence fees	2 266 ..	4.51	5.53	7.14	6.96	8.46	10.83	16.35	14.38
Other business services	2 268 ..	33.24	43.18	47.96	56.18	68.26	78.30	72.70	74.56
Personal, cultural, and recreational	2 287 ..	1.01	.98	1.17	.94	1.14	1.06	1.23	1.08
Government, n.i.e.	2 291 ..	7.44	8.04	6.37	6.35	6.38	5.13	4.67	4.47
Other services, debit	3 200 BA	**−72.46**	**−83.03**	**−90.74**	**−97.70**	**−115.79**	**−129.00**	**−123.20**	**−123.03**
Communications	3 245 ..	−4.07	−4.66	−5.02	−6.27	−6.64	−7.10	−6.56	−7.42
Construction	3 249 ..	−5.45	−5.86	−6.59	−7.35	−9.18	−11.34	−9.96	−7.81
Insurance	3 253 ..	−3.44	−5.30	−4.76	−2.66	−3.26	−4.16	−3.49	−4.01
Financial	3 260 ..	−2.41	−3.63	−4.56	−5.82	−8.10	−7.75	−6.95	−6.85
Computer and information	3 262 ..	−7.27	−8.14	−8.59	−9.24	−11.87	−13.76	−12.54	−14.11
Royalties and licence fees	3 266 ..	−5.33	−5.85	−8.50	−9.33	−11.19	−12.85	−15.02	−13.05
Other business services	3 268 ..	−39.83	−44.99	−47.46	−50.64	−60.90	−67.47	−64.51	−65.82
Personal, cultural, and recreational	3 287 ..	−2.95	−3.19	−3.49	−4.72	−2.80	−2.94	−2.77	−2.78
Government, n.i.e.	3 291 ..	−1.69	−1.40	−1.77	−1.66	−1.85	−1.64	−1.39	−1.19

Table 2 (Continued). STANDARD PRESENTATION, 2003–2010

(Billions of U.S. dollars)

	Code	2003	2004	2005	2006	2007	2008	2009	2010
C. INCOME	4 300	**−16.99**	**25.60**	**30.84**	**56.43**	**59.58**	**51.07**	**70.31**	**59.65**
Total credit	2 300	*118.53*	*170.23*	*200.02*	*251.69*	*328.31*	*288.35*	*248.68*	*230.54*
Total debit	3 300	*−135.52*	*−144.63*	*−169.18*	*−195.26*	*−268.73*	*−237.28*	*−178.37*	*−170.89*
Compensation of employees, credit	2 310	**5.74**	**6.51**	**6.87**	**7.48**	**9.77**	**10.69**	**11.06**	**11.16**
Compensation of employees, debit	3 310	**−7.10**	**−7.71**	**−8.41**	**−8.49**	**−9.46**	**−10.02**	**−11.38**	**−11.50**
Investment income, credit	2 320	**112.79**	**163.72**	**193.15**	**244.21**	**318.54**	**277.67**	**237.63**	**219.37**
Direct investment income	2 330	17.48	51.57	61.45	78.08	93.58	41.05	81.19	86.54
Dividends and distributed branch profits	2 332	20.21	25.39	32.16	37.62	43.27	55.50	39.11	45.27
Reinvested earnings and undistributed branch profits	2 333	−4.59	23.41	25.77	35.45	41.47	−25.12	32.40	31.25
Income on debt (interest)	2 334	1.86	2.76	3.52	5.01	8.84	10.67	9.68	10.02
Portfolio investment income	2 339	50.18	58.63	62.95	73.70	97.81	114.38	95.66	83.77
Income on equity	2 340	13.85	18.20	18.72	22.46	28.06	31.48	22.49	15.38
Income on bonds and notes	2 350	36.00	40.03	43.71	50.00	67.54	78.90	72.45	68.17
Income on money market instruments	2 360	.34	.40	.51	1.25	2.20	4.00	.71	.22
Other investment income	2 370	45.12	53.53	68.75	92.42	127.15	122.24	60.78	49.07
Investment income, debit	3 320	**−128.42**	**−136.91**	**−160.77**	**−186.77**	**−259.27**	**−227.26**	**−166.99**	**−159.38**
Direct investment income	3 330	−25.75	−26.64	−39.32	−42.11	−64.96	−24.95	−45.18	−52.23
Dividends and distributed branch profits	3 332	−13.77	−16.91	−20.31	−24.67	−33.64	−33.10	−21.30	−23.08
Reinvested earnings and undistributed branch profits	3 333	3.84	5.08	−4.13	.52	−7.16	31.73	−2.02	−7.25
Income on debt (interest)	3 334	−15.82	−14.81	−14.89	−17.96	−24.16	−23.58	−21.85	−21.90
Portfolio investment income	3 339	−63.46	−67.75	−70.31	−79.33	−105.55	−125.90	−87.02	−74.60
Income on equity	3 340	−9.26	−10.39	−11.82	−17.51	−27.60	−32.68	−23.58	−19.28
Income on bonds and notes	3 350	−50.64	−54.48	−56.52	−58.56	−72.09	−82.17	−57.73	−51.98
Income on money market instruments	3 360	−3.56	−2.88	−1.97	−3.26	−5.86	−11.05	−5.70	−3.33
Other investment income	3 370	−39.21	−42.52	−51.14	−65.34	−88.76	−76.41	−34.80	−32.56
D. CURRENT TRANSFERS	4 379	**−31.63**	**−34.38**	**−36.25**	**−35.77**	**−44.66**	**−49.14**	**−45.65**	**−50.79**
Credit	2 379	**17.50**	**19.04**	**20.77**	**24.55**	**25.03**	**27.20**	**24.25**	**22.73**
General government	2 380	13.28	15.52	16.23	20.64	20.12	22.03	19.04	17.41
Other sectors	2 390	4.22	3.51	4.54	3.91	4.91	5.17	5.21	5.32
Workers' remittances	2 391	....	....	....	....	....	....	....	....
Other current transfers	2 392	4.22	3.51	4.54	3.91	4.91	5.17	5.21	5.32
Debit	3 379	**−49.14**	**−53.42**	**−57.01**	**−60.32**	**−69.69**	**−76.34**	**−69.90**	**−73.52**
General government	3 380	−33.60	−36.07	−38.60	−40.44	−43.63	−47.07	−44.97	−48.19
Other sectors	3 390	−15.54	−17.35	−18.41	−19.88	−26.06	−29.27	−24.93	−25.33
Workers' remittances	3 391	−3.77	−3.95	−3.65	−3.68	−4.11	−4.53	−4.17	−4.03
Other current transfers	3 392	−11.77	−13.40	−14.76	−16.21	−21.96	−24.74	−20.75	−21.30
CAPITAL AND FINANCIAL ACCOUNT	4 996	**−70.57**	**−150.65**	**−163.64**	**−220.05**	**−290.66**	**−235.45**	**−207.25**	**−187.70**
CAPITAL ACCOUNT	4 994	**.35**	**.52**	**−1.82**	**−.34**	**.07**	**−.19**	**.07**	**−.82**
Total credit	2 994	*3.23*	*3.30*	*4.31*	*3.97*	*4.75*	*4.90*	*4.99*	*4.24*
Total debit	3 994	*−2.87*	*−2.78*	*−6.13*	*−4.31*	*−4.67*	*−5.09*	*−4.92*	*−5.07*
Capital transfers, credit	2 400	**3.23**	**3.30**	**4.31**	**3.97**	**4.75**	**4.90**	**4.99**	**4.24**
General government	2 401	....	....	....	....	....	....	....	....
Debt forgiveness	2 402	....	....	....	....	....	....	....	....
Other capital transfers	2 410	....	....	....	....	....	....	....	....
Other sectors	2 430	3.23	3.30	4.31	3.97	4.75	4.90	4.99	4.24
Migrants' transfers	2 431	.04	.07	.07	.09	.12	.20	.15	.17
Debt forgiveness	2 432	....	....	....	....	....	....	.63	.49
Other capital transfers	2 440	3.19	3.23	4.25	3.89	4.62	4.70	4.21	3.58
Capital transfers, debit	3 400	**−2.87**	**−2.78**	**−6.13**	**−4.31**	**−4.67**	**−5.09**	**−4.92**	**−5.07**
General government	3 401	−1.41	−1.37	−4.35	−2.46	−2.85	−2.67	−2.39	−2.72
Debt forgiveness	3 402	−.32	−.06	−2.88	−.90	−1.01	−.49	−.06	−.07
Other capital transfers	3 410	−1.09	−1.30	−1.47	−1.55	−1.84	−2.18	−2.33	−2.65
Other sectors	3 430	−1.46	−1.41	−1.77	−1.86	−1.82	−2.42	−2.53	−2.34
Migrants' transfers	3 431	−.33	−.40	−.44	−.38	−.44	−.47	−.40	−.38
Debt forgiveness	3 432	−.48	−.29	−.42	−.40	−.25	−.68	−.95	−.66
Other capital transfers	3 440	−.65	−.72	−.92	−1.08	−1.13	−1.27	−1.18	−1.31
Nonproduced nonfinancial assets, credit	2 480	....	....	....	....	....	....	....	....
Nonproduced nonfinancial assets, debit	3 480	....	....	....	....	....	....	....	....

Table 2 (Continued). STANDARD PRESENTATION, 2003–2010

(Billions of U.S. dollars)

	Code	2003	2004	2005	2006	2007	2008	2009	2010
FINANCIAL ACCOUNT	4 995	**−70.93**	**−151.17**	**−161.82**	**−219.70**	**−290.73**	**−235.26**	**−207.32**	**−186.88**
A. DIRECT INVESTMENT	4 500	**25.78**	**−29.76**	**−30.48**	**−62.57**	**−91.14**	**−76.45**	**−39.06**	**−62.23**
Direct investment abroad	4 505	**−5.15**	**−19.96**	**−76.96**	**−119.22**	**−171.73**	**−81.23**	**−77.97**	**−108.36**
Equity capital	4 510	−37.83	19.96	−35.22	−91.71	−68.97	−79.79	−69.78	−58.55
Claims on affiliated enterprises	4 515	−37.83	19.96	−35.22	−91.71	−68.97	−79.79	−69.78	−58.55
Liabilities to affiliated enterprises	4 520	....	....	....	....	....	....	....	....
Reinvested earnings	4 525	4.59	−23.41	−25.77	−35.45	−41.47	25.12	−32.40	−31.25
Other capital	4 530	28.08	−16.51	−15.97	7.94	−61.29	−26.57	24.22	−18.56
Claims on affiliated enterprises	4 535	−2.95	−8.46	−23.57	−16.51	−28.98	−43.30	−11.51	−30.55
Liabilities to affiliated enterprises	4 540	31.03	−8.05	7.60	24.45	−32.31	16.73	35.72	12.00
Direct investment in Germany	4 555	**30.93**	**−9.80**	**46.47**	**56.64**	**80.59**	**4.79**	**38.92**	**46.13**
Equity capital	4 560	53.08	43.98	35.90	37.93	56.57	34.34	12.43	10.14
Claims on direct investors	4 565	....	....	....	....	....	....	....	....
Liabilities to direct investors	4 570	53.08	43.98	35.90	37.93	56.57	34.34	12.43	10.14
Reinvested earnings	4 575	−3.84	−5.08	4.13	−.52	7.16	−31.73	2.02	7.25
Other capital	4 580	−18.31	−48.70	6.45	19.23	16.86	2.18	24.46	28.73
Claims on direct investors	4 585	−14.94	−51.30	12.22	25.55	19.42	7.84	20.17	35.50
Liabilities to direct investors	4 590	−3.37	2.59	−5.77	−6.32	−2.56	−5.66	4.29	−6.76
B. PORTFOLIO INVESTMENT	4 600	**60.60**	**19.25**	**−35.66**	**−22.37**	**215.36**	**73.42**	**−116.12**	**−169.76**
Assets	4 602	**−52.51**	**−128.60**	**−257.33**	**−203.39**	**−198.95**	**23.42**	**−96.13**	**−231.13**
Equity securities	4 610	3.89	−4.83	−78.46	−28.63	−27.93	42.88	−.61	−28.51
Monetary authorities	4 611	....	....	....	....	....	....	....	....
General government	4 612	....	....	....	....	....	....	....	....
Banks	4 613	−6.02	−3.57	−20.11	−15.09	−20.34	46.11	9.43	−10.59
Other sectors	4 614	9.92	−1.26	−58.35	−13.54	−7.59	−3.23	−10.04	−17.92
Debt securities	4 619	−56.40	−123.77	−178.87	−174.77	−171.02	−19.46	−95.52	−202.62
Bonds and notes	4 620	−61.17	−109.42	−173.02	−165.89	−134.32	−41.41	−113.41	−211.21
Monetary authorities	4 621	....	−.09	−.29	−.09	−2.28	−.07	−6.90	−24.82
General government	4 622	....	....	....	....	....	....	....	−145.73
Banks	4 623	−36.15	−80.88	−110.05	−126.12	−128.37	8.92	43.73	88.99
Other sectors	4 624	−25.02	−28.45	−62.68	−39.68	−3.67	−50.27	−150.25	−129.65
Money market instruments	4 630	4.77	−14.35	−5.85	−8.88	−36.70	21.95	17.90	8.58
Monetary authorities	4 631	....	....	....	....	....	....	....	−.15
General government	4 632	....	....	....	....	....	....	....	....
Banks	4 633	.78	−7.60	−1.48	−7.49	−40.44	19.12	18.96	6.34
Other sectors	4 634	3.99	−6.76	−4.36	−1.39	3.74	2.83	−1.06	2.40
Liabilities	4 652	**113.10**	**147.85**	**221.66**	**181.03**	**414.32**	**50.01**	**−19.99**	**61.37**
Equity securities	4 660	25.23	−7.88	22.06	35.66	76.96	−65.48	11.99	−1.99
Banks	4 663	1.56	−1.61	−10.30	−2.51	2.53	−11.76	.19	2.89
Other sectors	4 664	23.68	−6.27	32.36	38.17	74.43	−53.71	11.79	−4.88
Debt securities	4 669	87.87	155.73	199.60	145.37	337.36	115.48	−31.98	63.36
Bonds and notes	4 670	73.88	173.84	202.19	147.95	273.76	55.53	−99.78	62.67
Monetary authorities	4 671	....	....	....	....	....	....	....	....
General government	4 672	20.28	58.20	89.74	65.94	85.35	66.58	36.02	93.26
Banks	4 673	53.60	115.64	112.46	82.02	188.41	−11.05	−115.11	−59.40
Other sectors	4 674	....	....	....	....	....	....	−20.68	28.81
Money market instruments	4 680	13.99	−18.11	−2.59	−2.58	63.60	59.95	67.80	.69
Monetary authorities	4 681	....	....	....	....	....	....	....	....
General government	4 682	5.85	−1.80	3.92	−2.23	−1.24	14.36	76.55	−28.16
Banks	4 683	5.36	−15.86	−3.67	−2.29	40.39	3.37	9.60	21.41
Other sectors	4 684	2.78	−.45	−2.84	1.94	24.45	42.22	−18.35	7.44
C. FINANCIAL DERIVATIVES	4 910	**−2.38**	**−9.37**	**−12.02**	**−7.77**	**−119.86**	**−47.72**	**15.16**	**−22.92**
Monetary authorities	4 911	....	....	....	....	....	....	....	....
General government	4 912	....	....	....	....	....	....	....	....
Banks	4 913	....	....	....	....	....	....	....	....
Other sectors	4 914	....	....	....	....	....	....	....	....
Assets	4 900	....	....	....	....	....	....	....	....
Monetary authorities	4 901	....	....	....	....	....	....	....	....
General government	4 902	....	....	....	....	....	....	....	....
Banks	4 903	....	....	....	....	....	....	....	....
Other sectors	4 904	....	....	....	....	....	....	....	....
Liabilities	4 905	**−2.38**	**−9.37**	**−12.02**	**−7.77**	**−119.86**	**−47.72**	**15.16**	**−22.92**
Monetary authorities	4 906	....	....	....	....	....	....	....	....
General government	4 907	....	....	....	....	....	....	....	....
Banks	4 908	....	....	....	....	....	....	....	....
Other sectors	4 909	....	....	....	....	....	....	....	....

Table 2 (Concluded). STANDARD PRESENTATION, 2003–2010

(Billions of U.S. dollars)

	Code	2003	2004	2005	2006	2007	2008	2009	2010
D. OTHER INVESTMENT	4 700	**−155.61**	**−133.09**	**−86.25**	**−130.65**	**−293.87**	**−181.77**	**−54.96**	**70.17**
Assets	4 703	−170.90	−179.47	−161.90	−261.15	−455.26	−221.77	136.14	−163.59
Trade credits	4 706	2.65	−1.96	−8.63	−6.39	−6.43	−5.45	7.96	−3.02
General government	4 707	....	....	....	....	....	....	....	....
of which: Short-term	4 709	....	....	....	....	....	....	....	....
Other sectors	4 710	2.65	−1.96	−8.63	−6.39	−6.43	−5.45	7.96	−3.02
of which: Short-term	4 712	2.65	−1.96	−8.63	−6.39	−6.43	−5.45	7.96	−3.02
Loans	4 714	−139.43	−152.99	−106.48	−250.36	−291.62	−126.55	232.28	109.28
Monetary authorities	4 715	....	....	....	....	....	....	....	.42
of which: Short-term	4 718	....	....	....	....	....	....	....	....
General government	4 719	.77	1.01	10.52	10.24	.91	1.02	−.48	−67.88
of which: Short-term	4 721	....	.02	....	.01	−.35	.37	−.85	−6.82
Banks	4 722	−135.13	−151.86	−112.95	−256.18	−304.06	−122.31	239.01	188.08
of which: Short-term	4 724	−98.72	−159.42	−26.38	−166.12	−170.95	93.26	199.75	85.13
Other sectors	4 725	−5.07	−2.14	−4.05	−4.42	11.53	−5.26	−6.25	−11.35
of which: Short-term	4 727	−2.37	−1.06	1.32	−2.42	12.68	.09	3.17	−10.75
Currency and deposits	4 730	−30.86	−20.66	−41.54	1.61	−147.61	−83.80	−99.95	−266.72
Monetary authorities	4 731	−.21	−4.08	−26.00	29.12	−91.17	−64.60	−81.86	−193.52
General government	4 732	.33	2.20	−5.07	−8.40	11.14	4.12	4.91	−14.61
Banks	4 733	.02	.06	−.03	−.17	....	−.01	.04	−.10
Other sectors	4 734	−31.01	−18.84	−10.44	−18.95	−67.58	−23.32	−23.04	−58.49
Other assets	4 736	−3.26	−3.86	−5.24	−6.01	−9.60	−5.96	−4.15	−3.13
Monetary authorities	4 737	....	.05	−.05	....	−.02	....	.14	−.43
of which: Short-term	4 739	....	....	....	....	....	....	....	....
General government	4 740	−.27	−.53	−.63	−.69	−.82	−.95	−1.09	−.02
of which: Short-term	4 742	....	....	....	....	....	....	....	....
Banks	4 743	−.07	−.55	−.17	−.17	−3.25	2.23	−.14	.03
of which: Short-term	4 745	....	....	....	....	....	....	....	....
Other sectors	4 746	−2.92	−2.83	−4.40	−5.15	−5.52	−7.24	−3.05	−2.72
of which: Short-term	4 748	....	....	....	....	....	....	....	....
Liabilities	4 753	**15.30**	**46.37**	**75.64**	**130.50**	**161.40**	**40.00**	**−191.10**	**233.76**
Trade credits	4 756	1.82	4.89	6.92	10.42	15.55	10.85	1.46	.35
General government	4 757	....	....	....	....	....	....	....	....
of which: Short-term	4 759	....	....	....	....	....	....	....	....
Other sectors	4 760	1.82	4.89	6.92	10.42	15.55	10.85	1.46	.35
of which: Short-term	4 762	1.82	4.89	6.92	10.42	15.55	10.85	1.46	.35
Loans	4 764	−9.95	8.10	49.38	101.39	113.61	5.48	−139.42	224.50
Monetary authorities	4 765	....	....	....	....	....	....	....	....
of which: Use of Fund credit and loans from the Fund	4 766	....	....	....	....	....	....	....	....
of which: Short-term	4 768	....	....	....	....	....	....	....	....
General government	4 769	4.03	−5.65	4.83	−.19	−5.58	10.96	−9.46	126.25
of which: Short-term	4 771	−1.30	−1.67	1.35	−1.22	−1.25	12.76	−6.70	126.58
Banks	4 772	−12.72	6.60	12.37	48.99	79.77	−63.46	−120.68	96.58
of which: Short-term	4 774	−6.45	19.57	24.05	67.87	100.00	−78.51	−85.43	104.27
Other sectors	4 775	−1.26	7.15	32.18	52.58	39.43	57.97	−9.28	1.68
of which: Short-term	4 777	−1.20	−.85	8.56	12.38	10.08	18.49	−11.35	8.12
Currency and deposits	4 780	23.43	32.41	18.57	18.20	30.31	20.77	−71.41	9.19
Monetary authorities	4 781	2.13	−2.98	−2.72	−1.64	16.15	20.78	−28.30	7.36
General government	4 782	....	....	....	....	....	....	....	....
Banks	4 783	21.30	35.39	21.29	19.84	14.15	....	−43.10	1.83
Other sectors	4 784	....	....	....	....	....	....	....	....
Other liabilities	4 786	....	.97	.78	.50	1.92	2.90	18.28	−.27
Monetary authorities	4 787	....	....	....	....	....	....	16.95	....
of which: Short-term	4 789	....	....	....	....	....	....	....	....
General government	4 790	....	....	....	−.01	.01	....	....	....
of which: Short-term	4 792	....	....	....	....	....	....	....	....
Banks	4 793	.01	.06	.01	.33	.99	3.30	1.25	−.02
of which: Short-term	4 795	....	....	....	....	....	....	....	....
Other sectors	4 796	−.01	.91	.78	.18	.92	−.41	.09	−.25
of which: Short-term	4 798	....	....	....	....	....	....	....	....
E. RESERVE ASSETS	4 802	**.68**	**1.81**	**2.60**	**3.65**	**−1.23**	**−2.74**	**−12.36**	**−2.13**
Monetary gold	4 812	....	....	....	....	....	....	....	....
Special drawing rights	4 811	.21	−.03	....	−.02	−.05	−.09	−16.81	−.01
Reserve position in the Fund	4 810	−.28	1.08	2.91	1.65	.63	−1.00	−1.39	−2.30
Foreign exchange	4 803	.76	.75	−.31	2.02	−1.82	−1.65	5.84	.17
Other claims	4 813	....	....	....	....	....	....	....	....
NET ERRORS AND OMISSIONS	4 998	**23.64**	**22.65**	**23.02**	**37.37**	**41.56**	**7.33**	**18.62**	**−.24**

Table 3. INTERNATIONAL INVESTMENT POSITION (End-period stocks), 2003–2010

(Billions of U.S. dollars)

	Code	2003	2004	2005	2006	2007	2008	2009	2010
ASSETS..	8 995 C..	**4,061.54**	**4,750.35**	**4,811.84**	**6,013.62**	**7,387.17**	**6,835.87**	**7,263.54**	**8,473.78**
Direct investment abroad..............................	8 505 ..	**720.52**	**814.67**	**831.36**	**1,042.29**	**1,311.07**	**1,249.72**	**1,346.12**	**1,405.82**
Equity capital and reinvested earnings.................	8 506 ..	722.33	809.74	824.81	1,036.92	1,309.83	1,179.86	1,271.19	1,331.01
Claims on affiliated enterprises........................	8 507 ..	....	....	....	....	....	....	....	....
Liabilities to affiliated enterprises....................	8 508 ..	....	....	....	....	....	....	....	....
Other capital..	8 530 ..	−1.80	4.93	6.56	5.37	1.25	69.86	74.93	74.81
Claims on affiliated enterprises........................	8 535 ..	131.15	144.18	146.35	168.84	197.91	239.37	253.98	255.13
Liabilities to affiliated enterprises....................	8 540 ..	−132.96	−139.26	−139.79	−163.47	−196.67	−169.51	−179.05	−180.31
Portfolio investment......................................	8 602 ..	**1,381.82**	**1,676.48**	**1,817.91**	**2,266.37**	**2,624.81**	**2,149.16**	**2,507.87**	**2,555.69**
Equity securities...	8 610 ..	576.24	668.23	771.38	884.23	954.03	589.53	707.09	739.72
Monetary authorities.....................................	8 611 ..	....	....	....	....	....	....	....	....
General government......................................	8 612 ..	....	....	....	.57	1.05	1.24	1.39	1.23
Banks..	8 613 ..	31.35	36.07	52.18	65.29	79.53	29.68	29.28	30.13
Other sectors...	8 614 ..	544.89	632.16	719.20	818.37	873.46	558.62	676.42	708.35
Debt securities..	8 619 ..	805.58	1,008.25	1,046.53	1,382.14	1,670.78	1,559.63	1,800.78	1,815.97
Bonds and notes...	8 620 ..	786.89	978.03	1,019.05	1,350.07	1,596.27	1,510.20	1,767.38	1,791.84
Monetary authorities..................................	8 621 ..	.57	.91	1.06	1.22	3.72	3.58	10.74	32.82
General government....................................	8 622 ..	....	....	....	2.02	3.08	4.62	15.50	175.70
Banks...	8 623 ..	401.68	527.32	564.20	784.32	961.68	883.11	908.62	742.65
Other sectors..	8 624 ..	384.64	449.80	453.80	562.51	627.80	618.89	832.52	840.68
Money market instruments............................	8 630 ..	18.69	30.21	27.48	32.07	74.51	49.44	33.40	24.12
Monetary authorities..................................	8 631 ..	....	....	....	....	....	....	....	.15
General government....................................	8 632 ..	....	....	....	.01	.11	.01	....	....
Banks...	8 633 ..	13.29	22.46	21.67	26.39	64.02	41.13	24.41	15.72
Other sectors..	8 634 ..	5.40	7.75	5.81	5.67	10.38	8.30	8.99	8.26
Financial derivatives......................................	8 900 ..	....	....	....	....	....	....	....	**1,047.83**
Monetary authorities.......................................	8 901 ..	....	....	....	....	....	....	....	....
General government..	8 902 ..	....	....	....	....	....	....	....	....
Banks...	8 903 ..	....	....	....	....	....	....	....	1,047.83
Other sectors..	8 904 ..	....	....	....	....	....	....	....	....
Other investment...	8 703 ..	**1,862.36**	**2,162.03**	**2,060.89**	**2,593.32**	**3,315.06**	**3,298.95**	**3,228.71**	**3,247.94**
Trade credits..	8 706 ..	110.08	122.19	115.45	142.04	166.11	155.53	147.51	145.96
General government.......................................	8 707 ..	....	....	....	....	....	....	....	....
of which: Short-term..................................	8 709 ..	....	....	....	....	....	....	....	....
Other sectors...	8 710 ..	110.08	122.19	115.45	142.04	166.11	155.53	147.51	145.96
of which: Short-term..................................	8 712 ..	*110.08*	*122.19*	*115.45*	*142.04*	*166.11*	*155.53*	*147.51*	*145.96*
Loans...	8 714 ..	1,478.64	1,732.54	1,621.02	2,087.06	2,583.80	2,535.37	2,337.20	2,133.36
Monetary authorities.....................................	8 715 ..	21.50	16.43	14.23	15.89	17.84	16.87	16.15	14.58
of which: Short-term..................................	8 718 ..	....	....	....	....	....	....	....	....
General government......................................	8 719 ..	28.29	36.05	21.16	12.51	12.56	10.95	26.58	101.21
of which: Short-term..................................	8 721 ..	*.46*	*.48*	*.41*	*.46*	*.40*	*.04*	*1.14*	*8.63*
Banks..	8 722 ..	1,289.93	1,530.83	1,472.83	1,875.58	2,353.65	2,311.84	2,099.10	1,810.20
of which: Short-term..................................	8 724 ..	*792.40*	*1,013.88*	*922.48*	*1,186.18*	*1,473.69*	*1,279.50*	*1,097.45*	*963.27*
Other sectors...	8 725 ..	138.91	149.23	112.80	183.08	199.76	195.71	195.38	207.38
of which: Short-term..................................	8 727 ..	*87.75*	*97.35*	*80.80*	*122.20*	*122.93*	*114.99*	*107.40*	*116.02*
Currency and deposits....................................	8 730 ..	214.85	258.19	277.82	307.18	493.15	535.47	665.35	891.64
Monetary authorities.....................................	8 731 ..	....	10.70	35.26	7.11	104.60	160.95	256.34	435.01
General government......................................	8 732 ..	4.56	2.49	17.84	28.39	19.37	14.41	12.06	25.14
Banks..	8 733 ..	....	....	....	....	....	....	....	....
Other sectors...	8 734 ..	210.28	245.01	224.73	271.68	369.19	360.11	396.95	431.49
Other assets...	8 736 ..	58.80	49.11	46.60	57.04	71.99	72.58	78.65	76.99
Monetary authorities.....................................	8 737 ..	1.56	1.63	1.45	1.62	1.83	1.73	1.64	1.95
of which: Short-term..................................	8 739 ..	....	....	....	....	....	....	....	....
General government......................................	8 740 ..	20.19	3.84	3.57	3.82	4.11	4.01	4.14	3.79
of which: Short-term..................................	8 742 ..	....	....	....	....	....	....	....	....
Banks..	8 743 ..	2.12	2.90	2.67	3.23	6.93	4.15	4.46	4.17
of which: Short-term..................................	8 745 ..	....	....	....	....	....	....	....	....
Other sectors...	8 746 ..	34.92	40.75	38.90	48.37	59.12	62.68	68.41	67.08
of which: Short-term..................................	8 748 ..	*.08*	*.50*	*.39*	*.42*	*.14*	*.13*	*.13*	*.13*
Reserve assets..	8 802 ..	**96.84**	**97.17**	**101.67**	**111.64**	**136.23**	**138.04**	**180.85**	**216.50**
Monetary gold..	8 812 ..	46.14	48.35	56.54	69.95	91.91	94.91	120.92	154.20
Special drawing rights.....................................	8 811 ..	1.94	2.06	1.89	2.01	2.16	2.20	19.10	18.77
Reserve position in the Fund...........................	8 810 ..	7.66	6.86	3.48	1.96	1.40	2.38	3.90	6.17
Foreign exchange..	8 803 ..	41.10	39.90	39.76	37.72	40.77	38.56	36.93	37.35
Other claims...	8 813 ..	....	....	....	....	....	....	....	....

Table 3 (Concluded). INTERNATIONAL INVESTMENT POSITION (End-period stocks), 2003–2010

(Billions of U.S. dollars)

	Code	2003	2004	2005	2006	2007	2008	2009	2010
LIABILITIES	8 995 D.	**3,882.34**	**4,431.10**	**4,259.81**	**5,161.88**	**6,439.85**	**5,976.70**	**6,080.98**	**7,221.42**
Direct investment in Germany	8 555 ..	**666.19**	**719.26**	**647.81**	**836.23**	**1,012.73**	**927.37**	**944.67**	**910.39**
Equity capital and reinvested earnings	8 556 ..	352.49	423.50	401.81	513.48	649.61	571.70	586.03	561.90
Claims on direct investors	8 557 ..	....	....	....	....	....	....	....	....
Liabilities to direct investors	8 558 ..	....	....	....	....	....	....	....	....
Other capital	8 580 ..	313.70	295.76	246.00	322.75	363.12	355.67	358.64	348.50
Claims on direct investors	8 585 ..	−26.38	−28.56	−25.56	−30.20	−37.55	−40.35	−41.01	−45.32
Liabilities to direct investors	8 590 ..	340.08	324.33	271.56	352.95	400.66	396.02	399.65	393.81
Portfolio investment	8 652 ..	**1,732.88**	**2,082.82**	**2,114.04**	**2,507.97**	**3,294.35**	**2,968.71**	**3,124.65**	**3,088.05**
Equity securities	8 660 ..	362.45	399.72	445.16	622.86	908.92	474.38	580.03	598.75
Banks	8 663 ..	36.04	44.32	61.75	65.96	74.62	22.75	33.06	36.41
Other sectors	8 664 ..	326.41	355.40	383.40	556.90	834.30	451.63	546.96	562.35
Debt securities	8 669 ..	1,370.43	1,683.10	1,668.88	1,885.11	2,385.44	2,494.33	2,544.62	2,489.30
Bonds and notes	8 670 ..	1,250.19	1,572.99	1,576.95	1,784.38	2,204.93	2,268.11	2,237.87	2,205.09
Monetary authorities	8 671 ..	....	....	....	....	....	....	....	....
General government	8 672 ..	620.77	762.69	759.42	866.19	1,017.48	1,119.49	1,166.71	1,205.11
Banks	8 673 ..	599.84	772.30	781.39	880.46	1,135.89	1,096.42	1,039.75	941.48
Other sectors	8 674 ..	29.58	38.00	36.14	37.73	51.57	52.20	31.41	58.50
Money market instruments	8 680 ..	120.24	110.10	91.94	100.74	180.50	226.22	306.75	284.20
Monetary authorities	8 681 ..	....	....	....	....	....	....	....	....
General government	8 682 ..	32.88	33.49	32.59	34.06	36.65	47.91	131.52	93.25
Banks	8 683 ..	77.49	66.46	53.56	57.74	107.50	104.57	118.12	130.29
Other sectors	8 684 ..	9.86	10.15	5.79	8.93	36.35	73.75	57.11	60.66
Financial derivatives	8 905 ..	....	....	....	....	....	....	....	**1,050.82**
Monetary authorities	8 906 ..	....	....	....	....	....	....	....	....
General government	8 907 ..	....	....	....	....	....	....	....	....
Banks	8 908 ..	....	....	....	....	....	....	....	1,050.82
Other sectors	8 909 ..	....	....	....	....	....	....	....	....
Other investment	8 753 ..	**1,483.27**	**1,629.03**	**1,497.96**	**1,817.67**	**2,132.77**	**2,080.61**	**2,011.66**	**2,172.16**
Trade credits	8 756 ..	74.99	88.19	84.93	106.68	137.08	135.53	143.98	138.77
General government	8 757 ..	....	....	....	....	....	....	....	....
of which: Short-term	8 759 ..	....	....	....	....	....	....	....	....
Other sectors	8 760 ..	74.99	88.19	84.93	106.68	137.08	135.53	143.98	138.77
of which: Short-term	8 762 ..	*74.99*	*88.19*	*84.93*	*106.68*	*137.08*	*135.53*	*143.98*	*138.77*
Loans	8 764 ..	1,404.38	1,524.56	1,400.05	1,697.33	1,961.41	1,889.89	1,820.40	1,979.21
Monetary authorities	8 765 ..	13.19	....	....	....	....	....	....	....
of which: Use of Fund credit and loans from the Fund	8 766 ..	....	....	....	....	....	....	....	....
of which: Short-term	8 768 ..	....	....	....	....	....	....	....	....
General government	8 769 ..	21.07	25.52	26.10	29.12	29.61	38.18	33.13	157.65
of which: Short-term	8 771 ..	*6.06*	*5.26*	*8.10*	*7.72*	*8.14*	*17.99*	*13.93*	*138.58*
Banks	8 772 ..	1,136.43	1,248.06	1,144.41	1,319.49	1,538.09	1,382.29	1,258.34	1,299.83
of which: Short-term	8 774 ..	*782.81*	*888.73*	*833.78*	*1,002.46*	*1,217.15*	*1,072.51*	*973.46*	*1,031.83*
Other sectors	8 775 ..	233.68	250.98	229.54	348.72	393.71	469.42	528.93	521.73
of which: Short-term	8 777 ..	*112.96*	*122.79*	*115.38*	*162.40*	*179.65*	*203.10*	*209.12*	*203.52*
Currency and deposits	8 780 ..	....	10.81	7.41	6.35	23.56	41.99	13.15	19.54
Monetary authorities	8 781 ..	....	10.81	7.41	6.35	23.56	41.99	13.15	19.54
General government	8 782 ..	....	....	....	....	....	....	....	....
Banks	8 783 ..	....	....	....	....	....	....	....	....
Other sectors	8 784 ..	....	....	....	....	....	....	....	....
Other liabilities	8 786 ..	3.91	5.46	5.56	7.31	10.72	13.21	34.13	34.65
Monetary authorities	8 787 ..	....	....	....	....	....	....	18.91	18.57
of which: Short-term	8 789 ..	....	....	....	....	....	....	....	....
General government	8 790 ..	.57	.83	.73	1.28	1.82	1.91	2.11	3.86
of which: Short-term	8 792 ..	....	....	....	....	....	....	....	....
Banks	8 793 ..	1.03	1.16	1.01	1.47	2.69	5.63	7.10	6.69
of which: Short-term	8 795 ..	....	....	....	....	....	....	....	....
Other sectors	8 796 ..	2.32	3.46	3.82	4.56	6.21	5.67	6.02	5.53
of which: Short-term	8 798 ..	....	....	....	....	....	....	....	....
NET INTERNATIONAL INVESTMENT POSITION	8 995 ..	**179.20**	**319.25**	**552.03**	**851.74**	**947.32**	**859.18**	**1,182.57**	**1,252.35**
Conversion rates: euros per U.S. dollar (end of period)	0 104 ..	.7918	.7342	.8477	.7593	.6793	.7185	.6942	.7484

Table 1. ANALYTIC PRESENTATION, 2003–2010

(Millions of U.S. dollars)

	Code	2003	2004	2005	2006	2007	2008	2009	2010
A. Current Account[1]	4 993 Z.	**101.7**	**−590.2**	**−1,104.6**	**−1,042.6**	**−2,151.4**	**−3,543.1**	**−1,598.5**	**−2,700.5**
Goods: exports f.o.b.	2 100 ..	2,562.6	2,704.5	2,802.2	3,726.7	4,172.1	5,269.7	5,839.7	7,960.1
Goods: imports f.o.b.	3 100 ..	−3,232.8	−4,297.3	−5,347.3	−6,753.7	−8,066.1	−10,268.5	−8,046.3	−10,922.1
Balance on Goods	4 100 ..	*−670.3*	*−1,592.8*	*−2,545.1*	*−3,027.0*	*−3,894.0*	*−4,998.8*	*−2,206.6*	*−2,962.0*
Services: credit	2 200 ..	630.0	702.3	1,106.5	1,382.8	1,831.9	1,800.9	1,769.7	1,477.3
Services: debit	3 200 ..	−912.8	−1,081.8	−1,273.1	−1,519.4	−1,993.9	−2,298.2	−2,943.1	−3,003.2
Balance on Goods and Services	4 991 ..	*−953.1*	*−1,972.3*	*−2,711.7*	*−3,163.5*	*−4,056.0*	*−5,496.0*	*−3,380.0*	*−4,488.0*
Income: credit	2 300 ..	21.4	44.5	43.3	73.3	84.0	85.6	101.1	52.9
Income: debit	3 300 ..	−202.4	−242.3	−230.4	−200.6	−222.6	−344.2	−397.6	−587.9
Balance on Goods, Services, and Income	4 992 ..	*−1,134.0*	*−2,170.1*	*−2,898.8*	*−3,290.9*	*−4,194.6*	*−5,754.6*	*−3,676.5*	*−5,022.9*
Current transfers: credit	2 379 Z.	1,244.9	1,579.9	1,794.2	2,248.3	2,043.2	2,211.5	2,078.0	2,322.4
Current transfers: debit	3 379 ..	−9.2	....	....	....	....	....	....	....
B. Capital Account[1]	4 994 Z.	**154.3**	**251.0**	**331.2**	**229.9**	**188.1**	**463.3**	**563.9**	**337.5**
Capital account: credit	2 994 Z.	154.3	251.0	331.2	229.9	188.1	463.3	563.9	337.5
Capital account: debit	3 994 ..	....	....	....	....	....	....	....	....
Total, Groups A Plus B	4 981 ..	*256.0*	*−339.1*	*−773.4*	*−812.7*	*−1,963.3*	*−3,079.8*	*−1,034.6*	*−2,363.0*
C. Financial Account[1]	4 995 W.	**406.1**	**566.9**	**632.1**	**1,356.9**	**2,666.3**	**1,806.1**	**3,086.2**	**3,970.5**
Direct investment abroad	4 505 ..	....	....	....	....	....	−8.8	−6.9	....
Direct investment in Ghana	4 555 Z.	136.8	139.3	145.0	636.0	855.4	1,220.4	1,684.7	2,527.4
Portfolio investment assets	4 602 ..	....	....	....	65.8	373.3	....	41.3	723.0
Equity securities	4 610 ..	....	....	....	....	....	....	....	....
Debt securities	4 619 ..	....	....	....	65.8	373.3	....	41.3	723.0
Portfolio investment liabilities	4 652 Z.	....	....	....	....	666.1	−49.0	−84.9	−102.5
Equity securities	4 660 ..	....	....	....	....	....	....	....	....
Debt securities	4 669 Z.	....	....	....	....	666.1	−49.0	−84.9	−102.5
Financial derivatives	4 910 ..	....	....	....	....	....	....	....	....
Financial derivatives assets	4 900 ..	....	....	....	....	....	....	....	....
Financial derivatives liabilities	4 905 ..	....	....	....	....	....	....	....	....
Other investment assets	4 703 ..	....	....	....	....	....	....	....	....
Monetary authorities	4 701 ..	....	....	....	....	....	....	....	....
General government	4 704 ..	....	....	....	....	....	....	....	....
Banks	4 705 ..	....	....	....	....	....	....	....	....
Other sectors	4 728 ..	....	....	....	....	....	....	....	....
Other investment liabilities	4 753 W.	269.4	427.7	487.1	655.1	771.6	643.5	1,452.0	822.7
Monetary authorities	4 753 WA	95.1	337.1	−207.5	163.5	92.8	229.9	583.2	22.7
General government	4 753 ZB	124.3	−123.1	151.8	215.5	298.0	409.6	1,226.2	979.6
Banks	4 753 ZC	9.7	−94.6	27.4	−28.7	252.9	−148.0	−252.4	106.7
Other sectors	4 753 ZD	40.3	308.2	515.3	304.8	127.9	152.1	−104.9	−286.3
Total, Groups A Through C	4 983 ..	*662.1*	*227.8*	*−141.3*	*544.2*	*703.0*	*−1,273.7*	*2,051.7*	*1,607.6*
D. Net Errors and Omissions	4 998 ..	**−25.4**	**−115.7**	**64.7**	**−24.9**	**−150.7**	**515.3**	**−1,022.3**	**−163.0**
Total, Groups A Through D	4 984 ..	*636.8*	*112.1*	*−76.6*	*519.3*	*552.2*	*−758.5*	*1,029.4*	*1,444.6*
E. Reserves and Related Items	4 802 A.	**−636.8**	**−112.1**	**76.6**	**−519.3**	**−552.2**	**758.5**	**−1,029.4**	**−1,444.6**
Reserve assets	4 802 ..	−790.7	−302.8	−133.3	−373.7	−552.2	758.5	−1,134.4	−1,564.3
Use of Fund credit and loans	4 766 ..	54.6	−5.3	−15.1	−267.2	....	....	105.0	119.7
Exceptional financing	4 920 ..	99.4	196.0	225.0	121.6	....	....	....	....
Conversion rates: cedis per U.S. dollar	0 101 ..	**.8668**	**.8995**	**.9063**	**.9165**	**.9352**	**1.0579**	**1.4088**	**1.4310**

[1] Excludes components that have been classified in the categories of Group E.

Table 2. STANDARD PRESENTATION, 2003–2010

(Millions of U.S. dollars)

	Code	2003	2004	2005	2006	2007	2008	2009	2010
CURRENT ACCOUNT	4 993	101.7	−590.2	−1,104.6	−1,042.6	−2,151.4	−3,543.1	−1,598.5	−2,700.5
A. GOODS	4 100	−670.3	−1,592.8	−2,545.1	−3,027.0	−3,894.0	−4,998.8	−2,206.6	−2,962.0
Credit	2 100	2,562.6	2,704.5	2,802.2	3,726.7	4,172.1	5,269.7	5,839.7	7,960.1
General merchandise: exports f.o.b.	2 110	1,732.4	1,864.3	1,856.4	2,449.4	2,438.4	3,023.5	3,288.3	4,156.6
Goods for processing: exports f.o.b.	2 150	....	....	....	....	....	....	....	....
Repairs on goods	2 160	....	....	....	....	....	....	....	....
Goods procured in ports by carriers	2 170	....	....	....	....	....	....	....	....
Nonmonetary gold	2 180	830.1	840.2	945.8	1,277.3	1,733.8	2,246.3	2,551.4	3,803.5
Debit	3 100	−3,232.8	−4,297.3	−5,347.3	−6,753.7	−8,066.1	−10,268.5	−8,046.3	−10,922.1
General merchandise: imports f.o.b.	3 110	−3,232.8	−4,297.3	−5,347.3	−6,753.7	−8,066.1	−10,268.5	−8,046.3	−10,922.1
Goods for processing: imports f.o.b.	3 150	....	....	....	....	....	....	....	....
Repairs on goods	3 160	....	....	....	....	....	....	....	....
Goods procured in ports by carriers	3 170	....	....	....	....	....	....	....	....
Nonmonetary gold	3 180	....	....	....	....	....	....	....	....
B. SERVICES	4 200	−282.8	−379.5	−166.6	−136.5	−162.1	−497.3	−1,173.4	−1,525.9
Total credit	2 200	*630.0*	*702.3*	*1,106.5*	*1,382.8*	*1,831.9*	*1,800.9*	*1,769.7*	*1,477.3*
Total debit	3 200	*−912.8*	*−1,081.8*	*−1,273.1*	*−1,519.4*	*−1,993.9*	*−2,298.2*	*−2,943.1*	*−3,003.2*
Transportation services, credit	2 205	124.3	136.8	145.9	203.4	313.2	239.5	322.8	363.7
Passenger	2 850	*26.9*	*29.1*	*31.4*	*49.2*	*82.5*	*51.1*	*80.9*	*86.1*
Freight	2 851	*55.4*	*62.3*	*65.3*	*77.2*	*101.8*	*108.4*	*115.5*	*142.9*
Other	2 852	*42.0*	*45.4*	*49.2*	*77.0*	*129.0*	*80.0*	*126.5*	*134.7*
Sea transport, passenger	2 207	....	....	....	....	....	....	....	....
Sea transport, freight	2 208	55.4	62.3	65.3	77.2	101.8	108.4	115.5	142.9
Sea transport, other	2 209	42.0	45.4	49.2	77.0	129.0	80.0	126.5	134.7
Air transport, passenger	2 211	26.9	29.1	31.4	49.2	82.5	51.1	80.9	86.1
Air transport, freight	2 212	....	....	....	....	....	....	....	....
Air transport, other	2 213	....	....	....	....	....	....	....	....
Other transport, passenger	2 215	....	....	....	....	....	....	....	....
Other transport, freight	2 216	....	....	....	....	....	....	....	....
Other transport, other	2 217	....	....	....	....	....	....	....	....
Transportation services, debit	3 205	−323.1	−401.9	−580.9	−739.6	−855.2	−1,104.6	−894.3	−1,135.3
Passenger	3 850	*−77.6*	*−83.8*	*−169.1*	*−229.6*	*−257.8*	*−328.3*	*−263.5*	*−308.5*
Freight	3 851	*−218.3*	*−288.6*	*−352.4*	*−429.3*	*−506.8*	*−661.0*	*−538.3*	*−718.5*
Other	3 852	*−27.2*	*−29.5*	*−59.4*	*−80.7*	*−90.6*	*−115.3*	*−92.6*	*−108.4*
Sea transport, passenger	3 207	....	....	....	....	....	....	....	....
Sea transport, freight	3 208	−218.3	−288.6	−352.4	−429.3	−506.8	−661.0	−538.3	−718.5
Sea transport, other	3 209	−27.2	−29.5	−59.4	−80.7	−90.6	−115.3	−92.6	−108.4
Air transport, passenger	3 211	−77.6	−83.8	−169.1	−229.6	−257.8	−328.3	−263.5	−308.5
Air transport, freight	3 212	....	....	....	....	....	....	....	....
Air transport, other	3 213	....	....	....	....	....	....	....	....
Other transport, passenger	3 215	....	....	....	....	....	....	....	....
Other transport, freight	3 216	....	....	....	....	....	....	....	....
Other transport, other	3 217	....	....	....	....	....	....	....	....
Travel, credit	2 236	414.4	466.0	836.1	861.3	908.2	918.7	768.0	619.5
Business travel	2 237	290.1	326.2	585.3	602.9	635.8	643.1	537.6	433.7
Personal travel	2 240	124.3	139.8	250.8	258.4	272.5	275.6	230.4	185.9
Travel, debit	3 236	−138.1	−186.4	−302.8	−344.5	−558.0	−542.1	−684.4	−574.4
Business travel	3 237	−96.7	−130.5	−212.0	−241.2	−390.6	−379.4	−479.1	−402.1
Personal travel	3 240	−41.4	−55.9	−90.8	−103.4	−167.4	−162.6	−205.3	−172.3
Other services, credit	2 200 BA	91.3	99.5	124.5	318.1	610.4	642.7	678.9	494.1
Communications	2 245	....	....	....	....	....	....	....	....
Construction	2 249	....	....	....	....	....	....	....	....
Insurance	2 253	6.8	7.7	8.1	9.5	12.6	13.4	14.3	17.7
Financial	2 260	....	....	....	....	....	....	....	....
Computer and information	2 262	....	....	....	....	....	....	....	....
Royalties and licence fees	2 266	....	....	....	....	....	....	....	....
Other business services	2 268	66.8	73.2	92.8	168.6	380.4	387.2	416.9	342.7
Personal, cultural, and recreational	2 287	....	....	....	....	....	....	....	....
Government, n.i.e.	2 291	17.7	18.6	23.6	140.0	217.5	242.1	247.7	133.7
Other services, debit	3 200 BA	−451.6	−493.5	−389.4	−435.2	−580.8	−651.5	−1,364.3	−1,293.5
Communications	3 245	....	....	....	....	....	....	....	....
Construction	3 249	....	....	....	....	....	....	....	....
Insurance	3 253	−35.5	−47.0	−57.4	−69.9	−82.5	−107.6	−87.6	−117.0
Financial	3 260	....	....	....	....	....	....	....	....
Computer and information	3 262	....	....	....	....	....	....	....	....
Royalties and licence fees	3 266	....	....	....	....	....	....	....	....
Other business services	3 268	−246.7	−268.7	−199.0	−274.4	−312.0	−283.4	−700.0	−617.5
Personal, cultural, and recreational	3 287	....	....	....	....	....	....	....	....
Government, n.i.e.	3 291	−169.4	−177.8	−133.0	−91.0	−186.3	−260.5	−576.7	−559.1

Table 2 (Continued). STANDARD PRESENTATION, 2003–2010

(Millions of U.S. dollars)

	Code	2003	2004	2005	2006	2007	2008	2009	2010
C. INCOME	4 300	**−181.0**	**−197.8**	**−187.1**	**−127.4**	**−138.6**	**−258.6**	**−296.5**	**−535.0**
Total credit	2 300	*21.4*	*44.5*	*43.3*	*73.3*	*84.0*	*85.6*	*101.1*	*52.9*
Total debit	3 300	*−202.4*	*−242.3*	*−230.4*	*−200.6*	*−222.6*	*−344.2*	*−397.6*	*−587.9*
Compensation of employees, credit	2 310	....	....	....	....	....	....	....	....
Compensation of employees, debit	3 310	....	....	....	....	....	....	....	....
Investment income, credit	2 320	**21.4**	**44.5**	**43.3**	**73.3**	**84.0**	**85.6**	**101.1**	**52.9**
Direct investment income	2 330	....	....	....	....	....	....	....	....
Dividends and distributed branch profits	2 332	....	....	....	....	....	....	....	....
Reinvested earnings and undistributed branch profits	2 333	....	....	....	....	....	....	....	....
Income on debt (interest)	2 334	....	....	....	....	....	....	....	....
Portfolio investment income	2 339	....	....	....	....	....	....	....	....
Income on equity	2 340	....	....	....	....	....	....	....	....
Income on bonds and notes	2 350	....	....	....	....	....	....	....	....
Income on money market instruments	2 360	....	....	....	....	....	....	....	....
Other investment income	2 370	21.4	44.5	43.3	73.3	84.0	85.6	101.1	52.9
Investment income, debit	3 320	**−202.4**	**−242.3**	**−230.4**	**−200.6**	**−222.6**	**−344.2**	**−397.6**	**−587.9**
Direct investment income	3 330	−60.9	−92.0	−94.3	−91.5	−135.4	−172.5	−240.5	−395.6
Dividends and distributed branch profits	3 332	−60.0	−70.0	−71.1	−91.5	−135.4	−172.5	−240.5	−395.6
Reinvested earnings and undistributed branch profits	3 333	....	....	....	....	....	....	....	....
Income on debt (interest)	3 334	−.9	−22.0	−23.2	....	....	....	....	....
Portfolio investment income	3 339	−24.3	−4.5			−28.9	−106.6	−85.0	−102.8
Income on equity	3 340	....	....	....	....	....	....	....	....
Income on bonds and notes	3 350	−24.3	−4.5			−28.9	−106.6	−85.0	−102.8
Income on money market instruments	3 360	....	....	....	....	....	....	....	....
Other investment income	3 370	−117.2	−145.8	−136.1	−109.1	−58.3	−65.1	−72.1	−89.5
D. CURRENT TRANSFERS	4 379	**1,235.7**	**1,579.9**	**1,794.2**	**2,248.3**	**2,043.2**	**2,211.5**	**2,078.0**	**2,322.4**
Credit	2 379	**1,244.9**	**1,579.9**	**1,794.2**	**2,248.3**	**2,043.2**	**2,211.5**	**2,078.0**	**2,322.4**
General government	2 380	227.7	292.9	244.5	603.7	209.4	241.1	289.6	199.7
Other sectors	2 390	1,017.2	1,287.1	1,549.8	1,644.6	1,833.8	1,970.4	1,788.4	2,122.7
Workers' remittances	2 391	65.1	82.4	99.2	105.3	117.4	126.1	114.5	135.9
Other current transfers	2 392	952.1	1,204.7	1,450.6	1,539.3	1,716.4	1,844.3	1,673.9	1,986.8
Debit	3 379	**−9.2**	....	....	....	....	....	....	....
General government	3 380	−9.2	....	....	....	....	....	....	....
Other sectors	3 390	....	....	....	....	....	....	....	....
Workers' remittances	3 391	....	....	....	....	....	....	....	....
Other current transfers	3 392	....	....	....	....	....	....	....	....
CAPITAL AND FINANCIAL ACCOUNT	4 996	**−76.3**	**705.9**	**1,039.9**	**1,067.5**	**2,302.2**	**3,027.9**	**2,620.8**	**2,863.4**
CAPITAL ACCOUNT	4 994	**154.3**	**251.0**	**331.2**	**229.9**	**188.1**	**463.3**	**563.9**	**337.5**
Total credit	2 994	*154.3*	*251.0*	*331.2*	*229.9*	*188.1*	*463.3*	*563.9*	*337.5*
Total debit	3 994	....	....	....	....	....	....	....	....
Capital transfers, credit	2 400	**154.3**	**251.0**	**331.2**	**229.9**	**188.1**	**463.3**	**563.9**	**337.5**
General government	2 401	154.3	251.0	331.2	229.9	188.1	463.3	563.9	337.5
Debt forgiveness	2 402	....	....	....	....	....	....	....	....
Other capital transfers	2 410	154.3	251.0	331.2	229.9	188.1	463.3	563.9	337.5
Other sectors	2 430	....	....	....	....	....	....	....	....
Migrants' transfers	2 431	....	....	....	....	....	....	....	....
Debt forgiveness	2 432	....	....	....	....	....	....	....	....
Other capital transfers	2 440	....	....	....	....	....	....	....	....
Capital transfers, debit	3 400	....	....	....	....	....	....	....	....
General government	3 401	....	....	....	....	....	....	....	....
Debt forgiveness	3 402	....	....	....	....	....	....	....	....
Other capital transfers	3 410	....	....	....	....	....	....	....	....
Other sectors	3 430	....	....	....	....	....	....	....	....
Migrants' transfers	3 431	....	....	....	....	....	....	....	....
Debt forgiveness	3 432	....	....	....	....	....	....	....	....
Other capital transfers	3 440	....	....	....	....	....	....	....	....
Nonproduced nonfinancial assets, credit	2 480	....	....	....	....	....	....	....	....
Nonproduced nonfinancial assets, debit	3 480	....	....	....	....	....	....	....	....

Table 2 (Continued). STANDARD PRESENTATION, 2003–2010

(Millions of U.S. dollars)

	Code	2003	2004	2005	2006	2007	2008	2009	2010
FINANCIAL ACCOUNT	4 995	**−230.6**	**454.8**	**708.7**	**837.6**	**2,114.0**	**2,564.6**	**2,056.9**	**2,525.9**
A. DIRECT INVESTMENT	4 500	**136.8**	**139.3**	**145.0**	**636.0**	**855.4**	**1,211.6**	**1,677.8**	**2,527.4**
Direct investment abroad	4 505	....	....	....	....	....	**−8.8**	**−6.9**	....
Equity capital	4 510	....	....	....	....	....	....	....	....
Claims on affiliated enterprises	4 515	....	....	....	....	....	....	....	....
Liabilities to affiliated enterprises	4 520	....	....	....	....	....	....	....	....
Reinvested earnings	4 525	....	....	....	....	....	....	....	....
Other capital	4 530	....	....	....	....	....	−8.8	−6.9	....
Claims on affiliated enterprises	4 535	....	....	....	....	....	−8.8	−6.9	....
Liabilities to affiliated enterprises	4 540	....	....	....	....	....	....	....	....
Direct investment in Ghana	4 555	**136.8**	**139.3**	**145.0**	**636.0**	**855.4**	**1,220.4**	**1,684.7**	**2,527.4**
Equity capital	4 560	136.8	139.3	145.0	636.0	855.4	1,220.4	1,684.7	2,527.4
Claims on direct investors	4 565	....	....	....	....	....	....	....	....
Liabilities to direct investors	4 570	136.8	139.3	145.0	636.0	855.4	1,220.4	1,684.7	2,527.4
Reinvested earnings	4 575	....	....	....	....	....	....	....	....
Other capital	4 580	....	....	....	....	....	....	....	....
Claims on direct investors	4 585	....	....	....	....	....	....	....	....
Liabilities to direct investors	4 590	....	....	....	....	....	....	....	....
B. PORTFOLIO INVESTMENT	4 600	....	....	....	**65.8**	**1,039.3**	**−49.0**	**−43.6**	**620.5**
Assets	4 602	....	....	....	**65.8**	**373.3**	....	**41.3**	**723.0**
Equity securities	4 610	....	....	....	....	....	....	....	....
Monetary authorities	4 611	....	....	....	....	....	....	....	....
General government	4 612	....	....	....	....	....	....	....	....
Banks	4 613	....	....	....	....	....	....	....	....
Other sectors	4 614	....	....	....	....	....	....	....	....
Debt securities	4 619	....	....	....	65.8	373.3	....	41.3	723.0
Bonds and notes	4 620	....	....	....	....	....	....	....	....
Monetary authorities	4 621	....	....	....	....	....	....	....	....
General government	4 622	....	....	....	....	....	....	....	....
Banks	4 623	....	....	....	....	....	....	....	....
Other sectors	4 624	....	....	....	....	....	....	....	....
Money market instruments	4 630	....	....	....	65.8	373.3	....	41.3	723.0
Monetary authorities	4 631	....	....	....	....	....	....	....	....
General government	4 632	....	....	....	....	....	....	....	....
Banks	4 633	....	....	....	....	....	....	....	....
Other sectors	4 634	....	....	....	65.8	373.3	....	41.3	723.0
Liabilities	4 652	....	....	....	....	**666.1**	**−49.0**	**−84.9**	**−102.5**
Equity securities	4 660	....	....	....	....	....	....	....	....
Banks	4 663	....	....	....	....	....	....	....	....
Other sectors	4 664	....	....	....	....	....	....	....	....
Debt securities	4 669	....	....	....	....	666.1	−49.0	−84.9	−102.5
Bonds and notes	4 670	....	....	....	....	750.0	....	....	....
Monetary authorities	4 671	....	....	....	....	....	....	....	....
General government	4 672	....	....	....	....	750.0	....	....	....
Banks	4 673	....	....	....	....	....	....	....	....
Other sectors	4 674	....	....	....	....	....	....	....	....
Money market instruments	4 680	....	....	....	....	−83.9	−49.0	−84.9	−102.5
Monetary authorities	4 681	....	....	....	....	....	....	....	....
General government	4 682	....	....	....	....	....	....	....	....
Banks	4 683	....	....	....	....	....	....	....	....
Other sectors	4 684	....	....	....	....	−83.9	−49.0	−84.9	−102.5
C. FINANCIAL DERIVATIVES	4 910	....	....	....	....	....	....	....	....
Monetary authorities	4 911	....	....	....	....	....	....	....	....
General government	4 912	....	....	....	....	....	....	....	....
Banks	4 913	....	....	....	....	....	....	....	....
Other sectors	4 914	....	....	....	....	....	....	....	....
Assets	4 900	....	....	....	....	....	....	....	....
Monetary authorities	4 901	....	....	....	....	....	....	....	....
General government	4 902	....	....	....	....	....	....	....	....
Banks	4 903	....	....	....	....	....	....	....	....
Other sectors	4 904	....	....	....	....	....	....	....	....
Liabilities	4 905	....	....	....	....	....	....	....	....
Monetary authorities	4 906	....	....	....	....	....	....	....	....
General government	4 907	....	....	....	....	....	....	....	....
Banks	4 908	....	....	....	....	....	....	....	....
Other sectors	4 909	....	....	....	....	....	....	....	....

Table 2 (Concluded). STANDARD PRESENTATION, 2003–2010

(Millions of U.S. dollars)

	Code	2003	2004	2005	2006	2007	2008	2009	2010
D. OTHER INVESTMENT	4 700 ..	**423.3**	**618.4**	**697.0**	**509.5**	**771.6**	**643.5**	**1,557.0**	**942.4**
Assets	4 703 ..	....	....	....	....	....	....	....	....
Trade credits	4 706 ..	....	....	....	....	....	....	....	....
General government	4 707 ..	....	....	....	....	....	....	....	....
of which: Short-term	4 709 ..	....	....	....	....	....	....	....	....
Other sectors	4 710 ..	....	....	....	....	....	....	....	....
of which: Short-term	4 712 ..	....	....	....	....	....	....	....	....
Loans	4 714 ..	....	....	....	....	....	....	....	....
Monetary authorities	4 715 ..	....	....	....	....	....	....	....	....
of which: Short-term	4 718 ..	....	....	....	....	....	....	....	....
General government	4 719 ..	....	....	....	....	....	....	....	....
of which: Short-term	4 721 ..	....	....	....	....	....	....	....	....
Banks	4 722 ..	....	....	....	....	....	....	....	....
of which: Short-term	4 724 ..	....	....	....	....	....	....	....	....
Other sectors	4 725 ..	....	....	....	....	....	....	....	....
of which: Short-term	4 727 ..	....	....	....	....	....	....	....	....
Currency and deposits	4 730 ..	....	....	....	....	....	....	....	....
Monetary authorities	4 731 ..	....	....	....	....	....	....	....	....
General government	4 732 ..	....	....	....	....	....	....	....	....
Banks	4 733 ..	....	....	....	....	....	....	....	....
Other sectors	4 734 ..	....	....	....	....	....	....	....	....
Other assets	4 736 ..	....	....	....	....	....	....	....	....
Monetary authorities	4 737 ..	....	....	....	....	....	....	....	....
of which: Short-term	4 739 ..	....	....	....	....	....	....	....	....
General government	4 740 ..	....	....	....	....	....	....	....	....
of which: Short-term	4 742 ..	....	....	....	....	....	....	....	....
Banks	4 743 ..	....	....	....	....	....	....	....	....
of which: Short-term	4 745 ..	....	....	....	....	....	....	....	....
Other sectors	4 746 ..	....	....	....	....	....	....	....	....
of which: Short-term	4 748 ..	....	....	....	....	....	....	....	....
Liabilities	4 753 ..	**423.3**	**618.4**	**697.0**	**509.5**	**771.6**	**643.5**	**1,557.0**	**942.4**
Trade credits	4 756 ..	−23.0	86.7	96.0	−83.4	25.8	−39.8	30.4	211.3
General government	4 757 ..	....	....	....	....	....	....	....	....
of which: Short-term	4 759 ..	....	....	....	....	....	....	....	....
Other sectors	4 760 ..	−23.0	86.7	96.0	−83.4	25.8	−39.8	30.4	211.3
of which: Short-term	4 762 ..	*−23.0*	*86.7*	*96.0*	*−83.4*	*25.8*	*−39.8*	*30.4*	*211.3*
Loans	4 764 ..	270.0	102.5	592.1	392.4	1,186.6	1,101.6	2,105.5	1,567.2
Monetary authorities	4 765 ..	54.6	−5.3	−15.1	−267.2	....	....	105.0	119.7
of which: Use of Fund credit and loans from the Fund	4 766 ..	*54.6*	*−5.3*	*−15.1*	*−267.2*	....	....	*105.0*	*119.7*
of which: Short-term	4 768 ..	....	....	....	....	....	....	....	....
General government	4 769 ..	124.3	−123.1	151.8	215.5	298.0	409.6	1,226.2	979.6
of which: Short-term	4 771 ..	*68.0*	*−175.0*	*10.7*	*135.0*	*−119.7*	*−77.0*	*140.0*	*100.0*
Banks	4 772 ..	....	....	....	....	....	....	....	....
of which: Short-term	4 774 ..	....	....	....	....	....	....	....	....
Other sectors	4 775 ..	91.1	230.9	455.3	444.1	888.6	692.0	774.3	468.0
of which: Short-term	4 777 ..	....	....	....	....	....	....	....	....
Currency and deposits	4 780 ..	55.7	1.3	−70.5	58.6	366.2	−130.9	−324.7	198.3
Monetary authorities	4 781 ..	45.8	67.1	−103.0	82.4	102.3	20.9	−72.1	95.8
General government	4 782 ..	....	....	....	....	....	....	....	....
Banks	4 783 ..	9.7	−94.6	27.4	−28.7	252.9	−148.0	−252.4	106.7
Other sectors	4 784 ..	.2	28.8	5.1	4.8	11.0	−3.8	−.2	−4.2
Other liabilities	4 786 ..	120.7	427.9	79.5	141.9	−807.0	−287.4	−254.2	−1,034.5
Monetary authorities	4 787 ..	49.3	270.0	−104.5	81.1	−9.5	209.0	655.3	−73.1
of which: Short-term	4 789 ..	*49.3*	*270.0*	*−104.5*	*81.1*	*−9.5*	*209.0*	*201.2*	*−73.1*
General government	4 790 ..	99.4	196.0	225.0	121.6	....	....	....	....
of which: Short-term	4 792 ..	*99.4*	*196.0*	*225.0*	*121.6*	....	....	....	....
Banks	4 793 ..	....	....	....	....	....	....	....	....
of which: Short-term	4 795 ..	....	....	....	....	....	....	....	....
Other sectors	4 796 ..	−28.0	−38.2	−41.0	−60.8	−797.5	−496.4	−909.5	−961.3
of which: Short-term	4 798 ..	....	....	....	....	....	....	....	....
E. RESERVE ASSETS	4 802 ..	**−790.7**	**−302.8**	**−133.3**	**−373.7**	**−552.2**	**758.5**	**−1,134.4**	**−1,564.3**
Monetary gold	4 812 ..	−20.6	−5.8	−21.6	−33.7	....	−67.1	−64.0	−87.8
Special drawing rights	4 811 ..	−41.9	27.0	18.5	....	.6	.1	−453.1	−1.2
Reserve position in the Fund	4 810 ..	....	....	....	....	....	....	....	....
Foreign exchange	4 803 ..	−728.1	−324.0	−130.4	−339.9	−552.8	825.5	−617.2	−1,475.3
Other claims	4 813 ..	−.2	−.1	.1	−.1	−.1	....	....	....
NET ERRORS AND OMISSIONS	4 998 ..	**−25.4**	**−115.7**	**64.7**	**−24.9**	**−150.7**	**515.3**	**−1,022.3**	**−163.0**

Table 1. ANALYTIC PRESENTATION, 2003–2010

(Millions of U.S. dollars)

	Code	2003	2004	2005	2006	2007	2008	2009	2010
A. Current Account[1]	4 993 Z.	**−12,804**	**−13,476**	**−18,233**	**−29,565**	**−44,587**	**−51,313**	**−35,913**	**−32,335**
Goods: exports f.o.b.	2 100 ..	12,578	15,739	17,631	20,300	23,991	29,163	21,361	22,628
Goods: imports f.o.b.	3 100 ..	−38,184	−47,360	−51,900	−64,585	−81,041	−94,209	−64,197	−60,165
Balance on Goods	4 100 ..	*−25,606*	*−31,621*	*−34,268*	*−44,285*	*−57,050*	*−65,046*	*−42,836*	*−37,537*
Services: credit	2 200 ..	24,283	33,085	33,914	35,762	43,080	50,473	37,789	37,465
Services: debit	3 200 ..	−11,250	−14,020	−14,742	−16,367	−20,270	−24,903	−20,007	−20,187
Balance on Goods and Services	4 991 ..	*−12,573*	*−12,556*	*−15,096*	*−24,889*	*−34,240*	*−39,477*	*−25,054*	*−20,259*
Income: credit	2 300 ..	2,911	3,495	4,072	4,566	6,345	8,427	5,933	5,031
Income: debit	3 300 ..	−7,413	−8,920	−11,102	−13,524	−18,814	−24,442	−18,449	−17,226
Balance on Goods, Services, and IncomeU.S. dollar	4 992 ..	*−17,075*	*−17,980*	*−22,126*	*−33,847*	*−46,709*	*−55,492*	*−37,570*	*−32,454*
Current transfers: credit	2 379 Z.	7,202	7,901	8,615	8,587	9,053	10,189	7,328	6,053
Current transfers: debit	3 379 ..	−2,930	−3,396	−4,722	−4,305	−6,931	−6,010	−5,670	−5,935
B. Capital Account[1]	4 994 Z.	**1,411**	**2,990**	**2,563**	**3,822**	**5,957**	**5,995**	**2,818**	**2,776**
Capital account: credit	2 994 Z.	1,585	3,278	2,905	4,173	6,426	6,813	3,251	3,155
Capital account: debit	3 994 ..	−173	−288	−342	−351	−469	−818	−433	−379
Total, Groups A Plus B	4 981 ..	*−11,392*	*−10,486*	*−15,670*	*−25,743*	*−38,630*	*−45,318*	*−33,095*	*−29,559*
C. Financial Account[1]	4 995 W.	**6,417**	**6,836**	**15,633**	**25,661**	**38,027**	**44,243**	**35,095**	**15,722**
Direct investment abroad	4 505 ..	−375	−1,028	−1,476	−4,226	−5,262	−2,776	−2,097	−1,262
Direct investment in Greece	4 555 Z.	1,332	2,105	658	5,401	1,959	5,304	2,419	2,250
Portfolio investment assets	4 602 ..	−9,805	−13,835	−23,194	−9,374	−21,636	144	−4,146	17,078
Equity securities	4 610 ..	−505	−830	−2,189	−2,923	−593	4,030	−951	−1,551
Debt securities	4 619 ..	−9,300	−13,005	−21,004	−6,452	−21,043	−3,886	−3,195	18,629
Portfolio investment liabilities	4 652 Z.	23,456	31,301	32,308	18,738	45,545	24,891	43,145	−43,932
Equity securities	4 660 ..	2,568	4,290	6,293	7,529	10,865	−5,260	764	−1,459
Debt securities	4 669 Z.	20,887	27,010	26,015	11,208	34,680	30,151	42,382	−42,473
Financial derivatives	4 910 ..	111	−429	13	920	−623	−661	−1,151	416
Financial derivatives assets	4 900 ..	111	−429	13	920	−623	−661	−1,151	416
Financial derivatives liabilities	4 905 ..	....	....	....	....	....	....	....	....
Other investment assets	4 703 ..	−4,413	−7,463	−8,740	−7,336	−22,118	−40,679	−32,753	10,245
Monetary authorities	4 701 ..	−1,043	−1,078	−295	11	1,100	525	−119	−65
General government	4 704 ..	....	....	....	....	....	....	....	....
Banks	4 705 ..	−2,602	−5,068	−7,358	−7,514	−22,653	−43,229	−31,817	23,241
Other sectors	4 728 ..	−768	−1,317	−1,087	166	−565	2,025	−816	−12,930
Other investment liabilities	4 753 W.	−3,888	−3,813	16,064	21,539	40,161	58,021	29,678	30,926
Monetary authorities	4 753 WA	−2,311	−11,799	1,434	1,058	3,716	33,932	20,384	49,695
General government	4 753 ZB	−2,888	−1,271	−516	728	−3,132	−1,336	−3,179	24,676
Banks	4 753 ZC	2,773	10,661	17,833	20,019	40,386	26,088	2,902	−42,725
Other sectors	4 753 ZD	−1,462	−1,403	−2,686	−267	−809	−663	9,571	−719
Total, Groups A Through C	4 983 ..	*−4,975*	*−3,650*	*−37*	*−83*	*−603*	*−1,074*	*2,000*	*−13,837*
D. Net Errors and Omissions	4 998 ..	**253**	**373**	**−67**	**361**	**1,060**	**1,113**	**−788**	**−99**
Total, Groups A Through D	4 984 ..	*−4,722*	*−3,277*	*−104*	*279*	*457*	*39*	*1,213*	*−13,936*
E. Reserves and Related Items	4 802 A.	**4,722**	**3,277**	**104**	**−279**	**−457**	**−39**	**−1,213**	**13,936**
Reserve assets	4 802 ..	4,722	3,277	104	−279	−457	−39	−1,213	201
Use of Fund credit and loans	4 766 ..	....	....	....	....	....	....	....	13,735
Exceptional financing	4 920 ..	....	....	....	....	....	....	....	....
Conversion rates: euros per U.S. dollar	0 103 ..	**.8860**	**.8054**	**.8041**	**.7971**	**.7306**	**.6827**	**.7198**	**.7550**

[1] Excludes components that have been classified in the categories of Group E.

Table 2. STANDARD PRESENTATION, 2003–2010

(Millions of U.S. dollars)

	Code	2003	2004	2005	2006	2007	2008	2009	2010
CURRENT ACCOUNT	4 993	−12,804	−13,476	−18,233	−29,565	−44,587	−51,313	−35,913	−32,335
A. GOODS	4 100	−25,606	−31,621	−34,268	−44,285	−57,050	−65,046	−42,836	−37,537
Credit	2 100	12,578	15,739	17,631	20,300	23,991	29,163	21,361	22,628
General merchandise: exports f.o.b.	2 110	11,942	14,904	16,701	19,209	22,797	25,405	18,700	20,500
Goods for processing: exports f.o.b.	2 150	29	23	43	44	55	34	23	13
Repairs on goods	2 160	71	91	105	102	170	234	256	204
Goods procured in ports by carriers	2 170	535	721	782	945	969	3,489	2,383	1,912
Nonmonetary gold	2 180	....	....	....	....	....	....	....	....
Debit	3 100	−38,184	−47,360	−51,900	−64,585	−81,041	−94,209	−64,197	−60,165
General merchandise: imports f.o.b.	3 110	−37,861	−46,912	−51,350	−63,339	−79,668	−91,949	−62,672	−58,433
Goods for processing: imports f.o.b.	3 150	−34	−52	−49	−56	−65	−59	−47	−38
Repairs on goods	3 160	−97	−104	−146	−366	−299	−392	−231	−165
Goods procured in ports by carriers	3 170	−191	−292	−354	−825	−1,010	−1,810	−1,246	−1,529
Nonmonetary gold	3 180	....	....	....	....	....	....	....	....
B. SERVICES	4 200	13,033	19,065	19,172	19,396	22,810	25,569	17,782	17,278
Total credit	2 200	*24,283*	*33,085*	*33,914*	*35,762*	*43,080*	*50,473*	*37,789*	*37,465*
Total debit	3 200	*−11,250*	*−14,020*	*−14,742*	*−16,367*	*−20,270*	*−24,903*	*−20,007*	*−20,187*
Transportation services, credit	2 205	10,840	16,538	17,284	17,989	23,300	28,316	18,872	20,412
Passenger	2 850	*76*	*94*	*119*	*93*	*137*	*170*	*115*	*100*
Freight	2 851	*63*	*104*	*62*	*81*	*114*	*114*	*76*	*72*
Other	2 852	*10,701*	*16,340*	*17,103*	*17,815*	*23,049*	*28,033*	*18,680*	*20,240*
Sea transport, passenger	2 207	76	94	119	93	137	170	115	100
Sea transport, freight	2 208	50	64	43	48	90	92	60	48
Sea transport, other	2 209	10,023	15,258	15,983	16,530	21,334	25,751	16,894	18,403
Air transport, passenger	2 211	....	....	....	....	....	....	....	....
Air transport, freight	2 212	....	....	....	....	....	....	....	....
Air transport, other	2 213	386	746	769	863	1,169	1,599	1,219	1,265
Other transport, passenger	2 215	....	....	....	....	....	....	....	....
Other transport, freight	2 216	13	40	20	33	24	21	16	24
Other transport, other	2 217	292	336	351	422	547	682	567	572
Transportation services, debit	3 205	−5,578	−7,122	−7,751	−8,781	−10,681	−13,736	−9,868	−10,814
Passenger	3 850	*−8*	*−8*	*−6*	*−7*	*−7*	*−16*	*−20*	*−20*
Freight	3 851	*−177*	*−234*	*−242*	*−228*	*−284*	*−328*	*−248*	*−256*
Other	3 852	*−5,394*	*−6,880*	*−7,503*	*−8,547*	*−10,390*	*−13,391*	*−9,600*	*−10,538*
Sea transport, passenger	3 207	−8	−8	−6	−7	−7	−16	−20	−20
Sea transport, freight	3 208	−174	−233	−240	−226	−281	−327	−245	−251
Sea transport, other	3 209	−4,145	−5,335	−5,527	−6,077	−7,168	−9,224	−6,419	−7,585
Air transport, passenger	3 211	....	....	....	....	....	....	....	....
Air transport, freight	3 212	....	....	....	....	....	....	....	....
Air transport, other	3 213	−372	−495	−454	−483	−620	−862	−731	−535
Other transport, passenger	3 215	....	....	....	....	....	....	....	....
Other transport, freight	3 216	−3	−1	−2	−2	−3	−1	−3	−5
Other transport, other	3 217	−876	−1,050	−1,522	−1,987	−2,602	−3,306	−2,449	−2,418
Travel, credit	2 236	10,766	12,715	13,333	14,402	15,549	17,416	14,681	12,479
Business travel	2 237	1,034	1,405	1,176	1,156	1,346	1,336	976	983
Personal travel	2 240	9,732	11,309	12,157	13,246	14,204	16,081	13,705	11,497
Travel, debit	3 236	−2,431	−2,872	−3,039	−2,997	−3,423	−3,930	−3,381	−2,854
Business travel	3 237	−947	−1,167	−1,260	−1,354	−1,459	−1,592	−1,279	−1,182
Personal travel	3 240	−1,484	−1,705	−1,779	−1,643	−1,964	−2,338	−2,101	−1,672
Other services, credit	2 200 BA	2,678	3,832	3,297	3,372	4,231	4,740	4,235	4,574
Communications	2 245	322	393	395	386	461	496	418	415
Construction	2 249	195	216	286	305	361	387	393	708
Insurance	2 253	199	222	264	266	388	444	443	405
Financial	2 260	85	126	107	105	168	160	171	159
Computer and information	2 262	135	199	173	203	236	352	402	473
Royalties and licence fees	2 266	18	32	60	67	52	44	48	69
Other business services	2 268	1,310	1,577	1,737	1,795	2,251	2,540	2,049	2,027
Personal, cultural, and recreational	2 287	332	966	166	154	219	222	213	189
Government, n.i.e.	2 291	81	100	108	91	95	95	99	130
Other services, debit	3 200 BA	−3,241	−4,026	−3,952	−4,588	−6,165	−7,237	−6,759	−6,519
Communications	3 245	−336	−364	−324	−360	−562	−653	−684	−518
Construction	3 249	−108	−138	−99	−143	−138	−272	−303	−321
Insurance	3 253	−501	−598	−732	−935	−1,213	−1,476	−1,336	−1,454
Financial	3 260	−82	−75	−76	−141	−472	−262	−291	−443
Computer and information	3 262	−188	−224	−222	−254	−383	−469	−499	−546
Royalties and licence fees	3 266	−335	−466	−442	−406	−600	−713	−654	−627
Other business services	3 268	−988	−1,344	−1,424	−1,655	−1,958	−2,423	−2,160	−2,015
Personal, cultural, and recreational	3 287	−184	−357	−185	−227	−354	−456	−351	−300
Government, n.i.e.	3 291	−520	−460	−450	−467	−486	−511	−482	−295

Table 2 (Continued). STANDARD PRESENTATION, 2003–2010
(Millions of U.S. dollars)

	Code	2003	2004	2005	2006	2007	2008	2009	2010
C. INCOME	4 300	**−4,503**	**−5,425**	**−7,030**	**−8,958**	**−12,469**	**−16,015**	**−12,516**	**−12,195**
Total credit	2 300	*2,911*	*3,495*	*4,072*	*4,566*	*6,345*	*8,427*	*5,933*	*5,031*
Total debit	3 300	*−7,413*	*−8,920*	*−11,102*	*−13,524*	*−18,814*	*−24,442*	*−18,449*	*−17,226*
Compensation of employees, credit	2 310	**381**	**348**	**357**	**400**	**504**	**509**	**411**	**265**
Compensation of employees, debit	3 310	**−193**	**−235**	**−273**	**−353**	**−457**	**−596**	**−575**	**−501**
Investment income, credit	2 320	**2,530**	**3,148**	**3,715**	**4,166**	**5,841**	**7,918**	**5,522**	**4,766**
Direct investment income	2 330	481	578	657	681	841	1,140	753	760
Dividends and distributed branch profits	2 332	113	156	151	176	290	550	199	231
Reinvested earnings and undistributed branch profits	2 333	366	422	498	502	548	588	552	525
Income on debt (interest)	2 334	2	1	8	3	4	2	2	3
Portfolio investment income	2 339	1,197	1,586	1,719	1,839	2,657	3,004	2,882	2,663
Income on equity	2 340	26	33	53	51	81	128	38	43
Income on bonds and notes	2 350	1,169	1,551	1,664	1,783	2,549	2,853	2,631	2,532
Income on money market instruments	2 360	2	2	2	4	27	24	213	88
Other investment income	2 370	852	983	1,340	1,646	2,343	3,775	1,887	1,343
Investment income, debit	3 320	**−7,221**	**−8,685**	**−10,829**	**−13,171**	**−18,357**	**−23,846**	**−17,874**	**−16,725**
Direct investment income	3 330	−1,219	−1,307	−1,697	−1,569	−1,973	−2,632	−683	−882
Dividends and distributed branch profits	3 332	−545	−521	−726	−632	−922	−1,482	−1,095	−1,297
Reinvested earnings and undistributed branch profits	3 333	−615	−750	−871	−878	−959	−1,029	511	487
Income on debt (interest)	3 334	−59	−36	−100	−60	−92	−121	−100	−72
Portfolio investment income	3 339	−3,855	−5,112	−6,766	−8,203	−10,943	−13,256	−12,466	−11,322
Income on equity	3 340	−185	−337	−728	−998	−1,618	−1,491	−738	−642
Income on bonds and notes	3 350	−3,667	−4,773	−6,032	−7,191	−9,190	−11,473	−11,638	−10,679
Income on money market instruments	3 360	−2	−2	−6	−13	−134	−292	−90	−2
Other investment income	3 370	−2,148	−2,266	−2,366	−3,399	−5,442	−7,958	−4,725	−4,521
D. CURRENT TRANSFERS	4 379	**4,272**	**4,504**	**3,893**	**4,282**	**2,122**	**4,180**	**1,657**	**118**
Credit	2 379	**7,202**	**7,901**	**8,615**	**8,587**	**9,053**	**10,189**	**7,328**	**6,053**
General government	2 380	4,628	5,077	5,811	5,591	5,966	6,944	4,759	4,105
Other sectors	2 390	2,574	2,824	2,804	2,996	3,087	3,245	2,568	1,948
Workers' remittances	2 391	1,183	894	863	1,143	1,980	2,178	1,609	1,234
Other current transfers	2 392	1,391	1,929	1,941	1,853	1,107	1,067	959	713
Debit	3 379	**−2,930**	**−3,396**	**−4,722**	**−4,305**	**−6,931**	**−6,010**	**−5,670**	**−5,935**
General government	3 380	−2,453	−2,761	−3,660	−3,087	−5,296	−3,940	−3,705	−3,821
Other sectors	3 390	−478	−635	−1,063	−1,218	−1,636	−2,070	−1,965	−2,113
Workers' remittances	3 391	−187	−262	−630	−629	−1,003	−1,316	−1,268	−1,431
Other current transfers	3 392	−291	−374	−433	−589	−633	−754	−697	−682
CAPITAL AND FINANCIAL ACCOUNT	4 996	**12,551**	**13,103**	**18,300**	**29,204**	**43,528**	**50,200**	**36,700**	**32,435**
CAPITAL ACCOUNT	4 994	**1,411**	**2,990**	**2,563**	**3,822**	**5,957**	**5,995**	**2,818**	**2,776**
Total credit	2 994	*1,585*	*3,278*	*2,905*	*4,173*	*6,426*	*6,813*	*3,251*	*3,155*
Total debit	3 994	*−173*	*−288*	*−342*	*−351*	*−469*	*−818*	*−433*	*−379*
Capital transfers, credit	2 400	**1,560**	**3,251**	**2,879**	**4,124**	**6,375**	**6,499**	**3,104**	**3,094**
General government	2 401	1,397	3,086	2,672	3,917	6,050	6,247	2,980	3,000
Debt forgiveness	2 402	8	7	10	9	12	11	6	4
Other capital transfers	2 410	1,390	3,079	2,663	3,908	6,038	6,236	2,974	2,995
Other sectors	2 430	163	165	207	207	325	251	124	94
Migrants' transfers	2 431	....	....	....	....	....	....	....	....
Debt forgiveness	2 432	4	4	7	4	13	9	4	1
Other capital transfers	2 440	159	161	200	203	312	242	120	93
Capital transfers, debit	3 400	**−165**	**−276**	**−262**	**−302**	**−450**	**−750**	**−406**	**−334**
General government	3 401	−18	−86	−28	−40	−37	−298	−20	−21
Debt forgiveness	3 402	−4	−5	−9	−13	−9	−12	−6	−5
Other capital transfers	3 410	−13	−81	−19	−27	−28	−285	−14	−16
Other sectors	3 430	−147	−190	−233	−262	−413	−453	−385	−313
Migrants' transfers	3 431	....	....	....	....	....	....	....	....
Debt forgiveness	3 432	−7	−20	−19	−12	−23	−24	−10	−10
Other capital transfers	3 440	−140	−170	−214	−249	−390	−428	−375	−303
Nonproduced nonfinancial assets, credit	2 480	**24**	**27**	**26**	**48**	**51**	**314**	**147**	**61**
Nonproduced nonfinancial assets, debit	3 480	**−9**	**−12**	**−80**	**−49**	**−19**	**−67**	**−28**	**−44**

Table 2 (Continued). STANDARD PRESENTATION, 2003–2010

(Millions of U.S. dollars)

	Code	2003	2004	2005	2006	2007	2008	2009	2010
FINANCIAL ACCOUNT	4 995	**11,140**	**10,113**	**15,737**	**25,382**	**37,571**	**44,205**	**33,883**	**29,658**
A. DIRECT INVESTMENT	4 500	**957**	**1,077**	**–818**	**1,175**	**–3,303**	**2,527**	**322**	**988**
Direct investment abroad	4 505	**–375**	**–1,028**	**–1,476**	**–4,226**	**–5,262**	**–2,776**	**–2,097**	**–1,262**
Equity capital	4 510	51	–521	–947	–3,754	–4,611	–2,568	–1,899	–878
Claims on affiliated enterprises	4 515	25	–536	–953	–3,756	–4,612	–2,569	–1,899	–877
Liabilities to affiliated enterprises	4 520	26	15	6	1	....	....	–1	–1
Reinvested earnings	4 525	–366	–422	–498	–502	–546	–588	–552	–525
Other capital	4 530	–60	–85	–31	30	–104	380	354	142
Claims on affiliated enterprises	4 535	–79	–96	–50	29	–94	–38	15	–3
Liabilities to affiliated enterprises	4 540	19	11	19	1	–10	418	340	145
Direct investment in Greece	4 555	**1,332**	**2,105**	**658**	**5,401**	**1,959**	**5,304**	**2,419**	**2,250**
Equity capital	4 560	1,244	1,729	131	4,780	2,440	5,175	3,406	3,068
Claims on direct investors	4 565	–7	–10	–3	–6	–3	–2	–1	....
Liabilities to direct investors	4 570	1,251	1,739	134	4,786	2,443	5,176	3,408	3,069
Reinvested earnings	4 575	615	750	872	878	959	1,029	–511	–487
Other capital	4 580	–527	–374	–345	–257	–1,440	–900	–476	–331
Claims on direct investors	4 585	–23	–7	–4	....	–5	–10	–3	–2
Liabilities to direct investors	4 590	–504	–367	–341	–257	–1,435	–890	–472	–329
B. PORTFOLIO INVESTMENT	4 600	**13,651**	**17,465**	**9,114**	**9,363**	**23,910**	**25,035**	**38,999**	**–26,854**
Assets	4 602	**–9,805**	**–13,835**	**–23,194**	**–9,374**	**–21,636**	**144**	**–4,146**	**17,078**
Equity securities	4 610	–505	–830	–2,189	–2,923	–593	4,030	–951	–1,551
Monetary authorities	4 611	....	....	....	....	....	....	....	....
General government	4 612	....	....	....	....	....	....	....	....
Banks	4 613	–223	–267	–768	–1,111	–2,110	–985	–1,448	–1,283
Other sectors	4 614	–282	–563	–1,422	–1,812	1,517	5,016	497	–268
Debt securities	4 619	–9,300	–13,005	–21,004	–6,452	–21,043	–3,886	–3,195	18,629
Bonds and notes	4 620	–9,233	–12,734	–18,669	–5,648	–13,532	–2,911	–3,595	18,629
Monetary authorities	4 621	1,529	–3,853	–1,290	–114	–3,075	5,626	–5,318	3,554
General government	4 622	....	....	....	....	....	....	....	....
Banks	4 623	–8,137	–1,948	–2,679	–4,859	–8,774	–14,523	–3,139	14,771
Other sectors	4 624	–2,624	–6,933	–14,699	–674	–1,683	5,986	4,862	304
Money market instruments	4 630	–67	–272	–2,335	–804	–7,511	–976	400	....
Monetary authorities	4 631	....	....	....	....	–3,047	....	....	....
General government	4 632	....	....	....	....	....	....	....	....
Banks	4 633	60	–63	–65	....	....	–740	–882	....
Other sectors	4 634	–127	–209	–2,270	–804	–4,464	–235	1,282	....
Liabilities	4 652	**23,456**	**31,301**	**32,308**	**18,738**	**45,545**	**24,891**	**43,145**	**–43,932**
Equity securities	4 660	2,568	4,290	6,293	7,529	10,865	–5,260	764	–1,459
Banks	4 663	668	1,116	1,923	4,010	5,243	–2,932	1,034	–1,822
Other sectors	4 664	1,901	3,174	4,369	3,519	5,622	–2,328	–270	363
Debt securities	4 669	20,887	27,010	26,015	11,208	34,680	30,151	42,382	–42,473
Bonds and notes	4 670	20,820	26,738	25,989	11,458	33,558	24,589	41,206	–46,143
Monetary authorities	4 671	....	....	....	....	....	....	....	....
General government	4 672	20,820	26,738	25,464	10,368	32,677	20,869	41,206	–37,839
Banks	4 673	....	....	....	....	....	....	....	–7,763
Other sectors	4 674	....	....	526	1,090	881	3,720	....	–542
Money market instruments	4 680	68	272	26	–250	1,122	5,562	1,175	3,671
Monetary authorities	4 681	....	....	....	....	....	....	....	....
General government	4 682	68	272	26	–250	1,122	5,562	1,175	3,671
Banks	4 683	....	....	....	....	....	....	....	....
Other sectors	4 684	....	....	....	....	....	....	....	....
C. FINANCIAL DERIVATIVES	4 910	**111**	**–429**	**13**	**920**	**–623**	**–661**	**–1,151**	**416**
Monetary authorities	4 911	....	....	....	....	....	....	....	....
General government	4 912	....	....	....	....	....	....	....	....
Banks	4 913	111	–429	13	920	–623	–661	–1,151	416
Other sectors	4 914	....	....	....	....	....	....	....	....
Assets	4 900	**111**	**–429**	**13**	**920**	**–623**	**–661**	**–1,151**	**416**
Monetary authorities	4 901	....	....	....	....	....	....	....	....
General government	4 902	....	....	....	....	....	....	....	....
Banks	4 903	111	–429	13	920	–623	–661	–1,151	416
Other sectors	4 904	....	....	....	....	....	....	....	....
Liabilities	4 905	....	....	....	....	....	....	....	....
Monetary authorities	4 906	....	....	....	....	....	....	....	....
General government	4 907	....	....	....	....	....	....	....	....
Banks	4 908	....	....	....	....	....	....	....	....
Other sectors	4 909	....	....	....	....	....	....	....	....

Table 2 (Concluded). STANDARD PRESENTATION, 2003–2010
(Millions of U.S. dollars)

	Code	2003	2004	2005	2006	2007	2008	2009	2010
D. OTHER INVESTMENT	4 700	**−8,301**	**−11,277**	**7,324**	**14,202**	**18,043**	**17,343**	**−3,075**	**54,907**
Assets	4 703	**−4,413**	**−7,463**	**−8,740**	**−7,336**	**−22,118**	**−40,679**	**−32,753**	**10,245**
Trade credits	4 706	....	....	....	....	....	....	....	−136
General government	4 707	....	....	....	....	....	....	....	
of which: Short-term	4 709	....	....	....	....	....	....	....	
Other sectors	4 710	....	....	....	....	....	....	....	−136
of which: Short-term	4 712	....	....	....	....	....	....	....	
Loans	4 714	−20	8	35	−418	−607	−1,171	−453	133
Monetary authorities	4 715	....	....	....	....	....	....	....	
of which: Short-term	4 718	....	....	....	....	....	....	....	
General government	4 719	....	....	....	....	....	....	....	
of which: Short-term	4 721	....	....	....	....	....	....	....	
Banks	4 722	−20	8	35	−418	−607	−887	−443	264
of which: Short-term	4 724	....	....	....	....	....	....	....	
Other sectors	4 725	....	....	....	....	....	−284	−10	−132
of which: Short-term	4 727	....	....	....	....	....	....	....	
Currency and deposits	4 730	−4,448	−7,530	−8,775	−6,918	−21,511	−39,508	−32,299	10,293
Monetary authorities	4 731	−1,043	−1,078	−295	11	1,100	525	−119	−21
General government	4 732	....	....	....	....	....	....	....	
Banks	4 733	−2,582	−5,076	−7,393	−7,096	−22,046	−42,342	−31,374	22,976
Other sectors	4 734	−823	−1,375	−1,087	166	−565	2,309	−806	−12,663
Other assets	4 736	54	58	....	....	....	....	....	−45
Monetary authorities	4 737	....	....	....	....	....	....	....	−45
of which: Short-term	4 739	....	....	....	....	....	....	....	
General government	4 740	....	....	....	....	....	....	....	
of which: Short-term	4 742	....	....	....	....	....	....	....	
Banks	4 743	....	....	....	....	....	....	....	
of which: Short-term	4 745	....	....	....	....	....	....	....	
Other sectors	4 746	54	58	....	....	....	....	....	
of which: Short-term	4 748	....	....	....	....	....	....	....	
Liabilities	4 753	**−3,888**	**−3,813**	**16,064**	**21,539**	**40,161**	**58,021**	**29,678**	**44,661**
Trade credits	4 756	....	....	....	....	....	....	....	291
General government	4 757	....	....	....	....	....	....	....	
of which: Short-term	4 759	....	....	....	....	....	....	....	
Other sectors	4 760	....	....	....	....	....	....	....	291
of which: Short-term	4 762	....	....	....	....	....	....	....	
Loans	4 764	−4,329	−2,742	−2,433	598	−3,598	−1,282	6,587	39,119
Monetary authorities	4 765	....	....	....	....	....	....	....	13,735
of which: Use of Fund credit and loans from the Fund..	4 766	....	....	....	....	....	....	....	*13,735*
of which: Short-term	4 768	....	....	....	....	....	....	....	
General government	4 769	−2,888	−1,271	−516	728	−3,132	−1,336	−3,179	24,676
of which: Short-term	4 771	....	....	....	....	....	....	....	
Banks	4 772	−393	−687	−343	15	282	1,047	615	1,512
of which: Short-term	4 774	....	....	....	....	....	....	....	
Other sectors	4 775	−1,048	−784	−1,574	−145	−748	−993	9,151	−804
of which: Short-term	4 777	....	....	....	....	....	....	....	
Currency and deposits	4 780	392	−1,116	18,497	20,941	43,759	59,303	22,030	5,251
Monetary authorities	4 781	−2,311	−11,799	1,434	1,058	3,716	33,932	19,324	49,695
General government	4 782	....	....	....	....	....	....	....	
Banks	4 783	3,166	11,347	18,176	20,004	40,104	25,041	2,286	−44,237
Other sectors	4 784	−464	−665	−1,112	−121	−60	330	420	−206
Other liabilities	4 786	49	46	....	....	....	....	1,060	....
Monetary authorities	4 787	....	....	....	....	....	....	1,060	
of which: Short-term	4 789	....	....	....	....	....	....	....	
General government	4 790	....	....	....	....	....	....	....	
of which: Short-term	4 792	....	....	....	....	....	....	....	
Banks	4 793	....	....	....	....	....	....	....	
of which: Short-term	4 795	....	....	....	....	....	....	....	
Other sectors	4 796	49	46	....	....	....	....	....	
of which: Short-term	4 798	....	....	....	....	....	....	....	
E. RESERVE ASSETS	4 802	**4,722**	**3,277**	**104**	**−279**	**−457**	**−39**	**−1,213**	**201**
Monetary gold	4 812	161	31	−484	−277	−454	−320	−10	2
Special drawing rights	4 811	−5	−4	−4	1	3	3	−1,060	127
Reserve position in the Fund	4 810	−12	94	222	47	47	−76	−101	....
Foreign exchange	4 803	4,578	3,156	370	−50	−53	354	−41	72
Other claims	4 813	....	....	....	....	....	....	....	
NET ERRORS AND OMISSIONS	4 998	**253**	**373**	**−67**	**361**	**1,060**	**1,113**	**−788**	**−99**

2011, International Monetary Fund: *Balance of Payments Statistics Yearbook*

Table 3. INTERNATIONAL INVESTMENT POSITION (End-period stocks), 2003–2010

(Millions of U.S. dollars)

	Code	2003	2004	2005	2006	2007	2008	2009	2010
ASSETS....................	8 995 C.	**113,718**	**139,964**	**153,464**	**196,273**	**279,777**	**313,339**	**367,042**	**301,035**
Direct investment abroad..........	8 505 ..	**12,337**	**13,791**	**13,602**	**22,418**	**31,650**	**37,232**	**39,454**	**37,875**
Equity capital and reinvested earnings............	8 506 ..	11,178	12,969	13,056	21,898	30,578	35,725	40,332	38,839
Claims on affiliated enterprises............	8 507 ..	11,178	12,969	13,056	21,898	30,578	35,725	40,332	38,839
Liabilities to affiliated enterprises............	8 508 ..	....	....	....	....	....	....	....	....
Other capital............	8 530 ..	1,159	823	546	520	1,072	1,507	−879	−964
Claims on affiliated enterprises............	8 535 ..	1,159	823	546	520	1,072	1,507	−879	−964
Liabilities to affiliated enterprises............	8 540 ..	....	....	....	....	....	....	....	....
Portfolio investment............	8 602 ..	**34,966**	**52,666**	**69,979**	**88,496**	**127,849**	**122,770**	**132,845**	**104,503**
Equity securities............	8 610 ..	4,893	6,200	8,326	13,356	20,602	16,005	25,486	24,084
Monetary authorities............	8 611 ..	506	550	488	545	605	572	592	653
General government............	8 612 ..	....	....	....	....	....	....	....	....
Banks............	8 613 ..	1,786	2,109	2,612	4,687	10,495	11,612	17,377	16,113
Other sectors............	8 614 ..	2,601	3,541	5,226	8,123	9,502	3,820	7,517	7,317
Debt securities............	8 619 ..	30,073	46,465	61,652	75,140	107,247	106,766	107,359	80,419
Bonds and notes............	8 620 ..	29,471	45,820	59,834	72,305	96,130	95,521	99,452	75,622
Monetary authorities............	8 621 ..	5,973	11,150	10,479	11,911	16,748	12,211	21,600	16,437
General government............	8 622 ..	....	....	....	....	....	....	....	....
Banks............	8 623 ..	13,942	15,847	15,269	21,551	33,537	49,471	53,465	39,231
Other sectors............	8 624 ..	9,556	18,823	34,086	38,842	45,844	33,839	24,386	19,955
Money market instruments............	8 630 ..	602	646	1,818	2,836	11,117	11,245	7,907	4,797
Monetary authorities............	8 631 ..	....	....	....	....	3,094	2,925	....	4,452
General government............	8 632 ..	....	....	....	....				
Banks............	8 633 ..	109	78	61	46	184	657	1,393	....
Other sectors............	8 634 ..	494	568	1,757	2,789	7,839	7,663	6,514	345
Financial derivatives............	8 900 ..	**326**	**821**	**659**	**13**	**740**	**1,350**	**2,551**	**1,864**
Monetary authorities............	8 901 ..	....	....	....	....	....	....	....	....
General government............	8 902 ..	....	....	....	....	....	....		
Banks............	8 903 ..	326	821	659	13	740	1,350	2,551	1,864
Other sectors............	8 904 ..	....	....	....	....	....	....	....	....
Other investment............	8 703 ..	**60,288**	**69,978**	**66,937**	**82,497**	**115,880**	**148,487**	**186,646**	**150,425**
Trade credits............	8 706 ..	719	613	714	884	844	829	147	270
General government............	8 707 ..	....	....	....	....	....	....	....	....
of which: Short-term............	8 709 ..	....	....	....	....	....	....	....	....
Other sectors............	8 710 ..	719	613	714	884	844	829	147	270
of which: Short-term............	8 712 ..	....	....	....	....	....	....	....	....
Loans............	8 714 ..	39,490	45,316	44,555	58,753	90,067	126,074	164,152	24,163
Monetary authorities............	8 715 ..	2,708	3,328	3,217	3,569	2,779	2,140	2,358	1,558
of which: Short-term............	8 718 ..	....	....	....	....	....	....	....	....
General government............	8 719 ..	....	....	....	....	....	....	....	....
of which: Short-term............	8 721 ..	....	....	....	....	....	....	....	....
Banks............	8 722 ..	36,782	41,988	41,338	55,184	87,288	123,934	161,794	22,604
of which: Short-term............	8 724 ..	....	....	....	....	....	....	....	*5,453*
Other sectors............	8 725 ..	....	....	....	....	....	....	....	....
of which: Short-term............	8 727 ..	....	....	....	....	....	....	....	....
Currency and deposits............	8 730 ..	20,079	24,049	21,669	22,860	24,969	21,583	22,347	125,993
Monetary authorities............	8 731 ..	....	....	....	....	....	....	....	....
General government............	8 732 ..	....	....	....	....	....	....	....	....
Banks............	8 733 ..	....	....	....	....	....	....	....	92,756
Other sectors............	8 734 ..	20,079	24,049	21,669	22,860	24,969	21,583	22,347	33,236
Other assets............	8 736 ..	....	....	....	....	....	....	....	....
Monetary authorities............	8 737 ..	....	....	....	....	....	....	....	....
of which: Short-term............	8 739 ..	....	....	....	....	....	....	....	....
General government............	8 740 ..	....	....	....	....	....	....	....	....
of which: Short-term............	8 742 ..	....	....	....	....	....	....	....	....
Banks............	8 743 ..	....	....	....	....	....	....	....	....
of which: Short-term............	8 745 ..	....	....	....	....	....	....	....	....
Other sectors............	8 746 ..	....	....	....	....	....	....	....	....
of which: Short-term............	8 748 ..	....	....	....	....	....	....	....	....
Reserve assets............	8 802 ..	**5,801**	**2,708**	**2,287**	**2,850**	**3,658**	**3,500**	**5,547**	**6,368**
Monetary gold............	8 812 ..	1,440	1,517	1,780	2,284	3,027	3,156	3,992	5,059
Special drawing rights............	8 811 ..	21	27	29	29	28	24	1,088	938
Reserve position in the Fund............	8 810 ..	497	420	168	128	85	161	268	263
Foreign exchange............	8 803 ..	3,843	744	309	408	518	159	199	108
Other claims............	8 813 ..	....	....	....	....	....	....	....	....

Table 3 (Concluded). INTERNATIONAL INVESTMENT POSITION (End-period stocks), 2003–2010

(Millions of U.S. dollars)

	Code	2003	2004	2005	2006	2007	2008	2009	2010
LIABILITIES	8 995 D.	242,000	309,039	329,468	430,922	595,504	562,716	655,831	595,466
Direct investment in Greece	8 555	22,454	28,482	29,189	41,288	53,221	38,119	42,097	33,558
Equity capital and reinvested earnings	8 556	21,620	27,420	26,967	38,592	49,655	34,150	39,130	31,135
Claims on direct investors	8 557	....	....	....	....	....	....	....	....
Liabilities to direct investors	8 558	21,620	27,420	26,967	38,592	49,655	34,150	39,130	31,135
Other capital	8 580	834	1,061	2,223	2,696	3,565	3,969	2,968	2,423
Claims on direct investors	8 585	....	....	....	....	....	....	....	....
Liabilities to direct investors	8 590	834	1,061	2,223	2,696	3,565	3,969	2,968	2,423
Portfolio investment	8 652	133,865	188,456	202,113	255,983	348,059	290,836	343,677	213,433
Equity securities	8 660	16,140	28,386	37,963	60,247	93,548	23,893	28,115	17,106
Banks	8 663	5,302	10,837	14,104	25,290	40,830	8,558	12,585	4,462
Other sectors	8 664	10,838	17,549	23,858	34,957	52,717	15,335	15,530	12,644
Debt securities	8 669	117,725	160,070	164,151	195,735	254,512	266,943	315,562	196,327
Bonds and notes	8 670	117,709	159,999	164,061	195,503	252,736	259,310	303,768	194,765
Monetary authorities	8 671	....	....	....	....	....	....	....	....
General government	8 672	112,829	154,093	158,198	188,025	243,208	245,380	293,044	187,425
Banks	8 673	39	41	32	1	1	1,809	1,873	....
Other sectors	8 674	4,841	5,865	5,831	7,477	9,527	12,120	8,851	7,340
Money market instruments	8 680	16	71	90	232	1,775	7,633	11,794	1,562
Monetary authorities	8 681	....	....	....	....	....	....	....	....
General government	8 682	6	71	90	232	1,775	7,633	11,794	1,535
Banks	8 683	10	....	....	....	....	....	....	....
Other sectors	8 684	....	....	....	....	....	....	....	27
Financial derivatives	8 905	....	....	....	....	....	....	....	....
Monetary authorities	8 906	....	....	....	....	....	....	....	....
General government	8 907	....	....	....	....	....	....	....	....
Banks	8 908	....	....	....	....	....	....	....	....
Other sectors	8 909	....	....	....	....	....	....	....	....
Other investment	8 753	85,681	92,101	98,165	133,652	194,224	233,761	270,057	348,475
Trade credits	8 756	1,748	1,712	1,236	1,733	1,993	1,745	902	1,104
General government	8 757	51	10	6	7	7	6	4	4
of which: Short-term	8 759	....	....	....	....	....	....	....	....
Other sectors	8 760	1,697	1,703	1,230	1,727	1,986	1,740	897	1,100
of which: Short-term	8 762	....	....	....	....	....	....	....	....
Loans	8 764	83,933	90,389	96,929	131,919	192,231	232,016	267,929	346,167
Monetary authorities	8 765	19,391	8,916	8,514	10,777	15,894	49,194	70,641	130,429
of which: Use of Fund credit and loans from the Fund	8 766	....	....	....	....	....	....	....	14,062
of which: Short-term	8 768	19,391	8,916	8,514	10,777	15,894	49,194	70,641	116,367
General government	8 769	14,100	15,659	13,035	15,423	15,726	14,166	11,435	47,246
of which: Short-term	8 771	....	....	....	....	....	....	....	....
Banks	8 772	35,378	51,054	61,901	90,376	143,416	152,939	160,715	155,563
of which: Short-term	8 774	....	....	....	....	....	....	....	....
Other sectors	8 775	15,064	14,760	13,479	15,342	17,194	15,716	25,137	12,928
of which: Short-term	8 777	....	....	....	....	....	....	....	....
Currency and deposits	8 780	....	....	....	....	....	....	....	....
Monetary authorities	8 781	....	....	....	....	....	....	....	....
General government	8 782	....	....	....	....	....	....	....	....
Banks	8 783	....	....	....	....	....	....	....	....
Other sectors	8 784	....	....	....	....	....	....	....	....
Other liabilities	8 786	....	....	....	....	....	....	1,226	1,205
Monetary authorities	8 787	....	....	....	....	....	....	1,226	1,205
of which: Short-term	8 789	....	....	....	....	....	....	....	....
General government	8 790	....	....	....	....	....	....	....	....
of which: Short-term	8 792	....	....	....	....	....	....	....	....
Banks	8 793	....	....	....	....	....	....	....	....
of which: Short-term	8 795	....	....	....	....	....	....	....	....
Other sectors	8 796	....	....	....	....	....	....	....	....
of which: Short-term	8 798	....	....	....	....	....	....	....	....
NET INTERNATIONAL INVESTMENT POSITION U.S.	8 995	−128,281	−169,074	−176,004	−234,649	−315,727	−249,376	−288,789	−294,430
Conversion rates: euros per U.S. dollar (end of period)	0 104	.7918	.7342	.8477	.7593	.6793	.7185	.6942	.7484

Table 1. ANALYTIC PRESENTATION, 2003–2010
(Millions of U.S. dollars)

	Code	2003	2004	2005	2006	2007	2008	2009	2010
A. Current Account[1]...........................	4 993 Z.	**−145.94**	**−65.70**	**−193.26**	**−226.70**	**−264.27**	**−274.45**	**−213.95**	**−218.22**
Goods: exports f.o.b........................	2 100 ..	45.54	37.52	32.87	32.30	40.73	40.47	35.29	31.06
Goods: imports f.o.b........................	3 100 ..	−228.47	−226.75	−299.96	−297.09	−327.89	−338.76	−262.88	−284.42
Balance on Goods.........................	4 100 ..	*−182.93*	*−189.22*	*−267.10*	*−264.79*	*−287.16*	*−298.29*	*−227.58*	*−253.36*
Services: credit.............................	2 200 ..	133.99	160.21	116.00	130.01	148.21	149.32	140.17	138.21
Services: debit.............................	3 200 ..	−82.99	−92.37	−96.20	−105.31	−108.50	−113.38	−98.27	−101.00
Balance on Goods and Services.........	4 991 ..	*−131.93*	*−121.38*	*−247.29*	*−240.09*	*−247.45*	*−262.35*	*−185.68*	*−216.15*
Income: credit.............................	2 300 ..	3.73	5.69	11.43	13.26	13.66	8.08	8.30	8.72
Income: debit.............................	3 300 ..	−54.23	−70.88	−39.72	−42.14	−56.71	−57.34	−74.28	−55.06
Balance on Goods, Services, and Income.........	4 992 ..	*−182.42*	*−186.58*	*−275.57*	*−268.97*	*−290.49*	*−311.61*	*−251.65*	*−262.48*
Current transfers: credit..................	2 379 Z.	48.24	125.91	87.59	54.95	40.58	51.63	54.80	61.86
Current transfers: debit...................	3 379 ..	−11.76	−5.03	−5.29	−12.68	−14.35	−14.48	−17.10	−17.60
B. Capital Account[1]...........................	4 994 Z.	**43.19**	**39.83**	**47.00**	**61.76**	**38.83**	**41.00**	**38.67**	**49.51**
Capital account: credit....................	2 994 Z.	45.23	41.87	49.04	63.80	40.87	43.29	40.74	51.63
Capital account: debit.....................	3 994 ..	−2.04	−2.04	−2.04	−2.04	−2.04	−2.29	−2.07	−2.13
Total, Groups A Plus B....................	4 981 ..	*−102.75*	*−25.87*	*−146.26*	*−164.94*	*−225.44*	*−233.45*	*−175.28*	*−168.71*
C. Financial Account[1]........................	4 995 W.	**78.23**	**32.48**	**120.60**	**146.73**	**207.00**	**213.63**	**166.30**	**126.84**
Direct investment abroad..................	4 505 ..	....	....	....	....	....	....	....	....
Direct investment in Grenada.............	4 555 Z.	89.17	65.01	70.16	89.79	156.55	142.24	102.56	63.61
Portfolio investment assets................	4 602 ..	−2.59	−7.44	.59	−5.32	−2.61	−.19	6.78	2.76
Equity securities........................	4 610 ..	....	....	....	....	....	....	....	....
Debt securities..........................	4 619 ..	....	....	....	....	....	....	....	....
Portfolio investment liabilities............	4 652 Z.	31.68	37.48	17.21	4.57	.59	2.76	7.25	2.30
Equity securities........................	4 660 ..	....	....	....	....	....	....	....	....
Debt securities..........................	4 669 Z.	....	....	....	....	....	....	....	....
Financial derivatives......................	4 910 ..	....	....	....	....	....	....	....	....
Financial derivatives assets...............	4 900 ..	....	....	....	....	....	....	....	....
Financial derivatives liabilities...........	4 905 ..	....	....	....	....	....	....	....	....
Other investment assets..................	4 703 ..	−50.28	−100.06	−228.44	−17.79	−14.35	−14.28	−28.96	−15.29
Monetary authorities....................	4 701 ..	....	....	....	....	....	....	....	....
General government.....................	4 704 ..	....	....	....	....	....	....	....	....
Banks....................................	4 705 ..	−29.56	−77.76	....	....	....	....	−4.59	....
Other sectors............................	4 728 ..	−20.72	−22.29	−228.44	−17.79	−14.35	−14.28	−24.38	−15.29
Other investment liabilities...............	4 753 W.	10.25	37.49	261.09	75.49	66.81	83.10	78.69	73.47
Monetary authorities....................	4 753 WA	....	....	....	....	....	....	16.00	....
General government.....................	4 753 ZB	....	....	....	....	....	....	....	....
Banks....................................	4 753 ZC	....	....	38.22	46.34	16.52	51.70	....	5.70
Other sectors............................	4 753 ZD	10.25	37.49	222.87	29.15	50.29	31.40	62.69	67.77
Total, Groups A Through C................	4 983 ..	*−24.52*	*6.61*	*−25.66*	*−18.21*	*−18.44*	*−19.82*	*−8.98*	*−41.87*
D. Net Errors and Omissions....................	4 998 ..	**7.71**	**35.30**	**−1.74**	**23.31**	**31.36**	**7.45**	**22.97**	**25.84**
Total, Groups A Through D................	4 984 ..	*−16.82*	*41.91*	*−27.40*	*5.10*	*12.93*	*−12.37*	*13.99*	*−16.03*
E. Reserves and Related Items................	4 802 A.	**16.82**	**−41.91**	**27.40**	**−5.10**	**−12.93**	**12.37**	**−13.99**	**16.03**
Reserve assets.............................	4 802 ..	12.81	−46.34	27.40	−5.75	−10.69	6.72	−23.70	9.63
Use of Fund credit and loans.............	4 766 ..	4.00	4.43	....	.65	−2.23	5.65	9.70	6.40
Exceptional financing.....................	4 920 ..	....	....	....	....	....	....	....	....
Conversion rates: Eastern Caribbean dollars per U.S. dollar........................	0 101 ..	**2.7000**	**2.7000**	**2.7000**	**2.7000**	**2.7000**	**2.7000**	**2.7000**	**2.7000**

[1] Excludes components that have been classified in the categories of Group E.

Table 2. STANDARD PRESENTATION, 2003–2010

(Millions of U.S. dollars)

	Code	2003	2004	2005	2006	2007	2008	2009	2010
CURRENT ACCOUNT..	4 993 ..	**−145.94**	**−65.70**	**−193.26**	**−226.70**	**−264.27**	**−274.45**	**−213.95**	**−218.22**
A. GOODS...	4 100 ..	**−182.93**	**−189.22**	**−267.10**	**−264.79**	**−287.16**	**−298.29**	**−227.58**	**−253.36**
Credit..	2 100 ..	**45.54**	**37.52**	**32.87**	**32.30**	**40.73**	**40.47**	**35.29**	**31.06**
General merchandise: exports f.o.b.................	2 110 ..	41.82	32.04	27.64	25.37	33.41	30.25	29.19	24.16
Goods for processing: exports f.o.b...............	2 150 ..	....	....	....	....	....	....	....	....
Repairs on goods..	2 160 ..	....	.01	....	.01	....	....	....	....
Goods procured in ports by carriers.............	2 170 ..	3.72	5.47	5.22	6.91	7.32	10.22	6.10	6.90
Nonmonetary gold..	2 180 ..	....	....	....	....	....	....	....	....
Debit..	3 100 ..	**−228.47**	**−226.75**	**−299.96**	**−297.09**	**−327.89**	**−338.76**	**−262.88**	**−284.42**
General merchandise: imports f.o.b.................	3 110 ..	−228.47	−226.75	−299.96	−297.09	−327.89	−338.76	−262.88	−284.42
Goods for processing: imports f.o.b...............	3 150 ..	....	....	....	....	....	....	....	....
Repairs on goods..	3 160 ..	....	....	....	....	....	....	....	....
Goods procured in ports by carriers.............	3 170 ..	....	....	....	....	....	....	....	....
Nonmonetary gold..	3 180 ..	....	....	....	....	....	....	....	....
B. SERVICES..	4 200 ..	**51.00**	**67.84**	**19.81**	**24.70**	**39.71**	**35.94**	**41.91**	**37.21**
Total credit..	2 200 ..	*133.99*	*160.21*	*116.00*	*130.01*	*148.21*	*149.32*	*140.17*	*138.21*
Total debit...	3 200 ..	*−82.99*	*−92.37*	*−96.20*	*−105.31*	*−108.50*	*−113.38*	*−98.27*	*−101.00*
Transportation services, credit..................	2 205 ..	**8.96**	**9.29**	**11.28**	**11.59**	**11.27**	**10.41**	**9.71**	**9.84**
Passenger..	2 850 ..	....	....	....	....	....	....	....	....
Freight...	2 851 ..	....	....	....	....	....	....	....	....
Other...	2 852 ..	....	....	....	....	....	....	....	....
Sea transport, passenger................................	2 207 ..	....	....	....	....	....	....	....	....
Sea transport, freight......................................	2 208 ..	....	....	....	....	....	....	....	....
Sea transport, other..	2 209 ..	....	....	....	....	....	....	....	....
Air transport, passenger.................................	2 211 ..	....	....	....	....	....	....	....	....
Air transport, freight.......................................	2 212 ..	....	....	....	....	....	....	....	....
Air transport, other...	2 213 ..	....	....	....	....	....	....	....	....
Other transport, passenger............................	2 215 ..	....	....	....	....	....	....	....	....
Other transport, freight..................................	2 216 ..	....	....	....	....	....	....	....	....
Other transport, other....................................	2 217 ..	....	....	....	....	....	....	....	....
Transportation services, debit..................	3 205 ..	**−39.17**	**−40.33**	**−48.78**	**−49.60**	**−53.29**	**−54.68**	**−44.32**	**−46.61**
Passenger..	3 850 ..	....	....	....	....	....	....	....	....
Freight...	3 851 ..	....	....	....	....	....	....	....	....
Other...	3 852 ..	....	....	....	....	....	....	....	....
Sea transport, passenger................................	3 207 ..	....	....	....	....	....	....	....	....
Sea transport, freight......................................	3 208 ..	....	....	....	....	....	....	....	....
Sea transport, other..	3 209 ..	....	....	....	....	....	....	....	....
Air transport, passenger.................................	3 211 ..	....	....	....	....	....	....	....	....
Air transport, freight.......................................	3 212 ..	....	....	....	....	....	....	....	....
Air transport, other...	3 213 ..	....	....	....	....	....	....	....	....
Other transport, passenger............................	3 215 ..	....	....	....	....	....	....	....	....
Other transport, freight..................................	3 216 ..	....	....	....	....	....	....	....	....
Other transport, other....................................	3 217 ..	....	....	....	....	....	....	....	....
Travel, credit...	2 236 ..	**103.74**	**86.45**	**71.41**	**93.80**	**108.73**	**108.58**	**98.97**	**96.19**
Business travel...	2 237 ..	....	....	....	....	....	....	....	....
Personal travel..	2 240 ..	....	....	....	....	....	....	....	....
Travel, debit...	3 236 ..	**−8.40**	**−8.51**	**−10.04**	**−15.52**	**−15.79**	**−11.06**	**−10.37**	**−9.85**
Business travel...	3 237 ..	....	....	....	....	....	....	....	....
Personal travel..	3 240 ..	....	....	....	....	....	....	....	....
Other services, credit.................................	2 200 BA	**21.30**	**64.47**	**33.31**	**24.61**	**28.21**	**30.33**	**31.49**	**32.18**
Communications..	2 245 ..	7.69	9.14	9.30	10.59	11.12	12.71	13.37	13.55
Construction..	2 249 ..	....	....	....	....	....	....	....	....
Insurance...	2 253 ..	3.46	45.00	13.64	3.60	4.58	5.39	4.55	4.68
Financial..	2 260 ..	....	....	....	....	....	....	....	....
Computer and information..............................	2 262 ..	....	....	....	....	....	....	....	....
Royalties and licence fees..............................	2 266 ..	....	....	....	.06	.06	.07	.43	.44
Other business services..................................	2 268 ..	8.45	8.69	9.07	8.96	10.99	10.82	11.52	11.86
Personal, cultural, and recreational...............	2 287 ..	....	....	....	....	....	....	....	....
Government, n.i.e..	2 291 ..	1.70	1.64	1.30	1.40	1.45	1.35	1.63	1.67
Other services, debit...................................	3 200 BA	**−35.42**	**−43.53**	**−37.38**	**−40.19**	**−39.42**	**−47.64**	**−43.58**	**−44.54**
Communications..	3 245 ..	−4.19	−3.64	−1.88	−2.73	−2.94	−3.68	−2.75	−2.83
Construction..	3 249 ..	−4.91	−3.03	−4.08	−5.04	−4.27	−6.10	−4.26	−3.72
Insurance...	3 253 ..	−8.95	−9.33	−12.67	−14.49	−14.97	−15.08	−13.69	−14.53
Financial..	3 260 ..	....	....	....	....	....	....	....	....
Computer and information..............................	3 262 ..	....	....	....	−.10	−.06	−.01	−.02	−.02
Royalties and licence fees..............................	3 266 ..	−.57	−.79	−.89	−2.37	−2.53	−3.02	−3.49	−3.59
Other business services..................................	3 268 ..	−11.00	−13.97	−10.07	−11.22	−10.50	−12.55	−12.65	−13.00
Personal, cultural, and recreational...............	3 287 ..	....	....	....	....	....	....	....	....
Government, n.i.e..	3 291 ..	−5.80	−12.77	−7.80	−4.23	−4.14	−7.20	−6.71	−6.85

Table 2 (Continued). STANDARD PRESENTATION, 2003–2010

(Millions of U.S. dollars)

	Code	2003	2004	2005	2006	2007	2008	2009	2010
C. INCOME	4 300	**−50.49**	**−65.19**	**−28.28**	**−28.88**	**−43.05**	**−49.26**	**−65.98**	**−46.33**
Total credit	2 300	*3.73*	*5.69*	*11.43*	*13.26*	*13.66*	*8.08*	*8.30*	*8.72*
Total debit	3 300	*−54.23*	*−70.88*	*−39.72*	*−42.14*	*−56.71*	*−57.34*	*−74.28*	*−55.06*
Compensation of employees, credit	2 310	**.04**	**.04**	**.03**	**.81**	**.25**	**.19**	**.17**	**.18**
Compensation of employees, debit	3 310	....	....	....	....	....	....	....	....
Investment income, credit	2 320	**3.69**	**5.65**	**11.40**	**12.44**	**13.41**	**7.89**	**8.13**	**8.55**
Direct investment income	2 330	.02	....	....	.04	.03	.21	.26	.26
Dividends and distributed branch profits	2 332	....	....	....	....	....	....	....	....
Reinvested earnings and undistributed branch profits	2 333	....	....	....	....	....	....	....	....
Income on debt (interest)	2 334	.02	....	....	.04	.03	.21	.26	.26
Portfolio investment income	2 339	.53	.19	1.62	3.09	4.27	1.95	2.49	2.75
Income on equity	2 340	.53	.19	1.62	3.09	4.27	1.95	2.49	2.75
Income on bonds and notes	2 350	....	....	....	....	....	....	....	....
Income on money market instruments	2 360	....	....	....	....	....	....	....	....
Other investment income	2 370	3.15	5.46	9.77	9.31	9.11	5.73	5.38	5.54
Investment income, debit	3 320	**−54.23**	**−70.88**	**−39.72**	**−42.14**	**−56.71**	**−57.34**	**−74.28**	**−55.06**
Direct investment income	3 330	−26.14	−24.92	−22.74	−22.05	−35.68	−35.48	−55.36	−35.35
Dividends and distributed branch profits	3 332	−16.22	−11.46	−11.11	−7.85	−17.36	−21.56	−47.19	−26.95
Reinvested earnings and undistributed branch profits	3 333	−9.30	−12.61	−10.80	−12.47	−15.50	−12.10	−5.25	−5.40
Income on debt (interest)	3 334	−.62	−.85	−.84	−1.73	−2.81	−1.82	−2.92	−3.00
Portfolio investment income	3 339	−11.57	−16.39	−.47	−.13	−.39	−.32	−.38	−.33
Income on equity	3 340	−11.57	−16.39	−.47	−.13	−.39	−.32	−.38	−.33
Income on bonds and notes	3 350	....	....	....	....	....	....	....	....
Income on money market instruments	3 360	....	....	....	....	....	....	....	....
Other investment income	3 370	−16.51	−29.57	−16.50	−19.97	−20.64	−21.54	−18.54	−19.37
D. CURRENT TRANSFERS	4 379	**36.48**	**120.87**	**82.31**	**42.27**	**26.23**	**37.16**	**37.70**	**44.26**
Credit	2 379	**48.24**	**125.91**	**87.59**	**54.95**	**40.58**	**51.63**	**54.80**	**61.86**
General government	2 380	21.17	43.42	35.14	21.67	8.01	19.74	26.76	33.45
Other sectors	2 390	27.07	82.49	52.45	33.28	32.56	31.89	28.04	28.41
Workers' remittances	2 391	25.24	48.07	26.80	27.63	28.38	28.66	27.48	27.84
Other current transfers	2 392	1.83	34.41	25.65	5.65	4.19	3.23	.56	.57
Debit	3 379	**−11.76**	**−5.03**	**−5.29**	**−12.68**	**−14.35**	**−14.48**	**−17.10**	**−17.60**
General government	3 380	−3.37	−3.82	−3.86	−4.48	−3.03	−3.43	−3.73	−3.84
Other sectors	3 390	−8.39	−1.21	−1.42	−8.19	−11.32	−11.05	−13.37	−13.76
Workers' remittances	3 391	−1.21	−1.21	−1.42	−1.48	−1.60	−1.80	−1.50	−1.54
Other current transfers	3 392	−7.17	....	....	−6.71	−9.72	−9.26	−11.87	−12.22
CAPITAL AND FINANCIAL ACCOUNT	4 996	**138.23**	**30.40**	**195.00**	**203.40**	**232.90**	**267.01**	**190.98**	**192.39**
CAPITAL ACCOUNT	4 994	**43.19**	**39.83**	**47.00**	**61.76**	**38.83**	**41.00**	**38.67**	**49.51**
Total credit	2 994	*45.23*	*41.87*	*49.04*	*63.80*	*40.87*	*43.29*	*40.74*	*51.63*
Total debit	3 994	*−2.04*	*−2.04*	*−2.04*	*−2.04*	*−2.04*	*−2.29*	*−2.07*	*−2.13*
Capital transfers, credit	2 400	**45.23**	**41.87**	**49.04**	**63.80**	**40.87**	**43.29**	**40.74**	**51.63**
General government	2 401	21.94	17.79	24.31	38.30	14.68	16.77	15.01	25.15
Debt forgiveness	2 402	....	....	....	....	....	....	....	....
Other capital transfers	2 410	21.94	17.79	24.31	38.30	14.68	16.77	15.01	25.15
Other sectors	2 430	23.29	24.08	24.73	25.50	26.19	26.53	25.73	26.48
Migrants' transfers	2 431	23.29	24.08	24.73	25.50	26.19	26.53	25.73	26.48
Debt forgiveness	2 432	....	....	....	....	....	....	....	....
Other capital transfers	2 440	....	....	....	....	....	....	....	....
Capital transfers, debit	3 400	**−2.04**	**−2.04**	**−2.04**	**−2.04**	**−2.04**	**−2.29**	**−2.07**	**−2.13**
General government	3 401	....	....	....	....	....	....	....	....
Debt forgiveness	3 402	....	....	....	....	....	....	....	....
Other capital transfers	3 410	....	....	....	....	....	....	....	....
Other sectors	3 430	−2.04	−2.04	−2.04	−2.04	−2.04	−2.29	−2.07	−2.13
Migrants' transfers	3 431	−2.04	−2.04	−2.04	−2.04	−2.04	−2.29	−2.07	−2.13
Debt forgiveness	3 432	....	....	....	....	....	....	....	....
Other capital transfers	3 440	....	....	....	....	....	....	....	....
Nonproduced nonfinancial assets, credit	2 480	....	....	....	....	....	....	....	....
Nonproduced nonfinancial assets, debit	3 480	....	....	....	....	....	....	....	....

Table 2 (Continued). STANDARD PRESENTATION, 2003–2010

(Millions of U.S. dollars)

	Code	2003	2004	2005	2006	2007	2008	2009	2010
FINANCIAL ACCOUNT	4 995 ..	**95.04**	**−9.43**	**148.00**	**141.64**	**194.07**	**226.01**	**152.31**	**142.88**
A. DIRECT INVESTMENT	4 500 ..	**89.17**	**65.01**	**70.16**	**89.79**	**156.55**	**142.24**	**102.56**	**63.61**
Direct investment abroad	4 505 ..	....	....	....	....	....	....	....	....
Equity capital	4 510 ..	....	....	....	....	....	....	....	....
Claims on affiliated enterprises	4 515 ..	....	....	....	....	....	....	....	....
Liabilities to affiliated enterprises	4 520 ..	....	....	....	....	....	....	....	....
Reinvested earnings	4 525 ..	....	....	....	....	....	....	....	....
Other capital	4 530 ..	....	....	....	....	....	....	....	....
Claims on affiliated enterprises	4 535 ..	....	....	....	....	....	....	....	....
Liabilities to affiliated enterprises	4 540 ..	....	....	....	....	....	....	....	....
Direct investment in Grenada	4 555 ..	**89.17**	**65.01**	**70.16**	**89.79**	**156.55**	**142.24**	**102.56**	**63.61**
Equity capital	4 560 ..	57.14	33.87	38.82	54.85	108.81	110.97	77.50	37.19
Claims on direct investors	4 565 ..	....	....	....	....	....	....	....	....
Liabilities to direct investors	4 570 ..	57.14	33.87	38.82	54.85	108.81	110.97	77.50	37.19
Reinvested earnings	4 575 ..	9.30	12.61	10.80	12.47	15.50	12.10	5.25	5.40
Other capital	4 580 ..	22.73	18.53	20.54	22.46	32.25	19.16	19.80	21.02
Claims on direct investors	4 585 ..	....	....	....	....	....	....	....	....
Liabilities to direct investors	4 590 ..	22.73	18.53	20.54	22.46	32.25	19.16	19.80	21.02
B. PORTFOLIO INVESTMENT	4 600 ..	**29.09**	**30.03**	**17.80**	**−.75**	**−2.02**	**2.57**	**14.02**	**5.06**
Assets	4 602 ..	**−2.59**	**−7.44**	**.59**	**−5.32**	**−2.61**	**−.19**	**6.78**	**2.76**
Equity securities	4 610 ..	....	....	....	....	....	....	....	....
Monetary authorities	4 611 ..	....	....	....	....	....	....	....	....
General government	4 612 ..	....	....	....	....	....	....	....	....
Banks	4 613 ..	....	....	....	....	....	....	....	....
Other sectors	4 614 ..	....	....	....	....	....	....	....	....
Debt securities	4 619 ..	....	....	....	....	....	....	....	....
Bonds and notes	4 620 ..	....	....	....	....	....	....	....	....
Monetary authorities	4 621 ..	....	....	....	....	....	....	....	....
General government	4 622 ..	....	....	....	....	....	....	....	....
Banks	4 623 ..	....	....	....	....	....	....	....	....
Other sectors	4 624 ..	....	....	....	....	....	....	....	....
Money market instruments	4 630 ..	....	....	....	....	....	....	....	....
Monetary authorities	4 631 ..	....	....	....	....	....	....	....	....
General government	4 632 ..	....	....	....	....	....	....	....	....
Banks	4 633 ..	....	....	....	....	....	....	....	....
Other sectors	4 634 ..	....	....	....	....	....	....	....	....
Liabilities	4 652 ..	**31.68**	**37.48**	**17.21**	**4.57**	**.59**	**2.76**	**7.25**	**2.30**
Equity securities	4 660 ..	....	....	....	....	....	....	....	....
Banks	4 663 ..	....	....	....	....	....	....	....	....
Other sectors	4 664 ..	....	....	....	....	....	....	....	....
Debt securities	4 669 ..	....	....	....	....	....	....	....	....
Bonds and notes	4 670 ..	....	....	....	....	....	....	....	....
Monetary authorities	4 671 ..	....	....	....	....	....	....	....	....
General government	4 672 ..	....	....	....	....	....	....	....	....
Banks	4 673 ..	....	....	....	....	....	....	....	....
Other sectors	4 674 ..	....	....	....	....	....	....	....	....
Money market instruments	4 680 ..	....	....	....	....	....	....	....	....
Monetary authorities	4 681 ..	....	....	....	....	....	....	....	....
General government	4 682 ..	....	....	....	....	....	....	....	....
Banks	4 683 ..	....	....	....	....	....	....	....	....
Other sectors	4 684 ..	....	....	....	....	....	....	....	....
C. FINANCIAL DERIVATIVES	4 910 ..	....	....	....	....	....	....	....	....
Monetary authorities	4 911 ..	....	....	....	....	....	....	....	....
General government	4 912 ..	....	....	....	....	....	....	....	....
Banks	4 913 ..	....	....	....	....	....	....	....	....
Other sectors	4 914 ..	....	....	....	....	....	....	....	....
Assets	4 900 ..	....	....	....	....	....	....	....	....
Monetary authorities	4 901 ..	....	....	....	....	....	....	....	....
General government	4 902 ..	....	....	....	....	....	....	....	....
Banks	4 903 ..	....	....	....	....	....	....	....	....
Other sectors	4 904 ..	....	....	....	....	....	....	....	....
Liabilities	4 905 ..	....	....	....	....	....	....	....	....
Monetary authorities	4 906 ..	....	....	....	....	....	....	....	....
General government	4 907 ..	....	....	....	....	....	....	....	....
Banks	4 908 ..	....	....	....	....	....	....	....	....
Other sectors	4 909 ..	....	....	....	....	....	....	....	....

Table 2 (Concluded). STANDARD PRESENTATION, 2003–2010

(Millions of U.S. dollars)

	Code	2003	2004	2005	2006	2007	2008	2009	2010
D. OTHER INVESTMENT	4 700	−36.03	−58.14	32.65	58.34	50.23	74.47	59.42	64.58
Assets	4 703	−50.28	−100.06	−228.44	−17.79	−14.35	−14.28	−28.96	−15.29
Trade credits	4 706	....	....	....	....	....	....	....	....
General government	4 707	....	....	....	....	....	....	....	....
of which: Short-term	4 709	....	....	....	....	....	....	....	....
Other sectors	4 710	....	....	....	....	....	....	....	....
of which: Short-term	4 712	....	....	....	....	....	....	....	....
Loans	4 714	−29.56	−77.76	....	....	....	....	−4.59	....
Monetary authorities	4 715	....	....	....	....	....	....	....	....
of which: Short-term	4 718	....	....	....	....	....	....	....	....
General government	4 719	....	....	....	....	....	....	....	....
of which: Short-term	4 721	....	....	....	....	....	....	....	....
Banks	4 722	−29.56	−77.76	....	....	....	....	−4.59	....
of which: Short-term	4 724	....	....	....	....	....	....	....	....
Other sectors	4 725	....	....	....	....	....	....	....	....
of which: Short-term	4 727	....	....	....	....	....	....	....	....
Currency and deposits	4 730	....	....	....	....	....	....	....	....
Monetary authorities	4 731	....	....	....	....	....	....	....	....
General government	4 732	....	....	....	....	....	....	....	....
Banks	4 733	....	....	....	....	....	....	....	....
Other sectors	4 734	....	....	....	....	....	....	....	....
Other assets	4 736	−20.72	−22.29	−228.44	−17.79	−14.35	−14.28	−24.38	−15.29
Monetary authorities	4 737	....	....	....	....	....	....	....	....
of which: Short-term	4 739	....	....	....	....	....	....	....	....
General government	4 740	....	....	....	....	....	....	....	....
of which: Short-term	4 742	....	....	....	....	....	....	....	....
Banks	4 743	....	....	....	....	....	....	....	....
of which: Short-term	4 745	....	....	....	....	....	....	....	....
Other sectors	4 746	−20.72	−22.29	−228.44	−17.79	−14.35	−14.28	−24.38	−15.29
of which: Short-term	4 748	....	....	....	....	....	....	....	....
Liabilities	4 753	14.25	41.91	261.09	76.14	64.57	88.75	88.39	79.87
Trade credits	4 756	....	....	....	....	....	....	....	....
General government	4 757	....	....	....	....	....	....	....	....
of which: Short-term	4 759	....	....	....	....	....	....	....	....
Other sectors	4 760	....	....	....	....	....	....	....	....
of which: Short-term	4 762	....	....	....	....	....	....	....	....
Loans	4 764	4.00	4.43	....	.65	−2.23	5.65	9.70	6.40
Monetary authorities	4 765	4.00	4.43	....	.65	−2.23	5.65	9.70	6.40
of which: Use of Fund credit and loans from the Fund	4 766	4.00	4.43	....	.65	−2.23	5.65	9.70	6.40
of which: Short-term	4 768	....	....	....	....	....	....	....	....
General government	4 769	....	....	....	....	....	....	....	....
of which: Short-term	4 771	....	....	....	....	....	....	....	....
Banks	4 772	....	....	....	....	....	....	....	....
of which: Short-term	4 774	....	....	....	....	....	....	....	....
Other sectors	4 775	....	....	....	....	....	....	....	....
of which: Short-term	4 777	....	....	....	....	....	....	....	....
Currency and deposits	4 780	....	....	....	....	....	....	....	....
Monetary authorities	4 781	....	....	....	....	....	....	....	....
General government	4 782	....	....	....	....	....	....	....	....
Banks	4 783	....	....	....	....	....	....	....	....
Other sectors	4 784	....	....	....	....	....	....	....	....
Other liabilities	4 786	10.25	37.49	261.09	75.49	66.81	83.10	78.69	73.47
Monetary authorities	4 787	....	....	....	....	....	....	16.00	....
of which: Short-term	4 789	....	....	....	....	....	....	....	....
General government	4 790	....	....	....	....	....	....	....	....
of which: Short-term	4 792	....	....	....	....	....	....	....	....
Banks	4 793	....	....	38.22	46.34	16.52	51.70	....	5.70
of which: Short-term	4 795	....	....	....	....	....	....	....	....
Other sectors	4 796	10.25	37.49	222.87	29.15	50.29	31.40	62.69	67.77
of which: Short-term	4 798	....	....	....	....	....	....	....	....
E. RESERVE ASSETS	4 802	12.81	−46.34	27.40	−5.75	−10.69	6.72	−23.70	9.63
Monetary gold	4 812	....	....	....	....	....	....	....	....
Special drawing rights	4 811	....	−.01	−.01	−.11	.06	−1.15	−15.37	....
Reserve position in the Fund	4 810	....	....	....	....	....	....	....	....
Foreign exchange	4 803	8.20	−7.84	−.07	−.08	−.09	1.48	....	....
Other claims	4 813	4.62	−38.49	27.48	−5.56	−10.66	6.39	−8.33	9.62
NET ERRORS AND OMISSIONS	4 998	7.71	35.30	−1.74	23.31	31.36	7.45	22.97	25.84

Table 1. ANALYTIC PRESENTATION, 2003–2010

(Millions of U.S. dollars)

	Code	2003	2004	2005	2006	2007	2008	2009	2010
A. Current Account[1]	4 993 Z.	**−1,039.2**	**−1,235.7**	**−1,300.6**	**−1,585.3**	**−1,842.8**	**−1,751.0**	**−51.8**	**−878.3**
Goods: exports f.o.b.	2 100 ..	3,059.9	5,105.1	5,459.5	6,082.1	6,983.2	7,846.4	7,294.9	8,565.9
Goods: imports f.o.b.	3 100 ..	−6,175.7	−8,737.0	−9,650.1	−10,934.4	−12,470.2	−13,421.2	−10,643.1	−12,858.2
Balance on Goods	4 100 ..	*−3,115.9*	*−3,631.9*	*−4,190.6*	*−4,852.3*	*−5,487.0*	*−5,574.8*	*−3,348.2*	*−4,292.3*
Services: credit	2 200 ..	1,058.8	1,100.4	1,307.8	1,518.9	1,731.2	1,872.9	1,925.0	2,216.3
Services: debit	3 200 ..	−1,126.1	−1,344.3	−1,449.6	−1,778.4	−2,041.2	−2,149.0	−2,083.6	−2,369.9
Balance on Goods and Services	4 991 ..	*−3,183.2*	*−3,875.8*	*−4,332.4*	*−5,111.8*	*−5,797.0*	*−5,850.9*	*−3,506.8*	*−4,445.9*
Income: credit	2 300 ..	179.1	219.9	301.5	434.6	556.0	544.5	352.1	288.1
Income: debit	3 300 ..	−497.0	−630.0	−786.5	−1,115.0	−1,398.7	−1,482.1	−1,463.2	−1,488.0
Balance on Goods, Services, and Income	4 992 ..	*−3,501.0*	*−4,285.9*	*−4,817.4*	*−5,792.2*	*−6,639.7*	*−6,788.5*	*−4,617.9*	*−5,645.8*
Current transfers: credit	2 379 Z.	2,558.9	3,085.6	3,555.3	4,244.4	4,808.0	5,056.7	4,584.5	4,792.0
Current transfers: debit	3 379 ..	−97.0	−35.4	−38.5	−37.5	−11.1	−19.2	−18.4	−24.5
B. Capital Account[1]	4 994 Z.	**133.8**	....	....	**142.2**	....	**1.1**	**1.0**	**1.1**
Capital account: credit	2 994 Z.	133.8	....	....	142.2	....	1.1	1.0	1.1
Capital account: debit	3 994 ..	....	....	....	....	....	....	....	....
Total, Groups A Plus B	4 981 ..	*−905.4*	*−1,235.7*	*−1,300.6*	*−1,443.1*	*−1,842.8*	*−1,749.9*	*−50.8*	*−877.2*
C. Financial Account[1]	4 995 W.	**1,516.3**	**402.4**	**611.7**	**1,045.0**	**1,551.2**	**1,273.3**	**70.5**	**1,284.0**
Direct investment abroad	4 505 ..	....	−41.2	−38.4	−40.0	−25.4	−16.4	−26.3	−23.5
Direct investment in Guatemala	4 555 Z.	131.0	296.0	508.6	591.8	745.1	753.8	600.0	686.9
Portfolio investment assets	4 602 ..	18.1	11.6	−39.8	−59.8	16.7	−10.4	23.2	−15.4
Equity securities	4 610 ..	....	....	−.4	....	−.4	....	−.4	−.4
Debt securities	4 619 ..	18.1	11.6	−39.4	−59.8	17.1	−10.4	23.6	−15.0
Portfolio investment liabilities	4 652 Z.	−11.0	−143.8	−106.0	−131.3	−245.0	−118.3	−281.4	−27.6
Equity securities	4 660 ..	....	....	....	....	....	....	....	....
Debt securities	4 669 Z.	−11.0	−143.8	−106.0	−131.3	−245.0	−118.3	−281.4	−27.6
Financial derivatives	4 910 ..	....	....	....	....	....	....	....	....
Financial derivatives assets	4 900 ..	....	....	....	....	....	....	....	....
Financial derivatives liabilities	4 905 ..	....	....	....	....	....	....	....	....
Other investment assets	4 703 ..	173.5	−340.3	−434.5	−508.9	−597.5	−2.4	−260.6	82.8
Monetary authorities	4 701 ..	....	....	....	−.4	.2	−.4	2.0	....
General government	4 704 ..	....	....	....	....	....	....	....	....
Banks	4 705 ..	....	−93.1	−1.0	−250.6	−167.6	−3.1	−36.4	−.5
Other sectors	4 728 ..	173.5	−247.2	−433.5	−257.9	−430.1	1.1	−226.2	83.3
Other investment liabilities	4 753 W.	1,204.7	620.1	721.8	1,193.2	1,657.3	667.0	15.6	580.8
Monetary authorities	4 753 WA	−11.7	−69.9	−.5	−1.2	−.4	−2.7	270.3	−.6
General government	4 753 ZB	307.9	92.2	−43.5	356.3	392.9	121.8	533.4	617.4
Banks	4 753 ZC	....	99.1	191.2	293.4	521.2	−178.3	−306.6	19.2
Other sectors	4 753 ZD	908.5	498.7	574.6	544.7	743.6	726.2	−481.5	−55.2
Total, Groups A Through C	4 983 ..	*610.9*	*−833.3*	*−688.9*	*−398.1*	*−291.6*	*−476.6*	*19.7*	*406.8*
D. Net Errors and Omissions	4 998 ..	**−60.8**	**835.0**	**798.3**	**479.8**	**405.9**	**547.2**	**257.7**	**156.5**
Total, Groups A Through D	4 984 ..	*550.1*	*1.7*	*109.4*	*81.7*	*114.3*	*70.6*	*277.4*	*563.3*
E. Reserves and Related Items	4 802 A.	**−550.1**	**−1.7**	**−109.4**	**−81.7**	**−114.3**	**−70.6**	**−277.4**	**−563.3**
Reserve assets	4 802 ..	−550.1	−604.0	−238.0	−250.7	−214.9	−332.1	−470.6	−676.9
Use of Fund credit and loans	4 766 ..	....	....	....	....	....	....	....	....
Exceptional financing	4 920 ..	....	602.3	128.6	169.0	100.6	261.5	193.2	113.6
Conversion rates: quetzales per U.S. dollar	0 101 ..	**7.9408**	**7.9465**	**7.6339**	**7.6026**	**7.6733**	**7.5600**	**8.1616**	**8.0578**

[1] Excludes components that have been classified in the categories of Group E.

Table 2. STANDARD PRESENTATION, 2003–2010

(Millions of U.S. dollars)

	Code	2003	2004	2005	2006	2007	2008	2009	2010
CURRENT ACCOUNT	4 993	**−1,039.2**	**−1,164.4**	**−1,241.0**	**−1,524.0**	**−1,785.6**	**−1,680.5**	**7.7**	**−826.1**
A. GOODS	4 100	**−3,115.9**	**−3,631.9**	**−4,190.6**	**−4,852.3**	**−5,487.0**	**−5,574.8**	**−3,348.2**	**−4,292.3**
Credit	2 100	**3,059.9**	**5,105.1**	**5,459.5**	**6,082.1**	**6,983.2**	**7,846.4**	**7,294.9**	**8,565.9**
General merchandise: exports f.o.b.	2 110	2,631.7	5,057.5	5,403.7	6,021.7	6,907.7	7,746.8	7,221.5	8,473.9
Goods for processing: exports f.o.b.	2 150	428.1	....	....	....	....	....	....	....
Repairs on goods	2 160	....	....	....	....	....	....	....	....
Goods procured in ports by carriers	2 170	....	47.6	55.8	60.4	75.5	99.6	73.4	92.0
Nonmonetary gold	2 180	....	....	....	....	....	....	....	....
Debit	3 100	**−6,175.7**	**−8,737.0**	**−9,650.1**	**−10,934.4**	**−12,470.2**	**−13,421.2**	**−10,643.1**	**−12,858.2**
General merchandise: imports f.o.b.	3 110	−6,175.7	−8,735.8	−9,648.9	−10,932.0	−12,469.0	−13,418.6	−10,641.5	−12,856.4
Goods for processing: imports f.o.b.	3 150	....	....	....	....	....	....	....	....
Repairs on goods	3 160	....	....	....	....	....	....	....	....
Goods procured in ports by carriers	3 170	....	−1.2	−1.2	−2.4	−1.2	−2.6	−1.6	−1.8
Nonmonetary gold	3 180	....	....	....	....	....	....	....	....
B. SERVICES	4 200	**−67.3**	**−243.9**	**−141.8**	**−259.5**	**−310.0**	**−276.1**	**−158.6**	**−153.6**
Total credit	2 200	*1,058.8*	*1,100.4*	*1,307.8*	*1,518.9*	*1,731.2*	*1,872.9*	*1,925.0*	*2,216.3*
Total debit	3 200	*−1,126.1*	*−1,344.3*	*−1,449.6*	*−1,778.4*	*−2,041.2*	*−2,149.0*	*−2,083.6*	*−2,369.9*
Transportation services, credit	2 205	**84.2**	**150.3**	**152.4**	**166.7**	**187.8**	**254.6**	**255.5**	**314.1**
Passenger	2 850	*24.7*	*....*	*....*	*....*	*....*	*.1*	*.4*	*.4*
Freight	2 851	*3.6*	*53.6*	*57.8*	*63.4*	*79.6*	*79.4*	*60.5*	*80.7*
Other	2 852	*55.9*	*96.7*	*94.6*	*103.3*	*108.2*	*175.1*	*194.6*	*233.0*
Sea transport, passenger	2 207	1.1	....	....	....	....	....	....	....
Sea transport, freight	2 208	.3	....	....	....	....	....	....	....
Sea transport, other	2 209	6.6	87.4	86.5	96.2	100.5	142.9	174.6	210.0
Air transport, passenger	2 211	4.4	....	....	....	....	.1	.4	.4
Air transport, freight	2 212	....	....	....	....	....	....	....	....
Air transport, other	2 213	47.3	9.3	8.1	7.1	7.7	32.2	20.0	23.0
Other transport, passenger	2 215	19.3	....	....	....	....	....	....	....
Other transport, freight	2 216	3.3	53.6	57.8	63.4	79.6	79.4	60.5	80.7
Other transport, other	2 217	2.1	....	....	....	....	....	....	....
Transportation services, debit	3 205	**−560.4**	**−684.1**	**−787.5**	**−911.6**	**−1,073.2**	**−1,146.4**	**−955.6**	**−1,156.8**
Passenger	3 850	*−61.4*	*−102.9*	*−110.6*	*−125.5*	*−139.5*	*−134.3*	*−147.0*	*−250.3*
Freight	3 851	*−495.0*	*−578.9*	*−674.1*	*−783.4*	*−930.7*	*−1,004.1*	*−781.4*	*−875.7*
Other	3 852	*−4.0*	*−2.3*	*−2.8*	*−2.7*	*−3.0*	*−8.0*	*−27.2*	*−30.8*
Sea transport, passenger	3 207	−.2	....	....	....	....	....	....	....
Sea transport, freight	3 208	−331.6	−409.6	−476.6	−554.1	−645.5	−696.3	−549.3	−613.0
Sea transport, other	3 209	−.9	....	....	....	....	....	....	....
Air transport, passenger	3 211	−47.6	−102.9	−110.6	−125.5	−139.5	−134.3	−142.7	−245.8
Air transport, freight	3 212	−43.0	−58.5	−68.1	−79.1	−92.2	−99.4	−78.2	−94.7
Air transport, other	3 213	−1.4	....	....	....	....	....	....	....
Other transport, passenger	3 215	−13.6	....	....	....	....	....	−4.3	−4.5
Other transport, freight	3 216	−120.4	−110.8	−129.4	−150.2	−193.0	−208.4	−153.9	−168.0
Other transport, other	3 217	−1.8	−2.3	−2.8	−2.7	−3.0	−8.0	−27.2	−30.8
Travel, credit	2 236	**620.7**	**629.8**	**790.7**	**918.7**	**1,054.7**	**1,068.4**	**1,178.9**	**1,377.9**
Business travel	2 237	132.4	107.1	134.5	156.1	179.3	181.6	200.4	261.8
Personal travel	2 240	488.3	522.7	656.2	762.6	875.4	886.8	978.5	1,116.1
Travel, debit	3 236	**−312.0**	**−385.4**	**−420.8**	**−528.5**	**−597.2**	**−606.5**	**−715.3**	**−782.8**
Business travel	3 237	−122.3	−108.3	−117.7	−146.9	−165.8	−168.4	−200.8	−219.8
Personal travel	3 240	−189.7	−277.1	−303.1	−381.6	−431.4	−438.1	−514.5	−563.0
Other services, credit	2 200 BA	**353.9**	**320.3**	**364.7**	**433.5**	**488.7**	**549.9**	**490.6**	**524.3**
Communications	2 245	9.0	167.1	174.1	209.1	265.1	273.0	259.8	272.5
Construction	2 249	18.2	....	....	5.2	....	....	2.1	5.6
Insurance	2 253	59.4	12.9	13.9	18.4	20.7	21.9	19.0	41.9
Financial	2 260	4.7	5.2	5.2	8.8	14.7	5.8	10.0	10.2
Computer and information	2 262	1.9	2.4	9.5	13.4	10.9	11.0	11.4	11.7
Royalties and licence fees	2 266	....	2.2	4.5	7.9	10.8	11.9	13.1	13.4
Other business services	2 268	155.5	44.0	71.0	62.0	54.6	84.9	68.2	69.6
Personal, cultural, and recreational	2 287	.7	.9	.1					
Government, n.i.e.	2 291	104.6	85.6	86.4	108.7	111.9	141.4	107.0	99.4
Other services, debit	3 200 BA	**−253.7**	**−274.8**	**−241.3**	**−338.3**	**−370.8**	**−396.1**	**−412.7**	**−430.3**
Communications	3 245	−5.7	−14.8	−17.1	−30.0	−32.0	−32.4	−38.8	−43.2
Construction	3 249	−3.2	....	....	−1.2	....	....	−.4	−.5
Insurance	3 253	−128.3	−172.4	−124.6	−181.8	−201.8	−203.9	−198.0	−189.7
Financial	3 260	−13.7	−3.6	−6.0	−10.0	−8.2	−11.0	−3.1	−8.7
Computer and information	3 262	−1.1	−3.4	−1.7	−11.3	−9.5	−8.4	−9.4	−9.4
Royalties and licence fees	3 266	....	−39.9	−49.4	−60.2	−72.1	−62.2	−86.2	−92.2
Other business services	3 268	−60.5	−19.1	−21.6	−16.7	−18.7	−40.3	−48.8	−62.8
Personal, cultural, and recreational	3 287	−.4	−2.0	−.1	−5.1	−4.3	−4.5	−2.7	−4.4
Government, n.i.e.	3 291	−40.7	−19.6	−20.8	−22.0	−24.2	−33.4	−25.3	−19.4

Table 2 (Continued). STANDARD PRESENTATION, 2003–2010

(Millions of U.S. dollars)

	Code	2003	2004	2005	2006	2007	2008	2009	2010
C. INCOME	4 300	**−317.9**	**−410.1**	**−485.0**	**−680.4**	**−842.7**	**−937.6**	**−1,111.1**	**−1,199.9**
Total credit	2 300	*179.1*	*219.9*	*301.5*	*434.6*	*556.0*	*544.5*	*352.1*	*288.1*
Total debit	3 300	*−497.0*	*−630.0*	*−786.5*	*−1,115.0*	*−1,398.7*	*−1,482.1*	*−1,463.2*	*−1,488.0*
Compensation of employees, credit	2 310	**40.5**	**11.5**	**22.0**	**20.4**	**29.4**	**40.3**	**53.3**	**66.7**
Compensation of employees, debit	3 310	**−5.9**	**−1.2**	**−8.7**	**−10.8**	**−10.2**	**−9.8**	**−7.4**	**−5.2**
Investment income, credit	2 320	**138.6**	**208.4**	**279.5**	**414.2**	**526.6**	**504.2**	**298.8**	**221.4**
Direct investment income	2 330	100.4	41.2	38.4	43.1	67.3	52.1	58.5	49.0
Dividends and distributed branch profits	2 332	80.9	....	....	34.4	50.5	35.7	40.9	32.2
Reinvested earnings and undistributed branch profits	2 333	....	41.2	38.4	8.7	16.8	16.4	17.6	16.8
Income on debt (interest)	2 334	19.5	....	....	....	....	....	....	....
Portfolio investment income	2 339	....	3.8	7.5	11.4	11.1	2.5	11.8	11.3
Income on equity	2 340	....	2.1	2.5	3.1	....	....	....	....
Income on bonds and notes	2 350	....	1.7	5.0	8.3	11.1	2.5	11.8	11.3
Income on money market instruments	2 360	....	....	....	....	....	....	....	....
Other investment income	2 370	38.2	163.4	233.6	359.7	448.2	449.6	228.5	161.1
Investment income, debit	3 320	**−491.0**	**−628.8**	**−777.8**	**−1,104.2**	**−1,388.5**	**−1,472.3**	**−1,455.8**	**−1,482.8**
Direct investment income	3 330	−318.8	−270.2	−370.1	−607.6	−819.2	−886.0	−950.9	−997.4
Dividends and distributed branch profits	3 332	−213.6	−34.9	3.4	−77.4	−298.6	−400.2	−459.3	−529.3
Reinvested earnings and undistributed branch profits	3 333	−57.6	−234.6	−372.0	−525.8	−514.7	−481.8	−487.5	−464.4
Income on debt (interest)	3 334	−47.6	−.7	−1.5	−4.4	−5.9	−4.0	−4.1	−3.7
Portfolio investment income	3 339	−22.4	−87.0	−109.2	−107.5	−104.4	−87.4	−97.4	−96.3
Income on equity	3 340	....	....	....	....	....	....	....	....
Income on bonds and notes	3 350	−22.4	−87.0	−109.2	−107.5	−104.4	−87.4	−97.4	−96.3
Income on money market instruments	3 360	....	....	....	....	....	....	....	....
Other investment income	3 370	−149.8	−271.6	−298.5	−389.1	−464.9	−498.9	−407.5	−389.1
D. CURRENT TRANSFERS	4 379	**2,461.9**	**3,121.5**	**3,576.4**	**4,268.2**	**4,854.1**	**5,108.0**	**4,625.6**	**4,819.7**
Credit	2 379	**2,558.9**	**3,156.9**	**3,614.9**	**4,305.7**	**4,865.3**	**5,127.2**	**4,644.0**	**4,844.2**
General government	2 380	....	84.8	76.1	61.3	57.2	175.3	169.1	164.6
Other sectors	2 390	2,558.9	3,072.1	3,538.8	4,244.4	4,808.0	4,951.9	4,474.9	4,679.6
Workers' remittances	2 391	2,106.5	2,616.0	3,044.6	3,679.7	4,206.8	4,419.4	3,966.0	4,162.5
Other current transfers	2 392	452.3	456.1	494.2	564.7	601.2	532.5	508.9	517.1
Debit	3 379	**−97.0**	**−35.4**	**−38.5**	**−37.5**	**−11.1**	**−19.2**	**−18.4**	**−24.5**
General government	3 380	....	−2.9	−5.1	−2.8	−4.4	−2.9	−2.2	−6.9
Other sectors	3 390	−97.0	−32.5	−33.4	−34.7	−6.7	−16.3	−16.2	−17.6
Workers' remittances	3 391	−80.2	−32.5	−33.4	−34.7	−6.7	−16.3	−14.7	−15.5
Other current transfers	3 392	*−16.8	....	....	....	....	....	−1.5	−2.1
CAPITAL AND FINANCIAL ACCOUNT	4 996	**1,099.9**	**329.4**	**442.7**	**1,044.2**	**1,379.7**	**1,133.3**	**−265.4**	**669.6**
CAPITAL ACCOUNT	4 994	**133.8**	....	....	**142.2**	....	**1.1**	**1.0**	**1.1**
Total credit	2 994	*133.8*	....	....	*142.2*	....	*1.1*	*1.0*	*1.1*
Total debit	3 994	....	....	....	....	....	....	....	....
Capital transfers, credit	2 400	**133.8**	....	....	**142.2**	....	**1.1**	**1.0**	**1.1**
General government	2 401	133.8	....	....	21.7	....	....	....	....
Debt forgiveness	2 402	....	....	....	....	....	....	....	....
Other capital transfers	2 410	133.8	....	....	21.7	....	....	....	....
Other sectors	2 430	....	....	....	120.5	....	1.1	1.0	1.1
Migrants' transfers	2 431	....	....	....	....	....	....	....	....
Debt forgiveness	2 432	....	....	....	120.5	....	....	....	....
Other capital transfers	2 440	....	....	....	....	....	1.1	1.0	1.1
Capital transfers, debit	3 400	....	....	....	....	....	....	....	....
General government	3 401	....	....	....	....	....	....	....	....
Debt forgiveness	3 402	....	....	....	....	....	....	....	....
Other capital transfers	3 410	....	....	....	....	....	....	....	....
Other sectors	3 430	....	....	....	....	....	....	....	....
Migrants' transfers	3 431	....	....	....	....	....	....	....	....
Debt forgiveness	3 432	....	....	....	....	....	....	....	....
Other capital transfers	3 440	....	....	....	....	....	....	....	....
Nonproduced nonfinancial assets, credit	2 480	....	....	....	....	....	....	....	....
Nonproduced nonfinancial assets, debit	3 480	....	....	....	....	....	....	....	....

Table 2 (Continued). STANDARD PRESENTATION, 2003–2010

(Millions of U.S. dollars)

	Code	2003	2004	2005	2006	2007	2008	2009	2010
FINANCIAL ACCOUNT	4 995	966.2	329.4	442.7	902.0	1,379.7	1,132.2	−266.4	668.5
A. DIRECT INVESTMENT	4 500	131.0	254.8	470.2	551.8	719.7	737.4	573.7	663.4
Direct investment abroad	4 505	....	−41.2	−38.4	−40.0	−25.4	−16.4	−26.3	−23.5
Equity capital	4 510	....	....	....	−31.3	−8.6	....	−8.7	−6.7
Claims on affiliated enterprises	4 515	....	....	....	−31.3	−8.6	....	−8.7	−6.7
Liabilities to affiliated enterprises	4 520	....	....	....	....	....	....	....	....
Reinvested earnings	4 525	....	−41.2	−38.4	−8.7	−16.8	−16.4	−17.6	−16.8
Other capital	4 530	....	....	....	....	....	....	....	....
Claims on affiliated enterprises	4 535	....	....	....	....	....	....	....	....
Liabilities to affiliated enterprises	4 540	....	....	....	....	....	....	....	....
Direct investment in Guatemala	4 555	131.0	296.0	508.6	591.8	745.1	753.8	600.0	686.9
Equity capital	4 560	59.7	23.0	18.2	86.7	260.3	197.4	93.6	181.9
Claims on direct investors	4 565	111.5	3.0	−1.8	....	....	....	....	....
Liabilities to direct investors	4 570	−51.8	20.0	20.0	86.7	260.3	197.4	93.6	181.9
Reinvested earnings	4 575	57.6	234.6	372.0	525.8	514.7	481.8	487.5	464.4
Other capital	4 580	13.7	38.4	118.4	−20.7	−29.9	74.6	18.9	40.6
Claims on direct investors	4 585	....	−28.4	−29.6	−43.5	−114.1	2.7	−96.4	−72.6
Liabilities to direct investors	4 590	13.7	66.8	148.0	22.8	84.2	71.9	115.3	113.2
B. PORTFOLIO INVESTMENT	4 600	7.1	398.8	−76.8	−83.4	−184.9	62.3	−124.5	18.4
Assets	4 602	18.1	11.6	−39.8	−59.8	16.7	−10.4	23.2	−15.4
Equity securities	4 610	....	....	−.4	....	−.4	....	−.4	−.4
Monetary authorities	4 611	....	....	....	....	....	....	....	....
General government	4 612	....	....	....	....	....	....	....	....
Banks	4 613	....	....	....	....	....	....	....	....
Other sectors	4 614	....	....	−.4	....	−.4	....	−.4	−.4
Debt securities	4 619	18.1	11.6	−39.4	−59.8	17.1	−10.4	23.6	−15.0
Bonds and notes	4 620	18.1	11.6	−39.4	−59.8	17.1	−10.4	23.6	−15.0
Monetary authorities	4 621	....	....	....	....	....	....	....	....
General government	4 622	....	....	....	....	....	....	....	....
Banks	4 623	....	11.6	−42.1	−55.8	35.7	−11.4	8.5	−22.4
Other sectors	4 624	18.1	....	2.7	−4.0	−18.6	1.0	15.1	7.4
Money market instruments	4 630	....	....	....	....	....	....	....	....
Monetary authorities	4 631	....	....	....	....	....	....	....	....
General government	4 632	....	....	....	....	....	....	....	....
Banks	4 633	....	....	....	....	....	....	....	....
Other sectors	4 634	....	....	....	....	....	....	....	....
Liabilities	4 652	−11.0	387.2	−37.0	−23.6	−201.6	72.7	−147.7	33.8
Equity securities	4 660	....	....	....	....	....	....	....	....
Banks	4 663	....	....	....	....	....	....	....	....
Other sectors	4 664	....	....	....	....	....	....	....	....
Debt securities	4 669	−11.0	387.2	−37.0	−23.6	−201.6	72.7	−147.7	33.8
Bonds and notes	4 670	−11.0	387.2	−37.0	−23.6	−201.6	72.7	−147.7	33.8
Monetary authorities	4 671	....	....	....	....	....	....	....	....
General government	4 672	−11.0	237.9	−42.2	−30.2	−160.4	−1.2	−12.3	−5.5
Banks	4 673	....	39.6	−2.4	30.5	−41.2	85.2	−109.1	19.0
Other sectors	4 674	....	109.7	7.6	−23.9	....	−11.3	−26.3	20.3
Money market instruments	4 680	....	....	....	....	....	....	....	....
Monetary authorities	4 681	....	....	....	....	....	....	....	....
General government	4 682	....	....	....	....	....	....	....	....
Banks	4 683	....	....	....	....	....	....	....	....
Other sectors	4 684	....	....	....	....	....	....	....	....
C. FINANCIAL DERIVATIVES	4 910	....	....	....	....	....	....	....	....
Monetary authorities	4 911	....	....	....	....	....	....	....	....
General government	4 912	....	....	....	....	....	....	....	....
Banks	4 913	....	....	....	....	....	....	....	....
Other sectors	4 914	....	....	....	....	....	....	....	....
Assets	4 900	....	....	....	....	....	....	....	....
Monetary authorities	4 901	....	....	....	....	....	....	....	....
General government	4 902	....	....	....	....	....	....	....	....
Banks	4 903	....	....	....	....	....	....	....	....
Other sectors	4 904	....	....	....	....	....	....	....	....
Liabilities	4 905	....	....	....	....	....	....	....	....
Monetary authorities	4 906	....	....	....	....	....	....	....	....
General government	4 907	....	....	....	....	....	....	....	....
Banks	4 908	....	....	....	....	....	....	....	....
Other sectors	4 909	....	....	....	....	....	....	....	....

Table 2 (Concluded). STANDARD PRESENTATION, 2003–2010

(Millions of U.S. dollars)

	Code	2003	2004	2005	2006	2007	2008	2009	2010
D. OTHER INVESTMENT	4 700	**1,378.3**	**279.8**	**287.3**	**684.3**	**1,059.8**	**664.6**	**−245.0**	**663.6**
Assets	4 703	173.5	−340.3	−434.5	−508.9	−597.5	−2.4	−260.6	82.8
Trade credits	4 706	....	−72.7	−74.9	−99.7	−67.0	−35.6	−195.2	−101.9
General government	4 707	....	....	....	....	....	....	....	....
of which: Short-term	4 709	....	....	....	....	....	....	....	....
Other sectors	4 710	....	−72.7	−74.9	−99.7	−67.0	−35.6	−195.2	−101.9
of which: Short-term	4 712	....	−72.7	−74.9	−99.7	−67.0	−35.6	−195.2	−101.9
Loans	4 714	....	−62.7	−61.6	−229.4	−80.4	63.2	78.2	−33.2
Monetary authorities	4 715	....	....	....	....	....	....	....	....
of which: Short-term	4 718	....	....	....	....	....	....	....	....
General government	4 719	....	....	....	....	....	....	....	....
of which: Short-term	4 721	....	....	....	....	....	....	....	....
Banks	4 722	....	−62.7	−61.6	−229.4	−80.4	63.2	78.2	−33.2
of which: Short-term	4 724	....	....	....	....	....	....	....	....
Other sectors	4 725	....	....	....	....	....	....	....	....
of which: Short-term	4 727	....	....	....	....	....	....	....	....
Currency and deposits	4 730	....	−204.9	−298.0	−178.2	−450.3	−29.6	−145.6	217.9
Monetary authorities	4 731	....	....	....	....	....	....	....	....
General government	4 732	....	....	....	....	....	....	....	....
Banks	4 733	....	−30.4	60.6	−21.2	−87.2	−66.3	−114.6	32.7
Other sectors	4 734	....	−174.5	−358.6	−157.0	−363.1	36.7	−31.0	185.2
Other assets	4 736	173.5	....	....	−1.6	.2	−.4	2.0	....
Monetary authorities	4 737	....	....	....	−.4	.2	−.4	2.0	....
of which: Short-term	4 739	....	....	....	−.4	.2	−.4	2.0	....
General government	4 740	....	....	....	....	....	....	....	....
of which: Short-term	4 742	....	....	....	....	....	....	....	....
Banks	4 743	....	....	....	....	....	....	....	....
of which: Short-term	4 745	....	....	....	....	....	....	....	....
Other sectors	4 746	173.5	....	....	−1.2	....	....	....	....
of which: Short-term	4 748	....	....	....	−1.2	....	....	....	....
Liabilities	4 753	**1,204.7**	**620.1**	**721.8**	**1,193.2**	**1,657.3**	**667.0**	**15.6**	**580.8**
Trade credits	4 756	1,058.3	359.4	235.6	305.4	452.3	363.6	−149.6	84.8
General government	4 757	....	....	....	....	....	....	....	....
of which: Short-term	4 759	....	....	....	....	....	....	....	−.3
Other sectors	4 760	1,058.3	359.4	235.6	305.4	452.3	363.6	−149.6	84.8
of which: Short-term	4 762	1,058.3	359.4	235.6	305.4	452.3	363.6	−149.6	84.8
Loans	4 764	647.4	274.5	504.1	908.3	1,152.1	341.6	−175.8	570.4
Monetary authorities	4 765	−11.4	−68.2	−.5	−.3	....	....	....	....
of which: Use of Fund credit and loans from the Fund	4 766	....	....	....	....	....	....	....	....
of which: Short-term	4 768	....	....	....	....	....	....	....	....
General government	4 769	307.9	92.2	−43.5	356.3	392.9	121.8	533.4	617.4
of which: Short-term	4 771	....	....	....	....	....	....	....	....
Banks	4 772	....	111.2	209.1	313.0	467.9	−142.8	−377.3	93.0
of which: Short-term	4 774	....	....	....	....	....	....	....	....
Other sectors	4 775	351.0	139.3	339.0	239.3	291.3	362.6	−331.9	−140.0
of which: Short-term	4 777	−25.3	....	....	....	....	....	....	....
Currency and deposits	4 780	....	−13.8	−17.9	−20.5	52.9	−38.1	70.4	−74.4
Monetary authorities	4 781	....	−1.7	....	−.9	−.4	−2.6	−.3	−.6
General government	4 782	....	....	....	....	....	....	....	....
Banks	4 783	....	−12.1	−17.9	−19.6	53.3	−35.5	70.7	−73.8
Other sectors	4 784	....	....	....	....	....	....	....	....
Other liabilities	4 786	−501.0	....	....	....	....	−.1	270.6	....
Monetary authorities	4 787	−.2	....	....	....	....	−.1	270.6	....
of which: Short-term	4 789	−.2	....	....	....	....	....	....	....
General government	4 790	....	....	....	....	....	....	....	....
of which: Short-term	4 792	....	....	....	....	....	....	....	....
Banks	4 793	....	....	....	....	....	....	....	....
of which: Short-term	4 795	....	....	....	....	....	....	....	....
Other sectors	4 796	−500.8	....	....	....	....	....	....	....
of which: Short-term	4 798	−500.8	....	....	....	....	....	....	....
E. RESERVE ASSETS	4 802	**−550.1**	**−604.0**	**−238.0**	**−250.7**	**−214.9**	**−332.1**	**−470.6**	**−676.9**
Monetary gold	4 812	−16.4	....	....	....	....	....	....	−.3
Special drawing rights	4 811	.7	.6	.8	1.2	1.5	.7	−268.9	1.1
Reserve position in the Fund	4 810	....	....	....	....	....	....	....	....
Foreign exchange	4 803	−534.5	−593.2	−238.3	−252.4	−216.4	−332.8	−201.7	−677.7
Other claims	4 813	....	−11.4	−.5	.5	....	....	....	....
NET ERRORS AND OMISSIONS	4 998	**−60.8**	**835.0**	**798.3**	**479.8**	**405.9**	**547.2**	**257.7**	**156.5**

Table 3. INTERNATIONAL INVESTMENT POSITION (End-period stocks), 2003–2010

(Millions of U.S. dollars)

	Code	2003	2004	2005	2006	2007	2008	2009	2010
ASSETS	8 995 C.	....	....	**8,858.2**	**9,775.7**	**10,469.9**	**10,627.2**	**11,433.8**	**12,261.8**
Direct investment abroad	8 505	....	....	**250.3**	**293.4**	**315.6**	**332.0**	**358.3**	**381.7**
Equity capital and reinvested earnings	8 506			250.3	293.4	315.6	332.0	358.3	381.7
Claims on affiliated enterprises	8 507			250.3	293.4	315.6	332.0	358.3	381.7
Liabilities to affiliated enterprises	8 508			....	....	....	....	....	....
Other capital	8 530			....	....	....	....	....	....
Claims on affiliated enterprises	8 535			....	....	....	....	....	....
Liabilities to affiliated enterprises	8 540			....	....	....	....	....	....
Portfolio investment	8 602	....	....	**163.9**	**223.5**	**205.0**	**215.5**	**192.4**	**207.7**
Equity securities	8 610			....	....	....	....	....	....
Monetary authorities	8 611			....	....	....	....	....	....
General government	8 612			....	....	....	....	....	....
Banks	8 613			....	....	....	....	....	....
Other sectors	8 614			....	....	....	....	....	....
Debt securities	8 619			163.9	223.5	205.0	215.5	192.4	207.7
Bonds and notes	8 620			163.9	223.5	205.0	215.5	192.4	207.7
Monetary authorities	8 621			....	....	....	....	....	....
General government	8 622			....	....	....	....	....	....
Banks	8 623			101.3	156.9	121.2	132.7	124.2	146.5
Other sectors	8 624			62.6	66.6	83.8	82.8	68.2	61.2
Money market instruments	8 630			....	....	....	....	....	....
Monetary authorities	8 631			....	....	....	....	....	....
General government	8 632			....	....	....	....	....	....
Banks	8 633			....	....	....	....	....	....
Other sectors	8 634			....	....	....	....	....	....
Financial derivatives	8 900	....	....	....	....	....	....	....	....
Monetary authorities	8 901			....	....	....	....	....	....
General government	8 902			....	....	....	....	....	....
Banks	8 903			....	....	....	....	....	....
Other sectors	8 904			....	....	....	....	....	....
Other investment	8 703	....	....	**4,667.0**	**5,203.6**	**5,634.8**	**5,426.9**	**5,674.6**	**5,722.8**
Trade credits	8 706			549.3	649.0	582.0	351.1	546.3	648.2
General government	8 707			....	....	....	....	....	....
of which: Short-term	8 709			....	....	....	....	....	....
Other sectors	8 710			549.3	649.0	582.0	351.1	546.3	648.2
of which: Short-term	8 712			*549.3*	*649.0*	*582.0*	*351.1*	*546.3*	*648.2*
Loans	8 714			185.9	431.7	468.5	466.6	388.4	421.6
Monetary authorities	8 715			23.1	23.1	23.1	23.1	23.1	23.1
of which: Short-term	8 718			....	....	....	....	....	....
General government	8 719			....	....	....	....	....	....
of which: Short-term	8 721			....	....	....	....	....	....
Banks	8 722			162.8	408.6	445.4	443.5	365.3	398.5
of which: Short-term	8 724			....	....	....	....	....	....
Other sectors	8 725			....	....	....	....	....	....
of which: Short-term	8 727			....	....	....	....	....	....
Currency and deposits	8 730			3,800.7	3,989.9	4,451.2	4,475.7	4,608.4	4,521.5
Monetary authorities	8 731			....	....	....	....	....	....
General government	8 732			....	....	....	....	....	....
Banks	8 733			197.0	218.2	305.5	371.9	486.5	453.7
Other sectors	8 734			3,603.7	3,771.7	4,145.7	4,103.8	4,121.9	4,067.8
Other assets	8 736			131.1	133.0	133.1	133.5	131.5	131.4
Monetary authorities	8 737			130.7	131.4	131.5	131.9	129.9	129.9
of which: Short-term	8 739			*130.7*	*131.4*	*131.5*	*131.9*	*129.9*	*129.9*
General government	8 740			....	....	....	....	....	....
of which: Short-term	8 742			....	....	....	....	....	....
Banks	8 743			....	....	....	....	....	....
of which: Short-term	8 745			....	....	....	....	....	....
Other sectors	8 746			.4	1.6	1.6	1.6	1.6	1.6
of which: Short-term	8 748			*.4*	*1.6*	*1.6*	*1.6*	*1.6*	*1.6*
Reserve assets	8 802	....	....	**3,777.0**	**4,055.2**	**4,314.5**	**4,652.8**	**5,208.5**	**5,949.7**
Monetary gold	8 812			113.2	140.3	184.6	191.0	244.9	312.9
Special drawing rights	8 811	8.2	8.0	6.5	5.6	4.3	3.5	273.3	267.4
Reserve position in the Fund	8 810			....	....	....	....	....	....
Foreign exchange	8 803			3,656.8	3,909.2	4,125.6	4,458.3	4,690.3	5,369.4
Other claims	8 813			.5	.1	....	....	....	....

Table 3 (Concluded). INTERNATIONAL INVESTMENT POSITION (End-period stocks), 2003–2010

(Millions of U.S. dollars)

	Code	2003	2004	2005	2006	2007	2008	2009	2010
LIABILITIES	8 995 D.	....	....	**11,735.0**	**13,305.6**	**15,009.4**	**16,017.4**	**16,227.4**	**17,639.2**
Direct investment in Guatemala	8 555	....	....	**3,319.2**	**3,897.8**	**4,617.6**	**5,439.3**	**5,636.0**	**6,398.5**
Equity capital and reinvested earnings	8 556	....	....	2,545.8	4,034.2	4,802.3	4,900.8	5,461.3	6,180.9
Claims on direct investors	8 557	....	....	....	....	....	....	....	....
Liabilities to direct investors	8 558	....	....	2,545.8	4,034.2	4,802.3	4,900.8	5,461.3	6,180.9
Other capital	8 580	....	....	773.4	−136.4	−184.7	538.5	174.7	217.6
Claims on direct investors	8 585	....	....	−192.5	−288.4	−706.5	21.8	−907.4	−992.2
Liabilities to direct investors	8 590	....	....	965.9	152.0	521.8	516.7	1,082.1	1,209.8
Portfolio investment	8 652	....	....	**1,601.8**	**1,538.6**	**1,348.2**	**1,254.9**	**1,271.7**	**1,329.1**
Equity securities	8 660	....	....	....	....	....	....	....	....
Banks	8 663	....	....	....	....	....	....	....	....
Other sectors	8 664	....	....	....	....	....	....	....	....
Debt securities	8 669	....	....	1,601.8	1,538.6	1,348.2	1,254.9	1,271.7	1,329.1
Bonds and notes	8 670	....	....	1,601.8	1,538.6	1,348.2	1,254.9	1,271.7	1,329.1
Monetary authorities	8 671	....	....	....	....	....	....	....	....
General government	8 672	....	....	1,304.5	1,301.5	1,136.1	947.4	1,099.6	1,117.7
Banks	8 673	....	....	205.9	163.1	173.0	258.0	148.8	167.7
Other sectors	8 674	....	....	91.4	74.0	39.1	49.5	23.3	43.6
Money market instruments	8 680	....	....	....	....	....	....	....	....
Monetary authorities	8 681	....	....	....	....	....	....	....	....
General government	8 682	....	....	....	....	....	....	....	....
Banks	8 683	....	....	....	....	....	....	....	....
Other sectors	8 684	....	....	....	....	....	....	....	....
Financial derivatives	8 905	....	....	....	....	....	....	....	....
Monetary authorities	8 906	....	....	....	....	....	....	....	....
General government	8 907	....	....	....	....	....	....	....	....
Banks	8 908	....	....	....	....	....	....	....	....
Other sectors	8 909	....	....	....	....	....	....	....	....
Other investment	8 753	....	....	**6,814.0**	**7,869.2**	**9,043.6**	**9,323.2**	**9,319.7**	**9,911.7**
Trade credits	8 756	....	....	792.1	899.4	897.6	683.4	533.8	618.8
General government	8 757	....	....	....	....	....	....	....	....
of which: Short-term	8 759	....	....	....	....	....	....	....	....
Other sectors	8 760	....	....	792.1	899.4	897.6	683.4	533.8	618.8
of which: Short-term	8 762	....	....	*792.1*	*899.4*	*897.6*	*683.4*	*533.8*	*618.8*
Loans	8 764	....	....	5,863.5	6,797.3	7,986.9	8,361.0	8,153.1	8,751.4
Monetary authorities	8 765	....	....	.3	....	....	....	....	....
of which: Use of Fund credit and loans from the Fund	8 766	....	....	....	....	....	....	....	....
of which: Short-term	8 768	....	....	....	....	....	....	....	....
General government	8 769	....	....	2,402.5	2,773.6	3,195.0	3,330.3	3,834.8	4,472.0
of which: Short-term	8 771	....	....	....	....	....	....	....	....
Banks	8 772	....	....	1,052.6	1,365.5	1,833.4	1,690.7	1,313.4	1,406.4
of which: Short-term	8 774	....	....	....	....	....	....	....	....
Other sectors	8 775	....	....	2,408.1	2,658.2	2,958.5	3,340.0	3,004.9	2,873.1
of which: Short-term	8 777	....	....	....	....	....	....	....	....
Currency and deposits	8 780	....	....	118.8	130.9	114.5	236.1	306.4	232.1
Monetary authorities	8 781	....	....	9.3	8.3	7.9	5.3	5.0	4.4
General government	8 782	....	....	....	....	....	....	....	....
Banks	8 783	....	....	109.5	122.6	106.6	230.8	301.4	227.7
Other sectors	8 784	....	....	....	....	....	....	....	....
Other liabilities	8 786	....	....	39.6	41.6	44.6	42.7	326.4	309.4
Monetary authorities	8 787	....	....	39.6	41.6	44.6	42.7	326.4	309.4
of which: Short-term	8 789	....	....	....	....	....	....	....	....
General government	8 790	....	....	....	....	....	....	....	....
of which: Short-term	8 792	....	....	....	....	....	....	....	....
Banks	8 793	....	....	....	....	....	....	....	....
of which: Short-term	8 795	....	....	....	....	....	....	....	....
Other sectors	8 796	....	....	....	....	....	....	....	....
of which: Short-term	8 798	....	....	....	....	....	....	....	....
NET INTERNATIONAL INVESTMENT POSITION	8 995	....	....	**−2,876.8**	**−3,529.9**	**−4,539.5**	**−5,390.2**	**−4,793.5**	**−5,377.4**
Conversion rates: quetzales per U.S. dollar (end of period)	0 102	8.0407	7.7484	7.6103	7.6245	7.6308	7.7744	8.3471	8.0160

Table 1. ANALYTIC PRESENTATION, 2003–2010

(Millions of U.S. dollars)

	Code	2003	2004	2005	2006	2007	2008	2009	2010
A. Current Account[1]	4 993 Z.	**−187.5**	**−174.8**	**−160.3**	**−221.4**	**−462.4**	**−440.1**	**−426.7**	**−329.2**
Goods: exports f.o.b.	2 100 ..	609.3	725.6	846.5	1,032.6	1,203.2	1,342.0	1,049.7	1,471.2
Goods: imports f.o.b.	3 100 ..	−644.3	−688.4	−752.9	−956.0	−1,217.6	−1,366.1	−1,060.1	−1,404.9
Balance on Goods	4 100 ..	*−35.0*	*37.2*	*93.6*	*76.5*	*−14.4*	*−24.1*	*−10.4*	*66.3*
Services: credit	2 200 ..	133.7	85.4	82.9	63.5	48.7	102.9	72.2	62.4
Services: debit	3 200 ..	−307.3	−275.2	−278.3	−300.0	−295.1	−444.3	−330.7	−395.5
Balance on Goods and Services	4 991 ..	*−208.6*	*−152.7*	*−101.9*	*−159.9*	*−260.9*	*−365.5*	*−268.8*	*−266.9*
Income: credit	2 300 ..	12.6	9.8	3.2	1.4	61.0	9.9	22.2	14.9
Income: debit	3 300 ..	−124.3	−37.1	−51.6	−42.2	−124.1	−101.1	−190.4	−92.0
Balance on Goods, Services, and Income	4 992 ..	*−320.3*	*−180.0*	*−150.3*	*−200.7*	*−324.0*	*−456.7*	*−437.1*	*−344.0*
Current transfers: credit	2 379 Z.	194.6	55.1	49.2	56.0	35.3	102.6	61.9	81.5
Current transfers: debit	3 379 ..	−61.7	−49.9	−59.3	−76.6	−173.7	−86.0	−51.5	−66.8
B. Capital Account[1]	4 994 Z.	**57.6**	**−30.2**	**20.6**	**27.4**	**106.5**	**34.8**	**16.4**	**16.9**
Capital account: credit	2 994 Z.	57.6	....	13.0	44.6	187.5	40.9	16.4	19.3
Capital account: debit	3 994 ..	....	−30.2	7.6	−17.2	−81.0	−6.1	....	−2.4
Total, Groups A Plus B	4 981 ..	*−129.9*	*−205.0*	*−139.8*	*−193.9*	*−355.9*	*−405.4*	*−410.3*	*−312.3*
C. Financial Account[1]	4 995 W.	**58.6**	**77.7**	**90.7**	**239.2**	**457.8**	**436.5**	**515.9**	**313.4**
Direct investment abroad	4 505 ..	....	....	....	....	....	−63.6	....	....
Direct investment in Guinea	4 555 Z.	79.0	....	105.0	125.0	385.9	381.9	49.8	101.4
Portfolio investment assets	4 602 ..	−4.6	14.8	....	22.4	8.3	....	....	−.1
Equity securities	4 610 ..	....	....	....	....	....	....	....	....
Debt securities	4 619 ..	−4.6	14.8	....	22.4	8.3	....	....	−.1
Portfolio investment liabilities	4 652 Z.	....	....	....	....	....	....	....	....
Equity securities	4 660 ..	....	....	....	....	....	....	....	....
Debt securities	4 669 Z.	....	....	....	....	....	....	....	....
Financial derivatives	4 910 ..	....	....	....	....	....	....	....	....
Financial derivatives assets	4 900 ..	....	....	....	....	....	....	....	....
Financial derivatives liabilities	4 905 ..	....	....	....	....	....	....	....	....
Other investment assets	4 703 ..	−4.4	49.5	−89.7	37.4	33.2	−44.1	56.1	−77.4
Monetary authorities	4 701 ..	1.8	7.0	−5.4	9.5	−6.6	−2.5	−.8	9.1
General government	4 704 ..	....	....	....	....	....	....	....	....
Banks	4 705 ..	−6.1	42.5	−84.3	27.9	39.8	23.8	63.0	−62.2
Other sectors	4 728 ..	....	....	....	....	....	−65.4	−6.1	−24.3
Other investment liabilities	4 753 W.	−11.4	13.4	75.4	54.4	30.4	162.4	409.9	289.5
Monetary authorities	4 753 WA	2.0	2.9	−5.8	4.8	−69.2	48.6	132.4	.2
General government	4 753 ZB	−8.9	7.2	....	47.8	79.2	54.2	51.3	16.9
Banks	4 753 ZC	−4.2	3.3	−25.9	1.8	.4	6.7	−3.8	22.5
Other sectors	4 753 ZD	−.4	....	107.0	....	20.0	52.9	230.1	249.9
Total, Groups A Through C	4 983 ..	*−71.4*	*−127.3*	*−49.0*	*45.2*	*101.9*	*31.2*	*105.6*	*1.1*
D. Net Errors and Omissions	4 998 ..	**−157.1**	**68.6**	**120.2**	**37.2**	**88.3**	**−16.2**	**48.6**	**38.7**
Total, Groups A Through D	4 984 ..	*−228.5*	*−58.6*	*71.2*	*82.4*	*190.2*	*15.0*	*154.1*	*39.8*
E. Reserves and Related Items	4 802 A.	**228.5**	**58.6**	**−71.2**	**−82.4**	**−190.2**	**−15.0**	**−154.1**	**−39.8**
Reserve assets	4 802 ..	131.5	11.8	16.5	15.0	8.7	−10.6	−223.5	35.5
Use of Fund credit and loans	4 766 ..	−14.8	−19.5	−25.7	−19.5	−10.4	8.0	−12.9	−10.2
Exceptional financing	4 920 ..	111.8	66.3	−61.9	−77.9	−188.6	−12.4	82.2	−65.1
Conversion rates: Guinean francs per U.S. dollar	0 101 ..	**1,984.9**	**2,225.0**	**3,644.3**	**5,350.0**	**4,122.8**	**5,500.0**	**....**	**....**

[1] Excludes components that have been classified in the categories of Group E.

Table 2. STANDARD PRESENTATION, 2003–2010

(Millions of U.S. dollars)

	Code	2003	2004	2005	2006	2007	2008	2009	2010
CURRENT ACCOUNT...	4 993 ..	**−185.3**	**−162.4**	**−160.3**	**−221.4**	**−454.6**	**−438.2**	**−403.4**	**−326.9**
A. GOODS...	4 100 ..	**−35.0**	**37.2**	**93.6**	**76.5**	**−14.4**	**−24.1**	**−10.4**	**66.3**
Credit..	2 100 ..	**609.3**	**725.6**	**846.5**	**1,032.6**	**1,203.2**	**1,342.0**	**1,049.7**	**1,471.2**
General merchandise: exports f.o.b...............	2 110 ..	366.6	514.8	669.4	667.0	1,070.1	1,342.0	377.0	1,471.2
Goods for processing: exports f.o.b..............	2 150 ..	....	....	3.7	....	....	....	....	....
Repairs on goods..	2 160 ..	....	....	....	....	....	....	....	....
Goods procured in ports by carriers.............	2 170 ..	....	....	....	....	.3	....	....	....
Nonmonetary gold......................................	2 180 ..	242.7	210.7	173.4	365.6	132.8	....	672.7	....
Debit...	3 100 ..	**−644.3**	**−688.4**	**−752.9**	**−956.0**	**−1,217.6**	**−1,366.1**	**−1,060.1**	**−1,404.9**
General merchandise: imports f.o.b...............	3 110 ..	−617.0	−680.7	−739.5	−950.6	−1,206.4	−1,364.2	−1,054.5	−1,398.5
Goods for processing: imports f.o.b..............	3 150 ..	−27.1	−7.7	−13.4	−5.4	−11.2	−.6	−5.6	−6.4
Repairs on goods..	3 160 ..	−.1	−.1	....	....	....	−1.3	....	....
Goods procured in ports by carriers.............	3 170 ..	−.1	....	....	....	....	....	....	....
Nonmonetary gold......................................	3 180 ..	....	....	....	....	....	....	....	....
B. SERVICES...	4 200 ..	**−173.6**	**−189.9**	**−195.4**	**−236.5**	**−246.4**	**−341.4**	**−258.5**	**−333.1**
Total credit..	2 200 ..	*133.7*	*85.4*	*82.9*	*63.5*	*48.7*	*102.9*	*72.2*	*62.4*
Total debit..	3 200 ..	*−307.3*	*−275.2*	*−278.3*	*−300.0*	*−295.1*	*−444.3*	*−330.7*	*−395.5*
Transportation services, credit...............	2 205 ..	**6.7**	**6.7**	**12.0**	**7.1**	**6.0**	**11.6**	**14.9**	**3.8**
Passenger..	2 850 ..	*.6*	*....*	*5.6*	*....*	*.9*	*.9*	*2.1*	*....*
Freight..	2 851 ..	*4.9*	*5.7*	*6.0*	*2.3*	*2.0*	*6.1*	*6.1*	*2.3*
Other..	2 852 ..	*1.3*	*1.0*	*.5*	*4.8*	*3.1*	*4.6*	*6.7*	*1.6*
Sea transport, passenger............................	2 207 ..	....	....	....	....	....	....	....	....
Sea transport, freight..................................	2 208 ..	4.4	5.6	5.8	2.3	1.0	6.1	6.1	2.2
Sea transport, other....................................	2 209 ..	1.0	.1	.4	3.7	1.2	.6	6.6	.7
Air transport, passenger..............................	2 211 ..	.6	....	5.6	....	.9	.9	2.1	....
Air transport, freight...................................	2 212 ..	.5	.1	.2	....	1.0	....	....	....
Air transport, other.....................................	2 213 ..	.3	.9	.1	1.1	1.8	4.0	.1	.9
Other transport, passenger..........................	2 215 ..	....	....	....	....	....	....	....	....
Other transport, freight...............................	2 216 ..	....	....	....	....	....	....	....	....
Other transport, other.................................	2 217 ..	....	....	....	....	....	....	....	....
Transportation services, debit..............	3 205 ..	**−54.3**	**−92.5**	**−107.0**	**−116.6**	**−96.5**	**−267.0**	**−105.5**	**−227.8**
Passenger..	3 850 ..	*−10.2*	*−4.3*	*−8.6*	*−12.9*	*−66.5*	*−21.2*	*−14.5*	*−8.5*
Freight..	3 851 ..	*−37.5*	*−84.3*	*−66.5*	*−48.5*	*−26.5*	*−107.2*	*−66.6*	*−184.3*
Other..	3 852 ..	*−6.6*	*−3.9*	*−32.0*	*−55.2*	*−3.4*	*−138.6*	*−24.4*	*−35.0*
Sea transport, passenger............................	3 207 ..	....	....	....	....	−50.7	....	....	....
Sea transport, freight..................................	3 208 ..	−34.6	−75.7	−56.9	−29.3	−7.4	−107.2	−61.3	−165.9
Sea transport, other....................................	3 209 ..	−5.8	−3.3	−31.2	−55.2	−2.4	−138.6	−23.9	−25.2
Air transport, passenger..............................	3 211 ..	−10.2	−4.3	−8.6	−12.9	−15.9	−21.2	−14.5	−8.5
Air transport, freight...................................	3 212 ..	−2.9	−8.6	−9.5	−19.2	−19.2	....	−5.4	−18.4
Air transport, other.....................................	3 213 ..	−.8	−.6	−.7	....	−1.0	....	−.5	−9.7
Other transport, passenger..........................	3 215 ..	....	....	....	....	....	....	....	....
Other transport, freight...............................	3 216 ..	....	....	....	....	....	....	....	....
Other transport, other.................................	3 217 ..	....	....	....	....	....	....	....	....
Travel, credit..	2 236 ..	**....**	**....**	**....**	**....**	**.2**	**1.5**	**2.8**	**2.0**
Business travel...	2 237 ..	....	....	....	....	.1	.1	.2	.1
Personal travel...	2 240 ..	....	....	....	....	.1	1.4	2.6	1.9
Travel, debit..	3 236 ..	**−26.0**	**−25.1**	**−28.8**	**−28.0**	**−29.0**	**−9.2**	**−13.1**	**−7.5**
Business travel...	3 237 ..	−1.0	−.7	−5.9	−.7	−.8	−1.1	−1.5	−2.5
Personal travel...	3 240 ..	−25.0	−24.3	−23.0	−27.3	−28.2	−8.1	−11.6	−5.0
Other services, credit............................	2 200 BA	**127.0**	**78.7**	**70.9**	**56.5**	**42.6**	**89.8**	**54.5**	**56.5**
Communications...	2 245 ..	.1	.3	.6	....	10.7	11.7	15.5	32.7
Construction..	2 249 ..	42.0	18.2	20.2	25.1	13.6	40.5	15.6	6.7
Insurance..	2 253 ..	.3	.1	1.2	2.4	.4	.4	5.9	9.6
Financial...	2 260 ..	....	....	....	....	....	....	....	....
Computer and information...........................	2 262 ..	....	....	.1	....	....	.3	.1	....
Royalties and licence fees...........................	2 266 ..	.3	....	.3	....	.1	.1	....	....
Other business services..............................	2 268 ..	6.0	5.4	.3	3.3	12.1	26.3	8.2	.8
Personal, cultural, and recreational.............	2 287 ..	....	....	.4	....	1.1	2.4	4.0	5.1
Government, n.i.e.......................................	2 291 ..	78.3	54.7	47.9	25.7	4.6	8.1	5.4	1.6
Other services, debit.............................	3 200 BA	**−227.0**	**−157.7**	**−142.5**	**−155.4**	**−169.7**	**−168.1**	**−212.1**	**−160.2**
Communications...	3 245 ..	−5.0	−2.7	−6.9	−4.7	−23.8	−18.5	−12.2	−12.8
Construction..	3 249 ..	−27.6	−6.9	−7.7	−6.9	−46.4	−31.1	−18.2	−5.8
Insurance..	3 253 ..	−18.8	−24.8	−8.8	−30.2	−14.6	−15.2	−26.1	−27.5
Financial...	3 260 ..	....	....	....	....	....	....	....	....
Computer and information...........................	3 262 ..	−.4	−.3	−.6	−.3	−.4	−7.4	−3.7	−.6
Royalties and licence fees...........................	3 266 ..	−.9	−.2	−.9	−.2	....	−.4	−.2	−1.2
Other business services..............................	3 268 ..	−54.8	−42.6	−43.6	−46.3	−35.8	−49.6	−109.1	−97.6
Personal, cultural, and recreational.............	3 287 ..	−.2	−.5	−.2	−.1	−.9	....	....	....
Government, n.i.e.......................................	3 291 ..	−119.3	−79.8	−73.7	−66.9	−47.8	−45.9	−42.8	−14.7

Table 2 (Continued). STANDARD PRESENTATION, 2003–2010

(Millions of U.S. dollars)

	Code	2003	2004	2005	2006	2007	2008	2009	2010
C. INCOME	4 300	**−111.7**	**−27.3**	**−48.4**	**−40.8**	**−63.2**	**−91.2**	**−168.2**	**−77.1**
Total credit	2 300	*12.6*	*9.8*	*3.2*	*1.4*	*61.0*	*9.9*	*22.2*	*14.9*
Total debit	3 300	*−124.3*	*−37.1*	*−51.6*	*−42.2*	*−124.1*	*−101.1*	*−190.4*	*−92.0*
Compensation of employees, credit	2 310	....	....	....	....	....	1.8	1.5	1.4
Compensation of employees, debit	3 310	**−4.1**	**−1.7**	**−2.0**	**−2.9**	**−4.6**	**−19.6**	**−14.2**	**−8.9**
Investment income, credit	2 320	**12.6**	**9.8**	**3.2**	**1.4**	**61.0**	**8.1**	**20.7**	**13.5**
Direct investment income	2 330	....	....	1.5	....	.1	.1	2.2	2.0
Dividends and distributed branch profits	2 332	....	....	1.5	....	....	.1	2.2	2.0
Reinvested earnings and undistributed branch profits	2 333	....	....	....	....	....	....	....	....
Income on debt (interest)	2 334	....	....	....	....	.1	....	....	....
Portfolio investment income	2 339	....	....	....	....	....	2.4	3.9	....
Income on equity	2 340	....	....	....	....	....	2.4	3.9	....
Income on bonds and notes	2 350	....	....	....	....	....	....	....	....
Income on money market instruments	2 360	....	....	....	....	....	....	....	....
Other investment income	2 370	12.6	9.8	1.7	1.4	60.9	5.6	14.6	11.6
Investment income, debit	3 320	**−120.2**	**−35.4**	**−49.6**	**−39.4**	**−119.6**	**−81.5**	**−176.3**	**−83.2**
Direct investment income	3 330	−79.0	....	....	....	−54.0	−14.2	−87.6	−.3
Dividends and distributed branch profits	3 332	....	....	....	....	−54.0	−1.7	−78.7	−.3
Reinvested earnings and undistributed branch profits	3 333	−79.0	....	....	....	....	−10.7	....	....
Income on debt (interest)	3 334	....	....	....	....	....	−1.8	−8.9	....
Portfolio investment income	3 339	....	....	....	....	....	−47.8	−56.9	−54.7
Income on equity	3 340	....	....	....	....	....	−5.8	−5.0	−2.7
Income on bonds and notes	3 350	....	....	....	....	....	−42.0	−51.9	−52.0
Income on money market instruments	3 360	....	....	....	....	....	....	....	....
Other investment income	3 370	−41.3	−35.4	−49.6	−39.4	−65.6	−19.5	−31.8	−28.3
D. CURRENT TRANSFERS	4 379	**135.1**	**17.7**	**−10.1**	**−20.6**	**−130.6**	**18.5**	**33.7**	**17.1**
Credit	2 379	**196.8**	**67.6**	**49.2**	**56.0**	**43.1**	**104.5**	**85.3**	**83.8**
General government	2 380	85.8	25.9	7.6	26.5	7.8	1.9	23.4	2.3
Other sectors	2 390	111.0	41.6	41.6	29.5	35.3	102.6	61.9	81.5
Workers' remittances	2 391	111.0	41.6	41.6	29.5	15.1	59.8	50.5	44.8
Other current transfers	2 392	....	....	.1	....	20.3	42.8	11.4	36.7
Debit	3 379	**−61.7**	**−49.9**	**−59.3**	**−76.6**	**−173.7**	**−86.0**	**−51.5**	**−66.8**
General government	3 380	−8.1	−2.6	....	−26.9	−.4	−.4	−.3	−.1
Other sectors	3 390	−53.7	−47.3	−59.2	−49.8	−173.3	−85.6	−51.3	−66.6
Workers' remittances	3 391	−42.3	−46.3	−57.8	−48.7	−34.4	−35.9	−30.7	−32.1
Other current transfers	3 392	−11.4	−1.0	−1.4	−1.0	−138.9	−49.7	−20.6	−34.5
CAPITAL AND FINANCIAL ACCOUNT	4 996	**342.4**	**93.7**	**40.1**	**184.2**	**366.2**	**454.4**	**354.8**	**288.2**
CAPITAL ACCOUNT	4 994	**57.6**	**−30.2**	**20.6**	**27.4**	**106.5**	**34.8**	**39.5**	**47.3**
Total credit	2 994	*57.6*	*....*	*13.0*	*44.6*	*187.5*	*40.9*	*39.5*	*49.7*
Total debit	3 994	*....*	*−30.2*	*7.6*	*−17.2*	*−81.0*	*−6.1*	*....*	*−2.4*
Capital transfers, credit	2 400	**57.6**	**....**	**13.0**	**44.6**	**187.5**	**40.9**	**39.5**	**49.7**
General government	2 401	57.6	....	13.0	20.0	51.8	30.6	27.9	35.6
Debt forgiveness	2 402	4.1	....	....	....	16.2	....	23.1	30.4
Other capital transfers	2 410	53.5	....	13.0	20.0	35.7	30.6	4.7	5.2
Other sectors	2 430	....	....	....	24.6	135.7	10.3	11.7	14.1
Migrants' transfers	2 431	....	....	....	24.6	135.7	10.3	11.7	14.1
Debt forgiveness	2 432	....	....	....	....	....	....	....	....
Other capital transfers	2 440	....	....	....	....	....	....	....	....
Capital transfers, debit	3 400	**....**	**−30.2**	**7.6**	**−17.2**	**−81.0**	**−6.1**	**....**	**−2.4**
General government	3 401	....	....	....	....	....	....	....	....
Debt forgiveness	3 402	....	....	....	....	....	....	....	....
Other capital transfers	3 410	....	....	....	....	....	....	....	....
Other sectors	3 430	....	−30.2	7.6	−17.2	−81.0	−6.1	....	−2.4
Migrants' transfers	3 431	....	....	....	....	−80.5	....	....	−2.4
Debt forgiveness	3 432	....	....	....	....	....	....	....	....
Other capital transfers	3 440	....	−30.2	7.6	−17.2	−.5	−6.1	....	....
Nonproduced nonfinancial assets, credit	2 480	....	....	....	....	....	....	....	....
Nonproduced nonfinancial assets, debit	3 480	....	....	....	....	....	....	....	....

Table 2 (Continued). STANDARD PRESENTATION, 2003–2010

(Millions of U.S. dollars)

	Code	2003	2004	2005	2006	2007	2008	2009	2010
FINANCIAL ACCOUNT	4 995	**284.8**	**123.9**	**19.6**	**156.8**	**259.7**	**419.6**	**315.3**	**240.9**
A. DIRECT INVESTMENT	4 500	**79.0**	....	**105.0**	**125.0**	**385.9**	**318.2**	**140.9**	**101.4**
Direct investment abroad	4 505	....	....	....	....	....	−63.6	....	....
Equity capital	4 510	....	....	....	....	....	−63.6	....	....
Claims on affiliated enterprises	4 515	....	....	....	....	....	−63.6		
Liabilities to affiliated enterprises	4 520	....	....	....	....	....	....		
Reinvested earnings	4 525	....	....	....	....	....	....		
Other capital	4 530	....	....	....	....	....	....		
Claims on affiliated enterprises	4 535	....	....	....	....	....	....		
Liabilities to affiliated enterprises	4 540	....	....	....	....	....	....		
Direct investment in Guinea	4 555	**79.0**	....	**105.0**	**125.0**	**385.9**	**381.9**	**140.9**	**101.4**
Equity capital	4 560	....	....	105.0	125.0	385.9	367.9	140.9	101.4
Claims on direct investors	4 565	....	....	105.0	125.0	385.9	367.9	49.8	101.4
Liabilities to direct investors	4 570	....	....	....	....	....	....	91.0	....
Reinvested earnings	4 575	79.0	....	....	....	....	10.7	....	....
Other capital	4 580	....	....	....	....	....	3.4	....	....
Claims on direct investors	4 585	....	....	....	....	....	3.4	....	....
Liabilities to direct investors	4 590	....	....	....	....	....	....	....	....
B. PORTFOLIO INVESTMENT	4 600	**−4.6**	**14.8**	....	**22.4**	**−129.8**	....	....	**1.3**
Assets	4 602	**−4.6**	**14.8**	....	**22.4**	**8.3**	....	....	**−.1**
Equity securities	4 610	....	....	....	....	....	....	....	....
Monetary authorities	4 611	....	....	....	....	....	....	....	....
General government	4 612	....	....	....	....	....	....	....	....
Banks	4 613	....	....	....	....	....	....	....	....
Other sectors	4 614	....	....	....	....	....	....	....	....
Debt securities	4 619	−4.6	14.8	....	22.4	8.3	....	....	−.1
Bonds and notes	4 620	−4.6	14.8	....	22.4	8.3	....	....	
Monetary authorities	4 621	−4.6	14.8	....	22.4	8.3	....	....	
General government	4 622	....	....	....	....	....	....	....	
Banks	4 623	....	....	....	....	....	....	....	
Other sectors	4 624	....	....	....	....	....	....	....	
Money market instruments	4 630	....	....	....	....	....	....	....	−.1
Monetary authorities	4 631	....	....	....	....	....	....	....	−.1
General government	4 632	....	....	....	....	....	....	....	
Banks	4 633	....	....	....	....	....	....	....	
Other sectors	4 634	....	....	....	....	....	....	....	
Liabilities	4 652	....	....	....	....	**−138.1**	....	....	**1.4**
Equity securities	4 660	....	....	....	....	....	....	....	
Banks	4 663	....	....	....	....	....	....	....	
Other sectors	4 664	....	....	....	....	....	....	....	....
Debt securities	4 669	....	....	....	....	−138.1	....	....	1.4
Bonds and notes	4 670	....	....	....	....	−138.1	....	....	1.4
Monetary authorities	4 671	....	....	....	....	....	....	....	
General government	4 672	....	....	....	....	−138.1	....	....	
Banks	4 673	....	....	....	....	....	....	....	
Other sectors	4 674	....	....	....	....	....	....	....	1.4
Money market instruments	4 680	....	....	....	....	....	....	....	
Monetary authorities	4 681	....	....	....	....	....	....	....	
General government	4 682	....	....	....	....	....	....	....	
Banks	4 683	....	....	....	....	....	....	....	
Other sectors	4 684	....	....	....	....	....	....	....	
C. FINANCIAL DERIVATIVES	4 910	....	....	....	....	....	....	....	
Monetary authorities	4 911	....	....	....	....	....	....	....	
General government	4 912	....	....	....	....	....	....	....	
Banks	4 913	....	....	....	....	....	....	....	
Other sectors	4 914	....	....	....	....	....	....	....	
Assets	4 900	....	....	....	....	....	....	....	
Monetary authorities	4 901	....	....	....	....	....	....	....	
General government	4 902	....	....	....	....	....	....	....	
Banks	4 903	....	....	....	....	....	....	....	
Other sectors	4 904	....	....	....	....	....	....	....	
Liabilities	4 905	....	....	....	....	....	....	....	
Monetary authorities	4 906	....	....	....	....	....	....	....	
General government	4 907	....	....	....	....	....	....	....	
Banks	4 908	....	....	....	....	....	....	....	
Other sectors	4 909	....	....	....	....	....	....	....	

Table 2 (Concluded). STANDARD PRESENTATION, 2003–2010

(Millions of U.S. dollars)

	Code	2003	2004	2005	2006	2007	2008	2009	2010
D. OTHER INVESTMENT	4 700	**78.9**	**97.2**	**−101.9**	**−5.6**	**−5.1**	**112.0**	**397.9**	**102.7**
Assets	4 703	−4.4	49.5	−89.7	37.4	33.2	−44.1	56.1	−77.4
Trade credits	4 706	....	....	....	....	....	−65.2	−6.1	−24.3
General government	4 707	....	....	....	....	....	....	....	....
of which: Short-term	4 709	....	....	....	....	....	....	....	....
Other sectors	4 710	....	....	....	....	....	−65.2	−6.1	−24.3
of which: Short-term	4 712	....	....	....	....	....	−65.2	−6.1	−24.3
Loans	4 714	....	....	....	....	....	....	....	....
Monetary authorities	4 715	....	....	....	....	....	....	....	....
of which: Short-term	4 718	....	....	....	....	....	....	....	....
General government	4 719	....	....	....	....	....	....	....	....
of which: Short-term	4 721	....	....	....	....	....	....	....	....
Banks	4 722	....	....	....	....	....	....	....	....
of which: Short-term	4 724	....	....	....	....	....	....	....	....
Other sectors	4 725	....	....	....	....	....	....	....	....
of which: Short-term	4 727	....	....	....	....	....	....	....	....
Currency and deposits	4 730	−6.1	42.5	−84.3	27.9	39.8	23.5	63.0	−62.2
Monetary authorities	4 731	....	....	....	....	....	....	....	....
General government	4 732	....	....	....	....	....	....	....	....
Banks	4 733	−6.1	42.5	−84.3	27.9	39.8	23.8	63.0	−62.2
Other sectors	4 734	....	....	....	....	....	−.3	....	....
Other assets	4 736	1.8	7.0	−5.4	9.5	−6.6	−2.5	−.8	9.1
Monetary authorities	4 737	1.8	7.0	−5.4	9.5	−6.6	−2.5	−.8	9.1
of which: Short-term	4 739	1.8	7.0	−5.4	9.5	−6.6	−2.5	−.8	9.1
General government	4 740	....	....	....	....	....	....	....	....
of which: Short-term	4 742	....	....	....	....	....	....	....	....
Banks	4 743	....	....	....	....	....	....	....	....
of which: Short-term	4 745	....	....	....	....	....	....	....	....
Other sectors	4 746	....	....	....	....	....	....	....	....
of which: Short-term	4 748	....	....	....	....	....	....	....	....
Liabilities	4 753	**83.3**	**47.7**	**−12.3**	**−43.0**	**−38.3**	**156.1**	**341.8**	**180.1**
Trade credits	4 756	....	....	....	....	....	5.6	230.1	155.4
General government	4 757	....	....	....	....	....	....	....	....
of which: Short-term	4 759	....	....	....	....	....	....	....	....
Other sectors	4 760	....	....	....	....	....	5.6	230.1	155.4
of which: Short-term	4 762	....	....	....	....	....	5.6	230.1	155.4
Loans	4 764	122.0	38.8	−3.9	−21.7	75.0	162.9	−1.4	−7.9
Monetary authorities	4 765	−14.8	−19.5	−25.7	−19.5	−10.4	56.7	−11.0	−10.2
of which: Use of Fund credit and loans from the Fund	4 766	−14.8	−19.5	−25.7	−19.5	−10.4	8.0	−12.9	−10.2
of which: Short-term	4 768	....	....	....	....	....	....	....	....
General government	4 769	137.2	58.3	−74.7	−2.2	74.4	63.6	10.3	−68.1
of which: Short-term	4 771	....	....	....	....	....	....	....	....
Banks	4 772	....	....	....	....	....	−.2	−.7	....
of which: Short-term	4 774	....	....	....	....	....	....	....	....
Other sectors	4 775	−.4	....	96.5	....	11.0	42.8	....	70.4
of which: Short-term	4 777	26.5	....	107.0	....	20.0	47.3	....	70.4
Currency and deposits	4 780	−4.2	3.2	−25.2	.1	−.2	6.5	−3.8	22.5
Monetary authorities	4 781	....	−.1	.6	−1.7	−.6	−.2	....	....
General government	4 782	....	....	....	....	....	....	....	....
Banks	4 783	−4.2	3.3	−25.9	1.8	.4	6.7	−3.8	22.5
Other sectors	4 784	....	....	....	....	....	....	....	....
Other liabilities	4 786	−34.6	5.7	16.8	−21.4	−113.0	−19.0	116.9	10.2
Monetary authorities	4 787	2.0	3.0	−22.3	6.5	−68.5	.1	130.5	.2
of which: Short-term	4 789	2.0	3.0	−22.3	6.5	−68.5	.1	−2.0	.2
General government	4 790	−36.6	2.7	39.1	−28.0	−44.5	−19.1	−13.6	10.0
of which: Short-term	4 792	−32.5	2.7	39.1	−28.0	−44.5	−19.1	−13.6	10.0
Banks	4 793	....	....	....	....	....	....	....	....
of which: Short-term	4 795	....	....	....	....	....	....	....	....
Other sectors	4 796	....	....	....	....	....	....	....	....
of which: Short-term	4 798	....	....	....	....	....	....	....	....
E. RESERVE ASSETS	4 802	**131.5**	**11.8**	**16.5**	**15.0**	**8.7**	**−10.6**	**−223.5**	**35.5**
Monetary gold	4 812	90.7	−1.1	−1.9	−18.6	−1.8	7.1	−1.7	1.5
Special drawing rights	4 811	1.5	.2	−.2	.1	−12.0	9.6	−125.9	10.3
Reserve position in the Fund	4 810	....	....	....	....	....	....	....	....
Foreign exchange	4 803	39.4	12.7	18.6	4.5	22.5	−27.3	−95.9	23.7
Other claims	4 813	....	....	....	29.0	....	....	....	....
NET ERRORS AND OMISSIONS	4 998	**−157.1**	**68.6**	**120.2**	**37.2**	**88.3**	**−16.2**	**48.6**	**38.7**

Table 3. INTERNATIONAL INVESTMENT POSITION (End-period stocks), 2003–2010

(Millions of U.S. dollars)

	Code	2003	2004	2005	2006	2007	2008	2009	2010
ASSETS..	8 995 C.	....	....	....	....	....	**337.9**	**508.8**	**545.5**
Direct investment abroad.............	8 505 ..	....	....	....	....	....	**143.6**	**143.6**	**143.6**
Equity capital and reinvested earnings..............	8 506 ..	....	....	....	....	....	62.5	62.5	62.5
Claims on affiliated enterprises............	8 507 ..	....	....	....	....	....	62.5	62.5	62.5
Liabilities to affiliated enterprises.........	8 508 ..	....	....	....	....	....	....	....	....
Other capital............................	8 530 ..	....	....	....	....	....	81.1	81.1	81.1
Claims on affiliated enterprises............	8 535 ..	....	....	....	....	....	81.1	81.1	81.1
Liabilities to affiliated enterprises.........	8 540 ..	....	....	....	....	....	....	....	....
Portfolio investment......................	8 602 ..	....	....	....	....	....	....	....	**.1**
Equity securities........................	8 610 ..	....	....	....	....	....	....	....	....
Monetary authorities..................	8 611 ..	....	....	....	....	....	....	....	....
General government..................	8 612 ..	....	....	....	....	....	....	....	....
Banks..............................	8 613 ..	....	....	....	....	....	....	....	....
Other sectors.......................	8 614 ..	....	....	....	....	....	....	....	....
Debt securities.........................	8 619 ..	....	....	....	....	....	....	....	.1
Bonds and notes......................	8 620 ..	....	....	....	....	....	....	....	.1
Monetary authorities..............	8 621 ..	....	....	....	....	....	....	....	....
General government..............	8 622 ..	....	....	....	....	....	....	....	....
Banks..........................	8 623 ..	....	....	....	....	....	....	....	....
Other sectors...................	8 624 ..	....	....	....	....	....	....	....	.1
Money market instruments..............	8 630 ..	....	....	....	....	....	....	....	....
Monetary authorities..............	8 631 ..	....	....	....	....	....	....	....	....
General government..............	8 632 ..	....	....	....	....	....	....	....	....
Banks..........................	8 633 ..	....	....	....	....	....	....	....	....
Other sectors...................	8 634 ..	....	....	....	....	....	....	....	....
Financial derivatives....................	8 900 ..	....	....	....	....	....	....	....	....
Monetary authorities....................	8 901 ..	....	....	....	....	....	....	....	....
General government....................	8 902 ..	....	....	....	....	....	....	....	....
Banks................................	8 903 ..	....	....	....	....	....	....	....	....
Other sectors..........................	8 904 ..	....	....	....	....	....	....	....	....
Other investment......................	8 703 ..	....	....	....	....	....	**149.5**	**93.4**	**170.8**
Trade credits...........................	8 706 ..	....	....	....	....	....	21.2	27.2	51.5
General government..................	8 707 ..	....	....	....	....	....	....	....	....
of which: Short-term.................	8 709 ..	....	....	....	....	....	....	....	....
Other sectors........................	8 710 ..	....	....	....	....	....	21.2	27.2	51.5
of which: Short-term.................	8 712 ..	....	....	....	....	....	*21.2*	*27.2*	*51.5*
Loans................................	8 714 ..	....	....	....	....	....	....	....	....
Monetary authorities..................	8 715 ..	....	....	....	....	....	....	....	....
of which: Short-term...............	8 718 ..	....	....	....	....	....	....	....	....
General government..................	8 719 ..	....	....	....	....	....	....	....	....
of which: Short-term...............	8 721 ..	....	....	....	....	....	....	....	....
Banks..............................	8 722 ..	....	....	....	....	....	....	....	....
of which: Short-term...............	8 724 ..	....	....	....	....	....	....	....	....
Other sectors.......................	8 725 ..	....	....	....	....	....	....	....	....
of which: Short-term...............	8 727 ..	....	....	....	....	....	....	....	....
Currency and deposits...................	8 730 ..	....	....	....	....	....	100.9	37.9	100.1
Monetary authorities..................	8 731 ..	....	....	....	....	....	....	....	....
General government..................	8 732 ..	....	....	....	....	....	....	....	....
Banks..............................	8 733 ..	....	....	....	....	....	100.9	37.9	100.1
Other sectors.......................	8 734 ..	....	....	....	....	....	....	....	....
Other assets...........................	8 736 ..	....	....	....	....	....	27.5	28.3	19.2
Monetary authorities..................	8 737 ..	....	....	....	....	....	27.5	28.3	19.2
of which: Short-term...............	8 739 ..	....	....	....	....	....	*27.5*	*28.3*	*19.2*
General government..................	8 740 ..	....	....	....	....	....	....	....	....
of which: Short-term...............	8 742 ..	....	....	....	....	....	....	....	....
Banks..............................	8 743 ..	....	....	....	....	....	....	....	....
of which: Short-term...............	8 745 ..	....	....	....	....	....	....	....	....
Other sectors.......................	8 746 ..	....	....	....	....	....	....	....	....
of which: Short-term...............	8 748 ..	....	....	....	....	....	....	....	....
Reserve assets..........................	8 802 ..	....	....	....	....	....	**44.8**	**271.8**	**231.0**
Monetary gold.........................	8 812 ..	....	....	....	....	....	5.4	7.1	5.6
Special drawing rights...................	8 811 ..	.2	....	....	....	12.2	2.4	128.9	116.2
Reserve position in the Fund..............	8 810 ..	.1	.1	.1	.1	.1	.1	.1	.1
Foreign exchange.......................	8 803 ..	....	....	....	....	....	36.9	135.7	109.1
Other claims...........................	8 813 ..	....	....	....	....	....	....	....	....

Table 3 (Concluded). INTERNATIONAL INVESTMENT POSITION (End-period stocks), 2003–2010

(Millions of U.S. dollars)

	Code	2003	2004	2005	2006	2007	2008	2009	2010
LIABILITIES.............	8 995 D.	....	....	....	....	....	659.2	970.1	1,106.7
Direct investment in Guinea................	8 555 ..	....	....	....	....	....	243.9	384.7	486.1
Equity capital and reinvested earnings...............	8 556 ..	....	....	....	....	....	243.9	384.7	486.1
Claims on direct investors......................	8 557 ..	....	....	....	....	....	....	....	....
Liabilities to direct investors..................	8 558 ..	....	....	....	....	....	243.9	384.7	486.1
Other capital............................	8 580 ..	....	....	....	....	....	....	....	....
Claims on direct investors......................	8 585 ..	....	....	....	....	....	....	....	....
Liabilities to direct investors..................	8 590 ..	....	....	....	....	....	....	....	....
Portfolio investment................	8 652 ..	....	....	....	....	....	42.9	42.9	44.3
Equity securities........................	8 660 ..	....	....	....	....	....	42.9	42.9	42.9
Banks............................	8 663 ..	....	....	....	....	....	....	....	....
Other sectors......................	8 664 ..	....	....	....	....	....	42.9	42.9	42.9
Debt securities.........................	8 669 ..	....	....	....	....	....	....	....	1.4
Bonds and notes........................	8 670 ..	....	....	....	....	....	....	....	1.4
Monetary authorities...................	8 671 ..	....	....	....	....	....	....	....	....
General government...................	8 672 ..	....	....	....	....	....	....	....	....
Banks.........................	8 673 ..	....	....	....	....	....	....	....	....
Other sectors....................	8 674 ..	....	....	....	....	....	....	....	1.4
Money market instruments................	8 680 ..	....	....	....	....	....	....	....	....
Monetary authorities...................	8 681 ..	....	....	....	....	....	....	....	....
General government...................	8 682 ..	....	....	....	....	....	....	....	....
Banks.........................	8 683 ..	....	....	....	....	....	....	....	....
Other sectors....................	8 684 ..	....	....	....	....	....	....	....	....
Financial derivatives................	8 905 ..	....	....	....	....	....	....	....	....
Monetary authorities......................	8 906 ..	....	....	....	....	....	....	....	....
General government......................	8 907 ..	....	....	....	....	....	....	....	....
Banks............................	8 908 ..	....	....	....	....	....	....	....	....
Other sectors........................	8 909 ..	....	....	....	....	....	....	....	....
Other investment................	8 753 ..	....	....	....	....	....	372.5	542.5	576.3
Trade credits..........................	8 756 ..	....	....	....	....	....	52.1	76.9	92.0
General government......................	8 757 ..	....	....	....	....	....	....	....	....
of which: Short-term..................	8 759 ..	....	....	....	....	....	....	....	....
Other sectors........................	8 760 ..	....	....	....	....	....	52.1	76.9	92.0
of which: Short-term..................	8 762 ..	....	....	....	....	....	*52.1*	*76.9*	*92.0*
Loans................................	8 764 ..	....	....	....	....	....	296.3	296.8	287.7
Monetary authorities......................	8 765 ..	....	....	....	....	....	76.0	66.2	54.8
of which: Use of Fund credit and loans from the Fund....	8 766 ..	*136.3*	*121.9*	*87.3*	*72.1*	*64.7*	*70.7*	*59.0*	*47.6*
of which: Short-term..................	8 768 ..	....	....	....	....	....	....	....	....
General government......................	8 769 ..	....	....	....	....	....	220.3	230.6	162.5
of which: Short-term..................	8 771 ..	....	....	....	....	....	....	....	....
Banks............................	8 772 ..	....	....	....	....	....	....	....	....
of which: Short-term..................	8 774 ..	....	....	....	....	....	....	....	....
Other sectors........................	8 775 ..	....	....	....	....	....	....	....	70.4
of which: Short-term..................	8 777 ..	....	....	....	....	....	....	....	*70.4*
Currency and deposits....................	8 780 ..	....	....	....	....	....	2.5	.7	21.2
Monetary authorities......................	8 781 ..	....	....	....	....	....	....	....	....
General government......................	8 782 ..	....	....	....	....	....	....	....	....
Banks............................	8 783 ..	....	....	....	....	....	2.5	.7	21.2
Other sectors........................	8 784 ..	....	....	....	....	....	....	....	....
Other liabilities.......................	8 786 ..	....	....	....	....	....	21.5	168.1	175.4
Monetary authorities......................	8 787 ..	....	....	....	....	....	.5	160.6	158.0
of which: Short-term..................	8 789 ..	....	....	....	....	....	*.5*	....	*.2*
General government......................	8 790 ..	....	....	....	....	....	21.0	7.5	17.4
of which: Short-term..................	8 792 ..	....	....	....	....	....	*21.0*	*7.5*	*17.4*
Banks............................	8 793 ..	....	....	....	....	....	....	....	....
of which: Short-term..................	8 795 ..	....	....	....	....	....	....	....	....
Other sectors........................	8 796 ..	....	....	....	....	....	....	....	....
of which: Short-term..................	8 798 ..	....	....	....	....	....	....	....	....
NET INTERNATIONAL INVESTMENT POSITION........	8 995 ..	....	....	....	....	....	−321.3	−461.3	−561.2
Conversion rates: Guinean francs per U.S. dollar (end of period)................	0 102 ..	2,000.0	2,550.0	4,500.0	5,650.0	4,181.7	5,161.0	....	....

Table 1. ANALYTIC PRESENTATION, 2003–2010

(Millions of U.S. dollars)

	Code	2003	2004	2005	2006	2007	2008	2009	2010
A. Current Account[1]	4 993 Z.	**−6.47**	**−13.22**	**−45.55**	**−74.15**	**−66.10**	**−92.86**	**−113.57**	....
Goods: exports f.o.b.	2 100 ..	65.01	75.77	89.62	74.14	107.04	128.13	121.64	....
Goods: imports f.o.b.	3 100 ..	−65.30	−82.87	−105.93	−127.05	−167.90	−198.79	−202.32	....
Balance on Goods	4 100 ..	*−.29*	*−7.11*	*−16.31*	*−52.91*	*−60.87*	*−70.66*	*−80.68*	....
Services: credit	2 200 ..	6.00	7.70	5.17	3.43	33.39	43.78	33.12	....
Services: debit	3 200 ..	−36.21	−44.32	−41.74	−39.58	−68.23	−85.19	−86.87	....
Balance on Goods and Services	4 991 ..	*−30.50*	*−43.73*	*−52.88*	*−89.06*	*−95.70*	*−112.06*	*−134.43*	
Income: credit	2 300 ..	2.08	1.30	.44	.29	.44	.18	5.54	
Income: debit	3 300 ..	−10.91	−10.94	−9.26	−9.13	−10.34	−14.88	−16.65	
Balance on Goods, Services, and Income	4 992 ..	*−39.34*	*−53.36*	*−61.69*	*−97.89*	*−105.60*	*−126.76*	*−145.54*	
Current transfers: credit	2 379 Z.	39.69	47.36	25.07	32.46	43.71	50.37	52.24	
Current transfers: debit	3 379 ..	−6.83	−7.21	−8.93	−8.72	−4.22	−16.46	−20.28	
B. Capital Account[1]	4 994 Z.	**42.82**	**27.40**	**36.07**	**22.39**	**20.94**	**32.28**	**65.83**	....
Capital account: credit	2 994 Z.	42.82	27.44	36.07	22.39	20.94	32.29	65.83	....
Capital account: debit	3 994 ..	....	−.05	....	....	....	....	....	
Total, Groups A Plus B	4 981 ..	*36.35*	*14.18*	*−9.48*	*−51.76*	*−45.16*	*−60.57*	*−47.74*	
C. Financial Account[1]	4 995 W.	**−13.06**	**1.18**	**−8.78**	**−5.17**	**−8.97**	**−55.52**	**−11.79**	....
Direct investment abroad	4 505 ..	−.52	7.50	−.70	−.50	−.21	.83	.10	....
Direct investment in Guinea-Bissau	4 555 Z.	4.01	1.73	8.69	17.72	18.77	5.14	17.45	
Portfolio investment assets	4 602 ..	.60	.95	−4.55	.97	−5.22	−8.37	−19.14	
Equity securities	4 610 ..	....	.91	2.09	1.34	1.04	....	....	
Debt securities	4 619 ..	.60	.04	−6.64	−.37	−6.26	−8.37	−19.14	
Portfolio investment liabilities	4 652 Z.	.34	....	....	....	.21	....	−.21	
Equity securities	4 660 ..	.34	....	....	....	.21	....	−.21	
Debt securities	4 669 Z.	....	....	....	....	....	....	....	
Financial derivatives	4 910 ..	....	....	....	....	....	....	....	
Financial derivatives assets	4 900 ..	....	....	....	....	....	....	....	
Financial derivatives liabilities	4 905 ..	....	....	....	....	....	....	....	
Other investment assets	4 703 ..	−18.99	−7.65	4.33	−6.66	−5.02	−28.18	3.70	
Monetary authorities	4 701 ..	....	....	....	....	....	....	....	
General government	4 704 ..	....	....	....	....	....	....	....	
Banks	4 705 ..	−16.33	−2.68	7.23	−6.51	3.00	−24.47	3.62	
Other sectors	4 728 ..	−2.66	−4.98	−2.90	−.16	−8.02	−3.71	.08	
Other investment liabilities	4 753 W.	1.50	−1.35	−16.55	−16.69	−17.50	−24.93	−13.68	
Monetary authorities	4 753 WA	−.45	1.28	1.26	1.67	1.02	−1.95	18.32	
General government	4 753 ZB	7.63	.47	−23.77	−16.69	−23.26	−29.28	−23.90	
Banks	4 753 ZC	.46	.31	4.52	−2.77	.20	11.41	−8.13	
Other sectors	4 753 ZD	−6.14	−3.40	1.44	1.09	4.54	−5.11	.04	
Total, Groups A Through C	4 983 ..	*23.28*	*15.35*	*−18.26*	*−56.93*	*−54.13*	*−116.09*	*−59.53*	
D. Net Errors and Omissions	4 998 ..	**6.15**	**−4.16**	**−4.57**	**1.20**	**5.69**	**−7.59**	**−7.58**	....
Total, Groups A Through D	4 984 ..	*29.44*	*11.19*	*−22.83*	*−55.73*	*−48.45*	*−123.67*	*−67.10*	
E. Reserves and Related Items	4 802 A.	**−29.44**	**−11.19**	**22.83**	**55.73**	**48.45**	**123.67**	**67.10**	....
Reserve assets	4 802 ..	−38.22	−32.94	−18.41	6.27	−20.71	−18.75	−38.84	....
Use of Fund credit and loans	4 766 ..	−4.85	−5.33	−3.16	−3.82	−3.32	3.73	1.15	....
Exceptional financing	4 920 ..	13.64	27.08	44.40	53.28	72.48	138.70	104.79	....
Conversion rates: CFA francs per U.S. dollar	0 101 ..	**581.20**	**528.28**	**527.47**	**522.89**	**479.27**	**447.81**	**472.19**	**495.28**

[1] Excludes components that have been classified in the categories of Group E.

Table 2. STANDARD PRESENTATION, 2003–2010

(Millions of U.S. dollars)

	Code	2003	2004	2005	2006	2007	2008	2009	2010
CURRENT ACCOUNT..	4 993 ..	**−.29**	**13.86**	**−10.48**	**−40.08**	**−30.63**	**−28.76**	**−47.59**	....
A. GOODS	4 100 ..	**−.29**	**−7.11**	**−16.31**	**−52.91**	**−60.87**	**−70.66**	**−80.68**	....
Credit..	2 100 ..	**65.01**	**75.77**	**89.62**	**74.14**	**107.04**	**128.13**	**121.64**	....
General merchandise: exports f.o.b.	2 110 ..	64.97	75.71	89.56	72.87	105.73	126.45	120.48	....
Goods for processing: exports f.o.b.	2 150 ..	....	....	....	....	....	....	....	....
Repairs on goods	2 160 ..	....	....	....	....	....	....	....	....
Goods procured in ports by carriers	2 170 ..	.04	.05	.06	1.27	1.30	1.67	1.17	....
Nonmonetary gold	2 180 ..	....	....	....	....	....	....	....	....
Debit..	3 100 ..	**−65.30**	**−82.87**	**−105.93**	**−127.05**	**−167.90**	**−198.79**	**−202.32**	....
General merchandise: imports f.o.b.	3 110 ..	−65.30	−82.87	−105.93	−127.05	−167.90	−198.79	−202.32	....
Goods for processing: imports f.o.b.	3 150 ..	....	....	....	....	....	....	....	....
Repairs on goods	3 160 ..	....	....	....	....	....	....	....	....
Goods procured in ports by carriers	3 170 ..	....	....	....	....	....	....	....	....
Nonmonetary gold	3 180 ..	....	....	....	....	....	....	....	....
B. SERVICES..	4 200 ..	**−30.21**	**−36.62**	**−36.57**	**−36.15**	**−34.83**	**−41.40**	**−53.75**	....
Total credit	2 200 ..	*6.00*	*7.70*	*5.17*	*3.43*	*33.39*	*43.78*	*33.12*	....
Total debit	3 200 ..	*−36.21*	*−44.32*	*−41.74*	*−39.58*	*−68.23*	*−85.19*	*−86.87*	....
Transportation services, credit........................	2 205 ..	**.77**	**1.33**	**.49**	....	**.07**	**.07**	....	....
Passenger	2 850 ..	*.64*	*1.18*	....	....	....	....	....	....
Freight	2 851 ..	....	....	*.49*	....	....	....	....	....
Other	2 852 ..	*.13*	*.15*	....	....	*.07*	*.07*	....	....
Sea transport, passenger	2 207 ..	....	....	....	....	....	....	....	....
Sea transport, freight	2 208 ..	....	....	....	....	....	....	....	....
Sea transport, other	2 209 ..	....	....	....	....	....	....	....	....
Air transport, passenger	2 211 ..	....	....	....	....	....	....	....	....
Air transport, freight	2 212 ..	....	....	....	....	....	....	....	....
Air transport, other	2 213 ..	.13	.15	....	....	.07	.07	....	....
Other transport, passenger	2 215 ..	.64	1.18	....	....	....	....	....	....
Other transport, freight	2 216 ..	....	....	.49	....	....	....	....	....
Other transport, other	2 217 ..	....	....	....	....	....	....	....	....
Transportation services, debit........................	3 205 ..	**−21.29**	**−22.71**	**−25.44**	**−22.52**	**−23.99**	**−32.09**	**−30.39**	....
Passenger	3 850 ..	*−8.02*	*−9.21*	*−9.07*	*−2.34*	*−.45*	*−.48*	*−.32*	....
Freight	3 851 ..	*−13.26*	*−13.49*	*−16.37*	*−20.17*	*−23.52*	*−31.61*	*−30.07*	....
Other	3 852 ..	....	....	....	....	*−.03*	....	....	....
Sea transport, passenger	3 207 ..	....	....	....	....	....	....	....	....
Sea transport, freight	3 208 ..	−10.99	−8.35	−8.38	−11.94	−20.84	−28.25	−26.83	....
Sea transport, other	3 209 ..	....	....	....	....	....	....	....	....
Air transport, passenger	3 211 ..	−6.73	−7.93	−7.87	−2.34	−.45	−.48	−.32	....
Air transport, freight	3 212 ..	....	....	....	....	−.01	−.01	−.06	....
Air transport, other	3 213 ..	....	....	....	....	−.03	....	....	....
Other transport, passenger	3 215 ..	−1.29	−1.29	−1.21	....	....	....	....	....
Other transport, freight	3 216 ..	−2.28	−5.14	−7.99	−8.22	−2.68	−3.35	−3.18	....
Other transport, other	3 217 ..	....	....	....	....	....	....	....	....
Travel, credit..	2 236 ..	**1.84**	**.96**	**1.62**	**2.80**	**28.39**	**38.21**	**11.98**	....
Business travel	2 237 ..	.80	.77	.12	2.79	1.21	7.99	1.33	....
Personal travel	2 240 ..	1.03	.19	1.49	.01	27.18	30.21	10.65	....
Travel, debit..	3 236 ..	**−13.28**	**−13.13**	**−9.80**	**−15.54**	**−40.21**	**−45.58**	**−25.74**	....
Business travel	3 237 ..	−5.39	−2.81	−1.00	−9.35	−12.67	−10.85	−3.19	....
Personal travel	3 240 ..	−7.90	−10.32	−8.79	−6.19	−27.54	−34.72	−22.55	....
Other services, credit......................................	2 200 BA	**3.39**	**5.41**	**3.06**	**.63**	**4.93**	**5.50**	**21.14**	....
Communications	2 245 ..	.07	.08	....	....	.04	.10	12.14	....
Construction	2 249 ..	....	....	....	....	....	....	....	....
Insurance	2 253 ..	.01	.02	....	....	....	....	....	....
Financial	2 260 ..	.73	1.11	....	.15	1.43	.28	2.90	....
Computer and information	2 262 ..	....	....	....	....	....	....	....	....
Royalties and licence fees	2 266 ..	....	....	....	....	....	....	....	....
Other business services	2 268 ..	1.54	2.30	2.52	.48	3.46	5.12	4.83	....
Personal, cultural, and recreational	2 287 ..	....	....	....	....	....	....	....	....
Government, n.i.e.	2 291 ..	1.03	1.89	.54	....	....	....	1.27	....
Other services, debit..	3 200 BA	**−1.64**	**−8.49**	**−6.50**	**−1.52**	**−4.02**	**−7.52**	**−30.74**	....
Communications	3 245 ..	−.34	−3.97	−3.81	−.16	−.17	−.16	−4.66	....
Construction	3 249 ..	....	−.01	−.05	....	−.02	−.12	−.04	....
Insurance	3 253 ..	−.22	−.12	−1.74	−1.10	−1.23	−4.07	−4.12	....
Financial	3 260 ..	−.15	−.05	−.01	−.07	−.10	−.08	−.21	....
Computer and information	3 262 ..	....	−.06	−.65	−.01	−2.04	−2.56	−1.95	....
Royalties and licence fees	3 266 ..	....	....	....	....	....	....	....	....
Other business services	3 268 ..	−.58	−2.38	−.23	−.18	−.46	−.53	−17.43	....
Personal, cultural, and recreational	3 287 ..	....	....	....	....	....	....	....	....
Government, n.i.e.	3 291 ..	−.35	−1.89	....	....	....	....	−2.33	....

Table 2 (Continued). STANDARD PRESENTATION, 2003–2010

(Millions of U.S. dollars)

	Code	2003	2004	2005	2006	2007	2008	2009	2010
C. INCOME	4 300	**−8.83**	**−9.63**	**−8.82**	**−8.83**	**−9.90**	**−14.70**	**−11.11**	....
Total credit	2 300	*2.08*	*1.30*	*.44*	*.29*	*.44*	*.18*	*5.54*	....
Total debit	3 300	*−10.91*	*−10.94*	*−9.26*	*−9.13*	*−10.34*	*−14.88*	*−16.65*	....
Compensation of employees, credit	2 310	**1.83**	**.79**	**.30**	....	....	....	....	....
Compensation of employees, debit	3 310	**−.17**	**−.02**	**−.27**	**−.31**	**−.16**	**−.32**	**−.12**	....
Investment income, credit	2 320	**.25**	**.51**	**.14**	**.29**	**.44**	**.18**	**5.54**	....
Direct investment income	2 330	....	....	....	.10	−.08	....	....	
Dividends and distributed branch profits	2 332	....	....	....	....	−.10	....	....	
Reinvested earnings and undistributed branch profits	2 333	....	....	....	.10	.02	....	....	
Income on debt (interest)	2 334	....	....	....	....	....	....	....	
Portfolio investment income	2 339	....	....	....	....	.20	.10	.51	
Income on equity	2 340	....	....	....	....	....	....	....	
Income on bonds and notes	2 350	....	....	....	....	.09	....	.45	
Income on money market instruments	2 360	....	....	....	....	.11	.10	.06	
Other investment income	2 370	.25	.51	.14	.19	.32	.08	5.03	
Investment income, debit	3 320	**−10.74**	**−10.92**	**−8.99**	**−8.82**	**−10.18**	**−14.56**	**−16.54**	....
Direct investment income	3 330	−.16	−.05	....	....	....	−.26	−2.49	
Dividends and distributed branch profits	3 332	....	....	....	....	....	−.22	−2.49	
Reinvested earnings and undistributed branch profits	3 333	−.16	−.05	....	....	....	....	....	
Income on debt (interest)	3 334	....	....	....	....	....	−.04	....	
Portfolio investment income	3 339	−.60	....	−.43	−.41	−.20	−.01	−2.21	
Income on equity	3 340	−.60	....	−.30	−.41	−.10	....	....	
Income on bonds and notes	3 350	....	....	−.13	....	....	−.01	−.55	
Income on money market instruments	3 360	....	....	....	....	−.10	....	−1.66	
Other investment income	3 370	−9.98	−10.87	−8.55	−8.41	−9.98	−14.29	−11.83	
D. CURRENT TRANSFERS	4 379	**39.05**	**67.23**	**51.21**	**57.82**	**74.97**	**98.00**	**97.95**	....
Credit	2 379	**45.87**	**74.44**	**60.14**	**66.54**	**79.19**	**114.46**	**118.23**	....
General government	2 380	18.82	43.57	35.06	34.08	35.47	64.09	65.98	
Other sectors	2 390	27.06	30.87	25.07	32.46	43.71	50.37	52.24	
Workers' remittances	2 391	21.30	26.91	19.60	25.52	43.03	49.46	48.85	
Other current transfers	2 392	5.76	3.96	5.48	6.94	.68	.91	3.39	
Debit	3 379	**−6.83**	**−7.21**	**−8.93**	**−8.72**	**−4.22**	**−16.46**	**−20.28**	....
General government	3 380	....	....	....	....	....	....	....	
Other sectors	3 390	−6.83	−7.21	−8.93	−8.72	−4.22	−16.46	−20.28	
Workers' remittances	3 391	−6.32	−5.36	−5.08	−4.02	−4.17	−16.43	−20.07	
Other current transfers	3 392	−.51	−1.85	−3.84	−4.71	−.05	−.04	−.21	
CAPITAL AND FINANCIAL ACCOUNT	4 996	**−5.86**	**−9.70**	**15.05**	**38.87**	**24.94**	**36.35**	**55.16**	....
CAPITAL ACCOUNT	4 994	**42.82**	**27.40**	**45.40**	**32.20**	**32.11**	**36.77**	**70.46**	....
Total credit	2 994	*42.82*	*27.44*	*45.40*	*32.20*	*32.11*	*36.77*	*70.46*	....
Total debit	3 994	....	*−.05*	....	....	....	....	....	....
Capital transfers, credit	2 400	**42.82**	**27.44**	**45.40**	**32.20**	**32.11**	**36.77**	**70.46**	....
General government	2 401	36.01	23.15	41.60	29.33	32.03	36.77	68.39	
Debt forgiveness	2 402	....	....	9.33	9.81	11.17	4.49	4.63	
Other capital transfers	2 410	36.01	23.15	32.27	19.52	20.87	32.29	63.77	
Other sectors	2 430	6.81	4.29	3.79	2.87	.08	....	2.06	
Migrants' transfers	2 431	....	....	....	....	....	....	....	
Debt forgiveness	2 432	....	....	....	....	....	....	....	
Other capital transfers	2 440	6.81	4.29	3.79	2.87	.08	....	2.06	
Capital transfers, debit	3 400	....	....	....	....	....	....	....	....
General government	3 401	....	....	....	....	....	....	....	
Debt forgiveness	3 402	....	....	....	....	....	....	....	
Other capital transfers	3 410	....	....	....	....	....	....	....	
Other sectors	3 430	....	....	....	....	....	....	....	
Migrants' transfers	3 431	....	....	....	....	....	....	....	
Debt forgiveness	3 432	....	....	....	....	....	....	....	
Other capital transfers	3 440	....	....	....	....	....	....	....	
Nonproduced nonfinancial assets, credit	2 480	....	....	....	....	....	....	....	....
Nonproduced nonfinancial assets, debit	3 480	....	**−.05**	....	....	....	....	....	....

Table 2 (Continued). STANDARD PRESENTATION, 2003–2010

(Millions of U.S. dollars)

	Code	2003	2004	2005	2006	2007	2008	2009	2010
FINANCIAL ACCOUNT...............	4 995 ..	−48.68	−37.10	−30.35	6.68	−7.16	−.42	−15.29	....
A. DIRECT INVESTMENT...............	4 500 ..	3.49	9.23	8.00	17.22	18.56	5.97	17.55	....
Direct investment abroad...............	4 505 ..	−.52	7.50	−.70	−.50	−.21	.83	.10	....
Equity capital...............	4 510 ..	−.52	7.76	....	....	....	....	.88	....
Claims on affiliated enterprises...............	4 515 ..	−.52	8.04	....	....	....	....	.88	....
Liabilities to affiliated enterprises...............	4 520 ..	....	−.28	....	....	....	....	....	....
Reinvested earnings...............	4 525 ..	....	....	....	−.10	−.02	....	....	....
Other capital...............	4 530 ..	....	−.26	−.70	−.40	−.19	.83	−.78	....
Claims on affiliated enterprises...............	4 535 ..	....	−.26	−.70	−.40	−.19	−.66	.62	....
Liabilities to affiliated enterprises...............	4 540 ..	....	....	....	....	....	1.49	−1.41	....
Direct investment in Guinea-Bissau...............	4 555 ..	**4.01**	**1.73**	**8.69**	**17.72**	**18.77**	**5.14**	**17.45**	....
Equity capital...............	4 560 ..	1.24	2.08	5.92	17.89	18.77	5.14	17.45	....
Claims on direct investors...............	4 565 ..	....	....	....	....	....	....	....	....
Liabilities to direct investors...............	4 570 ..	1.24	2.08	5.92	17.89	18.77	5.14	17.45	....
Reinvested earnings...............	4 575 ..	.16	.05	....	....	....	....	....	....
Other capital...............	4 580 ..	2.61	−.40	2.77	−.16	....	....	....	....
Claims on direct investors...............	4 585 ..	....	−.47	....	−.16	....	....	....	....
Liabilities to direct investors...............	4 590 ..	2.61	.08	2.77	....	....	....	....	....
B. PORTFOLIO INVESTMENT...............	4 600 ..	**.94**	**.95**	**−4.55**	**.97**	**−5.01**	**.56**	**−5.75**	....
Assets...............	4 602 ..	**.60**	**.95**	**−4.55**	**.97**	**−5.22**	**−8.37**	**−19.14**	....
Equity securities...............	4 610 ..	....	.91	2.09	1.34	1.04	....	....	....
Monetary authorities...............	4 611 ..	....	....	....	....	....	....	....	....
General government...............	4 612 ..	....	....	....	....	....	....	....	....
Banks...............	4 613 ..	....	.91	....	....	....	....	....	....
Other sectors...............	4 614 ..	....	....	2.09	1.34	1.04	....	....	....
Debt securities...............	4 619 ..	.60	.04	−6.64	−.37	−6.26	−8.37	−19.14	....
Bonds and notes...............	4 620 ..	.60	.04	−6.64	.02	−6.26	−8.37	−19.12	....
Monetary authorities...............	4 621 ..	....	....	....	....	....	....	....	....
General government...............	4 622 ..	....	....	....	....	....	....	....	....
Banks...............	4 623 ..	.04	.04	−6.64	.02	−6.26	−8.93	−19.12	....
Other sectors...............	4 624 ..	.56	....	....	....	....	.56	....	....
Money market instruments...............	4 630 ..	....	....	....	−.40	....	....	−.03	....
Monetary authorities...............	4 631 ..	....	....	....	....	....	....	....	....
General government...............	4 632 ..	....	....	....	....	....	....	....	....
Banks...............	4 633 ..	....	....	....	−.40	....	....	....	....
Other sectors...............	4 634 ..	....	....	....	....	....	....	−.03	....
Liabilities...............	4 652 ..	**.34**	....	....	....	**.21**	**8.93**	**13.40**	....
Equity securities...............	4 660 ..	.34	....	....	....	.21	....	−.21	....
Banks...............	4 663 ..	.34	....	....	....	.21	....	−.21	....
Other sectors...............	4 664 ..	....	....	....	....	....	....	....	....
Debt securities...............	4 669 ..	....	....	....	....	....	8.93	13.61	....
Bonds and notes...............	4 670 ..	....	....	....	....	....	8.93	13.61	....
Monetary authorities...............	4 671 ..	....	....	....	....	....	....	....	....
General government...............	4 672 ..	....	....	....	....	....	....	....	....
Banks...............	4 673 ..	....	....	....	....	....	8.93	13.61	....
Other sectors...............	4 674 ..	....	....	....	....	....	....	....	....
Money market instruments...............	4 680 ..	....	....	....	....	....	....	....	....
Monetary authorities...............	4 681 ..	....	....	....	....	....	....	....	....
General government...............	4 682 ..	....	....	....	....	....	....	....	....
Banks...............	4 683 ..	....	....	....	....	....	....	....	....
Other sectors...............	4 684 ..	....	....	....	....	....	....	....	....
C. FINANCIAL DERIVATIVES...............	4 910 ..	....	....	....	....	....	....	....	....
Monetary authorities...............	4 911 ..	....	....	....	....	....	....	....	....
General government...............	4 912 ..	....	....	....	....	....	....	....	....
Banks...............	4 913 ..	....	....	....	....	....	....	....	....
Other sectors...............	4 914 ..	....	....	....	....	....	....	....	....
Assets...............	4 900 ..	....	....	....	....	....	....	....	....
Monetary authorities...............	4 901 ..	....	....	....	....	....	....	....	....
General government...............	4 902 ..	....	....	....	....	....	....	....	....
Banks...............	4 903 ..	....	....	....	....	....	....	....	....
Other sectors...............	4 904 ..	....	....	....	....	....	....	....	....
Liabilities...............	4 905 ..	....	....	....	....	....	....	....	....
Monetary authorities...............	4 906 ..	....	....	....	....	....	....	....	....
General government...............	4 907 ..	....	....	....	....	....	....	....	....
Banks...............	4 908 ..	....	....	....	....	....	....	....	....
Other sectors...............	4 909 ..	....	....	....	....	....	....	....	....

Table 2 (Concluded). STANDARD PRESENTATION, 2003–2010

(Millions of U.S. dollars)

	Code	2003	2004	2005	2006	2007	2008	2009	2010
D. OTHER INVESTMENT	4 700	**−14.89**	**−14.33**	**−15.39**	**−17.78**	....	**11.80**	**11.75**	....
Assets	4 703	**−18.99**	**−7.65**	**4.33**	**−6.66**	**−5.02**	**−28.18**	**3.70**	....
Trade credits	4 706	−.42	−.05	−2.23	.11	−.20	....	−.27	....
General government	4 707	....	....	....	....	....	....	....	....
of which: Short-term	4 709	....	....	....	....	....	....	....	....
Other sectors	4 710	−.42	−.05	−2.23	.11	−.20	....	−.27	....
of which: Short-term	4 712	*−.42*	*−.05*	*−2.23*	*.11*	*−.20*	....	*−.27*	....
Loans	4 714	....	....	....	−.02	....	−.01	−17.73	....
Monetary authorities	4 715	....	....	....	....	....	....	....	....
of which: Short-term	4 718	....	....	....	....	....	....	....	....
General government	4 719	....	....	....	....	....	....	....	....
of which: Short-term	4 721	....	....	....	....	....	....	....	....
Banks	4 722	....	....	....	....	....	....	−17.74	....
of which: Short-term	4 724	....	....	....	....	....	....	*−16.04*	....
Other sectors	4 725	....	....	....	−.02	....	−.01	.01	....
of which: Short-term	4 727	....	....	....	*−.02*	....	*−.01*	*.01*	....
Currency and deposits	4 730	−18.57	−7.53	7.26	−6.73	−4.57	−24.98	21.72	....
Monetary authorities	4 731	....	....	....	....	....	....	....	....
General government	4 732	....	....	....	....	....	....	....	....
Banks	4 733	−16.33	−2.61	7.64	−6.51	3.15	−24.63	21.39	....
Other sectors	4 734	−2.24	−4.92	−.38	−.22	−7.73	−.35	.33	....
Other assets	4 736	....	−.08	−.71	−.02	−.25	−3.18	−.03	....
Monetary authorities	4 737	....	....	....	....	....	....	....	....
of which: Short-term	4 739	....	....	....	....	....	....	....	....
General government	4 740	....	....	....	....	....	....	....	....
of which: Short-term	4 742	....	....	....	....	....	....	....	....
Banks	4 743	....	−.06	−.41	....	−.15	.17	−.03	....
of which: Short-term	4 745	....	*−.06*	*−.41*	....	*−.15*	*.17*	*−.03*	....
Other sectors	4 746	....	−.01	−.30	−.02	−.10	−3.35	....	....
of which: Short-term	4 748	....	*−.01*	*−.30*	*−.02*	*−.10*	*−3.35*	....	....
Liabilities	4 753	**4.10**	**−6.68**	**−19.71**	**−11.12**	**5.01**	**39.98**	**8.05**	....
Trade credits	4 756	−7.78	.33	1.44	....	2.30	3.38	−2.23	....
General government	4 757	....	....	....	....	....	....	....	....
of which: Short-term	4 759	....	....	....	....	....	....	....	....
Other sectors	4 760	−7.78	.33	1.44	....	2.30	3.38	−2.23	....
of which: Short-term	4 762	*−7.78*	*.33*	*1.44*	....	*2.30*	*3.38*	*−2.23*	....
Loans	4 764	10.19	−8.76	−26.93	−10.06	1.36	27.14	1.15	....
Monetary authorities	4 765	−4.85	−5.33	−3.16	−3.82	−3.32	3.73	1.15	....
of which: Use of Fund credit and loans from the Fund	4 766	*−4.85*	*−5.33*	*−3.16*	*−3.82*	*−3.32*	*3.73*	*1.15*	....
of which: Short-term	4 768	....	....	....	....	....	....	....	....
General government	4 769	15.08	.47	−23.77	−7.29	2.44	31.90	−2.22	....
of which: Short-term	4 771	*37.06*	....	....	*27.10*	*14.81*	*29.03*	*15.32*	....
Banks	4 772	−.03	....	....	....	....	....	....	....
of which: Short-term	4 774	*−.03*	....	....	....	....	....	....	....
Other sectors	4 775	....	−3.90	....	1.06	2.25	−8.49	2.21	....
of which: Short-term	4 777	....	*−3.90*	....	....	....	*−8.49*	....	....
Currency and deposits	4 780	1.58	−.89	4.93	−2.64	.99	8.19	−9.44	....
Monetary authorities	4 781	1.08	−.94	1.31	.21	.79	−1.98	−1.30	....
General government	4 782	....	....	....	....	....	....	....	....
Banks	4 783	.50	.05	3.63	−2.86	.20	10.17	−8.13	....
Other sectors	4 784	....	....	....	....	....	....	....	....
Other liabilities	4 786	.10	2.65	.85	1.59	.36	1.27	18.57	....
Monetary authorities	4 787	−1.53	2.21	−.05	1.46	.23	.03	19.62	....
of which: Short-term	4 789	*−1.53*	*2.21*	*−.05*	*1.46*	....	....	....	....
General government	4 790	....	....	....	....	....	....	....	....
of which: Short-term	4 792	....	....	....	....	....	....	....	....
Banks	4 793	....	.26	.89	.09	.14	1.24	−1.11	....
of which: Short-term	4 795	....	*.26*	*.89*	*.09*	*.14*	*1.24*	*−1.11*	....
Other sectors	4 796	1.63	.17	....	.04	....	....	.05	....
of which: Short-term	4 798	*1.63*	*.17*	....	*.04*	....	....	*.05*	....
E. RESERVE ASSETS	4 802	**−38.22**	**−32.94**	**−18.41**	**6.27**	**−20.71**	**−18.75**	**−38.84**	....
Monetary gold	4 812	....	....	....	....	....	....	....	....
Special drawing rights	4 811	−.74	.53	.06	.09	.46	−.03	−18.49	....
Reserve position in the Fund	4 810	....	....	....	....	−.02	−.06	−.06	....
Foreign exchange	4 803	−37.48	−33.48	−18.47	6.18	−21.14	−18.66	−20.28	....
Other claims	4 813	....	....	....	....	....	....	....	....
NET ERRORS AND OMISSIONS	4 998	**6.15**	**−4.16**	**−4.57**	**1.20**	**5.69**	**−7.59**	**−7.58**	....

Table 3. INTERNATIONAL INVESTMENT POSITION (End-period stocks), 2003–2010

(Millions of U.S. dollars)

	Code	2003	2004	2005	2006	2007	2008	2009	2010
ASSETS	8 995 C.	**180.14**	**88.49**	**95.68**	**103.56**	**142.63**	**179.44**	**247.15**	....
Direct investment abroad	8 505 ..	**.58**	**.60**	**.66**	**1.34**	**1.70**	....	....	....
Equity capital and reinvested earnings	8 506 ..	.58	.31	....	....	....	....	....	....
Claims on affiliated enterprises	8 507 ..	.58	.31	....	....	....	....	....	....
Liabilities to affiliated enterprises	8 508 ..	....	....	....	....	....	....	....	....
Other capital	8 530 ..	....	.28	.66	1.34	1.70	....	....	....
Claims on affiliated enterprises	8 535 ..	....	.28	.66	1.34	1.70	....	....	....
Liabilities to affiliated enterprises	8 540 ..	....	....	....	....	....	....	....	....
Portfolio investment	8 602 ..	....	....	**6.29**	**7.03**	**14.59**	**12.84**	**29.63**	....
Equity securities	8 610 ..	....	....	....	....	....	3.36	....	....
Monetary authorities	8 611 ..	....	....	....	....	....	....	....	....
General government	8 612 ..	....	....	....	....	....	....	....	....
Banks	8 613 ..	....	....	....	....	....	3.36	....	....
Other sectors	8 614 ..	....	....	....	....	....	....	....	....
Debt securities	8 619 ..	....	....	6.29	7.03	14.59	9.48	29.63	....
Bonds and notes	8 620 ..	....	....	6.29	7.03	14.59	9.48	29.63	....
Monetary authorities	8 621 ..	....	....	....	....	....	....	....	....
General government	8 622 ..	....	....	....	....	....	....	....	....
Banks	8 623 ..	....	....	6.29	7.03	14.59	9.48	29.63	....
Other sectors	8 624 ..	....	....	....	....	....	....	....	....
Money market instruments	8 630 ..	....	....	....	....	....	....	....	....
Monetary authorities	8 631 ..	....	....	....	....	....	....	....	....
General government	8 632 ..	....	....	....	....	....	....	....	....
Banks	8 633 ..	....	....	....	....	....	....	....	....
Other sectors	8 634 ..	....	....	....	....	....	....	....	....
Financial derivatives	8 900 ..	....	....	....	...	....	....	....	....
Monetary authorities	8 901 ..	....	....	....	....	....	....	....	....
General government	8 902 ..	....	....	....	....	....	....	....	....
Banks	8 903 ..	....	....	....	....	....	....	....	....
Other sectors	8 904 ..	....	....	....	....	....	....	....	....
Other investment	8 703 ..	**13.21**	**16.29**	**9.21**	**14.08**	**13.43**	**42.04**	**48.92**	....
Trade credits	8 706 ..	.47	....	2.16	....	2.61	1.15	.26	....
General government	8 707 ..	....	....	....	....	....	....	....	....
of which: Short-term	8 709 ..	....	....	....	....	....	....	....	....
Other sectors	8 710 ..	.47	....	2.16	....	2.61	1.15	.26	....
of which: Short-term	8 712 ..	*.47*	....	*2.16*	....	*2.61*	*1.15*	*.26*	....
Loans	8 714 ..	....	....	6.31	−.02	−.03	5.50	35.03	....
Monetary authorities	8 715 ..	....	....	....	−.02	−.03	5.50	18.40	....
of which: Short-term	8 718 ..	....	....	....	*−.02*	*−.03*	*5.50*	*18.40*	....
General government	8 719 ..	....	....	....	....	....	....	....	....
of which: Short-term	8 721 ..	....	....	....	....	....	....	....	....
Banks	8 722 ..	....	....	6.08	....	....	....	16.64	....
of which: Short-term	8 724 ..	....	....	*6.08*	....	....	....	....	....
Other sectors	8 725 ..	....	....	.22	....	....	....	....	....
of which: Short-term	8 727 ..	....	....	*.22*	....	....	....	....	....
Currency and deposits	8 730 ..	12.74	16.20	....	14.10	10.85	35.38	13.62	....
Monetary authorities	8 731 ..	....	....	....	....	....	....	....	....
General government	8 732 ..	....	....	....	....	....	....	....	....
Banks	8 733 ..	11.61	15.39	....	13.87	10.85	35.38	13.62	....
Other sectors	8 734 ..	1.13	.81	....	.23	....	....	....	....
Other assets	8 736 ..	....	.09	.74	....	....	....	....	....
Monetary authorities	8 737 ..	....	....	....	....	....	....	....	....
of which: Short-term	8 739 ..	....	....	....	....	....	....	....	....
General government	8 740 ..	....	....	....	....	....	....	....	....
of which: Short-term	8 742 ..	....	....	....	....	....	....	....	....
Banks	8 743 ..	....	.07	.45	....	....	....	....	....
of which: Short-term	8 745 ..	....	*.07*	*.45*	....	....	....	....	....
Other sectors	8 746 ..	....	.01	.29	....	....	....	....	....
of which: Short-term	8 748 ..	....	*.01*	*.29*	....	....	....	....	....
Reserve assets	8 802 ..	**166.35**	**71.61**	**79.52**	**81.11**	**112.91**	**124.56**	**168.59**	....
Monetary gold	8 812 ..	....	....	....	....	....	....	....	....
Special drawing rights	8 811 ..	1.18	.68	.57	.50	.05	.08	18.64	19.09
Reserve position in the Fund	8 810 ..	....	....	....	....	.02	.08	.15	.20
Foreign exchange	8 803 ..	165.16	70.93	78.95	80.60	112.83	124.40	149.80	....
Other claims	8 813 ..	....	....	....	....	....	....	....	....

Table 3 (Concluded). INTERNATIONAL INVESTMENT POSITION (End-period stocks), 2003–2010

(Millions of U.S. dollars)

	Code	2003	2004	2005	2006	2007	2008	2009	2010
LIABILITIES...	8 995 D.	**1,194.97**	**1,512.08**	**1,175.63**	**1,321.80**	**1,641.38**	**1,300.66**	**1,343.54**	....
Direct investment in Guinea-Bissau......................	8 555 ..	**1.55**	**.85**	**5.93**	**25.42**	**170.96**	**97.59**	**119.22**	....
Equity capital and reinvested earnings...............	8 556 ..	1.45	1.17	5.93	25.42	170.96	97.59	119.22	....
Claims on direct investors..........................	8 557 ..	....	....	....	....	....	....	....	
Liabilities to direct investors......................	8 558 ..	1.45	1.17	5.93	25.42	170.96	97.59	119.22	
Other capital......................................	8 580 ..	.10	−.33	....	....	....	....	....	
Claims on direct investors..........................	8 585 ..	....	−.33	....	....	....	....	....	
Liabilities to direct investors......................	8 590 ..	.10	....	....	....	....	....	....	
Portfolio investment..	8 652 ..	**1.26**	**1.36**	**1.17**	**2.72**	**3.26**	**9.22**	**14.90**	....
Equity securities....................................	8 660 ..	1.26	1.36	1.17	2.72	3.26	.73	.79	
Banks...	8 663 ..	1.26	1.36	1.17	2.72	3.26	.73	.79	
Other sectors.....................................	8 664 ..	....	....	....	....	....	....	....	
Debt securities.....................................	8 669 ..	....	....	....	....	....	8.49	14.11	
Bonds and notes.................................	8 670 ..	....	....	....	....	....	8.49	14.11	
Monetary authorities..........................	8 671 ..	....	....	....	....	....	....	....	
General government..........................	8 672 ..	....	....	....	....	....	....	....	
Banks.......................................	8 673 ..	....	....	....	....	....	8.49	14.11	
Other sectors................................	8 674 ..	....	....	....	....	....	....	....	
Money market instruments.......................	8 680 ..	....	....	....	....	....	....	....	
Monetary authorities..........................	8 681 ..	....	....	....	....	....	....	....	
General government..........................	8 682 ..	....	....	....	....	....	....	....	
Banks.......................................	8 683 ..	....	....	....	....	....	....	....	
Other sectors................................	8 684 ..	....	....	....	....	....	....	....	
Financial derivatives......................................	8 905 ..	....	....	....	....	....	....	....	
Monetary authorities...............................	8 906 ..	....	....	....	....	....	....	....	
General government................................	8 907 ..	....	....	....	....	....	....	....	
Banks..	8 908 ..	....	....	....	....	....	....	....	
Other sectors......................................	8 909 ..	....	....	....	....	....	....	....	
Other investment..	8 753 ..	**1,192.16**	**1,509.88**	**1,168.53**	**1,293.66**	**1,467.16**	**1,193.85**	**1,209.42**	....
Trade credits.......................................	8 756 ..	....	.36	1.36	3.04	4.17	4.33	4.75	....
General government..............................	8 757 ..	....	....	....	1.52	4.17	4.33	4.75	
of which: Short-term...........................	8 759 ..	....	....	....	*1.52*	*4.17*	*4.33*	*4.75*	
Other sectors.....................................	8 760 ..	....	.36	1.36	1.52	....	....	....	
of which: Short-term...........................	8 762 ..	....	*.36*	*1.36*	*1.52*	....	....	....	
Loans..	8 764 ..	1,190.00	1,507.46	1,161.94	1,285.99	1,456.36	1,175.24	1,199.75	
Monetary authorities..............................	8 765 ..	20.47	15.79	11.50	8.21	5.19	8.60	9.94	....
of which: Use of Fund credit and loans from the Fund....	8 766 ..	*20.47*	*15.79*	*11.50*	*8.21*	*5.19*	*8.60*	*9.94*	*3.72*
of which: Short-term...........................	8 768 ..	....	....	....	....	....	....	....	
General government..............................	8 769 ..	1,169.47	1,491.61	1,150.44	1,276.67	1,440.54	1,141.01	1,163.98	
of which: Short-term...........................	8 771 ..	*263.02*	*303.26*	*300.48*	*363.90*	*433.58*	....	....	
Banks...	8 772 ..	.06	.07	....	....	6.97	25.21	24.84	
of which: Short-term...........................	8 774 ..	*.03*	*.03*	....	....	*6.97*	*25.21*	*24.84*	
Other sectors.....................................	8 775 ..	....	....	....	1.11	3.66	.42	.99	
of which: Short-term...........................	8 777 ..	....	....	....	*1.11*	*3.66*	*.42*	*.99*	
Currency and deposits..............................	8 780 ..	3.05	2.43	5.75	3.65	5.14	13.01	3.30	
Monetary authorities..............................	8 781 ..	2.05	1.19	2.27	3.65	5.14	13.01	3.30	
General government..............................	8 782 ..	....	....	....	....	....	....	....	
Banks...	8 783 ..	1.00	1.24	3.49	....	....	....	....	
Other sectors.....................................	8 784 ..	....	....	....	....	....	....	....	
Other liabilities....................................	8 786 ..	−.90	−.38	−.53	.98	1.49	1.26	1.62	
Monetary authorities..............................	8 787 ..	−2.73	−.55	−.53	.98	1.49	1.26	1.62	
of which: Short-term...........................	8 789 ..	*−2.73*	*−.55*	*−.53*	*.98*	*1.49*	*1.26*	*1.62*	
General government..............................	8 790 ..	....	....	....	....	....	....	....	
of which: Short-term...........................	8 792 ..	....	....	....	....	....	....	....	
Banks...	8 793 ..	....	....	....	....	....	....	....	
of which: Short-term...........................	8 795 ..	....	....	....	....	....	....	....	
Other sectors.....................................	8 796 ..	1.83	.18	....	....	....	....	....	
of which: Short-term...........................	8 798 ..	*1.83*	*.18*	....	....	....	....	....	
NET INTERNATIONAL INVESTMENT POSITION.........	8 995 ..	**−1,014.83**	**−1,423.59**	**−1,079.95**	**−1,218.24**	**−1,498.75**	**−1,121.23**	**−1,096.40**	....
Conversion rates: CFA francs per U.S. dollar (end of period)...	0 102 ..	519.36	481.58	556.04	498.07	445.59	471.34	455.34	490.91

Table 1. ANALYTIC PRESENTATION, 2003–2010

(Millions of U.S. dollars)

	Code	2003	2004	2005	2006	2007	2008	2009	2010
A. Current Account[1]	4 993 Z.	**−44.6**	**−19.9**	**−96.3**	**−180.6**	**−112.3**	**−191.6**	**−165.3**	**−159.7**
Goods: exports f.o.b.	2 100 ..	508.0	584.0	545.6	579.6	689.3	789.0	768.2	884.5
Goods: imports f.o.b.	3 100 ..	−525.3	−591.8	−717.1	−809.8	−977.6	−1,183.4	−1,096.8	−1,299.3
Balance on Goods	4 100 ..	*−17.3*	*−7.8*	*−171.4*	*−230.2*	*−288.3*	*−394.4*	*−328.7*	*−414.9*
Services: credit	2 200 ..	156.8	160.9	147.9	147.6	172.9	211.9	170.3	248.0
Services: debit	3 200 ..	−172.1	−207.6	−200.9	−245.4	−272.5	−323.1	−272.4	−343.8
Balance on Goods and Services	4 991 ..	*−32.6*	*−54.5*	*−224.5*	*−327.9*	*−387.9*	*−505.6*	*−430.8*	*−510.7*
Income: credit	2 300 ..	4.7	4.0	3.3	2.8	27.2	34.3	14.9	23.3
Income: debit	3 300 ..	−59.9	−43.4	−42.3	−71.8	−38.3	−49.1	−49.0	−43.0
Balance on Goods, Services, and Income	4 992 ..	*−87.8*	*−93.9*	*−263.5*	*−396.9*	*−399.1*	*−520.4*	*−464.9*	*−530.4*
Current transfers: credit	2 379 Z.	127.4	193.9	261.9	310.9	423.8	470.0	471.7	555.5
Current transfers: debit	3 379 ..	−84.2	−119.9	−94.6	−94.6	−137.0	−141.2	−172.1	−184.8
B. Capital Account[1]	4 994 Z.	**43.8**	**45.9**	**52.1**	**319.3**	**426.6**	**38.7**	**37.2**	**27.1**
Capital account: credit	2 994 Z.	43.8	45.9	52.1	319.3	426.6	38.7	37.2	27.1
Capital account: debit	3 994 ..	....	....	....	....	....	....	....	....
Total, Groups A Plus B	4 981 ..	*−.8*	*26.0*	*−44.2*	*138.7*	*314.3*	*−152.9*	*−128.1*	*−132.6*
C. Financial Account[1]	4 995 W.	**35.0**	**38.5**	**126.7**	**−52.4**	**−235.7**	**268.3**	**446.3**	**355.7**
Direct investment abroad	4 505 ..	....	....	....	....	....	....	....	....
Direct investment in Guyana	4 555 Z.	26.1	30.0	76.8	102.4	152.4	168.0	208.0	269.6
Portfolio investment assets	4 602 ..	−26.8	−16.2	−34.1	−5.5	−95.3	−2.7	19.9	−11.9
Equity securities	4 610 ..	....	....	....	....	....	....	....	....
Debt securities	4 619 ..	−26.8	−16.2	−34.1	−5.5	−95.3	−2.7	19.9	−11.9
Portfolio investment liabilities	4 652 Z.	−.5	10.6	17.3	1.4	.2	9.3	12.7	9.0
Equity securities	4 660 ..	....	....	....	....	....	....	....	....
Debt securities	4 669 Z.	−.5	10.6	17.3	1.4	.2	9.3	12.7	9.0
Financial derivatives	4 910 ..	....	....	....	....	....	....	....	....
Financial derivatives assets	4 900 ..	....	....	....	....	....	....	....	....
Financial derivatives liabilities	4 905 ..	....	....	....	....	....	....	....	....
Other investment assets	4 703 ..	....	....	....	....	....	....	....	....
Monetary authorities	4 701 ..	....	....	....	....	....	....	....	....
General government	4 704 ..	....	....	....	....	....	....	....	....
Banks	4 705 ..	....	....	....	....	....	....	....	....
Other sectors	4 728 ..	....	....	....	....	....	....	....	....
Other investment liabilities	4 753 W.	36.2	14.1	66.7	−150.7	−293.0	93.7	205.7	89.1
Monetary authorities	4 753 WA							113.3	
General government	4 753 ZB	36.2	14.1	66.7	−150.7	−293.0	93.7	92.4	89.1
Banks	4 753 ZC	....	....	....	....	....	....	....	....
Other sectors	4 753 ZD	....	....	....	....	....	....	....	....
Total, Groups A Through C	4 983 ..	*34.2*	*64.5*	*82.5*	*86.3*	*78.6*	*115.4*	*318.2*	*223.1*
D. Net Errors and Omissions	4 998 ..	**−19.9**	**−43.4**	**−68.2**	**−52.9**	**−81.6**	**−56.8**	**−44.0**	**−68.6**
Total, Groups A Through D	4 984 ..	*14.3*	*21.1*	*14.3*	*33.3*	*−3.1*	*58.6*	*274.2*	*154.5*
E. Reserves and Related Items	4 802 A.	**−14.3**	**−21.1**	**−14.3**	**−33.3**	**3.1**	**−58.6**	**−274.2**	**−154.5**
Reserve assets	4 802 ..	−5.0	−9.8	−24.9	−25.3	−35.6	−58.6	−274.2	−153.1
Use of Fund credit and loans	4 766 ..	−9.3	−11.2	10.5	−38.2	....	....	....	−1.4
Exceptional financing	4 920 ..	....	....	....	30.2	38.7	....	....	....
Conversion rates: Guyana dollars per U.S. dollar	0 101 ..	**193.88**	**198.31**	**199.88**	**200.19**	**202.35**	**203.63**	**203.95**	**203.64**

[1] Excludes components that have been classified in the categories of Group E.

Table 2. STANDARD PRESENTATION, 2003–2010

(Millions of U.S. dollars)

	Code	2003	2004	2005	2006	2007	2008	2009	2010
CURRENT ACCOUNT	4 993	−44.6	−19.9	−96.3	−180.6	−112.3	−191.6	−165.3	−159.7
A. GOODS	4 100	−17.3	−7.8	−171.4	−230.2	−288.3	−394.4	−328.7	−414.9
Credit	2 100	508.0	584.0	545.6	579.6	689.3	789.0	768.2	884.5
General merchandise: exports f.o.b.	2 110	508.0	584.0	545.6	579.6	689.3	789.0	768.2	884.5
Goods for processing: exports f.o.b.	2 150	....	....	....	....	....	....	....	....
Repairs on goods	2 160	....	....	....	....	....	....	....	....
Goods procured in ports by carriers	2 170	....	....	....	....	....	....	....	....
Nonmonetary gold	2 180	....	....	....	....	....	....	....	....
Debit	3 100	−525.3	−591.8	−717.1	−809.8	−977.6	−1,183.4	−1,096.8	−1,299.3
General merchandise: imports f.o.b.	3 110	−525.3	−591.8	−717.1	−809.8	−977.6	−1,183.4	−1,096.8	−1,299.3
Goods for processing: imports f.o.b.	3 150	....	....	....	....	....	....	....	....
Repairs on goods	3 160	....	....	....	....	....	....	....	....
Goods procured in ports by carriers	3 170	....	....	....	....	....	....	....	....
Nonmonetary gold	3 180	....	....	....	....	....	....	....	....
B. SERVICES	4 200	−15.3	−46.7	−53.0	−97.8	−99.6	−111.2	−102.1	−95.8
Total credit	2 200	*156.8*	*160.9*	*147.9*	*147.6*	*172.9*	*211.9*	*170.3*	*248.0*
Total debit	3 200	*−172.1*	*−207.6*	*−200.9*	*−245.4*	*−272.5*	*−323.1*	*−272.4*	*−343.8*
Transportation services, credit	2 205	6.7	7.2	7.6	8.1	8.7	9.4	9.9	13.8
Passenger	2 850	*2.0*	....	....	....	....	....	....	....
Freight	2 851	*4.7*	*7.2*	*7.6*	*8.1*	*8.7*	*9.4*	*9.9*	*13.8*
Other	2 852	....	....	....	....	....	....	....	....
Sea transport, passenger	2 207	....	....	....	....	....	....	....	....
Sea transport, freight	2 208	4.7	7.2	7.6	8.1	8.7	9.4	9.9	13.8
Sea transport, other	2 209	....	....	....	....	....	....	....	....
Air transport, passenger	2 211	2.0	....	....	....	....	....	....	....
Air transport, freight	2 212	....	....	....	....	....	....	....	....
Air transport, other	2 213	....	....	....	....	....	....	....	....
Other transport, passenger	2 215	....	....	....	....	....	....	....	....
Other transport, freight	2 216	....	....	....	....	....	....	....	....
Other transport, other	2 217	....	....	....	....	....	....	....	....
Transportation services, debit	3 205	−50.7	−59.6	−71.6	−80.6	−85.5	−116.8	−82.6	−105.4
Passenger	3 850	*−4.3*	....	....	....	....	....	....	....
Freight	3 851	*−46.4*	*−59.6*	*−71.6*	*−80.6*	*−85.5*	*−116.8*	*−82.6*	*−105.4*
Other	3 852	....	....	....	....	....	....	....	....
Sea transport, passenger	3 207	....	....	....	....	....	....	....	....
Sea transport, freight	3 208	−46.4	−59.6	−71.6	−80.6	−85.5	−116.8	−82.6	−105.4
Sea transport, other	3 209	....	....	....	....	....	....	....	....
Air transport, passenger	3 211	−4.3	....	....	....	....	....	....	....
Air transport, freight	3 212	....	....	....	....	....	....	....	....
Air transport, other	3 213	....	....	....	....	....	....	....	....
Other transport, passenger	3 215	....	....	....	....	....	....	....	....
Other transport, freight	3 216	....	....	....	....	....	....	....	....
Other transport, other	3 217	....	....	....	....	....	....	....	....
Travel, credit	2 236	25.8	27.1	35.1	37.1	50.5	59.2	35.0	80.5
Business travel	2 237	....	....	....	....	....	....	....	....
Personal travel	2 240	25.8	27.1	35.1	37.1	50.5	59.2	35.0	80.5
Travel, debit	3 236	−26.3	−30.4	−39.6	−49.0	−57.5	−52.4	−52.4	−73.4
Business travel	3 237	....	....	....	....	....	....	....	....
Personal travel	3 240	−26.3	−30.4	−39.6	−49.0	−57.5	−52.4	−52.4	−73.4
Other services, credit	2 200 BA	124.3	126.6	105.2	102.5	113.7	143.3	125.4	153.8
Communications	2 245	26.4	27.7	29.1	30.6	32.1	33.7	35.4	44.2
Construction	2 249	....	....	....	....	....	....	....	....
Insurance	2 253	6.4	6.7	7.0	7.4	7.8	8.1	8.5	9.8
Financial	2 260	7.8	....	....	....	....	....	10.3	17.3
Computer and information	2 262	4.1	4.4	4.6	4.8	5.1	5.5	5.9	7.0
Royalties and licence fees	2 266	32.1	33.7	35.4	37.2	40.5	42.6	44.7	46.9
Other business services	2 268	47.5	54.0	29.0	22.5	28.2	53.4	20.5	28.5
Personal, cultural, and recreational	2 287	....	....	....	....	....	....	....	....
Government, n.i.e.	2 291	....	....	....	....	....	....	....	....
Other services, debit	3 200 BA	−95.1	−117.6	−89.7	−115.8	−129.5	−153.9	−137.5	−165.1
Communications	3 245	−17.6	−18.5	−19.4	−20.4	−21.4	−22.4	−23.6	−29.5
Construction	3 249	....	....	....	....	....	....	....	....
Insurance	3 253	−18.8	−19.7	−20.7	−21.8	−22.8	−24.0	−17.0	−23.0
Financial	3 260	−7.7	....	....	....	....	....	−5.7	−8.1
Computer and information	3 262	−3.2	−3.5	−3.8	−4.1	−4.4	−4.6	−4.9	−6.6
Royalties and licence fees	3 266	−17.6	−18.5	−19.4	−20.4	−21.4	−22.5	−23.0	−28.0
Other business services	3 268	−30.2	−57.4	−26.4	−49.1	−59.4	−80.3	−63.3	−69.9
Personal, cultural, and recreational	3 287	....	....	....	....	....	....	....	....
Government, n.i.e.	3 291	....	....	....	....	....	....	....	....

2011, International Monetary Fund: *Balance of Payments Statistics Yearbook*

Table 2 (Continued). STANDARD PRESENTATION, 2003–2010

(Millions of U.S. dollars)

	Code	2003	2004	2005	2006	2007	2008	2009	2010
C. INCOME	4 300	**−55.2**	**−39.4**	**−39.0**	**−69.0**	**−11.2**	**−14.8**	**−34.1**	**−19.7**
Total credit	2 300	*4.7*	*4.0*	*3.3*	*2.8*	*27.2*	*34.3*	*14.9*	*23.3*
Total debit	3 300	*−59.9*	*−43.4*	*−42.3*	*−71.8*	*−38.3*	*−49.1*	*−49.0*	*−43.0*
Compensation of employees, credit	2 310	....	....	....	....	4.2	4.5	4.9	5.3
Compensation of employees, debit	3 310	−5.5	−5.8	−5.9	−6.0	−7.5	−8.1	−7.6	−8.3
Investment income, credit	2 320	**4.7**	**4.0**	**3.3**	**2.8**	**23.0**	**29.8**	**10.0**	**18.0**
Direct investment income	2 330	....	....	....	....	....	....	....	....
Dividends and distributed branch profits	2 332	....	....	....	....	....	....	....	....
Reinvested earnings and undistributed branch profits	2 333	....	....	....	....	....	....	....	....
Income on debt (interest)	2 334	....	....	....	....	....	....	....	....
Portfolio investment income	2 339	4.7	....	....	....	....	....	....	....
Income on equity	2 340	....	....	....	....	....	....	....	....
Income on bonds and notes	2 350	4.7	....	....	....	....	....	....	....
Income on money market instruments	2 360	....	....	....	....	....	....	....	....
Other investment income	2 370	....	4.0	3.3	2.8	23.0	29.8	10.0	18.0
Investment income, debit	3 320	**−54.4**	**−37.6**	**−36.4**	**−65.8**	**−30.8**	**−41.0**	**−41.4**	**−34.8**
Direct investment income	3 330	−2.3	−2.7	−6.9	−9.2	7.2	−.4	−17.2	−12.0
Dividends and distributed branch profits	3 332	....	....	....	....	....	....	....	....
Reinvested earnings and undistributed branch profits	3 333	−2.3	−2.7	−6.9	−9.2	7.2	−.4	−17.2	−12.0
Income on debt (interest)	3 334	....	....	....	....	....	....	....	....
Portfolio investment income	3 339	....	....	....	....	....	....	....	....
Income on equity	3 340	....	....	....	....	....	....	....	....
Income on bonds and notes	3 350	....	....	....	....	....	....	....	....
Income on money market instruments	3 360	....	....	....	....	....	....	....	....
Other investment income	3 370	−52.1	−34.9	−29.5	−56.6	−38.0	−40.6	−24.2	−22.8
D. CURRENT TRANSFERS	4 379	**43.2**	**74.0**	**167.2**	**216.3**	**286.8**	**328.8**	**299.6**	**370.8**
Credit	2 379	**127.4**	**193.9**	**261.9**	**310.9**	**423.8**	**470.0**	**471.7**	**555.5**
General government	2 380	....	....	....	....	....	....	....	....
Other sectors	2 390	127.4	193.9	261.9	310.9	423.8	470.0	471.7	555.5
Workers' remittances	2 391	99.3	153.0	201.3	218.1	278.5	273.9	262.1	367.8
Other current transfers	2 392	28.1	40.8	60.6	92.8	145.3	196.1	209.6	187.7
Debit	3 379	**−84.2**	**−119.9**	**−94.6**	**−94.6**	**−137.0**	**−141.2**	**−172.1**	**−184.8**
General government	3 380	....	....	....	....	....	....	....	....
Other sectors	3 390	−84.2	−119.9	−94.6	−94.6	−137.0	−141.2	−172.1	−184.8
Workers' remittances	3 391	−44.9	−74.8	−48.9	−42.4	−54.1	−68.6	−82.9	−125.1
Other current transfers	3 392	−39.3	−45.1	−45.7	−52.2	−82.9	−72.6	−89.2	−59.6
CAPITAL AND FINANCIAL ACCOUNT	4 996	**64.5**	**63.4**	**164.5**	**233.6**	**194.0**	**248.4**	**209.3**	**228.3**
CAPITAL ACCOUNT	4 994	**43.8**	**45.9**	**52.1**	**349.5**	**465.3**	**38.7**	**37.2**	**27.1**
Total credit	2 994	*43.8*	*45.9*	*52.1*	*349.5*	*465.3*	*38.7*	*37.2*	*27.1*
Total debit	3 994	....	....	....	....	....	....	....	....
Capital transfers, credit	2 400	**43.8**	**45.9**	**52.1**	**349.5**	**465.3**	**38.7**	**37.2**	**27.1**
General government	2 401	43.8	....	....	251.0	356.5	....	....	....
Debt forgiveness	2 402	....	....	....	251.0	356.5	....	....	....
Other capital transfers	2 410	43.8	....	....	....	....	....	....	....
Other sectors	2 430	....	45.9	52.1	98.5	108.8	38.7	37.2	27.1
Migrants' transfers	2 431	....	....	....	....	....	....	....	....
Debt forgiveness	2 432	....	....	....	....	....	....	....	....
Other capital transfers	2 440	....	45.9	52.1	98.5	108.8	38.7	37.2	27.1
Capital transfers, debit	3 400	....	....	....	....	....	....	....	....
General government	3 401	....	....	....	....	....	....	....	....
Debt forgiveness	3 402	....	....	....	....	....	....	....	....
Other capital transfers	3 410	....	....	....	....	....	....	....	....
Other sectors	3 430	....	....	....	....	....	....	....	....
Migrants' transfers	3 431	....	....	....	....	....	....	....	....
Debt forgiveness	3 432	....	....	....	....	....	....	....	....
Other capital transfers	3 440	....	....	....	....	....	....	....	....
Nonproduced nonfinancial assets, credit	2 480	....	....	....	....	....	....	....	....
Nonproduced nonfinancial assets, debit	3 480	....	....	....	....	....	....	....	....

Table 2 (Continued). STANDARD PRESENTATION, 2003–2010

(Millions of U.S. dollars)

	Code	2003	2004	2005	2006	2007	2008	2009	2010
FINANCIAL ACCOUNT	4 995	**20.7**	**17.5**	**112.4**	**−115.9**	**−271.3**	**209.7**	**172.1**	**201.2**
A. DIRECT INVESTMENT	4 500	**26.1**	**30.0**	**76.8**	**102.4**	**152.4**	**168.0**	**208.0**	**269.6**
Direct investment abroad	4 505	....	....	....	....	....	....	....	....
Equity capital	4 510	....	....	....	....	....	....	....	....
Claims on affiliated enterprises	4 515	....	....	....	....	....	....	....	....
Liabilities to affiliated enterprises	4 520	....	....	....	....	....	....	....	....
Reinvested earnings	4 525	....	....	....	....	....	....	....	....
Other capital	4 530	....	....	....	....	....	....	....	....
Claims on affiliated enterprises	4 535	....	....	....	....	....	....	....	....
Liabilities to affiliated enterprises	4 540	....	....	....	....	....	....	....	....
Direct investment in Guyana	4 555	**26.1**	**30.0**	**76.8**	**102.4**	**152.4**	**168.0**	**208.0**	**269.6**
Equity capital	4 560	3.7	4.3	11.0	14.6	15.3	20.6	44.0	71.7
Claims on direct investors	4 565	....	....	....	....	....	....	....	....
Liabilities to direct investors	4 570	3.7	4.3	11.0	14.6	15.3	20.6	44.0	71.7
Reinvested earnings	4 575	2.3	2.7	6.9	9.2	−7.2	.4	17.2	12.0
Other capital	4 580	20.1	23.0	58.9	78.6	144.3	147.0	146.8	185.9
Claims on direct investors	4 585	....	....	....	....	....	....	....	....
Liabilities to direct investors	4 590	20.1	23.0	58.9	78.6	144.3	147.0	146.8	185.9
B. PORTFOLIO INVESTMENT	4 600	**−27.3**	**−5.6**	**−16.8**	**−4.1**	**−95.1**	**6.6**	**32.6**	**−2.9**
Assets	4 602	**−26.8**	**−16.2**	**−34.1**	**−5.5**	**−95.3**	**−2.7**	**19.9**	**−11.9**
Equity securities	4 610	....	....	....	....	....	....	....	....
Monetary authorities	4 611	....	....	....	....	....	....	....	....
General government	4 612	....	....	....	....	....	....	....	....
Banks	4 613	....	....	....	....	....	....	....	....
Other sectors	4 614	....	....	....	....	....	....	....	....
Debt securities	4 619	−26.8	−16.2	−34.1	−5.5	−95.3	−2.7	19.9	−11.9
Bonds and notes	4 620	−26.8	−16.2	−34.1	−5.5	−95.3	−2.7	19.9	−11.9
Monetary authorities	4 621	....	....	....	....	....	....	....	....
General government	4 622	....	....	....	....	....	....	....	....
Banks	4 623	....	−16.2	−34.1	−5.5	−95.3	−2.7	19.9	−11.9
Other sectors	4 624	−26.8	....	....	....	....	....	....	....
Money market instruments	4 630	....	....	....	....	....	....	....	....
Monetary authorities	4 631	....	....	....	....	....	....	....	....
General government	4 632	....	....	....	....	....	....	....	....
Banks	4 633	....	....	....	....	....	....	....	....
Other sectors	4 634	....	....	....	....	....	....	....	....
Liabilities	4 652	**−.5**	**10.6**	**17.3**	**1.4**	**.2**	**9.3**	**12.7**	**9.0**
Equity securities	4 660	....	....	....	....	....	....	....	....
Banks	4 663	....	....	....	....	....	....	....	....
Other sectors	4 664	....	....	....	....	....	....	....	....
Debt securities	4 669	−.5	10.6	17.3	1.4	.2	9.3	12.7	9.0
Bonds and notes	4 670	....	....	....	....	....	....	....	....
Monetary authorities	4 671	....	....	....	....	....	....	....	....
General government	4 672	....	....	....	....	....	....	....	....
Banks	4 673	....	....	....	....	....	....	....	....
Other sectors	4 674	....	....	....	....	....	....	....	....
Money market instruments	4 680	−.5	10.6	17.3	1.4	.2	9.3	12.7	9.0
Monetary authorities	4 681	....	....	....	....	....	....	....	....
General government	4 682	....	....	....	....	....	....	....	....
Banks	4 683	....	10.6	17.3	1.4	.2	9.3	12.7	9.0
Other sectors	4 684	−.5	....	....	....	....	....	....	....
C. FINANCIAL DERIVATIVES	4 910	....	....	....	....	....	....	....	....
Monetary authorities	4 911	....	....	....	....	....	....	....	....
General government	4 912	....	....	....	....	....	....	....	....
Banks	4 913	....	....	....	....	....	....	....	....
Other sectors	4 914	....	....	....	....	....	....	....	....
Assets	4 900	....	....	....	....	....	....	....	....
Monetary authorities	4 901	....	....	....	....	....	....	....	....
General government	4 902	....	....	....	....	....	....	....	....
Banks	4 903	....	....	....	....	....	....	....	....
Other sectors	4 904	....	....	....	....	....	....	....	....
Liabilities	4 905	....	....	....	....	....	....	....	....
Monetary authorities	4 906	....	....	....	....	....	....	....	....
General government	4 907	....	....	....	....	....	....	....	....
Banks	4 908	....	....	....	....	....	....	....	....
Other sectors	4 909	....	....	....	....	....	....	....	....

Table 2 (Concluded). STANDARD PRESENTATION, 2003–2010

(Millions of U.S. dollars)

	Code	2003	2004	2005	2006	2007	2008	2009	2010
D. OTHER INVESTMENT	4 700 ..	**26.9**	**2.9**	**77.2**	**−188.9**	**−293.0**	**93.7**	**205.7**	**87.7**
Assets	4 703 ..	....	....	....	....	....	....	....	....
Trade credits	4 706 ..	....	....	....	....	....	....	....	....
General government	4 707 ..	....	....	....	....	....	....	....	....
of which: Short-term	4 709 ..	....	....	....	....	....	....	....	....
Other sectors	4 710 ..	....	....	....	....	....	....	....	....
of which: Short-term	4 712 ..	....	....	....	....	....	....	....	....
Loans	4 714 ..	....	....	....	....	....	....	....	....
Monetary authorities	4 715 ..	....	....	....	....	....	....	....	....
of which: Short-term	4 718 ..	....	....	....	....	....	....	....	....
General government	4 719 ..	....	....	....	....	....	....	....	....
of which: Short-term	4 721 ..	....	....	....	....	....	....	....	....
Banks	4 722 ..	....	....	....	....	....	....	....	....
of which: Short-term	4 724 ..	....	....	....	....	....	....	....	....
Other sectors	4 725 ..	....	....	....	....	....	....	....	....
of which: Short-term	4 727 ..	....	....	....	....	....	....	....	....
Currency and deposits	4 730 ..	....	....	....	....	....	....	....	....
Monetary authorities	4 731 ..	....	....	....	....	....	....	....	....
General government	4 732 ..	....	....	....	....	....	....	....	....
Banks	4 733 ..	....	....	....	....	....	....	....	....
Other sectors	4 734 ..	....	....	....	....	....	....	....	....
Other assets	4 736 ..	....	....	....	....	....	....	....	....
Monetary authorities	4 737 ..	....	....	....	....	....	....	....	....
of which: Short-term	4 739 ..	....	....	....	....	....	....	....	....
General government	4 740 ..	....	....	....	....	....	....	....	....
of which: Short-term	4 742 ..	....	....	....	....	....	....	....	....
Banks	4 743 ..	....	....	....	....	....	....	....	....
of which: Short-term	4 745 ..	....	....	....	....	....	....	....	....
Other sectors	4 746 ..	....	....	....	....	....	....	....	....
of which: Short-term	4 748 ..	....	....	....	....	....	....	....	....
Liabilities	4 753 ..	**26.9**	**2.9**	**77.2**	**−188.9**	**−293.0**	**93.7**	**205.7**	**87.7**
Trade credits	4 756 ..	....	....	....	....	....	....	....	....
General government	4 757 ..	....	....	....	....	....	....	....	....
of which: Short-term	4 759 ..	....	....	....	....	....	....	....	....
Other sectors	4 760 ..	....	....	....	....	....	....	....	....
of which: Short-term	4 762 ..	....	....	....	....	....	....	....	....
Loans	4 764 ..	26.9	50.2	113.0	−153.7	−251.6	139.4	135.2	140.6
Monetary authorities	4 765 ..	−9.3	−11.2	10.5	−38.2	....	....	....	−1.4
of which: Use of Fund credit and loans from the Fund	4 766 ..	−9.3	−11.2	10.5	−38.2	....	....	....	−1.4
of which: Short-term	4 768 ..	....	....	....	....	....	....	....	....
General government	4 769 ..	36.2	61.4	102.5	−115.5	−251.6	139.4	135.2	142.0
of which: Short-term	4 771 ..	....	....	....	....	....	....	....	....
Banks	4 772 ..	....	....	....	....	....	....	....	....
of which: Short-term	4 774 ..	....	....	....	....	....	....	....	....
Other sectors	4 775 ..	....	....	....	....	....	....	....	....
of which: Short-term	4 777 ..	....	....	....	....	....	....	....	....
Currency and deposits	4 780 ..	....	....	....	....	....	....	....	....
Monetary authorities	4 781 ..	....	....	....	....	....	....	....	....
General government	4 782 ..	....	....	....	....	....	....	....	....
Banks	4 783 ..	....	....	....	....	....	....	....	....
Other sectors	4 784 ..	....	....	....	....	....	....	....	....
Other liabilities	4 786 ..	....	−47.3	−35.8	−35.2	−41.4	−45.6	70.6	−52.9
Monetary authorities	4 787 ..	....	....	....	....	....	....	113.3	....
of which: Short-term	4 789 ..	....	....	....	....	....	....	....	....
General government	4 790 ..	....	−47.3	−35.8	−35.2	−41.4	−45.6	−42.7	−52.9
of which: Short-term	4 792 ..	....	....	....	....	....	....	....	....
Banks	4 793 ..	....	....	....	....	....	....	....	....
of which: Short-term	4 795 ..	....	....	....	....	....	....	....	....
Other sectors	4 796 ..	....	....	....	....	....	....	....	....
of which: Short-term	4 798 ..	....	....	....	....	....	....	....	....
E. RESERVE ASSETS	4 802 ..	**−5.0**	**−9.8**	**−24.9**	**−25.3**	**−35.6**	**−58.6**	**−274.2**	**−153.1**
Monetary gold	4 812 ..	....	....	....	....	....	....	....	....
Special drawing rights	4 811 ..	.3	−1.8	6.2	−.6	1.2	.4	−2.7	1.8
Reserve position in the Fund	4 810 ..	....	....	....	....	....	....	....	....
Foreign exchange	4 803 ..	−5.3	−8.0	−31.0	−24.8	−36.8	−59.1	−271.4	−154.9
Other claims	4 813 ..	....	....	....	....	....	....	....	....
NET ERRORS AND OMISSIONS	4 998 ..	**−19.9**	**−43.4**	**−68.2**	**−52.9**	**−81.6**	**−56.8**	**−44.0**	**−68.6**

Table 1. ANALYTIC PRESENTATION, FISCAL YEARS 2003–2010 ENDING SEPTEMBER 30

(Millions of U.S. dollars)

	Code	2003	2004	2005	2006	2007	2008	2009	2010
A. Current Account[1]........................	4 993 Z.	**−181.8**	**−168.3**	**−360.9**	**−462.2**	**−480.1**	**−766.1**	**−624.2**	**−1,955.6**
Goods: exports f.o.b....................	2 100 ..	333.8	376.9	459.6	495.2	522.8	490.2	551.0	561.5
Goods: imports f.o.b....................	3 100 ..	−1,116.0	−1,210.0	−1,308.5	−1,548.2	−1,704.2	−2,107.8	−2,032.1	−2,809.1
Balance on Goods.....................	4 100 ..	*−782.2*	*−833.1*	*−848.9*	*−1,053.1*	*−1,181.4*	*−1,617.6*	*−1,481.1*	*−2,247.7*
Services: credit...........................	2 200 ..	136.0	135.7	141.0	190.2	253.7	339.5	375.5	238.0
Services: debit............................	3 200 ..	−301.0	−351.6	−544.4	−593.4	−683.5	−756.6	−772.1	−1,274.9
Balance on Goods and Services.......	4 991 ..	*−947.2*	*−1,049.0*	*−1,252.3*	*−1,456.2*	*−1,611.2*	*−2,034.8*	*−1,877.7*	*−3,284.6*
Income: credit............................	2 300 ..	....	....	....	18.7	25.0	28.2	31.1	32.6
Income: debit............................	3 300 ..	−14.3	−12.3	−35.0	−12.1	−19.6	−12.2	−18.3	−10.4
Balance on Goods, Services, and Income........	4 992 ..	*−961.4*	*−1,061.3*	*−1,287.3*	*−1,449.6*	*−1,605.8*	*−2,018.8*	*−1,864.9*	*−3,262.4*
Current transfers: credit...............	2 379 Z.	811.0	931.5	986.2	1,062.9	1,222.1	1,369.8	1,375.5	1,473.8
Current transfers: debit...............	3 379 ..	−31.4	−38.5	−59.7	−75.5	−96.4	−117.1	−134.8	−167.0
B. Capital Account[1].......................	4 994 Z.	....	....	....	....	....	....	**910.1**	**1,205.0**
Capital account: credit.................	2 994 Z.	....	....	....	....	....	....	910.1	1,205.0
Capital account: debit.................	3 994 ..	....	....	....	....	....	....	....	....
Total, Groups A Plus B................	4 981 ..	*−181.8*	*−168.3*	*−360.9*	*−462.2*	*−480.1*	*−766.1*	*285.9*	*−750.6*
C. Financial Account[1]........................	4 995 W.	**−60.1**	**39.6**	**−9.7**	**153.8**	**160.4**	**305.5**	**−520.4**	**−104.2**
Direct investment abroad..............	4 505 ..	....	....	....	....	....	....	....	....
Direct investment in Haiti..............	4 555 Z.	13.8	5.9	26.0	160.6	74.5	29.8	38.0	150.0
Portfolio investment assets............	4 602 ..	....	....	....	....	....	....	....	....
Equity securities..........................	4 610 ..	....	....	....	....	....	....	....	....
Debt securities............................	4 619 ..	....	....	....	....	....	....	....	....
Portfolio investment liabilities.........	4 652 Z.	....	....	....	....	....	....	....	....
Equity securities..........................	4 660 ..	....	....	....	....	....	....	....	....
Debt securities............................	4 669 Z.	....	....	....	....	....	....	....	....
Financial derivatives.....................	4 910 ..	....	....	....	....	....	....	....	....
Financial derivatives assets............	4 900 ..	....	....	....	....	....	....	....	....
Financial derivatives liabilities.........	4 905 ..	....	....	....	....	....	....	....	....
Other investment assets................	4 703 ..	−87.8	5.7	−52.5	−55.1	1.9	−75.0	36.0	58.8
Monetary authorities....................	4 701 ..	.3	.1	−.9	.1	−.1	.3	−19.3	16.5
General government......................	4 704 ..	....	....	....	....	....	....	....	....
Banks...	4 705 ..	−48.1	.6	−57.6	−75.1	4.1	−161.2	55.3	65.4
Other sectors..............................	4 728 ..	−40.0	5.0	6.0	19.8	−2.0	86.0	....	−23.0
Other investment liabilities............	4 753 W.	13.8	28.0	16.7	48.3	83.9	350.6	−594.4	−313.0
Monetary authorities....................	4 753 WA	1.4	4.0	−1.1	10.7	.5	50.4	141.9	−60.0
General government......................	4 753 ZB	11.3	.4	31.0	42.4	73.1	280.7	−735.9	−259.0
Banks...	4 753 ZC	1.1	23.6	−13.2	−4.7	10.3	19.5	−1.4	6.0
Other sectors..............................	4 753 ZD	....	....	....	....	....	....	1.0	....
Total, Groups A Through C............	4 983 ..	*−241.9*	*−128.7*	*−370.6*	*−308.4*	*−319.8*	*−460.6*	*−234.5*	*−854.8*
D. Net Errors and Omissions.................	4 998 ..	**101.5**	**62.6**	**35.6**	**31.0**	**82.1**	**83.1**	**−188.6**	**161.4**
Total, Groups A Through D............	4 984 ..	*−140.4*	*−66.2*	*−335.1*	*−277.3*	*−237.7*	*−377.5*	*−423.1*	*−693.4*
E. Reserves and Related Items..............	4 802 A.	**140.4**	**66.2**	**335.1**	**277.3**	**237.7**	**377.5**	**423.1**	**693.4**
Reserve assets..............................	4 802 ..	20.7	−50.0	−21.8	−108.1	−208.4	−170.5	−35.4	−951.8
Use of Fund credit and loans..........	4 766 ..	−14.5	−7.1	11.0	10.3	20.8	51.2	57.4	−144.8
Exceptional financing...................	4 920 ..	134.2	123.3	345.9	375.2	425.3	496.9	401.1	1,790.0
Conversion rates: gourdes per U.S. dollar.............	0 101 ..	**40.455**	**39.683**	**38.984**	**41.449**	**37.400**	**38.267**	**40.683**	**40.310**

[1] Excludes components that have been classified in the categories of Group E.

Table 2. STANDARD PRESENTATION, FISCAL YEARS 2003–2010 ENDING SEPTEMBER 30

(Millions of U.S. dollars)

	Code	2003	2004	2005	2006	2007	2008	2009	2010
CURRENT ACCOUNT	4 993	**−44.8**	**−62.4**	**7.0**	**−85.1**	**−85.1**	**−292.4**	**−226.7**	**−165.6**
A. GOODS	4 100	**−782.2**	**−833.1**	**−848.9**	**−1,053.1**	**−1,181.4**	**−1,617.6**	**−1,481.1**	**−2,247.7**
Credit	2 100	**333.8**	**376.9**	**459.6**	**495.2**	**522.8**	**490.2**	**551.0**	**561.5**
General merchandise: exports f.o.b.	2 110	333.8	376.9	459.6	495.2	522.8	490.2	551.0	561.5
Goods for processing: exports f.o.b.	2 150	....	....	....	....	....	....	....	....
Repairs on goods	2 160	....	....	....	....	....	....	....	....
Goods procured in ports by carriers	2 170	....	....	....	....	....	....	....	....
Nonmonetary gold	2 180	....	....	....	....	....	....	....	....
Debit	3 100	**−1,116.0**	**−1,210.0**	**−1,308.5**	**−1,548.2**	**−1,704.2**	**−2,107.8**	**−2,032.1**	**−2,809.1**
General merchandise: imports f.o.b.	3 110	−1,116.0	−1,210.0	−1,308.5	−1,548.2	−1,704.2	−2,107.8	−2,032.1	−2,809.1
Goods for processing: imports f.o.b.	3 150	....	....	....	....	....	....	....	....
Repairs on goods	3 160	....	....	....	....	....	....	....	....
Goods procured in ports by carriers	3 170	....	....	....	....	....	....	....	....
Nonmonetary gold	3 180	....	....	....	....	....	....	....	....
B. SERVICES	4 200	**−165.0**	**−215.8**	**−403.4**	**−403.1**	**−429.8**	**−417.2**	**−396.6**	**−1,036.9**
Total credit	2 200	*136.0*	*135.7*	*141.0*	*190.2*	*253.7*	*339.5*	*375.5*	*238.0*
Total debit	3 200	*−301.0*	*−351.6*	*−544.4*	*−593.4*	*−683.5*	*−756.6*	*−772.1*	*−1,274.9*
Transportation services, credit	2 205	....	....	....	....	....	....	....	....
Passenger	2 850	....	....	....	....	....	....	....	....
Freight	2 851	....	....	....	....	....	....	....	....
Other	2 852	....	....	....	....	....	....	....	....
Sea transport, passenger	2 207	....	....	....	....	....	....	....	....
Sea transport, freight	2 208	....	....	....	....	....	....	....	....
Sea transport, other	2 209	....	....	....	....	....	....	....	....
Air transport, passenger	2 211	....	....	....	....	....	....	....	....
Air transport, freight	2 212	....	....	....	....	....	....	....	....
Air transport, other	2 213	....	....	....	....	....	....	....	....
Other transport, passenger	2 215	....	....	....	....	....	....	....	....
Other transport, freight	2 216	....	....	....	....	....	....	....	....
Other transport, other	2 217	....	....	....	....	....	....	....	....
Transportation services, debit	3 205	**−243.5**	**−224.9**	**−217.3**	**−299.6**	**−396.4**	**−477.9**	**−522.6**	**−579.8**
Passenger	3 850	*−159.5*	*−133.8*	*−118.6*	*−183.1*	*−274.6*	*−319.4*	*−369.6*	*−368.4*
Freight	3 851	*−84.0*	*−91.1*	*−98.8*	*−116.5*	*−121.8*	*−158.6*	*−153.0*	*−211.4*
Other	3 852	....	....	....	....	....	....	....	....
Sea transport, passenger	3 207	....	....	....	....	....	....	....	....
Sea transport, freight	3 208	−84.0	−91.1	−98.8	−116.5	−121.8	−158.6	−153.0	−211.4
Sea transport, other	3 209	....	....	....	....	....	....	....	....
Air transport, passenger	3 211	−159.5	−133.8	−118.6	−183.1	−274.6	−319.4	−369.6	−368.4
Air transport, freight	3 212	....	....	....	....	....	....	....	....
Air transport, other	3 213	....	....	....	....	....	....	....	....
Other transport, passenger	3 215	....	....	....	....	....	....	....	....
Other transport, freight	3 216	....	....	....	....	....	....	....	....
Other transport, other	3 217	....	....	....	....	....	....	....	....
Travel, credit	2 236	**95.6**	**86.8**	**79.5**	**125.9**	**189.9**	**275.6**	**311.6**	**166.9**
Business travel	2 237	....	....	....	....	....	....	....	....
Personal travel	2 240	95.6	86.8	79.5	125.9	189.9	275.6	311.6	166.9
Travel, debit	3 236	....	**−71.9**	**−55.4**	**−55.6**	**−56.5**	**−63.7**	**−62.6**	**−63.3**
Business travel	3 237	....	....	....	....	....	....	....	....
Personal travel	3 240	....	−71.9	−55.4	−55.6	−56.5	−63.7	−62.6	−63.3
Other services, credit	2 200 BA	**40.4**	**48.9**	**61.5**	**64.3**	**63.8**	**63.8**	**63.9**	**71.1**
Communications	2 245	12.6	17.1	9.3	9.9	9.4	9.4	9.5	16.6
Construction	2 249	....	....	....	....	....	....	....	....
Insurance	2 253	....	....	....	....	....	....	....	....
Financial	2 260	....	....	....	....	....	....	....	....
Computer and information	2 262	....	....	....	....	....	....	....	....
Royalties and licence fees	2 266	5.8	....	....	....	....	....	....	....
Other business services	2 268	....	....	....	....	....	....	....	....
Personal, cultural, and recreational	2 287	....	....	....	....	....	....	....	....
Government, n.i.e.	2 291	22.0	31.8	52.2	54.4	54.4	54.4	54.4	54.5
Other services, debit	3 200 BA	**−57.5**	**−54.7**	**−271.7**	**−238.1**	**−230.6**	**−215.0**	**−186.9**	**−631.8**
Communications	3 245	−3.4	−12.4	−19.6	−9.0	−11.9	−12.0	−12.0	−12.0
Construction	3 249	....	....	....	....	....	....	....	−290.0
Insurance	3 253	....	....	....	....	....	....	....	....
Financial	3 260	....	−4.9	−5.8	−6.3	−7.0	−6.9	−6.1	−.3
Computer and information	3 262	....	....	....	....	....	....	....	....
Royalties and licence fees	3 266	−.4	−.4	−.4	−.5	−.4	−.4	−.4	....
Other business services	3 268	....	....	....	....	....	....	....	−28.0
Personal, cultural, and recreational	3 287	....	−21.4	−217.6	−191.2	−172.9	−157.2	−124.1	−250.0
Government, n.i.e.	3 291	−53.7	−15.6	−28.3	−31.1	−38.4	−38.5	−44.3	−51.5

Table 2 (Continued). STANDARD PRESENTATION, FISCAL YEARS 2003–2010 ENDING SEPTEMBER 30

(Millions of U.S. dollars)

	Code	2003	2004	2005	2006	2007	2008	2009	2010
C. INCOME	4 300	**−14.3**	**−12.3**	**−35.0**	**6.6**	**5.4**	**16.0**	**12.8**	**22.2**
Total credit	2 300	....	....	....	*18.7*	*25.0*	*28.2*	*31.1*	*32.6*
Total debit	3 300	*−14.3*	*−12.3*	*−35.0*	*−12.1*	*−19.6*	*−12.2*	*−18.3*	*−10.4*
Compensation of employees, credit	2 310	....	....	....	....	....	....	....	....
Compensation of employees, debit	3 310	....	....	....	....	....	....	....	....
Investment income, credit	2 320	....	....	....	18.7	25.0	28.2	31.1	32.6
Direct investment income	2 330	....	....	....	....	....	....	....	....
Dividends and distributed branch profits	2 332	....	....	....	....	....	....	....	....
Reinvested earnings and undistributed branch profits	2 333	....	....	....	....	....	....	....	....
Income on debt (interest)	2 334	....	....	....	....	....	....	....	....
Portfolio investment income	2 339	....	....	....	....	....	....	....	....
Income on equity	2 340	....	....	....	....	....	....	....	....
Income on bonds and notes	2 350	....	....	....	....	....	....	....	....
Income on money market instruments	2 360	....	....	....	....	....	....	....	....
Other investment income	2 370	....	....	....	18.7	25.0	28.2	31.1	32.6
Investment income, debit	3 320	**−14.3**	**−12.3**	**−35.0**	**−12.1**	**−19.6**	**−12.2**	**−18.3**	**−10.4**
Direct investment income	3 330	....	....	....	....	....	....	....	....
Dividends and distributed branch profits	3 332	....	....	....	....	....	....	....	....
Reinvested earnings and undistributed branch profits	3 333	....	....	....	....	....	....	....	....
Income on debt (interest)	3 334	....	....	....	....	....	....	....	....
Portfolio investment income	3 339	....	....	....	....	....	....	....	....
Income on equity	3 340	....	....	....	....	....	....	....	....
Income on bonds and notes	3 350	....	....	....	....	....	....	....	....
Income on money market instruments	3 360	....	....	....	....	....	....	....	....
Other investment income	3 370	−14.3	−12.3	−35.0	−12.1	−19.6	−12.2	−18.3	−10.4
D. CURRENT TRANSFERS	4 379	**916.7**	**998.9**	**1,294.4**	**1,364.5**	**1,520.7**	**1,726.4**	**1,638.2**	**3,096.8**
Credit	2 379	**948.0**	**1,037.4**	**1,354.1**	**1,440.0**	**1,617.1**	**1,843.5**	**1,773.1**	**3,263.8**
General government	2 380	137.0	105.9	367.9	377.1	395.0	473.7	397.5	1,790.0
Other sectors	2 390	811.0	931.5	986.2	1,062.9	1,222.1	1,369.8	1,375.5	1,473.8
Workers' remittances	2 391	811.0	931.5	986.2	1,062.9	1,222.1	1,369.8	1,375.5	1,473.8
Other current transfers	2 392	....	....	....	....	....	....	....	....
Debit	3 379	**−31.4**	**−38.5**	**−59.7**	**−75.5**	**−96.4**	**−117.1**	**−134.8**	**−167.0**
General government	3 380	....	....	....	....	....	....	....	....
Other sectors	3 390	−31.4	−38.5	−59.7	−75.5	−96.4	−117.1	−134.8	−167.0
Workers' remittances	3 391	−31.4	−38.5	−59.7	−75.5	−96.4	−117.1	−134.8	−167.0
Other current transfers	3 392	....	....	....	....	....	....	....	....
CAPITAL AND FINANCIAL ACCOUNT	4 996	**−56.7**	**−.2**	**−42.6**	**54.0**	**3.0**	**209.3**	**415.3**	**4.2**
CAPITAL ACCOUNT	4 994	....	....	....	....	....	....	**910.1**	**1,205.0**
Total credit	2 994	....	....	....	....	....	....	*910.1*	*1,205.0*
Total debit	3 994	....	....	....	....	....	....	....	....
Capital transfers, credit	2 400	....	....	....	....	....	....	**910.1**	**1,205.0**
General government	2 401	....	....	....	....	....	....	910.1	547.0
Debt forgiveness	2 402	....	....	....	....	....	....	910.1	547.0
Other capital transfers	2 410	....	....	....	....	....	....	....	....
Other sectors	2 430	....	....	....	....	....	....	....	658.0
Migrants' transfers	2 431	....	....	....	....	....	....	....	....
Debt forgiveness	2 432	....	....	....	....	....	....	....	....
Other capital transfers	2 440	....	....	....	....	....	....	....	658.0
Capital transfers, debit	3 400	....	....	....	....	....	....	....	....
General government	3 401	....	....	....	....	....	....	....	....
Debt forgiveness	3 402	....	....	....	....	....	....	....	....
Other capital transfers	3 410	....	....	....	....	....	....	....	....
Other sectors	3 430	....	....	....	....	....	....	....	....
Migrants' transfers	3 431	....	....	....	....	....	....	....	....
Debt forgiveness	3 432	....	....	....	....	....	....	....	....
Other capital transfers	3 440	....	....	....	....	....	....	....	....
Nonproduced nonfinancial assets, credit	2 480	....	....	....	....	....	....	....	....
Nonproduced nonfinancial assets, debit	3 480	....	....	....	....	....	....	....	....

Table 2 (Continued). STANDARD PRESENTATION, FISCAL YEARS 2003–2010 ENDING SEPTEMBER 30

(Millions of U.S. dollars)

	Code	2003	2004	2005	2006	2007	2008	2009	2010
FINANCIAL ACCOUNT	4 995	−56.7	−.2	−42.6	54.0	3.0	209.3	−494.9	−1,200.8
A. DIRECT INVESTMENT	4 500	13.8	5.9	26.0	160.6	74.5	29.8	38.0	150.0
Direct investment abroad	4 505	....	....	....	....	....	....	....	....
Equity capital	4 510	....	....	....	....	....	....	....	....
Claims on affiliated enterprises	4 515	....	....	....	....	....	....	....	....
Liabilities to affiliated enterprises	4 520	....	....	....	....	....	....	....	....
Reinvested earnings	4 525	....	....	....	....	....	....	....	....
Other capital	4 530	....	....	....	....	....	....	....	....
Claims on affiliated enterprises	4 535	....	....	....	....	....	....	....	....
Liabilities to affiliated enterprises	4 540	....	....	....	....	....	....	....	....
Direct investment in Haiti	4 555	13.8	5.9	26.0	160.6	74.5	29.8	38.0	150.0
Equity capital	4 560	13.8	5.9	26.0	160.6	74.5	29.8	38.0	150.0
Claims on direct investors	4 565	....	....	....	....	....	....	....	....
Liabilities to direct investors	4 570	13.8	5.9	26.0	160.6	74.5	29.8	38.0	150.0
Reinvested earnings	4 575	....	....	....	....	....	....	....	....
Other capital	4 580	....	....	....	....	....	....	....	....
Claims on direct investors	4 585	....	....	....	....	....	....	....	....
Liabilities to direct investors	4 590	....	....	....	....	....	....	....	....
B. PORTFOLIO INVESTMENT	4 600	....	....	....	....	....	....	....	....
Assets	4 602	....	....	....	....	....	....	....	....
Equity securities	4 610	....	....	....	....	....	....	....	....
Monetary authorities	4 611	....	....	....	....	....	....	....	....
General government	4 612	....	....	....	....	....	....	....	....
Banks	4 613	....	....	....	....	....	....	....	....
Other sectors	4 614	....	....	....	....	....	....	....	....
Debt securities	4 619	....	....	....	....	....	....	....	....
Bonds and notes	4 620	....	....	....	....	....	....	....	....
Monetary authorities	4 621	....	....	....	....	....	....	....	....
General government	4 622	....	....	....	....	....	....	....	....
Banks	4 623	....	....	....	....	....	....	....	....
Other sectors	4 624	....	....	....	....	....	....	....	....
Money market instruments	4 630	....	....	....	....	....	....	....	....
Monetary authorities	4 631	....	....	....	....	....	....	....	....
General government	4 632	....	....	....	....	....	....	....	....
Banks	4 633	....	....	....	....	....	....	....	....
Other sectors	4 634	....	....	....	....	....	....	....	....
Liabilities	4 652	....	....	....	....	....	....	....	....
Equity securities	4 660	....	....	....	....	....	....	....	....
Banks	4 663	....	....	....	....	....	....	....	....
Other sectors	4 664	....	....	....	....	....	....	....	....
Debt securities	4 669	....	....	....	....	....	....	....	....
Bonds and notes	4 670	....	....	....	....	....	....	....	....
Monetary authorities	4 671	....	....	....	....	....	....	....	....
General government	4 672	....	....	....	....	....	....	....	....
Banks	4 673	....	....	....	....	....	....	....	....
Other sectors	4 674	....	....	....	....	....	....	....	....
Money market instruments	4 680	....	....	....	....	....	....	....	....
Monetary authorities	4 681	....	....	....	....	....	....	....	....
General government	4 682	....	....	....	....	....	....	....	....
Banks	4 683	....	....	....	....	....	....	....	....
Other sectors	4 684	....	....	....	....	....	....	....	....
C. FINANCIAL DERIVATIVES	4 910	....	....	....	....	....	....	....	....
Monetary authorities	4 911	....	....	....	....	....	....	....	....
General government	4 912	....	....	....	....	....	....	....	....
Banks	4 913	....	....	....	....	....	....	....	....
Other sectors	4 914	....	....	....	....	....	....	....	....
Assets	4 900	....	....	....	160.6	74.5	29.8	....	150.0
Monetary authorities	4 901	....	....	....	....	....	....	....	....
General government	4 902	....	....	....	....	....	....	....	....
Banks	4 903	....	....	....	....	....	....	....	....
Other sectors	4 904	....	....	....	....	....	....	....	....
Liabilities	4 905	....	....	....	....	....	....	....	....
Monetary authorities	4 906	....	....	....	....	....	....	....	....
General government	4 907	....	....	....	....	....	....	....	....
Banks	4 908	....	....	....	....	....	....	....	....
Other sectors	4 909	....	....	....	....	....	....	....	....

Table 2 (Concluded). STANDARD PRESENTATION, FISCAL YEARS 2003–2010 ENDING SEPTEMBER 30

(Millions of U.S. dollars)

	Code	2003	2004	2005	2006	2007	2008	2009	2010
D. OTHER INVESTMENT	4 700	**−91.3**	**43.9**	**−46.8**	**1.5**	**136.9**	**350.0**	**−497.4**	**−399.0**
Assets	4 703	**−87.8**	**5.7**	**−52.5**	**−55.1**	**1.9**	**−75.0**	**36.0**	**58.8**
Trade credits	4 706	....	....	....	....	....	....	....	....
General government	4 707	....	....	....	....	....	....	....	....
of which: Short-term	4 709	....	....	....	....	....	....	....	....
Other sectors	4 710	....	....	....	....	....	....	....	....
of which: Short-term	4 712	....	....	....	....	....	....	....	....
Loans	4 714	....	....	....	....	....	....	....	....
Monetary authorities	4 715	....	....	....	....	....	....	....	....
of which: Short-term	4 718	....	....	....	....	....	....	....	....
General government	4 719	....	....	....	....	....	....	....	....
of which: Short-term	4 721	....	....	....	....	....	....	....	....
Banks	4 722	....	....	....	....	....	....	....	....
of which: Short-term	4 724	....	....	....	....	....	....	....	....
Other sectors	4 725	....	....	....	....	....	....	....	....
of which: Short-term	4 727	....	....	....	....	....	....	....	....
Currency and deposits	4 730	−26.3	11.0	−18.3	9.3	−18.4	14.7	−23.0	42.5
Monetary authorities	4 731	....	....	....	....	....	....	....	....
General government	4 732	....	....	....	....	....	....	....	....
Banks	4 733	13.7	6.0	−24.3	−10.5	−16.4	−71.3	−23.0	65.5
Other sectors	4 734	−40.0	5.0	6.0	19.8	−2.0	86.0	....	−23.0
Other assets	4 736	−61.5	−5.3	−34.2	−64.5	20.3	−89.7	59.1	16.3
Monetary authorities	4 737	.3	.1	−.9	.1	−.1	.3	−19.3	16.5
of which: Short-term	4 739	.3	.1	−.9	.1	−.1	.3	−19.3	16.5
General government	4 740	....	....	....	....	....	....	....	....
of which: Short-term	4 742	....	....	....	....	....	....	....	....
Banks	4 743	−61.8	−5.4	−33.3	−64.6	20.5	−90.0	78.4	−.2
of which: Short-term	4 745	−61.8	−5.4	−33.3	−64.6	20.5	−90.0	78.4	−.2
Other sectors	4 746	....	....	....	....	....	....	....	....
of which: Short-term	4 748	....	....	....	....	....	....	....	....
Liabilities	4 753	**−3.5**	**38.2**	**5.7**	**56.7**	**134.9**	**424.9**	**−533.4**	**−457.8**
Trade credits	4 756	....	....	....	....	....	....	....	....
General government	4 757	....	....	....	....	....	....	....	....
of which: Short-term	4 759	....	....	....	....	....	....	....	....
Other sectors	4 760	....	....	....	....	....	....	....	....
of which: Short-term	4 762	....	....	....	....	....	....	....	....
Loans	4 764	−5.6	−6.7	45.7	49.0	172.2	358.0	−664.5	−403.8
Monetary authorities	4 765	−14.5	−7.1	11.0	10.3	20.8	51.2	57.4	−144.8
of which: Use of Fund credit and loans from the Fund	4 766	−14.5	−7.1	11.0	10.3	20.8	51.2	57.4	−144.8
of which: Short-term	4 768	....	....	....	....	....	....	....	....
General government	4 769	11.3	.4	31.0	42.4	141.4	303.8	−732.2	−259.0
of which: Short-term	4 771	....	....	....	....	....	....	....	....
Banks	4 772	−2.4	....	3.6	−3.7	10.1	3.0	10.4	....
of which: Short-term	4 774	....	....	....	....	....	....	....	....
Other sectors	4 775	....	....	....	....	....	....	....	....
of which: Short-term	4 777	....	....	....	....	....	....	....	....
Currency and deposits	4 780	4.1	21.5	−13.6	−3.7	−2.5	7.6	2.1	.8
Monetary authorities	4 781	....	....	....	....	....	....	....	....
General government	4 782	....	....	....	....	....	....	....	....
Banks	4 783	4.1	21.5	−13.6	−3.7	−2.5	7.6	1.1	.8
Other sectors	4 784	....	....	....	....	....	....	1.0	....
Other liabilities	4 786	−1.9	23.5	−26.4	11.3	−34.8	59.4	129.0	−54.8
Monetary authorities	4 787	1.4	4.0	−1.1	10.7	.5	50.4	141.9	−60.0
of which: Short-term	4 789	1.4	1.2	1.6	.8	.5	28.6	3.6	....
General government	4 790	−2.8	17.4	−22.1	1.7	−38.0	....	....	....
of which: Short-term	4 792	−2.8	17.4	−22.1	1.7	−38.0	....	....	....
Banks	4 793	−.6	2.1	−3.2	−1.1	2.7	8.9	−12.9	5.2
of which: Short-term	4 795	....	2.1	−3.2	−1.1	2.7	8.9	−12.9	5.2
Other sectors	4 796	....	....	....	....	....	....	....	....
of which: Short-term	4 798	....	....	....	....	....	....	....	....
E. RESERVE ASSETS	4 802	**20.7**	**−50.0**	**−21.8**	**−108.1**	**−208.4**	**−170.5**	**−35.4**	**−951.8**
Monetary gold	4 812	....	−.2	−.1	−.2	−.2	−.2	−.2	−.4
Special drawing rights	4 811	.4	−.4	.7	−9.7	2.9	.3	102.1	−106.3
Reserve position in the Fund	4 810	....	....	....	....	....	....	.1	−.1
Foreign exchange	4 803	20.4	−49.3	−22.5	−98.3	−211.1	−170.5	−137.4	−845.0
Other claims	4 813	....	....	....	....	....	....	....	....
NET ERRORS AND OMISSIONS	4 998	**101.5**	**62.6**	**35.6**	**31.0**	**82.1**	**83.1**	**−188.6**	**161.4**

Table 3. INTERNATIONAL INVESTMENT POSITION (End-period stocks), 2003–2010

(Millions of U.S. dollars)

	Code	2003	2004	2005	2006	2007	2008	2009	2010
ASSETS	8 995 C.	534.1	537.5	649.9	1,038.4	1,246.8	1,647.4	1,721.1	2,941.1
Direct investment abroad	8 505	....	....	....	....	....	....	....	....
Equity capital and reinvested earnings	8 506	....	....	....	....	....	....	....	....
Claims on affiliated enterprises	8 507	....	....	....	....	....	....	....	....
Liabilities to affiliated enterprises	8 508	....	....	....	....	....	....	....	....
Other capital	8 530	....	....	....	....	....	....	....	....
Claims on affiliated enterprises	8 535	....	....	....	....	....	....	....	....
Liabilities to affiliated enterprises	8 540	....	....	....	....	....	....	....	....
Portfolio investment	8 602	....	....	....	....	....	....	....	....
Equity securities	8 610	....	....	....	....	....	....	....	....
Monetary authorities	8 611	....	....	....	....	....	....	....	....
General government	8 612	....	....	....	....	....	....	....	....
Banks	8 613	....	....	....	....	....	....	....	....
Other sectors	8 614	....	....	....	....	....	....	....	....
Debt securities	8 619	....	....	....	....	....	....	....	....
Bonds and notes	8 620	....	....	....	....	....	....	....	....
Monetary authorities	8 621	....	....	....	....	....	....	....	....
General government	8 622	....	....	....	....	....	....	....	....
Banks	8 623	....	....	....	....	....	....	....	....
Other sectors	8 624	....	....	....	....	....	....	....	....
Money market instruments	8 630	....	....	....	....	....	....	....	....
Monetary authorities	8 631	....	....	....	....	....	....	....	....
General government	8 632	....	....	....	....	....	....	....	....
Banks	8 633	....	....	....	....	....	....	....	....
Other sectors	8 634	....	....	....	....	....	....	....	....
Financial derivatives	8 900	....	....	....	....	....	....	....	....
Monetary authorities	8 901	....	....	....	....	....	....	....	....
General government	8 902	....	....	....	....	....	....	....	....
Banks	8 903	....	....	....	....	....	....	....	....
Other sectors	8 904	....	....	....	....	....	....	....	....
Other investment	8 703	327.4	280.8	371.4	651.5	651.0	888.6	813.2	1,147.4
Trade credits	8 706	....	....	....	....	....	....	....	....
General government	8 707	....	....	....	....	....	....	....	....
of which: Short-term	8 709	....	....	....	....	....	....	....	....
Other sectors	8 710	....	....	....	....	....	....	....	....
of which: Short-term	8 712	....	....	....	....	....	....	....	....
Loans	8 714	....	....	....	....	....	....	....	....
Monetary authorities	8 715	....	....	....	....	....	....	....	....
of which: Short-term	8 718	....	....	....	....	....	....	....	....
General government	8 719	....	....	....	....	....	....	....	....
of which: Short-term	8 721	....	....	....	....	....	....	....	....
Banks	8 722	....	....	....	....	....	....	....	....
of which: Short-term	8 724	....	....	....	....	....	....	....	....
Other sectors	8 725	....	....	....	....	....	....	....	....
of which: Short-term	8 727	....	....	....	....	....	....	....	....
Currency and deposits	8 730	193.1	141.1	198.4	413.9	433.9	581.5	586.0	645.9
Monetary authorities	8 731	....	....	....	....	....	....	....	....
General government	8 732	....	....	....	....	....	....	....	....
Banks	8 733	86.1	80.1	104.4	114.9	130.9	202.5	224.0	260.9
Other sectors	8 734	107.0	61.0	94.0	299.0	303.0	379.0	362.0	385.0
Other assets	8 736	134.3	139.7	173.0	237.6	217.1	307.1	227.2	501.5
Monetary authorities	8 737	....	....	....	....	....	....	....	....
of which: Short-term	8 739	....	....	....	....	....	....	....	....
General government	8 740	....	....	....	....	....	....	....	....
of which: Short-term	8 742	....	....	....	....	....	....	....	....
Banks	8 743	134.3	139.7	173.0	237.6	217.1	307.1	227.2	501.5
of which: Short-term	8 745	....	....	....	....	....	....	....	....
Other sectors	8 746	....	....	....	....	....	....	....	....
of which: Short-term	8 748	....	....	....	....	....	....	....	....
Reserve assets	8 802	206.7	256.6	278.5	386.9	595.8	758.8	907.9	1,793.6
Monetary gold	8 812	.3	.5	.6	.8	1.0	1.2	1.3	1.7
Special drawing rights	8 811	.3	.8	.1	10.1	7.6	7.3	....	107.2
Reserve position in the Fund	8 810	.1	.1	.1	.1	.1	.1	....	.1
Foreign exchange	8 803	156.6	205.9	227.6	325.9	536.9	700.3	837.8	1,632.3
Other claims	8 813	49.4	49.3	50.2	50.1	50.2	49.9	68.8	52.3

Table 3 (Concluded). INTERNATIONAL INVESTMENT POSITION (End-period stocks), 2003–2010

(Millions of U.S. dollars)

	Code	2003	2004	2005	2006	2007	2008	2009	2010
LIABILITIES	8 995 D.	**1,640.4**	**1,670.1**	**1,723.5**	**1,967.4**	**2,195.8**	**2,696.8**	**2,252.3**	**1,775.6**
Direct investment in Haiti	8 555 ..	**118.6**	**124.5**	**150.5**	**310.5**	**385.0**	**415.4**	**453.3**	**603.3**
Equity capital and reinvested earnings	8 556 ..	118.6	124.5	150.5	310.5	385.0	415.4	453.3	603.3
Claims on direct investors	8 557 ..	....	....	....	....	....	....	....	....
Liabilities to direct investors	8 558 ..	118.6	124.5	150.5	310.5	385.0	415.4	453.3	603.3
Other capital	8 580 ..	....	....	....	....	....	....	....	....
Claims on direct investors	8 585 ..	....	....	....	....	....	....	....	....
Liabilities to direct investors	8 590 ..	....	....	....	....	....	....	....	....
Portfolio investment	8 652 ..	....	....	....	....	....	....	....	....
Equity securities	8 660 ..	....	....	....	....	....	....	....	....
Banks	8 663 ..	....	....	....	....	....	....	....	....
Other sectors	8 664 ..	....	....	....	....	....	....	....	....
Debt securities	8 669 ..	....	....	....	....	....	....	....	....
Bonds and notes	8 670 ..	....	....	....	....	....	....	....	....
Monetary authorities	8 671 ..	....	....	....	....	....	....	....	....
General government	8 672 ..	....	....	....	....	....	....	....	....
Banks	8 673 ..	....	....	....	....	....	....	....	....
Other sectors	8 674 ..	....	....	....	....	....	....	....	....
Money market instruments	8 680 ..	....	....	....	....	....	....	....	....
Monetary authorities	8 681 ..	....	....	....	....	....	....	....	....
General government	8 682 ..	....	....	....	....	....	....	....	....
Banks	8 683 ..	....	....	....	....	....	....	....	....
Other sectors	8 684 ..	....	....	....	....	....	....	....	....
Financial derivatives	8 905 ..	....	....	....	....	....	....	....	....
Monetary authorities	8 906 ..	....	....	....	....	....	....	....	....
General government	8 907 ..	....	....	....	....	....	....	....	....
Banks	8 908 ..	....	....	....	....	....	....	....	....
Other sectors	8 909 ..	....	....	....	....	....	....	....	....
Other investment	8 753 ..	**1,521.8**	**1,545.6**	**1,573.0**	**1,657.0**	**1,810.8**	**2,281.4**	**1,799.0**	**1,172.3**
Trade credits	8 756 ..	....	....	....	....	....	....	....	....
General government	8 757 ..	....	....	....	....	....	....	....	....
of which: Short-term	8 759 ..	....	....	....	....	....	....	....	....
Other sectors	8 760 ..	....	....	....	....	....	....	....	....
of which: Short-term	8 762 ..	....	....	....	....	....	....	....	....
Loans	8 764 ..	1,307.2	1,329.3	1,364.8	1,453.6	1,598.5	2,004.5	1,387.6	831.6
Monetary authorities	8 765 ..	17.9	11.1	21.4	32.5	55.6	104.8	166.4	12.7
of which: Use of Fund credit and loans from the Fund	8 766 ..	*17.9*	*11.1*	*21.4*	*32.5*	*55.6*	*104.8*	*166.4*	*12.7*
of which: Short-term	8 768 ..	....	....	....	....	....	....	....	....
General government	8 769 ..	1,287.4	1,316.3	1,337.8	1,419.3	1,541.0	1,884.7	1,196.0	794.0
of which: Short-term	8 771 ..	....	....	....	....	....	....	....	....
Banks	8 772 ..	1.9	1.9	5.6	1.9	1.9	15.0	25.2	24.9
of which: Short-term	8 774 ..	....	....	....	....	....	....	....	....
Other sectors	8 775 ..	....	....	....	....	....	....	....	....
of which: Short-term	8 777 ..	....	....	....	....	....	....	....	....
Currency and deposits	8 780 ..	135.5	138.0	134.4	129.7	138.2	130.8	133.7	117.5
Monetary authorities	8 781 ..	....	....	....	....	....	....	....	....
General government	8 782 ..	....	....	....	....	....	....	....	....
Banks	8 783 ..	14.5	36.0	22.4	18.7	16.2	23.8	24.7	25.5
Other sectors	8 784 ..	121.0	102.0	112.0	111.0	122.0	107.0	109.0	92.0
Other liabilities	8 786 ..	79.1	78.3	73.8	73.6	74.1	146.1	277.7	223.2
Monetary authorities	8 787 ..	63.4	67.3	66.1	66.9	67.4	127.8	272.3	212.3
of which: Short-term	8 789 ..	....	....	....	....	....	....	....	....
General government	8 790 ..	....	....	....	....	....	....	....	....
of which: Short-term	8 792 ..	....	....	....	....	....	....	....	....
Banks	8 793 ..	15.0	11.0	7.8	6.7	6.7	18.3	5.4	10.9
of which: Short-term	8 795 ..	....	....	....	*6.7*	*6.7*	*18.3*	*5.4*	*10.9*
Other sectors	8 796 ..	.7	....	....	....	....	....	....	....
of which: Short-term	8 798 ..	*.7*	*.3*	....	....	....	....	....	....
NET INTERNATIONAL INVESTMENT POSITION	8 995 ..	**−1,106.2**	**−1,132.6**	**−1,073.5**	**−929.1**	**−949.0**	**−1,049.4**	**−531.3**	**1,165.4**
Conversion rates: gourdes per U.S. dollar (end of period)	0 102 ..	**42.025**	**36.823**	**43.043**	**39.129**	**36.381**	**39.954**	**41.774**	**39.941**

2011, International Monetary Fund: *Balance of Payments Statistics Yearbook*

Table 1. ANALYTIC PRESENTATION, 2003–2010

(Millions of U.S. dollars)

	Code	2003	2004	2005	2006	2007	2008	2009	2010
A. Current Account[1]............................	4 993 Z.	**−552.8**	**−683.4**	**−304.3**	**−403.9**	**−1,116.1**	**−1,781.6**	**−515.5**	**−954.8**
Goods: exports f.o.b..............................	2 100 ..	3,754.0	4,533.9	5,048.0	5,276.6	5,783.6	6,347.0	4,824.6	5,741.9
Goods: imports f.o.b..............................	3 100 ..	−4,774.1	−5,827.2	−6,544.6	−7,303.3	−8,887.7	−10,323.2	−7,299.2	−8,549.5
Balance on Goods.............................	4 100 ..	*−1,020.1*	*−1,293.3*	*−1,496.6*	*−2,026.7*	*−3,104.1*	*−3,976.2*	*−2,474.5*	*−2,807.6*
Services: credit................................	2 200 ..	591.1	644.7	699.6	744.9	780.7	885.4	953.4	1,021.6
Services: debit.................................	3 200 ..	−753.2	−848.9	−928.8	−1,035.7	−1,068.8	−1,213.1	−1,103.4	−1,331.3
Balance on Goods and Services.............	4 991 ..	*−1,182.2*	*−1,497.5*	*−1,725.8*	*−2,317.4*	*−3,392.2*	*−4,303.9*	*−2,624.4*	*−3,117.4*
Income: credit.................................	2 300 ..	67.9	87.5	145.1	198.2	257.2	148.1	73.9	54.6
Income: debit.................................	3 300 ..	−429.8	−538.7	−618.7	−735.0	−652.4	−605.3	−603.9	−652.5
Balance on Goods, Services, and Income.........	4 992 ..	*−1,544.0*	*−1,948.7*	*−2,199.5*	*−2,854.2*	*−3,787.4*	*−4,761.1*	*−3,154.5*	*−3,715.3*
Current transfers: credit........................	2 379 Z.	1,091.9	1,374.0	2,042.4	2,588.8	2,825.2	3,049.5	2,697.0	2,818.0
Current transfers: debit.........................	3 379 ..	−100.7	−108.6	−147.3	−138.4	−154.0	−69.9	−57.9	−57.5
B. Capital Account[1]...........................	4 994 Z.	**49.2**	**50.8**	**593.5**	**1,484.8**	**1,206.7**	**89.8**	**130.4**	**84.4**
Capital account: credit..........................	2 994 Z.	49.2	50.8	593.5	1,484.8	1,206.7	89.8	130.4	84.4
Capital account: debit...........................	3 994 ..	....	....	....	....	....	....	....	....
Total, Groups A Plus B.......................	4 981 ..	*−503.6*	*−632.6*	*289.2*	*1,080.9*	*90.6*	*−1,691.7*	*−385.0*	*−870.4*
C. Financial Account[1]........................	4 995 W.	**304.3**	**987.9**	**689.4**	**899.2**	**1,297.1**	**1,355.7**	**479.2**	**1,247.8**
Direct investment abroad........................	4 505 ..	−12.2	6.2	1.0	−.6	−1.5	1.0	−.7	1.4
Direct investment in Honduras..................	4 555 Z.	402.8	546.9	599.8	669.1	927.5	929.3	523.2	797.4
Portfolio investment assets.....................	4 602 ..	−7.3	−11.8	−23.1	−20.9	−22.4	−26.8	6.0	−15.0
Equity securities.............................	4 610 ..	−5.7	−1.2	−11.7	1.8	.6	−4.1	.4	2.4
Debt securities..............................	4 619 ..	−1.6	−10.6	−11.4	−22.7	−23.0	−22.6	5.6	−17.4
Portfolio investment liabilities.................	4 652 Z.	.2	.2	....	....	....	....	50.0	....
Equity securities.............................	4 660 ..	.2	.2	....	....	....	....	....	....
Debt securities..............................	4 669 Z.	....	....	....	....	....	....	50.0	....
Financial derivatives...........................	4 910 ..	....	....	....	....	....	....	....	....
Financial derivatives assets.....................	4 900 ..	....	....	....	....	....	....	....	....
Financial derivatives liabilities.................	4 905 ..	....	....	....	....	....	....	....	....
Other investment assets.......................	4 703 ..	−62.5	−59.3	12.3	84.4	−29.2	17.6	77.6	88.3
Monetary authorities.........................	4 701 ..	1.0	2.6	−.5	....	....	....	....	....
General government........................	4 704 ..	−.9	−1.0	....	−.1	−.1	−.1	−.1	−.1
Banks.......................................	4 705 ..	17.0	−96.1	6.0	23.7	−41.0	−6.8	94.0	84.1
Other sectors...............................	4 728 ..	−79.6	35.2	6.8	60.8	12.0	24.5	−16.3	4.4
Other investment liabilities....................	4 753 W.	−16.7	505.7	99.4	167.2	422.5	434.6	−176.9	375.7
Monetary authorities.........................	4 753 WA	−13.1	−11.0	−14.4	−6.1	−2.5	−13.1	148.3	−1.7
General government........................	4 753 ZB	34.8	247.2	66.4	65.4	192.2	340.4	33.3	380.6
Banks.......................................	4 753 ZC	−19.6	107.3	107.7	123.2	159.8	31.7	−298.6	16.7
Other sectors...............................	4 753 ZD	−18.8	162.2	−60.3	−15.2	73.0	75.6	−59.9	−19.9
Total, Groups A Through C.................	4 983 ..	*−199.3*	*355.3*	*978.6*	*1,980.2*	*1,387.6*	*−336.0*	*94.2*	*377.4*
D. Net Errors and Omissions.................	4 998 ..	**5.1**	**46.6**	**−190.4**	**−305.4**	**−353.2**	**205.1**	**−510.5**	**192.2**
Total, Groups A Through D..................	4 984 ..	*−194.2*	*401.9*	*788.2*	*1,674.8*	*1,034.4*	*−130.9*	*−416.4*	*569.5*
E. Reserves and Related Items................	4 802 A.	**194.2**	**−401.9**	**−788.2**	**−1,674.8**	**−1,034.4**	**130.9**	**416.4**	**−569.5**
Reserve assets.................................	4 802 ..	96.5	−510.4	−346.4	−282.1	108.5	77.8	346.8	−590.9
Use of Fund credit and loans....................	4 766 ..	−41.1	15.1	−11.5	−140.8	....	....	....	−1.6
Exceptional financing..........................	4 920 ..	138.8	93.4	−430.3	−1,251.9	−1,143.0	53.1	69.5	23.0
Conversion rates: lempiras per U.S. dollar............	0 101 ..	**17.3453**	**18.2062**	**18.8323**	**18.8952**	**18.8951**	**18.9038**	**18.8951**	**18.8951**

[1] Excludes components that have been classified in the categories of Group E.

Table 2. STANDARD PRESENTATION, 2003–2010

(Millions of U.S. dollars)

	Code	2003	2004	2005	2006	2007	2008	2009	2010
CURRENT ACCOUNT	4 993	**−552.8**	**−683.4**	**−304.3**	**−403.9**	**−1,116.1**	**−1,781.6**	**−515.5**	**−954.8**
A. GOODS	4 100	−1,020.1	−1,293.3	−1,496.6	−2,026.7	−3,104.1	−3,976.2	−2,474.5	−2,807.6
Credit	2 100	**3,754.0**	**4,533.9**	**5,048.0**	**5,276.6**	**5,783.6**	**6,347.0**	**4,824.6**	**5,741.9**
General merchandise: exports f.o.b.	2 110	1,288.3	1,566.8	1,829.2	2,016.3	2,461.4	2,808.9	2,238.2	2,664.8
Goods for processing: exports f.o.b.	2 150	2,389.9	2,888.1	3,149.8	3,167.6	3,240.8	3,473.2	2,506.8	2,979.1
Repairs on goods	2 160	.9	.5	.2	.2	.2	.2	.5	.6
Goods procured in ports by carriers	2 170	4.7	4.8	5.7	12.5	13.7	15.2	13.1	12.9
Nonmonetary gold	2 180	70.1	73.6	63.2	79.9	67.6	49.5	66.1	84.4
Debit	3 100	**−4,774.1**	**−5,827.2**	**−6,544.6**	**−7,303.3**	**−8,887.7**	**−10,323.2**	**−7,299.2**	**−8,549.5**
General merchandise: imports f.o.b.	3 110	−3,178.2	−3,883.6	−4,467.4	−5,218.3	−6,706.5	−8,161.8	−5,698.8	−6,659.2
Goods for processing: imports f.o.b.	3 150	−1,592.3	−1,940.8	−2,075.7	−2,084.2	−2,180.1	−2,160.9	−1,599.9	−1,889.8
Repairs on goods	3 160	−2.6	−.7	−.6	−.2	−.4	−.5	−.5	−.6
Goods procured in ports by carriers	3 170	−.9	−2.1	−.8	−.6	−.7	....	....	....
Nonmonetary gold	3 180	....	....	....	....	....	....	....	....
B. SERVICES	4 200	**−162.1**	**−204.2**	**−229.3**	**−290.7**	**−288.1**	**−327.7**	**−149.9**	**−309.7**
Total credit	2 200	*591.1*	*644.7*	*699.6*	*744.9*	*780.7*	*885.4*	*953.4*	*1,021.6*
Total debit	3 200	*−753.2*	*−848.9*	*−928.8*	*−1,035.7*	*−1,068.8*	*−1,213.1*	*−1,103.4*	*−1,331.3*
Transportation services, credit	2 205	**45.0**	**37.1**	**38.7**	**38.7**	**49.9**	**44.3**	**52.3**	**48.6**
Passenger	2 850	*7.9*	*6.2*	*2.3*	*.7*	*.6*	*.7*	*.1*	*1.7*
Freight	2 851	....	....	....	....	....	....	....	....
Other	2 852	*37.2*	*30.9*	*36.4*	*37.9*	*49.3*	*43.6*	*52.2*	*46.8*
Sea transport, passenger	2 207	....	....	....	....	....	....	....	....
Sea transport, freight	2 208	....	....	....	....	....	....	....	....
Sea transport, other	2 209	27.6	29.3	34.9	34.5	38.0	35.1	38.4	40.3
Air transport, passenger	2 211	7.6	5.9	1.7	....	.1	.1	.1	.1
Air transport, freight	2 212	....	....	....	....	....	....	....	....
Air transport, other	2 213	9.6	1.6	1.5	3.4	11.3	8.5	13.8	6.5
Other transport, passenger	2 215	.2	.3	.5	.7	.5	.6	....	1.6
Other transport, freight	2 216	....	....	....	....	....	....	....	....
Other transport, other	2 217	....	....	....	....	....	....	....	....
Transportation services, debit	3 205	**−373.8**	**−439.5**	**−499.9**	**−531.6**	**−625.1**	**−707.5**	**−459.8**	**−587.6**
Passenger	3 850	*−56.7*	*−56.1*	*−59.0*	*−70.1*	*−97.4*	*−94.3*	*−64.9*	*−84.6*
Freight	3 851	*−311.4*	*−378.9*	*−437.2*	*−461.5*	*−527.7*	*−613.2*	*−394.9*	*−503.0*
Other	3 852	*−5.6*	*−4.4*	*−3.7*	....	....	....	....	....
Sea transport, passenger	3 207	....	....	....	....	....	....	....	....
Sea transport, freight	3 208	−226.2	−280.6	−308.1	−377.4	−365.6	−420.8	−238.3	−327.8
Sea transport, other	3 209	−5.4	−4.0	−3.5	....	....	....	....	....
Air transport, passenger	3 211	−55.5	−55.0	−57.7	−69.0	−96.0	−92.8	−60.5	−83.1
Air transport, freight	3 212	−16.3	−18.2	−24.1	−19.6	−36.3	−43.3	−22.2	−32.4
Air transport, other	3 213	−.2	−.4	−.2	....	....	....	....	....
Other transport, passenger	3 215	−1.3	−1.2	−1.3	−1.1	−1.4	−1.5	−4.4	−1.5
Other transport, freight	3 216	−69.0	−80.1	−105.1	−64.4	−125.8	−149.1	−134.4	−142.8
Other transport, other	3 217	....	....	....	....	....	....	....	....
Travel, credit	2 236	**364.4**	**413.5**	**463.5**	**515.3**	**545.6**	**619.0**	**615.9**	**650.0**
Business travel	2 237	145.7	165.4	185.4	206.1	218.2	247.5	246.4	260.0
Personal travel	2 240	218.6	248.1	278.1	309.2	327.4	371.5	369.5	390.0
Travel, debit	3 236	**−217.5**	**−244.2**	**−262.1**	**−355.0**	**−212.0**	**−290.5**	**−296.0**	**−320.7**
Business travel	3 237	−87.0	−97.7	−104.9	−142.0	−84.8	−116.3	−118.4	−129.5
Personal travel	3 240	−130.5	−146.5	−157.3	−213.0	−127.2	−174.2	−177.6	−191.2
Other services, credit	2 200 BA	**181.7**	**194.0**	**197.4**	**191.0**	**185.3**	**222.1**	**285.2**	**323.1**
Communications	2 245	126.4	151.2	143.5	136.9	137.7	179.2	251.4	253.4
Construction	2 249	1.2	1.3	.1	....	....	....	....	....
Insurance	2 253	17.6	17.4	18.2	20.8	23.8	24.8	21.1	25.0
Financial	2 260	2.1	2.5	5.7	....	.4	.1	....	....
Computer and information	2 262	.3	.2	.1	1.3	.3	.1	.1	4.5
Royalties and licence fees	2 266	.8	....	....	....	....	....	....	....
Other business services	2 268	15.6	11.9	13.5	13.9	12.7	6.8	4.5	10.3
Personal, cultural, and recreational	2 287	....	....	.3	.1	....	....	2.5	11.7
Government, n.i.e.	2 291	17.7	9.5	15.9	18.1	10.3	11.0	5.6	18.1
Other services, debit	3 200 BA	**−162.0**	**−165.2**	**−166.8**	**−149.1**	**−231.7**	**−215.1**	**−347.5**	**−423.0**
Communications	3 245	−20.4	−18.1	−19.3	−36.2	−56.7	−79.2	−229.3	−219.7
Construction	3 249	−32.0	−36.0	−38.0	....	....	....	....	−3.1
Insurance	3 253	−7.2	−7.7	−8.8	−9.7	−80.0	−67.1	−50.1	−90.4
Financial	3 260	−22.6	−16.6	−12.5	−14.2	−7.4	−10.1	−9.2	−17.5
Computer and information	3 262	−1.7	−2.8	−4.7	−12.3	−15.4	−.7	−.8	−3.2
Royalties and licence fees	3 266	−19.1	−19.4	−20.9	−26.8	−27.7	−19.8	−25.7	−30.4
Other business services	3 268	−48.3	−50.7	−50.9	−35.0	−25.1	−14.0	−9.7	−33.4
Personal, cultural, and recreational	3 287	−3.6	−5.0	−6.1	−6.0	−8.1	−9.7	−6.0	−6.0
Government, n.i.e.	3 291	−7.1	−8.9	−5.6	−8.9	−11.2	−14.4	−16.8	−19.4

Table 2 (Continued). STANDARD PRESENTATION, 2003–2010

(Millions of U.S. dollars)

	Code	2003	2004	2005	2006	2007	2008	2009	2010
C. INCOME	4 300	**−361.8**	**−451.2**	**−473.6**	**−536.8**	**−395.2**	**−457.2**	**−530.1**	**−598.0**
Total credit	2 300	*67.9*	*87.5*	*145.1*	*198.2*	*257.2*	*148.1*	*73.9*	*54.6*
Total debit	3 300	*−429.8*	*−538.7*	*−618.7*	*−735.0*	*−652.4*	*−605.3*	*−603.9*	*−652.5*
Compensation of employees, credit	2 310	**23.1**	**31.1**	**29.4**	**29.9**	**32.9**	**13.9**	**9.4**	**8.7**
Compensation of employees, debit	3 310	**−12.0**	**−16.6**	**−.5**	**−2.1**	**−2.5**	**−19.1**	**−27.2**	**−10.1**
Investment income, credit	2 320	**44.9**	**56.4**	**115.6**	**168.3**	**224.3**	**134.2**	**64.5**	**45.8**
Direct investment income	2 330	....	....	....	.7	....	....	.1	....
Dividends and distributed branch profits	2 332	....	....	....	....	....	....	....	....
Reinvested earnings and undistributed branch profits	2 333	....	....	....	....	....	....	....	....
Income on debt (interest)	2 334	....	....	....	.7	....	....	.1	....
Portfolio investment income	2 339	5.0	5.6	6.3	4.8	4.3	3.8	4.5	11.4
Income on equity	2 340	.9	1.2	.6	....	....	....	....	....
Income on bonds and notes	2 350	4.1	4.4	5.6	4.8	4.3	3.8	4.5	11.4
Income on money market instruments	2 360	....	....	....	....	....	....	....	....
Other investment income	2 370	39.9	50.8	109.4	162.8	220.0	130.4	59.9	34.5
Investment income, debit	3 320	**−417.8**	**−522.1**	**−618.2**	**−732.9**	**−649.9**	**−586.1**	**−576.7**	**−642.5**
Direct investment income	3 330	−291.6	−390.4	−479.5	−620.7	−534.9	−488.2	−499.2	−566.6
Dividends and distributed branch profits	3 332	−66.4	−108.8	−103.9	−195.9	−23.9	−29.7	−148.5	−122.8
Reinvested earnings and undistributed branch profits	3 333	−225.2	−280.4	−367.6	−419.4	−504.7	−455.8	−348.0	−439.7
Income on debt (interest)	3 334	−.1	−1.2	−8.0	−5.4	−6.3	−2.7	−2.7	−4.1
Portfolio investment income	3 339	....	....	....	....	....	....	....	−1.0
Income on equity	3 340	....	....	....	....	....	....	....	....
Income on bonds and notes	3 350	....	....	....	....	....	....	....	−1.0
Income on money market instruments	3 360	....	....	....	....	....	....	....	....
Other investment income	3 370	−126.1	−131.7	−138.7	−112.2	−115.0	−97.9	−77.5	−74.8
D. CURRENT TRANSFERS	4 379	**991.2**	**1,265.3**	**1,895.1**	**2,450.3**	**2,671.3**	**2,979.6**	**2,639.0**	**2,760.5**
Credit	2 379	**1,091.9**	**1,374.0**	**2,042.4**	**2,588.8**	**2,825.2**	**3,049.5**	**2,697.0**	**2,818.0**
General government	2 380	201.0	185.5	181.4	195.4	144.3	165.8	131.4	131.3
Other sectors	2 390	890.9	1,188.4	1,861.1	2,393.3	2,681.0	2,883.7	2,565.6	2,686.7
Workers' remittances	2 391	842.3	1,138.0	1,775.8	2,307.4	2,580.7	2,807.5	2,467.9	2,594.1
Other current transfers	2 392	48.6	50.4	85.3	86.0	100.2	76.2	97.7	92.6
Debit	3 379	**−100.7**	**−108.6**	**−147.3**	**−138.4**	**−154.0**	**−69.9**	**−57.9**	**−57.5**
General government	3 380	−7.0	−4.5	−23.0	−4.5	−2.0	−6.3	−8.1	−9.9
Other sectors	3 390	−93.7	−104.1	−124.3	−134.0	−152.0	−63.6	−49.8	−47.7
Workers' remittances	3 391	....	....	....	....	....	....	....	....
Other current transfers	3 392	−93.7	−104.1	−124.3	−134.0	−152.0	−63.6	−49.8	−47.7
CAPITAL AND FINANCIAL ACCOUNT	4 996	**547.7**	**636.8**	**494.7**	**709.2**	**1,469.3**	**1,576.5**	**1,026.0**	**762.7**
CAPITAL ACCOUNT	4 994	**55.7**	**142.1**	**860.1**	**1,639.5**	**1,280.8**	**158.6**	**138.7**	**84.4**
Total credit	2 994	*55.7*	*142.1*	*860.1*	*1,639.5*	*1,280.8*	*158.6*	*138.7*	*84.4*
Total debit	3 994	....	....	....	....	....	....	....	....
Capital transfers, credit	2 400	**55.7**	**142.1**	**860.1**	**1,639.5**	**1,280.8**	**158.6**	**138.7**	**84.4**
General government	2 401	35.9	136.1	844.4	1,607.1	1,245.2	108.3	101.1	47.6
Debt forgiveness	2 402	6.5	91.3	266.6	154.7	74.1	68.8	8.3	....
Other capital transfers	2 410	29.4	44.8	577.8	1,452.4	1,171.1	39.6	92.9	47.6
Other sectors	2 430	19.8	6.0	15.7	32.4	35.6	50.3	37.6	36.9
Migrants' transfers	2 431	18.1	6.0	12.4	30.2	34.0	36.9	34.6	36.9
Debt forgiveness	2 432	....	....	....	....	1.2	....	....	....
Other capital transfers	2 440	1.8	....	3.3	2.2	.5	13.4	3.0	....
Capital transfers, debit	3 400	....	....	....	....	....	....	....	....
General government	3 401	....	....	....	....	....	....	....	....
Debt forgiveness	3 402	....	....	....	....	....	....	....	....
Other capital transfers	3 410	....	....	....	....	....	....	....	....
Other sectors	3 430	....	....	....	....	....	....	....	....
Migrants' transfers	3 431	....	....	....	....	....	....	....	....
Debt forgiveness	3 432	....	....	....	....	....	....	....	....
Other capital transfers	3 440	....	....	....	....	....	....	....	....
Nonproduced nonfinancial assets, credit	2 480	....	....	....	....	....	....	....	....
Nonproduced nonfinancial assets, debit	3 480	....	....	....	....	....	....	....	....

Table 2 (Continued). STANDARD PRESENTATION, 2003–2010

(Millions of U.S. dollars)

	Code	2003	2004	2005	2006	2007	2008	2009	2010
FINANCIAL ACCOUNT........................	4 995 ..	492.0	494.7	−365.4	−930.2	188.5	1,417.9	887.3	678.2
A. DIRECT INVESTMENT....................	4 500 ..	390.6	553.1	600.8	668.5	926.1	930.3	522.5	798.8
Direct investment abroad................	4 505 ..	−12.2	6.2	1.0	−.6	−1.5	1.0	−.7	1.4
Equity capital..............................	4 510 ..	−1.3	....	....	....	....	....	....	....
Claims on affiliated enterprises.......	4 515 ..	....	....	....	....	....	....	....	....
Liabilities to affiliated enterprises....	4 520 ..	−1.3	....	....	....	....	....	....	....
Reinvested earnings......................	4 525 ..	....	....	....	....	....	....	....	....
Other capital..............................	4 530 ..	−10.9	6.2	1.0	−.6	−1.5	1.0	−.7	1.4
Claims on affiliated enterprises.......	4 535 ..	....	6.2	1.0	−.6	−1.5	1.0	−.7	1.4
Liabilities to affiliated enterprises....	4 540 ..	−10.9	....	....	....	....	....	....	....
Direct investment in Honduras.........	4 555 ..	402.8	546.9	599.8	669.1	927.5	929.3	523.2	797.4
Equity capital..............................	4 560 ..	139.6	182.6	169.0	204.1	219.8	429.1	163.2	102.9
Claims on direct investors.............	4 565 ..	....	....	....	....	....	....	....	....
Liabilities to direct investors.........	4 570 ..	139.6	182.6	169.0	204.1	219.8	429.1	163.2	102.9
Reinvested earnings......................	4 575 ..	225.2	280.4	367.6	419.4	504.7	455.8	348.0	439.7
Other capital..............................	4 580 ..	38.1	83.9	63.2	45.6	203.0	44.5	12.1	254.8
Claims on direct investors.............	4 585 ..	.4	−45.5	−1.3	−48.5	−39.4	−116.5	34.6	4.9
Liabilities to direct investors.........	4 590 ..	37.6	129.4	64.5	94.1	242.4	161.0	−22.6	249.9
B. PORTFOLIO INVESTMENT..............	4 600 ..	−7.1	−11.6	−23.1	−20.9	−22.4	−26.8	56.0	−15.0
Assets.......................................	4 602 ..	−7.3	−11.8	−23.1	−20.9	−22.4	−26.8	6.0	−15.0
Equity securities.........................	4 610 ..	−5.7	−1.2	−11.7	1.8	.6	−4.1	.4	2.4
Monetary authorities.....................	4 611 ..	....	....	....	....	....	....	....	....
General government......................	4 612 ..	....	....	....	....	....	....	....	....
Banks.......................................	4 613 ..	....	....	−.4	1.8	.4	−4.1	.4	2.4
Other sectors.............................	4 614 ..	−5.7	−1.2	−11.3	....	.2	....	....	....
Debt securities............................	4 619 ..	−1.6	−10.6	−11.4	−22.7	−23.0	−22.6	5.6	−17.4
Bonds and notes.........................	4 620 ..	−1.6	−10.6	−11.4	−22.7	−23.0	−22.6	5.6	−17.4
Monetary authorities.................	4 621 ..	−1.9	−2.0	−2.2	−2.3	−2.4	−2.7	−2.9	−3.1
General government..................	4 622 ..	−4.1	−4.3	−4.6	−4.8	−10.4	−6.1	−5.8	−6.1
Banks....................................	4 623 ..	....	−4.5	−4.7	−14.5	−10.2	−13.8	14.3	−7.0
Other sectors..........................	4 624 ..	4.4	.2	....	−1.0	....	....	....	−1.2
Money market instruments.............	4 630 ..	....	....	....	....	....	....	....	....
Monetary authorities.................	4 631 ..	....	....	....	....	....	....	....	....
General government..................	4 632 ..	....	....	....	....	....	....	....	....
Banks....................................	4 633 ..	....	....	....	....	....	....	....	....
Other sectors..........................	4 634 ..	....	....	....	....	....	....	....	....
Liabilities..................................	4 652 ..	.2	.2	....	....	....	....	50.0	....
Equity securities.........................	4 660 ..	.2	.2	....	....	....	....	....	....
Banks.......................................	4 663 ..	....	....	....	....	....	....	....	....
Other sectors.............................	4 664 ..	.2	.2	....	....	....	....	....	....
Debt securities............................	4 669 ..	....	....	....	....	....	....	50.0	....
Bonds and notes.........................	4 670 ..	....	....	....	....	....	....	50.0	....
Monetary authorities.................	4 671 ..	....	....	....	....	....	....	....	....
General government..................	4 672 ..	....	....	....	....	....	....	50.0	....
Banks....................................	4 673 ..	....	....	....	....	....	....	....	....
Other sectors..........................	4 674 ..	....	....	....	....	....	....	....	....
Money market instruments.............	4 680 ..	....	....	....	....	....	....	....	....
Monetary authorities.................	4 681 ..	....	....	....	....	....	....	....	....
General government..................	4 682 ..	....	....	....	....	....	....	....	....
Banks....................................	4 683 ..	....	....	....	....	....	....	....	....
Other sectors..........................	4 684 ..	....	....	....	....	....	....	....	....
C. FINANCIAL DERIVATIVES...............	4 910 ..	....	....	....	....	....	....	....	....
Monetary authorities.....................	4 911 ..	....	....	....	....	....	....	....	....
General government......................	4 912 ..	....	....	....	....	....	....	....	....
Banks.......................................	4 913 ..	....	....	....	....	....	....	....	....
Other sectors.............................	4 914 ..	....	....	....	....	....	....	....	....
Assets.......................................	4 900 ..	....	....	....	....	....	....	....	....
Monetary authorities.....................	4 901 ..	....	....	....	....	....	....	....	....
General government......................	4 902 ..	....	....	....	....	....	....	....	....
Banks.......................................	4 903 ..	....	....	....	....	....	....	....	....
Other sectors.............................	4 904 ..	....	....	....	....	....	....	....	....
Liabilities..................................	4 905 ..	....	....	....	....	....	....	....	....
Monetary authorities.....................	4 906 ..	....	....	....	....	....	....	....	....
General government......................	4 907 ..	....	....	....	....	....	....	....	....
Banks.......................................	4 908 ..	....	....	....	....	....	....	....	....
Other sectors.............................	4 909 ..	....	....	....	....	....	....	....	....

2011, International Monetary Fund: *Balance of Payments Statistics Yearbook*

Table 2 (Concluded). STANDARD PRESENTATION, 2003–2010

(Millions of U.S. dollars)

	Code	2003	2004	2005	2006	2007	2008	2009	2010
D. OTHER INVESTMENT..............................	4 700 ..	**11.9**	**463.5**	**−596.7**	**−1,295.8**	**−823.8**	**436.5**	**−38.1**	**485.4**
Assets..	4 703 ..	−62.5	−59.3	12.3	84.4	−29.2	17.6	77.6	88.3
Trade credits...	4 706 ..	−66.3	33.8	12.6	37.9	9.7	2.9	−9.2	9.0
General government...............................	4 707 ..	....	....	....	....	....	....	....	....
of which: Short-term..........................	4 709 ..	....	....	....	....	....	....	....	....
Other sectors...	4 710 ..	−66.3	33.8	12.6	37.9	9.7	2.9	−9.2	9.0
of which: Short-term..........................	4 712 ..	*−66.3*	*33.8*	*12.6*	*37.9*	*9.7*	*2.9*	*−9.2*	*9.0*
Loans..	4 714 ..	−2.6	−17.3	5.9	2.8	−26.1	41.0	−3.6	22.7
Monetary authorities.............................	4 715 ..	....	....	....	....	....	....	....	....
of which: Short-term..........................	4 718 ..	....	....	....	....	....	....	....	....
General government...............................	4 719 ..	....	....	....	....	....	....	....	....
of which: Short-term..........................	4 721 ..	....	....	....	....	....	....	....	....
Banks..	4 722 ..	.2	−1.6	11.2	1.2	−29.3	20.5	−9.1	20.3
of which: Short-term..........................	4 724 ..	*.2*	*−1.6*	*11.2*	*1.2*	*−29.3*	*20.5*	*−9.1*	*20.3*
Other sectors...	4 725 ..	−2.8	−15.7	−5.3	1.6	3.3	20.6	5.5	2.4
of which: Short-term..........................	4 727 ..	....	*−15.9*	*−5.3*	*1.6*	*3.3*	*20.6*	*5.5*	*2.4*
Currency and deposits.............................	4 730 ..	10.9	−69.3	−4.3	55.4	−13.7	−26.3	100.9	63.7
Monetary authorities.............................	4 731 ..	....	....	....	....	....	....	....	....
General government...............................	4 732 ..	−.9	−1.0	....	−.1	−.1	−.1	−.1	−.1
Banks..	4 733 ..	16.8	−94.4	−5.3	22.5	−11.7	−27.3	103.1	63.8
Other sectors...	4 734 ..	−5.0	26.1	1.0	33.0	−1.9	1.1	−2.1	....
Other assets...	4 736 ..	−4.5	−6.5	−1.9	−11.7	1.0	....	−10.5	−7.1
Monetary authorities.............................	4 737 ..	1.0	2.6	−.5	....	....	....	....	....
of which: Short-term..........................	4 739 ..	*1.0*	*2.6*	*−.5*	....	....	....	....	....
General government...............................	4 740 ..	....	....	....	....	....	....	....	....
of which: Short-term..........................	4 742 ..	....	....	....	....	....	....	....	....
Banks..	4 743 ..	....	−.1	....	....	....	....	....	....
of which: Short-term..........................	4 745 ..	....	*−.1*	....	....	....	....	....	....
Other sectors...	4 746 ..	−5.5	−9.0	−1.5	−11.7	1.0	....	−10.5	−7.1
of which: Short-term..........................	4 748 ..	....	*−3.3*	*5.7*	*−.5*	*1.0*	....	*−10.5*	*−7.1*
Liabilities..	4 753 ..	**74.4**	**522.8**	**−609.0**	**−1,380.1**	**−794.6**	**419.0**	**−115.7**	**397.0**
Trade credits...	4 756 ..	.1	23.6	−1.0	−1.0	24.2	20.3	−10.2	−11.3
General government...............................	4 757 ..	....	....	....	....	....	....	....	....
of which: Short-term..........................	4 759 ..	....	....	....	....	....	....	....	....
Other sectors...	4 760 ..	.1	23.6	−1.0	−1.0	24.2	20.3	−10.2	−11.3
of which: Short-term..........................	4 762 ..	*10.9*	*19.6*	*−1.0*	*−1.0*	*24.2*	*19.5*	*−10.4*	*−14.2*
Loans..	4 764 ..	−60.4	413.8	−692.5	−1,388.4	−841.0	352.3	−296.5	397.2
Monetary authorities.............................	4 765 ..	−56.9	−6.3	−44.5	−175.5	−7.8	−18.4	−15.4	−6.6
of which: Use of Fund credit and loans from the Fund..	4 766 ..	*−41.1*	*15.1*	*−11.5*	*−140.8*	....	....	....	*−1.6*
of which: Short-term..........................	4 768 ..	....	....	−9.3	....	....	*−10.6*	*−7.4*	....
General government...............................	4 769 ..	34.8	201.1	−670.1	−1,320.3	−1,028.1	301.8	33.3	380.6
of which: Short-term..........................	4 771 ..	....	*−53.2*	*−141.3*	*−44.9*	*−2.4*	*−25.0*	....	....
Banks..	4 772 ..	−23.4	93.4	84.1	113.4	145.5	15.0	−282.8	29.4
of which: Short-term..........................	4 774 ..	*7.4*	*18.3*	*36.2*	*30.6*	*29.8*	*15.1*	*−173.1*	*60.8*
Other sectors...	4 775 ..	−14.9	125.6	−62.1	−6.0	49.4	53.9	−31.5	−6.1
of which: Short-term..........................	4 777 ..	*20.8*	*−65.8*	*−28.7*	*−40.1*	*−29.9*	*−63.1*	*−11.5*	*8.9*
Currency and deposits.............................	4 780 ..	4.6	12.0	25.6	11.8	16.9	22.0	−15.8	−9.5
Monetary authorities.............................	4 781 ..	3.5	4.8	2.0	2.0	2.6	5.3	.1	3.2
General government...............................	4 782 ..	....	....	....	....	....	....	....	....
Banks..	4 783 ..	1.1	7.2	23.6	9.8	14.3	16.7	−15.8	−12.7
Other sectors...	4 784 ..	....	....	....	....	....	....	....	....
Other liabilities.......................................	4 786 ..	130.1	73.3	58.9	−2.5	5.3	24.4	206.8	20.6
Monetary authorities.............................	4 787 ..	3.2	4.0	3.0	....	3.3	.3	163.7	.1
of which: Short-term..........................	4 789 ..	*3.2*	*4.0*	*3.0*	....	*3.3*	*.3*	....	*.1*
General government...............................	4 790 ..	128.3	49.5	53.2	5.7	2.6	22.7	61.3	23.0
of which: Short-term..........................	4 792 ..	*128.3*	*49.5*	*53.2*	*5.7*	*2.6*	*22.7*	*61.3*	*23.0*
Banks..	4 793 ..	2.6	6.7	....	....	....	....	....	....
of which: Short-term..........................	4 795 ..	*2.6*	*6.7*	....	....	....	....	....	....
Other sectors...	4 796 ..	−4.0	13.1	2.7	−8.2	−.6	1.4	−18.1	−2.4
of which: Short-term..........................	4 798 ..	*−4.0*	*13.1*	*2.7*	*−8.2*	*−.6*	*1.4*	*−18.1*	*−2.4*
E. RESERVE ASSETS..............................	4 802 ..	**96.5**	**−510.4**	**−346.4**	**−282.1**	**108.5**	**77.8**	**346.8**	**−590.9**
Monetary gold...	4 812 ..	....	....	....	....	−.7	.5	−.1	−.5
Special drawing rights.............................	4 811 ..	.4	....	−.2	.3	−.1	....	−163.5	1.8
Reserve position in the Fund....................	4 810 ..	....	....	....	....	....	....	....	....
Foreign exchange.....................................	4 803 ..	96.2	−510.4	−346.2	−282.4	109.3	77.3	510.5	−592.2
Other claims...	4 813 ..	....	....	....	....	....	....	....	....
NET ERRORS AND OMISSIONS..................	4 998 ..	**5.1**	**46.6**	**−190.4**	**−305.4**	**−353.2**	**205.1**	**−510.5**	**192.2**

Table 3. INTERNATIONAL INVESTMENT POSITION (End-period stocks), 2003–2010

(Millions of U.S. dollars)

	Code	2003	2004	2005	2006	2007	2008	2009	2010
ASSETS..	8 995 C.	....	**3,204.8**	**3,613.3**	**4,643.1**	**4,821.3**	**4,846.0**	**4,341.2**	**4,864.2**
Direct investment abroad.................................	8 505 ..	....	**24.6**	**23.6**	**24.8**	**26.3**	**40.1**	**43.7**	**42.3**
Equity capital and reinvested earnings...................	8 506 ..	....	....	....	....	....	....	....	....
Claims on affiliated enterprises......................	8 507 ..	....	....	....	....	....	....	....	....
Liabilities to affiliated enterprises..................	8 508 ..	....	....	....	....	....	....	....	....
Other capital..	8 530 ..	....	24.6	23.6	24.8	26.3	40.1	43.7	42.3
Claims on affiliated enterprises......................	8 535 ..	....	24.6	23.6	24.8	26.3	40.1	43.7	42.3
Liabilities to affiliated enterprises..................	8 540 ..	....	....	....	....	....	....	....	....
Portfolio investment..................................	8 602 ..	....	**174.3**	**193.5**	**218.6**	**241.1**	**272.9**	**260.4**	**275.6**
Equity securities......................................	8 610 ..	....	3.4	15.1	13.3	12.7	20.4	16.3	13.9
Monetary authorities.................................	8 611 ..	....	....	....	....	....	....	....	....
General government..................................	8 612 ..	....	....	....	....	....	....	....	....
Banks..	8 613 ..	....	3.4	3.8	2.0	1.6	9.3	5.2	2.8
Other sectors..	8 614 ..	....		11.3	11.3	11.1	11.1	11.1	11.1
Debt securities..	8 619 ..	....	171.0	178.4	205.3	228.4	252.5	244.1	261.8
Bonds and notes......................................	8 620 ..	....	171.0	178.4	205.3	228.4	252.5	244.1	261.8
Monetary authorities...............................	8 621 ..	....	30.4	32.6	34.9	37.3	40.0	42.9	46.0
General government................................	8 622 ..	....	130.5	133.0	137.9	148.4	154.5	159.8	166.1
Banks..	8 623 ..	....	10.1	12.8	31.5	41.8	57.0	40.4	47.6
Other sectors......................................	8 624 ..	....	....	....	1.0	1.0	1.0	1.0	2.2
Money market instruments............................	8 630 ..	....	....	....	....	....	....	....	....
Monetary authorities...............................	8 631 ..	....	....	....	....	....	....	....	....
General government................................	8 632 ..	....	....	....	....	....	....	....	....
Banks..	8 633 ..	....	....	....	....	....	....	....	....
Other sectors......................................	8 634 ..	....	....	....	....	....	....	....	....
Financial derivatives.................................	8 900 ..	....	....	....	....	....	....	....	....
Monetary authorities..................................	8 901 ..	....	....	....	....	....	....	....	....
General government....................................	8 902 ..	....	....	....	....	....	....	....	....
Banks..	8 903 ..	....	....	....	....	....	....	....	....
Other sectors..	8 904 ..	....	....	....	....	....	....	....	....
Other investment.....................................	8 703 ..	....	**1,056.0**	**1,090.7**	**1,792.2**	**2,045.7**	**2,083.4**	**1,927.9**	**1,845.8**
Trade credits..	8 706 ..	....	50.4	37.8	31.5	54.7	52.1	61.3	52.3
General government..................................	8 707 ..	....	....	....	....	....	....	....	....
of which: Short-term.............................	8 709 ..	....	....	....	....	....	....	....	....
Other sectors..	8 710 ..	....	50.4	37.8	31.5	54.7	52.1	61.3	52.3
of which: Short-term.............................	8 712 ..	....	*50.4*	*37.8*	*31.5*	*54.7*	*52.1*	*61.3*	*52.3*
Loans..	8 714 ..	....	130.7	135.7	131.7	180.4	140.3	141.6	118.0
Monetary authorities.................................	8 715 ..	....	105.5	105.5	105.5	105.5	105.5	105.5	105.5
of which: Short-term.............................	8 718 ..	....	....	....	....	....	....	....	....
General government..................................	8 719 ..	....	....	....	....	....	....	....	....
of which: Short-term.............................	8 721 ..	....	....	....	....	....	....	....	....
Banks..	8 722 ..	....	23.2	22.9	20.5	49.9	30.0	40.8	19.5
of which: Short-term.............................	8 724 ..	....	....	....	....	....	....	....	....
Other sectors..	8 725 ..	....	2.0	7.3	5.7	25.0	4.8	−4.7	−7.1
of which: Short-term.............................	8 727 ..	....	*2.0*	*7.3*	*5.7*	*25.0*	*4.8*	*−4.7*	*−7.1*
Currency and deposits..................................	8 730 ..	....	757.1	797.5	1,508.8	1,691.6	1,771.9	1,595.4	1,539.0
Monetary authorities.................................	8 731 ..	....	....	....	....	....	....	....	....
General government..................................	8 732 ..	....		.1	.3	.4			
Banks..	8 733 ..	....	620.1	626.4	612.5	624.2	652.0	549.5	486.0
Other sectors..	8 734 ..	....	137.0	170.9	896.0	1,067.0	1,120.0	1,046.0	1,053.0
Other assets...	8 736 ..	....	117.8	119.8	120.2	119.0	119.1	129.6	136.6
Monetary authorities.................................	8 737 ..	....	111.2	111.6	111.6	111.4	111.5	111.5	111.5
of which: Short-term.............................	8 739 ..	....	....	....	....	....	....	....	....
General government..................................	8 740 ..	....	....	....	....	....	....	....	....
of which: Short-term.............................	8 742 ..	....	....	....	....	....	....	....	....
Banks..	8 743 ..	....	.1	.1	.1	.1	....	....	....
of which: Short-term.............................	8 745 ..	....	*.1*	*.1*	*.1*	*.1*	....	....	....
Other sectors..	8 746 ..	....	6.6	8.0	8.5	7.5	7.6	18.1	25.1
of which: Short-term.............................	8 748 ..	....	*6.6*	*8.0*	*8.5*	*7.5*	*7.6*	*18.1*	*25.1*
Reserve assets.......................................	8 802 ..	....	**1,949.8**	**2,305.6**	**2,607.5**	**2,508.2**	**2,449.6**	**2,109.2**	**2,700.4**
Monetary gold...	8 812 ..	....	9.9	11.3	13.9	18.2	19.1	24.0	31.1
Special drawing rights.................................	8 811 ..	.1	.1	.3	....	.1	.1	164.3	159.6
Reserve position in the Fund..........................	8 810 ..	12.8	13.4	12.3	13.0	13.6	13.3	13.5	13.3
Foreign exchange......................................	8 803 ..	....	1,926.4	2,281.7	2,580.6	2,476.3	2,417.1	1,907.3	2,496.4
Other claims...	8 813 ..	....	....	....	....	....	....	....	....

Table 3 (Concluded). INTERNATIONAL INVESTMENT POSITION (End-period stocks), 2003–2010

(Millions of U.S. dollars)

	Code	2003	2004	2005	2006	2007	2008	2009	2010
LIABILITIES	8 995 D.	....	**8,675.1**	**8,338.4**	**7,773.2**	**7,888.3**	**9,371.2**	**10,038.9**	**11,224.8**
Direct investment in Honduras	8 555 ..	....	**2,270.1**	**2,838.3**	**3,512.4**	**4,440.0**	**5,472.8**	**5,996.1**	**6,793.4**
Equity capital and reinvested earnings	8 556 ..	....	1,921.6	2,539.7	3,272.9	4,200.1	4,852.6	5,363.8	5,906.4
Claims on direct investors	8 557 ..	....	....	....	....	....	....	....	....
Liabilities to direct investors	8 558 ..	....	1,921.6	2,539.7	3,272.9	4,200.1	4,852.6	5,363.8	5,906.4
Other capital	8 580 ..	....	348.5	298.6	239.5	239.9	620.2	632.3	887.0
Claims on direct investors	8 585 ..	....	....	....	....	....	....	....	....
Liabilities to direct investors	8 590 ..	....	348.5	298.6	239.5	239.9	620.2	632.3	887.0
Portfolio investment	8 652 ..	....	....	....	....	....	**78.3**	**112.1**	**90.0**
Equity securities	8 660 ..	....	....	....	....	....	....	....	....
Banks	8 663 ..	....	....	....	....	....	....	....	....
Other sectors	8 664 ..	....	....	....	....	....	....	....	....
Debt securities	8 669 ..	....	....	....	....	....	78.3	112.1	90.0
Bonds and notes	8 670 ..	....	....	....	....	....	78.3	112.1	90.0
Monetary authorities	8 671 ..	....	....	....	....	....	....	....	....
General government	8 672 ..	....	....	....	....	....	....	50.0	50.0
Banks	8 673 ..	....	....	....	....	....	78.3	62.1	40.0
Other sectors	8 674 ..	....	....	....	....	....	....	....	....
Money market instruments	8 680 ..	....	....	....	....	....	....	....	....
Monetary authorities	8 681 ..	....	....	....	....	....	....	....	....
General government	8 682 ..	....	....	....	....	....	....	....	....
Banks	8 683 ..	....	....	....	....	....	....	....	....
Other sectors	8 684 ..	....	....	....	....	....	....	....	....
Financial derivatives	8 905 ..	....	....	....	....	....	....	....	....
Monetary authorities	8 906 ..	....	....	....	....	....	....	....	....
General government	8 907 ..	....	....	....	....	....	....	....	....
Banks	8 908 ..	....	....	....	....	....	....	....	....
Other sectors	8 909 ..	....	....	....	....	....	....	....	....
Other investment	8 753 ..	....	**6,405.0**	**5,500.1**	**4,260.8**	**3,448.4**	**3,820.0**	**3,930.7**	**4,341.3**
Trade credits	8 756 ..	....	177.2	152.3	145.8	138.4	158.6	151.1	176.6
General government	8 757 ..	....	....	....	....	....	....	....	....
of which: Short-term	8 759 ..	....	....	....	....	....	....	....	....
Other sectors	8 760 ..	....	177.2	152.3	145.8	138.4	158.6	151.1	176.6
of which: Short-term	8 762 ..	....	*135.1*	*136.7*	*135.8*	*128.4*	*147.8*	*140.7*	*128.2*
Loans	8 764 ..	....	6,156.2	5,250.4	4,013.8	3,190.4	3,489.9	3,280.9	3,686.6
Monetary authorities	8 765 ..	....	368.5	323.8	178.6	172.4	164.0	139.5	129.7
of which: Use of Fund credit and loans from the Fund	8 766 ..	*171.5*	*195.2*	*168.1*	*30.6*	*32.1*	*31.3*	*31.9*	*29.8*
of which: Short-term	8 768 ..	....	....	....	....	....	....	....	....
General government	8 769 ..	....	4,909.1	4,024.0	2,815.8	1,801.3	2,120.5	2,226.9	2,601.0
of which: Short-term	8 771 ..	....	....	....	....	....	....	....	....
Banks	8 772 ..	....	346.4	434.3	559.1	705.8	650.5	390.4	439.4
of which: Short-term	8 774 ..	....	*101.3*	*155.3*	*185.9*	*215.7*	*233.0*	*47.9*	*108.6*
Other sectors	8 775 ..	....	532.2	468.4	460.4	510.8	555.0	524.0	516.4
of which: Short-term	8 777 ..	....	*181.6*	*165.9*	*158.8*	*169.7*	*158.6*	*147.1*	*156.0*
Currency and deposits	8 780 ..	....	48.8	72.0	85.5	102.4	124.4	108.6	99.2
Monetary authorities	8 781 ..	....	19.0	21.0	23.0	25.6	30.9	31.0	34.2
General government	8 782 ..	....	....	....	....	....	....	....	....
Banks	8 783 ..	....	29.8	51.0	62.6	76.9	93.5	77.6	64.9
Other sectors	8 784 ..	....	....	....	....	....	....	....	....
Other liabilities	8 786 ..	....	22.8	25.5	15.7	17.1	47.0	390.1	379.0
Monetary authorities	8 787 ..	....	.5	.4	.5	.5	29.0	390.2	381.5
of which: Short-term	8 789 ..	....	*.5*	*.4*	*.5*	*.5*	*29.0*	*196.0*	*190.7*
General government	8 790 ..	....	....	....	....	....	....	....	....
of which: Short-term	8 792 ..	....	....	....	....	....	....	....	....
Banks	8 793 ..	....	....	....	....	....	....	....	....
of which: Short-term	8 795 ..	....	....	....	....	....	....	....	....
Other sectors	8 796 ..	....	22.4	25.1	15.2	16.7	18.0	−.1	−2.5
of which: Short-term	8 798 ..	....	*22.4*	*25.1*	*15.2*	*16.7*	*18.0*	*−.1*	*−2.5*
NET INTERNATIONAL INVESTMENT POSITION	8 995 ..	....	−5,470.4	−4,725.1	−3,130.1	−3,067.0	−4,525.2	−5,697.7	−6,360.6
Conversion rates: lempiras per U.S. dollar (end of period)	0 102 ..	17.7482	18.6328	18.8952	18.8952	18.8951	18.8951	18.8951	18.8951

Table 1. ANALYTIC PRESENTATION, 2003–2010

(Millions of U.S. dollars)

	Code	2003	2004	2005	2006	2007	2008	2009	2010
A. Current Account[1]	4 993 Z.	**−6,721**	**−8,809**	**−8,343**	**−8,626**	**−9,578**	**−11,116**	**473**	**3,049**
Goods: exports f.o.b.	2 100 ..	42,943	55,343	61,687	73,455	93,844	107,239	81,563	93,294
Goods: imports f.o.b.	3 100 ..	−46,221	−59,204	−64,825	−76,539	−94,019	−108,031	−76,780	−87,082
Balance on Goods	4 100 ..	*−3,279*	*−3,861*	*−3,138*	*−3,084*	*−175*	*−792*	*4,782*	*6,212*
Services: credit	2 200 ..	9,211	10,769	12,857	13,704	17,281	20,277	18,578	19,056
Services: debit	3 200 ..	−9,150	−10,178	−11,448	−12,135	−15,846	−18,822	−16,669	−15,879
Balance on Goods and Services	4 991 ..	*−3,217*	*−3,269*	*−1,729*	*−1,515*	*1,259*	*663*	*6,691*	*9,389*
Income: credit	2 300 ..	1,371	3,277	3,533	8,339	12,840	16,296	16,982	15,552
Income: debit	3 300 ..	−5,541	−8,642	−9,778	−15,058	−22,995	−27,232	−23,711	−22,389
Balance on Goods, Services, and Income	4 992 ..	*−7,388*	*−8,635*	*−7,974*	*−8,234*	*−8,896*	*−10,273*	*−38*	*2,552*
Current transfers: credit	2 379 Z.	1,283	2,203	2,992	3,343	4,082	2,657	3,401	3,410
Current transfers: debit	3 379 ..	−616	−2,377	−3,361	−3,736	−4,764	−3,500	−2,890	−2,913
B. Capital Account[1]	4 994 Z.	**−27**	**98**	**740**	**748**	**979**	**1,649**	**1,493**	**2,295**
Capital account: credit	2 994 Z.	240	288	858	1,286	1,423	1,709	2,483	2,972
Capital account: debit	3 994 ..	−267	−190	−118	−538	−444	−61	−990	−677
Total, Groups A Plus B	4 981 ..	*−6,748*	*−8,711*	*−7,603*	*−7,878*	*−8,599*	*−9,467*	*1,965*	*5,343*
C. Financial Account[1]	4 995 W.	**6,858**	**12,791**	**14,982**	**11,477**	**9,486**	**17,133**	**2,775**	**2,078**
Direct investment abroad	4 505 ..	−1,661	−1,116	−2,230	−18,601	−67,679	−70,261	−3,482	45,187
Direct investment in Hungary	4 555 Z.	2,177	4,282	7,626	19,522	70,843	72,257	3,354	−41,989
Portfolio investment assets	4 602 ..	15	−526	−1,283	−2,427	−2,869	−3,854	−1,061	−437
Equity securities	4 610 ..	−42	−524	−747	−1,907	−2,574	−3,296	−1,132	−678
Debt securities	4 619 ..	57	−3	−536	−520	−295	−559	71	241
Portfolio investment liabilities	4 652 Z.	2,902	7,353	5,784	8,751	526	910	−3,724	604
Equity securities	4 660 ..	269	1,491	−16	912	−5,010	−197	954	−97
Debt securities	4 669 Z.	2,633	5,862	5,801	7,839	5,536	1,107	−4,678	701
Financial derivatives	4 910 ..	251	412	−151	187	1,121	−1,063	1,034	839
Financial derivatives assets	4 900 ..	2,320	4,214	3,621	4,570	6,336	12,981	7,766	6,518
Financial derivatives liabilities	4 905 ..	−2,069	−3,802	−3,771	−4,383	−5,215	−14,044	−6,732	−5,679
Other investment assets	4 703 ..	−2,827	−1,543	−2,324	−3,604	−7,977	−3,574	−1,049	−906
Monetary authorities	4 701 ..	−1,049	1,100	−11	....	....	....	....	....
General government	4 704 ..	198	−203	−212	431	−863	−141	−477	−173
Banks	4 705 ..	−951	−349	−165	−2,983	−3,898	−3,543	144	1,598
Other sectors	4 728 ..	−1,026	−2,090	−1,935	−1,052	−3,216	110	−715	−2,330
Other investment liabilities	4 753 W.	6,000	3,930	7,559	7,648	15,521	22,719	7,702	−1,220
Monetary authorities	4 753 WA	569	−916	−36	56	−112	785	2,722	3,377
General government	4 753 ZB	319	561	560	720	2,894	3,282	6,027	985
Banks	4 753 ZC	3,986	2,662	4,575	4,368	6,458	13,820	−3,148	−4,233
Other sectors	4 753 ZD	1,126	1,622	2,461	2,504	6,281	4,832	2,101	−1,348
Total, Groups A Through C	4 983 ..	*110*	*4,081*	*7,379*	*3,599*	*887*	*7,666*	*4,740*	*7,422*
D. Net Errors and Omissions	4 998 ..	**226**	**−2,100**	**−2,475**	**−2,497**	**−733**	**−3,493**	**−775**	**−3,259**
Total, Groups A Through D	4 984 ..	*336*	*1,981*	*4,904*	*1,102*	*154*	*4,173*	*3,965*	*4,162*
E. Reserves and Related Items	4 802 A.	**−336**	**−1,981**	**−4,904**	**−1,102**	**−154**	**−4,173**	**−3,965**	**−4,162**
Reserve assets	4 802 ..	−336	−1,981	−4,904	−1,102	−154	−10,424	−9,123	−4,162
Use of Fund credit and loans	4 766 ..	....	....	....	....	....	6,251	5,158	....
Exceptional financing	4 920 ..	....	....	....	....	....	....	....	....
Conversion rates: forint per U.S. dollar	0 101 ..	**224.31**	**202.75**	**199.58**	**210.39**	**183.63**	**172.11**	**202.34**	**207.94**

[1] Excludes components that have been classified in the categories of Group E.

Table 2. STANDARD PRESENTATION, 2003–2010

(Millions of U.S. dollars)

	Code	2003	2004	2005	2006	2007	2008	2009	2010
CURRENT ACCOUNT	4 993 ..	**−6,721**	**−8,809**	**−8,343**	**−8,626**	**−9,578**	**−11,116**	**473**	**3,049**
A. GOODS	4 100 ..	**−3,279**	**−3,861**	**−3,138**	**−3,084**	**−175**	**−792**	**4,782**	**6,212**
Credit	2 100 ..	**42,943**	**55,343**	**61,687**	**73,455**	**93,844**	**107,239**	**81,563**	**93,294**
General merchandise: exports f.o.b.	2 110 ..	41,321	53,822	60,368	72,119	92,362	105,707	80,446	92,077
Goods for processing: exports f.o.b.	2 150 ..	1,575	1,434	1,108	1,133	1,228	1,243	831	921
Repairs on goods	2 160 ..	47	86	211	203	255	289	285	295
Goods procured in ports by carriers	2 170 ..	....	....	....	....	....	....	....	....
Nonmonetary gold	2 180 ..	....	....	....	....	....	....	....	....
Debit	3 100 ..	**−46,221**	**−59,204**	**−64,825**	**−76,539**	**−94,019**	**−108,031**	**−76,780**	**−87,082**
General merchandise: imports f.o.b.	3 110 ..	−46,060	−58,982	−64,613	−76,239	−93,578	−107,488	−76,300	−86,801
Goods for processing: imports f.o.b.	3 150 ..	−110	−191	−172	−237	−359	−446	−380	−152
Repairs on goods	3 160 ..	−51	−32	−39	−64	−82	−97	−100	−129
Goods procured in ports by carriers	3 170 ..	....	....	....	....	....	....	....	....
Nonmonetary gold	3 180 ..	....	....	....	....	....	....	....	....
B. SERVICES	4 200 ..	**61**	**592**	**1,409**	**1,569**	**1,434**	**1,455**	**1,908**	**3,177**
Total credit	2 200 ..	*9,211*	*10,769*	*12,857*	*13,704*	*17,281*	*20,277*	*18,578*	*19,056*
Total debit	3 200 ..	*−9,150*	*−10,178*	*−11,448*	*−12,135*	*−15,846*	*−18,822*	*−16,669*	*−15,879*
Transportation services, credit	2 205 ..	**1,020**	**1,330**	**2,129**	**2,643**	**3,324**	**3,991**	**3,438**	**3,667**
Passenger	2 850 ..	*58*	*95*	*641*	*744*	*889*	*1,080*	*1,028*	*1,008*
Freight	2 851 ..	*615*	*849*	*706*	*909*	*1,258*	*1,440*	*1,280*	*1,378*
Other	2 852 ..	*346*	*386*	*783*	*990*	*1,176*	*1,472*	*1,130*	*1,281*
Sea transport, passenger	2 207 ..	....	....	....	....	....	....	....	....
Sea transport, freight	2 208 ..	....	....	17	11	8	7	7	8
Sea transport, other	2 209 ..	....	....	16	19	25	33	24	35
Air transport, passenger	2 211 ..	....	....	609	715	846	1,041	996	977
Air transport, freight	2 212 ..	....	....	22	41	48	50	39	40
Air transport, other	2 213 ..	....	....	266	265	284	414	335	365
Other transport, passenger	2 215 ..	....	....	31	29	43	39	32	31
Other transport, freight	2 216 ..	....	....	667	857	1,202	1,383	1,234	1,330
Other transport, other	2 217 ..	....	....	501	707	867	1,025	770	881
Transportation services, debit	3 205 ..	**−1,397**	**−1,567**	**−2,216**	**−2,475**	**−3,050**	**−3,604**	**−2,843**	**−3,099**
Passenger	3 850 ..	*−106*	*−61*	*−444*	*−440*	*−542*	*−608*	*−483*	*−455*
Freight	3 851 ..	*−795*	*−992*	*−974*	*−1,038*	*−1,308*	*−1,551*	*−1,170*	*−1,311*
Other	3 852 ..	*−496*	*−514*	*−797*	*−997*	*−1,200*	*−1,446*	*−1,190*	*−1,333*
Sea transport, passenger	3 207 ..	....	....	....	....	....	....	....	....
Sea transport, freight	3 208 ..	....	....	−40	−38	−38	−72	−55	−58
Sea transport, other	3 209 ..	....	....	−64	−57	−73	−101	−69	−95
Air transport, passenger	3 211 ..	....	....	−428	−424	−519	−590	−468	−441
Air transport, freight	3 212 ..	....	....	−54	−46	−42	−82	−64	−81
Air transport, other	3 213 ..	....	....	−320	−432	−491	−594	−549	−615
Other transport, passenger	3 215 ..	....	....	−16	−17	−24	−18	−15	−14
Other transport, freight	3 216 ..	....	....	−880	−955	−1,227	−1,397	−1,051	−1,172
Other transport, other	3 217 ..	....	....	−414	−508	−636	−751	−572	−623
Travel, credit	2 236 ..	**4,061**	**3,914**	**4,120**	**4,254**	**4,739**	**6,033**	**5,712**	**5,339**
Business travel	2 237 ..	376	570	763	788	903	987	830	785
Personal travel	2 240 ..	3,685	3,344	3,357	3,466	3,836	5,046	4,881	4,554
Travel, debit	3 236 ..	**−2,594**	**−2,421**	**−2,382**	**−2,126**	**−2,949**	**−4,037**	**−3,638**	**−2,958**
Business travel	3 237 ..	−341	−223	−353	−512	−760	−1,415	−1,570	−1,085
Personal travel	3 240 ..	−2,254	−2,198	−2,029	−1,614	−2,190	−2,622	−2,068	−1,874
Other services, credit	2 200 BA	**4,130**	**5,526**	**6,608**	**6,807**	**9,218**	**10,253**	**9,428**	**10,050**
Communications	2 245 ..	208	292	341	399	438	545	465	421
Construction	2 249 ..	198	167	173	392	527	612	491	418
Insurance	2 253 ..	33	38	7	14	22	29	19	27
Financial	2 260 ..	191	250	146	159	256	251	182	161
Computer and information	2 262 ..	244	338	382	511	842	1,132	1,160	1,220
Royalties and licence fees	2 266 ..	313	540	837	550	920	864	831	1,028
Other business services	2 268 ..	2,018	2,670	3,325	3,609	4,736	5,678	5,071	5,384
Personal, cultural, and recreational	2 287 ..	845	1,167	1,272	1,066	1,360	999	1,074	1,270
Government, n.i.e.	2 291 ..	80	65	125	106	118	143	135	122
Other services, debit	3 200 BA	**−5,158**	**−6,189**	**−6,851**	**−7,534**	**−9,847**	**−11,181**	**−10,188**	**−9,821**
Communications	3 245 ..	−181	−311	−355	−462	−582	−567	−501	−449
Construction	3 249 ..	−203	−62	−101	−237	−354	−408	−397	−372
Insurance	3 253 ..	−211	−215	−202	−205	−200	−202	−283	−163
Financial	3 260 ..	−277	−376	−186	−208	−292	−304	−256	−207
Computer and information	3 262 ..	−267	−392	−494	−563	−693	−804	−702	−717
Royalties and licence fees	3 266 ..	−464	−1,054	−1,108	−1,169	−1,752	−2,008	−1,438	−1,332
Other business services	3 268 ..	−2,582	−2,597	−3,088	−3,636	−4,768	−5,708	−5,490	−5,428
Personal, cultural, and recreational	3 287 ..	−845	−1,048	−1,144	−861	−976	−917	−905	−973
Government, n.i.e.	3 291 ..	−128	−134	−173	−192	−230	−262	−217	−181

Table 2 (Continued). STANDARD PRESENTATION, 2003–2010

(Millions of U.S. dollars)

	Code	2003	2004	2005	2006	2007	2008	2009	2010
C. INCOME	4 300	**−4,170**	**−5,365**	**−6,245**	**−6,719**	**−10,155**	**−10,936**	**−6,729**	**−6,837**
Total credit	2 300	*1,371*	*3,277*	*3,533*	*8,339*	*12,840*	*16,296*	*16,982*	*15,552*
Total debit	3 300	*−5,541*	*−8,642*	*−9,778*	*−15,058*	*−22,995*	*−27,232*	*−23,711*	*−22,389*
Compensation of employees, credit	2 310	**249**	**1,655**	**1,852**	**2,019**	**2,252**	**2,461**	**2,087**	**2,221**
Compensation of employees, debit	3 310	**−91**	**−728**	**−814**	**−874**	**−1,256**	**−1,405**	**−1,107**	**−1,143**
Investment income, credit	2 320	**1,122**	**1,622**	**1,682**	**6,320**	**10,588**	**13,835**	**14,894**	**13,331**
Direct investment income	2 330	150	697	649	4,867	8,493	11,399	12,818	11,374
Dividends and distributed branch profits	2 332	39	145	460	2,643	3,478	3,207	1,910	2,105
Reinvested earnings and undistributed branch profits	2 333	88	497	114	1,324	3,811	5,208	8,978	7,690
Income on debt (interest)	2 334	23	56	75	900	1,204	2,985	1,931	1,578
Portfolio investment income	2 339	606	434	567	773	997	1,262	1,302	1,364
Income on equity	2 340	18	23	53	64	95	207	206	243
Income on bonds and notes	2 350	525	344	426	553	668	846	866	948
Income on money market instruments	2 360	63	67	89	157	235	209	230	173
Other investment income	2 370	366	491	465	679	1,097	1,174	774	593
Investment income, debit	3 320	**−5,450**	**−7,914**	**−8,964**	**−14,184**	**−21,739**	**−25,827**	**−22,604**	**−21,246**
Direct investment income	3 330	−3,597	−5,495	−5,900	−10,636	−16,524	−18,725	−17,310	−16,597
Dividends and distributed branch profits	3 332	−1,426	−2,213	−3,028	−6,320	−8,394	−9,659	−9,321	−8,896
Reinvested earnings and undistributed branch profits	3 333	−2,057	−2,829	−2,308	−3,243	−6,918	−5,748	−4,129	−3,918
Income on debt (interest)	3 334	−113	−452	−564	−1,073	−1,212	−3,318	−3,859	−3,783
Portfolio investment income	3 339	−1,225	−1,671	−2,196	−2,406	−3,284	−3,691	−2,627	−2,485
Income on equity	3 340	−52	−194	−373	−415	−749	−592	−174	−165
Income on bonds and notes	3 350	−1,172	−1,477	−1,822	−1,989	−2,531	−3,008	−2,315	−2,216
Income on money market instruments	3 360	−1	....	−1	−1	−4	−91	−137	−104
Other investment income	3 370	−628	−748	−869	−1,142	−1,930	−3,411	−2,667	−2,163
D. CURRENT TRANSFERS	4 379	**667**	**−174**	**−369**	**−392**	**−682**	**−843**	**511**	**497**
Credit	2 379	**1,283**	**2,203**	**2,992**	**3,343**	**4,082**	**2,657**	**3,401**	**3,410**
General government	2 380	290	737	1,041	1,064	1,506	854	1,059	1,037
Other sectors	2 390	993	1,466	1,951	2,279	2,576	1,803	2,342	2,373
Workers' remittances	2 391	39	46	61	54	57	48	43	44
Other current transfers	2 392	954	1,421	1,890	2,225	2,519	1,755	2,299	2,329
Debit	3 379	**−616**	**−2,377**	**−3,361**	**−3,736**	**−4,764**	**−3,500**	**−2,890**	**−2,913**
General government	3 380	−162	−715	−1,431	−1,319	−1,569	−1,251	−1,126	−1,149
Other sectors	3 390	−454	−1,662	−1,930	−2,417	−3,195	−2,249	−1,764	−1,764
Workers' remittances	3 391	−20	−83	−98	−107	−111	−131	−116	−122
Other current transfers	3 392	−434	−1,579	−1,832	−2,310	−3,084	−2,118	−1,648	−1,642
CAPITAL AND FINANCIAL ACCOUNT	4 996	**6,495**	**10,908**	**10,818**	**11,123**	**10,311**	**14,608**	**303**	**210**
CAPITAL ACCOUNT	4 994	**−27**	**98**	**740**	**748**	**979**	**1,649**	**1,493**	**2,295**
Total credit	2 994	*240*	*288*	*858*	*1,286*	*1,423*	*1,709*	*2,483*	*2,972*
Total debit	3 994	*−267*	*−190*	*−118*	*−538*	*−444*	*−61*	*−990*	*−677*
Capital transfers, credit	2 400	**215**	**270**	**807**	**1,185**	**1,214**	**1,267**	**2,472**	**2,947**
General government	2 401	96	57	280	591	832	535	1,267	1,969
Debt forgiveness	2 402	....	....	....	....	....	....	....	....
Other capital transfers	2 410	96	57	280	591	832	535	1,267	1,969
Other sectors	2 430	119	214	527	595	381	732	1,205	978
Migrants' transfers	2 431	7	16	18	6	2	....	....	....
Debt forgiveness	2 432	....	....	....	....	....	....	....	....
Other capital transfers	2 440	112	197	509	589	379	732	1,205	978
Capital transfers, debit	3 400	**−164**	**−59**	**−84**	**−458**	**−122**	**−13**	**−112**	**−269**
General government	3 401	−132	−20	−23	−272	−34	....	−47	−59
Debt forgiveness	3 402	....	....	....	....	....	....	....	....
Other capital transfers	3 410	−132	−20	−23	−272	−34	....	−47	−59
Other sectors	3 430	−32	−39	−61	−187	−88	−13	−65	−210
Migrants' transfers	3 431	−3	−3	−3	−5	−7	....	....	....
Debt forgiveness	3 432	....	....	....	....	....	....	....	....
Other capital transfers	3 440	−28	−37	−58	−182	−82	−13	−65	−210
Nonproduced nonfinancial assets, credit	2 480	**25**	**18**	**51**	**100**	**209**	**443**	**10**	**26**
Nonproduced nonfinancial assets, debit	3 480	**−104**	**−131**	**−34**	**−80**	**−322**	**−48**	**−879**	**−408**

Table 2 (Continued). STANDARD PRESENTATION, 2003–2010

(Millions of U.S. dollars)

	Code	2003	2004	2005	2006	2007	2008	2009	2010
FINANCIAL ACCOUNT	4 995	**6,522**	**10,810**	**10,078**	**10,375**	**9,332**	**12,960**	**−1,190**	**−2,084**
A. DIRECT INVESTMENT	4 500	**516**	**3,166**	**5,396**	**922**	**3,165**	**1,995**	**−128**	**3,198**
Direct investment abroad	4 505	**−1,661**	**−1,116**	**−2,230**	**−18,601**	**−67,679**	**−70,261**	**−3,482**	**45,187**
Equity capital	4 510	−1,462	−533	−2,324	−15,933	−62,506	−65,613	4,513	52,326
Claims on affiliated enterprises	4 515	−1,462	−533	−2,324	−15,933	−62,506	−65,613	4,513	52,326
Liabilities to affiliated enterprises	4 520	....	....	....	....	....	....	....	....
Reinvested earnings	4 525	−88	−497	−114	−1,324	−3,811	−5,208	−8,978	−7,690
Other capital	4 530	−111	−86	208	−1,343	−1,362	559	982	551
Claims on affiliated enterprises	4 535	−170	−63	−113	−1,370	−1,353	552	−871	−81
Liabilities to affiliated enterprises	4 540	59	−23	321	27	−9	6	1,853	632
Direct investment in Hungary	4 555	**2,177**	**4,282**	**7,626**	**19,522**	**70,843**	**72,257**	**3,354**	**−41,989**
Equity capital	4 560	−862	1,322	4,833	9,770	53,529	36,084	−11,050	−13,208
Claims on direct investors	4 565	....	....	....	....	....	....	....	....
Liabilities to direct investors	4 570	−862	1,322	4,833	9,770	53,529	36,084	−11,050	−13,208
Reinvested earnings	4 575	2,057	2,829	2,308	3,243	6,918	5,748	4,129	3,918
Other capital	4 580	982	131	485	6,510	10,396	30,425	10,274	−32,699
Claims on direct investors	4 585	−1,921	−279	−558	871	203	−2,535	9,911	−14,760
Liabilities to direct investors	4 590	2,903	410	1,043	5,639	10,193	32,960	363	−17,939
B. PORTFOLIO INVESTMENT	4 600	**2,917**	**6,826**	**4,501**	**6,324**	**−2,343**	**−2,945**	**−4,785**	**167**
Assets	4 602	**15**	**−526**	**−1,283**	**−2,427**	**−2,869**	**−3,854**	**−1,061**	**−437**
Equity securities	4 610	−42	−524	−747	−1,907	−2,574	−3,296	−1,132	−678
Monetary authorities	4 611	....	....	....	....	....	....	....	....
General government	4 612	....	....	....	....	....	....	....	....
Banks	4 613	−22	−35	70	13	9	....	....	....
Other sectors	4 614	−20	−489	−817	−1,920	−2,582	−3,296	−1,132	−678
Debt securities	4 619	57	−3	−536	−520	−295	−559	71	241
Bonds and notes	4 620	73	16	−503	−532	−286	−540	88	225
Monetary authorities	4 621	....	....	....	....	....	....	....	....
General government	4 622	....	....	....	....	....	....	....	−38
Banks	4 623	−59	38	−51	−248	279	121	−41	−58
Other sectors	4 624	132	−22	−451	−284	−565	−660	129	322
Money market instruments	4 630	−16	−19	−34	12	−9	−19	−17	15
Monetary authorities	4 631	....	....	....	....	....	....	....	....
General government	4 632	....	....	....	....	....	....	....	....
Banks	4 633	9		−22	14	−4	5	−8	3
Other sectors	4 634	−25	−19	−11	−2	−5	−24	−9	12
Liabilities	4 652	**2,902**	**7,353**	**5,784**	**8,751**	**526**	**910**	**−3,724**	**604**
Equity securities	4 660	269	1,491	−16	912	−5,010	−197	954	−97
Banks	4 663	40	172	−277	799	−146	−1,306	755	−131
Other sectors	4 664	229	1,319	261	113	−4,864	1,109	199	33
Debt securities	4 669	2,633	5,862	5,801	7,839	5,536	1,107	−4,678	701
Bonds and notes	4 670	2,712	5,633	6,107	7,601	5,442	995	−4,641	−264
Monetary authorities	4 671	−1,739	−1,274	−868	−21	−382	−147	....	−87
General government	4 672	4,039	5,325	4,622	4,204	3,360	−1,100	−2,022	1,785
Banks	4 673	413	1,483	1,328	3,231	2,551	2,429	−2,567	−2,749
Other sectors	4 674	−1	99	1,025	187	−88	−186	−52	786
Money market instruments	4 680	−78	229	−306	238	94	112	−37	965
Monetary authorities	4 681	....	....	....	....	−12	....	76	844
General government	4 682	−85	230	−306	239	86	121	−113	122
Banks	4 683	7	....	....	....	22	40	....	1
Other sectors	4 684	....	−1	....	....	−2	−49	1	−1
C. FINANCIAL DERIVATIVES	4 910	**251**	**412**	**−151**	**187**	**1,121**	**−1,063**	**1,034**	**839**
Monetary authorities	4 911	139	35	−320	31	−103	−454	57	31
General government	4 912	....	24	52	48	10	−52	−115	158
Banks	4 913	267	714	125	−15	1,360	506	1,030	349
Other sectors	4 914	−155	−361	−8	124	−147	−1,063	61	302
Assets	4 900	**2,320**	**4,214**	**3,621**	**4,570**	**6,336**	**12,981**	**7,766**	**6,518**
Monetary authorities	4 901	324	277	153	284	249	305	438	420
General government	4 902	....	....	67	86	60	5	−42	198
Banks	4 903	2,049	3,414	2,974	3,930	5,844	10,732	6,474	4,109
Other sectors	4 904	−53	523	425	270	183	1,939	897	1,791
Liabilities	4 905	**−2,069**	**−3,802**	**−3,771**	**−4,383**	**−5,215**	**−14,044**	**−6,732**	**−5,679**
Monetary authorities	4 906	−185	−243	−473	−253	−351	−759	−381	−389
General government	4 907	....	24	−15	−38	−50	−57	−73	−40
Banks	4 908	−1,782	−2,700	−2,850	−3,946	−4,483	−10,226	−5,444	−3,760
Other sectors	4 909	−102	−884	−433	−146	−330	−3,002	−835	−1,490

Table 2 (Concluded). STANDARD PRESENTATION, 2003–2010

(Millions of U.S. dollars)

	Code	2003	2004	2005	2006	2007	2008	2009	2010
D. OTHER INVESTMENT	4 700	**3,173**	**2,387**	**5,236**	**4,044**	**7,543**	**25,396**	**11,812**	**−2,125**
Assets	4 703	**−2,827**	**−1,543**	**−2,324**	**−3,604**	**−7,977**	**−3,574**	**−1,049**	**−906**
Trade credits	4 706	−300	−416	−984	−1,159	−925	−19	131	−831
General government	4 707	199	−23	−13	481	34	1	....	....
of which: Short-term	4 709	....	....	....	....	....	....	....	....
Other sectors	4 710	−498	−394	−971	−1,640	−959	−20	131	−831
of which: Short-term	4 712	−584	−380	−777	−1,828	−911	−13	143	−827
Loans	4 714	−2,687	−236	−1,666	−95	−5,446	−4,533	682	1,740
Monetary authorities	4 715	−1,049	−7	....	....	....	....	....	....
of which: Short-term	4 718	−1,049	....	....	....	....	....	....	....
General government	4 719	....	−10	−57	−100	−428	−5	6	1
of which: Short-term	4 721	−9	−6	−57	−127	−425	....	....	....
Banks	4 722	−1,101	1,021	−729	−1,545	−4,167	−4,585	798	1,716
of which: Short-term	4 724	−727	741	−131	−170	−449	−151	181	−392
Other sectors	4 725	−537	−1,240	−880	1,551	−851	57	−121	23
of which: Short-term	4 727	−629	−1,074	−765	1,565	−595	21	−28	−11
Currency and deposits	4 730	159	−384	525	−2,098	−1,459	350	−1,199	−1,127
Monetary authorities	4 731	....	1,106	....	....	....	....	....	....
General government	4 732	....	....	....	....	....	67	−39	211
Banks	4 733	150	−1,370	579	−1,438	265	1,190	−707	63
Other sectors	4 734	9	−120	−54	−661	−1,724	−907	−452	−1,401
Other assets	4 736	....	−507	−198	−252	−148	629	−663	−688
Monetary authorities	4 737	....	....	−11	....	....	....	....	....
of which: Short-term	4 739	....	....	....	....	....	....	....	....
General government	4 740	....	−170	−142	50	−470	−204	−444	−386
of which: Short-term	4 742	....	−137	−105	86	−392	−120	−402	−382
Banks	4 743	....	....	−15	....	4	−148	53	−182
of which: Short-term	4 745	....	....	....	....	....	−147	53	−182
Other sectors	4 746	....	−337	−29	−302	318	981	−272	−120
of which: Short-term	4 748	....	−337	−29	−299	317	988	−217	−103
Liabilities	4 753	**6,000**	**3,930**	**7,559**	**7,648**	**15,521**	**28,969**	**12,860**	**−1,220**
Trade credits	4 756	20	294	791	1,367	830	−466	771	582
General government	4 757	....	....	....	....	....	....	....	....
of which: Short-term	4 759	....	....	....	....	....	....	....	....
Other sectors	4 760	20	294	791	1,367	830	−466	771	582
of which: Short-term	4 762	20	294	676	1,106	1,210	−437	770	571
Loans	4 764	6,096	2,498	2,995	3,155	7,696	19,025	12,926	−368
Monetary authorities	4 765	569	−787	43	59	−87	6,843	6,413	3,297
of which: Use of Fund credit and loans from the Fund..	4 766	....	....	....	....	....	6,251	5,158	....
of which: Short-term	4 768	625	−787	50	59	−87	592	1,255	3,297
General government	4 769	319	161	415	809	1,843	3,105	5,495	1,335
of which: Short-term	4 771	....	4	....	....	450	−84	−345	949
Banks	4 772	4,158	2,006	1,302	1,778	663	3,915	−390	−3,135
of which: Short-term	4 774	2,287	−128	265	−102	75	403	1,499	−1,105
Other sectors	4 775	1,051	1,119	1,234	509	5,277	5,162	1,407	−1,866
of which: Short-term	4 777	237	681	215	42	1,002	541	−51	−573
Currency and deposits	4 780	−116	912	3,622	3,180	6,002	10,185	−2,840	−1,001
Monetary authorities	4 781	1	−31	−39	−3	−25	192	−82	79
General government	4 782	....	....	....	....	....	....	....	....
Banks	4 783	−171	851	3,301	2,623	5,729	9,993	−2,758	−1,080
Other sectors	4 784	55	91	361	560	298	....	....	....
Other liabilities	4 786	....	227	152	−54	993	225	2,004	−432
Monetary authorities	4 787	....	−98	−40	....	....	....	1,550	....
of which: Short-term	4 789	....	−98	−40	....	....	....	....	....
General government	4 790	....	401	145	−89	1,051	177	532	−350
of which: Short-term	4 792	....	401	145	−89	1,051	177	532	−350
Banks	4 793	....	−195	−28	−33	65	−88	....	−18
of which: Short-term	4 795	....	−195	−28	−33	65	−88	....	−18
Other sectors	4 796	....	119	75	68	−123	136	−78	−64
of which: Short-term	4 798	....	128	74	−43	8	130	−72	−65
E. RESERVE ASSETS	4 802	**−336**	**−1,981**	**−4,904**	**−1,102**	**−154**	**−10,424**	**−9,123**	**−4,162**
Monetary gold	4 812	....	1	....	....	....	....	....	....
Special drawing rights	4 811	−10	−9	−10	−7	−6	25	−1,421	296
Reserve position in the Fund	4 810	−23	161	309	64	29	−4	....	....
Foreign exchange	4 803	92	−2,143	−4,898	−1,580	−186	−10,369	−6,849	−5,458
Other claims	4 813	−395	10	−304	420	9	−76	−853	999
NET ERRORS AND OMISSIONS	4 998	**226**	**−2,100**	**−2,475**	**−2,497**	**−733**	**−3,493**	**−775**	**−3,259**

Table 3. INTERNATIONAL INVESTMENT POSITION (End-period stocks), 2003–2010

(Millions of U.S. dollars)

	Code	2003	2004	2005	2006	2007	2008	2009	2010
ASSETS	8 995 C.	**32,540**	**47,213**	**51,878**	**116,675**	**210,450**	**264,558**	**273,550**	**231,047**
Direct investment abroad	8 505	**3,509**	**6,018**	**7,810**	**57,114**	**133,141**	**189,262**	**183,742**	**139,792**
Equity capital and reinvested earnings	8 506	3,205	5,603	7,636	55,103	129,076	185,875	181,336	138,331
Claims on affiliated enterprises	8 507	3,205	5,603	7,636	55,103	129,076	185,887	181,336	138,331
Liabilities to affiliated enterprises	8 508	....	....	....	....	....	−13	....	....
Other capital	8 530	304	415	174	2,011	4,065	3,387	2,406	1,461
Claims on affiliated enterprises	8 535	382	473	546	2,463	4,575	4,782	5,703	5,370
Liabilities to affiliated enterprises	8 540	−78	−58	−371	−453	−510	−1,394	−3,296	−3,909
Portfolio investment	8 602	**1,045**	**1,692**	**2,800**	**5,568**	**9,468**	**8,460**	**11,823**	**12,500**
Equity securities	8 610	425	1,017	1,663	3,828	7,256	6,238	9,602	10,718
Monetary authorities	8 611	....	....	....	....	....	....	....	....
General government	8 612	....	....	....	....	....	....	....	....
Banks	8 613	22	64	7	4	3	....	....	....
Other sectors	8 614	403	953	1,656	3,824	7,252	6,238	9,602	10,718
Debt securities	8 619	620	675	1,137	1,740	2,212	2,222	2,221	1,782
Bonds and notes	8 620	515	541	989	1,624	2,067	2,201	2,179	1,757
Monetary authorities	8 621	....	....	....	....	....	....	....	....
General government	8 622	....	....	....	....	....	....	....	43
Banks	8 623	323	308	330	625	378	259	314	360
Other sectors	8 624	192	233	659	998	1,689	1,942	1,865	1,354
Money market instruments	8 630	104	135	148	116	145	21	42	25
Monetary authorities	8 631	....	....	....	....	....	....	....	....
General government	8 632	....	....	....	....	....	....	....	....
Banks	8 633	1	2	17	3	6	1	9	5
Other sectors	8 634	103	133	130	114	139	20	33	20
Financial derivatives	8 900	**1,604**	**2,481**	**1,447**	**2,070**	**2,438**	**5,133**	**3,434**	**3,825**
Monetary authorities	8 901	249	195	138	83	72	295	114	178
General government	8 902	....	34	191	98	111	371	481	1,323
Banks	8 903	1,356	2,251	1,118	1,889	2,255	3,950	2,280	1,837
Other sectors	8 904	....	....	....	....	....	516	558	488
Other investment	8 703	**13,588**	**21,057**	**21,217**	**30,334**	**41,351**	**27,830**	**30,368**	**29,941**
Trade credits	8 706	2,756	7,377	7,252	9,601	11,496	3,767	3,883	4,553
General government	8 707	231	282	270	24	1	....	....	....
of which: Short-term	8 709	....	....	....	....	....	....	....	....
Other sectors	8 710	2,526	7,096	6,982	9,577	11,495	3,767	3,883	4,553
of which: Short-term	8 712	*2,268*	*7,041*	*6,746*	*9,527*	*11,481*	*3,695*	*3,799*	*4,471*
Loans	8 714	10,354	8,607	9,469	12,552	19,350	13,829	13,602	11,413
Monetary authorities	8 715	1,107	....	....	....	....	....	....	....
of which: Short-term	8 718	*1,095*	....	....	....	....	....	....	....
General government	8 719	131	27	55	181	732	71	54	47
of which: Short-term	8 721	*21*	*17*	*46*	*181*	*729*	....	....	....
Banks	8 722	4,991	2,414	2,883	4,708	9,401	13,578	12,992	10,853
of which: Short-term	8 724	*3,141*	*706*	*691*	*922*	*1,417*	*1,163*	*948*	*1,256*
Other sectors	8 725	4,124	6,166	6,531	7,663	9,217	181	555	513
of which: Short-term	8 727	*3,035*	*4,852*	*5,210*	*6,275*	*7,465*	*34*	*350*	*360*
Currency and deposits	8 730	478	4,313	3,678	7,012	9,146	7,810	9,688	10,515
Monetary authorities	8 731	....	....	....	....	....	....	....	....
General government	8 732	....	....	....	....	....	557	615	354
Banks	8 733	322	4,030	3,336	5,543	5,578	3,690	4,718	4,688
Other sectors	8 734	156	283	342	1,469	3,568	3,563	4,355	5,473
Other assets	8 736	....	760	818	1,169	1,360	2,424	3,195	3,460
Monetary authorities	8 737	....	23	31	33	35	36	37	37
of which: Short-term	8 739	....	....	....	....	....	....	....	....
General government	8 740	....	311	400	378	819	1,096	1,697	1,956
of which: Short-term	8 742	....	*160*	*229*	*154*	*487*	*638*	*1,188*	*1,472*
Banks	8 743	....	....	....	2	3	484	410	327
of which: Short-term	8 745	....	....	....	....	....	*480*	*407*	*325*
Other sectors	8 746	....	426	387	755	503	808	1,051	1,139
of which: Short-term	8 748	....	*375*	*343*	*704*	*447*	*789*	*970*	*1,046*
Reserve assets	8 802	**12,793**	**15,965**	**18,603**	**21,589**	**24,052**	**33,874**	**44,183**	**44,988**
Monetary gold	8 812	42	43	51	63	82	86	109	139
Special drawing rights	8 811	46	58	64	74	83	54	1,479	1,154
Reserve position in the Fund	8 810	676	538	192	137	113	114	116	114
Foreign exchange	8 803	11,426	14,723	17,466	20,857	23,197	33,198	41,082	43,146
Other claims	8 813	603	602	831	459	576	422	1,397	434

Table 3 (Concluded). INTERNATIONAL INVESTMENT POSITION (End-period stocks), 2003–2010

(Millions of U.S. dollars)

	Code	2003	2004	2005	2006	2007	2008	2009	2010
LIABILITIES.........................	8 995 D.	**102,881**	**145,066**	**149,220**	**237,528**	**343,011**	**413,977**	**439,464**	**381,669**
Direct investment in Hungary.............	8 555 ..	**48,340**	**61,567**	**61,110**	**119,821**	**195,828**	**256,724**	**264,628**	**214,507**
Equity capital and reinvested earnings.....	8 556 ..	41,921	55,144	55,225	147,598	214,554	234,551	231,132	213,802
Claims on direct investors.........	8 557 ..	....	....	....	....	....	....	....	....
Liabilities to direct investors.......	8 558 ..	41,921	55,144	55,225	147,598	214,554	234,551	231,133	213,802
Other capital.....................	8 580 ..	6,419	6,423	5,885	−27,776	−18,726	22,173	33,495	705
Claims on direct investors.........	8 585 ..	−4,634	−5,536	−5,368	−62,643	−66,499	−57,514	−48,879	−60,289
Liabilities to direct investors.......	8 590 ..	11,053	11,958	11,253	34,867	47,774	79,687	82,374	60,994
Portfolio investment.................	8 652 ..	**27,793**	**43,153**	**46,068**	**63,019**	**70,395**	**59,001**	**63,106**	**58,175**
Equity securities.................	8 660 ..	5,604	11,359	13,157	18,376	15,267	9,035	16,600	15,215
Banks........................	8 663 ..	947	1,957	1,998	3,373	2,420	2,541	6,090	4,821
Other sectors.................	8 664 ..	4,657	9,402	11,159	15,004	12,847	6,494	10,510	10,394
Debt securities..................	8 669 ..	22,189	31,794	32,911	44,643	55,128	49,967	46,507	42,961
Bonds and notes..............	8 670 ..	21,763	31,025	32,566	43,983	54,280	49,282	45,686	41,358
Monetary authorities.........	8 671 ..	3,130	2,035	964	935	579	515	506	464
General government..........	8 672 ..	17,248	25,678	26,450	33,653	40,541	35,253	34,025	32,415
Banks.....................	8 673 ..	1,349	3,162	3,978	7,884	11,566	12,237	10,035	6,610
Other sectors..............	8 674 ..	36	149	1,174	1,512	1,594	1,277	1,120	1,869
Money market instruments.....	8 680 ..	426	770	346	659	848	684	821	1,602
Monetary authorities.........	8 681 ..	....	....	....	....	....	....	188	933
General government..........	8 682 ..	331	660	253	555	711	676	624	662
Banks.....................	8 683 ..	9	10	9	10	33	5	5	5
Other sectors..............	8 684 ..	86	100	84	94	104	3	4	2
Financial derivatives...............	8 905 ..	**2,000**	**2,605**	**1,652**	**2,403**	**3,192**	**6,356**	**4,291**	**5,833**
Monetary authorities..............	8 906 ..	538	611	284	336	232	99	143	86
General government...............	8 907 ..	....	134	255	563	970	858	955	738
Banks.........................	8 908 ..	1,463	1,861	1,113	1,505	1,990	4,835	2,796	4,422
Other sectors...................	8 909 ..	....	....	....	....	....	564	398	587
Other investment..................	8 753 ..	**24,748**	**37,741**	**40,390**	**52,285**	**73,595**	**91,896**	**107,439**	**103,153**
Trade credits....................	8 756 ..	36	6,477	6,262	8,523	10,272	4,152	5,065	5,495
General government.............	8 757 ..	....	....	....	....	....	....	....	....
of which: Short-term.........	8 759 ..	....	....	....	....	....	....	....	....
Other sectors.................	8 760 ..	36	6,477	6,262	8,523	10,272	4,152	5,065	5,495
of which: Short-term.........	8 762 ..	*35*	*6,477*	*6,147*	*8,148*	*10,272*	*4,064*	*5,023*	*5,431*
Loans.........................	8 764 ..	23,646	22,362	22,922	28,360	39,403	55,448	70,396	67,783
Monetary authorities...........	8 765 ..	1,234	6	239	329	297	7,419	14,131	16,996
of which: Use of Fund credit and loans from the Fund....	8 766 ..	....	....	....	....	....	*6,492*	*11,972*	*11,761*
of which: Short-term.......	8 768 ..	*1,229*	....	*239*	*329*	*297*	*927*	*2,158*	*5,235*
General government...........	8 769 ..	2,806	3,212	3,224	4,427	6,817	9,805	15,757	15,994
of which: Short-term.......	8 771 ..	....	....	....	....	*482*	*419*	*107*	*1,056*
Banks.....................	8 772 ..	11,014	8,593	8,896	11,676	13,600	18,105	18,222	14,678
of which: Short-term.......	8 774 ..	*4,084*	*145*	*515*	*474*	*602*	*918*	*2,489*	*1,451*
Other sectors..............	8 775 ..	8,592	10,551	10,564	11,929	18,690	20,119	22,287	20,115
of which: Short-term.......	8 777 ..	*1,548*	*2,200*	*2,300*	*1,826*	*3,019*	*2,170*	*2,166*	*1,505*
Currency and deposits............	8 780 ..	1,066	7,471	10,167	14,251	21,596	29,963	27,421	25,948
Monetary authorities...........	8 781 ..	11	104	55	63	46	238	170	245
General government...........	8 782 ..	....	....	....	....	....	....	....	....
Banks.....................	8 783 ..	979	7,189	9,570	12,987	20,089	29,724	27,251	25,704
Other sectors..............	8 784 ..	75	178	542	1,200	1,461	....	....	....
Other liabilities................	8 786 ..	....	1,432	1,038	1,151	2,324	2,333	4,556	3,928
Monetary authorities...........	8 787 ..	....	247	....	....	....	....	1,554	1,526
of which: Short-term.......	8 789 ..	....	*247*	....	....	....	....	....	....
General government...........	8 790 ..	....	637	650	648	1,832	1,666	2,396	1,826
of which: Short-term.......	8 792 ..	....	*637*	*650*	*648*	*1,832*	*1,666*	*2,396*	*1,826*
Banks.....................	8 793 ..	....	268	69	70	142	43	47	33
of which: Short-term.......	8 795 ..	....	*268*	*69*	*70*	*142*	*43*	*47*	*33*
Other sectors..............	8 796 ..	....	280	318	433	349	623	559	542
of which: Short-term.......	8 798 ..	....	*277*	*315*	*303*	*344*	*610*	*548*	*531*
NET INTERNATIONAL INVESTMENT POSITION........	8 995 ..	**−70,342**	**−97,853**	**−97,342**	**−120,853**	**−132,561**	**−149,419**	**−165,914**	**−150,622**
Conversion rates: forint per U.S. dollar (end of period).............	0 102 ..	**207.92**	**180.29**	**213.58**	**191.62**	**172.61**	**187.91**	**188.07**	**208.65**

Table 1. ANALYTIC PRESENTATION, 2003–2010

(Millions of U.S. dollars)

	Code	2003	2004	2005	2006	2007	2008	2009	2010
A. Current Account[1]	4 993 Z.	**−534**	**−1,317**	**−2,648**	**−3,990**	**−3,195**	**−4,472**	**−1,436**	**−1,417**
Goods: exports f.o.b.	2 100 ..	2,386	2,896	3,107	3,477	4,793	5,399	4,051	4,603
Goods: imports f.o.b.	3 100 ..	−2,596	−3,415	−4,590	−5,716	−6,179	−5,699	−3,318	−3,620
Balance on Goods	4 100 ..	*−210*	*−519*	*−1,482*	*−2,239*	*−1,385*	*−300*	*733*	*983*
Services: credit	2 200 ..	1,378	1,623	2,037	1,871	2,277	2,190	2,311	2,464
Services: debit	3 200 ..	−1,503	−1,838	−2,554	−2,562	−2,968	−2,535	−2,029	−2,183
Balance on Goods and Services	4 991 ..	*−335*	*−735*	*−1,999*	*−2,930*	*−2,076*	*−645*	*1,016*	*1,264*
Income: credit	2 300 ..	376	470	1,455	2,595	4,469	1,328	−55	−420
Income: debit	3 300 ..	−559	−1,035	−2,078	−3,620	−5,528	−5,116	−2,325	−2,190
Balance on Goods, Services, and Income	4 992 ..	*−519*	*−1,300*	*−2,621*	*−3,955*	*−3,135*	*−4,433*	*−1,364*	*−1,346*
Current transfers: credit	2 379 Z.	12	10	11	8	16	20	4	7
Current transfers: debit	3 379 ..	−28	−27	−38	−43	−76	−60	−76	−78
B. Capital Account[1]	4 994 Z.	**−5**	**−3**	**−27**	**−26**	**−30**	**−13**	**−12**	**−3**
Capital account: credit	2 994 Z.	15	32	14	15	16	16	4	3
Capital account: debit	3 994 ..	−20	−35	−41	−41	−46	−29	−16	−6
Total, Groups A Plus B	4 981 ..	*−539*	*−1,320*	*−2,675*	*−4,016*	*−3,225*	*−4,485*	*−1,447*	*−1,420*
C. Financial Account[1]	4 995 W.	**444**	**1,925**	**2,354**	**7,089**	**4,375**	**13,942**	**−2,009**	**4,891**
Direct investment abroad	4 505 ..	−384	−2,587	−7,114	−5,555	−10,227	3,790	−2,267	2,630
Direct investment in Iceland	4 555 Z.	336	757	3,124	3,886	6,879	1,208	64	488
Portfolio investment assets	4 602 ..	−593	−1,675	−4,707	−3,042	−9,200	5,616	1,286	−22
Equity securities	4 610 ..	−531	−1,612	−3,279	−1,081	−4,430	2,393	350	990
Debt securities	4 619 ..	−62	−63	−1,428	−1,961	−4,770	3,223	936	−1,013
Portfolio investment liabilities	4 652 Z.	3,603	8,401	16,935	14,380	599	−1,217	−10,966	−10,540
Equity securities	4 660 ..	−46	302	83	1,166	211	−1,990	−13	−83
Debt securities	4 669 Z.	3,650	8,099	16,851	13,214	388	774	−10,953	−10,457
Financial derivatives	4 910 ..	....	....	....	....	....	....	....	....
Financial derivatives assets	4 900 ..	....	....	....	....	....	....	....	....
Financial derivatives liabilities	4 905 ..	....	....	....	....	....	....	....	....
Other investment assets	4 703 ..	−2,081	−3,460	−10,922	−11,371	−17,146	−2,617	−949	2,438
Monetary authorities	4 701 ..	....	....	....	....	....	....	....	....
General government	4 704 ..	....	....	....	....	....	....	....	....
Banks	4 705 ..	−2,157	−3,187	−10,466	−11,085	−18,022	−1,386	−249	−326
Other sectors	4 728 ..	76	−274	−456	−286	876	−1,231	−699	2,763
Other investment liabilities	4 753 W.	−437	491	5,038	8,791	33,470	7,162	10,823	9,898
Monetary authorities	4 753 WA	−206	....	1	−19	−4	285	−239	265
General government	4 753 ZB	−76	−51	−137	−75	−24	568	371	709
Banks	4 753 ZC	−37	668	3,487	7,114	31,579	5,609	−420	−669
Other sectors	4 753 ZD	−118	−126	1,687	1,771	1,919	700	11,111	9,593
Total, Groups A Through C	4 983 ..	*−95*	*606*	*−321*	*3,073*	*1,151*	*9,457*	*−3,457*	*3,471*
D. Net Errors and Omissions	4 998 ..	**401**	**−404**	**392**	**−1,822**	**−1,042**	**−9,101**	**3,516**	**−1,811**
Total, Groups A Through D	4 984 ..	*307*	*202*	*71*	*1,252*	*108*	*356*	*59*	*1,660*
E. Reserves and Related Items	4 802 A.	**−307**	**−202**	**−71**	**−1,252**	**−108**	**−356**	**−59**	**−1,660**
Reserve assets	4 802 ..	−307	−202	−71	−1,252	−108	−1,187	−226	−1,980
Use of Fund credit and loans	4 766 ..	....	....	....	....	....	830	167	321
Exceptional financing	4 920 ..	....	....	....	....	....	....	....	....
Conversion rates: krónur per U.S. dollar	0 101 ..	**76.709**	**70.192**	**62.982**	**70.180**	**64.055**	**87.948**	**123.638**	**122.242**

[1] Excludes components that have been classified in the categories of Group E.

Table 2. STANDARD PRESENTATION, 2003–2010

(Millions of U.S. dollars)

	Code	2003	2004	2005	2006	2007	2008	2009	2010
CURRENT ACCOUNT	4 993	**−534**	**−1,317**	**−2,648**	**−3,990**	**−3,195**	**−4,472**	**−1,436**	**−1,417**
A. GOODS	4 100	**−210**	**−519**	**−1,482**	**−2,239**	**−1,385**	**−300**	**733**	**983**
Credit	2 100	**2,386**	**2,896**	**3,107**	**3,477**	**4,793**	**5,399**	**4,051**	**4,603**
General merchandise: exports f.o.b.	2 110	2,386	2,896	3,107	3,477	4,793	5,399	4,051	4,603
Goods for processing: exports f.o.b.	2 150	....	....	....	....	....	....	....	....
Repairs on goods	2 160	....	....	....	....	....	....	....	....
Goods procured in ports by carriers	2 170	....	....	....	....	....	....	....	....
Nonmonetary gold	2 180	....	....	....	....	....	....	....	....
Debit	3 100	**−2,596**	**−3,415**	**−4,590**	**−5,716**	**−6,179**	**−5,699**	**−3,318**	**−3,620**
General merchandise: imports f.o.b.	3 110	−2,596	−3,415	−4,590	−5,716	−6,179	−5,699	−3,318	−3,620
Goods for processing: imports f.o.b.	3 150	....	....	....	....	....	....	....	....
Repairs on goods	3 160	....	....	....	....	....	....	....	....
Goods procured in ports by carriers	3 170	....	....	....	....	....	....	....	....
Nonmonetary gold	3 180	....	....	....	....	....	....	....	....
B. SERVICES	4 200	**−125**	**−215**	**−516**	**−691**	**−691**	**−345**	**283**	**281**
Total credit	2 200	*1,378*	*1,623*	*2,037*	*1,871*	*2,277*	*2,190*	*2,311*	*2,464*
Total debit	3 200	*−1,503*	*−1,838*	*−2,554*	*−2,562*	*−2,968*	*−2,535*	*−2,029*	*−2,183*
Transportation services, credit	2 205	**656**	**902**	**1,078**	**838**	**1,008**	**937**	**1,052**	**1,194**
Passenger	2 850	*167*	*188*	*222*	*224*	*247*	*257*	....	....
Freight	2 851	*153*	*219*	*182*	*139*	*165*	*132*	....	....
Other	2 852	*336*	*495*	*674*	*475*	*597*	*548*	....	....
Sea transport, passenger	2 207	....	....	....	....	....	....		
Sea transport, freight	2 208	107	121	132	116	140	120		
Sea transport, other	2 209	11	9	54	14	54	7		
Air transport, passenger	2 211	167	188	222	224	247	257		
Air transport, freight	2 212	46	99	50	23	25	12		
Air transport, other	2 213	325	486	620	461	542	541		
Other transport, passenger	2 215	....	....	....	....	....	....		
Other transport, freight	2 216	....	....	....	....	....	....		
Other transport, other	2 217	....	....	....	....	....	....		
Transportation services, debit	3 205	**−518**	**−698**	**−885**	**−766**	**−883**	**−805**	**−683**	**−631**
Passenger	3 850	*−1*	*−2*	*−11*	*−8*	*−10*	*−4*	....	....
Freight	3 851	*−14*	*−21*	*−28*	*−25*	*−32*	*−34*	....	....
Other	3 852	*−503*	*−675*	*−846*	*−733*	*−841*	*−767*	....	....
Sea transport, passenger	3 207	....	....	....	....	....	....		
Sea transport, freight	3 208	−14	−21	−28	−25	−32	−33		
Sea transport, other	3 209	−120	−140	−245	−221	−288	−244		
Air transport, passenger	3 211	−1	−2	−11	−8	−10	−4		
Air transport, freight	3 212	....	....	....	....	....	−1		
Air transport, other	3 213	−383	−534	−601	−511	−552	−523		
Other transport, passenger	3 215	....	....	....	....	....	....		
Other transport, freight	3 216	....	....	....	....	....	....		
Other transport, other	3 217	....	....	....	....	....	....		
Travel, credit	2 236	**319**	**370**	**413**	**478**	**601**	**624**	**541**	**557**
Business travel	2 237	....	....	....	....	....	....		
Personal travel	2 240	319	370	413	478	601	624	....	....
Travel, debit	3 236	**−523**	**−697**	**−980**	**−1,076**	**−1,326**	**−1,103**	**−535**	**−572**
Business travel	3 237	....	....	....	....	....	....		
Personal travel	3 240	−523	−697	−980	−1,076	−1,326	−1,103		
Other services, credit	2 200 BA	**403**	**351**	**546**	**555**	**668**	**630**	**718**	**713**
Communications	2 245	8	10	9	12	14	11	....	....
Construction	2 249	14	2	....	....	....	....		
Insurance	2 253	7	9	8	10	12	15	....	....
Financial	2 260	1	1	....	1	2	3		
Computer and information	2 262	44	56	69	89	92	85		
Royalties and licence fees	2 266	....	2	....	....	....	....		
Other business services	2 268	227	167	358	372	526	497	718	713
Personal, cultural, and recreational	2 287	4	9	16	12	9	12		
Government, n.i.e.	2 291	97	96	86	59	13	6	....	....
Other services, debit	3 200 BA	**−462**	**−444**	**−689**	**−721**	**−758**	**−627**	**−811**	**−980**
Communications	3 245	−45	−21	−43	−46	−45	−31	....	....
Construction	3 249	−24	−9	−7	−18	−25	−12		
Insurance	3 253	−24	−19	−41	−51	−36	−21		
Financial	3 260	−11	−38	−24	−19	−21	−16		
Computer and information	3 262	−14	−8	−12	−17	−23	−21		
Royalties and licence fees	3 266	−2	−2	−4	−4	−5	−4	....	....
Other business services	3 268	−309	−314	−522	−531	−560	−488	−811	−980
Personal, cultural, and recreational	3 287	−11	−12	−13	−14	−17	−10	....	....
Government, n.i.e.	3 291	−22	−21	−22	−20	−25	−24	....	....

Table 2 (Continued). STANDARD PRESENTATION, 2003–2010

(Millions of U.S. dollars)

	Code	2003	2004	2005	2006	2007	2008	2009	2010
C. INCOME	4 300	**−183**	**−565**	**−622**	**−1,024**	**−1,059**	**−3,788**	**−2,380**	**−2,610**
Total credit	2 300	*376*	*470*	*1,455*	*2,595*	*4,469*	*1,328*	*−55*	*−420*
Total debit	3 300	*−559*	*−1,035*	*−2,078*	*−3,620*	*−5,528*	*−5,116*	*−2,325*	*−2,190*
Compensation of employees, credit	2 310	**81**	**80**	**74**	**72**	**25**	**19**	**20**	**22**
Compensation of employees, debit	3 310	**−6**	**−12**	**−24**	**−39**	**−54**	**−27**	**−18**	**−7**
Investment income, credit	2 320	**295**	**390**	**1,381**	**2,523**	**4,444**	**1,309**	**−75**	**−442**
Direct investment income	2 330	209	212	966	1,331	1,912	−1,104	−541	−728
Dividends and distributed branch profits	2 332	18	50	70	29	1,264	318	27	242
Reinvested earnings and undistributed branch profits	2 333	182	137	870	1,156	488	−1,316	−20	−435
Income on debt (interest)	2 334	9	25	26	146	160	−106	−548	−535
Portfolio investment income	2 339	36	67	94	247	704	567	141	87
Income on equity	2 340	29	52	73	150	269	230	101	36
Income on bonds and notes	2 350	7	15	21	97	435	337	39	28
Income on money market instruments	2 360	....	....	....	....	....	....	2	23
Other investment income	2 370	49	110	321	945	1,828	1,846	325	198
Investment income, debit	3 320	**−553**	**−1,023**	**−2,053**	**−3,581**	**−5,474**	**−5,088**	**−2,306**	**−2,184**
Direct investment income	3 330	−160	−499	−1,044	−1,157	−938	713	250	−375
Dividends and distributed branch profits	3 332	−81	−23	−30	−83	−302	−116	−4	−5
Reinvested earnings and undistributed branch profits	3 333	−76	−458	−1,007	−1,068	−558	980	612	21
Income on debt (interest)	3 334	−2	−18	−7	−6	−78	−150	−358	−392
Portfolio investment income	3 339	−247	−376	−791	−1,797	−2,907	−3,220	−1,652	−1,362
Income on equity	3 340	−8	−16	−25	−49	−106	−75	−11	−15
Income on bonds and notes	3 350	−214	−319	−717	−1,639	−2,648	−3,009	−1,605	−1,334
Income on money market instruments	3 360	−24	−40	−49	−109	−153	−136	−36	−13
Other investment income	3 370	−146	−149	−219	−626	−1,629	−2,582	−904	−446
D. CURRENT TRANSFERS	4 379	**−15**	**−17**	**−27**	**−35**	**−60**	**−40**	**−72**	**−70**
Credit	2 379	**12**	**10**	**11**	**8**	**16**	**20**	**4**	**7**
General government	2 380	11	....	1	....	....	....	....	....
Other sectors	2 390	2	10	10	8	16	20	4	7
Workers' remittances	2 391	....	....	....	....	....	....	....	....
Other current transfers	2 392	2	10	10	8	16	20	4	7
Debit	3 379	**−28**	**−27**	**−38**	**−43**	**−76**	**−60**	**−76**	**−78**
General government	3 380	−19	−19	−26	−29	−56	−46	−45	−45
Other sectors	3 390	−9	−8	−12	−14	−20	−13	−31	−33
Workers' remittances	3 391	....	....	....	....	....	....	....	....
Other current transfers	3 392	−9	−8	−12	−14	−20	−13	−31	−33
CAPITAL AND FINANCIAL ACCOUNT	4 996	**133**	**1,720**	**2,256**	**5,812**	**4,237**	**13,573**	**−2,080**	**3,228**
CAPITAL ACCOUNT	4 994	**−5**	**−3**	**−27**	**−26**	**−30**	**−13**	**−12**	**−3**
Total credit	2 994	*15*	*32*	*14*	*15*	*16*	*16*	*4*	*3*
Total debit	3 994	*−20*	*−35*	*−41*	*−41*	*−46*	*−29*	*−16*	*−6*
Capital transfers, credit	2 400	**15**	**32**	**14**	**15**	**16**	**16**	**4**	**3**
General government	2 401	....	....	....	....	....	....	....	....
Debt forgiveness	2 402	....	....	....	....	....	....	....	....
Other capital transfers	2 410	....	....	....	....	....	....	....	....
Other sectors	2 430	15	32	14	15	16	16	4	3
Migrants' transfers	2 431	15	32	14	15	16	16	4	3
Debt forgiveness	2 432	....	....	....	....	....	....	....	....
Other capital transfers	2 440	....	....	....	....	....	....	....	....
Capital transfers, debit	3 400	**−20**	**−35**	**−41**	**−41**	**−46**	**−29**	**−16**	**−6**
General government	3 401	....	....	....	....	....	....	....	....
Debt forgiveness	3 402	....	....	....	....	....	....	....	....
Other capital transfers	3 410	....	....	....	....	....	....	....	....
Other sectors	3 430	−20	−35	−41	−41	−46	−29	−16	−6
Migrants' transfers	3 431	−20	−35	−41	−41	−46	−29	−16	−6
Debt forgiveness	3 432	....	....	....	....	....	....	....	....
Other capital transfers	3 440	....	....	....	....	....	....	....	....
Nonproduced nonfinancial assets, credit	2 480	....	....	....	....	....	....	....	....
Nonproduced nonfinancial assets, debit	3 480	....	....	....	....	....	....	....	....

Table 2 (Continued). STANDARD PRESENTATION, 2003–2010

(Millions of U.S. dollars)

	Code	2003	2004	2005	2006	2007	2008	2009	2010
FINANCIAL ACCOUNT............................	4 995 ..	**138**	**1,723**	**2,283**	**5,838**	**4,267**	**13,586**	**−2,068**	**3,231**
A. DIRECT INVESTMENT...........................	4 500 ..	**−48**	**−1,830**	**−3,990**	**−1,669**	**−3,348**	**4,998**	**−2,203**	**3,118**
Direct investment abroad.............................	4 505 ..	**−384**	**−2,587**	**−7,114**	**−5,555**	**−10,227**	**3,790**	**−2,267**	**2,630**
Equity capital...	4 510 ..	−274	−2,052	−5,158	−3,617	−10,104	1,331	−2,477	963
Claims on affiliated enterprises................	4 515 ..	....	....	....	....	....	....	....	....
Liabilities to affiliated enterprises...........	4 520 ..	....	....	....	....	....	....	....	....
Reinvested earnings..................................	4 525 ..	−182	−137	−870	−1,156	−488	1,316	20	435
Other capital..	4 530 ..	72	−399	−1,086	−782	366	1,144	190	1,231
Claims on affiliated enterprises................	4 535 ..	....	....	....	....	....	....	....	....
Liabilities to affiliated enterprises...........	4 540 ..	....	....	....	....	....	....	....	....
Direct investment in Iceland......................	4 555 ..	**336**	**757**	**3,124**	**3,886**	**6,879**	**1,208**	**64**	**488**
Equity capital...	4 560 ..	78	100	1,661	2,129	2,576	757	230	160
Claims on direct investors.......................	4 565 ..	....	....	....	....	....	....	....	....
Liabilities to direct investors....................	4 570 ..	....	....	....	....	....	....	....	....
Reinvested earnings..................................	4 575 ..	76	458	1,007	1,068	558	−980	−612	−21
Other capital..	4 580 ..	182	199	456	689	3,746	1,431	446	350
Claims on direct investors.......................	4 585 ..	....	....	....	....	....	....	....	....
Liabilities to direct investors....................	4 590 ..	....	....	....	....	....	....	....	....
B. PORTFOLIO INVESTMENT.....................	4 600 ..	**3,010**	**6,725**	**12,228**	**11,338**	**−8,601**	**4,400**	**−9,680**	**−10,563**
Assets...	4 602 ..	**−593**	**−1,675**	**−4,707**	**−3,042**	**−9,200**	**5,616**	**1,286**	**−22**
Equity securities......................................	4 610 ..	−531	−1,612	−3,279	−1,081	−4,430	2,393	350	990
Monetary authorities...........................	4 611 ..	−1	....	−1	....	....	....	....	....
General government............................	4 612 ..	....	....	....	....	....	....	....	....
Banks..	4 613 ..	−47	−366	−1,553	−29	−2,896	881	224	8
Other sectors.......................................	4 614 ..	−483	−1,247	−1,724	−1,052	−1,534	1,513	126	982
Debt securities..	4 619 ..	−62	−63	−1,428	−1,961	−4,770	3,223	936	−1,013
Bonds and notes..................................	4 620 ..	−66	−67	−1,430	−1,956	−4,767	3,223	1,110	188
Monetary authorities........................	4 621 ..	1	....	....	....	....	....	....	....
General government.........................	4 622 ..	....	....	....	....	....	....	....	....
Banks..	4 623 ..	−7	−22	−1,092	−1,829	−4,181	3,171	133	20
Other sectors....................................	4 624 ..	−60	−46	−338	−127	−586	52	977	167
Money market instruments....................	4 630 ..	4	4	2	−5	−3	....	−173	−1,200
Monetary authorities........................	4 631 ..	....	....	....	....	....	....	....	....
General government.........................	4 632 ..	....	....	....	....	....	....	−169	−64
Banks..	4 633 ..	4	4	2	....	....	....	−169	−64
Other sectors....................................	4 634 ..	....	....	....	−5	−3	....	−4	−1,137
Liabilities...	4 652 ..	**3,603**	**8,401**	**16,935**	**14,380**	**599**	**−1,217**	**−10,966**	**−10,540**
Equity securities......................................	4 660 ..	−46	302	83	1,166	211	−1,990	−13	−83
Banks..	4 663 ..	−12	54	379	629	1,139	−1,145	−34	....
Other sectors.......................................	4 664 ..	−35	248	−295	537	−928	−845	21	−83
Debt securities..	4 669 ..	3,650	8,099	16,851	13,214	388	774	−10,953	−10,457
Bonds and notes..................................	4 670 ..	2,885	7,789	16,733	13,962	−122	149	−10,385	−10,799
Monetary authorities........................	4 671 ..	....	....	....	....	....	....	....	....
General government.........................	4 672 ..	137	178	−217	969	138	2,717	−137	−1,334
Banks..	4 673 ..	2,554	7,427	16,949	12,456	−563	−1,648	....	−6
Other sectors....................................	4 674 ..	193	184	1	537	302	−920	−10,248	−9,460
Money market instruments....................	4 680 ..	765	310	118	−748	510	624	−569	341
Monetary authorities........................	4 681 ..	....	....	....	....	....	1,151	−876	....
General government.........................	4 682 ..	−203	12	−199	17	−5	295	306	341
Banks..	4 683 ..	968	298	317	−894	469	−1,061	....	....
Other sectors....................................	4 684 ..	....	....	....	129	45	239	1	....
C. FINANCIAL DERIVATIVES......................	4 910 ..	....	....	....	....	....	....	....	....
Monetary authorities................................	4 911 ..	....	....	....	....	....	....	....	....
General government.................................	4 912 ..	....	....	....	....	....	....	....	....
Banks...	4 913 ..	....	....	....	....	....	....	....	....
Other sectors..	4 914 ..	....	....	....	....	....	....	....	....
Assets...	4 900 ..	....	....	....	....	....	....	....	....
Monetary authorities............................	4 901 ..	....	....	....	....	....	....	....	....
General government.............................	4 902 ..	....	....	....	....	....	....	....	....
Banks..	4 903 ..	....	....	....	....	....	....	....	....
Other sectors.......................................	4 904 ..	....	....	....	....	....	....	....	....
Liabilities...	4 905 ..	....	....	....	....	....	....	....	....
Monetary authorities............................	4 906 ..	....	....	....	....	....	....	....	....
General government.............................	4 907 ..	....	....	....	....	....	....	....	....
Banks..	4 908 ..	....	....	....	....	....	....	....	....
Other sectors.......................................	4 909 ..	....	....	....	....	....	....	....	....

Table 2 (Concluded). STANDARD PRESENTATION, 2003–2010

(Millions of U.S. dollars)

	Code	2003	2004	2005	2006	2007	2008	2009	2010
D. OTHER INVESTMENT	4 700	**−2,518**	**−2,969**	**−5,884**	**−2,580**	**16,324**	**5,375**	**10,041**	**12,656**
Assets	4 703	−2,081	−3,460	−10,922	−11,371	−17,146	−2,617	−949	2,438
Trade credits	4 706	30	−69	14	−105	58	56	−20	−28
General government	4 707	....	....	....	....	....	....	....	....
of which: Short-term	4 709	....	....	....	....	....	....	....	....
Other sectors	4 710	30	−69	14	−105	58	56	−20	−28
of which: Short-term	4 712	....	....	....	....	....	....	....	....
Loans	4 714	−1,180	−2,460	−9,287	−9,322	−8,659	−3,871	−778	4,052
Monetary authorities	4 715	....	....	....	....	....	....	....	....
of which: Short-term	4 718	....	....	....	....	....	....	....	....
General government	4 719	....	....	....	....	....	....	....	....
of which: Short-term	4 721	....	....	....	....	....	....	....	....
Banks	4 722	−1,173	−2,257	−8,806	−9,438	−9,167	−2,597	200	−13
of which: Short-term	4 724	....	....	....	....	....	....	....	....
Other sectors	4 725	−7	−203	−481	116	507	−1,273	−978	4,065
of which: Short-term	4 727	....	....	....	....	....	....	....	....
Currency and deposits	4 730	−932	−932	−1,652	−1,917	−8,574	1,198	−127	−1,525
Monetary authorities	4 731	....	....	....	....	....	....	....	....
General government	4 732	....	....	....	....	....	....	....	....
Banks	4 733	−985	−930	−1,660	−1,647	−8,856	1,211	−450	−312
Other sectors	4 734	52	−2	7	−270	282	−13	322	−1,213
Other assets	4 736	....	....	3	−28	29	....	−24	−60
Monetary authorities	4 737	....	....	....	....	....	....	....	....
of which: Short-term	4 739	....	....	....	....	....	....	....	....
General government	4 740	....	....	....	....	....	....	....	....
of which: Short-term	4 742	....	....	....	....	....	....	....	....
Banks	4 743	....	....	....	....	....	....	....	....
of which: Short-term	4 745	....	....	....	....	....	....	....	....
Other sectors	4 746	....	....	3	−28	29	....	−24	−60
of which: Short-term	4 748	....	....	....	....	....	....	....	....
Liabilities	4 753	−437	491	5,038	8,791	33,470	7,992	10,990	10,218
Trade credits	4 756	34	34	69	8	45	−122	−76	18
General government	4 757	....	....	....	....	....	....	....	....
of which: Short-term	4 759	....	....	....	....	....	....	....	....
Other sectors	4 760	34	34	69	8	45	−122	−76	18
of which: Short-term	4 762	....	....	....	....	....	....	....	....
Loans	4 764	−537	190	4,583	4,690	17,788	9,185	−3,895	−1,351
Monetary authorities	4 765	−206	....	....	....	....	806	−300	309
of which: Use of Fund credit and loans from the Fund	4 766	....	....	....	....	....	830	167	321
of which: Short-term	4 768	−206	....	....	....	....	−24	−467	−11
General government	4 769	−76	−51	−137	−75	−24	568	371	709
of which: Short-term	4 771	....	....	....	....	....	....	....	....
Banks	4 772	−103	398	3,105	3,015	15,939	8,904	−123	−244
of which: Short-term	4 774	145	524	1,981	1,134	12,195	7,014	−31	−2
Other sectors	4 775	−152	−157	1,614	1,750	1,873	−1,094	−3,843	−2,125
of which: Short-term	4 777	−5	1	1	239	−240	−26	−3	23
Currency and deposits	4 780	65	270	383	4,079	15,636	−2,986	−219	−149
Monetary authorities	4 781	....	....	1	−19	−4	309	79	276
General government	4 782	....	....	....	....	....	....	....	....
Banks	4 783	66	270	382	4,098	15,640	−3,295	−298	−425
Other sectors	4 784	....	....	....	....	....	....	....	....
Other liabilities	4 786	....	−4	4	13	....	1,915	15,180	11,700
Monetary authorities	4 787	....	....	....	....	....	....	150	....
of which: Short-term	4 789	....	....	....	....	....	....	....	....
General government	4 790	....	....	....	....	....	....	....	....
of which: Short-term	4 792	....	....	....	....	....	....	....	....
Banks	4 793	....	....	....	....	....	....	....	....
of which: Short-term	4 795	....	....	....	....	....	....	....	....
Other sectors	4 796	....	−4	4	13	....	1,915	15,030	11,700
of which: Short-term	4 798	....	....	....	....	....	....	....	....
E. RESERVE ASSETS	4 802	**−307**	**−202**	**−71**	**−1,252**	**−108**	**−1,187**	**−226**	**−1,980**
Monetary gold	4 812	....	....	....	....	−11	−3	−14	−21
Special drawing rights	4 811	....	....	....	....	....	....	−144	29
Reserve position in the Fund	4 810	....	....	....	....	....	....	....	....
Foreign exchange	4 803	−306	−202	−71	−1,251	−97	−1,183	−68	−1,989
Other claims	4 813	....	....	....	....	....	....	....	....
NET ERRORS AND OMISSIONS	4 998	**401**	**−404**	**392**	**−1,822**	**−1,042**	**−9,101**	**3,516**	**−1,811**

Table 3. INTERNATIONAL INVESTMENT POSITION (End-period stocks), 2003–2010

(Millions of U.S. dollars)

	Code	2003	2004	2005	2006	2007	2008	2009	2010
ASSETS	8 995 C.	**9,983**	**18,920**	**39,330**	**65,551**	**108,388**	**35,870**	**32,138**	**35,542**
Direct investment abroad	8 505	**1,733**	**4,040**	**10,004**	**13,930**	**25,061**	**9,382**	**9,270**	**11,138**
Equity capital and reinvested earnings	8 506	1,559	3,463	8,470	11,789	23,358	9,088	6,882	6,468
Claims on affiliated enterprises	8 507	....	....	....	....	....	....	....	....
Liabilities to affiliated enterprises	8 508	....	....	....	....	....	....	....	....
Other capital	8 530	175	576	1,534	2,141	1,704	294	2,388	4,669
Claims on affiliated enterprises	8 535	386	851	1,940	2,817	5,646	4,011	6,556	5,562
Liabilities to affiliated enterprises	8 540	−211	−275	−407	−676	−3,942	−3,717	−4,168	−893
Portfolio investment	8 602	**3,695**	**6,130**	**10,874**	**18,596**	**31,127**	**8,514**	**7,102**	**7,027**
Equity securities	8 610	3,369	5,838	9,229	13,383	20,608	6,725	6,159	5,077
Monetary authorities	8 611	2	2	3	3	8	2	1	2
General government	8 612	5	5	5	23	27	26	26	24
Banks	8 613	235	695	2,387	2,969	6,466	293	44	27
Other sectors	8 614	3,127	5,137	6,834	10,389	14,107	6,405	6,087	5,024
Debt securities	8 619	326	292	1,646	5,213	10,520	1,789	943	1,950
Bonds and notes	8 620	320	290	1,646	5,207	10,511	1,787	706	454
Monetary authorities	8 621	1	1	1	1	....	....	....	....
General government	8 622	....	....	....	....	....	....	....	....
Banks	8 623	40	73	1,120	3,124	8,272	241	69	32
Other sectors	8 624	279	216	525	2,083	2,238	1,546	637	422
Money market instruments	8 630	6	2	....	5	9	1	237	1,496
Monetary authorities	8 631	....	....	....	....	....	....	....	....
General government	8 632	....	....	....	....	....	....	....	....
Banks	8 633	6	2	....	....	....	1	237	267
Other sectors	8 634	....	....	....	5	9	....	....	1,229
Financial derivatives	8 900	....	....	....	....	....	....	....	....
Monetary authorities	8 901								
General government	8 902								
Banks	8 903								
Other sectors	8 904								
Other investment	8 703	**3,736**	**7,676**	**17,392**	**30,688**	**49,573**	**14,412**	**11,884**	**11,588**
Trade credits	8 706	130	194	163	279	237	177	200	226
General government	8 707	....	....	....	....	....	....	....	....
of which: Short-term	8 709	....							
Other sectors	8 710	130	194	163	279	237	177	200	226
of which: Short-term	8 712	....							
Loans	8 714	2,280	5,047	13,461	24,218	33,937	11,464	8,832	7,010
Monetary authorities	8 715	....	....	....	....	....	....	....	....
of which: Short-term	8 718	....	....						
General government	8 719	....	....	....	....	....	....	....	....
of which: Short-term	8 721	....							
Banks	8 722	2,273	4,829	12,799	23,635	33,836	2,615	749	841
of which: Short-term	8 724	....							
Other sectors	8 725	7	218	662	583	101	8,849	8,083	6,169
of which: Short-term	8 727	....							
Currency and deposits	8 730	1,320	2,429	3,765	6,160	15,397	2,769	2,825	4,263
Monetary authorities	8 731	....	....	....	....	....	....	....	....
General government	8 732	....	....	....	....	....	....	....	....
Banks	8 733	1,238	2,335	3,708	5,824	15,336	654	967	1,257
Other sectors	8 734	83	93	57	336	61	2,115	1,858	3,006
Other assets	8 736	6	6	2	31	3	2	27	88
Monetary authorities	8 737	....	....	....	....	....	....	....	....
of which: Short-term	8 739	....							
General government	8 740	....	....	....	....	....	....	....	....
of which: Short-term	8 742	....							
Banks	8 743	....	....	....	....	....	....	....	....
of which: Short-term	8 745	....							
Other sectors	8 746	6	6	2	31	3	2	27	88
of which: Short-term	8 748	....							
Reserve assets	8 802	**819**	**1,074**	**1,060**	**2,337**	**2,626**	**3,562**	**3,883**	**5,790**
Monetary gold	8 812	26	28	33	41	53	55	69	91
Special drawing rights	8 811	....	....	....	....	....	....	145	113
Reserve position in the Fund	8 810	28	29	27	28	29	29	29	29
Foreign exchange	8 803	765	1,017	1,000	2,268	2,543	3,478	3,639	5,557
Other claims	8 813	....	....	....	....	....	....	....	....

Table 3 (Concluded). INTERNATIONAL INVESTMENT POSITION (End-period stocks), 2003–2010

(Millions of U.S. dollars)

	Code	2003	2004	2005	2006	2007	2008	2009	2010
LIABILITIES..................................	8 995 D.	**17,402**	**29,186**	**53,030**	**82,279**	**131,948**	**120,621**	**117,899**	**119,619**
Direct investment in Iceland................	8 555 ..	**1,193**	**2,088**	**4,668**	**7,649**	**16,379**	**9,184**	**8,629**	**11,767**
Equity capital and reinvested earnings..........	8 556 ..	869	1,542	3,728	5,949	10,654	2,162	912	1,444
Claims on direct investors....................	8 557 ..	....	....	....	....	....	....	....	....
Liabilities to direct investors................	8 558 ..	....	....	....	....	....	....	....	....
Other capital................................	8 580 ..	325	545	940	1,701	5,725	7,022	7,718	10,322
Claims on direct investors....................	8 585 ..	−98	−113	−145	−265	−454	−306	−327	−461
Liabilities to direct investors................	8 590 ..	422	658	1,085	1,966	6,178	7,328	8,044	10,783
Portfolio investment......................	8 652 ..	**10,626**	**20,697**	**37,587**	**54,558**	**59,698**	**50,219**	**39,720**	**27,605**
Equity securities............................	8 660 ..	293	781	3,690	4,980	5,831	103	89	100
Banks....................................	8 663 ..	213	379	1,621	2,206	3,442	18	....	....
Other sectors............................	8 664 ..	80	402	2,069	2,774	2,389	85	89	100
Debt securities.............................	8 669 ..	10,333	19,916	33,897	49,578	53,867	50,115	39,631	27,505
Bonds and notes.........................	8 670 ..	8,609	17,737	31,613	48,291	52,129	48,660	39,171	27,177
Monetary authorities...................	8 671 ..	....	....	....	....	....	....	....	....
General government...................	8 672 ..	2,202	2,574	2,187	3,217	3,782	3,635	3,642	2,176
Banks................................	8 673 ..	5,316	13,782	28,282	43,314	45,306	....	....	2
Other sectors.........................	8 674 ..	1,091	1,381	1,145	1,760	3,042	45,025	35,529	24,999
Money market instruments................	8 680 ..	1,725	2,179	2,284	1,287	1,738	1,455	459	328
Monetary authorities...................	8 681 ..	....	....	....	....	....	884	....	....
General government...................	8 682 ..	196	221	7	21	24	134	456	327
Banks................................	8 683 ..	1,528	1,958	2,277	1,142	1,523	....	....	....
Other sectors.........................	8 684 ..	....	....	....	124	191	438	3	1
Financial derivatives......................	8 905 ..	....	....	....	....	....	....	....	....
Monetary authorities........................	8 906 ..	....	....	....	....	....	....	....	....
General government.........................	8 907 ..	....	....	....	....	....	....	....	....
Banks......................................	8 908 ..	....	....	....	....	....	....	....	....
Other sectors..............................	8 909 ..	....	....	....	....	....	....	....	....
Other investment........................	8 753 ..	**5,582**	**6,401**	**10,776**	**20,072**	**55,871**	**61,218**	**69,550**	**80,248**
Trade credits...............................	8 756 ..	160	202	250	274	334	202	127	145
General government.......................	8 757 ..	....	....	....	....	....	....	....	....
of which: Short-term..................	8 759 ..	....	....	....	....	....	....	....	....
Other sectors............................	8 760 ..	160	202	250	274	334	202	127	145
of which: Short-term..................	8 762 ..	....	....	....	....	....	....	....	....
Loans......................................	8 764 ..	5,197	5,683	9,682	14,688	34,703	39,962	34,476	33,157
Monetary authorities......................	8 765 ..	....	....	....	....	....	1,343	1,176	1,673
of which: Use of Fund credit and loans from the Fund....	8 766 ..	....	....	....	....	....	*863*	*1,043*	*1,348*
of which: Short-term..................	8 768 ..	....	....	....	....	....	*480*	*17*	*5*
General government......................	8 769 ..	713	684	237	166	119	635	1,017	1,774
of which: Short-term..................	8 771 ..	....	....	....	....	....	....	....	....
Banks....................................	8 772 ..	3,147	3,756	6,475	9,817	28,510	3,089	336	....
of which: Short-term..................	8 774 ..	*1,539*	*2,180*	*3,919*	*5,244*	*18,092*	*275*	*77*	....
Other sectors............................	8 775 ..	1,337	1,243	2,970	4,705	6,075	34,895	31,946	29,710
of which: Short-term..................	8 777 ..	*8*	*9*	*60*	*277*	*101*	*22,619*	*20,831*	*21,222*
Currency and deposits.......................	8 780 ..	203	496	822	5,074	20,796	19,214	16,468	16,596
Monetary authorities......................	8 781 ..	2	2	2	1	2	215	277	578
General government......................	8 782 ..	....	....	....	....	....	....	....	....
Banks....................................	8 783 ..	202	493	820	5,073	20,794	2,526	2,090	1,760
Other sectors............................	8 784 ..	....	....	....	....	....	16,473	14,101	14,259
Other liabilities............................	8 786 ..	23	20	21	36	38	1,840	18,478	30,350
Monetary authorities......................	8 787 ..	....	....	....	....	....	....	176	173
of which: Short-term..................	8 789 ..	....	....	....	....	....	....	....	....
General government......................	8 790 ..	....	....	....	....	....	....	....	....
of which: Short-term..................	8 792 ..	....	....	....	....	....	....	....	....
Banks....................................	8 793 ..	....	....	....	....	....	....	....	....
of which: Short-term..................	8 795 ..	....	....	....	....	....	....	....	....
Other sectors............................	8 796 ..	23	20	21	36	38	1,840	18,302	30,177
of which: Short-term..................	8 798 ..	....	....	....	....	....	....	....	....
NET INTERNATIONAL INVESTMENT POSITION........	8 995 ..	**−7,419**	**−10,265**	**−13,700**	**−16,728**	**−23,560**	**−84,751**	**−85,760**	**−84,077**
Conversion rates: krónur per U.S. dollar (end of period)................	0 102 ..	70.990	61.040	62.980	71.660	61.850	120.580	124.900	115.050

Table 1. ANALYTIC PRESENTATION, 2003–2010
(Millions of U.S. dollars)

	Code	2003	2004	2005	2006	2007	2008	2009	2010
A. Current Account[1]	4 993 Z.	**8,773**	**780**	**−10,284**	**−9,299**	**−8,076**	**−30,972**	**−25,922**	**−51,781**
Goods: exports f.o.b.	2 100 ..	60,893	77,939	102,175	123,768	153,784	198,598	168,219	225,502
Goods: imports f.o.b.	3 100 ..	−68,081	−95,539	−134,692	−166,572	−208,611	−291,740	−247,883	−323,435
Balance on Goods	4 100 ..	*−7,188*	*−17,600*	*−32,517*	*−42,804*	*−54,827*	*−93,142*	*−79,665*	*−97,934*
Services: credit	2 200 ..	23,902	38,281	52,527	69,730	86,929	107,131	93,036	123,762
Services: debit	3 200 ..	−24,878	−35,641	−47,287	−58,696	−70,805	−88,348	−81,049	−116,842
Balance on Goods and Services	4 991 ..	*−8,164*	*−14,960*	*−27,276*	*−31,770*	*−38,704*	*−74,360*	*−67,678*	*−91,013*
Income: credit	2 300 ..	3,491	4,690	5,646	8,199	12,650	15,593	13,734	9,612
Income: debit	3 300 ..	−8,386	−8,742	−12,296	−14,445	−19,166	−20,958	−21,271	−22,538
Balance on Goods, Services, and Income	4 992 ..	*−13,059*	*−19,012*	*−33,926*	*−38,015*	*−45,220*	*−79,724*	*−75,214*	*−103,939*
Current transfers: credit	2 379 Z.	22,401	20,615	24,512	30,015	38,885	52,065	51,387	55,046
Current transfers: debit	3 379 ..	−570	−822	−869	−1,299	−1,742	−3,313	−2,095	−2,889
B. Capital Account[1]	4 994 Z.	....	....	....	....	....	....	....	**−1**
Capital account: credit	2 994 Z.	....	....	....	....	....	....	....	....
Capital account: debit	3 994 ..	....	....	....	....	....	....	....	−1
Total, Groups A Plus B	4 981 ..	*8,773*	*780*	*−10,284*	*−9,299*	*−8,076*	*−30,972*	*−25,922*	*−51,782*
C. Financial Account[1]	4 995 W.	**16,421**	**22,229**	**25,284**	**37,775**	**94,363**	**34,437**	**43,096**	**68,537**
Direct investment abroad	4 505 ..	−1,879	−2,179	−2,978	−14,344	−17,281	−19,257	−15,927	−13,151
Direct investment in India	4 555 Z.	4,323	5,771	7,606	20,336	25,483	43,406	35,596	24,159
Portfolio investment assets	4 602 ..	....	−17	−7	37	153	−45	−174	−1,110
Equity securities	4 610 ..	....	−17	−7	37	153	−45	−174	−1,110
Debt securities	4 619 ..	....	....	....	....	....	....	....	....
Portfolio investment liabilities	4 652 Z.	8,216	9,054	12,151	9,509	32,863	−15,030	21,112	39,972
Equity securities	4 660 ..	8,216	9,054	12,151	9,509	32,863	−15,030	21,112	39,972
Debt securities	4 669 Z.	....	....	....	....	....	....	....	....
Financial derivatives	4 910 ..	....	....	....	....	....	....	....	....
Financial derivatives assets	4 900 ..	....	....	....	....	....	....	....	....
Financial derivatives liabilities	4 905 ..	....	....	....	....	....	....	....	....
Other investment assets	4 703 ..	4,018	2,899	−4,432	−2,789	13,065	1,010	−9,484	−13,661
Monetary authorities	4 701 ..	....	....	....	....	....	....	....	....
General government	4 704 ..	−79	−104	−74	−25	−6	−259	−362	−110
Banks	4 705 ..	1,696	−14	−1,100	−4,489	4,510	1,487	96	449
Other sectors	4 728 ..	2,402	3,017	−3,258	1,725	8,562	−218	−9,218	−13,999
Other investment liabilities	4 753 W.	1,742	6,701	12,943	25,026	40,080	24,352	11,974	32,328
Monetary authorities	4 753 WA	−427	−45	598	453	−280	−533	5,404	−527
General government	4 753 ZB	−4,754	−578	1,882	1,417	1,908	2,659	2,910	5,236
Banks	4 753 ZC	7,589	1,860	4,562	3,839	3,385	4,888	−627	4,918
Other sectors	4 753 ZD	−666	5,464	5,901	19,317	35,068	17,339	4,287	22,701
Total, Groups A Through C	4 983 ..	*25,193*	*23,009*	*15,000*	*28,476*	*86,288*	*3,465*	*17,174*	*16,756*
D. Net Errors and Omissions	4 998 ..	**1,028**	**640**	**−446**	**694**	**1,200**	**21,908**	**−11,438**	**−15,789**
Total, Groups A Through D	4 984 ..	*26,222*	*23,649*	*14,554*	*29,170*	*87,488*	*25,373*	*5,736*	*966*
E. Reserves and Related Items	4 802 A.	**−26,222**	**−23,649**	**−14,554**	**−29,170**	**−87,488**	**−25,373**	**−5,736**	**−966**
Reserve assets	4 802 ..	−26,222	−23,649	−14,554	−29,170	−87,488	−25,373	−5,736	−966
Use of Fund credit and loans	4 766 ..	....	....	....	....	....	....	....	....
Exceptional financing	4 920 ..	....	....	....	....	....	....	....	....
Conversion rates: Indian rupees per U.S. dollar	0 101 ..	**46.583**	**45.316**	**44.100**	**45.307**	**41.349**	**43.505**	**48.405**	**45.726**

[1] Excludes components that have been classified in the categories of Group E.

2011, International Monetary Fund: *Balance of Payments Statistics Yearbook*

Table 2. STANDARD PRESENTATION, 2003–2010

(Millions of U.S. dollars)

	Code	2003	2004	2005	2006	2007	2008	2009	2010
CURRENT ACCOUNT	4 993	**8,773**	**780**	**−10,284**	**−9,299**	**−8,076**	**−30,972**	**−25,922**	**−51,781**
A. GOODS	4 100	**−7,188**	**−17,600**	**−32,517**	**−42,804**	**−54,827**	**−93,142**	**−79,665**	**−97,934**
Credit	2 100	**60,893**	**77,939**	**102,175**	**123,768**	**153,784**	**198,598**	**168,219**	**225,502**
General merchandise: exports f.o.b.	2 110	60,893	77,939	102,175	123,768	153,784	198,598	168,219	225,502
Goods for processing: exports f.o.b.	2 150	....	....	....	....	....	....	....	....
Repairs on goods	2 160	....	....	....	....	....	....	....	....
Goods procured in ports by carriers	2 170	....	....	....	....	....	....	....	....
Nonmonetary gold	2 180	....	....	....	....	....	....	....	....
Debit	3 100	**−68,081**	**−95,539**	**−134,692**	**−166,572**	**−208,611**	**−291,740**	**−247,883**	**−323,435**
General merchandise: imports f.o.b.	3 110	−68,081	−95,539	−134,692	−166,572	−208,611	−291,740	−247,883	−323,435
Goods for processing: imports f.o.b.	3 150	....	....	....	....	....	....	....	....
Repairs on goods	3 160	....	....	....	....	....	....	....	....
Goods procured in ports by carriers	3 170	....	....	....	....	....	....	....	....
Nonmonetary gold	3 180	....	....	....	....	....	....	....	....
B. SERVICES	4 200	**−976**	**2,640**	**5,241**	**11,034**	**16,124**	**18,782**	**11,987**	**6,921**
Total credit	2 200	*23,902*	*38,281*	*52,527*	*69,730*	*86,929*	*107,131*	*93,036*	*123,762*
Total debit	3 200	*−24,878*	*−35,641*	*−47,287*	*−58,696*	*−70,805*	*−88,348*	*−81,049*	*−116,842*
Transportation services, credit	2 205	**3,022**	**4,373**	**5,754**	**7,561**	**9,037**	**11,565**	**10,978**	**13,248**
Passenger	2 850	*97*	*137*	*166*	*281*	*504*	*630*	*373*	*513*
Freight	2 851	*2,284*	*3,317*	*4,245*	*5,251*	*6,216*	*7,910*	*7,508*	*9,502*
Other	2 852	*640*	*918*	*1,343*	*2,029*	*2,317*	*3,025*	*3,097*	*3,233*
Sea transport, passenger	2 207	....	....	....	....	....	....	....	....
Sea transport, freight	2 208	2,284	3,317	4,245	5,251	6,216	7,910	7,508	9,502
Sea transport, other	2 209	410	725	996	1,385	1,412	1,856	1,585	1,556
Air transport, passenger	2 211	97	137	166	281	504	630	373	513
Air transport, freight	2 212	....	....	....	....	....	....	....	....
Air transport, other	2 213	18	123	56	91	191	177	100	59
Other transport, passenger	2 215	....	....	....	....	....	....	....	....
Other transport, freight	2 216	....	....	....	....	....	....	....	....
Other transport, other	2 217	212	70	292	553	714	993	1,412	1,619
Transportation services, debit	3 205	**−9,312**	**−13,233**	**−20,678**	**−24,856**	**−30,836**	**−42,665**	**−35,449**	**−46,422**
Passenger	3 850	*−800*	*−967*	*−2,090*	*−1,893*	*−2,471*	*−2,477*	*−2,197*	*−3,118*
Freight	3 851	*−7,492*	*−10,728*	*−14,921*	*−18,572*	*−23,736*	*−33,606*	*−27,647*	*−36,742*
Other	3 852	*−1,020*	*−1,538*	*−3,667*	*−4,392*	*−4,628*	*−6,582*	*−5,604*	*−6,562*
Sea transport, passenger	3 207	....	....	....	....	....	....	....	....
Sea transport, freight	3 208	−4,637	−8,674	−13,760	−16,958	−20,338	−30,939	−26,379	−35,495
Sea transport, other	3 209	−741	−1,153	−2,253	−2,791	−2,605	−3,310	−2,752	−2,803
Air transport, passenger	3 211	−800	−967	−2,090	−1,893	−2,471	−2,477	−2,197	−3,118
Air transport, freight	3 212	−2,855	−2,054	−1,161	−1,613	−3,398	−2,668	−1,269	−1,247
Air transport, other	3 213	−217	−227	−350	−482	−816	−1,282	−996	−1,520
Other transport, passenger	3 215	....	....	....	....	....	....	....	....
Other transport, freight	3 216	....	....	....	....	....	....	....	....
Other transport, other	3 217	−62	−158	−1,064	−1,118	−1,207	−1,989	−1,856	−2,239
Travel, credit	2 236	**4,463**	**6,170**	**7,493**	**8,634**	**10,729**	**11,832**	**11,136**	**14,160**
Business travel	2 237	....	....	....	....	....	....	....	....
Personal travel	2 240	4,463	6,170	7,493	8,634	10,729	11,832	11,136	14,160
Travel, debit	3 236	**−3,585**	**−4,816**	**−6,187**	**−6,845**	**−8,219**	**−9,606**	**−9,310**	**−10,628**
Business travel	3 237	−2,402	−3,068	−1,601	−996	−894	−960	−2,961	−4,304
Personal travel	3 240	−1,183	−1,747	−4,586	−5,849	−7,325	−8,646	−6,349	−6,324
Other services, credit	2 200 BA	**16,417**	**27,738**	**39,280**	**53,535**	**67,162**	**83,734**	**70,922**	**96,354**
Communications	2 245	969	1,094	1,566	2,181	2,347	2,478	1,484	1,411
Construction	2 249	276	516	346	619	753	841	837	524
Insurance	2 253	408	842	941	1,113	1,506	1,561	1,528	1,782
Financial	2 260	367	341	1,143	2,357	3,379	4,291	3,662	6,003
Computer and information	2 262	11,876	16,344	21,875	29,088	37,492	49,111	46,657	56,701
Royalties and licence fees	2 266	24	53	206	61	163	148	193	129
Other business services	2 268	2,229	8,153	12,764	17,536	20,696	24,211	15,690	28,985
Personal, cultural, and recreational	2 287	....	46	111	306	509	707	468	335
Government, n.i.e.	2 291	269	350	328	274	317	386	405	485
Other services, debit	3 200 BA	**−11,981**	**−17,592**	**−20,422**	**−26,995**	**−31,751**	**−36,078**	**−36,290**	**−59,791**
Communications	3 245	−611	−579	−418	−606	−863	−1,045	−1,280	−1,194
Construction	3 249	−1,209	−829	−602	−794	−728	−704	−1,079	−991
Insurance	3 253	−1,164	−1,748	−2,330	−2,671	−3,189	−4,332	−4,021	−5,004
Financial	3 260	−488	−791	−869	−1,950	−3,236	−3,545	−3,759	−6,787
Computer and information	3 262	−686	−932	−1,266	−1,957	−3,583	−3,787	−2,266	−2,531
Royalties and licence fees	3 266	−550	−611	−672	−846	−1,160	−1,529	−1,860	−2,438
Other business services	3 268	−7,075	−11,693	−13,694	−17,593	−18,404	−20,309	−21,036	−39,678
Personal, cultural, and recreational	3 287	....	−61	−105	−104	−169	−325	−268	−467
Government, n.i.e.	3 291	−199	−348	−467	−474	−418	−501	−722	−702

Table 2 (Continued). STANDARD PRESENTATION, 2003–2010

(Millions of U.S. dollars)

	Code	2003	2004	2005	2006	2007	2008	2009	2010
C. INCOME..	4 300 ..	**−4,895**	**−4,052**	**−6,650**	**−6,245**	**−6,516**	**−5,364**	**−7,536**	**−12,926**
Total credit..	2 300 ..	*3,491*	*4,690*	*5,646*	*8,199*	*12,650*	*15,593*	*13,734*	*9,612*
Total debit...	3 300 ..	*−8,386*	*−8,742*	*−12,296*	*−14,445*	*−19,166*	*−20,958*	*−21,271*	*−22,538*
Compensation of employees, credit..............	2 310 ..	**115**	**353**	**266**	**309**	**447**	**798**	**873**	**991**
Compensation of employees, debit...............	3 310 ..	**−778**	**−1,200**	**−987**	**−858**	**−1,055**	**−1,330**	**−1,525**	**−2,007**
Investment income, credit.......................	2 320 ..	**3,376**	**4,337**	**5,380**	**7,891**	**12,203**	**14,796**	**12,862**	**8,621**
Direct investment income...................	2 330 ..	704	378	1,057	1,490	1,594	1,476	1,433	1,354
Dividends and distributed branch profits........	2 332 ..	14	54	176	411	512	393	350	270
Reinvested earnings and undistributed branch profits.....	2 333 ..	690	324	881	1,080	1,082	1,083	1,083	1,084
Income on debt (interest)................	2 334 ..	....	....	....	....	....	....	....	....
Portfolio investment income.............	2 339 ..	29	129	150	57	41	135	84	1,588
Income on equity.........................	2 340 ..	....	....	....	....	....	....	....	....
Income on bonds and notes.............	2 350 ..	29	129	150	57	41	135	84	1,588
Income on money market instruments......	2 360 ..	....	....	....	....	....	....	....	....
Other investment income..................	2 370 ..	2,643	3,830	4,172	6,343	10,569	13,185	11,345	5,679
Investment income, debit........................	3 320 ..	**−7,608**	**−7,542**	**−11,309**	**−13,587**	**−18,110**	**−19,628**	**−19,746**	**−20,530**
Direct investment income...................	3 330 ..	−2,413	−3,479	−5,244	−7,738	−10,910	−11,989	−12,278	−13,385
Dividends and distributed branch profits........	3 332 ..	−860	−1,686	−2,698	−2,677	−3,693	−3,295	−3,520	−4,515
Reinvested earnings and undistributed branch profits.....	3 333 ..	−1,553	−1,793	−2,546	−5,061	−7,217	−8,694	−8,758	−8,869
Income on debt (interest)................	3 334 ..	....	....	....	....	....	....	....	....
Portfolio investment income.............	3 339 ..	−31	−146	−612	−107	−53	−88	−201	−312
Income on equity.........................	3 340 ..	....	....	....	....	....	....	....	....
Income on bonds and notes.............	3 350 ..	−31	−146	−612	−107	−53	−88	−201	−312
Income on money market instruments......	3 360 ..	....	....	....	....	....	....	....	....
Other investment income..................	3 370 ..	−5,164	−3,917	−5,453	−5,743	−7,147	−7,551	−7,267	−6,834
D. CURRENT TRANSFERS............................	4 379 ..	**21,831**	**19,793**	**23,643**	**28,716**	**37,144**	**48,752**	**49,292**	**52,158**
Credit..	2 379 ..	**22,401**	**20,615**	**24,512**	**30,015**	**38,885**	**52,065**	**51,387**	**55,046**
General government.......................	2 380 ..	517	603	603	768	666	731	758	667
Other sectors..............................	2 390 ..	21,884	20,012	23,909	29,247	38,220	51,334	50,629	54,380
Workers' remittances..................	2 391 ..	20,884	18,397	21,859	28,025	36,770	49,180	48,596	53,044
Other current transfers...............	2 392 ..	1,000	1,615	2,050	1,223	1,450	2,155	2,033	1,336
Debit...	3 379 ..	**−570**	**−822**	**−869**	**−1,299**	**−1,742**	**−3,313**	**−2,095**	**−2,889**
General government.......................	3 380 ..	....	−266	−394	−442	−508	−418	−442	−619
Other sectors..............................	3 390 ..	−570	−556	−476	−857	−1,234	−2,895	−1,653	−2,270
Workers' remittances..................	3 391 ..	−487	−453	−361	−704	−1,004	−2,482	−1,366	−1,881
Other current transfers...............	3 392 ..	−82	−103	−114	−153	−230	−412	−287	−389
CAPITAL AND FINANCIAL ACCOUNT.............	4 996 ..	**−9,801**	**−1,420**	**10,730**	**8,605**	**6,875**	**9,064**	**37,360**	**67,570**
CAPITAL ACCOUNT...............................	4 994 ..	....	....	....	....	....	....	....	**−1**
Total credit..	2 994 ..	....	....	....	....	....	....	....	....
Total debit...	3 994 ..	....	....	....	....	....	....	....	*−1*
Capital transfers, credit.........................	2 400 ..	....	....	....	....	....	....	....	....
General government.......................	2 401 ..	....	....	....	....	....	....	....	....
Debt forgiveness......................	2 402 ..								
Other capital transfers...............	2 410 ..	....							
Other sectors..............................	2 430 ..								
Migrants' transfers....................	2 431 ..								
Debt forgiveness......................	2 432 ..								
Other capital transfers...............	2 440 ..								
Capital transfers, debit..........................	3 400 ..	....							
General government.......................	3 401 ..								
Debt forgiveness......................	3 402 ..								
Other capital transfers...............	3 410 ..								
Other sectors..............................	3 430 ..								
Migrants' transfers....................	3 431 ..								
Debt forgiveness......................	3 432 ..								
Other capital transfers...............	3 440 ..								
Nonproduced nonfinancial assets, credit............	2 480 ..	....							....
Nonproduced nonfinancial assets, debit.............	3 480 ..	....	....	....	....	....	....	....	**−1**

Table 2 (Continued). STANDARD PRESENTATION, 2003–2010

(Millions of U.S. dollars)

	Code	2003	2004	2005	2006	2007	2008	2009	2010
FINANCIAL ACCOUNT	4 995	**−9,801**	**−1,420**	**10,730**	**8,605**	**6,875**	**9,064**	**37,360**	**67,571**
A. DIRECT INVESTMENT	4 500	**2,444**	**3,592**	**4,629**	**5,992**	**8,202**	**24,150**	**19,669**	**11,008**
Direct investment abroad	4 505	**−1,879**	**−2,179**	**−2,978**	**−14,344**	**−17,281**	**−19,257**	**−15,927**	**−13,151**
Equity capital	4 510	−968	−1,601	−1,468	−11,741	−13,967	−14,127	−11,579	−6,580
Claims on affiliated enterprises	4 515	−968	−1,601	−1,468	−11,741	−13,967	−14,127	−11,579	−6,580
Liabilities to affiliated enterprises	4 520	....	....	....	....	....	....	....	....
Reinvested earnings	4 525	−690	−324	−881	−1,080	−1,082	−1,083	−1,083	−1,084
Other capital	4 530	−221	−254	−629	−1,523	−2,232	−4,046	−3,265	−5,487
Claims on affiliated enterprises	4 535	−221	−254	−629	−1,523	−2,232	−4,046	−3,265	−5,487
Liabilities to affiliated enterprises	4 540	....	....	....	....	....	....	....	....
Direct investment in India	4 555	**4,323**	**5,771**	**7,606**	**20,336**	**25,483**	**43,406**	**35,596**	**24,159**
Equity capital	4 560	2,129	3,636	4,723	14,968	17,711	33,996	25,355	15,364
Claims on direct investors	4 565	....	....	....	....	....	....	....	....
Liabilities to direct investors	4 570	2,129	3,636	4,723	14,968	17,711	33,996	25,355	15,364
Reinvested earnings	4 575	1,553	1,793	2,546	5,061	7,217	8,694	8,758	8,869
Other capital	4 580	641	342	337	307	554	716	1,483	−74
Claims on direct investors	4 585	641	342	337	307	255	....	....	....
Liabilities to direct investors	4 590	....	....	....	....	300	716	1,483	−74
B. PORTFOLIO INVESTMENT	4 600	**8,216**	**9,037**	**12,144**	**9,546**	**33,016**	**−15,075**	**20,937**	**38,862**
Assets	4 602	....	**−17**	**−7**	**37**	**153**	**−45**	**−174**	**−1,110**
Equity securities	4 610	....	−17	−7	37	153	−45	−174	−1,110
Monetary authorities	4 611	....	....	....	....	....	....	....	....
General government	4 612	....	....	....	....	....	....	....	....
Banks	4 613	....	....	....	....	....	....	....	....
Other sectors	4 614	....	−17	−7	37	153	−45	−174	−1,110
Debt securities	4 619	....	....	....	....	....	....	....	....
Bonds and notes	4 620	....	....	....	....	....	....	....	....
Monetary authorities	4 621	....	....	....	....	....	....	....	....
General government	4 622	....	....	....	....	....	....	....	....
Banks	4 623	....	....	....	....	....	....	....	....
Other sectors	4 624	....	....	....	....	....	....	....	....
Money market instruments	4 630	....	....	....	....	....	....	....	....
Monetary authorities	4 631	....	....	....	....	....	....	....	....
General government	4 632	....	....	....	....	....	....	....	....
Banks	4 633	....	....	....	....	....	....	....	....
Other sectors	4 634	....	....	....	....	....	....	....	....
Liabilities	4 652	**8,216**	**9,054**	**12,151**	**9,509**	**32,863**	**−15,030**	**21,112**	**39,972**
Equity securities	4 660	8,216	9,054	12,151	9,509	32,863	−15,030	21,112	39,972
Banks	4 663	....	....	....	....	....	....	....	....
Other sectors	4 664	....	....	....	....	....	....	....	....
Debt securities	4 669	....	....	....	....	....	....	....	....
Bonds and notes	4 670	....	....	....	....	....	....	....	....
Monetary authorities	4 671	....	....	....	....	....	....	....	....
General government	4 672	....	....	....	....	....	....	....	....
Banks	4 673	....	....	....	....	....	....	....	....
Other sectors	4 674	....	....	....	....	....	....	....	....
Money market instruments	4 680	....	....	....	....	....	....	....	....
Monetary authorities	4 681	....	....	....	....	....	....	....	....
General government	4 682	....	....	....	....	....	....	....	....
Banks	4 683	....	....	....	....	....	....	....	....
Other sectors	4 684	....	....	....	....	....	....	....	....
C. FINANCIAL DERIVATIVES	4 910	....	....	....	....	....	....	....	....
Monetary authorities	4 911	....	....	....	....	....	....	....	....
General government	4 912	....	....	....	....	....	....	....	....
Banks	4 913	....	....	....	....	....	....	....	....
Other sectors	4 914	....	....	....	....	....	....	....	....
Assets	4 900	....	....	....	....	....	....	....	....
Monetary authorities	4 901	....	....	....	....	....	....	....	....
General government	4 902	....	....	....	....	....	....	....	....
Banks	4 903	....	....	....	....	....	....	....	....
Other sectors	4 904	....	....	....	....	....	....	....	....
Liabilities	4 905	....	....	....	....	....	....	....	....
Monetary authorities	4 906	....	....	....	....	....	....	....	....
General government	4 907	....	....	....	....	....	....	....	....
Banks	4 908	....	....	....	....	....	....	....	....
Other sectors	4 909	....	....	....	....	....	....	....	....

Table 2 (Concluded). STANDARD PRESENTATION, 2003–2010

(Millions of U.S. dollars)

	Code	2003	2004	2005	2006	2007	2008	2009	2010
D. OTHER INVESTMENT	4 700	**5,761**	**9,600**	**8,511**	**22,237**	**53,146**	**25,362**	**2,490**	**18,667**
Assets	4 703	**4,018**	**2,899**	**−4,432**	**−2,789**	**13,065**	**1,010**	**−9,484**	**−13,661**
Trade credits	4 706	....	....	....	....	....	....	....	....
General government	4 707	....	....	....	....	....	....	....	....
of which: Short-term	4 709	....	....	....	....	....	....	....	....
Other sectors	4 710	....	....	....	....	....	....	....	....
of which: Short-term	4 712	....	....	....	....	....	....	....	....
Loans	4 714	−76	−236	−315	−247	−302	897	−710	−169
Monetary authorities	4 715	....	....	....	....	....	....	....	....
of which: Short-term	4 718	....	....	....	....	....	....	....	....
General government	4 719	−79	−104	−74	−25	−6	−259	−362	−110
of which: Short-term	4 721	....	....	....	....	....	....	....	....
Banks	4 722	....	....	....	....	....	....	....	....
of which: Short-term	4 724	....	....	....	....	....	....	....	....
Other sectors	4 725	3	−132	−241	−222	−295	1,156	−348	−59
of which: Short-term	4 727	....	....	....	....	....	....	....	....
Currency and deposits	4 730	1,696	−14	−1,100	−4,489	4,510	1,487	96	449
Monetary authorities	4 731	....	....	....	....	....	....	....	....
General government	4 732	....	....	....	....	....	....	....	....
Banks	4 733	1,696	−14	−1,100	−4,489	4,510	1,487	96	449
Other sectors	4 734	....	....	....	....	....	....	....	....
Other assets	4 736	2,399	3,149	−3,017	1,946	8,857	−1,374	−8,870	−13,940
Monetary authorities	4 737	....	....	....	....	....	....	....	....
of which: Short-term	4 739	....	....	....	....	....	....	....	....
General government	4 740	....	....	....	....	....	....	....	....
of which: Short-term	4 742	....	....	....	....	....	....	....	....
Banks	4 743	....	....	....	....	....	....	....	....
of which: Short-term	4 745	....	....	....	....	....	....	....	....
Other sectors	4 746	2,399	3,149	−3,017	1,946	8,857	−1,374	−8,870	−13,940
of which: Short-term	4 748	....	....	....	....	....	−1,374	−8,870	−13,940
Liabilities	4 753	**1,742**	**6,701**	**12,943**	**25,026**	**40,080**	**24,352**	**11,974**	**32,328**
Trade credits	4 756	2,883	2,016	4,543	5,663	11,056	6,416	510	12,947
General government	4 757	....	....	....	....	....	....	....	....
of which: Short-term	4 759	....	....	....	....	....	....	....	....
Other sectors	4 760	2,883	2,016	4,543	5,663	11,056	6,416	510	12,947
of which: Short-term	4 762	2,883	2,016	4,543	5,663	11,056	6,416	510	12,947
Loans	4 764	−5,059	6,136	6,342	13,562	29,588	15,245	409	18,109
Monetary authorities	4 765	....	....	....	....	....	....	....	....
of which: Use of Fund credit and loans from the Fund	4 766	....	....	....	....	....	....	....	....
of which: Short-term	4 768	....	....	....	....	....	....	....	....
General government	4 769	−4,754	−578	1,882	1,417	1,908	2,659	2,910	5,236
of which: Short-term	4 771	....	....	....	....	....	....	....	....
Banks	4 772	3,244	3,266	3,102	−1,509	3,668	1,664	−6,277	3,119
of which: Short-term	4 774	....	....	....	....	....	....	....	....
Other sectors	4 775	−3,549	3,448	1,358	13,654	24,011	10,922	3,776	9,754
of which: Short-term	4 777	....	....	....	....	....	....	....	....
Currency and deposits	4 780	3,918	−1,451	2,058	5,801	−564	2,691	5,906	1,272
Monetary authorities	4 781	−427	−45	598	453	−280	−533	256	−527
General government	4 782	....	....	....	....	....	....	....	....
Banks	4 783	4,345	−1,406	1,460	5,348	−283	3,224	5,650	1,799
Other sectors	4 784	....	....	....	....	....	....	....	....
Other liabilities	4 786	....	....	....	....	....	....	5,148	....
Monetary authorities	4 787	....	....	....	....	....	....	5,148	....
of which: Short-term	4 789	....	....	....	....	....	....	....	....
General government	4 790	....	....	....	....	....	....	....	....
of which: Short-term	4 792	....	....	....	....	....	....	....	....
Banks	4 793	....	....	....	....	....	....	....	....
of which: Short-term	4 795	....	....	....	....	....	....	....	....
Other sectors	4 796	....	....	....	....	....	....	....	....
of which: Short-term	4 798	....	....	....	....	....	....	....	....
E. RESERVE ASSETS	4 802	**−26,222**	**−23,649**	**−14,554**	**−29,170**	**−87,488**	**−25,373**	**−5,736**	**−966**
Monetary gold	4 812	....	....	....	....	....	....	....	....
Special drawing rights	4 811	4	−2	....	4	−2	....	−5,145	....
Reserve position in the Fund	4 810	−563	−46	405	388	140	−383	−591	−966
Foreign exchange	4 803	−25,663	−23,601	−14,959	−29,562	−87,626	−24,990	....	....
Other claims	4 813	....	....	....	....	....	....	....	....
NET ERRORS AND OMISSIONS	4 998	**1,028**	**640**	**−446**	**694**	**1,200**	**21,908**	**−11,438**	**−15,789**

Table 3. IIP: (End-March following year stocks) 2003–2005; (End-period stocks)2006-2010

(Millions of U.S. dollars)

	Code	2003	2004	2005	2006	2007	2008	2009	2010
ASSETS	8 995 C.	**129,520**	**167,482**	**181,093**	**231,642**	**335,780**	**332,167**	**380,843**	**410,409**
Direct investment abroad	8 505 ..	**7,392**	**10,072**	**12,832**	**27,036**	**44,080**	**62,451**	**79,164**	**93,904**
Equity capital and reinvested earnings	8 506 ..	6,859	9,121	11,176	24,110	38,948	53,442	66,737	74,955
Claims on affiliated enterprises	8 507 ..	6,859	9,121	11,176	24,110	38,948	53,442	66,737	74,955
Liabilities to affiliated enterprises	8 508 ..	....	....	....	....	....	....	....	....
Other capital	8 530 ..	532	951	1,657	2,925	5,132	9,009	12,426	18,949
Claims on affiliated enterprises	8 535 ..	532	951	1,657	2,925	5,132	9,009	12,426	18,949
Liabilities to affiliated enterprises	8 540 ..	....	....	....	....	....	....	....	....
Portfolio investment	8 602 ..	**359**	**471**	**962**	**1,115**	**724**	**514**	**1,029**	**1,611**
Equity securities	8 610 ..	169	244	491	656	566	494	987	1,572
Monetary authorities	8 611 ..	....	....	....	....	....	....	....	....
General government	8 612 ..	....	....	....	....	....	....	....	....
Banks	8 613 ..	143	212	438	334	361	327	256	507
Other sectors	8 614 ..	27	32	53	322	206	167	731	1,065
Debt securities	8 619 ..	190	227	471	459	158	20	42	39
Bonds and notes	8 620 ..	113	186	455	441	144	7	34	31
Monetary authorities	8 621 ..	....	....	....	....	....	....	....	....
General government	8 622 ..	....	....	....	....	....	....	....	....
Banks	8 623 ..	111	183	445	433	141	5	4	31
Other sectors	8 624 ..	2	2	10	8	3	3	30	....
Money market instruments	8 630 ..	77	41	16	18	14	13	8	8
Monetary authorities	8 631 ..	....	....	....	....	....	....	....	....
General government	8 632 ..	....	....	....	....	....	....	....	....
Banks	8 633 ..	77	41	16	18	14	13	8	8
Other sectors	8 634 ..	....	....	....	....	....	....	....	....
Financial derivatives	8 900 ..	....	....	....	....	....	....	....	....
Monetary authorities	8 901 ..	....	....	....	....	....	....	....	....
General government	8 902 ..	....	....	....	....	....	....	....	....
Banks	8 903 ..	....	....	....	....	....	....	....	....
Other sectors	8 904 ..	....	....	....	....	....	....	....	....
Other investment	8 703 ..	**14,224**	**14,909**	**17,053**	**26,297**	**15,695**	**13,324**	**17,177**	**17,147**
Trade credits	8 706 ..	544	1,111	−281	2,185	542	−4,474	−1,680	−5,257
General government	8 707 ..	....	....	....	....	....	....	....	....
of which: Short-term	8 709 ..	....	....	....	....	....	....	....	....
Other sectors	8 710 ..	544	1,111	−281	2,185	542	−4,474	−1,680	−5,257
of which: Short-term	8 712 ..	*544*	*1,111*	*−281*	*2,185*	*542*	*−4,474*	*−1,680*	*−5,257*
Loans	8 714 ..	1,682	1,869	2,554	3,710	3,734	4,631	3,891	3,973
Monetary authorities	8 715 ..	....	....	....	....	....	....	....	....
of which: Short-term	8 718 ..	....	....	....	....	....	....	....	....
General government	8 719 ..	659	791	826	842	956	744	912	970
of which: Short-term	8 721 ..	....	....	....	....	....	....	....	....
Banks	8 722 ..	762	794	1,405	2,519	1,909	3,055	1,866	1,840
of which: Short-term	8 724 ..	....	....	....	....	....	....	....	....
Other sectors	8 725 ..	261	284	322	349	869	832	1,113	1,163
of which: Short-term	8 727 ..	....	....	....	....	....	....	....	....
Currency and deposits	8 730 ..	9,079	8,484	11,499	16,584	6,753	6,478	7,745	9,121
Monetary authorities	8 731 ..	....	....	....	....	....	....	....	....
General government	8 732 ..	5	4	3	2	1	2	1	1
Banks	8 733 ..	8,377	7,582	10,303	15,586	5,872	5,793	7,127	8,476
Other sectors	8 734 ..	696	899	1,193	996	880	683	616	644
Other assets	8 736 ..	2,919	3,446	3,281	3,818	4,665	6,689	7,220	9,311
Monetary authorities	8 737 ..	....	....	....	....	....	....	....	....
of which: Short-term	8 739 ..	....	....	....	....	....	....	....	....
General government	8 740 ..	683	729	701	715	726	740	734	737
of which: Short-term	8 742 ..	....	....	....	....	....	....	....	....
Banks	8 743 ..	1,429	1,680	1,785	2,171	2,914	5,027	5,508	7,538
of which: Short-term	8 745 ..	....	....	....	....	....	....	....	....
Other sectors	8 746 ..	808	1,037	795	932	1,026	922	978	1,036
of which: Short-term	8 748 ..	....	....	....	....	....	....	....	....
Reserve assets	8 802 ..	**107,544**	**142,030**	**150,246**	**177,195**	**275,281**	**255,877**	**283,474**	**297,746**
Monetary gold	8 812 ..	3,994	4,517	5,697	6,515	8,327	8,484	18,292	22,470
Special drawing rights	8 811 ..	3	5	4	1	3	3	5,169	5,078
Reserve position in the Fund	8 810 ..	1,318	1,424	902	550	432	813	1,430	2,385
Foreign exchange	8 803 ..	102,229	136,084	143,643	170,130	266,519	246,577	258,583	267,815
Other claims	8 813 ..	....	....	....	....	....	....	....	....

Table 3 (Concluded). IIP: (End-March following year stocks) 2003–2005; (End-period stocks)2006-2010

(Millions of U.S. dollars)

	Code	2003	2004	2005	2006	2007	2008	2009	2010
LIABILITIES	8 995 D.	**175,761**	**210,728**	**228,529**	**291,324**	**410,546**	**418,047**	**513,424**	**633,457**
Direct investment in India	8 555	**36,374**	**44,669**	**50,614**	**70,870**	**105,790**	**123,294**	**167,022**	**198,405**
Equity capital and reinvested earnings	8 556	34,012	41,392	47,349	67,320	101,568	118,210	160,129	191,931
Claims on direct investors	8 557	....	....	....	....	....	....	....	....
Liabilities to direct investors	8 558	34,012	41,392	47,349	67,320	101,568	118,210	160,129	191,931
Other capital	8 580	2,362	3,276	3,265	3,550	4,222	5,084	6,893	6,474
Claims on direct investors	8 585	....	....	....	....	....	....	....	....
Liabilities to direct investors	8 590	2,362	3,276	3,265	3,550	4,222	5,084	6,893	6,474
Portfolio investment	8 652	**41,614**	**55,907**	**63,970**	**74,179**	**122,599**	**91,581**	**117,086**	**171,496**
Equity securities	8 660	32,322	43,323	54,184	60,512	101,680	69,026	93,320	138,216
Banks	8 663	....	....	....	....	....	....	....	....
Other sectors	8 664	32,322	43,323	54,184	60,512	101,680	69,026	93,320	138,216
Debt securities	8 669	9,291	12,583	9,786	13,667	20,919	22,555	23,766	33,279
Bonds and notes	8 670	9,291	12,583	9,719	13,178	19,974	20,261	21,557	29,295
Monetary authorities	8 671	....	....	....	....	....	....	....	....
General government	8 672	177	159	109	109	81	47	38	44
Banks	8 673	5,265	5,855	528	532	551	608	299	320
Other sectors	8 674	3,850	6,569	9,082	12,537	19,343	19,606	21,220	28,931
Money market instruments	8 680	....	....	67	488	945	2,293	2,209	3,984
Monetary authorities	8 681	....	....	....	....	....	....	....	....
General government	8 682	....	....	67	488	945	2,293	2,209	3,984
Banks	8 683	....	....	....	....	....	....	....	....
Other sectors	8 684	....	....	....	....	....	....	....	....
Financial derivatives	8 905	....	....	....	....	....	....	....	....
Monetary authorities	8 906	....	....	....	....	....	....	....	....
General government	8 907	....	....	....	....	....	....	....	....
Banks	8 908	....	....	....	....	....	....	....	....
Other sectors	8 909	....	....	....	....	....	....	....	....
Other investment	8 753	**97,773**	**110,153**	**113,945**	**146,275**	**182,156**	**203,172**	**229,317**	**263,556**
Trade credits	8 756	6,013	9,595	10,401	27,006	37,905	44,511	45,064	57,925
General government	8 757	1,101	1,141	1,051	1,061	1,125	1,358	1,370	1,536
of which: Short-term	8 759	....	....	....	....	....	....	....	....
Other sectors	8 760	4,912	8,454	9,350	25,945	36,780	43,153	43,694	56,389
of which: Short-term	8 762	*3,932*	*7,554*	*8,607*	*25,228*	*36,094*	*42,451*	*43,022*	*55,748*
Loans	8 764	60,170	65,589	67,164	76,057	97,280	114,832	121,941	140,029
Monetary authorities	8 765	....	....	....	....	....	....	....	....
of which: Use of Fund credit and loans from the Fund	8 766	....	....	....	....	....	....	....	....
of which: Short-term	8 768	....	....	....	....	....	....	....	....
General government	8 769	41,673	44,811	43,816	46,139	49,806	53,400	55,530	61,159
of which: Short-term	8 771	....	....	....	....	....	....	....	....
Banks	8 772	2,004	1,710	1,482	1,521	1,606	1,700	2,308	2,937
of which: Short-term	8 774	....	....	....	....	....	....	....	....
Other sectors	8 775	16,493	19,068	21,866	28,396	45,867	59,732	64,103	75,933
of which: Short-term	8 777	....	....	....	....	....	....	....	....
Currency and deposits	8 780	30,657	33,772	35,791	41,204	44,129	41,070	48,010	51,332
Monetary authorities	8 781	630	901	1,015	996	1,095	774	662	665
General government	8 782	....	....	....	....	....	....	....	....
Banks	8 783	30,027	32,871	34,775	40,208	43,034	40,296	47,348	50,667
Other sectors	8 784	....	....	....	....	....	....	....	....
Other liabilities	8 786	934	1,196	590	2,009	2,843	2,759	14,302	14,270
Monetary authorities	8 787	....	....	....	....	1,076	1,049	6,237	6,127
of which: Short-term	8 789	....	....	....	....	....	....	....	....
General government	8 790	....	....	....	....	....	....	6,237	6,127
of which: Short-term	8 792	....	....	....	....	....	....	....	....
Banks	8 793	15	165	69	1,059	802	596	694	692
of which: Short-term	8 795	*15*	*165*	*69*	*1,059*	*802*	*596*	*694*	*692*
Other sectors	8 796	919	1,032	521	950	965	1,114	1,134	1,325
of which: Short-term	8 798	*919*	*1,032*	*521*	*950*	*965*	*1,114*	*1,134*	*1,325*
NET INTERNATIONAL INVESTMENT POSITION	8 995	**−46,242**	**−43,246**	**−47,436**	**−59,682**	**−74,766**	**−85,880**	**−132,581**	**−223,048**
Conversion rates: Indian rupees per U.S. dollar (end of period)	0 102	**45.605**	**43.585**	**45.065**	**44.245**	**39.415**	**48.455**	**46.680**	**44.810**

Table 1. ANALYTIC PRESENTATION, 2003–2010

(Millions of U.S. dollars)

	Code	2003	2004	2005	2006	2007	2008	2009	2010
A. Current Account[1]	4 993 Z.	**8,107**	**1,563**	**278**	**10,859**	**10,493**	**125**	**10,628**	**5,643**
Goods: exports f.o.b.	2 100 ..	64,109	70,767	86,995	103,528	118,014	139,606	119,646	158,074
Goods: imports f.o.b.	3 100 ..	−39,546	−50,615	−69,462	−73,868	−85,260	−116,691	−88,714	−127,447
Balance on Goods	4 100 ..	*24,563*	*20,152*	*17,534*	*29,660*	*32,754*	*22,915*	*30,932*	*30,628*
Services: credit	2 200 ..	5,293	12,045	12,926	11,520	12,487	15,247	13,155	16,766
Services: debit	3 200 ..	−17,400	−20,856	−22,049	−21,394	−24,328	−28,245	−22,896	−26,090
Balance on Goods and Services	4 991 ..	*12,456*	*11,341*	*8,411*	*19,786*	*20,913*	*9,917*	*21,191*	*21,303*
Income: credit	2 300 ..	1,054	1,995	2,338	2,587	3,469	3,592	1,921	1,890
Income: debit	3 300 ..	−7,272	−12,912	−15,264	−16,377	−18,994	−18,747	−17,061	−22,181
Balance on Goods, Services, and Income	4 992 ..	*6,238*	*424*	*−4,515*	*5,996*	*5,389*	*−5,238*	*6,051*	*1,012*
Current transfers: credit	2 379 Z.	2,053	2,433	5,993	6,079	6,801	7,352	7,241	7,571
Current transfers: debit	3 379 ..	−184	−1,294	−1,200	−1,216	−1,697	−1,989	−2,663	−2,941
B. Capital Account[1]	4 994 Z.	....	....	**334**	**350**	**546**	**294**	**96**	**50**
Capital account: credit	2 994 Z.	....	....	334	350	546	294	96	50
Capital account: debit	3 994 ..	....	....	....	....	....	....	....	....
Total, Groups A Plus B	4 981 ..	*8,107*	*1,563*	*611*	*11,210*	*11,039*	*420*	*10,724*	*5,692*
C. Financial Account[1]	4 995 W.	**−949**	**−667**	**−2,587**	**2,674**	**3,045**	**−2,126**	**4,756**	**26,151**
Direct investment abroad	4 505 ..	....	−3,408	−3,065	−2,726	−4,675	−5,900	−2,249	−2,664
Direct investment in Indonesia	4 555 Z.	−597	1,896	8,336	4,914	6,928	9,318	4,877	13,371
Portfolio investment assets	4 602 ..	....	353	−1,080	−1,830	−4,415	−1,294	−144	−2,511
Equity securities	4 610 ..	....	−106	38	10	−217	−298	−363	−96
Debt securities	4 619 ..	....	459	−1,118	−1,841	−4,199	−996	219	−2,415
Portfolio investment liabilities	4 652 Z.	2,251	4,056	5,270	6,107	9,981	3,059	10,480	15,713
Equity securities	4 660 ..	1,130	2,043	−165	1,898	3,559	322	787	2,132
Debt securities	4 669 Z.	1,121	2,014	5,435	4,210	6,422	2,736	9,693	13,582
Financial derivatives	4 910 ..	....	....	....	....	....	....	....	....
Financial derivatives assets	4 900 ..	....	....	....	....	....	....	....	....
Financial derivatives liabilities	4 905 ..	....	....	....	....	....	....	....	....
Other investment assets	4 703 ..	−5	985	−8,646	−1,587	−4,486	−10,755	−12,002	−1,725
Monetary authorities	4 701 ..	....	....	....	....	....	....	101	1
General government	4 704 ..	....	....	....	....	....	....	....	....
Banks	4 705 ..	....	1,701	−4,662	1,719	2,334	−4,830	−6,800	2,695
Other sectors	4 728 ..	−5	−716	−3,984	−3,306	−6,820	−5,925	−5,303	−4,421
Other investment liabilities	4 753 W.	−2,599	−4,549	−3,401	−2,204	−289	3,446	3,794	3,968
Monetary authorities	4 753 WA	....	−12	....	−528	−45	−71	2,653	1,972
General government	4 753 ZB	−398	−5,201	−3,446	−1,967	−2,318	−1,365	−1,127	−215
Banks	4 753 ZC	−69	678	−1,150	924	796	2,048	−114	1,076
Other sectors	4 753 ZD	−2,132	−15	1,194	−632	1,279	2,834	2,382	1,136
Total, Groups A Through C	4 983 ..	*7,157*	*896*	*−1,975*	*13,884*	*14,084*	*−1,707*	*15,481*	*31,844*
D. Net Errors and Omissions	4 998 ..	**−3,510**	**−3,094**	**−136**	**1,074**	**−1,378**	**−212**	**−2,975**	**−1,559**
Total, Groups A Through D	4 984 ..	*3,647*	*−2,198*	*−2,111*	*14,958*	*12,706*	*−1,918*	*12,506*	*30,284*
E. Reserves and Related Items	4 802 A.	**−3,647**	**2,198**	**2,111**	**−14,958**	**−12,706**	**1,918**	**−12,506**	**−30,284**
Reserve assets	4 802 ..	−4,236	686	657	−6,903	−12,706	1,918	−12,506	−30,284
Use of Fund credit and loans	4 766 ..	588	−1,007	−1,144	−8,055	....	....	....	....
Exceptional financing	4 920 ..	....	2,519	2,598	....	....	....	....	....
Conversion rates: rupiah per U.S. dollar	0 101 ..	**8,577.1**	**8,938.9**	**9,704.7**	**9,159.3**	**9,141.0**	**9,699.0**	**10,389.9**	**9,090.4**

[1] Excludes components that have been classified in the categories of Group E.

Table 2. STANDARD PRESENTATION, 2003–2010

(Millions of U.S. dollars)

	Code	2003	2004	2005	2006	2007	2008	2009	2010
CURRENT ACCOUNT	4 993	8,107	1,563	278	10,859	10,493	125	10,628	5,643
A. GOODS	4 100	24,563	20,152	17,534	29,660	32,754	22,915	30,932	30,628
Credit	2 100	64,109	70,767	86,995	103,528	118,014	139,606	119,646	158,074
General merchandise: exports f.o.b.	2 110	64,109	65,855	80,948	97,490	110,384	130,448	111,515	147,629
Goods for processing: exports f.o.b.	2 150	....	4,683	5,269	5,213	6,637	7,242	6,307	8,043
Repairs on goods	2 160	....	....	44	64	74	154	72	65
Goods procured in ports by carriers	2 170	....	....	498	223	217	911	898	1,238
Nonmonetary gold	2 180	....	229	236	538	701	850	854	1,099
Debit	3 100	−39,546	−50,615	−69,462	−73,868	−85,260	−116,691	−88,714	−127,447
General merchandise: imports f.o.b.	3 110	−39,546	−46,616	−63,523	−65,609	−76,395	−107,017	−80,365	−118,179
Goods for processing: imports f.o.b.	3 150	....	−3,999	−5,242	−7,648	−8,234	−8,797	−7,479	−8,260
Repairs on goods	3 160	....	....	−148	−167	−250	−225	−256	−224
Goods procured in ports by carriers	3 170	....	....	−548	−444	−380	−625	−591	−700
Nonmonetary gold	3 180	....	....	....	....	....	−25	−23	−83
B. SERVICES	4 200	−12,108	−8,811	−9,122	−9,874	−11,841	−12,998	−9,741	−9,324
Total credit	2 200	*5,293*	*12,045*	*12,926*	*11,520*	*12,487*	*15,247*	*13,155*	*16,766*
Total debit	3 200	*−17,400*	*−20,856*	*−22,049*	*−21,394*	*−24,328*	*−28,245*	*−22,896*	*−26,090*
Transportation services, credit	2 205	856	2,279	2,842	2,102	2,206	2,800	2,439	2,665
Passenger	2 850	*424*	*428*	*572*	*442*	*485*	*773*	*456*	*660*
Freight	2 851	....	*1,288*	*1,733*	*1,331*	*1,365*	*1,565*	*1,498*	*1,479*
Other	2 852	*431*	*563*	*538*	*329*	*356*	*462*	*485*	*526*
Sea transport, passenger	2 207	....	....	....	....	....	....	....	....
Sea transport, freight	2 208	....	....	....	....	....	....	....	....
Sea transport, other	2 209	....	....	....	....	....	....	....	....
Air transport, passenger	2 211	....	....	....	....	....	....	....	....
Air transport, freight	2 212	....	....	....	....	....	....	....	....
Air transport, other	2 213	....	....	....	....	....	....	....	....
Other transport, passenger	2 215	....	....	....	....	....	....	....	....
Other transport, freight	2 216	....	....	....	....	....	....	....	....
Other transport, other	2 217	....	....	....	....	....	....	....	....
Transportation services, debit	3 205	−4,824	−5,474	−7,451	−8,181	−9,501	−13,895	−6,522	−8,673
Passenger	3 850	*−1,345*	*−1,062*	*−1,156*	*−1,428*	*−1,674*	*−3,247*	*−1,592*	*−2,037*
Freight	3 851	*−2,697*	*−4,213*	*−6,063*	*−6,478*	*−7,483*	*−10,260*	*−4,704*	*−6,327*
Other	3 852	*−781*	*−199*	*−231*	*−275*	*−343*	*−388*	*−226*	*−309*
Sea transport, passenger	3 207	....	....	....	....	....	....	....	....
Sea transport, freight	3 208	....	....	....	....	....	....	....	....
Sea transport, other	3 209	....	....	....	....	....	....	....	....
Air transport, passenger	3 211	....	....	....	....	....	....	....	....
Air transport, freight	3 212	....	....	....	....	....	....	....	....
Air transport, other	3 213	....	....	....	....	....	....	....	....
Other transport, passenger	3 215	....	....	....	....	....	....	....	....
Other transport, freight	3 216	....	....	....	....	....	....	....	....
Other transport, other	3 217	....	....	....	....	....	....	....	....
Travel, credit	2 236	4,037	4,798	4,522	4,448	5,346	7,377	5,598	6,958
Business travel	2 237	1,211	1,439	1,357	1,334	1,604	2,213	1,816	2,242
Personal travel	2 240	2,826	3,358	3,165	3,114	3,742	5,164	3,782	4,716
Travel, debit	3 236	−3,082	−3,507	−3,584	−4,030	−4,904	−5,554	−5,316	−6,395
Business travel	3 237	−1,053	−1,069	−1,076	−1,247	−1,536	−1,763	−1,554	−2,000
Personal travel	3 240	−2,029	−2,438	−2,509	−2,783	−3,368	−3,791	−3,762	−4,395
Other services, credit	2 200 BA	400	4,969	5,563	4,970	4,935	5,069	5,119	7,142
Communications	2 245	248	835	998	1,102	1,343	1,096	1,031	1,126
Construction	2 249	....	463	484	456	459	667	586	520
Insurance	2 253	3	8	15	32	19	20	21	22
Financial	2 260	....	297	367	183	289	304	178	332
Computer and information	2 262	....	138	147	118	141	178	126	114
Royalties and licence fees	2 266	....	221	263	13	31	27	38	60
Other business services	2 268	....	2,669	2,876	2,564	2,185	2,184	2,527	4,309
Personal, cultural, and recreational	2 287	....	47	57	74	55	77	75	104
Government, n.i.e.	2 291	150	291	355	427	414	515	537	555
Other services, debit	3 200 BA	−9,494	−11,876	−11,014	−9,183	−9,924	−8,796	−11,058	−11,023
Communications	3 245	−131	−359	−495	−571	−641	−776	−452	−547
Construction	3 249	....	−708	−726	−986	−740	−749	−798	−592
Insurance	3 253	−300	−353	−338	−384	−664	−683	−1,318	−1,153
Financial	3 260	....	−594	−539	−346	−373	−342	−405	−450
Computer and information	3 262	....	−468	−561	−595	−679	−713	−642	−585
Royalties and licence fees	3 266	....	−990	−961	−872	−1,085	−1,328	−1,530	−1,616
Other business services	3 268	−8,834	−7,984	−7,017	−5,086	−5,380	−3,829	−5,525	−5,456
Personal, cultural, and recreational	3 287	....	−184	−166	−124	−107	−126	−126	−133
Government, n.i.e.	3 291	−230	−236	−212	−219	−254	−251	−260	−490

Table 2 (Continued). STANDARD PRESENTATION, 2003–2010

(Millions of U.S. dollars)

	Code	2003	2004	2005	2006	2007	2008	2009	2010
C. INCOME	4 300	**−6,217**	**−10,917**	**−12,927**	**−13,790**	**−15,525**	**−15,155**	**−15,140**	**−20,291**
Total credit	2 300	*1,054*	*1,995*	*2,338*	*2,587*	*3,469*	*3,592*	*1,921*	*1,890*
Total debit	3 300	*−7,272*	*−12,912*	*−15,264*	*−16,377*	*−18,994*	*−18,747*	*−17,061*	*−22,181*
Compensation of employees, credit	2 310	....	**166**	**123**	**162**	**171**	**176**	**175**	**181**
Compensation of employees, debit	3 310	....	**−138**	**−344**	**−299**	**−483**	**−560**	**−953**	**−962**
Investment income, credit	2 320	**1,054**	**1,829**	**2,214**	**2,425**	**3,299**	**3,415**	**1,746**	**1,709**
Direct investment income	2 330	....	103	209	116	299	369	212	139
Dividends and distributed branch profits	2 332	....	....	....	....	....	....	....	....
Reinvested earnings and undistributed branch profits	2 333	....	....	....	....	....	....	....	....
Income on debt (interest)	2 334	....	3	6	10	60	26	15	19
Portfolio investment income	2 339	671	1,085	1,258	1,382	1,827	2,349	1,249	1,360
Income on equity	2 340	....	210	272	160	312	218	288	358
Income on bonds and notes	2 350	....	....	....	....	....	....	....	....
Income on money market instruments	2 360	....	....	....	....	....	....	....	....
Other investment income	2 370	384	641	747	928	1,173	698	285	209
Investment income, debit	3 320	**−7,272**	**−12,774**	**−14,920**	**−16,078**	**−18,511**	**−18,188**	**−16,108**	**−21,218**
Direct investment income	3 330	−2,754	−8,323	−9,525	−9,637	−10,813	−10,675	−8,848	−12,436
Dividends and distributed branch profits	3 332	−1,445	−7,237	....	....	....	....	....	....
Reinvested earnings and undistributed branch profits	3 333	....	....	....	....	....	....	....	....
Income on debt (interest)	3 334	−1,309	−1,087	−146	−129	−215	−180	−165	−262
Portfolio investment income	3 339	−9	−23	−1,715	−2,898	−3,779	−4,121	−4,509	−6,174
Income on equity	3 340	....	....	−1,495	−1,244	−1,775	−1,745	−2,102	−2,590
Income on bonds and notes	3 350	....	....	....	....	....	....	....	....
Income on money market instruments	3 360	....	....	....	....	....	....	....	....
Other investment income	3 370	−4,508	−4,428	−3,680	−3,542	−3,919	−3,391	−2,751	−2,608
D. CURRENT TRANSFERS	4 379	**1,869**	**1,139**	**4,793**	**4,863**	**5,104**	**5,364**	**4,578**	**4,630**
Credit	2 379	**2,053**	**2,433**	**5,993**	**6,079**	**6,801**	**7,352**	**7,241**	**7,571**
General government	2 380	139	296	44	22	180	189	89	287
Other sectors	2 390	1,914	2,136	5,949	6,057	6,621	7,163	7,152	7,285
Workers' remittances	2 391	1,489	1,700	5,296	5,560	6,004	6,618	6,618	6,735
Other current transfers	2 392	425	436	653	497	617	545	534	550
Debit	3 379	**−184**	**−1,294**	**−1,200**	**−1,216**	**−1,697**	**−1,989**	**−2,663**	**−2,941**
General government	3 380	....	....	....	....	....	....	....	....
Other sectors	3 390	−184	−1,294	−1,200	−1,216	−1,697	−1,989	−2,663	−2,941
Workers' remittances	3 391	....	−775	−834	−1,060	−1,171	−1,412	−1,748	−1,877
Other current transfers	3 392	−184	−519	−365	−156	−525	−577	−915	−1,063
CAPITAL AND FINANCIAL ACCOUNT	4 996	**−4,597**	**1,531**	**−141**	**−11,933**	**−9,115**	**86**	**−7,653**	**−4,083**
CAPITAL ACCOUNT	4 994	....	....	**334**	**350**	**546**	**294**	**96**	**50**
Total credit	2 994	....	....	*334*	*350*	*546*	*294*	*96*	*50*
Total debit	3 994	....	....	....	....	....	....	....	....
Capital transfers, credit	2 400	....	....	**334**	**350**	**546**	**294**	**96**	**50**
General government	2 401	....	....	27	89	81	21	11	32
Debt forgiveness	2 402	....	....	....	....	....	....	....	....
Other capital transfers	2 410	....	....	27	89	81	21	11	32
Other sectors	2 430	....	....	307	261	465	273	85	18
Migrants' transfers	2 431	....	....	....	....	....	....	....	....
Debt forgiveness	2 432	....	....	....	....	....	....	....	....
Other capital transfers	2 440	....	....	307	261	465	273	85	18
Capital transfers, debit	3 400	....	....	....	....	....	....	....	....
General government	3 401	....	....	....	....	....	....	....	....
Debt forgiveness	3 402	....	....	....	....	....	....	....	....
Other capital transfers	3 410	....	....	....	....	....	....	....	....
Other sectors	3 430	....	....	....	....	....	....	....	....
Migrants' transfers	3 431	....	....	....	....	....	....	....	....
Debt forgiveness	3 432	....	....	....	....	....	....	....	....
Other capital transfers	3 440	....	....	....	....	....	....	....	....
Nonproduced nonfinancial assets, credit	2 480	....	....	....	....	....	....	....	....
Nonproduced nonfinancial assets, debit	3 480	....	....	....	....	....	....	....	....

Table 2 (Continued). STANDARD PRESENTATION, 2003–2010

(Millions of U.S. dollars)

	Code	2003	2004	2005	2006	2007	2008	2009	2010
FINANCIAL ACCOUNT	4 995	**−4,597**	**1,531**	**−475**	**−12,283**	**−9,661**	**−208**	**−7,749**	**−4,133**
A. DIRECT INVESTMENT	4 500	**−597**	**−1,512**	**5,271**	**2,188**	**2,253**	**3,419**	**2,628**	**10,706**
Direct investment abroad	4 505	....	**−3,408**	**−3,065**	**−2,726**	**−4,675**	**−5,900**	**−2,249**	**−2,664**
Equity capital	4 510	....	−470	−331	−609	−997	−1,420	−1,524	−1,041
Claims on affiliated enterprises	4 515	....	....	....	−609	−997	−1,420	−1,524	−1,041
Liabilities to affiliated enterprises	4 520	....	....	....	....	....	....	....	....
Reinvested earnings	4 525	....	....	....	....	....	....	....	....
Other capital	4 530	....	−2,938	−2,734	−2,117	−3,678	−4,480	−725	−1,623
Claims on affiliated enterprises	4 535	....	....	....	−2,117	−3,678	−4,480	−725	−1,623
Liabilities to affiliated enterprises	4 540	....	....	....	....	....	....	....	....
Direct investment in Indonesia	4 555	**−597**	**1,896**	**8,336**	**4,914**	**6,928**	**9,318**	**4,877**	**13,371**
Equity capital	4 560	1,483	2,138	7,812	4,616	7,549	9,105	4,982	12,068
Claims on direct investors	4 565	....	....	....	....	....	....	....	....
Liabilities to direct investors	4 570	1,483	2,138	7,812	4,616	7,549	9,105	4,982	12,068
Reinvested earnings	4 575	....	....	....	....	....	....	....	....
Other capital	4 580	−2,080	−242	524	298	−621	213	−104	1,302
Claims on direct investors	4 585	....	....	....	....	....	....	....	....
Liabilities to direct investors	4 590	−2,080	−242	524	298	−621	213	−104	1,302
B. PORTFOLIO INVESTMENT	4 600	**2,251**	**4,409**	**4,190**	**4,277**	**5,566**	**1,764**	**10,336**	**13,202**
Assets	4 602	....	**353**	**−1,080**	**−1,830**	**−4,415**	**−1,294**	**−144**	**−2,511**
Equity securities	4 610	....	−106	38	10	−217	−298	−363	−96
Monetary authorities	4 611	....	....	....	....	....	....	....	....
General government	4 612	....	....	....	....	....	....	....	....
Banks	4 613	....	....	....	....	....	....	....	....
Other sectors	4 614	....	−106	38	10	−217	−298	−363	−96
Debt securities	4 619	....	459	−1,118	−1,841	−4,199	−996	219	−2,415
Bonds and notes	4 620	....	459	−1,118	....	....	....	....	....
Monetary authorities	4 621	....	....	....	....	....	....	....	....
General government	4 622	....	....	....	....	....	....	....	....
Banks	4 623	....	....	....	....	....	....	....	....
Other sectors	4 624	....	459	−1,118	....	....	....	....	....
Money market instruments	4 630	....	....	....	....	....	....	....	....
Monetary authorities	4 631	....	....	....	....	....	....	....	....
General government	4 632	....	....	....	....	....	....	....	....
Banks	4 633	....	....	....	....	....	....	....	....
Other sectors	4 634	....	....	....	....	....	....	....	....
Liabilities	4 652	**2,251**	**4,056**	**5,270**	**6,107**	**9,981**	**3,059**	**10,480**	**15,713**
Equity securities	4 660	1,130	2,043	−165	1,898	3,559	322	787	2,132
Banks	4 663	....	....	....	....	....	....	....	....
Other sectors	4 664	1,130	2,043	−165	....	....	....	....	....
Debt securities	4 669	1,121	2,014	5,435	4,210	6,422	2,736	9,693	13,582
Bonds and notes	4 670	1,121	1,241	4,758	3,834	5,190	4,765	5,938	11,086
Monetary authorities	4 671	1,121	....	....	....	....	....	....	....
General government	4 672	....	1,479	4,149	....	....	5,299	5,889	10,960
Banks	4 673	....	....	....	....	....	....	....	....
Other sectors	4 674	....	−238	609	....	....	−534	50	126
Money market instruments	4 680	....	773	677	375	1,233	−2,028	3,754	2,496
Monetary authorities	4 681	....	773	677	375	1,233	−1,980	3,558	1,281
General government	4 682	....	....	....	....	....	43	132	1,286
Banks	4 683	....	....	....	....	....	−91	65	−70
Other sectors	4 684	....	....	....	....	....	....	....	....
C. FINANCIAL DERIVATIVES	4 910	....	....	....	....	....	....	....	....
Monetary authorities	4 911	....	....	....	....	....	....	....	....
General government	4 912	....	....	....	....	....	....	....	....
Banks	4 913	....	....	....	....	....	....	....	....
Other sectors	4 914	....	....	....	....	....	....	....	....
Assets	4 900	....	....	....	....	....	....	....	....
Monetary authorities	4 901	....	....	....	....	....	....	....	....
General government	4 902	....	....	....	....	....	....	....	....
Banks	4 903	....	....	....	....	....	....	....	....
Other sectors	4 904	....	....	....	....	....	....	....	....
Liabilities	4 905	....	....	....	....	....	....	....	....
Monetary authorities	4 906	....	....	....	....	....	....	....	....
General government	4 907	....	....	....	....	....	....	....	....
Banks	4 908	....	....	....	....	....	....	....	....
Other sectors	4 909	....	....	....	....	....	....	....	....

Table 2 (Concluded). STANDARD PRESENTATION, 2003–2010

(Millions of U.S. dollars)

	Code	2003	2004	2005	2006	2007	2008	2009	2010
D. OTHER INVESTMENT	4 700 ..	−2,016	−2,052	−10,593	−11,845	−4,775	−7,309	−8,208	2,243
Assets	4 703 ..	−5	985	−8,646	−1,587	−4,486	−10,755	−12,002	−1,725
Trade credits	4 706 ..	....	−2,069	−3,664	−2,233	−4,853	−5,382	−2,866	−2,569
General government	4 707 ..	....	....	....	....	....	....	....	....
of which: Short-term	4 709 ..	....	....	....	....	....	....	....	....
Other sectors	4 710 ..	....	−2,069	−3,664	−2,233	−4,853	−5,382	−2,866	−2,569
of which: Short-term	4 712 ..		−2,069	−3,664	−2,233	−4,853	−5,382	−2,866	−2,569
Loans	4 714 ..	....	6	187	−71	349	−257	−188	−224
Monetary authorities	4 715 ..	....	....	....	....	....	....	....	....
of which: Short-term	4 718 ..	....	....	....	....	....	....	....	....
General government	4 719 ..	....	....	....	....	....	....	....	....
of which: Short-term	4 721 ..	....	....	....	....	....	....	....	....
Banks	4 722 ..	....	....	....	....	....	....	....	....
of which: Short-term	4 724 ..	....	....	....	....	....	....	....	....
Other sectors	4 725 ..	....	6	187	−71	349	−257	−188	−224
of which: Short-term	4 727 ..	....	....	....	....	....	....	....	....
Currency and deposits	4 730 ..	....	2,856	−5,512	690	278	−5,113	−9,033	1,103
Monetary authorities	4 731 ..	....	....	....	....	....	....	....	....
General government	4 732 ..	....	....	....	....	....	....	....	....
Banks	4 733 ..	....	1,701	−4,662	1,719	2,334	−4,830	−6,800	2,695
Other sectors	4 734 ..	....	1,155	−850	−1,029	−2,057	−283	−2,233	−1,592
Other assets	4 736 ..	−5	192	343	26	−259	−4	85	−36
Monetary authorities	4 737 ..	....	....	....	....	....	....	101	1
of which: Short-term	4 739 ..	....	....	....	....	....	....	....	....
General government	4 740 ..	....	....	....	....	....	....	....	....
of which: Short-term	4 742 ..	....	....	....	....	....	....	....	....
Banks	4 743 ..	....	....	....	....	....	....	....	....
of which: Short-term	4 745 ..	....	....	....	....	....	....	....	....
Other sectors	4 746 ..	−5	192	343	26	−259	−4	−16	−37
of which: Short-term	4 748 ..	....	....	....	....	....	....	....	....
Liabilities	4 753 ..	−2,011	−3,037	−1,948	−10,258	−289	3,446	3,794	3,968
Trade credits	4 756 ..	....	−127	170	168	147	8	−32	211
General government	4 757 ..	....	....	....	....	....	....	....	....
of which: Short-term	4 759 ..	....	....	....	....	....	....	....	....
Other sectors	4 760 ..	....	−127	170	168	147	8	−32	211
of which: Short-term	4 762 ..				168	147	8	−32	211
Loans	4 764 ..	−2,011	−3,147	−2,267	−10,937	−1,161	2,823	1,873	102
Monetary authorities	4 765 ..	588	−1,019	−1,144	−8,583	−45	−71	−68	−48
of which: Use of Fund credit and loans from the Fund	4 766 ..	588	−1,007	−1,144	−8,055	....	....	....	....
of which: Short-term	4 768 ..	....	....	....	....	....	....	....	....
General government	4 769 ..	−398	−2,682	−848	−1,967	−2,318	−1,365	−1,127	−215
of which: Short-term	4 771 ..	....	....	....	....	....	....	....	....
Banks	4 772 ..	−69	441	−1,299	413	71	1,433	653	−559
of which: Short-term	4 774 ..	115	....	....	145	−3	1	58	62
Other sectors	4 775 ..	−2,132	112	1,024	−800	1,131	2,826	2,415	925
of which: Short-term	4 777 ..	−717	....	....	−169	178	−129	−118	−788
Currency and deposits	4 780 ..	....	237	149	511	725	615	−767	1,635
Monetary authorities	4 781 ..	....	....	....	....	....	....	....	....
General government	4 782 ..	....	....	....	....	....	....	....	....
Banks	4 783 ..	....	237	149	511	725	615	−767	1,635
Other sectors	4 784 ..	....	....	....	....	....	....	....	....
Other liabilities	4 786 ..	....	....	....	....	....	....	2,721	2,020
Monetary authorities	4 787 ..	....	....	....	....	....	....	2,721	2,020
of which: Short-term	4 789 ..	....	....	....	....	....	....	....	....
General government	4 790 ..	....	....	....	....	....	....	....	....
of which: Short-term	4 792 ..	....	....	....	....	....	....	....	....
Banks	4 793 ..	....	....	....	....	....	....	....	....
of which: Short-term	4 795 ..	....	....	....	....	....	....	....	....
Other sectors	4 796 ..	....	....	....	....	....	....	....	....
of which: Short-term	4 798 ..	....	....	....	....	....	....	....	....
E. RESERVE ASSETS	4 802 ..	−4,236	686	657	−6,903	−12,706	1,918	−12,506	−30,284
Monetary gold	4 812 ..	−213	−147	143	307	....	....	....	....
Special drawing rights	4 811 ..	16	3	−7	−8	10	−26	−2,719	1
Reserve position in the Fund	4 810 ..	....	....	....	....	....	....	....	....
Foreign exchange	4 803 ..	−3,988	830	621	−7,202	−12,715	1,945	−9,786	−30,285
Other claims	4 813 ..	−50	....	−99	....	....	....	....	....
NET ERRORS AND OMISSIONS	4 998 ..	−3,510	−3,094	−136	1,074	−1,378	−212	−2,975	−1,559

Table 3. INTERNATIONAL INVESTMENT POSITION (End-period stocks), 2003–2010

(Millions of U.S. dollars)

	Code	2003	2004	2005	2006	2007	2008	2009	2010
ASSETS	8 995 C.	**56,383**	**56,514**	**60,614**	**74,432**	**97,539**	**80,324**	**99,943**	**133,118**
Direct investment abroad	8 505 ..	**−208**	**−102**	**−1,762**	**1,042**	**3,193**	**2,802**	**33**	**1,731**
Equity capital and reinvested earnings	8 506 ..	6	167	200	2,977	3,808	4,030	4,980	5,702
Claims on affiliated enterprises	8 507 ..	95	167	234	3,037	4,165	4,396	5,292	6,112
Liabilities to affiliated enterprises	8 508 ..	−89	....	−34	−60	−357	−366	−312	−410
Other capital	8 530 ..	−214	−269	−1,961	−1,935	−614	−1,228	−4,947	−3,971
Claims on affiliated enterprises	8 535 ..	96	59	190	4,328	5,347	5,319	6,009	6,420
Liabilities to affiliated enterprises	8 540 ..	−310	−327	−2,151	−6,263	−5,961	−6,547	−10,956	−10,392
Portfolio investment	8 602 ..	**2,888**	**2,802**	**2,510**	**3,744**	**3,598**	**4,312**	**4,193**	**6,496**
Equity securities	8 610 ..	31	51	94	354	865	488	852	948
Monetary authorities	8 611 ..	....	....	....	....	....	....	....	....
General government	8 612 ..	....	....	....	....	....	....	....	....
Banks	8 613 ..	3	3	....	....	....	....	....	....
Other sectors	8 614 ..	28	48	93	354	865	488	851	948
Debt securities	8 619 ..	2,857	2,751	2,416	3,390	2,733	3,823	3,341	5,549
Bonds and notes	8 620 ..	1,814	1,358	1,049	1,755	1,803	2,741	2,212	4,432
Monetary authorities	8 621 ..	....	....	....	....	....	....	....	2,021
General government	8 622 ..	....	....	....	....	....	....	....	....
Banks	8 623 ..	1,168	854	937	1,256	1,109	1,621	959	937
Other sectors	8 624 ..	646	503	112	498	694	1,120	1,253	1,474
Money market instruments	8 630 ..	1,043	1,394	1,367	1,635	930	1,082	1,129	1,117
Monetary authorities	8 631 ..	....	....	....	....	....	....	....	....
General government	8 632 ..	....	....	....	....	....	....	....	....
Banks	8 633 ..	961	1,351	1,366	1,597	833	625	1,002	878
Other sectors	8 634 ..	82	43	1	39	97	457	127	239
Financial derivatives	8 900 ..	**33**	**40**	**27**	**19**	**38**	**170**	**76**	**81**
Monetary authorities	8 901 ..	....	....	....	....	....	....	....	....
General government	8 902 ..	....	....	....	....	....	....	....	....
Banks	8 903 ..	33	40	27	19	38	170	76	81
Other sectors	8 904 ..	....	....	....	....	....	....	....	....
Other investment	8 703 ..	**17,372**	**17,452**	**25,115**	**27,040**	**33,788**	**21,402**	**29,525**	**28,603**
Trade credits	8 706 ..	2,545	2,041	3,184	3,276	4,061	2,723	5,107	6,387
General government	8 707 ..	....	....	....	....	....	....	....	....
of which: Short-term	8 709 ..	....	....	....	....	....	....	....	....
Other sectors	8 710 ..	2,545	2,041	3,184	3,276	4,061	2,723	5,107	6,387
of which: Short-term	8 712 ..	*2,545*	*2,041*	*3,184*	*3,276*	*4,061*	*2,723*	*5,107*	*6,387*
Loans	8 714 ..	524	201	124	231	282	628	666	1,320
Monetary authorities	8 715 ..	....	....	....	....	....	....	....	....
of which: Short-term	8 718 ..	....	....	....	....	....	....	....	....
General government	8 719 ..	....	....	....	....	....	....	....	....
of which: Short-term	8 721 ..	....	....	....	....	....	....	....	....
Banks	8 722 ..	208	43	74	136	162	149	134	751
of which: Short-term	8 724 ..	*128*	*25*	*43*	*72*	*85*	*108*	*119*	*615*
Other sectors	8 725 ..	316	158	49	95	120	479	532	569
of which: Short-term	8 727 ..	*225*	*79*	....	....	....	....	....	....
Currency and deposits	8 730 ..	9,969	8,780	14,007	12,102	10,362	14,548	20,046	17,760
Monetary authorities	8 731 ..	251	229	156	115	27	46	47	46
General government	8 732 ..	41	670	665	642	610	....	....	....
Banks	8 733 ..	5,497	3,796	8,458	6,739	4,405	9,234	16,188	12,310
Other sectors	8 734 ..	4,180	4,086	4,728	4,606	5,320	5,267	3,812	5,404
Other assets	8 736 ..	4,335	6,430	7,800	11,431	19,083	3,503	3,706	3,136
Monetary authorities	8 737 ..	1,658	2,101	3,999	8,500	14,857	143	106	105
of which: Short-term	8 739 ..	*1,471*	*1,912*	*3,820*	*8,319*	*14,791*	*78*	*40*	*40*
General government	8 740 ..	1	180	180	....	....	543	606	606
of which: Short-term	8 742 ..	*1*	*180*	*180*	....	....	*543*	*606*	*606*
Banks	8 743 ..	1,320	1,247	1,243	707	1,071	1,664	1,290	1,301
of which: Short-term	8 745 ..	*1,317*	*1,245*	*1,240*	*695*	*1,062*	*1,656*	*1,287*	*1,289*
Other sectors	8 746 ..	1,356	2,903	2,379	2,223	3,155	1,154	1,703	1,124
of which: Short-term	8 748 ..	*1,356*	*2,903*	*2,379*	*2,223*	*3,155*	*1,154*	*1,703*	*1,124*
Reserve assets	8 802 ..	**36,297**	**36,321**	**34,724**	**42,587**	**56,922**	**51,638**	**66,116**	**96,207**
Monetary gold	8 812 ..	1,284	1,316	1,583	1,483	1,946	2,041	2,552	3,299
Special drawing rights	8 811 ..	4	2	7	18	9	34	2,763	2,714
Reserve position in the Fund	8 810 ..	216	226	208	219	230	224	228	224
Foreign exchange	8 803 ..	34,742	34,724	32,774	40,697	54,556	49,164	60,369	89,751
Other claims	8 813 ..	50	52	151	169	182	175	203	219

Table 3 (Concluded). INTERNATIONAL INVESTMENT POSITION (End-period stocks), 2003–2010

(Millions of U.S. dollars)

	Code	2003	2004	2005	2006	2007	2008	2009	2010
LIABILITIES	8 995 D.	**162,345**	**173,272**	**185,469**	**211,288**	**266,707**	**228,079**	**317,143**	**422,384**
Direct investment in Indonesia	8 555 ..	**10,328**	**15,858**	**41,187**	**54,534**	**79,927**	**72,227**	**108,795**	**154,158**
Equity capital and reinvested earnings	8 556 ..	6,531	9,747	37,654	51,759	73,910	64,791	102,799	144,105
Claims on direct investors	8 557 ..	−16	−48	−75	−9	−7	−8	−10	−13
Liabilities to direct investors	8 558 ..	6,547	9,795	37,728	51,768	73,917	64,799	102,810	144,118
Other capital	8 580 ..	3,797	6,111	3,533	2,775	6,017	7,436	5,996	10,053
Claims on direct investors	8 585 ..	−353	−562	−1,416	−1,901	−658	−789	−1,551	−1,894
Liabilities to direct investors	8 590 ..	4,150	6,672	4,949	4,676	6,675	8,226	7,547	11,947
Portfolio investment	8 652 ..	**23,297**	**25,732**	**34,592**	**56,162**	**71,421**	**45,348**	**95,641**	**146,688**
Equity securities	8 660 ..	14,808	15,594	15,854	31,519	41,416	14,983	53,293	88,847
Banks	8 663 ..	3,759	5,110	6,021	10,635	13,629	5,506	16,334	25,443
Other sectors	8 664 ..	11,049	10,484	9,833	20,883	27,787	9,477	36,959	63,404
Debt securities	8 669 ..	8,489	10,138	18,738	24,643	30,005	30,365	42,348	57,841
Bonds and notes	8 670 ..	7,805	8,438	15,256	20,651	22,668	25,189	33,034	45,558
Monetary authorities	8 671 ..	....	....	....	....	....	....	....	....
General government	8 672 ..	1,060	2,469	6,683	11,030	14,668	18,433	25,661	37,265
Banks	8 673 ..	1,048	729	1,237	1,665	1,372	716	464	599
Other sectors	8 674 ..	5,697	5,240	7,336	7,956	6,628	6,041	6,910	7,695
Money market instruments	8 680 ..	684	1,699	3,482	3,992	7,336	5,176	9,313	12,283
Monetary authorities	8 681 ..	97	843	1,503	2,002	2,971	772	4,700	6,109
General government	8 682 ..	....	....	....	....	....	....	171	1,496
Banks	8 683 ..	388	592	1,487	1,200	2,797	2,439	2,463	2,789
Other sectors	8 684 ..	200	265	492	790	1,569	1,965	1,979	1,889
Financial derivatives	8 905 ..	**32**	**40**	**43**	**22**	**22**	**221**	**78**	**57**
Monetary authorities	8 906 ..	....	....	....	....	....	....	....	....
General government	8 907 ..	....	....	....	....	....	....	....	....
Banks	8 908 ..	32	40	43	22	22	221	78	57
Other sectors	8 909 ..	....	....	....	....	....	....	....	....
Other investment	8 753 ..	**128,687**	**131,642**	**109,647**	**100,570**	**115,336**	**110,283**	**112,629**	**121,481**
Trade credits	8 756 ..	268	428	356	515	467	649	552	691
General government	8 757 ..	....	....	....	....	....	....	....	....
of which: Short-term	8 759 ..	....	....	....	....	....	....	....	....
Other sectors	8 760 ..	268	428	356	515	467	649	552	691
of which: Short-term	8 762 ..	*107*	*155*	*232*	*452*	*388*	*620*	*511*	*659*
Loans	8 764 ..	125,156	125,388	104,268	94,439	93,513	103,240	104,543	108,143
Monetary authorities	8 765 ..	12,130	11,529	9,092	756	717	682	610	580
of which: Use of Fund credit and loans from the Fund	8 766 ..	*10,276*	*9,686*	*7,807*	....	....	....	....	....
of which: Short-term	8 768 ..	....	....	....	....	....	....	....	....
General government	8 769 ..	68,417	67,917	62,795	62,021	62,253	66,689	65,021	68,099
of which: Short-term	8 771 ..	....	....	....	....	....	....	....	....
Banks	8 772 ..	1,355	1,486	1,321	1,708	1,229	2,514	2,853	2,743
of which: Short-term	8 774 ..	*113*	*97*	*92*	*165*	*29*	*119*	....	*17*
Other sectors	8 775 ..	43,254	44,457	31,060	29,954	29,313	33,355	36,060	36,721
of which: Short-term	8 777 ..	*1,420*	*2,133*	*2,878*	*2,798*	*4,715*	*5,535*	*7,183*	*5,999*
Currency and deposits	8 780 ..	1,338	1,574	1,725	2,235	2,960	3,946	2,966	5,826
Monetary authorities	8 781 ..	3	2	4	3	4	11	7	4
General government	8 782 ..	....	....	....	....	....	....	....	....
Banks	8 783 ..	1,335	1,572	1,721	2,232	2,956	3,936	2,959	5,822
Other sectors	8 784 ..	....	....	....	....	....	....	....	....
Other liabilities	8 786 ..	1,927	4,252	3,298	3,381	18,396	2,448	4,568	6,821
Monetary authorities	8 787 ..	58	70	80	4	14,791	....	3,106	5,071
of which: Short-term	8 789 ..	*58*	*70*	*80*	*4*	*14,791*	....	*1*	*2,021*
General government	8 790 ..	3	11	11	....	....	....	....	....
of which: Short-term	8 792 ..	*3*	*11*	*11*	....	....	....	....	....
Banks	8 793 ..	1,069	2,106	2,020	1,655	1,579	1,980	792	1,093
of which: Short-term	8 795 ..	*1,069*	*2,106*	*2,014*	*1,655*	*1,568*	*1,966*	*791*	*1,093*
Other sectors	8 796 ..	796	2,065	1,188	1,722	2,026	468	670	657
of which: Short-term	8 798 ..	*796*	*2,065*	*368*	*898*	*1,181*	*468*	*670*	*657*
NET INTERNATIONAL INVESTMENT POSITION	8 995 ..	**−105,962**	**−116,758**	**−124,855**	**−136,857**	**−169,168**	**−147,755**	**−217,201**	**−289,265**
Conversion rates: rupiah per U.S. dollar (end of period)	0 102 ..	**8,465.0**	**9,290.0**	**9,830.0**	**9,020.0**	**9,419.0**	**10,950.0**	**9,400.0**	**8,991.0**

Table 1. ANALYTIC PRESENTATION, 2003–2010

(Millions of U.S. dollars)

	Code	2003	2004	2005	2006	2007	2008	2009	2010
A. Current Account[1]	4 993 Z.	....	....	**−7,513**	**1,252**	**14,056**	**26,973**	....	....
Goods: exports f.o.b.	2 100 ..	....	....	23,697	30,529	39,587	63,726	....	....
Goods: imports f.o.b.	3 100 ..	....	....	−20,002	−18,708	−16,623	−29,761	....	....
Balance on Goods	4 100 ..	....	....	*3,695*	*11,822*	*22,965*	*33,965*		
Services: credit	2 200 ..	....	....	355	357	868	1,969	....	
Services: debit	3 200 ..	....	....	−6,095	−5,490	−4,866	−7,969	....	
Balance on Goods and Services	4 991 ..	....	....	*−2,044*	*6,689*	*18,967*	*27,964*		
Income: credit	2 300 ..	....	....	680	1,206	1,923	4,039	....	
Income: debit	3 300 ..	....	....	−5,207	−4,751	−4,990	−1,934	....	
Balance on Goods, Services, and Income	4 992 ..	....	....	*−6,571*	*3,144*	*15,900*	*30,070*	....	
Current transfers: credit	2 379 Z.			552	261	89	188		
Current transfers: debit	3 379 ..			−1,493	−2,153	−1,932	−3,284		
B. Capital Account[1]	4 994 Z.	....	....	**3,889**	**2,769**	**675**	**441**	....	....
Capital account: credit	2 994 Z.	....	....	3,889	2,769	675	441		
Capital account: debit	3 994 ..	....	....	....	....	....	....		
C. Financial Account[1]	4 995 W.	....	...	**−1,350**	**−3,067**	**−5,274**	**−3,146**	....	....
Direct investment abroad	4 505 ..	....	....	−89	−305	−8	−34		
Direct investment in Iraq	4 555 Z.	....	....	515	383	972	1,856	....	
Portfolio investment assets	4 602 ..	....	....	−1,968	−3,670	−1,774	−2,799		
Equity securities	4 610 ..	....	....	....	....	....	....		
Debt securities	4 619 ..	....	....	−1,968	−3,670	−1,774	−2,799		
Portfolio investment liabilities	4 652 Z.	....	....	....	....	....	....		
Equity securities	4 660 ..	....	....	....	....	....	....		
Debt securities	4 669 Z.	....	....	....	....	....	....		
Financial derivatives	4 910 ..			....	....	....	....		
Financial derivatives assets	4 900 ..			....	....	....	....		
Financial derivatives liabilities	4 905 ..			....	....	....	....		
Other investment assets	4 703 ..	....	....	−283	1,847	−4,939	−850		
Monetary authorities	4 701 ..	....	....	....	41	....	....		
General government	4 704 ..	....	....	224	2,363	−3,266	−382		
Banks	4 705 ..	....	...	−506	−557	−1,673	−468		
Other sectors	4 728 ..	....		....	....	....	....		
Other investment liabilities	4 753 W.	....	....	474	−1,322	474	−1,320		
Monetary authorities	4 753 WA	....	....	203	−929	....	....		
General government	4 753 ZB	....	....	−115	−281	....	−313		
Banks	4 753 ZC	....	....	386	−112	474	−1,007		
Other sectors	4 753 ZD			....	....	....	....		
D. Net Errors and Omissions	4 998 ..	....	....	**451**	**579**	**−3,662**	**−5,777**	....	....
Total, Groups A Through D	4 984 ..	....	....	*−4,523*	*1,533*	*5,795*	*18,491*		
E. Reserves and Related Items	4 802 A.	....	....	**4,523**	**−1,533**	**−5,795**	**−18,491**	....	....
Reserve assets	4 802 ..			−4,338	−7,363	−11,340	−18,651		
Use of Fund credit and loans	4 766 ..	....	....	....	....	−468	....		
Exceptional financing	4 920 ..	....	....	8,861	5,830	6,013	160	....	
Conversion rates: New Iraqi dinars per U.S. dollar	0 101 ..	**2,133.78**	**1,453.42**	**1,472.00**	**1,467.42**	**1,254.57**	**1,193.08**	**1,170.00**	**1,170.00**

[1] Excludes components that have been classified in the categories of Group E.

Table 2. STANDARD PRESENTATION, 2003–2010

(Millions of U.S. dollars)

	Code	2003	2004	2005	2006	2007	2008	2009	2010
CURRENT ACCOUNT..........................	4 993 ..	....	....	**–3,335**	**2,681**	**15,519**	**27,133**	....	....
A. GOODS....................................	4 100 ..	....	....	**3,695**	**11,822**	**22,965**	**33,965**	....	....
Credit....................................	2 100 ..	....	....	**23,697**	**30,529**	**39,587**	**63,726**	....	....
General merchandise: exports f.o.b............	2 110 ..	....	....	23,697	30,529	39,587	63,726	....	....
Goods for processing: exports f.o.b...........	2 150 ..	....	....	....	....	....	....	....	....
Repairs on goods..............................	2 160 ..	....	....	....	....	....	....	....	....
Goods procured in ports by carriers...........	2 170 ..	....	....	....	....	....	....	....	....
Nonmonetary gold..............................	2 180 ..	....	....	....	....	....	....	....	....
Debit.....................................	3 100 ..	....	....	**–20,002**	**–18,708**	**–16,623**	**–29,761**	....	....
General merchandise: imports f.o.b............	3 110 ..	....	....	–20,002	–18,708	–16,623	–29,761	....	....
Goods for processing: imports f.o.b...........	3 150 ..	....	....	....	....	....	....	....	....
Repairs on goods..............................	3 160 ..	....	....	....	....	....	....	....	....
Goods procured in ports by carriers...........	3 170 ..	....	....	....	....	....	....	....	....
Nonmonetary gold..............................	3 180 ..	....	....	....	....	....	....	....	....
B. SERVICES................................	4 200 ..	....	....	**–5,739**	**–5,133**	**–3,998**	**–6,001**	....	....
Total credit................................	2 200 ..	....	....	*355*	*357*	*868*	*1,969*		
Total debit.................................	3 200 ..	....	....	*–6,095*	*–5,490*	*–4,866*	*–7,969*		
Transportation services, credit...........	2 205 ..	....	....	**170**	**204**	**258**	**375**	....	....
Passenger...................................	2 850 ..	....	....	*18*	*26*	*39*	*22*		
Freight.....................................	2 851 ..	....	....	*153*	*172*	*205*	*343*		
Other.......................................	2 852 ..	....	....		*6*	*13*	*11*		
Sea transport, passenger......................	2 207 ..	....	....	....	....		....	....	....
Sea transport, freight........................	2 208 ..	....	....	4	160	205	331	....	....
Sea transport, other..........................	2 209 ..	....	....		....	7	....	....	....
Air transport, passenger......................	2 211 ..	....	....	5			3	....	....
Air transport, freight........................	2 212 ..	....	....	3				....	....
Air transport, other..........................	2 213 ..	....	....					....	....
Other transport, passenger....................	2 215 ..	....	....	13	26	39	18	....	....
Other transport, freight......................	2 216 ..	....	....	146	12	....	11	....	....
Other transport, other........................	2 217 ..	....	....	....	6	7	11	....	....
Transportation services, debit............	3 205 ..	....	....	**–2,811**	**–2,581**	**–2,280**	**–4,013**	....	....
Passenger...................................	3 850 ..	....	....	*–188*	*–131*	*–66*	*–19*		
Freight.....................................	3 851 ..	....	....	*–2,612*	*–2,444*	*–2,215*	*–3,854*		
Other.......................................	3 852 ..	....	....	*–11*	*–6*	....	*–140*		
Sea transport, passenger......................	3 207 ..	....	....					....	....
Sea transport, freight........................	3 208 ..	....	....	–522	–8	–6	–1	....	....
Sea transport, other..........................	3 209 ..	....	....		....	....		....	....
Air transport, passenger......................	3 211 ..	....	....	–155	–131	–64	–19	....	....
Air transport, freight........................	3 212 ..	....	....	–10	....		–4	....	....
Air transport, other..........................	3 213 ..	....	....	–11	–6	....	–140	....	....
Other transport, passenger....................	3 215 ..	....	....	–33		–1		....	....
Other transport, freight......................	3 216 ..	....	....	–2,080	–2,436	–2,209	–3,849	....	....
Other transport, other........................	3 217 ..	....	....	....		....		....	....
Travel, credit............................	2 236 ..	....	....	**168**	**144**	**516**	**2**	....	....
Business travel...............................	2 237 ..	....	....	....	....	....	....	....	....
Personal travel...............................	2 240 ..	....	....	168	144	516	1	....	....
Travel, debit.............................	3 236 ..	....	....	**–439**	**–395**	**–639**	**–794**	....	....
Business travel...............................	3 237 ..	....	....	–338	–218	–123	–36	....	....
Personal travel...............................	3 240 ..	....	....	–101	–177	–516	–757	....	....
Other services, credit....................	2 200 BA	....	....	**17**	**9**	**95**	**1,592**	....	....
Communications................................	2 245 ..	....	....	6	4	19	9	....	....
Construction..................................	2 249 ..	....	....	....	....	....	....	....	....
Insurance.....................................	2 253 ..	....	....	....	....	....	2	....	....
Financial.....................................	2 260 ..	....	....	3	1	19	3	....	....
Computer and information......................	2 262 ..	....	....	1	....	10	2	....	....
Royalties and licence fees....................	2 266 ..	....	....	....	....	....	1,312	....	....
Other business services.......................	2 268 ..	....	....	....	....	17	15	....	....
Personal, cultural, and recreational..........	2 287 ..	....	....	....	....	1	3	....	....
Government, n.i.e.............................	2 291 ..	....	....	8	4	29	247	....	....
Other services, debit.....................	3 200 BA	....	....	**–2,845**	**–2,514**	**–1,946**	**–3,163**	....	....
Communications................................	3 245 ..	....	....	–236	–126	–110	–61	....	....
Construction..................................	3 249 ..	....	....	–394	–330	–112	–143	....	....
Insurance.....................................	3 253 ..	....	....	–941	–885	–784	–1,406	....	....
Financial.....................................	3 260 ..	....	....	–40	–93	–377	–621	....	....
Computer and information......................	3 262 ..	....	....	–205	–177	–65	–39	....	....
Royalties and licence fees....................	3 266 ..	....	....	–29	....	–204	–396	....	....
Other business services.......................	3 268 ..	....	....	–180	–327	–144	–65	....	....
Personal, cultural, and recreational..........	3 287 ..	....	....	–151	–118	–27	–28	....	....
Government, n.i.e.............................	3 291 ..	....	....	–668	–460	–125	–404	....	....

Table 2 (Continued). STANDARD PRESENTATION, 2003–2010

(Millions of U.S. dollars)

	Code	2003	2004	2005	2006	2007	2008	2009	2010
C. INCOME	4 300	....	....	**−4,527**	**−3,546**	**−3,067**	**2,106**	....	....
Total credit	2 300	....	....	*680*	*1,206*	*1,923*	*4,039*	....	....
Total debit	3 300	....	....	*−5,207*	*−4,751*	*−4,990*	*−1,934*	....	....
Compensation of employees, credit	2 310	....	....	**258**	**128**	**1**	**7**	....	....
Compensation of employees, debit	3 310	....	....	**−83**	**−153**	**−2**	**−2**	....	....
Investment income, credit	2 320	....	....	**423**	**1,078**	**1,923**	**4,032**	....	....
Direct investment income	2 330	....	....	6	27	1	5	....	....
Dividends and distributed branch profits	2 332	....	....	6	27	1	5	....	....
Reinvested earnings and undistributed branch profits	2 333	....	....	....	....	....	....	....	....
Income on debt (interest)	2 334	....	....	....	....	....	....	....	....
Portfolio investment income	2 339	....	....	185	592	1,047	2,466	....	....
Income on equity	2 340	....	....	6	....	....	....	....	....
Income on bonds and notes	2 350	....	....	179	592	1,047	2,465	....	....
Income on money market instruments	2 360	....	....	....	....	....	1	....	....
Other investment income	2 370	....	....	233	459	874	1,562	....	....
Investment income, debit	3 320	....	....	**−5,125**	**−4,598**	**−4,989**	**−1,932**	....	....
Direct investment income	3 330	....	....	−36	−67	−346	−267	....	....
Dividends and distributed branch profits	3 332	....	....	−36	−67	−346	−267	....	....
Reinvested earnings and undistributed branch profits	3 333	....	....	....	....	....	....	....	....
Income on debt (interest)	3 334	....	....	....	....	....	....	....	....
Portfolio investment income	3 339	....	....	....	....	−2	....	....	....
Income on equity	3 340	....	....	....	....	−2	....	....	....
Income on bonds and notes	3 350	....	....	....	....	....	....	....	....
Income on money market instruments	3 360	....	....	....	....	....	....	....	....
Other investment income	3 370	....	....	−5,089	−4,531	−4,640	−1,665	....	....
D. CURRENT TRANSFERS	4 379	....	....	**3,236**	**−462**	**−381**	**−2,936**	....	....
Credit	2 379	....	....	**4,729**	**1,691**	**1,551**	**348**	....	....
General government	2 380	....	....	4,178	1,429	1,463	163	....	....
Other sectors	2 390	....	....	552	261	89	185	....	....
Workers' remittances	2 391	....	....	454	261	3	64	....	....
Other current transfers	2 392	....	....	98	....	86	121	....	....
Debit	3 379	....	....	**−1,493**	**−2,153**	**−1,932**	**−3,284**	....	....
General government	3 380	....	....	−1,153	−1,520	−1,889	−3,166	....	....
Other sectors	3 390	....	....	−340	−632	−43	−118	....	....
Workers' remittances	3 391	....	....	....	−629	−16	−30	....	....
Other current transfers	3 392	....	....	−340	−4	−28	−88	....	....
CAPITAL AND FINANCIAL ACCOUNT	4 996	....	....	**2,884**	**−3,261**	**−11,857**	**−21,356**	....	....
CAPITAL ACCOUNT	4 994	....	....	**20,489**	**17,984**	**675**	**441**	....	....
Total credit	2 994	....	....	*20,489*	*17,984*	*675*	*441*	....	....
Total debit	3 994	....	....	....	....	....	....	....	....
Capital transfers, credit	2 400	....	....	**20,489**	**17,984**	**675**	**441**	....	....
General government	2 401	....	....	20,489	17,984	675	441	....	....
Debt forgiveness	2 402	....	....	16,952	15,215	....	....	....	....
Other capital transfers	2 410	....	....	3,537	2,769	675	441	....	....
Other sectors	2 430	....	....	....	....	....	....	....	....
Migrants' transfers	2 431	....	....	....	....	....	....	....	....
Debt forgiveness	2 432	....	....	....	....	....	....	....	....
Other capital transfers	2 440	....	....	....	....	....	....	....	....
Capital transfers, debit	3 400	....	....	....	....	....	....	....	....
General government	3 401	....	....	....	....	....	....	....	....
Debt forgiveness	3 402	....	....	....	....	....	....	....	....
Other capital transfers	3 410	....	....	....	....	....	....	....	....
Other sectors	3 430	....	....	....	....	....	....	....	....
Migrants' transfers	3 431	....	....	....	....	....	....	....	....
Debt forgiveness	3 432	....	....	....	....	....	....	....	....
Other capital transfers	3 440	....	....	....	....	....	....	....	....
Nonproduced nonfinancial assets, credit	2 480	....	....	....	....	....	....	....	....
Nonproduced nonfinancial assets, debit	3 480	....	....	....	....	....	....	....	....

Table 2 (Continued). STANDARD PRESENTATION, 2003–2010

(Millions of U.S. dollars)

	Code	2003	2004	2005	2006	2007	2008	2009	2010
FINANCIAL ACCOUNT..................................	4 995 ..	....	....	−17,604	−21,245	−12,532	−21,797	....	....
A. DIRECT INVESTMENT..........................	4 500 ..	....	....	427	78	964	1,822	....	....
Direct investment abroad........................	4 505 ..	....	....	−89	−305	−8	−34	....	....
Equity capital......................................	4 510 ..	....	....	−89	−305	−8	−34		
Claims on affiliated enterprises...........	4 515 ..	....	....	−89	−305	−8	−34		
Liabilities to affiliated enterprises........	4 520 ..	....	....	....	....	....	....		
Reinvested earnings...............................	4 525 ..	....	....	....	....	....	....		
Other capital.......................................	4 530 ..	....	....	....	....	....	....		
Claims on affiliated enterprises...........	4 535 ..	....	....	....	....	....	....		
Liabilities to affiliated enterprises........	4 540 ..	....	....	....	....	....	....		
Direct investment in Iraq........................	4 555 ..	....	....	515	383	972	1,856	....	....
Equity capital......................................	4 560 ..	....	....	515	383	972	1,856		
Claims on direct investors...................	4 565 ..	....	....	....					
Liabilities to direct investors..............	4 570 ..	....	....	515	383	972	1,856		
Reinvested earnings...............................	4 575 ..	....	....	....	....	....	....		
Other capital.......................................	4 580 ..	....	....	....	....	....	....		
Claims on direct investors...................	4 585 ..	....	....	....	....	....	....		
Liabilities to direct investors..............	4 590 ..	....	....	....	....	....	....		
B. PORTFOLIO INVESTMENT....................	4 600 ..	....	....	−1,968	−3,670	−1,774	−2,799	....	....
Assets...	4 602 ..	....	....	−1,968	−3,670	−1,774	−2,799	....	....
Equity securities..................................	4 610 ..	....	....	....	....	....	....		
Monetary authorities.........................	4 611 ..	....	....	....	....	....	....		
General government..........................	4 612 ..	....	....	....	....	....	....		
Banks..	4 613 ..	....	....	....	....	....	....		
Other sectors....................................	4 614 ..	....	....	....	....	....	....		
Debt securities....................................	4 619 ..	....	....	−1,968	−3,670	−1,774	−2,799		
Bonds and notes...............................	4 620 ..	....	....	−1,968	−3,617	−1,774	−2,799		
Monetary authorities......................	4 621 ..	....	....	....	....	....	....		
General government.......................	4 622 ..	....	....	−1,968	−3,617	−1,774	−2,814		
Banks...	4 623 ..	....	....	....	....	1	7		
Other sectors................................	4 624 ..	....	....	....	....	....	9		
Money market instruments..................	4 630 ..	....	....	....	−53	....	....		
Monetary authorities......................	4 631 ..	....	....	....	....	....	....		
General government.......................	4 632 ..	....	....	....	....	....	....		
Banks...	4 633 ..	....	....	....	−53	....	....		
Other sectors................................	4 634 ..	....	....	....	....	....	....		
Liabilities...	4 652 ..	....	....	....	....	....	....	....	....
Equity securities..................................	4 660 ..	....	....	....	....	....	....		
Banks..	4 663 ..	....	....	....	....	....	....		
Other sectors....................................	4 664 ..	....	....	....	....	....	....		
Debt securities....................................	4 669 ..	....	....	....	....	....	....		
Bonds and notes...............................	4 670 ..	....	....	....	....	....	....		
Monetary authorities......................	4 671 ..	....	....	....	....	....	....		
General government.......................	4 672 ..	....	....	....	....	....	....		
Banks...	4 673 ..	....	....	....	....	....	....		
Other sectors................................	4 674 ..	....	....	....	....	....	....		
Money market instruments..................	4 680 ..	....	....	....	....	....	....		
Monetary authorities......................	4 681 ..	....	....	....	....	....	....		
General government.......................	4 682 ..	....	....	....	....	....	....		
Banks...	4 683 ..	....	....	....	....	....	....		
Other sectors................................	4 684 ..	....	....	....	....	....	....		
C. FINANCIAL DERIVATIVES......................	4 910 ..	....	....	....	....	....	....	....	....
Monetary authorities.............................	4 911 ..	....	....	....	....	....	....		
General government..............................	4 912 ..	....	....	....	....	....	....		
Banks...	4 913 ..	....	....	....	....	....	....		
Other sectors..	4 914 ..	....	....	....	....	....	....		
Assets...	4 900 ..	....	....	....	....	....	....	....	....
Monetary authorities.........................	4 901 ..	....	....	....	....	....	....		
General government..........................	4 902 ..	....	....	....	....	....	....		
Banks..	4 903 ..	....	....	....	....	....	....		
Other sectors....................................	4 904 ..	....	....	....	....	....	....		
Liabilities...	4 905 ..	....	....	....	....	....	....	....	....
Monetary authorities.........................	4 906 ..	....	....	....	....	....	....		
General government..........................	4 907 ..	....	....	....	....	....	....		
Banks..	4 908 ..	....	....	....	....	....	....		
Other sectors....................................	4 909 ..	....	....	....	....	....	....		

Table 2 (Concluded). STANDARD PRESENTATION, 2003–2010

(Millions of U.S. dollars)

	Code	2003	2004	2005	2006	2007	2008	2009	2010
D. OTHER INVESTMENT	4 700	....	....	**−11,726**	**−10,290**	**−383**	**−2,170**	....	....
Assets	4 703	....	....	**−283**	**1,847**	**−4,939**	**−850**	....	....
Trade credits	4 706	....	....	−71	−55	−28	....		
General government	4 707	....	....	−71	−55	−28	....		
of which: Short-term	4 709	....	....	....	....	....	....		
Other sectors	4 710	....	....	....	....	....	....		
of which: Short-term	4 712	....	....	....	....	....	....		
Loans	4 714	....	....						
Monetary authorities	4 715								
of which: Short-term	4 718								
General government	4 719								
of which: Short-term	4 721								
Banks	4 722								
of which: Short-term	4 724								
Other sectors	4 725								
of which: Short-term	4 727								
Currency and deposits	4 730	....	....	−2,453	2,003	−4,911	42		
Monetary authorities	4 731	....	....	....	....	....	....		
General government	4 732	....	....	−1,947	2,561	−3,176	−382		
Banks	4 733	....	....	−506	−557	−1,735	424		
Other sectors	4 734								
Other assets	4 736	....	....	2,242	−102	....	−892		
Monetary authorities	4 737	....	....	....	41	....	....		
of which: Short-term	4 739								
General government	4 740	....	....	2,242	−143	−61	....		
of which: Short-term	4 742			*2,291*	*263*	....	....		
Banks	4 743	....	....	....	....	62	−892		
of which: Short-term	4 745					*62*	*−892*		
Other sectors	4 746								
of which: Short-term	4 748								
Liabilities	4 753	....	....	**−11,443**	**−12,137**	**4,556**	**−1,320**	....	....
Trade credits	4 756	....	....	....	....	....	....		
General government	4 757	....	....	....	....	....	....		
of which: Short-term	4 759	....	....	....	....	....	....		
Other sectors	4 760	....	....	....	....	....	....		
of which: Short-term	4 762	....	....	....	....	....	....		
Loans	4 764	....	....	5,591	3,191	3,672	147		
Monetary authorities	4 765	....	....	203	−929	−468	....		
of which: Use of Fund credit and loans from the Fund	4 766	....	....	....	....	*−468*	....		
of which: Short-term	4 768	....	....	....	....	....	....		
General government	4 769	....	....	4,920	4,120	4,550	−313		
of which: Short-term	4 771								
Banks	4 772	....	....	468	....	−410	460		
of which: Short-term	4 774					*−410*	*460*		
Other sectors	4 775					....	....		
of which: Short-term	4 777								
Currency and deposits	4 780	....	....	−82	−135	84	−655		
Monetary authorities	4 781	....	....	....	....	....	....		
General government	4 782	....	....	....	....	....	....		
Banks	4 783	....	....	−82	−135	84	−655		
Other sectors	4 784	....	....	....	....	....	....		
Other liabilities	4 786	....	....	−16,952	−15,192	800	−812		
Monetary authorities	4 787	....	....	....	....	....	....		
of which: Short-term	4 789								
General government	4 790	....	....	−16,952	−15,215	....	....		
of which: Short-term	4 792	....	....	*−16,952*	*−15,215*	....	....		
Banks	4 793	....	....	....	23	800	−812		
of which: Short-term	4 795				*12*				
Other sectors	4 796								
of which: Short-term	4 798								
E. RESERVE ASSETS	4 802	....	....	**−4,338**	**−7,363**	**−11,340**	**−18,651**	....	....
Monetary gold	4 812								
Special drawing rights	4 811	....	....	4	3	320	−7		
Reserve position in the Fund	4 810	....	....	....	....	....	....		
Foreign exchange	4 803	....	....	−4,342	−7,366	−11,660	−18,644		
Other claims	4 813	....	....	....	....	....	....		
NET ERRORS AND OMISSIONS	4 998	....	....	**451**	**579**	**−3,662**	**−5,777**	....	....

Table 3. INTERNATIONAL INVESTMENT POSITION (End-period stocks), 2003–2010

(Millions of U.S. dollars)

	Code	2003	2004	2005	2006	2007	2008	2009	2010
ASSETS	8 995 C.	....	....	....	33,908	48,744	68,391	67,820	68,963
Direct investment abroad	8 505 ..	....	....	....	....	....	....	....	....
Equity capital and reinvested earnings	8 506 ..	....	....	....	....	....	....	....	....
Claims on affiliated enterprises	8 507 ..	....	....	....	....	....	....	....	....
Liabilities to affiliated enterprises	8 508 ..	....	....	....	....	....	....	....	....
Other capital	8 530 ..	....	....	....	....	....	....	....	....
Claims on affiliated enterprises	8 535 ..	....	....	....	....	....	....	....	....
Liabilities to affiliated enterprises	8 540 ..	....	....	....	....	....	....	....	....
Portfolio investment	8 602 ..	....	....	....	8,117	7,466	10,274	6,627	5,925
Equity securities	8 610 ..	....	....	....	....	....	....	....	....
Monetary authorities	8 611 .	....	....	....	....	....	....	....	....
General government	8 612 ..	....	....	....	....	....	....	....	....
Banks	8 613 ..	....	....	....	....	....	....	....	....
Other sectors	8 614 ..	....	....	....	....	....	....	....	....
Debt securities	8 619 ..	....	....	....	8,117	7,466	10,274	6,627	5,925
Bonds and notes	8 620 ..	....	....	....	108	107	101	133	169
Monetary authorities	8 621 ..	....	....	....	....	....	....	....	....
General government	8 622 ..	....	....	....	....	....	....	....	....
Banks	8 623 ..	....	....	....	108	107	101	133	145
Other sectors	8 624 ..	....	....	....	....	....	....	....	25
Money market instruments	8 630 ..	....	....	....	8,008	7,359	10,173	6,495	5,756
Monetary authorities	8 631 ..	....	....	....	....	....	....	....	....
General government	8 632 ..	....	....	....	8,008	7,359	10,173	6,495	5,756
Banks	8 633 ..	....	....	....	....	....	....	....	....
Other sectors	8 634 ..	....	....	....	....	....	....	....	....
Financial derivatives	8 900 ..	....	....	....	....	....	....	....	....
Monetary authorities	8 901 ..	....	....	....	....	....	....	....	....
General government	8 902 ..	....	....	....	....	....	....	....	....
Banks	8 903 ..	....	....	....	....	....	....	....	....
Other sectors	8 904 ..	....	....	....	....	....	....	....	....
Other investment	8 703 ..	....	....	....	5,751	9,822	7,912	16,857	12,395
Trade credits	8 706 ..	....	....	....	....	....	....	....	....
General government	8 707 ..	....	....	....	....	....	....	....	....
of which: Short-term	8 709 ..	....	....	....	....	....	....	....	....
Other sectors	8 710 ..	....	....	....	....	....	....	....	....
of which: Short-term	8 712 ..	....	....	....	....	....	....	....	....
Loans	8 714 ..	....	....	....	....	....	....	....	....
Monetary authorities	8 715 ..	....	....	....	....	....	....	....	....
of which: Short-term	8 718 ..	....	....	....	....	....	....	....	....
General government	8 719 ..	....	....	....	....	....	....	....	....
of which: Short-term	8 721 ..	....	....	....	....	....	....	....	....
Banks	8 722 ..	....	....	....	....	....	....	....	....
of which: Short-term	8 724 ..	....	....	....	....	....	....	....	....
Other sectors	8 725 ..	....	....	....	....	....	....	....	....
of which: Short-term	8 727 ..	....	....	....	....	....	....	....	....
Currency and deposits	8 730 ..	....	....	....	4,489	8,623	5,821	14,841	10,658
Monetary authorities	8 731 ..	....	....	....	....	....	....	....	....
General government	8 732 ..	....	....	....	....	2,399	21	3,383	1,691
Banks	8 733 ..	....	....	....	4,489	6,224	5,800	11,458	8,967
Other sectors	8 734 ..	....	....	....	....	....	....	....	....
Other assets	8 736 ..	....	....	....	1,262	1,200	2,092	2,017	1,737
Monetary authorities	8 737 ..	....	....	....	....	....	....	....	....
of which: Short-term	8 739 ..	....	....	....	....	....	....	....	....
General government	8 740 ..	....	....	....	....	....	....	....	....
of which: Short-term	8 742 ..	....	....	....	....	....	....	....	....
Banks	8 743 ..	....	....	....	1,262	1,200	2,092	2,017	1,737
of which: Short-term	8 745 ..	....	....	....	*1,262*	*1,200*	*2,092*	*2,017*	*1,737*
Other sectors	8 746 ..	....	....	....	....	....	....	....	....
of which: Short-term	8 748 ..	....	....	....	....	....	....	....	....
Reserve assets	8 802 ..	....	....	....	20,041	31,455	50,206	44,336	50,643
Monetary gold	8 812 ..	....	....	....	120	158	163	208	266
Special drawing rights	8 811 ..	....	460	420	439	140	143	1,818	1,774
Reserve position in the Fund	8 810 ..	....	266	245	257	270	264	268	263
Foreign exchange	8 803 ..	....	....	....	19,225	30,888	49,636	42,041	48,340
Other claims	8 813 ..	....	....	....	....	....	....	....	....

Table 3 (Concluded). INTERNATIONAL INVESTMENT POSITION (End-period stocks), 2003–2010

(Millions of U.S. dollars)

	Code	2003	2004	2005	2006	2007	2008	2009	2010
LIABILITIES	8 995 D.	....	....	....	**83,892**	**84,670**	**75,482**	**80,876**	**73,538**
Direct investment in Iraq	8 555 ..	....	....	....	**898**	**1,870**	**3,726**	**5,582**	**7,033**
Equity capital and reinvested earnings	8 556 ..	....	....	....	....	....	....	....	....
Claims on direct investors	8 557 ..	....	....	....	....	....	....	....	....
Liabilities to direct investors	8 558 ..	....	....	....	....	....	....	....	....
Other capital	8 580 ..	....	....	....	898	1,870	3,726	5,582	7,033
Claims on direct investors	8 585 ..	....	....	....	....	....	....	....	....
Liabilities to direct investors	8 590 ..	....	....	....	898	1,870	3,726	5,582	7,033
Portfolio investment	8 652 ..	....	....	....	**1,177**	**799**	**889**	**1,338**	**1,152**
Equity securities	8 660 ..	....	....	....	16	40	40	117	117
Banks	8 663 ..	....	....	....	....	....	....	....	....
Other sectors	8 664 ..	....	....	....	16	40	40	117	117
Debt securities	8 669 ..	....	....	....	1,161	759	849	1,221	1,035
Bonds and notes	8 670 ..	....	....	....	1,161	759	849	1,221	1,035
Monetary authorities	8 671 ..	....	....	....	....	....	....	....	....
General government	8 672 ..	....	....	....	1,161	759	849	1,221	1,035
Banks	8 673 ..	....	....	....	....	....	....	....	....
Other sectors	8 674 ..	....	....	....	....	....	....	....	....
Money market instruments	8 680 ..	....	....	....	....	....	....	....	....
Monetary authorities	8 681 ..	....	....	....	....	....	....	....	....
General government	8 682 ..	....	....	....	....	....	....	....	....
Banks	8 683 ..	....	....	....	....	....	....	....	....
Other sectors	8 684 ..	....	....	....	....	....	....	....	....
Financial derivatives	8 905 ..	....	....	....	....	....	....	....	....
Monetary authorities	8 906 ..	....	....	....	....	....	....	....	....
General government	8 907 ..	....	....	....	....	....	....	....	....
Banks	8 908 ..	....	....	....	....	....	....	....	....
Other sectors	8 909 ..	....	....	....	....	....	....	....	....
Other investment	8 753 ..	....	....	....	**81,817**	**82,001**	**70,867**	**73,956**	**65,352**
Trade credits	8 756 ..	....	....	....	....	....	....	....	....
General government	8 757 ..	....	....	....	....	....	....	....	....
of which: Short-term	8 759 ..	....	....	....	....	....	....	....	....
Other sectors	8 760 ..	....	....	....	....	....	....	....	....
of which: Short-term	8 762 ..	....	....	....	....	....	....	....	....
Loans	8 764 ..	....	....	....	80,110	79,409	69,742	69,728	62,804
Monetary authorities	8 765 ..	....	....	....	447	....	....	....	1,190
of which: Use of Fund credit and loans from the Fund	8 766 ..	....	*461*	*425*	*447*	....	....	....	*1,190*
of which: Short-term	8 768 ..	....	....	....	....	....	....	....	....
General government	8 769 ..	....	....	....	73,085	73,241	63,114	63,068	54,801
of which: Short-term	8 771 ..	....	....	....	....	....	....	....	....
Banks	8 772 ..	....	....	....	6,578	6,168	6,628	6,660	6,814
of which: Short-term	8 774 ..	....	....	....	....	....	....	....	....
Other sectors	8 775 ..	....	....	....	....	....	....	....	....
of which: Short-term	8 777 ..	....	....	....	....	....	....	....	....
Currency and deposits	8 780 ..	....	....	....	1,692	1,775	1,120	2,439	784
Monetary authorities	8 781 ..	....	....	....	....	....	....	....	....
General government	8 782 ..	....	....	....	....	....	....	....	....
Banks	8 783 ..	....	....	....	1,692	1,775	1,120	2,439	784
Other sectors	8 784 ..	....	....	....	....	....	....	....	....
Other liabilities	8 786 ..	....	....	....	16	816	4	1,789	1,764
Monetary authorities	8 787 ..	....	....	....	....	....	....	1,779	1,747
of which: Short-term	8 789 ..	....	....	....	....	....	....	....	....
General government	8 790 ..	....	....	....	....	....	....	....	....
of which: Short-term	8 792 ..	....	....	....	....	....	....	....	....
Banks	8 793 ..	....	....	....	16	816	4	11	17
of which: Short-term	8 795 ..	....	....	....	....	....	....	....	....
Other sectors	8 796 ..	....	....	....	....	....	....	....	....
of which: Short-term	8 798 ..	....	....	....	....	....	....	....	....
NET INTERNATIONAL INVESTMENT POSITION	8 995 ..	....	....	....	**–49,985**	**–35,926**	**–7,090**	**–13,055**	**–4,574**
Conversion rates: New Iraqi dinars per U.S. dollar (end of period)	0 102 ..	**1,685.00**	**1,469.00**	**1,487.00**	**1,325.00**	**1,215.00**	**1,172.00**	**1,170.00**	**1,170.00**

2011, International Monetary Fund: *Balance of Payments Statistics Yearbook*

Table 1. ANALYTIC PRESENTATION, 2003–2010

(Millions of U.S. dollars)

	Code	2003	2004	2005	2006	2007	2008	2009	2010
A. Current Account[1]	4 993 Z.	**89**	**−1,081**	**−7,150**	**−7,859**	**−13,850**	**−15,297**	**−6,293**	**954**
Goods: exports f.o.b.	2 100 ..	88,590	100,116	102,825	104,512	115,248	119,038	107,880	109,856
Goods: imports f.o.b.	3 100 ..	−51,709	−61,102	−67,730	−73,075	−88,122	−84,325	−62,768	−61,583
Balance on Goods	4 100 ..	*36,882*	*39,014*	*35,096*	*31,437*	*27,126*	*34,713*	*45,112*	*48,273*
Services: credit	2 200 ..	42,061	52,718	59,920	71,729	93,289	99,872	93,652	97,833
Services: debit	3 200 ..	−54,596	−65,384	−71,437	−80,289	−94,912	−110,875	−104,741	−107,270
Balance on Goods and Services	4 991 ..	*24,346*	*26,348*	*23,579*	*22,877*	*25,503*	*23,711*	*34,022*	*38,837*
Income: credit	2 300 ..	34,095	43,457	53,862	83,138	116,528	123,774	76,471	76,418
Income: debit	3 300 ..	−58,879	−71,388	−84,876	−113,283	−154,622	−160,909	−115,253	−112,711
Balance on Goods, Services, and Income	4 992 ..	*−438*	*−1,583*	*−7,434*	*−7,267*	*−12,590*	*−13,424*	*−4,760*	*2,544*
Current transfers: credit	2 379 Z.	7,027	6,626	6,963	6,645	6,704	8,013	7,552	6,626
Current transfers: debit	3 379 ..	−6,500	−6,123	−6,679	−7,237	−7,964	−9,886	−9,085	−8,215
B. Capital Account[1]	4 994 Z.	**126**	**368**	**323**	**283**	**51**	**74**	**−1,844**	**−915**
Capital account: credit	2 994 Z.	617	797	534	392	167	197	103	131
Capital account: debit	3 994 ..	−491	−428	−211	−109	−116	−123	−1,946	−1,046
Total, Groups A Plus B	4 981 ..	*215*	*−712*	*−6,827*	*−7,576*	*−13,799*	*−15,223*	*−8,137*	*40*
C. Financial Account[1]	4 995 W.	**−3,481**	**3,301**	**−2,501**	**6,139**	**16,813**	**25,300**	**−704**	**15,439**
Direct investment abroad	4 505 ..	−5,594	−18,107	−14,491	−15,294	−20,567	−18,567	−26,836	−18,108
Direct investment in Ireland	4 555 Z.	22,411	−10,994	−30,334	−5,523	24,581	−16,339	26,551	27,085
Portfolio investment assets	4 602 ..	−163,841	−168,940	−151,139	−267,083	−232,631	−45,303	−749	28,611
Equity securities	4 610 ..	−29,545	−46,087	−59,602	−74,006	−29,415	32,388	−13,643	−36,745
Debt securities	4 619 ..	−134,296	−122,853	−91,537	−193,077	−203,216	−77,691	12,894	65,356
Portfolio investment liabilities	4 652 Z.	119,397	186,471	215,056	279,049	222,285	−17,190	35,184	101,137
Equity securities	4 660 ..	76,776	81,709	93,590	160,467	138,387	−7,844	30,815	152,236
Debt securities	4 669 Z.	42,621	104,761	121,466	118,581	83,898	−9,346	4,369	−51,099
Financial derivatives	4 910 ..	−525	1,042	−8,041	374	−16,331	1,388	−3,367	−16,038
Financial derivatives assets	4 900 ..	−406	−1,903	−5,347	3,046	−18,725	6,210	16,553	−8,006
Financial derivatives liabilities	4 905 ..	−120	2,945	−2,694	−2,672	2,393	−4,822	−19,921	−8,032
Other investment assets	4 703 ..	−65,871	−57,406	−133,298	−154,941	−196,846	−106,455	72,037	−21,004
Monetary authorities	4 701 ..	−1,576	308	−296	−1,093	3,402	−4,801	6,717	481
General government	4 704 ..	31	−381	−226	407	1,253	191	443	−378
Banks	4 705 ..	−35,458	−40,525	−85,843	−83,501	−110,378	−66,934	68,872	8,423
Other sectors	4 728 ..	−28,867	−16,809	−46,934	−70,753	−91,123	−34,912	−3,995	−29,530
Other investment liabilities	4 753 W.	90,542	71,236	119,746	169,557	236,323	227,766	−103,524	−86,244
Monetary authorities	4 753 WA	7,461	−4,349	−9	−2,577	−1,631	62,672	380	4
General government	4 753 ZB	−286	−9	−149	−5	360	395	−46	....
Banks	4 753 ZC	62,487	63,865	50,354	118,157	42,120	−12,885	−8,439	−44,624
Other sectors	4 753 ZD	20,881	11,729	27,555	53,982	66,064	37,258	5,188	27,337
Total, Groups A Through C	4 983 ..	*−3,266*	*2,588*	*−9,328*	*−1,437*	*3,014*	*10,077*	*−8,841*	*15,479*
D. Net Errors and Omissions	4 998 ..	**1,375**	**−4,023**	**7,552**	**1,324**	**−2,998**	**−9,921**	**9,874**	**−15,520**
Total, Groups A Through D	4 984 ..	*−1,890*	*−1,435*	*−1,776*	*−112*	*16*	*157*	*1,034*	*−42*
E. Reserves and Related Items	4 802 A.	**1,890**	**1,435**	**1,776**	**112**	**−16**	**−157**	**−1,034**	**42**
Reserve assets	4 802 ..	1,890	1,435	1,776	112	−16	−157	−1,034	42
Use of Fund credit and loans	4 766 ..	....	....	....	....	....	....	....	....
Exceptional financing	4 920 ..	....	....	....	....	....	....	....	....
Conversion rates: euros per U.S. dollar	0 103 ..	**.8860**	**.8054**	**.8041**	**.7971**	**.7306**	**.6827**	**.7198**	**.7550**

[1] Excludes components that have been classified in the categories of Group E.

Table 2. STANDARD PRESENTATION, 2003–2010

(Millions of U.S. dollars)

	Code	2003	2004	2005	2006	2007	2008	2009	2010
CURRENT ACCOUNT................................	4 993 ..	**89**	**−1,081**	**−7,150**	**−7,859**	**−13,850**	**−15,297**	**−6,293**	**954**
A. GOODS..	4 100 ..	**36,882**	**39,014**	**35,096**	**31,437**	**27,126**	**34,713**	**45,112**	**48,273**
Credit...	2 100 ..	**88,590**	**100,116**	**102,825**	**104,512**	**115,248**	**119,038**	**107,880**	**109,856**
General merchandise: exports f.o.b.........	2 110 ..	88,590	100,062	102,775	104,497	115,208	119,015	119,857	109,834
Goods for processing: exports f.o.b.........	2 150 ..	....	....	....	....	....	....	....	....
Repairs on goods...............................	2 160 ..	....	55	50	15	40	24	22	21
Goods procured in ports by carriers........	2 170 ..	....	....	....	....	....	....	....	....
Nonmonetary gold..............................	2 180 ..	....	....	....	....	....	....	....	....
Debit...	3 100 ..	**−51,709**	**−61,102**	**−67,730**	**−73,075**	**−88,122**	**−84,325**	**−62,768**	**−61,583**
General merchandise: imports f.o.b.........	3 110 ..	−51,709	−61,102	−67,730	−73,075	−88,122	−84,326	−62,768	−61,583
Goods for processing: imports f.o.b.........	3 150 ..	....	....	....	....	....	....	....	....
Repairs on goods...............................	3 160 ..	....	....	....	....	....	2	....	....
Goods procured in ports by carriers........	3 170 ..	....	....	....	....	....	....	....	....
Nonmonetary gold..............................	3 180 ..	....	....	....	....	....	....	....	....
B. SERVICES.......................................	4 200 ..	**−12,535**	**−12,666**	**−11,516**	**−8,560**	**−1,623**	**−11,003**	**−11,090**	**−9,437**
Total credit......................................	2 200 ..	*42,061*	*52,718*	*59,920*	*71,729*	*93,289*	*99,872*	*93,652*	*97,833*
Total debit.......................................	3 200 ..	*−54,596*	*−65,384*	*−71,437*	*−80,289*	*−94,912*	*−110,875*	*−104,741*	*−107,270*
Transportation services, credit............	2 205 ..	**1,932**	**2,346**	**2,646**	**2,938**	**3,984**	**4,464**	**4,257**	**4,746**
Passenger..	2 850 ..	*1,344*	*1,700*	*1,998*	*2,295*	*3,189*	*3,611*	*3,498*	*4,031*
Freight..	2 851 ..	*158*	*174*	*174*	*166*	*274*	*294*	*230*	*211*
Other..	2 852 ..	*429*	*472*	*473*	*477*	*521*	*559*	*529*	*504*
Sea transport, passenger......................	2 207 ..	82	85	81	74	87	84	67	76
Sea transport, freight..........................	2 208 ..	122	134	134	126	231	247	185	169
Sea transport, other...........................	2 209 ..	45	50	50	50	55	59	56	53
Air transport, passenger.......................	2 211 ..	1,262	1,615	1,918	2,221	3,102	3,528	3,432	3,955
Air transport, freight...........................	2 212 ..	36	40	40	40	44	47	45	42
Air transport, other............................	2 213 ..	384	422	423	427	466	500	473	451
Other transport, passenger...................	2 215 ..	....	....	....	....	....	....	....	....
Other transport, freight.......................	2 216 ..	....	....	....	....	....	....	....	....
Other transport, other.........................	2 217 ..	....	....	....	....	....	....	....	....
Transportation services, debit.............	3 205 ..	**−1,950**	**−2,224**	**−2,467**	**−2,547**	**−2,836**	**−2,809**	**−2,236**	**−2,141**
Passenger..	3 850 ..	*−96*	*−114*	*−112*	*−116*	*−129*	*−126*	*−114*	*−107*
Freight..	3 851 ..	*−1,461*	*−1,678*	*−1,921*	*−1,995*	*−2,230*	*−2,171*	*−1,637*	*−1,572*
Other..	3 852 ..	*−393*	*−432*	*−433*	*−437*	*−477*	*−512*	*−485*	*−461*
Sea transport, passenger......................	3 207 ..	−12	−22	−20	−23	−27	−18	−11	−9
Sea transport, freight..........................	3 208 ..	−1,022	−1,175	−1,344	−1,396	−1,560	−1,520	−1,146	−1,099
Sea transport, other...........................	3 209 ..	−118	−129	−130	−131	−143	−153	−145	−138
Air transport, passenger.......................	3 211 ..	−84	−92	−92	−93	−101	−109	−103	−98
Air transport, freight...........................	3 212 ..	−293	−336	−384	−399	−447	−435	−327	−315
Air transport, other............................	3 213 ..	−276	−303	−304	−306	−334	−359	−340	−324
Other transport, passenger...................	3 215 ..	....	....	....	....	....	....	....	....
Other transport, freight.......................	3 216 ..	−146	−167	−193	−200	−223	−217	−164	−158
Other transport, other.........................	3 217 ..	....	....	....	....	....	....	....	....
Travel, credit..................................	2 236 ..	**3,862**	**4,375**	**4,782**	**5,369**	**6,074**	**6,356**	**4,894**	**4,040**
Business travel...................................	2 237 ..	....	....	59	103	155	1,023	715	593
Personal travel..................................	2 240 ..	3,862	4,375	4,723	5,266	5,919	5,333	4,180	3,447
Travel, debit...................................	3 236 ..	**−4,736**	**−5,177**	**−6,074**	**−6,862**	**−8,656**	**−10,413**	**−8,773**	**−7,691**
Business travel...................................	3 237 ..	....	....	−82	−89	−93	−1,557	−1,163	−1,044
Personal travel..................................	3 240 ..	−4,736	−5,177	−5,992	−6,773	−8,563	−8,856	−7,611	−6,646
Other services, credit.......................	2 200 BA ..	**36,267**	**45,996**	**52,492**	**61,562**	**82,305**	**88,518**	**83,673**	**88,200**
Communications.................................	2 245 ..	705	427	538	543	708	879	593	726
Construction.....................................	2 249 ..	27	....	....	....	....	....	....	....
Insurance...	2 253 ..	8,731	9,726	8,611	10,969	12,045	11,980	10,148	10,329
Financial..	2 260 ..	3,817	5,303	6,029	7,810	10,213	9,726	8,072	7,925
Computer and information.....................	2 262 ..	14,238	18,774	19,586	22,994	29,825	35,035	33,984	37,385
Royalties and licence fees.....................	2 266 ..	211	352	773	925	1,185	1,475	1,698	2,252
Other business services........................	2 268 ..	7,862	10,498	16,232	18,276	28,279	29,422	29,177	29,583
Personal, cultural, and recreational..........	2 287 ..	400	....	413	....	....	....	....	....
Government, n.i.e................................	2 291 ..	276	505	518	45	49	....	....	....
Other services, debit........................	3 200 BA ..	**−47,910**	**−57,983**	**−62,896**	**−61,439**	**−83,221**	**−97,406**	**−93,501**	**−97,184**
Communications.................................	3 245 ..	−860	−773	−882	−970	−1,123	−1,569	−1,389	−1,603
Construction.....................................	3 249 ..	−47	....	....	....	....	....	....	....
Insurance...	3 253 ..	−6,301	−7,498	−7,434	−9,095	−9,778	−9,256	−8,628	−8,123
Financial..	3 260 ..	−2,052	−2,776	−3,303	−4,910	−6,357	−6,564	−5,968	−5,986
Computer and information.....................	3 262 ..	−371	−380	−437	−706	−907	−1,039	−871	−857
Royalties and licence fees.....................	3 266 ..	−16,077	−18,847	−19,223	−22,033	−24,017	−35,455	−35,014	−37,823
Other business services........................	3 268 ..	−22,038	−27,539	−31,421	−23,680	−40,996	−43,523	−41,632	−42,792
Personal, cultural, and recreational..........	3 287 ..	−87	....	−105	....	....	....	....	....
Government, n.i.e................................	3 291 ..	−77	−56	−51	−45	−41	....	....	....

Table 2 (Continued). STANDARD PRESENTATION, 2003–2010

(Millions of U.S. dollars)

	Code	2003	2004	2005	2006	2007	2008	2009	2010
C. INCOME	4 300	**−24,784**	**−27,931**	**−31,014**	**−30,144**	**−38,094**	**−37,134**	**−38,782**	**−36,293**
Total credit	2 300	*34,095*	*43,457*	*53,862*	*83,138*	*116,528*	*123,774*	*76,471*	*76,418*
Total debit	3 300	*−58,879*	*−71,388*	*−84,876*	*−113,283*	*−154,622*	*−160,909*	*−115,253*	*−112,711*
Compensation of employees, credit	2 310	**304**	**389**	**488**	**520**	**573**	**623**	**560**	**585**
Compensation of employees, debit	3 310	**−548**	**−734**	**−1,063**	**−1,278**	**−1,619**	**−1,576**	**−1,101**	**−979**
Investment income, credit	2 320	**33,791**	**43,068**	**53,374**	**82,618**	**115,955**	**123,152**	**75,911**	**75,833**
Direct investment income	2 330	5,003	7,489	8,017	10,887	14,376	15,042	12,901	19,336
Dividends and distributed branch profits	2 332	278	....	202	643	....	....	1,963	1,709
Reinvested earnings and undistributed branch profits	2 333	3,023	....	4,544	4,819	....	....	6,588	13,998
Income on debt (interest)	2 334	1,702	2,838	3,271	5,425	6,798	8,109	4,350	3,629
Portfolio investment income	2 339	18,435	23,014	27,708	41,974	56,497	60,142	35,483	32,966
Income on equity	2 340	2,386	3,406	4,411	7,841	8,502	8,995	5,605	7,141
Income on bonds and notes	2 350	13,061	15,959	18,062	25,431	34,016	39,451	26,977	24,024
Income on money market instruments	2 360	2,989	3,649	5,236	8,701	13,979	11,697	2,901	1,801
Other investment income	2 370	10,352	12,565	17,649	29,758	45,082	47,967	27,527	23,531
Investment income, debit	3 320	**−58,331**	**−70,655**	**−83,813**	**−112,005**	**−153,003**	**−159,332**	**−114,152**	**−111,732**
Direct investment income	3 330	−34,602	−39,681	−40,889	−39,375	−50,590	−45,306	−48,656	−51,296
Dividends and distributed branch profits	3 332	−15,023	−25,925	−32,446	−25,187	−23,142	−19,711	−22,208	−21,660
Reinvested earnings and undistributed branch profits	3 333	−17,886	−11,590	−5,680	−11,695	−24,840	−22,572	−23,921	−28,076
Income on debt (interest)	3 334	−1,693	−2,166	−2,763	−2,493	−2,608	−3,022	−2,527	−1,560
Portfolio investment income	3 339	−13,856	−18,434	−23,545	−42,018	−58,212	−63,396	−39,221	−39,772
Income on equity	3 340	−9,029	−10,829	−13,472	−21,455	−28,060	−27,573	−15,275	−18,764
Income on bonds and notes	3 350	−3,877	−6,501	−8,189	−16,951	−25,364	−33,448	−22,302	−20,118
Income on money market instruments	3 360	−950	−1,104	−1,884	−3,612	−4,788	−2,376	−1,645	−890
Other investment income	3 370	−9,873	−12,540	−19,379	−30,612	−44,201	−50,630	−26,275	−20,664
D. CURRENT TRANSFERS	4 379	**527**	**503**	**284**	**−592**	**−1,260**	**−1,873**	**−1,533**	**−1,589**
Credit	2 379	**7,027**	**6,626**	**6,963**	**6,645**	**6,704**	**8,013**	**7,552**	**6,626**
General government	2 380	167	303	271	239	220	118	67	75
Other sectors	2 390	6,860	6,323	6,693	6,407	6,484	7,894	7,485	6,551
Workers' remittances	2 391	33	25	25	19	16	10	13	16
Other current transfers	2 392	6,826	6,298	6,668	6,388	6,467	7,884	7,472	6,535
Debit	3 379	**−6,500**	**−6,123**	**−6,679**	**−7,237**	**−7,964**	**−9,886**	**−9,085**	**−8,215**
General government	3 380	−1,356	−1,663	−1,975	−2,258	−2,779	−2,885	−3,182	−2,796
Other sectors	3 390	−5,144	−4,460	−4,704	−4,979	−5,184	−7,001	−5,903	−5,419
Workers' remittances	3 391	−154	−169	−378	−575	−902	−1,096	−802	−684
Other current transfers	3 392	−4,991	−4,291	−4,327	−4,405	−4,283	−5,905	−5,101	−4,735
CAPITAL AND FINANCIAL ACCOUNT	4 996	**−1,464**	**5,104**	**−402**	**6,534**	**16,848**	**25,218**	**−3,581**	**14,566**
CAPITAL ACCOUNT	4 994	**126**	**368**	**323**	**283**	**51**	**74**	**−1,844**	**−915**
Total credit	2 994	*617*	*797*	*534*	*392*	*167*	*197*	*103*	*131*
Total debit	3 994	*−491*	*−428*	*−211*	*−109*	*−116*	*−123*	*−1,946*	*−1,046*
Capital transfers, credit	2 400	**588**	**670**	**381**	**357**	**167**	**197**	**103**	**110**
General government	2 401	584	665	376	355	167	197	103	110
Debt forgiveness	2 402	....	....	....	....	....	....	....	....
Other capital transfers	2 410	584	665	376	355	167	197	103	110
Other sectors	2 430	5	5	5	2	....	....	....	....
Migrants' transfers	2 431	....	....	....	....	....	....	....	....
Debt forgiveness	2 432	....	....	....	....	....	....	....	....
Other capital transfers	2 440	5	5	5	2	....	....	....	....
Capital transfers, debit	3 400	**−86**	**−94**	**−95**	**−95**	**−104**	**−106**	**−89**	**−88**
General government	3 401	....	....	....	....	....	....	....	....
Debt forgiveness	3 402	....	....	....	....	....	....	....	....
Other capital transfers	3 410	....	....	....	....	....	....	....	....
Other sectors	3 430	−86	−94	−95	−95	−104	−106	−89	−88
Migrants' transfers	3 431	−86	−94	−95	−95	−104	−106	−89	−88
Debt forgiveness	3 432	....	....	....	....	....	....	....	....
Other capital transfers	3 440	....	....	....	....	....	....	....	....
Nonproduced nonfinancial assets, credit	2 480	**29**	**127**	**153**	**35**	....	....	....	**21**
Nonproduced nonfinancial assets, debit	3 480	**−405**	**−334**	**−116**	**−14**	**−12**	**−16**	**−1,857**	**−959**

Table 2 (Continued). STANDARD PRESENTATION, 2003–2010

(Millions of U.S. dollars)

	Code	2003	2004	2005	2006	2007	2008	2009	2010
FINANCIAL ACCOUNT	4 995	−1,591	4,735	−724	6,251	16,797	25,144	−1,738	15,481
A. DIRECT INVESTMENT	4 500	16,817	−29,102	−44,824	−20,817	4,014	−34,905	−285	8,977
Direct investment abroad	4 505	−5,594	−18,107	−14,491	−15,294	−20,567	−18,567	−26,836	−18,108
Equity capital	4 510	−2,696	....	−4,426	−14,489	....	....	−14,395	2,747
Claims on affiliated enterprises	4 515	....	....	....	....	....	....	....	....
Liabilities to affiliated enterprises	4 520	....	....	....	....	....	....	....	....
Reinvested earnings	4 525	−3,023	....	−4,544	−4,819	....	....	−6,588	−13,998
Other capital	4 530	126	....	−5,520	4,014	−6,841	−4,785	−5,854	−6,858
Claims on affiliated enterprises	4 535	−299	....	....	966	−7,101	−5,999	−8,801	−2,084
Liabilities to affiliated enterprises	4 540	425	....	....	3,048	260	1,214	2,948	−4,773
Direct investment in Ireland	4 555	22,411	−10,994	−30,334	−5,523	24,581	−16,339	26,551	27,085
Equity capital	4 560	4,153	−5,952	4,703	−5,270	−2,908	−5,155	8,738	−5,481
Claims on direct investors	4 565	....	....	....	....	....	....	....	....
Liabilities to direct investors	4 570	....	−5,952	....	−5,270	−2,908	−5,155	8,738	−5,481
Reinvested earnings	4 575	17,886	11,590	5,680	11,695	24,840	22,577	23,921	28,073
Other capital	4 580	372	−16,632	−40,717	−11,948	2,649	−33,760	−6,109	4,494
Claims on direct investors	4 585	−32,576	−46,650	−78,014	−24,560	−35,100	−38,383	−24,652	−1,350
Liabilities to direct investors	4 590	32,948	30,018	37,297	12,612	37,749	4,622	18,543	5,844
B. PORTFOLIO INVESTMENT	4 600	−44,444	17,530	63,917	11,966	−10,346	−62,493	34,435	129,748
Assets	4 602	−163,841	−168,940	−151,139	−267,083	−232,631	−45,303	−749	28,611
Equity securities	4 610	−29,545	−46,087	−59,602	−74,006	−29,415	32,388	−13,643	−36,745
Monetary authorities	4 611	....	....	....	....	....	....	....	....
General government	4 612	....	....	−1,411	....	....	....	3,549	747
Banks	4 613	....	....	−610	....	....	....	−674	1,192
Other sectors	4 614	....	....	−57,580	....	−29,013	32,229	−16,519	−38,684
Debt securities	4 619	−134,296	−122,853	−91,537	−193,077	−203,216	−77,691	12,894	65,356
Bonds and notes	4 620	−93,015	−79,453	−92,303	−109,342	−116,326	−72,523	49,139	83,168
Monetary authorities	4 621	−220	−1,350	−2,808	33	−5,863	−2,903	2,365	−41
General government	4 622	−68	−69	−251	−953	−1,467	1,339	2,847	−232
Banks	4 623	−62,099	−64,807	−68,879	−80,715	−58,590	−22,089	82,835	159,834
Other sectors	4 624	−30,627	−13,227	−20,366	−27,707	−50,405	−48,870	−38,908	−76,393
Money market instruments	4 630	−41,281	−43,400	766	−83,735	−86,891	−5,168	−36,245	−17,812
Monetary authorities	4 631	−1,052	−732	99	−540	2,473	−3,363	−1,219	−1,916
General government	4 632	....	....	....	....	....	....	....	....
Banks	4 633	−21,761	−32,890	−21,473	−78,864	−77,037	−3,035	−37,894	−1,204
Other sectors	4 634	−18,469	−9,778	22,139	−4,331	−12,327	1,230	2,868	−14,692
Liabilities	4 652	119,397	186,471	215,056	279,049	222,285	−17,190	35,184	101,137
Equity securities	4 660	76,776	81,709	93,590	160,467	138,387	−7,844	30,815	152,236
Banks	4 663	....	37,954	32,051	87,902	93,651	10,987	−17,588	39,711
Other sectors	4 664	....	43,755	61,539	72,565	44,736	−18,831	48,403	112,525
Debt securities	4 669	42,621	104,761	121,466	118,581	83,898	−9,346	4,369	−51,099
Bonds and notes	4 670	....	80,422	76,548	109,490	69,022	−19,780	25,797	−9,441
Monetary authorities	4 671	....	....	....	....	....	....	....	....
General government	4 672	....	4,693	2,074	401	2,945	13,929	29,203	19,852
Banks	4 673	....	45,545	40,602	46,085	3,553	−90,351	−14,379	−32,164
Other sectors	4 674	....	30,184	33,872	63,003	62,524	56,641	10,972	2,871
Money market instruments	4 680	....	24,340	44,917	9,092	14,876	10,434	−21,427	−41,659
Monetary authorities	4 681	....	....	....	....	....	....	....	....
General government	4 682	....	−2,263	−282	....	252	25,922	....	....
Banks	4 683	....	18,328	32,424	15,297	20,364	....	....	....
Other sectors	4 684	....	8,275	12,776	−6,205	−5,741	....	....	....
C. FINANCIAL DERIVATIVES	4 910	−525	1,042	−8,041	374	−16,331	1,388	−3,367	−16,038
Monetary authorities	4 911	....	....	....	....	....	−330	348	....
General government	4 912	−31	−18	−19	−4	7	−9	−3	31
Banks	4 913	544	−1,056	−5,489	3,152	−9,541	6,311	−2,544	−17,258
Other sectors	4 914	−919	−1,710	−2,533	−2,775	−6,798	−4,584	−1,169	1,189
Assets	4 900	−406	−1,903	−5,347	3,046	−18,725	6,210	16,553	−8,006
Monetary authorities	4 901	....	....	....	....	....	−330	348	....
General government	4 902	−31	....	....	....	7	−9	−3	31
Banks	4 903	544	....	....	....	....	4,764	19,648	−7,254
Other sectors	4 904	−919	....	....	....	....	1,785	−3,439	−783
Liabilities	4 905	−120	2,945	−2,694	−2,672	2,393	−4,822	−19,921	−8,032
Monetary authorities	4 906	....	....	....	....	....	....	....	....
General government	4 907	....	....	....	....	....	....	....	....
Banks	4 908	....	....	....	....	....	1,547	−22,191	−10,004
Other sectors	4 909	....	....	....	....	....	−6,369	2,271	1,972

Table 2 (Concluded). STANDARD PRESENTATION, 2003–2010

(Millions of U.S. dollars)

	Code	2003	2004	2005	2006	2007	2008	2009	2010
D. OTHER INVESTMENT	4 700	**24,672**	**13,830**	**–13,552**	**14,616**	**39,477**	**121,310**	**–31,487**	**–107,248**
Assets	4 703	**–65,871**	**–57,406**	**–133,298**	**–154,941**	**–196,846**	**–106,455**	**72,037**	**–21,004**
Trade credits	4 706	–126	990	–2,445	–2,673	–892	3,403	1,754	–1,872
General government	4 707	....	....	....	....	....	....	....	....
of which: Short-term	4 709	....	....	....	....	....	....	....	....
Other sectors	4 710	–126	990	–2,445	–2,673	–892	3,403	1,754	–1,872
of which: Short-term	4 712	–126	990	–2,445	–2,673	–892	3,403	1,754	–1,872
Loans	4 714	–34,071	–42,180	–62,594	–134,903	–118,812	11,798	50,412	31,175
Monetary authorities	4 715	–1,006	146	127	85	784	–48	–1,121	471
of which: Short-term	4 718	–1,006	146	127	85	784	–48	–1,121	471
General government	4 719	....	....	....	....	....	....	....	–449
of which: Short-term	4 721	....	....	....	....	....	....	....	....
Banks	4 722	–14,223	–31,735	–34,561	–75,900	–40,352	54,793	49,299	39,791
of which: Short-term	4 724	–980	–6,341	–17,864	–26,537	–16,225	–6,264	28,085	27,311
Other sectors	4 725	–18,842	–10,591	–28,160	–59,089	–79,244	–42,946	2,233	–8,638
of which: Short-term	4 727	–4,368	4,658	–5,759	–11,425	–16,952	8,335	–2,923	–7,166
Currency and deposits	4 730	–30,102	–14,486	–47,321	–7,056	–71,523	–125,963	26,947	–38,570
Monetary authorities	4 731	–570	291	–423	–1,193	2,608	–5,578	7,836	10
General government	4 732	31	–381	–226	407	1,253	191	443	72
Banks	4 733	–22,859	–9,840	–47,415	–7,264	–70,198	–118,891	18,360	–30,973
Other sectors	4 734	–6,704	–4,556	743	994	–5,185	–1,685	307	–7,679
Other assets	4 736	–1,572	–1,730	–20,939	–10,309	–5,619	4,306	–7,075	–11,737
Monetary authorities	4 737	....	–129	....	15	10	825	2	....
of which: Short-term	4 739	....	–129	....	15	10	825	2	....
General government	4 740	....	....	....	....	....	....	....	....
of which: Short-term	4 742	....	....	....	....	....	....	....	....
Banks	4 743	1,624	1,050	–3,866	–338	172	–2,835	1,213	–396
of which: Short-term	4 745	....	....	....	....	....	....	1,266	55
Other sectors	4 746	–3,196	–2,652	–17,073	–9,986	–5,802	6,317	–8,290	–11,341
of which: Short-term	4 748	–2,124	–1,751	....	–5,681	1,101	....	–791	–7,476
Liabilities	4 753	**90,542**	**71,236**	**119,746**	**169,557**	**236,323**	**227,766**	**–103,524**	**–86,244**
Trade credits	4 756	2,450	1,442	3,368	6,138	2,807	7,953	–6,956	3,751
General government	4 757	....	....	....	....	....	....	....	....
of which: Short-term	4 759	....	....	....	....	....	....	....	....
Other sectors	4 760	2,450	1,442	3,368	6,138	2,807	7,953	–6,956	3,751
of which: Short-term	4 762	2,450	1,442	3,368	6,138	2,807	7,953	–6,956	3,751
Loans	4 764	64,412	19,841	67,627	119,045	86,816	19,534	–8,351	–46,244
Monetary authorities	4 765	....	....	....	....	....	....	–693	....
of which: Use of Fund credit and loans from the Fund	4 766	....	....	....	....	....	....	....	....
of which: Short-term	4 768	....	....	....	....	....	....	–693	....
General government	4 769	–286	–9	–149	–5	360	395	–46	....
of which: Short-term	4 771	–198	67	–144	–5	360	497	....	....
Banks	4 772	51,240	16,183	50,740	92,279	37,025	–14,746	–7,776	–45,506
of which: Short-term	4 774	42,015	23,679	32,667	....	4,483	–14,066	–2,235	–47,809
Other sectors	4 775	13,458	3,668	17,036	26,771	49,431	33,886	165	–738
of which: Short-term	4 777	10,013	–226	5,106	7,924	31,619	–12,733	9,225	2,501
Currency and deposits	4 780	20,560	43,905	41,994	16,539	–1,596	202,999	–100,606	–68,961
Monetary authorities	4 781	7,494	–4,345	....	–2,574	–1,596	62,673	....	....
General government	4 782	....	....	....	....	....	....	....	....
Banks	4 783	13,411	48,102	....	19,211	....	....	....	....
Other sectors	4 784	–345	148	....	–99	....	....	....	....
Other liabilities	4 786	3,121	6,048	6,757	27,836	18,886	–2,721	12,389	25,210
Monetary authorities	4 787	–33	–4	–9	–3	–35	–1	1,074	4
of which: Short-term	4 789	–33	–4	–9	–3	–35	–1	–1	4
General government	4 790	....	....	....	....	....	....	....	....
of which: Short-term	4 792	....	....	....	....	....	....	....	....
Banks	4 793	–2,164	–420	–385	6,667	5,095	1,861	–663	882
of which: Short-term	4 795	–2,164	–420	–385	....	5,095	....	–663	882
Other sectors	4 796	5,318	6,472	7,151	21,172	13,826	–4,581	11,978	24,323
of which: Short-term	4 798	5,186	....	....	....	....	....	12,346	....
E. RESERVE ASSETS	4 802	**1,890**	**1,435**	**1,776**	**112**	**–16**	**–157**	**–1,034**	**42**
Monetary gold	4 812	–1	8	18	....	5	1	–1	–1
Special drawing rights	4 811	–6	–6	–6	–2	–1	....	–1,075	54
Reserve position in the Fund	4 810	–59	175	212	52	48	–77	–75	6
Foreign exchange	4 803	1,956	1,258	1,552	63	–69	–81	119	–17
Other claims	4 813	....	....	....	....	....	....	....	....
NET ERRORS AND OMISSIONS	4 998	**1,375**	**–4,023**	**7,552**	**1,324**	**–2,998**	**–9,921**	**9,874**	**–15,520**

Table 3. INTERNATIONAL INVESTMENT POSITION (End-period stocks), 2003–2010

(Millions of U.S. dollars)

	Code	2003	2004	2005	2006	2007	2008	2009	2010
ASSETS	8 995 C.	**1,364,407**	**1,757,495**	**1,983,595**	**2,648,945**	**3,341,746**	**3,039,726**	**3,316,541**	**3,332,300**
Direct investment abroad	8 505	**73,321**	**106,692**	**104,152**	**120,728**	**150,060**	**168,926**	**273,296**	**317,711**
Equity capital and reinvested earnings	8 506	67,539	91,766	87,684	108,435	130,693	139,128	230,172	265,621
Claims on affiliated enterprises	8 507	68,076	91,849	87,692	108,475	....	139,688	232,281	266,359
Liabilities to affiliated enterprises	8 508	−537	−83	−8	−40	....	−559	−2,109	−739
Other capital	8 530	5,782	14,926	16,469	12,293	19,367	29,798	43,124	52,090
Claims on affiliated enterprises	8 535	14,605	26,318	24,880	25,053	34,906	47,954	68,995	73,355
Liabilities to affiliated enterprises	8 540	−8,823	−11,393	−8,411	−12,760	−15,539	−18,156	−25,870	−21,264
Portfolio investment	8 602	**834,518**	**1,072,312**	**1,182,212**	**1,620,218**	**1,970,468**	**1,621,055**	**1,802,055**	**1,764,344**
Equity securities	8 610	222,503	304,943	383,155	573,199	649,173	427,868	539,873	603,914
Monetary authorities	8 611	....	....	....	....	....	....	....	....
General government	8 612	8,528	11,955	14,382	19,823	24,119	14,972	14,553	14,753
Banks	8 613	201	1,146	1,811	3,959	2,885	2,628	3,769	861
Other sectors	8 614	213,774	291,842	366,962	549,417	622,168	410,269	521,552	588,301
Debt securities	8 619	612,016	767,369	799,057	1,047,019	1,321,295	1,193,187	1,262,182	1,160,430
Bonds and notes	8 620	379,235	474,982	535,258	682,305	978,855	892,547	949,664	809,045
Monetary authorities	8 621	3,740	5,447	7,354	8,065	15,491	17,121	15,177	14,017
General government	8 622	1,694	2,023	2,079	3,182	4,982	3,674	612	782
Banks	8 623	174,539	253,082	300,204	403,880	613,548	576,054	563,551	350,654
Other sectors	8 624	199,262	214,430	225,621	267,177	344,835	295,699	370,324	443,593
Money market instruments	8 630	232,781	292,387	263,799	364,714	342,440	300,639	312,518	351,385
Monetary authorities	8 631	1,163	2,091	1,765	2,576	218	3,570	4,999	6,554
General government	8 632	....	....	....	....	....	....	....	....
Banks	8 633	200,516	246,678	244,652	338,137	305,514	267,476	272,671	296,739
Other sectors	8 634	31,101	43,619	17,382	24,001	36,708	29,593	34,848	48,091
Financial derivatives	8 900	**7,317**	**9,138**	**11,048**	**11,326**	**37,793**	**51,325**	**67,473**	**82,565**
Monetary authorities	8 901	....	....	....	....	....	348	....	....
General government	8 902	162	−3	26	−36	−59	90	−213	−627
Banks	8 903	3,793	3,578	3,643	3,686	27,053	42,642	54,005	68,277
Other sectors	8 904	3,362	5,563	7,379	7,675	10,799	8,244	13,681	14,915
Other investment	8 703	**445,091**	**566,439**	**685,304**	**895,830**	**1,182,485**	**1,197,382**	**1,171,562**	**1,165,566**
Trade credits	8 706	28,873	29,037	32,878	43,192	49,960	36,211	41,194	42,166
General government	8 707	....	....	....	....	....	....	....	....
of which: Short-term	8 709	....	....	....	....	....	....	....	....
Other sectors	8 710	28,873	29,037	32,878	43,192	49,960	36,211	41,194	42,166
of which: Short-term	8 712	*28,873*	*29,037*	*32,878*	*43,192*	*49,960*	*36,211*	*41,194*	*42,166*
Loans	8 714	274,548	376,121	438,171	564,503	701,435	669,747	632,880	593,357
Monetary authorities	8 715	1,080	1,000	790	763	....	....	1,204	609
of which: Short-term	8 718	*1,080*	*1,000*	*790*	*763*	....	....	*1,204*	*609*
General government	8 719	....	....	....	....	....	....	....	....
of which: Short-term	8 721	....	....	....	....	....	....	....	....
Banks	8 722	104,227	142,709	160,956	217,154	245,667	198,835	162,063	138,926
of which: Short-term	8 724	*22,252*	*36,564*	*51,693*	*77,544*	*43,434*	*44,436*	*24,365*	*18,644*
Other sectors	8 725	169,242	232,412	276,425	346,587	455,768	470,912	469,613	453,822
of which: Short-term	8 727	*38,385*	*34,738*	*39,731*	*54,064*	*69,357*	*66,008*	*56,248*	*67,729*
Currency and deposits	8 730	114,391	134,611	164,245	221,571	351,577	423,327	422,318	443,927
Monetary authorities	8 731	1,920	1,801	1,948	3,435	1,038	7,014	....	....
General government	8 732	928	1,429	1,430	1,192	183	49	61	40
Banks	8 733	85,491	100,142	132,714	187,695	312,020	363,416	364,616	381,885
Other sectors	8 734	26,052	31,240	28,154	29,249	38,336	52,848	57,641	62,002
Other assets	8 736	27,278	26,670	50,010	66,564	79,513	68,097	75,171	86,115
Monetary authorities	8 737	590	776	672	735	811	1	....	....
of which: Short-term	8 739	*590*	*776*	*672*	*735*	*811*	*1*	....	....
General government	8 740	....	....	....	....	....	....	....	....
of which: Short-term	8 742	....	....	....	....	....	....	....	....
Banks	8 743	8,650	3,757	8,352	10,161	13,470	11,316	2,995	3,393
of which: Short-term	8 745	....	....	....	....	....	....	....	....
Other sectors	8 746	18,038	22,137	40,985	55,668	65,232	56,780	72,176	82,723
of which: Short-term	8 748	*7,483*	*8,228*	*8,850*	*15,039*	*17,567*	*13,181*	*25,131*	*35,127*
Reserve assets	8 802	**4,159**	**2,914**	**879**	**843**	**940**	**1,038**	**2,155**	**2,115**
Monetary gold	8 812	81	84	99	122	162	167	213	273
Special drawing rights	8 811	79	89	88	95	101	98	1,179	1,104
Reserve position in the Fund	8 810	575	418	176	131	87	164	245	237
Foreign exchange	8 803	3,425	2,322	516	494	590	610	517	501
Other claims	8 813	....	....	....	....	....	....	....	....

Table 3 (Concluded). INTERNATIONAL INVESTMENT POSITION (End-period stocks), 2003–2010

(Millions of U.S. dollars)

	Code	2003	2004	2005	2006	2007	2008	2009	2010
LIABILITIES..	8 995 D.	**1,399,964**	**1,794,149**	**2,030,767**	**2,661,394**	**3,396,110**	**3,218,667**	**3,544,039**	**3,532,961**
Direct investment in Ireland................	8 555 ..	**222,837**	**207,648**	**163,530**	**156,491**	**203,683**	**193,249**	**243,932**	**245,798**
Equity capital and reinvested earnings...........	8 556 ..	224,902	228,371	217,604	226,419	267,017	256,979	303,638	291,246
Claims on direct investors........................	8 557 ..	....	....	....	....	....	....	....	....
Liabilities to direct investors...................	8 558 ..	224,902	228,371	217,604	226,419	267,017	256,979	303,638	291,246
Other capital..	8 580 ..	−2,065	−20,723	−54,074	−69,927	−63,334	−63,730	−59,706	−45,448
Claims on direct investors........................	8 585 ..	−109,438	−157,125	−229,837	−268,390	−319,984	−334,895	−370,910	−360,389
Liabilities to direct investors...................	8 590 ..	107,373	136,402	175,764	198,463	256,650	271,164	311,204	314,941
Portfolio investment............................	8 652 ..	**684,799**	**982,009**	**1,210,257**	**1,611,591**	**1,957,758**	**1,643,932**	**1,948,581**	**2,074,155**
Equity securities.....................................	8 660 ..	481,712	613,830	712,330	950,795	1,155,092	889,191	1,177,526	1,407,712
Banks..	8 663 ..	201,419	257,536	277,517	377,673	470,033	411,303	438,738	464,022
Other sectors.......................................	8 664 ..	280,293	356,294	434,813	573,122	685,059	477,888	738,789	943,690
Debt securities.......................................	8 669 ..	203,087	368,178	497,927	660,796	802,665	754,741	771,055	666,443
Bonds and notes..................................	8 670 ..	149,495	286,034	382,288	526,380	728,748	682,451	693,384	633,500
Monetary authorities..........................	8 671 ..	....	....	....	....	....	....	....	....
General government...........................	8 672 ..	27,043	34,279	31,677	35,716	42,984	53,798	86,025	99,948
Banks...	8 673 ..	42,132	93,311	131,007	180,267	284,817	176,310	141,589	98,857
Other sectors....................................	8 674 ..	80,319	158,445	219,604	310,397	400,947	452,343	465,769	434,695
Money market instruments....................	8 680 ..	53,592	82,144	115,639	134,416	73,917	72,290	77,671	32,943
Monetary authorities..........................	8 681 ..	....	....	....	....	....	....	....	....
General government...........................	8 682 ..	2,516	278	....	....	867	26,508	22,276	7,688
Banks...	8 683 ..	34,678	56,328	80,405	102,676	44,120	33,132	43,415	15,743
Other sectors....................................	8 684 ..	16,398	25,538	35,234	31,740	28,930	12,651	11,980	9,511
Financial derivatives............................	8 905 ..	....	....	**2,895**	....	**42,139**	**65,606**	**73,707**	**73,372**
Monetary authorities................................	8 906 ..	....	....	....	....	....	....	....	....
General government................................	8 907 ..	....	....	....	....	....	....	....	....
Banks..	8 908 ..	....	....	....	....	....	65,262	71,490	71,198
Other sectors...	8 909 ..	....	....	....	54	....	344	2,217	2,174
Other investment................................	8 753 ..	....	....	**654,086**	....	**1,192,531**	**1,315,880**	**1,277,818**	**1,139,635**
Trade credits..	8 756 ..	17,856	18,233	20,002	28,795	32,679	36,996	27,709	31,804
General government................................	8 757 ..	....	....	....	....	....	....	....	....
of which: Short-term...........................	8 759 ..	....	....	....	....	....	....	....	....
Other sectors...	8 760 ..	17,856	18,233	20,002	28,795	32,679	36,996	27,709	31,804
of which: Short-term...........................	8 762 ..	*17,856*	*18,233*	*20,002*	*28,795*	*32,679*	*36,996*	*27,709*	*31,804*
Loans..	8 764 ..	284,347	318,628	357,843	510,489	476,447	404,889	413,444	380,518
Monetary authorities................................	8 765 ..	....	....	....	....	....	....	....	....
of which: Use of Fund credit and loans from the Fund....	8 766 ..	....	....	....	....	....	....	....	....
of which: Short-term...........................	8 768 ..	....	....	....	....	....	....	....	....
General government................................	8 769 ..	318	385	158	209	542	43	1	....
of which: Short-term...........................	8 771 ..	*63*	*196*	....	....	*368*	....	....	....
Banks..	8 772 ..	188,539	214,671	243,911	359,062	261,912	166,545	161,648	111,406
of which: Short-term...........................	8 774 ..	*139,214*	*186,172*	*201,949*	*264,002*	*144,406*	*68,454*	*65,481*	*19,253*
Other sectors...	8 775 ..	95,489	103,571	113,774	151,218	213,993	238,301	251,794	269,112
of which: Short-term...........................	8 777 ..	*50,184*	*49,590*	*51,016*	*64,591*	*103,539*	*85,751*	*106,377*	*104,522*
Currency and deposits..............................	8 780 ..	128,160	187,605	204,706	242,296	550,701	753,727	683,729	555,744
Monetary authorities................................	8 781 ..	13,059	9,100	5,319	3,352	876	61,741	77,099	193,996
General government................................	8 782 ..	....	....	....	....	....	....	....	....
Banks..	8 783 ..	112,814	174,076	196,724	236,245	547,587	687,109	601,551	356,177
Other sectors...	8 784 ..	2,287	4,428	2,663	2,700	2,238	4,877	5,078	5,571
Other liabilities......................................	8 786 ..	....	....	71,535	....	132,704	120,269	152,937	171,569
Monetary authorities................................	8 787 ..	141	157	137	144	135	143	1,226	1,208
of which: Short-term...........................	8 789 ..	*141*	*157*	*137*	*144*	*135*	*143*	*10*	*13*
General government................................	8 790 ..	....	....	....	....	....	....	....	....
of which: Short-term...........................	8 792 ..	....	....	....	....	....	....	....	....
Banks..	8 793 ..	....	....	....	....	....	4,824	4,149	4,218
of which: Short-term...........................	8 795 ..	....	....	....	....	....	*4,824*	*4,149*	*4,218*
Other sectors...	8 796 ..	50,774	63,079	....	98,884	....	115,302	147,562	166,143
of which: Short-term...........................	8 798 ..	*50,774*	*63,079*	....	*98,884*	....	*115,302*	*147,562*	*166,143*
NET INTERNATIONAL INVESTMENT POSITION........	8 995 ..	**−35,557**	**−36,654**	**−47,173**	**−12,449**	**−54,364**	**−178,940**	**−227,497**	**−200,660**
Conversion rates: euros per U.S. dollar (end of period)................	0 104 ..	.7918	.7342	.8477	.7593	.6793	.7185	.6942	.7484

Table 1. ANALYTIC PRESENTATION, 2003–2010

(Millions of U.S. dollars)

	Code	2003	2004	2005	2006	2007	2008	2009	2010
A. Current Account[1]	4 993 Z.	**746**	**2,341**	**4,246**	**7,387**	**4,882**	**1,526**	**7,061**	**6,396**
Goods: exports f.o.b.	2 100 ..	29,940	36,357	39,767	43,319	50,286	57,161	45,898	55,674
Goods: imports f.o.b.	3 100 ..	−33,316	−39,507	−43,887	−47,154	−55,969	−64,399	−45,993	−58,039
Balance on Goods	4 100 ..	*−3,376*	*−3,151*	*−4,120*	*−3,836*	*−5,684*	*−7,238*	*−96*	*−2,365*
Services: credit	2 200 ..	13,661	16,081	17,516	19,222	21,145	24,306	21,979	24,704
Services: debit	3 200 ..	−11,201	−12,822	−13,715	−14,654	−17,577	−19,909	−17,136	−18,056
Balance on Goods and Services	4 991 ..	*−916*	*109*	*−320*	*733*	*−2,115*	*−2,841*	*4,748*	*4,283*
Income: credit	2 300 ..	2,814	3,004	5,601	8,387	10,873	7,242	5,692	5,823
Income: debit	3 300 ..	−7,563	−7,046	−7,037	−9,174	−11,133	−11,357	−10,781	−12,135
Balance on Goods, Services, and Income	4 992 ..	*−5,665*	*−3,934*	*−1,756*	*−55*	*−2,375*	*−6,956*	*−341*	*−2,030*
Current transfers: credit	2 379 Z.	7,556	7,355	7,040	8,559	8,528	9,424	8,395	9,481
Current transfers: debit	3 379 ..	−1,145	−1,081	−1,038	−1,117	−1,271	−943	−993	−1,055
B. Capital Account[1]	4 994 Z.	**534**	**667**	**727**	**786**	**822**	**1,109**	**908**	**983**
Capital account: credit	2 994 Z.	534	667	727	786	822	1,109	908	983
Capital account: debit	3 994 ..	....	....	....	....	....	....	....	....
Total, Groups A Plus B	4 981 ..	*1,280*	*3,007*	*4,973*	*8,173*	*5,704*	*2,635*	*7,969*	*7,379*
C. Financial Account[1]	4 995 W.	**−4,330**	**−6,763**	**−8,725**	**−10,523**	**−2,510**	**13,753**	**6,148**	**1,248**
Direct investment abroad	4 505 ..	−2,086	−4,533	−2,946	−15,462	−8,604	−7,210	−1,695	−7,960
Direct investment in Israel	4 555 Z.	3,322	2,947	4,818	15,296	8,798	10,874	4,438	5,152
Portfolio investment assets	4 602 ..	−3,247	−2,854	−7,975	−6,347	−3,138	−1,634	−8,254	−8,901
Equity securities	4 610 ..	−1,054	−1,149	−3,373	−2,906	−2,034	−2,290	−7,126	−7,251
Debt securities	4 619 ..	−2,193	−1,704	−4,601	−3,441	−1,103	656	−1,128	−1,650
Portfolio investment liabilities	4 652 Z.	62	3,828	2,313	4,041	3,596	2,149	3,085	8,602
Equity securities	4 660 ..	−108	3,940	2,255	3,970	3,620	2,153	2,122	−612
Debt securities	4 669 Z.	170	−113	58	71	−24	−4	963	9,214
Financial derivatives	4 910 ..	14	50	35	−89	29	−116	230	30
Financial derivatives assets	4 900 ..	14	50	35	−89	29	−116	230	30
Financial derivatives liabilities	4 905 ..	....	....	....	....	....	....	....	....
Other investment assets	4 703 ..	−2,024	−6,584	−5,315	−10,719	−7,172	10,819	4,499	929
Monetary authorities	4 701 ..	....	....	....	....	....	....	....	....
General government	4 704 ..	−13	13	1,305	206	−180	39	−138	188
Banks	4 705 ..	−1,255	−3,658	−4,718	−7,153	784	6,992	5,055	1,469
Other sectors	4 728 ..	−756	−2,939	−1,902	−3,771	−7,776	3,788	−417	−728
Other investment liabilities	4 753 W.	−371	384	344	2,757	3,981	−1,129	3,844	3,396
Monetary authorities	4 753 WA	....	....	....	....	....	....	1,214	....
General government	4 753 ZB	−76	−276	−549	−467	−431	−1,449	236	−1,126
Banks	4 753 ZC	−558	−1,120	−132	1,215	1,315	472	650	2,312
Other sectors	4 753 ZD	263	1,781	1,025	2,009	3,097	−152	1,745	2,211
Total, Groups A Through C	4 983 ..	*−3,050*	*−3,755*	*−3,753*	*−2,350*	*3,194*	*16,388*	*14,117*	*8,627*
D. Net Errors and Omissions	4 998 ..	**2,821**	**799**	**5,279**	**−2,277**	**−2,937**	**−1,071**	**3,381**	**2,947**
Total, Groups A Through D	4 984 ..	*−229*	*−2,956*	*1,527*	*−4,626*	*258*	*15,317*	*17,497*	*11,573*
E. Reserves and Related Items	4 802 A.	**229**	**2,956**	**−1,527**	**4,626**	**−258**	**−15,317**	**−17,497**	**−11,573**
Reserve assets	4 802 ..	−1,023	−280	−1,970	−417	1,702	−14,164	−16,802	−12,000
Use of Fund credit and loans	4 766 ..	....	....	....	....	....	....	....	....
Exceptional financing	4 920 ..	1,252	3,236	443	5,043	−1,960	−1,153	−696	426
Conversion rates: new sheqalim per U.S. dollar	0 101 ..	**4.5541**	**4.4820**	**4.4877**	**4.4558**	**4.1081**	**3.5880**	**3.9323**	**3.7390**

[1] Excludes components that have been classified in the categories of Group E.

Table 2. STANDARD PRESENTATION, 2003–2010

(Millions of U.S. dollars)

	Code	2003	2004	2005	2006	2007	2008	2009	2010
CURRENT ACCOUNT...	4 993 ..	**746**	**2,341**	**4,246**	**7,387**	**4,882**	**1,526**	**7,061**	**6,396**
A. GOODS..	4 100 ..	**–3,376**	**–3,151**	**–4,120**	**–3,836**	**–5,684**	**–7,238**	**–96**	**–2,365**
Credit..	2 100 ..	**29,940**	**36,357**	**39,767**	**43,319**	**50,286**	**57,161**	**45,898**	**55,674**
General merchandise: exports f.o.b...................	2 110 ..	29,814	36,250	39,651	43,241	50,066	56,630	45,560	55,238
Goods for processing: exports f.o.b...................	2 150 ..	....	....	....	....	....	....	....	....
Repairs on goods..	2 160 ..	....	....	....	....	....	....	....	....
Goods procured in ports by carriers.................	2 170 ..	126	107	116	78	220	531	338	436
Nonmonetary gold...	2 180 ..	....	....	....	....	....	....	....	....
Debit..	3 100 ..	**–33,316**	**–39,507**	**–43,887**	**–47,154**	**–55,969**	**–64,399**	**–45,993**	**–58,039**
General merchandise: imports f.o.b...................	3 110 ..	–33,001	–39,107	–43,324	–46,431	–55,103	–63,099	–45,350	–57,085
Goods for processing: imports f.o.b...................	3 150 ..	....	....	....	....	....	....	....	....
Repairs on goods..	3 160 ..	....	....	....	....	....	....	....	....
Goods procured in ports by carriers.................	3 170 ..	–315	–400	–563	–723	–867	–1,300	–643	–954
Nonmonetary gold...	3 180 ..	....	....	....	....	....	....	....	....
B. SERVICES..	4 200 ..	**2,460**	**3,259**	**3,800**	**4,568**	**3,569**	**4,397**	**4,844**	**6,648**
Total credit..	2 200 ..	*13,661*	*16,081*	*17,516*	*19,222*	*21,145*	*24,306*	*21,979*	*24,704*
Total debit...	3 200 ..	*–11,201*	*–12,822*	*–13,715*	*–14,654*	*–17,577*	*–19,909*	*–17,136*	*–18,056*
Transportation services, credit......................	2 205 ..	**2,597**	**3,199**	**3,685**	**3,658**	**4,443**	**5,168**	**3,165**	**4,253**
Passenger...	2 850 ..	*341*	*432*	*561*	*540*	*653*	*751*	*591*	*745*
Freight..	2 851 ..	*1,899*	*2,374*	*2,680*	*2,685*	*3,335*	*3,764*	*2,132*	*3,041*
Other..	2 852 ..	*358*	*393*	*444*	*433*	*455*	*653*	*443*	*467*
Sea transport, passenger..................................	2 207 ..	....	....	....	....	....	....	....	....
Sea transport, freight.......................................	2 208 ..	1,752	2,172	2,477	2,467	3,120	3,589	2,040	2,921
Sea transport, other...	2 209 ..	217	249	289	306	316	503	296	316
Air transport, passenger...................................	2 211 ..	341	432	561	540	653	751	591	745
Air transport, freight..	2 212 ..	147	202	203	218	215	175	92	120
Air transport, other..	2 213 ..	114	117	125	99	91	95	92	89
Other transport, passenger..............................	2 215 ..	....	....	....	....	....	....	....	....
Other transport, freight....................................	2 216 ..	....	....	....	....	....	....	....	....
Other transport, other......................................	2 217 ..	27	27	31	28	48	55	55	62
Transportation services, debit.......................	3 205 ..	**–3,730**	**–4,347**	**–4,711**	**–4,785**	**–5,776**	**–6,623**	**–5,429**	**–5,786**
Passenger...	3 850 ..	*–791*	*–867*	*–885*	*–887*	*–991*	*–1,006*	*–960*	*–1,020*
Freight..	3 851 ..	*–1,038*	*–1,205*	*–1,293*	*–1,401*	*–1,639*	*–2,085*	*–1,701*	*–1,908*
Other..	3 852 ..	*–1,901*	*–2,276*	*–2,533*	*–2,497*	*–3,146*	*–3,532*	*–2,768*	*–2,858*
Sea transport, passenger..................................	3 207 ..	–7	–8	–8	–8	–9	–9	–8	–9
Sea transport, freight.......................................	3 208 ..	–896	–1,056	–1,121	–1,200	–1,390	–1,761	–1,440	–1,615
Sea transport, other...	3 209 ..	–1,544	–1,845	–2,055	–2,114	–2,743	–3,137	–2,387	–2,474
Air transport, passenger...................................	3 211 ..	–785	–859	–877	–879	–982	–997	–952	–1,011
Air transport, freight..	3 212 ..	–142	–149	–173	–201	–250	–324	–261	–293
Air transport, other..	3 213 ..	–352	–423	–461	–367	–380	–367	–357	–358
Other transport, passenger..............................	3 215 ..	....	....	....	....	....	....	....	....
Other transport, freight....................................	3 216 ..	....	....	....	....	....	....	....	....
Other transport, other......................................	3 217 ..	–5	–8	–16	–17	–23	–27	–25	–26
Travel, credit..	2 236 ..	**2,132**	**2,476**	**2,866**	**2,794**	**3,136**	**4,279**	**3,741**	**4,768**
Business travel...	2 237 ..	....	....	....	....	....	....	....	....
Personal travel...	2 240 ..	....	....	....	....	....	....	....	....
Travel, debit..	3 236 ..	**–2,550**	**–2,796**	**–2,895**	**–2,983**	**–3,260**	**–3,439**	**–2,909**	**–3,413**
Business travel...	3 237 ..	....	....	....	....	....	....	....	....
Personal travel...	3 240 ..	....	....	....	....	....	....	....	....
Other services, credit.....................................	2 200 BA	**8,932**	**10,407**	**10,966**	**12,771**	**13,567**	**14,860**	**15,074**	**15,683**
Communications...	2 245 ..	171	147	161	221	229	275	267	289
Construction...	2 249 ..	249	325	348	509	666	819	786	838
Insurance..	2 253 ..	16	15	16	21	24	24	25	25
Financial...	2 260 ..	....	....	....	....	....	....	....	....
Computer and information................................	2 262 ..	3,409	4,407	4,529	5,289	5,809	6,852	7,671	7,700
Royalties and licence fees................................	2 266 ..	425	505	574	593	785	804	761	849
Other business services....................................	2 268 ..	4,623	4,979	5,296	6,100	6,023	6,065	5,546	5,963
Personal, cultural, and recreational..................	2 287 ..	....	....	....	....	....	....	....	....
Government, n.i.e..	2 291 ..	39	31	42	38	31	23	18	19
Other services, debit.......................................	3 200 BA	**–4,921**	**–5,679**	**–6,110**	**–6,886**	**–8,541**	**–9,848**	**–8,798**	**–8,857**
Communications...	3 245 ..	–204	–242	–211	–318	–351	–283	–306	–298
Construction...	3 249 ..	....	....	....	....	....	....	....	....
Insurance..	3 253 ..	–435	–435	–412	–413	–392	–466	–388	–408
Financial...	3 260 ..	....	....	....	....	....	....	....	....
Computer and information................................	3 262 ..	....	....	....	....	....	....	....	....
Royalties and licence fees................................	3 266 ..	–433	–491	–542	–681	–948	–1,107	–897	–860
Other business services....................................	3 268 ..	–3,625	–4,301	–4,727	–5,245	–6,594	–7,711	–6,937	–7,023
Personal, cultural, and recreational..................	3 287 ..	....	....	....	....	....	....	....	....
Government, n.i.e..	3 291 ..	–224	–211	–218	–230	–255	–281	–271	–269

Table 2 (Continued). STANDARD PRESENTATION, 2003–2010

(Millions of U.S. dollars)

	Code	2003	2004	2005	2006	2007	2008	2009	2010
C. INCOME	4 300	**−4,749**	**−4,042**	**−1,436**	**−787**	**−260**	**−4,115**	**−5,089**	**−6,312**
Total credit	2 300	*2,814*	*3,004*	*5,601*	*8,387*	*10,873*	*7,242*	*5,692*	*5,823*
Total debit	3 300	*−7,563*	*−7,046*	*−7,037*	*−9,174*	*−11,133*	*−11,357*	*−10,781*	*−12,135*
Compensation of employees, credit	2 310	**171**	**298**	**377**	**463**	**546**	**513**	**507**	**572**
Compensation of employees, debit	3 310	**−2,502**	**−2,218**	**−2,206**	**−2,334**	**−2,798**	**−3,550**	**−3,283**	**−3,739**
Investment income, credit	2 320	**2,643**	**2,706**	**5,224**	**7,923**	**10,327**	**6,729**	**5,185**	**5,251**
Direct investment income	2 330	1,158	1,119	2,335	3,353	4,441	2,637	2,647	2,791
Dividends and distributed branch profits	2 332	732	495	760	1,379	1,593	1,221	1,469	764
Reinvested earnings and undistributed branch profits	2 333	314	476	1,311	1,513	2,174	920	856	1,745
Income on debt (interest)	2 334	112	148	265	461	673	497	322	283
Portfolio investment income	2 339	402	443	888	1,446	1,770	1,156	1,169	1,115
Income on equity	2 340	255	186	311	536	691	461	604	479
Income on bonds and notes	2 350	146	257	577	910	1,079	696	565	637
Income on money market instruments	2 360	....	....	....	....	....	....	....	....
Other investment income	2 370	1,084	1,144	2,000	3,124	4,117	2,935	1,370	1,345
Investment income, debit	3 320	**−5,061**	**−4,828**	**−4,832**	**−6,840**	**−8,335**	**−7,807**	**−7,498**	**−8,396**
Direct investment income	3 330	−1,737	−1,648	−654	−2,301	−3,237	−3,351	−4,074	−4,973
Dividends and distributed branch profits	3 332	−517	−456	−874	−567	−715	−959	−1,390	−844
Reinvested earnings and undistributed branch profits	3 333	−1,157	−1,108	369	−1,507	−2,295	−2,226	−2,578	−4,053
Income on debt (interest)	3 334	−64	−84	−149	−227	−227	−166	−107	−77
Portfolio investment income	3 339	−1,838	−1,914	−2,533	−2,250	−2,641	−2,493	−2,219	−2,510
Income on equity	3 340	−439	−385	−1,010	−460	−758	−610	−419	−856
Income on bonds and notes	3 350	−1,399	−1,530	−1,523	−1,789	−1,882	−1,883	−1,800	−1,654
Income on money market instruments	3 360	....	....	....	....	....	....	....	....
Other investment income	3 370	−1,487	−1,266	−1,645	−2,289	−2,457	−1,964	−1,205	−913
D. CURRENT TRANSFERS	4 379	**6,411**	**6,275**	**6,002**	**7,442**	**7,257**	**8,482**	**7,402**	**8,426**
Credit	2 379	**7,556**	**7,355**	**7,040**	**8,559**	**8,528**	**9,424**	**8,395**	**9,481**
General government	2 380	4,200	3,587	3,340	4,519	3,978	4,523	3,767	4,426
Other sectors	2 390	3,356	3,768	3,699	4,040	4,550	4,902	4,628	5,055
Workers' remittances	2 391	....	....	....	....	....	....	....	....
Other current transfers	2 392	3,356	3,768	3,699	4,040	4,550	4,902	4,628	5,055
Debit	3 379	**−1,145**	**−1,081**	**−1,038**	**−1,117**	**−1,271**	**−943**	**−993**	**−1,055**
General government	3 380	−85	−71	−104	−107	−111	−111	−110	−113
Other sectors	3 390	−1,060	−1,009	−934	−1,010	−1,161	−832	−883	−942
Workers' remittances	3 391	....	....	....	....	....	....	....	....
Other current transfers	3 392	−1,060	−1,009	−934	−1,010	−1,161	−832	−883	−942
CAPITAL AND FINANCIAL ACCOUNT	4 996	**−3,566**	**−3,140**	**−9,526**	**−5,110**	**−1,945**	**−455**	**−10,442**	**−9,343**
CAPITAL ACCOUNT	4 994	**534**	**667**	**727**	**786**	**822**	**1,109**	**908**	**983**
Total credit	2 994	*534*	*667*	*727*	*786*	*822*	*1,109*	*908*	*983*
Total debit	3 994	....	....	....	....	....	....	....	....
Capital transfers, credit	2 400	**534**	**667**	**727**	**786**	**822**	**1,109**	**908**	**983**
General government	2 401	191	173	163	203	201	145	101	112
Debt forgiveness	2 402	....	....	....	....	....	....	....	....
Other capital transfers	2 410	191	173	163	203	201	145	101	112
Other sectors	2 430	344	494	564	584	621	964	806	870
Migrants' transfers	2 431	252	417	473	481	495	909	760	840
Debt forgiveness	2 432	....	....	....	....	....	....	....	....
Other capital transfers	2 440	92	77	91	102	126	55	46	31
Capital transfers, debit	3 400	....	....	....	....	....	....	....	....
General government	3 401	....	....	....	....	....	....	....	....
Debt forgiveness	3 402	....	....	....	....	....	....	....	....
Other capital transfers	3 410	....	....	....	....	....	....	....	....
Other sectors	3 430	....	....	....	....	....	....	....	....
Migrants' transfers	3 431	....	....	....	....	....	....	....	....
Debt forgiveness	3 432	....	....	....	....	....	....	....	....
Other capital transfers	3 440	....	....	....	....	....	....	....	....
Nonproduced nonfinancial assets, credit	2 480	....	....	....	....	....	....	....	....
Nonproduced nonfinancial assets, debit	3 480	....	....	....	....	....	....	....	....

Table 2 (Continued). STANDARD PRESENTATION, 2003–2010

(Millions of U.S. dollars)

	Code	2003	2004	2005	2006	2007	2008	2009	2010
FINANCIAL ACCOUNT	4 995	−4,101	−3,807	−10,252	−5,896	−2,767	−1,564	−11,350	−10,325
A. DIRECT INVESTMENT	4 500	1,236	−1,586	1,873	−166	194	3,665	2,744	−2,808
Direct investment abroad	4 505	−2,086	−4,533	−2,946	−15,462	−8,604	−7,210	−1,695	−7,960
Equity capital	4 510	−810	−3,673	−1,435	−11,228	−4,581	−5,616	−53	−2,569
Claims on affiliated enterprises	4 515	....	....	....	....	....	....	....	....
Liabilities to affiliated enterprises	4 520	....	....	....	....	....	....	....	....
Reinvested earnings	4 525	−314	−476	−1,311	−1,513	−2,174	−920	−856	−1,745
Other capital	4 530	−962	−384	−200	−2,721	−1,848	−674	−786	−3,646
Claims on affiliated enterprises	4 535	....	....	....	....	....	....	....	....
Liabilities to affiliated enterprises	4 540	....	....	....	....	....	....	....	....
Direct investment in Israel	4 555	3,322	2,947	4,818	15,296	8,798	10,874	4,438	5,152
Equity capital	4 560	1,766	1,664	4,958	13,495	6,459	8,247	1,384	1,534
Claims on direct investors	4 565	....	....	....	....	....	....	....	....
Liabilities to direct investors	4 570	....	....	....	....	....	....	....	....
Reinvested earnings	4 575	1,157	1,108	−369	1,507	2,295	2,226	2,578	4,053
Other capital	4 580	400	175	230	293	44	401	476	−435
Claims on direct investors	4 585	....	....	....	....	....	....	....	....
Liabilities to direct investors	4 590	400	175	230	293	44	401	476	−435
B. PORTFOLIO INVESTMENT	4 600	−1,933	4,210	−5,219	2,737	−1,502	−638	−5,865	127
Assets	4 602	−3,247	−2,854	−7,975	−6,347	−3,138	−1,634	−8,254	−8,901
Equity securities	4 610	−1,054	−1,149	−3,373	−2,906	−2,034	−2,290	−7,126	−7,251
Monetary authorities	4 611	....	....	....	....	....	....	....	....
General government	4 612	....	....	....	....	....	....	....	....
Banks	4 613	....	....	....	....	....	....	....	....
Other sectors	4 614	−1,054	−1,149	−3,373	−2,906	−2,034	−2,290	−7,126	−7,251
Debt securities	4 619	−2,193	−1,704	−4,601	−3,441	−1,103	656	−1,128	−1,650
Bonds and notes	4 620	−2,193	−1,704	−4,601	−3,441	−1,103	656	−1,128	−1,650
Monetary authorities	4 621	....	....	....	....	....	....	....	....
General government	4 622	13	11	10	8	8	10	5	−3
Banks	4 623	−518	167	−1,555	−1,311	−1,111	99	−62	789
Other sectors	4 624	−1,687	−1,883	−3,056	−2,138	....	546	−1,071	−2,437
Money market instruments	4 630	....	....	....	....	....	....	....	....
Monetary authorities	4 631	....	....	....	....	....	....	....	....
General government	4 632	....	....	....	....	....	....	....	....
Banks	4 633	....	....	....	....	....	....	....	....
Other sectors	4 634	....	....	....	....	....	....	....	....
Liabilities	4 652	1,314	7,063	2,756	9,084	1,636	996	2,389	9,028
Equity securities	4 660	−108	3,940	2,255	3,970	3,620	2,153	2,122	−612
Banks	4 663	....	....	....	....	....	....	....	....
Other sectors	4 664	−108	3,940	2,255	3,970	3,620	2,153	2,122	−612
Debt securities	4 669	1,422	3,123	501	5,114	−1,984	−1,157	267	9,640
Bonds and notes	4 670	1,422	3,123	501	5,114	−1,984	−1,157	267	9,640
Monetary authorities	4 671	170	−113	58	71	−24	−4	963	9,214
General government	4 672	1,928	1,568	632	2,282	−1,454	−2,174	664	776
Banks	4 673	....	....	....	....	....	....	....	....
Other sectors	4 674	−676	1,668	−189	2,761	−506	1,021	−1,359	−350
Money market instruments	4 680	....	....	....	....	....	....	....	....
Monetary authorities	4 681	....	....	....	....	....	....	....	....
General government	4 682	....	....	....	....	....	....	....	....
Banks	4 683	....	....	....	....	....	....	....	....
Other sectors	4 684	....	....	....	....	....	....	....	....
C. FINANCIAL DERIVATIVES	4 910	14	50	35	−89	29	−116	230	30
Monetary authorities	4 911	....	....	....	....	....	....	....	....
General government	4 912	....	....	....	....	....	....	....	....
Banks	4 913	....	....	....	....	....	....	....	....
Other sectors	4 914	14	50	35	−89	29	−116	230	30
Assets	4 900	14	50	35	−89	29	−116	230	30
Monetary authorities	4 901	....	....	....	....	....	....	....	....
General government	4 902	....	....	....	....	....	....	....	....
Banks	4 903	....	....	....	....	....	....	....	....
Other sectors	4 904	14	50	35	−89	29	−116	230	30
Liabilities	4 905	....	....	....	....	....	....	....	....
Monetary authorities	4 906	....	....	....	....	....	....	....	....
General government	4 907	....	....	....	....	....	....	....	....
Banks	4 908	....	....	....	....	....	....	....	....
Other sectors	4 909	....	....	....	....	....	....	....	....

Table 2 (Concluded). STANDARD PRESENTATION, 2003–2010

(Millions of U.S. dollars)

	Code	2003	2004	2005	2006	2007	2008	2009	2010
D. OTHER INVESTMENT	4 700	**−2,395**	**−6,200**	**−4,971**	**−7,962**	**−3,191**	**9,690**	**8,343**	**4,325**
Assets	4 703	**−2,024**	**−6,584**	**−5,315**	**−10,719**	**−7,172**	**10,819**	**4,499**	**929**
Trade credits	4 706	−981	−1,679	420	−1,367	−3,116	2,890	129	−922
General government	4 707	−153	−71	11	11	11	11	11	11
of which: Short-term	4 709	....	....	....	....	....	....	....	....
Other sectors	4 710	−828	−1,608	409	−1,378	−3,127	2,880	118	−933
of which: Short-term	4 712	*−828*	*−1,608*	*409*	*−1,378*	*−3,127*	*2,880*	*118*	*−933*
Loans	4 714	507	610	−686	−888	−150	−2,207	1,229	−301
Monetary authorities	4 715	....	....	....	....	....	....	....	....
of which: Short-term	4 718	....	....	....	....	....	....	....	....
General government	4 719	....	....	....	....	....	....	....	....
of which: Short-term	4 721	....	....	....	....	....	....	....	....
Banks	4 722	507	610	−686	−888	−150	−2,207	1,229	−301
of which: Short-term	4 724	*507*	*610*	*−686*	*−888*	*−150*	*−2,207*	*1,229*	*−301*
Other sectors	4 725	....	....	....	....	....	....	....	....
of which: Short-term	4 727	....	....	....	....	....	....	....	....
Currency and deposits	4 730	−1,590	−5,551	−6,004	−7,747	−2,341	10,163	3,269	2,859
Monetary authorities	4 731	....	....	....	....	....	....	....	....
General government	4 732	....	....	....	....	....	....	....	....
Banks	4 733	−1,762	−4,267	−4,032	−6,265	934	9,199	3,825	1,770
Other sectors	4 734	172	−1,284	−1,972	−1,482	−3,274	964	−556	1,090
Other assets	4 736	40	37	955	−717	−1,566	−28	−128	−708
Monetary authorities	4 737	....	....	....	....	....	....	....	....
of which: Short-term	4 739	....	....	....	....	....	....	....	....
General government	4 740	140	84	1,295	195	−191	28	−149	177
of which: Short-term	4 742	*140*	*84*	*1,295*	*195*	*−191*	*28*	*−149*	*177*
Banks	4 743	....	....	....	....	....	....	....	....
of which: Short-term	4 745	....	....	....	....	....	....	....	....
Other sectors	4 746	−100	−47	−340	−912	−1,375	−55	21	−885
of which: Short-term	4 748	....	....	....	....	....	....	....	....
Liabilities	4 753	**−371**	**384**	**344**	**2,757**	**3,981**	**−1,129**	**3,844**	**3,396**
Trade credits	4 756	84	951	1,112	765	1,764	−1,553	1,301	1,379
General government	4 757	....	....	....	....	....	....	....	....
of which: Short-term	4 759	....	....	....	....	....	....	....	....
Other sectors	4 760	84	951	1,112	765	1,764	−1,553	1,301	1,379
of which: Short-term	4 762	*84*	*951*	*1,112*	*765*	*1,764*	*−1,553*	*1,301*	*1,379*
Loans	4 764	103	553	−636	778	902	−48	680	−294
Monetary authorities	4 765	....	....	....	....	....	....	....	....
of which: Use of Fund credit and loans from the Fund	4 766	....	....	....	....	....	....	....	....
of which: Short-term	4 768	....	....	....	....	....	....	....	....
General government	4 769	−76	−276	−549	−467	−431	−1,449	236	−1,126
of which: Short-term	4 771	....	*−25*	....	....	....	....	....	....
Banks	4 772	....	....	....	....	....	....	....	....
of which: Short-term	4 774	....	....	....	....	....	....	....	....
Other sectors	4 775	179	830	−87	1,244	1,333	1,401	444	832
of which: Short-term	4 777	*17*	*83*	*−10*	*124*	*133*	*139*	*44*	*82*
Currency and deposits	4 780	−558	−1,120	−132	1,215	1,315	472	650	2,312
Monetary authorities	4 781	....	....	....	....	....	....	....	....
General government	4 782	....	....	....	....	....	....	....	....
Banks	4 783	−558	−1,120	−132	1,215	1,315	472	650	2,312
Other sectors	4 784	....	....	....	....	....	....	....	....
Other liabilities	4 786	....	....	....	....	....	....	1,214	....
Monetary authorities	4 787	....	....	....	....	....	....	1,214	....
of which: Short-term	4 789	....	....	....	....	....	....	....	....
General government	4 790	....	....	....	....	....	....	....	....
of which: Short-term	4 792	....	....	....	....	....	....	....	....
Banks	4 793	....	....	....	....	....	....	....	....
of which: Short-term	4 795	....	....	....	....	....	....	....	....
Other sectors	4 796	....	....	....	....	....	....	....	....
of which: Short-term	4 798	....	....	....	....	....	....	....	....
E. RESERVE ASSETS	4 802	**−1,023**	**−280**	**−1,970**	**−417**	**1,702**	**−14,164**	**−16,802**	**−12,000**
Monetary gold	4 812	....	....	....	....	....	....	....	....
Special drawing rights	4 811	−4	−5	−5	....	3	3	−1,214	−109
Reserve position in the Fund	4 810	−69	84	229	86	32	−81	−108	−35
Foreign exchange	4 803	−887	−356	−2,123	−503	1,666	−14,087	−15,480	−11,842
Other claims	4 813	−62	−2	−71	....	....	....	....	−15
NET ERRORS AND OMISSIONS	4 998	**2,821**	**799**	**5,279**	**−2,277**	**−2,937**	**−1,071**	**3,381**	**2,947**

Table 3. INTERNATIONAL INVESTMENT POSITION (End-period stocks), 2003–2010

(Millions of U.S. dollars)

	Code	2003	2004	2005	2006	2007	2008	2009	2010
ASSETS	8 995 C.	**91,524**	**108,271**	**125,789**	**166,665**	**190,825**	**188,026**	**220,372**	**252,217**
Direct investment abroad	8 505 ..	**13,097**	**18,493**	**23,083**	**39,322**	**49,833**	**54,410**	**57,371**	**66,299**
Equity capital and reinvested earnings	8 506 ..	8,560	13,527	17,554	30,689	39,108	43,046	45,013	50,054
Claims on affiliated enterprises	8 507 ..	8,560	13,527	17,554	30,689	39,108	43,046	45,013	50,054
Liabilities to affiliated enterprises	8 508 ..	....	....	....	....	....	....	....	....
Other capital	8 530 ..	4,537	4,966	5,529	8,633	10,726	11,364	12,358	16,245
Claims on affiliated enterprises	8 535 ..	4,537	4,966	5,529	8,633	10,726	11,364	12,358	16,245
Liabilities to affiliated enterprises	8 540 ..	....	....	....	....	....	....	....	....
Portfolio investment	8 602 ..	**14,980**	**18,576**	**26,589**	**37,104**	**42,122**	**33,395**	**49,425**	**61,747**
Equity securities	8 610 ..	3,513	5,003	8,663	14,123	16,931	12,870	25,337	34,773
Monetary authorities	8 611 ..	....	....	....	....	....	....	....	....
General government	8 612 ..	....	....	....	....	....	....	....	....
Banks	8 613 ..	....	....	....	....	....	....	....	....
Other sectors	8 614 ..	3,513	5,003	8,663	14,123	16,931	12,870	25,337	34,773
Debt securities	8 619 ..	11,467	13,574	17,926	22,981	25,191	20,525	24,089	26,974
Bonds and notes	8 620 ..	11,467	13,574	17,926	22,981	25,191	20,525	24,089	26,974
Monetary authorities	8 621 ..	....	....	....	....	....	....	....	....
General government	8 622 ..	54	43	33	24	17	7	1	4
Banks	8 623 ..	3,054	2,961	4,339	5,932	7,449	6,549	7,026	6,021
Other sectors	8 624 ..	8,359	10,570	13,555	17,026	17,726	13,970	17,061	20,950
Money market instruments	8 630 ..	....	....	....	....	....	....	....	....
Monetary authorities	8 631 ..	....	....	....	....	....	....	....	....
General government	8 632 ..	....	....	....	....	....	....	....	....
Banks	8 633 ..	....	....	....	....	....	....	....	....
Other sectors	8 634 ..	....	....	....	....	....	....	....	....
Financial derivatives	8 900 ..	**99**	**37**	**10**	**107**	**73**	**−67**	**−68**	**−135**
Monetary authorities	8 901 ..	....	....	....	....	....	....	....	....
General government	8 902 ..	....	....	....	....	....	....	....	....
Banks	8 903 ..	....	....	....	....	....	....	....	....
Other sectors	8 904 ..	99	37	10	107	73	−67	−68	−135
Other investment	8 703 ..	**36,903**	**43,935**	**47,840**	**60,954**	**70,172**	**57,704**	**52,964**	**51,517**
Trade credits	8 706 ..	7,592	9,314	8,687	10,033	12,472	9,499	9,464	10,273
General government	8 707 ..	....	....	....	....	....	....	....	....
of which: Short-term	8 709 ..	....	....	....	....	....	....	....	....
Other sectors	8 710 ..	7,592	9,314	8,687	10,033	12,472	9,499	9,464	10,273
of which: Short-term	8 712 ..	*7,592*	*9,314*	*8,687*	*10,033*	*12,472*	*9,499*	*9,464*	*10,273*
Loans	8 714 ..	6,052	5,687	5,945	7,239	8,256	10,804	9,781	10,201
Monetary authorities	8 715 ..	....	....	....	....	....	....	....	....
of which: Short-term	8 718 ..	....	....	....	....	....	....	....	....
General government	8 719 ..	....	....	....	....	....	....	....	....
of which: Short-term	8 721 ..	....	....	....	....	....	....	....	....
Banks	8 722 ..	4,833	4,293	3,866	4,869	5,577	7,649	6,487	6,742
of which: Short-term	8 724 ..	....	....	....	....	....	....	....	....
Other sectors	8 725 ..	1,219	1,394	2,079	2,370	2,679	3,155	3,294	3,460
of which: Short-term	8 727 ..	....	....	....	....	....	....	....	....
Currency and deposits	8 730 ..	22,911	28,534	32,364	41,808	46,139	34,298	30,752	26,425
Monetary authorities	8 731 ..	....	....	....	....	....	....	....	....
General government	8 732 ..	1,999	1,986	680	474	534	495	633	473
Banks	8 733 ..	9,877	14,424	17,801	24,526	23,981	14,463	10,795	8,889
Other sectors	8 734 ..	11,035	12,125	13,883	16,808	21,624	19,340	19,324	17,064
Other assets	8 736 ..	348	400	844	1,875	3,305	3,103	2,967	4,618
Monetary authorities	8 737 ..	....	....	....	....	....	....	....	....
of which: Short-term	8 739 ..	....	....	....	....	....	....	....	....
General government	8 740 ..	147	149	220	220	220	220	220	234
of which: Short-term	8 742 ..	*147*	*149*	*220*	*220*	*220*	*220*	*220*	*234*
Banks	8 743 ..	....	....	....	....	....	....	....	....
of which: Short-term	8 745 ..	....	....	....	....	....	....	....	....
Other sectors	8 746 ..	201	251	624	1,656	3,085	2,884	2,748	4,384
of which: Short-term	8 748 ..	....	....	....	....	....	....	....	*1*
Reserve assets	8 802 ..	**26,446**	**27,229**	**28,266**	**29,178**	**28,625**	**42,583**	**60,679**	**72,789**
Monetary gold	8 812 ..	....	....	....	....	....	....	....	....
Special drawing rights	8 811 ..	9	15	19	19	17	13	1,231	1,323
Reserve position in the Fund	8 810 ..	527	463	202	123	96	176	289	319
Foreign exchange	8 803 ..	25,763	26,601	27,825	28,815	28,291	42,173	58,938	70,913
Other claims	8 813 ..	147	149	221	221	221	221	221	233

Table 3 (Concluded). INTERNATIONAL INVESTMENT POSITION (End-period stocks), 2003–2010

(Millions of U.S. dollars)

	Code	2003	2004	2005	2006	2007	2008	2009	2010
LIABILITIES	8 995 D.	**122,351**	**136,558**	**154,256**	**178,390**	**207,502**	**191,531**	**226,804**	**251,230**
Direct investment in Israel	8 555	**27,696**	**30,689**	**37,826**	**53,955**	**60,550**	**62,169**	**69,164**	**77,810**
Equity capital and reinvested earnings	8 556	25,040	27,858	34,765	50,600	57,151	58,369	64,888	73,969
Claims on direct investors	8 557	....	....	....	....	....	....	....	....
Liabilities to direct investors	8 558	25,040	27,858	34,765	50,600	57,151	58,369	64,888	73,969
Other capital	8 580	2,656	2,831	3,061	3,355	3,399	3,800	4,276	3,841
Claims on direct investors	8 585	....	....	....	....	....	....	....	....
Liabilities to direct investors	8 590	2,656	2,831	3,061	3,355	3,399	3,800	4,276	3,841
Portfolio investment	8 652	**43,642**	**53,866**	**65,077**	**69,523**	**87,053**	**71,367**	**95,146**	**107,858**
Equity securities	8 660	23,479	30,444	41,494	40,535	59,670	44,961	68,650	71,278
Banks	8 663	....	....	....	....	....	....	....	....
Other sectors	8 664	23,479	30,444	41,494	40,535	59,670	44,961	68,650	71,278
Debt securities	8 669	20,163	23,422	23,583	28,988	27,383	26,406	26,496	36,580
Bonds and notes	8 670	19,943	23,315	23,423	28,742	27,189	26,211	25,340	25,770
Monetary authorities	8 671	....	....	....	....	....	....	....	....
General government	8 672	16,380	18,053	18,463	20,975	19,835	17,658	18,183	18,814
Banks	8 673	....	....	....	....	....	....	....	....
Other sectors	8 674	3,562	5,263	4,960	7,767	7,355	8,553	7,157	6,956
Money market instruments	8 680	220	107	160	246	194	195	1,156	10,809
Monetary authorities	8 681	220	107	160	246	194	195	1,156	10,809
General government	8 682	....	....	....	....	....	....	....	....
Banks	8 683	....	....	....	....	....	....	....	....
Other sectors	8 684	....	....	....	....	....	....	....	....
Financial derivatives	8 905	....	....	....	....	....	....	....	....
Monetary authorities	8 906	....	....	....	....	....	....	....	....
General government	8 907	....	....	....	....	....	....	....	....
Banks	8 908	....	....	....	....	....	....	....	....
Other sectors	8 909	....	....	....	....	....	....	....	....
Other investment	8 753	**51,014**	**52,003**	**51,352**	**54,912**	**59,899**	**57,996**	**62,494**	**65,563**
Trade credits	8 756	5,961	7,033	7,931	8,828	10,772	9,285	10,614	11,928
General government	8 757	....	....	....	....	....	....	....	....
of which: Short-term	8 759	....	....	....	....	....	....	....	....
Other sectors	8 760	5,961	7,033	7,931	8,828	10,772	9,285	10,614	11,928
of which: Short-term	8 762	*5,961*	*7,033*	*7,931*	*8,828*	*10,772*	*9,285*	*10,614*	*11,928*
Loans	8 764	20,308	20,982	20,232	21,096	22,176	21,995	22,741	22,415
Monetary authorities	8 765	....	....	....	....	....	....	....	....
of which: Use of Fund credit and loans from the Fund	8 766	....	....	....	....	....	....	....	....
of which: Short-term	8 768	....	....	....	....	....	....	....	....
General government	8 769	13,208	13,054	12,391	12,011	11,758	10,176	10,477	9,318
of which: Short-term	8 771	*25*	....	....	....	....	....	*175*	....
Banks	8 772	....	....	....	....	....	....	....	....
of which: Short-term	8 774	....	....	....	....	....	....	....	....
Other sectors	8 775	7,099	7,928	7,841	9,085	10,418	11,819	12,264	13,097
of which: Short-term	8 777	*976*	*1,076*	*1,090*	*1,244*	*1,382*	*1,562*	*1,654*	*1,694*
Currency and deposits	8 780	24,745	23,989	23,189	24,988	26,951	26,716	27,754	29,859
Monetary authorities	8 781	....	....	....	....	....	....	....	....
General government	8 782	....	....	....	....	....	....	....	....
Banks	8 783	24,745	23,989	23,189	24,988	26,951	26,716	27,754	29,859
Other sectors	8 784	....	....	....	....	....	....	....	....
Other liabilities	8 786	....	....	....	....	....	....	1,385	1,360
Monetary authorities	8 787	....	....	....	....	....	....	1,385	1,360
of which: Short-term	8 789	....	....	....	....	....	....	....	....
General government	8 790	....	....	....	....	....	....	....	....
of which: Short-term	8 792	....	....	....	....	....	....	....	....
Banks	8 793	....	....	....	....	....	....	....	....
of which: Short-term	8 795	....	....	....	....	....	....	....	....
Other sectors	8 796	....	....	....	....	....	....	....	....
of which: Short-term	8 798	....	....	....	....	....	....	....	....
NET INTERNATIONAL INVESTMENT POSITION	8 995	**−30,827**	**−28,287**	**−28,467**	**−11,725**	**−16,677**	**−3,505**	**−6,432**	**987**
Conversion rates: new sheqalim per U.S. dollar (end of period)	0 102	**4.3790**	**4.3080**	**4.6030**	**4.2250**	**3.8460**	**3.8020**	**3.7750**	**3.5490**

Table 1. ANALYTIC PRESENTATION, 2003–2010

(Billions of U.S. dollars)

	Code	2003	2004	2005	2006	2007	2008	2009	2010
A. Current Account[1]	4 993 Z.	**−19.41**	**−16.45**	**−29.74**	**−47.83**	**−51.57**	**−66.25**	**−41.00**	**−71.23**
Goods: exports f.o.b.	2 100 ..	298.12	352.17	372.38	418.07	501.28	545.08	407.46	448.37
Goods: imports f.o.b.	3 100 ..	−286.64	−341.28	−371.81	−430.58	−496.70	−547.92	−406.00	−475.65
Balance on Goods	4 100 ..	*11.48*	*10.89*	*.56*	*−12.51*	*4.58*	*−2.84*	*1.46*	*−27.28*
Services: credit	2 200 ..	71.77	84.52	89.22	98.98	112.21	116.26	94.89	98.74
Services: debit	3 200 ..	−74.33	−83.25	−90.08	−100.51	−121.87	−128.83	−106.36	−110.65
Balance on Goods and Services	4 991 ..	*8.91*	*12.17*	*−.30*	*−14.04*	*−5.08*	*−15.41*	*−10.02*	*−39.19*
Income: credit	2 300 ..	48.78	53.12	61.32	72.35	88.21	103.50	80.39	73.61
Income: debit	3 300 ..	−69.00	−71.46	−78.43	−89.43	−115.01	−132.14	−94.64	−84.26
Balance on Goods, Services, and Income	4 992 ..	*−11.31*	*−6.17*	*−17.41*	*−31.11*	*−31.88*	*−44.04*	*−24.27*	*−49.84*
Current transfers: credit	2 379 Z.	20.65	21.83	23.54	22.22	26.62	28.99	29.17	23.15
Current transfers: debit	3 379 ..	−28.74	−32.12	−35.88	−38.94	−46.31	−51.20	−45.90	−44.54
B. Capital Account[1]	4 994 Z.	**2.67**	**2.17**	**1.63**	**2.36**	**3.15**	**−.35**	**−.05**	**−.72**
Capital account: credit	2 994 Z.	4.95	4.11	5.12	5.49	5.18	3.66	2.97	2.31
Capital account: debit	3 994 ..	−2.28	−1.94	−3.49	−3.12	−2.03	−4.01	−3.02	−3.04
Total, Groups A Plus B	4 981 ..	*−16.74*	*−14.28*	*−28.11*	*−45.46*	*−48.43*	*−66.60*	*−41.06*	*−71.95*
C. Financial Account[1]	4 995 W.	**20.44**	**8.35**	**25.29**	**30.94**	**37.74**	**53.83**	**56.06**	**117.72**
Direct investment abroad	4 505 ..	−8.99	−19.25	−40.78	−42.48	−92.12	−69.51	−19.76	−20.38
Direct investment in Italy	4 555 Z.	16.54	16.79	19.64	39.01	40.04	−9.49	16.58	9.60
Portfolio investment assets	4 602 ..	−57.41	−26.38	−108.09	−61.72	1.59	95.63	−55.94	−43.16
Equity securities	4 610 ..	−16.00	−16.17	−24.88	−23.04	17.02	118.45	−18.89	−54.53
Debt securities	4 619 ..	−41.41	−10.21	−83.21	−38.69	−15.44	−22.82	−37.05	11.37
Portfolio investment liabilities	4 652 Z.	60.15	58.55	164.40	115.29	24.06	11.24	88.66	94.03
Equity securities	4 660 ..	−2.01	17.18	2.63	13.56	−14.87	−29.01	20.90	3.83
Debt securities	4 669 Z.	62.16	41.37	161.77	101.73	38.93	40.25	67.76	90.20
Financial derivatives	4 910 ..	−5.47	2.28	3.12	−.59	.74	2.56	5.79	3.04
Financial derivatives assets	4 900 ..	−10.28	....	....	....	....	−3.51	12.16	9.58
Financial derivatives liabilities	4 905 ..	4.81	2.28	3.12	−.59	.74	6.07	−6.37	−6.54
Other investment assets	4 703 ..	−20.58	−47.94	−100.28	−142.42	−82.67	37.42	58.96	57.71
Monetary authorities	4 701 ..	−.07	−8.70	−4.35	−18.73	−18.29	21.09	−39.99	66.80
General government	4 704 ..	1.41	−.56	−1.23	−.36	.02	.03	−.07	.01
Banks	4 705 ..	.43	−27.29	−24.83	−58.87	−39.39	25.66	53.68	−4.54
Other sectors	4 728 ..	−22.35	−11.38	−69.87	−64.45	−25.01	−9.36	45.34	−4.56
Other investment liabilities	4 753 W.	36.20	24.29	87.28	123.86	146.10	−14.01	−38.24	16.89
Monetary authorities	4 753 WA	−2.55	.39	1.10	−.94	−1.14	.13	9.29	3.51
General government	4 753 ZB	−1.01	−.65	1.30	−.39	−1.29	−.12	−.16	−.14
Banks	4 753 ZC	43.75	14.72	59.50	113.40	152.67	−45.34	−61.81	15.53
Other sectors	4 753 ZD	−3.98	9.83	25.37	11.79	−4.14	31.33	14.44	−2.01
Total, Groups A Through C	4 983 ..	*3.70*	*−5.94*	*−2.83*	*−14.53*	*−10.69*	*−12.77*	*15.00*	*45.76*
D. Net Errors and Omissions	4 998 ..	**−2.58**	**3.09**	**1.80**	**13.96**	**12.58**	**20.97**	**−6.00**	**−44.42**
Total, Groups A Through D	4 984 ..	*1.11*	*−2.84*	*−1.03*	*−.57*	*1.89*	*8.20*	*9.00*	*1.34*
E. Reserves and Related Items	4 802 A.	**−1.11**	**2.84**	**1.03**	**.57**	**−1.89**	**−8.20**	**−9.00**	**−1.34**
Reserve assets	4 802 ..	−1.11	2.84	1.03	.57	−1.89	−8.20	−9.00	−1.34
Use of Fund credit and loans	4 766 ..	....	....	....	....	....	....	....	....
Exceptional financing	4 920 ..	....	....	....	....	....	....	....	....
Conversion rates: euros per U.S. dollar	0 103 ..	**.8860**	**.8054**	**.8041**	**.7971**	**.7306**	**.6827**	**.7198**	**.7550**

[1] Excludes components that have been classified in the categories of Group E.

Table 2. STANDARD PRESENTATION, 2003–2010

(Billions of U.S. dollars)

	Code	2003	2004	2005	2006	2007	2008	2009	2010
CURRENT ACCOUNT	4 993	**−19.41**	**−16.45**	**−29.74**	**−47.83**	**−51.57**	**−66.25**	**−41.00**	**−71.23**
A. GOODS	4 100	**11.48**	**10.89**	**.56**	**−12.51**	**4.58**	**−2.84**	**1.46**	**−27.28**
Credit	2 100	**298.12**	**352.17**	**372.38**	**418.07**	**501.28**	**545.08**	**407.46**	**448.37**
General merchandise: exports f.o.b.	2 110	286.56	338.41	357.51	400.43	479.52	520.75	386.54	424.83
Goods for processing: exports f.o.b.	2 150	10.98	12.80	13.79	16.42	19.67	20.42	16.43	17.96
Repairs on goods	2 160	.08	.16	.18	.16	.17	.14	.24	.22
Goods procured in ports by carriers	2 170	.28	.49	.55	.54	.91	2.54	1.27	1.37
Nonmonetary gold	2 180	.22	.31	.35	.52	1.02	1.23	2.99	3.99
Debit	3 100	**−286.64**	**−341.28**	**−371.81**	**−430.58**	**−496.70**	**−547.92**	**−406.00**	**−475.65**
General merchandise: imports f.o.b.	3 110	−272.46	−324.37	−353.85	−409.57	−470.06	−522.70	−382.63	−451.02
Goods for processing: imports f.o.b.	3 150	−10.82	−13.12	−13.61	−15.83	−19.60	−19.31	−17.64	−17.77
Repairs on goods	3 160	−.07	−.09	−.16	−.24	−.26	−.17	−.19	−.19
Goods procured in ports by carriers	3 170	−.69	−.89	−1.33	−1.65	−1.72	−1.62	−2.04	−2.14
Nonmonetary gold	3 180	−2.59	−2.81	−2.87	−3.29	−5.07	−4.12	−3.51	−4.53
B. SERVICES	4 200	**−2.57**	**1.28**	**−.87**	**−1.53**	**−9.66**	**−12.56**	**−11.48**	**−11.91**
Total credit	2 200	*71.77*	*84.52*	*89.22*	*98.98*	*112.21*	*116.26*	*94.89*	*98.74*
Total debit	3 200	*−74.33*	*−83.25*	*−90.08*	*−100.51*	*−121.87*	*−128.83*	*−106.36*	*−110.65*
Transportation services, credit	2 205	**10.58**	**14.89**	**14.76**	**16.20**	**18.04**	**18.13**	**12.81**	**14.53**
Passenger	2 850	*1.34*	*2.49*	*3.05*	*3.39*	*3.48*	*2.56*	*1.56*	*1.62*
Freight	2 851	*3.49*	*4.52*	*4.99*	*5.57*	*6.48*	*7.21*	*4.67*	*5.45*
Other	2 852	*5.74*	*7.88*	*6.72*	*7.25*	*8.08*	*8.36*	*6.57*	*7.47*
Sea transport, passenger	2 207	.02	.02	.05	.05	.05	.06	.05	.04
Sea transport, freight	2 208	2.19	2.68	2.97	3.23	3.78	4.25	2.66	3.16
Sea transport, other	2 209	2.87	3.74	2.84	2.95	3.12	3.27	2.51	3.10
Air transport, passenger	2 211	1.04	2.16	2.76	3.11	3.19	2.24	1.28	1.36
Air transport, freight	2 212	.12	.17	.22	.23	.37	.29	.10	.16
Air transport, other	2 213	1.86	2.81	2.70	2.97	3.36	3.38	2.75	2.81
Other transport, passenger	2 215	.28	.31	.24	.23	.24	.26	.23	.22
Other transport, freight	2 216	1.19	1.67	1.80	2.11	2.33	2.67	1.91	2.13
Other transport, other	2 217	1.01	1.33	1.17	1.33	1.60	1.71	1.31	1.56
Transportation services, debit	3 205	**−16.20**	**−21.03**	**−21.33**	**−22.69**	**−27.72**	**−29.91**	**−22.58**	**−25.62**
Passenger	3 850	*−3.14*	*−3.60*	*−4.40*	*−4.28*	*−5.43*	*−6.88*	*−6.45*	*−6.15*
Freight	3 851	*−6.71*	*−9.15*	*−10.11*	*−11.01*	*−13.80*	*−14.09*	*−9.10*	*−11.52*
Other	3 852	*−6.35*	*−8.28*	*−6.82*	*−7.40*	*−8.49*	*−8.95*	*−7.03*	*−7.95*
Sea transport, passenger	3 207	−.11	−.13	−.14	−.09	−.12	−.19	−.19	−.19
Sea transport, freight	3 208	−3.78	−5.16	−5.62	−6.05	−7.59	−7.32	−3.54	−5.29
Sea transport, other	3 209	−3.23	−4.18	−3.05	−3.37	−3.65	−3.80	−2.78	−3.46
Air transport, passenger	3 211	−2.89	−3.35	−4.18	−4.11	−5.23	−6.60	−6.19	−5.89
Air transport, freight	3 212	−.35	−.51	−.55	−.58	−.75	−.76	−.60	−.73
Air transport, other	3 213	−2.01	−2.50	−2.33	−2.45	−2.98	−3.16	−2.71	−2.66
Other transport, passenger	3 215	−.15	−.13	−.09	−.08	−.07	−.09	−.08	−.07
Other transport, freight	3 216	−2.58	−3.48	−3.94	−4.39	−5.46	−6.01	−4.96	−5.51
Other transport, other	3 217	−1.12	−1.59	−1.44	−1.58	−1.87	−1.98	−1.54	−1.83
Travel, credit	2 236	**31.25**	**35.38**	**35.32**	**38.26**	**42.66**	**46.19**	**40.38**	**38.44**
Business travel	2 237	6.80	7.34	7.15	8.20	9.36	10.12	8.68	8.44
Personal travel	2 240	24.45	28.04	28.17	30.06	33.30	36.07	31.70	29.99
Travel, debit	3 236	**−20.59**	**−20.46**	**−22.37**	**−23.15**	**−27.33**	**−30.93**	**−27.95**	**−26.91**
Business travel	3 237	−8.23	−7.40	−7.89	−8.15	−9.88	−10.23	−8.66	−8.32
Personal travel	3 240	−12.35	−13.06	−14.48	−15.00	−17.45	−20.70	−19.29	−18.59
Other services, credit	2 200 BA	**29.94**	**34.25**	**39.14**	**44.52**	**51.52**	**51.94**	**41.70**	**45.77**
Communications	2 245	1.89	2.00	2.19	3.20	3.05	6.26	5.31	6.79
Construction	2 249	2.09	2.05	2.21	2.43	3.17	.29	.37	.11
Insurance	2 253	1.16	1.60	1.62	1.70	1.54	3.86	3.12	2.91
Financial	2 260	.89	.94	1.25	2.00	3.89	3.00	2.15	2.51
Computer and information	2 262	.50	.59	.64	.93	.91	2.26	1.86	2.04
Royalties and licence fees	2 266	.52	.77	1.13	1.12	1.05	3.97	3.93	3.62
Other business services	2 268	21.00	24.35	28.22	30.77	35.20	30.27	23.29	26.23
Personal, cultural, and recreational	2 287	.72	.75	.76	.95	1.17	.26	.32	.33
Government, n.i.e.	2 291	1.16	1.22	1.12	1.43	1.53	1.78	1.34	1.22
Other services, debit	3 200 BA	**−37.55**	**−41.75**	**−46.38**	**−54.66**	**−66.82**	**−67.99**	**−55.84**	**−58.13**
Communications	3 245	−3.23	−2.77	−3.11	−4.64	−4.42	−6.58	−5.38	−6.57
Construction	3 249	−2.46	−2.69	−2.19	−2.57	−3.47	−.06	−.04	−.07
Insurance	3 253	−1.79	−2.29	−2.14	−2.89	−3.45	−5.84	−3.82	−3.98
Financial	3 260	−.81	−1.29	−1.22	−1.04	−1.43	−3.82	−4.17	−4.55
Computer and information	3 262	−1.05	−1.23	−1.53	−1.72	−1.79	−4.51	−3.52	−4.40
Royalties and licence fees	3 266	−1.70	−1.75	−1.94	−1.84	−1.68	−7.78	−6.85	−7.01
Other business services	3 268	−24.25	−26.65	−30.89	−35.92	−45.30	−36.40	−29.54	−28.61
Personal, cultural, and recreational	3 287	−1.03	−1.51	−1.64	−1.64	−2.10	−.71	−.66	−.74
Government, n.i.e.	3 291	−1.23	−1.57	−1.72	−2.40	−3.19	−2.28	−1.86	−2.19

Table 2 (Continued). STANDARD PRESENTATION, 2003–2010

(Billions of U.S. dollars)

	Code	2003	2004	2005	2006	2007	2008	2009	2010
C. INCOME	4 300	**−20.22**	**−18.34**	**−17.11**	**−17.08**	**−26.80**	**−28.64**	**−14.25**	**−10.65**
Total credit	2 300	*48.78*	*53.12*	*61.32*	*72.35*	*88.21*	*103.50*	*80.39*	*73.61*
Total debit	3 300	*−69.00*	*−71.46*	*−78.43*	*−89.43*	*−115.01*	*−132.14*	*−94.64*	*−84.26*
Compensation of employees, credit	2 310	**1.73**	**1.81**	**2.03**	**2.24**	**2.72**	**4.92**	**4.65**	**6.23**
Compensation of employees, debit	3 310	**−2.98**	**−2.07**	**−2.72**	**−2.65**	**−2.86**	**−3.70**	**−3.44**	**−3.49**
Investment income, credit	2 320	**47.05**	**51.31**	**59.29**	**70.11**	**85.49**	**98.58**	**75.75**	**67.38**
Direct investment income	2 330	5.51	5.00	4.97	7.65	10.71	33.26	28.59	27.75
Dividends and distributed branch profits	2 332	1.90	2.17	2.27	3.37	4.48	15.85	10.23	14.14
Reinvested earnings and undistributed branch profits	2 333	3.61	2.84	2.70	4.29	6.23	15.11	14.70	9.81
Income on debt (interest)	2 334	....	....	....	....	....	2.30	3.66	3.80
Portfolio investment income	2 339	30.10	35.79	40.25	47.92	52.67	41.65	35.32	33.20
Income on equity	2 340	5.03	8.22	10.33	11.22	17.46	13.04	8.45	8.17
Income on bonds and notes	2 350	24.67	27.12	29.81	36.60	35.02	28.18	26.47	25.00
Income on money market instruments	2 360	.40	.45	.10	.11	.19	.43	.40	.03
Other investment income	2 370	11.44	10.52	14.07	14.53	21.11	23.67	11.84	6.43
Investment income, debit	3 320	**−66.02**	**−69.39**	**−75.71**	**−86.78**	**−112.15**	**−128.44**	**−91.21**	**−80.77**
Direct investment income	3 330	−5.39	−5.50	−5.82	−6.80	−7.11	−21.31	−17.71	−15.54
Dividends and distributed branch profits	3 332	−.60	−.58	−.63	−.62	−.59	−8.50	−1.07	−4.05
Reinvested earnings and undistributed branch profits	3 333	−4.79	−4.92	−5.19	−6.18	−6.52	−5.01	−7.26	−5.78
Income on debt (interest)	3 334	....	....	....	....	....	−7.80	−9.37	−5.71
Portfolio investment income	3 339	−44.27	−49.04	−51.74	−54.86	−68.32	−81.11	−62.01	−59.38
Income on equity	3 340	−11.59	−12.75	−15.41	−18.56	−19.61	−17.49	−7.69	−7.19
Income on bonds and notes	3 350	−29.50	−32.79	−34.77	−34.91	−47.01	−62.15	−53.08	−51.29
Income on money market instruments	3 360	−3.19	−3.50	−1.56	−1.38	−1.70	−1.47	−1.24	−.90
Other investment income	3 370	−16.36	−14.84	−18.16	−25.12	−36.73	−26.02	−11.50	−5.85
D. CURRENT TRANSFERS	4 379	**−8.10**	**−10.29**	**−12.33**	**−16.71**	**−19.70**	**−22.21**	**−16.73**	**−21.39**
Credit	2 379	**20.65**	**21.83**	**23.54**	**22.22**	**26.62**	**28.99**	**29.17**	**23.15**
General government	2 380	11.73	12.20	12.32	12.37	15.83	14.63	15.90	10.76
Other sectors	2 390	8.92	9.63	11.22	9.85	10.79	14.37	13.27	12.39
Workers' remittances	2 391	.29	.28	.29	.31	.35	.64	.57	.58
Other current transfers	2 392	8.63	9.35	10.93	9.54	10.44	13.73	12.70	11.81
Debit	3 379	**−28.74**	**−32.12**	**−35.88**	**−38.94**	**−46.31**	**−51.20**	**−45.90**	**−44.54**
General government	3 380	−18.11	−20.63	−22.67	−22.21	−26.14	−28.51	−25.83	−24.75
Other sectors	3 390	−10.64	−11.49	−13.20	−16.73	−20.17	−22.69	−20.07	−19.79
Workers' remittances	3 391	−1.33	−3.37	−4.83	−5.70	−8.32	−9.36	−9.43	−8.71
Other current transfers	3 392	−9.31	−8.12	−8.37	−11.03	−11.85	−13.32	−10.64	−11.07
CAPITAL AND FINANCIAL ACCOUNT	4 996	**21.99**	**13.36**	**27.95**	**33.87**	**38.99**	**45.28**	**47.00**	**115.65**
CAPITAL ACCOUNT	4 994	**2.67**	**2.17**	**1.63**	**2.36**	**3.15**	**−.35**	**−.05**	**−.72**
Total credit	2 994	*4.95*	*4.11*	*5.12*	*5.49*	*5.18*	*3.66*	*2.97*	*2.31*
Total debit	3 994	*−2.28*	*−1.94*	*−3.49*	*−3.12*	*−2.03*	*−4.01*	*−3.02*	*−3.04*
Capital transfers, credit	2 400	**4.68**	**3.86**	**4.78**	**5.27**	**4.95**	**3.16**	**2.33**	**1.96**
General government	2 401	4.21	3.56	4.61	4.80	4.53	3.16	2.32	1.96
Debt forgiveness	2 402	....	....	....	....	....			
Other capital transfers	2 410	4.21	3.56	4.61	4.80	4.53	3.16	2.32	1.96
Other sectors	2 430	.47	.29	.17	.47	.42			
Migrants' transfers	2 431	.13	.08	.08	.07	.10			
Debt forgiveness	2 432	....	....	....	....				
Other capital transfers	2 440	.34	.21	.09	.40	.32			
Capital transfers, debit	3 400	**−1.92**	**−1.64**	**−3.23**	**−2.79**	**−1.70**	**−1.97**	**−1.57**	**−1.75**
General government	3 401	−1.70	−1.31	−2.98	−2.24	−1.39	−1.97	−1.54	−1.65
Debt forgiveness	3 402	−.75	−.29	−1.49	−1.28	−.15			
Other capital transfers	3 410	−.95	−1.02	−1.49	−.96	−1.24	−1.97	−1.54	−1.65
Other sectors	3 430	−.22	−.33	−.25	−.55	−.31		−.03	−.10
Migrants' transfers	3 431	−.06	−.07	−.08	−.09	−.10			
Debt forgiveness	3 432	....	....	−.01	....				
Other capital transfers	3 440	−.16	−.25	−.16	−.46	−.21		−.03	−.10
Nonproduced nonfinancial assets, credit	2 480	**.27**	**.26**	**.34**	**.22**	**.23**	**.50**	**.64**	**.35**
Nonproduced nonfinancial assets, debit	3 480	**−.36**	**−.30**	**−.26**	**−.34**	**−.33**	**−2.04**	**−1.45**	**−1.29**

Table 2 (Continued). STANDARD PRESENTATION, 2003–2010

(Billions of U.S. dollars)

	Code	2003	2004	2005	2006	2007	2008	2009	2010
FINANCIAL ACCOUNT	4 995	**19.32**	**11.19**	**26.32**	**31.51**	**35.85**	**45.63**	**47.05**	**116.38**
A. DIRECT INVESTMENT	4 500	**7.55**	**−2.46**	**−21.14**	**−3.47**	**−52.08**	**−79.00**	**−3.18**	**−10.78**
Direct investment abroad	4 505	**−8.99**	**−19.25**	**−40.78**	**−42.48**	**−92.12**	**−69.51**	**−19.76**	**−20.38**
Equity capital	4 510	−12.82	−.99	−26.54	−28.66	−67.49	−26.14	−12.30	−19.99
Claims on affiliated enterprises	4 515	....	....	....	....	....	....	....	....
Liabilities to affiliated enterprises	4 520	....	....	....	....	....	....	....	....
Reinvested earnings	4 525	−3.61	−2.84	−2.70	−4.29	−6.23	−15.11	−14.70	−9.82
Other capital	4 530	7.45	−15.42	−11.54	−9.53	−18.40	−28.27	7.24	9.43
Claims on affiliated enterprises	4 535	....	....	....	....	....	....	....	....
Liabilities to affiliated enterprises	4 540	....	....	....	....	....	....	....	....
Direct investment in Italy	4 555	**16.54**	**16.79**	**19.64**	**39.01**	**40.04**	**−9.49**	**16.58**	**9.60**
Equity capital	4 560	2.81	7.46	8.49	21.98	18.44	−4.87	7.47	7.93
Claims on direct investors	4 565	....	....	....	....	....	....	....	....
Liabilities to direct investors	4 570	....	....	....	....	....	....	....	....
Reinvested earnings	4 575	4.79	4.92	5.19	6.18	6.52	5.03	7.26	5.78
Other capital	4 580	8.94	4.41	5.96	10.85	15.08	−9.65	1.84	−4.11
Claims on direct investors	4 585	....	....	....	....	....	....	....	....
Liabilities to direct investors	4 590	....	....	....	....	....	....	....	....
B. PORTFOLIO INVESTMENT	4 600	**2.74**	**32.18**	**56.31**	**53.57**	**25.65**	**106.86**	**32.72**	**50.86**
Assets	4 602	**−57.41**	**−26.38**	**−108.09**	**−61.72**	**1.59**	**95.63**	**−55.94**	**−43.16**
Equity securities	4 610	−16.00	−16.17	−24.88	−23.04	17.02	118.45	−18.89	−54.53
Monetary authorities	4 611	.03	−.05	−.67	−.18	....	−1.00	−1.06	−.38
General government	4 612	−.38	.31	−.27	−.11	−.09	−.38	−.18	−.80
Banks	4 613	−.25	−1.25	2.23	−1.50	−11.44	17.61	.41	−1.90
Other sectors	4 614	−15.39	−15.17	−26.17	−21.25	28.55	102.22	−18.06	−51.45
Debt securities	4 619	−41.41	−10.21	−83.21	−38.69	−15.44	−22.82	−37.05	11.37
Bonds and notes	4 620	−44.59	−11.04	−80.92	−33.05	−9.10	−23.17	−39.10	11.23
Monetary authorities	4 621	−.34	.08	−.07	−15.24	−7.25	−3.67	−12.88	−34.91
General government	4 622	−.17	−.17	−.68	−.56	−.02	−.14	.17	.78
Banks	4 623	−11.30	−9.84	.18	1.30	−6.94	−39.40	−2.06	11.45
Other sectors	4 624	−32.78	−1.10	−80.35	−18.54	5.11	20.05	−24.33	33.91
Money market instruments	4 630	3.18	.83	−2.28	−5.64	−6.34	.34	2.05	.14
Monetary authorities	4 631	.18	−1.43	−.24	.82	2.34	.47	.05	....
General government	4 632	−.07	−.01	.02	.02	.08	.02	−.04	.04
Banks	4 633	−.19	.91	.59	−.43	.12	−.14	−1.14	.91
Other sectors	4 634	3.27	1.36	−2.65	−6.05	−8.87	....	3.18	−.81
Liabilities	4 652	**60.15**	**58.55**	**164.40**	**115.29**	**24.06**	**11.24**	**88.66**	**94.03**
Equity securities	4 660	−2.01	17.18	2.63	13.56	−14.87	−29.01	20.90	3.83
Banks	4 663	4.57	3.27	27.53	4.85	−14.40	−3.06	7.48	2.18
Other sectors	4 664	−6.58	13.91	−24.90	8.71	−.47	−25.95	13.42	1.65
Debt securities	4 669	62.16	41.37	161.77	101.73	38.93	40.25	67.76	90.20
Bonds and notes	4 670	53.11	58.35	149.58	120.88	33.04	18.70	17.97	86.63
Monetary authorities	4 671	....	....	....	....	....	....	....	....
General government	4 672	53.17	25.42	108.42	64.51	−12.88	23.54	35.70	82.83
Banks	4 673	−.89	18.98	35.27	53.47	42.93	13.47	−14.00	1.12
Other sectors	4 674	.83	13.95	5.88	2.89	3.00	−18.31	−3.73	2.68
Money market instruments	4 680	9.05	−16.97	12.20	−19.15	5.89	21.56	49.79	3.57
Monetary authorities	4 681	....	....	....	....	....	....	....	....
General government	4 682	15.27	−14.30	12.21	−19.08	5.42	22.03	49.98	3.61
Banks	4 683	−6.23	−2.68	−.02	−.07	.47	−.48	−.19	−.04
Other sectors	4 684	....	....	....	....	....	....	....	....
C. FINANCIAL DERIVATIVES	4 910	**−5.47**	**2.28**	**3.12**	**−.59**	**.74**	**2.56**	**5.79**	**3.04**
Monetary authorities	4 911	....	....	....	....	....	....	....	....
General government	4 912	−.04	−.02	−.07	−.02	−.05	−3.38	−2.04	−2.46
Banks	4 913	−4.42	−3.52	−6.86	−7.01	−5.96	1.47	5.63	.66
Other sectors	4 914	−1.00	5.82	10.05	6.43	6.74	4.47	2.20	4.84
Assets	4 900	**−10.28**	....	....	....	....	**−3.51**	**12.16**	**9.58**
Monetary authorities	4 901	....	....	....	....	....	....	....	....
General government	4 902	−.04	....	....	....	....	−.68	−.65	−.61
Banks	4 903	−6.93	....	....	....	....	−7.49	10.79	8.32
Other sectors	4 904	−3.31	....	....	....	....	4.65	2.02	1.87
Liabilities	4 905	**4.81**	**2.28**	**3.12**	**−.59**	**.74**	**6.07**	**−6.37**	**−6.54**
Monetary authorities	4 906	....	....	....	....	....	....	....	....
General government	4 907	....	−.02	−.07	−.02	−.05	−2.70	−1.39	−1.86
Banks	4 908	2.51	−3.52	−6.86	−7.01	−5.96	8.96	−5.16	−7.66
Other sectors	4 909	2.30	5.82	10.05	6.43	6.74	−.18	.18	2.97

Table 2 (Concluded). STANDARD PRESENTATION, 2003–2010

(Billions of U.S. dollars)

	Code	2003	2004	2005	2006	2007	2008	2009	2010
D. OTHER INVESTMENT	4 700	**15.61**	**−23.65**	**−13.00**	**−18.57**	**63.43**	**23.41**	**20.72**	**74.60**
Assets	4 703	**−20.58**	**−47.94**	**−100.28**	**−142.42**	**−82.67**	**37.42**	**58.96**	**57.71**
Trade credits	4 706	.34	−2.95	−.38	.79	.57	3.86	−5.95	4.16
General government	4 707	−.01	−.01	.01	....	−.01	....	....	....
of which: Short-term	4 709	....	....	....	....	....	....	....	....
Other sectors	4 710	.35	−2.94	−.39	.79	.58	3.86	−5.95	4.16
of which: Short-term	4 712	....	....	....	....	....	....	....	....
Loans	4 714	16.31	−14.64	−47.08	−66.58	−62.33	35.96	37.58	−4.56
Monetary authorities	4 715	....	.23	....	....	.06	....	.02	....
of which: Short-term	4 718	....	....	....	....	....	....	....	....
General government	4 719	.57	.44	−.38	−.06	−.15	.03	−.07	.01
of which: Short-term	4 721	....	....	....	....	....	....	....	....
Banks	4 722	−.07	−13.95	2.83	−22.16	−19.65	35.92	34.79	−3.41
of which: Short-term	4 724	....	−10.54	11.79	−28.60	.29	44.57	26.85	1.49
Other sectors	4 725	15.82	−1.36	−49.53	−44.36	−42.58	....	2.83	−1.16
of which: Short-term	4 727	....	....	....	....	....	....	....	....
Currency and deposits	4 730	−31.17	−17.88	−39.13	−58.34	−4.93	12.81	22.39	53.66
Monetary authorities	4 731	−.06	−8.96	−4.34	−18.73	−18.29	21.01	−39.22	66.75
General government	4 732	1.02	−.64	−.45	−.28	.19	....	....	....
Banks	4 733	4.01	−6.83	−19.95	−24.48	−12.39	−3.08	17.60	−3.53
Other sectors	4 734	−36.14	−1.45	−14.39	−14.85	25.56	−5.12	44.01	−9.57
Other assets	4 736	−6.07	−12.47	−13.69	−18.30	−15.97	−15.21	4.95	4.46
Monetary authorities	4 737	....	.02	....	....	−.06	.07	−.79	.05
of which: Short-term	4 739	....	....	....	....	....	....	....	....
General government	4 740	−.17	−.35	−.42	−.03	....	....	....	....
of which: Short-term	4 742	....	....	....	....	....	....	....	....
Banks	4 743	−3.51	−6.51	−7.71	−12.23	−7.35	−7.19	1.29	2.40
of which: Short-term	4 745	....	−4.69	−8.56	6.36	−12.44	−7.19	1.29	2.40
Other sectors	4 746	−2.39	−5.63	−5.56	−6.03	−8.56	−8.10	4.45	2.01
of which: Short-term	4 748	....	....	....	....	....	....	....	....
Liabilities	4 753	**36.20**	**24.29**	**87.28**	**123.86**	**146.10**	**−14.01**	**−38.24**	**16.89**
Trade credits	4 756	−.49	1.05	3.25	1.60	−.76	.69	−7.58	4.99
General government	4 757	−.01	....	−.01	−.01	.01	....	....	....
of which: Short-term	4 759	....	....	....	....	....	....	....	....
Other sectors	4 760	−.48	1.04	3.26	1.61	−.77	.69	−7.58	4.99
of which: Short-term	4 762	....	....	....	....	....	....	....	....
Loans	4 764	5.87	26.72	12.42	23.54	18.30	4.40	42.60	26.24
Monetary authorities	4 765	−2.64	.40	1.01	−.80	−1.11	−.01	−.01	−.03
of which: Use of Fund credit and loans from the Fund	4 766	....	....	....	....	....	....	....	....
of which: Short-term	4 768	−2.64	.40	1.01	−.80	−1.11	−.01	−.01	−.03
General government	4 769	−.99	−.60	1.70	−.31	−.87	−.12	−.16	−.14
of which: Short-term	4 771	....	....	....	....	....	....	....	....
Banks	4 772	13.97	20.65	5.63	16.40	25.92	−22.09	21.10	34.72
of which: Short-term	4 774	....	12.74	2.08	9.44	35.41	−.87	3.64	29.91
Other sectors	4 775	−4.48	6.27	4.08	8.24	−5.64	26.63	21.67	−8.32
of which: Short-term	4 777	....	....	....	....	....	....	....	....
Currency and deposits	4 780	30.36	−5.57	47.93	91.23	111.01	−25.81	−82.73	−18.90
Monetary authorities	4 781	−.01	.01	.07	−.02	−.01	.08	−.08	.03
General government	4 782	....	....	....	....	....	....	....	....
Banks	4 783	30.38	−5.58	47.86	91.25	111.02	−25.89	−82.65	−18.93
Other sectors	4 784	−.01	....	....	....	....	....	....	....
Other liabilities	4 786	.46	2.10	23.68	7.49	17.54	6.71	9.47	4.56
Monetary authorities	4 787	.09	−.01	.02	−.12	−.02	.06	9.39	3.51
of which: Short-term	4 789	....	....	....	....	....	....	....	....
General government	4 790	−.02	−.05	−.39	−.07	−.43	....	....	....
of which: Short-term	4 792	....	....	....	....	....	....	....	....
Banks	4 793	−.61	−.35	6.01	5.74	15.73	2.64	−.26	−.27
of which: Short-term	4 795	....	−.31	2.20	6.69	−6.92	2.64	−.26	−.27
Other sectors	4 796	.99	2.52	18.03	1.94	2.27	4.00	.35	1.32
of which: Short-term	4 798	....	....	....	....	....	....	....	....
E. RESERVE ASSETS	4 802	**−1.11**	**2.84**	**1.03**	**.57**	**−1.89**	**−8.20**	**−9.00**	**−1.34**
Monetary gold	4 812	....	....	....	....	....	....	....	....
Special drawing rights	4 811	−.04	.02	−.10	−.03	−.04	.07	−9.12	−.30
Reserve position in the Fund	4 810	.13	.61	1.69	.85	.28	−.78	−.25	−.65
Foreign exchange	4 803	−1.21	2.22	−.56	−.25	−2.13	−7.49	.36	−.39
Other claims	4 813	....	....	....	....	....	....	....	....
NET ERRORS AND OMISSIONS	4 998	**−2.58**	**3.09**	**1.80**	**13.96**	**12.58**	**20.97**	**−6.00**	**−44.42**

Table 3. INTERNATIONAL INVESTMENT POSITION (End-period stocks), 2003–2010

(Billions of U.S. dollars)

	Code	2003	2004	2005	2006	2007	2008	2009	2010
ASSETS	8 995 C.	**1,561.71**	**1,829.15**	**1,920.15**	**2,397.61**	**2,637.45**	**2,345.90**	**2,544.79**	**2,451.88**
Direct investment abroad	8 505	**238.89**	**280.48**	**293.48**	**378.93**	**417.87**	**442.39**	**486.39**	**475.60**
Equity capital and reinvested earnings	8 506	213.49	248.47	253.04	320.73	421.06	423.35	472.83	472.60
Claims on affiliated enterprises	8 507	....	....	....	....	....	....	....	....
Liabilities to affiliated enterprises	8 508	....	....	....	....	....	....	....	....
Other capital	8 530	25.40	32.01	40.44	58.21	−3.19	19.04	13.56	3.00
Claims on affiliated enterprises	8 535	....	....	....	....	100.15	101.19	121.17	110.16
Liabilities to affiliated enterprises	8 540	....	....	....	....	−103.33	−82.15	−107.62	−107.16
Portfolio investment	8 602	**790.97**	**933.58**	**982.07**	**1,153.00**	**1,295.66**	**1,003.53**	**1,173.57**	**1,154.63**
Equity securities	8 610	331.05	399.68	416.45	534.84	589.97	318.13	400.07	454.32
Monetary authorities	8 611	.62	.69	1.67	2.07	2.45	3.23	5.02	5.45
General government	8 612	.95	1.15	1.64	2.92	3.38	2.45	3.12	3.99
Banks	8 613	15.11	18.05	17.18	22.72	35.99	9.94	14.24	14.85
Other sectors	8 614	314.37	379.79	395.96	507.14	548.15	302.52	377.69	430.03
Debt securities	8 619	459.92	533.90	565.62	618.16	705.68	685.40	773.50	700.31
Bonds and notes	8 620	453.54	521.25	558.54	611.35	689.18	677.58	769.62	696.86
Monetary authorities	8 621	.41	.35	.40	16.22	25.91	30.99	45.24	76.69
General government	8 622	3.96	4.22	4.84	6.03	6.26	6.88	7.08	5.74
Banks	8 623	60.56	80.49	70.11	73.89	86.39	107.64	120.98	99.67
Other sectors	8 624	388.60	436.19	483.19	515.20	570.62	532.07	596.32	514.76
Money market instruments	8 630	6.38	12.65	7.08	6.81	16.50	7.82	3.88	3.45
Monetary authorities	8 631	2.05	3.47	3.64	2.90	.57	.05	....	....
General government	8 632	.06	.03	.02	.01	....	.02	.04	....
Banks	8 633	1.02	1.03	.08	.41	2.22	.51	1.27	.30
Other sectors	8 634	3.26	8.12	3.34	3.50	13.72	7.24	2.57	3.15
Financial derivatives	8 900	**22.70**	**28.49**	**30.23**	**31.28**	**34.30**	**161.51**	**146.81**	**149.28**
Monetary authorities	8 901	....	....	....	....	4.19	6.97	12.00	14.55
General government	8 902	.11	.14	.18	.22	16.17	141.37	121.21	123.98
Banks	8 903	8.63	13.31	15.38	12.66	13.93	13.18	13.60	10.75
Other sectors	8 904	13.97	15.04	14.66	18.40				
Other investment	8 703	**445.88**	**524.21**	**548.42**	**758.62**	**795.30**	**633.19**	**605.22**	**513.51**
Trade credits	8 706	57.75	65.48	57.08	62.94	68.24	60.66	69.18	61.31
General government	8 707	.02	.04	.02	.01	....	....	....	....
of which: Short-term	8 709	....	....	....	....	....	....	....	....
Other sectors	8 710	57.73	65.45	57.06	62.93	68.24	60.66	69.18	61.31
of which: Short-term	8 712	....	....	....	....	....	....	....	....
Loans	8 714	291.68	332.87	359.39	535.01	528.52	480.57	445.44	372.51
Monetary authorities	8 715	13.76	22.72	21.11	44.47	68.00	42.11	90.72	15.96
of which: Short-term	8 718	....	....	....	....	....	....	....	....
General government	8 719	21.63	23.21	25.09	28.10	35.95	33.99	35.28	37.94
of which: Short-term	8 721	....	....	....	....	....	....	....	....
Banks	8 722	187.59	220.43	199.10	272.52	318.26	301.25	256.49	250.61
of which: Short-term	8 724	....	....	....	....	....	....	....	....
Other sectors	8 725	68.71	66.51	114.09	189.92	106.31	103.22	62.95	68.00
of which: Short-term	8 727	....	....	....	....	....	....	....	....
Currency and deposits	8 730	....	....	....	....	....	....	....	....
Monetary authorities	8 731	....	....	....	....	....	....	....	....
General government	8 732	....	....	....	....	....	....	....	....
Banks	8 733	....	....	....	....	....	....	....	....
Other sectors	8 734	....	....	....	....	....	....	....	....
Other assets	8 736	96.45	125.86	131.94	160.67	198.54	91.96	90.61	79.68
Monetary authorities	8 737	.94	.99	.86	.96	1.13	1.75	1.81	1.65
of which: Short-term	8 739	....	....	....	....	....	....	....	....
General government	8 740	7.28	8.24	7.54	8.45	12.02	11.36	11.76	10.91
of which: Short-term	8 742	....	....	....	....	....	....	....	....
Banks	8 743	37.83	56.19	65.88	80.48	119.18	9.68	9.43	6.58
of which: Short-term	8 745	....	....	....	....	....	....	....	....
Other sectors	8 746	50.39	60.44	57.66	70.78	66.20	69.18	67.60	60.54
of which: Short-term	8 748	....	....	....	....	....	....	....	....
Reserve assets	8 802	**63.26**	**62.39**	**65.95**	**75.77**	**94.32**	**105.27**	**132.80**	**158.86**
Monetary gold	8 812	32.89	34.53	40.44	50.11	65.94	68.19	87.03	111.17
Special drawing rights	8 811	.16	.14	.23	.27	.33	.26	9.41	9.55
Reserve position in the Fund	8 810	4.15	3.70	1.76	.98	.73	1.52	1.83	2.46
Foreign exchange	8 803	26.06	24.01	23.53	24.41	27.32	35.30	34.52	35.68
Other claims	8 813	....	....	....	....	....	....	....	....

2011, International Monetary Fund: *Balance of Payments Statistics Yearbook*

Table 3 (Concluded). INTERNATIONAL INVESTMENT POSITION (End-period stocks), 2003–2010

(Billions of U.S. dollars)

	Code	2003	2004	2005	2006	2007	2008	2009	2010
LIABILITIES	8 995 D.	**1,816.67**	**2,137.73**	**2,184.39**	**2,800.09**	**3,198.37**	**2,874.26**	**3,110.00**	**2,960.26**
Direct investment in Italy	8 555 ..	**180.89**	**220.72**	**224.08**	**294.87**	**376.51**	**327.91**	**364.43**	**337.40**
Equity capital and reinvested earnings	8 556 ..	147.00	184.94	185.65	240.70	277.20	246.18	274.43	257.51
Claims on direct investors	8 557 ..	....	....	....	....	....	....	....	....
Liabilities to direct investors	8 558 ..	....	....	....	....	....	....	....	....
Other capital	8 580 ..	33.89	35.77	38.43	54.17	99.31	81.73	90.00	79.90
Claims on direct investors	8 585 ..	....	....	....	....	−14.34	−15.53	−15.39	−11.25
Liabilities to direct investors	8 590 ..	....	....	....	....	113.65	97.27	105.39	91.14
Portfolio investment	8 652 ..	**1,086.74**	**1,286.36**	**1,308.24**	**1,657.76**	**1,862.08**	**1,586.44**	**1,810.91**	**1,697.32**
Equity securities	8 660 ..	201.65	285.35	292.20	412.91	419.41	186.16	245.72	203.89
Banks	8 663 ..	46.14	59.74	98.28	144.40	130.98	52.40	74.29	48.15
Other sectors	8 664 ..	155.51	225.61	193.92	268.51	288.43	133.75	171.43	155.74
Debt securities	8 669 ..	885.09	1,001.02	1,016.04	1,244.85	1,442.67	1,400.28	1,565.20	1,493.43
Bonds and notes	8 670 ..	853.13	985.42	991.84	1,237.59	1,426.93	1,364.50	1,473.52	1,405.15
Monetary authorities	8 671 ..	....	....	....	....	....	....	....	....
General government	8 672 ..	655.36	722.57	713.52	854.62	960.87	929.74	1,029.19	991.82
Banks	8 673 ..	70.61	96.72	116.77	186.49	242.27	240.98	237.17	219.00
Other sectors	8 674 ..	127.16	166.12	161.54	196.49	223.80	193.79	207.16	194.34
Money market instruments	8 680 ..	31.95	15.60	24.20	7.26	15.73	35.78	91.68	88.28
Monetary authorities	8 681 ..	....	....	....	....	....	....	....	....
General government	8 682 ..	29.06	15.44	24.08	7.20	15.18	35.69	91.68	88.25
Banks	8 683 ..	2.89	.16	.12	.06	.55	.09	....	....
Other sectors	8 684 ..	....	....	....	....	....	....	....	.03
Financial derivatives	8 905 ..	**15.90**	**26.35**	**37.73**	**47.60**	**29.03**	**177.17**	**160.68**	**178.52**
Monetary authorities	8 906 ..	....	....	....	....	....	....	....	....
General government	8 907 ..	.01	.01	.01	.01	.02	4.90	10.73	15.56
Banks	8 908 ..	6.38	9.95	12.57	10.70	12.46	156.79	131.21	142.21
Other sectors	8 909 ..	9.51	16.38	25.15	36.89	16.55	15.48	18.75	20.75
Other investment	8 753 ..	**533.15**	**604.30**	**614.34**	**799.85**	**930.74**	**782.74**	**773.97**	**747.01**
Trade credits	8 756 ..	29.83	33.09	31.88	37.46	42.66	40.64	35.84	39.00
General government	8 758 ..	....	....	....	....	....	....	....	....
of which: Short-term	8 759 ..	....	....	....	....	....	....	....	....
Other sectors	8 760 ..	29.81	33.07	31.86	37.45	42.66	40.64	35.84	39.00
of which: Short-term	8 762 ..	....	....	....	....	....	....	....	....
Loans	8 764 ..	473.46	524.93	514.95	684.78	807.97	734.76	718.90	685.08
Monetary authorities	8 765 ..	2.95	.92	2.01	1.22	.11	.21	.13	.15
of which: Use of Fund credit and loans from the Fund	8 766 ..	....	....	....	....	....	....	....	....
of which: Short-term	8 768 ..	....	....	....	....	....	....	....	....
General government	8 769 ..	6.27	6.08	6.85	6.16	4.93	4.66	4.83	4.48
of which: Short-term	8 771 ..	....	....	....	....	....	....	....	....
Banks	8 772 ..	361.80	403.91	402.37	553.24	745.60	651.00	610.26	592.18
of which: Short-term	8 774 ..	....	....	....	....	....	....	....	....
Other sectors	8 775 ..	102.44	114.02	103.72	124.16	57.33	78.89	103.68	88.27
of which: Short-term	8 777 ..	....	....	....	....	....	....	....	....
Currency and deposits	8 780 ..	....	....	....	....	....	....	....	....
Monetary authorities	8 781 ..	....	....	....	....	....	....	....	....
General government	8 782 ..	....	....	....	....	....	....	....	....
Banks	8 783 ..	....	....	....	....	....	....	....	....
Other sectors	8 784 ..	....	....	....	....	....	....	....	....
Other liabilities	8 786 ..	29.86	46.28	67.51	77.61	80.11	7.34	19.23	22.93
Monetary authorities	8 787 ..	.14	.13	.15	.03	.03	.08	10.63	13.92
of which: Short-term	8 789 ..	....	....	....	....	....	....	....	....
General government	8 790 ..	.22	.17	.10	.45	.21	.20	.21	.19
of which: Short-term	8 792 ..	....	....	....	....	....	....	....	....
Banks	8 793 ..	25.18	38.27	43.78	49.27	79.44	2.06	2.96	2.56
of which: Short-term	8 795 ..	....	....	....	....	....	....	....	....
Other sectors	8 796 ..	4.33	7.71	23.48	27.86	.44	5.00	5.44	6.26
of which: Short-term	8 798 ..	....	....	....	....	....	....	....	....
NET INTERNATIONAL INVESTMENT POSITION	8 995 ..	**−254.96**	**−308.58**	**−264.24**	**−402.48**	**−560.92**	**−528.36**	**−565.21**	**−508.37**
Conversion rates: euros per U.S. dollar (end of period)	0 104 ..	.7918	.7342	.8477	.7593	.6793	.7185	.6942	.7484

Table 1. ANALYTIC PRESENTATION, 2003–2010

(Millions of U.S. dollars)

	Code	2003	2004	2005	2006	2007	2008	2009	2010
A. Current Account[1]	4 993 Z.	**−773.4**	**−501.6**	**−1,071.3**	**−1,182.9**	**−2,038.1**	**−2,793.3**	**−1,127.5**	**−934.0**
Goods: exports f.o.b.	2 100 ..	1,385.6	1,601.6	1,664.3	2,133.6	2,362.6	2,743.9	1,387.7	1,370.4
Goods: imports f.o.b.	3 100 ..	−3,328.2	−3,545.3	−4,245.5	−5,077.0	−6,203.9	−7,546.8	−4,475.7	−4,629.4
Balance on Goods	4 100 ..	*−1,942.6*	*−1,943.7*	*−2,581.2*	*−2,943.4*	*−3,841.3*	*−4,802.9*	*−3,087.9*	*−3,259.0*
Services: credit	2 200 ..	2,137.7	2,297.1	2,329.7	2,648.7	2,706.6	2,795.2	2,650.6	2,634.0
Services: debit	3 200 ..	−1,586.1	−1,718.7	−1,722.0	−2,021.1	−2,281.7	−2,367.1	−1,880.6	−1,824.4
Balance on Goods and Services	4 991 ..	*−1,391.1*	*−1,365.3*	*−1,973.5*	*−2,315.8*	*−3,416.4*	*−4,374.8*	*−2,318.0*	*−2,449.4*
Income: credit	2 300 ..	217.6	269.6	327.9	378.4	520.7	487.9	235.0	243.2
Income: debit	3 300 ..	−789.0	−852.1	−1,004.1	−994.0	−1,182.3	−1,056.2	−902.9	−737.8
Balance on Goods, Services, and Income	4 992 ..	*−1,962.5*	*−1,947.8*	*−2,649.8*	*−2,931.4*	*−4,078.0*	*−4,943.1*	*−2,985.9*	*−2,944.0*
Current transfers: credit	2 379 Z.	1,523.5	1,892.1	1,935.5	2,088.5	2,385.7	2,488.8	2,122.0	2,292.9
Current transfers: debit	3 379 ..	−334.4	−445.9	−357.0	−339.9	−345.8	−339.0	−263.6	−282.9
B. Capital Account[1]	4 994 Z.	**.1**	**2.2**	**−18.3**	**−27.7**	**−35.5**	**18.1**	**20.7**	**−22.1**
Capital account: credit	2 994 Z.	19.3	35.8	22.5	26.8	22.2	72.6	64.2	21.4
Capital account: debit	3 994 ..	−19.2	−33.6	−40.8	−54.5	−57.7	−54.5	−43.4	−43.4
Total, Groups A Plus B	4 981 ..	*−773.3*	*−499.4*	*−1,089.6*	*−1,210.5*	*−2,073.7*	*−2,775.2*	*−1,106.8*	*−956.1*
C. Financial Account[1]	4 995 W.	**314.4**	**1,215.8**	**1,309.7**	**1,338.1**	**1,294.4**	**3,020.5**	**1,280.8**	**437.0**
Direct investment abroad	4 505 ..	−116.3	−60.0	−101.0	−85.4	−115.0	−75.9	−61.1	−58.2
Direct investment in Jamaica	4 555 Z.	720.7	601.6	682.5	882.2	866.5	1,436.6	540.9	227.7
Portfolio investment assets	4 602 ..	−1,105.2	−1,132.8	−1,406.4	−506.4	−1,768.6	−813.8	−731.7	−1,107.9
Equity securities	4 610 ..	....	....	....	....	....	....	....	....
Debt securities	4 619 ..	−1,105.2	−1,132.8	−1,406.4	−506.4	−1,768.6	−813.8	−731.7	−1,107.9
Portfolio investment liabilities	4 652 Z.	819.6	1,228.8	1,280.4	377.9	1,128.1	781.1	379.5	755.7
Equity securities	4 660 ..	....	....	....	....	....	....	....	....
Debt securities	4 669 Z.	819.6	1,228.8	1,280.4	377.9	1,128.1	781.1	379.5	755.7
Financial derivatives	4 910 ..	....	....	....	....	....	....	....	....
Financial derivatives assets	4 900 ..	....	....	....	....	....	....	....	....
Financial derivatives liabilities	4 905 ..	....	....	....	....	....	....	....	....
Other investment assets	4 703 ..	−307.6	−127.4	−290.8	−269.0	−238.3	−242.2	21.0	−1,143.4
Monetary authorities	4 701 ..	....	....	−61.3	.1	53.5	5.6	334.8	−798.7
General government	4 704 ..	1.2	−1.0	−1.8	.1	−.8	−.4	−15.2	9.6
Banks	4 705 ..	−362.8	−175.5	−274.2	−317.5	−338.2	−287.4	−334.8	−401.6
Other sectors	4 728 ..	54.0	49.1	46.5	48.4	47.2	40.1	36.2	47.3
Other investment liabilities	4 753 W.	303.1	705.6	1,145.0	938.9	1,421.6	1,934.7	1,132.1	1,763.1
Monetary authorities	4 753 WA	....	....	....	....	....	....	345.2	....
General government	4 753 ZB	−362.7	481.2	117.8	72.0	106.6	188.9	−200.4	663.5
Banks	4 753 ZC	395.5	143.2	405.8	357.7	252.8	765.7	152.7	195.4
Other sectors	4 753 ZD	270.3	81.2	621.4	509.2	1,062.2	980.1	834.7	904.2
Total, Groups A Through C	4 983 ..	*−458.9*	*716.4*	*220.1*	*127.6*	*−779.3*	*245.3*	*174.0*	*−519.1*
D. Net Errors and Omissions	4 998 ..	**28.3**	**−21.7**	**9.8**	**102.8**	**339.5**	**−350.3**	**−203.3**	**171.0**
Total, Groups A Through D	4 984 ..	*−430.5*	*694.7*	*229.9*	*230.3*	*−439.8*	*−105.0*	*−29.3*	*−348.1*
E. Reserves and Related Items	4 802 A.	**430.5**	**−694.7**	**−229.9**	**−230.3**	**439.8**	**105.0**	**29.3**	**348.1**
Reserve assets	4 802 ..	447.7	−685.6	−227.9	−230.3	439.8	105.0	29.3	−431.4
Use of Fund credit and loans	4 766 ..	−16.1	−8.0	−.9	....	....	....	....	779.5
Exceptional financing	4 920 ..	−1.0	−1.1	−1.1	....	....	....	....	....
Conversion rates: Jamaica dollars per U.S. dollar	0 101 ..	**57.741**	**61.197**	**62.281**	**65.744**	**69.192**	**72.756**	**87.894**	**87.196**

[1] Excludes components that have been classified in the categories of Group E.

Table 2. STANDARD PRESENTATION, 2003–2010

(Millions of U.S. dollars)

	Code	2003	2004	2005	2006	2007	2008	2009	2010
CURRENT ACCOUNT	4 993	−773.4	−501.6	−1,071.3	−1,182.9	−2,038.1	−2,793.3	−1,127.5	−934.0
A. GOODS	4 100	−1,942.6	−1,943.7	−2,581.2	−2,943.4	−3,841.3	−4,802.9	−3,087.9	−3,259.0
Credit	2 100	1,385.6	1,601.6	1,664.3	2,133.6	2,362.6	2,743.9	1,387.7	1,370.4
General merchandise: exports f.o.b.	2 110	1,337.6	1,531.3	1,588.3	2,037.6	2,259.3	2,592.1	1,281.1	1,234.7
Goods for processing: exports f.o.b.	2 150	....	....	....	....	....	....	....	....
Repairs on goods	2 160	....	....	....	....	....	....	....	....
Goods procured in ports by carriers	2 170	48.0	70.3	76.0	96.0	103.3	151.8	106.6	135.7
Nonmonetary gold	2 180	....	....	....	....	....	....	....	....
Debit	3 100	−3,328.2	−3,545.3	−4,245.5	−5,077.0	−6,203.9	−7,546.8	−4,475.7	−4,629.4
General merchandise: imports f.o.b.	3 110	−3,252.0	−3,433.0	−4,134.3	−4,945.0	−6,066.9	−7,402.1	−4,419.0	−4,559.0
Goods for processing: imports f.o.b.	3 150	....	....	....	....	....	....	....	....
Repairs on goods	3 160	....	....	....	....	....	....	....	....
Goods procured in ports by carriers	3 170	−76.2	−112.3	−111.2	−132.0	−137.0	−144.7	−56.7	−70.4
Nonmonetary gold	3 180	....	....	....	....	....	....	....	....
B. SERVICES	4 200	**551.6**	**578.4**	**607.6**	**627.6**	**424.9**	**428.1**	**769.9**	**809.6**
Total credit	2 200	*2,137.7*	*2,297.1*	*2,329.7*	*2,648.7*	*2,706.6*	*2,795.2*	*2,650.6*	*2,634.0*
Total debit	3 200	*−1,586.1*	*−1,718.7*	*−1,722.0*	*−2,021.1*	*−2,281.7*	*−2,367.1*	*−1,880.6*	*−1,824.4*
Transportation services, credit	2 205	**474.3**	**497.3**	**451.1**	**459.0**	**447.2**	**469.0**	**344.2**	**295.2**
Passenger	2 850	*266.2*	*295.2*	*237.8*	*224.2*	*231.5*	*245.7*	*145.1*	*94.2*
Freight	2 851	*3.6*	*7.6*	*14.6*	*17.8*	*15.3*	*14.6*	*4.4*	*3.8*
Other	2 852	*204.5*	*194.5*	*198.7*	*217.0*	*200.3*	*208.7*	*194.7*	*197.2*
Sea transport, passenger	2 207	....	....	....	....	....	....	....	....
Sea transport, freight	2 208	....	....	....	....	....	....	....	....
Sea transport, other	2 209	....	....	....	....	....	....	....	....
Air transport, passenger	2 211	....	....	....	....	....	....	....	....
Air transport, freight	2 212	....	....	....	....	....	....	....	....
Air transport, other	2 213	....	....	....	....	....	....	....	....
Other transport, passenger	2 215	....	....	....	....	....	....	....	....
Other transport, freight	2 216	....	....	....	....	....	....	....	....
Other transport, other	2 217	....	....	....	....	....	....	....	....
Transportation services, debit	3 205	**−617.9**	**−641.0**	**−717.7**	**−885.4**	**−987.6**	**−1,113.6**	**−785.4**	**−725.2**
Passenger	3 850	*−17.4*	*−31.7*	*−40.8*	*−41.5*	*−41.7*	*−43.9*	*−43.0*	*−42.2*
Freight	3 851	*−467.1*	*−499.6*	*−572.1*	*−666.4*	*−775.1*	*−894.0*	*−611.5*	*−614.8*
Other	3 852	*−133.4*	*−109.7*	*−104.9*	*−177.5*	*−170.8*	*−175.7*	*−130.9*	*−68.3*
Sea transport, passenger	3 207	....	....	....	....	....	....	....	....
Sea transport, freight	3 208	....	....	....	....	....	....	....	....
Sea transport, other	3 209	....	....	....	....	....	....	....	....
Air transport, passenger	3 211	....	....	....	....	....	....	....	....
Air transport, freight	3 212	....	....	....	....	....	....	....	....
Air transport, other	3 213	....	....	....	....	....	....	....	....
Other transport, passenger	3 215	....	....	....	....	....	....	....	....
Other transport, freight	3 216	....	....	....	....	....	....	....	....
Other transport, other	3 217	....	....	....	....	....	....	....	....
Travel, credit	2 236	**1,355.1**	**1,438.0**	**1,545.2**	**1,870.1**	**1,910.0**	**1,975.8**	**1,925.5**	**2,001.3**
Business travel	2 237	....	....	....	....	....	....	....	....
Personal travel	2 240	....	....	....	....	....	....	....	....
Travel, debit	3 236	**−252.4**	**−286.2**	**−249.5**	**−273.4**	**−298.2**	**−268.2**	**−216.4**	**−192.5**
Business travel	3 237	....	....	....	....	....	....	....	....
Personal travel	3 240	....	....	....	....	....	....	....	....
Other services, credit	2 200 BA	**308.3**	**361.8**	**333.4**	**319.7**	**349.4**	**350.4**	**380.9**	**337.5**
Communications	2 245	144.6	192.8	148.4	147.8	157.2	136.0	151.1	129.0
Construction	2 249	....	....	....	....	....	....	....	....
Insurance	2 253	7.8	9.1	14.2	13.8	12.4	10.6	8.4	5.5
Financial	2 260	26.3	27.7	50.4	40.4	66.9	42.5	52.6	34.1
Computer and information	2 262	36.0	33.1	34.5	28.8	27.3	29.2	36.6	38.4
Royalties and licence fees	2 266	12.0	9.7	12.7	12.0	14.9	16.6	9.1	4.9
Other business services	2 268	26.4	26.3	9.6	10.5	4.7	44.6	53.6	54.7
Personal, cultural, and recreational	2 287	20.4	28.4	29.6	31.2	29.1	38.6	34.5	37.3
Government, n.i.e.	2 291	34.8	34.6	34.1	35.2	37.0	32.4	35.0	33.6
Other services, debit	3 200 BA	**−715.8**	**−791.5**	**−754.8**	**−862.2**	**−995.9**	**−985.3**	**−878.8**	**−906.7**
Communications	3 245	−45.9	−48.4	−47.2	−79.6	−72.4	−56.4	−74.8	−70.3
Construction	3 249	−4.8	−4.8	−4.8	−4.8	−4.8	−4.8	−4.8	−72.6
Insurance	3 253	−97.3	−124.3	−133.8	−168.2	−180.2	−194.6	−154.2	−152.5
Financial	3 260	−16.3	−32.0	−34.2	−42.7	−54.9	−42.2	−46.3	−47.1
Computer and information	3 262	−20.4	−75.1	−17.2	−23.7	−25.8	−24.1	−42.3	−36.4
Royalties and licence fees	3 266	−10.8	−9.1	−11.0	−11.2	−60.4	−48.2	−44.8	−36.3
Other business services	3 268	−469.5	−447.1	−458.3	−476.1	−539.3	−546.4	−445.2	−420.2
Personal, cultural, and recreational	3 287	−2.4	−2.5	−2.0	−4.4	−2.2	−5.9	−9.8	−13.5
Government, n.i.e.	3 291	−48.4	−48.2	−46.4	−51.6	−56.1	−62.8	−56.6	−57.9

Table 2 (Continued). STANDARD PRESENTATION, 2003–2010

(Millions of U.S. dollars)

	Code	2003	2004	2005	2006	2007	2008	2009	2010
C. INCOME	4 300	**−571.4**	**−582.5**	**−676.2**	**−615.6**	**−661.6**	**−568.3**	**−667.9**	**−494.6**
Total credit	2 300	*217.6*	*269.6*	*327.9*	*378.4*	*520.7*	*487.9*	*235.0*	*243.2*
Total debit	3 300	*−789.0*	*−852.1*	*−1,004.1*	*−994.0*	*−1,182.3*	*−1,056.2*	*−902.9*	*−737.8*
Compensation of employees, credit	2 310	**110.1**	**135.4**	**140.4**	**154.3**	**157.8**	**135.1**	**99.2**	**120.3**
Compensation of employees, debit	3 310	**−39.4**	**−51.0**	**−51.8**	**−58.3**	**−93.0**	**−51.4**	**−31.6**	**−31.2**
Investment income, credit	2 320	**107.5**	**134.2**	**187.5**	**224.0**	**363.0**	**352.8**	**135.8**	**122.9**
Direct investment income	2 330	8.4	24.9	24.4	−.3	9.6	13.9	10.9	5.2
Dividends and distributed branch profits	2 332	8.4	24.9	24.4	−.3	9.6	13.9	10.9	5.2
Reinvested earnings and undistributed branch profits	2 333	....	....	....	....	....	....	....	....
Income on debt (interest)	2 334	....	....	....	....	....	....	....	....
Portfolio investment income	2 339	14.8	35.9	56.3	73.8	176.7	209.6	71.2	71.6
Income on equity	2 340	....	....	....	....	....	....	....	....
Income on bonds and notes	2 350	....	....	....	....	....	....	....	....
Income on money market instruments	2 360	....	....	....	....	....	....	....	....
Other investment income	2 370	84.3	73.3	106.9	150.6	176.7	129.4	53.7	46.2
Investment income, debit	3 320	**−749.6**	**−801.1**	**−952.4**	**−935.7**	**−1,089.3**	**−1,004.8**	**−871.3**	**−706.6**
Direct investment income	3 330	−326.3	−361.6	−453.7	−375.6	−532.6	−376.2	−231.8	−127.0
Dividends and distributed branch profits	3 332	−128.6	−175.8	−241.0	−228.8	−316.6	−250.1	−51.3	−61.2
Reinvested earnings and undistributed branch profits	3 333	−158.1	−178.0	−201.6	−132.1	−177.3	−117.5	−161.8	−60.1
Income on debt (interest)	3 334	−39.6	−7.8	−11.0	−14.7	−38.7	−8.6	−18.7	−5.7
Portfolio investment income	3 339	−25.2	−18.6	−35.2	−42.3	−27.1	−19.5	−13.3	−15.0
Income on equity	3 340	....	....	....	....	....	....	....	....
Income on bonds and notes	3 350	....	....	....	....	....	....	....	....
Income on money market instruments	3 360	....	....	....	....	....	....	....	....
Other investment income	3 370	−398.1	−421.0	−463.5	−517.8	−529.6	−609.1	−626.2	−564.7
D. CURRENT TRANSFERS	4 379	**1,189.1**	**1,446.3**	**1,578.4**	**1,748.6**	**2,039.9**	**2,149.8**	**1,858.4**	**2,010.0**
Credit	2 379	**1,523.5**	**1,892.1**	**1,935.5**	**2,088.5**	**2,385.7**	**2,488.8**	**2,122.0**	**2,292.9**
General government	2 380	110.0	163.5	141.8	152.1	141.2	107.2	155.9	209.9
Other sectors	2 390	1,413.5	1,728.6	1,793.7	1,936.4	2,244.4	2,381.6	1,966.2	2,083.0
Workers' remittances	2 391	1,269.5	1,465.8	1,621.2	1,769.4	1,964.3	2,021.5	1,790.3	1,906.2
Other current transfers	2 392	144.0	262.8	172.4	167.0	280.1	360.1	175.9	176.8
Debit	3 379	**−334.4**	**−445.9**	**−357.0**	**−339.9**	**−345.8**	**−339.0**	**−263.6**	**−282.9**
General government	3 380	−4.8	−3.6	−4.8	−6.7	−8.3	−6.5	−12.0	−15.6
Other sectors	3 390	−329.6	−442.3	−352.2	−333.2	−337.5	−332.5	−251.6	−267.2
Workers' remittances	3 391	−282.8	−339.9	−316.9	−299.6	−303.2	−313.2	−237.4	−248.1
Other current transfers	3 392	−46.8	−102.3	−35.3	−33.6	−34.3	−19.3	−14.2	−19.1
CAPITAL AND FINANCIAL ACCOUNT	4 996	**745.0**	**523.3**	**1,061.5**	**1,080.1**	**1,698.6**	**3,143.6**	**1,330.8**	**763.0**
CAPITAL ACCOUNT	4 994	**.1**	**2.2**	**−18.3**	**−27.7**	**−35.5**	**18.1**	**20.7**	**−22.1**
Total credit	2 994	*19.3*	*35.8*	*22.5*	*26.8*	*22.2*	*72.6*	*64.2*	*21.4*
Total debit	3 994	*−19.2*	*−33.6*	*−40.8*	*−54.5*	*−57.7*	*−54.5*	*−43.4*	*−43.4*
Capital transfers, credit	2 400	**18.9**	**35.8**	**22.5**	**26.8**	**22.2**	**72.6**	**64.2**	**21.4**
General government	2 401	.1	13.8	.3	4.1	.7	48.6	45.3	4.2
Debt forgiveness	2 402	....	....	....	....	....	....	....	....
Other capital transfers	2 410	.1	13.8	.3	4.1	.7	48.6	45.3	4.2
Other sectors	2 430	18.8	22.0	22.2	22.7	21.5	24.0	18.9	17.1
Migrants' transfers	2 431	18.8	22.0	22.2	22.7	21.5	24.0	18.9	17.1
Debt forgiveness	2 432	....	....	....	....	....	....	....	....
Other capital transfers	2 440	....	....	....	....	....	....	....	....
Capital transfers, debit	3 400	**−19.2**	**−33.6**	**−40.8**	**−54.5**	**−57.7**	**−54.5**	**−43.4**	**−43.4**
General government	3 401	....	....	....	....	....	....	....	....
Debt forgiveness	3 402	....	....	....	....	....	....	....	....
Other capital transfers	3 410	....	....	....	....	....	....	....	....
Other sectors	3 430	−19.2	−33.6	−40.8	−54.5	−57.7	−54.5	−43.4	−43.4
Migrants' transfers	3 431	−19.2	−33.6	−40.8	−54.5	−57.7	−54.5	−43.4	−43.4
Debt forgiveness	3 432	....	....	....	....	....	....	....	....
Other capital transfers	3 440	....	....	....	....	....	....	....	....
Nonproduced nonfinancial assets, credit	2 480	**.4**	....	....	....	....	....	....	....
Nonproduced nonfinancial assets, debit	3 480	....	....	....	....	....	....	....	....

Jamaica 343

Table 2 (Continued). STANDARD PRESENTATION, 2003–2010

(Millions of U.S. dollars)

	Code	2003	2004	2005	2006	2007	2008	2009	2010
FINANCIAL ACCOUNT	4 995	**744.9**	**521.1**	**1,079.8**	**1,107.8**	**1,734.1**	**3,125.5**	**1,310.1**	**785.1**
A. DIRECT INVESTMENT	4 500	**604.4**	**541.6**	**581.5**	**796.8**	**751.5**	**1,360.7**	**479.8**	**169.5**
Direct investment abroad	4 505	**−116.3**	**−60.0**	**−101.0**	**−85.4**	**−115.0**	**−75.9**	**−61.1**	**−58.2**
Equity capital	4 510	−79.1	−17.7	−56.4	−45.6	−60.4	−15.9	−5.4	−16.3
Claims on affiliated enterprises	4 515	−79.1	−17.7	−56.4	−45.6	−60.4	−15.9	−5.4	−16.3
Liabilities to affiliated enterprises	4 520	....	....	....	....	....	....	....	....
Reinvested earnings	4 525	....	....	....	....	....	....	....	....
Other capital	4 530	−37.2	−42.2	−44.6	−39.8	−54.6	−60.0	−55.7	−41.9
Claims on affiliated enterprises	4 535	....	....	....	....	....	....	....	....
Liabilities to affiliated enterprises	4 540	−37.2	−42.2	−44.6	−39.8	−54.6	−60.0	−55.7	−41.9
Direct investment in Jamaica	4 555	**720.7**	**601.6**	**682.5**	**882.2**	**866.5**	**1,436.6**	**540.9**	**227.7**
Equity capital	4 560	538.7	336.3	458.3	740.1	540.5	1,204.2	278.5	123.2
Claims on direct investors	4 565	....	....	....	....	....	....	....	....
Liabilities to direct investors	4 570	538.7	336.3	458.3	740.1	540.5	1,204.2	278.5	123.2
Reinvested earnings	4 575	158.1	178.0	201.6	132.1	177.3	117.5	161.8	60.1
Other capital	4 580	23.9	87.3	22.7	10.0	148.7	114.9	100.6	44.4
Claims on direct investors	4 585	....	....	....	....	....	....	....	....
Liabilities to direct investors	4 590	23.9	87.3	22.7	10.0	148.7	114.9	100.6	44.4
B. PORTFOLIO INVESTMENT	4 600	**−285.6**	**96.0**	**−126.0**	**−128.5**	**−640.4**	**−32.8**	**−352.1**	**−352.2**
Assets	4 602	**−1,105.2**	**−1,132.8**	**−1,406.4**	**−506.4**	**−1,768.6**	**−813.8**	**−731.7**	**−1,107.9**
Equity securities	4 610	....	....	....	....	....	....	....	....
Monetary authorities	4 611	....	....	....	....	....	....	....	....
General government	4 612	....	....	....	....	....	....	....	....
Banks	4 613	....	....	....	....	....	....	....	....
Other sectors	4 614	....	....	....	....	....	....	....	....
Debt securities	4 619	−1,105.2	−1,132.8	−1,406.4	−506.4	−1,768.6	−813.8	−731.7	−1,107.9
Bonds and notes	4 620	−1,105.2	−1,132.8	−1,406.4	−506.4	−1,768.6	−813.8	−731.7	−1,107.9
Monetary authorities	4 621	....	....	....	....	....	....	....	....
General government	4 622	....	....	....	....	....	....	....	....
Banks	4 623	....	....	....	....	....	....	....	....
Other sectors	4 624	−1,105.2	−1,132.8	−1,406.4	−506.4	−1,768.6	−813.8	−731.7	−1,107.9
Money market instruments	4 630	....	....	....	....	....	....	....	....
Monetary authorities	4 631	....	....	....	....	....	....	....	....
General government	4 632	....	....	....	....	....	....	....	....
Banks	4 633	....	....	....	....	....	....	....	....
Other sectors	4 634	....	....	....	....	....	....	....	....
Liabilities	4 652	**819.6**	**1,228.8**	**1,280.4**	**377.9**	**1,128.1**	**781.1**	**379.5**	**755.7**
Equity securities	4 660	....	....	....	....	....	....	....	....
Banks	4 663	....	....	....	....	....	....	....	....
Other sectors	4 664	....	....	....	....	....	....	....	....
Debt securities	4 669	819.6	1,228.8	1,280.4	377.9	1,128.1	781.1	379.5	755.7
Bonds and notes	4 670	819.6	1,228.8	1,280.4	377.9	1,128.1	781.1	379.5	755.7
Monetary authorities	4 671	....	....	....	....	....	....	....	....
General government	4 672	....	....	....	....	....	....	....	....
Banks	4 673	....	....	....	....	....	....	....	....
Other sectors	4 674	819.6	1,228.8	1,280.4	377.9	1,128.1	781.1	379.5	755.7
Money market instruments	4 680	....	....	....	....	....	....	....	....
Monetary authorities	4 681	....	....	....	....	....	....	....	....
General government	4 682	....	....	....	....	....	....	....	....
Banks	4 683	....	....	....	....	....	....	....	....
Other sectors	4 684	....	....	....	....	....	....	....	....
C. FINANCIAL DERIVATIVES	4 910	....	....	....	....	....	....	....	....
Monetary authorities	4 911	....	....	....	....	....	....	....	....
General government	4 912	....	....	....	....	....	....	....	....
Banks	4 913	....	....	....	....	....	....	....	....
Other sectors	4 914	....	....	....	....	....	....	....	....
Assets	4 900	....	....	....	....	....	....	....	....
Monetary authorities	4 901	....	....	....	....	....	....	....	....
General government	4 902	....	....	....	....	....	....	....	....
Banks	4 903	....	....	....	....	....	....	....	....
Other sectors	4 904	....	....	....	....	....	....	....	....
Liabilities	4 905	....	....	....	....	....	....	....	....
Monetary authorities	4 906	....	....	....	....	....	....	....	....
General government	4 907	....	....	....	....	....	....	....	....
Banks	4 908	....	....	....	....	....	....	....	....
Other sectors	4 909	....	....	....	....	....	....	....	....

Table 2 (Concluded). STANDARD PRESENTATION, 2003–2010

(Millions of U.S. dollars)

	Code	2003	2004	2005	2006	2007	2008	2009	2010
D. OTHER INVESTMENT	4 700	−21.6	569.1	852.3	669.9	1,183.3	1,692.5	1,153.1	1,399.2
Assets	4 703	−307.6	−127.4	−290.8	−269.0	−238.3	−242.2	21.0	−1,143.4
Trade credits	4 706	....	....	....	....	....	....	....	....
General government	4 707	....	....	....	....	....	....	....	....
of which: Short-term	4 709	....	....	....	....	....	....	....	....
Other sectors	4 710	....	....	....	....	....	....	....	....
of which: Short-term	4 712	....	....	....	....	....	....	....	....
Loans	4 714	....	....	....	....	....	....	....	....
Monetary authorities	4 715	....	....	....	....	....	....	....	....
of which: Short-term	4 718	....	....	....	....	....	....	....	....
General government	4 719	....	....	....	....	....	....	....	....
of which: Short-term	4 721	....	....	....	....	....	....	....	....
Banks	4 722	....	....	....	....	....	....	....	....
of which: Short-term	4 724	....	....	....	....	....	....	....	....
Other sectors	4 725	....	....	....	....	....	....	....	....
of which: Short-term	4 727	....	....	....	....	....	....	....	....
Currency and deposits	4 730	−362.8	−175.5	−274.2	−317.5	−338.2	−287.4	−334.8	−401.6
Monetary authorities	4 731	....	....	....	....	....	....	....	....
General government	4 732	....	....	....	....	....	....	....	....
Banks	4 733	−362.8	−175.5	−274.2	−317.5	−338.2	−287.4	−334.8	−401.6
Other sectors	4 734	....	....	....	....	....	....	....	....
Other assets	4 736	55.2	48.1	−16.6	48.5	99.9	45.2	355.8	−741.8
Monetary authorities	4 737	....	....	−61.3	.1	53.5	5.6	334.8	−798.7
of which: Short-term	4 739	....	....	*−61.3*	*.1*	*53.5*	*5.6*	*334.8*	*−13.4*
General government	4 740	1.2	−1.0	−1.8	.1	−.8	−.4	−15.2	9.6
of which: Short-term	4 742	....	....	....	....	....	....	....	....
Banks	4 743	....	....	....	....	....	....	....	....
of which: Short-term	4 745	....	....	....	....	....	....	....	....
Other sectors	4 746	54.0	49.1	46.5	48.4	47.2	40.1	36.2	47.3
of which: Short-term	4 748	*55.2*	*50.8*	*48.3*	*50.8*	*50.8*	*50.8*	*50.8*	*50.8*
Liabilities	4 753	**286.0**	**696.5**	**1,143.0**	**938.9**	**1,421.6**	**1,934.7**	**1,132.1**	**2,542.6**
Trade credits	4 756	10.5	−19.8	16.2	−149.9	65.8	57.0	−12.2	86.2
General government	4 757	....	....	....	....	....	....	....	....
of which: Short-term	4 759	....	....	....	....	....	....	....	....
Other sectors	4 760	10.5	−19.8	16.2	−149.9	65.8	57.0	−12.2	86.2
of which: Short-term	4 762	*10.5*	*−19.8*	*16.2*	*−149.9*	*65.8*	*57.0*	*−12.2*	*86.2*
Loans	4 764	−77.4	737.9	640.3	1,029.8	524.7	981.4	−39.3	1,523.8
Monetary authorities	4 765	−17.1	−9.1	−2.0	....	....	....	....	779.5
of which: Use of Fund credit and loans from the Fund	4 766	*−16.1*	*−8.0*	*−.9*	....	....	....	....	*779.5*
of which: Short-term	4 768	....	....	....	....	....	....	....	....
General government	4 769	−362.7	481.2	117.8	72.0	106.6	188.9	−200.4	663.5
of which: Short-term	4 771	....	....	....	....	....	....	....	....
Banks	4 772	....	....	....	....	....	....	....	....
of which: Short-term	4 774	....	....	....	....	....	....	....	....
Other sectors	4 775	302.4	265.8	524.5	957.8	418.1	792.6	161.2	80.9
of which: Short-term	4 777	....	....	....	....	....	....	....	....
Currency and deposits	4 780	350.5	−24.2	484.9	57.2	829.4	893.8	836.8	930.7
Monetary authorities	4 781	....	....	....	....	....	....	....	....
General government	4 782	....	....	....	....	....	....	....	....
Banks	4 783	395.5	143.2	405.8	357.7	252.8	765.7	152.7	195.4
Other sectors	4 784	−45.0	−167.4	79.1	−300.5	576.5	128.0	684.1	735.3
Other liabilities	4 786	2.4	2.6	1.6	1.8	1.8	2.5	346.8	1.9
Monetary authorities	4 787	....	....	....	....	....	....	345.2	....
of which: Short-term	4 789	....	....	....	....	....	....	....	....
General government	4 790	....	....	....	....	....	....	....	....
of which: Short-term	4 792	....	....	....	....	....	....	....	....
Banks	4 793	....	....	....	....	....	....	....	....
of which: Short-term	4 795	....	....	....	....	....	....	....	....
Other sectors	4 796	2.4	2.6	1.6	1.8	1.8	2.5	1.7	1.9
of which: Short-term	4 798	....	....	....	....	....	....	....	....
E. RESERVE ASSETS	4 802	**447.7**	**−685.6**	**−227.9**	**−230.3**	**439.8**	**105.0**	**29.3**	**−431.4**
Monetary gold	4 812	....	....	....	....	....	....	....	....
Special drawing rights	4 811	.9	....	.1	−.2	....	.2	−345.1	10.6
Reserve position in the Fund	4 810	....	....	....	....	....	....	....	....
Foreign exchange	4 803	446.8	−685.6	−228.0	−230.1	439.8	104.8	374.4	−442.0
Other claims	4 813	....	....	....	....	....	....	....	....
NET ERRORS AND OMISSIONS	4 998	**28.3**	**−21.7**	**9.8**	**102.8**	**339.5**	**−350.3**	**−203.3**	**171.0**

Table 3. INTERNATIONAL INVESTMENT POSITION (End-period stocks), 2003–2010

(Millions of U.S. dollars)

	Code	2003	2004	2005	2006	2007	2008	2009	2010
ASSETS..	8 995 C.	....	....	**3,616.4**	**4,463.6**	**5,105.5**	**5,181.7**	**4,271.9**	**5,775.0**
Direct investment abroad........................	8 505 ..	....	....	**48.6**	**96.0**	**69.0**	**62.2**	**220.1**	**151.5**
Equity capital and reinvested earnings............	8 506 ..	....	....	....	....	....	....	....	....
Claims on affiliated enterprises..................	8 507 ..	....	....	....	....	....	....	....	....
Liabilities to affiliated enterprises..............	8 508 ..	....	....	....	....	....	....	....	....
Other capital..	8 530 ..	....	....	....	....	....	....	....	....
Claims on affiliated enterprises..................	8 535 ..	....	....	....	....	....	....	....	....
Liabilities to affiliated enterprises..............	8 540 ..	....	....	....	....	....	....	....	....
Portfolio investment................................	8 602 ..	....	....	**602.6**	**1,114.8**	**1,895.5**	**2,072.2**	**1,430.4**	**1,590.6**
Equity securities.....................................	8 610 ..	....	....	....	....	....	....	55.8	56.7
Monetary authorities............................	8 611 ..	....	....	....	....	....	....	....	....
General government.............................	8 612 ..	....	....	....	....	....	....	....	....
Banks..	8 613 ..	....	....	....	....	....	....	....	....
Other sectors....................................	8 614 ..	....	....	....	....	....	....	....	....
Debt securities......................................	8 619 ..	....	....					1,374.5	1,533.9
Bonds and notes.................................	8 620 ..	....	....						
Monetary authorities..........................	8 621 ..	....	....						
General government...........................	8 622 ..	....	....						
Banks..	8 623 ..	....	....						
Other sectors..................................	8 624 ..	....	....						
Money market instruments.....................	8 630 ..	....	....						
Monetary authorities..........................	8 631 ..	....	....						
General government...........................	8 632 ..	....	....						
Banks..	8 633 ..	....	....						
Other sectors..................................	8 634 ..	....							
Financial derivatives...............................	8 900 ..	....	....	**19.4**	**2.8**	**31.0**	**61.2**	**2.4**	**8.9**
Monetary authorities..............................	8 901 ..	....	....	....	....	....	....	....	....
General government...............................	8 902 ..	....	....	....	....	....	....	....	....
Banks..	8 903 ..	....	....	....	....	....	....	....	....
Other sectors.......................................	8 904 ..	....	....	....	....	....	....	....	....
Other investment...................................	8 703 ..	....	....	**858.5**	**932.3**	**1,232.0**	**1,213.0**	**873.9**	**1,853.8**
Trade credits..	8 706 ..	....	....	30.5	37.6	120.3	37.2	63.2	113.6
General government.............................	8 707 ..	....	....	....	....	....	....	....	....
of which: Short-term.........................	8 709 ..	....	....	....	....	....	....	....	....
Other sectors....................................	8 710 ..	....	....	....	....	....	....	....	....
of which: Short-term.........................	8 712 ..	....	....	....	....	....	....	....	....
Loans..	8 714 ..	....	....	26.9	29.4	67.2	357.2	64.2	44.4
Monetary authorities............................	8 715 ..	....	....	....	....	....	....	....	....
of which: Short-term.........................	8 718 ..	....	....	....	....	....	....	....	....
General government.............................	8 719 ..	....	....	....	....	....	....	....	....
of which: Short-term.........................	8 721 ..	....	....	....	....	....	....	....	....
Banks..	8 722 ..	....	....	....	....	....	....	....	....
of which: Short-term.........................	8 724 ..	....	....	....	....	....	....	....	....
Other sectors....................................	8 725 ..	....	....	....	....	....	....	....	....
of which: Short-term.........................	8 727 ..	....	....	....	....	....	....	....	....
Currency and deposits.............................	8 730 ..	....	....	623.2	594.4	959.6	755.5	575.4	736.8
Monetary authorities............................	8 731 ..	....	....	....	....	....	....	....	....
General government.............................	8 732 ..	....	....	....	....	....	....	....	....
Banks..	8 733 ..	....	....	....	....	....	....	....	....
Other sectors....................................	8 734 ..	....	....	....	....	....	....	....	....
Other assets..	8 736 ..	....	....	177.9	270.9	84.8	63.1	171.1	958.9
Monetary authorities............................	8 737 ..	....	....	....	....	....	....	....	....
of which: Short-term.........................	8 739 ..	....	....	....	....	....	....	....	....
General government.............................	8 740 ..	....	....	....	....	....	....	....	....
of which: Short-term.........................	8 742 ..	....	....	....	....	....	....	....	....
Banks..	8 743 ..	....	....	....	....	....	....	....	....
of which: Short-term.........................	8 745 ..	....	....	....	....	....	....	....	....
Other sectors....................................	8 746 ..	....	....	....	....	....	....	....	....
of which: Short-term.........................	8 748 ..	....	....	....	....	....	....	....	....
Reserve assets.....................................	8 802 ..	....	....	**2,087.4**	**2,317.8**	**1,878.1**	**1,773.0**	**1,745.1**	**2,170.3**
Monetary gold.......................................	8 812 ..	....	....	....	....	....	....	....	....
Special drawing rights..............................	8 811 ..	.1	.1	....	.3	.3	.1	346.5	329.7
Reserve position in the Fund......................	8 810 ..	....	....	....	....	....	....	....	....
Foreign exchange....................................	8 803 ..	....	....	2,087.4	2,317.6	1,877.7	1,772.9	1,398.6	1,840.6
Other claims...	8 813 ..	....	....	....	....	....	....	....	....

Table 3 (Concluded). INTERNATIONAL INVESTMENT POSITION (End-period stocks), 2003–2010

(Millions of U.S. dollars)

	Code	2003	2004	2005	2006	2007	2008	2009	2010
LIABILITIES..	8 995 D	....	....	**14,440.9**	**16,696.3**	**18,550.7**	**20,488.7**	**21,196.3**	**23,693.6**
Direct investment in Jamaica..................	8 555	....	....	**6,918.5**	**7,800.7**	**8,667.2**	**10,103.8**	**10,627.5**	**10,855.2**
Equity capital and reinvested earnings..........	8 556	....	....	....	....	....	....	....	....
Claims on direct investors..........................	8 557	....	....	....	....	....	....	....	....
Liabilities to direct investors......................	8 558	....	....	....	....	....	....	....	....
Other capital..	8 580	....	....	....	....	....	....	....	....
Claims on direct investors..........................	8 585	....	....	....	....	....	....	....	....
Liabilities to direct investors......................	8 590	....	....	....	....	....	....	....	....
Portfolio investment...............................	8 652	....	....	**357.5**	**518.5**	**633.4**	**422.5**	**414.4**	**586.8**
Equity securities..	8 660	....	....	....	....	....	....	414.4	507.0
Banks..	8 663	....	....	....	....	....	....	....	....
Other sectors..	8 664	....	....	....	....	....	....	....	....
Debt securities..	8 669	....	....	....	....	....	....	....	79.8
Bonds and notes..	8 670	....	....	....	....	....	....	....	....
Monetary authorities..............................	8 671	....	....	....	....	....	....	....	....
General government................................	8 672	....	....	....	....	....	....	....	....
Banks..	8 673	....	....	....	....	....	....	....	....
Other sectors..	8 674	....	....	....	....	....	....	....	....
Money market instruments........................	8 680	....	....	....	....	....	....	....	....
Monetary authorities..............................	8 681	....	....	....	....	....	....	....	....
General government................................	8 682	....	....	....	....	....	....	....	....
Banks..	8 683	....	....	....	....	....	....	....	....
Other sectors..	8 684	....	....	....	....	....	....	....	....
Financial derivatives..............................	8 905	....	....	**11.3**	....	**23.3**	**70.3**	**19.4**	**20.6**
Monetary authorities....................................	8 906	....	....	....	....	....	....	....	....
General government......................................	8 907	....	....	....	....	....	....	....	....
Banks..	8 908	....	....	....	....	....	....	....	....
Other sectors..	8 909	....	....	....	....	....	....	....	....
Other investment....................................	8 753	....	....	**7,153.5**	**8,377.1**	**9,226.8**	**9,892.1**	**10,135.0**	**12,231.1**
Trade credits..	8 756	....	....	48.4	654.9	601.4	738.1	915.6	1,311.3
General government......................................	8 757	....	....	....	....	....	....	....	....
of which: Short-term..............................	8 759	....	....	....	....	....	....	....	....
Other sectors..	8 760	....	....	....	....	....	....	....	....
of which: Short-term..............................	8 762	....	....	....	....	....	....	....	....
Loans..	8 764	....	....	6,545.1	6,879.7	7,674.4	8,030.9	7,891.8	9,668.1
Monetary authorities....................................	8 765	....	....	....	....	....	....	....	785.3
of which: Use of Fund credit and loans from the Fund....	8 766	*8.9*	*.9*	....	....	....	....	....	*785.3*
of which: Short-term..............................	8 768	....	....	....	....	....	....	....	....
General government......................................	8 769	....	....	....	....	....	....	....	....
of which: Short-term..............................	8 771	....	....	....	....	....	....	....	....
Banks..	8 772	....	....	....	....	....	....	....	....
of which: Short-term..............................	8 774	....	....	....	....	....	....	....	....
Other sectors..	8 775	....	....	....	....	....	....	....	....
of which: Short-term..............................	8 777	....	....	....	....	....	....	....	....
Currency and deposits................................	8 780	....	....	386.7	777.9	863.1	882.8	734.1	789.6
Monetary authorities....................................	8 781	....	....	....	....	....	....	....	....
General government......................................	8 782	....	....	....	....	....	....	....	....
Banks..	8 783	....	....	....	....	....	....	....	....
Other sectors..	8 784	....	....	....	....	....	....	....	....
Other liabilities..	8 786	....	....	173.3	64.6	87.9	240.4	593.5	462.1
Monetary authorities....................................	8 787	....	....	....	....	....	....	303.4	303.4
of which: Short-term..............................	8 789	....	....	....	....	....	....	....	....
General government......................................	8 790	....	....	....	....	....	....	....	....
of which: Short-term..............................	8 792	....	....	....	....	....	....	....	....
Banks..	8 793	....	....	....	....	....	....	....	....
of which: Short-term..............................	8 795	....	....	....	....	....	....	....	....
Other sectors..	8 796	....	....	....	....	....	....	....	....
of which: Short-term..............................	8 798	....	....	....	....	....	....	....	....
NET INTERNATIONAL INVESTMENT POSITION........	8 995	....	....	**−10,824.4**	**−12,232.7**	**−13,445.3**	**−15,307.0**	**−16,924.5**	**−17,918.6**
Conversion rates: Jamaica dollars per U.S. dollar (end of period)...........................	0 102	60.517	61.450	64.381	67.032	70.397	80.217	89.328	85.601

Table 1. ANALYTIC PRESENTATION, 2003–2010

(Billions of U.S. dollars)

	Code	2003	2004	2005	2006	2007	2008	2009	2010
A. Current Account[1]	4 993 Z.	**136.22**	**172.06**	**165.78**	**170.52**	**210.49**	**156.63**	**142.19**	**195.75**
Goods: exports f.o.b.	2 100 ..	449.12	539.00	567.57	615.81	678.09	746.47	545.28	730.08
Goods: imports f.o.b.	3 100 ..	−342.72	−406.87	−473.61	−534.51	−573.34	−708.34	−501.65	−639.10
Balance on Goods	4 100 ..	*106.40*	*132.13*	*93.96*	*81.30*	*104.75*	*38.13*	*43.63*	*90.97*
Services: credit	2 200 ..	77.62	97.61	110.21	117.30	129.12	148.75	128.34	141.46
Services: debit	3 200 ..	−111.53	−135.51	−134.26	−135.56	−150.37	−169.54	−148.72	−157.57
Balance on Goods and Services	4 991 ..	*72.49*	*94.23*	*69.91*	*63.05*	*83.50*	*17.34*	*23.25*	*74.86*
Income: credit	2 300 ..	95.21	113.33	141.06	165.80	199.46	212.10	175.22	173.68
Income: debit	3 300 ..	−23.97	−27.63	−37.62	−47.65	−60.96	−59.76	−43.88	−40.39
Balance on Goods, Services, and Income	4 992 ..	*143.73*	*179.93*	*173.36*	*181.20*	*222.00*	*169.68*	*154.59*	*208.15*
Current transfers: credit	2 379 Z.	6.51	6.91	9.74	6.18	6.77	9.10	9.52	10.09
Current transfers: debit	3 379 ..	−14.02	−14.78	−17.31	−16.87	−18.28	−22.15	−21.91	−22.48
B. Capital Account[1]	4 994 Z.	**−4.00**	**−4.79**	**−4.88**	**−4.76**	**−4.03**	**−5.47**	**−4.99**	**−4.96**
Capital account: credit	2 994 Z.	.39	.44	.83	.75	.69	.63	1.11	.88
Capital account: debit	3 994 ..	−4.39	−5.23	−5.71	−5.51	−4.72	−6.10	−6.10	−5.85
Total, Groups A Plus B	4 981 ..	*132.22*	*167.27*	*160.91*	*165.76*	*206.46*	*151.17*	*137.20*	*190.79*
C. Financial Account[1]	4 995 W.	**71.92**	**22.51**	**−122.68**	**−102.34**	**−187.24**	**−172.62**	**−130.15**	**−130.47**
Direct investment abroad	4 505 ..	−28.77	−30.96	−45.44	−50.17	−73.49	−130.82	−74.62	−57.22
Direct investment in Japan	4 555 Z.	6.24	7.81	3.21	−6.78	22.18	24.55	11.83	−1.36
Portfolio investment assets	4 602 ..	−176.29	−173.77	−196.40	−71.04	−123.45	−189.64	−160.25	−262.64
Equity securities	4 610 ..	−4.47	−31.47	−22.97	−25.04	−26.09	−65.56	−29.69	−21.46
Debt securities	4 619 ..	−171.82	−142.30	−173.43	−46.00	−97.36	−124.08	−130.56	−241.18
Portfolio investment liabilities	4 652 Z.	81.18	196.72	183.13	198.56	196.58	−102.96	−56.26	111.64
Equity securities	4 660 ..	87.78	98.28	131.32	71.44	45.45	−69.69	12.43	40.33
Debt securities	4 669 Z.	−6.59	98.44	51.81	127.12	151.13	−33.27	−68.69	71.31
Financial derivatives	4 910 ..	5.58	2.41	−6.53	2.46	2.80	24.79	10.55	11.94
Financial derivatives assets	4 900 ..	64.96	56.44	230.59	143.48	188.50	271.95	333.85	403.46
Financial derivatives liabilities	4 905 ..	−59.38	−54.04	−237.12	−141.03	−185.71	−247.16	−323.30	−391.51
Other investment assets	4 703 ..	149.89	−48.00	−106.60	−86.24	−260.78	139.46	202.75	−130.14
Monetary authorities	4 701 ..	....	....	....	....	....	....	....	....
General government	4 704 ..	4.49	3.88	14.29	3.48	−.36	−6.90	−9.78	−13.01
Banks	4 705 ..	140.78	3.24	−29.80	−7.50	−195.65	−39.12	202.63	−116.65
Other sectors	4 728 ..	4.62	−55.12	−91.08	−82.22	−64.78	185.48	9.90	−.49
Other investment liabilities	4 753 W.	34.10	68.31	45.94	−89.12	48.92	61.99	−64.15	197.30
Monetary authorities	4 753 WA	....	....	....	....	....	....	17.80	....
General government	4 753 ZB	5.14	.99	12.24	−25.44	1.28	120.36	−108.95	−10.74
Banks	4 753 ZC	−26.22	42.73	−9.38	−48.83	.32	60.87	49.54	93.24
Other sectors	4 753 ZD	55.17	24.59	43.07	−14.85	47.31	−119.24	−22.55	114.80
Total, Groups A Through C	4 983 ..	*204.14*	*189.78*	*38.22*	*63.42*	*19.22*	*−21.46*	*7.05*	*60.32*
D. Net Errors and Omissions	4 998 ..	**−16.99**	**−28.92**	**−15.90**	**−31.44**	**17.30**	**52.34**	**19.87**	**−16.46**
Total, Groups A Through D	4 984 ..	*187.15*	*160.85*	*22.33*	*31.98*	*36.52*	*30.88*	*26.92*	*43.85*
E. Reserves and Related Items	4 802 A.	**−187.15**	**−160.85**	**−22.33**	**−31.98**	**−36.52**	**−30.88**	**−26.92**	**−43.85**
Reserve assets	4 802 ..	−187.15	−160.85	−22.33	−31.98	−36.52	−30.88	−26.92	−43.85
Use of Fund credit and loans	4 766 ..	....	....	....	....	....	....	....	....
Exceptional financing	4 920 ..	....	....	....	....	....	....	....	....
Conversion rates: yen per U.S. dollar	0 101 ..	**115.93**	**108.19**	**110.22**	**116.30**	**117.75**	**103.36**	**93.57**	**87.78**

[1] Excludes components that have been classified in the categories of Group E.

Table 2. STANDARD PRESENTATION, 2003–2010

(Billions of U.S. dollars)

	Code	2003	2004	2005	2006	2007	2008	2009	2010
CURRENT ACCOUNT	4 993	**136.22**	**172.06**	**165.78**	**170.52**	**210.49**	**156.63**	**142.19**	**195.75**
A. GOODS	4 100	**106.40**	**132.13**	**93.96**	**81.30**	**104.75**	**38.13**	**43.63**	**90.97**
Credit	2 100	**449.12**	**539.00**	**567.57**	**615.81**	**678.09**	**746.47**	**545.28**	**730.08**
General merchandise: exports f.o.b.	2 110	441.70	530.97	558.70	605.02	664.95	729.81	532.74	714.07
Goods for processing: exports f.o.b.	2 150	5.03	5.27	4.84	4.55	5.00	5.07	4.56	4.88
Repairs on goods	2 160	.21	.20	.27	.30	.34	.42	.31	.22
Goods procured in ports by carriers	2 170	1.31	1.68	2.36	2.97	4.22	6.23	3.33	4.86
Nonmonetary gold	2 180	.87	.88	1.41	2.98	3.57	4.94	4.34	6.04
Debit	3 100	**−342.72**	**−406.87**	**−473.61**	**−534.51**	**−573.34**	**−708.34**	**−501.65**	**−639.10**
General merchandise: imports f.o.b.	3 110	−327.21	−389.14	−453.43	−523.19	−545.76	−675.85	−481.57	−615.24
Goods for processing: imports f.o.b.	3 150	−8.99	−9.73	−9.03	−4.64	−12.78	−13.70	−11.12	−11.73
Repairs on goods	3 160	−.37	−.46	−.57	−.27	−.54	−.80	−.47	−.47
Goods procured in ports by carriers	3 170	−5.62	−6.58	−9.48	−6.20	−13.55	−17.08	−7.99	−10.98
Nonmonetary gold	3 180	−.54	−.94	−1.11	−.21	−.71	−.91	−.49	−.69
B. SERVICES	4 200	**−33.91**	**−37.90**	**−24.05**	**−18.26**	**−21.25**	**−20.79**	**−20.38**	**−16.11**
Total credit	2 200	*77.62*	*97.61*	*110.21*	*117.30*	*129.12*	*148.75*	*128.34*	*141.46*
Total debit	3 200	*−111.53*	*−135.51*	*−134.26*	*−135.56*	*−150.37*	*−169.54*	*−148.72*	*−157.57*
Transportation services, credit	2 205	**26.50**	**32.15**	**35.75**	**37.65**	**42.02**	**46.84**	**31.61**	**38.95**
Passenger	2 850	*2.63*	*3.08*	*3.12*	*3.02*	*3.08*	*2.96*	*2.21*	*2.13*
Freight	2 851	*18.38*	*22.52*	*25.62*	*28.10*	*32.50*	*37.67*	*23.98*	*30.42*
Other	2 852	*5.50*	*6.55*	*7.01*	*6.53*	*6.44*	*6.20*	*5.42*	*6.40*
Sea transport, passenger	2 207	.01	.01	.02	.01	.02	.02	.01	.02
Sea transport, freight	2 208	15.85	19.44	22.61	25.05	29.21	34.41	21.54	27.54
Sea transport, other	2 209	2.48	2.70	2.88	2.59	2.70	2.49	2.15	2.58
Air transport, passenger	2 211	2.62	3.07	3.11	3.01	3.06	2.94	2.20	2.12
Air transport, freight	2 212	2.52	3.08	3.00	3.04	3.29	3.25	2.43	2.87
Air transport, other	2 213	3.02	3.85	4.13	3.93	3.74	3.71	3.27	3.82
Other transport, passenger	2 215	....	....	....	....	....	....	....	....
Other transport, freight	2 216	.01	....	....	.01	....	.02	.02	.01
Other transport, other	2 217	....	....	....	....	....	.01	....	....
Transportation services, debit	3 205	**−34.20**	**−42.72**	**−40.38**	**−42.84**	**−49.04**	**−53.95**	**−40.56**	**−46.53**
Passenger	3 850	*−7.55*	*−9.92*	*−10.54*	*−10.78*	*−10.75*	*−11.07*	*−9.59*	*−11.36*
Freight	3 851	*−20.05*	*−24.87*	*−20.71*	*−22.48*	*−27.94*	*−31.80*	*−22.52*	*−25.73*
Other	3 852	*−6.59*	*−7.93*	*−9.13*	*−9.57*	*−10.35*	*−11.07*	*−8.45*	*−9.44*
Sea transport, passenger	3 207	....	....	−.01	−.05	−.05	−.06	−.05	−.05
Sea transport, freight	3 208	−17.76	−22.38	−18.06	−19.80	−25.29	−29.40	−20.87	−23.65
Sea transport, other	3 209	−5.65	−6.87	−8.00	−8.53	−9.33	−10.02	−7.88	−8.81
Air transport, passenger	3 211	−7.54	−9.91	−10.52	−10.73	−10.69	−11.01	−9.54	−11.31
Air transport, freight	3 212	−2.18	−2.44	−2.60	−2.60	−2.51	−2.28	−1.58	−1.99
Air transport, other	3 213	−.94	−1.07	−1.12	−1.04	−1.01	−1.04	−.56	−.62
Other transport, passenger	3 215	....	−.01	−.01	....	....	....	....	....
Other transport, freight	3 216	−.11	−.05	−.05	−.07	−.13	−.12	−.07	−.09
Other transport, other	3 217	....	....	−.01	....	−.01	−.01	−.01	−.01
Travel, credit	2 236	**8.85**	**11.26**	**12.43**	**8.47**	**9.35**	**10.82**	**10.33**	**13.22**
Business travel	2 237	....	3.84	4.07	2.43	2.51	2.75	1.88	2.16
Personal travel	2 240	....	7.43	8.36	6.04	6.84	8.07	8.45	11.07
Travel, debit	3 236	**−28.96**	**−38.25**	**−37.56**	**−26.88**	**−26.51**	**−27.90**	**−25.20**	**−27.95**
Business travel	3 237	....	−6.74	−7.40	−5.38	−4.94	−5.53	−5.32	−5.07
Personal travel	3 240	....	−31.51	−30.16	−21.49	−21.57	−22.37	−19.88	−22.88
Other services, credit	2 200 BA	**42.27**	**54.20**	**62.03**	**71.18**	**77.75**	**91.10**	**86.40**	**89.28**
Communications	2 245	.66	.45	.39	.44	.55	.65	.67	.73
Construction	2 249	4.55	6.87	7.22	8.98	10.32	13.81	12.44	10.66
Insurance	2 253	.37	1.07	.87	1.58	1.34	.94	.86	1.27
Financial	2 260	3.47	4.41	5.04	6.15	6.21	5.45	4.80	3.61
Computer and information	2 262	1.08	1.04	1.13	.97	.97	.95	.86	1.05
Royalties and licence fees	2 266	12.27	15.70	17.66	20.10	23.23	25.70	21.70	26.68
Other business services	2 268	18.04	21.91	27.28	30.68	32.92	41.13	42.49	42.55
Personal, cultural, and recreational	2 287	.14	.07	.10	.14	.16	.15	.16	.15
Government, n.i.e.	2 291	1.69	2.68	2.33	2.16	2.06	2.31	2.42	2.58
Other services, debit	3 200 BA	**−48.37**	**−54.54**	**−56.31**	**−65.84**	**−74.82**	**−87.69**	**−82.96**	**−83.10**
Communications	3 245	−.80	−.62	−.62	−.73	−1.03	−1.08	−1.12	−1.02
Construction	3 249	−3.38	−4.80	−4.77	−6.20	−7.94	−11.36	−11.41	−7.86
Insurance	3 253	−3.54	−3.44	−1.89	−4.57	−4.12	−5.13	−5.14	−6.82
Financial	3 260	−2.18	−2.65	−2.69	−2.99	−3.61	−3.98	−3.06	−3.15
Computer and information	3 262	−2.11	−2.19	−2.43	−3.12	−3.61	−3.97	−3.76	−3.57
Royalties and licence fees	3 266	−11.00	−13.64	−14.65	−15.50	−16.68	−18.31	−16.83	−18.77
Other business services	3 268	−23.15	−24.61	−26.50	−29.77	−34.84	−40.55	−38.82	−39.19
Personal, cultural, and recreational	3 287	−.95	−1.08	−1.11	−1.30	−1.32	−1.21	−1.06	−.93
Government, n.i.e.	3 291	−1.27	−1.50	−1.66	−1.66	−1.68	−2.10	−1.75	−1.77

Table 2 (Continued). STANDARD PRESENTATION, 2003–2010

(Billions of U.S. dollars)

	Code	2003	2004	2005	2006	2007	2008	2009	2010
C. INCOME	4 300	**71.24**	**85.70**	**103.44**	**118.16**	**138.50**	**152.34**	**131.34**	**133.29**
Total credit	2 300	*95.21*	*113.33*	*141.06*	*165.80*	*199.46*	*212.10*	*175.22*	*173.68*
Total debit	3 300	*–23.97*	*–27.63*	*–37.62*	*–47.65*	*–60.96*	*–59.76*	*–43.88*	*–40.39*
Compensation of employees, credit	2 310	**.15**	**.17**	**.17**	**.15**	**.12**	**.18**	**.17**	**.17**
Compensation of employees, debit	3 310	**–.27**	**–.29**	**–.30**	**–.18**	**–.18**	**–.20**	**–.21**	**–.23**
Investment income, credit	2 320	**95.06**	**113.16**	**140.89**	**165.65**	**199.34**	**211.92**	**175.05**	**173.50**
Direct investment income	2 330	13.11	18.96	30.37	35.12	45.09	48.39	45.36	38.30
Dividends and distributed branch profits	2 332	7.89	12.27	16.35	17.84	24.40	23.17	32.13	35.47
Reinvested earnings and undistributed branch profits	2 333	4.58	5.97	13.23	16.39	19.61	24.15	12.16	2.00
Income on debt (interest)	2 334	.64	.72	.80	.90	1.09	1.07	1.06	.83
Portfolio investment income	2 339	68.79	81.33	95.28	111.28	129.22	137.56	113.53	121.43
Income on equity	2 340	10.26	13.72	18.62	22.72	27.28	29.04	19.93	27.79
Income on bonds and notes	2 350	56.52	65.89	73.72	84.30	98.05	106.03	92.76	92.88
Income on money market instruments	2 360	2.01	1.72	2.94	4.26	3.89	2.49	.84	.76
Other investment income	2 370	13.16	12.87	15.24	19.25	25.03	25.97	16.16	13.78
Investment income, debit	3 320	**–23.70**	**–27.34**	**–37.32**	**–47.47**	**–60.78**	**–59.56**	**–43.67**	**–40.16**
Direct investment income	3 330	–5.04	–6.34	–9.48	–9.01	–14.89	–11.77	–8.77	–5.82
Dividends and distributed branch profits	3 332	–3.25	–3.99	–7.51	–6.50	–10.69	–7.41	–6.98	–8.28
Reinvested earnings and undistributed branch profits	3 333	–1.41	–1.95	–1.70	–2.25	–3.84	–3.75	–1.19	2.91
Income on debt (interest)	3 334	–.38	–.41	–.28	–.26	–.36	–.61	–.59	–.45
Portfolio investment income	3 339	–10.09	–12.63	–16.90	–21.14	–26.49	–31.39	–24.37	–27.11
Income on equity	3 340	–3.41	–6.02	–9.93	–13.88	–17.32	–20.98	–14.51	–17.19
Income on bonds and notes	3 350	–6.67	–6.61	–6.97	–7.26	–9.16	–10.41	–9.83	–9.89
Income on money market instruments	3 360	–.01	....	....	....	....	....	–.02	–.04
Other investment income	3 370	–8.57	–8.37	–10.93	–17.32	–19.40	–16.40	–10.54	–7.23
D. CURRENT TRANSFERS	4 379	**–7.51**	**–7.88**	**–7.57**	**–10.68**	**–11.51**	**–13.04**	**–12.40**	**–12.40**
Credit	2 379	**6.51**	**6.91**	**9.74**	**6.18**	**6.77**	**9.10**	**9.52**	**10.09**
General government	2 380	.19	.18	1.21	.14	.23	.30	.35	.45
Other sectors	2 390	6.32	6.73	8.53	6.05	6.54	8.80	9.17	9.64
Workers' remittances	2 391	.66	.60	.73	1.03	1.26	1.56	1.42	1.51
Other current transfers	2 392	5.66	6.13	7.80	5.02	5.28	7.25	7.75	8.13
Debit	3 379	**–14.02**	**–14.78**	**–17.31**	**–16.87**	**–18.28**	**–22.15**	**–21.91**	**–22.48**
General government	3 380	–3.88	–5.61	–5.21	–4.82	–5.13	–5.46	–6.10	–5.83
Other sectors	3 390	–10.14	–9.17	–12.10	–12.05	–13.16	–16.69	–15.82	–16.65
Workers' remittances	3 391	–1.23	–.93	–.85	–3.15	–3.46	–4.35	–3.72	–4.14
Other current transfers	3 392	–8.91	–8.25	–11.25	–8.89	–9.70	–12.34	–12.10	–12.51
CAPITAL AND FINANCIAL ACCOUNT	4 996	**–119.23**	**–143.13**	**–149.89**	**–139.08**	**–227.79**	**–208.97**	**–162.06**	**–179.29**
CAPITAL ACCOUNT	4 994	**–4.00**	**–4.79**	**–4.88**	**–4.76**	**–4.03**	**–5.47**	**–4.99**	**–4.96**
Total credit	2 994	*.39*	*.44*	*.83*	*.75*	*.69*	*.63*	*1.11*	*.88*
Total debit	3 994	*–4.39*	*–5.23*	*–5.71*	*–5.51*	*–4.72*	*–6.10*	*–6.10*	*–5.85*
Capital transfers, credit	2 400	**.28**	**.17**	**.62**	**.42**	**.20**	**.20**	**.20**	**.13**
General government	2 401	....	....	....	....	....	....	....	....
Debt forgiveness	2 402	....	....	....	....	....	....	....	....
Other capital transfers	2 410	....	....	....	....	....	....	....	....
Other sectors	2 430	.28	.16	.61	.42	.20	.20	.20	.13
Migrants' transfers	2 431	.27	.16	.18	.20	.19	.20	.18	.12
Debt forgiveness	2 432	....	....	.43	.21	....	....	....	....
Other capital transfers	2 440	.01	.01	.01	.01	.01	.01	.02	.01
Capital transfers, debit	3 400	**–2.54**	**–4.53**	**–4.57**	**–4.43**	**–3.05**	**–4.01**	**–2.76**	**–3.87**
General government	3 401	–1.55	–3.71	–4.25	–4.13	–2.23	–3.48	–2.31	–3.54
Debt forgiveness	3 402	....	....	–2.81	–3.03	–1.18	–2.29	–.10	–.03
Other capital transfers	3 410	–1.55	–3.71	–1.44	–1.10	–1.05	–1.19	–2.22	–3.51
Other sectors	3 430	–.99	–.82	–.31	–.30	–.81	–.53	–.45	–.33
Migrants' transfers	3 431	–.27	–.20	–.13	–.14	–.40	–.19	–.14	–.11
Debt forgiveness	3 432	–.70	–.61	–.17	–.15	–.38	–.31	–.30	–.20
Other capital transfers	3 440	–.02	–.01	–.01	–.01	–.04	–.03	–.01	–.02
Nonproduced nonfinancial assets, credit	2 480	**.12**	**.28**	**.21**	**.33**	**.49**	**.43**	**.91**	**.75**
Nonproduced nonfinancial assets, debit	3 480	**–1.85**	**–.70**	**–1.14**	**–1.08**	**–1.68**	**–2.08**	**–3.33**	**–1.98**

Table 2 (Continued). STANDARD PRESENTATION, 2003–2010

(Billions of U.S. dollars)

	Code	2003	2004	2005	2006	2007	2008	2009	2010
FINANCIAL ACCOUNT	4 995	−115.23	−138.35	−145.01	−134.32	−223.76	−203.50	−157.07	−174.33
A. DIRECT INVESTMENT	4 500	−22.53	−23.15	−42.22	−56.95	−51.31	−106.27	−62.79	−58.58
Direct investment abroad	4 505	−28.77	−30.96	−45.44	−50.17	−73.49	−130.82	−74.62	−57.22
Equity capital	4 510	−20.79	−20.95	−28.92	−28.74	−51.80	−96.58	−57.33	−54.74
Claims on affiliated enterprises	4 515	−20.79	−20.95	−28.92	−28.74	−51.80	−96.58	−57.33	−54.88
Liabilities to affiliated enterprises	4 520	....	....	....	....	....	....	....	.15
Reinvested earnings	4 525	−4.58	−5.97	−13.23	−16.39	−19.61	−24.15	−12.16	−2.00
Other capital	4 530	−3.40	−4.04	−3.29	−5.04	−2.08	−10.09	−5.13	−.49
Claims on affiliated enterprises	4 535	−3.94	−2.76	−4.42	−6.24	−2.68	−12.83	−8.24	−1.57
Liabilities to affiliated enterprises	4 540	.54	−1.28	1.13	1.20	.61	2.74	3.11	1.08
Direct investment in Japan	4 555	6.24	7.81	3.21	−6.78	22.18	24.55	11.83	−1.36
Equity capital	4 560	7.51	7.02	3.78	−8.93	10.53	24.14	10.73	7.51
Claims on direct investors	4 565	....	....	....	....	....	−.73	....	....
Liabilities to direct investors	4 570	7.51	7.02	3.78	−8.92	10.53	24.87	10.73	7.52
Reinvested earnings	4 575	1.41	1.95	1.70	2.25	3.84	3.75	1.19	−2.91
Other capital	4 580	−2.69	−1.16	−2.27	−.11	7.81	−3.34	−.08	−5.96
Claims on direct investors	4 585	−1.55	−1.27	.02	−.96	−.13	−1.34	−.54	−1.21
Liabilities to direct investors	4 590	−1.14	.11	−2.28	.85	7.93	−2.00	.45	−4.76
B. PORTFOLIO INVESTMENT	4 600	−95.11	22.95	−13.27	127.52	73.13	−292.60	−216.50	−151.00
Assets	4 602	−176.29	−173.77	−196.40	−71.04	−123.45	−189.64	−160.25	−262.64
Equity securities	4 610	−4.47	−31.47	−22.97	−25.04	−26.09	−65.56	−29.69	−21.46
Monetary authorities	4 611	....	....	....	....	....	....	....	....
General government	4 612	....	....	−.02	−.02	....	−.04	−.07	−.05
Banks	4 613	−.37	−1.29	−1.80	−1.38	−1.67	−3.51	.41	−.02
Other sectors	4 614	−4.10	−30.18	−21.15	−23.63	−24.42	−62.02	−30.03	−21.40
Debt securities	4 619	−171.82	−142.30	−173.43	−46.00	−97.36	−124.08	−130.56	−241.18
Bonds and notes	4 620	−177.77	−148.54	−182.88	−55.55	−102.31	−118.54	−129.56	−243.76
Monetary authorities	4 621	....	....	....	....	....	....	....	....
General government	4 622	6.56	3.02	.35	.13	−.64	−.10	.22	−.07
Banks	4 623	−63.50	−61.15	−56.44	17.10	−16.33	−10.24	−79.28	−98.50
Other sectors	4 624	−120.83	−90.41	−126.78	−72.79	−85.34	−108.19	−50.51	−145.19
Money market instruments	4 630	5.94	6.24	9.45	9.55	4.95	−5.54	−1.00	2.58
Monetary authorities	4 631	....	....	....	....	....	....	....	....
General government	4 632	.18	.31	....	....	....	....	....	....
Banks	4 633	−12.85	−10.84	5.21	3.20	−.77	−5.04	−1.62	2.11
Other sectors	4 634	18.62	16.76	4.24	6.36	5.72	−.50	.63	.47
Liabilities	4 652	81.18	196.72	183.13	198.56	196.58	−102.96	−56.26	111.64
Equity securities	4 660	87.78	98.28	131.32	71.44	45.45	−69.69	12.43	40.33
Banks	4 663	8.41	16.67	13.00	15.51	.39	−4.54	3.37	8.02
Other sectors	4 664	79.37	81.61	118.31	55.92	45.07	−65.15	9.07	32.31
Debt securities	4 669	−6.59	98.44	51.81	127.12	151.13	−33.27	−68.69	71.31
Bonds and notes	4 670	−18.30	53.47	61.01	78.33	66.62	−42.05	−68.42	6.05
Monetary authorities	4 671	....	....	....	....	....	....	....	....
General government	4 672	−17.14	43.62	55.80	58.76	68.59	−25.37	−64.44	8.60
Banks	4 673	4.68	9.31	6.73	4.89	.99	−2.72	7.13	.46
Other sectors	4 674	−5.84	.54	−1.52	14.68	−2.95	−13.96	−11.10	−3.01
Money market instruments	4 680	11.71	44.97	−9.20	48.78	84.50	8.78	−.27	65.27
Monetary authorities	4 681	....	....	....	....	....	....	....	....
General government	4 682	10.68	43.19	−9.30	48.61	84.53	9.00	.39	66.25
Banks	4 683	.17	.11	−.02	....	−.01	....	....	....
Other sectors	4 684	.85	1.67	.12	.18	−.02	−.21	−.67	−.98
C. FINANCIAL DERIVATIVES	4 910	5.58	2.41	−6.53	2.46	2.80	24.79	10.55	11.94
Monetary authorities	4 911	....	....	....	....	....	....	....	....
General government	4 912	.04	.11	.09	−.17	−.25	.08	.36	.12
Banks	4 913	5.49	4.12	3.47	.48	−.79	15.49	9.17	11.30
Other sectors	4 914	.04	−1.82	−10.08	2.14	3.84	9.22	1.02	.53
Assets	4 900	64.96	56.44	230.59	143.48	188.50	271.95	333.85	403.46
Monetary authorities	4 901	....	....	....	....	....	....	....	....
General government	4 902	.56	.14	.19	.07	.13	.37	.55	.32
Banks	4 903	60.63	56.57	78.34	88.50	121.62	162.53	139.44	119.32
Other sectors	4 904	3.76	−.27	152.06	54.90	66.75	109.05	193.86	283.82
Liabilities	4 905	−59.38	−54.04	−237.12	−141.03	−185.71	−247.16	−323.30	−391.51
Monetary authorities	4 906	....	....	....	....	....	....	....	....
General government	4 907	−.52	−.03	−.10	−.25	−.38	−.30	−.19	−.20
Banks	4 908	−55.14	−52.45	−74.87	−88.02	−122.41	−147.04	−130.27	−108.02
Other sectors	4 909	−3.72	−1.55	−162.14	−52.76	−62.91	−99.82	−192.84	−283.30

Table 2 (Concluded). STANDARD PRESENTATION, 2003–2010

(Billions of U.S. dollars)

	Code	2003	2004	2005	2006	2007	2008	2009	2010
D. OTHER INVESTMENT	4 700	**183.99**	**20.30**	**−60.66**	**−175.36**	**−211.86**	**201.45**	**138.59**	**67.16**
Assets	4 703	**149.89**	**−48.00**	**−106.60**	**−86.24**	**−260.78**	**139.46**	**202.75**	**−130.14**
Trade credits	4 706	−1.82	−1.80	−2.65	−5.05	−3.40	5.78	.02	−5.51
General government	4 707	.34	.30	.53	−.52	.68	1.62	.66	.12
of which: Short-term	4 709	....	....	.12	....	.02	−.04	.05	−.12
Other sectors	4 710	−2.16	−2.10	−3.17	−4.53	−4.08	4.15	−.64	−5.63
of which: Short-term	4 712	−3.42	−3.40	−3.49	−5.33	−4.52	4.86	−.92	−5.57
Loans	4 714	86.80	−38.30	−79.10	−62.29	−144.13	92.96	220.68	−62.58
Monetary authorities	4 715	....	....	....	....	....	....	....	....
of which: Short-term	4 718	....	....	....	....	....	....	....	....
General government	4 719	5.03	3.82	2.29	.13	−1.82	−7.44	−10.03	−10.20
of which: Short-term	4 721	....	....	....	....	....	....	−2.68	−5.78
Banks	4 722	87.97	7.59	−30.28	8.79	−105.05	−43.08	222.45	−60.96
of which: Short-term	4 724	92.48	3.97	−36.52	13.14	−96.08	−16.74	245.56	−28.97
Other sectors	4 725	−6.20	−49.71	−51.11	−71.20	−37.26	143.49	8.26	8.58
of which: Short-term	4 727	−10.77	−60.32	−38.71	−70.23	−39.01	142.21	11.46	3.94
Currency and deposits	4 730	5.12	−14.08	−5.35	−20.49	−117.14	55.84	43.65	−6.31
Monetary authorities	4 731	....	....	....	....	....	....	....	....
General government	4 732	....	....	....	....	....	....	....	....
Banks	4 733	−7.57	−11.64	9.26	−8.24	−96.65	40.90	32.70	.21
Other sectors	4 734	12.69	−2.44	−14.61	−12.25	−20.49	14.94	10.96	−6.52
Other assets	4 736	59.79	6.17	−19.50	1.59	3.89	−15.12	−61.61	−55.74
Monetary authorities	4 737	....	....	....	....	....	....	....	....
of which: Short-term	4 739	....	....	....	....	....	....	....	....
General government	4 740	−.88	−.24	11.47	3.87	.78	−1.08	−.42	−2.93
of which: Short-term	4 742	−.01	.70	12.40	6.41	.91	.35	−.23	.16
Banks	4 743	60.38	7.30	−8.78	−8.04	6.06	−36.94	−52.51	−55.90
of which: Short-term	4 745	62.12	−.28	2.13	2.78	−4.89	−35.05	−42.52	−35.30
Other sectors	4 746	.29	−.89	−22.19	5.77	−2.95	22.90	−8.68	3.08
of which: Short-term	4 748	.99	−.21	−21.23	6.00	−2.88	23.35	−9.19	2.26
Liabilities	4 753	**34.10**	**68.31**	**45.94**	**−89.12**	**48.92**	**61.99**	**−64.15**	**197.30**
Trade credits	4 756	.80	.68	4.82	3.24	4.24	−.69	2.66	1.62
General government	4 757	....	....	....	....	....	....	....	....
of which: Short-term	4 759	....	....	....	....	....	....	....	....
Other sectors	4 760	.80	.68	4.82	3.24	4.24	−.69	2.66	1.62
of which: Short-term	4 762	1.39	1.36	4.99	3.70	4.63	−.63	2.69	1.99
Loans	4 764	22.66	81.81	9.83	−74.73	51.90	−59.52	43.02	174.72
Monetary authorities	4 765	....	....	....	....	....	....	....	....
of which: Use of Fund credit and loans from the Fund..	4 766	....	....	....	....	....	....	....	....
of which: Short-term	4 768	....	....	....	....	....	....	....	....
General government	4 769	....	14.81	18.66	−21.15	1.63	.12	15.07	−10.96
of which: Short-term	4 771	....	14.80	18.66	−21.15	1.63	.12	15.07	−10.96
Banks	4 772	−36.88	35.24	−5.76	−44.42	−6.54	39.38	60.33	78.26
of which: Short-term	4 774	−34.84	44.60	1.80	−56.11	−16.35	22.04	63.12	86.57
Other sectors	4 775	59.54	31.76	−3.08	−9.16	56.81	−99.01	−32.38	107.41
of which: Short-term	4 777	68.30	22.40	9.02	−13.57	50.16	−98.34	−29.08	117.65
Currency and deposits	4 780	17.00	−4.15	2.98	−9.32	6.55	122.91	−122.70	13.08
Monetary authorities	4 781	....	....	....	....	....	....	....	....
General government	4 782	5.83	−13.29	−.92	−3.89	.03	119.27	−123.84	−.67
Banks	4 783	11.17	9.14	3.90	−5.42	6.52	3.64	1.14	13.76
Other sectors	4 784	....	....	....	....	....	....	....	....
Other liabilities	4 786	−6.36	−10.04	28.31	−8.31	−13.76	−.71	12.87	7.88
Monetary authorities	4 787	....	....	....	....	....	....	17.80	....
of which: Short-term	4 789	....	....	....	....	....	....	....	....
General government	4 790	−.68	−.53	−5.50	−.40	−.37	.98	−.18	.90
of which: Short-term	4 792	−.68	−.53	−5.50	−.40	−.37	.98	−.18	.90
Banks	4 793	−.51	−1.65	−7.52	1.01	.35	17.85	−11.92	1.22
of which: Short-term	4 795	1.63	−1.60	−6.22	1.01	.34	17.83	−11.90	1.25
Other sectors	4 796	−5.17	−7.86	41.33	−8.93	−13.73	−19.53	7.17	5.76
of which: Short-term	4 798	−4.77	−7.69	39.62	−8.61	−8.63	−19.30	6.81	3.65
E. RESERVE ASSETS	4 802	**−187.15**	**−160.85**	**−22.33**	**−31.98**	**−36.52**	**−30.88**	**−26.92**	**−43.85**
Monetary gold	4 812	....	....	....	....	....	....	....	....
Special drawing rights	4 811	−.01	.05	.03	−.09	−.08	−.08	−17.83	−.03
Reserve position in the Fund	4 810	.18	1.24	3.44	1.06	.61	−1.26	−1.55	−.36
Foreign exchange	4 803	−187.33	−162.14	−25.80	−32.95	−37.06	−29.54	−6.83	−43.46
Other claims	4 813	....	....	....	....	....	....	−.71	....
NET ERRORS AND OMISSIONS	4 998	**−16.99**	**−28.92**	**−15.90**	**−31.44**	**17.30**	**52.34**	**19.87**	**−16.46**

Table 3. INTERNATIONAL INVESTMENT POSITION (End-period stocks), 2003–2010

(Billions of U.S. dollars)

	Code	2003	2004	2005	2006	2007	2008	2009	2010
ASSETS	8 995 C.	**3,599.80**	**4,166.99**	**4,290.87**	**4,691.94**	**5,355.23**	**5,721.01**	**6,026.77**	**6,918.65**
Direct investment abroad	8 505	**335.50**	**370.54**	**386.59**	**449.57**	**542.62**	**680.33**	**740.93**	**831.08**
Equity capital and reinvested earnings	8 506	315.03	351.27	368.46	429.18	518.91	644.06	704.01	795.69
Claims on affiliated enterprises	8 507	315.06	351.33	368.51	429.28	518.96	644.10	704.12	795.86
Liabilities to affiliated enterprises	8 508	−.03	−.05	−.05	−.10	−.05	−.04	−.12	−.17
Other capital	8 530	20.47	19.27	18.12	20.39	23.70	36.27	36.92	35.38
Claims on affiliated enterprises	8 535	24.04	21.84	20.67	23.32	26.44	42.35	44.49	43.76
Liabilities to affiliated enterprises	8 540	−3.57	−2.57	−2.54	−2.94	−2.73	−6.08	−7.57	−8.38
Portfolio investment	8 602	**1,721.32**	**2,009.67**	**2,114.89**	**2,343.48**	**2,523.57**	**2,376.66**	**2,845.85**	**3,345.83**
Equity securities	8 610	274.46	364.69	408.57	510.42	573.47	394.67	594.04	678.48
Monetary authorities	8 611	....	....	....	....	....	....	....	....
General government	8 612	.03	....	....	....	....	.26	.08	.12
Banks	8 613	5.15	5.85	6.86	10.22	13.54	14.47	14.08	16.76
Other sectors	8 614	269.28	358.84	401.72	500.20	559.93	379.94	579.88	661.60
Debt securities	8 619	1,446.86	1,644.98	1,706.31	1,833.06	1,950.10	1,981.99	2,251.81	2,667.35
Bonds and notes	8 620	1,407.17	1,610.02	1,681.11	1,811.99	1,924.83	1,952.66	2,224.77	2,636.11
Monetary authorities	8 621	....	....	....	....	....	....	....	....
General government	8 622	17.98	16.07	7.36	6.39	4.96	5.08	5.10	6.30
Banks	8 623	422.95	491.32	565.25	558.60	573.11	590.50	697.09	876.14
Other sectors	8 624	966.24	1,102.63	1,108.50	1,247.00	1,346.76	1,357.08	1,522.57	1,753.67
Money market instruments	8 630	39.69	34.97	25.20	21.08	25.27	29.32	27.05	31.24
Monetary authorities	8 631	....	....	....	....	....	....	....	....
General government	8 632	.12	.07	.02	.03	.06	.04	.04	.01
Banks	8 633	14.96	12.99	10.18	6.39	11.85	14.25	12.38	10.94
Other sectors	8 634	24.61	21.91	15.01	14.66	13.36	15.04	14.63	20.28
Financial derivatives	8 900	**4.90**	**5.75**	**26.31**	**23.03**	**38.96**	**77.38**	**46.18**	**52.63**
Monetary authorities	8 901	....	....	....	....	....	....	....	....
General government	8 902	....	....	....	....	....	....	....	....
Banks	8 903	2.90	3.08	7.62	12.65	16.47	47.77	24.81	24.61
Other sectors	8 904	2.00	2.67	18.70	10.38	22.49	29.61	21.37	28.01
Other investment	8 703	**865.03**	**938.51**	**920.10**	**981.07**	**1,282.69**	**1,562.01**	**1,342.59**	**1,592.39**
Trade credits	8 706	47.89	50.62	51.80	52.47	56.58	54.94	54.40	61.99
General government	8 707	12.41	12.16	11.65	7.85	7.24	8.00	7.71	8.53
of which: Short-term	8 709	*.51*	*.53*	*.58*	*.22*	*.05*	*.11*	*.05*	*.20*
Other sectors	8 710	35.48	38.46	40.15	44.62	49.34	46.94	46.68	53.45
of which: Short-term	8 712	*28.05*	*32.27*	*33.22*	*38.97*	*44.09*	*41.18*	*41.22*	*47.50*
Loans	8 714	656.94	693.57	671.70	699.16	852.55	1,004.06	782.33	875.01
Monetary authorities	8 715	....	....	....	....	....	....	....	....
of which: Short-term	8 718	....	....	....	....	....	....	....	....
General government	8 719	157.75	158.25	138.26	138.48	144.92	181.51	189.55	217.63
of which: Short-term	8 721	....	....	....	....	....	....	*2.66*	*8.50*
Banks	8 722	385.52	375.80	371.83	349.47	457.90	588.82	380.04	436.93
of which: Short-term	8 724	*295.08*	*289.93*	*296.16*	*269.57*	*367.27*	*457.88*	*226.44*	*240.91*
Other sectors	8 725	113.67	159.52	161.61	211.20	249.73	233.73	212.74	220.46
of which: Short-term	8 727	*40.09*	*94.95*	*97.78*	*144.98*	*178.16*	*156.91*	*131.36*	*135.46*
Currency and deposits	8 730	64.07	79.98	79.73	102.81	221.84	196.65	154.59	176.29
Monetary authorities	8 731	....	....	....	....	....	....	....	....
General government	8 732	....	....	....	....	....	....	....	....
Banks	8 733	40.52	52.06	40.61	48.73	147.42	123.79	91.98	97.98
Other sectors	8 734	23.55	27.92	39.12	54.08	74.41	72.86	62.61	78.31
Other assets	8 736	96.13	114.34	116.87	126.63	151.73	306.37	351.28	479.10
Monetary authorities	8 737	....	....	....	....	....	....	....	....
of which: Short-term	8 739	....	....	....	....	....	....	....	....
General government	8 740	58.64	62.69	48.89	50.84	52.35	65.85	63.77	74.31
of which: Short-term	8 742	*15.75*	*15.81*	*5.83*	*5.56*	*5.24*	*6.88*	*7.07*	*7.84*
Banks	8 743	21.31	34.22	50.57	58.46	81.67	219.65	268.23	386.88
of which: Short-term	8 745	*−2.02*	*18.17*	*11.54*	*12.80*	*38.78*	*159.29*	*197.39*	*278.20*
Other sectors	8 746	16.18	17.43	17.40	17.34	17.70	20.86	19.28	17.92
of which: Short-term	8 748	*3.78*	*4.07*	*4.29*	*4.07*	*3.99*	*3.97*	*3.03*	*.52*
Reserve assets	8 802	**673.06**	**842.52**	**842.98**	**894.79**	**967.39**	**1,024.64**	**1,051.21**	**1,096.72**
Monetary gold	8 812	10.23	10.74	12.57	15.64	20.42	21.17	27.18	34.72
Special drawing rights	8 811	2.77	2.84	2.58	2.81	3.03	3.03	20.97	20.63
Reserve position in the Fund	8 810	7.73	6.79	2.88	1.93	1.39	2.66	4.31	4.61
Foreign exchange	8 803	652.33	822.15	824.95	874.07	942.18	997.41	998.35	1,036.33
Other claims	8 813	....	....	....	.34	.37	.37	.40	.44

Table 3 (Concluded). INTERNATIONAL INVESTMENT POSITION (End-period stocks), 2003–2010

(Billions of U.S. dollars)

	Code	2003	2004	2005	2006	2007	2008	2009	2010
LIABILITIES...	8 995 D.	**1,986.18**	**2,382.51**	**2,759.11**	**2,883.77**	**3,160.27**	**3,236.04**	**3,134.93**	**3,830.95**
Direct investment in Japan........................	8 555 ..	**89.73**	**96.99**	**100.90**	**107.64**	**132.85**	**203.37**	**200.14**	**214.88**
Equity capital and reinvested earnings............................	8 556 ..	70.69	76.42	82.49	90.70	107.51	173.61	174.21	203.32
Claims on direct investors............................	8 557 ..	−.08	−.04	−.21	−.25	−.37	−.56	−.28	−.52
Liabilities to direct investors......................	8 558 ..	70.77	76.46	82.70	90.95	107.88	174.17	174.49	203.84
Other capital....................................	8 580 ..	19.03	20.57	18.41	16.94	25.35	29.76	25.94	11.56
Claims on direct investors............................	8 585 ..	−3.00	−2.48	−1.21	−1.98	−1.74	−3.81	−4.31	−6.07
Liabilities to direct investors......................	8 590 ..	22.04	23.05	19.62	18.92	27.09	33.57	30.24	17.63
Portfolio investment..............................	8 652 ..	**867.17**	**1,153.39**	**1,542.42**	**1,762.89**	**1,942.87**	**1,546.09**	**1,541.35**	**1,871.72**
Equity securities...	8 660 ..	561.02	743.30	1,126.07	1,254.95	1,245.89	756.20	829.59	988.79
Banks...	8 663 ..	31.45	61.33	101.97	110.08	80.57	58.56	55.25	78.85
Other sectors......................................	8 664 ..	529.57	681.98	1,024.10	1,144.87	1,165.32	697.64	774.34	909.94
Debt securities..	8 669 ..	306.14	410.09	416.35	507.94	696.98	789.89	711.76	882.93
Bonds and notes..................................	8 670 ..	253.11	325.07	351.17	416.80	528.10	558.13	458.78	526.42
Monetary authorities...........................	8 671 ..	....	....	....	....	....	....	....	....
General government............................	8 672 ..	169.56	232.03	261.76	311.68	419.14	458.24	366.62	430.43
Banks.......................................	8 673 ..	16.43	19.60	23.34	28.10	29.66	25.83	31.57	34.04
Other sectors..................................	8 674 ..	67.12	73.45	66.08	77.02	79.30	74.06	60.59	61.95
Money market instruments....................	8 680 ..	53.04	85.02	65.18	91.13	168.88	231.76	252.97	356.51
Monetary authorities...........................	8 681 ..	....	....	....	....	....	....	....	....
General government............................	8 682 ..	53.04	84.25	64.97	90.59	168.09	231.10	251.85	356.35
Banks.......................................	8 683 ..	....	.01	....	....	....	....	....	....
Other sectors..................................	8 684 ..	....	.76	.21	.55	.79	.66	1.12	.16
Financial derivatives..............................	8 905 ..	**6.79**	**10.77**	**33.23**	**30.16**	**43.55**	**85.52**	**56.63**	**64.66**
Monetary authorities................................	8 906 ..	....	....	....	....	....	....	....	....
General government................................	8 907 ..	....	....	....	....	....	....	....	....
Banks...	8 908 ..	3.75	6.07	10.83	16.45	21.23	53.32	32.47	32.89
Other sectors......................................	8 909 ..	3.04	4.70	22.41	13.70	22.32	32.20	24.16	31.77
Other investment..................................	8 753 ..	**1,022.50**	**1,121.36**	**1,082.55**	**983.09**	**1,041.00**	**1,401.06**	**1,336.81**	**1,679.69**
Trade credits......................................	8 756 ..	10.37	13.22	16.00	20.36	23.47	25.11	25.98	29.20
General government............................	8 757 ..	....	....	....	....	....	....	....	....
of which: Short-term...........................	8 759 ..	....	....	....	....	....	....	....	....
Other sectors......................................	8 760 ..	10.37	13.22	16.00	20.36	23.47	25.11	25.98	29.20
of which: Short-term...........................	8 762 ..	*10.35*	*12.01*	*14.69*	*18.21*	*22.37*	*23.45*	*24.30*	*27.45*
Loans..	8 764 ..	781.19	871.84	803.64	717.57	744.82	842.74	887.99	1,119.49
Monetary authorities...........................	8 765 ..	....	....	....	....	....	....	....	....
of which: Use of Fund credit and loans from the Fund....	8 766 ..	....	....	....	....	....	....	....	....
of which: Short-term...........................	8 768 ..	....	....	....	....	....	....	....	....
General government............................	8 769 ..	....	15.22	31.33	10.66	12.94	17.49	32.18	24.09
of which: Short-term...........................	8 771 ..	....	*15.22*	*31.33*	*10.66*	*12.94*	*17.49*	*32.18*	*24.09*
Banks.......................................	8 772 ..	465.68	507.54	482.04	438.80	422.96	505.67	563.59	666.05
of which: Short-term...........................	8 774 ..	*380.95*	*430.67*	*418.57*	*363.89*	*336.68*	*386.39*	*448.55*	*549.27*
Other sectors..................................	8 775 ..	315.51	349.08	290.27	268.11	308.91	319.57	292.22	429.35
of which: Short-term...........................	8 777 ..	*262.13*	*283.29*	*246.15*	*219.89*	*251.39*	*247.68*	*225.83*	*364.30*
Currency and deposits............................	8 780 ..	102.51	100.03	93.76	84.26	92.24	240.73	111.91	131.74
Monetary authorities...........................	8 781 ..	....	....	....	....	....	....	....	....
General government............................	8 782 ..	....	....	....	....	....	....	.76	.12
Banks.......................................	8 783 ..	102.51	100.03	93.76	84.26	92.24	240.73	111.15	131.62
Other sectors..................................	8 784 ..	....	....	....	....	....	....	....	....
Other liabilities..................................	8 786 ..	128.43	136.26	169.16	160.89	180.47	292.49	310.94	399.26
Monetary authorities...........................	8 787 ..	....	....	....	....	....	....	19.26	....
of which: Short-term...........................	8 789 ..	....	....	....	....	....	....	....	....
General government............................	8 790 ..	5.14	4.74	3.97	3.61	3.39	4.88	3.05	23.50
of which: Short-term...........................	8 792 ..	*5.14*	*4.74*	*3.97*	*3.61*	*3.39*	*4.88*	*3.05*	*4.57*
Banks.......................................	8 793 ..	92.21	101.74	127.09	120.71	147.28	255.37	259.68	346.03
of which: Short-term...........................	8 795 ..	*90.92*	*100.51*	*111.17*	*107.78*	*134.12*	*231.21*	*236.84*	*321.45*
Other sectors..................................	8 796 ..	31.08	29.78	38.10	36.58	29.80	32.24	28.95	29.73
of which: Short-term...........................	8 798 ..	*31.23*	*25.57*	*32.79*	*31.63*	*29.91*	*31.96*	*28.29*	*26.33*
NET INTERNATIONAL INVESTMENT POSITION........	8 995 ..	**1,613.63**	**1,784.49**	**1,531.76**	**1,808.17**	**2,194.96**	**2,484.97**	**2,891.84**	**3,087.70**
Conversion rates: yen per U.S. dollar (end of period)..	0 102 ..	**107.10**	**104.12**	**117.97**	**118.95**	**114.00**	**90.75**	**92.06**	**81.45**

Table 1. ANALYTIC PRESENTATION, 2003–2010
(Millions of U.S. dollars)

	Code	2003	2004	2005	2006	2007	2008	2009	2010
A. Current Account¹......................................	4 993 Z.	**1,198.5**	**39.1**	**−2,271.7**	**−1,726.0**	**−2,874.8**	**−2,038.1**	**−1,125.5**	**−1,311.5**
Goods: exports f.o.b..	2 100 ..	3,081.7	3,882.9	4,301.4	5,204.4	5,731.5	7,937.1	6,375.1	7,028.3
Goods: imports f.o.b..	3 100 ..	−5,077.9	−7,261.1	−9,317.3	−10,260.2	−12,183.2	−15,102.0	−12,641.1	−13,678.7
Balance on Goods..	4 100 ..	*−1,996.2*	*−3,378.1*	*−5,015.9*	*−5,055.9*	*−6,451.8*	*−7,164.9*	*−6,266.0*	*−6,650.4*
Services: credit...	2 200 ..	1,748.2	2,072.8	2,333.6	2,907.5	3,548.4	4,478.0	4,552.5	5,161.1
Services: debit..	3 200 ..	−1,889.3	−2,145.8	−2,542.0	−2,970.7	−3,517.3	−4,126.5	−3,812.8	−4,270.6
Balance on Goods and Services.......................	4 991 ..	*−2,137.3*	*−3,451.2*	*−5,224.4*	*−5,119.0*	*−6,420.7*	*−6,813.4*	*−5,526.3*	*−5,759.8*
Income: credit..	2 300 ..	550.5	649.2	791.3	1,031.9	1,403.8	1,335.7	1,170.2	1,078.5
Income: debit...	3 300 ..	−420.6	−375.2	−454.9	−578.8	−720.5	−641.1	−567.0	−571.5
Balance on Goods, Services, and Income........	4 992 ..	*−2,007.4*	*−3,177.2*	*−4,888.0*	*−4,666.0*	*−5,737.4*	*−6,118.8*	*−4,923.2*	*−5,252.9*
Current transfers: credit....................................	2 379 Z.	3,501.0	3,562.5	3,029.9	3,378.8	3,594.8	4,715.0	4,453.0	4,491.8
Current transfers: debit.....................................	3 379 ..	−295.1	−346.3	−413.5	−438.8	−732.2	−634.3	−655.4	−550.4
B. Capital Account¹.....................................	4 994 Z.	**93.5**	**2.1**	**8.5**	**62.8**	**12.8**	**283.9**	**.6**	**.3**
Capital account: credit......................................	2 994 Z.	93.5	2.1	8.5	62.8	12.8	283.9	.6	.3
Capital account: debit.......................................	3 994 ..	....	....	....	....	....	....	....	....
Total, Groups A Plus B....................................	4 981 ..	*1,292.1*	*41.2*	*−2,263.2*	*−1,663.2*	*−2,861.9*	*−1,754.2*	*−1,125.0*	*−1,311.2*
C. Financial Account¹..................................	4 995 W.	**−106.8**	**17.2**	**1,848.7**	**3,318.9**	**3,220.2**	**2,746.6**	**3,715.6**	**1,595.4**
Direct investment abroad..................................	4 505 ..	3.7	−18.2	−163.2	138.1	−48.1	−12.8	−72.4	−28.5
Direct investment in Jordan...............................	4 555 Z.	547.0	936.8	1,984.5	3,544.0	2,622.1	2,826.7	2,426.6	1,701.4
Portfolio investment assets...............................	4 602 ..	−122.6	−199.0	143.6	−180.4	494.4	51.9	−600.0	41.0
Equity securities...	4 610 ..	−122.6	−199.0	143.6	−180.4	13.3	2.7	4.4	32.8
Debt securities..	4 619 ..	....	....	....	....	481.1	49.2	−604.4	8.2
Portfolio investment liabilities...........................	4 652 Z.	−349.1	−89.8	169.1	143.6	346.0	521.1	−29.6	−20.4
Equity securities...	4 660 Z.	−57.8	−89.8	169.1	143.6	346.0	521.1	−29.6	−20.4
Debt securities..	4 669 Z.	−291.3	....	....	....	....	....	....	....
Financial derivatives..	4 910 ..	....	....	....	....	....	....	....	....
Financial derivatives assets...............................	4 900 ..	....	....	....	....	....	....	....	....
Financial derivatives liabilities..........................	4 905 ..	....	....	....	....	....	....	....	....
Other investment assets....................................	4 703 ..	252.9	−680.8	−615.9	−1,148.0	−939.6	734.6	1,503.4	−1,228.7
Monetary authorities......................................	4 701 ..	−22.6	−23.4	−36.0	−58.7	−58.3	−41.9	−26.8	−32.0
General government.......................................	4 704 ..	....	....	....	....	....	....	....	....
Banks..	4 705 ..	275.5	−657.4	−580.0	−1,089.3	−881.4	939.5	1,386.2	−1,120.7
Other sectors..	4 728 ..	....	....	....	....	....	−163.1	143.9	−76.1
Other investment liabilities...............................	4 753 W.	−438.6	68.3	330.6	821.6	745.4	−1,375.0	487.5	1,130.6
Monetary authorities......................................	4 753 WA	−13.4	−29.3	−9.2	97.7	2.3	104.5	168.7	598.7
General government.......................................	4 753 ZB	−275.7	−114.2	74.6	−183.9	−146.4	−2,577.5	217.6	−223.0
Banks..	4 753 ZC	−99.4	329.3	272.6	804.5	814.2	1,027.2	214.8	445.4
Other sectors..	4 753 ZD	−50.1	−117.5	−7.5	103.2	75.3	70.8	−113.5	309.4
Total, Groups A Through C...............................	4 983 ..	*1,185.3*	*58.4*	*−414.5*	*1,655.7*	*358.3*	*992.4*	*2,590.6*	*284.1*
D. Net Errors and Omissions.................................	4 998 ..	**91.4**	**121.5**	**675.3**	**−214.0**	**531.8**	**204.7**	**536.9**	**425.7**
Total, Groups A Through D...............................	4 984 ..	*1,276.7*	*179.8*	*260.8*	*1,441.7*	*890.0*	*1,197.1*	*3,127.5*	*709.8*
E. Reserves and Related Items...........................	4 802 A.	**−1,276.7**	**−179.8**	**−260.8**	**−1,441.7**	**−890.0**	**−1,197.1**	**−3,127.5**	**−709.8**
Reserve assets..	4 802 ..	−1,176.7	−81.8	−183.5	−1,353.3	−813.6	−1,137.6	−3,112.0	−1,455.9
Use of Fund credit and loans.............................	4 766 ..	−100.0	−98.1	−77.2	−88.4	−76.4	−59.4	−15.5	−3.9
Exceptional financing..	4 920 ..	....	....	....	....	....	....	....	750.0
Conversion rates: Jordanian dinar per U.S. dollar...	0 101 ..	**.7090**	**.7090**	**.7090**	**.7090**	**.7090**	**.7097**	**.7100**	**.7100**

¹ Excludes components that have been classified in the categories of Group E.

Table 2. STANDARD PRESENTATION, 2003–2010

(Millions of U.S. dollars)

	Code	2003	2004	2005	2006	2007	2008	2009	2010
CURRENT ACCOUNT	4 993	**1,198.5**	**39.1**	**−2,271.7**	**−1,726.0**	**−2,874.8**	**−2,038.1**	**−1,125.5**	**−1,311.5**
A. GOODS	4 100	**−1,996.2**	**−3,378.1**	**−5,015.9**	**−5,055.9**	**−6,451.8**	**−7,164.9**	**−6,266.0**	**−6,650.4**
Credit	2 100	**3,081.7**	**3,882.9**	**4,301.4**	**5,204.4**	**5,731.5**	**7,937.1**	**6,375.1**	**7,028.3**
General merchandise: exports f.o.b.	2 110	2,871.2	3,831.9	4,297.6	4,927.5	5,685.1	7,855.1	6,138.0	6,828.2
Goods for processing: exports f.o.b.	2 150	....	....	....	....	....	....	....	....
Repairs on goods	2 160	....	....	....	....	....	....	....	....
Goods procured in ports by carriers	2 170	....	....	....	....	....	....	....	....
Nonmonetary gold	2 180	210.4	51.1	3.8	276.9	46.4	82.0	237.1	200.1
Debit	3 100	**−5,077.9**	**−7,261.1**	**−9,317.3**	**−10,260.2**	**−12,183.2**	**−15,102.0**	**−12,641.1**	**−13,678.7**
General merchandise: imports f.o.b.	3 110	−5,006.5	−7,159.1	−9,248.7	−10,223.7	−12,089.0	−14,948.4	−12,618.3	−13,664.5
Goods for processing: imports f.o.b.	3 150	....	....	....	....	....	....	....	....
Repairs on goods	3 160	....	....	....	....	....	....	....	....
Goods procured in ports by carriers	3 170	....	....	....	....	....	....	....	....
Nonmonetary gold	3 180	−71.4	−102.0	−68.7	−36.5	−94.2	−153.5	−22.9	−14.2
B. SERVICES	4 200	**−141.0**	**−73.1**	**−208.5**	**−63.2**	**31.0**	**351.5**	**739.7**	**890.6**
Total credit	2 200	*1,748.2*	*2,072.8*	*2,333.6*	*2,907.5*	*3,548.4*	*4,478.0*	*4,552.5*	*5,161.1*
Total debit	3 200	*−1,889.3*	*−2,145.8*	*−2,542.0*	*−2,970.7*	*−3,517.3*	*−4,126.5*	*−3,812.8*	*−4,270.6*
Transportation services, credit	2 205	**303.2**	**426.0**	**469.8**	**527.6**	**660.6**	**835.7**	**793.4**	**851.7**
Passenger	2 850	*203.5*	*291.4*	*317.8*	*366.0*	*443.3*	*595.6*	*559.6*	*604.8*
Freight	2 851	*32.0*	*37.7*	*46.1*	*39.8*	*69.7*	*41.7*	*47.5*	*45.5*
Other	2 852	*67.7*	*96.9*	*105.9*	*121.9*	*147.7*	*198.4*	*186.3*	*201.4*
Sea transport, passenger	2 207	....	....	....	....	....	....	....	....
Sea transport, freight	2 208	....	....	....	....	....	....	....	....
Sea transport, other	2 209	....	....	....	....	....	....	....	....
Air transport, passenger	2 211	....	....	....	....	....	....	....	....
Air transport, freight	2 212	....	....	....	....	....	....	....	....
Air transport, other	2 213	....	....	....	....	....	....	....	....
Other transport, passenger	2 215	....	....	....	....	....	....	....	....
Other transport, freight	2 216	....	....	....	....	....	....	....	....
Other transport, other	2 217	....	....	....	....	....	....	....	....
Transportation services, debit	3 205	**−825.9**	**−1,106.6**	**−1,341.6**	**−1,536.0**	**−1,814.0**	**−2,240.0**	**−1,941.7**	**−2,120.6**
Passenger	3 850	*−51.3*	*−61.4*	*−68.0*	*−119.2*	*−141.3*	*−136.4*	*−138.5*	*−173.5*
Freight	3 851	*−513.5*	*−734.3*	*−942.2*	*−1,037.5*	*−1,232.2*	*−1,527.2*	*−1,278.5*	*−1,383.4*
Other	3 852	*−261.1*	*−311.0*	*−331.5*	*−379.3*	*−440.5*	*−576.4*	*−524.8*	*−563.7*
Sea transport, passenger	3 207	....	....	....	....	....	....	....	....
Sea transport, freight	3 208	....	....	....	....	....	....	....	....
Sea transport, other	3 209	....	....	....	....	....	....	....	....
Air transport, passenger	3 211	....	....	....	....	....	....	....	....
Air transport, freight	3 212	....	....	....	....	....	....	....	....
Air transport, other	3 213	....	....	....	....	....	....	....	....
Other transport, passenger	3 215	....	....	....	....	....	....	....	....
Other transport, freight	3 216	....	....	....	....	....	....	....	....
Other transport, other	3 217	....	....	....	....	....	....	....	....
Travel, credit	2 236	**1,061.5**	**1,329.8**	**1,440.6**	**2,060.4**	**2,310.7**	**2,942.6**	**2,911.0**	**3,413.0**
Business travel	2 237	....	....	....	....	....	....	....	....
Personal travel	2 240	....	....	....	....	....	....	....	....
Travel, debit	3 236	**−451.9**	**−523.8**	**−585.2**	**−837.0**	**−882.7**	**−1,003.6**	**−1,063.9**	**−1,431.4**
Business travel	3 237	....	....	....	....	....	....	....	....
Personal travel	3 240	−451.9	−523.8	−585.2	−837.0	−882.7	−1,003.6	−1,063.9	−1,431.4
Other services, credit	2 200 BA	**383.5**	**317.1**	**423.1**	**319.5**	**577.0**	**699.8**	**848.2**	**896.5**
Communications	2 245	....	....	....	....	....	....	....	....
Construction	2 249	....	....	....	....	....	....	....	....
Insurance	2 253	....	....	....	....	....	....	....	....
Financial	2 260	....	....	....	....	....	....	....	....
Computer and information	2 262	....	....	....	....	....	....	....	....
Royalties and licence fees	2 266	....	....	....	....	....	....	....	....
Other business services	2 268	351.9	295.9	328.6	262.2	464.7	575.0	490.6	517.0
Personal, cultural, and recreational	2 287	....	....	....	....	....	....	....	....
Government, n.i.e.	2 291	31.6	21.2	94.5	57.3	112.3	124.8	357.6	379.4
Other services, debit	3 200 BA	**−611.4**	**−515.4**	**−615.2**	**−597.7**	**−820.7**	**−882.9**	**−807.2**	**−718.6**
Communications	3 245	....	....	....	....	....	....	....	....
Construction	3 249	....	....	....	....	....	....	....	....
Insurance	3 253	−114.1	−163.2	−209.4	−230.6	−273.8	−339.3	−284.1	−307.5
Financial	3 260	....	....	....	....	....	....	....	....
Computer and information	3 262	....	....	....	....	....	....	....	....
Royalties and licence fees	3 266	....	....	....	....	....	....	....	....
Other business services	3 268	−297.7	−178.7	−328.6	−250.5	−385.8	−343.2	−377.7	−304.4
Personal, cultural, and recreational	3 287	....	....	....	....	....	....	....	....
Government, n.i.e.	3 291	−199.6	−173.5	−77.2	−116.6	−161.2	−200.4	−145.4	−106.8

Table 2 (Continued). STANDARD PRESENTATION, 2003–2010

(Millions of U.S. dollars)

	Code	2003	2004	2005	2006	2007	2008	2009	2010
C. INCOME	4 300	**129.9**	**274.0**	**336.4**	**453.0**	**683.4**	**694.6**	**603.2**	**506.9**
Total credit	2 300	*550.5*	*649.2*	*791.3*	*1,031.9*	*1,403.8*	*1,335.7*	*1,170.2*	*1,078.5*
Total debit	3 300	*–420.6*	*–375.2*	*–454.9*	*–578.8*	*–720.5*	*–641.1*	*–567.0*	*–571.5*
Compensation of employees, credit	2 310	**220.2**	**271.7**	**320.9**	**369.0**	**440.5**	**634.9**	**478.5**	**475.4**
Compensation of employees, debit	3 310	**–26.8**	**–32.2**	**–41.2**	**–47.4**	**–56.7**	**–55.7**	**–59.2**	**–58.5**
Investment income, credit	2 320	**330.3**	**377.6**	**470.4**	**662.9**	**963.3**	**700.8**	**691.7**	**603.1**
Direct investment income	2 330	....	....	....	....	....	....	....	....
Dividends and distributed branch profits	2 332	....	....	....	....	....	....	....	....
Reinvested earnings and undistributed branch profits	2 333	....	....	....	....	....	....	....	....
Income on debt (interest)	2 334	....	....	....	....	....	....	....	....
Portfolio investment income	2 339	....	....	....	....	....	....	....	....
Income on equity	2 340	....	....	....	....	....	....	....	....
Income on bonds and notes	2 350	....	....	....	....	....	....	....	....
Income on money market instruments	2 360	....	....	....	....	....	....	....	....
Other investment income	2 370	330.3	377.6	470.4	662.9	963.3	700.8	691.7	603.1
Investment income, debit	3 320	**–393.8**	**–343.0**	**–413.7**	**–531.5**	**–663.8**	**–585.5**	**–507.9**	**–513.1**
Direct investment income	3 330	–48.4	–50.6	–73.6	–130.0	–160.4	–255.7	–294.4	–283.4
Dividends and distributed branch profits	3 332	....	....	....	....	–160.4	–255.7	–294.4	–283.4
Reinvested earnings and undistributed branch profits	3 333	....	....	....	....	....	....	....	....
Income on debt (interest)	3 334	....	....	....	....	....	....	....	....
Portfolio investment income	3 339	–1.7	–.6	....	....	....	....	....	....
Income on equity	3 340	....	....	....	....	....	....	....	....
Income on bonds and notes	3 350	–1.7	–.6	....	....	....	....	....	....
Income on money market instruments	3 360	....	....	....	....	....	....	....	....
Other investment income	3 370	–343.7	–291.8	–340.1	–401.4	–503.4	–329.8	–213.5	–229.7
D. CURRENT TRANSFERS	4 379	**3,205.9**	**3,216.2**	**2,616.4**	**2,940.1**	**2,862.6**	**4,080.7**	**3,797.6**	**3,941.4**
Credit	2 379	**3,501.0**	**3,562.5**	**3,029.9**	**3,378.8**	**3,594.8**	**4,715.0**	**4,453.0**	**4,491.8**
General government	2 380	1,406.5	1,334.1	752.0	844.6	462.5	1,341.6	982.7	1,203.8
Other sectors	2 390	2,094.5	2,228.3	2,277.9	2,534.3	3,132.3	3,373.5	3,470.3	3,288.0
Workers' remittances	2 391	1,981.0	2,058.7	2,178.8	2,514.4	2,993.7	3,159.2	3,118.6	3,165.2
Other current transfers	2 392	113.5	169.7	99.0	19.9	138.6	214.3	351.7	122.8
Debit	3 379	**–295.1**	**–346.3**	**–413.5**	**–438.8**	**–732.2**	**–634.3**	**–655.4**	**–550.4**
General government	3 380	–2.0	–8.9	–6.6	–34.1	–4.9	–2.5	–17.9	–3.7
Other sectors	3 390	–293.1	–337.4	–406.9	–404.7	–727.2	–631.8	–637.5	–546.8
Workers' remittances	3 391	–200.1	–239.9	–308.0	–354.2	–422.6	–416.1	–443.1	–436.3
Other current transfers	3 392	–92.9	–97.5	–98.9	–50.5	–304.7	–215.7	–194.4	–110.4
CAPITAL AND FINANCIAL ACCOUNT	4 996	**–1,290.0**	**–160.5**	**1,596.4**	**1,939.9**	**2,343.0**	**1,833.4**	**588.6**	**885.9**
CAPITAL ACCOUNT	4 994	**93.5**	**2.1**	**8.5**	**62.8**	**12.8**	**283.9**	**.6**	**.3**
Total credit	2 994	*93.5*	*2.1*	*8.5*	*62.8*	*12.8*	*283.9*	*.6*	*.3*
Total debit	3 994	....	....	....	....	....	....	....	....
Capital transfers, credit	2 400	**93.5**	**2.1**	**8.5**	**62.8**	**12.8**	**283.9**	**.6**	**.3**
General government	2 401	....	....	....	....	....	....	....	....
Debt forgiveness	2 402	....	....	....	....	....	....	....	....
Other capital transfers	2 410	....	....	....	....	....	....	....	....
Other sectors	2 430	93.5	2.1	8.5	62.8	12.8	283.9	.6	.3
Migrants' transfers	2 431	....	....	....	....	....	....	....	....
Debt forgiveness	2 432	....	....	....	....	....	....	....	....
Other capital transfers	2 440	93.5	2.1	8.5	62.8	12.8	283.9	.6	.3
Capital transfers, debit	3 400	....	....	....	....	....	....	....	....
General government	3 401	....	....	....	....	....	....	....	....
Debt forgiveness	3 402	....	....	....	....	....	....	....	....
Other capital transfers	3 410	....	....	....	....	....	....	....	....
Other sectors	3 430	....	....	....	....	....	....	....	....
Migrants' transfers	3 431	....	....	....	....	....	....	....	....
Debt forgiveness	3 432	....	....	....	....	....	....	....	....
Other capital transfers	3 440	....	....	....	....	....	....	....	....
Nonproduced nonfinancial assets, credit	2 480	....	....	....	....	....	....	....	....
Nonproduced nonfinancial assets, debit	3 480	....	....	....	....	....	....	....	....

Table 2 (Continued). STANDARD PRESENTATION, 2003–2010

(Millions of U.S. dollars)

	Code	2003	2004	2005	2006	2007	2008	2009	2010
FINANCIAL ACCOUNT...............................	4 995 ..	−1,383.5	−162.6	1,587.9	1,877.2	2,330.2	1,549.5	588.0	885.6
A. DIRECT INVESTMENT.........................	4 500 ..	550.6	918.6	1,821.3	3,682.1	2,574.0	2,813.9	2,354.2	1,673.0
Direct investment abroad......................	4 505 ..	3.7	−18.2	−163.2	138.1	−48.1	−12.8	−72.4	−28.5
Equity capital...	4 510 ..	....	....	....	....	....	....	....	....
Claims on affiliated enterprises...................	4 515 ..	....	....	....	....	....	....	....	....
Liabilities to affiliated enterprises..............	4 520 ..	....	....	....	....	....	....	....	....
Reinvested earnings....................................	4 525 ..	....	....	....	....	....	....	....	....
Other capital..	4 530 ..	....	....	....	....	....	....	....	....
Claims on affiliated enterprises...................	4 535 ..	....	....	....	....	....	....	....	....
Liabilities to affiliated enterprises..............	4 540 ..	....	....	....	....	....	....	....	....
Direct investment in Jordan....................	4 555 ..	547.0	936.8	1,984.5	3,544.0	2,622.1	2,826.7	2,426.6	1,701.4
Equity capital...	4 560 ..	....	....	....	....	....	....	....	....
Claims on direct investors...........................	4 565 ..	....	....	....	....	....	....	....	....
Liabilities to direct investors.....................	4 570 ..	....	....	....	....	....	....	....	....
Reinvested earnings....................................	4 575 ..	....	....	....	....	....	....	....	....
Other capital..	4 580 ..	....	....	....	....	....	....	....	....
Claims on direct investors...........................	4 585 ..	....	....	....	....	....	....	....	....
Liabilities to direct investors.....................	4 590 ..	....	....	....	....	....	....	....	....
B. PORTFOLIO INVESTMENT......................	4 600 ..	−471.7	−288.9	312.7	−36.8	840.3	573.1	−629.6	770.6
Assets..	4 602 ..	−122.6	−199.0	143.6	−180.4	494.4	51.9	−600.0	41.0
Equity securities..	4 610 ..	−122.6	−199.0	143.6	−180.4	13.3	2.7	4.4	32.8
Monetary authorities.................................	4 611 ..	....	....	....	....	....	....	....	....
General government..................................	4 612 ..	....	....	....	....	....	....	....	....
Banks..	4 613 ..	−122.6	−199.0	143.6	−180.4	13.3	2.7	4.4	32.8
Other sectors..	4 614 ..	....	....	....	....	....	....	....	....
Debt securities...	4 619 ..	....	....	....	....	481.1	49.2	−604.4	8.2
Bonds and notes...	4 620 ..	....	....	....	....	481.1	49.2	−604.4	8.2
Monetary authorities.................................	4 621 ..	....	....	....	....	....	....	....	....
General government..................................	4 622 ..	....	....	....	....	....	....	....	....
Banks..	4 623 ..	....	....	....	....	481.1	49.2	−604.4	8.2
Other sectors..	4 624 ..	....	....	....	....	....	....	....	....
Money market instruments.........................	4 630 ..	....	....	....	....	....	....	....	....
Monetary authorities.................................	4 631 ..	....	....	....	....	....	....	....	....
General government..................................	4 632 ..	....	....	....	....	....	....	....	....
Banks..	4 633 ..	....	....	....	....	....	....	....	....
Other sectors..	4 634 ..	....	....	....	....	....	....	....	....
Liabilities..	4 652 ..	−349.1	−89.8	169.1	143.6	346.0	521.1	−29.6	729.6
Equity securities..	4 660 ..	−57.8	−89.8	169.1	143.6	346.0	521.1	−29.6	−20.4
Banks..	4 663 ..	....	....	....	....	....	....	....	....
Other sectors..	4 664 ..	−57.8	−89.8	169.1	143.6	346.0	521.1	−29.6	−20.4
Debt securities...	4 669 ..	−291.3	....	....	....	....	....	....	750.0
Bonds and notes...	4 670 ..	−291.3	....	....	....	....	....	....	750.0
Monetary authorities.................................	4 671 ..	....	....	....	....	....	....	....	....
General government..................................	4 672 ..	−291.3	....	....	....	....	....	....	750.0
Banks..	4 673 ..	....	....	....	....	....	....	....	....
Other sectors..	4 674 ..	....	....	....	....	....	....	....	....
Money market instruments.........................	4 680 ..	....	....	....	....	....	....	....	....
Monetary authorities.................................	4 681 ..	....	....	....	....	....	....	....	....
General government..................................	4 682 ..	....	....	....	....	....	....	....	....
Banks..	4 683 ..	....	....	....	....	....	....	....	....
Other sectors..	4 684 ..	....	....	....	....	....	....	....	....
C. FINANCIAL DERIVATIVES.......................	4 910 ..	....	....	....	....	....	....	....	....
Monetary authorities.................................	4 911 ..	....	....	....	....	....	....	....	....
General government..................................	4 912 ..	....	....	....	....	....	....	....	....
Banks..	4 913 ..	....	....	....	....	....	....	....	....
Other sectors..	4 914 ..	....	....	....	....	....	....	....	....
Assets..	4 900 ..	....	....	....	....	....	....	....	....
Monetary authorities.................................	4 901 ..	....	....	....	....	....	....	....	....
General government..................................	4 902 ..	....	....	....	....	....	....	....	....
Banks..	4 903 ..	....	....	....	....	....	....	....	....
Other sectors..	4 904 ..	....	....	....	....	....	....	....	....
Liabilities..	4 905 ..	....	....	....	....	....	....	....	....
Monetary authorities.................................	4 906 ..	....	....	....	....	....	....	....	....
General government..................................	4 907 ..	....	....	....	....	....	....	....	....
Banks..	4 908 ..	....	....	....	....	....	....	....	....
Other sectors..	4 909 ..	....	....	....	....	....	....	....	....

Table 2 (Concluded). STANDARD PRESENTATION, 2003–2010

(Millions of U.S. dollars)

	Code	2003	2004	2005	2006	2007	2008	2009	2010
D. OTHER INVESTMENT	4 700	−285.8	−710.6	−362.6	−414.8	−270.6	−699.9	1,975.4	−102.1
Assets	4 703	252.9	−680.8	−615.9	−1,148.0	−939.6	734.6	1,503.4	−1,228.7
Trade credits	4 706	....	....	....	....	....	−163.1	143.9	−76.1
General government	4 707	....	....	....	....	....	....	....	....
of which: Short-term	4 709	....	....	....	....	....	....	....	....
Other sectors	4 710	....	....	....	....	....	−163.1	143.9	−76.1
of which: Short-term	4 712	....	....	....	....	....	....	....	....
Loans	4 714	−26.2	50.5	34.7	−117.6	4.5	−319.5	−575.9	−105.4
Monetary authorities	4 715	11.3	....	....	....	....	....	....	....
of which: Short-term	4 718	....	....	....	....	....	....	....	....
General government	4 719	....	....	....	....	....	....	....	....
of which: Short-term	4 721	....	....	....	....	....	....	....	....
Banks	4 722	−37.5	50.5	34.7	−117.6	4.5	−319.5	−575.9	−105.4
of which: Short-term	4 724	....	....	....	....	....	....	....	....
Other sectors	4 725	....	....	....	....	....	....	....	....
of which: Short-term	4 727	....	....	....	....	....	....	....	....
Currency and deposits	4 730	285.9	−682.5	−583.2	−838.6	−857.5	1,034.6	1,925.2	−1,016.2
Monetary authorities	4 731	....	....	....	....	....	....	....	....
General government	4 732	....	....	....	....	....	....	....	....
Banks	4 733	285.9	−682.5	−583.2	−838.6	−857.5	1,034.6	1,925.2	−1,016.2
Other sectors	4 734	....	....	....	....	....	....	....	....
Other assets	4 736	−6.8	−48.8	−67.4	−191.7	−86.6	182.5	10.1	−31.1
Monetary authorities	4 737	−33.9	−23.4	−36.0	−58.7	−58.3	−41.9	−26.8	−32.0
of which: Short-term	4 739	−33.9	−23.4	−36.0	−58.7	−58.3	−41.9	−26.8	−32.0
General government	4 740	....	....	....	....	....	....	....	....
of which: Short-term	4 742	....	....	....	....	....	....	....	....
Banks	4 743	27.1	−25.4	−31.5	−133.0	−28.3	224.3	36.9	.8
of which: Short-term	4 745	....	....	....	....	....	....	....	....
Other sectors	4 746	....	....	....	....	....	....	....	....
of which: Short-term	4 748	....	....	....	....	....	....	....	....
Liabilities	4 753	−538.6	−29.8	253.4	733.2	669.0	−1,434.4	472.0	1,126.7
Trade credits	4 756	3.7	−37.4	−7.9	47.5	29.9	61.6	−125.1	27.3
General government	4 757	....	....	....	....	....	....	....	....
of which: Short-term	4 759	....	....	....	....	....	....	....	....
Other sectors	4 760	3.7	−37.4	−7.9	47.5	29.9	61.6	−125.1	27.3
of which: Short-term	4 762	3.7	−37.4	−7.9	47.5	29.9	61.6	−125.1	27.3
Loans	4 764	−265.3	−269.2	−40.0	−54.7	−181.1	−2,682.3	313.7	155.1
Monetary authorities	4 765	−109.2	−109.7	−86.5	−88.4	−76.4	−59.4	121.8	107.1
of which: Use of Fund credit and loans from the Fund	4 766	−100.0	−98.1	−77.2	−88.4	−76.4	−59.4	−15.5	−3.9
of which: Short-term	4 768	....	....	....	....	....	....	....	....
General government	4 769	−101.0	−83.1	6.1	−92.0	−146.4	−2,577.5	217.6	−223.0
of which: Short-term	4 771	....	....	....	....	....	....	....	....
Banks	4 772	−1.4	3.7	40.1	70.0	−3.7	−54.5	−37.2	−11.1
of which: Short-term	4 774	....	....	....	....	....	....	....	....
Other sectors	4 775	−53.7	−80.1	.4	55.7	45.4	9.2	11.5	282.1
of which: Short-term	4 777	....	....	....	....	....	....	....	....
Currency and deposits	4 780	−102.3	307.9	232.7	832.3	782.2	1,196.7	53.8	934.6
Monetary authorities	4 781	−4.2	−17.8	.1	97.7	2.3	104.5	−195.5	487.7
General government	4 782	....	....	....	....	....	....	....	....
Banks	4 783	−98.0	325.7	232.6	734.6	780.0	1,092.2	249.3	446.9
Other sectors	4 784	....	....	....	....	....	....	....	....
Other liabilities	4 786	−174.8	−31.2	68.5	−92.0	37.9	−10.5	229.5	9.6
Monetary authorities	4 787	....	....	....	....	....	....	226.8	....
of which: Short-term	4 789	....	....	....	....	....	....	....	....
General government	4 790	−174.8	−31.2	68.5	−92.0	....	....	....	....
of which: Short-term	4 792	....	....	....	....	....	....	....	....
Banks	4 793	....	....	....	....	37.9	−10.5	2.7	9.6
of which: Short-term	4 795	....	....	....	....	....	....	....	....
Other sectors	4 796	....	....	....	....	....	....	....	....
of which: Short-term	4 798	....	....	....	....	....	....	....	....
E. RESERVE ASSETS	4 802	−1,176.7	−81.8	−183.5	−1,353.3	−813.6	−1,137.6	−3,112.0	−1,455.9
Monetary gold	4 812	−.4	....	....	1.0	−40.6	39.7	....	....
Special drawing rights	4 811	....	−.5	.9	−.5	−.8	−1.2	−226.0	.2
Reserve position in the Fund	4 810	....	−.1	−.1	−.1	−.1	....	−.1	....
Foreign exchange	4 803	−1,176.3	−81.2	−184.3	−1,353.7	−772.1	−1,176.1	−2,885.9	−1,456.1
Other claims	4 813	....	....	....	....	....	....	....	....
NET ERRORS AND OMISSIONS	4 998	91.4	121.5	675.3	−214.0	531.8	204.7	536.9	425.7

Table 3. INTERNATIONAL INVESTMENT POSITION (End-period stocks), 2003–2010

(Millions of U.S. dollars)

	Code	2003	2004	2005	2006	2007	2008	2009	2010
ASSETS..	8 995 C.	**12,684.4**	**13,849.4**	**14,452.6**	**17,138.0**	**18,681.5**	**18,972.5**	**21,323.2**	**24,017.5**
Direct investment abroad...................	8 505 ..	**80.3**	**286.6**	**449.6**	**311.6**	**359.7**	**372.4**	**444.4**	**473.1**
Equity capital and reinvested earnings............	8 506 ..	80.3	286.6	449.6	311.6	359.7	372.4	444.4	473.1
Claims on affiliated enterprises................	8 507 ..	80.3	286.6	449.6	311.6	359.7	372.4	444.4	473.1
Liabilities to affiliated enterprises............	8 508 ..	....	....	....	....	....	....	....	....
Other capital..	8 530 ..	....	....	....	....	....	....	....	....
Claims on affiliated enterprises................	8 535 ..	....	....	....	....	....	....	....	....
Liabilities to affiliated enterprises............	8 540 ..	....	....	....	....	....	....	....	....
Portfolio investment............................	8 602 ..	**642.3**	**862.6**	**719.2**	**902.0**	**410.7**	**353.6**	**960.1**	**930.6**
Equity securities......................................	8 610 ..	22.7	49.1	92.1	61.2	71.1	69.1	88.0	96.1
Monetary authorities............................	8 611 ..	....	....	....	....	....	....	....	....
General government.............................	8 612 ..	....	....	....	....	....	....	....	....
Banks..	8 613 ..	22.7	24.0	60.8	27.4	40.9	40.9	61.3	69.3
Other sectors......................................	8 614 ..	....	25.1	31.3	33.9	30.2	28.2	26.8	26.8
Debt securities..	8 619 ..	619.6	813.5	627.1	840.8	339.6	284.5	872.1	834.5
Bonds and notes..................................	8 620 ..	619.6	813.5	627.1	840.8	339.6	284.5	872.1	834.5
Monetary authorities.........................	8 621 ..	....	....	....	....	....	....	....	....
General government..........................	8 622 ..	....	....	....	....	....	....	....	....
Banks..	8 623 ..	619.6	813.5	627.1	840.8	339.6	284.5	872.1	834.5
Other sectors....................................	8 624 ..	....	....	....	....	....	....	....	....
Money market instruments...................	8 630 ..	....	....	....	....	....	....	....	....
Monetary authorities.........................	8 631 ..	....	....	....	....	....	....	....	....
General government..........................	8 632 ..	....	....	....	....	....	....	....	....
Banks..	8 633 ..	....	....	....	....	....	....	....	....
Other sectors....................................	8 634 ..	....	....	....	....	....	....	....	....
Financial derivatives...........................	8 900 ..	....	....	....	....	....	....	....	....
Monetary authorities..............................	8 901 ..	....	....	....	....	....	....	....	....
General government...............................	8 902 ..	....	....	....	....	....	....	....	....
Banks..	8 903 ..	....	....	....	....	....	....	....	....
Other sectors...	8 904 ..	....	....	....	....	....	....	....	....
Other investment................................	8 703 ..	**6,596.2**	**7,253.9**	**7,835.8**	**8,946.1**	**9,982.1**	**9,331.0**	**7,795.8**	**8,996.5**
Trade credits..	8 706 ..	....	....	....	....	151.6	314.9	170.6	246.5
General government.............................	8 707 ..	....	....	....	....	....	....	....	....
of which: Short-term.......................	8 709 ..	....	....	....	....	....	....	....	....
Other sectors......................................	8 710 ..	....	....	....	....	151.6	314.9	170.6	246.5
of which: Short-term.......................	8 712 ..	....	....	....	....	....	....	....	....
Loans..	8 714 ..	1,490.7	1,440.2	1,405.5	1,523.0	1,518.5	1,837.7	2,411.5	2,516.9
Monetary authorities............................	8 715 ..	1,081.7	1,081.7	1,081.7	1,081.7	1,081.7	1,081.3	1,080.1	1,080.1
of which: Short-term.......................	8 718 ..	....	....	....	....	....	....	....	....
General government.............................	8 719 ..	....	....	....	....	....	....	....	....
of which: Short-term.......................	8 721 ..	....	....	....	....	....	....	....	....
Banks..	8 722 ..	409.0	358.5	323.8	441.3	436.8	756.3	1,331.4	1,436.8
of which: Short-term.......................	8 724 ..	*387.2*	*315.4*	*245.3*	*327.1*	*301.3*	*634.4*	*1,183.2*	*1,301.1*
Other sectors......................................	8 725 ..	....	....	....	....	....	....	....	....
of which: Short-term.......................	8 727 ..	....	....	....	....	....	....	....	....
Currency and deposits..............................	8 730 ..	4,642.9	5,325.5	5,908.6	6,747.3	7,604.8	6,566.8	4,634.5	5,650.7
Monetary authorities............................	8 731 ..	....	....	....	....	....	....	....	....
General government.............................	8 732 ..	....	....	....	....	....	....	....	....
Banks..	8 733 ..	4,642.9	5,325.5	5,908.6	6,747.3	7,604.8	6,566.8	4,634.5	5,650.7
Other sectors......................................	8 734 ..	....	....	....	....	....	....	....	....
Other assets...	8 736 ..	462.6	488.2	521.7	675.9	707.2	611.7	579.2	582.4
Monetary authorities............................	8 737 ..	56.8	57.0	59.1	80.3	83.2	212.5	217.3	221.4
of which: Short-term.......................	8 739 ..	....	....	....	....	....	....	....	....
General government.............................	8 740 ..	....	....	....	....	....	....	....	....
of which: Short-term.......................	8 742 ..	....	....	....	....	....	....	....	....
Banks..	8 743 ..	405.8	431.2	462.6	595.6	624.0	399.2	361.8	361.0
of which: Short-term.......................	8 745 ..	....	....	....	....	....	....	....	....
Other sectors......................................	8 746 ..	....	....	....	....	....	....	....	....
of which: Short-term.......................	8 748 ..	....	....	....	....	....	....	....	....
Reserve assets...................................	8 802 ..	**5,365.7**	**5,446.3**	**5,447.9**	**6,978.3**	**7,929.0**	**8,915.5**	**12,122.9**	**13,617.4**
Monetary gold..	8 812 ..	171.4	179.5	212.3	257.1	387.0	356.4	449.9	579.6
Special drawing rights..............................	8 811 ..	1.1	1.7	.6	1.3	2.2	3.2	230.0	225.8
Reserve position in the Fund.....................	8 810 ..	.1	.1	.2	.3	.4	.4	.5	.5
Foreign exchange....................................	8 803 ..	5,193.1	5,264.9	5,234.8	6,719.6	7,539.4	8,555.5	11,442.5	12,811.5
Other claims..	8 813 ..	....	....	....	....	....	....	....	....

Table 3 (Concluded). INTERNATIONAL INVESTMENT POSITION (End-period stocks), 2003–2010

(Millions of U.S. dollars)

	Code	2003	2004	2005	2006	2007	2008	2009	2010
LIABILITIES..	8 995 D.	**19,878.7**	**24,602.9**	**34,342.5**	**32,618.4**	**40,517.3**	**38,662.1**	**38,364.5**	**41,572.1**
Direct investment in Jordan..................	8 555 ..	**5,004.2**	**8,315.7**	**13,228.8**	**12,713.1**	**19,012.7**	**20,405.8**	**20,761.4**	**21,898.6**
Equity capital and reinvested earnings...........	8 556 ..	5,004.2	8,315.7	13,228.8	12,713.1	19,012.7	20,405.8	20,761.4	21,898.6
Claims on direct investors........................	8 557 ..	....	....	....	....	....	....	....	....
Liabilities to direct investors....................	8 558 ..	5,004.2	8,315.7	13,228.8	12,713.1	19,012.7	20,405.8	20,761.4	21,898.6
Other capital..	8 580 ..	....	....	....	....	....	....	....	....
Claims on direct investors........................	8 585 ..	....	....	....	....	....	....	....	....
Liabilities to direct investors....................	8 590 ..	....	....	....	....	....	....	....	....
Portfolio investment..........................	8 652 ..	**2,210.3**	**3,260.4**	**8,210.0**	**5,896.5**	**6,531.9**	**4,385.1**	**3,329.6**	**4,116.5**
Equity securities.....................................	8 660 ..	2,210.3	3,260.4	8,210.0	5,896.5	6,531.9	4,385.1	3,329.6	3,397.0
Banks..	8 663 ..	1,808.6	2,804.8	7,382.2	5,063.9	5,557.6	3,562.6	2,549.4	2,694.6
Other sectors.......................................	8 664 ..	401.7	455.6	827.8	832.6	974.3	822.5	780.1	702.4
Debt securities.......................................	8 669 ..	....	....	....	....	....	....	....	719.4
Bonds and notes...................................	8 670 ..	....	....	....	....	....	....	....	719.4
Monetary authorities...........................	8 671 ..	....	....	....	....	....	....	....	....
General government............................	8 672 ..	....	....	....	....	....	....	....	719.4
Banks...	8 673 ..	....	....	....	....	....	....	....	....
Other sectors.....................................	8 674 ..	....	....	....	....	....	....	....	....
Money market instruments.....................	8 680 ..	....	....	....	....	....	....	....	....
Monetary authorities...........................	8 681 ..	....	....	....	....	....	....	....	....
General government............................	8 682 ..	....	....	....	....	....	....	....	....
Banks...	8 683 ..	....	....	....	....	....	....	....	....
Other sectors.....................................	8 684 ..	....	....	....	....	....	....	....	....
Financial derivatives..........................	8 905 ..	....	....	....	....	....	....	....	....
Monetary authorities..............................	8 906 ..	....	....	....	....	....	....	....	....
General government...............................	8 907 ..	....	....	....	....	....	....	....	....
Banks..	8 908 ..	....	....	....	....	....	....	....	....
Other sectors..	8 909 ..	....	....	....	....	....	....	....	....
Other investment..............................	8 753 ..	**12,664.1**	**13,026.9**	**12,903.7**	**14,008.8**	**14,972.6**	**13,871.2**	**14,273.5**	**15,557.0**
Trade credits...	8 756 ..	395.2	357.8	349.9	397.5	427.4	488.8	363.2	390.6
General government...............................	8 757 ..	....	....	....	....	....	....	....	....
of which: Short-term.........................	8 759 ..	....	....	....	....	....	....	....	....
Other sectors.......................................	8 760 ..	395.2	357.8	349.9	397.5	427.4	488.8	363.2	390.6
of which: Short-term.........................	8 762 ..	*395.2*	*357.8*	*349.9*	*397.5*	*427.4*	*488.8*	*363.2*	*390.6*
Loans..	8 764 ..	7,723.4	7,631.4	7,214.8	7,506.8	7,619.5	5,272.2	5,524.5	5,840.9
Monetary authorities............................	8 765 ..	442.2	347.6	236.3	158.3	87.6	27.6	154.3	245.1
of which: Use of Fund credit and loans from the Fund....	8 766 ..	*421.4*	*337.7*	*236.3*	*158.3*	*87.6*	*27.6*	*11.9*	*7.8*
of which: Short-term.......................	8 768 ..	....	....	....	....	....	....	....	....
General government............................	8 769 ..	6,907.6	7,055.2	6,561.2	6,784.4	6,915.4	4,677.1	4,840.7	4,783.7
of which: Short-term.......................	8 771 ..	....	....	....	....	....	....	....	....
Banks..	8 772 ..	9.4	13.1	53.2	123.1	119.5	64.9	27.6	16.5
of which: Short-term.......................	8 774 ..	*9.4*	*13.1*	*53.2*	*123.1*	*119.5*	*64.9*	*27.6*	*16.5*
Other sectors.....................................	8 775 ..	364.0	215.5	364.2	441.0	497.0	502.7	501.8	795.6
of which: Short-term.......................	8 777 ..	....	....	....	....	....	....	....	....
Currency and deposits............................	8 780 ..	4,309.9	4,833.2	5,065.9	5,897.9	6,680.1	7,875.7	7,920.8	8,855.5
Monetary authorities............................	8 781 ..	176.0	158.3	158.4	256.0	258.1	362.5	166.6	654.4
General government............................	8 782 ..	....	....	....	....	....	....	....	....
Banks..	8 783 ..	4,133.9	4,674.9	4,907.5	5,641.9	6,422.0	7,513.2	7,754.2	8,201.1
Other sectors.....................................	8 784 ..	....	....	....	....	....	....	....	....
Other liabilities.....................................	8 786 ..	235.7	204.5	273.1	206.6	245.7	234.5	464.9	470.0
Monetary authorities............................	8 787 ..	....	....	....	25.4	26.7	26.1	254.1	249.6
of which: Short-term.......................	8 789 ..	....	....	....	....	....	....	....	....
General government............................	8 790 ..	....	....	....	....	....	....	....	....
of which: Short-term.......................	8 792 ..	....	....	....	....	....	....	....	....
Banks..	8 793 ..	235.7	204.5	273.1	181.2	219.0	208.4	210.8	220.4
of which: Short-term.......................	8 795 ..	*235.7*	*204.5*	*273.1*	*181.2*	*219.0*	*208.4*	*210.8*	*220.4*
Other sectors.....................................	8 796 ..	....	....	....	....	....	....	....	....
of which: Short-term.......................	8 798 ..	....	....	....	....	....	....	....	....
NET INTERNATIONAL INVESTMENT POSITION........	8 995 ..	**–7,194.2**	**–10,753.6**	**–19,889.9**	**–15,480.4**	**–21,835.8**	**–19,689.6**	**–17,041.3**	**–17,554.6**
Conversion rates: Jordanian dinar per U.S. dollar (end of period)...........................	0 102 ..	.7090	.7090	.7090	.7090	.7090	.7092	.7100	.7100

Table 1. ANALYTIC PRESENTATION, 2003–2010

(Millions of U.S. dollars)

	Code	2003	2004	2005	2006	2007	2008	2009	2010
A. Current Account[1]	4 993 Z.	**−272.6**	**335.4**	**−1,055.8**	**−1,998.6**	**−8,321.9**	**6,325.5**	**−4,359.2**	**4,319.0**
Goods: exports f.o.b.	2 100 ..	13,232.6	20,603.1	28,300.6	38,762.1	48,351.1	71,970.8	43,931.1	60,837.9
Goods: imports f.o.b.	3 100 ..	−9,553.6	−13,817.7	−17,978.8	−24,120.4	−33,260.2	−38,452.0	−28,961.7	−31,956.5
Balance on Goods	4 100 ..	*3,679.0*	*6,785.4*	*10,321.8*	*14,641.7*	*15,091.0*	*33,518.8*	*14,969.4*	*28,881.4*
Services: credit	2 200 ..	1,712.3	2,009.2	2,228.4	2,818.7	3,564.3	4,425.6	4,233.8	4,244.6
Services: debit	3 200 ..	−3,752.7	−5,107.9	−7,495.7	−8,760.4	−11,729.8	−11,119.2	−10,044.5	−11,297.7
Balance on Goods and Services	4 991 ..	*1,638.6*	*3,686.7*	*5,054.5*	*8,700.1*	*6,925.5*	*26,825.3*	*9,158.7*	*21,828.4*
Income: credit	2 300 ..	255.3	422.5	680.3	1,430.5	3,463.5	3,240.7	2,500.3	1,834.8
Income: debit	3 300 ..	−2,001.9	−3,285.6	−6,377.2	−10,922.0	−16,551.4	−22,755.8	−15,335.5	−18,909.5
Balance on Goods, Services, and Income	4 992 ..	*−108.0*	*823.6*	*−642.4*	*−791.3*	*−6,162.4*	*7,310.2*	*−3,676.4*	*4,753.6*
Current transfers: credit	2 379 Z.	278.6	352.9	810.0	904.2	903.8	1,104.2	992.4	1,510.7
Current transfers: debit	3 379 ..	−443.3	−841.1	−1,223.5	−2,111.4	−3,063.3	−2,088.8	−1,675.2	−1,945.4
B. Capital Account[1]	4 994 Z.	**−27.8**	**−21.3**	**14.0**	**31.9**	**24.6**	**−12.6**	**−29.5**	**7,888.2**
Capital account: credit	2 994 Z.	123.1	113.1	120.9	106.6	116.3	85.1	94.4	7,965.4
Capital account: debit	3 994 ..	−150.9	−134.3	−106.9	−74.7	−91.7	−97.7	−123.9	−77.3
Total, Groups A Plus B	4 981 ..	*−300.4*	*314.1*	*−1,041.8*	*−1,966.6*	*−8,297.3*	*6,312.9*	*−4,388.7*	*12,207.2*
C. Financial Account[1]	4 995 W.	**2,765.8**	**4,700.7**	**898.0**	**16,168.9**	**8,235.0**	**1,622.3**	**7,901.5**	**−8,878.9**
Direct investment abroad	4 505 ..	121.3	1,278.9	145.9	384.7	−3,153.1	−1,203.9	−3,118.1	−7,805.9
Direct investment in Kazakhstan	4 555 Z.	2,092.0	4,157.2	1,971.2	6,278.2	11,119.0	14,321.8	13,771.4	9,961.0
Portfolio investment assets	4 602 ..	−2,073.1	−1,092.1	−5,157.1	−9,176.7	−4,101.3	−7,277.6	1,875.6	−7,166.0
Equity securities	4 610 ..	−311.8	−362.8	−423.8	−1,847.4	−1,531.6	593.5	−619.8	−798.3
Debt securities	4 619 ..	−1,761.2	−729.3	−4,733.3	−7,329.3	−2,569.7	−7,871.1	2,495.4	−6,367.7
Portfolio investment liabilities	4 652 Z.	182.1	675.0	1,204.4	4,675.4	−481.8	−2,099.9	1,120.5	15,878.0
Equity securities	4 660 ..	63.8	−12.8	149.7	2,788.9	828.3	−1,280.4	37.8	96.2
Debt securities	4 669 Z.	118.3	687.7	1,054.7	1,886.5	−1,310.2	−819.5	1,082.8	15,781.8
Financial derivatives	4 910 ..	15.9	−46.4	−112.6	−67.8	−366.6	187.3	56.8	13.0
Financial derivatives assets	4 900 ..	....	−44.6	−119.7	−91.6	−614.0	−363.3	367.2	261.8
Financial derivatives liabilities	4 905 ..	15.9	−1.8	7.0	23.8	247.3	550.5	−310.4	−248.8
Other investment assets	4 703 ..	−977.5	−4,466.0	−4,310.4	−8,032.6	−11,910.9	−3,633.5	−1,060.4	−6,351.8
Monetary authorities	4 701 ..	−128.9	−9.3	−73.5	−110.7	−369.0	151.4	−113.4	130.3
General government	4 704 ..	275.0	....	....	−212.8	−189.6	−94.0	1.0	.2
Banks	4 705 ..	−314.3	−1,755.1	−3,172.4	−6,081.5	−6,466.9	−1,953.8	401.9	−1,374.7
Other sectors	4 728 ..	−809.3	−2,701.6	−1,064.5	−1,627.5	−4,885.4	−1,737.1	−1,349.9	−5,107.6
Other investment liabilities	4 753 W.	3,405.0	4,194.2	7,156.7	22,107.7	17,129.7	1,328.1	−4,744.5	−13,407.3
Monetary authorities	4 753 WA	85.5	−67.4	−17.2	....	−1.8	.1	639.6	127.7
General government	4 753 ZB	57.4	−65.7	−827.3	−.5	−57.9	33.5	607.6	1,424.0
Banks	4 753 ZC	2,147.5	2,997.7	6,574.1	16,884.0	11,591.7	−5,950.1	−9,145.9	−17,848.9
Other sectors	4 753 ZD	1,114.7	1,329.6	1,427.1	5,224.2	5,597.7	7,244.7	3,154.2	2,889.9
Total, Groups A Through C	4 983 ..	*2,465.4*	*5,014.9*	*−143.8*	*14,202.3*	*−62.3*	*7,935.2*	*3,512.8*	*3,328.2*
D. Net Errors and Omissions	4 998 ..	**−931.9**	**−1,015.9**	**−1,800.0**	**−3,127.7**	**−2,966.4**	**−5,746.5**	**−1,055.6**	**1,406.5**
Total, Groups A Through D	4 984 ..	*1,533.5*	*3,999.0*	*−1,943.8*	*11,074.6*	*−3,028.7*	*2,188.8*	*2,457.1*	*4,734.7*
E. Reserves and Related Items	4 802 A.	**−1,533.5**	**−3,999.0**	**1,943.8**	**−11,074.6**	**3,028.7**	**−2,188.8**	**−2,457.1**	**−4,734.7**
Reserve assets	4 802 ..	−1,533.5	−3,999.0	1,943.8	−11,074.6	3,028.7	−2,188.8	−2,457.1	−4,734.7
Use of Fund credit and loans	4 766 ..	....	....	....	....	....	....	....	....
Exceptional financing	4 920 ..	....	....	....	....	....	....	....	....
Conversion rates: tenge per U.S. dollar	0 101 ..	**149.58**	**136.04**	**132.88**	**126.09**	**122.55**	**120.30**	**147.50**	**147.36**

[1] Excludes components that have been classified in the categories of Group E.

Table 2. STANDARD PRESENTATION, 2003–2010

(Millions of U.S. dollars)

	Code	2003	2004	2005	2006	2007	2008	2009	2010
CURRENT ACCOUNT	4 993	−272.6	335.4	−1,055.8	−1,998.6	−8,321.9	6,325.5	−4,359.2	4,319.0
A. GOODS	4 100	3,679.0	6,785.4	10,321.8	14,641.7	15,091.0	33,518.8	14,969.4	28,881.4
Credit	2 100	13,232.6	20,603.1	28,300.6	38,762.1	48,351.1	71,970.8	43,931.1	60,837.9
General merchandise: exports f.o.b.	2 110	13,201.4	20,536.9	28,180.8	38,608.7	48,197.0	71,770.1	43,809.1	60,618.6
Goods for processing: exports f.o.b.	2 150	....	....	....	....	....	....	....	....
Repairs on goods	2 160	9.3	7.4	1.4	.7	3.0	6.6	7.7	5.5
Goods procured in ports by carriers	2 170	22.0	58.8	118.4	152.7	151.1	194.1	114.3	213.9
Nonmonetary gold	2 180	....	....	....	....	....	....	....	....
Debit	3 100	−9,553.6	−13,817.7	−17,978.8	−24,120.4	−33,260.2	−38,452.0	−28,961.7	−31,956.5
General merchandise: imports f.o.b.	3 110	−9,439.9	−13,783.4	−17,929.4	−24,038.3	−33,076.9	−38,280.3	−28,880.0	−31,883.2
Goods for processing: imports f.o.b.	3 150	....	....	....	....	....	....	....	....
Repairs on goods	3 160	−92.7	−12.8	−25.6	−50.7	−138.3	−99.8	−42.3	−33.9
Goods procured in ports by carriers	3 170	−21.1	−21.5	−23.8	−31.4	−45.0	−71.9	−39.5	−39.4
Nonmonetary gold	3 180	....	....	....	....	....	....	....	....
B. SERVICES	4 200	−2,040.4	−3,098.7	−5,267.3	−5,941.6	−8,165.5	−6,693.6	−5,810.7	−7,053.1
Total credit	2 200	*1,712.3*	*2,009.2*	*2,228.4*	*2,818.7*	*3,564.3*	*4,425.6*	*4,233.8*	*4,244.6*
Total debit	3 200	*−3,752.7*	*−5,107.9*	*−7,495.7*	*−8,760.4*	*−11,729.8*	*−11,119.2*	*−10,044.5*	*−11,297.7*
Transportation services, credit	2 205	712.9	837.3	1,021.4	1,457.9	1,735.5	2,241.5	2,165.9	2,271.0
Passenger	2 850	*74.0*	*85.1*	*100.2*	*134.5*	*199.7*	*242.7*	*222.0*	*230.7*
Freight	2 851	*545.7*	*616.1*	*757.2*	*1,113.8*	*1,311.4*	*1,751.3*	*1,690.1*	*1,759.0*
Other	2 852	*93.3*	*136.0*	*163.9*	*209.5*	*224.5*	*247.5*	*253.7*	*281.3*
Sea transport, passenger	2 207	....	....	....	....	....	....	....	....
Sea transport, freight	2 208	....	....	.1	1.2	.4	.1	....	.1
Sea transport, other	2 209	15.8	21.3	30.0	37.4	24.0	32.1	46.3	34.2
Air transport, passenger	2 211	45.6	49.2	57.5	76.1	123.0	143.2	136.9	162.2
Air transport, freight	2 212	15.8	22.6	25.4	50.4	63.0	88.9	63.2	78.7
Air transport, other	2 213	69.6	94.2	116.5	146.0	175.6	183.1	172.6	209.6
Other transport, passenger	2 215	28.4	35.9	42.7	58.5	76.7	99.5	85.1	68.4
Other transport, freight	2 216	529.8	593.5	731.8	1,062.2	1,247.9	1,662.4	1,626.9	1,680.2
Other transport, other	2 217	7.9	20.6	17.4	26.1	24.9	32.3	34.8	37.4
Transportation services, debit	3 205	−583.3	−871.1	−1,167.5	−1,513.4	−2,120.4	−2,369.2	−1,862.6	−1,853.0
Passenger	3 850	*−114.3*	*−153.2*	*−186.6*	*−238.9*	*−314.0*	*−283.2*	*−187.4*	*−216.0*
Freight	3 851	*−433.3*	*−672.7*	*−898.5*	*−1,207.7*	*−1,670.6*	*−1,886.3*	*−1,509.6*	*−1,468.8*
Other	3 852	*−35.7*	*−45.3*	*−82.4*	*−66.9*	*−135.8*	*−199.6*	*−165.6*	*−168.3*
Sea transport, passenger	3 207	−.7	−.8	−.7	−.3	−.5	−.5	−.1	−.1
Sea transport, freight	3 208	−22.4	−34.7	−42.6	−55.9	−76.6	−85.4	−74.0	−69.8
Sea transport, other	3 209	....	−9.2	−18.2	−7.9	−8.7	−9.8	−9.3	−4.7
Air transport, passenger	3 211	−96.7	−132.2	−163.9	−207.7	−271.1	−228.0	−137.9	−168.7
Air transport, freight	3 212	−80.9	−125.8	−168.5	−226.2	−313.3	−352.4	−284.5	−271.7
Air transport, other	3 213	−31.8	−30.6	−45.2	−52.5	−52.7	−64.4	−61.2	−67.8
Other transport, passenger	3 215	−17.0	−20.2	−22.1	−30.9	−42.3	−54.7	−49.4	−47.2
Other transport, freight	3 216	−330.0	−512.2	−687.4	−925.6	−1,280.8	−1,448.6	−1,151.1	−1,127.3
Other transport, other	3 217	−3.9	−5.5	−19.0	−6.5	−74.5	−125.5	−95.1	−95.9
Travel, credit	2 236	564.0	717.8	700.9	837.9	1,013.0	1,011.6	962.8	1,004.8
Business travel	2 237	103.3	171.7	132.8	153.1	167.2	156.4	140.9	125.7
Personal travel	2 240	460.7	546.1	568.1	684.8	845.8	855.2	821.9	879.1
Travel, debit	3 236	−668.7	−843.6	−753.0	−820.7	−1,081.9	−1,077.8	−1,113.2	−1,220.7
Business travel	3 237	−43.5	−156.2	−160.1	−125.1	−151.4	−116.7	−130.6	−82.7
Personal travel	3 240	−625.3	−687.5	−592.9	−695.6	−930.5	−961.1	−982.5	−1,138.0
Other services, credit	2 200 BA	435.4	454.1	506.2	523.0	815.8	1,172.5	1,105.2	968.9
Communications	2 245	60.8	63.1	73.1	79.6	87.8	98.4	120.4	89.6
Construction	2 249	19.3	3.3	2.0	3.5	5.5	18.2	6.4	23.2
Insurance	2 253	2.0	3.3	3.8	8.9	35.4	83.2	114.6	74.9
Financial	2 260	14.1	18.9	18.3	22.0	75.6	112.5	48.8	28.6
Computer and information	2 262	.6	.9	1.0	1.3	2.2	8.1	9.1	11.3
Royalties and licence fees	2 266	....	....	....	....	....	....	....	....
Other business services	2 268	153.8	172.1	178.6	172.5	294.9	407.1	384.1	382.0
Personal, cultural, and recreational	2 287	....	.1	.2	.3	1.1	.8	.8	.8
Government, n.i.e.	2 291	184.8	192.4	229.1	235.0	313.3	444.3	420.9	358.5
Other services, debit	3 200 BA	−2,500.6	−3,393.1	−5,575.2	−6,426.3	−8,527.5	−7,672.1	−7,068.8	−8,224.0
Communications	3 245	−60.7	−67.7	−72.4	−94.3	−106.5	−120.9	−122.8	−134.4
Construction	3 249	−813.3	−733.5	−1,941.4	−3,237.7	−4,352.1	−3,187.7	−2,057.1	−1,666.0
Insurance	3 253	−88.7	−93.8	−173.4	−253.7	−246.1	−263.3	−325.1	−322.5
Financial	3 260	−21.2	−31.9	−47.5	−182.4	−193.1	−323.5	−285.5	−257.9
Computer and information	3 262	−20.6	−29.4	−52.9	−58.3	−78.5	−88.6	−118.9	−100.3
Royalties and licence fees	3 266	−19.6	−25.7	−30.9	−48.4	−68.0	−86.7	−64.4	−86.5
Other business services	3 268	−1,423.1	−2,354.6	−3,119.8	−2,397.3	−3,209.2	−3,371.6	−3,883.2	−5,449.2
Personal, cultural, and recreational	3 287	−12.4	−6.5	−16.5	−15.2	−17.5	−25.1	−28.5	−37.0
Government, n.i.e.	3 291	−41.0	−50.1	−120.4	−138.9	−256.4	−204.6	−183.3	−170.2

Table 2 (Continued). STANDARD PRESENTATION, 2003–2010

(Millions of U.S. dollars)

	Code	2003	2004	2005	2006	2007	2008	2009	2010
C. INCOME	4 300	**−1,746.6**	**−2,863.1**	**−5,696.9**	**−9,491.4**	**−13,087.9**	**−19,515.1**	**−12,835.1**	**−17,074.7**
Total credit	2 300	*255.3*	*422.5*	*680.3*	*1,430.5*	*3,463.5*	*3,240.7*	*2,500.3*	*1,834.8*
Total debit	3 300	*−2,001.9*	*−3,285.6*	*−6,377.2*	*−10,922.0*	*−16,551.4*	*−22,755.8*	*−15,335.5*	*−18,909.5*
Compensation of employees, credit	2 310	**3.9**	**3.9**	**6.3**	**10.6**	**11.1**	**5.4**	**5.0**	**4.6**
Compensation of employees, debit	3 310	**−229.8**	**−413.7**	**−734.7**	**−959.0**	**−1,214.4**	**−1,457.5**	**−1,309.9**	**−1,350.3**
Investment income, credit	2 320	**251.4**	**418.7**	**674.1**	**1,420.0**	**3,452.4**	**3,235.3**	**2,495.3**	**1,830.1**
Direct investment income	2 330	−16.7	−29.7	−162.4	−193.6	59.4	−188.8	−469.9	−428.6
Dividends and distributed branch profits	2 332	....	.2	7.7	1.4	226.1	120.7	48.0	237.5
Reinvested earnings and undistributed branch profits	2 333	....	7.6	−7.9	.5	31.1	.2	.3	3.5
Income on debt (interest)	2 334	−16.7	−37.6	−162.3	−195.4	−197.8	−309.7	−518.3	−669.5
Portfolio investment income	2 339	225.6	294.1	445.7	883.9	1,459.0	1,181.5	1,054.8	964.4
Income on equity	2 340	7.3	18.6	25.4	51.8	102.6	119.2	105.2	100.5
Income on bonds and notes	2 350	204.1	255.3	356.3	663.9	1,341.7	1,039.6	949.4	863.9
Income on money market instruments	2 360	14.2	20.2	63.9	168.1	14.6	22.7	.2	....
Other investment income	2 370	42.5	154.3	390.8	729.6	1,934.1	2,242.6	1,910.4	1,294.3
Investment income, debit	3 320	**−1,772.1**	**−2,871.9**	**−5,642.6**	**−9,963.0**	**−15,337.0**	**−21,298.4**	**−14,025.6**	**−17,559.2**
Direct investment income	3 330	−1,431.6	−2,346.6	−4,633.1	−7,693.7	−11,304.9	−16,956.0	−10,710.9	−14,922.9
Dividends and distributed branch profits	3 332	−288.2	−1,369.6	−3,601.0	−5,685.4	−7,769.5	−14,391.7	−7,068.9	−12,126.3
Reinvested earnings and undistributed branch profits	3 333	−769.5	−515.6	−206.4	−783.0	−2,038.4	−1,064.1	−2,234.2	−1,261.7
Income on debt (interest)	3 334	−373.9	−461.4	−825.7	−1,225.3	−1,497.1	−1,500.2	−1,407.7	−1,534.9
Portfolio investment income	3 339	−36.5	−84.8	−154.3	−341.9	−394.5	−321.4	−245.6	−897.5
Income on equity	3 340	−5.2	−11.5	−25.1	−116.3	−100.4	−26.2	−21.5	−108.1
Income on bonds and notes	3 350	−31.4	−73.3	−129.2	−225.6	−290.2	−295.2	−224.1	−789.4
Income on money market instruments	3 360	....	....	−.1	....	−3.9	....	....	....
Other investment income	3 370	−304.0	−440.5	−855.2	−1,927.4	−3,637.6	−4,021.0	−3,069.1	−1,738.7
D. CURRENT TRANSFERS	4 379	**−164.7**	**−488.2**	**−413.5**	**−1,207.2**	**−2,159.5**	**−984.7**	**−682.8**	**−434.6**
Credit	2 379	**278.6**	**352.9**	**810.0**	**904.2**	**903.8**	**1,104.2**	**992.4**	**1,510.7**
General government	2 380	211.7	275.8	726.2	810.3	739.7	950.9	776.5	1,268.5
Other sectors	2 390	66.9	77.1	83.8	93.9	164.1	153.3	215.9	242.2
Workers' remittances	2 391	38.3	53.5	55.8	73.0	131.9	120.2	193.2	220.9
Other current transfers	2 392	28.6	23.6	28.0	20.9	32.2	33.1	22.8	21.3
Debit	3 379	**−443.3**	**−841.1**	**−1,223.5**	**−2,111.4**	**−3,063.3**	**−2,088.8**	**−1,675.2**	**−1,945.4**
General government	3 380	−8.4	−14.5	−16.2	−23.8	−18.9	−30.2	−24.0	−316.9
Other sectors	3 390	−434.9	−826.6	−1,207.2	−2,087.6	−3,044.4	−2,058.6	−1,651.2	−1,628.4
Workers' remittances	3 391	−421.1	−805.8	−1,158.5	−1,999.5	−2,997.9	−2,004.2	−1,624.2	−1,594.8
Other current transfers	3 392	−13.8	−20.8	−48.8	−88.1	−46.5	−54.4	−27.0	−33.7
CAPITAL AND FINANCIAL ACCOUNT	4 996	**1,204.5**	**680.5**	**2,855.8**	**5,126.2**	**11,288.3**	**−579.0**	**5,414.9**	**−5,725.5**
CAPITAL ACCOUNT	4 994	**−27.8**	**−21.3**	**14.0**	**31.9**	**24.6**	**−12.6**	**−29.5**	**7,888.2**
Total credit	2 994	*123.1*	*113.1*	*120.9*	*106.6*	*116.3*	*85.1*	*94.4*	*7,965.4*
Total debit	3 994	*−150.9*	*−134.3*	*−106.9*	*−74.7*	*−91.7*	*−97.7*	*−123.9*	*−77.3*
Capital transfers, credit	2 400	**123.1**	**113.1**	**120.9**	**106.6**	**116.3**	**85.1**	**92.4**	**7,965.4**
General government	2 401	9.7	2.4	1.1	2.0	3.4	4.2	.8	.9
Debt forgiveness	2 402	....	....	....	....	....	....	....	....
Other capital transfers	2 410	9.7	2.4	1.1	2.0	3.4	4.2	.8	.9
Other sectors	2 430	113.4	110.7	119.9	104.6	112.9	81.0	91.6	7,964.5
Migrants' transfers	2 431	105.3	108.5	116.4	102.8	80.0	65.9	62.6	65.1
Debt forgiveness	2 432	....	....	....	....	31.6	14.8	28.3	7,898.9
Other capital transfers	2 440	8.1	2.2	3.4	1.8	1.3	.2	.7	.5
Capital transfers, debit	3 400	**−150.9**	**−134.3**	**−106.9**	**−74.7**	**−91.7**	**−97.7**	**−123.9**	**−77.3**
General government	3 401	....	−.1	....	....	....	....	....	....
Debt forgiveness	3 402	....	....	....	....	....	....	....	....
Other capital transfers	3 410	....	−.1	....	....	....	....	....	....
Other sectors	3 430	−150.8	−134.2	−106.9	−74.7	−91.7	−97.7	−123.9	−77.2
Migrants' transfers	3 431	−150.8	−134.2	−106.9	−74.7	−91.2	−97.5	−123.5	−75.8
Debt forgiveness	3 432	....	....	....	....	−.5	−.2	−.4	−1.4
Other capital transfers	3 440	....	....	....	....	....	....	....	....
Nonproduced nonfinancial assets, credit	2 480	....	....	....	....	....	....	**2.0**	....
Nonproduced nonfinancial assets, debit	3 480	....	....	....	....	....	....	....	....

Table 2 (Continued). STANDARD PRESENTATION, 2003–2010

(Millions of U.S. dollars)

	Code	2003	2004	2005	2006	2007	2008	2009	2010
FINANCIAL ACCOUNT	4 995	**1,232.3**	**701.8**	**2,841.8**	**5,094.3**	**11,263.7**	**−566.4**	**5,444.3**	**−13,613.7**
A. DIRECT INVESTMENT	4 500	**2,213.4**	**5,436.2**	**2,117.1**	**6,662.9**	**7,965.9**	**13,117.9**	**10,653.4**	**2,155.1**
Direct investment abroad	4 505	**121.3**	**1,278.9**	**145.9**	**384.7**	**−3,153.1**	**−1,203.9**	**−3,118.1**	**−7,805.9**
Equity capital	4 510	−7.9	−69.8	−124.5	−821.8	−2,204.7	−4,105.0	−1,755.6	−6,157.7
Claims on affiliated enterprises	4 515	−7.9	−69.7	−124.5	−821.9	−2,204.5	−4,105.0	−1,755.6	−6,157.7
Liabilities to affiliated enterprises	4 520	....	....	....	.2	−.2	....	....	....
Reinvested earnings	4 525	....	−7.6	7.9	−.5	−31.1	−.2	−.3	−3.5
Other capital	4 530	129.2	1,356.3	262.5	1,207.0	−917.4	2,901.4	−1,362.1	−1,644.7
Claims on affiliated enterprises	4 535	4.3	−164.9	−83.2	−29.0	−92.1	−21.7	−2,660.9	2,429.7
Liabilities to affiliated enterprises	4 540	125.0	1,521.2	345.7	1,235.9	−825.3	2,923.1	1,298.8	−4,074.5
Direct investment in Kazakhstan	4 555	**2,092.0**	**4,157.2**	**1,971.2**	**6,278.2**	**11,119.0**	**14,321.8**	**13,771.4**	**9,961.0**
Equity capital	4 560	409.1	374.7	40.1	556.8	5,286.5	5,881.6	2,455.7	1,202.6
Claims on direct investors	4 565	....	−19.1	9.8	−35.0	3.1	−3.6	−12.5	−48.4
Liabilities to direct investors	4 570	409.1	393.8	30.3	591.8	5,283.4	5,885.2	2,468.2	1,251.0
Reinvested earnings	4 575	769.5	515.6	206.4	783.0	2,038.4	1,064.1	2,234.2	1,261.7
Other capital	4 580	913.4	3,266.9	1,724.8	4,938.4	3,794.2	7,376.1	9,081.5	7,496.8
Claims on direct investors	4 585	−266.2	82.3	−239.0	−61.9	−1,682.3	429.5	285.2	76.3
Liabilities to direct investors	4 590	1,179.6	3,184.6	1,963.7	5,000.3	5,476.5	6,946.5	8,796.3	7,420.5
B. PORTFOLIO INVESTMENT	4 600	**−1,891.0**	**−417.2**	**−3,952.7**	**−4,501.4**	**−4,583.1**	**−9,377.5**	**2,996.1**	**8,712.0**
Assets	4 602	**−2,073.1**	**−1,092.1**	**−5,157.1**	**−9,176.7**	**−4,101.3**	**−7,277.6**	**1,875.6**	**−7,166.0**
Equity securities	4 610	−311.8	−362.8	−423.8	−1,847.4	−1,531.6	593.5	−619.8	−798.3
Monetary authorities	4 611	−256.3	−391.7	−418.3	−1,781.4	−1,036.2	1,335.4	−700.0	−846.2
General government	4 612	....	....	....	....	....	....	....	....
Banks	4 613	....	....	....	....	.1	−3.4	−3.1	−14.9
Other sectors	4 614	−55.6	28.9	−5.6	−65.9	−495.5	−738.5	83.3	62.9
Debt securities	4 619	−1,761.2	−729.3	−4,733.3	−7,329.3	−2,569.7	−7,871.1	2,495.4	−6,367.7
Bonds and notes	4 620	−1,257.7	−363.1	−3,495.1	−7,392.6	−2,032.3	−316.1	−1,724.3	−3,752.3
Monetary authorities	4 621	−963.8	−428.2	−1,338.0	−4,101.8	−4,642.4	−177.3	−180.2	−3,943.6
General government	4 622	....	....	....	....	....	....	....	....
Banks	4 623	−414.1	−45.7	−1,738.9	−1,910.5	1,875.4	339.0	−160.0	−46.7
Other sectors	4 624	120.2	110.8	−418.2	−1,380.2	734.7	−477.8	−1,384.0	238.0
Money market instruments	4 630	−503.5	−366.2	−1,238.2	63.2	−537.4	−7,555.0	4,219.6	−2,615.4
Monetary authorities	4 631	−496.0	−369.2	−1,214.6	35.7	−466.2	−7,566.9	4,195.5	−2,615.0
General government	4 632	....	....	....	....	....	....	....	....
Banks	4 633	−.6	−3.3	−23.6	27.5	....	....	....	....
Other sectors	4 634	−7.0	6.3	....	.1	−71.2	11.9	24.1	−.4
Liabilities	4 652	**182.1**	**675.0**	**1,204.4**	**4,675.4**	**−481.8**	**−2,099.9**	**1,120.5**	**15,878.0**
Equity securities	4 660	63.8	−12.8	149.7	2,788.9	828.3	−1,280.4	37.8	96.2
Banks	4 663	46.8	50.9	167.6	1,762.2	361.9	−932.8	−296.0	−1.0
Other sectors	4 664	17.0	−63.7	−17.9	1,026.7	466.4	−347.6	333.8	97.2
Debt securities	4 669	118.3	687.7	1,054.7	1,886.5	−1,310.2	−819.5	1,082.8	15,781.8
Bonds and notes	4 670	118.4	687.1	955.2	1,115.6	795.9	−682.8	748.1	15,889.7
Monetary authorities	4 671	....	....	....	....	....	....	....	....
General government	4 672	54.3	21.2	−59.8	.5	−6.9	....	....	....
Banks	4 673	60.2	624.5	1,026.6	1,186.1	248.3	−607.9	718.2	8,236.3
Other sectors	4 674	3.9	41.4	−11.5	−71.0	554.5	−74.9	29.8	7,653.4
Money market instruments	4 680	−.1	.6	99.5	770.9	−2,106.0	−136.7	334.7	−107.8
Monetary authorities	4 681	....	....	99.4	740.3	−2,122.5	−97.9	362.2	−156.3
General government	4 682	−.1	....	−.1	33.1	18.0	−38.4	−27.4	48.5
Banks	4 683	....	....	....	....	....	....	....	....
Other sectors	4 684	....	.6	.1	−2.4	−1.5	−.4	−.1	....
C. FINANCIAL DERIVATIVES	4 910	**15.9**	**−46.4**	**−112.6**	**−67.8**	**−366.6**	**187.3**	**56.8**	**13.0**
Monetary authorities	4 911	15.9	−7.7	−38.8	−4.6	11.3	−9.2	24.9	8.9
General government	4 912	....	....	....	....	....	....	....	....
Banks	4 913	....	1.9	−.2	−41.2	−367.8	313.8	40.5	40.2
Other sectors	4 914	....	−40.7	−73.7	−21.9	−10.1	−117.3	−8.6	−36.1
Assets	4 900	....	**−44.6**	**−119.7**	**−91.6**	**−614.0**	**−363.3**	**367.2**	**261.8**
Monetary authorities	4 901	....	....	−5.6	−4.6	10.2	−31.7	31.7	−8.1
General government	4 902	....	....	....	....	....	....	....	....
Banks	4 903	....	.7	−2.6	−73.7	−621.7	−169.0	327.9	271.9
Other sectors	4 904	....	−45.3	−111.5	−13.3	−2.5	−162.5	7.6	−2.0
Liabilities	4 905	**15.9**	**−1.8**	**7.0**	**23.8**	**247.3**	**550.5**	**−310.4**	**−248.8**
Monetary authorities	4 906	15.9	−7.7	−33.2	....	1.1	22.5	−6.8	17.0
General government	4 907	....	....	....	....	....	....	....	....
Banks	4 908	....	1.2	2.4	32.5	253.9	482.8	−287.4	−231.7
Other sectors	4 909	....	4.7	37.8	−8.7	−7.7	45.3	−16.2	−34.1

Table 2 (Concluded). STANDARD PRESENTATION, 2003–2010

(Millions of U.S. dollars)

	Code	2003	2004	2005	2006	2007	2008	2009	2010
D. OTHER INVESTMENT	4 700 ..	**2,427.6**	**−271.9**	**2,846.3**	**14,075.2**	**5,218.8**	**−2,305.4**	**−5,804.9**	**−19,759.1**
Assets	4 703 ..	**−977.5**	**−4,466.0**	**−4,310.4**	**−8,032.6**	**−11,910.9**	**−3,633.5**	**−1,060.4**	**−6,351.8**
Trade credits	4 706 ..	−617.0	−1,029.4	−1,034.4	−1,641.4	−2,510.0	−207.7	868.3	−1,957.2
General government	4 707 ..	....	....	....	....	....	....	....	....
of which: Short-term	4 709 ..	....	....	....	....	....	....	....	....
Other sectors	4 710 ..	−617.0	−1,029.4	−1,034.4	−1,641.4	−2,510.0	−207.7	868.3	−1,957.2
of which: Short-term	4 712 ..	−620.1	−899.6	−958.4	−1,592.7	−1,864.1	−76.6	677.0	−1,696.8
Loans	4 714 ..	−415.0	−1,394.8	−1,082.1	−5,147.5	−5,268.3	−2,232.2	1,922.0	3,664.2
Monetary authorities	4 715 ..	....	....	....	....	....	....	....	....
of which: Short-term	4 718 ..	....	....	....	....	....	....	....	....
General government	4 719 ..	....	....	....	1.2	1.2	1.2	1.2	1.2
of which: Short-term	4 721 ..	....	....	....	....	....	....	....	....
Banks	4 722 ..	−358.4	−1,423.6	−865.3	−4,990.1	−4,348.9	−1,492.2	2,762.1	3,446.2
of which: Short-term	4 724 ..	−101.5	−183.5	−314.9	−1,136.8	−597.6	−360.3	1,347.9	−49.7
Other sectors	4 725 ..	−56.6	28.9	−216.9	−158.6	−920.6	−741.2	−841.3	216.8
of which: Short-term	4 727 ..	−21.0	22.4	−202.0	−46.7	−559.9	−17.7	43.9	−395.8
Currency and deposits	4 730 ..	−218.0	−1,815.9	−1,893.1	−762.0	−3,879.0	−1,156.4	−631.5	−3,458.1
Monetary authorities	4 731 ..	−168.1	−9.3	−26.6	−122.3	−404.3	151.4	−113.4	133.5
General government	4 732 ..	....	....	....	....	....	....	....	....
Banks	4 733 ..	65.0	−263.9	−2,316.4	−928.2	−2,155.3	−340.9	666.4	−381.6
Other sectors	4 734 ..	−114.9	−1,542.8	449.9	288.5	−1,319.4	−967.0	−1,184.5	−3,210.0
Other assets	4 736 ..	272.5	−225.9	−300.7	−481.7	−253.7	−37.3	−3,219.1	−4,600.8
Monetary authorities	4 737 ..	39.2	....	−46.8	11.6	35.3	....	....	−3.2
of which: Short-term	4 739 ..	39.2	....	−46.8	11.6	35.3	....	....	−3.2
General government	4 740 ..	275.0	....	....	−214.0	−190.8	−95.2	−.3	−1.0
of which: Short-term	4 742 ..	....	....	....	....	....	....	....	....
Banks	4 743 ..	−21.0	−67.6	9.2	−163.2	37.2	−120.8	−3,026.5	−4,439.3
of which: Short-term	4 745 ..	−21.0	−67.6	9.2	−163.2	37.2	−120.8	−3,026.5	−4,439.3
Other sectors	4 746 ..	−20.7	−158.3	−263.2	−116.0	−135.4	178.7	−192.3	−157.3
of which: Short-term	4 748 ..	−20.7	−158.3	−263.2	−116.0	−135.4	178.7	−192.3	−157.3
Liabilities	4 753 ..	**3,405.0**	**4,194.2**	**7,156.7**	**22,107.7**	**17,129.7**	**1,328.1**	**−4,744.5**	**−13,407.3**
Trade credits	4 756 ..	224.8	413.6	279.0	1,507.3	1,401.0	395.6	−525.9	1,178.1
General government	4 757 ..	....	....	....	....	....	....	....	....
of which: Short-term	4 759 ..	....	....	....	....	....	....	....	....
Other sectors	4 760 ..	224.8	413.6	279.0	1,507.3	1,401.0	395.6	−525.9	1,178.1
of which: Short-term	4 762 ..	180.7	267.3	115.3	1,370.4	973.5	253.9	−364.8	1,229.2
Loans	4 764 ..	2,919.4	3,666.5	6,406.0	19,781.4	14,802.3	2,396.6	−7,338.2	−12,587.8
Monetary authorities	4 765 ..	....	....	....	....	....	....	....	....
of which: Use of Fund credit and loans from the Fund..	4 766 ..	....	....	....	....	....	....	....	....
of which: Short-term	4 768 ..	....	....	....	....	....	....	....	....
General government	4 769 ..	57.4	−65.7	−827.3	−.5	−57.9	33.5	607.6	1,424.0
of which: Short-term	4 771 ..	....	....	....	....	....	....	....	....
Banks	4 772 ..	2,007.1	2,763.8	6,078.2	16,038.2	10,707.1	−4,505.7	−11,585.6	−15,682.1
of which: Short-term	4 774 ..	675.2	401.2	3,601.8	494.0	−1,448.7	−1,769.2	−1,620.2	−107.5
Other sectors	4 775 ..	855.0	968.4	1,155.2	3,743.8	4,153.1	6,868.8	3,639.8	1,670.2
of which: Short-term	4 777 ..	85.6	71.5	123.0	766.5	366.9	837.3	−1,316.1	265.7
Currency and deposits	4 780 ..	126.4	93.4	497.6	652.6	757.1	−1,320.3	131.0	617.9
Monetary authorities	4 781 ..	....	.2	.1	−.3	−.8	.1	103.1	127.7
General government	4 782 ..	....	....	....	....	....	....	....	....
Banks	4 783 ..	126.4	93.2	497.5	652.9	757.9	−1,320.5	27.9	490.2
Other sectors	4 784 ..	....	....	....	....	....	....	....	....
Other liabilities	4 786 ..	134.5	20.6	−25.9	166.4	169.4	−143.7	2,988.6	−2,615.4
Monetary authorities	4 787 ..	85.5	−67.6	−17.3	.3	−1.0	....	536.5	....
of which: Short-term	4 789 ..	85.5	−67.6	−17.3	.3	−1.0	....	....	....
General government	4 790 ..	....	....	....	....	....	....	....	....
of which: Short-term	4 792 ..	....	....	....	....	....	....	....	....
Banks	4 793 ..	14.1	140.7	−1.5	192.9	126.7	−123.9	2,411.8	−2,657.0
of which: Short-term	4 795 ..	14.1	140.7	−1.5	192.9	126.7	−123.9	2,411.8	−2,657.0
Other sectors	4 796 ..	34.9	−52.4	−7.1	−26.9	43.6	−19.7	40.3	41.6
of which: Short-term	4 798 ..	34.9	−52.4	−7.1	−26.9	43.6	−19.7	40.3	41.6
E. RESERVE ASSETS	4 802 ..	**−1,533.5**	**−3,999.0**	**1,943.8**	**−11,074.6**	**3,028.7**	**−2,188.8**	**−2,457.1**	**−4,734.7**
Monetary gold	4 812 ..	....	....	....	....	....	....	....	....
Special drawing rights	4 811 ..	....	....	....	....	−.1	....	−537.5	....
Reserve position in the Fund	4 810 ..	....	....	....	....	....	....	....	....
Foreign exchange	4 803 ..	−1,538.5	−3,997.2	1,950.3	−11,077.2	3,017.8	−2,188.7	−1,919.7	−4,734.7
Other claims	4 813 ..	5.0	−1.8	−6.5	2.7	10.9	....	....	....
NET ERRORS AND OMISSIONS	4 998 ..	**−931.9**	**−1,015.9**	**−1,800.0**	**−3,127.7**	**−2,966.4**	**−5,746.5**	**−1,055.6**	**1,406.5**

Kazakhstan   916

Table 3. INTERNATIONAL INVESTMENT POSITION (End-period stocks), 2003–2010

(Millions of U.S. dollars)

	Code	2003	2004	2005	2006	2007	2008	2009	2010
ASSETS....................	8 995 C.	**14,283.7**	**23,070.7**	**30,174.2**	**59,425.5**	**77,610.8**	**92,786.2**	**97,367.5**	**117,625.5**
Direct investment abroad..........	8 505 ..	**300.4**	**−971.7**	**−1,141.8**	**−1,006.7**	**2,161.1**	**3,252.7**	**7,036.6**	**16,175.8**
Equity capital and reinvested earnings..	8 506 ..	475.8	558.3	673.8	1,999.2	4,221.9	8,171.7	10,590.7	18,061.5
Claims on affiliated enterprises..........	8 507 ..	475.8	558.3	673.8	1,999.4	4,221.9	8,171.7	10,590.7	18,061.5
Liabilities to affiliated enterprises........	8 508 ..	....	....	....	−.2	....	....	....	....
Other capital..........	8 530 ..	−175.4	−1,529.9	−1,815.6	−3,005.9	−2,060.8	−4,919.1	−3,554.1	−1,885.6
Claims on affiliated enterprises..........	8 535 ..	2.1	171.8	231.4	277.6	398.0	418.6	3,089.6	684.2
Liabilities to affiliated enterprises........	8 540 ..	−177.4	−1,701.7	−2,047.0	−3,283.5	−2,458.8	−5,337.6	−6,643.7	−2,569.8
Portfolio investment..........	8 602 ..	**4,563.6**	**5,903.3**	**10,962.2**	**20,104.8**	**24,842.0**	**31,591.1**	**28,110.0**	**34,038.7**
Equity securities..........	8 610 ..	641.5	1,075.2	1,512.7	3,271.1	4,901.2	3,491.7	4,439.6	5,197.7
Monetary authorities..........	8 611 ..	544.0	1,010.4	1,439.5	3,205.0	4,229.4	2,698.9	3,460.9	4,321.0
General government..........	8 612 ..	....	....	....	....	....	....	....	....
Banks..........	8 613 ..	....	....	....	....	....	2.6	26.0	38.1
Other sectors..........	8 614 ..	97.6	64.8	73.2	66.2	671.8	790.3	952.7	838.6
Debt securities..........	8 619 ..	3,922.0	4,828.1	9,449.5	16,833.6	19,940.8	28,099.4	23,670.4	28,841.0
Bonds and notes..........	8 620 ..	2,862.7	3,406.0	6,788.9	14,218.8	16,840.4	18,100.2	17,942.2	20,514.8
Monetary authorities..........	8 621 ..	2,011.8	2,560.5	3,729.9	7,888.8	12,942.4	14,107.1	14,586.9	17,817.6
General government..........	8 622 ..	....	....	....	....	....	....	....	....
Banks..........	8 623 ..	677.2	785.3	2,557.4	4,493.1	2,671.4	2,301.6	955.9	778.7
Other sectors..........	8 624 ..	173.7	60.2	501.6	1,836.9	1,226.7	1,691.4	2,399.4	1,918.5
Money market instruments..........	8 630 ..	1,059.3	1,422.2	2,660.6	2,614.8	3,100.4	9,999.2	5,728.2	8,326.2
Monetary authorities..........	8 631 ..	1,051.3	1,418.9	2,634.1	2,614.8	3,090.4	9,999.2	5,725.6	8,323.3
General government..........	8 632 ..	....	....	....	....	....	....	....	....
Banks..........	8 633 ..	1.8	3.3	26.5	....	....	....	....	....
Other sectors..........	8 634 ..	6.2	....	....	....	10.0	....	2.6	2.8
Financial derivatives..........	8 900 ..	**....**	**48.4**	**164.3**	**258.1**	**866.5**	**1,296.9**	**754.3**	**386.6**
Monetary authorities..........	8 901 ..	....	....	5.6	10.2	....	31.7	....	8.1
General government..........	8 902 ..	....	....	....	....	....	....	....	....
Banks..........	8 903 ..	....	3.0	1.9	77.8	696.2	948.9	583.8	205.3
Other sectors..........	8 904 ..	....	45.3	156.9	170.1	170.4	316.3	170.5	173.2
Other investment..........	8 703 ..	**4,457.6**	**8,810.1**	**13,119.8**	**20,942.2**	**32,111.9**	**36,773.4**	**38,373.2**	**38,733.5**
Trade credits..........	8 706 ..	1,878.5	2,957.4	3,949.9	5,614.1	8,496.3	8,639.2	7,498.9	9,658.9
General government..........	8 707 ..	....	....	....	....	....	....	....	....
of which: Short-term..........	8 709 ..	....	....	....	....	....	....	....	....
Other sectors..........	8 710 ..	1,878.5	2,957.4	3,949.9	5,614.1	8,496.3	8,639.2	7,498.9	9,658.9
of which: Short-term..........	8 712 ..	*1,725.0*	*2,694.2*	*3,648.0*	*5,258.6*	*7,384.1*	*7,438.6*	*6,504.3*	*8,365.4*
Loans..........	8 714 ..	580.6	1,855.6	3,022.3	8,287.1	13,719.5	17,195.3	15,233.6	11,404.8
Monetary authorities..........	8 715 ..	....	....	....	....	....	....	....	....
of which: Short-term..........	8 718 ..	....	....	....	....	....	....	....	....
General government..........	8 719 ..	39.9	39.9	39.9	38.7	37.5	36.3	35.1	33.8
of which: Short-term..........	8 721 ..	....	....	....	....	....	....	....	....
Banks..........	8 722 ..	478.1	1,765.2	2,636.3	7,734.3	12,155.9	13,579.3	10,793.6	7,225.6
of which: Short-term..........	8 724 ..	*191.9*	*326.0*	*632.8*	*1,886.8*	*2,505.4*	*2,833.5*	*1,453.6*	*1,468.6*
Other sectors..........	8 725 ..	62.6	50.5	346.1	514.1	1,526.1	3,579.7	4,405.0	4,145.4
of which: Short-term..........	8 727 ..	*24.0*	*18.3*	*290.2*	*342.4*	*917.4*	*927.4*	*225.9*	*614.1*
Currency and deposits..........	8 730 ..	1,848.4	3,630.4	5,499.3	6,118.8	8,695.4	9,767.5	10,045.5	11,667.2
Monetary authorities..........	8 731 ..	183.3	192.6	219.2	341.8	746.5	577.6	695.2	562.4
General government..........	8 732 ..	....	....	....	....	....	....	....	....
Banks..........	8 733 ..	798.3	1,062.8	3,355.0	4,321.5	6,751.1	7,050.8	6,447.5	6,724.9
Other sectors..........	8 734 ..	866.7	2,375.0	1,925.0	1,455.5	1,197.8	2,139.1	2,902.8	4,379.9
Other assets..........	8 736 ..	150.1	366.8	648.3	922.1	1,200.7	1,171.4	5,595.2	6,002.6
Monetary authorities..........	8 737 ..	....	....	46.8	35.3	....	....	....	3.2
of which: Short-term..........	8 739 ..	....	....	*46.8*	*35.3*	....	....	....	*3.2*
General government..........	8 740 ..	....	....	....	214.0	404.8	500.0	500.3	501.3
of which: Short-term..........	8 742 ..	....	....	....	....	....	....	....	....
Banks..........	8 743 ..	63.5	130.3	102.2	266.3	253.9	382.8	4,615.2	4,863.3
of which: Short-term..........	8 745 ..	*63.5*	*130.3*	*102.2*	*266.3*	*253.9*	*382.8*	*4,615.2*	*4,863.3*
Other sectors..........	8 746 ..	86.5	236.5	499.3	406.6	541.9	288.5	479.8	634.8
of which: Short-term..........	8 748 ..	*86.5*	*236.5*	*499.3*	*406.6*	*541.9*	*288.5*	*479.8*	*634.8*
Reserve assets..........	8 802 ..	**4,962.1**	**9,280.5**	**7,069.7**	**19,127.1**	**17,629.3**	**19,872.1**	**23,093.4**	**28,290.8**
Monetary gold..........	8 812 ..	725.9	803.6	985.5	1,376.2	1,852.5	2,000.7	2,500.7	3,052.2
Special drawing rights..........	8 811 ..	1.2	1.2	1.2	1.3	1.4	1.4	540.2	530.6
Reserve position in the Fund..........	8 810 ..	....	....	....	....	....	....	....	....
Foreign exchange..........	8 803 ..	4,229.4	8,468.7	6,069.5	17,738.6	15,775.4	17,870.1	20,052.6	24,707.9
Other claims..........	8 813 ..	5.6	7.1	13.6	10.9	....	....	....	....

Table 3 (Concluded). INTERNATIONAL INVESTMENT POSITION (End-period stocks), 2003–2010

(Millions of U.S. dollars)

	Code	2003	2004	2005	2006	2007	2008	2009	2010
LIABILITIES	8 995 D.	**29,041.5**	**38,772.8**	**50,451.5**	**88,390.9**	**121,928.3**	**131,628.2**	**140,681.6**	**151,600.7**
Direct investment in Kazakhstan	8 555	**17,587.1**	**22,376.5**	**25,607.4**	**32,879.4**	**44,590.0**	**59,034.7**	**72,547.1**	**81,351.8**
Equity capital and reinvested earnings	8 556	6,101.6	7,640.4	8,921.0	11,217.1	19,276.8	24,678.6	29,202.2	30,827.8
Claims on direct investors	8 557	....	−19.1	−9.0	−43.6	−41.5	−45.8	−54.5	−365.2
Liabilities to direct investors	8 558	6,101.6	7,659.5	8,930.1	11,260.6	19,318.4	24,724.3	29,256.7	31,193.0
Other capital	8 580	11,485.5	14,736.1	16,686.4	21,662.3	25,313.2	34,356.1	43,344.9	50,524.1
Claims on direct investors	8 585	−320.1	−237.1	−488.6	−567.2	−2,308.7	−505.0	−224.6	−152.9
Liabilities to direct investors	8 590	11,805.6	14,973.3	17,175.0	22,229.5	27,621.9	34,861.1	43,569.5	50,677.0
Portfolio investment	8 652	**581.0**	**1,310.8**	**2,721.1**	**11,142.1**	**14,313.3**	**7,077.6**	**8,414.6**	**23,890.6**
Equity securities	8 660	221.6	291.5	593.2	6,942.5	10,212.2	3,923.4	4,486.2	3,841.4
Banks	8 663	137.4	189.8	476.9	5,466.0	5,915.0	1,898.1	796.8	630.2
Other sectors	8 664	84.2	101.7	116.3	1,476.5	4,297.2	2,025.3	3,689.3	3,211.2
Debt securities	8 669	359.4	1,019.3	2,127.9	4,199.6	4,101.1	3,154.2	3,928.4	20,049.2
Bonds and notes	8 670	359.4	1,015.3	2,024.0	3,086.2	3,935.7	3,120.4	3,552.2	19,769.1
Monetary authorities	8 671	....	....	....	....	....	....	....	....
General government	8 672	129.1	113.4	52.3	14.3	....	....	....	....
Banks	8 673	120.2	754.1	1,824.8	2,984.1	3,266.2	2,518.3	2,752.0	10,715.7
Other sectors	8 674	110.0	147.8	146.8	87.8	669.5	602.1	800.2	9,053.4
Money market instruments	8 680	....	4.0	103.9	1,113.4	165.4	33.8	376.2	280.0
Monetary authorities	8 681	....	....	99.8	1,073.0	104.8	10.0	376.1	230.9
General government	8 682	....	....	....	38.8	60.3	23.8	....	49.1
Banks	8 683	....	....	....	....	....	....	....	....
Other sectors	8 684	....	4.0	4.2	1.6	.3	.1	.1	....
Financial derivatives	8 905	**40.9**	**38.8**	**44.3**	**67.9**	**313.6**	**935.6**	**620.3**	**411.7**
Monetary authorities	8 906	40.9	33.2	....	....	1.1	23.6	16.8	33.8
General government	8 907	....	....	....	....	....	....	....	....
Banks	8 908	....	1.0	1.8	34.1	278.7	775.9	547.8	323.4
Other sectors	8 909	....	4.7	42.5	33.8	33.8	136.1	55.6	54.6
Other investment	8 753	**10,832.5**	**15,046.7**	**22,078.7**	**44,301.5**	**62,711.3**	**64,580.4**	**59,099.6**	**45,946.6**
Trade credits	8 756	2,165.1	2,628.1	2,915.5	4,469.0	5,891.3	6,326.6	5,832.1	7,341.4
General government	8 757	....	....	....	....	....	....	....	....
of which: Short-term	8 759	....	....	....	....	....	....	....	....
Other sectors	8 760	2,165.1	2,628.1	2,915.5	4,469.0	5,891.3	6,326.6	5,832.1	7,341.4
of which: Short-term	8 762	*1,006.9*	*1,222.3*	*1,259.4*	*2,684.0*	*3,704.2*	*4,001.8*	*3,786.3*	*5,332.8*
Loans	8 764	7,841.8	11,564.2	17,801.2	37,620.7	53,581.1	56,507.5	48,614.8	35,946.6
Monetary authorities	8 765	....	....	....	....	....	....	....	....
of which: Use of Fund credit and loans from the Fund	8 766	....	....	....	....	....	....	....	....
of which: Short-term	8 768	....	....	....	....	....	....	....	....
General government	8 769	2,423.2	2,382.7	1,426.6	1,442.1	1,431.2	1,618.1	2,218.1	3,751.2
of which: Short-term	8 771	....	....	....	....	....	....	....	....
Banks	8 772	3,404.1	6,165.2	12,204.2	28,187.9	39,623.3	35,092.9	23,455.5	7,582.5
of which: Short-term	8 774	*1,359.7*	*1,728.7*	*5,318.2*	*5,801.4*	*3,747.5*	*2,010.9*	*353.1*	*227.7*
Other sectors	8 775	2,014.4	3,016.3	4,170.4	7,990.8	12,526.6	19,796.5	22,941.2	24,612.9
of which: Short-term	8 777	*212.9*	*275.0*	*369.2*	*1,162.7*	*1,437.3*	*2,247.2*	*927.5*	*1,141.9*
Currency and deposits	8 780	577.5	587.6	1,113.5	1,785.9	2,565.3	1,230.6	1,230.8	1,844.8
Monetary authorities	8 781	.1	.3	1.0	.8	....	.3	103.6	239.5
General government	8 782	....	....	....	....	....	....	....	....
Banks	8 783	577.4	587.3	1,112.5	1,785.2	2,565.3	1,230.3	1,127.3	1,605.2
Other sectors	8 784	....	....	....	....	....	....	....	....
Other liabilities	8 786	248.1	266.8	248.5	425.9	673.6	515.7	3,421.9	813.8
Monetary authorities	8 787	87.9	20.4	2.8	3.1	2.1	1.9	539.7	530.2
of which: Short-term	8 789	*86.0*	*18.5*	*.9*	*1.2*	*.2*	....	....	....
General government	8 790	....	....	....	....	....	....	....	....
of which: Short-term	8 792	....	....	....	....	....	....	....	....
Banks	8 793	17.6	174.9	174.8	366.2	491.4	379.7	2,747.7	120.4
of which: Short-term	8 795	*17.6*	*174.9*	*174.8*	*366.2*	*491.4*	*379.7*	*2,747.7*	*120.4*
Other sectors	8 796	142.6	71.5	70.9	56.6	180.1	134.1	134.4	163.2
of which: Short-term	8 798	*142.6*	*71.5*	*70.9*	*56.6*	*180.1*	*134.1*	*134.4*	*163.2*
NET INTERNATIONAL INVESTMENT POSITION	8 995	**−14,757.8**	**−15,702.1**	**−20,277.3**	**−28,965.4**	**−44,317.5**	**−38,842.0**	**−43,314.2**	**−33,975.2**
Conversion rates: tenge per U.S. dollar (end of period)	0 102	**144.22**	**130.00**	**133.98**	**127.00**	**120.30**	**120.79**	**148.46**	**147.50**

Table 1. ANALYTIC PRESENTATION, 2003–2010

(Millions of U.S. dollars)

	Code	2003	2004	2005	2006	2007	2008	2009	2010
A. Current Account[1]	4 993 Z.	**132.4**	**–131.8**	**–252.3**	**–510.4**	**–1,032.0**	**–1,982.6**	**–1,688.5**	**–2,512.2**
Goods: exports f.o.b.	2 100 ..	2,412.2	2,726.0	3,462.1	3,516.2	4,132.2	5,039.8	4,502.3	5,224.7
Goods: imports f.o.b.	3 100 ..	–3,568.6	–4,350.6	–5,601.7	–6,769.5	–8,388.2	–10,689.0	–9,489.8	–11,527.7
Balance on Goods	4 100 ..	*–1,156.4*	*–1,624.7*	*–2,139.5*	*–3,253.2*	*–4,256.0*	*–5,649.2*	*–4,987.6*	*–6,303.0*
Services: credit	2 200 ..	1,197.6	1,556.5	1,880.1	2,429.5	2,930.6	3,250.8	2,882.8	3,675.5
Services: debit	3 200 ..	–690.6	–939.2	–1,137.1	–1,401.5	–1,670.8	–1,870.2	–1,811.8	–2,015.7
Balance on Goods and Services	4 991 ..	*–649.3*	*–1,007.3*	*–1,396.6*	*–2,225.3*	*–2,996.2*	*–4,268.6*	*–3,916.5*	*–4,643.2*
Income: credit	2 300 ..	59.6	45.0	73.3	99.4	160.6	176.2	181.9	136.4
Income: debit	3 300 ..	–148.2	–171.5	–181.7	–169.5	–304.8	–221.4	–212.4	–291.8
Balance on Goods, Services, and Income	4 992 ..	*–737.9*	*–1,133.8*	*–1,505.0*	*–2,295.3*	*–3,140.4*	*–4,313.8*	*–3,947.0*	*–4,798.6*
Current transfers: credit	2 379 Z.	884.5	1,044.7	1,319.2	1,832.8	2,148.8	2,419.3	2,341.3	2,368.4
Current transfers: debit	3 379 ..	–14.1	–42.6	–66.6	–47.9	–40.4	–88.1	–82.8	–82.0
B. Capital Account[1]	4 994 Z.	**163.0**	**145.2**	**103.3**	**168.4**	**156.8**	**94.5**	**260.9**	**240.2**
Capital account: credit	2 994 Z.	163.0	145.2	103.3	168.4	156.8	94.5	260.9	240.2
Capital account: debit	3 994 ..	....	....	....	....	....	....	....	....
Total, Groups A Plus B	4 981 ..	*295.5*	*13.4*	*–149.0*	*–342.0*	*–875.2*	*–1,888.1*	*–1,427.7*	*–2,272.1*
C. Financial Account[1]	4 995 W.	**406.3**	**40.2**	**511.4**	**673.6**	**1,936.4**	**1,095.4**	**2,465.8**	**2,145.9**
Direct investment abroad	4 505 ..	–2.1	–4.4	–9.7	–24.0	–36.0	–43.8	–46.0	–1.6
Direct investment in Kenya	4 555 Z.	81.7	46.1	21.2	50.7	729.0	95.6	116.3	185.8
Portfolio investment assets	4 602 ..	–38.6	–71.7	–45.9	–23.6	–25.5	–35.9	–23.7	–51.2
Equity securities	4 610 ..	–12.2	–25.8	–27.9	–20.5	–24.8	–35.9	–8.8	–8.5
Debt securities	4 619 ..	–26.4	–45.9	–18.0	–3.1	–.7	....	–14.8	–42.7
Portfolio investment liabilities	4 652 Z.	.9	5.4	15.4	3.0	.8	9.8	2.8	33.5
Equity securities	4 660 ..	.6	3.2	3.1	1.8	.5	5.0	2.6	33.3
Debt securities	4 669 Z.	.3	2.1	12.3	1.2	.3	4.8	.2	.3
Financial derivatives	4 910 ..	....	....	....	....	....	....	....	....
Financial derivatives assets	4 900 ..	....	....	....	....	....	....	....	....
Financial derivatives liabilities	4 905 ..	....	....	....	....	....	....	....	....
Other investment assets	4 703 ..	–67.4	–307.1	–200.6	–259.6	–346.7	–631.6	544.6	97.2
Monetary authorities	4 701 ..	....	....	....	....	....	....	....	....
General government	4 704 ..	....	....	....	....	....	....	....	....
Banks	4 705 ..	–11.0	....	....	....	....	....	....	....
Other sectors	4 728 ..	–56.4	–307.1	–200.6	–259.6	–346.7	–631.6	544.6	97.2
Other investment liabilities	4 753 W.	431.7	372.0	730.9	927.1	1,614.8	1,701.3	1,871.9	1,882.1
Monetary authorities	4 753 WA	....	....	....	....	....	....	347.8	....
General government	4 753 ZB	–81.3	–171.4	–46.1	61.9	134.8	100.5	740.7	585.0
Banks	4 753 ZC	....	....	....	....	281.2	578.4	–55.1	–35.0
Other sectors	4 753 ZD	513.0	543.4	777.0	865.2	1,198.8	1,022.4	838.6	1,332.2
Total, Groups A Through C	4 983 ..	*701.8*	*53.7*	*362.4*	*331.6*	*1,061.2*	*–792.7*	*1,038.2*	*–126.1*
D. Net Errors and Omissions	4 998 ..	**–276.5**	**–66.8**	**–245.4**	**249.7**	**–249.9**	**297.4**	**79.8**	**267.7**
Total, Groups A Through D	4 984 ..	*425.2*	*–13.1*	*117.0*	*581.3*	*811.3*	*–495.3*	*1,118.0*	*141.6*
E. Reserves and Related Items	4 802 A.	**–425.2**	**13.1**	**–117.0**	**–581.3**	**–811.3**	**495.3**	**–1,118.0**	**–141.6**
Reserve assets	4 802 ..	–412.6	–36.6	–281.2	–615.8	–938.2	475.9	–1,317.7	–129.1
Use of Fund credit and loans	4 766 ..	16.7	–14.1	69.1	–13.5	106.2	–10.6	191.5	–25.4
Exceptional financing	4 920 ..	–29.3	63.8	95.1	48.1	20.7	30.0	8.2	12.8
Conversion rates: Kenya shillings per U.S. dollar	0 101 ..	**75.936**	**79.174**	**75.554**	**72.101**	**67.318**	**69.175**	**77.352**	**79.233**

[1] Excludes components that have been classified in the categories of Group E.

Table 2. STANDARD PRESENTATION, 2003–2010

(Millions of U.S. dollars)

	Code	2003	2004	2005	2006	2007	2008	2009	2010
CURRENT ACCOUNT	4 993	**132.4**	**−131.8**	**−252.3**	**−510.4**	**−1,032.0**	**−1,982.6**	**−1,688.5**	**−2,512.2**
A. GOODS	4 100	**−1,156.4**	**−1,624.7**	**−2,139.5**	**−3,253.2**	**−4,256.0**	**−5,649.2**	**−4,987.6**	**−6,303.0**
Credit	2 100	**2,412.2**	**2,726.0**	**3,462.1**	**3,516.2**	**4,132.2**	**5,039.8**	**4,502.3**	**5,224.7**
General merchandise: exports f.o.b.	2 110	2,334.5	2,617.6	3,347.1	3,355.1	3,991.8	4,949.9	4,413.9	5,032.5
Goods for processing: exports f.o.b.	2 150	....	....	....	....	....	....	....	....
Repairs on goods	2 160	2.6	2.5	2.7	7.2	9.0	11.1	10.2	12.0
Goods procured in ports by carriers	2 170	61.3	100.6	104.8	147.1	77.2	70.9	51.6	67.9
Nonmonetary gold	2 180	13.8	5.2	7.6	6.8	54.2	7.9	26.6	112.4
Debit	3 100	**−3,568.6**	**−4,350.6**	**−5,601.7**	**−6,769.5**	**−8,388.2**	**−10,689.0**	**−9,489.8**	**−11,527.7**
General merchandise: imports f.o.b.	3 110	−3,514.3	−4,299.3	−5,548.6	−6,712.8	−8,368.7	−10,409.7	−9,438.6	−11,155.4
Goods for processing: imports f.o.b.	3 150	....	....	....	....	....	....	....	....
Repairs on goods	3 160	−15.5	−16.1	−15.1	−17.4	−19.5	−53.3	−28.6	−73.0
Goods procured in ports by carriers	3 170	−38.8	−35.3	−38.0	−39.3	....	−225.8	−22.6	−299.1
Nonmonetary gold	3 180	....	....	....	....	−.1	−.1	....	−.2
B. SERVICES	4 200	**507.0**	**617.4**	**743.0**	**1,028.0**	**1,259.8**	**1,380.5**	**1,071.0**	**1,659.8**
Total credit	2 200	*1,197.6*	*1,556.5*	*1,880.1*	*2,429.5*	*2,930.6*	*3,250.8*	*2,882.8*	*3,675.5*
Total debit	3 200	*−690.6*	*−939.2*	*−1,137.1*	*−1,401.5*	*−1,670.8*	*−1,870.2*	*−1,811.8*	*−2,015.7*
Transportation services, credit	2 205	**487.8**	**598.5**	**736.5**	**990.0**	**1,129.8**	**1,284.9**	**1,082.3**	**1,562.6**
Passenger	2 850	*271.8*	*312.8*	*390.0*	*493.5*	*596.5*	*646.3*	*433.5*	*820.1*
Freight	2 851	*153.9*	*211.0*	*265.2*	*360.3*	*351.3*	*458.8*	*478.1*	*584.0*
Other	2 852	*62.2*	*74.7*	*81.3*	*136.1*	*182.0*	*179.7*	*170.7*	*158.5*
Sea transport, passenger	2 207	....	....	....	....	....	....	....	....
Sea transport, freight	2 208	....	....	....	....	....	....	....	....
Sea transport, other	2 209	49.2	59.8	62.7	110.2	138.3	140.4	139.1	145.0
Air transport, passenger	2 211	271.8	312.8	390.0	493.5	596.5	646.3	433.5	820.1
Air transport, freight	2 212	17.2	19.7	24.6	71.8	72.7	66.3	53.4	61.4
Air transport, other	2 213	12.9	14.9	18.6	25.9	43.7	39.3	31.6	13.5
Other transport, passenger	2 215	....	....	....	....	....	....	....	....
Other transport, freight	2 216	136.8	191.2	240.6	288.5	278.6	392.5	424.7	522.6
Other transport, other	2 217	....	....	....	....	....	....	....	....
Transportation services, debit	3 205	**−249.7**	**−346.3**	**−426.3**	**−670.4**	**−776.8**	**−859.8**	**−840.8**	**−933.0**
Passenger	3 850	....	....	....	....	....	....	....	....
Freight	3 851	*−223.1*	*−287.2*	*−347.1*	*−573.2*	*−694.3*	*−805.6*	*−783.6*	*−828.7*
Other	3 852	*−26.6*	*−59.0*	*−79.2*	*−97.2*	*−82.5*	*−54.2*	*−57.2*	*−104.3*
Sea transport, passenger	3 207	....	....	....	....	....	....	....	....
Sea transport, freight	3 208	−192.8	−253.5	−301.7	−507.0	−655.2	−765.1	−748.3	−797.7
Sea transport, other	3 209	−6.0	−35.3	−41.4	−14.9	−14.5	−8.1	−14.2	−19.6
Air transport, passenger	3 211	....	....	....	....	....	....	....	....
Air transport, freight	3 212	....	....	....	....	....	....	....	....
Air transport, other	3 213	−20.6	−23.7	−37.8	−82.3	−68.0	−46.2	−42.9	−84.7
Other transport, passenger	3 215	....	....	....	....	....	....	....	....
Other transport, freight	3 216	−30.4	−33.7	−45.4	−66.2	−39.1	−40.5	−35.3	−31.0
Other transport, other	3 217	....	....	....	....	....	....	....	....
Travel, credit	2 236	**347.4**	**485.7**	**579.1**	**687.5**	**916.7**	**752.2**	**689.9**	**799.9**
Business travel	2 237	48.5	56.7	64.3	97.7	107.3	84.1	55.8	104.4
Personal travel	2 240	298.9	429.0	514.8	589.8	809.4	668.1	634.2	695.6
Travel, debit	3 236	**−127.1**	**−107.5**	**−123.9**	**−177.8**	**−264.5**	**−265.6**	**−226.7**	**−211.9**
Business travel	3 237	−81.6	−49.3	−53.9	−66.6	−96.7	−118.9	−112.9	−120.3
Personal travel	3 240	−45.5	−58.2	−69.9	−111.2	−167.8	−146.7	−113.8	−91.6
Other services, credit	2 200 BA	**362.4**	**472.3**	**564.5**	**752.1**	**884.1**	**1,213.7**	**1,110.6**	**1,313.0**
Communications	2 245	15.2	113.2	177.7	283.3	328.7	436.6	378.4	359.6
Construction	2 249	....	....	....	....	....	....	....	....
Insurance	2 253	13.8	12.4	10.5	7.3	7.6	10.4	14.1	31.8
Financial	2 260	....	....	....	....	....	....	....	109.5
Computer and information	2 262	....	.4	1.1	.7	.8	1.1	.4	.3
Royalties and licence fees	2 266	11.6	16.6	17.5	9.9	23.0	32.8	19.5	53.8
Other business services	2 268	....	....	....	....	....	....	....	....
Personal, cultural, and recreational	2 287	.3	.3	.4	.7	2.1	1.9	3.0	2.1
Government, n.i.e.	2 291	321.5	329.5	357.4	450.2	522.0	730.9	695.1	756.0
Other services, debit	3 200 BA	**−313.8**	**−485.4**	**−587.0**	**−553.3**	**−629.5**	**−744.8**	**−744.3**	**−870.9**
Communications	3 245	−6.2	−108.4	−107.5	−130.4	−153.5	−188.8	−188.1	−164.8
Construction	3 249	....	....	....	....	....	....	....	....
Insurance	3 253	−40.9	−39.5	−58.9	−72.7	−47.2	−80.2	−90.7	−114.9
Financial	3 260	−31.7	−69.4	−17.9	−23.1	−27.5	−34.4	−37.2	−65.2
Computer and information	3 262	−1.6	−.7	−1.5	−1.8	−2.3	−2.3	−1.6	−1.5
Royalties and licence fees	3 266	−39.2	−50.3	−36.9	−19.7	−23.6	−28.4	−21.2	−17.8
Other business services	3 268	−76.5	−79.6	−180.7	−137.1	−183.1	−202.7	−212.7	−299.9
Personal, cultural, and recreational	3 287	−2.5	−1.2	−1.1	−1.6	−.8	−.6	−4.9	−7.4
Government, n.i.e.	3 291	−115.2	−136.3	−182.5	−166.8	−191.5	−207.3	−187.9	−199.3

Table 2 (Continued). STANDARD PRESENTATION, 2003–2010
(Millions of U.S. dollars)

	Code	2003	2004	2005	2006	2007	2008	2009	2010
C. INCOME	4 300	**−88.6**	**−126.5**	**−108.5**	**−70.1**	**−144.2**	**−45.2**	**−30.5**	**−155.4**
Total credit	2 300	*59.6*	*45.0*	*73.3*	*99.4*	*160.6*	*176.2*	*181.9*	*136.4*
Total debit	3 300	*−148.2*	*−171.5*	*−181.7*	*−169.5*	*−304.8*	*−221.4*	*−212.4*	*−291.8*
Compensation of employees, credit	2 310	....	....	....	....	....	....	....	....
Compensation of employees, debit	3 310	....	....	....	....	....	....	....	....
Investment income, credit	2 320	**59.6**	**45.0**	**73.3**	**99.4**	**160.6**	**176.2**	**181.9**	**136.4**
Direct investment income	2 330	....	....	....	....	....	....	....	....
Dividends and distributed branch profits	2 332	....	....	....	....	....	....	....	....
Reinvested earnings and undistributed branch profits	2 333	....	....	....	....	....	....	....	....
Income on debt (interest)	2 334	....	....	....	....	....	....	....	....
Portfolio investment income	2 339	....	....	....	....	....	....	....	....
Income on equity	2 340	....	....	....	....	....	....	....	....
Income on bonds and notes	2 350	....	....	....	....	....	....	....	....
Income on money market instruments	2 360	....	....	....	....	....	....	....	....
Other investment income	2 370	59.6	45.0	73.3	99.4	160.6	176.2	181.9	136.4
Investment income, debit	3 320	**−148.2**	**−171.5**	**−181.7**	**−169.5**	**−304.8**	**−221.4**	**−212.4**	**−291.8**
Direct investment income	3 330	−32.5	−30.6	−34.9	−38.9	−124.0	−52.0	−60.3	−66.8
Dividends and distributed branch profits	3 332	−31.1	−29.8	−34.1	−38.4	−108.5	−43.1	−59.4	−60.4
Reinvested earnings and undistributed branch profits	3 333	....	....	....	....	....	....	....	....
Income on debt (interest)	3 334	−1.3	−.8	−.8	−.5	−15.5	−8.9	−.9	−6.4
Portfolio investment income	3 339	−2.2	−6.8	−3.8	−5.4	−5.3	−15.6	−34.2	−51.2
Income on equity	3 340	−1.6	−5.3	−2.9	−3.3	−4.0	−13.5	−30.8	−45.4
Income on bonds and notes	3 350	−.7	−1.6	−.9	−2.1	−1.2	−2.0	−3.4	−5.9
Income on money market instruments	3 360	....	....	....	....	....	....	....	....
Other investment income	3 370	−113.5	−134.1	−143.0	−125.2	−175.5	−153.9	−117.8	−173.8
D. CURRENT TRANSFERS	4 379	**870.3**	**1,002.1**	**1,252.7**	**1,784.9**	**2,108.4**	**2,331.2**	**2,258.5**	**2,286.4**
Credit	2 379	**884.5**	**1,044.7**	**1,319.2**	**1,832.8**	**2,148.8**	**2,419.3**	**2,341.3**	**2,368.4**
General government	2 380	69.5	106.1	100.3	123.8	220.1	220.3	339.2	244.4
Other sectors	2 390	815.0	938.5	1,218.9	1,709.0	1,928.7	2,199.0	2,002.1	2,124.0
Workers' remittances	2 391	65.8	375.8	425.0	570.5	645.2	667.3	631.5	683.7
Other current transfers	2 392	749.1	562.7	793.9	1,138.5	1,283.5	1,531.7	1,370.6	1,440.3
Debit	3 379	**−14.1**	**−42.6**	**−66.6**	**−47.9**	**−40.4**	**−88.1**	**−82.8**	**−82.0**
General government	3 380	−7.5	−8.6	−10.1	−22.5	−24.1	−23.6	−22.0	−24.1
Other sectors	3 390	−6.6	−34.0	−56.4	−25.4	−16.4	−64.5	−60.8	−57.9
Workers' remittances	3 391	−6.6	−34.0	−56.4	−25.4	−16.4	−64.5	−60.8	−57.9
Other current transfers	3 392	....	....	....	....	....	....	....	....
CAPITAL AND FINANCIAL ACCOUNT	4 996	**144.1**	**198.6**	**497.7**	**260.7**	**1,281.9**	**1,685.2**	**1,608.7**	**2,244.5**
CAPITAL ACCOUNT	4 994	**163.0**	**145.2**	**103.3**	**168.4**	**156.8**	**94.5**	**260.9**	**240.2**
Total credit	2 994	*163.0*	*145.2*	*103.3*	*168.4*	*156.8*	*94.5*	*260.9*	*240.2*
Total debit	3 994	....	....	....	....	....	....	....	....
Capital transfers, credit	2 400	**163.0**	**145.2**	**103.3**	**168.4**	**156.8**	**94.5**	**260.9**	**240.2**
General government	2 401	163.0	145.2	103.3	168.4	156.8	94.5	260.9	240.2
Debt forgiveness	2 402	....	....	....	....	....	....	....	....
Other capital transfers	2 410	163.0	145.2	103.3	168.4	156.8	94.5	260.9	240.2
Other sectors	2 430	....	....	....	....	....	....	....	....
Migrants' transfers	2 431	....	....	....	....	....	....	....	....
Debt forgiveness	2 432	....	....	....	....	....	....	....	....
Other capital transfers	2 440	....	....	....	....	....	....	....	....
Capital transfers, debit	3 400	....	....	....	....	....	....	....	....
General government	3 401	....	....	....	....	....	....	....	....
Debt forgiveness	3 402	....	....	....	....	....	....	....	....
Other capital transfers	3 410	....	....	....	....	....	....	....	....
Other sectors	3 430	....	....	....	....	....	....	....	....
Migrants' transfers	3 431	....	....	....	....	....	....	....	....
Debt forgiveness	3 432	....	....	....	....	....	....	....	....
Other capital transfers	3 440	....	....	....	....	....	....	....	....
Nonproduced nonfinancial assets, credit	2 480	....	....	....	....	....	....	....	....
Nonproduced nonfinancial assets, debit	3 480	....	....	....	....	....	....	....	....

Table 2 (Continued). STANDARD PRESENTATION, 2003–2010

(Millions of U.S. dollars)

	Code	2003	2004	2005	2006	2007	2008	2009	2010
FINANCIAL ACCOUNT	4 995	**−18.9**	**53.4**	**394.4**	**92.3**	**1,125.1**	**1,590.7**	**1,347.9**	**2,004.3**
A. DIRECT INVESTMENT	4 500	**79.7**	**41.6**	**11.5**	**26.7**	**693.0**	**51.8**	**70.3**	**184.2**
Direct investment abroad	4 505	**−2.1**	**−4.4**	**−9.7**	**−24.0**	**−36.0**	**−43.8**	**−46.0**	**−1.6**
Equity capital	4 510	−2.1	−4.4	−9.7	−24.0	−36.0	−43.8	−46.0	−1.6
Claims on affiliated enterprises	4 515	−2.1	−4.4	−9.7	−24.0	−36.0	−43.8	−46.0	−1.6
Liabilities to affiliated enterprises	4 520	....	....	....	....	....	....	....	....
Reinvested earnings	4 525	....	....	....	....	....	....	....	....
Other capital	4 530	....	....	....	....	....	....	....	....
Claims on affiliated enterprises	4 535	....	....	....	....	....	....	....	....
Liabilities to affiliated enterprises	4 540	....	....	....	....	....	....	....	....
Direct investment in Kenya	4 555	**81.7**	**46.1**	**21.2**	**50.7**	**729.0**	**95.6**	**116.3**	**185.8**
Equity capital	4 560	27.0	29.9	5.6	3.0	665.3	22.8	31.6	89.4
Claims on direct investors	4 565	....	....	....	....	....	....	....	....
Liabilities to direct investors	4 570	27.0	29.9	5.6	3.0	665.3	22.8	31.6	89.4
Reinvested earnings	4 575	....	....	....	....	....	....	....	....
Other capital	4 580	54.7	16.2	15.6	47.7	63.7	72.8	84.7	96.4
Claims on direct investors	4 585	....	....	....	....	....	....	....	....
Liabilities to direct investors	4 590	54.7	16.2	15.6	47.7	63.7	72.8	84.7	96.4
B. PORTFOLIO INVESTMENT	4 600	**−37.7**	**−66.3**	**−30.5**	**−20.6**	**−24.7**	**−26.1**	**−20.9**	**−17.6**
Assets	4 602	**−38.6**	**−71.7**	**−45.9**	**−23.6**	**−25.5**	**−35.9**	**−23.7**	**−51.2**
Equity securities	4 610	−12.2	−25.8	−27.9	−20.5	−24.8	−35.9	−8.8	−8.5
Monetary authorities	4 611	....	....	....	....	....	....	....	....
General government	4 612	....	....	....	....	....	....	....	....
Banks	4 613	....	....	....	....	....	....	....	....
Other sectors	4 614	−12.2	−25.8	−27.9	−20.5	−24.8	−35.9	−8.8	−8.5
Debt securities	4 619	−26.4	−45.9	−18.0	−3.1	−.7	....	−14.8	−42.7
Bonds and notes	4 620	−26.4	−45.9	−18.0	−3.1	−.7	....	−14.8	−42.7
Monetary authorities	4 621	−.1	....	....	....	....	....	....	....
General government	4 622	....	....	....	....	....	....	....	....
Banks	4 623	....	....	....	....	....	....	....	....
Other sectors	4 624	−26.3	−45.9	−18.0	−3.1	−.7	....	−14.8	−42.7
Money market instruments	4 630	....	....	....	....	....	....	....	....
Monetary authorities	4 631	....	....	....	....	....	....	....	....
General government	4 632	....	....	....	....	....	....	....	....
Banks	4 633	....	....	....	....	....	....	....	....
Other sectors	4 634	....	....	....	....	....	....	....	....
Liabilities	4 652	**.9**	**5.4**	**15.4**	**3.0**	**.8**	**9.8**	**2.8**	**33.5**
Equity securities	4 660	.6	3.2	3.1	1.8	.5	5.0	2.6	33.3
Banks	4 663	.6	3.2	3.1	1.8	.5	5.0	2.6	33.3
Other sectors	4 664	....	....	....	....	....	....	....	....
Debt securities	4 669	.3	2.1	12.3	1.2	.3	4.8	.2	.3
Bonds and notes	4 670	.3	2.1	12.3	1.2	.3	4.8	.2	.3
Monetary authorities	4 671	.3	2.1	12.3	1.2	.3	4.8	.2	.3
General government	4 672	....	....	....	....	....	....	....	....
Banks	4 673	....	....	....	....	....	....	....	....
Other sectors	4 674	....	....	....	....	....	....	....	....
Money market instruments	4 680	....	....	....	....	....	....	....	....
Monetary authorities	4 681	....	....	....	....	....	....	....	....
General government	4 682	....	....	....	....	....	....	....	....
Banks	4 683	....	....	....	....	....	....	....	....
Other sectors	4 684	....	....	....	....	....	....	....	....
C. FINANCIAL DERIVATIVES	4 910	....	....	....	....	....	....	....	....
Monetary authorities	4 911	....	....	....	....	....	....	....	....
General government	4 912	....	....	....	....	....	....	....	....
Banks	4 913	....	....	....	....	....	....	....	....
Other sectors	4 914	....	....	....	....	....	....	....	....
Assets	4 900	....	....	....	....	....	....	....	....
Monetary authorities	4 901	....	....	....	....	....	....	....	....
General government	4 902	....	....	....	....	....	....	....	....
Banks	4 903	....	....	....	....	....	....	....	....
Other sectors	4 904	....	....	....	....	....	....	....	....
Liabilities	4 905	....	....	....	....	....	....	....	....
Monetary authorities	4 906	....	....	....	....	....	....	....	....
General government	4 907	....	....	....	....	....	....	....	....
Banks	4 908	....	....	....	....	....	....	....	....
Other sectors	4 909	....	....	....	....	....	....	....	....

Table 2 (Concluded). STANDARD PRESENTATION, 2003–2010

(Millions of U.S. dollars)

	Code	2003	2004	2005	2006	2007	2008	2009	2010
D. OTHER INVESTMENT	4 700	**351.7**	**114.6**	**694.5**	**702.1**	**1,395.0**	**1,089.0**	**2,616.2**	**1,966.8**
Assets	4 703	−67.4	−307.1	−200.6	−259.6	−346.7	−631.6	544.6	97.2
Trade credits	4 706	....	....	....	....	....	....	....	....
General government	4 707	....	....	....	....	....	....	....	....
of which: Short-term	4 709	....	....	....	....	....	....	....	....
Other sectors	4 710	....	....	....	....	....	....	....	....
of which: Short-term	4 712	....	....	....	....	....	....	....	....
Loans	4 714	....	....	....	....	....	....	....	....
Monetary authorities	4 715	....	....	....	....	....	....	....	....
of which: Short-term	4 718	....	....	....	....	....	....	....	....
General government	4 719	....	....	....	....	....	....	....	....
of which: Short-term	4 721	....	....	....	....	....	....	....	....
Banks	4 722	....	....	....	....	....	....	....	....
of which: Short-term	4 724	....	....	....	....	....	....	....	....
Other sectors	4 725	....	....	....	....	....	....	....	....
of which: Short-term	4 727	....	....	....	....	....	....	....	....
Currency and deposits	4 730	....	−211.3	−117.0	−180.8	−286.1	−563.2	548.7	95.8
Monetary authorities	4 731	....	....	....	....	....	....	....	....
General government	4 732	....	....	....	....	....	....	....	....
Banks	4 733	....	....	....	....	....	....	....	....
Other sectors	4 734	....	−211.3	−117.0	−180.8	−286.1	−563.2	548.7	95.8
Other assets	4 736	−67.4	−95.8	−83.6	−78.8	−60.5	−68.4	−4.1	1.4
Monetary authorities	4 737	....	....	....	....	....	....	....	....
of which: Short-term	4 739	....	....	....	....	....	....	....	....
General government	4 740	....	....	....	....	....	....	....	....
of which: Short-term	4 742	....	....	....	....	....	....	....	....
Banks	4 743	−11.0	....	....	....	....	....	....	....
of which: Short-term	4 745	−11.0	....	....	....	....	....	....	....
Other sectors	4 746	−56.4	−95.8	−83.6	−78.8	−60.5	−68.4	−4.1	1.4
of which: Short-term	4 748	12.5	13.4	15.8	18.5	22.2	24.2	21.6	23.6
Liabilities	4 753	**419.1**	**421.7**	**895.1**	**961.6**	**1,741.7**	**1,720.7**	**2,071.6**	**1,869.6**
Trade credits	4 756	....	....	....	....	....	....	....	....
General government	4 757	....	....	....	....	....	....	....	....
of which: Short-term	4 759	....	....	....	....	....	....	....	....
Other sectors	4 760	....	....	....	....	....	....	....	....
of which: Short-term	4 762	....	....	....	....	....	....	....	....
Loans	4 764	−135.3	−265.2	146.7	58.7	217.0	53.3	894.4	515.6
Monetary authorities	4 765	16.7	−14.1	69.1	−13.5	106.2	−10.6	191.5	−25.4
of which: Use of Fund credit and loans from the Fund	4 766	16.7	−14.1	69.1	−13.5	106.2	−10.6	191.5	−25.4
of which: Short-term	4 768	....	....	....	....	....	....	....	....
General government	4 769	−81.3	−171.4	−46.1	61.9	134.8	100.5	740.7	585.0
of which: Short-term	4 771	....	....	....	....	....	....	....	....
Banks	4 772	....	....	....	....	....	....	....	....
of which: Short-term	4 774	....	....	....	....	....	....	....	....
Other sectors	4 775	−70.7	−79.7	123.7	10.3	−23.9	−36.6	−37.9	−44.0
of which: Short-term	4 777	....	....	....	....	....	....	....	....
Currency and deposits	4 780	109.5	53.3	−42.7	26.4	324.6	546.8	−31.1	−40.9
Monetary authorities	4 781	....	....	....	....	....	....	....	....
General government	4 782	....	....	....	....	....	....	....	....
Banks	4 783	....	....	....	....	281.2	578.4	−55.1	−35.0
Other sectors	4 784	109.5	53.3	−42.7	26.4	43.4	−31.6	24.0	−5.9
Other liabilities	4 786	444.9	633.6	791.1	876.5	1,200.0	1,120.5	1,208.4	1,395.0
Monetary authorities	4 787	....	....	....	....	....	....	347.8	....
of which: Short-term	4 789	....	....	....	....	....	....	....	....
General government	4 790	−29.3	63.8	95.1	48.1	20.7	30.0	8.2	12.8
of which: Short-term	4 792	−29.3	63.8	95.1	48.1	20.7	30.0	8.2	12.8
Banks	4 793	....	....	....	....	....	....	....	....
of which: Short-term	4 795	....	....	....	....	....	....	....	....
Other sectors	4 796	474.2	569.8	696.0	828.5	1,179.3	1,090.6	852.4	1,382.1
of which: Short-term	4 798	474.2	569.8	696.0	828.5	1,179.3	1,090.6	852.4	1,382.1
E. RESERVE ASSETS	4 802	**−412.6**	**−36.6**	**−281.2**	**−615.8**	**−938.2**	**475.9**	**−1,317.7**	**−129.1**
Monetary gold	4 812	....	....	....	....	....	....	....	....
Special drawing rights	4 811	−.8	1.4	.5	−.3	.4	−2.9	−346.1	25.6
Reserve position in the Fund	4 810	−.1	....	−.1	−.1	....	....	−.1	−.1
Foreign exchange	4 803	−411.3	−38.3	−281.3	−615.4	−938.3	478.9	−971.2	−155.3
Other claims	4 813	−.3	.3	−.3	−.1	−.3	....	−.3	.7
NET ERRORS AND OMISSIONS	4 998	**−276.5**	**−66.8**	**−245.4**	**249.7**	**−249.9**	**297.4**	**79.8**	**267.7**

Table 1. ANALYTIC PRESENTATION, 2003–2010

(Millions of U.S. dollars)

	Code	2003	2004	2005	2006	2007	2008	2009	2010
A. Current Account[1]	4 993 Z.	**15,584**	**32,312**	**18,607**	**14,083**	**21,770**	**3,197**	**32,791**	**28,214**
Goods: exports f.o.b.	2 100 ..	199,709	260,242	289,892	336,576	389,645	434,699	358,217	464,301
Goods: imports f.o.b.	3 100 ..	−175,670	−220,567	−257,052	−305,079	−352,468	−429,525	−320,355	−422,425
Balance on Goods	4 100 ..	*24,039*	*39,675*	*32,840*	*31,497*	*37,177*	*5,174*	*37,862*	*41,876*
Services: credit	2 200 ..	34,958	44,441	49,726	56,761	72,918	90,587	73,553	82,706
Services: debit	3 200 ..	−40,761	−50,414	−59,660	−70,156	−84,933	−96,326	−80,190	−93,907
Balance on Goods and Services	4 991 ..	*18,236*	*33,703*	*22,905*	*18,102*	*25,162*	*−565*	*31,226*	*30,675*
Income: credit	2 300 ..	7,103	9,369	10,177	14,088	18,915	21,653	14,514	15,879
Income: debit	3 300 ..	−6,850	−8,328	−11,994	−14,014	−18,780	−17,218	−12,238	−15,111
Balance on Goods, Services, and Income	4 992 ..	*18,489*	*34,744*	*21,088*	*18,176*	*25,297*	*3,871*	*33,502*	*31,443*
Current transfers: credit	2 379 Z.	7,859	9,151	10,004	9,588	11,158	14,070	12,700	13,396
Current transfers: debit	3 379 ..	−10,764	−11,583	−12,486	−13,680	−14,685	−14,744	−13,412	−16,626
B. Capital Account[1]	4 994 Z.	**−1,398**	**−1,753**	**−2,340**	**−3,126**	**−2,388**	**109**	**290**	**−174**
Capital account: credit	2 994 Z.	59	72	147	290	526	1,863	1,856	1,931
Capital account: debit	3 994 ..	−1,457	−1,825	−2,487	−3,416	−2,914	−1,754	−1,566	−2,105
Total, Groups A Plus B	4 981 ..	*14,186*	*30,560*	*16,266*	*10,957*	*19,382*	*3,306*	*33,080*	*28,039*
C. Financial Account[1]	4 995 W.	**10,900**	**4,997**	**2,617**	**11,088**	**−6,361**	**−57,709**	**33,768**	**1,937**
Direct investment abroad	4 505 ..	−4,135	−5,651	−6,366	−11,175	−19,720	−20,251	−17,197	−19,230
Direct investment in Republic of Korea	4 555 Z.	3,526	9,246	6,309	3,586	1,784	3,311	2,249	−150
Portfolio investment assets	4 602 ..	−5,403	−11,776	−17,632	−31,286	−56,436	23,484	1,436	−3,542
Equity securities	4 610 ..	−1,993	−3,622	−3,686	−15,262	−52,550	7,124	−2,109	−4,896
Debt securities	4 619 ..	−3,410	−8,154	−13,946	−16,024	−3,886	16,360	3,544	1,355
Portfolio investment liabilities	4 652 Z.	22,690	18,375	14,114	8,056	30,378	−25,890	48,292	42,094
Equity securities	4 660 ..	14,419	9,469	3,282	−8,391	−28,728	−33,623	24,856	23,026
Debt securities	4 669 Z.	8,272	8,906	10,831	16,447	59,106	7,733	23,436	19,069
Financial derivatives	4 910 ..	619	2,020	1,790	484	5,445	−14,770	−3,093	−7
Financial derivatives assets	4 900 ..	1,813	4,380	6,957	8,933	12,109	54,978	74,846	49,550
Financial derivatives liabilities	4 905 ..	−1,194	−2,360	−5,167	−8,449	−6,665	−69,748	−77,939	−49,557
Other investment assets	4 703 ..	−5,132	−8,138	−2,658	−7,945	−14,836	−13,742	1,688	−12,258
Monetary authorities	4 701 ..	−48	−55	−8	−1,299	−132	−99	−104	−153
General government	4 704 ..	−27	−1,577	−394	−390	−269	−246	−405	−655
Banks	4 705 ..	−4,210	−5,666	−1,525	−3,747	−10,169	−10,827	5,550	−5,456
Other sectors	4 728 ..	−848	−841	−732	−2,510	−4,266	−2,570	−3,355	−5,993
Other investment liabilities	4 753 W.	−1,264	920	7,061	49,367	47,023	−9,851	394	−4,971
Monetary authorities	4 753 WA	−35	−10	433	1,596	305	10,898	−8,957	−107
General government	4 753 ZB	−5,255	−2,549	−2,602	−924	−872	−839	−761	−660
Banks	4 753 ZC	669	1,154	5,733	42,378	45,013	−23,314	7,480	−7,987
Other sectors	4 753 ZD	3,357	2,325	3,497	6,317	2,577	3,404	2,632	3,783
Total, Groups A Through C	4 983 ..	*25,086*	*35,556*	*18,883*	*22,045*	*13,022*	*−54,403*	*66,848*	*29,976*
D. Net Errors and Omissions	4 998 ..	**705**	**3,119**	**981**	**45**	**2,088**	**−2,044**	**1,804**	**−2,805**
Total, Groups A Through D	4 984 ..	*25,791*	*38,675*	*19,864*	*22,090*	*15,109*	*−56,447*	*68,652*	*27,172*
E. Reserves and Related Items	4 802 A.	**−25,791**	**−38,675**	**−19,864**	**−22,090**	**−15,109**	**56,447**	**−68,652**	**−27,172**
Reserve assets	4 802 ..	−25,791	−38,675	−19,864	−22,090	−15,109	56,447	−68,652	−27,172
Use of Fund credit and loans	4 766 ..	....	....	....	....	....	....	....	....
Exceptional financing	4 920 ..	....	....	....	....	....	....	....	....
Conversion rates: won per U.S. dollar	0 101 ..	**1,191.6**	**1,145.3**	**1,024.1**	**954.8**	**929.3**	**1,102.0**	**1,276.9**	**1,156.1**

[1] Excludes components that have been classified in the categories of Group E.

Table 2. STANDARD PRESENTATION, 2003–2010

(Millions of U.S. dollars)

	Code	2003	2004	2005	2006	2007	2008	2009	2010
CURRENT ACCOUNT..	4 993 ..	**15,584**	**32,312**	**18,607**	**14,083**	**21,770**	**3,197**	**32,791**	**28,214**
A. GOODS..	4 100 ..	**24,039**	**39,675**	**32,840**	**31,497**	**37,177**	**5,174**	**37,862**	**41,876**
Credit...	2 100 ..	**199,709**	**260,242**	**289,892**	**336,576**	**389,645**	**434,699**	**358,217**	**464,301**
General merchandise: exports f.o.b........................	2 110 ..	185,825	243,045	269,061	311,112	359,320	399,741	321,280	418,677
Goods for processing: exports f.o.b.	2 150 ..	11,920	14,153	20,596	24,605	29,624	33,694	34,153	42,694
Repairs on goods...	2 160 ..	17	99	19	82	77	47	27	14
Goods procured in ports by carriers.......................	2 170 ..	....	....	....	....	....	....	....	....
Nonmonetary gold...	2 180 ..	1,947	2,945	216	777	625	1,217	2,757	2,916
Debit...	3 100 ..	**−175,670**	**−220,567**	**−257,052**	**−305,079**	**−352,468**	**−429,525**	**−320,355**	**−422,425**
General merchandise: imports f.o.b........................	3 110 ..	−164,092	−206,382	−242,528	−288,303	−333,313	−409,355	−303,384	−399,922
Goods for processing: imports f.o.b.	3 150 ..	−8,805	−10,739	−13,730	−16,016	−17,899	−18,941	−15,860	−20,955
Repairs on goods...	3 160 ..	−6	−85	−36	−18	−29	−44	−31	−42
Goods procured in ports by carriers.......................	3 170 ..	....	....	....	....	....	....	....	....
Nonmonetary gold...	3 180 ..	−2,767	−3,361	−757	−742	−1,227	−1,185	−1,079	−1,506
B. SERVICES..	4 200 ..	**−5,803**	**−5,972**	**−9,935**	**−13,396**	**−12,015**	**−5,738**	**−6,637**	**−11,201**
Total credit...	2 200 ..	*34,958*	*44,441*	*49,726*	*56,761*	*72,918*	*90,587*	*73,553*	*82,706*
Total debit..	3 200 ..	*−40,761*	*−50,414*	*−59,660*	*−70,156*	*−84,933*	*−96,326*	*−80,190*	*−93,907*
Transportation services, credit.........................	2 205 ..	**17,180**	**22,529**	**23,877**	**25,807**	**33,556**	**44,768**	**28,693**	**38,044**
Passenger...	2 850 ..	*1,647*	*2,157*	*2,484*	*2,720*	*3,150*	*3,705*	*3,485*	*4,040*
Freight..	2 851 ..	*13,502*	*17,422*	*18,360*	*20,099*	*27,742*	*38,011*	*23,243*	*31,281*
Other...	2 852 ..	*2,031*	*2,951*	*3,033*	*2,989*	*2,664*	*3,052*	*1,965*	*2,723*
Sea transport, passenger...................................	2 207 ..	....	....	....	....	....	9	10	11
Sea transport, freight.......................................	2 208 ..	....	....	....	....	....	35,093	21,025	27,817
Sea transport, other..	2 209 ..	....	....	....	....	....	2,855	1,907	2,447
Air transport, passenger....................................	2 211 ..	....	....	....	....	....	3,696	3,476	4,029
Air transport, freight..	2 212 ..	....	....	....	....	....	2,918	2,219	3,464
Air transport, other...	2 213 ..	....	....	....	....	....	198	58	277
Other transport, passenger................................	2 215 ..	....	....	....	....	....	....	....	....
Other transport, freight....................................	2 216 ..	....	....	....	....	....	....	....	....
Other transport, other......................................	2 217 ..	....	....	....	....	....	....	....	....
Transportation services, debit..........................	3 205 ..	**−13,613**	**−17,655**	**−20,144**	**−23,133**	**−29,076**	**−36,770**	**−23,451**	**−28,791**
Passenger...	3 850 ..	*−960*	*−1,157*	*−1,518*	*−2,138*	*−2,474*	*−2,391*	*−1,320*	*−2,026*
Freight..	3 851 ..	*−4,566*	*−6,930*	*−7,997*	*−9,623*	*−13,178*	*−19,132*	*−11,914*	*−12,977*
Other...	3 852 ..	*−8,087*	*−9,568*	*−10,629*	*−11,372*	*−13,424*	*−15,247*	*−10,218*	*−13,788*
Sea transport, passenger...................................	3 207 ..	....	....	....	....	....	−28	−17	−11
Sea transport, freight.......................................	3 208 ..	....	....	....	....	....	−18,770	−11,713	−12,661
Sea transport, other..	3 209 ..	....	....	....	....	....	−11,926	−7,813	−10,971
Air transport, passenger....................................	3 211 ..	....	....	....	....	....	−2,363	−1,303	−2,015
Air transport, freight..	3 212 ..	....	....	....	....	....	−362	−200	−316
Air transport, other...	3 213 ..	....	....	....	....	....	−3,321	−2,405	−2,817
Other transport, passenger................................	3 215 ..	....	....	....	....	....	....	....	....
Other transport, freight....................................	3 216 ..	....	....	....	....	....	....	....	....
Other transport, other......................................	3 217 ..	....	....	....	....	....	....	....	....
Travel, credit...	2 236 ..	**5,358**	**6,069**	**5,806**	**5,788**	**6,138**	**9,774**	**9,819**	**9,765**
Business travel...	2 237 ..	....	....	....	....	....	4,082	3,617	4,086
Personal travel...	2 240 ..	....	....	....	....	....	5,692	6,202	5,679
Travel, debit..	3 236 ..	**−10,103**	**−12,350**	**−15,406**	**−18,851**	**−21,975**	**−19,065**	**−15,040**	**−17,669**
Business travel...	3 237 ..	....	....	....	....	....	−4,433	−2,561	−4,008
Personal travel...	3 240 ..	....	....	....	....	....	−14,633	−12,478	−13,661
Other services, credit....................................	2 200 BA	**12,420**	**15,843**	**20,043**	**25,166**	**33,224**	**36,046**	**35,041**	**34,898**
Communications...	2 245 ..	341	446	443	642	547	724	725	742
Construction..	2 249 ..	2,038	2,659	4,707	7,003	9,698	13,686	14,553	11,842
Insurance...	2 253 ..	34	139	169	274	415	466	340	391
Financial..	2 260 ..	699	1,083	1,651	2,543	4,001	3,785	2,280	2,847
Computer and information.................................	2 262 ..	30	25	57	248	340	304	218	235
Royalties and licence fees..................................	2 266 ..	1,311	1,861	1,908	2,046	1,735	2,382	3,199	3,146
Other business services.....................................	2 268 ..	6,687	8,125	9,422	10,532	14,421	12,965	12,088	13,910
Personal, cultural, and recreational.......................	2 287 ..	76	128	268	369	448	527	523	635
Government, n.i.e..	2 291 ..	1,203	1,377	1,418	1,509	1,620	1,206	1,115	1,150
Other services, debit.....................................	3 200 BA	**−17,045**	**−20,409**	**−24,110**	**−28,173**	**−33,882**	**−40,491**	**−41,700**	**−47,447**
Communications...	3 245 ..	−693	−636	−773	−1,012	−913	−1,149	−1,227	−1,317
Construction..	3 249 ..	−394	−490	−879	−1,308	−1,828	−2,608	−2,806	−2,235
Insurance...	3 253 ..	−390	−461	−733	−854	−1,000	−744	−735	−860
Financial..	3 260 ..	−101	−127	−235	−547	−696	−691	−708	−860
Computer and information.................................	3 262 ..	−134	−157	−183	−598	−544	−571	−401	−477
Royalties and licence fees..................................	3 266 ..	−3,570	−4,446	−4,561	−4,650	−5,134	−5,656	−7,188	−8,965
Other business services.....................................	3 268 ..	−11,049	−13,163	−15,538	−17,705	−21,829	−27,245	−27,094	−30,746
Personal, cultural, and recreational.......................	3 287 ..	−261	−376	−477	−671	−929	−891	−846	−1,016
Government, n.i.e..	3 291 ..	−453	−554	−733	−828	−1,009	−936	−696	−971

Table 2 (Continued). STANDARD PRESENTATION, 2003–2010

(Millions of U.S. dollars)

	Code	2003	2004	2005	2006	2007	2008	2009	2010
C. INCOME	4 300	**253**	**1,042**	**−1,817**	**75**	**135**	**4,435**	**2,277**	**768**
Total credit	2 300	*7,103*	*9,369*	*10,177*	*14,088*	*18,915*	*21,653*	*14,514*	*15,879*
Total debit	3 300	*−6,850*	*−8,328*	*−11,994*	*−14,014*	*−18,780*	*−17,218*	*−12,238*	*−15,111*
Compensation of employees, credit	2 310	**732**	**713**	**745**	**685**	**692**	**745**	**594**	**599**
Compensation of employees, debit	3 310	**−97**	**−126**	**−119**	**−141**	**−186**	**−556**	**−647**	**−1,075**
Investment income, credit	2 320	**6,371**	**8,656**	**9,432**	**13,403**	**18,223**	**20,908**	**13,920**	**15,281**
Direct investment income	2 330	749	1,518	1,493	1,547	1,925	2,612	1,827	2,147
Dividends and distributed branch profits	2 332	....	....	....	....	....	2,593	1,832	2,142
Reinvested earnings and undistributed branch profits	2 333	....	....	....	....	....	−61	−101	−61
Income on debt (interest)	2 334	57	16	24	28	48	80	96	67
Portfolio investment income	2 339	5,172	5,786	6,567	9,726	13,387	16,220	10,894	12,398
Income on equity	2 340	114	163	326	779	849	2,608	921	1,327
Income on bonds and notes	2 350	....	....	....	....	....	13,334	9,813	10,951
Income on money market instruments	2 360	....	....	....	....	....	278	160	119
Other investment income	2 370	451	1,352	1,372	2,131	2,911	2,076	1,199	736
Investment income, debit	3 320	**−6,752**	**−8,202**	**−11,875**	**−13,873**	**−18,594**	**−16,662**	**−11,590**	**−14,036**
Direct investment income	3 330	−2,240	−2,533	−4,351	−4,176	−5,253	−5,020	−3,986	−6,238
Dividends and distributed branch profits	3 332	....	....	....	....	....	−4,996	−3,952	−6,218
Reinvested earnings and undistributed branch profits	3 333	....	....	....	....	....	....	....	....
Income on debt (interest)	3 334	−17	−8	−57	−61	−71	−24	−35	−21
Portfolio investment income	3 339	−2,468	−3,612	−5,014	−6,012	−7,483	−6,198	−4,592	−5,883
Income on equity	3 340	−1,343	−2,489	−3,025	−3,041	−3,853	−3,262	−1,261	−1,382
Income on bonds and notes	3 350	....	....	....	....	....	−2,227	−3,261	−4,416
Income on money market instruments	3 360	....	....	....	....	....	−708	−70	−85
Other investment income	3 370	−2,044	−2,057	−2,510	−3,685	−5,858	−5,444	−3,012	−1,915
D. CURRENT TRANSFERS	4 379	**−2,905**	**−2,432**	**−2,482**	**−4,093**	**−3,527**	**−674**	**−712**	**−3,229**
Credit	2 379	**7,859**	**9,151**	**10,004**	**9,588**	**11,158**	**14,070**	**12,700**	**13,396**
General government	2 380	76	98	188	313	271	323	149	175
Other sectors	2 390	7,784	9,053	9,816	9,275	10,887	13,747	12,552	13,221
Workers' remittances	2 391	5,553	5,836	5,759	5,369	5,907	8,329	6,684	6,400
Other current transfers	2 392	2,231	3,217	4,057	3,906	4,980	5,418	5,868	6,821
Debit	3 379	**−10,764**	**−11,583**	**−12,486**	**−13,680**	**−14,685**	**−14,744**	**−13,412**	**−16,626**
General government	3 380	−989	−1,005	−1,252	−1,402	−1,459	−1,472	−1,569	−1,682
Other sectors	3 390	−9,775	−10,578	−11,234	−12,278	−13,227	−13,271	−11,843	−14,944
Workers' remittances	3 391	−6,882	−6,844	−6,895	−7,421	−7,926	−7,424	−6,964	−8,894
Other current transfers	3 392	−2,893	−3,734	−4,339	−4,857	−5,300	−5,847	−4,879	−6,050
CAPITAL AND FINANCIAL ACCOUNT	4 996	**−16,289**	**−35,431**	**−19,588**	**−14,129**	**−23,858**	**−1,153**	**−34,594**	**−25,409**
CAPITAL ACCOUNT	4 994	**−1,398**	**−1,753**	**−2,340**	**−3,126**	**−2,388**	**109**	**290**	**−174**
Total credit	2 994	*59*	*72*	*147*	*290*	*526*	*1,863*	*1,856*	*1,931*
Total debit	3 994	*−1,457*	*−1,825*	*−2,487*	*−3,416*	*−2,914*	*−1,754*	*−1,566*	*−2,105*
Capital transfers, credit	2 400	**53**	**56**	**38**	**171**	**297**	**1,771**	**1,706**	**1,793**
General government	2 401	....	....	....	....	....	....	....	....
Debt forgiveness	2 402	....	....	....	....	....	....	....	....
Other capital transfers	2 410	....	....	....	....	....	....	....	....
Other sectors	2 430	53	56	38	171	297	1,771	1,706	1,793
Migrants' transfers	2 431	19	21	4	126	213	1,658	1,634	1,710
Debt forgiveness	2 432	....	....	....	....	....	....	....	....
Other capital transfers	2 440	33	36	34	45	85	113	72	83
Capital transfers, debit	3 400	**−1,396**	**−1,812**	**−2,378**	**−3,190**	**−2,638**	**−1,539**	**−1,408**	**−1,838**
General government	3 401	....	....	....	....	....	....	....	....
Debt forgiveness	3 402	....	....	....	....	....	....	....	....
Other capital transfers	3 410	....	....	....	....	....	....	....	....
Other sectors	3 430	−1,396	−1,812	−2,378	−3,190	−2,638	−1,539	−1,408	−1,838
Migrants' transfers	3 431	−955	−1,343	−1,755	−2,600	−2,090	−1,134	−1,037	−1,416
Debt forgiveness	3 432	....	....	....	....	....	....	....	....
Other capital transfers	3 440	−441	−469	−623	−590	−549	−406	−371	−423
Nonproduced nonfinancial assets, credit	2 480	**6**	**16**	**109**	**119**	**229**	**92**	**150**	**138**
Nonproduced nonfinancial assets, debit	3 480	**−61**	**−12**	**−109**	**−226**	**−275**	**−215**	**−158**	**−267**

Table 2 (Continued). STANDARD PRESENTATION, 2003–2010

(Millions of U.S. dollars)

	Code	2003	2004	2005	2006	2007	2008	2009	2010
FINANCIAL ACCOUNT	4 995	−14,891	−33,678	−17,247	−11,003	−21,470	−1,262	−34,884	−25,235
A. DIRECT INVESTMENT	4 500	−610	3,595	−58	−7,588	−17,935	−16,941	−14,948	−19,380
Direct investment abroad	4 505	−4,135	−5,651	−6,366	−11,175	−19,720	−20,251	−17,197	−19,230
Equity capital	4 510	−4,372	−5,213	−5,973	−9,719	−17,717	−17,203	−14,632	−16,698
Claims on affiliated enterprises	4 515	−4,372	−5,213	−5,973	−9,719	−17,717	−17,203	−14,632	−16,698
Liabilities to affiliated enterprises	4 520	....	....	....	....	....	....		
Reinvested earnings	4 525	....	....	....	....	....	61	101	61
Other capital	4 530	237	−438	−394	−1,455	−2,002	−3,109	−2,666	−2,593
Claims on affiliated enterprises	4 535	237	−438	−394	−1,455	−2,002	−3,109	−2,666	−2,593
Liabilities to affiliated enterprises	4 540	....	....	....	....	....	....		
Direct investment in Republic of Korea	4 555	3,526	9,246	6,309	3,586	1,784	3,311	2,249	−150
Equity capital	4 560	2,975	7,880	5,775	2,400	676	1,282	1,383	−578
Claims on direct investors	4 565	....	....	....	....	....	....		
Liabilities to direct investors	4 570	2,975	7,880	5,775	2,400	676	1,282	1,383	−578
Reinvested earnings	4 575	....	....	....	....	....	....		
Other capital	4 580	551	1,366	534	1,186	1,109	2,029	866	428
Claims on direct investors	4 585	....	....	....	....	....	....		
Liabilities to direct investors	4 590	551	1,366	534	1,186	1,109	2,029	866	428
B. PORTFOLIO INVESTMENT	4 600	17,287	6,599	−3,518	−23,230	−26,058	−2,406	49,728	38,552
Assets	4 602	−5,403	−11,776	−17,632	−31,286	−56,436	23,484	1,436	−3,542
Equity securities	4 610	−1,993	−3,622	−3,686	−15,262	−52,550	7,124	−2,109	−4,896
Monetary authorities	4 611								
General government	4 612	....	....	....	−82	....	−2,857	−3,389	−5,571
Banks	4 613	−434	−3,303	−3,456	−12,769	−53,039	8,133	−2,200	3,412
Other sectors	4 614	−1,559	−319	−230	−2,411	489	1,848	3,480	−2,738
Debt securities	4 619	−3,410	−8,154	−13,946	−16,024	−3,886	16,360	3,544	1,355
Bonds and notes	4 620	−3,236	−7,938	−14,059	−15,950	−3,554	16,265	3,423	1,323
Monetary authorities	4 621	....	....	....	....	....	....		
General government	4 622	....	−3,203	−7,795	−3,557	−200	9,199	1	−435
Banks	4 623	209	−691	−1,269	−4,453	−167	1,363	412	620
Other sectors	4 624	−3,445	−4,043	−4,995	−7,940	−3,187	5,703	3,009	1,138
Money market instruments	4 630	−174	−217	113	−75	−332	96	122	32
Monetary authorities	4 631	....	....	....	....	....	....		
General government	4 632	....	....	....	....	....	....		
Banks	4 633	−162	−227	142	−106	−1	94	−20	−9
Other sectors	4 634	−12	11	−29	31	−332	2	142	41
Liabilities	4 652	22,690	18,375	14,114	8,056	30,378	−25,890	48,292	42,094
Equity securities	4 660	14,419	9,469	3,282	−8,391	−28,728	−33,623	24,856	23,026
Banks	4 663	....	....	....	....	....	....		
Other sectors	4 664	....	....	....	....	....	....		
Debt securities	4 669	8,272	8,906	10,831	16,447	59,106	7,733	23,436	19,069
Bonds and notes	4 670	8,084	9,185	9,222	16,319	49,353	6,353	16,721	20,593
Monetary authorities	4 671	....	....	....	....	....	....		
General government	4 672	....	....	....	....	....	....		
Banks	4 673	....	....	....	....	....	....		
Other sectors	4 674	....	....	....	....	....	....		
Money market instruments	4 680	188	−279	1,610	128	9,753	1,380	6,715	−1,524
Monetary authorities	4 681	....	....	....	....	....	....		
General government	4 682	....	....	....	....	....	....		
Banks	4 683	....	....	....	....	....	....		
Other sectors	4 684	....	....	....	....	....	....		
C. FINANCIAL DERIVATIVES	4 910	619	2,020	1,790	484	5,445	−14,770	−3,093	−7
Monetary authorities	4 911	....	....	....	....	....	....		
General government	4 912	....	....	....	....	....	....		
Banks	4 913	....	....	....	....	....	....		
Other sectors	4 914	....	....	....	....	....	....		
Assets	4 900	1,813	4,380	6,957	8,933	12,109	54,978	74,846	49,550
Monetary authorities	4 901	....	....	....	....	....	....		
General government	4 902	....	....	....	....	....	....		
Banks	4 903	....	....	....	....	....	....		
Other sectors	4 904	....	....	....	....	....	....		
Liabilities	4 905	−1,194	−2,360	−5,167	−8,449	−6,665	−69,748	−77,939	−49,557
Monetary authorities	4 906	....	....	....	....	....	....		
General government	4 907	....	....	....	....	....	....		
Banks	4 908	....	....	....	....	....	....		
Other sectors	4 909	....	....	....	....	....	....		

Table 2 (Concluded). STANDARD PRESENTATION, 2003–2010

(Millions of U.S. dollars)

	Code	2003	2004	2005	2006	2007	2008	2009	2010
D. OTHER INVESTMENT	4 700 ..	**−6,396**	**−7,218**	**4,403**	**41,421**	**32,188**	**−23,593**	**2,082**	**−17,228**
Assets	4 703 ..	**−5,132**	**−8,138**	**−2,658**	**−7,945**	**−14,836**	**−13,742**	**1,688**	**−12,258**
Trade credits	4 706 ..	23	−987	454	−1,591	−926	76	−2,532	−2,912
General government	4 707 ..	....	....	....	....	....	....	....	....
of which: Short-term	4 709 ..	....	....	....	....	....	....	....	....
Other sectors	4 710 ..	23	−987	454	−1,591	−926	76	−2,532	−2,912
of which: Short-term	4 712 ..	*−47*	*−999*	*292*	*−1,613*	*−953*	*45*	*−2,128*	*−1,179*
Loans	4 714 ..	−4,493	−2,386	246	−1,275	−9,191	−10,158	361	−3,577
Monetary authorities	4 715 ..	12	8	10	31	....	....	....	....
of which: Short-term	4 718 ..	....	....	....	....	....	....	....	....
General government	4 719 ..	−99	−1,408	−131	−116	−177	−161	−212	−318
of which: Short-term	4 721 ..	....	....	....	....	....	....	....	....
Banks	4 722 ..	−4,497	−1,045	786	−751	−8,659	−9,445	1,414	−2,590
of which: Short-term	4 724 ..	*−4,705*	*−1,316*	*1,758*	*3,472*	*−825*	*−5,658*	*3,793*	*−2,337*
Other sectors	4 725 ..	91	59	−418	−439	−355	−552	−841	−670
of which: Short-term	4 727 ..	*91*	*59*	*−418*	*−301*	*234*	*−214*	*−524*	*−512*
Currency and deposits	4 730 ..	−1,326	−130	−1,247	−1,354	−3,478	−6,320	2,270	−3,228
Monetary authorities	4 731 ..	....	....	....	....	....	....	....	....
General government	4 732 ..	72	−169	−262	−274	−92	−85	−192	−338
Banks	4 733 ..	−431	−49	−183	−465	−435	−4,355	2,517	−377
Other sectors	4 734 ..	−967	87	−802	−615	−2,951	−1,880	−54	−2,513
Other assets	4 736 ..	663	−4,636	−2,111	−3,725	−1,241	2,661	1,589	−2,541
Monetary authorities	4 737 ..	−60	−63	−17	−1,331	−132	−99	−104	−153
of which: Short-term	4 739 ..	....	....	....	....	....	....	....	....
General government	4 740 ..	....	....	....	....	....	....	....	....
of which: Short-term	4 742 ..	....	....	....	....	....	....	....	....
Banks	4 743 ..	718	−4,573	−2,128	−2,530	−1,075	2,973	1,620	−2,490
of which: Short-term	4 745 ..	....	....	....	....	....	....	....	....
Other sectors	4 746 ..	5	....	35	136	−33	−214	73	102
of which: Short-term	4 748 ..	....	....	....	....	....	....	....	....
Liabilities	4 753 ..	**−1,264**	**920**	**7,061**	**49,367**	**47,023**	**−9,851**	**394**	**−4,971**
Trade credits	4 756 ..	2,603	4,726	5,369	6,128	−133	−25	1,293	414
General government	4 757 ..	....	....	....	....	....	....	....	....
of which: Short-term	4 759 ..	....	....	....	....	....	....	....	....
Other sectors	4 760 ..	2,603	4,726	5,369	6,128	−133	−25	1,293	414
of which: Short-term	4 762 ..	*1,410*	*3,160*	*5,018*	*7,073*	*679*	*1,886*	*1,304*	*1,581*
Loans	4 764 ..	−5,032	−935	1,022	44,180	41,968	−24,140	7,848	−7,684
Monetary authorities	4 765 ..	....	....	....	....	....	....	....	....
of which: Use of Fund credit and loans from the Fund..	4 766 ..	....	....	....	....	....	....	....	....
of which: Short-term	4 768 ..	....	....	....	....	....	....	....	....
General government	4 769 ..	−5,255	−2,549	−2,602	−924	−872	−839	−761	−660
of which: Short-term	4 771 ..	....	....	....	....	....	....	....	....
Banks	4 772 ..	1,075	2,027	4,410	44,914	40,130	−26,734	7,264	−10,401
of which: Short-term	4 774 ..	*648*	*3,515*	*5,538*	*42,568*	*33,518*	*−26,106*	*3,198*	*−13,835*
Other sectors	4 775 ..	−852	−414	−787	189	2,710	3,433	1,345	3,377
of which: Short-term	4 777 ..	*−582*	*−220*	*186*	*−128*	*943*	*1,832*	*525*	*793*
Currency and deposits	4 780 ..	840	−2,650	−717	−2,416	5,105	13,509	−12,347	2,040
Monetary authorities	4 781 ..	....	....	....	....	35	10,350	−12,370	....
General government	4 782 ..	....	....	....	....	....	....	....	....
Banks	4 783 ..	239	−440	64	−2,416	5,070	3,163	30	2,048
Other sectors	4 784 ..	601	−2,211	−780	....	....	−5	−7	−9
Other liabilities	4 786 ..	325	−220	1,387	1,475	84	805	3,599	259
Monetary authorities	4 787 ..	−35	−10	433	1,596	270	548	3,413	−107
of which: Short-term	4 789 ..	....	....	....	....	....	....	....	....
General government	4 790 ..	....	....	....	....	....	....	....	....
of which: Short-term	4 792 ..	....	....	....	....	....	....	....	....
Banks	4 793 ..	−645	−434	1,259	−121	−186	257	187	367
of which: Short-term	4 795 ..	....	....	....	....	....	....	....	....
Other sectors	4 796 ..	1,005	224	−305	....	....	....	....	....
of which: Short-term	4 798 ..	....	....	....	....	....	....	....	....
E. RESERVE ASSETS	4 802 ..	**−25,791**	**−38,675**	**−19,864**	**−22,090**	**−15,109**	**56,447**	**−68,652**	**−27,172**
Monetary gold	4 812 ..	−2	−1	−1	−1	....	−1	−3	−1
Special drawing rights	4 811 ..	−8	−10	−14	−8	−11	−20	−3,644	128
Reserve position in the Fund	4 810 ..	−175	....	425	−114	146	−269	−387	−57
Foreign exchange	4 803 ..	−25,607	−38,663	−20,274	−21,968	−15,243	56,737	−64,618	−27,243
Other claims	4 813 ..	....	....	....	....	....	....	....	....
NET ERRORS AND OMISSIONS	4 998 ..	**705**	**3,119**	**981**	**45**	**2,088**	**−2,044**	**1,804**	**−2,805**

Table 3. INTERNATIONAL INVESTMENT POSITION (End-period stocks), 2003–2010

(Millions of U.S. dollars)

	Code	2003	2004	2005	2006	2007	2008	2009	2010
ASSETS	8 995 C.	**258,148**	**329,736**	**368,434**	**465,561**	**596,793**	**489,468**	**623,493**	**688,137**
Direct investment abroad	8 505	**24,986**	**32,166**	**38,683**	**49,187**	**74,777**	**97,911**	**120,441**	**138,984**
Equity capital and reinvested earnings	8 506	23,045	30,041	35,741	45,652	68,074	88,371	109,140	125,151
Claims on affiliated enterprises	8 507	23,045	30,041	35,741	45,652	68,074	88,371	109,140	125,151
Liabilities to affiliated enterprises	8 508	....	....	....	....	....	....	....	....
Other capital	8 530	1,942	2,124	2,942	3,535	6,703	9,539	11,301	13,833
Claims on affiliated enterprises	8 535	1,942	2,124	2,942	3,535	6,703	9,539	11,301	13,833
Liabilities to affiliated enterprises	8 540	....	....	....	....	....	....	....	....
Portfolio investment	8 602	**19,546**	**33,086**	**52,134**	**97,766**	**158,606**	**75,113**	**99,675**	**113,481**
Equity securities	8 610	3,416	9,009	13,914	36,819	104,858	47,879	73,945	85,815
Monetary authorities	8 611	....	....	....	....	....	....	....	....
General government	8 612	....	....	....	....	....	....	....	....
Banks	8 613	....	....	....	....	....	....	....	....
Other sectors	8 614	....	....	....	....	....	....	....	....
Debt securities	8 619	16,130	24,077	38,221	60,947	53,749	27,234	25,730	27,666
Bonds and notes	8 620	16,030	23,812	38,049	60,736	53,256	26,906	25,303	27,559
Monetary authorities	8 621	....	....	....	....	....	....	....	....
General government	8 622	49	3,057	10,365	13,829	16,636	6,266	5,607	6,159
Banks	8 623	2,847	3,204	4,211	9,044	9,078	4,960	5,173	4,457
Other sectors	8 624	13,133	17,551	23,473	37,863	27,542	15,680	14,523	16,942
Money market instruments	8 630	101	265	171	211	493	328	426	107
Monetary authorities	8 631	....	....	....	....	....	....	....	....
General government	8 632	....	....	....	....	....	....	....	....
Banks	8 633	22	229	123	185	143	1	48	72
Other sectors	8 634	79	37	49	26	350	327	379	35
Financial derivatives	8 900	**777**	**1,078**	**1,009**	**1,392**	**2,338**	**10,356**	**28,682**	**27,605**
Monetary authorities	8 901	....	....	....	....	....	....	....	....
General government	8 902	....	....	....	....	....	....	....	....
Banks	8 903	....	....	....	....	....	....	....	....
Other sectors	8 904	....	....	....	....	....	....	....	....
Other investment	8 703	**57,483**	**64,337**	**66,217**	**78,260**	**98,847**	**104,868**	**104,683**	**116,496**
Trade credits	8 706	9,766	8,787	9,526	12,792	15,164	14,161	16,762	19,463
General government	8 707	....	....	....	....	....	....	....	....
of which: Short-term	8 709	....	....	....	....	....	....	....	....
Other sectors	8 710	9,766	8,787	9,526	12,792	15,164	14,161	16,762	19,463
of which: Short-term	8 712	*9,412*	*8,445*	*9,374*	*12,667*	*15,068*	*14,098*	*16,294*	*17,366*
Loans	8 714	21,160	23,911	23,213	25,471	35,856	45,325	45,213	50,302
Monetary authorities	8 715	49	41	31	....	....	....	....	....
of which: Short-term	8 718	....	....	....	....	....	....	....	....
General government	8 719	869	2,346	2,470	2,666	2,715	2,387	2,659	2,966
of which: Short-term	8 721	....	....	....	....	....	....	....	....
Banks	8 722	19,845	21,277	20,580	21,717	31,104	40,347	39,125	43,299
of which: Short-term	8 724	*11,163*	*12,453*	*10,549*	*7,127*	*8,781*	*14,111*	*10,348*	*13,538*
Other sectors	8 725	398	248	132	1,088	2,037	2,592	3,429	4,036
of which: Short-term	8 727	....	....	....	....	*403*	*622*	*1,148*	*1,679*
Currency and deposits	8 730	4,556	4,064	4,108	5,599	11,150	11,777	9,608	11,742
Monetary authorities	8 731	....	....	....	....	....	....	....	....
General government	8 732	315	348	381	431	525	636	981	896
Banks	8 733	3,164	3,237	3,419	4,331	6,198	9,963	7,469	7,906
Other sectors	8 734	1,077	479	307	836	4,426	1,178	1,158	2,940
Other assets	8 736	22,001	27,575	29,370	34,398	36,677	33,605	33,100	34,989
Monetary authorities	8 737	2,141	2,493	3,019	4,980	5,236	4,354	5,123	4,663
of which: Short-term	8 739	*1,384*	*1,605*	*2,003*	*3,882*	*4,048*	*3,303*	*3,919*	*3,321*
General government	8 740	27	29	29	30	30	27	28	28
of which: Short-term	8 742	*17*	*18*	*18*	*19*	*20*	*17*	*18*	*18*
Banks	8 743	18,977	24,207	25,403	28,679	30,817	28,371	26,862	29,175
of which: Short-term	8 745	*18,532*	*23,810*	*25,241*	*28,533*	*30,653*	*28,230*	*26,472*	*29,019*
Other sectors	8 746	856	847	919	710	594	853	1,088	1,123
of which: Short-term	8 748	*544*	*293*	*485*	*393*	*555*	*843*	*1,073*	*1,088*
Reserve assets	8 802	**155,355**	**199,069**	**210,391**	**238,957**	**262,224**	**201,220**	**270,012**	**291,571**
Monetary gold	8 812	71	72	74	74	74	76	79	80
Special drawing rights	8 811	21	33	44	54	69	86	3,745	3,540
Reserve position in the Fund	8 810	754	788	306	440	311	580	985	1,025
Foreign exchange	8 803	154,509	198,175	209,968	238,388	261,771	200,479	265,202	286,926
Other claims	8 813	....	....	....	....	....	....	....	....

Table 3 (Concluded). INTERNATIONAL INVESTMENT POSITION (End-period stocks), 2003–2010

(Millions of U.S. dollars)

	Code	2003	2004	2005	2006	2007	2008	2009	2010
LIABILITIES.........................	8 995 D.	**337,755**	**413,494**	**539,444**	**652,264**	**826,331**	**547,913**	**726,483**	**824,969**
Direct investment in Republic of Korea...............	8 555 ..	**66,070**	**87,766**	**104,879**	**115,774**	**121,957**	**94,679**	**117,732**	**127,047**
Equity capital and reinvested earnings...........................	8 556 ..	62,704	83,914	100,768	113,393	118,203	90,151	112,056	121,321
Claims on direct investors............................	8 557 ..	....	....	....	....	....	....	....	....
Liabilities to direct investors............................	8 558 ..	62,704	83,914	100,768	113,393	118,203	90,151	112,056	121,321
Other capital..	8 580 ..	3,366	3,852	4,112	2,381	3,754	4,528	5,677	5,726
Claims on direct investors............................	8 585 ..	....	....	....	....	....	....	....	....
Liabilities to direct investors............................	8 590 ..	3,366	3,852	4,112	2,381	3,754	4,528	5,677	5,726
Portfolio investment..	8 652 ..	**165,029**	**210,313**	**310,456**	**352,393**	**456,654**	**252,152**	**389,687**	**490,777**
Equity securities..	8 660 ..	116,758	156,417	249,475	276,388	320,065	124,640	236,424	316,366
Banks..	8 663 ..	....	....	....	....	....	....	....	....
Other sectors...	8 664 ..	....	....	....	....	....	....	....	....
Debt securities..	8 669 ..	48,271	53,897	60,981	76,005	136,588	127,512	153,263	174,411
Bonds and notes......................................	8 670 ..	47,265	53,306	59,638	73,577	127,717	122,723	142,673	166,286
Monetary authorities..............................	8 671 ..	2,745	3,512	4,292	5,194	11,801	12,457	23,987	21,050
General government...............................	8 672 ..	1,261	2,237	3,005	5,664	27,949	18,109	25,512	42,525
Banks..	8 673 ..	17,161	22,559	26,001	32,007	45,591	45,721	47,141	50,308
Other sectors..	8 674 ..	26,099	24,999	26,339	30,712	42,377	46,437	46,033	52,404
Money market instruments......................	8 680 ..	1,005	591	1,343	2,428	8,871	4,790	10,590	8,125
Monetary authorities..............................	8 681 ..	669	311	300	150	5,634	3,637	7,877	7,195
General government...............................	8 682 ..	2	....	....	2	1	2	1	....
Banks..	8 683 ..	260	171	1,026	2,226	3,113	1,020	2,448	793
Other sectors..	8 684 ..	73	109	17	50	123	131	264	137
Financial derivatives..............................	8 905 ..	**899**	**904**	**1,319**	**2,423**	**4,911**	**15,753**	**32,599**	**27,298**
Monetary authorities.............................	8 906 ..	....	....	....	....	....	....	....	....
General government...............................	8 907 ..	....	....	....	....	....	....	....	....
Banks..	8 908 ..	....	....	....	....	....	....	....	....
Other sectors...	8 909 ..	....	....	....	....	....	....	....	....
Other investment...................................	8 753 ..	**105,758**	**114,510**	**122,789**	**181,674**	**242,810**	**185,330**	**186,465**	**179,848**
Trade credits..	8 756 ..	20,225	27,307	33,210	42,351	57,995	9,802	11,861	13,406
General government...............................	8 757 ..	....	....	....	....	....	....	....	....
of which: Short-term............................	8 759 ..	....	....	....	....	....	....	....	....
Other sectors...	8 760 ..	20,225	27,307	33,210	42,351	57,995	9,802	11,861	13,406
of which: Short-term............................	8 762 ..	*4,442*	*5,625*	*6,680*	*7,386*	*8,156*	*9,706*	*11,775*	*13,302*
Loans...	8 764 ..	73,780	73,968	75,635	122,837	162,906	140,980	146,399	138,661
Monetary authorities..............................	8 765 ..	....	....	....	....	....	....	....	....
of which: Use of Fund credit and loans from the Fund....	8 766 ..	....	....	....	....	....	....	....	....
of which: Short-term............................	8 768 ..	....	....	....	....	....	....	....	....
General government...............................	8 769 ..	10,300	8,143	5,448	4,601	3,787	3,022	2,277	1,638
of which: Short-term............................	8 771 ..	....	....	....	....	....	....	....	....
Banks..	8 772 ..	46,077	46,993	51,181	96,182	135,369	112,601	120,634	111,454
of which: Short-term............................	8 774 ..	*36,285*	*39,511*	*45,030*	*87,748*	*122,067*	*99,281*	*103,169*	*89,339*
Other sectors..	8 775 ..	17,402	18,832	19,006	22,054	23,750	25,357	23,489	25,568
of which: Short-term............................	8 777 ..	*1,505*	*1,812*	*2,238*	*2,188*	*2,377*	*4,687*	*2,351*	*3,347*
Currency and deposits.............................	8 780 ..	6,408	7,722	9,027	11,806	15,885	26,897	17,432	16,776
Monetary authorities..............................	8 781 ..	1,433	1,665	1,923	3,756	3,923	14,635	3,850	3,098
General government...............................	8 782 ..	....	....	....	....	....	....	....	....
Banks..	8 783 ..	3,772	4,026	4,361	4,625	6,453	7,386	7,868	8,771
Other sectors..	8 784 ..	1,203	2,031	2,743	3,424	5,509	4,876	5,715	4,907
Other liabilities.......................................	8 786 ..	5,345	5,514	4,917	4,680	6,024	7,651	10,773	11,005
Monetary authorities..............................	8 787 ..	452	496	553	510	511	602	4,302	4,230
of which: Short-term............................	8 789 ..	....	....	....	....	....	....	....	....
General government...............................	8 790 ..	10	9	11	12	12	9	10	10
of which: Short-term............................	8 792 ..	....	....	....	....	....	....	....	....
Banks..	8 793 ..	459	743	860	1,493	2,354	2,692	2,172	2,429
of which: Short-term............................	8 795 ..	*459*	*743*	*860*	*1,493*	*2,354*	*2,692*	*2,172*	*2,429*
Other sectors..	8 796 ..	4,425	4,267	3,493	2,665	3,147	4,348	4,290	4,336
of which: Short-term............................	8 798 ..	*702*	*344*	*734*	*698*	*540*	*1,841*	*1,705*	*1,678*
NET INTERNATIONAL INVESTMENT POSITION........	8 995 ..	**−79,608**	**−83,759**	**−171,010**	**−186,703**	**−229,538**	**−58,445**	**−102,991**	**−136,833**
Conversion rates: won per U.S. dollar (end of period)..................	0 102 ..	**1,192.6**	**1,035.1**	**1,011.6**	**929.8**	**936.1**	**1,259.5**	**1,164.5**	**1,134.8**

Table 1. ANALYTIC PRESENTATION, 2003–2010

(Millions of U.S. dollars)

	Code	2003	2004	2005	2006	2007	2008	2009	2010
A. Current Account[1]	4 993 Z.	....	−258.5	−307.7	−283.6	−484.6	−920.9	−843.6	−859.8
Goods: exports f.o.b.	2 100 ..	....	79.2	84.3	153.7	242.5	318.5	249.5	402.6
Goods: imports f.o.b.	3 100 ..	....	−1,299.9	−1,425.6	−1,625.3	−2,114.9	−2,762.2	−2,593.8	−2,679.0
Balance on Goods	4 100 ..	....	*−1,220.7*	*−1,341.3*	*−1,471.6*	*−1,872.4*	*−2,443.6*	*−2,344.4*	*−2,276.3*
Services: credit	2 200 ..	....	306.4	329.6	400.1	458.6	515.0	597.5	690.2
Services: debit	3 200 ..	....	−329.2	−339.9	−363.7	−378.4	−396.2	−431.2	−624.6
Balance on Goods and Services	4 991 ..	....	*−1,243.4*	*−1,351.6*	*−1,435.2*	*−1,792.2*	*−2,324.9*	*−2,178.0*	*−2,210.7*
Income: credit	2 300 ..	....	196.6	212.0	235.6	322.5	341.8	253.8	250.3
Income: debit	3 300 ..	....	−25.0	−39.0	−36.4	−67.6	−101.5	−139.2	−78.2
Balance on Goods, Services, and Income	4 992 ..	....	*−1,071.8*	*−1,178.7*	*−1,236.1*	*−1,537.3*	*−2,084.6*	*−2,063.5*	*−2,038.6*
Current transfers: credit	2 379 Z.	....	1,022.9	1,068.2	1,110.4	1,180.1	1,316.8	1,392.2	1,318.1
Current transfers: debit	3 379 ..	....	−209.7	−197.3	−157.9	−127.4	−153.1	−172.3	−139.3
B. Capital Account[1]	4 994 Z.	....	**27.2**	**23.6**	**26.1**	**22.6**	**15.3**	**26.9**	**33.6**
Capital account: credit	2 994 Z.	....	27.2	23.6	26.5	25.3	20.9	50.6	52.6
Capital account: debit	3 994 ..	....	....	....	−.4	−2.6	−5.6	−23.7	−19.0
Total, Groups A Plus B	4 981 ..	....	*−231.4*	*−284.2*	*−257.5*	*−462.0*	*−905.6*	*−816.7*	*−826.2*
C. Financial Account[1]	4 995 W.	....	**−68.5**	**26.6**	**52.9**	**499.6**	**696.5**	**459.9**	**685.5**
Direct investment abroad	4 505 ..	....	....	....	−7.0	−13.3	−36.6	−14.6	−4.5
Direct investment in the Republic of Kosovo	4 555 Z.	....	53.3	133.8	369.8	603.2	536.8	408.1	413.4
Portfolio investment assets	4 602 ..	....	−39.8	−21.8	−82.0	−50.1	24.6	−85.6	−308.7
Equity securities	4 610 ..	....	....	....	....	....	....	....	−58.5
Debt securities	4 619 ..	....	−39.8	−21.8	−82.0	−50.1	24.6	−85.6	−250.2
Portfolio investment liabilities	4 652 Z.	....	....	....	....	....	....	....	....
Equity securities	4 660 ..	....	....	....	....	....	....	....	....
Debt securities	4 669 Z.	....	....	....	....	....	....	....	....
Financial derivatives	4 910 ..	....	....	....	....	....	....	....	....
Financial derivatives assets	4 900 ..	....	....	....	....	....	....	....	....
Financial derivatives liabilities	4 905 ..	....	....	....	....	....	....	....	....
Other investment assets	4 703 ..	....	−159.0	−175.8	−274.3	−148.3	−29.0	2.7	351.4
Monetary authorities	4 701 ..	....	−10.0	−99.5	−207.9	−172.7	−43.9	−185.1	15.0
General government	4 704 ..	....	−.9	4.3	1.3	....	....	....	12.9
Banks	4 705 ..	....	−90.5	−47.6	−38.9	7.4	−104.6	−158.6	−71.1
Other sectors	4 728 ..	....	−57.7	−33.0	−28.7	17.0	119.5	346.5	394.6
Other investment liabilities	4 753 W.	....	77.0	90.3	46.4	108.0	200.7	149.3	233.9
Monetary authorities	4 753 WA	....	6.1	−2.6	−3.8	−.1	....	86.6	....
General government	4 753 ZB	....	....	....	....	....	....	−194.9	13.4
Banks	4 753 ZC	....	3.8	15.2	17.4	−15.7	39.7	89.5	35.2
Other sectors	4 753 ZD	....	67.2	77.7	32.8	123.9	161.0	168.1	185.3
Total, Groups A Through C	4 983 ..	....	*−299.9*	*−257.6*	*−204.6*	*37.6*	*−209.1*	*−356.8*	*−140.7*
D. Net Errors and Omissions	4 998 ..	....	**159.9**	**217.3**	**302.3**	**359.7**	**243.0**	**79.2**	**138.6**
Total, Groups A Through D	4 984 ..	....	*−140.0*	*−40.2*	*97.7*	*397.3*	*33.8*	*−277.7*	*−2.1*
E. Reserves and Related Items	4 802 A.	....	**140.0**	**40.2**	**−97.7**	**−397.3**	**−33.8**	**277.7**	**2.1**
Reserve assets	4 802 ..	....	140.0	40.2	−97.7	−397.3	−33.8	146.0	−26.3
Use of Fund credit and loans	4 766 ..	....	....	....	....	....	....	....	28.5
Exceptional financing	4 920 ..	....	....	....	....	....	....	131.7	....
Conversion rates: euros per U.S. dollar	0 103 ..	.8860	.8054	.8041	.7971	.7306	.6827	.7198	.7550

[1] Excludes components that have been classified in the categories of Group E.

Table 2. STANDARD PRESENTATION, 2003–2010

(Millions of U.S. dollars)

	Code	2003	2004	2005	2006	2007	2008	2009	2010
CURRENT ACCOUNT..............................	4 993 ..	....	**−258.5**	**−307.7**	**−283.6**	**−484.6**	**−920.9**	**−843.6**	**−859.8**
A. GOODS..	4 100 ..	....	**−1,220.7**	**−1,341.3**	**−1,471.6**	**−1,872.4**	**−2,443.6**	**−2,344.4**	**−2,276.3**
Credit..	2 100 ..	....	**79.2**	**84.3**	**153.7**	**242.5**	**318.5**	**249.5**	**402.6**
General merchandise: exports f.o.b..........	2 110 ..	....	67.0	65.3	108.7	165.0	149.2	118.1	185.9
Goods for processing: exports f.o.b..........	2 150 ..	....	.4	1.1	26.1	57.3	134.1	92.4	181.3
Repairs on goods..............................	2 160 ..	....	2.7	3.5	4.0	3.7	8.7	22.5	20.8
Goods procured in ports by carriers........	2 170 ..	....	9.0	14.3	14.9	16.5	26.5	16.5	14.6
Nonmonetary gold.............................	2 180 ..	....	....	....	....	....	....	....	....
Debit..	3 100 ..	....	**−1,299.9**	**−1,425.6**	**−1,625.3**	**−2,114.9**	**−2,762.2**	**−2,593.8**	**−2,679.0**
General merchandise: imports f.o.b..........	3 110 ..	....	−1,287.9	−1,411.3	−1,572.3	−2,062.8	−2,694.3	−2,549.8	−2,603.2
Goods for processing: imports f.o.b..........	3 150 ..	....	−.4	−1.0	−38.9	−34.1	−38.8	−17.4	−44.9
Repairs on goods..............................	3 160 ..	....	−4.8	−1.8	−2.9	−5.4	−8.6	−16.9	−20.7
Goods procured in ports by carriers........	3 170 ..	....	−6.9	−11.4	−11.2	−12.5	−20.5	−9.8	−10.1
Nonmonetary gold.............................	3 180 ..	....	....	....	....	....	....	....	....
B. SERVICES.......................................	4 200 ..	....	**−22.7**	**−10.3**	**36.4**	**80.2**	**118.8**	**166.3**	**65.6**
Total credit..	2 200 ..	....	*306.4*	*329.6*	*400.1*	*458.6*	*515.0*	*597.5*	*690.2*
Total debit..	3 200 ..	....	*−329.2*	*−339.9*	*−363.7*	*−378.4*	*−396.2*	*−431.2*	*−624.6*
Transportation services, credit............	2 205 ..	....	**27.8**	**27.8**	**28.7**	**43.3**	**42.4**	**42.0**	**43.5**
Passenger..	2 850 ..	....	....	....	....	*1.3*	*3.0*	*1.5*	*2.0*
Freight..	2 851 ..	....	....	....	....				
Other..	2 852 ..	....	*27.8*	*27.8*	*28.7*	*42.0*	*39.4*	*40.5*	*41.4*
Sea transport, passenger...................	2 207 ..	....	....	....	....	....	....	....	....
Sea transport, freight........................	2 208 ..	....	....	....	....	....	....	....	....
Sea transport, other..........................	2 209 ..	....	....	....	....	....	....	....	....
Air transport, passenger.....................	2 211 ..	....	....	....	....	....	....	....	....
Air transport, freight.........................	2 212 ..	....	....	....	....	....	....	....	....
Air transport, other..........................	2 213 ..	....	26.7	27.7	27.7	42.0	39.4	40.5	41.4
Other transport, passenger..................	2 215 ..	....	....	....	....	....	....	....	....
Other transport, freight......................	2 216 ..	....	....	....	....	1.3	3.0	1.5	2.0
Other transport, other.......................	2 217 ..	....	1.1	.1	.9	....	....	....	....
Transportation services, debit............	3 205 ..	....	**−62.7**	**−64.3**	**−62.3**	**−92.9**	**−132.8**	**−128.3**	**−127.1**
Passenger..	3 850 ..	....	*−15.5*	*−15.6*	*−10.1*	*−15.2*	*−26.9*	*−25.8*	*−25.9*
Freight..	3 851 ..	....	*−.3*	*−.4*		*−77.7*	*−105.8*	*−102.5*	*−101.3*
Other..	3 852 ..	....	*−46.9*	*−48.4*	*−52.2*	....	....	....	....
Sea transport, passenger...................	3 207 ..	....	....	....	....	....	....	....	....
Sea transport, freight........................	3 208 ..	....	....	....	....	....	....	....	....
Sea transport, other..........................	3 209 ..	....	....	....	....	....	....	....	....
Air transport, passenger.....................	3 211 ..	....	−15.5	−15.6	−10.1	−15.2	−26.9	−25.8	−25.9
Air transport, freight.........................	3 212 ..	....	−.3	−.4	....	....	....	....	....
Air transport, other..........................	3 213 ..	....	−1.4	−1.1	....	....	....	....	....
Other transport, passenger..................	3 215 ..	....	....	....	....	....	....	....	....
Other transport, freight......................	3 216 ..	....	....	....	....	−77.7	−105.8	−102.5	−101.3
Other transport, other.......................	3 217 ..	....	−45.5	−47.3	−52.2	....	....	....	....
Travel, credit................................	2 236 ..	....	**91.2**	**109.7**	**137.1**	**152.6**	**200.4**	**262.7**	**302.7**
Business travel................................	2 237 ..	....	1.2	.6	4.0	....	.2	.5	1.2
Personal travel...............................	2 240 ..	....	90.0	109.0	133.1	152.6	200.2	262.2	301.5
Travel, debit................................	3 236 ..	....	**−57.6**	**−63.8**	**−65.9**	**−68.1**	**−77.1**	**−115.2**	**−136.9**
Business travel................................	3 237 ..	....	−1.9	−3.0	−3.1	−7.2	−2.6	−4.3	−3.0
Personal travel...............................	3 240 ..	....	−55.7	−60.8	−62.8	−60.9	−74.5	−110.9	−133.9
Other services, credit......................	2 200 BA	....	**187.4**	**192.1**	**234.4**	**262.7**	**272.2**	**292.8**	**344.0**
Communications...............................	2 245 ..	....	33.9	39.1	61.4	77.4	81.9	98.5	102.1
Construction..................................	2 249 ..	....	12.6	18.2	17.6	4.0	13.1	21.8	69.0
Insurance......................................	2 253 ..	....	9.4	9.4	12.9	15.7	17.7	20.8	19.3
Financial.......................................	2 260 ..	....	2.4	2.2	2.6	2.0	3.9	7.0	4.9
Computer and information..................	2 262 ..	....	1.7	2.5	3.5	2.4	2.0	2.8	3.5
Royalties and licence fees..................	2 266 ..	....	....	....	.4	.1	.8	1.6	.8
Other business services....................	2 268 ..	....	20.8	13.1	27.9	44.3	19.9	26.1	55.4
Personal, cultural, and recreational.......	2 287 ..	....	.9	.8	1.1	.7	1.2	1.2	6.0
Government, n.i.e.............................	2 291 ..	....	105.8	106.9	107.1	116.0	131.8	113.1	83.1
Other services, debit......................	3 200 BA	....	**−208.9**	**−211.8**	**−235.5**	**−217.3**	**−186.3**	**−187.7**	**−360.5**
Communications...............................	3 245 ..	....	−19.1	−29.9	−25.1	−19.9	−20.3	−16.8	−37.2
Construction..................................	3 249 ..	....	−11.3	−17.4	−18.6	−27.6	−8.4	−6.8	−123.0
Insurance......................................	3 253 ..	....	−18.3	−18.5	−19.9	−27.7	−35.4	−34.1	−36.7
Financial.......................................	3 260 ..	....	−4.4	−4.5	−5.6	−8.0	−3.7	−2.5	−.6
Computer and information..................	3 262 ..	....	−5.3	−7.6	−3.2	−6.2	−9.6	−4.9	−8.4
Royalties and licence fees..................	3 266 ..	....	−2.1	−1.7	−.1	−2.4	−5.5	−5.7	−3.7
Other business services....................	3 268 ..	....	−143.6	−126.4	−157.9	−119.8	−99.1	−114.4	−136.2
Personal, cultural, and recreational.......	3 287 ..	....	−1.3	−2.1	−1.4	−.9	−1.0	−.1	−6.3
Government, n.i.e.............................	3 291 ..	....	−3.5	−3.6	−3.7	−4.8	−3.5	−2.4	−8.5

Table 2 (Continued). STANDARD PRESENTATION, 2003–2010

(Millions of U.S. dollars)

	Code	2003	2004	2005	2006	2007	2008	2009	2010
C. INCOME	4 300	....	**171.7**	**173.0**	**199.2**	**254.9**	**240.2**	**114.5**	**172.1**
Total credit	2 300	....	*196.6*	*212.0*	*235.6*	*322.5*	*341.8*	*253.8*	*250.3*
Total debit	3 300	....	*–25.0*	*–39.0*	*–36.4*	*–67.6*	*–101.5*	*–139.2*	*–78.2*
Compensation of employees, credit	2 310	....	**177.5**	**181.5**	**184.8**	**213.0**	**258.1**	**236.3**	**233.9**
Compensation of employees, debit	3 310	....	**–.9**	**–.9**	**–.9**	**–1.0**	**–1.1**	**–1.3**	**–6.0**
Investment income, credit	2 320	....	**19.1**	**30.5**	**50.9**	**109.6**	**83.7**	**17.5**	**16.4**
Direct investment income	2 330	....	....	....	....	....	....	....	.1
Dividends and distributed branch profits	2 332	....	....	....	....	....	....	....	.1
Reinvested earnings and undistributed branch profits	2 333	....	....	....	....	....	....	....	....
Income on debt (interest)	2 334	....	....	....	....	....	....	....	....
Portfolio investment income	2 339	....	5.9	16.6	23.2	47.2	3.4	1.7	4.5
Income on equity	2 340	....	....	....	....	....	....	....	....
Income on bonds and notes	2 350	....	....	....	....	....	....	....	....
Income on money market instruments	2 360	....	5.9	16.6	23.2	47.2	3.4	1.7	4.5
Other investment income	2 370	....	13.2	14.0	27.6	62.3	80.3	15.8	11.8
Investment income, debit	3 320	....	**–24.1**	**–38.1**	**–35.5**	**–66.6**	**–100.4**	**–137.9**	**–72.2**
Direct investment income	3 330	....	–18.8	–28.1	–31.2	–59.0	–88.4	–102.0	–38.2
Dividends and distributed branch profits	3 332	....	–7.6	–7.2	–.1	–2.1	–6.1	–22.5	–5.0
Reinvested earnings and undistributed branch profits	3 333	....	–11.3	–20.9	–31.1	–57.0	–82.3	–79.4	–33.1
Income on debt (interest)	3 334	....	....	....	....	....	....	....	....
Portfolio investment income	3 339	....	–3.6	–7.2	–.1	–2.1	–.2	....	....
Income on equity	3 340	....	....	....	....	....	....	....	....
Income on bonds and notes	3 350	....	....	....	....	....	....	....	....
Income on money market instruments	3 360	....	–3.6	–7.2	–.1	–2.1	–.2	....	....
Other investment income	3 370	....	–1.7	–2.9	–4.2	–5.5	–11.7	–35.9	–34.0
D. CURRENT TRANSFERS	4 379	....	**813.2**	**870.9**	**952.5**	**1,052.6**	**1,163.7**	**1,219.9**	**1,178.8**
Credit	2 379	....	**1,022.9**	**1,068.2**	**1,110.4**	**1,180.1**	**1,316.8**	**1,392.2**	**1,318.1**
General government	2 380	....	471.3	440.4	410.7	344.1	383.3	569.5	480.0
Other sectors	2 390	....	551.6	627.8	699.6	836.0	933.5	822.7	838.1
Workers' remittances	2 391	....	443.3	519.8	586.0	705.7	784.2	707.8	677.2
Other current transfers	2 392	....	108.3	108.0	113.6	130.3	149.3	114.8	160.9
Debit	3 379	....	**–209.7**	**–197.3**	**–157.9**	**–127.4**	**–153.1**	**–172.3**	**–139.3**
General government	3 380	....	–9.4	–7.7	–9.4	–8.6	–8.0	....	....
Other sectors	3 390	....	–200.2	–189.6	–148.5	–118.8	–145.1	–172.3	–139.3
Workers' remittances	3 391	....	–171.2	–160.9	–119.0	–95.0	–125.4	–154.2	–121.2
Other current transfers	3 392	....	–29.0	–28.7	–29.5	–23.9	–19.7	–18.1	–18.1
CAPITAL AND FINANCIAL ACCOUNT	4 996	....	**98.6**	**90.4**	**–18.7**	**124.9**	**678.0**	**764.5**	**721.2**
CAPITAL ACCOUNT	4 994	....	**27.2**	**23.6**	**26.1**	**22.6**	**15.3**	**158.6**	**33.6**
Total credit	2 994	....	*27.2*	*23.6*	*26.5*	*25.3*	*20.9*	*182.2*	*52.6*
Total debit	3 994	....	....	....	*–.4*	*–2.6*	*–5.6*	*–23.7*	*–19.0*
Capital transfers, credit	2 400	....	**27.2**	**23.6**	**26.5**	**25.3**	**20.9**	**182.2**	**52.6**
General government	2 401	....	24.0	19.6	23.5	21.9	17.7	153.4	32.1
Debt forgiveness	2 402	....	....	....	....	....	....	131.7	....
Other capital transfers	2 410	....	24.0	19.6	23.5	21.9	17.7	21.7	32.1
Other sectors	2 430	....	3.2	3.9	3.1	3.4	3.3	28.8	20.5
Migrants' transfers	2 431	....	3.2	3.9	3.1	3.4	3.3	28.8	20.5
Debt forgiveness	2 432	....	....	....	....	....	....	....	....
Other capital transfers	2 440	....	....	....	....	....	....	....	....
Capital transfers, debit	3 400	....	....	....	**–.4**	**–2.6**	**–5.6**	**–23.7**	**–19.0**
General government	3 401	....	....	....	....	....	....	....	....
Debt forgiveness	3 402	....	....	....	....	....	....	....	....
Other capital transfers	3 410	....	....	....	....	....	....	....	....
Other sectors	3 430	....	....	....	–.4	–2.6	–5.6	–23.7	–19.0
Migrants' transfers	3 431	....	....	....	–.4	–2.6	–5.6	–23.7	–19.0
Debt forgiveness	3 432	....	....	....	....	....	....	....	....
Other capital transfers	3 440	....	....	....	....	....	....	....	....
Nonproduced nonfinancial assets, credit	2 480	....	....	....	....	....	....	....	....
Nonproduced nonfinancial assets, debit	3 480	....	....	....	....	....	....	....	....

Table 2 (Continued). STANDARD PRESENTATION, 2003–2010

(Millions of U.S. dollars)

	Code	2003	2004	2005	2006	2007	2008	2009	2010
FINANCIAL ACCOUNT	4 995	....	71.5	66.8	−44.8	102.3	662.7	605.9	687.6
A. DIRECT INVESTMENT	4 500	....	53.3	133.8	362.8	590.0	500.2	393.5	408.9
Direct investment abroad	4 505	....	....	....	−7.0	−13.3	−36.6	−14.6	−4.5
Equity capital	4 510				−7.0	−13.3	−36.6	−14.6	−4.5
Claims on affiliated enterprises	4 515	....	....	....	−7.0	−13.3	−36.6	−14.6	−4.5
Liabilities to affiliated enterprises	4 520	....	....	....	....	....	....	....	....
Reinvested earnings	4 525	....	....	....	....	....	....	....	....
Other capital	4 530	....	....	....	....	....	....	....	....
Claims on affiliated enterprises	4 535	....	....	....	....	....	....	....	....
Liabilities to affiliated enterprises	4 540	....	....	....	....	....	....	....	....
Direct investment in the Republic of Kosovo	4 555	....	53.3	133.8	369.8	603.2	536.8	408.1	413.4
Equity capital	4 560		37.7	81.6	239.9	391.6	325.6	296.5	307.2
Claims on direct investors	4 565	....	....	....	....	....	....	....	....
Liabilities to direct investors	4 570	....	37.7	81.6	239.9	391.6	325.6	296.5	307.2
Reinvested earnings	4 575		11.3	20.9	31.1	57.0	82.3	79.4	33.1
Other capital	4 580		4.3	31.3	98.8	154.6	128.9	32.1	73.1
Claims on direct investors	4 585	....	....	....	....	....	....	....	....
Liabilities to direct investors	4 590		4.3	31.3	98.8	154.6	128.9	32.1	73.1
B. PORTFOLIO INVESTMENT	4 600	....	−39.8	−21.8	−82.0	−50.1	24.6	−85.6	−308.7
Assets	4 602	....	−39.8	−21.8	−82.0	−50.1	24.6	−85.6	−308.7
Equity securities	4 610	....	....	....	....	....	....	....	−58.5
Monetary authorities	4 611	....	....	....	....	....	....	....	....
General government	4 612	....	....	....	....	....	....	....	....
Banks	4 613	....	....	....	....	....	....	....	....
Other sectors	4 614	....	....	....	....	....	....	....	−58.5
Debt securities	4 619	....	−39.8	−21.8	−82.0	−50.1	24.6	−85.6	−250.2
Bonds and notes	4 620	....	....	....	....	....	....	....	−52.3
Monetary authorities	4 621	....	....	....	....	....	....	....	....
General government	4 622	....	....	....	....	....	....	....	....
Banks	4 623	....	....	....	....	....	....	....	....
Other sectors	4 624	....	....	....	....	....	....	....	−52.3
Money market instruments	4 630	....	−39.8	−21.8	−82.0	−50.1	24.6	−85.6	−197.9
Monetary authorities	4 631	....	....	....	....	....	....	....	....
General government	4 632	....	....	....	....	....	....	....	....
Banks	4 633	....	9.1	36.5	−20.7	28.1	56.3	−85.6	−103.2
Other sectors	4 634	....	−49.0	−58.3	−61.4	−78.2	−31.6	....	−94.7
Liabilities	4 652	....	....	....	....	....	....	....	....
Equity securities	4 660	....	....	....	....	....	....	....	....
Banks	4 663	....	....	....	....	....	....	....	....
Other sectors	4 664	....	....	....	....	....	....	....	....
Debt securities	4 669	....	....	....	....	....	....	....	....
Bonds and notes	4 670	....	....	....	....	....	....	....	....
Monetary authorities	4 671	....	....	....	....	....	....	....	....
General government	4 672	....	....	....	....	....	....	....	....
Banks	4 673	....	....	....	....	....	....	....	....
Other sectors	4 674	....	....	....	....	....	....	....	....
Money market instruments	4 680	....	....	....	....	....	....	....	....
Monetary authorities	4 681	....	....	....	....	....	....	....	....
General government	4 682	....	....	....	....	....	....	....	....
Banks	4 683	....	....	....	....	....	....	....	....
Other sectors	4 684	....	....	....	....	....	....	....	....
C. FINANCIAL DERIVATIVES	4 910	....	....	....	....	....	....	....	....
Monetary authorities	4 911	....	....	....	....	....	....	....	....
General government	4 912	....	....	....	....	....	....	....	....
Banks	4 913	....	....	....	....	....	....	....	....
Other sectors	4 914	....	....	....	....	....	....	....	....
Assets	4 900	....	....	....	....	....	....	....	....
Monetary authorities	4 901	....	....	....	....	....	....	....	....
General government	4 902	....	....	....	....	....	....	....	....
Banks	4 903	....	....	....	....	....	....	....	....
Other sectors	4 904	....	....	....	....	....	....	....	....
Liabilities	4 905	....	....	....	....	....	....	....	....
Monetary authorities	4 906	....	....	....	....	....	....	....	....
General government	4 907	....	....	....	....	....	....	....	....
Banks	4 908	....	....	....	....	....	....	....	....
Other sectors	4 909	....	....	....	....	....	....	....	....

Table 2 (Concluded). STANDARD PRESENTATION, 2003–2010

(Millions of U.S. dollars)

	Code	2003	2004	2005	2006	2007	2008	2009	2010
D. OTHER INVESTMENT	4 700	....	−82.0	−85.5	−227.9	−40.3	171.7	152.0	613.8
Assets	4 703	....	−159.0	−175.8	−274.3	−148.3	−29.0	2.7	351.4
Trade credits	4 706	....	17.7	15.2	6.5	−1.3	−15.8	−4.0	−6.4
General government	4 707	....	....	....	....	....	....	....	....
of which: Short-term	4 709	....	....	....	....	....	....	....	....
Other sectors	4 710	....	17.7	15.2	6.5	−1.3	−15.8	−4.0	−6.4
of which: Short-term	4 712	....	....	....	....	....	....	....	....
Loans	4 714	....	−14.5	8.6	−3.7	−6.1	−2.0	5.9	−24.3
Monetary authorities	4 715	....	....	....	....	....	....	....	....
of which: Short-term	4 718	....	....	....	....	....	....	....	....
General government	4 719	....	....	....	....	....	....	....	....
of which: Short-term	4 721	....	....	....	....	....	....	....	....
Banks	4 722	....	−14.5	8.6	−3.7	−6.1	−2.0	5.9	−26.3
of which: Short-term	4 724	....	−14.5	8.6	−3.7	−6.1	−2.0	5.9	−26.3
Other sectors	4 725	....	....	....	....	....	....	....	2.0
of which: Short-term	4 727	....	....	....	....	....	....	....	−1.7
Currency and deposits	4 730	....	−162.2	−199.6	−277.1	−140.8	−11.2	.8	382.1
Monetary authorities	4 731	....	−10.0	−99.5	−207.9	−172.7	−43.9	−185.1	15.0
General government	4 732	....	−.9	4.3	1.3				12.9
Banks	4 733	....	−76.0	−56.3	−35.3	13.6	−102.6	−164.5	−44.8
Other sectors	4 734	....	−75.3	−48.1	−35.2	18.3	135.3	350.5	399.0
Other assets	4 736	....	....	....	....	....	....	....	....
Monetary authorities	4 737	....	....	....	....	....	....	....	....
of which: Short-term	4 739	....	....	....	....	....	....	....	....
General government	4 740	....	....	....	....	....	....	....	....
of which: Short-term	4 742	....	....	....	....	....	....	....	....
Banks	4 743	....	....	....	....	....	....	....	....
of which: Short-term	4 745	....	....	....	....	....	....	....	....
Other sectors	4 746	....	....	....	....	....	....	....	....
of which: Short-term	4 748	....	....	....	....	....	....	....	....
Liabilities	4 753	....	77.0	90.3	46.4	108.0	200.7	149.3	262.4
Trade credits	4 756	....	61.0	64.5	33.0	94.0	94.2	143.3	128.6
General government	4 757	....	....	....	....	....	....	....	....
of which: Short-term	4 759	....	....	....	....	....	....	....	....
Other sectors	4 760	....	61.0	64.5	33.0	94.0	94.2	143.3	128.6
of which: Short-term	4 762	....	....	....	....	....	....	....	....
Loans	4 764	....	19.1	21.3	13.4	18.9	71.0	−113.7	78.2
Monetary authorities	4 765	....	....	....	....	....	....	....	28.5
of which: Use of Fund credit and loans from the Fund	4 766	....	....	....	....	....	....	....	28.5
of which: Short-term	4 768	....	....	....	....	....	....	....	....
General government	4 769	....	....	....	....	....	....	−194.9	13.4
of which: Short-term	4 771	....	....	....	....	....	....	....	....
Banks	4 772	....	12.9	8.2	13.6	−10.9	4.4	56.4	7.3
of which: Short-term	4 774	....	12.9	8.2	13.6	−10.9	4.4	56.4	7.3
Other sectors	4 775	....	6.2	13.2	−.2	29.9	66.6	24.9	29.0
of which: Short-term	4 777	....	−1.7	5.2	−3.0	29.7	35.3	37.8	4.0
Currency and deposits	4 780	....	−3.0	4.5	.1	−4.9	35.5	33.1	55.5
Monetary authorities	4 781	....	6.1	−2.6	−3.8	−.1	....	....	....
General government	4 782	....	....	....	....	....	....	....	....
Banks	4 783	....	−9.1	7.1	3.8	−4.8	35.3	33.1	27.9
Other sectors	4 784	....	....	....	....	....	.1	−.1	27.6
Other liabilities	4 786	....	....	....	....	....	....	86.6	....
Monetary authorities	4 787	....	....	....	....	....	....	86.6	....
of which: Short-term	4 789	....	....	....	....	....	....	....	....
General government	4 790	....	....	....	....	....	....	....	....
of which: Short-term	4 792	....	....	....	....	....	....	....	....
Banks	4 793	....	....	....	....	....	....	....	....
of which: Short-term	4 795	....	....	....	....	....	....	....	....
Other sectors	4 796	....	....	....	....	....	....	....	....
of which: Short-term	4 798	....	....	....	....	....	....	....	....
E. RESERVE ASSETS	4 802	....	140.0	40.2	−97.7	−397.3	−33.8	146.0	−26.3
Monetary gold	4 812	....	....	....	....	....	....	....	....
Special drawing rights	4 811	....	....	....	....	....	....	−86.6	.3
Reserve position in the Fund	4 810	....	....	....	....	....	....	−22.4	.1
Foreign exchange	4 803	....	140.0	40.2	−97.7	−397.3	−33.8	255.0	−26.8
Other claims	4 813	....	....	....	....	....	....	....	....
NET ERRORS AND OMISSIONS	4 998	....	159.9	217.3	302.3	359.7	243.0	79.2	138.6

Table 1. ANALYTIC PRESENTATION, 2003–2010

(Millions of U.S. dollars)

	Code	2003	2004	2005	2006	2007	2008	2009	2010
A. Current Account[1]	4 993 Z.	**9,424**	**15,508**	**30,071**	**45,312**	**41,330**	**60,239**	**25,774**	**36,822**
Goods: exports f.o.b.	2 100 ..	21,794	29,001	45,303	56,453	62,526	86,944	51,675	66,973
Goods: imports f.o.b.	3 100 ..	−9,880	−12,402	−15,053	−16,240	−19,962	−22,939	−17,285	−19,065
Balance on Goods	4 100 ..	*11,914*	*16,598*	*30,249*	*40,213*	*42,564*	*64,004*	*34,390*	*47,908*
Services: credit	2 200 ..	3,144	3,771	4,775	8,444	10,169	11,959	11,309	7,716
Services: debit	3 200 ..	−6,615	−7,495	−8,715	−10,638	−13,344	−15,777	−13,850	−13,617
Balance on Goods and Services	4 991 ..	*8,443*	*12,874*	*26,309*	*38,019*	*39,389*	*60,186*	*31,849*	*42,007*
Income: credit	2 300 ..	3,733	5,888	8,023	12,499	16,327	13,962	8,599	9,619
Income: debit	3 300 ..	−372	−700	−841	−1,533	−3,932	−3,219	−1,671	−1,801
Balance on Goods, Services, and Income	4 992 ..	*11,804*	*18,062*	*33,491*	*48,986*	*51,784*	*70,929*	*38,776*	*49,825*
Current transfers: credit	2 379 Z.	66	....	....	....	....	....	....	....
Current transfers: debit	3 379 ..	−2,446	−2,554	−3,421	−3,674	−10,453	−10,689	−13,002	−13,003
B. Capital Account[1]	4 994 Z.	**1,431**	**348**	**710**	**744**	**1,488**	**1,729**	**1,065**	**2,158**
Capital account: credit	2 994 Z.	1,463	431	781	851	1,554	1,855	1,192	2,263
Capital account: debit	3 994 ..	−32	−82	−71	−107	−66	−127	−126	−105
Total, Groups A Plus B	4 981 ..	*10,856*	*15,856*	*30,780*	*46,055*	*42,818*	*61,968*	*26,840*	*38,980*
C. Financial Account[1]	4 995 W.	**−12,106**	**−16,765**	**−32,762**	**−49,559**	**−34,862**	**−51,281**	**−26,457**	**−34,686**
Direct investment abroad	4 505 ..	4,960	−2,581	−5,142	−8,211	−9,784	−9,091	−8,635	−2,068
Direct investment in Kuwait	4 555 Z.	−67	24	234	121	112	−6	1,114	81
Portfolio investment assets	4 602 ..	−13,708	−14,168	−12,675	−29,171	−35,581	−32,085	−8,674	−6,921
Equity securities	4 610 ..	....	−1,513	−2,088	−3,249	−3,849	−2,182	−3,920	−1,456
Debt securities	4 619 ..	−13,708	−12,655	−10,587	−25,921	−31,732	−29,902	−4,754	−5,465
Portfolio investment liabilities	4 652 Z.	334	288	−459	44	677	3,955	480	−815
Equity securities	4 660 ..	....	....	....	44	677	3,955	501	−815
Debt securities	4 669 Z.	334	288	−459	....	....	....	−21	....
Financial derivatives	4 910 ..	....	....	....	....	....	....	−48	−3
Financial derivatives assets	4 900 ..	....	....	....	....	....	....	−252	−40
Financial derivatives liabilities	4 905 ..	....	....	....	....	....	....	204	37
Other investment assets	4 703 ..	−3,391	−559	−19,323	−22,735	−14,483	−18,281	3,148	−14,498
Monetary authorities	4 701 ..	....	....	....	....	....	....	....	....
General government	4 704 ..	−3,319	3,132	−16,496	−15,382	−2,956	−11,215	−7,195	−7,940
Banks	4 705 ..	58	−2,148	−1,622	−4,382	−6,336	−4,169	5,228	1,158
Other sectors	4 728 ..	−130	−1,543	−1,205	−2,972	−5,191	−2,897	5,115	−7,717
Other investment liabilities	4 753 W.	−234	232	4,603	10,392	24,197	4,227	−13,842	−10,461
Monetary authorities	4 753 WA	30	34	259	100	67	−156	1,902	2
General government	4 753 ZB	−179	−28	836	352	2,606	1,263	−3,227	−932
Banks	4 753 ZC	−549	−419	1,988	2,985	10,941	−1,738	−6,255	512
Other sectors	4 753 ZD	464	645	1,520	6,955	10,582	4,858	−6,261	−10,043
Total, Groups A Through C	4 983 ..	*−1,250*	*−908*	*−1,982*	*−3,503*	*7,955*	*10,687*	*382*	*4,294*
D. Net Errors and Omissions	4 998 ..	**−574**	**1,534**	**2,601**	**7,087**	**−4,737**	**−10,040**	**3,376**	**−3,683**
Total, Groups A Through D	4 984 ..	*−1,824*	*626*	*619*	*3,584*	*3,219*	*647*	*3,759*	*611*
E. Reserves and Related Items	4 802 A.	**1,824**	**−626**	**−619**	**−3,584**	**−3,219**	**−647**	**−3,759**	**−611**
Reserve assets	4 802 ..	1,824	−626	−619	−3,584	−3,219	−647	−3,759	−611
Use of Fund credit and loans	4 766 ..	....	....	....	....	....	....	....	....
Exceptional financing	4 920 ..	....	....	....	....	....	....	....	....
Conversion rates: Kuwaiti dinar per U.S. dollar	0 101 ..	**.2980**	**.2947**	**.2920**	**.2902**	**.2842**	**.2688**	**.2878**	**.2866**

[1] Excludes components that have been classified in the categories of Group E.

Table 2. STANDARD PRESENTATION, 2003–2010

(Millions of U.S. dollars)

	Code	2003	2004	2005	2006	2007	2008	2009	2010
CURRENT ACCOUNT	4 993	9,424	15,508	30,071	45,312	41,330	60,239	25,774	36,822
A. GOODS	4 100	11,914	16,598	30,249	40,213	42,564	64,004	34,390	47,908
Credit	2 100	21,794	29,001	45,303	56,453	62,526	86,944	51,675	66,973
General merchandise: exports f.o.b.	2 110	21,794	29,001	45,303	56,453	62,526	86,944	51,675	66,973
Goods for processing: exports f.o.b.	2 150	....	....	....	....	....	....	....	....
Repairs on goods	2 160	....	....	....	....	....	....	....	....
Goods procured in ports by carriers	2 170	....	....	....	....	....	....	....	....
Nonmonetary gold	2 180	....	....	....	....	....	....	....	....
Debit	3 100	−9,880	−12,402	−15,053	−16,240	−19,962	−22,939	−17,285	−19,065
General merchandise: imports f.o.b.	3 110	−9,880	−12,402	−15,053	−16,240	−19,962	−22,939	−17,285	−19,065
Goods for processing: imports f.o.b.	3 150	....	....	....	....	....	....	....	....
Repairs on goods	3 160	....	....	....	....	....	....	....	....
Goods procured in ports by carriers	3 170	....	....	....	....	....	....	....	....
Nonmonetary gold	3 180	....	....	....	....	....	....	....	....
B. SERVICES	4 200	−3,471	−3,724	−3,940	−2,194	−3,175	−3,818	−2,541	−5,901
Total credit	2 200	*3,144*	*3,771*	*4,775*	*8,444*	*10,169*	*11,959*	*11,309*	*7,716*
Total debit	3 200	*−6,615*	*−7,495*	*−8,715*	*−10,638*	*−13,344*	*−15,777*	*−13,850*	*−13,617*
Transportation services, credit	2 205	1,516	1,713	2,260	3,179	3,458	4,585	3,218	3,191
Passenger	2 850	*210*	*220*	*248*	*303*	*307*	*353*	*305*	*285*
Freight	2 851	*1,200*	*1,386*	*1,903*	*2,768*	*3,071*	*3,756*	*2,515*	*2,689*
Other	2 852	*106*	*107*	*108*	*109*	*80*	*476*	*398*	*217*
Sea transport, passenger	2 207	....	....	....	....	....	....	....	....
Sea transport, freight	2 208	....	....	....	....	....	....	....	....
Sea transport, other	2 209	....	....	....	....	....	....	....	....
Air transport, passenger	2 211	....	....	....	....	....	....	....	....
Air transport, freight	2 212	....	....	....	....	....	....	....	....
Air transport, other	2 213	....	....	....	....	....	....	....	....
Other transport, passenger	2 215	....	....	....	....	....	....	....	....
Other transport, freight	2 216	....	....	....	....	....	....	....	....
Other transport, other	2 217	....	....	....	....	....	....	....	....
Transportation services, debit	3 205	−2,026	−2,206	−2,646	−2,957	−3,556	−5,562	−4,570	−4,885
Passenger	3 850	*−402*	*−446*	*−465*	*−501*	*−631*	*−771*	*−611*	*−672*
Freight	3 851	*−1,573*	*−1,703*	*−2,125*	*−2,402*	*−2,855*	*−4,492*	*−3,689*	*−3,945*
Other	3 852	*−51*	*−57*	*−55*	*−54*	*−70*	*−299*	*−271*	*−268*
Sea transport, passenger	3 207	....	....	....	....	....	....	....	....
Sea transport, freight	3 208	....	....	....	....	....	....	....	....
Sea transport, other	3 209	....	....	....	....	....	....	....	....
Air transport, passenger	3 211	....	....	....	....	....	....	....	....
Air transport, freight	3 212	....	....	....	....	....	....	....	....
Air transport, other	3 213	....	....	....	....	....	....	....	....
Other transport, passenger	3 215	....	....	....	....	....	....	....	....
Other transport, freight	3 216	....	....	....	....	....	....	....	....
Other transport, other	3 217	....	....	....	....	....	....	....	....
Travel, credit	2 236	118	178	165	205	223	257	355	225
Business travel	2 237	118	178	165	205	223	257	355	225
Personal travel	2 240	....	....	....	....	....	....	....	....
Travel, debit	3 236	−3,348	−3,701	−4,532	−5,573	−6,636	−7,570	−6,443	−6,747
Business travel	3 237	−3,348	−3,701	−4,532	−5,573	−6,636	−7,570	−6,443	−6,747
Personal travel	3 240	....	....	....	....	....	....	....	....
Other services, credit	2 200 BA	1,509	1,880	2,349	5,060	6,488	7,117	7,735	4,299
Communications	2 245	....	504	1,295	3,397	4,667	6,073	6,886	3,557
Construction	2 249	....	....	....	....	....	....	....	....
Insurance	2 253	83	79	85	64	66	63	187	57
Financial	2 260	46	42	35	35	53	385	105	106
Computer and information	2 262	....	....	....	....	....	....	....	....
Royalties and licence fees	2 266	....	....	....	....	....	....	....	....
Other business services	2 268	....	....	....	....	615	637	....	....
Personal, cultural, and recreational	2 287	....	....	....	....	....	....	....	....
Government, n.i.e.	2 291	1,380	1,255	934	949	1,064	597	557	578
Other services, debit	3 200 BA	−1,242	−1,588	−1,537	−2,108	−3,152	−2,645	−2,836	−1,985
Communications	3 245	....	−123	−95	−92	−89	−52	−62	−99
Construction	3 249	−42	−41	−42	−43	−45	−1,116	−1,158	−47
Insurance	3 253	−88	−101	−126	−138	−163	−201	−402	−300
Financial	3 260	−31	−29	−2	−2	−6	−171	−137	−84
Computer and information	3 262	....	....	....	....	....	....	....	....
Royalties and licence fees	3 266	....	....	....	....	....	....	....	....
Other business services	3 268	....	....	....	....	....	−126	−243	−97
Personal, cultural, and recreational	3 287	....	....	....	....	....	....	....	....
Government, n.i.e.	3 291	−1,081	−1,294	−1,271	−1,833	−2,850	−978	−834	−1,357

2011, International Monetary Fund: *Balance of Payments Statistics Yearbook*

Table 2 (Continued). STANDARD PRESENTATION, 2003–2010

(Millions of U.S. dollars)

	Code	2003	2004	2005	2006	2007	2008	2009	2010
C. INCOME	4 300	**3,361**	**5,188**	**7,182**	**10,967**	**12,395**	**10,743**	**6,928**	**7,818**
Total credit	2 300	*3,733*	*5,888*	*8,023*	*12,499*	*16,327*	*13,962*	*8,599*	*9,619*
Total debit	3 300	*−372*	*−700*	*−841*	*−1,533*	*−3,932*	*−3,219*	*−1,671*	*−1,801*
Compensation of employees, credit	2 310	....	....	....	....	....	....	....	....
Compensation of employees, debit	3 310	....	....	....	....	....	....	−100	−48
Investment income, credit	2 320	**3,733**	**5,888**	**8,023**	**12,499**	**16,327**	**13,962**	**8,599**	**9,619**
Direct investment income	2 330	....	....	....	....	....	....	....	....
Dividends and distributed branch profits	2 332	....	....	....	....	....	....	....	....
Reinvested earnings and undistributed branch profits	2 333	....	....	....	....	....	....	....	....
Income on debt (interest)	2 334	....	....	....	....	....	....	....	....
Portfolio investment income	2 339	....	....	....	....	....	....	....	....
Income on equity	2 340	....	....	....	....	....	....	....	....
Income on bonds and notes	2 350	....	....	....	....	....	....	....	....
Income on money market instruments	2 360	....	....	....	....	....	....	....	....
Other investment income	2 370	3,733	5,888	8,023	12,499	16,327	13,962	8,599	9,619
Investment income, debit	3 320	**−372**	**−700**	**−841**	**−1,533**	**−3,932**	**−3,219**	**−1,571**	**−1,752**
Direct investment income	3 330	....	....	....	....	....	....	....	....
Dividends and distributed branch profits	3 332	....	....	....	....	....	....	....	....
Reinvested earnings and undistributed branch profits	3 333	....	....	....	....	....	....	....	....
Income on debt (interest)	3 334	....	....	....	....	....	....	....	....
Portfolio investment income	3 339	....	....	....	....	....	....	....	....
Income on equity	3 340	....	....	....	....	....	....	....	....
Income on bonds and notes	3 350	....	....	....	....	....	....	....	....
Income on money market instruments	3 360	....	....	....	....	....	....	....	....
Other investment income	3 370	−372	−700	−841	−1,533	−3,932	−3,219	−1,571	−1,752
D. CURRENT TRANSFERS	4 379	**−2,379**	**−2,554**	**−3,421**	**−3,674**	**−10,453**	**−10,689**	**−13,002**	**−13,003**
Credit	2 379	**66**	....	....	....	....	....	....	....
General government	2 380	66	....	....	....	....	....	....	....
Other sectors	2 390	....	....	....	....	....	....	....	....
Workers' remittances	2 391	....	....	....	....	....	....	....	....
Other current transfers	2 392	....	....	....	....	....	....	....	....
Debit	3 379	**−2,446**	**−2,554**	**−3,421**	**−3,674**	**−10,453**	**−10,689**	**−13,002**	**−13,003**
General government	3 380	−189	−104	−715	−405	−574	−267	−530	−363
Other sectors	3 390	−2,257	−2,450	−2,705	−3,269	−9,880	−10,422	−12,472	−12,640
Workers' remittances	3 391	−2,144	−2,404	−2,648	−3,183	−9,764	−10,323	−11,649	−11,722
Other current transfers	3 392	−113	−46	−58	−86	−116	−100	−823	−918
CAPITAL AND FINANCIAL ACCOUNT	4 996	**−8,850**	**−17,042**	**−32,671**	**−52,399**	**−36,593**	**−50,199**	**−29,150**	**−33,139**
CAPITAL ACCOUNT	4 994	**1,431**	**348**	**710**	**744**	**1,488**	**1,729**	**1,065**	**2,158**
Total credit	2 994	*1,463*	*431*	*781*	*851*	*1,554*	*1,855*	*1,192*	*2,263*
Total debit	3 994	*−32*	*−82*	*−71*	*−107*	*−66*	*−127*	*−126*	*−105*
Capital transfers, credit	2 400	**1,463**	**431**	**781**	**851**	**1,554**	**1,855**	**1,192**	**2,263**
General government	2 401	703	3	55	498	1,361	1,785	1,152	997
Debt forgiveness	2 402	....	....	....	....	....	....	....	....
Other capital transfers	2 410	703	3	55	498	1,361	1,785	1,152	997
Other sectors	2 430	761	428	726	353	194	71	40	1,267
Migrants' transfers	2 431	....	....	....	....	....	....	....	....
Debt forgiveness	2 432	....	....	....	....	....	....	....	....
Other capital transfers	2 440	761	428	726	353	194	71	40	1,267
Capital transfers, debit	3 400	**−32**	**−82**	**−71**	**−107**	**−66**	**−127**	**−126**	**−105**
General government	3 401	−32	−40	−27	−34	−23	−19	−16	−22
Debt forgiveness	3 402	....	....	....	....	....	....	....	....
Other capital transfers	3 410	−32	−40	−27	−34	−23	−19	−16	−22
Other sectors	3 430	....	−42	−43	−72	−44	−108	−110	−84
Migrants' transfers	3 431	....	....	....	....	....	....	....	....
Debt forgiveness	3 432	....	....	....	....	....	....	....	....
Other capital transfers	3 440	....	−42	−43	−72	−44	−108	−110	−84
Nonproduced nonfinancial assets, credit	2 480	....	....	....	....	....	....	....	....
Nonproduced nonfinancial assets, debit	3 480	....	....	....	....	....	....	....	....

Table 2 (Continued). STANDARD PRESENTATION, 2003–2010

(Millions of U.S. dollars)

	Code	2003	2004	2005	2006	2007	2008	2009	2010
FINANCIAL ACCOUNT	4 995	−10,281	−17,391	−33,381	−53,142	−38,081	−51,928	−30,216	−35,297
A. DIRECT INVESTMENT	4 500	4,893	−2,558	−4,908	−8,089	−9,673	−9,097	−7,522	−1,988
Direct investment abroad	4 505	4,960	−2,581	−5,142	−8,211	−9,784	−9,091	−8,635	−2,068
Equity capital	4 510	−789	−2,581	−5,157	−8,211	−9,784	−9,099	−8,417	−2,068
Claims on affiliated enterprises	4 515	−789	−2,581	−5,157	−8,211	−9,784	−9,099	−8,417	−2,068
Liabilities to affiliated enterprises	4 520	....	....	....	....	....	....		
Reinvested earnings	4 525	....	....	....	....	....	....		
Other capital	4 530	5,749	....	15	....	....	9	−219	
Claims on affiliated enterprises	4 535	5,749	....	15	....	....	9	−219	
Liabilities to affiliated enterprises	4 540	....	....	....	....	....			
Direct investment in Kuwait	4 555	−67	24	234	121	112	−6	1,114	81
Equity capital	4 560	−67	24	234	121	112	−6	1,114	81
Claims on direct investors	4 565	....							
Liabilities to direct investors	4 570	−67	24	234	121	112	−6	1,114	81
Reinvested earnings	4 575	....	....	....					
Other capital	4 580		....	....					
Claims on direct investors	4 585			....					
Liabilities to direct investors	4 590	....		....					
B. PORTFOLIO INVESTMENT	4 600	−13,374	−13,880	−13,134	−29,126	−34,904	−28,130	−8,194	−7,736
Assets	4 602	−13,708	−14,168	−12,675	−29,171	−35,581	−32,085	−8,674	−6,921
Equity securities	4 610		−1,513	−2,088	−3,249	−3,849	−2,182	−3,920	−1,456
Monetary authorities	4 611	....		....					
General government	4 612	....	....	....	....	....	....	−3,725	−3,302
Banks	4 613	....	−316	−370	−430	−1,487	−1,297	−67	16
Other sectors	4 614	....	−1,197	−1,718	−2,819	−2,362	−886	−128	1,830
Debt securities	4 619	−13,708	−12,655	−10,587	−25,921	−31,732	−29,902	−4,754	−5,465
Bonds and notes	4 620	−13,708	−12,655	−10,587	−25,921	−31,732	−29,902	−4,754	−5,465
Monetary authorities	4 621	....		....					
General government	4 622	−12,073	−12,501	−5,546	−20,604	−27,061	−28,012	−5,925	−4,765
Banks	4 623	−6	−61	−70	−82	−284	−246	145	−201
Other sectors	4 624	−1,629	−93	−4,972	−5,235	−4,388	−1,645	1,025	−499
Money market instruments	4 630	....	....	....	....	....	....	....	....
Monetary authorities	4 631	....	....	....	....	....	....	....	....
General government	4 632	....	....	....	....	....	....	....	....
Banks	4 633	....	....	....	....	....	....	....	....
Other sectors	4 634	....	....	....	....	....	....	....	....
Liabilities	4 652	334	288	−459	44	677	3,955	480	−815
Equity securities	4 660	....		....	44	677	3,955	501	−815
Banks	4 663	....		....	−35	−11	−212	8	24
Other sectors	4 664	....	....		80	688	4,167	493	−839
Debt securities	4 669	334	288	−459	....	....	....	−21	....
Bonds and notes	4 670	334	288	−459	....	....	....	−21	
Monetary authorities	4 671	....		....					
General government	4 672	....	....	....	....				
Banks	4 673	191	71	−487					
Other sectors	4 674	143	217	28				−21	
Money market instruments	4 680	....	....	....					
Monetary authorities	4 681	....	....						
General government	4 682	....	....	....					
Banks	4 683	....	....	....					
Other sectors	4 684	....	....	....					
C. FINANCIAL DERIVATIVES	4 910	....	....	....	....	....	....	−48	−3
Monetary authorities	4 911	....	....	....	....	....	....		
General government	4 912	....	....	....	....	....	....		
Banks	4 913	....	....	....	....	....	....		
Other sectors	4 914	....	....	....	....	....	....	−48	−3
Assets	4 900	....	....	....	....	....	....	−252	−40
Monetary authorities	4 901	....	....	....	....	....	....		
General government	4 902	....	....	....	....	....	....		
Banks	4 903	....	....	....	....	....	....		
Other sectors	4 904	....	....	....	....	....	....	−252	−40
Liabilities	4 905	....	....	....	....	....	....	204	37
Monetary authorities	4 906	....	....	....	....	....	....		
General government	4 907	....	....	....	....	....	....		
Banks	4 908	....	....	....	....	....	....		
Other sectors	4 909	....	....	....	....	....	....	204	37

Table 2 (Concluded). STANDARD PRESENTATION, 2003–2010

(Millions of U.S. dollars)

	Code	2003	2004	2005	2006	2007	2008	2009	2010
D. OTHER INVESTMENT	4 700	**−3,624**	**−327**	**−14,720**	**−12,344**	**9,714**	**−14,054**	**−10,693**	**−24,960**
Assets	4 703	**−3,391**	**−559**	**−19,323**	**−22,735**	**−14,483**	**−18,281**	**3,148**	**−14,498**
Trade credits	4 706	−846	−657	−1,473	−441	−1,611	3,453	−2,462	−1,181
General government	4 707	−846	−657	−1,473	−441	−1,611	3,453	−2,462	−1,181
of which: Short-term	4 709	*−846*	*−657*	*−1,473*	*−441*	*−1,611*	*3,453*	*−2,462*	*−1,181*
Other sectors	4 710	....	....	....	....	....	....	....	....
of which: Short-term	4 712	....	....	....	....	....	....	....	....
Loans	4 714	952	90	−939	−356	−1,320	−1,074	−576	1,252
Monetary authorities	4 715	....	....	....	....	....	....	....	....
of which: Short-term	4 718	....	....	....	....	....	....	....	....
General government	4 719	−343	−428	−513	410	226	−873	−264	−72
of which: Short-term	4 721	....	....	....	....	....	....	....	....
Banks	4 722	1,317	496	−365	−716	−1,203	−363	−126	1,254
of which: Short-term	4 724	*1,317*	*496*	*−365*	*−716*	*−1,203*	*−363*	*−126*	*1,254*
Other sectors	4 725	−21	23	−62	−51	−343	162	−186	70
of which: Short-term	4 727	*−21*	....	*−62*	*−51*	*−343*	*162*	*−186*	*70*
Currency and deposits	4 730	−3,274	−77	−17,055	−20,866	−9,108	−18,649	4,909	−10,919
Monetary authorities	4 731	....	....	....	....	....	....	....	....
General government	4 732	−1,921	4,279	−14,392	−14,657	−1,104	−13,218	−4,950	−6,660
Banks	4 733	−1,198	−2,509	−1,366	−3,640	−4,251	−3,590	5,473	189
Other sectors	4 734	−155	−1,847	−1,297	−2,569	−3,753	−1,841	4,387	−4,447
Other assets	4 736	−223	84	145	−1,072	−2,443	−2,012	1,277	−3,651
Monetary authorities	4 737	....	....	....	....	....	....	....	....
of which: Short-term	4 739	....	....	....	....	....	....	....	....
General government	4 740	−209	−62	−118	−694	−466	−577	481	−27
of which: Short-term	4 742	....	....	....	....	....	....	....	....
Banks	4 743	−61	−135	109	−27	−882	−216	−119	−285
of which: Short-term	4 745	*−61*	*−135*	*109*	*−27*	*−882*	*−216*	*−119*	*−285*
Other sectors	4 746	47	281	154	−352	−1,095	−1,219	915	−3,339
of which: Short-term	4 748	*47*	*281*	*154*	*−352*	*−1,095*	*−1,219*	*915*	*−3,339*
Liabilities	4 753	**−234**	**232**	**4,603**	**10,392**	**24,197**	**4,227**	**−13,842**	**−10,461**
Trade credits	4 756	....	....	....	....	....	....	....	....
General government	4 757	....	....	....	....	....	....	....	....
of which: Short-term	4 759	....	....	....	....	....	....	....	....
Other sectors	4 760	....	....	....	....	....	....	....	....
of which: Short-term	4 762	....	....	....	....	....	....	....	....
Loans	4 764	357	494	1,319	6,224	10,204	3,529	−4,115	−7,030
Monetary authorities	4 765	....	....	....	....	....	....	....	....
of which: Use of Fund credit and loans from the Fund	4 766	....	....	....	....	....	....	....	....
of which: Short-term	4 768	....	....	....	....	....	....	....	....
General government	4 769	−36	−37	−41	−38	−24	200	1	−57
of which: Short-term	4 771	....	....	....	....	....	....	....	....
Banks	4 772	....	....	....	....	....	....	....	527
of which: Short-term	4 774	....	....	....	....	....	....	....	*527*
Other sectors	4 775	393	531	1,360	6,262	10,228	3,329	−4,116	−7,500
of which: Short-term	4 777	....	....	....	....	....	....	*−4,116*	*−7,500*
Currency and deposits	4 780	−534	−437	1,926	3,036	10,701	−1,747	−4,293	314
Monetary authorities	4 781	....	....	....	....	....	....	....	....
General government	4 782	....	....	....	....	....	....	....	....
Banks	4 783	−534	−469	1,878	3,039	10,780	−1,807	−4,293	314
Other sectors	4 784	....	32	48	−3	−79	60		
Other liabilities	4 786	−57	176	1,358	1,132	3,292	2,445	−5,433	−3,745
Monetary authorities	4 787	30	34	259	100	67	−156	1,902	2
of which: Short-term	4 789	*30*	*34*	*259*	*100*	*67*	*−156*	*−114*	*2*
General government	4 790	−143	9	877	390	2,630	1,062	−3,228	−875
of which: Short-term	4 792	*−143*	*9*	*877*	*390*	*2,630*	*1,062*	*−3,228*	*−875*
Banks	4 793	−15	51	110	−54	161	70	−1,961	−329
of which: Short-term	4 795	*−15*	*51*	*110*	*−54*	*161*	*70*	*−1,961*	*−329*
Other sectors	4 796	71	82	112	696	433	1,469	−2,145	−2,543
of which: Short-term	4 798	*71*	*82*	*112*	*696*	*433*	*1,469*	*−2,145*	*−2,543*
E. RESERVE ASSETS	4 802	**1,824**	**−626**	**−619**	**−3,584**	**−3,219**	**−647**	**−3,759**	**−611**
Monetary gold	4 812	....	....	....	....	....	....	....	....
Special drawing rights	4 811	−14	−14	−17	−13	−13	−9	−2,018	−1
Reserve position in the Fund	4 810	9	94	363	129	45	−124	−122	....
Foreign exchange	4 803	1,829	−706	−965	−3,699	−3,251	−514	−1,619	−609
Other claims	4 813	....	....	....	....	....	....	....	....
NET ERRORS AND OMISSIONS	4 998	**−574**	**1,534**	**2,601**	**7,087**	**−4,737**	**−10,040**	**3,376**	**−3,683**

Table 3. INTERNATIONAL INVESTMENT POSITION (End-period stocks), 2003–2010

(Millions of U.S. dollars)

	Code	2003	2004	2005	2006	2007	2008	2009	2010
ASSETS	8 995 C.	**46,186**	**53,625**	**70,771**	**96,641**	**131,612**	**172,999**	**165,488**	**135,438**
Direct investment abroad	8 505 ..	**766**	**1,468**	**5,893**	**10,845**	**14,665**	**22,436**	**22,990**	**19,068**
Equity capital and reinvested earnings	8 506 ..	766	1,468	5,893	10,845	14,665	20,710	21,067	18,676
Claims on affiliated enterprises	8 507 ..	766	1,468	5,893	10,845	14,665	20,710	21,067	18,676
Liabilities to affiliated enterprises	8 508 ..	....	....	....	....	....			....
Other capital	8 530 ..	....	....	....		....	1,727	1,923	392
Claims on affiliated enterprises	8 535 ..	....		....		....	1,727	1,923	392
Liabilities to affiliated enterprises	8 540 ..	....		....	....	....			....
Portfolio investment	8 602 ..	**9,756**	**11,407**	**18,642**	**27,424**	**37,915**	**59,169**	**55,388**	**24,724**
Equity securities	8 610 ..	4,367	5,875	8,017	11,357	16,036	50,887	48,214	21,447
Monetary authorities	8 611 ..	....	....	....	....	....			....
General government	8 612 ..			....					....
Banks	8 613 ..	1,853	2,168	2,559	3,015	4,741	7,575	7,425	2,050
Other sectors	8 614 ..	2,514	3,707	5,459	8,342	11,294	43,312	40,789	19,397
Debt securities	8 619 ..	5,389	5,532	10,625	16,067	21,880	8,282	7,174	3,277
Bonds and notes	8 620 ..	5,389	5,532	10,625	16,067	21,880	8,282	7,174	3,277
Monetary authorities	8 621 ..	....		....		....			....
General government	8 622 ..	....		....	....	....			
Banks	8 623 ..	353	414	487	575	904	1,295	1,161	1,238
Other sectors	8 624 ..	5,036	5,118	10,138	15,492	20,976	6,986	6,013	2,039
Money market instruments	8 630 ..	....		....		....			....
Monetary authorities	8 631 ..	....		....	....	....			....
General government	8 632 ..	....		....	....	....			....
Banks	8 633 ..	....		....	....	....			....
Other sectors	8 634 ..	....		....	....	....			
Financial derivatives	8 900 ..	**....**	**....**	**....**	**....**	**....**	**14**	**242**	**278**
Monetary authorities	8 901 ..	....		....	....	....			....
General government	8 902 ..	....		....	....	....			....
Banks	8 903 ..	....		....	....	....			....
Other sectors	8 904 ..	....		....	....	....	14	242	278
Other investment	8 703 ..	**27,983**	**32,405**	**37,267**	**45,702**	**62,265**	**74,161**	**66,500**	**70,032**
Trade credits	8 706 ..	1,692	2,349	3,843	4,323	6,257	2,826	5,190	6,031
General government	8 707 ..	1,692	2,349	3,843	4,323	6,257	2,826	5,190	6,031
of which: Short-term	8 709 ..	*1,692*	*2,349*	*3,843*	*4,323*	*6,257*	*2,826*	*5,190*	*6,031*
Other sectors	8 710 ..	....	....	....	....	....			....
of which: Short-term	8 712 ..	....	....	....	....	....			....
Loans	8 714 ..	6,528	6,071	6,758	7,739	9,936	20,381	20,306	19,508
Monetary authorities	8 715 ..	....	....	....	....	....			....
of which: Short-term	8 718 ..	....	....	....	....	....			....
General government	8 719 ..	4,280	4,342	4,587	4,777	5,186	5,386	5,404	5,695
of which: Short-term	8 721 ..	....	....	....	....	....			....
Banks	8 722 ..	1,958	1,462	1,841	2,577	3,982	4,298	4,419	3,077
of which: Short-term	8 724 ..	*1,958*	*1,462*	*1,841*	*2,577*	*3,982*	*4,298*	*4,419*	*3,077*
Other sectors	8 725 ..	290	266	330	386	767	10,697	10,484	10,735
of which: Short-term	8 727 ..	....	*266*	*330*	*386*	*767*	*10,697*	*10,484*	*10,735*
Currency and deposits	8 730 ..	18,603	22,971	25,905	32,489	42,863	45,678	36,674	37,595
Monetary authorities	8 731 ..	....	....	....	....	....			....
General government	8 732 ..	....	....	....	....	....			....
Banks	8 733 ..	3,890	6,411	7,851	11,678	17,028	18,925	13,836	10,227
Other sectors	8 734 ..	14,712	16,561	18,054	20,810	25,834	26,753	22,838	27,368
Other assets	8 736 ..	1,161	1,015	761	1,150	3,210	5,277	4,330	6,898
Monetary authorities	8 737 ..	....	....	....	....	....			....
of which: Short-term	8 739 ..	....	....	....	....	....			....
General government	8 740 ..	....	....	....	....	....			....
of which: Short-term	8 742 ..	....	....	....	....	....			....
Banks	8 743 ..	187	321	215	244	1,177	1,403	1,521	1,760
of which: Short-term	8 745 ..	*187*	*321*	*215*	*244*	*1,177*	*1,403*	*1,521*	*1,760*
Other sectors	8 746 ..	974	693	546	906	2,033	3,873	2,809	5,138
of which: Short-term	8 748 ..	*974*	*693*	*546*	*906*	*2,033*	*3,873*	*2,809*	*5,138*
Reserve assets	8 802 ..	**7,681**	**8,345**	**8,967**	**12,670**	**16,766**	**17,219**	**20,369**	**21,337**
Monetary gold	8 812 ..	108	108	109	110	116	115	111	113
Special drawing rights	8 811 ..	160	182	184	207	231	234	2,261	2,223
Reserve position in the Fund	8 810 ..	777	713	298	181	144	268	398	391
Foreign exchange	8 803 ..	6,637	7,343	8,376	12,172	16,276	16,602	17,599	18,610
Other claims	8 813 ..	....	....	....	....	....	....	....	....

Table 3 (Concluded). INTERNATIONAL INVESTMENT POSITION (End-period stocks), 2003–2010

(Millions of U.S. dollars)

	Code	2003	2004	2005	2006	2007	2008	2009	2010
LIABILITIES	8 995 D.	**16,493**	**17,078**	**21,609**	**32,421**	**60,035**	**68,715**	**56,833**	**51,155**
Direct investment in Kuwait	8 555 ..	**384**	**408**	**645**	**773**	**945**	**8,722**	**9,486**	**6,560**
Equity capital and reinvested earnings	8 556 ..	384	408	645	773	945	8,526	9,249	6,514
Claims on direct investors	8 557 ..	....	....	....	....	....	....	....	....
Liabilities to direct investors	8 558 ..	384	408	645	773	945	8,526	9,249	6,514
Other capital	8 580 ..	....	....	....	....	....	196	237	45
Claims on direct investors	8 585 ..	....	....	....	....	....	....	....	....
Liabilities to direct investors	8 590 ..	....	....	....	....	....	196	237	45
Portfolio investment	8 652 ..	**882**	**1,170**	**722**	**780**	**1,360**	**7,042**	**6,261**	**13,171**
Equity securities	8 660 ..	....	....	....	....	....	6,925	6,169	13,171
Banks	8 663 ..	....	....	....	....	....	48	54	80
Other sectors	8 664 ..	....	....	....	....	....	6,877	6,115	13,091
Debt securities	8 669 ..	882	1,170	722	780	1,360	118	93	....
Bonds and notes	8 670 ..	882	1,170	722	780	1,360	118	93	....
Monetary authorities	8 671 ..	....	....	....	....	....	....	....	
General government	8 672 ..	....	....	....	....	....	....	....	
Banks	8 673 ..	652	722	241	209	209	....	....	
Other sectors	8 674 ..	231	448	480	572	1,152	118	93	
Money market instruments	8 680 ..	....	....	....	....	....	....	....	
Monetary authorities	8 681 ..	....	....	....	....	....	....	....	
General government	8 682 ..	....	....	....	....	....	....	....	
Banks	8 683 ..	....	....	....	....	....	....	....	
Other sectors	8 684 ..	....	....	....	....	....	....	....	
Financial derivatives	8 905 ..	**....**	**....**	**....**	**....**	**....**	**24**	**231**	**281**
Monetary authorities	8 906 ..	....	....	....	....	....	....	....	....
General government	8 907 ..	....	....	....	....	....	....	....	....
Banks	8 908 ..	....	....	....	....	....	....	....	....
Other sectors	8 909 ..	....	....	....	....	....	24	231	281
Other investment	8 753 ..	**15,227**	**15,500**	**20,242**	**30,868**	**57,729**	**52,927**	**40,855**	**31,144**
Trade credits	8 756 ..	....	....	....	....	....	....	....	....
General government	8 757 ..	....	....	....	....	....	....	....	....
of which: Short-term	8 759 ..	....	....	....	....	....	....	....	....
Other sectors	8 760 ..	....	....	....	....	....	....	....	....
of which: Short-term	8 762 ..	....	....	....	....	....	....	....	....
Loans	8 764 ..	8,182	8,675	10,075	16,421	27,622	23,977	22,173	15,845
Monetary authorities	8 765 ..	....	....	....	....	....	....	....	....
of which: Use of Fund credit and loans from the Fund	8 766 ..	....	....	....	....	....	....	....	....
of which: Short-term	8 768 ..	....	....	....	....	....	....	....	....
General government	8 769 ..	141	104	64	27	4	199	203	146
of which: Short-term	8 771 ..	*141*	*104*	*64*	*27*	....	....	....	....
Banks	8 772 ..	....	....	....	....	....	....	644	1,189
of which: Short-term	8 774 ..	....	....	....	....	....	....	*644*	*1,189*
Other sectors	8 775 ..	8,040	8,571	10,010	16,394	27,618	23,778	21,326	14,509
of which: Short-term	8 777 ..	*8,040*	*8,571*	*10,010*	*16,394*	*27,618*	*23,778*	*21,326*	*14,509*
Currency and deposits	8 780 ..	5,841	5,404	7,379	10,499	22,263	8,543	4,023	8,536
Monetary authorities	8 781 ..	....	....	....	....	....	....	....	....
General government	8 782 ..	....	....	....	....	....	....	....	....
Banks	8 783 ..	5,841	5,372	7,299	10,421	22,263	8,543	4,023	8,536
Other sectors	8 784 ..	....	32	80	78	....	....	....	....
Other liabilities	8 786 ..	1,204	1,421	2,789	3,948	7,844	20,406	14,659	6,763
Monetary authorities	8 787 ..	74	149	406	506	585	415	2,308	2,279
of which: Short-term	8 789 ..	*74*	*108*	*367*	*466*	*543*	*374*	*245*	*253*
General government	8 790 ..	521	530	1,412	1,817	4,914	5,566	2,116	3,527
of which: Short-term	8 792 ..	*521*	*530*	*1,412*	*1,817*	*4,914*	*5,566*	*2,116*	*3,527*
Banks	8 793 ..	39	90	201	148	325	8,177	5,917	253
of which: Short-term	8 795 ..	*39*	*90*	*201*	*148*	*325*	*8,177*	*5,917*	*253*
Other sectors	8 796 ..	570	652	770	1,476	2,020	6,248	4,318	704
of which: Short-term	8 798 ..	*570*	*652*	*770*	*1,476*	*2,020*	*6,248*	*4,318*	*704*
NET INTERNATIONAL INVESTMENT POSITION	8 995 ..	**29,693**	**36,547**	**49,161**	**64,220**	**71,577**	**104,284**	**108,655**	**84,283**
Conversion rates: Kuwaiti dinar per U.S. dollar (end of period)	0 102 ..	**.2947**	**.2947**	**.2920**	**.2891**	**.2730**	**.2760**	**.2868**	**.2806**

Table 1. ANALYTIC PRESENTATION, 2003–2010

(Millions of U.S. dollars)

	Code	2003	2004	2005	2006	2007	2008	2009	2010
A. Current Account[1]	4 993 Z.	**−60.5**	**3.7**	**−62.1**	**−303.2**	**−261.3**	**−750.3**	**−300.2**	**−467.0**
Goods: exports f.o.b.	2 100 ..	590.3	733.2	686.8	906.0	1,337.8	1,874.4	1,700.4	1,778.7
Goods: imports f.o.b.	3 100 ..	−723.1	−903.8	−1,105.5	−1,792.4	−2,613.6	−3,753.5	−2,813.6	−2,980.9
Balance on Goods	4 100 ..	*−132.8*	*−170.6*	*−418.7*	*−886.5*	*−1,275.8*	*−1,879.2*	*−1,113.2*	*−1,202.2*
Services: credit	2 200 ..	158.2	209.8	259.4	378.7	684.8	896.1	859.8	693.1
Services: debit	3 200 ..	−159.6	−222.6	−290.3	−459.7	−604.5	−992.9	−866.9	−924.2
Balance on Goods and Services	4 991 ..	*−134.2*	*−183.5*	*−449.5*	*−967.4*	*−1,195.5*	*−1,975.9*	*−1,120.2*	*−1,433.3*
Income: credit	2 300 ..	5.2	7.8	16.5	41.6	42.6	41.7	21.7	70.7
Income: debit	3 300 ..	−67.2	−109.9	−104.7	−89.8	−94.5	−243.3	−211.6	−413.9
Balance on Goods, Services, and Income	4 992 ..	*−196.2*	*−285.6*	*−537.7*	*−1,015.6*	*−1,247.4*	*−2,177.6*	*−1,310.1*	*−1,776.5*
Current transfers: credit	2 379 Z.	142.7	306.9	513.6	762.4	1,065.2	1,507.7	1,095.0	1,450.9
Current transfers: debit	3 379 ..	−7.0	−17.6	−37.9	−50.0	−79.0	−80.5	−85.1	−141.4
B. Capital Account[1]	4 994 Z.	**−.9**	**−19.9**	**−20.5**	**−43.9**	**−74.9**	**−44.9**	**−14.0**	**−62.1**
Capital account: credit	2 994 Z.	36.0	33.7	51.6	37.8	54.3	52.7	65.0	66.9
Capital account: debit	3 994 ..	−36.9	−53.6	−72.2	−81.7	−129.1	−97.6	−78.9	−129.0
Total, Groups A Plus B	4 981 ..	*−61.3*	*−16.2*	*−82.6*	*−347.1*	*−336.1*	*−795.3*	*−314.2*	*−529.0*
C. Financial Account[1]	4 995 W.	**27.7**	**180.1**	**85.4**	**339.4**	**363.8**	**218.9**	**448.0**	**646.0**
Direct investment abroad	4 505 ..	....	−43.9	....	....	.2	.1	.3	....
Direct investment in Kyrgyz Republic	4 555 Z.	45.5	175.5	42.6	182.0	207.9	377.0	189.4	437.6
Portfolio investment assets	4 602 ..	1.1	−9.5	2.3	−3.0	−19.2	−31.8	−21.7	182.5
Equity securities	4 610 ..	....	....	....	....	−.2	....	....	22.9
Debt securities	4 619 ..	1.1	−9.5	2.3	−3.0	−19.0	−31.8	−21.7	159.5
Portfolio investment liabilities	4 652 Z.	5.0	....	....	....	1.5	6.2	.7	−18.2
Equity securities	4 660 ..	5.0	....	....	....	1.5	6.2	.7	−18.2
Debt securities	4 669 Z.	....	....	....	....	....	....	....	....
Financial derivatives	4 910 ..	−20.0	−20.5	....	....	....	....	....	....
Financial derivatives assets	4 900 ..	−20.0	−20.5	....	....	....	....	....	....
Financial derivatives liabilities	4 905 ..	....	....	....	....	....	....	....	....
Other investment assets	4 703 ..	−76.6	−35.8	−47.5	−24.0	19.4	−362.7	−215.8	106.8
Monetary authorities	4 701 ..	1.7	9.3	18.7	1.0	20.0	−19.3	−2.3	....
General government	4 704 ..	−.2	....	....	....	....	....	....	....
Banks	4 705 ..	−50.2	−63.2	−15.1	−17.0	37.7	−115.9	−156.5	199.9
Other sectors	4 728 ..	−28.0	18.1	−51.1	−8.0	−38.3	−227.4	−57.0	−93.1
Other investment liabilities	4 753 W.	72.8	114.3	88.1	184.4	154.1	230.0	495.1	−62.7
Monetary authorities	4 753 WA	....	....	....	....	....	....	132.5	....
General government	4 753 ZB	76.7	101.5	81.1	63.1	41.3	16.3	340.4	117.1
Banks	4 753 ZC	36.6	42.2	−11.9	−26.6	66.6	48.4	50.4	−204.0
Other sectors	4 753 ZD	−40.5	−29.5	19.0	147.9	46.2	165.3	−28.2	24.2
Total, Groups A Through C	4 983 ..	*−33.6*	*163.9*	*2.8*	*−7.7*	*27.7*	*−576.4*	*133.8*	*116.9*
D. Net Errors and Omissions	4 998 ..	**80.4**	**−19.4**	**65.6**	**184.4**	**265.4**	**629.6**	**−67.0**	**−95.5**
Total, Groups A Through D	4 984 ..	*46.8*	*144.5*	*68.4*	*176.7*	*293.1*	*53.2*	*66.8*	*21.4*
E. Reserves and Related Items	4 802 A.	**−46.8**	**−144.5**	**−68.4**	**−176.7**	**−293.1**	**−53.2**	**−66.8**	**−21.4**
Reserve assets	4 802 ..	−64.2	−166.2	−80.5	−170.3	−306.7	−121.0	−264.6	−115.7
Use of Fund credit and loans	4 766 ..	−.9	−3.9	−12.5	−23.5	−20.7	18.3	−.2	12.4
Exceptional financing	4 920 ..	18.3	25.6	24.6	17.1	34.3	49.5	198.0	81.8
Conversion rates: soms per U.S. dollar	0 101 ..	**43.648**	**42.650**	**41.012**	**40.153**	**37.316**	**36.575**	**42.904**	**45.964**

[1] Excludes components that have been classified in the categories of Group E.

Table 2. STANDARD PRESENTATION, 2003–2010

(Millions of U.S. dollars)

	Code	2003	2004	2005	2006	2007	2008	2009	2010
CURRENT ACCOUNT...	4 993 ..	**−42.2**	**29.3**	**−37.4**	**−286.1**	**−226.9**	**−700.9**	**−102.2**	**−385.2**
A. GOODS..	4 100 ..	**−132.8**	**−170.6**	**−418.7**	**−886.5**	**−1,275.8**	**−1,879.2**	**−1,113.2**	**−1,202.2**
Credit..	2 100 ..	**590.3**	**733.2**	**686.8**	**906.0**	**1,337.8**	**1,874.4**	**1,700.4**	**1,778.7**
General merchandise: exports f.o.b..............	2 110 ..	330.7	445.8	456.1	700.0	1,113.1	1,410.9	1,170.9	1,110.4
Goods for processing: exports f.o.b............	2 150 ..	....	....	....	....	....	....	....	....
Repairs on goods.......................................	2 160 ..	....	....	....	....	....	....	....	....
Goods procured in ports by carriers............	2 170 ..	....	....	....	....	....	....	....	....
Nonmonetary gold.....................................	2 180 ..	259.6	287.4	230.7	206.0	224.7	463.5	529.5	668.3
Debit..	3 100 ..	**−723.1**	**−903.8**	**−1,105.5**	**−1,792.4**	**−2,613.6**	**−3,753.5**	**−2,813.6**	**−2,980.9**
General merchandise: imports f.o.b..............	3 110 ..	−720.2	−900.4	−1,102.7	−1,790.0	−2,605.2	−3,737.3	−2,806.3	−2,978.6
Goods for processing: imports f.o.b...........	3 150 ..	....	....	....	....	....	....	....	....
Repairs on goods.......................................	3 160 ..	....	....	....	....	....	....	....	....
Goods procured in ports by carriers............	3 170 ..	−2.9	−3.4	−2.8	−2.4	−8.4	−16.3	−7.3	−2.4
Nonmonetary gold.....................................	3 180 ..	....	....	....	....	....	....	....	....
B. SERVICES..	4 200 ..	**−1.4**	**−12.8**	**−30.8**	**−81.0**	**80.3**	**−96.8**	**−7.0**	**−231.1**
Total credit...	2 200 ..	*158.2*	*209.8*	*259.4*	*378.7*	*684.8*	*896.1*	*859.8*	*693.1*
Total debit..	3 200 ..	*−159.6*	*−222.6*	*−290.3*	*−459.7*	*−604.5*	*−992.9*	*−866.9*	*−924.2*
Transportation services, credit....................	2 205 ..	**41.9**	**50.8**	**60.6**	**56.6**	**139.3**	**146.4**	**134.9**	**150.4**
Passenger..	2 850 ..	*13.5*	*15.6*	*20.9*	*22.1*	*45.9*	*54.7*	*46.9*	*51.7*
Freight..	2 851 ..	*16.5*	*20.5*	*20.8*	*17.6*	*43.7*	*44.7*	*43.9*	*49.2*
Other..	2 852 ..	*11.9*	*14.6*	*18.9*	*16.8*	*49.8*	*47.0*	*44.1*	*49.5*
Sea transport, passenger............................	2 207 ..	....	....	....	....	....	....	....	....
Sea transport, freight.................................	2 208 ..	....	....	....	....	....	....	....	....
Sea transport, other...................................	2 209 ..	....	....	....	....	....	....	....	....
Air transport, passenger.............................	2 211 ..	5.6	7.0	7.8	6.8	19.7	19.8	20.4	22.9
Air transport, freight..................................	2 212 ..	10.1	12.6	14.1	12.4	35.6	35.7	36.8	41.4
Air transport, other....................................	2 213 ..	10.5	13.2	14.7	12.9	37.2	37.3	38.4	43.2
Other transport, passenger.........................	2 215 ..	8.0	8.6	13.1	15.3	26.2	34.9	26.6	28.8
Other transport, freight..............................	2 216 ..	6.4	7.9	6.7	5.3	8.1	8.9	7.1	7.9
Other transport, other................................	2 217 ..	1.4	1.5	4.2	3.9	12.6	9.7	5.7	6.3
Transportation services, debit.....................	3 205 ..	**−64.2**	**−88.7**	**−125.5**	**−178.0**	**−337.1**	**−488.7**	**−412.5**	**−417.0**
Passenger..	3 850 ..	*−17.9*	*−23.2*	*−36.1*	*−50.2*	*−103.3*	*−147.0*	*−126.0*	*−127.3*
Freight..	3 851 ..	*−25.4*	*−33.7*	*−43.8*	*−62.9*	*−92.5*	*−140.1*	*−118.5*	*−129.6*
Other..	3 852 ..	*−20.9*	*−31.8*	*−45.5*	*−64.8*	*−141.4*	*−201.6*	*−168.0*	*−160.1*
Sea transport, passenger............................	3 207 ..	....	....	....	....	....	....	....	....
Sea transport, freight.................................	3 208 ..	....	....	....	....	....	....	....	....
Sea transport, other...................................	3 209 ..	....	....	....	....	....	....	....	....
Air transport, passenger.............................	3 211 ..	−4.8	−6.1	−10.1	−12.0	−29.0	−31.7	−28.8	−29.1
Air transport, freight..................................	3 212 ..	−.9	−1.1	−1.9	−2.2	−5.3	−5.8	−5.3	−5.3
Air transport, other....................................	3 213 ..	−7.6	−9.6	−15.9	−18.8	−45.6	−49.8	−45.2	−45.7
Other transport, passenger.........................	3 215 ..	−13.0	−17.2	−26.0	−38.2	−74.3	−115.3	−97.2	−98.2
Other transport, freight..............................	3 216 ..	−24.5	−32.6	−42.0	−60.7	−87.2	−134.3	−113.3	−124.3
Other transport, other................................	3 217 ..	−13.4	−22.2	−29.6	−46.0	−95.8	−151.8	−122.8	−114.4
Travel, credit..	2 236 ..	**47.8**	**75.6**	**73.0**	**167.0**	**346.0**	**514.5**	**458.8**	**283.6**
Business travel...	2 237 ..	25.8	40.7	39.1	86.4	176.5	261.6	204.2	122.0
Personal travel...	2 240 ..	21.9	35.0	33.9	80.6	169.5	252.9	254.6	161.7
Travel, debit...	3 236 ..	**−16.6**	**−50.3**	**−58.4**	**−91.6**	**−112.4**	**−304.4**	**−264.8**	**−271.1**
Business travel...	3 237 ..	−11.6	−35.2	−40.9	−64.2	−78.7	−213.1	−149.7	−143.7
Personal travel...	3 240 ..	−5.0	−15.1	−17.5	−27.5	−33.7	−91.3	−115.1	−127.4
Other services, credit................................	2 200 BA	**68.6**	**83.4**	**125.8**	**155.2**	**199.4**	**235.2**	**266.1**	**259.1**
Communications...	2 245 ..	8.7	8.0	6.4	10.1	12.0	16.4	9.3	19.9
Construction..	2 249 ..	5.7	8.3	19.0	19.7	16.8	20.8	18.8	32.8
Insurance...	2 253 ..	1.3	.2	.2	1.4	5.0	8.3	3.6	6.7
Financial..	2 260 ..	.6	1.9	3.8	2.0	3.7	13.5	10.9	.6
Computer and information..........................	2 262 ..	1.5	.7	1.2	1.3	1.1	1.4	1.3	3.1
Royalties and licence fees...........................	2 266 ..	.5	1.0	1.7	2.4	2.4	2.8	3.7	1.1
Other business services..............................	2 268 ..	23.6	37.4	61.0	80.8	82.5	90.9	122.0	112.2
Personal, cultural, and recreational.............	2 287 ..	5.6	8.6	6.7	10.2	45.3	69.4	86.2	68.1
Government, n.i.e.......................................	2 291 ..	21.2	17.3	25.9	27.3	30.7	11.6	10.3	14.6
Other services, debit.................................	3 200 BA	**−78.9**	**−83.7**	**−106.4**	**−190.1**	**−155.0**	**−199.7**	**−189.5**	**−236.1**
Communications...	3 245 ..	−8.2	−6.1	−6.0	−5.9	−7.4	−12.6	−9.2	−12.8
Construction..	3 249 ..	−2.7	−1.6	−2.1	−3.3	−11.8	−10.5	−18.3	−11.9
Insurance...	3 253 ..	−15.0	−13.2	−14.9	−18.3	−9.4	−10.8	−12.0	−14.1
Financial..	3 260 ..	−4.4	−12.7	−4.4	−3.6	−9.0	−9.1	−4.0	−17.1
Computer and information..........................	3 262 ..	−3.5	−3.3	−2.2	−1.7	−4.4	−14.6	−16.2	−13.6
Royalties and licence fees...........................	3 266 ..	−3.5	−3.0	−6.0	−19.5	−11.7	−14.9	−12.1	−2.6
Other business services..............................	3 268 ..	−35.7	−32.8	−45.5	−103.1	−69.9	−83.6	−72.3	−136.7
Personal, cultural, and recreational.............	3 287 ..	−3.1	−6.3	−21.0	−29.9	−26.2	−38.1	−36.2	−18.3
Government, n.i.e.......................................	3 291 ..	−2.6	−4.8	−4.2	−4.8	−5.2	−5.5	−9.2	−9.1

Table 2 (Continued). STANDARD PRESENTATION, 2003–2010

(Millions of U.S. dollars)

	Code	2003	2004	2005	2006	2007	2008	2009	2010
C. INCOME	4 300	**−62.0**	**−102.2**	**−88.2**	**−48.2**	**−51.9**	**−201.6**	**−189.9**	**−343.1**
Total credit	2 300	*5.2*	*7.8*	*16.5*	*41.6*	*42.6*	*41.7*	*21.7*	*70.7*
Total debit	3 300	*−67.2*	*−109.9*	*−104.7*	*−89.8*	*−94.5*	*−243.3*	*−211.6*	*−413.9*
Compensation of employees, credit	2 310	....	....	....	....	....	....	....	....
Compensation of employees, debit	3 310	**−13.3**	**−14.2**	**−20.4**	**−24.2**	**−20.8**	**−22.3**	**−27.0**	**−32.3**
Investment income, credit	2 320	**5.2**	**7.8**	**16.5**	**41.6**	**42.6**	**41.7**	**21.7**	**70.7**
Direct investment income	2 330	....	....	....	....	....	....	....	41.1
Dividends and distributed branch profits	2 332	....	....	....	....	....	....	....	41.1
Reinvested earnings and undistributed branch profits	2 333	....	....	....	....	....	....	....	....
Income on debt (interest)	2 334	....	....	....	....	....	....	....	....
Portfolio investment income	2 339	.3	.1	....	.1	.2	.5	4.2	.2
Income on equity	2 340	....	....	....	....	....	....	....	....
Income on bonds and notes	2 350	.3	.1	....	.1	.2	.5	4.2	.2
Income on money market instruments	2 360	....	....	....	....	....	....	....	....
Other investment income	2 370	4.9	7.6	16.5	41.5	42.4	41.2	17.5	29.5
Investment income, debit	3 320	**−54.0**	**−95.7**	**−84.3**	**−65.6**	**−73.8**	**−221.0**	**−184.5**	**−381.6**
Direct investment income	3 330	−26.7	−57.6	−36.0	−39.8	−39.5	−172.8	−126.0	−327.5
Dividends and distributed branch profits	3 332	−.1	....	−2.3	−14.0	−.2	−1.6	....	−50.2
Reinvested earnings and undistributed branch profits	3 333	−21.8	−48.0	−30.7	−21.0	−33.6	−152.9	−108.0	−238.7
Income on debt (interest)	3 334	−4.9	−9.5	−3.0	−4.8	−5.8	−18.2	−18.1	−38.6
Portfolio investment income	3 339	....	....	....	....	....	....	....	....
Income on equity	3 340	....	....	....	....	....	....	....	....
Income on bonds and notes	3 350	....	....	....	....	....	....	....	....
Income on money market instruments	3 360	....	....	....	....	....	....	....	....
Other investment income	3 370	−27.2	−38.2	−48.3	−25.8	−34.2	−48.2	−58.5	−54.1
D. CURRENT TRANSFERS	4 379	**154.0**	**314.9**	**500.3**	**729.5**	**1,020.5**	**1,476.7**	**1,207.9**	**1,391.3**
Credit	2 379	**161.0**	**332.5**	**538.2**	**779.5**	**1,099.5**	**1,557.2**	**1,293.0**	**1,532.7**
General government	2 380	18.3	25.6	24.6	17.1	34.3	49.5	198.0	81.8
Other sectors	2 390	142.7	306.9	513.6	762.4	1,065.2	1,507.7	1,095.0	1,450.9
Workers' remittances	2 391	70.3	179.1	313.3	473.1	705.4	1,224.1	982.7	1,266.2
Other current transfers	2 392	72.4	127.9	200.3	289.3	359.8	283.6	112.3	184.7
Debit	3 379	**−7.0**	**−17.6**	**−37.9**	**−50.0**	**−79.0**	**−80.5**	**−85.1**	**−141.4**
General government	3 380	−1.3	−1.9	−1.6	−4.7	−3.4	−3.6	−3.0	−3.6
Other sectors	3 390	−5.7	−15.7	−36.3	−45.3	−75.6	−76.9	−82.1	−137.8
Workers' remittances	3 391	−5.2	−15.4	−32.8	−43.9	−69.8	−76.5	−81.7	−135.5
Other current transfers	3 392	−.6	−.3	−3.4	−1.4	−5.8	−.4	−.3	−2.3
CAPITAL AND FINANCIAL ACCOUNT	4 996	**−38.3**	**−9.9**	**−28.1**	**101.8**	**−38.5**	**71.3**	**169.2**	**480.7**
CAPITAL ACCOUNT	4 994	**−.9**	**−19.9**	**−20.5**	**−43.9**	**−74.9**	**−44.9**	**−14.0**	**−62.1**
Total credit	2 994	*36.0*	*33.7*	*51.6*	*37.8*	*54.3*	*52.7*	*65.0*	*66.9*
Total debit	3 994	*−36.9*	*−53.6*	*−72.2*	*−81.7*	*−129.1*	*−97.6*	*−78.9*	*−129.0*
Capital transfers, credit	2 400	**36.0**	**33.7**	**51.6**	**37.8**	**54.3**	**52.7**	**65.0**	**66.9**
General government	2 401	27.5	22.7	23.1	29.4	36.3	36.6	50.7	20.0
Debt forgiveness	2 402	....	....	....	....	....	....	....	....
Other capital transfers	2 410	27.5	22.7	23.1	29.4	36.3	36.6	50.7	20.0
Other sectors	2 430	8.6	11.0	28.5	8.4	18.0	16.1	14.3	46.9
Migrants' transfers	2 431	7.8	9.6	8.7	8.1	9.4	8.3	9.1	9.2
Debt forgiveness	2 432	....	....	19.0	....	....	....	....	....
Other capital transfers	2 440	.7	1.4	.8	.3	8.6	7.9	5.2	37.7
Capital transfers, debit	3 400	**−36.9**	**−53.6**	**−72.2**	**−81.7**	**−129.1**	**−97.6**	**−78.9**	**−129.0**
General government	3 401	....	....	....	....	....	....	....	....
Debt forgiveness	3 402	....	....	....	....	....	....	....	....
Other capital transfers	3 410	....	....	....	....	....	....	....	....
Other sectors	3 430	−36.9	−53.6	−72.2	−81.7	−129.1	−97.6	−78.9	−129.0
Migrants' transfers	3 431	−36.8	−53.4	−72.2	−81.7	−129.1	−97.6	−78.9	−129.0
Debt forgiveness	3 432	....	....	....	....	....	....	....	....
Other capital transfers	3 440	−.1	−.2	....	....	....	....	....	....
Nonproduced nonfinancial assets, credit	2 480	....	....	....	....	....	....	....	....
Nonproduced nonfinancial assets, debit	3 480	....	....	....	....	....	....	....	....

Table 2 (Continued). STANDARD PRESENTATION, 2003–2010

(Millions of U.S. dollars)

	Code	2003	2004	2005	2006	2007	2008	2009	2010
FINANCIAL ACCOUNT	4 995 ..	**−37.4**	**10.0**	**−7.6**	**145.6**	**36.4**	**116.2**	**183.2**	**542.8**
A. DIRECT INVESTMENT	4 500 ..	**45.5**	**131.5**	**42.6**	**182.0**	**208.1**	**377.1**	**189.6**	**437.6**
Direct investment abroad	4 505 ..	....	**−43.9**	....	....	.2	.1	.3	....
Equity capital	4 510 ..	....	−43.9	....	....	.2	.1	.3	....
Claims on affiliated enterprises	4 515 ..	....	−43.9	....	....	.2	.1	.3	....
Liabilities to affiliated enterprises	4 520 ..	....	....	....	....	....	....	....	....
Reinvested earnings	4 525 ..	....	....	....	....	....	....	....	....
Other capital	4 530 ..	....	....	....	....	....	....	....	....
Claims on affiliated enterprises	4 535 ..	....	....	....	....	....	....	....	....
Liabilities to affiliated enterprises	4 540 ..	....	....	....	....	....	....	....	....
Direct investment in Kyrgyz Republic	4 555 ..	**45.5**	**175.5**	**42.6**	**182.0**	**207.9**	**377.0**	**189.4**	**437.6**
Equity capital	4 560 ..	14.9	149.5	16.2	31.5	16.4	25.3	69.7	−7.9
Claims on direct investors	4 565 ..	....	....	....	....	....	....	....	....
Liabilities to direct investors	4 570 ..	14.9	149.5	16.2	31.5	16.4	25.3	69.7	−7.9
Reinvested earnings	4 575 ..	21.8	48.0	30.7	21.0	33.6	152.9	108.0	238.7
Other capital	4 580 ..	8.8	−22.1	−4.3	129.5	157.9	198.8	11.7	206.8
Claims on direct investors	4 585 ..	....	....	....	....	....	....	....	....
Liabilities to direct investors	4 590 ..	8.8	−22.1	−4.3	129.5	157.9	198.8	11.7	206.8
B. PORTFOLIO INVESTMENT	4 600 ..	**6.0**	**−9.5**	**2.3**	**−3.0**	**−17.7**	**−25.6**	**−21.0**	**164.3**
Assets	4 602 ..	**1.1**	**−9.5**	**2.3**	**−3.0**	**−19.2**	**−31.8**	**−21.7**	**182.5**
Equity securities	4 610 ..	....	....	....	....	−.2	....	....	22.9
Monetary authorities	4 611 ..	....	....	....	....	....	....	....	....
General government	4 612 ..	....	....	....	....	....	....	....	....
Banks	4 613 ..	....	....	....	....	....	....	....	−4.2
Other sectors	4 614 ..	....	....	....	....	−.2	....	....	27.1
Debt securities	4 619 ..	1.1	−9.5	2.3	−3.0	−19.0	−31.8	−21.7	159.5
Bonds and notes	4 620 ..	1.1	−9.5	2.3	−3.0	−19.0	−31.8	−21.7	159.5
Monetary authorities	4 621 ..	....	....	....	....	....	....	....	....
General government	4 622 ..	....	....	....	....	....	....	....	....
Banks	4 623 ..	1.1	−9.5	2.3	−3.0	−19.0	−31.8	−21.7	22.3
Other sectors	4 624 ..	....	....	....	....	....	....	....	137.2
Money market instruments	4 630 ..	....	....	....	....	....	....	....	....
Monetary authorities	4 631 ..	....	....	....	....	....	....	....	....
General government	4 632 ..	....	....	....	....	....	....	....	....
Banks	4 633 ..	....	....	....	....	....	....	....	....
Other sectors	4 634 ..	....	....	....	....	....	....	....	....
Liabilities	4 652 ..	**5.0**	....	....	....	**1.5**	**6.2**	**.7**	**−18.2**
Equity securities	4 660 ..	5.0	....	....	....	1.5	6.2	.7	−18.2
Banks	4 663 ..	3.5	....	....	....	1.0	4.4	.5	−12.7
Other sectors	4 664 ..	1.5	....	....	....	.4	1.9	.2	−5.4
Debt securities	4 669 ..	....	....	....	....	....	....	....	....
Bonds and notes	4 670 ..	....	....	....	....	....	....	....	....
Monetary authorities	4 671 ..	....	....	....	....	....	....	....	....
General government	4 672 ..	....	....	....	....	....	....	....	....
Banks	4 673 ..	....	....	....	....	....	....	....	....
Other sectors	4 674 ..	....	....	....	....	....	....	....	....
Money market instruments	4 680 ..	....	....	....	....	....	....	....	....
Monetary authorities	4 681 ..	....	....	....	....	....	....	....	....
General government	4 682 ..	....	....	....	....	....	....	....	....
Banks	4 683 ..	....	....	....	....	....	....	....	....
Other sectors	4 684 ..	....	....	....	....	....	....	....	....
C. FINANCIAL DERIVATIVES	4 910 ..	**−20.0**	**−20.5**	....	....	....	....	....	....
Monetary authorities	4 911 ..	....	....	....	....	....	....	....	....
General government	4 912 ..	....	....	....	....	....	....	....	....
Banks	4 913 ..	....	....	....	....	....	....	....	....
Other sectors	4 914 ..	−20.0	−20.5	....	....	....	....	....	....
Assets	4 900 ..	**−20.0**	**−20.5**	....	....	....	....	....	....
Monetary authorities	4 901 ..	....	....	....	....	....	....	....	....
General government	4 902 ..	....	....	....	....	....	....	....	....
Banks	4 903 ..	....	....	....	....	....	....	....	....
Other sectors	4 904 ..	−20.0	−20.5	....	....	....	....	....	....
Liabilities	4 905 ..	....	....	....	....	....	....	....	....
Monetary authorities	4 906 ..	....	....	....	....	....	....	....	....
General government	4 907 ..	....	....	....	....	....	....	....	....
Banks	4 908 ..	....	....	....	....	....	....	....	....
Other sectors	4 909 ..	....	....	....	....	....	....	....	....

Table 2 (Concluded). STANDARD PRESENTATION, 2003–2010

(Millions of U.S. dollars)

	Code	2003	2004	2005	2006	2007	2008	2009	2010
D. OTHER INVESTMENT	4 700	**−4.7**	**74.6**	**28.1**	**136.9**	**152.8**	**−114.4**	**279.1**	**56.5**
Assets	4 703	**−76.6**	**−35.8**	**−47.5**	**−24.0**	**19.4**	**−362.7**	**−215.8**	**106.8**
Trade credits	4 706	−18.2	8.4	−45.1	−13.5	−27.6	−224.0	−7.5	−82.3
General government	4 707	....	....	....	....	....	....	....	....
of which: Short-term	4 709	....	....	....	....	....	....	....	....
Other sectors	4 710	−18.2	8.4	−45.1	−13.5	−27.6	−224.0	−7.5	−82.3
of which: Short-term	4 712	*−6.0*	*2.8*	*−14.9*	*−4.5*	*−9.1*	*−73.9*	*−2.5*	*−27.2*
Loans	4 714	.1	−8.3	−2.9	.5	−3.3	6.8	7.2	−1.2
Monetary authorities	4 715	....	....	....	....	....	....	....	....
of which: Short-term	4 718	....	....	....	....	....	....	....	....
General government	4 719	....	....	....	....	....	....	....	....
of which: Short-term	4 721	....	....	....	....	....	....	....	....
Banks	4 722	.1	−8.3	−2.9	.5	−3.3	6.8	7.2	−1.2
of which: Short-term	4 724	*.1*	*−8.3*	*−2.9*	*.5*	*−3.3*	*6.8*	*7.2*	*−1.2*
Other sectors	4 725	....	....	....	....	....	....	....	....
of which: Short-term	4 727	....	....	....	....	....	....	....	....
Currency and deposits	4 730	−60.3	−45.4	−18.5	−12.2	30.0	−126.1	−213.2	190.3
Monetary authorities	4 731	....	....	....	....	....	....	....	....
General government	4 732	....	....	....	....	....	....	....	....
Banks	4 733	−50.3	−54.9	−12.2	−17.5	40.9	−122.7	−163.7	201.1
Other sectors	4 734	−10.0	9.5	−6.3	5.2	−10.9	−3.4	−49.5	−10.8
Other assets	4 736	1.8	9.6	19.0	1.3	20.3	−19.3	−2.3	....
Monetary authorities	4 737	1.7	9.3	18.7	1.0	20.0	−19.3	−2.3	....
of which: Short-term	4 739	....	....	....	....	....	....	....	....
General government	4 740	−.2	....	....	....	....	....	....	....
of which: Short-term	4 742	....	....	....	....	....	....	....	....
Banks	4 743	....	....	....	....	....	....	....	....
of which: Short-term	4 745	....	....	....	....	....	....	....	....
Other sectors	4 746	.3	.3	.3	.3	.3	....	....	....
of which: Short-term	4 748	*.3*	*.3*	*.3*	*.3*	*.3*	....	....	....
Liabilities	4 753	**71.9**	**110.4**	**75.6**	**160.9**	**133.4**	**248.3**	**494.9**	**−50.3**
Trade credits	4 756	9.9	−21.2	19.8	132.7	13.3	121.6	−41.0	17.3
General government	4 757	....	....	....	....	....	....	....	....
of which: Short-term	4 759	....	....	....	....	....	....	....	....
Other sectors	4 760	9.9	−21.2	19.8	132.7	13.3	121.6	−41.0	17.3
of which: Short-term	4 762	*4.5*	*−9.5*	*8.9*	*59.7*	*6.0*	*54.7*	*−18.5*	*7.8*
Loans	4 764	−19.7	46.9	12.1	54.7	19.7	60.6	306.4	86.2
Monetary authorities	4 765	−.9	−3.9	−12.5	−23.5	−20.7	18.3	−.2	12.4
of which: Use of Fund credit and loans from the Fund	4 766	*−.9*	*−3.9*	*−12.5*	*−23.5*	*−20.7*	*18.3*	*−.2*	*12.4*
of which: Short-term	4 768	....	....	....	....	....	....	....	....
General government	4 769	34.0	56.3	17.2	56.5	38.5	12.9	332.7	110.8
of which: Short-term	4 771	....	....	....	....	....	....	....	....
Banks	4 772	−4.9	1.5	6.2	9.7	−14.5	1.6	−4.3	−1.5
of which: Short-term	4 774	*−4.9*	*1.5*	*6.2*	*9.7*	*−14.5*	*1.6*	*−4.3*	*−1.5*
Other sectors	4 775	−47.9	−7.0	1.2	12.1	16.4	27.8	−21.8	−35.4
of which: Short-term	4 777	....	....	....	....	....	....	....	....
Currency and deposits	4 780	41.5	40.7	−18.2	−36.3	81.1	46.8	54.7	−202.5
Monetary authorities	4 781	....	....	....	....	....	....	....	....
General government	4 782	....	....	....	....	....	....	....	....
Banks	4 783	41.5	40.7	−18.2	−36.3	81.1	46.8	54.7	−202.5
Other sectors	4 784	....	....	....	....	....	....	....	....
Other liabilities	4 786	40.1	44.0	61.8	9.7	19.2	19.4	174.8	48.6
Monetary authorities	4 787	....	....	....	....	....	....	132.5	....
of which: Short-term	4 789	....	....	....	....	....	....	....	....
General government	4 790	42.7	45.2	63.8	6.6	2.8	3.5	7.7	6.4
of which: Short-term	4 792	*42.7*	*45.2*	*63.8*	*6.6*	*2.8*	*3.5*	*7.7*	*6.4*
Banks	4 793	....	....	....	....	....	....	....	....
of which: Short-term	4 795	....	....	....	....	....	....	....	....
Other sectors	4 796	−2.6	−1.3	−2.0	3.1	16.5	15.9	34.6	42.2
of which: Short-term	4 798	*−.5*	*.5*	*.1*	*3.1*	*16.5*	*15.9*	*34.6*	*42.2*
E. RESERVE ASSETS	4 802	**−64.2**	**−166.2**	**−80.5**	**−170.3**	**−306.7**	**−121.0**	**−264.6**	**−115.7**
Monetary gold	4 812	....	....	−18.7	....	....	....	....	....
Special drawing rights	4 811	−8.7	−8.6	13.0	−27.2	20.4	−43.0	−106.0	−12.5
Reserve position in the Fund	4 810	....	....	....	....	....	....	....	....
Foreign exchange	4 803	−55.5	−157.6	−74.8	−143.1	−327.1	−77.9	−158.6	−103.2
Other claims	4 813	....	....	....	....	....	....	....	....
NET ERRORS AND OMISSIONS	4 998	**80.4**	**−19.4**	**65.6**	**184.4**	**265.4**	**629.6**	**−67.0**	**−95.5**

Table 3. INTERNATIONAL INVESTMENT POSITION (End-period stocks), 2003–2010

(Millions of U.S. dollars)

	Code	2003	2004	2005	2006	2007	2008	2009	2010
ASSETS	8 995 C.	**711.5**	**991.5**	**1,165.2**	**1,270.3**	**1,696.0**	**2,086.9**	**3,081.8**	**2,678.3**
Direct investment abroad	8 505 ..	**39.3**	**83.2**	**147.5**	**3.4**	**17.9**	**17.8**	**1.0**	**1.5**
Equity capital and reinvested earnings	8 506 ..	39.3	83.2	147.5	3.4	17.9	17.8	1.0	1.5
Claims on affiliated enterprises	8 507 ..	39.3	83.2	147.5	3.4	17.9	17.8	1.0	1.5
Liabilities to affiliated enterprises	8 508 ..	....	....	....	....	....	....	....	....
Other capital	8 530 ..	....	....	....	....	....	....	....	....
Claims on affiliated enterprises	8 535 ..	....	....	....	....	....	....	....	....
Liabilities to affiliated enterprises	8 540 ..	....	....	....	....	....	....	....	....
Portfolio investment	8 602 ..	**7.6**	**17.4**	**14.9**	**19.3**	**50.5**	**78.7**	**570.3**	**182.6**
Equity securities	8 610 ..	....	....	....	....	27.7	27.7	27.7	−33.9
Monetary authorities	8 611 ..	....	....	....	....	....	....	....	....
General government	8 612 ..	....	....	....	....	....	....	....	....
Banks	8 613 ..	....	....	....	....	....	....	.6	....
Other sectors	8 614 ..	....	....	....	....	27.7	27.7	27.1	−33.9
Debt securities	8 619 ..	7.6	17.4	14.9	19.3	22.8	51.0	542.6	216.4
Bonds and notes	8 620 ..	7.6	17.4	14.9	19.3	22.8	51.0	542.6	216.4
Monetary authorities	8 621 ..	....	....	....	....	....	....	....	....
General government	8 622 ..	....	....	....	....	....	....	....	....
Banks	8 623 ..	....	....	....	....	....	....	72.5	....
Other sectors	8 624 ..	7.6	17.4	14.9	19.3	22.8	51.0	470.1	216.4
Money market instruments	8 630 ..	....	....	....	....	....	....	....	....
Monetary authorities	8 631 ..	....	....	....	....	....	....	....	....
General government	8 632 ..	....	....	....	....	....	....	....	....
Banks	8 633 ..	....	....	....	....	....	....	....	....
Other sectors	8 634 ..	....	....	....	....	....	....	....	....
Financial derivatives	8 900 ..	....	....	....	....	....	....	....	....
Monetary authorities	8 901 ..	....	....	....	....	....	....	....	....
General government	8 902 ..	....	....	....	....	....	....	....	....
Banks	8 903 ..	....	....	....	....	....	....	....	....
Other sectors	8 904 ..	....	....	....	....	....	....	....	....
Other investment	8 703 ..	**305.4**	**347.0**	**394.3**	**433.3**	**433.8**	**767.8**	**929.6**	**777.7**
Trade credits	8 706 ..	117.8	110.1	155.9	177.0	221.5	417.8	366.3	420.2
General government	8 707 ..	....	....	....	....	....	....	....	....
of which: Short-term	8 709 ..	....	....	....	....	....	....	....	....
Other sectors	8 710 ..	117.8	110.1	155.9	177.0	221.5	417.8	366.3	420.2
of which: Short-term	8 712 ..	*40.0*	*37.4*	*53.0*	*60.2*	*75.3*	*142.0*	*124.5*	*142.9*
Loans	8 714 ..	6.5	15.0	17.9	17.4	20.6	13.5	10.8	1.0
Monetary authorities	8 715 ..	....	....	....	....	....	....	....	....
of which: Short-term	8 718 ..	....	....	....	....	....	....	....	....
General government	8 719 ..	1.1	.8	.6	.3	....	....	....	....
of which: Short-term	8 721 ..	....	....	....	....	....	....	....	....
Banks	8 722 ..	5.4	14.2	17.3	17.1	20.6	13.5	10.8	1.0
of which: Short-term	8 724 ..	....	....	....	....	....	....	*2.1*	*.1*
Other sectors	8 725 ..	....	....	....	....	....	....	....	....
of which: Short-term	8 727 ..	....	....	....	....	....	....	....	....
Currency and deposits	8 730 ..	151.3	200.4	216.7	236.0	208.8	334.3	548.6	352.7
Monetary authorities	8 731 ..	....	....	....	....	....	....	....	....
General government	8 732 ..	....	....	....	....	....	....	....	....
Banks	8 733 ..	151.3	200.4	216.7	236.0	208.8	334.3	548.6	352.7
Other sectors	8 734 ..	....	....	....	....	....	....	....	....
Other assets	8 736 ..	29.8	21.4	3.9	2.9	−17.1	2.2	3.9	3.9
Monetary authorities	8 737 ..	29.8	21.4	3.9	2.9	−17.1	2.2	3.9	3.9
of which: Short-term	8 739 ..	....	....	....	....	....	....	....	....
General government	8 740 ..	....	....	....	....	....	....	....	....
of which: Short-term	8 742 ..	....	....	....	....	....	....	....	....
Banks	8 743 ..	....	....	....	....	....	....	....	....
of which: Short-term	8 745 ..	....	....	....	....	....	....	....	....
Other sectors	8 746 ..	....	....	....	....	....	....	....	....
of which: Short-term	8 748 ..	....	....	....	....	....	....	....	....
Reserve assets	8 802 ..	**359.3**	**543.9**	**608.5**	**814.3**	**1,193.8**	**1,222.5**	**1,580.9**	**1,716.5**
Monetary gold	8 812 ..	9.6	18.9	42.6	52.8	69.5	71.9	90.8	116.8
Special drawing rights	8 811 ..	10.3	19.9	5.3	33.3	13.8	55.3	162.1	171.7
Reserve position in the Fund	8 810 ..	....	....	....	....	....	....	....	....
Foreign exchange	8 803 ..	339.3	505.1	560.6	728.2	1,110.5	1,095.4	1,328.0	1,428.0
Other claims	8 813 ..	....	....	....	....	....	....	....	....

Table 3 (Concluded). INTERNATIONAL INVESTMENT POSITION (End-period stocks), 2003–2010

(Millions of U.S. dollars)

	Code	2003	2004	2005	2006	2007	2008	2009	2010
LIABILITIES.........................	8 995 D.	**2,603.5**	**2,945.5**	**2,798.3**	**3,061.0**	**3,505.1**	**3,919.4**	**4,483.6**	**4,473.8**
Direct investment in Kyrgyz Republic..................	8 555 ..	**523.4**	**712.4**	**517.7**	**619.8**	**818.5**	**1,062.5**	**1,003.8**	**1,033.9**
Equity capital and reinvested earnings.............................	8 556 ..	260.7	459.0	257.9	301.3	316.4	359.6	462.9	411.6
Claims on direct investors........................	8 557 ..	....	....	....	....	....	....	....	....
Liabilities to direct investors.......................	8 558 ..	260.7	459.0	257.9	301.3	316.4	359.6	462.9	411.6
Other capital...	8 580 ..	262.7	253.4	259.7	318.6	502.2	702.9	540.9	622.3
Claims on direct investors........................	8 585 ..	....	6.2	10.5	12.4	15.3	9.7	−23.7	−41.8
Liabilities to direct investors.......................	8 590 ..	262.7	247.2	249.3	306.2	486.9	693.2	564.6	664.1
Portfolio investment.........................	8 652 ..	**5.7**	**6.0**	**6.1**	**6.6**	**8.7**	**21.2**	**20.1**	**.3**
Equity securities...	8 660 ..	5.7	6.0	6.1	6.6	8.7	21.2	20.1	.3
Banks..	8 663 ..	5.7	6.0	6.1	6.6	8.7	21.2	20.1	.3
Other sectors......................................	8 664 ..	....	....	....	....	....	....	....	....
Debt securities...	8 669 ..	....	....	....	....	....	....	....	....
Bonds and notes.................................	8 670 ..	....	....	....	....	....	....	....	....
Monetary authorities........................	8 671 ..	....	....	....	....	....	....	....	....
General government........................	8 672 ..	....	....	....	....	....	....	....	....
Banks..	8 673 ..	....	....	....	....	....	....	....	....
Other sectors................................	8 674 ..	....	....	....	....	....	....	....	....
Money market instruments.................	8 680 ..	....	....	....	....	....	....	....	....
Monetary authorities........................	8 681 ..	....	....	....	....	....	....	....	....
General government........................	8 682 ..	....	....	....	....	....	....	....	....
Banks..	8 683 ..	....	....	....	....	....	....	....	....
Other sectors................................	8 684 ..	....	....	....	....	....	....	....	....
Financial derivatives.........................	8 905 ..	**24.6**	....	....	....	....	....	....	....
Monetary authorities..................................	8 906 ..	....	....	....	....	....	....	....	....
General government..................................	8 907 ..	....	....	....	....	....	....	....	....
Banks..	8 908 ..	....	....	....	....	....	....	....	....
Other sectors...	8 909 ..	24.6	....	....	....	....	....	....	....
Other investment.........................	8 753 ..	**2,049.8**	**2,227.1**	**2,274.5**	**2,434.5**	**2,677.9**	**2,835.7**	**3,459.7**	**3,439.6**
Trade credits...	8 756 ..	148.0	110.7	218.9	283.2	326.4	405.1	327.8	328.2
General government..................................	8 757 ..	....	....	....	....	....	....	....	....
of which: Short-term............................	8 759 ..	....	....	....	....	....	....	....	....
Other sectors...	8 760 ..	148.0	110.7	218.9	283.2	326.4	405.1	327.8	328.2
of which: Short-term............................	8 762 ..	*48.8*	*36.5*	*72.2*	*93.5*	*107.7*	*133.7*	*108.2*	*108.3*
Loans...	8 764 ..	1,831.7	2,003.9	1,902.9	2,031.7	2,147.1	2,180.9	2,690.3	2,905.0
Monetary authorities..................................	8 765 ..	201.9	206.9	177.9	163.1	149.8	164.5	167.1	176.7
of which: Use of Fund credit and loans from the Fund....	8 766 ..	*201.9*	*206.9*	*177.9*	*163.1*	*149.8*	*164.5*	*167.1*	*176.7*
of which: Short-term............................	8 768 ..	....	....	....	....	....	....	....	....
General government..................................	8 769 ..	1,574.5	1,752.3	1,681.8	1,813.9	1,929.7	1,919.2	2,335.8	2,469.1
of which: Short-term............................	8 771 ..	....	....	....	....	....	....	....	....
Banks..	8 772 ..	5.4	7.2	8.3	18.0	22.1	33.6	30.6	54.7
of which: Short-term............................	8 774 ..	....	....	....	....	....	*1.6*	*4.3*	....
Other sectors...	8 775 ..	49.9	37.5	34.9	36.8	45.4	63.5	156.8	204.6
of which: Short-term............................	8 777 ..	....	....	....	....	....	....	....	....
Currency and deposits..............................	8 780 ..	70.1	112.4	152.7	119.6	204.5	249.7	308.8	75.8
Monetary authorities..................................	8 781 ..	....	....	....	....	....	....	....	....
General government..................................	8 782 ..	....	....	....	....	....	....	....	....
Banks..	8 783 ..	70.1	112.4	152.7	119.6	204.5	249.7	308.8	75.8
Other sectors...	8 784 ..	....	....	....	....	....	....	....	....
Other liabilities...	8 786 ..	....	....	....	....	....	....	132.8	130.5
Monetary authorities..................................	8 787 ..	....	....	....	....	....	....	132.8	130.5
of which: Short-term............................	8 789 ..	....	....	....	....	....	....	....	....
General government..................................	8 790 ..	....	....	....	....	....	....	....	....
of which: Short-term............................	8 792 ..	....	....	....	....	....	....	....	....
Banks..	8 793 ..	....	....	....	....	....	....	....	....
of which: Short-term............................	8 795 ..	....	....	....	....	....	....	....	....
Other sectors...	8 796 ..	....	....	....	....	....	....	....	....
of which: Short-term............................	8 798 ..	....	....	....	....	....	....	....	....
NET INTERNATIONAL INVESTMENT POSITION........	8 995 ..	**−1,892.0**	**−1,954.0**	**−1,633.1**	**−1,790.7**	**−1,809.1**	**−1,832.5**	**−1,401.8**	**−1,795.5**
Conversion rates: soms per U.S. dollar (end of period)...	0 102 ..	**44.190**	**41.625**	**41.301**	**38.124**	**35.499**	**39.418**	**44.092**	**47.099**

Table 1. ANALYTIC PRESENTATION, 2003–2010

(Millions of U.S. dollars)

	Code	2003	2004	2005	2006	2007	2008	2009	2010
A. Current Account[1]............................	4 993 Z.	**−29.7**	**−178.2**	**−173.8**	**75.3**	**139.4**	**77.5**	**−60.9**	**29.3**
Goods: exports f.o.b........................	2 100 ..	335.5	363.3	553.1	882.0	922.7	1,091.9	1,052.7	1,746.4
Goods: imports f.o.b........................	3 100 ..	−462.1	−712.7	−882.0	−1,060.2	−1,064.6	−1,403.2	−1,461.1	−2,060.4
Balance on Goods........................	4 100 ..	*−126.7*	*−349.4*	*−328.9*	*−178.2*	*−141.9*	*−311.3*	*−408.4*	*−314.0*
Services: credit.............................	2 200 ..	127.4	178.8	204.2	223.4	278.1	401.6	397.3	511.0
Services: debit..............................	3 200 ..	−28.4	−31.4	−39.0	−37.4	−43.8	−107.9	−135.6	−263.1
Balance on Goods and Services........	4 991 ..	*−27.6*	*−202.0*	*−163.6*	*7.8*	*92.4*	*−17.5*	*−146.8*	*−66.1*
Income: credit..............................	2 300 ..	3.6	4.0	5.0	16.2	43.6	32.1	41.7	50.3
Income: debit...............................	3 300 ..	−45.5	−58.8	−82.4	−75.4	−94.0	−77.7	−88.8	−133.5
Balance on Goods, Services, and Income...	4 992 ..	*−69.5*	*−256.9*	*−240.9*	*−51.3*	*42.0*	*−63.2*	*−193.8*	*−149.3*
Current transfers: credit..................	2 379 Z.	111.0	119.2	124.2	151.5	139.1	198.9	178.4	218.7
Current transfers: debit...................	3 379 ..	−71.2	−40.6	−57.0	−24.9	−41.7	−58.2	−45.5	−40.1
B. Capital Account[1]............................	4 994 Z.	....	....	....	....	....	....	....	....
Capital account: credit....................	2 994 Z.	....	....	....	....	....	....	....	....
Capital account: debit.....................	3 994 ..	....	....	....	....	....	....	....	....
Total, Groups A Plus B...................	4 981 ..	*−29.7*	*−178.2*	*−173.8*	*75.3*	*139.4*	*77.5*	*−60.9*	*29.3*
C. Financial Account[1]..........................	4 995 W.	**118.5**	**100.5**	**161.8**	**231.8**	**399.2**	**433.4**	**635.1**	**476.5**
Direct investment abroad.................	4 505 ..	....	....	....	....	....	....	....	....
Direct investment in Lao PDR............	4 555 Z.	19.5	16.9	27.7	187.3	323.5	227.8	318.6	278.8
Portfolio investment assets..............	4 602 ..	....	....	....	....	....	....	....	....
Equity securities........................	4 610 ..	....	....	....	....	....	....	....	....
Debt securities..........................	4 619 ..	....	....	....	....	....	....	....	....
Portfolio investment liabilities..........	4 652 Z.	....	....	....	....	....	....	....	53.8
Equity securities........................	4 660 ..	....	....	....	....	....	....	....	53.8
Debt securities..........................	4 669 Z.	....	....	....	....	....	....	....	....
Financial derivatives......................	4 910 ..	....	....	....	....	....	....	....	....
Financial derivatives assets..............	4 900 ..	....	....	....	....	....	....	....	....
Financial derivatives liabilities..........	4 905 ..	....	....	....	....	....	....	....	....
Other investment assets..................	4 703 ..	−47.2	−53.0	−3.4	−111.0	−134.9	−3.0	142.7	−173.9
Monetary authorities....................	4 701 ..	....	....	....	....	....	....	....	....
General government.....................	4 704 ..	....	....	....	....	....	....	....	....
Banks....................................	4 705 ..	−47.2	−53.0	−3.4	−111.0	−134.9	−3.0	142.7	−173.9
Other sectors............................	4 728 ..	....	....	....	....	....	....	....	....
Other investment liabilities..............	4 753 W.	146.1	136.6	137.5	155.5	210.7	208.7	173.7	317.8
Monetary authorities....................	4 753 WA	....	....	....	....	....	....	64.4	....
General government.....................	4 753 ZB	117.1	117.6	124.0	130.8	192.8	133.9	119.2	114.3
Banks....................................	4 753 ZC	29.1	19.0	13.5	24.7	17.9	74.7	−9.9	203.5
Other sectors............................	4 753 ZD	....	....	....	....	....	....	....	....
Total, Groups A Through C..............	4 983 ..	*88.8*	*−77.7*	*−12.0*	*307.1*	*538.7*	*511.0*	*574.1*	*505.8*
D. Net Errors and Omissions..................	4 998 ..	**−81.7**	**65.3**	**5.9**	**−400.7**	**−750.2**	**−407.8**	**−507.9**	**−403.2**
Total, Groups A Through D..............	4 984 ..	*7.1*	*−12.4*	*−6.0*	*−93.6*	*−211.5*	*103.2*	*66.3*	*102.6*
E. Reserves and Related Items..............	4 802 A.	**−7.1**	**12.4**	**6.0**	**93.6**	**211.5**	**−103.2**	**−66.3**	**−102.6**
Reserve assets.............................	4 802 ..	−4.4	20.3	12.1	96.9	214.5	−98.9	−60.7	−97.0
Use of Fund credit and loans............	4 766 ..	−2.7	−7.9	−6.1	−3.3	−3.0	−4.3	−5.5	−5.6
Exceptional financing.....................	4 920 ..	....	....	....	....	....	....	....	....
Conversion rates: kip per U.S. dollar..............	0 101 ..	**10,569.0**	**10,585.4**	**10,655.2**	**10,159.9**	**9,603.2**	**8,744.2**	**8,516.1**	**8,258.8**

[1] Excludes components that have been classified in the categories of Group E.

Table 2. STANDARD PRESENTATION, 2003–2010

(Millions of U.S. dollars)

	Code	2003	2004	2005	2006	2007	2008	2009	2010
CURRENT ACCOUNT	4 993	**−29.7**	**−178.2**	**−173.8**	**75.3**	**139.4**	**77.5**	**−60.9**	**29.3**
A. GOODS	4 100	**−126.7**	**−349.4**	**−328.9**	**−178.2**	**−141.9**	**−311.3**	**−408.4**	**−314.0**
Credit	2 100	**335.5**	**363.3**	**553.1**	**882.0**	**922.7**	**1,091.9**	**1,052.7**	**1,746.4**
General merchandise: exports f.o.b.	2 110	335.5	363.3	553.1	882.0	922.7	1,010.3	958.7	1,602.5
Goods for processing: exports f.o.b.	2 150	....	....	....	....	....			
Repairs on goods	2 160	....	....	....	....	....			
Goods procured in ports by carriers	2 170	....	....	....	....	....	1.0	3.4	12.5
Nonmonetary gold	2 180	....	....	....	....	....	80.6	90.6	131.4
Debit	3 100	**−462.1**	**−712.7**	**−882.0**	**−1,060.2**	**−1,064.6**	**−1,403.2**	**−1,461.1**	**−2,060.4**
General merchandise: imports f.o.b.	3 110	−462.1	−712.7	−882.0	−1,060.2	−1,064.6	−1,381.1	−1,399.7	−1,847.8
Goods for processing: imports f.o.b.	3 150	....	....	....	....	....			
Repairs on goods	3 160	....	....	....	....	....			
Goods procured in ports by carriers	3 170	....	....	....	....	....	−1.9	−1.7	−2.9
Nonmonetary gold	3 180	....	....	....	....	....	−20.2	−59.7	−209.8
B. SERVICES	4 200	**99.0**	**147.4**	**165.3**	**186.0**	**234.3**	**293.7**	**261.6**	**247.9**
Total credit	2 200	*127.4*	*178.8*	*204.2*	*223.4*	*278.1*	*401.6*	*397.3*	*511.0*
Total debit	3 200	*−28.4*	*−31.4*	*−39.0*	*−37.4*	*−43.8*	*−107.9*	*−135.6*	*−263.1*
Transportation services, credit	2 205	**25.3**	**29.7**	**32.6**	**31.5**	**30.1**	**43.4**	**36.1**	**51.1**
Passenger	2 850	*3.2*	*3.2*	*3.5*	*1.8*	*1.4*	*4.0*	*2.8*	*3.4*
Freight	2 851	*2.6*	*2.8*	*3.1*	*4.9*	*1.9*	*2.6*	*2.4*	*3.3*
Other	2 852	*19.5*	*23.7*	*26.0*	*24.8*	*26.8*	*36.9*	*30.9*	*44.4*
Sea transport, passenger	2 207	....	....	....	....	....	....	....	....
Sea transport, freight	2 208	....	....	....	....	....	....	....	....
Sea transport, other	2 209	....	....	....	....	....	....	....	....
Air transport, passenger	2 211	3.2	3.2	3.5	1.8	1.4	4.0	2.8	3.4
Air transport, freight	2 212	2.6	2.8	3.1	4.9	1.9	2.6	2.4	3.3
Air transport, other	2 213	....	....	....	....	....	....	....	....
Other transport, passenger	2 215	....	....	....	....	....	....	....	....
Other transport, freight	2 216	....	....	....	....	....	....	....	....
Other transport, other	2 217	19.5	23.7	26.0	24.8	26.8	36.9	30.9	44.4
Transportation services, debit	3 205	**−5.4**	**−5.7**	**−6.9**	**−7.2**	**−6.5**	**−14.0**	**−13.4**	**−16.4**
Passenger	3 850	*−4.0*	*−4.2*	*−5.1*	*−5.6*	*−5.7*	*−10.1*	*−7.5*	*−12.0*
Freight	3 851	....	....	....	....	....	....	....	....
Other	3 852	*−1.4*	*−1.5*	*−1.8*	*−1.6*	*−.8*	*−3.8*	*−5.9*	*−4.4*
Sea transport, passenger	3 207	....	....	....	....	....	....	....	....
Sea transport, freight	3 208	....	....	....	....	....	....	....	....
Sea transport, other	3 209	....	....	....	....	....	....	....	....
Air transport, passenger	3 211	−4.0	−4.2	−5.1	−5.6	−5.7	−10.1	−7.5	−12.0
Air transport, freight	3 212	....	....	....	....	....	....	....	....
Air transport, other	3 213	....	....	....	....	....	....	....	....
Other transport, passenger	3 215	....	....	....	....	....	....	....	....
Other transport, freight	3 216	....	....	....	....	....	....	....	....
Other transport, other	3 217	−1.4	−1.5	−1.8	−1.6	−.8	−3.8	−5.9	−4.4
Travel, credit	2 236	**74.0**	**119.0**	**139.2**	**157.7**	**189.4**	**275.5**	**267.7**	**381.7**
Business travel	2 237	....	....	....	....	....	....	....	....
Personal travel	2 240	74.0	119.0	139.2	157.7	189.4	275.5	267.7	381.7
Travel, debit	3 236	**−1.2**	**−3.8**	**−5.0**	**−8.9**	**−8.4**	**−41.3**	**−82.5**	**−202.7**
Business travel	3 237	....	....	....	....	....	....	....	....
Personal travel	3 240	−1.2	−3.8	−5.0	−8.9	−8.4	−41.3	−82.5	−202.7
Other services, credit	2 200 BA	**28.1**	**30.2**	**32.5**	**34.2**	**58.7**	**82.7**	**93.5**	**78.2**
Communications	2 245	9.1	8.4	9.7	10.2	28.7	32.2	33.3	32.0
Construction	2 249	....	....	....	....	....	....	27.0	13.1
Insurance	2 253	2.2	2.6	2.9	3.2	7.2	8.3	10.0	10.9
Financial	2 260	....	....	....	....	....	....	....	....
Computer and information	2 262	....	....	....	....	....	....	....	....
Royalties and licence fees	2 266	....	....	....	....	....	....	....	....
Other business services	2 268	....	....	....	....	....	....	....	....
Personal, cultural, and recreational	2 287	....	....	....	....	....	....	....	....
Government, n.i.e.	2 291	16.8	19.2	19.8	20.8	22.8	42.2	23.3	22.2
Other services, debit	3 200 BA	**−21.8**	**−21.9**	**−27.0**	**−21.4**	**−29.0**	**−52.6**	**−39.7**	**−44.1**
Communications	3 245	−1.3	−2.2	−2.5	−2.7	−4.1	−9.4	−11.2	−14.6
Construction	3 249	−18.8	−17.2	−22.8	−24.4	−34.9	−26.3	−11.8	−10.7
Insurance	3 253	4.3	4.8	8.7	12.4	16.1	−11.3	−11.0	−13.2
Financial	3 260	....	....	....	....	....	....	....	....
Computer and information	3 262	....	....	....	....	....	....	....	....
Royalties and licence fees	3 266	....	....	....	....	....	....	....	....
Other business services	3 268	....	....	....	....	....	....	....	....
Personal, cultural, and recreational	3 287	....	....	....	....	....	....	....	....
Government, n.i.e.	3 291	−6.0	−7.3	−10.4	−6.6	−6.1	−5.6	−5.8	−5.6

Table 2 (Continued). STANDARD PRESENTATION, 2003–2010

(Millions of U.S. dollars)

	Code	2003	2004	2005	2006	2007	2008	2009	2010
C. INCOME	4 300	**−41.9**	**−54.9**	**−77.3**	**−59.2**	**−50.3**	**−45.6**	**−47.0**	**−83.2**
Total credit	2 300	*3.6*	*4.0*	*5.0*	*16.2*	*43.6*	*32.1*	*41.7*	*50.3*
Total debit	3 300	*−45.5*	*−58.8*	*−82.4*	*−75.4*	*−94.0*	*−77.7*	*−88.8*	*−133.5*
Compensation of employees, credit	2 310	**.8**	**.8**	**.8**	**4.2**	**6.2**	**11.6**	**27.7**	**35.1**
Compensation of employees, debit	3 310	**−1.0**	**−.8**	**−.8**	**−5.4**	**−6.0**	**−5.5**	**−8.0**	**−13.5**
Investment income, credit	2 320	**2.8**	**3.2**	**4.2**	**12.0**	**37.4**	**20.5**	**14.0**	**15.2**
Direct investment income	2 330	....	....	....	....	....	....	....	2.0
Dividends and distributed branch profits	2 332	....	....	....	....	....	....	....	2.0
Reinvested earnings and undistributed branch profits	2 333	....	....	....	....	....	....	....	....
Income on debt (interest)	2 334	....	....	....	....	....	....	....	....
Portfolio investment income	2 339	....	....	....	....	....	....	....	....
Income on equity	2 340	....	....	....	....	....	....	....	....
Income on bonds and notes	2 350	....	....	....	....	....	....	....	....
Income on money market instruments	2 360	....	....	....	....	....	....	....	....
Other investment income	2 370	2.8	3.2	4.2	12.0	37.4	20.5	14.0	13.2
Investment income, debit	3 320	**−44.5**	**−58.0**	**−81.5**	**−70.0**	**−88.0**	**−72.2**	**−80.8**	**−120.0**
Direct investment income	3 330	−7.2	−11.3	−24.9	−23.4	−47.7	−25.6	−43.1	−44.2
Dividends and distributed branch profits	3 332	−7.2	−11.3	−24.9	−23.4	−47.7	−25.6	−43.1	−44.2
Reinvested earnings and undistributed branch profits	3 333	....	....	....	....	....	....	....	....
Income on debt (interest)	3 334	....	....	....	....	....	....	....	....
Portfolio investment income	3 339	−33.7	−43.0	−51.3	−40.6	−38.0	−28.5	−35.2	−69.1
Income on equity	3 340	....	....	....	....	....	....	....	....
Income on bonds and notes	3 350	−11.3	−20.5	−27.8	−17.0	−15.3	−22.0	−24.2	−34.9
Income on money market instruments	3 360	−22.3	−22.5	−23.5	−23.7	−22.7	−6.5	−11.0	−34.2
Other investment income	3 370	−3.6	−3.7	−5.3	−6.0	−2.3	−18.2	−2.5	−6.7
D. CURRENT TRANSFERS	4 379	**39.8**	**78.6**	**67.2**	**126.6**	**97.4**	**140.7**	**132.9**	**178.6**
Credit	2 379	**111.0**	**119.2**	**124.2**	**151.5**	**139.1**	**198.9**	**178.4**	**218.7**
General government	2 380	25.0	37.9	34.2	67.5	46.3	77.1	97.5	108.6
Other sectors	2 390	86.0	81.3	90.0	84.0	92.8	121.8	80.9	110.1
Workers' remittances	2 391	....	....	....	....	....	6.2	9.9	6.7
Other current transfers	2 392	86.0	81.3	90.0	84.0	92.8	115.6	71.0	103.4
Debit	3 379	**−71.2**	**−40.6**	**−57.0**	**−24.9**	**−41.7**	**−58.2**	**−45.5**	**−40.1**
General government	3 380	....	....	....	....	....	....	....	....
Other sectors	3 390	−71.2	−40.6	−57.0	−24.9	−41.7	−58.2	−45.5	−40.1
Workers' remittances	3 391	....	....	....	....	....	−3.8	−14.4	−5.8
Other current transfers	3 392	−71.2	−40.6	−57.0	−24.9	−41.7	−54.3	−31.1	−34.3
CAPITAL AND FINANCIAL ACCOUNT	4 996	**111.4**	**112.9**	**167.8**	**325.4**	**610.7**	**330.2**	**568.8**	**373.9**
CAPITAL ACCOUNT	4 994	....	....	....	....	....	....	....	....
Total credit	2 994	....	....	....	....	....	....	....	....
Total debit	3 994	....	....	....	....	....	....	....	....
Capital transfers, credit	2 400	....	....	....	....	....	....	....	....
General government	2 401	....	....	....	....	....	....	....	....
Debt forgiveness	2 402	....	....	....	....	....	....	....	....
Other capital transfers	2 410	....	....	....	....	....	....	....	....
Other sectors	2 430	....	....	....	....	....	....	....	....
Migrants' transfers	2 431	....	....	....	....	....	....	....	....
Debt forgiveness	2 432	....	....	....	....	....	....	....	....
Other capital transfers	2 440	....	....	....	....	....	....	....	....
Capital transfers, debit	3 400	....	....	....	....	....	....	....	....
General government	3 401	....	....	....	....	....	....	....	....
Debt forgiveness	3 402	....	....	....	....	....	....	....	....
Other capital transfers	3 410	....	....	....	....	....	....	....	....
Other sectors	3 430	....	....	....	....	....	....	....	....
Migrants' transfers	3 431	....	....	....	....	....	....	....	....
Debt forgiveness	3 432	....	....	....	....	....	....	....	....
Other capital transfers	3 440	....	....	....	....	....	....	....	....
Nonproduced nonfinancial assets, credit	2 480	....	....	....	....	....	....	....	....
Nonproduced nonfinancial assets, debit	3 480	....	....	....	....	....	....	....	....

Table 2 (Continued). STANDARD PRESENTATION, 2003–2010

(Millions of U.S. dollars)

	Code	2003	2004	2005	2006	2007	2008	2009	2010
FINANCIAL ACCOUNT....................................	4 995 ..	**111.4**	**112.9**	**167.8**	**325.4**	**610.7**	**330.2**	**568.8**	**373.9**
A. DIRECT INVESTMENT........................	4 500 ..	**19.5**	**16.9**	**27.7**	**187.3**	**323.5**	**227.8**	**318.6**	**278.8**
Direct investment abroad..............	4 505 ..	....	....	....	....	....	....	....	....
Equity capital..	4 510 ..								
Claims on affiliated enterprises..........	4 515 ..	....	....	....	....	....	....		
Liabilities to affiliated enterprises......	4 520 ..	....	....	....	....	....			
Reinvested earnings.............................	4 525 ..	....	....						
Other capital..	4 530 ..	....	....						
Claims on affiliated enterprises..........	4 535 ..	....	....						
Liabilities to affiliated enterprises......	4 540 ..	....	....						
Direct investment in Lao PDR...........	4 555 ..	**19.5**	**16.9**	**27.7**	**187.3**	**323.5**	**227.8**	**318.6**	**278.8**
Equity capital..	4 560 ..	19.5	16.9	27.7	187.3	323.5	227.8	318.6	278.8
Claims on direct investors...................	4 565 ..	....	....						
Liabilities to direct investors...............	4 570 ..	19.5	16.9	27.7	187.3	323.5	227.8	318.6	278.8
Reinvested earnings.............................	4 575 ..	....	....						
Other capital..	4 580 ..	....	....						
Claims on direct investors...................	4 585 ..	....	....						
Liabilities to direct investors...............	4 590 ..	....							
B. PORTFOLIO INVESTMENT....................	4 600 ..	....	....	....	....	....	....	....	**53.8**
Assets..	4 602 ..	....	....	....	....	....	....	....	....
Equity securities...................................	4 610 ..	....	....	....	....	....	....	....	....
Monetary authorities........................	4 611 ..	....	....	....	....	....	....	....	....
General government.........................	4 612 ..	....	....	....	....	....	....	....	....
Banks...	4 613 ..	....	....	....	....	....	....	....	....
Other sectors....................................	4 614 ..	....	....	....	....	....	....	....	....
Debt securities.....................................	4 619 ..	....	....	....	....	....	....	....	....
Bonds and notes................................	4 620 ..	....	....	....	....	....	....	....	....
Monetary authorities.....................	4 621 ..	....	....	....	....	....	....	....	....
General government......................	4 622 ..	....	....	....	....	....	....	....	....
Banks..	4 623 ..	....	....	....	....	....	....	....	....
Other sectors.................................	4 624 ..	....	....	....	....	....	....	....	....
Money market instruments...............	4 630 ..	....	....	....	....	....	....	....	....
Monetary authorities.....................	4 631 ..	....	....	....	....	....	....	....	....
General government......................	4 632 ..	....	....	....	....	....	....	....	....
Banks..	4 633 ..	....	....	....	....	....	....	....	....
Other sectors.................................	4 634 ..	....	....	....	....	....	....	....	....
Liabilities...	4 652 ..	....	....	....	....	....	....	....	**53.8**
Equity securities...................................	4 660 ..	....	....	....	....	....	....	....	53.8
Banks...	4 663 ..	....	....	....	....	....	....	....	....
Other sectors....................................	4 664 ..	....	....	....	....	....	....	....	53.8
Debt securities.....................................	4 669 ..	....	....	....	....	....	....	....	....
Bonds and notes................................	4 670 ..	....	....	....	....	....	....	....	....
Monetary authorities.....................	4 671 ..	....	....	....	....	....	....	....	....
General government......................	4 672 ..	....	....	....	....	....	....	....	....
Banks..	4 673 ..	....	....	....	....	....	....	....	....
Other sectors.................................	4 674 ..	....	....	....	....	....	....	....	....
Money market instruments...............	4 680 ..	....	....	....	....	....	....	....	....
Monetary authorities.....................	4 681 ..	....	....	....	....	....	....	....	....
General government......................	4 682 ..	....	....	....	....	....	....	....	....
Banks..	4 683 ..	....	....	....	....	....	....	....	....
Other sectors.................................	4 684 ..	....	....	....	....	....	....	....	....
C. FINANCIAL DERIVATIVES......................	4 910 ..	....	....	....	....	....	....	....	....
Monetary authorities...........................	4 911 ..	....	....	....	....	....	....	....	....
General government............................	4 912 ..	....	....	....	....	....	....	....	....
Banks..	4 913 ..	....	....	....	....	....	....	....	....
Other sectors.......................................	4 914 ..	....	....	....	....	....	....	....	....
Assets..	4 900 ..	....	....	....	....	....	....	....	....
Monetary authorities...........................	4 901 ..	....	....	....	....	....	....	....	....
General government............................	4 902 ..	....	....	....	....	....	....	....	....
Banks..	4 903 ..	....	....	....	....	....	....	....	....
Other sectors.......................................	4 904 ..	....	....	....	....	....	....	....	....
Liabilities...	4 905 ..	....	....	....	....	....	....	....	....
Monetary authorities...........................	4 906 ..	....	....	....	....	....	....	....	....
General government............................	4 907 ..	....	....	....	....	....	....	....	....
Banks..	4 908 ..	....	....	....	....	....	....	....	....
Other sectors.......................................	4 909 ..	....	....	....	....	....	....	....	....

Table 2 (Concluded). STANDARD PRESENTATION, 2003–2010

(Millions of U.S. dollars)

	Code	2003	2004	2005	2006	2007	2008	2009	2010
D. OTHER INVESTMENT	4 700 ..	**96.3**	**75.7**	**128.0**	**41.2**	**72.8**	**201.3**	**310.9**	**138.4**
Assets	4 703 ..	−47.2	−53.0	−3.4	−111.0	−134.9	−3.0	142.7	−173.9
Trade credits	4 706 ..	....	....	....	....	....	....	....	....
General government	4 707 ..	....	....	....	....	....	....	....	....
of which: Short-term	4 709 ..	....	....	....	....	....	....	....	....
Other sectors	4 710 ..	....	....	....	....	....	....	....	....
of which: Short-term	4 712 ..	....	....	....	....	....	....	....	....
Loans	4 714 ..	....	....	....	....	....	....	....	....
Monetary authorities	4 715 ..	....	....	....	....	....	....	....	....
of which: Short-term	4 718 ..	....	....	....	....	....	....	....	....
General government	4 719 ..	....	....	....	....	....	....	....	....
of which: Short-term	4 721 ..	....	....	....	....	....	....	....	....
Banks	4 722 ..	....	....	....	....	....	....	....	....
of which: Short-term	4 724 ..	....	....	....	....	....	....	....	....
Other sectors	4 725 ..	....	....	....	....	....	....	....	....
of which: Short-term	4 727 ..	....	....	....	....	....	....	....	....
Currency and deposits	4 730 ..	−47.2	−53.0	−3.4	−111.0	−134.9	−3.0	142.7	−173.9
Monetary authorities	4 731 ..	....	....	....	....	....	....	....	....
General government	4 732 ..	....	....	....	....	....	....	....	....
Banks	4 733 ..	−47.2	−53.0	−3.4	−111.0	−134.9	−3.0	142.7	−173.9
Other sectors	4 734 ..	....	....	....	....	....	....	....	....
Other assets	4 736 ..	....	....	....	....	....	....	....	....
Monetary authorities	4 737 ..	....	....	....	....	....	....	....	....
of which: Short-term	4 739 ..	....	....	....	....	....	....	....	....
General government	4 740 ..	....	....	....	....	....	....	....	....
of which: Short-term	4 742 ..	....	....	....	....	....	....	....	....
Banks	4 743 ..	....	....	....	....	....	....	....	....
of which: Short-term	4 745 ..	....	....	....	....	....	....	....	....
Other sectors	4 746 ..	....	....	....	....	....	....	....	....
of which: Short-term	4 748 ..	....	....	....	....	....	....	....	....
Liabilities	4 753 ..	**143.4**	**128.8**	**131.5**	**152.2**	**207.7**	**204.4**	**168.2**	**312.3**
Trade credits	4 756 ..	....	....	....	....	....	133.9	119.2	114.3
General government	4 757 ..	....	....	....	....	....	133.9	119.2	114.3
of which: Short-term	4 759 ..	....	....	....	....	....	....	....	....
Other sectors	4 760 ..	....	....	....	....	....	....	....	....
of which: Short-term	4 762 ..	....	....	....	....	....	....	....	....
Loans	4 764 ..	114.3	109.8	118.0	127.6	189.8	−4.3	−5.5	−5.6
Monetary authorities	4 765 ..	−2.7	−7.9	−6.1	−3.3	−3.0	−4.3	−5.5	−5.6
of which: Use of Fund credit and loans from the Fund..	4 766 ..	−2.7	−7.9	−6.1	−3.3	−3.0	−4.3	−5.5	−5.6
of which: Short-term	4 768 ..	....	....	....	....	....	....	....	....
General government	4 769 ..	117.1	117.6	124.0	130.8	192.8	....	....	....
of which: Short-term	4 771 ..	....	....	....	....	....	....	....	....
Banks	4 772 ..	....	....	....	....	....	....	....	....
of which: Short-term	4 774 ..	....	....	....	....	....	....	....	....
Other sectors	4 775 ..	....	....	....	....	....	....	....	....
of which: Short-term	4 777 ..	....	....	....	....	....	....	....	....
Currency and deposits	4 780 ..	29.1	19.0	13.5	24.7	17.9	74.7	−9.9	203.5
Monetary authorities	4 781 ..	....	....	....	....	....	....	....	....
General government	4 782 ..	....	....	....	....	....	....	....	....
Banks	4 783 ..	29.1	19.0	13.5	24.7	17.9	74.7	−9.9	203.5
Other sectors	4 784 ..	....	....	....	....	....	....	64.4	....
Other liabilities	4 786 ..	....	....	....	....	....	....	64.4	....
Monetary authorities	4 787 ..	....	....	....	....	....	....	....	....
of which: Short-term	4 789 ..	....	....	....	....	....	....	....	....
General government	4 790 ..	....	....	....	....	....	....	....	....
of which: Short-term	4 792 ..	....	....	....	....	....	....	....	....
Banks	4 793 ..	....	....	....	....	....	....	....	....
of which: Short-term	4 795 ..	....	....	....	....	....	....	....	....
Other sectors	4 796 ..	....	....	....	....	....	....	....	....
of which: Short-term	4 798 ..	....	....	....	....	....	....	....	....
E. RESERVE ASSETS	4 802 ..	**−4.4**	**20.3**	**12.1**	**96.9**	**214.5**	**−98.9**	**−60.7**	**−97.0**
Monetary gold	4 812 ..	1.6	....	1.0	2.3	1.7	.8	....	.2
Special drawing rights	4 811 ..	−11.7	4.4	.1	.1	....	....	−64.4	....
Reserve position in the Fund	4 810 ..	....	....	....	....	....	....	....	....
Foreign exchange	4 803 ..	5.8	15.9	11.0	94.5	212.8	−99.7	3.7	−97.2
Other claims	4 813 ..	....	....	....	....	....	....	....	....
NET ERRORS AND OMISSIONS	4 998 ..	**−81.7**	**65.3**	**5.9**	**−400.7**	**−750.2**	**−407.8**	**−507.9**	**−403.2**

Table 1. ANALYTIC PRESENTATION, 2003–2010

(Millions of U.S. dollars)

	Code	2003	2004	2005	2006	2007	2008	2009	2010
A. Current Account[1]........................	4 993 Z.	**−921**	**−1,762**	**−1,992**	**−4,522**	**−6,425**	**−4,492**	**2,284**	**731**
Goods: exports f.o.b..........................	2 100 ..	3,171	4,221	5,361	6,140	8,227	9,634	7,387	9,107
Goods: imports f.o.b..........................	3 100 ..	−5,173	−7,002	−8,379	−11,271	−15,125	−15,648	−9,209	−10,799
Balance on Goods........................	4 100 ..	*−2,003*	*−2,781*	*−3,018*	*−5,131*	*−6,898*	*−6,014*	*−1,822*	*−1,691*
Services: credit................................	2 200 ..	1,506	1,779	2,163	2,642	3,705	4,538	3,844	3,693
Services: debit................................	3 200 ..	−929	−1,178	−1,557	−1,980	−2,703	−3,190	−2,278	−2,226
Balance on Goods and Services........	4 991 ..	*−1,427*	*−2,180*	*−2,413*	*−4,469*	*−5,896*	*−4,666*	*−255*	*−225*
Income: credit................................	2 300 ..	368	500	772	1,078	1,487	1,785	1,324	1,116
Income: debit................................	3 300 ..	−393	−775	−948	−1,610	−2,396	−2,381	331	−1,031
Balance on Goods, Services, and Income........	4 992 ..	*−1,451*	*−2,455*	*−2,589*	*−5,001*	*−6,804*	*−5,261*	*1,400*	*−140*
Current transfers: credit....................	2 379 Z.	924	1,289	1,373	1,789	2,023	2,191	1,984	1,643
Current transfers: debit....................	3 379 ..	−394	−595	−776	−1,310	−1,644	−1,422	−1,100	−772
B. Capital Account[1]........................	4 994 Z.	**76**	**144**	**212**	**239**	**578**	**513**	**622**	**470**
Capital account: credit......................	2 994 Z.	80	151	220	249	588	535	637	485
Capital account: debit......................	3 994 ..	−4	−7	−8	−10	−10	−23	−15	−15
Total, Groups A Plus B....................	4 981 ..	*−844*	*−1,618*	*−1,780*	*−4,283*	*−5,847*	*−3,979*	*2,906*	*1,201*
C. Financial Account[1]......................	4 995 W.	**937**	**2,013**	**2,600**	**6,141**	**7,042**	**3,255**	**−1,801**	**−745**
Direct investment abroad................	4 505 ..	−50	−110	−128	−173	−371	−265	57	−20
Direct investment in Latvia............	4 555 Z.	304	637	714	1,664	2,316	1,357	94	369
Portfolio investment assets..............	4 602 ..	−286	−21	−270	−246	−607	222	161	−178
Equity securities........................	4 610 ..	7	−29	−73	−73	−170	433	−166	−113
Debt securities..........................	4 619 ..	−292	8	−197	−174	−437	−211	327	−65
Portfolio investment liabilities..........	4 652 Z.	70	255	131	294	−52	151	11	−34
Equity securities........................	4 660 ..	39	32	12	22	−12	−50	−8	9
Debt securities..........................	4 669 Z.	31	223	119	272	−39	201	19	−43
Financial derivatives......................	4 910 ..	6	−47	−76	60	229	−67	403	−220
Financial derivatives assets............	4 900 ..	−5	−35	58	130	334	325	639	256
Financial derivatives liabilities........	4 905 ..	11	−13	−134	−70	−105	−392	−236	−476
Other investment assets..................	4 703 ..	−687	−1,776	−398	−1,953	−6,063	−504	−1,046	−875
Monetary authorities....................	4 701 ..	1	−2	−1	−1	−1	−1	....	....
General government....................	4 704 ..	....	−31	−23	1	−32	16	....	....
Banks..	4 705 ..	−635	−1,601	169	−687	−3,896	1,126	−248	−828
Other sectors............................	4 728 ..	−53	−143	−542	−1,267	−2,135	−1,645	−799	−47
Other investment liabilities..............	4 753 W.	1,580	3,076	2,626	6,495	11,590	2,361	−1,481	214
Monetary authorities....................	4 753 WA	....	44	−36	33	−21	715	−424	−60
General government....................	4 753 ZB	−66	19	−50	56	201	93	3,483	1,224
Banks..	4 753 ZC	1,480	2,533	2,482	5,131	8,477	805	−4,186	−945
Other sectors............................	4 753 ZD	165	480	230	1,275	2,933	748	−353	−4
Total, Groups A Through C..............	4 983 ..	*92*	*395*	*820*	*1,858*	*1,195*	*−724*	*1,104*	*456*
D. Net Errors and Omissions................	4 998 ..	**−13**	**8**	**−296**	**120**	**−212**	**−577**	**180**	**114**
Total, Groups A Through D..............	4 984 ..	*79*	*403*	*524*	*1,979*	*982*	*−1,301*	*1,285*	*570*
E. Reserves and Related Items..........	4 802 A.	**−79**	**−403**	**−524**	**−1,979**	**−982**	**1,301**	**−1,285**	**−570**
Reserve assets..............................	4 802 ..	−68	−398	−524	−1,979	−982	487	−1,563	−981
Use of Fund credit and loans..........	4 766 ..	−11	−6	....	....	....	814	278	411
Exceptional financing....................	4 920 ..	....	....	....	....	....	....	....	....
Conversion rates: lats per U.S. dollar..........	0 101 ..	**.5715**	**.5402**	**.5647**	**.5604**	**.5138**	**.4808**	**.5056**	**.5305**

[1] Excludes components that have been classified in the categories of Group E.

Table 2. STANDARD PRESENTATION, 2003–2010

(Millions of U.S. dollars)

	Code	2003	2004	2005	2006	2007	2008	2009	2010
CURRENT ACCOUNT............................	4 993 ..	**−921**	**−1,762**	**−1,992**	**−4,522**	**−6,425**	**−4,492**	**2,284**	**731**
A. GOODS............................	4 100 ..	**−2,003**	**−2,781**	**−3,018**	**−5,131**	**−6,898**	**−6,014**	**−1,822**	**−1,691**
Credit............................	2 100 ..	**3,171**	**4,221**	**5,361**	**6,140**	**8,227**	**9,634**	**7,387**	**9,107**
General merchandise: exports f.o.b.............	2 110 ..	2,307	3,393	4,647	5,469	7,535	8,835	6,878	8,653
Goods for processing: exports f.o.b.............	2 150 ..	765	708	530	509	520	550	361	271
Repairs on goods............................	2 160 ..	49	65	94	71	77	109	54	66
Goods procured in ports by carriers.............	2 170 ..	49	56	90	92	96	140	94	117
Nonmonetary gold............................	2 180 ..	....	....	....	....	....	....	....	....
Debit............................	3 100 ..	**−5,173**	**−7,002**	**−8,379**	**−11,271**	**−15,125**	**−15,648**	**−9,209**	**−10,799**
General merchandise: imports f.o.b.............	3 110 ..	−4,580	−6,429	−7,860	−10,716	−14,600	−14,910	−8,765	−10,385
Goods for processing: imports f.o.b.............	3 150 ..	−485	−456	−383	−376	−296	−355	−213	−163
Repairs on goods............................	3 160 ..	−17	−19	−10	−23	−39	−45	−17	−12
Goods procured in ports by carriers.............	3 170 ..	−91	−97	−127	−157	−190	−337	−214	−239
Nonmonetary gold............................	3 180 ..	....	....	....	....	....	....	....	....
B. SERVICES............................	4 200 ..	**576**	**601**	**606**	**662**	**1,002**	**1,348**	**1,567**	**1,466**
Total credit............................	2 200 ..	*1,506*	*1,779*	*2,163*	*2,642*	*3,705*	*4,538*	*3,844*	*3,693*
Total debit............................	3 200 ..	*−929*	*−1,178*	*−1,557*	*−1,980*	*−2,703*	*−3,190*	*−2,278*	*−2,226*
Transportation services, credit............	2 205 ..	**892**	**991**	**1,219**	**1,414**	**1,874**	**2,303**	**1,943**	**1,817**
Passenger............................	2 850 ..	*49*	*76*	*105*	*142*	*209*	*331*	*290*	*323*
Freight............................	2 851 ..	*560*	*592*	*714*	*845*	*1,068*	*1,292*	*1,040*	*939*
Other............................	2 852 ..	*284*	*323*	*400*	*426*	*598*	*681*	*613*	*556*
Sea transport, passenger...............	2 207 ..	3	3	3	....	6	11	8	4
Sea transport, freight...............	2 208 ..	212	199	222	238	271	283	230	135
Sea transport, other...............	2 209 ..	209	248	319	321	400	457	447	397
Air transport, passenger...............	2 211 ..	36	61	89	125	180	291	261	295
Air transport, freight...............	2 212 ..	5	6	6	8	11	12	17	13
Air transport, other...............	2 213 ..	25	35	41	54	83	61	41	34
Other transport, passenger...............	2 215 ..	10	11	14	17	23	29	21	24
Other transport, freight...............	2 216 ..	343	388	485	599	786	998	794	791
Other transport, other...............	2 217 ..	49	39	41	52	114	164	125	125
Transportation services, debit............	3 205 ..	**−301**	**−413**	**−501**	**−639**	**−786**	**−823**	**−576**	**−657**
Passenger............................	3 850 ..	*−37*	*−51*	*−71*	*−84*	*−94*	*−108*	*−107*	*−124*
Freight............................	3 851 ..	*−134*	*−201*	*−245*	*−323*	*−440*	*−461*	*−280*	*−337*
Other............................	3 852 ..	*−130*	*−161*	*−185*	*−232*	*−252*	*−254*	*−190*	*−195*
Sea transport, passenger...............	3 207 ..	−1	−1	−1	−2	−2	−2	−44	−50
Sea transport, freight...............	3 208 ..	−27	−46	−54	−79	−118	−113	−80	−85
Sea transport, other...............	3 209 ..	−66	−61	−53	−70	−68	−70	−47	−33
Air transport, passenger...............	3 211 ..	−35	−48	−69	−81	−89	−104	−61	−72
Air transport, freight...............	3 212 ..	−17	−23	−23	−30	−40	−49	−28	−44
Air transport, other...............	3 213 ..	−22	−54	−84	−111	−130	−114	−98	−119
Other transport, passenger...............	3 215 ..	−1	−2	−1	−1	−2	−2	−2	−3
Other transport, freight...............	3 216 ..	−91	−132	−169	−214	−283	−299	−172	−209
Other transport, other...............	3 217 ..	−42	−46	−47	−51	−55	−70	−45	−43
Travel, credit............................	2 236 ..	**222**	**267**	**341**	**480**	**672**	**803**	**723**	**640**
Business travel............................	2 237 ..	93	103	109	142	200	236	201	199
Personal travel............................	2 240 ..	130	164	232	337	471	567	522	441
Travel, debit............................	3 236 ..	**−328**	**−377**	**−584**	**−704**	**−927**	**−1,142**	**−799**	**−647**
Business travel............................	3 237 ..	−77	−114	−160	−141	−155	−216	−172	−139
Personal travel............................	3 240 ..	−251	−263	−423	−564	−772	−927	−627	−509
Other services, credit............................	2 200 BA ..	**391**	**521**	**603**	**749**	**1,159**	**1,432**	**1,178**	**1,235**
Communications............................	2 245 ..	36	53	61	82	81	99	101	95
Construction............................	2 249 ..	32	47	14	25	53	87	37	79
Insurance............................	2 253 ..	10	12	11	10	17	16	27	27
Financial............................	2 260 ..	93	115	129	179	264	288	248	227
Computer and information............................	2 262 ..	33	43	54	73	99	139	126	133
Royalties and licence fees............................	2 266 ..	4	8	10	11	13	13	7	12
Other business services............................	2 268 ..	162	214	290	332	585	736	592	615
Personal, cultural, and recreational...............	2 287 ..	4	3	5	6	9	12	9	12
Government, n.i.e............................	2 291 ..	18	28	29	30	38	43	32	35
Other services, debit............................	3 200 BA ..	**−301**	**−387**	**−472**	**−637**	**−989**	**−1,225**	**−902**	**−922**
Communications............................	3 245 ..	−22	−47	−58	−81	−106	−113	−107	−104
Construction............................	3 249 ..	−17	−18	−12	−42	−157	−216	−90	−68
Insurance............................	3 253 ..	−51	−40	−28	−27	−53	−40	−26	−25
Financial............................	3 260 ..	−25	−28	−31	−30	−55	−105	−82	−111
Computer and information............................	3 262 ..	−23	−28	−51	−63	−88	−101	−100	−99
Royalties and licence fees............................	3 266 ..	−10	−14	−14	−20	−40	−36	−26	−33
Other business services............................	3 268 ..	−134	−184	−249	−343	−447	−555	−432	−451
Personal, cultural, and recreational...............	3 287 ..	−7	−15	−13	−15	−21	−32	−21	−17
Government, n.i.e............................	3 291 ..	−12	−14	−16	−18	−24	−27	−18	−16

Table 2 (Continued). STANDARD PRESENTATION, 2003–2010

(Millions of U.S. dollars)

	Code	2003	2004	2005	2006	2007	2008	2009	2010
C. INCOME	4 300	**−24**	**−275**	**−176**	**−532**	**−908**	**−596**	**1,655**	**85**
Total credit	2 300	*368*	*500*	*772*	*1,078*	*1,487*	*1,785*	*1,324*	*1,116*
Total debit	3 300	*−393*	*−775*	*−948*	*−1,610*	*−2,396*	*−2,381*	*331*	*−1,031*
Compensation of employees, credit	2 310	**172**	**228**	**379**	**481**	**551**	**600**	**589**	**614**
Compensation of employees, debit	3 310	**−5**	**−10**	**−16**	**−25**	**−40**	**−54**	**−43**	**−43**
Investment income, credit	2 320	**197**	**272**	**392**	**597**	**937**	**1,186**	**735**	**502**
Direct investment income	2 330	5	6	35	35	68	55	−72	−30
Dividends and distributed branch profits	2 332	1	2	13	14	18	22	16	7
Reinvested earnings and undistributed branch profits	2 333	4	4	21	20	49	31	−93	−42
Income on debt (interest)	2 334	....	....	....	....	1	2	4	4
Portfolio investment income	2 339	131	163	186	302	377	511	355	295
Income on equity	2 340	....	1	1	2	2	4	1	3
Income on bonds and notes	2 350	98	109	132	189	295	347	315	235
Income on money market instruments	2 360	33	54	54	112	81	160	38	57
Other investment income	2 370	61	103	171	261	492	620	452	237
Investment income, debit	3 320	**−388**	**−766**	**−932**	**−1,585**	**−2,356**	**−2,328**	**374**	**−987**
Direct investment income	3 330	−211	−529	−617	−983	−1,240	−611	1,462	−129
Dividends and distributed branch profits	3 332	−85	−200	−250	−216	−509	−500	−624	−417
Reinvested earnings and undistributed branch profits	3 333	−95	−304	−335	−735	−663	−11	2,184	370
Income on debt (interest)	3 334	−31	−26	−32	−32	−69	−101	−99	−82
Portfolio investment income	3 339	−73	−110	−110	−190	−150	−308	−189	−168
Income on equity	3 340	−3	−2	−3	−4	−7	−7	−9	....
Income on bonds and notes	3 350	−40	−57	−62	−89	−108	−199	−166	−132
Income on money market instruments	3 360	−29	−51	−45	−97	−35	−102	−14	−36
Other investment income	3 370	−104	−127	−205	−413	−966	−1,408	−899	−690
D. CURRENT TRANSFERS	4 379	**530**	**694**	**596**	**479**	**380**	**769**	**883**	**871**
Credit	2 379	**924**	**1,289**	**1,373**	**1,789**	**2,023**	**2,191**	**1,984**	**1,643**
General government	2 380	98	218	251	254	363	416	625	761
Other sectors	2 390	826	1,071	1,122	1,535	1,661	1,776	1,358	883
Workers' remittances	2 391	2	2	2	2	2	2	2	....
Other current transfers	2 392	825	1,069	1,120	1,534	1,659	1,774	1,356	883
Debit	3 379	**−394**	**−595**	**−776**	**−1,310**	**−1,644**	**−1,422**	**−1,100**	**−772**
General government	3 380	−15	−101	−183	−224	−295	−343	−303	−261
Other sectors	3 390	−380	−494	−594	−1,086	−1,348	−1,079	−797	−511
Workers' remittances	3 391	−3	−4	−4	−4	−5	−4	−3	....
Other current transfers	3 392	−376	−491	−590	−1,081	−1,343	−1,075	−795	−511
CAPITAL AND FINANCIAL ACCOUNT	4 996	**934**	**1,754**	**2,288**	**4,401**	**6,637**	**5,069**	**−2,464**	**−845**
CAPITAL ACCOUNT	4 994	**76**	**144**	**212**	**239**	**578**	**513**	**622**	**470**
Total credit	2 994	*80*	*151*	*220*	*249*	*588*	*535*	*637*	*485*
Total debit	3 994	*−4*	*−7*	*−8*	*−10*	*−10*	*−23*	*−15*	*−15*
Capital transfers, credit	2 400	**80**	**151**	**220**	**242**	**586**	**529**	**637**	**485**
General government	2 401	69	149	218	242	586	528	604	466
Debt forgiveness	2 402	....	....	....	....	....	....	....	....
Other capital transfers	2 410	69	149	218	242	586	528	604	466
Other sectors	2 430	10	2	2	....	1	1	33	18
Migrants' transfers	2 431	....	....	....	....	....	....	....	....
Debt forgiveness	2 432	....	....	....	....	....	....	33	....
Other capital transfers	2 440	10	2	2	....	1	1	1	18
Capital transfers, debit	3 400	**−4**	**−6**	**−5**	**−9**	**−10**	**−22**	**−15**	**−14**
General government	3 401	....	....	....	....	....	....	....	....
Debt forgiveness	3 402	....	....	....	....	....	....	....	....
Other capital transfers	3 410	....	....	....	....	....	....	....	....
Other sectors	3 430	−3	−6	−5	−9	−10	−22	−15	−14
Migrants' transfers	3 431	....	....	....	....	....	....	....	....
Debt forgiveness	3 432	....	....	....	....	....	....	....	....
Other capital transfers	3 440	−3	−6	−5	−9	−10	−22	−15	−14
Nonproduced nonfinancial assets, credit	2 480	....	....	....	7	1	6	....	....
Nonproduced nonfinancial assets, debit	3 480	....	−1	−2	−1	....	....	....	−1

Table 2 (Continued). STANDARD PRESENTATION, 2003–2010

(Millions of U.S. dollars)

	Code	2003	2004	2005	2006	2007	2008	2009	2010
FINANCIAL ACCOUNT	4 995	**857**	**1,610**	**2,076**	**4,162**	**6,059**	**4,556**	**−3,086**	**−1,315**
A. DIRECT INVESTMENT	4 500	**254**	**527**	**585**	**1,491**	**1,945**	**1,092**	**150**	**349**
Direct investment abroad	4 505	**−50**	**−110**	**−128**	**−173**	**−371**	**−265**	**57**	**−20**
Equity capital	4 510	−42	−60	−62	−98	−240	−143	−147	−12
Claims on affiliated enterprises	4 515	−42	−60	−62	−98	−240	−144	−147	−12
Liabilities to affiliated enterprises	4 520	....	....	....	....	....	1	....	....
Reinvested earnings	4 525	−4	−4	−21	−20	−49	−31	93	42
Other capital	4 530	−4	−46	−45	−55	−82	−91	111	−50
Claims on affiliated enterprises	4 535	−5	−46	−49	−66	−103	−81	107	−55
Liabilities to affiliated enterprises	4 540	1	....	4	11	21	−10	4	6
Direct investment in Latvia	4 555	**304**	**637**	**714**	**1,664**	**2,316**	**1,357**	**94**	**369**
Equity capital	4 560	177	246	237	532	1,281	572	1,567	654
Claims on direct investors	4 565	−22	29	−22	21	....	−3	−22	8
Liabilities to direct investors	4 570	199	217	260	511	1,281	574	1,588	647
Reinvested earnings	4 575	95	304	335	735	663	11	−2,184	−370
Other capital	4 580	31	88	141	398	372	775	711	84
Claims on direct investors	4 585	−19	−8	−72	−48	−377	−84	163	−66
Liabilities to direct investors	4 590	51	95	213	446	749	859	548	151
B. PORTFOLIO INVESTMENT	4 600	**−216**	**234**	**−138**	**48**	**−659**	**373**	**172**	**−212**
Assets	4 602	**−286**	**−21**	**−270**	**−246**	**−607**	**222**	**161**	**−178**
Equity securities	4 610	7	−29	−73	−73	−170	433	−166	−113
Monetary authorities	4 611	....	....	....	....	....	....	....	....
General government	4 612	....	....	....	....	....	....	....	....
Banks	4 613	15	−1	−13	−23	1	12	26	20
Other sectors	4 614	−9	−28	−60	−50	−171	421	−192	−133
Debt securities	4 619	−292	8	−197	−174	−437	−211	327	−65
Bonds and notes	4 620	−290	23	−207	−159	−402	−175	470	−1
Monetary authorities	4 621	....	....	....	....	....	....	....	....
General government	4 622	....	....	....	....	....	....	....	....
Banks	4 623	−276	37	−183	−134	−207	−18	504	−11
Other sectors	4 624	−14	−13	−24	−26	−196	−156	−34	10
Money market instruments	4 630	−3	−16	10	−14	−35	−37	−143	−64
Monetary authorities	4 631	....	....	....	....	....	....	....	....
General government	4 632	....	....	....	....	....	−15	....	....
Banks	4 633	−1	−16	11	−9	−21	15	−114	−98
Other sectors	4 634	−2	....	−2	−5	−14	−36	−29	34
Liabilities	4 652	**70**	**255**	**131**	**294**	**−52**	**151**	**11**	**−34**
Equity securities	4 660	39	32	12	22	−12	−50	−8	9
Banks	4 663	25	−1	−10	13	20	−35	34	4
Other sectors	4 664	15	32	23	9	−32	−16	−41	6
Debt securities	4 669	31	223	119	272	−39	201	19	−43
Bonds and notes	4 670	31	221	120	271	−49	215	−2	−36
Monetary authorities	4 671	....	....	....	....	....	....	....	....
General government	4 672	30	185	....	13	14	378	−3	−4
Banks	4 673	1	36	119	258	−61	−160	1	−32
Other sectors	4 674	....	....	....	....	−2	−3	−1	....
Money market instruments	4 680	....	2	−1	1	10	−14	21	−8
Monetary authorities	4 681	....	....	....	....	....	....	....	....
General government	4 682	....	2	−1	1	−3	....	21	−15
Banks	4 683	....	....	....	....	11	−12	....	2
Other sectors	4 684	....	....	....	....	1	−2	....	5
C. FINANCIAL DERIVATIVES	4 910	**6**	**−47**	**−76**	**60**	**229**	**−67**	**403**	**−220**
Monetary authorities	4 911	2	−42	−55	55	245	−79	387	−194
General government	4 912	....	....	....	1	−2	1	−16	21
Banks	4 913	3	−5	−6	2	−8	18	44	−52
Other sectors	4 914	1	....	−15	2	−6	−7	−11	4
Assets	4 900	**−5**	**−35**	**58**	**130**	**334**	**325**	**639**	**256**
Monetary authorities	4 901	−2	−36	76	136	373	390	587	225
General government	4 902	....	....	....	1	−1	3	....	22
Banks	4 903	−3	2	−3	−9	−32	−61	64	5
Other sectors	4 904	1	....	−15	2	−6	−7	−12	4
Liabilities	4 905	**11**	**−13**	**−134**	**−70**	**−105**	**−392**	**−236**	**−476**
Monetary authorities	4 906	4	−6	−131	−81	−128	−469	−200	−418
General government	4 907	....	....	....	1	−1	−2	−16	−1
Banks	4 908	6	−7	−3	11	24	79	−20	−57
Other sectors	4 909	....	....	....	....	....	....	....	....

Table 2 (Concluded). STANDARD PRESENTATION, 2003–2010

(Millions of U.S. dollars)

	Code	2003	2004	2005	2006	2007	2008	2009	2010
D. OTHER INVESTMENT	4 700	**882**	**1,294**	**2,229**	**4,542**	**5,526**	**2,672**	**−2,249**	**−250**
Assets	4 703	−687	−1,776	−398	−1,953	−6,063	−504	−1,046	−875
Trade credits	4 706	−20	−125	−168	−133	−222	−1	120	−224
General government	4 707	....	....	....	....	....	....	....	....
of which: Short-term	4 709	....	....	....	....	....	....	....	....
Other sectors	4 710	−20	−125	−168	−133	−222	−1	120	−224
of which: Short-term	4 712	*−20*	*−125*	*−168*	*−133*	*−222*	*−1*	*120*	*−224*
Loans	4 714	−122	−990	35	−632	−2,219	−317	−71	598
Monetary authorities	4 715	....	....	....	....	....	....	....	....
of which: Short-term	4 718	....	....	....	....	....	....	....	....
General government	4 719	....	....	....	....	....	....	....	....
of which: Short-term	4 721	....	....	....	....	....	....	....	....
Banks	4 722	−98	−943	119	−549	−1,635	−208	−149	582
of which: Short-term	4 724	*13*	*−523*	*220*	*−53*	*−1,066*	*221*	*−259*	*229*
Other sectors	4 725	−24	−47	−84	−83	−584	−109	78	16
of which: Short-term	4 727	*−11*	*−4*	*−46*	*−53*	*−72*	*−68*	*−55*	*−28*
Currency and deposits	4 730	−551	−619	−219	−1,158	−3,598	−146	−1,038	−1,205
Monetary authorities	4 731	....	....	....	....	....	....	....	....
General government	4 732	....	1	....	1	−32	16	....	....
Banks	4 733	−531	−650	55	−112	−2,238	1,349	−59	−1,375
Other sectors	4 734	−21	30	−275	−1,047	−1,328	−1,511	−978	171
Other assets	4 736	6	−41	−45	−31	−25	−40	−57	−44
Monetary authorities	4 737	1	−2	−1	−1	−1	−1	....	....
of which: Short-term	4 739	*1*	....	*1*	*−1*	*−1*	*−1*	....	....
General government	4 740	....	−32	−23	....	....	....	....	....
of which: Short-term	4 742	....	....	....	....	....	....	....	....
Banks	4 743	−6	−8	−6	−27	−23	−15	−40	−34
of which: Short-term	4 745	*−6*	*−8*	*−6*	*−27*	*−23*	*−15*	*−40*	*−34*
Other sectors	4 746	11	....	−15	−3	−1	−24	−18	−10
of which: Short-term	4 748	*11*	....	*−15*	*−3*	*5*	*−23*	*−8*	*−9*
Liabilities	4 753	**1,569**	**3,070**	**2,626**	**6,495**	**11,590**	**3,175**	**−1,203**	**625**
Trade credits	4 756	54	192	122	128	308	−56	−282	540
General government	4 757	....	....	....	....	....	....	....	....
of which: Short-term	4 759	....	....	....	....	....	....	....	....
Other sectors	4 760	54	192	122	128	308	−56	−282	540
of which: Short-term	4 762	*54*	*192*	*122*	*128*	*308*	*−56*	*−282*	*540*
Loans	4 764	579	1,676	2,810	5,732	7,841	5,307	465	−2,567
Monetary authorities	4 765	−11	−6	....	....	....	1,052	41	411
of which: Use of Fund credit and loans from the Fund	4 766	*−11*	*−6*	....	....	....	*814*	*278*	*411*
of which: Short-term	4 768	....	....	....	....	....	*238*	*−237*	....
General government	4 769	−66	−5	−71	62	212	105	3,424	1,184
of which: Short-term	4 771	....	....	....	....	*37*	*−37*	....	....
Banks	4 772	543	1,417	2,777	4,542	5,049	3,356	−2,918	−3,735
of which: Short-term	4 774	*287*	*349*	*573*	*1,703*	*1,391*	*−564*	*−1,601*	*−701*
Other sectors	4 775	113	269	105	1,128	2,580	793	−83	−427
of which: Short-term	4 777	*−20*	*43*	*−19*	*144*	*124*	*206*	*−99*	*−34*
Currency and deposits	4 780	937	1,112	−300	561	3,337	−2,090	−1,640	2,691
Monetary authorities	4 781	....	43	−35	33	−21	474	−375	−60
General government	4 782	....	....	....	....	....	....	....	....
Banks	4 783	937	1,068	−265	528	3,358	−2,564	−1,265	2,751
Other sectors	4 784	....	....	....	....	....	....	....	....
Other liabilities	4 786	−1	90	−6	73	105	14	255	−39
Monetary authorities	4 787	....	1	−1	....	....	3	188	....
of which: Short-term	4 789	....	*1*	*−1*	....	....	*3*	*−1*	....
General government	4 790	....	23	21	−6	−11	−12	59	39
of which: Short-term	4 792	....	....	....	....	....	....	*69*	*43*
Banks	4 793	....	48	−30	61	70	13	−3	40
of which: Short-term	4 795	....	*48*	*−30*	*61*	*70*	*13*	*−3*	*40*
Other sectors	4 796	−2	18	4	18	46	11	11	−118
of which: Short-term	4 798	*−2*	*18*	*4*	*18*	*46*	*11*	*11*	*−118*
E. RESERVE ASSETS	4 802	**−68**	**−398**	**−524**	**−1,979**	**−982**	**487**	**−1,563**	**−981**
Monetary gold	4 812	....	....	....	....	....	....	....	....
Special drawing rights	4 811	....	....	....	....	....	....	−186	−3
Reserve position in the Fund	4 810	....	....	....	....	....	....	....	....
Foreign exchange	4 803	−68	−398	−524	−1,979	−982	487	−1,377	−978
Other claims	4 813	....	....	....	....	....	....	....	....
NET ERRORS AND OMISSIONS	4 998	**−13**	**8**	**−296**	**120**	**−212**	**−577**	**180**	**114**

Table 3. INTERNATIONAL INVESTMENT POSITION (End-period stocks), 2003–2010

(Millions of U.S. dollars)

	Code	2003	2004	2005	2006	2007	2008	2009	2010
ASSETS	8 995 C.	**6,674**	**9,380**	**10,045**	**15,174**	**24,548**	**24,653**	**27,298**	**27,938**
Direct investment abroad	8 505 ..	**114**	**239**	**282**	**475**	**926**	**1,054**	**891**	**880**
Equity capital and reinvested earnings	8 506 ..	83	152	169	293	626	686	630	584
Claims on affiliated enterprises	8 507 ..	84	153	169	293	626	686	630	584
Liabilities to affiliated enterprises	8 508 ..	....	....	....	....	....	−1	....	....
Other capital	8 530 ..	31	86	114	182	300	368	261	296
Claims on affiliated enterprises	8 535 ..	37	94	124	205	344	411	309	332
Liabilities to affiliated enterprises	8 540 ..	−6	−8	−10	−23	−44	−43	−48	−36
Portfolio investment	8 602 ..	**1,255**	**1,340**	**1,601**	**2,041**	**2,807**	**2,920**	**2,989**	**3,221**
Equity securities	8 610 ..	48	83	168	300	530	522	771	915
Monetary authorities	8 611 ..	....	....	....	....	....	....	....	....
General government	8 612 ..	....	....	....	....	....	....	....	....
Banks	8 613 ..	29	30	51	94	106	62	53	40
Other sectors	8 614 ..	19	52	117	206	424	460	718	875
Debt securities	8 619 ..	1,207	1,258	1,433	1,742	2,277	2,398	2,217	2,306
Bonds and notes	8 620 ..	1,194	1,228	1,417	1,709	2,204	2,301	1,985	2,014
Monetary authorities	8 621 ..	....	....	....	....	....	....	....	....
General government	8 622 ..	....	....	....	....	....	....	....	....
Banks	8 623 ..	1,170	1,173	1,338	1,580	1,862	1,766	1,368	1,337
Other sectors	8 624 ..	24	55	79	129	342	535	617	677
Money market instruments	8 630 ..	13	30	16	33	73	97	233	292
Monetary authorities	8 631 ..	....	....	....	....	....	....	....	....
General government	8 632 ..	....	....	....	....	....	....	....	....
Banks	8 633 ..	2	18	7	16	40	26	138	234
Other sectors	8 634 ..	11	12	10	17	33	71	95	58
Financial derivatives	8 900 ..	**18**	**52**	**21**	**80**	**101**	**415**	**133**	**87**
Monetary authorities	8 901 ..	9	46	6	58	34	269	10	5
General government	8 902 ..	....	....	4	....	1	9	37	6
Banks	8 903 ..	7	6	8	18	52	111	46	39
Other sectors	8 904 ..	3	....	4	5	13	26	40	38
Other investment	8 703 ..	**3,752**	**5,726**	**5,780**	**8,068**	**14,956**	**15,015**	**16,379**	**16,144**
Trade credits	8 706 ..	625	808	874	1,152	1,654	1,569	1,626	1,633
General government	8 707 ..	....	....	....	....	....	....	....	....
of which: Short-term	8 709 ..	....	....	....	....	....	....	....	....
Other sectors	8 710 ..	625	808	874	1,152	1,654	1,569	1,626	1,633
of which: Short-term	8 712 ..	*625*	*808*	*874*	*1,152*	*1,654*	*1,569*	*1,626*	*1,633*
Loans	8 714 ..	1,301	2,352	2,199	2,913	5,387	5,579	5,620	3,553
Monetary authorities	8 715 ..	....	....	....	....	....	....	....	....
of which: Short-term	8 718 ..	....	....	....	....	....	....	....	....
General government	8 719 ..	....	....	....	....	....	....	....	....
of which: Short-term	8 721 ..	....	....	....	....	....	....	....	....
Banks	8 722 ..	1,184	2,173	1,978	2,567	4,368	4,515	4,669	2,722
of which: Short-term	8 724 ..	*802*	*1,339*	*1,098*	*1,151*	*2,282*	*2,056*	*2,316*	*882*
Other sectors	8 725 ..	118	179	221	346	1,020	1,064	951	831
of which: Short-term	8 727 ..	*74*	*82*	*103*	*155*	*226*	*265*	*215*	*206*
Currency and deposits	8 730 ..	1,755	2,444	2,561	3,826	7,718	7,630	8,827	10,613
Monetary authorities	8 731 ..	....	....	....	....	....	....	....	....
General government	8 732 ..	2	....	....	....	35	....	....	....
Banks	8 733 ..	1,641	2,346	2,211	2,361	4,659	3,185	3,285	5,681
Other sectors	8 734 ..	113	97	350	1,465	3,024	4,444	5,542	4,931
Other assets	8 736 ..	70	122	146	177	198	237	307	346
Monetary authorities	8 737 ..	2	4	5	6	7	7	7	7
of which: Short-term	8 739 ..	*1*	*1*	....	*1*	*2*	*2*	*2*	*2*
General government	8 740 ..	18	55	70	77	84	84	84	82
of which: Short-term	8 742 ..	....	....	....	....	....	....	....	....
Banks	8 743 ..	18	26	31	58	82	94	133	181
of which: Short-term	8 745 ..	*18*	*26*	*31*	*58*	*82*	*94*	*133*	*171*
Other sectors	8 746 ..	32	36	41	37	25	52	82	76
of which: Short-term	8 748 ..	*32*	*35*	*40*	*35*	*17*	*44*	*64*	*59*
Reserve assets	8 802 ..	**1,535**	**2,022**	**2,361**	**4,509**	**5,758**	**5,248**	**6,905**	**7,606**
Monetary gold	8 812 ..	103	110	128	156	205	220	275	350
Special drawing rights	8 811 ..	....	....	....	....	....	....	187	187
Reserve position in the Fund	8 810 ..	....	....	....	....	....	....	....	....
Foreign exchange	8 803 ..	1,432	1,912	2,232	4,353	5,553	5,028	6,444	7,070
Other claims	8 813 ..	....	....	....	....	....	....	....	....

Table 3 (Concluded). INTERNATIONAL INVESTMENT POSITION (End-period stocks), 2003–2010

(Millions of U.S. dollars)

	Code	2003	2004	2005	2006	2007	2008	2009	2010
LIABILITIES	8 995 D.	**11,836**	**16,900**	**19,096**	**29,693**	**47,279**	**50,325**	**49,585**	**47,217**
Direct investment in Latvia	8 555 ..	**3,277**	**4,529**	**4,929**	**7,476**	**10,842**	**11,537**	**11,602**	**10,751**
Equity capital and reinvested earnings	8 556 ..	2,406	3,433	3,836	5,791	8,592	8,559	8,041	8,162
Claims on direct investors	8 557 ..	−51	−26	−28	−11	−14	−17	−41	−21
Liabilities to direct investors	8 558 ..	2,458	3,460	3,865	5,802	8,606	8,576	8,081	8,183
Other capital	8 580 ..	870	1,095	1,093	1,685	2,249	2,978	3,561	2,588
Claims on direct investors	8 585 ..	−129	−154	−174	−232	−733	−852	−774	−796
Liabilities to direct investors	8 590 ..	999	1,250	1,266	1,917	2,982	3,831	4,335	3,384
Portfolio investment	8 652 ..	**687**	**1,035**	**1,118**	**1,599**	**1,787**	**1,735**	**1,741**	**1,616**
Equity securities	8 660 ..	121	152	233	329	388	227	202	221
Banks	8 663 ..	45	46	55	98	144	77	88	79
Other sectors	8 664 ..	76	106	178	230	244	150	114	141
Debt securities	8 669 ..	566	882	885	1,271	1,399	1,508	1,539	1,396
Bonds and notes	8 670 ..	566	881	885	1,270	1,385	1,505	1,517	1,388
Monetary authorities	8 671 ..	....	....	....	....	....	....	....	....
General government	8 672 ..	537	810	706	794	914	1,191	1,200	1,094
Banks	8 673 ..	28	70	179	463	448	294	298	276
Other sectors	8 674 ..	....	....	....	13	23	20	19	17
Money market instruments	8 680 ..	....	2	....	1	14	3	22	8
Monetary authorities	8 681 ..	....	....	....	....	....	....	....	....
General government	8 682 ..	....	2	....	1	....	....	21	3
Banks	8 683 ..	....	....	....	....	12	....	....	....
Other sectors	8 684 ..	....	....	....	....	2	3	1	5
Financial derivatives	8 905 ..	**43**	**27**	**31**	**60**	**110**	**178**	**155**	**92**
Monetary authorities	8 906 ..	15	9	17	25	39	32	38	35
General government	8 907 ..	....	....	....	9	18	13	....	....
Banks	8 908 ..	24	18	14	26	53	134	118	57
Other sectors	8 909 ..	4	....	....	....	....	....	....	....
Other investment	8 753 ..	**7,828**	**11,309**	**13,018**	**20,558**	**34,541**	**36,874**	**36,087**	**34,759**
Trade credits	8 756 ..	788	1,044	1,004	1,272	1,796	1,639	1,450	1,845
General government	8 757 ..	....	....	....	....	....	....	....	....
of which: Short-term	8 759 ..	....	....	....	....	....	....	....	....
Other sectors	8 760 ..	788	1,044	1,004	1,272	1,796	1,639	1,450	1,845
of which: Short-term	8 762 ..	*788*	*1,044*	*1,004*	*1,272*	*1,796*	*1,639*	*1,450*	*1,845*
Loans	8 764 ..	3,443	5,373	7,618	14,204	23,918	28,641	29,475	12,276
Monetary authorities	8 765 ..	6	....	....	....	....	1,075	1,119	1,513
of which: Use of Fund credit and loans from the Fund	8 766 ..	*6*	....	....	....	....	*825*	*1,119*	*1,513*
of which: Short-term	8 768 ..	....	....	....	....	....	*250*	....	....
General government	8 769 ..	314	327	264	355	601	740	4,352	5,131
of which: Short-term	8 771 ..	....	....	....	....	*36*	....	....	....
Banks	8 772 ..	1,841	3,423	5,800	10,950	17,374	20,282	17,463	....
of which: Short-term	8 774 ..	*1,114*	*1,535*	*1,996*	*3,840*	*5,617*	*5,066*	*3,421*	....
Other sectors	8 775 ..	1,282	1,623	1,554	2,899	5,943	6,544	6,541	5,632
of which: Short-term	8 777 ..	*181*	*263*	*129*	*322*	*449*	*613*	*442*	*395*
Currency and deposits	8 780 ..	3,519	4,714	4,263	4,863	8,381	6,105	4,422	20,057
Monetary authorities	8 781 ..	2	47	8	43	24	527	106	43
General government	8 782 ..	....	....	....	....	....	....	....	....
Banks	8 783 ..	3,518	4,667	4,254	4,820	8,358	5,578	4,316	20,014
Other sectors	8 784 ..	....	....	....	....	....	....	....	....
Other liabilities	8 786 ..	79	178	132	218	445	489	739	581
Monetary authorities	8 787 ..	1	1	....	....	1	3	191	188
of which: Short-term	8 789 ..	*1*	*1*	....	....	*1*	*3*	*2*	*2*
General government	8 790 ..	....	27	43	41	34	22	85	118
of which: Short-term	8 792 ..	....	....	....	....	....	....	*74*	*111*
Banks	8 793 ..	21	69	38	100	171	181	175	144
of which: Short-term	8 795 ..	*21*	*69*	*38*	*100*	*171*	*181*	*175*	*144*
Other sectors	8 796 ..	57	81	51	77	240	284	288	132
of which: Short-term	8 798 ..	*57*	*81*	*51*	*77*	*240*	*284*	*288*	*132*
NET INTERNATIONAL INVESTMENT POSITION	8 995 ..	**−5,162**	**−7,520**	**−9,051**	**−14,519**	**−22,731**	**−25,673**	**−22,288**	**−19,279**
Conversion rates: lats per U.S. dollar (end of period)	0 102 ..	.5410	.5160	.5930	.5360	.4840	.4950	.4890	.5350

2011, International Monetary Fund: *Balance of Payments Statistics Yearbook*

Table 1. ANALYTIC PRESENTATION, 2003–2010

(Millions of U.S. dollars)

	Code	2003	2004	2005	2006	2007	2008	2009	2010
A. Current Account[1].....................	4 993 Z.	**–5,138**	**–4,406**	**–2,748**	**–1,221**	**–1,605**	**–4,103**	**–6,741**	**–9,415**
Goods: exports f.o.b..........................	2 100 ..	1,998	2,397	2,652	3,229	4,046	5,251	4,716	5,466
Goods: imports f.o.b..........................	3 100 ..	–7,001	–9,175	–9,239	–9,345	–11,926	–16,261	–15,895	–17,728
Balance on Goods........................	4 100 ..	*–5,003*	*–6,778*	*–6,588*	*–6,115*	*–7,880*	*–11,010*	*–11,179*	*–12,263*
Services: credit................................	2 200 ..	9,462	9,704	10,858	11,581	12,755	17,574	16,889	15,268
Services: debit.................................	3 200 ..	–6,488	–8,230	–7,895	–8,734	–9,988	–13,464	–14,051	–13,009
Balance on Goods and Services........*	4 991 ..	*–2,029*	*–5,304*	*–3,624*	*–3,269*	*–5,114*	*–6,900*	*–8,340*	*–10,004*
Income: credit..................................	2 300 ..	1,399	1,060	1,733	2,440	3,113	2,723	2,040	1,495
Income: debit...................................	3 300 ..	–4,836	–1,878	–1,919	–2,256	–2,373	–2,286	–2,268	–1,450
Balance on Goods, Services, and Income........	4 992 ..	*–5,467*	*–6,121*	*–3,811*	*–3,085*	*–4,373*	*–6,463*	*–8,568*	*–9,959*
Current transfers: credit....................	2 379 Z.	4,079	5,325	4,399	5,053	5,219	6,070	6,642	5,069
Current transfers: debit.....................	3 379 ..	–3,751	–3,609	–3,337	–3,189	–2,450	–3,709	–4,815	–4,525
B. Capital Account[1]........................	4 994 Z.	**29**	**50**	**27**	**1,940**	**590**	**410**	**18**	**345**
Capital account: credit......................	2 994 Z.	30	54	27	1,944	591	410	25	910
Capital account: debit.......................	3 994 ..	–1	–3	....	–4	–1	....	–7	–565
Total, Groups A Plus B.....................	4 981 ..	*–5,109*	*–4,355*	*–2,721*	*720*	*–1,015*	*–3,693*	*–6,723*	*–9,071*
C. Financial Account[1]......................	4 995 W.	**6,344**	**4,309**	**3,786**	**2,240**	**6,424**	**12,693**	**18,700**	**5,719**
Direct investment abroad...................	4 505 ..	–611	–827	–715	–875	–848	–987	–1,126	–574
Direct investment in Lebanon.............	4 555 Z.	2,860	1,899	2,624	2,675	3,376	4,333	4,804	4,955
Portfolio investment assets................	4 602 ..	–773	–614	–112	–358	–1,560	–566	–826	–1,016
Equity securities............................	4 610 ..	–254	–349	–152	–206	–472	–403	–707	1,083
Debt securities..............................	4 619 ..	–519	–265	40	–152	–1,088	–163	–119	–2,099
Portfolio investment liabilities............	4 652 Z.	644	–93	648	2,024	1,730	1,203	2,690	–108
Equity securities............................	4 660 ..	207	148	1,436	551	791	466	929	–50
Debt securities..............................	4 669 Z.	437	–241	–788	1,473	939	738	1,761	–58
Financial derivatives..........................	4 910 ..	....	....	....	....	....	....	....	....
Financial derivatives assets................	4 900 ..	....	....	....	....	....	....	....	....
Financial derivatives liabilities............	4 905 ..	....	....	....	....	....	....	....	....
Other investment assets....................	4 703 ..	2,803	3,125	2,638	–1,598	529	7,819	5,083	2,074
Monetary authorities......................	4 701 ..	....	....	....	....	....	....	....	....
General government.......................	4 704 ..	–25	45	65	44	29	12	27	....
Banks...	4 705 ..	3,212	3,565	3,783	1,617	877	6,254	2,820	2,697
Other sectors.................................	4 728 ..	–384	–485	–1,211	–3,259	–377	1,553	2,236	–623
Other investment liabilities................	4 753 W.	1,421	819	–1,296	373	3,197	890	8,075	388
Monetary authorities......................	4 753 WA	....	....	–22	2	244	93	244	–160
General government.......................	4 753 ZB	612	–13	–73	–51	299	169	–226	–142
Banks...	4 753 ZC	–3	–7	–463	482	1,481	2,256	5,701	1,970
Other sectors.................................	4 753 ZD	812	839	–738	–59	1,174	–1,628	2,355	–1,280
Total, Groups A Through C...............	4 983 ..	*1,235*	*–46*	*1,066*	*2,960*	*5,409*	*9,000*	*11,977*	*–3,351*
D. Net Errors and Omissions...............	4 998 ..	**3,802**	**–734**	**–608**	**–2,814**	**–6,074**	**–1,664**	**–3,042**	**6,411**
Total, Groups A Through D...............	4 984 ..	*5,037*	*–780*	*458*	*146*	*–665*	*7,336*	*8,935*	*3,059*
E. Reserves and Related Items............	4 802 A.	**–5,037**	**780**	**–458**	**–146**	**665**	**–7,336**	**–8,935**	**–3,059**
Reserve assets..................................	4 802 ..	–5,037	780	–458	–250	588	–7,374	–8,935	–3,040
Use of Fund credit and loans.............	4 766 ..	....	....	....	....	77	38	....	–20
Exceptional financing.........................	4 920 ..	....	....	....	105	....	....	....	....
Conversion rates: Lebanese pounds per U.S. dollar................	0 101 ..	**1,507.5**	**1,507.5**	**1,507.5**	**1,507.5**	**1,507.5**	**1,507.5**	**1,507.5**	**1,507.5**

[1] Excludes components that have been classified in the categories of Group E.

Table 2. STANDARD PRESENTATION, 2003–2010
(Millions of U.S. dollars)

	Code	2003	2004	2005	2006	2007	2008	2009	2010
CURRENT ACCOUNT	4 993	**−5,138**	**−4,406**	**−2,748**	**−1,116**	**−1,605**	**−4,103**	**−6,741**	**−9,415**
A. GOODS	4 100	**−5,003**	**−6,778**	**−6,588**	**−6,115**	**−7,880**	**−11,010**	**−11,179**	**−12,263**
Credit	2 100	**1,998**	**2,397**	**2,652**	**3,229**	**4,046**	**5,251**	**4,716**	**5,466**
General merchandise: exports f.o.b.	2 110	1,378	1,868	2,158	2,301	3,171	3,978	3,251	3,850
Goods for processing: exports f.o.b.	2 150	225	301	291	416	472	797	529	738
Repairs on goods	2 160	....	....	....	....	....	....	....	39
Goods procured in ports by carriers	2 170	40	46	83	68	89	157	95	9
Nonmonetary gold	2 180	355	182	120	445	315	319	842	830
Debit	3 100	**−7,001**	**−9,175**	**−9,239**	**−9,345**	**−11,926**	**−16,261**	**−15,895**	**−17,728**
General merchandise: imports f.o.b.	3 110	−6,645	−8,576	−8,625	−8,879	−11,197	−15,018	−14,945	−16,386
Goods for processing: imports f.o.b.	3 150	−191	−264	−278	−319	−463	−730	−500	−494
Repairs on goods	3 160	−2	−2	−2	−1	....	....	....	−46
Goods procured in ports by carriers	3 170	....	....	....	....	....	....	....	....
Nonmonetary gold	3 180	−164	−332	−334	−146	−266	−513	−450	−802
B. SERVICES	4 200	**2,974**	**1,474**	**2,963**	**2,846**	**2,766**	**4,110**	**2,839**	**2,258**
Total credit	2 200	*9,462*	*9,704*	*10,858*	*11,581*	*12,755*	*17,574*	*16,889*	*15,268*
Total debit	3 200	*−6,488*	*−8,230*	*−7,895*	*−8,734*	*−9,988*	*−13,464*	*−14,051*	*−13,009*
Transportation services, credit	2 205	**408**	**520**	**438**	**477**	**580**	**499**	**383**	**622**
Passenger	2 850	*408*	*520*	*437*	*476*	*580*	*498*	*383*	*162*
Freight	2 851	....	....	....	....	....	....	....	*243*
Other	2 852	....	....	....	....	....	....	....	*216*
Sea transport, passenger	2 207	....	....	....	....	....	....	....	41
Sea transport, freight	2 208	....	....	....	....	....	....	....	189
Sea transport, other	2 209	....	....	....	....	....	....	....	118
Air transport, passenger	2 211	408	520	437	476	580	498	383	113
Air transport, freight	2 212	....	....	....	....	....	....	....	27
Air transport, other	2 213	....	....	....	....	....	....	....	32
Other transport, passenger	2 215	....	....	....	....	....	....	....	9
Other transport, freight	2 216	....	....	....	....	....	....	....	27
Other transport, other	2 217	....	....	....	....	....	....	....	67
Transportation services, debit	3 205	**−902**	**−1,229**	**−1,332**	**−1,500**	**−1,719**	**−1,943**	**−2,160**	**−1,911**
Passenger	3 850	*−376*	*−549*	*−657*	*−777*	*−800*	*−733*	*−916*	*−346*
Freight	3 851	*−525*	*−680*	*−675*	*−724*	*−919*	*−1,211*	*−1,244*	*−1,385*
Other	3 852	....	....	....	....	....	....	....	*−181*
Sea transport, passenger	3 207	....	....	....	....	....	....	....	−86
Sea transport, freight	3 208	−388	−513	−516	−553	−708	−933	−916	−1,023
Sea transport, other	3 209	....	....	....	....	....	....	....	−100
Air transport, passenger	3 211	−376	−549	−657	−777	−800	−733	−916	−256
Air transport, freight	3 212	−103	−124	−117	−119	−150	−197	−253	−266
Air transport, other	3 213	....	....	....	....	....	....	....	−40
Other transport, passenger	3 215	....	....	....	....	....	....	....	−4
Other transport, freight	3 216	−34	−43	−42	−51	−61	−80	−76	−95
Other transport, other	3 217	....	....	....	....	....	....	....	−40
Travel, credit	2 236	**6,374**	**5,411**	**5,532**	**4,981**	**5,216**	**5,819**	**6,774**	**8,012**
Business travel	2 237	1,690	89	529	72	100	178	234	173
Personal travel	2 240	4,683	5,322	5,002	4,909	5,116	5,641	6,541	7,839
Travel, debit	3 236	**−2,943**	**−3,170**	**−2,908**	**−3,006**	**−3,114**	**−3,564**	**−4,012**	**−4,734**
Business travel	3 237	−76	−111	−179	−82	−94	−269	−197	−135
Personal travel	3 240	−2,867	−3,059	−2,729	−2,924	−3,020	−3,296	−3,815	−4,600
Other services, credit	2 200 BA	**2,680**	**3,773**	**4,889**	**6,123**	**6,959**	**11,256**	**9,732**	**6,634**
Communications	2 245	163	229	241	305	250	329	483	379
Construction	2 249	....	....	....	....	....	....	....	596
Insurance	2 253	124	141	209	189	265	266	242	67
Financial	2 260	27	40	58	129	105	100	115	2,114
Computer and information	2 262	....	....	....	....	....	....	....	93
Royalties and licence fees	2 266	....	....	....	....	....	....	....	7
Other business services	2 268	2,351	3,340	4,362	5,485	6,328	10,545	8,878	3,107
Personal, cultural, and recreational	2 287	....	....	....	....	....	....	....	202
Government, n.i.e.	2 291	16	22	19	16	11	16	15	68
Other services, debit	3 200 BA	**−2,644**	**−3,831**	**−3,655**	**−4,228**	**−5,155**	**−7,956**	**−7,878**	**−6,364**
Communications	3 245	−97	−203	−138	−217	−210	−249	−244	−291
Construction	3 249	....	....	....	....	....	....	....	−516
Insurance	3 253	−217	−176	−248	−260	−287	−301	16	−164
Financial	3 260	−6	−9	−10	−19	−19	−27	−28	−1,074
Computer and information	3 262	....	....	....	....	−1	....	−2	−97
Royalties and licence fees	3 266	....	....	....	....	....	....	−1	−12
Other business services	3 268	−2,310	−3,426	−3,242	−3,717	−4,622	−7,360	−7,600	−4,064
Personal, cultural, and recreational	3 287	....	....	....	....	....	....	....	−123
Government, n.i.e.	3 291	−14	−16	−16	−15	−16	−19	−19	−24

Table 2 (Continued). STANDARD PRESENTATION, 2003–2010

(Millions of U.S. dollars)

	Code	2003	2004	2005	2006	2007	2008	2009	2010
C. INCOME	4 300	**−3,438**	**−818**	**−186**	**184**	**740**	**437**	**−228**	**45**
Total credit	2 300	*1,399*	*1,060*	*1,733*	*2,440*	*3,113*	*2,723*	*2,040*	*1,495*
Total debit	3 300	*−4,836*	*−1,878*	*−1,919*	*−2,256*	*−2,373*	*−2,286*	*−2,268*	*−1,450*
Compensation of employees, credit	2 310	**779**	**409**	**667**	**579**	**747**	**1,405**	**1,173**	**569**
Compensation of employees, debit	3 310	**−387**	**−660**	**−731**	**−661**	**−597**	**−790**	**−1,034**	**−544**
Investment income, credit	2 320	**619**	**651**	**1,066**	**1,860**	**2,366**	**1,318**	**867**	**926**
Direct investment income	2 330	87	63	122	79	68	121	137	192
Dividends and distributed branch profits	2 332	87	63	122	79	68	121	137	192
Reinvested earnings and undistributed branch profits	2 333	....	....	....	....	....	....	....	....
Income on debt (interest)	2 334	....	....	....	....	....	....	....	....
Portfolio investment income	2 339	213	135	64	70	75	60	64	41
Income on equity	2 340	....	....	....	....	....	....	....	25
Income on bonds and notes	2 350	....	....	....	....	....	....	....	3
Income on money market instruments	2 360	213	135	64	70	75	60	64	12
Other investment income	2 370	319	453	881	1,712	2,223	1,137	666	693
Investment income, debit	3 320	**−4,449**	**−1,218**	**−1,188**	**−1,595**	**−1,776**	**−1,496**	**−1,234**	**−906**
Direct investment income	3 330	−69	−91	−95	−96	−64	−121	−95	−208
Dividends and distributed branch profits	3 332	−69	−91	−95	−96	−64	−121	−95	−208
Reinvested earnings and undistributed branch profits	3 333	....	....	....	....	....	....	....	....
Income on debt (interest)	3 334	....	....	....	....	....	....	....	....
Portfolio investment income	3 339	−3,876	−573	−447	−467	−519	−430	−382	−354
Income on equity	3 340	....	....	....	....	....	....	....	−19
Income on bonds and notes	3 350	−417	−377	−377	−357	−385	−272	−281	−323
Income on money market instruments	3 360	−3,460	−196	−70	−110	−135	−158	−102	−13
Other investment income	3 370	−503	−555	−646	−1,032	−1,192	−945	−757	−344
D. CURRENT TRANSFERS	4 379	**328**	**1,716**	**1,063**	**1,969**	**2,769**	**2,360**	**1,827**	**544**
Credit	2 379	**4,079**	**5,325**	**4,399**	**5,157**	**5,219**	**6,070**	**6,642**	**5,069**
General government	2 380	8	11	8	113	13	55	21	27
Other sectors	2 390	4,071	5,314	4,392	5,045	5,205	6,015	6,621	5,042
Workers' remittances	2 391	3,964	5,183	4,257	4,623	5,022	5,775	6,385	3,429
Other current transfers	2 392	108	132	134	422	183	240	236	1,613
Debit	3 379	**−3,751**	**−3,609**	**−3,337**	**−3,189**	**−2,450**	**−3,709**	**−4,815**	**−4,525**
General government	3 380	−4	−5	−8	−3	−10	−25	−24	−39
Other sectors	3 390	−3,747	−3,604	−3,329	−3,185	−2,440	−3,684	−4,791	−4,486
Workers' remittances	3 391	−3,694	−3,573	−3,281	−2,784	−2,365	−3,576	−4,715	−2,909
Other current transfers	3 392	−53	−31	−48	−401	−75	−108	−76	−1,577
CAPITAL AND FINANCIAL ACCOUNT	4 996	**1,336**	**5,139**	**3,356**	**3,931**	**7,679**	**5,766**	**9,783**	**3,005**
CAPITAL ACCOUNT	4 994	**29**	**50**	**27**	**1,940**	**590**	**410**	**18**	**345**
Total credit	2 994	*30*	*54*	*27*	*1,944*	*591*	*410*	*25*	*910*
Total debit	3 994	*−1*	*−3*	*....*	*−4*	*−1*	*....*	*−7*	*−565*
Capital transfers, credit	2 400	**30**	**54**	**27**	**1,944**	**591**	**410**	**24**	**410**
General government	2 401	30	54	27	1,944	591	410	24	26
Debt forgiveness	2 402	....	....	....	....	....	....	....	....
Other capital transfers	2 410	30	54	27	1,944	591	410	24	26
Other sectors	2 430	....	....	....	....	....	....	....	385
Migrants' transfers	2 431	....	....	....	....	....	....	....	271
Debt forgiveness	2 432	....	....	....	....	....	....	....	....
Other capital transfers	2 440	....	....	....	....	....	....	....	113
Capital transfers, debit	3 400	**−1**	**−3**	**....**	**−4**	**−1**	**....**	**−6**	**−207**
General government	3 401	−1	−3	....	−4	−1	....	−6	....
Debt forgiveness	3 402	....	....	....	....	....	....	....	....
Other capital transfers	3 410	−1	−3	....	−4	−1	....	−6	....
Other sectors	3 430	....	....	....	....	....	....	....	−207
Migrants' transfers	3 431	....	....	....	....	....	....	....	−52
Debt forgiveness	3 432	....	....	....	....	....	....	....	....
Other capital transfers	3 440	....	....	....	....	....	....	....	−154
Nonproduced nonfinancial assets, credit	2 480	**....**	**....**	**....**	**....**	**....**	**....**	**1**	**500**
Nonproduced nonfinancial assets, debit	3 480	**....**	**....**	**....**	**....**	**....**	**....**	**−1**	**−359**

Table 2 (Continued). STANDARD PRESENTATION, 2003–2010

(Millions of U.S. dollars)

	Code	2003	2004	2005	2006	2007	2008	2009	2010
FINANCIAL ACCOUNT	4 995	1,307	5,089	3,329	1,990	7,089	5,357	9,765	2,660
A. DIRECT INVESTMENT	4 500	2,249	1,072	1,908	1,800	2,528	3,346	3,678	4,381
Direct investment abroad	4 505	−611	−827	−715	−875	−848	−987	−1,126	−574
Equity capital	4 510	−611	−827	−715	−875	−848	−987	−1,126	−574
Claims on affiliated enterprises	4 515	−611	−827	−715	−875	−848	−987	−1,126	−574
Liabilities to affiliated enterprises	4 520	....	....	....	....	....	....	....	....
Reinvested earnings	4 525	....	....	....	....	....	....	....	....
Other capital	4 530	....	....	....	....	....	....	....	....
Claims on affiliated enterprises	4 535	....	....	....	....	....	....	....	....
Liabilities to affiliated enterprises	4 540	....	....	....	....	....	....	....	....
Direct investment in Lebanon	4 555	2,860	1,899	2,624	2,675	3,376	4,333	4,804	4,955
Equity capital	4 560	2,860	1,899	2,624	2,675	3,376	4,333	4,804	4,955
Claims on direct investors	4 565	....	....	....	....	....	....	....	....
Liabilities to direct investors	4 570	2,860	1,899	2,624	2,675	3,376	4,333	4,804	4,955
Reinvested earnings	4 575	....	....	....	....	....	....	....	....
Other capital	4 580	....	....	....	....	....	....	....	....
Claims on direct investors	4 585	....	....	....	....	....	....	....	....
Liabilities to direct investors	4 590	....	....	....	....	....	....	....	....
B. PORTFOLIO INVESTMENT	4 600	−129	−707	536	1,665	170	637	1,865	−1,124
Assets	4 602	−773	−614	−112	−358	−1,560	−566	−826	−1,016
Equity securities	4 610	−254	−349	−152	−206	−472	−403	−707	1,083
Monetary authorities	4 611	....	....	....	....	....	....	....	....
General government	4 612	−107	....	−1	−1	−3	....	....	....
Banks	4 613	−89	−294	−115	−201	46	−257	−241	33
Other sectors	4 614	−58	−55	−36	−3	−515	−146	−465	1,050
Debt securities	4 619	−519	−265	40	−152	−1,088	−163	−119	−2,099
Bonds and notes	4 620	−514	−274	39	−139	−989	−220	−53	−2,137
Monetary authorities	4 621	....	....	....	....	....	....	....	....
General government	4 622	....	....	....	....	....	....	....	....
Banks	4 623	−452	−218	64	−89	−995	−242	61	−876
Other sectors	4 624	−62	−55	−25	−51	6	22	−114	−1,260
Money market instruments	4 630	−5	8	1	−13	−99	57	−66	38
Monetary authorities	4 631	....	....	....	....	....	....	....	....
General government	4 632	....	....	....	....	....	....	....	....
Banks	4 633	−2	4	2	−12	−100	62	−71	37
Other sectors	4 634	−2	5	−1	−1	2	−5	5	1
Liabilities	4 652	644	−93	648	2,024	1,730	1,203	2,690	−108
Equity securities	4 660	207	148	1,436	551	791	466	929	−50
Banks	4 663	22	42	153	163	183	127	464	−13
Other sectors	4 664	185	106	1,283	388	609	339	465	−37
Debt securities	4 669	437	−241	−788	1,473	939	738	1,761	−58
Bonds and notes	4 670	563	−272	−642	1,448	925	738	1,627	−348
Monetary authorities	4 671	−50	−253	−313	1,752	35	−333	−108	−11
General government	4 672	−323	−1,285	−600	−1,073	−634	−435	−843	−430
Banks	4 673	93	171	152	143	112	276	1,215	87
Other sectors	4 674	843	1,095	119	625	1,412	1,231	1,362	6
Money market instruments	4 680	−127	32	−146	25	15	....	135	290
Monetary authorities	4 681	....	....	....	....	....	....	....	....
General government	4 682	−127	32	−146	25	15	....	135	142
Banks	4 683	....	....	....	....	....	....	....	−1
Other sectors	4 684	....	....	....	....	....	....	....	148
C. FINANCIAL DERIVATIVES	4 910	....	....	....	....	....	....	....	....
Monetary authorities	4 911	....	....	....	....	....	....	....	....
General government	4 912	....	....	....	....	....	....	....	....
Banks	4 913	....	....	....	....	....	....	....	....
Other sectors	4 914	....	....	....	....	....	....	....	....
Assets	4 900	....	....	....	....	....	....	....	....
Monetary authorities	4 901	....	....	....	....	....	....	....	....
General government	4 902	....	....	....	....	....	....	....	....
Banks	4 903	....	....	....	....	....	....	....	....
Other sectors	4 904	....	....	....	....	....	....	....	....
Liabilities	4 905	....	....	....	....	....	....	....	....
Monetary authorities	4 906	....	....	....	....	....	....	....	....
General government	4 907	....	....	....	....	....	....	....	....
Banks	4 908	....	....	....	....	....	....	....	....
Other sectors	4 909	....	....	....	....	....	....	....	....

Table 2 (Concluded). STANDARD PRESENTATION, 2003–2010

(Millions of U.S. dollars)

	Code	2003	2004	2005	2006	2007	2008	2009	2010
D. OTHER INVESTMENT	4 700 ..	**4,224**	**3,945**	**1,342**	**−1,225**	**3,803**	**8,747**	**13,158**	**2,443**
Assets	4 703 ..	**2,803**	**3,125**	**2,638**	**−1,598**	**529**	**7,819**	**5,083**	**2,074**
Trade credits	4 706 ..	....	....	....	....	....	....	....	....
General government	4 707 ..	....	....	....	....	....	....	....	....
of which: Short-term	4 709 ..	....	....	....	....	....	....	....	....
Other sectors	4 710 ..	....	....	....	....	....	....	....	....
of which: Short-term	4 712 ..	....	....	....	....	....	....	....	....
Loans	4 714 ..	1,562	4,541	3,645	4,981	5,205	4,943	7,496	4,723
Monetary authorities	4 715 ..	....	....	....	....	....	....	....	....
of which: Short-term	4 718 ..	....	....	....	....	....	....	....	....
General government	4 719 ..	−1	....	....	1	−6	−1	−8	....
of which: Short-term	4 721 ..	....	....	....	....	....	....	....	....
Banks	4 722 ..	1,561	4,515	3,599	4,687	5,213	4,663	7,559	4,790
of which: Short-term	4 724 ..	....	....	....	....	....	....	....	*4,790*
Other sectors	4 725 ..	2	26	46	293	−2	281	−56	−67
of which: Short-term	4 727 ..	....	....	....	....	....	....	....	*21*
Currency and deposits	4 730 ..	1,240	−1,415	−1,007	−6,579	−4,676	2,876	−2,413	−2,648
Monetary authorities	4 731 ..	....	....	....	....	....	....	....	....
General government	4 732 ..	−24	45	65	43	35	13	34	....
Banks	4 733 ..	1,651	−949	184	−3,070	−4,336	1,591	−4,739	−2,093
Other sectors	4 734 ..	−386	−511	−1,257	−3,552	−375	1,272	2,292	−555
Other assets	4 736 ..	....	....	....	....	....	....	....	....
Monetary authorities	4 737 ..	....	....	....	....	....	....	....	....
of which: Short-term	4 739 ..	....	....	....	....	....	....	....	....
General government	4 740 ..	....	....	....	....	....	....	....	....
of which: Short-term	4 742 ..	....	....	....	....	....	....	....	....
Banks	4 743 ..	....	....	....	....	....	....	....	....
of which: Short-term	4 745 ..	....	....	....	....	....	....	....	....
Other sectors	4 746 ..	....	....	....	....	....	....	....	....
of which: Short-term	4 748 ..	....	....	....	....	....	....	....	....
Liabilities	4 753 ..	**1,421**	**819**	**−1,296**	**373**	**3,274**	**928**	**8,075**	**368**
Trade credits	4 756 ..	....	....	....	....	....	....	....	....
General government	4 757 ..	....	....	....	....	....	....	....	....
of which: Short-term	4 759 ..	....	....	....	....	....	....	....	....
Other sectors	4 760 ..	....	....	....	....	....	....	....	....
of which: Short-term	4 762 ..	....	....	....	....	....	....	....	....
Loans	4 764 ..	488	−105	−368	−171	313	135	35	−182
Monetary authorities	4 765 ..	....	....	....	....	77	38	....	−20
of which: Use of Fund credit and loans from the Fund	4 766 ..	....	....	....	....	*77*	*38*	....	*−20*
of which: Short-term	4 768 ..	....	....	....	....	....	....	....	....
General government	4 769 ..	581	−12	−73	−49	290	164	−95	−149
of which: Short-term	4 771 ..	....	....	....	....	....	....	....	....
Banks	4 772 ..	−3	−7	−10	−41	12	26	168	....
of which: Short-term	4 774 ..	....	....	....	....	....	....	....	....
Other sectors	4 775 ..	−91	−86	−285	−81	−67	−94	−38	−14
of which: Short-term	4 777 ..	....	....	....	....	....	....	....	*−21*
Currency and deposits	4 780 ..	934	924	−928	544	2,962	793	7,744	550
Monetary authorities	4 781 ..	....	....	−22	2	244	93	−52	−160
General government	4 782 ..	31	−1	....	−2	10	5	−131	7
Banks	4 783 ..	....	....	−453	523	1,469	2,230	5,533	1,969
Other sectors	4 784 ..	903	925	−453	22	1,240	−1,534	2,393	−1,266
Other liabilities	4 786 ..	....	....	....	....	....	....	295	....
Monetary authorities	4 787 ..	....	....	....	....	....	....	295	....
of which: Short-term	4 789 ..	....	....	....	....	....	....	....	....
General government	4 790 ..	....	....	....	....	....	....	....	....
of which: Short-term	4 792 ..	....	....	....	....	....	....	....	....
Banks	4 793 ..	....	....	....	....	....	....	....	....
of which: Short-term	4 795 ..	....	....	....	....	....	....	....	....
Other sectors	4 796 ..	....	....	....	....	....	....	....	....
of which: Short-term	4 798 ..	....	....	....	....	....	....	....	....
E. RESERVE ASSETS	4 802 ..	**−5,037**	**780**	**−458**	**−250**	**588**	**−7,374**	**−8,935**	**−3,040**
Monetary gold	4 812 ..	....	....	....	....	....	....	....	....
Special drawing rights	4 811 ..	−1	−1	−1	−2	1	1	−294	1
Reserve position in the Fund	4 810 ..	....	....	....	....	....	....	....	....
Foreign exchange	4 803 ..	−5,037	781	−456	−248	587	−7,376	−8,641	−3,041
Other claims	4 813 ..	....	....	....	....	....	....	....	....
NET ERRORS AND OMISSIONS	4 998 ..	**3,802**	**−734**	**−608**	**−2,814**	**−6,074**	**−1,664**	**−3,042**	**6,411**

Table 1. ANALYTIC PRESENTATION, 2003–2010
(Millions of U.S. dollars)

	Code	2003	2004	2005	2006	2007	2008	2009	2010
A. Current Account[1]	4 993 Z.	**50.5**	**107.6**	**−16.9**	**82.6**	**98.5**	**143.7**	**−2.4**	**−421.4**
Goods: exports f.o.b.	2 100 ..	561.1	664.4	634.3	718.2	829.7	884.0	734.1	851.8
Goods: imports f.o.b.	3 100 ..	−1,032.1	−1,234.2	−1,289.4	−1,359.1	−1,506.2	−1,531.7	−1,587.2	−1,998.3
Balance on Goods	4 100 ..	*−471.0*	*−569.7*	*−655.1*	*−640.9*	*−676.5*	*−647.6*	*−853.0*	*−1,146.5*
Services: credit	2 200 ..	26.8	34.9	36.1	41.7	42.5	43.0	43.8	48.0
Services: debit	3 200 ..	−327.5	−372.1	−369.0	−351.8	−380.3	−371.3	−384.6	−516.2
Balance on Goods and Services	4 991 ..	*−771.8*	*−906.9*	*−988.1*	*−951.0*	*−1,014.2*	*−975.9*	*−1,193.9*	*−1,614.8*
Income: credit	2 300 ..	641.3	758.8	727.2	717.2	782.6	768.7	772.3	878.3
Income: debit	3 300 ..	−138.9	−185.1	−230.1	−259.9	−365.4	−341.8	−304.6	−346.3
Balance on Goods, Services, and Income	4 992 ..	*−269.4*	*−333.3*	*−490.9*	*−493.7*	*−597.0*	*−549.0*	*−726.2*	*−1,082.7*
Current transfers: credit	2 379 Z.	338.8	465.1	497.3	598.4	719.5	716.8	748.7	688.0
Current transfers: debit	3 379 ..	−19.0	−24.2	−23.3	−22.1	−24.0	−24.1	−24.8	−26.8
B. Capital Account[1]	4 994 Z.	**36.6**	**22.4**	**14.9**	**6.7**	**24.2**	**18.6**	**74.6**	**123.3**
Capital account: credit	2 994 Z.	46.7	33.4	21.3	11.0	32.0	23.6	79.6	142.6
Capital account: debit	3 994 ..	−10.1	−11.0	−6.4	−4.3	−7.9	−4.9	−4.9	−19.3
Total, Groups A Plus B	4 981 ..	*87.1*	*129.9*	*−2.0*	*89.3*	*122.7*	*162.3*	*72.3*	*−298.1*
C. Financial Account[1]	4 995 W.	**−80.7**	**−155.6**	**−46.5**	**−209.6**	**−95.1**	**−77.1**	**3.0**	**−135.6**
Direct investment abroad	4 505 ..	....	−.9	.9	−3.3	1.9	1.8	1.9	2.3
Direct investment in Lesotho	4 555 Z.	43.9	55.6	69.1	58.5	104.5	110.0	100.9	117.0
Portfolio investment assets	4 602 ..	−.7	−2.1	−.9	−1.6	−.2	−.2	−.2	−.2
Equity securities	4 610 ..	−.7	−1.6	....	....	.2	.2	.2	.2
Debt securities	4 619 ..	....	−.6	−.9	−1.7	−.4	−.3	−.3	−.4
Portfolio investment liabilities	4 652 Z.	.3	.8	....	1.3	.1	.1	.1	.2
Equity securities	4 660 ..	.3	.7	....	1.3	....	....	....	....
Debt securities	4 669 Z.	....	.1	....	....	.1	.1	.1	.1
Financial derivatives	4 910 ..	....	....	....	....	....	....	....	....
Financial derivatives assets	4 900 ..	....	....	....	....	....	....	....	....
Financial derivatives liabilities	4 905 ..	....	....	....	....	....	....	....	....
Other investment assets	4 703 ..	−126.4	−218.2	−151.0	−243.5	−225.7	−218.4	−174.7	−245.2
Monetary authorities	4 701 ..	....	....	....	....	....	....	....	....
General government	4 704 ..	....	....	....	....	....	....	....	....
Banks	4 705 ..	−8.8	−48.9	−.1	−87.8	−62.2	−73.4	−24.1	−82.9
Other sectors	4 728 ..	−117.6	−169.3	−150.9	−155.8	−163.5	−145.1	−150.6	−162.3
Other investment liabilities	4 753 W.	2.2	9.3	35.3	−20.9	24.2	29.6	74.9	−9.6
Monetary authorities	4 753 WA	−17.8	.9	94.2	−1.0	9.3	15.8	38.8	−10.4
General government	4 753 ZB	−10.0	1.6	−46.1	−13.0	7.4	5.2	−.3	18.1
Banks	4 753 ZC	19.2	−13.7	−13.6	−7.7	−.3	1.2	28.7	−26.5
Other sectors	4 753 ZD	10.9	20.5	.8	.8	7.8	7.4	7.7	9.2
Total, Groups A Through C	4 983 ..	*6.4*	*−25.7*	*−48.6*	*−120.3*	*27.6*	*85.2*	*75.2*	*−433.7*
D. Net Errors and Omissions	4 998 ..	**−71.2**	**29.4**	**92.2**	**311.0**	**242.3**	**188.2**	**−102.8**	**219.9**
Total, Groups A Through D	4 984 ..	*−64.8*	*3.8*	*43.7*	*190.8*	*269.9*	*273.4*	*−27.5*	*−213.8*
E. Reserves and Related Items	4 802 A.	**64.8**	**−3.8**	**−43.7**	**−190.8**	**−269.9**	**−273.4**	**27.5**	**213.8**
Reserve assets	4 802 ..	62.3	−13.6	−43.7	−190.3	−267.2	−268.4	33.5	209.9
Use of Fund credit and loans	4 766 ..	2.5	9.8	....	−.5	−2.7	−5.0	−5.9	4.0
Exceptional financing	4 920 ..	....	....	....	....	....	....	....	....
Conversion rates: maloti per U.S. dollar	0 101 ..	**7.565**	**6.460**	**6.359**	**6.772**	**7.045**	**8.261**	**8.474**	**7.321**

[1] Excludes components that have been classified in the categories of Group E.

2011, International Monetary Fund: *Balance of Payments Statistics Yearbook*

Table 2. STANDARD PRESENTATION, 2003–2010

(Millions of U.S. dollars)

	Code	2003	2004	2005	2006	2007	2008	2009	2010
CURRENT ACCOUNT	4 993	50.5	107.6	−16.9	82.6	98.5	143.7	−2.4	−421.4
A. GOODS	4 100	−471.0	−569.7	−655.1	−640.9	−676.5	−647.6	−853.0	−1,146.5
Credit	2 100	561.1	664.4	634.3	718.2	829.7	884.0	734.1	851.8
General merchandise: exports f.o.b.	2 110	561.1	664.4	634.3	718.2	829.7	884.0	734.1	851.8
Goods for processing: exports f.o.b.	2 150	....	....	....	....	....	....	....	....
Repairs on goods	2 160	....	....	....	....	....	....	....	....
Goods procured in ports by carriers	2 170	....	....	....	....	....	....	....	....
Nonmonetary gold	2 180	....	....	....	....	....	....	....	....
Debit	3 100	−1,032.1	−1,234.2	−1,289.4	−1,359.1	−1,506.2	−1,531.7	−1,587.2	−1,998.3
General merchandise: imports f.o.b.	3 110	−1,032.1	−1,234.2	−1,289.4	−1,359.1	−1,506.2	−1,531.7	−1,587.2	−1,998.3
Goods for processing: imports f.o.b.	3 150	....	....	....	....	....	....	....	....
Repairs on goods	3 160	....	....	....	....	....	....	....	....
Goods procured in ports by carriers	3 170	....	....	....	....	....	....	....	....
Nonmonetary gold	3 180	....	....	....	....	....	....	....	....
B. SERVICES	4 200	−300.8	−337.2	−333.0	−310.2	−337.7	−328.3	−340.9	−468.2
Total credit	2 200	*26.8*	*34.9*	*36.1*	*41.7*	*42.5*	*43.0*	*43.8*	*48.0*
Total debit	3 200	*−327.5*	*−372.1*	*−369.0*	*−351.8*	*−380.3*	*−371.3*	*−384.6*	*−516.2*
Transportation services, credit	2 205	.5	.6	.8	.7	.7	.6	.6	.7
Passenger	2 850	....	....	....	....	....	....	....	....
Freight	2 851	....	....	....	....	....	....	....	....
Other	2 852	*.5*	*.6*	*.8*	*.7*	*.7*	*.6*	*.6*	*.7*
Sea transport, passenger	2 207	....	....	....	....	....	....	....	....
Sea transport, freight	2 208	....	....	....	....	....	....	....	....
Sea transport, other	2 209	....	....	....	....	....	....	....	....
Air transport, passenger	2 211	....	....	....	....	....	....	....	....
Air transport, freight	2 212	....	....	....	....	....	....	....	....
Air transport, other	2 213	.5	.6	.8	.7	.7	.6	.6	.7
Other transport, passenger	2 215	....	....	....	....	....	....	....	....
Other transport, freight	2 216	....	....	....	....	....	....	....	....
Other transport, other	2 217	....	....	....	....	....	....	....	....
Transportation services, debit	3 205	−30.9	−38.5	−40.5	−37.1	−43.3	−47.5	−42.3	−68.7
Passenger	3 850	*−3.9*	*−6.6*	*−8.9*	*−3.0*	*−7.7*	*−5.4*	*−7.7*	*−8.4*
Freight	3 851	*−27.0*	*−31.9*	*−31.5*	*−34.1*	*−35.6*	*−42.1*	*−34.6*	*−60.4*
Other	3 852	....	....	....	....	....	....	....	....
Sea transport, passenger	3 207	....	....	....	....	....	....	....	....
Sea transport, freight	3 208	....	....	....	....	....	....	....	....
Sea transport, other	3 209	....	....	....	....	....	....	....	....
Air transport, passenger	3 211	−3.9	−6.6	−8.9	−3.0	−7.7	−5.4	−7.7	−8.4
Air transport, freight	3 212	....	....	....	....	....	....	....	....
Air transport, other	3 213	....	....	....	....	....	....	....	....
Other transport, passenger	3 215	....	....	....	....	....	....	....	....
Other transport, freight	3 216	−27.0	−31.9	−31.5	−34.1	−35.6	−42.1	−34.6	−60.4
Other transport, other	3 217	....	....	....	....	....	....	....	....
Travel, credit	2 236	20.7	25.8	27.1	29.4	30.8	30.2	29.9	34.4
Business travel	2 237	....	....	....	....	....	....	....	....
Personal travel	2 240	20.7	25.8	27.1	29.4	30.8	30.2	29.9	34.4
Travel, debit	3 236	−237.8	−271.0	−261.2	−246.7	−259.2	−245.5	−256.1	−309.8
Business travel	3 237	−213.4	−242.6	−236.1	−230.1	−244.6	−233.4	−244.4	−294.1
Personal travel	3 240	−24.3	−28.4	−25.1	−16.6	−14.6	−12.0	−11.7	−15.7
Other services, credit	2 200 BA	5.5	8.4	8.2	11.6	11.0	12.2	13.3	12.9
Communications	2 245	....	....	1.3	4.7	4.1	5.2	2.1	.9
Construction	2 249	....	....	....	....	....	....	....	....
Insurance	2 253	.1	.1	....	....	....	.3	.7	....
Financial	2 260	....	....	....	....	....	....	....	.1
Computer and information	2 262	.4	.6	.6	.6	.6	.6	.6	1.2
Royalties and licence fees	2 266	....	....	....	....	....	....	....	....
Other business services	2 268	1.7	3.7	2.1	2.2	2.2	2.4	4.0	6.3
Personal, cultural, and recreational	2 287	....	....	....	....	....	....	....	....
Government, n.i.e.	2 291	3.2	3.9	4.1	4.0	4.0	3.7	5.8	4.3
Other services, debit	3 200 BA	−58.8	−62.6	−67.3	−68.1	−77.8	−78.4	−86.2	−137.7
Communications	3 245	....	....	−2.0	−1.5	−2.7	−4.0	−5.0	−1.9
Construction	3 249	....	....	....	....	....	....	....	....
Insurance	3 253	−8.0	−10.7	−12.9	−11.9	−12.9	−14.6	−11.4	−14.1
Financial	3 260	−2.2	−2.7	−2.9	−2.9	−3.0	−2.9	−3.0	−5.9
Computer and information	3 262	−.8	−1.0	−1.1	−1.1	−1.1	−1.1	−1.1	−2.2
Royalties and licence fees	3 266	−1.3	−1.6	−1.7	−1.7	−1.7	−1.6	−1.7	−3.4
Other business services	3 268	−31.1	−36.5	−31.7	−28.9	−34.5	−29.4	−30.5	−73.1
Personal, cultural, and recreational	3 287	....	....	....	....	....	....	....	....
Government, n.i.e.	3 291	−15.5	−10.2	−15.1	−20.2	−21.8	−24.8	−33.5	−37.1

Table 2 (Continued). STANDARD PRESENTATION, 2003–2010

(Millions of U.S. dollars)

	Code	2003	2004	2005	2006	2007	2008	2009	2010
C. INCOME	4 300	**502.4**	**573.6**	**497.2**	**457.3**	**417.2**	**426.8**	**467.7**	**532.1**
Total credit	2 300	*641.3*	*758.8*	*727.2*	*717.2*	*782.6*	*768.7*	*772.3*	*878.3*
Total debit	3 300	*−138.9*	*−185.1*	*−230.1*	*−259.9*	*−365.4*	*−341.8*	*−304.6*	*−346.3*
Compensation of employees, credit	2 310	**551.4**	**621.0**	**597.6**	**580.2**	**618.9**	**590.3**	**616.8**	**738.5**
Compensation of employees, debit	3 310	....	....	....	....	....	....	....	....
Investment income, credit	2 320	**89.9**	**137.8**	**129.7**	**137.0**	**163.7**	**178.3**	**155.5**	**139.8**
Direct investment income	2 330	....	....	....	....	....	....	....	....
Dividends and distributed branch profits	2 332	....	....	....	....	....	....	....	....
Reinvested earnings and undistributed branch profits	2 333	....	....	....	....	....	....	....	....
Income on debt (interest)	2 334	....	....	....	....	....	....	....	....
Portfolio investment income	2 339	....	....	....	....	....	....	....	....
Income on equity	2 340	....	....	....	....	....	....	....	....
Income on bonds and notes	2 350	....	....	....	....	....	....	....	....
Income on money market instruments	2 360	....	....	....	....	....	....	....	....
Other investment income	2 370	89.9	137.8	129.7	137.0	163.7	178.3	155.5	....
Investment income, debit	3 320	**−138.9**	**−185.1**	**−230.1**	**−259.9**	**−365.4**	**−341.8**	**−304.6**	**−346.3**
Direct investment income	3 330	−125.4	−158.3	−191.6	−249.4	−301.2	−333.9	−296.4	−338.9
Dividends and distributed branch profits	3 332	−123.7	−156.1	−148.1	−193.8	−234.7	−260.3	−233.2	−266.7
Reinvested earnings and undistributed branch profits	3 333	−1.7	−2.1	−43.5	−55.6	−66.4	−73.6	−63.1	−72.2
Income on debt (interest)	3 334	....	....	....	....	....	....	....	....
Portfolio investment income	3 339	....	....	....	....	....	....	....	....
Income on equity	3 340	....	....	....	....	....	....	....	....
Income on bonds and notes	3 350	....	....	....	....	....	....	....	....
Income on money market instruments	3 360	....	....	....	....	....	....	....	....
Other investment income	3 370	−13.5	−26.9	−38.5	−10.5	−64.2	−7.9	−8.2	−7.4
D. CURRENT TRANSFERS	4 379	**319.8**	**440.9**	**474.0**	**576.3**	**695.5**	**692.7**	**723.8**	**661.2**
Credit	2 379	**338.8**	**465.1**	**497.3**	**598.4**	**719.5**	**716.8**	**748.7**	**688.0**
General government	2 380	229.6	334.0	362.4	458.2	592.6	594.2	614.8	524.4
Other sectors	2 390	109.2	131.0	134.8	140.2	126.9	122.6	133.9	163.6
Workers' remittances	2 391	5.5	6.2	6.0	5.8	6.2	5.9	6.2	7.4
Other current transfers	2 392	103.7	124.8	128.9	134.4	120.7	116.7	127.7	156.2
Debit	3 379	**−19.0**	**−24.2**	**−23.3**	**−22.1**	**−24.0**	**−24.1**	**−24.8**	**−26.8**
General government	3 380	−18.8	−24.0	−23.1	−22.0	−23.9	−24.0	−24.5	−26.1
Other sectors	3 390	−.2	−.2	−.1	....	−.1	−.1	−.3	−.7
Workers' remittances	3 391	....	....	....	....	....	....	....	....
Other current transfers	3 392	−.2	−.2	−.1	....	−.1	−.1	−.3	−.7
CAPITAL AND FINANCIAL ACCOUNT	4 996	**20.8**	**−137.0**	**−75.3**	**−393.6**	**−340.8**	**−331.8**	**105.1**	**201.6**
CAPITAL ACCOUNT	4 994	**36.6**	**22.4**	**14.9**	**6.7**	**24.2**	**18.6**	**74.6**	**123.3**
Total credit	2 994	*46.7*	*33.4*	*21.3*	*11.0*	*32.0*	*23.6*	*79.6*	*142.6*
Total debit	3 994	*−10.1*	*−11.0*	*−6.4*	*−4.3*	*−7.9*	*−4.9*	*−4.9*	*−19.3*
Capital transfers, credit	2 400	**46.7**	**33.4**	**21.3**	**11.0**	**32.0**	**23.6**	**79.6**	**142.6**
General government	2 401	46.7	33.4	21.3	11.0	32.0	23.6	79.6	142.6
Debt forgiveness	2 402	....	....	....	....	....	....	....	....
Other capital transfers	2 410	46.7	33.4	21.3	11.0	32.0	23.6	79.6	142.6
Other sectors	2 430	....	....	....	....	....	....	....	....
Migrants' transfers	2 431	....	....	....	....	....	....	....	....
Debt forgiveness	2 432	....	....	....	....	....	....	....	....
Other capital transfers	2 440	....	....	....	....	....	....	....	....
Capital transfers, debit	3 400	**−10.1**	**−11.0**	**−6.4**	**−4.3**	**−7.9**	**−4.9**	**−4.9**	**−19.3**
General government	3 401	....	....	....	....	....	....	....	....
Debt forgiveness	3 402	....	....	....	....	....	....	....	....
Other capital transfers	3 410	....	....	....	....	....	....	....	....
Other sectors	3 430	−10.1	−11.0	−6.4	−4.3	−7.9	−4.9	−4.9	−19.3
Migrants' transfers	3 431	−10.1	−11.0	−6.4	−4.3	−7.9	−4.9	−4.9	−19.3
Debt forgiveness	3 432	....	....	....	....	....	....	....	....
Other capital transfers	3 440	....	....	....	....	....	....	....	....
Nonproduced nonfinancial assets, credit	2 480	....	....	....	....	....	....	....	....
Nonproduced nonfinancial assets, debit	3 480	....	....	....	....	....	....	....	....

Table 2 (Continued). STANDARD PRESENTATION, 2003–2010

(Millions of U.S. dollars)

	Code	2003	2004	2005	2006	2007	2008	2009	2010
FINANCIAL ACCOUNT	4 995	−15.9	−159.3	−90.2	−400.4	−365.0	−350.5	30.5	78.3
A. DIRECT INVESTMENT	4 500	43.9	54.7	70.0	55.2	106.4	111.8	102.8	119.3
Direct investment abroad	4 505	....	−.9	.9	−3.3	1.9	1.8	1.9	2.3
Equity capital	4 510	....	−.8	.9	−3.3	.2	.2	.2	.3
Claims on affiliated enterprises	4 515	....	−.8	.9	−3.3	.2	.2	.2	.3
Liabilities to affiliated enterprises	4 520	....	....	....	....	....	....	....	....
Reinvested earnings	4 525	....	....	....	....	....	....	....	....
Other capital	4 530	....	−.1	....	....	1.7	1.6	1.7	2.0
Claims on affiliated enterprises	4 535	....	−.1	....	....	1.7	1.6	1.7	2.0
Liabilities to affiliated enterprises	4 540	....	....	....	....	....	....	....	....
Direct investment in Lesotho	4 555	43.9	55.6	69.1	58.5	104.5	110.0	100.9	117.0
Equity capital	4 560	42.2	53.5	26.5	....	34.4	32.9	34.2	40.5
Claims on direct investors	4 565	....	....	....	....	....	....	....	....
Liabilities to direct investors	4 570	42.2	53.5	26.5	....	34.4	32.9	34.2	40.5
Reinvested earnings	4 575	1.7	2.1	43.5	55.6	66.4	73.6	63.1	72.2
Other capital	4 580	....	....	−.8	3.0	3.7	3.5	3.6	4.3
Claims on direct investors	4 585	....	....	....	....	....	....	....	....
Liabilities to direct investors	4 590	....	....	....	....	....	....	....	....
B. PORTFOLIO INVESTMENT	4 600	−.3	−1.4	−.8	−.3	....	....	....	−.1
Assets	4 602	−.7	−2.1	−.9	−1.6	−.2	−.2	−.2	−.2
Equity securities	4 610	−.7	−1.6	....	....	.2	.2	.2	.2
Monetary authorities	4 611	....	....	....	....	....	....	....	....
General government	4 612	....	....	....	....	....	....	....	....
Banks	4 613	....	....	....	....	....	....	....	....
Other sectors	4 614	−.7	−1.6	....	....	.2	.2	.2	.2
Debt securities	4 619	....	−.6	−.9	−1.7	−.4	−.3	−.3	−.4
Bonds and notes	4 620	....	....	....	....	....	....	....	....
Monetary authorities	4 621	....	....	....	....	....	....	....	....
General government	4 622	....	....	....	....	....	....	....	....
Banks	4 623	....	....	....	....	....	....	....	....
Other sectors	4 624	....	....	....	....	....	....	....	....
Money market instruments	4 630	....	....	....	....	....	....	....	....
Monetary authorities	4 631	....	....	....	....	....	....	....	....
General government	4 632	....	....	....	....	....	....	....	....
Banks	4 633	....	....	....	....	....	....	....	....
Other sectors	4 634	....	....	....	....	....	....	....	....
Liabilities	4 652	.3	.8	....	1.3	.1	.1	.1	.2
Equity securities	4 660	.3	.7	....	1.3	....	....	....	....
Banks	4 663	....	....	....	....	....	....	....	....
Other sectors	4 664	.3	.7	....	1.3	....	....	....	....
Debt securities	4 669	....	.1	....	....	.1	.1	.1	.1
Bonds and notes	4 670	....	....	....	....	....	....	....	....
Monetary authorities	4 671	....	....	....	....	....	....	....	....
General government	4 672	....	....	....	....	....	....	....	....
Banks	4 673	....	....	....	....	....	....	....	....
Other sectors	4 674	....	....	....	....	....	....	....	....
Money market instruments	4 680	....	....	....	....	....	....	....	....
Monetary authorities	4 681	....	....	....	....	....	....	....	....
General government	4 682	....	....	....	....	....	....	....	....
Banks	4 683	....	....	....	....	....	....	....	....
Other sectors	4 684	....	....	....	....	....	....	....	....
C. FINANCIAL DERIVATIVES	4 910	....	....	....	....	....	....	....	....
Monetary authorities	4 911	....	....	....	....	....	....	....	....
General government	4 912	....	....	....	....	....	....	....	....
Banks	4 913	....	....	....	....	....	....	....	....
Other sectors	4 914	....	....	....	....	....	....	....	....
Assets	4 900	....	....	....	....	....	....	....	....
Monetary authorities	4 901	....	....	....	....	....	....	....	....
General government	4 902	....	....	....	....	....	....	....	....
Banks	4 903	....	....	....	....	....	....	....	....
Other sectors	4 904	....	....	....	....	....	....	....	....
Liabilities	4 905	....	....	....	....	....	....	....	....
Monetary authorities	4 906	....	....	....	....	....	....	....	....
General government	4 907	....	....	....	....	....	....	....	....
Banks	4 908	....	....	....	....	....	....	....	....
Other sectors	4 909	....	....	....	....	....	....	....	....

Table 2 (Concluded). STANDARD PRESENTATION, 2003–2010

(Millions of U.S. dollars)

	Code	2003	2004	2005	2006	2007	2008	2009	2010
D. OTHER INVESTMENT	4 700	**−121.7**	**−199.1**	**−115.7**	**−264.9**	**−204.1**	**−193.9**	**−105.8**	**−250.9**
Assets	4 703	**−126.4**	**−218.2**	**−151.0**	**−243.5**	**−225.7**	**−218.4**	**−174.7**	**−245.2**
Trade credits	4 706	−4.6	−10.6	−20.9	....	−2.8	−2.7	−2.8	−3.3
General government	4 707	....	....	....	....	....	....	....	....
of which: Short-term	4 709	....	....	....	....	....	....	....	....
Other sectors	4 710	−4.6	−10.6	−20.9	....	−2.8	−2.7	−2.8	−3.3
of which: Short-term	4 712	....	....	....	....	....	....	....	....
Loans	4 714	....	....	....	−.8	−1.0	−.9	−1.0	−1.9
Monetary authorities	4 715	....	....	....	....	....	....	....	....
of which: Short-term	4 718	....	....	....	....	....	....	....	....
General government	4 719	....	....	....	....	....	....	....	....
of which: Short-term	4 721	....	....	....	....	....	....	....	....
Banks	4 722	....	....	....	....	....	....	....	....
of which: Short-term	4 724	....	....	....	....	....	....	....	....
Other sectors	4 725	....	....	....	−.8	−1.0	−.9	−1.0	−1.9
of which: Short-term	4 727	....	....	....	....	....	....	....	....
Currency and deposits	4 730	−120.8	−205.2	−131.4	−242.4	−222.3	−215.2	−171.4	−240.7
Monetary authorities	4 731	....	....	....	....	....	....	....	....
General government	4 732	....	....	....	....	....	....	....	....
Banks	4 733	−8.8	−48.9	−.1	−87.8	−62.2	−73.4	−24.1	−82.9
Other sectors	4 734	−112.0	−156.2	−131.3	−154.7	−160.1	−141.8	−147.3	−157.8
Other assets	4 736	−1.0	−2.4	1.3	−.3	.4	.4	.4	.7
Monetary authorities	4 737	....	....	....	....	....	....	....	....
of which: Short-term	4 739	....	....	....	....	....	....	....	....
General government	4 740	....	....	....	....	....	....	....	....
of which: Short-term	4 742	....	....	....	....	....	....	....	....
Banks	4 743	....	....	....	....	....	....	....	....
of which: Short-term	4 745	....	....	....	....	....	....	....	....
Other sectors	4 746	−1.0	−2.4	1.3	−.3	.4	.4	.4	.7
of which: Short-term	4 748	....	....	....	....	....	....	....	....
Liabilities	4 753	**4.7**	**19.1**	**35.3**	**−21.4**	**21.6**	**24.6**	**69.0**	**−5.7**
Trade credits	4 756	6.3	14.7	21.5	−.1	4.3	4.1	4.3	5.1
General government	4 757	....	....	....	....	....	....	....	....
of which: Short-term	4 759	....	....	....	....	....	....	....	....
Other sectors	4 760	6.3	14.7	21.5	−.1	4.3	4.1	4.3	5.1
of which: Short-term	4 762	....	....	....	....	....	....	....	....
Loans	4 764	−3.3	16.4	−66.7	−13.2	7.0	2.4	−4.0	24.8
Monetary authorities	4 765	2.5	9.8	....	−.5	−2.7	−5.0	−5.9	4.0
of which: Use of Fund credit and loans from the Fund	4 766	2.5	9.8	....	−.5	−2.7	−5.0	−5.9	4.0
of which: Short-term	4 768	....	....	....	....	....	....	....	....
General government	4 769	−10.0	1.6	−46.1	−13.0	7.4	5.2	−.3	18.1
of which: Short-term	4 771	....	....	....	....	....	....	....	....
Banks	4 772	....	....	....	....	....	....	....	....
of which: Short-term	4 774	....	....	....	....	....	....	....	....
Other sectors	4 775	4.2	5.0	−20.7	.4	2.3	2.2	2.3	2.7
of which: Short-term	4 777	....	....	....	....	....	....	....	....
Currency and deposits	4 780	1.4	−12.8	80.6	−8.7	9.1	17.0	22.0	−36.9
Monetary authorities	4 781	−17.8	.9	94.2	−1.0	9.3	15.8	−6.8	−10.4
General government	4 782	....	....	....	....	....	....	....	....
Banks	4 783	19.2	−13.7	−13.6	−7.7	−.3	1.2	28.7	−26.5
Other sectors	4 784	....	....	....	....	....	....	....	....
Other liabilities	4 786	.3	.8	−.1	.5	1.2	1.1	46.7	1.4
Monetary authorities	4 787	....	....	....	....	....	....	45.5	....
of which: Short-term	4 789	....	....	....	....	....	....	....	....
General government	4 790	....	....	....	....	....	....	....	....
of which: Short-term	4 792	....	....	....	....	....	....	....	....
Banks	4 793	....	....	....	....	....	....	....	....
of which: Short-term	4 795	....	....	....	....	....	....	....	....
Other sectors	4 796	.3	.8	−.1	.5	1.2	1.1	1.2	1.4
of which: Short-term	4 798	.3	.8	−.1	.5	1.2	1.1	1.2	1.4
E. RESERVE ASSETS	4 802	**62.3**	**−13.6**	**−43.7**	**−190.3**	**−267.2**	**−268.4**	**33.5**	**209.9**
Monetary gold	4 812	....	....	....	....	....	....	....	....
Special drawing rights	4 811	....	....	.1	.2	−6.0	.6	−43.2	−4.0
Reserve position in the Fund	4 810	....	....	−.1	....	....	....	....	....
Foreign exchange	4 803	63.2	−14.7	−40.4	−190.7	−259.0	−267.9	75.9	212.1
Other claims	4 813	−.9	1.1	−3.4	.2	−2.3	−1.1	.7	1.8
NET ERRORS AND OMISSIONS	4 998	**−71.2**	**29.4**	**92.2**	**311.0**	**242.3**	**188.2**	**−102.8**	**219.9**

Table 3. INTERNATIONAL INVESTMENT POSITION (End-period stocks), 2003–2010

(Millions of U.S. dollars)

	Code	2003	2004	2005	2006	2007	2008	2009	2010
ASSETS	8 995 C.	**629.4**	**818.0**	**769.4**	**970.4**	**1,336.6**	**1,295.4**	**1,626.6**	**1,666.5**
Direct investment abroad	8 505 ..	....	....	....	....	....	....	....	....
Equity capital and reinvested earnings	8 506 ..	....	....	....	....	....	....	....	....
Claims on affiliated enterprises	8 507 ..	....	....	....	....	....	....	....	....
Liabilities to affiliated enterprises	8 508 ..	....	....	....	....	....	....	....	....
Other capital	8 530 ..	....	....	....	....	....	....	....	....
Claims on affiliated enterprises	8 535 ..	....	....	....	....	....	....	....	....
Liabilities to affiliated enterprises	8 540 ..	....	....	....	....	....	....	....	....
Portfolio investment	8 602 ..	....	....	....	....	....	....	....	....
Equity securities	8 610 ..	....	....	....	....	....	....	....	....
Monetary authorities	8 611 ..	....	....	....	....	....	....	....	....
General government	8 612 ..	....	....	....	....	....	....	....	....
Banks	8 613 ..	....	....	....	....	....	....	....	....
Other sectors	8 614 ..	....	....	....	....	....	....	....	....
Debt securities	8 619 ..	....	....	....	....	....	....	....	....
Bonds and notes	8 620 ..	....	....	....	....	....	....	....	....
Monetary authorities	8 621 ..	....	....	....	....	....	....	....	....
General government	8 622 ..	....	....	....	....	....	....	....	....
Banks	8 623 ..	....	....	....	....	....	....	....	....
Other sectors	8 624 ..	....	....	....	....	....	....	....	....
Money market instruments	8 630 ..	....	....	....	....	....	....	....	....
Monetary authorities	8 631 ..	....	....	....	....	....	....	....	....
General government	8 632 ..	....	....	....	....	....	....	....	....
Banks	8 633 ..	....	....	....	....	....	....	....	....
Other sectors	8 634 ..	....	....	....	....	....	....	....	....
Financial derivatives	8 900 ..	....	....	....	....	....	....	....	....
Monetary authorities	8 901 ..	....	....	....	....	....	....	....	....
General government	8 902 ..	....	....	....	....	....	....	....	....
Banks	8 903 ..	....	....	....	....	....	....	....	....
Other sectors	8 904 ..	....	....	....	....	....	....	....	....
Other investment	8 703 ..	**126.1**	**222.7**	**196.3**	**264.8**	**333.9**	**323.9**	**446.8**	**590.7**
Trade credits	8 706 ..	....	....	....	....	....	....	....	....
General government	8 707 ..	....	....	....	....	....	....	....	....
of which: Short-term	8 709 ..	....	....	....	....	....	....	....	....
Other sectors	8 710 ..	....	....	....	....	....	....	....	....
of which: Short-term	8 712 ..	....	....	....	....	....	....	....	....
Loans	8 714 ..	....	....	....	....	....	....	....	....
Monetary authorities	8 715 ..	....	....	....	....	....	....	....	....
of which: Short-term	8 718 ..	....	....	....	....	....	....	....	....
General government	8 719 ..	....	....	....	....	....	....	....	....
of which: Short-term	8 721 ..	....	....	....	....	....	....	....	....
Banks	8 722 ..	....	....	....	....	....	....	....	....
of which: Short-term	8 724 ..	....	....	....	....	....	....	....	....
Other sectors	8 725 ..	....	....	....	....	....	....	....	....
of which: Short-term	8 727 ..	....	....	....	....	....	....	....	....
Currency and deposits	8 730 ..	....	....	....	....	....	....	....	....
Monetary authorities	8 731 ..	....	....	....	....	....	....	....	....
General government	8 732 ..	....	....	....	....	....	....	....	....
Banks	8 733 ..	....	....	....	....	....	....	....	....
Other sectors	8 734 ..	....	....	196.3	264.8	333.9	323.9	446.8	590.7
Other assets	8 736 ..	126.1	222.7	196.3	264.8	333.9	323.9	446.8	590.7
Monetary authorities	8 737 ..	....	....	....	....	....	....	....	....
of which: Short-term	8 739 ..	....	....	....	....	....	....	....	....
General government	8 740 ..	....	....	....	....	....	....	....	....
of which: Short-term	8 742 ..	....	....	....	....	....	....	....	....
Banks	8 743 ..	126.1	222.7	196.3	264.8	333.9	323.9	446.8	590.7
of which: Short-term	8 745 ..	*126.1*	*222.7*	*196.3*	*264.8*	*333.9*	*323.9*	*446.8*	*590.7*
Other sectors	8 746 ..	....	....	....	....	....	....	....	....
of which: Short-term	8 748 ..	....	....	....	....	....	....	....	....
Reserve assets	8 802 ..	**503.2**	**595.3**	**573.1**	**705.6**	**1,002.8**	**971.5**	**1,179.8**	**1,075.8**
Monetary gold	8 812 ..	....	....	....	....	....	....	....	....
Special drawing rights	8 811 ..	.6	.6	.4	.2	6.3	5.5	49.0	52.6
Reserve position in the Fund	8 810 ..	5.3	5.5	5.1	5.4	5.7	5.6	5.7	5.6
Foreign exchange	8 803 ..	384.9	431.5	299.0	300.8	411.2	431.1	611.1	456.6
Other claims	8 813 ..	112.4	157.7	268.5	399.2	579.5	529.3	514.1	561.0

Table 3 (Concluded). INTERNATIONAL INVESTMENT POSITION (End-period stocks), 2003–2010

(Millions of U.S. dollars)

	Code	2003	2004	2005	2006	2007	2008	2009	2010
LIABILITIES	8 995 D.	**802.1**	**881.0**	**773.0**	**772.2**	**822.9**	**812.8**	**906.9**	**935.3**
Direct investment in Lesotho	8 555 ..	....	....	....	....	....	....	....	....
Equity capital and reinvested earnings	8 556 ..	....	....	....	....	....	....	....	....
Claims on direct investors	8 557 ..	....	....	....	....	....	....	....	....
Liabilities to direct investors	8 558 ..	....	....	....	....	....	....	....	....
Other capital	8 580 ..	....	....	....	....	....	....	....	....
Claims on direct investors	8 585 ..	....	....	....	....	....	....	....	....
Liabilities to direct investors	8 590 ..	....	....	....	....	....	....	....	....
Portfolio investment	8 652 ..	....	....	....	....	....	....	....	....
Equity securities	8 660 ..	....	....	....	....	....	....	....	....
Banks	8 663 ..	....	....	....	....	....	....	....	....
Other sectors	8 664 ..	....	....	....	....	....	....	....	....
Debt securities	8 669 ..	....	....	....	....	....	....	....	....
Bonds and notes	8 670 ..	....	....	....	....	....	....	....	....
Monetary authorities	8 671 ..	....	....	....	....	....	....	....	....
General government	8 672 ..	....	....	....	....	....	....	....	....
Banks	8 673 ..	....	....	....	....	....	....	....	....
Other sectors	8 674 ..	....	....	....	....	....	....	....	....
Money market instruments	8 680 ..	....	....	....	....	....	....	....	....
Monetary authorities	8 681 ..	....	....	....	....	....	....	....	....
General government	8 682 ..	....	....	....	....	....	....	....	....
Banks	8 683 ..	....	....	....	....	....	....	....	....
Other sectors	8 684 ..	....	....	....	....	....	....	....	....
Financial derivatives	8 905 ..	....	....	....	....	....	....	....	....
Monetary authorities	8 906 ..	....	....	....	....	....	....	....	....
General government	8 907 ..	....	....	....	....	....	....	....	....
Banks	8 908 ..	....	....	....	....	....	....	....	....
Other sectors	8 909 ..	....	....	....	....	....	....	....	....
Other investment	8 753 ..	**802.1**	**881.0**	**773.0**	**772.2**	**822.9**	**812.8**	**906.9**	**935.3**
Trade credits	8 756 ..	....	....	....	....	....	....	....	....
General government	8 757 ..	....	....	....	....	....	....	....	....
of which: Short-term	8 759 ..	....	....	....	....	....	....	....	....
Other sectors	8 760 ..	....	....	....	....	....	....	....	....
of which: Short-term	8 762 ..	....	....	....	....	....	....	....	....
Loans	8 764 ..	694.0	768.6	669.3	684.0	722.7	723.6	721.0	774.8
Monetary authorities	8 765 ..	26.6	38.0	35.0	36.3	35.4	29.7	24.1	28.2
of which: Use of Fund credit and loans from the Fund	8 766 ..	*26.6*	*38.0*	*35.0*	*36.3*	*35.4*	*29.7*	*24.1*	*28.2*
of which: Short-term	8 768 ..	....	....	....	....	....	....	....	....
General government	8 769 ..	667.5	730.5	634.2	647.7	687.3	693.9	696.9	746.6
of which: Short-term	8 771 ..	....	....	....	....	....	....	....	....
Banks	8 772 ..	....	....	....	....	....	....	....	....
of which: Short-term	8 774 ..	....	....	....	....	....	....	....	....
Other sectors	8 775 ..	....	....	....	....	....	....	....	....
of which: Short-term	8 777 ..	....	....	....	....	....	....	....	....
Currency and deposits	8 780 ..	34.6	24.1	16.9	10.5	10.8	10.0	42.1	17.7
Monetary authorities	8 781 ..	....	....	....	....	....	....	....	....
General government	8 782 ..	....	....	....	....	....	....	....	....
Banks	8 783 ..	34.6	24.1	16.9	10.5	10.8	10.0	42.1	17.7
Other sectors	8 784 ..	....	....	....	....	....	....	....	....
Other liabilities	8 786 ..	73.5	88.3	86.9	77.7	89.4	79.3	143.8	142.7
Monetary authorities	8 787 ..	73.5	88.3	86.9	77.7	89.4	79.3	143.8	142.7
of which: Short-term	8 789 ..	*73.5*	*88.3*	*86.9*	*77.7*	*89.4*	*79.3*	*92.2*	*92.1*
General government	8 790 ..	....	....	....	....	....	....	....	....
of which: Short-term	8 792 ..	....	....	....	....	....	....	....	....
Banks	8 793 ..	....	....	....	....	....	....	....	....
of which: Short-term	8 795 ..	....	....	....	....	....	....	....	....
Other sectors	8 796 ..	....	....	....	....	....	....	....	....
of which: Short-term	8 798 ..	....	....	....	....	....	....	....	....
NET INTERNATIONAL INVESTMENT POSITION	8 995 ..	**−172.8**	**−63.0**	**−3.6**	**198.2**	**513.7**	**482.6**	**719.7**	**731.2**
Conversion rates: maloti per U.S. dollar (end of period)	0 102 ..	**6.640**	**5.630**	**6.325**	**6.970**	**6.810**	**9.305**	**7.380**	**6.632**

Table 1. ANALYTIC PRESENTATION, 2003–2010

(Millions of U.S. dollars)

	Code	2003	2004	2005	2006	2007	2008	2009	2010
A. Current Account[1]	4 993 Z.	....	−172.5	−207.5	−368.9	−395.1	−618.2	−541.1	−737.8
Goods: exports f.o.b.	2 100 ..	....	104.8	132.3	154.6	196.2	249.0	180.0	241.5
Goods: imports f.o.b.	3 100 ..	....	−278.9	−306.4	−441.1	−498.5	−728.8	−559.0	−719.9
Balance on Goods	4 100 ..	....	*−174.1*	*−174.1*	*−286.5*	*−302.3*	*−479.8*	*−379.0*	*−478.4*
Services: credit	2 200 ..	....	212.4	213.2	336.5	346.2	509.6	274.1	158.2
Services: debit	3 200 ..	....	−779.8	−855.5	−1,274.6	−1,248.8	−1,411.1	−1,145.2	−1,079.9
Balance on Goods and Services	4 991 ..	....	*−741.5*	*−816.4*	*−1,224.6*	*−1,204.9*	*−1,381.4*	*−1,250.1*	*−1,400.1*
Income: credit	2 300 ..	....	5.0	9.2	18.3	19.9	22.4	18.1	31.3
Income: debit	3 300 ..	....	−167.6	−155.8	−166.7	−176.9	−170.7	−145.9	−7.0
Balance on Goods, Services, and Income	4 992 ..	....	*−904.1*	*−963.0*	*−1,372.9*	*−1,361.9*	*−1,529.7*	*−1,377.9*	*−1,375.8*
Current transfers: credit	2 379 Z.	....	731.6	755.4	1,004.1	966.8	911.5	836.8	638.1
Current transfers: debit	3 379 ..	....	....	....	....	....	....	....	....
B. Capital Account[1]	4 994 Z.	....	....	....	....	....	1,197.0	1,526.0	1,596.1
Capital account: credit	2 994 Z.	....	....	....	....	....	1,197.0	1,526.0	1,596.1
Capital account: debit	3 994 ..	....	....	....	....	....	....	....	....
Total, Groups A Plus B	4 981 ..	....	*−172.5*	*−207.5*	*−368.9*	*−395.1*	*578.8*	*984.9*	*858.4*
C. Financial Account[1]	4 995 W.	....	**52.2**	**61.1**	**86.6**	**113.5**	**347.9**	**576.7**	**447.4**
Direct investment abroad	4 505 ..	....	....	....	....	....	....	....	....
Direct investment in Liberia	4 555 Z.	....	75.4	82.8	107.9	131.6	394.5	217.8	452.9
Portfolio investment assets	4 602 ..	....	....	....	....	....	....	....	....
Equity securities	4 610 ..	....	....	....	....	....	....	....	....
Debt securities	4 619 ..	....	....	....	....	....	....	....	....
Portfolio investment liabilities	4 652 Z.	....	....	....	....	....	....	....	....
Equity securities	4 660 ..	....	....	....	....	....	....	....	....
Debt securities	4 669 Z.	....	....	....	....	....	....	....	....
Financial derivatives	4 910 ..	....	....	....	....	....	....	....	....
Financial derivatives assets	4 900 ..	....	....	....	....	....	....	....	....
Financial derivatives liabilities	4 905 ..	....	....	....	....	....	....	....	....
Other investment assets	4 703 ..	....	−3.3	−3.1	−15.5	−13.2	−33.2	200.4	1.4
Monetary authorities	4 701 ..	....	−3.3	−3.1	−15.5	−13.2	−33.2	200.4	1.4
General government	4 704 ..	....	....	....	....	....	....	....	....
Banks	4 705 ..	....	....	....	....	....	....	....	....
Other sectors	4 728 ..	....	....	....	....	....	....	....	....
Other investment liabilities	4 753 W.	....	−19.9	−18.7	−5.7	−4.9	−13.4	158.5	−6.8
Monetary authorities	4 753 WA	....	....	....	....	....	....	160.8	....
General government	4 753 ZB	....	−19.9	−18.7	−5.7	−4.9	−13.4	−2.3	−6.8
Banks	4 753 ZC	....	....	....	....	....	....	....	....
Other sectors	4 753 ZD	....	....	....	....	....	....	....	....
Total, Groups A Through C	4 983 ..	....	*−120.4*	*−146.5*	*−282.2*	*−281.6*	*926.7*	*1,561.6*	*1,305.8*
D. Net Errors and Omissions	4 998 ..	....	**−46.9**	**−34.5**	**−20.5**	**2.4**	**−465.1**	**10.8**	**847.1**
Total, Groups A Through D	4 984 ..	....	*−167.3*	*−181.0*	*−302.8*	*−279.2*	*461.6*	*1,572.4*	*2,152.9*
E. Reserves and Related Items	4 802 A.	....	**167.3**	**181.0**	**302.8**	**279.2**	**−461.6**	**−1,572.4**	**−2,152.9**
Reserve assets	4 802 ..	....	−5.3	−2.3	−38.6	−38.8	−72.4	−328.0	−87.0
Use of Fund credit and loans	4 766 ..	....	....	−.1	−.7	−.7	545.0	17.7	−791.9
Exceptional financing	4 920 ..	....	172.6	183.4	342.1	318.7	−934.1	−1,262.1	−1,274.1
Conversion rates: Liberian dollar per U.S. dollar	0 101 ..	59.3788	54.9058	57.0958	58.0133	61.2722	63.2075	68.2867	71.3200

[1] Excludes components that have been classified in the categories of Group E.

Table 2. STANDARD PRESENTATION, 2003–2010

(Millions of U.S. dollars)

	Code	2003	2004	2005	2006	2007	2008	2009	2010
CURRENT ACCOUNT............................	4 993	....	**−159.7**	**−183.5**	**−172.8**	**−223.2**	**−354.3**	**−277.2**	**−415.7**
A. GOODS..	4 100	....	**−174.1**	**−174.1**	**−286.5**	**−302.3**	**−479.8**	**−379.0**	**−478.4**
Credit..	2 100	....	**104.8**	**132.3**	**154.6**	**196.2**	**249.0**	**180.0**	**241.5**
General merchandise: exports f.o.b..........	2 110	....	103.8	131.3	153.0	189.1	233.6	155.2	218.6
Goods for processing: exports f.o.b..........	2 150	....	....	....	....	....	....	....	....
Repairs on goods..................................	2 160	....	....	....	....	....	....	....	....
Goods procured in ports by carriers.........	2 170	....	.9	1.0	1.5	1.6	2.1	10.6	2.9
Nonmonetary gold................................	2 180	....	....	....		.2	5.5	13.3	14.2	20.0
Debit...	3 100	....	**−278.9**	**−306.4**	**−441.1**	**−498.5**	**−728.8**	**−559.0**	**−719.9**
General merchandise: imports f.o.b..........	3 110	....	−278.9	−306.4	−441.1	−498.5	−728.8	−559.0	−719.9
Goods for processing: imports f.o.b..........	3 150	....	....	....	....	....	....	....	....
Repairs on goods..................................	3 160	....	....	....	....	....	....	....	....
Goods procured in ports by carriers.........	3 170	....	....	....	....	....	....	....	....
Nonmonetary gold................................	3 180	....	....	....	....	....	....	....	....
B. SERVICES.....................................	4 200	....	**−567.4**	**−642.2**	**−938.1**	**−902.6**	**−901.5**	**−871.1**	**−921.7**
Total credit..	2 200	....	*212.4*	*213.2*	*336.5*	*346.2*	*509.6*	*274.1*	*158.2*
Total debit...	3 200	....	*−779.8*	*−855.5*	*−1,274.6*	*−1,248.8*	*−1,411.1*	*−1,145.2*	*−1,079.9*
Transportation services, credit..........	2 205	....	**7.1**	**11.1**	**15.0**	**20.2**	**19.2**	**14.9**	**22.2**
Passenger..	2 850	....	....	....	....	....	....	....	....
Freight..	2 851	....	....	....	....	....	....	....	....
Other..	2 852	....	*7.1*	*11.1*	*15.0*	*20.2*	*19.2*	*14.9*	*22.2*
Sea transport, passenger.......................	2 207	....	....	....	....	....	....	....	....
Sea transport, freight............................	2 208	....	....	....	....	....	....	....	....
Sea transport, other..............................	2 209	....	6.4	10.0	13.6	18.4	19.2	14.9	18.5
Air transport, passenger........................	2 211	....	....	....	....	....	....	....	....
Air transport, freight.............................	2 212	....	....	....	....	....	....	....	....
Air transport, other...............................	2 213	....	.7	1.1	1.5	1.7	....	....	1.9
Other transport, passenger....................	2 215	....	....	....	....	....	....	....	....
Other transport, freight.........................	2 216	....	....	....	....	....	....	....	....
Other transport, other...........................	2 217	....	....	....	....	....	....	....	1.9
Transportation services, debit...........	3 205	....	**−72.6**	**−80.3**	**−114.5**	**−127.2**	**−230.7**	**−84.9**	**−126.6**
Passenger..	3 850	....	*−15.3*	*−17.4*	*−23.7*	*−27.3*	*−28.4*	*−22.4*	*−70.6*
Freight..	3 851	....	*−57.4*	*−62.9*	*−90.8*	*−99.9*	*−202.4*	*−62.5*	*−56.0*
Other..	3 852	....	....	....	....	....	....	....	....
Sea transport, passenger.......................	3 207	....	....	....	....	....	....	....	....
Sea transport, freight............................	3 208	....	−54.5	−59.7	−86.3	−94.9	−192.2	−59.3	−53.2
Sea transport, other..............................	3 209	....	....	....	....	....	....	....	....
Air transport, passenger........................	3 211	....	−15.3	−17.4	−23.7	−27.3	−28.4	−22.4	−70.6
Air transport, freight.............................	3 212	....	−2.9	−3.1	−4.5	−5.0	−10.1	−3.1	−2.8
Air transport, other...............................	3 213	....	....	....	....	....	....	....	....
Other transport, passenger....................	3 215	....	....	....	....	....	....	....	....
Other transport, freight.........................	3 216	....	....	....	....	....	....	....	....
Other transport, other...........................	3 217	....	....	....	....	....	....	....	....
Travel, credit..................................	2 236	....	**58.6**	**67.2**	**124.4**	**131.1**	**158.0**	**123.3**	**12.4**
Business travel....................................	2 237	....	58.6	67.2	124.4	131.1	158.0	123.3	12.4
Personal travel....................................	2 240	....	....	....	....	....	....	....	....
Travel, debit...................................	3 236	....	**−13.9**	**−15.7**	**−17.3**	**−20.9**	**−30.3**	**−28.7**	**−63.2**
Business travel....................................	3 237	....	−4.5	−4.9	−2.7	−3.3	−3.5	−4.2	−2.4
Personal travel....................................	3 240	....	−9.4	−10.7	−14.6	−17.7	−26.9	−24.5	−60.8
Other services, credit......................	2 200 BA	....	**146.6**	**134.9**	**197.1**	**194.9**	**332.4**	**135.9**	**123.6**
Communications..................................	2 245	....	....	....	....	....	....	....	....
Construction.......................................	2 249	....	....	....	....	....	....	....	....
Insurance...	2 253	....	....	....	....	....	....	....	....
Financial..	2 260	....	....	....	....	....	....	....	....
Computer and information.....................	2 262	....	....	....	....	....	....	....	....
Royalties and licence fees.....................	2 266	....	....	....	....	....	....	....	....
Other business services.........................	2 268	....	2.5	2.8	3.8	4.3	4.5	4.3	5.2
Personal, cultural, and recreational.........	2 287	....	....	....	....	....	....	....	....
Government, n.i.e.................................	2 291	....	144.2	132.1	193.3	190.6	327.8	131.6	118.3
Other services, debit........................	3 200 BA	....	**−693.3**	**−759.5**	**−1,142.8**	**−1,100.6**	**−1,150.1**	**−1,031.5**	**−890.1**
Communications..................................	3 245	....	....	....	....	....	....	....	....
Construction.......................................	3 249	....	....	....	....	....	....	....	....
Insurance...	3 253	....	−3.1	−3.5	−4.8	−5.3	−10.7	−3.3	−2.9
Financial..	3 260	....	....	....	....	....	....	....	....
Computer and information.....................	3 262	....	....	....	....	....	....	....	....
Royalties and licence fees.....................	3 266	....	....	....	....	....	....	....	....
Other business services.........................	3 268	....	....	....	−44.8	−42.4	−46.7	−31.1	−27.9
Personal, cultural, and recreational.........	3 287	....	....	....	−35.5	−23.1	−26.1	7.3	−13.2
Government, n.i.e.................................	3 291	....	−690.2	−756.0	−1,057.7	−1,029.9	−1,066.7	−1,004.5	−846.0

Table 2 (Continued). STANDARD PRESENTATION, 2003–2010

(Millions of U.S. dollars)

	Code	2003	2004	2005	2006	2007	2008	2009	2010
C. INCOME................................	4 300 ..	....	−162.6	−146.6	−148.3	−157.0	−148.3	−127.8	24.3
Total credit................................	2 300 ..	....	*5.0*	*9.2*	*18.3*	*19.9*	*22.4*	*18.1*	*31.3*
Total debit................................	3 300 ..	....	*−167.6*	*−155.8*	*−166.7*	*−176.9*	*−170.7*	*−145.9*	*−7.0*
Compensation of employees, credit..................	2 310 ..	....	5.0	9.2	18.3	19.9	22.4	18.1	31.3
Compensation of employees, debit..................	3 310 ..	....	−.2	−.2	−.2	−.3	−.5	−1.0	−1.1
Investment income, credit........................	2 320 ..	....	....	....	....	....	....	....	....
Direct investment income........................	2 330 ..	....	....	....	....	....	....	....	....
Dividends and distributed branch profits.......................	2 332 ..	....	....	....	....	....	....	....	....
Reinvested earnings and undistributed branch profits.....	2 333 ..	....	....	....	....	....	....	....	....
Income on debt (interest).........................	2 334 ..	....	....	....	....	....	....	....	....
Portfolio investment income.........................	2 339 ..	....	....	....	....	....	....	....	....
Income on equity................................	2 340 ..	....	....	....	....	....	....	....	....
Income on bonds and notes......................	2 350 ..	....	....	....	....	....	....	....	....
Income on money market instruments....................	2 360 ..	....	....	....	....	....	....	....	....
Other investment income.........................	2 370 ..	....	....	....	....	....	....	....	....
Investment income, debit........................	3 320 ..	....	−167.4	−155.6	−166.4	−176.6	−170.2	−144.9	−5.9
Direct investment income........................	3 330 ..	....	−5.7	−7.1	−14.0	−14.7	−22.5	−5.8	−.1
Dividends and distributed branch profits......................	3 332 ..	....	−2.8	−3.5	−7.0	−7.3	−11.3	−2.9	
Reinvested earnings and undistributed branch profits.....	3 333 ..	....	−2.8	−3.5	−7.0	−7.3	−11.3	−2.9	
Income on debt (interest).........................	3 334 ..	....	....	....	....	....	....	....	
Portfolio investment income.........................	3 339 ..	....	....	....	....	....	....	....	
Income on equity................................	3 340 ..	....	....	....	....	....	....	....	
Income on bonds and notes......................	3 350 ..	....	....	....	....	....	....	....	
Income on money market instruments....................	3 360 ..	....	....	....	....	....	....	....	
Other investment income.........................	3 370 ..	....	−161.8	−148.6	−152.4	−161.9	−147.7	−139.1	−5.8
D. CURRENT TRANSFERS........................	4 379 ..	....	744.4	779.4	1,200.1	1,138.8	1,175.4	1,100.7	960.1
Credit..	2 379 ..	....	744.4	779.4	1,200.1	1,138.8	1,175.4	1,100.7	960.1
General government........................	2 380 ..	....	689.3	755.0	1,137.0	1,094.1	1,137.0	1,091.0	959.9
Other sectors........................	2 390 ..	....	55.1	24.4	63.1	44.7	38.3	9.7	.2
Workers' remittances........................	2 391 ..	....	53.4	22.6	60.5	42.1	35.7	7.0	.2
Other current transfers........................	2 392 ..	....	1.6	1.8	2.7	2.6	2.6	2.6	....
Debit..	3 379 ..	....	....	....	....	....	....	....	....
General government........................	3 380 ..	....	....	....	....	....	....	....	....
Other sectors........................	3 390 ..	....	....	....	....	....	....	....	....
Workers' remittances........................	3 391 ..	....	....	....	....	....	....	....	....
Other current transfers........................	3 392 ..	....	....	....	....	....	....	....	....
CAPITAL AND FINANCIAL ACCOUNT........................	4 996 ..	....	206.7	218.1	193.3	220.7	819.5	266.4	−431.4
CAPITAL ACCOUNT........................	4 994 ..	....	....	....	....	....	1,197.0	1,526.0	1,596.1
Total credit........................	2 994 ..	....	....	....	....	....	*1,197.0*	*1,526.0*	*1,596.1*
Total debit........................	3 994 ..	....	....	....	....	....	....	....	....
Capital transfers, credit........................	2 400 ..	....	....	....	....	....	1,197.0	1,526.0	1,596.1
General government........................	2 401 ..	....				....	1,197.0	1,526.0	1,596.1
Debt forgiveness........................	2 402 ..	....					1,197.0	1,526.0	1,596.1
Other capital transfers........................	2 410 ..	....					....	....	....
Other sectors........................	2 430 ..	....					....	....	....
Migrants' transfers........................	2 431 ..	....					....	....	....
Debt forgiveness........................	2 432 ..	....					....	....	....
Other capital transfers........................	2 440 ..	....					....	....	....
Capital transfers, debit........................	3 400 ..	....	....	....	....	....	....	....	....
General government........................	3 401 ..	....					....	....	....
Debt forgiveness........................	3 402 ..	....					....	....	....
Other capital transfers........................	3 410 ..	....					....	....	....
Other sectors........................	3 430 ..	....					....	....	....
Migrants' transfers........................	3 431 ..	....					....	....	....
Debt forgiveness........................	3 432 ..	....					....	....	....
Other capital transfers........................	3 440 ..	....					....	....	....
Nonproduced nonfinancial assets, credit............	2 480 ..	....	....	....	....	....	....	....	....
Nonproduced nonfinancial assets, debit............	3 480 ..	....	....	....	....	....	....	....	....

Table 2 (Continued). STANDARD PRESENTATION, 2003–2010

(Millions of U.S. dollars)

	Code	2003	2004	2005	2006	2007	2008	2009	2010
FINANCIAL ACCOUNT..	4 995 ..	....	206.7	218.1	193.3	220.7	−377.5	−1,259.6	−2,027.5
A. DIRECT INVESTMENT.................................	4 500 ..	....	75.4	82.8	107.9	131.6	394.5	217.8	452.9
Direct investment abroad...................................	4 505 ..	....	....	....	....	....	....	....	....
Equity capital...	4 510 ..	....	....	....	....	....	....	....	....
Claims on affiliated enterprises.............................	4 515 ..	....	....	....	....	....	....	....	....
Liabilities to affiliated enterprises.........................	4 520 ..	....	....	....	....	....	....	....	....
Reinvested earnings...	4 525 ..	....	....	....	....	....	....	....	....
Other capital..	4 530 ..	....	....	....	....	....	....	....	....
Claims on affiliated enterprises.............................	4 535 ..	....	....	....	....	....	....	....	....
Liabilities to affiliated enterprises.........................	4 540 ..	....	....	....	....	....	....	....	....
Direct investment in Liberia......................	4 555 ..	....	75.4	82.8	107.9	131.6	394.5	217.8	452.9
Equity capital...	4 560 ..	....	....	....	....	....	....	....	....
Claims on direct investors.....................................	4 565 ..	....	....	....	....	....	....	....	....
Liabilities to direct investors.................................	4 570 ..	....	....	....	....	....	....	....	....
Reinvested earnings...	4 575 ..	....	2.8	3.5	7.0	7.3	11.3	2.9	....
Other capital..	4 580 ..	....	72.5	79.3	100.8	124.3	383.3	214.9	452.8
Claims on direct investors.....................................	4 585 ..	....	....	....	....	....	111.0	90.0	....
Liabilities to direct investors.................................	4 590 ..	....	72.5	79.3	100.8	124.3	272.3	124.9	452.8
B. PORTFOLIO INVESTMENT...........................	4 600 ..	....	....	....	....	....	....	....	....
Assets..	4 602 ..	....	....	....	....	....	....	....	....
Equity securities..	4 610 ..	....	....	....	....	....	....	....	....
Monetary authorities...	4 611 ..	....	....	....	....	....	....	....	....
General government..	4 612 ..	....	....	....	....	....	....	....	....
Banks..	4 613 ..	....	....	....	....	....	....	....	....
Other sectors...	4 614 ..	....	....	....	....	....	....	....	....
Debt securities...	4 619 ..	....	....	....	....	....	....	....	....
Bonds and notes..	4 620 ..	....	....	....	....	....	....	....	....
Monetary authorities...	4 621 ..	....	....	....	....	....	....	....	....
General government..	4 622 ..	....	....	....	....	....	....	....	....
Banks..	4 623 ..	....	....	....	....	....	....	....	....
Other sectors...	4 624 ..	....	....	....	....	....	....	....	....
Money market instruments....................................	4 630 ..	....	....	....	....	....	....	....	....
Monetary authorities...	4 631 ..	....	....	....	....	....	....	....	....
General government..	4 632 ..	....	....	....	....	....	....	....	....
Banks..	4 633 ..	....	....	....	....	....	....	....	....
Other sectors...	4 634 ..	....	....	....	....	....	....	....	....
Liabilities..	4 652 ..	....	....	....	....	....	....	....	....
Equity securities..	4 660 ..	....	....	....	....	....	....	....	....
Banks..	4 663 ..	....	....	....	....	....	....	....	....
Other sectors...	4 664 ..	....	....	....	....	....	....	....	....
Debt securities...	4 669 ..	....	....	....	....	....	....	....	....
Bonds and notes..	4 670 ..	....	....	....	....	....	....	....	....
Monetary authorities...	4 671 ..	....	....	....	....	....	....	....	....
General government..	4 672 ..	....	....	....	....	....	....	....	....
Banks..	4 673 ..	....	....	....	....	....	....	....	....
Other sectors...	4 674 ..	....	....	....	....	....	....	....	....
Money market instruments....................................	4 680 ..	....	....	....	....	....	....	....	....
Monetary authorities...	4 681 ..	....	....	....	....	....	....	....	....
General government..	4 682 ..	....	....	....	....	....	....	....	....
Banks..	4 683 ..	....	....	....	....	....	....	....	....
Other sectors...	4 684 ..	....	....	....	....	....	....	....	....
C. FINANCIAL DERIVATIVES.............................	4 910 ..	....	....	....	....	....	....	....	....
Monetary authorities...	4 911 ..	....	....	....	....	....	....	....	....
General government..	4 912 ..	....	....	....	....	....	....	....	....
Banks..	4 913 ..	....	....	....	....	....	....	....	....
Other sectors...	4 914 ..	....	....	....	....	....	....	....	....
Assets..	4 900 ..	....	....	....	....	....	....	....	....
Monetary authorities...	4 901 ..	....	....	....	....	....	....	....	....
General government..	4 902 ..	....	....	....	....	....	....	....	....
Banks..	4 903 ..	....	....	....	....	....	....	....	....
Other sectors...	4 904 ..	....	....	....	....	....	....	....	....
Liabilities..	4 905 ..	....	....	....	....	....	333.	....	....
Monetary authorities...	4 906 ..	....	....	....	....	....	....	....	....
General government..	4 907 ..	....	....	....	....	....	....	....	....
Banks..	4 908 ..	....	....	....	....	....	....	....	....
Other sectors...	4 909 ..	....	....	....	....	....	....	....	....

2011, International Monetary Fund: *Balance of Payments Statistics Yearbook*

Table 2 (Concluded). STANDARD PRESENTATION, 2003–2010

(Millions of U.S. dollars)

	Code	2003	2004	2005	2006	2007	2008	2009	2010
D. OTHER INVESTMENT	4 700	. . . .	136.6	137.6	124.1	127.9	−699.6	−1,149.4	−2,393.5
Assets	4 703	. . . .	−3.3	−3.1	−15.5	−13.2	−33.2	200.4	1.4
Trade credits	4 706	. . . .	. . . .	. . . .	. . . .	. . . .	. . . .	. . . .	. . . .
General government	4 707	. . . .	. . . .	. . . .	. . . .	. . . .	. . . .	. . . .	. . . .
of which: Short-term	4 709	. . . .	. . . .	. . . .	. . . .	. . . .	. . . .	. . . .	. . . .
Other sectors	4 710	. . . .	. . . .	. . . .	. . . .	. . . .	. . . .	. . . .	. . . .
of which: Short-term	4 712	. . . .	. . . .	. . . .	. . . .	. . . .	. . . .	. . . .	. . . .
Loans	4 714	. . . .	. . . .	. . . .	. . . .	. . . .	. . . .	. . . .	. . . .
Monetary authorities	4 715	. . . .	. . . .	. . . .	. . . .	. . . .	. . . .	. . . .	. . . .
of which: Short-term	4 718	. . . .	. . . .	. . . .	. . . .	. . . .	. . . .	. . . .	. . . .
General government	4 719	. . . .	. . . .	. . . .	. . . .	. . . .	. . . .	. . . .	. . . .
of which: Short-term	4 721	. . . .	. . . .	. . . .	. . . .	. . . .	. . . .	. . . .	. . . .
Banks	4 722	. . . .	. . . .	. . . .	. . . .	. . . .	. . . .	. . . .	. . . .
of which: Short-term	4 724	. . . .	. . . .	. . . .	. . . .	. . . .	. . . .	. . . .	. . . .
Other sectors	4 725	. . . .	. . . .	. . . .	. . . .	. . . .	. . . .	. . . .	. . . .
of which: Short-term	4 727	. . . .	. . . .	. . . .	. . . .	. . . .	. . . .	. . . .	. . . .
Currency and deposits	4 730	. . . .	−3.3	−3.1	−15.5	−13.2	−33.2	200.4	1.4
Monetary authorities	4 731	. . . .	−3.3	−3.1	−15.5	−13.2	−33.2	200.4	1.4
General government	4 732	. . . .	. . . .	. . . .	. . . .	. . . .	. . . .	. . . .	. . . .
Banks	4 733	. . . .	. . . .	. . . .	. . . .	. . . .	. . . .	. . . .	. . . .
Other sectors	4 734	. . . .	. . . .	. . . .	. . . .	. . . .	. . . .	. . . .	. . . .
Other assets	4 736	. . . .	. . . .	. . . .	. . . .	. . . .	. . . .	. . . .	. . . .
Monetary authorities	4 737	. . . .	. . . .	. . . .	. . . .	. . . .	. . . .	. . . .	. . . .
of which: Short-term	4 739	. . . .	. . . .	. . . .	. . . .	. . . .	. . . .	. . . .	. . . .
General government	4 740	. . . .	. . . .	. . . .	. . . .	. . . .	. . . .	. . . .	. . . .
of which: Short-term	4 742	. . . .	. . . .	. . . .	. . . .	. . . .	. . . .	. . . .	. . . .
Banks	4 743	. . . .	. . . .	. . . .	. . . .	. . . .	. . . .	. . . .	. . . .
of which: Short-term	4 745	. . . .	. . . .	. . . .	. . . .	. . . .	. . . .	. . . .	. . . .
Other sectors	4 746	. . . .	. . . .	. . . .	. . . .	. . . .	. . . .	. . . .	. . . .
of which: Short-term	4 748	. . . .	. . . .	. . . .	. . . .	. . . .	. . . .	. . . .	. . . .
Liabilities	4 753	. . . .	140.0	140.7	139.6	141.1	−666.4	−1,349.8	−2,394.9
Trade credits	4 756	. . . .	. . . .	. . . .	. . . .	. . . .	. . . .	. . . .	. . . .
General government	4 757	. . . .	. . . .	. . . .	. . . .	. . . .	. . . .	. . . .	. . . .
of which: Short-term	4 759	. . . .	. . . .	. . . .	. . . .	. . . .	. . . .	. . . .	. . . .
Other sectors	4 760	. . . .	. . . .	. . . .	. . . .	. . . .	. . . .	. . . .	. . . .
of which: Short-term	4 762	. . . .	. . . .	. . . .	. . . .	. . . .	. . . .	. . . .	. . . .
Loans	4 764	. . . .	−19.9	−18.8	−6.4	−5.7	530.6	15.4	−798.7
Monetary authorities	4 765	. . . .	. . . .	−.1	−.7	−.7	545.0	17.7	−791.9
of which: Use of Fund credit and loans from the Fund	4 766	. . . .	. . . .	−.1	−.7	−.7	545.0	17.7	−791.9
of which: Short-term	4 768	. . . .	. . . .	. . . .	. . . .	. . . .	. . . .	. . . .	. . . .
General government	4 769	. . . .	−19.9	−18.7	−5.7	−4.9	−13.4	−2.3	−6.8
of which: Short-term	4 771	. . . .	. . . .	. . . .	. . . .	. . . .	. . . .	. . . .	. . . .
Banks	4 772	. . . .	. . . .	. . . .	. . . .	. . . .	−1.0	. . . .	. . . .
of which: Short-term	4 774	. . . .	. . . .	. . . .	. . . .	. . . .	−1.0	. . . .	. . . .
Other sectors	4 775	. . . .	. . . .	. . . .	. . . .	. . . .	. . . .	. . . .	. . . .
of which: Short-term	4 777	. . . .	. . . .	. . . .	. . . .	. . . .	. . . .	. . . .	. . . .
Currency and deposits	4 780	. . . .	. . . .	. . . .	. . . .	. . . .	. . . .	. . . .	. . . .
Monetary authorities	4 781	. . . .	. . . .	. . . .	. . . .	. . . .	. . . .	. . . .	. . . .
General government	4 782	. . . .	. . . .	. . . .	. . . .	. . . .	. . . .	. . . .	. . . .
Banks	4 783	. . . .	. . . .	. . . .	. . . .	. . . .	. . . .	. . . .	. . . .
Other sectors	4 784	. . . .	. . . .	. . . .	. . . .	. . . .	. . . .	. . . .	. . . .
Other liabilities	4 786	. . . .	159.8	159.4	146.0	146.8	−1,197.0	−1,365.2	−1,596.1
Monetary authorities	4 787	. . . .	. . . .	. . . .	. . . .	. . . .	. . . .	160.8	. . . .
of which: Short-term	4 789	. . . .	. . . .	. . . .	. . . .	. . . .	. . . .	. . . .	. . . .
General government	4 790	. . . .	159.8	159.4	146.0	146.8	−1,197.0	−1,526.0	−1,596.1
of which: Short-term	4 792	. . . .	159.8	159.4	146.0	146.8	−1,197.0	−1,526.0	−1,596.1
Banks	4 793	. . . .	. . . .	. . . .	. . . .	. . . .	. . . .	. . . .	. . . .
of which: Short-term	4 795	. . . .	. . . .	. . . .	. . . .	. . . .	. . . .	. . . .	. . . .
Other sectors	4 796	. . . .	. . . .	. . . .	. . . .	. . . .	. . . .	. . . .	. . . .
of which: Short-term	4 798	. . . .	. . . .	. . . .	. . . .	. . . .	. . . .	. . . .	. . . .
E. RESERVE ASSETS	4 802	. . . .	−5.3	−2.3	−38.6	−38.8	−72.4	−328.0	−87.0
Monetary gold	4 812	. . . .	. . . .	. . . .	. . . .	. . . .	. . . .	. . . .	. . . .
Special drawing rights	4 811	. . . .	. . . .	. . . .	. . . .	. . . .	−22.4	−178.3	−12.4
Reserve position in the Fund	4 810	. . . .	. . . .	. . . .	. . . .	. . . .	. . . .	. . . .	. . . .
Foreign exchange	4 803	. . . .	−5.3	−2.3	−38.6	−38.8	−50.1	−149.7	−74.5
Other claims	4 813	. . . .	. . . .	. . . .	. . . .	. . . .	. . . .	. . . .	. . . .
NET ERRORS AND OMISSIONS	4 998	. . . .	−46.9	−34.5	−20.5	2.4	−465.1	10.8	847.1

Table 1. ANALYTIC PRESENTATION, 2003–2010

(Millions of U.S. dollars)

	Code	2003	2004	2005	2006	2007	2008	2009	2010
A. Current Account[1]	4 993 Z.	**3,402**	**4,616**	**14,945**	**22,170**	**28,510**	**35,702**	**9,381**	**16,801**
Goods: exports f.o.b.	2 100 ..	12,878	17,425	28,849	37,473	46,970	61,950	37,055	48,935
Goods: imports f.o.b.	3 100 ..	−7,200	−8,768	−11,174	−13,219	−17,701	−21,658	−22,002	−24,559
Balance on Goods	4 100 ..	*5,678*	*8,657*	*17,675*	*24,254*	*29,269*	*40,292*	*15,053*	*24,376*
Services: credit	2 200 ..	442	437	534	489	109	208	385	410
Services: debit	3 200 ..	−1,597	−1,914	−2,349	−2,564	−2,665	−4,344	−5,063	−6,127
Balance on Goods and Services	4 991 ..	*4,523*	*7,180*	*15,860*	*22,179*	*26,712*	*36,155*	*10,375*	*18,659*
Income: credit	2 300 ..	1,689	1,339	1,837	2,180	4,517	4,471	2,461	2,318
Income: debit	3 300 ..	−1,149	−1,394	−2,118	−2,775	−2,500	−3,885	−1,883	−2,348
Balance on Goods, Services, and Income	4 992 ..	*5,063*	*7,125*	*15,579*	*21,584*	*28,729*	*36,742*	*10,953*	*18,629*
Current transfers: credit	2 379 Z.	255	254	418	1,646	598	45	....	....
Current transfers: debit	3 379 ..	−1,916	−2,763	−1,052	−1,060	−817	−1,085	−1,572	−1,828
B. Capital Account[1]	4 994 Z.	....	....	....	....	....	....	....	....
Capital account: credit	2 994 Z.	....	....	....	....	....	....	....	....
Capital account: debit	3 994 ..	....	....	....	....	....	....	....	....
Total, Groups A Plus B	4 981 ..	*3,402*	*4,616*	*14,945*	*22,170*	*28,510*	*35,702*	*9,381*	*16,801*
C. Financial Account[1]	4 995 W.	**−166**	**−238**	**392**	**−4,731**	**−9,542**	**−21,039**	**−5,525**	**−10,339**
Direct investment abroad	4 505 ..	−63	−286	−128	−474	−3,933	−5,888	−1,165	−2,722
Direct investment in Libya	4 555 Z.	143	357	1,038	2,064	4,689	4,111	1,371	1,784
Portfolio investment assets	4 602 ..	−607	−187	−393	−5,198	−1,440	−10,964	−3,352	−4,396
Equity securities	4 610 ..	−18	27	−47	−60	−1,440	−10,964	−3,352	−4,396
Debt securities	4 619 ..	−589	−214	−346	−5,138	....	....	....	....
Portfolio investment liabilities	4 652 Z.	....	....	....	....	....	....	....	....
Equity securities	4 660 ..	....	....	....	....	....	....	....	....
Debt securities	4 669 Z.	....	....	....	....	....	....	....	....
Financial derivatives	4 910 ..	....	....	....	....	....	....	....	....
Financial derivatives assets	4 900 ..	....	....	....	....	....	....	....	....
Financial derivatives liabilities	4 905 ..	....	....	....	....	....	....	....	....
Other investment assets	4 703 ..	−163	−1,767	−416	−1,194	−8,947	−8,280	−3,952	−4,889
Monetary authorities	4 701 ..	....	....	....	....	....	....	....	....
General government	4 704 ..	6	....	....	....	−8,263	−8,753	−3,668	−3,670
Banks	4 705 ..	−152	−2,077	328	291	1,969	254	−284	−1,219
Other sectors	4 728 ..	−17	310	−744	−1,485	−2,653	220	....	....
Other investment liabilities	4 753 W.	524	1,645	291	71	88	−19	1,573	−116
Monetary authorities	4 753 WA	−7	....	....	....	4	....	1,611	26
General government	4 753 ZB	....	....	....	....	....	....	....	....
Banks	4 753 ZC	548	1,855	224	387	−4	....	139	−143
Other sectors	4 753 ZD	−17	−210	67	−316	88	−19	−177	1
Total, Groups A Through C	4 983 ..	*3,236*	*4,378*	*15,337*	*17,439*	*18,968*	*14,662*	*3,856*	*6,462*
D. Net Errors and Omissions	4 998 ..	**1,890**	**1,733**	**−1,497**	**2,008**	**1,076**	**−1,715**	**1,333**	**−2,292**
Total, Groups A Through D	4 984 ..	*5,126*	*6,111*	*13,840*	*19,447*	*20,044*	*12,948*	*5,188*	*4,170*
E. Reserves and Related Items	4 802 A.	**−5,126**	**−6,111**	**−13,840**	**−19,447**	**−20,044**	**−12,948**	**−5,188**	**−4,170**
Reserve assets	4 802 ..	−5,126	−6,040	−13,840	−19,447	−20,044	−12,948	−5,188	−4,170
Use of Fund credit and loans	4 766 ..	....	....	....	....	....	....	....	....
Exceptional financing	4 920 ..	....	−71	....	....	....	....	....	....
Conversion rates: Libyan dinars per U.S. dollar	0 101 ..	**1.29294**	**1.30497**	**1.30838**	**1.31357**	**1.26264**	**1.22356**	**1.25353**	**1.26679**

[1] Excludes components that have been classified in the categories of Group E.

Table 2. STANDARD PRESENTATION, 2003–2010

(Millions of U.S. dollars)

	Code	2003	2004	2005	2006	2007	2008	2009	2010
CURRENT ACCOUNT..	4 993 ..	**3,402**	**4,616**	**14,945**	**22,170**	**28,510**	**35,702**	**9,381**	**16,801**
A. GOODS...	4 100 ..	**5,678**	**8,657**	**17,675**	**24,254**	**29,269**	**40,292**	**15,053**	**24,376**
Credit..	2 100 ..	**12,878**	**17,425**	**28,849**	**37,473**	**46,970**	**61,950**	**37,055**	**48,935**
General merchandise: exports f.o.b................	2 110 ..	12,878	17,425	28,849	37,473	46,929	61,950	37,055	48,935
Goods for processing: exports f.o.b...............	2 150 ..	....	....	....	....	41	....	....	....
Repairs on goods..	2 160 ..	....	....	....	....	....	....	....	....
Goods procured in ports by carriers...............	2 170 ..	....	....	....	....	....	....	....	....
Nonmonetary gold...	2 180 ..	....	....	....	....	....	....	....	....
Debit..	3 100 ..	**−7,200**	**−8,768**	**−11,174**	**−13,219**	**−17,701**	**−21,658**	**−22,002**	**−24,559**
General merchandise: imports f.o.b................	3 110 ..	−7,200	−8,768	−11,174	−13,219	−17,701	−21,658	−22,002	−24,559
Goods for processing: imports f.o.b...............	3 150 ..	....	....	....	....	....	....	....	....
Repairs on goods..	3 160 ..	....	....	....	....	....	....	....	....
Goods procured in ports by carriers...............	3 170 ..	....	....	....	....	....	....	....	....
Nonmonetary gold...	3 180 ..	....	....	....	....	....	....	....	....
B. SERVICES..	4 200 ..	**−1,155**	**−1,477**	**−1,815**	**−2,075**	**−2,557**	**−4,137**	**−4,678**	**−5,717**
Total credit...	2 200 ..	*442*	*437*	*534*	*489*	*109*	*208*	*385*	*410*
Total debit..	3 200 ..	*−1,597*	*−1,914*	*−2,349*	*−2,564*	*−2,665*	*−4,344*	*−5,063*	*−6,127*
Transportation services, credit............	2 205 ..	**58**	**63**	**116**	**128**	**25**	**118**	**262**	**263**
Passenger..	2 850 ..	*38*	*43*	*51*	*54*	*25*	*25*	*109*	*110*
Freight..	2 851 ..	*20*	*20*	*65*	*74*	....	*93*	*153*	*153*
Other..	2 852 ..	....	....	....	....	....	....	....	....
Sea transport, passenger..............................	2 207 ..	2	2	2	2	....	....	....	....
Sea transport, freight...................................	2 208 ..	20	20	25	30	....	93	153	153
Sea transport, other.....................................	2 209 ..	....	....	....	....	....	....	....	....
Air transport, passenger...............................	2 211 ..	16	16	19	20	25	25	109	110
Air transport, freight....................................	2 212 ..	....	....	....	....	....	....	....	....
Air transport, other......................................	2 213 ..	....	....	....	....	....	....	....	....
Other transport, passenger...........................	2 215 ..	20	25	30	32	....	....	....	....
Other transport, freight................................	2 216 ..	....	....	40	44	....	....	....	....
Other transport, other..................................	2 217 ..	....	....	....	....	....	....	....	....
Transportation services, debit.............	3 205 ..	**−661**	**−766**	**−1,016**	**−1,182**	**−1,263**	**−1,485**	**−2,070**	**−2,340**
Passenger..	3 850 ..	*−132*	*−186*	*−240*	*−247*	*−121*	*−62*	*−96*	*−137*
Freight..	3 851 ..	*−529*	*−580*	*−776*	*−935*	*−1,142*	*−1,397*	*−1,958*	*−2,186*
Other..	3 852 ..	....	....	....	....	....	*−26*	*−16*	*−16*
Sea transport, passenger..............................	3 207 ..	....	....	....	....	....	....	....	....
Sea transport, freight...................................	3 208 ..	−481	−522	−691	−840	−952	−1,164	−1,713	−1,913
Sea transport, other.....................................	3 209 ..	....	....	....	....	....	−26	−16	−16
Air transport, passenger...............................	3 211 ..	−132	−186	−225	−230	−121	−62	−96	−137
Air transport, freight....................................	3 212 ..	−48	−58	−60	−65	−190	−233	−245	−273
Air transport, other......................................	3 213 ..	....	....	....	....	....	....	....	....
Other transport, passenger...........................	3 215 ..	....	....	−15	−17	....	....	....	....
Other transport, freight................................	3 216 ..	....	....	−25	−30	....	....	....	....
Other transport, other..................................	3 217 ..	....	....	....	....	....	....	....	....
Travel, credit.......................................	2 236 ..	**205**	**218**	**250**	**190**	**74**	**74**	**50**	**60**
Business travel...	2 237 ..	200	211	241	180	....	....	....	....
Personal travel...	2 240 ..	5	7	9	10	74	74	50	60
Travel, debit...	3 236 ..	**−557**	**−603**	**−680**	**−668**	**−889**	**−1,277**	**−1,587**	**−2,047**
Business travel...	3 237 ..	−23	−21	−25	−30	−130	−213	−288	−394
Personal travel...	3 240 ..	−534	−582	−655	−638	−759	−1,065	−1,299	−1,653
Other services, credit...........................	2 200 BA	**179**	**156**	**168**	**171**	**9**	**16**	**73**	**88**
Communications...	2 245 ..	11	10	10	12	9	11	10	12
Construction..	2 249 ..	....	....	....	....	....	....	....	....
Insurance..	2 253 ..	55	60	43	55	....	5	63	76
Financial...	2 260 ..	....	....	....	....	....	....	....	....
Computer and information............................	2 262 ..	....	....	....	....	....	....	....	....
Royalties and licence fees............................	2 266 ..	....	....	....	....	....	....	....	....
Other business services...............................	2 268 ..	....	....	....	....	....	....	....	....
Personal, cultural, and recreational...............	2 287 ..	....	....	....	....	....	....	....	....
Government, n.i.e...	2 291 ..	113	86	115	104	....	....	....	....
Other services, debit............................	3 200 BA	**−379**	**−545**	**−653**	**−714**	**−513**	**−1,582**	**−1,406**	**−1,740**
Communications...	3 245 ..	−13	−15	−18	−22	−31	−36	−41	−49
Construction..	3 249 ..	−168	−183	−149	−160	−87	−531	−32	−165
Insurance..	3 253 ..	−59	−104	−160	−182	−190	−242	−594	−651
Financial...	3 260 ..	−10	−13	−20	−16	....	....	....	....
Computer and information............................	3 262 ..	−12	−15	−25	−30	....	....	....	....
Royalties and licence fees............................	3 266 ..	....	....	....	....	....	....	....	....
Other business services...............................	3 268 ..	−39	−45	−50	−52	−36	....	....	....
Personal, cultural, and recreational...............	3 287 ..	−9	−9	−10	−12	....	....	....	....
Government, n.i.e...	3 291 ..	−69	−161	−221	−240	−169	−773	−740	−876

Table 2 (Continued). STANDARD PRESENTATION, 2003–2010
(Millions of U.S. dollars)

	Code	2003	2004	2005	2006	2007	2008	2009	2010
C. INCOME	4 300	**540**	**−55**	**−281**	**−595**	**2,017**	**586**	**578**	**−30**
Total credit	2 300	*1,689*	*1,339*	*1,837*	*2,180*	*4,517*	*4,471*	*2,461*	*2,318*
Total debit	3 300	*−1,149*	*−1,394*	*−2,118*	*−2,775*	*−2,500*	*−3,885*	*−1,883*	*−2,348*
Compensation of employees, credit	2 310	**5**	**5**	**8**	**10**	....	....	....	....
Compensation of employees, debit	3 310	**−32**	**−35**	**−60**	**−65**	....	....	....	....
Investment income, credit	2 320	**1,684**	**1,334**	**1,829**	**2,170**	**4,517**	**4,471**	**2,461**	**2,318**
Direct investment income	2 330	232	156	224	320	175	248	407	596
Dividends and distributed branch profits	2 332	232	156	224	320	175	236	395	573
Reinvested earnings and undistributed branch profits	2 333	....	....	....	....	....	....	....	....
Income on debt (interest)	2 334	....	....	....	....	....	12	12	23
Portfolio investment income	2 339	1,452	1,178	1,605	1,850	813	664	1,495	1,161
Income on equity	2 340	1,452	1,178	1,605	1,850	813	664	1,495	1,161
Income on bonds and notes	2 350	....	....	....	....	....	....	....	....
Income on money market instruments	2 360	....	....	....	....	....	....	....	....
Other investment income	2 370	....	....	....	....	3,529	3,560	559	561
Investment income, debit	3 320	**−1,117**	**−1,359**	**−2,058**	**−2,710**	**−2,500**	**−3,885**	**−1,883**	**−2,348**
Direct investment income	3 330	−1,078	−1,359	−2,058	−2,710	−2,500	−3,616	−1,834	−2,348
Dividends and distributed branch profits	3 332	−935	−1,146	−1,895	−2,460	−740	−1,808	−1,410	−1,729
Reinvested earnings and undistributed branch profits	3 333	−143	−213	−163	−250	−1,760	−1,808	−424	−619
Income on debt (interest)	3 334	....	....	....	....	....	....	....	....
Portfolio investment income	3 339	−39	....	....	....	....	−263	−50	....
Income on equity	3 340	−39	....	....	....	....	−263	−50	....
Income on bonds and notes	3 350	....	....	....	....	....	....	....	....
Income on money market instruments	3 360	....	....	....	....	....	....	....	....
Other investment income	3 370	....	....	....	....	....	−6	....	....
D. CURRENT TRANSFERS	4 379	**−1,661**	**−2,509**	**−634**	**586**	**−219**	**−1,040**	**−1,572**	**−1,828**
Credit	2 379	**255**	**254**	**418**	**1,646**	**598**	**45**	....	....
General government	2 380	12	15	18	1,300	598	45	....	....
Other sectors	2 390	243	239	400	346	....	....	....	....
Workers' remittances	2 391	3	5	7	6	....	....	....	....
Other current transfers	2 392	240	234	393	340	....	....	....	....
Debit	3 379	**−1,916**	**−2,763**	**−1,052**	**−1,060**	**−817**	**−1,085**	**−1,572**	**−1,828**
General government	3 380	−1,186	−1,756	−130	−110	−55	−121	−211	−219
Other sectors	3 390	−730	−1,007	−922	−950	−762	−964	−1,361	−1,609
Workers' remittances	3 391	−644	−940	−854	−880	−762	−964	−1,361	−1,609
Other current transfers	3 392	−86	−67	−68	−70	....	....	....	....
CAPITAL AND FINANCIAL ACCOUNT	4 996	**−5,292**	**−6,349**	**−13,448**	**−24,178**	**−29,587**	**−33,987**	**−10,713**	**−14,509**
CAPITAL ACCOUNT	4 994	....	....	....	....	....	....	....	....
Total credit	2 994	....	....	....	....	....	....	....	....
Total debit	3 994	....	....	....	....	....	....	....	....
Capital transfers, credit	2 400	....	....	....	....	....	....	....	....
General government	2 401	....	....	....	....	....	....	....	....
Debt forgiveness	2 402	....	....	....	....	....	....	....	....
Other capital transfers	2 410	....	....	....	....	....	....	....	....
Other sectors	2 430	....	....	....	....	....	....	....	....
Migrants' transfers	2 431	....	....	....	....	....	....	....	....
Debt forgiveness	2 432	....	....	....	....	....	....	....	....
Other capital transfers	2 440	....	....	....	....	....	....	....	....
Capital transfers, debit	3 400	....	....	....	....	....	....	....	....
General government	3 401	....	....	....	....	....	....	....	....
Debt forgiveness	3 402	....	....	....	....	....	....	....	....
Other capital transfers	3 410	....	....	....	....	....	....	....	....
Other sectors	3 430	....	....	....	....	....	....	....	....
Migrants' transfers	3 431	....	....	....	....	....	....	....	....
Debt forgiveness	3 432	....	....	....	....	....	....	....	....
Other capital transfers	3 440	....	....	....	....	....	....	....	....
Nonproduced nonfinancial assets, credit	2 480	....	....	....	....	....	....	....	....
Nonproduced nonfinancial assets, debit	3 480	....	....	....	....	....	....	....	....

Table 2 (Continued). STANDARD PRESENTATION, 2003–2010

(Millions of U.S. dollars)

	Code	2003	2004	2005	2006	2007	2008	2009	2010
FINANCIAL ACCOUNT	4 995	**−5,292**	**−6,349**	**−13,448**	**−24,178**	**−29,587**	**−33,987**	**−10,713**	**−14,509**
A. DIRECT INVESTMENT	4 500	**80**	**71**	**910**	**1,590**	**756**	**−1,777**	**206**	**−938**
Direct investment abroad	4 505	**−63**	**−286**	**−128**	**−474**	**−3,933**	**−5,888**	**−1,165**	**−2,722**
Equity capital	4 510	−63	−286	−128	−474	−3,933	−5,888	−1,165	−2,722
Claims on affiliated enterprises	4 515	−63	−286	−128	−474	−3,933	−5,888	−1,165	−2,722
Liabilities to affiliated enterprises	4 520	....	....	....	....	....	....	....	....
Reinvested earnings	4 525	....	....	....	....	....	....	....	....
Other capital	4 530	....	....	....	....	....	....	....	....
Claims on affiliated enterprises	4 535	....	....	....	....	....	....	....	....
Liabilities to affiliated enterprises	4 540	....	....	....	....	....	....	....	....
Direct investment in Libya	4 555	**143**	**357**	**1,038**	**2,064**	**4,689**	**4,111**	**1,371**	**1,784**
Equity capital	4 560	....	....	....	....	2,929	2,303	947	1,165
Claims on direct investors	4 565	....	....	....	....	....	....	....	....
Liabilities to direct investors	4 570	....	....	....	....	2,929	2,303	947	1,165
Reinvested earnings	4 575	143	213	163	250	1,760	1,808	424	619
Other capital	4 580	....	144	875	1,814	....	....	....	....
Claims on direct investors	4 585	....	....	....	....	....	....	....	....
Liabilities to direct investors	4 590	....	144	875	1,814	....	....	....	....
B. PORTFOLIO INVESTMENT	4 600	**−607**	**−187**	**−393**	**−5,198**	**−1,440**	**−10,964**	**−3,352**	**−4,396**
Assets	4 602	**−607**	**−187**	**−393**	**−5,198**	**−1,440**	**−10,964**	**−3,352**	**−4,396**
Equity securities	4 610	−18	27	−47	−60	−1,440	−10,964	−3,352	−4,396
Monetary authorities	4 611	....	....	....	....			....	....
General government	4 612	....	....	....	....	....	....	−3,106	−3,723
Banks	4 613	....	....	....	....	−172	500	405	−22
Other sectors	4 614	−18	27	−47	−60	−1,268	−11,464	−651	−651
Debt securities	4 619	−589	−214	−346	−5,138	....	....	....	....
Bonds and notes	4 620	−333	61	−333	−5,125	....	....	....	....
Monetary authorities	4 621	....	....	....	....	....	....	....	....
General government	4 622	....	....	....	....	....	....	....	....
Banks	4 623	−333	61	−333	−5,125	....	....	....	....
Other sectors	4 624	....	....	....	....	....	....	....	....
Money market instruments	4 630	−256	−275	−13	−13	....	....	....	....
Monetary authorities	4 631	....	....	....	....	....	....	....	....
General government	4 632	....	....	....	....	....	....	....	....
Banks	4 633	....	....	....	....	....	....	....	....
Other sectors	4 634	−256	−275	−13	−13	....	....	....	....
Liabilities	4 652	**....**	**....**	**....**	**....**	**....**	**....**	**....**	**....**
Equity securities	4 660	....	....	....	....	....	....	....	....
Banks	4 663	....	....	....	....	....	....	....	....
Other sectors	4 664	....	....	....	....	....	....	....	....
Debt securities	4 669	....	....	....	....	....	....	....	....
Bonds and notes	4 670	....	....	....	....	....	....	....	....
Monetary authorities	4 671	....	....	....	....	....	....	....	....
General government	4 672	....	....	....	....	....	....	....	....
Banks	4 673	....	....	....	....	....	....	....	....
Other sectors	4 674	....	....	....	....	....	....	....	....
Money market instruments	4 680	....	....	....	....	....	....	....	....
Monetary authorities	4 681	....	....	....	....	....	....	....	....
General government	4 682	....	....	....	....	....	....	....	....
Banks	4 683	....	....	....	....	....	....	....	....
Other sectors	4 684	....	....	....	....	....	....	....	....
C. FINANCIAL DERIVATIVES	4 910	**....**	**....**	**....**	**....**	**....**	**....**	**....**	**....**
Monetary authorities	4 911	....	....	....	....	....	....	....	....
General government	4 912	....	....	....	....	....	....	....	....
Banks	4 913	....	....	....	....	....	....	....	....
Other sectors	4 914	....	....	....	....	....	....	....	....
Assets	4 900	**....**	**....**	**....**	**....**	**....**	**....**	**....**	**....**
Monetary authorities	4 901	....	....	....	....	....	....	....	....
General government	4 902	....	....	....	....	....	....	....	....
Banks	4 903	....	....	....	....	....	....	....	....
Other sectors	4 904	....	....	....	....	....	....	....	....
Liabilities	4 905	**....**	**....**	**....**	**....**	**....**	**....**	**....**	**....**
Monetary authorities	4 906	....	....	....	....	....	....	....	....
General government	4 907	....	....	....	....	....	....	....	....
Banks	4 908	....	....	....	....	....	....	....	....
Other sectors	4 909	....	....	....	....	....	....	....	....

Table 2 (Concluded). STANDARD PRESENTATION, 2003–2010

(Millions of U.S. dollars)

	Code	2003	2004	2005	2006	2007	2008	2009	2010
D. OTHER INVESTMENT	4 700	**361**	**−193**	**−125**	**−1,123**	**−8,859**	**−8,299**	**−2,379**	**−5,005**
Assets	4 703	**−163**	**−1,767**	**−416**	**−1,194**	**−8,947**	**−8,280**	**−3,952**	**−4,889**
Trade credits	4 706	....	....	....	....	−8,378	−8,710	−3,170	−3,487
General government	4 707	....	....	....	....	−8,331	−8,710	−3,170	−3,487
of which: Short-term	4 709	....	....	....	....	*−8,331*	*−8,710*	*−3,170*	*−3,487*
Other sectors	4 710	....	....	....	....	−47	....	....	....
of which: Short-term	4 712	....	....	....	....	....	....	....	....
Loans	4 714	−78	446	156	156	−716	−43	−498	−183
Monetary authorities	4 715	....	....	....	....	....	....	....	....
of which: Short-term	4 718	....	....	....	....	....	....	....	....
General government	4 719	4	....	....	....	....	−43	−498	−183
of which: Short-term	4 721	....	....	....	....	....	....	....	....
Banks	4 722	−82	446	141	141	−108	....	....	....
of which: Short-term	4 724	*−82*	*446*	*141*	*141*	....	....	....	....
Other sectors	4 725	....	....	15	15	−608	....	....	....
of which: Short-term	4 727	....	....	*15*	*15*	....	....	....	....
Currency and deposits	4 730	−85	−2,213	−572	−1,350	137	473	−284	−1,219
Monetary authorities	4 731	....	....	....	....	....	....	....	....
General government	4 732	2	....	....	....	68	....	....	....
Banks	4 733	−70	−2,523	187	150	2,066	254	−284	−1,219
Other sectors	4 734	−17	310	−759	−1,500	−1,997	220	....	....
Other assets	4 736	....	....	....	....	11	....	....	....
Monetary authorities	4 737	....	....	....	....	....	....	....	....
of which: Short-term	4 739	....	....	....	....	....	....	....	....
General government	4 740	....	....	....	....	....	....	....	....
of which: Short-term	4 742	....	....	....	....	....	....	....	....
Banks	4 743	....	....	....	....	11	....	....	....
of which: Short-term	4 745	....	....	....	....	*11*	....	....	....
Other sectors	4 746	....	....	....	....	....	....	....	....
of which: Short-term	4 748	....	....	....	....	....	....	....	....
Liabilities	4 753	**524**	**1,574**	**291**	**71**	**88**	**−19**	**1,573**	**−116**
Trade credits	4 756	....	....	....	....	....	....	....	....
General government	4 757	....	....	....	....	....	....	....	....
of which: Short-term	4 759	....	....	....	....	....	....	....	....
Other sectors	4 760	....	....	....	....	....	....	....	....
of which: Short-term	4 762	....	....	....	....	....	....	....	....
Loans	4 764	....	−71	....	....	50	−19	−173	5
Monetary authorities	4 765	....	....	....	....	....	....	....	....
of which: Use of Fund credit and loans from the Fund	4 766	....	....	....	....	....	....	....	....
of which: Short-term	4 768	....	....	....	....	....	....	....	....
General government	4 769	....	....	....	....	....	....	....	....
of which: Short-term	4 771	....	....	....	....	....	....	....	....
Banks	4 772	....	−71	....	....	....	....	....	....
of which: Short-term	4 774	....	....	....	....	....	....	....	....
Other sectors	4 775	....	....	....	....	50	−19	−173	5
of which: Short-term	4 777	....	....	....	....	....	*−19*	*−173*	*5*
Currency and deposits	4 780	221	....	−63	−63	....	....	135	−147
Monetary authorities	4 781	−7	....	....	....	4	....	....	....
General government	4 782	....	....	....	....	....	....	....	....
Banks	4 783	228	....	−63	−63	−4	....	139	−143
Other sectors	4 784	....	....	....	....	....	....	−4	−4
Other liabilities	4 786	303	1,645	354	134	38	....	1,611	26
Monetary authorities	4 787	....	....	....	....	....	....	1,611	26
of which: Short-term	4 789	....	....	....	....	....	....	*26*	*26*
General government	4 790	....	....	....	....	....	....	....	....
of which: Short-term	4 792	....	....	....	....	....	....	....	....
Banks	4 793	320	1,855	287	450	....	....	....	....
of which: Short-term	4 795	....	....	....	....	....	....	....	....
Other sectors	4 796	−17	−210	67	−316	38	....	....	....
of which: Short-term	4 798	*−17*	*−210*	*67*	*−316*	*38*	....	....	....
E. RESERVE ASSETS	4 802	**−5,126**	**−6,040**	**−13,840**	**−19,447**	**−20,044**	**−12,948**	**−5,188**	**−4,170**
Monetary gold	4 812	....	....	....	....	....	....	....	....
Special drawing rights	4 811	−18	−20	−29	−42	−54	−41	−1,593	−3
Reserve position in the Fund	4 810	....	....	....	....	....	....	25	207
Foreign exchange	4 803	−5,108	−6,018	−13,814	−19,400	−19,990	−12,906	−3,621	−4,373
Other claims	4 813	1	−2	3	−5	....	....	....	....
NET ERRORS AND OMISSIONS	4 998	**1,890**	**1,733**	**−1,497**	**2,008**	**1,076**	**−1,715**	**1,333**	**−2,292**

Table 1. ANALYTIC PRESENTATION, 2003–2010

(Millions of U.S. dollars)

	Code	2003	2004	2005	2006	2007	2008	2009	2010
A. Current Account[1]	4 993 Z.	**−1,278.4**	**−1,724.6**	**−1,831.2**	**−3,218.1**	**−5,692.4**	**−6,355.9**	**1,648.3**	**667.2**
Goods: exports f.o.b.	2 100 ..	7,657.8	9,306.3	11,774.4	14,150.6	17,162.0	23,745.0	16,484.2	20,815.8
Goods: imports f.o.b.	3 100 ..	−9,362.0	−11,688.9	−14,690.4	−18,359.8	−23,035.8	−29,952.5	−17,638.0	−22,375.7
Balance on Goods	4 100 ..	*−1,704.2*	*−2,382.6*	*−2,916.0*	*−4,209.3*	*−5,873.8*	*−6,207.5*	*−1,153.8*	*−1,560.0*
Services: credit	2 200 ..	1,878.0	2,444.4	3,104.3	3,623.2	4,025.0	4,767.1	3,710.1	4,120.0
Services: debit	3 200 ..	−1,263.6	−1,632.1	−2,054.6	−2,540.0	−3,392.7	−4,199.6	−2,983.6	−2,824.5
Balance on Goods and Services	4 991 ..	*−1,089.8*	*−1,570.2*	*−1,866.3*	*−3,126.0*	*−5,241.6*	*−5,640.0*	*−427.3*	*−264.5*
Income: credit	2 300 ..	235.2	354.9	448.3	589.9	793.5	1,055.3	754.2	808.8
Income: debit	3 300 ..	−717.4	−967.3	−1,075.4	−1,406.9	−2,407.2	−2,852.3	−326.5	−1,711.5
Balance on Goods, Services, and Income	4 992 ..	*−1,572.0*	*−2,182.5*	*−2,493.4*	*−3,943.0*	*−6,855.3*	*−7,437.0*	*.4*	*−1,167.3*
Current transfers: credit	2 379 Z.	301.5	612.1	951.3	1,425.1	2,071.2	2,167.2	2,677.3	2,794.9
Current transfers: debit	3 379 ..	−7.8	−154.2	−289.1	−700.2	−908.3	−1,086.1	−1,029.4	−960.4
B. Capital Account[1]	4 994 Z.	**67.5**	**287.2**	**331.1**	**351.4**	**690.1**	**880.6**	**1,261.5**	**985.8**
Capital account: credit	2 994 Z.	68.3	288.1	331.2	351.6	690.1	880.7	1,261.9	985.8
Capital account: debit	3 994 ..	−.8	−1.0	−.1	−.2	....	−.1	−.5	....
Total, Groups A Plus B	4 981 ..	*−1,210.8*	*−1,437.5*	*−1,500.1*	*−2,866.7*	*−5,002.3*	*−5,475.3*	*2,909.8*	*1,653.0*
C. Financial Account[1]	4 995 W.	**1,642.3**	**1,141.2**	**2,261.8**	**4,662.6**	**6,271.9**	**4,353.6**	**−2,773.7**	**−957.7**
Direct investment abroad	4 505 ..	−37.2	−262.6	−343.0	−289.5	−608.4	−355.5	−200.7	−132.3
Direct investment in Lithuania	4 555 Z.	179.2	773.2	1,031.8	1,840.2	2,017.0	2,069.8	126.1	622.2
Portfolio investment assets	4 602 ..	29.8	−219.9	−778.5	−1,105.8	−838.0	−101.0	−1,162.2	−532.6
Equity securities	4 610 ..	−1.8	−18.8	−185.1	−286.4	−357.0	26.5	−425.9	−523.5
Debt securities	4 619 ..	31.6	−201.0	−593.4	−819.4	−481.0	−127.5	−736.2	−9.1
Portfolio investment liabilities	4 652 Z.	222.3	431.1	541.6	852.1	608.8	−236.0	2,293.6	2,456.7
Equity securities	4 660 ..	4.2	7.9	130.0	72.0	−166.3	2.6	−2.2	36.5
Debt securities	4 669 Z.	218.0	423.1	411.6	780.1	775.0	−238.5	2,295.7	2,420.2
Financial derivatives	4 910 ..	−28.0	2.6	12.9	−11.0	−2.4	14.8	38.2	−89.0
Financial derivatives assets	4 900 ..	28.1	60.0	27.4	9.5	4.8	40.4	61.6	−141.2
Financial derivatives liabilities	4 905 ..	−56.2	−57.4	−14.5	−20.5	−7.1	−25.6	−23.5	52.2
Other investment assets	4 703 ..	−100.9	−683.8	−785.6	−475.7	−1,561.1	−607.6	−709.0	−158.8
Monetary authorities	4 701 ..	....	....	....	....	....	....	....	....
General government	4 704 ..	....	−7.3	....	....	....	....	−147.8	−269.9
Banks	4 705 ..	−161.0	−671.1	−394.7	−335.3	−720.4	−122.6	−1,234.9	538.0
Other sectors	4 728 ..	60.1	−5.4	−390.9	−140.4	−840.7	−484.9	673.7	−427.0
Other investment liabilities	4 753 W.	1,377.2	1,100.7	2,582.6	3,852.4	6,656.0	3,569.2	−3,159.8	−3,124.0
Monetary authorities	4 753 WA	−8.0	−66.7	5.5	75.3	323.4	−399.8	336.0	52.5
General government	4 753 ZB	−9.4	−308.2	−191.0	−24.5	−120.1	115.0	908.2	472.2
Banks	4 753 ZC	737.6	870.3	2,577.3	2,560.0	4,702.7	3,882.6	−2,586.3	−2,667.5
Other sectors	4 753 ZD	657.0	605.3	190.8	1,241.6	1,750.0	−28.7	−1,817.7	−981.3
Total, Groups A Through C	4 983 ..	*431.5*	*−296.3*	*761.7*	*1,795.9*	*1,269.7*	*−1,121.6*	*136.1*	*695.3*
D. Net Errors and Omissions	4 998 ..	**181.2**	**191.8**	**−49.4**	**−289.1**	**−53.9**	**−39.8**	**8.3**	**4.0**
Total, Groups A Through D	4 984 ..	*612.7*	*−104.4*	*712.3*	*1,506.7*	*1,215.7*	*−1,161.4*	*144.4*	*699.3*
E. Reserves and Related Items	4 802 A.	**−612.7**	**104.4**	**−712.3**	**−1,506.7**	**−1,215.7**	**1,161.4**	**−144.4**	**−699.3**
Reserve assets	4 802 ..	−531.2	124.2	−686.8	−1,506.7	−1,215.7	1,161.4	−144.4	−699.3
Use of Fund credit and loans	4 766 ..	−81.4	−19.8	−25.5	....	....	....	....	....
Exceptional financing	4 920 ..	....	....	....	....	....	....	....	....
Conversion rates: litai per U.S. dollar	0 101 ..	**3.0609**	**2.7806**	**2.7740**	**2.7522**	**2.5237**	**2.3571**	**2.4840**	**2.6063**

---

[1] Excludes components that have been classified in the categories of Group E.

Table 2. STANDARD PRESENTATION, 2003–2010

(Millions of U.S. dollars)

	Code	2003	2004	2005	2006	2007	2008	2009	2010
CURRENT ACCOUNT	4 993	−1,278.4	−1,724.6	−1,831.2	−3,218.1	−5,692.4	−6,355.9	1,648.3	667.2
A. GOODS	4 100	−1,704.2	−2,382.6	−2,916.0	−4,209.3	−5,873.8	−6,207.5	−1,153.8	−1,560.0
Credit	2 100	7,657.8	9,306.3	11,774.4	14,150.6	17,162.0	23,745.0	16,484.2	20,815.8
General merchandise: exports f.o.b.	2 110	5,761.4	7,879.4	10,622.4	12,869.8	15,654.2	22,347.5	15,356.9	19,663.8
Goods for processing: exports f.o.b.	2 150	1,880.1	1,409.7	1,120.6	1,237.4	1,421.7	1,305.8	1,083.9	1,084.2
Repairs on goods	2 160	....	....	....	....	....	....	....	....
Goods procured in ports by carriers	2 170	4.8	.3	7.5	.3	.9	1.2	1.9	1.0
Nonmonetary gold	2 180	11.5	17.0	23.9	43.0	85.2	90.6	41.4	66.7
Debit	3 100	−9,362.0	−11,688.9	−14,690.4	−18,359.8	−23,035.8	−29,952.5	−17,638.0	−22,375.7
General merchandise: imports f.o.b.	3 110	−7,864.6	−10,475.2	−13,610.5	−17,048.8	−21,468.6	−28,410.1	−16,656.6	−21,359.6
Goods for processing: imports f.o.b.	3 150	−1,419.7	−1,068.2	−899.0	−999.3	−1,199.1	−1,034.3	−661.5	−681.1
Repairs on goods	3 160	....	....	....	....	....	....	....	....
Goods procured in ports by carriers	3 170	−62.4	−127.5	−158.6	−274.6	−305.3	−438.1	−296.6	−298.1
Nonmonetary gold	3 180	−15.3	−18.0	−22.3	−37.0	−62.9	−70.0	−23.2	−36.9
B. SERVICES	4 200	614.4	812.4	1,049.7	1,083.3	632.3	567.4	726.5	1,295.5
Total credit	2 200	*1,878.0*	*2,444.4*	*3,104.3*	*3,623.2*	*4,025.0*	*4,767.1*	*3,710.1*	*4,120.0*
Total debit	3 200	*−1,263.6*	*−1,632.1*	*−2,054.6*	*−2,540.0*	*−3,392.7*	*−4,199.6*	*−2,983.6*	*−2,824.5*
Transportation services, credit	2 205	932.6	1,353.4	1,587.2	1,945.2	2,347.6	2,878.5	2,096.9	2,421.8
Passenger	2 850	*61.9*	*57.9*	*54.3*	*38.5*	*38.9*	*67.1*	*90.6*	*75.6*
Freight	2 851	*625.6*	*960.9*	*1,181.8*	*1,476.0*	*1,801.5*	*2,073.0*	*1,441.0*	*1,692.1*
Other	2 852	*245.1*	*334.5*	*351.1*	*430.7*	*507.2*	*738.5*	*565.3*	*654.1*
Sea transport, passenger	2 207	3.8	6.3	5.5	7.5	8.0	10.0	8.3	7.6
Sea transport, freight	2 208	105.3	127.8	191.5	184.1	167.9	154.5	136.4	127.1
Sea transport, other	2 209	114.3	49.0	43.3	36.3	50.0	63.6	21.9	24.2
Air transport, passenger	2 211	37.6	40.4	36.5	18.3	13.8	38.1	65.3	46.6
Air transport, freight	2 212	4.5	6.9	6.2	5.6	8.3	10.2	8.7	14.1
Air transport, other	2 213	25.2	35.0	43.9	43.1	52.1	74.8	84.3	85.3
Other transport, passenger	2 215	20.6	11.2	12.4	12.7	17.1	19.0	17.0	21.4
Other transport, freight	2 216	515.8	826.2	984.1	1,286.2	1,625.2	1,908.2	1,295.9	1,550.9
Other transport, other	2 217	105.6	250.6	263.9	351.3	405.2	600.1	459.1	544.5
Transportation services, debit	3 205	−509.6	−663.5	−896.7	−1,111.2	−1,565.5	−1,890.5	−1,111.2	−1,419.6
Passenger	3 850	*−5.0*	*−6.9*	*−12.7*	*−21.8*	*−24.2*	*−36.3*	*−8.7*	*−5.3*
Freight	3 851	*−371.3*	*−505.1*	*−659.7*	*−801.1*	*−1,212.2*	*−1,431.9*	*−786.6*	*−1,082.2*
Other	3 852	*−133.2*	*−151.5*	*−224.3*	*−288.3*	*−329.1*	*−422.3*	*−315.9*	*−332.1*
Sea transport, passenger	3 207	....	−.1	....	−.4	....	−.1	....	−.1
Sea transport, freight	3 208	−107.7	−131.9	−203.6	−243.5	−363.8	−666.2	−361.9	−502.9
Sea transport, other	3 209	−16.2	−6.4	−10.9	−18.9	−22.1	−21.5	−13.4	−15.2
Air transport, passenger	3 211	−.2	−.4	−5.4	−12.7	−13.5	−24.8	−.3	−.1
Air transport, freight	3 212	−10.8	−11.7	−12.6	−16.9	−30.6	−27.1	−14.4	−16.9
Air transport, other	3 213	−17.7	−19.7	−31.4	−25.4	−31.4	−48.9	−20.1	−18.4
Other transport, passenger	3 215	−4.8	−6.4	−7.3	−8.7	−10.7	−11.4	−8.4	−5.1
Other transport, freight	3 216	−252.8	−361.5	−443.6	−540.7	−817.8	−738.6	−410.3	−562.4
Other transport, other	3 217	−99.4	−125.5	−181.9	−244.0	−275.6	−351.8	−282.4	−298.4
Travel, credit	2 236	638.0	776.4	921.1	1,038.0	1,153.0	1,248.9	1,010.9	1,021.3
Business travel	2 237	111.2	135.3	170.6	277.2	358.1	424.7	309.3	322.5
Personal travel	2 240	526.8	641.1	750.5	760.8	795.0	824.3	701.6	698.8
Travel, debit	3 236	−470.6	−635.8	−744.0	−909.1	−1,143.5	−1,530.8	−1,121.9	−780.9
Business travel	3 237	−140.0	−189.2	−207.4	−266.7	−160.5	−217.2	−141.6	−98.4
Personal travel	3 240	−330.6	−446.6	−536.6	−642.4	−983.0	−1,313.5	−980.3	−682.4
Other services, credit	2 200 BA	307.4	314.7	595.9	640.0	524.4	639.6	602.2	676.9
Communications	2 245	59.5	64.2	76.8	87.4	99.9	107.2	104.8	113.3
Construction	2 249	24.2	30.2	34.0	31.4	67.7	97.1	66.9	84.9
Insurance	2 253	.1	.7	−.6	−10.0	−13.0	5.1	.3	1.8
Financial	2 260	7.1	11.1	16.5	29.3	37.8	54.2	39.6	36.5
Computer and information	2 262	28.6	31.0	28.4	18.4	23.9	41.4	39.9	38.8
Royalties and licence fees	2 266	.5	.8	1.9	.7	.2	.9	.4	.9
Other business services	2 268	154.9	153.5	398.9	426.6	246.9	256.0	283.4	328.5
Personal, cultural, and recreational	2 287	18.3	9.4	10.3	15.7	16.3	18.5	15.8	16.3
Government, n.i.e.	2 291	14.0	13.8	29.8	40.4	44.6	59.2	51.1	56.1
Other services, debit	3 200 BA	−283.4	−332.8	−413.9	−519.6	−683.8	−778.4	−750.4	−624.0
Communications	3 245	−50.4	−57.1	−66.3	−79.4	−94.0	−113.5	−110.6	−121.2
Construction	3 249	−8.2	−7.6	−13.4	−19.5	−88.1	−64.7	−133.6	−30.1
Insurance	3 253	−12.3	−21.5	−27.1	−44.8	−82.0	−73.3	−27.1	−41.3
Financial	3 260	−3.7	−5.0	−5.9	−17.5	−22.5	−46.4	−23.6	−16.1
Computer and information	3 262	−15.9	−20.1	−22.8	−22.9	−26.9	−39.0	−37.6	−37.9
Royalties and licence fees	3 266	−18.1	−18.0	−20.7	−24.4	−21.6	−34.5	−29.1	−34.8
Other business services	3 268	−125.7	−147.6	−190.0	−230.7	−236.2	−279.6	−238.4	−217.7
Personal, cultural, and recreational	3 287	−1.0	−1.5	−2.4	−2.4	−2.2	−8.4	−9.9	−10.0
Government, n.i.e.	3 291	−48.2	−54.5	−65.2	−78.0	−110.3	−119.0	−140.6	−115.0

Table 2 (Continued). STANDARD PRESENTATION, 2003–2010

(Millions of U.S. dollars)

	Code	2003	2004	2005	2006	2007	2008	2009	2010
C. INCOME	4 300	**−482.3**	**−612.4**	**−627.1**	**−817.0**	**−1,613.7**	**−1,797.0**	**427.7**	**−902.8**
Total credit	2 300	*235.2*	*354.9*	*448.3*	*589.9*	*793.5*	*1,055.3*	*754.2*	*808.8*
Total debit	3 300	*−717.4*	*−967.3*	*−1,075.4*	*−1,406.9*	*−2,407.2*	*−2,852.3*	*−326.5*	*−1,711.5*
Compensation of employees, credit	2 310	**81.6**	**162.7**	**224.5**	**248.1**	**255.7**	**225.4**	**190.2**	**279.6**
Compensation of employees, debit	3 310	**−36.1**	**−25.9**	**−45.2**	**−51.3**	**−85.4**	**−78.6**	**−127.2**	**−81.7**
Investment income, credit	2 320	**153.6**	**192.2**	**223.9**	**341.8**	**537.8**	**829.9**	**564.0**	**529.2**
Direct investment income	2 330	8.0	16.3	10.5	42.6	9.5	59.6	−25.8	40.1
Dividends and distributed branch profits	2 332	....	.1	.3	1.8	.3	4.3	31.0	8.9
Reinvested earnings and undistributed branch profits	2 333	−1.1	5.1	4.3	2.6	−20.5	17.6	−82.2	12.0
Income on debt (interest)	2 334	9.1	11.1	5.9	38.2	29.7	37.7	25.4	19.2
Portfolio investment income	2 339	105.1	127.0	138.0	187.8	336.1	404.6	251.0	225.3
Income on equity	2 340	.4	.4	.4	.5	.6	.7	.6	1.3
Income on bonds and notes	2 350	93.8	119.4	128.8	172.2	310.7	372.7	241.0	212.2
Income on money market instruments	2 360	10.9	7.3	8.8	15.0	24.7	31.2	9.4	11.8
Other investment income	2 370	40.5	48.9	75.4	111.5	192.2	365.6	338.8	263.8
Investment income, debit	3 320	**−681.4**	**−941.4**	**−1,030.2**	**−1,355.6**	**−2,321.8**	**−2,773.7**	**−199.3**	**−1,629.9**
Direct investment income	3 330	−401.4	−649.1	−711.2	−877.6	−1,423.1	−1,298.2	943.9	−499.4
Dividends and distributed branch profits	3 332	−166.6	−229.7	−396.0	−177.7	−287.4	−851.3	−470.8	−584.6
Reinvested earnings and undistributed branch profits	3 333	−222.1	−409.0	−299.2	−678.1	−1,058.1	−321.4	1,508.3	151.5
Income on debt (interest)	3 334	−12.7	−10.4	−16.0	−21.8	−77.6	−125.5	−93.7	−66.3
Portfolio investment income	3 339	−144.5	−178.4	−170.1	−183.2	−217.8	−265.6	−334.4	−557.8
Income on equity	3 340	−8.5	−6.1	−11.3	−12.6	−21.6	−23.2	−15.1	−12.5
Income on bonds and notes	3 350	−134.2	−170.2	−158.5	−169.6	−185.8	−235.1	−318.8	−543.7
Income on money market instruments	3 360	−1.8	−2.2	−.3	−1.0	−10.4	−7.3	−.6	−1.6
Other investment income	3 370	−135.5	−113.8	−148.9	−294.8	−680.9	−1,209.8	−808.8	−572.7
D. CURRENT TRANSFERS	4 379	**293.7**	**457.9**	**662.2**	**724.8**	**1,162.9**	**1,081.1**	**1,647.9**	**1,834.5**
Credit	2 379	**301.5**	**612.1**	**951.3**	**1,425.1**	**2,071.2**	**2,167.2**	**2,677.3**	**2,794.9**
General government	2 380	99.4	229.5	405.5	464.0	789.1	696.6	1,445.5	1,233.3
Other sectors	2 390	202.1	382.6	545.8	961.1	1,282.1	1,470.6	1,231.8	1,561.7
Workers' remittances	2 391	33.2	161.8	309.8	745.9	1,177.0	1,262.8	982.2	1,295.3
Other current transfers	2 392	168.9	220.8	235.9	215.1	105.1	207.8	249.6	266.3
Debit	3 379	**−7.8**	**−154.2**	**−289.1**	**−700.2**	**−908.3**	**−1,086.1**	**−1,029.4**	**−960.4**
General government	3 380	−1.6	−151.6	−285.5	−323.2	−394.0	−514.4	−453.1	−366.8
Other sectors	3 390	−6.3	−2.6	−3.6	−377.0	−514.3	−571.7	−576.3	−593.6
Workers' remittances	3 391	−5.9	−1.7	−2.2	−374.5	−481.3	−536.5	−492.5	−456.6
Other current transfers	3 392	−.4	−.9	−1.5	−2.5	−33.0	−35.2	−83.8	−137.0
CAPITAL AND FINANCIAL ACCOUNT	4 996	**1,097.2**	**1,532.8**	**1,880.6**	**3,507.2**	**5,746.4**	**6,395.6**	**−1,656.6**	**−671.2**
CAPITAL ACCOUNT	4 994	**67.5**	**287.2**	**331.1**	**351.4**	**690.1**	**880.6**	**1,261.5**	**985.8**
Total credit	2 994	*68.3*	*288.1*	*331.2*	*351.6*	*690.1*	*880.7*	*1,261.9*	*985.8*
Total debit	3 994	*−.8*	*−1.0*	*−.1*	*−.2*	*....*	*−.1*	*−.5*	*....*
Capital transfers, credit	2 400	**68.3**	**288.1**	**331.2**	**351.6**	**690.1**	**880.7**	**1,261.9**	**985.8**
General government	2 401	68.0	287.8	331.2	351.1	690.1	880.7	1,260.3	985.8
Debt forgiveness	2 402	....	....	....	....	....	....	....	....
Other capital transfers	2 410	68.0	287.8	331.2	351.1	690.1	880.7	1,260.3	985.8
Other sectors	2 430	.3	.4	....	.5	....	....	1.6	....
Migrants' transfers	2 431	....	....	....	....	....	....	....	....
Debt forgiveness	2 432	.3	.4	....	....	....	....	1.6	....
Other capital transfers	2 440	....	....	....	.5	....	....	....	....
Capital transfers, debit	3 400	**−.8**	**−1.0**	**−.1**	**−.2**	**....**	**−.1**	**−.5**	**....**
General government	3 401	....	....	....	....	....	....	....	....
Debt forgiveness	3 402	....	....	....	....	....	....	....	....
Other capital transfers	3 410	....	....	....	....	....	....	....	....
Other sectors	3 430	−.8	−1.0	−.1	−.2	....	−.1	−.5	....
Migrants' transfers	3 431	....	....	....	....	....	....	....	....
Debt forgiveness	3 432	−.8	−1.0	−.1	....	....	−.1	−.5	....
Other capital transfers	3 440	....	....	....	−.2	....	....	....	....
Nonproduced nonfinancial assets, credit	2 480	....	....	....	....	....	....	....	....
Nonproduced nonfinancial assets, debit	3 480	....	....	....	....	....	....	....	....

Table 2 (Continued). STANDARD PRESENTATION, 2003–2010
(Millions of U.S. dollars)

	Code	2003	2004	2005	2006	2007	2008	2009	2010
FINANCIAL ACCOUNT...............	4 995 ..	**1,029.6**	**1,245.6**	**1,549.4**	**3,155.8**	**5,056.2**	**5,515.0**	**−2,918.0**	**−1,657.0**
A. DIRECT INVESTMENT..............	4 500 ..	**142.0**	**510.5**	**688.8**	**1,550.6**	**1,408.6**	**1,714.2**	**−74.5**	**490.0**
Direct investment abroad............	4 505 ..	**−37.2**	**−262.6**	**−343.0**	**−289.5**	**−608.4**	**−355.5**	**−200.7**	**−132.3**
Equity capital............	4 510 ..	−10.4	−194.6	−204.1	−104.5	−676.5	−382.1	−177.5	−135.7
Claims on affiliated enterprises....	4 515 ..	−10.4	−197.1	−201.7	−104.5	−676.5	−382.1	−177.5	−135.7
Liabilities to affiliated enterprises..	4 520 ..	....	2.5	−2.4	....	....	....	....	....
Reinvested earnings............	4 525 ..	1.1	−5.1	−4.3	−2.6	20.5	−17.6	82.2	−12.0
Other capital............	4 530 ..	−27.8	−62.9	−134.6	−182.5	47.7	44.2	−105.4	15.4
Claims on affiliated enterprises....	4 535 ..	−26.3	−63.9	−147.4	−192.5	9.3	−82.7	14.9	−24.4
Liabilities to affiliated enterprises..	4 540 ..	−1.5	1.0	12.8	10.0	38.4	126.9	−120.4	39.8
Direct investment in Lithuania...........	4 555 ..	**179.2**	**773.2**	**1,031.8**	**1,840.2**	**2,017.0**	**2,069.8**	**126.1**	**622.2**
Equity capital............	4 560 ..	192.4	315.6	432.0	1,076.0	408.0	798.6	1,251.9	224.2
Claims on direct investors....	4 565 ..	....	−.1	....	....	.4	....	....	....
Liabilities to direct investors....	4 570 ..	192.4	315.7	432.0	1,076.0	407.6	798.6	1,251.9	224.2
Reinvested earnings............	4 575 ..	222.1	409.0	299.2	678.1	1,058.1	321.4	−1,508.3	−151.5
Other capital............	4 580 ..	−235.3	48.5	300.6	86.0	550.9	949.8	382.6	549.6
Claims on direct investors....	4 585 ..	−39.7	−31.3	−146.9	−201.9	−270.2	211.5	−192.8	55.2
Liabilities to direct investors....	4 590 ..	−195.6	79.8	447.4	287.9	821.1	738.3	575.4	494.4
B. PORTFOLIO INVESTMENT..............	4 600 ..	**252.1**	**211.2**	**−236.9**	**−253.7**	**−229.2**	**−337.0**	**1,131.4**	**1,924.1**
Assets............	4 602 ..	**29.8**	**−219.9**	**−778.5**	**−1,105.8**	**−838.0**	**−101.0**	**−1,162.2**	**−532.6**
Equity securities............	4 610 ..	−1.8	−18.8	−185.1	−286.4	−357.0	26.5	−425.9	−523.5
Monetary authorities............	4 611 ..	....	−2.1	−1.4	....	.1	....	....	....
General government............	4 612 ..	....	....	....	....	....	....	....	.3
Banks............	4 613 ..	....	.3	−31.6	−33.8	14.2	−1.8	4.3	−11.0
Other sectors............	4 614 ..	−1.8	−17.0	−152.1	−252.6	−371.2	28.3	−430.2	−512.7
Debt securities............	4 619 ..	31.6	−201.0	−593.4	−819.4	−481.0	−127.5	−736.2	−9.1
Bonds and notes............	4 620 ..	3.0	−219.7	−439.2	−543.9	−220.4	−303.4	−295.7	−28.3
Monetary authorities............	4 621 ..	....	....	....	....	....	....	....	....
General government............	4 622 ..	....	....	....	....	....	....	....	....
Banks............	4 623 ..	4.0	−182.1	−319.7	−365.1	57.9	97.1	−127.9	33.5
Other sectors............	4 624 ..	−.9	−37.6	−119.5	−178.8	−278.3	−400.4	−167.8	−61.8
Money market instruments............	4 630 ..	28.6	18.6	−154.3	−275.5	−260.6	175.9	−440.5	19.1
Monetary authorities............	4 631 ..	....	....	....	....	....	....	....	....
General government............	4 632 ..	....	....	....	....	....	....	....	....
Banks............	4 633 ..	29.1	19.4	−154.1	−277.2	−253.6	169.5	−269.2	−97.9
Other sectors............	4 634 ..	−.5	−.7	−.2	1.7	−7.0	6.3	−171.3	117.0
Liabilities............	4 652 ..	**222.3**	**431.1**	**541.6**	**852.1**	**608.8**	**−236.0**	**2,293.6**	**2,456.7**
Equity securities............	4 660 ..	4.2	7.9	130.0	72.0	−166.3	2.6	−2.2	36.5
Banks............	4 663 ..	6.3	−12.9	−10.0	34.2	−115.0	5.0	−1.5	−1.1
Other sectors............	4 664 ..	−2.1	20.8	140.0	37.8	−51.3	−2.5	−.6	37.7
Debt securities............	4 669 ..	218.0	423.1	411.6	780.1	775.0	−238.5	2,295.7	2,420.2
Bonds and notes............	4 670 ..	191.1	455.8	349.4	881.9	772.6	−237.4	2,262.1	2,422.9
Monetary authorities............	4 671 ..	....	....	....	....	....	....	....	....
General government............	4 672 ..	161.7	405.2	313.0	924.2	569.4	−163.9	2,270.6	2,472.7
Banks............	4 673 ..	57.4	63.6	38.3	−46.9	199.7	−78.6	−1.2	−50.3
Other sectors............	4 674 ..	−27.9	−13.0	−1.8	4.7	3.6	5.0	−7.3	.5
Money market instruments............	4 680 ..	26.9	−32.6	62.2	−101.9	2.4	−1.1	33.6	−2.7
Monetary authorities............	4 681 ..	....	....	....	....	....	....	....	....
General government............	4 682 ..	27.1	−14.0	88.1	−89.1	....	....	3.3	16.8
Banks............	4 683 ..	−.2	34.1	−24.4	−12.7	2.4	−1.1	28.4	−26.1
Other sectors............	4 684 ..	....	−52.7	−1.6	−.1	....	....	2.0	6.6
C. FINANCIAL DERIVATIVES..............	4 910 ..	**−28.0**	**2.6**	**12.9**	**−11.0**	**−2.4**	**14.8**	**38.2**	**−89.0**
Monetary authorities............	4 911 ..	....	....	....	....	....	....	....	....
General government............	4 912 ..	....	....	....	....	....	....	....	....
Banks............	4 913 ..	−31.2	2.6	12.9	−11.1	−2.4	14.8	38.2	−89.0
Other sectors............	4 914 ..	3.2	−.1	....	....	....	....	....	....
Assets............	4 900 ..	**28.1**	**60.0**	**27.4**	**9.5**	**4.8**	**40.4**	**61.6**	**−141.2**
Monetary authorities............	4 901 ..	....	....	....	....	....	....	....	....
General government............	4 902 ..	....	....	....	....	....	....	....	....
Banks............	4 903 ..	28.1	60.1	27.4	9.4	4.8	40.4	61.6	−141.2
Other sectors............	4 904 ..	.1	−.1	....	....	....	....	....	....
Liabilities............	4 905 ..	**−56.2**	**−57.4**	**−14.5**	**−20.5**	**−7.1**	**−25.6**	**−23.5**	**52.2**
Monetary authorities............	4 906 ..	....	....	....	....	....	....	....	....
General government............	4 907 ..	....	....	....	....	....	....	....	....
Banks............	4 908 ..	−59.3	−57.4	−14.5	−20.5	−7.1	−25.6	−23.5	52.2
Other sectors............	4 909 ..	3.2	....	....	....	....	....	....	....

Table 2 (Concluded). STANDARD PRESENTATION, 2003–2010

(Millions of U.S. dollars)

	Code	2003	2004	2005	2006	2007	2008	2009	2010
D. OTHER INVESTMENT	4 700 ..	**1,194.8**	**397.1**	**1,771.5**	**3,376.6**	**5,094.9**	**2,961.6**	**−3,868.7**	**−3,282.8**
Assets	4 703 ..	**−100.9**	**−683.8**	**−785.6**	**−475.7**	**−1,561.1**	**−607.6**	**−709.0**	**−158.8**
Trade credits	4 706 ..	61.5	−58.3	−392.9	−52.6	−404.0	−333.1	508.7	−198.6
General government	4 707 ..	....	....	....	....	....	....	....	....
of which: Short-term	4 709 ..	....	....	....	....	....	....	....	....
Other sectors	4 710 ..	61.5	−58.3	−392.9	−52.6	−404.0	−333.1	508.7	−198.6
of which: Short-term	4 712 ..	*61.5*	*−58.3*	*−392.9*	*−52.6*	*−404.0*	*−333.1*	*508.7*	*−198.6*
Loans	4 714 ..	−9.7	−429.5	−271.2	41.1	−991.4	110.0	−541.8	−1.7
Monetary authorities	4 715 ..	....	....	....	....	....	....	....	....
of which: Short-term	4 718 ..	....	....	....	....	....	....	....	....
General government	4 719 ..	....	....	....	....	....	....	....	....
of which: Short-term	4 721 ..	....	....	....	....	....	....	....	....
Banks	4 722 ..	16.3	−431.0	−220.6	115.5	−962.8	257.5	−705.3	54.5
of which: Short-term	4 724 ..	*31.3*	*−408.2*	*−228.2*	*215.7*	*−733.4*	*250.8*	*−611.0*	*71.4*
Other sectors	4 725 ..	−26.0	1.4	−50.6	−74.4	−28.6	−147.5	163.5	−56.2
of which: Short-term	4 727 ..	*−23.7*	*11.3*	*−23.3*	*−43.2*	*−48.3*	*−110.8*	*110.5*	*−56.0*
Currency and deposits	4 730 ..	−143.8	−208.0	−106.2	−473.4	−155.7	−151.3	−765.2	68.7
Monetary authorities	4 731 ..	....	....	....	....	....	....	....	....
General government	4 732 ..	....	−7.3	....	....	....	....	−147.8	−269.9
Banks	4 733 ..	−171.3	−243.3	−163.2	−459.7	245.3	−376.2	−527.2	484.4
Other sectors	4 734 ..	27.5	42.5	57.0	−13.7	−401.0	224.9	−90.3	−145.8
Other assets	4 736 ..	−8.9	12.0	−15.3	9.2	−10.0	−233.1	89.3	−27.3
Monetary authorities	4 737 ..	....	....	....	....	....	....	....	....
of which: Short-term	4 739 ..	....	....	....	....	....	....	....	....
General government	4 740 ..	....	....	....	....	....	....	....	....
of which: Short-term	4 742 ..	....	....	....	....	....	....	....	....
Banks	4 743 ..	−6.0	3.1	−10.9	8.9	−2.9	−3.9	−2.4	−1.0
of which: Short-term	4 745 ..	*−6.0*	*3.1*	*−10.9*	*8.9*	*−2.9*	*−3.9*	*−2.4*	*−1.0*
Other sectors	4 746 ..	−2.9	8.9	−4.4	.3	−7.1	−229.2	91.8	−26.4
of which: Short-term	4 748 ..	*−2.9*	*8.9*	*−4.4*	*.3*	*−7.1*	*−229.2*	*91.8*	*−26.4*
Liabilities	4 753 ..	**1,295.7**	**1,081.0**	**2,557.0**	**3,852.4**	**6,656.0**	**3,569.2**	**−3,159.8**	**−3,124.0**
Trade credits	4 756 ..	272.7	243.4	530.1	−1.1	268.0	−410.8	−740.3	272.3
General government	4 757 ..	....	....	....	....	....	....	....	....
of which: Short-term	4 759 ..	....	....	....	....	....	....	....	....
Other sectors	4 760 ..	272.7	243.4	530.1	−1.1	268.0	−410.8	−740.3	272.3
of which: Short-term	4 762 ..	*272.7*	*243.4*	*530.1*	*−1.1*	*268.0*	*−410.8*	*−740.3*	*272.3*
Loans	4 764 ..	995.2	648.7	1,880.7	3,549.6	6,099.7	4,567.1	−3,020.2	−3,828.0
Monetary authorities	4 765 ..	−81.4	−19.8	−25.5	....	....	....	....	....
of which: Use of Fund credit and loans from the Fund	4 766 ..	*−81.4*	*−19.8*	*−25.5*	....	....	....	....	....
of which: Short-term	4 768 ..	....	....	....	....	....	....	....	....
General government	4 769 ..	−9.4	−308.2	−191.0	−24.5	−120.1	115.0	908.2	472.2
of which: Short-term	4 771 ..	*80.0*	*−85.3*	....	....	....	....	....	....
Banks	4 772 ..	683.2	594.4	2,434.4	2,336.3	4,771.7	4,069.9	−2,893.9	−3,059.0
of which: Short-term	4 774 ..	*455.6*	*27.9*	*953.9*	*264.7*	*810.9*	*1,757.4*	*−1,861.1*	*−632.8*
Other sectors	4 775 ..	402.9	382.2	−337.1	1,237.9	1,448.1	382.1	−1,034.5	−1,241.3
of which: Short-term	4 777 ..	*1.3*	*65.4*	*−62.4*	*34.3*	*82.1*	*20.8*	*−61.4*	*−138.1*
Currency and deposits	4 780 ..	80.6	286.8	156.2	260.8	−110.7	−192.3	323.8	410.9
Monetary authorities	4 781 ..	−.2	1.8	5.5	77.9	−27.0	−12.6	113.5	−119.2
General government	4 782 ..	....	....	....	....	....	....	....	....
Banks	4 783 ..	80.8	285.0	150.6	182.8	−83.7	−179.7	210.3	530.1
Other sectors	4 784 ..	....	....	....	....	....	....	....	....
Other liabilities	4 786 ..	−52.8	−97.9	−9.9	43.2	399.1	−394.7	276.9	20.9
Monetary authorities	4 787 ..	−7.8	−68.6	....	−2.7	350.4	−387.2	222.5	171.7
of which: Short-term	4 789 ..	*−7.8*	*−68.6*	....	*−2.7*	*350.4*	*−387.2*	*7.8*	*171.7*
General government	4 790 ..	....	....	....	....	....	....	....	....
of which: Short-term	4 792 ..	....	....	....	....	....	....	....	....
Banks	4 793 ..	−26.4	−9.1	−7.7	40.9	14.7	−7.6	97.4	−138.5
of which: Short-term	4 795 ..	*−26.4*	*−9.1*	*−7.7*	*40.9*	*14.7*	*−7.6*	*97.4*	*−138.5*
Other sectors	4 796 ..	−18.6	−20.2	−2.2	4.9	34.0	....	−42.9	−12.2
of which: Short-term	4 798 ..	*−18.6*	*−20.2*	*−2.2*	*4.9*	*34.0*	....	*−42.9*	*−12.2*
E. RESERVE ASSETS	4 802 ..	**−531.2**	**124.2**	**−686.8**	**−1,506.7**	**−1,215.7**	**1,161.4**	**−144.4**	**−699.3**
Monetary gold	4 812 ..	....	.1	....	....	−.4	−.3	−.3	....
Special drawing rights	4 811 ..	53.6	....	....	....	....	....	−214.7	....
Reserve position in the Fund	4 810 ..	....	....	....	....	....	....	....	....
Foreign exchange	4 803 ..	−584.9	124.1	−686.8	−1,506.7	−1,215.3	1,161.7	70.6	−699.3
Other claims	4 813 ..	....	....	....	....	....	....	....	....
NET ERRORS AND OMISSIONS	4 998 ..	**181.2**	**191.8**	**−49.4**	**−289.1**	**−53.9**	**−39.8**	**8.3**	**4.0**

Table 3. INTERNATIONAL INVESTMENT POSITION (End-period stocks), 2003–2010

(Millions of U.S. dollars)

	Code	2003	2004	2005	2006	2007	2008	2009	2010
ASSETS	8 995 C.	**5,717.0**	**7,413.0**	**9,129.0**	**13,457.3**	**19,195.5**	**18,081.9**	**20,360.1**	**20,268.4**
Direct investment abroad	8 505	**119.7**	**422.8**	**721.1**	**1,041.4**	**1,570.5**	**1,990.1**	**2,310.6**	**2,091.6**
Equity capital and reinvested earnings	8 506	62.7	287.2	490.7	558.8	1,074.3	1,547.4	1,754.6	1,610.0
Claims on affiliated enterprises	8 507	62.7	289.9	490.7	558.8	1,074.3	1,547.4	1,754.6	1,610.0
Liabilities to affiliated enterprises	8 508	....	−2.6	....	....	....	....	....	....
Other capital	8 530	57.0	135.6	230.4	482.6	496.1	442.8	556.0	481.6
Claims on affiliated enterprises	8 535	57.2	136.9	243.6	507.3	563.9	637.8	599.8	558.4
Liabilities to affiliated enterprises	8 540	−.2	−1.3	−13.1	−24.7	−67.8	−195.0	−43.7	−76.8
Portfolio investment	8 602	**268.8**	**516.7**	**1,255.2**	**2,517.2**	**3,617.0**	**3,451.3**	**4,424.1**	**4,606.7**
Equity securities	8 610	11.8	36.2	220.5	561.4	1,038.6	833.4	1,287.0	1,793.7
Monetary authorities	8 611	2.8	5.4	6.0	6.6	7.4	7.1	7.3	6.7
General government	8 612	....	....	....	....	....	....	....	.1
Banks	8 613	1.6	1.5	5.2	40.9	29.3	12.6	4.6	15.1
Other sectors	8 614	7.3	29.3	209.3	513.9	1,001.9	813.7	1,275.2	1,771.7
Debt securities	8 619	257.0	480.5	1,034.8	1,955.8	2,578.4	2,617.9	3,137.1	2,813.1
Bonds and notes	8 620	91.2	345.0	756.9	1,363.7	1,626.4	2,562.5	2,687.8	2,449.3
Monetary authorities	8 621	....	....	....	....	....	....	....	....
General government	8 622	....	....	....	....	....	....	....	....
Banks	8 623	59.4	252.3	547.2	968.5	987.1	1,444.8	1,486.1	1,357.0
Other sectors	8 624	31.9	92.7	209.7	395.2	639.3	1,117.7	1,201.7	1,092.2
Money market instruments	8 630	165.7	135.5	277.8	592.1	952.1	55.4	449.4	363.8
Monetary authorities	8 631	....	....	....	....	....	....	....	....
General government	8 632	....	....	....	....	....	....	....	....
Banks	8 633	147.3	134.3	276.4	587.6	939.6	48.9	309.9	361.0
Other sectors	8 634	18.5	1.2	1.4	4.5	12.5	6.5	139.5	2.8
Financial derivatives	8 900	**.2**	**....**	**9.6**	**69.0**	**222.0**	**39.2**	**46.3**	**149.6**
Monetary authorities	8 901	....	....	....	....	....	....	....	....
General government	8 902	....	....	....	....	....	....	....	....
Banks	8 903	....	....	9.5	69.0	222.0	39.2	46.3	149.6
Other sectors	8 904	.2	....	....	....	....	....	....	....
Other investment	8 703	**1,878.7**	**2,879.5**	**3,327.5**	**4,057.1**	**6,064.9**	**6,158.2**	**6,919.5**	**6,583.3**
Trade credits	8 706	828.7	1,115.5	1,355.1	1,518.3	2,118.5	2,143.8	1,651.2	1,731.7
General government	8 707	....	....	....	....	....	....	....	....
of which: Short-term	8 709	....	....	....	....	....	....	....	....
Other sectors	8 710	828.7	1,115.5	1,355.1	1,518.3	2,118.5	2,143.8	1,651.2	1,731.7
of which: Short-term	8 712	*828.7*	*1,115.5*	*1,355.1*	*1,518.3*	*2,118.5*	*2,143.8*	*1,651.2*	*1,731.7*
Loans	8 714	328.9	786.5	992.9	998.2	2,068.0	2,051.0	2,588.0	2,403.0
Monetary authorities	8 715	....	....	....	....	....	....	....	....
of which: Short-term	8 718	....	....	....	....	....	....	....	....
General government	8 719	....	....	....	....	....	....	....	....
of which: Short-term	8 721	....	....	....	....	....	....	....	....
Banks	8 722	257.5	733.7	867.2	789.0	1,802.7	1,572.0	2,284.2	2,132.4
of which: Short-term	8 724	*172.9*	*613.3*	*774.9*	*589.2*	*1,345.3*	*1,124.8*	*1,741.9*	*1,463.9*
Other sectors	8 725	71.4	52.9	125.7	209.2	265.3	479.0	303.8	270.6
of which: Short-term	8 727	*43.9*	*33.2*	*55.7*	*105.2*	*169.8*	*347.1*	*229.1*	*219.7*
Currency and deposits	8 730	684.6	957.6	944.2	1,511.3	1,815.0	1,800.4	2,609.9	2,369.6
Monetary authorities	8 731	....	....	....	....	....	....	....	....
General government	8 732	....	....	....	....	....	....	143.6	372.7
Banks	8 733	463.6	731.6	784.2	1,324.3	1,197.0	1,414.4	1,976.9	1,390.3
Other sectors	8 734	221.0	226.0	160.0	187.0	618.0	386.0	489.4	606.6
Other assets	8 736	36.5	19.9	35.3	29.3	63.5	163.0	70.4	79.0
Monetary authorities	8 737	....	....	....	....	....	....	....	....
of which: Short-term	8 739	....	....	....	....	....	....	....	....
General government	8 740	....	....	....	....	....	....	....	....
of which: Short-term	8 742	....	....	....	....	....	....	....	....
Banks	8 743	15.2	13.8	19.1	11.4	15.4	13.2	17.4	12.1
of which: Short-term	8 745	*15.2*	*13.8*	*19.1*	*11.4*	*15.4*	*13.2*	*17.4*	*12.1*
Other sectors	8 746	21.3	6.0	16.1	17.9	48.0	149.8	52.9	66.9
of which: Short-term	8 748	*21.3*	*6.0*	*16.1*	*17.9*	*48.0*	*149.8*	*52.9*	*66.9*
Reserve assets	8 802	**3,449.7**	**3,594.0**	**3,815.6**	**5,772.6**	**7,721.1**	**6,443.0**	**6,659.7**	**6,837.3**
Monetary gold	8 812	77.7	81.4	95.3	118.1	155.4	161.5	206.4	263.7
Special drawing rights	8 811	.1	.1	.1	.1	.1	.1	215.3	211.5
Reserve position in the Fund	8 810	....	....	....	.1	.1	.1	.1	.1
Foreign exchange	8 803	3,371.9	3,512.5	3,720.1	5,654.3	7,565.6	6,281.3	6,237.9	6,362.0
Other claims	8 813	....	....	....	....	....	....	....	....

Table 3 (Concluded). INTERNATIONAL INVESTMENT POSITION (End-period stocks), 2003–2010

(Millions of U.S. dollars)

	Code	2003	2004	2005	2006	2007	2008	2009	2010
LIABILITIES............	8 995 D.	**12,575.8**	**15,956.7**	**19,717.0**	**28,931.5**	**42,683.0**	**41,819.7**	**43,278.4**	**40,788.5**
Direct investment in Lithuania............	8 555 ..	**4,959.8**	**6,388.9**	**8,211.0**	**10,996.3**	**15,061.9**	**13,074.0**	**14,009.6**	**13,448.6**
Equity capital and reinvested earnings....	8 556 ..	4,193.9	5,475.9	7,129.0	9,663.6	12,714.2	9,829.9	10,334.9	9,606.1
Claims on direct investors............	8 557 ..	....	−.1	−.1	−.5	....	....	....	....
Liabilities to direct investors........	8 558 ..	4,193.9	5,476.0	7,129.1	9,664.1	12,714.2	9,829.9	10,334.9	9,606.1
Other capital............	8 580 ..	765.9	913.0	1,082.0	1,332.7	2,347.8	3,244.1	3,674.7	3,842.5
Claims on direct investors............	8 585 ..	−110.0	−165.0	−282.6	−504.0	−845.2	−630.3	−916.0	−796.8
Liabilities to direct investors........	8 590 ..	875.9	1,077.9	1,364.7	1,836.7	3,193.0	3,874.4	4,590.7	4,639.3
Portfolio investment............	8 652 ..	**2,077.3**	**2,812.0**	**2,981.6**	**4,572.3**	**5,705.0**	**4,007.3**	**7,175.9**	**9,879.0**
Equity securities............	8 660 ..	144.0	172.5	319.5	809.4	743.5	233.2	335.1	493.2
Banks............	8 663 ..	51.8	42.8	27.8	205.3	128.3	26.1	36.4	39.3
Other sectors............	8 664 ..	92.1	129.7	291.8	604.0	615.3	207.0	298.7	453.8
Debt securities............	8 669 ..	1,933.3	2,639.5	2,662.1	3,762.9	4,961.5	3,774.2	6,840.8	9,385.8
Bonds and notes............	8 670 ..	1,834.0	2,535.8	2,560.9	3,762.9	4,958.8	3,772.6	6,807.4	9,359.8
Monetary authorities............	8 671 ..	....	....	....	....	....	....	....	....
General government............	8 672 ..	1,756.8	2,395.2	2,402.4	3,628.9	4,609.6	3,567.9	6,547.1	9,174.5
Banks............	8 673 ..	62.3	138.5	158.5	128.6	339.4	190.8	253.8	180.1
Other sectors............	8 674 ..	15.0	2.1	....	5.4	9.9	13.9	6.5	5.2
Money market instruments............	8 680 ..	99.2	103.7	101.2	....	2.7	1.6	33.4	26.0
Monetary authorities............	8 681 ..	....	....	....	....	....	....	....	....
General government............	8 682 ..	39.9	62.0	87.8	....	....	....	3.3	19.5
Banks............	8 683 ..	1.4	39.9	13.3	....	2.7	1.6	28.0	....
Other sectors............	8 684 ..	57.9	1.8	.1	....	....	....	2.1	6.5
Financial derivatives............	8 905 ..	**10.2**	**2.9**	**4.0**	**30.1**	**41.0**	**131.6**	**156.1**	**150.9**
Monetary authorities............	8 906 ..	....	....	....	....	....	....	....	....
General government............	8 907 ..	....	....	....	....	....	....	....	....
Banks............	8 908 ..	....	....	3.1	30.1	41.0	131.6	156.1	150.9
Other sectors............	8 909 ..	10.2	2.9	.9	....	....	....	....	....
Other investment............	8 753 ..	**5,528.6**	**6,752.9**	**8,520.4**	**13,332.8**	**21,875.1**	**24,606.9**	**21,936.9**	**17,310.0**
Trade credits............	8 756 ..	1,437.3	1,644.2	1,945.5	2,169.2	2,719.8	2,413.3	1,698.7	1,819.3
General government............	8 757 ..	....	....	....	....	....	....	....	....
of which: Short-term............	8 759 ..	....	....	....	....	....	....	....	....
Other sectors............	8 760 ..	1,437.3	1,644.2	1,945.5	2,169.2	2,719.8	2,413.3	1,698.7	1,819.3
of which: Short-term............	8 762 ..	*1,437.3*	*1,644.2*	*1,945.5*	*2,169.2*	*2,719.8*	*2,413.3*	*1,698.7*	*1,819.3*
Loans............	8 764 ..	3,524.8	4,321.3	5,720.3	9,933.5	17,498.5	21,184.9	18,603.1	13,622.7
Monetary authorities............	8 765 ..	44.9	26.1	....	....	....	....	....	....
of which: Use of Fund credit and loans from the Fund....	8 766 ..	*44.9*	*26.1*	....	....	....	....	....	....
of which: Short-term............	8 768 ..	....	....	....	....	....	....	....	....
General government............	8 769 ..	717.7	478.0	254.7	256.2	153.1	269.2	1,216.4	1,580.0
of which: Short-term............	8 771 ..	*87.5*	....	....	....	....	....	....	....
Banks............	8 772 ..	1,470.6	2,097.6	4,274.4	7,124.3	12,900.9	16,361.5	13,800.9	9,893.9
of which: Short-term............	8 774 ..	*1,006.3*	*985.4*	*1,805.2*	*2,080.4*	*3,063.9*	*4,453.8*	*2,586.1*	*1,886.5*
Other sectors............	8 775 ..	1,291.5	1,719.6	1,191.2	2,553.0	4,444.4	4,554.1	3,585.8	2,148.7
of which: Short-term............	8 777 ..	*79.7*	*245.4*	*165.8*	*192.3*	*319.9*	*295.7*	*224.5*	*81.0*
Currency and deposits............	8 780 ..	387.8	695.2	785.7	1,101.7	1,053.5	826.6	1,194.5	1,428.2
Monetary authorities............	8 781 ..	.2	4.0	8.9	89.9	64.3	53.7	164.4	44.3
General government............	8 782 ..	....	....	....	....	....	....	....	....
Banks............	8 783 ..	387.6	691.1	776.9	1,011.8	989.2	772.9	1,030.1	1,383.9
Other sectors............	8 784 ..	....	....	....	....	....	....	....	....
Other liabilities............	8 786 ..	178.8	92.3	68.9	128.4	603.4	182.2	440.6	439.8
Monetary authorities............	8 787 ..	67.1	....	....	....	391.5	....	222.7	388.0
of which: Short-term............	8 789 ..	*67.1*	....	....	....	*391.5*	....	*7.6*	*176.6*
General government............	8 790 ..	....	....	....	....	....	....	....	....
of which: Short-term............	8 792 ..	....	....	....	....	....	....	....	....
Banks............	8 793 ..	51.9	50.4	35.6	86.4	123.1	100.3	181.3	34.8
of which: Short-term............	8 795 ..	*51.9*	*50.4*	*35.6*	*86.4*	*123.1*	*100.3*	*181.3*	*34.8*
Other sectors............	8 796 ..	59.7	41.9	33.3	42.0	88.7	81.9	36.5	17.0
of which: Short-term............	8 798 ..	*59.7*	*41.9*	*33.3*	*42.0*	*88.7*	*81.9*	*36.5*	*17.0*
NET INTERNATIONAL INVESTMENT POSITION........	8 995 ..	**−6,858.9**	**−8,543.7**	**−10,588.0**	**−15,474.2**	**−23,487.5**	**−23,737.8**	**−22,918.3**	**−20,520.1**
Conversion rates: litai per U.S. dollar (end of period)............	0 102 ..	**2.7621**	**2.5345**	**2.9102**	**2.6304**	**2.3572**	**2.4507**	**2.4052**	**2.6099**

Table 1. ANALYTIC PRESENTATION, 2003–2010
(Millions of U.S. dollars)

	Code	2003	2004	2005	2006	2007	2008	2009	2010
A. Current Account[1]	4 993 Z.	**2,409**	**4,088**	**4,406**	**4,397**	**5,215**	**3,040**	**3,307**	**4,122**
Goods: exports f.o.b.	2 100 ..	10,942	13,526	14,709	16,497	18,405	21,370	15,384	16,662
Goods: imports f.o.b.	3 100 ..	−13,937	−17,078	−18,849	−20,805	−23,206	−28,063	−19,973	−22,105
Balance on Goods	4 100 ..	*−2,995*	*−3,552*	*−4,140*	*−4,308*	*−4,801*	*−6,692*	*−4,588*	*−5,443*
Services: credit	2 200 ..	25,499	33,957	40,416	50,698	65,057	68,523	58,474	66,767
Services: debit	3 200 ..	−15,531	−20,940	−24,196	−29,861	−37,746	−39,079	−33,395	−36,678
Balance on Goods and Services	4 991 ..	*6,973*	*9,465*	*12,080*	*16,529*	*22,510*	*22,752*	*20,490*	*24,646*
Income: credit	2 300 ..	69,291	76,855	99,464	128,706	167,831	203,250	134,904	137,630
Income: debit	3 300 ..	−73,247	−81,166	−106,012	−139,689	−183,114	−220,220	−150,683	−157,255
Balance on Goods, Services, and Income	4 992 ..	*3,017*	*5,154*	*5,533*	*5,546*	*7,228*	*5,782*	*4,711*	*5,021*
Current transfers: credit	2 379 Z.	3,889	4,025	4,744	5,778	5,994	7,284	6,654	6,621
Current transfers: debit	3 379 ..	−4,497	−5,090	−5,871	−6,928	−8,007	−10,026	−8,058	−7,521
B. Capital Account[1]	4 994 Z.	**−140**	**−772**	**1,248**	**−366**	**−197**	**−373**	**−386**	**−306**
Capital account: credit	2 994 Z.	63	51	1,576	36	58	125	141	122
Capital account: debit	3 994 ..	−204	−823	−329	−402	−254	−499	−527	−428
Total, Groups A Plus B	4 981 ..	*2,268*	*3,316*	*5,654*	*4,030*	*5,018*	*2,667*	*2,921*	*3,815*
C. Financial Account[1]	4 995 W.	**−2,084**	**−3,528**	**−5,633**	**−4,034**	**−4,969**	**−2,432**	**−2,328**	**−3,493**
Direct investment abroad	4 505 ..	−100,458	−85,310	−123,371	−115,562	−269,230	−129,848	−229,528	−185,132
Direct investment in Luxembourg	4 555 Z.	89,784	80,098	115,151	129,879	193,765	102,113	207,130	207,871
Portfolio investment assets	4 602 ..	−78,422	−87,546	−267,098	−176,160	−174,516	164,735	−252,532	−135,253
Equity securities	4 610 ..	−35,857	−45,835	−123,620	−102,723	−52,572	85,754	−89,026	−62,031
Debt securities	4 619 ..	−42,565	−41,711	−143,477	−73,437	−121,944	78,981	−163,507	−73,222
Portfolio investment liabilities	4 652 Z.	99,486	139,610	315,158	250,713	307,662	−126,994	180,437	195,646
Equity securities	4 660 ..	70,443	121,546	275,580	220,277	279,314	−132,109	148,625	209,858
Debt securities	4 669 Z.	29,043	18,064	39,577	30,436	28,348	5,116	31,812	−14,212
Financial derivatives	4 910 ..	6,158	−2,998	−3,190	9,850	14,177	−21,730	−12,732	24,083
Financial derivatives assets	4 900 ..	....	....	....	....	....	....	....	....
Financial derivatives liabilities	4 905 ..	....	....	....	....	....	....	....	....
Other investment assets	4 703 ..	−33,924	−117,163	−191,871	−267,184	−249,183	−49,105	121,440	−166,008
Monetary authorities	4 701 ..	−7,641	−7,210	−5,755	3,281	−18,671	−30,614	−15,747	−19,401
General government	4 704 ..	−1	....	−1	−9	−317	−1	−6	−137
Banks	4 705 ..	−3,623	−43,871	−36,573	−57,181	−118,631	−18,822	147,565	−7,757
Other sectors	4 728 ..	−22,658	−66,081	−149,541	−213,276	−111,563	332	−10,373	−138,713
Other investment liabilities	4 753 W.	15,292	69,781	149,588	164,429	172,356	58,397	−16,543	55,301
Monetary authorities	4 753 WA	−5,824	6,208	322	−343	454	1,147	605	69
General government	4 753 ZB	−1	−16	....	....	−1	....	....	....
Banks	4 753 ZC	17,866	31,295	41,383	43,908	75,326	−14,656	−78,187	−9,637
Other sectors	4 753 ZD	3,251	32,294	107,883	120,863	96,576	71,906	61,039	64,868
Total, Groups A Through C	4 983 ..	*184*	*−212*	*21*	*−4*	*49*	*235*	*593*	*323*
D. Net Errors and Omissions	4 998 ..	**−76**	**220**	**−69**	**−24**	**−138**	**−64**	**−147**	**−290**
Total, Groups A Through D	4 984 ..	*108*	*8*	*−48*	*−28*	*−89*	*171*	*446*	*33*
E. Reserves and Related Items	4 802 A.	**−108**	**−8**	**48**	**28**	**89**	**−171**	**−446**	**−33**
Reserve assets	4 802 ..	−108	−8	48	28	89	−171	−446	−33
Use of Fund credit and loans	4 766 ..	....	....	....	....	....	....	....	....
Exceptional financing	4 920 ..	....	....	....	....	....	....	....	....
Conversion rates: euros per U.S. dollar	0 103 ..	**.8860**	**.8054**	**.8041**	**.7971**	**.7306**	**.6827**	**.7198**	**.7550**

[1] Excludes components that have been classified in the categories of Group E.

Table 2. STANDARD PRESENTATION, 2003–2010

(Millions of U.S. dollars)

	Code	2003	2004	2005	2006	2007	2008	2009	2010
CURRENT ACCOUNT..	4 993 ..	**2,409**	**4,088**	**4,406**	**4,397**	**5,215**	**3,040**	**3,307**	**4,122**
A. GOODS...	4 100 ..	**−2,995**	**−3,552**	**−4,140**	**−4,308**	**−4,801**	**−6,692**	**−4,588**	**−5,443**
Credit..	2 100 ..	**10,942**	**13,526**	**14,709**	**16,497**	**18,405**	**21,370**	**15,384**	**16,662**
General merchandise: exports f.o.b.................	2 110 ..	9,487	11,705	12,672	13,890	15,761	16,728	12,054	13,552
Goods for processing: exports f.o.b...............	2 150 ..	194	199	192	149	246	548	316	237
Repairs on goods..	2 160 ..	1	3	2	4	3	42	25	14
Goods procured in ports by carriers..............	2 170 ..	799	1,043	1,340	1,422	1,534	1,963	1,339	1,556
Nonmonetary gold..	2 180 ..	461	576	503	1,032	862	2,089	1,650	1,303
Debit...	3 100 ..	**−13,937**	**−17,078**	**−18,849**	**−20,805**	**−23,206**	**−28,063**	**−19,973**	**−22,105**
General merchandise: imports f.o.b................	3 110 ..	−12,988	−16,140	−17,159	−18,992	−21,598	−24,949	−18,210	−20,268
Goods for processing: imports f.o.b..............	3 150 ..	−191	−202	−184	−156	−223	−214	−161	−170
Repairs on goods..	3 160 ..	−13	−15	−12	−12	−9	−46	−106	−121
Goods procured in ports by carriers..............	3 170 ..	−206	−266	−433	−589	−654	−942	−497	−584
Nonmonetary gold..	3 180 ..	−541	−455	−1,061	−1,056	−722	−1,911	−997	−962
B. SERVICES...	4 200 ..	**9,968**	**13,017**	**16,220**	**20,837**	**27,311**	**29,444**	**25,079**	**30,089**
Total credit...	2 200 ..	*25,499*	*33,957*	*40,416*	*50,698*	*65,057*	*68,523*	*58,474*	*66,767*
Total debit..	3 200 ..	*−15,531*	*−20,940*	*−24,196*	*−29,861*	*−37,746*	*−39,079*	*−33,395*	*−36,678*
Transportation services, credit...............	2 205 ..	**1,765**	**2,179**	**2,667**	**2,903**	**3,476**	**4,170**	**3,143**	**3,387**
Passenger...	2 850 ..	....	....	....	....	....	....	....	....
Freight...	2 851 ..	....	....	....	....	....	....	....	....
Other..	2 852 ..	....	....	....	....	....	....	....	....
Sea transport, passenger...............................	2 207 ..	....	....	....	....	....	....	....	....
Sea transport, freight.....................................	2 208 ..	....	....	....	....	....	....	....	....
Sea transport, other.......................................	2 209 ..	....	....	....	....	....	....	....	....
Air transport, passenger................................	2 211 ..	....	....	....	....	....	....	....	....
Air transport, freight......................................	2 212 ..	....	....	....	....	....	....	....	....
Air transport, other..	2 213 ..	....	....	....	....	....	....	....	....
Other transport, passenger...........................	2 215 ..	....	....	....	....	....	....	....	....
Other transport, freight..................................	2 216 ..	....	....	....	....	....	....	....	....
Other transport, other....................................	2 217 ..	....	....	....	....	....	....	....	....
Transportation services, debit................	3 205 ..	**−784**	**−1,062**	**−1,266**	**−1,356**	**−1,760**	**−2,019**	**−1,560**	**−1,655**
Passenger...	3 850 ..	....	....	....	....	....	....	....	....
Freight...	3 851 ..	....	....	....	....	....	....	....	....
Other..	3 852 ..	....	....	....	....	....	....	....	....
Sea transport, passenger...............................	3 207 ..	....	....	....	....	....	....	....	....
Sea transport, freight.....................................	3 208 ..	....	....	....	....	....	....	....	....
Sea transport, other.......................................	3 209 ..	....	....	....	....	....	....	....	....
Air transport, passenger................................	3 211 ..	....	....	....	....	....	....	....	....
Air transport, freight......................................	3 212 ..	....	....	....	....	....	....	....	....
Air transport, other..	3 213 ..	....	....	....	....	....	....	....	....
Other transport, passenger...........................	3 215 ..	....	....	....	....	....	....	....	....
Other transport, freight..................................	3 216 ..	....	....	....	....	....	....	....	....
Other transport, other....................................	3 217 ..	....	....	....	....	....	....	....	....
Travel, credit..	2 236 ..	**2,994**	**3,650**	**3,612**	**3,636**	**4,032**	**4,486**	**4,176**	**4,107**
Business travel..	2 237 ..	....	....	....	....	....	....	....	....
Personal travel..	2 240 ..	....	....	....	....	....	....	....	....
Travel, debit..	3 236 ..	**−2,423**	**−2,911**	**−2,977**	**−3,138**	**−3,476**	**−3,801**	**−3,612**	**−3,517**
Business travel..	3 237 ..	....	....	....	....	....	....	....	....
Personal travel..	3 240 ..	....	....	....	....	....	....	....	....
Other services, credit.............................	2 200 BA ..	**20,739**	**28,127**	**34,138**	**44,159**	**57,549**	**59,866**	**51,155**	**59,273**
Communications...	2 245 ..	828	951	1,101	1,360	2,096	2,842	3,340	2,638
Construction..	2 249 ..	165	232	286	339	482	610	462	438
Insurance...	2 253 ..	1,300	1,671	1,956	2,433	2,576	3,171	3,203	3,551
Financial..	2 260 ..	14,323	19,449	24,423	32,818	43,097	41,784	33,492	40,546
Computer and information............................	2 262 ..	1,199	2,283	2,405	2,287	1,398	1,226	1,027	757
Royalties and licence fees.............................	2 266 ..	128	200	297	395	399	342	377	473
Other business services.................................	2 268 ..	2,371	2,834	3,137	3,869	6,428	8,419	7,443	8,390
Personal, cultural, and recreational..............	2 287 ..	162	189	240	331	626	887	1,256	1,983
Government, n.i.e...	2 291 ..	262	319	275	326	446	584	554	498
Other services, debit..............................	3 200 BA ..	**−12,324**	**−16,966**	**−19,954**	**−25,368**	**−32,510**	**−33,259**	**−28,223**	**−31,506**
Communications...	3 245 ..	−584	−1,083	−1,158	−1,326	−1,224	−1,397	−1,479	−842
Construction..	3 249 ..	−318	−399	−425	−486	−637	−776	−602	−560
Insurance...	3 253 ..	−842	−1,134	−1,232	−1,643	−1,487	−1,885	−1,840	−2,107
Financial..	3 260 ..	−7,549	−10,125	−12,678	−16,831	−21,798	−20,328	−16,022	−18,938
Computer and information............................	3 262 ..	−366	−582	−680	−670	−759	−773	−752	−832
Royalties and licence fees.............................	3 266 ..	−109	−147	−138	−162	−401	−542	−467	−406
Other business services.................................	3 268 ..	−2,118	−2,992	−3,281	−3,792	−5,553	−6,701	−5,852	−6,201
Personal, cultural, and recreational..............	3 287 ..	−418	−477	−332	−428	−617	−812	−1,163	−1,571
Government, n.i.e...	3 291 ..	−20	−27	−30	−29	−34	−44	−46	−51

Table 2 (Continued). STANDARD PRESENTATION, 2003–2010

(Millions of U.S. dollars)

	Code	2003	2004	2005	2006	2007	2008	2009	2010
C. INCOME	4 300	**−3,956**	**−4,311**	**−6,548**	**−10,983**	**−15,282**	**−16,970**	**−15,779**	**−19,625**
Total credit	2 300	*69,291*	*76,855*	*99,464*	*128,706*	*167,831*	*203,250*	*134,904*	*137,630*
Total debit	3 300	*−73,247*	*−81,166*	*−106,012*	*−139,689*	*−183,114*	*−220,220*	*−150,683*	*−157,255*
Compensation of employees, credit	2 310	**994**	**1,115**	**1,258**	**1,345**	**1,424**	**1,599**	**1,568**	**1,551**
Compensation of employees, debit	3 310	**−4,930**	**−5,928**	**−6,488**	**−7,302**	**−8,963**	**−10,698**	**−10,460**	**−10,321**
Investment income, credit	2 320	**68,297**	**75,740**	**98,206**	**127,361**	**166,408**	**201,651**	**133,336**	**136,079**
Direct investment income	2 330	19,976	20,518	34,361	37,889	48,755	66,016	34,795	37,497
Dividends and distributed branch profits	2 332	14,862	13,803	25,412	29,730	35,644	51,860	39,128	35,164
Reinvested earnings and undistributed branch profits	2 333	−534	1,912	2,605	676	4,212	3,061	−5,968	650
Income on debt (interest)	2 334	5,647	4,803	6,345	7,483	8,900	11,095	1,635	1,683
Portfolio investment income	2 339	35,345	41,766	49,081	68,329	86,460	98,735	70,254	73,504
Income on equity	2 340	8,355	9,601	14,681	22,027	26,527	34,452	19,962	23,737
Income on bonds and notes	2 350	24,740	29,457	30,915	40,912	50,682	53,179	40,890	45,462
Income on money market instruments	2 360	2,250	2,708	3,485	5,390	9,252	11,104	9,402	4,306
Other investment income	2 370	12,977	13,456	14,764	21,143	31,192	36,900	28,287	25,078
Investment income, debit	3 320	**−68,317**	**−75,238**	**−99,523**	**−132,387**	**−174,151**	**−209,521**	**−140,222**	**−146,934**
Direct investment income	3 330	−26,299	−26,145	−39,328	−43,279	−57,837	−75,367	−46,693	−52,872
Dividends and distributed branch profits	3 332	−21,359	−21,655	−33,513	−38,628	−48,525	−61,514	−40,480	−41,246
Reinvested earnings and undistributed branch profits	3 333	−2,002	−2,491	−1,949	−110	−3,532	−5,531	677	−7,123
Income on debt (interest)	3 334	−2,939	−2,000	−3,867	−4,541	−5,780	−8,321	−6,890	−4,504
Portfolio investment income	3 339	−31,542	−38,223	−46,183	−64,836	−82,553	−96,236	−83,579	−86,521
Income on equity	3 340	−29,706	−36,354	−43,995	−62,813	−80,040	−94,152	−63,520	−67,120
Income on bonds and notes	3 350	−1,347	−1,345	−1,455	−1,240	−1,498	−1,209	−19,268	−18,856
Income on money market instruments	3 360	−490	−524	−733	−783	−1,015	−875	−791	−546
Other investment income	3 370	−10,475	−10,869	−14,012	−24,272	−33,760	−37,919	−9,950	−7,540
D. CURRENT TRANSFERS	4 379	**−608**	**−1,065**	**−1,126**	**−1,149**	**−2,013**	**−2,742**	**−1,404**	**−900**
Credit	2 379	**3,889**	**4,025**	**4,744**	**5,778**	**5,994**	**7,284**	**6,654**	**6,621**
General government	2 380	1,626	1,804	1,991	2,417	2,729	3,412	3,204	3,139
Other sectors	2 390	2,263	2,221	2,753	3,361	3,265	3,872	3,451	3,482
Workers' remittances	2 391	1	4	4	4	5	3	3	3
Other current transfers	2 392	2,262	2,216	2,749	3,356	3,260	3,868	3,448	3,480
Debit	3 379	**−4,497**	**−5,090**	**−5,871**	**−6,928**	**−8,007**	**−10,026**	**−8,058**	**−7,521**
General government	3 380	−1,397	−1,637	−1,864	−1,947	−2,292	−2,845	−2,721	−2,740
Other sectors	3 390	−3,100	−3,453	−4,007	−4,981	−5,715	−7,181	−5,337	−4,781
Workers' remittances	3 391	−53	−65	−68	−81	−92	−108	−94	−92
Other current transfers	3 392	−3,047	−3,388	−3,939	−4,899	−5,623	−7,073	−5,243	−4,689
CAPITAL AND FINANCIAL ACCOUNT	4 996	**−2,332**	**−4,308**	**−4,337**	**−4,372**	**−5,077**	**−2,976**	**−3,160**	**−3,832**
CAPITAL ACCOUNT	4 994	**−140**	**−772**	**1,248**	**−366**	**−197**	**−373**	**−386**	**−306**
Total credit	2 994	*63*	*51*	*1,576*	*36*	*58*	*125*	*141*	*122*
Total debit	3 994	*−204*	*−823*	*−329*	*−402*	*−254*	*−499*	*−527*	*−428*
Capital transfers, credit	2 400	**48**	**37**	**55**	**30**	**46**	**34**	**28**	**48**
General government	2 401	20	26	38	18	16	15	14	15
Debt forgiveness	2 402	....	....	....	....	....	....	....	....
Other capital transfers	2 410	20	26	38	18	16	15	14	15
Other sectors	2 430	28	11	16	12	30	19	14	32
Migrants' transfers	2 431	28	11	5	12	23	19	14	32
Debt forgiveness	2 432	....	....		....		....	....	....
Other capital transfers	2 440	....	....	11	....	7	....	....	....
Capital transfers, debit	3 400	**−144**	**−247**	**−190**	**−225**	**−222**	**−259**	**−229**	**−245**
General government	3 401	−109	−235	−164	−184	−199	−213	−207	−212
Debt forgiveness	3 402	....	....	....	....	....	....	....	....
Other capital transfers	3 410	−109	−235	−164	−184	−199	−213	−207	−212
Other sectors	3 430	−35	−13	−26	−41	−23	−45	−22	−33
Migrants' transfers	3 431	−27	−7	−17	−30	−13	−32	−9	−20
Debt forgiveness	3 432	....	....	....	....	....	....	....	....
Other capital transfers	3 440	−8	−5	−9	−11	−10	−13	−13	−14
Nonproduced nonfinancial assets, credit	2 480	**16**	**14**	**1,522**	**6**	**12**	**91**	**113**	**74**
Nonproduced nonfinancial assets, debit	3 480	**−60**	**−575**	**−139**	**−178**	**−32**	**−240**	**−298**	**−183**

Table 2 (Continued). STANDARD PRESENTATION, 2003–2010

(Millions of U.S. dollars)

	Code	2003	2004	2005	2006	2007	2008	2009	2010
FINANCIAL ACCOUNT	4 995	**−2,192**	**−3,536**	**−5,585**	**−4,006**	**−4,880**	**−2,603**	**−2,774**	**−3,525**
A. DIRECT INVESTMENT	4 500	**−10,674**	**−5,212**	**−8,220**	**14,318**	**−75,465**	**−27,736**	**−22,398**	**22,739**
Direct investment abroad	4 505	**−100,458**	**−85,310**	**−123,371**	**−115,562**	**−269,230**	**−129,848**	**−229,528**	**−185,132**
Equity capital	4 510	−88,178	−103,908	−108,839	−87,715	−227,760	−85,666	−128,905	−163,399
Claims on affiliated enterprises	4 515	....	....	....	....	....	....	....	....
Liabilities to affiliated enterprises	4 520	....	....	....	....	....	....	....	....
Reinvested earnings	4 525	534	−1,912	−2,605	−676	−4,212	−3,061	5,968	−650
Other capital	4 530	−12,815	20,510	−11,927	−27,171	−37,259	−41,121	−106,591	−21,083
Claims on affiliated enterprises	4 535	....	....	....	....	....	....	....	....
Liabilities to affiliated enterprises	4 540	....	....	....	....	....	....	....	....
Direct investment in Luxembourg	4 555	**89,784**	**80,098**	**115,151**	**129,879**	**193,765**	**102,113**	**207,130**	**207,871**
Equity capital	4 560	81,288	66,743	46,036	115,174	157,852	45,518	236,501	286,719
Claims on direct investors	4 565	....	....	....	....	....	....	....	....
Liabilities to direct investors	4 570	....	....	....	....	....	....	....	....
Reinvested earnings	4 575	2,002	2,491	1,949	110	3,532	5,531	−677	7,123
Other capital	4 580	6,494	10,863	67,166	14,595	32,380	51,064	−28,694	−85,971
Claims on direct investors	4 585	....	....	....	....	....	....	....	....
Liabilities to direct investors	4 590	....	....	....	....	....	....	....	....
B. PORTFOLIO INVESTMENT	4 600	**21,064**	**52,064**	**48,060**	**74,553**	**133,146**	**37,742**	**−72,095**	**60,393**
Assets	4 602	**−78,422**	**−87,546**	**−267,098**	**−176,160**	**−174,516**	**164,735**	**−252,532**	**−135,253**
Equity securities	4 610	−35,857	−45,835	−123,620	−102,723	−52,572	85,754	−89,026	−62,031
Monetary authorities	4 611	....	....	....	....	....	....	....	....
General government	4 612	....	....	....	....	....	....	−855	−1
Banks	4 613	1,318	−1,023	192	−4,697	−1,591	1,471	−1,553	−380
Other sectors	4 614	−37,175	−44,811	−123,812	−98,025	−50,981	84,283	−86,618	−61,650
Debt securities	4 619	−42,565	−41,711	−143,477	−73,437	−121,944	78,981	−163,507	−73,222
Bonds and notes	4 620	−64,746	−50,817	−124,442	−53,197	−90,315	117,331	−84,900	−114,789
Monetary authorities	4 621	−180	−659	−2,060	−1,338	−254	−356	−579	108
General government	4 622	116	124	95	−155	−156	62	−29	443
Banks	4 623	−22,630	−4,228	−14,181	−24,774	−23,587	18,635	32,106	38,694
Other sectors	4 624	−42,053	−46,055	−108,297	−26,930	−66,317	98,990	−116,399	−154,035
Money market instruments	4 630	22,182	9,105	−19,035	−20,240	−31,629	−38,350	−78,606	41,567
Monetary authorities	4 631	....	−499	473	−534	182	−912	1,266	−197
General government	4 632	....	....	....	....	....	....	....	....
Banks	4 633	−9,936	−1,478	−1,009	−2,636	−22,434	−58,879	−72,609	62,486
Other sectors	4 634	32,118	11,082	−18,499	−17,069	−9,377	21,442	−7,263	−20,722
Liabilities	4 652	**99,486**	**139,610**	**315,158**	**250,713**	**307,662**	**−126,994**	**180,437**	**195,646**
Equity securities	4 660	70,443	121,546	275,580	220,277	279,314	−132,109	148,625	209,858
Banks	4 663	7,331	2,575	557	13,994	81,906	101,476	−5,577	−57,187
Other sectors	4 664	63,112	118,971	275,023	206,283	197,408	−233,586	154,202	267,044
Debt securities	4 669	29,043	18,064	39,577	30,436	28,348	5,116	31,812	−14,212
Bonds and notes	4 670	21,852	20,578	37,387	26,366	22,701	16,291	24,964	−15,023
Monetary authorities	4 671	....	....	....	....	....	....	....	....
General government	4 672	−48	−9	−2	1	−5	687	80	1,731
Banks	4 673	8,644	10,889	8,726	603	6,284	−11,489	−7,525	−15,830
Other sectors	4 674	13,257	9,698	28,663	25,763	16,422	27,093	32,409	−923
Money market instruments	4 680	7,191	−2,515	2,190	4,070	5,647	−11,175	6,848	811
Monetary authorities	4 681	....	....	....	....	....	....	....	....
General government	4 682	−30	1	....	−320	−112	9	....	....
Banks	4 683	−5,429	−7,715	−5,452	3,578	7,794	−13,163	6,080	2,909
Other sectors	4 684	12,650	5,200	7,642	812	−2,035	1,979	769	−2,098
C. FINANCIAL DERIVATIVES	4 910	**6,158**	**−2,998**	**−3,190**	**9,850**	**14,177**	**−21,730**	**−12,732**	**24,083**
Monetary authorities	4 911	....	−5	7	13	....	−9	3	13
General government	4 912	....	....	....	....	....	....	....	....
Banks	4 913	1,733	−1,990	807	3,609	5,442	−1,979	−1,670	2,178
Other sectors	4 914	4,424	−1,002	−4,004	6,229	8,735	−19,742	−11,065	21,892
Assets	4 900	....	....	....	....	....	....	....	....
Monetary authorities	4 901	....	....	....	....	....	....	....	....
General government	4 902	....	....	....	....	....	....	....	....
Banks	4 903	....	....	....	....	....	....	....	....
Other sectors	4 904	....	....	....	....	....	....	....	....
Liabilities	4 905	....	....	....	....	....	....	....	....
Monetary authorities	4 906	....	....	....	....	....	....	....	....
General government	4 907	....	....	....	....	....	....	....	....
Banks	4 908	....	....	....	....	....	....	....	....
Other sectors	4 909	....	....	....	....	....	....	....	....

Table 2 (Concluded). STANDARD PRESENTATION, 2003–2010
(Millions of U.S. dollars)

	Code	2003	2004	2005	2006	2007	2008	2009	2010
D. OTHER INVESTMENT	4 700	**−18,632**	**−47,382**	**−42,283**	**−102,756**	**−76,827**	**9,292**	**104,897**	**−110,707**
Assets	4 703	−33,924	−117,163	−191,871	−267,184	−249,183	−49,105	121,440	−166,008
Trade credits	4 706	−363	−626	−153	−547	−558	1,144	−1,199	−1,359
General government	4 707	....	....	....	....	....	....	....	....
of which: Short-term	4 709	....	....	....	....	....	....	....	....
Other sectors	4 710	−363	−626	−153	−547	−558	1,144	−1,199	−1,359
of which: Short-term	4 712	....	....	....	....	....	....	....	....
Loans	4 714	−22,586	−105,652	−179,929	−236,297	−263,599	−72,076	121,807	−61,837
Monetary authorities	4 715	−7,641	−7,210	−5,755	3,281	−18,671	−30,614	−15,741	−19,397
of which: Short-term	4 718	−7,641	−7,210	−5,755	3,281	−18,671	−30,614	−15,741	−19,397
General government	4 719	....	....	....	....	....	....	....	−71
of which: Short-term	4 721	....	....	....	....	....	....	....	−70
Banks	4 722	−3,623	−43,871	−36,573	−57,181	−118,631	−18,822	147,565	−7,757
of which: Short-term	4 724	4,017	−39,319	−22,173	−41,262	−93,729	498	130,335	−15,091
Other sectors	4 725	−11,322	−54,571	−137,601	−182,397	−126,297	−22,640	−10,018	−34,611
of which: Short-term	4 727	−6,326	−38,785	−120,601	−155,144	−91,705	2,164	−5,623	−27,538
Currency and deposits	4 730	−12,701	−9,939	−11,118	−28,438	15,148	23,532	−15,777	−52,568
Monetary authorities	4 731	....	....	....	....	....	....	....	....
General government	4 732	....	....	....	−1	−9	−1	−6	−65
Banks	4 733	....	....	....	....	....	....	....	....
Other sectors	4 734	−12,701	−9,939	−11,118	−28,438	15,157	23,533	−15,771	−52,503
Other assets	4 736	1,727	−945	−671	−1,903	−173	−1,706	16,609	−50,245
Monetary authorities	4 737	....	....	....	....	....	....	−5	−4
of which: Short-term	4 739	....	....	....	....	....	....	....	....
General government	4 740	−1	....	−1	−7	−308	....	....	−1
of which: Short-term	4 742	....	....	....	....	....	....	....	....
Banks	4 743	....	....	....	....	....	....	....	....
of which: Short-term	4 745	....	....	....	....	....	....	....	....
Other sectors	4 746	1,728	−945	−670	−1,895	135	−1,706	16,615	−50,240
of which: Short-term	4 748	....	....	....	....	....	....	16,724	−49,067
Liabilities	4 753	**15,292**	**69,781**	**149,588**	**164,429**	**172,356**	**58,397**	**−16,543**	**55,301**
Trade credits	4 756	121	595	−365	−227	211	−155	458	2,378
General government	4 757	....	....	....	....	....	....	....	....
of which: Short-term	4 759	....	....	....	....	....	....	....	....
Other sectors	4 760	121	595	−365	−227	211	−155	458	2,378
of which: Short-term	4 762	....	....	....	....	....	....	....	....
Loans	4 764	19,171	57,785	143,141	155,591	162,570	48,584	−73,964	15,289
Monetary authorities	4 765	....	....	....	....	....	....	....	....
of which: Use of Fund credit and loans from the Fund	4 766	....	....	....	....	....	....	....	....
of which: Short-term	4 768	....	....	....	....	....	....	....	....
General government	4 769	−1	−16	....	....	−1	....	....	....
of which: Short-term	4 771	....	....	....	....	−1	....	....	....
Banks	4 772	17,866	31,295	41,383	43,908	75,326	−14,656	−78,187	−9,637
of which: Short-term	4 774	12,379	7,404	23,807	39,252	68,795	−1,604	−84,310	−14,825
Other sectors	4 775	1,306	26,506	101,759	111,683	87,244	63,240	4,222	24,926
of which: Short-term	4 777	490	27,266	101,859	112,019	67,459	48,421	13,622	33,124
Currency and deposits	4 780	−5,824	6,208	322	−343	454	1,147	246	69
Monetary authorities	4 781	−5,824	6,208	322	−343	454	1,147	246	69
General government	4 782	....	....	....	....	....	....	....	....
Banks	4 783	....	....	....	....	....	....	....	....
Other sectors	4 784	....	....	....	....	....	....	....	....
Other liabilities	4 786	1,824	5,193	6,490	9,407	9,121	8,821	56,718	37,564
Monetary authorities	4 787	....	....	....	....	....	....	359	....
of which: Short-term	4 789	....	....	....	....	....	....	....	....
General government	4 790	....	....	....	....	....	....	....	....
of which: Short-term	4 792	....	....	....	....	....	....	....	....
Banks	4 793	....	....	....	....	....	....	....	....
of which: Short-term	4 795	....	....	....	....	....	....	....	....
Other sectors	4 796	1,824	5,193	6,490	9,407	9,121	8,821	56,359	37,564
of which: Short-term	4 798	....	....	....	....	....	....	42,861	26,604
E. RESERVE ASSETS	4 802	**−108**	**−8**	**48**	**28**	**89**	**−171**	**−446**	**−33**
Monetary gold	4 812	2	....	....	....	....	1	1	....
Special drawing rights	4 811	−2	−2	−2	−1	−1	−1	−359	....
Reserve position in the Fund	4 810	−21	45	72	17	16	−26	−25	−22
Foreign exchange	4 803	−86	−52	−21	13	74	−145	−63	−11
Other claims	4 813	....	....	....	....	....	....	....	....
NET ERRORS AND OMISSIONS	4 998	**−76**	**220**	**−69**	**−24**	**−138**	**−64**	**−147**	**−290**

Table 3. INTERNATIONAL INVESTMENT POSITION (End-period stocks), 2003–2010

(Millions of U.S. dollars)

	Code	2003	2004	2005	2006	2007	2008	2009	2010
ASSETS	8 995 C.	**2,803,822**	**3,413,908**	**3,773,818**	**4,907,644**	**6,199,267**	**5,561,720**	**6,217,246**	**6,560,383**
Direct investment abroad	8 505 ..	**739,969**	**884,760**	**896,848**	**1,093,670**	**1,467,731**	**1,491,255**	**1,798,698**	**1,902,344**
Equity capital and reinvested earnings	8 506 ..	608,768	764,303	780,091	930,071	1,250,437	1,262,774	1,448,724	1,545,026
Claims on affiliated enterprises	8 507 ..	....	....	....	....	....	....	....	....
Liabilities to affiliated enterprises	8 508 ..	....	....	....	....	....	....	....	....
Other capital	8 530 ..	131,201	120,457	116,756	163,598	217,294	228,481	349,974	357,318
Claims on affiliated enterprises	8 535 ..	....	....	....	....	....	....	....	....
Liabilities to affiliated enterprises	8 540 ..	....	....	....	....	....	....	....	....
Portfolio investment	8 602 ..	**1,333,204**	**1,616,314**	**1,840,921**	**2,432,433**	**2,882,607**	**2,182,754**	**2,717,159**	**2,876,459**
Equity securities	8 610 ..	488,241	637,837	807,866	1,149,652	1,413,236	763,820	1,065,969	1,225,702
Monetary authorities	8 611 ..	....	....	....	....	....			
General government	8 612 ..	....	....	....	....	....	6	1,039	834
Banks	8 613 ..	8,257	12,142	10,540	16,394	19,431	7,409	7,772	7,940
Other sectors	8 614 ..	479,983	625,694	797,326	1,133,258	1,393,805	756,404	1,057,158	1,216,928
Debt securities	8 619 ..	844,963	978,477	1,033,055	1,282,781	1,469,371	1,418,935	1,651,190	1,650,757
Bonds and notes	8 620 ..	749,929	868,571	915,332	1,128,293	1,257,695	1,102,674	1,273,321	1,327,776
Monetary authorities	8 621 ..	1,892	2,767	4,260	6,105	7,011	6,454	7,685	6,859
General government	8 622 ..	576	481	308	568	717	683	771	303
Banks	8 623 ..	302,659	335,108	344,708	402,758	473,123	359,517	345,964	288,167
Other sectors	8 624 ..	444,801	530,216	566,056	718,862	776,844	736,020	918,901	1,032,446
Money market instruments	8 630 ..	95,034	109,906	117,723	154,488	211,676	316,260	377,869	322,981
Monetary authorities	8 631 ..	32	578	82	639	564	1,439	179	365
General government	8 632 ..	....	....	....	....	....			
Banks	8 633 ..	58,911	64,975	62,518	70,361	101,301	230,956	296,149	225,711
Other sectors	8 634 ..	36,092	44,353	55,123	83,488	109,810	83,865	81,541	96,905
Financial derivatives	8 900 ..	**22,653**	**23,734**	**31,077**	**26,678**	**30,259**	**92,917**	**76,837**	**91,234**
Monetary authorities	8 901 ..	....	....	....	....	....	46	75	163
General government	8 902 ..	....	....	....	....	....			
Banks	8 903 ..	17,100	20,477	18,852	22,614	18,816	26,272	14,476	13,194
Other sectors	8 904 ..	5,553	3,257	12,224	4,064	11,443	66,598	62,286	77,877
Other investment	8 703 ..	**707,686**	**888,769**	**1,004,693**	**1,354,598**	**1,818,465**	**1,794,396**	**1,623,741**	**1,689,498**
Trade credits	8 706 ..	2,555	3,448	3,127	4,103	5,168	3,711	4,714	5,853
General government	8 707 ..	....	....	....	....	....	....	....	....
of which: Short-term	8 709 ..	....	....	....	....	....	....	....	....
Other sectors	8 710 ..	2,555	3,448	3,127	4,103	5,168	3,711	4,714	5,853
of which: Short-term	8 712 ..	....	....	....	....	....	....	....	....
Loans	8 714 ..	574,977	708,743	826,319	1,117,988	1,483,506	1,513,011	1,418,398	1,485,817
Monetary authorities	8 715 ..	3,057	4,755	9,295	7,003	27,112	58,746	75,799	90,894
of which: Short-term	8 718 ..	....	....	....	....	....	....	....	....
General government	8 719 ..	....	....	109	155	174	331	370	405
of which: Short-term	8 721 ..	....	....	....	....	....	....	....	....
Banks	8 722 ..	487,900	562,010	538,125	640,400	810,054	799,559	666,913	636,459
of which: Short-term	8 724 ..	*416,654*	*70,655*	*78,092*	*108,819*	*131,594*	*593,066*	*467,893*	*451,031*
Other sectors	8 725 ..	84,019	141,979	278,791	470,429	646,167	654,375	675,317	758,058
of which: Short-term	8 727 ..	....	....	....	....	....	....	....	....
Currency and deposits	8 730 ..	79,888	113,172	107,478	142,302	219,821	205,467	155,902	132,085
Monetary authorities	8 731 ..	....	....	....	....	....	....	....	....
General government	8 732 ..	....	....	....	....	....	....	....	....
Banks	8 733 ..	....	....	....	....	....	....	....	....
Other sectors	8 734 ..	79,888	113,172	107,478	142,302	219,821	205,467	155,902	132,085
Other assets	8 736 ..	50,266	63,406	67,769	90,205	109,969	72,207	44,727	65,744
Monetary authorities	8 737 ..	10	14	11	13	16	15	23	25
of which: Short-term	8 739 ..	....	....	....	....	....	....	....	....
General government	8 740 ..	42	50	47	54	53	55	55	54
of which: Short-term	8 742 ..	....	....	....	....	....	....	....	....
Banks	8 743 ..	....	....	....	....	....	....	....	....
of which: Short-term	8 745 ..	....	....	....	....	....	....	....	....
Other sectors	8 746 ..	50,214	63,342	67,712	90,138	109,901	72,137	44,650	65,665
of which: Short-term	8 748 ..	....	....	....	....	....	....	....	....
Reserve assets	8 802 ..	**311**	**331**	**278**	**265**	**206**	**398**	**810**	**849**
Monetary gold	8 812 ..	31	33	38	47	62	63	80	102
Special drawing rights	8 811 ..	12	15	16	18	20	21	381	375
Reserve position in the Fund	8 810 ..	179	139	58	44	30	56	82	102
Foreign exchange	8 803 ..	89	144	166	156	94	258	268	271
Other claims	8 813 ..	....	....	....	....	....	....	....	....

Table 3 (Concluded). INTERNATIONAL INVESTMENT POSITION (End-period stocks), 2003–2010

(Millions of U.S. dollars)

	Code	2003	2004	2005	2006	2007	2008	2009	2010
LIABILITIES	8 995 D.	2,758,058	3,371,641	3,728,179	4,848,880	6,146,543	5,509,651	6,164,188	6,508,834
Direct investment in Luxembourg	8 555	768,405	950,233	913,244	1,150,660	1,502,080	1,514,258	1,772,077	1,865,465
Equity capital and reinvested earnings	8 556	672,053	834,064	749,493	953,253	1,257,612	1,217,660	1,494,257	1,686,515
Claims on direct investors	8 557	....	....	....	....	....	....	....	....
Liabilities to direct investors	8 558	....	....	....	....	....	....	....	....
Other capital	8 580	96,352	116,169	163,750	197,407	244,468	296,597	277,820	178,950
Claims on direct investors	8 585	....	....	....	....	....	....	....	....
Liabilities to direct investors	8 590	....	....	....	....	....	....	....	....
Portfolio investment	8 652	1,337,144	1,661,113	1,944,049	2,530,490	3,166,601	2,465,226	3,053,468	3,259,572
Equity securities	8 660	1,143,406	1,436,258	1,698,464	2,233,555	2,821,021	2,087,299	2,589,294	2,832,992
Banks	8 663	183,871	196,070	187,957	231,765	355,935	418,871	427,641	353,039
Other sectors	8 664	959,535	1,240,188	1,510,508	2,001,791	2,465,086	1,668,429	2,161,653	2,479,953
Debt securities	8 669	193,739	224,856	245,584	296,935	345,579	377,927	464,174	426,579
Bonds and notes	8 670	151,267	196,108	218,891	261,740	306,041	358,357	437,255	399,535
Monetary authorities	8 671	....	....	....	....	....	....	....	....
General government	8 672	....	....	....	....	....	1,232	1,416	3,165
Banks	8 673	52,873	69,175	75,327	85,759	96,847	79,279	75,025	59,294
Other sectors	8 674	98,394	126,933	143,564	175,980	209,194	277,846	360,814	337,076
Money market instruments	8 680	42,472	28,747	26,693	35,195	39,538	19,570	26,918	27,044
Monetary authorities	8 681	....	....	....	....	....	....	....	....
General government	8 682	....	....	....	....	....	....	....	....
Banks	8 683	31,179	25,947	18,792	23,639	31,386	12,843	17,257	18,399
Other sectors	8 684	11,293	2,800	7,901	11,557	8,152	6,726	9,662	8,645
Financial derivatives	8 905	27,920	30,891	26,095	28,582	41,229	71,675	42,117	73,005
Monetary authorities	8 906	....	....	....	....	....	....	....	....
General government	8 907	....	....	....	....	....	....	....	....
Banks	8 908	20,315	22,691	18,975	21,948	26,862	35,010	19,946	20,307
Other sectors	8 909	7,605	8,200	7,120	6,635	14,368	36,665	22,171	52,698
Other investment	8 753	624,589	729,404	844,792	1,139,147	1,436,633	1,458,492	1,296,526	1,310,792
Trade credits	8 756	1,248	1,992	1,422	1,316	1,632	1,677	1,631	2,445
General government	8 757	....	....	....	....	....	....	....	....
of which: Short-term	8 759	....	....	....	....	....	....	....	....
Other sectors	8 760	1,248	1,992	1,422	1,316	1,632	1,677	1,631	2,445
of which: Short-term	8 762	....	....	....	....	....	....	....	....
Loans	8 764	569,735	659,492	766,835	1,035,934	1,310,672	1,342,563	1,152,738	1,118,664
Monetary authorities	8 765	....	....	....	....	....	....	....	....
of which: Use of Fund credit and loans from the Fund	8 766	....	....	....	....	....	....	....	....
of which: Short-term	8 768	....	....	....	....	....	....	....	....
General government	8 769	15	....	30	60	67	192	208	197
of which: Short-term	8 771	....	....	....	....	....	....	....	....
Banks	8 772	450,011	499,059	486,735	572,958	697,033	658,447	593,750	555,599
of which: Short-term	8 774	385,512	451,783	441,037	516,880	631,121	598,172	528,387	487,826
Other sectors	8 775	119,709	160,434	280,070	462,916	613,571	683,923	558,779	562,867
of which: Short-term	8 777	83,923	114,078	210,052	347,187	460,179	512,942	419,084	450,294
Currency and deposits	8 780	91	154	427	92	557	1,489	1,798	1,744
Monetary authorities	8 781	91	154	427	92	557	1,489	1,798	1,744
General government	8 782	....	....	....	....	....	....	....	....
Banks	8 783	....	....	....	....	....	....	....	....
Other sectors	8 784	....	....	....	....	....	....	....	....
Other liabilities	8 786	53,516	67,766	76,109	101,805	123,772	112,764	140,360	187,940
Monetary authorities	8 787	....	....	....	....	....	....	387	380
of which: Short-term	8 789	....	....	....	....	....	....	....	....
General government	8 790	....	....	....	....	....	....	....	....
of which: Short-term	8 792	....	....	....	....	....	....	....	....
Banks	8 793	....	....	....	....	....	....	....	....
of which: Short-term	8 795	....	....	....	....	....	....	....	....
Other sectors	8 796	53,516	67,766	76,109	101,805	123,772	112,764	139,973	187,560
of which: Short-term	8 798	13,971	17,554	20,222	26,452	31,261	50,909	58,704	186,085
NET INTERNATIONAL INVESTMENT POSITION	8 995	45,764	42,267	45,639	58,765	52,724	52,069	53,058	51,549
Conversion rates: euros per U.S. dollar (end of period)	0 104	.7918	.7342	.8477	.7593	.6793	.7185	.6942	.7484

Table 1. ANALYTIC PRESENTATION, 2003–2010

(Millions of U.S. dollars)

	Code	2003	2004	2005	2006	2007	2008	2009	2010
A. Current Account[1]	4 993 Z.	**−185.5**	**−451.6**	**−159.3**	**−28.5**	**−605.7**	**−1,235.8**	**−598.8**	**−261.8**
Goods: exports f.o.b.	2 100 ..	1,362.7	1,674.9	2,040.6	2,410.7	3,391.5	3,983.3	2,685.5	3,295.6
Goods: imports f.o.b.	3 100 ..	−2,213.7	−2,813.8	−3,103.6	−3,671.2	−5,030.0	−6,573.2	−4,842.5	−5,241.0
Balance on Goods	4 100 ..	*−851.0*	*−1,139.0*	*−1,063.0*	*−1,260.5*	*−1,638.5*	*−2,589.9*	*−2,157.1*	*−1,945.4*
Services: credit	2 200 ..	380.3	452.5	515.5	601.3	818.4	1,011.5	862.8	915.9
Services: debit	3 200 ..	−386.9	−506.9	−549.1	−572.8	−784.0	−1,000.7	−822.7	−837.6
Balance on Goods and Services	4 991 ..	*−857.6*	*−1,193.3*	*−1,096.7*	*−1,232.0*	*−1,604.1*	*−2,579.1*	*−2,117.0*	*−1,867.1*
Income: credit	2 300 ..	60.4	84.6	97.5	134.9	213.1	272.7	178.2	190.8
Income: debit	3 300 ..	−124.2	−122.6	−212.4	−168.6	−598.1	−387.4	−260.6	−388.8
Balance on Goods, Services, and Income	4 992 ..	*−921.4*	*−1,231.3*	*−1,211.5*	*−1,265.7*	*−1,989.2*	*−2,693.8*	*−2,199.4*	*−2,065.1*
Current transfers: credit	2 379 Z.	773.8	824.5	1,094.9	1,279.2	1,480.9	1,528.0	1,666.9	1,866.7
Current transfers: debit	3 379 ..	−37.9	−44.8	−42.7	−42.1	−97.5	−70.0	−66.4	−63.4
B. Capital Account[1]	4 994 Z.	**−6.7**	**−4.6**	**−2.0**	**−1.1**	**4.9**	**−17.6**	**28.6**	**12.0**
Capital account: credit	2 994 Z.	....	....	....	....	....	....	35.8	30.2
Capital account: debit	3 994 ..	−6.7	−4.6	−2.0	−1.1	4.9	−17.6	−7.1	−18.2
Total, Groups A Plus B	4 981 ..	*−192.2*	*−456.2*	*−161.3*	*−29.7*	*−600.8*	*−1,253.3*	*−570.2*	*−249.8*
C. Financial Account[1]	4 995 W.	**280.6**	**466.8**	**577.6**	**409.5**	**841.9**	**1,204.2**	**671.5**	**302.9**
Direct investment abroad	4 505 ..	−.3	−1.2	−2.8	−.2	1.1	13.5	−11.6	−2.0
Direct investment in Macedonia, FYR	4 555 Z.	117.8	323.0	97.0	424.2	699.1	587.0	197.1	295.8
Portfolio investment assets	4 602 ..	.3	−.9	.8	−.5	−2.8	−1.1	−51.3	−29.0
Equity securities	4 610 ..	.1	.2	.1	.1	−2.3	−.4	−29.2	−18.5
Debt securities	4 619 ..	.3	−1.1	.7	−.5	−.5	−.7	−22.1	−10.5
Portfolio investment liabilities	4 652 Z.	5.3	12.4	237.8	92.8	157.9	−71.4	198.5	−54.4
Equity securities	4 660 ..	2.7	13.0	53.8	86.3	169.8	−49.4	−14.0	−3.9
Debt securities	4 669 Z.	2.6	−.7	184.0	6.5	−11.9	−22.0	212.5	−50.6
Financial derivatives	4 910 ..	....	....	....	....	....	....	....	....
Financial derivatives assets	4 900 ..	....	....	....	....	....	....	....	....
Financial derivatives liabilities	4 905 ..	....	....	....	....	....	....	....	....
Other investment assets	4 703 ..	18.2	8.5	−47.0	−148.6	−80.9	297.7	−144.6	−209.4
Monetary authorities	4 701 ..	17.8	26.4	.8	−3.3	−.2	24.2	.1	.8
General government	4 704 ..	....	....	....	....	....	....	....	....
Banks	4 705 ..	−37.9	−94.8	7.8	−66.4	5.7	334.4	−131.0	−90.7
Other sectors	4 728 ..	38.3	76.8	−55.6	−78.9	−86.3	−60.9	−13.7	−119.5
Other investment liabilities	4 753 W.	139.3	125.0	291.9	41.9	67.4	378.4	483.4	301.9
Monetary authorities	4 753 WA	....	....	....	....	....	....	89.4	....
General government	4 753 ZB	28.3	38.9	44.3	−157.7	−155.1	49.0	10.8	50.5
Banks	4 753 ZC	−34.0	−24.1	82.6	104.2	169.2	−7.5	121.9	136.0
Other sectors	4 753 ZD	145.0	110.2	165.0	95.3	53.4	337.0	261.3	115.4
Total, Groups A Through C	4 983 ..	*88.4*	*10.6*	*416.3*	*379.9*	*241.0*	*−49.1*	*101.3*	*53.2*
D. Net Errors and Omissions	4 998 ..	**−33.1**	**17.5**	**−5.8**	**5.4**	**−42.0**	**2.0**	**34.8**	**−.1**
Total, Groups A Through D	4 984 ..	*55.4*	*28.0*	*410.6*	*385.3*	*199.0*	*−47.2*	*136.1*	*53.1*
E. Reserves and Related Items	4 802 A.	**−55.4**	**−28.0**	**−410.6**	**−385.3**	**−199.0**	**47.2**	**−136.1**	**−53.1**
Reserve assets	4 802 ..	−50.7	−19.4	−415.3	−375.7	−142.9	47.2	−136.1	−53.1
Use of Fund credit and loans	4 766 ..	−4.7	−8.6	4.7	−9.6	−56.1	....	....	....
Exceptional financing	4 920 ..	....	....	....	....	....	....	....	....
Conversion rates: denars per U.S. dollar	0 101 ..	**54.322**	**49.410**	**49.284**	**48.802**	**44.730**	**41.868**	**44.101**	**46.485**

[1] Excludes components that have been classified in the categories of Group E.

Table 2. STANDARD PRESENTATION, 2003–2010

(Millions of U.S. dollars)

	Code	2003	2004	2005	2006	2007	2008	2009	2010
CURRENT ACCOUNT	4 993	−185.5	−451.6	−159.3	−28.5	−605.7	−1,235.8	−598.8	−261.8
A. GOODS	4 100	−851.0	−1,139.0	−1,063.0	−1,260.5	−1,638.5	−2,589.9	−2,157.1	−1,945.4
Credit	2 100	1,362.7	1,674.9	2,040.6	2,410.7	3,391.5	3,983.3	2,685.5	3,295.6
General merchandise: exports f.o.b.	2 110	751.9	1,033.5	1,385.3	1,772.8	2,548.2	2,972.3	1,875.7	2,524.1
Goods for processing: exports f.o.b.	2 150	607.6	635.4	649.3	632.7	838.6	1,003.9	805.7	767.2
Repairs on goods	2 160	.9	2.8	2.1	1.3	1.3	1.9	1.2	1.1
Goods procured in ports by carriers	2 170	2.3	3.2	3.9	4.0	3.4	5.2	2.9	3.1
Nonmonetary gold	2 180	....	....	....	....	....	....	....	....
Debit	3 100	−2,213.7	−2,813.8	−3,103.6	−3,671.2	−5,030.0	−6,573.2	−4,842.5	−5,241.0
General merchandise: imports f.o.b.	3 110	−1,766.4	−2,353.6	−2,638.2	−3,202.9	−4,429.2	−5,833.4	−4,304.8	−4,642.2
Goods for processing: imports f.o.b.	3 150	−441.6	−453.2	−457.7	−462.7	−594.7	−733.0	−536.6	−597.4
Repairs on goods	3 160	−2.5	−3.4	−3.8	−2.4	−.9	−1.3	−.7	−1.4
Goods procured in ports by carriers	3 170	−3.1	−3.7	−3.9	−3.2	−5.2	−5.4	−.5	....
Nonmonetary gold	3 180	....	....	....	....	....	....	....	−.1
B. SERVICES	4 200	−6.6	−54.4	−33.6	28.5	34.4	10.8	40.1	78.3
Total credit	2 200	*380.3*	*452.5*	*515.5*	*601.3*	*818.4*	*1,011.5*	*862.8*	*915.9*
Total debit	3 200	*−386.9*	*−506.9*	*−549.1*	*−572.8*	*−784.0*	*−1,000.7*	*−822.7*	*−837.6*
Transportation services, credit	2 205	125.7	143.4	160.2	186.3	253.1	327.4	252.0	288.6
Passenger	2 850	*29.2*	*30.7*	*27.2*	*27.4*	*32.6*	*34.3*	*13.7*	*12.4*
Freight	2 851	*67.9*	*77.8*	*93.9*	*115.8*	*167.8*	*236.3*	*192.7*	*235.9*
Other	2 852	*28.6*	*34.9*	*39.1*	*43.1*	*52.8*	*56.9*	*45.6*	*40.3*
Sea transport, passenger	2 207	....	....	....	....	.1	.1	.1	....
Sea transport, freight	2 208	.1	.2	.7	.3	.4	2.3	2.8	4.9
Sea transport, other	2 209	....	....	.2	....	.3	.1	.3	.5
Air transport, passenger	2 211	28.4	29.3	25.8	25.2	30.5	31.5	10.8	10.1
Air transport, freight	2 212	.3	.5	.5	.5	.6	1.0	.7	.5
Air transport, other	2 213	6.0	6.7	9.1	9.9	9.7	12.5	15.0	18.0
Other transport, passenger	2 215	.9	1.4	1.4	2.2	2.0	2.7	2.8	2.2
Other transport, freight	2 216	67.5	77.0	92.8	115.0	166.8	233.0	189.2	230.4
Other transport, other	2 217	22.6	28.2	29.8	33.2	42.8	44.3	30.3	21.8
Transportation services, debit	3 205	−162.8	−209.2	−218.9	−228.9	−312.6	−397.8	−305.3	−316.0
Passenger	3 850	*−23.5*	*−29.7*	*−34.8*	*−38.6*	*−44.7*	*−54.5*	*−49.7*	*−49.0*
Freight	3 851	*−95.5*	*−132.6*	*−138.5*	*−141.0*	*−191.2*	*−238.8*	*−178.6*	*−175.5*
Other	3 852	*−43.9*	*−46.9*	*−45.6*	*−49.3*	*−76.7*	*−104.5*	*−77.1*	*−91.6*
Sea transport, passenger	3 207	−.1	−.2	....	−.2	−.2	−.1	....	−.1
Sea transport, freight	3 208	−5.9	−12.7	−13.2	−12.4	−21.2	−41.7	−20.5	−25.8
Sea transport, other	3 209	−2.9	−4.7	−6.1	−8.9	−19.7	−27.1	−17.7	−24.5
Air transport, passenger	3 211	−22.2	−28.1	−33.5	−36.3	−42.2	−52.0	−47.4	−46.7
Air transport, freight	3 212	−2.8	−2.9	−2.7	−2.6	−4.1	−4.4	−3.8	−2.6
Air transport, other	3 213	−18.9	−18.0	−11.6	−10.9	−14.5	−16.7	−3.3	−2.3
Other transport, passenger	3 215	−1.2	−1.5	−1.3	−2.0	−2.2	−2.4	−2.2	−2.2
Other transport, freight	3 216	−86.7	−117.0	−122.5	−125.9	−165.9	−192.8	−154.2	−147.0
Other transport, other	3 217	−22.1	−24.1	−28.0	−29.5	−42.6	−60.7	−56.1	−64.7
Travel, credit	2 236	56.7	71.9	89.5	129.2	185.8	228.5	217.8	197.3
Business travel	2 237	....	....	....	....	....	....	....	....
Personal travel	2 240	56.7	71.9	89.5	129.2	185.8	228.5	217.8	197.3
Travel, debit	3 236	−48.0	−54.5	−61.9	−70.7	−101.6	−136.3	−100.2	−92.0
Business travel	3 237	−15.9	−17.8	−20.3	−20.8	−24.2	−29.0	−21.2	−19.9
Personal travel	3 240	−32.0	−36.7	−41.6	−50.0	−77.4	−107.4	−79.0	−72.0
Other services, credit	2 200 BA	197.9	237.2	265.7	285.8	379.4	455.7	393.0	430.1
Communications	2 245	55.0	48.0	44.9	61.0	69.8	80.0	86.3	79.4
Construction	2 249	41.3	56.4	59.4	48.5	75.9	64.3	44.8	18.3
Insurance	2 253	2.3	4.6	4.9	5.9	5.7	7.7	8.8	6.2
Financial	2 260	2.9	3.2	3.5	5.2	8.6	5.2	4.2	3.4
Computer and information	2 262	4.6	8.9	16.7	23.6	33.0	50.1	36.7	49.5
Royalties and licence fees	2 266	2.3	3.1	3.1	2.7	4.6	5.8	6.2	6.9
Other business services	2 268	64.6	82.3	99.9	109.2	146.1	204.7	168.9	230.9
Personal, cultural, and recreational	2 287	4.4	7.0	7.1	10.1	16.6	18.1	19.9	21.0
Government, n.i.e.	2 291	20.6	23.8	26.3	19.9	18.9	19.8	17.4	14.5
Other services, debit	3 200 BA	−176.1	−243.2	−268.3	−273.2	−369.8	−466.7	−417.1	−429.6
Communications	3 245	−19.9	−20.9	−20.6	−27.7	−31.9	−47.7	−59.1	−48.9
Construction	3 249	−4.0	−2.9	−8.9	−2.8	−2.3	−11.9	−12.8	−8.8
Insurance	3 253	−10.7	−13.5	−16.3	−20.9	−22.1	−25.8	−21.2	−27.1
Financial	3 260	−2.8	−3.4	−4.5	−3.1	−6.7	−6.8	−6.7	−7.1
Computer and information	3 262	−13.0	−20.9	−24.4	−40.4	−41.6	−62.5	−57.0	−54.3
Royalties and licence fees	3 266	−7.0	−9.4	−10.4	−8.7	−19.3	−24.9	−20.2	−17.8
Other business services	3 268	−96.3	−144.5	−154.9	−134.0	−197.8	−231.4	−184.1	−207.1
Personal, cultural, and recreational	3 287	−5.6	−5.3	−6.3	−7.7	−9.8	−16.4	−22.0	−22.0
Government, n.i.e.	3 291	−16.9	−22.4	−22.1	−27.9	−38.3	−39.1	−34.0	−36.5

2011, International Monetary Fund: *Balance of Payments Statistics Yearbook*

Table 2 (Continued). STANDARD PRESENTATION, 2003–2010

(Millions of U.S. dollars)

	Code	2003	2004	2005	2006	2007	2008	2009	2010
C. INCOME	4 300	**−63.8**	**−38.0**	**−114.8**	**−33.7**	**−385.0**	**−114.7**	**−82.4**	**−198.0**
Total credit	2 300	*60.4*	*84.6*	*97.5*	*134.9*	*213.1*	*272.7*	*178.2*	*190.8*
Total debit	3 300	*−124.2*	*−122.6*	*−212.4*	*−168.6*	*−598.1*	*−387.4*	*−260.6*	*−388.8*
Compensation of employees, credit	2 310	**27.9**	**52.0**	**57.2**	**68.9**	**105.8**	**140.5**	**121.0**	**128.0**
Compensation of employees, debit	3 310	**−.6**	**−1.4**	**−1.5**	**−2.2**	**−2.5**	**−4.8**	**−4.0**	**−3.4**
Investment income, credit	2 320	**32.5**	**32.6**	**40.3**	**66.0**	**107.3**	**132.2**	**57.2**	**62.8**
Direct investment income	2 330	.9	.4	.6	.5	2.5	3.5	2.4	2.1
Dividends and distributed branch profits	2 332	.9	.4	.6	.5	2.5	3.5	2.4	2.1
Reinvested earnings and undistributed branch profits	2 333	....	....	....	....	....	....	....	....
Income on debt (interest)	2 334	....	....	....	....	....	....	....	....
Portfolio investment income	2 339	5.5	2.7	1.1	3.0	13.0	77.1	45.9	52.4
Income on equity	2 340	....	....	....	....	....	....	....	....
Income on bonds and notes	2 350	5.5	2.7	1.1	3.0	13.0	77.1	45.9	52.4
Income on money market instruments	2 360	....	....	....	....	....	....	....	....
Other investment income	2 370	26.1	29.4	38.6	62.5	91.8	51.7	8.9	8.3
Investment income, debit	3 320	**−123.5**	**−121.1**	**−210.8**	**−166.4**	**−595.6**	**−382.6**	**−256.6**	**−385.4**
Direct investment income	3 330	−64.3	−67.5	−141.8	−58.6	−469.5	−253.4	−138.4	−238.8
Dividends and distributed branch profits	3 332	−34.4	−66.5	−86.0	−39.2	−218.5	−229.1	−296.4	−156.3
Reinvested earnings and undistributed branch profits	3 333	−30.0	−.9	−55.9	−19.5	−251.1	−24.4	158.0	−82.5
Income on debt (interest)	3 334	....	....	....	....	....	....	....	....
Portfolio investment income	3 339	−2.2	1.5	−4.5	−20.9	−9.0	−9.4	−8.6	−24.8
Income on equity	3 340	−2.1	2.1	−3.8	−10.9	....	....	....	....
Income on bonds and notes	3 350	−.1	−.6	−.7	−10.0	−9.0	−9.4	−8.6	−24.8
Income on money market instruments	3 360	....	....	....	....	....	....	....	....
Other investment income	3 370	−57.0	−55.1	−64.5	−86.8	−117.1	−119.8	−109.6	−121.8
D. CURRENT TRANSFERS	4 379	**735.9**	**779.7**	**1,052.2**	**1,237.1**	**1,383.4**	**1,458.0**	**1,600.5**	**1,803.3**
Credit	2 379	**773.8**	**824.5**	**1,094.9**	**1,279.2**	**1,480.9**	**1,528.0**	**1,666.9**	**1,866.7**
General government	2 380	108.0	76.0	75.0	83.3	84.0	93.8	59.0	47.5
Other sectors	2 390	665.8	748.5	1,019.9	1,195.9	1,396.9	1,434.2	1,608.0	1,819.3
Workers' remittances	2 391	145.7	161.1	169.4	197.6	239.2	266.1	260.1	259.9
Other current transfers	2 392	520.0	587.5	850.6	998.3	1,157.7	1,168.1	1,347.8	1,559.4
Debit	3 379	**−37.9**	**−44.8**	**−42.7**	**−42.1**	**−97.5**	**−70.0**	**−66.4**	**−63.4**
General government	3 380	−4.1	−5.9	−9.5	−9.4	−53.1	−19.2	−8.2	−5.3
Other sectors	3 390	−33.8	−38.9	−33.2	−32.7	−44.4	−50.8	−58.2	−58.1
Workers' remittances	3 391	−15.4	−14.7	−14.0	−15.6	−22.3	−28.2	−22.3	−19.3
Other current transfers	3 392	−18.4	−24.2	−19.2	−17.0	−22.0	−22.6	−35.9	−38.9
CAPITAL AND FINANCIAL ACCOUNT	4 996	**218.6**	**434.1**	**165.1**	**23.1**	**647.8**	**1,233.8**	**564.0**	**261.9**
CAPITAL ACCOUNT	4 994	**−6.7**	**−4.6**	**−2.0**	**−1.1**	**4.9**	**−17.6**	**28.6**	**12.0**
Total credit	2 994	....	....	....	....	....	....	*35.8*	*30.2*
Total debit	3 994	*−6.7*	*−4.6*	*−2.0*	*−1.1*	*4.9*	*−17.6*	*−7.1*	*−18.2*
Capital transfers, credit	2 400	....	....	....	....	....	....	**35.8**	**30.2**
General government	2 401	....	....	....	....	....	....	....	....
Debt forgiveness	2 402	....	....	....	....	....	....	....	....
Other capital transfers	2 410	....	....	....	....	....	....	....	....
Other sectors	2 430	....	....	....	....	....	....	35.8	30.2
Migrants' transfers	2 431	....	....	....	....	....	....	....	....
Debt forgiveness	2 432	....	....	....	....	....	....	4.5	....
Other capital transfers	2 440	....	....	....	....	....	....	31.3	30.2
Capital transfers, debit	3 400	**−6.6**	**−4.6**	**−2.0**	**−1.1**	**1.6**	**−1.3**	**−17.9**	**−18.2**
General government	3 401	....	....	....	....	....	....	....	....
Debt forgiveness	3 402	....	....	....	....	....	....	....	....
Other capital transfers	3 410	....	....	....	....	....	....	....	....
Other sectors	3 430	−6.6	−4.6	−2.0	−1.1	1.6	−1.3	−17.9	−18.2
Migrants' transfers	3 431	....	....	....	....	....	....	....	....
Debt forgiveness	3 432	....	....	....	....	....	....	....	....
Other capital transfers	3 440	−6.6	−4.6	−2.0	−1.1	1.6	−1.3	−17.9	−18.2
Nonproduced nonfinancial assets, credit	2 480	....	....	....	....	....	....	....	....
Nonproduced nonfinancial assets, debit	3 480	**−.1**	....	....	....	**3.3**	**−16.3**	**10.8**	....

Table 2 (Continued). STANDARD PRESENTATION, 2003–2010

(Millions of U.S. dollars)

	Code	2003	2004	2005	2006	2007	2008	2009	2010
FINANCIAL ACCOUNT	4 995	225.2	438.8	167.1	24.2	642.8	1,251.4	535.4	249.9
A. DIRECT INVESTMENT	4 500	117.5	321.9	94.2	424.0	700.2	600.5	185.5	293.8
Direct investment abroad	4 505	−.3	−1.2	−2.8	−.2	1.1	13.5	−11.6	−2.0
Equity capital	4 510	−.3	−1.2	−2.8	−.2	1.1	13.5	−11.6	−2.0
Claims on affiliated enterprises	4 515	−.3	−1.2	−2.8	−.2	1.1	13.5	−11.6	−2.0
Liabilities to affiliated enterprises	4 520	....	....	....	....	....	....	....	....
Reinvested earnings	4 525	....	....	....	....	....	....	....	....
Other capital	4 530	....	....	....	....	....	....	....	....
Claims on affiliated enterprises	4 535	....	....	....	....	....	....	....	....
Liabilities to affiliated enterprises	4 540	....	....	....	....	....	....	....	....
Direct investment in Macedonia, FYR	4 555	117.8	323.0	97.0	424.2	699.1	587.0	197.1	295.8
Equity capital	4 560	97.7	152.9	98.9	353.9	259.3	299.7	214.9	167.1
Claims on direct investors	4 565	....	....	....	....	....	....	....	....
Liabilities to direct investors	4 570	97.7	152.9	98.9	353.9	259.3	299.7	214.9	167.1
Reinvested earnings	4 575	30.0	.9	55.9	19.5	251.1	24.4	−158.0	82.5
Other capital	4 580	−9.9	169.2	−57.7	50.8	188.7	262.9	140.2	46.2
Claims on direct investors	4 585	−1.3	13.9	−48.3	−3.3	−34.4	−24.7	−62.4	−84.9
Liabilities to direct investors	4 590	−8.6	155.3	−9.4	54.0	223.1	287.6	202.6	131.1
B. PORTFOLIO INVESTMENT	4 600	5.7	11.5	238.6	92.4	155.2	−72.5	147.2	−83.4
Assets	4 602	.3	−.9	.8	−.5	−2.8	−1.1	−51.3	−29.0
Equity securities	4 610	.1	.2	.1	.1	−2.3	−.4	−29.2	−18.5
Monetary authorities	4 611	....	....	....	....	....	....	....	....
General government	4 612	....	....	....	....	....	....	....	....
Banks	4 613	....	....	....	....	....	....	....	....
Other sectors	4 614	.1	.2	.1	.1	−2.3	−.4	−29.2	−18.5
Debt securities	4 619	.3	−1.1	.7	−.5	−.5	−.7	−22.1	−10.5
Bonds and notes	4 620	.3	−1.1	.7	−.5	−.5	−.7	−22.1	−10.5
Monetary authorities	4 621	....	....	....	....	....	....	....	....
General government	4 622	....	....	....	....	....	....	....	....
Banks	4 623	.2	−1.1	.7	−.5	−.4	.1	−3.9	....
Other sectors	4 624	.1	....	....	....	....	−.8	−18.2	−10.5
Money market instruments	4 630	....	....	....	....	....	....	....	....
Monetary authorities	4 631	....	....	....	....	....	....	....	....
General government	4 632	....	....	....	....	....	....	....	....
Banks	4 633	....	....	....	....	....	....	....	....
Other sectors	4 634	....	....	....	....	....	....	....	....
Liabilities	4 652	5.3	12.4	237.8	92.8	157.9	−71.4	198.5	−54.4
Equity securities	4 660	2.7	13.0	53.8	86.3	169.8	−49.4	−14.0	−3.9
Banks	4 663	....	....	....	32.9	88.7	−19.6	−4.9	−.2
Other sectors	4 664	2.7	13.0	53.8	53.4	81.1	−29.7	−9.1	−3.6
Debt securities	4 669	2.6	−.7	184.0	6.5	−11.9	−22.0	212.5	−50.6
Bonds and notes	4 670	2.6	−.7	184.0	6.5	−11.9	−22.0	212.5	−50.6
Monetary authorities	4 671	....	....	....	....	....	....	....	....
General government	4 672	2.6	−.7	184.0	6.5	−11.9	−22.0	212.5	−49.2
Banks	4 673	....	....	....	....	....	....	....	....
Other sectors	4 674	....	....	....	....	....	....	....	−1.4
Money market instruments	4 680	....	....	....	....	....	....	....	....
Monetary authorities	4 681	....	....	....	....	....	....	....	....
General government	4 682	....	....	....	....	....	....	....	....
Banks	4 683	....	....	....	....	....	....	....	....
Other sectors	4 684	....	....	....	....	....	....	....	....
C. FINANCIAL DERIVATIVES	4 910	....	....	....	....	....	....	....	....
Monetary authorities	4 911	....	....	....	....	....	....	....	....
General government	4 912	....	....	....	....	....	....	....	....
Banks	4 913	....	....	....	....	....	....	....	....
Other sectors	4 914	....	....	....	....	....	....	....	....
Assets	4 900	....	....	....	....	....	....	....	....
Monetary authorities	4 901	....	....	....	....	....	....	....	....
General government	4 902	....	....	....	....	....	....	....	....
Banks	4 903	....	....	....	....	....	....	....	....
Other sectors	4 904	....	....	....	....	....	....	....	....
Liabilities	4 905	....	....	....	....	....	....	....	....
Monetary authorities	4 906	....	....	....	....	....	....	....	....
General government	4 907	....	....	....	....	....	....	....	....
Banks	4 908	....	....	....	....	....	....	....	....
Other sectors	4 909	....	....	....	....	....	....	....	....

Table 2 (Concluded). STANDARD PRESENTATION, 2003–2010

(Millions of U.S. dollars)

	Code	2003	2004	2005	2006	2007	2008	2009	2010
D. OTHER INVESTMENT	4 700	**152.8**	**124.9**	**249.5**	**−116.4**	**−69.6**	**676.2**	**338.8**	**92.6**
Assets	4 703	**18.2**	**8.5**	**−47.0**	**−148.6**	**−80.9**	**297.7**	**−144.6**	**−209.4**
Trade credits	4 706	....	....	....	....	....	....	....	....
General government	4 707	....	....	....	....	....	....	....	....
of which: Short-term	4 709	....	....	....	....	....	....	....	....
Other sectors	4 710	....	....	....	....	....	....	....	....
of which: Short-term	4 712	....	....	....	....	....	....	....	....
Loans	4 714	1.0	1.9	−7.4	7.5	....	−7.1	−26.9	6.0
Monetary authorities	4 715	....	....	....	....	....	....	....	....
of which: Short-term	4 718	....	....	....	....	....	....	....	....
General government	4 719	....	....	....	....	....	....	....	....
of which: Short-term	4 721	....	....	....	....	....	....	....	....
Banks	4 722	2.6	....	−3.4	2.3	.8	−.6	−22.4	8.4
of which: Short-term	4 724	1.7	....	−.1	−.5	.4	.1	−17.8	7.7
Other sectors	4 725	−1.7	1.9	−4.0	5.2	−.8	−6.5	−4.4	−2.4
of which: Short-term	4 727	−1.7	1.9	−4.0	5.2	−.8	−1.2	.2	.2
Currency and deposits	4 730	19.1	7.2	−42.8	−155.1	−81.4	303.5	−117.9	−215.7
Monetary authorities	4 731	17.8	26.4	.8	−3.3	−.2	24.2	.1	.8
General government	4 732	....	....	....	....	....	....	....	....
Banks	4 733	−38.6	−94.2	8.0	−67.7	4.4	333.7	−108.7	−99.4
Other sectors	4 734	39.9	74.9	−51.6	−84.1	−85.5	−54.4	−9.3	−117.1
Other assets	4 736	−1.9	−.6	3.2	−1.0	.5	1.3	.2	.3
Monetary authorities	4 737	....	....	....	....	....	....	....	....
of which: Short-term	4 739	....	....	....	....	....	....	....	....
General government	4 740	....	....	....	....	....	....	....	....
of which: Short-term	4 742	....	....	....	....	....	....	....	....
Banks	4 743	−1.9	−.6	3.2	−1.0	.5	1.3	.2	.3
of which: Short-term	4 745	−1.9	−.6	3.2	−1.0	.5	1.3	.2	.3
Other sectors	4 746	....	....	....	....	....	....	....	....
of which: Short-term	4 748	....	....	....	....	....	....	....	....
Liabilities	4 753	**134.7**	**116.4**	**296.6**	**32.2**	**11.3**	**378.4**	**483.4**	**301.9**
Trade credits	4 756	72.1	90.4	131.5	−21.1	−22.9	5.7	222.9	58.9
General government	4 757	....	....	....	....	....	....	....	....
of which: Short-term	4 759	....	....	....	....	....	....	....	....
Other sectors	4 760	72.1	90.4	131.5	−21.1	−22.9	5.7	222.9	58.9
of which: Short-term	4 762	72.1	90.4	131.5	−21.1	−22.9	5.7	222.9	58.9
Loans	4 764	58.6	14.0	127.8	−7.4	−121.6	343.4	102.2	159.9
Monetary authorities	4 765	−4.7	−8.6	4.7	−9.6	−56.1	....	....	....
of which: Use of Fund credit and loans from the Fund	4 766	−4.7	−8.6	4.7	−9.6	−56.1	....	....	....
of which: Short-term	4 768	....	....	....	....	....	....	....	....
General government	4 769	36.0	38.9	44.3	−157.7	−155.1	48.7	10.8	50.2
of which: Short-term	4 771	....	....	....	....	....	....	....	....
Banks	4 772	−44.3	−22.5	56.5	50.1	95.1	−27.5	87.3	141.3
of which: Short-term	4 774	−20.7	−6.5	−6.8	−1.5	20.3	−24.1	58.8	−8.9
Other sectors	4 775	71.6	6.2	22.2	109.7	−5.5	322.2	4.1	−31.6
of which: Short-term	4 777	2.3	−26.2	17.6	40.2	36.6	−41.8	−15.3	51.1
Currency and deposits	4 780	9.5	−2.7	24.9	52.9	72.7	18.6	33.7	−6.3
Monetary authorities	4 781	....	....	....	....	....	....	....	....
General government	4 782	....	....	....	....	....	....	....	....
Banks	4 783	9.5	−2.7	24.9	52.9	72.7	18.6	33.7	−6.3
Other sectors	4 784	....	....	....	....	....	....	....	....
Other liabilities	4 786	−5.6	14.6	12.4	7.9	83.1	10.7	124.6	89.4
Monetary authorities	4 787	....	....	....	....	....	....	89.4	....
of which: Short-term	4 789	....	....	....	....	....	....	....	....
General government	4 790	−7.7	....	....	....	....	.3	....	.3
of which: Short-term	4 792	−7.7	....	....	....	....	.3	....	.3
Banks	4 793	.8	1.1	1.1	1.2	1.4	1.3	.9	1.0
of which: Short-term	4 795	.8	1.1	1.1	1.2	1.4	1.3	.9	1.0
Other sectors	4 796	1.3	13.5	11.2	6.7	81.7	9.1	34.3	88.0
of which: Short-term	4 798	1.3	13.5	11.2	6.7	81.7	9.1	34.3	88.0
E. RESERVE ASSETS	4 802	**−50.7**	**−19.4**	**−415.3**	**−375.7**	**−142.9**	**47.2**	**−136.1**	**−53.1**
Monetary gold	4 812	40.2	−39.5	....	....	....	....	....	....
Special drawing rights	4 811	6.1	−.4	−.1	−2.1	1.6	....	−89.3	87.5
Reserve position in the Fund	4 810	....	....	....	....	....	....	....	....
Foreign exchange	4 803	−97.0	20.4	−415.1	−373.6	−144.5	47.1	−46.8	−140.5
Other claims	4 813	....	....	....	....	....	....	....	....
NET ERRORS AND OMISSIONS	4 998	**−33.1**	**17.5**	**−5.8**	**5.4**	**−42.0**	**2.0**	**34.8**	**−.1**

Table 3. INTERNATIONAL INVESTMENT POSITION (End-period stocks), 2003–2010

(Millions of U.S. dollars)

	Code	2003	2004	2005	2006	2007	2008	2009	2010
ASSETS	8 995 C.	**1,868.4**	**2,161.7**	**2,455.6**	**3,255.2**	**3,946.3**	**3,463.5**	**3,737.3**	**3,918.1**
Direct investment abroad	8 505 ..	**42.0**	**54.2**	**62.1**	**38.4**	**67.6**	**85.8**	**95.6**	**95.4**
Equity capital and reinvested earnings	8 506 ..	35.7	43.9	43.6	36.4	51.6	69.0	71.1	63.4
Claims on affiliated enterprises	8 507 ..	35.7	43.9	43.6	36.4	51.6	69.0	71.1	63.4
Liabilities to affiliated enterprises	8 508 ..	....	....	....	....	....	....	....	....
Other capital	8 530 ..	6.3	10.3	18.5	2.0	16.0	16.8	24.5	32.0
Claims on affiliated enterprises	8 535 ..	10.8	15.3	25.2	19.3	25.0	27.3	35.3	47.9
Liabilities to affiliated enterprises	8 540 ..	−4.5	−5.0	−6.7	−17.3	−9.0	−10.4	−10.7	−15.9
Portfolio investment	8 602 ..	**3.8**	**4.1**	**3.6**	**4.2**	**4.4**	**3.1**	**6.2**	**31.7**
Equity securities	8 610 ..	3.8	4.1	3.6	4.2	4.4	3.1	6.2	23.9
Monetary authorities	8 611 ..	....	....	....	....	....	....	....	....
General government	8 612 ..	....	....	....	....	....	....	....	....
Banks	8 613 ..	3.0	3.3	2.9	3.4	3.6	2.1	2.2	2.2
Other sectors	8 614 ..	.8	.8	.7	.8	.8	1.0	4.0	21.7
Debt securities	8 619 ..	....	....	....	....	....	....	....	7.9
Bonds and notes	8 620 ..	....	....	....	....	....	....	....	7.9
Monetary authorities	8 621 ..	....	....	....	....	....	....	....	....
General government	8 622 ..	....	....	....	....	....	....	....	....
Banks	8 623 ..	....	....	....	....	....	....	....	....
Other sectors	8 624 ..	....	....	....	....	....	....	....	7.9
Money market instruments	8 630 ..	....	....	....	....	....	....	....	....
Monetary authorities	8 631 ..	....	....	....	....	....	....	....	....
General government	8 632 ..	....	....	....	....	....	....	....	....
Banks	8 633 ..	....	....	....	....	....	....	....	....
Other sectors	8 634 ..	....	....	....	....	....	....	....	....
Financial derivatives	8 900 ..	....	....	....	....	....	....	....	....
Monetary authorities	8 901 ..	....	....	....	....	....	....	....	....
General government	8 902 ..	....	....	....	....	....	....	....	....
Banks	8 903 ..	....	....	....	....	....	....	....	....
Other sectors	8 904 ..	....	....	....	....	....	....	....	....
Other investment	8 703 ..	**929.3**	**1,128.1**	**1,065.3**	**1,346.9**	**1,634.7**	**1,267.1**	**1,344.9**	**1,513.1**
Trade credits	8 706 ..	194.3	266.8	298.7	441.8	652.7	674.0	586.1	721.8
General government	8 707 ..	....	....	....	....	....	....	....	....
of which: Short-term	8 709 ..	....	....	....	....	....	....	....	....
Other sectors	8 710 ..	194.3	266.8	298.7	441.8	652.7	674.0	586.1	721.8
of which: Short-term	8 712 ..	*193.9*	*266.8*	*298.2*	*441.0*	*651.6*	*672.7*	*585.3*	*721.8*
Loans	8 714 ..	25.5	2.8	4.5	2.3	3.9	8.5	31.5	19.7
Monetary authorities	8 715 ..	....	....	....	....	....	....	....	....
of which: Short-term	8 718 ..	....	....	....	....	....	....	....	....
General government	8 719 ..	....	....	....	....	....	....	....	....
of which: Short-term	8 721 ..	....	....	....	....	....	....	....	....
Banks	8 722 ..	24.0	1.1	4.1	2.0	1.1	1.5	23.4	13.6
of which: Short-term	8 724 ..	*8.8*	....	*2.6*	*.5*	....	....	*16.0*	*8.8*
Other sectors	8 725 ..	1.5	1.7	.4	.3	2.8	7.0	8.1	6.1
of which: Short-term	8 727 ..	*1.5*	....	*.2*	....	*.5*	*1.2*	*.4*	....
Currency and deposits	8 730 ..	706.4	827.7	733.3	868.7	937.0	541.1	679.3	737.0
Monetary authorities	8 731 ..	41.4	16.2	15.5	23.6	25.3	1.6	1.4	....
General government	8 732 ..	....	....	....	....	....	....	....	....
Banks	8 733 ..	664.6	811.5	717.8	844.8	911.2	539.2	677.9	737.0
Other sectors	8 734 ..	.4	....	....	.3	.6	.3	....	.1
Other assets	8 736 ..	3.1	30.8	28.8	34.1	41.2	43.4	48.0	34.6
Monetary authorities	8 737 ..	....	....	....	....	....	....	....	....
of which: Short-term	8 739 ..	....	....	....	....	....	....	....	....
General government	8 740 ..	....	....	....	....	....	....	....	....
of which: Short-term	8 742 ..	....	....	....	....	....	....	....	....
Banks	8 743 ..	....	30.2	28.2	33.4	39.9	10.1	11.1	10.0
of which: Short-term	8 745 ..	....	*30.2*	*28.2*	*33.4*	*39.9*	*10.1*	*11.1*	*10.0*
Other sectors	8 746 ..	3.1	.6	.5	.8	1.3	33.3	36.9	24.6
of which: Short-term	8 748 ..	*3.1*	*.6*	*.5*	*.8*	*1.3*	*33.3*	*36.9*	*24.6*
Reserve assets	8 802 ..	**893.3**	**975.2**	**1,324.7**	**1,865.7**	**2,239.6**	**2,107.6**	**2,290.5**	**2,277.8**
Monetary gold	8 812 ..	37.1	86.5	112.0	138.8	182.6	188.8	241.0	307.8
Special drawing rights	8 811 ..	.3	.8	.8	3.0	1.5	1.4	91.1	1.2
Reserve position in the Fund	8 810 ..	....	....	....	....	....	....	....	....
Foreign exchange	8 803 ..	856.0	888.0	1,212.0	1,724.0	2,055.6	1,917.4	1,958.5	1,968.8
Other claims	8 813 ..	....	....	....	....	....	....	....	....

Table 3 (Concluded). INTERNATIONAL INVESTMENT POSITION (End-period stocks), 2003–2010

(Millions of U.S. dollars)

	Code	2003	2004	2005	2006	2007	2008	2009	2010
LIABILITIES...	8 995 D.	**3,867.5**	**4,673.3**	**4,804.2**	**5,741.0**	**7,475.3**	**8,069.0**	**8,919.1**	**8,860.0**
Direct investment in Macedonia, FYR..................	8 555 ..	**1,614.7**	**2,190.5**	**2,086.9**	**2,763.8**	**3,739.4**	**4,185.3**	**4,504.1**	**4,449.7**
Equity capital and reinvested earnings.............................	8 556 ..	1,477.0	1,858.5	1,863.5	2,454.0	3,271.3	3,394.0	3,557.6	3,509.5
Claims on direct investors...	8 557 ..	....	....	....	....	....	....	....	....
Liabilities to direct investors...	8 558 ..	1,477.0	1,858.5	1,863.5	2,454.0	3,271.3	3,394.0	3,557.6	3,509.5
Other capital...	8 580 ..	137.7	332.1	223.4	309.8	468.0	791.4	946.5	940.2
Claims on direct investors...	8 585 ..	−60.0	−49.9	−87.9	−106.6	−155.9	−160.7	−243.7	−305.2
Liabilities to direct investors...	8 590 ..	197.6	382.0	311.3	416.4	623.9	952.0	1,190.2	1,245.4
Portfolio investment..	8 652 ..	**107.2**	**71.6**	**273.9**	**364.7**	**445.2**	**373.5**	**590.7**	**524.7**
Equity securities..	8 660 ..	80.5	40.0	52.8	114.0	194.8	187.9	195.6	181.8
Banks...	8 663 ..	12.6	19.1	29.5	106.2	90.9	99.7	107.1	107.5
Other sectors..	8 664 ..	67.9	20.9	23.2	7.8	103.9	88.2	88.4	74.3
Debt securities...	8 669 ..	26.8	31.6	221.2	250.7	250.5	185.6	395.1	343.0
Bonds and notes...	8 670 ..	26.8	31.6	221.2	250.7	250.5	185.6	395.1	343.0
Monetary authorities...	8 671 ..	....	....	....	....	....	....	....	....
General government..	8 672 ..	26.8	31.6	221.2	250.7	250.5	185.6	395.1	343.0
Banks..	8 673 ..	....	....	....	....	....	....	....	....
Other sectors...	8 674 ..	....	....	....	....	....	....	....	....
Money market instruments.....................................	8 680 ..	....	....	....	....	....	....	....	....
Monetary authorities...	8 681 ..	....	....	....	....	....	....	....	....
General government..	8 682 ..	....	....	....	....	....	....	....	....
Banks..	8 683 ..	....	....	....	....	....	....	....	....
Other sectors...	8 684 ..	....	....	....	....	....	....	....	....
Financial derivatives..	8 905 ..	....	....	....	....	....	....	....	....
Monetary authorities..	8 906 ..	....	....	....	....	....	....	....	....
General government...	8 907 ..	....	....	....	....	....	....	....	....
Banks..	8 908 ..	....	....	....	....	....	....	....	....
Other sectors..	8 909 ..	....	....	....	....	....	....	....	....
Other investment...	8 753 ..	**2,145.6**	**2,411.2**	**2,443.4**	**2,612.4**	**3,290.7**	**3,510.2**	**3,824.3**	**3,885.5**
Trade credits...	8 756 ..	398.2	469.8	441.1	486.2	854.5	914.4	914.6	877.9
General government..	8 757 ..	....	....	....	....	....	4.9	3.5	2.2
of which: Short-term...	8 759 ..	....	....	....	....	....	....	....	....
Other sectors..	8 760 ..	398.2	469.8	441.1	486.2	854.5	909.5	911.0	875.7
of which: Short-term...	8 762 ..	*336.4*	*438.8*	*428.1*	*460.4*	*833.1*	*876.3*	*883.6*	*857.6*
Loans...	8 764 ..	1,657.2	1,788.1	1,820.2	1,853.1	1,991.9	2,180.9	2,338.1	2,420.4
Monetary authorities...	8 765 ..	68.3	62.5	62.2	55.7	....	....	....	....
of which: Use of Fund credit and loans from the Fund....	8 766 ..	*68.3*	*62.5*	*62.2*	*55.7*	....	....	....	....
of which: Short-term..	8 768 ..	....	....	....	....	....	....	....	....
General government..	8 769 ..	1,256.5	1,351.2	1,292.2	1,152.6	1,068.4	1,087.3	1,114.9	1,132.2
of which: Short-term..	8 771 ..	....	....	....	....	....	....	....	....
Banks..	8 772 ..	90.9	85.5	127.1	192.7	317.8	283.6	372.9	498.9
of which: Short-term..	8 774 ..	*10.9*	*9.6*	*1.5*	....	*24.2*	....	*57.4*	*4.9*
Other sectors...	8 775 ..	241.4	289.0	338.8	452.2	605.7	810.0	850.3	789.3
of which: Short-term..	8 777 ..	*21.5*	*6.5*	*62.6*	*15.3*	*57.8*	*21.0*	*10.9*	*59.3*
Currency and deposits...	8 780 ..	68.9	70.6	86.9	148.6	238.3	245.4	285.0	260.0
Monetary authorities...	8 781 ..	....	....	....	....	....	....	....	....
General government..	8 782 ..	....	....	....	....	....	....	....	....
Banks..	8 783 ..	68.9	70.6	86.9	148.6	238.3	245.4	285.0	260.0
Other sectors...	8 784 ..	....	....	....	....	....	....	....	....
Other liabilities..	8 786 ..	21.4	82.7	95.3	124.5	206.0	169.6	286.6	327.2
Monetary authorities...	8 787 ..	....	13.0	12.0	12.6	13.2	12.9	102.9	101.5
of which: Short-term..	8 789 ..	....	....	....	....	....	....	....	....
General government..	8 790 ..	....	....	....	....	....	....	.3	.6
of which: Short-term..	8 792 ..	....	....	....	....	....	....	*.3*	*.6*
Banks..	8 793 ..	....	11.7	12.6	14.1	13.8	12.5	13.4	6.0
of which: Short-term..	8 795 ..	....	*11.7*	*12.6*	*14.1*	*13.8*	*12.5*	*13.4*	*6.0*
Other sectors...	8 796 ..	21.4	58.0	70.7	97.7	179.0	144.1	170.0	219.1
of which: Short-term..	8 798 ..	*21.4*	*58.0*	*70.7*	*97.7*	*178.5*	*143.6*	*169.5*	*204.7*
NET INTERNATIONAL INVESTMENT POSITION........	8 995 ..	**−1,999.1**	**−2,511.6**	**−2,348.6**	**−2,485.7**	**−3,529.0**	**−4,605.5**	**−5,181.8**	**−4,941.9**
Conversion rates: denars per U.S. dollar (end of period)...	0 102 ..	**49.050**	**45.068**	**51.859**	**46.450**	**41.656**	**43.561**	**42.665**	**46.314**

Table 1. ANALYTIC PRESENTATION, 2003–2010

(Millions of U.S. dollars)

	Code	2003	2004	2005	2006	2007	2008	2009	2010
A. Current Account[1]	4 993 Z.	**−458**	**−541**	**−626**	....	....	....	....	....
Goods: exports f.o.b.	2 100 ..	854	990	834	....	....	....	....	....
Goods: imports f.o.b.	3 100 ..	−1,111	−1,427	−1,427	....	....	....	....	....
Balance on Goods	4 100 ..	*−258*	*−437*	*−592*	....	....	....	....	....
Services: credit	2 200 ..	322	425	498	....	....	....	....	....
Services: debit	3 200 ..	−619	−637	−615	....	....	....	....	....
Balance on Goods and Services	4 991 ..	*−555*	*−649*	*−710*	....	....	....	....	....
Income: credit	2 300 ..	16	15	24	....	....	....	....	....
Income: debit	3 300 ..	−94	−89	−104	....	....	....	....	....
Balance on Goods, Services, and Income	4 992 ..	*−632*	*−723*	*−790*	....	....	....	....	....
Current transfers: credit	2 379 Z.	357	245	208	....	....	....	....	....
Current transfers: debit	3 379 ..	−183	−62	−45	....	....	....	....	....
B. Capital Account[1]	4 994 Z.	**143**	**182**	**192**	....	....	....	....	....
Capital account: credit	2 994 Z.	143	182	192	....	....	....	....	....
Capital account: debit	3 994 ..	....	....	....	....	....	....	....	....
Total, Groups A Plus B	4 981 ..	*−315*	*−359*	*−435*	....	....	....	....	....
C. Financial Account[1]	4 995 W.	**−126**	**251**	**−6**	....	....	....	....	....
Direct investment abroad	4 505 ..	....	....		....	....	....	....	....
Direct investment in Madagascar	4 555 Z.	13	53	85	....	....	....	....	....
Portfolio investment assets	4 602 ..	....	....		....	....	....	....	....
Equity securities	4 610 ..	....	....		....	....	....	....	....
Debt securities	4 619 ..	....	....		....	....	....	....	....
Portfolio investment liabilities	4 652 Z.	....	....		....	....	....	....	....
Equity securities	4 660 ..	....	....		....	....	....	....	....
Debt securities	4 669 Z.	....	....		....	....	....	....	....
Financial derivatives	4 910 ..	....	....		....	....	....	....	....
Financial derivatives assets	4 900 ..	....	....		....	....	....	....	....
Financial derivatives liabilities	4 905 ..	....	....		....	....	....	....	....
Other investment assets	4 703 ..	−29	295	11	....	....	....	....	....
Monetary authorities	4 701 ..	4	315	....	....	....	....	....	....
General government	4 704 ..	....	....		....	....	....	....	....
Banks	4 705 ..	−32	−20	11	....	....	....	....	....
Other sectors	4 728 ..	....	....		....	....	....	....	....
Other investment liabilities	4 753 W.	−110	−97	−102	....	....	....	....	....
Monetary authorities	4 753 WA	−1	−1	....	....	....	....	....	....
General government	4 753 ZB	−100	−101	−89	....	....	....	....	....
Banks	4 753 ZC	3	6	−14	....	....	....	....	....
Other sectors	4 753 ZD	−13	....		....	....	....	....	....
Total, Groups A Through C	4 983 ..	*−441*	*−108*	*−440*	....	....	....	....	....
D. Net Errors and Omissions	4 998 ..	**67**	**−35**	**91**	....	....	....	....	....
Total, Groups A Through D	4 984 ..	*−374*	*−143*	*−349*	....	....	....	....	....
E. Reserves and Related Items	4 802 A.	**374**	**143**	**349**	....	....	....	....	....
Reserve assets	4 802 ..	−25	−384	−10	....	....	....	....	....
Use of Fund credit and loans	4 766 ..	8	44	5	....	....	....	....	....
Exceptional financing	4 920 ..	391	483	354	....	....	....	....	....
Conversion rates: Malagasy ariary per U.S. dollar	0 101 ..	**1,238.3**	**1,868.9**	**2,003.0**	**2,142.3**	**1,873.9**	**1,708.4**	**1,956.2**	**2,090.0**

[1] Excludes components that have been classified in the categories of Group E.

Table 2. STANDARD PRESENTATION, 2003–2010

(Millions of U.S. dollars)

	Code	2003	2004	2005	2006	2007	2008	2009	2010
CURRENT ACCOUNT	4 993	**−328**	**−399**	**−554**	....	....	....	....	....
A. GOODS	4 100	**−258**	**−437**	**−592**	....	....	....	....	....
Credit	2 100	**854**	**990**	**834**	....	....	....	....	....
General merchandise: exports f.o.b.	2 110	449	450	352	....	....	....	....	....
Goods for processing: exports f.o.b.	2 150	405	540	482	....	....	....	....	....
Repairs on goods	2 160	....	....	....	....	....	....	....	....
Goods procured in ports by carriers	2 170	....	....	....	....	....	....	....	....
Nonmonetary gold	2 180	....	....	....	....	....	....	....	....
Debit	3 100	**−1,111**	**−1,427**	**−1,427**	....	....	....	....	....
General merchandise: imports f.o.b.	3 110	−748	−929	−1,024	....	....	....	....	....
Goods for processing: imports f.o.b.	3 150	−363	−498	−402	....	....	....	....	....
Repairs on goods	3 160	....	....	....	....	....	....	....	....
Goods procured in ports by carriers	3 170	....	....	....	....	....	....	....	....
Nonmonetary gold	3 180	....	....	....	....	....	....	....	....
B. SERVICES	4 200	**−297**	**−212**	**−117**	....	....	....	....	....
Total credit	2 200	*322*	*425*	*498*	....	....	....	....	....
Total debit	3 200	*−619*	*−637*	*−615*	....	....	....	....	....
Transportation services, credit	2 205	**58**	**100**	**118**	....	....	....	....	....
Passenger	2 850	*43*	*82*	*107*	....	....	....	....	....
Freight	2 851	*7*	*10*	*9*	....	....	....	....	....
Other	2 852	*8*	*8*	*3*	....	....	....	....	....
Sea transport, passenger	2 207	....	....	....	....	....	....	....	....
Sea transport, freight	2 208	7	9	9	....	....	....	....	....
Sea transport, other	2 209	4	6	1	....	....	....	....	....
Air transport, passenger	2 211	43	82	107	....	....	....	....	....
Air transport, freight	2 212	....	2	....	....	....	....	....	....
Air transport, other	2 213	4	2	2	....	....	....	....	....
Other transport, passenger	2 215	....	....	....	....	....	....	....	....
Other transport, freight	2 216	....	....	....	....	....	....	....	....
Other transport, other	2 217	....	....	....	....	....	....	....	....
Transportation services, debit	3 205	**−230**	**−237**	**−224**	....	....	....	....	....
Passenger	3 850	*−3*	*−15*	*−6*	....	....	....	....	....
Freight	3 851	*−167*	*−214*	*−214*	....	....	....	....	....
Other	3 852	*−61*	*−8*	*−4*	....	....	....	....	....
Sea transport, passenger	3 207	....	....	....	....	....	....	....	....
Sea transport, freight	3 208	−167	−214	−214	....	....	....	....	....
Sea transport, other	3 209	−1	−4	−1	....	....	....	....	....
Air transport, passenger	3 211	−3	−15	−6	....	....	....	....	....
Air transport, freight	3 212	....	....	....	....	....	....	....	....
Air transport, other	3 213	−60	−4	−3	....	....	....	....	....
Other transport, passenger	3 215	....	....	....	....	....	....	....	....
Other transport, freight	3 216	....	....	....	....	....	....	....	....
Other transport, other	3 217	....	....	....	....	....	....	....	....
Travel, credit	2 236	**76**	**157**	**183**	....	....	....	....	....
Business travel	2 237	1	1	....	....	....	....	....	....
Personal travel	2 240	75	156	183	....	....	....	....	....
Travel, debit	3 236	**−64**	**−93**	**−74**	....	....	....	....	....
Business travel	3 237	−7	−8	....	....	....	....	....	....
Personal travel	3 240	−57	−86	−73	....	....	....	....	....
Other services, credit	2 200 BA	**188**	**168**	**197**	....	....	....	....	....
Communications	2 245	6	7	2	....	....	....	....	....
Construction	2 249	74	10	2	....	....	....	....	....
Insurance	2 253	1	3	....	....	....	....	....	....
Financial	2 260	4	1	....	....	....	....	....	....
Computer and information	2 262	1	1	....	....	....	....	....	....
Royalties and licence fees	2 266	1	....	2	....	....	....	....	....
Other business services	2 268	32	79	111	....	....	....	....	....
Personal, cultural, and recreational	2 287	....	....	....	....	....	....	....	....
Government, n.i.e.	2 291	69	66	78	....	....	....	....	....
Other services, debit	3 200 BA	**−325**	**−307**	**−318**	....	....	....	....	....
Communications	3 245	−5	−4	−6	....	....	....	....	....
Construction	3 249	−39	−5	−2	....	....	....	....	....
Insurance	3 253	−10	−7	−5	....	....	....	....	....
Financial	3 260	−5	−5	....	....	....	....	....	....
Computer and information	3 262	−2	−3	−1	....	....	....	....	....
Royalties and licence fees	3 266	−7	−23	−9	....	....	....	....	....
Other business services	3 268	−118	−97	−143	....	....	....	....	....
Personal, cultural, and recreational	3 287	....	....	....	....	....	....	....	....
Government, n.i.e.	3 291	−139	−164	−153	....	....	....	....	....

Table 2 (Continued). STANDARD PRESENTATION, 2003–2010
(Millions of U.S. dollars)

	Code	2003	2004	2005	2006	2007	2008	2009	2010
C. INCOME	4 300	−77	−74	−80	....	....	....	....	....
Total credit	2 300	16	15	24	....	....	....	....	....
Total debit	3 300	−94	−89	−104	....	....	....	....	....
Compensation of employees, credit	2 310	8	7	10	....	....	....	....	....
Compensation of employees, debit	3 310	−5	−6	−13	....	....	....	....	....
Investment income, credit	2 320	8	8	14	....	....	....	....	....
Direct investment income	2 330	....	....	....					
Dividends and distributed branch profits	2 332	....	....	....					
Reinvested earnings and undistributed branch profits	2 333	....	....	....					
Income on debt (interest)	2 334	....	....	....					
Portfolio investment income	2 339	....	....	....					
Income on equity	2 340	....	....	....					
Income on bonds and notes	2 350	....	....	....					
Income on money market instruments	2 360	....	....	....					
Other investment income	2 370	8	8	14					
Investment income, debit	3 320	−89	−83	−90	....	....	....	....	....
Direct investment income	3 330	−32	−21	−38	....	....	....	....	....
Dividends and distributed branch profits	3 332	−32	−21	−38					
Reinvested earnings and undistributed branch profits	3 333	....	....	....					
Income on debt (interest)	3 334	....	....	....					
Portfolio investment income	3 339	....	....	....					
Income on equity	3 340	....	....	....					
Income on bonds and notes	3 350	....	....	....					
Income on money market instruments	3 360	....	....	....					
Other investment income	3 370	−57	−63	−52					
D. CURRENT TRANSFERS	4 379	304	324	236	....	....	....	....	....
Credit	2 379	487	387	281	....	....	....	....	....
General government	2 380	149	162	72	....	....	....	....	....
Other sectors	2 390	338	224	208	....	....	....	....	....
Workers' remittances	2 391	8	4	1	....	....	....	....	....
Other current transfers	2 392	330	220	207	....	....	....	....	....
Debit	3 379	−183	−62	−45	....	....	....	....	....
General government	3 380	−5	....	−14	....	....	....	....	....
Other sectors	3 390	−178	−62	−31	....	....	....	....	....
Workers' remittances	3 391	−13	−3	−8	....	....	....	....	....
Other current transfers	3 392	−165	−59	−23	....	....	....	....	....
CAPITAL AND FINANCIAL ACCOUNT	4 996	261	434	463	....	....	....	....	....
CAPITAL ACCOUNT	4 994	143	182	192	....	....	....	....	....
Total credit	2 994	143	182	192	....	....	....	....	....
Total debit	3 994	....	....	....	....	....	....	....	....
Capital transfers, credit	2 400	143	182	192	....	....	....	....	....
General government	2 401	143	182	192	....	....	....	....	....
Debt forgiveness	2 402	....	....	....	....	....	....	....	....
Other capital transfers	2 410	143	182	192	....	....	....	....	....
Other sectors	2 430	....	....	....	....	....	....	....	....
Migrants' transfers	2 431	....	....	....	....	....	....	....	....
Debt forgiveness	2 432	....	....	....	....	....	....	....	....
Other capital transfers	2 440	....	....	....	....	....	....	....	....
Capital transfers, debit	3 400	....	....	....	....	....	....	....	....
General government	3 401	....	....	....	....	....	....	....	....
Debt forgiveness	3 402	....	....	....	....	....	....	....	....
Other capital transfers	3 410	....	....	....	....	....	....	....	....
Other sectors	3 430	....	....	....	....	....	....	....	....
Migrants' transfers	3 431	....	....	....	....	....	....	....	....
Debt forgiveness	3 432	....	....	....	....	....	....	....	....
Other capital transfers	3 440	....	....	....	....	....	....	....	....
Nonproduced nonfinancial assets, credit	2 480	....	....	....	....	....	....	....	....
Nonproduced nonfinancial assets, debit	3 480	....	....	....	....	....	....	....	....

Table 2 (Continued). STANDARD PRESENTATION, 2003–2010

(Millions of U.S. dollars)

	Code	2003	2004	2005	2006	2007	2008	2009	2010
FINANCIAL ACCOUNT	4 995 ..	**118**	**252**	**271**	....	....	....	....	....
A. DIRECT INVESTMENT	4 500 ..	**13**	**53**	**85**	....	....	....	....	....
Direct investment abroad	4 505 ..	....	....	....	....	....	....	....	....
Equity capital	4 510 ..	....	....	....	....	....	....	....	....
Claims on affiliated enterprises	4 515 ..	....	....	....	....	....	....	....	....
Liabilities to affiliated enterprises	4 520 ..	....	....	....	....	....	....	....	....
Reinvested earnings	4 525 ..	....	....	....	....	....	....	....	....
Other capital	4 530 ..	....	....	....	....	....	....	....	....
Claims on affiliated enterprises	4 535 ..	....	....	....	....	....	....	....	....
Liabilities to affiliated enterprises	4 540 ..	....	....	....	....	....	....	....	....
Direct investment in Madagascar	4 555 ..	**13**	**53**	**85**	....	....	....	....	....
Equity capital	4 560 ..	13	53	85	....	....	....	....	....
Claims on direct investors	4 565 ..	....	....	....	....	....	....	....	....
Liabilities to direct investors	4 570 ..	13	53	85	....	....	....	....	....
Reinvested earnings	4 575 ..	....	....	....	....	....	....	....	....
Other capital	4 580 ..	....	....	....	....	....	....	....	....
Claims on direct investors	4 585 ..	....	....	....	....	....	....	....	....
Liabilities to direct investors	4 590 ..	....	....	....	....	....	....	....	....
B. PORTFOLIO INVESTMENT	4 600 ..	....	....	....	....	....	....	....	....
Assets	4 602 ..	....	....	....	....	....	....	....	....
Equity securities	4 610 ..	....	....	....	....	....	....	....	....
Monetary authorities	4 611 ..	....	....	....	....	....	....	....	....
General government	4 612 ..	....	....	....	....	....	....	....	....
Banks	4 613 ..	....	....	....	....	....	....	....	....
Other sectors	4 614 ..	....	....	....	....	....	....	....	....
Debt securities	4 619 ..	....	....	....	....	....	....	....	....
Bonds and notes	4 620 ..	....	....	....	....	....	....	....	....
Monetary authorities	4 621 ..	....	....	....	....	....	....	....	....
General government	4 622 ..	....	....	....	....	....	....	....	....
Banks	4 623 ..	....	....	....	....	....	....	....	....
Other sectors	4 624 ..	....	....	....	....	....	....	....	....
Money market instruments	4 630 ..	....	....	....	....	....	....	....	....
Monetary authorities	4 631 ..	....	....	....	....	....	....	....	....
General government	4 632 ..	....	....	....	....	....	....	....	....
Banks	4 633 ..	....	....	....	....	....	....	....	....
Other sectors	4 634 ..	....	....	....	....	....	....	....	....
Liabilities	4 652 ..	....	....	....	....	....	....	....	....
Equity securities	4 660 ..	....	....	....	....	....	....	....	....
Banks	4 663 ..	....	....	....	....	....	....	....	....
Other sectors	4 664 ..	....	....	....	....	....	....	....	....
Debt securities	4 669 ..	....	....	....	....	....	....	....	....
Bonds and notes	4 670 ..	....	....	....	....	....	....	....	....
Monetary authorities	4 671 ..	....	....	....	....	....	....	....	....
General government	4 672 ..	....	....	....	....	....	....	....	....
Banks	4 673 ..	....	....	....	....	....	....	....	....
Other sectors	4 674 ..	....	....	....	....	....	....	....	....
Money market instruments	4 680 ..	....	....	....	....	....	....	....	....
Monetary authorities	4 681 ..	....	....	....	....	....	....	....	....
General government	4 682 ..	....	....	....	....	....	....	....	....
Banks	4 683 ..	....	....	....	....	....	....	....	....
Other sectors	4 684 ..	....	....	....	....	....	....	....	....
C. FINANCIAL DERIVATIVES	4 910 ..	....	....	....	....	....	....	....	....
Monetary authorities	4 911 ..	....	....	....	....	....	....	....	....
General government	4 912 ..	....	....	....	....	....	....	....	....
Banks	4 913 ..	....	....	....	....	....	....	....	....
Other sectors	4 914 ..	....	....	....	....	....	....	....	....
Assets	4 900 ..	....	....	....	....	....	....	....	....
Monetary authorities	4 901 ..	....	....	....	....	....	....	....	....
General government	4 902 ..	....	....	....	....	....	....	....	....
Banks	4 903 ..	....	....	....	....	....	....	....	....
Other sectors	4 904 ..	....	....	....	....	....	....	....	....
Liabilities	4 905 ..	....	....	....	....	....	....	....	....
Monetary authorities	4 906 ..	....	....	....	....	....	....	....	....
General government	4 907 ..	....	....	....	....	....	....	....	....
Banks	4 908 ..	....	....	....	....	....	....	....	....
Other sectors	4 909 ..	....	....	....	....	....	....	....	....

Table 2 (Concluded). STANDARD PRESENTATION, 2003–2010

(Millions of U.S. dollars)

	Code	2003	2004	2005	2006	2007	2008	2009	2010
D. OTHER INVESTMENT............................	4 700 ..	**131**	**583**	**196**	....	....	....	....	....
Assets...	4 703 ..	**−29**	**295**	**11**	....	....	....	....	....
Trade credits......................................	4 706 ..	....	....	....	....	....	....	....	....
General government...........................	4 707 ..	....	....	....	....	....	....	....	....
of which: Short-term......................	4 709 ..	....	....	....	....	....	....	....	....
Other sectors..................................	4 710 ..	....	....	....	....	....	....	....	....
of which: Short-term......................	4 712 ..	....	....	....	....	....	....	....	....
Loans...	4 714 ..	−23	4	5	....	....	....	....	....
Monetary authorities.........................	4 715 ..	....	....	....	....	....	....	....	....
of which: Short-term......................	4 718 ..	....	....	....	....	....	....	....	....
General government...........................	4 719 ..	....	....	....	....	....	....	....	....
of which: Short-term......................	4 721 ..	....	....	....	....	....	....	....	....
Banks..	4 722 ..	−23	4	5	....	....	....	....	....
of which: Short-term......................	4 724 ..	....	....	....	....	....	....	....	....
Other sectors..................................	4 725 ..	....	....	....	....	....	....	....	....
of which: Short-term......................	4 727 ..	....	....	....	....	....	....	....	....
Currency and deposits..........................	4 730 ..	−6	−26	9	....	....	....	....	....
Monetary authorities.........................	4 731 ..	....	....	....	....	....	....	....	....
General government...........................	4 732 ..	....	....	....	....	....	....	....	....
Banks..	4 733 ..	−6	−26	9	....	....	....	....	....
Other sectors..................................	4 734 ..	....	....	....	....	....	....	....	....
Other assets......................................	4 736 ..	....	317	−4	....	....	....	....	....
Monetary authorities.........................	4 737 ..	4	315		....	....	....	....	....
of which: Short-term......................	4 739 ..	*4*	*−13*		....	....	....	....	....
General government...........................	4 740 ..	....	....	....	....	....	....	....	....
of which: Short-term......................	4 742 ..	....	....	....	....	....	....	....	....
Banks..	4 743 ..	−3	2	−4	....	....	....	....	....
of which: Short-term......................	4 745 ..	*−3*	*2*	*−4*	....	....	....	....	....
Other sectors..................................	4 746 ..	....	....	....	....	....	....	....	....
of which: Short-term......................	4 748 ..	....	....	....	....	....	....	....	....
Liabilities...	4 753 ..	**159**	**288**	**184**	....	....	....	....	....
Trade credits......................................	4 756 ..	....	....	....	....	....	....	....	....
General government...........................	4 757 ..	....	....	....	....	....	....	....	....
of which: Short-term......................	4 759 ..	....	....	....	....	....	....	....	....
Other sectors..................................	4 760 ..	....	....	....	....	....	....	....	....
of which: Short-term......................	4 762 ..	....	....	....	....	....	....	....	....
Loans...	4 764 ..	171	298	206	....	....	....	....	....
Monetary authorities.........................	4 765 ..	8	44	5	....	....	....	....	....
of which: Use of Fund credit and loans from the Fund..	4 766 ..	*8*	*44*	*5*	....	....	....	....	....
of which: Short-term......................	4 768 ..	....	....	....	....	....	....	....	....
General government...........................	4 769 ..	175	268	208	....	....	....	....	....
of which: Short-term......................	4 771 ..	....	....	....	....	....	....	....	....
Banks..	4 772 ..	....	....	....	....	....	....	....	....
of which: Short-term......................	4 774 ..	....	....	....	....	....	....	....	....
Other sectors..................................	4 775 ..	−13	−14	−7	....	....	....	....	....
of which: Short-term......................	4 777 ..	....	....	....	....	....	....	....	....
Currency and deposits..........................	4 780 ..	2	−3	−6	....	....	....	....	....
Monetary authorities.........................	4 781 ..	−3	−1	....	....	....	....	....	....
General government...........................	4 782 ..	....	....	....	....	....	....	....	....
Banks..	4 783 ..	4	−2	−6	....	....	....	....	....
Other sectors..................................	4 784 ..	....	....	....	....	....	....	....	....
Other liabilities..................................	4 786 ..	−13	−7	−15	....	....	....	....	....
Monetary authorities.........................	4 787 ..	1	....	....	....	....	....	....	....
of which: Short-term......................	4 789 ..	*1*	....	....	....	....	....	....	....
General government...........................	4 790 ..	−13	−14	−7	....	....	....	....	....
of which: Short-term......................	4 792 ..	*−13*	*−14*	*−7*	....	....	....	....	....
Banks..	4 793 ..	−1	7	−7	....	....	....	....	....
of which: Short-term......................	4 795 ..	*−1*	*7*	*−7*	....	....	....	....	....
Other sectors..................................	4 796 ..	....	....	....	....	....	....	....	....
of which: Short-term......................	4 798 ..	....	....	....	....	....	....	....	....
E. RESERVE ASSETS..............................	4 802 ..	**−25**	**−384**	**−10**	....	....	....	....	....
Monetary gold....................................	4 812 ..	....	....	....	....	....	....	....	....
Special drawing rights...........................	4 811 ..	....	....	....	....	....	....	....	....
Reserve position in the Fund....................	4 810 ..	....	....	....	....	....	....	....	....
Foreign exchange.................................	4 803 ..	−25	−384	−10	....	....	....	....	....
Other claims......................................	4 813 ..	....	....	....	....	....	....	....	....
NET ERRORS AND OMISSIONS...................	4 998 ..	**67**	**−35**	**91**	....	....	....	....	....

Table 1. ANALYTIC PRESENTATION, 2003–2010

(Millions of U.S. dollars)

	Code	2003	2004	2005	2006	2007	2008	2009	2010
A. Current Account[1]	4 993 Z.	**−306.5**	**−450.5**	**−620.4**	**−448.1**	**−704.4**	**−807.8**	**−562.6**	....
Goods: exports f.o.b.	2 100 ..	567.5	517.5	541.4	721.0	761.8	950.1	1,268.4	....
Goods: imports f.o.b.	3 100 ..	−864.4	−1,024.9	−1,300.5	−1,312.6	−1,565.6	−1,897.4	−1,995.3	....
Balance on Goods	4 100 ..	*−296.9*	*−507.4*	*−759.1*	*−591.6*	*−803.8*	*−947.3*	*−726.9*	....
Services: credit	2 200 ..	86.0	93.6	106.5	107.0	119.9	124.4	130.7	....
Services: debit	3 200 ..	−134.5	−138.8	−143.3	−141.8	−78.6	−98.6	−109.5	....
Balance on Goods and Services	4 991 ..	*−345.4*	*−552.6*	*−795.9*	*−626.4*	*−762.6*	*−921.5*	*−705.8*	....
Income: credit	2 300 ..	.7	.3	.3	.3	.3	.5	.8	....
Income: debit	3 300 ..	−69.5	−75.0	−61.5	−61.5	−61.5	−157.8	−110.4	....
Balance on Goods, Services, and Income	4 992 ..	*−414.2*	*−627.3*	*−857.1*	*−687.6*	*−823.8*	*−1,078.7*	*−815.3*	....
Current transfers: credit	2 379 Z.	114.0	185.0	247.5	253.0	123.5	276.2	260.2	....
Current transfers: debit	3 379 ..	−6.3	−8.2	−10.8	−13.4	−4.1	−5.4	−7.5	....
B. Capital Account[1]	4 994 Z.	**158.5**	**267.9**	**363.1**	**312.6**	**182.7**	**432.8**	**398.8**	....
Capital account: credit	2 994 Z.	158.7	268.1	363.3	312.7	182.7	432.8	398.8	....
Capital account: debit	3 994 ..	−.2	−.2	−.1	−.1	....	....	....	....
Total, Groups A Plus B	4 981 ..	*−148.0*	*−182.5*	*−257.2*	*−135.5*	*−521.7*	*−375.0*	*−163.8*	....
C. Financial Account[1]	4 995 W.	**127.5**	**121.2**	**75.1**	**131.4**	**112.0**	**264.3**	**275.7**	....
Direct investment abroad	4 505 ..	−1.3	−1.7	−1.4	−1.4	−1.4	19.2	19.2	....
Direct investment in Malawi	4 555 Z.	83.2	129.7	38.1	92.6	52.7	175.8	75.8	....
Portfolio investment assets	4 602 ..	....	....	−.1	−.1	−.1	−.1	−.1	....
Equity securities	4 610 ..	....	....	−.1	−.1	−.1	−.1	−.1	....
Debt securities	4 619 ..	....	....	....	....	....	....	....	....
Portfolio investment liabilities	4 652 Z.	.1	−.1	−.1	−.1	−.1	....	....	....
Equity securities	4 660 ..	.1	−.1	−.1	−.1	−.1	....	....	....
Debt securities	4 669 Z.	....	....	....	....	....	....	....	....
Financial derivatives	4 910 ..	....	....	....	....	....	....	....	....
Financial derivatives assets	4 900 ..	....	....	....	....	....	....	....	....
Financial derivatives liabilities	4 905 ..	....	....	....	....	....	....	....	....
Other investment assets	4 703 ..	7.9	−14.5	−.3	−.3	−.3	6.8	6.8	....
Monetary authorities	4 701 ..	....	....	....	....	....	....	....	....
General government	4 704 ..	....	....	....	....	....	....	....	....
Banks	4 705 ..	....	....	....	....	....	....	....	....
Other sectors	4 728 ..	7.9	−14.5	−.3	−.3	−.3	6.8	6.8	....
Other investment liabilities	4 753 W.	37.7	7.8	38.7	40.6	61.1	62.6	174.0	....
Monetary authorities	4 753 WA	....	....	....	....	....	....	86.5	....
General government	4 753 ZB	33.0	5.1	36.0	37.9	58.4	59.9	84.8	....
Banks	4 753 ZC	....	....	....	....	....	....	....	....
Other sectors	4 753 ZD	4.7	2.7	2.7	2.7	2.7	2.7	2.7	....
Total, Groups A Through C	4 983 ..	*−20.5*	*−61.3*	*−182.2*	*−4.2*	*−409.7*	*−110.7*	*111.9*	....
D. Net Errors and Omissions	4 998 ..	**−18.0**	**81.1**	**223.1**	**38.1**	**517.8**	**21.0**	**−233.8**	....
Total, Groups A Through D	4 984 ..	*−38.5*	*19.8*	*40.9*	*33.9*	*108.0*	*−89.7*	*−121.9*	....
E. Reserves and Related Items	4 802 A.	**38.5**	**−19.8**	**−40.9**	**−33.9**	**−108.0**	**89.7**	**121.9**	....
Reserve assets	4 802 ..	39.4	−6.0	−30.9	25.1	−118.1	−6.0	121.9	....
Use of Fund credit and loans	4 766 ..	−1.0	−13.7	−10.1	−59.1	10.1	95.7	....	....
Exceptional financing	4 920 ..	....	....	....	....	....	....	....	....
Conversion rates: Malawi kwacha per U.S. dollar	0 101 ..	**97.432**	**108.898**	**118.420**	**136.014**	**139.957**	**140.523**	**141.167**	**150.487**

[1] Excludes components that have been classified in the categories of Group E.

Table 2. STANDARD PRESENTATION, 2003–2010

(Millions of U.S. dollars)

	Code	2003	2004	2005	2006	2007	2008	2009	2010
CURRENT ACCOUNT	4 993	−306.5	−450.5	−620.4	−448.1	−704.4	−807.8	−562.6	....
A. GOODS	4 100	−296.9	−507.4	−759.1	−591.6	−803.8	−947.3	−726.9	....
Credit	2 100	567.5	517.5	541.4	721.0	761.8	950.1	1,268.4	....
General merchandise: exports f.o.b.	2 110	566.3	516.2	538.8	717.1	753.0	940.5	1,263.4	....
Goods for processing: exports f.o.b.	2 150	....	....	....	....	....	....	....	....
Repairs on goods	2 160	....	....	....	....	....	....	....	
Goods procured in ports by carriers	2 170	1.2	1.3	2.6	4.0	8.8	9.7	5.0	....
Nonmonetary gold	2 180	....	....	....	....	....	....	....	
Debit	3 100	−864.4	−1,024.9	−1,300.5	−1,312.6	−1,565.6	−1,897.4	−1,995.3	....
General merchandise: imports f.o.b.	3 110	−863.8	−1,024.0	−1,299.8	−1,311.9	−1,556.4	−1,886.8	−1,984.3	....
Goods for processing: imports f.o.b.	3 150	....	....	....	....	....	....	....	....
Repairs on goods	3 160	....	....	....	....	....	....	....	
Goods procured in ports by carriers	3 170	−.7	−.9	−.8	−.8	−9.2	−10.6	−11.0	....
Nonmonetary gold	3 180	....	....	....	....	....	....	....	
B. SERVICES	4 200	−48.5	−45.2	−36.7	−34.8	41.3	25.8	21.2	....
Total credit	2 200	*86.0*	*93.6*	*106.5*	*107.0*	*119.9*	*124.4*	*130.7*	....
Total debit	3 200	*−134.5*	*−138.8*	*−143.3*	*−141.8*	*−78.6*	*−98.6*	*−109.5*	....
Transportation services, credit	2 205	22.0	22.7	29.9	30.1	21.2	21.0	22.9	....
Passenger	2 850	*12.1*	*12.5*	*19.2*	*19.1*	*11.8*	*12.1*	*13.0*	
Freight	2 851	*7.3*	*7.3*	*7.6*	*8.2*	*6.2*	*4.9*	*5.2*	
Other	2 852	*2.7*	*2.8*	*3.1*	*2.8*	*3.2*	*4.0*	*4.7*	
Sea transport, passenger	2 207	....	....	....	....	....	....	....	
Sea transport, freight	2 208	....	....	....	....	....	....	....	
Sea transport, other	2 209	....	....	....	....	....	....	....	
Air transport, passenger	2 211	11.7	12.2	18.8	18.7	11.5	9.7	8.6	
Air transport, freight	2 212	1.5	1.5	1.8	2.4	.4	.4	.4	
Air transport, other	2 213	2.5	2.7	2.9	2.6	3.1	3.8	3.8	
Other transport, passenger	2 215	.4	.4	.4	.4	.4	2.4	4.4	
Other transport, freight	2 216	5.8	5.8	5.8	5.8	5.8	4.5	4.9	
Other transport, other	2 217	.1	.1	.1	.1	.1	.2	.9	
Transportation services, debit	3 205	−27.6	−26.2	−27.3	−27.4	−10.9	−11.9	−14.7	....
Passenger	3 850	*−12.9*	*−9.6*	*−10.1*	*−10.1*	*−5.8*	*−6.8*	*−9.2*	
Freight	3 851	*−7.3*	*−8.6*	*−10.9*	*−11.0*	*−.1*	*−.2*	*−.1*	
Other	3 852	*−7.4*	*−8.0*	*−6.2*	*−6.2*	*−5.0*	*−4.9*	*−5.4*	
Sea transport, passenger	3 207	....	....	....	....	....	....	....	
Sea transport, freight	3 208	....	....	....	....	....	....	....	
Sea transport, other	3 209	....	....	....	....	....	....	....	
Air transport, passenger	3 211	−12.7	−9.3	−9.9	−9.9	−5.6	−6.1	−7.8	
Air transport, freight	3 212	−1.9	−2.2	−2.8	−2.8	−.1	−.2	−.1	
Air transport, other	3 213	−3.8	−4.4	−2.6	−2.6	−1.3	−1.1	−1.1	
Other transport, passenger	3 215	−.3	−.3	−.3	−.3	−.3	−.7	−1.5	
Other transport, freight	3 216	−5.4	−6.4	−8.1	−8.2	....	....	....	
Other transport, other	3 217	−3.6	−3.6	−3.6	−3.6	−3.6	−3.8	−4.3	....
Travel, credit	2 236	53.9	62.0	68.1	68.1	70.1	69.7	70.2	....
Business travel	2 237	26.6	30.3	36.6	36.6	36.6	36.6	36.6	
Personal travel	2 240	27.3	31.7	31.5	31.5	33.5	33.1	33.6	
Travel, debit	3 236	−57.2	−60.3	−53.9	−53.9	−45.8	−46.3	−46.7	....
Business travel	3 237	−40.5	−42.1	−36.2	−36.2	−36.2	−36.2	−36.2	
Personal travel	3 240	−16.7	−18.1	−17.8	−17.8	−9.6	−10.2	−10.6	
Other services, credit	2 200 BA	10.1	8.9	8.6	8.8	28.6	33.7	37.6	....
Communications	2 245	2.4	1.6	2.0	2.0	19.6	21.0	26.5	....
Construction	2 249	.8	.8	.8	.8	.8	1.5	.7	
Insurance	2 253	.1	.2	.2	.2	.2	3.4	.2	
Financial	2 260	1.5	1.1	.4	.6	1.2	.3	.2	
Computer and information	2 262	....	....	....	....	....	....	....	
Royalties and licence fees	2 266	....	....	....	....	....	....	....	
Other business services	2 268	2.6	2.6	2.6	2.6	4.2	4.4	5.3	
Personal, cultural, and recreational	2 287	.3	.3	.3	.3	.3	.3	.5	
Government, n.i.e.	2 291	2.4	2.4	2.4	2.4	2.4	2.8	4.2	
Other services, debit	3 200 BA	−49.7	−52.4	−62.1	−60.4	−21.9	−40.4	−48.1	....
Communications	3 245	−2.0	−.2	−6.4	−6.4	−.6	−3.4	−3.4	
Construction	3 249	....	....	....	....	....	....	....	
Insurance	3 253	−3.9	−4.3	−5.0	−5.0	−3.9	−1.9	−5.6	
Financial	3 260	....	....	....	....	....	....	....	
Computer and information	3 262	−1.0	−1.0	−1.0	−1.0	−1.0	−1.2	−1.0	
Royalties and licence fees	3 266	−.4	−1.0	−.4	−.4	−.4	−.4	−.4	
Other business services	3 268	−21.9	−23.2	−20.9	−20.9	−3.8	−7.3	−6.6	
Personal, cultural, and recreational	3 287	−8.3	−8.2	−9.3	−9.3	−.1	−.2	−.2	
Government, n.i.e.	3 291	−12.2	−14.5	−19.0	−17.4	−12.0	−26.0	−30.7	....

Table 2 (Continued). STANDARD PRESENTATION, 2003–2010

(Millions of U.S. dollars)

	Code	2003	2004	2005	2006	2007	2008	2009	2010
C. INCOME	4 300 ..	**−68.8**	**−74.7**	**−61.2**	**−61.2**	**−61.2**	**−157.2**	**−109.6**	....
Total credit	2 300 ..	*.7*	*.3*	*.3*	*.3*	*.3*	*.5*	*.8*	....
Total debit	3 300 ..	*−69.5*	*−75.0*	*−61.5*	*−61.5*	*−61.5*	*−157.8*	*−110.4*	....
Compensation of employees, credit	2 310 ..	**.2**	**.2**	**.2**	**.2**	**.2**	**.3**	**.5**	....
Compensation of employees, debit	3 310 ..	**−6.9**	**−6.9**	**−6.9**	**−6.9**	**−6.9**	**−6.0**	**−7.2**	....
Investment income, credit	2 320 ..	**.5**	**.1**	**.1**	**.1**	**.1**	**.3**	**.3**	....
Direct investment income	2 330 ..	.5	.1	.1	.1	.1	.3	.3	....
Dividends and distributed branch profits	2 332 ..	....	....	....	....	....	....	....	
Reinvested earnings and undistributed branch profits	2 333 ..	.5	.1	.1	.1	.1	.3	.3	
Income on debt (interest)	2 334 ..	....	....	....	....	....	....	....	
Portfolio investment income	2 339 ..	....	....	....	....	....	....	....	
Income on equity	2 340 ..	....	....	....	....	....	....	....	
Income on bonds and notes	2 350 ..	....	....	....	....	....	....	....	
Income on money market instruments	2 360 ..	....	....	....	....	....	....	....	
Other investment income	2 370 ..	....	....	....	....	....	....	....	
Investment income, debit	3 320 ..	**−62.6**	**−68.1**	**−54.6**	**−54.6**	**−54.6**	**−151.8**	**−103.2**	....
Direct investment income	3 330 ..	−62.6	−68.1	−54.6	−54.6	−54.6	−151.8	−103.2	....
Dividends and distributed branch profits	3 332 ..	−23.3	−26.3	−23.9	−23.9	−23.9	−42.5	−33.2	
Reinvested earnings and undistributed branch profits	3 333 ..	−34.7	−34.5	−26.0	−26.0	−26.0	−104.6	−65.3	
Income on debt (interest)	3 334 ..	−4.6	−7.3	−4.7	−4.7	−4.7	−4.7	−4.7	
Portfolio investment income	3 339 ..	....	....	....	....	....	....	....	
Income on equity	3 340 ..	....	....	....	....	....	....	....	
Income on bonds and notes	3 350 ..	....	....	....	....	....	....	....	
Income on money market instruments	3 360 ..	....	....	....	....	....	....	....	
Other investment income	3 370 ..	....	....	....	....	....	....	....	
D. CURRENT TRANSFERS	4 379 ..	**107.7**	**176.8**	**236.7**	**239.5**	**119.4**	**270.9**	**252.7**	....
Credit	2 379 ..	**114.0**	**185.0**	**247.5**	**253.0**	**123.5**	**276.2**	**260.2**	....
General government	2 380 ..	59.2	118.4	162.8	136.3	97.7	232.3	213.2	....
Other sectors	2 390 ..	54.8	66.6	84.8	116.7	25.8	44.0	47.1	....
Workers' remittances	2 391 ..	13.7	18.1	22.3	14.6	13.7	16.4	16.1	....
Other current transfers	2 392 ..	41.1	48.5	62.4	102.1	12.1	27.6	30.9	....
Debit	3 379 ..	**−6.3**	**−8.2**	**−10.8**	**−13.4**	**−4.1**	**−5.4**	**−7.5**	....
General government	3 380 ..	....	....	....	....	−.5	−.6	−.6	....
Other sectors	3 390 ..	−6.3	−8.2	−10.8	−13.4	−3.6	−4.8	−6.9	....
Workers' remittances	3 391 ..	−.1	−.4	−.4	−.4	−3.3	−4.4	−6.2	....
Other current transfers	3 392 ..	−6.2	−7.8	−10.4	−13.0	−.4	−.4	−.7	....
CAPITAL AND FINANCIAL ACCOUNT	4 996 ..	**324.5**	**369.4**	**397.3**	**410.0**	**186.6**	**786.8**	**796.4**	....
CAPITAL ACCOUNT	4 994 ..	**158.5**	**267.9**	**363.1**	**312.6**	**182.7**	**432.8**	**398.8**	....
Total credit	2 994 ..	*158.7*	*268.1*	*363.3*	*312.7*	*182.7*	*432.8*	*398.8*	....
Total debit	3 994 ..	*−.2*	*−.2*	*−.1*	*−.1*	....	....	....	....
Capital transfers, credit	2 400 ..	**158.7**	**268.1**	**363.3**	**312.7**	**182.7**	**432.8**	**398.8**	....
General government	2 401 ..	157.5	266.9	362.1	311.5	181.5	431.3	395.9	....
Debt forgiveness	2 402 ..	47.6	47.1	59.8	58.5	....	....	....	
Other capital transfers	2 410 ..	109.9	219.9	302.3	253.1	181.5	431.3	395.9	
Other sectors	2 430 ..	1.2	1.2	1.2	1.2	1.2	1.5	2.9	
Migrants' transfers	2 431 ..	....	....	....	....	....	....	....	
Debt forgiveness	2 432 ..	....	....	....	....	....	....	....	
Other capital transfers	2 440 ..	1.2	1.2	1.2	1.2	1.2	1.5	2.9	
Capital transfers, debit	3 400 ..	**−.2**	**−.2**	**−.1**	**−.1**	....	....	....	....
General government	3 401 ..	....	....	....	....	....	....	....	
Debt forgiveness	3 402 ..	....	....	....	....	....	....	....	
Other capital transfers	3 410 ..	....	....	....	....	....	....	....	
Other sectors	3 430 ..	−.2	−.2	−.1	−.1	....	....	....	
Migrants' transfers	3 431 ..	−.2	−.2	−.1	−.1	....	....	....	
Debt forgiveness	3 432 ..	....	....	....	....	....	....	....	
Other capital transfers	3 440 ..	....	....	....	....	....	....	....	
Nonproduced nonfinancial assets, credit	2 480 ..	....	....	....	....	....	....	....	....
Nonproduced nonfinancial assets, debit	3 480 ..	....	....	....	....	....	....	....	....

Table 2 (Continued). STANDARD PRESENTATION, 2003–2010

(Millions of U.S. dollars)

	Code	2003	2004	2005	2006	2007	2008	2009	2010
FINANCIAL ACCOUNT.....................................	4 995 ..	**166.0**	**101.5**	**34.1**	**97.4**	**4.0**	**354.0**	**397.6**	....
A. DIRECT INVESTMENT.............................	4 500 ..	81.8	128.0	36.7	91.1	51.2	195.0	95.0	....
Direct investment abroad........................	4 505 ..	–1.3	–1.7	–1.4	–1.4	–1.4	19.2	19.2	....
Equity capital..	4 510 ..	–.4	–1.1	–.8	–.8	–.8	–2.5	–2.5	....
Claims on affiliated enterprises..............	4 515 ..	–.4	–1.1	–.8	–.8	–.8	–2.5	–2.5	....
Liabilities to affiliated enterprises..........	4 520 ..	....	....	....	....	....	....	....	....
Reinvested earnings...............................	4 525 ..	–.5	–.1	–.1	–.1	–.1	–.3	–.3	....
Other capital...	4 530 ..	–.4	–.5	–.5	–.5	–.5	22.0	22.0	....
Claims on affiliated enterprises..............	4 535 ..	–.4	–.5	–.5	–.5	–.5	22.0	22.0	....
Liabilities to affiliated enterprises..........	4 540 ..	....	....	....	....	....	....	....	....
Direct investment in Malawi............................	4 555 ..	83.2	129.7	38.1	92.6	52.7	175.8	75.8	....
Equity capital..	4 560 ..	18.0	26.3	12.1	66.6	26.7	71.2	10.5	....
Claims on direct investors.....................	4 565 ..	....	....	....	....	....	....	....	....
Liabilities to direct investors.................	4 570 ..	18.0	26.3	12.1	66.6	26.7	71.2	10.5	....
Reinvested earnings...............................	4 575 ..	34.7	34.5	26.0	26.0	26.0	104.6	65.3	....
Other capital...	4 580 ..	30.5	69.0	....	....	....	....	....	....
Claims on direct investors.....................	4 585 ..	....	....	....	....	....	....	....	....
Liabilities to direct investors.................	4 590 ..	30.5	69.0	....	....	....	....	....	....
B. PORTFOLIO INVESTMENT............................	4 600 ..	.1	–.1	–.1	–.1	–.1	–.1	–.1	....
Assets...	4 602 ..	....	....	–.1	–.1	–.1	–.1	–.1	....
Equity securities...................................	4 610 ..	....	....	–.1	–.1	–.1	–.1	–.1	....
Monetary authorities...........................	4 611 ..	....	....	....	....	....	....	....	....
General government............................	4 612 ..	....	....	....	....	....	....	....	....
Banks..	4 613 ..	....	....	....	....	....	....	....	....
Other sectors.....................................	4 614 ..	....	....	–.1	–.1	–.1	–.1	–.1	....
Debt securities......................................	4 619 ..	....	....	....	....	....	....	....	....
Bonds and notes.................................	4 620 ..	....	....	....	....	....	....	....	....
Monetary authorities...........................	4 621 ..	....	....	....	....	....	....	....	....
General government............................	4 622 ..	....	....	....	....	....	....	....	....
Banks..	4 623 ..	....	....	....	....	....	....	....	....
Other sectors.....................................	4 624 ..	....	....	....	....	....	....	....	....
Money market instruments...................	4 630 ..	....	....	....	....	....	....	....	....
Monetary authorities...........................	4 631 ..	....	....	....	....	....	....	....	....
General government............................	4 632 ..	....	....	....	....	....	....	....	....
Banks..	4 633 ..	....	....	....	....	....	....	....	....
Other sectors.....................................	4 634 ..	....	....	....	....	....	....	....	....
Liabilities...	4 652 ..	.1	–.1	–.1	–.1	–.1	....	....	....
Equity securities...................................	4 660 ..	.1	–.1	–.1	–.1	–.1	....	....	....
Banks..	4 663 ..	....	....	....	....	....	....	....	....
Other sectors.....................................	4 664 ..	.1	–.1	–.1	–.1	–.1	....	....	....
Debt securities......................................	4 669 ..	....	....	....	....	....	....	....	....
Bonds and notes.................................	4 670 ..	....	....	....	....	....	....	....	....
Monetary authorities...........................	4 671 ..	....	....	....	....	....	....	....	....
General government............................	4 672 ..	....	....	....	....	....	....	....	....
Banks..	4 673 ..	....	....	....	....	....	....	....	....
Other sectors.....................................	4 674 ..	....	....	....	....	....	....	....	....
Money market instruments...................	4 680 ..	....	....	....	....	....	....	....	....
Monetary authorities...........................	4 681 ..	....	....	....	....	....	....	....	....
General government............................	4 682 ..	....	....	....	....	....	....	....	....
Banks..	4 683 ..	....	....	....	....	....	....	....	....
Other sectors.....................................	4 684 ..	....	....	....	....	....	....	....	....
C. FINANCIAL DERIVATIVES...........................	4 910 ..	....	....	....	....	....	....	....	....
Monetary authorities...............................	4 911 ..	....	....	....	....	....	....	....	....
General government................................	4 912 ..	....	....	....	....	....	....	....	....
Banks..	4 913 ..	....	....	....	....	....	....	....	....
Other sectors...	4 914 ..	....	....	....	....	....	....	....	....
Assets...	4 900 ..	....	....	....	....	....	....	....	....
Monetary authorities...............................	4 901 ..	....	....	....	....	....	....	....	....
General government................................	4 902 ..	....	....	....	....	....	....	....	....
Banks..	4 903 ..	....	....	....	....	....	....	....	....
Other sectors...	4 904 ..	....	....	....	....	....	....	....	....
Liabilities...	4 905 ..	....	....	....	....	....	....	....	....
Monetary authorities...............................	4 906 ..	....	....	....	....	....	....	....	....
General government................................	4 907 ..	....	....	....	....	....	....	....	....
Banks..	4 908 ..	....	....	....	....	....	....	....	....
Other sectors...	4 909 ..	....	....	....	....	....	....	....	....

Table 2 (Concluded). STANDARD PRESENTATION, 2003–2010

(Millions of U.S. dollars)

	Code	2003	2004	2005	2006	2007	2008	2009	2010
D. OTHER INVESTMENT..................................	4 700 ..	**44.6**	**−20.4**	**28.4**	**−18.7**	**70.9**	**165.1**	**180.8**	....
Assets..	4 703 ..	**7.9**	**−14.5**	**−.3**	**−.3**	**−.3**	**6.8**	**6.8**	....
Trade credits..	4 706 ..	7.8	−14.3	−.2	−.2	−.2	6.8	6.8	....
General government............................	4 707 ..	....	....	....	....	....	....	....	....
of which: Short-term.........................	4 709 ..	....	....	....	....	....	....	....	....
Other sectors......................................	4 710 ..	7.8	−14.3	−.2	−.2	−.2	6.8	6.8	....
of which: Short-term.........................	4 712 ..	*7.8*	*−14.3*	*−.2*	*−.2*	*−.2*	*6.8*	*6.8*	....
Loans...	4 714 ..	.2	−.2	....	....	....	....	−.1	....
Monetary authorities............................	4 715 ..	....	....	....	....	....	....	....	....
of which: Short-term.........................	4 718 ..	....	....	....	....	....	....	....	....
General government............................	4 719 ..	....	....	....	....	....	....	....	....
of which: Short-term.........................	4 721 ..	....	....	....	....	....	....	....	....
Banks..	4 722 ..	....	....	....	....	....	....	....	....
of which: Short-term.........................	4 724 ..	....	....	....	....	....	....	....	....
Other sectors......................................	4 725 ..	.2	−.2	....	....	....	....	−.1	....
of which: Short-term.........................	4 727 ..	....	....	....	....	....	....	....	....
Currency and deposits.............................	4 730 ..	....	....	....	....	....	....	....	....
Monetary authorities............................	4 731 ..	....	....	....	....	....	....	....	....
General government............................	4 732 ..	....	....	....	....	....	....	....	....
Banks..	4 733 ..	....	....	....	....	....	....	....	....
Other sectors......................................	4 734 ..	....	....	....	....	....	....	....	....
Other assets...	4 736 ..	....	....	....	....	....	....	....	....
Monetary authorities............................	4 737 ..	....	....	....	....	....	....	....	....
of which: Short-term.........................	4 739 ..	....	....	....	....	....	....	....	....
General government............................	4 740 ..	....	....	....	....	....	....	....	....
of which: Short-term.........................	4 742 ..	....	....	....	....	....	....	....	....
Banks..	4 743 ..	....	....	....	....	....	....	....	....
of which: Short-term.........................	4 745 ..	....	....	....	....	....	....	....	....
Other sectors......................................	4 746 ..	....	....	....	....	....	....	....	....
of which: Short-term.........................	4 748 ..	....	....	....	....	....	....	....	....
Liabilities..	4 753 ..	**36.7**	**−6.0**	**28.7**	**−18.5**	**71.2**	**158.3**	**174.0**	....
Trade credits..	4 756 ..	....	....	....	....	....	....	....	....
General government............................	4 757 ..	....	....	....	....	....	....	....	....
of which: Short-term.........................	4 759 ..	....	....	....	....	....	....	....	....
Other sectors......................................	4 760 ..	....	....	....	....	....	....	....	....
of which: Short-term.........................	4 762 ..	....	....	....	....	....	....	....	....
Loans...	4 764 ..	32.7	−8.1	26.6	−20.6	69.1	156.2	85.4	....
Monetary authorities............................	4 765 ..	−1.0	−13.7	−10.1	−59.1	10.1	95.7	....	....
of which: Use of Fund credit and loans from the Fund..	4 766 ..	*−1.0*	*−13.7*	*−10.1*	*−59.1*	*10.1*	*95.7*	....	....
of which: Short-term.........................	4 768 ..	....	....	....	....	....	....	....	....
General government............................	4 769 ..	33.0	5.1	36.0	37.9	58.4	59.9	84.8	....
of which: Short-term.........................	4 771 ..	....	....	....	....	....	....	....	....
Banks..	4 772 ..	....	....	....	....	....	....	....	....
of which: Short-term.........................	4 774 ..	....	....	....	....	....	....	....	....
Other sectors......................................	4 775 ..	.7	.6	.6	.6	.6	.6	.6	....
of which: Short-term.........................	4 777 ..	....	*.2*	*.2*	*.2*	*.2*	*.2*	*.2*	....
Currency and deposits.............................	4 780 ..	....	....	....	....	....	....	....	....
Monetary authorities............................	4 781 ..	....	....	....	....	....	....	....	....
General government............................	4 782 ..	....	....	....	....	....	....	....	....
Banks..	4 783 ..	....	....	....	....	....	....	....	....
Other sectors......................................	4 784 ..	....	....	....	....	....	....	....	....
Other liabilities.......................................	4 786 ..	4.0	2.1	2.1	2.1	2.1	2.1	88.6	....
Monetary authorities............................	4 787 ..	....	....	....	....	....	....	86.5	....
of which: Short-term.........................	4 789 ..	....	....	....	....	....	....	....	....
General government............................	4 790 ..	.2	....	....	....	....	....	....	....
of which: Short-term.........................	4 792 ..	....	....	....	....	....	....	....	....
Banks..	4 793 ..	....	....	....	....	....	....	....	....
of which: Short-term.........................	4 795 ..	....	....	....	....	....	....	....	....
Other sectors......................................	4 796 ..	4.0	2.1	2.1	2.1	2.1	2.1	2.1	....
of which: Short-term.........................	4 798 ..	*4.0*	*2.1*	*2.1*	*2.1*	*2.1*	*2.1*	*2.1*	....
E. RESERVE ASSETS.......................................	4 802 ..	**39.4**	**−6.0**	**−30.9**	**25.1**	**−118.1**	**−6.0**	**121.9**	....
Monetary gold...	4 812 ..	....	....	....	....	....	....	....	....
Special drawing rights................................	4 811 ..	−.3	−.7	.1	.4	.7	−.1	.2	....
Reserve position in the Fund......................	4 810 ..	....	....	....	....	....	....	−.1	....
Foreign exchange.......................................	4 803 ..	39.8	−5.3	−30.9	24.7	−118.8	−5.9	121.8	....
Other claims..	4 813 ..	....	....	....	....	....	....	....	....
NET ERRORS AND OMISSIONS...........................	4 998 ..	**−18.0**	**81.1**	**223.1**	**38.1**	**517.8**	**21.0**	**−233.8**	....

Table 1. ANALYTIC PRESENTATION, 2003–2010

(Millions of U.S. dollars)

	Code	2003	2004	2005	2006	2007	2008	2009	2010
A. Current Account[1]	4 993 Z.	**13,381**	**15,079**	**19,980**	**26,200**	**29,770**	**38,914**	**31,801**	**27,290**
Goods: exports f.o.b.	2 100 ..	104,999	126,817	141,808	160,916	176,220	199,733	157,655	198,954
Goods: imports f.o.b.	3 100 ..	−79,289	−99,244	−108,653	−123,474	−138,493	−148,472	−117,402	−157,283
Balance on Goods	4 100 ..	*25,711*	*27,572*	*33,156*	*37,441*	*37,727*	*51,261*	*40,253*	*41,672*
Services: credit	2 200 ..	13,577	17,111	19,576	21,681	29,462	30,321	28,769	32,760
Services: debit	3 200 ..	−17,532	−19,269	−21,956	−23,651	−28,668	−30,270	−27,472	−32,216
Balance on Goods and Services	4 991 ..	*21,757*	*25,415*	*30,776*	*35,472*	*38,520*	*51,313*	*41,551*	*42,215*
Income: credit	2 300 ..	3,448	4,329	5,373	8,494	11,380	12,081	11,213	11,978
Income: debit	3 300 ..	−9,376	−10,751	−11,691	−13,206	−15,462	−19,218	−15,382	−20,120
Balance on Goods, Services, and Income	4 992 ..	*15,829*	*18,993*	*24,457*	*30,760*	*34,438*	*44,176*	*37,381*	*34,073*
Current transfers: credit	2 379 Z.	508	422	299	314	391	419	1,077	578
Current transfers: debit	3 379 ..	−2,955	−4,335	−4,776	−4,874	−5,059	−5,681	−6,657	−7,361
B. Capital Account[1]	4 994 Z.	....	....	....	**−72**	**−54**	**187**	**−45**	**−51**
Capital account: credit	2 994 Z.	....	....	....	9	14	268	3	26
Capital account: debit	3 994 ..	....	....	....	−82	−68	−81	−48	−77
Total, Groups A Plus B	4 981 ..	*13,381*	*15,079*	*19,980*	*26,127*	*29,716*	*39,101*	*31,756*	*27,239*
C. Financial Account[1]	4 995 W.	**−3,196**	**5,091**	**−9,806**	**−11,812**	**−11,377**	**−33,974**	**−22,639**	**−5,919**
Direct investment abroad	4 505 ..	−1,369	−2,061	−2,972	−6,023	−11,334	−15,203	−8,014	−13,513
Direct investment in Malaysia	4 555 Z.	2,473	4,624	3,966	6,076	8,590	7,376	1,387	9,167
Portfolio investment assets	4 602 ..	−196	−287	−715	−2,121	−3,932	−2,878	−6,339	....
Equity securities	4 610 ..	−18	23	7	−1,887	−4,093	−2,291	−3,760	....
Debt securities	4 619 ..	−178	−309	−722	−234	161	−587	−2,580	....
Portfolio investment liabilities	4 652 Z.	1,174	8,675	−2,985	5,557	9,320	−21,083	6,048	....
Equity securities	4 660 ..	1,339	4,509	−1,200	2,355	−669	−10,716	−449	....
Debt securities	4 669 Z.	−165	4,166	−1,786	3,202	9,989	−10,367	6,497	....
Financial derivatives	4 910 ..	119	294	−58	29	−48	−659	683	−212
Financial derivatives assets	4 900 ..	−24	−1,520	−59	8	198	−1,165	32	....
Financial derivatives liabilities	4 905 ..	142	1,814	1	21	−246	506	651	....
Other investment assets	4 703 ..	−4,502	−10,756	−4,877	−8,562	−17,400	3,826	−17,667	....
Monetary authorities	4 701 ..	....	....	....	....	....	....	....	....
General government	4 704 ..	5	....	8	−1	−4	....	1	....
Banks	4 705 ..	904	−4,698	1,579	−4,291	−13,041	11,922	−2,974	....
Other sectors	4 728 ..	−5,411	−6,058	−6,464	−4,271	−4,355	−8,096	−14,695	....
Other investment liabilities	4 753 W.	−895	4,602	−2,164	−6,769	3,427	−5,352	1,263	....
Monetary authorities	4 753 WA	−62	....	....	....	....	....	1,885	....
General government	4 753 ZB	−2,891	633	−841	−2,194	−653	−142	−151	....
Banks	4 753 ZC	1,715	1,684	−134	−3,613	6,425	1,920	−247	....
Other sectors	4 753 ZD	343	2,284	−1,188	−962	−2,344	−7,130	−225	....
Total, Groups A Through C	4 983 ..	*10,185*	*20,170*	*10,174*	*14,315*	*18,338*	*5,127*	*9,117*	*21,321*
D. Net Errors and Omissions	4 998 ..	**−4**	**1,880**	**−6,555**	**−7,451**	**−5,195**	**−8,578**	**−5,199**	**−21,358**
Total, Groups A Through D	4 984 ..	*10,181*	*22,050*	*3,620*	*6,864*	*13,144*	*−3,450*	*3,918*	*−37*
E. Reserves and Related Items	4 802 A.	**−10,181**	**−22,050**	**−3,620**	**−6,864**	**−13,144**	**3,450**	**−3,918**	**37**
Reserve assets	4 802 ..	−10,181	−22,050	−3,620	−6,864	−13,144	3,450	−3,918	37
Use of Fund credit and loans	4 766 ..	....	....	....	....	....	....	....	....
Exceptional financing	4 920 ..	....	....	....	....	....	....	....	....
Conversion rates: ringgit per U.S. dollar	0 101 ..	**3.800**	**3.800**	**3.787**	**3.668**	**3.438**	**3.336**	**3.525**	**3.221**

[1] Excludes components that have been classified in the categories of Group E.

Table 2. STANDARD PRESENTATION, 2003–2010

(Millions of U.S. dollars)

	Code	2003	2004	2005	2006	2007	2008	2009	2010
CURRENT ACCOUNT.....................................	4 993 ..	**13,381**	**15,079**	**19,980**	**26,200**	**29,770**	**38,914**	**31,801**	**27,290**
A. GOODS..	4 100 ..	**25,711**	**27,572**	**33,156**	**37,441**	**37,727**	**51,261**	**40,253**	**41,672**
Credit..	2 100 ..	**104,999**	**126,817**	**141,808**	**160,916**	**176,220**	**199,733**	**157,655**	**198,954**
General merchandise: exports f.o.b.................	2 110 ..	104,563	126,134	141,068	159,739	175,472	198,597	156,798	....
Goods for processing: exports f.o.b..............	2 150 ..	14	29	34	33	67	80	75	....
Repairs on goods..	2 160 ..	56	199	172	218	210	290	244	....
Goods procured in ports by carriers..............	2 170 ..	141	207	275	649	308	420	313	....
Nonmonetary gold.......................................	2 180 ..	226	248	260	278	164	346	225	....
Debit..	3 100 ..	**−79,289**	**−99,244**	**−108,653**	**−123,474**	**−138,493**	**−148,472**	**−117,402**	**−157,283**
General merchandise: imports f.o.b................	3 110 ..	−78,175	−97,758	−106,645	−121,295	−135,592	−144,743	−114,916	....
Goods for processing: imports f.o.b..............	3 150 ..	−7	−27	−31	−31	−61	−80	−75	....
Repairs on goods..	3 160 ..	....	....	....	....	....	....	....	....
Goods procured in ports by carriers..............	3 170 ..	−250	−470	−816	−894	−1,077	−1,272	−722	....
Nonmonetary gold.......................................	3 180 ..	−857	−989	−1,161	−1,254	−1,762	−2,377	−1,689	....
B. SERVICES..	4 200 ..	**−3,954**	**−2,158**	**−2,380**	**−1,970**	**794**	**51**	**1,298**	**544**
Total credit...	2 200 ..	*13,577*	*17,111*	*19,576*	*21,681*	*29,462*	*30,321*	*28,769*	*32,760*
Total debit..	3 200 ..	*−17,532*	*−19,269*	*−21,956*	*−23,651*	*−28,668*	*−30,270*	*−27,472*	*−32,216*
Transportation services, credit...............	2 205 ..	**2,767**	**3,196**	**4,056**	**4,153**	**7,145**	**6,766**	**4,408**	**4,692**
Passenger..	2 850 ..	*898*	*980*	*1,543*	*1,853*	*3,898*	*3,260*	*1,433*	....
Freight..	2 851 ..	*1,406*	*1,756*	*2,011*	*1,732*	*2,445*	*2,523*	*2,043*	....
Other..	2 852 ..	*463*	*461*	*501*	*568*	*802*	*983*	*932*	....
Sea transport, passenger..............................	2 207 ..	....	....	....	....	1	1	3	....
Sea transport, freight...................................	2 208 ..	1,203	1,455	1,731	1,465	1,740	1,870	1,590	....
Sea transport, other.....................................	2 209 ..	382	376	404	461	696	809	694	....
Air transport, passenger...............................	2 211 ..	898	980	1,543	1,853	3,897	3,259	1,430	....
Air transport, freight....................................	2 212 ..	203	301	280	267	705	652	453	....
Air transport, other......................................	2 213 ..	81	85	97	107	103	105	162	....
Other transport, passenger...........................	2 215 ..	....	....	....	....				
Other transport, freight................................	2 216 ..	....	....	....	....				
Other transport, other..................................	2 217 ..	....	....	....	....	3	68	76	....
Transportation services, debit................	3 205 ..	**−6,260**	**−7,814**	**−8,396**	**−9,533**	**−10,942**	**−11,391**	**−9,265**	**−11,905**
Passenger..	3 850 ..	*−555*	*−644*	*−628*	*−828*	*−999*	*−1,015*	*−688*	....
Freight..	3 851 ..	*−5,029*	*−6,301*	*−6,938*	*−7,890*	*−8,816*	*−9,492*	*−7,490*	....
Other..	3 852 ..	*−675*	*−868*	*−830*	*−815*	*−1,127*	*−885*	*−1,087*	....
Sea transport, passenger..............................	3 207 ..	....	....	....	....	−5	−11	−8	....
Sea transport, freight...................................	3 208 ..	−5,029	−6,301	−6,938	−7,890	−8,816	−9,492	−7,490	....
Sea transport, other.....................................	3 209 ..	−435	−515	−513	−493	−607	−426	−629	....
Air transport, passenger...............................	3 211 ..	−555	−644	−628	−828	−994	−1,004	−681	....
Air transport, freight....................................	3 212 ..	....	....	....	....				
Air transport, other......................................	3 213 ..	−241	−353	−316	−321	−521	−458	−456	....
Other transport, passenger...........................	3 215 ..	....	....	....	....				
Other transport, freight................................	3 216 ..	....	....	....	....				
Other transport, other..................................	3 217 ..	....	....	....	....	....	−1	−2	....
Travel, credit...	2 236 ..	**5,901**	**8,203**	**8,846**	**10,427**	**14,050**	**15,293**	**15,797**	**18,315**
Business travel...	2 237 ..	5,820	8,082	8,738	10,247	13,808	15,056	15,582	....
Personal travel...	2 240 ..	80	121	108	180	241	237	215	....
Travel, debit..	3 236 ..	**−2,846**	**−3,178**	**−3,711**	**−4,257**	**−5,601**	**−6,709**	**−6,508**	**−7,943**
Business travel...	3 237 ..	−2,150	−2,323	−2,771	−3,134	−4,225	−5,006	−4,834	....
Personal travel...	3 240 ..	−697	−855	−940	−1,123	−1,376	−1,703	−1,674	....
Other services, credit.............................	2 200 BA	**4,910**	**5,712**	**6,674**	**7,102**	**8,267**	**8,262**	**8,563**	**9,754**
Communications..	2 245 ..	201	395	615	551	611	602	560	9,754
Construction..	2 249 ..	262	453	811	992	1,359	1,212	909	....
Insurance..	2 253 ..	223	280	278	290	357	371	379	....
Financial...	2 260 ..	109	97	60	71	88	87	90	....
Computer and information............................	2 262 ..	216	348	435	574	848	1,025	1,454	....
Royalties and licence fees.............................	2 266 ..	20	42	27	26	37	199	266	....
Other business services................................	2 268 ..	1,924	2,315	2,773	3,625	4,047	3,857	4,218	....
Personal, cultural, and recreational...............	2 287 ..	1,835	1,670	1,562	863	832	872	646	....
Government, n.i.e...	2 291 ..	119	112	113	110	87	38	42	....
Other services, debit..............................	3 200 BA	**−8,426**	**−8,277**	**−9,849**	**−9,861**	**−12,125**	**−12,170**	**−11,698**	**−12,368**
Communications..	3 245 ..	−252	−503	−680	−660	−857	−817	−772	−12,368
Construction..	3 249 ..	−410	−518	−1,087	−1,146	−1,689	−1,412	−1,034	....
Insurance..	3 253 ..	−480	−494	−518	−611	−684	−728	−734	....
Financial...	3 260 ..	−117	−121	−119	−129	−204	−301	−307	....
Computer and information............................	3 262 ..	−197	−325	−379	−531	−646	−896	−1,206	....
Royalties and licence fees.............................	3 266 ..	−782	−896	−1,370	−954	−1,185	−1,268	−1,133	....
Other business services................................	3 268 ..	−3,057	−3,219	−3,636	−4,171	−4,733	−5,363	−5,400	....
Personal, cultural, and recreational...............	3 287 ..	−2,922	−1,899	−1,855	−1,431	−1,933	−1,177	−897	....
Government, n.i.e...	3 291 ..	−209	−302	−205	−230	−193	−210	−215	....

Table 2 (Continued). STANDARD PRESENTATION, 2003–2010

(Millions of U.S. dollars)

	Code	2003	2004	2005	2006	2007	2008	2009	2010
C. INCOME	4 300	**−5,928**	**−6,422**	**−6,318**	**−4,712**	**−4,082**	**−7,137**	**−4,170**	**−8,142**
Total credit	2 300	*3,448*	*4,329*	*5,373*	*8,494*	*11,380*	*12,081*	*11,213*	*11,978*
Total debit	3 300	*−9,376*	*−10,751*	*−11,691*	*−13,206*	*−15,462*	*−19,218*	*−15,382*	*−20,120*
Compensation of employees, credit	2 310	**571**	**802**	**1,117**	**1,365**	**1,556**	**1,329**	**1,131**	**1,102**
Compensation of employees, debit	3 310	**−821**	**−1,064**	**−1,244**	**−1,449**	**−1,738**	**−1,547**	**−1,554**	**−1,754**
Investment income, credit	2 320	**2,877**	**3,527**	**4,256**	**7,129**	**9,824**	**10,752**	**10,082**	**10,876**
Direct investment income	2 330	517	1,126	1,087	3,254	4,368	4,723	5,065	5,875
Dividends and distributed branch profits	2 332	....	....	....	....	....	....	....	....
Reinvested earnings and undistributed branch profits	2 333	....	....	....	....	....	....	....	....
Income on debt (interest)	2 334	128	78	118	295	484	1,082	1,242	....
Portfolio investment income	2 339	89	103	100	193	150	248	238	495
Income on equity	2 340	50	76	43	125	97	205	175	....
Income on bonds and notes	2 350	6	9	26	16	20	41	62	....
Income on money market instruments	2 360	33	17	31	51	33	2	1	....
Other investment income	2 370	2,271	2,299	3,068	3,683	5,305	5,780	4,780	4,506
Investment income, debit	3 320	**−8,555**	**−9,687**	**−10,446**	**−11,757**	**−13,724**	**−17,671**	**−13,829**	**−18,366**
Direct investment income	3 330	−6,735	−7,757	−8,330	−8,858	−9,932	−13,838	−11,119	−15,338
Dividends and distributed branch profits	3 332	....	....	....	....	....	....	....	....
Reinvested earnings and undistributed branch profits	3 333	....	....	....	....	....	....	....	....
Income on debt (interest)	3 334	−70	−104	−89	−84	−64	−252	−222	....
Portfolio investment income	3 339	−196	−380	−528	−1,001	−1,854	−3,221	−2,295	−2,639
Income on equity	3 340	−183	−322	−396	−632	−1,532	−1,925	−1,099	....
Income on bonds and notes	3 350	−11	−58	−132	−369	−322	−1,257	−1,196	....
Income on money market instruments	3 360	−1	....	....	....	....	−39	....	....
Other investment income	3 370	−1,624	−1,551	−1,589	−1,898	−1,938	−611	−415	−389
D. CURRENT TRANSFERS	4 379	**−2,447**	**−3,914**	**−4,477**	**−4,560**	**−4,668**	**−5,262**	**−5,580**	**−6,783**
Credit	2 379	**508**	**422**	**299**	**314**	**391**	**419**	**1,077**	**578**
General government	2 380	92	120	134	134	140	90	81	....
Other sectors	2 390	416	302	164	180	251	329	996	....
Workers' remittances	2 391	....	....	....	....	....	....	....	....
Other current transfers	2 392	416	302	164	180	251	329	996	....
Debit	3 379	**−2,955**	**−4,335**	**−4,776**	**−4,874**	**−5,059**	**−5,681**	**−6,657**	**−7,361**
General government	3 380	−46	−63	−152	−228	−105	−142	−127	....
Other sectors	3 390	−2,909	−4,272	−4,624	−4,646	−4,954	−5,539	−6,531	....
Workers' remittances	3 391	−2,643	−4,001	−4,435	−4,147	−4,650	−5,238	−4,975	....
Other current transfers	3 392	−267	−271	−189	−499	−304	−301	−1,556	....
CAPITAL AND FINANCIAL ACCOUNT	4 996	**−13,377**	**−16,959**	**−13,425**	**−18,749**	**−24,575**	**−30,337**	**−26,602**	**−5,933**
CAPITAL ACCOUNT	4 994	....	....	....	**−72**	**−54**	**187**	**−45**	**−51**
Total credit	2 994	....	....	....	*9*	*14*	*268*	*3*	*26*
Total debit	3 994	....	....	....	*−82*	*−68*	*−81*	*−48*	*−77*
Capital transfers, credit	2 400	....	....	....	**7**	**14**	**4**	**3**	**17**
General government	2 401	....	....	....	....	....	....	....	....
Debt forgiveness	2 402	....	....	....	....	....	....	....	....
Other capital transfers	2 410	....	....	....	....	....	....	....	....
Other sectors	2 430	....	....	....	....	....	....	....	....
Migrants' transfers	2 431	....	....	....	....	....	....	....	....
Debt forgiveness	2 432	....	....	....	....	....	....	....	....
Other capital transfers	2 440	....	....	....	....	....	....	....	....
Capital transfers, debit	3 400	....	....	....	**−67**	**−34**	**−53**	**−30**	**−43**
General government	3 401	....	....	....	....	....	....	....	....
Debt forgiveness	3 402	....	....	....	....	....	....	....	....
Other capital transfers	3 410	....	....	....	....	....	....	....	....
Other sectors	3 430	....	....	....	....	....	....	....	....
Migrants' transfers	3 431	....	....	....	....	....	....	....	....
Debt forgiveness	3 432	....	....	....	....	....	....	....	....
Other capital transfers	3 440	....	....	....	....	....	....	....	....
Nonproduced nonfinancial assets, credit	2 480	....	....	....	**2**	....	**264**	....	**9**
Nonproduced nonfinancial assets, debit	3 480	....	....	....	**−15**	**−34**	**−28**	**−19**	**−34**

Table 2 (Continued). STANDARD PRESENTATION, 2003–2010

(Millions of U.S. dollars)

	Code	2003	2004	2005	2006	2007	2008	2009	2010
FINANCIAL ACCOUNT	4 995 ..	**−13,377**	**−16,959**	**−13,425**	**−18,676**	**−24,521**	**−30,523**	**−26,557**	**−5,882**
A. DIRECT INVESTMENT	4 500 ..	**1,104**	**2,563**	**994**	**53**	**−2,744**	**−7,828**	**−6,626**	**−4,346**
Direct investment abroad	4 505 ..	**−1,369**	**−2,061**	**−2,972**	**−6,023**	**−11,334**	**−15,203**	**−8,014**	**−13,513**
Equity capital	4 510 ..	−1,089	−957	−1,867	−4,583	−9,216	−8,816	−5,413	....
Claims on affiliated enterprises	4 515 ..	−1,089	−957	−1,867	−4,583	−9,216	−8,782	−5,405	....
Liabilities to affiliated enterprises	4 520 ..	....	....	....	....	....	−34	−8	....
Reinvested earnings	4 525 ..	....	....	....	....	....			
Other capital	4 530 ..	−280	−1,104	−1,105	−1,440	−2,118	−6,387	−2,600	....
Claims on affiliated enterprises	4 535 ..	−504	−987	−1,021	−1,185	−1,997	−6,364	−3,085	
Liabilities to affiliated enterprises	4 540 ..	224	−117	−84	−255	−121	−23	485	....
Direct investment in Malaysia	4 555 ..	**2,473**	**4,624**	**3,966**	**6,076**	**8,590**	**7,376**	**1,387**	**9,167**
Equity capital	4 560 ..	3,317	4,438	4,232	7,609	8,688	5,209	715	
Claims on direct investors	4 565 ..	....	....	....	....	....	8	....	
Liabilities to direct investors	4 570 ..	3,317	4,438	4,232	7,609	8,688	5,201	715	
Reinvested earnings	4 575 ..	....	....	....	....	....			
Other capital	4 580 ..	−843	186	−266	−1,533	−97	2,167	673	....
Claims on direct investors	4 585 ..	−522	131	−43	−1,869	−602	−262	1,749	
Liabilities to direct investors	4 590 ..	−322	56	−223	337	505	2,429	−1,077	....
B. PORTFOLIO INVESTMENT	4 600 ..	**978**	**8,389**	**−3,700**	**3,436**	**5,388**	**−23,961**	**−291**	**14,991**
Assets	4 602 ..	**−196**	**−287**	**−715**	**−2,121**	**−3,932**	**−2,878**	**−6,339**	....
Equity securities	4 610 ..	−18	23	7	−1,887	−4,093	−2,291	−3,760	
Monetary authorities	4 611 ..	....	....	....	....	1	....	−2	
General government	4 612 ..	....	....	....	....	....	274	−3	
Banks	4 613 ..	....	−6	1	1	−33	38	−122	....
Other sectors	4 614 ..	−19	28	7	−1,888	−4,061	−2,603	−3,633	
Debt securities	4 619 ..	−178	−309	−722	−234	161	−587	−2,580	
Bonds and notes	4 620 ..	−191	−111	−398	−602	289	−754	−1,747	
Monetary authorities	4 621 ..	....	....	....	....	....	1		
General government	4 622 ..	19	91	15	−16	7	9	1	
Banks	4 623 ..	−213	−180	−256	−409	417	−257	−279	
Other sectors	4 624 ..	3	−21	−157	−177	−135	−506	−1,468	
Money market instruments	4 630 ..	13	−198	−325	368	−127	166	−833	....
Monetary authorities	4 631 ..	....	....	....	....	1	....	....	
General government	4 632 ..	....	....	....	....	1	....		
Banks	4 633 ..	8	....	....	....	....	146	−690	
Other sectors	4 634 ..	5	−198	−325	369	−129	20	−143	
Liabilities	4 652 ..	**1,174**	**8,675**	**−2,985**	**5,557**	**9,320**	**−21,083**	**6,048**	....
Equity securities	4 660 ..	1,339	4,509	−1,200	2,355	−669	−10,716	−449	
Banks	4 663 ..	612	466	−928	32	716	−1,129	−21	
Other sectors	4 664 ..	728	4,043	−272	2,323	−1,385	−9,587	−428	
Debt securities	4 669 ..	−165	4,166	−1,786	3,202	9,989	−10,367	6,497	
Bonds and notes	4 670 ..	−113	3,666	−630	2,661	3,860	979	3,795	
Monetary authorities	4 671 ..	....	....	−894	−188	−76	−151	−41	
General government	4 672 ..	41	2,373	595	1,890	3,017	281	1,382	....
Banks	4 673 ..	150	478	497	165	−4	231	−672	
Other sectors	4 674 ..	−304	816	−828	794	922	618	3,125	
Money market instruments	4 680 ..	−52	500	−1,156	541	6,129	−11,346	2,702	
Monetary authorities	4 681 ..	....	....	−260	1,000	365	−11,319	−222	
General government	4 682 ..	....	472	−198	47	−495	−439	113	
Banks	4 683 ..	1	−1	−697	−813	95	−150	−52	
Other sectors	4 684 ..	−53	28	−1	307	6,164	563	2,862	
C. FINANCIAL DERIVATIVES	4 910 ..	**119**	**294**	**−58**	**29**	**−48**	**−659**	**683**	**−212**
Monetary authorities	4 911 ..	....	....	....	....	....	....	....	
General government	4 912 ..	....	....	....	....	....	....	....	
Banks	4 913 ..	116	293	−62	38	19	−532	470	....
Other sectors	4 914 ..	3	1	3	−8	−67	−128	213	
Assets	4 900 ..	**−24**	**−1,520**	**−59**	**8**	**198**	**−1,165**	**32**	....
Monetary authorities	4 901 ..	....	....	....	....	....	....	....	
General government	4 902 ..	....	....	....	....	....	....	....	
Banks	4 903 ..	−17	−1,519	−59	13	155	−1,036	−157	
Other sectors	4 904 ..	−6	−1	−1	−5	43	−129	189	
Liabilities	4 905 ..	**142**	**1,814**	**1**	**21**	**−246**	**506**	**651**	....
Monetary authorities	4 906 ..	....	....	....	....	....	....	....	
General government	4 907 ..	....	....	....	....	....	....	....	
Banks	4 908 ..	133	1,812	−3	25	−136	504	627	....
Other sectors	4 909 ..	9	2	4	−4	−110	2	24	....

Table 2 (Concluded). STANDARD PRESENTATION, 2003–2010

(Millions of U.S. dollars)

	Code	2003	2004	2005	2006	2007	2008	2009	2010
D. OTHER INVESTMENT	4 700	**–5,397**	**–6,154**	**–7,041**	**–15,331**	**–13,973**	**–1,526**	**–16,404**	**–16,351**
Assets	4 703	**–4,502**	**–10,756**	**–4,877**	**–8,562**	**–17,400**	**3,826**	**–17,667**	....
Trade credits	4 706	–2,024	–2,508	–10,166	–1,731	–1,716	–8,110	–10,463	....
General government	4 707	5	1	9	....	–4	....	1	....
of which: Short-term	4 709	*5*	*1*	*9*	....	*–4*	....	*1*	....
Other sectors	4 710	–2,029	–2,509	–10,175	–1,731	–1,712	–8,110	–10,464	....
of which: Short-term	4 712	*–2,029*	*–2,509*	*–10,175*	*–1,731*	*–1,712*	*–8,256*	*–10,436*	....
Loans	4 714	237	–685	–306	–310	–848	–2,180	–1,979	....
Monetary authorities	4 715	....	....	....	....	....	....	....	
of which: Short-term	4 718	....	....	....	....	....	....	....	
General government	4 719	....	....	....	....	....	....	....	
of which: Short-term	4 721	....	....						
Banks	4 722	127	–798	–85	–1	–662	–2,162	–1,898	
of which: Short-term	4 724	*209*	*–690*	*–85*	*19*	*–27*	*3*	*106*	
Other sectors	4 725	111	113	–221	–308	–186	–18	–81	
of which: Short-term	4 727	*119*	*–36*	*–65*	*–130*	*–9*	*–5*	*–23*	
Currency and deposits	4 730	456	–4,722	2,549	–5,445	–12,522	14,593	–2,231	
Monetary authorities	4 731	....	....	....	....				
General government	4 732	....	....						
Banks	4 733	777	–3,891	1,670	–4,278	–12,320	14,283	–1,410	
Other sectors	4 734	–320	–830	879	–1,167	–203	310	–821	
Other assets	4 736	–3,172	–2,842	3,046	–1,076	–2,314	–478	–2,994	
Monetary authorities	4 737	....	....	....	....				
of which: Short-term	4 739	....	....						
General government	4 740	....	–2	–1	–1	....			
of which: Short-term	4 742	*–1*	*–2*	*–1*	*–1*				
Banks	4 743	1	–9	–6	–12	–60	–199	334	
of which: Short-term	4 745	*1*	*–9*	*–6*	*–12*	*–60*			
Other sectors	4 746	–3,172	–2,831	3,053	–1,064	–2,254	–279	–3,328	
of which: Short-term	4 748	*525*	*–2,247*	*2,696*	*–752*	*–2,391*	....		
Liabilities	4 753	**–895**	**4,602**	**–2,164**	**–6,769**	**3,427**	**–5,352**	**1,263**	....
Trade credits	4 756	–856	551	–434	–877	–232	–7,720	299	....
General government	4 757	....	....	....	....	....			
of which: Short-term	4 759	....	....	....	....				
Other sectors	4 760	–856	551	–434	–877	–232	–7,720	299	
of which: Short-term	4 762	*–856*	*551*	*–434*	*–877*	*–232*	*–7,794*	*182*	
Loans	4 764	–3,011	21	–1,116	–2,460	–2,110	797	636	
Monetary authorities	4 765	–62	....	....	....	....			
of which: Use of Fund credit and loans from the Fund	4 766	....	....	....	....	....			
of which: Short-term	4 768	....	....	....	....				
General government	4 769	–2,891	633	–840	–2,194	–653	–142	–151	
of which: Short-term	4 771	*–3,163*	*–754*	*–630*	*–2,360*	*–338*	....		
Banks	4 772	298	–279	–65	–302	–170	376	259	....
of which: Short-term	4 774	*305*	*–276*	*–65*	*–252*	*–48*	....	....	
Other sectors	4 775	–355	–333	–212	36	–1,287	562	528	
of which: Short-term	4 777	*–44*	*–152*	*–39*	*24*	*–417*	*–182*	*102*	
Currency and deposits	4 780	1,411	1,920	–66	–3,373	6,688	1,591	–518	
Monetary authorities	4 781	....	....	....	....	....			
General government	4 782	....	....						
Banks	4 783	1,412	1,920	–66	–3,373	6,679	1,591	–518	
Other sectors	4 784	–1	....	....	–1	9			
Other liabilities	4 786	1,561	2,109	–547	–58	–919	–20	847	
Monetary authorities	4 787	....	....	....	....	....		1,885	
of which: Short-term	4 789	....	....	....	....				
General government	4 790	....	....	–2	....	....			
of which: Short-term	4 792	....	....						
Banks	4 793	5	43	–3	62	–84	–48	13	
of which: Short-term	4 795	*5*	*43*	*–3*	*62*	*–84*	....		
Other sectors	4 796	1,556	2,066	–543	–120	–835	28	–1,052	....
of which: Short-term	4 798	*–1,545*	*1,110*	*276*	*262*	*–291*	*2*	....	
E. RESERVE ASSETS	4 802	**–10,181**	**–22,050**	**–3,620**	**–6,864**	**–13,144**	**3,450**	**–3,918**	**37**
Monetary gold	4 812	....	....	....	....	....	....	....	....
Special drawing rights	4 811	–12	–12	–13	–7	–5	–3	–1,887	–1
Reserve position in the Fund	4 810	–5	128	437	103	48	–162	–115	–35
Foreign exchange	4 803	–10,164	–22,166	–4,044	–6,959	–13,187	3,615	–1,916	73
Other claims	4 813	....	....	....	....	....	....	....	....
NET ERRORS AND OMISSIONS	4 998	**–4**	**1,880**	**–6,555**	**–7,451**	**–5,195**	**–8,578**	**–5,199**	**–21,358**

Table 3. INTERNATIONAL INVESTMENT POSITION (End-period stocks), 2003–2010

(Millions of U.S. dollars)

	Code	2003	2004	2005	2006	2007	2008	2009	2010
ASSETS	8 995 C.	**77,625**	**106,132**	**116,846**	**157,297**	**224,898**	**219,182**	**251,339**	**292,270**
Direct investment abroad	8 505	**12,019**	**12,794**	**22,035**	**36,127**	**58,436**	**67,580**	**80,488**	**96,758**
Equity capital and reinvested earnings	8 506	7,033	8,008	13,499	20,189	34,318	43,018	54,161	65,487
Claims on affiliated enterprises	8 507	....	....	....	....	....	....	....	....
Liabilities to affiliated enterprises	8 508	....	....	....	....	....	....	....	....
Other capital	8 530	4,986	4,787	8,536	15,938	24,117	24,561	26,326	31,271
Claims on affiliated enterprises	8 535	....	....	....	....	....	....	....	....
Liabilities to affiliated enterprises	8 540	....	....	....	....	....	....	....	....
Portfolio investment	8 602	**2,490**	**2,509**	**4,183**	**8,269**	**15,320**	**16,215**	**27,801**	**35,893**
Equity securities	8 610	1,083	917	1,715	5,512	12,524	11,592	20,152	25,050
Monetary authorities	8 611	....	....	....	....	....	....	....	....
General government	8 612	....	....	....	....	....	....	....	....
Banks	8 613	....	....	....	....	....	....	....	....
Other sectors	8 614	....	....	....	....	....	....	....	....
Debt securities	8 619	1,407	1,592	2,468	2,758	2,796	4,623	7,649	10,843
Bonds and notes	8 620	....	....	....	....	....	....	....	....
Monetary authorities	8 621	....	....	....	....	....	....	....	....
General government	8 622	....	....	....	....	....	....	....	....
Banks	8 623	....	....	....	....	....	....	....	....
Other sectors	8 624	....	....	....	....	....	....	....	....
Money market instruments	8 630	....	....	....	....	....	....	....	....
Monetary authorities	8 631	....	....	....	....	....	....	....	....
General government	8 632	....	....	....	....	....	....	....	....
Banks	8 633	....	....	....	....	....	....	....	....
Other sectors	8 634	....	....	....	....	....	....	....	....
Financial derivatives	8 900	**319**	**166**	**233**	**586**	**541**	**2,235**	**2,273**	**1,701**
Monetary authorities	8 901	....	....	....	....	....	....	....	....
General government	8 902	....	....	....	....	....	....	....	....
Banks	8 903	....	....	....	....	....	....	....	....
Other sectors	8 904	....	....	....	....	....	....	....	....
Other investment	8 703	**18,689**	**24,462**	**20,256**	**30,114**	**49,109**	**41,520**	**44,042**	**51,337**
Trade credits	8 706	....	....	....	....	....	....	....	....
General government	8 707	....	....	....	....	....	....	....	....
of which: Short-term	8 709	....	....	....	....	....	....	....	....
Other sectors	8 710	....	....	....	....	....	....	....	....
of which: Short-term	8 712	....	....	....	....	....	....	....	....
Loans	8 714	....	....	....	....	....	....	....	....
Monetary authorities	8 715	....	....	....	....	....	....	....	....
of which: Short-term	8 718	....	....	....	....	....	....	....	....
General government	8 719	....	....	....	....	....	....	....	....
of which: Short-term	8 721	....	....	....	....	....	....	....	....
Banks	8 722	....	....	....	....	....	....	....	....
of which: Short-term	8 724	....	....	....	....	....	....	....	....
Other sectors	8 725	....	....	....	....	....	....	....	....
of which: Short-term	8 727	....	....	....	....	....	....	....	....
Currency and deposits	8 730	....	....	....	....	....	....	....	....
Monetary authorities	8 731	....	....	....	....	....	....	....	....
General government	8 732	....	....	....	....	....	....	....	....
Banks	8 733	....	....	....	....	....	....	....	....
Other sectors	8 734	....	....	....	....	....	....	....	....
Other assets	8 736	....	....	....	....	....	....	....	....
Monetary authorities	8 737	....	....	....	....	....	....	....	....
of which: Short-term	8 739	....	....	....	....	....	....	....	....
General government	8 740	....	....	....	....	....	....	....	....
of which: Short-term	8 742	....	....	....	....	....	....	....	....
Banks	8 743	....	....	....	....	....	....	....	....
of which: Short-term	8 745	....	....	....	....	....	....	....	....
Other sectors	8 746	....	....	....	....	....	....	....	....
of which: Short-term	8 748	....	....	....	....	....	....	....	....
Reserve assets	8 802	**44,109**	**66,201**	**70,139**	**82,201**	**101,493**	**91,632**	**96,736**	**106,581**
Monetary gold	8 812	294	294	294	293	294	379	1,282	1,643
Special drawing rights	8 811	178	199	196	214	229	226	2,124	2,088
Reserve position in the Fund	8 810	871	776	285	195	155	317	442	471
Foreign exchange	8 803	40,556	61,744	66,203	78,101	95,062	85,766	86,532	95,941
Other claims	8 813	2,209	3,187	3,160	3,398	5,753	4,944	6,355	6,438

Table 3 (Concluded). INTERNATIONAL INVESTMENT POSITION (End-period stocks), 2003–2010

(Millions of U.S. dollars)

	Code	2003	2004	2005	2006	2007	2008	2009	2010
LIABILITIES	8 995 D.	**115,084**	**139,645**	**136,699**	**163,947**	**229,471**	**186,200**	**216,271**	**287,967**
Direct investment in Malaysia	8 555	**41,188**	**43,047**	**44,460**	**53,710**	**75,763**	**73,262**	**78,838**	**101,339**
Equity capital and reinvested earnings	8 556	37,312	39,754	41,346	51,246	71,667	68,781	73,244	95,248
Claims on direct investors	8 557	....	....	....	....	....	....	....	....
Liabilities to direct investors	8 558	....	....	....	....	....	....	....	....
Other capital	8 580	3,876	3,293	3,113	2,464	4,096	4,481	5,594	6,091
Claims on direct investors	8 585	....	....	....	....	....	....	....	....
Liabilities to direct investors	8 590	....	....	....	....	....	....	....	....
Portfolio investment	8 652	**22,822**	**50,938**	**46,054**	**65,927**	**103,208**	**64,357**	**84,797**	**128,531**
Equity securities	8 660	20,818	31,285	30,498	46,031	68,162	27,689	41,716	65,902
Banks	8 663	....	....	....	....	....	....	....	....
Other sectors	8 664	....	....	....	....	....	....	....	....
Debt securities	8 669	2,003	19,653	15,556	19,897	35,045	36,669	43,081	62,629
Bonds and notes	8 670	....	....	....	....	....	....	....	....
Monetary authorities	8 671	....	....	....	....	....	....	....	....
General government	8 672	....	....	....	....	....	....	....	....
Banks	8 673	....	....	....	....	....	....	....	....
Other sectors	8 674	....	....	....	....	....	....	....	....
Money market instruments	8 680	....	....	....	....	....	....	....	....
Monetary authorities	8 681	....	....	....	....	....	....	....	....
General government	8 682	....	....	....	....	....	....	....	....
Banks	8 683	....	....	....	....	....	....	....	....
Other sectors	8 684	....	....	....	....	....	....	....	....
Financial derivatives	8 905	**208**	**223**	**317**	**515**	**536**	**2,135**	**2,539**	**1,499**
Monetary authorities	8 906	....	....	....	....	....	....	....	....
General government	8 907	....	....	....	....	....	....	....	....
Banks	8 908	....	....	....	....	....	....	....	....
Other sectors	8 909	....	....	....	....	....	....	....	....
Other investment	8 753	**50,866**	**45,436**	**45,869**	**43,794**	**49,965**	**46,446**	**50,097**	**56,599**
Trade credits	8 756	....	....	....	....	....	....	....	....
General government	8 757	....	....	....	....	....	....	....	....
of which: Short-term	8 759	....	....	....	....	....	....	....	....
Other sectors	8 760	....	....	....	....	....	....	....	....
of which: Short-term	8 762	....	....	....	....	....	....	....	....
Loans	8 764	....	....	....	....	....	....	....	....
Monetary authorities	8 765	....	....	....	....	....	....	....	....
of which: Use of Fund credit and loans from the Fund	8 766	....	....	....	....	....	....	....	....
of which: Short-term	8 768	....	....	....	....	....	....	....	....
General government	8 769	....	....	....	....	....	....	....	....
of which: Short-term	8 771	....	....	....	....	....	....	....	....
Banks	8 772	....	....	....	....	....	....	....	....
of which: Short-term	8 774	....	....	....	....	....	....	....	....
Other sectors	8 775	....	....	....	....	....	....	....	....
of which: Short-term	8 777	....	....	....	....	....	....	....	....
Currency and deposits	8 780	....	....	....	....	....	....	....	....
Monetary authorities	8 781	....	....	....	....	....	....	....	....
General government	8 782	....	....	....	....	....	....	....	....
Banks	8 783	....	....	....	....	....	....	....	....
Other sectors	8 784	....	....	....	....	....	....	....	....
Other liabilities	8 786	....	....	....	....	....	....	....	....
Monetary authorities	8 787	....	....	....	....	....	....	....	....
of which: Short-term	8 789	....	....	....	....	....	....	....	....
General government	8 790	....	....	....	....	....	....	....	....
of which: Short-term	8 792	....	....	....	....	....	....	....	....
Banks	8 793	....	....	....	....	....	....	....	....
of which: Short-term	8 795	....	....	....	....	....	....	....	....
Other sectors	8 796	....	....	....	....	....	....	....	....
of which: Short-term	8 798	....	....	....	....	....	....	....	....
NET INTERNATIONAL INVESTMENT POSITION	8 995	**−37,459**	**−33,513**	**−19,853**	**−6,650**	**−4,573**	**32,982**	**35,068**	**4,303**
Conversion rates: ringgit per U.S. dollar (end of period)	0 102	**3.800**	**3.800**	**3.780**	**3.532**	**3.307**	**3.464**	**3.425**	**3.084**

Table 1. ANALYTIC PRESENTATION, 2003–2010

(Millions of U.S. dollars)

	Code	2003	2004	2005	2006	2007	2008	2009	2010
A. Current Account[1].....................	4 993 Z.	−31.3	−122.3	−273.0	−302.0	−437.8	−647.3	−418.7	−462.7
Goods: exports f.o.b...............	2 100 ..	152.0	181.0	161.6	225.2	228.0	331.1	169.0	180.0
Goods: imports f.o.b...............	3 100 ..	−414.3	−564.8	−655.5	−815.3	−964.7	−1,221.0	−851.3	−978.0
Balance on Goods................	4 100 ..	*−262.3*	*−383.8*	*−493.8*	*−590.1*	*−736.8*	*−889.9*	*−682.2*	*−798.0*
Services: credit.....................	2 200 ..	431.9	507.7	322.9	551.9	649.1	720.8	659.7	768.5
Services: debit......................	3 200 ..	−120.3	−157.4	−213.1	−231.2	−269.3	−350.5	−286.3	−306.3
Balance on Goods and Services................	4 991 ..	*49.4*	*−33.6*	*−384.0*	*−269.4*	*−356.9*	*−519.6*	*−308.9*	*−335.7*
Income: credit.......................	2 300 ..	6.2	9.8	10.9	15.6	21.7	11.2	5.0	4.9
Income: debit........................	3 300 ..	−44.6	−44.9	−41.8	−56.3	−88.9	−75.4	−58.2	−65.2
Balance on Goods, Services, and Income............	4 992 ..	*11.0*	*−68.8*	*−415.0*	*−310.1*	*−424.1*	*−583.8*	*−362.0*	*−396.0*
Current transfers: credit...........	2 379 Z.	12.7	7.6	211.5	91.3	91.5	65.0	58.9	43.1
Current transfers: debit...........	3 379 ..	−54.9	−61.1	−69.5	−83.2	−105.2	−128.4	−115.6	−109.8
B. Capital Account[1].....................	4 994 Z.	....	....	....	....	....	....	....	....
Capital account: credit...........	2 994 Z.	....	....	....	....	....	....	....	....
Capital account: debit...........	3 994 ..	....	....	....	....	....	....	....	....
Total, Groups A Plus B..........	4 981 ..	*−31.3*	*−122.3*	*−273.0*	*−302.0*	*−437.8*	*−647.3*	*−418.7*	*−462.7*
C. Financial Account[1].....................	4 995 W.	**47.1**	**119.9**	**222.6**	**238.9**	**349.3**	**380.9**	**329.9**	**350.1**
Direct investment abroad............	4 505 ..	....	....	....	....	....	....	....	....
Direct investment in Maldives............	4 555 Z.	31.8	52.9	53.0	63.8	90.6	134.8	112.3	163.8
Portfolio investment assets............	4 602 ..	....	....	....	....	....	....	....	....
Equity securities..................	4 610 ..	....	....	....	....	....	....	....	....
Debt securities...................	4 619 ..	....	....	....	....	....	....	....	....
Portfolio investment liabilities............	4 652 Z.	....	....	....	....	....	....	....	....
Equity securities..................	4 660 ..	....	....	....	....	....	....	....	....
Debt securities...................	4 669 Z.	....	....	....	....	....	....	....	....
Financial derivatives...............	4 910 ..	....	....	....	....	....	....	....	....
Financial derivatives assets............	4 900 ..	....	....	....	....	....	....	....	....
Financial derivatives liabilities............	4 905 ..	....	....	....	....	....	....	....	....
Other investment assets............	4 703 ..	−30.2	−15.5	32.2	−20.9	−14.3	22.4	−11.2	−1.8
Monetary authorities............	4 701 ..	....	....	....	....	....	....	....	....
General government............	4 704 ..	....	....	....	....	....	....	....	....
Banks............................	4 705 ..	−30.2	−15.5	32.2	−20.9	−14.3	22.4	−11.2	−1.8
Other sectors....................	4 728 ..	....	....	....	....	....	....	....	....
Other investment liabilities............	4 753 W.	45.4	82.4	137.4	196.0	273.0	223.8	228.8	188.1
Monetary authorities............	4 753 WA	....	.1	6.3	....	....	−2.3	16.4	10.1
General government............	4 753 ZB	29.9	25.0	18.6	38.6	36.0	66.6	88.7	56.6
Banks............................	4 753 ZC	−19.3	3.6	67.2	125.2	207.6	77.3	−15.6	−7.2
Other sectors....................	4 753 ZD	34.9	53.8	45.3	32.2	29.4	82.2	139.2	128.5
Total, Groups A Through C............	4 983 ..	*15.8*	*−2.5*	*−50.4*	*−63.1*	*−88.5*	*−266.3*	*−88.8*	*−112.6*
D. Net Errors and Omissions...............	4 998 ..	**10.4**	**46.5**	**27.1**	**108.1**	**165.3**	**201.0**	**104.1**	**158.6**
Total, Groups A Through D............	4 984 ..	*26.2*	*44.1*	*−23.3*	*45.0*	*76.8*	*−65.3*	*15.3*	*46.0*
E. Reserves and Related Items...............	4 802 A.	**−26.2**	**−44.1**	**23.3**	**−45.0**	**−76.8**	**65.3**	**−15.3**	**−46.0**
Reserve assets......................	4 802 ..	−26.2	−44.1	17.1	−45.0	−76.8	67.7	−20.3	−53.1
Use of Fund credit and loans............	4 766 ..	....	....	6.3	....	....	−2.4	4.9	7.0
Exceptional financing............	4 920 ..	....	....	....	....	....	....	....	....
Conversion rates: rufiyaa per U.S. dollar...............	0 101 ..	**12.800**	**12.800**	**12.800**	**12.800**	**12.800**	**12.800**	**12.800**	**12.800**

[1] Excludes components that have been classified in the categories of Group E.

Table 2. STANDARD PRESENTATION, 2003–2010

(Millions of U.S. dollars)

	Code	2003	2004	2005	2006	2007	2008	2009	2010
CURRENT ACCOUNT	4 993	−31.3	−122.3	−273.0	−302.0	−437.8	−647.3	−418.7	−462.7
A. GOODS	4 100	−262.3	−383.8	−493.8	−590.1	−736.8	−889.9	−682.2	−798.0
Credit	2 100	152.0	181.0	161.6	225.2	228.0	331.1	169.0	180.0
General merchandise: exports f.o.b.	2 110	118.1	127.9	112.8	144.5	129.7	197.3	91.6	76.5
Goods for processing: exports f.o.b.	2 150	....	....	....	....	....	....	....	....
Repairs on goods	2 160	....	....	....	....	....	....	....	....
Goods procured in ports by carriers	2 170	33.9	53.1	48.8	80.8	98.2	133.8	77.5	103.5
Nonmonetary gold	2 180	....	....	....	....	....	....	....	....
Debit	3 100	−414.3	−564.8	−655.5	−815.3	−964.7	−1,221.0	−851.3	−978.0
General merchandise: imports f.o.b.	3 110	−414.3	−564.8	−655.5	−815.3	−964.7	−1,221.0	−851.3	−978.0
Goods for processing: imports f.o.b.	3 150	....	....	....	....	....	....	....	....
Repairs on goods	3 160	....	....	....	....	....	....	....	....
Goods procured in ports by carriers	3 170	....	....	....	....	....	....	....	....
Nonmonetary gold	3 180	....	....	....	....	....	....	....	....
B. SERVICES	4 200	311.7	350.2	109.8	320.7	379.8	370.3	373.3	462.2
Total credit	2 200	*431.9*	*507.7*	*322.9*	*551.9*	*649.1*	*720.8*	*659.7*	*768.5*
Total debit	3 200	*−120.3*	*−157.4*	*−213.1*	*−231.2*	*−269.3*	*−350.5*	*−286.3*	*−306.3*
Transportation services, credit	2 205	20.1	23.3	22.0	26.0	28.6	40.3	36.2	39.7
Passenger	2 850	....	....	....	....	....	....	....	....
Freight	2 851	*3.6*	*3.6*	*5.0*	*5.9*	*7.3*	*9.7*	*6.8*	*8.9*
Other	2 852	*16.5*	*19.7*	*17.0*	*20.1*	*21.3*	*30.5*	*29.4*	*30.8*
Sea transport, passenger	2 207	....	....	....	....	....	....	....	....
Sea transport, freight	2 208	....	....	....	....	....	....	....	....
Sea transport, other	2 209	....	....	....	....	....	....	....	....
Air transport, passenger	2 211	....	....	....	....	....	....	....	....
Air transport, freight	2 212	....	....	....	....	....	....	....	....
Air transport, other	2 213	16.5	19.7	17.0	20.1	21.3	30.5	29.4	30.8
Other transport, passenger	2 215	....	....	....	....	....	....	....	....
Other transport, freight	2 216	....	....	....	....	....	....	....	....
Other transport, other	2 217	....	....	....	....	....	....	....	....
Transportation services, debit	3 205	−58.8	−80.1	−94.5	−115.5	−137.0	−191.9	−142.1	−161.5
Passenger	3 850	*−13.8*	*−19.3*	*−24.3*	*−28.2*	*−34.1*	*−39.8*	*−35.8*	*−39.4*
Freight	3 851	*−43.2*	*−58.9*	*−68.4*	*−85.1*	*−100.6*	*−149.9*	*−104.5*	*−120.0*
Other	3 852	*−1.8*	*−1.8*	*−1.8*	*−2.2*	*−2.2*	*−2.3*	*−1.8*	*−2.1*
Sea transport, passenger	3 207	....	....	....	....	....	....	....	....
Sea transport, freight	3 208	....	....	....	....	....	....	....	....
Sea transport, other	3 209	−1.3	−1.3	−1.3	−1.7	−1.7	−1.8	−1.2	−1.4
Air transport, passenger	3 211	−13.8	−19.3	−24.3	−28.2	−34.1	−39.8	−35.8	−39.4
Air transport, freight	3 212	....	....	....	....	....	....	....	....
Air transport, other	3 213	−.5	−.5	−.5	−.5	−.5	−.5	−.6	−.7
Other transport, passenger	3 215	....	....	....	....	....	....	....	....
Other transport, freight	3 216	....	....	....	....	....	....	....	....
Other transport, other	3 217	....	....	....	....	....	....	....	....
Travel, credit	2 236	401.6	470.9	286.6	512.4	602.4	663.6	608.3	713.6
Business travel	2 237	....	....	....	....	....	....	....	....
Personal travel	2 240	401.6	470.9	286.6	512.4	602.4	663.6	608.3	713.6
Travel, debit	3 236	−46.3	−55.5	−69.9	−78.3	−93.2	−108.6	−100.4	−102.7
Business travel	3 237	−1.5	−1.6	−2.5	−2.5	−2.5	−2.5	−4.7	−2.0
Personal travel	3 240	−44.8	−53.9	−67.4	−75.8	−90.7	−106.0	−95.7	−100.7
Other services, credit	2 200 BA	10.2	13.4	14.2	13.4	18.1	17.0	15.2	15.2
Communications	2 245	....	....	....	....	....	....	....	....
Construction	2 249	....	....	....	....	....	....	....	....
Insurance	2 253	.4	.4	.6	.7	.8	1.1	1.1	1.1
Financial	2 260	....	....	....	....	....	....	....	....
Computer and information	2 262	....	....	....	....	....	....	....	....
Royalties and licence fees	2 266	6.7	9.9	7.5	10.0	6.5	11.0	8.7	8.4
Other business services	2 268	....	....	....	....	....	....	....	....
Personal, cultural, and recreational	2 287	....	....	....	....	....	....	....	....
Government, n.i.e.	2 291	3.1	3.1	6.1	2.8	10.8	5.0	5.4	5.7
Other services, debit	3 200 BA	−15.2	−21.9	−48.6	−37.4	−39.1	−50.1	−43.9	−42.0
Communications	3 245	....	....	....	....	....	....	....	....
Construction	3 249	....	....	....	....	....	....	....	....
Insurance	3 253	−4.8	−6.5	−7.6	−9.5	−11.2	−16.7	−11.6	−13.3
Financial	3 260	....	....	....	....	....	....	....	....
Computer and information	3 262	....	....	....	....	....	....	....	....
Royalties and licence fees	3 266	....	....	....	....	....	....	....	....
Other business services	3 268	−8.9	−13.0	−38.1	−23.1	−23.5	−24.9	−28.1	−21.6
Personal, cultural, and recreational	3 287	....	....	....	....	....	....	....	....
Government, n.i.e.	3 291	−1.5	−2.3	−2.9	−4.8	−4.4	−8.5	−4.2	−7.1

Table 2 (Continued). STANDARD PRESENTATION, 2003–2010

(Millions of U.S. dollars)

	Code	2003	2004	2005	2006	2007	2008	2009	2010
C. INCOME	4 300 ..	**−38.4**	**−35.2**	**−31.0**	**−40.8**	**−67.2**	**−64.2**	**−53.2**	**−60.2**
Total credit	2 300 ..	*6.2*	*9.8*	*10.9*	*15.6*	*21.7*	*11.2*	*5.0*	*4.9*
Total debit	3 300 ..	*−44.6*	*−44.9*	*−41.8*	*−56.3*	*−88.9*	*−75.4*	*−58.2*	*−65.2*
Compensation of employees, credit	2 310 ..	**2.0**	**2.9**	**2.3**	**2.8**	**3.0**	**3.4**	**3.7**	**4.1**
Compensation of employees, debit	3 310 ..	**−.4**	**−.4**	**−.4**	**−.4**	**−.4**	**−.4**	**−.5**	**−.5**
Investment income, credit	2 320 ..	**4.2**	**6.9**	**8.6**	**12.8**	**18.8**	**7.8**	**1.3**	**.8**
Direct investment income	2 330 ..	....	....	....	....	....	....	....	....
Dividends and distributed branch profits	2 332 ..	....	....	....	....	....	....	....	....
Reinvested earnings and undistributed branch profits	2 333 ..	....	....	....	....	....	....	....	....
Income on debt (interest)	2 334 ..	....	....	....	....	....	....	....	....
Portfolio investment income	2 339 ..	....	....	....	....	....	....	....	....
Income on equity	2 340 ..	....	....	....	....	....	....	....	....
Income on bonds and notes	2 350 ..	....	....	....	....	....	....	....	....
Income on money market instruments	2 360 ..	....	....	....	....	....	....	....	....
Other investment income	2 370 ..	4.2	6.9	8.6	12.8	18.8	7.8	1.3	.8
Investment income, debit	3 320 ..	**−44.2**	**−44.5**	**−41.4**	**−55.9**	**−88.5**	**−74.9**	**−57.7**	**−64.7**
Direct investment income	3 330 ..	−39.0	−36.4	−31.0	−41.0	−44.9	−35.9	−26.4	−30.8
Dividends and distributed branch profits	3 332 ..	−25.5	−21.7	−21.5	−27.2	−29.9	−23.9	−16.8	−19.6
Reinvested earnings and undistributed branch profits	3 333 ..	−13.5	−14.7	−9.5	−13.9	−15.0	−12.0	−9.6	−11.2
Income on debt (interest)	3 334 ..	....	....	....	....	....	....	....	....
Portfolio investment income	3 339 ..	....	....	....	....	....	....	....	....
Income on equity	3 340 ..	....	....	....	....	....	....	....	....
Income on bonds and notes	3 350 ..	....	....	....	....	....	....	....	....
Income on money market instruments	3 360 ..	....	....	....	....	....	....	....	....
Other investment income	3 370 ..	−5.2	−8.1	−10.5	−14.9	−43.6	−39.0	−31.4	−33.8
D. CURRENT TRANSFERS	4 379 ..	**−42.3**	**−53.6**	**142.0**	**8.2**	**−13.7**	**−63.5**	**−56.7**	**−66.7**
Credit	2 379 ..	**12.7**	**7.6**	**211.5**	**91.3**	**91.5**	**65.0**	**58.9**	**43.1**
General government	2 380 ..	12.7	7.6	211.5	91.3	91.5	65.0	58.9	43.1
Other sectors	2 390 ..	....	....	....	....	....	....	....	....
Workers' remittances	2 391 ..	....	....	....	....	....	....	....	....
Other current transfers	2 392 ..	....	....	....	....	....	....	....	....
Debit	3 379 ..	**−54.9**	**−61.1**	**−69.5**	**−83.2**	**−105.2**	**−128.4**	**−115.6**	**−109.8**
General government	3 380 ..	....	....	....	....	....	....	....	....
Other sectors	3 390 ..	−54.9	−61.1	−69.5	−83.2	−105.2	−128.4	−115.6	−109.8
Workers' remittances	3 391 ..	−54.9	−61.1	−69.5	−83.2	−105.2	−128.4	−115.6	−109.8
Other current transfers	3 392 ..	....	....	....	....	....	....	....	....
CAPITAL AND FINANCIAL ACCOUNT	4 996 ..	**20.9**	**75.8**	**245.9**	**193.9**	**272.5**	**446.2**	**314.6**	**304.1**
CAPITAL ACCOUNT	4 994 ..	....	....	....	....	....	....	....	....
Total credit	2 994 ..	....	....	....	....	....	....	....	....
Total debit	3 994 ..	....	....	....	....	....	....	....	....
Capital transfers, credit	2 400 ..	....	....	....	....	....	....	....	....
General government	2 401 ..	....	....	....	....	....	....	....	....
Debt forgiveness	2 402 ..	....	....	....	....	....	....	....	....
Other capital transfers	2 410 ..	....	....	....	....	....	....	....	....
Other sectors	2 430 ..	....	....	....	....	....	....	....	....
Migrants' transfers	2 431 ..	....	....	....	....	....	....	....	....
Debt forgiveness	2 432 ..	....	....	....	....	....	....	....	....
Other capital transfers	2 440 ..	....	....	....	....	....	....	....	....
Capital transfers, debit	3 400 ..	....	....	....	....	....	....	....	....
General government	3 401 ..	....	....	....	....	....	....	....	....
Debt forgiveness	3 402 ..	....	....	....	....	....	....	....	....
Other capital transfers	3 410 ..	....	....	....	....	....	....	....	....
Other sectors	3 430 ..	....	....	....	....	....	....	....	....
Migrants' transfers	3 431 ..	....	....	....	....	....	....	....	....
Debt forgiveness	3 432 ..	....	....	....	....	....	....	....	....
Other capital transfers	3 440 ..	....	....	....	....	....	....	....	....
Nonproduced nonfinancial assets, credit	2 480 ..	....	....	....	....	....	....	....	....
Nonproduced nonfinancial assets, debit	3 480 ..	....	....	....	....	....	....	....	....

Table 2 (Continued). STANDARD PRESENTATION, 2003–2010
(Millions of U.S. dollars)

	Code	2003	2004	2005	2006	2007	2008	2009	2010
FINANCIAL ACCOUNT	4 995	**20.9**	**75.8**	**245.9**	**193.9**	**272.5**	**446.2**	**314.6**	**304.1**
A. DIRECT INVESTMENT	4 500	**31.8**	**52.9**	**53.0**	**63.8**	**90.6**	**134.8**	**112.3**	**163.8**
Direct investment abroad	4 505	....	....	....	....	....	....	....	....
Equity capital	4 510	....	....	....	....	....	....	....	....
Claims on affiliated enterprises	4 515	....	....	....	....	....	....	....	....
Liabilities to affiliated enterprises	4 520	....	....	....	....	....	....	....	....
Reinvested earnings	4 525	....	....	....	....	....	....	....	....
Other capital	4 530	....	....	....	....	....	....	....	....
Claims on affiliated enterprises	4 535	....	....	....	....	....	....	....	....
Liabilities to affiliated enterprises	4 540	....	....	....	....	....	....	....	....
Direct investment in Maldives	4 555	**31.8**	**52.9**	**53.0**	**63.8**	**90.6**	**134.8**	**112.3**	**163.8**
Equity capital	4 560	18.3	38.2	43.5	50.0	75.6	122.8	102.7	152.6
Claims on direct investors	4 565	....	....	....	....	....	....	....	....
Liabilities to direct investors	4 570	18.3	38.2	43.5	50.0	75.6	122.8	102.7	152.6
Reinvested earnings	4 575	13.5	14.7	9.5	13.9	15.0	12.0	9.6	11.2
Other capital	4 580	....	....	....	....	....	....	....	....
Claims on direct investors	4 585	....	....	....	....	....	....	....	....
Liabilities to direct investors	4 590	....	....	....	....	....	....	....	....
B. PORTFOLIO INVESTMENT	4 600	....	....	....	....	....	....	....	....
Assets	4 602	....	....	....	....	....	....	....	....
Equity securities	4 610	....	....	....	....	....	....	....	....
Monetary authorities	4 611	....	....	....	....	....	....	....	....
General government	4 612	....	....	....	....	....	....	....	....
Banks	4 613	....	....	....	....	....	....	....	....
Other sectors	4 614	....	....	....	....	....	....	....	....
Debt securities	4 619	....	....	....	....	....	....	....	....
Bonds and notes	4 620	....	....	....	....	....	....	....	....
Monetary authorities	4 621	....	....	....	....	....	....	....	....
General government	4 622	....	....	....	....	....	....	....	....
Banks	4 623	....	....	....	....	....	....	....	....
Other sectors	4 624	....	....	....	....	....	....	....	....
Money market instruments	4 630	....	....	....	....	....	....	....	....
Monetary authorities	4 631	....	....	....	....	....	....	....	....
General government	4 632	....	....	....	....	....	....	....	....
Banks	4 633	....	....	....	....	....	....	....	....
Other sectors	4 634	....	....	....	....	....	....	....	....
Liabilities	4 652	....	....	....	....	....	....	....	....
Equity securities	4 660	....	....	....	....	....	....	....	....
Banks	4 663	....	....	....	....	....	....	....	....
Other sectors	4 664	....	....	....	....	....	....	....	....
Debt securities	4 669	....	....	....	....	....	....	....	....
Bonds and notes	4 670	....	....	....	....	....	....	....	....
Monetary authorities	4 671	....	....	....	....	....	....	....	....
General government	4 672	....	....	....	....	....	....	....	....
Banks	4 673	....	....	....	....	....	....	....	....
Other sectors	4 674	....	....	....	....	....	....	....	....
Money market instruments	4 680	....	....	....	....	....	....	....	....
Monetary authorities	4 681	....	....	....	....	....	....	....	....
General government	4 682	....	....	....	....	....	....	....	....
Banks	4 683	....	....	....	....	....	....	....	....
Other sectors	4 684	....	....	....	....	....	....	....	....
C. FINANCIAL DERIVATIVES	4 910	....	....	....	....	....	....	....	....
Monetary authorities	4 911	....	....	....	....	....	....	....	....
General government	4 912	....	....	....	....	....	....	....	....
Banks	4 913	....	....	....	....	....	....	....	....
Other sectors	4 914	....	....	....	....	....	....	....	....
Assets	4 900	....	....	....	....	....	....	....	....
Monetary authorities	4 901	....	....	....	....	....	....	....	....
General government	4 902	....	....	....	....	....	....	....	....
Banks	4 903	....	....	....	....	....	....	....	....
Other sectors	4 904	....	....	....	....	....	....	....	....
Liabilities	4 905	....	....	....	....	....	....	....	....
Monetary authorities	4 906	....	....	....	....	....	....	....	....
General government	4 907	....	....	....	....	....	....	....	....
Banks	4 908	....	....	....	....	....	....	....	....
Other sectors	4 909	....	....	....	....	....	....	....	....

Table 2 (Concluded). STANDARD PRESENTATION, 2003–2010

(Millions of U.S. dollars)

	Code	2003	2004	2005	2006	2007	2008	2009	2010
D. OTHER INVESTMENT	4 700 ..	**15.3**	**66.9**	**175.8**	**175.0**	**258.7**	**243.7**	**222.5**	**193.3**
Assets	4 703 ..	**−30.2**	**−15.5**	**32.2**	**−20.9**	**−14.3**	**22.4**	**−11.2**	**−1.8**
Trade credits	4 706 ..	....	....	....	....	....	....	....	....
General government	4 707 ..	....	....	....	....	....	....	....	....
of which: Short-term	4 709 ..	....	....	....	....	....	....	....	....
Other sectors	4 710 ..	....	....	....	....	....	....	....	....
of which: Short-term	4 712 ..	....	....	....	....	....	....	....	....
Loans	4 714 ..	−4.3	4.7	−1.8	−11.6	6.1	9.5	1.3	....
Monetary authorities	4 715 ..	....	....	....	....	....	....	....	....
of which: Short-term	4 718 ..	....	....	....	....	....	....	....	....
General government	4 719 ..	....	....	....	....	....	....	....	....
of which: Short-term	4 721 ..	....	....	....	....	....	....	....	....
Banks	4 722 ..	−4.3	4.7	−1.8	−11.6	6.1	9.5	1.3	....
of which: Short-term	4 724 ..	....	....	....	....	....	....	....	....
Other sectors	4 725 ..	....	....	....	....	....	....	....	....
of which: Short-term	4 727 ..	....	....	....	....	....	....	....	....
Currency and deposits	4 730 ..	−25.9	−20.1	34.0	−9.3	−20.4	12.8	−12.5	−1.8
Monetary authorities	4 731 ..	....	....	....	....	....	....	....	....
General government	4 732 ..	....	....	....	....	....	....	....	....
Banks	4 733 ..	−25.9	−20.1	34.0	−9.3	−20.4	12.8	−12.5	−1.8
Other sectors	4 734 ..	....	....	....	....	....	....	....	....
Other assets	4 736 ..	....	....	....	....	....	....	....	....
Monetary authorities	4 737 ..	....	....	....	....	....	....	....	....
of which: Short-term	4 739 ..	....	....	....	....	....	....	....	....
General government	4 740 ..	....	....	....	....	....	....	....	....
of which: Short-term	4 742 ..	....	....	....	....	....	....	....	....
Banks	4 743 ..	....	....	....	....	....	....	....	....
of which: Short-term	4 745 ..	....	....	....	....	....	....	....	....
Other sectors	4 746 ..	....	....	....	....	....	....	....	....
of which: Short-term	4 748 ..	....	....	....	....	....	....	....	....
Liabilities	4 753 ..	**45.4**	**82.4**	**143.6**	**196.0**	**273.0**	**221.4**	**233.7**	**195.1**
Trade credits	4 756 ..	....	....	....	....	....	....	....	....
General government	4 757 ..	....	....	....	....	....	....	....	....
of which: Short-term	4 759 ..	....	....	....	....	....	....	....	....
Other sectors	4 760 ..	....	....	....	....	....	....	....	....
of which: Short-term	4 762 ..	....	....	....	....	....	....	....	....
Loans	4 764 ..	40.7	77.9	135.3	196.2	274.2	228.6	210.6	185.0
Monetary authorities	4 765 ..	....	....	6.3	....	....	−2.4	4.9	7.0
of which: Use of Fund credit and loans from the Fund	4 766 ..	....	....	*6.3*	....	....	*−2.4*	*4.9*	*7.0*
of which: Short-term	4 768 ..	....	....	....	....	....	....	....	....
General government	4 769 ..	29.9	25.0	18.6	38.6	36.0	66.6	88.7	56.6
of which: Short-term	4 771 ..	....	....	....	....	....	....	....	....
Banks	4 772 ..	−24.1	−.9	65.2	125.4	208.8	82.2	−22.3	−7.2
of which: Short-term	4 774 ..	....	....	....	....	....	....	....	....
Other sectors	4 775 ..	34.9	53.8	45.3	32.2	29.4	82.2	139.2	128.5
of which: Short-term	4 777 ..	....	....	....	....	....	....	....	....
Currency and deposits	4 780 ..	4.7	4.5	2.0	−.3	−1.2	−4.9	6.7	....
Monetary authorities	4 781 ..	....	....	....	....	....	....	....	....
General government	4 782 ..	....	....	....	....	....	....	....	....
Banks	4 783 ..	4.7	4.5	2.0	−.3	−1.2	−4.9	6.7	....
Other sectors	4 784 ..	....	....	....	....	....	....	....	....
Other liabilities	4 786 ..	....	.1	6.3	....	....	−2.3	16.4	10.1
Monetary authorities	4 787 ..	....	.1	6.3	....	....	−2.3	16.4	10.1
of which: Short-term	4 789 ..	....	*.1*	*6.3*	....	....	*−2.3*	*4.9*	*10.1*
General government	4 790 ..	....	....	....	....	....	....	....	....
of which: Short-term	4 792 ..	....	....	....	....	....	....	....	....
Banks	4 793 ..	....	....	....	....	....	....	....	....
of which: Short-term	4 795 ..	....	....	....	....	....	....	....	....
Other sectors	4 796 ..	....	....	....	....	....	....	....	....
of which: Short-term	4 798 ..	....	....	....	....	....	....	....	....
E. RESERVE ASSETS	4 802 ..	**−26.2**	**−44.1**	**17.1**	**−45.0**	**−76.8**	**67.7**	**−20.3**	**−53.1**
Monetary gold	4 812 ..	−.1	....	....	....	....	....	....	....
Special drawing rights	4 811 ..	....	....	....	....	....	−.1	−11.5	.2
Reserve position in the Fund	4 810 ..	....	....	....	....	....	....	....	....
Foreign exchange	4 803 ..	−26.1	−43.9	17.1	−45.0	−76.8	67.7	−8.8	−53.3
Other claims	4 813 ..	.1	−.1	....	....	.1	....	.1	....
NET ERRORS AND OMISSIONS	4 998 ..	**10.4**	**46.5**	**27.1**	**108.1**	**165.3**	**201.0**	**104.1**	**158.6**

Table 3. INTERNATIONAL INVESTMENT POSITION (End-period stocks), 2003–2010

(Millions of U.S. dollars)

	Code	2003	2004	2005	2006	2007	2008	2009	2010
ASSETS	8 995 C.	**224.9**	**284.5**	**234.2**	**300.3**	**391.5**	**301.3**	**331.1**	**385.6**
Direct investment abroad	8 505 ..	....	....	....	....	....	....	....	....
Equity capital and reinvested earnings	8 506 ..	....	....	....	....	....	....	....	....
Claims on affiliated enterprises	8 507 ..	....	....	....	....	....	....	....	....
Liabilities to affiliated enterprises	8 508 ..	....	....	....	....	....	....	....	....
Other capital	8 530 ..	....	....	....	....	....	....	....	....
Claims on affiliated enterprises	8 535 ..	....	....	....	....	....	....	....	....
Liabilities to affiliated enterprises	8 540 ..	....	....	....	....	....	....	....	....
Portfolio investment	8 602 ..	....	....	....	....	....	....	....	....
Equity securities	8 610 ..								
Monetary authorities	8 611 ..								
General government	8 612 ..	....	....	....	....	....	....	....	....
Banks	8 613 ..	....	....	....	....	....	....	....	....
Other sectors	8 614 ..	....	....	....	....	....	....	....	....
Debt securities	8 619 ..	....	....	....	....	....	....	....	....
Bonds and notes	8 620 ..	....	....	....	....	....	....	....	....
Monetary authorities	8 621 ..	....	....	....	....	....	....	....	....
General government	8 622 ..	....	....	....	....	....	....	....	....
Banks	8 623 ..	....	....	....	....	....	....	....	....
Other sectors	8 624 ..	....	....	....	....	....	....	....	....
Money market instruments	8 630 ..	....	....	....	....	....	....	....	....
Monetary authorities	8 631 ..	....	....	....	....	....	....	....	....
General government	8 632 ..	....	....	....	....	....	....	....	....
Banks	8 633 ..	....	....	....	....	....	....	....	....
Other sectors	8 634 ..	....	....	....	....	....	....	....	....
Financial derivatives	8 900 ..	....	....	....	....	....	....	....	....
Monetary authorities	8 901 ..	....	....	....	....	....	....	....	....
General government	8 902 ..	....	....	....	....	....	....	....	....
Banks	8 903 ..	....	....	....	....	....	....	....	....
Other sectors	8 904 ..	....	....	....	....	....	....	....	....
Other investment	8 703 ..	**63.9**	**79.4**	**47.1**	**68.1**	**82.4**	**60.0**	**69.4**	**71.2**
Trade credits	8 706 ..	....	....	....	....	....	....	....	....
General government	8 707 ..	....	....	....	....	....	....	....	....
of which: Short-term	8 709 ..	....	....	....	....	....	....	....	....
Other sectors	8 710 ..	....	....	....	....	....	....	....	....
of which: Short-term	8 712 ..	....	....	....	....	....	....	....	....
Loans	8 714 ..	7.2	2.5	4.3	16.0	9.8	.3	1.3	1.3
Monetary authorities	8 715 ..	....	....	....	....	....	....	....	....
of which: Short-term	8 718 ..	....	....	....	....	....	....	....	....
General government	8 719 ..	....	....	....	....	....	....	....	....
of which: Short-term	8 721 ..	....	....	....	....	....	....	....	....
Banks	8 722 ..	7.2	2.5	4.3	16.0	9.8	.3	1.3	1.3
of which: Short-term	8 724 ..	....	....	....	....	....	....	....	....
Other sectors	8 725 ..	....	....	....	....	....	....	....	....
of which: Short-term	8 727 ..	....	....	....	....	....	....	....	....
Currency and deposits	8 730 ..	56.7	76.8	42.8	52.1	72.5	59.7	68.1	69.8
Monetary authorities	8 731 ..	....	....	....	....	....	....	....	....
General government	8 732 ..	....	....	....	....	....	....	....	....
Banks	8 733 ..	56.7	76.8	42.8	52.1	72.5	59.7	68.1	69.8
Other sectors	8 734 ..	....	....	....	....	....	....	....	....
Other assets	8 736 ..	....	....	....	....	....	....	....	....
Monetary authorities	8 737 ..	....	....	....	....	....	....	....	....
of which: Short-term	8 739 ..	....	....	....	....	....	....	....	....
General government	8 740 ..	....	....	....	....	....	....	....	....
of which: Short-term	8 742 ..	....	....	....	....	....	....	....	....
Banks	8 743 ..	....	....	....	....	....	....	....	....
of which: Short-term	8 745 ..	....	....	....	....	....	....	....	....
Other sectors	8 746 ..	....	....	....	....	....	....	....	....
of which: Short-term	8 748 ..	....	....	....	....	....	....	....	....
Reserve assets	8 802 ..	**161.0**	**205.2**	**187.1**	**232.2**	**309.1**	**241.3**	**261.7**	**314.5**
Monetary gold	8 812 ..	.7	.7	....	....	....	....	....	....
Special drawing rights	8 811 ..	.4	.5	.5	.5	.6	.6	12.2	11.7
Reserve position in the Fund	8 810 ..	2.3	2.4	2.2	2.3	2.5	2.4	2.4	2.4
Foreign exchange	8 803 ..	156.7	200.7	183.6	228.5	305.3	237.6	246.4	299.6
Other claims	8 813 ..	.8	.8	.8	.8	.8	.8	.7	.7

2011, International Monetary Fund: *Balance of Payments Statistics Yearbook*

Table 3 (Concluded). INTERNATIONAL INVESTMENT POSITION (End-period stocks), 2003–2010

(Millions of U.S. dollars)

	Code	2003	2004	2005	2006	2007	2008	2009	2010
LIABILITIES..	8 995 D.	**290.3**	**332.6**	**410.1**	**588.1**	**853.7**	**977.1**	**977.1**	**1,066.9**
Direct investment in Maldives...............	8 555 ..	....	....	....	....	....	....	....	....
Equity capital and reinvested earnings............................	8 556 ..	....	....	....	....	....	....	....	....
Claims on direct investors..................................	8 557 ..	....	....	....	....	....	....	....	....
Liabilities to direct investors.............................	8 558 ..	....	....	....	....	....	....	....	....
Other capital..	8 580 ..	....	....	....	....	....	....	....	....
Claims on direct investors..................................	8 585 ..	....	....	....	....	....	....	....	....
Liabilities to direct investors.............................	8 590 ..	....	....	....	....	....	....	....	....
Portfolio investment...............................	8 652 ..	....	....	....	....	....	....	....	....
Equity securities...	8 660 ..	....	....	....	....	....	....	....	....
Banks..	8 663 ..	....	....	....	....	....	....	....	....
Other sectors..	8 664 ..	....	....	....	....	....	....	....	....
Debt securities..	8 669 ..	....	....	....	....	....	....	....	....
Bonds and notes..	8 670 ..	....	....	....	....	....	....	....	....
Monetary authorities....................................	8 671 ..	....	....	....	....	....	....	....	....
General government.....................................	8 672 ..	....	....	....	....	....	....	....	....
Banks..	8 673 ..	....	....	....	....	....	....	....	....
Other sectors...	8 674 ..	....	....	....	....	....	....	....	....
Money market instruments.................................	8 680 ..	....	....	....	....	....	....	....	....
Monetary authorities....................................	8 681 ..	....	....	....	....	....	....	....	....
General government.....................................	8 682 ..	....	....	....	....	....	....	....	....
Banks..	8 683 ..	....	....	....	....	....	....	....	....
Other sectors...	8 684 ..	....	....	....	....	....	....	....	....
Financial derivatives...............................	8 905 ..	....	....	....	....	....	....	....	....
Monetary authorities..	8 906 ..	....	....	....	....	....	....	....	....
General government...	8 907 ..	....	....	....	....	....	....	....	....
Banks..	8 908 ..	....	....	....	....	....	....	....	....
Other sectors...	8 909 ..	....	....	....	....	....	....	....	....
Other investment...................................	8 753 ..	**290.3**	**332.6**	**410.1**	**588.1**	**853.7**	**977.1**	**977.1**	**1,066.9**
Trade credits...	8 756 ..	....	....	....	....	....	....	....	....
General government...	8 757 ..	....	....	....	....	....	....	....	....
of which: Short-term....................................	8 759 ..	....	....	....	....	....	....	....	....
Other sectors..	8 760 ..	....	....	....	....	....	....	....	....
of which: Short-term....................................	8 762 ..	....	....	....	....	....	....	....	....
Loans...	8 764 ..	283.4	321.2	390.3	568.6	835.5	966.0	942.4	1,021.7
Monetary authorities.......................................	8 765 ..	....	....	5.9	6.2	6.5	3.9	8.8	15.8
of which: Use of Fund credit and loans from the Fund....	8 766 ..	....	....	*5.9*	*6.2*	*6.5*	*3.9*	*8.8*	*15.8*
of which: Short-term....................................	8 768 ..	....	....	....	....	....	....	....	....
General government..	8 769 ..	272.9	311.6	309.6	362.3	420.0	470.8	533.1	598.3
of which: Short-term....................................	8 771 ..	....	....	....	....	....	....	....	....
Banks...	8 772 ..	10.5	9.6	74.8	200.2	409.0	491.3	400.4	407.6
of which: Short-term....................................	8 774 ..	....	....	....	....	....	....	....	....
Other sectors..	8 775 ..	....	....	....	....	....	....	....	....
of which: Short-term....................................	8 777 ..	....	....	....	....	....	....	....	....
Currency and deposits......................................	8 780 ..	6.1	10.6	12.6	12.3	11.2	6.2	13.1	13.1
Monetary authorities.......................................	8 781 ..	....	....	....	....	....	....	....	....
General government..	8 782 ..	....	....	....	....	....	....	....	....
Banks...	8 783 ..	6.1	10.6	12.6	12.3	11.2	6.2	13.1	13.1
Other sectors..	8 784 ..	....	....	....	....	....	....	....	....
Other liabilities..	8 786 ..	.8	.9	7.1	7.1	7.1	4.8	21.7	32.1
Monetary authorities.......................................	8 787 ..	.8	.9	7.1	7.1	7.1	4.8	21.7	32.1
of which: Short-term....................................	8 789 ..	*.8*	*.9*	*7.1*	*7.1*	*7.1*	*4.8*	*9.6*	*20.2*
General government..	8 790 ..	....	....	....	....	....	....	....	....
of which: Short-term....................................	8 792 ..	....	....	....	....	....	....	....	....
Banks...	8 793 ..	....	....	....	....	....	....	....	....
of which: Short-term....................................	8 795 ..	....	....	....	....	....	....	....	....
Other sectors..	8 796 ..	....	....	....	....	....	....	....	....
of which: Short-term....................................	8 798 ..	....	....	....	....	....	....	....	....
NET INTERNATIONAL INVESTMENT POSITION........	8 995 ..	**−65.4**	**−48.1**	**−175.8**	**−287.9**	**−462.2**	**−675.7**	**−646.1**	**−681.3**
Conversion rates: rufiyaa per U.S. dollar (end of period)...........................	0 102 ..	12.800	12.800	12.800	12.800	12.800	12.800	12.800	12.800

Table 1. ANALYTIC PRESENTATION, 2003–2010
(Millions of U.S. dollars)

	Code	2003	2004	2005	2006	2007	2008	2009	2010
A. Current Account[1]............................	4 993 Z.	**−271.0**	**−409.0**	**−437.7**	**−218.6**	**−581.1**	**−1,066.4**	**−654.9**	....
Goods: exports f.o.b........................	2 100 ..	927.8	976.4	1,100.9	1,550.4	1,556.3	2,097.2	1,773.7	....
Goods: imports f.o.b........................	3 100 ..	−988.3	−1,092.9	−1,245.5	−1,475.4	−1,846.0	−2,735.9	−1,986.3	....
Balance on Goods.....................	4 100 ..	*−60.5*	*−116.4*	*−144.6*	*75.0*	*−289.7*	*−638.7*	*−212.6*	....
Services: credit.............................	2 200 ..	224.3	241.1	274.3	313.3	376.7	454.3	354.4	....
Services: debit..............................	3 200 ..	−482.2	−531.8	−588.0	−674.5	−776.6	−1,024.3	−825.6	....
Balance on Goods and Services......	4 991 ..	*−318.5*	*−407.1*	*−458.3*	*−286.2*	*−689.6*	*−1,208.7*	*−683.9*	....
Income: credit...............................	2 300 ..	21.3	24.0	32.0	33.2	52.4	53.0	51.7	....
Income: debit...............................	3 300 ..	−181.2	−218.8	−239.0	−290.7	−343.9	−365.6	−509.1	....
Balance on Goods, Services, and Income......	4 992 ..	*−478.4*	*−601.9*	*−665.3*	*−543.7*	*−981.1*	*−1,521.3*	*−1,141.2*	....
Current transfers: credit.................	2 379 Z.	265.5	251.3	286.0	380.9	482.8	554.0	648.3	....
Current transfers: debit..................	3 379 ..	−58.1	−58.3	−58.5	−55.8	−82.9	−99.2	−162.0	....
B. Capital Account[1].............................	4 994 Z.	**113.7**	**151.4**	**148.9**	**140.6**	**301.8**	**328.8**	**384.1**	....
Capital account: credit...................	2 994 Z.	113.7	151.5	149.5	141.2	302.4	329.6	384.8	....
Capital account: debit....................	3 994 ..	....	....	−.6	−.6	−.7	−.8	−.8	....
Total, Groups A Plus B...............	4 981 ..	*−157.3*	*−257.5*	*−288.8*	*−78.0*	*−279.3*	*−737.6*	*−270.8*	....
C. Financial Account[1]...........................	4 995 W.	**288.7**	**99.9**	**333.4**	**−1,910.2**	**229.6**	**620.1**	**892.3**	....
Direct investment abroad................	4 505 ..	−1.4	−.8	36.6	34.5	11.7	48.0	30.9	....
Direct investment in Mali...............	4 555 Z.	132.3	101.0	188.1	47.6	53.8	131.7	718.5	....
Portfolio investment assets.............	4 602 ..	−27.1	−3.2	−18.0	−6.9	−31.0	−117.9	−60.3	....
Equity securities.......................	4 610 ..	.2	−5.1	....	−.3	.1	−2.2	−6.3	....
Debt securities.........................	4 619 ..	−27.2	1.9	−18.0	−6.6	−31.0	−115.7	−54.0	....
Portfolio investment liabilities........	4 652 Z.	27.6	.6	2.9	−4.2	−15.5	22.6	21.3	....
Equity securities.......................	4 660 ..	.9	−.7	8.9	2.8	−6.4	−3.0	−3.0	....
Debt securities.........................	4 669 Z.	26.7	1.3	−5.9	−6.9	−9.1	25.6	24.3	....
Financial derivatives.....................	4 910 ..	....	−.4	−.1	....	−.1	3.6	−1.6	....
Financial derivatives assets.............	4 900 ..	....	−.4	−.1	....	−.1	3.6	−1.6	....
Financial derivatives liabilities........	4 905 ..	....	....	....	....	....	....	....	....
Other investment assets................	4 703 ..	3.7	−130.9	−109.2	−209.3	−68.4	205.5	−370.7	....
Monetary authorities..................	4 701 ..	....	....	....	....	....	....	....	....
General government..................	4 704 ..	....	−.5	....	−3.7	.7	3.5	....	....
Banks....................................	4 705 ..	15.6	−22.9	.9	−85.9	−60.3	187.4	−141.8	....
Other sectors...........................	4 728 ..	−11.9	−107.5	−110.0	−119.7	−8.9	14.5	−228.9	....
Other investment liabilities............	4 753 W.	153.7	133.5	232.9	−1,771.9	279.1	326.7	554.3	....
Monetary authorities..................	4 753 WA	.3	.3	−.1	1.4	−2.4	15.7	104.8	....
General government..................	4 753 ZB	104.4	86.7	158.1	−1,745.5	182.2	158.1	333.1	....
Banks....................................	4 753 ZC	11.1	21.0	81.9	45.0	128.9	−23.2	185.0	....
Other sectors...........................	4 753 ZD	37.9	25.5	−7.0	−72.8	−29.5	176.1	−68.6	....
Total, Groups A Through C...........	4 983 ..	*131.4*	*−157.7*	*44.5*	*−1,988.2*	*−49.7*	*−117.5*	*621.5*	....
D. Net Errors and Omissions....................	4 998 ..	**45.2**	**−26.3**	**−29.0**	**−46.8**	**30.1**	**34.0**	**−175.2**	....
Total, Groups A Through D...........	4 984 ..	*176.5*	*−184.0*	*15.5*	*−2,035.0*	*−19.7*	*−83.4*	*446.3*	....
E. Reserves and Related Items...................	4 802 A.	**−176.5**	**184.0**	**−15.5**	**2,035.0**	**19.7**	**83.4**	**−446.3**	....
Reserve assets..............................	4 802 ..	−216.6	159.9	−122.7	−14.9	−4.6	−46.3	−481.5	....
Use of Fund credit and loans............	4 766 ..	−11.8	−30.1	−24.8	−102.8	4.1	28.6	3.1	....
Exceptional financing....................	4 920 ..	51.9	54.2	132.0	2,152.7	20.1	101.1	32.1	....
Conversion rates: CFA francs per U.S. dollar..........	0 101 ..	**581.20**	**528.28**	**527.47**	**522.89**	**479.27**	**447.81**	**472.19**	**495.28**

[1] Excludes components that have been classified in the categories of Group E.

Table 2. STANDARD PRESENTATION, 2003–2010

(Millions of U.S. dollars)

	Code	2003	2004	2005	2006	2007	2008	2009	2010
CURRENT ACCOUNT	4 993 ..	**−271.0**	**−409.0**	**−437.7**	**−218.6**	**−581.1**	**−1,066.4**	**−654.9**	....
A. GOODS	4 100 ..	**−60.5**	**−116.4**	**−144.6**	**75.0**	**−289.7**	**−638.7**	**−212.6**	....
Credit	2 100 ..	**927.8**	**976.4**	**1,100.9**	**1,550.4**	**1,556.3**	**2,097.2**	**1,773.7**	....
General merchandise: exports f.o.b.	2 110 ..	361.7	458.4	419.1	422.2	473.8	646.0	418.7	....
Goods for processing: exports f.o.b.	2 150 ..	....	....	....	....	....	....	....	....
Repairs on goods	2 160 ..	.2	....	....	....	.6	1.5	1.4	....
Goods procured in ports by carriers	2 170 ..	3.7	5.9	7.8	4.6	7.0	7.4	7.7	....
Nonmonetary gold	2 180 ..	562.3	512.2	674.0	1,123.5	1,074.9	1,442.3	1,345.9	....
Debit	3 100 ..	**−988.3**	**−1,092.9**	**−1,245.5**	**−1,475.4**	**−1,846.0**	**−2,735.9**	**−1,986.3**	....
General merchandise: imports f.o.b.	3 110 ..	−977.0	−1,088.9	−1,243.5	−1,473.2	−1,838.9	−2,727.6	−1,977.8	....
Goods for processing: imports f.o.b.	3 150 ..	....	....	....	....	....	....	....	....
Repairs on goods	3 160 ..	−3.1	−2.0	−1.9	−2.2	−1.5	−2.3	−4.0	....
Goods procured in ports by carriers	3 170 ..	−8.3	−2.0	....	....	−5.6	−6.0	−4.5	....
Nonmonetary gold	3 180 ..	....	....	....	....	....	....	....	....
B. SERVICES	4 200 ..	**−258.0**	**−290.7**	**−313.7**	**−361.2**	**−399.9**	**−570.0**	**−471.2**	....
Total credit	2 200 ..	*224.3*	*241.1*	*274.3*	*313.3*	*376.7*	*454.3*	*354.4*	....
Total debit	3 200 ..	*−482.2*	*−531.8*	*−588.0*	*−674.5*	*−776.6*	*−1,024.3*	*−825.6*	....
Transportation services, credit	2 205 ..	**42.7**	**30.6**	**35.1**	**39.1**	**25.9**	**32.5**	**19.6**	....
Passenger	2 850 ..	*7.9*	*2.3*	*1.2*	*.4*	*6.3*	*10.5*	*4.0*	....
Freight	2 851 ..	*30.8*	*25.2*	*25.3*	*32.4*	*14.5*	*16.8*	*10.6*	....
Other	2 852 ..	*3.9*	*3.1*	*8.6*	*6.3*	*5.1*	*5.1*	*5.0*	....
Sea transport, passenger	2 207 ..	....	....	....	....	....	....	....	....
Sea transport, freight	2 208 ..	....	....	....	....	....	....	....	....
Sea transport, other	2 209 ..	....	.1	2.3	.6	....	....	....	....
Air transport, passenger	2 211 ..	6.4	2.1	....	....	5.9	7.0	3.6	....
Air transport, freight	2 212 ..	....	....	....	....	1.3	1.4	....	....
Air transport, other	2 213 ..	3.9	3.0	6.3	5.7	5.1	5.1	5.0	....
Other transport, passenger	2 215 ..	1.5	.2	1.2	.4	.4	3.6	.5	....
Other transport, freight	2 216 ..	30.8	25.2	25.3	32.4	13.3	15.4	10.6	....
Other transport, other	2 217 ..	....	....	....	....	....	....	....	....
Transportation services, debit	3 205 ..	**−312.3**	**−342.8**	**−361.0**	**−405.4**	**−454.8**	**−644.6**	**−459.9**	....
Passenger	3 850 ..	*−46.4*	*−58.6*	*−56.4*	*−75.7*	*−63.6*	*−80.8*	*−88.9*	....
Freight	3 851 ..	*−263.2*	*−277.4*	*−297.2*	*−327.4*	*−387.8*	*−560.1*	*−367.0*	....
Other	3 852 ..	*−2.7*	*−6.8*	*−7.5*	*−2.3*	*−3.5*	*−3.7*	*−4.0*	....
Sea transport, passenger	3 207 ..	....	....	....	....	....	....	....	....
Sea transport, freight	3 208 ..	−144.7	−152.6	−163.5	−180.1	−224.8	−309.7	−201.9	....
Sea transport, other	3 209 ..	....	−2.2	−2.5	....	....	....	....	....
Air transport, passenger	3 211 ..	−46.4	−58.6	−56.4	−75.7	−63.6	−80.8	−88.9	....
Air transport, freight	3 212 ..	−19.7	−20.8	−22.3	−24.6	−30.6	−39.3	−27.5	....
Air transport, other	3 213 ..	−2.7	−1.9	−2.1	−2.3	−3.5	−3.7	−4.0	....
Other transport, passenger	3 215 ..	....	....	....	....	....	....	....	....
Other transport, freight	3 216 ..	−98.8	−104.0	−111.4	−122.8	−132.4	−211.1	−137.6	....
Other transport, other	3 217 ..	....	−2.7	−2.8	....	....	....	....	....
Travel, credit	2 236 ..	**127.9**	**140.4**	**148.4**	**175.0**	**221.0**	**274.9**	**191.6**	....
Business travel	2 237 ..	53.6	60.8	67.0	91.6	132.9	116.5	82.1	....
Personal travel	2 240 ..	74.3	79.6	81.4	83.5	88.1	158.4	109.5	....
Travel, debit	3 236 ..	**−47.6**	**−66.5**	**−76.9**	**−120.2**	**−137.2**	**−147.2**	**−101.6**	....
Business travel	3 237 ..	−27.7	−43.9	−53.5	−73.4	−82.9	−89.6	−57.7	....
Personal travel	3 240 ..	−19.9	−22.5	−23.4	−46.7	−54.3	−57.6	−43.9	....
Other services, credit	2 200 BA	**53.7**	**70.1**	**90.8**	**99.2**	**129.8**	**147.0**	**143.1**	....
Communications	2 245 ..	12.2	37.8	44.2	60.8	86.4	105.1	100.5	....
Construction	2 249 ..	5.9	2.3	2.0	3.4	1.4	2.3	5.0	....
Insurance	2 253 ..	1.2	1.7	3.2	4.3	1.6	.6	2.1	....
Financial	2 260 ..	2.0	3.6	4.2	2.7	3.1	1.8	4.9	....
Computer and information	2 262 ..	....	....	....	....	....	....	....	....
Royalties and licence fees	2 266 ..	....	.2	.2	.2	.1	.2	....	....
Other business services	2 268 ..	15.7	10.1	15.9	5.6	19.0	24.0	10.7	....
Personal, cultural, and recreational	2 287 ..	.2	....	.3	.3	.6	.3	.6	....
Government, n.i.e.	2 291 ..	16.5	14.4	20.8	21.9	17.5	12.6	19.4	....
Other services, debit	3 200 BA	**−122.4**	**−122.5**	**−150.1**	**−149.0**	**−184.5**	**−232.5**	**−264.0**	....
Communications	3 245 ..	−9.7	−12.9	−22.9	−24.1	−45.7	−54.8	−51.4	....
Construction	3 249 ..	−22.0	−15.6	−18.8	−16.4	−38.3	−45.2	−50.5	....
Insurance	3 253 ..	−19.1	−32.2	−35.5	−29.5	−28.8	−42.9	−36.0	....
Financial	3 260 ..	−8.1	−2.3	−4.2	−4.2	−4.8	−4.6	−12.2	....
Computer and information	3 262 ..	−2.1	−6.2	−8.3	−6.1	−4.0	−6.0	−6.0	....
Royalties and licence fees	3 266 ..	−.9	−.6	−1.1	−1.1	−1.0	−1.6	−2.6	....
Other business services	3 268 ..	−56.0	−36.2	−39.5	−49.4	−55.2	−72.7	−90.6	....
Personal, cultural, and recreational	3 287 ..	−.2	−12.9	−14.4	−15.3	−4.4	−2.3	−2.5	....
Government, n.i.e.	3 291 ..	−4.2	−3.6	−5.2	−2.8	−2.3	−2.4	−12.2	....

Table 2 (Continued). STANDARD PRESENTATION, 2003–2010

(Millions of U.S. dollars)

	Code	2003	2004	2005	2006	2007	2008	2009	2010
C. INCOME	4 300	**−159.9**	**−194.8**	**−206.9**	**−257.5**	**−291.4**	**−312.6**	**−457.4**	....
Total credit	2 300	*21.3*	*24.0*	*32.0*	*33.2*	*52.4*	*53.0*	*51.7*	....
Total debit	3 300	*−181.2*	*−218.8*	*−239.0*	*−290.7*	*−343.9*	*−365.6*	*−509.1*	....
Compensation of employees, credit	2 310	**14.9**	**17.4**	**23.9**	**19.1**	**20.8**	**24.8**	**29.9**	....
Compensation of employees, debit	3 310	**−9.7**	**−12.3**	**−18.5**	**−9.9**	**−13.5**	**−14.2**	**−27.6**	....
Investment income, credit	2 320	**6.4**	**6.6**	**8.1**	**14.1**	**31.6**	**28.2**	**21.9**	....
Direct investment income	2 330	.6	.1	.3	.1	....	.6	−.1	....
Dividends and distributed branch profits	2 332	.6	.1	.3	....	.1	.3	.2	....
Reinvested earnings and undistributed branch profits	2 333	....	....	....	....	−.1	.3	−.3	....
Income on debt (interest)	2 334	....	....	....	.1	....	....	....	....
Portfolio investment income	2 339	2.3	3.2	4.2	7.1	17.8	10.8	9.7	....
Income on equity	2 340	....	.1	.2	.2	.1	.2	.7	....
Income on bonds and notes	2 350	2.2	3.1	3.3	4.9	17.4	9.6	8.7	....
Income on money market instruments	2 360	.1	....	.7	1.9	.3	1.0	.2	....
Other investment income	2 370	3.4	3.2	3.7	6.9	13.8	16.8	12.3	....
Investment income, debit	3 320	**−171.6**	**−206.5**	**−220.5**	**−280.8**	**−330.4**	**−351.4**	**−481.5**	....
Direct investment income	3 330	−120.0	−152.0	−154.7	−215.0	−243.2	−277.6	−429.5	....
Dividends and distributed branch profits	3 332	−128.7	−60.2	−110.1	−182.7	−180.4	−179.9	−337.9	....
Reinvested earnings and undistributed branch profits	3 333	9.6	−93.9	−38.9	−23.4	−52.5	−89.5	−91.6	....
Income on debt (interest)	3 334	−1.0	2.1	−5.6	−8.9	−10.3	−8.2	....	....
Portfolio investment income	3 339	−19.6	−21.2	−16.7	−16.9	−43.2	−31.4	−11.8	....
Income on equity	3 340	−7.5	−5.7	−5.1	−3.0	−21.4	−1.8	−2.6	....
Income on bonds and notes	3 350	−12.0	−15.5	−11.6	−13.9	−21.8	−27.8	−8.5	....
Income on money market instruments	3 360	....	....	....	....	−.1	−1.9	−.7	....
Other investment income	3 370	−32.0	−33.3	−49.1	−48.8	−44.0	−42.3	−40.2	....
D. CURRENT TRANSFERS	4 379	**207.4**	**193.0**	**227.6**	**325.1**	**399.9**	**454.9**	**486.4**	....
Credit	2 379	**265.5**	**251.3**	**286.0**	**380.9**	**482.8**	**554.0**	**648.3**	....
General government	2 380	119.9	101.6	119.9	169.1	125.9	110.3	189.3	....
Other sectors	2 390	145.6	149.7	166.2	211.8	356.9	443.7	459.0	....
Workers' remittances	2 391	138.9	138.1	153.3	192.7	323.1	406.1	423.9	....
Other current transfers	2 392	6.7	11.6	12.9	19.0	33.8	37.6	35.2	....
Debit	3 379	**−58.1**	**−58.3**	**−58.5**	**−55.8**	**−82.9**	**−99.2**	**−162.0**	....
General government	3 380	−4.0	−4.4	−4.0	−4.4	−7.5	−4.2	−14.9	....
Other sectors	3 390	−54.1	−54.0	−54.4	−51.4	−75.4	−94.9	−147.1	....
Workers' remittances	3 391	−47.9	−51.6	−50.8	−47.2	−69.2	−90.6	−139.3	....
Other current transfers	3 392	−6.1	−2.4	−3.6	−4.1	−6.2	−4.4	−7.8	....
CAPITAL AND FINANCIAL ACCOUNT	4 996	**225.8**	**435.3**	**466.7**	**265.4**	**551.1**	**1,032.4**	**830.1**	....
CAPITAL ACCOUNT	4 994	**165.5**	**205.7**	**205.9**	**2,258.5**	**324.1**	**353.2**	**411.6**	....
Total credit	2 994	*165.6*	*205.7*	*206.5*	*2,259.1*	*324.8*	*354.0*	*412.4*	....
Total debit	3 994	....	....	*−.6*	*−.6*	*−.7*	*−.8*	*−.8*	....
Capital transfers, credit	2 400	**165.6**	**205.7**	**206.5**	**2,259.1**	**324.8**	**354.0**	**412.4**	....
General government	2 401	156.3	186.7	194.4	2,247.8	294.0	268.2	332.1	....
Debt forgiveness	2 402	51.9	54.2	57.0	2,117.9	22.3	24.4	27.6	....
Other capital transfers	2 410	104.4	132.5	137.4	129.9	271.7	243.9	304.5	....
Other sectors	2 430	9.3	19.0	12.0	11.3	30.8	85.8	80.3	....
Migrants' transfers	2 431	....	....	....	....	....	....	....	....
Debt forgiveness	2 432	....	....	....	....	....	....	....	....
Other capital transfers	2 440	9.3	19.0	12.0	11.3	30.8	85.8	80.3	....
Capital transfers, debit	3 400	....	....	....	....	....	....	....	....
General government	3 401	....	....	....	....	....	....	....	....
Debt forgiveness	3 402	....	....	....	....	....	....	....	....
Other capital transfers	3 410	....	....	....	....	....	....	....	....
Other sectors	3 430	....	....	....	....	....	....	....	....
Migrants' transfers	3 431	....	....	....	....	....	....	....	....
Debt forgiveness	3 432	....	....	....	....	....	....	....	....
Other capital transfers	3 440	....	....	....	....	....	....	....	....
Nonproduced nonfinancial assets, credit	2 480	....	....	....	....	....	....	....	....
Nonproduced nonfinancial assets, debit	3 480	....	....	**−.6**	**−.6**	**−.7**	**−.8**	**−.8**	....

Table 2 (Continued). STANDARD PRESENTATION, 2003–2010

(Millions of U.S. dollars)

	Code	2003	2004	2005	2006	2007	2008	2009	2010
FINANCIAL ACCOUNT............................	4 995 ..	60.3	229.7	260.9	−1,993.1	227.0	679.2	418.5	....
A. DIRECT INVESTMENT.....................	4 500 ..	130.8	100.2	224.7	82.1	65.5	179.7	749.4	....
Direct investment abroad...............	4 505 ..	−1.4	−.8	36.6	34.5	11.7	48.0	30.9	....
Equity capital................................	4 510 ..	−.4	−1.7	−1.5	−6.1	−1.8	−1.8	−5.3	....
Claims on affiliated enterprises..........	4 515 ..	....	....	....	1.0	.5	1.8	.5	....
Liabilities to affiliated enterprises.......	4 520 ..	−.4	−1.7	−1.5	−7.1	−2.3	−3.5	−5.7	....
Reinvested earnings........................	4 525 ..	....	....	....	....	.1	−.3	.3	....
Other capital................................	4 530 ..	−1.0	.9	38.1	40.6	13.4	50.0	35.8	....
Claims on affiliated enterprises.........	4 535 ..	−2.6	−1.5	.8	1.1	−3.3	−1.8	1.4	....
Liabilities to affiliated enterprises.......	4 540 ..	1.6	2.4	37.2	39.6	16.7	51.8	34.4	....
Direct investment in Mali...............	4 555 ..	132.3	101.0	188.1	47.6	53.8	131.7	718.5	....
Equity capital................................	4 560 ..	56.5	−2.1	46.0	49.3	6.6	12.3	285.7	....
Claims on direct investors...............	4 565 ..	64.8	24.2	85.8	86.4	137.3	128.4	674.1	....
Liabilities to direct investors...........	4 570 ..	−8.4	−26.3	−39.8	−37.1	−130.7	−116.1	−388.4	....
Reinvested earnings........................	4 575 ..	−9.6	93.9	38.9	23.4	52.5	89.5	91.6	....
Other capital................................	4 580 ..	85.4	9.2	103.2	−25.1	−5.4	29.8	341.1	....
Claims on direct investors...............	4 585 ..	−3.7	−7.3	−1.0	.6	....	−.2	.1	....
Liabilities to direct investors...........	4 590 ..	89.1	16.5	104.3	−25.7	−5.4	30.0	340.9	....
B. PORTFOLIO INVESTMENT...............	4 600 ..	.5	−2.6	−15.1	−11.1	−46.5	−95.3	−39.0	....
Assets...	4 602 ..	−27.1	−3.2	−18.0	−6.9	−31.0	−117.9	−60.3	....
Equity securities............................	4 610 ..	.2	−5.1	....	−.3	.1	−2.2	−6.3	....
Monetary authorities......................	4 611 ..	....	....	....	....	....	....	....	
General government.......................	4 612 ..	....	....	....	....	....	....	....	
Banks..	4 613 ..	....	....	....	−.3	....	−1.8	−6.0	
Other sectors..............................	4 614 ..	.2	−5.1	....	....	.1	−.4	−.3	
Debt securities..............................	4 619 ..	−27.2	1.9	−18.0	−6.6	−31.0	−115.7	−54.0	
Bonds and notes..........................	4 620 ..	−27.2	1.9	−17.7	−6.6	−31.0	−110.3	−18.2	
Monetary authorities....................	4 621 ..	....	....	....	....	....	....	....	
General government.....................	4 622 ..	....	....	....	−1.9	....	−24.6	5.0	
Banks......................................	4 623 ..	−12.5	−7.2	−16.2	−5.7	−31.1	−83.0	−30.5	
Other sectors............................	4 624 ..	−14.7	9.1	−1.5	1.1	.1	−2.7	7.3	
Money market instruments.............	4 630 ..	....	....	−.3	....	....	−5.4	−35.8	
Monetary authorities....................	4 631 ..	....	....	....	....	....	....	....	
General government.....................	4 632 ..	....	....	....	....	....	....	....	
Banks......................................	4 633 ..	.2	....	....	....	....	−3.0	−35.8	
Other sectors............................	4 634 ..	−.2	....	−.3	....	....	−2.4	....	
Liabilities.....................................	4 652 ..	27.6	.6	2.9	−4.2	−15.5	22.6	21.3	....
Equity securities............................	4 660 ..	.9	−.7	8.9	2.8	−6.4	−3.0	−3.0	
Banks..	4 663 ..	−.4	.5	4.7	3.1	1.5	−6.5	−2.5	
Other sectors..............................	4 664 ..	1.3	−1.2	4.2	−.4	−7.9	3.5	−.5	
Debt securities..............................	4 669 ..	26.7	1.3	−5.9	−6.9	−9.1	25.6	24.3	
Bonds and notes..........................	4 670 ..	26.7	1.3	−2.5	−6.9	−16.2	31.2	24.3	
Monetary authorities....................	4 671 ..	....	....	....	....	....	....	....	
General government.....................	4 672 ..	....	....	....	....	....	....	54.1	
Banks......................................	4 673 ..	....	1.2	−4.5	−4.9	−16.2	25.2	−26.0	
Other sectors............................	4 674 ..	26.7	.2	2.0	−2.0	....	6.0	−3.8	
Money market instruments.............	4 680 ..	....	....	−3.4	....	7.1	−5.6	....	
Monetary authorities....................	4 681 ..	....	....	....	....	....	....	....	
General government.....................	4 682 ..	....	....	....	....	....	....	....	
Banks......................................	4 683 ..	....	....	−3.4	....	7.1	−5.6	....	
Other sectors............................	4 684 ..	....	....	....	....	....	....	....	
C. FINANCIAL DERIVATIVES...............	4 910 ..	....	−.4	−.1	....	−.1	3.6	−1.6	....
Monetary authorities......................	4 911 ..	....	....	....	....	....	....	....	
General government.......................	4 912 ..	....	....	....	....	....	....	....	
Banks..	4 913 ..	....	−.1	....	....	....	....	−1.5	
Other sectors..............................	4 914 ..	....	−.3	−.1	....	−.1	3.6	−.1	
Assets...	4 900 ..	....	−.4	−.1	....	−.1	3.6	−1.6	....
Monetary authorities......................	4 901 ..	....	....	....	....	....	....	....	
General government.......................	4 902 ..	....	....	....	....	....	....	....	
Banks..	4 903 ..	....	−.1	....	....	....	....	−1.5	
Other sectors..............................	4 904 ..	....	−.3	−.1	....	−.1	3.6	−.1	
Liabilities.....................................	4 905 ..	....	....	....	....	....	....	....	....
Monetary authorities......................	4 906 ..	....	....	....	....	....	....	....	
General government.......................	4 907 ..	....	....	....	....	....	....	....	
Banks..	4 908 ..	....	....	....	....	....	....	....	
Other sectors..............................	4 909 ..	....	....	....	....	....	....	....	

Table 2 (Concluded). STANDARD PRESENTATION, 2003–2010

(Millions of U.S. dollars)

	Code	2003	2004	2005	2006	2007	2008	2009	2010
D. OTHER INVESTMENT	4 700	**145.5**	**−27.4**	**174.0**	**−2,049.3**	**212.6**	**637.6**	**191.2**	....
Assets	4 703	3.7	−130.9	−109.2	−209.3	−68.4	205.5	−370.7	....
Trade credits	4 706	−4.8	−55.3	−4.2	3.3	−2.9	−1.5	−27.7	....
General government	4 707	....	....	....	....	....	....	....	....
of which: Short-term	4 709	....	....	....	....	....	....	....	....
Other sectors	4 710	−4.8	−55.3	−4.2	3.3	−2.9	−1.5	−27.7	....
of which: Short-term	4 712	*−4.8*	*−55.3*	*−4.2*	*3.3*	*−2.9*	*−1.5*	*−27.7*	
Loans	4 714	−22.9	−4.9	6.0	−19.1	−16.1	40.6	−25.1	....
Monetary authorities	4 715	....	....	....	....	....	....	....	
of which: Short-term	4 718	....	....	....	....	....	....	....	
General government	4 719	....	....	....	....	....	....	....	
of which: Short-term	4 721	....	....	....	....	....	....	....	
Banks	4 722	−22.9	−4.8	6.1	−19.1	−16.1	40.6	−21.2	
of which: Short-term	4 724	*−13.1*	*.6*	*.6*	*−2.1*	*6.2*	*21.4*	*−13.4*	
Other sectors	4 725	....	....	−.1	....	....	....	−3.9	
of which: Short-term	4 727	....	....	−.1	....	....	....	−3.9	
Currency and deposits	4 730	34.1	−72.9	−84.0	−148.3	−16.9	102.1	−118.2	
Monetary authorities	4 731	....	....	....	....	....	....	....	
General government	4 732	....	....	....	....	....	....	....	
Banks	4 733	34.5	−21.6	−2.1	−57.0	−9.6	96.8	−27.2	
Other sectors	4 734	−.5	−51.3	−81.9	−91.4	−7.3	5.3	−91.0	
Other assets	4 736	−2.7	2.2	−26.9	−45.2	−32.6	64.3	−199.7	
Monetary authorities	4 737	....	....	....	....	....	....	....	
of which: Short-term	4 739	....	....	....	....	....	....	....	
General government	4 740	....	−.5	....	−3.7	.7	3.5	....	
of which: Short-term	4 742	....	−.5	....	−3.7	.7	3.5	....	
Banks	4 743	3.9	3.6	−3.1	−9.9	−34.6	50.0	−93.5	
of which: Short-term	4 745	*4.1*	*3.6*	*−3.1*	*−9.9*	*−34.6*	*50.0*	*−93.5*	
Other sectors	4 746	−6.7	−.8	−23.8	−31.7	1.3	10.7	−106.3	
of which: Short-term	4 748	*−6.7*	*−.8*	*−23.8*	*−31.7*	*1.3*	*10.7*	*−106.3*	....
Liabilities	4 753	**141.8**	**103.4**	**283.1**	**−1,840.0**	**281.1**	**432.1**	**561.9**	....
Trade credits	4 756	10.6	−1.8	15.4	2.2	7.6	188.2	39.6	
General government	4 757	....	....	....	....	....	....	....	
of which: Short-term	4 759	....	....	....	....	....	....	....	
Other sectors	4 760	10.6	−1.8	15.4	2.2	7.6	188.2	39.6	
of which: Short-term	4 762	*10.6*	*−1.8*	*15.4*	*2.2*	*7.6*	*188.2*	*39.6*	
Loans	4 764	113.0	100.5	213.5	−1,832.6	147.5	240.5	261.9	
Monetary authorities	4 765	−11.8	−30.1	−24.8	−102.8	4.1	28.6	3.1	
of which: Use of Fund credit and loans from the Fund	4 766	*−11.8*	*−30.1*	*−24.8*	*−102.8*	*4.1*	*28.6*	*3.1*	
of which: Short-term	4 768	....	....	....	....	....	....	....	
General government	4 769	104.4	86.7	158.1	−1,745.5	182.2	230.8	333.1	
of which: Short-term	4 771	....	....	....	....	....	72.7	....	
Banks	4 772	3.2	17.9	9.9	13.2	2.7	−13.6	1.5	
of which: Short-term	4 774	*1.5*	*8.4*	*−2.5*	*2.0*	*−7.9*	*.4*	....	
Other sectors	4 775	17.2	26.0	70.3	2.4	−41.4	−5.2	−75.8	
of which: Short-term	4 777	....	....	....	....	−29.9	3.7	−70.2	
Currency and deposits	4 780	13.0	−10.1	76.6	32.4	32.7	−150.5	23.6	
Monetary authorities	4 781	1.3	−3.7	4.2	−1.2	−.8	−3.2	5.9	
General government	4 782	....	....	....	....	....	....	....	
Banks	4 783	11.8	−6.4	72.5	33.6	33.6	−147.3	17.7	
Other sectors	4 784	....	....	....	....	....	....	....	
Other liabilities	4 786	5.3	14.8	−22.5	−42.0	93.2	153.9	236.8	
Monetary authorities	4 787	−1.0	4.0	−4.3	2.6	−1.6	18.9	98.9	
of which: Short-term	4 789	....	*4.0*	*−4.3*	*2.6*	*−1.6*	*18.9*	*−15.8*	
General government	4 790	....	....	....	....	....	....	....	
of which: Short-term	4 792	....	....	....	....	....	....	....	
Banks	4 793	−3.9	9.4	−.5	−1.9	84.8	138.1	165.8	
of which: Short-term	4 795	*−3.9*	*9.4*	*−.5*	*−1.9*	*84.8*	*138.1*	*165.8*	
Other sectors	4 796	10.1	1.3	−17.7	−42.7	10.0	−3.1	−27.9	
of which: Short-term	4 798	*10.1*	*1.3*	*−17.7*	*−42.7*	*10.0*	*−3.1*	*−27.9*	....
E. RESERVE ASSETS	4 802	**−216.6**	**159.9**	**−122.7**	**−14.9**	**−4.6**	**−46.3**	**−481.5**	....
Monetary gold	4 812	....	....	....	....	....	....	....	
Special drawing rights	4 811	−.8	.3	.3	.2	....	....	−114.5	
Reserve position in the Fund	4 810	−.1	−.1	−.2	−.3	−.4	−.2	−.3	
Foreign exchange	4 803	−215.7	159.7	−122.7	−14.9	−4.2	−46.1	−366.7	
Other claims	4 813	....	....	....	....	....	....	....	....
NET ERRORS AND OMISSIONS	4 998	**45.2**	**−26.3**	**−29.0**	**−46.8**	**30.1**	**34.0**	**−175.2**	....

Table 3. INTERNATIONAL INVESTMENT POSITION (End-period stocks), 2003–2010

(Millions of U.S. dollars)

	Code	2003	2004	2005	2006	2007	2008	2009	2010
ASSETS	8 995 C.	**1,358.3**	**1,409.7**	**1,347.7**	**1,592.3**	**1,728.7**	**1,673.0**	**2,364.6**	....
Direct investment abroad	8 505 ..	**6.6**	**10.2**	**7.9**	**3.8**	**12.1**	**11.0**	**10.6**	....
Equity capital and reinvested earnings	8 506 ..	5.2	7.5	6.6	7.5	10.3	11.4	17.3	....
Claims on affiliated enterprises	8 507 ..	5.2	7.5	6.6	7.5	10.3	11.4	17.3	....
Liabilities to affiliated enterprises	8 508 ..	....	....	....	....	....	....	....	....
Other capital	8 530 ..	1.4	2.7	1.3	−3.7	1.9	−.4	−6.7	....
Claims on affiliated enterprises	8 535 ..	1.4	2.7	1.3	....	1.9	−.4	−6.7	....
Liabilities to affiliated enterprises	8 540 ..	....	....	....	−3.7	....	....	....	....
Portfolio investment	8 602 ..	**98.3**	**96.8**	**65.7**	**120.7**	**76.4**	**221.1**	**285.5**	....
Equity securities	8 610 ..	1.1	6.4	6.8	3.3	1.1	1.3	2.8	....
Monetary authorities	8 611 ..	....	....	....	....	....	....	....	....
General government	8 612 ..	....	....	....	....	....	....	....	....
Banks	8 613 ..	.4	....	6.6	3.2	1.0	.8	2.0	....
Other sectors	8 614 ..	.7	6.4	.1	.2	.1	.4	.8	....
Debt securities	8 619 ..	97.2	90.4	59.0	117.3	75.3	219.8	282.6	....
Bonds and notes	8 620 ..	95.9	90.1	58.7	104.4	75.3	172.0	213.3	....
Monetary authorities	8 621 ..	....	....	....	....	....	....	....	....
General government	8 622 ..	....	....	....	....	....	....	....	....
Banks	8 623 ..	57.4	58.6	56.3	100.2	70.7	154.1	205.8	....
Other sectors	8 624 ..	38.5	31.5	2.4	4.3	4.6	17.9	7.5	....
Money market instruments	8 630 ..	1.2	.3	.3	12.9	....	47.9	69.3	....
Monetary authorities	8 631 ..	....	....	....	....	....	....	....	....
General government	8 632 ..	....	....	....	....	....	....	....	....
Banks	8 633 ..	1.0	.3	....	12.5	....	45.6	67.0	....
Other sectors	8 634 ..	.3	....	.3	.3	....	2.3	2.3	....
Financial derivatives	8 900 ..	**.1**	**.5**	**.4**	**.4**	**.5**	**.3**	**.3**	....
Monetary authorities	8 901 ..	....	....	....	....	....	....	....	....
General government	8 902 ..	....	....	....	....	....	....	....	....
Banks	8 903 ..	....	....	.3	....	....	....	....	....
Other sectors	8 904 ..	.1	.5	.2	.4	.5	.3	.3	....
Other investment	8 703 ..	**300.8**	**450.9**	**419.2**	**498.7**	**552.8**	**368.7**	**463.3**	....
Trade credits	8 706 ..	33.3	87.1	52.4	58.0	64.4	57.5	88.1	....
General government	8 707 ..	....	....	....	....	....	....	....	....
of which: Short-term	8 709 ..	....	....	....	....	....	....	....	....
Other sectors	8 710 ..	33.3	87.1	52.4	58.0	64.4	57.5	88.1	....
of which: Short-term	8 712 ..	....	....	....	....	....	....	....	....
Loans	8 714 ..	59.0	68.9	54.0	80.2	106.9	62.5	26.0	....
Monetary authorities	8 715 ..	....	....	....	....	....	....	....	....
of which: Short-term	8 718 ..	....	....	....	....	....	....	....	....
General government	8 719 ..	....	....	....	....	....	....	....	....
of which: Short-term	8 721 ..	....	....	....	....	....	....	....	....
Banks	8 722 ..	58.9	68.9	53.9	80.2	106.9	62.5	22.0	....
of which: Short-term	8 724 ..	*46.1*	*49.1*	*41.9*	*49.1*	*48.2*	*25.2*	*13.9*	....
Other sectors	8 725 ..	....	....	.1	....	....	....	4.1	....
of which: Short-term	8 727 ..	....	....	....	....	....	....	....	....
Currency and deposits	8 730 ..	183.9	272.4	292.8	301.5	290.3	228.5	155.8	....
Monetary authorities	8 731 ..	....	....	....	....	....	....	....	....
General government	8 732 ..	....	....	....	....	....	....	....	....
Banks	8 733 ..	140.8	175.5	146.5	223.4	260.0	153.8	28.2	....
Other sectors	8 734 ..	43.1	96.8	146.3	78.2	30.3	74.6	127.6	....
Other assets	8 736 ..	24.7	22.6	20.0	59.1	91.2	20.3	193.4	....
Monetary authorities	8 737 ..	....	....	....	....	....	....	....	....
of which: Short-term	8 739 ..	....	....	....	....	....	....	....	....
General government	8 740 ..	....	.6	....	3.9	3.5	....	....	....
of which: Short-term	8 742 ..	....	....	....	....	....	....	....	....
Banks	8 743 ..	−6.5	−11.0	−6.6	3.0	40.6	−9.2	96.9	....
of which: Short-term	8 745 ..	*−6.6*	*−11.0*	*−6.6*	*3.0*	*40.6*	*−9.2*	*96.9*	....
Other sectors	8 746 ..	31.2	33.0	26.6	52.3	47.1	29.4	96.5	....
of which: Short-term	8 748 ..	....	....	....	....	....	....	....	....
Reserve assets	8 802 ..	**952.5**	**851.3**	**854.5**	**968.8**	**1,086.8**	**1,071.9**	**1,604.9**	....
Monetary gold	8 812 ..	....	....	....	....	....	....	....	....
Special drawing rights	8 811 ..	.9	.6	.3	.1	.1	.1	115.0	113.1
Reserve position in the Fund	8 810 ..	13.2	13.9	13.1	14.1	15.1	14.9	15.5	15.4
Foreign exchange	8 803 ..	938.4	836.8	841.2	954.7	1,071.6	1,056.9	1,474.3	....
Other claims	8 813 ..	....	....	....	....	....	....	....	....

Table 3 (Concluded). INTERNATIONAL INVESTMENT POSITION (End-period stocks), 2003–2010

(Millions of U.S. dollars)

	Code	2003	2004	2005	2006	2007	2008	2009	2010
LIABILITIES	8 995 D.	**4,459.1**	**4,956.7**	**4,440.8**	**2,887.5**	**3,203.4**	**3,427.7**	**4,300.6**	....
Direct investment in Mali	8 555	**682.6**	**756.4**	**871.6**	**965.6**	**966.7**	**977.6**	**1,882.8**	....
Equity capital and reinvested earnings	8 556	551.4	682.9	654.6	680.5	655.1	608.6	574.1	....
Claims on direct investors	8 557	....	....	....	....	....	....	....	
Liabilities to direct investors	8 558	....	....	....	....	....	....	....	
Other capital	8 580	131.2	73.5	217.0	285.1	311.6	369.1	1,308.7	....
Claims on direct investors	8 585	....	....	....	....	....	....	....	
Liabilities to direct investors	8 590	....	....	....	....	....	....	....	
Portfolio investment	8 652	**46.9**	**16.4**	**33.5**	**38.1**	**72.1**	**80.6**	**92.1**	....
Equity securities	8 660	17.1	16.2	22.4	28.7	24.1	19.8	17.4	
Banks	8 663	1.7	1.7	6.5	10.6	13.2	6.2	3.8	
Other sectors	8 664	15.4	14.5	15.9	18.1	10.9	13.6	13.5	
Debt securities	8 669	29.8	.2	11.0	9.4	48.0	60.8	74.7	
Bonds and notes	8 670	29.8	.2	11.0	9.4	6.9	40.5	59.4	
Monetary authorities	8 671	....	....	....	....	....	....	....	
General government	8 672	....	....	....	....	....	....	56.1	
Banks	8 673	....	....	9.1	9.4	6.9	34.8	1.3	
Other sectors	8 674	29.8	.2	1.9	....	....	5.7	2.0	
Money market instruments	8 680	....	....	....	....	41.1	20.3	15.3	
Monetary authorities	8 681	....	....	....	....	....	....	....	
General government	8 682	....	....	....	....	....	....	....	
Banks	8 683	....	....	....	....	41.1	17.1	15.3	
Other sectors	8 684	....	....	....	....	....	3.2	....	
Financial derivatives	8 905	....	....	....	....	....	**3.2**	**3.3**	....
Monetary authorities	8 906	....	....	....	....	....	....	....	
General government	8 907	....	....	....	....	....	....	....	
Banks	8 908	....	....	....	....	....	....	....	
Other sectors	8 909	....	....	....	....	....	3.2	3.3	
Other investment	8 753	**3,729.5**	**4,183.9**	**3,535.7**	**1,883.8**	**2,164.6**	**2,366.2**	**2,322.4**	....
Trade credits	8 756	67.5	62.0	58.3	97.9	84.0	117.3	171.1	....
General government	8 757	....	....	....	....	....	....	....	
of which: Short-term	8 759	....	....	....	....	....	....	....	
Other sectors	8 760	67.5	62.0	58.3	97.9	84.0	117.3	171.1	
of which: Short-term	8 762	....	....	....	....	....	....	....	
Loans	8 764	3,457.6	3,920.5	3,259.7	1,486.6	1,715.8	2,031.8	1,958.3	....
Monetary authorities	8 765	168.8	144.8	109.2	8.0	12.6	40.0	43.9	
of which: Use of Fund credit and loans from the Fund	8 766	*168.8*	*144.8*	*109.2*	*8.0*	*12.6*	*40.0*	*43.9*	*49.1*
of which: Short-term	8 768	....	....	....	....	....	....	....	
General government	8 769	3,170.3	3,612.8	3,011.5	1,262.9	1,507.4	1,799.1	1,897.6	
of which: Short-term	8 771	....	....	....	....	....	....	....	
Banks	8 772	40.1	63.0	63.9	85.2	98.1	79.8	1.5	
of which: Short-term	8 774	*15.5*	*25.9*	*20.0*	*24.5*	*18.8*	*18.2*	....	
Other sectors	8 775	78.4	99.9	75.1	130.5	97.6	112.9	15.3	
of which: Short-term	8 777	....	....	....	....	....	....	....	
Currency and deposits	8 780	174.5	163.4	231.7	276.9	341.7	179.9	31.6	
Monetary authorities	8 781	7.4	4.0	7.4	8.4	7.5	4.0	10.9	
General government	8 782	....	....	....	....	....	....	....	
Banks	8 783	167.1	159.5	224.3	268.5	334.2	175.9	20.7	
Other sectors	8 784	....	....	....	....	....	....	....	
Other liabilities	8 786	29.9	38.0	−14.1	22.4	23.1	37.1	161.4	
Monetary authorities	8 787	.3	4.7	....	2.7	1.3	19.2	143.6	
of which: Short-term	8 789	*.3*	*4.7*		*2.7*	*1.3*	*19.2*	*3.5*	
General government	8 790	....	....	....	....	....	....	....	
of which: Short-term	8 792	....	....	....	....	....	....	....	
Banks	8 793	....	....	....	....	....	....	....	
of which: Short-term	8 795	....	....	....	....	....	....	....	
Other sectors	8 796	29.6	33.3	−14.0	19.6	21.8	17.9	17.7	
of which: Short-term	8 798	....	....	....	....	....	....	....	
NET INTERNATIONAL INVESTMENT POSITION	8 995	−3,100.8	−3,547.0	−3,093.1	−1,295.2	−1,474.8	−1,754.7	−1,936.0	....
Conversion rates: CFA francs per U.S. dollar (end of period)	0 102	519.36	481.58	556.04	498.07	445.59	471.34	455.34	490.91

Table 1. ANALYTIC PRESENTATION, 2003–2010

(Millions of U.S. dollars)

	Code	2003	2004	2005	2006	2007	2008	2009	2010
A. Current Account[1]	4 993 Z.	**−156.3**	**−337.6**	**−523.5**	**−617.8**	**−605.6**	**−663.1**	**−599.9**	**−415.3**
Goods: exports f.o.b.	2 100 ..	2,591.8	2,719.9	2,586.9	2,937.7	3,304.5	3,188.9	2,426.7	3,088.0
Goods: imports f.o.b.	3 100 ..	−3,232.0	−3,583.3	−3,709.4	−4,146.5	−4,655.7	−5,038.1	−3,797.1	−4,317.3
Balance on Goods	4 100 ..	*−640.2*	*−863.4*	*−1,122.5*	*−1,208.9*	*−1,351.1*	*−1,849.3*	*−1,370.4*	*−1,229.3*
Services: credit	2 200 ..	1,452.0	1,689.2	2,006.6	2,585.3	3,411.7	4,198.2	3,887.1	3,940.0
Services: debit	3 200 ..	−894.3	−1,051.5	−1,204.0	−1,769.3	−2,358.5	−2,664.5	−2,612.7	−2,577.2
Balance on Goods and Services	4 991 ..	*−82.6*	*−225.7*	*−320.0*	*−392.9*	*−297.9*	*−315.5*	*−96.0*	*133.5*
Income: credit	2 300 ..	905.3	971.3	1,207.8	1,839.8	2,710.9	3,249.2	2,288.2	2,180.2
Income: debit	3 300 ..	−934.4	−1,025.1	−1,454.9	−2,053.2	−2,981.9	−3,586.1	−2,856.0	−2,766.4
Balance on Goods, Services, and Income	4 992 ..	*−111.7*	*−279.5*	*−567.1*	*−606.3*	*−569.0*	*−652.5*	*−663.8*	*−452.8*
Current transfers: credit	2 379 Z.	203.4	221.6	343.4	523.5	882.2	1,358.1	1,982.7	1,718.2
Current transfers: debit	3 379 ..	−247.9	−279.7	−299.9	−535.0	−918.8	−1,368.7	−1,918.8	−1,680.7
B. Capital Account[1]	4 994 Z.	**17.2**	**83.6**	**193.2**	**193.1**	**95.4**	**41.3**	**109.7**	**106.3**
Capital account: credit	2 994 Z.	18.6	87.3	205.5	200.1	104.7	50.8	120.5	119.0
Capital account: debit	3 994 ..	−1.4	−3.8	−12.3	−7.0	−9.4	−9.5	−10.8	−12.6
Total, Groups A Plus B	4 981 ..	*−139.1*	*−254.0*	*−330.3*	*−424.7*	*−510.2*	*−621.8*	*−490.2*	*−309.0*
C. Financial Account[1]	4 995 W.	**259.2**	**−36.7**	**610.7**	**492.5**	**878.3**	**136.1**	**223.1**	**−92.7**
Direct investment abroad	4 505 ..	−575.2	−7.3	24.3	−30.0	−15.9	−309.6	−134.2	−86.2
Direct investment in Malta	4 555 Z.	1,007.0	395.2	678.7	1,841.4	996.2	833.5	753.4	998.6
Portfolio investment assets	4 602 ..	−1,571.0	−2,094.1	−2,608.1	−2,454.1	535.0	−267.2	−2,754.2	−4,248.1
Equity securities	4 610 ..	−11.6	−51.4	−98.4	−72.0	−116.7	−174.9	−5.3	−60.3
Debt securities	4 619 ..	−1,559.5	−2,042.7	−2,509.7	−2,382.2	651.8	−92.3	−2,748.9	−4,187.9
Portfolio investment liabilities	4 652 Z.	−20.2	4.5	36.1	−18.5	.4	254.1	−43.7	1.0
Equity securities	4 660 ..	−13.5	7.6	35.5	−9.1	−.1	13.3	−6.7	23.1
Debt securities	4 669 Z.	−6.7	−3.1	.6	−9.4	.4	240.8	−37.0	−22.1
Financial derivatives	4 910 ..	25.1	−18.2	−23.9	30.3	167.4	−452.5	−88.6	31.1
Financial derivatives assets	4 900 ..	−5.0	−17.6	−19.2	51.3	−196.1	15.0	−3.2	−62.5
Financial derivatives liabilities	4 905 ..	30.0	−.5	−4.7	−21.0	363.5	−467.6	−85.4	93.5
Other investment assets	4 703 ..	−68.7	−1,277.8	−2,805.2	−4,075.7	−10,313.0	−6,966.6	5,237.1	623.2
Monetary authorities	4 701 ..	....	−.1	6.9	....	....	1,479.3	243.5	3.0
General government	4 704 ..	....	−.4	.3	−.3	5.0	5.5	−15.2	−34.3
Banks	4 705 ..	−92.8	−1,168.2	−2,743.2	−3,940.7	−10,235.5	−7,993.7	5,152.0	662.9
Other sectors	4 728 ..	24.1	−109.1	−69.2	−134.8	−82.6	−457.7	−143.2	−8.4
Other investment liabilities	4 753 W.	1,462.2	2,961.0	5,308.8	5,199.2	9,508.2	7,044.4	−2,746.7	2,587.8
Monetary authorities	4 753 WA	51.3	−71.1	18.6	9.9	7.7	1,031.1	449.8	527.8
General government	4 753 ZB	43.0	−4.7	−26.7	−34.7	−19.6	−14.7	12.5	−8.4
Banks	4 753 ZC	1,278.0	2,993.2	5,037.1	5,203.0	9,178.0	5,709.0	−3,328.5	1,715.8
Other sectors	4 753 ZD	89.8	43.5	279.9	21.0	342.1	319.1	119.5	352.6
Total, Groups A Through C	4 983 ..	*120.1*	*−290.7*	*280.4*	*67.8*	*368.1*	*−485.7*	*−267.1*	*−401.7*
D. Net Errors and Omissions	4 998 ..	**23.8**	**83.4**	**−63.6**	**43.5**	**127.3**	**293.8**	**397.2**	**432.0**
Total, Groups A Through D	4 984 ..	*144.0*	*−207.3*	*216.8*	*111.3*	*495.4*	*−191.9*	*130.1*	*30.3*
E. Reserves and Related Items	4 802 A.	**−144.0**	**207.3**	**−216.8**	**−111.3**	**−495.4**	**191.9**	**−130.1**	**−30.3**
Reserve assets	4 802 ..	−144.0	207.3	−216.8	−111.3	−495.4	191.9	−130.1	−30.3
Use of Fund credit and loans	4 766 ..	....	....	....	....	....	....	....	....
Exceptional financing	4 920 ..	....	....	....	....	....	....	....	....
Conversion rates: Maltese liri per U.S. dollar	0 101 ..	**.3772**	**.3447**	**.3458**	**.3409**	**.3117**	**....**	**....**	**....**
Conversion rates: euros per U.S. dollar	0 103 ..	**.8860**	**.8054**	**.8041**	**.7971**	**.7306**	**.6827**	**.7198**	**.7550**

[1] Excludes components that have been classified in the categories of Group E.

Table 2. STANDARD PRESENTATION, 2003–2010

(Millions of U.S. dollars)

	Code	2003	2004	2005	2006	2007	2008	2009	2010
CURRENT ACCOUNT...............................	4 993 ..	**−156.3**	**−337.6**	**−523.5**	**−617.8**	**−605.6**	**−663.1**	**−599.9**	**−415.3**
A. GOODS................................	4 100 ..	**−640.2**	**−863.4**	**−1,122.5**	**−1,208.9**	**−1,351.1**	**−1,849.3**	**−1,370.4**	**−1,229.3**
Credit..................................	2 100 ..	**2,591.8**	**2,719.9**	**2,586.9**	**2,937.7**	**3,304.5**	**3,188.9**	**2,426.7**	**3,088.0**
General merchandise: exports f.o.b..............	2 110 ..	2,435.7	2,565.8	2,420.2	2,777.7	3,116.1	2,961.9	2,270.6	2,746.0
Goods for processing: exports f.o.b.............	2 150 ..	....	....	....	....	....	....	....	....
Repairs on goods................................	2 160 ..	....	49.0	118.0	110.7	127.3	140.0	108.0	141.7
Goods procured in ports by carriers...........	2 170 ..	156.1	104.2	48.2	47.0	58.9	82.8	46.3	189.1
Nonmonetary gold...............................	2 180 ..	....	.9	.4	2.2	2.3	4.2	1.8	11.3
Debit...................................	3 100 ..	**−3,232.0**	**−3,583.3**	**−3,709.4**	**−4,146.5**	**−4,655.7**	**−5,038.1**	**−3,797.1**	**−4,317.3**
General merchandise: imports f.o.b..............	3 110 ..	−3,171.3	−3,526.4	−3,636.4	−4,051.7	−4,527.9	−4,899.8	−3,727.9	−4,218.4
Goods for processing: imports f.o.b.............	3 150 ..	....	....	....	....	....	....	....	....
Repairs on goods................................	3 160 ..	−23.3	−10.7	−12.8	−10.6	−8.3	−7.1	−6.1	−7.0
Goods procured in ports by carriers...........	3 170 ..	−14.2	−26.1	−38.6	−51.4	−82.9	−93.6	−34.9	−39.8
Nonmonetary gold...............................	3 180 ..	−23.2	−20.0	−21.7	−32.8	−36.5	−37.6	−28.2	−52.1
B. SERVICES...............................	4 200 ..	**557.6**	**637.7**	**802.5**	**816.0**	**1,053.2**	**1,533.7**	**1,274.4**	**1,362.8**
Total credit................................	2 200 ..	*1,452.0*	*1,689.2*	*2,006.6*	*2,585.3*	*3,411.7*	*4,198.2*	*3,887.1*	*3,940.0*
Total debit.................................	3 200 ..	*−894.3*	*−1,051.5*	*−1,204.0*	*−1,769.3*	*−2,358.5*	*−2,664.5*	*−2,612.7*	*−2,577.2*
Transportation services, credit............	2 205 ..	**329.0**	**350.3**	**312.0**	**391.8**	**423.5**	**515.0**	**431.7**	**390.3**
Passenger..................................	2 850 ..	*146.9*	*182.1*	*168.8*	*198.8*	*229.4*	*254.7*	*197.4*	*187.1*
Freight....................................	2 851 ..	*24.2*	*14.9*	*12.0*	*16.0*	*14.6*	*17.1*	*10.3*	*7.4*
Other......................................	2 852 ..	*157.9*	*153.3*	*131.2*	*177.0*	*179.5*	*243.2*	*224.0*	*195.8*
Sea transport, passenger......................	2 207 ..	....	....	....	....	....	....	....	....
Sea transport, freight.........................	2 208 ..	....	....	....	....	....	....	....	....
Sea transport, other..........................	2 209 ..	....	....	....	....	....	....	....	....
Air transport, passenger......................	2 211 ..	146.9	182.1	168.8	198.8	229.4	254.7	197.4	187.1
Air transport, freight.........................	2 212 ..	24.2	14.9	12.0	16.0	14.6	17.1	10.3	7.4
Air transport, other..........................	2 213 ..	157.9	153.3	131.2	177.0	179.5	243.2	224.0	195.8
Other transport, passenger...................	2 215 ..	....	....	....	....	....	....	....	....
Other transport, freight......................	2 216 ..	....	....	....	....	....	....	....	....
Other transport, other........................	2 217 ..	....	....	....	....	....	....	....	....
Transportation services, debit.............	3 205 ..	**−353.7**	**−272.3**	**−232.0**	**−291.5**	**−306.3**	**−311.3**	**−273.3**	**−362.9**
Passenger..................................	3 850 ..	*−23.0*	*−35.7*	*−42.9*	*−42.3*	*−43.3*	*−48.3*	*−68.4*	*−90.0*
Freight....................................	3 851 ..	*−210.1*	*−156.2*	*−144.7*	*−162.8*	*−210.1*	*−233.7*	*−182.3*	*−245.9*
Other......................................	3 852 ..	*−120.7*	*−80.3*	*−44.4*	*−86.4*	*−52.8*	*−29.4*	*−22.6*	*−27.0*
Sea transport, passenger......................	3 207 ..	....	....	....	....	....	....	....	....
Sea transport, freight.........................	3 208 ..	....	....	....	....	....	....	....	....
Sea transport, other..........................	3 209 ..	....	....	....	....	....	....	....	....
Air transport, passenger......................	3 211 ..	−23.0	−35.7	−42.9	−42.3	−43.3	−48.3	−68.4	−90.0
Air transport, freight.........................	3 212 ..	−210.1	−156.2	−144.7	−162.8	−210.1	−233.7	−182.3	−245.9
Air transport, other..........................	3 213 ..	−120.7	−80.3	−44.4	−86.4	−52.8	−29.4	−22.6	−27.0
Other transport, passenger...................	3 215 ..	....	....	....	....	....	....	....	....
Other transport, freight......................	3 216 ..	....	....	....	....	....	....	....	....
Other transport, other........................	3 217 ..	....	....	....	....	....	....	....	....
Travel, credit.............................	2 236 ..	**722.1**	**766.6**	**754.9**	**767.0**	**965.0**	**1,077.0**	**896.3**	**1,065.8**
Business travel................................	2 237 ..	722.1	766.6	754.9	767.0	965.0	1,077.0	896.3	1,065.8
Personal travel................................	2 240 ..	....	....	....	....	....	....	....	....
Travel, debit..............................	3 236 ..	**−215.1**	**−255.5**	**−268.0**	**−319.7**	**−375.5**	**−444.8**	**−436.3**	**−464.4**
Business travel................................	3 237 ..	−215.1	−255.5	−268.0	−319.7	−375.5	−444.8	−436.3	−464.4
Personal travel................................	3 240 ..	....	....	....	....	....	....	....	....
Other services, credit....................	2 200 BA	**400.8**	**572.3**	**939.6**	**1,426.5**	**2,023.3**	**2,606.2**	**2,559.1**	**2,483.9**
Communications...............................	2 245 ..	31.8	48.5	61.8	56.4	77.3	59.4	46.8	45.9
Construction..................................	2 249 ..	....	....	....	....	....	....	....	....
Insurance.....................................	2 253 ..	27.7	42.8	46.0	40.9	39.8	41.4	47.3	48.4
Financial.....................................	2 260 ..	....	65.4	65.4	115.6	235.1	203.6	199.0	269.3
Computer and information.....................	2 262 ..	5.1	15.4	45.3	52.0	47.7	66.2	63.7	56.5
Royalties and licence fees.....................	2 266 ..	1.2	3.2	48.0	143.5	52.1	45.3	41.2	29.7
Other business services.......................	2 268 ..	231.8	209.6	282.2	514.2	817.0	791.8	685.7	619.8
Personal, cultural, and recreational...........	2 287 ..	72.6	161.4	361.7	473.4	721.2	1,364.6	1,437.5	1,385.2
Government, n.i.e..............................	2 291 ..	30.7	26.0	29.2	30.6	33.2	34.0	37.8	29.2
Other services, debit......................	3 200 BA	**−325.5**	**−523.8**	**−704.1**	**−1,158.1**	**−1,676.7**	**−1,908.4**	**−1,903.1**	**−1,750.0**
Communications...............................	3 245 ..	−13.1	−33.4	−33.7	−40.9	−54.8	−52.4	−52.4	−70.5
Construction..................................	3 249 ..	....	....	....	....	....	....	....	....
Insurance.....................................	3 253 ..	−72.9	−85.6	−97.2	−89.5	−96.6	−120.4	−117.5	−118.6
Financial.....................................	3 260 ..	....	−106.0	−75.0	−122.3	−349.7	−355.2	−183.5	−163.4
Computer and information.....................	3 262 ..	−3.6	−15.7	−30.2	−53.0	−80.8	−157.6	−175.8	−159.2
Royalties and licence fees.....................	3 266 ..	−15.2	−17.7	−53.7	−34.3	−88.2	−127.0	−168.5	−163.6
Other business services.......................	3 268 ..	−179.3	−238.2	−388.3	−789.4	−964.2	−1,053.8	−1,157.0	−1,032.0
Personal, cultural, and recreational...........	3 287 ..	−7.7	−6.5	−7.8	−11.7	−16.3	−19.1	−26.9	−22.2
Government, n.i.e..............................	3 291 ..	−33.7	−20.7	−18.1	−17.0	−26.1	−23.0	−21.4	−20.4

2011, International Monetary Fund: *Balance of Payments Statistics Yearbook*

Table 2 (Continued). STANDARD PRESENTATION, 2003–2010

(Millions of U.S. dollars)

	Code	2003	2004	2005	2006	2007	2008	2009	2010
C. INCOME	4 300	**−29.1**	**−53.8**	**−247.1**	**−213.4**	**−271.0**	**−337.0**	**−567.9**	**−586.2**
Total credit	2 300	*905.3*	*971.3*	*1,207.8*	*1,839.8*	*2,710.9*	*3,249.2*	*2,288.2*	*2,180.2*
Total debit	3 300	*−934.4*	*−1,025.1*	*−1,454.9*	*−2,053.2*	*−2,981.9*	*−3,586.1*	*−2,856.0*	*−2,766.4*
Compensation of employees, credit	2 310	**25.2**	**30.9**	**33.3**	**35.3**	**49.3**	**53.3**	**50.0**	**47.3**
Compensation of employees, debit	3 310	**−10.2**	**−15.8**	**−21.8**	**−39.0**	**−44.8**	**−45.5**	**−34.4**	**−33.3**
Investment income, credit	2 320	**880.1**	**940.4**	**1,174.4**	**1,804.5**	**2,661.6**	**3,195.8**	**2,238.2**	**2,132.9**
Direct investment income	2 330	880.1	32.9	28.4	15.8	58.5	32.0	19.5	26.6
Dividends and distributed branch profits	2 332	1.4	26.4	22.1	12.8	59.1	11.4	18.9	11.9
Reinvested earnings and undistributed branch profits	2 333	.8	3.9	2.8	−.6	−4.9	16.0	−4.9	9.3
Income on debt (interest)	2 334	877.8	2.6	3.6	3.6	4.3	4.6	5.5	5.4
Portfolio investment income	2 339	....	481.8	624.2	986.9	1,243.7	1,292.7	811.1	981.6
Income on equity	2 340	....	6.3	6.6	10.0	11.9	16.6	8.3	8.4
Income on bonds and notes	2 350	....	475.4	617.6	976.8	1,231.8	1,275.9	792.3	962.5
Income on money market instruments	2 360	....	....	....	....	....	.2	10.4	10.7
Other investment income	2 370	....	425.7	521.8	801.9	1,359.4	1,871.1	1,407.6	1,124.7
Investment income, debit	3 320	**−924.2**	**−1,009.3**	**−1,433.1**	**−2,014.2**	**−2,937.1**	**−3,540.6**	**−2,821.6**	**−2,733.1**
Direct investment income	3 330	−922.4	−320.5	−556.1	−585.6	−841.4	−950.3	−1,240.8	−1,186.1
Dividends and distributed branch profits	3 332	−204.4	−235.3	−455.3	−493.3	−551.9	−711.2	−772.4	−1,171.8
Reinvested earnings and undistributed branch profits	3 333	−92.9	−82.1	−95.4	−85.7	−278.1	−215.7	−446.7	14.6
Income on debt (interest)	3 334	−625.1	−3.1	−5.4	−6.6	−11.3	−23.4	−21.7	−28.8
Portfolio investment income	3 339	....	−22.4	−24.7	−24.0	−20.9	−25.4	−32.2	−29.2
Income on equity	3 340	....	−3.9	−6.4	−5.6	−.6	−.2	−3.3	−.5
Income on bonds and notes	3 350	....	−18.5	−18.3	−18.3	−20.3	−25.3	−28.8	−28.6
Income on money market instruments	3 360	....	....	....	....	−.1	....	−.1	....
Other investment income	3 370	−1.8	−666.4	−852.3	−1,404.6	−2,074.8	−2,564.9	−1,548.6	−1,517.9
D. CURRENT TRANSFERS	4 379	**−44.5**	**−58.1**	**43.5**	**−11.5**	**−36.6**	**−10.6**	**63.9**	**37.5**
Credit	2 379	**203.4**	**221.6**	**343.4**	**523.5**	**882.2**	**1,358.1**	**1,982.7**	**1,718.2**
General government	2 380	54.8	85.4	154.1	350.0	702.9	1,137.3	1,753.6	1,489.3
Other sectors	2 390	148.6	136.2	189.3	173.5	179.3	220.8	229.1	228.8
Workers' remittances	2 391	.6	.1	.2	.3	.3	.3	.3	.2
Other current transfers	2 392	148.0	136.1	189.1	173.1	179.0	220.5	228.8	228.7
Debit	3 379	**−247.9**	**−279.7**	**−299.9**	**−535.0**	**−918.8**	**−1,368.7**	**−1,918.8**	**−1,680.7**
General government	3 380	−30.9	−71.6	−128.9	−351.2	−704.9	−1,119.7	−1,686.5	−1,452.9
Other sectors	3 390	−217.0	−208.0	−171.0	−183.7	−213.9	−249.0	−232.3	−227.8
Workers' remittances	3 391	−1.3	−2.2	−6.7	−4.2	−4.1	−5.0	−5.3	−6.5
Other current transfers	3 392	−215.7	−205.9	−164.3	−179.5	−209.7	−244.0	−227.0	−221.2
CAPITAL AND FINANCIAL ACCOUNT	4 996	**132.5**	**254.2**	**587.2**	**574.3**	**478.3**	**369.3**	**202.7**	**−16.7**
CAPITAL ACCOUNT	4 994	**17.2**	**83.6**	**193.2**	**193.1**	**95.4**	**41.3**	**109.7**	**106.3**
Total credit	2 994	*18.6*	*87.3*	*205.5*	*200.1*	*104.7*	*50.8*	*120.5*	*119.0*
Total debit	3 994	*−1.4*	*−3.8*	*−12.3*	*−7.0*	*−9.4*	*−9.5*	*−10.8*	*−12.6*
Capital transfers, credit	2 400	**18.6**	**87.3**	**205.5**	**181.9**	**96.6**	**50.8**	**120.4**	**118.9**
General government	2 401	6.7	87.1	192.7	176.9	93.3	46.6	116.4	115.2
Debt forgiveness	2 402	....	....	....	....	....	....	....	....
Other capital transfers	2 410	6.7	87.1	192.7	176.9	93.3	46.6	116.4	115.2
Other sectors	2 430	11.9	.2	12.8	5.0	3.4	4.2	4.0	3.7
Migrants' transfers	2 431	1.0	.1	....	.4	.2	.2	.2	.1
Debt forgiveness	2 432	10.9	....	12.6	3.0	.3	.7	.7	.6
Other capital transfers	2 440	....	.1	.1	1.7	2.9	3.3	3.1	3.0
Capital transfers, debit	3 400	**−1.4**	**−3.2**	**−11.6**	**−5.8**	**−7.5**	**−4.6**	**−6.1**	**−8.2**
General government	3 401	....	....	....	−.2	....	....	....	....
Debt forgiveness	3 402	....	....	....	....	....	....	....	....
Other capital transfers	3 410	....	....	....	−.2	....	....	....	....
Other sectors	3 430	−1.4	−3.2	−11.6	−5.6	−7.5	−4.6	−6.1	−8.2
Migrants' transfers	3 431	−1.4	−3.1	−4.0	−3.1	−3.8	−3.9	−4.0	−6.1
Debt forgiveness	3 432	....	−.2	−7.6	−2.5	−3.6	−.7	−2.2	−2.1
Other capital transfers	3 440	....	....	....	....	....	....	....	....
Nonproduced nonfinancial assets, credit	2 480	....	....	....	**18.2**	**8.1**	....	**.1**	....
Nonproduced nonfinancial assets, debit	3 480	....	**−.5**	**−.7**	**−1.3**	**−1.9**	**−4.9**	**−4.6**	**−4.4**

Table 2 (Continued). STANDARD PRESENTATION, 2003–2010

(Millions of U.S. dollars)

	Code	2003	2004	2005	2006	2007	2008	2009	2010
FINANCIAL ACCOUNT	4 995	**115.3**	**170.6**	**394.0**	**381.2**	**382.9**	**328.0**	**92.9**	**−123.0**
A. DIRECT INVESTMENT	4 500	**431.8**	**387.9**	**703.0**	**1,811.4**	**980.4**	**523.9**	**619.2**	**912.4**
Direct investment abroad	4 505	**−575.2**	**−7.3**	**24.3**	**−30.0**	**−15.9**	**−309.6**	**−134.2**	**−86.2**
Equity capital	4 510	−579.8	−33.7	−26.1	−10.5	7.8	−241.7	−113.5	−14.5
Claims on affiliated enterprises	4 515	−579.8	−33.7	−26.1	−10.5	7.8	−241.7	−113.5	−14.5
Liabilities to affiliated enterprises	4 520	....	....	....	....	....	....	....	....
Reinvested earnings	4 525	−.8	−3.9	−2.8	.6	4.9	−16.0	4.9	−9.3
Other capital	4 530	5.5	30.3	53.2	−20.1	−28.6	−51.9	−25.6	−62.4
Claims on affiliated enterprises	4 535	1.7	19.3	−27.5	−6.3	−24.3	−83.3	−40.0	−87.2
Liabilities to affiliated enterprises	4 540	3.8	10.9	80.8	−13.8	−4.3	31.5	14.3	24.8
Direct investment in Malta	4 555	**1,007.0**	**395.2**	**678.7**	**1,841.4**	**996.2**	**833.5**	**753.4**	**998.6**
Equity capital	4 560	819.7	317.8	391.8	1,154.1	725.3	471.7	287.3	1,010.9
Claims on direct investors	4 565	....	....	....	....	....	....	....	....
Liabilities to direct investors	4 570	819.7	317.8	391.8	1,154.1	725.3	471.7	287.3	1,010.9
Reinvested earnings	4 575	92.9	82.1	95.4	85.7	278.1	215.7	446.7	−14.6
Other capital	4 580	94.4	−4.7	191.5	601.5	−7.1	146.1	19.4	2.3
Claims on direct investors	4 585	99.3	−23.0	66.2	50.2	−239.9	−85.5	−94.0	−226.1
Liabilities to direct investors	4 590	−5.0	18.3	125.2	551.4	232.8	231.6	113.5	228.4
B. PORTFOLIO INVESTMENT	4 600	**−1,591.2**	**−2,089.6**	**−2,571.9**	**−2,472.6**	**535.4**	**−13.1**	**−2,797.9**	**−4,247.1**
Assets	4 602	**−1,571.0**	**−2,094.1**	**−2,608.1**	**−2,454.1**	**535.0**	**−267.2**	**−2,754.2**	**−4,248.1**
Equity securities	4 610	−11.6	−51.4	−98.4	−72.0	−116.7	−174.9	−5.3	−60.3
Monetary authorities	4 611	....	....	....	....	....	....	....	....
General government	4 612	....	....	3.1	....	−2.0	....	−2.0	....
Banks	4 613	−15.6	2.3	−27.0	11.7	7.0	−76.0	24.8	5.1
Other sectors	4 614	4.0	−53.8	−74.5	−83.6	−121.7	−98.9	−28.0	−65.4
Debt securities	4 619	−1,559.5	−2,042.7	−2,509.7	−2,382.2	651.8	−92.3	−2,748.9	−4,187.9
Bonds and notes	4 620	−970.7	−2,116.1	−2,504.9	−2,389.2	643.6	−108.1	−2,440.4	−3,959.4
Monetary authorities	4 621	....	....	....	....	....	−215.9	−134.5	−661.6
General government	4 622	....	....	....	....	....	....	....	....
Banks	4 623	−910.0	−2,070.3	−2,476.9	−2,228.5	671.6	143.4	−2,122.6	−3,217.8
Other sectors	4 624	−60.7	−45.8	−28.0	−160.7	−28.0	−35.6	−183.3	−80.0
Money market instruments	4 630	−588.8	73.4	−4.8	7.1	8.2	15.8	−308.5	−228.5
Monetary authorities	4 631	....	....	....	....	....	....	....	....
General government	4 632	....	....	....	....	....	....	....	....
Banks	4 633	−539.7	63.8	−14.7	....	....	14.0	−311.9	−228.3
Other sectors	4 634	−49.0	9.7	10.0	7.1	8.2	1.8	3.4	−.2
Liabilities	4 652	**−20.2**	**4.5**	**36.1**	**−18.5**	**.4**	**254.1**	**−43.7**	**1.0**
Equity securities	4 660	−13.5	7.6	35.5	−9.1	−.1	13.3	−6.7	23.1
Banks	4 663	−9.8	8.3	34.3	−18.6	1.5	6.3	−4.2	.1
Other sectors	4 664	−3.7	−.7	1.2	9.5	−1.6	7.0	−2.5	23.1
Debt securities	4 669	−6.7	−3.1	.6	−9.4	.4	240.8	−37.0	−22.1
Bonds and notes	4 670	1.5	−4.1	3.3	−7.3	.4	125.8	22.2	19.2
Monetary authorities	4 671	....	....	....	....	....	....	....	....
General government	4 672	....	.8	.2	−.1	−2.5	117.9	22.0	18.2
Banks	4 673	1.4	−6.1	1.1	−9.6	5.0	1.6	.8	1.2
Other sectors	4 674	.1	1.2	2.0	2.4	−2.1	6.3	−.6	−.2
Money market instruments	4 680	−8.2	1.0	−2.7	−2.1	....	115.0	−59.2	−41.3
Monetary authorities	4 681	....	....	....	....	....	....	....	....
General government	4 682	....	....	....	....	....	116.1	−64.2	−36.6
Banks	4 683	−8.2	1.0	−2.7	−2.1	....	−1.0	5.0	−4.8
Other sectors	4 684	....	....	....	....	....	....	....	....
C. FINANCIAL DERIVATIVES	4 910	**25.1**	**−18.2**	**−23.9**	**30.3**	**167.4**	**−452.5**	**−88.6**	**31.1**
Monetary authorities	4 911	....	....	....	....	....	27.4	−.3	−6.4
General government	4 912	....	....	....	....	....	....	....	....
Banks	4 913	25.1	−18.1	−24.0	30.3	167.3	−482.2	−90.0	37.3
Other sectors	4 914	....	−.1	.1	....	.1	2.2	1.7	.1
Assets	4 900	**−5.0**	**−17.6**	**−19.2**	**51.3**	**−196.1**	**15.0**	**−3.2**	**−62.5**
Monetary authorities	4 901	....	....	....	....	....	1.5	11.0	3.1
General government	4 902	....	....	....	....	....	....	....	....
Banks	4 903	−5.0	−17.6	−19.3	51.3	−196.2	11.3	−15.9	−65.7
Other sectors	4 904	....	−.1	.1	....	.1	2.2	1.7	.1
Liabilities	4 905	**30.0**	**−.5**	**−4.7**	**−21.0**	**363.5**	**−467.6**	**−85.4**	**93.5**
Monetary authorities	4 906	....	....	....	....	....	25.9	−11.3	−9.5
General government	4 907	....	....	....	....	....	....	....	....
Banks	4 908	30.0	−.5	−4.7	−21.0	363.5	−493.5	−74.1	103.0
Other sectors	4 909	....	....	....	....	....	....	....	....

Table 2 (Concluded). STANDARD PRESENTATION, 2003–2010

(Millions of U.S. dollars)

	Code	2003	2004	2005	2006	2007	2008	2009	2010
D. OTHER INVESTMENT...	4 700 ..	**1,393.5**	**1,683.2**	**2,503.6**	**1,123.4**	**−804.8**	**77.8**	**2,490.4**	**3,211.0**
Assets...	4 703 ..	**−68.7**	**−1,277.8**	**−2,805.2**	**−4,075.7**	**−10,313.0**	**−6,966.6**	**5,237.1**	**623.2**
Trade credits..	4 706 ..	6.4	−49.8	−123.6	−39.7	−75.2	−418.2	−156.9	−5.9
General government...........................	4 707 ..	....	....	−.5	.1	4.9	5.6	−15.2	−8.7
of which: Short-term..................	4 709 ..	....	....	*−.5*	*.1*	*4.9*	*5.6*	*−15.2*	*8.2*
Other sectors...................................	4 710 ..	6.4	−49.8	−123.2	−39.8	−80.1	−423.8	−141.6	2.8
of which: Short-term..................	4 712 ..	*6.4*	*−36.5*	*−122.2*	*−37.9*	*−130.0*	*−395.7*	*−109.0*	*39.1*
Loans..	4 714 ..	−357.2	−1,304.6	−2,233.3	−3,605.9	−8,789.6	−5,023.7	5,710.3	2,085.3
Monetary authorities.........................	4 715 ..	....	....	....	....	....	....	....	....
of which: Short-term..................	4 718 ..	....	....	....	....	....	....	....	....
General government...........................	4 719 ..	....	....	....	....	....	....	....	−25.2
of which: Short-term..................	4 721 ..	....	....	....	....	....	....	....	....
Banks...	4 722 ..	−346.8	−1,212.2	−2,224.6	−3,574.3	−8,790.1	−4,995.9	5,721.4	2,128.0
of which: Short-term..................	4 724 ..	*−45.8*	*−4.3*	*−69.5*	*−87.3*	*−520.5*	*1,619.7*	*446.6*	*−432.5*
Other sectors...................................	4 725 ..	−10.4	−92.4	−8.7	−31.6	.5	−27.8	−11.1	−17.5
of which: Short-term..................	4 727 ..	*−9.1*	*−13.6*	*−11.5*	*−32.3*	*1.1*	*−18.5*	*−4.5*	*−19.5*
Currency and deposits............................	4 730 ..	348.0	119.2	−394.2	−473.1	−1,405.4	−1,425.3	−245.4	−1,507.0
Monetary authorities.........................	4 731 ..	....	−.2	6.9	....	....	1,496.9	244.9	1.1
General government...........................	4 732 ..	....	−.4	.8	−.4	.2	....	....	−.4
Banks...	4 733 ..	308.3	74.2	−477.4	−421.8	−1,414.7	−2,924.2	−508.3	−1,528.7
Other sectors...................................	4 734 ..	39.7	45.6	75.6	−50.9	9.1	2.0	18.0	20.9
Other assets..	4 736 ..	−65.9	−42.5	−54.1	43.0	−42.8	−99.4	−70.9	50.8
Monetary authorities.........................	4 737 ..	....	.2	....	....	....	−17.6	−1.4	1.8
of which: Short-term..................	4 739 ..	....	....	....	....	....	*−.9*	*1.0*	*.4*
General government...........................	4 740 ..	....	....	....	....	....	....	....	....
of which: Short-term..................	4 742 ..	....	....	....	....	....	....	....	....
Banks...	4 743 ..	−54.3	−30.2	−41.1	55.5	−30.7	−73.6	−61.0	63.6
of which: Short-term..................	4 745 ..	*15.1*	*−29.7*	*−41.2*	*20.4*	*−30.0*	*40.9*	*−95.2*	*39.4*
Other sectors...................................	4 746 ..	−11.6	−12.5	−12.9	−12.6	−12.1	−8.2	−8.5	−14.6
of which: Short-term..................	4 748 ..	*1.7*	*.8*	*−2.8*	*−1.3*	*.7*	*.4*	*−.8*	*−8.4*
Liabilities..	4 753 ..	**1,462.2**	**2,961.0**	**5,308.8**	**5,199.2**	**9,508.2**	**7,044.4**	**−2,746.7**	**2,587.8**
Trade credits..	4 756 ..	20.3	76.5	162.6	1.2	126.5	267.2	56.6	197.4
General government...........................	4 757 ..	....	12.5	−11.5	.9	−3.4	3.1	37.7	9.3
of which: Short-term..................	4 759 ..	....	*12.5*	*−11.5*	*.9*	*−3.4*	*3.1*	*37.7*	*9.3*
Other sectors...................................	4 760 ..	20.3	64.0	174.1	.3	129.9	264.1	18.9	188.1
of which: Short-term..................	4 762 ..	*20.3*	*59.6*	*174.0*	*1.8*	*129.1*	*256.0*	*13.5*	*202.1*
Loans..	4 764 ..	1,692.3	1,086.6	3,651.6	3,982.9	3,839.9	1,041.8	−2,292.6	1,402.2
Monetary authorities.........................	4 765 ..	52.5	−55.5	13.7	−.7	....	....	....	....
of which: Use of Fund credit and loans from the Fund..	4 766 ..	....	....	....	....	....	....	....	....
of which: Short-term..................	4 768 ..	*52.5*	*−56.0*	*13.7*	*−.7*	....	....	....	....
General government...........................	4 769 ..	43.0	−17.2	−15.2	−35.7	−16.1	−17.8	−25.2	−17.8
of which: Short-term..................	4 771 ..	....	....	....	....	....	....	....	*−1.2*
Banks...	4 772 ..	1,544.7	1,189.9	3,560.2	4,033.4	3,673.5	1,056.8	−2,366.4	1,257.3
of which: Short-term..................	4 774 ..	*587.8*	*−568.0*	*3,592.3*	*1,832.9*	*955.6*	*−1,550.3*	*−2,590.1*	*−1,543.5*
Other sectors...................................	4 775 ..	52.1	−30.7	92.9	−14.0	182.5	2.8	98.9	162.7
of which: Short-term..................	4 777 ..	*2.7*	*−19.0*	*−11.2*	*−17.4*	*2.7*	*55.5*	*−1.4*	*6.2*
Currency and deposits............................	4 780 ..	−235.6	1,711.4	1,518.3	1,180.9	4,813.7	5,043.4	−715.7	1,051.8
Monetary authorities.........................	4 781 ..	−1.1	−15.6	4.9	10.6	7.7	1,028.6	318.5	527.8
General government...........................	4 782 ..	....	....	....	....	....	....	....	....
Banks...	4 783 ..	−234.5	1,722.5	1,502.0	1,141.2	4,776.4	3,962.6	−1,035.8	522.1
Other sectors...................................	4 784 ..	....	4.5	11.4	29.1	29.7	52.1	1.7	1.8
Other liabilities......................................	4 786 ..	−14.8	86.6	−23.6	34.1	728.1	692.1	205.0	−63.6
Monetary authorities.........................	4 787 ..	....	....	....	....	....	2.5	131.4	....
of which: Short-term..................	4 789 ..	....	....	....	....	....	*2.5*	....	....
General government...........................	4 790 ..	....	....	....	....	....	....	....	....
of which: Short-term..................	4 792 ..	....	....	....	....	....	....	....	....
Banks...	4 793 ..	−32.2	80.8	−25.1	28.4	728.1	689.6	73.6	−63.6
of which: Short-term..................	4 795 ..	*−78.8*	*16.2*	*12.7*	*10.8*	*537.7*	*627.0*	*258.3*	*7.5*
Other sectors...................................	4 796 ..	17.4	5.8	1.5	5.7	....	....	....	....
of which: Short-term..................	4 798 ..	*4.4*	*5.8*	*1.5*	*5.7*	....	....	....	....
E. RESERVE ASSETS...	4 802 ..	**−144.0**	**207.3**	**−216.8**	**−111.3**	**−495.4**	**191.9**	**−130.1**	**−30.3**
Monetary gold.......................................	4 812 ..	....	.1	....	−1.1	−8.0	49.8	2.1	4.9
Special drawing rights.............................	4 811 ..	−1.3	−1.4	−2.0	−2.9	−5.8	39.5	−131.7	.2
Reserve position in the Fund......................	4 810 ..	....	....	....	....	....	....	11.1	3.2
Foreign exchange..................................	4 803 ..	−135.2	208.8	−214.8	−107.4	−481.4	102.6	−11.6	−38.6
Other claims..	4 813 ..	−7.5	−.3	....	....	−.2	....	....	....
NET ERRORS AND OMISSIONS...........................	4 998 ..	**23.8**	**83.4**	**−63.6**	**43.5**	**127.3**	**293.8**	**397.2**	**432.0**

Table 3. INTERNATIONAL INVESTMENT POSITION (End-period stocks), 2003–2010

(Millions of U.S. dollars)

	Code	2003	2004	2005	2006	2007	2008	2009	2010
ASSETS	8 995 C.	**17,980.6**	**22,816.9**	**26,804.5**	**35,347.7**	**49,417.3**	**51,939.1**	**51,924.1**	**59,731.6**
Direct investment abroad	8 505 ..	**923.5**	**1,121.1**	**991.6**	**1,150.4**	**1,197.9**	**970.4**	**1,533.7**	**1,532.0**
Equity capital and reinvested earnings	8 506 ..	837.4	921.2	854.5	1,022.0	1,054.7	756.2	1,129.7	1,088.6
Claims on affiliated enterprises	8 507 ..	837.4	921.2	854.5	1,022.0	1,054.7	756.2	1,129.7	1,088.6
Liabilities to affiliated enterprises	8 508 ..	....	....	....	....	....	....	....	....
Other capital	8 530 ..	86.1	199.9	137.1	128.4	143.2	214.2	404.0	443.4
Claims on affiliated enterprises	8 535 ..	101.3	231.4	225.4	223.7	238.6	313.9	518.9	567.5
Liabilities to affiliated enterprises	8 540 ..	−15.2	−31.5	−88.3	−95.3	−95.3	−99.7	−114.9	−124.1
Portfolio investment	8 602 ..	**7,020.0**	**9,731.3**	**11,860.6**	**14,975.6**	**15,742.2**	**14,179.0**	**17,933.1**	**20,851.7**
Equity securities	8 610 ..	462.0	605.5	775.4	1,059.9	1,319.4	1,123.8	1,216.3	1,234.6
Monetary authorities	8 611 ..	....	....	....	....	....	....	....	....
General government	8 612 ..	....	....	....	....	....	....	2.2	2.1
Banks	8 613 ..	23.4	9.4	36.6	35.0	39.5	108.2	76.3	54.5
Other sectors	8 614 ..	438.6	596.1	738.8	1,024.9	1,279.9	1,015.6	1,137.8	1,178.1
Debt securities	8 619 ..	6,558.0	9,125.9	11,085.2	13,915.7	14,422.9	13,055.2	16,716.9	19,617.1
Bonds and notes	8 620 ..	5,840.7	8,543.0	10,520.2	13,914.7	14,422.3	13,042.4	16,424.5	19,384.3
Monetary authorities	8 621 ..	....	....	....	....	....	1,342.6	1,551.0	2,045.4
General government	8 622 ..	....	....	....	....	....	....	....	....
Banks	8 623 ..	5,407.9	7,837.2	9,781.4	13,039.6	13,499.2	10,803.1	13,756.3	16,243.1
Other sectors	8 624 ..	432.8	705.8	738.9	875.1	923.0	896.7	1,117.1	1,095.8
Money market instruments	8 630 ..	717.2	582.9	565.0	1.0	.6	12.8	292.4	232.8
Monetary authorities	8 631 ..	....	....	....	....	....	....	....	....
General government	8 632 ..	....	....	....	....	....	....	....	....
Banks	8 633 ..	577.0	582.4	564.8	....	....	12.8	291.3	231.6
Other sectors	8 634 ..	140.3	.5	.2	1.0	.6	....	1.1	1.1
Financial derivatives	8 900 ..	**5.2**	**14.6**	**49.9**	**45.3**	**157.2**	**385.2**	**198.9**	**290.4**
Monetary authorities	8 901 ..	....	....	....	....	....	26.9	....	2.0
General government	8 902 ..	....	....	....	....	....	....	....	....
Banks	8 903 ..	5.2	14.3	49.7	43.2	154.9	358.3	198.2	284.9
Other sectors	8 904 ..	....	.3	.1	2.2	2.2	....	.8	3.6
Other investment	8 703 ..	**7,274.1**	**9,187.7**	**11,320.3**	**16,226.0**	**28,550.0**	**36,031.1**	**31,719.7**	**36,517.3**
Trade credits	8 706 ..	219.7	449.0	540.9	643.3	739.7	1,196.0	1,475.8	1,343.2
General government	8 707 ..	.3	....	.5	.7	7.7	2.1	17.9	26.5
of which: Short-term	8 709 ..	*.3*	....	*.5*	*.7*	*7.7*	*2.1*	*17.9*	*8.6*
Other sectors	8 710 ..	219.4	449.0	540.4	642.5	731.9	1,193.9	1,458.0	1,316.7
of which: Short-term	8 712 ..	*219.4*	*408.3*	*539.3*	*638.9*	*669.2*	*1,066.1*	*1,310.2*	*1,143.6*
Loans	8 714 ..	5,074.8	6,717.1	8,371.9	12,570.6	22,709.2	26,920.0	21,740.0	34,055.2
Monetary authorities	8 715 ..	....	....	....	....	....	....	....	....
of which: Short-term	8 718 ..	....	....	....	....	....	....	....	....
General government	8 719 ..	.1	....	....	....	....	....	....	26.4
of which: Short-term	8 721 ..	....	....	....	....	....	....	....	....
Banks	8 722 ..	5,024.0	6,613.9	8,259.4	12,408.6	22,548.6	26,730.1	21,551.2	33,830.2
of which: Short-term	8 724 ..	*2,132.5*	*213.2*	*151.4*	*567.0*	*1,220.7*	*2,118.2*	*1,801.3*	*12,365.8*
Other sectors	8 725 ..	50.8	103.2	112.5	162.0	160.7	189.8	188.9	198.6
of which: Short-term	8 727 ..	*34.4*	*25.3*	*35.4*	*78.2*	*78.8*	*143.8*	*92.4*	*105.6*
Currency and deposits	8 730 ..	1,676.8	1,924.2	2,307.6	2,959.9	4,985.5	7,684.5	8,246.8	950.4
Monetary authorities	8 731 ..	....	6.6	....	....	....	435.1	205.8	199.5
General government	8 732 ..	.8	1.1	.4	.4	.1	.1	.1	....
Banks	8 733 ..	1,280.8	1,376.3	1,701.7	2,187.0	4,060.9	6,458.5	7,222.6	7.2
Other sectors	8 734 ..	395.2	540.2	605.5	772.5	924.5	790.8	818.3	743.7
Other assets	8 736 ..	302.8	97.3	100.0	52.2	115.6	230.7	257.0	168.5
Monetary authorities	8 737 ..	....	.3	.5	.5	.6	17.1	19.0	18.9
of which: Short-term	8 739 ..	....	....	....	....	....	*1.1*	....	....
General government	8 740 ..	3.5	....	....	....	....	....	....	....
of which: Short-term	8 742 ..	....	....	....	....	....	....	....	....
Banks	8 743 ..	207.9	60.6	65.7	42.9	105.3	204.3	228.4	140.7
of which: Short-term	8 745 ..	*207.9*	*60.0*	*65.3*	*29.0*	*87.4*	*58.3*	*134.5*	*140.7*
Other sectors	8 746 ..	91.4	36.5	33.7	8.7	9.8	9.2	9.6	8.9
of which: Short-term	8 748 ..	*35.4*	*29.6*	*25.9*	....	....	....	....	....
Reserve assets	8 802 ..	**2,757.7**	**2,762.3**	**2,582.1**	**2,950.4**	**3,770.0**	**373.4**	**538.6**	**540.2**
Monetary gold	8 812 ..	1.8	1.9	2.3	4.1	13.0	5.1	6.5	4.4
Special drawing rights	8 811 ..	44.3	47.8	45.9	51.2	59.8	18.0	150.5	147.6
Reserve position in the Fund	8 810 ..	59.8	62.5	57.5	60.6	63.6	62.0	51.9	47.7
Foreign exchange	8 803 ..	2,651.8	2,649.9	2,474.2	2,834.6	3,633.6	288.3	329.7	340.5
Other claims	8 813 ..	....	.1	2.3	....	....	....	....	....

Table 3 (Concluded). INTERNATIONAL INVESTMENT POSITION (End-period stocks), 2003–2010

(Millions of U.S. dollars)

	Code	2003	2004	2005	2006	2007	2008	2009	2010
LIABILITIES...	8 995 D.	**15,745.1**	**20,346.2**	**24,705.4**	**33,471.6**	**47,962.5**	**51,645.3**	**50,883.9**	**59,124.2**
Direct investment in Malta........................	8 555 ..	**3,281.0**	**4,061.4**	**4,300.5**	**6,539.4**	**8,299.3**	**7,977.8**	**9,335.7**	**16,556.5**
Equity capital and reinvested earnings...............	8 556 ..	3,605.5	4,294.3	4,338.6	6,056.4	7,761.8	7,396.5	8,755.8	15,960.8
Claims on direct investors..........................	8 557 ..	....	....	....	....	....	....	....	....
Liabilities to direct investors......................	8 558 ..	3,605.5	4,294.3	4,338.6	6,056.4	7,761.8	7,396.5	8,755.8	15,960.8
Other capital..	8 580 ..	−324.5	−232.9	−38.1	483.0	537.4	581.3	579.9	595.7
Claims on direct investors..........................	8 585 ..	−655.1	−638.4	−556.3	−619.1	−985.5	−747.8	−833.3	−960.6
Liabilities to direct investors......................	8 590 ..	330.5	405.5	518.2	1,102.1	1,523.0	1,329.1	1,413.2	1,556.4
Portfolio investment................................	8 652 ..	**412.7**	**483.0**	**487.2**	**537.5**	**598.9**	**766.8**	**718.2**	**639.2**
Equity securities....................................	8 660 ..	47.2	160.8	214.3	245.4	262.4	220.0	203.1	196.8
Banks..	8 663 ..	....	105.9	177.3	180.4	185.7	173.8	159.3	117.3
Other sectors......................................	8 664 ..	47.2	55.0	37.0	65.1	76.7	46.2	43.8	79.5
Debt securities.....................................	8 669 ..	365.5	322.2	272.9	292.1	336.5	546.8	515.1	442.4
Bonds and notes..................................	8 670 ..	363.0	317.8	272.0	292.1	335.5	440.2	464.8	442.4
Monetary authorities............................	8 671 ..	....	....	....	....	....	....	....	....
General government.............................	8 672 ..	3.7	3.3	2.9	4.7	8.3	125.1	141.3	138.8
Banks...	8 673 ..	30.0	25.6	23.2	14.1	19.5	19.0	20.1	19.9
Other sectors....................................	8 674 ..	329.3	288.9	245.9	273.2	307.7	296.1	303.5	283.7
Money market instruments........................	8 680 ..	2.5	4.4	.9	....	1.0	106.6	50.2	....
Monetary authorities............................	8 681 ..	....	....	....	....	....	....	....	....
General government.............................	8 682 ..	....	....	....	....	....	106.6	45.3	....
Banks...	8 683 ..	2.5	4.4	.9	....	1.0	....	5.0	....
Other sectors....................................	8 684 ..	....	....	....	....	....	....	....	....
Financial derivatives...............................	8 905 ..	**31.6**	**51.9**	**52.1**	**65.0**	**116.4**	**392.0**	**256.2**	**410.6**
Monetary authorities................................	8 906 ..	....	....	....	....	....	1.6	3.1	....
General government................................	8 907 ..	....	....	....	....	....	....	....	....
Banks..	8 908 ..	31.6	51.9	52.1	65.0	116.4	390.4	253.1	406.2
Other sectors.......................................	8 909 ..	....	....	....	....	....	....	....	4.4
Other investment...................................	8 753 ..	**12,019.8**	**15,749.9**	**19,865.5**	**26,329.7**	**38,947.8**	**42,508.7**	**40,573.8**	**41,517.9**
Trade credits.......................................	8 756 ..	234.3	343.9	524.5	604.6	714.2	902.5	979.4	1,093.7
General government................................	8 757 ..	12.7	22.0	8.3	10.0	7.0	10.3	46.7	48.5
of which: Short-term............................	8 759 ..	*12.7*	*22.0*	*8.3*	*10.0*	*7.0*	*10.3*	*46.7*	*48.5*
Other sectors......................................	8 760 ..	221.6	321.9	516.3	594.6	707.2	892.2	932.7	1,045.3
of which: Short-term............................	8 762 ..	*221.6*	*316.3*	*510.6*	*583.0*	*696.2*	*868.0*	*899.6*	*1,026.3*
Loans..	8 764 ..	6,344.6	7,880.6	10,793.1	15,441.0	20,791.4	20,741.2	18,791.7	1,010.3
Monetary authorities..............................	8 765 ..	55.2	.6	....	....	....	....	....	....
of which: Use of Fund credit and loans from the Fund....	8 766 ..	....	....	....	....	....	....	....	....
of which: Short-term............................	8 768 ..	*55.2*	....	....	....	....	....	....	....
General government.............................	8 769 ..	250.1	251.7	202.1	187.4	192.8	165.6	147.4	117.2
of which: Short-term............................	8 771 ..	....	....	....	....	....	....	....	....
Banks...	8 772 ..	5,702.9	7,246.9	10,117.5	14,784.0	19,864.7	19,869.5	17,879.3	....
of which: Short-term............................	8 774 ..	*4,562.3*	*4,561.9*	*7,867.8*	*6,652.6*	*8,211.8*	*12,930.3*	*10,516.3*	....
Other sectors....................................	8 775 ..	336.4	381.4	473.5	469.6	733.9	706.0	765.0	893.1
of which: Short-term............................	8 777 ..	*31.2*	*39.9*	*33.1*	*29.5*	*62.1*	*103.8*	*48.9*	*53.1*
Currency and deposits..............................	8 780 ..	5,207.3	7,300.5	8,381.6	10,134.1	16,497.3	19,340.1	20,328.2	39,024.4
Monetary authorities..............................	8 781 ..	19.8	8.7	20.0	35.2	46.2	943.3	1,190.3	1,642.1
General government.............................	8 782 ..	....	....	....	....	....	....	....	....
Banks...	8 783 ..	5,187.5	7,265.7	8,326.6	10,026.7	16,338.5	18,254.7	18,989.1	37,242.5
Other sectors....................................	8 784 ..	....	26.1	35.0	72.2	112.5	142.1	148.8	139.8
Other liabilities....................................	8 786 ..	233.5	224.9	166.3	150.0	944.9	1,524.9	474.5	389.6
Monetary authorities..............................	8 787 ..	....	....	....	....	....	....	149.6	146.9
of which: Short-term............................	8 789 ..	....	....	....	....	....	....	....	....
General government.............................	8 790 ..	....	....	....	....	....	....	....	....
of which: Short-term............................	8 792 ..	....	....	....	....	....	....	....	....
Banks...	8 793 ..	217.0	209.9	151.8	150.0	944.9	1,524.9	324.9	242.6
of which: Short-term............................	8 795 ..	*217.0*	*110.4*	*95.3*	*44.8*	*662.6*	*1,202.2*	*190.3*	*242.6*
Other sectors....................................	8 796 ..	16.5	15.0	14.4	....	....	....	....	....
of which: Short-term............................	8 798 ..	*16.5*	*15.0*	*14.4*	....	....	....	....	....
NET INTERNATIONAL INVESTMENT POSITION........	8 995 ..	**2,235.5**	**2,470.7**	**2,099.1**	**1,876.1**	**1,454.8**	**293.7**	**1,040.2**	**607.4**
Conversion rates: Maltese liris per U.S. dollar (end of period)...............................	0 102 ..	**.3425**	**.3185**	**.3627**	**.3257**	**.2916**	....	....	....
Conversion rates: euros per U.S. dollar (end of period)..	0 104 ..	**.7918**	**.7342**	**.8477**	**.7593**	**.6793**	**.7185**	**.6942**	**.7484**

Table 1. ANALYTIC PRESENTATION, 2003–2010
(Millions of U.S. dollars)

	Code	2003	2004	2005	2006	2007	2008	2009	2010
A. Current Account[1]	4 993 Z.	**93.2**	**–111.8**	**–324.0**	**–604.4**	**–433.9**	**–975.8**	**–655.0**	**–799.6**
Goods: exports f.o.b.	2 100	1,898.1	1,993.1	2,138.4	2,328.8	2,237.9	2,383.9	1,938.5	2,261.5
Goods: imports f.o.b.	3 100	–2,201.1	–2,572.6	–2,935.2	–3,408.8	–3,655.7	–4,386.0	–3,503.9	–4,157.3
Balance on Goods	4 100	*–303.0*	*–579.5*	*–796.8*	*–1,080.0*	*–1,417.8*	*–2,002.1*	*–1,565.4*	*–1,895.8*
Services: credit	2 200	1,280.1	1,455.6	1,618.1	1,671.3	2,205.2	2,543.9	2,239.0	2,695.1
Services: debit	3 200	–906.3	–1,023.3	–1,197.7	–1,316.9	–1,569.4	–1,919.9	–1,607.3	–1,983.8
Balance on Goods and Services	4 991	*70.8*	*–147.2*	*–376.5*	*–725.5*	*–782.0*	*–1,378.1*	*–933.7*	*–1,184.5*
Income: credit	2 300	47.0	51.7	142.9	373.9	816.4	819.9	457.6	456.8
Income: debit	3 300	–77.1	–65.7	–151.3	–323.8	–593.3	–641.7	–402.6	–255.1
Balance on Goods, Services, and Income	4 992	*40.8*	*–161.1*	*–385.0*	*–675.5*	*–558.9*	*–1,200.0*	*–878.7*	*–982.9*
Current transfers: credit	2 379 Z.	163.0	168.1	162.3	179.3	250.1	411.2	413.1	404.4
Current transfers: debit	3 379	–110.6	–118.7	–101.3	–108.2	–125.2	–187.0	–189.4	–221.1
B. Capital Account[1]	4 994 Z.	**–.9**	**–1.6**	**–1.8**	**–2.7**	**–1.6**	**–1.4**	**–1.9**	**–4.8**
Capital account: credit	2 994 Z.	....	....	....	....	....	....	....	....
Capital account: debit	3 994	–.9	–1.6	–1.8	–2.7	–1.6	–1.4	–1.9	–4.8
Total, Groups A Plus B	4 981	*92.3*	*–113.4*	*–325.7*	*–607.1*	*–435.6*	*–977.2*	*–656.9*	*–804.4*
C. Financial Account[1]	4 995 W.	**89.7**	**8.1**	**142.1**	**172.8**	**494.9**	**943.2**	**753.7**	**840.5**
Direct investment abroad	4 505	6.0	–31.8	–47.0	–9.6	–59.6	–52.4	–37.8	–129.4
Direct investment in Mauritius	4 555 Z.	62.6	13.9	41.8	106.8	340.8	377.7	256.7	431.0
Portfolio investment assets	4 602	–27.1	–52.4	–41.6	–110.5	–95.3	–92.9	–261.1	–138.6
Equity securities	4 610	–27.1	–52.4	–41.6	–110.5	–95.3	–92.9	–261.1	–138.6
Debt securities	4 619	....	....	....	....	....	....	....	....
Portfolio investment liabilities	4 652 Z.	8.9	15.3	25.4	80.6	153.7	–76.8	204.8	–45.4
Equity securities	4 660	8.1	19.3	35.6	35.1	49.8	33.9	206.0	–40.3
Debt securities	4 669 Z.	.8	–3.9	–10.2	45.5	104.0	–110.6	–1.3	–5.2
Financial derivatives	4 910	....	....	....	....	....	....	....	....
Financial derivatives assets	4 900	....	....	....	....	....	....	....	....
Financial derivatives liabilities	4 905	....	....	....	....	....	....	....	....
Other investment assets	4 703	–22.8	–49.4	–230.9	–371.0	–2,972.8	631.8	–357.7	–3,851.4
Monetary authorities	4 701	....	....	....	....	....	....	....	....
General government	4 704	....	....	....	....	....	....	....	....
Banks	4 705	14.1	–44.2	–195.5	–338.6	–2,852.6	616.2	–362.7	–3,841.2
Other sectors	4 728	–36.9	–5.2	–35.4	–32.4	–120.3	15.6	5.0	–10.2
Other investment liabilities	4 753 W.	62.0	112.4	394.3	476.5	3,128.2	155.7	948.9	4,574.2
Monetary authorities	4 753 WA	....	....	....	....	....	....	126.6	....
General government	4 753 ZB	–8.2	–7.3	10.3	–19.7	46.1	54.5	152.8	183.8
Banks	4 753 ZC	6.1	56.7	7.1	–5.0	2,633.7	–259.1	307.3	4,035.9
Other sectors	4 753 ZD	64.1	63.0	377.0	501.3	448.4	360.3	362.2	354.5
Total, Groups A Through C	4 983	*182.0*	*–105.3*	*–183.6*	*–434.3*	*59.4*	*–34.0*	*96.8*	*36.1*
D. Net Errors and Omissions	4 998	**40.4**	**77.9**	**18.7**	**294.2**	**376.6**	**211.9**	**287.8**	**172.9**
Total, Groups A Through D	4 984	*222.4*	*–27.5*	*–165.0*	*–140.1*	*436.0*	*177.9*	*384.7*	*209.0*
E. Reserves and Related Items	4 802 A.	**–222.4**	**27.5**	**165.0**	**140.1**	**–436.0**	**–177.9**	**–384.7**	**–209.0**
Reserve assets	4 802	–222.4	27.5	165.0	140.1	–436.0	–177.9	–384.7	–209.0
Use of Fund credit and loans	4 766	....	....	....	....	....	....	....	....
Exceptional financing	4 920	....	....	....	....	....	....	....	....
Conversion rates: Mauritian rupees per U.S. dollar	0 101	**27.901**	**27.499**	**29.496**	**31.708**	**31.314**	**28.453**	**31.960**	**30.784**

[1] Excludes components that have been classified in the categories of Group E.

Table 2. STANDARD PRESENTATION, 2003–2010

(Millions of U.S. dollars)

	Code	2003	2004	2005	2006	2007	2008	2009	2010
CURRENT ACCOUNT...	4 993 ..	**93.2**	**−111.8**	**−324.0**	**−604.4**	**−433.9**	**−975.8**	**−655.0**	**−799.6**
A. GOODS..	4 100 ..	**−303.0**	**−579.5**	**−796.8**	**−1,080.0**	**−1,417.8**	**−2,002.1**	**−1,565.4**	**−1,895.8**
Credit...	2 100 ..	**1,898.1**	**1,993.1**	**2,138.4**	**2,328.8**	**2,237.9**	**2,383.9**	**1,938.5**	**2,261.5**
General merchandise: exports f.o.b.............	2 110 ..	1,824.8	1,913.2	1,999.2	2,168.9	2,063.1	2,070.0	1,763.9	2,015.0
Goods for processing: exports f.o.b..............	2 150 ..	....	....	....	....	....	....	....	....
Repairs on goods..	2 160 ..	....	....	....	....	....	....	....	....
Goods procured in ports by carriers.............	2 170 ..	73.3	79.9	139.1	159.9	174.8	314.0	174.6	246.5
Nonmonetary gold......................................	2 180 ..	....	....	....	....	....	....	....	....
Debit..	3 100 ..	**−2,201.1**	**−2,572.6**	**−2,935.2**	**−3,408.8**	**−3,655.7**	**−4,386.0**	**−3,503.9**	**−4,157.3**
General merchandise: imports f.o.b.............	3 110 ..	−2,164.7	−2,517.4	−2,865.2	−3,326.4	−3,563.3	−4,257.5	−3,447.2	−4,079.2
Goods for processing: imports f.o.b..............	3 150 ..	....	....	....	....	....	....	....	....
Repairs on goods..	3 160 ..	....	....	....	....	....	....	....	....
Goods procured in ports by carriers.............	3 170 ..	−36.4	−55.2	−70.0	−82.5	−92.4	−128.5	−56.7	−78.1
Nonmonetary gold......................................	3 180 ..	....	....	....	....	....	....	....	....
B. SERVICES..	4 200 ..	**373.8**	**432.3**	**420.4**	**354.4**	**635.8**	**623.9**	**631.7**	**711.3**
Total credit..	2 200 ..	*1,280.1*	*1,455.6*	*1,618.1*	*1,671.3*	*2,205.2*	*2,543.9*	*2,239.0*	*2,695.1*
Total debit..	3 200 ..	*−906.3*	*−1,023.3*	*−1,197.7*	*−1,316.9*	*−1,569.4*	*−1,919.9*	*−1,607.3*	*−1,983.8*
Transportation services, credit.........................	2 205 ..	**335.1**	**372.9**	**384.1**	**362.5**	**430.7**	**445.8**	**337.8**	**375.6**
Passenger..	2 850 ..	*263.3*	*300.2*	*317.6*	*297.5*	*359.1*	*369.3*	*269.8*	*300.2*
Freight...	2 851 ..	*24.0*	*28.1*	*29.0*	*27.0*	*24.2*	*27.7*	*21.5*	*24.3*
Other..	2 852 ..	*47.8*	*44.5*	*37.5*	*38.1*	*47.3*	*48.8*	*46.6*	*51.1*
Sea transport, passenger...........................	2 207 ..	....	....	....	....	....	....	....	....
Sea transport, freight.................................	2 208 ..	....	....	....	....	....	....	....	....
Sea transport, other...................................	2 209 ..	....	....	....	....	....	....	....	....
Air transport, passenger.............................	2 211 ..	....	....	....	....	....	....	....	....
Air transport, freight..................................	2 212 ..	....	....	....	....	....	....	....	....
Air transport, other....................................	2 213 ..	....	....	....	....	....	....	....	....
Other transport, passenger........................	2 215 ..	....	....	....	....	....	....	....	....
Other transport, freight..............................	2 216 ..	....	....	....	....	....	....	....	....
Other transport, other................................	2 217 ..	....	....	....	....	....	....	....	....
Transportation services, debit.........................	3 205 ..	**−400.3**	**−469.0**	**−522.5**	**−534.1**	**−601.4**	**−645.7**	**−512.0**	**−549.2**
Passenger..	3 850 ..	*−19.8*	*−21.9*	*−20.4*	*−20.4*	*−27.2*	*−36.9*	*−29.6*	*−25.2*
Freight...	3 851 ..	*−164.6*	*−212.8*	*−246.8*	*−256.6*	*−283.7*	*−341.4*	*−247.0*	*−279.1*
Other..	3 852 ..	*−215.9*	*−234.3*	*−255.2*	*−257.1*	*−290.5*	*−267.4*	*−235.4*	*−244.8*
Sea transport, passenger...........................	3 207 ..	....	....	....	....	....	....	....	....
Sea transport, freight.................................	3 208 ..	....	....	....	....	....	....	....	....
Sea transport, other...................................	3 209 ..	....	....	....	....	....	....	....	....
Air transport, passenger.............................	3 211 ..	....	....	....	....	....	....	....	....
Air transport, freight..................................	3 212 ..	....	....	....	....	....	....	....	....
Air transport, other....................................	3 213 ..	....	....	....	....	....	....	....	....
Other transport, passenger........................	3 215 ..	....	....	....	....	....	....	....	....
Other transport, freight..............................	3 216 ..	....	....	....	....	....	....	....	....
Other transport, other................................	3 217 ..	....	....	....	....	....	....	....	....
Travel, credit..	2 236 ..	**696.7**	**856.1**	**871.0**	**1,005.3**	**1,303.7**	**1,453.8**	**1,120.1**	**1,285.3**
Business travel..	2 237 ..	244.8	330.7	368.0	367.0	450.2	517.2	389.2	452.2
Personal travel..	2 240 ..	452.0	525.4	503.0	638.3	853.5	936.6	730.9	833.1
Travel, debit...	3 236 ..	**−216.1**	**−254.8**	**−275.0**	**−326.8**	**−356.8**	**−451.7**	**−354.3**	**−398.0**
Business travel..	3 237 ..	−26.1	−14.0	−24.7	−14.4	−24.5	−45.0	−46.5	−33.6
Personal travel..	3 240 ..	−190.0	−240.8	−250.3	−312.4	−332.3	−406.6	−307.8	−364.4
Other services, credit.................................	2 200 BA	**248.2**	**226.7**	**363.0**	**303.5**	**470.8**	**644.3**	**781.0**	**1,034.1**
Communications..	2 245 ..	20.5	19.9	19.9	26.1	42.0	76.8	51.3	73.3
Construction..	2 249 ..	3.3	4.6	24.0	17.7	7.5	9.7	7.2	34.9
Insurance..	2 253 ..	8.6	6.5	3.4	6.5	9.4	15.0	26.8	28.9
Financial..	2 260 ..	12.7	17.9	17.1	20.8	32.6	47.9	72.3	55.6
Computer and information..........................	2 262 ..	9.2	12.3	16.9	24.3	20.3	15.9	30.8	29.4
Royalties and licence fees..........................	2 266 ..	....	.1	....	.2	.5	....	.1	.6
Other business services..............................	2 268 ..	182.3	155.5	265.2	197.8	343.0	459.0	574.2	757.8
Personal, cultural, and recreational.............	2 287 ..	5.3	3.6	2.4	1.9	4.2	5.8	4.2	14.5
Government, n.i.e......................................	2 291 ..	6.3	6.3	13.9	8.2	11.3	14.3	14.1	39.2
Other services, debit..................................	3 200 BA	**−289.9**	**−299.5**	**−400.3**	**−455.9**	**−611.1**	**−822.6**	**−741.0**	**−1,036.7**
Communications..	3 245 ..	−22.5	−20.0	−18.3	−30.3	−25.9	−31.1	−39.5	−56.1
Construction..	3 249 ..	−7.1	−3.5	−10.4	−4.3	−10.2	−20.9	−11.8	−49.3
Insurance..	3 253 ..	−39.7	−55.7	−59.6	−58.7	−62.4	−70.0	−54.5	−64.4
Financial..	3 260 ..	−6.3	−5.5	−4.2	−12.2	−24.2	−36.2	−32.1	−84.7
Computer and information..........................	3 262 ..	−8.0	−8.4	−6.4	−8.0	−7.4	−5.9	−8.0	−11.7
Royalties and licence fees..........................	3 266 ..	−1.7	−4.3	−4.7	−4.4	−6.0	−5.9	−5.2	−12.1
Other business services..............................	3 268 ..	−160.0	−162.6	−261.4	−299.7	−428.3	−602.6	−512.9	−667.7
Personal, cultural, and recreational.............	3 287 ..	−13.8	−21.3	−30.6	−33.5	−39.3	−39.6	−55.5	−62.7
Government, n.i.e......................................	3 291 ..	−30.8	−18.3	−4.7	−4.7	−7.3	−10.4	−21.6	−28.1

Table 2 (Continued). STANDARD PRESENTATION, 2003–2010

(Millions of U.S. dollars)

	Code	2003	2004	2005	2006	2007	2008	2009	2010
C. INCOME	4 300	**−30.0**	**−14.0**	**−8.5**	**50.1**	**223.1**	**178.2**	**55.0**	**201.6**
Total credit	2 300	*47.0*	*51.7*	*142.9*	*373.9*	*816.4*	*819.9*	*457.6*	*456.8*
Total debit	3 300	*−77.1*	*−65.7*	*−151.3*	*−323.8*	*−593.3*	*−641.7*	*−402.6*	*−255.1*
Compensation of employees, credit	2 310	**.6**	**.7**	**.6**	**.7**	**.7**	**.6**	**.7**	**.8**
Compensation of employees, debit	3 310	**−9.1**	**−9.3**	**−9.2**	**−10.1**	**−9.9**	**−12.7**	**−10.3**	**−8.5**
Investment income, credit	2 320	**46.5**	**51.0**	**142.2**	**373.2**	**815.7**	**819.2**	**456.9**	**456.0**
Direct investment income	2 330	2.7	3.9	4.5	2.4	4.1	6.0	25.7	28.6
Dividends and distributed branch profits	2 332	2.7	3.9	4.5	2.4	4.1	6.0	25.7	28.6
Reinvested earnings and undistributed branch profits	2 333	....	....	....	....	....	....	....	....
Income on debt (interest)	2 334	....	....	....	....	....	....	....	....
Portfolio investment income	2 339	3.4	3.5	3.4	3.6	9.9	10.0	26.9	17.0
Income on equity	2 340	3.4	3.5	3.4	3.6	9.9	10.0	26.9	17.0
Income on bonds and notes	2 350	....	....	....	....	....	....	....	....
Income on money market instruments	2 360	....	....	....	....	....	....	....	....
Other investment income	2 370	40.4	43.6	134.4	367.2	801.6	803.3	404.3	410.3
Investment income, debit	3 320	**−68.0**	**−56.4**	**−142.1**	**−313.8**	**−583.3**	**−629.0**	**−392.3**	**−246.7**
Direct investment income	3 330	−23.6	−13.6	−33.6	−88.1	−90.1	−163.2	−194.7	−91.9
Dividends and distributed branch profits	3 332	−23.6	−13.6	−33.6	−88.1	−90.1	−163.2	−194.7	−91.9
Reinvested earnings and undistributed branch profits	3 333	....	....	....	....	....	....	....	....
Income on debt (interest)	3 334	....	....	....	....	....	....	....	....
Portfolio investment income	3 339	−6.7	−9.0	−17.0	−23.0	−65.3	−62.3	−54.9	−72.7
Income on equity	3 340	−4.5	−8.1	−17.0	−23.0	−65.3	−62.3	−54.9	−72.7
Income on bonds and notes	3 350	....	....	....	....	....	....	....	....
Income on money market instruments	3 360	−2.3	−.8	....	....	....	....	....	....
Other investment income	3 370	−37.6	−33.8	−91.4	−202.7	−427.9	−403.4	−142.7	−82.2
D. CURRENT TRANSFERS	4 379	**52.4**	**49.3**	**61.0**	**71.1**	**124.9**	**224.2**	**223.7**	**183.3**
Credit	2 379	**163.0**	**168.1**	**162.3**	**179.3**	**250.1**	**411.2**	**413.1**	**404.4**
General government	2 380	15.1	22.0	16.4	17.7	22.8	91.7	115.2	66.6
Other sectors	2 390	147.9	146.0	145.9	161.6	227.3	319.5	297.9	337.8
Workers' remittances	2 391	....	....	....	....	....	....	....	....
Other current transfers	2 392	147.9	146.0	145.9	161.6	227.3	319.5	297.9	337.8
Debit	3 379	**−110.6**	**−118.7**	**−101.3**	**−108.2**	**−125.2**	**−187.0**	**−189.4**	**−221.1**
General government	3 380	−.5	−4.0	−5.9	−6.1	−5.3	−5.1	−12.6	−10.7
Other sectors	3 390	−110.1	−114.7	−95.4	−102.1	−119.9	−182.0	−176.8	−210.4
Workers' remittances	3 391	....	....	....	....	....	....	....	....
Other current transfers	3 392	−110.1	−114.7	−95.4	−102.1	−119.9	−182.0	−176.8	−210.4
CAPITAL AND FINANCIAL ACCOUNT	4 996	**−133.5**	**33.9**	**305.3**	**310.2**	**57.3**	**763.9**	**367.1**	**626.7**
CAPITAL ACCOUNT	4 994	**−.9**	**−1.6**	**−1.8**	**−2.7**	**−1.6**	**−1.4**	**−1.9**	**−4.8**
Total credit	2 994	....	....	....	....	....	....	....	....
Total debit	3 994	*−.9*	*−1.6*	*−1.8*	*−2.7*	*−1.6*	*−1.4*	*−1.9*	*−4.8*
Capital transfers, credit	2 400	....	....	....	....	....	....	....	....
General government	2 401	....	....	....	....	....	....	....	....
Debt forgiveness	2 402	....	....	....	....	....	....	....	....
Other capital transfers	2 410	....	....	....	....	....	....	....	....
Other sectors	2 430	....	....	....	....	....	....	....	....
Migrants' transfers	2 431	....	....	....	....	....	....	....	....
Debt forgiveness	2 432	....	....	....	....	....	....	....	....
Other capital transfers	2 440	....	....	....	....	....	....	....	....
Capital transfers, debit	3 400	**−.9**	**−1.6**	**−1.8**	**−2.7**	**−1.6**	**−1.4**	**−1.9**	**−4.8**
General government	3 401	....	....	....	....	....	....	....	....
Debt forgiveness	3 402	....	....	....	....	....	....	....	....
Other capital transfers	3 410	....	....	....	....	....	....	....	....
Other sectors	3 430	−.9	−1.6	−1.8	−2.7	−1.6	−1.4	−1.9	−4.8
Migrants' transfers	3 431	−.9	−1.6	−1.8	−2.7	−1.6	−1.4	−1.9	−4.8
Debt forgiveness	3 432	....	....	....	....	....	....	....	....
Other capital transfers	3 440	....	....	....	....	....	....	....	....
Nonproduced nonfinancial assets, credit	2 480	....	....	....	....	....	....	....	....
Nonproduced nonfinancial assets, debit	3 480	....	....	....	....	....	....	....	....

Table 2 (Continued). STANDARD PRESENTATION, 2003–2010

(Millions of U.S. dollars)

	Code	2003	2004	2005	2006	2007	2008	2009	2010
FINANCIAL ACCOUNT	4 995	**−132.7**	**35.5**	**307.0**	**312.9**	**58.9**	**765.3**	**369.1**	**631.5**
A. DIRECT INVESTMENT	4 500	**68.6**	**−17.9**	**−5.2**	**97.2**	**281.2**	**325.3**	**218.8**	**301.7**
Direct investment abroad	4 505	**6.0**	**−31.8**	**−47.0**	**−9.6**	**−59.6**	**−52.4**	**−37.8**	**−129.4**
Equity capital	4 510	6.0	−31.8	−47.0	−9.6	−59.6	−52.4	−37.8	−129.4
Claims on affiliated enterprises	4 515	....	....	....	....	....	....	....	....
Liabilities to affiliated enterprises	4 520	....	....	....	....	....	....	....	....
Reinvested earnings	4 525	....	....	....	....	....	....	....	....
Other capital	4 530	....	....	....	....	....	....	....	....
Claims on affiliated enterprises	4 535	....	....	....	....	....	....	....	....
Liabilities to affiliated enterprises	4 540	....	....	....	....	....	....	....	....
Direct investment in Mauritius	4 555	**62.6**	**13.9**	**41.8**	**106.8**	**340.8**	**377.7**	**256.7**	**431.0**
Equity capital	4 560	62.6	13.9	41.8	106.8	340.8	377.7	256.7	431.0
Claims on direct investors	4 565	....	....	....	....	....	....	....	....
Liabilities to direct investors	4 570	....	....	....	....	....	....	....	....
Reinvested earnings	4 575	....	....	....	....	....	....	....	....
Other capital	4 580	....	....	....	....	....	....	....	....
Claims on direct investors	4 585	....	....	....	....	....	....	....	....
Liabilities to direct investors	4 590	....	....	....	....	....	....	....	....
B. PORTFOLIO INVESTMENT	4 600	**−18.1**	**−37.0**	**−16.2**	**−29.9**	**58.4**	**−169.7**	**−56.3**	**−184.0**
Assets	4 602	**−27.1**	**−52.4**	**−41.6**	**−110.5**	**−95.3**	**−92.9**	**−261.1**	**−138.6**
Equity securities	4 610	−27.1	−52.4	−41.6	−110.5	−95.3	−92.9	−261.1	−138.6
Monetary authorities	4 611	....	....	....	....	....	....	....	....
General government	4 612	....	....	....	....	....	....	....	....
Banks	4 613	....	....	....	....	....	....	....	....
Other sectors	4 614	−27.1	−52.4	−41.6	−110.5	−95.3	−92.9	−261.1	−138.6
Debt securities	4 619	....	....	....	....	....	....	....	....
Bonds and notes	4 620	....	....	....	....	....	....	....	....
Monetary authorities	4 621	....	....	....	....	....	....	....	....
General government	4 622	....	....	....	....	....	....	....	....
Banks	4 623	....	....	....	....	....	....	....	....
Other sectors	4 624	....	....	....	....	....	....	....	....
Money market instruments	4 630	....	....	....	....	....	....	....	....
Monetary authorities	4 631	....	....	....	....	....	....	....	....
General government	4 632	....	....	....	....	....	....	....	....
Banks	4 633	....	....	....	....	....	....	....	....
Other sectors	4 634	....	....	....	....	....	....	....	....
Liabilities	4 652	**8.9**	**15.3**	**25.4**	**80.6**	**153.7**	**−76.8**	**204.8**	**−45.4**
Equity securities	4 660	8.1	19.3	35.6	35.1	49.8	33.9	206.0	−40.3
Banks	4 663	....	....	....	....	....	....	....	....
Other sectors	4 664	8.1	19.3	35.6	35.1	49.8	33.9	206.0	−40.3
Debt securities	4 669	.8	−3.9	−10.2	45.5	104.0	−110.6	−1.3	−5.2
Bonds and notes	4 670	....	....	1.1	46.0	....	....	....	....
Monetary authorities	4 671	....	....	....	....	....	....	....	....
General government	4 672	....	....	....	....	....	....	....	....
Banks	4 673	....	....	1.1	46.0	....	....	....	....
Other sectors	4 674	....	....	....	....	....	....	....	....
Money market instruments	4 680	.8	−3.9	−11.3	−.6	104.0	−110.6	−1.3	−5.2
Monetary authorities	4 681	1.5	.7	−2.1	....	1.5	−2.7	....	....
General government	4 682	−.7	−4.7	−9.3	−.6	102.5	−107.9	−1.3	−5.2
Banks	4 683	....	....	....	....	....	....	....	....
Other sectors	4 684	....	....	....	....	....	....	....	....
C. FINANCIAL DERIVATIVES	4 910	....	....	....	....	....	....	....	....
Monetary authorities	4 911	....	....	....	....	....	....	....	....
General government	4 912	....	....	....	....	....	....	....	....
Banks	4 913	....	....	....	....	....	....	....	....
Other sectors	4 914	....	....	....	....	....	....	....	....
Assets	4 900	....	....	....	....	....	....	....	....
Monetary authorities	4 901	....	....	....	....	....	....	....	....
General government	4 902	....	....	....	....	....	....	....	....
Banks	4 903	....	....	....	....	....	....	....	....
Other sectors	4 904	....	....	....	....	....	....	....	....
Liabilities	4 905	....	....	....	....	....	....	....	....
Monetary authorities	4 906	....	....	....	....	....	....	....	....
General government	4 907	....	....	....	....	....	....	....	....
Banks	4 908	....	....	....	....	....	....	....	....
Other sectors	4 909	....	....	....	....	....	....	....	....

Table 2 (Concluded). STANDARD PRESENTATION, 2003–2010

(Millions of U.S. dollars)

	Code	2003	2004	2005	2006	2007	2008	2009	2010
D. OTHER INVESTMENT	4 700	**39.2**	**63.0**	**163.4**	**105.5**	**155.3**	**787.5**	**591.2**	**722.8**
Assets	4 703	−22.8	−49.4	−230.9	−371.0	−2,972.8	631.8	−357.7	−3,851.4
Trade credits	4 706	....	....	....	....	....	....	....	....
General government	4 707	....	....	....	....	....	....	....	....
of which: Short-term	4 709	....	....	....	....	....	....	....	....
Other sectors	4 710	....	....	....	....	....	....	....	....
of which: Short-term	4 712	....	....	....	....	....	....	....	....
Loans	4 714	....	....	−92.6	5.3	−2,399.0	−1,425.0	1,166.8	1,078.5
Monetary authorities	4 715	....	....	....	....	....	....	....	....
General government	4 719	....	....	....	....	....	....	....	....
of which: Short-term	4 721	....	....	....	....	....	....	....	....
Banks	4 722	....	....	−92.6	5.3	−2,399.0	−1,425.0	1,166.8	1,078.5
of which: Short-term	4 724	....	....	*−92.6*	*5.3*	*−2,399.0*	*−1,425.0*	*1,166.8*	*1,078.5*
Other sectors	4 725	....	....	....	....	....	....	....	....
of which: Short-term	4 727	....	....	....	....	....	....	....	....
Currency and deposits	4 730	−4.3	−63.4	−133.9	−330.3	129.5	2,629.0	3,497.1	−1,860.0
Monetary authorities	4 731	....	....	....	....	....	....	....	....
General government	4 732	....	....	....	....	....	....	....	....
Banks	4 733	14.1	−44.2	−92.6	−306.9	129.5	2,629.0	3,497.1	−1,860.0
Other sectors	4 734	−18.3	−19.2	−41.3	−23.3	....	....	....	....
Other assets	4 736	−18.5	14.1	−4.4	−46.0	−703.4	−572.1	−5,021.7	−3,069.9
Monetary authorities	4 737	....	....	....	....	....	....	....	....
of which: Short-term	4 739	....	....	....	....	....	....	....	....
General government	4 740	....	....	....	....	....	....	....	....
of which: Short-term	4 742	....	....	....	....	....	....	....	....
Banks	4 743	....	....	−10.3	−36.9	−583.1	−587.8	−5,026.7	−3,059.7
of which: Short-term	4 745	....	....	*−10.3*	*−36.9*	*−583.1*	*−587.8*	*−5,026.7*	*−3,059.7*
Other sectors	4 746	−18.5	14.1	5.8	−9.1	−120.3	15.6	5.0	−10.2
of which: Short-term	4 748	*−18.5*	*14.1*	*5.8*	*−9.1*	*−120.3*	*15.6*	*5.0*	*−10.2*
Liabilities	4 753	**62.0**	**112.4**	**394.3**	**476.5**	**3,128.2**	**155.7**	**948.9**	**4,574.2**
Trade credits	4 756	....	80.8	210.3	231.2	244.4	292.4	191.1	283.4
General government	4 757	....	....	....	....	....	....	....	....
of which: Short-term	4 759	....	....	....	....	....	....	....	....
Other sectors	4 760	....	80.8	210.3	231.2	244.4	292.4	191.1	283.4
of which: Short-term	4 762	....	*80.8*	*210.3*	*231.2*	*244.4*	*292.4*	*191.1*	*283.4*
Loans	4 764	−90.7	−82.7	49.9	−3.0	1,040.3	98.6	−208.6	583.2
Monetary authorities	4 765	....	....	....	....	....	....	....	....
of which: Use of Fund credit and loans from the Fund	4 766	....	....	....	....	....	....	....	....
of which: Short-term	4 768	....	....	....	....	....	....	....	....
General government	4 769	−8.2	−7.3	10.3	−19.7	46.1	54.5	152.8	183.8
of which: Short-term	4 771	....	....	....	....	....	....	....	....
Banks	4 772	....	....	7.1	−5.0	960.2	116.0	−420.7	328.3
of which: Short-term	4 774	....	....	*7.1*	*−5.0*	*960.2*	*116.0*	*−420.7*	*328.3*
Other sectors	4 775	−82.5	−75.4	32.5	21.8	34.0	−72.0	59.3	71.1
of which: Short-term	4 777	....	....	....	....	....	....	....	....
Currency and deposits	4 780	152.7	114.3	134.1	248.3	1,260.5	−278.6	−1,136.5	−83.2
Monetary authorities	4 781	....	....	....	....	....	....	....	....
General government	4 782	....	....	....	....	....	....	....	....
Banks	4 783	6.1	56.7	....	....	1,090.5	−418.4	−1,248.4	−83.2
Other sectors	4 784	146.6	57.6	134.1	248.3	169.9	139.8	111.9	....
Other liabilities	4 786	....	....	....	....	583.0	43.3	2,103.0	3,790.8
Monetary authorities	4 787	....	....	....	....	....	....	126.6	....
of which: Short-term	4 789	....	....	....	....	....	....	....	....
General government	4 790	....	....	....	....	....	....	....	....
of which: Short-term	4 792	....	....	....	....	....	....	....	....
Banks	4 793	....	....	....	....	583.0	43.3	1,976.4	3,790.8
of which: Short-term	4 795	....	....	....	....	*583.0*	*43.3*	*1,976.4*	*3,790.8*
Other sectors	4 796	....	....	....	....	....	....	....	....
of which: Short-term	4 798	....	....	....	....	....	....	....	....
E. RESERVE ASSETS	4 802	**−222.4**	**27.5**	**165.0**	**140.1**	**−436.0**	**−177.9**	**−384.7**	**−209.0**
Monetary gold	4 812	....	....	....	....	....	....	−73.5	....
Special drawing rights	4 811	−.3	−.4	−.6	−.5	−.3	−.5	−126.7	.2
Reserve position in the Fund	4 810	−10.5	....	6.2	10.2	5.2	−9.1	....	−13.3
Foreign exchange	4 803	−211.6	27.9	159.4	130.4	−440.9	−168.3	−184.5	−195.9
Other claims	4 813	....	....	....	....	....	....	....	....
NET ERRORS AND OMISSIONS	4 998	**40.4**	**77.9**	**18.7**	**294.2**	**376.6**	**211.9**	**287.8**	**172.9**

Table 3. INTERNATIONAL INVESTMENT POSITION (End-period stocks), 2003–2010

(Millions of U.S. dollars)

	Code	2003	2004	2005	2006	2007	2008	2009	2010
ASSETS	8 995 C.	**2,159.2**	**2,184.3**	**2,139.0**	**2,484.7**	**3,561.6**	**11,714.7**	**12,709.5**	**16,360.5**
Direct investment abroad	8 505 ..	....	....	....	....	....	....	....	....
Equity capital and reinvested earnings	8 506 ..	....	....	....	....	....	....	....	....
Claims on affiliated enterprises	8 507 ..	....	....	....	....	....	....	....	....
Liabilities to affiliated enterprises	8 508 ..	....	....	....	....	....	....	....	....
Other capital	8 530 ..	....	....	....	....	....	....	....	....
Claims on affiliated enterprises	8 535 ..	....	....	....	....	....	....	....	....
Liabilities to affiliated enterprises	8 540 ..	....	....	....	....	....	....	....	....
Portfolio investment	8 602 ..	....	....	....	....	....	**1,434.6**	**1,914.8**	**2,559.0**
Equity securities	8 610 ..	....	....	....	....	....	349.6	375.1	106.1
Monetary authorities	8 611 ..	....	....	....	....	....	....	....	....
General government	8 612 ..	....	....	....	....	....	....	....	....
Banks	8 613 ..	....	....	....	....	....	117.2	118.8	106.1
Other sectors	8 614 ..	....	....	....	....	....	232.4	256.3	....
Debt securities	8 619 ..	....	....	....	....	....	1,084.9	1,539.7	2,452.9
Bonds and notes	8 620 ..	....	....	....	....	....	1,084.9	1,539.7	2,452.9
Monetary authorities	8 621 ..	....	....	....	....	....	....	....	....
General government	8 622 ..	....	....	....	....	....	....	....	....
Banks	8 623 ..	....	....	....	....	....	1,075.6	1,512.8	2,452.9
Other sectors	8 624 ..	....	....	....	....	....	9.3	26.9	....
Money market instruments	8 630 ..	....	....	....	....	....	....	....	....
Monetary authorities	8 631 ..	....	....	....	....	....	....	....	....
General government	8 632 ..	....	....	....	....	....	....	....	....
Banks	8 633 ..	....	....	....	....	....	....	....	....
Other sectors	8 634 ..	....	....	....	....	....	....	....	....
Financial derivatives	8 900 ..	....	....	....	....	....	**1,223.4**	**3,019.2**	**6,449.3**
Monetary authorities	8 901 ..	....	....	....	....	....	....	....	....
General government	8 902 ..	....	....	....	....	....	....	....	....
Banks	8 903 ..	....	....	....	....	....	1,223.4	3,019.2	6,449.3
Other sectors	8 904 ..	....	....	....	....	....	....	....	....
Other investment	8 703 ..	**560.7**	**554.4**	**773.2**	**1,183.8**	**1,739.9**	**7,271.4**	**5,471.9**	**4,750.7**
Trade credits	8 706 ..	....	....	....	....	....	....	....	....
General government	8 707 ..	....	....	....	....	....	....	....	....
of which: Short-term	8 709 ..	....	....	....	....	....	....	....	....
Other sectors	8 710 ..	....	....	....	....	....	....	....	....
of which: Short-term	8 712 ..	....	....	....	....	....	....	....	....
Loans	8 714 ..	....	....	204.7	195.3	338.3	3,721.7	4,052.4	3,612.7
Monetary authorities	8 715 ..	....	....	....	....	....	....	....	....
of which: Short-term	8 718 ..	....	....	....	....	....	....	....	....
General government	8 719 ..	....	....	....	....	....	....	....	....
of which: Short-term	8 721 ..	....	....	....	....	....	....	....	....
Banks	8 722 ..	....	....	204.7	195.3	338.3	3,721.7	4,052.4	3,612.7
of which: Short-term	8 724 ..	....	....	*204.7*	*195.3*	*338.3*	*3,721.7*	*4,052.4*	*3,612.7*
Other sectors	8 725 ..	....	....	....	....	....	....	....	....
of which: Short-term	8 727 ..	....	....	....	....	....	....	....	....
Currency and deposits	8 730 ..	503.1	512.5	416.1	766.3	1,148.2	3,488.1	1,365.6	916.2
Monetary authorities	8 731 ..	....	....	....	....	....	....	....	....
General government	8 732 ..	....	....	....	....	....	....	....	....
Banks	8 733 ..	503.1	512.5	416.1	766.3	1,148.2	3,488.1	1,365.6	916.2
Other sectors	8 734 ..	....	....	....	....	....	....	....	....
Other assets	8 736 ..	57.6	41.9	152.5	222.2	253.3	61.7	53.8	221.8
Monetary authorities	8 737 ..	....	....	....	....	....	....	....	....
of which: Short-term	8 739 ..	....	....	....	....	....	....	....	....
General government	8 740 ..	....	....	....	....	....	....	....	....
of which: Short-term	8 742 ..	....	....	....	....	....	....	....	....
Banks	8 743 ..	....	....	109.2	140.1	196.2	22.9	18.9	175.6
of which: Short-term	8 745 ..	....	....	*109.2*	*140.1*	*196.2*	*22.9*	*18.9*	*175.6*
Other sectors	8 746 ..	57.6	41.9	43.3	82.1	57.1	38.8	34.9	46.2
of which: Short-term	8 748 ..	*57.6*	*41.9*	*43.3*	*82.1*	*57.1*	*38.8*	*34.9*	*46.2*
Reserve assets	8 802 ..	**1,598.4**	**1,629.9**	**1,365.8**	**1,300.9**	**1,821.8**	**1,785.3**	**2,303.7**	**2,601.4**
Monetary gold	8 812 ..	21.1	23.9	25.9	31.3	41.5	42.7	124.9	159.6
Special drawing rights	8 811 ..	25.6	27.2	25.7	27.5	29.3	29.0	156.7	153.7
Reserve position in the Fund	8 810 ..	32.5	34.0	25.0	15.8	11.1	20.3	20.6	34.0
Foreign exchange	8 803 ..	1,519.2	1,544.7	1,289.2	1,226.3	1,739.9	1,693.4	2,001.5	2,254.2
Other claims	8 813 ..	....	....	....	....	....	....	....	....

Table 3 (Concluded). INTERNATIONAL INVESTMENT POSITION (End-period stocks), 2003–2010

(Millions of U.S. dollars)

	Code	2003	2004	2005	2006	2007	2008	2009	2010
LIABILITIES........	8 995 D.	**1,281.5**	**1,262.8**	**1,233.6**	**1,134.2**	**1,322.8**	**9,545.4**	**10,356.2**	**14,350.6**
Direct investment in Mauritius..........	8 555 ..	....	....	....	....	....	....	....	....
Equity capital and reinvested earnings........	8 556 ..	....	....	....	....	....	....	....	....
Claims on direct investors........	8 557 ..	....	....	....	....	....	....	....	....
Liabilities to direct investors........	8 558 ..	....	....	....	....	....	....	....	....
Other capital........	8 580 ..	....	....	....	....	....	....	....	....
Claims on direct investors........	8 585 ..	....	....	....	....	....	....	....	....
Liabilities to direct investors........	8 590 ..	....	....	....	....	....	....	....	....
Portfolio investment........	8 652 ..	**51.6**	**62.5**	**82.1**	**149.9**	**236.6**	**259.5**	**471.3**	**425.1**
Equity securities........	8 660 ..	33.8	49.9	80.3	104.0	180.8	188.2	406.1	363.1
Banks........	8 663 ..	....	....	....	....	....	....	....	....
Other sectors........	8 664 ..	33.8	49.9	80.3	104.0	180.8	188.2	406.1	363.1
Debt securities........	8 669 ..	17.8	12.7	1.8	45.9	55.8	71.3	65.2	62.0
Bonds and notes........	8 670 ..	....	....	1.1	45.9	55.8	49.6	50.8	50.7
Monetary authorities........	8 671 ..	....	....	....	....	....	....	....	....
General government........	8 672 ..	....	....	....	....	....	....	....	....
Banks........	8 673 ..	....	....	....	....	....	....	....	....
Other sectors........	8 674 ..	....	....	1.1	45.9	55.8	49.6	50.8	50.7
Money market instruments........	8 680 ..	17.8	12.7	.6	....	....	21.7	14.4	11.3
Monetary authorities........	8 681 ..	1.6	2.1	....	....	....	....	....	....
General government........	8 682 ..	16.2	10.5	.6	....	....	9.3	8.7	3.4
Banks........	8 683 ..	....	....	....	....	....	12.4	5.7	7.9
Other sectors........	8 684 ..	....	....	....	....	....	....	....	....
Financial derivatives........	8 905 ..	....	....	....	....	....	**1,238.9**	**2,998.7**	**6,430.7**
Monetary authorities........	8 906 ..	....	....	....	....	....	....	....	....
General government........	8 907 ..	....	....	....	....	....	....	....	....
Banks........	8 908 ..	....	....	....	....	....	1,238.9	2,998.7	6,430.7
Other sectors........	8 909 ..	....	....	....	....	....	....	....	....
Other investment........	8 753 ..	**1,229.9**	**1,200.3**	**1,151.5**	**984.3**	**1,086.1**	**8,047.0**	**6,886.1**	**7,494.9**
Trade credits........	8 756 ..	....	....	....	....	....	....	....	....
General government........	8 757 ..	....	....	....	....	....	....	....	....
of which: Short-term........	8 759 ..	....	....	....	....	....	....	....	....
Other sectors........	8 760 ..	....	....	....	....	....	....	....	....
of which: Short-term........	8 762 ..	....	....	....	....	....	....	....	....
Loans........	8 764 ..	1,004.6	933.0	1,151.5	984.3	1,086.1	4,111.0	3,984.3	4,459.3
Monetary authorities........	8 765 ..	....	....	....	....	....	....	....	....
of which: Use of Fund credit and loans from the Fund....	8 766 ..	....	....	....	....	....	....	....	....
of which: Short-term........	8 768 ..	....	....	....	....	....	....	....	....
General government........	8 769 ..	300.4	294.4	285.9	260.3	343.3	655.1	892.5	1,057.4
of which: Short-term........	8 771 ..	....	....	....	....	....	....	....	....
Banks........	8 772 ..	....	....	251.8	242.0	329.3	3,406.9	3,011.1	3,300.2
of which: Short-term........	8 774 ..	....	....	*251.8*	*242.0*	*329.3*	*3,406.9*	*3,011.1*	*3,300.2*
Other sectors........	8 775 ..	704.2	638.7	613.8	482.0	413.5	49.0	80.7	101.7
of which: Short-term........	8 777 ..	....	....	....	....	....	....	....	....
Currency and deposits........	8 780 ..	225.3	267.3	....	....	....	3,808.8	2,642.4	2,558.4
Monetary authorities........	8 781 ..	....	....	....	....	....	....	....	....
General government........	8 782 ..	....	....	....	....	....	....	....	....
Banks........	8 783 ..	225.3	267.3	....	....	....	3,808.8	2,642.4	2,558.4
Other sectors........	8 784 ..	....	....	....	....	....	....	....	....
Other liabilities........	8 786 ..	....	....	....	....	....	127.2	259.4	477.2
Monetary authorities........	8 787 ..	....	....	....	....	....	....	151.7	149.1
of which: Short-term........	8 789 ..	....	....	....	....	....	....	....	....
General government........	8 790 ..	....	....	....	....	....	....	....	....
of which: Short-term........	8 792 ..	....	....	....	....	....	....	....	....
Banks........	8 793 ..	....	....	....	....	....	127.2	107.7	328.1
of which: Short-term........	8 795 ..	....	....	....	....	....	*127.2*	*107.7*	*328.1*
Other sectors........	8 796 ..	....	....	....	....	....	....	....	....
of which: Short-term........	8 798 ..	....	....	....	....	....	....	....	....
NET INTERNATIONAL INVESTMENT POSITION........	8 995 ..	**877.7**	**921.5**	**905.4**	**1,350.6**	**2,238.9**	**2,169.3**	**2,353.3**	**2,009.9**
Conversion rates: Mauritian rupees per U.S. dollar (end of period)........	0 102 ..	**26.088**	**28.204**	**30.667**	**34.337**	**28.216**	**31.756**	**30.291**	**30.391**

Table 1. ANALYTIC PRESENTATION, 2003–2010

(Millions of U.S. dollars)

	Code	2003	2004	2005	2006	2007	2008	2009	2010
A. Current Account[1]	4 993 Z.	**−7,177**	**−5,253**	**−5,095**	**−4,502**	**−8,865**	**−16,353**	**−6,368**	**−5,679**
Goods: exports f.o.b.	2 100 ..	164,986	188,294	214,633	250,319	272,293	291,886	229,975	298,860
Goods: imports f.o.b.	3 100 ..	−170,925	−197,270	−222,484	−256,777	−282,802	−309,672	−235,042	−301,940
Balance on Goods	4 100 ..	*−5,938*	*−8,976*	*−7,851*	*−6,457*	*−10,509*	*−17,786*	*−5,067*	*−3,080*
Services: credit	2 200 ..	12,397	13,711	15,666	15,827	17,072	17,496	14,496	14,937
Services: debit	3 200 ..	−17,763	−19,319	−20,776	−22,115	−23,212	−24,466	−22,935	−25,137
Balance on Goods and Services	4 991 ..	*−11,304*	*−14,584*	*−12,960*	*−12,745*	*−16,649*	*−24,756*	*−13,506*	*−13,280*
Income: credit	2 300 ..	3,858	5,657	5,110	6,244	7,749	7,566	5,269	5,290
Income: debit	3 300 ..	−15,316	−15,073	−19,367	−23,935	−26,347	−24,612	−19,648	−19,179
Balance on Goods, Services, and Income	4 992 ..	*−22,762*	*−24,000*	*−27,217*	*−30,436*	*−35,246*	*−41,802*	*−27,885*	*−27,169*
Current transfers: credit	2 379 Z.	15,622	18,827	22,179	26,022	26,489	25,576	21,578	21,577
Current transfers: debit	3 379 ..	−37	−80	−57	−88	−108	−128	−60	−86
B. Capital Account[1]	4 994 Z.	....	....	....	....	....	....	....	....
Capital account: credit	2 994 Z.	....	....	....	....	....	....	....	....
Capital account: debit	3 994 ..	....	....	....	....	....	....	....	....
Total, Groups A Plus B	4 981 ..	*−7,177*	*−5,253*	*−5,095*	*−4,502*	*−8,865*	*−16,353*	*−6,368*	*−5,679*
C. Financial Account[1]	4 995 W.	**18,997**	**14,166**	**16,757**	**−2,479**	**22,812**	**28,280**	**23,237**	**36,661**
Direct investment abroad	4 505 ..	−1,253	−4,432	−6,474	−5,758	−8,256	−1,157	−7,019	−13,570
Direct investment in Mexico	4 555 Z.	16,246	24,818	24,280	19,951	30,070	26,948	15,575	19,627
Portfolio investment assets	4 602 ..	1,215	−1,754	−3,316	−6,008	−4,730	−2,131	3,885	2,340
Equity securities	4 610 ..	....	....	....	....	....	....	....	....
Debt securities	4 619 ..	1,215	−1,754	−3,316	−6,008	−4,730	−2,131	3,885	2,340
Portfolio investment liabilities	4 652 Z.	3,006	5,094	7,713	137	13,349	4,826	15,275	37,137
Equity securities	4 660 ..	−123	−2,522	3,353	2,805	−482	−3,503	4,169	641
Debt securities	4 669 Z.	3,129	7,616	4,360	−2,668	13,831	8,329	11,106	36,496
Financial derivatives	4 910 ..	....	....	....	....	....	....	....	....
Financial derivatives assets	4 900 ..	....	....	....	....	....	....	....	....
Financial derivatives liabilities	4 905 ..	....	....	....	....	....	....	....	....
Other investment assets	4 703 ..	3,503	−5,579	−4,403	−6,148	−17,046	−5,791	−14,849	−20,758
Monetary authorities	4 701 ..	....	....	....	....	....	....	....	....
General government	4 704 ..	....	....	....	....	....	....	....	....
Banks	4 705 ..	3,332	748	−1,940	−2,420	−3,746	−10,380	6,355	−3,372
Other sectors	4 728 ..	171	−6,328	−2,463	−3,728	−13,300	4,589	−21,204	−17,386
Other investment liabilities	4 753 W.	−3,719	−3,981	−1,044	−4,653	9,426	5,586	10,371	11,885
Monetary authorities	4 753 WA	....	....	....	....	....	....	11,229	−3,221
General government	4 753 ZB	1,861	752	1,494	−1,497	1,643	1,982	5,353	4,268
Banks	4 753 ZC	−1,160	−2,728	−5,321	−7,774	1,765	−1,636	999	10,215
Other sectors	4 753 ZD	−4,419	−2,004	2,783	4,618	6,019	5,240	−7,211	623
Total, Groups A Through C	4 983 ..	*11,820*	*8,913*	*11,662*	*−6,981*	*13,947*	*11,927*	*16,870*	*30,982*
D. Net Errors and Omissions	4 998 ..	**−2,003**	**−4,809**	**−4,698**	**5,678**	**−3,697**	**−4,196**	**−11,180**	**−8,044**
Total, Groups A Through D	4 984 ..	*9,817*	*4,104*	*6,964*	*−1,303*	*10,250*	*7,731*	*5,690*	*22,938*
E. Reserves and Related Items	4 802 A.	**−9,817**	**−4,104**	**−6,964**	**1,303**	**−10,250**	**−7,731**	**−5,690**	**−22,938**
Reserve assets	4 802 ..	−9,833	−4,120	−6,980	1,288	−10,264	−7,745	−5,703	−22,952
Use of Fund credit and loans	4 766 ..	....	....	....	....	....	....	....	....
Exceptional financing	4 920 ..	16	15	15	15	14	14	14	13
Conversion rates: Mexican pesos per U.S. dollar	0 101 ..	**10.7890**	**11.2860**	**10.8979**	**10.8992**	**10.9282**	**11.1297**	**13.5135**	**12.6360**

[1] Excludes components that have been classified in the categories of Group E.

Table 2. STANDARD PRESENTATION, 2003–2010

(Millions of U.S. dollars)

	Code	2003	2004	2005	2006	2007	2008	2009	2010
CURRENT ACCOUNT..............................	4 993 ..	**−7,161**	**−5,237**	**−5,079**	**−4,487**	**−8,851**	**−16,339**	**−6,354**	**−5,665**
A. GOODS..........................	4 100 ..	**−5,938**	**−8,976**	**−7,851**	**−6,457**	**−10,509**	**−17,786**	**−5,067**	**−3,080**
Credit..................................	2 100 ..	**164,986**	**188,294**	**214,633**	**250,319**	**272,293**	**291,886**	**229,975**	**298,860**
General merchandise: exports f.o.b....................	2 110 ..	164,600	187,838	213,919	248,882	270,297	288,669	225,699	292,720
Goods for processing: exports f.o.b....................	2 150 ..	....	....	....	....	....	....	....	....
Repairs on goods................................	2 160 ..	....	....	....	....	....	....	....	....
Goods procured in ports by carriers...................	2 170 ..	220	296	400	394	418	544	271	387
Nonmonetary gold...............................	2 180 ..	167	161	314	1,043	1,578	2,673	4,004	5,753
Debit..................................	3 100 ..	**−170,925**	**−197,270**	**−222,484**	**−256,777**	**−282,802**	**−309,672**	**−235,042**	**−301,940**
General merchandise: imports f.o.b....................	3 110 ..	−170,285	−196,604	−221,696	−255,787	−281,573	−308,267	−234,232	−301,308
Goods for processing: imports f.o.b....................	3 150 ..	....	....	....	....	....	....	....	....
Repairs on goods................................	3 160 ..	−147	−132	−141	−145	−197	−172	−141	−120
Goods procured in ports by carriers...................	3 170 ..	−232	−328	−524	−573	−655	−898	−516	−338
Nonmonetary gold...............................	3 180 ..	−261	−205	−123	−271	−376	−336	−153	−174
B. SERVICES.........................	4 200 ..	**−5,365**	**−5,608**	**−5,109**	**−6,288**	**−6,140**	**−6,969**	**−8,439**	**−10,200**
Total credit..................................	2 200 ..	*12,397*	*13,711*	*15,666*	*15,827*	*17,072*	*17,496*	*14,496*	*14,937*
Total debit..................................	3 200 ..	*−17,763*	*−19,319*	*−20,776*	*−22,115*	*−23,212*	*−24,466*	*−22,935*	*−25,137*
Transportation services, credit....................	2 205 ..	**893**	**1,066**	**1,353**	**1,518**	**1,512**	**1,768**	**1,342**	**1,062**
Passenger..................................	2 850 ..	*696*	*813*	*998*	*1,152*	*1,136*	*1,358*	*1,034*	*657*
Freight..................................	2 851 ..	....	....	....	....	....	....	....	....
Other..................................	2 852 ..	*197*	*253*	*355*	*366*	*376*	*411*	*309*	*405*
Sea transport, passenger.....................	2 207 ..	....	....	....	....	....	....	....	....
Sea transport, freight.....................	2 208 ..	....	....	....	....	....	....	....	....
Sea transport, other.....................	2 209 ..	77	67	122	86	76	64	55	54
Air transport, passenger.....................	2 211 ..	696	813	998	1,152	1,136	1,358	1,034	657
Air transport, freight.....................	2 212 ..	....	....	....	....	....	....	....	....
Air transport, other.....................	2 213 ..	121	186	233	280	300	347	254	350
Other transport, passenger.....................	2 215 ..	....	....	....	....	....	....	....	....
Other transport, freight.....................	2 216 ..	....	....	....	....	....	....	....	....
Other transport, other.....................	2 217 ..	....	....	....	....	....	....	....	....
Transportation services, debit....................	3 205 ..	**−5,713**	**−6,747**	**−8,070**	**−8,940**	**−9,936**	**−11,847**	**−9,267**	**−10,707**
Passenger..................................	3 850 ..	*−999*	*−1,075*	*−1,351*	*−1,279*	*−1,456*	*−1,659*	*−1,494*	*−1,791*
Freight..................................	3 851 ..	*−4,445*	*−5,378*	*−6,374*	*−7,301*	*−8,172*	*−9,841*	*−7,453*	*−8,585*
Other..................................	3 852 ..	*−269*	*−295*	*−345*	*−359*	*−307*	*−347*	*−320*	*−331*
Sea transport, passenger.....................	3 207 ..	....	....	....	....	....	....	....	....
Sea transport, freight.....................	3 208 ..	−2,355	−3,031	−3,807	−4,426	−5,111	−6,354	−4,514	−6,141
Sea transport, other.....................	3 209 ..	−6							
Air transport, passenger.....................	3 211 ..	−999	−1,075	−1,351	−1,279	−1,456	−1,659	−1,494	−1,791
Air transport, freight.....................	3 212 ..	−2,090	−2,347	−2,567	−2,875	−3,061	−3,487	−2,939	−2,444
Air transport, other.....................	3 213 ..	−262	−295	−345	−359	−307	−347	−320	−331
Other transport, passenger.....................	3 215 ..	....	....	....	....	....	....	....	....
Other transport, freight.....................	3 216 ..	....	....	....	....	....	....	....	....
Other transport, other.....................	3 217 ..	....	....	....	....	....	....	....	....
Travel, credit............................	2 236 ..	**9,362**	**10,796**	**11,803**	**12,177**	**12,852**	**13,289**	**11,275**	**11,760**
Business travel................................	2 237 ..	439	511	716	732	745	751	617	743
Personal travel................................	2 240 ..	8,922	10,285	11,088	11,445	12,107	12,538	10,658	11,017
Travel, debit............................	3 236 ..	**−6,253**	**−6,959**	**−7,600**	**−8,108**	**−8,375**	**−8,526**	**−7,132**	**−7,284**
Business travel................................	3 237 ..	−614	−702	−827	−806	−970	−1,041	−970	−1,101
Personal travel................................	3 240 ..	−5,640	−6,257	−6,773	−7,303	−7,404	−7,485	−6,161	−6,183
Other services, credit........................	2 200 BA	**2,143**	**1,849**	**2,510**	**2,132**	**2,708**	**2,439**	**1,878**	**2,115**
Communications...............................	2 245 ..	423	423	548	466	400	336	203	202
Construction..................................	2 249 ..	....	....	....	....	....	....	....	....
Insurance..................................	2 253 ..	1,163	864	1,550	1,263	1,999	2,010	1,594	1,831
Financial..................................	2 260 ..	....	....	....	....	....	....	....	....
Computer and information.....................	2 262 ..	....	....	....	....	....	....	....	....
Royalties and licence fees.....................	2 266 ..	84	52	....	....	....	....	....	....
Other business services.....................	2 268 ..	41	80	....	....	−11	....	−1	....
Personal, cultural, and recreational...............	2 287 ..	293	358	373	383	308	87	80	80
Government, n.i.e...............................	2 291 ..	140	74	39	20	11	6	3	2
Other services, debit........................	3 200 BA	**−5,797**	**−5,612**	**−5,106**	**−5,067**	**−4,901**	**−4,093**	**−6,536**	**−7,146**
Communications...............................	3 245 ..	−310	−175	−119	−107	−99	−94	−72	−80
Construction..................................	3 249 ..	....	....	....	....	....	....	....	....
Insurance..................................	3 253 ..	−2,316	−2,288	−2,340	−1,977	−2,764	−2,732	−3,199	−2,625
Financial..................................	3 260 ..	−400	−412	−550	−374	−270	−116	−419	−548
Computer and information.....................	3 262 ..	....	....	....	....	....	....	....	....
Royalties and licence fees.....................	3 266 ..	−608	−805	−111	−503	....	....	....	....
Other business services.....................	3 268 ..	−1,372	−1,178	−1,186	−1,277	−672	−389	−384	−302
Personal, cultural, and recreational...............	3 287 ..	−220	−225	−275	−326	−259	−227	−272	−272
Government, n.i.e...............................	3 291 ..	−570	−529	−525	−504	−837	−534	−2,190	−3,319

2011, International Monetary Fund: *Balance of Payments Statistics Yearbook*

Table 2 (Continued). STANDARD PRESENTATION, 2003–2010

(Millions of U.S. dollars)

	Code	2003	2004	2005	2006	2007	2008	2009	2010
C. INCOME	4 300	**−11,458**	**−9,416**	**−14,257**	**−17,691**	**−18,598**	**−17,046**	**−14,379**	**−13,889**
Total credit	2 300	*3,858*	*5,657*	*5,110*	*6,244*	*7,749*	*7,566*	*5,269*	*5,290*
Total debit	3 300	*−15,316*	*−15,073*	*−19,367*	*−23,935*	*−26,347*	*−24,612*	*−19,648*	*−19,179*
Compensation of employees, credit	2 310	**1,515**	**1,530**	**1,054**	**976**	**821**	**897**	**769**	**776**
Compensation of employees, debit	3 310	....	....	....	....	....	....	....	....
Investment income, credit	2 320	**2,343**	**4,127**	**4,056**	**5,268**	**6,928**	**6,670**	**4,500**	**4,513**
Direct investment income	2 330	....	1,916	1,046	171	616	825	687	795
Dividends and distributed branch profits	2 332	....	40	70	171	120	440	656	....
Reinvested earnings and undistributed branch profits	2 333	....	1,876	975	....	497	385	31	795
Income on debt (interest)	2 334	....	....	....	....	....	....	....	....
Portfolio investment income	2 339	....	....	....	....	....	....	....	....
Income on equity	2 340	....	....	....	....	....	....	....	....
Income on bonds and notes	2 350	....	....	....	....	....	....	....	....
Income on money market instruments	2 360	....	....	....	....	....	....	....	....
Other investment income	2 370	2,343	2,211	3,011	5,097	6,312	5,845	3,813	3,718
Investment income, debit	3 320	**−15,316**	**−15,073**	**−19,367**	**−23,935**	**−26,347**	**−24,612**	**−19,648**	**−19,179**
Direct investment income	3 330	−3,646	−3,851	−7,107	−10,173	−11,609	−10,091	−7,893	−6,495
Dividends and distributed branch profits	3 332	−1,541	−1,326	−3,075	−2,423	−3,529	−2,295	−3,514	−3,839
Reinvested earnings and undistributed branch profits	3 333	−2,105	−2,525	−4,032	−7,750	−8,080	−7,796	−4,379	−2,657
Income on debt (interest)	3 334	....	....	....	....	....	....	....	....
Portfolio investment income	3 339	−197	−269	−625	−887	−1,318	−1,908	−1,791	−2,891
Income on equity	3 340	....	....	....	....	....	....	....	....
Income on bonds and notes	3 350	....	....	....	....	....	....	....	....
Income on money market instruments	3 360	−197	−269	−625	−887	−1,318	−1,908	−1,791	−2,891
Other investment income	3 370	−11,473	−10,953	−11,634	−12,875	−13,420	−12,613	−9,965	−9,793
D. CURRENT TRANSFERS	4 379	**15,601**	**18,763**	**22,137**	**25,949**	**26,396**	**25,462**	**21,531**	**21,504**
Credit	2 379	**15,638**	**18,843**	**22,194**	**26,037**	**26,503**	**25,591**	**21,592**	**21,590**
General government	2 380	54	54	54	53	53	52	52	52
Other sectors	2 390	15,583	18,789	22,141	25,983	26,451	25,538	21,539	21,538
Workers' remittances	2 391	15,139	18,332	21,688	25,567	26,050	25,139	21,245	21,271
Other current transfers	2 392	445	457	452	417	401	399	295	267
Debit	3 379	**−37**	**−80**	**−57**	**−88**	**−108**	**−128**	**−60**	**−86**
General government	3 380	....	....	....	....	....	....	....	....
Other sectors	3 390	−37	−80	−57	−88	−108	−128	−60	−86
Workers' remittances	3 391	....	....	....	....	....	....	....	....
Other current transfers	3 392	−37	−80	−57	−88	−108	−128	−60	−86
CAPITAL AND FINANCIAL ACCOUNT	4 996	**9,164**	**10,046**	**9,777**	**−1,191**	**12,548**	**20,535**	**17,534**	**13,709**
CAPITAL ACCOUNT	4 994	....	....	....	....	....	....	....	....
Total credit	2 994	....	....	....	....	....	....	....	....
Total debit	3 994	....	....	....	....	....	....	....	....
Capital transfers, credit	2 400	....	....	....	....	....	....	....	....
General government	2 401	....	....	....	....	....	....	....	....
Debt forgiveness	2 402	....	....	....	....	....	....	....	....
Other capital transfers	2 410	....	....	....	....	....	....	....	....
Other sectors	2 430	....	....	....	....	....	....	....	....
Migrants' transfers	2 431	....	....	....	....	....	....	....	....
Debt forgiveness	2 432	....	....	....	....	....	....	....	....
Other capital transfers	2 440	....	....	....	....	....	....	....	....
Capital transfers, debit	3 400	....	....	....	....	....	....	....	....
General government	3 401	....	....	....	....	....	....	....	....
Debt forgiveness	3 402	....	....	....	....	....	....	....	....
Other capital transfers	3 410	....	....	....	....	....	....	....	....
Other sectors	3 430	....	....	....	....	....	....	....	....
Migrants' transfers	3 431	....	....	....	....	....	....	....	....
Debt forgiveness	3 432	....	....	....	....	....	....	....	....
Other capital transfers	3 440	....	....	....	....	....	....	....	....
Nonproduced nonfinancial assets, credit	2 480	....	....	....	....	....	....	....	....
Nonproduced nonfinancial assets, debit	3 480	....	....	....	....	....	....	....	....

Table 2 (Continued). STANDARD PRESENTATION, 2003–2010

(Millions of U.S. dollars)

	Code	2003	2004	2005	2006	2007	2008	2009	2010
FINANCIAL ACCOUNT........................	4 995 ..	**9,164**	**10,046**	**9,777**	**−1,191**	**12,548**	**20,535**	**17,534**	**13,709**
A. DIRECT INVESTMENT.....................	4 500 ..	**14,993**	**20,386**	**17,806**	**14,193**	**21,813**	**25,791**	**8,556**	**6,056**
Direct investment abroad...................	4 505 ..	**−1,253**	**−4,432**	**−6,474**	**−5,758**	**−8,256**	**−1,157**	**−7,019**	**−13,570**
Equity capital............................	4 510 ..	−1,253	−1,901	−3,726	−5,452	−4,239	−1,253	−6,093	−11,845
Claims on affiliated enterprises............	4 515 ..	−1,253	−1,901	−3,726	−5,452	−4,239	−1,253	−6,093	−11,845
Liabilities to affiliated enterprises.........	4 520 ..	....	....	....	....	....	....	....	....
Reinvested earnings......................	4 525 ..	....	−1,876	−975	....	−497	−385	−31	−795
Other capital............................	4 530 ..	....	−655	−1,772	−307	−3,520	481	−895	−930
Claims on affiliated enterprises............	4 535 ..	....	−655	−1,772	−307	−3,520	481	−895	−930
Liabilities to affiliated enterprises.........	4 540 ..	....	....	....	....	....	....	....	....
Direct investment in Mexico...............	4 555 ..	**16,246**	**24,818**	**24,280**	**19,951**	**30,070**	**26,948**	**15,575**	**19,627**
Equity capital............................	4 560 ..	7,008	14,859	12,929	6,045	16,238	11,290	6,972	12,995
Claims on direct investors................	4 565 ..	....	....	....	....	....	....	....	....
Liabilities to direct investors.............	4 570 ..	7,008	14,859	12,929	6,045	16,238	11,290	6,972	12,995
Reinvested earnings......................	4 575 ..	2,105	2,525	4,032	7,750	8,080	7,796	4,379	2,657
Other capital............................	4 580 ..	7,134	7,434	7,320	6,156	5,752	7,862	4,224	3,975
Claims on direct investors................	4 585 ..	....	....	....	....	....	....	....	....
Liabilities to direct investors.............	4 590 ..	7,134	7,434	7,320	6,156	5,752	7,862	4,224	3,975
B. PORTFOLIO INVESTMENT.................	4 600 ..	**4,220**	**3,340**	**4,397**	**−5,871**	**8,618**	**2,695**	**19,159**	**39,478**
Assets..................................	4 602 ..	**1,215**	**−1,754**	**−3,316**	**−6,008**	**−4,730**	**−2,131**	**3,885**	**2,340**
Equity securities.........................	4 610 ..	....	....	....	....	....	....	....	....
Monetary authorities....................	4 611 ..	....	....	....	....	....	....	....	....
General government.....................	4 612 ..	....	....	....	....	....	....	....	....
Banks.................................	4 613 ..	....	....	....	....	....	....	....	....
Other sectors..........................	4 614 ..	....	....	....	....	....	....	....	....
Debt securities..........................	4 619 ..	1,215	−1,754	−3,316	−6,008	−4,730	−2,131	3,885	2,340
Bonds and notes........................	4 620 ..	1,215	−1,754	−3,316	−6,008	−4,730	−2,131	3,885	2,340
Monetary authorities..................	4 621 ..	....	....	....	....	....	....	....	....
General government...................	4 622 ..	91	1,718						
Banks................................	4 623 ..	....	....	....	....	....	....	....	....
Other sectors.........................	4 624 ..	1,124	−3,472	−3,316	−6,008	−4,730	−2,131	3,885	2,340
Money market instruments................	4 630 ..	....	....	....	....	....	....	....	....
Monetary authorities..................	4 631 ..	....	....	....	....	....	....	....	....
General government...................	4 632 ..	....	....	....	....	....	....	....	....
Banks................................	4 633 ..	....	....	....	....	....	....	....	....
Other sectors.........................	4 634 ..	....	....	....	....	....	....	....	....
Liabilities..............................	4 652 ..	**3,006**	**5,094**	**7,713**	**137**	**13,349**	**4,826**	**15,275**	**37,137**
Equity securities.........................	4 660 ..	−123	−2,522	3,353	2,805	−482	−3,503	4,169	641
Banks.................................	4 663 ..	....	....	....	....	....	....	....	....
Other sectors..........................	4 664 ..	−123	−2,522	3,353	2,805	−482	−3,503	4,169	641
Debt securities..........................	4 669 ..	3,129	7,616	4,360	−2,668	13,831	8,329	11,106	36,496
Bonds and notes........................	4 670 ..	2,369	2,567	1,667	−5,181	6,020	2,396	7,627	13,369
Monetary authorities..................	4 671 ..	....	....	....	....	....	....	....	....
General government...................	4 672 ..	−258	1,976	−1,550	−9,516	−3,066	−2,052	1,938	4,533
Banks................................	4 673 ..	−1,025	−900	−347	260	220	....	−233	....
Other sectors.........................	4 674 ..	3,652	1,491	3,563	4,074	8,866	4,448	5,922	8,836
Money market instruments................	4 680 ..	760	5,050	2,693	2,513	7,811	5,933	3,479	23,127
Monetary authorities..................	4 681 ..	....	....	....	....	....	....	....	....
General government...................	4 682 ..	744	5,007	2,774	2,512	7,810	5,953	3,479	23,126
Banks................................	4 683 ..	15	42	−81	1	1	−20	....	1
Other sectors.........................	4 684 ..	....	....	....	....	....	....	....	....
C. FINANCIAL DERIVATIVES................	4 910 ..	....	....	....	....	....	....	....	....
Monetary authorities.....................	4 911 ..	....	....	....	....	....	....	....	....
General government......................	4 912 ..	....	....	....	....	....	....	....	....
Banks...................................	4 913 ..	....	....	....	....	....	....	....	....
Other sectors............................	4 914 ..	....	....	....	....	....	....	....	....
Assets..................................	4 900 ..	....	....	....	....	....	....	....	....
Monetary authorities.....................	4 901 ..	....	....	....	....	....	....	....	....
General government......................	4 902 ..	....	....	....	....	....	....	....	....
Banks...................................	4 903 ..	....	....	....	....	....	....	....	....
Other sectors............................	4 904 ..	....	....	....	....	....	....	....	....
Liabilities..............................	4 905 ..	....	....	....	....	....	....	....	....
Monetary authorities.....................	4 906 ..	....	....	....	....	....	....	....	....
General government......................	4 907 ..	....	....	....	....	....	....	....	....
Banks...................................	4 908 ..	....	....	....	....	....	....	....	....
Other sectors............................	4 909 ..	....	....	....	....	....	....	....	....

Table 2 (Concluded). STANDARD PRESENTATION, 2003–2010

(Millions of U.S. dollars)

	Code	2003	2004	2005	2006	2007	2008	2009	2010
D. OTHER INVESTMENT	4 700	−216	−9,560	−5,447	−10,801	−7,620	−205	−4,478	−8,873
Assets	4 703	3,503	−5,579	−4,403	−6,148	−17,046	−5,791	−14,849	−20,758
Trade credits	4 706	46	....	....	....	....	....	....	....
General government	4 707	....	....	....	....	....	....	....	....
of which: Short-term	4 709	....	....	....	....	....	....	....	....
Other sectors	4 710	46	....	....	....	....	....	....	....
of which: Short-term	4 712	46	....	....	....	....	....	....	....
Loans	4 714	....	....	....	....	....	....	....	....
Monetary authorities	4 715	....	....	....	....	....	....	....	....
of which: Short-term	4 718	....	....	....	....	....	....	....	....
General government	4 719	....	....	....	....	....	....	....	....
of which: Short-term	4 721	....	....	....	....	....	....	....	....
Banks	4 722	....	....	....	....	....	....	....	....
of which: Short-term	4 724	....	....	....	....	....	....	....	....
Other sectors	4 725	....	....	....	....	....	....	....	....
of which: Short-term	4 727	....	....	....	....	....	....	....	....
Currency and deposits	4 730	3,457	−5,579	−4,403	−6,148	−17,046	−5,791	−14,849	−20,758
Monetary authorities	4 731	....	....	....	....	....	....	....	....
General government	4 732	....	....	....	....	....	....	....	....
Banks	4 733	3,332	748	−1,940	−2,420	−3,746	−10,380	6,355	−3,372
Other sectors	4 734	125	−6,328	−2,463	−3,728	−13,300	4,589	−21,204	−17,386
Other assets	4 736	....	....	....	....	....	....	....	....
Monetary authorities	4 737	....	....	....	....	....	....	....	....
of which: Short-term	4 739	....	....	....	....	....	....	....	....
General government	4 740	....	....	....	....	....	....	....	....
of which: Short-term	4 742	....	....	....	....	....	....	....	....
Banks	4 743	....	....	....	....	....	....	....	....
of which: Short-term	4 745	....	....	....	....	....	....	....	....
Other sectors	4 746	....	....	....	....	....	....	....	....
of which: Short-term	4 748	....	....	....	....	....	....	....	....
Liabilities	4 753	−3,719	−3,981	−1,044	−4,653	9,426	5,586	10,371	11,885
Trade credits	4 756	....	....	....	....	....	....	....	....
General government	4 757	....	....	....	....	....	....	....	....
of which: Short-term	4 759	....	....	....	....	....	....	....	....
Other sectors	4 760	....	....	....	....	....	....	....	....
of which: Short-term	4 762	....	....	....	....	....	....	....	....
Loans	4 764	−3,719	−3,981	−1,044	−4,653	9,426	5,586	6,371	11,885
Monetary authorities	4 765	....	....	....	....	....	....	7,229	−3,221
of which: Use of Fund credit and loans from the Fund	4 766	....	....	....	....	....	....	....	....
of which: Short-term	4 768	....	....	....	....	....	....	....	....
General government	4 769	1,861	752	1,494	−1,497	1,643	1,982	5,353	4,268
of which: Short-term	4 771	....	....	....	....	....	....	....	....
Banks	4 772	−1,160	−2,728	−5,321	−7,774	1,765	−1,636	999	10,215
of which: Short-term	4 774	379	−693	−1,909	−120	2,824	660	135	5,760
Other sectors	4 775	−4,419	−2,004	2,783	4,618	6,019	5,240	−7,211	623
of which: Short-term	4 777	−3,054	−2,743	−3,530	−2,734	−5,220	−1,581	−1,806	−3,163
Currency and deposits	4 780	....	....	....	....	....	....	....	....
Monetary authorities	4 781	....	....	....	....	....	....	....	....
General government	4 782	....	....	....	....	....	....	....	....
Banks	4 783	....	....	....	....	....	....	....	....
Other sectors	4 784	....	....	....	....	....	....	....	....
Other liabilities	4 786	....	....	....	....	....	....	4,000	....
Monetary authorities	4 787	....	....	....	....	....	....	4,000	....
of which: Short-term	4 789	....	....	....	....	....	....	....	....
General government	4 790	....	....	....	....	....	....	....	....
of which: Short-term	4 792	....	....	....	....	....	....	....	....
Banks	4 793	....	....	....	....	....	....	....	....
of which: Short-term	4 795	....	....	....	....	....	....	....	....
Other sectors	4 796	....	....	....	....	....	....	....	....
of which: Short-term	4 798	....	....	....	....	....	....	....	....
E. RESERVE ASSETS	4 802	−9,833	−4,120	−6,980	1,288	−10,264	−7,745	−5,703	−22,952
Monetary gold	4 812	7	10	5	−3	−40	−73	−131	−20
Special drawing rights	4 811	−5	−11	−18	−13	39	−69	−3,985	120
Reserve position in the Fund	4 810	−419	−77	229	275	24	−280	−327	−112
Foreign exchange	4 803	−8,307	−5,140	−9,914	−2,152	−10,785	−8,085	−481	−20,854
Other claims	4 813	−1,109	1,099	2,718	3,181	498	762	−779	−2,086
NET ERRORS AND OMISSIONS	4 998	−2,003	−4,809	−4,698	5,678	−3,697	−4,196	−11,180	−8,044

Table 3. INTERNATIONAL INVESTMENT POSITION (End-period stocks), 2003–2010

(Millions of U.S. dollars)

	Code	2003	2004	2005	2006	2007	2008	2009	2010
ASSETS	8 995 C.	**132,296**	**148,127**	**171,593**	**188,518**	**228,862**	**245,392**	**245,626**	**303,092**
Direct investment abroad	8 505 ..	**30,938**	**35,370**	**41,844**	**47,602**	**55,859**	**57,016**	**64,035**	**78,379**
Equity capital and reinvested earnings	8 506 ..	30,938	35,370	41,844	47,602	55,859	57,016	64,035	78,379
Claims on affiliated enterprises	8 507 ..	30,938	35,370	41,844	47,602	55,859	57,016	64,035	78,379
Liabilities to affiliated enterprises	8 508 ..	....	....	....	....	....	....	....	....
Other capital	8 530 ..	....	....	....	....	....	....	....	....
Claims on affiliated enterprises	8 535 ..	....	....	....	....	....	....	....	....
Liabilities to affiliated enterprises	8 540 ..	....	....	....	....	....	....	....	....
Portfolio investment	8 602 ..	**2,472**	**2,204**	**5,880**	**10,291**	**12,490**	**13,268**	**17,942**	**15,633**
Equity securities	8 610 ..	....	....	....	....	....	....	....	....
Monetary authorities	8 611 ..	....	....	....	....	....	....	....	....
General government	8 612 ..	....	....	....	....	....	....	....	....
Banks	8 613 ..	....	....	....	....	....	....	....	....
Other sectors	8 614 ..	....	....	....	....	....	....	....	....
Debt securities	8 619 ..	2,472	2,204	5,880	10,291	12,490	13,268	17,942	15,633
Bonds and notes	8 620 ..	2,472	2,204	5,880	10,291	12,490	13,268	17,942	15,633
Monetary authorities	8 621 ..	....	....	....	....	....	....	....	....
General government	8 622 ..	....	....	....	....	....	....	....	....
Banks	8 623 ..	2,472	2,204	2,966	3,378	1,417	2,442	3,832	4,003
Other sectors	8 624 ..	....	....	2,914	6,913	11,073	10,826	14,110	11,630
Money market instruments	8 630 ..	....	....	....	....	....	....	....	....
Monetary authorities	8 631 ..	....	....	....	....	....	....	....	....
General government	8 632 ..	....	....	....	....	....	....	....	....
Banks	8 633 ..	....	....	....	....	....	....	....	....
Other sectors	8 634 ..	....	....	....	....	....	....	....	....
Financial derivatives	8 900 ..	....	....	....	....	....	....	....	....
Monetary authorities	8 901 ..	....	....	....	....	....	....	....	....
General government	8 902 ..	....	....	....	....	....	....	....	....
Banks	8 903 ..	....	....	....	....	....	....	....	....
Other sectors	8 904 ..	....	....	....	....	....	....	....	....
Other investment	8 703 ..	**41,451**	**49,053**	**55,200**	**62,945**	**82,522**	**89,667**	**72,811**	**95,483**
Trade credits	8 706 ..	....	....	....	....	....	....	....	....
General government	8 707 ..	....	....	....	....	....	....	....	....
of which: Short-term	8 709 ..	....	....	....	....	....	....	....	....
Other sectors	8 710 ..	....	....	....	....	....	....	....	....
of which: Short-term	8 712 ..	....	....	....	....	....	....	....	....
Loans	8 714 ..	....	....	....	....	....	....	....	....
Monetary authorities	8 715 ..	....	....	....	....	....	....	....	....
of which: Short-term	8 718 ..	....	....	....	....	....	....	....	....
General government	8 719 ..	....	....	....	....	....	....	....	....
of which: Short-term	8 721 ..	....	....	....	....	....	....	....	....
Banks	8 722 ..	....	....	....	....	....	....	....	....
of which: Short-term	8 724 ..	....	....	....	....	....	....	....	....
Other sectors	8 725 ..	....	....	....	....	....	....	....	....
of which: Short-term	8 727 ..	....	....	....	....	....	....	....	....
Currency and deposits	8 730 ..	....	....	....	....	....	....	....	....
Monetary authorities	8 731 ..	....	....	....	....	....	....	....	....
General government	8 732 ..	....	....	....	....	....	....	....	....
Banks	8 733 ..	....	....	....	....	....	....	....	....
Other sectors	8 734 ..	....	....	....	....	....	....	....	....
Other assets	8 736 ..	41,451	49,053	55,200	62,945	82,522	89,667	72,811	95,483
Monetary authorities	8 737 ..	....	....	....	....	....	....	....	....
of which: Short-term	8 739 ..	....	....	....	....	....	....	....	....
General government	8 740 ..	....	....	....	....	....	....	....	....
of which: Short-term	8 742 ..	....	....	....	....	....	....	....	....
Banks	8 743 ..	8,076	12,548	13,536	15,544	19,801	19,054	17,521	18,377
of which: Short-term	8 745 ..	....	....	....	....	....	....	....	....
Other sectors	8 746 ..	33,375	36,505	41,664	47,401	62,721	70,613	55,290	77,106
of which: Short-term	8 748 ..	....	....	....	....	....	....	....	....
Reserve assets	8 802 ..	**57,435**	**61,501**	**68,669**	**67,680**	**77,992**	**85,441**	**90,838**	**113,597**
Monetary gold	8 812 ..	71	61	56	59	99	172	302	322
Special drawing rights	8 811 ..	433	465	445	482	466	519	4,525	4,325
Reserve position in the Fund	8 810 ..	782	898	594	340	334	613	961	1,057
Foreign exchange	8 803 ..	56,148	60,077	67,574	66,798	77,093	84,138	85,049	107,893
Other claims	8 813 ..	....	....	....	....	....	....	....	....

Table 3 (Concluded). INTERNATIONAL INVESTMENT POSITION (End-period stocks), 2003–2010

(Millions of U.S. dollars)

	Code	2003	2004	2005	2006	2007	2008	2009	2010
LIABILITIES	8 995 D.	**354,489**	**401,396**	**461,577**	**497,722**	**579,159**	**607,226**	**598,277**	**665,823**
Direct investment in Mexico	8 555 ..	**139,734**	**164,552**	**188,589**	**209,009**	**238,723**	**264,587**	**279,793**	**298,472**
Equity capital and reinvested earnings	8 556 ..	139,734	164,552	188,589	209,009	238,723	264,587	279,793	298,472
Claims on direct investors	8 557 ..	....	....	....	....	....	....	....	....
Liabilities to direct investors	8 558 ..	139,734	164,552	188,589	209,009	238,723	264,587	279,793	298,472
Other capital	8 580 ..	....	....	....	....	....	....	....	....
Claims on direct investors	8 585 ..	....	....	....	....	....	....	....	....
Liabilities to direct investors	8 590 ..	....	....	....	....	....	....	....	....
Portfolio investment	8 652 ..	**144,488**	**170,334**	**207,984**	**228,238**	**270,711**	**267,127**	**236,230**	**273,145**
Equity securities	8 660 ..	56,516	73,967	106,555	128,015	154,445	148,697	134,384	135,025
Banks	8 663 ..	....	....	....	....	....	....	....	....
Other sectors	8 664 ..	56,516	73,967	106,555	128,015	154,445	148,697	134,384	135,025
Debt securities	8 669 ..	87,972	96,367	101,429	100,223	116,266	118,430	101,846	138,120
Bonds and notes	8 670 ..	85,864	89,385	91,312	87,781	96,027	98,446	78,384	91,531
Monetary authorities	8 671 ..	....	....	....	....	....	....	....	....
General government	8 672 ..	42,604	45,511	44,152	36,289	35,429	33,325	35,325	40,109
Banks	8 673 ..	5,252	3,906	3,510	3,766	4,007	4,086	3,684	3,684
Other sectors	8 674 ..	38,009	39,968	43,651	47,725	56,592	61,035	39,375	47,738
Money market instruments	8 680 ..	2,107	6,982	10,117	12,443	20,239	19,984	23,462	46,590
Monetary authorities	8 681 ..	....	....	....	....	....	....	....	....
General government	8 682 ..	2,107	6,982	10,117	12,443	20,239	19,984	23,462	46,590
Banks	8 683 ..	....	....	....	....	....	....	....	....
Other sectors	8 684 ..	....	....	....	....	....	....	....	....
Financial derivatives	8 905 ..	....	....	....	....	....	....	....	....
Monetary authorities	8 906 ..	....	....	....	....	....	....	....	....
General government	8 907 ..	....	....	....	....	....	....	....	....
Banks	8 908 ..	....	....	....	....	....	....	....	....
Other sectors	8 909 ..	....	....	....	....	....	....	....	....
Other investment	8 753 ..	**70,267**	**66,511**	**65,004**	**60,475**	**69,725**	**75,511**	**82,254**	**94,206**
Trade credits	8 756 ..	....	....	....	....	....	....	....	....
General government	8 757 ..	....	....	....	....	....	....	....	....
of which: Short-term	8 759 ..	....	....	....	....	....	....	....	....
Other sectors	8 760 ..	....	....	....	....	....	....	....	....
of which: Short-term	8 762 ..	....	....	....	....	....	....	....	....
Loans	8 764 ..	....	....	....	....	....	....	3,221	....
Monetary authorities	8 765 ..	....	....	....	....	....	....	3,221	....
of which: Use of Fund credit and loans from the Fund	8 766 ..	....	....	....	....	....	....	....	....
of which: Short-term	8 768 ..	....	....	....	....	....	....	....	....
General government	8 769 ..	....	....	....	....	....	....	....	....
of which: Short-term	8 771 ..	....	....	....	....	....	....	....	....
Banks	8 772 ..	....	....	....	....	....	....	....	....
of which: Short-term	8 774 ..	....	....	....	....	....	....	....	....
Other sectors	8 775 ..	....	....	....	....	....	....	....	....
of which: Short-term	8 777 ..	....	....	....	....	....	....	....	....
Currency and deposits	8 780 ..	....	....	....	....	....	....	....	....
Monetary authorities	8 781 ..	....	....	....	....	....	....	....	....
General government	8 782 ..	....	....	....	....	....	....	....	....
Banks	8 783 ..	....	....	....	....	....	....	....	....
Other sectors	8 784 ..	....	....	....	....	....	....	....	....
Other liabilities	8 786 ..	70,267	66,511	65,004	60,475	69,725	75,511	79,033	94,206
Monetary authorities	8 787 ..	....	....	....	....	....	....	4,470	4,391
of which: Short-term	8 789 ..	....	....	....	....	....	....	....	....
General government	8 790 ..	2,294	3,051	4,538	3,041	4,685	6,672	12,025	20,332
of which: Short-term	8 792 ..	....	....	....	....	....	....	....	....
Banks	8 793 ..	25,704	23,599	17,935	10,263	12,163	10,589	11,602	12,250
of which: Short-term	8 795 ..	....	....	....	....	....	....	....	....
Other sectors	8 796 ..	42,269	39,861	42,530	47,171	52,877	58,250	50,935	57,233
of which: Short-term	8 798 ..	....	....	....	....	....	....	....	....
NET INTERNATIONAL INVESTMENT POSITION	8 995 ..	**−222,192**	**−253,269**	**−289,984**	**−309,203**	**−350,297**	**−361,834**	**−352,652**	**−362,732**
Conversion rates: Mexican pesos per U.S. dollar (end of period)	0 102 ..	**11.2360**	**11.2648**	**10.7777**	**10.8810**	**10.8662**	**13.5383**	**13.0587**	**12.3571**

Table 1. ANALYTIC PRESENTATION, 2003–2010

(Millions of U.S. dollars)

	Code	2003	2004	2005	2006	2007	2008	2009	2010
A. Current Account[1]	4 993 Z.	**−130.3**	**−47.1**	**−247.7**	**−391.1**	**−723.3**	**−1,040.9**	**−534.4**	**−591.6**
Goods: exports f.o.b.	2 100 ..	805.1	994.1	1,104.6	1,060.8	1,373.3	1,645.9	1,326.9	1,590.4
Goods: imports f.o.b.	3 100 ..	−1,428.1	−1,748.2	−2,296.1	−2,643.5	−3,671.4	−4,869.1	−3,275.7	−3,810.0
Balance on Goods	4 100 ..	*−623.0*	*−754.2*	*−1,191.5*	*−1,582.7*	*−2,298.1*	*−3,223.2*	*−1,948.8*	*−2,219.5*
Services: credit	2 200 ..	250.0	332.1	398.9	467.1	628.4	843.9	673.1	701.2
Services: debit	3 200 ..	−294.3	−353.1	−419.7	−487.6	−650.1	−837.1	−712.9	−771.0
Balance on Goods and Services	4 991 ..	*−667.3*	*−775.1*	*−1,212.2*	*−1,603.2*	*−2,319.8*	*−3,216.4*	*−1,988.6*	*−2,289.3*
Income: credit	2 300 ..	340.8	490.0	539.3	605.9	710.1	905.0	590.0	749.2
Income: debit	3 300 ..	−110.0	−133.0	−128.4	−203.4	−293.7	−306.4	−287.1	−262.6
Balance on Goods, Services, and Income	4 992 ..	*−436.5*	*−418.1*	*−801.4*	*−1,200.7*	*−1,903.4*	*−2,617.8*	*−1,685.6*	*−1,802.6*
Current transfers: credit	2 379 Z.	334.0	406.8	596.8	859.6	1,245.1	1,688.4	1,254.6	1,296.8
Current transfers: debit	3 379 ..	−27.8	−35.8	−43.2	−50.0	−65.1	−111.5	−103.4	−85.8
B. Capital Account[1]	4 994 Z.	**−19.0**	**−18.3**	**−16.9**	**−22.8**	**−8.0**	**−14.6**	**−17.5**	**−28.4**
Capital account: credit	2 994 Z.	4.6	7.2	5.2	6.1	7.0	9.3	12.2	13.4
Capital account: debit	3 994 ..	−23.6	−25.5	−22.1	−28.9	−14.9	−23.9	−29.7	−41.8
Total, Groups A Plus B	4 981 ..	*−149.3*	*−65.4*	*−264.6*	*−413.9*	*−731.3*	*−1,055.5*	*−551.9*	*−620.0*
C. Financial Account[1]	4 995 W.	**84.3**	**113.0**	**200.5**	**359.5**	**1,013.4**	**1,286.5**	**108.1**	**414.5**
Direct investment abroad	4 505 ..	−.1	−3.2	.2	.9	−17.4	−16.1	−6.8	−3.5
Direct investment in Moldova	4 555 Z.	73.8	87.7	190.7	258.5	541.3	711.5	145.3	192.8
Portfolio investment assets	4 602 ..	.4	−1.5	−1.2	−.2	−.1	....	−.3	−.2
Equity securities	4 610 ..	−.1	−.2	....	−.2	−.1	....	−.3	−.2
Debt securities	4 619 ..	.5	−1.3	−1.2	....	....	....	....	....
Portfolio investment liabilities	4 652 Z.	−24.2	−8.3	−5.8	−4.6	−4.4	6.4	−5.6	5.8
Equity securities	4 660 ..	.7	−.8	.6	1.8	1.7	11.4	2.4	5.8
Debt securities	4 669 Z.	−24.9	−7.5	−6.4	−6.4	−6.2	−4.9	−8.0	....
Financial derivatives	4 910 ..	.1	.6	−1.6	.2	−.5	.9	.3	−.6
Financial derivatives assets	4 900 ..	....	−.5	−1.7	−.1	−.5	−.1	−.1	−.6
Financial derivatives liabilities	4 905 ..	.1	1.0	.1	.3	.1	1.0	.4	....
Other investment assets	4 703 ..	6.5	−31.6	−78.2	−49.4	35.3	52.1	−210.6	75.5
Monetary authorities	4 701 ..	....	−18.8	−14.1	....	....	....	....	....
General government	4 704 ..	−.2	.3	−.2	....	....	....	....	....
Banks	4 705 ..	−19.6	5.8	−50.7	−77.6	49.2	−36.2	−186.8	39.1
Other sectors	4 728 ..	26.4	−18.9	−13.1	28.2	−13.9	88.3	−23.8	36.4
Other investment liabilities	4 753 W.	27.8	69.3	96.3	154.0	459.1	531.6	185.5	144.8
Monetary authorities	4 753 WA	....	....	....	....	....	....	184.1	....
General government	4 753 ZB	−25.1	−19.1	−14.8	−29.9	−14.6	−21.3	−3.4	4.0
Banks	4 753 ZC	14.1	17.0	13.8	60.3	192.8	208.9	−101.6	−30.5
Other sectors	4 753 ZD	38.8	71.4	97.3	123.6	281.0	344.0	106.4	171.3
Total, Groups A Through C	4 983 ..	*−65.0*	*47.5*	*−64.1*	*−54.4*	*282.1*	*231.0*	*−443.8*	*−205.4*
D. Net Errors and Omissions	4 998 ..	**47.4**	**100.6**	**178.3**	**81.9**	**107.8**	**65.2**	**49.9**	**62.8**
Total, Groups A Through D	4 984 ..	*−17.6*	*148.2*	*114.2*	*27.5*	*389.9*	*296.2*	*−393.9*	*−142.6*
E. Reserves and Related Items	4 802 A.	**17.6**	**−148.2**	**−114.2**	**−27.5**	**−389.9**	**−296.2**	**393.9**	**142.6**
Reserve assets	4 802 ..	−14.1	−148.0	−128.6	−140.7	−528.9	−452.0	202.1	−294.4
Use of Fund credit and loans	4 766 ..	−22.2	−21.6	−21.7	41.1	11.2	13.5	−16.3	174.6
Exceptional financing	4 920 ..	53.9	21.4	36.1	72.1	127.8	142.3	208.1	262.4
Conversion rates: Moldovan lei per U.S. dollar	0 101 ..	**13.945**	**12.330**	**12.600**	**13.131**	**12.140**	**10.392**	**11.110**	**12.369**

[1] Excludes components that have been classified in the categories of Group E.

Table 2. STANDARD PRESENTATION, 2003–2010

(Millions of U.S. dollars)

	Code	2003	2004	2005	2006	2007	2008	2009	2010
CURRENT ACCOUNT	4 993	−130.1	−46.1	−225.8	−386.4	−671.1	−979.0	−465.0	−483.6
A. GOODS	4 100	−623.0	−754.2	−1,191.5	−1,582.7	−2,298.1	−3,223.2	−1,948.8	−2,219.5
Credit	2 100	805.1	994.1	1,104.6	1,060.8	1,373.3	1,645.9	1,326.9	1,590.4
General merchandise: exports f.o.b.	2 110	655.9	793.9	885.7	779.0	1,013.3	1,152.6	902.8	1,146.8
Goods for processing: exports f.o.b.	2 150	149.1	199.2	217.9	273.3	346.8	464.9	396.2	414.7
Repairs on goods	2 160	.1	.5	.6	.5	.6	1.3	.9	.7
Goods procured in ports by carriers	2 170	....	.5	.4	7.9	12.7	27.2	26.8	28.0
Nonmonetary gold	2 180	....	....	....	....	....	....	.3	.3
Debit	3 100	−1,428.1	−1,748.2	−2,296.1	−2,643.5	−3,671.4	−4,869.1	−3,275.7	−3,810.0
General merchandise: imports f.o.b.	3 110	−1,305.9	−1,589.1	−2,113.9	−2,428.0	−3,401.6	−4,508.2	−2,974.1	−3,472.5
Goods for processing: imports f.o.b.	3 150	−117.4	−152.0	−172.0	−208.8	−261.7	−341.7	−287.8	−312.4
Repairs on goods	3 160	−1.4	−3.3	−5.3	−.6	−.8	−.6	−1.4	−5.8
Goods procured in ports by carriers	3 170	−3.3	−3.9	−4.5	−5.6	−6.6	−18.4	−12.5	−19.2
Nonmonetary gold	3 180	−.1	....	−.4	−.5	−.7	−.3	....	−.1
B. SERVICES	4 200	−44.3	−21.0	−20.7	−20.5	−21.7	6.9	−39.8	−69.8
Total credit	2 200	*250.0*	*332.1*	*398.9*	*467.1*	*628.4*	*843.9*	*673.1*	*701.2*
Total debit	3 200	*−294.3*	*−353.1*	*−419.7*	*−487.6*	*−650.1*	*−837.1*	*−712.9*	*−771.0*
Transportation services, credit	2 205	**127.1**	**142.6**	**169.6**	**197.0**	**263.8**	**357.0**	**253.5**	**244.5**
Passenger	2 850	*25.2*	*20.6*	*34.7*	*32.8*	*57.5*	*76.7*	*66.8*	*59.2*
Freight	2 851	*97.3*	*116.4*	*127.7*	*156.6*	*192.9*	*259.9*	*167.8*	*163.9*
Other	2 852	*4.7*	*5.7*	*7.1*	*7.6*	*13.4*	*21.2*	*18.9*	*21.3*
Sea transport, passenger	2 207	....	....	....	....	....	....	....	....
Sea transport, freight	2 208	.1	....	.1	.2	.5	12.5	2.1	1.2
Sea transport, other	2 209	....	....	....	....	....	....	.1	.1
Air transport, passenger	2 211	17.2	13.6	27.9	24.2	45.4	59.9	53.7	47.9
Air transport, freight	2 212	3.2	11.7	7.7	14.9	12.0	12.6	11.9	14.1
Air transport, other	2 213	1.6	2.4	3.1	1.1	4.6	9.7	11.4	14.4
Other transport, passenger	2 215	8.0	7.0	6.9	8.6	12.1	16.8	13.1	11.3
Other transport, freight	2 216	94.0	104.7	119.9	141.5	180.4	234.2	153.8	148.6
Other transport, other	2 217	3.0	3.3	4.0	6.5	8.7	11.4	7.4	6.8
Transportation services, debit	3 205	**−99.9**	**−116.0**	**−147.1**	**−172.1**	**−245.3**	**−324.9**	**−256.8**	**−285.1**
Passenger	3 850	*−19.1*	*−22.2*	*−28.9*	*−33.9*	*−57.2*	*−71.4*	*−63.9*	*−64.3*
Freight	3 851	*−68.2*	*−77.6*	*−99.8*	*−119.3*	*−163.4*	*−222.0*	*−158.2*	*−185.2*
Other	3 852	*−12.6*	*−16.2*	*−18.4*	*−18.9*	*−24.7*	*−31.6*	*−34.7*	*−35.6*
Sea transport, passenger	3 207	....	....	−.1	....	....	....	....	....
Sea transport, freight	3 208	−.1	−.2	....	−2.1	....	−.6	−10.9	−18.5
Sea transport, other	3 209	....	....	....	....	−.2	−.3	−1.7	−1.6
Air transport, passenger	3 211	−14.4	−16.9	−25.2	−28.3	−48.8	−59.9	−51.8	−52.6
Air transport, freight	3 212	−2.2	−3.0	−1.7	−5.9	−6.0	−7.8	−5.8	−8.4
Air transport, other	3 213	−9.7	−13.1	−15.1	−14.5	−17.6	−20.7	−25.7	−28.0
Other transport, passenger	3 215	−4.7	−5.3	−3.6	−5.6	−8.4	−11.5	−12.1	−11.6
Other transport, freight	3 216	−66.0	−74.4	−98.0	−111.3	−157.3	−213.6	−141.6	−158.4
Other transport, other	3 217	−2.9	−3.1	−3.3	−4.4	−7.0	−10.6	−7.3	−6.0
Travel, credit	2 236	**54.4**	**91.2**	**103.2**	**116.6**	**170.6**	**216.4**	**172.5**	**173.7**
Business travel	2 237	18.4	20.8	23.9	30.3	43.3	60.9	56.3	53.1
Personal travel	2 240	36.0	70.4	79.3	86.4	127.3	155.6	116.2	120.5
Travel, debit	3 236	**−99.4**	**−113.2**	**−141.2**	**−189.6**	**−232.6**	**−287.7**	**−243.0**	**−264.8**
Business travel	3 237	−54.5	−70.1	−82.7	−100.2	−107.4	−134.8	−111.6	−124.8
Personal travel	3 240	−44.9	−43.0	−58.6	−89.3	−125.2	−152.9	−131.5	−140.1
Other services, credit	2 200 BA	**68.5**	**98.2**	**126.2**	**153.5**	**194.0**	**270.5**	**247.1**	**283.1**
Communications	2 245	24.4	45.3	59.4	71.2	85.7	114.6	105.2	126.1
Construction	2 249	.6	4.3	6.1	10.7	15.0	15.4	26.8	14.5
Insurance	2 253	1.0	.8	.6	.8	2.1	4.0	2.1	1.2
Financial	2 260	1.8	1.7	3.2	4.0	4.1	4.6	3.1	3.1
Computer and information	2 262	1.2	2.6	3.6	8.0	14.3	26.3	29.8	33.4
Royalties and licence fees	2 266	1.4	2.2	1.6	1.7	6.2	3.9	4.3	4.9
Other business services	2 268	18.3	28.4	36.2	38.3	47.4	81.4	54.0	62.1
Personal, cultural, and recreational	2 287	.5	.8	.8	.6	.3	.4	....	.1
Government, n.i.e.	2 291	19.3	12.1	14.8	18.3	19.1	19.9	21.7	37.8
Other services, debit	3 200 BA	**−94.9**	**−123.8**	**−131.4**	**−126.0**	**−172.3**	**−224.5**	**−213.1**	**−221.0**
Communications	3 245	−19.0	−18.8	−27.3	−29.0	−37.6	−47.4	−39.2	−38.1
Construction	3 249	−2.1	−3.4	−2.5	−4.2	−7.3	−9.6	−24.3	−24.4
Insurance	3 253	−2.4	−2.2	−3.1	−5.6	−5.2	−13.0	−11.9	−15.7
Financial	3 260	−2.9	−2.9	−3.6	−4.9	−6.7	−6.9	−5.2	−6.5
Computer and information	3 262	−2.7	−6.1	−4.4	−5.9	−15.7	−16.0	−24.0	−23.6
Royalties and licence fees	3 266	−3.0	−2.6	−2.3	−4.0	−7.2	−14.9	−10.6	−12.7
Other business services	3 268	−35.8	−65.7	−58.2	−41.4	−54.5	−70.1	−61.9	−56.6
Personal, cultural, and recreational	3 287	−.6	−.5	−.6	−.7	−.7	−.9	−.9	−1.1
Government, n.i.e.	3 291	−26.3	−21.6	−29.5	−30.3	−37.4	−45.7	−35.1	−42.3

Table 2 (Continued). STANDARD PRESENTATION, 2003–2010

(Millions of U.S. dollars)

	Code	2003	2004	2005	2006	2007	2008	2009	2010
C. INCOME	4 300	**230.8**	**357.0**	**410.9**	**402.5**	**416.4**	**598.6**	**302.9**	**486.7**
Total credit	2 300	*340.8*	*490.0*	*539.3*	*605.9*	*710.1*	*905.0*	*590.0*	*749.2*
Total debit	3 300	*–110.0*	*–133.0*	*–128.4*	*–203.4*	*–293.7*	*–306.4*	*–287.1*	*–262.6*
Compensation of employees, credit	2 310	**332.0**	**480.0**	**520.0**	**573.0**	**649.0**	**842.0**	**563.4**	**730.8**
Compensation of employees, debit	3 310	**–43.0**	**–41.1**	**–43.2**	**–50.4**	**–56.1**	**–79.0**	**–66.3**	**–59.4**
Investment income, credit	2 320	**8.8**	**10.0**	**19.3**	**32.9**	**61.1**	**63.0**	**26.6**	**18.4**
Direct investment income	2 330	....	....	....	.1	.1	....	.3	1.5
Dividends and distributed branch profits	2 332	....	....	....	....	....	....	.1	.6
Reinvested earnings and undistributed branch profits	2 333	....	....	....	....	....	....	....	....
Income on debt (interest)	2 334	....	....	....	.1	.1	....	.2	.9
Portfolio investment income	2 339	2.8	2.4	5.1	10.9	15.0	16.4	19.2	13.7
Income on equity	2 340	....	....	....	....	....	....	....	.1
Income on bonds and notes	2 350	2.8	2.4	5.1	10.9	15.0	16.4	19.2	13.7
Income on money market instruments	2 360	....	....	....	....	....	....	....	....
Other investment income	2 370	6.0	7.7	14.2	22.0	46.0	46.5	7.1	3.2
Investment income, debit	3 320	**–67.0**	**–91.9**	**–85.2**	**–153.0**	**–237.6**	**–227.4**	**–220.8**	**–203.2**
Direct investment income	3 330	–24.7	–49.5	–44.9	–107.8	–182.2	–152.0	–156.0	–147.3
Dividends and distributed branch profits	3 332	–3.3	–3.9	–6.1	–55.1	–52.8	–37.8	–136.9	–124.5
Reinvested earnings and undistributed branch profits	3 333	–15.3	–38.1	–27.4	–41.6	–112.8	–98.7	11.6	–14.6
Income on debt (interest)	3 334	–6.1	–7.5	–11.4	–11.1	–16.7	–15.4	–30.7	–8.3
Portfolio investment income	3 339	–2.8	–2.3	–2.4	–2.5	–3.2	–4.8	–1.6	–2.6
Income on equity	3 340	–.6	–.2	....	–.2	–1.4	–3.7	–1.2	–2.6
Income on bonds and notes	3 350	–2.2	–2.0	–2.4	–2.3	–1.8	–1.1	–.4	....
Income on money market instruments	3 360	....	....	....	....	....	....	....	....
Other investment income	3 370	–39.5	–40.2	–37.9	–42.7	–52.1	–70.7	–63.3	–53.3
D. CURRENT TRANSFERS	4 379	**306.4**	**372.0**	**575.5**	**814.3**	**1,232.3**	**1,638.8**	**1,220.6**	**1,319.0**
Credit	2 379	**334.2**	**407.8**	**618.8**	**864.3**	**1,297.3**	**1,750.3**	**1,324.0**	**1,404.8**
General government	2 380	67.4	64.1	81.3	75.5	143.9	204.3	186.2	252.2
Other sectors	2 390	266.8	343.7	537.5	788.8	1,153.4	1,546.0	1,137.8	1,152.6
Workers' remittances	2 391	152.0	221.4	395.1	602.8	842.3	1,046.0	635.2	648.7
Other current transfers	2 392	114.8	122.3	142.4	185.9	311.2	499.9	502.6	503.9
Debit	3 379	**–27.8**	**–35.8**	**–43.2**	**–50.0**	**–65.1**	**–111.5**	**–103.4**	**–85.8**
General government	3 380	–5.3	–5.4	–5.4	–6.5	–4.9	–6.3	–13.7	–6.9
Other sectors	3 390	–22.6	–30.4	–37.9	–43.5	–60.2	–105.2	–89.6	–78.9
Workers' remittances	3 391	–.8	–.8	–3.1	–6.5	–15.8	–13.3	–8.0	–16.2
Other current transfers	3 392	–21.7	–29.7	–34.8	–37.0	–44.4	–91.9	–81.7	–62.8
CAPITAL AND FINANCIAL ACCOUNT	4 996	**82.7**	**–54.5**	**47.5**	**304.5**	**563.3**	**913.7**	**415.1**	**420.7**
CAPITAL ACCOUNT	4 994	**–19.0**	**–12.8**	**–3.8**	**–22.8**	**–8.0**	**–14.6**	**–17.5**	**–28.4**
Total credit	2 994	*4.6*	*12.7*	*18.3*	*6.1*	*7.0*	*9.3*	*12.2*	*13.4*
Total debit	3 994	*–23.6*	*–25.5*	*–22.1*	*–28.9*	*–14.9*	*–23.9*	*–29.7*	*–41.8*
Capital transfers, credit	2 400	**4.6**	**12.7**	**18.3**	**6.1**	**7.0**	**9.3**	**12.2**	**13.4**
General government	2 401	....	5.5	13.0	....	....	....	....	....
Debt forgiveness	2 402	....	5.5	13.0	....	....	....	....	....
Other capital transfers	2 410	....	....	....	....	....	....	....	....
Other sectors	2 430	4.6	7.2	5.2	6.1	7.0	9.3	12.2	13.4
Migrants' transfers	2 431	2.6	3.9	5.2	5.9	7.0	9.3	12.1	12.1
Debt forgiveness	2 432	....	.4	....	....	....	....	....	....
Other capital transfers	2 440	2.0	2.9	....	.2	....	.1	.1	1.3
Capital transfers, debit	3 400	**–23.6**	**–25.5**	**–22.1**	**–28.9**	**–14.9**	**–23.9**	**–29.7**	**–41.8**
General government	3 401	....	....	....	....	....	....	....	....
Debt forgiveness	3 402	....	....	....	....	....	....	....	....
Other capital transfers	3 410	....	....	....	....	....	....	....	....
Other sectors	3 430	–23.6	–25.5	–22.1	–28.9	–14.9	–23.9	–29.7	–41.8
Migrants' transfers	3 431	–23.6	–25.5	–22.1	–28.8	–14.8	–23.2	–29.7	–41.2
Debt forgiveness	3 432	....	....	....	....	....	....	....	....
Other capital transfers	3 440	....	–.1	....	....	–.1	–.8	....	–.6
Nonproduced nonfinancial assets, credit	2 480	....	....	....	....	....	....	....	....
Nonproduced nonfinancial assets, debit	3 480	....	....	....	....	....	....	....	....

Table 2 (Continued). STANDARD PRESENTATION, 2003–2010

(Millions of U.S. dollars)

	Code	2003	2004	2005	2006	2007	2008	2009	2010
FINANCIAL ACCOUNT	4 995 ..	**101.7**	**−41.7**	**51.3**	**327.3**	**571.2**	**928.3**	**432.6**	**449.1**
A. DIRECT INVESTMENT	4 500 ..	**73.6**	**147.8**	**190.9**	**259.4**	**523.9**	**695.4**	**138.6**	**193.9**
Direct investment abroad	4 505 ..	−.1	−3.2	.2	.9	−17.4	−16.1	−6.8	−3.5
Equity capital	4 510 ..	−.1	−.2	.2	−.8	−12.6	−16.1	−8.2	−3.4
Claims on affiliated enterprises	4 515 ..	−.1	−.2	.2	−.8	−12.6	−16.1	−8.2	−3.4
Liabilities to affiliated enterprises	4 520 ..	....	....	....	....	....	....	....	....
Reinvested earnings	4 525 ..	....	....	....	....	....	....	....	....
Other capital	4 530 ..	....	−3.0	−.1	1.8	−4.7	.1	1.4	−.1
Claims on affiliated enterprises	4 535 ..	....	−3.0	−.1	1.8	−4.7	.1	1.4	−.1
Liabilities to affiliated enterprises	4 540 ..	....	....	....	....	....	....	....	....
Direct investment in Moldova	4 555 ..	**73.8**	**151.0**	**190.7**	**258.5**	**541.3**	**711.5**	**145.3**	**197.4**
Equity capital	4 560 ..	39.7	114.1	79.6	119.0	227.4	441.7	161.6	157.0
Claims on direct investors	4 565 ..	....	....	....	....	....	....	....	....
Liabilities to direct investors	4 570 ..	39.7	114.1	79.6	119.0	227.4	441.7	161.6	157.0
Reinvested earnings	4 575 ..	15.3	38.1	27.4	41.6	112.8	98.7	−11.6	14.6
Other capital	4 580 ..	18.8	−1.2	83.7	97.9	201.1	171.1	−4.7	25.9
Claims on direct investors	4 585 ..	....	....	....	−.2	5.2	−15.2	10.2	−4.1
Liabilities to direct investors	4 590 ..	18.8	−1.2	83.7	98.1	195.8	186.2	−14.9	30.0
B. PORTFOLIO INVESTMENT	4 600 ..	**−23.8**	**−9.8**	**−7.0**	**−4.8**	**−4.5**	**6.4**	**−5.8**	**5.6**
Assets	4 602 ..	.4	−1.5	−1.2	−.2	−.1	....	−.3	−.2
Equity securities	4 610 ..	−.1	−.2	....	−.2	−.1	....	−.3	−.2
Monetary authorities	4 611 ..	....	....	....	....	....	....	....	....
General government	4 612 ..	....	....	....	....	....	....	....	....
Banks	4 613 ..	....	....	....	....	....	....	....	....
Other sectors	4 614 ..	−.1	−.2	....	−.2	....	....	−.3	−.2
Debt securities	4 619 ..	.5	−1.3	−1.2	....	....	....	....	....
Bonds and notes	4 620 ..	.5	−1.3	−1.2	....	....	....	....	....
Monetary authorities	4 621 ..	....	....	....	....	....	....	....	....
General government	4 622 ..	....	....	....	....	....	....	....	....
Banks	4 623 ..	.5	−1.3	−1.2	....	....	....	....	....
Other sectors	4 624 ..	....	....	....	....	....	....	....	....
Money market instruments	4 630 ..	....	....	....	....	....	....	....	....
Monetary authorities	4 631 ..	....	....	....	....	....	....	....	....
General government	4 632 ..	....	....	....	....	....	....	....	....
Banks	4 633 ..	....	....	....	....	....	....	....	....
Other sectors	4 634 ..	....	....	....	....	....	....	....	....
Liabilities	4 652 ..	**−24.2**	**−8.3**	**−5.8**	**−4.6**	**−4.4**	**6.4**	**−5.6**	**5.8**
Equity securities	4 660 ..	.7	−.8	.6	1.8	1.7	11.4	2.4	5.8
Banks	4 663 ..	−.3	−.6	.6	1.7	1.5	11.0	−.5	5.8
Other sectors	4 664 ..	1.0	−.2	....	.1	.3	.4	2.9	.1
Debt securities	4 669 ..	−24.9	−7.5	−6.4	−6.4	−6.2	−4.9	−8.0	....
Bonds and notes	4 670 ..	−24.9	−7.5	−6.4	−6.4	−6.4	−6.4	−6.4	....
Monetary authorities	4 671 ..	....	....	....	....	....	....	....	....
General government	4 672 ..	−24.9	−7.5	−6.4	−6.4	−6.4	−6.4	−6.4	....
Banks	4 673 ..	....	....	....	....	....	....	....	....
Other sectors	4 674 ..	....	....	....	....	....	....	....	....
Money market instruments	4 680 ..	....	....	....	....	.2	1.4	−1.6	....
Monetary authorities	4 681 ..	....	....	....	....	....	....	....	....
General government	4 682 ..	....	....	....	....	.2	1.4	−1.6	....
Banks	4 683 ..	....	....	....	....	....	....	....	....
Other sectors	4 684 ..	....	....	....	....	....	....	....	....
C. FINANCIAL DERIVATIVES	4 910 ..	**.1**	**.6**	**−1.6**	**.2**	**−.5**	**.9**	**.3**	**−.6**
Monetary authorities	4 911 ..	....	....	....	....	....	....	....	....
General government	4 912 ..	....	....	....	....	....	....	....	....
Banks	4 913 ..	.1	.6	−1.6	.2	−.5	.9	.3	−.6
Other sectors	4 914 ..	....	....	....	....	....	....	....	....
Assets	4 900 ..	....	−.5	−1.7	−.1	−.5	−.1	−.1	−.6
Monetary authorities	4 901 ..	....	....	....	....	....	....	....	....
General government	4 902 ..	....	....	....	....	....	....	....	....
Banks	4 903 ..	....	−.5	−1.7	−.1	−.5	−.1	−.1	−.6
Other sectors	4 904 ..	....	....	....	....	....	....	....	....
Liabilities	4 905 ..	**.1**	**1.0**	**.1**	**.3**	**.1**	**1.0**	**.4**	....
Monetary authorities	4 906 ..	....	....	....	....	....	....	....	....
General government	4 907 ..	....	....	....	....	....	....	....	....
Banks	4 908 ..	.1	1.0	.1	.3	.1	1.0	.4	....
Other sectors	4 909 ..	....	....	....	....	....	....	....	....

Table 2 (Concluded). STANDARD PRESENTATION, 2003–2010

(Millions of U.S. dollars)

	Code	2003	2004	2005	2006	2007	2008	2009	2010
D. OTHER INVESTMENT	4 700	**65.8**	**−32.3**	**−2.4**	**213.2**	**581.2**	**677.7**	**97.4**	**544.6**
Assets	4 703	6.5	−31.6	−78.2	−49.4	35.3	52.1	−210.6	75.5
Trade credits	4 706	−17.4	−27.4	−25.7	17.4	−7.6	76.3	44.9	21.2
General government	4 707	....	....	....	....	....	....	....	....
of which: Short-term	4 709	....	....	....	....	....	....	....	....
Other sectors	4 710	−17.4	−27.4	−25.7	17.4	−7.6	76.3	44.9	21.2
of which: Short-term	4 712	*−17.4*	*−27.4*	*−25.7*	*17.4*	*−7.6*	*76.3*	*44.9*	*21.2*
Loans	4 714	....	....	....	....	−6.0	1.8	4.2	−7.4
Monetary authorities	4 715	....	....	....	....	....	....	....	....
of which: Short-term	4 718	....	....	....	....	....	....	....	....
General government	4 719								
of which: Short-term	4 721								
Banks	4 722	....	....	....	....	....	....	....	−4.9
of which: Short-term	4 724	....	....	....	....	....	....	....	....
Other sectors	4 725	....	....	....	....	−6.0	1.8	4.2	−2.5
of which: Short-term	4 727								
Currency and deposits	4 730	24.0	−5.6	−52.5	−66.8	48.9	−26.0	−259.6	61.6
Monetary authorities	4 731	....	−18.8	−14.1					
General government	4 732	−.2	.3	−.2					
Banks	4 733	−19.6	5.8	−50.7	−77.6	49.2	−36.2	−186.8	44.0
Other sectors	4 734	43.8	7.1	12.6	10.8	−.3	10.2	−72.9	17.6
Other assets	4 736	....	1.3	....	....	....	....	....	....
Monetary authorities	4 737	....	....	....	....	....	....	....	....
of which: Short-term	4 739	....	....	....	....	....	....	....	....
General government	4 740	....	....	....	....	....	....	....	....
of which: Short-term	4 742	....	....	....	....	....	....	....	....
Banks	4 743	....	....	....	....	....	....	....	....
of which: Short-term	4 745	....	....	....	....	....	....	....	....
Other sectors	4 746	....	1.3	....	....	....	....	....	....
of which: Short-term	4 748	....	....	....	....	....	....	....	....
Liabilities	4 753	**59.3**	**−.7**	**75.8**	**262.6**	**545.8**	**625.5**	**308.0**	**469.1**
Trade credits	4 756	27.3	36.6	60.1	44.9	107.1	131.2	90.7	128.6
General government	4 757								
of which: Short-term	4 759								
Other sectors	4 760	27.3	36.6	60.1	44.9	107.1	131.2	90.7	128.6
of which: Short-term	4 762	*27.3*	*36.6*	*60.1*	*44.9*	*107.1*	*131.2*	*90.7*	*128.6*
Loans	4 764	−23.8	−4.7	−7.6	184.2	334.6	412.5	−58.9	284.0
Monetary authorities	4 765	−22.2	−21.6	−21.7	41.1	11.2	13.5	−16.3	174.6
of which: Use of Fund credit and loans from the Fund	4 766	*−22.2*	*−21.6*	*−21.7*	*41.1*	*11.2*	*13.5*	*−16.3*	*174.6*
of which: Short-term	4 768	....	....	....	....	....	....	....	....
General government	4 769	−22.6	−19.1	−14.8	57.8	27.6	20.1	−3.4	44.4
of which: Short-term	4 771	....	....	....	....	....	....	....	....
Banks	4 772	9.5	2.3	1.2	7.0	121.9	166.0	−55.0	33.9
of which: Short-term	4 774	*8.6*	*−6.1*	*−2.0*		*10.1*	*46.6*	*−46.2*	....
Other sectors	4 775	11.5	33.7	27.7	78.3	173.9	212.9	15.7	31.1
of which: Short-term	4 777	*.7*	*−.7*	*1.6*	*−.2*	*29.8*	*−13.8*	*.2*	*23.8*
Currency and deposits	4 780	4.6	14.7	12.6	53.3	60.6	53.1	−46.6	−69.6
Monetary authorities	4 781	....	....	....	....	....	....	....	....
General government	4 782	....	....	....	....	....	....	....	....
Banks	4 783	4.6	14.7	12.6	53.3	60.6	53.1	−46.6	−69.6
Other sectors	4 784	....	....	....	....	....	....	....	....
Other liabilities	4 786	51.2	−47.3	10.6	−19.8	43.6	28.8	322.8	126.1
Monetary authorities	4 787	....	....	....	....	....	....	184.1	....
of which: Short-term	4 789	....	....	....	....	....	....	....	....
General government	4 790	37.6	−39.9	16.9	−60.9	−.1	....	....	....
of which: Short-term	4 792	*37.6*	*−39.9*	*16.9*	*−60.9*	*−.1*			
Banks	4 793	....	....	....	....	10.3	−10.3	....	.6
of which: Short-term	4 795	....	....	....	....	*10.3*	*−10.3*		*.6*
Other sectors	4 796	13.6	−7.4	−6.3	41.1	33.4	39.1	138.7	125.5
of which: Short-term	4 798	*13.6*	*−7.4*	*−6.3*	*41.1*	*33.4*	*39.1*	*138.7*	*125.5*
E. RESERVE ASSETS	4 802	**−14.1**	**−148.0**	**−128.6**	**−140.7**	**−528.9**	**−452.0**	**202.1**	**−294.4**
Monetary gold	4 812	....	....	....	....	....	....	....	....
Special drawing rights	4 811	.3	....	....	−.1	....	....	−1.8	3.2
Reserve position in the Fund	4 810	....	....	....	....	....	....	....	....
Foreign exchange	4 803	−14.3	−148.0	−128.7	−140.6	−528.9	−452.0	203.9	−297.5
Other claims	4 813	....	....	....	....	....	....	....	....
NET ERRORS AND OMISSIONS	4 998	**47.4**	**100.6**	**178.3**	**81.9**	**107.8**	**65.2**	**49.9**	**62.8**

Table 3. INTERNATIONAL INVESTMENT POSITION (End-period stocks), 2003–2010

(Millions of U.S. dollars)

	Code	2003	2004	2005	2006	2007	2008	2009	2010
ASSETS	8 995 C.	**798.0**	**1,007.1**	**1,180.6**	**1,414.9**	**1,996.5**	**2,290.3**	**2,320.7**	**2,453.7**
Direct investment abroad	8 505 ..	**23.6**	**23.9**	**25.1**	**24.1**	**41.5**	**57.6**	**64.3**	**67.9**
Equity capital and reinvested earnings	8 506 ..	23.3	23.5	24.6	25.5	38.1	54.2	62.4	65.8
Claims on affiliated enterprises	8 507 ..	23.3	23.5	24.6	25.5	38.1	54.2	62.4	65.8
Liabilities to affiliated enterprises	8 508 ..	....	....	....	....	....	....	....	....
Other capital	8 530 ..	.4	.4	.4	−1.3	3.4	3.3	1.9	2.0
Claims on affiliated enterprises	8 535 ..	.4	.4	.4	−1.3	3.4	3.3	1.9	2.0
Liabilities to affiliated enterprises	8 540 ..	....	....	....	....	....	....	....	....
Portfolio investment	8 602 ..	**4.7**	**6.1**	**7.3**	**7.5**	**7.6**	**7.6**	**8.1**	**8.3**
Equity securities	8 610 ..	.5	.7	.7	.9	.9	1.0	1.4	1.6
Monetary authorities	8 611 ..	....	....	....	....	....	....	....	....
General government	8 612 ..	.4	.4	.4	.4	.4	.4	.4	.4
Banks	8 613 ..	....	....	....	....	....	....	....	....
Other sectors	8 614 ..	.1	.3	.3	.5	.5	.6	1.0	1.2
Debt securities	8 619 ..	4.2	5.5	6.7	6.7	6.7	6.7	6.7	6.7
Bonds and notes	8 620 ..	4.2	5.5	6.7	6.7	6.7	6.7	6.7	6.7
Monetary authorities	8 621 ..	....	....	....	....	....	....	....	....
General government	8 622 ..	....	....	....	....	....	....	....	....
Banks	8 623 ..	4.0	5.3	6.5	6.5	6.5	6.5	6.5	6.5
Other sectors	8 624 ..	.1	.1	.1	.1	.1	.1	.1	.1
Money market instruments	8 630 ..	....	....	....	....	....	....	....	....
Monetary authorities	8 631 ..	....	....	....	....	....	....	....	....
General government	8 632 ..	....	....	....	....	....	....	....	....
Banks	8 633 ..	....	....	....	....	....	....	....	....
Other sectors	8 634 ..	....	....	....	....	....	....	....	....
Financial derivatives	8 900 ..	**....**	**.4**	**2.1**	**2.2**	**2.8**	**2.8**	**2.9**	**3.5**
Monetary authorities	8 901 ..	....	....	....	....	....	....	....	....
General government	8 902 ..	....	....	....	....	....	....	....	....
Banks	8 903 ..	....	.4	2.1	2.2	2.8	2.8	2.9	3.5
Other sectors	8 904 ..	....	....	....	....	....	....	....	....
Other investment	8 703 ..	**467.4**	**506.5**	**548.6**	**605.7**	**610.9**	**549.9**	**765.2**	**656.4**
Trade credits	8 706 ..	283.2	314.4	345.3	330.5	355.5	277.6	233.4	211.0
General government	8 707 ..	....	....	....	....	....	....	....	....
of which: Short-term	8 709 ..	....	....	....	....	....	....	....	....
Other sectors	8 710 ..	283.2	314.4	345.3	330.5	355.5	277.6	233.4	211.0
of which: Short-term	8 712 ..	*283.2*	*314.4*	*345.3*	*330.5*	*355.5*	*277.6*	*233.4*	*211.0*
Loans	8 714 ..	....	....	....	....	6.0	4.2	....	7.3
Monetary authorities	8 715 ..	....	....	....	....	....	....	....	....
of which: Short-term	8 718 ..	....	....	....	....	....	....	....	....
General government	8 719 ..	....	....	....	....	....	....	....	....
of which: Short-term	8 721 ..	....	....	....	....	....	....	....	....
Banks	8 722 ..	....	....	....	....	....	....	....	4.9
of which: Short-term	8 724 ..	....	....	....	....	....	....	....	....
Other sectors	8 725 ..	....	....	....	....	6.0	4.2	....	2.5
of which: Short-term	8 727 ..	....	....	....	....	....	....	....	....
Currency and deposits	8 730 ..	173.9	183.1	194.3	266.2	240.4	259.1	522.8	429.0
Monetary authorities	8 731 ..	....	19.4	....	....	....	....	....	....
General government	8 732 ..	1.1	.8	....	....	....	....	....	....
Banks	8 733 ..	115.2	112.5	156.5	244.2	218.0	246.7	437.5	372.7
Other sectors	8 734 ..	57.6	50.5	37.8	22.0	22.4	12.5	85.3	56.3
Other assets	8 736 ..	10.4	9.0	9.0	9.0	9.0	9.0	9.0	9.0
Monetary authorities	8 737 ..	....	....	....	....	....	....	....	....
of which: Short-term	8 739 ..	....	....	....	....	....	....	....	....
General government	8 740 ..	....	....	....	....	....	....	....	....
of which: Short-term	8 742 ..	....	....	....	....	....	....	....	....
Banks	8 743 ..	....	....	....	....	....	....	....	....
of which: Short-term	8 745 ..	....	....	....	....	....	....	....	....
Other sectors	8 746 ..	10.4	9.0	9.0	9.0	9.0	9.0	9.0	9.0
of which: Short-term	8 748 ..	....	....	....	....	....	....	....	....
Reserve assets	8 802 ..	**302.3**	**470.3**	**597.4**	**775.3**	**1,333.7**	**1,672.4**	**1,480.3**	**1,717.7**
Monetary gold	8 812 ..	....	....	....	....	....	....	....	....
Special drawing rights	8 811 ..	....	.1	....	.2	.2	.1	3.6	.3
Reserve position in the Fund	8 810 ..	....	....	....	....	....	....	....	....
Foreign exchange	8 803 ..	302.2	470.2	597.4	775.1	1,333.5	1,672.3	1,476.7	1,717.3
Other claims	8 813 ..	....	....	....	....	....	....	....	....

Moldova 921

Table 3 (Concluded). INTERNATIONAL INVESTMENT POSITION (End-period stocks), 2003–2010

(Millions of U.S. dollars)

	Code	2003	2004	2005	2006	2007	2008	2009	2010
LIABILITIES	8 995 D.	2,473.4	2,578.9	2,880.4	3,460.3	4,686.3	6,003.4	6,408.3	7,010.5
Direct investment in Moldova	8 555 ..	713.9	843.9	1,020.2	1,278.1	1,876.5	2,596.3	2,697.0	2,879.6
Equity capital and reinvested earnings	8 556 ..	527.9	680.7	785.4	943.1	1,325.5	1,885.2	2,001.7	2,175.6
Claims on direct investors	8 557 ..	....	....	....	....	....	....	....	....
Liabilities to direct investors	8 558 ..	527.9	680.7	785.4	943.1	1,325.5	1,885.2	2,001.7	2,175.6
Other capital	8 580 ..	186.0	163.2	234.8	335.0	551.0	711.1	695.3	704.1
Claims on direct investors	8 585 ..	....	−4.8	−4.8	−5.0	.2	−14.9	−5.8	−9.8
Liabilities to direct investors	8 590 ..	186.0	168.0	239.6	340.0	550.8	726.0	701.1	713.9
Portfolio investment	8 652 ..	110.9	51.5	46.1	51.1	53.9	56.9	49.3	55.5
Equity securities	8 660 ..	16.5	19.7	20.7	32.0	41.0	48.9	49.3	55.5
Banks	8 663 ..	4.7	7.1	8.3	19.6	26.8	33.1	31.2	37.4
Other sectors	8 664 ..	11.9	12.7	12.4	12.4	14.2	15.9	18.0	18.1
Debt securities	8 669 ..	94.3	31.8	25.4	19.0	12.9	8.0	....	....
Bonds and notes	8 670 ..	94.3	31.8	25.4	19.0	12.7	6.4	....	....
Monetary authorities	8 671 ..	....	....	....	....	....	....		
General government	8 672 ..	94.3	31.8	25.4	19.0	12.7	6.4		
Banks	8 673 ..	....	....	....	....	....	....		
Other sectors	8 674 ..	....	....	....	....	....	....		
Money market instruments	8 680 ..	....	....	....	....	.2	1.6		
Monetary authorities	8 681 ..	....	....	....	....	....	....		
General government	8 682 ..	....	....	....	....	.2	1.6		
Banks	8 683 ..	....	....	....	....	....	....		
Other sectors	8 684 ..	....	....	....	....	....	....		
Financial derivatives	8 905 ..	....	1.1	1.2	1.5	1.5	2.5	3.0	3.0
Monetary authorities	8 906 ..	....	....	....	....	....	....	....	....
General government	8 907 ..	....	....	....	....	....	....	....	....
Banks	8 908 ..	....	1.1	1.2	1.5	1.5	2.5	3.0	3.0
Other sectors	8 909 ..	....	....	....	....	....	....	....	....
Other investment	8 753 ..	1,648.6	1,682.5	1,813.0	2,129.6	2,754.4	3,347.7	3,659.0	4,072.4
Trade credits	8 756 ..	137.7	175.0	338.6	387.4	501.7	623.0	714.2	834.7
General government	8 757 ..	....	....	....	....	....	....	....	....
of which: Short-term	8 759 ..	....	....	....	....	....	....	....	....
Other sectors	8 760 ..	137.7	175.0	338.6	387.4	501.7	623.0	714.2	834.7
of which: Short-term	8 762 ..	*137.7*	*175.0*	*338.6*	*387.4*	*501.7*	*623.0*	*714.2*	*834.7*
Loans	8 764 ..	1,035.6	1,076.9	1,025.8	1,232.7	1,627.8	2,023.3	1,988.8	2,235.9
Monetary authorities	8 765 ..	142.6	126.4	95.5	141.1	159.5	167.6	153.9	327.4
of which: Use of Fund credit and loans from the Fund	8 766 ..	*142.6*	*126.4*	*95.5*	*141.1*	*159.5*	*167.6*	*153.9*	*327.4*
of which: Short-term	8 768 ..	....	....	....	....	....	....	....	....
General government	8 769 ..	644.2	646.8	595.9	699.0	753.1	771.9	773.6	811.7
of which: Short-term	8 771 ..	....	....	....	....	....	....	....	....
Banks	8 772 ..	33.0	34.8	35.8	43.5	170.2	335.0	278.2	304.0
of which: Short-term	8 774 ..	*8.6*	*2.0*	....	....	*10.1*	*56.8*	*10.6*	*10.6*
Other sectors	8 775 ..	215.8	269.0	298.7	349.1	545.0	748.9	783.1	792.7
of which: Short-term	8 777 ..	*.8*	*.1*	*1.4*	*.8*	*30.9*	*16.9*	*17.0*	*40.8*
Currency and deposits	8 780 ..	24.6	39.6	51.0	106.8	178.5	226.4	179.4	102.0
Monetary authorities	8 781 ..	....	....	....	....	....	....	....	....
General government	8 782 ..	....	....	....	....	....	....	....	....
Banks	8 783 ..	24.6	39.6	51.0	106.8	178.5	226.4	179.4	102.0
Other sectors	8 784 ..	....	....	....	....	....	....	....	....
Other liabilities	8 786 ..	450.8	391.0	397.6	402.7	446.3	475.1	776.7	899.9
Monetary authorities	8 787 ..	....	....	....	....	....	....	184.5	181.3
of which: Short-term	8 789 ..	....	....	....	....	....	....	....	....
General government	8 790 ..	70.4	20.9	36.3	.1	....	....	....	....
of which: Short-term	8 792 ..	*70.4*	*20.9*	*36.3*	*.1*	....	....	....	....
Banks	8 793 ..	....	....	....	....	10.3	....	....	.6
of which: Short-term	8 795 ..	....	....	....	....	*10.3*	....	....	*.6*
Other sectors	8 796 ..	380.4	370.1	361.4	402.6	436.0	475.1	592.1	718.0
of which: Short-term	8 798 ..	*380.4*	*370.1*	*361.4*	*402.6*	*436.0*	*475.1*	*592.1*	*718.0*
NET INTERNATIONAL INVESTMENT POSITION	8 995 ..	−1,675.4	−1,571.8	−1,699.9	−2,045.4	−2,689.8	−3,713.1	−4,087.5	−4,556.8
Conversion rates: Moldovan lei per U.S. dollar (end of period)	0 102 ..	13.220	12.461	12.832	12.905	11.319	10.400	12.302	12.154

Table 1. ANALYTIC PRESENTATION, 2003–2010

(Millions of U.S. dollars)

	Code	2003	2004	2005	2006	2007	2008	2009	2010
A. Current Account[1].....................	4 993 Z.	**−148.1**	**−24.6**	**−4.5**	**109.0**	**171.8**	**−690.1**	**−341.8**	**−886.5**
Goods: exports f.o.b........................	2 100 ..	627.3	872.1	1,068.6	1,545.2	1,950.7	2,529.1	1,885.4	2,908.5
Goods: imports f.o.b........................	3 100 ..	−826.9	−901.0	−1,097.4	−1,356.7	−2,003.1	−3,156.3	−2,074.2	−3,088.9
Balance on Goods........................	4 100 ..	*−199.6*	*−28.9*	*−28.8*	*188.5*	*−52.4*	*−627.2*	*−188.8*	*−180.4*
Services: credit...............................	2 200 ..	207.9	338.4	414.5	485.8	581.8	499.4	414.5	485.9
Services: debit................................	3 200 ..	−257.1	−503.7	−475.9	−523.2	−472.4	−610.2	−557.8	−780.3
Balance on Goods and Services........	4 991 ..	*−248.8*	*−194.2*	*−90.2*	*151.0*	*57.0*	*−738.0*	*−332.0*	*−474.7*
Income: credit................................	2 300 ..	13.9	16.5	10.7	17.4	53.5	16.5	24.3	28.9
Income: debit.................................	3 300 ..	−25.4	−27.7	−61.4	−161.9	−151.0	−189.3	−219.8	−627.8
Balance on Goods, Services, and Income.........	4 992 ..	*−260.3*	*−205.3*	*−140.9*	*6.5*	*−40.5*	*−910.8*	*−527.4*	*−1,073.5*
Current transfers: credit..................	2 379 Z.	167.1	230.9	177.6	179.8	303.8	378.4	260.3	309.4
Current transfers: debit...................	3 379 ..	−54.9	−50.2	−41.2	−77.4	−91.5	−157.7	−74.6	−122.4
B. Capital Account[1].....................	4 994 Z.	....	....	....	....	....	**84.1**	**160.5**	**152.2**
Capital account: credit....................	2 994 Z.	....	....	....	....	....	84.5	160.5	152.7
Capital account: debit.....................	3 994 ..	....	....	....	....	....	−.5	....	−.5
Total, Groups A Plus B..................	4 981 ..	*−148.1*	*−24.6*	*−4.5*	*109.0*	*171.8*	*−606.1*	*−181.3*	*−734.3*
C. Financial Account[1]..................	4 995 W.	**5.0**	**−23.2**	**45.6**	**181.4**	**276.0**	**1,147.6**	**608.5**	**1,369.9**
Direct investment abroad................	4 505 ..	....	....	....	....	−12.8	−6.2	−53.8	−46.6
Direct investment in Mongolia.........	4 555 Z.	131.5	92.9	184.6	344.0	372.8	844.7	623.6	1,454.7
Portfolio investment assets.............	4 602 ..	50.0	−2.5	....	....	−1.2	−51.2	−138.8	143.3
Equity securities........................	4 610 ..	....	−2.5	....	....	−.3	−25.1	−6.4	−12.9
Debt securities..........................	4 619 ..	50.0	....	....	....	−.9	−26.1	−132.4	156.2
Portfolio investment liabilities.........	4 652 Z.	....	−50.0	....	....	76.0	14.8	56.7	751.0
Equity securities........................	4 660 ..	....	....	....	....	.8	13.4	3.6	680.3
Debt securities..........................	4 669 Z.	....	−50.0	....	....	75.2	1.3	53.1	70.7
Financial derivatives.......................	4 910 ..	....	....	....	....	....	....	....	....
Financial derivatives assets.............	4 900 ..	....	....	....	....	....	....	....	....
Financial derivatives liabilities.........	4 905 ..	....	....	....	....	....	....	....	....
Other investment assets..................	4 703 ..	9.6	−132.2	−124.8	−223.4	−207.8	64.5	−144.8	−1,040.2
Monetary authorities...................	4 701 ..	....	....	....	....	....	....	....	....
General government...................	4 704 ..	....	....	....	....	....	....	....	....
Banks...	4 705 ..	46.8	15.0	−1.5	−1.0	−114.2	113.0	−74.5	−197.4
Other sectors.............................	4 728 ..	−37.2	−147.2	....	....	−93.7	−48.5	−70.4	−842.8
Other investment liabilities.............	4 753 W.	−186.1	68.6	−14.2	60.8	49.0	281.2	265.6	107.8
Monetary authorities...................	4 753 WA	....	....	....	....	....	....	74.7	−1.3
General government...................	4 753 ZB	−144.5	112.9	79.6	63.0	....	38.6	149.7	9.6
Banks...	4 753 ZC	2.4	27.3	2.5	1.5	50.2	171.3	15.4	−.1
Other sectors.............................	4 753 ZD	−44.0	−71.6	−96.3	−3.7	−1.2	71.3	25.9	99.6
Total, Groups A Through C............	4 983 ..	*−143.1*	*−47.7*	*41.1*	*290.4*	*447.8*	*541.6*	*427.2*	*635.6*
D. Net Errors and Omissions...............	4 998 ..	**−5.9**	**1.4**	**−75.5**	**−7.9**	**−158.7**	**−774.7**	**127.6**	**239.3**
Total, Groups A Through D............	4 984 ..	*−149.0*	*−46.3*	*−34.4*	*282.5*	*289.1*	*−233.1*	*554.7*	*874.8*
E. Reserves and Related Items............	4 802 A.	**149.0**	**46.3**	**34.4**	**−282.5**	**−289.1**	**233.1**	**−554.7**	**−874.8**
Reserve assets...............................	4 802 ..	96.8	−34.4	−48.5	−389.2	−282.6	237.7	−712.5	−893.6
Use of Fund credit and loans...........	4 766 ..	2.8	−7.2	−5.9	−5.9	−6.6	−5.1	157.8	18.7
Exceptional financing......................	4 920 ..	49.4	88.0	88.8	112.6	....	.4	....	....
Conversion rates: togrogs per U.S. dollar.............	0 101 ..	**1,146.5**	**1,185.3**	**1,205.2**	**1,179.7**	**1,170.4**	**1,165.8**	**1,437.8**	**1,357.1**

[1] Excludes components that have been classified in the categories of Group E.

Table 2. STANDARD PRESENTATION, 2003–2010

(Millions of U.S. dollars)

	Code	2003	2004	2005	2006	2007	2008	2009	2010
CURRENT ACCOUNT	4 993	**−98.7**	**63.4**	**84.3**	**221.6**	**171.8**	**−690.1**	**−341.8**	**−886.5**
A. GOODS	4 100	**−199.6**	**−28.9**	**−28.8**	**188.5**	**−52.4**	**−627.2**	**−188.8**	**−180.4**
Credit	2 100	**627.3**	**872.1**	**1,068.6**	**1,545.2**	**1,950.7**	**2,529.1**	**1,885.4**	**2,908.5**
General merchandise: exports f.o.b.	2 110	627.3	872.1	737.2	1,275.1	1,715.8	1,908.7	1,572.4	2,729.5
Goods for processing: exports f.o.b.	2 150	....	....	....	....	....	20.5	4.5	.6
Repairs on goods	2 160	....	....	....	....	....	....	....	....
Goods procured in ports by carriers	2 170	....	....	....	....	....	....	....	....
Nonmonetary gold	2 180	....	....	331.4	270.1	234.9	599.9	308.5	178.3
Debit	3 100	**−826.9**	**−901.0**	**−1,097.4**	**−1,356.7**	**−2,003.1**	**−3,156.3**	**−2,074.2**	**−3,088.9**
General merchandise: imports f.o.b.	3 110	−826.9	−901.0	−1,097.4	−1,356.7	−2,003.1	−3,121.9	−2,044.2	−3,067.6
Goods for processing: imports f.o.b.	3 150	....	....	....	....	....	....	−1.9	−.8
Repairs on goods	3 160	....	....	....	....	....	−18.3	−13.2	−8.2
Goods procured in ports by carriers	3 170	....	....	....	....	....	−16.1	−14.9	−12.3
Nonmonetary gold	3 180	....	....	....	....	....	....	....	....
B. SERVICES	4 200	**−49.2**	**−165.3**	**−61.4**	**−37.5**	**109.4**	**−110.8**	**−143.2**	**−294.3**
Total credit	2 200	*207.9*	*338.4*	*414.5*	*485.8*	*581.8*	*499.4*	*414.5*	*485.9*
Total debit	3 200	*−257.1*	*−503.7*	*−475.9*	*−523.2*	*−472.4*	*−610.2*	*−557.8*	*−780.3*
Transportation services, credit	2 205	**40.5**	**107.6**	**199.2**	**214.4**	**218.3**	**165.4**	**135.6**	**174.6**
Passenger	2 850	*11.0*	*19.6*	*26.4*	*36.2*	*42.5*	*24.6*	*17.7*	*43.7*
Freight	2 851	....	*37.0*	*77.9*	*97.6*	*86.0*	*67.5*	*62.6*	*66.9*
Other	2 852	*29.5*	*51.1*	*95.0*	*80.6*	*89.8*	*73.2*	*55.2*	*64.1*
Sea transport, passenger	2 207	....	....	....	....	....	....	....	....
Sea transport, freight	2 208	....	....	....	....	....	....	....	....
Sea transport, other	2 209	....	....	....	....	....	....	....	....
Air transport, passenger	2 211	6.9	10.4	....	....	42.5	22.4	16.0	41.8
Air transport, freight	2 212	....	7.4	....	....	....	19.0	3.8	4.5
Air transport, other	2 213	24.1	29.0	....	....	....	66.6	49.5	60.8
Other transport, passenger	2 215	4.1	9.2	....	....	....	2.2	1.7	1.9
Other transport, freight	2 216	....	29.6	....	....	86.0	48.5	58.9	62.3
Other transport, other	2 217	5.4	22.1	....	....	89.8	6.6	5.8	3.3
Transportation services, debit	3 205	**−44.2**	**−199.4**	**−216.1**	**−254.6**	**−151.5**	**−258.9**	**−203.3**	**−285.1**
Passenger	3 850	*−5.9*	*−13.6*	*−16.3*	*−24.2*	*−21.9*	*−32.0*	*−31.9*	*−54.4*
Freight	3 851	....	*−107.2*	*−129.3*	*−151.5*	*−101.1*	*−197.5*	*−145.5*	*−214.8*
Other	3 852	*−38.3*	*−78.6*	*−70.6*	*−78.9*	*−28.5*	*−29.3*	*−25.9*	*−16.0*
Sea transport, passenger	3 207	....	....	....	....	....	....	....	....
Sea transport, freight	3 208	....	....	....	....	....	....	....	....
Sea transport, other	3 209	....	....	....	....	....	....	....	....
Air transport, passenger	3 211	−4.4	−7.2	....	....	−21.9	−4.7	−4.6	−50.4
Air transport, freight	3 212	....	−21.4	....	....	....	....	.4	....
Air transport, other	3 213	−10.5	−12.9	....	....	....	−10.5	−14.5	−9.4
Other transport, passenger	3 215	−1.5	−6.4	....	....	....	−27.3	−27.3	−4.0
Other transport, freight	3 216	....	−85.8	....	....	−101.1	−197.5	−145.9	−214.8
Other transport, other	3 217	−27.8	−65.7	....	....	−28.5	−18.8	−11.4	−6.6
Travel, credit	2 236	**143.0**	**185.1**	**176.8**	**225.1**	**311.5**	**246.9**	**235.3**	**244.0**
Business travel	2 237	....	.4	.7	2.3	5.1	14.2	34.0	31.2
Personal travel	2 240	143.0	184.7	176.1	222.8	306.4	232.7	201.3	212.9
Travel, debit	3 236	**−137.5**	**−192.7**	**−156.6**	**−187.9**	**−204.6**	**−217.3**	**−210.4**	**−265.3**
Business travel	3 237	....	−7.6	−4.7	−5.6	−4.5	−3.9	−2.4	−3.0
Personal travel	3 240	−137.5	−185.1	−151.9	−182.4	−200.1	−213.4	−208.0	−262.3
Other services, credit	2 200 BA	**24.4**	**45.7**	**38.5**	**46.3**	**52.0**	**87.1**	**43.7**	**67.3**
Communications	2 245	4.8	4.8	14.5	17.9	19.4	18.6	11.3	9.0
Construction	2 249	....	....	.8	.4	2.7	4.8	2.2	2.9
Insurance	2 253	1.2	2.0	2.3	.7	.2	3.6	3.2	4.2
Financial	2 260	.5	2.0	5.0	9.0	2.8	.6	1.5	6.6
Computer and information	2 262	1.8	1.2	.8	.2	1.2	.6	1.2	.8
Royalties and licence fees	2 266	....	....	....	....	....	12.5	.2	.5
Other business services	2 268	10.7	25.4	9.7	15.2	19.4	43.3	21.8	39.9
Personal, cultural, and recreational	2 287	.2	1.1	.1	....	−.2	.5	.2	.3
Government, n.i.e.	2 291	5.2	9.2	5.4	2.9	6.5	2.5	2.1	3.0
Other services, debit	3 200 BA	**−75.4**	**−111.6**	**−103.1**	**−80.7**	**−116.3**	**−134.0**	**−144.1**	**−229.8**
Communications	3 245	−7.4	−9.1	−23.4	−9.9	−15.4	−24.0	−23.5	−26.1
Construction	3 249	−.6	−.6	−2.9	−1.5	−22.6	−3.0	−1.3	−6.8
Insurance	3 253	−1.2	−32.9	−15.2	−16.9	−10.5	−15.3	−13.4	−19.4
Financial	3 260	−3.2	−7.9	−7.9	−3.0	−2.7	−1.4	−4.6	−10.0
Computer and information	3 262	−.5	−1.3	−2.3	−.5	−1.5	−5.7	−3.8	−4.8
Royalties and licence fees	3 266	....	....	....	....	....	−1.3	−.8	−2.6
Other business services	3 268	−53.7	−52.6	−43.3	−42.4	−47.2	−70.6	−83.5	−139.2
Personal, cultural, and recreational	3 287	−.2	....	−.2	2.2	....	−.7	−.2	−.4
Government, n.i.e.	3 291	−8.6	−7.2	−8.0	−9.0	−16.5	−12.2	−12.9	−20.3

2011, International Monetary Fund: *Balance of Payments Statistics Yearbook*

Table 2 (Continued). STANDARD PRESENTATION, 2003–2010

(Millions of U.S. dollars)

	Code	2003	2004	2005	2006	2007	2008	2009	2010
C. INCOME	4 300 ..	**−11.5**	**−11.1**	**−50.8**	**−144.5**	**−97.5**	**−172.7**	**−195.4**	**−598.8**
Total credit	2 300 ..	*13.9*	*16.5*	*10.7*	*17.4*	*53.5*	*16.5*	*24.3*	*28.9*
Total debit	3 300 ..	*−25.4*	*−27.7*	*−61.4*	*−161.9*	*−151.0*	*−189.3*	*−219.8*	*−627.8*
Compensation of employees, credit	2 310 ..	....	**7.1**	**2.8**	**1.6**	**3.8**	**6.4**	**8.1**	**18.3**
Compensation of employees, debit	3 310 ..	....	....	....	....	....	**−22.8**	**−12.1**	**−50.6**
Investment income, credit	2 320 ..	**13.9**	**9.4**	**7.9**	**15.8**	**49.7**	**10.2**	**16.2**	**10.6**
Direct investment income	2 330 ..	....	....	....	....	....	2.2	4.8	.2
Dividends and distributed branch profits	2 332 ..	....	....	....	....	....	....	....	.8
Reinvested earnings and undistributed branch profits	2 333 ..	....	....	....	....	....	....	....	−.6
Income on debt (interest)	2 334 ..	....	....	....	....	....	2.2	4.8	....
Portfolio investment income	2 339 ..	7.4	1.0	....	....	....	4.7	5.0	3.0
Income on equity	2 340 ..	....	....	....	....	....	....	....	....
Income on bonds and notes	2 350 ..	1.5	1.0	....	....	....	4.7	5.0	2.2
Income on money market instruments	2 360 ..	5.9	....	....	....	....	....	....	.8
Other investment income	2 370 ..	6.5	8.4	7.9	15.8	49.7	3.3	6.4	7.4
Investment income, debit	3 320 ..	**−25.4**	**−27.7**	**−61.4**	**−161.9**	**−151.0**	**−166.5**	**−207.7**	**−577.2**
Direct investment income	3 330 ..	−5.0	−9.5	−41.0	−145.4	−125.8	−109.1	−121.0	−465.2
Dividends and distributed branch profits	3 332 ..	−5.0	−9.5	−41.0	−145.4	−125.8	−91.3	−133.8	−340.1
Reinvested earnings and undistributed branch profits	3 333 ..	....	....	....	....	....	−17.5	16.1	−113.8
Income on debt (interest)	3 334 ..	....	....	....	....	....	−.2	−3.3	−11.3
Portfolio investment income	3 339 ..	....	....	....	....	−6.2	−16.8	−20.0	−13.5
Income on equity	3 340 ..	....	....	....	....	....	....	....	....
Income on bonds and notes	3 350 ..	....	....	....	....	−6.2	−16.8	−20.0	−13.5
Income on money market instruments	3 360 ..	....	....	....	....	....	....	....	....
Other investment income	3 370 ..	−20.4	−18.2	−20.4	−16.5	−19.0	−40.6	−66.7	−98.5
D. CURRENT TRANSFERS	4 379 ..	**161.6**	**268.7**	**225.2**	**215.1**	**212.3**	**220.7**	**185.7**	**187.0**
Credit	2 379 ..	**216.5**	**318.9**	**266.4**	**292.5**	**303.8**	**378.4**	**260.3**	**309.4**
General government	2 380 ..	49.4	88.0	88.8	112.6	109.0	33.4	62.2	35.0
Other sectors	2 390 ..	167.1	230.9	177.6	179.8	194.8	345.0	198.1	274.4
Workers' remittances	2 391 ..	128.6	195.4	177.6	179.8	174.3	218.2	191.5	247.9
Other current transfers	2 392 ..	38.5	35.5	....	....	20.5	126.8	6.6	26.4
Debit	3 379 ..	**−54.9**	**−50.2**	**−41.2**	**−77.4**	**−91.5**	**−157.7**	**−74.6**	**−122.4**
General government	3 380 ..	−.6	−1.1	−.8	−.8	−.8	−.9	−2.7	−2.1
Other sectors	3 390 ..	−54.3	−49.1	−40.4	−76.6	−90.7	−156.8	−72.0	−120.3
Workers' remittances	3 391 ..	−54.3	−49.1	−40.4	−76.6	−90.3	−149.4	−71.4	−118.5
Other current transfers	3 392 ..	....	....	....	....	−.4	−7.5	−.6	−1.7
CAPITAL AND FINANCIAL ACCOUNT	4 996 ..	**104.6**	**−64.9**	**−8.8**	**−213.7**	**−13.1**	**1,464.8**	**214.2**	**647.3**
CAPITAL ACCOUNT	4 994 ..	....	....	....	....	....	**84.1**	**160.5**	**152.2**
Total credit	2 994 ..	....	....	....	....	....	*84.5*	*160.5*	*152.7*
Total debit	3 994 ..	....	....	....	....	....	*−.5*	....	*−.5*
Capital transfers, credit	2 400 ..	....	....	....	....	....	**84.5**	**160.5**	**152.7**
General government	2 401 ..	....	....	....	....	....	78.8	145.1	81.8
Debt forgiveness	2 402 ..	....	....	....	....	....	....	....	....
Other capital transfers	2 410 ..	....	....	....	....	....	78.8	145.1	81.8
Other sectors	2 430 ..	....	....	....	....	....	5.8	15.4	70.9
Migrants' transfers	2 431 ..	....	....	....	....	....	.7	....	10.3
Debt forgiveness	2 432 ..	....	....	....	....	....	....	....	....
Other capital transfers	2 440 ..	....	....	....	....	....	5.0	15.4	60.6
Capital transfers, debit	3 400 ..	....	....	....	....	....	**−.5**	....	....
General government	3 401 ..	....	....	....	....	....	....	....	....
Debt forgiveness	3 402 ..	....	....	....	....	....	....	....	....
Other capital transfers	3 410 ..	....	....	....	....	....	....	....	....
Other sectors	3 430 ..	....	....	....	....	....	−.5	....	....
Migrants' transfers	3 431 ..	....	....	....	....	....	....	....	−.1
Debt forgiveness	3 432 ..	....	....	....	....	....	....	....	....
Other capital transfers	3 440 ..	....	....	....	....	....	−.5	....	.1
Nonproduced nonfinancial assets, credit	2 480 ..	....	....	....	....	....	....	....	....
Nonproduced nonfinancial assets, debit	3 480 ..	....	....	....	....	....	....	....	**−.5**

Table 2 (Continued). STANDARD PRESENTATION, 2003–2010

(Millions of U.S. dollars)

	Code	2003	2004	2005	2006	2007	2008	2009	2010
FINANCIAL ACCOUNT........................	4 995 ..	**104.6**	**−64.9**	**−8.8**	**−213.7**	**−13.1**	**1,380.7**	**53.7**	**495.0**
A. DIRECT INVESTMENT.....................	4 500 ..	**131.5**	**92.9**	**184.6**	**344.0**	**360.0**	**838.5**	**569.8**	**1,408.1**
Direct investment abroad.....................	4 505 ..	....	....	....	....	−12.8	−6.2	−53.8	−46.6
Equity capital..........................	4 510 ..	....	....	....	....	−1.1	−6.4	.4	−46.7
Claims on affiliated enterprises..........	4 515 ..	....	....	....	....	−1.1	−6.4	.4	−46.7
Liabilities to affiliated enterprises.......	4 520 ..	....	....	....	....	....	....	....	....
Reinvested earnings.....................	4 525 ..	....	....	....	....	....	....	....	.6
Other capital..........................	4 530 ..	....	....	....	....	−11.7	.2	−54.2	−.5
Claims on affiliated enterprises..........	4 535 ..	....	....	....	....	−11.7	.2	−54.2	−.5
Liabilities to affiliated enterprises.......	4 540 ..	....	....	....	....	....	....	....	....
Direct investment in Mongolia..............	4 555 ..	131.5	92.9	184.6	344.0	372.8	844.7	623.6	1,454.7
Equity capital..........................	4 560 ..	131.5	92.9	184.6	344.0	322.8	811.0	504.1	1,218.0
Claims on direct investors...............	4 565 ..	....	....	....	....	....	....	....	....
Liabilities to direct investors............	4 570 ..	131.5	92.9	184.6	344.0	322.8	811.0	504.1	1,218.0
Reinvested earnings.....................	4 575 ..	....	....	....	....	....	17.5	−16.1	113.8
Other capital..........................	4 580 ..	....	....	....	....	49.9	16.2	135.6	122.9
Claims on direct investors...............	4 585 ..	....	....	....	....	....	....	....	....
Liabilities to direct investors............	4 590 ..	....	....	....	....	49.9	16.2	135.6	122.9
B. PORTFOLIO INVESTMENT.................	4 600 ..	**50.0**	**−52.5**	....	....	**74.9**	**−36.0**	**−82.1**	**894.3**
Assets.................................	4 602 ..	**50.0**	**−2.5**	....	....	**−1.2**	**−51.2**	**−138.8**	**143.3**
Equity securities.......................	4 610 ..	....	−2.5	....	....	−.3	−25.1	−6.4	−12.9
Monetary authorities..................	4 611 ..	....	....	....	....	....	....	....	....
General government..................	4 612 ..	....	....	....	....	....	....	....	....
Banks.............................	4 613 ..	....	−2.5	....	....	−.3	−4.2	....	−3.3
Other sectors.......................	4 614 ..	....	....	....	....	....	−20.9	−6.4	−9.6
Debt securities........................	4 619 ..	50.0	....	....	....	−.9	−26.1	−132.4	156.2
Bonds and notes.....................	4 620 ..	50.0	....	....	....	−.9	−1.7	....	2.1
Monetary authorities..............	4 621 ..	....	....	....	....	....	....	....	....
General government..............	4 622 ..	50.0	....	....	....	....	....	....	....
Banks...........................	4 623 ..	....	....	....	....	−.9	−1.6	....	....
Other sectors.....................	4 624 ..	....	....	....	....	....	....	....	2.1
Money market instruments............	4 630 ..	....	....	....	....	....	−24.4	−132.4	154.1
Monetary authorities..............	4 631 ..	....	....	....	....	....	....	....	....
General government..............	4 632 ..	....	....	....	....	....	....	....	....
Banks...........................	4 633 ..	....	....	....	....	....	....	.7	....
Other sectors.....................	4 634 ..	....	....	....	....	....	−24.4	−133.1	154.1
Liabilities............................	4 652 ..	....	**−50.0**	....	....	**76.0**	**15.2**	**56.7**	**751.0**
Equity securities.......................	4 660 ..	....	....	....	....	.8	13.4	3.6	680.3
Banks.............................	4 663 ..	....	....	....	....	....	.5	−.4	....
Other sectors.......................	4 664 ..	....	....	....	....	.8	12.9	4.0	680.3
Debt securities........................	4 669 ..	....	−50.0	....	....	75.2	1.8	53.1	70.7
Bonds and notes.....................	4 670 ..	....	−50.0	....	....	75.2	1.8	53.1	70.7
Monetary authorities..............	4 671 ..	....	....	....	....	....	....	....	....
General government..............	4 672 ..	....	−50.0	....	....	....	....	70.6	−52.7
Banks...........................	4 673 ..	....	....	....	....	74.8	8.4	−17.5	123.5
Other sectors.....................	4 674 ..	....	....	....	....	.4	−6.7	....	−.1
Money market instruments............	4 680 ..	....	....	....	....	....	....	....	....
Monetary authorities..............	4 681 ..	....	....	....	....	....	....	....	....
General government..............	4 682 ..	....	....	....	....	....	....	....	....
Banks...........................	4 683 ..	....	....	....	....	....	....	....	....
Other sectors.....................	4 684 ..	....	....	....	....	....	....	....	....
C. FINANCIAL DERIVATIVES................	4 910 ..	....	....	....	....	....	....	....	....
Monetary authorities....................	4 911 ..	....	....	....	....	....	....	....	....
General government.....................	4 912 ..	....	....	....	....	....	....	....	....
Banks................................	4 913 ..	....	....	....	....	....	....	....	....
Other sectors..........................	4 914 ..	....	....	....	....	....	....	....	....
Assets.................................	4 900 ..	....	....	....	....	....	....	....	....
Monetary authorities....................	4 901 ..	....	....	....	....	....	....	....	....
General government.....................	4 902 ..	....	....	....	....	....	....	....	....
Banks................................	4 903 ..	....	....	....	....	....	....	....	....
Other sectors..........................	4 904 ..	....	....	....	....	....	....	....	....
Liabilities............................	4 905 ..	....	....	....	....	....	....	....	....
Monetary authorities....................	4 906 ..	....	....	....	....	....	....	....	....
General government.....................	4 907 ..	....	....	....	....	....	....	....	....
Banks................................	4 908 ..	....	....	....	....	....	....	....	....
Other sectors..........................	4 909 ..	....	....	....	....	....	....	....	....

Table 2 (Concluded). STANDARD PRESENTATION, 2003–2010
(Millions of U.S. dollars)

	Code	2003	2004	2005	2006	2007	2008	2009	2010
D. OTHER INVESTMENT	4 700 ..	**−173.7**	**−70.8**	**−144.9**	**−168.5**	**−165.4**	**340.6**	**278.5**	**−913.7**
Assets	4 703 ..	9.6	−132.2	−124.8	−223.4	−207.8	64.5	−144.8	−1,040.2
Trade credits	4 706 ..	−1.0	3.4	16.2	10.6	−15.5	....	10.8	−4.0
General government	4 707 ..	....	....	....	....	....	....	....	....
of which: Short-term	4 709 ..	....	....	....	....	....	....	....	....
Other sectors	4 710 ..	−1.0	3.4	....	....	−15.5	....	10.8	−4.0
of which: Short-term	4 712 ..	−1.0	3.4	....	....	−15.5	....	10.8	−4.0
Loans	4 714 ..	....	3.2	−1.5	−1.0	−70.2	7.6	5.2	4.4
Monetary authorities	4 715 ..	....	....	....	....	....	....	....	....
of which: Short-term	4 718 ..	....	....	....	....	....	....	....	....
General government	4 719 ..	....	....	....	....	....	....	....	....
of which: Short-term	4 721 ..	....	....	....	....	....	....	....	....
Banks	4 722 ..	....	3.2	−1.5	−1.0	7.7	7.6	5.2	8.6
of which: Short-term	4 724 ..	....	.1	−1.5	−1.0	7.7	....	....	....
Other sectors	4 725 ..	....	....	....	....	−77.8	....	....	−4.2
of which: Short-term	4 727 ..	....	....	....	....	−78.7	....	....	−4.2
Currency and deposits	4 730 ..	10.6	−135.8	−139.6	−233.0	−121.8	57.1	−160.8	−1,040.6
Monetary authorities	4 731 ..	....	....	....	....	....	....	....	....
General government	4 732 ..	....	....	....	....	....	....	....	....
Banks	4 733 ..	46.8	14.8	....	....	−121.8	105.4	−79.6	−206.0
Other sectors	4 734 ..	−36.2	−150.6	....	....	....	−48.2	−81.2	−834.6
Other assets	4 736 ..	....	−3.0	....	....	−.3	−.3	....	....
Monetary authorities	4 737 ..	....	....	....	....	....	....	....	....
of which: Short-term	4 739 ..	....	....	....	....	....	....	....	....
General government	4 740 ..	....	....	....	....	....	....	....	....
of which: Short-term	4 742 ..	....	....	....	....	....	....	....	....
Banks	4 743 ..	....	−3.0	....	....	....	....	....	....
of which: Short-term	4 745 ..	....	−3.0	....	....	....	....	....	....
Other sectors	4 746 ..	....	....	....	....	−.3	−.3	....	....
of which: Short-term	4 748 ..	....	....	....	....	−.3	−.3	....	....
Liabilities	4 753 ..	−183.3	61.4	−20.1	54.9	42.4	276.1	423.4	126.5
Trade credits	4 756 ..	−2.5	.8	−9.4	24.7	2.3	....	3.6	63.1
General government	4 757 ..	....	....	....	....	....	....	....	....
of which: Short-term	4 759 ..	....	....	....	....	....	....	....	....
Other sectors	4 760 ..	−2.5	.8	−9.4	24.7	2.3	....	3.6	63.1
of which: Short-term	4 762 ..	−2.5	.8	−9.4	24.7	2.3	....	3.6	63.1
Loans	4 764 ..	−180.1	43.8	−7.9	45.1	56.0	218.6	388.4	132.3
Monetary authorities	4 765 ..	2.8	−7.2	−5.9	−5.9	−6.6	−5.1	156.2	17.4
of which: Use of Fund credit and loans from the Fund	4 766 ..	2.8	−7.2	−5.9	−5.9	−6.6	−5.1	157.8	18.7
of which: Short-term	4 768 ..	....	....	....	....	....	....	....	....
General government	4 769 ..	−144.5	112.9	79.6	63.0	....	38.6	149.7	9.6
of which: Short-term	4 771 ..	....	....	....	....	....	....	....	....
Banks	4 772 ..	3.1	10.5	5.4	16.3	38.0	113.8	60.3	−8.9
of which: Short-term	4 774 ..	....	....	4.4	....	5.2	5.5	28.9	−51.5
Other sectors	4 775 ..	−41.5	−72.4	−87.0	−28.3	24.6	71.3	22.2	114.2
of which: Short-term	4 777 ..	−21.0	−26.6	−78.0	−17.3	35.2	....	5.0	−18.7
Currency and deposits	4 780 ..	−.7	16.5	−2.9	−14.9	12.2	57.5	−44.9	−68.9
Monetary authorities	4 781 ..	....	....	....	....	....	....	....	....
General government	4 782 ..	....	....	....	....	....	....	....	....
Banks	4 783 ..	−.7	16.5	−2.9	−14.9	12.2	57.5	−44.9	8.8
Other sectors	4 784 ..	....	....	....	....	....	....	....	−77.7
Other liabilities	4 786 ..	....	.3	....	....	−28.1	....	76.3	....
Monetary authorities	4 787 ..	....	....	....	....	....	....	76.3	....
of which: Short-term	4 789 ..	....	....	....	....	....	....	....	....
General government	4 790 ..	....	....	....	....	....	....	....	....
of which: Short-term	4 792 ..	....	....	....	....	....	....	....	....
Banks	4 793 ..	....	.3	....	....	....	....	....	....
of which: Short-term	4 795 ..	....	.3	....	....	....	....	....	....
Other sectors	4 796 ..	....	....	....	....	−28.1	....	....	....
of which: Short-term	4 798 ..	....	....	....	....	−28.1	....	....	....
E. RESERVE ASSETS	4 802 ..	**96.8**	**−34.4**	**−48.5**	**−389.2**	**−282.6**	**237.7**	**−712.5**	**−893.6**
Monetary gold	4 812 ..	43.1	−7.4	14.1	−134.7	−64.2	....	27.0	....
Special drawing rights	4 811 ..	....	....	....	....	....	....	−76.2	2.3
Reserve position in the Fund	4 810 ..	....	....	....	....	....	....	....	....
Foreign exchange	4 803 ..	21.6	3.2	76.8	−33.7	....	237.7	−656.6	−905.9
Other claims	4 813 ..	32.1	−30.2	−139.4	−220.9	−218.3	....	−6.7	10.0
NET ERRORS AND OMISSIONS	4 998 ..	**−5.9**	**1.4**	**−75.5**	**−7.9**	**−158.7**	**−774.7**	**127.6**	**239.3**

Table 3. INTERNATIONAL INVESTMENT POSITION (End-period stocks), 2003–2010

(Millions of U.S. dollars)

	Code	2003	2004	2005	2006	2007	2008	2009	2010
ASSETS	8 995 C.	....	....	....	....	....	....	....	**3,482.5**
Direct investment abroad	8 505 ..	....	....	....	....	....	....	....	**112.8**
Equity capital and reinvested earnings	8 506 ..	....	....	....	....	....	....	....	110.8
Claims on affiliated enterprises	8 507 ..	....	....	....	....	....	....	....	110.8
Liabilities to affiliated enterprises	8 508 ..	....	....	....	....	....	....	....	....
Other capital	8 530 ..	....	....	....	....	....	....	....	1.9
Claims on affiliated enterprises	8 535 ..	....	....	....	....	....	....	....	1.9
Liabilities to affiliated enterprises	8 540 ..	....	....	....	....	....	....	....	....
Portfolio investment	8 602 ..	....	....	....	....	....	....	....	**45.3**
Equity securities	8 610 ..	....	....	....	....	....	....	....	.4
Monetary authorities	8 611 ..	....	....	....	....	....	....	....	....
General government	8 612 ..	....	....	....	....	....	....	....	....
Banks	8 613 ..	....	....	....	....	....	....	....	....
Other sectors	8 614 ..	....	....	....	....	....	....	....	.4
Debt securities	8 619 ..	....	....	....	....	....	....	....	45.0
Bonds and notes	8 620 ..	....	....	....	....	....	....	....	45.0
Monetary authorities	8 621 ..	....	....	....	....	....	....	....	....
General government	8 622 ..	....	....	....	....	....	....	....	....
Banks	8 623 ..	....	....	....	....	....	....	....	.2
Other sectors	8 624 ..	....	....	....	....	....	....	....	44.8
Money market instruments	8 630 ..	....	....	....	....	....	....	....	....
Monetary authorities	8 631 ..	....	....	....	....	....	....	....	....
General government	8 632 ..	....	....	....	....	....	....	....	....
Banks	8 633 ..	....	....	....	....	....	....	....	....
Other sectors	8 634 ..	....	....	....	....	....	....	....	....
Financial derivatives	8 900 ..	....	....	....	....	....	....	....	....
Monetary authorities	8 901 ..	....	....	....	....	....	....	....	....
General government	8 902 ..	....	....	....	....	....	....	....	....
Banks	8 903 ..	....	....	....	....	....	....	....	....
Other sectors	8 904 ..	....	....	....	....	....	....	....	....
Other investment	8 703 ..	....	....	....	....	....	....	....	**1,016.0**
Trade credits	8 706 ..	....	....	....	....	....	....	....	101.9
General government	8 707 ..	....	....	....	....	....	....	....	....
of which: Short-term	8 709 ..	....	....	....	....	....	....	....	....
Other sectors	8 710 ..	....	....	....	....	....	....	....	101.9
of which: Short-term	8 712 ..	....	....	....	....	....	....	....	*101.9*
Loans	8 714 ..	....	....	....	....	....	....	....	18.4
Monetary authorities	8 715 ..	....	....	....	....	....	....	....	....
of which: Short-term	8 718 ..	....	....	....	....	....	....	....	....
General government	8 719 ..	....	....	....	....	....	....	....	....
of which: Short-term	8 721 ..	....	....	....	....	....	....	....	....
Banks	8 722 ..	....	....	....	....	....	....	....	18.4
of which: Short-term	8 724 ..	....	....	....	....	....	....	....	*18.4*
Other sectors	8 725 ..	....	....	....	....	....	....	....	....
of which: Short-term	8 727 ..	....	....	....	....	....	....	....	....
Currency and deposits	8 730 ..	....	....	....	....	....	....	....	895.6
Monetary authorities	8 731 ..	....	....	....	....	....	....	....	....
General government	8 732 ..	....	....	....	....	....	....	....	....
Banks	8 733 ..	....	....	....	....	....	....	....	503.4
Other sectors	8 734 ..	....	....	....	....	....	....	....	392.2
Other assets	8 736 ..	....	....	....	....	....	....	....	....
Monetary authorities	8 737 ..	....	....	....	....	....	....	....	....
of which: Short-term	8 739 ..	....	....	....	....	....	....	....	....
General government	8 740 ..	....	....	....	....	....	....	....	....
of which: Short-term	8 742 ..	....	....	....	....	....	....	....	....
Banks	8 743 ..	....	....	....	....	....	....	....	....
of which: Short-term	8 745 ..	....	....	....	....	....	....	....	....
Other sectors	8 746 ..	....	....	....	....	....	....	....	....
of which: Short-term	8 748 ..	....	....	....	....	....	....	....	....
Reserve assets	8 802 ..	....	....	....	....	....	....	....	**2,308.4**
Monetary gold	8 812 ..	....	....	....	....	....	....	....	39.1
Special drawing rights	8 811 ..	....	....	....	....	....	.1	76.4	72.7
Reserve position in the Fund	8 810 ..	.1	.2	.2	.2	.2	.2	.2	.2
Foreign exchange	8 803 ..	....	....	....	....	....	....	....	2,196.3
Other claims	8 813 ..	....	....	....	....	....	....	....	....

Table 3 (Concluded). INTERNATIONAL INVESTMENT POSITION (End-period stocks), 2003–2010

(Millions of U.S. dollars)

	Code	2003	2004	2005	2006	2007	2008	2009	2010
LIABILITIES	8 995 D.	....	....	....	....	....	....	....	**8,350.9**
Direct investment in Mongolia	8 555 ..	....	....	....	....	....	....	....	**4,426.0**
Equity capital and reinvested earnings	8 556 ..	....	....	....	....	....	....	....	3,532.6
Claims on direct investors	8 557 ..	....	....	....	....	....	....	....	....
Liabilities to direct investors	8 558 ..	....	....	....	....	....	....	....	3,532.6
Other capital	8 580 ..	....	....	....	....	....	....	....	893.4
Claims on direct investors	8 585 ..	....	....	....	....	....	....	....	....
Liabilities to direct investors	8 590 ..	....	....	....	....	....	....	....	893.4
Portfolio investment	8 652 ..	....	....	....	....	....	....	....	**1,082.3**
Equity securities	8 660 ..	....	....	....	....	....	....	....	872.2
Banks	8 663 ..	....	....	....	....	....	....	....	....
Other sectors	8 664 ..	....	....	....	....	....	....	....	872.2
Debt securities	8 669 ..	....	....	....	....	....	....	....	210.1
Bonds and notes	8 670 ..	....	....	....	....	....	....	....	210.1
Monetary authorities	8 671 ..	....	....	....	....	....	....	....	....
General government	8 672 ..	....	....	....	....	....	....	....	19.0
Banks	8 673 ..	....	....	....	....	....	....	....	191.1
Other sectors	8 674 ..	....	....	....	....	....	....	....	....
Money market instruments	8 680 ..	....	....	....	....	....	....	....	....
Monetary authorities	8 681 ..	....	....	....	....	....	....	....	....
General government	8 682 ..	....	....	....	....	....	....	....	....
Banks	8 683 ..	....	....	....	....	....	....	....	....
Other sectors	8 684 ..	....	....	....	....	....	....	....	....
Financial derivatives	8 905 ..	....	....	....	....	....	....	....	....
Monetary authorities	8 906 ..	....	....	....	....	....	....	....	....
General government	8 907 ..	....	....	....	....	....	....	....	....
Banks	8 908 ..	....	....	....	....	....	....	....	....
Other sectors	8 909 ..	....	....	....	....	....	....	....	....
Other investment	8 753 ..	....	....	....	....	....	....	....	**2,842.5**
Trade credits	8 756 ..	....	....	....	....	....	....	....	70.7
General government	8 757 ..	....	....	....	....	....	....	....	....
of which: Short-term	8 759 ..	....	....	....	....	....	....	....	....
Other sectors	8 760 ..	....	....	....	....	....	....	....	70.7
of which: Short-term	8 762 ..	....	....	....	....	....	....	....	*46.7*
Loans	8 764 ..	....	....	....	....	....	....	....	2,645.6
Monetary authorities	8 765 ..	....	....	....	....	....	....	....	198.5
of which: Use of Fund credit and loans from the Fund	8 766 ..	*49.6*	*44.3*	*35.0*	*30.8*	*25.5*	*20.0*	*181.9*	*197.6*
of which: Short-term	8 768 ..	....	....	....	....	....	....	....	....
General government	8 769 ..	....	....	....	....	....	....	....	1,768.7
of which: Short-term	8 771 ..	....	....	....	....	....	....	....	....
Banks	8 772 ..	....	....	....	....	....	....	....	262.5
of which: Short-term	8 774 ..	....	....	....	....	....	....	....	*64.5*
Other sectors	8 775 ..	....	....	....	....	....	....	....	415.8
of which: Short-term	8 777 ..	....	....	....	....	....	....	....	*87.4*
Currency and deposits	8 780 ..	....	....	....	....	....	....	....	34.6
Monetary authorities	8 781 ..	....	....	....	....	....	....	....	....
General government	8 782 ..	....	....	....	....	....	....	....	....
Banks	8 783 ..	....	....	....	....	....	....	....	34.6
Other sectors	8 784 ..	....	....	....	....	....	....	....	....
Other liabilities	8 786 ..	....	....	....	....	....	....	....	91.6
Monetary authorities	8 787 ..	....	....	....	....	....	....	....	75.1
of which: Short-term	8 789 ..	....	....	....	....	....	....	....	....
General government	8 790 ..	....	....	....	....	....	....	....	....
of which: Short-term	8 792 ..	....	....	....	....	....	....	....	....
Banks	8 793 ..	....	....	....	....	....	....	....	16.5
of which: Short-term	8 795 ..	....	....	....	....	....	....	....	*16.5*
Other sectors	8 796 ..	....	....	....	....	....	....	....	....
of which: Short-term	8 798 ..	....	....	....	....	....	....	....	....
NET INTERNATIONAL INVESTMENT POSITION	8 995 ..	....	....	....	....	....	....	....	**−4,868.4**
Conversion rates: togrogs per U.S. dollar (end of period)	0 102 ..	**1,168.0**	**1,209.0**	**1,221.0**	**1,165.0**	**1,170.0**	**1,267.5**	**1,442.8**	**1,256.5**

Table 1. ANALYTIC PRESENTATION, 2003–2010

(Millions of U.S. dollars)

	Code	2003	2004	2005	2006	2007	2008	2009	2010
A. Current Account[1]	4 993 Z.	....	....	....	....	−1,475	−2,320	−1,245	−1,031
Goods: exports f.o.b.	2 100 ..	....	....	....	....	662	660	412	472
Goods: imports f.o.b.	3 100 ..	....	....	....	....	−2,861	−3,739	−2,317	−2,217
Balance on Goods	4 100 ..	....	....	....	....	*−2,200*	*−3,079*	*−1,906*	*−1,745*
Services: credit	2 200 ..	....	....	....	....	921	1,099	945	989
Services: debit	3 200 ..	....	....	....	....	−320	−514	−411	−398
Balance on Goods and Services	4 991 ..	....	....	....	....	*−1,599*	*−2,494*	*−1,371*	*−1,154*
Income: credit	2 300 ..	....	....	....	....	144	247	226	220
Income: debit	3 300 ..	....	....	....	....	−101	−180	−219	−248
Balance on Goods, Services, and Income	4 992 ..	....	....	....	....	*−1,556*	*−2,427*	*−1,364*	*−1,182*
Current transfers: credit	2 379 Z.	....	....	....	....	138	160	163	194
Current transfers: debit	3 379	....	....	....	....	−57	−53	−45	−42
B. Capital Account[1]	4 994 Z.	....	....	....	....	−2	−1	3	−1
Capital account: credit	2 994 Z.	....	....	....	....	1	....	3	....
Capital account: debit	3 994 ..	....	....	....	....	−3	−1	....	−1
Total, Groups A Plus B	4 981 ..	....	....	....	....	*−1,477*	*−2,321*	*−1,242*	*−1,031*
C. Financial Account[1]	4 995 W.	....	....	....	....	1,650	1,715	889	513
Direct investment abroad	4 505 ..	....	....	....	....	−157	−108	−46	−29
Direct investment in Montenegro	4 555 Z.	....	....	....	....	934	960	1,527	760
Portfolio investment assets	4 602 ..	....	....	....	....	−4	−17	−53	−5
Equity securities	4 610 ..	....	....	....	....	−18	−13	−49	2
Debt securities	4 619 ..	....	....	....	....	15	−4	−4	−6
Portfolio investment liabilities	4 652 Z.	....	....	....	....	11	−6	−5	254
Equity securities	4 660 ..	....	....	....	....	5	−6	−5	−8
Debt securities	4 669 Z.	....	....	....	....	6	....	....	262
Financial derivatives	4 910 ..	....	....	....	....	....	....	....	....
Financial derivatives assets	4 900 ..	....	....	....	....	....	....	....	....
Financial derivatives liabilities	4 905 ..	....	....	....	....	....	....	....	....
Other investment assets	4 703 ..	....	....	....	....	−417	−269	−448	−447
Monetary authorities	4 701 ..	....	....	....	....	....	....	....	....
General government	4 704 ..	....	....	....	....	....	....	....	....
Banks	4 705 ..	....	....	....	....	−86	135	−118	−95
Other sectors	4 728 ..	....	....	....	....	−331	−403	−330	−352
Other investment liabilities	4 753 W.	....	....	....	....	1,283	1,154	−87	−21
Monetary authorities	4 753 WA	....	....	....	....	....	....	79	....
General government	4 753 ZB	....	....	....	....	−84	−10	199	10
Banks	4 753 ZC	....	....	....	....	655	672	−303	−139
Other sectors	4 753 ZD	....	....	....	....	712	492	−63	108
Total, Groups A Through C	4 983 ..	....	....	....	....	*173*	*−606*	*−354*	*−518*
D. Net Errors and Omissions	4 998 ..	....	....	....	....	1	378	473	540
Total, Groups A Through D	4 984 ..	....	....	....	....	*174*	*−227*	*119*	*22*
E. Reserves and Related Items	4 802 A.	....	....	....	....	−174	227	−119	−22
Reserve assets	4 802 ..	....	....	....	....	−174	227	−119	−22
Use of Fund credit and loans	4 766 ..	....	....	....	....	....	....	....	....
Exceptional financing	4 920 ..	....	....	....	....	....	....	....	....
Conversion rates: euros per U.S. dollar	0 103 ..	**.8860**	**.8054**	**.8041**	**.7971**	**.7306**	**.6827**	**.7198**	**.7550**

[1] Excludes components that have been classified in the categories of Group E.

Table 2. STANDARD PRESENTATION, 2003–2010

(Millions of U.S. dollars)

	Code	2003	2004	2005	2006	2007	2008	2009	2010
CURRENT ACCOUNT...............................	4 993 ..	....	....	....	....	**−1,475**	**−2,320**	**−1,245**	**−1,031**
A. GOODS...............................	4 100 ..	....	....	....	....	**−2,200**	**−3,079**	**−1,906**	**−1,745**
Credit...............................	2 100 ..	....	....	....	....	**662**	**660**	**412**	**472**
General merchandise: exports f.o.b.......	2 110 ..	....	....	....	....	633	620	389	452
Goods for processing: exports f.o.b.......	2 150 ..	....	....	....	....	....	....	....	....
Repairs on goods...........................	2 160 ..	....	....	....	....	29	40	23	20
Goods procured in ports by carriers.......	2 170 ..	....	....	....	....	....	....	....	....
Nonmonetary gold...........................	2 180 ..	....	....	....	....	....	....	....	....
Debit...............................	3 100 ..	....	....	....	....	**−2,861**	**−3,739**	**−2,317**	**−2,217**
General merchandise: imports f.o.b.......	3 110 ..	....	....	....	....	−2,846	−3,718	−2,302	−2,201
Goods for processing: imports f.o.b.......	3 150 ..	....	....	....	....	....	....	....	....
Repairs on goods...........................	3 160 ..	....	....	....	....	−15	−21	−15	−16
Goods procured in ports by carriers.......	3 170 ..	....	....	....	....	....	....	....	....
Nonmonetary gold...........................	3 180 ..	....	....	....	....	....	....	....	....
B. SERVICES...............................	4 200 ..	....	....	....	....	**601**	**585**	**534**	**591**
Total credit...........................	2 200 ..	....	....	....	....	*921*	*1,099*	*945*	*989*
Total debit...........................	3 200 ..	....	....	....	....	*−320*	*−514*	*−411*	*−398*
Transportation services, credit...........	2 205 ..	....	....	....	....	**99**	**135**	**138**	**172**
Passenger...........................	2 850 ..	....	....	....	....	*30*	*46*	*46*	*53*
Freight...........................	2 851 ..	....	....	....	....	*14*	*18*	*26*	*36*
Other...........................	2 852 ..	....	....	....	....	*54*	*71*	*65*	*84*
Sea transport, passenger...................	2 207 ..	....	....	....	....	5	5	2	1
Sea transport, freight...................	2 208 ..	....	....	....	....	1	1	....	....
Sea transport, other...................	2 209 ..	....	....	....	....	38	46	47	53
Air transport, passenger...................	2 211 ..	....	....	....	....	24	40	43	50
Air transport, freight...................	2 212 ..	....	....	....	....	....	....	....	....
Air transport, other...................	2 213 ..	....	....	....	....	10	15	8	13
Other transport, passenger...................	2 215 ..	....	....	....	....	1	1	1	1
Other transport, freight...................	2 216 ..	....	....	....	....	13	17	26	36
Other transport, other...................	2 217 ..	....	....	....	....	7	10	10	17
Transportation services, debit...........	3 205 ..	....	....	....	....	**−77**	**−121**	**−92**	**−98**
Passenger...........................	3 850 ..	....	....	....	....	*−21*	*−37*	*−27*	*−26*
Freight...........................	3 851 ..	....	....	....	....	*−36*	*−49*	*−36*	*−44*
Other...........................	3 852 ..	....	....	....	....	*−20*	*−35*	*−29*	*−28*
Sea transport, passenger...................	3 207 ..	....	....	....	....	....	....	....	....
Sea transport, freight...................	3 208 ..	....	....	....	....	−1	−1	−1	−4
Sea transport, other...................	3 209 ..	....	....	....	....	−6	−11	−10	−9
Air transport, passenger...................	3 211 ..	....	....	....	....	−20	−36	−26	−26
Air transport, freight...................	3 212 ..	....	....	....	....	....	−1	....	−1
Air transport, other...................	3 213 ..	....	....	....	....	−12	−21	−16	−16
Other transport, passenger...................	3 215 ..	....	....	....	....	−1	−1	−1	−1
Other transport, freight...................	3 216 ..	....	....	....	....	−34	−47	−35	−39
Other transport, other...................	3 217 ..	....	....	....	....	−2	−3	−3	−2
Travel, credit...........................	2 236 ..	....	....	....	....	**629**	**755**	**659**	**660**
Business travel...........................	2 237 ..	....	....	....	....	....	....	....	....
Personal travel...........................	2 240 ..	....	....	....	....	629	755	659	660
Travel, debit...........................	3 236 ..	....	....	....	....	**−37**	**−43**	**−49**	**−45**
Business travel...........................	3 237 ..	....	....	....	....	−3	−2	−1	−1
Personal travel...........................	3 240 ..	....	....	....	....	−34	−41	−48	−44
Other services, credit...................	2 200 BA	....	....	....	....	**194**	**210**	**148**	**157**
Communications...........................	2 245 ..	....	....	....	....	40	45	37	36
Construction...........................	2 249 ..	....	....	....	....	67	74	38	35
Insurance...........................	2 253 ..	....	....	....	....	2	3	5	6
Financial...........................	2 260 ..	....	....	....	....	4	5	9	6
Computer and information...................	2 262 ..	....	....	....	....	5	4	5	4
Royalties and licence fees...................	2 266 ..	....	....	....	....	1	2	1	3
Other business services...................	2 268 ..	....	....	....	....	64	58	40	53
Personal, cultural, and recreational.......	2 287 ..	....	....	....	....	11	18	13	15
Government, n.i.e.......................	2 291 ..	....	....	....	....	....	....	....	....
Other services, debit...................	3 200 BA	....	....	....	....	**−206**	**−350**	**−270**	**−255**
Communications...........................	3 245 ..	....	....	....	....	−10	−12	−24	−21
Construction...........................	3 249 ..	....	....	....	....	−49	−95	−58	−58
Insurance...........................	3 253 ..	....	....	....	....	−16	−18	−19	−18
Financial...........................	3 260 ..	....	....	....	....	−13	−6	−6	−6
Computer and information...................	3 262 ..	....	....	....	....	−11	−22	−17	−21
Royalties and licence fees...................	3 266 ..	....	....	....	....	−9	−11	−12	−9
Other business services...................	3 268 ..	....	....	....	....	−79	−138	−102	−94
Personal, cultural, and recreational.......	3 287 ..	....	....	....	....	−12	−34	−17	−17
Government, n.i.e.......................	3 291 ..	....	....	....	....	−8	−13	−15	−12

Table 2 (Continued). STANDARD PRESENTATION, 2003–2010

(Millions of U.S. dollars)

	Code	2003	2004	2005	2006	2007	2008	2009	2010
C. INCOME	4 300	....	....	....	....	**43**	**67**	**7**	**−29**
Total credit	2 300	....	....	....	....	*144*	*247*	*226*	*220*
Total debit	3 300	....	....	....	....	*−101*	*−180*	*−219*	*−248*
Compensation of employees, credit	2 310	....	....	....	....	**109**	**208**	**216**	**210**
Compensation of employees, debit	3 310	....	....	....	....	**−7**	**−8**	**−8**	**−11**
Investment income, credit	2 320	....	....	....	....	**35**	**40**	**10**	**9**
Direct investment income	2 330	....	....	....	....	2	1	2	2
Dividends and distributed branch profits	2 332	....	....	....	....	2	1	2	2
Reinvested earnings and undistributed branch profits	2 333	....	....	....	....	....	....	....	....
Income on debt (interest)	2 334	....	....	....	....	....	....	....	....
Portfolio investment income	2 339	....	....	....	....	....	....	....	....
Income on equity	2 340	....	....	....	....	....	....	....	....
Income on bonds and notes	2 350	....	....	....	....	....	....	....	....
Income on money market instruments	2 360	....	....	....	....	....	....	....	....
Other investment income	2 370	....	....	....	....	33	39	8	7
Investment income, debit	3 320	....	....	....	....	**−94**	**−172**	**−210**	**−237**
Direct investment income	3 330	....	....	....	....	−16	−43	−90	−100
Dividends and distributed branch profits	3 332	....	....	....	....	−16	−43	−90	−100
Reinvested earnings and undistributed branch profits	3 333	....	....	....	....	....	....	....	....
Income on debt (interest)	3 334	....	....	....	....	....	....	....	....
Portfolio investment income	3 339	....	....	....	....	....	−1	....	....
Income on equity	3 340	....	....	....	....	....	....	....	....
Income on bonds and notes	3 350	....	....	....	....	....	....	....	....
Income on money market instruments	3 360	....	....	....	....	....	....	....	....
Other investment income	3 370	....	....	....	....	−79	−129	−120	−137
D. CURRENT TRANSFERS	4 379	....	....	....	....	**81**	**107**	**119**	**152**
Credit	2 379	....	....	....	....	**138**	**160**	**163**	**194**
General government	2 380	....	....	....	....	11	20	21	32
Other sectors	2 390	....	....	....	....	127	140	143	162
Workers' remittances	2 391	....	....	....	....	87	90	86	90
Other current transfers	2 392	....	....	....	....	41	50	57	72
Debit	3 379	....	....	....	....	**−57**	**−53**	**−45**	**−42**
General government	3 380	....	....	....	....	−8	−6	−13	−10
Other sectors	3 390	....	....	....	....	−49	−47	−32	−32
Workers' remittances	3 391	....	....	....	....	−20	−19	−17	−16
Other current transfers	3 392	....	....	....	....	−29	−28	−14	−16
CAPITAL AND FINANCIAL ACCOUNT	4 996	....	....	....	....	**1,474**	**1,942**	**773**	**491**
CAPITAL ACCOUNT	4 994	....	....	....	....	**−2**	**−1**	**3**	**−1**
Total credit	2 994	....	....	....	....	*1*	....	*3*	....
Total debit	3 994	....	....	....	....	*−3*	*−1*	....	*−1*
Capital transfers, credit	2 400	....	....	....	....	**1**	....	....	....
General government	2 401	....	....	....	....	....	....	....	....
Debt forgiveness	2 402	....	....	....	....	....	....	....	....
Other capital transfers	2 410	....	....	....	....	....	....	....	....
Other sectors	2 430	....	....	....	....	1	....	....	....
Migrants' transfers	2 431	....	....	....	....	....	....	....	....
Debt forgiveness	2 432	....	....	....	....	....	....	....	....
Other capital transfers	2 440	....	....	....	....	1	....	....	....
Capital transfers, debit	3 400	....	....	....	....	**−3**	**−1**	....	**−1**
General government	3 401	....	....	....	....	....	....	....	....
Debt forgiveness	3 402	....	....	....	....	....	....	....	....
Other capital transfers	3 410	....	....	....	....	....	....	....	....
Other sectors	3 430	....	....	....	....	−3	−1	....	−1
Migrants' transfers	3 431	....	....	....	....	....	....	....	....
Debt forgiveness	3 432	....	....	....	....	....	....	....	....
Other capital transfers	3 440	....	....	....	....	−3	....	....	−1
Nonproduced nonfinancial assets, credit	2 480	....	....	....	....	....	....	**3**	....
Nonproduced nonfinancial assets, debit	3 480	....	....	....	....	....	....	....	....

Table 2 (Continued). STANDARD PRESENTATION, 2003–2010

(Millions of U.S. dollars)

	Code	2003	2004	2005	2006	2007	2008	2009	2010
FINANCIAL ACCOUNT	4 995 ..	....	....	....	....	**1,476**	**1,942**	**770**	**491**
A. DIRECT INVESTMENT	4 500 ..	....	....	....	....	**777**	**852**	**1,482**	**731**
Direct investment abroad	4 505 ..	....	....	....	....	**−157**	**−108**	**−46**	**−29**
Equity capital	4 510 ..	....	....	....	....	−157	−108	−46	−14
Claims on affiliated enterprises	4 515 ..	....	....	....	....	....	....	....	....
Liabilities to affiliated enterprises	4 520 ..	....	....	....	....	....	....	....	....
Reinvested earnings	4 525 ..	....	....	....	....	....	....	....	....
Other capital	4 530 ..	....	....	....	....	....	....	....	−15
Claims on affiliated enterprises	4 535 ..	....	....	....	....	....	....	....	−15
Liabilities to affiliated enterprises	4 540 ..	....	....	....	....	....	....	....	....
Direct investment in Montenegro	4 555 ..	....	....	....	....	**934**	**960**	**1,527**	**760**
Equity capital	4 560 ..	....	....	....	....	720	615	1,339	568
Claims on direct investors	4 565 ..	....	....	....	....	....	....	....	....
Liabilities to direct investors	4 570 ..	....	....	....	....	....	....	....	....
Reinvested earnings	4 575 ..	....	....	....	....	....	....	....	....
Other capital	4 580 ..	....	....	....	....	214	346	188	192
Claims on direct investors	4 585 ..	....	....	....	....	....	....	....	....
Liabilities to direct investors	4 590 ..	....	....	....	....	214	346	188	192
B. PORTFOLIO INVESTMENT	4 600 ..	....	....	....	....	**7**	**−23**	**−58**	**249**
Assets	4 602 ..	....	....	....	....	**−4**	**−17**	**−53**	**−5**
Equity securities	4 610 ..	....	....	....	....	−18	−13	−49	2
Monetary authorities	4 611 ..	....	....	....	....	....	....	....	....
General government	4 612 ..	....	....	....	....	....	....	....	....
Banks	4 613 ..	....	....	....	....	....	....	....	....
Other sectors	4 614 ..	....	....	....	....	....	....	....	....
Debt securities	4 619 ..	....	....	....	....	15	−4	−4	−6
Bonds and notes	4 620 ..	....	....	....	....	15	−2	−4	−6
Monetary authorities	4 621 ..	....	....	....	....	....	....	....	....
General government	4 622 ..	....	....	....	....	....	....	....	....
Banks	4 623 ..	....	....	....	....	8	....	....	....
Other sectors	4 624 ..	....	....	....	....	7	−2	−4	−6
Money market instruments	4 630 ..	....	....	....	....	....	−1	....	....
Monetary authorities	4 631 ..	....	....	....	....	....	....	....	....
General government	4 632 ..	....	....	....	....	....	....	....	....
Banks	4 633 ..	....	....	....	....	....	....	....	....
Other sectors	4 634 ..	....	....	....	....	....	−1	....	....
Liabilities	4 652 ..	....	....	....	....	**11**	**−6**	**−5**	**254**
Equity securities	4 660 ..	....	....	....	....	5	−6	−5	−8
Banks	4 663 ..	....	....	....	....	....	....	....	....
Other sectors	4 664 ..	....	....	....	....	....	....	....	....
Debt securities	4 669 ..	....	....	....	....	6	....	....	262
Bonds and notes	4 670 ..	....	....	....	....	6	....	....	262
Monetary authorities	4 671 ..	....	....	....	....	....	....	....	....
General government	4 672 ..	....	....	....	....	....	....	....	262
Banks	4 673 ..	....	....	....	....	6	....	....	−4
Other sectors	4 674 ..	....	....	....	....	....	....	....	4
Money market instruments	4 680 ..	....	....	....	....	....	....	....	....
Monetary authorities	4 681 ..	....	....	....	....	....	....	....	....
General government	4 682 ..	....	....	....	....	....	....	....	....
Banks	4 683 ..	....	....	....	....	....	....	....	....
Other sectors	4 684 ..	....	....	....	....	....	....	....	....
C. FINANCIAL DERIVATIVES	4 910 ..	....	....	....	....	....	....	....	....
Monetary authorities	4 911 ..	....	....	....	....	....	....	....	....
General government	4 912 ..	....	....	....	....	....	....	....	....
Banks	4 913 ..	....	....	....	....	....	....	....	....
Other sectors	4 914 ..	....	....	....	....	....	....	....	....
Assets	4 900 ..	....	....	....	....	....	....	....	....
Monetary authorities	4 901 ..	....	....	....	....	....	....	....	....
General government	4 902 ..	....	....	....	....	....	....	....	....
Banks	4 903 ..	....	....	....	....	....	....	....	....
Other sectors	4 904 ..	....	....	....	....	....	....	....	....
Liabilities	4 905 ..	....	....	....	....	....	....	....	....
Monetary authorities	4 906 ..	....	....	....	....	....	....	....	....
General government	4 907 ..	....	....	....	....	....	....	....	....
Banks	4 908 ..	....	....	....	....	....	....	....	....
Other sectors	4 909 ..	....	....	....	....	....	....	....	....

Table 2 (Concluded). STANDARD PRESENTATION, 2003–2010

(Millions of U.S. dollars)

	Code	2003	2004	2005	2006	2007	2008	2009	2010
D. OTHER INVESTMENT	4 700	....	....	....	....	**866**	**885**	**−534**	**−467**
Assets	4 703	....	....	....	....	**−417**	**−269**	**−448**	**−447**
Trade credits	4 706	....	....	....	....	....	....	....	....
General government	4 707	....	....	....	....	....	....	....	....
of which: Short-term	4 709	....	....	....	....	....	....	....	....
Other sectors	4 710	....	....	....	....	....	....	....	....
of which: Short-term	4 712	....	....	....	....	....	....	....	....
Loans	4 714	....	....	....	....	−42	−37	−8	−12
Monetary authorities	4 715	....	....	....	....	....	....	....	....
of which: Short-term	4 718	....	....	....	....	....	....	....	....
General government	4 719	....	....	....	....	....	....	....	....
of which: Short-term	4 721	....	....	....	....	....	....	....	....
Banks	4 722	....	....	....	....	−33	−21	−7	−10
of which: Short-term	4 724	....	....	....	....	....	....	....	....
Other sectors	4 725	....	....	....	....	−9	−16	....	−1
of which: Short-term	4 727	....	....	....	....	−9	−7	....	−1
Currency and deposits	4 730	....	....	....	....	−375	−231	−440	−435
Monetary authorities	4 731	....	....	....	....	....	....	....	....
General government	4 732	....	....	....	....	....	....	....	....
Banks	4 733	....	....	....	....	−53	156	−110	−84
Other sectors	4 734	....	....	....	....	−322	−387	−330	−351
Other assets	4 736	....	....	....	....	....	....	....	....
Monetary authorities	4 737	....	....	....	....	....	....	....	....
of which: Short-term	4 739	....	....	....	....	....	....	....	....
General government	4 740	....	....	....	....	....	....	....	....
of which: Short-term	4 742	....	....	....	....	....	....	....	....
Banks	4 743	....	....	....	....	....	....	....	....
of which: Short-term	4 745	....	....	....	....	....	....	....	....
Other sectors	4 746	....	....	....	....	....	....	....	....
of which: Short-term	4 748	....	....	....	....	....	....	....	....
Liabilities	4 753	....	....	....	....	**1,283**	**1,154**	**−87**	**−21**
Trade credits	4 756	....	....	....	....	32	6	3	−10
General government	4 757	....	....	....	....	....	....	4	−1
of which: Short-term	4 759	....	....	....	....	....	....	....	....
Other sectors	4 760	....	....	....	....	32	6	....	−9
of which: Short-term	4 762	....	....	....	....	....	....	....	....
Loans	4 764	....	....	....	....	1,091	956	−45	86
Monetary authorities	4 765	....	....	....	....	....	....	....	....
of which: Use of Fund credit and loans from the Fund	4 766	....	....	....	....	....	....	....	....
of which: Short-term	4 768	....	....	....	....	....	....	....	....
General government	4 769	....	....	....	....	−84	−10	195	11
of which: Short-term	4 771	....	....	....	....	....	....	....	....
Banks	4 772	....	....	....	....	488	463	−186	−48
of which: Short-term	4 774	....	....	....	....	....	....	−139	2
Other sectors	4 775	....	....	....	....	686	503	−54	122
of which: Short-term	4 777	....	....	....	....	−16	35	−16	21
Currency and deposits	4 780	....	....	....	....	167	208	−117	−91
Monetary authorities	4 781	....	....	....	....	....	....	....	....
General government	4 782	....	....	....	....	....	....	....	....
Banks	4 783	....	....	....	....	167	208	−117	−91
Other sectors	4 784	....	....	....	....	....	....	....	....
Other liabilities	4 786	....	....	....	....	−6	−16	71	−6
Monetary authorities	4 787	....	....	....	....	....	....	79	....
of which: Short-term	4 789	....	....	....	....	....	....	....	....
General government	4 790	....	....	....	....	....	....	....	....
of which: Short-term	4 792	....	....	....	....	....	....	....	....
Banks	4 793	....	....	....	....	....	....	....	....
of which: Short-term	4 795	....	....	....	....	....	....	....	....
Other sectors	4 796	....	....	....	....	−6	−16	−8	−6
of which: Short-term	4 798	....	....	....	....	....	....	....	....
E. RESERVE ASSETS	4 802	....	....	....	....	**−174**	**227**	**−119**	**−22**
Monetary gold	4 812	....	....	....	....	−1	....	....	....
Special drawing rights	4 811	....	....	....	....	....	....	−40	....
Reserve position in the Fund	4 810	....	....	....	....	−10	....	....	....
Foreign exchange	4 803	....	....	....	....	−38	227	−79	−22
Other claims	4 813	....	....	....	....	−125	....	....	....
NET ERRORS AND OMISSIONS	4 998	....	....	....	....	**1**	**378**	**473**	**540**

Table 1. ANALYTIC PRESENTATION, 2003–2010

(Millions of U.S. dollars)

	Code	2003	2004	2005	2006	2007	2008	2009	2010
A. Current Account[1]	4 993 Z.	**−7.87**	**−10.54**	**−15.83**	**−7.54**	**−10.42**	**−19.69**	**−12.71**	**−10.92**
Goods: exports f.o.b.	2 100 ..	2.87	5.34	1.88	1.79	3.08	4.07	3.23	1.13
Goods: imports f.o.b.	3 100 ..	−25.01	−25.28	−26.19	−26.57	−26.09	−33.54	−26.07	−19.90
Balance on Goods	4 100 ..	*−22.14*	*−19.94*	*−24.31*	*−24.78*	*−23.01*	*−29.47*	*−22.84*	*−18.77*
Services: credit	2 200 ..	11.96	14.87	14.80	14.75	14.72	13.90	11.80	10.74
Services: debit	3 200 ..	−18.53	−25.28	−25.74	−17.31	−19.01	−23.36	−17.60	−16.67
Balance on Goods and Services	4 991 ..	*−28.71*	*−30.34*	*−35.25*	*−27.35*	*−27.30*	*−38.93*	*−28.64*	*−24.70*
Income: credit	2 300 ..	.84	1.24	2.12	2.51	2.08	1.13	1.05	1.04
Income: debit	3 300 ..	−2.05	−4.65	−4.93	−4.42	−5.82	−5.57	−4.66	−4.50
Balance on Goods, Services, and Income	4 992 ..	*−29.92*	*−33.75*	*−38.07*	*−29.26*	*−31.04*	*−43.38*	*−32.25*	*−28.17*
Current transfers: credit	2 379 Z.	26.93	28.30	28.04	25.44	25.28	27.91	24.24	21.85
Current transfers: debit	3 379 ..	−4.89	−5.09	−5.80	−3.72	−4.66	−4.22	−4.70	−4.61
B. Capital Account[1]	4 994 Z.	**14.37**	**11.84**	**5.39**	**3.62**	**5.08**	**7.63**	**18.74**	**15.42**
Capital account: credit	2 994 Z.	16.52	14.12	7.81	6.18	7.66	10.39	21.57	18.19
Capital account: debit	3 994 ..	−2.16	−2.29	−2.42	−2.56	−2.58	−2.76	−2.83	−2.78
Total, Groups A Plus B	4 981 ..	*6.49*	*1.30*	*−10.44*	*−3.92*	*−5.34*	*−12.06*	*6.03*	*4.50*
C. Financial Account[1]	4 995 W.	**−8.26**	**−1.72**	**10.08**	**4.31**	**5.20**	**9.01**	**−1.38**	**3.69**
Direct investment abroad	4 505 ..	....	....	....	....	....	....	....	....
Direct investment in Montserrat	4 555 Z.	2.08	2.34	5.44	3.99	6.85	12.68	2.56	2.23
Portfolio investment assets	4 602 ..	....	....	....	....	....	....	....	....
Equity securities	4 610 ..	....	....	....	....	....	....	....	....
Debt securities	4 619 ..	....	....	....	....	....	....	....	....
Portfolio investment liabilities	4 652 Z.	.08	.05	−.13	.06	.10	−.53	.48	....
Equity securities	4 660 ..	....	....	....	....	....	....	....	....
Debt securities	4 669 Z.	....	....	....	....	....	....	....	....
Financial derivatives	4 910 ..	....	....	....	....	....	....	....	....
Financial derivatives assets	4 900 ..	....	....	....	....	....	....	....	....
Financial derivatives liabilities	4 905 ..	....	....	....	....	....	....	....	....
Other investment assets	4 703 ..	−10.03	−5.47	−3.67	−3.25	−4.55	−3.77	−8.13	−4.17
Monetary authorities	4 701 ..	....	....	....	....	....	....	....	....
General government	4 704 ..	....	....	....	....	....	....	....	....
Banks	4 705 ..	−9.27	−4.67	....	−.38	−.64	−1.39	−3.88	....
Other sectors	4 728 ..	−.75	−.81	−3.67	−2.87	−3.91	−2.38	−4.25	−4.17
Other investment liabilities	4 753 W.	−.40	1.37	8.44	3.51	2.79	.63	3.71	5.63
Monetary authorities	4 753 WA	−.73	−.19	−.19	−.18	−.38	−.23	−.23	−.22
General government	4 753 ZB	....	....	....	....	....	....	....	....
Banks	4 753 ZC	....	....	2.88	....	....	....	....	1.98
Other sectors	4 753 ZD	.33	1.56	5.74	3.69	3.17	.86	3.94	3.87
Total, Groups A Through C	4 983 ..	*−1.77*	*−.42*	*−.36*	*.39*	*−.14*	*−3.04*	*4.66*	*8.19*
D. Net Errors and Omissions	4 998 ..	**2.73**	**−1.04**	**.25**	**.26**	**.05**	**.22**	**−2.03**	**−5.67**
Total, Groups A Through D	4 984 ..	*.96*	*−1.46*	*−.11*	*.65*	*−.09*	*−2.82*	*2.63*	*2.52*
E. Reserves and Related Items	4 802 A.	**−.96**	**1.46**	**.11**	**−.65**	**.09**	**2.82**	**−2.63**	**−2.52**
Reserve assets	4 802 ..	−.96	1.46	.11	−.65	.09	2.82	−2.63	−2.52
Use of Fund credit and loans	4 766 ..	....	....	....	....	....	....	....	....
Exceptional financing	4 920 ..	....	....	....	....	....	....	....	....
Conversion rates: Eastern Caribbean dollars per U.S. dollar	0 101 ..	**2.7000**	**2.7000**	**2.7000**	**2.7000**	**2.7000**	**2.7000**	**2.7000**	**2.7000**

[1] Excludes components that have been classified in the categories of Group E.

Table 2. STANDARD PRESENTATION, 2003–2010

(Millions of U.S. dollars)

	Code	2003	2004	2005	2006	2007	2008	2009	2010
CURRENT ACCOUNT....................................	4 993 ..	**−7.87**	**−10.54**	**−15.83**	**−7.54**	**−10.42**	**−19.69**	**−12.71**	**−10.92**
A. GOODS..	4 100 ..	**−22.14**	**−19.94**	**−24.31**	**−24.78**	**−23.01**	**−29.47**	**−22.84**	**−18.77**
Credit..	2 100 ..	**2.87**	**5.34**	**1.88**	**1.79**	**3.08**	**4.07**	**3.23**	**1.13**
General merchandise: exports f.o.b...........	2 110 ..	2.32	4.79	1.47	1.38	2.64	4.06	3.15	1.10
Goods for processing: exports f.o.b...........	2 150 ..	....	....	....	....	....	....	....	....
Repairs on goods.....................................	2 160 ..	....	....	....	....	....	....	....	....
Goods procured in ports by carriers...........	2 170 ..	.55	.56	.41	.41	.44	.01	.08	.03
Nonmonetary gold....................................	2 180 ..	....	....	....	....	....	....	....	....
Debit...	3 100 ..	**−25.01**	**−25.28**	**−26.19**	**−26.57**	**−26.09**	**−33.54**	**−26.07**	**−19.90**
General merchandise: imports f.o.b...........	3 110 ..	−25.01	−25.28	−26.19	−26.57	−26.09	−33.54	−26.07	−19.90
Goods for processing: imports f.o.b...........	3 150 ..	....	....	....	....	....	....	....	....
Repairs on goods.....................................	3 160 ..	....	....	....	....	....	....	....	....
Goods procured in ports by carriers...........	3 170 ..	....	....	....	....	....	....	....	....
Nonmonetary gold....................................	3 180 ..	....	....	....	....	....	....	....	....
B. SERVICES..	4 200 ..	**−6.57**	**−10.40**	**−10.94**	**−2.56**	**−4.30**	**−9.46**	**−5.80**	**−5.93**
Total credit...	2 200 ..	*11.96*	*14.87*	*14.80*	*14.75*	*14.72*	*13.90*	*11.80*	*10.74*
Total debit..	3 200 ..	*−18.53*	*−25.28*	*−25.74*	*−17.31*	*−19.01*	*−23.36*	*−17.60*	*−16.67*
Transportation services, credit............	2 205 ..	**1.44**	**1.40**	**1.40**	**1.46**	**1.14**	**1.18**	**1.18**	**1.10**
Passenger...	2 850 ..	....	....	....	....	....	....	....	....
Freight...	2 851 ..	....	....	....	....	....	....	....	....
Other...	2 852 ..	....	....	....	....	....	....	....	....
Sea transport, passenger.........................	2 207 ..	....	....	....	....	....	....	....	....
Sea transport, freight...............................	2 208 ..	....	....	....	....	....	....	....	....
Sea transport, other................................	2 209 ..	....	....	....	....	....	....	....	....
Air transport, passenger..........................	2 211 ..	....	....	....	....	....	....	....	....
Air transport, freight...............................	2 212 ..	....	....	....	....	....	....	....	....
Air transport, other.................................	2 213 ..	....	....	....	....	....	....	....	....
Other transport, passenger......................	2 215 ..	....	....	....	....	....	....	....	....
Other transport, freight...........................	2 216 ..	....	....	....	....	....	....	....	....
Other transport, other.............................	2 217 ..	....	....	....	....	....	....	....	....
Transportation services, debit............	3 205 ..	**−4.54**	**−4.66**	**−4.79**	**−5.41**	**−6.13**	**−7.37**	**−6.54**	**−5.77**
Passenger...	3 850 ..	....	....	....	....	....	....	....	....
Freight...	3 851 ..	....	....	....	....	....	....	....	....
Other...	3 852 ..	....	....	....	....	....	....	....	....
Sea transport, passenger.........................	3 207 ..	....	....	....	....	....	....	....	....
Sea transport, freight...............................	3 208 ..	....	....	....	....	....	....	....	....
Sea transport, other................................	3 209 ..	....	....	....	....	....	....	....	....
Air transport, passenger..........................	3 211 ..	....	....	....	....	....	....	....	....
Air transport, freight...............................	3 212 ..	....	....	....	....	....	....	....	....
Air transport, other.................................	3 213 ..	....	....	....	....	....	....	....	....
Other transport, passenger......................	3 215 ..	....	....	....	....	....	....	....	....
Other transport, freight...........................	3 216 ..	....	....	....	....	....	....	....	....
Other transport, other.............................	3 217 ..	....	....	....	....	....	....	....	....
Travel, credit....................................	2 236 ..	**7.33**	**9.19**	**8.98**	**7.75**	**7.44**	**7.04**	**6.07**	**5.17**
Business travel..	2 237 ..	....	....	....	....	....	....	....	....
Personal travel..	2 240 ..	....	....	....	....	....	....	....	....
Travel, debit......................................	3 236 ..	**−1.96**	**−2.11**	**−2.61**	**−2.84**	**−2.88**	**−3.22**	**−2.96**	**−2.91**
Business travel..	3 237 ..	....	....	....	....	....	....	....	....
Personal travel..	3 240 ..	....	....	....	....	....	....	....	....
Other services, credit........................	2 200 BA ..	**3.19**	**4.28**	**4.43**	**5.55**	**6.13**	**5.68**	**4.55**	**4.47**
Communications......................................	2 245 ..	1.87	3.00	3.00	3.03	3.15	3.20	3.28	3.22
Construction..	2 249 ..	....	....	....	....	....	....	....	....
Insurance..	2 253 ..	.30	.41	.56	.46	.44	.49	.36	.35
Financial...	2 260 ..	....	....	....	....	....	....	....	....
Computer and information........................	2 262 ..	....	....	....	....	....	....	....	....
Royalties and licence fees........................	2 266 ..	....	....	....	....	....	....	....	....
Other business services...........................	2 268 ..	.81	.68	.60	1.74	2.30	1.80	.74	.73
Personal, cultural, and recreational...........	2 287 ..	....	....	....	....	....	....	....	....
Government, n.i.e.....................................	2 291 ..	.20	.18	.27	.31	.24	.19	.17	.18
Other services, debit.........................	3 200 BA ..	**−12.03**	**−18.50**	**−18.34**	**−9.06**	**−10.00**	**−12.77**	**−8.09**	**−7.99**
Communications......................................	3 245 ..	−1.08	−2.47	−2.47	−2.50	−2.60	−2.61	−2.68	−2.75
Construction..	3 249 ..	−1.87	−5.69	−2.93	....	....	....	....	....
Insurance..	3 253 ..	−.67	−.84	−.98	−1.01	−1.16	−1.27	−.94	−.79
Financial...	3 260 ..	....	....	....	....	....	....	....	....
Computer and information........................	3 262 ..	−.06	−.07	−.01	−.01	−.01	....	....	....
Royalties and licence fees........................	3 266 ..	−.05	−.06	−.06	−.08	−.08	−.11	−.11	−.10
Other business services...........................	3 268 ..	−2.67	−2.87	−2.59	−2.86	−3.01	−2.73	−3.04	−2.98
Personal, cultural, and recreational...........	3 287 ..	....	....	....	....	....	....	....	....
Government, n.i.e.....................................	3 291 ..	−5.62	−6.50	−9.31	−2.61	−3.14	−6.05	−1.33	−1.36

Table 2 (Continued). STANDARD PRESENTATION, 2003–2010

(Millions of U.S. dollars)

	Code	2003	2004	2005	2006	2007	2008	2009	2010
C. INCOME	4 300	**−1.21**	**−3.41**	**−2.82**	**−1.91**	**−3.74**	**−4.45**	**−3.61**	**−3.47**
Total credit	2 300	*.84*	*1.24*	*2.12*	*2.51*	*2.08*	*1.13*	*1.05*	*1.04*
Total debit	3 300	*−2.05*	*−4.65*	*−4.93*	*−4.42*	*−5.82*	*−5.57*	*−4.66*	*−4.50*
Compensation of employees, credit	2 310	....	....	....	....	....	....	....	....
Compensation of employees, debit	3 310	**−.21**	**−.86**	**−.73**	....	**−.58**	**−.50**	**−.76**	**−.67**
Investment income, credit	2 320	**.84**	**1.24**	**2.12**	**2.51**	**2.08**	**1.13**	**1.05**	**1.04**
Direct investment income	2 330	....	....	....	....	....	....	....	....
Dividends and distributed branch profits	2 332	....	....	....	....	....	....	....	....
Reinvested earnings and undistributed branch profits	2 333	....	....	....	....	....	....	....	....
Income on debt (interest)	2 334	....	....	....	....	....	....	....	....
Portfolio investment income	2 339	.66	.68	.96	1.00	.38	.65	.66	.65
Income on equity	2 340	.66	.68	.96	1.00	.38	.65	.66	.65
Income on bonds and notes	2 350	....	....	....	....	....	....	....	....
Income on money market instruments	2 360	....	....	....	....	....	....	....	....
Other investment income	2 370	.18	.56	1.16	1.51	1.70	.48	.39	.38
Investment income, debit	3 320	**−1.84**	**−3.80**	**−4.21**	**−4.42**	**−5.24**	**−5.07**	**−3.91**	**−3.83**
Direct investment income	3 330	−1.23	−2.31	−2.46	−2.49	−2.91	−3.22	−3.34	−3.27
Dividends and distributed branch profits	3 332	−.86	−1.55	−1.65	−1.74	−2.03	−2.43	−2.53	−2.48
Reinvested earnings and undistributed branch profits	3 333	−.36	−.76	−.80	−.75	−.89	−.80	−.81	−.79
Income on debt (interest)	3 334	−.01	....	....	....	....	....	....	....
Portfolio investment income	3 339	....	....	....	....	....	....	....	....
Income on equity	3 340	....	....	....	....	....	....	....	....
Income on bonds and notes	3 350	....	....	....	....	....	....	....	....
Income on money market instruments	3 360	....	....	....	....	....	....	....	....
Other investment income	3 370	−.61	−1.48	−1.75	−1.92	−2.33	−1.84	−.57	−.56
D. CURRENT TRANSFERS	4 379	**22.05**	**23.21**	**22.24**	**21.72**	**20.63**	**23.69**	**19.55**	**17.24**
Credit	2 379	**26.93**	**28.30**	**28.04**	**25.44**	**25.28**	**27.91**	**24.24**	**21.85**
General government	2 380	25.95	27.47	27.37	24.91	24.71	27.32	23.71	21.30
Other sectors	2 390	.99	.83	.68	.53	.58	.59	.53	.55
Workers' remittances	2 391	.48	.49	.51	.52	.54	.54	.53	.54
Other current transfers	2 392	.51	.33	.17	.01	.04	.04	.01	.01
Debit	3 379	**−4.89**	**−5.09**	**−5.80**	**−3.72**	**−4.66**	**−4.22**	**−4.70**	**−4.61**
General government	3 380	−1.96	−2.24	−2.63	−.59	−1.34	−.92	−1.92	−1.89
Other sectors	3 390	−2.92	−2.84	−3.17	−3.13	−3.32	−3.30	−2.77	−2.72
Workers' remittances	3 391	−1.60	−1.70	−1.75	−1.75	−1.83	−1.81	−1.38	−1.36
Other current transfers	3 392	−1.32	−1.14	−1.43	−1.38	−1.49	−1.50	−1.39	−1.36
CAPITAL AND FINANCIAL ACCOUNT	4 996	**5.14**	**11.58**	**15.58**	**7.28**	**10.37**	**19.47**	**14.73**	**16.59**
CAPITAL ACCOUNT	4 994	**14.37**	**11.84**	**5.39**	**3.62**	**5.08**	**7.63**	**18.74**	**15.42**
Total credit	2 994	*16.52*	*14.12*	*7.81*	*6.18*	*7.66*	*10.39*	*21.57*	*18.19*
Total debit	3 994	*−2.16*	*−2.29*	*−2.42*	*−2.56*	*−2.58*	*−2.76*	*−2.83*	*−2.78*
Capital transfers, credit	2 400	**16.52**	**14.12**	**7.81**	**6.18**	**7.66**	**10.39**	**21.57**	**18.19**
General government	2 401	15.95	13.53	7.20	5.57	7.04	9.76	20.96	17.57
Debt forgiveness	2 402	....	....	....	....	....	....	....	....
Other capital transfers	2 410	15.95	13.53	7.20	5.57	7.04	9.76	20.96	17.57
Other sectors	2 430	.58	.59	.61	.61	.62	.63	.61	.63
Migrants' transfers	2 431	.58	.59	.61	.61	.62	.63	.61	.63
Debt forgiveness	2 432	....	....	....	....	....	....	....	....
Other capital transfers	2 440	....	....	....	....	....	....	....	....
Capital transfers, debit	3 400	**−2.16**	**−2.29**	**−2.42**	**−2.56**	**−2.58**	**−2.76**	**−2.83**	**−2.78**
General government	3 401	....	....	....	....	....	....	....	....
Debt forgiveness	3 402	....	....	....	....	....	....	....	....
Other capital transfers	3 410	....	....	....	....	....	....	....	....
Other sectors	3 430	−2.16	−2.29	−2.42	−2.56	−2.58	−2.76	−2.83	−2.78
Migrants' transfers	3 431	−2.16	−2.29	−2.42	−2.56	−2.58	−2.76	−2.83	−2.78
Debt forgiveness	3 432	....	....	....	....	....	....	....	....
Other capital transfers	3 440	....	....	....	....	....	....	....	....
Nonproduced nonfinancial assets, credit	2 480	....	....	....	....	....	....	....	....
Nonproduced nonfinancial assets, debit	3 480	....	....	....	....	....	....	....	....

Table 2 (Continued). STANDARD PRESENTATION, 2003–2010

(Millions of U.S. dollars)

	Code	2003	2004	2005	2006	2007	2008	2009	2010
FINANCIAL ACCOUNT................................	4 995 ..	**−9.22**	**−.26**	**10.19**	**3.66**	**5.29**	**11.84**	**−4.01**	**1.17**
A. DIRECT INVESTMENT..........................	4 500 ..	**2.08**	**2.34**	**5.44**	**3.99**	**6.85**	**12.68**	**2.56**	**2.23**
Direct investment abroad........................	4 505 ..	....	....	....	....	....	....	....	....
Equity capital..	4 510 ..	....	....	....	....	....	....	....	....
Claims on affiliated enterprises..................	4 515 ..	....	....	....	....	....	....	....	....
Liabilities to affiliated enterprises...............	4 520 ..	....	....	....	....	....	....	....	....
Reinvested earnings..................................	4 525 ..	....	....	....	....	....	....	....	....
Other capital...	4 530 ..	....	....	....	....	....	....	....	....
Claims on affiliated enterprises..................	4 535 ..	....	....	....	....	....	....	....	....
Liabilities to affiliated enterprises...............	4 540 ..	....	....	....	....	....	....	....	....
Direct investment in Montserrat..........................	4 555 ..	**2.08**	**2.34**	**5.44**	**3.99**	**6.85**	**12.68**	**2.56**	**2.23**
Equity capital..	4 560 ..	1.45	....	....	....	....	....	....	....
Claims on direct investors.........................	4 565 ..	....	....	....	....	....	....	....	....
Liabilities to direct investors.....................	4 570 ..	1.45	....	....	....	....	....	....	....
Reinvested earnings..................................	4 575 ..	.36	.76	.80	.75	.89	.80	.81	.79
Other capital...	4 580 ..	.27	1.58	4.64	3.24	5.97	11.88	1.75	1.43
Claims on direct investors.........................	4 585 ..	....	....	....	....	....	....	....	....
Liabilities to direct investors.....................	4 590 ..	.27	1.58	4.64	3.24	5.97	11.88	1.75	1.43
B. PORTFOLIO INVESTMENT......................	4 600 ..	**.08**	**.05**	**−.13**	**.06**	**.10**	**−.53**	**.48**	**....**
Assets..	4 602 ..	....	....	....	....	....	....	....	....
Equity securities......................................	4 610 ..	....	....	....	....	....	....	....	....
Monetary authorities................................	4 611 ..	....	....	....	....	....	....	....	....
General government................................	4 612 ..	....	....	....	....	....	....	....	....
Banks..	4 613 ..	....	....	....	....	....	....	....	....
Other sectors...	4 614 ..	....	....	....	....	....	....	....	....
Debt securities...	4 619 ..	....	....	....	....	....	....	....	....
Bonds and notes.....................................	4 620 ..	....	....	....	....	....	....	....	....
Monetary authorities............................	4 621 ..	....	....	....	....	....	....	....	....
General government............................	4 622 ..	....	....	....	....	....	....	....	....
Banks..	4 623 ..	....	....	....	....	....	....	....	....
Other sectors......................................	4 624 ..	....	....	....	....	....	....	....	....
Money market instruments........................	4 630 ..	....	....	....	....	....	....	....	....
Monetary authorities............................	4 631 ..	....	....	....	....	....	....	....	....
General government............................	4 632 ..	....	....	....	....	....	....	....	....
Banks..	4 633 ..	....	....	....	....	....	....	....	....
Other sectors......................................	4 634 ..	....	....	....	....	....	....	....	....
Liabilities...	4 652 ..	**.08**	**.05**	**−.13**	**.06**	**.10**	**−.53**	**.48**	**....**
Equity securities......................................	4 660 ..	....	....	....	....	....	....	....	....
Banks..	4 663 ..	....	....	....	....	....	....	....	....
Other sectors...	4 664 ..	....	....	....	....	....	....	....	....
Debt securities...	4 669 ..	....	....	....	....	....	....	....	....
Bonds and notes.....................................	4 670 ..	....	....	....	....	....	....	....	....
Monetary authorities............................	4 671 ..	....	....	....	....	....	....	....	....
General government............................	4 672 ..	....	....	....	....	....	....	....	....
Banks..	4 673 ..	....	....	....	....	....	....	....	....
Other sectors......................................	4 674 ..	....	....	....	....	....	....	....	....
Money market instruments........................	4 680 ..	....	....	....	....	....	....	....	....
Monetary authorities............................	4 681 ..	....	....	....	....	....	....	....	....
General government............................	4 682 ..	....	....	....	....	....	....	....	....
Banks..	4 683 ..	....	....	....	....	....	....	....	....
Other sectors......................................	4 684 ..	....	....	....	....	....	....	....	....
C. FINANCIAL DERIVATIVES......................	4 910 ..	....	....	....	....	....	....	....	....
Monetary authorities................................	4 911 ..	....	....	....	....	....	....	....	....
General government................................	4 912 ..	....	....	....	....	....	....	....	....
Banks..	4 913 ..	....	....	....	....	....	....	....	....
Other sectors...	4 914 ..	....	....	....	....	....	....	....	....
Assets..	4 900 ..	....	....	....	....	....	....	....	....
Monetary authorities................................	4 901 ..	....	....	....	....	....	....	....	....
General government................................	4 902 ..	....	....	....	....	....	....	....	....
Banks..	4 903 ..	....	....	....	....	....	....	....	....
Other sectors...	4 904 ..	....	....	....	....	....	....	....	....
Liabilities...	4 905 ..	....	....	....	....	....	....	....	....
Monetary authorities................................	4 906 ..	....	....	....	....	....	....	....	....
General government................................	4 907 ..	....	....	....	....	....	....	....	....
Banks..	4 908 ..	....	....	....	....	....	....	....	....
Other sectors...	4 909 ..	....	....	....	....	....	....	....	....

Table 2 (Concluded). STANDARD PRESENTATION, 2003–2010

(Millions of U.S. dollars)

	Code	2003	2004	2005	2006	2007	2008	2009	2010
D. OTHER INVESTMENT	4 700	**−10.43**	**−4.10**	**4.77**	**.26**	**−1.76**	**−3.14**	**−4.42**	**1.46**
Assets	4 703	**−10.03**	**−5.47**	**−3.67**	**−3.25**	**−4.55**	**−3.77**	**−8.13**	**−4.17**
Trade credits	4 706	....	....	....	....	....	....	....	....
General government	4 707	....	....	....	....	....	....	....	....
of which: Short-term	4 709	....	....	....	....	....	....	....	....
Other sectors	4 710	....	....	....	....	....	....	....	....
of which: Short-term	4 712	....	....	....	....	....	....	....	....
Loans	4 714	−9.27	−4.67	....	−.38	−.64	−1.39	−3.88	....
Monetary authorities	4 715	....	....	....	....	....	....	....	....
of which: Short-term	4 718	....	....	....	....	....	....	....	....
General government	4 719	....	....	....	....	....	....	....	....
of which: Short-term	4 721	....	....	....	....	....	....	....	....
Banks	4 722	−9.27	−4.67	....	−.38	−.64	−1.39	−3.88	....
of which: Short-term	4 724	....	....	....	....	....	....	....	....
Other sectors	4 725	....	....	....	....	....	....	....	....
of which: Short-term	4 727	....	....	....	....	....	....	....	....
Currency and deposits	4 730	....	....	....	....	....	....	....	....
Monetary authorities	4 731	....	....	....	....	....	....	....	....
General government	4 732	....	....	....	....	....	....	....	....
Banks	4 733	....	....	....	....	....	....	....	....
Other sectors	4 734	....	....	....	....	....	....	....	....
Other assets	4 736	−.75	−.81	−3.67	−2.87	−3.91	−2.38	−4.25	−4.17
Monetary authorities	4 737	....	....	....	....	....	....	....	....
of which: Short-term	4 739	....	....	....	....	....	....	....	....
General government	4 740	....	....	....	....	....	....	....	....
of which: Short-term	4 742	....	....	....	....	....	....	....	....
Banks	4 743	....	....	....	....	....	....	....	....
of which: Short-term	4 745	....	....	....	....	....	....	....	....
Other sectors	4 746	−.75	−.81	−3.67	−2.87	−3.91	−2.38	−4.25	−4.17
of which: Short-term	4 748	....	....	....	....	....	....	....	....
Liabilities	4 753	**−.40**	**1.37**	**8.44**	**3.51**	**2.79**	**.63**	**3.71**	**5.63**
Trade credits	4 756	....	....	....	....	....	....	....	....
General government	4 757	....	....	....	....	....	....	....	....
of which: Short-term	4 759	....	....	....	....	....	....	....	....
Other sectors	4 760	....	....	....	....	....	....	....	....
of which: Short-term	4 762	....	....	....	....	....	....	....	....
Loans	4 764	−.73	−.19	−.19	−.18	−.38	−.23	−.23	−.22
Monetary authorities	4 765	−.73	−.19	−.19	−.18	−.38	−.23	−.23	−.22
of which: Use of Fund credit and loans from the Fund	4 766	....	....	....	....	....	....	....	....
of which: Short-term	4 768	....	....	....	....	....	....	....	....
General government	4 769	....	....	....	....	....	....	....	....
of which: Short-term	4 771	....	....	....	....	....	....	....	....
Banks	4 772	....	....	....	....	....	....	....	....
of which: Short-term	4 774	....	....	....	....	....	....	....	....
Other sectors	4 775	....	....	....	....	....	....	....	....
of which: Short-term	4 777	....	....	....	....	....	....	....	....
Currency and deposits	4 780	....	....	....	....	....	....	....	....
Monetary authorities	4 781	....	....	....	....	....	....	....	....
General government	4 782	....	....	....	....	....	....	....	....
Banks	4 783	....	....	....	....	....	....	....	....
Other sectors	4 784	....	....	....	....	....	....	....	....
Other liabilities	4 786	.33	1.56	8.62	3.69	3.17	.86	3.94	5.85
Monetary authorities	4 787	....	....	....	....	....	....	....	....
of which: Short-term	4 789	....	....	....	....	....	....	....	....
General government	4 790	....	....	....	....	....	....	....	....
of which: Short-term	4 792	....	....	....	....	....	....	....	....
Banks	4 793	....	....	2.88	....	....	....	....	1.98
of which: Short-term	4 795	....	....	....	....	....	....	....	....
Other sectors	4 796	.33	1.56	5.74	3.69	3.17	.86	3.94	3.87
of which: Short-term	4 798	....	....	....	....	....	....	....	....
E. RESERVE ASSETS	4 802	**−.96**	**1.46**	**.11**	**−.65**	**.09**	**2.82**	**−2.63**	**−2.52**
Monetary gold	4 812	....	....	....	....	....	....	....	....
Special drawing rights	4 811	....	....	....	....	....	....	....	....
Reserve position in the Fund	4 810	....	....	....	....	....	....	....	....
Foreign exchange	4 803	−.14	.33	−.04	−.04	.03	....	....	....
Other claims	4 813	−.83	1.13	.15	−.61	.06	2.82	−2.63	−2.52
NET ERRORS AND OMISSIONS	4 998	**2.73**	**−1.04**	**.25**	**.26**	**.05**	**.22**	**−2.03**	**−5.67**

Table 1. ANALYTIC PRESENTATION, 2003–2010

(Millions of U.S. dollars)

	Code	2003	2004	2005	2006	2007	2008	2009	2010
A. Current Account[1]	4 993 Z.	**1,552**	**922**	**949**	**1,315**	**−224**	**−5,659**	**−5,362**	**−4,209**
Goods: exports f.o.b.	2 100 ..	8,771	9,922	10,690	11,926	15,146	20,330	14,044	17,584
Goods: imports f.o.b.	3 100 ..	−13,117	−16,408	−18,894	−21,683	−29,316	−39,827	−30,408	−32,646
Balance on Goods	4 100 ..	*−4,345*	*−6,487*	*−8,204*	*−9,756*	*−14,170*	*−19,497*	*−16,363*	*−15,062*
Services: credit	2 200 ..	5,478	6,710	8,098	9,789	12,165	13,416	12,336	12,545
Services: debit	3 200 ..	−2,861	−3,451	−3,845	−4,473	−5,416	−6,694	−6,899	−7,436
Balance on Goods and Services	4 991 ..	*−1,728*	*−3,228*	*−3,951*	*−4,441*	*−7,421*	*−12,775*	*−10,927*	*−9,953*
Income: credit	2 300 ..	370	505	689	750	961	1,059	925	868
Income: debit	3 300 ..	−1,162	−1,176	−1,072	−1,227	−1,365	−1,581	−2,421	−2,110
Balance on Goods, Services, and Income	4 992 ..	*−2,520*	*−3,898*	*−4,335*	*−4,918*	*−7,825*	*−13,297*	*−12,422*	*−11,196*
Current transfers: credit	2 379 Z.	4,214	4,974	5,441	6,410	7,786	7,849	7,278	7,240
Current transfers: debit	3 379 ..	−141	−154	−158	−177	−185	−211	−218	−254
B. Capital Account[1]	4 994 Z.	**−10**	**−8**	**−5**	**−3**	**−3**	**−2**	**....**	**....**
Capital account: credit	2 994 Z.	....	....	....	....	....	1	....	....
Capital account: debit	3 994 ..	−10	−8	−5	−3	−3	−3	−1	....
Total, Groups A Plus B	4 981 ..	*1,542*	*914*	*944*	*1,312*	*−227*	*−5,661*	*−5,362*	*−4,209*
C. Financial Account[1]	4 995 W.	**−1,091**	**102**	**−88**	**−185**	**−718**	**371**	**1,481**	**1,364**
Direct investment abroad	4 505 ..	−13	−31	−74	−451	−632	−316	−479	−580
Direct investment in Morocco	4 555 Z.	2,313	787	1,620	2,366	2,807	2,466	1,970	1,241
Portfolio investment assets	4 602 ..	....	....	−4	3	−16	−257	−12	−22
Equity securities	4 610 ..	....	....	−4	3	−16	−257	−12	−22
Debt securities	4 619 ..	....	....	....	....	....	....	....	....
Portfolio investment liabilities	4 652 Z.	8	597	64	−298	−64	148	−4	132
Equity securities	4 660 ..	8	597	64	−298	−64	148	−4	132
Debt securities	4 669 Z.	....	....	....	....	....	....	....	....
Financial derivatives	4 910 ..	....	....	....	....	....	....	....	....
Financial derivatives assets	4 900 ..	....	....	....	....	....	....	....	....
Financial derivatives liabilities	4 905 ..	....	....	....	....	....	....	....	....
Other investment assets	4 703 ..	−869	−454	−891	−762	−1,617	−413	−56	880
Monetary authorities	4 701 ..	....	....	....	....	....	....	....	....
General government	4 704 ..	....	....	....	....	....	....	....	....
Banks	4 705 ..	−529	....	−193	....	65	−9	140	934
Other sectors	4 728 ..	−340	−454	−699	−762	−1,682	−404	−196	−54
Other investment liabilities	4 753 W.	−2,529	−797	−803	−1,043	−1,195	−1,257	63	−287
Monetary authorities	4 753 WA	....	....	....	....	....	....	803	21
General government	4 753 ZB	−1,830	−1,321	−1,227	−1,108	−1,542	−1,236	−620	−679
Banks	4 753 ZC	−214	−213	−177	−76	−25	−52	−47	516
Other sectors	4 753 ZD	−486	737	602	141	372	32	−73	−144
Total, Groups A Through C	4 983 ..	*451*	*1,015*	*856*	*1,127*	*−945*	*−5,290*	*−3,881*	*−2,846*
D. Net Errors and Omissions	4 998 ..	**−297**	**−282**	**−407**	**−499**	**105**	**−414**	**−523**	**−167**
Total, Groups A Through D	4 984 ..	*154*	*733*	*449*	*628*	*−840*	*−5,704*	*−4,404*	*−3,012*
E. Reserves and Related Items	4 802 A.	**−154**	**−733**	**−449**	**−628**	**840**	**5,704**	**4,404**	**3,012**
Reserve assets	4 802 ..	−1,649	−1,901	−2,352	−2,711	−2,034	1,306	148	−1,211
Use of Fund credit and loans	4 766 ..	....	....	....	....	....	....	....	....
Exceptional financing	4 920 ..	1,495	1,168	1,904	2,083	2,874	4,398	4,256	4,224
Conversion rates: Moroccan dirhams per U.S. dollar	0 101 ..	**9.574**	**8.868**	**8.865**	**8.796**	**8.192**	**7.750**	**8.057**	**8.417**

[1] Excludes components that have been classified in the categories of Group E.

Table 2. STANDARD PRESENTATION, 2003–2010

(Millions of U.S. dollars)

	Code	2003	2004	2005	2006	2007	2008	2009	2010
CURRENT ACCOUNT	4 993	**1,582**	**970**	**1,041**	**1,411**	**−122**	**−4,528**	**−4,971**	**−3,925**
A. GOODS	4 100	**−4,345**	**−6,487**	**−8,204**	**−9,756**	**−14,170**	**−19,497**	**−16,363**	**−15,062**
Credit	2 100	**8,771**	**9,922**	**10,690**	**11,926**	**15,146**	**20,330**	**14,044**	**17,584**
General merchandise: exports f.o.b.	2 110	5,481	6,422	7,239	7,904	9,741	14,963	9,014	12,165
Goods for processing: exports f.o.b.	2 150	3,241	3,438	3,362	3,888	5,262	5,078	4,886	5,238
Repairs on goods	2 160	....	....	....	....	....	....	....	....
Goods procured in ports by carriers	2 170	49	62	89	135	144	289	144	182
Nonmonetary gold	2 180	....	....	....	....	....	....	....	....
Debit	3 100	**−13,117**	**−16,408**	**−18,894**	**−21,683**	**−29,316**	**−39,827**	**−30,408**	**−32,646**
General merchandise: imports f.o.b.	3 110	−11,194	−14,269	−16,687	−19,372	−25,941	−36,635	−28,014	−29,623
Goods for processing: imports f.o.b.	3 150	−1,916	−2,134	−2,196	−2,300	−3,362	−3,176	−2,381	−3,019
Repairs on goods	3 160	....	....	....	....	....	....	....	....
Goods procured in ports by carriers	3 170	−7	−5	−10	−11	−13	−15	−14	−5
Nonmonetary gold	3 180	....	....	....	....	....	....	....	....
B. SERVICES	4 200	**2,617**	**3,259**	**4,253**	**5,316**	**6,749**	**6,722**	**5,437**	**5,109**
Total credit	2 200	*5,478*	*6,710*	*8,098*	*9,789*	*12,165*	*13,416*	*12,336*	*12,545*
Total debit	3 200	*−2,861*	*−3,451*	*−3,845*	*−4,473*	*−5,416*	*−6,694*	*−6,899*	*−7,436*
Transportation services, credit	2 205	**910**	**1,025**	**1,300**	**1,489**	**1,818**	**2,500**	**2,099**	**2,152**
Passenger	2 850	*581*	*618*	*816*	*916*	*1,126*	*1,664*	*1,354*	*1,474*
Freight	2 851	*329*	*407*	*485*	*572*	*692*	*836*	*745*	*679*
Other	2 852	....	....	....	....	....	....	....	....
Sea transport, passenger	2 207	22	27	39	35	9	106	82	49
Sea transport, freight	2 208	237	326	386	472	549	428	472	369
Sea transport, other	2 209	....	....	....	....	....	....	....	....
Air transport, passenger	2 211	558	587	773	876	1,114	1,553	1,269	1,421
Air transport, freight	2 212	54	29	19	13	23	13	11	10
Air transport, other	2 213	....	....	....	....	....	....	....	....
Other transport, passenger	2 215	1	3	4	5	3	6	3	4
Other transport, freight	2 216	38	53	79	87	120	395	262	299
Other transport, other	2 217	....	....	....	....	....	....	....	....
Transportation services, debit	3 205	**−1,127**	**−1,375**	**−1,580**	**−1,754**	**−2,211**	**−2,647**	**−2,340**	**−2,640**
Passenger	3 850	*−297*	*−338*	*−387*	*−420*	*−538*	*−820*	*−607*	*−676*
Freight	3 851	*−830*	*−1,037*	*−1,193*	*−1,333*	*−1,673*	*−1,827*	*−1,732*	*−1,963*
Other	3 852	....	....	....	....	....	....	....	....
Sea transport, passenger	3 207	−15	−16	−21	−25	−20	−92	−92	−94
Sea transport, freight	3 208	−662	−879	−1,027	−1,173	−1,487	−1,617	−1,476	−1,647
Sea transport, other	3 209	....	....	....	....	....	....	....	....
Air transport, passenger	3 211	−280	−319	−363	−392	−517	−726	−515	−581
Air transport, freight	3 212	−108	−103	−90	−75	−58	−49	−31	−35
Air transport, other	3 213	....	....	....	....	....	....	....	....
Other transport, passenger	3 215	−2	−3	−3	−4	−2	−2	....	−1
Other transport, freight	3 216	−61	−55	−76	−85	−128	−160	−225	−282
Other transport, other	3 217	....	....	....	....	....	....	....	....
Travel, credit	2 236	**3,221**	**3,922**	**4,610**	**5,984**	**7,181**	**7,221**	**6,626**	**6,702**
Business travel	2 237	....	....	....	....	....	....	....	....
Personal travel	2 240	3,221	3,922	4,610	5,984	7,181	7,221	6,626	6,702
Travel, debit	3 236	**−548**	**−574**	**−612**	**−693**	**−880**	**−1,090**	**−1,106**	**−1,203**
Business travel	3 237	−88	−96	−97	−99	−150	−223	−181	−173
Personal travel	3 240	−460	−479	−515	−593	−731	−867	−925	−1,030
Other services, credit	2 200 BA	**1,347**	**1,763**	**2,188**	**2,316**	**3,166**	**3,695**	**3,611**	**3,691**
Communications	2 245	250	342	328	387	401	641	679	713
Construction	2 249	....	....	....	....	....	61	49	50
Insurance	2 253	76	95	72	76	72	112	181	153
Financial	2 260	....	....	....	....	....	40	31	37
Computer and information	2 262	....	....	....	....	....	156	248	297
Royalties and licence fees	2 266	26	16	13	3	4	....	2	4
Other business services	2 268	643	904	1,247	1,330	2,014	2,016	1,920	1,994
Personal, cultural, and recreational	2 287	....	....	....	....	....	93	56	37
Government, n.i.e.	2 291	353	406	529	520	675	577	444	407
Other services, debit	3 200 BA	**−1,186**	**−1,502**	**−1,654**	**−2,027**	**−2,324**	**−2,957**	**−3,454**	**−3,594**
Communications	3 245	−22	−48	−44	−64	−108	−92	−87	−76
Construction	3 249	....	....	....	....	....	−6	−7	−5
Insurance	3 253	−57	−82	−80	−93	−113	−135	−182	−186
Financial	3 260	....	....	....	....	....	−31	−65	−58
Computer and information	3 262	....	....	....	....	....	−35	−41	−72
Royalties and licence fees	3 266	−29	−37	−45	−49	−36	−15	−49	−30
Other business services	3 268	−567	−689	−742	−909	−1,178	−1,549	−1,400	−1,431
Personal, cultural, and recreational	3 287	....	....	....	....	....	−28	−26	−25
Government, n.i.e.	3 291	−512	−646	−742	−911	−889	−1,066	−1,597	−1,712

Table 2 (Continued). STANDARD PRESENTATION, 2003–2010

(Millions of U.S. dollars)

	Code	2003	2004	2005	2006	2007	2008	2009	2010
C. INCOME	4 300	−792	−671	−384	−477	−405	−522	−1,495	−1,242
Total credit	2 300	370	505	689	750	961	1,059	925	868
Total debit	3 300	−1,162	−1,176	−1,072	−1,227	−1,365	−1,581	−2,421	−2,110
Compensation of employees, credit	2 310	....	....	....	....	....	....	....	....
Compensation of employees, debit	3 310	....	....	....	....	....	....	....	....
Investment income, credit	2 320	370	505	689	750	961	1,059	925	868
Direct investment income	2 330	13	60	59	72	78	44	40	74
Dividends and distributed branch profits	2 332	11	16	21	25	17	44	36	74
Reinvested earnings and undistributed branch profits	2 333	....	10	....	....	....	....	....	....
Income on debt (interest)	2 334	2	33	38	47	61	....	4	....
Portfolio investment income	2 339	....	....	....	....	....	12	....	....
Income on equity	2 340	....	....	....	....	....	12	....	....
Income on bonds and notes	2 350	....	....	....	....	....			
Income on money market instruments	2 360	....	....	....	....	....	....	....	....
Other investment income	2 370	357	445	630	678	883	1,004	886	794
Investment income, debit	3 320	−1,162	−1,176	−1,072	−1,227	−1,365	−1,581	−2,421	−2,110
Direct investment income	3 330	−593	−670	−594	−674	−730	−835	−1,753	−1,445
Dividends and distributed branch profits	3 332	−504	−572	−435	−533	−544	−773	−1,147	−1,025
Reinvested earnings and undistributed branch profits	3 333	−8	....	−69	−56	−115	−60	−605	−419
Income on debt (interest)	3 334	−81	−98	−90	−85	−71	−2	−1	−1
Portfolio investment income	3 339	−3	−10	−32	−65	−51	−83	−60	−83
Income on equity	3 340	−3	−10	−32	−65	−51	−83	−60	−83
Income on bonds and notes	3 350	....	....	....	....	....	....		
Income on money market instruments	3 360	....	....	....	....	....	....	....	....
Other investment income	3 370	−566	−496	−447	−488	−585	−664	−608	−582
D. CURRENT TRANSFERS	4 379	4,102	4,868	5,375	6,329	7,703	8,768	7,451	7,270
Credit	2 379	4,243	5,022	5,533	6,506	7,888	8,980	7,669	7,524
General government	2 380	142	193	273	328	349	1,235	463	333
Other sectors	2 390	4,101	4,829	5,260	6,177	7,539	7,745	7,205	7,192
Workers' remittances	2 391	3,614	4,221	4,589	5,451	6,730	6,894	6,269	6,423
Other current transfers	2 392	488	608	671	726	809	851	936	769
Debit	3 379	−141	−154	−158	−177	−185	−211	−218	−254
General government	3 380	−59	−54	−37	−63	−61	−78	−77	−85
Other sectors	3 390	−82	−101	−120	−114	−124	−134	−141	−169
Workers' remittances	3 391	−34	−34	−35	−38	−49	−54	−60	−62
Other current transfers	3 392	−48	−67	−85	−76	−75	−79	−81	−107
CAPITAL AND FINANCIAL ACCOUNT	4 996	−1,285	−688	−633	−912	17	4,943	5,494	4,092
CAPITAL ACCOUNT	4 994	−10	−8	−5	−3	−3	−2	....	....
Total credit	2 994	....	....	....	....	....	1		
Total debit	3 994	−10	−8	−5	−3	−3	−3	−1	....
Capital transfers, credit	2 400	....	....	....	....	....	1	....	....
General government	2 401	....	....	....	....	....	....		
Debt forgiveness	2 402								
Other capital transfers	2 410	....	....						
Other sectors	2 430	....	....	....	....	....	1		
Migrants' transfers	2 431	....	....	....	....	....	1		
Debt forgiveness	2 432								
Other capital transfers	2 440	....	....						
Capital transfers, debit	3 400	−10	−8	−5	−3	−3	−3	−1	....
General government	3 401	....	....	....	....	....	....		
Debt forgiveness	3 402								
Other capital transfers	3 410	....							
Other sectors	3 430	−10	−8	−5	−3	−3	−3	−1	....
Migrants' transfers	3 431	−10	−8	−5	−3	−3	−3	−1	....
Debt forgiveness	3 432								
Other capital transfers	3 440	....	....	....	....	....	....		
Nonproduced nonfinancial assets, credit	2 480	....	....	....	....	....	....	....	....
Nonproduced nonfinancial assets, debit	3 480	....	....	....	....	....	....	....	....

Table 2 (Continued). STANDARD PRESENTATION, 2003–2010

(Millions of U.S. dollars)

	Code	2003	2004	2005	2006	2007	2008	2009	2010
FINANCIAL ACCOUNT	4 995 ..	**−1,275**	**−680**	**−629**	**−909**	**20**	**4,945**	**5,495**	**4,092**
A. DIRECT INVESTMENT	4 500 ..	**2,300**	**862**	**1,596**	**2,010**	**2,194**	**2,150**	**1,491**	**661**
Direct investment abroad	4 505 ..	−13	−31	−74	−451	−632	−316	−479	−580
Equity capital	4 510 ..	−13	−20	−74	−451	−632	−316	−479	−580
Claims on affiliated enterprises	4 515 ..	−13	−20	−74	−451	−632	−316	−479	−580
Liabilities to affiliated enterprises	4 520 ..	....	....	....	....	....	....	....	....
Reinvested earnings	4 525 ..	....	−10	....	....	....	....	....	....
Other capital	4 530 ..	....	....	....	....	....	....	....	....
Claims on affiliated enterprises	4 535 ..	....	....	....	....	....	....	....	....
Liabilities to affiliated enterprises	4 540 ..	....	....	....	....	....	....	....	....
Direct investment in Morocco	4 555 ..	**2,313**	**893**	**1,671**	**2,461**	**2,826**	**2,466**	**1,970**	**1,241**
Equity capital	4 560 ..	2,225	764	880	2,629	2,443	2,362	1,851	950
Claims on direct investors	4 565 ..	....	....	....	....	....	....	....	....
Liabilities to direct investors	4 570 ..	2,225	764	880	2,629	2,443	2,362	1,851	950
Reinvested earnings	4 575 ..	8	....	69	56	115	60	605	419
Other capital	4 580 ..	81	130	721	−224	267	44	−486	−129
Claims on direct investors	4 585 ..	....	....	....	....	....	....	....	....
Liabilities to direct investors	4 590 ..	81	130	721	−224	267	44	−486	−129
B. PORTFOLIO INVESTMENT	4 600 ..	**8**	**597**	**60**	**−295**	**−80**	**−109**	**−17**	**110**
Assets	4 602 ..	....	....	**−4**	**3**	**−16**	**−257**	**−12**	**−22**
Equity securities	4 610 ..	....	....	−4	3	−16	−257	−12	−22
Monetary authorities	4 611 ..	....	....	....	....	....	....	....	....
General government	4 612 ..	....	....	....	....	....	....	....	....
Banks	4 613 ..	....	....	....	....	....	....	....	....
Other sectors	4 614 ..	....	....	−4	3	−16	−257	−12	−22
Debt securities	4 619 ..	....	....	....	....	....	....	....	....
Bonds and notes	4 620 ..	....	....	....	....	....	....	....	....
Monetary authorities	4 621 ..	....	....	....	....	....	....	....	....
General government	4 622 ..	....	....	....	....	....	....	....	....
Banks	4 623 ..	....	....	....	....	....	....	....	....
Other sectors	4 624 ..	....	....	....	....	....	....	....	....
Money market instruments	4 630 ..	....	....	....	....	....	....	....	....
Monetary authorities	4 631 ..	....	....	....	....	....	....	....	....
General government	4 632 ..	....	....	....	....	....	....	....	....
Banks	4 633 ..	....	....	....	....	....	....	....	....
Other sectors	4 634 ..	....	....	....	....	....	....	....	....
Liabilities	4 652 ..	**8**	**597**	**64**	**−298**	**−64**	**148**	**−4**	**132**
Equity securities	4 660 ..	8	597	64	−298	−64	148	−4	132
Banks	4 663 ..	....	....	....	....	....	....	....	....
Other sectors	4 664 ..	8	597	64	−298	−64	148	−4	132
Debt securities	4 669 ..	....	....	....	....	....	....	....	....
Bonds and notes	4 670 ..	....	....	....	....	....	....	....	....
Monetary authorities	4 671 ..	....	....	....	....	....	....	....	....
General government	4 672 ..	....	....	....	....	....	....	....	....
Banks	4 673 ..	....	....	....	....	....	....	....	....
Other sectors	4 674 ..	....	....	....	....	....	....	....	....
Money market instruments	4 680 ..	....	....	....	....	....	....	....	....
Monetary authorities	4 681 ..	....	....	....	....	....	....	....	....
General government	4 682 ..	....	....	....	....	....	....	....	....
Banks	4 683 ..	....	....	....	....	....	....	....	....
Other sectors	4 684 ..	....	....	....	....	....	....	....	....
C. FINANCIAL DERIVATIVES	4 910 ..	....	....	....	....	....	....	....	....
Monetary authorities	4 911 ..	....	....	....	....	....	....	....	....
General government	4 912 ..	....	....	....	....	....	....	....	....
Banks	4 913 ..	....	....	....	....	....	....	....	....
Other sectors	4 914 ..	....	....	....	....	....	....	....	....
Assets	4 900 ..	....	....	....	....	....	....	....	....
Monetary authorities	4 901 ..	....	....	....	....	....	....	....	....
General government	4 902 ..	....	....	....	....	....	....	....	....
Banks	4 903 ..	....	....	....	....	....	....	....	....
Other sectors	4 904 ..	....	....	....	....	....	....	....	....
Liabilities	4 905 ..	....	....	....	....	....	....	....	....
Monetary authorities	4 906 ..	....	....	....	....	....	....	....	....
General government	4 907 ..	....	....	....	....	....	....	....	....
Banks	4 908 ..	....	....	....	....	....	....	....	....
Other sectors	4 909 ..	....	....	....	....	....	....	....	....

Table 2 (Concluded). STANDARD PRESENTATION, 2003–2010

(Millions of U.S. dollars)

	Code	2003	2004	2005	2006	2007	2008	2009	2010
D. OTHER INVESTMENT................................	4 700 ..	**−1,934**	**−237**	**67**	**87**	**−60**	**1,598**	**3,872**	**4,533**
Assets................................	4 703 ..	**−869**	**−454**	**−891**	**−762**	**−1,617**	**−413**	**−56**	**880**
Trade credits................................	4 706 ..	−340	−451	−694	−758	−1,668	−422	−196	−54
General government................................	4 707 ..	....	....	....	....	....	....	....	....
of which: Short-term................................	4 709 ..	....	....	....	....	....	....	....	....
Other sectors................................	4 710 ..	−340	−451	−694	−758	−1,668	−422	−196	−54
of which: Short-term................................	4 712 ..	−340	−451	−694	−758	−1,668	−422	−196	−54
Loans................................	4 714 ..	−529	....	−193	....	65	−9	180	171
Monetary authorities................................	4 715 ..	....	....	....	....	....	....	....	....
of which: Short-term................................	4 718 ..	....	....	....	....	....	....	....	....
General government................................	4 719 ..	....	....	....	....	....	....	....	....
of which: Short-term................................	4 721 ..	....	....	....	....	....	....	....	....
Banks................................	4 722 ..	−529	....	−193	....	65	−9	180	171
of which: Short-term................................	4 724 ..	....	....	....	....	....	....	....	....
Other sectors................................	4 725 ..	....	....	....	....	....	....	....	....
of which: Short-term................................	4 727 ..	....	....	....	....	....	....	....	....
Currency and deposits................................	4 730 ..	....	−4	−5	−4	−14	18	−41	763
Monetary authorities................................	4 731 ..	....	....	....	....	....	....	....	....
General government................................	4 732 ..	....	....	....	....	....	....	....	....
Banks................................	4 733 ..	....	....	....	....	....	....	−41	763
Other sectors................................	4 734 ..	....	−4	−5	−4	−14	18	....	....
Other assets................................	4 736 ..	....	....	....	....	....	....	....	....
Monetary authorities................................	4 737 ..	....	....	....	....	....	....	....	....
of which: Short-term................................	4 739 ..	....	....	....	....	....	....	....	....
General government................................	4 740 ..	....	....	....	....	....	....	....	....
of which: Short-term................................	4 742 ..	....	....	....	....	....	....	....	....
Banks................................	4 743 ..	....	....	....	....	....	....	....	....
of which: Short-term................................	4 745 ..	....	....	....	....	....	....	....	....
Other sectors................................	4 746 ..	....	....	....	....	....	....	....	....
of which: Short-term................................	4 748 ..	....	....	....	....	....	....	....	....
Liabilities................................	4 753 ..	**−1,064**	**217**	**958**	**849**	**1,557**	**2,011**	**3,928**	**3,653**
Trade credits................................	4 756 ..	392	1,260	1,041	1,154	1,270	533	449	465
General government................................	4 757 ..	....	....	....	....	....	....	....	....
of which: Short-term................................	4 759 ..	....	....	....	....	....	....	....	....
Other sectors................................	4 760 ..	392	1,260	1,041	1,154	1,270	533	449	465
of which: Short-term................................	4 762 ..	392	1,260	1,041	1,154	1,270	533	449	465
Loans................................	4 764 ..	−1,388	−1,288	−279	−301	312	1,299	2,669	2,607
Monetary authorities................................	4 765 ..	....	....	....	....	....	....	....	....
of which: Use of Fund credit and loans from the Fund..	4 766 ..	....	....	....	....	....	....	....	....
of which: Short-term................................	4 768 ..	....	....	....	....	....	....	....	....
General government................................	4 769 ..	−991	−936	−393	−376	−16	249	1,271	1,899
of which: Short-term................................	4 771 ..	....	....	....	....	....	....	....	....
Banks................................	4 772 ..	−211	−213	−174	−76	−25	−52	−55	−45
of which: Short-term................................	4 774 ..	....	....	....	....	....	....	....	....
Other sectors................................	4 775 ..	−185	−139	289	151	354	1,102	1,453	753
of which: Short-term................................	4 777 ..	....	....	....	....	....	....	....	....
Currency and deposits................................	4 780 ..	−68	245	196	−4	−25	180	68	581
Monetary authorities................................	4 781 ..	....	....	....	....	....	....	60	21
General government................................	4 782 ..	....	....	....	....	....	....	....	....
Banks................................	4 783 ..	....	....	....	....	....	....	8	561
Other sectors................................	4 784 ..	−68	245	196	−4	−25	180	....	....
Other liabilities................................	4 786 ..	....	....	....	....	....	....	743	....
Monetary authorities................................	4 787 ..	....	....	....	....	....	....	743	....
of which: Short-term................................	4 789 ..	....	....	....	....	....	....	....	....
General government................................	4 790 ..	....	....	....	....	....	....	....	....
of which: Short-term................................	4 792 ..	....	....	....	....	....	....	....	....
Banks................................	4 793 ..	....	....	....	....	....	....	....	....
of which: Short-term................................	4 795 ..	....	....	....	....	....	....	....	....
Other sectors................................	4 796 ..	....	....	....	....	....	....	....	....
of which: Short-term................................	4 798 ..	....	....	....	....	....	....	....	....
E. RESERVE ASSETS................................	4 802 ..	**−1,649**	**−1,901**	**−2,352**	**−2,711**	**−2,034**	**1,306**	**148**	**−1,211**
Monetary gold................................	4 812 ..	....	....	....	....	....	−52	....	....
Special drawing rights................................	4 811 ..	20	−3	33	29	23	12	−741	7
Reserve position in the Fund................................	4 810 ..	....	....	....	....	....	....	....	....
Foreign exchange................................	4 803 ..	−1,789	−1,899	−2,385	−2,740	−2,056	1,346	889	−1,219
Other claims................................	4 813 ..	120	....	....	....	....	....	....	....
NET ERRORS AND OMISSIONS................................	4 998 ..	**−297**	**−282**	**−407**	**−499**	**105**	**−414**	**−523**	**−167**

Table 3. INTERNATIONAL INVESTMENT POSITION (End-period stocks), 2003–2010

(Millions of U.S. dollars)

	Code	2003	2004	2005	2006	2007	2008	2009	2010
ASSETS	8 995 C.	**17,022**	**20,207**	**20,823**	**26,411**	**32,455**	**30,287**	**30,750**	**29,718**
Direct investment abroad	8 505 ..	**560**	**676**	**666**	**1,054**	**1,337**	**1,699**	**1,861**	**1,851**
Equity capital and reinvested earnings	8 506 ..	520	490	535	984	1,246	1,552	1,799	1,801
Claims on affiliated enterprises	8 507 ..	520	490	535	984	1,246	1,552	1,799	1,801
Liabilities to affiliated enterprises	8 508 ..	....	....	....	....	....	....	....	....
Other capital	8 530 ..	41	185	131	70	92	147	62	50
Claims on affiliated enterprises	8 535 ..	41	185	131	70	92	147	62	50
Liabilities to affiliated enterprises	8 540 ..	....	....	....	....	....	....	....	....
Portfolio investment	8 602 ..	**116**	**156**	**176**	**178**	**916**	**1,022**	**724**	**891**
Equity securities	8 610 ..	116	156	176	171	907	946	707	877
Monetary authorities	8 611 ..	....	....	....	....	....	....	....	....
General government	8 612 ..	....	....	....	....	....	....	....	....
Banks	8 613 ..	56	67	60	69	76	74	93	185
Other sectors	8 614 ..	60	89	116	101	831	872	614	691
Debt securities	8 619 ..	....	....	....	8	9	76	17	14
Bonds and notes	8 620 ..	....	....	....	8	9	76	17	14
Monetary authorities	8 621 ..	....	....	....	....	....	....	....	....
General government	8 622 ..	....	....	....	....	....	....	....	....
Banks	8 623 ..	....	....	....	....	....	....	....	....
Other sectors	8 624 ..	....	....	....	8	9	76	17	14
Money market instruments	8 630 ..	....	....	....	....	....	....	....	....
Monetary authorities	8 631 ..	....	....	....	....	....	....	....	....
General government	8 632 ..	....	....	....	....	....	....	....	....
Banks	8 633 ..	....	....	....	....	....	....	....	....
Other sectors	8 634 ..	....	....	....	....	....	....	....	....
Financial derivatives	8 900 ..	....	....	....	....	....	....	....	....
Monetary authorities	8 901 ..	....	....	....	....	....	....	....	....
General government	8 902 ..	....	....	....	....	....	....	....	....
Banks	8 903 ..	....	....	....	....	....	....	....	....
Other sectors	8 904 ..	....	....	....	....	....	....	....	....
Other investment	8 703 ..	**1,305**	**1,221**	**1,335**	**1,559**	**1,906**	**1,790**	**4,585**	**3,362**
Trade credits	8 706 ..	390	450	453	583	845	1,038	1,271	1,340
General government	8 707 ..	....	....	....	....	....	....	....	....
of which: Short-term	8 709 ..	....	....	....	....	....	....	....	....
Other sectors	8 710 ..	390	450	453	583	845	1,038	1,271	1,340
of which: Short-term	8 712 ..	*390*	*450*	*453*	*583*	*845*	*1,038*	*1,271*	*1,340*
Loans	8 714 ..	603	614	720	788	783	591	450	315
Monetary authorities	8 715 ..	....	....	....	....	....	....	....	....
of which: Short-term	8 718 ..	....	....	....	....	....	....	....	....
General government	8 719 ..	....	....	....	....	....	....	....	....
of which: Short-term	8 721 ..	....	....	....	....	....	....	....	....
Banks	8 722 ..	603	614	613	670	654	468	323	196
of which: Short-term	8 724 ..	....	....	....	....	....	....	....	....
Other sectors	8 725 ..	....	....	107	118	129	123	126	119
of which: Short-term	8 727 ..	....	....	....	....	....	....	....	....
Currency and deposits	8 730 ..	235	73	85	106	190	73	2,772	1,620
Monetary authorities	8 731 ..	....	....	....	....	....	....	....	....
General government	8 732 ..	....	....	....	....	....	....	....	....
Banks	8 733 ..	25	....	....	....	....	....	2,670	1,546
Other sectors	8 734 ..	210	73	85	106	190	73	102	74
Other assets	8 736 ..	77	84	77	83	89	88	92	87
Monetary authorities	8 737 ..	....	....	....	....	....	....	....	....
of which: Short-term	8 739 ..	....	....	....	....	....	....	....	....
General government	8 740 ..	77	84	77	83	89	88	92	87
of which: Short-term	8 742 ..	....	....	....	....	....	....	....	....
Banks	8 743 ..	....	....	....	....	....	....	....	....
of which: Short-term	8 745 ..	....	....	....	....	....	....	....	....
Other sectors	8 746 ..	....	....	....	....	....	....	....	....
of which: Short-term	8 748 ..	....	....	....	....	....	....	....	....
Reserve assets	8 802 ..	**15,040**	**18,154**	**18,646**	**23,620**	**28,296**	**25,775**	**23,579**	**23,614**
Monetary gold	8 812 ..	224	239	280	450	593	613	783	1,000
Special drawing rights	8 811 ..	112	120	79	53	32	19	763	743
Reserve position in the Fund	8 810 ..	105	109	101	106	111	109	110	108
Foreign exchange	8 803 ..	14,599	17,686	18,187	23,011	27,560	25,035	21,923	21,764
Other claims	8 813 ..	....	....	....	....	....	....	....	....

Table 3 (Concluded). INTERNATIONAL INVESTMENT POSITION (End-period stocks), 2003–2010

(Millions of U.S. dollars)

	Code	2003	2004	2005	2006	2007	2008	2009	2010
LIABILITIES	8 995 D.	**34,727**	**38,675**	**38,119**	**48,686**	**61,173**	**62,998**	**71,518**	**76,471**
Direct investment in Morocco	8 555	**17,106**	**19,883**	**20,752**	**29,939**	**38,613**	**39,388**	**42,581**	**45,255**
Equity capital and reinvested earnings	8 556	16,037	18,675	19,017	28,214	36,531	37,348	40,750	43,647
Claims on direct investors	8 557	....	....	....	....	....	....	....	....
Liabilities to direct investors	8 558	16,037	18,675	19,017	28,214	36,531	37,348	40,750	43,647
Other capital	8 580	1,069	1,208	1,735	1,725	2,082	2,041	1,831	1,607
Claims on direct investors	8 585	....	....	....	....	....	....	....	....
Liabilities to direct investors	8 590	1,069	1,208	1,735	1,725	2,082	2,041	1,831	1,607
Portfolio investment	8 652	**840**	**1,720**	**2,037**	**2,110**	**3,277**	**3,210**	**3,664**	**3,574**
Equity securities	8 660	799	1,679	2,017	2,108	3,271	3,210	3,664	3,574
Banks	8 663	156	251	348	433	952	1,084	1,356	1,351
Other sectors	8 664	643	1,428	1,669	1,675	2,319	2,126	2,307	2,223
Debt securities	8 669	41	41	20	2	6	....	....	....
Bonds and notes	8 670	41	41	20	2	6	....	....	....
Monetary authorities	8 671	....	....	....	....	....	....	....	....
General government	8 672	14	18	2	....	....	....	....	....
Banks	8 673	....	....	....	....	....	....	....	....
Other sectors	8 674	27	23	19	2	6	....	....	....
Money market instruments	8 680	....	....	....	....	....	....	....	....
Monetary authorities	8 681	....	....	....	....	....	....	....	....
General government	8 682	....	....	....	....	....	....	....	....
Banks	8 683	....	....	....	....	....	....	....	....
Other sectors	8 684	....	....	....	....	....	....	....	....
Financial derivatives	8 905	....	....	....	....	....	....	....	....
Monetary authorities	8 906	....	....	....	....	....	....	....	....
General government	8 907	....	....	....	....	....	....	....	....
Banks	8 908	....	....	....	....	....	....	....	....
Other sectors	8 909	....	....	....	....	....	....	....	....
Other investment	8 753	**16,780**	**17,073**	**15,330**	**16,637**	**19,283**	**20,400**	**25,273**	**27,642**
Trade credits	8 756	362	745	661	818	1,130	1,316	1,385	1,494
General government	8 757	....	....	....	....	....	....	....	....
of which: Short-term	8 759	....	....	....	....	....	....	....	....
Other sectors	8 760	362	745	661	818	1,130	1,316	1,385	1,494
of which: Short-term	8 762	*362*	*745*	*661*	*818*	*1,130*	*1,316*	*1,385*	*1,494*
Loans	8 764	15,834	15,657	13,866	14,752	16,708	17,311	20,326	21,884
Monetary authorities	8 765	....	....	....	....	....	....	....	....
of which: Use of Fund credit and loans from the Fund	8 766	....	....	....	....	....	....	....	....
of which: Short-term	8 768	....	....	....	....	....	....	....	....
General government	8 769	9,020	8,562	7,464	7,693	8,550	8,429	10,017	11,048
of which: Short-term	8 771	....	....	....	....	....	....	....	....
Banks	8 772	853	677	432	341	318	432	387	329
of which: Short-term	8 774	....	....	....	....	....	....	....	....
Other sectors	8 775	5,962	6,418	5,970	6,717	7,840	8,451	9,921	10,507
of which: Short-term	8 777	....	....	....	....	....	....	....	....
Currency and deposits	8 780	584	671	803	1,067	1,445	1,773	2,682	3,399
Monetary authorities	8 781	135	217	261	262	323	460	326	327
General government	8 782	....	....	....	....	....	....	....	....
Banks	8 783	449	454	542	805	1,122	1,313	2,356	3,072
Other sectors	8 784	....	....	....	....	....	....	....	....
Other liabilities	8 786	....	....	....	....	....	....	880	865
Monetary authorities	8 787	....	....	....	....	....	....	880	865
of which: Short-term	8 789	....	....	....	....	....	....	....	....
General government	8 790	....	....	....	....	....	....	....	....
of which: Short-term	8 792	....	....	....	....	....	....	....	....
Banks	8 793	....	....	....	....	....	....	....	....
of which: Short-term	8 795	....	....	....	....	....	....	....	....
Other sectors	8 796	....	....	....	....	....	....	....	....
of which: Short-term	8 798	....	....	....	....	....	....	....	....
NET INTERNATIONAL INVESTMENT POSITION	8 995	**−17,705**	**−18,468**	**−17,297**	**−22,275**	**−28,718**	**−32,712**	**−40,768**	**−46,753**
Conversion rates: Moroccan dirhams per U.S. dollar (end of period)	0 102	**8.750**	**8.218**	**9.249**	**8.457**	**7.713**	**8.098**	**7.860**	**8.357**

Table 1. ANALYTIC PRESENTATION, 2003–2010

(Millions of U.S. dollars)

	Code	2003	2004	2005	2006	2007	2008	2009	2010
A. Current Account[1]	4 993 Z.	**−816.5**	**−607.4**	**−760.6**	**−773.2**	**−785.3**	**−1,179.4**	**−1,220.1**	**−1,113.3**
Goods: exports f.o.b.	2 100 ..	1,043.9	1,503.9	1,745.3	2,381.1	2,412.1	2,653.3	2,147.2	2,333.3
Goods: imports f.o.b.	3 100 ..	−1,648.1	−1,849.7	−2,242.3	−2,648.8	−2,811.1	−3,643.4	−3,422.0	−3,512.4
Balance on Goods	4 100 ..	*−604.2*	*−345.8*	*−497.1*	*−267.7*	*−399.0*	*−990.2*	*−1,274.8*	*−1,179.2*
Services: credit	2 200 ..	303.9	255.6	342.0	386.3	458.7	555.0	611.7	646.9
Services: debit	3 200 ..	−573.9	−531.4	−648.6	−758.1	−855.6	−965.3	−1,069.0	−1,153.2
Balance on Goods and Services	4 991 ..	*−874.1*	*−621.7*	*−803.7*	*−639.5*	*−795.8*	*−1,400.5*	*−1,732.1*	*−1,685.5*
Income: credit	2 300 ..	55.9	74.5	98.9	159.8	193.6	167.1	176.2	162.4
Income: debit	3 300 ..	−221.4	−374.0	−458.8	−794.3	−785.2	−798.5	−427.2	−247.0
Balance on Goods, Services, and Income	4 992 ..	*−1,039.6*	*−921.2*	*−1,163.6*	*−1,273.9*	*−1,387.5*	*−2,031.9*	*−1,983.2*	*−1,770.1*
Current transfers: credit	2 379 Z.	293.2	370.5	480.7	574.5	667.6	977.5	931.7	817.2
Current transfers: debit	3 379 ..	−70.0	−56.7	−77.8	−73.8	−65.4	−125.1	−168.6	−160.4
B. Capital Account[1]	4 994 Z.	**270.7**	**578.1**	**187.9**	**488.5**	**415.1**	**419.9**	**422.3**	**345.5**
Capital account: credit	2 994 Z.	271.2	581.2	191.8	490.8	416.1	427.9	428.9	350.9
Capital account: debit	3 994 ..	−.5	−3.1	−3.9	−2.3	−1.0	−8.0	−6.6	−5.4
Total, Groups A Plus B	4 981 ..	*−545.8*	*−29.2*	*−572.8*	*−284.7*	*−370.1*	*−759.5*	*−797.8*	*−767.8*
C. Financial Account[1]	4 995 W.	**372.8**	**−46.5**	**95.2**	**−1,501.7**	**442.0**	**772.6**	**1,035.5**	**768.9**
Direct investment abroad	4 505 ..	....	....	....	−.4	.3	....	−2.8	.8
Direct investment in Mozambique	4 555 Z.	336.7	244.7	107.9	153.7	427.4	591.6	892.5	789.0
Portfolio investment assets	4 602 ..	5.0	−25.4	−88.8	−124.2	−3.5	−8.4	4.4	.3
Equity securities	4 610 ..	5.0	−25.4	−7.3	−.2	−1.4	−.3	−.5	−.1
Debt securities	4 619 ..	....	....	−81.5	−124.0	−2.1	−8.0	4.9	.3
Portfolio investment liabilities	4 652 Z.	....	....	.3	.4	−2.1	.3	.1	1.1
Equity securities	4 660 ..	....	....	.3	.4	.3	.4	....	.3
Debt securities	4 669 Z.	....	....	....	....	−2.4	−.1	.1	.8
Financial derivatives	4 910 ..	....	....	....	....	−16.0	....	....	....
Financial derivatives assets	4 900 ..	....	....	....	....	−16.0	....	....	....
Financial derivatives liabilities	4 905 ..	....	....	....	....	....	....	....	....
Other investment assets	4 703 ..	−77.1	−88.7	−78.5	−13.8	−411.5	−80.7	−118.6	−179.5
Monetary authorities	4 701 ..	6.9	−186.4	40.9	17.5	13.1	50.0	−33.1	23.7
General government	4 704 ..	....	....	....	....	....	....	....	....
Banks	4 705 ..	13.1	57.8	−76.3	−106.9	−273.4	90.2	−31.5	−146.4
Other sectors	4 728 ..	−97.1	39.9	−43.1	75.5	−151.3	−220.9	−53.9	−56.8
Other investment liabilities	4 753 W.	108.2	−177.1	154.3	−1,517.5	447.4	269.7	260.0	157.2
Monetary authorities	4 753 WA	22.3	−48.4	−.3	.3	2.9	.1	178.0	3.6
General government	4 753 ZB	53.0	−47.6	95.8	−1,475.5	216.2	342.1	434.0	468.4
Banks	4 753 ZC	15.7	9.6	6.4	−35.6	66.4	24.5	134.6	33.1
Other sectors	4 753 ZD	17.3	−90.8	52.4	−6.7	161.8	−96.9	−486.5	−347.9
Total, Groups A Through C	4 983 ..	*−172.9*	*−75.7*	*−477.5*	*−1,786.5*	*71.9*	*13.1*	*237.7*	*1.1*
D. Net Errors and Omissions	4 998 ..	**208.2**	**216.4**	**280.9**	**143.8**	**65.2**	**107.5**	**−42.7**	**66.5**
Total, Groups A Through D	4 984 ..	*35.3*	*140.7*	*−196.6*	*−1,642.6*	*137.1*	*120.6*	*195.0*	*67.7*
E. Reserves and Related Items	4 802 A.	**−35.3**	**−140.7**	**196.6**	**1,642.6**	**−137.1**	**−120.6**	**−195.0**	**−67.7**
Reserve assets	4 802 ..	−181.5	−169.1	129.9	−29.3	−285.1	−140.0	−351.6	−98.6
Use of Fund credit and loans	4 766 ..	−9.1	−20.4	−25.3	−149.4	4.9	....	154.7	20.6
Exceptional financing	4 920 ..	155.3	48.8	92.1	1,821.4	143.1	19.5	1.9	10.4
Conversion rates: meticais per U.S. dollar	0 101 ..	**23.7823**	**22.5813**	**23.0610**	**25.4008**	**25.8403**	**24.3006**	**27.5183**	**33.9601**

[1] Excludes components that have been classified in the categories of Group E.

Table 2. STANDARD PRESENTATION, 2003–2010

(Millions of U.S. dollars)

	Code	2003	2004	2005	2006	2007	2008	2009	2010
CURRENT ACCOUNT	4 993	**−816.5**	**−607.4**	**−760.6**	**−773.2**	**−785.3**	**−1,179.4**	**−1,220.1**	**−1,113.3**
A. GOODS	4 100	**−604.2**	**−345.8**	**−497.1**	**−267.7**	**−399.0**	**−990.2**	**−1,274.8**	**−1,179.2**
Credit	2 100	**1,043.9**	**1,503.9**	**1,745.3**	**2,381.1**	**2,412.1**	**2,653.3**	**2,147.2**	**2,333.3**
General merchandise: exports f.o.b.	2 110	1,043.9	1,503.9	1,745.3	2,381.1	2,412.1	2,653.3	2,147.2	2,333.3
Goods for processing: exports f.o.b.	2 150	....	....	....	....	....	....	....	....
Repairs on goods	2 160	....	....	....	....	....	....	....	....
Goods procured in ports by carriers	2 170	....	....	....	....	....	....	....	....
Nonmonetary gold	2 180	....	....	....	....	....	....	....	....
Debit	3 100	**−1,648.1**	**−1,849.7**	**−2,242.3**	**−2,648.8**	**−2,811.1**	**−3,643.4**	**−3,422.0**	**−3,512.4**
General merchandise: imports f.o.b.	3 110	−1,648.1	−1,849.7	−2,242.3	−2,648.8	−2,811.1	−3,643.4	−3,422.0	−3,512.4
Goods for processing: imports f.o.b.	3 150	....	....	....	....	....	....	....	....
Repairs on goods	3 160	....	....	....	....	....	....	....	....
Goods procured in ports by carriers	3 170	....	....	....	....	....	....	....	....
Nonmonetary gold	3 180	....	....	....	....	....	....	....	....
B. SERVICES	4 200	**−270.0**	**−275.8**	**−306.6**	**−371.8**	**−396.8**	**−410.4**	**−457.3**	**−506.3**
Total credit	2 200	*303.9*	*255.6*	*342.0*	*386.3*	*458.7*	*555.0*	*611.7*	*646.9*
Total debit	3 200	*−573.9*	*−531.4*	*−648.6*	*−758.1*	*−855.6*	*−965.3*	*−1,069.0*	*−1,153.2*
Transportation services, credit	2 205	**90.5**	**80.0**	**89.4**	**105.0**	**128.6**	**157.9**	**153.1**	**162.8**
Passenger	2 850	*8.0*	*.5*	*7.8*	*5.2*	*19.2*	*23.0*	*20.5*	*33.5*
Freight	2 851	*32.1*	*27.7*	*54.5*	*69.1*	*46.2*	*39.8*	*45.4*	*38.3*
Other	2 852	*50.5*	*51.9*	*27.1*	*30.8*	*63.2*	*95.0*	*87.1*	*91.0*
Sea transport, passenger	2 207	....	....	....	....	....	....	....	....
Sea transport, freight	2 208	11.5	27.6	33.7	34.8	3.2	3.0	3.2	2.4
Sea transport, other	2 209	34.3	7.3	13.5	7.6	44.6	66.8	63.1	56.0
Air transport, passenger	2 211	....	.5	7.7	5.1	19.2	22.4	19.7	27.1
Air transport, freight	2 212	....	....	.2	2.4	.1	....	....	....
Air transport, other	2 213	1.5	2.5	5.3	10.7	8.5	13.9	4.4	15.9
Other transport, passenger	2 215	8.0	....	.1	....	....	.7	.8	6.3
Other transport, freight	2 216	20.5	....	20.7	31.9	42.9	36.8	42.2	35.9
Other transport, other	2 217	14.6	42.0	8.3	12.5	10.1	14.4	19.6	19.1
Transportation services, debit	3 205	**−190.4**	**−190.7**	**−230.0**	**−273.1**	**−294.7**	**−377.3**	**−363.6**	**−308.1**
Passenger	3 850	*−.8*	*−6.1*	*−11.3*	*−25.6*	*−29.3*	*−33.4*	*−35.1*	*−34.2*
Freight	3 851	*−163.7*	*−168.6*	*−204.8*	*−242.2*	*−253.2*	*−328.5*	*−308.5*	*−232.3*
Other	3 852	*−25.9*	*−16.0*	*−13.9*	*−5.4*	*−12.2*	*−15.4*	*−20.0*	*−41.6*
Sea transport, passenger	3 207	....	....	....	....	....	....	....	....
Sea transport, freight	3 208	−.1	−2.1	−2.3	−3.5	....	....	....	....
Sea transport, other	3 209	−7.4	−.9	−5.2	−1.1	−6.1	−7.4	−4.3	−22.4
Air transport, passenger	3 211	....	−6.1	−11.0	−25.5	−29.2	−30.5	−31.7	−34.2
Air transport, freight	3 212	−.6	....	−.7	....	....	....	....	....
Air transport, other	3 213	−5.0	....	−7.7	−3.6	−3.7	−4.9	−6.0	−13.5
Other transport, passenger	3 215	−.7	....	−.3	....	−.1	−2.9	−3.4	....
Other transport, freight	3 216	−163.1	−166.5	−201.8	−238.7	−253.2	−328.5	−308.5	−232.2
Other transport, other	3 217	−13.6	−15.1	−.9	−.7	−2.5	−3.2	−9.7	−5.7
Travel, credit	2 236	**97.6**	**95.3**	**129.6**	**139.7**	**163.4**	**190.0**	**195.6**	**197.3**
Business travel	2 237	38.0	18.8	5.8	3.7	11.3	1.8	.5	.8
Personal travel	2 240	59.6	76.4	123.9	135.9	152.1	188.1	195.1	196.6
Travel, debit	3 236	**−139.8**	**−134.2**	**−176.0**	**−179.5**	**−180.0**	**−208.3**	**−211.8**	**−250.5**
Business travel	3 237	−51.4	−7.6	−5.1	−17.5	−34.9	−53.8	−42.2	−85.4
Personal travel	3 240	−88.4	−126.6	−170.9	−162.0	−145.1	−154.5	−169.6	−165.1
Other services, credit	2 200 BA	**115.8**	**80.2**	**123.0**	**141.6**	**166.8**	**207.1**	**263.0**	**286.8**
Communications	2 245	7.4	8.5	10.8	15.3	19.0	31.3	30.5	38.9
Construction	2 249	11.8	11.1	22.1	24.9	18.5	18.1	15.0	24.6
Insurance	2 253	.7	.4	.1	....	2.0	1.1	2.7	3.9
Financial	2 260	4.0	1.5	1.3	1.7	4.3	3.1	4.1	4.0
Computer and information	2 262	....	1.0	1.6	2.7	3.9	2.8	4.9	6.7
Royalties and licence fees	2 266	15.0	.5	2.2	1.0	....	....	.2	....
Other business services	2 268	73.1	48.0	58.2	61.8	64.2	83.4	137.6	137.0
Personal, cultural, and recreational	2 287	.1	.2	.4	2.3	.5	.7	.3	1.2
Government, n.i.e.	2 291	3.7	9.1	26.3	31.8	54.4	66.7	67.7	70.4
Other services, debit	3 200 BA	**−243.6**	**−206.5**	**−242.6**	**−305.5**	**−380.8**	**−379.7**	**−493.6**	**−594.6**
Communications	3 245	−10.6	−8.5	−11.2	−16.9	−17.0	−27.7	−27.7	−46.2
Construction	3 249	−60.9	−52.2	−78.6	−93.7	−61.4	−34.3	−109.8	−117.5
Insurance	3 253	−4.5	−.4	−2.4	−1.8	−3.8	−3.9	−7.6	−18.8
Financial	3 260	−3.2	−7.7	−17.6	−12.5	−19.5	−9.4	−12.6	−16.8
Computer and information	3 262	−.1	−1.1	−4.3	−6.4	−6.8	−6.2	−9.9	−12.0
Royalties and licence fees	3 266	−1.4	−3.1	−5.7	−2.3	−2.4	−1.9	−3.6	−4.2
Other business services	3 268	−142.5	−113.3	−100.8	−141.1	−233.2	−248.4	−263.0	−326.2
Personal, cultural, and recreational	3 287	....	−.4	−.8	−1.1	−.7	−.7	−1.7	−1.5
Government, n.i.e.	3 291	−20.4	−19.9	−21.3	−29.6	−36.1	−47.2	−57.7	−51.2

Table 2 (Continued). STANDARD PRESENTATION, 2003–2010

(Millions of U.S. dollars)

	Code	2003	2004	2005	2006	2007	2008	2009	2010
C. INCOME	4 300	**−165.5**	**−299.5**	**−359.8**	**−634.5**	**−591.6**	**−631.3**	**−251.0**	**−84.6**
Total credit	2 300	*55.9*	*74.5*	*98.9*	*159.8*	*193.6*	*167.1*	*176.2*	*162.4*
Total debit	3 300	*−221.4*	*−374.0*	*−458.8*	*−794.3*	*−785.2*	*−798.5*	*−427.2*	*−247.0*
Compensation of employees, credit	2 310	**39.5**	**55.0**	**50.9**	**64.2**	**68.5**	**81.7**	**79.7**	**98.4**
Compensation of employees, debit	3 310	**−9.0**	**−9.0**	**−10.4**	**−13.8**	**−19.3**	**−19.0**	**−24.9**	**−32.8**
Investment income, credit	2 320	**16.4**	**19.5**	**48.1**	**95.6**	**125.1**	**85.5**	**96.5**	**64.0**
Direct investment income	2 330	....	....	....	....	4.1	2.9	2.0	.6
Dividends and distributed branch profits	2 332	....	....	....	....	4.1	2.9	2.0	.6
Reinvested earnings and undistributed branch profits	2 333	....	....	....	....	....	....	....	....
Income on debt (interest)	2 334	....	....	....	....	....	....	....	....
Portfolio investment income	2 339	6.8	6.6	15.5	28.5	41.8	14.1	22.6	28.5
Income on equity	2 340	6.6	6.1	1.7	.1	.1	....	.1	.4
Income on bonds and notes	2 350	.2	.5	13.8	28.4	41.8	14.0	22.6	28.0
Income on money market instruments	2 360	....	....	....	....	....	....	....	....
Other investment income	2 370	9.6	12.9	32.5	67.1	79.2	68.5	71.8	34.9
Investment income, debit	3 320	**−212.4**	**−365.0**	**−448.3**	**−780.5**	**−765.9**	**−779.5**	**−402.3**	**−214.2**
Direct investment income	3 330	−42.1	−167.6	−284.0	−471.4	−553.6	−544.5	−239.9	−69.6
Dividends and distributed branch profits	3 332	−42.1	−162.7	−267.1	−390.4	−523.8	−416.8	−219.3	−68.8
Reinvested earnings and undistributed branch profits	3 333	....	....	....	−77.2	−24.2	−123.9	−19.5	−.2
Income on debt (interest)	3 334	....	−4.9	−16.9	−3.8	−5.6	−3.8	−1.1	−.5
Portfolio investment income	3 339	....	−.5	−.7	−.6	−.4	−.1	−12.4	−16.6
Income on equity	3 340	....	....	−.7	−.6	−.4	−.1	−.4	−.4
Income on bonds and notes	3 350	....	−.5	....	....	....	....	−11.9	−16.2
Income on money market instruments	3 360	....	....	....	....	....	....	....	....
Other investment income	3 370	−170.3	−197.0	−163.6	−308.5	−212.0	−234.9	−150.0	−128.0
D. CURRENT TRANSFERS	4 379	**223.1**	**313.8**	**402.9**	**500.7**	**602.2**	**852.5**	**763.1**	**656.8**
Credit	2 379	**293.2**	**370.5**	**480.7**	**574.5**	**667.6**	**977.5**	**931.7**	**817.2**
General government	2 380	232.4	325.3	373.9	454.9	518.4	778.3	687.6	606.1
Other sectors	2 390	60.7	45.2	106.8	119.6	149.2	199.3	244.1	211.0
Workers' remittances	2 391	29.9	2.5	8.0	15.8	30.9	34.1	31.5	33.4
Other current transfers	2 392	30.8	42.7	98.8	103.7	118.3	165.2	212.6	177.6
Debit	3 379	**−70.0**	**−56.7**	**−77.8**	**−73.8**	**−65.4**	**−125.1**	**−168.6**	**−160.4**
General government	3 380	....	−1.6	−.1	−1.9	−3.6	−10.1	−5.5	−1.2
Other sectors	3 390	−70.0	−55.1	−77.7	−71.8	−61.8	−115.0	−163.1	−159.1
Workers' remittances	3 391	−20.5	−11.3	−14.1	−12.3	−25.9	−37.8	−40.9	−47.2
Other current transfers	3 392	−49.5	−43.8	−63.6	−59.5	−35.8	−77.2	−122.3	−111.9
CAPITAL AND FINANCIAL ACCOUNT	4 996	**608.3**	**391.0**	**479.7**	**629.4**	**720.1**	**1,071.9**	**1,262.9**	**1,046.8**
CAPITAL ACCOUNT	4 994	**284.1**	**578.1**	**193.2**	**2,277.9**	**541.9**	**421.5**	**424.2**	**348.1**
Total credit	2 994	*284.6*	*581.2*	*197.1*	*2,280.3*	*542.9*	*429.4*	*430.8*	*353.4*
Total debit	3 994	*−.5*	*−3.1*	*−3.9*	*−2.3*	*−1.0*	*−8.0*	*−6.6*	*−5.4*
Capital transfers, credit	2 400	**284.6**	**581.2**	**197.1**	**2,280.3**	**542.8**	**429.4**	**430.8**	**353.4**
General government	2 401	272.8	512.9	86.1	1,957.3	386.8	255.2	270.2	189.5
Debt forgiveness	2 402	13.3	315.1	5.4	1,789.4	126.8	1.6	1.9	2.5
Other capital transfers	2 410	259.5	197.8	80.8	167.9	260.1	253.6	268.3	187.0
Other sectors	2 430	11.7	68.3	111.0	322.9	156.0	174.3	160.6	163.9
Migrants' transfers	2 431	....	....	....	....	....	....	....	....
Debt forgiveness	2 432	....	....	....	....	....	....	....	....
Other capital transfers	2 440	11.7	68.3	111.0	322.9	156.0	174.3	160.6	163.9
Capital transfers, debit	3 400	**−.5**	**−3.0**	**−3.9**	**−2.3**	**−.9**	**−8.0**	**−6.6**	**−5.4**
General government	3 401	....	....	....	....	....	....	....	−.1
Debt forgiveness	3 402	....	....	....	....	....	....	....	....
Other capital transfers	3 410	....	....	....	....	....	....	....	−.1
Other sectors	3 430	−.5	−3.0	−3.9	−2.3	−.9	−8.0	−6.6	−5.3
Migrants' transfers	3 431	....	....	....	....	....	....	....	....
Debt forgiveness	3 432	....	....	....	....	....	....	....	....
Other capital transfers	3 440	−.5	−3.0	−3.9	−2.3	−.9	−8.0	−6.6	−5.3
Nonproduced nonfinancial assets, credit	2 480	....	....	....	....	....	....	....	....
Nonproduced nonfinancial assets, debit	3 480	....	....	....	....	....	....	....	....

Table 2 (Continued). STANDARD PRESENTATION, 2003–2010

(Millions of U.S. dollars)

	Code	2003	2004	2005	2006	2007	2008	2009	2010
FINANCIAL ACCOUNT	4 995	324.2	−187.2	286.4	−1,648.5	178.1	650.5	838.7	698.7
A. DIRECT INVESTMENT	4 500	336.7	244.7	107.9	153.3	427.7	591.6	889.7	789.8
Direct investment abroad	4 505	....	....	....	−.4	.3	....	−2.8	.8
Equity capital	4 510	....	....	....	−.4	....	....	−2.8	.6
Claims on affiliated enterprises	4 515	....	....	....	−.4	....	....	−1.4	.6
Liabilities to affiliated enterprises	4 520	....	....	....	....	....	....	−1.4	....
Reinvested earnings	4 525	....	....	....	....	....	....	....	....
Other capital	4 530	....	....	....	....	.3	....	−.1	.2
Claims on affiliated enterprises	4 535	....	....	....	....	.3	....	−.1	.2
Liabilities to affiliated enterprises	4 540	....	....	....	....	....	....	....	....
Direct investment in Mozambique	4 555	336.7	244.7	107.9	153.7	427.4	591.6	892.5	789.0
Equity capital	4 560	336.7	234.6	59.8	111.8	167.3	130.5	225.6	105.6
Claims on direct investors	4 565	....	....	....	....	−.8	....	....	....
Liabilities to direct investors	4 570	336.7	234.6	59.8	111.8	168.1	130.5	225.6	105.6
Reinvested earnings	4 575	....	....	....	77.2	24.2	123.9	19.5	.2
Other capital	4 580	....	10.1	48.1	−35.2	235.9	337.2	647.3	683.2
Claims on direct investors	4 585	....	....	−14.6	−31.6	11.5	32.5	−4.6	−16.4
Liabilities to direct investors	4 590	....	10.1	62.6	−3.6	224.5	304.7	651.9	699.6
B. PORTFOLIO INVESTMENT	4 600	5.0	−25.4	−88.5	−123.8	−5.6	−8.0	4.5	1.4
Assets	4 602	5.0	−25.4	−88.8	−124.2	−3.5	−8.4	4.4	.3
Equity securities	4 610	5.0	−25.4	−7.3	−.2	−1.4	−.3	−.5	−.1
Monetary authorities	4 611	−.8	....	....	....	−1.3	....	....	....
General government	4 612	....	....	....	....	....	....	....	....
Banks	4 613	5.8	−25.4	−7.2	....	....	....	....	....
Other sectors	4 614	....	....	−.1	−.2	−.1	−.3	−.5	−.1
Debt securities	4 619	....	....	−81.5	−124.0	−2.1	−8.0	4.9	.3
Bonds and notes	4 620	....	....	−81.5	−124.0	−2.1	−8.0	4.9	.3
Monetary authorities	4 621	....	....	−69.9	−84.1	....	....	....	....
General government	4 622	....	....	....	....	....	....	....	....
Banks	4 623	....	....	−11.6	−39.9	−2.1	−8.0	6.0	.3
Other sectors	4 624	....	....	....	....	....	....	−1.1	....
Money market instruments	4 630	....	....	....	....	....	....	....	....
Monetary authorities	4 631	....	....	....	....	....	....	....	....
General government	4 632	....	....	....	....	....	....	....	....
Banks	4 633	....	....	....	....	....	....	....	....
Other sectors	4 634	....	....	....	....	....	....	....	....
Liabilities	4 652	....	....	.3	.4	−2.1	.3	.1	1.1
Equity securities	4 660	....	....	.3	.4	.3	.4	....	.3
Banks	4 663	....	....	....	....	....	....	....	....
Other sectors	4 664	....	....	.3	.4	.3	.4	....	.3
Debt securities	4 669	....	....	....	....	−2.4	−.1	.1	.8
Bonds and notes	4 670	....	....	....	....	−2.4	−.1	.1	.8
Monetary authorities	4 671	....	....	....	....	−2.4	−.2	.1	.8
General government	4 672	....	....	....	....	....	....	....	....
Banks	4 673	....	....	....	....	....	....	....	....
Other sectors	4 674	....	....	....	....	....	.1	....	....
Money market instruments	4 680	....	....	....	....	....	....	....	....
Monetary authorities	4 681	....	....	....	....	....	....	....	....
General government	4 682	....	....	....	....	....	....	....	....
Banks	4 683	....	....	....	....	....	....	....	....
Other sectors	4 684	....	....	....	....	....	....	....	....
C. FINANCIAL DERIVATIVES	4 910	....	....	....	....	−16.0	....	....	....
Monetary authorities	4 911	....	....	....	....	....	....	....	....
General government	4 912	....	....	....	....	....	....	....	....
Banks	4 913	....	....	....	....	....	....	....	....
Other sectors	4 914	....	....	....	....	−16.0	....	....	....
Assets	4 900	....	....	....	....	−16.0	....	....	....
Monetary authorities	4 901	....	....	....	....	....	....	....	....
General government	4 902	....	....	....	....	....	....	....	....
Banks	4 903	....	....	....	....	....	....	....	....
Other sectors	4 904	....	....	....	....	−16.0	....	....	....
Liabilities	4 905	....	....	....	....	....	....	....	....
Monetary authorities	4 906	....	....	....	....	....	....	....	....
General government	4 907	....	....	....	....	....	....	....	....
Banks	4 908	....	....	....	....	....	....	....	....
Other sectors	4 909	....	....	....	....	....	....	....	....

Table 2 (Concluded). STANDARD PRESENTATION, 2003–2010

(Millions of U.S. dollars)

	Code	2003	2004	2005	2006	2007	2008	2009	2010
D. OTHER INVESTMENT	4 700 ..	**164.0**	**−237.4**	**137.2**	**−1,648.8**	**57.1**	**207.0**	**296.1**	**6.2**
Assets	4 703 ..	**−77.1**	**−88.7**	**−78.5**	**−13.8**	**−411.5**	**−80.7**	**−118.6**	**−179.5**
Trade credits	4 706 ..	−3.3	−2.8	−3.7	−27.8	−65.8	−14.3	−21.3	−79.1
General government	4 707 ..	....	....	....	....	....	....	....	....
of which: Short-term	4 709 ..	....	....	....	....	....	....	....	....
Other sectors	4 710 ..	−3.3	−2.8	−3.7	−27.8	−65.8	−14.3	−21.3	−79.1
of which: Short-term	4 712 ..	*−3.3*	*−2.8*	*−3.7*	*−27.8*	*−65.8*	*−14.3*	*−21.3*	*−79.1*
Loans	4 714 ..	....	....	....	6.7	−34.4	91.4	−18.6	−19.5
Monetary authorities	4 715 ..	....	....	....	....	....	....	.1	....
of which: Short-term	4 718 ..	....	....	....	....	....	....	*.1*	....
General government	4 719 ..	....	....	....	....	....	....	....	....
of which: Short-term	4 721 ..	....	....	....	....	....	....	....	....
Banks	4 722 ..	....	....	....	....	−32.9	92.0	−18.6	−39.6
of which: Short-term	4 724 ..	....	....	....	....	*−32.9*	*92.0*	*−18.6*	*−39.6*
Other sectors	4 725 ..	....	....	....	6.7	−1.5	−.6	....	20.0
of which: Short-term	4 727 ..	....	....	....	*6.7*	*−.9*	*.9*	....	*−.2*
Currency and deposits	4 730 ..	20.0	−66.6	−108.8	−30.0	−328.4	−210.5	−6.3	−88.6
Monetary authorities	4 731 ..	6.9	−122.8	....	....	7.2	48.1	−31.3	29.4
General government	4 732 ..	....	....	....	....	....	....	....	....
Banks	4 733 ..	13.1	56.2	−76.6	−105.9	−240.0	9.4	−19.1	−112.0
Other sectors	4 734 ..	....	....	−32.2	75.8	−95.6	−268.0	44.0	−6.0
Other assets	4 736 ..	−93.8	−19.4	34.0	37.3	17.1	52.7	−72.4	7.7
Monetary authorities	4 737 ..	....	−63.6	40.9	17.5	5.9	1.8	−1.9	−5.7
of which: Short-term	4 739 ..	....	*−63.6*	*40.9*	*17.5*	*5.9*	*1.8*	*−1.9*	*−5.7*
General government	4 740 ..	....	....	....	....	....	....	....	....
of which: Short-term	4 742 ..	....	....	....	....	....	....	....	....
Banks	4 743 ..	....	1.6	.3	−1.0	−.4	−11.3	6.2	5.2
of which: Short-term	4 745 ..	....	*1.6*	*.3*	*−1.0*	*−.4*	*−11.3*	*6.2*	*5.2*
Other sectors	4 746 ..	−93.8	42.6	−7.3	20.8	11.6	62.1	−76.6	8.3
of which: Short-term	4 748 ..	....	*42.6*	*−7.3*	*20.8*	*11.6*	*62.1*	*−76.6*	*8.3*
Liabilities	4 753 ..	**241.1**	**−148.7**	**215.7**	**−1,635.0**	**468.6**	**287.7**	**414.7**	**185.6**
Trade credits	4 756 ..	.1	1.3	8.8	−3.8	36.6	1.1	−243.0	−158.4
General government	4 757 ..	....	....	....	....	....	....	....	....
of which: Short-term	4 759 ..	....	....	....	....	....	....	....	....
Other sectors	4 760 ..	.1	1.3	8.8	−3.8	36.6	1.1	−243.0	−158.4
of which: Short-term	4 762 ..	....	*1.3*	*8.8*	*−3.8*	*36.6*	*1.1*	*−243.0*	*−158.4*
Loans	4 764 ..	94.6	−206.2	126.9	−1,866.5	368.8	218.1	443.1	343.2
Monetary authorities	4 765 ..	13.2	−68.8	−25.6	−149.1	5.4	−.2	156.7	20.6
of which: Use of Fund credit and loans from the Fund	4 766 ..	*−9.1*	*−20.4*	*−25.3*	*−149.4*	*4.9*	....	*154.7*	*20.6*
of which: Short-term	4 768 ..	....	....	*.1*	....	....	*−.2*	*2.1*	....
General government	4 769 ..	53.0	−47.6	95.8	−1,475.5	216.2	342.1	434.0	468.4
of which: Short-term	4 771 ..	....	....	....	....	....	....	....	....
Banks	4 772 ..	11.2	2.3	18.5	−31.7	29.9	−21.2	79.6	43.7
of which: Short-term	4 774 ..	*12.0*	*−2.8*	*23.7*	*−30.8*	....	....	....	....
Other sectors	4 775 ..	17.2	−92.1	38.3	−210.1	117.3	−102.6	−227.2	−189.5
of which: Short-term	4 777 ..	....	....	....	....	*−4.0*	*−50.0*	....	....
Currency and deposits	4 780 ..	.9	7.3	−12.0	−3.9	31.5	48.9	60.6	−7.8
Monetary authorities	4 781 ..	....	....	....	....	2.5	.2	5.7	2.8
General government	4 782 ..	....	....	....	....	....	....	....	....
Banks	4 783 ..	.9	7.3	−12.0	−3.9	29.0	48.7	54.9	−10.6
Other sectors	4 784 ..	....	....	....	....	....	....	....	....
Other liabilities	4 786 ..	145.5	48.8	91.9	239.2	31.6	19.6	154.0	8.6
Monetary authorities	4 787 ..	....	....	....	....	....	....	170.2	.8
of which: Short-term	4 789 ..	....	....	....	....	....	....	....	....
General government	4 790 ..	141.9	48.8	86.7	32.0	16.3	17.9	.1	7.8
of which: Short-term	4 792 ..	*141.9*	*48.8*	*86.7*	*32.0*	*16.3*	*17.9*	*.1*	*7.8*
Banks	4 793 ..	3.5	....	....	....	7.5	−3.0	....	....
of which: Short-term	4 795 ..	*3.5*	....	....	....	*7.5*	*−3.0*	....	....
Other sectors	4 796 ..	....	....	5.3	207.2	7.9	4.6	−16.3	....
of which: Short-term	4 798 ..	....	....	*5.3*	*207.2*	*8.1*	*5.1*	*−15.1*	....
E. RESERVE ASSETS	4 802 ..	**−181.5**	**−169.1**	**129.9**	**−29.3**	**−285.1**	**−140.0**	**−351.6**	**−98.6**
Monetary gold	4 812 ..	12.3	−18.6	−20.0	−11.5	−18.7	−3.5	−.3	−23.2
Special drawing rights	4 811 ..	....	....	−.2	....	.1	.1	−169.9	.3
Reserve position in the Fund	4 810 ..	....	....	....	....	....	....	....	....
Foreign exchange	4 803 ..	−193.8	−150.5	150.1	−17.8	−266.5	−136.6	−181.4	−75.7
Other claims	4 813 ..	....	....	....	....	....	....	....	....
NET ERRORS AND OMISSIONS	4 998 ..	**208.2**	**216.4**	**280.9**	**143.8**	**65.2**	**107.5**	**−42.7**	**66.5**

Table 3. INTERNATIONAL INVESTMENT POSITION (End-period stocks), 2003–2010

(Millions of U.S. dollars)

	Code	2003	2004	2005	2006	2007	2008	2009	2010
ASSETS	8 995 C.	....	2,109.5	2,242.1	2,541.1	3,264.8	3,659.3	4,126.9	4,420.1
Direct investment abroad	8 505	....	....	....	.4	.5	.6	2.0	1.3
Equity capital and reinvested earnings	8 506	....	....	....	.4	.4	.4	1.8	1.3
Claims on affiliated enterprises	8 507	....	....	....	.4	.4	.4	1.8	1.2
Liabilities to affiliated enterprises	8 508	....	....	....	....	....	....	....	.1
Other capital	8 530	....	....	....	....	.1	.2	.2	.1
Claims on affiliated enterprises	8 535	....	....	....	....	.1	.2	.2	.1
Liabilities to affiliated enterprises	8 540	....	....	....	....	....	....	....	.1
Portfolio investment	8 602	....	68.5	157.2	281.3	284.8	293.2	288.8	288.6
Equity securities	8 610	....	....	7.2	7.2	8.6	9.0	9.5	9.5
Monetary authorities	8 611	....	....	....	....	1.3	1.3	1.3	1.3
General government	8 612	....	....	....	....	....	....	....	....
Banks	8 613	....	....	7.2	7.2	7.2	7.2	7.2	7.2
Other sectors	8 614	....	....	....	.1	.1	.5	.9	1.0
Debt securities	8 619	....	68.5	150.1	274.1	276.2	284.2	279.3	279.0
Bonds and notes	8 620	....	68.5	150.1	274.1	276.2	284.2	279.3	279.0
Monetary authorities	8 621	....	....	69.9	154.0	154.0	154.0	154.0	154.0
General government	8 622	....	....	....	....	....	....	....	....
Banks	8 623	....	68.5	80.1	120.1	122.1	130.1	124.1	123.8
Other sectors	8 624	....	....	....	....	....	....	1.2	1.2
Money market instruments	8 630	....	....	....	....	....	....	....	....
Monetary authorities	8 631	....	....	....	....	....	....	....	....
General government	8 632	....	....	....	....	....	....	....	....
Banks	8 633	....	....	....	....	....	....	....	....
Other sectors	8 634	....	....	....	....	....	....	....	....
Financial derivatives	8 900	....	....	....	....	16.0	16.0	16.0	16.0
Monetary authorities	8 901	....	....	....	....	....	....	....	....
General government	8 902	....	....	....	....	....	....	....	....
Banks	8 903	....	....	....	....	....	....	....	....
Other sectors	8 904	....	....	....	....	16.0	16.0	16.0	16.0
Other investment	8 703	....	884.3	982.6	1,024.5	1,443.4	1,689.5	1,808.0	2,006.5
Trade credits	8 706	....	10.8	14.5	39.4	105.2	119.5	140.8	219.9
General government	8 707	....	....	....	....	....	....	....	....
of which: Short-term	8 709	....	....	....	....	....	....	....	....
Other sectors	8 710	....	10.8	14.5	39.4	105.2	119.5	140.8	219.9
of which: Short-term	8 712	....	*10.8*	*14.5*	*39.4*	*105.2*	*119.5*	*140.8*	*219.9*
Loans	8 714	....	....	6.7	1.5	35.9	4.7	23.3	61.8
Monetary authorities	8 715	....	....	....	....	....	.1	.1	....
of which: Short-term	8 718	....	....	....	....	....	*.1*	*.1*	....
General government	8 719	....	....	....	....	....	....	....	....
of which: Short-term	8 721	....	....	....	....	....	....	....	....
Banks	8 722	....	....	....	....	32.9	.9	19.6	59.2
of which: Short-term	8 724	....	....	....	....	*32.9*	*.9*	*19.6*	*59.1*
Other sectors	8 725	....	....	6.7	1.5	3.0	3.6	3.6	2.6
of which: Short-term	8 727	....	....	*6.7*	*1.5*	*2.3*	*1.5*	*1.5*	*1.6*
Currency and deposits	8 730	....	655.2	764.0	823.4	1,159.2	1,417.8	1,424.1	1,512.7
Monetary authorities	8 731	....	....	....	....	.2	.2	31.5	2.1
General government	8 732	....	....	....	....	....	....	....	....
Banks	8 733	....	261.2	337.9	443.7	683.8	674.3	693.4	805.4
Other sectors	8 734	....	394.0	426.1	379.6	475.3	743.3	699.3	705.3
Other assets	8 736	....	218.3	197.5	160.2	143.0	147.5	219.8	212.1
Monetary authorities	8 737	....	197.5	156.5	139.0	133.1	131.3	133.2	138.9
of which: Short-term	8 739	....	*197.5*	*156.5*	*139.0*	*133.1*	*131.3*	*133.2*	*138.9*
General government	8 740	....	....	....	....	....	....	....	....
of which: Short-term	8 742	....	....	....	....	....	....	....	....
Banks	8 743	....	1.8	1.5	2.5	3.0	14.2	8.1	2.9
of which: Short-term	8 745	....	*1.8*	*1.5*	*2.5*	*3.0*	*14.2*	*8.1*	*2.9*
Other sectors	8 746	....	19.0	39.4	18.7	7.0	2.0	78.6	70.3
of which: Short-term	8 748	....	*19.0*	*39.4*	*18.7*	*7.0*	*2.0*	*78.6*	*70.3*
Reserve assets	8 802	....	1,156.6	1,102.3	1,234.9	1,520.0	1,660.0	2,012.0	2,107.6
Monetary gold	8 812	....	28.9	49.0	60.5	79.3	82.7	83.1	106.3
Special drawing rights	8 811	.1	.1	.2	.2	.2	.1	170.3	167.1
Reserve position in the Fund	8 810	....	....	....	....	....	....	....	....
Foreign exchange	8 803	....	1,127.6	1,053.0	1,174.2	1,440.5	1,577.2	1,758.6	1,834.3
Other claims	8 813	....	....	....	....	....	....	....	....

Table 3 (Concluded). INTERNATIONAL INVESTMENT POSITION (End-period stocks), 2003–2010

(Millions of U.S. dollars)

	Code	2003	2004	2005	2006	2007	2008	2009	2010
LIABILITIES	8 995 D.	....	**11,492.4**	**12,068.2**	**10,657.4**	**9,458.9**	**10,192.0**	**11,555.3**	**12,009.5**
Direct investment in Mozambique	8 555 ..	....	**2,441.5**	**2,665.0**	**2,777.3**	**3,181.4**	**3,649.1**	**4,522.1**	**5,310.9**
Equity capital and reinvested earnings	8 556 ..	....	2,380.9	2,440.7	2,552.5	2,720.6	2,851.2	3,076.8	3,182.4
Claims on direct investors	8 557 ..	....	....	....	....	....	....	....	....
Liabilities to direct investors	8 558 ..	....	2,380.9	2,440.7	2,552.5	2,720.6	2,851.2	3,076.8	3,182.4
Other capital	8 580 ..	....	60.6	224.3	224.8	460.8	798.0	1,445.3	2,128.5
Claims on direct investors	8 585 ..	....	−14.2	6.2	5.1	16.6	49.1	44.5	28.0
Liabilities to direct investors	8 590 ..	....	74.8	218.0	219.7	444.2	748.9	1,400.8	2,100.4
Portfolio investment	8 652 ..	....	....	**.3**	**.7**	**1.0**	**1.5**	**1.6**	**2.7**
Equity securities	8 660 ..	....	....	.3	.7	1.0	1.4	1.3	1.6
Banks	8 663 ..	....	....	....	....	....	....	....	....
Other sectors	8 664 ..	....	....	.3	.7	1.0	1.4	1.3	1.6
Debt securities	8 669 ..	....	....	....	....	....	.1	.3	1.1
Bonds and notes	8 670 ..	....	....	....	....	....	.1	.3	1.1
Monetary authorities	8 671 ..	....	....	....	....	....	....	.1	.9
General government	8 672 ..	....	....	....	....	....	....	....	....
Banks	8 673 ..	....	....	....	....	....	....	....	....
Other sectors	8 674 ..	....	....	....	....	....	.1	.1	.1
Money market instruments	8 680 ..	....	....	....	....	....	....	....	....
Monetary authorities	8 681 ..	....	....	....	....	....	....	....	....
General government	8 682 ..	....	....	....	....	....	....	....	....
Banks	8 683 ..	....	....	....	....	....	....	....	....
Other sectors	8 684 ..	....	....	....	....	....	....	....	....
Financial derivatives	8 905 ..	....	....	....	....	....	....	....	....
Monetary authorities	8 906 ..	....	....	....	....	....	....	....	....
General government	8 907 ..	....	....	....	....	....	....	....	....
Banks	8 908 ..	....	....	....	....	....	....	....	....
Other sectors	8 909 ..	....	....	....	....	....	....	....	....
Other investment	8 753 ..	....	**9,050.9**	**9,402.9**	**7,879.3**	**6,276.5**	**6,541.4**	**7,031.6**	**6,695.9**
Trade credits	8 756 ..	....	6.5	16.3	12.5	49.2	50.3	3.2	1.8
General government	8 757 ..	....	....	....	....	....	....	....	....
of which: Short-term	8 759 ..	....	....	....	....	....	....	....	....
Other sectors	8 760 ..	....	6.5	16.3	12.5	49.2	50.3	3.2	1.8
of which: Short-term	8 762 ..	....	*6.5*	*16.3*	*12.5*	*49.2*	*50.3*	*3.2*	*1.8*
Loans	8 764 ..	....	8,950.4	9,199.3	7,444.2	5,878.4	6,073.7	6,394.9	6,063.6
Monetary authorities	8 765 ..	....	200.3	159.6	12.8	18.9	18.3	176.5	195.1
of which: Use of Fund credit and loans from the Fund	8 766 ..	209.2	*197.3*	*156.9*	*9.7*	*15.4*	*15.0*	*171.1*	*189.7*
of which: Short-term	8 768 ..	....	....	*.1*	*.1*	*.2*	....	*2.1*	*2.1*
General government	8 769 ..	....	4,416.1	4,648.9	3,282.0	3,316.9	3,637.1	3,947.7	3,743.6
of which: Short-term	8 771 ..	....	....	....	....	....	....	....	....
Banks	8 772 ..	....	22.2	40.7	8.9	38.9	17.7	97.3	141.0
of which: Short-term	8 774 ..	....	*11.0*	*34.7*	*3.8*	*3.8*	*3.8*	*3.8*	*3.8*
Other sectors	8 775 ..	....	4,311.8	4,350.1	4,140.5	2,503.8	2,400.6	2,173.4	1,983.9
of which: Short-term	8 777 ..	....	....	....	*.5*	*1.0*	*.5*	*.5*	*.5*
Currency and deposits	8 780 ..	....	45.2	33.1	29.2	60.8	109.7	170.3	162.5
Monetary authorities	8 781 ..	....	....	....	....	2.5	2.7	8.4	11.2
General government	8 782 ..	....	....	....	....	....	....	....	....
Banks	8 783 ..	....	45.2	33.1	29.2	58.3	107.0	161.9	151.3
Other sectors	8 784 ..	....	....	....	....	....	....	....	....
Other liabilities	8 786 ..	....	48.8	154.2	393.4	288.1	307.7	463.1	467.9
Monetary authorities	8 787 ..	....	....	....	....	.1	.1	170.7	167.7
of which: Short-term	8 789 ..	....	....	....	....	....	....	....	....
General government	8 790 ..	....	48.8	135.5	167.4	183.8	201.7	201.7	209.5
of which: Short-term	8 792 ..	....	*48.8*	*135.5*	*167.4*	*183.8*	*201.7*	*201.7*	*209.5*
Banks	8 793 ..	....	....	....	....	7.5	4.5	4.5	4.5
of which: Short-term	8 795 ..	....	....	....	....	*7.5*	*4.5*	*4.5*	*4.5*
Other sectors	8 796 ..	....	....	18.7	225.9	96.8	101.5	86.2	86.2
of which: Short-term	8 798 ..	....	....	*17.7*	*224.9*	*96.1*	*101.2*	*86.1*	*86.1*
NET INTERNATIONAL INVESTMENT POSITION	8 995 ..	....	**−9,382.9**	**−9,826.0**	**−8,116.2**	**−6,194.1**	**−6,532.7**	**−7,428.4**	**−7,589.4**
Conversion rates: meticais per U.S. dollar (end of period)	0 102 ..	23.8567	18.8993	24.1830	25.9700	23.8200	25.5000	29.1900	32.5800

Table 1. ANALYTIC PRESENTATION, 2003–2010

(Millions of U.S. dollars)

	Code	2003	2004	2005	2006	2007	2008	2009	2010
A. Current Account[1]	4 993 Z.	**−19.3**	**111.5**	**587.7**	**802.0**	**1,851.4**	**1,547.5**	**1,086.5**	**1,526.9**
Goods: exports f.o.b.	2 100 ..	2,709.7	2,926.6	3,787.8	4,554.7	6,302.7	7,197.6	6,700.4	7,831.3
Goods: imports f.o.b.	3 100 ..	−1,911.6	−1,998.7	−1,759.4	−2,343.4	−3,038.0	−3,885.5	−3,959.1	−4,375.5
Balance on Goods	4 100 ..	*798.1*	*927.9*	*2,028.4*	*2,211.3*	*3,264.7*	*3,312.0*	*2,741.3*	*3,455.8*
Services: credit	2 200 ..	249.1	254.7	259.1	279.5	307.3	305.6	316.6	366.6
Services: debit	3 200 ..	−420.0	−459.6	−502.0	−562.9	−659.9	−623.4	−623.6	−797.1
Balance on Goods and Services	4 991 ..	*627.3*	*723.0*	*1,785.5*	*1,928.0*	*2,912.1*	*2,994.2*	*2,434.3*	*3,025.4*
Income: credit	2 300 ..	29.4	40.4	55.5	97.8	175.9	178.7	95.7	149.0
Income: debit	3 300 ..	−771.0	−785.8	−1,427.3	−1,346.2	−1,443.1	−1,936.3	−1,881.1	−1,888.6
Balance on Goods, Services, and Income	4 992 ..	*−114.2*	*−22.4*	*413.8*	*679.6*	*1,644.9*	*1,236.6*	*648.9*	*1,285.8*
Current transfers: credit	2 379 Z.	118.0	160.6	197.8	161.4	234.0	364.1	501.6	349.2
Current transfers: debit	3 379 ..	−23.0	−26.7	−23.8	−39.0	−27.5	−53.1	−64.1	−108.2
B. Capital Account[1]	4 994 Z.	....	....	....	....	....	....	....	....
Capital account: credit	2 994 Z.	....	....	....	....	....	....	....	....
Capital account: debit	3 994 ..	....	....	....	....	....	....	....	....
Total, Groups A Plus B	4 981 ..	*−19.3*	*111.5*	*587.7*	*802.0*	*1,851.4*	*1,547.5*	*1,086.5*	*1,526.9*
C. Financial Account[1]	4 995 W.	**137.1**	**125.2**	**166.2**	**253.0**	**649.9**	**1,003.4**	**1,551.2**	**1,128.7**
Direct investment abroad	4 505 ..	....	....	....	....	....	....	....	....
Direct investment in Myanmar	4 555 Z.	251.5	213.5	237.2	278.6	717.3	872.7	1,090.2	910.3
Portfolio investment assets	4 602 ..	....	....	....	....	....	....	....	....
Equity securities	4 610 ..	....	....	....	....	....	....	....	....
Debt securities	4 619 ..	....	....	....	....	....	....	....	....
Portfolio investment liabilities	4 652 Z.	....	....	....	....	....	....	....	....
Equity securities	4 660 Z.	....	....	....	....	....	....	....	....
Debt securities	4 669 Z.	....	....	....	....	....	....	....	....
Financial derivatives	4 910 ..	....	....	....	....	....	....	....	....
Financial derivatives assets	4 900 ..	....	....	....	....	....	....	....	....
Financial derivatives liabilities	4 905 ..	....	....	....	....	....	....	....	....
Other investment assets	4 703 ..	....	....	....	....	....	....	....	....
Monetary authorities	4 701 ..	....	....	....	....	....	....	....	....
General government	4 704 ..	....	....	....	....	....	....	....	....
Banks	4 705 ..	....	....	....	....	....	....	....	....
Other sectors	4 728 ..	....	....	....	....	....	....	....	....
Other investment liabilities	4 753 W.	−114.3	−88.3	−71.1	−25.6	−67.3	130.7	461.0	218.4
Monetary authorities	4 753 WA	−21.2	−13.4	10.5	−8.0	−47.7	−24.3	274.4	−26.7
General government	4 753 ZB	−91.2	−85.2	−88.1	−31.8	−20.6	162.0	147.1	227.4
Banks	4 753 ZC	5.3	12.4	9.4	17.8	1.2	−6.9	39.5	17.7
Other sectors	4 753 ZD	−7.2	−2.2	−2.9	−3.6	−.2	....	....	....
Total, Groups A Through C	4 983 ..	*117.9*	*236.7*	*753.9*	*1,055.0*	*2,501.4*	*2,550.9*	*2,637.7*	*2,655.6*
D. Net Errors and Omissions	4 998 ..	**−78.9**	**−142.7**	**−610.3**	**−632.1**	**−795.6**	**−1,663.5**	**−1,426.9**	**−2,089.9**
Total, Groups A Through D	4 984 ..	*38.9*	*94.0*	*143.6*	*422.9*	*1,705.8*	*887.4*	*1,210.8*	*565.7*
E. Reserves and Related Items	4 802 A.	**−38.9**	**−94.0**	**−143.6**	**−422.9**	**−1,705.8**	**−887.4**	**−1,210.8**	**−565.7**
Reserve assets	4 802 ..	−38.9	−94.0	−143.6	−422.9	−1,705.8	−887.4	−1,210.8	−565.7
Use of Fund credit and loans	4 766 ..	....	....	....	....	....	....	....	....
Exceptional financing	4 920 ..	....	....	....	....	....	....	....	....
Conversion rates: kyats per U.S. dollar	0 101 ..	**6.0764**	**5.7459**	**5.7610**	**5.7838**	**5.5597**	**5.3875**	**5.5195**	**5.5778**

[1] Excludes components that have been classified in the categories of Group E.

Table 2. STANDARD PRESENTATION, 2003–2010

(Millions of U.S. dollars)

	Code	2003	2004	2005	2006	2007	2008	2009	2010
CURRENT ACCOUNT............................	4 993 ..	**−19.3**	**111.5**	**587.7**	**802.0**	**1,851.4**	**1,547.5**	**1,086.5**	**1,526.9**
A. GOODS....................................	4 100 ..	**798.1**	**927.9**	**2,028.4**	**2,211.3**	**3,264.7**	**3,312.0**	**2,741.3**	**3,455.8**
Credit....................................	2 100 ..	**2,709.7**	**2,926.6**	**3,787.8**	**4,554.7**	**6,302.7**	**7,197.6**	**6,700.4**	**7,831.3**
General merchandise: exports f.o.b................	2 110 ..	2,353.0	2,697.2	3,537.3	4,264.9	6,012.4	7,083.1	6,644.8	7,535.2
Goods for processing: exports f.o.b...............	2 150 ..	356.7	229.4	250.5	289.8	290.3	114.4	55.7	296.1
Repairs on goods..............................	2 160 ..	....	....	....	....	....	....	....	....
Goods procured in ports by carriers.............	2 170 ..	....	....	....	....	....	....	....	....
Nonmonetary gold.............................	2 180 ..	....	....	....	....	....	....	....	....
Debit.....................................	3 100 ..	**−1,911.6**	**−1,998.7**	**−1,759.4**	**−2,343.4**	**−3,038.0**	**−3,885.5**	**−3,959.1**	**−4,375.5**
General merchandise: imports f.o.b................	3 110 ..	−1,589.0	−1,768.1	−1,533.4	−2,090.8	−2,742.8	−3,607.0	−3,687.7	−4,021.4
Goods for processing: imports f.o.b...............	3 150 ..	−322.6	−230.7	−226.0	−252.5	−295.2	−278.5	−271.4	−354.1
Repairs on goods..............................	3 160 ..	....	....	....	....	....	....	....	....
Goods procured in ports by carriers.............	3 170 ..	....	....	....	....	....	....	....	....
Nonmonetary gold.............................	3 180 ..	....	....	....	....	....	....	....	....
B. SERVICES................................	4 200 ..	**−170.8**	**−204.9**	**−242.9**	**−283.4**	**−352.5**	**−317.8**	**−307.0**	**−430.4**
Total credit.................................	2 200 ..	*249.1*	*254.7*	*259.1*	*279.5*	*307.3*	*305.6*	*316.6*	*366.6*
Total debit..................................	3 200 ..	*−420.0*	*−459.6*	*−502.0*	*−562.9*	*−659.9*	*−623.4*	*−623.6*	*−797.1*
Transportation services, credit...............	2 205 ..	**72.3**	**85.3**	**119.6**	**130.1**	**112.7**	**122.9**	**140.1**	**149.7**
Passenger...................................	2 850 ..	*14.3*	*13.5*	*16.5*	*13.1*	*12.1*	*11.9*	*19.2*	*19.0*
Freight.....................................	2 851 ..	*14.1*	*13.0*	*45.2*	*48.3*	*37.1*	*27.1*	*34.7*	*24.6*
Other......................................	2 852 ..	*43.8*	*58.9*	*57.9*	*68.8*	*63.4*	*83.9*	*86.2*	*106.1*
Sea transport, passenger.......................	2 207 ..	....	....	....	....	....	....	....	....
Sea transport, freight.........................	2 208 ..	....	....	....	....	....	....	....	....
Sea transport, other..........................	2 209 ..	....	....	....	....	....	....	....	....
Air transport, passenger.......................	2 211 ..	....	....	....	....	....	....	....	....
Air transport, freight.........................	2 212 ..	....	....	....	....	....	....	....	....
Air transport, other..........................	2 213 ..	....	....	....	....	....	....	....	....
Other transport, passenger....................	2 215 ..	....	....	....	....	....	....	....	....
Other transport, freight.......................	2 216 ..	....	....	....	....	....	....	....	....
Other transport, other........................	2 217 ..	....	....	....	....	....	....	....	....
Transportation services, debit................	3 205 ..	**−215.6**	**−227.2**	**−197.0**	**−254.1**	**−308.9**	**−460.9**	**−463.5**	**−453.3**
Passenger...................................	3 850 ..	*−3.5*	*−2.8*	*−2.6*	*−2.9*	*−3.0*	*−.7*	....	....
Freight.....................................	3 851 ..	*−211.2*	*−219.9*	*−189.7*	*−249.4*	*−304.2*	*−457.2*	*−459.6*	*−451.7*
Other......................................	3 852 ..	*−.8*	*−4.5*	*−4.7*	*−1.9*	*−1.7*	*−3.0*	*−3.9*	*−1.6*
Sea transport, passenger.......................	3 207 ..	....	....	....	....	....	....	....	....
Sea transport, freight.........................	3 208 ..	....	....	....	....	....	....	....	....
Sea transport, other..........................	3 209 ..	....	....	....	....	....	....	....	....
Air transport, passenger.......................	3 211 ..	....	....	....	....	....	....	....	....
Air transport, freight.........................	3 212 ..	....	....	....	....	....	....	....	....
Air transport, other..........................	3 213 ..	....	....	....	....	....	....	....	....
Other transport, passenger....................	3 215 ..	....	....	....	....	....	....	....	....
Other transport, freight.......................	3 216 ..	....	....	....	....	....	....	....	....
Other transport, other........................	3 217 ..	....	....	....	....	....	....	....	....
Travel, credit.............................	2 236 ..	**56.4**	**83.9**	**67.6**	**46.3**	**86.0**	**69.0**	**56.2**	**72.6**
Business travel...............................	2 237 ..	....	....	....	....	....	....	....	....
Personal travel...............................	2 240 ..	....	....	....	....	....	....	....	....
Travel, debit..............................	3 236 ..	**−32.0**	**−28.9**	**−31.1**	**−37.0**	**−36.6**	**−49.2**	**−52.4**	**−53.9**
Business travel...............................	3 237 ..	....	....	....	....	....	....	....	....
Personal travel...............................	3 240 ..	....	....	....	....	....	....	....	....
Other services, credit......................	2 200 BA	**120.5**	**85.5**	**71.8**	**103.0**	**108.6**	**113.7**	**120.3**	**144.3**
Communications..............................	2 245 ..	....	....	....	....	....	....	....	....
Construction.................................	2 249 ..	....	....	....	....	....	....	....	....
Insurance....................................	2 253 ..	....	....	....	....	....	....	....	....
Financial....................................	2 260 ..	....	....	....	....	....	....	....	....
Computer and information......................	2 262 ..	....	....	....	....	....	....	....	....
Royalties and licence fees......................	2 266 ..	....	....	....	....	....	....	....	....
Other business services........................	2 268 ..	99.1	62.7	50.2	79.9	86.3	84.9	85.8	112.1
Personal, cultural, and recreational..............	2 287 ..	....	....	....	....	....	....	....	....
Government, n.i.e.............................	2 291 ..	21.4	22.8	21.7	23.2	22.3	28.8	34.5	32.1
Other services, debit.......................	3 200 BA	**−172.3**	**−203.6**	**−273.8**	**−271.8**	**−314.3**	**−113.4**	**−107.6**	**−289.8**
Communications..............................	3 245 ..	....	....	....	....	....	....	....	....
Construction.................................	3 249 ..	....	....	....	....	....	....	....	....
Insurance....................................	3 253 ..	....	....	....	....	....	....	....	....
Financial....................................	3 260 ..	....	....	....	....	....	....	....	....
Computer and information......................	3 262 ..	....	....	....	....	....	....	....	....
Royalties and licence fees......................	3 266 ..	....	....	....	....	....	....	....	....
Other business services........................	3 268 ..	−149.9	−185.0	−255.2	−249.2	−282.2	−79.7	−62.6	−243.3
Personal, cultural, and recreational..............	3 287 ..	−5.7	−3.1	−2.5	−6.7	−8.0	−14.8	−20.9	−10.8
Government, n.i.e.............................	3 291 ..	−16.7	−15.5	−16.1	−15.9	−24.1	−18.8	−24.2	−35.7

Table 2 (Continued). STANDARD PRESENTATION, 2003–2010
(Millions of U.S. dollars)

	Code	2003	2004	2005	2006	2007	2008	2009	2010
C. INCOME	4 300	**−741.5**	**−745.4**	**−1,371.7**	**−1,248.4**	**−1,267.2**	**−1,757.6**	**−1,785.4**	**−1,739.5**
Total credit	2 300	*29.4*	*40.4*	*55.5*	*97.8*	*175.9*	*178.7*	*95.7*	*149.0*
Total debit	3 300	*−771.0*	*−785.8*	*−1,427.3*	*−1,346.2*	*−1,443.1*	*−1,936.3*	*−1,881.1*	*−1,888.6*
Compensation of employees, credit	2 310	**26.0**	**36.5**	**43.7**	**50.6**	**81.8**	**55.3**	**55.0**	**116.0**
Compensation of employees, debit	3 310	....	....	....	....	....	....	....	....
Investment income, credit	2 320	**3.4**	**3.9**	**11.8**	**47.1**	**94.1**	**123.4**	**40.7**	**33.0**
Direct investment income	2 330	....	....	....	....	3.7	11.1	8.6	19.1
Dividends and distributed branch profits	2 332	....	....	....	....	....	....	....	....
Reinvested earnings and undistributed branch profits	2 333	....	....	....	....	....	....	....	....
Income on debt (interest)	2 334	....	....	....	....	....	....	....	....
Portfolio investment income	2 339	....	....	....	....	....	....	....	....
Income on equity	2 340	....	....	....	....	....	....	....	....
Income on bonds and notes	2 350	....	....	....	....	....	....	....	....
Income on money market instruments	2 360	....	....	....	....	....	....	....	....
Other investment income	2 370	3.4	3.9	11.8	47.1	90.4	112.3	32.1	13.9
Investment income, debit	3 320	**−771.0**	**−785.8**	**−1,427.3**	**−1,346.2**	**−1,443.1**	**−1,936.3**	**−1,881.1**	**−1,888.6**
Direct investment income	3 330	−751.6	−761.6	−1,402.4	−1,317.0	−1,401.7	−1,902.3	−1,829.2	−1,834.7
Dividends and distributed branch profits	3 332	....	....	....	....	....	....	....	....
Reinvested earnings and undistributed branch profits	3 333	....	....	....	....	....	....	....	....
Income on debt (interest)	3 334	....	....	....	....	....	....	....	....
Portfolio investment income	3 339	....	....	....	....	....	....	....	....
Income on equity	3 340	....	....	....	....	....	....	....	....
Income on bonds and notes	3 350	....	....	....	....	....	....	....	....
Income on money market instruments	3 360	....	....	....	....	....	....	....	....
Other investment income	3 370	−19.3	−24.2	−24.8	−29.2	−41.4	−34.0	−51.9	−53.8
D. CURRENT TRANSFERS	4 379	**95.0**	**133.9**	**173.9**	**122.4**	**206.5**	**311.0**	**437.6**	**241.0**
Credit	2 379	**118.0**	**160.6**	**197.8**	**161.4**	**234.0**	**364.1**	**501.6**	**349.2**
General government	2 380	27.4	26.0	48.6	32.2	35.9	55.0	203.3	80.0
Other sectors	2 390	90.6	134.6	149.1	129.2	198.1	309.1	298.4	269.3
Workers' remittances	2 391	59.3	81.3	87.0	65.7	....	....	....	....
Other current transfers	2 392	31.4	53.3	62.1	63.5	....	....	....	....
Debit	3 379	**−23.0**	**−26.7**	**−23.8**	**−39.0**	**−27.5**	**−53.1**	**−64.1**	**−108.2**
General government	3 380	−.2	−.2	....	....	....	....	....	....
Other sectors	3 390	−22.8	−26.5	−23.8	−39.0	−27.5	−53.1	−64.1	−108.2
Workers' remittances	3 391	−22.8	−24.5	−19.0	−31.7	....	....	....	....
Other current transfers	3 392	....	−2.0	−4.8	−7.4	....	....	....	....
CAPITAL AND FINANCIAL ACCOUNT	4 996	**98.2**	**31.2**	**22.6**	**−169.9**	**−1,055.8**	**115.9**	**340.4**	**563.1**
CAPITAL ACCOUNT	4 994	....	....	....	....	....	....	....	....
Total credit	2 994	....	....	....	....	....	....	....	....
Total debit	3 994	....	....	....	....	....	....	....	....
Capital transfers, credit	2 400	....	....	....	....	....	....	....	....
General government	2 401	....	....	....	....	....	....	....	....
Debt forgiveness	2 402	....	....	....	....	....	....	....	....
Other capital transfers	2 410	....	....	....	....	....	....	....	....
Other sectors	2 430	....	....	....	....	....	....	....	....
Migrants' transfers	2 431	....	....	....	....	....	....	....	....
Debt forgiveness	2 432	....	....	....	....	....	....	....	....
Other capital transfers	2 440	....	....	....	....	....	....	....	....
Capital transfers, debit	3 400	....	....	....	....	....	....	....	....
General government	3 401	....	....	....	....	....	....	....	....
Debt forgiveness	3 402	....	....	....	....	....	....	....	....
Other capital transfers	3 410	....	....	....	....	....	....	....	....
Other sectors	3 430	....	....	....	....	....	....	....	....
Migrants' transfers	3 431	....	....	....	....	....	....	....	....
Debt forgiveness	3 432	....	....	....	....	....	....	....	....
Other capital transfers	3 440	....	....	....	....	....	....	....	....
Nonproduced nonfinancial assets, credit	2 480	....	....	....	....	....	....	....	....
Nonproduced nonfinancial assets, debit	3 480	....	....	....	....	....	....	....	....

2011, International Monetary Fund: *Balance of Payments Statistics Yearbook*

Table 2 (Continued). STANDARD PRESENTATION, 2003–2010
(Millions of U.S. dollars)

	Code	2003	2004	2005	2006	2007	2008	2009	2010
FINANCIAL ACCOUNT	4 995	98.2	31.2	22.6	−169.9	−1,055.8	115.9	340.4	563.1
A. DIRECT INVESTMENT	4 500	251.5	213.5	237.2	278.6	717.3	872.7	1,090.2	910.3
Direct investment abroad	4 505	....	....	....	....	....	....	....	....
Equity capital	4 510	....	....	....	....	....	....	....	....
Claims on affiliated enterprises	4 515	....	....	....	....	....	....	....	....
Liabilities to affiliated enterprises	4 520	....	....	....	....	....	....	....	....
Reinvested earnings	4 525	....	....	....	....	....	....	....	....
Other capital	4 530	....	....	....	....	....	....	....	....
Claims on affiliated enterprises	4 535	....	....	....	....	....	....	....	....
Liabilities to affiliated enterprises	4 540	....	....	....	....	....	....	....	....
Direct investment in Myanmar	4 555	251.5	213.5	237.2	278.6	717.3	872.7	1,090.2	910.3
Equity capital	4 560	251.5	213.5	237.2	278.6	717.3	872.7	1,090.2	910.3
Claims on direct investors	4 565	....	....	....	....	....	....	....	....
Liabilities to direct investors	4 570	....	....	....	....	....	....	....	....
Reinvested earnings	4 575	....	....	....	....	....	....	....	....
Other capital	4 580	....	....	....	....	....	....	....	....
Claims on direct investors	4 585	....	....	....	....	....	....	....	....
Liabilities to direct investors	4 590	....	....	....	....	....	....	....	....
B. PORTFOLIO INVESTMENT	4 600	....	....	....	....	....	....	....	....
Assets	4 602	....	....	....	....	....	....	....	....
Equity securities	4 610	....	....	....	....	....	....	....	....
Monetary authorities	4 611	....	....	....	....	....	....	....	....
General government	4 612	....	....	....	....	....	....	....	....
Banks	4 613	....	....	....	....	....	....	....	....
Other sectors	4 614	....	....	....	....	....	....	....	....
Debt securities	4 619	....	....	....	....	....	....	....	....
Bonds and notes	4 620	....	....	....	....	....	....	....	....
Monetary authorities	4 621	....	....	....	....	....	....	....	....
General government	4 622	....	....	....	....	....	....	....	....
Banks	4 623	....	....	....	....	....	....	....	....
Other sectors	4 624	....	....	....	....	....	....	....	....
Money market instruments	4 630	....	....	....	....	....	....	....	....
Monetary authorities	4 631	....	....	....	....	....	....	....	....
General government	4 632	....	....	....	....	....	....	....	....
Banks	4 633	....	....	....	....	....	....	....	....
Other sectors	4 634	....	....	....	....	....	....	....	....
Liabilities	4 652	....	....	....	....	....	....	....	....
Equity securities	4 660	....	....	....	....	....	....	....	....
Banks	4 663	....	....	....	....	....	....	....	....
Other sectors	4 664	....	....	....	....	....	....	....	....
Debt securities	4 669	....	....	....	....	....	....	....	....
Bonds and notes	4 670	....	....	....	....	....	....	....	....
Monetary authorities	4 671	....	....	....	....	....	....	....	....
General government	4 672	....	....	....	....	....	....	....	....
Banks	4 673	....	....	....	....	....	....	....	....
Other sectors	4 674	....	....	....	....	....	....	....	....
Money market instruments	4 680	....	....	....	....	....	....	....	....
Monetary authorities	4 681	....	....	....	....	....	....	....	....
General government	4 682	....	....	....	....	....	....	....	....
Banks	4 683	....	....	....	....	....	....	....	....
Other sectors	4 684	....	....	....	....	....	....	....	....
C. FINANCIAL DERIVATIVES	4 910	....	....	....	....	....	....	....	....
Monetary authorities	4 911	....	....	....	....	....	....	....	....
General government	4 912	....	....	....	....	....	....	....	....
Banks	4 913	....	....	....	....	....	....	....	....
Other sectors	4 914	....	....	....	....	....	....	....	....
Assets	4 900	....	....	....	....	....	....	....	....
Monetary authorities	4 901	....	....	....	....	....	....	....	....
General government	4 902	....	....	....	....	....	....	....	....
Banks	4 903	....	....	....	....	....	....	....	....
Other sectors	4 904	....	....	....	....	....	....	....	....
Liabilities	4 905	....	....	....	....	....	....	....	....
Monetary authorities	4 906	....	....	....	....	....	....	....	....
General government	4 907	....	....	....	....	....	....	....	....
Banks	4 908	....	....	....	....	....	....	....	....
Other sectors	4 909	....	....	....	....	....	....	....	....

Table 2 (Concluded). STANDARD PRESENTATION, 2003–2010

(Millions of U.S. dollars)

	Code	2003	2004	2005	2006	2007	2008	2009	2010
D. OTHER INVESTMENT	4 700	−114.3	−88.3	−71.1	−25.6	−67.3	130.7	461.0	218.4
Assets	4 703	....	....	....	....	....	....	....	....
Trade credits	4 706	....	....	....	....	....	....	....	....
General government	4 707	....	....	....	....	....	....	....	....
of which: Short-term	4 709	....	....	....	....	....	....	....	....
Other sectors	4 710	....	....	....	....	....	....	....	....
of which: Short-term	4 712	....	....	....	....	....	....	....	....
Loans	4 714	....	....	....	....	....	....	....	....
Monetary authorities	4 715	....	....	....	....	....	....	....	....
of which: Short-term	4 718	....	....	....	....	....	....	....	....
General government	4 719	....	....	....	....	....	....	....	....
of which: Short-term	4 721	....	....	....	....	....	....	....	....
Banks	4 722	....	....	....	....	....	....	....	....
of which: Short-term	4 724	....	....	....	....	....	....	....	....
Other sectors	4 725	....	....	....	....	....	....	....	....
of which: Short-term	4 727	....	....	....	....	....	....	....	....
Currency and deposits	4 730	....	....	....	....	....	....	....	....
Monetary authorities	4 731	....	....	....	....	....	....	....	....
General government	4 732	....	....	....	....	....	....	....	....
Banks	4 733	....	....	....	....	....	....	....	....
Other sectors	4 734	....	....	....	....	....	....	....	....
Other assets	4 736	....	....	....	....	....	....	....	....
Monetary authorities	4 737	....	....	....	....	....	....	....	....
of which: Short-term	4 739	....	....	....	....	....	....	....	....
General government	4 740	....	....	....	....	....	....	....	....
of which: Short-term	4 742	....	....	....	....	....	....	....	....
Banks	4 743	....	....	....	....	....	....	....	....
of which: Short-term	4 745	....	....	....	....	....	....	....	....
Other sectors	4 746	....	....	....	....	....	....	....	....
of which: Short-term	4 748	....	....	....	....	....	....	....	....
Liabilities	4 753	−114.3	−88.3	−71.1	−25.6	−67.3	130.7	461.0	218.4
Trade credits	4 756	....	....	....	....	....	....	....	....
General government	4 757	....	....	....	....	....	....	....	....
of which: Short-term	4 759	....	....	....	....	....	....	....	....
Other sectors	4 760	....	....	....	....	....	....	....	....
of which: Short-term	4 762	....	....	....	....	....	....	....	....
Loans	4 764	−98.4	−87.4	−91.0	−35.5	−20.8	165.0	156.5	230.7
Monetary authorities	4 765	....	....	....	....	....	....	....	....
of which: Use of Fund credit and loans from the Fund	4 766	....	....	....	....	....	....	....	....
of which: Short-term	4 768	....	....	....	....	....	....	....	....
General government	4 769	−91.2	−85.2	−88.1	−31.8	−20.6	165.0	156.5	230.7
of which: Short-term	4 771	....	....	....	....	....	....	....	....
Banks	4 772	....	....	....	....	....	....	....	....
of which: Short-term	4 774	....	....	....	....	....	....	....	....
Other sectors	4 775	−7.2	−2.2	−2.9	−3.6	−.2	....	....	....
of which: Short-term	4 777	....	....	....	....	....	....	....	....
Currency and deposits	4 780	.9	4.0	2.9	3.6	−8.6	.7	−.4	−1.6
Monetary authorities	4 781	....	....	....	....	....	....	....	....
General government	4 782	....	....	....	....	....	....	....	....
Banks	4 783	.9	4.0	2.9	3.6	−8.6	.7	−.4	−1.6
Other sectors	4 784	....	....	....	....	....	....	....	....
Other liabilities	4 786	−16.8	−5.0	17.1	6.2	−37.9	−35.0	304.9	−10.7
Monetary authorities	4 787	−21.2	−13.4	10.5	−8.0	−47.7	−24.3	274.4	−26.7
of which: Short-term	4 789	....	....	....	....	....	....	....	....
General government	4 790	....	....	....	....	....	−3.1	−9.4	−3.2
of which: Short-term	4 792	....	....	....	....	....	....	....	....
Banks	4 793	4.4	8.4	6.6	14.2	9.9	−7.6	39.9	19.3
of which: Short-term	4 795	....	....	....	....	....	....	....	....
Other sectors	4 796	....	....	....	....	....	....	....	....
of which: Short-term	4 798	....	....	....	....	....	....	....	....
E. RESERVE ASSETS	4 802	−38.9	−94.0	−143.6	−422.9	−1,705.8	−887.4	−1,210.8	−565.7
Monetary gold	4 812	....	....	....	....	....	....	....	....
Special drawing rights	4 811	....	.1	−.2	.1	−.2	.3	−109.1	108.6
Reserve position in the Fund	4 810	....	....	....	....	....	....	....	....
Foreign exchange	4 803	15.6	40.1	−144.1	−421.4	−1,702.7	−890.1	−1,099.0	−669.6
Other claims	4 813	−54.6	−134.2	.6	−1.6	−2.9	2.4	−2.8	−4.6
NET ERRORS AND OMISSIONS	4 998	−78.9	−142.7	−610.3	−632.1	−795.6	−1,663.5	−1,426.9	−2,089.9

Table 3. INTERNATIONAL INVESTMENT POSITION (End-period stocks), 2003–2010

(Millions of U.S. dollars)

	Code	2003	2004	2005	2006	2007	2008	2009	2010
ASSETS...	8 995 C.	**665.5**	**792.5**	**890.7**	**1,390.4**	....	....	....	....
Direct investment abroad..........................	8 505 ..	....	....	....	....	....	....	....	....
Equity capital and reinvested earnings..........	8 506 ..	....	....	....	....	....	....	....	....
Claims on affiliated enterprises..............	8 507 ..	....	....	....	....	....	....	....	....
Liabilities to affiliated enterprises...........	8 508 ..	....	....	....	....	....	....	....	....
Other capital...	8 530 ..	....	....	....	....	....	....	....	....
Claims on affiliated enterprises..............	8 535 ..	....	....	....	....	....	....	....	....
Liabilities to affiliated enterprises...........	8 540 ..	....	....	....	....	....	....	....	....
Portfolio investment...............................	8 602 ..	....	....	....	....	....	....	....	....
Equity securities.....................................	8 610 ..	....	....	....	....	....	....	....	....
Monetary authorities............................	8 611 ..	....	....	....	....	....	....	....	....
General government.............................	8 612 ..	....	....	....	....	....	....	....	....
Banks..	8 613 ..	....	....	....	....	....	....	....	....
Other sectors......................................	8 614 ..	....	....	....	....	....	....	....	....
Debt securities.......................................	8 619 ..	....	....	....	....	....	....	....	....
Bonds and notes..................................	8 620 ..	....	....	....	....	....	....	....	....
Monetary authorities.........................	8 621 ..	....	....	....	....	....	....	....	....
General government..........................	8 622 ..	....	....	....	....	....	....	....	....
Banks..	8 623 ..	....	....	....	....	....	....	....	....
Other sectors...................................	8 624 ..	....	....	....	....	....	....	....	....
Money market instruments....................	8 630 ..	....	....	....	....	....	....	....	....
Monetary authorities.........................	8 631 ..	....	....	....	....	....	....	....	....
General government..........................	8 632 ..	....	....	....	....	....	....	....	....
Banks..	8 633 ..	....	....	....	....	....	....	....	....
Other sectors...................................	8 634 ..	....	....	....	....	....	....	....	....
Financial derivatives..............................	8 900 ..	....	....	....	....	....	....	....	....
Monetary authorities...............................	8 901 ..	....	....	....	....	....	....	....	....
General government................................	8 902 ..	....	....	....	....	....	....	....	....
Banks..	8 903 ..	....	....	....	....	....	....	....	....
Other sectors...	8 904 ..	....	....	....	....	....	....	....	....
Other investment..................................	8 703 ..	....	....	....	....	....	....	....	....
Trade credits..	8 706 ..	....	....	....	....	....	....	....	....
General government.............................	8 707 ..	....	....	....	....	....	....	....	....
of which: Short-term.........................	8 709 ..	....	....	....	....	....	....	....	....
Other sectors......................................	8 710 ..	....	....	....	....	....	....	....	....
of which: Short-term.........................	8 712 ..	....	....	....	....	....	....	....	....
Loans..	8 714 ..	....	....	....	....	....	....	....	....
Monetary authorities............................	8 715 ..	....	....	....	....	....	....	....	....
of which: Short-term.........................	8 718 ..	....	....	....	....	....	....	....	....
General government.............................	8 719 ..	....	....	....	....	....	....	....	....
of which: Short-term.........................	8 721 ..	....	....	....	....	....	....	....	....
Banks..	8 722 ..	....	....	....	....	....	....	....	....
of which: Short-term.........................	8 724 ..	....	....	....	....	....	....	....	....
Other sectors......................................	8 725 ..	....	....	....	....	....	....	....	....
of which: Short-term.........................	8 727 ..	....	....	....	....	....	....	....	....
Currency and deposits..............................	8 730 ..	....	....	....	....	....	....	....	....
Monetary authorities............................	8 731 ..	....	....	....	....	....	....	....	....
General government.............................	8 732 ..	....	....	....	....	....	....	....	....
Banks..	8 733 ..	....	....	....	....	....	....	....	....
Other sectors......................................	8 734 ..	....	....	....	....	....	....	....	....
Other assets...	8 736 ..	....	....	....	....	....	....	....	....
Monetary authorities............................	8 737 ..	....	....	....	....	....	....	....	....
of which: Short-term.........................	8 739 ..	....	....	....	....	....	....	....	....
General government.............................	8 740 ..	....	....	....	....	....	....	....	....
of which: Short-term.........................	8 742 ..	....	....	....	....	....	....	....	....
Banks..	8 743 ..	....	....	....	....	....	....	....	....
of which: Short-term.........................	8 745 ..	....	....	....	....	....	....	....	....
Other sectors......................................	8 746 ..	....	....	....	....	....	....	....	....
of which: Short-term.........................	8 748 ..	....	....	....	....	....	....	....	....
Reserve assets.......................................	8 802 ..	**665.5**	**792.5**	**890.7**	**1,390.4**	....	....		....
Monetary gold..	8 812 ..	99.8	104.0	119.0	146.2	....	....		
Special drawing rights..............................	8 811 ..	.1	....	.2	.2	.4	.1	113.3	2.6
Reserve position in the Fund......................	8 810 ..					....	....	....	....
Foreign exchange....................................	8 803 ..	210.1	177.9	765.2	1,235.8	....	....	....	....
Other claims..	8 813 ..	355.5	510.7	6.3	8.2	....	....	....	....

Table 3 (Concluded). INTERNATIONAL INVESTMENT POSITION (End-period stocks), 2003–2010

(Millions of U.S. dollars)

	Code	2003	2004	2005	2006	2007	2008	2009	2010
LIABILITIES	8 995 D.	**10,101.4**	**10,688.3**	**10,081.1**	**10,868.9**	....	....	....	....
Direct investment in Myanmar	8 555 ..	**4,392.6**	**4,814.6**	**4,714.9**	**5,247.4**	....	....	....	....
Equity capital and reinvested earnings	8 556 ..	4,392.6	4,814.6	4,714.9	5,247.4	....	....	....	....
Claims on direct investors	8 557 ..	....	....	....	5,247.4	....	....	....	....
Liabilities to direct investors	8 558 ..	4,392.6	4,814.6	4,714.9	....	....	....	....	....
Other capital	8 580 ..								
Claims on direct investors	8 585 ..	....	....						
Liabilities to direct investors	8 590 ..	....	....						
Portfolio investment	8 652 ..	....	....	....	....	....	....	....	....
Equity securities	8 660 ..	....	....	....	....				
Banks	8 663 ..	....	....	....	....				
Other sectors	8 664 ..	....	....	....	....				
Debt securities	8 669 ..	....	....	....	....				
Bonds and notes	8 670 ..	....	....	....	....				
Monetary authorities	8 671 ..	....	....	....	....				
General government	8 672 ..	....	....	....	....				
Banks	8 673 ..	....	....	....	....				
Other sectors	8 674 ..	....	....	....	....				
Money market instruments	8 680 ..	....	....	....	....				
Monetary authorities	8 681 ..	....	....	....	....				
General government	8 682 ..	....	....	....	....				
Banks	8 683 ..	....	....	....	....				
Other sectors	8 684 ..	....	....	....	....				
Financial derivatives	8 905 ..	....	....	....	....	....	....	....	....
Monetary authorities	8 906 ..	....	....	....	....				
General government	8 907 ..	....	....	....	....				
Banks	8 908 ..	....	....	....	....				
Other sectors	8 909 ..	....	....	....	....				
Other investment	8 753 ..	**5,708.7**	**5,873.6**	**5,366.3**	**5,621.5**	....	....	....	....
Trade credits	8 756 ..	....	....	....	....				
General government	8 757 ..	....	....	....	....				
of which: Short-term	8 759 ..	....	....	....	....				
Other sectors	8 760 ..	....	....	....	....				
of which: Short-term	8 762 ..	....	....	....	....				
Loans	8 764 ..	5,365.0	5,515.4	5,016.8	5,243.5	....	....		
Monetary authorities	8 765 ..	....	....	....	....				
of which: Use of Fund credit and loans from the Fund	8 766 ..	....	....	....	....				
of which: Short-term	8 768 ..	....	....	....	....				
General government	8 769 ..	....	....	....	....				
of which: Short-term	8 771 ..	....	....	....	....				
Banks	8 772 ..	....	....	....	....				
of which: Short-term	8 774 ..	....	....	....	....				
Other sectors	8 775 ..	....	....	....	....				
of which: Short-term	8 777 ..	....	....	....	....				
Currency and deposits	8 780 ..	2.5	6.8	9.0	13.3	....	....		
Monetary authorities	8 781 ..	....	....	....	....				
General government	8 782 ..	....	....	....	....				
Banks	8 783 ..	2.5	6.8	9.0	13.3				
Other sectors	8 784 ..	....	....	....	....				
Other liabilities	8 786 ..	341.2	351.4	340.5	364.7	....			
Monetary authorities	8 787 ..	315.9	316.1	301.6	309.3	....			
of which: Short-term	8 789 ..	....	....	....	....				
General government	8 790 ..	....	....	....	....				
of which: Short-term	8 792 ..	....	....	....	....				
Banks	8 793 ..	25.3	35.3	38.9	55.4				
of which: Short-term	8 795 ..	....	....	....	....				
Other sectors	8 796 ..	....	....	....	....				
of which: Short-term	8 798 ..	....	....	....	....				
NET INTERNATIONAL INVESTMENT POSITION	8 995 ..	**–9,435.8**	**–9,895.7**	**–9,190.4**	**–9,478.5**	....	....	....	....
Conversion rates: kyats per U.S. dollar (end of period)	0 102 ..	**5.7259**	**5.4787**	**5.9530**	**5.6558**	**5.3842**	**5.5240**	**5.4274**	**5.5249**

Table 1. ANALYTIC PRESENTATION, 2003–2010

(Millions of U.S. dollars)

	Code	2003	2004	2005	2006	2007	2008	2009	2010
A. Current Account[1]	4 993 Z.	**204.4**	**384.5**	**266.8**	**1,015.8**	**692.6**	**44.9**	**−161.0**	**−314.2**
Goods: exports f.o.b.	2 100 ..	1,262.0	1,827.5	2,069.9	2,646.6	2,921.6	3,116.4	3,535.3	4,129.0
Goods: imports f.o.b.	3 100 ..	−1,726.0	−2,110.3	−2,326.2	−2,544.2	−3,101.6	−3,833.2	−4,518.8	−4,914.7
Balance on Goods	4 100 ..	*−464.0*	*−282.8*	*−256.3*	*102.4*	*−180.0*	*−716.9*	*−983.5*	*−785.7*
Services: credit	2 200 ..	414.5	475.4	412.6	525.7	598.6	554.7	521.5	853.3
Services: debit	3 200 ..	−276.3	−420.2	−368.8	−429.7	−513.6	−588.7	−609.0	−705.1
Balance on Goods and Services	4 991 ..	*−325.9*	*−227.7*	*−212.4*	*198.4*	*−95.0*	*−750.9*	*−1,071.0*	*−637.5*
Income: credit	2 300 ..	184.8	217.0	225.4	256.0	273.2	303.1	339.3	228.5
Income: debit	3 300 ..	−53.6	−212.1	−352.6	−318.9	−431.5	−457.6	−409.3	−792.4
Balance on Goods, Services, and Income	4 992 ..	*−194.6*	*−222.8*	*−339.6*	*135.6*	*−253.3*	*−905.4*	*−1,141.0*	*−1,201.5*
Current transfers: credit	2 379 Z.	426.2	642.1	651.1	925.6	998.3	1,009.3	1,063.9	974.8
Current transfers: debit	3 379 ..	−27.2	−34.9	−44.7	−45.4	−52.3	−59.0	−83.8	−87.5
B. Capital Account[1]	4 994 Z.	**68.3**	**77.2**	**79.6**	**83.3**	**83.4**	**77.2**	**66.7**	**112.5**
Capital account: credit	2 994 Z.	68.6	77.6	80.2	83.8	83.9	77.6	75.1	122.3
Capital account: debit	3 994 ..	−.4	−.5	−.5	−.5	−.5	−.4	−8.3	−9.8
Total, Groups A Plus B	4 981 ..	*272.7*	*461.6*	*346.4*	*1,099.1*	*776.0*	*122.1*	*−94.2*	*−201.7*
C. Financial Account[1]	4 995 W.	**−581.9**	**−779.0**	**−874.8**	**−1,525.3**	**−1,467.0**	**−898.1**	**−671.9**	**−470.4**
Direct investment abroad	4 505 ..	11.5	22.7	12.3	12.6	−2.7	−6.2	3.0	−4.4
Direct investment in Namibia	4 555 Z.	33.3	88.2	166.1	−30.9	169.9	409.0	490.2	795.9
Portfolio investment assets	4 602 ..	−612.3	−825.5	−1,052.8	−1,133.0	−1,482.9	−1,023.4	−533.2	−695.1
Equity securities	4 610 ..	−400.9	−500.4	−754.2	−785.7	−1,210.6	−753.7	−495.5	−400.6
Debt securities	4 619 ..	−211.5	−325.0	−298.7	−347.3	−272.3	−269.7	−37.7	−294.4
Portfolio investment liabilities	4 652 Z.	3.9	4.5	5.1	4.7	4.5	3.9	−58.7	4.4
Equity securities	4 660 ..	3.9	4.5	5.1	4.7	4.5	3.9	3.7	4.4
Debt securities	4 669 Z.	....	....	....	....	....	....	−62.4	....
Financial derivatives	4 910 ..	....	....	....	....	....	....	.1	....
Financial derivatives assets	4 900 ..	....	....	....	....	....	....	.1	....
Financial derivatives liabilities	4 905 ..	....	....	....	....	....	....	....	....
Other investment assets	4 703 ..	23.3	44.6	43.2	−353.7	136.2	−111.8	−401.1	−470.2
Monetary authorities	4 701 ..	....	....	....	....	....	....	−2.7	....
General government	4 704 ..	−4.3	−6.2	−6.3	−5.9	−5.6	−4.9	−4.7	−5.5
Banks	4 705 ..	28.1	59.6	51.1	−356.2	191.4	−44.2	−394.3	−535.8
Other sectors	4 728 ..	−.5	−8.8	−1.6	8.3	−49.6	−62.8	.6	71.1
Other investment liabilities	4 753 W.	−41.5	−113.6	−48.6	−25.0	−292.0	−169.5	−172.1	−101.0
Monetary authorities	4 753 WA	....	....	....	....	....	....	199.1	−7.5
General government	4 753 ZB	−7.3	−4.5	−16.5	−11.5	−19.2	−18.2	−73.4	21.6
Banks	4 753 ZC	....	....	.9	51.6	−2.7	−17.9	−61.6	.1
Other sectors	4 753 ZD	−34.2	−109.1	−32.9	−65.1	−270.1	−133.5	−236.2	−115.2
Total, Groups A Through C	4 983 ..	*−309.2*	*−317.4*	*−528.4*	*−426.2*	*−691.0*	*−776.0*	*−766.1*	*−672.1*
D. Net Errors and Omissions	4 998 ..	**−88.8**	**115.3**	**127.9**	**121.6**	**490.5**	**676.1**	**186.3**	**−378.9**
Total, Groups A Through D	4 984 ..	*−398.1*	*−202.1*	*−400.5*	*−304.5*	*−200.5*	*−99.9*	*−579.8*	*−1,051.0*
E. Reserves and Related Items	4 802 A.	**398.1**	**202.1**	**400.5**	**304.5**	**200.5**	**99.9**	**579.8**	**1,051.0**
Reserve assets	4 802 ..	107.2	14.2	−1.1	−163.1	−570.8	−766.3	−119.0	529.1
Use of Fund credit and loans	4 766 ..	....	....	....	....	....	....	....	....
Exceptional financing	4 920 ..	290.8	187.9	401.6	467.6	771.4	866.2	698.8	521.9
Conversion rates: Namibia dollars per U.S. dollar	0 101 ..	**7.565**	**6.460**	**6.359**	**6.772**	**7.045**	**8.261**	**8.474**	**7.321**

[1] Excludes components that have been classified in the categories of Group E.

Table 2. STANDARD PRESENTATION, 2003–2010

(Millions of U.S. dollars)

	Code	2003	2004	2005	2006	2007	2008	2009	2010
CURRENT ACCOUNT...........................	4 993 ..	**265.7**	**446.3**	**333.4**	**1,081.7**	**747.0**	**224.7**	**119.9**	**30.5**
A. GOODS.........................	4 100 ..	**−464.0**	**−282.8**	**−256.3**	**102.4**	**−180.0**	**−716.9**	**−983.5**	**−785.7**
Credit..........................	2 100 ..	**1,262.0**	**1,827.5**	**2,069.9**	**2,646.6**	**2,921.6**	**3,116.4**	**3,535.3**	**4,129.0**
General merchandise: exports f.o.b.	2 110 ..	1,262.0	1,827.5	2,069.9	2,646.6	2,921.6	3,116.4	3,535.3	4,129.0
Goods for processing: exports f.o.b.	2 150 ..	....	....	....	....	....	....	....	....
Repairs on goods..........................	2 160 ..	....	....	....	....	....	....	....	....
Goods procured in ports by carriers..........	2 170 ..	....	....	....	....	....	....	....	....
Nonmonetary gold..........................	2 180 ..	....	....	....	....	....	....	....	....
Debit..........................	3 100 ..	**−1,726.0**	**−2,110.3**	**−2,326.2**	**−2,544.2**	**−3,101.6**	**−3,833.2**	**−4,518.8**	**−4,914.7**
General merchandise: imports f.o.b.	3 110 ..	−1,726.0	−2,110.3	−2,326.2	−2,544.2	−3,101.6	−3,833.2	−4,518.8	−4,914.7
Goods for processing: imports f.o.b.	3 150 ..	....	....	....	....	....	....	....	....
Repairs on goods..........................	3 160 ..	....	....	....	....	....	....	....	....
Goods procured in ports by carriers..........	3 170 ..	....	....	....	....	....	....	....	....
Nonmonetary gold..........................	3 180 ..	....	....	....	....	....	....	....	....
B. SERVICES.........................	4 200 ..	**138.2**	**55.2**	**43.8**	**96.0**	**85.0**	**−34.0**	**−87.5**	**148.2**
Total credit..........................	2 200 ..	*414.5*	*475.4*	*412.6*	*525.7*	*598.6*	*554.7*	*521.5*	*853.3*
Total debit..........................	3 200 ..	*−276.3*	*−420.2*	*−368.8*	*−429.7*	*−513.6*	*−588.7*	*−609.0*	*−705.1*
Transportation services, credit..........	2 205 ..	**54.1**	**25.5**	**22.5**	**101.5**	**119.8**	**115.1**	**117.0**	**136.6**
Passenger..........................	2 850 ..	*49.6*	*20.8*	*14.1*	*92.4*	*108.4*	*101.6*	*106.0*	*121.4*
Freight..........................	2 851 ..	....	....	....	....	....	....	....	....
Other..........................	2 852 ..	*4.5*	*4.8*	*8.4*	*9.1*	*11.4*	*13.5*	*11.0*	*15.2*
Sea transport, passenger..........	2 207 ..	....	....	....	....	....	....	....	....
Sea transport, freight..........	2 208 ..	....	....	....	....	....	....	....	....
Sea transport, other..........	2 209 ..	....	....	....	....	....	....	....	....
Air transport, passenger..........	2 211 ..	49.6	20.8	14.1	92.4	108.4	101.6	106.0	121.4
Air transport, freight..........	2 212 ..	....	....	....	....	....	....	....	....
Air transport, other..........	2 213 ..	4.5	4.8	8.4	9.1	11.4	13.5	11.0	15.2
Other transport, passenger..........	2 215 ..	....	....	....	....	....	....	....	....
Other transport, freight..........	2 216 ..	....	....	....	....	....	....	....	....
Other transport, other..........	2 217 ..	....	....	....	....	....	....	....	....
Transportation services, debit..........	3 205 ..	**−61.1**	**−135.5**	**−130.7**	**−149.8**	**−241.0**	**−237.3**	**−220.4**	**−223.3**
Passenger..........................	3 850 ..	....	....	....	....	....	....	....	....
Freight..........................	3 851 ..	*−61.1*	*−135.5*	*−130.7*	*−149.8*	*−241.0*	*−237.3*	*−220.4*	*−223.3*
Other..........................	3 852 ..	....	....	....	....	....	....	....	....
Sea transport, passenger..........	3 207 ..	....	....	....	....	....	....	....	....
Sea transport, freight..........	3 208 ..	−15.3	−33.9	−32.7	−37.4	−60.3	−59.3	−55.1	−55.8
Sea transport, other..........	3 209 ..	....	....	....	....	....	....	....	....
Air transport, passenger..........	3 211 ..	....	....	....	....	....	....	....	....
Air transport, freight..........	3 212 ..	−15.3	−33.9	−32.7	−37.4	−60.3	−59.3	−55.1	−55.8
Air transport, other..........	3 213 ..	....	....	....	....	....	....	....	....
Other transport, passenger..........	3 215 ..	....	....	....	....	....	....	....	....
Other transport, freight..........	3 216 ..	−30.6	−67.8	−65.4	−74.9	−120.5	−118.6	−110.2	−111.6
Other transport, other..........	3 217 ..	....	....	....	....	....	....	....	....
Travel, credit..........................	2 236 ..	**332.5**	**404.8**	**349.0**	**381.3**	**434.1**	**382.5**	**363.5**	**439.0**
Business travel..........................	2 237 ..	81.5	89.9	89.4	60.7	48.6	49.3	49.0	56.1
Personal travel..........................	2 240 ..	251.0	314.9	259.6	320.6	385.5	333.2	314.5	383.0
Travel, debit..........................	3 236 ..	**−101.0**	**−122.8**	**−108.2**	**−118.3**	**−132.2**	**−114.3**	**−108.8**	**−144.8**
Business travel..........................	3 237 ..	−12.2	−13.5	−13.4	−9.1	−7.3	−6.4	−6.2	−7.1
Personal travel..........................	3 240 ..	−88.8	−109.3	−94.8	−109.2	−124.9	−107.9	−102.6	−137.7
Other services, credit..........................	2 200 BA	**27.9**	**45.0**	**41.1**	**42.8**	**44.8**	**57.1**	**41.0**	**277.6**
Communications..........................	2 245 ..	8.5	15.5	16.8	15.7	15.0	12.9	12.6	14.2
Construction..........................	2 249 ..	....	....	....	....	....	....	....	....
Insurance..........................	2 253 ..	....	....	.1	1.7	5.1	3.2	2.8	5.7
Financial..........................	2 260 ..	....	....	....	....	....	15.5	2.5	2.7
Computer and information..........................	2 262 ..	....	.1	....	1.2	1.2	.1	.1	.4
Royalties and licence fees..........................	2 266 ..	....	....	....	....	....	....	....	....
Other business services..........................	2 268 ..	3.4	9.7	2.4	4.0	4.2	8.8	6.8	236.0
Personal, cultural, and recreational..........................	2 287 ..	....	....	....	....	....	....	....	....
Government, n.i.e...........................	2 291 ..	16.0	19.8	21.7	20.2	19.3	16.7	16.3	18.6
Other services, debit..........................	3 200 BA	**−114.2**	**−161.9**	**−129.9**	**−161.6**	**−140.3**	**−237.1**	**−279.8**	**−337.0**
Communications..........................	3 245 ..	−.2	−.3	−.3	−.3	−.3	−.2	−.2	....
Construction..........................	3 249 ..	−2.7	−4.4	−3.9	−24.6	−9.0	−23.7	−98.2	−52.9
Insurance..........................	3 253 ..	−17.5	−17.7	−9.4	−18.8	−27.0	−17.8	−25.8	−33.2
Financial..........................	3 260 ..	−5.4	−3.1	−9.5	−4.4	−4.9	−4.8	−.9	−15.0
Computer and information..........................	3 262 ..	−12.3	−14.6	−13.1	−21.1	−15.5	−19.1	−30.4	−31.4
Royalties and licence fees..........................	3 266 ..	−3.6	−3.2	−1.7	−3.0	−1.9	−15.2	−5.8	−7.6
Other business services..........................	3 268 ..	−65.1	−109.5	−82.7	−80.6	−73.2	−149.0	−111.5	−189.2
Personal, cultural, and recreational..........................	3 287 ..	....	....	....	....	....	....	....	....
Government, n.i.e...........................	3 291 ..	−7.5	−9.2	−9.3	−8.8	−8.4	−7.3	−7.1	−7.7

Table 2 (Continued). STANDARD PRESENTATION, 2003–2010

(Millions of U.S. dollars)

	Code	2003	2004	2005	2006	2007	2008	2009	2010
C. INCOME	4 300	**131.3**	**4.9**	**−127.2**	**−62.9**	**−158.4**	**−154.5**	**−70.0**	**−563.9**
Total credit	2 300	*184.8*	*217.0*	*225.4*	*256.0*	*273.2*	*303.1*	*339.3*	*228.5*
Total debit	3 300	*−53.6*	*−212.1*	*−352.6*	*−318.9*	*−431.5*	*−457.6*	*−409.3*	*−792.4*
Compensation of employees, credit	2 310	**7.0**	**8.7**	**10.5**	**9.9**	**9.5**	**8.2**	**8.0**	**9.3**
Compensation of employees, debit	3 310	**−11.1**	**−12.9**	**−14.1**	**−15.7**	**−11.8**	**−39.1**	**−12.3**	**−28.2**
Investment income, credit	2 320	**177.8**	**208.3**	**214.9**	**246.1**	**263.7**	**294.9**	**331.3**	**219.2**
Direct investment income	2 330	−.5	1.4	7.8	.7	.8	5.7	.1	2.5
Dividends and distributed branch profits	2 332	.2	.3	.3	.2	.2	.2	.2	....
Reinvested earnings and undistributed branch profits	2 333	−1.8	−2.2	2.1	−1.3	−.5	2.6	−1.2	1.2
Income on debt (interest)	2 334	1.1	3.4	5.5	1.7	1.1	2.9	1.2	1.2
Portfolio investment income	2 339	139.4	165.0	163.9	207.6	204.3	202.9	176.3	148.6
Income on equity	2 340	80.8	84.0	88.0	145.0	134.8	111.9	92.2	75.5
Income on bonds and notes	2 350	2.8	2.8	3.4	3.1	3.0	2.6	2.0	2.2
Income on money market instruments	2 360	55.8	78.2	72.5	59.6	66.6	88.4	82.1	71.0
Other investment income	2 370	38.9	41.9	43.2	37.8	58.6	86.3	154.9	68.1
Investment income, debit	3 320	**−42.5**	**−199.2**	**−338.5**	**−303.2**	**−419.8**	**−418.5**	**−397.0**	**−764.2**
Direct investment income	3 330	2.7	−143.5	−285.2	−257.3	−369.5	−372.6	−352.2	−719.9
Dividends and distributed branch profits	3 332	−64.8	−68.8	−73.6	−96.0	−183.8	−247.2	−202.0	−205.7
Reinvested earnings and undistributed branch profits	3 333	69.8	−70.0	−206.3	−156.2	−185.8	−135.6	−157.5	−492.1
Income on debt (interest)	3 334	−2.4	−4.7	−5.3	−5.1	.1	10.1	7.3	−22.1
Portfolio investment income	3 339	−11.0	−23.6	−25.4	−24.9	−24.2	−20.8	−20.5	−25.5
Income on equity	3 340	....	....	....	−.6	−.8	−.7	−.7	−.5
Income on bonds and notes	3 350	−10.0	−21.5	−22.5	−21.7	−20.8	−18.0	−17.7	−20.2
Income on money market instruments	3 360	−1.0	−2.1	−2.9	−2.6	−2.5	−2.2	−2.1	−4.7
Other investment income	3 370	−34.2	−32.1	−27.9	−21.1	−26.1	−25.1	−24.3	−18.8
D. CURRENT TRANSFERS	4 379	**460.3**	**669.1**	**673.0**	**946.1**	**1,000.3**	**1,130.1**	**1,260.9**	**1,231.9**
Credit	2 379	**487.5**	**703.9**	**717.7**	**991.5**	**1,052.7**	**1,189.1**	**1,344.7**	**1,319.4**
General government	2 380	462.1	676.8	692.0	964.3	1,029.7	1,168.4	1,324.9	1,299.5
Other sectors	2 390	25.4	27.1	25.8	27.2	22.9	20.7	19.8	20.0
Workers' remittances	2 391	4.8	5.9	7.1	6.5	6.2	5.4	5.3	6.0
Other current transfers	2 392	20.6	21.2	18.7	20.7	16.7	15.3	14.5	14.0
Debit	3 379	**−27.2**	**−34.9**	**−44.7**	**−45.4**	**−52.3**	**−59.0**	**−83.8**	**−87.5**
General government	3 380	−23.0	−30.0	−39.9	−40.8	−47.9	−55.2	−80.1	−83.1
Other sectors	3 390	−4.2	−4.8	−4.8	−4.6	−4.4	−3.8	−3.7	−4.4
Workers' remittances	3 391	−3.6	−4.2	−4.2	−4.0	−3.8	−3.3	−3.2	−3.8
Other current transfers	3 392	−.5	−.6	−.6	−.6	−.6	−.5	−.5	−.5
CAPITAL AND FINANCIAL ACCOUNT	4 996	**−176.9**	**−561.6**	**−461.3**	**−1,203.3**	**−1,237.5**	**−900.8**	**−306.2**	**348.4**
CAPITAL ACCOUNT	4 994	**68.3**	**77.2**	**79.6**	**83.3**	**83.4**	**77.2**	**66.7**	**112.5**
Total credit	2 994	*68.6*	*77.6*	*80.2*	*83.8*	*83.9*	*77.6*	*75.1*	*122.3*
Total debit	3 994	*−.4*	*−.5*	*−.5*	*−.5*	*−.5*	*−.4*	*−8.3*	*−9.8*
Capital transfers, credit	2 400	**68.6**	**77.6**	**80.2**	**83.8**	**83.9**	**77.6**	**75.1**	**122.3**
General government	2 401	65.1	73.6	76.0	80.0	80.2	74.4	72.0	118.5
Debt forgiveness	2 402	....	....	....	....	....	....	....	....
Other capital transfers	2 410	65.1	73.6	76.0	80.0	80.2	74.4	72.0	118.5
Other sectors	2 430	3.5	4.0	4.1	3.8	3.7	3.2	3.1	3.8
Migrants' transfers	2 431	.4	.6	.5	.5	.5	.4	.4	.5
Debt forgiveness	2 432	....	....	....	....	....	....	....	....
Other capital transfers	2 440	3.0	3.4	3.6	3.4	3.2	2.8	2.7	3.3
Capital transfers, debit	3 400	**−.4**	**−.5**	**−.5**	**−.5**	**−.5**	**−.4**	**−8.3**	**−9.8**
General government	3 401	....	....	....	....	....	....	−7.9	−9.3
Debt forgiveness	3 402	....	....	....	....	....	....	....	....
Other capital transfers	3 410	....	....	....	....	....	....	−7.9	−9.3
Other sectors	3 430	−.4	−.5	−.5	−.5	−.5	−.4	−.4	−.5
Migrants' transfers	3 431	−.4	−.5	−.5	−.5	−.5	−.4	−.4	−.5
Debt forgiveness	3 432	....	....	....	....	....	....	....	....
Other capital transfers	3 440	....	....	....	....	....	....	....	....
Nonproduced nonfinancial assets, credit	2 480	....	....	....	....	....	....	....	....
Nonproduced nonfinancial assets, debit	3 480	....	....	....	....	....	....	....	....

Table 2 (Continued). STANDARD PRESENTATION, 2003–2010

(Millions of U.S. dollars)

	Code	2003	2004	2005	2006	2007	2008	2009	2010
FINANCIAL ACCOUNT	4 995	−245.1	−638.7	−540.9	−1,286.6	−1,320.8	−978.0	−372.9	236.0
A. DIRECT INVESTMENT	4 500	157.6	246.1	403.1	403.5	718.5	742.6	528.1	802.7
Direct investment abroad	4 505	11.5	22.7	12.3	12.6	−2.7	−6.2	3.0	−4.4
Equity capital	4 510	1.2	1.2	1.5	5.4	−2.8	.3	....	−2.8
Claims on affiliated enterprises	4 515	1.2	1.2	1.5	5.4	−2.8	.3	....	−2.8
Liabilities to affiliated enterprises	4 520	....	....	....	....	....	....	....	....
Reinvested earnings	4 525	1.8	2.2	−2.1	1.3	.5	−2.6	1.2	−1.2
Other capital	4 530	8.6	19.2	12.8	5.9	−.5	−3.9	1.7	−.4
Claims on affiliated enterprises	4 535	8.6	19.2	12.8	5.9	−.5	−3.9	1.7	−.4
Liabilities to affiliated enterprises	4 540	....	....	....	....	....	....	....	....
Direct investment in Namibia	4 555	146.1	223.4	390.8	391.0	721.3	748.8	525.1	807.1
Equity capital	4 560	111.3	133.3	222.9	420.1	549.6	338.4	33.5	9.6
Claims on direct investors	4 565	....	....	....	....	....	....	....	....
Liabilities to direct investors	4 570	111.3	133.3	222.9	420.1	549.6	338.4	33.5	9.6
Reinvested earnings	4 575	−69.8	70.0	206.3	156.2	185.8	135.6	157.5	492.1
Other capital	4 580	104.7	20.0	−38.3	−185.3	−14.2	274.9	334.1	305.4
Claims on direct investors	4 585	81.0	−.2	−1.9	−218.8	51.5	−.9	9.7	30.8
Liabilities to direct investors	4 590	23.7	20.2	−36.4	33.5	−65.7	275.8	324.4	274.5
B. PORTFOLIO INVESTMENT	4 600	−635.2	−845.4	−1,045.6	−1,125.8	−1,476.6	−1,018.2	−590.7	−689.1
Assets	4 602	−612.3	−825.5	−1,052.8	−1,133.0	−1,482.9	−1,023.4	−533.2	−695.1
Equity securities	4 610	−400.9	−500.4	−754.2	−785.7	−1,210.6	−753.7	−495.5	−400.6
Monetary authorities	4 611	....	....	....	....	....	....	....	....
General government	4 612	....	....	....	....	....	....	....	....
Banks	4 613	....	....	....	....	....	....	−.4	−4.4
Other sectors	4 614	−400.9	−500.4	−754.2	−785.7	−1,210.6	−753.7	−495.1	−396.3
Debt securities	4 619	−211.5	−325.0	−298.7	−347.3	−272.3	−269.7	−37.7	−294.4
Bonds and notes	4 620	....	....	....	....	....	....	−7.2	24.9
Monetary authorities	4 621	....	....	....	....	....	....	....	....
General government	4 622	....	....	....	....	....	....	....	....
Banks	4 623	....	....	....	....	....	....	−7.2	24.9
Other sectors	4 624	....	....	....	....	....	....	....	....
Money market instruments	4 630	−211.5	−325.0	−298.7	−347.3	−272.3	−269.7	−30.5	−319.3
Monetary authorities	4 631	....	....	....	....	....	....	....	....
General government	4 632	....	....	....	....	....	....	....	....
Banks	4 633	....	....	....	....	....	....	....	24.9
Other sectors	4 634	−211.5	−325.0	−298.7	−347.3	−272.3	−269.7	−30.5	−344.2
Liabilities	4 652	−22.9	−19.9	7.3	7.1	6.3	5.2	−57.5	6.0
Equity securities	4 660	3.9	4.5	5.1	4.7	4.5	3.9	3.7	4.4
Banks	4 663	.1	.1	.1	.1	.1	.1	....	....
Other sectors	4 664	3.8	4.4	4.9	4.6	4.4	3.8	3.7	4.4
Debt securities	4 669	−26.8	−24.5	2.2	2.4	1.8	1.3	−61.2	1.6
Bonds and notes	4 670	−26.8	−24.5	2.2	2.4	1.8	1.3	−61.2	1.6
Monetary authorities	4 671	....	....	....	....	....	....	....	....
General government	4 672	−26.8	−24.5	2.2	2.4	1.8	1.3	1.3	1.6
Banks	4 673	....	....	....	....	....	....	−62.4	....
Other sectors	4 674	....	....	....	....	....	....	....	....
Money market instruments	4 680	....	....	....	....	....	....	....	....
Monetary authorities	4 681	....	....	....	....	....	....	....	....
General government	4 682	....	....	....	....	....	....	....	....
Banks	4 683	....	....	....	....	....	....	....	....
Other sectors	4 684	....	....	....	....	....	....	....	....
C. FINANCIAL DERIVATIVES	4 910	....	....	....	....	....	....	.1	....
Monetary authorities	4 911	....	....	....	....	....	....	....	....
General government	4 912	....	....	....	....	....	....	....	....
Banks	4 913	....	....	....	....	....	....	.1	....
Other sectors	4 914	....	....	....	....	....	....	....	....
Assets	4 900	....	....	....	....	....	....	.1	....
Monetary authorities	4 901	....	....	....	....	....	....	....	....
General government	4 902	....	....	....	....	....	....	....	....
Banks	4 903	....	....	....	....	....	....	.1	....
Other sectors	4 904	....	....	....	....	....	....	....	....
Liabilities	4 905	....	....	....	....	....	....	....	....
Monetary authorities	4 906	....	....	....	....	....	....	....	....
General government	4 907	....	....	....	....	....	....	....	....
Banks	4 908	....	....	....	....	....	....	....	....
Other sectors	4 909	....	....	....	....	....	....	....	....

Table 2 (Concluded). STANDARD PRESENTATION, 2003–2010

(Millions of U.S. dollars)

	Code	2003	2004	2005	2006	2007	2008	2009	2010
D. OTHER INVESTMENT	4 700 ..	**125.3**	**−53.6**	**102.6**	**−401.3**	**8.1**	**63.9**	**−191.4**	**−406.8**
Assets	4 703 ..	**23.3**	**44.6**	**43.2**	**−353.7**	**136.2**	**−111.8**	**−401.1**	**−470.2**
Trade credits	4 706 ..	....	....	....	....	....	....	....	....
General government	4 707 ..	....	....	....	....	....	....	....	....
of which: Short-term	4 709 ..	....	....	....	....	....	....	....	....
Other sectors	4 710 ..	....	....	....	....	....	....	....	....
of which: Short-term	4 712 ..	....	....	....	....	....	....	....	....
Loans	4 714 ..	4.4	24.5	37.3	−6.1	−11.5	−71.5	−216.5	−512.5
Monetary authorities	4 715 ..	....	....	....	....	....	....	−2.7	....
of which: Short-term	4 718 ..	....	....	....	....	....	....	....	....
General government	4 719 ..	....	....	....	....	....	....	....	....
of which: Short-term	4 721 ..	....	....	....	....	....	....	....	....
Banks	4 722 ..	6.0	6.9	14.5	−1.6	36.5	−8.6	−217.4	−556.5
of which: Short-term	4 724 ..	*5.2*	*−10.9*	*18.3*	*−2.7*	*36.0*	*−6.7*	*−148.5*	*−499.0*
Other sectors	4 725 ..	−1.6	17.6	22.8	−4.6	−48.0	−62.9	3.7	44.0
of which: Short-term	4 727 ..	*−1.6*	*17.6*	*22.8*	*−4.6*	*−48.0*	*−62.9*	*3.7*	*44.0*
Currency and deposits	4 730 ..	21.7	53.3	35.2	−357.1	152.0	−38.2	−177.5	41.3
Monetary authorities	4 731 ..	....	....	....	....	....	....	....	....
General government	4 732 ..	....	....	....	....	....	....	....	....
Banks	4 733 ..	22.3	54.0	36.0	−356.4	152.7	−37.6	−176.9	18.9
Other sectors	4 734 ..	−.6	−.7	−.8	−.7	−.7	−.6	−.6	22.4
Other assets	4 736 ..	−2.9	−33.1	−29.3	9.5	−4.3	−2.2	−7.2	1.1
Monetary authorities	4 737 ..	....	....	....	....	....	....	....	....
of which: Short-term	4 739 ..	....	....	....	....	....	....	....	....
General government	4 740 ..	−4.3	−6.2	−6.3	−5.9	−5.6	−4.9	−4.7	−5.5
of which: Short-term	4 742 ..	....	....	....	....	....	....	....	....
Banks	4 743 ..	−.3	−1.2	.6	1.8	2.3	2.0	....	1.9
of which: Short-term	4 745 ..	*−.3*	*−1.2*	*.6*	*1.8*	*2.3*	*2.0*	....	*1.9*
Other sectors	4 746 ..	1.7	−25.7	−23.7	13.6	−.9	.7	−2.5	4.7
of which: Short-term	4 748 ..	....	....	....	....	....	....	....	....
Liabilities	4 753 ..	**102.0**	**−98.2**	**59.4**	**−47.5**	**−128.1**	**175.8**	**209.7**	**63.4**
Trade credits	4 756 ..	....	....	....	....	....	....	....	....
General government	4 757 ..	....	....	....	....	....	....	....	....
of which: Short-term	4 759 ..	....	....	....	....	....	....	....	....
Other sectors	4 760 ..	....	....	....	....	....	....	....	....
of which: Short-term	4 762 ..	....	....	....	....	....	....	....	....
Loans	4 764 ..	102.0	−98.2	59.4	−47.5	−128.1	175.8	9.5	71.6
Monetary authorities	4 765 ..	....	....	....	....	....	....	....	....
of which: Use of Fund credit and loans from the Fund	4 766 ..	....	....	....	....	....	....	....	....
of which: Short-term	4 768 ..	....	....	....	....	....	....	....	....
General government	4 769 ..	42.2	14.1	14.2	18.5	6.8	6.3	−5.6	22.0
of which: Short-term	4 771 ..	....	....	....	....	....	....	....	....
Banks	4 772 ..	36.2	−4.1	61.6	−77.3	−11.7	2.0	−151.4	47.2
of which: Short-term	4 774 ..	*36.2*	*−5.0*	*8.7*	*−191.6*	*−9.2*	*6.5*	*−89.3*	*47.5*
Other sectors	4 775 ..	23.6	−108.2	−16.3	11.3	−123.2	167.5	166.5	2.4
of which: Short-term	4 777 ..	*7.9*	*−28.5*	*−18.3*	*−33.2*	*48.4*	*−90.6*	*−54.3*	*−45.3*
Currency and deposits	4 780 ..	....	....	....	....	....	....	−3.1	−.4
Monetary authorities	4 781 ..	....	....	....	....	....	....	−4.4	.4
General government	4 782 ..	....	....	....	....	....	....	....	−.4
Banks	4 783 ..	....	....	....	....	....	....	1.3	....
Other sectors	4 784 ..	....	....	....	....	....	....	....	−.4
Other liabilities	4 786 ..	....	....	....	....	....	....	203.4	−7.9
Monetary authorities	4 787 ..	....	....	....	....	....	....	203.5	−7.9
of which: Short-term	4 789 ..	....	....	....	....	....	....	−.5	−3.9
General government	4 790 ..	....	....	....	....	....	....	....	....
of which: Short-term	4 792 ..	....	....	....	....	....	....	....	....
Banks	4 793 ..	....	....	....	....	....	....	−.1	....
of which: Short-term	4 795 ..	....	....	....	....	....	....	*−.1*	....
Other sectors	4 796 ..	....	....	....	....	....	....	....	....
of which: Short-term	4 798 ..	....	....	....	....	....	....	....	....
E. RESERVE ASSETS	4 802 ..	**107.2**	**14.2**	**−1.1**	**−163.1**	**−570.8**	**−766.3**	**−119.0**	**529.1**
Monetary gold	4 812 ..	....	....	....	....	....	....	....	....
Special drawing rights	4 811 ..	....	....	....	....	....	....	−203.9	....
Reserve position in the Fund	4 810 ..	....	....	....	....	....	....	....	....
Foreign exchange	4 803 ..	107.2	14.2	−1.0	−163.1	−570.8	−766.3	84.9	529.1
Other claims	4 813 ..	....	....	....	....	....	....	....	....
NET ERRORS AND OMISSIONS	4 998 ..	**−88.8**	**115.3**	**127.9**	**121.6**	**490.5**	**676.1**	**186.3**	**−378.9**

Table 3. INTERNATIONAL INVESTMENT POSITION (End-period stocks), 2003–2010

(Millions of U.S. dollars)

	Code	2003	2004	2005	2006	2007	2008	2009	2010
ASSETS..	8 995 C.	2,937.1	3,720.8	4,717.9	5,966.2	8,419.3	6,842.4	8,388.5	8,684.1
Direct investment abroad............................	8 505 ..	33.2	57.2	25.7	7.3	15.6	11.4	68.4	50.5
Equity capital and reinvested earnings..........	8 506 ..	9.3	33.1	21.6	5.4	12.7	8.1	24.8	32.3
Claims on affiliated enterprises................	8 507 ..	....	33.1	21.6	5.4	12.7	8.1	24.8	32.3
Liabilities to affiliated enterprises.............	8 508 ..	....	....	....	....	....	....	....	....
Other capital..	8 530 ..	23.9	24.2	4.1	1.9	2.9	3.2	43.6	18.2
Claims on affiliated enterprises................	8 535 ..	....	24.2	4.1	1.9	2.9	3.2	43.6	18.2
Liabilities to affiliated enterprises.............	8 540 ..	....	....	....	....	....	....	....	....
Portfolio investment.....................................	8 602 ..	2,354.4	3,025.6	4,095.0	4,493.4	6,022.8	4,258.9	5,756.1	5,058.7
Equity securities...	8 610 ..	....	1,706.4	2,977.2	3,304.3	3,643.4	2,181.8	3,366.5	2,334.0
Monetary authorities................................	8 611 ..	....	....	....	....	....	....	....	....
General government.................................	8 612 ..	....	....	....	....	....	....	....	....
Banks..	8 613 ..	....	....	....	....	....	....	1.9	1.5
Other sectors..	8 614 ..	....	1,706.4	2,977.2	3,304.3	3,643.4	2,181.8	3,364.6	2,332.5
Debt securities...	8 619 ..	....	1,319.2	1,117.8	1,189.0	2,379.5	2,077.2	2,389.6	2,724.7
Bonds and notes......................................	8 620 ..	....	1,319.2	1,117.8	1,189.0	2,379.5	2,077.2	2,389.6	2,724.7
Monetary authorities............................	8 621 ..	....	....	....	....	....	....	....	....
General government.............................	8 622 ..	....	....	....	....	....	....	....	....
Banks..	8 623 ..	....	....	....	....	....	....	30.9	7.6
Other sectors..	8 624 ..	....	1,319.2	1,117.8	1,189.0	2,379.5	2,077.2	2,358.7	2,717.1
Money market instruments.......................	8 630 ..	....	....	....	....	....	....	....	....
Monetary authorities............................	8 631 ..	....	....	....	....	....	....	....	....
General government.............................	8 632 ..	....	....	....	....	....	....	....	....
Banks..	8 633 ..	....	....	....	....	....	....	....	....
Other sectors..	8 634 ..	....	....	....	....	....	....	....	....
Financial derivatives...................................	8 900 ..	....	....	....	....	....	....	....	....
Monetary authorities...................................	8 901 ..	....	....	....	....	....	....	....	....
General government.....................................	8 902 ..	....	....	....	....	....	....	....	....
Banks..	8 903 ..	....	....	....	....	....	....	....	....
Other sectors...	8 904 ..	....	....	....	....	....	....	....	....
Other investment...	8 703 ..	230.5	309.8	302.9	1,043.7	1,440.7	1,205.7	650.1	1,993.9
Trade credits..	8 706 ..	....	....	....	....	....	....	....	....
General government.................................	8 707 ..	....	....	....	....	....	....	....	....
of which: Short-term............................	8 709 ..	....	....	....	....	....	....	....	....
Other sectors..	8 710 ..	....	....	....	....	....	....	....	....
of which: Short-term............................	8 712 ..	....	....	....	....	....	....	....	....
Loans..	8 714 ..	172.2	174.3	114.9	525.7	251.0	185.7	85.5	462.2
Monetary authorities................................	8 715 ..	....	....	....	....	....	....	....	....
of which: Short-term............................	8 718 ..	....	....	....	....	....	....	....	....
General government.................................	8 719 ..	....	2.4	1.4	4.7	6.0	8.8	12.2	13.8
of which: Short-term............................	8 721 ..	....	*1.7*	....	*4.2*	*5.4*	*8.4*	*11.7*	*13.2*
Banks..	8 722 ..	62.7	69.9	46.1	489.2	144.3	99.1	14.1	19.9
of which: Short-term............................	8 724 ..	....	*67.0*	*40.3*	*335.7*	*47.3*	*39.4*	....	....
Other sectors..	8 725 ..	109.5	102.0	67.4	31.8	100.7	77.7	59.2	428.5
of which: Short-term............................	8 727 ..	*101.9*	*93.0*	*56.9*	*20.3*	*79.9*	*42.4*	*49.8*	*414.0*
Currency and deposits..................................	8 730 ..	.1	7.1	36.4	357.5	1,157.3	878.7	375.8	403.5
Monetary authorities................................	8 731 ..	....	....	....	....	....	....	....	....
General government.................................	8 732 ..	....	....	....	....	....	....	....	....
Banks..	8 733 ..	.1	7.1	36.4	357.5	1,157.3	878.7	375.8	403.5
Other sectors..	8 734 ..	....	....	....	....	....	....	....	....
Other assets...	8 736 ..	58.2	128.4	151.5	160.4	32.5	141.3	188.8	1,128.2
Monetary authorities................................	8 737 ..	....	....	....	....	....	....	....	....
of which: Short-term............................	8 739 ..	....	....	....	....	....	....	....	....
General government.................................	8 740 ..	....	....	....	....	....	....	....	....
of which: Short-term............................	8 742 ..	....	....	....	....	....	....	....	....
Banks..	8 743 ..	47.8	....	....	....	....	....	....	....
of which: Short-term............................	8 745 ..	....	....	....	....	....	....	....	....
Other sectors..	8 746 ..	10.4	128.4	151.5	160.4	32.5	141.3	188.8	1,128.2
of which: Short-term............................	8 748 ..	....	....	....	....	....	....	....	....
Reserve assets..	8 802 ..	319.1	328.2	294.4	421.8	940.1	1,366.4	1,913.9	1,581.0
Monetary gold..	8 812 ..	....	....	....	....	....	....	....	....
Special drawing rights..................................	8 811 ..	....	....	....	....	....	....	204.4	200.8
Reserve position in the Fund........................	8 810 ..	.1	.1	.1	.1	.1	.1	.1	.1
Foreign exchange..	8 803 ..	319.0	328.1	294.2	421.7	940.0	1,366.2	1,691.8	1,354.5
Other claims...	8 813 ..	....	....	....	....	....	....	17.5	25.5

2011, International Monetary Fund: *Balance of Payments Statistics Yearbook*

Table 3 (Concluded). INTERNATIONAL INVESTMENT POSITION (End-period stocks), 2003–2010

(Millions of U.S. dollars)

	Code	2003	2004	2005	2006	2007	2008	2009	2010
LIABILITIES................................	8 995 D.	**4,019.3**	**5,231.7**	**4,123.9**	**4,641.2**	**5,126.5**	**4,451.1**	**4,285.4**	**6,815.4**
Direct investment in Namibia............	8 555 ..	**2,951.9**	**4,120.4**	**2,453.4**	**2,785.7**	**3,854.4**	**3,542.6**	**3,132.5**	**5,333.9**
Equity capital and reinvested earnings........	8 556 ..	2,393.6	3,368.4	2,260.0	2,381.6	2,851.3	2,438.8	1,870.9	3,546.4
Claims on direct investors................	8 557 ..	....	....	....	....	....	....	....	....
Liabilities to direct investors.............	8 558 ..	....	3,368.4	2,260.0	2,381.6	2,851.3	2,438.8	1,870.9	3,546.4
Other capital.................................	8 580 ..	558.3	752.1	193.5	404.1	1,003.1	1,103.9	1,261.5	1,787.5
Claims on direct investors................	8 585 ..	....	....	....	....	....	....	....	....
Liabilities to direct investors.............	8 590 ..	....	752.1	193.5	404.1	1,003.1	1,103.9	1,261.5	1,787.5
Portfolio investment.....................	8 652 ..	**57.7**	**68.7**	**92.4**	**83.8**	**85.8**	**62.8**	**92.8**	**103.2**
Equity securities...........................	8 660 ..	5.8	6.9	15.6	14.1	14.4	10.5	13.3	14.8
Banks......................................	8 663 ..	....	....	....	....	....	....	....	....
Other sectors.............................	8 664 ..	....	6.9	15.6	14.1	14.4	10.5	13.3	14.8
Debt securities.............................	8 669 ..	51.8	61.8	76.9	69.7	71.4	52.2	79.5	88.5
Bonds and notes..........................	8 670 ..	....	61.8	76.9	69.7	71.4	52.2	79.5	88.5
Monetary authorities...................	8 671 ..	....	....	....	....	....	....	....	....
General government....................	8 672 ..	....	61.8	76.9	69.7	71.4	52.2	65.9	73.3
Banks....................................	8 673 ..	....	....	....	....	....	....	13.6	15.2
Other sectors............................	8 674 ..	....	....	....	....	....	....	....	....
Money market instruments...............	8 680 ..	....	....	....	....	....	....	....	....
Monetary authorities...................	8 681 ..	....	....	....	....	....	....	....	....
General government....................	8 682 ..	....	....	....	....	....	....	....	....
Banks....................................	8 683 ..	....	....	....	....	....	....	....	....
Other sectors............................	8 684 ..	....	....	....	....	....	....	....	....
Financial derivatives.....................	8 905 ..	....	....	....	....	....	....	....	....
Monetary authorities.......................	8 906 ..	....	....	....	....	....	....	....	....
General government........................	8 907 ..	....	....	....	....	....	....	....	....
Banks.......................................	8 908 ..	....	....	....	....	....	....	....	....
Other sectors..............................	8 909 ..	....	....	....	....	....	....	....	....
Other investment.........................	8 753 ..	**1,009.7**	**1,042.6**	**1,578.0**	**1,771.7**	**1,186.3**	**845.7**	**1,060.2**	**1,378.2**
Trade credits...............................	8 756 ..	....	....	....	....	....	....	....	....
General government........................	8 757 ..	....	....	....	....	....	....	....	....
of which: Short-term....................	8 759 ..	....	....	....	....	....	....	....	....
Other sectors..............................	8 760 ..	....	....	....	....	....	....	....	....
of which: Short-term....................	8 762 ..	....	....	....	....	....	....	....	....
Loans.......................................	8 764 ..	873.3	1,042.6	1,395.7	1,607.7	1,032.5	809.8	802.2	1,050.2
Monetary authorities.......................	8 765 ..	....	....	....	....	....	....	....	....
of which: Use of Fund credit and loans from the Fund....	8 766 ..	....	....	....	....	....	....	....	....
of which: Short-term....................	8 768 ..	....	....	....	....	....	....	....	....
General government........................	8 769 ..	302.0	597.1	575.3	615.9	626.5	597.1	677.8	705.1
of which: Short-term....................	8 771 ..	*15.9*	*91.7*	*250.3*	*238.7*	*22.5*	*41.9*	*27.6*	*32.2*
Banks.......................................	8 772 ..	222.4	307.0	115.3	200.7	239.1	129.4	....	....
of which: Short-term....................	8 774 ..	....	*185.6*	*98.8*	*135.0*	*174.4*	*67.8*	....	....
Other sectors..............................	8 775 ..	348.9	138.6	705.0	791.1	166.9	83.3	124.4	345.1
of which: Short-term....................	8 777 ..	*121.7*	*114.8*	*43.6*	*124.0*	*143.5*	*47.1*	*88.9*	*103.5*
Currency and deposits......................	8 780 ..	....	....	182.3	164.0	153.8	36.0	42.6	120.2
Monetary authorities.......................	8 781 ..	....	....	....	....	....	....	.7	1.3
General government........................	8 782 ..	....	....	....	....	....	....	....	....
Banks.......................................	8 783 ..	....	....	182.3	164.0	153.8	36.0	41.9	119.0
Other sectors..............................	8 784 ..	....	....	....	....	....	....	....	....
Other liabilities............................	8 786 ..	136.4	....	....	....	....	....	215.4	207.7
Monetary authorities.......................	8 787 ..	....	....	....	....	....	....	215.4	207.7
of which: Short-term....................	8 789 ..	....	....	....	....	....	....	*10.9*	*6.9*
General government........................	8 790 ..	....	....	....	....	....	....	....	....
of which: Short-term....................	8 792 ..	....	....	....	....	....	....	....	....
Banks.......................................	8 793 ..	136.4	....	....	....	....	....	....	....
of which: Short-term....................	8 795 ..	....	....	....	....	....	....	....	....
Other sectors..............................	8 796 ..	....	....	....	....	....	....	....	....
of which: Short-term....................	8 798 ..	....	....	....	....	....	....	....	....
NET INTERNATIONAL INVESTMENT POSITION........	8 995 ..	**−1,082.2**	**−1,510.9**	**594.0**	**1,325.0**	**3,292.8**	**2,391.2**	**4,103.2**	**1,868.7**
Conversion rates: Namibia dollars per U.S. dollar (end of period)...........................	0 102 ..	**6.640**	**5.630**	**6.325**	**6.970**	**6.810**	**9.305**	**7.380**	**6.632**

Table 1. ANALYTIC PRESENTATION, 2003–2010

(Millions of U.S. dollars)

	Code	2003	2004	2005	2006	2007	2008	2009	2010
A. Current Account[1]	4 993 Z.	**119.9**	**−45.0**	**1.1**	**−10.4**	**−130.0**	**384.5**	**−227.5**	**−438.0**
Goods: exports f.o.b.	2 100 ..	703.2	773.1	902.9	848.8	924.9	986.6	837.4	901.9
Goods: imports f.o.b.	3 100 ..	−1,665.9	−1,908.0	−2,276.5	−2,441.0	−2,932.6	−3,519.3	−4,265.4	−5,016.4
Balance on Goods	4 100 ..	*−962.7*	*−1,134.9*	*−1,373.6*	*−1,592.2*	*−2,007.6*	*−2,532.8*	*−3,428.1*	*−4,114.5*
Services: credit	2 200 ..	372.1	460.9	380.3	385.7	511.3	723.7	705.3	671.9
Services: debit	3 200 ..	−266.2	−385.0	−434.7	−492.8	−722.6	−851.7	−842.2	−871.0
Balance on Goods and Services	4 991 ..	*−856.8*	*−1,059.1*	*−1,428.0*	*−1,699.4*	*−2,218.9*	*−2,660.9*	*−3,564.9*	*−4,313.6*
Income: credit	2 300 ..	48.7	63.0	139.9	158.2	224.3	235.6	210.1	209.8
Income: debit	3 300 ..	−69.0	−78.0	−91.6	−96.1	−87.6	−84.6	−52.4	−116.3
Balance on Goods, Services, and Income	4 992 ..	*−877.1*	*−1,074.1*	*−1,379.7*	*−1,637.3*	*−2,082.2*	*−2,509.8*	*−3,407.2*	*−4,220.0*
Current transfers: credit	2 379 Z.	1,022.5	1,091.8	1,441.3	1,695.7	1,993.7	2,945.5	3,289.5	3,835.4
Current transfers: debit	3 379 ..	−25.4	−62.8	−60.5	−68.9	−41.5	−51.2	−109.8	−53.4
B. Capital Account[1]	4 994 Z.	**24.8**	**15.7**	**40.3**	**46.3**	**75.4**	**113.6**	**132.4**	**185.5**
Capital account: credit	2 994 Z.	24.8	15.7	40.5	46.4	75.5	115.0	132.9	186.4
Capital account: debit	3 994 ..	....	....	−.2	−.1	−.1	−1.4	−.6	−1.0
Total, Groups A Plus B	4 981 ..	*144.8*	*−29.4*	*41.4*	*35.9*	*−54.7*	*498.1*	*−95.1*	*−252.5*
C. Financial Account[1]	4 995 W.	**−354.1**	**−488.5**	**−276.5**	**−117.5**	**−269.4**	**−86.4**	**−184.4**	**167.5**
Direct investment abroad	4 505 ..	....	....	....	....	....	....	....	....
Direct investment in Nepal	4 555 Z.	14.8	−.4	2.5	−6.6	5.7	1.0	38.2	87.8
Portfolio investment assets	4 602 ..	....	....	....	....	....	....	....	....
Equity securities	4 610 ..	....	....	....	....	....	....	....	....
Debt securities	4 619 ..	....	....	....	....	....	....	....	....
Portfolio investment liabilities	4 652 Z.	....	....	....	....	....	....	....	....
Equity securities	4 660 ..	....	....	....	....	....	....	....	....
Debt securities	4 669 Z.	....	....	....	....	....	....	....	....
Financial derivatives	4 910 ..	....	....	....	....	....	....	....	....
Financial derivatives assets	4 900 ..	....	....	....	....	....	....	....	....
Financial derivatives liabilities	4 905 ..	....	....	....	....	....	....	....	....
Other investment assets	4 703 ..	−436.7	−348.0	−242.4	−250.9	−161.0	−386.7	−306.2	−355.2
Monetary authorities	4 701 ..	....	....	....	....	....	....	....	....
General government	4 704 ..	....	....	....	....	....	....	....	....
Banks	4 705 ..	....	....	....	−15.3	−61.8	−262.5	−21.6	2.3
Other sectors	4 728 ..	−436.7	−348.0	−242.4	−235.5	−99.2	−124.2	−284.6	−357.6
Other investment liabilities	4 753 W.	67.8	−140.0	−36.5	140.0	−114.2	299.3	83.7	434.8
Monetary authorities	4 753 WA	.2	−1.6	−2.3	−.2	.1	−.1	175.5	6.6
General government	4 753 ZB	−67.6	−90.7	−84.3	−103.5	−111.5	−128.2	−138.3	−150.6
Banks	4 753 ZC	19.2	4.7	22.3	39.1	56.0	233.5	22.5	43.5
Other sectors	4 753 ZD	116.0	−52.5	27.8	204.6	−58.7	194.0	24.0	535.3
Total, Groups A Through C	4 983 ..	*−209.3*	*−517.8*	*−235.1*	*−81.6*	*−324.1*	*411.7*	*−279.5*	*−85.0*
D. Net Errors and Omissions	4 998 ..	**309.9**	**415.9**	**139.0**	**108.5**	**19.1**	**−107.5**	**−72.6**	**−186.3**
Total, Groups A Through D	4 984 ..	*100.6*	*−101.9*	*−96.1*	*26.9*	*−305.0*	*304.2*	*−352.1*	*−271.3*
E. Reserves and Related Items	4 802 A.	**−100.6**	**101.9**	**96.1**	**−26.9**	**305.0**	**−304.2**	**352.1**	**271.3**
Reserve assets	4 802 ..	−218.1	−178.0	−170.9	−329.0	−1.1	−831.2	1.8	−198.6
Use of Fund credit and loans	4 766 ..	7.1	10.0	....	21.2	33.1	....	−2.2	37.5
Exceptional financing	4 920 ..	110.4	270.0	267.0	280.8	273.0	526.9	352.5	432.4
Conversion rates: Nepalese rupees per U.S. dollar	0 101 ..	**76.141**	**73.674**	**71.368**	**72.756**	**66.415**	**69.762**	**77.545**	**73.155**

[1] Excludes components that have been classified in the categories of Group E.

Table 2. STANDARD PRESENTATION, 2003–2010

(Millions of U.S. dollars)

	Code	2003	2004	2005	2006	2007	2008	2009	2010
CURRENT ACCOUNT...	4 993 ..	**180.3**	**100.0**	**153.1**	**150.1**	**5.7**	**733.3**	**18.4**	**−128.2**
A. GOODS...	4 100 ..	**−962.7**	**−1,134.9**	**−1,373.6**	**−1,592.2**	**−2,007.6**	**−2,532.8**	**−3,428.1**	**−4,114.5**
Credit...	2 100 ..	**703.2**	**773.1**	**902.9**	**848.8**	**924.9**	**986.6**	**837.4**	**901.9**
General merchandise: exports f.o.b.................	2 110 ..	703.2	773.1	902.9	848.8	924.9	986.6	837.4	901.9
Goods for processing: exports f.o.b...............	2 150 ..	....	....	....	....	....	....	....	....
Repairs on goods...	2 160 ..	....	....	....	....	....	....	....	....
Goods procured in ports by carriers...............	2 170 ..	....	....	....	....	....	....	....	....
Nonmonetary gold...	2 180 ..	....	....	....	....	....	....	....	....
Debit...	3 100 ..	**−1,665.9**	**−1,908.0**	**−2,276.5**	**−2,441.0**	**−2,932.6**	**−3,519.3**	**−4,265.4**	**−5,016.4**
General merchandise: imports f.o.b.................	3 110 ..	−1,665.9	−1,908.0	−2,276.5	−2,441.0	−2,932.6	−3,519.3	−4,265.4	−5,016.4
Goods for processing: imports f.o.b...............	3 150 ..	....	....	....	....	....	....	....	....
Repairs on goods...	3 160 ..	....	....	....	....	....	....	....	....
Goods procured in ports by carriers...............	3 170 ..	....	....	....	....	....	....	....	....
Nonmonetary gold...	3 180 ..	....	....	....	....	....	....	....	....
B. SERVICES...	4 200 ..	**105.9**	**75.9**	**−54.4**	**−107.1**	**−211.3**	**−128.1**	**−136.9**	**−199.1**
Total credit...	2 200 ..	*372.1*	*460.9*	*380.3*	*385.7*	*511.3*	*723.7*	*705.3*	*671.9*
Total debit...	3 200 ..	*−266.2*	*−385.0*	*−434.7*	*−492.8*	*−722.6*	*−851.7*	*−842.2*	*−871.0*
Transportation services, credit...............	2 205 ..	**35.9**	**32.5**	**32.6**	**35.1**	**37.0**	**27.3**	**38.3**	**39.9**
Passenger...	2 850 ..	*32.6*	*30.2*	*29.3*	*29.2*	*34.4*	*18.4*	*26.0*	*34.3*
Freight...	2 851 ..	....	....	....	....	....	....	....	....
Other...	2 852 ..	*3.3*	*2.3*	*3.3*	*5.9*	*2.7*	*8.9*	*12.3*	*5.6*
Sea transport, passenger.............................	2 207 ..	....	....	....	....	....	....	....	....
Sea transport, freight.............................	2 208 ..	....	....	....	....	....	....	....	....
Sea transport, other.............................	2 209 ..	....	....	....	....	....	....	....	....
Air transport, passenger.............................	2 211 ..	....	....	....	....	....	....	....	....
Air transport, freight.............................	2 212 ..	....	....	....	....	....	....	....	....
Air transport, other.............................	2 213 ..	....	....	....	....	....	....	....	....
Other transport, passenger.............................	2 215 ..	....	....	....	....	....	....	....	....
Other transport, freight.............................	2 216 ..	....	....	....	....	....	....	....	....
Other transport, other.............................	2 217 ..	....	....	....	....	....	....	....	....
Transportation services, debit...............	3 205 ..	**−115.0**	**−141.5**	**−160.8**	**−186.3**	**−287.3**	**−331.9**	**−271.4**	**−281.3**
Passenger...	3 850 ..	*−38.1*	*−51.1*	*−57.7*	*−76.4*	*−127.5*	*−163.6*	*−138.2*	*−125.8*
Freight...	3 851 ..	*−58.6*	*−69.3*	*−78.0*	*−78.9*	*−85.4*	*−118.2*	*−102.3*	*−125.0*
Other...	3 852 ..	*−18.3*	*−21.0*	*−25.1*	*−31.1*	*−74.5*	*−50.1*	*−31.0*	*−30.6*
Sea transport, passenger.............................	3 207 ..	....	....	....	....	....	....	....	....
Sea transport, freight.............................	3 208 ..	....	....	....	....	....	....	....	....
Sea transport, other.............................	3 209 ..	....	....	....	....	....	....	....	....
Air transport, passenger.............................	3 211 ..	....	....	....	....	....	....	....	....
Air transport, freight.............................	3 212 ..	....	....	....	....	....	....	....	....
Air transport, other.............................	3 213 ..	....	....	....	....	....	....	....	....
Other transport, passenger.............................	3 215 ..	....	....	....	....	....	....	....	....
Other transport, freight.............................	3 216 ..	....	....	....	....	....	....	....	....
Other transport, other.............................	3 217 ..	....	....	....	....	....	....	....	....
Travel, credit...	2 236 ..	**199.5**	**230.2**	**131.3**	**127.8**	**199.9**	**334.8**	**413.3**	**344.2**
Business travel...	2 237 ..	....	....	....	....	....	....	....	....
Personal travel...	2 240 ..	....	....	....	....	....	....	....	....
Travel, debit...	3 236 ..	**−81.2**	**−153.8**	**−163.2**	**−185.3**	**−273.6**	**−380.7**	**−433.9**	**−402.3**
Business travel...	3 237 ..	....	....	....	....	....	....	....	....
Personal travel...	3 240 ..	....	....	....	....	....	....	....	....
Other services, credit...	2 200 BA ..	**136.7**	**198.2**	**216.4**	**222.7**	**274.4**	**361.6**	**253.7**	**287.8**
Communications...	2 245 ..	17.2	31.8	39.7	34.7	38.2	44.6	39.2	57.9
Construction...	2 249 ..	....	....	....	....	....	....	....	....
Insurance...	2 253 ..	.6	.2	3.9	1.6	3.1	.7	1.5	.4
Financial...	2 260 ..	....	....	....	....	....	....	....	....
Computer and information.............................	2 262 ..	....	....	....	....	....	....	....	....
Royalties and licence fees.............................	2 266 ..	....	....	....	....	....	....	....	....
Other business services.............................	2 268 ..	49.3	61.1	63.9	52.4	61.3	87.0	108.6	141.3
Personal, cultural, and recreational...............	2 287 ..	....	....	....	....	....	....	....	....
Government, n.i.e...	2 291 ..	69.7	105.1	109.0	134.0	171.8	229.3	104.5	88.1
Other services, debit...	3 200 BA ..	**−70.0**	**−89.8**	**−110.7**	**−121.2**	**−161.6**	**−139.1**	**−136.9**	**−187.3**
Communications...	3 245 ..	−5.3	−8.2	−4.1	−4.1	−5.0	−3.6	−23.1	−54.8
Construction...	3 249 ..	....	....	....	....	....	....	....	....
Insurance...	3 253 ..	−17.2	−18.2	−26.3	−28.7	−30.7	−30.5	−26.9	−30.0
Financial...	3 260 ..	....	....	....	....	....	....	....	....
Computer and information.............................	3 262 ..	....	....	....	....	....	....	....	....
Royalties and licence fees.............................	3 266 ..	....	....	....	....	....	....	....	....
Other business services.............................	3 268 ..	−39.0	−54.0	−69.4	−83.8	−119.5	−93.4	−72.8	−78.1
Personal, cultural, and recreational...............	3 287 ..	....	....	....	....	....	....	....	....
Government, n.i.e...	3 291 ..	−8.5	−9.3	−10.9	−4.6	−6.4	−11.6	−14.2	−24.5

Table 2 (Continued). STANDARD PRESENTATION, 2003–2010

(Millions of U.S. dollars)

	Code	2003	2004	2005	2006	2007	2008	2009	2010
C. INCOME	4 300	**−20.3**	**−15.0**	**48.3**	**62.1**	**136.7**	**151.0**	**157.7**	**93.5**
Total credit	2 300	*48.7*	*63.0*	*139.9*	*158.2*	*224.3*	*235.6*	*210.1*	*209.8*
Total debit	3 300	*−69.0*	*−78.0*	*−91.6*	*−96.1*	*−87.6*	*−84.6*	*−52.4*	*−116.3*
Compensation of employees, credit	2 310	**26.7**	**30.0**	**85.5**	**79.9**	**86.7**	**145.8**	**127.1**	**132.4**
Compensation of employees, debit	3 310	**−.8**	**−.8**	**−5.3**	**−10.3**	**−4.0**	**−5.3**	**−12.3**	**−32.4**
Investment income, credit	2 320	**22.0**	**33.0**	**54.4**	**78.2**	**137.6**	**89.8**	**83.1**	**77.4**
Direct investment income	2 330	....	....	....	....	....	....	....	....
Dividends and distributed branch profits	2 332	....	....	....	....	....	....	....	....
Reinvested earnings and undistributed branch profits	2 333	....	....	....	....	....	....	....	....
Income on debt (interest)	2 334	....	....	....	....	....	....	....	....
Portfolio investment income	2 339	....	....	....	....	....	....	....	....
Income on equity	2 340	....	....	....	....	....	....	....	....
Income on bonds and notes	2 350	....	....	....	....	....	....	....	....
Income on money market instruments	2 360	....	....	....	....	....	....	....	....
Other investment income	2 370	22.0	33.0	54.4	78.2	137.6	89.8	83.1	77.4
Investment income, debit	3 320	**−68.2**	**−77.2**	**−86.3**	**−85.8**	**−83.7**	**−79.3**	**−40.0**	**−83.9**
Direct investment income	3 330	−42.1	−44.9	−56.6	−55.7	−54.0	−44.1	−8.8	−49.8
Dividends and distributed branch profits	3 332	−42.1	−44.9	−56.6	−55.7	−54.0	−44.1	−8.8	−49.8
Reinvested earnings and undistributed branch profits	3 333	....	....	....	....	....	....	....	....
Income on debt (interest)	3 334	....	....	....	....	....	....	....	....
Portfolio investment income	3 339	....	....	....	....	....	....	....	....
Income on equity	3 340	....	....	....	....	....	....	....	....
Income on bonds and notes	3 350	....	....	....	....	....	....	....	....
Income on money market instruments	3 360	....	....	....	....	....	....	....	....
Other investment income	3 370	−26.2	−32.3	−29.7	−30.0	−29.7	−35.2	−31.3	−34.0
D. CURRENT TRANSFERS	4 379	**1,057.4**	**1,174.0**	**1,532.8**	**1,787.4**	**2,087.9**	**3,243.2**	**3,425.6**	**4,091.8**
Credit	2 379	**1,082.8**	**1,236.8**	**1,593.3**	**1,856.2**	**2,129.4**	**3,294.4**	**3,535.4**	**4,145.2**
General government	2 380	92.7	190.7	167.1	160.5	182.3	384.5	285.7	350.7
Other sectors	2 390	990.1	1,046.1	1,426.2	1,695.7	1,947.2	2,909.8	3,249.7	3,794.5
Workers' remittances	2 391	744.4	792.6	1,126.3	1,373.3	1,647.1	2,581.3	2,858.0	3,336.1
Other current transfers	2 392	245.7	253.5	299.8	322.4	300.0	328.6	391.7	458.4
Debit	3 379	**−25.4**	**−62.8**	**−60.5**	**−68.9**	**−41.5**	**−51.2**	**−109.8**	**−53.4**
General government	3 380	....	....	....	....	−.1	−.1	−.4	....
Other sectors	3 390	−25.4	−62.8	−60.5	−68.9	−41.4	−51.1	−109.4	−53.4
Workers' remittances	3 391	−25.4	−62.8	−60.5	−68.9	....	....	....	....
Other current transfers	3 392	....	....	....	....	....	....	....	....
CAPITAL AND FINANCIAL ACCOUNT	4 996	**−490.2**	**−515.9**	**−292.1**	**−258.6**	**−24.7**	**−625.9**	**54.1**	**314.5**
CAPITAL ACCOUNT	4 994	**24.8**	**15.7**	**40.3**	**46.3**	**75.4**	**113.6**	**132.4**	**185.5**
Total credit	2 994	*24.8*	*15.7*	*40.5*	*46.4*	*75.5*	*115.0*	*132.9*	*186.4*
Total debit	3 994	....	....	*−.2*	*−.1*	*−.1*	*−1.4*	*−.6*	*−1.0*
Capital transfers, credit	2 400	**24.8**	**15.7**	**40.5**	**46.4**	**75.5**	**115.0**	**132.9**	**186.4**
General government	2 401	24.8	15.7	40.5	46.4	75.5	114.9	132.4	186.4
Debt forgiveness	2 402	....	....	....	....	....	....	....	....
Other capital transfers	2 410	24.8	15.7	40.5	46.4	75.5	114.9	132.4	186.4
Other sectors	2 430	....	....	....	....	....	....	.6	....
Migrants' transfers	2 431	....	....	....	....	....	....	.5	....
Debt forgiveness	2 432	....	....	....	....	....	....	....	....
Other capital transfers	2 440	....	....	....	....	....	....	....	....
Capital transfers, debit	3 400	....	....	**−.2**	**−.1**	**−.1**	**−1.4**	**−.6**	**−1.0**
General government	3 401	....	....	....	....	....	....	....	−.3
Debt forgiveness	3 402	....	....	....	....	....	....	....	....
Other capital transfers	3 410	....	....	....	....	....	....	....	−.3
Other sectors	3 430	....	....	−.2	−.1	−.1	−1.4	−.6	−.6
Migrants' transfers	3 431	....	....	....	....	....	....	....	....
Debt forgiveness	3 432	....	....	....	....	....	....	....	....
Other capital transfers	3 440	....	....	−.2	−.1	−.1	−1.4	−.6	−.6
Nonproduced nonfinancial assets, credit	2 480	....	....	....	....	....	....	....	....
Nonproduced nonfinancial assets, debit	3 480	....	....	....	....	....	....	....	....

2011, International Monetary Fund: *Balance of Payments Statistics Yearbook*

Table 2 (Continued). STANDARD PRESENTATION, 2003–2010
(Millions of U.S. dollars)

	Code	2003	2004	2005	2006	2007	2008	2009	2010
FINANCIAL ACCOUNT...............................	4 995 ..	−515.0	−531.5	−332.4	−304.9	−100.1	−739.5	−78.2	129.0
A. DIRECT INVESTMENT.......................	4 500 ..	14.8	−.4	2.5	−6.6	5.7	1.0	38.2	87.8
Direct investment abroad........................	4 505 ..	....	....	....	....	....	....	....	....
Equity capital..	4 510 ..	....	....	....	....	....	....	....	....
Claims on affiliated enterprises......................	4 515 ..	....	....	....	....	....	....	....	....
Liabilities to affiliated enterprises..................	4 520 ..	....	....	....	....	....	....	....	....
Reinvested earnings....................................	4 525 ..	....	....	....	....	....	....	....	....
Other capital..	4 530 ..	....	....	....	....	....	....	....	....
Claims on affiliated enterprises......................	4 535 ..	....	....	....	....	....	....	....	....
Liabilities to affiliated enterprises..................	4 540 ..	....	....	....	....	....	....	....	....
Direct investment in Nepal.......................	4 555 ..	14.8	−.4	2.5	−6.6	5.7	1.0	38.2	87.8
Equity capital..	4 560 ..	14.8	−.4	2.5	−6.6	5.3	−5.3	....	....
Claims on direct investors...........................	4 565 ..	....	....	....	....	....	....	....	....
Liabilities to direct investors.......................	4 570 ..	14.8	−.4	2.5	−6.6	5.3	−5.3	....	....
Reinvested earnings....................................	4 575 ..	....	....	....	....	....	....	....	....
Other capital..	4 580 ..	....	....	....	....	.5	6.3	38.2	87.8
Claims on direct investors...........................	4 585 ..	....	....	....	....	....	....	....	....
Liabilities to direct investors.......................	4 590 ..	....	....	....	....	....	6.3	38.2	87.8
B. PORTFOLIO INVESTMENT................	4 600 ..	....	....	....	....	....	....	....	....
Assets..	4 602 ..	....	....	....	....	....	....	....	....
Equity securities..	4 610 ..	....	....	....	....	....	....	....	....
Monetary authorities..................................	4 611 ..	....	....	....	....	....	....	....	....
General government...................................	4 612 ..	....	....	....	....	....	....	....	....
Banks...	4 613 ..	....	....	....	....	....	....	....	....
Other sectors...	4 614 ..	....	....	....	....	....	....	....	....
Debt securities..	4 619 ..	....	....	....	....	....	....	....	....
Bonds and notes.......................................	4 620 ..	....	....	....	....	....	....	....	....
Monetary authorities..................................	4 621 ..	....	....	....	....	....	....	....	....
General government...................................	4 622 ..	....	....	....	....	....	....	....	....
Banks...	4 623 ..	....	....	....	....	....	....	....	....
Other sectors...	4 624 ..	....	....	....	....	....	....	....	....
Money market instruments...........................	4 630 ..	....	....	....	....	....	....	....	....
Monetary authorities..................................	4 631 ..	....	....	....	....	....	....	....	....
General government...................................	4 632 ..	....	....	....	....	....	....	....	....
Banks...	4 633 ..	....	....	....	....	....	....	....	....
Other sectors...	4 634 ..	....	....	....	....	....	....	....	....
Liabilities..	4 652 ..	....	....	....	....	....	....	....	....
Equity securities..	4 660 ..	....	....	....	....	....	....	....	....
Banks...	4 663 ..	....	....	....	....	....	....	....	....
Other sectors...	4 664 ..	....	....	....	....	....	....	....	....
Debt securities..	4 669 ..	....	....	....	....	....	....	....	....
Bonds and notes.......................................	4 670 ..	....	....	....	....	....	....	....	....
Monetary authorities..................................	4 671 ..	....	....	....	....	....	....	....	....
General government...................................	4 672 ..	....	....	....	....	....	....	....	....
Banks...	4 673 ..	....	....	....	....	....	....	....	....
Other sectors...	4 674 ..	....	....	....	....	....	....	....	....
Money market instruments...........................	4 680 ..	....	....	....	....	....	....	....	....
Monetary authorities..................................	4 681 ..	....	....	....	....	....	....	....	....
General government...................................	4 682 ..	....	....	....	....	....	....	....	....
Banks...	4 683 ..	....	....	....	....	....	....	....	....
Other sectors...	4 684 ..	....	....	....	....	....	....	....	....
C. FINANCIAL DERIVATIVES................	4 910 ..	....	....	....	....	....	....	....	....
Monetary authorities..................................	4 911 ..	....	....	....	....	....	....	....	....
General government...................................	4 912 ..	....	....	....	....	....	....	....	....
Banks...	4 913 ..	....	....	....	....	....	....	....	....
Other sectors...	4 914 ..	....	....	....	....	....	....	....	....
Assets..	4 900 ..	....	....	....	−6.6	....	....	....	....
Monetary authorities..................................	4 901 ..	....	....	....	....	....	....	....	....
General government...................................	4 902 ..	....	....	....	....	....	....	....	....
Banks...	4 903 ..	....	....	....	....	....	....	....	....
Other sectors...	4 904 ..	....	....	....	....	....	....	....	....
Liabilities..	4 905 ..	....	....	....	....	....	....	....	....
Monetary authorities..................................	4 906 ..	....	....	....	....	....	....	....	....
General government...................................	4 907 ..	....	....	....	....	....	....	....	....
Banks...	4 908 ..	....	....	....	....	....	....	....	....
Other sectors...	4 909 ..	....	....	....	....	....	....	....	....

Table 2 (Concluded). STANDARD PRESENTATION, 2003–2010

(Millions of U.S. dollars)

	Code	2003	2004	2005	2006	2007	2008	2009	2010
D. OTHER INVESTMENT	4 700	−311.7	−353.1	−164.0	30.7	−104.7	90.7	−118.2	239.8
Assets	4 703	−436.7	−348.0	−242.4	−250.9	−161.0	−386.7	−306.2	−355.2
Trade credits	4 706	−34.9	17.6	−39.7	−94.9	−44.9	41.5	−74.4	−47.0
General government	4 707	....	....	....	....	....	....	....	....
of which: Short-term	4 709	....	....	....	....	....	....	....	....
Other sectors	4 710	−34.9	17.6	−39.7	−94.9	−44.9	41.5	−74.4	−47.0
of which: Short-term	4 712	*−34.9*	*17.6*	*−39.7*	*−94.9*	*−44.9*	*41.5*	*−74.4*	*−47.0*
Loans	4 714	....	....	....	....	....	....	....	....
Monetary authorities	4 715	....	....	....	....	....	....	....	....
of which: Short-term	4 718	....	....	....	....	....	....	....	....
General government	4 719	....	....	....	....	....	....	....	....
of which: Short-term	4 721	....	....	....	....	....	....	....	....
Banks	4 722	....	....	....	....	....	....	....	....
of which: Short-term	4 724	....	....	....	....	....	....	....	....
Other sectors	4 725	....	....	....	....	....	....	....	....
of which: Short-term	4 727	....	....	....	....	....	....	....	....
Currency and deposits	4 730	....	....	....	−15.3	−61.8	−262.5	−21.6	2.3
Monetary authorities	4 731	....	....	....	....	....	....	....	....
General government	4 732	....	....	....	....	....	....	....	....
Banks	4 733	....	....	....	−15.3	−61.8	−262.5	−21.6	2.3
Other sectors	4 734	....	....	....	....	....	....	....	....
Other assets	4 736	−401.8	−365.6	−202.7	−140.6	−54.2	−165.7	−210.2	−310.5
Monetary authorities	4 737	....	....	....	....	....	....	....	....
of which: Short-term	4 739	....	....	....	....	....	....	....	....
General government	4 740	....	....	....	....	....	....	....	....
of which: Short-term	4 742	....	....	....	....	....	....	....	....
Banks	4 743	....	....	....	....	....	....	....	....
of which: Short-term	4 745	....	....	....	....	....	....	....	....
Other sectors	4 746	−401.8	−365.6	−202.7	−140.6	−54.2	−165.7	−210.2	−310.5
of which: Short-term	4 748	*−401.8*	*−365.6*	*−202.7*	*−140.6*	*−54.2*	*−165.7*	*−210.2*	*−310.5*
Liabilities	4 753	**125.0**	**−5.1**	**78.5**	**281.6**	**56.3**	**477.3**	**188.0**	**595.1**
Trade credits	4 756	119.8	−47.4	37.6	219.1	−54.6	196.9	25.7	536.9
General government	4 757	....	....	....	....	....	....	....	....
of which: Short-term	4 759	....	....	....	....	....	....	....	....
Other sectors	4 760	119.8	−47.4	37.6	219.1	−54.6	196.9	25.7	536.9
of which: Short-term	4 762	*119.8*	*−47.4*	*37.6*	*219.1*	*−54.6*	*196.9*	*25.7*	*536.9*
Loans	4 764	−14.9	39.2	20.8	23.5	54.8	47.0	−35.7	8.0
Monetary authorities	4 765	6.4	10.0	....	21.2	33.1	....	−2.2	37.5
of which: Use of Fund credit and loans from the Fund	4 766	*7.1*	*10.0*	....	*21.2*	*33.1*	....	*−2.2*	*37.5*
of which: Short-term	4 768	....	....	....	....	....	....	....	....
General government	4 769	−26.4	32.0	28.8	10.9	24.3	48.4	−33.2	−29.1
of which: Short-term	4 771	....	....	....	....	....	....	....	....
Banks	4 772	....	....	....	....	....	....	....	....
of which: Short-term	4 774	....	....	....	....	....	....	....	....
Other sectors	4 775	5.0	−2.8	−8.0	−8.6	−2.6	−1.3	−.2	−.4
of which: Short-term	4 777	....	....	....	....	....	....	....	....
Currency and deposits	4 780	20.1	3.1	20.0	39.0	56.1	233.4	22.5	43.8
Monetary authorities	4 781	.9	−1.6	−2.3	−.2	.1	−.1	....	.3
General government	4 782	....	....	....	....	....	....	....	....
Banks	4 783	19.2	4.7	22.3	39.1	56.0	233.5	22.5	43.5
Other sectors	4 784	....	....	....	....	....	....	....	....
Other liabilities	4 786	....	....	....	....	....	....	175.5	6.3
Monetary authorities	4 787	....	....	....	....	....	....	175.5	6.3
of which: Short-term	4 789	....	....	....	....	....	....	*81.7*	*6.3*
General government	4 790	....	....	....	....	....	....	....	....
of which: Short-term	4 792	....	....	....	....	....	....	....	....
Banks	4 793	....	....	....	....	....	....	....	....
of which: Short-term	4 795	....	....	....	....	....	....	....	....
Other sectors	4 796	....	....	....	....	....	....	....	....
of which: Short-term	4 798	....	....	....	....	....	....	....	....
E. RESERVE ASSETS	4 802	**−218.1**	**−178.0**	**−170.9**	**−329.0**	**−1.1**	**−831.2**	**1.8**	**−198.6**
Monetary gold	4 812	....	....	....	....	....	....	....	....
Special drawing rights	4 811	−.8	−8.4	.1	.2	.4	.5	−91.1	4.4
Reserve position in the Fund	4 810	....	8.5	....	....	....	....	....	....
Foreign exchange	4 803	−217.3	−178.1	−171.0	−329.2	−1.5	−831.7	92.9	−203.0
Other claims	4 813	....	....	....	....	....	....	....	....
NET ERRORS AND OMISSIONS	4 998	**309.9**	**415.9**	**139.0**	**108.5**	**19.1**	**−107.5**	**−72.6**	**−186.3**

Table 1. ANALYTIC PRESENTATION, 2003–2010

(Millions of U.S. dollars)

	Code	2003	2004	2005	2006	2007	2008	2009	2010
A. Current Account[1]..............	4 993 Z.	**29,867**	**46,100**	**46,618**	**63,069**	**52,526**	**38,036**	**34,026**	**51,635**
Goods: exports f.o.b..........	2 100 ..	264,966	313,429	344,734	389,678	466,246	530,955	420,200	480,296
Goods: imports f.o.b..........	3 100 ..	−228,447	−272,590	−297,088	−342,152	−408,828	−469,794	−373,337	−428,419
Balance on Goods..........	4 100 ..	*36,519*	*40,839*	*47,647*	*47,525*	*57,419*	*61,162*	*46,863*	*51,877*
Services: credit..........	2 200 ..	63,227	73,772	80,085	84,810	96,737	105,573	93,314	95,812
Services: debit..........	3 200 ..	−63,897	−69,444	−73,307	−75,484	−84,527	−92,673	−85,449	−85,120
Balance on Goods and Services..........	4 991 ..	*35,850*	*45,167*	*54,425*	*56,852*	*69,628*	*74,062*	*54,728*	*62,569*
Income: credit..........	2 300 ..	59,006	80,671	98,776	130,556	158,612	133,589	89,390	98,054
Income: debit..........	3 300 ..	−57,773	−69,306	−94,839	−113,974	−159,426	−152,523	−99,788	−94,484
Balance on Goods, Services, and Income..........	4 992 ..	*37,082*	*56,533*	*58,362*	*73,434*	*68,815*	*55,129*	*44,330*	*66,139*
Current transfers: credit..........	2 379 Z.	8,444	9,764	11,177	17,729	15,669	17,524	20,611	16,999
Current transfers: debit..........	3 379 ..	−15,659	−20,197	−22,921	−28,095	−31,957	−34,616	−30,916	−31,503
B. Capital Account[1]..............	4 994 Z.	**−3,069**	**−1,614**	**−1,764**	**−2,617**	**−2,067**	**−4,474**	**−3,134**	**−5,836**
Capital account: credit..........	2 994 Z.	1,682	1,734	2,127	3,152	3,640	2,279	3,284	3,071
Capital account: debit..........	3 994 ..	−4,750	−3,349	−3,891	−5,769	−5,707	−6,753	−6,418	−8,907
Total, Groups A Plus B..........	4 981 ..	*26,798*	*44,485*	*44,854*	*60,452*	*50,458*	*33,562*	*30,891*	*45,799*
C. Financial Account[1]..............	4 995 W.	**−23,963**	**−46,181**	**−39,415**	**−66,341**	**−35,586**	**−31,486**	**−44,535**	**−24,303**
Direct investment abroad..........	4 505 ..	−44,641	−28,849	−129,925	−64,083	−53,735	−67,561	−25,878	−49,267
Direct investment in the Netherlands..........	4 555 Z.	20,441	4,379	47,328	7,054	124,756	10,008	36,738	−15,597
Portfolio investment assets..........	4 602 ..	−63,372	−105,084	−83,831	−46,141	−40,197	7,520	−73,506	10,988
Equity securities..........	4 610 ..	−15,394	−34,534	−11,531	−4,886	−28,340	−23,609	−25,849	1,157
Debt securities..........	4 619 ..	−47,978	−70,551	−72,301	−41,255	−11,857	31,129	−47,657	9,831
Portfolio investment liabilities..........	4 652 Z.	85,229	74,104	160,315	70,800	−81,746	67,702	33,092	48,352
Equity securities..........	4 660 ..	898	3,379	82,931	15,521	−100,035	−12,556	19,590	11,327
Debt securities..........	4 669 Z.	84,331	70,725	77,384	55,279	18,288	80,257	13,502	37,024
Financial derivatives..........	4 910 ..	−230	−1,518	−4,181	−11,072	3,245	−22,332	26,880	−15,531
Financial derivatives assets..........	4 900 ..	126,911	165,590	150,955	132,229	172,022	186,245	206,175	431,224
Financial derivatives liabilities..........	4 905 ..	−127,141	−167,108	−155,136	−143,301	−168,778	−208,578	−179,295	−446,755
Other investment assets..........	4 703 ..	−66,500	−67,053	−65,310	−214,025	−222,248	99,455	93,894	−41,746
Monetary authorities..........	4 701 ..	277	−335	196	−693	1,008	−2,105	−23,496	−31,830
General government..........	4 704 ..	−1,660	650	321	1,249	−98	−1,095	−9,066	−1,684
Banks..........	4 705 ..	−56,184	−57,572	−45,783	−197,202	−193,366	120,363	116,323	−5,871
Other sectors..........	4 728 ..	−8,934	−9,795	−20,044	−17,379	−29,791	−17,707	10,132	−2,362
Other investment liabilities..........	4 753 W.	45,110	77,840	36,189	191,125	234,340	−126,277	−135,755	38,498
Monetary authorities..........	4 753 WA	−3,544	2,085	−3,182	−8,788	46,126	−6,344	−24,973	3,402
General government..........	4 753 ZB	−133	−1,845	259	426	771	1,750	23,057	−2,959
Banks..........	4 753 ZC	41,211	77,337	39,026	161,198	182,576	−154,407	−38,954	41,592
Other sectors..........	4 753 ZD	7,576	263	85	38,289	4,867	32,724	−94,885	−3,536
Total, Groups A Through C..........	4 983 ..	*2,835*	*−1,696*	*5,439*	*−5,890*	*14,873*	*2,076*	*−13,644*	*21,496*
D. Net Errors and Omissions..........	4 998 ..	**−3,272**	**785**	**−7,229**	**6,670**	**−16,282**	**−1,229**	**20,603**	**−21,315**
Total, Groups A Through D..........	4 984 ..	*−437*	*−911*	*−1,790*	*780*	*−1,409*	*847*	*6,959*	*181*
E. Reserves and Related Items..........	4 802 A.	**437**	**911**	**1,790**	**−780**	**1,409**	**−847**	**−6,959**	**−181**
Reserve assets..........	4 802 ..	437	911	1,790	−780	1,409	−847	−6,959	−181
Use of Fund credit and loans..........	4 766 ..	....	....	....	....	....	....	....	....
Exceptional financing..........	4 920 ..	....	....	....	....	....	....	....	....
Conversion rates: euros per U.S. dollar..........	0 103 ..	**.8860**	**.8054**	**.8041**	**.7971**	**.7306**	**.6827**	**.7198**	**.7550**

[1] Excludes components that have been classified in the categories of Group E.

Table 2. STANDARD PRESENTATION, 2003–2010

(Millions of U.S. dollars)

	Code	2003	2004	2005	2006	2007	2008	2009	2010
CURRENT ACCOUNT	4 993	**29,867**	**46,100**	**46,618**	**63,069**	**52,526**	**38,036**	**34,026**	**51,635**
A. GOODS	4 100	**36,519**	**40,839**	**47,647**	**47,525**	**57,419**	**61,162**	**46,863**	**51,877**
Credit	2 100	**264,966**	**313,429**	**344,734**	**389,678**	**466,246**	**530,955**	**420,200**	**480,296**
General merchandise: exports f.o.b.	2 110	254,746	302,795	331,983	376,674	452,213	505,407	405,283	464,440
Goods for processing: exports f.o.b.	2 150	8,683	8,675	10,345	9,961	10,028	19,400	10,562	10,347
Repairs on goods	2 160	....	....	....	....	....	....	....	....
Goods procured in ports by carriers	2 170	1,454	1,920	2,281	2,692	3,524	5,100	3,218	4,114
Nonmonetary gold	2 180	83	39	125	351	481	1,048	1,137	1,395
Debit	3 100	**−228,447**	**−272,590**	**−297,088**	**−342,152**	**−408,828**	**−469,794**	**−373,337**	**−428,419**
General merchandise: imports f.o.b.	3 110	−221,000	−263,939	−287,199	−331,405	−395,221	−450,218	−358,984	−414,096
Goods for processing: imports f.o.b.	3 150	−6,258	−7,110	−7,780	−8,311	−10,586	−15,615	−10,628	−10,283
Repairs on goods	3 160	....	....	....	....	....	....	....	....
Goods procured in ports by carriers	3 170	−1,089	−1,435	−1,925	−2,049	−2,506	−2,838	−2,565	−2,521
Nonmonetary gold	3 180	−100	−106	−183	−388	−514	−1,123	−1,160	−1,520
B. SERVICES	4 200	**−670**	**4,328**	**6,779**	**9,327**	**12,210**	**12,900**	**7,865**	**10,692**
Total credit	2 200	*63,227*	*73,772*	*80,085*	*84,810*	*96,737*	*105,573*	*93,314*	*95,812*
Total debit	3 200	*−63,897*	*−69,444*	*−73,307*	*−75,484*	*−84,527*	*−92,673*	*−85,449*	*−85,120*
Transportation services, credit	2 205	**16,271**	**19,402**	**21,441**	**24,886**	**27,504**	**31,003**	**24,636**	**25,589**
Passenger	2 850	....	....	*6,078*	*6,147*	*6,583*	*7,180*	*5,467*	*5,829*
Freight	2 851	....	....	*12,760*	*14,198*	*15,608*	*17,648*	*14,565*	*14,833*
Other	2 852	....	....	*2,603*	*4,540*	*5,313*	*6,174*	*4,604*	*4,927*
Sea transport, passenger	2 207	....	....	75	87	66	62	53	58
Sea transport, freight	2 208	....	....	7,808	6,781	6,920	7,569	5,937	5,600
Sea transport, other	2 209	....	....	1,645	2,195	2,481	2,619	1,711	1,705
Air transport, passenger	2 211	....	....	5,892	5,852	6,327	6,906	5,341	5,722
Air transport, freight	2 212	....	....	2,566	1,622	1,765	2,341	1,421	1,861
Air transport, other	2 213	....	....	414	366	407	490	503	620
Other transport, passenger	2 215	....	....	112	208	190	212	73	49
Other transport, freight	2 216	....	....	2,387	5,796	6,923	7,738	7,207	7,373
Other transport, other	2 217	....	....	544	1,979	2,426	3,066	2,390	2,602
Transportation services, debit	3 205	**−12,188**	**−13,715**	**−14,952**	**−18,787**	**−20,821**	**−22,617**	**−17,951**	**−18,845**
Passenger	3 850	....	....	*−481*	*−366*	*−367*	*−389*	*−322*	*−283*
Freight	3 851	....	....	*−8,312*	*−14,519*	*−16,533*	*−18,180*	*−13,984*	*−14,702*
Other	3 852	....	....	*−6,159*	*−3,902*	*−3,921*	*−4,049*	*−3,645*	*−3,861*
Sea transport, passenger	3 207	....	....					−4	−6
Sea transport, freight	3 208	....	....	−4,581	−6,324	−6,646	−7,259	−4,695	−4,511
Sea transport, other	3 209	....	....	−1,828	−1,228	−1,267	−1,283	−1,061	−1,157
Air transport, passenger	3 211	....	....	−332	−196	−210	−234	−183	−175
Air transport, freight	3 212	....	....	−742	−1,624	−1,778	−2,270	−2,046	−2,358
Air transport, other	3 213	....	....	−3,928	−2,003	−1,895	−1,873	−1,659	−1,713
Other transport, passenger	3 215	....	....	−149	−170	−157	−155	−134	−102
Other transport, freight	3 216	....	....	−2,988	−6,572	−8,109	−8,651	−7,243	−7,833
Other transport, other	3 217	....	....	−403	−671	−759	−892	−926	−991
Travel, credit	2 236	**9,163**	**10,308**	**10,450**	**11,382**	**13,339**	**13,343**	**12,401**	**12,861**
Business travel	2 237	....	3,382	3,464	3,627	4,328	4,389	3,862	4,109
Personal travel	2 240	....	6,926	6,987	7,755	9,011	8,955	8,539	8,752
Travel, debit	3 236	**−15,265**	**−16,348**	**−16,140**	**−17,087**	**−19,109**	**−21,828**	**−20,758**	**−19,489**
Business travel	3 237	....	−4,058	−3,921	−4,156	−4,682	−5,205	−4,995	−4,760
Personal travel	3 240	....	−12,289	−12,219	−12,931	−14,427	−16,623	−15,764	−14,730
Other services, credit	2 200 BA	**37,793**	**44,062**	**48,194**	**48,543**	**55,894**	**61,227**	**56,278**	**57,362**
Communications	2 245	2,588	3,310	3,762	3,792	4,200	4,514	4,427	4,935
Construction	2 249	2,145	2,129	2,751	2,272	2,539	3,233	2,954	2,789
Insurance	2 253	380	414	452	512	613	703	564	626
Financial	2 260	738	836	910	1,047	1,368	1,499	1,303	1,333
Computer and information	2 262	2,884	3,702	3,723	4,969	6,419	6,684	6,121	6,320
Royalties and licence fees	2 266	2,930	4,205	3,866	3,481	4,322	4,873	5,474	5,491
Other business services	2 268	23,599	26,704	29,924	29,642	33,246	36,110	32,176	32,715
Personal, cultural, and recreational	2 287	618	771	902	717	671	752	796	702
Government, n.i.e.	2 291	1,910	1,990	1,904	2,110	2,515	2,859	2,462	2,450
Other services, debit	3 200 BA	**−36,444**	**−39,382**	**−42,216**	**−39,609**	**−44,597**	**−48,228**	**−46,740**	**−46,786**
Communications	3 245	−2,498	−2,868	−3,194	−3,771	−3,834	−3,958	−3,817	−4,085
Construction	3 249	−1,002	−1,071	−1,417	−1,189	−1,368	−1,732	−2,174	−2,009
Insurance	3 253	−1,011	−761	−802	−889	−1,037	−1,198	−995	−1,066
Financial	3 260	−887	−888	−1,011	−1,135	−1,627	−1,731	−1,390	−1,382
Computer and information	3 262	−2,352	−3,107	−3,697	−4,448	−5,470	−5,730	−5,757	−5,352
Royalties and licence fees	3 266	−3,360	−3,339	−3,692	−2,879	−3,662	−3,532	−4,073	−3,707
Other business services	3 268	−23,646	−25,590	−26,561	−23,762	−26,125	−28,875	−26,906	−27,747
Personal, cultural, and recreational	3 287	−746	−880	−949	−730	−706	−726	−799	−702
Government, n.i.e.	3 291	−943	−879	−894	−805	−767	−746	−828	−736

Table 2 (Continued). STANDARD PRESENTATION, 2003–2010

(Millions of U.S. dollars)

	Code	2003	2004	2005	2006	2007	2008	2009	2010
C. INCOME	4 300 ..	**1,233**	**11,366**	**3,937**	**16,582**	**−814**	**−18,933**	**−10,397**	**3,570**
Total credit	2 300 ..	*59,006*	*80,671*	*98,776*	*130,556*	*158,612*	*133,589*	*89,390*	*98,054*
Total debit	3 300 ..	*−57,773*	*−69,306*	*−94,839*	*−113,974*	*−159,426*	*−152,523*	*−99,788*	*−94,484*
Compensation of employees, credit	2 310 ..	**1,120**	**1,251**	**1,203**	**1,186**	**1,319**	**1,385**	**1,461**	**1,457**
Compensation of employees, debit	3 310 ..	**−1,812**	**−2,290**	**−2,670**	**−2,972**	**−6,626**	**−8,817**	**−8,159**	**−7,185**
Investment income, credit	2 320 ..	**57,886**	**79,420**	**97,573**	**129,370**	**157,293**	**132,204**	**87,929**	**96,597**
Direct investment income	2 330 ..	25,973	40,787	50,359	68,807	78,333	47,209	34,558	50,230
Dividends and distributed branch profits	2 332 ..	11,889	15,105	46,375	57,171	51,083	52,796	34,531	50,192
Reinvested earnings and undistributed branch profits	2 333 ..	7,923	17,548	−4,507	757	16,224	−18,123	−10,190	−9,365
Income on debt (interest)	2 334 ..	6,161	8,134	8,491	10,879	11,026	12,536	10,216	9,404
Portfolio investment income	2 339 ..	20,909	26,743	30,846	35,699	40,234	43,575	38,462	36,672
Income on equity	2 340 ..	4,826	6,491	8,589	9,783	11,810	12,685	8,303	8,927
Income on bonds and notes	2 350 ..	16,043	20,211	22,116	25,773	28,315	30,832	29,804	27,701
Income on money market instruments	2 360 ..	40	41	140	142	109	58	355	44
Other investment income	2 370 ..	11,004	11,890	16,368	24,864	38,726	41,420	14,910	9,695
Investment income, debit	3 320 ..	**−55,960**	**−67,016**	**−92,170**	**−111,002**	**−152,800**	**−143,706**	**−91,628**	**−87,299**
Direct investment income	3 330 ..	−18,099	−23,002	−31,665	−35,019	−49,435	−34,687	−24,728	−27,041
Dividends and distributed branch profits	3 332 ..	−8,749	−8,343	−25,350	−14,032	−33,871	−18,160	−15,756	−17,248
Reinvested earnings and undistributed branch profits	3 333 ..	−4,501	−8,698	499	−12,816	−5,925	−5,008	750	−2,079
Income on debt (interest)	3 334 ..	−4,849	−5,960	−6,815	−8,171	−9,639	−11,519	−9,721	−7,714
Portfolio investment income	3 339 ..	−23,953	−27,721	−38,156	−45,074	−56,088	−58,985	−45,957	−47,017
Income on equity	3 340 ..	−6,681	−7,949	−13,856	−16,951	−22,127	−22,862	−15,186	−15,366
Income on bonds and notes	3 350 ..	−16,628	−18,893	−23,464	−27,022	−31,972	−33,951	−29,848	−31,207
Income on money market instruments	3 360 ..	−644	−879	−836	−1,102	−1,988	−2,172	−923	−445
Other investment income	3 370 ..	−13,908	−16,294	−22,348	−30,909	−47,278	−50,033	−20,944	−13,241
D. CURRENT TRANSFERS	4 379 ..	**−7,216**	**−10,433**	**−11,744**	**−10,366**	**−16,289**	**−17,093**	**−10,305**	**−14,504**
Credit	2 379 ..	**8,444**	**9,764**	**11,177**	**17,729**	**15,669**	**17,524**	**20,611**	**16,999**
General government	2 380 ..	3,090	4,271	5,191	6,102	6,524	6,817	9,561	5,376
Other sectors	2 390 ..	5,354	5,493	5,986	11,628	9,145	10,707	11,050	11,624
Workers' remittances	2 391 ..	....	....	....	310	312	265	251	239
Other current transfers	2 392 ..	5,354	5,493	5,986	11,318	8,832	10,442	10,799	11,385
Debit	3 379 ..	**−15,659**	**−20,197**	**−22,921**	**−28,095**	**−31,957**	**−34,616**	**−30,916**	**−31,503**
General government	3 380 ..	−9,488	−12,374	−13,630	−15,165	−14,750	−17,626	−14,300	−14,635
Other sectors	3 390 ..	−6,171	−7,823	−9,290	−12,930	−17,207	−16,991	−16,616	−16,868
Workers' remittances	3 391 ..	−656	−644	−849	−783	−2,089	−2,303	−2,077	−1,978
Other current transfers	3 392 ..	−5,515	−7,179	−8,441	−12,147	−15,119	−14,687	−14,538	−14,890
CAPITAL AND FINANCIAL ACCOUNT	4 996 ..	**−26,595**	**−46,884**	**−39,389**	**−69,738**	**−36,244**	**−36,807**	**−54,628**	**−30,320**
CAPITAL ACCOUNT	4 994 ..	**−3,069**	**−1,614**	**−1,764**	**−2,617**	**−2,067**	**−4,474**	**−3,134**	**−5,836**
Total credit	2 994 ..	*1,682*	*1,734*	*2,127*	*3,152*	*3,640*	*2,279*	*3,284*	*3,071*
Total debit	3 994 ..	*−4,750*	*−3,349*	*−3,891*	*−5,769*	*−5,707*	*−6,753*	*−6,418*	*−8,907*
Capital transfers, credit	2 400 ..	**1,675**	**1,593**	**2,049**	**2,467**	**3,502**	**2,125**	**3,181**	**2,999**
General government	2 401 ..	250	256	308	409	17	....	....	....
Debt forgiveness	2 402 ..	....	....	....	....	....	....	....	....
Other capital transfers	2 410 ..	....	....	....	....	....	....	....	....
Other sectors	2 430 ..	1,425	1,338	1,741	2,058	3,485	2,125	3,181	2,999
Migrants' transfers	2 431 ..	904	913	994	1,289	1,229	1,650	1,986	2,138
Debt forgiveness	2 432 ..	....	....	....	....	....	....	....	....
Other capital transfers	2 440 ..	520	425	747	769	2,256	475	1,195	860
Capital transfers, debit	3 400 ..	**−2,955**	**−3,263**	**−3,855**	**−5,738**	**−5,635**	**−6,613**	**−6,354**	**−8,779**
General government	3 401 ..	−565	−743	−951	−1,650	−912	−2,322	−1,897	−4,586
Debt forgiveness	3 402 ..	....	....	....	....	....	....	....	....
Other capital transfers	3 410 ..	....	....	....	....	....	....	....	....
Other sectors	3 430 ..	−2,390	−2,520	−2,904	−4,087	−4,723	−4,291	−4,457	−4,193
Migrants' transfers	3 431 ..	−1,770	−2,098	−2,409	−2,855	−3,920	−3,794	−4,000	−3,760
Debt forgiveness	3 432 ..	....	....	....	....	....	....	....	....
Other capital transfers	3 440 ..	−620	−423	−495	−1,232	−803	−497	−457	−433
Nonproduced nonfinancial assets, credit	2 480 ..	**7**	**141**	**78**	**685**	**137**	**155**	**104**	**73**
Nonproduced nonfinancial assets, debit	3 480 ..	**−1,796**	**−85**	**−37**	**−31**	**−72**	**−140**	**−64**	**−128**

Table 2 (Continued). STANDARD PRESENTATION, 2003–2010
(Millions of U.S. dollars)

	Code	2003	2004	2005	2006	2007	2008	2009	2010
FINANCIAL ACCOUNT	4 995	−23,526	−45,270	−37,625	−67,121	−34,177	−32,333	−51,494	−24,484
A. DIRECT INVESTMENT	4 500	−24,200	−24,471	−82,597	−57,029	71,021	−57,553	10,860	−64,864
Direct investment abroad	4 505	−44,641	−28,849	−129,925	−64,083	−53,735	−67,561	−25,878	−49,267
Equity capital	4 510	−33,241	−31,276	−109,801	−53,400	−22,805	−43,960	−44,154	−64,403
Claims on affiliated enterprises	4 515	....	−31,276	−109,800	−53,399	−22,789	−43,948	−44,154	−64,403
Liabilities to affiliated enterprises	4 520	....	....	−1	....	−16	−12	....	....
Reinvested earnings	4 525	−7,923	−17,548	4,507	−754	−16,223	18,123	10,190	9,365
Other capital	4 530	−3,477	19,975	−24,631	−9,929	−14,707	−41,725	8,086	5,772
Claims on affiliated enterprises	4 535	....	10,362	−21,952	−19,332	−19,427	−39,981	7,662	3,581
Liabilities to affiliated enterprises	4 540	....	9,612	−2,679	9,402	4,720	−1,744	424	2,190
Direct investment in the Netherlands	4 555	20,441	4,379	47,328	7,054	124,756	10,008	36,738	−15,597
Equity capital	4 560	16,637	6,600	4,917	6,536	134,873	−13,256	28,590	−2,682
Claims on direct investors	4 565	....	553	−27	−58	....	1	....	....
Liabilities to direct investors	4 570	....	6,046	4,944	6,594	134,873	−13,258	28,590	−2,682
Reinvested earnings	4 575	4,501	8,698	−499	12,820	5,923	5,011	−750	2,079
Other capital	4 580	−698	−10,920	42,911	−12,302	−16,040	18,253	8,897	−14,993
Claims on direct investors	4 585	....	−1,742	314	−3,631	2,345	−3,080	5,612	516
Liabilities to direct investors	4 590	....	−9,177	42,597	−8,671	−18,385	21,333	3,285	−15,510
B. PORTFOLIO INVESTMENT	4 600	21,857	−30,980	76,484	24,659	−121,943	75,222	−40,413	59,340
Assets	4 602	−63,372	−105,084	−83,831	−46,141	−40,197	7,520	−73,506	10,988
Equity securities	4 610	−15,394	−34,534	−11,531	−4,886	−28,340	−23,609	−25,849	1,157
Monetary authorities	4 611	....	23	39	....	−4	−964	320	286
General government	4 612	....	....	....	....	....	....	....	....
Banks	4 613	....	−4,439	−6,322	17,062	−8,889	2,108	2,057	−6,520
Other sectors	4 614	....	−30,118	−5,248	−21,948	−19,447	−24,752	−28,227	7,391
Debt securities	4 619	−47,978	−70,551	−72,301	−41,255	−11,857	31,129	−47,657	9,831
Bonds and notes	4 620	−50,239	−61,081	−73,197	−64,826	−20,373	13,450	−53,467	1,519
Monetary authorities	4 621	....	121	−1,153	−351	−5,091	−6,565	−998	−2,862
General government	4 622	....	....	....	....	....	....	−24,307	2,950
Banks	4 623	....	−6,323	−15,951	−27,553	4,257	20,986	−24,414	−4,346
Other sectors	4 624	....	−54,879	−56,093	−36,921	−19,539	−971	−3,748	5,777
Money market instruments	4 630	2,262	−9,470	897	23,571	8,516	17,678	5,811	8,312
Monetary authorities	4 631	....	....	....	23	−802	1,025	−616	908
General government	4 632	....	....	....	....	....	....	....	....
Banks	4 633	....	−7,732	−1,257	22,701	8,910	6,177	−171	1,866
Other sectors	4 634	....	−1,738	2,153	847	408	10,476	6,598	5,539
Liabilities	4 652	85,229	74,104	160,315	70,800	−81,746	67,702	33,092	48,352
Equity securities	4 660	898	3,379	82,931	15,521	−100,035	−12,556	19,590	11,327
Banks	4 663	....	....	....	....	....	....	....	....
Other sectors	4 664	....	....	....	....	....	....	....	....
Debt securities	4 669	84,331	70,725	77,384	55,279	18,288	80,257	13,502	37,024
Bonds and notes	4 670	81,011	75,715	83,421	73,915	14,064	−10,503	22,735	35,934
Monetary authorities	4 671	....	....	....	....	....	....	....	....
General government	4 672	13,113	22,525	13,756	−252	−19,867	25,681	3,915	−6,405
Banks	4 673	43,965	48,866	53,227	41,315	27,131	−7,453	20,086	41,158
Other sectors	4 674	23,933	4,324	16,438	32,853	6,799	−28,731	−1,266	1,182
Money market instruments	4 680	3,320	−4,991	−6,037	−18,636	4,225	90,761	−9,233	1,090
Monetary authorities	4 681	....	....	....	....	....	....	....	....
General government	4 682	2,444	−2,455	586	−5,765	994	77,107	−25,253	−10,188
Banks	4 683	−3,702	269	−7,565	−7,666	5,215	13,021	23,708	7,457
Other sectors	4 684	4,578	−2,804	942	−5,205	−1,985	633	−7,688	3,821
C. FINANCIAL DERIVATIVES	4 910	−230	−1,518	−4,181	−11,072	3,245	−22,332	26,880	−15,531
Monetary authorities	4 911	8	....	....	....	....	....	....	44
General government	4 912	....	....	....	−3	1	2,125	538	5,446
Banks	4 913	−362	−1,241	−1,293	−7,066	−10,296	−5,130	2,053	−10,553
Other sectors	4 914	123	−278	−2,888	−4,003	13,539	−19,327	24,288	−10,468
Assets	4 900	126,911	165,590	150,955	132,229	172,022	186,245	206,175	431,224
Monetary authorities	4 901	8	....	....	....	....	....	....	44
General government	4 902	....	....	....	−3	1	2,125	538	5,446
Banks	4 903	96,650	118,004	120,015	111,487	114,530	137,530	127,667	300,787
Other sectors	4 904	30,252	47,586	30,941	20,745	57,491	46,590	77,969	124,947
Liabilities	4 905	−127,141	−167,108	−155,136	−143,301	−168,778	−208,578	−179,295	−446,755
Monetary authorities	4 906	....	....	....	....	....	....	....	....
General government	4 907	....	....	....	....	....	....	....	....
Banks	4 908	−97,012	−119,245	−121,308	−118,554	−124,826	−142,661	−125,614	−311,340
Other sectors	4 909	−30,129	−47,864	−33,828	−24,747	−43,951	−65,917	−53,681	−135,414

Table 2 (Concluded). STANDARD PRESENTATION, 2003–2010

(Millions of U.S. dollars)

	Code	2003	2004	2005	2006	2007	2008	2009	2010
D. OTHER INVESTMENT	4 700 ..	**−21,390**	**10,788**	**−29,122**	**−22,900**	**12,092**	**−26,822**	**−41,861**	**−3,248**
Assets	4 703 ..	**−66,500**	**−67,053**	**−65,310**	**−214,025**	**−222,248**	**99,455**	**93,894**	**−41,746**
Trade credits	4 706 ..	−1,487	−3,266	−2,616	−3,238	−3,582	1,887	915	−9,192
General government	4 707 ..	....	....	....	....	....	....	....	....
of which: Short-term	4 709 ..	....	....	....	....	....	....	....	....
Other sectors	4 710 ..	−1,487	−3,266	−2,616	−3,238	−3,582	1,887	915	−9,192
of which: Short-term	4 712 ..	*−1,787*	*−3,256*	*−2,537*	*−3,420*	*−3,301*	*2,340*	*1,223*	*−9,095*
Loans	4 714 ..	−18,306	−4,198	−18,133	−16,273	−78,200	−38,299	5,833	−307
Monetary authorities	4 715 ..	....	....	....	....	....	....	....	....
of which: Short-term	4 718 ..	....	....	....	....	....	....	....	....
General government	4 719 ..	−1,492	568	−50	455	471	−1,595	−9,027	−1,976
of which: Short-term	4 721 ..	*−1,625*	....	*−119*	*300*	*188*	*−1,715*	....	....
Banks	4 722 ..	−13,695	−5,771	−14,569	−12,872	−68,972	−17,957	16,397	−5,099
of which: Short-term	4 724 ..	....	....	....	....	....	....	....	....
Other sectors	4 725 ..	−3,119	1,004	−3,514	−3,856	−9,699	−18,747	−1,537	6,768
of which: Short-term	4 727 ..	*−2,378*	*1,148*	*−3,428*	*−4,003*	*−9,302*	*−16,438*	*9,718*	*6,123*
Currency and deposits	4 730 ..	−48,139	−58,334	−40,191	−186,079	−132,312	145,265	78,601	−28,684
Monetary authorities	4 731 ..	277	−314	220	−693	1,014	−2,072	−23,319	−31,640
General government	4 732 ..	....	....	....	....	....	....	....	....
Banks	4 733 ..	−42,489	−51,801	−31,215	−184,329	−124,394	138,320	99,926	−772
Other sectors	4 734 ..	−5,928	−6,219	−9,196	−1,057	−8,932	9,018	1,994	3,728
Other assets	4 736 ..	1,433	−1,254	−4,371	−8,435	−8,154	−9,398	8,544	−3,563
Monetary authorities	4 737 ..	....	−21	−24	....	−7	−34	−177	−190
of which: Short-term	4 739 ..	....	....	....	....	....	....	....	....
General government	4 740 ..	−167	82	371	794	−569	500	−39	292
of which: Short-term	4 742 ..	....	....	....	....	*−764*	*452*	*−96*	*173*
Banks	4 743 ..	....	....	....	....	....	....	....	....
of which: Short-term	4 745 ..	....	....	....	....	....	....	....	....
Other sectors	4 746 ..	1,600	−1,315	−4,718	−9,229	−7,578	−9,865	8,760	−3,666
of which: Short-term	4 748 ..	*1,563*	*−1,316*	*−4,721*	*−9,238*	*−7,577*	*−16,626*	*8,210*	*−3,648*
Liabilities	4 753 ..	**45,110**	**77,840**	**36,189**	**191,125**	**234,340**	**−126,277**	**−135,755**	**38,498**
Trade credits	4 756 ..	913	2,039	1,742	1,846	1,872	−1,101	−430	5,434
General government	4 757 ..	....	....	....	....	....	....	....	....
of which: Short-term	4 759 ..	....	....	....	....	....	....	....	....
Other sectors	4 760 ..	913	2,039	1,742	1,846	1,872	−1,101	−430	5,434
of which: Short-term	4 762 ..	*932*	*2,039*	*1,742*	*1,847*	*1,872*	*−1,101*	*−430*	*5,435*
Loans	4 764 ..	19,033	4,145	12,691	23,572	45,989	−3,357	−6,689	10,227
Monetary authorities	4 765 ..	103	−1,192	292	1,284	−905	−324	132	−128
of which: Use of Fund credit and loans from the Fund	4 766 ..	....	....	....	....	....	....	....	....
of which: Short-term	4 768 ..	*103*	*−1,192*	*292*	*1,284*	*−905*	*−324*	*132*	*−128*
General government	4 769 ..	−187	−954	6	....	610	60	23,384	−2,835
of which: Short-term	4 771 ..	*−185*	*−944*	*4*	....	*743*	*59*	*−43*	*−29*
Banks	4 772 ..	19,604	3,018	22,270	4,223	31,495	−16,036	−13,996	16,817
of which: Short-term	4 774 ..	....	....	....	....	....	....	....	....
Other sectors	4 775 ..	−487	3,273	−9,877	18,065	14,789	12,944	−16,209	−3,627
of which: Short-term	4 777 ..	*413*	*1,132*	*−3,058*	*19,695*	*1,764*	*5,811*	*−11,863*	*−11,481*
Currency and deposits	4 780 ..	25,404	66,893	18,874	159,164	198,933	−142,047	−70,675	24,168
Monetary authorities	4 781 ..	−3,647	3,277	−3,474	−10,072	47,030	−6,020	−31,833	3,530
General government	4 782 ..	99	−890	391	228	133	1,251	−359	−323
Banks	4 783 ..	20,613	70,716	18,863	159,099	151,868	−136,374	−21,154	26,400
Other sectors	4 784 ..	8,339	−6,210	3,094	9,908	−99	−904	−17,330	−5,438
Other liabilities	4 786 ..	−240	4,763	2,881	6,544	−12,454	20,228	−57,961	−1,331
Monetary authorities	4 787 ..	....	....	....	....	....	....	6,727	....
of which: Short-term	4 789 ..	....	....	....	....	....	....	....	....
General government	4 790 ..	−45	−1	−138	198	28	439	32	199
of which: Short-term	4 792 ..	*−45*	*−1*	*−138*	*198*	*28*	*439*	*32*	*199*
Banks	4 793 ..	995	3,603	−2,107	−2,124	−787	−1,997	−3,804	−1,624
of which: Short-term	4 795 ..	*995*	*3,603*	*−2,107*	*−2,124*	*−787*	*−1,997*	*−3,804*	*−1,624*
Other sectors	4 796 ..	−1,189	1,161	5,126	8,470	−11,695	21,785	−60,917	94
of which: Short-term	4 798 ..	*−1,823*	*1,172*	*5,135*	*8,485*	*−11,714*	*28,633*	*−60,714*	*−292*
E. RESERVE ASSETS	4 802 ..	**437**	**911**	**1,790**	**−780**	**1,409**	**−847**	**−6,959**	**−181**
Monetary gold	4 812 ..	930	....	1,190	1,000	481	227	....	....
Special drawing rights	4 811 ..	−13	34	....	−31	−153	−66	−6,600	24
Reserve position in the Fund	4 810 ..	69	500	1,295	550	180	−549	−470	−475
Foreign exchange	4 803 ..	−549	377	−695	−2,299	901	−460	111	270
Other claims	4 813 ..	....	....	....	....	....	....	....	....
NET ERRORS AND OMISSIONS	4 998 ..	**−3,272**	**785**	**−7,229**	**6,670**	**−16,282**	**−1,229**	**20,603**	**−21,315**

Table 3. INTERNATIONAL INVESTMENT POSITION (End-period stocks), 2003–2010

(Billions of U.S. dollars)

	Code	2003	2004	2005	2006	2007	2008	2009	2010
ASSETS..........................	8 995 C.	**2,000.21**	**2,394.19**	**2,467.54**	**3,088.09**	**3,782.04**	**3,345.01**	**3,522.39**	**3,576.70**
Direct investment abroad..........................	8 505 ..	**521.30**	**587.25**	**615.73**	**763.40**	**942.09**	**889.89**	**956.45**	**954.40**
Equity capital and reinvested earnings..........................	8 506 ..	318.97	388.77	406.24	520.27	612.09	534.43	588.72	627.72
Claims on affiliated enterprises..........................	8 507 ..	319.03	389.16	406.56	520.39	612.26	534.56	588.72	627.72
Liabilities to affiliated enterprises..........................	8 508 ..	−.06	−.39	−.32	−.11	−.17	−.13	....	....
Other capital..........................	8 530 ..	202.33	198.48	209.49	243.13	329.99	355.46	367.73	326.68
Claims on affiliated enterprises..........................	8 535 ..	241.31	249.50	250.98	298.75	355.66	369.14	382.60	342.06
Liabilities to affiliated enterprises..........................	8 540 ..	−38.98	−51.02	−41.50	−55.62	−25.67	−13.68	−14.87	−15.38
Portfolio investment..........................	8 602 ..	**832.42**	**1,058.94**	**1,098.14**	**1,269.85**	**1,477.63**	**1,146.00**	**1,405.97**	**1,389.22**
Equity securities..........................	8 610 ..	349.82	442.99	474.96	554.98	644.10	408.68	561.25	613.21
Monetary authorities..........................	8 611 ..	1.40	1.51	1.55	1.59	1.76	1.89	2.08	1.91
General government..........................	8 612 ..	....	....	....	....	....	....	....	....
Banks..........................	8 613 ..	6.96	12.75	17.07	−17.78	−7.45	−1.77	−4.03	4.19
Other sectors..........................	8 614 ..	341.46	428.74	456.34	571.18	649.80	408.57	563.20	607.11
Debt securities..........................	8 619 ..	482.60	615.95	623.18	714.87	833.53	737.32	844.71	776.01
Bonds and notes..........................	8 620 ..	476.17	597.76	607.56	704.53	814.41	722.42	826.16	761.72
Monetary authorities..........................	8 621 ..	11.67	12.07	10.90	11.89	17.80	24.17	26.03	27.12
General government..........................	8 622 ..	....	....	....	....	....	....	23.81	19.62
Banks..........................	8 623 ..	143.14	161.49	158.14	182.81	183.99	149.07	172.29	154.57
Other sectors..........................	8 624 ..	321.36	424.20	438.51	509.83	612.61	549.18	604.03	560.40
Money market instruments..........................	8 630 ..	6.43	18.19	15.62	10.33	19.12	14.89	18.56	14.29
Monetary authorities..........................	8 631 ..	....	....	....	....	1.00	....	.93	.20
General government..........................	8 632 ..	....	....	....	....	....	....	....	....
Banks..........................	8 633 ..	5.01	14.21	13.32	6.01	2.17	.86	3.28	3.52
Other sectors..........................	8 634 ..	1.42	3.98	2.31	4.32	15.95	14.03	14.34	10.57
Financial derivatives..........................	8 900 ..	**86.71**	**85.89**	**70.36**	**77.63**	**119.64**	**248.67**	**157.90**	**204.97**
Monetary authorities..........................	8 901 ..	....	.01	.23	.03	.04	.09	....	.04
General government..........................	8 902 ..	....	....	....	....	....	....	....	3.21
Banks..........................	8 903 ..	60.66	68.42	59.15	63.14	96.66	181.48	117.76	159.73
Other sectors..........................	8 904 ..	26.05	17.46	10.97	14.46	22.93	67.10	40.14	41.99
Other investment..........................	8 703 ..	**538.18**	**640.51**	**662.85**	**953.30**	**1,215.70**	**1,031.95**	**962.47**	**981.87**
Trade credits..........................	8 706 ..	28.01	33.64	31.58	38.77	47.25	42.39	41.61	47.65
General government..........................	8 707 ..	.12	....	....	....	....	....	....	....
of which: Short-term..........................	8 709 ..								
Other sectors..........................	8 710 ..	27.89	33.64	31.58	38.77	47.25	42.39	41.61	47.65
of which: Short-term..........................	8 712 ..	*27.56*	*33.27*	*31.20*	*38.53*	*46.69*	*41.42*	*41.27*	*47.24*
Loans..........................	8 714 ..	117.60	128.80	151.94	185.50	251.51	265.74	265.59	275.76
Monetary authorities..........................	8 715 ..	....	....	....	....	....	....	....	....
of which: Short-term..........................	8 718 ..								
General government..........................	8 719 ..	2.57	2.17	1.82	1.87	1.78	1.56	10.71	10.68
of which: Short-term..........................	8 721 ..								
Banks..........................	8 722 ..	74.42	84.44	92.21	110.89	192.46	201.97	189.92	214.28
of which: Short-term..........................	8 724 ..								
Other sectors..........................	8 725 ..	40.61	42.19	57.92	72.74	57.27	62.21	64.97	50.80
of which: Short-term..........................	8 727 ..	*12.42*	*12.42*	*19.61*	*25.43*	*23.83*	*26.14*	*17.52*	*9.39*
Currency and deposits..........................	8 730 ..	352.88	433.78	436.30	671.22	864.06	661.67	599.26	602.00
Monetary authorities..........................	8 731 ..	3.74	4.30	3.62	4.84	4.32	3.90	26.79	57.73
General government..........................	8 732 ..	3.22	3.64	8.03	2.32	6.55	7.64	4.43	4.11
Banks..........................	8 733 ..	326.72	398.32	391.87	623.47	788.44	599.69	518.79	493.48
Other sectors..........................	8 734 ..	19.21	27.51	32.78	40.59	64.74	50.45	49.25	46.68
Other assets..........................	8 736 ..	39.68	44.29	43.02	57.81	52.88	62.15	56.01	56.47
Monetary authorities..........................	8 737 ..	.31	.36	.33	.37	.42	.40	.46	.52
of which: Short-term..........................	8 739 ..	....	....	....	....	....	....	....	....
General government..........................	8 740 ..	3.54	3.70	2.89	2.38	3.19	2.45	2.43	3.08
of which: Short-term..........................	8 742 ..	....	....	....	....	.77	.22	.18	....
Banks..........................	8 743 ..	2.35	3.94	6.83	11.43	14.42	18.95	13.17	9.21
of which: Short-term..........................	8 745 ..	*2.35*	*3.94*	*6.83*	*11.43*	*14.42*	*18.95*	*13.17*	*9.21*
Other sectors..........................	8 746 ..	33.48	36.28	32.97	43.63	34.85	40.35	39.94	43.66
of which: Short-term..........................	8 748 ..	*27.94*	*30.31*	*27.46*	*37.48*	*27.97*	*39.92*	*39.93*	*43.63*
Reserve assets..........................	8 802 ..	**21.60**	**21.60**	**20.46**	**23.90**	**26.98**	**28.51**	**39.61**	**46.24**
Monetary gold..........................	8 812 ..	10.43	10.95	11.46	13.10	16.71	17.03	21.74	27.77
Special drawing rights..........................	8 811 ..	.78	.78	.72	.78	.98	1.02	7.66	7.50
Reserve position in the Fund..........................	8 810 ..	3.05	2.67	1.19	.69	.54	1.09	1.60	2.07
Foreign exchange..........................	8 803 ..	7.34	7.21	7.09	9.33	8.75	9.37	8.61	8.90
Other claims..........................	8 813 ..	....	....	....	....	....	....	....	....

Table 3 (Concluded). INTERNATIONAL INVESTMENT POSITION (End-period stocks), 2003–2010

(Billions of U.S. dollars)

	Code	2003	2004	2005	2006	2007	2008	2009	2010
LIABILITIES..	8 995 D.	**2,013.86**	**2,369.41**	**2,483.42**	**3,065.19**	**3,832.73**	**3,310.48**	**3,352.22**	**3,364.16**
Direct investment in the Netherlands.................	8 555 ..	**428.05**	**477.22**	**451.23**	**515.69**	**766.62**	**645.60**	**660.45**	**594.93**
Equity capital and reinvested earnings...........................	8 556 ..	249.25	295.09	242.97	295.04	483.52	359.00	384.80	354.94
Claims on direct investors.............................	8 557 ..	−.04	−.02	−.24	−.18	−.08	−.07	−.01	−.01
Liabilities to direct investors..........................	8 558 ..	249.29	295.11	243.22	295.22	483.60	359.07	384.81	354.95
Other capital..	8 580 ..	178.79	182.13	208.26	220.64	283.10	286.60	275.65	239.99
Claims on direct investors.............................	8 585 ..	−11.01	−12.80	−10.72	−14.63	−14.93	−17.18	−34.40	−31.70
Liabilities to direct investors..........................	8 590 ..	189.80	194.93	218.98	235.27	298.03	303.78	310.05	271.68
Portfolio investment.............................	8 652 ..	**866.12**	**1,045.45**	**1,219.82**	**1,470.56**	**1,572.82**	**1,268.50**	**1,442.12**	**1,503.00**
Equity securities...	8 660 ..	314.56	368.43	536.65	658.50	667.41	333.82	437.18	450.66
Banks...	8 663 ..	25.60	31.72	35.37	43.32	1.40	.36	.28	.86
Other sectors...	8 664 ..	288.95	336.72	501.29	615.18	666.01	333.46	436.90	449.80
Debt securities...	8 669 ..	551.57	677.02	683.17	812.06	905.41	934.68	1,004.94	1,052.34
Bonds and notes......................................	8 670 ..	504.12	627.93	638.92	777.99	855.14	789.46	855.13	907.53
Monetary authorities...............................	8 671 ..	....	....	....	....	....	....	....	....
General government...............................	8 672 ..	159.39	198.19	187.58	209.34	206.05	230.61	252.53	235.49
Banks...	8 673 ..	230.81	299.14	323.10	395.45	455.07	417.22	447.88	484.69
Other sectors.......................................	8 674 ..	113.93	130.60	128.24	173.20	194.03	141.63	154.73	187.35
Money market instruments........................	8 680 ..	47.45	49.09	44.24	34.07	50.27	145.22	149.81	144.82
Monetary authorities...............................	8 681 ..	....	....	....	....	....	....	....	....
General government...............................	8 682 ..	23.20	22.67	20.02	17.08	21.82	102.49	77.10	62.00
Banks...	8 683 ..	18.64	21.74	17.53	13.66	23.37	33.45	69.79	76.38
Other sectors.......................................	8 684 ..	5.61	4.68	6.69	3.33	5.08	9.27	2.92	6.44
Financial derivatives.............................	8 905 ..	**94.85**	**98.66**	**86.95**	**84.24**	**122.66**	**241.75**	**183.78**	**215.31**
Monetary authorities.................................	8 906 ..	.01	....	....	.01	.01	.06	.02	.03
General government..................................	8 907 ..	....	....	....	....	....	....	....	.21
Banks...	8 908 ..	78.74	92.94	76.03	76.76	102.82	215.13	152.23	183.33
Other sectors...	8 909 ..	16.10	5.72	10.92	7.47	19.82	26.56	31.53	31.74
Other investment.............................	8 753 ..	**624.84**	**748.07**	**725.42**	**994.70**	**1,370.64**	**1,154.64**	**1,065.87**	**1,050.92**
Trade credits...	8 756 ..	18.45	22.10	20.83	25.77	30.97	27.93	28.38	31.71
General government..................................	8 757 ..	....	....	....	....	....	....	....	....
of which: Short-term..............................	8 759 ..	....	....	....	....	....	....	....	....
Other sectors...	8 760 ..	18.45	22.10	20.83	25.77	30.97	27.93	28.38	31.71
of which: Short-term..............................	8 762 ..	*17.92*	*21.54*	*20.35*	*24.77*	*29.85*	*26.87*	*27.22*	*30.63*
Loans...	8 764 ..	150.38	162.32	176.58	237.23	308.53	278.20	280.28	314.97
Monetary authorities...............................	8 765 ..	1.34	.13	.39	1.71	.83	....	.14	....
of which: Use of Fund credit and loans from the Fund....	8 766 ..	....	....	....	....	....	....	....	....
of which: Short-term.............................	8 768 ..	*1.34*	*.13*	*.39*	*1.71*	*.83*	....	*.14*	....
General government...............................	8 769 ..	3.81	2.73	2.54	2.72	3.66	2.99	26.18	21.69
of which: Short-term.............................	8 771 ..	*1.06*	*.06*	*.05*	....	*.78*	*.26*	*.41*	*.34*
Banks...	8 772 ..	67.64	74.44	94.71	116.90	163.98	136.59	126.49	177.00
of which: Short-term.............................	8 774 ..	....	....	....	....	....	....	....	....
Other sectors.......................................	8 775 ..	77.59	85.02	78.93	115.90	140.05	138.62	127.47	116.28
of which: Short-term.............................	8 777 ..	*17.65*	*19.70*	*17.95*	*45.99*	*39.83*	*49.78*	*54.08*	*38.37*
Currency and deposits.................................	8 780 ..	433.08	534.73	499.35	691.34	947.99	743.44	709.27	654.91
Monetary authorities...............................	8 781 ..	1.25	4.97	1.22	−9.22	39.14	34.92	3.24	6.53
General government...............................	8 782 ..	1.23	.39	.73	1.01	1.21	1.29	.89	.54
Banks...	8 783 ..	428.57	526.58	494.67	692.76	903.69	698.27	698.43	642.25
Other sectors.......................................	8 784 ..	2.02	2.79	2.72	6.78	3.95	8.96	6.71	5.58
Other liabilities.......................................	8 786 ..	22.92	28.93	28.66	40.36	83.15	105.07	47.93	49.33
Monetary authorities...............................	8 787 ..	....	....	....	....	....	....	7.58	7.45
of which: Short-term.............................	8 789 ..	....	....	....	....	....	....	....	....
General government...............................	8 790 ..	.58	.63	.42	.66	.78	.97	1.09	1.22
of which: Short-term.............................	8 792 ..	*.58*	*.63*	*.42*	*.66*	*.78*	*.97*	*1.09*	*1.22*
Banks...	8 793 ..	12.52	17.27	12.96	12.24	14.55	14.16	10.66	15.34
of which: Short-term.............................	8 795 ..	*12.52*	*17.27*	*12.96*	*12.24*	*14.55*	*14.16*	*10.66*	*15.34*
Other sectors.......................................	8 796 ..	9.83	11.04	15.29	27.46	67.83	89.94	28.60	25.33
of which: Short-term.............................	8 798 ..	*3.96*	*4.75*	*9.50*	*21.07*	*60.72*	*89.73*	*28.59*	*24.94*
NET INTERNATIONAL INVESTMENT POSITION........	8 995 ..	**−13.65**	**24.78**	**−15.88**	**22.90**	**−50.70**	**34.53**	**170.17**	**212.54**
Conversion rates: euros per U.S. dollar (end of period)..	0 104 ..	**.7918**	**.7342**	**.8477**	**.7593**	**.6793**	**.7185**	**.6942**	**.7484**

Table 1. ANALYTIC PRESENTATION, 2003–2010

(Millions of U.S. dollars)

	Code	2003	2004	2005	2006	2007	2008	2009	2010
A. Current Account[1]	4 993 Z.	**2.5**	**−88.1**	**−105.8**	**−260.0**	**−593.8**	**−872.1**	**−827.4**	....
Goods: exports f.o.b.	2 100 ..	429.4	521.3	608.0	694.7	676.4	1,088.4	810.1	....
Goods: imports f.o.b.	3 100 ..	−1,472.0	−1,722.9	−1,950.1	−2,209.3	−2,548.8	−3,079.0	−2,606.9	....
Balance on Goods	4 100 ..	*−1,042.6*	*−1,201.6*	*−1,342.1*	*−1,514.6*	*−1,872.4*	*−1,990.6*	*−1,796.9*	....
Services: credit	2 200 ..	1,691.6	1,800.1	1,875.1	1,991.1	2,098.4	2,054.8	2,035.4	....
Services: debit	3 200 ..	−758.6	−724.8	−734.0	−758.3	−797.3	−871.5	−929.7	....
Balance on Goods and Services	4 991 ..	*−109.7*	*−126.3*	*−201.1*	*−281.8*	*−571.2*	*−807.3*	*−691.1*	....
Income: credit	2 300 ..	90.0	88.5	106.2	137.0	170.2	139.6	109.6	....
Income: debit	3 300 ..	−97.1	−105.0	−121.3	−138.1	−167.3	−181.0	−206.1	....
Balance on Goods, Services, and Income	4 992 ..	*−116.7*	*−142.8*	*−216.1*	*−282.9*	*−568.3*	*−848.7*	*−787.7*	....
Current transfers: credit	2 379 Z.	396.9	323.2	415.1	328.8	301.2	374.2	375.0	....
Current transfers: debit	3 379 ..	−277.7	−268.5	−304.7	−305.9	−326.8	−397.7	−414.8	....
B. Capital Account[1]	4 994 Z.	**26.2**	**79.4**	**95.6**	**100.3**	**122.3**	**136.8**	**112.1**	....
Capital account: credit	2 994 Z.	32.8	80.2	96.1	102.6	126.9	137.4	115.5	....
Capital account: debit	3 994 ..	−6.6	−.8	−.5	−2.3	−4.6	−.6	−3.4	....
Total, Groups A Plus B	4 981 ..	*28.7*	*−8.7*	*−10.2*	*−159.7*	*−471.5*	*−735.4*	*−715.4*	....
C. Financial Account[1]	4 995 W.	**−6.1**	**−11.2**	**26.8**	**139.7**	**523.0**	**858.3**	**464.7**	....
Direct investment abroad	4 505 ..	.5	−22.1	−65.4	−56.6	3.2	−15.1	−7.3	....
Direct investment in the Netherlands Antilles	4 555 Z.	10.9	21.7	41.9	−21.9	234.3	266.0	116.9	....
Portfolio investment assets	4 602 ..	−1.3	−94.1	−25.8	67.3	−67.9	−47.4	−39.4	....
Equity securities	4 610 ..	−31.8	−13.6	−2.3	−12.5	−71.6	5.9	5.2	....
Debt securities	4 619 ..	30.5	−80.6	−23.5	79.8	3.7	−53.4	−44.6	....
Portfolio investment liabilities	4 652 Z.	5.0	93.3	1.6	−8.9	−11.2	−23.1	−66.2	....
Equity securities	4 660 ..	....	....	....	....	....	....	....	....
Debt securities	4 669 Z.	5.0	93.3	1.6	−8.9	−11.2	−23.1	−66.2	....
Financial derivatives	4 910 ..	....	....	.4	−1.6	−4.2	−.2	.2	....
Financial derivatives assets	4 900 ..	....	....	.4	−1.6	−4.2	−.2	.2	....
Financial derivatives liabilities	4 905 ..	....	....	....	....	....	....	....	....
Other investment assets	4 703 ..	−37.8	−4.7	40.5	193.3	407.8	707.1	504.7	....
Monetary authorities	4 701 ..	....	....	....	....	.3	−.4	....	....
General government	4 704 ..	−5.7	....	.2	−.1	−.2	7.5	.3	....
Banks	4 705 ..	−3.1	39.1	19.2	6.5	16.8	26.0	62.7	....
Other sectors	4 728 ..	−29.1	−43.7	21.1	186.8	390.9	674.0	441.6	....
Other investment liabilities	4 753 W.	16.5	−5.3	33.7	−31.8	−39.0	−29.0	−44.2	....
Monetary authorities	4 753 WA	....	....	....	....	....	....	....	....
General government	4 753 ZB	−37.8	−26.8	−34.8	−36.3	−22.0	−23.5	−19.2	....
Banks	4 753 ZC	−5.8	−25.1	5.6	−.3	−24.8	34.2	25.0	....
Other sectors	4 753 ZD	60.1	46.6	62.9	4.8	7.8	−39.6	−50.0	....
Total, Groups A Through C	4 983 ..	*22.5*	*−19.9*	*16.5*	*−20.0*	*51.5*	*122.9*	*−250.7*	....
D. Net Errors and Omissions	4 998 ..	**4.6**	**27.6**	**31.7**	**35.6**	**77.6**	**57.0**	**74.7**	....
Total, Groups A Through D	4 984 ..	*27.1*	*7.6*	*48.3*	*15.6*	*129.2*	*179.9*	*−176.0*	....
E. Reserves and Related Items	4 802 A.	**−27.1**	**−7.6**	**−48.3**	**−15.6**	**−129.2**	**−179.9**	**176.0**	....
Reserve assets	4 802 ..	−49.8	−36.9	−74.0	−47.1	−155.0	−207.6	−301.1	....
Use of Fund credit and loans	4 766 ..	....	....	....	....	....	....	....	....
Exceptional financing	4 920 ..	22.7	29.3	25.7	31.5	25.8	27.6	477.0	....
Conversion rates: Netherlands Antillean guilders per U.S. dollar	0 101 ..	**1.7900**	**1.7900**	**1.7900**	**1.7900**	**1.7900**	**1.7900**	**1.7900**	....

[1] Excludes components that have been classified in the categories of Group E.

Table 2. STANDARD PRESENTATION, 2003–2010

(Millions of U.S. dollars)

	Code	2003	2004	2005	2006	2007	2008	2009	2010
CURRENT ACCOUNT	4 993	2.5	−88.1	−105.8	−260.0	−593.8	−872.1	−373.9	....
A. GOODS	4 100	−1,042.6	−1,201.6	−1,342.1	−1,514.6	−1,872.4	−1,990.6	−1,796.9	....
Credit	2 100	429.4	521.3	608.0	694.7	676.4	1,088.4	810.1	....
General merchandise: exports f.o.b.	2 110	318.4	397.9	447.6	484.9	414.0	557.1	503.3	....
Goods for processing: exports f.o.b.	2 150	12.9	11.0	10.5	9.5	8.0	15.1	7.6	....
Repairs on goods	2 160	35.2	48.5	43.6	55.0	63.1	61.9	56.6	....
Goods procured in ports by carriers	2 170	62.9	64.0	106.3	145.3	191.3	454.3	242.6	....
Nonmonetary gold	2 180	....	....	....	....	....	....	....	....
Debit	3 100	−1,472.0	−1,722.9	−1,950.1	−2,209.3	−2,548.8	−3,079.0	−2,606.9	....
General merchandise: imports f.o.b.	3 110	−1,443.8	−1,699.6	−1,939.5	−2,203.2	−2,532.1	−3,064.6	−2,593.7	....
Goods for processing: imports f.o.b.	3 150	−19.9	−16.9	−9.4	−4.0	−13.6	−9.6	−6.6	....
Repairs on goods	3 160	−.2	−.4	....	−1.0	−.1	−.4	−1.3	....
Goods procured in ports by carriers	3 170	−8.2	−6.0	−1.2	−1.1	−2.9	−4.4	−5.3	....
Nonmonetary gold	3 180	....	....	....	....	....	....	....	....
B. SERVICES	4 200	933.0	1,075.3	1,141.1	1,232.8	1,301.2	1,183.3	1,105.7	....
Total credit	2 200	*1,691.6*	*1,800.1*	*1,875.1*	*1,991.1*	*2,098.4*	*2,054.8*	*2,035.4*	....
Total debit	3 200	*−758.6*	*−724.8*	*−734.0*	*−758.3*	*−797.3*	*−871.5*	*−929.7*	....
Transportation services, credit	2 205	130.8	123.3	126.8	132.0	144.4	162.3	173.9	....
Passenger	2 850	*65.3*	*34.5*	*7.1*	*4.8*	*5.9*	*9.7*	*20.3*	....
Freight	2 851	*2.6*	*1.4*	*1.0*	*1.0*	*1.8*	*3.1*	*3.5*	....
Other	2 852	*62.8*	*87.4*	*118.7*	*126.2*	*136.6*	*149.5*	*150.1*	....
Sea transport, passenger	2 207	.2	.2	.5	....	.7	1.0	.4	....
Sea transport, freight	2 208	....	....	....	....	....	....	....	....
Sea transport, other	2 209	60.0	80.5	109.7	118.5	127.1	138.0	135.9	....
Air transport, passenger	2 211	65.1	34.3	6.6	4.8	5.3	8.7	19.9	....
Air transport, freight	2 212	2.6	1.4	1.0	1.0	1.8	3.1	3.5	....
Air transport, other	2 213	2.8	6.9	8.9	7.7	9.5	11.5	14.3	....
Other transport, passenger	2 215	....	....	....	....	....	....	....	....
Other transport, freight	2 216	....	....	....	....	....	....	....	....
Other transport, other	2 217	....	....	....	....	....	....	....	....
Transportation services, debit	3 205	−69.1	−78.0	−85.7	−83.0	−92.0	−118.4	−158.1	....
Passenger	3 850	*−19.0*	*−21.5*	*−30.8*	*−22.1*	*−20.2*	*−26.4*	*−71.5*	....
Freight	3 851	*−37.2*	*−43.8*	*−50.0*	*−56.8*	*−65.3*	*−79.0*	*−66.8*	....
Other	3 852	*−12.9*	*−12.8*	*−4.9*	*−4.1*	*−6.6*	*−13.0*	*−19.8*	....
Sea transport, passenger	3 207	−.5	−.4	−.3	−.3	−.6	−.5	−.4	....
Sea transport, freight	3 208	−33.5	−39.4	−45.0	−51.1	−58.7	−71.1	−60.2	....
Sea transport, other	3 209	−2.1	−3.6	−1.9	−1.1	−3.2	−10.3	−13.7	....
Air transport, passenger	3 211	−18.5	−21.0	−30.5	−21.8	−19.6	−25.9	−71.1	....
Air transport, freight	3 212	−3.7	−4.4	−5.0	−5.7	−6.5	−7.9	−6.7	....
Air transport, other	3 213	−10.8	−9.2	−2.9	−3.0	−3.4	−2.7	−6.1	....
Other transport, passenger	3 215	....	....	....	....	....	....	....	....
Other transport, freight	3 216	....	....	....	....	....	....	....	....
Other transport, other	3 217	....	....	....	....	....	....	....	....
Travel, credit	2 236	855.2	936.4	989.5	1,019.3	1,098.3	1,162.7	1,083.5	....
Business travel	2 237	....	....	....	....	....	....	....	....
Personal travel	2 240	855.2	936.4	989.5	1,019.3	1,098.3	1,162.7	1,083.5	....
Travel, debit	3 236	−308.7	−280.6	−263.3	−281.6	−295.4	−299.0	−296.5	....
Business travel	3 237	....	....	....	....	....	....	....	....
Personal travel	3 240	−308.7	−280.6	−263.3	−281.6	−295.4	−299.0	−296.5	....
Other services, credit	2 200 BA	705.7	740.4	758.8	839.8	855.7	729.8	778.0	....
Communications	2 245	9.3	19.3	12.5	11.0	14.9	24.5	25.7	....
Construction	2 249	17.7	15.7	22.2	35.5	51.0	54.9	43.3	....
Insurance	2 253	3.3	4.6	.5	.5	.6	.6	.7	....
Financial	2 260	2.8	2.7	5.7	5.5	2.0	1.3	3.0	....
Computer and information	2 262	1.3	2.5	1.7	3.5	4.1	5.9	6.2	....
Royalties and licence fees	2 266	.5	.2	.3	.2	3.0	2.4	6.3	....
Other business services	2 268	617.8	648.8	659.3	727.8	729.4	612.2	660.8	....
Personal, cultural, and recreational	2 287	.6	.5	.2	.7	.2	.5	....	....
Government, n.i.e.	2 291	52.3	46.1	56.3	55.1	50.6	27.6	32.0	....
Other services, debit	3 200 BA	−380.8	−366.1	−385.0	−393.8	−409.9	−454.1	−475.1	....
Communications	3 245	−16.7	−15.2	−20.3	−23.2	−20.7	−33.0	−34.8	....
Construction	3 249	−15.6	−8.9	−33.3	−35.3	−51.8	−86.6	−60.1	....
Insurance	3 253	−12.1	−9.2	−10.1	−11.6	−13.3	−16.0	−13.7	....
Financial	3 260	−5.8	−4.9	−5.3	−5.0	−7.5	−4.5	−6.8	....
Computer and information	3 262	−9.2	−8.9	−13.9	−12.9	−15.2	−20.9	−27.0	....
Royalties and licence fees	3 266	−5.3	−5.0	−5.9	−7.0	−12.6	−18.5	−22.1	....
Other business services	3 268	−303.7	−298.7	−286.8	−288.6	−279.9	−267.0	−298.6	....
Personal, cultural, and recreational	3 287	−2.1	−1.1	−.7	−1.0	−.4	−1.6	−7.5	....
Government, n.i.e.	3 291	−10.4	−14.2	−8.6	−9.3	−8.5	−6.1	−4.5	....

Table 2 (Continued). STANDARD PRESENTATION, 2003–2010

(Millions of U.S. dollars)

	Code	2003	2004	2005	2006	2007	2008	2009	2010
C. INCOME	4 300	**−7.0**	**−16.5**	**−15.1**	**−1.1**	**2.9**	**−41.4**	**−96.5**	....
Total credit	2 300	*90.0*	*88.5*	*106.2*	*137.0*	*170.2*	*139.6*	*109.6*	....
Total debit	3 300	*−97.1*	*−105.0*	*−121.3*	*−138.1*	*−167.3*	*−181.0*	*−206.1*	....
Compensation of employees, credit	2 310	**5.6**	**3.9**	**9.5**	**17.5**	**21.6**	**27.5**	**30.9**	....
Compensation of employees, debit	3 310	**−34.3**	**−35.0**	**−42.1**	**−38.0**	**−43.7**	**−47.4**	**−43.7**	....
Investment income, credit	2 320	**84.5**	**84.6**	**96.8**	**119.6**	**148.6**	**112.1**	**78.7**	....
Direct investment income	2 330	15.4	27.4	15.9	31.1	19.3	21.5	24.8	....
Dividends and distributed branch profits	2 332	12.9	25.3	14.8	30.5	19.1	18.8	21.8	....
Reinvested earnings and undistributed branch profits	2 333	....	....	....	....	....	.9	....	....
Income on debt (interest)	2 334	2.5	2.1	1.1	.6	.2	1.8	3.1	....
Portfolio investment income	2 339	53.2	37.5	45.3	44.4	71.9	47.5	28.3	....
Income on equity	2 340	7.7	3.7	6.9	7.6	9.9	7.4	5.5	....
Income on bonds and notes	2 350	....	....	....	....	....	....	....	....
Income on money market instruments	2 360	45.5	33.8	38.4	36.7	61.9	40.0	22.8	....
Other investment income	2 370	15.8	19.7	35.6	44.1	57.5	43.1	25.5	....
Investment income, debit	3 320	**−62.8**	**−70.0**	**−79.2**	**−100.2**	**−123.6**	**−133.6**	**−162.4**	....
Direct investment income	3 330	−22.3	−27.3	−29.5	−48.9	−61.6	−61.2	−79.1	....
Dividends and distributed branch profits	3 332	−21.2	−24.5	−26.0	−46.9	−61.8	−53.2	−71.1	....
Reinvested earnings and undistributed branch profits	3 333	.4	−.3	−.9	−.1	2.6	−.4	−1.5	....
Income on debt (interest)	3 334	−1.5	−2.5	−2.7	−1.9	−2.3	−7.6	−6.4	....
Portfolio investment income	3 339	−25.1	−20.8	−22.0	−21.2	−31.6	−43.4	−61.2	....
Income on equity	3 340	−21.5	−18.8	−18.8	−19.2	−22.5	−35.6	−51.8	....
Income on bonds and notes	3 350	....	....	....	....	....	....	....	....
Income on money market instruments	3 360	−3.6	−2.0	−3.2	−2.1	−9.1	−7.9	−9.4	....
Other investment income	3 370	−15.4	−21.9	−27.7	−30.0	−30.5	−29.0	−22.2	....
D. CURRENT TRANSFERS	4 379	**119.2**	**54.7**	**110.3**	**22.9**	**−25.5**	**−23.5**	**413.8**	....
Credit	2 379	**396.9**	**323.2**	**415.1**	**328.8**	**301.2**	**374.2**	**828.6**	....
General government	2 380	86.7	70.5	177.2	85.4	52.4	91.7	541.0	....
Other sectors	2 390	310.1	252.6	237.9	243.4	248.8	282.4	287.6	....
Workers' remittances	2 391	.8	1.0	1.0	.4	.5	.7	2.8	....
Other current transfers	2 392	309.3	251.6	236.9	242.9	248.3	281.8	284.8	....
Debit	3 379	**−277.7**	**−268.5**	**−304.7**	**−305.9**	**−326.8**	**−397.7**	**−414.8**	....
General government	3 380	−11.5	−9.0	−18.9	−12.4	−15.0	−15.3	−13.9	....
Other sectors	3 390	−266.2	−259.5	−285.8	−293.5	−311.8	−382.4	−400.9	....
Workers' remittances	3 391	−18.1	−16.5	−16.5	−21.0	−23.8	−46.0	−58.8	....
Other current transfers	3 392	−248.2	−242.9	−269.3	−272.5	−288.1	−336.4	−342.1	....
CAPITAL AND FINANCIAL ACCOUNT	4 996	**−7.0**	**60.6**	**74.1**	**224.4**	**516.2**	**815.1**	**299.2**	....
CAPITAL ACCOUNT	4 994	**26.2**	**79.4**	**95.6**	**100.3**	**122.3**	**136.8**	**112.1**	....
Total credit	2 994	*32.8*	*80.2*	*96.1*	*102.6*	*126.9*	*137.4*	*115.5*	....
Total debit	3 994	*−6.6*	*−.8*	*−.5*	*−2.3*	*−4.6*	*−.6*	*−3.4*	....
Capital transfers, credit	2 400	**32.3**	**80.2**	**96.1**	**102.6**	**126.9**	**137.4**	**115.5**	....
General government	2 401	30.3	79.7	96.1	101.3	122.3	127.1	111.3	....
Debt forgiveness	2 402	....	....	....	....	....	....	....	....
Other capital transfers	2 410	30.3	79.7	96.1	101.3	122.3	127.1	111.3	....
Other sectors	2 430	2.0	.6	....	1.3	4.5	10.3	4.2	....
Migrants' transfers	2 431	1.5	.6	....	1.3	3.1	3.7	3.8	....
Debt forgiveness	2 432	....	....	....	....	....	....	....	....
Other capital transfers	2 440	.5	....	....	....	1.4	6.6	.4	....
Capital transfers, debit	3 400	**−6.6**	**−.8**	**−.5**	**−2.3**	**−4.6**	**−.6**	**−3.4**	....
General government	3 401	....	....	....	....	....	....	....	....
Debt forgiveness	3 402	....	....	....	....	....	....	....	....
Other capital transfers	3 410	....	....	....	....	....	....	....	....
Other sectors	3 430	−6.6	−.8	−.5	−2.3	−4.6	−.6	−3.4	....
Migrants' transfers	3 431	−6.3	−.8	−.5	−2.2	−4.6	−.6	−3.4	....
Debt forgiveness	3 432	....	....	....	....	....	....	....	....
Other capital transfers	3 440	−.3	−.1	....	−.1	....	....	....	....
Nonproduced nonfinancial assets, credit	2 480	**.4**	....	....	....	**.1**	....	....	....
Nonproduced nonfinancial assets, debit	3 480	....	....	....	....	....	....	....	....

Table 2 (Continued). STANDARD PRESENTATION, 2003–2010

(Millions of U.S. dollars)

	Code	2003	2004	2005	2006	2007	2008	2009	2010
FINANCIAL ACCOUNT..	4 995 ..	**−33.2**	**−18.8**	**−21.5**	**124.1**	**393.9**	**678.4**	**187.1**	....
A. DIRECT INVESTMENT..	4 500 ..	**11.5**	**−.4**	**−23.5**	**−78.5**	**237.5**	**250.9**	**109.6**	....
Direct investment abroad...............................	4 505 ..	.5	−22.1	−65.4	−56.6	3.2	−15.1	−7.3	....
Equity capital..	4 510 ..	.5	−7.1	−71.4	−43.9	−8.8	−15.1	−8.0	....
Claims on affiliated enterprises.................	4 515 ..	.5	−7.1	−71.4	−43.9	−8.8	−15.1	−8.0	....
Liabilities to affiliated enterprises..........	4 520 ..	....	....	....	....	....	....	....	
Reinvested earnings....................................	4 525 ..	....	....	....	....	....	−.9	....	
Other capital...	4 530 ..	.1	−15.0	6.1	−12.7	12.1	.9	.7	....
Claims on affiliated enterprises.................	4 535 ..	.1	−15.0	6.1	−12.7	12.1	.9	.7	....
Liabilities to affiliated enterprises..........	4 540 ..	....	....	....	....	....	....	....	
Direct investment in the Netherlands Antilles...	4 555 ..	**10.9**	**21.7**	**41.9**	**−21.9**	**234.3**	**266.0**	**116.9**	....
Equity capital..	4 560 ..	16.3	52.7	120.8	−8.0	205.4	224.8	47.9	
Claims on direct investors.........................	4 565 ..	....	....	....	....	....	....	....	
Liabilities to direct investors....................	4 570 ..	16.3	52.7	120.8	−8.0	205.4	224.8	47.9	
Reinvested earnings....................................	4 575 ..	−.4	.3	.9	....	−2.6	.4	1.5	
Other capital...	4 580 ..	−4.9	−31.3	−79.8	−13.9	31.5	40.8	67.5	
Claims on direct investors.........................	4 585 ..	1.6	−.5	.6	1.0	....	....		
Liabilities to direct investors....................	4 590 ..	−6.6	−31.3	−79.3	−14.5	30.5	40.8	67.5	
B. PORTFOLIO INVESTMENT.................................	4 600 ..	**3.7**	**−.9**	**−24.3**	**58.3**	**−79.2**	**−70.5**	**−105.6**	....
Assets...	4 602 ..	**−1.3**	**−94.1**	**−25.8**	**67.3**	**−67.9**	**−47.4**	**−39.4**	
Equity securities...	4 610 ..	−31.8	−13.6	−2.3	−12.5	−71.6	5.9	5.2	
Monetary authorities...............................	4 611 ..	....	....	....	....	....	....	....	
General government................................	4 612 ..	.1	−16.3	−18.3	−3.1	−5.1	−13.8	−.1	
Banks...	4 613 ..	−2.9	....	.5	.4	−.9	15.5	4.8	
Other sectors..	4 614 ..	−29.0	2.7	15.5	−9.8	−65.6	4.2	.5	
Debt securities..	4 619 ..	30.5	−80.6	−23.5	79.8	3.7	−53.4	−44.6	
Bonds and notes......................................	4 620 ..	23.9	−77.6	−32.3	74.9	−7.7	−47.1	−65.6	
Monetary authorities...........................	4 621 ..	−2.8	....	....	....	....	....	....	
General government.............................	4 622 ..	.5	−13.9	−.1	.1	−1.1	−1.7	−45.7	
Banks...	4 623 ..	1.5	1.3	.1	2.1	2.1	.2	−5.5	
Other sectors......................................	4 624 ..	24.7	−65.0	−32.3	72.7	−8.7	−45.6	−14.3	
Money market instruments......................	4 630 ..	6.6	−2.9	8.8	4.9	11.4	−6.3	21.0	
Monetary authorities...........................	4 631 ..	....	....	.1	....	....	....	....	
General government.............................	4 632 ..	....	....	−4.3	....	1.9	....	....	
Banks...	4 633 ..	....	....	−.5	−2.8	17.7	−11.8	.1	
Other sectors......................................	4 634 ..	6.6	−2.9	13.5	7.7	−8.2	5.5	21.0	
Liabilities..	4 652 ..	**5.0**	**93.3**	**1.6**	**−8.9**	**−11.2**	**−23.1**	**−66.2**	....
Equity securities...	4 660 ..	....	....	....	....	....	....	....	
Banks...	4 663 ..	....	....	....	....	....	....	....	
Other sectors..	4 664 ..	....	....	....	....	....	....	....	
Debt securities..	4 669 ..	5.0	93.3	1.6	−8.9	−11.2	−23.1	−66.2	
Bonds and notes......................................	4 670 ..	5.2	4.1	.9	−1.0	29.5	−3.8	−28.6	
Monetary authorities...........................	4 671 ..	....	....	....	....	....	....	....	
General government.............................	4 672 ..	.3	4.0	−.1	−.9	22.5	−4.6	−12.3	
Banks...	4 673 ..	5.3	.1	....	....	2.8	....	−16.3	
Other sectors......................................	4 674 ..	−.3	−.1	.9	−.1	4.2	.8	....	
Money market instruments......................	4 680 ..	−.3	89.2	.7	−7.9	−40.8	−19.2	−37.6	
Monetary authorities...........................	4 681 ..	....	....	....	....	....	....	....	
General government.............................	4 682 ..	....	....	....	....	....	....	−.2	
Banks...	4 683 ..	−.1	−3.4	....	....	−15.3	.2	−.6	
Other sectors......................................	4 684 ..	−.2	92.6	.7	−7.9	−25.5	−19.5	−36.7	
C. FINANCIAL DERIVATIVES..............................	4 910 ..	....	....	**.4**	**−1.6**	**−4.2**	**−.2**	**.2**	....
Monetary authorities..................................	4 911 ..	....	....	....	....	....	....	....	
General government....................................	4 912 ..	....	....	....	....	....	....	....	
Banks..	4 913 ..	....	....	....	.3	−4.2	....	....	
Other sectors...	4 914 ..	....	....	.4	−1.9	.1	−.2	.2	
Assets...	4 900 ..	....	....	**.4**	**−1.6**	**−4.2**	**−.2**	**.2**	....
Monetary authorities..................................	4 901 ..	....	....	....	....	....	....	....	
General government....................................	4 902 ..	....	....	....	....	....	....	....	
Banks..	4 903 ..	....	....	....	.3	−4.2	....	....	
Other sectors...	4 904 ..	....	....	.4	−1.9	.1	−.2	.2	
Liabilities..	4 905 ..	....	....	....	....	....	....	....	....
Monetary authorities..................................	4 906 ..	....	....	....	....	....	....	....	
General government....................................	4 907 ..	....	....	....	....	....	....	....	
Banks..	4 908 ..	....	....	....	....	....	....	....	
Other sectors...	4 909 ..	....	....	....	....	....	....	....	

Table 2 (Concluded). STANDARD PRESENTATION, 2003–2010

(Millions of U.S. dollars)

	Code	2003	2004	2005	2006	2007	2008	2009	2010
D. OTHER INVESTMENT	4 700	**1.4**	**19.4**	**99.9**	**193.0**	**394.7**	**705.7**	**483.9**	....
Assets	4 703	−37.8	−4.7	40.5	193.3	407.8	707.1	504.7	....
Trade credits	4 706	−34.9	−35.7	−56.4	−48.8	174.6	145.5	60.7	
General government	4 707	....	....	....	....	....	....	....	
of which: Short-term	4 709	....	....	....	....	....	....	....	
Other sectors	4 710	−34.9	−35.7	−56.4	−48.8	174.6	145.5	60.7	
of which: Short-term	4 712	−35.4	−35.4	−56.1	−48.7	174.6	145.5	60.7	....
Loans	4 714	−2.4	3.7	.2	8.8	21.8	5.5	2.6	
Monetary authorities	4 715	....	....	....	....	....	....	....	
of which: Short-term	4 718	....	....	....	....	....	....	....	
General government	4 719	....	....	....	....	....	....	....	
of which: Short-term	4 721	....	....	....	....	....	....	....	
Banks	4 722	....	2.5	2.0	6.6	15.7	5.0	.3	
of which: Short-term	4 724	....	....	....	....	.5			
Other sectors	4 725	−2.4	1.1	−1.8	2.2	6.2	.4	2.3	
of which: Short-term	4 727	....	....	−.1	−.1	−.3		−.5	
Currency and deposits	4 730	−14.7	5.5	90.8	157.8	61.1	325.6	246.7	
Monetary authorities	4 731	....	....	....	....	....	....	....	
General government	4 732	....	....	....	....	....	....	....	
Banks	4 733								
Other sectors	4 734	−14.7	5.5	90.8	157.8	61.1	325.6	246.7	
Other assets	4 736	14.2	21.9	5.9	75.4	150.3	230.5	194.7	
Monetary authorities	4 737	....	....	....	....	.3	−.4		
of which: Short-term	4 739	....	....	....	....	.3	−.4		
General government	4 740	−5.7	....	.2	−.1	−.2	7.5	.3	
of which: Short-term	4 742	−5.7	....	.2	−.1	−.2	7.5	.3	
Banks	4 743	−3.1	36.5	17.2	−.1	1.2	21.0	62.4	
of which: Short-term	4 745	1.8	36.7	16.3	....	1.5	21.0	62.4	
Other sectors	4 746	23.0	−14.6	−11.5	75.6	149.0	202.5	131.9	
of which: Short-term	4 748	29.4	3.6	3.5	82.6	167.4	208.0	148.0	
Liabilities	4 753	**39.3**	**24.0**	**59.4**	**−.3**	**−13.2**	**−1.3**	**−20.7**	....
Trade credits	4 756	97.3	58.6	71.9	16.6	−36.2	1.9	63.4	
General government	4 757	....	....	....	....	....	....	....	
of which: Short-term	4 759	....	....	....	....	....	....	....	
Other sectors	4 760	97.3	58.6	71.9	16.6	−36.2	1.9	63.4	
of which: Short-term	4 762	97.3	57.8	71.7	16.2	−42.0	7.8	61.7	
Loans	4 764	−33.0	−83.2	−51.9	−89.3	.7	−50.1	−132.5	
Monetary authorities	4 765	....	....	....	....	....	....	....	
of which: Use of Fund credit and loans from the Fund	4 766	....	....	....	....	....	....	....	
of which: Short-term	4 768	....	....	....	....	....	....	....	
General government	4 769	−21.4	−22.6	−23.7	−40.1	−18.0	−18.8	−16.0	
of which: Short-term	4 771	....	−.8	....	....	....	....	....	
Banks	4 772	−5.8	−23.8	−.4	−.3	2.7	2.1	−1.2	
of which: Short-term	4 774	....	−1.8	−.6	....	....	....	....	
Other sectors	4 775	−5.9	−36.8	−27.8	−48.9	16.0	−33.3	−115.4	
of which: Short-term	4 777	−.1	.1	3.1	.1	.3	2.1	.2	
Currency and deposits	4 780	....	....	....	....	....	....	....	
Monetary authorities	4 781	....	....	....	....	....	....	....	
General government	4 782	....	....	....	....	....	....	....	
Banks	4 783	....	....	....	....	....	....	....	
Other sectors	4 784	....	....	....	....	....	....	....	
Other liabilities	4 786	−25.0	48.6	39.4	72.4	22.3	46.9	48.4	
Monetary authorities	4 787	....	....	....	....	....	....	....	
of which: Short-term	4 789	....	....	....	....	....	....	....	
General government	4 790	6.4	25.1	14.6	35.3	21.8	22.9	20.2	
of which: Short-term	4 792	22.1	29.3	25.7	35.3	21.8	22.9	20.2	
Banks	4 793	....	−1.3	6.0	....	−27.5	32.2	26.2	
of which: Short-term	4 795	....	....	....	....	2.3	10.3	20.4	
Other sectors	4 796	−31.3	24.8	18.8	37.1	28.0	−8.1	2.0	
of which: Short-term	4 798	3.6	−10.7	14.5	10.3	21.6	−12.2	6.3	
E. RESERVE ASSETS	4 802	**−49.8**	**−36.9**	**−74.0**	**−47.1**	**−155.0**	**−207.6**	**−301.1**	....
Monetary gold	4 812	....	....	....	....	....	....	....	
Special drawing rights	4 811	....	....	....	....	....	....	....	
Reserve position in the Fund	4 810	....	....	....	....	....	....	....	
Foreign exchange	4 803	−49.8	−36.9	−74.0	−47.1	−155.0	−207.6	−301.1	
Other claims	4 813	....	....	....	....	....	....	....	
NET ERRORS AND OMISSIONS	4 998	**4.6**	**27.6**	**31.7**	**35.6**	**77.6**	**57.0**	**74.7**	....

2011, International Monetary Fund: *Balance of Payments Statistics Yearbook*

Table 1. ANALYTIC PRESENTATION, 2003–2010

(Millions of U.S. dollars)

	Code	2003	2004	2005	2006	2007	2008	2009	2010
A. Current Account[1]	4 993 Z.	**−3,170**	**−5,679**	**−8,777**	**−8,933**	**−10,825**	**−11,567**	**−3,248**	**−4,994**
Goods: exports f.o.b.	2 100 ..	16,804	20,466	22,006	22,576	27,288	31,192	25,336	31,883
Goods: imports f.o.b.	3 100 ..	−17,315	−21,888	−24,583	−24,573	−29,113	−32,922	−24,029	−29,539
Balance on Goods	4 100 ..	*−511*	*−1,422*	*−2,577*	*−1,997*	*−1,825*	*−1,730*	*1,307*	*2,344*
Services: credit	2 200 ..	6,892	8,243	8,691	8,159	9,448	9,476	8,164	9,033
Services: debit	3 200 ..	−5,747	−7,212	−8,239	−7,881	−9,224	−9,869	−8,065	−9,343
Balance on Goods and Services	4 991 ..	*634*	*−390*	*−2,125*	*−1,719*	*−1,602*	*−2,123*	*1,406*	*2,034*
Income: credit	2 300 ..	2,670	3,180	3,429	3,455	4,782	3,992	2,968	3,771
Income: debit	3 300 ..	−6,636	−8,555	−10,281	−11,079	−14,395	−14,083	−7,856	−10,771
Balance on Goods, Services, and Income	4 992 ..	*−3,332*	*−5,766*	*−8,976*	*−9,343*	*−11,214*	*−12,214*	*−3,482*	*−4,965*
Current transfers: credit	2 379 Z.	855	900	1,242	1,292	1,435	1,714	1,205	1,014
Current transfers: debit	3 379 ..	−693	−813	−1,043	−882	−1,046	−1,066	−972	−1,043
B. Capital Account[1]	4 994 Z.	**502**	**156**	**−197**	**−216**	**−553**	**−446**	**275**	**2,162**
Capital account: credit	2 994 Z.	1,065	963	740	650	656	766	1,165	3,232
Capital account: debit	3 994 ..	−563	−807	−937	−866	−1,209	−1,213	−890	−1,070
Total, Groups A Plus B	4 981 ..	*−2,667*	*−5,522*	*−8,974*	*−9,148*	*−11,378*	*−12,013*	*−2,974*	*−2,832*
C. Financial Account[1]	4 995 W.	**3,232**	**7,924**	**11,035**	**12,491**	**11,971**	**2,025**	**4,761**	**2,824**
Direct investment abroad	4 505 ..	−917	440	1,504	−159	−3,642	−904	1,399	−573
Direct investment in New Zealand	4 555 Z.	2,267	2,340	1,564	4,562	3,191	4,890	−719	701
Portfolio investment assets	4 602 ..	−865	−1,780	−631	−990	−2,537	1,867	−4,086	−2,331
Equity securities	4 610 ..	....	−1,572	−1,153	−760	−2,205	2,555	−2,265	−1,996
Debt securities	4 619 ..	....	−208	521	−230	−331	−688	−1,820	−334
Portfolio investment liabilities	4 652 Z.	1,896	8,271	581	38	12,019	−5,679	6,128	4,685
Equity securities	4 660 ..	719	99	−98	−397	229	170	967	−298
Debt securities	4 669 Z.	1,178	8,172	678	436	11,789	−5,850	5,161	4,983
Financial derivatives	4 910 ..	....	....	....	....	....	....	....	....
Financial derivatives assets	4 900 ..	....	....	....	....	....	....	....	....
Financial derivatives liabilities	4 905 ..	....	....	....	....	....	....	....	....
Other investment assets	4 703 ..	57	482	4,090	−1,761	−1,634	1,208	−993	−990
Monetary authorities	4 701 ..	....	....	....	....	....	....	....	....
General government	4 704 ..	....	....	....	....	....	....	....	....
Banks	4 705 ..	....	....	....	....	....	....	....	....
Other sectors	4 728 ..	....	....	....	....	....	....	....	....
Other investment liabilities	4 753 W.	794	−1,830	3,926	10,801	4,574	642	3,033	1,332
Monetary authorities	4 753 WA	....	....	....	....	....	....	....	....
General government	4 753 ZB	....	....	....	....	....	....	....	....
Banks	4 753 ZC	....	....	....	....	....	....	....	....
Other sectors	4 753 ZD	....	....	....	....	....	....	....	....
Total, Groups A Through C	4 983 ..	*565*	*2,402*	*2,061*	*3,343*	*594*	*−9,988*	*1,788*	*−8*
D. Net Errors and Omissions	4 998 ..	**218**	**−1,771**	**356**	**912**	**2,494**	**4,991**	**1,560**	**855**
Total, Groups A Through D	4 984 ..	*783*	*630*	*2,417*	*4,255*	*3,088*	*−4,997*	*3,348*	*848*
E. Reserves and Related Items	4 802 A.	**−783**	**−630**	**−2,417**	**−4,255**	**−3,088**	**4,997**	**−3,348**	**−848**
Reserve assets	4 802 ..	−783	−630	−2,417	−4,255	−3,088	4,997	−3,348	−848
Use of Fund credit and loans	4 766 ..	....	....	....	....	....	....	....	....
Exceptional financing	4 920 ..	....	....	....	....	....	....	....	....
Conversion rates: New Zealand dollars per U.S. dollar	0 101 ..	**1.7221**	**1.5087**	**1.4203**	**1.5421**	**1.3607**	**1.4227**	**1.6002**	**1.3874**

[1] Excludes components that have been classified in the categories of Group E.

Table 2. STANDARD PRESENTATION, 2003–2010

(Millions of U.S. dollars)

	Code	2003	2004	2005	2006	2007	2008	2009	2010
CURRENT ACCOUNT....................................	4 993 ..	**−3,170**	**−5,679**	**−8,777**	**−8,933**	**−10,825**	**−11,567**	**−3,248**	**−4,994**
A. GOODS...	4 100 ..	−511	−1,422	−2,577	−1,997	−1,825	−1,730	1,307	2,344
Credit..	2 100 ..	16,804	20,466	22,006	22,576	27,288	31,192	25,336	31,883
General merchandise: exports f.o.b............	2 110 ..	16,404	20,005	21,358	21,867	26,518	30,063	24,409	30,824
Goods for processing: exports f.o.b...........	2 150 ..	....	....	....	....	....	....	....	....
Repairs on goods..................................	2 160 ..	....	....	....	....	....	....	....	....
Goods procured in ports by carriers.........	2 170 ..	....	....	....	....	....	....	....	....
Nonmonetary gold................................	2 180 ..	130	158	173	186	202	364	338	382
Debit..	3 100 ..	−17,315	−21,888	−24,583	−24,573	−29,113	−32,922	−24,029	−29,539
General merchandise: imports f.o.b...........	3 110 ..	−17,162	−21,660	−24,226	−24,182	−28,554	−32,058	−23,585	−28,971
Goods for processing: imports f.o.b...........	3 150 ..	....	....	....	....	....	....	....	....
Repairs on goods..................................	3 160 ..	....	....	....	....	....	....	....	....
Goods procured in ports by carriers.........	3 170 ..	....	....	....	....	....	....	....	....
Nonmonetary gold................................	3 180 ..	−13	−13	−12	−14	−19	−32	−29	−30
B. SERVICES..	4 200 ..	**1,145**	**1,032**	**452**	**278**	**223**	**−393**	**99**	**−310**
Total credit......................................	2 200 ..	*6,892*	*8,243*	*8,691*	*8,159*	*9,448*	*9,476*	*8,164*	*9,033*
Total debit.......................................	3 200 ..	*−5,747*	*−7,212*	*−8,239*	*−7,881*	*−9,224*	*−9,869*	*−8,065*	*−9,343*
Transportation services, credit..........	2 205 ..	**1,353**	**1,531**	**1,694**	**1,689**	**1,986**	**1,965**	**1,477**	**1,780**
Passenger.......................................	2 850 ..	....	....	....	....	....	....	....	....
Freight..	2 851 ..	....	....	....	....	....	....	....	....
Other..	2 852 ..	....	....	....	....	....	....	....	....
Sea transport, passenger.......................	2 207 ..	....	....	....	....	....	....	....	....
Sea transport, freight...........................	2 208 ..	....	....	....	....	....	....	....	....
Sea transport, other.............................	2 209 ..	....	....	....	....	....	....	....	....
Air transport, passenger........................	2 211 ..	....	....	....	....	....	....	....	....
Air transport, freight............................	2 212 ..	....	....	....	....	....	....	....	....
Air transport, other..............................	2 213 ..	....	....	....	....	....	....	....	....
Other transport, passenger....................	2 215 ..	....	....	....	....	....	....	....	....
Other transport, freight.........................	2 216 ..	....	....	....	....	....	....	....	....
Other transport, other..........................	2 217 ..	....	....	....	....	....	....	....	....
Transportation services, debit...........	3 205 ..	**−2,000**	**−2,531**	**−2,801**	**−2,659**	**−2,970**	**−3,182**	**−2,235**	**−2,748**
Passenger.......................................	3 850 ..	....	....	....	....	....	....	....	....
Freight..	3 851 ..	....	....	....	....	....	....	....	....
Other..	3 852 ..	....	....	....	....	....	....	....	....
Sea transport, passenger.......................	3 207 ..	....	....	....	....	....	....	....	....
Sea transport, freight...........................	3 208 ..	....	....	....	....	....	....	....	....
Sea transport, other.............................	3 209 ..	....	....	....	....	....	....	....	....
Air transport, passenger........................	3 211 ..	....	....	....	....	....	....	....	....
Air transport, freight............................	3 212 ..	....	....	....	....	....	....	....	....
Air transport, other..............................	3 213 ..	....	....	....	....	....	....	....	....
Other transport, passenger....................	3 215 ..	....	....	....	....	....	....	....	....
Other transport, freight.........................	3 216 ..	....	....	....	....	....	....	....	....
Other transport, other..........................	3 217 ..	....	....	....	....	....	....	....	....
Travel, credit.................................	2 236 ..	**4,232**	**5,098**	**5,211**	**4,792**	**5,414**	**5,152**	**4,593**	**4,907**
Business travel....................................	2 237 ..	435	440	517	462	592	606	404	425
Personal travel....................................	2 240 ..	3,797	4,657	4,693	4,328	4,820	4,546	4,188	4,481
Travel, debit..................................	3 236 ..	**−1,649**	**−2,229**	**−2,671**	**−2,534**	**−3,077**	**−3,006**	**−2,581**	**−3,038**
Business travel....................................	3 237 ..	−353	−452	−546	−517	−607	−605	−484	−608
Personal travel....................................	3 240 ..	−1,297	−1,778	−2,124	−2,017	−2,470	−2,401	−2,097	−2,430
Other services, credit.......................	2 200 BA	**1,306**	**1,616**	**985**	**838**	**1,025**	**2,320**	**2,057**	**2,311**
Communications..................................	2 245 ..	209	225	274	152	186	198	153	157
Construction.......................................	2 249 ..	38	36	37	10	7	....	....	....
Insurance...	2 253 ..	25	29	27	27	30	....	....	....
Financial..	2 260 ..	33	59	87	80	80	88	81	101
Computer and information......................	2 262 ..	129	168	193	191	218	227	202	262
Royalties and licence fees......................	2 266 ..	108	105	93	123	140	179	159	183
Other business services.........................	2 268 ..	540	681	....	....	....	1,153	1,001	1,139
Personal, cultural, and recreational..........	2 287 ..	152	220	173	158	250	352	352	345
Government, n.i.e.................................	2 291 ..	72	94	102	97	114	122	108	125
Other services, debit........................	3 200 BA	**−2,096**	**−2,453**	**−2,769**	**−1,467**	**−1,722**	**−3,681**	**−3,249**	**−3,277**
Communications..................................	3 245 ..	−199	−226	−302	−195	−212	−186	−167	−180
Construction.......................................	3 249 ..	−6	−14	−29	−89	−107	−120	−109	....
Insurance...	3 253 ..	−183	−221	−240	−209	−218	−185	−186	....
Financial..	3 260 ..	−59	−88	−126	−75	−118	−104	−89	−109
Computer and information......................	3 262 ..	−134	−197	−248	−276	−316	−370	−331	−349
Royalties and licence fees......................	3 266 ..	−466	−529	−554	−497	−602	−603	−560	−669
Other business services.........................	3 268 ..	−897	−1,040	−1,138	....	....	−1,934	−1,635	−1,783
Personal, cultural, and recreational..........	3 287 ..	−72	−57	−43	−41	−51	−71	−65	−71
Government, n.i.e.................................	3 291 ..	−80	−82	−89	−85	−98	−108	−107	−117

Table 2 (Continued). STANDARD PRESENTATION, 2003–2010

(Millions of U.S. dollars)

	Code	2003	2004	2005	2006	2007	2008	2009	2010
C. INCOME	4 300	**−3,966**	**−5,376**	**−6,852**	**−7,623**	**−9,613**	**−10,091**	**−4,887**	**−6,999**
Total credit	2 300	*2,670*	*3,180*	*3,429*	*3,455*	*4,782*	*3,992*	*2,968*	*3,771*
Total debit	3 300	*−6,636*	*−8,555*	*−10,281*	*−11,079*	*−14,395*	*−14,083*	*−7,856*	*−10,771*
Compensation of employees, credit	2 310	....	....	....	....	....	....	....	....
Compensation of employees, debit	3 310	−44	−52	−55	−53	−66	−93	−82	−100
Investment income, credit	2 320	2,670	3,180	3,429	3,455	4,782	3,992	2,968	3,771
Direct investment income	2 330	606	564	372	422	852	265	217	585
Dividends and distributed branch profits	2 332	....	....	....	....	....	....	....	374
Reinvested earnings and undistributed branch profits	2 333	....	....	....	....	....	....	....	272
Income on debt (interest)	2 334	8	28	−10	38	26	−20	−12	−59
Portfolio investment income	2 339	443	594	594	834	1,412	1,447	980	1,223
Income on equity	2 340	98	187	271	370	547	591	488	558
Income on bonds and notes	2 350	323	379	222	202	257	415	424	632
Income on money market instruments	2 360	22	28	101	262	609	441	57	35
Other investment income	2 370	1,623	2,022	2,463	2,200	2,517	2,281	1,771	1,963
Investment income, debit	3 320	−6,593	−8,502	−10,226	−11,026	−14,330	−13,990	−7,773	−10,669
Direct investment income	3 330	−3,362	−4,363	−4,981	−4,957	−6,360	−6,081	−3,288	−5,560
Dividends and distributed branch profits	3 332	−1,874	−1,521	−2,041	−2,707	−3,871	−4,631	−2,376	−2,582
Reinvested earnings and undistributed branch profits	3 333	−1,244	−2,357	−2,382	−1,556	−1,319	24	220	−1,768
Income on debt (interest)	3 334	−244	−485	−558	−693	−1,171	−1,474	−1,133	−1,210
Portfolio investment income	3 339	−1,402	−1,911	−2,540	−2,788	−3,626	−3,393	−1,889	−2,236
Income on equity	3 340	−345	−568	−775	−692	−813	−732	−486	−574
Income on bonds and notes	3 350	−825	−1,053	−1,337	−1,615	−1,908	−1,859	−1,221	−1,525
Income on money market instruments	3 360	−232	−291	−427	−480	−905	−801	−181	−138
Other investment income	3 370	−1,830	−2,228	−2,705	−3,281	−4,344	−4,517	−2,596	−2,873
D. CURRENT TRANSFERS	4 379	**162**	**88**	**200**	**410**	**389**	**648**	**234**	**−29**
Credit	2 379	**855**	**900**	**1,242**	**1,292**	**1,435**	**1,714**	**1,205**	**1,014**
General government	2 380	548	558	872	939	1,029	1,263	846	613
Other sectors	2 390	308	343	370	352	407	451	359	402
Workers' remittances	2 391	....	....	....	....	....	....	....	....
Other current transfers	2 392	....	....	....	....	....	....	....	....
Debit	3 379	**−693**	**−813**	**−1,043**	**−882**	**−1,046**	**−1,066**	**−972**	**−1,043**
General government	3 380	−237	−282	−336	−308	−367	−374	−354	−396
Other sectors	3 390	−456	−530	−707	−573	−679	−693	−618	−647
Workers' remittances	3 391	....	....	....	....	....	....	....	....
Other current transfers	3 392	....	....	....	....	....	....	....	....
CAPITAL AND FINANCIAL ACCOUNT	4 996	**2,952**	**7,450**	**8,421**	**8,020**	**8,331**	**6,575**	**1,688**	**4,139**
CAPITAL ACCOUNT	4 994	**502**	**156**	**−197**	**−216**	**−553**	**−446**	**275**	**2,162**
Total credit	2 994	*1,065*	*963*	*740*	*650*	*656*	*766*	*1,165*	*3,232*
Total debit	3 994	*−563*	*−807*	*−937*	*−866*	*−1,209*	*−1,213*	*−890*	*−1,070*
Capital transfers, credit	2 400	**1,065**	**958**	**739**	**650**	**654**	**641**	**628**	**3,208**
General government	2 401	....	....	....	....	....	....	....	....
Debt forgiveness	2 402	....	....	....	....	....	....	....	....
Other capital transfers	2 410	....	....	....	....	....	....	....	....
Other sectors	2 430	1,065	958	739	650	654	641	628	2,060
Migrants' transfers	2 431	1,065	958	739	650	654	641	628	843
Debt forgiveness	2 432	....	....	....	....	....	....	....	....
Other capital transfers	2 440	....	....	....	....	....	....	....	....
Capital transfers, debit	3 400	**−561**	**−806**	**−936**	**−865**	**−1,207**	**−1,202**	**−871**	**−1,057**
General government	3 401	....	....	....	....	....	....	....	....
Debt forgiveness	3 402	....	....	....	....	....	....	....	....
Other capital transfers	3 410	....	....	....	....	....	....	....	....
Other sectors	3 430	−561	−806	−936	−865	−1,207	−1,202	−871	−1,057
Migrants' transfers	3 431	−561	−806	−936	−865	−1,207	−1,202	−871	−1,057
Debt forgiveness	3 432	....	....	....	....	....	....	....	....
Other capital transfers	3 440	....	....	....	....	....	....	....	....
Nonproduced nonfinancial assets, credit	2 480	....	4	1	....	2	126	537	24
Nonproduced nonfinancial assets, debit	3 480	−2	−1	−1	−1	−2	−11	−19	−13

Table 2 (Continued). STANDARD PRESENTATION, 2003–2010

(Millions of U.S. dollars)

	Code	2003	2004	2005	2006	2007	2008	2009	2010
FINANCIAL ACCOUNT	4 995	**2,449**	**7,294**	**8,618**	**8,236**	**8,883**	**7,022**	**1,413**	**1,976**
A. DIRECT INVESTMENT	4 500	**1,350**	**2,781**	**3,068**	**4,403**	**−451**	**3,986**	**680**	**128**
Direct investment abroad	4 505	**−917**	**440**	**1,504**	**−159**	**−3,642**	**−904**	**1,399**	**−573**
Equity capital	4 510	....	....	....	....	....	....	....	29
Claims on affiliated enterprises	4 515	....	....						
Liabilities to affiliated enterprises	4 520		....	....	....				
Reinvested earnings	4 525	....	....						−272
Other capital	4 530	126	24	....	....	−416	409	1,401	−333
Claims on affiliated enterprises	4 535	....			....				
Liabilities to affiliated enterprises	4 540		....		....				
Direct investment in New Zealand	4 555	**2,267**	**2,340**	**1,564**	**4,562**	**3,191**	**4,890**	**−719**	**701**
Equity capital	4 560	−2,801	−2,207	−1,889	961	1,494	139	748	16
Claims on direct investors	4 565								
Liabilities to direct investors	4 570	....	....	....					....
Reinvested earnings	4 575	1,244	2,357	2,382	1,556	1,319	−24	−220	1,768
Other capital	4 580	3,824	2,192	1,071	2,046	378	4,776	−1,246	−1,084
Claims on direct investors	4 585								
Liabilities to direct investors	4 590	....	....						
B. PORTFOLIO INVESTMENT	4 600	**1,031**	**6,491**	**−50**	**−952**	**9,482**	**−3,812**	**2,042**	**2,354**
Assets	4 602	**−865**	**−1,780**	**−631**	**−990**	**−2,537**	**1,867**	**−4,086**	**−2,331**
Equity securities	4 610	....	−1,572	−1,153	−760	−2,205	2,555	−2,265	−1,996
Monetary authorities	4 611								
General government	4 612								
Banks	4 613								
Other sectors	4 614					....			
Debt securities	4 619	....	−208	521	−230	−331	−688	−1,820	−334
Bonds and notes	4 620								
Monetary authorities	4 621								
General government	4 622								
Banks	4 623								
Other sectors	4 624								
Money market instruments	4 630								
Monetary authorities	4 631								
General government	4 632								
Banks	4 633								
Other sectors	4 634								
Liabilities	4 652	**1,896**	**8,271**	**581**	**38**	**12,019**	**−5,679**	**6,128**	**4,685**
Equity securities	4 660	719	99	−98	−397	229	170	967	−298
Banks	4 663								
Other sectors	4 664								
Debt securities	4 669	1,178	8,172	678	436	11,789	−5,850	5,161	4,983
Bonds and notes	4 670								
Monetary authorities	4 671								
General government	4 672								
Banks	4 673								
Other sectors	4 674								
Money market instruments	4 680								
Monetary authorities	4 681								
General government	4 682								
Banks	4 683								
Other sectors	4 684								
C. FINANCIAL DERIVATIVES	4 910	....	....	....	....	....	....	....	....
Monetary authorities	4 911	....	....						
General government	4 912	....	....						
Banks	4 913	....	....						
Other sectors	4 914	....	....						
Assets	4 900	....	....	....			....		
Monetary authorities	4 901	....	....						
General government	4 902	....	....						
Banks	4 903	....	....						
Other sectors	4 904	....	....						
Liabilities	4 905	....	....	....	....	....	....	....	....
Monetary authorities	4 906	....	....						
General government	4 907	....	....						
Banks	4 908	....	....						
Other sectors	4 909	....	....						

Table 2 (Concluded). STANDARD PRESENTATION, 2003–2010

(Millions of U.S. dollars)

	Code	2003	2004	2005	2006	2007	2008	2009	2010
D. OTHER INVESTMENT................................	4 700 ..	**851**	**−1,348**	**8,016**	**9,040**	**2,941**	**1,850**	**2,040**	**342**
Assets..	4 703 ..	**57**	**482**	**4,090**	**−1,761**	**−1,634**	**1,208**	**−993**	**−990**
Trade credits................................	4 706 ..	....	....	−347	−452	−163	....	....	−3,021
General government....................	4 707 ..	....	....	....	....	....	....	....	....
of which: Short-term..............	4 709 ..	....	....	....	....	....	....	....	....
Other sectors............................	4 710 ..	....	....	....	....	....	....	....	....
of which: Short-term..............	4 712 ..	....	....	....	....	....	....	....	....
Loans.......................................	4 714 ..	−175	747	5,101	−240	−1,759	1,640	−161	919
Monetary authorities..................	4 715 ..	....	....	....	....	....	....	....	....
of which: Short-term..............	4 718 ..	....	....	....	....	....	....	....	....
General government....................	4 719 ..	....	....	....	....	....	....	....	....
of which: Short-term..............	4 721 ..	....	....	....	....	....	....	....	....
Banks.......................................	4 722 ..	....	....	....	....	....	....	....	....
of which: Short-term..............	4 724 ..	....	....	....	....	....	....	....	....
Other sectors............................	4 725 ..	....	....	....	....	....	....	....	....
of which: Short-term..............	4 727 ..	....	....	....	....	....	....	....	....
Currency and deposits....................	4 730 ..	−117	−16	−579	−1,316	485	−379	−1,088	1,031
Monetary authorities..................	4 731 ..	....	....	....	....	....	....	....	....
General government....................	4 732 ..	....	....	....	....	....	....	....	....
Banks.......................................	4 733 ..	....	....	....	....	....	....	....	....
Other sectors............................	4 734 ..	....	....	....	....	....	....	....	....
Other assets................................	4 736 ..	....	....	−85	247	−196	....	....	81
Monetary authorities..................	4 737 ..	....	....	....	....	....	....	....	....
of which: Short-term..............	4 739 ..	....	....	....	....	....	....	....	....
General government....................	4 740 ..	....	....	....	....	....	....	....	....
of which: Short-term..............	4 742 ..	....	....	....	....	....	....	....	....
Banks.......................................	4 743 ..	....	....	....	....	....	....	....	....
of which: Short-term..............	4 745 ..	....	....	....	....	....	....	....	....
Other sectors............................	4 746 ..	....	....	....	....	....	....	....	....
of which: Short-term..............	4 748 ..	....	....	....	....	....	....	....	....
Liabilities....................................	4 753 ..	**794**	**−1,830**	**3,926**	**10,801**	**4,574**	**642**	**3,033**	**1,332**
Trade credits................................	4 756 ..	−151	−57	....	105	−44	−31	29	38
General government....................	4 757 ..	....	....	....	....	....	....	....	....
of which: Short-term..............	4 759 ..	....	....	....	....	....	....	....	....
Other sectors............................	4 760 ..	....	....	....	....	....	....	....	....
of which: Short-term..............	4 762 ..	....	....	....	....	....	....	....	....
Loans.......................................	4 764 ..	−83	−2,441	2,661	5,802	3,964	1,650	3,103	875
Monetary authorities..................	4 765 ..	....	....	....	....	....	....	....	....
of which: Use of Fund credit and loans from the Fund..	4 766 ..	....	....	....	....	....	....	....	....
of which: Short-term..............	4 768 ..	....	....	....	....	....	....	....	....
General government....................	4 769 ..	....	....	....	....	....	....	....	....
of which: Short-term..............	4 771 ..	....	....	....	....	....	....	....	....
Banks.......................................	4 772 ..	....	....	....	....	....	....	....	....
of which: Short-term..............	4 774 ..	....	....	....	....	....	....	....	....
Other sectors............................	4 775 ..	....	....	....	....	....	....	....	....
of which: Short-term..............	4 777 ..	....	....	....	....	....	....	....	....
Currency and deposits....................	4 780 ..	1,070	599	1,280	4,735	681	−836	−1,269	208
Monetary authorities..................	4 781 ..	....	....	....	....	....	....	....	....
General government....................	4 782 ..	....	....	....	....	....	....	....	....
Banks.......................................	4 783 ..	....	....	....	....	....	....	....	....
Other sectors............................	4 784 ..	....	....	....	....	....	....	....	....
Other liabilities............................	4 786 ..	−40	70	....	160	−27	−83	1,183	352
Monetary authorities..................	4 787 ..	....	....	....	....	....	....	....	....
of which: Short-term..............	4 789 ..	....	....	....	....	....	....	....	....
General government....................	4 790 ..	....	....	....	....	....	....	....	....
of which: Short-term..............	4 792 ..	....	....	....	....	....	....	....	....
Banks.......................................	4 793 ..	....	....	....	....	....	....	....	....
of which: Short-term..............	4 795 ..	....	....	....	....	....	....	....	....
Other sectors............................	4 796 ..	....	....	....	....	....	....	....	....
of which: Short-term..............	4 798 ..	....	....	....	....	....	....	....	....
E. RESERVE ASSETS............................	4 802 ..	**−783**	**−630**	**−2,417**	**−4,255**	**−3,088**	**4,997**	**−3,348**	**−848**
Monetary gold............................	4 812 ..	....	....	....	....	....	....	....	....
Special drawing rights....................	4 811 ..	−4	−5	−3	3	6	5	−1,314	....
Reserve position in the Fund............	4 810 ..	−135	189	277	53	29	−81	−93	−5
Foreign exchange........................	4 803 ..	244	−625	−2,549	−1,973	−6,544	5,102	−2,601	8
Other claims............................	4 813 ..	−888	−188	−142	−2,337	3,420	−30	660	−850
NET ERRORS AND OMISSIONS...................	4 998 ..	**218**	**−1,771**	**356**	**912**	**2,494**	**4,991**	**1,560**	**855**

Table 3. INTERNATIONAL INVESTMENT POSITION

(Millions of U.S. dollars)

	Code	2003	2004	2005	2006	2007	2008	2009	2010
ASSETS...	8 995 C.	**60,404**	**69,463**	**65,693**	**81,771**	**103,452**	**79,371**	**97,059**	**113,525**
Direct investment abroad.............................	8 505 ..	**11,883**	**13,957**	**11,807**	**13,416**	**16,094**	**14,122**	**14,075**	**16,767**
Equity capital and reinvested earnings..............	8 506 ..	10,538	12,045	10,243	11,173	13,150	12,210	12,922	14,604
Claims on affiliated enterprises.....................	8 507 ..	....	....	....	....	....	....	....	....
Liabilities to affiliated enterprises.................	8 508 ..	....	....	....	....	....	....	....	....
Other capital.......................................	8 530 ..	1,346	1,912	1,564	2,243	2,944	1,912	1,153	2,163
Claims on affiliated enterprises.....................	8 535 ..	....	....	....	....	....	....	....	....
Liabilities to affiliated enterprises.................	8 540 ..	....	....	....	....	....	....	....	....
Portfolio investment..............................	8 602 ..	**24,122**	**29,418**	**31,536**	**36,917**	**45,869**	**27,272**	**40,685**	**47,917**
Equity securities...................................	8 610 ..	18,112	22,761	25,613	30,421	37,083	19,552	30,013	35,604
Monetary authorities...............................	8 611 ..	....	....	....	....	....	....	....	....
General government................................	8 612 ..	....	....	....	....	....	....	....	....
Banks...	8 613 ..	....	....	....	....	....	....	....	....
Other sectors......................................	8 614 ..	....	....	....	....	....	....	....	....
Debt securities.....................................	8 619 ..	6,009	6,657	5,923	6,496	8,786	7,720	10,672	12,313
Bonds and notes...................................	8 620 ..	....	....	....	....	....	....	....	....
Monetary authorities.............................	8 621 ..	....	....	....	....	....	....	....	....
General government...............................	8 622 ..	....	....	....	....	....	....	....	....
Banks...	8 623 ..	....	....	....	....	....	....	....	....
Other sectors....................................	8 624 ..	....	....	....	....	....	....	....	....
Money market instruments.........................	8 630 ..	....	....	....	....	....	....	....	....
Monetary authorities.............................	8 631 ..	....	....	....	....	....	....	....	....
General government...............................	8 632 ..	....	....	....	....	....	....	....	....
Banks...	8 633 ..	....	....	....	....	....	....	....	....
Other sectors....................................	8 634 ..	....	....	....	....	....	....	....	....
Financial derivatives.............................	8 900 ..	**4,678**	**3,922**	**2,758**	**4,151**	**7,262**	**14,240**	**10,116**	**12,906**
Monetary authorities...............................	8 901 ..	....	....	....	....	....	....	....	....
General government................................	8 902 ..	....	....	....	....	....	....	....	....
Banks...	8 903 ..	....	....	....	....	....	....	....	....
Other sectors......................................	8 904 ..	....	....	....	....	....	....	....	....
Other investment................................	8 703 ..	**13,673**	**15,219**	**10,696**	**13,219**	**16,980**	**12,685**	**16,588**	**19,213**
Trade credits......................................	8 706 ..	1,567	1,614	1,821	2,302	2,769	1,947	2,399	5,843
General government................................	8 707 ..	....	....	....	....	....	....	....	....
of which: Short-term..............................	8 709 ..	....	....	....	....	....	....	....	....
Other sectors......................................	8 710 ..	....	....	....	....	....	....	....	....
of which: Short-term..............................	8 712 ..	....	....	....	....	....	....	....	....
Loans...	8 714 ..	10,472	11,379	5,881	5,987	9,089	6,104	7,426	7,164
Monetary authorities...............................	8 715 ..	....	....	....	....	....	....	....	....
of which: Short-term..............................	8 718 ..	....	....	....	....	....	....	....	....
General government................................	8 719 ..	....	....	....	....	....	....	....	....
of which: Short-term..............................	8 721 ..	....	....	....	....	....	....	....	....
Banks...	8 722 ..	....	....	....	....	....	....	....	....
of which: Short-term..............................	8 724 ..	....	....	....	....	....	....	....	....
Other sectors......................................	8 725 ..	....	....	....	....	....	....	....	....
of which: Short-term..............................	8 727 ..	....	....	....	....	....	....	....	....
Currency and deposits..............................	8 730 ..	1,488	1,879	2,114	3,867	3,976	3,610	5,727	5,037
Monetary authorities...............................	8 731 ..	....	....	....	....	....	....	....	....
General government................................	8 732 ..	....	....	....	....	....	....	....	....
Banks...	8 733 ..	....	....	....	....	....	....	....	....
Other sectors......................................	8 734 ..	....	....	....	....	....	....	....	....
Other assets.......................................	8 736 ..	147	347	880	1,062	1,146	1,023	1,035	1,169
Monetary authorities...............................	8 737 ..	....	....	....	....	....	....	....	....
of which: Short-term..............................	8 739 ..	....	....	....	....	....	....	....	....
General government................................	8 740 ..	....	....	....	....	....	....	....	....
of which: Short-term..............................	8 742 ..	....	....	....	....	....	....	....	....
Banks...	8 743 ..	....	....	....	....	....	....	....	....
of which: Short-term..............................	8 745 ..	....	....	....	....	....	....	....	....
Other sectors......................................	8 746 ..	....	....	....	....	....	....	....	....
of which: Short-term..............................	8 748 ..	....	....	....	....	....	....	....	....
Reserve assets..................................	8 802 ..	**6,048**	**6,947**	**8,896**	**14,069**	**17,247**	**11,052**	**15,595**	**16,722**
Monetary gold.....................................	8 812 ..	....	....	....	....	....	....	....	....
Special drawing rights..............................	8 811 ..	28	34	34	33	28	22	1,340	1,317
Reserve position in the Fund........................	8 810 ..	644	474	165	119	95	175	273	273
Foreign exchange...................................	8 803 ..	3,367	4,119	6,257	8,935	15,526	9,401	13,078	13,274
Other claims.......................................	8 813 ..	2,009	2,320	2,439	4,982	1,598	1,453	904	1,858

Table 3 (Concluded). INTERNATIONAL INVESTMENT POSITION

(Millions of U.S. dollars)

	Code	2003	2004	2005	2006	2007	2008	2009	2010
LIABILITIES..	8 995 D.	**122,806**	**149,446**	**147,544**	**172,761**	**207,208**	**167,623**	**206,610**	**227,113**
Direct investment in New Zealand..............	8 555 ..	**43,659**	**51,437**	**51,615**	**59,994**	**68,544**	**52,267**	**65,849**	**70,508**
Equity capital and reinvested earnings.............	8 556 ..	27,528	31,454	30,506	34,778	38,775	25,772	33,937	37,341
Claims on direct investors.........................	8 557 ..	....	....	....	....	....	....	....	....
Liabilities to direct investors.....................	8 558 ..	....	....	....	....	....	....	....	....
Other capital...	8 580 ..	16,131	19,983	21,108	25,216	29,769	26,495	31,911	33,167
Claims on direct investors.........................	8 585 ..	....	....	....	....	....	....	....	....
Liabilities to direct investors.....................	8 590 ..	....	....	....	....	....	....	....	....
Portfolio investment.................................	8 652 ..	**43,022**	**58,070**	**54,076**	**56,869**	**71,864**	**52,574**	**66,542**	**75,004**
Equity securities.......................................	8 660 ..	8,965	12,078	11,489	11,818	12,533	5,738	9,240	9,243
Banks..	8 663 ..	....	....	....	....	....	....	....	....
Other sectors.......................................	8 664 ..	....	....	....	....	....	....	....	....
Debt securities...	8 669 ..	34,057	45,993	42,587	45,051	59,330	46,836	57,302	65,761
Bonds and notes..................................	8 670 ..	....	....	....	....	....	....	....	....
Monetary authorities.........................	8 671 ..	....	....	....	....	....	....	....	....
General government..........................	8 672 ..	....	....	....	....	....	....	....	....
Banks..	8 673 ..	....	....	....	....	....	....	....	....
Other sectors...................................	8 674 ..	....	....	....	....	....	....	....	....
Money market instruments....................	8 680 ..	....	....	....	....	....	....	....	....
Monetary authorities.........................	8 681 ..	....	....	....	....	....	....	....	....
General government..........................	8 682 ..	....	....	....	....	....	....	....	....
Banks..	8 683 ..	....	....	....	....	....	....	....	....
Other sectors...................................	8 684 ..	....	....	....	....	....	....	....	....
Financial derivatives.................................	8 905 ..	**5,466**	**5,206**	**3,553**	**5,185**	**7,112**	**13,406**	**11,673**	**13,285**
Monetary authorities................................	8 906 ..	....	....	....	....	....	....	....	....
General government..................................	8 907 ..	....	....	....	....	....	....	....	....
Banks..	8 908 ..	....	....	....	....	....	....	....	....
Other sectors..	8 909 ..	....	....	....	....	....	....	....	....
Other investment....................................	8 753 ..	**30,659**	**34,732**	**38,301**	**50,713**	**59,688**	**49,376**	**62,547**	**68,315**
Trade credits...	8 756 ..	1,173	1,191	1,242	1,323	1,256	1,044	1,342	1,511
General government..............................	8 758 ..	....	....	....	....	....	....	....	....
of which: Short-term.........................	8 759 ..	....	....	....	....	....	....	....	....
Other sectors.......................................	8 760 ..	....	....	....	....	....	....	....	....
of which: Short-term.........................	8 762 ..	....	....	....	....	....	....	....	....
Loans...	8 764 ..	19,987	22,196	24,870	32,412	39,137	34,245	43,217	47,209
Monetary authorities.............................	8 765 ..	....	....	....	....	....	....	....	....
of which: Use of Fund credit and loans from the Fund....	8 766 ..	....	....	....	....	....	....	....	....
of which: Short-term.........................	8 768 ..	....	....	....	....	....	....	....	....
General government..............................	8 769 ..	....	....	....	....	....	....	....	....
of which: Short-term.........................	8 771 ..	....	....	....	....	....	....	....	....
Banks..	8 772 ..	....	....	....	....	....	....	....	....
of which: Short-term.........................	8 774 ..	....	....	....	....	....	....	....	....
Other sectors.......................................	8 775 ..	....	....	....	....	....	....	....	....
of which: Short-term.........................	8 777 ..	....	....	....	....	....	....	....	....
Currency and deposits...............................	8 780 ..	9,283	11,037	11,875	16,591	18,897	14,002	16,434	17,701
Monetary authorities.............................	8 781 ..	....	....	....	....	....	....	....	....
General government..............................	8 782 ..	....	....	....	....	....	....	....	....
Banks..	8 783 ..	....	....	....	....	....	....	....	....
Other sectors.......................................	8 784 ..	....	....	....	....	....	....	....	....
Other liabilities..	8 786 ..	216	308	313	386	398	84	1,554	1,894
Monetary authorities.............................	8 787 ..	....	....	....	....	....	....	....	....
of which: Short-term.........................	8 789 ..	....	....	....	....	....	....	....	....
General government..............................	8 790 ..	....	....	....	....	....	....	....	....
of which: Short-term.........................	8 792 ..	....	....	....	....	....	....	....	....
Banks..	8 793 ..	....	....	....	....	....	....	....	....
of which: Short-term.........................	8 795 ..	....	....	....	....	....	....	....	....
Other sectors.......................................	8 796 ..	....	....	....	....	....	....	....	....
of which: Short-term.........................	8 798 ..	....	....	....	....	....	....	....	....
NET INTERNATIONAL INVESTMENT POSITION........	8 995 ..	**−62,402**	**−79,983**	**−81,851**	**−90,990**	**−103,755**	**−88,253**	**−109,552**	**−113,588**
Conversion rates: New Zealand dollars per U.S. dollar (end of period)..................................	0 102 ..	1.5385	1.3920	1.4676	1.4166	1.2920	1.7286	1.3856	1.2977

Table 1. ANALYTIC PRESENTATION, 2003–2010

(Millions of U.S. dollars)

	Code	2003	2004	2005	2006	2007	2008	2009	2010
A. Current Account[1]	4 993 Z.	**−705.5**	**−687.4**	**−783.6**	**−838.4**	**−1,223.6**	**−1,570.3**	**−827.9**	**−963.4**
Goods: exports f.o.b.	2 100 ..	1,056.0	1,369.0	1,654.1	1,932.1	2,186.2	2,530.1	2,389.6	3,156.6
Goods: imports f.o.b.	3 100 ..	−2,027.0	−2,457.4	−2,956.1	−3,404.3	−3,989.2	−4,731.0	−3,929.1	−4,792.2
Balance on Goods	4 100 ..	*−971.0*	*−1,088.4*	*−1,302.0*	*−1,472.2*	*−1,803.0*	*−2,200.9*	*−1,539.5*	*−1,635.6*
Services: credit	2 200 ..	257.6	285.8	308.5	345.4	373.6	460.4	496.0	471.5
Services: debit	3 200 ..	−376.8	−409.0	−448.2	−501.5	−656.5	−729.4	−644.1	−693.7
Balance on Goods and Services	4 991 ..	*−1,090.2*	*−1,211.6*	*−1,441.7*	*−1,628.3*	*−2,085.9*	*−2,469.9*	*−1,687.6*	*−1,857.8*
Income: credit	2 300 ..	6.8	9.4	22.7	41.4	48.2	22.9	5.7	9.0
Income: debit	3 300 ..	−247.5	−240.2	−222.0	−254.8	−260.5	−263.2	−264.4	−287.4
Balance on Goods, Services, and Income	4 992 ..	*−1,330.9*	*−1,442.4*	*−1,641.0*	*−1,841.7*	*−2,298.2*	*−2,710.2*	*−1,946.3*	*−2,136.2*
Current transfers: credit	2 379 Z.	625.4	755.0	857.4	1,003.3	1,074.6	1,139.9	1,118.4	1,172.8
Current transfers: debit	3 379 ..	....	....	....	....	....	....	....	....
B. Capital Account[1]	4 994 Z.	**265.2**	**294.2**	**297.1**	**359.8**	**383.5**	**377.9**	**394.0**	**256.2**
Capital account: credit	2 994 Z.	265.2	294.2	297.1	359.8	383.5	377.9	394.0	256.2
Capital account: debit	3 994 ..	....	....	....	....	....	....	....	....
Total, Groups A Plus B	4 981 ..	*−440.3*	*−393.2*	*−486.5*	*−478.6*	*−840.1*	*−1,192.4*	*−433.9*	*−707.2*
C. Financial Account[1]	4 995 W.	**36.3**	**361.4**	**190.9**	**672.7**	**700.4**	**826.4**	**531.7**	**752.0**
Direct investment abroad	4 505 ..	....	....	....	....	....	....	....	....
Direct investment in Nicaragua	4 555 Z.	201.3	250.0	241.1	286.8	381.7	626.1	434.2	508.0
Portfolio investment assets	4 602 ..	....	....	....	....	....	....	....	....
Equity securities	4 610 ..	....	....	....	....	....	....	....	....
Debt securities	4 619 ..	....	....	....	....	....	....	....	....
Portfolio investment liabilities	4 652 Z.	....	....	....	....	....	....	....	....
Equity securities	4 660 ..	....	....	....	....	....	....	....	....
Debt securities	4 669 Z.	....	....	....	....	....	....	....	....
Financial derivatives	4 910 ..	....	....	....	....	....	....	....	....
Financial derivatives assets	4 900 ..	....	....	....	....	....	....	....	....
Financial derivatives liabilities	4 905 ..	....	....	....	....	....	....	....	....
Other investment assets	4 703 ..	−105.5	275.2	−182.3	4.9	−186.3	−276.6	−223.7	−202.3
Monetary authorities	4 701 ..	3.5	−.2	−53.8	−8.5	−6.6	−7.3	−6.4	−7.2
General government	4 704 ..	....	....	....	....	....	....	....	....
Banks	4 705 ..	−16.0	−8.3	−20.6	9.2	−7.3	−40.5	−193.8	−265.7
Other sectors	4 728 ..	−93.0	283.7	−107.9	4.2	−172.4	−228.8	−23.5	70.6
Other investment liabilities	4 753 W.	−59.5	−163.8	132.1	381.0	505.0	476.9	321.1	446.3
Monetary authorities	4 753 WA	2.9	−6.8	−25.4	2.1	−4.4	−16.9	153.0	−18.7
General government	4 753 ZB	−186.0	−155.0	−79.3	−69.1	−77.6	−52.7	−60.1	−52.4
Banks	4 753 ZC	−5.4	3.5	91.9	166.2	36.0	23.5	−80.7	−74.5
Other sectors	4 753 ZD	129.0	−5.5	144.9	281.8	551.0	523.0	308.9	591.9
Total, Groups A Through C	4 983 ..	*−404.0*	*−31.8*	*−295.6*	*194.1*	*−139.7*	*−366.0*	*97.8*	*44.7*
D. Net Errors and Omissions	4 998 ..	**−100.4**	**−403.0**	**−62.6**	**−230.6**	**−37.1**	**139.1**	**−39.2**	**−138.8**
Total, Groups A Through D	4 984 ..	*−504.4*	*−434.8*	*−358.1*	*−36.5*	*−176.8*	*−226.9*	*58.5*	*−94.1*
E. Reserves and Related Items	4 802 A.	**504.4**	**434.8**	**358.1**	**36.5**	**176.8**	**226.9**	**−58.5**	**94.1**
Reserve assets	4 802 ..	−55.0	−159.9	−5.7	−178.8	−167.1	−31.5	−422.8	−221.6
Use of Fund credit and loans	4 766 ..	21.6	23.9	−28.4	−141.5	18.5	28.6	38.1	19.7
Exceptional financing	4 920 ..	537.9	570.9	392.3	356.8	325.4	229.8	326.2	296.0
Conversion rates: córdobas per U.S. dollar	0 101 ..	**15.105**	**15.937**	**16.733**	**17.570**	**18.449**	**19.372**	**20.339**	**21.356**

[1] Excludes components that have been classified in the categories of Group E.

Table 2. STANDARD PRESENTATION, 2003–2010

(Millions of U.S. dollars)

	Code	2003	2004	2005	2006	2007	2008	2009	2010
CURRENT ACCOUNT....................................	4 993 ..	**−705.5**	**−687.4**	**−783.6**	**−838.4**	**−1,223.6**	**−1,570.3**	**−827.9**	**−963.4**
A. GOODS...	4 100 ..	**−971.0**	**−1,088.4**	**−1,302.0**	**−1,472.2**	**−1,803.0**	**−2,200.9**	**−1,539.5**	**−1,635.6**
Credit..	2 100 ..	**1,056.0**	**1,369.0**	**1,654.1**	**1,932.1**	**2,186.2**	**2,530.1**	**2,389.6**	**3,156.6**
General merchandise: exports f.o.b...............	2 110 ..	575.9	714.6	823.6	988.6	1,160.7	1,397.2	1,312.6	1,642.8
Goods for processing: exports f.o.b...............	2 150 ..	433.7	596.7	773.7	870.2	941.3	1,021.5	972.1	1,277.2
Repairs on goods...	2 160 ..	....	....	....	....	....	....	....	....
Goods procured in ports by carriers...............	2 170 ..	11.4	12.5	14.4	18.0	22.8	33.3	23.7	28.3
Nonmonetary gold..	2 180 ..	35.0	45.2	42.4	55.3	61.4	78.1	81.2	208.3
Debit...	3 100 ..	**−2,027.0**	**−2,457.4**	**−2,956.1**	**−3,404.3**	**−3,989.2**	**−4,731.0**	**−3,929.1**	**−4,792.2**
General merchandise: imports f.o.b...............	3 110 ..	−1,726.1	−2,027.7	−2,404.6	−2,777.6	−3,311.3	−3,995.4	−3,229.1	−3,872.5
Goods for processing: imports f.o.b...............	3 150 ..	−300.9	−429.7	−551.5	−626.7	−677.9	−735.6	−700.0	−919.7
Repairs on goods...	3 160 ..	....	....	....	....	....	....	....	....
Goods procured in ports by carriers...............	3 170 ..	....	....	....	....	....	....	....	....
Nonmonetary gold..	3 180 ..	....	....	....	....	....	....	....	....
B. SERVICES..	4 200 ..	**−119.2**	**−123.2**	**−139.7**	**−156.1**	**−282.9**	**−269.0**	**−148.1**	**−222.2**
Total credit..	2 200 ..	*257.6*	*285.8*	*308.5*	*345.4*	*373.6*	*460.4*	*496.0*	*471.5*
Total debit..	3 200 ..	*−376.8*	*−409.0*	*−448.2*	*−501.5*	*−656.5*	*−729.4*	*−644.1*	*−693.7*
Transportation services, credit..........	2 205 ..	**33.0**	**28.1**	**33.8**	**42.8**	**44.1**	**45.4**	**45.2**	**47.3**
Passenger..	2 850 ..	....	....	....	....	....	....	....	....
Freight..	2 851 ..	*13.9*	*7.9*	*11.3*	*12.8*	*14.5*	*15.7*	*15.0*	*12.9*
Other..	2 852 ..	*19.1*	*20.2*	*22.5*	*30.0*	*29.6*	*29.7*	*30.2*	*34.4*
Sea transport, passenger..............................	2 207 ..	....	....	....	....	....	....	....	....
Sea transport, freight.................................	2 208 ..	....	....	....	....	....	....	....	....
Sea transport, other...................................	2 209 ..	5.3	5.3	6.7	9.5	10.7	11.7	9.9	12.4
Air transport, passenger..............................	2 211 ..	....	....	....	....	....	....	....	....
Air transport, freight..................................	2 212 ..	....	....	....	....	....	....	....	....
Air transport, other....................................	2 213 ..	13.8	14.9	15.8	20.5	18.9	18.0	20.3	22.0
Other transport, passenger..........................	2 215 ..	....	....	....	....	....	....	....	....
Other transport, freight...............................	2 216 ..	13.9	7.9	11.3	12.8	14.5	15.7	15.0	12.9
Other transport, other.................................	2 217 ..	....	....	....	....	....	....	....	....
Transportation services, debit...........	3 205 ..	**−186.0**	**−196.4**	**−233.9**	**−266.9**	**−322.9**	**−342.8**	**−286.2**	**−328.3**
Passenger..	3 850 ..	*−63.6*	*−65.4*	*−70.9*	*−91.1*	*−101.1*	*−109.2*	*−104.9*	*−118.2*
Freight..	3 851 ..	*−122.4*	*−131.0*	*−163.0*	*−175.8*	*−221.8*	*−233.6*	*−181.3*	*−210.1*
Other..	3 852 ..	....	....	....	....	....	....	....	....
Sea transport, passenger..............................	3 207 ..	....	....	....	....	....	....	....	....
Sea transport, freight.................................	3 208 ..	−52.6	−58.6	−75.0	−83.1	−126.2	−130.9	−96.5	−107.9
Sea transport, other...................................	3 209 ..	....	....	....	....	....	....	....	....
Air transport, passenger..............................	3 211 ..	−63.6	−65.4	−70.9	−91.1	−101.1	−109.2	−104.9	−118.2
Air transport, freight..................................	3 212 ..	−13.1	−14.0	−16.0	−17.1	−21.0	−21.0	−15.8	−22.1
Air transport, other....................................	3 213 ..	....	....	....	....	....	....	....	....
Other transport, passenger..........................	3 215 ..	....	....	....	....	....	....	....	....
Other transport, freight...............................	3 216 ..	−56.7	−58.4	−72.0	−75.6	−74.6	−81.7	−69.0	−80.1
Other transport, other.................................	3 217 ..	....	....	....	....	....	....	....	....
Travel, credit...	2 236 ..	**160.2**	**192.0**	**206.3**	**230.6**	**255.1**	**301.0**	**334.4**	**308.5**
Business travel..	2 237 ..	....	....	....	....	....	....	....	....
Personal travel..	2 240 ..	160.2	192.0	206.3	230.6	255.1	301.0	334.4	308.5
Travel, debit..	3 236 ..	**−75.0**	**−89.3**	**−90.8**	**−97.0**	**−177.8**	**−219.8**	**−191.6**	**−205.3**
Business travel..	3 237 ..	....	....	....	....	....	....	....	....
Personal travel..	3 240 ..	−75.0	−89.3	−90.8	−97.0	−177.8	−219.8	−191.6	−205.3
Other services, credit............................	2 200 BA	**64.4**	**65.7**	**68.4**	**72.0**	**74.4**	**114.0**	**116.4**	**115.7**
Communications...	2 245 ..	26.4	27.1	28.3	29.4	30.5	64.9	57.7	54.9
Construction...	2 249 ..	....	....	....	....	....	....	....	....
Insurance...	2 253 ..	2.3	2.4	2.8	3.5	3.7	4.3	4.9	4.3
Financial..	2 260 ..	....	....	....	....	....	....	....	....
Computer and information............................	2 262 ..	....	....	....	....	....	....	....	....
Royalties and licence fees............................	2 266 ..	....	....	....	....	....	....	....	....
Other business services...............................	2 268 ..	....	....	....	....	....	3.6	13.0	15.3
Personal, cultural, and recreational...............	2 287 ..	....	....	....	....	....	....	....	....
Government, n.i.e..	2 291 ..	35.7	36.2	37.3	39.1	40.2	41.2	40.8	41.2
Other services, debit.............................	3 200 BA	**−115.8**	**−123.3**	**−123.5**	**−137.6**	**−155.8**	**−166.8**	**−166.3**	**−160.1**
Communications...	3 245 ..	−4.3	−4.7	−5.1	−5.3	−5.6	−9.3	−7.3	−8.6
Construction...	3 249 ..	....	....	....	....	....	....	....	....
Insurance...	3 253 ..	−28.6	−39.2	−40.8	−43.9	−56.4	−57.9	−55.6	−66.2
Financial..	3 260 ..	....	....	....	−6.8	−5.6	−5.9	−6.2	−6.2
Computer and information............................	3 262 ..	....	....	....	....	....	....	....	....
Royalties and licence fees............................	3 266 ..	....	....	....	....	....	....	....	....
Other business services...............................	3 268 ..	−59.4	−55.5	−53.0	−55.0	−57.0	−57.9	−59.9	−45.3
Personal, cultural, and recreational...............	3 287 ..	....	....	....	....	....	....	....	....
Government, n.i.e..	3 291 ..	−23.5	−23.9	−24.6	−26.6	−31.2	−35.8	−37.3	−33.8

Table 2 (Continued). STANDARD PRESENTATION, 2003–2010

(Millions of U.S. dollars)

	Code	2003	2004	2005	2006	2007	2008	2009	2010
C. INCOME	4 300	**−240.7**	**−230.8**	**−199.3**	**−213.4**	**−212.3**	**−240.3**	**−258.7**	**−278.4**
Total credit	2 300	*6.8*	*9.4*	*22.7*	*41.4*	*48.2*	*22.9*	*5.7*	*9.0*
Total debit	3 300	*−247.5*	*−240.2*	*−222.0*	*−254.8*	*−260.5*	*−263.2*	*−264.4*	*−287.4*
Compensation of employees, credit	2 310	....	....	....	....	....	....	....	....
Compensation of employees, debit	3 310	....	....	....	....	....	....	....	....
Investment income, credit	2 320	**6.8**	**9.4**	**22.7**	**41.4**	**48.2**	**22.9**	**5.7**	**9.0**
Direct investment income	2 330	....	....	....	....	....	....	....	....
Dividends and distributed branch profits	2 332	....	....	....	....	....	....	....	....
Reinvested earnings and undistributed branch profits	2 333	....	....	....	....	....	....	....	....
Income on debt (interest)	2 334	....	....	....	....	....	....	....	....
Portfolio investment income	2 339	....	....	....	....	....	....	....	....
Income on equity	2 340	....	....	....	....	....	....	....	....
Income on bonds and notes	2 350	....	....	....	....	....	....	....	....
Income on money market instruments	2 360	....	....	....	....	....	....	....	....
Other investment income	2 370	6.8	9.4	22.7	41.4	48.2	22.9	5.7	9.0
Investment income, debit	3 320	**−247.5**	**−240.2**	**−222.0**	**−254.8**	**−260.5**	**−263.2**	**−264.4**	**−287.4**
Direct investment income	3 330	−76.9	−80.0	−82.4	−84.9	−92.6	−112.9	−121.3	−135.2
Dividends and distributed branch profits	3 332	−76.9	−80.0	−82.4	−84.9	−92.6	−112.9	−121.3	−135.2
Reinvested earnings and undistributed branch profits	3 333	....	....	....	....	....	....	....	....
Income on debt (interest)	3 334	....	....	....	....	....	....	....	....
Portfolio investment income	3 339	....	....	....	....	....	....	....	....
Income on equity	3 340	....	....	....	....	....	....	....	....
Income on bonds and notes	3 350	....	....	....	....	....	....	....	....
Income on money market instruments	3 360	....	....	....	....	....	....	....	....
Other investment income	3 370	−170.6	−160.2	−139.6	−169.9	−167.9	−150.3	−143.1	−152.2
D. CURRENT TRANSFERS	4 379	**625.4**	**755.0**	**857.4**	**1,003.3**	**1,074.6**	**1,139.9**	**1,118.4**	**1,172.8**
Credit	2 379	**625.4**	**755.0**	**857.4**	**1,003.3**	**1,074.6**	**1,139.9**	**1,118.4**	**1,172.8**
General government	2 380	....	....	....	....	80.0	....	....	....
Other sectors	2 390	625.4	755.0	857.4	1,003.3	994.6	1,139.9	1,118.4	1,172.8
Workers' remittances	2 391	438.8	518.8	615.7	697.5	739.6	818.1	768.4	822.8
Other current transfers	2 392	186.6	236.2	241.7	305.8	255.0	321.8	350.0	350.0
Debit	3 379	....	....	....	....	....	....	....	....
General government	3 380	....	....	....	....	....	....	....	....
Other sectors	3 390	....	....	....	....	....	....	....	....
Workers' remittances	3 391	....	....	....	....	....	....	....	....
Other current transfers	3 392	....	....	....	....	....	....	....	....
CAPITAL AND FINANCIAL ACCOUNT	4 996	**805.9**	**1,090.4**	**846.1**	**1,069.0**	**1,260.7**	**1,431.2**	**867.1**	**1,102.2**
CAPITAL ACCOUNT	4 994	**752.8**	**1,909.0**	**479.1**	**1,590.2**	**2,903.4**	**437.0**	**557.2**	**267.3**
Total credit	2 994	*752.8*	*1,909.0*	*479.1*	*1,590.2*	*2,903.4*	*437.0*	*557.2*	*267.3*
Total debit	3 994	....	....	....	....	....	....	....	....
Capital transfers, credit	2 400	**752.8**	**1,909.0**	**479.1**	**1,590.2**	**2,903.4**	**437.0**	**557.2**	**267.3**
General government	2 401	609.3	1,764.1	345.1	1,440.2	2,732.5	243.3	314.8	133.3
Debt forgiveness	2 402	487.6	1,614.8	182.0	1,230.4	2,519.9	59.1	163.2	11.1
Other capital transfers	2 410	121.7	149.3	163.1	209.8	212.6	184.2	151.6	122.2
Other sectors	2 430	143.5	144.9	134.0	150.0	170.9	193.7	242.4	134.0
Migrants' transfers	2 431	....	....	....	....	....	....	....	....
Debt forgiveness	2 432	....	....	....	....	....	....	....	....
Other capital transfers	2 440	143.5	144.9	134.0	150.0	170.9	193.7	242.4	134.0
Capital transfers, debit	3 400	....	....	....	....	....	....	....	....
General government	3 401	....	....	....	....	....	....	....	....
Debt forgiveness	3 402	....	....	....	....	....	....	....	....
Other capital transfers	3 410	....	....	....	....	....	....	....	....
Other sectors	3 430	....	....	....	....	....	....	....	....
Migrants' transfers	3 431	....	....	....	....	....	....	....	....
Debt forgiveness	3 432	....	....	....	....	....	....	....	....
Other capital transfers	3 440	....	....	....	....	....	....	....	....
Nonproduced nonfinancial assets, credit	2 480	....	....	....	....	....	....	....	....
Nonproduced nonfinancial assets, debit	3 480	....	....	....	....	....	....	....	....

Table 2 (Continued). STANDARD PRESENTATION, 2003–2010

(Millions of U.S. dollars)

	Code	2003	2004	2005	2006	2007	2008	2009	2010
FINANCIAL ACCOUNT...	4 995 ..	**53.1**	**−818.6**	**367.0**	**−521.2**	**−1,642.7**	**994.2**	**309.9**	**834.9**
A. DIRECT INVESTMENT..	4 500 ..	**201.3**	**250.0**	**241.1**	**286.8**	**381.7**	**626.1**	**434.2**	**508.0**
Direct investment abroad..............................	4 505 ..	....	....	....	....	....	....	....	....
Equity capital...	4 510 ..	....	....	....	....	....	....	....	....
Claims on affiliated enterprises.............	4 515 ..	....	....	....	....	....	....	....	....
Liabilities to affiliated enterprises.........	4 520 ..	....	....	....	....	....	....	....	....
Reinvested earnings..................................	4 525 ..	....	....	....	....	....	....	....	....
Other capital...	4 530 ..	....	....	....	....	....	....	....	....
Claims on affiliated enterprises.............	4 535 ..	....	....	....	....	....	....	....	....
Liabilities to affiliated enterprises.........	4 540 ..	....	....	....	....	....	....	....	....
Direct investment in Nicaragua......................	4 555 ..	**201.3**	**250.0**	**241.1**	**286.8**	**381.7**	**626.1**	**434.2**	**508.0**
Equity capital...	4 560 ..	201.3	250.0	241.1	286.8	381.7	626.1	434.2	508.0
Claims on direct investors......................	4 565 ..	....	....	....	....	....	....	....	....
Liabilities to direct investors.................	4 570 ..	201.3	250.0	241.1	286.8	381.7	626.1	434.2	508.0
Reinvested earnings..................................	4 575 ..	....	....	....	....	....	....	....	....
Other capital...	4 580 ..	....	....	....	....	....	....	....	....
Claims on direct investors......................	4 585 ..	....	....	....	....	....	....	....	....
Liabilities to direct investors.................	4 590 ..	....	....	....	....	....	....	....	....
B. PORTFOLIO INVESTMENT.................................	4 600 ..	....	....	....	....	....	....		....
Assets...	4 602 ..	....	....	....	....	....	....		....
Equity securities...	4 610 ..	....	....	....	....	....	....		....
Monetary authorities...............................	4 611 ..	....	....	....	....	....	....		....
General government................................	4 612 ..	....	....	....	....	....	....		....
Banks...	4 613 ..	....	....	....	....	....	....		....
Other sectors..	4 614 ..	....	....	....	....	....	....		....
Debt securities..	4 619 ..	....	....	....	....	....	....		....
Bonds and notes......................................	4 620 ..	....	....	....	....	....	....		....
Monetary authorities...........................	4 621 ..	....	....	....	....	....	....		....
General government............................	4 622 ..	....	....	....	....	....	....		....
Banks...	4 623 ..	....	....	....	....	....	....		....
Other sectors..	4 624 ..	....	....	....	....	....	....		....
Money market instruments.....................	4 630 ..	....	....	....	....	....	....		....
Monetary authorities...........................	4 631 ..	....	....	....	....	....	....		....
General government............................	4 632 ..	....	....	....	....	....	....		....
Banks...	4 633 ..	....	....	....	....	....	....		....
Other sectors..	4 634 ..	....	....	....	....	....	....		....
Liabilities...	4 652 ..	....	....	....	....	....	....		....
Equity securities...	4 660 ..	....	....	....	....	....	....		....
Banks...	4 663 ..	....	....	....	....	....	....		....
Other sectors..	4 664 ..	....	....	....	....	....	....		....
Debt securities..	4 669 ..	....	....	....	....	....	....		....
Bonds and notes......................................	4 670 ..	....	....	....	....	....	....		....
Monetary authorities...........................	4 671 ..	....	....	....	....	....	....		....
General government............................	4 672 ..	....	....	....	....	....	....		....
Banks...	4 673 ..	....	....	....	....	....	....		....
Other sectors..	4 674 ..	....	....	....	....	....	....		....
Money market instruments.....................	4 680 ..	....	....	....	....	....	....		....
Monetary authorities...........................	4 681 ..	....	....	....	....	....	....		....
General government............................	4 682 ..	....	....	....	....	....	....		....
Banks...	4 683 ..	....	....	....	....	....	....		....
Other sectors..	4 684 ..	....	....	....	....	....	....		....
C. FINANCIAL DERIVATIVES.................................	4 910 ..	....	....	....	....	....	....		....
Monetary authorities...................................	4 911 ..	....	....	....	....	....	....		....
General government....................................	4 912 ..	....	....	....	....	....	....		....
Banks..	4 913 ..	....	....	....	....	....	....		....
Other sectors..	4 914 ..	....	....	....	....	....	....		....
Assets...	4 900 ..	201.3	....	241.1	....	381.7	....		....
Monetary authorities...............................	4 901 ..	201.3	....	....	....	....	....		....
General government................................	4 902 ..	....	....	....	....	....	....		....
Banks...	4 903 ..	....	....	....	....	....	....		....
Other sectors..	4 904 ..	....	....	....	....	....	....		....
Liabilities...	4 905 ..	....	....	....	....	....	....		....
Monetary authorities...............................	4 906 ..	....	....	....	....	....	....		....
General government................................	4 907 ..	....	....	....	....	....	....		....
Banks...	4 908 ..	....	....	....	....	....	....		....
Other sectors..	4 909 ..	....	....	....	....	....	....		....

Table 2 (Concluded). STANDARD PRESENTATION, 2003–2010

(Millions of U.S. dollars)

	Code	2003	2004	2005	2006	2007	2008	2009	2010
D. OTHER INVESTMENT	4 700	−93.1	−908.6	131.7	−629.2	−1,857.3	399.6	298.5	548.5
Assets	4 703	−105.5	275.2	−182.3	4.9	−186.3	−276.6	−223.7	−202.3
Trade credits	4 706	....	....	....	....	....	....	....	....
General government	4 707	....	....	....	....	....	....	....	....
of which: Short-term	4 709	....	....	....	....	....	....	....	....
Other sectors	4 710	....	....	....	....	....	....	....	....
of which: Short-term	4 712	....	....	....	....	....	....	....	....
Loans	4 714	....	−.3	−1.9	−.8	−21.4	−9.8	−5.5	−3.4
Monetary authorities	4 715	....	....	....	....	....	....	....	....
of which: Short-term	4 718	....	....	....	....	....	....	....	....
General government	4 719	....	....	....	....	....	....	....	....
of which: Short-term	4 721	....	....	....	....	....	....	....	....
Banks	4 722	....	....	....	....	....	....	....	....
of which: Short-term	4 724	....	....	....	....	....	....	....	....
Other sectors	4 725	....	−.3	−1.9	−.8	−21.4	−9.8	−5.5	−3.4
of which: Short-term	4 727	....	....	....	....	....	....	....	....
Currency and deposits	4 730	−104.8	275.2	−127.0	13.8	−155.9	−259.6	−206.8	−127.0
Monetary authorities	4 731	3.5	−.2	.2	−.2	2.3	....	....	....
General government	4 732	....	....	....	....	....	....	....	....
Banks	4 733	−15.3	−8.6	−21.2	9.0	−7.2	−40.6	−188.8	−201.0
Other sectors	4 734	−93.0	284.0	−106.0	5.0	−151.0	−219.0	−18.0	74.0
Other assets	4 736	−.7	.3	−53.4	−8.1	−9.0	−7.2	−11.4	−71.9
Monetary authorities	4 737	....	....	−54.0	−8.3	−8.9	−7.3	−6.4	−7.2
of which: Short-term	4 739	....	....	....	−8.3	−8.9	−7.3	−6.4	−7.2
General government	4 740	....	....	....	....	....	....	....	....
of which: Short-term	4 742	....	....	....	....	....	....	....	....
Banks	4 743	−.7	.3	.6	.2	−.1	.1	−5.0	−64.7
of which: Short-term	4 745	....	....	....	....	....	....	....	....
Other sectors	4 746	....	....	....	....	....	....	....	....
of which: Short-term	4 748	....	....	....	....	....	....	....	....
Liabilities	4 753	12.4	−1,183.8	314.0	−634.1	−1,671.0	676.2	522.2	750.8
Trade credits	4 756	117.8	−6.8	122.0	102.0	276.3	15.3	50.2	78.5
General government	4 757	....	....	....	....	....	....	....	....
of which: Short-term	4 759	....	....	....	....	....	....	....	....
Other sectors	4 760	117.8	−6.8	122.0	102.0	276.3	15.3	50.2	78.5
of which: Short-term	4 762	117.8	−6.8	122.0	102.0	276.3	15.3	50.2	78.5
Loans	4 764	−172.9	−1,231.3	147.7	−834.6	−2,021.0	614.9	275.1	657.7
Monetary authorities	4 765	5.8	6.3	−38.7	−322.9	−14.5	14.4	−125.6	2.7
of which: Use of Fund credit and loans from the Fund	4 766	21.6	23.9	−28.4	−141.5	18.5	28.6	38.1	19.7
of which: Short-term	4 768	.6	.5	....	−169.1	−20.0	....	−147.5	....
General government	4 769	−178.8	−1,238.6	81.7	−836.6	−2,321.9	61.2	225.9	213.2
of which: Short-term	4 771	−245.0	−1,376.4	−83.8	−978.8	−2,433.5	−43.4	....	....
Banks	4 772	−5.9	1.3	91.0	154.5	41.6	30.0	−83.1	−71.4
of which: Short-term	4 774	1.7	−6.5	11.8	54.2	−31.0	−17.6	−22.8	−8.2
Other sectors	4 775	6.0	−.3	13.7	170.4	273.8	509.3	257.9	513.2
of which: Short-term	4 777	20.2	10.7	21.7	172.7	277.2	517.5	262.6	514.1
Currency and deposits	4 780	18.4	10.4	−13.5	24.0	4.6	−7.2	10.4	−3.6
Monetary authorities	4 781	19.4	10.5	−13.8	11.8	11.2	−3.0	5.4	−1.7
General government	4 782	....	....	....	....	....	....	....	....
Banks	4 783	−1.0	−.1	.3	12.2	−6.6	−4.2	5.0	−1.9
Other sectors	4 784	....	....	....	....	....	....	....	....
Other liabilities	4 786	49.1	43.9	57.8	74.5	69.1	53.2	186.5	18.2
Monetary authorities	4 787	40.2	37.7	44.0	60.6	64.8	55.2	187.9	18.9
of which: Short-term	4 789	40.2	37.7	44.0	60.6	64.8	55.2	23.8	18.9
General government	4 790	2.2	2.3	4.0	5.0	2.4	1.9	.4	.4
of which: Short-term	4 792	2.2	2.3	4.0	5.0	2.4	1.9	.4	.4
Banks	4 793	1.5	2.3	.6	−.5	1.0	−2.3	−2.6	−1.3
of which: Short-term	4 795	1.5	2.3	.6	−.5	1.0	−2.3	−2.6	−1.3
Other sectors	4 796	5.2	1.6	9.2	9.4	.9	−1.6	.8	.2
of which: Short-term	4 798	5.2	1.6	9.2	9.4	.9	−1.6	.8	.2
E. RESERVE ASSETS	4 802	−55.0	−159.9	−5.7	−178.8	−167.1	−31.5	−422.8	−221.6
Monetary gold	4 812	−1.1	6.2	....	....	....	....	....	....
Special drawing rights	4 811	....	−.4	.2	−.1	.3	....	−163.7	.1
Reserve position in the Fund	4 810	....	....	....	....	....	....	....	....
Foreign exchange	4 803	−53.9	−165.7	−5.9	−178.7	−167.4	−31.5	−259.1	−221.7
Other claims	4 813	....	....	....	....	....	....	....	....
NET ERRORS AND OMISSIONS	4 998	−100.4	−403.0	−62.6	−230.6	−37.1	139.1	−39.2	−138.8

Table 3. INTERNATIONAL INVESTMENT POSITION (End-period stocks), 2003–2010

(Millions of U.S. dollars)

	Code	2003	2004	2005	2006	2007	2008	2009	2010
ASSETS	8 995 C.	777.3	991.1	1,172.9	1,440.8	1,708.3	1,970.4	2,647.0	3,304.0
Direct investment abroad	8 505 ..	....	....	....	....	....	....	....	....
Equity capital and reinvested earnings	8 506 ..	....	....	....	....	....	....	....	....
Claims on affiliated enterprises	8 507 ..	....	....	....	....	....	....	....	....
Liabilities to affiliated enterprises	8 508 ..	....	....	....	....	....	....	....	....
Other capital	8 530 ..	....	....	....	....	....	....	....	....
Claims on affiliated enterprises	8 535 ..	....	....	....	....	....	....	....	....
Liabilities to affiliated enterprises	8 540 ..	....	....	....	....	....	....	....	....
Portfolio investment	8 602 ..	....	....	....	....	....	....	....	....
Equity securities	8 610 ..	....	....	....	....	....	....	....	....
Monetary authorities	8 611 ..	....	....	....	....	....	....	....	....
General government	8 612 ..	....	....	....	....	....	....	....	....
Banks	8 613 ..	....	....	....	....	....	....	....	....
Other sectors	8 614 ..	....	....	....	....	....	....	....	....
Debt securities	8 619 ..	....	....	....	....	....	....	....	....
Bonds and notes	8 620 ..	....	....	....	....	....	....	....	....
Monetary authorities	8 621 ..	....	....	....	....	....	....	....	....
General government	8 622 ..	....	....	....	....	....	....	....	....
Banks	8 623 ..	....	....	....	....	....	....	....	....
Other sectors	8 624 ..	....	....	....	....	....	....	....	....
Money market instruments	8 630 ..	....	....	....	....	....	....	....	....
Monetary authorities	8 631 ..	....	....	....	....	....	....	....	....
General government	8 632 ..	....	....	....	....	....	....	....	....
Banks	8 633 ..	....	....	....	....	....	....	....	....
Other sectors	8 634 ..	....	....	....	....	....	....	....	....
Financial derivatives	8 900 ..	....	....	....	....	....	....	....	....
Monetary authorities	8 901 ..	....	....	....	....	....	....	....	....
General government	8 902 ..	....	....	....	....	....	....	....	....
Banks	8 903 ..	....	....	....	....	....	....	....	....
Other sectors	8 904 ..	....	....	....	....	....	....	....	....
Other investment	8 703 ..	269.0	322.9	499.1	581.2	676.2	908.1	1,158.8	1,597.1
Trade credits	8 706 ..	....	....	....	....	....	....	....	....
General government	8 707 ..	....	....	....	....	....	....	....	....
of which: Short-term	8 709 ..	....	....	....	....	....	....	....	....
Other sectors	8 710 ..	....	....	....	....	....	....	....	....
of which: Short-term	8 712 ..	....	....	....	....	....	....	....	....
Loans	8 714 ..	....	.3	2.2	3.0	24.4	34.2	39.7	43.1
Monetary authorities	8 715 ..	....	....	....	....	....	....	....	....
of which: Short-term	8 718 ..	....	....	....	....	....	....	....	....
General government	8 719 ..	....	....	....	....	....	....	....	....
of which: Short-term	8 721 ..	....	....	....	....	....	....	....	....
Banks	8 722 ..	....	....	....	....	....	....	....	....
of which: Short-term	8 724 ..	....	....	....	....	....	....	....	....
Other sectors	8 725 ..	....	.3	2.2	3.0	24.4	34.2	39.7	43.1
of which: Short-term	8 727 ..	....	....	....	....	....	....	....	....
Currency and deposits	8 730 ..	267.8	321.7	442.6	515.8	580.4	795.3	1,029.1	1,392.1
Monetary authorities	8 731 ..	2.1	2.3	2.1	2.3	....	....	....	....
General government	8 732 ..	....	....	....	....	....	....	....	....
Banks	8 733 ..	99.7	108.4	129.5	120.5	128.4	168.3	357.1	558.1
Other sectors	8 734 ..	166.0	211.0	311.0	393.0	452.0	627.0	672.0	834.0
Other assets	8 736 ..	1.2	.9	54.3	62.4	71.4	78.6	90.0	161.9
Monetary authorities	8 737 ..	....	....	54.0	62.3	71.2	78.5	84.9	92.1
of which: Short-term	8 739 ..	....	....	*54.0*	*62.3*	*71.2*	*78.5*	*84.9*	*92.1*
General government	8 740 ..	....	....	....	....	....	....	....	....
of which: Short-term	8 742 ..	....	....	....	....	....	....	....	....
Banks	8 743 ..	1.2	.9	.3	.1	.2	.1	5.1	69.8
of which: Short-term	8 745 ..	....	....	....	....	....	....	....	....
Other sectors	8 746 ..	....	....	....	....	....	....	....	....
of which: Short-term	8 748 ..	....	....	....	....	....	....	....	....
Reserve assets	8 802 ..	508.3	668.2	673.8	859.6	1,032.1	1,062.3	1,488.2	1,706.9
Monetary gold	8 812 ..	6.2	....	....	....	....	....	....	....
Special drawing rights	8 811 ..	.1	.5	.3	.4	.1	.1	164.5	161.5
Reserve position in the Fund	8 810 ..	....	....	....	....	....	....	....	....
Foreign exchange	8 803 ..	502.0	667.7	673.5	859.2	1,032.0	1,062.2	1,323.7	1,545.4
Other claims	8 813 ..	....	....	....	....	....	....	....	....

Table 3 (Concluded). INTERNATIONAL INVESTMENT POSITION (End-period stocks), 2003–2010

(Millions of U.S. dollars)

	Code	2003	2004	2005	2006	2007	2008	2009	2010
LIABILITIES..........	8 995 D.	**9,921.4**	**8,977.6**	**9,382.8**	**9,142.5**	**8,798.2**	**9,898.3**	**11,495.3**	**12,806.7**
Direct investment in Nicaragua..........	8 555 ..	**1,969.9**	**2,219.9**	**2,461.0**	**2,747.8**	**3,129.5**	**3,755.6**	**4,189.8**	**4,697.8**
Equity capital and reinvested earnings..........	8 556 ..	1,969.9	2,219.9	2,461.0	2,747.8	3,129.5	3,755.6	4,189.8	4,697.8
Claims on direct investors..........	8 557 ..	....	....	....	....	....	....	....	....
Liabilities to direct investors..........	8 558 ..	1,969.9	2,219.9	2,461.0	2,747.8	3,129.5	3,755.6	4,189.8	4,697.8
Other capital..........	8 580 ..	....	....	....	....	....	....	....	....
Claims on direct investors..........	8 585 ..	....	....	....	....	....	....	....	....
Liabilities to direct investors..........	8 590 ..	....	....	....	....	....	....	....	....
Portfolio investment..........	8 652 ..	....	....	....	....	....	....	....	....
Equity securities..........	8 660 ..	....	....	....	....	....	....	....	....
Banks..........	8 663 ..	....	....	....	....	....	....	....	....
Other sectors..........	8 664 ..	....	....	....	....	....	....	....	....
Debt securities..........	8 669 ..	....	....	....	....	....	....	....	....
Bonds and notes..........	8 670 ..	....	....	....	....	....	....	....	....
Monetary authorities..........	8 671 ..	....	....	....	....	....	....	....	....
General government..........	8 672 ..	....	....	....	....	....	....	....	....
Banks..........	8 673 ..	....	....	....	....	....	....	....	....
Other sectors..........	8 674 ..	....	....	....	....	....	....	....	....
Money market instruments..........	8 680 ..	....	....	....	....	....	....	....	....
Monetary authorities..........	8 681 ..	....	....	....	....	....	....	....	....
General government..........	8 682 ..	....	....	....	....	....	....	....	....
Banks..........	8 683 ..	....	....	....	....	....	....	....	....
Other sectors..........	8 684 ..	....	....	....	....	....	....	....	....
Financial derivatives..........	8 905 ..	....	....	....	....	....	....	....	....
Monetary authorities..........	8 906 ..	....	....	....	....	....	....	....	....
General government..........	8 907 ..	....	....	....	....	....	....	....	....
Banks..........	8 908 ..	....	....	....	....	....	....	....	....
Other sectors..........	8 909 ..	....	....	....	....	....	....	....	....
Other investment..........	8 753 ..	**7,951.5**	**6,757.7**	**6,921.8**	**6,394.7**	**5,668.7**	**6,142.7**	**7,305.5**	**8,108.9**
Trade credits..........	8 756 ..	1,034.9	1,028.1	1,150.1	1,252.0	1,528.3	1,543.6	1,593.8	1,672.3
General government..........	8 757 ..	....	....	....	....	....	....	....	....
of which: Short-term..........	8 759 ..	....	....	....	....	....	....	....	....
Other sectors..........	8 760 ..	1,034.9	1,028.1	1,150.1	1,252.0	1,528.3	1,543.6	1,593.8	1,672.3
of which: Short-term..........	8 762 ..	*1,034.9*	*1,028.1*	*1,150.1*	*1,252.0*	*1,528.3*	*1,543.6*	*1,593.8*	*1,672.3*
Loans..........	8 764 ..	6,698.4	5,498.6	5,555.0	4,899.9	3,894.6	4,362.6	5,467.6	6,197.4
Monetary authorities..........	8 765 ..	1,987.5	1,927.8	1,921.0	1,835.6	1,886.9	1,924.9	1,824.3	1,843.2
of which: Use of Fund credit and loans from the Fund....	8 766 ..	*213.2*	*247.7*	*200.8*	*62.9*	*84.8*	*111.0*	*150.3*	*167.4*
of which: Short-term..........	8 768 ..	*551.5*	*551.0*	*570.6*	*597.4*	*624.8*	*640.6*	*484.8*	*492.7*
General government..........	8 769 ..	4,590.3	3,447.0	3,399.7	2,637.3	1,422.5	1,491.2	1,737.0	1,936.4
of which: Short-term..........	8 771 ..	*1.2*	*1.0*	*1.0*	*1.1*	*1.3*	*1.1*	*1.2*	*1.3*
Banks..........	8 772 ..	94.1	96.6	187.8	342.2	383.8	414.4	331.4	260.0
of which: Short-term..........	8 774 ..	*22.5*	*16.0*	*27.8*	*82.0*	*51.0*	*33.4*	*10.7*	*2.5*
Other sectors..........	8 775 ..	26.5	27.2	46.5	84.8	201.4	532.1	1,574.9	2,157.8
of which: Short-term..........	8 777 ..	*17.0*	*15.4*	*21.9*	*32.9*	*40.9*	*38.1*	*40.2*	*47.0*
Currency and deposits..........	8 780 ..	211.5	221.9	208.4	232.4	237.0	229.7	240.2	236.6
Monetary authorities..........	8 781 ..	211.4	221.8	208.1	219.9	231.1	228.0	233.5	231.8
General government..........	8 782 ..	....	....	....	....	....	....	....	....
Banks..........	8 783 ..	.1	.1	.3	12.5	5.9	1.7	6.7	4.8
Other sectors..........	8 784 ..	....	....	....	....	....	....	....	....
Other liabilities..........	8 786 ..	6.7	9.1	8.3	10.4	8.8	6.8	3.9	2.6
Monetary authorities..........	8 787 ..	....	1.3	....	2.6	....	.3	....	....
of which: Short-term..........	8 789 ..	....	*1.3*	....	*2.6*	....	*.3*	....	....
General government..........	8 790 ..	....	....	....	....	....	....	....	....
of which: Short-term..........	8 792 ..	....	....	....	....	....	....	....	....
Banks..........	8 793 ..	6.7	7.8	8.3	7.8	8.8	6.5	3.9	2.6
of which: Short-term..........	8 795 ..	*5.4*	*7.7*	*8.3*	*7.8*	*8.8*	*6.5*	*3.9*	*2.6*
Other sectors..........	8 796 ..	....	....	....	....	....	....	....	....
of which: Short-term..........	8 798 ..	....	....	....	....	....	....	....	....
NET INTERNATIONAL INVESTMENT POSITION..........	8 995 ..	**–9,144.2**	**–7,986.5**	**–8,209.9**	**–7,701.7**	**–7,089.9**	**–7,927.9**	**–8,848.3**	**–9,502.7**
Conversion rates: córdobas per U.S. dollar (end of period)..........	0 102 ..	**15.552**	**16.329**	**17.146**	**18.003**	**18.903**	**19.848**	**20.841**	**21.883**

Table 1. ANALYTIC PRESENTATION, 2003–2010

(Millions of U.S. dollars)

	Code	2003	2004	2005	2006	2007	2008	2009	2010
A. Current Account[1]	4 993 Z.	**−218.7**	**−230.9**	**−311.5**	**−313.7**	**−351.3**	**−651.4**	**−1,320.1**	....
Goods: exports f.o.b.	2 100 ..	351.8	436.7	477.6	508.0	663.3	912.3	996.9	....
Goods: imports f.o.b.	3 100 ..	−488.5	−589.7	−769.5	−748.3	−914.6	−1,349.7	−1,794.2	....
Balance on Goods	4 100 ..	*−136.7*	*−153.0*	*−291.9*	*−240.3*	*−251.3*	*−437.4*	*−797.3*	....
Services: credit	2 200 ..	63.3	93.4	87.5	90.6	84.6	130.8	99.9	....
Services: debit	3 200 ..	−192.5	−262.2	−279.3	−328.5	−369.4	−600.9	−734.7	....
Balance on Goods and Services	4 991 ..	*−265.9*	*−321.8*	*−483.7*	*−478.3*	*−536.1*	*−907.5*	*−1,432.1*	....
Income: credit	2 300 ..	17.3	26.5	37.1	42.0	59.2	81.3	88.9	....
Income: debit	3 300 ..	−43.4	−39.4	−46.6	−40.8	−59.6	−55.6	−127.7	....
Balance on Goods, Services, and Income	4 992 ..	*−292.0*	*−334.7*	*−493.2*	*−477.1*	*−536.5*	*−881.8*	*−1,470.9*	....
Current transfers: credit	2 379 Z.	82.9	128.6	217.1	199.5	207.9	253.9	170.2	....
Current transfers: debit	3 379 ..	−9.5	−24.7	−35.4	−36.1	−22.6	−23.6	−19.3	....
B. Capital Account[1]	4 994 Z.	**92.3**	**249.2**	**49.4**	**220.2**	**268.8**	**532.1**	**247.1**	....
Capital account: credit	2 994 Z.	92.4	384.5	188.3	220.2	268.8	532.1	247.2	....
Capital account: debit	3 994 ..	−.1	−135.3	−138.9	....	....	....	−.1	....
Total, Groups A Plus B	4 981 ..	*−126.4*	*18.4*	*−262.1*	*−93.6*	*−82.4*	*−119.4*	*−1,072.9*	....
C. Financial Account[1]	4 995 W.	**97.1**	**−173.0**	**174.0**	**37.0**	**95.7**	**287.6**	**886.8**	....
Direct investment abroad	4 505 ..	....	−13.1	−9.3	1.0	−8.1	−24.4	−89.4	....
Direct investment in Niger	4 555 Z.	14.9	26.3	44.0	50.5	129.0	340.4	815.3	....
Portfolio investment assets	4 602 ..	−4.4	−.2	−.8	.2	....	−20.7	−29.7	....
Equity securities	4 610 ..	−4.3	−.3	−.7	.4	.2	4.1	2.2	....
Debt securities	4 619 ..	−.2	.1	−.1	−.2	−.2	−24.8	−31.8	....
Portfolio investment liabilities	4 652 Z.	6.9	5.0	42.5	−4.1	−8.2	−9.5	10.2	....
Equity securities	4 660 ..	....	3.8	.6	....	−.5	1.5	9.5	....
Debt securities	4 669 Z.	6.9	1.1	41.9	−4.1	−7.7	−10.9	.8	....
Financial derivatives	4 910 ..	....	1.1	....	....	1.8	−2.3	....	....
Financial derivatives assets	4 900 ..	....	....	....	....	....	−.3	....	....
Financial derivatives liabilities	4 905 ..	....	1.1	....	....	1.8	−2.0	....	....
Other investment assets	4 703 ..	−42.4	−72.8	−19.4	−30.1	−44.4	67.3	112.4	....
Monetary authorities	4 701 ..	....	....	....	....	....	....	....	....
General government	4 704 ..	.7	....	....	....	....	....	....	....
Banks	4 705 ..	−5.0	−10.9	−6.4	6.2	−29.4	−8.2	55.0	....
Other sectors	4 728 ..	−38.1	−61.9	−13.0	−36.3	−15.0	75.5	57.4	....
Other investment liabilities	4 753 W.	122.1	−119.3	117.0	19.4	25.5	−63.3	68.0	....
Monetary authorities	4 753 WA	.4	1.3	1.5	−1.6	3.9	13.1	67.3	....
General government	4 753 ZB	93.7	−148.9	87.2	....	....	....	....	....
Banks	4 753 ZC	17.0	−8.5	16.6	9.4	6.5	3.9	−14.8	....
Other sectors	4 753 ZD	11.0	36.8	11.7	11.6	15.1	−80.4	15.5	....
Total, Groups A Through C	4 983 ..	*−29.2*	*−154.6*	*−88.1*	*−56.6*	*13.3*	*168.2*	*−186.1*	....
D. Net Errors and Omissions	4 998 ..	**−14.6**	**115.9**	**120.9**	**1,501.1**	**−16.3**	**−66.4**	**2.9**	....
Total, Groups A Through D	4 984 ..	*−43.8*	*−38.7*	*32.8*	*1,444.5*	*−3.0*	*101.8*	*−183.3*	....
E. Reserves and Related Items	4 802 A.	**43.8**	**38.7**	**−32.8**	**−1,444.5**	**3.0**	**−101.8**	**183.3**	....
Reserve assets	4 802 ..	29.2	40.6	−35.4	−87.5	−166.7	−151.8	68.9	....
Use of Fund credit and loans	4 766 ..	14.6	−1.9	2.6	−103.5	11.7	11.9	5.0	....
Exceptional financing	4 920 ..	....	....	....	−1,253.5	158.0	38.1	109.4	....
Conversion rates: CFA francs per U.S. dollar	0 101 ..	**581.20**	**528.28**	**527.47**	**522.89**	**479.27**	**447.81**	**472.19**	**495.28**

[1] Excludes components that have been classified in the categories of Group E.

Table 2. STANDARD PRESENTATION, 2003–2010

(Millions of U.S. dollars)

	Code	2003	2004	2005	2006	2007	2008	2009	2010
CURRENT ACCOUNT	4 993	−218.7	−230.9	−311.5	−313.7	−351.3	−651.4	−1,320.1	....
A. GOODS	4 100	−136.7	−153.0	−291.9	−240.3	−251.3	−437.4	−797.3	....
Credit	2 100	351.8	436.7	477.6	508.0	663.3	912.3	996.9	....
General merchandise: exports f.o.b.	2 110	345.5	409.2	397.0	440.3	586.6	827.2	913.0	....
Goods for processing: exports f.o.b.	2 150	....	....	....	....	....	.1	....	....
Repairs on goods	2 160	....	....	....	....	....	....	....	....
Goods procured in ports by carriers	2 170	6.3	7.1	15.7	21.2	23.4	26.1	22.1	....
Nonmonetary gold	2 180	....	20.4	64.9	46.4	53.3	58.9	61.7	....
Debit	3 100	−488.5	−589.7	−769.5	−748.3	−914.6	−1,349.7	−1,794.2	....
General merchandise: imports f.o.b.	3 110	−470.9	−573.5	−748.7	−740.4	−901.4	−1,327.4	−1,772.9	....
Goods for processing: imports f.o.b.	3 150	....	....	....	....	....	....	....	....
Repairs on goods	3 160	−1.1	−.8	−.9	−.8	−.7	−.4	−1.0	....
Goods procured in ports by carriers	3 170	−16.3	−15.4	−19.8	−7.1	−12.5	−21.9	−20.3	....
Nonmonetary gold	3 180	−.1	....	....	....	....	....	....	....
B. SERVICES	4 200	−129.2	−168.8	−191.8	−238.0	−284.7	−470.1	−634.8	....
Total credit	2 200	*63.3*	*93.4*	*87.5*	*90.6*	*84.6*	*130.8*	*99.9*	....
Total debit	3 200	*−192.5*	*−262.2*	*−279.3*	*−328.5*	*−369.4*	*−600.9*	*−734.7*	....
Transportation services, credit	2 205	5.0	7.5	8.5	8.8	11.8	12.0	7.8	....
Passenger	2 850	*.5*	*1.3*	*.9*	*3.1*	*3.3*	*6.8*	*2.5*	....
Freight	2 851	*3.8*	*4.4*	*5.8*	*4.2*	*6.2*	*4.5*	*5.0*	....
Other	2 852	*.8*	*1.8*	*1.8*	*1.5*	*2.3*	*.6*	*.3*	....
Sea transport, passenger	2 207	....	....	....	....	....	....	....	....
Sea transport, freight	2 208	....	....	....	....	....	....	....	....
Sea transport, other	2 209	.1	....	.6	.1	.1	....	....	....
Air transport, passenger	2 211	....	....	....	....	....	....	....	....
Air transport, freight	2 212	....	....	....	....	....	....	....	....
Air transport, other	2 213	.7	1.8	1.3	1.4	2.2	.6	.3	....
Other transport, passenger	2 215	.5	1.3	.9	3.1	3.3	6.8	2.5	....
Other transport, freight	2 216	3.8	4.3	5.8	4.2	6.2	4.5	5.0	....
Other transport, other	2 217	....	....	....	....	....	....	....	....
Transportation services, debit	3 205	−134.7	−163.5	−213.4	−226.7	−274.3	−399.5	−533.1	....
Passenger	3 850	*−16.6*	*−19.8*	*−11.7*	*−13.5*	*−19.0*	*−30.4*	*−30.4*	....
Freight	3 851	*−117.3*	*−142.9*	*−200.5*	*−212.2*	*−253.5*	*−369.0*	*−502.6*	....
Other	3 852	*−.7*	*−.8*	*−1.1*	*−1.0*	*−1.8*	*−.1*	*....*	....
Sea transport, passenger	3 207	....	....	....	....	....	....	....	....
Sea transport, freight	3 208	−105.6	−130.2	−27.9	−168.8	−124.5	−147.6	−224.7	....
Sea transport, other	3 209	....	....	....	....	....	....	....	....
Air transport, passenger	3 211	−16.6	−19.8	−11.7	−13.5	−19.0	−30.4	−30.4	....
Air transport, freight	3 212	−3.5	−4.3	−120.7	−5.6	−35.8	−36.9	−46.4	....
Air transport, other	3 213	−.7	−.8	−1.1	−1.0	−1.8	−.1	....	....
Other transport, passenger	3 215	....	....	....	....	....	....	....	....
Other transport, freight	3 216	−8.2	−8.3	−51.9	−37.7	−93.2	−184.5	−231.6	....
Other transport, other	3 217	....	....	....	....	....	....	....	....
Travel, credit	2 236	27.5	31.2	43.2	36.1	41.2	78.6	66.0	....
Business travel	2 237	19.1	21.3	30.8	23.4	20.8	49.3	38.6	....
Personal travel	2 240	8.4	10.0	12.4	12.7	20.4	29.3	27.3	....
Travel, debit	3 236	−22.2	−22.4	−30.4	−27.6	−29.4	−68.2	−53.7	....
Business travel	3 237	−15.2	−14.3	−20.6	−18.7	−14.8	−37.7	−30.3	....
Personal travel	3 240	−7.0	−8.1	−9.8	−8.9	−14.6	−30.5	−23.4	....
Other services, credit	2 200 BA	30.8	54.7	35.8	45.6	31.7	40.3	26.2	....
Communications	2 245	16.2	29.2	22.5	29.6	13.0	15.1	12.7	....
Construction	2 249	....	11.4	1.6	.8	....	....	....	....
Insurance	2 253	.6	1.0	.6	.8	.5	1.3	.8	....
Financial	2 260	.2	.2	.3	2.9	5.0	7.3	2.1	....
Computer and information	2 262	.2	.1	....	.1	....	.1	.1	....
Royalties and licence fees	2 266	....	....	....	....	....	....	....	....
Other business services	2 268	7.0	7.0	7.5	4.6	7.8	10.6	10.3	....
Personal, cultural, and recreational	2 287	....	....	....	....	....	1.1	....	....
Government, n.i.e.	2 291	6.7	5.7	3.2	6.8	5.4	4.7	.2	....
Other services, debit	3 200 BA	−35.7	−76.3	−35.6	−74.2	−65.7	−133.2	−147.9	....
Communications	3 245	−4.5	−7.9	−12.9	−24.0	−9.9	−14.4	−12.1	....
Construction	3 249	....	−27.8	−.6	−.8	−10.4	−41.8	−55.0	....
Insurance	3 253	−3.2	−5.9	−4.6	−7.0	−9.9	−15.9	−15.8	....
Financial	3 260	−.4	−1.5	−1.4	−3.2	−2.2	−6.0	−10.1	....
Computer and information	3 262	−5.6	−6.9	−7.4	−9.2	−1.3	−5.5	−12.5	....
Royalties and licence fees	3 266	−.2	−.5	−1.1	−.5	−.1	−.3	−2.0	....
Other business services	3 268	−4.2	−14.0	−5.0	−21.3	−31.5	−47.6	−40.4	....
Personal, cultural, and recreational	3 287	−.4	....	....	−6.3	−.3	−.1	....	....
Government, n.i.e.	3 291	−17.1	−11.8	−2.6	−2.0	....	−1.6	....	....

Table 2 (Continued). STANDARD PRESENTATION, 2003–2010

(Millions of U.S. dollars)

	Code	2003	2004	2005	2006	2007	2008	2009	2010
C. INCOME	4 300 ..	**−26.1**	**−12.9**	**−9.5**	**1.2**	**−.4**	**25.7**	**−38.8**	....
Total credit	2 300 ..	*17.3*	*26.5*	*37.1*	*42.0*	*59.2*	*81.3*	*88.9*	....
Total debit	3 300 ..	*−43.4*	*−39.4*	*−46.6*	*−40.8*	*−59.6*	*−55.6*	*−127.7*	....
Compensation of employees, credit	2 310 ..	**14.0**	**16.8**	**20.9**	**29.0**	**36.7**	**40.6**	**41.4**	....
Compensation of employees, debit	3 310 ..	**−1.9**	**−3.2**	**−2.4**	**−2.0**	**−6.3**	**−7.5**	**−9.4**	....
Investment income, credit	2 320 ..	**3.3**	**9.6**	**16.2**	**12.9**	**22.5**	**40.7**	**47.6**	....
Direct investment income	2 330 ..	.1	6.1	13.7	−.3	6.0	15.8	30.3	....
Dividends and distributed branch profits	2 332 ..	....	.1	....	....	.3	....	....	....
Reinvested earnings and undistributed branch profits	2 333 ..	....	6.0	13.7	−.3	5.7	15.8	30.2	....
Income on debt (interest)	2 334 ..	.1	....	....	....	....	....	.1	....
Portfolio investment income	2 339 ..	.9	1.2	.8	.7	.9	3.0	5.2	....
Income on equity	2 340 ..	.1	.1	.1	.2	.3	1.6	2.3	....
Income on bonds and notes	2 350 ..	.8	.6	.7	.2	.6	.9	1.8	....
Income on money market instruments	2 360 ..	.1	.5	....	.3	....	.5	1.1	....
Other investment income	2 370 ..	2.3	2.4	1.7	12.6	15.6	22.0	12.1	....
Investment income, debit	3 320 ..	**−41.5**	**−36.1**	**−44.1**	**−38.7**	**−53.3**	**−48.1**	**−118.3**	....
Direct investment income	3 330 ..	−9.3	−15.8	−20.9	−12.5	−28.2	−23.2	−83.5	....
Dividends and distributed branch profits	3 332 ..	−1.4	−2.1	−3.3	−5.1	−5.9	−38.5	−37.2	....
Reinvested earnings and undistributed branch profits	3 333 ..	−7.6	−13.0	−16.5	−5.2	−12.9	35.2	−25.0	....
Income on debt (interest)	3 334 ..	−.3	−.7	−1.2	−2.3	−9.4	−20.0	−21.3	....
Portfolio investment income	3 339 ..	−2.5	−4.1	−5.6	−5.8	−6.7	−5.2	−12.0	....
Income on equity	3 340 ..	−2.0	−2.2	−1.9	−2.5	−1.0	−2.3	−4.7	....
Income on bonds and notes	3 350 ..	−.4	−1.9	−3.0	−3.2	−4.7	−2.9	−5.7	....
Income on money market instruments	3 360 ..	−.1	....	−.7	....	−1.0	....	−1.6	....
Other investment income	3 370 ..	−29.7	−16.2	−17.6	−20.5	−18.5	−19.7	−22.9	....
D. CURRENT TRANSFERS	4 379 ..	**73.3**	**103.9**	**181.7**	**163.4**	**185.3**	**230.3**	**150.9**	....
Credit	2 379 ..	**82.9**	**128.6**	**217.1**	**199.5**	**207.9**	**253.9**	**170.2**	....
General government	2 380 ..	58.2	74.6	113.7	91.9	102.6	127.9	39.1	....
Other sectors	2 390 ..	24.7	54.0	103.4	107.5	105.3	126.0	131.1	....
Workers' remittances	2 391 ..	11.5	42.9	45.5	49.1	42.7	53.1	60.3	....
Other current transfers	2 392 ..	13.1	11.1	57.9	58.5	62.6	72.9	70.7	....
Debit	3 379 ..	**−9.5**	**−24.7**	**−35.4**	**−36.1**	**−22.6**	**−23.6**	**−19.3**	....
General government	3 380 ..	−1.7	−1.4	−3.0	−8.1	−9.1	−8.3	−2.5	....
Other sectors	3 390 ..	−7.9	−23.3	−32.4	−28.0	−13.5	−15.3	−16.9	....
Workers' remittances	3 391 ..	−7.1	−21.6	−26.9	−27.2	−11.7	−14.8	−15.8	....
Other current transfers	3 392 ..	−.8	−1.7	−5.6	−.8	−1.7	−.5	−1.1	....
CAPITAL AND FINANCIAL ACCOUNT	4 996 ..	**233.3**	**115.0**	**190.6**	**−1,187.3**	**367.6**	**717.8**	**1,317.2**	....
CAPITAL ACCOUNT	4 994 ..	**92.3**	**249.2**	**49.4**	**220.2**	**268.8**	**532.1**	**254.9**	....
Total credit	2 994 ..	*92.4*	*384.5*	*188.3*	*220.2*	*268.8*	*532.1*	*255.0*	....
Total debit	3 994 ..	*−.1*	*−135.3*	*−138.9*	....	....	....	*−.1*	....
Capital transfers, credit	2 400 ..	**92.4**	**384.5**	**188.3**	**162.0**	**211.5**	**256.6**	**255.0**	....
General government	2 401 ..	87.6	373.6	181.0	148.5	197.0	247.6	231.2	....
Debt forgiveness	2 402 ..	19.8	285.6	34.5	.7	....	....	7.8	....
Other capital transfers	2 410 ..	67.8	88.0	146.5	147.8	197.0	247.6	223.4	....
Other sectors	2 430 ..	4.8	10.9	7.3	13.5	14.5	9.0	23.8	....
Migrants' transfers	2 431 ..	....	....	....	....	....	....	....	....
Debt forgiveness	2 432 ..	....	....	....	....	....	....	....	....
Other capital transfers	2 440 ..	4.8	10.9	7.3	13.5	14.5	9.0	23.8	....
Capital transfers, debit	3 400 ..	....	....	....	....	....	....	....	....
General government	3 401 ..	....	....	....	....	....	....	....	....
Debt forgiveness	3 402 ..	....	....	....	....	....	....	....	....
Other capital transfers	3 410 ..	....	....	....	....	....	....	....	....
Other sectors	3 430 ..	....	....	....	....	....	....	....	....
Migrants' transfers	3 431 ..	....	....	....	....	....	....	....	....
Debt forgiveness	3 432 ..	....	....	....	....	....	....	....	....
Other capital transfers	3 440 ..	....	....	....	....	....	....	....	....
Nonproduced nonfinancial assets, credit	2 480 ..	....	....	....	58.1	57.3	275.5	....	....
Nonproduced nonfinancial assets, debit	3 480 ..	**−.1**	**−135.3**	**−138.9**	....	....	....	**−.1**	....

Table 2 (Continued). STANDARD PRESENTATION, 2003–2010

(Millions of U.S. dollars)

	Code	2003	2004	2005	2006	2007	2008	2009	2010
FINANCIAL ACCOUNT	4 995 ..	**141.0**	**−134.3**	**141.2**	**−1,407.5**	**98.8**	**185.7**	**1,062.3**	....
A. DIRECT INVESTMENT	4 500 ..	**14.9**	**13.2**	**34.7**	**51.5**	**121.0**	**316.1**	**725.9**	....
Direct investment abroad	4 505 ..	....	**−13.1**	**−9.3**	**1.0**	**−8.1**	**−24.4**	**−89.4**	....
Equity capital	4 510 ..	−3.8	−2.3	−.9	−1.1	1.9	−12.5	−31.4	
Claims on affiliated enterprises	4 515 ..	....	....	....	....	2.3	.1	....	
Liabilities to affiliated enterprises	4 520 ..	....	....	....	−1.2	−.3	−12.6	−31.4	
Reinvested earnings	4 525 ..	....	−6.0	−13.7	.3	−5.7	−15.8	−30.2	
Other capital	4 530 ..	3.8	−4.8	5.3	1.8	−4.3	3.9	−27.9	
Claims on affiliated enterprises	4 535 ..	1.7	−2.1	−.3	−.8	−6.3	6.6	−33.7	
Liabilities to affiliated enterprises	4 540 ..	2.1	−2.8	5.6	2.6	2.0	−2.6	5.8	
Direct investment in Niger	4 555 ..	**14.9**	**26.3**	**44.0**	**50.5**	**129.0**	**340.4**	**815.3**	....
Equity capital	4 560 ..	4.9	12.8	6.1	12.4	34.5	45.0	163.7	
Claims on direct investors	4 565 ..	....	....	....	12.4	34.5	45.0	163.7	
Liabilities to direct investors	4 570 ..	....	....	....	....	....	....	....	
Reinvested earnings	4 575 ..	7.6	13.0	16.5	5.2	12.9	−35.2	25.0	
Other capital	4 580 ..	2.4	.6	21.3	33.0	81.7	330.6	626.7	
Claims on direct investors	4 585 ..	−1.4	−.8	−.1	−.7	−2.7	−1.8	−5.2	
Liabilities to direct investors	4 590 ..	3.9	1.4	21.4	33.7	84.4	332.4	631.8	
B. PORTFOLIO INVESTMENT	4 600 ..	**2.5**	**4.8**	**41.7**	**−3.9**	**−8.1**	**−30.2**	**−19.5**	....
Assets	4 602 ..	**−4.4**	**−.2**	**−.8**	**.2**	....	**−20.7**	**−29.7**	....
Equity securities	4 610 ..	−4.3	−.3	−.7	.4	.2	4.1	2.2	
Monetary authorities	4 611 ..								
General government	4 612 ..								
Banks	4 613 ..					.2		−6.4	
Other sectors	4 614 ..	−4.3	−.3	−.7	.4	....	4.1	8.5	
Debt securities	4 619 ..	−.2	.1	−.1	−.2	−.2	−24.8	−31.8	
Bonds and notes	4 620 ..	−.2	.1	−.1	−.2	−.2	−16.0	−31.6	
Monetary authorities	4 621 ..								
General government	4 622 ..							−.1	
Banks	4 623 ..						−13.0	−31.5	
Other sectors	4 624 ..	−.2	.1	−.1	−.2	−.2	−3.0	....	
Money market instruments	4 630 ..						−8.8	−.2	
Monetary authorities	4 631 ..								
General government	4 632 ..								
Banks	4 633 ..						−8.8	−.2	
Other sectors	4 634 ..								
Liabilities	4 652 ..	**6.9**	**5.0**	**42.5**	**−4.1**	**−8.2**	**−9.5**	**10.2**	....
Equity securities	4 660 ..	....	3.8	.6	....	−.5	1.5	9.5	
Banks	4 663 ..	....				−.3	1.5	2.4	
Other sectors	4 664 ..	....	3.8	.6		−.2		7.1	
Debt securities	4 669 ..	6.9	1.1	41.9	−4.1	−7.7	−10.9	.8	
Bonds and notes	4 670 ..	6.9	....	18.2	−4.1	−8.6	....	1.1	
Monetary authorities	4 671 ..								
General government	4 672 ..			−1.9					
Banks	4 673 ..			....				1.1	
Other sectors	4 674 ..	6.9	....	20.1	−4.1	−8.6			
Money market instruments	4 680 ..			23.7		.9	−10.9	−.3	
Monetary authorities	4 681 ..								
General government	4 682 ..			23.7		.9	−10.9		
Banks	4 683 ..							−.3	
Other sectors	4 684 ..								
C. FINANCIAL DERIVATIVES	4 910 ..	....	**1.1**	....	....	**1.8**	**−2.3**	....	....
Monetary authorities	4 911 ..								
General government	4 912 ..								
Banks	4 913 ..								
Other sectors	4 914 ..	....	1.1	....	....	1.8	−2.3		
Assets	4 900 ..	....	....	....	....	....	**−.3**	....	....
Monetary authorities	4 901 ..								
General government	4 902 ..								
Banks	4 903 ..								
Other sectors	4 904 ..						−.3		
Liabilities	4 905 ..	....	**1.1**	....	....	**1.8**	**−2.0**	....	....
Monetary authorities	4 906 ..								
General government	4 907 ..								
Banks	4 908 ..								
Other sectors	4 909 ..	....	1.1	....	....	1.8	−2.0	....	....

Table 2 (Concluded). STANDARD PRESENTATION, 2003–2010

(Millions of U.S. dollars)

	Code	2003	2004	2005	2006	2007	2008	2009	2010
D. OTHER INVESTMENT	4 700 ..	**94.4**	**−194.1**	**100.1**	**−1,367.7**	**150.8**	**54.0**	**287.0**	....
Assets	4 703 ..	**−42.4**	**−72.8**	**−19.4**	**−30.1**	**−44.4**	**67.3**	**112.4**	....
Trade credits	4 706 ..	−37.6	−29.2	−6.6	−9.2	−12.9	68.0	65.0	....
General government	4 707 ..	....	....	....	....	....	....	....	....
of which: Short-term	4 709 ..	....	....	....	....	....	....	....	....
Other sectors	4 710 ..	−37.6	−29.2	−6.6	−9.2	−12.9	68.0	65.0	....
of which: Short-term	4 712 ..	....	....	....	....	....	....	*65.0*	....
Loans	4 714 ..	−5.0	−3.5	−10.7	6.7	−14.8	−16.4	24.5	....
Monetary authorities	4 715 ..	....	....	....	....	....	....	....	....
of which: Short-term	4 718 ..	....	....	....	....	....	....	....	....
General government	4 719 ..	....	....	....	....	....	....	....	....
of which: Short-term	4 721 ..	....	....	....	....	....	....	....	....
Banks	4 722 ..	−4.9	−1.0	−7.5	6.7	−14.7	−16.3	24.5	....
of which: Short-term	4 724 ..	*−.9*	*−6.7*	*−6.0*	*6.4*	*−7.1*	*−.2*	*18.4*	....
Other sectors	4 725 ..	....	−2.5	−3.1	....	−.1	....	....	....
of which: Short-term	4 727 ..	....	....	....	....	....	....	....	....
Currency and deposits	4 730 ..	−1.4	−26.3	−1.8	−2.6	−14.2	9.9	29.2	....
Monetary authorities	4 731 ..	....	....	....	....	....	....	....	....
General government	4 732 ..	....	....	....	....	....	....	....	....
Banks	4 733 ..	−.6	−10.1	1.3	.3	−15.7	8.1	35.1	....
Other sectors	4 734 ..	−.8	−16.2	−3.1	−2.9	1.5	1.8	−5.9	....
Other assets	4 736 ..	1.6	−13.9	−.3	−25.1	−2.5	5.8	−6.3	....
Monetary authorities	4 737 ..	....	....	....	....	....	....	....	....
of which: Short-term	4 739 ..	....	....	....	....	....	....	....	....
General government	4 740 ..	.7	....	....	....	....	....	....	....
of which: Short-term	4 742 ..	....	....	....	....	....	....	....	....
Banks	4 743 ..	.5	.2	−.2	−.9	.9	.1	−4.6	....
of which: Short-term	4 745 ..	*.5*	*.5*	*−.2*	*.1*	*−.1*	*.1*	*−4.6*	....
Other sectors	4 746 ..	.4	−14.1	−.1	−24.2	−3.4	5.7	−1.7	....
of which: Short-term	4 748 ..	....	....	....	....	....	....	*−1.7*	....
Liabilities	4 753 ..	**136.7**	**−121.2**	**119.5**	**−1,337.6**	**195.2**	**−13.4**	**174.6**	....
Trade credits	4 756 ..	13.5	15.0	2.4	3.8	13.3	−76.6	−28.5	....
General government	4 757 ..	....	....	....	....	....	....	....	....
of which: Short-term	4 759 ..	....	....	....	....	....	....	....	....
Other sectors	4 760 ..	13.5	15.0	2.4	3.8	13.3	−76.6	−28.5	....
of which: Short-term	4 762 ..	....	....	....	....	....	....	*−28.5*	....
Loans	4 764 ..	114.5	−144.3	103.8	−1,354.6	164.6	44.6	126.3	....
Monetary authorities	4 765 ..	14.6	−1.9	2.6	−103.5	11.7	11.9	5.0	....
of which: Use of Fund credit and loans from the Fund	4 766 ..	*14.6*	*−1.9*	*2.6*	*−103.5*	*11.7*	*11.9*	*5.0*	....
of which: Short-term	4 768 ..	....	....	....	....	....	....	....	....
General government	4 769 ..	93.7	−148.9	87.2	−1,268.1	95.0	45.3	65.7	....
of which: Short-term	4 771 ..	....	....	....	....	....	....	....	....
Banks	4 772 ..	3.1	−2.3	6.2	12.5	24.6	−7.4	36.1	....
of which: Short-term	4 774 ..	*2.6*	*−6.7*	*3.4*	*2.4*	*−5.1*	*−5.4*	*.2*	....
Other sectors	4 775 ..	3.1	8.9	7.8	4.5	33.3	−5.2	19.4	....
of which: Short-term	4 777 ..	....	....	*9.4*	*−.5*	*−31.3*	*−68.3*	....	....
Currency and deposits	4 780 ..	11.6	−4.8	10.6	7.0	14.5	5.2	−15.9	....
Monetary authorities	4 781 ..	−2.4	1.3	.2	....	3.0	−4.1	−.9	....
General government	4 782 ..	....	....	....	....	....	....	....	....
Banks	4 783 ..	14.0	−6.2	10.4	7.0	11.6	9.3	−15.0	....
Other sectors	4 784 ..	....	....	....	....	....	....	....	....
Other liabilities	4 786 ..	−2.8	12.8	2.7	6.2	2.7	13.5	92.7	....
Monetary authorities	4 787 ..	2.7	....	1.3	−1.6	1.0	17.3	68.1	....
of which: Short-term	4 789 ..	....	....	....	....	....	....	....	....
General government	4 790 ..	....	....	....	....	....	....	....	....
of which: Short-term	4 792 ..	....	....	....	....	....	....	....	....
Banks	4 793 ..	....	....	....	....	....	....	....	....
of which: Short-term	4 795 ..	....	....	....	....	....	....	....	....
Other sectors	4 796 ..	−5.5	12.8	1.4	7.8	1.8	−3.8	24.5	....
of which: Short-term	4 798 ..	....	....	....	....	....	....	....	....
E. RESERVE ASSETS	4 802 ..	**29.2**	**40.6**	**−35.4**	**−87.5**	**−166.7**	**−151.8**	**68.9**	....
Monetary gold	4 812 ..	....	....	....	....	....	....	....	....
Special drawing rights	4 811 ..	−1.8	1.8	.6	.2	.1	−1.5	−83.3	....
Reserve position in the Fund	4 810 ..	....	....	−.1	....	....	....	....	....
Foreign exchange	4 803 ..	31.0	38.8	−35.9	−87.6	−166.7	−150.3	152.2	....
Other claims	4 813 ..	....	....	....	....	....	....	....	....
NET ERRORS AND OMISSIONS	4 998 ..	**−14.6**	**115.9**	**120.9**	**1,501.1**	**−16.3**	**−66.4**	**2.9**	....

Table 3. INTERNATIONAL INVESTMENT POSITION (End-period stocks), 2003–2010

(Millions of U.S. dollars)

	Code	2003	2004	2005	2006	2007	2008	2009	2010
ASSETS	8 995 C.	**343.0**	**411.9**	**362.8**	**536.0**	**778.8**	**964.0**	**925.4**	....
Direct investment abroad	8 505 ..	**−4.6**	**8.2**	**1.9**	**6.0**	**5.0**	**12.9**	**74.8**	....
Equity capital and reinvested earnings	8 506 ..	9.6	9.5	7.6	9.2	.6	12.4	45.8	....
Claims on affiliated enterprises	8 507 ..	....	....	....	....	....	....	....	....
Liabilities to affiliated enterprises	8 508 ..	....	....	....	....	....	....	....	....
Other capital	8 530 ..	−14.3	−1.3	−5.7	−3.2	4.5	.5	29.0	....
Claims on affiliated enterprises	8 535 ..	....	....	....	....	....	....	....	....
Liabilities to affiliated enterprises	8 540 ..	....	....	....	....	....	....	....	....
Portfolio investment	8 602 ..	**5.6**	**3.0**	**15.3**	**31.2**	**19.1**	**37.7**	**39.5**	....
Equity securities	8 610 ..	....	2.2	2.4	11.9	11.3	1.8	19.3	....
Monetary authorities	8 611 ..	....	....	....	....	....	....	....	....
General government	8 612 ..	....	....	....	....	....	....	....	....
Banks	8 613 ..	....	1.8	1.6	11.9	11.3	1.8	19.3	....
Other sectors	8 614 ..	....	.4	.7	....	....	....	....	....
Debt securities	8 619 ..	5.6	.8	12.9	19.3	7.8	35.9	20.1	....
Bonds and notes	8 620 ..	....	....	12.8	9.4	7.8	23.7	6.2	....
Monetary authorities	8 621 ..	....	....	....	....	....	....	....	....
General government	8 622 ..	....	....	....	....	....	....	....	....
Banks	8 623 ..	....	....	10.0	8.7	7.6	20.7	6.2	....
Other sectors	8 624 ..	....	....	2.8	.7	.2	3.1	....	....
Money market instruments	8 630 ..	5.6	.8	.1	10.0	....	12.2	14.0	....
Monetary authorities	8 631 ..	....	....	....	10.0	....	....	....	....
General government	8 632 ..	....	....	....	....	....	....	....	....
Banks	8 633 ..	5.6	.8	....	....	....	12.2	14.0	....
Other sectors	8 634 ..	....	....	.1	....	....	....	....	....
Financial derivatives	8 900 ..	....	....	**1.1**	....	....	**.3**	....	....
Monetary authorities	8 901 ..	....	....	....	....	....	....	....	....
General government	8 902 ..	....	....	....	....	....	....	....	....
Banks	8 903 ..	....	....	1.1	....	....	.3	....	....
Other sectors	8 904 ..	....	....	....	....	....	....	....	....
Other investment	8 703 ..	**68.7**	**150.8**	**93.8**	**127.8**	**161.6**	**207.8**	**155.6**	....
Trade credits	8 706 ..	10.5	40.3	19.9	30.5	43.5	81.2	5.8	....
General government	8 707 ..	....	....	....	....	....	....	....	....
of which: Short-term	8 709 ..	....	....	....	....	....	....	....	....
Other sectors	8 710 ..	10.5	40.3	19.9	30.5	43.5	81.2	5.8	....
of which: Short-term	8 712 ..	....	....	....	....	....	....	....	....
Loans	8 714 ..	14.4	19.3	24.5	17.0	34.8	48.3	24.6	....
Monetary authorities	8 715 ..	....	....	....	....	....	....	....	....
of which: Short-term	8 718 ..	....	....	....	....	....	....	....	....
General government	8 719 ..	....	....	....	....	....	....	....	....
of which: Short-term	8 721 ..	....	....	....	....	....	....	....	....
Banks	8 722 ..	14.3	16.6	21.5	16.9	34.7	48.3	24.6	....
of which: Short-term	8 724 ..	*6.1*	*13.9*	*17.7*	*13.0*	*22.2*	*21.1*	*2.7*	....
Other sectors	8 725 ..	....	2.7	3.0	....	.1	....	....	....
of which: Short-term	8 727 ..	....	....	....	....	....	....	....	....
Currency and deposits	8 730 ..	42.3	74.4	48.2	53.2	74.7	64.6	32.9	....
Monetary authorities	8 731 ..	....	....	....	....	....	....	....	....
General government	8 732 ..	....	....	....	....	....	....	....	....
Banks	8 733 ..	40.0	54.2	45.6	50.6	73.4	61.7	27.5	....
Other sectors	8 734 ..	2.3	20.2	2.6	2.6	1.2	2.9	5.3	....
Other assets	8 736 ..	1.6	16.9	1.1	27.1	8.6	13.7	92.3	....
Monetary authorities	8 737 ..	....	....	....	....	....	....	....	....
of which: Short-term	8 739 ..	....	....	....	....	....	....	....	....
General government	8 740 ..	....	....	....	....	....	....	....	....
of which: Short-term	8 742 ..	....	....	....	....	....	....	....	....
Banks	8 743 ..	.5	.3	.5	1.5	.7	.5	5.3	....
of which: Short-term	8 745 ..	*.5*	....	*.2*	*.2*	*.3*	*.2*	*5.0*	....
Other sectors	8 746 ..	1.1	16.6	.6	25.7	8.0	13.1	87.0	....
of which: Short-term	8 748 ..	....	....	....	....	....	....	....	....
Reserve assets	8 802 ..	**273.4**	**249.8**	**250.7**	**370.9**	**593.0**	**705.2**	**655.5**	....
Monetary gold	8 812 ..	....	....	....	....	....	....	....	....
Special drawing rights	8 811 ..	2.7	.9	.3	.1	.1	1.5	85.1	83.6
Reserve position in the Fund	8 810 ..	12.7	13.3	12.3	13.0	13.6	13.3	13.5	13.3
Foreign exchange	8 803 ..	258.0	235.6	238.1	357.8	579.3	690.5	556.9	....
Other claims	8 813 ..	....	....	....	....	....	....	....	....

Table 3 (Concluded). INTERNATIONAL INVESTMENT POSITION (End-period stocks), 2003–2010

(Millions of U.S. dollars)

	Code	2003	2004	2005	2006	2007	2008	2009	2010
LIABILITIES..	8 995 D.	**2,080.3**	**2,227.4**	**2,073.4**	**896.2**	**1,249.3**	**1,768.6**	**2,697.1**	....
Direct investment in Niger...............................	8 555 ..	**78.8**	**115.5**	**100.0**	**161.1**	**276.6**	**623.8**	**1,404.3**	....
Equity capital and reinvested earnings................	8 556 ..	74.6	110.7	76.3	103.8	126.8	192.6	262.0	....
Claims on direct investors..............................	8 557 ..	....	....	....	....	....	....	....	....
Liabilities to direct investors.........................	8 558 ..	....	....	....	....	....	....	....	....
Other capital..	8 580 ..	4.3	4.8	23.7	57.3	149.9	431.2	1,142.3	....
Claims on direct investors..............................	8 585 ..	....	....	....	....	....	....	....	....
Liabilities to direct investors.........................	8 590 ..	....	....	....	....	....	....	....	....
Portfolio investment.......................................	8 652 ..	**14.4**	**5.3**	**24.9**	**18.7**	**.7**	**1.6**	**12.2**	....
Equity securities...	8 660 ..	5.2	5.3	5.1	5.1	.7	1.6	11.3	....
Banks...	8 663 ..	.9	.6	.5	.3	....	1.4	3.9	....
Other sectors...	8 664 ..	4.3	4.6	4.6	4.8	.6	.2	7.5	....
Debt securities...	8 669 ..	9.2	....	19.8	13.6	....	....	.9	....
Bonds and notes..	8 670 ..	9.2	....	19.1	8.3	....	....	.9	....
Monetary authorities.................................	8 671 ..	....	....	....	....	....	....	....	....
General government.................................	8 672 ..	....	....	....	....	....	....	....	....
Banks..	8 673 ..	....	....	....	....	....	....	.9	....
Other sectors..	8 674 ..	9.2	....	19.1	8.3	....	....	....	....
Money market instruments..........................	8 680 ..	....	....	.7	5.3	....	....	....	....
Monetary authorities.................................	8 681 ..	....	....	....	....	....	....	....	....
General government.................................	8 682 ..	....	....	....	....	....	....	....	....
Banks..	8 683 ..	....	....	.7	5.3	....	....	....	....
Other sectors..	8 684 ..	....	....	....	....	....	....	....	....
Financial derivatives......................................	8 905 ..	....	....	....	....	**2.0**	....	....	....
Monetary authorities......................................	8 906 ..	....	....	....	....	....	....	....	....
General government..	8 907 ..	....	....	....	....	....	....	....	....
Banks...	8 908 ..	....	....	....	....	....	....	....	....
Other sectors...	8 909 ..	....	....	....	....	2.0	....	....	....
Other investment..	8 753 ..	**1,987.1**	**2,106.6**	**1,948.6**	**716.4**	**970.0**	**1,143.2**	**1,280.5**	....
Trade credits..	8 756 ..	49.8	52.5	35.0	38.5	60.3	122.2	79.3	....
General government......................................	8 757 ..	....	....	....	....	....	....	....	....
of which: Short-term.................................	8 759 ..	....	....	....	....	....	....	....	....
Other sectors...	8 760 ..	49.8	52.5	35.0	38.5	60.3	122.2	79.3	....
of which: Short-term.................................	8 762 ..	....	....	....	....	....	....	....	....
Loans...	8 764 ..	1,895.3	2,002.3	1,867.3	613.4	820.8	920.0	1,005.0	....
Monetary authorities.....................................	8 765 ..	131.4	135.4	127.6	26.5	40.1	50.7	56.7	....
of which: Use of Fund credit and loans from the Fund....	8 766 ..	*131.4*	*135.4*	*127.6*	*26.5*	*40.1*	*50.7*	*56.7*	*60.7*
of which: Short-term.................................	8 768 ..	....	....	....	....	....	....	....	....
General government......................................	8 769 ..	1,753.1	1,843.9	1,704.3	536.7	678.8	783.2	898.9	....
of which: Short-term.................................	8 771 ..	*7.2*	....	....	....	....	....	....	....
Banks...	8 772 ..	10.8	9.2	13.8	28.6	58.3	48.1	87.3	....
of which: Short-term.................................	8 774 ..	*10.3*	*3.8*	*6.5*	*9.8*	*5.5*	....	*.2*	....
Other sectors...	8 775 ..	....	13.7	21.5	21.6	43.5	37.9	−37.9	....
of which: Short-term.................................	8 777 ..	....	....	....	....	....	....	....	....
Currency and deposits....................................	8 780 ..	37.4	35.1	40.6	52.3	74.9	75.0	61.1	....
Monetary authorities.....................................	8 781 ..	1.2	2.7	2.2	2.4	5.9	1.7	.8	....
General government......................................	8 782 ..	....	....	....	....	....	....	....	....
Banks...	8 783 ..	36.3	32.4	38.4	49.9	69.0	73.4	60.3	....
Other sectors...	8 784 ..	....	....	....	....	....	....	....	....
Other liabilities..	8 786 ..	4.6	16.7	5.6	12.1	14.0	26.0	135.0	....
Monetary authorities.....................................	8 787 ..	3.1	1.9	2.9	1.6	2.8	19.0	102.3	....
of which: Short-term.................................	8 789 ..	....	....	....	....	....	....	....	....
General government......................................	8 790 ..	....	....	....	....	....	....	....	....
of which: Short-term.................................	8 792 ..	....	....	....	....	....	....	....	....
Banks...	8 793 ..	....	....	....	....	....	....	....	....
of which: Short-term.................................	8 795 ..	....	....	....	....	....	....	....	....
Other sectors...	8 796 ..	1.5	14.7	2.7	10.6	11.2	7.0	32.7	....
of which: Short-term.................................	8 798 ..	....	....	....	....	....	....	....	....
NET INTERNATIONAL INVESTMENT POSITION........	8 995 ..	**−1,737.3**	**−1,815.5**	**−1,710.6**	**−360.2**	**−470.5**	**−804.6**	**−1,771.6**	....
Conversion rates: CFA francs per U.S. dollar (end of period)..	0 102 ..	519.36	481.58	556.04	498.07	445.59	471.34	455.34	490.91

Table 1. ANALYTIC PRESENTATION, 2003–2010
(Millions of U.S. dollars)

	Code	2003	2004	2005	2006	2007	2008	2009	2010
A. Current Account[1]	4 993 Z.	**3,391**	**16,840**	**36,529**	**36,518**	**27,643**	**28,079**	**13,153**	**2,476**
Goods: exports f.o.b.	2 100 ..	23,976	34,766	55,201	56,935	66,040	85,729	56,121	73,698
Goods: imports f.o.b.	3 100 ..	−16,152	−15,009	−26,003	−21,988	−28,291	−39,844	−30,779	−53,461
Balance on Goods	4 100 ..	*7,824*	*19,757*	*29,198*	*34,947*	*37,748*	*45,885*	*25,341*	*20,237*
Services: credit	2 200 ..	3,473	3,336	1,793	2,299	1,443	2,264	2,218	3,076
Services: debit	3 200 ..	−5,715	−5,973	−6,623	−13,924	−18,345	−24,377	−18,697	−22,307
Balance on Goods and Services	4 991 ..	*5,582*	*17,120*	*24,367*	*23,322*	*20,846*	*23,772*	*8,863*	*1,007*
Income: credit	2 300 ..	82	157	155	1,875	2,564	2,352	935	982
Income: debit	3 300 ..	−3,325	−2,689	−3,146	−6,477	−14,311	−17,411	−15,339	−19,605
Balance on Goods, Services, and Income	4 992 ..	*2,339*	*14,588*	*21,377*	*18,720*	*9,099*	*8,713*	*−5,541*	*−17,616*
Current transfers: credit	2 379 Z.	1,063	2,273	15,284	17,975	18,695	19,897	19,158	20,583
Current transfers: debit	3 379 ..	−12	−21	−131	−177	−150	−531	−464	−491
B. Capital Account[1]	4 994 Z.	....	....	**7,336**	**10,556**	....	....	....	....
Capital account: credit	2 994 Z.	....	....	7,336	10,556	....	....	....	....
Capital account: debit	3 994 ..	....	....	....	....	....	....	....	....
Total, Groups A Plus B	4 981 ..	*3,391*	*16,841*	*43,865*	*47,074*	*27,643*	*28,079*	*13,153*	*2,476*
C. Financial Account[1]	4 995 W.	**−10,285**	**−13,061**	**−15,184**	**−16,028**	**−1,804**	**−6,718**	**2,615**	**−6,999**
Direct investment abroad	4 505 ..	....	....	−15	−320	−868	−1,052	−1,525	−915
Direct investment in Nigeria	4 555 Z.	2,005	1,874	4,983	4,854	6,035	8,197	8,555	6,049
Portfolio investment assets	4 602 ..	183	178	−1,372	−1,513	−1,843	−4,729	−822	−1,121
Equity securities	4 610 ..	....	....	−1,240	−1,364	−1,706	−4,041	−753	−1,027
Debt securities	4 619 ..	183	178	−132	−148	−137	−688	−68	−93
Portfolio investment liabilities	4 652 Z.	....	....	884	2,801	2,643	1,326	476	3,717
Equity securities	4 660 ..	....	....	751	1,769	1,447	−954	487	2,161
Debt securities	4 669 Z.	....	....	133	1,031	1,196	2,280	−11	1,556
Financial derivatives	4 910 ..	....	....	....	....	....	....	....	....
Financial derivatives assets	4 900 ..	....	....	....	....	....	....	....	....
Financial derivatives liabilities	4 905 ..	....	....	....	....	....	....	....	....
Other investment assets	4 703 ..	−5,845	−7,301	−1,487	−6,199	−9,841	−10,636	−6,482	−14,524
Monetary authorities	4 701 ..	....	....	....	....	....	....	....	....
General government	4 704 ..	....	....	....	119	−1,263	−2,071	−2,279	−2,018
Banks	4 705 ..	818	1,022	−111	−1,532	−914	−3,746	2,496	−368
Other sectors	4 728 ..	−6,663	−8,323	−1,376	−4,786	−7,664	−4,819	−6,698	−12,139
Other investment liabilities	4 753 W.	−6,628	−7,812	−18,177	−15,652	2,069	176	2,412	−204
Monetary authorities	4 753 WA	....	....	....	....	....	....	2,373	....
General government	4 753 ZB	−4,186	−5,079	−15,235	−16,284	−509	−26	198	716
Banks	4 753 ZC	....	....	124	203	2,215	−495	−747	−316
Other sectors	4 753 ZD	−2,442	−2,733	−3,066	430	363	697	589	−605
Total, Groups A Through C	4 983 ..	*−6,894*	*3,780*	*28,680*	*31,046*	*25,839*	*21,361*	*15,768*	*−4,523*
D. Net Errors and Omissions	4 998 ..	**5,634**	**4,711**	**−17,344**	**−17,151**	**−16,881**	**−19,704**	**−26,283**	**−5,207**
Total, Groups A Through D	4 984 ..	*−1,260*	*8,491*	*11,336*	*13,895*	*8,959*	*1,657*	*−10,515*	*−9,730*
E. Reserves and Related Items	4 802 A.	**1,260**	**−8,491**	**−11,336**	**−13,895**	**−8,959**	**−1,657**	**10,515**	**9,730**
Reserve assets	4 802 ..	214	−9,531	−11,336	−13,895	−8,959	−1,657	10,515	9,730
Use of Fund credit and loans	4 766 ..	....	....	....	....	....	....	....	....
Exceptional financing	4 920 ..	1,047	1,040	....	....	....	....	....	....
Conversion rates: naira per U.S. dollar	0 101 ..	**129.220**	**132.890**	**131.274**	**128.650**	**125.830**	**118.530**	**148.900**	**149.743**

[1] Excludes components that have been classified in the categories of Group E.

Table 2. STANDARD PRESENTATION, 2003–2010

(Millions of U.S. dollars)

	Code	2003	2004	2005	2006	2007	2008	2009	2010
CURRENT ACCOUNT	4 993 ..	**3,391**	**16,840**	**36,529**	**36,518**	**27,643**	**28,079**	**13,153**	**2,476**
A. GOODS	4 100 ..	**7,824**	**19,757**	**29,198**	**34,947**	**37,748**	**45,885**	**25,341**	**20,237**
Credit	2 100 ..	**23,976**	**34,766**	**55,201**	**56,935**	**66,040**	**85,729**	**56,121**	**73,698**
General merchandise: exports f.o.b.	2 110 ..	23,976	34,766	55,201	56,935	66,040	85,729	56,121	73,698
Goods for processing: exports f.o.b.	2 150 ..	....	....	....	....	....	....	....	....
Repairs on goods	2 160 ..	....	....	....	....	....	....	....	....
Goods procured in ports by carriers	2 170 ..	....	....	....	....	....	....	....	....
Nonmonetary gold	2 180 ..	....	....	....	....	....	....	....	....
Debit	3 100 ..	**−16,152**	**−15,009**	**−26,003**	**−21,988**	**−28,291**	**−39,844**	**−30,779**	**−53,461**
General merchandise: imports f.o.b.	3 110 ..	−16,152	−15,009	−26,003	−21,988	−28,291	−39,844	−30,779	−53,461
Goods for processing: imports f.o.b.	3 150 ..	....	....	....	....	....	....	....	....
Repairs on goods	3 160 ..	....	....	....	....	....	....	....	....
Goods procured in ports by carriers	3 170 ..	....	....	....	....	....	....	....	....
Nonmonetary gold	3 180 ..	....	....	....	....	....	....	....	....
B. SERVICES	4 200 ..	**−2,242**	**−2,637**	**−4,831**	**−11,625**	**−16,902**	**−22,113**	**−16,479**	**−19,231**
Total credit	2 200 ..	*3,473*	*3,336*	*1,793*	*2,299*	*1,443*	*2,264*	*2,218*	*3,076*
Total debit	3 200 ..	*−5,715*	*−5,973*	*−6,623*	*−13,924*	*−18,345*	*−24,377*	*−18,697*	*−22,307*
Transportation services, credit	2 205 ..	**361**	**673**	**1,338**	**1,827**	**830**	**1,209**	**1,098**	**1,961**
Passenger	2 850 ..	*28*	*28*	*85*	*25*	*124*	*390*	*189*	*167*
Freight	2 851 ..	*83*	*69*	*72*	*372*	*375*	*416*	*567*	*1,427*
Other	2 852 ..	*250*	*575*	*1,181*	*1,429*	*330*	*404*	*343*	*367*
Sea transport, passenger	2 207 ..	....	....	....	....	....	....	....	....
Sea transport, freight	2 208 ..	....	....	....	....	....	....	....	....
Sea transport, other	2 209 ..	....	....	....	....	....	....	....	....
Air transport, passenger	2 211 ..	....	....	....	....	....	....	....	....
Air transport, freight	2 212 ..	....	....	....	....	....	....	....	....
Air transport, other	2 213 ..	....	....	....	....	....	....	....	....
Other transport, passenger	2 215 ..	....	....	....	....	....	....	....	....
Other transport, freight	2 216 ..	....	....	....	....	....	....	....	....
Other transport, other	2 217 ..	....	....	....	....	....	....	....	....
Transportation services, debit	3 205 ..	**−1,284**	....	**−2,801**	**−3,298**	**−4,982**	**−6,869**	**−6,091**	**−8,717**
Passenger	3 850 ..	*−281*	....	*−261*	*−257*	*−1,075*	*−1,230*	*−1,224*	*−2,792*
Freight	3 851 ..	*−1,002*	....	*−2,507*	*−3,016*	*−3,825*	*−5,547*	*−4,707*	*−5,752*
Other	3 852 ..	....	....	*−34*	*−25*	*−83*	*−92*	*−161*	*−173*
Sea transport, passenger	3 207 ..	....	....	....	....	....	....	....	....
Sea transport, freight	3 208 ..	....	....	....	....	....	....	....	....
Sea transport, other	3 209 ..	....	....	....	....	....	....	....	....
Air transport, passenger	3 211 ..	....	....	....	....	....	....	....	....
Air transport, freight	3 212 ..	....	....	....	....	....	....	....	....
Air transport, other	3 213 ..	....	....	....	....	....	....	....	....
Other transport, passenger	3 215 ..	....	....	....	....	....	....	....	....
Other transport, freight	3 216 ..	....	....	....	....	....	....	....	....
Other transport, other	3 217 ..	....	....	....	....	....	....	....	....
Travel, credit	2 236 ..	**30**	**21**	**54**	**184**	**213**	**569**	**602**	**571**
Business travel	2 237 ..	....	....	....	....	....	....	....	....
Personal travel	2 240 ..	....	....	54	184	213	569	602	571
Travel, debit	3 236 ..	**−1,795**	....	**−240**	**−3,279**	**−5,589**	**−9,779**	**−5,012**	**−5,587**
Business travel	3 237 ..	....	....	−89	−241	−554	−928	−727	−758
Personal travel	3 240 ..	....	....	−151	−3,038	−5,035	−8,851	−4,285	−4,829
Other services, credit	2 200 BA	**3,082**	**2,642**	**401**	**288**	**400**	**486**	**518**	**544**
Communications	2 245 ..	....	....	20	24	27	30	37	48
Construction	2 249 ..	....	....	....	....	....	....	....	....
Insurance	2 253 ..	4	6	1	1	5	....	1	1
Financial	2 260 ..	....	....	11	12	13	15	8	14
Computer and information	2 262 ..	....	....	....	....	....	....	....	....
Royalties and licence fees	2 266 ..	....	....	....	....	....	....	....	....
Other business services	2 268 ..	3,078	2,637	9	9	10	10	14	18
Personal, cultural, and recreational	2 287 ..	....	....	....	....	....	....	....	....
Government, n.i.e.	2 291 ..	....	....	360	242	345	430	458	463
Other services, debit	3 200 BA	**−2,637**	....	**−3,582**	**−7,347**	**−7,774**	**−7,729**	**−7,593**	**−8,003**
Communications	3 245 ..	....	....	−159	−185	−211	−234	−343	−286
Construction	3 249 ..	....	....	−46	−53	−60	−67	−43	−129
Insurance	3 253 ..	....	....	−4	−275	−210	−1,014	−392	−532
Financial	3 260 ..	....	....	−26	−31	−9	−32	−49	−34
Computer and information	3 262 ..	....	....	−151	−176	−200	−222	−186	−124
Royalties and licence fees	3 266 ..	−50	....	−67	−84	−173	−190	−208	−224
Other business services	3 268 ..	−2,587	....	−2,890	−4,734	−4,120	−4,169	−4,150	−4,477
Personal, cultural, and recreational	3 287 ..	....	....	....	....	....	....	−11	−53
Government, n.i.e.	3 291 ..	....	....	−240	−1,809	−2,792	−1,800	−2,209	−2,144

Table 2 (Continued). STANDARD PRESENTATION, 2003–2010

(Millions of U.S. dollars)

	Code	2003	2004	2005	2006	2007	2008	2009	2010
C. INCOME	4 300	**−3,243**	**−2,532**	**−2,991**	**−4,602**	**−11,748**	**−15,059**	**−14,403**	**−18,623**
Total credit	2 300	*82*	*157*	*155*	*1,875*	*2,564*	*2,352*	*935*	*982*
Total debit	3 300	*−3,325*	*−2,689*	*−3,146*	*−6,477*	*−14,311*	*−17,411*	*−15,339*	*−19,605*
Compensation of employees, credit	2 310	....	....	155	192	218	127	138	167
Compensation of employees, debit	3 310	....	....	−54	−66	−28	−35	−19	−19
Investment income, credit	2 320	82	157	....	1,683	2,346	2,225	797	815
Direct investment income	2 330	82	157	....	15	22	72	105	119
Dividends and distributed branch profits	2 332	....	....	....	8	14	63	92	103
Reinvested earnings and undistributed branch profits	2 333	....	....	....	6	7	8	11	13
Income on debt (interest)	2 334	82	157	....	1	1	2	2	3
Portfolio investment income	2 339	....	....	....	54	53	73	19	24
Income on equity	2 340	....	....	....	....	....	....	....	....
Income on bonds and notes	2 350	....	....	....	....	....	....	....	....
Income on money market instruments	2 360	....	....	....	54	53	73	19	24
Other investment income	2 370	....	....	....	1,615	2,271	2,079	673	672
Investment income, debit	3 320	**−3,325**	**−2,689**	**−3,092**	**−6,410**	**−14,284**	**−17,376**	**−15,320**	**−19,586**
Direct investment income	3 330	−3,325	−2,689	−2,603	−5,768	−13,056	−17,000	−15,042	−19,121
Dividends and distributed branch profits	3 332	....	....	−800	−3,882	−10,888	−13,713	−11,873	−16,264
Reinvested earnings and undistributed branch profits	3 333	−1,807	−1,616	−1,758	−1,834	−2,094	−3,206	−3,144	−2,816
Income on debt (interest)	3 334	−1,518	−1,074	−45	−53	−74	−82	−24	−42
Portfolio investment income	3 339	....	....	−305	−481	−584	−279	−159	−341
Income on equity	3 340	....	....	−305	−361	−468	−261	−104	−236
Income on bonds and notes	3 350	....	....	....	....	....	....	....	....
Income on money market instruments	3 360	....	....	....	−120	−117	−18	−55	−105
Other investment income	3 370	....	....	−184	−161	−643	−96	−120	−124
D. CURRENT TRANSFERS	4 379	**1,051**	**2,252**	**15,152**	**17,798**	**18,545**	**19,366**	**18,694**	**20,093**
Credit	2 379	**1,063**	**2,273**	**15,284**	**17,975**	**18,695**	**19,897**	**19,158**	**20,583**
General government	2 380	....	....	120	1,023	860	816	923	927
Other sectors	2 390	1,063	2,273	15,164	16,952	17,835	19,081	18,235	19,656
Workers' remittances	2 391	1,063	2,273	14,485	16,740	17,793	19,079	18,230	19,651
Other current transfers	2 392	....	....	679	212	41	2	4	6
Debit	3 379	**−12**	**−21**	**−131**	**−177**	**−150**	**−531**	**−464**	**−491**
General government	3 380	....	....	−61	−48	−83	−119	−117	−169
Other sectors	3 390	−12	−21	−71	−129	−67	−412	−346	−322
Workers' remittances	3 391	−12	−21	−14	−35	−26	−23	−28	−29
Other current transfers	3 392	....	....	−56	−94	−41	−389	−318	−293
CAPITAL AND FINANCIAL ACCOUNT	4 996	**−9,024**	**−21,552**	**−19,185**	**−19,367**	**−10,763**	**−8,376**	**13,129**	**2,730**
CAPITAL ACCOUNT	4 994	....	....	**7,336**	**10,556**	....	....	....	....
Total credit	2 994	....	....	*7,336*	*10,556*	....	....	....	....
Total debit	3 994	....	....	....	....	....	....	....	....
Capital transfers, credit	2 400	....	....	**7,336**	**10,556**	....	....	....	....
General government	2 401	....	....	7,336	10,556	....	....	....	....
Debt forgiveness	2 402	....	....	7,336	10,556	....	....	....	....
Other capital transfers	2 410	....	....	....	....	....	....	....	....
Other sectors	2 430	....	....	....	....	....	....	....	....
Migrants' transfers	2 431	....	....	....	....	....	....	....	....
Debt forgiveness	2 432	....	....	....	....	....	....	....	....
Other capital transfers	2 440	....	....	....	....	....	....	....	....
Capital transfers, debit	3 400	....	....	....	....	....	....	....	....
General government	3 401	....	....	....	....	....	....	....	....
Debt forgiveness	3 402	....	....	....	....	....	....	....	....
Other capital transfers	3 410	....	....	....	....	....	....	....	....
Other sectors	3 430	....	....	....	....	....	....	....	....
Migrants' transfers	3 431	....	....	....	....	....	....	....	....
Debt forgiveness	3 432	....	....	....	....	....	....	....	....
Other capital transfers	3 440	....	....	....	....	....	....	....	....
Nonproduced nonfinancial assets, credit	2 480	....	....	....	....	....	....	....	....
Nonproduced nonfinancial assets, debit	3 480	....	....	....	....	....	....	....	....

Table 2 (Continued). STANDARD PRESENTATION, 2003–2010

(Millions of U.S. dollars)

	Code	2003	2004	2005	2006	2007	2008	2009	2010
FINANCIAL ACCOUNT	4 995 ..	**−9,025**	**−21,552**	**−26,520**	**−29,922**	**−10,763**	**−8,376**	**13,129**	**2,730**
A. DIRECT INVESTMENT	4 500 ..	**2,005**	**1,874**	**4,968**	**4,535**	**5,167**	**7,145**	**7,030**	**5,133**
Direct investment abroad	4 505 ..	....	....	−15	−320	−868	−1,052	−1,525	−915
Equity capital	4 510 ..	....	....	−15	−314	−861	−1,044	−1,514	−902
Claims on affiliated enterprises	4 515 ..	....	....	−15	−314	−861	−1,044	−1,514	−902
Liabilities to affiliated enterprises	4 520 ..	....	....	....	....	....	....	....	....
Reinvested earnings	4 525 ..	....	....	....	−6	−7	−8	−11	−13
Other capital	4 530 ..	....	....	....	....	....	....	....	....
Claims on affiliated enterprises	4 535 ..	....	....	....	....	....	....	....	....
Liabilities to affiliated enterprises	4 540 ..	....	....	....	....	....	....	....	....
Direct investment in Nigeria	4 555 ..	**2,005**	**1,874**	**4,983**	**4,854**	**6,035**	**8,197**	**8,555**	**6,049**
Equity capital	4 560 ..	....	....	3,225	3,021	3,903	4,927	5,390	3,173
Claims on direct investors	4 565 ..	....	....	....	....	....	....	....	....
Liabilities to direct investors	4 570 ..	....	....	3,225	3,021	3,903	4,927	5,390	3,173
Reinvested earnings	4 575 ..	1,807	1,616	1,758	1,834	2,094	3,206	3,144	2,816
Other capital	4 580 ..	198	259	....	....	38	63	20	60
Claims on direct investors	4 585 ..	....	....	....	....	....	....	....	....
Liabilities to direct investors	4 590 ..	....	....	....	....	38	63	20	60
B. PORTFOLIO INVESTMENT	4 600 ..	**183**	**178**	**−488**	**1,288**	**800**	**−3,403**	**−345**	**2,596**
Assets	4 602 ..	**183**	**178**	**−1,372**	**−1,513**	**−1,843**	**−4,729**	**−822**	**−1,121**
Equity securities	4 610 ..	....	....	−1,240	−1,364	−1,706	−4,041	−753	−1,027
Monetary authorities	4 611 ..	....	....	....	....	....	....	....	....
General government	4 612 ..	....	....	....	....	....	....	....	....
Banks	4 613 ..	....	....	−1,240	−1,364	−1,706	−4,041	−753	−1,027
Other sectors	4 614 ..	....	....	....	....	....	....	....	....
Debt securities	4 619 ..	183	178	−132	−148	−137	−688	−68	−93
Bonds and notes	4 620 ..	....	....	....	....	....	....	....	....
Monetary authorities	4 621 ..	....	....	....	....	....	....	....	....
General government	4 622 ..	....	....	....	....	....	....	....	....
Banks	4 623 ..	....	....	....	....	....	....	....	....
Other sectors	4 624 ..	....	....	....	....	....	....	....	....
Money market instruments	4 630 ..	....	....	−132	−148	−137	−688	−68	−93
Monetary authorities	4 631 ..	....	....	....	....	....	....	....	....
General government	4 632 ..	....	....	....	....	....	....	....	....
Banks	4 633 ..	....	....	−132	−148	−137	−688	−68	−93
Other sectors	4 634 ..	....	....	....	....	....	....	....	....
Liabilities	4 652 ..	....	....	**884**	**2,801**	**2,643**	**1,326**	**476**	**3,717**
Equity securities	4 660 ..	....	....	751	1,769	1,447	−954	487	2,161
Banks	4 663 ..	....	....	....	....	....	....	....	....
Other sectors	4 664 ..	....	....	751	1,769	1,447	−954	487	2,161
Debt securities	4 669 ..	....	....	133	1,031	1,196	2,280	−11	1,556
Bonds and notes	4 670 ..	....	....	133	1,003	1,049	1,349	−91	679
Monetary authorities	4 671 ..	....	....	....	....	....	....	....	....
General government	4 672 ..	....	....	133	1,003	1,049	1,349	−91	679
Banks	4 673 ..	....	....	....	....	....	....	....	....
Other sectors	4 674 ..	....	....	....	....	....	....	....	....
Money market instruments	4 680 ..	....	....	....	29	147	931	80	876
Monetary authorities	4 681 ..	....	....	....	....	....	....	....	....
General government	4 682 ..	....	....	....	....	....	....	....	....
Banks	4 683 ..	....	....	....	29	147	931	80	876
Other sectors	4 684 ..	....	....	....	....	....	....	....	....
C. FINANCIAL DERIVATIVES	4 910 ..	....	....	....	....	....	....	....	....
Monetary authorities	4 911 ..	....	....	....	....	....	....	....	....
General government	4 912 ..	....	....	....	....	....	....	....	....
Banks	4 913 ..	....	....	....	....	....	....	....	....
Other sectors	4 914 ..	....	....	....	....	....	....	....	....
Assets	4 900 ..	....	....	....	....	....	....	....	....
Monetary authorities	4 901 ..	....	....	....	....	....	....	....	....
General government	4 902 ..	....	....	....	....	....	....	....	....
Banks	4 903 ..	....	....	....	....	....	....	....	....
Other sectors	4 904 ..	....	....	....	....	....	....	....	....
Liabilities	4 905 ..	....	....	....	....	....	....	....	....
Monetary authorities	4 906 ..	....	....	....	....	....	....	....	....
General government	4 907 ..	....	....	....	....	....	....	....	....
Banks	4 908 ..	....	....	....	....	....	....	....	....
Other sectors	4 909 ..	....	....	....	....	....	....	....	....

Table 2 (Concluded). STANDARD PRESENTATION, 2003–2010

(Millions of U.S. dollars)

	Code	2003	2004	2005	2006	2007	2008	2009	2010
D. OTHER INVESTMENT	4 700	**−11,426**	**−14,073**	**−19,664**	**−21,851**	**−7,771**	**−10,461**	**−4,070**	**−14,729**
Assets	4 703	**−5,845**	**−7,301**	**−1,487**	**−6,199**	**−9,841**	**−10,636**	**−6,482**	**−14,524**
Trade credits	4 706	....	....	−1,376	−4,655	−7,162	−2,837	−6,653	−6,936
General government	4 707	....	....	....	....	....	....	....	....
of which: Short-term	4 709	....	....	....	....	....	....	....	....
Other sectors	4 710	....	....	−1,376	−4,655	−7,162	−2,837	−6,653	−6,936
of which: Short-term	4 712			*−1,376*	*−4,655*	*−7,162*	*−2,837*	*−6,653*	*−6,936*
Loans	4 714	....	....	−111	−125	−116	−290	−378	−226
Monetary authorities	4 715	....	....	....	....	....	....	....	....
of which: Short-term	4 718	....	....	....	....	....	....	....	....
General government	4 719	....	....	....	....	....	....	....	....
of which: Short-term	4 721	....	....	....	....	....	....	....	....
Banks	4 722	....	....	−111	−125	−116	−290	−378	−226
of which: Short-term	4 724	....	....	....	....	....	....	....	....
Other sectors	4 725	....	....	....	....	....	....	....	....
of which: Short-term	4 727	....	....	....	....	....	....	....	....
Currency and deposits	4 730	−5,845	−7,301	....	−1,419	−2,563	−7,509	549	−7,363
Monetary authorities	4 731	....	....	....	....	....	....	....	....
General government	4 732	....	....	....	119	−1,263	−2,071	−2,279	−2,018
Banks	4 733	818	1,022	....	−1,407	−798	−3,456	2,874	−142
Other sectors	4 734	−6,663	−8,323	....	−131	−502	−1,982	−45	−5,203
Other assets	4 736	....	....	....	....	....	....	....	....
Monetary authorities	4 737	....	....	....	....	....	....	....	....
of which: Short-term	4 739	....	....	....	....	....	....	....	....
General government	4 740	....	....	....	....	....	....	....	....
of which: Short-term	4 742	....	....	....	....	....	....	....	....
Banks	4 743	....	....	....	....	....	....	....	....
of which: Short-term	4 745	....	....	....	....	....	....	....	....
Other sectors	4 746	....	....	....	....	....	....	....	....
of which: Short-term	4 748	....	....	....	....	....	....	....	....
Liabilities	4 753	**−5,582**	**−6,772**	**−18,177**	**−15,652**	**2,069**	**176**	**2,412**	**−204**
Trade credits	4 756	−2,791	−3,386	....	....	....	....	....	....
General government	4 757	−2,791	−3,386	....	....	....	....	....	....
of which: Short-term	4 759	....	....	....	....	....	....	....	....
Other sectors	4 760	....	....	....	....	....	....	....	....
of which: Short-term	4 762	....	....	....	....	....	....	....	....
Loans	4 764	−1,395	−1,693	−18,214	−15,756	1,227	448	449	19
Monetary authorities	4 765	....	....	....	....	....	....	....	....
of which: Use of Fund credit and loans from the Fund	4 766	....	....	....	....	....	....	....	....
of which: Short-term	4 768	....	....	....	....	....	....	....	....
General government	4 769	−1,395	−1,693	−15,235	−16,284	−509	−26	198	716
of which: Short-term	4 771	....	....	....	....	....	....	....	....
Banks	4 772	....	....	87	98	1,372	−223	−338	−92
of which: Short-term	4 774			*87*	*98*	*1,372*	*−223*	*−338*	*−92*
Other sectors	4 775	....	....	−3,066	430	363	697	589	−605
of which: Short-term	4 777	....	....	....	....	....	....	....	....
Currency and deposits	4 780	....	....	36	104	843	−272	−409	−223
Monetary authorities	4 781	....	....	....	....	....	....	....	....
General government	4 782	....	....	....	....	....	....	....	....
Banks	4 783	....	....	36	104	843	−272	−409	−223
Other sectors	4 784	....	....	....	....	....	....	....	....
Other liabilities	4 786	−1,395	−1,693	....	....	....	....	2,373	....
Monetary authorities	4 787	1,047	1,040	....	....	....	....	2,373	....
of which: Short-term	4 789	*1,047*	*1,040*	....	....	....	....	....	....
General government	4 790	....	....	....	....	....	....	....	....
of which: Short-term	4 792	....	....	....	....	....	....	....	....
Banks	4 793	....	....	....	....	....	....	....	....
of which: Short-term	4 795	....	....	....	....	....	....	....	....
Other sectors	4 796	−2,442	−2,733	....	....	....	....	....	....
of which: Short-term	4 798	*−2,442*	*−2,733*	....	....	....	....	....	....
E. RESERVE ASSETS	4 802	**214**	**−9,531**	**−11,336**	**−13,895**	**−8,959**	**−1,657**	**10,515**	**9,730**
Monetary gold	4 812	....	....	....	....	....	....	....	....
Special drawing rights	4 811	....	....	....	....	....	....	−2,371	−231
Reserve position in the Fund	4 810	....	....	....	....	....	....	....	....
Foreign exchange	4 803	214	−9,531	−11,336	−13,895	−8,958	−1,657	12,886	9,960
Other claims	4 813	....	....	....	....	....	....	....	....
NET ERRORS AND OMISSIONS	4 998	**5,634**	**4,711**	**−17,344**	**−17,151**	**−16,881**	**−19,704**	**−26,283**	**−5,207**

Table 3. INTERNATIONAL INVESTMENT POSITION (End-period stocks), 2003–2010

(Millions of U.S. dollars)

	Code	2003	2004	2005	2006	2007	2008	2009	2010
ASSETS	8 995 C.	....	....	41,832	60,495	77,500	88,462	83,885	83,668
Direct investment abroad	8 505	....	....	305	624	1,506	2,565	4,118	5,041
Equity capital and reinvested earnings	8 506	....	....	305	624	1,506	2,565	4,118	5,041
Claims on affiliated enterprises	8 507	....	....	305	624	1,506	2,565	4,118	5,041
Liabilities to affiliated enterprises	8 508	....	....	....	....	....	....	....	....
Other capital	8 530	....	....	....	....	....	....	....	....
Claims on affiliated enterprises	8 535	....	....	....	....	....	....	....	....
Liabilities to affiliated enterprises	8 540	....	....	....	....	....	....	....	....
Portfolio investment	8 602	....	....	2,851	4,349	6,208	10,967	11,798	12,740
Equity securities	8 610	....	....	2,572	3,923	5,644	9,710	10,472	11,508
Monetary authorities	8 611	....	....	....	....	....	....	....	....
General government	8 612	....	....	....	....	....	....	....	....
Banks	8 613	....	....	2,572	3,923	5,644	9,710	10,472	11,508
Other sectors	8 614	....	....	....	....	....	....	....	....
Debt securities	8 619	....	....	279	426	564	1,257	1,326	1,232
Bonds and notes	8 620	....	....	....	....	....	....	....	....
Monetary authorities	8 621	....	....	....	....	....	....	....	....
General government	8 622	....	....	....	....	....	....	....	....
Banks	8 623	....	....	....	....	....	....	....	....
Other sectors	8 624	....	....	....	....	....	....	....	....
Money market instruments	8 630	....	....	279	426	564	1,257	1,326	1,232
Monetary authorities	8 631	....	....	....	....	....	....	....	....
General government	8 632	....	....	....	....	....	....	....	....
Banks	8 633	....	....	279	426	564	1,257	1,326	1,232
Other sectors	8 634	....	....	....	....	....	....	....	....
Financial derivatives	8 900	....	....	....	....	....	....	....	....
Monetary authorities	8 901	....	....	....	....	....	....	....	....
General government	8 902	....	....	....	....	....	....	....	....
Banks	8 903	....	....	....	....	....	....	....	....
Other sectors	8 904	....	....	....	....	....	....	....	....
Other investment	8 703	....	....	10,318	13,223	18,451	21,931	25,630	33,548
Trade credits	8 706	....	....	3,279	4,697	7,223	2,855	6,727	6,994
General government	8 707	....	....	....	....	....	....	....	....
of which: Short-term	8 709	....	....	....	....	....	....	....	....
Other sectors	8 710	....	....	3,279	4,697	7,223	2,855	6,727	6,994
of which: Short-term	8 712	....	....	....	....	....	....	....	....
Loans	8 714	....	....	934	1,051	1,168	1,460	1,842	2,070
Monetary authorities	8 715	....	....	....	....	....	....	....	....
of which: Short-term	8 718	....	....	....	....	....	....	....	....
General government	8 719	....	....	....	....	....	....	....	....
of which: Short-term	8 721	....	....	....	....	....	....	....	....
Banks	8 722	....	....	934	1,051	1,168	1,460	1,842	2,070
of which: Short-term	8 724	....	....	*934*	*1,051*	*1,168*	*1,460*	*1,842*	*2,070*
Other sectors	8 725	....	....	....	....	....	....	....	....
of which: Short-term	8 727	....	....	....	....	....	....	....	....
Currency and deposits	8 730	....	....	6,105	7,476	10,060	17,616	17,061	24,485
Monetary authorities	8 731	....	....	....	....	....	....	....	....
General government	8 732	....	....	874	746	2,019	4,104	6,408	8,443
Banks	8 733	....	....	3,591	4,975	5,780	9,257	6,351	6,494
Other sectors	8 734	....	....	1,640	1,755	2,261	4,255	4,301	9,547
Other assets	8 736	....	....	....	....	....	....	....	....
Monetary authorities	8 737	....	....	....	....	....	....	....	....
of which: Short-term	8 739	....	....	....	....	....	....	....	....
General government	8 740	....	....	....	....	....	....	....	....
of which: Short-term	8 742	....	....	....	....	....	....	....	....
Banks	8 743	....	....	....	....	....	....	....	....
of which: Short-term	8 745	....	....	....	....	....	....	....	....
Other sectors	8 746	....	....	....	....	....	....	....	....
of which: Short-term	8 748	....	....	....	....	....	....	....	....
Reserve assets	8 802	....	....	28,358	42,298	51,334	53,000	42,339	32,339
Monetary gold	8 812	....	....	....	....	....	....	....	....
Special drawing rights	8 811	....	....	....	....	1	1	2,380	2,580
Reserve position in the Fund	8 810	....	....	....	....	....	....	....	....
Foreign exchange	8 803	....	....	28,357	42,298	51,333	52,998	39,959	29,759
Other claims	8 813	....	....	....	....	....	....	....	....

Table 3 (Concluded). INTERNATIONAL INVESTMENT POSITION (End-period stocks), 2003–2010

(Millions of U.S. dollars)

	Code	2003	2004	2005	2006	2007	2008	2009	2010
LIABILITIES	8 995 D.	....	....	**63,997**	**54,966**	**66,291**	**75,621**	**87,278**	**97,257**
Direct investment in Nigeria	8 555 ..	....	....	**26,608**	**31,243**	**37,330**	**45,577**	**54,227**	**60,326**
Equity capital and reinvested earnings	8 556 ..	....	....	25,278	29,926	35,975	44,158	52,788	58,826
Claims on direct investors	8 557 ..	....	....	....	....	....	....	....	....
Liabilities to direct investors	8 558 ..	....	....	25,278	29,926	35,975	44,158	52,788	58,826
Other capital	8 580 ..	....	....	1,330	1,317	1,355	1,419	1,440	1,500
Claims on direct investors	8 585 ..	....	....	....	....	....	....	....	....
Liabilities to direct investors	8 590 ..	....	....	1,330	1,317	1,355	1,419	1,440	1,500
Portfolio investment	8 652 ..	....	....	**6,946**	**9,703**	**12,369**	**13,703**	**14,369**	**18,117**
Equity securities	8 660 ..	....	....	3,586	5,335	6,795	5,835	6,327	8,507
Banks	8 663 ..	....	....	....	....	....	....	....	....
Other sectors	8 664 ..	....	....	3,586	5,335	6,795	5,835	6,327	8,507
Debt securities	8 669 ..	....	....	3,361	4,368	5,574	7,868	8,041	9,610
Bonds and notes	8 670 ..	....	....	3,094	4,075	5,133	6,490	6,582	7,267
Monetary authorities	8 671 ..	....	....	....	....	....	....	....	....
General government	8 672 ..	....	....	3,094	4,075	5,133	6,490	6,582	7,267
Banks	8 673 ..	....	....	....	....	....	....	....	....
Other sectors	8 674 ..	....	....	....	....	....	....	....	....
Money market instruments	8 680 ..	....	....	267	293	441	1,378	1,459	2,343
Monetary authorities	8 681 ..	....	....	....	....	....	....	....	....
General government	8 682 ..	....	....	....	....	....	....	....	....
Banks	8 683 ..	....	....	267	293	441	1,378	1,459	2,343
Other sectors	8 684 ..	....	....	....	....	....	....	....	....
Financial derivatives	8 905 ..	....	....	....	....	....	....	....	....
Monetary authorities	8 906 ..	....	....	....	....	....	....	....	....
General government	8 907 ..	....	....	....	....	....	....	....	....
Banks	8 908 ..	....	....	....	....	....	....	....	....
Other sectors	8 909 ..	....	....	....	....	....	....	....	....
Other investment	8 753 ..	....	....	**30,442**	**14,020**	**16,592**	**16,341**	**18,682**	**18,814**
Trade credits	8 756 ..	....	....	....	....	....	....	....	....
General government	8 757 ..	....	....	....	....	....	....	....	....
of which: Short-term	8 759 ..	....	....	....	....	....	....	....	....
Other sectors	8 760 ..	....	....	....	....	....	....	....	....
of which: Short-term	8 762 ..	....	....	....	....	....	....	....	....
Loans	8 764 ..	....	....	24,878	8,406	10,127	10,150	10,279	10,682
Monetary authorities	8 765 ..	....	....	....	....	....	....	....	....
of which: Use of Fund credit and loans from the Fund....	8 766 ..	....	....	....	....	....	....	....	....
of which: Short-term	8 768 ..	....	....	....	....	....	....	....	....
General government	8 769 ..	....	....	20,681	4,046	3,533	3,507	3,707	4,429
of which: Short-term	8 771 ..	....	....	....	....	....	....	....	....
Banks	8 772 ..	....	....	995	1,084	2,469	2,244	2,586	2,493
of which: Short-term	8 774 ..	....	....	....	....	....	....	....	....
Other sectors	8 775 ..	....	....	3,202	3,275	4,125	4,399	3,985	3,760
of which: Short-term	8 777 ..	....	....	....	....	....	....	....	....
Currency and deposits	8 780 ..	....	....	5,564	5,614	6,464	6,190	5,777	5,552
Monetary authorities	8 781 ..	....	....	....	....	....	....	....	....
General government	8 782 ..	....	....	....	....	....	....	....	....
Banks	8 783 ..	....	....	5,564	5,614	6,464	6,190	5,777	5,552
Other sectors	8 784 ..	....	....	....	....	....	....	....	....
Other liabilities	8 786 ..	....	....	....	....	....	....	2,626	2,580
Monetary authorities	8 787 ..	....	....	....	....	....	....	2,626	2,580
of which: Short-term	8 789 ..	....	....	....	....	....	....	....	....
General government	8 790 ..	....	....	....	....	....	....	....	....
of which: Short-term	8 792 ..	....	....	....	....	....	....	....	....
Banks	8 793 ..	....	....	....	....	....	....	....	....
of which: Short-term	8 795 ..	....	....	....	....	....	....	....	....
Other sectors	8 796 ..	....	....	....	....	....	....	....	....
of which: Short-term	8 798 ..	....	....	....	....	....	....	....	....
NET INTERNATIONAL INVESTMENT POSITION	8 995 ..	....	....	−22,164	5,529	11,209	12,841	−3,393	−13,589
Conversion rates: naira per U.S. dollar (end of period)	0 102 ..	136.500	132.350	129.000	128.270	117.968	132.563	149.581	150.662

2011, International Monetary Fund: *Balance of Payments Statistics Yearbook*

Table 1. ANALYTIC PRESENTATION, 2003–2010

(Millions of U.S. dollars)

	Code	2003	2004	2005	2006	2007	2008	2009	2010
A. Current Account[1]	4 993 Z.	**27,698**	**33,000**	**49,003**	**58,166**	**55,430**	**79,235**	**44,543**	**51,444**
Goods: exports f.o.b.	2 100 ..	68,666	83,164	104,011	122,582	136,952	172,746	116,031	132,691
Goods: imports f.o.b.	3 100 ..	−40,504	−49,035	−55,094	−63,716	−78,631	−87,127	−67,212	−74,300
Balance on Goods	4 100 ..	*28,162*	*34,129*	*48,917*	*58,866*	*58,321*	*85,620*	*48,819*	*58,391*
Services: credit	2 200 ..	21,663	25,263	29,928	33,118	40,552	45,388	38,758	39,734
Services: debit	3 200 ..	−20,569	−24,304	−29,182	−31,318	−39,125	−45,154	−36,965	−42,842
Balance on Goods and Services	4 991 ..	*29,256*	*35,088*	*49,664*	*60,666*	*59,749*	*85,853*	*50,612*	*55,283*
Income: credit	2 300 ..	14,077	17,117	24,557	30,936	42,549	43,884	27,089	28,052
Income: debit	3 300 ..	−12,712	−16,570	−22,586	−30,456	−43,261	−47,031	−28,750	−27,180
Balance on Goods, Services, and Income	4 992 ..	*30,622*	*35,635*	*51,635*	*61,146*	*59,037*	*82,706*	*48,951*	*56,154*
Current transfers: credit	2 379 Z.	2,049	2,553	3,458	2,655	3,228	3,560	3,229	3,337
Current transfers: debit	3 379 ..	−4,972	−5,188	−6,090	−5,635	−6,835	−7,031	−7,637	−8,047
B. Capital Account[1]	4 994 Z.	**678**	**−154**	**−290**	**−146**	**−163**	**−210**	**−173**	**−213**
Capital account: credit	2 994 Z.	964	105	....	....	....	....	....	....
Capital account: debit	3 994 ..	−286	−260	−290	−146	−163	−210	−173	−213
Total, Groups A Plus B	4 981 ..	*28,376*	*32,846*	*48,713*	*58,020*	*55,266*	*79,025*	*44,370*	*51,231*
C. Financial Account[1]	4 995 W.	**−21,745**	**−22,300**	**−38,694**	**−39,738**	**−23,252**	**−74,120**	**−71,384**	**−42,181**
Direct investment abroad	4 505 ..	−6,052	−5,250	−21,820	−20,841	−12,895	−23,708	−30,135	−12,251
Direct investment in Norway	4 555 Z.	3,550	2,544	5,350	7,218	6,533	7,512	15,000	11,747
Portfolio investment assets	4 602 ..	−19,283	−38,031	−38,107	−113,529	−67,924	−132,330	−1,855	−52,712
Equity securities	4 610 ..	−8,498	−7,270	−18,286	−19,442	−51,743	−88,663	−57,105	−17,338
Debt securities	4 619 ..	−10,785	−30,761	−19,821	−94,087	−16,181	−43,666	55,250	−35,374
Portfolio investment liabilities	4 652 Z.	13,123	9,353	32,321	39,310	46,727	20,544	4,850	32,647
Equity securities	4 660 ..	2,040	4,493	11,661	8,197	9,452	−12,136	2,744	1,993
Debt securities	4 669 Z.	11,083	4,860	20,660	31,113	37,274	32,680	2,106	30,653
Financial derivatives	4 910 ..	−126	144	....	....	....	....	....	....
Financial derivatives assets	4 900 ..	35	−636	....	....	....	....	....	....
Financial derivatives liabilities	4 905 ..	−161	780	....	....	....	....	....	....
Other investment assets	4 703 ..	−25,212	−16,517	−38,085	−29,056	−43,446	36,560	26,178	−27,202
Monetary authorities	4 701 ..	−127	243	221	−16	6	−639	−308	−343
General government	4 704 ..	−14,642	−17,858	−20,779	−8,729	−22,384	94,993	6,053	−10,214
Banks	4 705 ..	−4,291	963	−9,850	−17,702	−14,690	−45,960	17,836	4,238
Other sectors	4 728 ..	−6,151	135	−7,678	−2,610	−6,378	−11,835	2,597	−20,883
Other investment liabilities	4 753 W.	12,256	25,458	21,648	77,160	47,753	17,301	−85,422	5,590
Monetary authorities	4 753 WA	−1,721	382	1,298	5,840	−680	4,464	−18,550	1,094
General government	4 753 ZB	9,992	22,306	−437	46,444	12,221	−48,271	−62,039	8,486
Banks	4 753 ZC	377	4,266	19,704	21,518	28,092	45,453	4,671	−15,913
Other sectors	4 753 ZD	3,608	−1,496	1,084	3,357	8,120	15,655	−9,505	11,923
Total, Groups A Through C	4 983 ..	*6,631*	*10,546*	*10,019*	*18,282*	*32,015*	*4,905*	*−27,014*	*9,050*
D. Net Errors and Omissions	4 998 ..	**−6,303**	**−5,319**	**−5,508**	**−12,807**	**−30,970**	**−292**	**9,946**	**−4,832**
Total, Groups A Through D	4 984 ..	*328*	*5,227*	*4,511*	*5,475*	*1,045*	*4,612*	*−17,068*	*4,218*
E. Reserves and Related Items	4 802 A.	**−328**	**−5,227**	**−4,511**	**−5,475**	**−1,045**	**−4,612**	**17,068**	**−4,218**
Reserve assets	4 802 ..	−328	−5,227	−4,511	−5,475	−1,045	−4,612	17,068	−4,218
Use of Fund credit and loans	4 766 ..	....	....	....	....	....	....	....	....
Exceptional financing	4 920 ..	....	....	....	....	....	....	....	....
Conversion rates: Norwegian kroner per U.S. dollar	0 101 ..	**7.0802**	**6.7408**	**6.4425**	**6.4133**	**5.8617**	**5.6400**	**6.2883**	**6.0442**

[1] Excludes components that have been classified in the categories of Group E.

Table 2. STANDARD PRESENTATION, 2003–2010

(Millions of U.S. dollars)

	Code	2003	2004	2005	2006	2007	2008	2009	2010
CURRENT ACCOUNT..	4 993 ..	**27,698**	**33,000**	**49,003**	**58,166**	**55,430**	**79,235**	**44,543**	**51,444**
A. GOODS..	4 100 ..	**28,162**	**34,129**	**48,917**	**58,866**	**58,321**	**85,620**	**48,819**	**58,391**
Credit...	2 100 ..	**68,666**	**83,164**	**104,011**	**122,582**	**136,952**	**172,746**	**116,031**	**132,691**
General merchandise: exports f.o.b..................	2 110 ..	68,250	82,674	103,642	122,002	136,303	171,402	114,930	131,326
Goods for processing: exports f.o.b..............	2 150 ..	....	....	....	....	....	....	....	....
Repairs on goods.....................................	2 160 ..	298	334	369	581	649	1,344	1,101	1,365
Goods procured in ports by carriers.............	2 170 ..	117	156	....	....	....	....	....	....
Nonmonetary gold.....................................	2 180 ..	....	....	....	....	....	....	....	....
Debit...	3 100 ..	**−40,504**	**−49,035**	**−55,094**	**−63,716**	**−78,631**	**−87,127**	**−67,212**	**−74,300**
General merchandise: imports f.o.b..............	3 110 ..	−38,848	−47,329	−53,179	−60,834	−75,378	−83,838	−64,909	−71,606
Goods for processing: imports f.o.b..............	3 150 ..	....	....	....	....	....	....	....	....
Repairs on goods.....................................	3 160 ..	−512	−461	−624	−629	−821	−969	−885	−858
Goods procured in ports by carriers.............	3 170 ..	−1,144	−1,245	−1,291	−2,253	−2,432	−2,320	−1,418	−1,836
Nonmonetary gold.....................................	3 180 ..	....	....	....	....	....	....	....	....
B. SERVICES...	4 200 ..	**1,094**	**959**	**747**	**1,800**	**1,428**	**233**	**1,793**	**−3,108**
Total credit..	2 200 ..	*21,663*	*25,263*	*29,928*	*33,118*	*40,552*	*45,388*	*38,758*	*39,734*
Total debit..	3 200 ..	*−20,569*	*−24,304*	*−29,182*	*−31,318*	*−39,125*	*−45,154*	*−36,965*	*−42,842*
Transportation services, credit.................	2 205 ..	**12,232**	**13,917**	**16,248**	**16,267**	**18,879**	**21,027**	**15,626**	**15,679**
Passenger..	2 850 ..	*489*	*551*	*698*	*647*	*735*	*1,050*	*362*	*405*
Freight...	2 851 ..	*8,000*	*9,162*	*10,398*	*11,295*	*12,361*	*14,557*	*11,308*	*10,719*
Other..	2 852 ..	*3,744*	*4,203*	*5,152*	*4,325*	*5,783*	*5,420*	*3,957*	*4,554*
Sea transport, passenger..........................	2 207 ..	240	251	362	334	351	410	227	269
Sea transport, freight..............................	2 208 ..	6,375	7,391	8,328	8,990	10,042	11,671	8,774	8,105
Sea transport, other................................	2 209 ..	2,771	3,082	3,783	3,048	4,097	3,742	2,075	2,459
Air transport, passenger...........................	2 211 ..	233	281	313	289	340	585	87	85
Air transport, freight...............................	2 212 ..	29	36	40	93	100	131	114	123
Air transport, other................................	2 213 ..	95	86	204	37	45	95	82	89
Other transport, passenger.......................	2 215 ..	16	19	23	24	43	55	48	51
Other transport, freight............................	2 216 ..	1,595	1,735	2,030	2,213	2,219	2,754	2,420	2,492
Other transport, other.............................	2 217 ..	879	1,035	1,165	1,240	1,642	1,584	1,800	2,006
Transportation services, debit.................	3 205 ..	**−7,156**	**−8,458**	**−9,682**	**−9,649**	**−13,850**	**−14,386**	**−9,470**	**−11,684**
Passenger..	3 850 ..	*−373*	*−405*	*−480*	*−231*	*−669*	*....*	*....*	*....*
Freight...	3 851 ..	*−773*	*−1,062*	*−1,753*	*−2,601*	*−4,515*	*−6,167*	*−3,702*	*−4,745*
Other..	3 852 ..	*−6,009*	*−6,991*	*−7,448*	*−6,817*	*−8,667*	*−8,219*	*−5,769*	*−6,939*
Sea transport, passenger..........................	3 207 ..	−37	−38	−48	−48	−50	....	....	....
Sea transport, freight..............................	3 208 ..	−452	−711	−799	−1,095	−2,069	−3,426	−1,391	−2,184
Sea transport, other................................	3 209 ..	−5,467	−6,421	−6,823	−6,539	−8,256	−7,721	−5,415	−6,509
Air transport, passenger...........................	3 211 ..	−315	−355	−413	−163	−583	....	....	....
Air transport, freight...............................	3 212 ..	−68	−60	−95	−196	−440	−432	−324	−372
Air transport, other................................	3 213 ..	−516	−529	−580	−231	−339	−414	−294	−357
Other transport, passenger.......................	3 215 ..	−22	−12	−19	−19	−36	....	....	....
Other transport, freight............................	3 216 ..	−254	−290	−860	−1,310	−2,006	−2,309	−1,987	−2,189
Other transport, other.............................	3 217 ..	−25	−41	−45	−47	−72	−84	−60	−73
Travel, credit......................................	2 236 ..	**2,500**	**2,980**	**3,332**	**3,617**	**4,367**	**4,807**	**4,082**	**4,576**
Business travel.......................................	2 237 ..	....	....	....	....	....	....	....	....
Personal travel.......................................	2 240 ..	2,500	2,980	3,332	3,617	4,367	4,807	4,082	4,576
Travel, debit.......................................	3 236 ..	**−6,716**	**−8,489**	**−10,111**	**−11,121**	**−11,822**	**−14,228**	**−12,366**	**−13,974**
Business travel.......................................	3 237 ..	−2,080	−2,649	−3,204	−3,302	−2,858	−3,235	−2,812	−2,886
Personal travel.......................................	3 240 ..	−4,636	−5,840	−6,907	−7,819	−8,964	−10,993	−9,554	−11,088
Other services, credit...........................	2 200 BA	**6,931**	**8,366**	**10,349**	**13,233**	**17,306**	**19,554**	**19,050**	**19,479**
Communications......................................	2 245 ..	309	321	378	400	578	787	683	737
Construction..	2 249 ..	116	116	254	330	364	465	430	336
Insurance..	2 253 ..	394	335	367	321	243	234	243	212
Financial...	2 260 ..	558	594	707	820	1,126	1,447	1,586	1,374
Computer and information........................	2 262 ..	373	566	899	1,376	1,831	2,166	2,643	3,023
Royalties and licence fees.........................	2 266 ..	195	242	414	489	540	690	637	498
Other business services............................	2 268 ..	4,470	5,708	6,670	8,752	11,842	12,957	12,131	12,672
Personal, cultural, and recreational.............	2 287 ..	210	185	351	422	438	561	477	398
Government, n.i.e....................................	2 291 ..	306	298	308	323	344	246	221	228
Other services, debit............................	3 200 BA	**−6,698**	**−7,357**	**−9,389**	**−10,548**	**−13,453**	**−16,541**	**−15,129**	**−17,184**
Communications......................................	3 245 ..	−217	−233	−286	−310	−448	−1,146	−891	−1,620
Construction..	3 249 ..	−48	−39	−42	−44	−55	−68	−49	−48
Insurance..	3 253 ..	−522	−439	−289	−174	−171	−102	−112	−63
Financial...	3 260 ..	−1,153	−1,180	−1,137	−959	−1,214	−1,133	−1,179	−1,260
Computer and information........................	3 262 ..	−507	−573	−1,006	−1,268	−1,597	−1,695	−1,579	−1,674
Royalties and licence fees.........................	3 266 ..	−394	−442	−469	−498	−614	−767	−553	−536
Other business services............................	3 268 ..	−3,399	−3,634	−5,180	−5,977	−7,828	−10,162	−9,722	−10,887
Personal, cultural, and recreational.............	3 287 ..	−304	−383	−508	−588	−729	−675	−577	−612
Government, n.i.e....................................	3 291 ..	−154	−433	−472	−730	−797	−792	−468	−485

2011, International Monetary Fund: *Balance of Payments Statistics Yearbook*

Table 2 (Continued). STANDARD PRESENTATION, 2003–2010

(Millions of U.S. dollars)

	Code	2003	2004	2005	2006	2007	2008	2009	2010
C. INCOME	4 300	**1,365**	**547**	**1,971**	**480**	**−712**	**−3,147**	**−1,660**	**872**
Total credit	2 300	*14,077*	*17,117*	*24,557*	*30,936*	*42,549*	*43,884*	*27,089*	*28,052*
Total debit	3 300	*−12,712*	*−16,570*	*−22,586*	*−30,456*	*−43,261*	*−47,031*	*−28,750*	*−27,180*
Compensation of employees, credit	2 310	**392**	**465**	**505**	**529**	**617**	**685**	**631**	**680**
Compensation of employees, debit	3 310	**−1,430**	**−1,749**	**−2,174**	**−2,597**	**−3,577**	**−4,750**	**−4,174**	**−4,045**
Investment income, credit	2 320	**13,686**	**16,652**	**24,052**	**30,407**	**41,933**	**43,199**	**26,458**	**27,372**
Direct investment income	2 330	4,128	4,892	13,914	12,561	15,161	13,838	10,349	11,933
Dividends and distributed branch profits	2 332	1,686	2,792	7,418	7,010	13,569	15,473	11,805	13,441
Reinvested earnings and undistributed branch profits	2 333	2,442	2,100	6,496	5,551	1,591	−1,636	−1,456	−1,508
Income on debt (interest)	2 334	....	....	....	....	....	....	....	....
Portfolio investment income	2 339	879	946	7,891	14,286	21,641	23,095	12,747	11,989
Income on equity	2 340	....	....	....	....	....	....	....	....
Income on bonds and notes	2 350	879	946	7,891	14,286	21,641	23,095	12,747	11,989
Income on money market instruments	2 360	....	....	....	....	....	....	....	....
Other investment income	2 370	8,679	10,814	2,247	3,560	5,132	6,266	3,362	3,451
Investment income, debit	3 320	**−11,282**	**−14,821**	**−20,412**	**−27,859**	**−39,684**	**−42,281**	**−24,575**	**−23,135**
Direct investment income	3 330	−4,050	−6,202	−12,290	−14,031	−18,264	−18,047	−13,076	−10,836
Dividends and distributed branch profits	3 332	−3,030	−4,611	−7,834	−11,565	−12,428	−16,739	−11,913	−9,631
Reinvested earnings and undistributed branch profits	3 333	−1,021	−1,592	−4,456	−2,466	−5,836	−1,307	−1,164	−1,205
Income on debt (interest)	3 334	....	....	....	....	....	....	....	....
Portfolio investment income	3 339	−502	−735	−3,576	−6,267	−9,856	−12,155	−6,225	−6,750
Income on equity	3 340	....	....	....	....	....	....	....	....
Income on bonds and notes	3 350	−502	−735	−3,576	−6,267	−9,856	−12,155	−6,225	−6,750
Income on money market instruments	3 360	....	....	....	....	....	....	....	....
Other investment income	3 370	−6,729	−7,884	−4,546	−7,562	−11,563	−12,079	−5,274	−5,549
D. CURRENT TRANSFERS	4 379	**−2,924**	**−2,635**	**−2,632**	**−2,980**	**−3,607**	**−3,471**	**−4,408**	**−4,711**
Credit	2 379	**2,049**	**2,553**	**3,458**	**2,655**	**3,228**	**3,560**	**3,229**	**3,337**
General government	2 380	22	25	279	223	378	575	242	273
Other sectors	2 390	2,027	2,528	3,179	2,432	2,850	2,985	2,987	3,064
Workers' remittances	2 391	....	....	....	....	....	....	....	....
Other current transfers	2 392	2,027	2,528	3,179	2,432	2,850	2,985	2,987	3,064
Debit	3 379	**−4,972**	**−5,188**	**−6,090**	**−5,635**	**−6,835**	**−7,031**	**−7,637**	**−8,047**
General government	3 380	−1,892	−2,030	−2,481	−2,748	−3,435	−3,691	−4,151	−4,614
Other sectors	3 390	−3,081	−3,158	−3,608	−2,887	−3,401	−3,340	−3,487	−3,434
Workers' remittances	3 391	....	....	....	....	....	....	....	....
Other current transfers	3 392	−3,081	−3,158	−3,608	−2,887	−3,401	−3,340	−3,487	−3,434
CAPITAL AND FINANCIAL ACCOUNT	4 996	**−21,395**	**−27,681**	**−43,495**	**−45,359**	**−24,460**	**−78,943**	**−54,489**	**−46,612**
CAPITAL ACCOUNT	4 994	**678**	**−154**	**−290**	**−146**	**−163**	**−210**	**−173**	**−213**
Total credit	2 994	*964*	*105*	....	....	....	....	....	....
Total debit	3 994	*−286*	*−260*	*−290*	*−146*	*−163*	*−210*	*−173*	*−213*
Capital transfers, credit	2 400	**963**	**105**	....	....	....	....	....	....
General government	2 401	....	....	....	....	....	....	....	....
Debt forgiveness	2 402	....	....	....	....	....	....	....	....
Other capital transfers	2 410	....	....	....	....	....	....	....	....
Other sectors	2 430	963	105	....	....	....	....	....	....
Migrants' transfers	2 431	....	....	....	....	....	....	....	....
Debt forgiveness	2 432	....	....	....	....	....	....	....	....
Other capital transfers	2 440	963	105	....	....	....	....	....	....
Capital transfers, debit	3 400	**−285**	**−258**	**−290**	**−146**	**−163**	**−210**	**−173**	**−213**
General government	3 401	....	....	....	....	....	....	....	....
Debt forgiveness	3 402	....	....	....	....	....	....	....	....
Other capital transfers	3 410	....	....	....	....	....	....	....	....
Other sectors	3 430	−285	−258	−290	−146	−163	−210	−173	−213
Migrants' transfers	3 431	....	....	....	....	....	....	....	....
Debt forgiveness	3 432	....	....	....	....	....	....	....	....
Other capital transfers	3 440	−285	−258	−290	−146	−163	−210	−173	−213
Nonproduced nonfinancial assets, credit	2 480	**1**	....	....	....	....	....	....	....
Nonproduced nonfinancial assets, debit	3 480	**−1**	**−1**	....	....	....	....	....	....

Table 2 (Continued). STANDARD PRESENTATION, 2003–2010

(Millions of U.S. dollars)

	Code	2003	2004	2005	2006	2007	2008	2009	2010
FINANCIAL ACCOUNT	4 995	−22,073	−27,527	−43,205	−45,214	−24,297	−78,732	−54,316	−46,398
A. DIRECT INVESTMENT	4 500	−2,503	−2,706	−16,471	−13,623	−6,362	−16,196	−15,135	−504
Direct investment abroad	4 505	−6,052	−5,250	−21,820	−20,841	−12,895	−23,708	−30,135	−12,251
Equity capital	4 510	−3,576	−3,356	−13,644	−15,717	−20,943	−24,243	−7,978	−17,650
Claims on affiliated enterprises	4 515	....	....	....	....	....	....	....	....
Liabilities to affiliated enterprises	4 520	....	....	....	....	....	....	....	....
Reinvested earnings	4 525	−2,442	−2,100	−6,496	−5,551	−1,591	1,636	1,456	1,508
Other capital	4 530	−35	206	−1,681	427	9,639	−1,100	−23,613	3,891
Claims on affiliated enterprises	4 535	−1,018	−2,569	−5,132	376	−3,023	−13,301	−13,651	−2,529
Liabilities to affiliated enterprises	4 540	983	2,775	3,452	50	12,663	12,201	−9,962	6,420
Direct investment in Norway	4 555	3,550	2,544	5,350	7,218	6,533	7,512	15,000	11,747
Equity capital	4 560	1,232	−2,882	1,800	2,287	−440	−940	1,246	1,423
Claims on direct investors	4 565	....	....	....	....	....	....	....	....
Liabilities to direct investors	4 570	....	....	....	....	....	....	....	....
Reinvested earnings	4 575	1,021	1,592	4,456	2,466	5,836	1,307	1,164	1,205
Other capital	4 580	1,297	3,834	−906	2,465	1,136	7,145	12,591	9,118
Claims on direct investors	4 585	353	400	−2,623	−2,150	−3,370	−1,641	2,711	4,314
Liabilities to direct investors	4 590	944	3,434	1,717	4,615	4,506	8,786	9,880	4,804
B. PORTFOLIO INVESTMENT	4 600	−6,160	−28,678	−5,786	−74,219	−21,197	−111,785	2,995	−20,065
Assets	4 602	−19,283	−38,031	−38,107	−113,529	−67,924	−132,330	−1,855	−52,712
Equity securities	4 610	−8,498	−7,270	−18,286	−19,442	−51,743	−88,663	−57,105	−17,338
Monetary authorities	4 611	....	....	....	....	....	....	....	....
General government	4 612	−7,821	−7,249	−10,242	−10,708	−45,874	−96,563	−48,829	−11,791
Banks	4 613	−21	−87	67	−202	−677	−625	221	−2
Other sectors	4 614	−656	66	−8,111	−8,531	−5,192	8,525	−8,498	−5,545
Debt securities	4 619	−10,785	−30,761	−19,821	−94,087	−16,181	−43,666	55,250	−35,374
Bonds and notes	4 620	−13,371	−29,665	−18,366	−94,187	−14,300	−45,457	56,071	−34,359
Monetary authorities	4 621	....	....	....	....	....	....	....	....
General government	4 622	−7,348	−23,035	−7,284	−82,004	−10,910	−36,518	61,448	−32,263
Banks	4 623	−1,892	−969	−3,416	−6,070	−318	−2,265	−3,676	586
Other sectors	4 624	−4,131	−5,660	−7,666	−6,112	−3,072	−6,674	−1,700	−2,682
Money market instruments	4 630	2,585	−1,096	−1,455	100	−1,881	1,791	−821	−1,015
Monetary authorities	4 631	....	....	....	....	....	....	....	....
General government	4 632	225	1,197	−804	−545	739	1,378	−47	−5
Banks	4 633	4	−36	−77	73	−2	−64	−2,059	177
Other sectors	4 634	2,356	−2,257	−574	572	−2,618	477	1,285	−1,186
Liabilities	4 652	13,123	9,353	32,321	39,310	46,727	20,544	4,850	32,647
Equity securities	4 660	2,040	4,493	11,661	8,197	9,452	−12,136	2,744	1,993
Banks	4 663	−1	36	219	−8	7	−165	109	53
Other sectors	4 664	2,042	4,457	11,442	8,204	9,446	−11,971	2,635	1,940
Debt securities	4 669	11,083	4,860	20,660	31,113	37,274	32,680	2,106	30,653
Bonds and notes	4 670	10,875	3,927	17,559	30,622	25,569	26,354	6,827	29,282
Monetary authorities	4 671	....	....	....	....	....	....	....	....
General government	4 672	1,361	−752	2,016	4,288	3,438	1,798	4,000	4,157
Banks	4 673	6,859	975	7,242	17,678	1,807	4,721	−7,953	−4,195
Other sectors	4 674	2,655	3,705	8,300	8,656	20,325	19,835	10,780	29,320
Money market instruments	4 680	208	932	3,100	491	11,705	6,327	−4,721	1,371
Monetary authorities	4 681	....	....	....	....	....	....	....	....
General government	4 682	−735	−772	31	717	845	1,572	−163	4,592
Banks	4 683	1,332	1,532	3,127	−486	5,812	4,833	−3,293	335
Other sectors	4 684	−389	172	−58	261	5,048	−78	−1,264	−3,557
C. FINANCIAL DERIVATIVES	4 910	−126	144	....	....	....	....	....	....
Monetary authorities	4 911	....	....	....	....	....	....	....	....
General government	4 912	82	−5	....	....	....	....	....	....
Banks	4 913	683	−163	....	....	....	....	....	....
Other sectors	4 914	−891	312	....	....	....	....	....	....
Assets	4 900	35	−636	....	....	....	....	....	....
Monetary authorities	4 901	....	....	....	....	....	....	....	....
General government	4 902	58	−45	....	....	....	....	....	....
Banks	4 903	18	−304	....	....	....	....	....	....
Other sectors	4 904	−41	−288	....	....	....	....	....	....
Liabilities	4 905	−161	780	....	....	....	....	....	....
Monetary authorities	4 906	....	....	....	....	....	....	....	....
General government	4 907	25	40	....	....	....	....	....	....
Banks	4 908	665	141	....	....	....	....	....	....
Other sectors	4 909	−851	600	....	....	....	....	....	....

2011, International Monetary Fund: *Balance of Payments Statistics Yearbook*

Table 2 (Concluded). STANDARD PRESENTATION, 2003–2010

(Millions of U.S. dollars)

	Code	2003	2004	2005	2006	2007	2008	2009	2010
D. OTHER INVESTMENT	4 700 ..	−12,956	8,940	−16,437	48,104	4,307	53,861	−59,245	−21,611
Assets	4 703 ..	−25,212	−16,517	−38,085	−29,056	−43,446	36,560	26,178	−27,202
Trade credits	4 706 ..	−709	683	−3,418	−1,393	−660	−556	−2,570	−9,699
General government	4 707 ..	....	....	....	....	....	....	....	....
of which: Short-term	4 709 ..	....	....	....	....	....	....	....	....
Other sectors	4 710 ..	−709	683	−3,418	−1,393	−660	−556	−2,570	−9,699
of which: Short-term	4 712 ..	−710	671	−3,418	−1,393	−660	−556	−2,570	−9,699
Loans	4 714 ..	−13,861	−19,590	−27,665	−15,165	−26,671	91,922	9,344	−15,584
Monetary authorities	4 715 ..	....	....	....	....	....	....	....	....
of which: Short-term	4 718 ..	....	....	....	....	....	....	....	....
General government	4 719 ..	−12,900	−18,403	−22,745	−10,965	−20,487	96,813	8,630	−10,850
of which: Short-term	4 721 ..	....	....	−22,872	−10,984	−20,387	96,659	9,054	−10,395
Banks	4 722 ..	−467	−402	−3,550	−2,995	−5,138	−2,669	1,967	−4,618
of which: Short-term	4 724 ..	....	....	−436	−1,034	−3,890	2,662	2,507	−2,763
Other sectors	4 725 ..	−494	−784	−1,371	−1,205	−1,046	−2,221	−1,253	−115
of which: Short-term	4 727 ..	−418	−631	102	−123	−164	−211	−10	58
Currency and deposits	4 730 ..	−6,405	242	−7,712	−11,319	−10,951	−24,612	12,639	3,013
Monetary authorities	4 731 ..	....	....	....	....	....	....	....	....
General government	4 732 ..	−1,199	1,586	−778	1,069	−1,461	2,376	2,165	−381
Banks	4 733 ..	−3,824	1,365	−5,380	−12,834	−9,958	−27,877	11,788	5,609
Other sectors	4 734 ..	−1,382	−2,709	−1,555	447	469	888	−1,314	−2,215
Other assets	4 736 ..	−4,236	2,148	710	−1,180	−5,164	−30,195	6,764	−4,933
Monetary authorities	4 737 ..	−127	243	221	−16	6	−639	−308	−343
of which: Short-term	4 739 ..	....	....	....	....	....	....	....	....
General government	4 740 ..	−543	−1,041	2,744	1,167	−435	−4,196	−4,742	1,018
of which: Short-term	4 742 ..	....	....	....	....	....	....	....	....
Banks	4 743 ..	....	....	−920	−1,872	406	−15,414	4,080	3,247
of which: Short-term	4 745 ..	....	....	....	....	....	....	....	....
Other sectors	4 746 ..	−3,566	2,946	−1,334	−459	−5,141	−9,946	7,735	−8,855
of which: Short-term	4 748 ..	....	....	....	....	....	....	....	....
Liabilities	4 753 ..	12,256	25,458	21,648	77,160	47,753	17,301	−85,422	5,590
Trade credits	4 756 ..	−817	−1,350	−550	430	566	−303	−170	8,065
General government	4 757 ..	....	....	....	....	....	....	....	....
of which: Short-term	4 759 ..	....	....	....	....	....	....	....	....
Other sectors	4 760 ..	−817	−1,350	−550	430	566	−303	−170	8,065
of which: Short-term	4 762 ..	−817	−1,350	−550	430	566	−303	−170	8,065
Loans	4 764 ..	8,963	23,976	6,315	58,075	14,605	−45,581	−78,812	8,680
Monetary authorities	4 765 ..	−1,397	265	1,765	5,886	−1,337	−2,637	−12,303	1,150
of which: Use of Fund credit and loans from the Fund	4 766 ..	....	....	....	....	....	....	....	....
of which: Short-term	4 768 ..	....	....	....	....	....	....	....	....
General government	4 769 ..	9,893	20,434	3,135	46,596	7,511	−47,761	−59,923	6,233
of which: Short-term	4 771 ..	9,893	20,434	3,135	46,584	7,511	−47,744	−60,469	6,233
Banks	4 772 ..	65	−331	1,031	3,534	2,851	−315	−3,388	−1,081
of which: Short-term	4 774 ..	....	....	−51	310	1,390	−789	−913	281
Other sectors	4 775 ..	401	3,609	384	2,059	5,580	5,131	−3,199	2,378
of which: Short-term	4 777 ..	....	....	....	....	....	....	....	....
Currency and deposits	4 780 ..	−12	4,715	16,998	16,860	22,156	42,670	6,564	−11,623
Monetary authorities	4 781 ..	−324	117	16	−43	....	8,207	−8,898	−45
General government	4 782 ..	....	....	....	....	....	....	....	....
Banks	4 783 ..	311	4,597	16,982	16,903	22,156	34,463	15,462	−11,578
Other sectors	4 784 ..	....	....	....	....	....	....	....	....
Other liabilities	4 786 ..	4,122	−1,883	−1,115	1,795	10,426	20,515	−13,003	468
Monetary authorities	4 787 ..	....	....	−483	−3	656	−1,106	2,652	−11
of which: Short-term	4 789 ..	....	....	....	....	....	....	....	....
General government	4 790 ..	99	1,872	−3,572	−152	4,709	−510	−2,116	2,253
of which: Short-term	4 792 ..	....	....	....	....	....	....	....	....
Banks	4 793 ..	....	....	1,691	1,081	3,085	11,305	−7,403	−3,254
of which: Short-term	4 795 ..	....	....	....	....	....	....	....	....
Other sectors	4 796 ..	4,023	−3,755	1,249	869	1,975	10,827	−6,135	1,480
of which: Short-term	4 798 ..	....	....	....	....	....	....	....	....
E. RESERVE ASSETS	4 802 ..	−328	−5,227	−4,511	−5,475	−1,045	−4,612	17,068	−4,218
Monetary gold	4 812 ..	....	475	....	....	....	....	....	....
Special drawing rights	4 811 ..	10	−12	28	−130	104	−83	−2,055	9
Reserve position in the Fund	4 810 ..	86	163	505	105	38	−122	−319	21
Foreign exchange	4 803 ..	340	−3,912	−2,047	−3,988	−1,732	−4,603	13,112	−2,332
Other claims	4 813 ..	−763	−1,941	−2,997	−1,463	545	196	6,330	−1,916
NET ERRORS AND OMISSIONS	4 998 ..	−6,303	−5,319	−5,508	−12,807	−30,970	−292	9,946	−4,832

Table 3. INTERNATIONAL INVESTMENT POSITION (End-period stocks), 2003–2010

(Millions of U.S. dollars)

	Code	2003	2004	2005	2006	2007	2008	2009	2010
ASSETS	8 995 C.	**369,891**	**499,303**	**568,534**	**794,790**	**1,012,761**	**916,524**	**1,048,368**	**1,173,614**
Direct investment abroad	8 505 ..	**45,912**	**88,915**	**95,851**	**118,480**	**155,197**	**145,015**	**168,880**	**186,708**
Equity capital and reinvested earnings	8 506 ..	....	....	....	96,671	139,355	128,071	152,906	170,682
Claims on affiliated enterprises	8 507 ..	....	....	....	....	....	....	....	....
Liabilities to affiliated enterprises	8 508 ..	....	....	....	....	....	....	....	....
Other capital	8 530 ..	....	....	....	21,809	15,842	16,945	15,974	16,026
Claims on affiliated enterprises	8 535 ..	....	....	....	....	....	....	....	....
Liabilities to affiliated enterprises	8 540 ..	....	....	....	....	....	....	....	....
Portfolio investment	8 602 ..	**175,584**	**251,967**	**280,637**	**434,333**	**545,818**	**523,337**	**650,083**	**730,606**
Equity securities	8 610 ..	67,157	99,440	125,959	174,890	248,248	203,333	353,414	404,519
Monetary authorities	8 611 ..	....	....	....	....	....	....	....	....
General government	8 612 ..	....	....	....	....	....	....	....	....
Banks	8 613 ..	....	....	....	....	....	....	....	....
Other sectors	8 614 ..	....	....	....	....	....	....	....	....
Debt securities	8 619 ..	108,426	152,527	154,679	259,443	297,570	320,004	296,669	326,087
Bonds and notes	8 620 ..	....	....	....	....	....	....	....	....
Monetary authorities	8 621 ..	....	....	....	....	....	....	....	....
General government	8 622 ..	....	....	....	....	....	....	....	....
Banks	8 623 ..	....	....	....	....	....	....	....	....
Other sectors	8 624 ..	....	....	....	....	....	....	....	....
Money market instruments	8 630 ..	....	....	....	....	....	....	....	....
Monetary authorities	8 631 ..	....	....	....	....	....	....	....	....
General government	8 632 ..	....	....	....	....	....	....	....	....
Banks	8 633 ..	....	....	....	....	....	....	....	....
Other sectors	8 634 ..	....	....	....	....	....	....	....	....
Financial derivatives	8 900 ..	....	....	....	....	....	....	....	....
Monetary authorities	8 901 ..	....	....	....	....	....	....	....	....
General government	8 902 ..	....	....	....	....	....	....	....	....
Banks	8 903 ..	....	....	....	....	....	....	....	....
Other sectors	8 904 ..	....	....	....	....	....	....	....	....
Other investment	8 703 ..	**110,830**	**113,606**	**144,983**	**185,483**	**250,606**	**188,679**	**180,516**	**203,096**
Trade credits	8 706 ..	....	....	....	15,395	18,653	14,924	20,078	27,502
General government	8 707 ..	....	....	....	....	....	....	....	....
of which: Short-term	8 709 ..	....	....	....	....	....	....	....	....
Other sectors	8 710 ..	....	....	....	....	....	....	....	....
of which: Short-term	8 712 ..	....	....	....	....	....	....	....	....
Loans	8 714 ..	....	....	....	120,093	156,307	73,206	68,116	83,140
Monetary authorities	8 715 ..	....	....	....	....	....	....	....	....
of which: Short-term	8 718 ..	....	....	....	....	....	....	....	....
General government	8 719 ..	....	....	....	....	....	....	....	....
of which: Short-term	8 721 ..	....	....	....	....	....	....	....	....
Banks	8 722 ..	....	....	....	....	....	....	....	....
of which: Short-term	8 724 ..	....	....	....	....	....	....	....	....
Other sectors	8 725 ..	....	....	....	....	....	....	....	....
of which: Short-term	8 727 ..	....	....	....	....	....	....	....	....
Currency and deposits	8 730 ..	....	....	....	32,948	49,690	64,921	55,291	52,478
Monetary authorities	8 731 ..	....	....	....	....	....	....	....	....
General government	8 732 ..	....	....	....	....	....	....	....	....
Banks	8 733 ..	....	....	....	....	....	....	....	....
Other sectors	8 734 ..	....	....	....	....	....	....	....	....
Other assets	8 736 ..	....	....	....	17,047	25,956	35,628	37,031	39,975
Monetary authorities	8 737 ..	....	....	....	....	....	....	....	....
of which: Short-term	8 739 ..	....	....	....	....	....	....	....	....
General government	8 740 ..	....	....	....	....	....	....	....	....
of which: Short-term	8 742 ..	....	....	....	....	....	....	....	....
Banks	8 743 ..	....	....	....	....	....	....	....	....
of which: Short-term	8 745 ..	....	....	....	....	....	....	....	....
Other sectors	8 746 ..	....	....	....	....	....	....	....	....
of which: Short-term	8 748 ..	....	....	....	....	....	....	....	....
Reserve assets	8 802 ..	**37,566**	**44,815**	**47,062**	**56,494**	**61,140**	**59,493**	**48,890**	**53,204**
Monetary gold	8 812 ..	....	....	....	....	....	....	....	....
Special drawing rights	8 811 ..	335	361	307	453	368	437	2,509	2,456
Reserve position in the Fund	8 810 ..	995	869	301	207	178	299	632	602
Foreign exchange	8 803 ..	36,236	43,586	46,454	55,834	60,594	58,757	45,749	50,146
Other claims	8 813 ..	....	....	....	....	....	....	....	....

2011, International Monetary Fund: *Balance of Payments Statistics Yearbook*

Table 3 (Concluded). INTERNATIONAL INVESTMENT POSITION (End-period stocks), 2003–2010

(Millions of U.S. dollars)

	Code	2003	2004	2005	2006	2007	2008	2009	2010
LIABILITIES..	8 995 D.	**269,546**	**373,962**	**402,681**	**591,090**	**786,603**	**697,374**	**724,529**	**768,021**
Direct investment in Norway..............................	8 555 ..	**26,106**	**85,028**	**81,474**	**97,577**	**132,441**	**118,518**	**148,322**	**155,291**
Equity capital and reinvested earnings............................	8 556 ..	....	....	....	59,061	84,083	68,976	84,117	80,954
Claims on direct investors............................	8 557 ..	....	....	....	....	....	....	....	....
Liabilities to direct investors............................	8 558 ..	....	....	....	....	....	....	....	....
Other capital............................	8 580 ..	....	....	....	38,516	48,358	49,542	64,206	74,338
Claims on direct investors............................	8 585 ..	....	....	....	....	....	....	....	....
Liabilities to direct investors............................	8 590 ..	....	....	....	....	....	....	....	....
Portfolio investment............................	8 652 ..	**103,017**	**131,047**	**158,210**	**238,509**	**323,426**	**246,316**	**299,344**	**335,304**
Equity securities............................	8 660 ..	21,498	40,549	58,822	100,857	132,994	40,755	76,560	86,376
Banks............................	8 663 ..	....	....	....	....	....	....	....	....
Other sectors............................	8 664 ..	....	....	....	....	....	....	....	....
Debt securities............................	8 669 ..	81,519	90,497	99,388	137,652	190,431	205,562	222,785	248,928
Bonds and notes............................	8 670 ..	....	....	....	....	....	....	....	....
Monetary authorities............................	8 671 ..	....	....	....	....	....	....	....	....
General government............................	8 672 ..	....	....	....	....	....	....	....	....
Banks............................	8 673 ..	....	....	....	....	....	....	....	....
Other sectors............................	8 674 ..	....	....	....	....	....	....	....	....
Money market instruments............................	8 680 ..	....	....	....	....	....	....	....	....
Monetary authorities............................	8 681 ..	....	....	....	....	....	....	....	....
General government............................	8 682 ..	....	....	....	....	....	....	....	....
Banks............................	8 683 ..	....	....	....	....	....	....	....	....
Other sectors............................	8 684 ..	....	....	....	....	....	....	....	....
Financial derivatives............................	8 905 ..	....	....	....	....	....	....	....	....
Monetary authorities............................	8 906 ..	....	....	....	....	....	....	....	....
General government............................	8 907 ..	....	....	....	....	....	....	....	....
Banks............................	8 908 ..	....	....	....	....	....	....	....	....
Other sectors............................	8 909 ..	....	....	....	....	....	....	....	....
Other investment............................	8 753 ..	**140,424**	**157,887**	**162,997**	**255,003**	**330,736**	**332,540**	**276,862**	**277,425**
Trade credits............................	8 756 ..	....	....	....	6,440	8,414	5,750	4,697	12,480
General government............................	8 757 ..	....	....	....	....	....	....	....	....
of which: Short-term............................	8 759 ..	....	....	....	....	....	....	....	....
Other sectors............................	8 760 ..	....	....	....	....	....	....	....	....
of which: Short-term............................	8 762 ..	....	....	....	....	....	....	....	....
Loans............................	8 764 ..	....	....	....	167,020	193,448	160,880	95,944	103,683
Monetary authorities............................	8 765 ..	....	....	....	....	....	....	....	....
of which: Use of Fund credit and loans from the Fund....	8 766 ..	....	....	....	....	....	....	....	....
of which: Short-term............................	8 768 ..	....	....	....	....	....	....	....	....
General government............................	8 769 ..	....	....	....	....	....	....	....	....
of which: Short-term............................	8 771 ..	....	....	....	....	....	....	....	....
Banks............................	8 772 ..	....	....	....	....	....	....	....	....
of which: Short-term............................	8 774 ..	....	....	....	....	....	....	....	....
Other sectors............................	8 775 ..	....	....	....	....	....	....	....	....
of which: Short-term............................	8 777 ..	....	....	....	....	....	....	....	....
Currency and deposits............................	8 780 ..	....	....	....	66,561	99,424	123,526	141,938	128,320
Monetary authorities............................	8 781 ..	....	....	....	....	....	....	....	....
General government............................	8 782 ..	....	....	....	....	....	....	....	....
Banks............................	8 783 ..	....	....	....	....	....	....	....	....
Other sectors............................	8 784 ..	....	....	....	....	....	....	....	....
Other liabilities............................	8 786 ..	....	....	....	14,982	29,450	42,384	31,832	30,535
Monetary authorities............................	8 787 ..	....	....	....	....	....	....	....	....
of which: Short-term............................	8 789 ..	....	....	....	....	....	....	....	....
General government............................	8 790 ..	....	....	....	....	....	....	....	....
of which: Short-term............................	8 792 ..	....	....	....	....	....	....	....	....
Banks............................	8 793 ..	....	....	....	....	....	....	....	....
of which: Short-term............................	8 795 ..	....	....	....	....	....	....	....	....
Other sectors............................	8 796 ..	....	....	....	....	....	....	....	....
of which: Short-term............................	8 798 ..	....	....	....	....	....	....	....	....
NET INTERNATIONAL INVESTMENT POSITION........	8 995 ..	**100,345**	**125,341**	**165,853**	**203,700**	**226,158**	**219,150**	**323,839**	**405,593**
Conversion rates: Norwegian kroner per U.S. dollar (end of period)............................	0 102 ..	**6.6800**	**6.0400**	**6.7700**	**6.2600**	**5.4100**	**7.0000**	**5.7800**	**5.8600**

Table 1. ANALYTIC PRESENTATION, 2003–2010

(Millions of U.S. dollars)

	Code	2003	2004	2005	2006	2007	2008	2009	2010
A. Current Account[1]................	4 993 Z.	**1,454**	**877**	**5,178**	**5,664**	**2,462**	**5,016**	**−603**	**5,096**
Goods: exports f.o.b................	2 100 ..	11,670	13,381	18,692	21,586	24,692	37,719	27,651	36,601
Goods: imports f.o.b................	3 100 ..	−6,086	−7,873	−8,029	−9,881	−14,343	−20,707	−16,052	−17,874
Balance on Goods................	4 100 ..	*5,584*	*5,508*	*10,663*	*11,705*	*10,349*	*17,012*	*11,600*	*18,726*
Services: credit................	2 200 ..	655	736	939	1,311	1,683	1,823	1,620	1,761
Services: debit................	3 200 ..	−2,573	−3,152	−3,145	−3,896	−5,095	−5,878	−5,488	−6,525
Balance on Goods and Services................	4 991 ..	*3,666*	*3,092*	*8,457*	*9,120*	*6,936*	*12,957*	*7,732*	*13,962*
Income: credit................	2 300 ..	317	762	765	1,742	2,162	1,097	652	626
Income: debit................	3 300 ..	−857	−1,152	−1,787	−2,409	−2,966	−3,857	−3,671	−3,788
Balance on Goods, Services, and Income................	4 992 ..	*3,126*	*2,702*	*7,435*	*8,452*	*6,132*	*10,197*	*4,713*	*10,800*
Current transfers: credit................	2 379 Z.	....	....	....	....	....	....	....	....
Current transfers: debit................	3 379 ..	−1,672	−1,826	−2,257	−2,788	−3,670	−5,181	−5,316	−5,704
B. Capital Account[1]................	4 994 Z.	**10**	**21**	**−16**	**−96**	**827**	**−52**	**55**	**−65**
Capital account: credit................	2 994 Z.	10	21	....	....	861	....	55	....
Capital account: debit................	3 994 ..	....	....	−16	−96	−34	−52	....	−65
Total, Groups A Plus B................	4 981 ..	*1,464*	*897*	*5,162*	*5,568*	*3,289*	*4,964*	*−548*	*5,031*
C. Financial Account[1]................	4 995 W.	**−261**	**360**	**−1,501**	**−3,352**	**2,753**	**−3,763**	**2,677**	**−2,372**
Direct investment abroad................	4 505 ..	−88	−42	−234	−275	37	−584	−73	−390
Direct investment in Oman................	4 555 Z.	25	111	1,538	1,596	3,332	2,952	1,509	2,333
Portfolio investment assets................	4 602 ..	−242	−174	−437	−1,020	−123	−150	−156	250
Equity securities................	4 610 ..	−242	−174	−437	−1,020	−123	−150	−156	250
Debt securities................	4 619 ..	....	....	....	....	....	....	....	....
Portfolio investment liabilities................	4 652 Z.	12	162	565	1,181	1,605	−1,523	246	703
Equity securities................	4 660 ..	51	32	573	1,181	1,629	−1,460	333	703
Debt securities................	4 669 Z.	−39	130	−8	....	−25	−63	−87	....
Financial derivatives................	4 910 ..	....	....	....	....	....	....	....	....
Financial derivatives assets................	4 900 ..	....	....	....	....	....	....	....	....
Financial derivatives liabilities................	4 905 ..	....	....	....	....	....	....	....	....
Other investment assets................	4 703 ..	−136	−977	−3,226	−6,938	−4,960	−7,660	2,165	−3,765
Monetary authorities................	4 701 ..	....	....	....	....	....	....	....	....
General government................	4 704 ..	....	....	....	....	....	....	....	....
Banks................	4 705 ..	−44	−593	−422	−1,221	−492	−681	518	530
Other sectors................	4 728 ..	−9	−39	−146	−1,041	99	−73	704	−4
Other investment liabilities................	4 753 W.	169	1,280	292	2,104	2,861	3,202	−1,015	−1,502
Monetary authorities................	4 753 WA	....	....	....	....	....	....	270	....
General government................	4 753 ZB	−421	195	−440	508	8	114	364	139
Banks................	4 753 ZC	−226	29	−273	1,028	1,657	2,086	−655	−1,310
Other sectors................	4 753 ZD	760	989	929	389	909	764	−707	431
Total, Groups A Through C................	4 983 ..	*1,204*	*1,258*	*3,660*	*2,217*	*6,042*	*1,202*	*2,129*	*2,660*
D. Net Errors and Omissions................	4 998 ..	**−565**	**−396**	**−851**	**−11**	**209**	**625**	**−1,053**	**−1,161**
Total, Groups A Through D................	4 984 ..	*638*	*861*	*2,809*	*2,206*	*6,250*	*1,827*	*1,076*	*1,499*
E. Reserves and Related Items................	4 802 A.	**−638**	**−861**	**−2,809**	**−2,206**	**−6,250**	**−1,827**	**−1,076**	**−1,499**
Reserve assets................	4 802 ..	−638	−861	−2,809	−2,206	−6,250	−1,827	−1,076	−1,499
Use of Fund credit and loans................	4 766 ..	....	....	....	....	....	....	....	....
Exceptional financing................	4 920 ..	....	....	....	....	....	....	....	....
Conversion rates: rial Omani per U.S. dollar........	0 101 ..	**.3845**	**.3845**	**.3845**	**.3845**	**.3845**	**.3845**	**.3845**	**.3845**

[1] Excludes components that have been classified in the categories of Group E.

2011, International Monetary Fund: *Balance of Payments Statistics Yearbook*

Table 2. STANDARD PRESENTATION, 2003–2010
(Millions of U.S. dollars)

	Code	2003	2004	2005	2006	2007	2008	2009	2010
CURRENT ACCOUNT	4 993	**1,454**	**877**	**5,178**	**5,664**	**2,462**	**5,016**	**−603**	**5,096**
A. GOODS	4 100	**5,584**	**5,508**	**10,663**	**11,705**	**10,349**	**17,012**	**11,600**	**18,726**
Credit	2 100	**11,670**	**13,381**	**18,692**	**21,586**	**24,692**	**37,719**	**27,651**	**36,601**
General merchandise: exports f.o.b.	2 110	11,670	13,381	18,692	21,586	24,692	37,719	27,651	36,601
Goods for processing: exports f.o.b.	2 150	....	....	....	....	....	....	....	....
Repairs on goods	2 160	....	....	....	....	....	....	....	....
Goods procured in ports by carriers	2 170	....	....	....	....	....	....	....	....
Nonmonetary gold	2 180	....	....	....	....	....	....	....	....
Debit	3 100	**−6,086**	**−7,873**	**−8,029**	**−9,881**	**−14,343**	**−20,707**	**−16,052**	**−17,874**
General merchandise: imports f.o.b.	3 110	−6,086	−7,873	−8,029	−9,881	−14,343	−20,707	−16,052	−17,874
Goods for processing: imports f.o.b.	3 150	....	....	....	....	....	....	....	....
Repairs on goods	3 160	....	....	....	....	....	....	....	....
Goods procured in ports by carriers	3 170	....	....	....	....	....	....	....	....
Nonmonetary gold	3 180	....	....	....	....	....	....	....	....
B. SERVICES	4 200	**−1,918**	**−2,416**	**−2,207**	**−2,586**	**−3,412**	**−4,055**	**−3,867**	**−4,765**
Total credit	2 200	*655*	*736*	*939*	*1,311*	*1,683*	*1,823*	*1,620*	*1,761*
Total debit	3 200	*−2,573*	*−3,152*	*−3,145*	*−3,896*	*−5,095*	*−5,878*	*−5,488*	*−6,525*
Transportation services, credit	2 205	**239**	**289**	**299**	**317**	**388**	**471**	**562**	**635**
Passenger	2 850	*161*	*190*	*198*	*205*	*257*	*309*	*403*	*476*
Freight	2 851	*78*	*99*	*101*	*112*	*130*	*161*	*159*	*159*
Other	2 852	....	....	....	....	....	....	....	....
Sea transport, passenger	2 207	....	....	....	....	....	....	....	....
Sea transport, freight	2 208	78	99	101	112	130	161	159	159
Sea transport, other	2 209	....	....	....	....	....	....	....	....
Air transport, passenger	2 211	161	190	198	205	257	309	403	476
Air transport, freight	2 212	....	....	....	....	....	....	....	....
Air transport, other	2 213	....	....	....	....	....	....	....	....
Other transport, passenger	2 215	....	....	....	....	....	....	....	....
Other transport, freight	2 216	....	....	....	....	....	....	....	....
Other transport, other	2 217	....	....	....	....	....	....	....	....
Transportation services, debit	3 205	**−820**	**−1,072**	**−1,051**	**−1,233**	**−1,722**	**−2,538**	**−2,096**	**−2,666**
Passenger	3 850	*−174*	*−179*	*−195*	*−182*	*−200*	*−341*	*−393*	*−767*
Freight	3 851	*−646*	*−892*	*−856*	*−1,051*	*−1,521*	*−2,198*	*−1,704*	*−1,899*
Other	3 852	....	....	....	....	....	....	....	....
Sea transport, passenger	3 207	....	....	....	....	....	....	....	....
Sea transport, freight	3 208	−646	−892	−856	−1,051	−1,521	−2,198	−1,704	−1,899
Sea transport, other	3 209	....	....	....	....	....	....	....	....
Air transport, passenger	3 211	−174	−179	−195	−182	−200	−341	−393	−767
Air transport, freight	3 212	....	....	....	....	....	....	....	....
Air transport, other	3 213	....	....	....	....	....	....	....	....
Other transport, passenger	3 215	....	....	....	....	....	....	....	....
Other transport, freight	3 216	....	....	....	....	....	....	....	....
Other transport, other	3 217	....	....	....	....	....	....	....	....
Travel, credit	2 236	**385**	**411**	**429**	**544**	**648**	**796**	**689**	**775**
Business travel	2 237	116	125	130	166	198	242	211	237
Personal travel	2 240	269	286	300	377	450	554	479	538
Travel, debit	3 236	**−630**	**−644**	**−668**	**−712**	**−752**	**−856**	**−902**	**−1,001**
Business travel	3 237	−83	−83	−94	−107	−120	−134	−151	−169
Personal travel	3 240	−546	−560	−575	−606	−631	−721	−752	−832
Other services, credit	2 200 BA	**31**	**36**	**211**	**450**	**648**	**557**	**369**	**351**
Communications	2 245	18	21	36	52	75	99	112	78
Construction	2 249	....	....	....	....	....	....	....	....
Insurance	2 253	3	3	5	5	8	16	23	26
Financial	2 260	....	....	....	....	....	....	....	....
Computer and information	2 262	....	....	....	....	....	....	....	....
Royalties and licence fees	2 266	....	....	....	....	....	....	....	....
Other business services	2 268	10	13	169	393	564	442	234	247
Personal, cultural, and recreational	2 287	....	....	....	....	....	....	....	....
Government, n.i.e.	2 291	....	....	....	....	....	....	....	....
Other services, debit	3 200 BA	**−1,124**	**−1,437**	**−1,426**	**−1,951**	**−2,622**	**−2,484**	**−2,489**	**−2,858**
Communications	3 245	−29	−36	−42	−44	−47	−55	−44	−36
Construction	3 249	....	....	....	....	....	....	....	....
Insurance	3 253	−221	−238	−285	−334	−562	−590	−624	−715
Financial	3 260	....	....	....	....	....	....	....	....
Computer and information	3 262	....	....	....	....	....	....	....	....
Royalties and licence fees	3 266	....	....	....	....	....	....	....	....
Other business services	3 268	−874	−1,163	−1,100	−1,573	−2,013	−1,839	−1,821	−2,107
Personal, cultural, and recreational	3 287	....	....	....	....	....	....	....	....
Government, n.i.e.	3 291	....	....	....	....	....	....	....	....

Table 2 (Continued). STANDARD PRESENTATION, 2003–2010

(Millions of U.S. dollars)

	Code	2003	2004	2005	2006	2007	2008	2009	2010
C. INCOME	4 300	**−540**	**−390**	**−1,022**	**−667**	**−804**	**−2,760**	**−3,019**	**−3,162**
Total credit	2 300	*317*	*762*	*765*	*1,742*	*2,162*	*1,097*	*652*	*626*
Total debit	3 300	*−857*	*−1,152*	*−1,787*	*−2,409*	*−2,966*	*−3,857*	*−3,671*	*−3,788*
Compensation of employees, credit	2 310	**39**	**39**	**39**	**39**	**39**	**39**	**39**	**39**
Compensation of employees, debit	3 310	....	....	....	....	....	....	....	....
Investment income, credit	2 320	**278**	**723**	**726**	**1,703**	**2,122**	**1,058**	**613**	**587**
Direct investment income	2 330	39	39	51	118	128	145	58	58
Dividends and distributed branch profits	2 332	....	....	....	....	....	....	....	....
Reinvested earnings and undistributed branch profits	2 333	....	....	....	....	....	....	....	....
Income on debt (interest)	2 334	....	....	....	....	....	....	....	....
Portfolio investment income	2 339	....	....	....	....	....	....	....	....
Income on equity	2 340	....	....	....	....	....	....	....	....
Income on bonds and notes	2 350	....	....	....	....	....	....	....	....
Income on money market instruments	2 360	....	....	....	....	....	....	....	....
Other investment income	2 370	239	684	675	1,585	1,995	912	555	530
Investment income, debit	3 320	**−857**	**−1,152**	**−1,787**	**−2,409**	**−2,966**	**−3,857**	**−3,671**	**−3,788**
Direct investment income	3 330	−717	−925	−1,529	−2,019	−2,346	−3,345	−3,096	−3,186
Dividends and distributed branch profits	3 332	....	....	....	....	....	....	....	....
Reinvested earnings and undistributed branch profits	3 333	....	....	....	....	....	....	....	....
Income on debt (interest)	3 334	....	....	....	....	....	....	....	....
Portfolio investment income	3 339	....	....	....	....	....	....	....	....
Income on equity	3 340	....	....	....	....	....	....	....	....
Income on bonds and notes	3 350	....	....	....	....	....	....	....	....
Income on money market instruments	3 360	....	....	....	....	....	....	....	....
Other investment income	3 370	−140	−227	−257	−391	−620	−512	−575	−602
D. CURRENT TRANSFERS	4 379	**−1,672**	**−1,826**	**−2,257**	**−2,788**	**−3,670**	**−5,181**	**−5,316**	**−5,704**
Credit	2 379	....	....	....	....	....	....	....	....
General government	2 380	....	....	....	....	....	....	....	....
Other sectors	2 390	....	....	....	....	....	....	....	....
Workers' remittances	2 391	....	....	....	....	....	....	....	....
Other current transfers	2 392	....	....	....	....	....	....	....	....
Debit	3 379	**−1,672**	**−1,826**	**−2,257**	**−2,788**	**−3,670**	**−5,181**	**−5,316**	**−5,704**
General government	3 380	....	....	....	....	....	....	....	....
Other sectors	3 390	−1,672	−1,826	−2,257	−2,788	−3,670	−5,181	−5,316	−5,704
Workers' remittances	3 391	−1,672	−1,826	−2,257	−2,788	−3,670	−5,181	−5,316	−5,704
Other current transfers	3 392	....	....	....	....	....	....	....	....
CAPITAL AND FINANCIAL ACCOUNT	4 996	**−888**	**−480**	**−4,326**	**−5,654**	**−2,671**	**−5,642**	**1,656**	**−3,936**
CAPITAL ACCOUNT	4 994	**10**	**21**	**−16**	**−96**	**827**	**−52**	**55**	**−65**
Total credit	2 994	*10*	*21*	....	....	*861*	....	*55*	....
Total debit	3 994	....	....	*−16*	*−96*	*−34*	*−52*	....	*−65*
Capital transfers, credit	2 400	**10**	**21**	....	....	**861**	....	**55**	....
General government	2 401	10	21	....	....	861	....	55	....
Debt forgiveness	2 402	....	....	....	....	....	....	....	....
Other capital transfers	2 410	10	21	....	....	861	....	55	....
Other sectors	2 430	....	....	....	....	....	....	....	....
Migrants' transfers	2 431	....	....	....	....	....	....	....	....
Debt forgiveness	2 432	....	....	....	....	....	....	....	....
Other capital transfers	2 440	....	....	....	....	....	....	....	....
Capital transfers, debit	3 400	....	....	**−16**	**−96**	**−34**	**−52**	....	**−65**
General government	3 401	....	....	−16	−96	−34	−52	....	−65
Debt forgiveness	3 402	....	....	....	....	....	....	....	....
Other capital transfers	3 410	....	....	−16	−96	−34	−52	....	−65
Other sectors	3 430	....	....	....	....	....	....	....	....
Migrants' transfers	3 431	....	....	....	....	....	....	....	....
Debt forgiveness	3 432	....	....	....	....	....	....	....	....
Other capital transfers	3 440	....	....	....	....	....	....	....	....
Nonproduced nonfinancial assets, credit	2 480	....	....	....	....	....	....	....	....
Nonproduced nonfinancial assets, debit	3 480	....	....	....	....	....	....	....	....

Table 2 (Continued). STANDARD PRESENTATION, 2003–2010

(Millions of U.S. dollars)

	Code	2003	2004	2005	2006	2007	2008	2009	2010
FINANCIAL ACCOUNT	4 995 ..	**−899**	**−501**	**−4,310**	**−5,557**	**−3,498**	**−5,590**	**1,601**	**−3,871**
A. DIRECT INVESTMENT	4 500 ..	**−63**	**69**	**1,305**	**1,321**	**3,369**	**2,367**	**1,436**	**1,943**
Direct investment abroad	4 505 ..	**−88**	**−42**	**−234**	**−275**	**37**	**−584**	**−73**	**−390**
Equity capital	4 510 ..	−88	−42	−234	−275	37	−584	−73	−390
Claims on affiliated enterprises	4 515 ..	−88	−42	−234	−275	37	−584	−73	−390
Liabilities to affiliated enterprises	4 520 ..	....	....	....	....	....	....	....	....
Reinvested earnings	4 525 ..	....	....	....	....	....	....	....	....
Other capital	4 530 ..	....	....	....	....	....	....	....	....
Claims on affiliated enterprises	4 535 ..	....	....	....	....	....	....	....	....
Liabilities to affiliated enterprises	4 540 ..	....	....	....	....	....	....	....	....
Direct investment in Oman	4 555 ..	**25**	**111**	**1,538**	**1,596**	**3,332**	**2,952**	**1,509**	**2,333**
Equity capital	4 560 ..	25	111	1,538	1,596	3,332	2,952	1,509	2,333
Claims on direct investors	4 565 ..	....	....	....	....	....	....	....	....
Liabilities to direct investors	4 570 ..	25	111	1,538	1,596	3,332	2,952	1,509	2,333
Reinvested earnings	4 575 ..	....	....	....	....	....	....	....	....
Other capital	4 580 ..	....	....	....	....	....	....	....	....
Claims on direct investors	4 585 ..	....	....	....	....	....	....	....	....
Liabilities to direct investors	4 590 ..	....	....	....	....	....	....	....	....
B. PORTFOLIO INVESTMENT	4 600 ..	**−229**	**−12**	**128**	**161**	**1,482**	**−1,673**	**91**	**953**
Assets	4 602 ..	**−242**	**−174**	**−437**	**−1,020**	**−123**	**−150**	**−156**	**250**
Equity securities	4 610 ..	−242	−174	−437	−1,020	−123	−150	−156	250
Monetary authorities	4 611 ..	....	....	....	....	....	....	....	....
General government	4 612 ..	....	....	....	....	....	....	....	....
Banks	4 613 ..	....	....	....	....	....	....	....	....
Other sectors	4 614 ..	....	....	....	....	....	....	....	....
Debt securities	4 619 ..	....	....	....	....	....	....	....	....
Bonds and notes	4 620 ..	....	....	....	....	....	....	....	....
Monetary authorities	4 621 ..	....	....	....	....	....	....	....	....
General government	4 622 ..	....	....	....	....	....	....	....	....
Banks	4 623 ..	....	....	....	....	....	....	....	....
Other sectors	4 624 ..	....	....	....	....	....	....	....	....
Money market instruments	4 630 ..	....	....	....	....	....	....	....	....
Monetary authorities	4 631 ..	....	....	....	....	....	....	....	....
General government	4 632 ..	....	....	....	....	....	....	....	....
Banks	4 633 ..	....	....	....	....	....	....	....	....
Other sectors	4 634 ..	....	....	....	....	....	....	....	....
Liabilities	4 652 ..	**12**	**162**	**565**	**1,181**	**1,605**	**−1,523**	**246**	**703**
Equity securities	4 660 ..	51	32	573	1,181	1,629	−1,460	333	703
Banks	4 663 ..	....	....	139	42	244	12	−33	82
Other sectors	4 664 ..	51	32	435	1,139	1,386	−1,472	365	621
Debt securities	4 669 ..	−39	130	−8	....	−25	−63	−87	....
Bonds and notes	4 670 ..	−39	130	−8	....	−25	−63	−87	....
Monetary authorities	4 671 ..	....	....	....	....	....	....	....	....
General government	4 672 ..	−39	130	−8	....	−25	−63	−87	....
Banks	4 673 ..	....	....	....	....	....	....	....	....
Other sectors	4 674 ..	....	....	....	....	....	....	....	....
Money market instruments	4 680 ..	....	....	....	....	....	....	....	....
Monetary authorities	4 681 ..	....	....	....	....	....	....	....	....
General government	4 682 ..	....	....	....	....	....	....	....	....
Banks	4 683 ..	....	....	....	....	....	....	....	....
Other sectors	4 684 ..	....	....	....	....	....	....	....	....
C. FINANCIAL DERIVATIVES	4 910 ..	....	....	....	....	....	....	....	....
Monetary authorities	4 911 ..	....	....	....	....	....	....	....	....
General government	4 912 ..	....	....	....	....	....	....	....	....
Banks	4 913 ..	....	....	....	....	....	....	....	....
Other sectors	4 914 ..	....	....	....	....	....	....	....	....
Assets	4 900 ..	....	....	....	....	....	....	....	....
Monetary authorities	4 901 ..	....	....	....	....	....	....	....	....
General government	4 902 ..	....	....	....	....	....	....	....	....
Banks	4 903 ..	....	....	....	....	....	....	....	....
Other sectors	4 904 ..	....	....	....	....	....	....	....	....
Liabilities	4 905 ..	....	....	....	....	....	....	....	....
Monetary authorities	4 906 ..	....	....	....	....	....	....	....	....
General government	4 907 ..	....	....	....	....	....	....	....	....
Banks	4 908 ..	....	....	....	....	....	....	....	....
Other sectors	4 909 ..	....	....	....	....	....	....	....	....

Table 2 (Concluded). STANDARD PRESENTATION, 2003–2010

(Millions of U.S. dollars)

	Code	2003	2004	2005	2006	2007	2008	2009	2010
D. OTHER INVESTMENT	4 700	32	303	−2,934	−4,834	−2,099	−4,457	1,151	−5,267
Assets	4 703	−136	−977	−3,226	−6,938	−4,960	−7,660	2,165	−3,765
Trade credits	4 706	−3	1	−48	−73	−24	−51	60	−47
General government	4 707	....	....	....	....	....	....	....	....
of which: Short-term	4 709	....	....	....	....	....	....	....	....
Other sectors	4 710	−3	1	−48	−73	−24	−51	60	−47
of which: Short-term	4 712	−3	1	−48	−73	−24	−51	60	−47
Loans	4 714	....	....	....	....	....	....	....	....
Monetary authorities	4 715	....	....	....	....	....	....	....	....
of which: Short-term	4 718	....	....	....	....	....	....	....	....
General government	4 719	....	....	....	....	....	....	....	....
of which: Short-term	4 721	....	....	....	....	....	....	....	....
Banks	4 722	....	....	....	....	....	....	....	....
of which: Short-term	4 724	....	....	....	....	....	....	....	....
Other sectors	4 725	....	....	....	....	....	....	....	....
of which: Short-term	4 727	....	....	....	....	....	....	....	....
Currency and deposits	4 730	−51	−633	−520	−2,189	−369	−703	1,163	573
Monetary authorities	4 731	....	....	....	....	....	....	....	....
General government	4 732	....	....	....	....	....	....	....	....
Banks	4 733	−44	−593	−422	−1,221	−492	−681	518	530
Other sectors	4 734	−7	−40	−97	−968	123	−22	644	43
Other assets	4 736	−83	−345	−2,658	−4,676	−4,566	−6,906	943	−4,291
Monetary authorities	4 737	....	....	....	....	....	....	....	....
of which: Short-term	4 739	....	....	....	....	....	....	....	....
General government	4 740	....	....	....	....	....	....	....	....
of which: Short-term	4 742	....	....	....	....	....	....	....	....
Banks	4 743	....	....	....	....	....	....	....	....
of which: Short-term	4 745	....	....	....	....	....	....	....	....
Other sectors	4 746	....	....	....	....	....	....	....	....
of which: Short-term	4 748	....	....	....	....	....	....	....	....
Liabilities	4 753	169	1,280	292	2,104	2,861	3,202	−1,015	−1,502
Trade credits	4 756	56	67	75	178	287	239	−286	−762
General government	4 757	....	....	....	....	....	....	....	....
of which: Short-term	4 759	....	....	....	....	....	....	....	....
Other sectors	4 760	....	....	....	....	....	....	....	....
of which: Short-term	4 762	....	....	....	....	....	....	....	....
Loans	4 764	−135	583	−59	804	837	672	−121	518
Monetary authorities	4 765	....	....	....	....	....	....	....	....
of which: Use of Fund credit and loans from the Fund	4 766	....	....	....	....	....	....	....	....
of which: Short-term	4 768	....	....	....	....	....	....	....	....
General government	4 769	−421	195	−440	508	8	114	364	139
of which: Short-term	4 771	....	....	....	....	....	....	....	....
Banks	4 772	....	....	....	....	....	....	....	....
of which: Short-term	4 774	....	....	....	....	....	....	....	....
Other sectors	4 775	286	388	380	295	829	558	−485	379
of which: Short-term	4 777	....	....	....	....	....	....	....	....
Currency and deposits	4 780	−226	29	−273	1,028	1,657	2,086	−655	−1,310
Monetary authorities	4 781	....	....	....	....	....	....	....	....
General government	4 782	....	....	....	....	....	....	....	....
Banks	4 783	−226	29	−273	1,028	1,657	2,086	−655	−1,310
Other sectors	4 784	....	....	....	....	....	....	....	....
Other liabilities	4 786	473	601	549	94	80	205	48	52
Monetary authorities	4 787	....	....	....	....	....	....	270	....
of which: Short-term	4 789	....	....	....	....	....	....	....	....
General government	4 790	....	....	....	....	....	....	....	....
of which: Short-term	4 792	....	....	....	....	....	....	....	....
Banks	4 793	....	....	....	....	....	....	....	....
of which: Short-term	4 795	....	....	....	....	....	....	....	....
Other sectors	4 796	473	601	549	94	80	205	−222	52
of which: Short-term	4 798	....	....	....	....	....	....	....	....
E. RESERVE ASSETS	4 802	−638	−861	−2,809	−2,206	−6,250	−1,827	−1,076	−1,499
Monetary gold	4 812	....	....	....	....	....	....	....	....
Special drawing rights	4 811	−2	−2	−2	−1	−1	−2	−270	....
Reserve position in the Fund	4 810	−5	20	57	9	8	−2	−34	−12
Foreign exchange	4 803	−632	−880	−2,864	−2,214	−6,258	−1,823	−772	−1,486
Other claims	4 813	....	....	....	....	....	....	....	....
NET ERRORS AND OMISSIONS	4 998	−565	−396	−851	−11	209	625	−1,053	−1,161

Table 1. ANALYTIC PRESENTATION, 2003–2010

(Millions of U.S. dollars)

	Code	2003	2004	2005	2006	2007	2008	2009	2010
A. Current Account[1]............................	4 993 Z.	**3,573**	**−817**	**−3,606**	**−6,750**	**−8,286**	**−15,655**	**−3,993**	**−1,490**
Goods: exports f.o.b............	2 100 ..	11,869	13,297	15,433	17,049	18,188	21,214	18,347	21,463
Goods: imports f.o.b............	3 100 ..	−11,978	−16,693	−21,773	−26,696	−28,775	−38,216	−28,617	−32,879
Balance on Goods.............	4 100 ..	*−109*	*−3,396*	*−6,340*	*−9,647*	*−10,587*	*−17,003*	*−10,270*	*−11,416*
Services: credit................	2 200 ..	2,968	2,749	3,678	3,506	3,767	4,263	3,983	6,410
Services: debit................	3 200 ..	−3,294	−5,333	−7,508	−8,418	−8,811	−9,717	−6,551	−7,088
Balance on Goods and Services.........	4 991 ..	*−435*	*−5,980*	*−10,170*	*−14,559*	*−15,631*	*−22,457*	*−12,838*	*−12,094*
Income: credit................	2 300 ..	180	221	657	864	1,357	1,285	607	681
Income: debit.................	3 300 ..	−2,404	−2,584	−3,172	−3,995	−5,097	−5,619	−4,221	−3,859
Balance on Goods, Services, and Income.........	4 992 ..	*−2,659*	*−8,343*	*−12,685*	*−17,691*	*−19,371*	*−26,791*	*−16,452*	*−15,272*
Current transfers: credit........	2 379 Z.	6,300	7,666	9,169	11,030	11,216	11,252	12,552	13,869
Current transfers: debit.........	3 379 ..	−68	−140	−90	−89	−131	−116	−93	−87
B. Capital Account[1]........................	4 994 Z.	**1,138**	**591**	**202**	**345**	**176**	**146**	**484**	**132**
Capital account: credit...........	2 994 Z.	1,140	596	214	351	182	151	490	132
Capital account: debit...........	3 994 ..	−2	−5	−12	−6	−6	−5	−6	....
Total, Groups A Plus B.........	4 981 ..	*4,711*	*−226*	*−3,404*	*−6,405*	*−8,110*	*−15,509*	*−3,509*	*−1,358*
C. Financial Account[1].......................	4 995 W.	**−1,751**	**−1,810**	**4,079**	**7,436**	**10,656**	**6,671**	**4,469**	**2,580**
Direct investment abroad...........	4 505 ..	−19	−56	−44	−109	−98	−49	−71	−46
Direct investment in Pakistan.......	4 555 Z.	534	1,118	2,201	4,273	5,590	5,438	2,338	2,016
Portfolio investment assets.........	4 602 ..	−2	9	19	−4	5	−26	−26	6
Equity securities.............	4 610 ..	−2	9	19	−4	5	−26	−26	6
Debt securities..............	4 619 ..	....	....	....	....	....	....	....	....
Portfolio investment liabilities......	4 652 Z.	−119	392	906	1,973	2,081	−243	−582	−114
Equity securities.............	4 660 ..	−26	49	451	1,152	1,276	−270	−37	524
Debt securities..............	4 669 Z.	−93	343	455	821	805	27	−545	−638
Financial derivatives.............	4 910 ..	....	....	....	....	....	....	....	....
Financial derivatives assets........	4 900 ..	....	....	....	....	....	....	....	....
Financial derivatives liabilities.....	4 905 ..	....	....	....	....	....	....	....	....
Other investment assets...........	4 703 ..	−542	−1,339	126	−242	284	−494	−3	−295
Monetary authorities..........	4 701 ..	....	....	....	....	....	....	....	....
General government...........	4 704 ..	19	−1	1	−1	6	1	2	1
Banks..................	4 705 ..	−247	−984	471	−41	375	−278	268	−50
Other sectors..............	4 728 ..	−314	−354	−346	−200	−97	−217	−273	−246
Other investment liabilities........	4 753 W.	−1,603	−1,934	871	1,545	2,794	2,045	2,813	1,013
Monetary authorities..........	4 753 WA	....	−15	8	2	−10	500	1,272	12
General government...........	4 753 ZB	−1,571	−1,335	661	921	1,767	1,179	1,569	508
Banks..................	4 753 ZC	29	22	68	−3	186	278	−182	−67
Other sectors..............	4 753 ZD	−61	−606	134	625	851	88	154	560
Total, Groups A Through C.........	4 983 ..	*2,960*	*−2,036*	*675*	*1,031*	*2,546*	*−8,838*	*960*	*1,222*
D. Net Errors and Omissions................	4 998 ..	**−44**	**676**	**−200**	**356**	**−29**	**−167**	**703**	**−528**
Total, Groups A Through D.........	4 984 ..	*2,916*	*−1,360*	*475*	*1,387*	*2,517*	*−9,005*	*1,662*	*694*
E. Reserves and Related Items..............	4 802 A.	**−2,916**	**1,360**	**−475**	**−1,387**	**−2,517**	**9,005**	**−1,662**	**−694**
Reserve assets................	4 802 ..	−3,003	1,728	−176	−1,380	−2,366	6,122	−5,017	−2,319
Use of Fund credit and loans........	4 766 ..	−120	−314	−244	−106	−151	2,882	3,032	1,325
Exceptional financing............	4 920 ..	207	−55	−55	100	....	....	323	300
Conversion rates: Pakistan rupees per U.S. dollar..............	0 101 ..	**57.752**	**58.258**	**59.514**	**60.271**	**60.739**	**70.408**	**81.713**	**85.194**

[1] Excludes components that have been classified in the categories of Group E.

Table 2. STANDARD PRESENTATION, 2003–2010

(Millions of U.S. dollars)

	Code	2003	2004	2005	2006	2007	2008	2009	2010
CURRENT ACCOUNT................................	4 993 ..	**3,573**	**−817**	**−3,606**	**−6,750**	**−8,286**	**−15,655**	**−3,993**	**−1,490**
A. GOODS..	4 100 ..	**−109**	**−3,396**	**−6,340**	**−9,647**	**−10,587**	**−17,003**	**−10,270**	**−11,416**
Credit...	2 100 ..	**11,869**	**13,297**	**15,433**	**17,049**	**18,188**	**21,214**	**18,347**	**21,463**
General merchandise: exports f.o.b................	2 110 ..	11,785	13,237	15,284	16,910	18,011	20,963	18,161	21,248
Goods for processing: exports f.o.b...............	2 150 ..	....	....	....	....	....	....	....	....
Repairs on goods..................................	2 160 ..	....	6	1	....	....	3	7	4
Goods procured in ports by carriers..............	2 170 ..	84	54	148	139	177	248	179	211
Nonmonetary gold.................................	2 180 ..	....	....	....	....	....	....	....	....
Debit..	3 100 ..	**−11,978**	**−16,693**	**−21,773**	**−26,696**	**−28,775**	**−38,216**	**−28,617**	**−32,879**
General merchandise: imports f.o.b................	3 110 ..	−11,929	−16,498	−21,456	−26,314	−28,409	−37,815	−28,366	−32,573
Goods for processing: imports f.o.b...............	3 150 ..	....	....	....	....	....	....	....	....
Repairs on goods..................................	3 160 ..	....	−50	−90	−99	−129	−84	−81	−75
Goods procured in ports by carriers..............	3 170 ..	−49	−145	−227	−283	−237	−317	−170	−231
Nonmonetary gold.................................	3 180 ..	....	....	....	....	....	....	....	....
B. SERVICES......................................	4 200 ..	**−326**	**−2,584**	**−3,830**	**−4,912**	**−5,044**	**−5,454**	**−2,568**	**−678**
Total credit......................................	2 200 ..	*2,968*	*2,749*	*3,678*	*3,506*	*3,767*	*4,263*	*3,983*	*6,410*
Total debit.......................................	3 200 ..	*−3,294*	*−5,333*	*−7,508*	*−8,418*	*−8,811*	*−9,717*	*−6,551*	*−7,088*
Transportation services, credit..............	2 205 ..	**836**	**940**	**1,076**	**1,112**	**1,068**	**1,227**	**1,155**	**1,333**
Passenger..	2 850 ..	*498*	*586*	*646*	*664*	*636*	*670*	*678*	*694*
Freight..	2 851 ..	*122*	*100*	*118*	*135*	*127*	*136*	*100*	*117*
Other..	2 852 ..	*216*	*254*	*312*	*313*	*305*	*421*	*377*	*522*
Sea transport, passenger...........................	2 207 ..	....	....	....	....	....	....	....	....
Sea transport, freight.............................	2 208 ..	26	25	27	29	30	49	29	31
Sea transport, other...............................	2 209 ..	113	103	151	145	129	194	100	305
Air transport, passenger...........................	2 211 ..	498	586	646	664	636	670	678	694
Air transport, freight..............................	2 212 ..	96	75	91	106	97	87	67	75
Air transport, other...............................	2 213 ..	103	151	161	168	176	227	277	217
Other transport, passenger.........................	2 215 ..	....	....	....	....	....	....	....	....
Other transport, freight............................	2 216 ..	....	....	....	....	....	....	4	11
Other transport, other.............................	2 217 ..	....	....	....	....	....	....	....	....
Transportation services, debit...............	3 205 ..	**−1,585**	**−2,076**	**−2,614**	**−3,027**	**−3,270**	**−4,210**	**−3,227**	**−3,755**
Passenger..	3 850 ..	*−238*	*−344*	*−473*	*−484*	*−490*	*−645*	*−413*	*−445*
Freight..	3 851 ..	*−1,015*	*−1,438*	*−1,837*	*−2,192*	*−2,415*	*−3,173*	*−2,352*	*−2,819*
Other..	3 852 ..	*−332*	*−294*	*−304*	*−351*	*−365*	*−392*	*−462*	*−491*
Sea transport, passenger...........................	3 207 ..	....	....	....	....	....	....	....	....
Sea transport, freight.............................	3 208 ..	−955	−1,285	−1,635	−1,935	−2,070	−2,748	−2,091	−2,505
Sea transport, other...............................	3 209 ..	−30	−21	−31	−47	−54	−76	−95	−73
Air transport, passenger...........................	3 211 ..	−238	−344	−473	−484	−490	−645	−413	−445
Air transport, freight..............................	3 212 ..	−54	−136	−180	−230	−327	−356	−226	−288
Air transport, other...............................	3 213 ..	−302	−275	−275	−304	−311	−316	−361	−418
Other transport, passenger.........................	3 215 ..	....	....	....	....	....	....	....	....
Other transport, freight............................	3 216 ..	−6	−17	−22	−27	−18	−69	−35	−26
Other transport, other.............................	3 217 ..	....	2	2	....	....	....	−6	....
Travel, credit.................................	2 236 ..	**122**	**179**	**182**	**255**	**276**	**316**	**272**	**304**
Business travel....................................	2 237 ..	1	2	8	13	14	19	9	4
Personal travel....................................	2 240 ..	121	177	174	242	262	297	263	300
Travel, debit..................................	3 236 ..	**−925**	**−1,268**	**−1,280**	**−1,545**	**−1,593**	**−1,518**	**−685**	**−925**
Business travel....................................	3 237 ..	−23	−102	−121	−71	−46	−29	−23	−30
Personal travel....................................	3 240 ..	−902	−1,166	−1,159	−1,474	−1,547	−1,489	−662	−895
Other services, credit........................	2 200 BA	**2,010**	**1,630**	**2,420**	**2,139**	**2,423**	**2,720**	**2,556**	**4,773**
Communications...................................	2 245 ..	190	233	284	157	128	91	284	242
Construction......................................	2 249 ..	4	24	18	31	66	42	17	20
Insurance...	2 253 ..	22	19	32	19	36	72	45	44
Financial..	2 260 ..	12	40	47	65	67	55	101	50
Computer and information.........................	2 262 ..	34	38	59	87	126	187	182	193
Royalties and licence fees.........................	2 266 ..	8	10	15	53	37	38	5	3
Other business services............................	2 268 ..	247	236	328	465	419	500	485	599
Personal, cultural, and recreational................	2 287 ..	1	....	2	1	1	3	2	4
Government, n.i.e.................................	2 291 ..	1,492	1,030	1,635	1,261	1,543	1,732	1,435	3,618
Other services, debit.........................	3 200 BA	**−784**	**−1,989**	**−3,614**	**−3,846**	**−3,948**	**−3,989**	**−2,640**	**−2,408**
Communications...................................	3 245 ..	−45	−46	−84	−89	−101	−128	−173	−158
Construction......................................	3 249 ..	−12	−8	−132	−58	−43	−55	−60	−29
Insurance...	3 253 ..	−73	−91	−126	−125	−141	−129	−145	−143
Financial..	3 260 ..	−73	−75	−124	−132	−125	−214	−114	−102
Computer and information.........................	3 262 ..	−6	−18	−34	−65	−122	−113	−138	−168
Royalties and licence fees.........................	3 266 ..	−36	−86	−109	−106	−107	−117	−90	−124
Other business services............................	3 268 ..	−347	−1,431	−2,695	−2,944	−2,924	−2,801	−1,255	−1,049
Personal, cultural, and recreational................	3 287 ..	....	−2	−8	−3	....	−1	−16	−13
Government, n.i.e.................................	3 291 ..	−192	−232	−302	−324	−385	−431	−649	−622

Table 2 (Continued). STANDARD PRESENTATION, 2003–2010

(Millions of U.S. dollars)

	Code	2003	2004	2005	2006	2007	2008	2009	2010
C. INCOME	4 300	**−2,224**	**−2,363**	**−2,515**	**−3,131**	**−3,740**	**−4,334**	**−3,614**	**−3,178**
Total credit	2 300	*180*	*221*	*657*	*864*	*1,357*	*1,285*	*607*	*681*
Total debit	3 300	*−2,404*	*−2,584*	*−3,172*	*−3,995*	*−5,097*	*−5,619*	*−4,221*	*−3,859*
Compensation of employees, credit	2 310	**1**	**2**	**3**	**8**	**6**	**14**	**16**	**23**
Compensation of employees, debit	3 310	....	**−1**	**−1**	**−2**	....	....	**−8**	**−9**
Investment income, credit	2 320	**179**	**219**	**654**	**856**	**1,351**	**1,271**	**591**	**658**
Direct investment income	2 330	3	18	18	48	20	44	38	23
Dividends and distributed branch profits	2 332	3	18	18	48	19	44	38	23
Reinvested earnings and undistributed branch profits	2 333	....	....	....	....	....	....	....	....
Income on debt (interest)	2 334	....	....	....	....	1	....	....	....
Portfolio investment income	2 339	5	17	328	357	671	768	433	500
Income on equity	2 340	3	7	1	4	10	15	....	1
Income on bonds and notes	2 350	2	9	27	7	5	28	1	1
Income on money market instruments	2 360	....	1	300	346	656	725	432	498
Other investment income	2 370	171	184	308	451	660	459	120	135
Investment income, debit	3 320	**−2,404**	**−2,583**	**−3,171**	**−3,993**	**−5,097**	**−5,619**	**−4,213**	**−3,850**
Direct investment income	3 330	−893	−1,486	−1,871	−2,580	−2,974	−3,203	−2,548	−2,131
Dividends and distributed branch profits	3 332	−739	−1,238	−1,447	−1,886	−2,003	−2,172	−2,179	−1,992
Reinvested earnings and undistributed branch profits	3 333	−154	−248	−424	−695	−971	−1,031	−333	−122
Income on debt (interest)	3 334	....	....	....	....	....	....	−36	−17
Portfolio investment income	3 339	−360	−197	−468	−473	−983	−1,191	−677	−813
Income on equity	3 340	−257	−104	−137	−155	−270	−230	−141	−205
Income on bonds and notes	3 350	−79	−43	−135	−140	−232	−220	−170	−148
Income on money market instruments	3 360	−24	−50	−196	−178	−481	−741	−366	−460
Other investment income	3 370	−1,151	−900	−832	−940	−1,140	−1,225	−988	−906
D. CURRENT TRANSFERS	4 379	**6,232**	**7,526**	**9,079**	**10,941**	**11,085**	**11,136**	**12,459**	**13,782**
Credit	2 379	**6,300**	**7,666**	**9,169**	**11,030**	**11,216**	**11,252**	**12,552**	**13,869**
General government	2 380	813	163	455	677	424	530	249	745
Other sectors	2 390	5,487	7,503	8,714	10,353	10,792	10,722	12,303	13,124
Workers' remittances	2 391	3,963	3,943	4,277	5,113	5,992	7,025	8,701	9,667
Other current transfers	2 392	1,524	3,560	4,437	5,240	4,800	3,697	3,602	3,457
Debit	3 379	**−68**	**−140**	**−90**	**−89**	**−131**	**−116**	**−93**	**−87**
General government	3 380	−14	−35	−22	−26	−55	−47	−51	−23
Other sectors	3 390	−54	−105	−68	−63	−76	−69	−42	−64
Workers' remittances	3 391	−5	−9	−2	−1	−2	....	....	−10
Other current transfers	3 392	−49	−96	−66	−62	−74	−69	−42	−54
CAPITAL AND FINANCIAL ACCOUNT	4 996	**−3,529**	**141**	**3,806**	**6,394**	**8,315**	**15,821**	**3,291**	**2,018**
CAPITAL ACCOUNT	4 994	**1,138**	**591**	**202**	**345**	**176**	**146**	**484**	**132**
Total credit	2 994	*1,140*	*596*	*214*	*351*	*182*	*151*	*490*	*132*
Total debit	3 994	*−2*	*−5*	*−12*	*−6*	*−6*	*−5*	*−6*	....
Capital transfers, credit	2 400	**1,140**	**596**	**202**	**331**	**182**	**149**	**490**	**132**
General government	2 401	1,135	576	161	301	165	118	481	128
Debt forgiveness	2 402	1,000	495	....	....	....	....	....	....
Other capital transfers	2 410	135	81	161	301	165	118	481	128
Other sectors	2 430	5	20	41	30	17	31	9	4
Migrants' transfers	2 431	....	....	....	....	....	....	....	....
Debt forgiveness	2 432	....	....	....	....	....	....	....	....
Other capital transfers	2 440	5	20	41	30	17	31	9	4
Capital transfers, debit	3 400	**−2**	**−5**	**−12**	**−6**	**−3**	**−5**	**−6**	....
General government	3 401	−2	....	−10	−5	....	....	−5	....
Debt forgiveness	3 402	....	....	....	....	....	....	....	....
Other capital transfers	3 410	−2	....	−10	−5	....	....	−5	....
Other sectors	3 430	....	−5	−2	−1	−3	−5	−1	....
Migrants' transfers	3 431	....	....	....	....	....	....	....	....
Debt forgiveness	3 432	....	....	....	....	....	....	....	....
Other capital transfers	3 440	....	−5	−2	−1	−3	−5	−1	....
Nonproduced nonfinancial assets, credit	2 480	....	....	**12**	**20**	....	**2**	....	....
Nonproduced nonfinancial assets, debit	3 480	....	....	....	....	**−3**	....	....	....

Table 2 (Continued). STANDARD PRESENTATION, 2003–2010
(Millions of U.S. dollars)

	Code	2003	2004	2005	2006	2007	2008	2009	2010
FINANCIAL ACCOUNT	4 995	−4,667	−450	3,604	6,049	8,139	15,675	2,807	1,886
A. DIRECT INVESTMENT	4 500	515	1,062	2,157	4,164	5,492	5,389	2,267	1,970
Direct investment abroad	4 505	−19	−56	−44	−109	−98	−49	−71	−46
Equity capital	4 510	....	....	....	....	....	−8	−71	−46
Claims on affiliated enterprises	4 515	....	....	....	....	....	−8	−71	−46
Liabilities to affiliated enterprises	4 520	....	....	....	....	....	....		
Reinvested earnings	4 525	....	....		....	....	....		
Other capital	4 530	−19	−56	−44	−109	−98	−41	....	....
Claims on affiliated enterprises	4 535	−19	−56	−44	−109	−98	−41		
Liabilities to affiliated enterprises	4 540	....	....		....				
Direct investment in Pakistan	4 555	**534**	**1,118**	**2,201**	**4,273**	**5,590**	**5,438**	**2,338**	**2,016**
Equity capital	4 560	379	867	1,777	3,518	4,617	4,407	2,005	1,894
Claims on direct investors	4 565								
Liabilities to direct investors	4 570	379	867	1,777	3,518	4,617	4,407	2,005	1,894
Reinvested earnings	4 575	154	248	424	695	971	1,031	333	122
Other capital	4 580	1	3	....	61	2	....	....	....
Claims on direct investors	4 585	....	....		....	....			
Liabilities to direct investors	4 590	1	3	....	61	2			
B. PORTFOLIO INVESTMENT	4 600	**−276**	**246**	**770**	**1,969**	**2,086**	**−269**	**−608**	**−108**
Assets	4 602	**−2**	**9**	**19**	**−4**	**5**	**−26**	**−26**	**6**
Equity securities	4 610	−2	9	19	−4	5	−26	−26	6
Monetary authorities	4 611	....	....	....	....	....	....	....	....
General government	4 612	....	....	....	....	....	....	....	....
Banks	4 613	....	....	....	....	....	−1	−34	6
Other sectors	4 614	−2	9	19	−4	5	−25	8	....
Debt securities	4 619	....	....	....	....	....	....	....	....
Bonds and notes	4 620	....	....	....	....	....	....	....	....
Monetary authorities	4 621	....	....	....	....	....	....	....	....
General government	4 622	....	....	....	....	....	....	....	....
Banks	4 623	....	....	....	....	....	....	....	....
Other sectors	4 624	....	....	....	....	....	....	....	....
Money market instruments	4 630	....	....	....	....	....	....	....	....
Monetary authorities	4 631	....	....	....	....	....	....	....	....
General government	4 632	....	....	....	....	....	....	....	....
Banks	4 633	....	....	....	....	....	....	....	....
Other sectors	4 634	....	....	....	....	....	....	....	....
Liabilities	4 652	**−274**	**237**	**751**	**1,973**	**2,081**	**−243**	**−582**	**−114**
Equity securities	4 660	−26	49	451	1,152	1,276	−270	−37	524
Banks	4 663	....	....	....	150	647	....	....	....
Other sectors	4 664	−26	49	451	1,002	629	−270	−37	524
Debt securities	4 669	−248	188	300	821	805	27	−545	−638
Bonds and notes	4 670	−248	188	300	821	805	27	−543	−638
Monetary authorities	4 671	....	....	....	....	....	−14	....	....
General government	4 672	−248	188	300	623	755	41	−543	−638
Banks	4 673	....	....	....	....	....	....	....	....
Other sectors	4 674	....	....	....	198	50	....	....	....
Money market instruments	4 680	....	....	....	....	....	....	−2	....
Monetary authorities	4 681	....	....	....	....	....	....	....	....
General government	4 682	....	....	....	....	....	....	−2	....
Banks	4 683	....	....	....	....	....	....	....	....
Other sectors	4 684	....	....	....	....	....	....	....	....
C. FINANCIAL DERIVATIVES	4 910	....	....	....	....	....	....	....	....
Monetary authorities	4 911	....	....	....	....	....	....	....	....
General government	4 912	....	....	....	....	....	....	....	....
Banks	4 913	....	....	....	....	....	....	....	....
Other sectors	4 914	....	....	....	....	....	....	....	....
Assets	4 900	....	....	....	....	....	....	....	....
Monetary authorities	4 901	....	....	....	....	....	....	....	....
General government	4 902	....	....	....	....	....	....	....	....
Banks	4 903	....	....	....	....	....	....	....	....
Other sectors	4 904	....	....	....	....	....	....	....	....
Liabilities	4 905	....	....	....	....	....	....	....	....
Monetary authorities	4 906	....	....	....	....	....	....	....	....
General government	4 907	....	....	....	....	....	....	....	....
Banks	4 908	....	....	....	....	....	....	....	....
Other sectors	4 909	....	....	....	....	....	....	....	....

Table 2 (Concluded). STANDARD PRESENTATION, 2003–2010

(Millions of U.S. dollars)

	Code	2003	2004	2005	2006	2007	2008	2009	2010
D. OTHER INVESTMENT	4 700	**−1,903**	**−3,487**	**853**	**1,297**	**2,927**	**4,433**	**6,165**	**2,343**
Assets	4 703	**−542**	**−1,339**	**126**	**−242**	**284**	**−494**	**−3**	**−295**
Trade credits	4 706	−198	−265	−301	−282	−267	−308	−192	−280
General government	4 707	....	....	....	....	....	....	....	....
of which: Short-term	4 709	....	....	....	....	....	....	....	....
Other sectors	4 710	−198	−265	−301	−282	−267	−308	−192	−280
of which: Short-term	4 712	*−198*	*−265*	*−301*	*−282*	*−267*	*−308*	*−192*	*−280*
Loans	4 714	....	....	....	....	....	....	....	....
Monetary authorities	4 715	....	....	....	....	....	....	....	....
of which: Short-term	4 718	....	....	....	....	....	....	....	....
General government	4 719	....	....	....	....	....	....	....	....
of which: Short-term	4 721	....	....	....	....	....	....	....	....
Banks	4 722	....	....	....	....	....	....	....	....
of which: Short-term	4 724	....	....	....	....	....	....	....	....
Other sectors	4 725	....	....	....	....	....	....	....	....
of which: Short-term	4 727	....	....	....	....	....	....	....	....
Currency and deposits	4 730	−243	−961	524	125	504	−274	129	334
Monetary authorities	4 731	....	....	....	....	....	....	....	....
General government	4 732	2	−1	....	−2	5	1	2	1
Banks	4 733	−171	−871	569	45	329	−366	208	299
Other sectors	4 734	−74	−89	−45	82	170	91	−81	34
Other assets	4 736	−101	−113	−97	−85	47	88	60	−349
Monetary authorities	4 737	....	....	....	....	....	....	....	....
of which: Short-term	4 739	....	....	....	....	....	....	....	....
General government	4 740	17	....	1	1	1	....	....	....
of which: Short-term	4 742	*17*							
Banks	4 743	−76	−113	−98	−86	46	88	60	−349
of which: Short-term	4 745	*−76*	*−113*	*−98*	*−86*	*46*	*88*	*60*	*−349*
Other sectors	4 746	−42	....	....	....	....	....	....	....
of which: Short-term	4 748	*−42*	....	....	....	....	....	....	....
Liabilities	4 753	**−1,361**	**−2,148**	**727**	**1,539**	**2,643**	**4,927**	**6,168**	**2,638**
Trade credits	4 756	....	....	....	....	....	....	....	....
General government	4 757	....	....	....	....	....	....	....	....
of which: Short-term	4 759	....	....	....	....	....	....	....	....
Other sectors	4 760	....	....	....	....	....	....	....	....
of which: Short-term	4 762	....	....	....	....	....	....	....	....
Loans	4 764	−1,496	−1,584	355	1,340	2,100	4,993	4,465	2,269
Monetary authorities	4 765	−120	−314	−244	−106	−151	2,882	3,032	1,325
of which: Use of Fund credit and loans from the Fund	4 766	*−120*	*−314*	*−244*	*−106*	*−151*	*2,882*	*3,032*	*1,325*
of which: Short-term	4 768	....	....	....	....	....	....	....	....
General government	4 769	−994	−1,211	792	1,044	1,789	1,201	1,188	930
of which: Short-term	4 771	*−215*	*−14*	*230*	*−132*	*434*	*97*	*−582*	*790*
Banks	4 772	....	....	....	....	50	....	−4	−7
of which: Short-term	4 774	....	....	....	....	....	....	....	*−7*
Other sectors	4 775	−382	−59	−193	402	412	910	249	21
of which: Short-term	4 777	*−78*	....	....	....	....	*6*	*−24*	*−14*
Currency and deposits	4 780	328	−421	393	127	464	−373	323	576
Monetary authorities	4 781	....	−15	5	2	....	....	−6	12
General government	4 782	....	−2	−10	−1	....	....	....	....
Banks	4 783	18	−8	−3	−1	43	344	411	38
Other sectors	4 784	310	−396	401	127	421	−717	−82	526
Other liabilities	4 786	−193	−143	−21	72	79	307	1,380	−207
Monetary authorities	4 787	....	....	3	....	−10	500	1,278	....
of which: Short-term	4 789	....	....	*3*	....	....	....	....	....
General government	4 790	−24	−22	−21	−22	−22	−22	704	−122
of which: Short-term	4 792	*1*	....	*1*	....	....	....	*26*	*−100*
Banks	4 793	−180	30	71	−2	93	−66	−589	−98
of which: Short-term	4 795	*−150*	*40*	*81*	*−45*	*105*	*−65*	*−574*	*−92*
Other sectors	4 796	11	−151	−74	96	18	−105	−13	13
of which: Short-term	4 798	*27*	*−105*	*−97*	*−29*	*−18*	*−170*	*−33*	*−70*
E. RESERVE ASSETS	4 802	**−3,003**	**1,728**	**−176**	**−1,380**	**−2,366**	**6,122**	**−5,017**	**−2,319**
Monetary gold	4 812	....	....	....	....	....	....	....	....
Special drawing rights	4 811	−230	13	10	12	11	26	−1,190	125
Reserve position in the Fund	4 810	....	....	....	....	....	....	....	....
Foreign exchange	4 803	−3,134	2,045	−206	−1,402	−2,377	6,096	−3,827	−2,444
Other claims	4 813	361	−330	20	10	....	....	....	....
NET ERRORS AND OMISSIONS	4 998	**−44**	**676**	**−200**	**356**	**−29**	**−167**	**703**	**−528**

Table 3. INTERNATIONAL INVESTMENT POSITION (End-period stocks), 2003–2010

(Millions of U.S. dollars)

	Code	2003	2004	2005	2006	2007	2008	2009	2010
ASSETS	8 995 C.	**16,981**	**17,071**	**17,681**	**19,735**	**22,701**	**16,773**	**23,380**	**26,552**
Direct investment abroad	8 505	**604**	**702**	**870**	**1,010**	**1,249**	**1,269**	**1,850**	**1,727**
Equity capital and reinvested earnings	8 506	604	702	870	1,010	1,249	1,269	1,797	1,673
Claims on affiliated enterprises	8 507	604	702	870	1,010	1,249	1,269	1,797	1,673
Liabilities to affiliated enterprises	8 508	....	....	....	....	....	....	....	....
Other capital	8 530	....	....	....	....	....	....	54	54
Claims on affiliated enterprises	8 535	....	....	....	....	....	....	54	54
Liabilities to affiliated enterprises	8 540	....	....	....	....	....	....	....	....
Portfolio investment	8 602	**155**	**158**	**452**	**311**	**330**	**111**	**153**	**151**
Equity securities	8 610	154	155	447	307	316	97	120	114
Monetary authorities	8 611	....	....	....	....	....	....	....	....
General government	8 612	....	....	....	....	....	....	....	....
Banks	8 613	55	98	375	234	254	95	78	74
Other sectors	8 614	99	57	72	73	62	2	42	40
Debt securities	8 619	1	3	5	4	14	14	33	37
Bonds and notes	8 620	1	3	5	4	14	14	33	37
Monetary authorities	8 621	....	....	....	....	....	....	....	....
General government	8 622	....	....	....	....	....	....	....	....
Banks	8 623	1	3	4	3	13	13	33	33
Other sectors	8 624	....	....	1	1	1	1	....	4
Money market instruments	8 630	....	....	....	....	....	....	....	....
Monetary authorities	8 631	....	....	....	....	....	....	....	....
General government	8 632	....	....	....	....	....	....	....	....
Banks	8 633	....	....	....	....	....	....	....	....
Other sectors	8 634	....	....	....	....	....	....	....	....
Financial derivatives	8 900	....	....	....	....	....	....	**27**	**20**
Monetary authorities	8 901	....	....	....	....	....	....	....	....
General government	8 902	....	....	....	....	....	....	....	....
Banks	8 903	....	....	....	....	....	....	27	20
Other sectors	8 904	....	....	....	....	....	....	....	....
Other investment	8 703	**3,526**	**5,492**	**5,336**	**5,752**	**5,651**	**6,255**	**6,204**	**6,704**
Trade credits	8 706	1,692	1,957	2,258	2,500	2,765	3,073	3,090	3,365
General government	8 707	....	....	....	....	....	....	....	....
of which: Short-term	8 709	....	....	....	....	....	....	....	....
Other sectors	8 710	1,692	1,957	2,258	2,500	2,765	3,073	3,090	3,365
of which: Short-term	8 712	*1,692*	*1,957*	*2,258*	*2,500*	*2,765*	*3,073*	*3,090*	*3,365*
Loans	8 714	80	83	86	89	92	95	99	101
Monetary authorities	8 715	....	....	....	....	....	....	....	....
of which: Short-term	8 718	....	....	....	....	....	....	....	....
General government	8 719	80	83	86	89	92	95	99	101
of which: Short-term	8 721	....	....	....	....	....	....	....	....
Banks	8 722	....	....	....	....	....	....	....	....
of which: Short-term	8 724	....	....	....	....	....	....	....	....
Other sectors	8 725	....	....	....	....	....	....	....	....
of which: Short-term	8 727	....	....	....	....	....	....	....	....
Currency and deposits	8 730	867	2,452	1,894	1,939	1,617	1,970	1,811	1,761
Monetary authorities	8 731	....	....	....	....	....	....	....	....
General government	8 732	4	5	3	5	5	2	6	8
Banks	8 733	807	2,322	1,738	1,848	1,518	1,885	1,680	1,578
Other sectors	8 734	56	125	153	86	94	83	125	175
Other assets	8 736	887	1,000	1,098	1,224	1,177	1,117	1,204	1,477
Monetary authorities	8 737	....	....	....	....	....	....	3	3
of which: Short-term	8 739	....	....	....	....	....	....	*3*	*3*
General government	8 740	....	....	....	....	....	....	....	....
of which: Short-term	8 742	....	....	....	....	....	....	....	....
Banks	8 743	887	1,000	1,098	1,224	1,177	1,117	1,201	1,474
of which: Short-term	8 745	*887*	*1,000*	*1,098*	*1,224*	*1,177*	*1,117*	*1,201*	*1,353*
Other sectors	8 746	....	....	....	....	....	....	....	....
of which: Short-term	8 748	....	....	....	....	....	....	....	....
Reserve assets	8 802	**12,696**	**10,719**	**11,023**	**12,662**	**15,471**	**9,138**	**15,146**	**17,950**
Monetary gold	8 812	860	904	1,059	1,313	1,732	1,791	2,286	2,910
Special drawing rights	8 811	248	245	216	216	215	183	1,381	1,230
Reserve position in the Fund	8 810	....	....	....	....	....	....	....	....
Foreign exchange	8 803	11,588	9,570	9,748	11,133	13,524	7,164	11,479	13,809
Other claims	8 813	....	....	....	....	....	....	....	....

Table 3 (Concluded). INTERNATIONAL INVESTMENT POSITION (End-period stocks), 2003–2010

(Millions of U.S. dollars)

	Code	2003	2004	2005	2006	2007	2008	2009	2010
LIABILITIES................................	8 995 D.	**43,568**	**44,873**	**46,868**	**55,197**	**73,473**	**86,962**	**79,026**	**87,060**
Direct investment in Pakistan..........................	8 555 ..	**7,195**	**7,606**	**10,209**	**13,682**	**25,621**	**31,059**	**17,386**	**22,642**
Equity capital and reinvested earnings....................	8 556 ..	6,269	6,628	9,109	12,241	23,065	28,503	15,582	20,752
Claims on direct investors....................	8 557 ..	....	....	....	....	....	....	....	....
Liabilities to direct investors....................	8 558 ..	6,269	6,628	9,109	12,241	23,065	28,503	15,582	20,752
Other capital....................	8 580 ..	926	978	1,100	1,441	2,556	2,556	1,804	1,890
Claims on direct investors....................	8 585 ..	....	....	....	....	....	....	−46	−46
Liabilities to direct investors....................	8 590 ..	926	978	1,100	1,441	2,556	2,556	1,850	1,936
Portfolio investment..........................	8 652 ..	**542**	**1,162**	**2,173**	**4,064**	**6,767**	**6,784**	**3,548**	**3,904**
Equity securities....................	8 660 ..	217	495	1,064	1,960	3,859	3,859	1,258	2,167
Banks....................	8 663 ..	50	92	283	669	1,559	1,559	513	661
Other sectors....................	8 664 ..	167	403	781	1,291	2,300	2,300	745	1,506
Debt securities....................	8 669 ..	325	667	1,109	2,104	2,908	2,925	2,290	1,737
Bonds and notes....................	8 670 ..	325	667	1,109	2,104	2,908	2,925	2,287	1,674
Monetary authorities....................	8 671 ..	....	....	....	....	....	....	....	....
General government....................	8 672 ..	310	655	1,100	1,900	2,655	2,650	2,150	1,550
Banks....................	8 673 ..	....	....	....	....	....	....	....	....
Other sectors....................	8 674 ..	15	12	9	204	253	275	137	124
Money market instruments....................	8 680 ..	....	....	....	....	....	....	3	63
Monetary authorities....................	8 681 ..	....	....	....	....	....	....	....	....
General government....................	8 682 ..	....	....	....	....	....	....	3	63
Banks....................	8 683 ..	....	....	....	....	....	....	....	....
Other sectors....................	8 684 ..	....	....	....	....	....	....	....	....
Financial derivatives..........................	8 905 ..	....	....	....	....	....	....	**57**	**51**
Monetary authorities....................	8 906 ..	....	....	....	....	....	....	....	....
General government....................	8 907 ..	....	....	....	....	....	....	....	....
Banks....................	8 908 ..	....	....	....	....	....	....	57	51
Other sectors....................	8 909 ..	....	....	....	....	....	....	....	....
Other investment..........................	8 753 ..	**35,831**	**36,105**	**34,486**	**37,451**	**41,085**	**49,119**	**58,035**	**60,463**
Trade credits....................	8 756 ..	162	140	221	506	445	445	1,365	1,365
General government....................	8 757 ..	....	....	....	....	....	....	....	....
of which: Short-term....................	8 759 ..	....	....	....	....	....	....	....	....
Other sectors....................	8 760 ..	162	140	221	506	445	445	1,365	1,365
of which: Short-term....................	8 762 ..	*162*	*140*	*221*	*506*	*445*	*445*	*1,365*	*1,365*
Loans....................	8 764 ..	33,841	34,161	32,414	35,109	38,988	46,620	52,723	55,193
Monetary authorities....................	8 765 ..	2,108	1,876	1,492	1,462	1,381	4,352	7,495	8,736
of which: Use of Fund credit and loans from the Fund....	8 766 ..	*2,108*	*1,876*	*1,492*	*1,462*	*1,381*	*4,352*	*7,495*	*8,736*
of which: Short-term....................	8 768 ..	....	....	....	....	....	....	....	....
General government....................	8 769 ..	29,342	30,510	29,352	31,605	35,006	38,810	41,597	42,588
of which: Short-term....................	8 771 ..	*95*	*111*	*343*	*51*	*601*	*663*	*322*	*863*
Banks....................	8 772 ..	....	....	....	....	....	50	126	112
of which: Short-term....................	8 774 ..	....	....	....	....	....	....	....	....
Other sectors....................	8 775 ..	2,391	1,775	1,570	2,042	2,601	3,408	3,505	3,757
of which: Short-term....................	8 777 ..	*22*	....	....	*78*	*267*	*283*	*211*	*353*
Currency and deposits....................	8 780 ..	1,143	1,152	1,200	1,182	1,159	1,606	2,130	2,243
Monetary authorities....................	8 781 ..	707	704	701	701	701	1,201	1,201	1,101
General government....................	8 782 ..	2	3	1	....	1	1	501	501
Banks....................	8 783 ..	434	445	498	481	457	404	428	641
Other sectors....................	8 784 ..	....	....	....	....	....	....	....	....
Other liabilities....................	8 786 ..	685	652	651	654	493	448	1,817	1,662
Monetary authorities....................	8 787 ..	....	....	....	....	....	....	1,550	1,522
of which: Short-term....................	8 789 ..	....	....	....	....	....	....	....	....
General government....................	8 790 ..	656	631	609	588	466	344	222	100
of which: Short-term....................	8 792 ..	*500*	*500*	*500*	*500*	*400*	*300*	*200*	*100*
Banks....................	8 793 ..	....	....	....	....	....	....	....	....
of which: Short-term....................	8 795 ..	....	....	....	....	....	....	....	....
Other sectors....................	8 796 ..	29	21	42	66	27	104	45	40
of which: Short-term....................	8 798 ..	*29*	*21*	*42*	*66*	*27*	*104*	*45*	*40*
NET INTERNATIONAL INVESTMENT POSITION........	8 995 ..	**−26,587**	**−27,802**	**−29,187**	**−35,463**	**−50,772**	**−70,189**	**−55,646**	**−60,508**
Conversion rates: Pakistan rupees per U.S. dollar (end of period)..........................	0 102 ..	**57.215**	**59.124**	**59.830**	**60.918**	**61.221**	**79.098**	**84.263**	**85.711**

Table 1. ANALYTIC PRESENTATION, 2003–2010

(Millions of U.S. dollars)

	Code	2003	2004	2005	2006	2007	2008	2009	2010
A. Current Account[1]	4 993 Z.	**−536.5**	**−1,003.2**	**−1,021.8**	**−448.4**	**−1,407.0**	**−2,722.1**	**−43.5**	**−2,953.2**
Goods: exports f.o.b.	2 100 ..	5,072.4	6,079.9	7,375.2	8,475.3	9,333.7	10,323.2	11,133.1	11,330.4
Goods: imports f.o.b.	3 100 ..	−6,274.4	−7,616.5	−8,933.0	−10,190.4	−12,523.8	−14,869.1	−13,255.6	−15,945.8
Balance on Goods	4 100 ..	*−1,202.0*	*−1,536.6*	*−1,557.8*	*−1,715.1*	*−3,190.1*	*−4,545.9*	*−2,122.5*	*−4,615.4*
Services: credit	2 200 ..	2,539.6	2,793.7	3,231.3	4,000.2	4,958.1	5,787.9	5,519.2	6,092.7
Services: debit	3 200 ..	−1,299.8	−1,457.0	−1,811.4	−1,727.7	−2,121.8	−2,632.5	−2,190.7	−2,760.1
Balance on Goods and Services	4 991 ..	*37.8*	*−199.9*	*−137.9*	*557.4*	*−353.8*	*−1,390.5*	*1,206.0*	*−1,282.8*
Income: credit	2 300 ..	805.3	790.9	1,054.8	1,403.0	1,864.2	1,893.1	1,504.6	1,525.0
Income: debit	3 300 ..	−1,614.0	−1,811.3	−2,180.4	−2,661.3	−3,170.6	−3,462.6	−2,964.5	−3,386.3
Balance on Goods, Services, and Income	4 992 ..	*−770.9*	*−1,220.3*	*−1,263.5*	*−700.9*	*−1,660.2*	*−2,960.0*	*−253.9*	*−3,144.1*
Current transfers: credit	2 379 Z.	298.6	297.6	338.2	388.4	416.4	449.5	463.1	458.1
Current transfers: debit	3 379 ..	−64.2	−80.5	−96.5	−135.9	−163.2	−211.6	−252.7	−267.2
B. Capital Account[1]	4 994 Z.	....	....	**15.8**	**15.2**	**43.7**	**56.9**	**23.1**	**42.5**
Capital account: credit	2 994 Z.	....	....	15.8	15.2	43.7	56.9	23.1	42.5
Capital account: debit	3 994 ..	....	....	....	....	....	....	....	....
Total, Groups A Plus B	4 981 ..	*−536.5*	*−1,003.2*	*−1,006.0*	*−433.2*	*−1,363.3*	*−2,665.2*	*−20.4*	*−2,910.7*
C. Financial Account[1]	4 995 W.	**178.0**	**496.7**	**2,040.1**	**463.6**	**2,459.1**	**2,655.4**	**852.6**	**1,819.3**
Direct investment abroad	4 505 ..	....	....	....	....	....	....	....	....
Direct investment in Panama	4 555 Z.	817.5	1,019.1	917.6	2,557.1	1,776.5	2,196.2	1,772.8	2,362.5
Portfolio investment assets	4 602 ..	−75.4	−650.9	−1,102.8	−755.9	−1,081.6	−411.6	−915.7	−849.6
Equity securities	4 610 ..	8.7	6.8	−16.9	−142.8	130.3	−3.1	7.9	−69.6
Debt securities	4 619 ..	−84.1	−657.7	−1,085.9	−613.1	−1,211.9	−408.5	−923.6	−780.0
Portfolio investment liabilities	4 652 Z.	139.6	775.9	545.7	254.9	450.0	−62.3	1,323.0	....
Equity securities	4 660 ..	....	....	....	....	....	....	....	....
Debt securities	4 669 Z.	139.6	775.9	545.7	254.9	450.0	−62.3	1,323.0	....
Financial derivatives	4 910 ..	....	....	....	....	....	....	....	....
Financial derivatives assets	4 900 ..	....	....	....	....	....	....	....	....
Financial derivatives liabilities	4 905 ..	....	....	....	....	....	....	....	....
Other investment assets	4 703 ..	631.2	−1,542.8	−334.4	−3,790.4	−5,118.5	−2,844.9	−1,519.5	−4,384.0
Monetary authorities	4 701 ..	....	....	....	....	....	....	....	....
General government	4 704 ..	32.1	−598.5	496.7	−309.1	....	....	....	....
Banks	4 705 ..	529.2	−710.8	−276.1	−2,848.1	−4,817.5	−2,964.7	−396.0	−3,917.4
Other sectors	4 728 ..	69.9	−233.5	−555.0	−633.2	−301.0	119.8	−1,123.5	−466.6
Other investment liabilities	4 753 W.	−1,334.9	895.4	2,014.0	2,197.9	6,432.7	3,778.0	192.0	4,690.4
Monetary authorities	4 753 WA	1.6	....	....	9.5	10.0	7.2	264.5	5.3
General government	4 753 ZB	10.2	−37.0	−54.2	23.6	34.8	243.8	335.4	266.3
Banks	4 753 ZC	−1,349.3	820.8	1,866.4	2,100.8	6,111.6	3,404.7	−543.0	4,087.9
Other sectors	4 753 ZD	2.6	111.6	201.8	64.0	276.3	122.3	135.1	330.9
Total, Groups A Through C	4 983 ..	*−358.5*	*−506.5*	*1,034.1*	*30.4*	*1,095.8*	*−9.8*	*832.2*	*−1,091.4*
D. Net Errors and Omissions	4 998 ..	**89.9**	**110.4**	**−357.9**	**141.3**	**−475.9**	**595.1**	**−218.0**	**748.7**
Total, Groups A Through D	4 984 ..	*−268.6*	*−396.1*	*676.2*	*171.7*	*619.9*	*585.3*	*614.2*	*−342.7*
E. Reserves and Related Items	4 802 A.	**268.6**	**396.1**	**−676.2**	**−171.7**	**−619.9**	**−585.3**	**−614.2**	**342.7**
Reserve assets	4 802 ..	268.2	397.0	−522.8	−161.8	−609.6	−580.0	−614.2	342.7
Use of Fund credit and loans	4 766 ..	−9.5	−10.0	−9.7	−9.9	−10.3	−5.3	....	....
Exceptional financing	4 920 ..	10.0	9.1	−143.7	....	....	....	....	....
Conversion rates: balboas per U.S. dollar	0 101 ..	**1.0000**	**1.0000**	**1.0000**	**1.0000**	**1.0000**	**1.0000**	**1.0000**	**1.0000**

[1] Excludes components that have been classified in the categories of Group E.

Table 2. STANDARD PRESENTATION, 2003–2010

(Millions of U.S. dollars)

	Code	2003	2004	2005	2006	2007	2008	2009	2010
CURRENT ACCOUNT................................	4 993 ..	**−536.5**	**−1,003.2**	**−1,021.8**	**−448.4**	**−1,407.0**	**−2,722.1**	**−43.5**	**−2,953.2**
A. GOODS..	4 100 ..	**−1,202.0**	**−1,536.6**	**−1,557.8**	**−1,715.1**	**−3,190.1**	**−4,545.9**	**−2,122.5**	**−4,615.4**
Credit...	2 100 ..	**5,072.4**	**6,079.9**	**7,375.2**	**8,475.3**	**9,333.7**	**10,323.2**	**11,133.1**	**11,330.4**
General merchandise: exports f.o.b.............	2 110 ..	4,953.5	5,909.0	7,160.2	8,151.5	8,967.1	9,920.8	10,846.1	11,126.2
Goods for processing: exports f.o.b............	2 150 ..	2.6	.7	1.1	.8	.4	.6	....	....
Repairs on goods..................................	2 160 ..	2.6	3.5	1.5	1.8	3.4	3.8	3.3	3.4
Goods procured in ports by carriers...........	2 170 ..	113.7	166.7	212.4	321.2	362.8	398.0	283.7	200.8
Nonmonetary gold..............................	2 180 ..	....	....	....	....	....	....	....	....
Debit..	3 100 ..	**−6,274.4**	**−7,616.5**	**−8,933.0**	**−10,190.4**	**−12,523.8**	**−14,869.1**	**−13,255.6**	**−15,945.8**
General merchandise: imports f.o.b............	3 110 ..	−6,243.8	−7,578.3	−8,869.0	−10,108.3	−12,427.0	−14,710.3	−13,147.1	−15,811.0
Goods for processing: imports f.o.b...........	3 150 ..	−1.8	−.8	−.9	−1.1	−.6	....	....	....
Repairs on goods..................................	3 160 ..	....	....	....	....	−2.5	−2.7	−3.9	−4.5
Goods procured in ports by carriers...........	3 170 ..	−28.8	−37.4	−63.1	−81.0	−93.7	−156.1	−104.6	−130.3
Nonmonetary gold..............................	3 180 ..	....	....	....	....	....	....	....	....
B. SERVICES.......................................	4 200 ..	**1,239.8**	**1,336.7**	**1,419.9**	**2,272.5**	**2,836.3**	**3,155.4**	**3,328.5**	**3,332.6**
Total credit......................................	2 200 ..	*2,539.6*	*2,793.7*	*3,231.3*	*4,000.2*	*4,958.1*	*5,787.9*	*5,519.2*	*6,092.7*
Total debit.......................................	3 200 ..	*−1,299.8*	*−1,457.0*	*−1,811.4*	*−1,727.7*	*−2,121.8*	*−2,632.5*	*−2,190.7*	*−2,760.1*
Transportation services, credit............	2 205 ..	**1,357.3**	**1,524.0**	**1,791.0**	**2,217.3**	**2,619.7**	**3,112.0**	**3,086.1**	**3,332.2**
Passenger..	2 850 ..	*218.5*	*252.0*	*327.7*	*464.6*	*620.9*	*799.8*	*795.5*	*876.1*
Freight...	2 851 ..	*8.3*	*10.0*	*11.5*	*13.1*	*21.7*	*25.9*	*22.1*	*25.3*
Other...	2 852 ..	*1,130.5*	*1,262.0*	*1,451.8*	*1,739.6*	*1,977.1*	*2,286.3*	*2,268.5*	*2,430.8*
Sea transport, passenger......................	2 207 ..	....	....	....	....	....	....	....	....
Sea transport, freight..........................	2 208 ..	....	....	....	....	....	....	....	....
Sea transport, other...........................	2 209 ..	1,110.3	1,240.2	1,420.6	1,708.6	1,942.4	2,248.2	2,230.7	2,393.1
Air transport, passenger.......................	2 211 ..	218.5	252.0	327.7	464.6	620.9	799.8	795.5	876.1
Air transport, freight...........................	2 212 ..	8.3	10.0	11.5	13.1	21.7	25.9	22.1	25.3
Air transport, other............................	2 213 ..	20.2	21.8	31.2	31.0	34.7	38.1	37.8	37.7
Other transport, passenger....................	2 215 ..	....	....	....	....	....	....	....	....
Other transport, freight........................	2 216 ..	....	....	....	....	....	....	....	....
Other transport, other.........................	2 217 ..	....	....	....	....	....	....	....	....
Transportation services, debit.............	3 205 ..	**−611.9**	**−746.7**	**−959.1**	**−952.8**	**−1,211.1**	**−1,543.2**	**−1,230.1**	**−1,541.4**
Passenger..	3 850 ..	*−58.6*	*−54.8*	*−116.7*	*−132.2*	*−149.9*	*−193.9*	*−164.6*	*−176.8*
Freight...	3 851 ..	*−497.3*	*−631.5*	*−768.4*	*−725.2*	*−935.1*	*−1,204.4*	*−908.3*	*−1,198.4*
Other...	3 852 ..	*−56.0*	*−60.4*	*−74.0*	*−95.4*	*−126.1*	*−144.9*	*−157.2*	*−166.2*
Sea transport, passenger......................	3 207 ..	....	....	....	....	....	....	....	....
Sea transport, freight..........................	3 208 ..	−497.3	−631.5	−768.4	−725.2	−935.1	−1,204.4	−908.3	−1,198.4
Sea transport, other...........................	3 209 ..	....	....	....	....	....	....	....	....
Air transport, passenger.......................	3 211 ..	−58.6	−54.8	−116.7	−132.2	−149.9	−193.9	−164.6	−176.8
Air transport, freight...........................	3 212 ..	....	....	....	....	....	....	....	....
Air transport, other............................	3 213 ..	−56.0	−60.4	−74.0	−95.4	−126.1	−144.9	−157.2	−166.2
Other transport, passenger....................	3 215 ..	....	....	....	....	....	....	....	....
Other transport, freight........................	3 216 ..	....	....	....	....	....	....	....	....
Other transport, other.........................	3 217 ..	....	....	....	....	....	....	....	....
Travel, credit..................................	2 236 ..	**584.6**	**651.0**	**779.8**	**960.0**	**1,184.8**	**1,408.1**	**1,483.5**	**1,676.3**
Business travel...................................	2 237 ..	99.7	108.4	124.0	151.8	197.1	229.1	223.1	247.4
Personal travel...................................	2 240 ..	484.9	542.6	655.8	808.2	987.7	1,179.0	1,260.4	1,428.9
Travel, debit...................................	3 236 ..	**−207.7**	**−238.9**	**−271.1**	**−271.2**	**−307.0**	**−365.8**	**−337.9**	**−397.8**
Business travel...................................	3 237 ..	−25.2	−28.9	−33.1	−33.4	−39.8	−48.2	−46.3	−54.1
Personal travel...................................	3 240 ..	−182.5	−210.0	−238.0	−237.8	−267.2	−317.6	−291.6	−343.7
Other services, credit........................	2 200 BA	**597.7**	**618.7**	**660.5**	**822.9**	**1,153.6**	**1,267.8**	**949.6**	**1,084.2**
Communications.................................	2 245 ..	72.9	103.3	126.8	161.5	215.6	223.4	238.8	249.3
Construction.....................................	2 249 ..	....	....	....	....	.6	2.5	1.5	1.7
Insurance...	2 253 ..	27.6	32.6	31.4	43.9	55.0	91.4	91.1	96.4
Financial..	2 260 ..	292.8	240.0	197.8	273.2	337.9	434.0	303.3	429.2
Computer and information.....................	2 262 ..	....	14.4	11.7	13.8	17.9	30.2	25.9	24.8
Royalties and licence fees......................	2 266 ..	....	....	....	....	....	....	....	....
Other business services........................	2 268 ..	167.8	193.0	254.6	287.6	455.9	416.7	232.9	202.6
Personal, cultural, and recreational..........	2 287 ..	....	....	....	....	....	....	....	....
Government, n.i.e................................	2 291 ..	36.6	35.4	38.2	42.9	70.7	69.6	56.1	80.2
Other services, debit.........................	3 200 BA	**−480.2**	**−471.4**	**−581.2**	**−503.7**	**−603.7**	**−723.5**	**−622.7**	**−820.9**
Communications.................................	3 245 ..	−21.2	−12.3	−25.1	−33.5	−54.3	−75.8	−44.6	−42.7
Construction.....................................	3 249 ..	....	....	....	....	....	....	....	....
Insurance...	3 253 ..	−67.4	−81.5	−105.3	−94.2	−72.2	−85.8	−79.0	−161.3
Financial..	3 260 ..	−169.1	−138.0	−157.4	−141.9	−220.1	−316.9	−231.7	−354.6
Computer and information.....................	3 262 ..	....	....	....	....	....	....	....	−2.2
Royalties and licence fees......................	3 266 ..	−42.4	−45.5	−44.6	−42.6	−56.1	−59.4	−25.0	−46.3
Other business services........................	3 268 ..	−133.6	−149.1	−195.9	−136.3	−144.6	−114.3	−169.6	−134.9
Personal, cultural, and recreational..........	3 287 ..	....	....	....	....	....	....	....	....
Government, n.i.e................................	3 291 ..	−46.5	−45.0	−52.9	−55.2	−56.4	−71.3	−72.8	−78.9

Table 2 (Continued). STANDARD PRESENTATION, 2003–2010

(Millions of U.S. dollars)

	Code	2003	2004	2005	2006	2007	2008	2009	2010
C. INCOME..	4 300	**−808.7**	**−1,020.4**	**−1,125.6**	**−1,258.3**	**−1,306.4**	**−1,569.5**	**−1,459.9**	**−1,861.3**
Total credit..	2 300	*805.3*	*790.9*	*1,054.8*	*1,403.0*	*1,864.2*	*1,893.1*	*1,504.6*	*1,525.0*
Total debit..	3 300	*−1,614.0*	*−1,811.3*	*−2,180.4*	*−2,661.3*	*−3,170.6*	*−3,462.6*	*−2,964.5*	*−3,386.3*
Compensation of employees, credit..................	2 310	**12.7**	**3.9**	**5.2**	**7.8**	**7.1**	**9.4**	**8.3**	**27.2**
Compensation of employees, debit..................	3 310	....	....	....	....	....	....	....	....
Investment income, credit.................................	2 320	**792.6**	**787.0**	**1,049.6**	**1,395.2**	**1,857.1**	**1,883.7**	**1,496.3**	**1,497.8**
Direct investment income..................................	2 330	....	....	....	....	....	....	....	....
Dividends and distributed branch profits.....................	2 332	....	....	....	....	....	....	....	....
Reinvested earnings and undistributed branch profits.....	2 333	....	....	....	....	....	....	....	....
Income on debt (interest).................................	2 334	....	....	....	....	....	....	....	....
Portfolio investment income...............................	2 339	329.1	358.4	421.4	435.3	588.2	599.1	438.8	475.2
Income on equity..	2 340	.9	4.0	1.0	5.6	3.2	6.4	1.6	1.9
Income on bonds and notes.................................	2 350	328.2	354.4	419.9	425.9	583.2	589.9	436.6	471.8
Income on money market instruments........................	2 360	....	....	.5	3.8	1.8	2.8	.6	1.5
Other investment income..................................	2 370	463.5	428.6	628.2	959.9	1,268.9	1,284.6	1,057.5	1,022.6
Investment income, debit.................................	3 320	**−1,614.0**	**−1,811.3**	**−2,180.4**	**−2,661.3**	**−3,170.6**	**−3,462.6**	**−2,964.5**	**−3,386.3**
Direct investment income..................................	3 330	−738.7	−967.4	−1,047.8	−1,196.7	−1,520.6	−1,748.1	−1,397.2	−1,815.0
Dividends and distributed branch profits.....................	3 332	−310.6	−403.5	−624.6	−1,010.2	−641.3	−578.4	−607.3	−941.2
Reinvested earnings and undistributed branch profits.....	3 333	−428.1	−563.9	−423.2	−186.5	−879.3	−1,169.7	−789.9	−873.8
Income on debt (interest).................................	3 334	....	....	....	....	....	....	....	....
Portfolio investment income...............................	3 339	−401.4	−427.4	−504.0	−488.5	−526.1	−548.3	−544.3	−591.7
Income on equity..	3 340	....	....	....	....	....	....	....	....
Income on bonds and notes.................................	3 350	−401.4	−427.4	−504.0	−488.5	−526.1	−548.3	−544.3	−591.7
Income on money market instruments........................	3 360	....	....	....	....	....	....	....	....
Other investment income..................................	3 370	−473.9	−416.5	−628.6	−976.1	−1,123.9	−1,166.2	−1,023.0	−979.6
D. CURRENT TRANSFERS...........................	4 379	**234.4**	**217.1**	**241.7**	**252.5**	**253.2**	**237.9**	**210.4**	**190.9**
Credit..	2 379	**298.6**	**297.6**	**338.2**	**388.4**	**416.4**	**449.5**	**463.1**	**458.1**
General government..	2 380	85.9	82.0	101.8	119.9	114.6	133.9	146.3	123.8
Other sectors...	2 390	212.7	215.6	236.4	268.5	301.8	315.6	316.8	334.3
Workers' remittances......................................	2 391	94.1	105.0	124.4	149.3	173.2	186.9	167.1	204.0
Other current transfers...................................	2 392	118.6	110.6	112.0	119.2	128.6	128.7	149.7	130.3
Debit..	3 379	**−64.2**	**−80.5**	**−96.5**	**−135.9**	**−163.2**	**−211.6**	**−252.7**	**−267.2**
General government..	3 380	−2.7	−3.2	−3.9	−10.4	−7.2	−8.7	−18.1	−14.3
Other sectors...	3 390	−61.5	−77.3	−92.6	−125.5	−156.0	−202.9	−234.6	−252.9
Workers' remittances......................................	3 391	−56.6	−72.3	−87.6	−120.5	−150.9	−197.7	−229.4	−247.7
Other current transfers...................................	3 392	−4.9	−5.0	−5.0	−5.0	−5.1	−5.2	−5.2	−5.2
CAPITAL AND FINANCIAL ACCOUNT......................	4 996	**446.6**	**892.8**	**1,379.7**	**307.1**	**1,882.9**	**2,127.0**	**261.5**	**2,204.5**
CAPITAL ACCOUNT.................................	4 994	**10.0**	**9.1**	**15.8**	**15.2**	**43.7**	**56.9**	**23.1**	**42.5**
Total credit..	2 994	*10.0*	*9.1*	*15.8*	*15.2*	*43.7*	*56.9*	*23.1*	*42.5*
Total debit..	3 994	....	....	....	....	....	....	....	....
Capital transfers, credit.................................	2 400	**10.0**	**9.1**	**15.8**	**15.2**	**43.7**	**56.9**	**23.1**	**42.5**
General government..	2 401	10.0	9.1	15.8	15.2	43.7	56.9	23.1	42.5
Debt forgiveness..	2 402	10.0	9.1	....	....	....	....	....	....
Other capital transfers...................................	2 410	....	....	15.8	15.2	43.7	56.9	23.1	42.5
Other sectors...	2 430	....	....	....	....	....	....	....	....
Migrants' transfers.......................................	2 431	....	....	....	....	....	....	....	....
Debt forgiveness..	2 432	....	....	....	....	....	....	....	....
Other capital transfers...................................	2 440	....	....	....	....	....	....	....	....
Capital transfers, debit.................................	3 400	....	....	....	....	....	....	....	....
General government..	3 401	....	....	....	....	....	....	....	....
Debt forgiveness..	3 402	....	....	....	....	....	....	....	....
Other capital transfers...................................	3 410	....	....	....	....	....	....	....	....
Other sectors...	3 430	....	....	....	....	....	....	....	....
Migrants' transfers.......................................	3 431	....	....	....	....	....	....	....	....
Debt forgiveness..	3 432	....	....	....	....	....	....	....	....
Other capital transfers...................................	3 440	....	....	....	....	....	....	....	....
Nonproduced nonfinancial assets, credit.............	2 480	....	....	....	....	....	....	....	....
Nonproduced nonfinancial assets, debit.............	3 480	....	....	....	....	....	....	....	....

Table 2 (Continued). STANDARD PRESENTATION, 2003–2010

(Millions of U.S. dollars)

	Code	2003	2004	2005	2006	2007	2008	2009	2010
FINANCIAL ACCOUNT	4 995	**436.6**	**883.7**	**1,363.9**	**291.9**	**1,839.2**	**2,070.1**	**238.4**	**2,162.0**
A. DIRECT INVESTMENT	4 500	**817.5**	**1,019.1**	**917.6**	**2,557.1**	**1,776.5**	**2,196.2**	**1,772.8**	**2,362.5**
Direct investment abroad	4 505	....	....	....	....	....	....	....	....
Equity capital	4 510	....	....	....	....	....	....	....	....
Claims on affiliated enterprises	4 515	....	....	....	....	....	....	....	....
Liabilities to affiliated enterprises	4 520	....	....	....	....	....	....	....	....
Reinvested earnings	4 525	....	....	....	....	....	....	....	....
Other capital	4 530	....	....	....	....	....	....	....	....
Claims on affiliated enterprises	4 535	....	....	....	....	....	....	....	....
Liabilities to affiliated enterprises	4 540	....	....	....	....	....	....	....	....
Direct investment in Panama	4 555	817.5	1,019.1	917.6	2,557.1	1,776.5	2,196.2	1,772.8	2,362.5
Equity capital	4 560	331.5	421.0	46.4	2,077.7	719.4	880.5	969.3	948.4
Claims on direct investors	4 565	....	....	....	....	....	....	....	....
Liabilities to direct investors	4 570	331.5	421.0	46.4	2,077.7	719.4	880.5	969.3	948.4
Reinvested earnings	4 575	428.1	563.9	423.2	186.5	879.3	1,169.7	789.9	873.8
Other capital	4 580	57.9	34.2	448.0	292.9	177.8	146.0	13.6	540.3
Claims on direct investors	4 585	−233.1	−258.8	−186.8	−379.2	−246.9	−337.8	−5.8	167.9
Liabilities to direct investors	4 590	291.0	293.0	634.8	672.1	424.7	483.8	19.4	372.4
B. PORTFOLIO INVESTMENT	4 600	**64.2**	**125.0**	**−700.8**	**−501.0**	**−631.6**	**−473.9**	**407.3**	**−849.6**
Assets	4 602	**−75.4**	**−650.9**	**−1,102.8**	**−755.9**	**−1,081.6**	**−411.6**	**−915.7**	**−849.6**
Equity securities	4 610	8.7	6.8	−16.9	−142.8	130.3	−3.1	7.9	−69.6
Monetary authorities	4 611	....	....	....	....	....	....	....	....
General government	4 612	....	....	....	....	....	....	....	....
Banks	4 613	....	....	....	....	....	....	....	....
Other sectors	4 614	8.7	6.8	−16.9	−142.8	130.3	−3.1	7.9	−69.6
Debt securities	4 619	−84.1	−657.7	−1,085.9	−613.1	−1,211.9	−408.5	−923.6	−780.0
Bonds and notes	4 620	−92.1	−657.7	−1,085.1	−539.4	−1,252.3	−428.5	−932.7	−766.7
Monetary authorities	4 621	....	....	....	....	....	....	....	....
General government	4 622	5.3	−5.1						
Banks	4 623	−36.9	−641.7	−1,087.6	−319.4	−1,450.5	−432.1	−986.0	−692.8
Other sectors	4 624	−60.5	−10.9	2.5	−220.0	198.2	3.6	53.3	−73.9
Money market instruments	4 630	8.0	....	−.8	−73.7	40.4	20.0	9.1	−13.3
Monetary authorities	4 631	....	....	....	....	....	....	....	....
General government	4 632	....	....	....	....	....	....	....	....
Banks	4 633	....	....	....	....	....	....	....	....
Other sectors	4 634	8.0	....	−.8	−73.7	40.4	20.0	9.1	−13.3
Liabilities	4 652	**139.6**	**775.9**	**402.0**	**254.9**	**450.0**	**−62.3**	**1,323.0**	....
Equity securities	4 660	....	....	....	....	....	....	....	....
Banks	4 663	....	....	....	....	....	....	....	....
Other sectors	4 664	....	....	....	....	....	....	....	....
Debt securities	4 669	139.6	775.9	402.0	254.9	450.0	−62.3	1,323.0	....
Bonds and notes	4 670	139.6	775.9	402.0	254.9	450.0	−62.3	1,323.0	....
Monetary authorities	4 671	....	....	....	....	....	....	....	....
General government	4 672	139.6	775.9	402.0	254.9	450.0	−62.3	1,323.0	....
Banks	4 673	....	....	....	....	....	....	....	....
Other sectors	4 674	....	....	....	....	....	....	....	....
Money market instruments	4 680	....	....	....	....	....	....	....	....
Monetary authorities	4 681	....	....	....	....	....	....	....	....
General government	4 682	....	....	....	....	....	....	....	....
Banks	4 683	....	....	....	....	....	....	....	....
Other sectors	4 684	....	....	....	....	....	....	....	....
C. FINANCIAL DERIVATIVES	4 910	....	....	....	....	....	....	....	....
Monetary authorities	4 911	....	....	....	....	....	....	....	....
General government	4 912	....	....	....	....	....	....	....	....
Banks	4 913	....	....	....	....	....	....	....	....
Other sectors	4 914	....	....	....	....	....	....	....	....
Assets	4 900	....	....	....	....	....	....	....	....
Monetary authorities	4 901	....	....	....	....	....	....	....	....
General government	4 902	....	....	....	....	....	....	....	....
Banks	4 903	....	....	....	....	....	....	....	....
Other sectors	4 904	....	....	....	....	....	....	....	....
Liabilities	4 905	....	....	....	....	....	....	....	....
Monetary authorities	4 906	....	....	....	....	....	....	....	....
General government	4 907	....	....	....	....	....	....	....	....
Banks	4 908	....	....	....	....	....	....	....	....
Other sectors	4 909	....	....	....	....	....	....	....	....

Table 2 (Concluded). STANDARD PRESENTATION, 2003–2010

(Millions of U.S. dollars)

	Code	2003	2004	2005	2006	2007	2008	2009	2010
D. OTHER INVESTMENT....................................	4 700 ..	**−713.2**	**−657.4**	**1,669.9**	**−1,602.4**	**1,303.9**	**927.8**	**−1,327.5**	**306.4**
Assets..	4 703 ..	**631.2**	**−1,542.8**	**−334.4**	**−3,790.4**	**−5,118.5**	**−2,844.9**	**−1,519.5**	**−4,384.0**
Trade credits..	4 706 ..	178.5	−133.2	−214.3	−308.9	−270.3	−83.2	−225.4	−104.3
General government...............................	4 707 ..	....	....	....	....	....	....	....	....
of which: Short-term.............................	4 709 ..	....	....	....	....	....	....	....	....
Other sectors.......................................	4 710 ..	178.5	−133.2	−214.3	−308.9	−270.3	−83.2	−225.4	−104.3
of which: Short-term...........................	4 712 ..	*123.3*	*−132.6*	*−252.8*	*−305.6*	*−254.2*	*−88.6*	*−218.1*	*−74.1*
Loans..	4 714 ..	822.0	−886.7	−1,388.1	−1,788.2	−4,521.8	−1,034.7	148.5	−3,525.7
Monetary authorities............................	4 715 ..	....	....	....	....	....	....	....	....
of which: Short-term...........................	4 718 ..	....	....	....	....	....	....	....	....
General government...............................	4 719 ..	....	....	....	....	....	....	....	....
of which: Short-term.............................	4 721 ..	....	....	....	....	....	....	....	....
Banks...	4 722 ..	822.0	−886.7	−1,388.1	−1,788.2	−4,521.8	−1,034.7	148.5	−3,525.7
of which: Short-term...........................	4 724 ..	*822.0*	*−886.7*	*−1,388.1*	*−1,788.2*	*−4,521.8*	*−1,034.7*	*148.5*	*−3,525.7*
Other sectors.......................................	4 725 ..	....	....	....	....	....	....	....	....
of which: Short-term...........................	4 727 ..	....	....	....	....	....	....	....	....
Currency and deposits..............................	4 730 ..	−318.1	−549.0	2,073.4	−1,508.7	−296.3	−1,971.2	−562.0	−299.1
Monetary authorities............................	4 731 ..	....	....	....	....	....	....	....	....
General government...............................	4 732 ..	32.1	−598.5	496.7	−309.1	....	....	....	....
Banks...	4 733 ..	−350.2	49.5	1,576.7	−1,199.6	−296.3	−1,971.2	−562.0	−299.1
Other sectors.......................................	4 734 ..	....	....	....	....	....	....	....	....
Other assets..	4 736 ..	−51.2	26.1	−805.4	−184.6	−30.1	244.2	−880.6	−454.9
Monetary authorities............................	4 737 ..	....	....	....	....	....	....	....	....
of which: Short-term...........................	4 739 ..	....	....	....	....	....	....	....	....
General government...............................	4 740 ..	....	....	....	....	....	....	....	....
of which: Short-term.............................	4 742 ..	....	....	....	....	....	....	....	....
Banks...	4 743 ..	57.4	126.4	−464.7	139.7	.6	41.2	17.5	−92.6
of which: Short-term...........................	4 745 ..	*57.4*	*126.4*	*−464.7*	*139.7*	*.6*	*41.2*	*17.5*	*−92.6*
Other sectors.......................................	4 746 ..	−108.6	−100.3	−340.7	−324.3	−30.7	203.0	−898.1	−362.3
of which: Short-term...........................	4 748 ..	*−108.6*	*−100.3*	*−340.7*	*−324.3*	*−30.7*	*203.0*	*−898.1*	*−362.3*
Liabilities..	4 753 ..	**−1,344.4**	**885.4**	**2,004.3**	**2,188.0**	**6,422.4**	**3,772.7**	**192.0**	**4,690.4**
Trade credits..	4 756 ..	24.1	54.9	107.7	73.7	79.8	59.5	−13.8	138.9
General government...............................	4 757 ..	....	....	....	....	....	....	....	....
of which: Short-term.............................	4 759 ..	....	....	....	....	....	....	....	....
Other sectors.......................................	4 760 ..	24.1	54.9	107.7	73.7	79.8	59.5	−13.8	138.9
of which: Short-term...........................	4 762 ..	*5.7*	*65.1*	*103.7*	*73.7*	*70.5*	*40.8*	*−23.1*	*111.6*
Loans..	4 764 ..	−701.0	602.8	853.7	851.8	1,631.4	−808.6	−282.6	5,130.5
Monetary authorities............................	4 765 ..	−9.5	−10.0	−9.7	−9.9	−10.3	−5.3	....	....
of which: Use of Fund credit and loans from the Fund..	4 766 ..	*−9.5*	*−10.0*	*−9.7*	*−9.9*	*−10.3*	*−5.3*	....	....
of which: Short-term.............................	4 768 ..	....	....	....	....	....	....	....	....
General government...............................	4 769 ..	10.2	−37.0	−54.2	23.6	34.8	243.8	335.4	266.3
of which: Short-term.............................	4 771 ..	....	....	....	....	....	....	....	....
Banks...	4 772 ..	−670.7	607.2	838.1	840.5	1,418.8	−1,106.8	−760.5	4,677.4
of which: Short-term...........................	4 774 ..	*−365.1*	*287.2*	*295.6*	*446.0*	*752.0*	*−586.6*	*−403.2*	*2,479.1*
Other sectors.......................................	4 775 ..	−31.0	42.6	79.5	−2.4	188.1	59.7	142.5	186.8
of which: Short-term...........................	4 777 ..	*−23.1*	*49.4*	*15.6*	*68.3*	*191.7*	*54.3*	*124.7*	*183.1*
Currency and deposits..............................	4 780 ..	−433.8	278.7	875.0	1,354.2	4,705.9	4,187.4	352.2	−686.2
Monetary authorities............................	4 781 ..	1.6	....	....	9.5	10.1	7.4	−2.0	1.7
General government...............................	4 782 ..	....	....	....	....	....	....	....	....
Banks...	4 783 ..	−435.4	278.7	875.0	1,344.7	4,695.8	4,180.0	354.2	−687.9
Other sectors.......................................	4 784 ..	....	....	....	....	....	....	....	....
Other liabilities.......................................	4 786 ..	−233.7	−51.0	167.9	−91.7	5.3	334.4	136.2	107.2
Monetary authorities............................	4 787 ..	....	....	....	....	−.1	−.2	266.5	3.6
of which: Short-term...........................	4 789 ..	....	....	....	....	....	....	....	....
General government...............................	4 790 ..	....	....	....	....	....	....	....	....
of which: Short-term.............................	4 792 ..	....	....	....	....	....	....	....	....
Banks...	4 793 ..	−243.2	−65.1	153.3	−84.4	−3.0	331.5	−136.7	98.4
of which: Short-term...........................	4 795 ..	*−243.2*	*−65.1*	*153.3*	*−84.4*	*−3.0*	*331.5*	*−136.7*	*98.4*
Other sectors.......................................	4 796 ..	9.5	14.1	14.6	−7.3	8.4	3.1	6.4	5.2
of which: Short-term...........................	4 798 ..	*9.5*	*14.1*	*14.6*	*−7.3*	*8.4*	*3.1*	*6.4*	*5.2*
E. RESERVE ASSETS.....................................	4 802 ..	**268.2**	**397.0**	**−522.8**	**−161.8**	**−609.6**	**−580.0**	**−614.2**	**342.7**
Monetary gold..	4 812 ..	....	....	....	....	....	....	....	....
Special drawing rights................................	4 811 ..	.3	....	−.3	−.1	.5	....	−266.4	.1
Reserve position in the Fund.......................	4 810 ..	....	....	....	....	....	....	....	....
Foreign exchange......................................	4 803 ..	277.6	421.5	−520.8	−148.5	−620.5	−543.4	−302.8	602.4
Other claims...	4 813 ..	−9.7	−24.5	−1.7	−13.2	10.4	−36.6	−45.0	−259.8
NET ERRORS AND OMISSIONS.............................	4 998 ..	**89.9**	**110.4**	**−357.9**	**141.3**	**−475.9**	**595.1**	**−218.0**	**748.7**

Table 3. INTERNATIONAL INVESTMENT POSITION (End-period stocks), 2003–2010

(Millions of U.S. dollars)

	Code	2003	2004	2005	2006	2007	2008	2009	2010
ASSETS............	8 995 C.	**20,515.9**	**22,345.0**	**24,303.4**	**29,012.5**	**35,823.2**	**39,684.1**	**42,734.8**	**47,620.7**
Direct investment abroad............	8 505 ..	....	....	....	....	....	....	....	....
Equity capital and reinvested earnings............	8 506 ..	....	....	....	....	....	....	....	....
Claims on affiliated enterprises............	8 507 ..	....	....	....	....	....	....	....	....
Liabilities to affiliated enterprises............	8 508 ..	....	....	....	....	....	....	....	....
Other capital............	8 530 ..	....	....	....	....	....	....	....	....
Claims on affiliated enterprises............	8 535 ..	....	....	....	....	....	....	....	....
Liabilities to affiliated enterprises............	8 540 ..	....	....	....	....	....	....	....	....
Portfolio investment............	8 602 ..	**3,525.7**	**4,206.1**	**5,308.9**	**6,064.8**	**7,146.4**	**7,566.0**	**8,481.7**	**9,331.3**
Equity securities............	8 610 ..	44.9	38.1	55.0	197.8	67.5	75.5	67.6	137.2
Monetary authorities............	8 611 ..	....	....	....	....	....	....	....	....
General government............	8 612 ..	....	....	....	....	....	....	....	....
Banks............	8 613 ..	....	....	....	....	....	....	....	....
Other sectors............	8 614 ..	44.9	38.1	55.0	197.8	67.5	75.5	67.6	137.2
Debt securities............	8 619 ..	3,480.8	4,168.0	5,253.9	5,867.0	7,078.9	7,490.5	8,414.1	9,194.1
Bonds and notes............	8 620 ..	3,480.8	4,168.0	5,253.1	5,792.5	7,044.8	7,476.4	8,409.1	9,175.8
Monetary authorities............	8 621 ..	....	....	....	....	....	....	....	....
General government............	8 622 ..	12.9	18.0	18.0	18.0	18.0	18.0	18.0	18.0
Banks............	8 623 ..	3,325.0	3,996.2	5,083.8	5,403.2	6,853.7	7,285.8	8,271.8	8,964.6
Other sectors............	8 624 ..	142.9	153.8	151.3	371.3	173.1	172.6	119.3	193.2
Money market instruments............	8 630 ..	....	....	.8	74.5	34.1	14.1	5.0	18.3
Monetary authorities............	8 631 ..	....	....	....	....	....	....	....	....
General government............	8 632 ..	....	....	....	....	....	....	....	....
Banks............	8 633 ..	....	....	....	....	....	....	....	....
Other sectors............	8 634 ..	....	....	.8	74.5	34.1	14.1	5.0	18.3
Financial derivatives............	8 900 ..	....	....	....	....	....	....	....	....
Monetary authorities............	8 901 ..	....	....	....	....	....	....	....	....
General government............	8 902 ..	....	....	....	....	....	....	....	....
Banks............	8 903 ..	....	....	....	....	....	....	....	....
Other sectors............	8 904 ..	....	....	....	....	....	....	....	....
Other investment............	8 703 ..	**14,683.7**	**16,228.6**	**16,562.9**	**20,353.3**	**25,471.8**	**28,333.7**	**29,853.2**	**34,237.2**
Trade credits............	8 706 ..	2,004.7	2,137.9	2,352.2	2,661.1	2,931.4	3,028.4	3,253.8	3,358.1
General government............	8 707 ..	....	....	....	....	....	....	....	....
of which: Short-term............	8 709 ..	....	....	....	....	....	....	....	....
Other sectors............	8 710 ..	2,004.7	2,137.9	2,352.2	2,661.1	2,931.4	3,028.4	3,253.8	3,358.1
of which: Short-term............	8 712 ..	*1,898.5*	*2,031.1*	*2,283.9*	*2,589.5*	*2,843.7*	*2,909.6*	*3,127.7*	*3,201.8*
Loans............	8 714 ..	6,419.5	7,312.5	8,700.6	10,488.7	15,010.4	16,045.1	15,896.6	19,422.3
Monetary authorities............	8 715 ..	....	....	....	....	....	....	....	....
of which: Short-term............	8 718 ..	....	....	....	....	....	....	....	....
General government............	8 719 ..	....	....	....	....	....	....	....	....
of which: Short-term............	8 721 ..	....	....	....	....	....	....	....	....
Banks............	8 722 ..	6,419.5	7,312.5	8,700.6	10,488.7	15,010.4	16,045.1	15,896.6	19,422.3
of which: Short-term............	8 724 ..	*6,419.5*	*7,312.5*	*8,700.6*	*10,488.7*	*15,010.4*	*16,045.1*	*15,896.6*	*19,422.3*
Other sectors............	8 725 ..	....	....	....	....	....	....	....	....
of which: Short-term............	8 727 ..	....	....	....	....	....	....	....	....
Currency and deposits............	8 730 ..	5,453.9	6,001.4	3,927.9	5,436.6	5,732.9	7,704.1	8,266.1	8,565.2
Monetary authorities............	8 731 ..	....	....	....	....	....	....	....	....
General government............	8 732 ..	7.5	606.0	109.3	418.4	418.4	418.4	418.4	418.4
Banks............	8 733 ..	5,446.4	5,395.4	3,818.6	5,018.2	5,314.5	7,285.7	7,847.7	8,146.8
Other sectors............	8 734 ..	....	....	....	....	....	....	....	....
Other assets............	8 736 ..	805.6	776.8	1,582.2	1,766.9	1,797.1	1,556.1	2,436.7	2,891.6
Monetary authorities............	8 737 ..	....	....	....	....	....	....	....	....
of which: Short-term............	8 739 ..	....	....	....	....	....	....	....	....
General government............	8 740 ..	29.2	29.2	29.2	29.2	29.2	29.2	29.2	29.2
of which: Short-term............	8 742 ..	....	....	....	....	....	....	....	....
Banks............	8 743 ..	353.9	224.8	689.5	549.9	549.4	508.2	490.7	583.3
of which: Short-term............	8 745 ..	*353.9*	*224.8*	*689.5*	*549.9*	*549.4*	*508.2*	*490.7*	*583.3*
Other sectors............	8 746 ..	422.5	522.8	863.5	1,187.8	1,218.5	1,018.7	1,916.8	2,279.1
of which: Short-term............	8 748 ..	*422.5*	*522.8*	*863.5*	*1,187.8*	*1,218.5*	*1,018.7*	*1,916.8*	*2,279.1*
Reserve assets............	8 802 ..	**2,306.5**	**1,910.4**	**2,431.6**	**2,594.4**	**3,205.0**	**3,784.4**	**4,399.9**	**4,052.2**
Monetary gold............	8 812 ..	....	....	....	....	....	....	....	....
Special drawing rights............	8 811 ..	.8	.9	1.1	1.3	.9	.8	268.2	263.3
Reserve position in the Fund............	8 810 ..	17.6	18.4	17.0	17.8	18.7	18.3	18.6	18.3
Foreign exchange............	8 803 ..	2,278.3	1,856.8	2,377.6	2,526.1	3,146.6	3,690.0	3,992.8	3,390.4
Other claims............	8 813 ..	9.8	34.3	36.0	49.2	38.8	75.4	120.4	380.2

Table 3 (Concluded). INTERNATIONAL INVESTMENT POSITION (End-period stocks), 2003–2010

(Millions of U.S. dollars)

	Code	2003	2004	2005	2006	2007	2008	2009	2010
LIABILITIES	8 995 D.	**29,806.3**	**32,512.5**	**35,795.3**	**40,809.0**	**49,450.3**	**55,428.9**	**58,677.2**	**65,721.1**
Direct investment in Panama	8 555	**8,230.4**	**9,249.5**	**10,167.1**	**12,724.2**	**14,500.7**	**16,809.2**	**18,582.0**	**20,944.5**
Equity capital and reinvested earnings	8 556	7,116.5	8,101.4	8,571.0	10,835.2	12,433.9	14,438.0	16,197.2	18,019.4
Claims on direct investors	8 557	....	....	....	....	....	....	....	....
Liabilities to direct investors	8 558	7,116.5	8,101.4	8,571.0	10,835.2	12,433.9	14,438.0	16,197.2	18,019.4
Other capital	8 580	1,113.9	1,148.1	1,596.1	1,889.0	2,066.8	2,371.2	2,384.8	2,925.1
Claims on direct investors	8 585	−1,209.4	−1,468.2	−1,655.0	−2,034.2	−2,281.1	−2,715.2	−2,721.0	−2,553.1
Liabilities to direct investors	8 590	2,323.3	2,616.3	3,251.1	3,923.2	4,347.9	5,086.4	5,105.8	5,478.2
Portfolio investment	8 652	**4,956.8**	**5,702.8**	**6,104.8**	**6,359.7**	**6,809.7**	**6,747.4**	**7,970.9**	**7,970.9**
Equity securities	8 660	....	....	....	....	....	....	....	....
Banks	8 663	....	....	....	....	....	....	....	....
Other sectors	8 664	....	....	....	....	....	....	....	....
Debt securities	8 669	4,956.8	5,702.8	6,104.8	6,359.7	6,809.7	6,747.4	7,970.9	7,970.9
Bonds and notes	8 670	4,956.8	5,702.8	6,104.8	6,359.7	6,809.7	6,747.4	7,970.9	7,970.9
Monetary authorities	8 671	....	....	....	....	....	....	....	....
General government	8 672	4,956.8	5,702.8	6,104.8	6,359.7	6,809.7	6,747.4	7,970.9	7,970.9
Banks	8 673	....	....	....	....	....	....	....	....
Other sectors	8 674	....	....	....	....	....	....	....	....
Money market instruments	8 680	....	....	....	....	....	....	....	....
Monetary authorities	8 681	....	....	....	....	....	....	....	....
General government	8 682	....	....	....	....	....	....	....	....
Banks	8 683	....	....	....	....	....	....	....	....
Other sectors	8 684	....	....	....	....	....	....	....	....
Financial derivatives	8 905	....	....	....	....	....	....	....	....
Monetary authorities	8 906	....	....	....	....	....	....	....	....
General government	8 907	....	....	....	....	....	....	....	....
Banks	8 908	....	....	....	....	....	....	....	....
Other sectors	8 909	....	....	....	....	....	....	....	....
Other investment	8 753	**16,619.1**	**17,560.2**	**19,523.4**	**21,725.1**	**28,139.9**	**31,872.3**	**32,124.3**	**36,805.7**
Trade credits	8 756	740.8	795.7	903.4	977.1	1,056.9	1,086.0	1,072.2	1,211.1
General government	8 757	....	....	....	....	....	....	....	....
of which: Short-term	8 759	....	....	....	....	....	....	....	....
Other sectors	8 760	740.8	795.7	903.4	977.1	1,056.9	1,086.0	1,072.2	1,211.1
of which: Short-term	8 762	*691.5*	*756.6*	*860.3*	*934.0*	*1,004.5*	*1,019.1*	*996.0*	*1,107.6*
Loans	8 764	5,008.0	5,660.0	6,472.2	7,337.8	8,961.7	8,143.4	7,878.7	13,009.2
Monetary authorities	8 765	127.3	118.9	106.5	97.7	88.0	82.7	82.7	82.7
of which: Use of Fund credit and loans from the Fund	8 766	*44.6*	*36.2*	*23.8*	*15.0*	*5.3*	....	....	....
of which: Short-term	8 768	....	....	....	....	....	....	....	....
General government	8 769	1,433.2	1,440.8	1,349.5	1,385.9	1,412.9	1,656.7	2,010.0	2,276.3
of which: Short-term	8 771	....	....	....	....	....	....	....	....
Banks	8 772	2,867.0	3,474.2	4,312.3	5,152.8	6,571.6	5,464.8	4,704.3	9,381.7
of which: Short-term	8 774	*1,014.0*	*1,301.2*	*1,596.8*	*2,042.8*	*2,794.8*	*2,208.2*	*1,805.0*	*4,284.1*
Other sectors	8 775	580.5	626.0	703.9	701.3	889.2	939.2	1,081.7	1,268.5
of which: Short-term	8 777	*532.9*	*582.3*	*597.9*	*666.2*	*857.9*	*902.5*	*1,027.2*	*1,210.3*
Currency and deposits	8 780	10,313.7	10,592.8	11,468.1	12,822.3	17,528.2	21,715.6	22,067.8	21,381.6
Monetary authorities	8 781	46.8	46.8	46.8	56.3	66.4	73.8	71.8	73.5
General government	8 782	....	....	....	....	....	....	....	....
Banks	8 783	10,266.9	10,546.0	11,421.3	12,766.0	17,461.8	21,641.8	21,996.0	21,308.1
Other sectors	8 784	....	....	....	....	....	....	....	....
Other liabilities	8 786	556.6	511.7	679.6	587.9	593.1	927.2	1,105.6	1,203.7
Monetary authorities	8 787	31.2	31.2	31.2	31.2	31.0	31.4	340.1	334.6
of which: Short-term	8 789	*31.2*	*31.2*	*31.2*	*31.2*	*31.2*	*31.2*	*31.2*	*31.2*
General government	8 790	2.1	2.1	2.1	2.1	2.1	2.1	2.1	2.1
of which: Short-term	8 792	*2.1*	*2.1*	*2.1*	*2.1*	*2.1*	*2.1*	*2.1*	*2.1*
Banks	8 793	490.0	431.0	584.3	499.9	496.9	828.4	691.7	790.1
of which: Short-term	8 795	*490.0*	*431.0*	*584.3*	*499.9*	*496.9*	*828.4*	*691.7*	*790.1*
Other sectors	8 796	33.3	47.4	62.0	54.7	63.1	65.3	71.7	76.9
of which: Short-term	8 798	*33.3*	*47.4*	*62.0*	*54.7*	*63.1*	*65.3*	*71.7*	*76.9*
NET INTERNATIONAL INVESTMENT POSITION	8 995	**−9,290.4**	**−10,167.5**	**−11,491.9**	**−11,796.5**	**−13,627.2**	**−15,744.8**	**−15,942.4**	**−18,100.4**
Conversion rates: balboas per U.S. dollar (end of period)	0 102	**1.0000**	**1.0000**	**1.0000**	**1.0000**	**1.0000**	**1.0000**	**1.0000**	**1.0000**

Table 1. ANALYTIC PRESENTATION, 2003–2010

(Millions of U.S. dollars)

	Code	2003	2004	2005	2006	2007	2008	2009	2010
A. Current Account[1]	4 993 Z.	**42.8**	**85.6**	**539.4**	**332.7**	**56.3**	**707.9**	**−851.8**	**−913.6**
Goods: exports f.o.b.	2 100 ..	2,200.8	2,618.1	3,317.6	4,204.3	4,747.8	5,805.5	4,391.9	5,744.7
Goods: imports f.o.b.	3 100 ..	−1,187.3	−1,459.3	−1,525.3	−1,990.5	−2,629.3	−3,140.2	−2,870.7	−3,528.9
Balance on Goods	4 100 ..	*1,013.5*	*1,158.8*	*1,792.4*	*2,213.8*	*2,118.5*	*2,665.4*	*1,521.2*	*2,215.8*
Services: credit	2 200 ..	235.5	211.1	304.9	322.5	352.6	368.7	185.4	310.4
Services: debit	3 200 ..	−967.2	−1,105.3	−1,277.9	−1,595.8	−1,945.4	−1,843.4	−1,840.0	−2,756.7
Balance on Goods and Services	4 991 ..	*281.8*	*264.5*	*819.4*	*940.5*	*525.8*	*1,190.7*	*−133.4*	*−230.5*
Income: credit	2 300 ..	16.2	19.8	26.1	70.3	104.4	85.1	46.3	41.6
Income: debit	3 300 ..	−492.9	−456.0	−564.6	−875.8	−824.0	−729.2	−671.1	−634.0
Balance on Goods, Services, and Income	4 992 ..	*−194.9*	*−171.6*	*280.9*	*135.1*	*−193.8*	*546.6*	*−758.1*	*−822.9*
Current transfers: credit	2 379 Z.	319.0	334.5	352.1	327.0	411.0	392.2	112.7	157.8
Current transfers: debit	3 379 ..	−81.2	−77.3	−93.6	−129.4	−160.9	−230.9	−206.5	−248.4
B. Capital Account[1]	4 994 Z.	....	....	**32.6**	**44.2**	**38.3**	**18.6**	**26.7**	**37.2**
Capital account: credit	2 994 Z.	....	....	32.6	44.2	38.3	26.0	33.9	44.5
Capital account: debit	3 994 ..	....	....	....	....	....	−7.4	−7.3	−7.4
Total, Groups A Plus B	4 981 ..	*42.8*	*85.6*	*572.0*	*376.9*	*94.6*	*726.5*	*−825.1*	*−876.4*
C. Financial Account[1]	4 995 W.	**−303.2**	**−280.4**	**−605.8**	**175.8**	**305.1**	**−1,059.2**	**1,156.4**	**1,037.3**
Direct investment abroad	4 505 ..	−8.2	−.6	−6.6	−1.1	−7.7	−.1	−4.4	−.2
Direct investment in Papua New Guinea	4 555 Z.	117.7	30.5	38.4	12.9	102.3	−30.5	423.2	28.9
Portfolio investment assets	4 602 ..	−46.6	−104.0	23.1	125.1	408.0	349.0	150.4	−104.4
Equity securities	4 610 ..	−64.0	−16.0	−15.3	382.9	96.4	176.4	4.9	−12.4
Debt securities	4 619 ..	17.4	−88.0	38.5	−257.8	311.6	172.7	145.5	−91.9
Portfolio investment liabilities	4 652 Z.	....	....	−1.8	....	....	....	....	....
Equity securities	4 660 ..	....	....	....	....	....	....	....	....
Debt securities	4 669 Z.	....	....	−1.8	....	....	....	....	....
Financial derivatives	4 910 ..	23.0	−9.4	−1.9	−11.2	−92.6	−131.6	21.1	−7.5
Financial derivatives assets	4 900 ..	23.0	−9.4	−1.9	−11.2	−92.6	−131.6	21.1	−7.5
Financial derivatives liabilities	4 905 ..	....	....	....	....	....	....	....	....
Other investment assets	4 703 ..	−221.3	−38.1	−679.6	250.6	8.9	−954.9	447.2	1,182.0
Monetary authorities	4 701 ..	....	....	....	....	....	....	....	....
General government	4 704 ..	....	....	....	....	....	....	....	....
Banks	4 705 ..	−106.9	−149.9	−141.1	60.9	−324.5	82.7	−113.1	−95.2
Other sectors	4 728 ..	−114.4	111.9	−538.4	189.6	333.5	−1,037.6	560.3	1,277.3
Other investment liabilities	4 753 W.	−167.8	−158.9	22.5	−200.4	−113.7	−291.2	118.8	−61.6
Monetary authorities	4 753 WA	....	....	....	....	....	....	181.6	....
General government	4 753 ZB	−118.5	−121.3	−94.5	−98.8	−149.9	−159.2	−35.2	−38.6
Banks	4 753 ZC	1.7	5.3	8.7	−19.4	12.8	−59.0	27.6	.4
Other sectors	4 753 ZD	−51.0	−42.9	108.3	−82.2	23.3	−72.9	−55.2	−23.3
Total, Groups A Through C	4 983 ..	*−260.4*	*−194.9*	*−33.8*	*552.7*	*399.8*	*−332.7*	*331.2*	*160.9*
D. Net Errors and Omissions	4 998 ..	**150.8**	**306.4**	**3.5**	**−15.1**	**9.7**	**−73.2**	**−162.6**	**−75.9**
Total, Groups A Through D	4 984 ..	*−109.6*	*111.5*	*−30.4*	*537.6*	*409.4*	*−406.0*	*168.6*	*85.0*
E. Reserves and Related Items	4 802 A.	**109.6**	**−111.5**	**30.4**	**−537.6**	**−409.4**	**406.0**	**−168.6**	**−85.0**
Reserve assets	4 802 ..	−103.3	−102.3	−95.4	−640.5	−537.5	221.8	−629.3	−406.9
Use of Fund credit and loans	4 766 ..	−5.4	−60.0	−62.2	....	....	....	....	....
Exceptional financing	4 920 ..	218.3	50.8	187.9	102.8	128.1	184.1	460.7	321.9
Conversion rates: kina per U.S. dollar	0 101 ..	**3.5635**	**3.2225**	**3.1019**	**3.0567**	**2.9653**	**2.7001**	**2.7551**	**2.7193**

[1] Excludes components that have been classified in the categories of Group E.

Table 2. STANDARD PRESENTATION, 2003–2010

(Millions of U.S. dollars)

	Code	2003	2004	2005	2006	2007	2008	2009	2010
CURRENT ACCOUNT	4 993	**42.8**	**85.6**	**539.4**	**332.7**	**56.3**	**707.9**	**−585.1**	**−633.0**
A. GOODS	4 100	**1,013.5**	**1,158.8**	**1,792.4**	**2,213.8**	**2,118.5**	**2,665.4**	**1,521.2**	**2,215.8**
Credit	2 100	**2,200.8**	**2,618.1**	**3,317.6**	**4,204.3**	**4,747.8**	**5,805.5**	**4,391.9**	**5,744.7**
General merchandise: exports f.o.b.	2 110	1,411.9	1,755.6	2,404.0	3,193.1	3,508.7	4,076.2	2,425.0	3,398.4
Goods for processing: exports f.o.b.	2 150	....	....	....	....	....	....	....	....
Repairs on goods	2 160	....	....	....	....	....	....	....	....
Goods procured in ports by carriers	2 170	....	....	....	....	....	....	....	....
Nonmonetary gold	2 180	788.9	862.5	913.7	1,011.2	1,239.1	1,729.3	1,966.9	2,346.3
Debit	3 100	**−1,187.3**	**−1,459.3**	**−1,525.3**	**−1,990.5**	**−2,629.3**	**−3,140.2**	**−2,870.7**	**−3,528.9**
General merchandise: imports f.o.b.	3 110	−1,187.3	−1,459.3	−1,525.3	−1,990.5	−2,629.3	−3,140.2	−2,870.7	−3,528.9
Goods for processing: imports f.o.b.	3 150	....	....	....	....	....	....	....	....
Repairs on goods	3 160	....	....	....	....	....	....	....	....
Goods procured in ports by carriers	3 170	....	....	....	....	....	....	....	....
Nonmonetary gold	3 180	....	....	....	....	....	....	....	....
B. SERVICES	4 200	**−731.6**	**−894.2**	**−973.0**	**−1,273.3**	**−1,592.8**	**−1,474.7**	**−1,654.6**	**−2,446.3**
Total credit	2 200	*235.5*	*211.1*	*304.9*	*322.5*	*352.6*	*368.7*	*185.4*	*310.4*
Total debit	3 200	*−967.2*	*−1,105.3*	*−1,277.9*	*−1,595.8*	*−1,945.4*	*−1,843.4*	*−1,840.0*	*−2,756.7*
Transportation services, credit	2 205	**16.6**	**20.8**	**31.1**	**21.4**	**27.2**	**26.0**	**13.8**	**20.9**
Passenger	2 850	*.9*	*1.3*	*5.8*	....	*.3*	*1.6*	....	*.1*
Freight	2 851	*15.7*	*19.5*	*25.3*	*21.4*	*26.9*	*24.4*	*13.8*	*20.7*
Other	2 852	....	....	....	....	....	....	....	....
Sea transport, passenger	2 207	....	....	....	....	....	....	....	.1
Sea transport, freight	2 208	15.7	19.1	19.7	21.0	20.9	20.4	13.5	19.7
Sea transport, other	2 209	....	....	....	....	....	....	....	....
Air transport, passenger	2 211	.9	1.3	5.8	....	.3	1.6	....	....
Air transport, freight	2 212	....	....	....	.4	1.1	3.6	.3	1.0
Air transport, other	2 213	....	....	....	....	....	....	....	....
Other transport, passenger	2 215	....	....	....	....	....	....	....	....
Other transport, freight	2 216	....	.4	5.6	....	4.9	.4	.1	.1
Other transport, other	2 217	....	....	....	....	....	....	....	....
Transportation services, debit	3 205	**−227.5**	**−270.8**	**−278.7**	**−354.3**	**−457.1**	**−516.5**	**−442.8**	**−590.3**
Passenger	3 850	*−.1*	*−.7*	*−.5*	*−26.7*	*−60.2*	*−45.5*	*−18.8*	*−18.5*
Freight	3 851	*−227.4*	*−270.1*	*−278.1*	*−327.6*	*−396.9*	*−470.9*	*−424.0*	*−571.8*
Other	3 852	....	....	....	....	....	....	....	....
Sea transport, passenger	3 207	....	−.1	−.5	....	−32.4	−4.5	−.1	−1.7
Sea transport, freight	3 208	−187.1	−233.4	−236.3	−314.7	−382.2	−454.1	−407.3	−542.1
Sea transport, other	3 209	....	....	....	....	....	....	....	....
Air transport, passenger	3 211	....	....	....	−26.6	−27.8	−40.7	−18.6	−16.8
Air transport, freight	3 212	−40.3	−36.6	−41.8	−12.8	−14.4	−16.2	−15.9	−28.5
Air transport, other	3 213	....	....	....	....	....	....	....	....
Other transport, passenger	3 215	....	−.7	....	−.1	−.1	−.3	−.1	....
Other transport, freight	3 216	−.1	....	....	−.1	−.3	−.6	−.9	−1.3
Other transport, other	3 217	....	....	....	....	....	....	....	....
Travel, credit	2 236	**4.0**	**5.8**	**3.6**	**3.9**	**4.2**	**2.1**	**2.1**	**2.3**
Business travel	2 237	3.7	4.3	2.4	2.7	2.9	1.5	1.2	1.9
Personal travel	2 240	.3	1.5	1.2	1.2	1.3	.6	.9	.3
Travel, debit	3 236	**−51.9**	**−71.2**	**−55.6**	**−15.7**	**−20.8**	**−28.9**	**−113.1**	**−118.8**
Business travel	3 237	−15.6	−20.6	−18.1	−11.0	−14.6	−20.2	−29.1	−40.5
Personal travel	3 240	−36.2	−50.6	−37.5	−4.7	−6.2	−8.7	−84.0	−78.3
Other services, credit	2 200 BA	**214.8**	**184.5**	**270.2**	**297.2**	**321.2**	**340.6**	**169.5**	**287.2**
Communications	2 245	.4	3.9	5.7	13.0	12.6	4.1	2.0	.5
Construction	2 249	96.3	28.1	15.3	17.0	8.2	3.0	40.4	95.4
Insurance	2 253	5.9	8.9	13.0	1.9	3.2	4.7	5.3	1.3
Financial	2 260	6.2	5.9	2.5	2.9	8.9	8.9	6.5	6.2
Computer and information	2 262	.1	.2	.9	1.9	.8	.1	.3	1.8
Royalties and licence fees	2 266	....	....	....	....	....	....	....	....
Other business services	2 268	92.1	115.1	215.4	242.0	248.1	268.6	89.7	150.8
Personal, cultural, and recreational	2 287	....	.2	.4	.5	.2	.2	....	....
Government, n.i.e.	2 291	13.8	22.2	17.0	17.9	39.2	50.8	25.3	31.3
Other services, debit	3 200 BA	**−687.8**	**−763.3**	**−943.6**	**−1,225.8**	**−1,467.5**	**−1,298.1**	**−1,284.0**	**−2,047.6**
Communications	3 245	−4.3	−11.1	−7.7	−7.4	−20.1	−23.0	−16.4	−40.2
Construction	3 249	−39.9	−37.9	−58.4	−55.5	−55.3	−54.0	−221.4	−676.1
Insurance	3 253	−64.5	−65.2	−64.6	−48.9	−51.8	−76.0	−91.2	−91.4
Financial	3 260	−16.0	−45.4	−53.4	−69.7	−233.0	−208.7	−160.2	−260.3
Computer and information	3 262	−10.4	−14.5	−11.7	−12.5	−15.0	−11.3	−15.1	−11.4
Royalties and licence fees	3 266	....	....	....	....	....	....	....	....
Other business services	3 268	−547.5	−560.0	−731.6	−1,019.7	−1,092.0	−898.6	−762.7	−947.6
Personal, cultural, and recreational	3 287	....	−.2	−.1	−.1	−.1	−.6	−.4	−.7
Government, n.i.e.	3 291	−5.3	−29.1	−16.2	−12.0	−.1	−25.9	−16.7	−19.8

Table 2 (Continued). STANDARD PRESENTATION, 2003–2010

(Millions of U.S. dollars)

	Code	2003	2004	2005	2006	2007	2008	2009	2010
C. INCOME	4 300	**−476.7**	**−436.2**	**−538.5**	**−805.4**	**−719.6**	**−644.1**	**−624.8**	**−592.4**
Total credit	2 300	*16.2*	*19.8*	*26.1*	*70.3*	*104.4*	*85.1*	*46.3*	*41.6*
Total debit	3 300	*−492.9*	*−456.0*	*−564.6*	*−875.8*	*−824.0*	*−729.2*	*−671.1*	*−634.0*
Compensation of employees, credit	2 310	**2.9**	**1.6**	**1.2**	**1.0**	**2.2**	**2.4**	**2.6**	**2.9**
Compensation of employees, debit	3 310	**−49.9**	**−55.6**	**−53.7**	**−61.1**	**−150.3**	**−118.6**	**−134.5**	**−168.1**
Investment income, credit	2 320	**13.3**	**18.2**	**25.0**	**69.3**	**102.2**	**82.7**	**43.7**	**38.6**
Direct investment income	2 330	6.9	2.2	.9	2.1	2.9	2.0	7.8	14.0
Dividends and distributed branch profits	2 332	6.9	2.2	.9	2.1	2.9	2.0	7.8	14.0
Reinvested earnings and undistributed branch profits	2 333	....	....	....	....	....	....	....	....
Income on debt (interest)	2 334	....	....	....	....	....	....	....	....
Portfolio investment income	2 339	6.4	16.0	24.1	67.2	99.3	80.8	35.9	24.6
Income on equity	2 340	....	....	....	....	....	....	....	....
Income on bonds and notes	2 350	6.2	14.0	21.1	53.6	74.5	64.3	28.3	10.9
Income on money market instruments	2 360	.2	2.0	3.0	13.6	24.8	16.5	7.5	13.7
Other investment income	2 370	....	....	....	....	....	....	....	....
Investment income, debit	3 320	**−443.0**	**−400.4**	**−510.9**	**−814.6**	**−673.7**	**−610.6**	**−536.6**	**−465.9**
Direct investment income	3 330	−443.0	−400.4	−510.9	−814.6	−673.7	−610.6	−536.6	−465.9
Dividends and distributed branch profits	3 332	−364.0	−328.6	−437.6	−725.1	−579.1	−541.5	−479.7	−418.0
Reinvested earnings and undistributed branch profits	3 333	−16.8	−18.6	−19.3	−19.6	−20.2	−22.2	−21.8	−22.1
Income on debt (interest)	3 334	−62.2	−53.1	−54.0	−69.9	−74.3	−46.9	−35.1	−25.8
Portfolio investment income	3 339	....	....	....	....	....	....	....	....
Income on equity	3 340	....	....	....	....	....	....	....	....
Income on bonds and notes	3 350	....	....	....	....	....	....	....	....
Income on money market instruments	3 360	....	....	....	....	....	....	....	....
Other investment income	3 370	....	....	....	....	....	....	....	....
D. CURRENT TRANSFERS	4 379	**237.7**	**257.2**	**258.5**	**197.6**	**250.1**	**161.3**	**173.0**	**189.9**
Credit	2 379	**319.0**	**334.5**	**352.1**	**327.0**	**411.0**	**392.2**	**379.4**	**438.3**
General government	2 380	174.7	204.0	185.2	269.0	302.5	171.5	266.7	280.6
Other sectors	2 390	144.2	130.5	166.9	58.0	108.5	220.6	112.7	157.8
Workers' remittances	2 391	4.0	7.9	5.7	3.4	5.4	5.0	2.1	.6
Other current transfers	2 392	140.2	122.5	161.2	54.6	103.1	215.7	110.6	157.2
Debit	3 379	**−81.2**	**−77.3**	**−93.6**	**−129.4**	**−160.9**	**−230.9**	**−206.5**	**−248.4**
General government	3 380	....	....	....	....	....	....	....	....
Other sectors	3 390	−81.2	−77.3	−93.6	−129.4	−160.9	−230.9	−206.5	−248.4
Workers' remittances	3 391	−41.2	−61.1	−74.5	−97.4	−133.7	−202.3	−180.8	−226.0
Other current transfers	3 392	−40.0	−16.2	−19.1	−32.0	−27.2	−28.6	−25.6	−22.4
CAPITAL AND FINANCIAL ACCOUNT	4 996	**−193.6**	**−391.9**	**−542.9**	**−317.6**	**−66.0**	**−634.7**	**747.7**	**708.9**
CAPITAL ACCOUNT	4 994	**....**	**....**	**32.6**	**44.2**	**38.3**	**18.6**	**26.7**	**37.2**
Total credit	2 994	*....*	*....*	*32.6*	*44.2*	*38.3*	*26.0*	*33.9*	*44.5*
Total debit	3 994	*....*	*....*	*....*	*....*	*....*	*−7.4*	*−7.3*	*−7.4*
Capital transfers, credit	2 400	**....**	**....**	**32.6**	**44.2**	**38.3**	**26.0**	**33.9**	**44.5**
General government	2 401	....	....	32.6	44.2	38.3	18.6	26.7	37.2
Debt forgiveness	2 402	....	....	....	....	....	....	....	....
Other capital transfers	2 410	....	....	32.6	44.2	38.3	18.6	26.7	37.2
Other sectors	2 430	....	....	....	....	....	7.4	7.3	7.4
Migrants' transfers	2 431	....	....	....	....	....	7.4	7.3	7.4
Debt forgiveness	2 432	....	....	....	....	....	....	....	....
Other capital transfers	2 440	....	....	....	....	....	....	....	....
Capital transfers, debit	3 400	**....**	**....**	**....**	**....**	**....**	**−7.4**	**−7.3**	**−7.4**
General government	3 401	....	....	....	....	....	....	....	....
Debt forgiveness	3 402	....	....	....	....	....	....	....	....
Other capital transfers	3 410	....	....	....	....	....	....	....	....
Other sectors	3 430	....	....	....	....	....	−7.4	−7.3	−7.4
Migrants' transfers	3 431	....	....	....	....	....	−7.4	−7.3	−7.4
Debt forgiveness	3 432	....	....	....	....	....	....	....	....
Other capital transfers	3 440	....	....	....	....	....	....	....	....
Nonproduced nonfinancial assets, credit	2 480	**....**	**....**	**....**	**....**	**....**	**....**	**....**	**....**
Nonproduced nonfinancial assets, debit	3 480	**....**	**....**	**....**	**....**	**....**	**....**	**....**	**....**

Table 2 (Continued). STANDARD PRESENTATION, 2003–2010

(Millions of U.S. dollars)

	Code	2003	2004	2005	2006	2007	2008	2009	2010
FINANCIAL ACCOUNT	4 995	**−193.6**	**−391.9**	**−575.4**	**−361.8**	**−104.3**	**−653.2**	**721.1**	**671.7**
A. DIRECT INVESTMENT	4 500	**109.5**	**29.9**	**31.8**	**11.8**	**94.6**	**−30.6**	**418.8**	**28.7**
Direct investment abroad	4 505	**−8.2**	**−.6**	**−6.6**	**−1.1**	**−7.7**	**−.1**	**−4.4**	**−.2**
Equity capital	4 510	−8.2	−.6	−6.6	−1.1	−7.7	−.1	−4.4	−.2
Claims on affiliated enterprises	4 515	....	....	....	....	....	....	....	....
Liabilities to affiliated enterprises	4 520	−8.2	−.6	−6.6	−1.1	−7.7	−.1	−4.4	−.2
Reinvested earnings	4 525	....	....	....	....	....	....	....	....
Other capital	4 530	....	....	....	....	....	....	....	....
Claims on affiliated enterprises	4 535	....	....	....	....	....	....	....	....
Liabilities to affiliated enterprises	4 540	....	....	....	....	....	....	....	....
Direct investment in Papua New Guinea	4 555	**117.7**	**30.5**	**38.4**	**12.9**	**102.3**	**−30.5**	**423.2**	**28.9**
Equity capital	4 560	101.0	12.6	18.4	−7.4	83.1	−47.6	402.1	6.6
Claims on direct investors	4 565	....	....	....	....	....	....	....	....
Liabilities to direct investors	4 570	101.0	12.6	18.4	−7.4	83.1	−47.6	402.1	6.6
Reinvested earnings	4 575	16.8	18.6	19.3	19.6	20.2	22.2	21.8	22.1
Other capital	4 580	−.1	−.7	.6	.6	−1.0	−5.1	−.6	.3
Claims on direct investors	4 585	....	....	....	....	....	....	....	....
Liabilities to direct investors	4 590	−.1	−.7	.6	.6	−1.0	−5.1	−.6	.3
B. PORTFOLIO INVESTMENT	4 600	**−46.6**	**−104.0**	**21.4**	**125.1**	**408.0**	**349.0**	**150.1**	**−104.4**
Assets	4 602	**−46.6**	**−104.0**	**23.1**	**125.1**	**408.0**	**349.0**	**150.4**	**−104.4**
Equity securities	4 610	−64.0	−16.0	−15.3	382.9	96.4	176.4	4.9	−12.4
Monetary authorities	4 611	....	....	....	....	....	....	....	....
General government	4 612	....	....	....	....	....	....	....	....
Banks	4 613	....	....	....	....	....	....	....	−1.2
Other sectors	4 614	−64.0	−16.0	−15.3	382.9	96.4	176.4	4.9	−11.3
Debt securities	4 619	17.4	−88.0	38.5	−257.8	311.6	172.7	145.5	−91.9
Bonds and notes	4 620	−2.4	20.2	−.4	−14.6	−29.0	9.0	−10.8	−17.1
Monetary authorities	4 621	....	....	....	....	....	....	....	....
General government	4 622	....	....	....	....	....	....	....	....
Banks	4 623	....	....	....	....	....	....	....	....
Other sectors	4 624	−2.4	20.2	−.4	−14.6	−29.0	9.0	−10.8	−17.1
Money market instruments	4 630	19.9	−108.2	38.8	−243.2	340.6	163.7	156.3	−74.9
Monetary authorities	4 631	....	....	....	....	....	....	....	....
General government	4 632	....	....	....	....	....	....	....	....
Banks	4 633	−10.4	....	....	....	....	....	....	....
Other sectors	4 634	30.3	−108.2	38.8	−243.2	340.6	163.7	156.3	−74.9
Liabilities	4 652	**....**	**....**	**−1.8**	**....**	**....**	**....**	**−.4**	**....**
Equity securities	4 660	....	....	....	....	....	....	....	....
Banks	4 663	....	....	....	....	....	....	....	....
Other sectors	4 664	....	....	....	....	....	....	....	....
Debt securities	4 669	....	....	−1.8	....	....	....	−.4	....
Bonds and notes	4 670	....	....	....	....	....	....	−.4	....
Monetary authorities	4 671	....	....	....	....	....	....	....	....
General government	4 672	....	....	....	....	....	....	....	....
Banks	4 673	....	....	....	....	....	....	....	....
Other sectors	4 674	....	....	....	....	....	....	−.4	....
Money market instruments	4 680	....	....	−1.8	....	....	....	....	....
Monetary authorities	4 681	....	....	....	....	....	....	....	....
General government	4 682	....	....	−1.8	....	....	....	....	....
Banks	4 683	....	....	....	....	....	....	....	....
Other sectors	4 684	....	....	....	....	....	....	....	....
C. FINANCIAL DERIVATIVES	4 910	**23.0**	**−9.4**	**−1.9**	**−11.2**	**−92.6**	**−131.6**	**21.1**	**−7.5**
Monetary authorities	4 911	....	....	....	....	....	....	....	....
General government	4 912	....	....	....	....	....	....	....	....
Banks	4 913	....	....	....	....	....	....	....	....
Other sectors	4 914	23.0	−9.4	−1.9	−11.2	−92.6	−131.6	21.1	−7.5
Assets	4 900	**23.0**	**−9.4**	**−1.9**	**−11.2**	**−92.6**	**−131.6**	**21.1**	**−7.5**
Monetary authorities	4 901	....	....	....	....	....	....	....	....
General government	4 902	....	....	....	....	....	....	....	....
Banks	4 903	....	....	....	....	....	....	....	....
Other sectors	4 904	23.0	−9.4	−1.9	−11.2	−92.6	−131.6	21.1	−7.5
Liabilities	4 905	**....**	**....**	**....**	**....**	**....**	**....**	**....**	**....**
Monetary authorities	4 906	....	....	....	....	....	....	....	....
General government	4 907	....	....	....	....	....	....	....	....
Banks	4 908	....	....	....	....	....	....	....	....
Other sectors	4 909	....	....	....	....	....	....	....	....

Table 2 (Concluded). STANDARD PRESENTATION, 2003–2010

(Millions of U.S. dollars)

	Code	2003	2004	2005	2006	2007	2008	2009	2010
D. OTHER INVESTMENT	4 700 ..	−176.2	−206.1	−531.3	153.0	23.3	−1,061.9	760.4	1,161.8
Assets	4 703 ..	−221.3	−38.1	−679.6	250.6	8.9	−954.9	447.2	1,182.0
Trade credits	4 706 ..	−183.4	−156.1	−229.9	−361.2	−551.1	−735.7	−478.2	−275.3
General government	4 707 ..	....	....	....	....	....	....	....	....
of which: Short-term	4 709 ..	....	....	....	....	....	....	....	....
Other sectors	4 710 ..	−183.4	−156.1	−229.9	−361.2	−551.1	−735.7	−478.2	−275.3
of which: Short-term	4 712 ..	*−183.4*	*−156.1*	*−229.9*	*−361.2*	*−551.1*	*−735.7*	*−478.2*	*−275.3*
Loans	4 714 ..	....	....	....	.2	....	−35.9	5.7	.5
Monetary authorities	4 715 ..	....	....	....	....	....	....	....	....
of which: Short-term	4 718 ..	....	....	....	....	....	....	....	....
General government	4 719 ..	....	....	....	....	....	....	....	....
of which: Short-term	4 721 ..	....	....	....	....	....	....	....	....
Banks	4 722 ..	....	....	....	....	....	....	....	....
of which: Short-term	4 724 ..	....	....	....	....	....	....	....	....
Other sectors	4 725 ..	....	....	....	.2	....	−35.9	5.7	.5
of which: Short-term	4 727 ..	....	....	....	....	....	....	....	....
Currency and deposits	4 730 ..	−173.4	−107.1	−223.6	136.9	−468.0	45.1	−494.3	42.7
Monetary authorities	4 731 ..	....	....	....	....	....	....	....	....
General government	4 732 ..	....	....	....	....	....	....	....	....
Banks	4 733 ..	−106.9	−149.9	−141.1	60.9	−324.5	82.7	−113.1	−95.2
Other sectors	4 734 ..	−66.5	42.9	−82.5	76.0	−143.5	−37.6	−381.2	137.9
Other assets	4 736 ..	135.5	225.0	−226.1	474.7	1,028.0	−228.4	1,414.0	1,414.2
Monetary authorities	4 737 ..	....	....	....	....	....	....	....	....
of which: Short-term	4 739 ..	....	....	....	....	....	....	....	....
General government	4 740 ..	....	....	....	....	....	....	....	....
of which: Short-term	4 742 ..	....	....	....	....	....	....	....	....
Banks	4 743 ..	....	....	....	....	....	....	....	....
of which: Short-term	4 745 ..	....	....	....	....	....	....	....	....
Other sectors	4 746 ..	135.5	225.0	−226.1	474.7	1,028.0	−228.4	1,414.0	1,414.2
of which: Short-term	4 748 ..	*135.5*	*225.0*	*−226.1*	*474.7*	*1,028.0*	*−228.4*	*1,414.0*	*1,414.2*
Liabilities	4 753 ..	**45.1**	**−168.1**	**148.2**	**−97.6**	**14.4**	**−107.0**	**313.2**	**−20.2**
Trade credits	4 756 ..	....	....	....	....	....	....	....	....
General government	4 757 ..	....	....	....	....	....	....	....	....
of which: Short-term	4 759 ..	....	....	....	....	....	....	....	....
Other sectors	4 760 ..	....	....	....	....	....	....	....	....
of which: Short-term	4 762 ..	....	....	....	....	....	....	....	....
Loans	4 764 ..	39.5	−176.4	142.6	−72.3	−1.9	−47.4	104.0	−20.6
Monetary authorities	4 765 ..	−5.4	−60.0	−62.2	....	....	....	....	....
of which: Use of Fund credit and loans from the Fund	4 766 ..	*−5.4*	*−60.0*	*−62.2*	....	....	....	....	....
of which: Short-term	4 768 ..	....	....	....	....	....	....	....	....
General government	4 769 ..	−118.5	−121.3	−94.5	−98.8	−149.9	−159.2	−35.2	−38.6
of which: Short-term	4 771 ..	....	....	....	....	....	....	....	....
Banks	4 772 ..	....	....	....	....	....	....	....	....
of which: Short-term	4 774 ..	....	....	....	....	....	....	....	....
Other sectors	4 775 ..	163.4	4.8	299.3	26.5	148.0	111.8	139.1	18.1
of which: Short-term	4 777 ..	*−15.4*	*−.4*	*−2.8*	*−3.3*	*.8*	*−2.2*	*48.7*	*36.1*
Currency and deposits	4 780 ..	1.7	5.3	7.8	−19.4	12.8	−59.0	27.6	.4
Monetary authorities	4 781 ..	....	....	....	....	....	....	....	....
General government	4 782 ..	....	....	....	....	....	....	....	....
Banks	4 783 ..	1.7	5.3	8.7	−19.4	12.8	−59.0	27.6	.4
Other sectors	4 784 ..	....	....	−1.0	....	....	....	....	....
Other liabilities	4 786 ..	3.9	3.0	−2.2	−5.9	3.5	−.6	181.6	....
Monetary authorities	4 787 ..	....	....	....	....	....	....	181.6	....
of which: Short-term	4 789 ..	....	....	....	....	....	....	....	....
General government	4 790 ..	....	....	....	....	....	....	....	....
of which: Short-term	4 792 ..	....	....	....	....	....	....	....	....
Banks	4 793 ..	....	....	....	....	....	....	....	....
of which: Short-term	4 795 ..	....	....	....	....	....	....	....	....
Other sectors	4 796 ..	3.9	3.0	−2.2	−5.9	3.5	−.6	....	....
of which: Short-term	4 798 ..	*3.9*	*3.0*	*−2.2*	*−5.9*	*3.5*	*−.6*	....	....
E. RESERVE ASSETS	4 802 ..	**−103.3**	**−102.3**	**−95.4**	**−640.5**	**−537.5**	**221.8**	**−629.3**	**−406.9**
Monetary gold	4 812 ..	.5	....	−4.2	6.0	−4.1	1.0	−12.7	−10.6
Special drawing rights	4 811 ..	2.8	3.0	.7	....	....	....	−181.5	155.9
Reserve position in the Fund	4 810 ..	−.1	....	....	....	....	....	....	....
Foreign exchange	4 803 ..	−106.6	−105.3	−91.8	−646.4	−533.4	220.8	−435.0	−552.2
Other claims	4 813 ..	....	....	....	....	....	....	....	....
NET ERRORS AND OMISSIONS	4 998 ..	**150.8**	**306.4**	**3.5**	**−15.1**	**9.7**	**−73.2**	**−162.6**	**−75.9**

Table 1. ANALYTIC PRESENTATION, 2003–2010

(Millions of U.S. dollars)

	Code	2003	2004	2005	2006	2007	2008	2009	2010
A. Current Account[1].....	4 993 Z.	**129.5**	**143.0**	**16.0**	**127.7**	**184.2**	**−304.1**	**66.6**	**−641.2**
Goods: exports f.o.b..........	2 100 ..	2,170.0	2,861.2	3,351.8	4,401.2	5,652.1	7,798.2	5,866.5	8,519.7
Goods: imports f.o.b..........	3 100 ..	−2,446.1	−3,105.3	−3,814.3	−5,022.2	−6,185.0	−8,844.3	−6,909.6	−9,916.3
Balance on Goods..........	*4 100 ..*	*−276.1*	*−244.1*	*−462.5*	*−621.0*	*−532.9*	*−1,046.1*	*−1,043.1*	*−1,396.5*
Services: credit..........	2 200 ..	573.8	627.6	655.9	798.1	961.9	1,149.9	1,429.0	1,468.9
Services: debit..........	3 200 ..	−328.6	−301.0	−343.4	−383.8	−463.3	−591.6	−538.3	−754.5
Balance on Goods and Services..........	*4 991 ..*	*−30.8*	*82.5*	*−150.0*	*−206.8*	*−34.4*	*−487.8*	*−152.4*	*−682.2*
Income: credit..........	2 300 ..	166.3	165.4	205.7	297.7	336.7	389.8	349.8	340.9
Income: debit..........	3 300 ..	−170.5	−299.1	−263.5	−389.3	−491.4	−620.3	−649.7	−842.5
Balance on Goods, Services, and Income..........	*4 992 ..*	*−35.0*	*−51.2*	*−207.8*	*−298.3*	*−189.0*	*−718.3*	*−452.3*	*−1,183.7*
Current transfers: credit..........	2 379 Z.	166.0	195.7	225.3	430.0	374.8	415.6	520.3	543.9
Current transfers: debit..........	3 379 ..	−1.5	−1.5	−1.5	−4.0	−1.5	−1.4	−1.4	−1.4
B. Capital Account[1]..........	4 994 Z.	**15.0**	**16.0**	**20.0**	**30.0**	**28.0**	**33.0**	**47.0**	**40.0**
Capital account: credit..........	2 994 Z.	15.0	16.0	20.0	30.0	28.0	33.0	47.0	40.0
Capital account: debit..........	3 994 ..	....	....	....	....	....	....	....	....
Total, Groups A Plus B..........	*4 981 ..*	*144.5*	*159.0*	*36.0*	*157.7*	*212.2*	*−271.1*	*113.6*	*−601.2*
C. Financial Account[1]..........	4 995 W.	**132.2**	**18.6**	**338.1**	**147.5**	**722.6**	**613.8**	**506.5**	**757.8**
Direct investment abroad..........	4 505 ..	−5.5	−6.0	−6.4	−6.8	−7.2	−4.0	−7.2	−7.2
Direct investment in Paraguay..........	4 555 Z.	27.4	37.7	53.5	173.3	206.3	278.7	200.7	344.5
Portfolio investment assets..........	4 602 ..	....	....	....	....	....	....	....	....
Equity securities..........	4 610 ..	....	....	....	....	....	....	....	....
Debt securities..........	4 619 ..	....	....	....	....	....	....	....	....
Portfolio investment liabilities..........	4 652 Z.	−.4	−.1	....	....	....	....	....	....
Equity securities..........	4 660 ..	....	....	....	....	....	....	....	....
Debt securities..........	4 669 Z.	−.4	−.1	....	....	....	....	....	....
Financial derivatives..........	4 910 ..	....	....	....	....	....	....	....	....
Financial derivatives assets..........	4 900 ..	....	....	....	....	....	....	....	....
Financial derivatives liabilities..........	4 905 ..	....	....	....	....	....	....	....	....
Other investment assets..........	4 703 ..	184.0	−39.5	423.4	90.0	470.4	−99.0	184.0	115.7
Monetary authorities..........	4 701 ..	....	....	....	....	....	....	....	....
General government..........	4 704 ..	−52.8	−56.1	−29.8	−51.7	−109.3	52.7	−14.3	−21.8
Banks..........	4 705 ..	−109.7	7.4	65.5	−7.8	−34.1	−295.2	−78.0	−159.4
Other sectors..........	4 728 ..	346.5	9.3	387.7	149.5	613.8	143.5	276.3	296.9
Other investment liabilities..........	4 753 W.	−73.3	26.5	−132.4	−109.0	53.1	438.1	129.0	304.8
Monetary authorities..........	4 753 WA	−4.4	−4.3	−2.5	−2.5	−2.6	−2.5	128.0	−2.2
General government..........	4 753 ZB	53.1	5.4	−48.9	−39.1	−61.1	−55.3	23.1	69.2
Banks..........	4 753 ZC	−23.9	18.9	−13.8	−12.9	126.2	144.6	25.8	171.6
Other sectors..........	4 753 ZD	−98.1	6.5	−67.2	−54.5	−9.4	351.3	−47.8	66.3
Total, Groups A Through C..........	*4 983 ..*	*276.7*	*177.6*	*374.1*	*305.2*	*934.8*	*342.7*	*620.2*	*156.6*
D. Net Errors and Omissions..........	4 998 ..	**−40.7**	**95.6**	**−210.8**	**77.5**	**−309.8**	**53.7**	**307.2**	**162.8**
Total, Groups A Through D..........	*4 984 ..*	*236.0*	*273.2*	*163.2*	*382.7*	*625.0*	*396.4*	*927.3*	*319.4*
E. Reserves and Related Items..........	4 802 A.	**−236.0**	**−273.2**	**−163.2**	**−382.7**	**−625.0**	**−396.4**	**−927.3**	**−319.4**
Reserve assets..........	4 802 ..	−303.2	−181.2	−149.2	−386.8	−629.5	−396.0	−927.2	−319.3
Use of Fund credit and loans..........	4 766 ..	....	....	....	....	....	....	....	....
Exceptional financing..........	4 920 ..	67.2	−92.0	−14.0	4.1	4.5	−.4	−.1	−.1
Conversion rates: guaraníes per U.S. dollar..........	0 101 ..	**6,424.3**	**5,974.6**	**6,178.0**	**5,635.5**	**5,032.7**	**4,363.2**	**4,965.4**	**4,735.5**

[1] Excludes components that have been classified in the categories of Group E.

Table 2. STANDARD PRESENTATION, 2003–2010

(Millions of U.S. dollars)

	Code	2003	2004	2005	2006	2007	2008	2009	2010
CURRENT ACCOUNT	4 993 ..	**129.5**	**143.0**	**16.0**	**127.7**	**184.2**	**−304.1**	**66.6**	**−641.2**
A. GOODS	4 100 ..	**−276.1**	**−244.1**	**−462.5**	**−621.0**	**−532.9**	**−1,046.1**	**−1,043.1**	**−1,396.5**
Credit	2 100 ..	**2,170.0**	**2,861.2**	**3,351.8**	**4,401.2**	**5,652.1**	**7,798.2**	**5,866.5**	**8,519.7**
General merchandise: exports f.o.b.	2 110 ..	2,163.1	2,854.3	3,315.6	4,337.9	5,408.9	7,710.2	5,795.5	8,404.0
Goods for processing: exports f.o.b.	2 150 ..	....	....	29.3	56.4	236.1	79.5	62.5	107.3
Repairs on goods	2 160 ..	.5	.5	.5	.5	.5	.5	.5	.5
Goods procured in ports by carriers	2 170 ..	6.4	6.4	6.4	6.4	6.6	8.0	8.0	8.0
Nonmonetary gold	2 180 ..								
Debit	3 100 ..	**−2,446.1**	**−3,105.3**	**−3,814.3**	**−5,022.2**	**−6,185.0**	**−8,844.3**	**−6,909.6**	**−9,916.3**
General merchandise: imports f.o.b.	3 110 ..	−2,442.7	−3,101.9	−3,799.9	−4,995.1	−6,056.8	−8,802.5	−6,875.4	−9,863.2
Goods for processing: imports f.o.b.	3 150 ..	....	....	−11.0	−23.7	−91.8	−36.0	−28.4	−47.3
Repairs on goods	3 160 ..	−.7	−.7	−.7	−.7	−.7	−.8	−.8	−.8
Goods procured in ports by carriers	3 170 ..	−2.7	−2.7	−2.7	−2.7	−35.8	−5.0	−5.0	−5.0
Nonmonetary gold	3 180 ..	....	....	....	....	....	....	....	....
B. SERVICES	4 200 ..	**245.2**	**326.6**	**312.5**	**414.2**	**498.6**	**558.3**	**890.6**	**714.4**
Total credit	2 200 ..	*573.8*	*627.6*	*655.9*	*798.1*	*961.9*	*1,149.9*	*1,429.0*	*1,468.9*
Total debit	3 200 ..	*−328.6*	*−301.0*	*−343.4*	*−383.8*	*−463.3*	*−591.6*	*−538.3*	*−754.5*
Transportation services, credit	2 205 ..	**84.5**	**86.7**	**86.7**	**97.2**	**124.2**	**203.6**	**161.8**	**230.4**
Passenger	2 850 ..	*16.5*	*16.5*	*18.0*	*20.0*	*18.6*	*18.6*	*20.4*	*26.4*
Freight	2 851 ..	*58.0*	*62.2*	*60.6*	*68.2*	*92.8*	*166.2*	*112.8*	*159.4*
Other	2 852 ..	*10.0*	*8.0*	*8.1*	*9.0*	*12.8*	*18.8*	*28.6*	*44.6*
Sea transport, passenger	2 207 ..	....	....	....	....	....	....	....	....
Sea transport, freight	2 208 ..	....	....	....	....	....	....	....	....
Sea transport, other	2 209 ..	....	....	....	....	....	....	....	....
Air transport, passenger	2 211 ..	10.0	10.0	10.0	12.0	12.0	12.0	12.0	18.0
Air transport, freight	2 212 ..								
Air transport, other	2 213 ..								
Other transport, passenger	2 215 ..	6.5	6.5	8.0	8.0	6.6	6.6	8.4	8.4
Other transport, freight	2 216 ..	58.0	62.2	60.6	68.2	92.8	166.2	112.8	159.4
Other transport, other	2 217 ..	10.0	8.0	8.1	9.0	12.8	18.8	28.6	44.6
Transportation services, debit	3 205 ..	**−180.4**	**−164.0**	**−181.3**	**−208.8**	**−264.7**	**−372.9**	**−313.7**	**−480.4**
Passenger	3 850 ..	*−48.3*	*−50.3*	*−51.1*	*−52.0*	*−74.6*	*−85.8*	*−100.1*	*−115.8*
Freight	3 851 ..	*−127.2*	*−107.3*	*−122.4*	*−146.5*	*−177.5*	*−271.7*	*−194.9*	*−341.8*
Other	3 852 ..	*−4.9*	*−6.4*	*−7.8*	*−10.3*	*−12.6*	*−15.3*	*−18.7*	*−22.8*
Sea transport, passenger	3 207 ..	....	....	....	....	....	....	....	....
Sea transport, freight	3 208 ..	−22.6	−19.4	−26.3	−35.0	−42.6	−64.7	−46.7	−83.5
Sea transport, other	3 209 ..	....	....	....	....	....	....	....	....
Air transport, passenger	3 211 ..	−40.0	−42.0	−42.8	−42.0	−63.0	−74.2	−87.5	−103.2
Air transport, freight	3 212 ..	−27.4	−22.8	−25.4	−33.7	−40.8	−61.9	−44.8	−86.0
Air transport, other	3 213 ..	....	....	....	....	....	....	....	....
Other transport, passenger	3 215 ..	−8.3	−8.3	−8.3	−10.0	−11.6	−11.6	−12.6	−12.6
Other transport, freight	3 216 ..	−77.2	−65.1	−70.7	−77.8	−94.1	−145.1	−103.4	−172.3
Other transport, other	3 217 ..	−4.9	−6.4	−7.8	−10.3	−12.6	−15.3	−18.7	−22.8
Travel, credit	2 236 ..	**63.6**	**69.7**	**77.5**	**91.5**	**101.8**	**109.3**	**204.7**	**217.4**
Business travel	2 237 ..	....	....	....	....	....	....	....	....
Personal travel	2 240 ..	63.6	69.7	77.5	91.5	101.8	109.3	204.7	217.4
Travel, debit	3 236 ..	**−66.9**	**−70.7**	**−78.6**	**−92.2**	**−108.8**	**−121.5**	**−128.5**	**−152.9**
Business travel	3 237 ..	....	....	....	....	....	....	....	....
Personal travel	3 240 ..	−66.9	−70.7	−78.6	−92.2	−108.8	−121.5	−128.5	−152.9
Other services, credit	2 200 BA	**425.7**	**471.2**	**491.8**	**609.4**	**735.9**	**837.0**	**1,062.5**	**1,021.1**
Communications	2 245 ..	13.0	16.0	17.0	17.0	14.0	13.0	17.0	16.5
Construction	2 249 ..	....	....	....	....	....	....	....	....
Insurance	2 253 ..	14.2	16.0	16.4	27.0	32.0	20.0	24.0	24.0
Financial	2 260 ..	6.1	10.5	10.2	3.5	1.6	3.3	3.1	3.4
Computer and information	2 262 ..	.2	.4	.4	2.4	2.6	.4	3.4	4.4
Royalties and licence fees	2 266 ..	193.4	207.9	218.7	254.7	287.2	282.3	263.9	254.1
Other business services	2 268 ..	175.4	190.3	182.9	232.2	319.3	428.0	591.1	559.7
Personal, cultural, and recreational	2 287 ..	....	....	....	....	....	....	....	14.0
Government, n.i.e.	2 291 ..	23.4	30.1	46.2	72.5	79.2	90.0	160.0	145.0
Other services, debit	3 200 BA	**−81.3**	**−66.3**	**−83.5**	**−82.8**	**−89.8**	**−97.3**	**−96.1**	**−121.2**
Communications	3 245 ..	−.2	−.2	−6.0	−2.7	−4.0	−4.0	−4.0	−4.0
Construction	3 249 ..	....	....	....	....	....	....	....	....
Insurance	3 253 ..	−40.8	−41.1	−51.2	−46.1	−44.6	−45.2	−46.2	−47.1
Financial	3 260 ..	−4.3	−3.4	−3.6	−3.7	−8.2	−7.3	−9.5	−8.7
Computer and information	3 262 ..	−1.2	−.9	−1.8	−1.5	−2.1	−2.1	−2.1	−2.1
Royalties and licence fees	3 266 ..	−4.6	−1.9	−1.7	−3.1	−1.2	−1.9	−1.7	−2.5
Other business services	3 268 ..	−19.2	−4.5	−4.3	−6.5	−8.7	−6.8	−6.6	−9.4
Personal, cultural, and recreational	3 287 ..	....	....	....	....	....	....	....	....
Government, n.i.e.	3 291 ..	−11.0	−14.3	−14.9	−19.2	−21.0	−30.0	−26.0	−47.4

Table 2 (Continued). STANDARD PRESENTATION, 2003–2010

(Millions of U.S. dollars)

	Code	2003	2004	2005	2006	2007	2008	2009	2010
C. INCOME	4 300	**−4.2**	**−133.7**	**−57.8**	**−91.6**	**−154.7**	**−230.5**	**−299.8**	**−501.5**
Total credit	2 300	*166.3*	*165.4*	*205.7*	*297.7*	*336.7*	*389.8*	*349.8*	*340.9*
Total debit	3 300	*−170.5*	*−299.1*	*−263.5*	*−389.3*	*−491.4*	*−620.3*	*−649.7*	*−842.5*
Compensation of employees, credit	2 310	**112.6**	**106.2**	**108.0**	**127.2**	**143.1**	**225.2**	**241.9**	**254.1**
Compensation of employees, debit	3 310	....	....	....	....	....	....	....	....
Investment income, credit	2 320	**53.7**	**59.2**	**97.7**	**170.5**	**193.6**	**164.6**	**107.9**	**86.8**
Direct investment income	2 330	24.0	29.0	25.2	26.7	25.4	25.3	29.9	28.9
Dividends and distributed branch profits	2 332	17.5	18.8	18.6	19.7	18.0	21.1	22.5	21.5
Reinvested earnings and undistributed branch profits	2 333	5.5	6.0	6.4	6.8	7.2	4.0	7.2	7.2
Income on debt (interest)	2 334	1.0	4.2	.2	.2	.2	.2	.2	.2
Portfolio investment income	2 339	2.3	2.3	2.3	1.1	2.9	....	....	....
Income on equity	2 340	....	....	....	....	....	....	....	....
Income on bonds and notes	2 350	2.3	2.3	2.3	1.1	2.9	....	....	....
Income on money market instruments	2 360	....	....	....	....	....	....	....	....
Other investment income	2 370	27.4	27.9	70.2	142.7	165.3	139.3	78.0	57.9
Investment income, debit	3 320	**−170.5**	**−299.1**	**−263.5**	**−389.3**	**−491.4**	**−620.3**	**−649.7**	**−842.5**
Direct investment income	3 330	−60.0	−192.3	−158.2	−271.0	−364.5	−505.4	−554.8	−763.5
Dividends and distributed branch profits	3 332	−86.1	−101.0	−172.0	−224.0	−332.2	−447.5	−530.1	−648.8
Reinvested earnings and undistributed branch profits	3 333	32.5	−85.8	15.2	−45.6	−30.9	−56.7	−23.5	−113.5
Income on debt (interest)	3 334	−6.4	−5.5	−1.4	−1.4	−1.4	−1.2	−1.2	−1.2
Portfolio investment income	3 339	....	....	....	....	....	....	....	....
Income on equity	3 340	....	....	....	....	....	....	....	....
Income on bonds and notes	3 350	....	....	....	....	....	....	....	....
Income on money market instruments	3 360	....	....	....	....	....	....	....	....
Other investment income	3 370	−110.5	−106.8	−105.3	−118.3	−126.9	−114.9	−94.9	−79.0
D. CURRENT TRANSFERS	4 379	**164.5**	**194.2**	**223.8**	**426.0**	**373.3**	**414.2**	**518.9**	**542.5**
Credit	2 379	**166.0**	**195.7**	**225.3**	**430.0**	**374.8**	**415.6**	**520.3**	**543.9**
General government	2 380	8.0	11.0	8.0	16.0	8.0	8.0	8.0	8.0
Other sectors	2 390	158.0	184.7	217.3	414.0	366.8	407.6	512.3	535.9
Workers' remittances	2 391	109.5	132.0	161.3	336.0	340.8	362.6	377.3	409.9
Other current transfers	2 392	48.5	52.7	56.0	78.0	26.0	45.0	135.0	126.0
Debit	3 379	**−1.5**	**−1.5**	**−1.5**	**−4.0**	**−1.5**	**−1.4**	**−1.4**	**−1.4**
General government	3 380	−1.5	−1.5	−1.5	−4.0	−1.5	−1.4	−1.4	−1.4
Other sectors	3 390	....	....	....	....	....	....	....	....
Workers' remittances	3 391	....	....	....	....	....	....	....	....
Other current transfers	3 392	....	....	....	....	....	....	....	....
CAPITAL AND FINANCIAL ACCOUNT	4 996	**−88.8**	**−238.6**	**194.8**	**−205.2**	**125.6**	**250.4**	**−373.8**	**478.4**
CAPITAL ACCOUNT	4 994	**15.0**	**16.0**	**20.0**	**30.0**	**28.0**	**33.0**	**47.0**	**40.0**
Total credit	2 994	*15.0*	*16.0*	*20.0*	*30.0*	*28.0*	*33.0*	*47.0*	*40.0*
Total debit	3 994	....	....	....	....	....	....	....	....
Capital transfers, credit	2 400	**15.0**	**16.0**	**20.0**	**30.0**	**28.0**	**33.0**	**47.0**	**40.0**
General government	2 401	15.0	16.0	20.0	30.0	28.0	33.0	47.0	40.0
Debt forgiveness	2 402	....	....	....	....	....	....	....	....
Other capital transfers	2 410	15.0	16.0	20.0	30.0	28.0	33.0	47.0	40.0
Other sectors	2 430	....	....	....	....	....	....	....	....
Migrants' transfers	2 431	....	....	....	....	....	....	....	....
Debt forgiveness	2 432	....	....	....	....	....	....	....	....
Other capital transfers	2 440	....	....	....	....	....	....	....	....
Capital transfers, debit	3 400	....	....	....	....	....	....	....	....
General government	3 401	....	....	....	....	....	....	....	....
Debt forgiveness	3 402	....	....	....	....	....	....	....	....
Other capital transfers	3 410	....	....	....	....	....	....	....	....
Other sectors	3 430	....	....	....	....	....	....	....	....
Migrants' transfers	3 431	....	....	....	....	....	....	....	....
Debt forgiveness	3 432	....	....	....	....	....	....	....	....
Other capital transfers	3 440	....	....	....	....	....	....	....	....
Nonproduced nonfinancial assets, credit	2 480	....	....	....	....	....	....	....	....
Nonproduced nonfinancial assets, debit	3 480	....	....	....	....	....	....	....	....

Table 2 (Continued). STANDARD PRESENTATION, 2003–2010

(Millions of U.S. dollars)

	Code	2003	2004	2005	2006	2007	2008	2009	2010
FINANCIAL ACCOUNT.....................	4 995 ..	**−103.8**	**−254.6**	**174.8**	**−235.2**	**97.6**	**217.4**	**−420.8**	**438.4**
A. DIRECT INVESTMENT.....................	4 500 ..	**21.9**	**31.7**	**47.1**	**166.5**	**199.1**	**274.7**	**193.5**	**337.3**
Direct investment abroad...................	4 505 ..	**−5.5**	**−6.0**	**−6.4**	**−6.8**	**−7.2**	**−4.0**	**−7.2**	**−7.2**
Equity capital....................................	4 510 ..	....	....	....	....	....	....	....	....
Claims on affiliated enterprises...........	4 515 ..	....	....	....	....	....	....	....	....
Liabilities to affiliated enterprises........	4 520 ..	....	....	....	....	....	....	....	....
Reinvested earnings............................	4 525 ..	−5.5	−6.0	−6.4	−6.8	−7.2	−4.0	−7.2	−7.2
Other capital....................................	4 530 ..	....	....	....	....	....	....	....	....
Claims on affiliated enterprises...........	4 535 ..	....	....	....	....	....	....	....	....
Liabilities to affiliated enterprises........	4 540 ..	....	....	....	....	....	....	....	....
Direct investment in Paraguay...........	4 555 ..	**27.4**	**37.7**	**53.5**	**173.3**	**206.3**	**278.7**	**200.7**	**344.5**
Equity capital....................................	4 560 ..	32.4	10.1	65.3	119.6	46.9	90.4	279.4	37.3
Claims on direct investors..................	4 565 ..	....	....	....	....	....	....	....	....
Liabilities to direct investors..............	4 570 ..	32.4	10.1	65.3	119.6	46.9	90.4	279.4	37.3
Reinvested earnings............................	4 575 ..	−32.5	85.8	−15.2	45.6	30.9	56.7	23.5	113.5
Other capital....................................	4 580 ..	27.5	−58.2	3.4	8.1	128.5	131.6	−102.2	193.7
Claims on direct investors..................	4 585 ..	82.6	−66.3	28.2	−73.6	97.3	−52.2	45.6	−78.1
Liabilities to direct investors..............	4 590 ..	−55.1	8.1	−24.8	81.7	31.2	183.8	−147.8	271.8
B. PORTFOLIO INVESTMENT................	4 600 ..	**−.4**	**−.1**	....	....	....	....	....	....
Assets...	4 602 ..	....	....	....	....	....	....	....	....
Equity securities...............................	4 610 ..	....	....	....	....	....	....	....	....
Monetary authorities.......................	4 611 ..	....	....	....	....	....	....	....	....
General government........................	4 612 ..	....	....	....	....	....	....	....	....
Banks...	4 613 ..	....	....	....	....	....	....	....	....
Other sectors................................	4 614 ..	....	....	....	....	....	....	....	....
Debt securities.................................	4 619 ..	....	....	....	....	....	....	....	....
Bonds and notes............................	4 620 ..	....	....	....	....	....	....	....	....
Monetary authorities.....................	4 621 ..	....	....	....	....	....	....	....	....
General government......................	4 622 ..	....	....	....	....	....	....	....	....
Banks...	4 623 ..	....	....	....	....	....	....	....	....
Other sectors..............................	4 624 ..	....	....	....	....	....	....	....	....
Money market instruments...............	4 630 ..	....	....	....	....	....	....	....	....
Monetary authorities.....................	4 631 ..	....	....	....	....	....	....	....	....
General government......................	4 632 ..	....	....	....	....	....	....	....	....
Banks...	4 633 ..	....	....	....	....	....	....	....	....
Other sectors..............................	4 634 ..	....	....	....	....	....	....	....	....
Liabilities.......................................	4 652 ..	**−.4**	**−.1**	....	....	....	....	....	....
Equity securities...............................	4 660 ..	....	....	....	....	....	....	....	....
Banks...	4 663 ..	....	....	....	....	....	....	....	....
Other sectors................................	4 664 ..	....	....	....	....	....	....	....	....
Debt securities.................................	4 669 ..	−.4	−.1	....	....	....	....	....	....
Bonds and notes............................	4 670 ..	−.4	−.1	....	....	....	....	....	....
Monetary authorities.....................	4 671 ..	....	....	....	....	....	....	....	....
General government......................	4 672 ..	....	....	....	....	....	....	....	....
Banks...	4 673 ..	....	....	....	....	....	....	....	....
Other sectors..............................	4 674 ..	−.4	−.1	....	....	....	....	....	....
Money market instruments...............	4 680 ..	....	....	....	....	....	....	....	....
Monetary authorities.....................	4 681 ..	....	....	....	....	....	....	....	....
General government......................	4 682 ..	....	....	....	....	....	....	....	....
Banks...	4 683 ..	....	....	....	....	....	....	....	....
Other sectors..............................	4 684 ..	....	....	....	....	....	....	....	....
C. FINANCIAL DERIVATIVES................	4 910 ..	....	....	....	....	....	....	....	....
Monetary authorities.........................	4 911 ..	....	....	....	....	....	....	....	....
General government..........................	4 912 ..	....	....	....	....	....	....	....	....
Banks...	4 913 ..	....	....	....	....	....	....	....	....
Other sectors..................................	4 914 ..	....	....	....	....	....	....	....	....
Assets...	4 900 ..	....	....	....	....	....	....	....	....
Monetary authorities.........................	4 901 ..	....	....	....	....	....	....	....	....
General government..........................	4 902 ..	....	....	....	....	....	....	....	....
Banks...	4 903 ..	....	....	....	....	....	....	....	....
Other sectors..................................	4 904 ..	....	....	....	....	....	....	....	....
Liabilities.......................................	4 905 ..	....	....	....	....	....	....	....	....
Monetary authorities.........................	4 906 ..	....	....	....	....	....	....	....	....
General government..........................	4 907 ..	....	....	....	....	....	....	....	....
Banks...	4 908 ..	....	....	....	....	....	....	....	....
Other sectors..................................	4 909 ..	....	....	....	....	....	....	....	....

Table 2 (Concluded). STANDARD PRESENTATION, 2003–2010

(Millions of U.S. dollars)

	Code	2003	2004	2005	2006	2007	2008	2009	2010
D. OTHER INVESTMENT	4 700	**177.9**	**−105.0**	**277.0**	**−14.9**	**528.0**	**338.7**	**312.9**	**420.4**
Assets	4 703	**184.0**	**−39.5**	**423.4**	**90.0**	**470.4**	**−99.0**	**184.0**	**115.7**
Trade credits	4 706	11.4	−7.5	....	−11.5	.8	19.3	1.1	−18.6
General government	4 707	....	....	....	....	....	....	....	....
of which: Short-term	4 709	....	....	....	....	....	....	....	....
Other sectors	4 710	11.4	−7.5	....	−11.5	.8	19.3	1.1	−18.6
of which: Short-term	4 712	*11.4*	*−7.5*	....	*−11.5*	*.8*	*19.3*	*1.1*	*−18.6*
Loans	4 714	−151.6	−28.6	−3.9	−34.6	−47.3	−98.0	137.5	31.6
Monetary authorities	4 715	....	....	....	....	....	....	....	....
of which: Short-term	4 718	....	....	....	....	....	....	....	....
General government	4 719	−46.7	−24.5	−28.0	−36.2	−75.2	39.6	78.0	73.0
of which: Short-term	4 721	....	....	....	....	....	....	....	....
Banks	4 722	−103.5	−1.7	27.9	2.1	25.8	−140.5	56.6	−44.3
of which: Short-term	4 724	*−103.5*	*−1.7*	*27.9*	*2.1*	*25.8*	*−140.5*	*56.6*	*−44.3*
Other sectors	4 725	−1.4	−2.4	−3.8	−.5	2.1	2.9	2.9	2.9
of which: Short-term	4 727	....	....	....	....	....	....	....	....
Currency and deposits	4 730	331.9	29.8	430.2	160.6	577.9	12.5	100.4	190.2
Monetary authorities	4 731	....	....	....	....	....	....	....	....
General government	4 732	....	....	....	....	....	....	....	....
Banks	4 733	−5.9	10.2	36.1	−5.1	−39.5	−116.2	−174.9	−109.2
Other sectors	4 734	337.8	19.6	394.1	165.7	617.4	128.7	275.3	299.4
Other assets	4 736	−7.8	−33.2	−3.0	−24.4	−61.0	−32.8	−55.0	−87.5
Monetary authorities	4 737	....	....	....	....	....	....	....	....
of which: Short-term	4 739	....	....	....	....	....	....	....	....
General government	4 740	−6.1	−31.6	−1.8	−15.5	−34.1	13.1	−92.3	−94.8
of which: Short-term	4 742	*−6.1*	*−31.6*	*−1.8*	*−15.5*	*−34.1*	*13.1*	*−92.3*	*−94.8*
Banks	4 743	−.3	−1.1	1.5	−4.8	−20.4	−38.5	40.3	−5.9
of which: Short-term	4 745	*−.3*	*−1.1*	*1.5*	*−4.8*	*−20.4*	*−38.5*	*40.3*	*−5.9*
Other sectors	4 746	−1.4	−.4	−2.7	−4.1	−6.5	−7.4	−3.0	13.2
of which: Short-term	4 748	*−1.5*	*−.4*	*−2.9*	*−4.2*	*−6.5*	*−7.4*	*−3.0*	*13.2*
Liabilities	4 753	**−6.1**	**−65.5**	**−146.4**	**−104.9**	**57.6**	**437.7**	**128.9**	**304.7**
Trade credits	4 756	−22.5	13.3	−19.1	−53.6	11.1	217.7	−18.2	48.8
General government	4 757	....	....	....	....	....	....	....	....
of which: Short-term	4 759	....	....	....	....	....	....	....	....
Other sectors	4 760	−22.5	13.3	−19.1	−53.6	11.1	217.7	−18.2	48.8
of which: Short-term	4 762	*−22.5*	*13.3*	*−19.1*	*−53.6*	*11.1*	*217.7*	*−18.2*	*48.8*
Loans	4 764	−19.0	−7.4	−121.4	−54.0	−91.2	−6.8	16.9	193.2
Monetary authorities	4 765	−3.2	−3.2	−3.2	−3.2	−3.3	−3.2	....	−2.9
of which: Use of Fund credit and loans from the Fund	4 766	....	....	....	....	....	....	....	....
of which: Short-term	4 768	....	....	....	....	....	....	....	....
General government	4 769	83.1	5.4	−48.9	−39.1	−61.1	−55.3	23.1	69.2
of which: Short-term	4 771	....	....	....	....	....	....	....	....
Banks	4 772	−17.3	1.1	−4.2	−.4	−2.1	7.5	5.4	93.5
of which: Short-term	4 774	*−16.3*	*2.1*	*−2.9*	*.7*	*−1.1*	*8.1*	*6.0*	*94.1*
Other sectors	4 775	−81.6	−10.7	−65.1	−11.3	−24.7	44.2	−11.6	33.4
of which: Short-term	4 777	*−7.6*	*5.1*	*2.6*	*.6*	*1.0*	*1.0*	*2.2*	*.8*
Currency and deposits	4 780	3.3	−.5	−7.2	4.6	117.8	64.8	63.7	51.7
Monetary authorities	4 781	....	....	....	....	....	....	....	....
General government	4 782	....	....	....	....	....	....	....	....
Banks	4 783	2.9	.3	−9.4	2.4	115.6	62.6	56.5	47.8
Other sectors	4 784	.4	−.8	2.2	2.2	2.2	2.2	7.2	3.9
Other liabilities	4 786	32.2	−70.9	1.3	−1.9	19.9	162.0	66.5	11.1
Monetary authorities	4 787	−3.3	−1.1	.7	.7	.7	.7	128.0	.7
of which: Short-term	4 789	*−3.3*	*−1.1*	*.7*	*.7*	*.7*	*.7*	*.7*	*.7*
General government	4 790	40.6	−80.8	−5.1	.2	....	−.3	....	....
of which: Short-term	4 792	*40.6*	*−80.8*	*−5.1*	*.2*	....	*−.3*	....	....
Banks	4 793	−9.3	17.1	−.4	−14.9	12.7	74.5	−36.1	30.3
of which: Short-term	4 795	*−9.3*	*17.1*	*−.4*	*−14.9*	*12.7*	*74.5*	*−36.1*	*30.3*
Other sectors	4 796	4.1	−6.1	6.1	12.1	6.5	87.1	−25.3	−19.9
of which: Short-term	4 798	*2.2*	*−7.3*	*4.9*	*10.9*	*5.3*	*85.9*	*−26.5*	*−21.1*
E. RESERVE ASSETS	4 802	**−303.2**	**−181.2**	**−149.2**	**−386.8**	**−629.5**	**−396.0**	**−927.2**	**−319.3**
Monetary gold	4 812	....	....	....	....	....	−19.7	....	....
Special drawing rights	4 811	−1.9	−2.1	−3.2	−5.0	97.9	−1.7	−127.5	−.1
Reserve position in the Fund	4 810	....	....	....	....	....	....	....	....
Foreign exchange	4 803	−301.2	−179.1	−152.3	−381.8	−727.4	−374.6	−799.7	−319.2
Other claims	4 813	−.1	....	6.3	....	....	....	....	....
NET ERRORS AND OMISSIONS	4 998	**−40.7**	**95.6**	**−210.8**	**77.5**	**−309.8**	**53.7**	**307.2**	**162.8**

2011, International Monetary Fund: *Balance of Payments Statistics Yearbook*

Table 3. INTERNATIONAL INVESTMENT POSITION (End-period stocks), 2003–2010

(Millions of U.S. dollars)

	Code	2003	2004	2005	2006	2007	2008	2009	2010
ASSETS..	8 995 C.	**2,483.9**	**2,854.8**	**3,434.8**	**4,515.1**	**4,842.0**	**5,340.9**	**7,677.2**	**8,547.3**
Direct investment abroad...........................	8 505 ..	**150.7**	**149.2**	**155.8**	**189.1**	**225.4**	**229.4**	**239.7**	**246.9**
Equity capital and reinvested earnings............................	8 506 ..	150.7	149.2	155.8	189.1	225.4	229.4	239.7	246.9
Claims on affiliated enterprises...............	8 507 ..	150.7	149.2	155.8	189.1	225.4	229.4	239.7	246.9
Liabilities to affiliated enterprises...........	8 508 ..	. . . .	. . . .	. . . .	. . . .	. . . .	. . . .	. . . .	. . . .
Other capital..	8 530 ..	. . . .	. . . .	. . . .	. . . .	. . . .	. . . .	. . . .	. . . .
Claims on affiliated enterprises...............	8 535 ..	. . . .	. . . .	. . . .	. . . .	. . . .	. . . .	. . . .	. . . .
Liabilities to affiliated enterprises...........	8 540 ..	. . . .	. . . .	. . . .	. . . .	. . . .	. . . .	. . . .	. . . .
Portfolio investment.................................	8 602 ..	**4.0**	**4.0**	**4.0**	**4.0**	**4.0**	**4.0**	**4.0**	**4.0**
Equity securities..	8 610 ..	4.0	4.0	4.0	4.0	4.0	4.0	4.0	4.0
Monetary authorities.................................	8 611 ..	3.8	3.8	3.8	3.8	3.8	3.8	3.8	3.8
General government..................................	8 612 ..	. . . .	. . . .	. . . .	. . . .	. . . .	. . . .	. . . .	. . . .
Banks...	8 613 ..	. . . .	. . . .	. . . .	. . . .	. . . .	. . . .	. . . .	. . . .
Other sectors...	8 614 ..	.2	.2	.2	.2	.2	.2	.2	.2
Debt securities...	8 619 ..	. . . .	. . . .	. . . .	. . . .	. . . .	. . . .	. . . .	. . . .
Bonds and notes...	8 620 ..	. . . .	. . . .	. . . .	. . . .	. . . .	. . . .	. . . .	. . . .
Monetary authorities.............................	8 621 ..	. . . .	. . . .	. . . .	. . . .	. . . .	. . . .	. . . .	. . . .
General government.............................	8 622 ..	. . . .	. . . .	. . . .	. . . .	. . . .	. . . .	. . . .	. . . .
Banks...	8 623 ..	. . . .	. . . .	. . . .	. . . .	. . . .	. . . .	. . . .	. . . .
Other sectors...	8 624 ..	. . . .	. . . .	. . . .	. . . .	. . . .	. . . .	. . . .	. . . .
Money market instruments.........................	8 630 ..	. . . .	. . . .	. . . .	. . . .	. . . .	. . . .	. . . .	. . . .
Monetary authorities.............................	8 631 ..	. . . .	. . . .	. . . .	. . . .	. . . .	. . . .	. . . .	. . . .
General government.............................	8 632 ..	. . . .	. . . .	. . . .	. . . .	. . . .	. . . .	. . . .	. . . .
Banks...	8 633 ..	. . . .	. . . .	. . . .	. . . .	. . . .	. . . .	. . . .	. . . .
Other sectors...	8 634 ..	. . . .	. . . .	. . . .	. . . .	. . . .	. . . .	. . . .	. . . .
Financial derivatives..................................	8 900 ..	. . . .	. . . .	. . . .	. . . .	. . . .	. . . .	. . . .	. . . .
Monetary authorities.....................................	8 901 ..	. . . .	. . . .	. . . .	. . . .	. . . .	. . . .	. . . .	. . . .
General government.......................................	8 902 ..	. . . .	. . . .	. . . .	. . . .	. . . .	. . . .	. . . .	. . . .
Banks..	8 903 ..	. . . .	. . . .	. . . .	. . . .	. . . .	. . . .	. . . .	. . . .
Other sectors..	8 904 ..	. . . .	. . . .	. . . .	. . . .	. . . .	. . . .	. . . .	. . . .
Other investment.......................................	8 703 ..	**1,336.2**	**1,513.7**	**1,957.9**	**2,597.7**	**2,147.5**	**2,244.3**	**3,573.1**	**4,119.8**
Trade credits..	8 706 ..	47.9	55.4	51.5	63.0	62.2	43.2	42.2	61.0
General government.....................................	8 707 ..	. . . .	. . . .	. . . .	. . . .	. . . .	. . . .	. . . .	. . . .
of which: Short-term.............................	8 709 ..	. . . .	. . . .	. . . .	. . . .	. . . .	. . . .	. . . .	. . . .
Other sectors...	8 710 ..	47.9	55.4	51.5	63.0	62.2	43.2	42.2	61.0
of which: Short-term.............................	8 712 ..	*47.9*	*55.4*	*51.5*	*63.0*	*62.2*	*43.2*	*42.2*	*61.0*
Loans..	8 714 ..	693.8	722.4	726.3	844.1	911.4	1,009.4	871.9	840.3
Monetary authorities...................................	8 715 ..	. . . .	. . . .	. . . .	. . . .	. . . .	. . . .	. . . .	. . . .
of which: Short-term.............................	8 718 ..	. . . .	. . . .	. . . .	. . . .	. . . .	. . . .	. . . .	. . . .
General government....................................	8 719 ..	405.2	429.7	457.7	577.1	672.3	632.7	554.7	481.7
of which: Short-term.............................	8 721 ..	. . . .	. . . .	. . . .	. . . .	. . . .	. . . .	. . . .	. . . .
Banks..	8 722 ..	275.9	277.6	249.7	247.6	221.8	362.3	305.7	350.0
of which: Short-term.............................	8 724 ..	*275.9*	*277.6*	*249.7*	*247.6*	*221.8*	*362.3*	*305.7*	*350.0*
Other sectors..	8 725 ..	12.7	15.1	18.9	19.4	17.3	14.4	11.5	8.6
of which: Short-term.............................	8 727 ..	*.7*	*.7*	*.7*	*.7*	*.7*	*.7*	*.7*	*.7*
Currency and deposits..................................	8 730 ..	529.2	637.4	1,076.2	1,561.1	983.3	968.2	2,380.5	2,852.4
Monetary authorities...................................	8 731 ..	. . . .	. . . .	. . . .	. . . .	. . . .	. . . .	. . . .	. . . .
General government....................................	8 732 ..	. . . .	. . . .	. . . .	. . . .	. . . .	. . . .	. . . .	. . . .
Banks..	8 733 ..	113.3	102.0	86.9	92.0	131.5	247.7	422.6	531.8
Other sectors..	8 734 ..	415.9	535.4	989.3	1,469.1	851.8	720.5	1,957.9	2,320.6
Other assets...	8 736 ..	65.3	98.5	103.8	129.5	190.6	223.4	278.5	366.0
Monetary authorities...................................	8 737 ..	. . . .	. . . .	. . . .	. . . .	. . . .	. . . .	. . . .	. . . .
of which: Short-term.............................	8 739 ..	. . . .	. . . .	. . . .	. . . .	. . . .	. . . .	. . . .	. . . .
General government....................................	8 740 ..	58.0	89.7	91.6	107.1	141.3	128.2	220.6	315.4
of which: Short-term.............................	8 742 ..	*58.0*	*89.7*	*91.6*	*107.1*	*141.3*	*128.2*	*220.6*	*315.4*
Banks..	8 743 ..	1.0	2.1	2.9	7.7	28.1	66.6	26.3	32.2
of which: Short-term.............................	8 745 ..	*1.0*	*2.1*	*2.9*	*7.7*	*28.1*	*66.6*	*26.3*	*32.2*
Other sectors..	8 746 ..	6.3	6.7	9.3	14.7	21.2	28.6	31.6	18.4
of which: Short-term.............................	8 748 ..	*5.9*	*6.3*	*9.1*	*14.6*	*21.1*	*28.5*	*31.5*	*18.3*
Reserve assets..	8 802 ..	**993.1**	**1,187.9**	**1,317.1**	**1,724.4**	**2,465.1**	**2,863.2**	**3,860.4**	**4,176.7**
Monetary gold...	8 812 ..	14.1	13.4	. . . .	. . . .	. . . .	18.4	23.2	26.4
Special drawing rights...................................	8 811 ..	125.8	133.6	126.1	137.8	43.6	44.2	173.0	170.1
Reserve position in the Fund........................	8 810 ..	31.9	33.4	30.7	32.3	33.9	33.1	33.7	33.1
Foreign exchange..	8 803 ..	815.0	1,001.3	1,160.3	1,554.2	2,387.4	2,767.4	3,630.4	3,947.0
Other claims..	8 813 ..	6.3	6.3	. . . .	. . . .	. . . .	. . . .	. . . .	. . . .

Table 3 (Concluded). INTERNATIONAL INVESTMENT POSITION (End-period stocks), 2003–2010

(Millions of U.S. dollars)

	Code	2003	2004	2005	2006	2007	2008	2009	2010
LIABILITIES...	8 995 D.	**4,218.6**	**4,228.0**	**4,111.7**	**4,585.0**	**5,118.0**	**6,024.4**	**6,578.1**	**7,106.8**
Direct investment in Paraguay............................	8 555 ..	**1,089.7**	**1,149.5**	**1,281.6**	**1,829.5**	**2,244.7**	**2,657.1**	**3,048.9**	**3,236.8**
Equity capital and reinvested earnings..........................	8 556 ..	916.2	1,034.3	1,161.5	1,714.8	2,001.5	2,282.3	2,776.3	2,770.5
Claims on direct investors..........................	8 557 ..	....	....	....	....	....	....	....	....
Liabilities to direct investors..........................	8 558 ..	916.2	1,034.3	1,161.5	1,714.8	2,001.5	2,282.3	2,776.3	2,770.5
Other capital..........................	8 580 ..	173.5	115.2	120.1	114.7	243.2	374.8	272.6	466.3
Claims on direct investors..........................	8 585 ..	−69.0	−136.2	−108.0	−195.1	−97.8	−150.0	−104.4	−182.5
Liabilities to direct investors..........................	8 590 ..	242.5	251.4	228.1	309.8	341.0	524.8	377.0	648.8
Portfolio investment............................	8 652 ..	....	....	.1	.2	.2	.2	.2	.2
Equity securities..........................	8 660 ..	....	....	....	....	....	....	....	....
Banks..........................	8 663 ..	....	....	....	....	....	....	....	....
Other sectors..........................	8 664 ..	....	....	....	....	....	....	....	....
Debt securities..........................	8 669 ..	....	....	.1	.2	.2	.2	.2	.2
Bonds and notes..........................	8 670 ..	....	....	.1	.2	.2	.2	.2	.2
Monetary authorities..........................	8 671 ..	....	....	....	....	....	....	....	....
General government..........................	8 672 ..	....	....	....	....	....	....	....	....
Banks..........................	8 673 ..	....	....	....	....	....	....	....	....
Other sectors..........................	8 674 ..	....	....	.1	.2	.2	.2	.2	.2
Money market instruments..........................	8 680 ..	....	....	....	....	....	....	....	....
Monetary authorities..........................	8 681 ..	....	....	....	....	....	....	....	....
General government..........................	8 682 ..	....	....	....	....	....	....	....	....
Banks..........................	8 683 ..	....	....	....	....	....	....	....	....
Other sectors..........................	8 684 ..	....	....	....	....	....	....	....	....
Financial derivatives............................	8 905 ..	....	....	....	....	....	....	....	....
Monetary authorities..........................	8 906 ..	....	....	....	....	....	....	....	....
General government..........................	8 907 ..	....	....	....	....	....	....	....	....
Banks..........................	8 908 ..	....	....	....	....	....	....	....	....
Other sectors..........................	8 909 ..	....	....	....	....	....	....	....	....
Other investment............................	8 753 ..	**3,128.9**	**3,078.6**	**2,830.1**	**2,755.4**	**2,873.2**	**3,367.2**	**3,529.0**	**3,869.8**
Trade credits..........................	8 756 ..	392.9	406.3	322.4	268.8	279.9	481.7	472.1	520.9
General government..........................	8 757 ..	....	....	....	....	....	....	....	....
of which: Short-term..........................	8 759 ..	....	....	....	....	....	....	....	....
Other sectors..........................	8 760 ..	392.9	406.3	322.4	268.8	279.9	481.7	472.1	520.9
of which: Short-term..........................	8 762 ..	*392.9*	*406.3*	*322.4*	*268.8*	*279.9*	*481.7*	*472.1*	*520.9*
Loans..........................	8 764 ..	2,524.8	2,530.2	2,355.4	2,330.9	2,278.4	2,343.8	2,381.9	2,616.0
Monetary authorities..........................	8 765 ..	20.7	17.3	13.9	10.6	7.3	2.9	2.9	....
of which: Use of Fund credit and loans from the Fund....	8 766 ..	....	....	....	....	....	....	....	....
of which: Short-term..........................	8 768 ..	....	....	....	....	....	....	....	....
General government..........................	8 769 ..	2,215.0	2,243.9	2,135.0	2,120.2	2,099.1	2,115.3	2,159.3	2,277.7
of which: Short-term..........................	8 771 ..	....	....	....	....	....	....	....	....
Banks..........................	8 772 ..	11.0	13.9	9.9	7.7	5.5	12.4	17.9	103.4
of which: Short-term..........................	8 774 ..	*1.3*	*3.4*	*.5*	*1.2*	*.1*	*8.2*	*14.2*	*100.3*
Other sectors..........................	8 775 ..	278.0	255.0	196.5	192.3	166.5	213.2	201.8	235.0
of which: Short-term..........................	8 777 ..	*8.9*	*14.0*	*16.6*	*17.3*	*18.3*	*19.3*	*21.5*	*22.3*
Currency and deposits..........................	8 780 ..	15.8	15.3	8.1	12.7	130.5	195.3	259.0	310.7
Monetary authorities..........................	8 781 ..	....	....	....	....	....	....	....	....
General government..........................	8 782 ..	....	....	....	....	....	....	....	....
Banks..........................	8 783 ..	14.6	14.9	5.5	7.9	123.5	186.1	242.6	290.4
Other sectors..........................	8 784 ..	1.2	.4	2.6	4.8	7.0	9.2	16.4	20.3
Other liabilities..........................	8 786 ..	195.5	126.8	144.2	143.0	184.4	346.4	416.0	422.2
Monetary authorities..........................	8 787 ..	1.6	.6	1.3	2.0	24.1	24.6	155.7	151.4
of which: Short-term..........................	8 789 ..	*1.6*	*.6*	*1.3*	*2.0*	*2.7*	*3.4*	*4.1*	*4.8*
General government..........................	8 790 ..	87.8	7.3	7.2	7.4	7.4	7.1	7.1	7.1
of which: Short-term..........................	8 792 ..	*87.8*	*7.3*	*7.2*	*7.4*	*7.4*	*7.1*	*7.1*	*7.1*
Banks..........................	8 793 ..	17.1	34.4	20.9	6.0	18.7	93.2	57.1	87.5
of which: Short-term..........................	8 795 ..	*17.1*	*34.4*	*20.9*	*6.0*	*18.7*	*93.2*	*57.1*	*87.5*
Other sectors..........................	8 796 ..	89.1	84.6	114.9	127.7	134.2	221.5	196.2	176.3
of which: Short-term..........................	8 798 ..	*80.0*	*74.3*	*103.4*	*115.0*	*120.3*	*206.4*	*179.9*	*158.8*
NET INTERNATIONAL INVESTMENT POSITION........	8 995 ..	**−1,734.7**	**−1,373.2**	**−677.0**	**−69.9**	**−276.0**	**−683.6**	**1,099.1**	**1,440.6**
Conversion rates: guaraníes per U.S. dollar (end of period)...	0 102 ..	**6,115.0**	**6,250.0**	**6,120.0**	**5,190.0**	**4,875.0**	**4,945.0**	**4,610.0**	**4,573.8**

Table 1. ANALYTIC PRESENTATION, 2003–2010

(Millions of U.S. dollars)

	Code	2003	2004	2005	2006	2007	2008	2009	2010
A. Current Account[1].............................	4 993 Z.	**−949**	**19**	**1,148**	**2,872**	**1,460**	**−5,318**	**211**	**−2,315**
Goods: exports f.o.b....................	2 100 ..	9,091	12,809	17,368	23,830	28,094	31,018	26,962	35,565
Goods: imports f.o.b.....................	3 100 ..	−8,205	−9,805	−12,082	−14,844	−19,591	−28,449	−21,011	−28,815
Balance on Goods..................	4 100 ..	*886*	*3,004*	*5,286*	*8,986*	*8,503*	*2,569*	*5,951*	*6,750*
Services: credit........................	2 200 ..	1,716	1,993	2,289	2,660	3,152	3,649	3,645	3,956
Services: debit.........................	3 200 ..	−2,616	−2,725	−3,123	−3,397	−4,344	−5,704	−4,789	−5,993
Balance on Goods and Services.........	4 991 ..	*−14*	*2,273*	*4,452*	*8,249*	*7,312*	*514*	*4,807*	*4,713*
Income: credit.........................	2 300 ..	322	332	625	1,050	1,587	1,837	1,433	1,175
Income: debit..........................	3 300 ..	−2,466	−4,017	−5,701	−8,612	−9,945	−10,611	−8,917	−11,228
Balance on Goods, Services, and Income.........	4 992 ..	*−2,158*	*−1,413*	*−624*	*687*	*−1,047*	*−8,261*	*−2,677*	*−5,341*
Current transfers: credit..............	2 379 Z.	1,215	1,439	1,781	2,195	2,517	2,950	2,894	3,033
Current transfers: debit...............	3 379 ..	−6	−6	−10	−10	−10	−7	−7	−7
B. Capital Account[1].............................	4 994 Z.	**−112**	**−86**	**−123**	**−126**	**−134**	**−121**	**−78**	**−115**
Capital account: credit................	2 994 Z.	4	27	6	6	3	12	8	7
Capital account: debit.................	3 994 ..	−116	−113	−129	−133	−137	−133	−85	−122
Total, Groups A Plus B...............	4 981 ..	*−1,060*	*−67*	*1,025*	*2,746*	*1,326*	*−5,439*	*133*	*−2,429*
C. Financial Account[1].............................	4 995 W.	**820**	**2,286**	**24**	**844**	**9,136**	**9,017**	**3,208**	**12,366**
Direct investment abroad...............	4 505 ..	−60	....	....	....	−66	−736	−398	−215
Direct investment in Peru..............	4 555 Z.	1,335	1,599	2,579	3,467	5,491	6,924	5,576	7,328
Portfolio investment assets............	4 602 ..	−1,287	−425	−817	−1,992	−390	462	−3,584	−820
Equity securities..................	4 610 ..	−1,287	−426	−818	−1,993	−391	461	−3,584	−821
Debt securities....................	4 619 ..	....	1	1	1	1	1	1	1
Portfolio investment liabilities........	4 652 Z.	1,211	1,244	2,579	380	4,030	−1	1,247	5,748
Equity securities..................	4 660 ..	1	−47	769	−45	70	85	47	87
Debt securities....................	4 669 Z.	1,210	1,291	1,810	425	3,960	−86	1,200	5,662
Financial derivatives..................	4 910 ..	....	....	....	....	....	....	....	....
Financial derivatives assets...........	4 900 ..	....	....	....	....	....	....	....	....
Financial derivatives liabilities.......	4 905 ..	....	....	....	....	....	....	....	....
Other investment assets................	4 703 ..	127	14	−1,084	−508	−443	860	95	−1,111
Monetary authorities...............	4 701 ..	119	86	−162	425	760	338	896	−222
General government................	4 704 ..	−203	−64	−214	−33	−16	32	−47	40
Banks.............................	4 705 ..	186	71	−324	−122	−19	−702	106	−173
Other sectors......................	4 728 ..	25	−79	−384	−778	−1,167	1,191	−860	−756
Other investment liabilities...........	4 753 W.	−506	−146	−3,233	−502	515	1,509	272	1,437
Monetary authorities...............	4 753 WA	−8	6	5	32	−23	5	814	5
General government................	4 753 ZB	−294	−130	−2,692	−545	−4,568	−1,439	−651	−3,587
Banks.............................	4 753 ZC	−84	53	327	−139	3,596	860	−352	3,684
Other sectors......................	4 753 ZD	−119	−75	−872	149	1,510	2,083	462	1,335
Total, Groups A Through C...........	4 983 ..	*−240*	*2,219*	*1,049*	*3,590*	*10,463*	*3,579*	*3,341*	*9,937*
D. Net Errors and Omissions.......................	4 998 ..	**801**	**236**	**362**	**−369**	**−119**	**−122**	**−1,439**	**1,033**
Total, Groups A Through D...........	4 984 ..	*561*	*2,456*	*1,411*	*3,221*	*10,343*	*3,457*	*1,902*	*10,970*
E. Reserves and Related Items...........................	4 802 A.	**−561**	**−2,456**	**−1,411**	**−3,221**	**−10,343**	**−3,457**	**−1,902**	**−10,970**
Reserve assets.........................	4 802 ..	−515	−2,442	−1,472	−3,209	−10,390	−3,513	−1,938	−10,989
Use of Fund credit and loans...........	4 766 ..	−110	−40	−40	−39	−20	....	....	....
Exceptional financing..................	4 920 ..	64	26	100	27	67	57	36	19
Conversion rates: nuevos soles per U.S. dollar......	0 101 ..	**3.4785**	**3.4132**	**3.2958**	**3.2740**	**3.1280**	**2.9244**	**3.0115**	**2.8251**

[1] Excludes components that have been classified in the categories of Group E.

Table 2. STANDARD PRESENTATION, 2003–2010
(Millions of U.S. dollars)

	Code	2003	2004	2005	2006	2007	2008	2009	2010
CURRENT ACCOUNT	4 993	−949	19	1,148	2,872	1,460	−5,318	211	−2,315
A. GOODS	4 100	886	3,004	5,286	8,986	8,503	2,569	5,951	6,750
Credit	2 100	9,091	12,809	17,368	23,830	28,094	31,018	26,962	35,565
General merchandise: exports f.o.b.	2 110	6,875	10,253	14,131	19,707	23,792	25,242	20,002	27,554
Goods for processing: exports f.o.b.	2 150	....	....	....	....	....	....	....	....
Repairs on goods	2 160	2	2	2	....	1	....	....	....
Goods procured in ports by carriers	2 170	112	129	139	90	114	190	154	254
Nonmonetary gold	2 180	2,102	2,424	3,095	4,032	4,187	5,586	6,805	7,756
Debit	3 100	−8,205	−9,805	−12,082	−14,844	−19,591	−28,449	−21,011	−28,815
General merchandise: imports f.o.b.	3 110	−7,986	−9,549	−11,747	−14,429	−19,218	−28,034	−20,764	−28,342
Goods for processing: imports f.o.b.	3 150	−188	−214	−275	−365	−322	−361	−196	−420
Repairs on goods	3 160	−6	−9	−24	−11	−10	−10	−6	−5
Goods procured in ports by carriers	3 170	−25	−33	−35	−39	−40	−44	−44	−46
Nonmonetary gold	3 180	....	....	....	....	....	....	....	−2
B. SERVICES	4 200	−900	−732	−834	−737	−1,192	−2,056	−1,144	−2,037
Total credit	2 200	*1,716*	*1,993*	*2,289*	*2,660*	*3,152*	*3,649*	*3,645*	*3,956*
Total debit	3 200	*−2,616*	*−2,725*	*−3,123*	*−3,397*	*−4,344*	*−5,704*	*−4,789*	*−5,993*
Transportation services, credit	2 205	309	373	449	545	646	818	758	854
Passenger	2 850	*60*	*90*	*130*	*205*	*284*	*405*	*426*	*467*
Freight	2 851	*26*	*43*	*60*	*64*	*80*	*84*	*32*	*37*
Other	2 852	*224*	*240*	*259*	*275*	*281*	*330*	*300*	*350*
Sea transport, passenger	2 207	....	....	....	....	....	....	....	....
Sea transport, freight	2 208	2	1	....	....	....	....	....	....
Sea transport, other	2 209	88	100	114	137	143	182	149	193
Air transport, passenger	2 211	60	90	130	205	284	405	426	467
Air transport, freight	2 212	24	42	60	64	80	84	32	37
Air transport, other	2 213	136	140	144	139	139	147	151	157
Other transport, passenger	2 215	....	....	....	....	....	....	....	....
Other transport, freight	2 216	....	....	....	....	....	....	....	....
Other transport, other	2 217	....	....	....	....	....	....	....	....
Transportation services, debit	3 205	−931	−1,087	−1,312	−1,419	−1,844	−2,560	−1,737	−2,453
Passenger	3 850	*−206*	*−209*	*−218*	*−249*	*−275*	*−310*	*−316*	*−372*
Freight	3 851	*−615*	*−784*	*−978*	*−1,074*	*−1,450*	*−2,126*	*−1,298*	*−1,919*
Other	3 852	*−110*	*−94*	*−116*	*−96*	*−119*	*−123*	*−124*	*−162*
Sea transport, passenger	3 207	....	....	....	....	....	....	....	....
Sea transport, freight	3 208	−549	−711	−900	−974	−1,314	−1,936	−1,154	−1,732
Sea transport, other	3 209	−35	−30	−27	−33	−37	−39	−56	−83
Air transport, passenger	3 211	−206	−209	−218	−249	−275	−310	−316	−372
Air transport, freight	3 212	−67	−73	−78	−99	−136	−191	−143	−187
Air transport, other	3 213	−75	−65	−89	−63	−81	−84	−68	−79
Other transport, passenger	3 215	....	....	....	....	....	....	....	....
Other transport, freight	3 216	....	....	....	....	....	....	....	....
Other transport, other	3 217	....	....	....	....	....	....	....	....
Travel, credit	2 236	963	1,142	1,308	1,570	1,723	1,991	2,014	2,274
Business travel	2 237	....	....	....	....	....	....	....	....
Personal travel	2 240	963	1,142	1,308	1,570	1,723	1,991	2,014	2,274
Travel, debit	3 236	−641	−643	−752	−798	−968	−1,121	−1,088	−1,274
Business travel	3 237	....	....	....	....	....	....	....	....
Personal travel	3 240	−641	−643	−752	−798	−968	−1,121	−1,088	−1,274
Other services, credit	2 200 BA	443	479	532	545	783	839	873	828
Communications	2 245	46	60	69	82	88	125	91	102
Construction	2 249	....	....	....	....	....	....	....	....
Insurance	2 253	89	82	118	103	289	227	271	166
Financial	2 260	7	6	6	30	38	47	48	59
Computer and information	2 262	....	....	....	....	13	20	18	21
Royalties and licence fees	2 266	1	....	2	3	1	2	2	3
Other business services	2 268	185	210	212	200	219	280	303	333
Personal, cultural, and recreational	2 287	....	....	....	....	3	4	3	4
Government, n.i.e.	2 291	116	121	125	128	131	135	137	140
Other services, debit	3 200 BA	−1,043	−995	−1,060	−1,180	−1,532	−2,023	−1,964	−2,266
Communications	3 245	−80	−81	−96	−109	−110	−133	−161	−180
Construction	3 249	....	....	....	....	−124	−156	−49	−56
Insurance	3 253	−267	−209	−233	−265	−311	−379	−447	−491
Financial	3 260	−18	−19	−20	−32	−29	−86	−72	−37
Computer and information	3 262	....	....	....	....	−122	−169	−153	−206
Royalties and licence fees	3 266	−74	−78	−82	−95	−111	−159	−152	−197
Other business services	3 268	−481	−485	−501	−547	−569	−784	−767	−929
Personal, cultural, and recreational	3 287	....	....	....	....	−24	−19	−18	−19
Government, n.i.e.	3 291	−122	−122	−128	−131	−130	−138	−146	−150

2011, International Monetary Fund: *Balance of Payments Statistics Yearbook*

Table 2 (Continued). STANDARD PRESENTATION, 2003–2010

(Millions of U.S. dollars)

	Code	2003	2004	2005	2006	2007	2008	2009	2010
C. INCOME	4 300	**−2,144**	**−3,686**	**−5,076**	**−7,562**	**−8,359**	**−8,774**	**−7,484**	**−10,053**
Total credit	2 300	*322*	*332*	*625*	*1,050*	*1,587*	*1,837*	*1,433*	*1,175*
Total debit	3 300	*−2,466*	*−4,017*	*−5,701*	*−8,612*	*−9,945*	*−10,611*	*−8,917*	*−11,228*
Compensation of employees, credit	2 310	....	....	....	....	....	....	....	....
Compensation of employees, debit	3 310	....	....	....	....	....	....	....	....
Investment income, credit	2 320	**322**	**332**	**625**	**1,050**	**1,587**	**1,837**	**1,433**	**1,175**
Direct investment income	2 330	....	....	....	....	....	....	....	....
Dividends and distributed branch profits	2 332	....	....	....	....	....	....	....	....
Reinvested earnings and undistributed branch profits	2 333	....	....	....	....	....	....	....	....
Income on debt (interest)	2 334	....	....	....	....	....	....	....	....
Portfolio investment income	2 339	....	....	....	....	....	....	....	....
Income on equity	2 340	....	....	....	....	....	....	....	....
Income on bonds and notes	2 350	....	....	....	....	....	....	....	....
Income on money market instruments	2 360	....	....	....	....	....	....	....	....
Other investment income	2 370	322	332	625	1,050	1,587	1,837	1,433	1,175
Investment income, debit	3 320	**−2,466**	**−4,017**	**−5,701**	**−8,612**	**−9,945**	**−10,611**	**−8,917**	**−11,228**
Direct investment income	3 330	−1,112	−2,567	−4,030	−6,741	−7,788	−8,346	−7,173	−9,478
Dividends and distributed branch profits	3 332	−474	−704	−1,306	−4,387	−3,953	−5,059	−2,222	−3,747
Reinvested earnings and undistributed branch profits	3 333	−638	−1,864	−2,724	−2,353	−3,835	−3,287	−4,951	−5,731
Income on debt (interest)	3 334	....	....	....	....	....	....	....	....
Portfolio investment income	3 339	−314	−433	−554	−734	−832	−903	−763	−926
Income on equity	3 340	....	....	....	....	....	....	....	....
Income on bonds and notes	3 350	−314	−433	−554	−734	−818	−812	−754	−923
Income on money market instruments	3 360	....	....	....	....	−14	−91	−9	−3
Other investment income	3 370	−1,039	−1,018	−1,117	−1,137	−1,326	−1,362	−981	−824
D. CURRENT TRANSFERS	4 379	**1,209**	**1,433**	**1,772**	**2,185**	**2,508**	**2,943**	**2,887**	**3,026**
Credit	2 379	**1,215**	**1,439**	**1,781**	**2,195**	**2,517**	**2,950**	**2,894**	**3,033**
General government	2 380	1	2	7	5	13	15	6	5
Other sectors	2 390	1,215	1,437	1,774	2,190	2,505	2,935	2,888	3,028
Workers' remittances	2 391	869	1,133	1,440	1,837	2,131	2,444	2,409	2,534
Other current transfers	2 392	346	304	334	353	374	491	480	495
Debit	3 379	**−6**	**−6**	**−10**	**−10**	**−10**	**−7**	**−7**	**−7**
General government	3 380	−6	−6	−10	−10	−10	−7	−7	−7
Other sectors	3 390	....	....	....	....	....	....	....	....
Workers' remittances	3 391	....	....	....	....	....	....	....	....
Other current transfers	3 392	....	....	....	....	....	....	....	....
CAPITAL AND FINANCIAL ACCOUNT	4 996	**147**	**−256**	**−1,510**	**−2,504**	**−1,341**	**5,439**	**1,228**	**1,281**
CAPITAL ACCOUNT	4 994	**−48**	**−59**	**−22**	**−100**	**−67**	**−64**	**−42**	**−96**
Total credit	2 994	*68*	*54*	*106*	*33*	*70*	*68*	*44*	*26*
Total debit	3 994	*−116*	*−113*	*−129*	*−133*	*−137*	*−133*	*−85*	*−122*
Capital transfers, credit	2 400	**68**	**54**	**106**	**33**	**70**	**68**	**44**	**26**
General government	2 401	65	28	103	29	68	63	38	20
Debt forgiveness	2 402	64	26	100	27	67	57	36	19
Other capital transfers	2 410	1	2	3	3	1	6	2	1
Other sectors	2 430	3	26	3	3	2	6	6	6
Migrants' transfers	2 431	....	....	....	....	....	....	....	....
Debt forgiveness	2 432	....	23	....	....	....	....	....	....
Other capital transfers	2 440	3	3	3	3	2	6	6	6
Capital transfers, debit	3 400	**−116**	**−113**	**−129**	**−133**	**−137**	**−133**	**−85**	**−122**
General government	3 401	....	....	....	....	....	....	....	....
Debt forgiveness	3 402	....	....	....	....	....	....	....	....
Other capital transfers	3 410	....	....	....	....	....	....	....	....
Other sectors	3 430	−116	−113	−129	−133	−137	−133	−85	−122
Migrants' transfers	3 431	−116	−113	−129	−133	−137	−133	−85	−122
Debt forgiveness	3 432	....	....	....	....	....	....	....	....
Other capital transfers	3 440	....	....	....	....	....	....	....	....
Nonproduced nonfinancial assets, credit	2 480	....	....	....	....	....	....	....	....
Nonproduced nonfinancial assets, debit	3 480	....	....	....	....	....	....	....	....

Table 2 (Continued). STANDARD PRESENTATION, 2003–2010

(Millions of U.S. dollars)

	Code	2003	2004	2005	2006	2007	2008	2009	2010
FINANCIAL ACCOUNT....................	4 995 ..	**195**	**−196**	**−1,488**	**−2,404**	**−1,274**	**5,504**	**1,270**	**1,377**
A. DIRECT INVESTMENT....................	4 500 ..	**1,275**	**1,599**	**2,579**	**3,467**	**5,425**	**6,188**	**5,178**	**7,113**
Direct investment abroad....................	4 505 ..	**−60**	....	....	....	**−66**	**−736**	**−398**	**−215**
Equity capital....................	4 510 ..	−60	....	....	....	−66	−736	−398	−215
Claims on affiliated enterprises....................	4 515 ..	−60	....	....	....	−66	−736	−398	−215
Liabilities to affiliated enterprises....................	4 520 ..	....	....	....	....	....	....	....	....
Reinvested earnings....................	4 525 ..	....	....	....	....	....	....	....	....
Other capital....................	4 530 ..	....	....	....	....	....	....	....	....
Claims on affiliated enterprises....................	4 535 ..	....	....	....	....	....	....	....	....
Liabilities to affiliated enterprises....................	4 540 ..	....	....	....	....	....	....	....	....
Direct investment in Peru....................	4 555 ..	**1,335**	**1,599**	**2,579**	**3,467**	**5,491**	**6,924**	**5,576**	**7,328**
Equity capital....................	4 560 ..	697	−265	−145	874	733	2,981	1,531	1,533
Claims on direct investors....................	4 565 ..	....	....	....	....	....	....	....	....
Liabilities to direct investors....................	4 570 ..	697	−265	−145	874	733	2,981	1,531	1,533
Reinvested earnings....................	4 575 ..	638	1,864	2,724	2,353	3,835	3,287	4,951	5,731
Other capital....................	4 580 ..	....	....	....	240	924	656	−906	64
Claims on direct investors....................	4 585 ..	....	....	....	....	....	....	....	....
Liabilities to direct investors....................	4 590 ..	....	....	....	240	924	656	−906	64
B. PORTFOLIO INVESTMENT....................	4 600 ..	**−76**	**820**	**1,762**	**−1,612**	**3,639**	**461**	**−2,337**	**4,928**
Assets....................	4 602 ..	**−1,287**	**−425**	**−817**	**−1,992**	**−390**	**462**	**−3,584**	**−820**
Equity securities....................	4 610 ..	−1,287	−426	−818	−1,993	−391	461	−3,584	−821
Monetary authorities....................	4 611 ..	....	....	....	....	....	....	....	....
General government....................	4 612 ..	−56	−58	−60	−56	−2	....	−2	....
Banks....................	4 613 ..	−234	120	56	−399	−55	−170	−668	742
Other sectors....................	4 614 ..	−997	−487	−814	−1,538	−334	631	−2,915	−1,564
Debt securities....................	4 619 ..	....	1	1	1	1	1	1	1
Bonds and notes....................	4 620 ..	....	1	1	1	1	1	1	1
Monetary authorities....................	4 621 ..	....	1	1	1	1	1	1	1
General government....................	4 622 ..	....	....	....	....	....	....	....	....
Banks....................	4 623 ..	....	....	....	....	....	....	....	....
Other sectors....................	4 624 ..	....	....	....	....	....	....	....	....
Money market instruments....................	4 630 ..	....	....	....	....	....	....	....	....
Monetary authorities....................	4 631 ..	....	....	....	....	....	....	....	....
General government....................	4 632 ..	....	....	....	....	....	....	....	....
Banks....................	4 633 ..	....	....	....	....	....	....	....	....
Other sectors....................	4 634 ..	....	....	....	....	....	....	....	....
Liabilities....................	4 652 ..	**1,211**	**1,244**	**2,579**	**380**	**4,030**	**−1**	**1,247**	**5,748**
Equity securities....................	4 660 ..	1	−47	769	−45	70	85	47	87
Banks....................	4 663 ..	....	....	....	....	....	....	....	....
Other sectors....................	4 664 ..	1	−47	769	−45	70	85	47	87
Debt securities....................	4 669 ..	1,210	1,291	1,810	425	3,960	−86	1,200	5,662
Bonds and notes....................	4 670 ..	1,210	1,291	1,810	425	3,110	95	1,783	5,742
Monetary authorities....................	4 671 ..	....	....	....	....	....	....	....	....
General government....................	4 672 ..	1,246	1,295	1,682	227	2,975	95	1,783	5,567
Banks....................	4 673 ..	....	....	....	....	....	....	....	....
Other sectors....................	4 674 ..	−36	−4	127	198	135	....	....	175
Money market instruments....................	4 680 ..	....	....	....	....	850	−181	−583	−80
Monetary authorities....................	4 681 ..	....	....	....	....	850	−181	−583	−80
General government....................	4 682 ..	....	....	....	....	....	....	....	....
Banks....................	4 683 ..	....	....	....	....	....	....	....	....
Other sectors....................	4 684 ..	....	....	....	....	....	....	....	....
C. FINANCIAL DERIVATIVES....................	4 910 ..	....	....	....	....	....	....	....	....
Monetary authorities....................	4 911 ..	....	....	....	....	....	....	....	....
General government....................	4 912 ..	....	....	....	....	....	....	....	....
Banks....................	4 913 ..	....	....	....	....	....	....	....	....
Other sectors....................	4 914 ..	....	....	....	....	....	....	....	....
Assets....................	4 900 ..	....	....	....	....	....	....	....	....
Monetary authorities....................	4 901 ..	....	....	....	....	....	....	....	....
General government....................	4 902 ..	....	....	....	....	....	....	....	....
Banks....................	4 903 ..	....	....	....	....	....	....	....	....
Other sectors....................	4 904 ..	....	....	....	....	....	....	....	....
Liabilities....................	4 905 ..	....	....	....	....	....	....	....	....
Monetary authorities....................	4 906 ..	....	....	....	....	....	....	....	....
General government....................	4 907 ..	....	....	....	....	....	....	....	....
Banks....................	4 908 ..	....	....	....	....	....	....	....	....
Other sectors....................	4 909 ..	....	....	....	....	....	....	....	....

Table 2 (Concluded). STANDARD PRESENTATION, 2003–2010

(Millions of U.S. dollars)

	Code	2003	2004	2005	2006	2007	2008	2009	2010
D. OTHER INVESTMENT	4 700	**−489**	**−172**	**−4,357**	**−1,050**	**52**	**2,369**	**367**	**325**
Assets	4 703	**127**	**14**	**−1,084**	**−508**	**−443**	**860**	**95**	**−1,111**
Trade credits	4 706	....	....	....	....	....	....	....	....
General government	4 707	....	....	....	....	....	....	....	....
of which: Short-term	4 709	....	....	....	....	....	....	....	....
Other sectors	4 710	....	....	....	....	....	....	....	....
of which: Short-term	4 712	....	....	....	....	....	....	....	....
Loans	4 714	....	....	....	....	....	....	....	....
Monetary authorities	4 715	....	....	....	....	....	....	....	....
of which: Short-term	4 718	....	....	....	....	....	....	....	....
General government	4 719	....	....	....	....	....	....	....	....
of which: Short-term	4 721	....	....	....	....	....	....	....	....
Banks	4 722	....	....	....	....	....	....	....	....
of which: Short-term	4 724	....	....	....	....	....	....	....	....
Other sectors	4 725	....	....	....	....	....	....	....	....
of which: Short-term	4 727	....	....	....	....	....	....	....	....
Currency and deposits	4 730	1	−72	−886	−949	−1,082	448	−669	−967
Monetary authorities	4 731	....	....	....	....	....	....	....	....
General government	4 732	−203	−64	−214	−33	−16	32	−47	40
Banks	4 733	179	71	−288	−138	102	−776	238	−251
Other sectors	4 734	25	−79	−384	−778	−1,167	1,191	−860	−756
Other assets	4 736	126	86	−198	440	639	412	764	−144
Monetary authorities	4 737	119	86	−162	425	760	338	896	−222
of which: Short-term	4 739	*119*	*86*	*−162*	*425*	*760*	*338*	*896*	*−222*
General government	4 740	....	....	....	....	....	....	....	....
of which: Short-term	4 742	....	....	....	....	....	....	....	....
Banks	4 743	7	....	−36	15	−121	73	−132	78
of which: Short-term	4 745	....	....	....	....	....	....	....	....
Other sectors	4 746	....	....	....	....	....	....	....	....
of which: Short-term	4 748	....	....	....	....	....	....	....	....
Liabilities	4 753	**−616**	**−186**	**−3,273**	**−541**	**495**	**1,509**	**272**	**1,437**
Trade credits	4 756	....	....	....	....	....	....	....	....
General government	4 757	....	....	....	....	....	....	....	....
of which: Short-term	4 759	....	....	....	....	....	....	....	....
Other sectors	4 760	....	....	....	....	....	....	....	....
of which: Short-term	4 762	....	....	....	....	....	....	....	....
Loans	4 764	−616	−186	−3,258	−541	495	1,509	−537	1,437
Monetary authorities	4 765	−118	−33	−35	−7	−43	5	4	5
of which: Use of Fund credit and loans from the Fund	4 766	*−110*	*−40*	*−40*	*−39*	*−20*	....	....	....
of which: Short-term	4 768	*−8*	*6*	*5*	*32*	*−23*	*5*	*4*	*5*
General government	4 769	−294	−130	−2,677	−545	−4,568	−1,439	−651	−3,587
of which: Short-term	4 771	....	....	....	....	....	....	....	....
Banks	4 772	−84	53	327	−139	3,596	860	−352	3,684
of which: Short-term	4 774	*−61*	*32*	*352*	*−265*	*1,495*	*−560*	*−265*	*669*
Other sectors	4 775	−119	−75	−872	149	1,510	2,083	462	1,335
of which: Short-term	4 777	*5*	*206*	*83*	*102*	*785*	*893*	*−743*	*681*
Currency and deposits	4 780	....	....	....	....	....	....	....	....
Monetary authorities	4 781	....	....	....	....	....	....	....	....
General government	4 782	....	....	....	....	....	....	....	....
Banks	4 783	....	....	....	....	....	....	....	....
Other sectors	4 784	....	....	....	....	....	....	....	....
Other liabilities	4 786	....	....	−15	....	....	....	810	....
Monetary authorities	4 787	....	....	....	....	....	....	810	....
of which: Short-term	4 789	....	....	....	....	....	....	....	....
General government	4 790	....	....	−15	....	....	....	....	....
of which: Short-term	4 792	....	....	*−15*	....	....	....	....	....
Banks	4 793	....	....	....	....	....	....	....	....
of which: Short-term	4 795	....	....	....	....	....	....	....	....
Other sectors	4 796	....	....	....	....	....	....	....	....
of which: Short-term	4 798	....	....	....	....	....	....	....	....
E. RESERVE ASSETS	4 802	**−515**	**−2,442**	**−1,472**	**−3,209**	**−10,390**	**−3,513**	**−1,938**	**−10,989**
Monetary gold	4 812	−76	−26	−87	−130	−222	−55	−235	−347
Special drawing rights	4 811	....	....	....	....	−3	−6	−809	....
Reserve position in the Fund	4 810	....	....	....	....	....	....	−187	....
Foreign exchange	4 803	−469	−2,406	−1,379	−3,066	−10,164	−3,432	−712	−10,623
Other claims	4 813	29	−11	−5	−13	−1	−20	5	−19
NET ERRORS AND OMISSIONS	4 998	**801**	**236**	**362**	**−369**	**−119**	**−122**	**−1,439**	**1,033**

Table 3. INTERNATIONAL INVESTMENT POSITION (End-period stocks), 2003–2010

(Millions of U.S. dollars)

	Code	2003	2004	2005	2006	2007	2008	2009	2010
ASSETS..	8 995 C.	**18,029**	**21,204**	**24,962**	**32,747**	**47,615**	**48,253**	**57,851**	**73,032**
Direct investment abroad........................	8 505 ..	**814**	**874**	**1,047**	**1,476**	**2,284**	**1,694**	**2,282**	**3,319**
Equity capital and reinvested earnings............	8 506 ..	814	874	1,047	1,476	2,284	1,694	2,282	3,319
Claims on affiliated enterprises.................	8 507 ..	814	874	1,047	1,476	2,284	1,694	2,282	3,319
Liabilities to affiliated enterprises..............	8 508 ..	....	....	....	....	....	....	....	....
Other capital..	8 530 ..	....	....	....	....	....	....	....	....
Claims on affiliated enterprises.................	8 535 ..	....	....	....	....	....	....	....	....
Liabilities to affiliated enterprises..............	8 540 ..	....	....	....	....	....	....	....	....
Portfolio investment................................	8 602 ..	**4,573**	**5,238**	**6,643**	**9,637**	**12,120**	**10,323**	**16,633**	**18,878**
Equity securities.....................................	8 610 ..	3,896	4,346	5,576	8,380	10,739	9,006	15,231	17,565
Monetary authorities.............................	8 611 ..	....	....	....	....	....	....	....	....
General government..............................	8 612 ..	....	....	....	....	....	....	....	....
Banks..	8 613 ..	612	492	436	835	915	1,110	1,751	1,025
Other sectors.......................................	8 614 ..	3,284	3,854	5,140	7,545	9,824	7,896	13,480	16,540
Debt securities......................................	8 619 ..	677	892	1,068	1,257	1,381	1,317	1,403	1,313
Bonds and notes...................................	8 620 ..	677	892	1,068	1,257	1,381	1,317	1,403	1,313
Monetary authorities..........................	8 621 ..	....	....	....	....	....	....	....	....
General government...........................	8 622 ..	677	892	1,068	1,257	1,381	1,317	1,403	1,313
Banks...	8 623 ..	....	....	....	....	....	....	....	....
Other sectors.....................................	8 624 ..	....	....	....	....	....	....	....	....
Money market instruments......................	8 630 ..	....	....	....	....	....	....	....	....
Monetary authorities..........................	8 631 ..	....	....	....	....	....	....	....	....
General government...........................	8 632 ..	....	....	....	....	....	....	....	....
Banks...	8 633 ..	....	....	....	....	....	....	....	....
Other sectors.....................................	8 634 ..	....	....	....	....	....	....	....	....
Financial derivatives................................	8 900 ..	....	....	....	....	....	....	....	....
Monetary authorities................................	8 901 ..	....	....	....	....	....	....	....	....
General government.................................	8 902 ..	....	....	....	....	....	....	....	....
Banks..	8 903 ..	....	....	....	....	....	....	....	....
Other sectors..	8 904 ..	....	....	....	....	....	....	....	....
Other investment....................................	8 703 ..	**2,445**	**2,453**	**3,161**	**4,315**	**5,501**	**5,012**	**5,766**	**6,695**
Trade credits..	8 706 ..	....	....	....	....	....	....	....	....
General government..............................	8 707 ..	....	....	....	....	....	....	....	....
of which: Short-term........................	8 709 ..	....	....	....	....	....	....	....	....
Other sectors.......................................	8 710 ..	....	....	....	....	....	....	....	....
of which: Short-term........................	8 712 ..	....	....	....	....	....	....	....	....
Loans..	8 714 ..	....	....	....	....	....	....	....	....
Monetary authorities.............................	8 715 ..	....	....	....	....	....	....	....	....
of which: Short-term........................	8 718 ..	....	....	....	....	....	....	....	....
General government..............................	8 719 ..	....	....	....	....	....	....	....	....
of which: Short-term........................	8 721 ..	....	....	....	....	....	....	....	....
Banks..	8 722 ..	....	....	....	....	....	....	....	....
of which: Short-term........................	8 724 ..	....	....	....	....	....	....	....	....
Other sectors.......................................	8 725 ..	....	....	....	....	....	....	....	....
of which: Short-term........................	8 727 ..	....	....	....	....	....	....	....	....
Currency and deposits.............................	8 730 ..	2,432	2,440	3,111	4,281	5,346	4,931	5,553	6,560
Monetary authorities.............................	8 731 ..	....	....	....	....	....	....	....	....
General government..............................	8 732 ..	....	....	....	....	....	....	....	....
Banks..	8 733 ..	644	573	860	998	896	1,672	1,434	1,685
Other sectors.......................................	8 734 ..	1,788	1,867	2,251	3,283	4,450	3,259	4,119	4,875
Other assets..	8 736 ..	13	13	50	34	155	82	213	136
Monetary authorities.............................	8 737 ..	....	....	....	....	....	....	....	....
of which: Short-term........................	8 739 ..	....	....	....	....	....	....	....	....
General government..............................	8 740 ..	....	....	....	....	....	....	....	....
of which: Short-term........................	8 742 ..	....	....	....	....	....	....	....	....
Banks..	8 743 ..	13	13	50	34	155	82	213	136
of which: Short-term........................	8 745 ..	....	....	....	....	....	....	....	....
Other sectors.......................................	8 746 ..	....	....	....	....	....	....	....	....
of which: Short-term........................	8 748 ..	....	....	....	....	....	....	....	....
Reserve assets..	8 802 ..	**10,197**	**12,639**	**14,111**	**17,320**	**27,710**	**31,223**	**33,169**	**44,140**
Monetary gold...	8 812 ..	463	489	576	706	928	983	1,218	1,565
Special drawing rights...............................	8 811 ..	....	....	....	1	4	9	822	807
Reserve position in the Fund.......................	8 810 ..	....	....	....	....	....	....	191	188
Foreign exchange.....................................	8 803 ..	9,387	11,793	13,172	16,238	26,402	29,834	30,546	41,169
Other claims..	8 813 ..	347	358	362	376	377	397	392	411

Table 3 (Concluded). INTERNATIONAL INVESTMENT POSITION (End-period stocks), 2003–2010

(Millions of U.S. dollars)

	Code	2003	2004	2005	2006	2007	2008	2009	2010
LIABILITIES	8 995 D.	**46,308**	**48,483**	**51,250**	**58,425**	**78,779**	**78,498**	**90,677**	**111,119**
Direct investment in Peru	8 555 ..	**12,876**	**13,310**	**15,889**	**20,484**	**26,808**	**32,340**	**34,356**	**41,684**
Equity capital and reinvested earnings	8 556 ..	12,876	13,310	15,889	20,484	26,808	32,340	34,356	41,684
Claims on direct investors	8 557 ..	....	....	....	....	....	....	....	....
Liabilities to direct investors	8 558 ..	12,876	13,310	15,889	20,484	26,808	32,340	34,356	41,684
Other capital	8 580 ..	....	....	....	....	....	....	....	....
Claims on direct investors	8 585 ..	....	....	....	....	....	....	....	....
Liabilities to direct investors	8 590 ..	....	....	....	....	....	....	....	....
Portfolio investment	8 652 ..	**9,570**	**10,963**	**15,316**	**17,851**	**28,781**	**19,451**	**29,176**	**38,295**
Equity securities	8 660 ..	3,845	3,928	6,705	9,043	19,077	11,319	19,634	28,260
Banks	8 663 ..	....	....	....	....	....	....	....	....
Other sectors	8 664 ..	3,845	3,928	6,705	9,043	19,077	11,319	19,634	28,260
Debt securities	8 669 ..	5,724	7,035	8,612	8,808	9,703	8,132	9,543	10,035
Bonds and notes	8 670 ..	5,724	7,035	8,612	8,808	8,813	7,432	9,458	10,035
Monetary authorities	8 671 ..	....	....	....	....	....	....	....	....
General government	8 672 ..	5,630	6,944	8,393	8,392	8,262	6,880	8,906	9,308
Banks	8 673 ..	....	....	....	....	....	....	....	....
Other sectors	8 674 ..	94	91	218	417	552	552	552	727
Money market instruments	8 680 ..	....	....	....	....	890	700	85	....
Monetary authorities	8 681 ..	....	....	....	....	890	700	85	....
General government	8 682 ..	....	....	....	....	....	....	....	....
Banks	8 683 ..	....	....	....	....	....	....	....	....
Other sectors	8 684 ..	....	....	....	....	....	....	....	....
Financial derivatives	8 905 ..	**....**	**....**	**....**	**....**	**....**	**....**	**....**	**....**
Monetary authorities	8 906 ..	....	....	....	....	....	....	....	....
General government	8 907 ..	....	....	....	....	....	....	....	....
Banks	8 908 ..	....	....	....	....	....	....	....	....
Other sectors	8 909 ..	....	....	....	....	....	....	....	....
Other investment	8 753 ..	**23,863**	**24,209**	**20,045**	**20,089**	**23,191**	**26,707**	**27,145**	**31,140**
Trade credits	8 756 ..	....	....	....	....	....	....	....	....
General government	8 757 ..	....	....	....	....	....	....	....	....
of which: Short-term	8 759 ..	....	....	....	....	....	....	....	....
Other sectors	8 760 ..	....	....	....	....	....	....	....	....
of which: Short-term	8 762 ..	....	....	....	....	....	....	....	....
Loans	8 764 ..	23,863	24,209	20,045	20,089	23,191	26,707	26,189	30,200
Monetary authorities	8 765 ..	151	122	80	75	31	36	39	45
of which: Use of Fund credit and loans from the Fund	8 766 ..	*139*	*104*	*57*	*20*	....	....	....	....
of which: Short-term	8 768 ..	*12*	*18*	*23*	*54*	*31*	*36*	*39*	*45*
General government	8 769 ..	16,593	16,977	13,415	13,177	11,457	11,802	11,173	10,062
of which: Short-term	8 771 ..	....	....	....	....	....	....	....	....
Banks	8 772 ..	909	961	1,288	1,149	4,745	5,605	5,253	8,937
of which: Short-term	8 774 ..	*702*	*733*	*1,085*	*820*	*2,315*	*1,755*	*1,490*	*2,159*
Other sectors	8 775 ..	6,210	6,149	5,262	5,688	6,958	9,263	9,723	11,155
of which: Short-term	8 777 ..	*1,812*	*2,018*	*2,100*	*2,484*	*3,018*	*3,911*	*3,168*	*3,849*
Currency and deposits	8 780 ..	....	....	....	....	....	....	....	....
Monetary authorities	8 781 ..	....	....	....	....	....	....	....	....
General government	8 782 ..	....	....	....	....	....	....	....	....
Banks	8 783 ..	....	....	....	....	....	....	....	....
Other sectors	8 784 ..	....	....	....	....	....	....	....	....
Other liabilities	8 786 ..	....	....	....	....	....	....	956	939
Monetary authorities	8 787 ..	....	....	....	....	....	....	956	939
of which: Short-term	8 789 ..	....	....	....	....	....	....	....	....
General government	8 790 ..	....	....	....	....	....	....	....	....
of which: Short-term	8 792 ..	....	....	....	....	....	....	....	....
Banks	8 793 ..	....	....	....	....	....	....	....	....
of which: Short-term	8 795 ..	....	....	....	....	....	....	....	....
Other sectors	8 796 ..	....	....	....	....	....	....	....	....
of which: Short-term	8 798 ..	....	....	....	....	....	....	....	....
NET INTERNATIONAL INVESTMENT POSITION	8 995 ..	**−28,279**	**−27,278**	**−26,288**	**−25,678**	**−31,164**	**−30,245**	**−32,826**	**−38,087**
Conversion rates: nuevos soles per U.S. dollar (end of period)	0 102 ..	3.4630	3.2815	3.4300	3.1955	2.9960	3.1395	2.8895	2.8085

Table 1. ANALYTIC PRESENTATION, 2003–2010

(Millions of U.S. dollars)

	Code	2003	2004	2005	2006	2007	2008	2009	2010
A. Current Account[1]	4 993 Z	**285**	**1,625**	**1,980**	**5,341**	**7,112**	**3,627**	**9,358**	**8,924**
Goods: exports f.o.b.	2 100	35,339	38,794	40,263	46,526	49,512	48,253	37,610	50,748
Goods: imports f.o.b.	3 100	−41,190	−44,478	−48,036	−53,258	−57,903	−61,138	−46,452	−61,714
Balance on Goods	4 100	*−5,851*	*−5,684*	*−7,773*	*−6,732*	*−8,391*	*−12,885*	*−8,842*	*−10,966*
Services: credit	2 200	3,389	4,043	4,525	6,444	9,766	9,717	11,014	14,358
Services: debit	3 200	−5,352	−5,820	−5,865	−6,307	−7,517	−8,557	−8,900	−11,419
Balance on Goods and Services	4 991	*−7,814*	*−7,461*	*−9,113*	*−6,595*	*−6,142*	*−11,725*	*−6,728*	*−8,027*
Income: credit	2 300	3,330	3,725	3,937	4,388	5,351	5,973	5,712	6,093
Income: debit	3 300	−3,617	−3,799	−4,235	−5,649	−6,250	−5,868	−5,905	−5,746
Balance on Goods, Services, and Income	4 992	*−8,101*	*−7,535*	*−9,411*	*−7,856*	*−7,041*	*−11,620*	*−6,921*	*−7,680*
Current transfers: credit	2 379 Z	8,626	9,420	11,711	13,511	14,573	15,780	16,910	17,434
Current transfers: debit	3 379	−240	−260	−320	−314	−420	−533	−631	−830
B. Capital Account[1]	4 994 Z	**54**	**17**	**40**	**138**	**24**	**53**	**104**	**98**
Capital account: credit	2 994 Z	82	46	58	181	108	114	166	170
Capital account: debit	3 994	−28	−29	−18	−43	−84	−61	−62	−72
Total, Groups A Plus B	4 981	*339*	*1,642*	*2,020*	*5,479*	*7,136*	*3,680*	*9,462*	*9,022*
C. Financial Account[1]	4 995 W	**480**	**−1,671**	**1,440**	**1,351**	**3,653**	**−1,694**	**−3,740**	**9,530**
Direct investment abroad	4 505	−303	−579	−189	−103	−3,536	−259	−359	−487
Direct investment in the Philippines	4 555 Z	491	688	1,854	2,921	2,916	1,544	1,963	1,713
Portfolio investment assets	4 602	−818	−910	−146	−1,567	834	789	−2,715	−3,460
Equity securities	4 610	−48	−18	−5	1	−79	75	−44	−11
Debt securities	4 619	−770	−892	−141	−1,568	913	714	−2,671	−3,449
Portfolio investment liabilities	4 652 Z	1,380	288	3,446	6,144	3,922	−4,416	2,090	9,845
Equity securities	4 660	500	518	1,465	2,525	3,178	−1,289	−1,096	503
Debt securities	4 669 Z	880	−230	1,981	3,619	744	−3,127	3,186	9,342
Financial derivatives	4 910	−64	−27	−43	−138	−288	−113	32	−191
Financial derivatives assets	4 900	54	58	98	159	170	541	403	429
Financial derivatives liabilities	4 905	−118	−85	−141	−297	−458	−654	−371	−620
Other investment assets	4 703	743	−859	−4,791	−3,512	−4,840	4,305	−1,967	−2,979
Monetary authorities	4 701	....	....	....	....	....	....	....	....
General government	4 704	....	....	....	....	....	....	....	....
Banks	4 705	370	−543	−3,741	−1,391	−2,244	2,402	−1,369	2,204
Other sectors	4 728	373	−316	−1,050	−2,121	−2,596	1,903	−598	−5,183
Other investment liabilities	4 753 W	−949	−272	1,309	−2,394	4,645	−3,544	−2,784	5,089
Monetary authorities	4 753 WA	3	−1,119	−514	−708	−177	8	−883	−1
General government	4 753 ZB	−64	−362	−500	256	438	58	957	−177
Banks	4 753 ZC	−453	1,233	1,105	−1,229	1,076	−647	−1,731	3,450
Other sectors	4 753 ZD	−435	−24	1,218	−713	3,308	−2,963	−1,127	1,817
Total, Groups A Through C	4 983	*819*	*−29*	*3,460*	*6,830*	*10,789*	*1,986*	*5,722*	*18,552*
D. Net Errors and Omissions	4 998	**−898**	**−274**	**−1,798**	**−1,588**	**−2,082**	**−1,889**	**−1,310**	**−1,959**
Total, Groups A Through D	4 984	*−79*	*−303*	*1,662*	*5,242*	*8,707*	*97*	*4,411*	*16,593*
E. Reserves and Related Items	4 802 A	**79**	**303**	**−1,662**	**−5,242**	**−8,707**	**−97**	**−4,411**	**−16,593**
Reserve assets	4 802	356	1,637	−1,622	−2,935	−8,550	−1,597	−4,911	−14,308
Use of Fund credit and loans	4 766	−607	−472	−321	−404	....	....	....	....
Exceptional financing	4 920	330	−862	281	−1,902	−157	1,500	500	−2,285
Conversion rates: Philippine pesos per U.S. dollar	0 101	**54.203**	**56.040**	**55.085**	**51.314**	**46.148**	**44.323**	**47.680**	**45.110**

[1] Excludes components that have been classified in the categories of Group E.

Table 2. STANDARD PRESENTATION, 2003–2010

(Millions of U.S. dollars)

	Code	2003	2004	2005	2006	2007	2008	2009	2010
CURRENT ACCOUNT	4 993 ..	**285**	**1,625**	**1,980**	**5,341**	**7,112**	**3,627**	**9,358**	**8,924**
A. GOODS	4 100 ..	**−5,851**	**−5,684**	**−7,773**	**−6,732**	**−8,391**	**−12,885**	**−8,842**	**−10,966**
Credit	2 100 ..	**35,339**	**38,794**	**40,263**	**46,526**	**49,512**	**48,253**	**37,610**	**50,748**
General merchandise: exports f.o.b.	2 110 ..	23,345	25,642	25,892	31,994	33,585	34,545	29,480	37,322
Goods for processing: exports f.o.b.	2 150 ..	11,802	12,992	14,231	14,136	15,429	13,113	7,849	13,215
Repairs on goods	2 160 ..	3	....	....	....	12	....	....	....
Goods procured in ports by carriers	2 170 ..	58	91	70	122	221	157	31	22
Nonmonetary gold	2 180 ..	131	69	70	274	265	438	250	189
Debit	3 100 ..	**−41,190**	**−44,478**	**−48,036**	**−53,258**	**−57,903**	**−61,138**	**−46,452**	**−61,714**
General merchandise: imports f.o.b.	3 110 ..	−31,526	−34,044	−36,049	−41,063	−44,007	−48,840	−39,080	−49,410
Goods for processing: imports f.o.b.	3 150 ..	−9,520	−10,275	−11,694	−11,833	−13,402	−11,551	−7,019	−11,831
Repairs on goods	3 160 ..	−55	−45	−42	....	−56	−50	....	....
Goods procured in ports by carriers	3 170 ..	−51	−77	−189	−244	−438	−697	−353	−473
Nonmonetary gold	3 180 ..	−38	−37	−62	−118	....	....	....	....
B. SERVICES	4 200 ..	**−1,963**	**−1,777**	**−1,340**	**137**	**2,249**	**1,160**	**2,114**	**2,939**
Total credit	2 200 ..	*3,389*	*4,043*	*4,525*	*6,444*	*9,766*	*9,717*	*11,014*	*14,358*
Total debit	3 200 ..	*−5,352*	*−5,820*	*−5,865*	*−6,307*	*−7,517*	*−8,557*	*−8,900*	*−11,419*
Transportation services, credit	2 205 ..	**951**	**1,001**	**962**	**1,151**	**1,323**	**1,295**	**1,153**	**1,351**
Passenger	2 850 ..	*277*	*373*	*490*	*518*	*587*	*525*	*523*	*598*
Freight	2 851 ..	*543*	*499*	*353*	*474*	*503*	*482*	*374*	*507*
Other	2 852 ..	*131*	*129*	*119*	*159*	*233*	*288*	*256*	*246*
Sea transport, passenger	2 207 ..	....	11	3	1	2	....	....	....
Sea transport, freight	2 208 ..	....	....	....	....	....	....	....	....
Sea transport, other	2 209 ..	41	49	54	71	94	135	99	94
Air transport, passenger	2 211 ..	277	362	487	517	585	525	523	598
Air transport, freight	2 212 ..	543	499	353	474	503	482	374	507
Air transport, other	2 213 ..	90	80	65	88	139	153	157	152
Other transport, passenger	2 215 ..	....	....	....	....	....	....	....	....
Other transport, freight	2 216 ..	....	....	....	....	....	....	....	....
Other transport, other	2 217 ..	....	....	....	....	....	....	....	....
Transportation services, debit	3 205 ..	**−2,419**	**−3,095**	**−3,125**	**−3,452**	**−3,844**	**−4,209**	**−3,661**	**−4,965**
Passenger	3 850 ..	*−236*	*−251*	*−268*	*−326*	*−392*	*−496*	*−553*	*−778*
Freight	3 851 ..	*−1,940*	*−2,677*	*−2,691*	*−2,966*	*−3,215*	*−3,421*	*−2,632*	*−3,428*
Other	3 852 ..	*−243*	*−167*	*−166*	*−160*	*−237*	*−292*	*−476*	*−759*
Sea transport, passenger	3 207 ..	....	....	....	....	....	....	....	....
Sea transport, freight	3 208 ..	....	....	....	....	....	....	....	....
Sea transport, other	3 209 ..	−113	−61	−39	−29	−38	−59	−61	−92
Air transport, passenger	3 211 ..	−236	−251	−268	−326	−392	−496	−553	−778
Air transport, freight	3 212 ..	−1,940	−2,677	−2,691	−2,966	−3,215	−3,421	−2,632	−3,428
Air transport, other	3 213 ..	−130	−106	−127	−131	−199	−233	−415	−667
Other transport, passenger	3 215 ..	....	....	....	....	....	....	....	....
Other transport, freight	3 216 ..	....	....	....	....	....	....	....	....
Other transport, other	3 217 ..	....	....	....	....	....	....	....	....
Travel, credit	2 236 ..	**1,544**	**2,017**	**2,265**	**3,501**	**4,933**	**2,499**	**2,330**	**2,630**
Business travel	2 237 ..	....	....	....	....	....	....	....	11
Personal travel	2 240 ..	1,544	2,017	2,265	3,501	4,933	2,499	2,330	2,619
Travel, debit	3 236 ..	**−1,413**	**−1,275**	**−1,279**	**−1,232**	**−1,663**	**−2,057**	**−2,698**	**−3,475**
Business travel	3 237 ..	−74	−49	−36	−38	−51	−65	−48	−74
Personal travel	3 240 ..	−1,339	−1,226	−1,243	−1,194	−1,612	−1,992	−2,650	−3,401
Other services, credit	2 200 BA	**894**	**1,025**	**1,298**	**1,792**	**3,510**	**5,923**	**7,531**	**10,377**
Communications	2 245 ..	433	487	522	575	517	404	354	305
Construction	2 249 ..	48	71	66	69	113	90	78	121
Insurance	2 253 ..	12	12	17	21	22	19	59	77
Financial	2 260 ..	38	43	53	101	87	59	70	38
Computer and information	2 262 ..	28	33	89	95	305	1,148	1,748	1,503
Royalties and licence fees	2 266 ..	4	11	6	6	5	....	2	4
Other business services	2 268 ..	322	361	525	898	2,439	4,182	5,186	8,288
Personal, cultural, and recreational	2 287 ..	9	7	20	27	22	21	34	41
Government, n.i.e.	2 291 ..	....	....	....	....	....	....	....	....
Other services, debit	3 200 BA	**−1,520**	**−1,450**	**−1,461**	**−1,623**	**−2,010**	**−2,291**	**−2,541**	**−2,979**
Communications	3 245 ..	−81	−128	−115	−98	−99	−147	−123	−154
Construction	3 249 ..	−64	−48	−7	−15	−21	−33	−20	−21
Insurance	3 253 ..	−182	−199	−203	−230	−251	−262	−235	−311
Financial	3 260 ..	−54	−77	−93	−125	−210	−82	−125	−74
Computer and information	3 262 ..	−46	−49	−62	−67	−62	−80	−91	−109
Royalties and licence fees	3 266 ..	−278	−273	−265	−349	−385	−382	−421	−445
Other business services	3 268 ..	−770	−610	−639	−635	−834	−1,070	−1,263	−1,575
Personal, cultural, and recreational	3 287 ..	−15	−15	−9	−8	−22	−26	−42	−59
Government, n.i.e.	3 291 ..	−30	−51	−68	−96	−126	−209	−221	−231

Table 2 (Continued). STANDARD PRESENTATION, 2003–2010

(Millions of U.S. dollars)

	Code	2003	2004	2005	2006	2007	2008	2009	2010
C. INCOME	4 300 ..	**−287**	**−74**	**−298**	**−1,261**	**−899**	**105**	**−193**	**347**
Total credit	2 300 ..	*3,330*	*3,725*	*3,937*	*4,388*	*5,351*	*5,973*	*5,712*	*6,093*
Total debit	3 300 ..	*−3,617*	*−3,799*	*−4,235*	*−5,649*	*−6,250*	*−5,868*	*−5,905*	*−5,746*
Compensation of employees, credit	2 310 ..	**2,558**	**2,851**	**2,893**	**2,758**	**3,030**	**4,092**	**4,585**	**5,127**
Compensation of employees, debit	3 310 ..	....	....	....	....	....	....	....	....
Investment income, credit	2 320 ..	**772**	**874**	**1,044**	**1,630**	**2,321**	**1,881**	**1,127**	**966**
Direct investment income	2 330 ..	20	27	19	53	48	32	72	116
Dividends and distributed branch profits	2 332 ..	20	18	17	53	44	28	70	116
Reinvested earnings and undistributed branch profits	2 333 ..	....	....	....	....	....	....	....	....
Income on debt (interest)	2 334 ..	....	9	2	....	4	4	2	....
Portfolio investment income	2 339 ..	532	596	625	802	1,359	1,259	887	688
Income on equity	2 340 ..	....	....	1	2	7	9	....	....
Income on bonds and notes	2 350 ..	476	487	575	740	1,338	1,249	886	688
Income on money market instruments	2 360 ..	56	109	49	60	14	1	1	....
Other investment income	2 370 ..	220	251	400	775	914	590	168	162
Investment income, debit	3 320 ..	**−3,617**	**−3,799**	**−4,235**	**−5,649**	**−6,250**	**−5,868**	**−5,905**	**−5,746**
Direct investment income	3 330 ..	−1,067	−1,373	−1,391	−2,015	−2,133	−1,675	−2,150	−2,234
Dividends and distributed branch profits	3 332 ..	−839	−1,172	−1,158	−1,443	−1,338	−1,518	−1,940	−1,865
Reinvested earnings and undistributed branch profits	3 333 ..	−168	−141	−140	−485	−620	−53	−155	−291
Income on debt (interest)	3 334 ..	−60	−60	−93	−87	−175	−104	−55	−78
Portfolio investment income	3 339 ..	−1,298	−1,281	−1,549	−1,855	−2,325	−2,580	−2,625	−2,619
Income on equity	3 340 ..	−50	−70	−164	−393	−672	−961	−1,049	−915
Income on bonds and notes	3 350 ..	−1,248	−1,210	−1,385	−1,462	−1,652	−1,619	−1,576	−1,704
Income on money market instruments	3 360 ..	....	−1	....	....	−1	....	....	....
Other investment income	3 370 ..	−1,252	−1,145	−1,295	−1,779	−1,792	−1,613	−1,130	−893
D. CURRENT TRANSFERS	4 379 ..	**8,386**	**9,160**	**11,391**	**13,197**	**14,153**	**15,247**	**16,279**	**16,604**
Credit	2 379 ..	**8,626**	**9,420**	**11,711**	**13,511**	**14,573**	**15,780**	**16,910**	**17,434**
General government	2 380 ..	620	460	530	424	625	451	640	310
Other sectors	2 390 ..	8,006	8,960	11,181	13,087	13,948	15,329	16,270	17,124
Workers' remittances	2 391 ..	7,681	8,617	10,668	12,481	13,255	14,536	15,141	16,238
Other current transfers	2 392 ..	325	343	513	606	693	793	1,129	886
Debit	3 379 ..	**−240**	**−260**	**−320**	**−314**	**−420**	**−533**	**−631**	**−830**
General government	3 380 ..	−65	−73	−93	−111	−119	−149	−186	−103
Other sectors	3 390 ..	−175	−187	−227	−203	−301	−384	−445	−727
Workers' remittances	3 391 ..	....	....	....	....	....	....	....	....
Other current transfers	3 392 ..	−175	−187	−227	−203	−301	−384	−445	−727
CAPITAL AND FINANCIAL ACCOUNT	4 996 ..	**613**	**−1,351**	**−182**	**−3,753**	**−5,030**	**−1,738**	**−8,048**	**−6,965**
CAPITAL ACCOUNT	4 994 ..	**54**	**17**	**40**	**138**	**24**	**53**	**104**	**98**
Total credit	2 994 ..	*82*	*46*	*58*	*181*	*108*	*114*	*166*	*170*
Total debit	3 994 ..	*−28*	*−29*	*−18*	*−43*	*−84*	*−61*	*−62*	*−72*
Capital transfers, credit	2 400 ..	**82**	**46**	**58**	**181**	**108**	**114**	**165**	**170**
General government	2 401 ..	41	41	41	61	81	91	118	109
Debt forgiveness	2 402 ..	....	....	....	....	....	....	....	....
Other capital transfers	2 410 ..	41	41	41	61	81	91	118	109
Other sectors	2 430 ..	41	5	17	120	27	23	47	61
Migrants' transfers	2 431 ..	4	3	5	12	17	14	39	58
Debt forgiveness	2 432 ..	....	....	....	91	....	3	....	....
Other capital transfers	2 440 ..	37	2	12	17	10	6	8	3
Capital transfers, debit	3 400 ..	**−28**	**−21**	**−16**	**−43**	**−42**	**−59**	**−62**	**−69**
General government	3 401 ..	....	....	....	....	....	....	....	....
Debt forgiveness	3 402 ..	....	....	....	....	....	....	....	....
Other capital transfers	3 410 ..	....	....	....	....	....	....	....	....
Other sectors	3 430 ..	−28	−21	−16	−43	−42	−59	−62	−69
Migrants' transfers	3 431 ..	−18	−17	−15	−20	−35	−44	−54	−62
Debt forgiveness	3 432 ..	....	....	....	....	....	....	....	....
Other capital transfers	3 440 ..	−10	−4	−1	−23	−7	−15	−8	−7
Nonproduced nonfinancial assets, credit	2 480 ..	....	....	....	....	....	....	1	....
Nonproduced nonfinancial assets, debit	3 480 ..	....	−8	−2	....	−42	−2	....	−3

Table 2 (Continued). STANDARD PRESENTATION, 2003–2010

(Millions of U.S. dollars)

	Code	2003	2004	2005	2006	2007	2008	2009	2010
FINANCIAL ACCOUNT	4 995	**559**	**−1,368**	**−222**	**−3,891**	**−5,054**	**−1,791**	**−8,152**	**−7,063**
A. DIRECT INVESTMENT	4 500	**188**	**109**	**1,665**	**2,818**	**−620**	**1,285**	**1,604**	**1,226**
Direct investment abroad	4 505	**−303**	**−579**	**−189**	**−103**	**−3,536**	**−259**	**−359**	**−487**
Equity capital	4 510	−303	−579	−189	−103	−3,536	−259	−359	−487
Claims on affiliated enterprises	4 515	−303	−579	−189	−103	−3,536	−259	−359	−487
Liabilities to affiliated enterprises	4 520	....	....	....	....	....	....	....	....
Reinvested earnings	4 525	....	....	....	....	....	....	....	....
Other capital	4 530	....	....	....	....	....	....	....	....
Claims on affiliated enterprises	4 535	....	....	....	....	....	....	....	....
Liabilities to affiliated enterprises	4 540	....	....	....	....	....	....	....	....
Direct investment in the Philippines	4 555	**491**	**688**	**1,854**	**2,921**	**2,916**	**1,544**	**1,963**	**1,713**
Equity capital	4 560	249	750	1,181	1,324	1,949	1,235	1,731	848
Claims on direct investors	4 565	....	....	....	....	....	....	....	....
Liabilities to direct investors	4 570	249	750	1,181	1,324	1,949	1,235	1,731	848
Reinvested earnings	4 575	168	141	140	485	620	53	155	291
Other capital	4 580	74	−203	533	1,112	347	256	77	574
Claims on direct investors	4 585	−1	96	190	214	−329	108	−749	−337
Liabilities to direct investors	4 590	75	−299	343	898	676	148	826	911
B. PORTFOLIO INVESTMENT	4 600	**562**	**−1,713**	**3,475**	**3,043**	**4,623**	**−3,627**	**−625**	**4,100**
Assets	4 602	**−818**	**−910**	**−146**	**−1,567**	**834**	**789**	**−2,715**	**−3,460**
Equity securities	4 610	−48	−18	−5	1	−79	75	−44	−11
Monetary authorities	4 611	....	....	....	....	....	....	....	....
General government	4 612	....	....	....	....	....	....	....	....
Banks	4 613	−2	−6	−1	2	5	14	−8	....
Other sectors	4 614	−46	−12	−4	−1	−84	61	−36	−11
Debt securities	4 619	−770	−892	−141	−1,568	913	714	−2,671	−3,449
Bonds and notes	4 620	−698	−183	−428	−1,272	87	160	−2,089	−3,342
Monetary authorities	4 621	....	....	....	....	....	....	....	....
General government	4 622	....	....	....	....	....	....	....	....
Banks	4 623	−613	−155	353	−1,224	−430	625	−465	−1,883
Other sectors	4 624	−85	−28	−781	−48	517	−465	−1,624	−1,459
Money market instruments	4 630	−72	−709	287	−296	826	554	−582	−107
Monetary authorities	4 631	....	....	....	....	....	....	....	....
General government	4 632	....	....	....	....	....	....	....	....
Banks	4 633	49	−668	352	−693	758	605	−254	467
Other sectors	4 634	−121	−41	−65	397	68	−51	−328	−574
Liabilities	4 652	**1,380**	**−803**	**3,621**	**4,610**	**3,789**	**−4,416**	**2,090**	**7,560**
Equity securities	4 660	500	518	1,465	2,525	3,178	−1,289	−1,096	503
Banks	4 663	3	1	−1	324	115	−48	18	162
Other sectors	4 664	497	517	1,466	2,201	3,063	−1,241	−1,114	341
Debt securities	4 669	880	−1,321	2,156	2,085	611	−3,127	3,186	7,057
Bonds and notes	4 670	880	−1,321	2,145	2,055	629	−3,126	3,139	7,056
Monetary authorities	4 671	−206	−542	−723	−41	91	−34	−102	−200
General government	4 672	1,281	−506	2,712	1,272	385	−1,068	2,846	6,005
Banks	4 673	5	125	225	122	−89	−182	49	778
Other sectors	4 674	−200	−398	−69	702	242	−1,842	346	473
Money market instruments	4 680	....	....	11	30	−18	−1	47	1
Monetary authorities	4 681	....	....	....	....	....	....	....	....
General government	4 682	....	....	....	....	....	....	....	....
Banks	4 683	....	....	....	....	....	....	....	....
Other sectors	4 684	....	....	11	30	−18	−1	47	1
C. FINANCIAL DERIVATIVES	4 910	**−64**	**−27**	**−43**	**−138**	**−288**	**−113**	**32**	**−191**
Monetary authorities	4 911	....	....	....	....	....	....	....	....
General government	4 912	....	....	....	....	....	....	....	....
Banks	4 913	−64	−27	−43	−138	−288	86	30	−184
Other sectors	4 914	....	....	....	....	....	−199	2	−7
Assets	4 900	**54**	**58**	**98**	**159**	**170**	**541**	**403**	**429**
Monetary authorities	4 901	....	....	....	....	....	....	....	....
General government	4 902	....	....	....	....	....	....	....	....
Banks	4 903	54	58	98	159	170	439	234	385
Other sectors	4 904	....	....	....	....	....	102	169	44
Liabilities	4 905	**−118**	**−85**	**−141**	**−297**	**−458**	**−654**	**−371**	**−620**
Monetary authorities	4 906	....	....	....	....	....	....	....	....
General government	4 907	....	....	....	....	....	....	....	....
Banks	4 908	−118	−85	−141	−297	−458	−353	−204	−569
Other sectors	4 909	....	....	....	....	....	−301	−167	−51

Table 2 (Concluded). STANDARD PRESENTATION, 2003–2010

(Millions of U.S. dollars)

	Code	2003	2004	2005	2006	2007	2008	2009	2010
D. OTHER INVESTMENT	4 700	**−483**	**−1,374**	**−3,697**	**−6,678**	**−219**	**2,261**	**−4,251**	**2,110**
Assets	4 703	**743**	**−859**	**−4,791**	**−3,512**	**−4,840**	**4,305**	**−1,967**	**−2,979**
Trade credits	4 706	−9	−3	−17	−3	−29	−8	−6	−4
General government	4 707	....	....	....	....	....	....	....	....
of which: Short-term	4 709	....	....	....	....	....	....	....	....
Other sectors	4 710	−9	−3	−17	−3	−29	−8	−6	−4
of which: Short-term	4 712	*−9*	*−3*	*−17*	*−3*	*−29*	*−8*	*−6*	*−4*
Loans	4 714	233	156	−1,857	−3,129	−1,259	3,197	−1,600	2,953
Monetary authorities	4 715	....	....	....	....	....	....	....	....
of which: Short-term	4 718	....	....	....	....	....	....	....	....
General government	4 719	....	....	....	....	....	....	....	....
of which: Short-term	4 721	....	....	....	....	....	....	....	....
Banks	4 722	225	351	−1,407	−1,937	−501	1,378	−2,183	2,942
of which: Short-term	4 724	*257*	*294*	*−1,454*	*−1,757*	*−97*	*1,180*	*−2,194*	*2,942*
Other sectors	4 725	8	−195	−450	−1,192	−758	1,819	583	11
of which: Short-term	4 727	*−11*	*−179*	*−457*	*−538*	*−746*	*1,228*	*561*	*12*
Currency and deposits	4 730	1,286	−937	−3,321	−2,257	−3,768	−3,600	4,551	−2,947
Monetary authorities	4 731	....	....	....	....	....	....	....	....
General government	4 732	....	....	....	....	....	....	....	....
Banks	4 733	907	−818	−2,750	−1,329	−1,958	−3,688	5,733	2,242
Other sectors	4 734	379	−119	−571	−928	−1,810	88	−1,182	−5,189
Other assets	4 736	−767	−75	404	1,877	216	4,716	−4,912	−2,981
Monetary authorities	4 737	....	....	....	....	....	....	....	....
of which: Short-term	4 739	....	....	....	....	....	....	....	....
General government	4 740	....	....	....	....	....	....	....	....
of which: Short-term	4 742	....	....	....	....	....	....	....	....
Banks	4 743	−762	−76	416	1,875	215	4,712	−4,919	−2,980
of which: Short-term	4 745	*−762*	*−76*	*416*	*1,875*	*215*	*4,712*	*−4,919*	*−2,980*
Other sectors	4 746	−5	1	−12	2	1	4	7	−1
of which: Short-term	4 748	*−5*	*1*	*−12*	*2*	*1*	*4*	*7*	*−1*
Liabilities	4 753	**−1,226**	**−515**	**1,094**	**−3,166**	**4,621**	**−2,044**	**−2,284**	**5,089**
Trade credits	4 756	125	380	−59	239	632	−668	3	1,047
General government	4 757	....	....	....	....	....	....	....	....
of which: Short-term	4 759	....	....	....	....	....	....	....	....
Other sectors	4 760	125	380	−59	239	632	−668	3	1,047
of which: Short-term	4 762	*311*	*391*	*−112*	*264*	*712*	*−528*	*15*	*1,058*
Loans	4 764	−1,012	−1,838	792	−3,141	3,286	−1,818	−2,267	1,835
Monetary authorities	4 765	−274	−1,362	−729	−1,400	−201	1,508	−1,510	−1
of which: Use of Fund credit and loans from the Fund	4 766	*−607*	*−472*	*−321*	*−404*	....	....	....	....
of which: Short-term	4 768	*138*	*−886*	*−468*	*−433*	*−7*	*1,508*	*−1,510*	*−1*
General government	4 769	−64	−362	−500	176	438	58	957	−177
of which: Short-term	4 771	....	....	....	....	....	....	....	....
Banks	4 772	−79	276	1,099	−1,182	415	−883	−1,009	1,209
of which: Short-term	4 774	*−604*	*226*	*1,099*	*−1,410*	*390*	*513*	*−430*	*−62*
Other sectors	4 775	−595	−390	922	−735	2,634	−2,501	−705	804
of which: Short-term	4 777	*94*	*−103*	*1,024*	*893*	*−217*	*−1,672*	*−120*	*−116*
Currency and deposits	4 780	−341	868	147	−339	552	−140	−530	1,876
Monetary authorities	4 781	....	....	....	....	....	....	....	....
General government	4 782	....	....	....	....	....	....	....	....
Banks	4 783	−373	883	−192	−126	537	−358	−126	1,908
Other sectors	4 784	32	−15	339	−213	15	218	−404	−32
Other liabilities	4 786	2	75	214	75	151	582	510	331
Monetary authorities	4 787	....	....	....	....	....	....	1,127	....
of which: Short-term	4 789	....	....	....	....	....	....	....	....
General government	4 790	....	....	....	....	....	....	....	....
of which: Short-term	4 792	....	....	....	....	....	....	....	....
Banks	4 793	−1	74	198	79	124	594	−596	333
of which: Short-term	4 795	*−1*	*74*	*198*	*79*	*124*	*594*	*−596*	*333*
Other sectors	4 796	3	1	16	−4	27	−12	−21	−2
of which: Short-term	4 798	*3*	*1*	*16*	*−4*	*27*	*−12*	*−21*	*−2*
E. RESERVE ASSETS	4 802	**356**	**1,637**	**−1,622**	**−2,935**	**−8,550**	**−1,597**	**−4,911**	**−14,308**
Monetary gold	4 812	460	955	1,415	944	912	385	854	1,235
Special drawing rights	4 811	9	1	....	−1	2	−11	−1,126	....
Reserve position in the Fund	4 810	....	....	....	....	....	....	....	−118
Foreign exchange	4 803	−113	681	−3,037	−3,878	−9,464	−1,971	−4,639	−15,425
Other claims	4 813	....	....	....	....	....	....	....	....
NET ERRORS AND OMISSIONS	4 998	**−898**	**−274**	**−1,798**	**−1,588**	**−2,082**	**−1,889**	**−1,310**	**−1,959**

Table 3. INTERNATIONAL INVESTMENT POSITION (End-period stocks), 2003–2010

(Millions of U.S. dollars)

	Code	2003	2004	2005	2006	2007	2008	2009	2010
ASSETS	8 995 C.	**32,300**	**33,820**	**40,629**	**50,423**	**66,831**	**65,486**	**77,166**	**96,126**
Direct investment abroad	8 505 ..	**1,260**	**1,839**	**2,028**	**2,131**	**5,667**	**5,736**	**6,095**	**6,581**
Equity capital and reinvested earnings	8 506 ..	1,260	1,839	2,028	2,131	5,667	5,736	6,095	6,581
Claims on affiliated enterprises	8 507 ..	1,260	1,839	2,028	2,131	5,667	5,736	6,095	6,581
Liabilities to affiliated enterprises	8 508 ..	....	....	....	....	....	....	....	....
Other capital	8 530 ..	....	....	....	....	....	....	....	....
Claims on affiliated enterprises	8 535 ..	....	....	....	....	....	....	....	....
Liabilities to affiliated enterprises	8 540 ..	....	....	....	....	....	....	....	....
Portfolio investment	8 602 ..	**4,112**	**5,022**	**5,303**	**6,830**	**5,907**	**4,730**	**8,591**	**12,050**
Equity securities	8 610 ..	167	185	190	119	198	145	165	177
Monetary authorities	8 611 ..	....	....	....	....	....	....	....	....
General government	8 612 ..	....	....	....	....	....	....	....	....
Banks	8 613 ..	25	31	32	30	25	33	17	18
Other sectors	8 614 ..	142	154	158	89	173	112	148	159
Debt securities	8 619 ..	3,945	4,837	5,113	6,711	5,709	4,585	8,426	11,873
Bonds and notes	8 620 ..	2,633	2,816	3,379	4,759	4,583	2,259	6,856	10,197
Monetary authorities	8 621 ..	167	167	5	6	6	....	....	....
General government	8 622 ..	264	264	345	83	....	....	....	....
Banks	8 623 ..	1,940	2,095	1,958	3,182	3,396	1,121	3,494	5,376
Other sectors	8 624 ..	262	290	1,071	1,488	1,181	1,138	3,362	4,821
Money market instruments	8 630 ..	1,312	2,021	1,734	1,952	1,126	2,326	1,570	1,676
Monetary authorities	8 631 ..	....	....	....	....	....	....	....	....
General government	8 632 ..	....	....	....	....	....	....	....	....
Banks	8 633 ..	675	1,343	991	1,684	926	2,126	991	523
Other sectors	8 634 ..	637	678	743	268	200	200	579	1,153
Financial derivatives	8 900 ..	**....**	**....**	**....**	**....**	**....**	**298**	**127**	**148**
Monetary authorities	8 901 ..	....	....	....	....	....	....	....	....
General government	8 902 ..	....	....	....	....	....	....	....	....
Banks	8 903 ..	....	....	....	....	....	231	119	146
Other sectors	8 904 ..	....	....	....	....	....	67	8	2
Other investment	8 703 ..	**9,865**	**10,730**	**14,804**	**18,495**	**21,506**	**17,171**	**18,110**	**14,975**
Trade credits	8 706 ..	15	18	35	38	67	75	81	85
General government	8 707 ..	....	....	....	....	....	....	....	....
of which: Short-term	8 709 ..	....	....	....	....	....	....	....	....
Other sectors	8 710 ..	15	18	35	38	67	75	81	85
of which: Short-term	8 712 ..	*15*	*18*	*35*	*38*	*67*	*75*	*81*	*85*
Loans	8 714 ..	3,159	3,003	4,860	8,273	9,322	6,109	7,709	4,752
Monetary authorities	8 715 ..	....	....	....	....	....	....	....	....
of which: Short-term	8 718 ..	....	....	....	....	....	....	....	....
General government	8 719 ..	....	....	....	....	....	....	....	....
of which: Short-term	8 721 ..	....	....	....	....	....	....	....	....
Banks	8 722 ..	3,104	2,753	4,160	6,097	6,598	5,292	7,475	4,529
of which: Short-term	8 724 ..	*2,919*	*2,625*	*4,079*	*5,836*	*5,933*	*5,170*	*7,364*	*4,529*
Other sectors	8 725 ..	55	250	700	2,176	2,724	817	234	223
of which: Short-term	8 727 ..	*27*	*206*	*663*	*1,485*	*2,021*	*705*	*144*	*132*
Currency and deposits	8 730 ..	5,998	6,814	8,192	9,042	9,633	8,857	9,438	9,056
Monetary authorities	8 731 ..	....	....	....	....	....	....	....	....
General government	8 732 ..	....	....	....	....	....	....	....	....
Banks	8 733 ..	1,974	2,671	3,564	3,571	4,189	3,501	3,573	3,638
Other sectors	8 734 ..	4,024	4,143	4,628	5,471	5,444	5,356	5,865	5,418
Other assets	8 736 ..	693	895	1,717	1,142	2,484	2,130	882	1,082
Monetary authorities	8 737 ..	59	65	64	67	83	69	70	69
of which: Short-term	8 739 ..	....	....	....	....	....	....	....	....
General government	8 740 ..	....	....	....	....	....	....	....	....
of which: Short-term	8 742 ..	....	....	....	....	....	....	....	....
Banks	8 743 ..	626	823	1,634	1,062	2,389	2,053	815	1,015
of which: Short-term	8 745 ..	*626*	*823*	*1,634*	*1,062*	*2,389*	*2,053*	*815*	*1,015*
Other sectors	8 746 ..	8	7	19	13	12	8	−3	−2
of which: Short-term	8 748 ..	*8*	*7*	*19*	*13*	*12*	*8*	*−3*	*−2*
Reserve assets	8 802 ..	**17,063**	**16,229**	**18,494**	**22,967**	**33,751**	**37,551**	**44,243**	**62,372**
Monetary gold	8 812 ..	3,408	3,112	2,568	2,941	3,541	4,358	5,460	7,010
Special drawing rights	8 811 ..	2	1	1	2	1	11	1,141	1,121
Reserve position in the Fund	8 810 ..	130	136	125	132	138	135	138	251
Foreign exchange	8 803 ..	13,523	12,980	15,800	19,892	30,071	33,047	37,504	53,991
Other claims	8 813 ..	....	....	....	....	....	....	....	....

Table 3 (Concluded). INTERNATIONAL INVESTMENT POSITION (End-period stocks), 2003–2010

(Millions of U.S. dollars)

	Code	2003	2004	2005	2006	2007	2008	2009	2010
LIABILITIES	8 995 D.	**72,790**	**72,617**	**77,573**	**82,267**	**95,897**	**92,919**	**92,535**	**106,715**
Direct investment in the Philippines	8 555	**11,411**	**12,737**	**14,978**	**16,914**	**20,463**	**21,746**	**22,931**	**26,319**
Equity capital and reinvested earnings	8 556	8,044	8,920	10,226	12,020	14,412	15,558	17,226	18,381
Claims on direct investors	8 557	....	....	....	....	....	....	....	....
Liabilities to direct investors	8 558	8,044	8,920	10,226	12,020	14,412	15,558	17,226	18,381
Other capital	8 580	3,367	3,817	4,752	4,894	6,051	6,188	5,705	7,938
Claims on direct investors	8 585	−793	−697	−507	−293	−622	−514	−1,263	−1,600
Liabilities to direct investors	8 590	4,160	4,514	5,259	5,187	6,673	6,702	6,968	9,538
Portfolio investment	8 652	**20,524**	**19,890**	**23,923**	**29,152**	**34,305**	**28,849**	**30,156**	**36,316**
Equity securities	8 660	2,362	2,880	4,345	6,870	10,263	8,913	8,386	9,021
Banks	8 663	15	16	15	339	669	560	1,147	1,441
Other sectors	8 664	2,347	2,864	4,330	6,531	9,594	8,353	7,239	7,580
Debt securities	8 669	18,162	17,010	19,578	22,282	24,042	19,936	21,770	27,295
Bonds and notes	8 670	18,162	17,010	19,521	22,264	23,966	19,929	21,770	27,295
Monetary authorities	8 671	777	392	289	248	338	306	202	174
General government	8 672	10,806	10,143	12,362	13,808	14,287	12,874	14,769	19,951
Banks	8 673	612	639	993	1,812	2,172	730	429	556
Other sectors	8 674	5,967	5,836	5,877	6,396	7,169	6,019	6,370	6,614
Money market instruments	8 680	....	....	57	18	76	7	....	....
Monetary authorities	8 681	....	....	....	....	....	....	....	....
General government	8 682	....	....	....	....	....	....	....	....
Banks	8 683	....	....	....	....	....	....	....	....
Other sectors	8 684	....	....	57	18	76	7	....	....
Financial derivatives	8 905	**....**	**....**	**....**	**....**	**....**	**352**	**236**	**309**
Monetary authorities	8 906	....	....	....	....	....	....	....	....
General government	8 907	....	....	....	....	....	....	....	....
Banks	8 908	....	....	....	....	....	209	210	308
Other sectors	8 909	....	....	....	....	....	143	26	1
Other investment	8 753	**40,855**	**39,990**	**38,672**	**36,201**	**41,129**	**41,972**	**39,212**	**43,771**
Trade credits	8 756	1,320	1,793	1,717	2,036	2,316	2,405	2,438	3,497
General government	8 757	11	8	4	1	....	....	....	....
of which: Short-term	8 759	....	....	....	....	....	....	....	....
Other sectors	8 760	1,309	1,785	1,713	2,035	2,316	2,405	2,438	3,497
of which: Short-term	8 762	*772*	*1,282*	*1,188*	*1,551*	*2,153*	*1,746*	*1,771*	*2,817*
Loans	8 764	38,547	36,873	35,650	32,830	36,931	37,470	34,436	37,744
Monetary authorities	8 765	3,648	2,330	1,535	192	....	1,500	....	....
of which: Use of Fund credit and loans from the Fund	8 766	*1,197*	*756*	*389*	....	....	....	....	....
of which: Short-term	8 768	*1,750*	*875*	*375*	....	....	*1,500*	....	....
General government	8 769	15,608	15,752	13,810	14,018	15,033	17,126	17,996	19,083
of which: Short-term	8 771	....	....	....	....	....	....	....	....
Banks	8 772	5,294	5,020	6,301	5,458	6,329	5,061	3,726	4,985
of which: Short-term	8 774	*2,089*	*1,724*	*2,580*	*456*	*2,054*	*2,141*	*889*	*2,037*
Other sectors	8 775	13,997	13,771	14,004	13,162	15,569	13,783	12,714	13,676
of which: Short-term	8 777	*576*	*640*	*1,696*	*2,466*	*1,907*	*527*	*448*	*326*
Currency and deposits	8 780	731	1,066	1,024	1,031	1,532	1,084	985	1,193
Monetary authorities	8 781	....	....	41	....	....	....	....	....
General government	8 782	....	....	....	....	....	....	....	....
Banks	8 783	705	1,044	965	1,009	1,516	1,068	973	1,187
Other sectors	8 784	26	22	18	22	16	16	12	6
Other liabilities	8 786	257	258	281	304	350	1,013	1,353	1,337
Monetary authorities	8 787	173	181	167	175	183	180	1,314	1,290
of which: Short-term	8 789	....	....	....	....	....	....	....	....
General government	8 790	....	....	....	....	....	....	....	....
of which: Short-term	8 792	....	....	....	....	....	....	....	....
Banks	8 793	78	73	97	109	120	798	22	32
of which: Short-term	8 795	*78*	*73*	*97*	*109*	*120*	*798*	*22*	*32*
Other sectors	8 796	6	4	17	20	47	35	17	15
of which: Short-term	8 798	*6*	*4*	*17*	*20*	*47*	*35*	*17*	*15*
NET INTERNATIONAL INVESTMENT POSITION	8 995	**−40,491**	**−38,797**	**−36,944**	**−31,844**	**−29,066**	**−27,433**	**−15,369**	**−10,589**
Conversion rates: Philippine pesos per U.S. dollar (end of period)	0 102	**55.569**	**56.267**	**53.067**	**49.132**	**41.401**	**47.485**	**46.356**	**43.885**

Table 1. ANALYTIC PRESENTATION, 2003–2010

(Millions of U.S. dollars)

	Code	2003	2004	2005	2006	2007	2008	2009	2010
A. Current Account[1]	4 993 Z.	**−5,473**	**−13,259**	**−7,242**	**−13,156**	**−26,499**	**−34,957**	**−17,155**	**−20,982**
Goods: exports f.o.b.	2 100 ..	61,007	81,862	96,395	117,468	145,337	178,427	142,085	162,267
Goods: imports f.o.b.	3 100 ..	−66,732	−87,823	−99,490	−124,840	−164,403	−209,086	−149,702	−173,681
Balance on Goods	4 100 ..	*−5,725*	*−5,961*	*−3,095*	*−7,372*	*−19,066*	*−30,659*	*−7,617*	*−11,414*
Services: credit	2 200 ..	11,174	13,471	16,258	20,592	28,914	35,549	28,986	32,480
Services: debit	3 200 ..	−10,931	−13,392	−15,520	−19,856	−24,156	−30,543	−24,191	−28,987
Balance on Goods and Services	4 991 ..	*−5,482*	*−5,882*	*−2,357*	*−6,636*	*−14,308*	*−25,653*	*−2,822*	*−7,921*
Income: credit	2 300 ..	3,284	5,305	6,998	9,043	10,141	11,126	6,625	7,589
Income: debit	3 300 ..	−5,745	−13,743	−13,841	−18,800	−26,526	−24,008	−23,176	−24,292
Balance on Goods, Services, and Income	4 992 ..	*−7,943*	*−14,320*	*−9,200*	*−16,393*	*−30,693*	*−38,535*	*−19,373*	*−24,624*
Current transfers: credit	2 379 Z.	3,769	4,011	6,452	8,235	10,397	11,172	10,349	9,873
Current transfers: debit	3 379 ..	−1,299	−2,950	−4,494	−4,998	−6,203	−7,594	−8,131	−6,231
B. Capital Account[1]	4 994 Z.	**−46**	**1,180**	**995**	**2,105**	**4,771**	**6,115**	**7,040**	**8,668**
Capital account: credit	2 994 Z.	60	1,326	1,185	2,573	5,410	7,089	7,438	9,233
Capital account: debit	3 994 ..	−106	−146	−190	−468	−639	−974	−398	−565
Total, Groups A Plus B	4 981 ..	*−5,519*	*−12,079*	*−6,247*	*−11,051*	*−21,728*	*−28,842*	*−10,115*	*−12,314*
C. Financial Account[1]	4 995 W.	**8,686**	**7,997**	**15,180**	**13,261**	**38,067**	**39,039**	**34,927**	**37,713**
Direct investment abroad	4 505 ..	−305	−955	−3,392	−9,168	−5,664	−4,613	−4,562	−5,646
Direct investment in Poland	4 555 Z.	4,589	12,716	10,309	19,876	23,651	14,978	13,022	9,056
Portfolio investment assets	4 602 ..	−1,296	−1,331	−2,509	−4,649	−6,340	2,358	−1,448	−965
Equity securities	4 610 ..	183	−57	−575	−2,996	−5,882	1,457	−1,862	−927
Debt securities	4 619 ..	−1,479	−1,274	−1,934	−1,653	−458	901	414	−38
Portfolio investment liabilities	4 652 Z.	3,740	10,571	15,095	1,706	113	−4,723	16,202	26,371
Equity securities	4 660 ..	−837	1,660	1,333	−2,128	−470	564	1,579	7,822
Debt securities	4 669 Z.	4,577	8,911	13,762	3,834	583	−5,287	14,623	18,549
Financial derivatives	4 910 ..	−870	200	193	−689	−2,046	−993	−1,692	−572
Financial derivatives assets	4 900 ..	....	....	....	....	....	....	....	....
Financial derivatives liabilities	4 905 ..	−870	200	193	−689	−2,046	−993	−1,692	−572
Other investment assets	4 703 ..	−493	−11,999	−2,784	−3,919	−1,771	5,217	5,275	−4,254
Monetary authorities	4 701 ..	....	−29	−17	9	−225	−699	−1,023	28
General government	4 704 ..	−47	−39	−160	−30	−323	−116	−174	−928
Banks	4 705 ..	351	−10,559	−836	−1,937	2,677	7,236	7,232	−1,895
Other sectors	4 728 ..	−797	−1,372	−1,771	−1,961	−3,900	−1,204	−760	−1,459
Other investment liabilities	4 753 W.	3,321	−1,205	−1,732	10,104	30,124	26,815	8,130	13,723
Monetary authorities	4 753 WA	−68	−106	1,910	−765	7,253	−6,178	2,923	1,709
General government	4 753 ZB	−1,236	−2,286	−6,443	−1,192	−1,429	−1,529	2,751	2,636
Banks	4 753 ZC	2,063	1,224	543	5,589	14,555	23,602	−471	6,246
Other sectors	4 753 ZD	2,562	−37	2,258	6,472	9,745	10,920	2,927	3,132
Total, Groups A Through C	4 983 ..	*3,167*	*−4,082*	*8,933*	*2,210*	*16,339*	*10,197*	*24,812*	*25,399*
D. Net Errors and Omissions	4 998 ..	**−1,961**	**4,883**	**−787**	**279**	**−3,295**	**−12,154**	**−10,050**	**−10,291**
Total, Groups A Through D	4 984 ..	*1,206*	*801*	*8,146*	*2,489*	*13,044*	*−1,957*	*14,761*	*15,108*
E. Reserves and Related Items	4 802 A.	**−1,206**	**−801**	**−8,146**	**−2,489**	**−13,044**	**1,957**	**−14,761**	**−15,108**
Reserve assets	4 802 ..	−1,206	−801	−8,146	−2,489	−13,044	1,957	−14,761	−15,108
Use of Fund credit and loans	4 766 ..	....	....	....	....	....	....	....	....
Exceptional financing	4 920 ..	....	....	....	....	....	....	....	....
Conversion rates: zlotys per U.S. dollar	0 101 ..	**3.8891**	**3.6576**	**3.2355**	**3.1032**	**2.7680**	**2.4092**	**3.1201**	**3.0153**

[1] Excludes components that have been classified in the categories of Group E.

Table 2. STANDARD PRESENTATION, 2003–2010

(Millions of U.S. dollars)

	Code	2003	2004	2005	2006	2007	2008	2009	2010
CURRENT ACCOUNT	4 993	−5,473	−13,259	−7,242	−13,156	−26,499	−34,957	−17,155	−20,982
A. GOODS	4 100	−5,725	−5,961	−3,095	−7,372	−19,066	−30,659	−7,617	−11,414
Credit	2 100	61,007	81,862	96,395	117,468	145,337	178,427	142,085	162,267
General merchandise: exports f.o.b.	2 110	....	....	....	....	....	....	....	....
Goods for processing: exports f.o.b.	2 150	....	....	....	....	....	....	....	....
Repairs on goods	2 160	....	....	....	....	....	....	....	....
Goods procured in ports by carriers	2 170	....	....	....	....	....	....	....	....
Nonmonetary gold	2 180	....	....	....	....	....	....	....	....
Debit	3 100	−66,732	−87,823	−99,490	−124,840	−164,403	−209,086	−149,702	−173,681
General merchandise: imports f.o.b.	3 110	....	....	....	....	....	....	....	....
Goods for processing: imports f.o.b.	3 150	....	....	....	....	....	....	....	....
Repairs on goods	3 160	....	....	....	....	....	....	....	....
Goods procured in ports by carriers	3 170	....	....	....	....	....	....	....	....
Nonmonetary gold	3 180	....	....	....	....	....	....	....	....
B. SERVICES	4 200	243	79	738	736	4,758	5,006	4,795	3,493
Total credit	2 200	*11,174*	*13,471*	*16,258*	*20,592*	*28,914*	*35,549*	*28,986*	*32,480*
Total debit	3 200	*−10,931*	*−13,392*	*−15,520*	*−19,856*	*−24,156*	*−30,543*	*−24,191*	*−28,987*
Transportation services, credit	2 205	3,995	4,200	5,457	6,995	9,303	10,954	8,711	8,792
Passenger	2 850	*664*	*666*	*854*	*883*	*1,087*	*1,069*	*832*	*759*
Freight	2 851	*3,101*	*3,194*	*4,142*	*5,505*	*7,453*	*8,599*	*6,851*	*6,398*
Other	2 852	*230*	*340*	*461*	*607*	*763*	*1,286*	*1,028*	*1,635*
Sea transport, passenger	2 207	11	15	18	32	36	41	52	16
Sea transport, freight	2 208	1,286	621	680	811	1,046	1,204	881	290
Sea transport, other	2 209	32	135	210	180	146	178	180	58
Air transport, passenger	2 211	567	604	773	750	906	929	666	677
Air transport, freight	2 212	46	78	67	81	114	128	94	109
Air transport, other	2 213	37	48	66	145	186	344	263	346
Other transport, passenger	2 215	86	47	63	101	145	99	114	66
Other transport, freight	2 216	1,769	2,495	3,395	4,613	6,293	7,267	5,876	5,999
Other transport, other	2 217	161	157	185	282	431	764	585	1,231
Transportation services, debit	3 205	−2,296	−2,948	−3,328	−4,255	−5,697	−7,187	−5,239	−6,112
Passenger	3 850	*−201*	*−316*	*−346*	*−430*	*−589*	*−786*	*−516*	*−423*
Freight	3 851	*−1,569*	*−2,076*	*−2,313*	*−3,063*	*−4,005*	*−4,839*	*−3,541*	*−4,616*
Other	3 852	*−526*	*−556*	*−669*	*−762*	*−1,103*	*−1,562*	*−1,182*	*−1,073*
Sea transport, passenger	3 207	....	−16	−12	−14	−29	−28	−18	−23
Sea transport, freight	3 208	−699	−612	−646	−837	−1,179	−1,309	−846	−975
Sea transport, other	3 209	−24	−122	−134	−116	−149	−223	−143	−98
Air transport, passenger	3 211	−160	−277	−313	−390	−535	−728	−454	−364
Air transport, freight	3 212	−35	−101	−116	−171	−208	−266	−178	−253
Air transport, other	3 213	−320	−289	−303	−334	−382	−479	−438	−350
Other transport, passenger	3 215	−41	−23	−21	−26	−25	−30	−44	−36
Other transport, freight	3 216	−835	−1,363	−1,551	−2,055	−2,618	−3,264	−2,517	−3,388
Other transport, other	3 217	−182	−145	−232	−312	−572	−860	−601	−625
Travel, credit	2 236	4,069	5,833	6,274	7,239	10,599	11,768	9,011	9,446
Business travel	2 237	....	....	....	....	....	....	....	....
Personal travel	2 240	....	....	....	....	....	....	....	....
Travel, debit	3 236	−3,085	−4,776	−5,548	−7,224	−7,753	−9,903	−7,372	−8,140
Business travel	3 237	....	....	....	....	....	....	....	....
Personal travel	3 240	....	....	....	....	....	....	....	....
Other services, credit	2 200 BA	3,110	3,438	4,527	6,358	9,012	12,827	11,264	14,242
Communications	2 245	243	298	308	396	506	621	646	560
Construction	2 249	731	660	862	1,230	1,618	1,903	1,509	1,296
Insurance	2 253	219	65	67	96	20	155	28	190
Financial	2 260	161	159	219	218	395	564	420	554
Computer and information	2 262	134	195	196	407	663	942	885	1,547
Royalties and licence fees	2 266	28	30	62	38	103	207	103	248
Other business services	2 268	1,532	1,906	2,673	3,763	5,418	8,079	7,401	9,544
Personal, cultural, and recreational	2 287	58	91	94	148	193	207	142	285
Government, n.i.e.	2 291	4	34	46	62	96	149	130	18
Other services, debit	3 200 BA	−5,550	−5,668	−6,644	−8,377	−10,706	−13,453	−11,580	−14,735
Communications	3 245	−245	−313	−364	−469	−703	−782	−808	−649
Construction	3 249	−791	−640	−512	−730	−915	−1,250	−992	−586
Insurance	3 253	−412	−256	−387	−398	−461	−500	−446	−314
Financial	3 260	−286	−371	−384	−378	−519	−856	−880	−881
Computer and information	3 262	−351	−420	−421	−585	−874	−996	−847	−1,672
Royalties and licence fees	3 266	−745	−883	−1,037	−1,313	−1,575	−1,773	−1,542	−2,244
Other business services	3 268	−2,471	−2,475	−3,169	−3,852	−4,981	−6,442	−5,328	−7,359
Personal, cultural, and recreational	3 287	−128	−131	−160	−234	−302	−328	−335	−859
Government, n.i.e.	3 291	−121	−179	−210	−418	−376	−526	−402	−171

Table 2 (Continued). STANDARD PRESENTATION, 2003–2010

(Millions of U.S. dollars)

	Code	2003	2004	2005	2006	2007	2008	2009	2010
C. INCOME	4 300	**−2,461**	**−8,438**	**−6,843**	**−9,757**	**−16,385**	**−12,882**	**−16,551**	**−16,703**
Total credit	2 300	*3,284*	*5,305*	*6,998*	*9,043*	*10,141*	*11,126*	*6,625*	*7,589*
Total debit	3 300	*−5,745*	*−13,743*	*−13,841*	*−18,800*	*−26,526*	*−24,008*	*−23,176*	*−24,292*
Compensation of employees, credit	2 310	**1,543**	**3,600**	**4,649**	**5,531**	**6,226**	**5,708**	**4,442**	**4,075**
Compensation of employees, debit	3 310	**−292**	**−632**	**−717**	**−796**	**−1,177**	**−1,690**	**−1,332**	**−1,514**
Investment income, credit	2 320	**1,741**	**1,705**	**2,349**	**3,512**	**3,915**	**5,418**	**2,183**	**3,514**
Direct investment income	2 330	3	80	126	670	134	970	−799	787
Dividends and distributed branch profits	2 332	14	37	43	62	149	615	351	299
Reinvested earnings and undistributed branch profits	2 333	−12	23	56	582	−85	225	−1,399	−97
Income on debt (interest)	2 334	1	20	27	26	70	130	249	585
Portfolio investment income	2 339	430	404	413	543	701	668	596	317
Income on equity	2 340	12	8	17	43	91	113	167	103
Income on bonds and notes	2 350	404	390	391	481	589	469	382	210
Income on money market instruments	2 360	14	6	5	19	21	86	47	4
Other investment income	2 370	1,308	1,221	1,810	2,299	3,080	3,780	2,386	2,410
Investment income, debit	3 320	**−5,453**	**−13,111**	**−13,124**	**−18,004**	**−25,349**	**−22,318**	**−21,844**	**−22,778**
Direct investment income	3 330	−2,093	−9,562	−9,283	−13,217	−18,908	−13,029	−14,396	−15,019
Dividends and distributed branch profits	3 332	−1,630	−2,683	−5,134	−6,464	−8,114	−12,097	−7,591	−6,392
Reinvested earnings and undistributed branch profits	3 333	84	−6,211	−3,416	−5,752	−9,339	1,116	−5,011	−6,374
Income on debt (interest)	3 334	−547	−668	−733	−1,001	−1,455	−2,048	−1,794	−2,253
Portfolio investment income	3 339	−1,529	−1,851	−2,174	−3,033	−3,564	−4,225	−3,791	−4,740
Income on equity	3 340	−306	−145	−325	−494	−728	−1,101	−859	−658
Income on bonds and notes	3 350	−1,172	−1,640	−1,747	−2,434	−2,772	−3,058	−2,875	−4,052
Income on money market instruments	3 360	−51	−66	−102	−105	−64	−66	−57	−30
Other investment income	3 370	−1,831	−1,698	−1,667	−1,754	−2,877	−5,064	−3,657	−3,019
D. CURRENT TRANSFERS	4 379	**2,470**	**1,061**	**1,958**	**3,237**	**4,194**	**3,578**	**2,218**	**3,642**
Credit	2 379	**3,769**	**4,011**	**6,452**	**8,235**	**10,397**	**11,172**	**10,349**	**9,873**
General government	2 380	718	2,460	4,231	4,784	5,545	5,587	5,869	5,970
Other sectors	2 390	3,051	1,551	2,221	3,451	4,852	5,585	4,480	3,903
Workers' remittances	2 391	741	1,124	1,822	2,955	4,242	4,700	3,652	3,539
Other current transfers	2 392	2,310	427	399	496	610	885	828	364
Debit	3 379	**−1,299**	**−2,950**	**−4,494**	**−4,998**	**−6,203**	**−7,594**	**−8,131**	**−6,231**
General government	3 380	−169	−1,867	−3,225	−3,413	−4,248	−5,367	−6,021	−5,119
Other sectors	3 390	−1,130	−1,083	−1,269	−1,585	−1,955	−2,227	−2,110	−1,112
Workers' remittances	3 391	−33	−20	−21	−24	−31	−51	−46	−61
Other current transfers	3 392	−1,097	−1,063	−1,248	−1,561	−1,924	−2,176	−2,064	−1,051
CAPITAL AND FINANCIAL ACCOUNT	4 996	**7,434**	**8,376**	**8,029**	**12,877**	**29,794**	**47,111**	**27,205**	**31,273**
CAPITAL ACCOUNT	4 994	**−46**	**1,180**	**995**	**2,105**	**4,771**	**6,115**	**7,040**	**8,668**
Total credit	2 994	*60*	*1,326*	*1,185*	*2,573*	*5,410*	*7,089*	*7,438*	*9,233*
Total debit	3 994	*−106*	*−146*	*−190*	*−468*	*−639*	*−974*	*−398*	*−565*
Capital transfers, credit	2 400	**51**	**1,315**	**1,174**	**2,395**	**5,322**	**6,651**	**7,307**	**9,002**
General government	2 401	45	1,256	1,140	2,371	5,282	6,597	7,259	9,002
Debt forgiveness	2 402	43	....	55	....	....	15	....	....
Other capital transfers	2 410	2	1,256	1,085	2,371	5,282	6,582	7,259	9,002
Other sectors	2 430	6	59	34	24	40	54	48	....
Migrants' transfers	2 431	....	4	11	10	28	39	32	....
Debt forgiveness	2 432	2	....	....	....	....	....	....	....
Other capital transfers	2 440	4	55	23	14	12	15	16	....
Capital transfers, debit	3 400	**−8**	**−19**	**−34**	**−115**	**−73**	**−203**	**−39**	**....**
General government	3 401	−4	−10	....	−96	−28	−145	−23	....
Debt forgiveness	3 402	−4	−9	....	−95	−15	−145	....	....
Other capital transfers	3 410	....	−1	....	−1	−13	....	−23	....
Other sectors	3 430	−4	−9	−34	−19	−45	−58	−16	....
Migrants' transfers	3 431	....	−6	−18	−13	−24	−34	−10	....
Debt forgiveness	3 432	....	....	−15	....	−15	....	....	....
Other capital transfers	3 440	−4	−3	−1	−6	−6	−24	−6	....
Nonproduced nonfinancial assets, credit	2 480	**9**	**11**	**11**	**178**	**88**	**438**	**131**	**231**
Nonproduced nonfinancial assets, debit	3 480	**−98**	**−127**	**−156**	**−353**	**−566**	**−771**	**−359**	**−565**

Table 2 (Continued). STANDARD PRESENTATION, 2003–2010

(Millions of U.S. dollars)

	Code	2003	2004	2005	2006	2007	2008	2009	2010
FINANCIAL ACCOUNT	4 995 ..	**7,480**	**7,196**	**7,034**	**10,772**	**25,023**	**40,996**	**20,165**	**22,605**
A. DIRECT INVESTMENT	4 500 ..	**4,284**	**11,761**	**6,917**	**10,708**	**17,987**	**10,365**	**8,460**	**3,410**
Direct investment abroad	4 505 ..	**−305**	**−955**	**−3,392**	**−9,168**	**−5,664**	**−4,613**	**−4,562**	**−5,646**
Equity capital	4 510 ..	−105	−565	−2,734	−7,848	−4,131	−2,854	−4,959	−3,403
Claims on affiliated enterprises	4 515 ..	−105	−565	−2,734	−7,848	−4,131	−2,854	−4,959	−3,403
Liabilities to affiliated enterprises	4 520 ..	....	....	....	....	....	....	....	....
Reinvested earnings	4 525 ..	12	−22	−55	−582	87	−225	1,399	97
Other capital	4 530 ..	−212	−368	−603	−738	−1,620	−1,534	−1,002	−2,340
Claims on affiliated enterprises	4 535 ..	−245	−394	−664	−735	−1,770	−1,601	−1,121	−3,125
Liabilities to affiliated enterprises	4 540 ..	33	26	61	−3	150	67	119	785
Direct investment in Poland	4 555 ..	**4,589**	**12,716**	**10,309**	**19,876**	**23,651**	**14,978**	**13,022**	**9,056**
Equity capital	4 560 ..	4,561	7,321	4,482	7,382	7,728	9,873	5,282	1,874
Claims on direct investors	4 565 ..	....	....	....	....	....	....	....	....
Liabilities to direct investors	4 570 ..	4,561	7,321	4,482	7,382	7,728	9,873	5,282	1,874
Reinvested earnings	4 575 ..	−84	6,210	3,416	5,753	9,340	−1,116	5,011	6,374
Other capital	4 580 ..	112	−815	2,411	6,741	6,583	6,221	2,729	808
Claims on direct investors	4 585 ..	−749	−1,162	−681	−1,645	−1,772	14	−1,247	−1,866
Liabilities to direct investors	4 590 ..	861	347	3,092	8,386	8,355	6,207	3,976	2,674
B. PORTFOLIO INVESTMENT	4 600 ..	**2,444**	**9,240**	**12,586**	**−2,943**	**−6,227**	**−2,365**	**14,754**	**25,406**
Assets	4 602 ..	**−1,296**	**−1,331**	**−2,509**	**−4,649**	**−6,340**	**2,358**	**−1,448**	**−965**
Equity securities	4 610 ..	183	−57	−575	−2,996	−5,882	1,457	−1,862	−927
Monetary authorities	4 611 ..	....	....	....	....	....	....	....	....
General government	4 612 ..	....	5	−4	−2	−3	1	....	....
Banks	4 613 ..	11	6	77	−84	−61	−193	−220	30
Other sectors	4 614 ..	172	−68	−648	−2,910	−5,818	1,649	−1,642	−957
Debt securities	4 619 ..	−1,479	−1,274	−1,934	−1,653	−458	901	414	−38
Bonds and notes	4 620 ..	−1,376	−934	−2,175	−1,541	−440	−1,492	100	−194
Monetary authorities	4 621 ..	....	....	....	....	....	....	....	....
General government	4 622 ..	−22	−7	−4	4	−21	−1	....	−9
Banks	4 623 ..	−284	−237	−1,166	59	431	676	171	27
Other sectors	4 624 ..	−1,070	−690	−1,005	−1,604	−850	−2,167	−71	−212
Money market instruments	4 630 ..	−103	−340	241	−112	−18	2,393	314	156
Monetary authorities	4 631 ..	....	....	....	....	....	....	....	....
General government	4 632 ..	1	....	4	−2	....	....	....	....
Banks	4 633 ..	26	−293	−36	−187	169	163	207	69
Other sectors	4 634 ..	−130	−47	273	77	−187	2,230	107	87
Liabilities	4 652 ..	**3,740**	**10,571**	**15,095**	**1,706**	**113**	**−4,723**	**16,202**	**26,371**
Equity securities	4 660 ..	−837	1,660	1,333	−2,128	−470	564	1,579	7,822
Banks	4 663 ..	−181	454	166	−1,096	−775	1,171	929	1,442
Other sectors	4 664 ..	−656	1,206	1,167	−1,032	305	−607	650	6,380
Debt securities	4 669 ..	4,577	8,911	13,762	3,834	583	−5,287	14,623	18,549
Bonds and notes	4 670 ..	4,741	8,909	13,999	4,275	610	−5,483	13,718	18,276
Monetary authorities	4 671 ..	....	....	....	....	....	....	−1	....
General government	4 672 ..	5,346	8,471	13,300	4,402	2,471	−4,679	13,370	18,109
Banks	4 673 ..	51	356	754	776	−1,724	−81	−14	55
Other sectors	4 674 ..	−656	82	−55	−903	−137	−723	363	112
Money market instruments	4 680 ..	−164	2	−237	−441	−27	196	905	273
Monetary authorities	4 681 ..	....	−1	....	....	....	....	....	....
General government	4 682 ..	−120	27	27	−251	13	263	970	507
Banks	4 683 ..	−3	−8	−40	5	−18	−14	....	1
Other sectors	4 684 ..	−41	−16	−224	−195	−22	−53	−65	−235
C. FINANCIAL DERIVATIVES	4 910 ..	**−870**	**200**	**193**	**−689**	**−2,046**	**−993**	**−1,692**	**−572**
Monetary authorities	4 911 ..	....	....	....	....	....	....	....	....
General government	4 912 ..	....	1	−7	9	−873	669	307	−542
Banks	4 913 ..	−192	1,018	230	195	87	−578	−678	−377
Other sectors	4 914 ..	−678	−819	−30	−893	−1,260	−1,084	−1,321	347
Assets	4 900 ..	....	....	....	....	....	....	....	....
Monetary authorities	4 901 ..	....	....	....	....	....	....	....	....
General government	4 902 ..	....	....	....	....	....	....	....	....
Banks	4 903 ..	....	....	....	....	....	....	....	....
Other sectors	4 904 ..	....	....	....	....	....	....	....	....
Liabilities	4 905 ..	**−870**	**200**	**193**	**−689**	**−2,046**	**−993**	**−1,692**	**−572**
Monetary authorities	4 906 ..	....	....	....	....	....	....	....	....
General government	4 907 ..	....	1	−7	9	−873	669	307	−542
Banks	4 908 ..	−192	1,018	230	195	87	−578	−678	−377
Other sectors	4 909 ..	−678	−819	−30	−893	−1,260	−1,084	−1,321	347

Table 2 (Concluded). STANDARD PRESENTATION, 2003–2010

(Millions of U.S. dollars)

	Code	2003	2004	2005	2006	2007	2008	2009	2010
D. OTHER INVESTMENT	4 700 ..	**2,828**	**–13,204**	**–4,516**	**6,185**	**28,353**	**32,032**	**13,405**	**9,469**
Assets	4 703 ..	**–493**	**–11,999**	**–2,784**	**–3,919**	**–1,771**	**5,217**	**5,275**	**–4,254**
Trade credits	4 706 ..	–777	–1,245	–1,613	–2,073	–3,028	857	855	–1,350
General government	4 707 ..	....	....	....	....	....	....	....	....
of which: Short-term	4 709 ..	....	....	....	....	....	....	....	....
Other sectors	4 710 ..	–777	–1,245	–1,613	–2,073	–3,028	857	855	–1,350
of which: Short-term	4 712 ..	*–777*	*–1,245*	*–1,613*	*–2,073*	*–3,028*	*857*	*855*	*–1,350*
Loans	4 714 ..	–438	–59	–308	–347	–1,036	–954	604	426
Monetary authorities	4 715 ..	....	....	....	....	....	....	....	....
of which: Short-term	4 718 ..	....	....	....	....	....	....	....	....
General government	4 719 ..	–28	–50	–36	14	–106	–6	–45	–127
of which: Short-term	4 721 ..	....	....	....	....	....	....	....	*–16*
Banks	4 722 ..	–261	–92	–226	–241	–764	–790	641	540
of which: Short-term	4 724 ..	*–90*	*58*	*–64*	*–7*	*–44*	*–10*	*251*	*–74*
Other sectors	4 725 ..	–149	83	–46	–120	–166	–158	8	13
of which: Short-term	4 727 ..	*–92*	*96*	*–22*	*–23*	*–5*	*–53*	*–6*	*82*
Currency and deposits	4 730 ..	746	–10,646	–731	–1,459	2,721	6,117	4,964	–1,774
Monetary authorities	4 731 ..	....	....	....	....	....	....	....	....
General government	4 732 ..	....	....	1	....	–3	–3	....	–684
Banks	4 733 ..	612	–10,425	–625	–1,691	3,430	8,026	6,595	–1,389
Other sectors	4 734 ..	134	–221	–107	232	–706	–1,906	–1,631	299
Other assets	4 736 ..	–24	–49	–132	–40	–428	–803	–1,148	–1,556
Monetary authorities	4 737 ..	....	–29	–17	9	–225	–699	–1,023	28
of which: Short-term	4 739 ..	....	....	*–25*	*–9*	*–245*	*–720*	*–1,041*	*28*
General government	4 740 ..	–19	11	–125	–44	–214	–107	–129	–117
of which: Short-term	4 742 ..	*–19*	*13*	*–32*	*66*	*5*	*124*	*–26*	....
Banks	4 743 ..	....	–42	15	–5	11	....	–4	–1,046
of which: Short-term	4 745 ..	....	*–42*	*15*	*–5*	*11*	....	*–4*	*–659*
Other sectors	4 746 ..	–5	11	–5	....	....	3	8	–421
of which: Short-term	4 748 ..	*–5*	*11*	*–5*	....	....	*3*	*8*	*–207*
Liabilities	4 753 ..	**3,321**	**–1,205**	**–1,732**	**10,104**	**30,124**	**26,815**	**8,130**	**13,723**
Trade credits	4 756 ..	1,466	1,250	1,618	1,918	2,510	734	95	1,824
General government	4 757 ..	....	....	....	....	....	....	....	....
of which: Short-term	4 759 ..	....	....	....	....	....	....	....	....
Other sectors	4 760 ..	1,466	1,250	1,618	1,918	2,510	734	95	1,824
of which: Short-term	4 762 ..	*1,466*	*1,250*	*1,618*	*1,918*	*2,510*	*734*	*95*	*1,824*
Loans	4 764 ..	69	–2,516	–4,805	7,238	13,351	20,039	5,188	4,904
Monetary authorities	4 765 ..	–4	–2	–1	....	....	....	....	....
of which: Use of Fund credit and loans from the Fund..	4 766 ..	....	....	....	....	....	....	....	....
of which: Short-term	4 768 ..	....	*–1*	....	....	....	....	....	....
General government	4 769 ..	–1,236	–2,286	–6,443	–1,192	–1,429	–1,529	2,751	2,637
of which: Short-term	4 771 ..	*–298*	....	....	*1*	*–1*	*3*	....	*86*
Banks	4 772 ..	233	1,040	1,038	3,872	7,532	11,406	–384	1,174
of which: Short-term	4 774 ..	....	*676*	*–691*	*84*	*571*	*469*	*–274*	*–169*
Other sectors	4 775 ..	1,076	–1,268	601	4,558	7,248	10,162	2,821	1,093
of which: Short-term	4 777 ..	*221*	*152*	*–178*	*–24*	*267*	*302*	*37*	*–70*
Currency and deposits	4 780 ..	1,766	80	1,416	952	14,276	6,018	749	6,817
Monetary authorities	4 781 ..	–64	–104	1,911	–765	7,253	–6,178	882	1,671
General government	4 782 ..	....	....	....	....	....	....	....	....
Banks	4 783 ..	1,830	184	–495	1,717	7,023	12,196	–133	5,146
Other sectors	4 784 ..	....	....	....	....	....	....	....	....
Other liabilities	4 786 ..	20	–19	39	–4	–13	24	2,098	178
Monetary authorities	4 787 ..	....	....	....	....	....	....	2,041	38
of which: Short-term	4 789 ..	....	....	....	....	....	....	....	*19*
General government	4 790 ..	....	....	....	....	....	....	....	–1
of which: Short-term	4 792 ..	....	....	....	....	....	....	....	*–1*
Banks	4 793 ..	....	....	....	....	....	....	46	–74
of which: Short-term	4 795 ..	....	....	....	....	....	....	*46*	*–200*
Other sectors	4 796 ..	20	–19	39	–4	–13	24	11	215
of which: Short-term	4 798 ..	*20*	*–19*	*39*	*–4*	*–13*	*24*	*11*	*129*
E. RESERVE ASSETS	4 802 ..	**–1,206**	**–801**	**–8,146**	**–2,489**	**–13,044**	**1,957**	**–14,761**	**–15,108**
Monetary gold	4 812 ..	....	....	....	....	....	–1	....	....
Special drawing rights	4 811 ..	–11	–12	–14	–7	–7	–11	–1,986	55
Reserve position in the Fund	4 810 ..	–80	130	353	134	36	–120	–156	–75
Foreign exchange	4 803 ..	–2,456	–918	–6,831	–3,259	–5,812	–4,673	–10,787	–13,665
Other claims	4 813 ..	1,341	....	–1,654	643	–7,261	6,762	–1,832	–1,423
NET ERRORS AND OMISSIONS	4 998 ..	**–1,961**	**4,883**	**–787**	**279**	**–3,295**	**–12,154**	**–10,050**	**–10,291**

Table 3. INTERNATIONAL INVESTMENT POSITION (End-period stocks), 2003–2010

(Millions of U.S. dollars)

	Code	2003	2004	2005	2006	2007	2008	2009	2010
ASSETS	8 995 C.	**58,539**	**79,765**	**92,129**	**117,956**	**156,877**	**136,866**	**156,156**	**181,554**
Direct investment abroad	8 505 ..	**2,145**	**3,351**	**6,308**	**14,393**	**21,317**	**24,095**	**29,306**	**39,266**
Equity capital and reinvested earnings	8 506 ..	1,621	2,341	4,699	11,834	16,731	18,340	22,418	21,557
Claims on affiliated enterprises	8 507 ..	1,621	2,341	4,699	11,834	16,731	18,340	22,418	21,557
Liabilities to affiliated enterprises	8 508 ..	....	....	....	....	....	....	....	....
Other capital	8 530 ..	524	1,010	1,609	2,559	4,586	5,755	6,888	17,709
Claims on affiliated enterprises	8 535 ..	635	1,162	1,813	2,781	4,977	6,168	7,448	23,249
Liabilities to affiliated enterprises	8 540 ..	−111	−152	−204	−222	−391	−413	−560	−5,540
Portfolio investment	8 602 ..	**4,143**	**6,710**	**8,781**	**13,840**	**21,982**	**10,588**	**14,073**	**14,017**
Equity securities	8 610 ..	229	744	1,681	5,214	12,037	4,225	8,759	10,125
Monetary authorities	8 611 ..	....	....	....	....	....	....	....	....
General government	8 612 ..	....	....	....	....	....	....	....	....
Banks	8 613 ..	7	9	8	9	19	14	15	8
Other sectors	8 614 ..	222	735	1,673	5,205	12,018	4,211	8,744	10,117
Debt securities	8 619 ..	3,914	5,966	7,100	8,626	9,945	6,363	5,314	3,892
Bonds and notes	8 620 ..	3,713	5,580	5,675	5,028	5,029	3,702	2,917	3,745
Monetary authorities	8 621 ..	....	....	....	....	....	....	....	....
General government	8 622 ..	412	465	530	266	268	215	159	179
Banks	8 623 ..	1,107	1,316	1,944	2,360	2,475	1,160	614	499
Other sectors	8 624 ..	2,194	3,799	3,201	2,402	2,286	2,327	2,144	3,067
Money market instruments	8 630 ..	201	386	1,425	3,598	4,916	2,661	2,397	147
Monetary authorities	8 631 ..	....	....	....	....	....	....	....	....
General government	8 632 ..	....	....	....	....	....	....	....	....
Banks	8 633 ..	5	5	....	175	6	....	....	135
Other sectors	8 634 ..	196	381	1,425	3,423	4,910	2,661	2,397	12
Financial derivatives	8 900 ..	**....**	**303**	**499**	**551**	**1,284**	**2,365**	**981**	**4,135**
Monetary authorities	8 901 ..	....	....	....	....	....	....	....	....
General government	8 902 ..	....	....	....	....	....	....	....	131
Banks	8 903 ..	....	....	316	392	1,023	1,755	661	2,499
Other sectors	8 904 ..	....	303	183	159	261	610	320	1,505
Other investment	8 703 ..	**18,097**	**32,617**	**33,970**	**40,688**	**46,549**	**37,639**	**32,208**	**30,637**
Trade credits	8 706 ..	4,452	6,180	7,100	9,901	14,152	12,280	11,673	10,644
General government	8 707 ..	....	....	....	....	....	....	....	43
of which: Short-term	8 709 ..	....	....	....	....	....	....	....	*43*
Other sectors	8 710 ..	4,452	6,180	7,100	9,901	14,152	12,280	11,673	10,601
of which: Short-term	8 712 ..	*4,174*	*5,903*	*6,830*	*9,510*	*13,515*	*11,493*	*11,180*	*10,601*
Loans	8 714 ..	1,194	1,299	1,480	1,880	3,020	3,767	3,173	3,384
Monetary authorities	8 715 ..	....	....	....	....	....	....	....	....
of which: Short-term	8 718 ..	....	....	....	....	....	....	....	....
General government	8 719 ..	182	225	262	242	347	352	395	502
of which: Short-term	8 721 ..	....	....	....	....	....	....	....	*15*
Banks	8 722 ..	800	917	1,071	1,384	2,298	2,931	2,292	2,345
of which: Short-term	8 724 ..	*227*	*170*	*227*	*244*	*305*	*304*	*53*	*523*
Other sectors	8 725 ..	212	157	147	254	375	484	486	537
of which: Short-term	8 727 ..	*102*	*15*	*33*	*41*	*19*	*64*	*68*	*254*
Currency and deposits	8 730 ..	11,201	23,499	23,627	27,046	27,187	19,686	15,273	12,523
Monetary authorities	8 731 ..	....	....	....	....	....	....	....	....
General government	8 732 ..	7	8	8	11	12	9	9	668
Banks	8 733 ..	10,626	22,354	22,061	25,088	24,206	14,596	7,937	8,203
Other sectors	8 734 ..	568	1,137	1,558	1,947	2,969	5,081	7,327	3,652
Other assets	8 736 ..	1,250	1,639	1,763	1,861	2,190	1,906	2,089	4,086
Monetary authorities	8 737 ..	15	129	164	172	183	71	75	28
of which: Short-term	8 739 ..	....	*86*	*126*	*131*	*138*	*28*	*31*	*1*
General government	8 740 ..	1,217	1,455	1,556	1,637	1,961	1,795	1,975	2,060
of which: Short-term	8 742 ..	*1,142*	*1,241*	*1,262*	*1,197*	*1,193*	*984*	*1,011*	....
Banks	8 743 ..	7	53	36	45	38	32	39	1,306
of which: Short-term	8 745 ..	*7*	*53*	*36*	*45*	*38*	*32*	*39*	*806*
Other sectors	8 746 ..	11	2	7	7	8	8	....	692
of which: Short-term	8 748 ..	*11*	*2*	*7*	*7*	*8*	*8*	....	*438*
Reserve assets	8 802 ..	**34,154**	**36,784**	**42,571**	**48,484**	**65,745**	**62,179**	**79,588**	**93,499**
Monetary gold	8 812 ..	1,381	1,449	1,697	2,103	2,768	2,862	3,653	4,667
Special drawing rights	8 811 ..	55	70	78	89	101	109	2,100	2,007
Reserve position in the Fund	8 810 ..	799	701	299	175	146	266	430	498
Foreign exchange	8 803 ..	31,919	34,539	38,825	45,085	54,636	57,247	69,741	81,431
Other claims	8 813 ..	....	25	1,672	1,032	8,095	1,695	3,664	4,897

Table 3 (Concluded). INTERNATIONAL INVESTMENT POSITION (End-period stocks), 2003–2010

(Millions of U.S. dollars)

	Code	2003	2004	2005	2006	2007	2008	2009	2010
LIABILITIES................................	8 995 D.	**152,527**	**208,379**	**220,050**	**284,316**	**398,212**	**379,511**	**433,663**	**482,035**
Direct investment in Poland..................	8 555 ..	**57,877**	**86,756**	**90,876**	**125,782**	**178,408**	**164,307**	**185,202**	**198,297**
Equity capital and reinvested earnings..................	8 556 ..	41,917	69,284	73,116	98,573	140,468	123,631	140,446	145,169
Claims on direct investors..................	8 557 ..	....	....	....	....	....	....	....	....
Liabilities to direct investors..................	8 558 ..	41,917	69,284	73,116	98,573	140,468	123,631	140,446	145,169
Other capital..................	8 580 ..	15,960	17,472	17,760	27,209	37,940	40,676	44,756	53,128
Claims on direct investors..................	8 585 ..	−3,257	−4,821	−4,997	−7,170	−9,729	−8,962	−10,574	−11,399
Liabilities to direct investors..................	8 590 ..	19,217	22,293	22,757	34,379	47,669	49,638	55,330	64,527
Portfolio investment..................	8 652 ..	**34,392**	**56,629**	**71,383**	**84,787**	**104,866**	**77,832**	**102,099**	**128,991**
Equity securities..................	8 660 ..	6,705	13,714	18,739	22,753	32,928	16,026	22,788	32,853
Banks..................	8 663 ..	2,220	5,285	6,666	8,835	14,511	7,027	9,661	8,822
Other sectors..................	8 664 ..	4,485	8,429	12,073	13,918	18,417	8,999	13,127	24,031
Debt securities..................	8 669 ..	27,687	42,915	52,644	62,034	71,938	61,806	79,311	96,138
Bonds and notes..................	8 670 ..	27,333	42,529	52,307	61,898	71,417	61,110	78,040	94,894
Monetary authorities..................	8 671 ..	....	....	....	....	....	....	....	....
General government..................	8 672 ..	22,041	36,218	45,459	54,773	65,382	55,711	71,571	92,212
Banks..................	8 673 ..	682	1,182	2,303	3,545	1,571	1,190	1,150	755
Other sectors..................	8 674 ..	4,610	5,129	4,545	3,580	4,464	4,209	5,319	1,927
Money market instruments..................	8 680 ..	354	386	337	136	521	696	1,271	1,244
Monetary authorities..................	8 681 ..	....	....	....	....	....	....	....	....
General government..................	8 682 ..	214	90	84	2	7	209	1,144	1,168
Banks..................	8 683 ..	30	90	92	103	137	100	14	....
Other sectors..................	8 684 ..	110	206	161	31	377	387	113	76
Financial derivatives..................	8 905 ..	**....**	**416**	**524**	**619**	**1,591**	**4,481**	**1,384**	**6,390**
Monetary authorities..................	8 906 ..	....	....	....	....	....	....	....	....
General government..................	8 907 ..	....	....	....	....	....	....	....	116
Banks..................	8 908 ..	....	....	191	243	1,030	3,613	797	4,925
Other sectors..................	8 909 ..	....	416	333	376	561	868	587	1,349
Other investment..................	8 753 ..	**60,258**	**64,578**	**57,267**	**73,128**	**113,347**	**132,891**	**144,978**	**148,357**
Trade credits..................	8 756 ..	7,319	9,256	9,968	12,773	16,629	16,285	16,642	15,059
General government..................	8 757 ..	....	....	....	....	....	....	....	1
of which: Short-term..................	8 759 ..	....	....	....	....	....	....	....	*1*
Other sectors..................	8 760 ..	7,319	9,256	9,968	12,773	16,629	16,285	16,642	15,058
of which: Short-term..................	8 762 ..	*7,010*	*8,830*	*9,668*	*12,395*	*16,161*	*15,848*	*16,057*	*15,058*
Loans..................	8 764 ..	46,924	48,066	38,887	49,764	70,117	85,692	92,129	91,988
Monetary authorities..................	8 765 ..	3	....	....	....	....	....	....	....
of which: Use of Fund credit and loans from the Fund....	8 766 ..	....	....	....	....	....	....	....	....
of which: Short-term..................	8 768 ..	....	....	....	....	....	....	....	....
General government..................	8 769 ..	22,805	21,477	13,240	13,130	13,081	11,041	14,131	16,163
of which: Short-term..................	8 771 ..	....	....	....	*1*	....	*3*	*4*	....
Banks..................	8 772 ..	4,855	6,491	6,772	11,431	20,817	31,149	30,734	33,971
of which: Short-term..................	8 774 ..	*16*	*793*	*67*	*163*	*809*	*2,909*	*1,801*	*1,670*
Other sectors..................	8 775 ..	19,261	20,098	18,875	25,203	36,219	43,502	47,264	41,854
of which: Short-term..................	8 777 ..	*542*	*560*	*300*	*292*	*808*	*921*	*968*	*3,408*
Currency and deposits..................	8 780 ..	5,662	6,698	7,445	9,047	24,815	28,588	31,346	36,343
Monetary authorities..................	8 781 ..	196	102	1,973	1,226	8,278	2,409	3,294	4,827
General government..................	8 782 ..	....	....	....	....	....	....	....	....
Banks..................	8 783 ..	5,466	6,596	5,472	7,821	16,537	26,179	28,052	31,516
Other sectors..................	8 784 ..	....	....	....	....	....	....	....	....
Other liabilities..................	8 786 ..	353	558	967	1,544	1,786	2,326	4,861	4,967
Monetary authorities..................	8 787 ..	....	6	3	1	2	....	2,076	2,055
of which: Short-term..................	8 789 ..	....	*6*	*3*	*1*	*2*	....	*31*	*46*
General government..................	8 790 ..	9	....	....	....	....	....	....	55
of which: Short-term..................	8 792 ..	*9*	....	....	....	....	....	....	....
Banks..................	8 793 ..	....	....	....	....	....	....	46	1,981
of which: Short-term..................	8 795 ..	....	....	....	....	....	....	*46*	*944*
Other sectors..................	8 796 ..	344	552	964	1,543	1,784	2,326	2,739	876
of which: Short-term..................	8 798 ..	*344*	*552*	*964*	*1,543*	*1,784*	*2,326*	*2,739*	*370*
NET INTERNATIONAL INVESTMENT POSITION........	8 995 ..	**−93,988**	**−128,614**	**−127,921**	**−166,360**	**−241,335**	**−242,645**	**−277,507**	**−300,481**
Conversion rates: zlotys per U.S. dollar (end of period)..................	0 102 ..	**3.7408**	**2.9904**	**3.2613**	**2.9105**	**2.4350**	**2.9618**	**2.8503**	**2.9641**

Table 1. ANALYTIC PRESENTATION, 2003–2010

(Millions of U.S. dollars)

	Code	2003	2004	2005	2006	2007	2008	2009	2010
A. Current Account[1]	4 993 Z.	**−10,477**	**−15,499**	**−19,821**	**−21,534**	**−23,516**	**−31,852**	**−25,596**	**−22,850**
Goods: exports f.o.b.	2 100 ..	33,090	38,449	38,762	45,017	52,801	57,871	44,670	48,905
Goods: imports f.o.b.	3 100 ..	−48,332	−58,789	−61,403	−68,124	−79,251	−91,659	−69,500	−73,016
Balance on Goods	4 100 ..	*−15,242*	*−20,340*	*−22,641*	*−23,107*	*−26,450*	*−33,787*	*−24,831*	*−24,111*
Services: credit	2 200 ..	12,382	14,655	15,158	18,459	23,308	26,299	22,810	23,220
Services: debit	3 200 ..	−8,256	−9,654	−10,335	−12,107	−14,315	−16,566	−14,387	−14,395
Balance on Goods and Services	4 991 ..	*−11,116*	*−15,339*	*−17,818*	*−16,755*	*−17,458*	*−24,054*	*−16,408*	*−15,286*
Income: credit	2 300 ..	6,638	8,058	9,325	13,593	17,149	18,403	11,531	13,473
Income: debit	3 300 ..	−9,260	−11,747	−14,151	−21,537	−26,781	−29,845	−23,712	−23,896
Balance on Goods, Services, and Income	4 992 ..	*−13,739*	*−19,029*	*−22,644*	*−24,699*	*−27,090*	*−35,496*	*−28,588*	*−25,709*
Current transfers: credit	2 379 Z.	6,544	7,297	7,226	8,054	8,705	9,423	8,931	8,811
Current transfers: debit	3 379 ..	−3,282	−3,767	−4,403	−4,890	−5,131	−5,779	−5,939	−5,952
B. Capital Account[1]	4 994 Z.	**2,977**	**2,773**	**2,114**	**1,546**	**2,889**	**3,869**	**1,923**	**2,591**
Capital account: credit	2 994 Z.	3,246	3,131	2,485	2,064	3,367	4,480	2,498	3,191
Capital account: debit	3 994 ..	−269	−358	−371	−518	−479	−611	−576	−600
Total, Groups A Plus B	4 981 ..	*−7,500*	*−12,726*	*−17,707*	*−19,989*	*−20,628*	*−27,983*	*−23,674*	*−20,259*
C. Financial Account[1]	4 995 W.	**627**	**10,661**	**15,745**	**16,826**	**18,916**	**28,148**	**25,338**	**22,060**
Direct investment abroad	4 505 ..	−6,575	−7,377	−2,252	−7,175	−5,465	−2,774	−766	8,164
Direct investment in Portugal	4 555 Z.	7,255	1,661	4,059	10,969	2,970	4,681	2,702	1,476
Portfolio investment assets	4 602 ..	−21,471	−13,598	−19,659	−7,991	−10,731	−17,149	−22,418	−3,756
Equity securities	4 610 ..	−622	−1,708	−1,845	−4,105	−2,192	580	−1,554	90
Debt securities	4 619 ..	−20,849	−11,890	−17,814	−3,885	−8,539	−17,728	−20,864	−3,846
Portfolio investment liabilities	4 652 Z.	15,886	14,826	19,263	13,514	24,712	39,990	43,011	−8,423
Equity securities	4 660 ..	9,863	7,233	5,594	3,829	292	8,679	3,499	−1,628
Debt securities	4 669 Z.	6,023	7,593	13,669	9,685	24,420	31,311	39,512	−6,796
Financial derivatives	4 910 ..	71	−90	−211	−263	236	215	210	505
Financial derivatives assets	4 900 ..	4,590	4,135	4,865	6,790	11,513	33,180	32,526	33,851
Financial derivatives liabilities	4 905 ..	−4,518	−4,226	−5,076	−7,053	−11,277	−32,965	−32,316	−33,346
Other investment assets	4 703 ..	−8,897	597	−724	−17,044	−15,795	14,626	−1,961	−8,937
Monetary authorities	4 701 ..	345	−954	−717	−1,251	−2,178	5,163	−1,614	−294
General government	4 704 ..	−190	47	−151	60	701	−333	163	180
Banks	4 705 ..	−8,713	−1,453	−1,342	−12,234	−8,583	12,069	−2,173	−2,411
Other sectors	4 728 ..	−338	2,957	1,485	−3,619	−5,736	−2,274	1,662	−6,412
Other investment liabilities	4 753 W.	14,357	14,643	15,270	24,816	22,990	−11,440	4,561	33,032
Monetary authorities	4 753 WA	−6,725	7,229	5,595	−7,926	−1,095	18,386	8,195	46,877
General government	4 753 ZB	567	578	−711	154	1,625	−2,837	314	−538
Banks	4 753 ZC	19,391	3,468	9,489	30,792	19,743	−26,045	−5,667	−16,203
Other sectors	4 753 ZD	1,124	3,369	897	1,795	2,717	−944	1,720	2,896
Total, Groups A Through C	4 983 ..	*−6,874*	*−2,065*	*−1,962*	*−3,163*	*−1,712*	*166*	*1,664*	*1,801*
D. Net Errors and Omissions	4 998 ..	**419**	**202**	**221**	**806**	**750**	**−50**	**−570**	**−530**
Total, Groups A Through D	4 984 ..	*−6,455*	*−1,863*	*−1,741*	*−2,357*	*−962*	*115*	*1,095*	*1,271*
E. Reserves and Related Items	4 802 A.	**6,455**	**1,863**	**1,741**	**2,357**	**962**	**−115**	**−1,095**	**−1,271**
Reserve assets	4 802 ..	6,455	1,863	1,741	2,357	962	−115	−1,095	−1,271
Use of Fund credit and loans	4 766 ..	....	....	....	....	....	....	....	....
Exceptional financing	4 920 ..	....	....	....	....	....	....	....	....
Conversion rates: euros per U.S. dollar	0 103 ..	**.8860**	**.8054**	**.8041**	**.7971**	**.7306**	**.6827**	**.7198**	**.7550**

[1] Excludes components that have been classified in the categories of Group E.

Table 2. STANDARD PRESENTATION, 2003–2010

(Millions of U.S. dollars)

	Code	2003	2004	2005	2006	2007	2008	2009	2010
CURRENT ACCOUNT	4 993 ..	−10,477	−15,499	−19,821	−21,534	−23,516	−31,852	−25,596	−22,850
A. GOODS	4 100 ..	−15,242	−20,340	−22,641	−23,107	−26,450	−33,787	−24,831	−24,111
Credit	2 100 ..	33,090	38,449	38,762	45,017	52,801	57,871	44,670	48,905
General merchandise: exports f.o.b.	2 110 ..	32,700	37,933	38,042	44,262	52,019	56,664	43,596	47,920
Goods for processing: exports f.o.b.	2 150 ..	104	113	134	155	116	216	195	202
Repairs on goods	2 160 ..	153	207	237	236	274	346	297	140
Goods procured in ports by carriers	2 170 ..	133	196	349	358	392	627	552	630
Nonmonetary gold	2 180 ..	....	....	....	5	....	19	30	14
Debit	3 100 ..	−48,332	−58,789	−61,403	−68,124	−79,251	−91,659	−69,500	−73,016
General merchandise: imports f.o.b.	3 110 ..	−48,084	−58,539	−61,087	−67,597	−78,605	−90,748	−68,965	−72,366
Goods for processing: imports f.o.b.	3 150 ..	....	−4	−4	−2	−3	−2	−11	−4
Repairs on goods	3 160 ..	−22	−13	−25	−15	−32	−35	−57	−45
Goods procured in ports by carriers	3 170 ..	−175	−180	−241	−473	−599	−858	−459	−550
Nonmonetary gold	3 180 ..	−51	−53	−46	−36	−12	−16	−8	−51
B. SERVICES	4 200 ..	**4,126**	**5,000**	**4,822**	**6,353**	**8,992**	**9,733**	**8,423**	**8,825**
Total credit	2 200 ..	*12,382*	*14,655*	*15,158*	*18,459*	*23,308*	*26,299*	*22,810*	*23,220*
Total debit	3 200 ..	*−8,256*	*−9,654*	*−10,335*	*−12,107*	*−14,315*	*−16,566*	*−14,387*	*−14,395*
Transportation services, credit	2 205 ..	**2,371**	**2,834**	**3,160**	**4,537**	**5,891**	**6,963**	**5,772**	**6,190**
Passenger	2 850 ..	*1,012*	*1,186*	*1,332*	*2,022*	*2,742*	*3,067*	*2,622*	*2,962*
Freight	2 851 ..	*779*	*950*	*1,083*	*1,420*	*1,746*	*2,137*	*1,776*	*1,825*
Other	2 852 ..	*580*	*698*	*745*	*1,095*	*1,404*	*1,758*	*1,373*	*1,403*
Sea transport, passenger	2 207 ..	1	3	4	3	2	2	2	2
Sea transport, freight	2 208 ..	127	114	174	335	425	541	472	484
Sea transport, other	2 209 ..	121	153	166	233	326	414	351	319
Air transport, passenger	2 211 ..	1,003	1,170	1,317	2,006	2,700	3,024	2,585	2,927
Air transport, freight	2 212 ..	82	114	128	144	170	195	131	164
Air transport, other	2 213 ..	354	418	460	681	836	1,043	807	880
Other transport, passenger	2 215 ..	8	12	11	13	40	42	35	34
Other transport, freight	2 216 ..	570	722	781	941	1,150	1,401	1,174	1,177
Other transport, other	2 217 ..	106	127	119	181	241	301	215	203
Transportation services, debit	3 205 ..	**−2,542**	**−3,054**	**−3,251**	**−3,789**	**−4,547**	**−5,199**	**−4,233**	**−4,259**
Passenger	3 850 ..	*−573*	*−606*	*−693*	*−802*	*−927*	*−955*	*−828*	*−786*
Freight	3 851 ..	*−1,532*	*−1,921*	*−2,063*	*−2,186*	*−2,564*	*−2,916*	*−2,271*	*−2,393*
Other	3 852 ..	*−436*	*−527*	*−494*	*−801*	*−1,057*	*−1,327*	*−1,133*	*−1,080*
Sea transport, passenger	3 207 ..	−1	−6	−6	−10	−9	−18	−18	−22
Sea transport, freight	3 208 ..	−810	−1,083	−1,245	−1,179	−1,393	−1,602	−1,238	−1,302
Sea transport, other	3 209 ..	−67	−73	−54	−89	−127	−146	−100	−94
Air transport, passenger	3 211 ..	−564	−586	−679	−781	−896	−922	−790	−756
Air transport, freight	3 212 ..	−107	−115	−109	−210	−253	−289	−224	−236
Air transport, other	3 213 ..	−362	−444	−418	−683	−895	−1,139	−988	−939
Other transport, passenger	3 215 ..	−8	−13	−8	−11	−21	−16	−20	−9
Other transport, freight	3 216 ..	−616	−723	−709	−798	−918	−1,025	−810	−856
Other transport, other	3 217 ..	−8	−10	−22	−29	−35	−43	−46	−46
Travel, credit	2 236 ..	**6,622**	**7,672**	**7,676**	**8,416**	**10,175**	**10,980**	**9,693**	**10,007**
Business travel	2 237 ..	....	....	....	849	1,028	1,109	1,000	1,001
Personal travel	2 240 ..	....	....	....	7,567	9,147	9,871	8,693	9,007
Travel, debit	3 236 ..	**−2,409**	**−2,763**	**−3,050**	**−3,340**	**−3,937**	**−4,328**	**−3,776**	**−3,905**
Business travel	3 237 ..	....	....	....	−1,164	−1,446	−1,583	−1,376	−937
Personal travel	3 240 ..	....	....	....	−2,176	−2,491	−2,745	−2,401	−2,968
Other services, credit	2 200 BA	**3,389**	**4,149**	**4,322**	**5,506**	**7,241**	**8,356**	**7,345**	**7,023**
Communications	2 245 ..	343	448	535	592	754	845	672	620
Construction	2 249 ..	309	434	365	538	830	960	712	663
Insurance	2 253 ..	94	137	101	116	134	151	147	128
Financial	2 260 ..	155	220	200	238	327	331	211	211
Computer and information	2 262 ..	108	142	149	213	321	393	378	363
Royalties and licence fees	2 266 ..	29	27	46	71	85	64	148	41
Other business services	2 268 ..	2,051	2,356	2,557	3,289	4,294	5,059	4,529	4,373
Personal, cultural, and recreational	2 287 ..	134	191	204	254	260	298	314	360
Government, n.i.e.	2 291 ..	166	194	164	196	237	254	235	263
Other services, debit	3 200 BA	**−3,305**	**−3,837**	**−4,034**	**−4,977**	**−5,831**	**−7,039**	**−6,378**	**−6,231**
Communications	3 245 ..	−266	−372	−388	−499	−682	−762	−620	−576
Construction	3 249 ..	−160	−159	−109	−135	−171	−235	−166	−125
Insurance	3 253 ..	−174	−246	−211	−235	−258	−297	−267	−314
Financial	3 260 ..	−180	−177	−227	−260	−276	−380	−249	−320
Computer and information	3 262 ..	−226	−208	−246	−328	−402	−505	−510	−489
Royalties and licence fees	3 266 ..	−305	−352	−339	−391	−450	−492	−513	−548
Other business services	3 268 ..	−1,556	−1,789	−2,007	−2,377	−2,797	−3,524	−3,208	−3,053
Personal, cultural, and recreational	3 287 ..	−264	−360	−342	−474	−512	−606	−674	−647
Government, n.i.e.	3 291 ..	−175	−173	−165	−279	−282	−238	−170	−159

Table 2 (Continued). STANDARD PRESENTATION, 2003–2010

(Millions of U.S. dollars)

	Code	2003	2004	2005	2006	2007	2008	2009	2010
C. INCOME	4 300	**−2,622**	**−3,689**	**−4,826**	**−7,944**	**−9,632**	**−11,442**	**−12,180**	**−10,423**
Total credit	2 300	*6,638*	*8,058*	*9,325*	*13,593*	*17,149*	*18,403*	*11,531*	*13,473*
Total debit	3 300	*−9,260*	*−11,747*	*−14,151*	*−21,537*	*−26,781*	*−29,845*	*−23,712*	*−23,896*
Compensation of employees, credit	2 310	**237**	**230**	**235**	**265**	**340**	**343**	**333**	**302**
Compensation of employees, debit	3 310	**−259**	**−378**	**−436**	**−445**	**−346**	**−388**	**−516**	**−491**
Investment income, credit	2 320	**6,401**	**7,828**	**9,090**	**13,328**	**16,810**	**18,060**	**11,198**	**13,171**
Direct investment income	2 330	1,309	1,926	2,770	3,356	3,579	3,812	3,066	5,459
Dividends and distributed branch profits	2 332	1,210	1,459	2,030	1,951	2,890	2,549	1,952	4,402
Reinvested earnings and undistributed branch profits	2 333	−84	348	606	1,174	424	1,058	905	940
Income on debt (interest)	2 334	184	119	134	231	265	205	209	118
Portfolio investment income	2 339	2,308	3,022	3,322	6,069	7,046	7,127	5,877	5,939
Income on equity	2 340	185	237	370	997	1,563	1,674	1,173	1,328
Income on bonds and notes	2 350	1,890	2,519	2,649	4,697	5,201	5,263	4,651	4,531
Income on money market instruments	2 360	232	266	303	375	282	190	53	80
Other investment income	2 370	2,783	2,880	2,999	3,903	6,185	7,121	2,255	1,773
Investment income, debit	3 320	**−9,002**	**−11,369**	**−13,715**	**−21,092**	**−26,435**	**−29,457**	**−23,195**	**−23,405**
Direct investment income	3 330	−2,126	−2,903	−4,342	−6,204	−6,321	−5,907	−8,192	−9,320
Dividends and distributed branch profits	3 332	−1,537	−2,158	−3,298	−3,248	−4,749	−4,351	−6,269	−7,335
Reinvested earnings and undistributed branch profits	3 333	−454	−643	−896	−2,797	−1,185	−1,295	−1,561	−1,720
Income on debt (interest)	3 334	−135	−103	−148	−159	−388	−262	−362	−264
Portfolio investment income	3 339	−2,979	−3,762	−4,153	−6,986	−8,769	−11,194	−10,666	−10,510
Income on equity	3 340	−578	−856	−1,271	−1,968	−2,448	−2,816	−2,570	−2,795
Income on bonds and notes	3 350	−2,206	−2,592	−2,454	−4,455	−5,513	−7,197	−7,341	−7,216
Income on money market instruments	3 360	−195	−314	−428	−563	−808	−1,182	−754	−499
Other investment income	3 370	−3,897	−4,704	−5,220	−7,902	−11,344	−12,356	−4,338	−3,574
D. CURRENT TRANSFERS	4 379	**3,262**	**3,530**	**2,823**	**3,164**	**3,573**	**3,644**	**2,991**	**2,858**
Credit	2 379	**6,544**	**7,297**	**7,226**	**8,054**	**8,705**	**9,423**	**8,931**	**8,811**
General government	2 380	2,654	2,826	2,813	2,991	2,762	2,848	3,357	3,269
Other sectors	2 390	3,890	4,471	4,412	5,064	5,943	6,575	5,574	5,541
Workers' remittances	2 391	2,752	3,032	2,826	3,045	3,551	3,647	3,190	3,181
Other current transfers	2 392	1,137	1,440	1,587	2,019	2,391	2,929	2,383	2,360
Debit	3 379	**−3,282**	**−3,767**	**−4,403**	**−4,890**	**−5,131**	**−5,779**	**−5,939**	**−5,952**
General government	3 380	−1,900	−2,015	−2,291	−2,646	−2,709	−3,057	−3,245	−3,323
Other sectors	3 390	−1,382	−1,752	−2,112	−2,244	−2,422	−2,722	−2,695	−2,630
Workers' remittances	3 391	−529	−604	−695	−766	−783	−847	−781	−752
Other current transfers	3 392	−853	−1,148	−1,417	−1,477	−1,640	−1,875	−1,913	−1,878
CAPITAL AND FINANCIAL ACCOUNT	4 996	**10,058**	**15,297**	**19,600**	**20,728**	**22,767**	**31,902**	**26,166**	**23,380**
CAPITAL ACCOUNT	4 994	**2,977**	**2,773**	**2,114**	**1,546**	**2,889**	**3,869**	**1,923**	**2,591**
Total credit	2 994	*3,246*	*3,131*	*2,485*	*2,064*	*3,367*	*4,480*	*2,498*	*3,191*
Total debit	3 994	*−269*	*−358*	*−371*	*−518*	*−479*	*−611*	*−576*	*−600*
Capital transfers, credit	2 400	**3,187**	**2,992**	**2,336**	**1,941**	**3,031**	**3,748**	**2,236**	**2,970**
General government	2 401	3,116	2,925	2,270	1,876	2,957	3,632	2,167	2,908
Debt forgiveness	2 402	....	....	....	....	....	....	....	....
Other capital transfers	2 410	3,116	2,925	2,270	1,876	2,957	3,632	2,167	2,908
Other sectors	2 430	70	68	66	65	73	116	68	62
Migrants' transfers	2 431	53	43	41	24	50	67	61	57
Debt forgiveness	2 432	2	2	1	....	1	1	1	1
Other capital transfers	2 440	16	23	24	41	22	48	7	4
Capital transfers, debit	3 400	**−224**	**−266**	**−282**	**−407**	**−367**	**−451**	**−293**	**−358**
General government	3 401	−60	−60	−89	−219	−79	−255	−123	−185
Debt forgiveness	3 402	....	....	....	....	....	−147	−17	−18
Other capital transfers	3 410	−60	−60	−89	−219	−79	−108	−106	−167
Other sectors	3 430	−164	−205	−193	−188	−288	−196	−171	−173
Migrants' transfers	3 431	−148	−182	−175	−166	−155	−176	−161	−163
Debt forgiveness	3 432	....	....	−1	−1	−87	−2	−1	−6
Other capital transfers	3 440	−17	−24	−17	−21	−46	−18	−8	−4
Nonproduced nonfinancial assets, credit	2 480	**59**	**138**	**149**	**123**	**337**	**732**	**262**	**221**
Nonproduced nonfinancial assets, debit	3 480	**−45**	**−92**	**−89**	**−111**	**−112**	**−160**	**−282**	**−242**

Table 2 (Continued). STANDARD PRESENTATION, 2003–2010

(Millions of U.S. dollars)

	Code	2003	2004	2005	2006	2007	2008	2009	2010
FINANCIAL ACCOUNT	4 995	**7,082**	**12,524**	**17,486**	**19,183**	**19,878**	**28,033**	**24,243**	**20,789**
A. DIRECT INVESTMENT	4 500	**680**	**−5,716**	**1,806**	**3,794**	**−2,495**	**1,907**	**1,936**	**9,640**
Direct investment abroad	4 505	**−6,575**	**−7,377**	**−2,252**	**−7,175**	**−5,465**	**−2,774**	**−766**	**8,164**
Equity capital	4 510	−7,332	−6,483	−62	−5,184	−1,869	−2,285	822	10,756
Claims on affiliated enterprises	4 515	−7,332	−6,484	−62	−5,184	−1,869	−2,285	822	10,757
Liabilities to affiliated enterprises	4 520	....	1	....	....	....	....	....	−1
Reinvested earnings	4 525	84	−348	−606	−1,174	−424	−1,058	−905	−940
Other capital	4 530	673	−547	−1,585	−817	−3,172	569	−684	−1,653
Claims on affiliated enterprises	4 535	478	−242	−1,216	−827	−3,139	137	−591	−1,090
Liabilities to affiliated enterprises	4 540	195	−305	−368	10	−33	432	−93	−563
Direct investment in Portugal	4 555	**7,255**	**1,661**	**4,059**	**10,969**	**2,970**	**4,681**	**2,702**	**1,476**
Equity capital	4 560	7,476	5,311	2,710	7,001	2,113	2,885	934	1,134
Claims on direct investors	4 565	....	1	....	4	....	....	....	....
Liabilities to direct investors	4 570	7,476	5,310	2,710	6,997	2,113	2,885	934	1,134
Reinvested earnings	4 575	454	643	896	2,797	1,185	1,295	1,561	1,720
Other capital	4 580	−675	−4,293	453	1,171	−328	502	207	−1,378
Claims on direct investors	4 585	−2,041	−1,141	−738	−1,668	−3,047	−2,406	−2,710	−4,635
Liabilities to direct investors	4 590	1,366	−3,152	1,191	2,838	2,719	2,908	2,917	3,258
B. PORTFOLIO INVESTMENT	4 600	**−5,585**	**1,228**	**−397**	**5,523**	**13,981**	**22,841**	**20,593**	**−12,179**
Assets	4 602	**−21,471**	**−13,598**	**−19,659**	**−7,991**	**−10,731**	**−17,149**	**−22,418**	**−3,756**
Equity securities	4 610	−622	−1,708	−1,845	−4,105	−2,192	580	−1,554	90
Monetary authorities	4 611	....	....	....	....	....	....	....	....
General government	4 612	−202	−299	476	49	−59	−2,134	−231	−383
Banks	4 613	252	−283	−677	−726	200	−119	326	1,104
Other sectors	4 614	−673	−1,127	−1,644	−3,429	−2,332	2,833	−1,649	−631
Debt securities	4 619	−20,849	−11,890	−17,814	−3,885	−8,539	−17,728	−20,864	−3,846
Bonds and notes	4 620	−15,445	−14,501	−14,401	−7,204	−11,744	−18,278	−23,188	695
Monetary authorities	4 621	−885	−1,156	1,479	−4,115	−625	−6,980	−1,825	−6,586
General government	4 622	−115	103	−641	−439	−224	882	−495	193
Banks	4 623	−6,162	−6,135	−3,051	5,690	−7,204	−19,053	−13,651	1,992
Other sectors	4 624	−8,283	−7,313	−12,189	−8,341	−3,691	6,873	−7,217	5,095
Money market instruments	4 630	−5,404	2,612	−3,413	3,319	3,205	550	2,324	−4,540
Monetary authorities	4 631	−4,749	2,349	−2,696	4,201	1,772	2,104	2,002	181
General government	4 632	−21	24	−2	....	1	−23	7	−11
Banks	4 633	−439	379	−147	−702	210	−565	828	−3,662
Other sectors	4 634	−195	−140	−567	−180	1,222	−967	−512	−1,048
Liabilities	4 652	**15,886**	**14,826**	**19,263**	**13,514**	**24,712**	**39,990**	**43,011**	**−8,423**
Equity securities	4 660	9,863	7,233	5,594	3,829	292	8,679	3,499	−1,628
Banks	4 663	−103	−156	805	669	−449	1,998	42	−170
Other sectors	4 664	9,966	7,389	4,789	3,160	740	6,681	3,457	−1,458
Debt securities	4 669	6,023	7,593	13,669	9,685	24,420	31,311	39,512	−6,796
Bonds and notes	4 670	3,384	895	7,866	15,041	22,762	21,439	33,368	1,211
Monetary authorities	4 671	....	....	....	....	....	....	....	....
General government	4 672	934	545	10,054	8,822	2,600	5,776	7,624	5,510
Banks	4 673	−163	−305	−6,102	1,199	16,046	15,353	24,380	−6,729
Other sectors	4 674	2,613	656	3,914	5,020	4,116	310	1,364	2,431
Money market instruments	4 680	2,640	6,697	5,802	−5,355	1,658	9,872	6,144	−8,007
Monetary authorities	4 681	....	....	....	....	....	....	....	....
General government	4 682	2,980	6,092	3,715	−4,426	1,358	6,830	5,470	−8,339
Banks	4 683	602	−663	−1,224	−19	459	2,291	−559	−824
Other sectors	4 684	−942	1,268	3,311	−910	−159	751	1,233	1,156
C. FINANCIAL DERIVATIVES	4 910	**71**	**−90**	**−211**	**−263**	**236**	**215**	**210**	**505**
Monetary authorities	4 911	5	1	3	....	....	−6	4	−12
General government	4 912	−95	−23	−52	−138	307	412	124	573
Banks	4 913	104	−34	−128	−316	−220	−336	185	−243
Other sectors	4 914	57	−34	−34	191	150	146	−103	187
Assets	4 900	**4,590**	**4,135**	**4,865**	**6,790**	**11,513**	**33,180**	**32,526**	**33,851**
Monetary authorities	4 901	6	5	6	5	7	45	83	110
General government	4 902	700	555	714	1,420	1,406	9,432	9,790	15,767
Banks	4 903	2,913	2,547	2,860	3,527	7,509	20,817	18,963	14,372
Other sectors	4 904	971	1,029	1,285	1,838	2,591	2,886	3,690	3,602
Liabilities	4 905	**−4,518**	**−4,226**	**−5,076**	**−7,053**	**−11,277**	**−32,965**	**−32,316**	**−33,346**
Monetary authorities	4 906	....	−3	−4	−5	−7	−51	−79	−121
General government	4 907	−795	−578	−766	−1,558	−1,100	−9,021	−9,666	−15,195
Banks	4 908	−2,809	−2,581	−2,987	−3,843	−7,729	−21,153	−18,778	−14,616
Other sectors	4 909	−914	−1,063	−1,319	−1,647	−2,441	−2,741	−3,793	−3,415

Table 2 (Concluded). STANDARD PRESENTATION, 2003–2010

(Millions of U.S. dollars)

	Code	2003	2004	2005	2006	2007	2008	2009	2010
D. OTHER INVESTMENT	4 700	**5,461**	**15,240**	**14,546**	**7,772**	**7,194**	**3,186**	**2,600**	**24,095**
Assets	4 703	**–8,897**	**597**	**–724**	**–17,044**	**–15,795**	**14,626**	**–1,961**	**–8,937**
Trade credits	4 706	–782	–746	–283	–1,240	–601	820	–909	–13
General government	4 707	....	....	....	....	....	....	....	1,085
of which: Short-term	4 709	....	....	....	....	....	....	....	....
Other sectors	4 710	–782	–746	–283	–1,240	–601	820	–909	–1,098
of which: Short-term	4 712	....	....	....	....	....	....	....	....
Loans	4 714	543	5,068	5,732	113	–5,654	–3,771	–7,780	–4,502
Monetary authorities	4 715	–6	16	–7	....	–12	–34	–73	118
of which: Short-term	4 718	–6	16	–7	....	–12	–34	–73	118
General government	4 719	–183	101	–153	69	749	–286	409	–837
of which: Short-term	4 721	....	....	....	....	....	–401	395	–109
Banks	4 722	–747	569	5,932	–1,508	–6,316	–1,407	–9,029	–1,738
of which: Short-term	4 724	....	....	....	....	....	....	....	....
Other sectors	4 725	1,480	4,381	–41	1,553	–75	–2,045	912	–2,045
of which: Short-term	4 727	615	–93	–73	16	–191	–2,102	1,027	514
Currency and deposits	4 730	–8,142	–2,832	–5,179	–14,729	–8,026	19,176	8,141	–2,766
Monetary authorities	4 731	351	–965	–699	–1,250	–2,165	5,198	–1,541	–293
General government	4 732	–6	–55	2	–4	–48	–34	–221	–14
Banks	4 733	–7,966	–2,022	–7,274	–10,727	–2,262	13,483	6,864	–614
Other sectors	4 734	–521	210	2,792	–2,748	–3,551	529	3,038	–1,845
Other assets	4 736	–515	–893	–995	–1,188	–1,515	–1,599	–1,413	–1,656
Monetary authorities	4 737	....	–5	–11	....	–1	....	....	–119
of which: Short-term	4 739	....	....	....	....	....	....	....	....
General government	4 740	....	....	....	–4	....	–14	–26	–53
of which: Short-term	4 742	....	....	....	....	....	....	....	–53
Banks	4 743	....	....	....	....	–4	–7	–8	–59
of which: Short-term	4 745	....	....	....	....	–4	....	....	–53
Other sectors	4 746	–515	–888	–983	–1,184	–1,509	–1,578	–1,379	–1,424
of which: Short-term	4 748	–517	–881	–980	–1,179	–1,496	–1,569	–1,346	–1,397
Liabilities	4 753	**14,357**	**14,643**	**15,270**	**24,816**	**22,990**	**–11,440**	**4,561**	**33,032**
Trade credits	4 756	550	1,581	–617	135	912	–1,526	857	1,689
General government	4 757	....	....	....	....	....	....	....	....
of which: Short-term	4 759	....	....	....	....	....	....	....	....
Other sectors	4 760	550	1,581	–617	135	912	–1,526	857	1,689
of which: Short-term	4 762	....	....	....	....	....	....	....	....
Loans	4 764	14,731	4,536	8,956	13,966	10,046	–11,367	–5,787	–12,229
Monetary authorities	4 765	–1,043	–1,635	–123	–856	–125	1	....	92
of which: Use of Fund credit and loans from the Fund	4 766	....	....	....	....	....	....	....	....
of which: Short-term	4 768	–2,780	–467	–72	–124	–19	1	....	52
General government	4 769	567	578	–711	154	1,625	–2,837	314	–538
of which: Short-term	4 771	449	445	–763	1,619	1,403	–2,782	–195	111
Banks	4 772	14,666	3,844	8,318	13,075	6,789	–9,107	–6,959	–12,978
of which: Short-term	4 774	....	....	....	....	....	....	....	....
Other sectors	4 775	541	1,748	1,472	1,593	1,757	577	858	1,196
of which: Short-term	4 777	179	406	493	–201	298	–1,315	–2	–150
Currency and deposits	4 780	–957	8,489	6,886	10,648	11,987	1,442	8,328	43,544
Monetary authorities	4 781	–5,682	8,866	5,715	–7,069	–966	18,379	7,035	46,769
General government	4 782	....	....	....	....	....	....	....	....
Banks	4 783	4,725	–377	1,171	17,718	12,954	–16,937	1,293	–3,225
Other sectors	4 784	....	....	....	....	....	....	....	....
Other liabilities	4 786	33	37	45	67	43	11	1,163	28
Monetary authorities	4 787	....	–3	3	–1	–4	5	1,160	16
of which: Short-term	4 789	....	–3	3	–1	–4	5	–17	16
General government	4 790	....	....	....	....	....	....	....	....
of which: Short-term	4 792	....	....	....	....	....	....	....	....
Banks	4 793	....	....	....	....	....	....	–1	....
of which: Short-term	4 795	....	....	....	....	....	....	–1	....
Other sectors	4 796	33	40	43	67	48	6	4	12
of which: Short-term	4 798	....	....	....	....	3	45	....	6
E. RESERVE ASSETS	4 802	**6,455**	**1,863**	**1,741**	**2,357**	**962**	**–115**	**–1,095**	**–1,271**
Monetary gold	4 812	860	727	636	719	....	....	....	....
Special drawing rights	4 811	–7	–8	–8	–5	–4	–3	–1,178	....
Reserve position in the Fund	4 810	–45	115	205	95	29	–75	–167	–22
Foreign exchange	4 803	5,647	1,028	908	1,548	937	–38	250	–1,249
Other claims	4 813	....	....	....	....	....	....	....	....
NET ERRORS AND OMISSIONS	4 998	**419**	**202**	**221**	**806**	**750**	**–50**	**–570**	**–530**

Table 3. INTERNATIONAL INVESTMENT POSITION (End-period stocks), 2003–2010

(Millions of U.S. dollars)

	Code	2003	2004	2005	2006	2007	2008	2009	2010
ASSETS	8 995 C.	**268,465**	**311,153**	**303,568**	**369,511**	**443,828**	**403,451**	**452,130**	**437,429**
Direct investment abroad	8 505	**34,443**	**43,941**	**41,965**	**53,984**	**67,708**	**63,006**	**68,471**	**64,253**
Equity capital and reinvested earnings	8 506	30,499	39,845	37,603	47,718	58,592	55,593	60,790	56,252
Claims on affiliated enterprises	8 507	30,499	39,845	37,603	47,718	58,592	55,593	60,790	56,252
Liabilities to affiliated enterprises	8 508	....	....	....	....	....	....	....	....
Other capital	8 530	3,944	4,096	4,362	6,265	9,116	7,413	7,681	8,001
Claims on affiliated enterprises	8 535	5,605	5,593	5,515	7,331	11,000	9,932	9,913	10,267
Liabilities to affiliated enterprises	8 540	−1,660	−1,497	−1,153	−1,066	−1,884	−2,519	−2,231	−2,266
Portfolio investment	8 602	**97,727**	**124,949**	**134,738**	**160,337**	**190,592**	**176,347**	**210,684**	**196,096**
Equity securities	8 610	11,018	16,556	27,495	39,544	50,953	32,396	38,463	35,871
Monetary authorities	8 611	....	....	....	....	....			
General government	8 612	610	1,058	539	658	869	2,129	2,532	3,044
Banks	8 613	1,518	2,544	4,254	6,437	8,666	6,069	7,225	5,570
Other sectors	8 614	8,890	12,953	22,702	32,449	41,418	24,198	28,705	27,257
Debt securities	8 619	86,709	108,394	107,243	120,793	139,639	143,951	172,221	160,226
Bonds and notes	8 620	72,194	96,385	95,209	111,275	133,026	138,087	168,321	152,039
Monetary authorities	8 621	3,477	5,726	3,505	8,212	9,753	16,640	19,231	24,488
General government	8 622	1,866	1,960	2,007	2,553	3,000	2,030	2,554	2,263
Banks	8 623	14,403	22,497	22,956	18,823	27,607	44,290	60,299	52,885
Other sectors	8 624	52,448	66,202	66,740	81,688	92,667	75,127	86,237	72,403
Money market instruments	8 630	14,515	12,009	12,034	9,518	6,613	5,864	3,901	8,187
Monetary authorities	8 631	10,175	7,661	9,261	5,869	4,462	2,349	346	149
General government	8 632	321	322	7	8	9	14	7	7
Banks	8 633	1,046	698	604	1,378	966	1,433	657	4,303
Other sectors	8 634	2,973	3,327	2,162	2,263	1,176	2,068	2,891	3,728
Financial derivatives	8 900	**2,671**	**2,097**	**1,858**	**2,094**	**2,772**	**8,125**	**7,729**	**8,516**
Monetary authorities	8 901	6	....	....	1	....	....	5	1
General government	8 902	296	....	....	....	....	....	....	152
Banks	8 903	2,370	2,096	1,857	2,094	2,762	8,059	7,602	8,295
Other sectors	8 904	....	....	1	....	9	66	122	68
Other investment	8 703	**120,810**	**128,483**	**114,643**	**143,213**	**171,209**	**144,025**	**149,260**	**147,568**
Trade credits	8 706	10,227	11,810	10,587	13,875	16,380	14,712	16,099	14,842
General government	8 707	....	....	....	747	1,090	1,105	1,190	....
of which: Short-term	8 709	....	....	....	*747*	*1,090*	*1,105*	*1,190*	....
Other sectors	8 710	10,227	11,810	10,587	13,128	15,289	13,607	14,909	14,842
of which: Short-term	8 712	*10,227*	*11,810*	*10,587*	*13,128*	*15,289*	*13,607*	*14,909*	*14,842*
Loans	8 714	78,793	81,111	74,514	91,883	106,188	91,436	95,273	94,602
Monetary authorities	8 715	....	....	....	....	....	....	....	....
of which: Short-term	8 718	....	....	....	....	....	....	....	....
General government	8 719	4,353	4,315	4,342	4,375	1,521	1,827	1,393	2,264
of which: Short-term	8 721	*1*	*1*	*1*	*1*	*1*	*424*	*1*	*108*
Banks	8 722	68,142	73,363	66,783	84,830	101,752	84,982	89,730	85,907
of which: Short-term	8 724	*52,553*	*56,939*	*58,256*	*73,642*	*82,827*	*65,382*	*60,581*	*56,858*
Other sectors	8 725	6,298	3,433	3,389	2,678	2,916	4,627	4,151	6,431
of which: Short-term	8 727	*112*	*217*	*450*	*502*	*760*	*2,571*	*1,682*	*1,431*
Currency and deposits	8 730	27,287	30,429	24,520	31,638	41,802	31,139	31,049	31,469
Monetary authorities	8 731	1,580	2,843	3,138	4,944	8,077	1,938	3,511	3,535
General government	8 732	133	204	163	178	246	266	498	484
Banks	8 733	....	....	....	....	....	....	....	....
Other sectors	8 734	25,574	27,383	21,218	26,516	33,479	28,935	27,041	27,450
Other assets	8 736	4,503	5,132	5,022	5,818	6,839	6,739	6,838	6,655
Monetary authorities	8 737	138	154	143	160	180	171	196	299
of which: Short-term	8 739	....	....	....	....	....	....	....	....
General government	8 740	2,828	2,979	2,701	2,914	3,149	3,041	3,142	3,039
of which: Short-term	8 742	*36*	*39*	*34*	*37*	*42*	*40*	*64*	*116*
Banks	8 743	89	94	107	138	152	152	164	214
of which: Short-term	8 745	*88*	*91*	*85*	*90*	*98*	*95*	*96*	*145*
Other sectors	8 746	1,449	1,907	2,070	2,607	3,358	3,375	3,336	3,103
of which: Short-term	8 748	*1,449*	*1,899*	*2,061*	*2,590*	*3,324*	*3,335*	*3,261*	*3,006*
Reserve assets	8 802	**12,813**	**11,684**	**10,364**	**9,883**	**11,546**	**11,948**	**15,985**	**20,995**
Monetary gold	8 812	6,938	6,510	6,885	7,819	10,288	10,639	13,577	17,343
Special drawing rights	8 811	91	103	103	113	123	123	1,306	1,283
Reserve position in the Fund	8 810	536	440	202	115	90	165	337	356
Foreign exchange	8 803	5,249	4,631	3,173	1,835	1,044	1,022	764	2,013
Other claims	8 813	....	....	....	....	....	....	....	....

Table 3 (Concluded). INTERNATIONAL INVESTMENT POSITION (End-period stocks), 2003–2010

(Millions of U.S. dollars)

	Code	2003	2004	2005	2006	2007	2008	2009	2010
LIABILITIES	8 995 D.	**373,942**	**439,448**	**426,192**	**536,524**	**665,378**	**633,472**	**721,800**	**687,493**
Direct investment in Portugal	8 555	**60,584**	**66,971**	**63,340**	**88,461**	**115,314**	**99,970**	**114,710**	**110,241**
Equity capital and reinvested earnings	8 556	51,096	62,533	59,730	82,160	106,159	90,676	104,565	102,129
Claims on direct investors	8 557	....	....	....	....	....	....	....	....
Liabilities to direct investors	8 558	51,096	62,533	59,730	82,160	106,159	90,676	104,565	102,129
Other capital	8 580	9,489	4,438	3,610	6,301	9,155	9,294	10,145	8,112
Claims on direct investors	8 585	−4,985	−5,905	−5,648	−6,836	−8,771	−9,308	−12,261	−16,001
Liabilities to direct investors	8 590	14,473	10,343	9,258	13,137	17,926	18,601	22,406	24,113
Portfolio investment	8 652	**127,057**	**156,523**	**159,339**	**194,298**	**244,825**	**250,708**	**311,598**	**264,707**
Equity securities	8 660	34,661	47,722	48,506	64,123	75,980	58,448	71,580	62,566
Banks	8 663	4,884	5,762	7,105	10,432	11,932	4,692	4,386	2,093
Other sectors	8 664	29,778	41,959	41,401	53,690	64,048	53,756	67,194	60,473
Debt securities	8 669	92,396	108,801	110,833	130,175	168,844	192,260	240,017	202,142
Bonds and notes	8 670	78,543	87,316	88,236	110,619	146,624	162,164	203,107	175,991
Monetary authorities	8 671	....	....	....	....	....	....	....	....
General government	8 672	63,430	70,571	72,107	89,814	102,216	106,032	119,859	103,592
Banks	8 673	9,259	9,639	4,738	6,333	24,500	37,634	63,998	52,065
Other sectors	8 674	5,854	7,106	11,392	14,471	19,909	18,498	19,250	20,333
Money market instruments	8 680	13,853	21,485	22,597	19,556	22,220	30,096	36,910	26,151
Monetary authorities	8 681	....	....	....	....	....	....	....	....
General government	8 682	4,213	11,067	12,773	10,011	12,771	18,657	24,113	14,214
Banks	8 683	2,136	1,466	17	....	483	2,318	1,712	467
Other sectors	8 684	7,504	8,952	9,807	9,545	8,966	9,121	11,086	11,469
Financial derivatives	8 905	**2,706**	**2,932**	**1,933**	**1,856**	**2,652**	**7,898**	**8,368**	**10,005**
Monetary authorities	8 906	....	....	....	....	....	....	....	....
General government	8 907	....	357	364	78	84	96	68	3
Banks	8 908	2,706	2,562	1,495	1,704	2,489	7,774	8,153	9,840
Other sectors	8 909	....	12	73	75	79	27	148	162
Other investment	8 753	**183,594**	**213,022**	**201,580**	**251,910**	**302,587**	**274,896**	**287,125**	**302,539**
Trade credits	8 756	11,699	14,284	11,842	13,396	15,887	13,519	14,871	15,410
General government	8 757	....	....	....	....	....	....	....	....
of which: Short-term	8 759	....	....	....	....	....	....	....	....
Other sectors	8 760	11,699	14,284	11,842	13,396	15,887	13,519	14,871	15,410
of which: Short-term	8 762	*11,699*	*14,284*	*11,842*	*13,396*	*15,887*	*13,519*	*14,871*	*15,410*
Loans	8 764	86,500	98,726	94,831	121,084	144,312	125,462	123,242	102,417
Monetary authorities	8 765	2,714	1,147	928	118	....	....	....	78
of which: Use of Fund credit and loans from the Fund	8 766	....	....	....	....	....	....	....	....
of which: Short-term	8 768	*902*	*343*	*270*	*51*				*39*
General government	8 769	3,983	4,981	3,444	11,040	14,448	11,101	12,430	11,112
of which: Short-term	8 771	*527*	*1,095*	*29*	*1,701*	*3,406*	*541*	*339*	*519*
Banks	8 772	61,819	71,421	70,722	92,447	109,544	94,923	90,378	71,340
of which: Short-term	8 774								
Other sectors	8 775	17,985	21,176	19,738	17,480	20,320	19,437	20,434	19,887
of which: Short-term	8 777	*1,595*	*2,161*	*2,384*	*2,454*	*3,074*	*1,787*	*1,839*	*1,686*
Currency and deposits	8 780	85,141	99,706	94,582	117,011	141,883	135,430	147,245	182,982
Monetary authorities	8 781	572	10,504	14,090	8,707	9,148	26,382	33,768	80,055
General government	8 782	....	....	....	....	....	....	....	....
Banks	8 783	84,569	89,202	80,491	108,304	132,734	109,048	113,478	102,927
Other sectors	8 784	....	....	....	....	....	....	....	....
Other liabilities	8 786	254	308	324	419	505	485	1,767	1,730
Monetary authorities	8 787	....	....	....	....	....	....	1,264	1,242
of which: Short-term	8 789	....	....	....	....	....	....	....	....
General government	8 790	....	....	....	....	....	....	....	....
of which: Short-term	8 792	....	....	....	....	....	....	....	....
Banks	8 793	110	111	108	110	113	111	111	109
of which: Short-term	8 795	*109*	*110*	*108*	*109*	*112*	*110*	*110*	*109*
Other sectors	8 796	144	197	216	308	393	374	392	379
of which: Short-term	8 798	*104*	*110*	*100*	*108*	*121*	*156*	*161*	*158*
NET INTERNATIONAL INVESTMENT POSITION	8 995	**−105,477**	**−128,295**	**−122,624**	**−167,013**	**−221,550**	**−230,021**	**−269,671**	**−250,064**
Conversion rates: euros per U.S. dollar (end of period)	0 104	.7918	.7342	.8477	.7593	.6793	.7185	.6942	.7484

Table 1. ANALYTIC PRESENTATION, 2003–2010

(Millions of U.S. dollars)

	Code	2003	2004	2005	2006	2007	2008	2009	2010
A. Current Account[1]	4 993 Z.	**−3,311**	**−6,382**	**−8,621**	**−12,785**	**−23,080**	**−23,719**	**−6,955**	**−6,480**
Goods: exports f.o.b.	2 100 ..	17,618	23,485	27,730	32,336	40,555	49,760	40,672	49,411
Goods: imports f.o.b.	3 100 ..	−22,155	−30,150	−37,348	−47,172	−65,121	−77,942	−50,278	−57,216
Balance on Goods	4 100 ..	*−4,537*	*−6,665*	*−9,618*	*−14,836*	*−24,566*	*−28,182*	*−9,606*	*−7,805*
Services: credit	2 200 ..	3,028	3,614	5,083	7,032	9,439	12,856	9,836	8,575
Services: debit	3 200 ..	−2,958	−3,879	−5,518	−7,027	−8,909	−11,905	−10,258	−9,411
Balance on Goods and Services	4 991 ..	*−4,467*	*−6,930*	*−10,053*	*−14,831*	*−24,036*	*−27,231*	*−10,028*	*−8,641*
Income: credit	2 300 ..	372	433	1,533	2,176	3,321	3,330	1,654	1,386
Income: debit	3 300 ..	−1,077	−3,582	−4,432	−6,255	−8,983	−8,702	−4,289	−3,747
Balance on Goods, Services, and Income	4 992 ..	*−5,172*	*−10,079*	*−12,952*	*−18,910*	*−29,698*	*−32,603*	*−12,663*	*−11,002*
Current transfers: credit	2 379 Z.	2,200	4,188	4,939	6,995	9,867	13,074	9,278	7,683
Current transfers: debit	3 379 ..	−339	−491	−607	−870	−3,249	−4,190	−3,570	−3,161
B. Capital Account[1]	4 994 Z.	**213**	**643**	**731**	**−34**	**1,145**	**912**	**928**	**294**
Capital account: credit	2 994 Z.	223	669	829	925	1,708	1,462	1,409	718
Capital account: debit	3 994 ..	−10	−26	−98	−959	−563	−550	−481	−424
Total, Groups A Plus B	4 981 ..	*−3,098*	*−5,739*	*−7,890*	*−12,819*	*−21,935*	*−22,807*	*−6,027*	*−6,186*
C. Financial Account[1]	4 995 W.	**4,400**	**10,761**	**14,089**	**18,899**	**29,533**	**25,027**	**1,427**	**6,135**
Direct investment abroad	4 505 ..	−39	−70	30	−422	−278	−277	88	−190
Direct investment in Romania	4 555 Z.	1,844	6,443	6,482	11,393	9,925	13,883	4,846	3,453
Portfolio investment assets	4 602 ..	9	−559	−140	−828	142	−310	−196	−165
Equity securities	4 610 ..	14	−559	−136	−390	−237	−274	204	−184
Debt securities	4 619 ..	−5	....	−3	−438	379	−36	−400	19
Portfolio investment liabilities	4 652 Z.	569	28	1,089	589	481	−412	959	1,779
Equity securities	4 660 ..	69	111	229	301	746	23	7	4
Debt securities	4 669 Z.	500	−83	860	289	−265	−435	952	1,775
Financial derivatives	4 910 ..	....	....	−26	−108	−415	−387	−61	4
Financial derivatives assets	4 900 ..	....	....	36	48	338	889	525	586
Financial derivatives liabilities	4 905 ..	....	....	−62	−156	−753	−1,276	−586	−582
Other investment assets	4 703 ..	72	−212	−1,078	−1,323	−1,173	−841	−2,916	−554
Monetary authorities	4 701 ..	−1	....	−11	....	−13	....	....	....
General government	4 704 ..	−36	−22	−15	758	161	−68	−39	−69
Banks	4 705 ..	229	−43	−198	−433	−50	101	−1,789	815
Other sectors	4 728 ..	−120	−147	−853	−1,648	−1,271	−874	−1,088	−1,300
Other investment liabilities	4 753 W.	1,945	5,131	7,731	9,598	20,851	13,371	−1,293	1,808
Monetary authorities	4 753 WA	....	99	−100	−3	185	211	1,041	−80
General government	4 753 ZB	889	1,015	568	28	−5	309	2,551	2,736
Banks	4 753 ZC	918	2,329	3,833	4,879	11,393	9,926	−4,051	1,399
Other sectors	4 753 ZD	138	1,688	3,430	4,694	9,278	2,925	−834	−2,247
Total, Groups A Through C	4 983 ..	*1,302*	*5,022*	*6,199*	*6,080*	*7,598*	*2,220*	*−4,600*	*−51*
D. Net Errors and Omissions	4 998 ..	**−289**	**1,167**	**612**	**521**	**−1,319**	**−2,065**	**−1,769**	**−922**
Total, Groups A Through D	4 984 ..	*1,013*	*6,189*	*6,811*	*6,602*	*6,279*	*155*	*−6,369*	*−973*
E. Reserves and Related Items	4 802 A.	**−1,013**	**−6,189**	**−6,811**	**−6,602**	**−6,279**	**−155**	**6,369**	**973**
Reserve assets	4 802 ..	−1,134	−6,018	−6,777	−6,435	−6,174	−155	−2,987	−4,702
Use of Fund credit and loans	4 766 ..	120	−171	−152	−166	−105	....	9,356	5,675
Exceptional financing	4 920 ..	....	....	117	....	....	....	....	....
Conversion rates: Romanian lei per U.S. dollar	0 101 ..	**3.320**	**3.264**	**2.914**	**2.809**	**2.438**	**2.519**	**3.049**	**3.178**

[1] Excludes components that have been classified in the categories of Group E.

Table 2. STANDARD PRESENTATION, 2003–2010

(Millions of U.S. dollars)

	Code	2003	2004	2005	2006	2007	2008	2009	2010
CURRENT ACCOUNT	4 993	−3,311	−6,382	−8,504	−12,785	−23,080	−23,719	−6,955	−6,480
A. GOODS	4 100	−4,537	−6,665	−9,618	−14,836	−24,566	−28,182	−9,606	−7,805
Credit	2 100	17,618	23,485	27,730	32,336	40,555	49,760	40,672	49,411
General merchandise: exports f.o.b.	2 110	16,819	22,477	14,466	17,830	30,078	40,008	33,693	43,296
Goods for processing: exports f.o.b.	2 150	716	861	13,243	14,496	10,466	9,736	6,979	6,115
Repairs on goods	2 160	81	146	....	....	....	....	....	....
Goods procured in ports by carriers	2 170	2	1	....	....	....	....	....	....
Nonmonetary gold	2 180	....	....	20	10	11	16	....	....
Debit	3 100	−22,155	−30,150	−37,348	−47,172	−65,121	−77,942	−50,278	−57,216
General merchandise: imports f.o.b.	3 110	−22,134	−30,128	−28,757	−37,915	−58,393	−71,902	−45,745	−53,077
Goods for processing: imports f.o.b.	3 150	−3	−5	−8,591	−9,256	−6,720	−6,030	−4,533	−4,139
Repairs on goods	3 160	−10	−7	....	....	....	....	....	....
Goods procured in ports by carriers	3 170	−8	−10	....	....	....	....	....	....
Nonmonetary gold	3 180	....	....	....	−1	−8	−10	....	....
B. SERVICES	4 200	70	−265	−435	5	530	951	−422	−836
Total credit	2 200	*3,028*	*3,614*	*5,083*	*7,032*	*9,439*	*12,856*	*9,836*	*8,575*
Total debit	3 200	*−2,958*	*−3,879*	*−5,518*	*−7,027*	*−8,909*	*−11,905*	*−10,258*	*−9,411*
Transportation services, credit	2 205	1,205	1,559	1,474	1,883	2,486	3,942	2,892	2,553
Passenger	2 850	*74*	*104*	*273*	*368*	*463*	*634*	*458*	*498*
Freight	2 851	*842*	*1,076*	*831*	*1,129*	*1,636*	*2,509*	*1,806*	*1,704*
Other	2 852	*289*	*379*	*370*	*386*	*387*	*799*	*628*	*351*
Sea transport, passenger	2 207	1	1	1	1	20	1	3	2
Sea transport, freight	2 208	51	51	69	106	144	203	112	106
Sea transport, other	2 209	103	157	186	259	237	514	402	192
Air transport, passenger	2 211	45	70	230	306	372	506	387	426
Air transport, freight	2 212	4	4	37	56	71	99	92	69
Air transport, other	2 213	167	205	151	83	90	135	127	94
Other transport, passenger	2 215	28	33	42	60	71	127	68	70
Other transport, freight	2 216	787	1,021	726	968	1,421	2,207	1,602	1,529
Other transport, other	2 217	19	17	33	44	60	150	99	65
Transportation services, debit	3 205	−1,133	−1,500	−1,966	−2,404	−3,282	−3,978	−2,792	−2,782
Passenger	3 850	*−93*	*−133*	*−148*	*−149*	*−182*	*−233*	*−297*	*−262*
Freight	3 851	*−954*	*−1,277*	*−1,683*	*−2,088*	*−2,924*	*−3,500*	*−2,256*	*−2,338*
Other	3 852	*−86*	*−90*	*−134*	*−167*	*−176*	*−245*	*−239*	*−182*
Sea transport, passenger	3 207	−1	−1	−1	−1	−4	−9	....	....
Sea transport, freight	3 208	−183	−287	−469	−551	−789	−951	−610	−587
Sea transport, other	3 209	−20	−29	−27	−52	−45	−48	−38	−62
Air transport, passenger	3 211	−89	−129	−138	−135	−160	−194	−285	−245
Air transport, freight	3 212	−41	−48	−72	−88	−124	−147	−95	−110
Air transport, other	3 213	−54	−51	−69	−77	−83	−119	−124	−82
Other transport, passenger	3 215	−3	−3	−10	−14	−18	−30	−12	−17
Other transport, freight	3 216	−730	−942	−1,143	−1,449	−2,011	−2,402	−1,551	−1,641
Other transport, other	3 217	−12	−10	−37	−38	−48	−78	−77	−38
Travel, credit	2 236	449	503	1,052	1,308	1,610	1,991	1,229	1,135
Business travel	2 237	34	50	514	828	1,157	1,577	894	740
Personal travel	2 240	415	453	538	481	453	414	335	395
Travel, debit	3 236	−479	−539	−925	−1,310	−1,543	−2,176	−1,472	−1,638
Business travel	3 237	−282	−320	−640	−937	−796	−1,105	−930	−1,096
Personal travel	3 240	−197	−219	−285	−373	−747	−1,071	−542	−542
Other services, credit	2 200 BA	1,374	1,552	2,558	3,841	5,343	6,923	5,715	4,887
Communications	2 245	238	296	674	1,102	1,081	1,153	865	567
Construction	2 249	106	120	195	264	216	462	510	660
Insurance	2 253	48	26	28	24	66	45	54	44
Financial	2 260	51	74	104	115	513	485	178	149
Computer and information	2 262	108	143	332	474	620	880	1,013	895
Royalties and licence fees	2 266	3	8	48	35	41	240	193	466
Other business services	2 268	674	647	1,058	1,716	2,654	3,543	2,782	1,982
Personal, cultural, and recreational	2 287	118	214	92	83	105	77	79	92
Government, n.i.e.	2 291	28	24	27	27	47	38	41	32
Other services, debit	3 200 BA	−1,346	−1,840	−2,627	−3,314	−4,084	−5,751	−5,994	−4,991
Communications	3 245	−86	−203	−361	−487	−578	−850	−1,115	−405
Construction	3 249	−32	−84	−197	−232	−531	−591	−529	−498
Insurance	3 253	−124	−109	−132	−142	−186	−240	−251	−222
Financial	3 260	−83	−117	−160	−228	−260	−280	−454	−394
Computer and information	3 262	−45	−83	−351	−422	−463	−738	−765	−749
Royalties and licence fees	3 266	−80	−108	−173	−236	−248	−346	−368	−428
Other business services	3 268	−750	−943	−1,053	−1,346	−1,592	−2,376	−2,181	−1,898
Personal, cultural, and recreational	3 287	−101	−143	−108	−94	−104	−201	−211	−269
Government, n.i.e.	3 291	−45	−50	−93	−126	−122	−129	−120	−128

2011, International Monetary Fund: *Balance of Payments Statistics Yearbook*

Table 2 (Continued). STANDARD PRESENTATION, 2003–2010

(Millions of U.S. dollars)

	Code	2003	2004	2005	2006	2007	2008	2009	2010
C. INCOME	4 300 ..	**−705**	**−3,149**	**−2,900**	**−4,079**	**−5,662**	**−5,372**	**−2,635**	**−2,361**
Total credit	2 300 ..	*372*	*433*	*1,533*	*2,176*	*3,321*	*3,330*	*1,654*	*1,386*
Total debit	3 300 ..	*−1,077*	*−3,582*	*−4,432*	*−6,255*	*−8,983*	*−8,702*	*−4,289*	*−3,747*
Compensation of employees, credit	2 310 ..	**110**	**113**	**954**	**1,165**	**1,626**	**1,705**	**683**	**639**
Compensation of employees, debit	3 310 ..	**−7**	**−5**	**−24**	**−42**	**−55**	**−169**	**−63**	**−87**
Investment income, credit	2 320 ..	**262**	**320**	**579**	**1,012**	**1,695**	**1,625**	**971**	**747**
Direct investment income	2 330 ..	11	9	−76	−21	60	21	31	20
Dividends and distributed branch profits	2 332 ..	10	5	....	5	13	20	13	8
Reinvested earnings and undistributed branch profits	2 333 ..	....	....	−78	−33	12	−64	−232	....
Income on debt (interest)	2 334 ..	1	4	1	7	35	65	250	12
Portfolio investment income	2 339 ..	173	230	488	589	1,130	1,227	751	579
Income on equity	2 340 ..	....	1	9	21	101	36	27	27
Income on bonds and notes	2 350 ..	103	32	464	563	1,028	1,182	718	534
Income on money market instruments	2 360 ..	70	197	15	4	1	9	6	18
Other investment income	2 370 ..	78	81	167	444	505	377	189	148
Investment income, debit	3 320 ..	**−1,070**	**−3,577**	**−4,409**	**−6,213**	**−8,928**	**−8,533**	**−4,226**	**−3,660**
Direct investment income	3 330 ..	−254	−2,594	−2,926	−4,164	−5,988	−4,362	−1,212	−747
Dividends and distributed branch profits	3 332 ..	−242	−707	−1,369	−733	−3,773	−3,942	−2,235	−2,228
Reinvested earnings and undistributed branch profits	3 333 ..	....	−1,805	−1,447	−3,354	−1,816	573	1,932	1,600
Income on debt (interest)	3 334 ..	−12	−82	−110	−77	−399	−993	−909	−119
Portfolio investment income	3 339 ..	−261	−340	−574	−718	−886	−987	−436	−586
Income on equity	3 340 ..	−1	−10	−191	−123	−226	−378	−164	−154
Income on bonds and notes	3 350 ..	−260	−327	−384	−595	−660	−609	−272	−431
Income on money market instruments	3 360 ..	....	−3	....	....	....	....	....	−1
Other investment income	3 370 ..	−555	−643	−909	−1,331	−2,054	−3,184	−2,578	−2,327
D. CURRENT TRANSFERS	4 379 ..	**1,861**	**3,697**	**4,449**	**6,125**	**6,618**	**8,884**	**5,708**	**4,522**
Credit	2 379 ..	**2,200**	**4,188**	**5,056**	**6,995**	**9,867**	**13,074**	**9,278**	**7,683**
General government	2 380 ..	264	213	190	367	1,290	3,358	3,212	2,639
Other sectors	2 390 ..	1,936	3,975	4,866	6,628	8,577	9,716	6,066	5,044
Workers' remittances	2 391 ..	14	18	3,754	5,509	6,835	7,580	4,198	3,171
Other current transfers	2 392 ..	1,922	3,957	1,112	1,119	1,742	2,136	1,868	1,873
Debit	3 379 ..	**−339**	**−491**	**−607**	**−870**	**−3,249**	**−4,190**	**−3,570**	**−3,161**
General government	3 380 ..	−41	−56	−107	−102	−1,686	−1,907	−2,213	−1,785
Other sectors	3 390 ..	−298	−435	−500	−767	−1,563	−2,283	−1,357	−1,376
Workers' remittances	3 391 ..	−1	−1	−4	−6	−289	−482	−236	−267
Other current transfers	3 392 ..	−297	−434	−496	−761	−1,274	−1,801	−1,121	−1,109
CAPITAL AND FINANCIAL ACCOUNT	4 996 ..	**3,600**	**5,215**	**7,891**	**12,263**	**24,399**	**25,784**	**8,724**	**7,402**
CAPITAL ACCOUNT	4 994 ..	**213**	**643**	**731**	**−34**	**1,145**	**912**	**928**	**294**
Total credit	2 994 ..	*223*	*669*	*829*	*925*	*1,708*	*1,462*	*1,409*	*718*
Total debit	3 994 ..	*−10*	*−26*	*−98*	*−959*	*−563*	*−550*	*−481*	*−424*
Capital transfers, credit	2 400 ..	**223**	**669**	**811**	**860**	**1,379**	**1,291**	**1,126**	**665**
General government	2 401 ..	115	549	478	569	948	699	809	370
Debt forgiveness	2 402 ..	115	549	....	....	....	....	....	....
Other capital transfers	2 410 ..	....	....	478	569	948	699	809	370
Other sectors	2 430 ..	108	120	333	291	431	592	317	295
Migrants' transfers	2 431 ..	....	1	25	44	81	96	71	73
Debt forgiveness	2 432 ..	95	90	24	18	11	25	13	4
Other capital transfers	2 440 ..	13	29	285	229	339	471	233	218
Capital transfers, debit	3 400 ..	**−10**	**−26**	**−80**	**−897**	**−386**	**−391**	**−384**	**−332**
General government	3 401 ..	....	....	....	−750	−95	−1	−202	−148
Debt forgiveness	3 402 ..	....	....	....	−750	−95	....	−3	....
Other capital transfers	3 410 ..	....	....	....	....	....	−1	−199	−148
Other sectors	3 430 ..	−10	−26	−80	−147	−291	−390	−182	−184
Migrants' transfers	3 431 ..	....	−2	−6	−8	−9	−13	−6	−1
Debt forgiveness	3 432 ..	....	....	....	....	....	....	....	....
Other capital transfers	3 440 ..	−10	−24	−74	−139	−282	−377	−176	−183
Nonproduced nonfinancial assets, credit	2 480 ..	....	....	**18**	**65**	**329**	**171**	**283**	**53**
Nonproduced nonfinancial assets, debit	3 480 ..	....	....	**−18**	**−62**	**−177**	**−159**	**−97**	**−92**

Table 2 (Continued). STANDARD PRESENTATION, 2003–2010

(Millions of U.S. dollars)

	Code	2003	2004	2005	2006	2007	2008	2009	2010
FINANCIAL ACCOUNT............................	4 995 ..	**3,387**	**4,572**	**7,160**	**12,297**	**23,254**	**24,872**	**7,796**	**7,108**
A. DIRECT INVESTMENT............................	4 500 ..	**1,805**	**6,373**	**6,512**	**10,971**	**9,647**	**13,606**	**4,934**	**3,263**
Direct investment abroad............................	4 505 ..	**−39**	**−70**	**30**	**−422**	**−278**	**−277**	**88**	**−190**
Equity capital............................	4 510 ..	−39	−70	−8	−269	−24	−112	−63	−137
Claims on affiliated enterprises............................	4 515 ..	−39	−70	−8	−269	−24	−112	−63	−142
Liabilities to affiliated enterprises............................	4 520 ..	....	....	....	....	....	....	....	5
Reinvested earnings............................	4 525 ..	....	....	78	33	−12	64	232	....
Other capital............................	4 530 ..	....	....	−39	−186	−242	−229	−81	−53
Claims on affiliated enterprises............................	4 535 ..	....	....	−39	−186	−242	−243	−81	....
Liabilities to affiliated enterprises............................	4 540 ..	....	....	....	....	....	14	....	−53
Direct investment in Romania............................	4 555 ..	**1,844**	**6,443**	**6,482**	**11,393**	**9,925**	**13,883**	**4,846**	**3,453**
Equity capital............................	4 560 ..	1,366	3,768	3,343	5,245	3,040	7,697	4,334	4,195
Claims on direct investors............................	4 565 ..	....	....	....	....	3	....	....	4
Liabilities to direct investors............................	4 570 ..	1,366	3,768	3,343	5,245	3,037	7,697	4,334	4,191
Reinvested earnings............................	4 575 ..	....	1,805	1,447	3,354	1,816	−573	−1,932	−1,600
Other capital............................	4 580 ..	478	870	1,692	2,795	5,069	6,759	2,444	858
Claims on direct investors............................	4 585 ..	....	....	−384	−58	−368	48	−80	−17
Liabilities to direct investors............................	4 590 ..	478	870	2,077	2,852	5,437	6,711	2,524	875
B. PORTFOLIO INVESTMENT............................	4 600 ..	**578**	**−531**	**949**	**−239**	**623**	**−722**	**763**	**1,614**
Assets............................	4 602 ..	**9**	**−559**	**−140**	**−828**	**142**	**−310**	**−196**	**−165**
Equity securities............................	4 610 ..	14	−559	−136	−390	−237	−274	204	−184
Monetary authorities............................	4 611 ..	....	....	....	....	....	....	....	....
General government............................	4 612 ..	....	....	....	....	....	....	....	....
Banks............................	4 613 ..	....	−546	....	−18	−96	19	....	−7
Other sectors............................	4 614 ..	14	−13	−136	−372	−141	−293	204	−177
Debt securities............................	4 619 ..	−5	....	−3	−438	379	−36	−400	19
Bonds and notes............................	4 620 ..	−5	....	−6	−290	260	−67	−400	130
Monetary authorities............................	4 621 ..	....	....	....	....	....	....	....	....
General government............................	4 622 ..	....	....	....	....	....	....	....	....
Banks............................	4 623 ..	−5	....	338	29	−17	−11	−232	180
Other sectors............................	4 624 ..	....	....	−344	−319	277	−56	−168	−50
Money market instruments............................	4 630 ..	....	....	2	−148	119	31	....	−111
Monetary authorities............................	4 631 ..	....	....	....	....	....	....	....	....
General government............................	4 632 ..	....	....	....	....	....	....	....	....
Banks............................	4 633 ..	....	....	....	....	−4	4	....	−61
Other sectors............................	4 634 ..	....	....	2	−148	123	27	....	−50
Liabilities............................	4 652 ..	**569**	**28**	**1,089**	**589**	**481**	**−412**	**959**	**1,779**
Equity securities............................	4 660 ..	69	111	229	301	746	23	7	4
Banks............................	4 663 ..	....	....	2	−4	59	19	−12	−25
Other sectors............................	4 664 ..	69	111	227	304	687	4	19	29
Debt securities............................	4 669 ..	500	−83	860	289	−265	−435	952	1,775
Bonds and notes............................	4 670 ..	497	−112	858	303	−371	−455	217	618
Monetary authorities............................	4 671 ..	....	....	....	....	....	....	....	....
General government............................	4 672 ..	608	22	240	72	−251	254	252	585
Banks............................	4 673 ..	−5	40	604	381	−119	−707	−34	32
Other sectors............................	4 674 ..	−106	−174	14	−150	−1	−2	−1	1
Money market instruments............................	4 680 ..	3	29	2	−15	106	20	735	1,157
Monetary authorities............................	4 681 ..	3	29	....	....	....	....	....	....
General government............................	4 682 ..	....	....	2	....	106	31	717	1,137
Banks............................	4 683 ..	....	....	....	....	....	....	....	....
Other sectors............................	4 684 ..	....	....	....	−15	....	−11	18	20
C. FINANCIAL DERIVATIVES............................	4 910 ..	....	....	**−26**	**−108**	**−415**	**−387**	**−61**	**4**
Monetary authorities............................	4 911 ..	....	....	....	....	....	....	....	....
General government............................	4 912 ..	....	....	....	....	....	1	....	....
Banks............................	4 913 ..	....	....	−34	−103	−405	−450	−94	−12
Other sectors............................	4 914 ..	....	....	7	−5	−10	62	33	16
Assets............................	4 900 ..	....	....	**36**	**48**	**338**	**889**	**525**	**586**
Monetary authorities............................	4 901 ..	....	....	....	....	....	....	....	....
General government............................	4 902 ..	....	....	....	....	....	1	....	....
Banks............................	4 903 ..	....	....	28	42	242	730	294	169
Other sectors............................	4 904 ..	....	....	7	6	96	158	231	417
Liabilities............................	4 905 ..	....	....	**−62**	**−156**	**−753**	**−1,276**	**−586**	**−582**
Monetary authorities............................	4 906 ..	....	....	....	....	....	....	....	....
General government............................	4 907 ..	....	....	....	....	....	....	....	....
Banks............................	4 908 ..	....	....	−62	−145	−647	−1,180	−388	−181
Other sectors............................	4 909 ..	....	....	....	−11	−106	−96	−198	−401

Table 2 (Concluded). STANDARD PRESENTATION, 2003–2010

(Millions of U.S. dollars)

	Code	2003	2004	2005	2006	2007	2008	2009	2010
D. OTHER INVESTMENT	4 700 ..	**2,137**	**4,748**	**6,502**	**8,109**	**19,573**	**12,530**	**5,147**	**6,929**
Assets	4 703 ..	72	−212	−1,078	−1,323	−1,173	−841	−2,916	−554
Trade credits	4 706 ..	−44	−97	101	506	−400	−306	−1,084	−384
General government	4 707 ..	−46	−37	−3	753	187	−37	−11	−17
of which: Short-term	4 709 ..	....	....	....	....	....	....	....	....
Other sectors	4 710 ..	2	−60	104	−246	−587	−269	−1,073	−367
of which: Short-term	4 712 ..	−16	−55	109	−311	−685	−444	−1,155	−662
Loans	4 714 ..	−31	29	−684	−1,131	−663	−727	−463	−580
Monetary authorities	4 715 ..	....	....	....	....	....	....	....	....
of which: Short-term	4 718 ..	....	....	....	....	....	....	....	....
General government	4 719 ..	....	....	....	....	....	....	....	....
of which: Short-term	4 721 ..	....	....	....	....	....	....	....	....
Banks	4 722 ..	−9	28	29	−27	−132	−53	−145	30
of which: Short-term	4 724 ..	1	....	−1	−27	−53	−48	−26	19
Other sectors	4 725 ..	−22	1	−713	−1,104	−531	−674	−318	−610
of which: Short-term	4 727 ..	....	23	−706	−939	−497	−634	−295	−563
Currency and deposits	4 730 ..	134	−148	−480	−659	−75	105	−1,433	499
Monetary authorities	4 731 ..	....	....	....	....	....	....	....	....
General government	4 732 ..	....	....	....	....	3	....	−2	3
Banks	4 733 ..	234	−60	−204	−314	18	55	−1,654	801
Other sectors	4 734 ..	−100	−88	−276	−345	−96	50	223	−305
Other assets	4 736 ..	13	4	−14	−39	−35	87	64	−89
Monetary authorities	4 737 ..	−1	....	−11	....	−13	....	....	....
of which: Short-term	4 739 ..	....	....	....	....	....	....	....	....
General government	4 740 ..	10	15	−12	5	−29	−31	−26	−55
of which: Short-term	4 742 ..	10	15	2	5	....	1	2	....
Banks	4 743 ..	4	−11	−23	−92	64	99	10	−16
of which: Short-term	4 745 ..	4	−11	−1	−37	21	77	30	−20
Other sectors	4 746 ..	....	....	32	47	−57	19	80	−18
of which: Short-term	4 748 ..	....	....	34	40	−60	−35	66	−29
Liabilities	4 753 ..	**2,065**	**4,960**	**7,579**	**9,431**	**20,746**	**13,371**	**8,063**	**7,483**
Trade credits	4 756 ..	−135	53	620	1,361	1,837	−2,230	−2,155	−628
General government	4 757 ..	−14	−27	−1	−46	−30	−9	−7	....
of which: Short-term	4 759 ..	....	....	....	....	....	....	....	....
Other sectors	4 760 ..	−121	80	621	1,407	1,867	−2,221	−2,148	−628
of which: Short-term	4 762 ..	−29	118	800	1,660	1,875	−1,752	−1,263	228
Loans	4 764 ..	1,767	4,041	4,884	7,761	8,271	9,097	11,400	7,040
Monetary authorities	4 765 ..	120	−72	−252	−166	−105	....	9,356	5,675
of which: Use of Fund credit and loans from the Fund	4 766 ..	120	−171	−152	−166	−105	....	9,356	5,675
of which: Short-term	4 768 ..	....	99	−100	....	....	....	....	....
General government	4 769 ..	903	1,042	569	74	−19	352	2,485	2,703
of which: Short-term	4 771 ..	....	....	....	....	3	15	9	....
Banks	4 772 ..	472	1,445	2,228	3,916	989	3,329	−1,802	233
of which: Short-term	4 774 ..	94	85	396	2,425	−1,753	248	−875	1,553
Other sectors	4 775 ..	272	1,626	2,339	3,938	7,406	5,416	1,361	−1,571
of which: Short-term	4 777 ..	381	1,018	471	2,306	2,781	−62	−2,697	−86
Currency and deposits	4 780 ..	463	616	882	1,063	7,495	900	−4,118	344
Monetary authorities	4 781 ..	....	....	....	....	185	211	−380	−80
General government	4 782 ..	....	....	....	....	44	−34	73	33
Banks	4 783 ..	463	616	882	1,063	7,266	723	−3,811	391
Other sectors	4 784 ..	....	....	....	....	....	....	....	....
Other liabilities	4 786 ..	−30	250	1,193	−754	3,143	5,604	2,936	727
Monetary authorities	4 787 ..	....	....	....	−3	....	....	1,421	....
of which: Short-term	4 789 ..	....	....	....	−3	....	....	....	....
General government	4 790 ..	....	....	−1	....	....	....	....	....
of which: Short-term	4 792 ..	....	....	....	....	....	....	....	....
Banks	4 793 ..	−17	268	724	−100	3,138	5,874	1,562	775
of which: Short-term	4 795 ..	....	....	70	−10	−23	469	−215	−212
Other sectors	4 796 ..	−13	−18	470	−651	5	−270	−47	−48
of which: Short-term	4 798 ..	−13	−18	488	−584	28	−224	−14	−26
E. RESERVE ASSETS	4 802 ..	**−1,134**	**−6,018**	**−6,777**	**−6,435**	**−6,174**	**−155**	**−2,987**	**−4,702**
Monetary gold	4 812 ..	....	....	....	....	....	....	....	....
Special drawing rights	4 811 ..	2	....	....	....	....	−128	−1,285	326
Reserve position in the Fund	4 810 ..	....	....	....	....	....	....	....	....
Foreign exchange	4 803 ..	−1,136	−6,018	−6,776	−6,436	−6,174	−27	−1,702	−5,028
Other claims	4 813 ..	....	....	....	....	....	....	....	....
NET ERRORS AND OMISSIONS	4 998 ..	**−289**	**1,167**	**612**	**521**	**−1,319**	**−2,065**	**−1,769**	**−922**

Table 3. INTERNATIONAL INVESTMENT POSITION (End-period stocks), 2003–2010

(Millions of U.S. dollars)

	Code	2003	2004	2005	2006	2007	2008	2009	2010
ASSETS	8 995 C.	**15,755**	**24,142**	**30,422**	**42,228**	**54,184**	**54,893**	**62,950**	**67,802**
Direct investment abroad	8 505 ..	**208**	**273**	**214**	**879**	**1,238**	**1,481**	**1,396**	**1,487**
Equity capital and reinvested earnings	8 506 ..	208	243	150	514	589	643	447	573
Claims on affiliated enterprises	8 507 ..	208	243	150	514	589	643	447	580
Liabilities to affiliated enterprises	8 508 ..	....	....	....	....	....	....	....	−7
Other capital	8 530 ..	....	30	63	365	649	838	949	913
Claims on affiliated enterprises	8 535 ..	....	34	67	368	652	863	959	926
Liabilities to affiliated enterprises	8 540 ..	....	−4	−4	−3	−3	−25	−9	−13
Portfolio investment	8 602 ..	**13**	**607**	**725**	**1,663**	**1,705**	**1,520**	**1,720**	**1,776**
Equity securities	8 610 ..	10	30	174	594	917	781	582	733
Monetary authorities	8 611 ..	....	....	....	....	....	....	....	....
General government	8 612 ..	....	....	....	....	....	....	....	....
Banks	8 613 ..	3	10	17	38	145	2	3	14
Other sectors	8 614 ..	7	20	157	556	772	778	579	720
Debt securities	8 619 ..	4	577	550	1,069	787	739	1,137	1,043
Bonds and notes	8 620 ..	4	573	546	910	738	720	1,120	885
Monetary authorities	8 621 ..	....	....	....	....	....	....	....	....
General government	8 622 ..	....	....	....	....	....	....	....	....
Banks	8 623 ..	....	572	189	179	218	201	431	203
Other sectors	8 624 ..	3	1	357	731	519	519	689	682
Money market instruments	8 630 ..	....	4	4	160	50	19	17	157
Monetary authorities	8 631 ..	....	....	....	....	....	....	....	....
General government	8 632 ..	....	....	....	....	....	....	....	....
Banks	8 633 ..	....	....	....	....	4	1	....	93
Other sectors	8 634 ..	....	4	4	160	46	18	17	64
Financial derivatives	8 900 ..	**....**	**....**	**−34**	**....**	**....**	**....**	**....**	**....**
Monetary authorities	8 901 ..	....	....	....	....	....	....	....	....
General government	8 902 ..	....	....	....	....	....	....	....	....
Banks	8 903 ..	....	....	−27	....	....	....	....	....
Other sectors	8 904 ..	....	....	−7	....	....	....	....	....
Other investment	8 703 ..	**6,083**	**6,978**	**7,914**	**9,478**	**11,285**	**12,142**	**15,397**	**16,474**
Trade credits	8 706 ..	3,324	3,785	3,878	3,288	3,319	3,892	4,860	5,858
General government	8 707 ..	2,961	3,402	3,446	2,702	2,290	2,326	2,338	2,354
of which: Short-term	8 709 ..	....	....	....	....	....	....	....	....
Other sectors	8 710 ..	363	383	432	586	1,029	1,566	2,522	3,504
of which: Short-term	8 712 ..	*249*	*333*	*359*	*559*	*1,029*	*1,566*	*2,522*	*3,504*
Loans	8 714 ..	214	201	850	2,134	2,956	3,551	4,083	4,434
Monetary authorities	8 715 ..	....	....	....	....	....	....	....	....
of which: Short-term	8 718 ..	....	....	....	....	....	....	....	....
General government	8 719 ..	....	....	....	....	....	....	....	....
of which: Short-term	8 721 ..	....	....	....	....	....	....	....	....
Banks	8 722 ..	151	135	98	145	253	282	427	373
of which: Short-term	8 724 ..	*15*	*16*	*24*	*59*	*80*	*118*	*141*	*111*
Other sectors	8 725 ..	63	65	752	1,989	2,703	3,269	3,656	4,061
of which: Short-term	8 727 ..	*39*	*19*	*705*	*1,760*	*2,416*	*2,930*	*3,272*	*3,687*
Currency and deposits	8 730 ..	1,475	1,921	2,085	2,846	3,737	3,477	5,243	4,885
Monetary authorities	8 731 ..	....	....	....	....	....	....	....	....
General government	8 732 ..	5	5	5	10	20	10	13	10
Banks	8 733 ..	903	1,074	1,091	1,436	1,743	1,571	3,338	2,301
Other sectors	8 734 ..	567	842	989	1,400	1,974	1,896	1,891	2,574
Other assets	8 736 ..	1,069	1,071	1,101	1,210	1,273	1,221	1,211	1,297
Monetary authorities	8 737 ..	15	15	24	27	42	41	42	41
of which: Short-term	8 739 ..	....	....	....	....	....	....	....	....
General government	8 740 ..	1,004	1,007	989	1,039	1,004	1,025	1,056	1,103
of which: Short-term	8 742 ..	*229*	*217*	*205*	*228*	*152*	*151*	*148*	*148*
Banks	8 743 ..	50	3	24	117	133	30	50	66
of which: Short-term	8 745 ..	*50*	*3*	*2*	*40*	*78*	....	....	*21*
Other sectors	8 746 ..	....	46	64	26	95	124	62	88
of which: Short-term	8 748 ..	....	*40*	*57*	*25*	*93*	*124*	*60*	*85*
Reserve assets	8 802 ..	**9,450**	**16,284**	**21,604**	**30,207**	**39,957**	**39,750**	**44,437**	**48,065**
Monetary gold	8 812 ..	1,410	1,481	1,728	2,140	2,762	2,882	3,680	4,704
Special drawing rights	8 811 ..	....	1	1	....	1	121	1,412	1,058
Reserve position in the Fund	8 810 ..	....	....	....	....	....	....	....	....
Foreign exchange	8 803 ..	8,040	14,802	19,875	28,066	37,194	36,747	39,345	42,303
Other claims	8 813 ..	....	....	....	....	....	....	....	....

Table 3 (Concluded). INTERNATIONAL INVESTMENT POSITION (End-period stocks), 2003–2010

(Millions of U.S. dollars)

	Code	2003	2004	2005	2006	2007	2008	2009	2010
LIABILITIES..	8 995 D.	**32,168**	**46,594**	**57,785**	**90,816**	**133,876**	**151,924**	**170,633**	**173,559**
Direct investment in Romania............................	8 555 ..	**12,187**	**20,523**	**25,893**	**45,454**	**62,861**	**68,614**	**71,981**	**70,059**
Equity capital and reinvested earnings...............................	8 556 ..	8,946	16,384	20,693	35,582	46,297	49,061	51,266	49,719
Claims on direct investors..................................	8 557 ..	....	....	....	−3	....	....	....	−14
Liabilities to direct investors...............................	8 558 ..	8,946	16,384	20,693	35,585	46,297	49,061	51,266	49,733
Other capital...	8 580 ..	3,241	4,139	5,200	9,872	16,563	19,553	20,714	20,340
Claims on direct investors..................................	8 585 ..	−16	−46	−444	−581	−973	−952	−1,090	−1,026
Liabilities to direct investors...............................	8 590 ..	3,258	4,185	5,644	10,454	17,537	20,505	21,805	21,367
Portfolio investment.....................................	8 652 ..	**4,503**	**4,832**	**5,251**	**6,292**	**7,247**	**6,211**	**7,083**	**7,727**
Equity securities...	8 660 ..	700	877	984	1,525	2,350	2,061	1,998	1,836
Banks...	8 663 ..	....	19	18	23	89	94	80	49
Other sectors...	8 664 ..	700	858	966	1,503	2,261	1,966	1,918	1,787
Debt securities...	8 669 ..	3,803	3,954	4,267	4,767	4,897	4,150	5,085	5,891
Bonds and notes..	8 670 ..	3,787	3,881	4,201	4,709	4,699	4,038	4,249	3,996
Monetary authorities...................................	8 671 ..	....	....	....	....	....	....	....	....
General government....................................	8 672 ..	3,089	3,304	3,100	3,451	3,585	3,712	3,994	3,828
Banks..	8 673 ..	4	128	770	1,166	1,114	326	255	168
Other sectors..	8 674 ..	694	449	331	91	....	....	....	....
Money market instruments..............................	8 680 ..	15	74	66	58	198	112	837	1,895
Monetary authorities...................................	8 681 ..	....	....	....	....	....	....	....	....
General government....................................	8 682 ..	....	25	23	26	162	93	801	1,840
Banks..	8 683 ..	....	....	....	....	....	....	....	....
Other sectors..	8 684 ..	15	49	43	32	36	19	36	55
Financial derivatives.....................................	8 905 ..	....	....	**−59**	....	....	....	....	....
Monetary authorities..	8 906 ..	....	....	....	....	....	....	....	....
General government...	8 907 ..	....	....	....	....	....	....	....	....
Banks..	8 908 ..	....	....	−58	....	....	....	....	....
Other sectors..	8 909 ..	....	....	....	....	....	....	....	....
Other investment..	8 753 ..	**15,478**	**21,240**	**26,700**	**39,070**	**63,768**	**77,100**	**91,569**	**95,773**
Trade credits...	8 756 ..	962	1,083	2,108	3,656	5,589	3,900	2,037	2,334
General government...	8 757 ..	79	56	82	40	17	5	1	2
of which: Short-term.....................................	8 759 ..	....	....	....	....	....	....	....	....
Other sectors...	8 760 ..	883	1,027	2,026	3,615	5,573	3,895	2,036	2,332
of which: Short-term.....................................	8 762 ..	*518*	*692*	*1,707*	*3,245*	*5,044*	*3,474*	*1,799*	*2,183*
Loans...	8 764 ..	13,135	17,907	20,484	30,057	41,433	51,649	69,156	73,463
Monetary authorities.......................................	8 765 ..	595	443	261	104	....	....	9,544	15,092
of which: Use of Fund credit and loans from the Fund....	8 766 ..	*595*	*443*	*261*	*104*	....	....	*9,544*	*15,092*
of which: Short-term...................................	8 768 ..	....	....	....	....	....	....	....	....
General government.......................................	8 769 ..	6,909	8,860	8,776	9,448	10,346	10,556	13,301	15,762
of which: Short-term...................................	8 771 ..	....	....	....	....	....	....	....	....
Banks..	8 772 ..	847	2,505	4,367	9,174	11,070	13,551	12,121	11,928
of which: Short-term...................................	8 774 ..	*82*	*212*	*545*	*3,047*	*1,328*	*1,486*	*632*	*2,154*
Other sectors..	8 775 ..	4,783	6,098	7,080	11,332	20,017	27,542	34,189	30,681
of which: Short-term...................................	8 777 ..	*303*	*1,130*	*1,429*	*3,910*	*7,265*	*6,936*	*4,322*	*3,952*
Currency and deposits.......................................	8 780 ..	1,294	2,204	3,546	5,248	11,903	13,311	8,063	7,359
Monetary authorities.......................................	8 781 ..	....	100	....	....	213	427	114	29
General government.......................................	8 782 ..	....	....	....	....	44	52	115	154
Banks..	8 783 ..	1,294	2,104	3,546	5,248	11,646	12,833	7,834	7,176
Other sectors..	8 784 ..	....	....	....	....	....	....	....	....
Other liabilities..	8 786 ..	87	46	562	109	4,843	8,240	12,313	12,616
Monetary authorities.......................................	8 787 ..	38	38	37	35	36	36	1,580	1,552
of which: Short-term...................................	8 789 ..	....	....	....	....	....	....	....	....
General government.......................................	8 790 ..	....	1	....	1	....	....	....	....
of which: Short-term...................................	8 792 ..	....	*1*	....	*1*	....	....	....	....
Banks..	8 793 ..	....	7	73	73	4,769	8,199	10,734	11,064
of which: Short-term...................................	8 795 ..	....	*7*	*73*	*73*	*39*	*511*	*304*	*63*
Other sectors..	8 796 ..	48	....	450	....	38	5	....	....
of which: Short-term...................................	8 798 ..	*48*	....	*450*	....	*36*	....	....	....
NET INTERNATIONAL INVESTMENT POSITION........	8 995 ..	**−16,413**	**−22,452**	**−27,363**	**−48,588**	**−79,692**	**−97,031**	**−107,683**	**−105,757**
Conversion rates: Romanian lei per U.S. dollar (end of period)...	0 102 ..	**3.260**	**2.907**	**3.108**	**2.568**	**2.456**	**2.834**	**2.936**	**3.205**

Table 1. ANALYTIC PRESENTATION, 2003–2010

(Millions of U.S. dollars)

	Code	2003	2004	2005	2006	2007	2008	2009	2010
A. Current Account[1]	4 993 Z.	**35,410**	**59,512**	**84,602**	**94,686**	**77,768**	**103,530**	**48,605**	**70,253**
Goods: exports f.o.b.	2 100 ..	135,929	183,207	243,798	303,550	354,401	471,603	303,388	400,419
Goods: imports f.o.b.	3 100 ..	−76,070	−97,382	−125,434	−164,281	−223,486	−291,861	−191,803	−248,738
Balance on Goods	4 100 ..	*59,860*	*85,825*	*118,364*	*139,269*	*130,915*	*179,742*	*111,585*	*151,681*
Services: credit	2 200 ..	16,229	20,595	24,970	31,102	39,257	51,178	41,594	45,120
Services: debit	3 200 ..	−27,122	−33,287	−38,745	−44,716	−58,145	−75,468	−61,429	−74,332
Balance on Goods and Services	4 991 ..	*48,966*	*73,133*	*104,589*	*125,656*	*112,027*	*155,453*	*91,750*	*122,470*
Income: credit	2 300 ..	11,057	11,998	17,475	29,757	47,397	61,778	33,184	37,359
Income: debit	3 300 ..	−24,228	−24,769	−36,424	−59,189	−78,149	−110,936	−73,467	−85,975
Balance on Goods, Services, and Income	4 992 ..	*35,795*	*60,361*	*85,640*	*96,224*	*81,275*	*106,295*	*51,467*	*73,853*
Current transfers: credit	2 379 Z.	2,537	3,467	4,490	6,403	8,423	10,969	8,908	9,953
Current transfers: debit	3 379 ..	−2,922	−4,317	−5,528	−7,940	−11,929	−13,734	−11,770	−13,552
B. Capital Account[1]	4 994 Z.	**−993**	**−1,624**	**−12,764**	**191**	**−10,224**	**496**	**−11,869**	**73**
Capital account: credit	2 994 Z.	616	862	678	1,023	1,393	1,647	1,649	1,024
Capital account: debit	3 994 ..	−1,609	−2,486	−13,442	−832	−11,617	−1,152	−13,518	−951
Total, Groups A Plus B	4 981 ..	*34,417*	*57,888*	*71,838*	*94,877*	*67,544*	*104,026*	*36,736*	*70,326*
C. Financial Account[1]	4 995 W.	**3,024**	**−5,128**	**1,025**	**3,071**	**94,730**	**−131,674**	**−31,648**	**−25,956**
Direct investment abroad	4 505 ..	−9,727	−13,782	−12,767	−23,151	−45,916	−55,594	−43,665	−52,476
Direct investment in the Russian Federation	4 555 Z.	7,958	15,444	12,886	29,701	55,073	75,002	36,500	42,846
Portfolio investment assets	4 602 ..	−2,180	−3,820	−10,666	6,248	−9,992	−7,843	−10,375	−3,470
Equity securities	4 610 ..	−47	−25	−733	116	−3,435	−135	−739	−1,447
Debt securities	4 619 ..	−2,133	−3,794	−9,933	6,131	−6,557	−7,708	−9,636	−2,023
Portfolio investment liabilities	4 652 Z.	−2,329	4,443	−713	9,455	15,545	−27,594	8,195	1,810
Equity securities	4 660 ..	422	270	−100	6,480	18,675	−15,005	3,369	−4,808
Debt securities	4 669 Z.	−2,750	4,173	−613	2,975	−3,130	−12,588	4,826	6,619
Financial derivatives	4 910 ..	640	−100	−233	−99	332	−1,370	−3,244	−1,841
Financial derivatives assets	4 900 ..	1,017	758	858	1,242	2,762	9,117	9,890	8,840
Financial derivatives liabilities	4 905 ..	−377	−857	−1,091	−1,342	−2,430	−10,487	−13,134	−10,682
Other investment assets	4 703 ..	−15,886	−26,644	−33,328	−49,422	−60,062	−177,515	6,141	−22,834
Monetary authorities	4 701 ..	467	306	205	175	−477	−56	57	−30
General government	4 704 ..	−299	−237	11,478	−1,338	7,242	−2,460	10,208	−311
Banks	4 705 ..	−837	−1,964	−9,905	−24,034	−22,678	−66,823	11,897	−4,721
Other sectors	4 728 ..	−15,216	−24,748	−35,107	−24,226	−44,149	−108,177	−16,021	−17,771
Other investment liabilities	4 753 W.	24,547	19,331	45,846	30,340	139,751	63,239	−25,201	10,010
Monetary authorities	4 753 WA	1,636	1,909	6,309	−7,331	882	1,440	11,889	−2,403
General government	4 753 ZB	−3,705	−5,485	−19,244	−27,053	−3,637	−1,538	−1,850	−1,165
Banks	4 753 ZC	11,546	6,709	18,087	48,272	51,768	12,884	−37,630	20,037
Other sectors	4 753 ZD	15,070	16,197	40,693	16,452	90,738	50,452	2,391	−6,458
Total, Groups A Through C	4 983 ..	*37,441*	*52,760*	*72,863*	*97,948*	*162,275*	*−27,648*	*5,088*	*44,370*
D. Net Errors and Omissions	4 998 ..	**−9,179**	**−5,870**	**−7,895**	**9,518**	**−13,347**	**−11,271**	**−1,724**	**−7,621**
Total, Groups A Through D	4 984 ..	*28,262*	*46,890*	*64,968*	*107,466*	*148,928*	*−38,919*	*3,363*	*36,749*
E. Reserves and Related Items	4 802 A.	**−28,262**	**−46,890**	**−64,968**	**−107,466**	**−148,928**	**38,919**	**−3,363**	**−36,749**
Reserve assets	4 802 ..	−26,365	−45,236	−61,461	−107,466	−148,928	38,919	−3,363	−36,749
Use of Fund credit and loans	4 766 ..	−1,897	−1,655	−3,506	....	....	....	....	....
Exceptional financing	4 920 ..	....	....	....	....	....	....	....	....
Conversion rates: rubles per U.S. dollar	0 101 ..	**30.692**	**28.814**	**28.284**	**27.191**	**25.581**	**24.853**	**31.740**	**30.368**

[1] Excludes components that have been classified in the categories of Group E.

Table 2. STANDARD PRESENTATION, 2003–2010

(Millions of U.S. dollars)

	Code	2003	2004	2005	2006	2007	2008	2009	2010
CURRENT ACCOUNT	4 993 ..	**35,410**	**59,512**	**84,602**	**94,686**	**77,768**	**103,530**	**48,605**	**70,253**
A. GOODS	4 100 ..	**59,860**	**85,825**	**118,364**	**139,269**	**130,915**	**179,742**	**111,585**	**151,681**
Credit	2 100 ..	**135,929**	**183,207**	**243,798**	**303,550**	**354,401**	**471,603**	**303,388**	**400,419**
General merchandise: exports f.o.b.	2 110 ..	128,888	177,556	236,193	294,880	342,059	457,462	293,976	388,586
Goods for processing: exports f.o.b.	2 150 ..	6,478	4,793	5,878	6,492	9,398	10,309	6,577	8,040
Repairs on goods	2 160 ..	205	371	849	673	465	585	683	1,165
Goods procured in ports by carriers	2 170 ..	358	487	878	1,505	2,480	3,248	2,152	2,628
Nonmonetary gold	2 180 ..	....	....	....	....	....	....	....	....
Debit	3 100 ..	**−76,070**	**−97,382**	**−125,434**	**−164,281**	**−223,486**	**−291,861**	**−191,803**	**−248,738**
General merchandise: imports f.o.b.	3 110 ..	−72,097	−93,312	−120,419	−158,574	−216,280	−282,876	−186,681	−242,360
Goods for processing: imports f.o.b.	3 150 ..	−2,964	−2,790	−3,214	−3,885	−4,797	−6,142	−3,111	−3,879
Repairs on goods	3 160 ..	−312	−426	−609	−262	−271	−332	−218	−344
Goods procured in ports by carriers	3 170 ..	−697	−854	−1,192	−1,559	−2,138	−2,511	−1,794	−2,155
Nonmonetary gold	3 180 ..	....	....	....	....	....	....	....	....
B. SERVICES	4 200 ..	**−10,894**	**−12,693**	**−13,775**	**−13,614**	**−18,888**	**−24,289**	**−19,836**	**−29,211**
Total credit	2 200 ..	*16,229*	*20,595*	*24,970*	*31,102*	*39,257*	*51,178*	*41,594*	*45,120*
Total debit	3 200 ..	*−27,122*	*−33,287*	*−38,745*	*−44,716*	*−58,145*	*−75,468*	*−61,429*	*−74,332*
Transportation services, credit	2 205 ..	**6,119**	**7,792**	**9,113**	**10,081**	**11,829**	**15,024**	**12,369**	**14,911**
Passenger	2 850 ..	*1,377*	*1,732*	*1,936*	*2,092*	*2,980*	*3,979*	*3,003*	*4,409*
Freight	2 851 ..	*2,660*	*3,598*	*4,256*	*4,669*	*5,156*	*6,688*	*5,048*	*5,746*
Other	2 852 ..	*2,082*	*2,462*	*2,921*	*3,320*	*3,693*	*4,357*	*4,318*	*4,755*
Sea transport, passenger	2 207 ..	1	1	1	....	1	3	3	1
Sea transport, freight	2 208 ..	820	1,041	1,171	1,042	1,016	1,129	764	854
Sea transport, other	2 209 ..	1,112	1,436	1,658	1,742	2,080	2,563	2,341	2,514
Air transport, passenger	2 211 ..	1,242	1,566	1,737	1,821	2,607	3,507	2,661	4,022
Air transport, freight	2 212 ..	518	718	881	1,093	1,234	1,522	1,454	1,743
Air transport, other	2 213 ..	610	640	880	1,154	1,061	1,136	1,315	1,575
Other transport, passenger	2 215 ..	135	165	198	270	372	470	340	386
Other transport, freight	2 216 ..	1,323	1,840	2,204	2,535	2,906	4,037	2,830	3,149
Other transport, other	2 217 ..	361	385	382	424	552	657	662	667
Transportation services, debit	3 205 ..	**−3,103**	**−3,886**	**−5,137**	**−6,722**	**−9,348**	**−12,960**	**−9,451**	**−12,058**
Passenger	3 850 ..	*−547*	*−797*	*−991*	*−1,366*	*−2,031*	*−3,232*	*−2,766*	*−3,477*
Freight	3 851 ..	*−1,359*	*−1,784*	*−2,683*	*−3,693*	*−5,205*	*−6,915*	*−4,427*	*−5,868*
Other	3 852 ..	*−1,197*	*−1,305*	*−1,462*	*−1,663*	*−2,111*	*−2,814*	*−2,258*	*−2,714*
Sea transport, passenger	3 207 ..	−1	−2	−1	−2	−5	−8	−4	−5
Sea transport, freight	3 208 ..	−475	−602	−926	−1,250	−1,774	−2,404	−1,656	−2,224
Sea transport, other	3 209 ..	−451	−421	−477	−525	−663	−987	−816	−925
Air transport, passenger	3 211 ..	−371	−579	−752	−1,057	−1,596	−2,662	−2,260	−2,918
Air transport, freight	3 212 ..	−598	−843	−1,329	−1,880	−2,751	−3,598	−2,170	−2,870
Air transport, other	3 213 ..	−494	−582	−704	−916	−1,176	−1,477	−1,174	−1,508
Other transport, passenger	3 215 ..	−175	−216	−238	−307	−430	−562	−502	−554
Other transport, freight	3 216 ..	−286	−339	−428	−563	−681	−913	−601	−774
Other transport, other	3 217 ..	−252	−301	−280	−223	−271	−350	−267	−281
Travel, credit	2 236 ..	**4,502**	**5,530**	**5,870**	**7,628**	**9,447**	**11,842**	**9,366**	**8,970**
Business travel	2 237 ..	1,450	1,936	2,379	3,809	4,929	7,002	5,346	5,095
Personal travel	2 240 ..	3,052	3,595	3,490	3,819	4,518	4,840	4,020	3,875
Travel, debit	3 236 ..	**−12,880**	**−15,285**	**−17,314**	**−18,112**	**−21,216**	**−23,778**	**−20,905**	**−26,516**
Business travel	3 237 ..	−2,458	−2,273	−2,455	−2,405	−2,479	−2,421	−1,743	−1,810
Personal travel	3 240 ..	−10,422	−13,012	−14,860	−15,707	−18,738	−21,356	−19,162	−24,706
Other services, credit	2 200 BA	**5,608**	**7,272**	**9,988**	**13,393**	**17,980**	**24,312**	**19,858**	**21,239**
Communications	2 245 ..	443	471	658	803	1,272	1,493	1,337	1,351
Construction	2 249 ..	1,050	1,577	2,209	3,050	3,450	4,663	3,293	2,625
Insurance	2 253 ..	148	242	323	377	379	644	443	462
Financial	2 260 ..	176	270	390	589	1,174	1,320	1,032	1,053
Computer and information	2 262 ..	175	256	422	632	1,097	1,644	1,291	1,359
Royalties and licence fees	2 266 ..	174	227	260	299	396	453	494	625
Other business services	2 268 ..	3,177	3,940	5,309	7,174	9,624	13,102	11,181	12,775
Personal, cultural, and recreational	2 287 ..	125	164	187	232	291	389	348	474
Government, n.i.e.	2 291 ..	140	126	230	237	297	605	440	515
Other services, debit	3 200 BA	**−11,139**	**−14,117**	**−16,294**	**−19,882**	**−27,581**	**−38,730**	**−31,073**	**−35,758**
Communications	3 245 ..	−555	−691	−746	−917	−1,298	−1,879	−1,898	−2,100
Construction	3 249 ..	−2,459	−3,047	−4,034	−4,603	−6,454	−8,839	−4,470	−5,102
Insurance	3 253 ..	−774	−1,157	−698	−716	−846	−1,249	−948	−1,037
Financial	3 260 ..	−314	−695	−892	−904	−1,472	−2,080	−1,486	−1,720
Computer and information	3 262 ..	−458	−320	−482	−613	−956	−1,424	−1,429	−1,884
Royalties and licence fees	3 266 ..	−711	−1,094	−1,593	−2,002	−2,806	−4,595	−4,107	−5,066
Other business services	3 268 ..	−5,046	−5,732	−6,459	−8,548	−11,618	−15,975	−13,742	−15,796
Personal, cultural, and recreational	3 287 ..	−188	−309	−440	−542	−753	−838	−806	−1,000
Government, n.i.e.	3 291 ..	−635	−1,071	−950	−1,036	−1,377	−1,851	−2,188	−2,053

Table 2 (Continued). STANDARD PRESENTATION, 2003–2010

(Millions of U.S. dollars)

	Code	2003	2004	2005	2006	2007	2008	2009	2010
C. INCOME................................	4 300 ..	**−13,171**	**−12,771**	**−18,949**	**−29,432**	**−30,752**	**−49,158**	**−40,283**	**−48,617**
Total credit....................................	2 300 ..	*11,057*	*11,998*	*17,475*	*29,757*	*47,397*	*61,778*	*33,184*	*37,359*
Total debit.....................................	3 300 ..	*−24,228*	*−24,769*	*−36,424*	*−59,189*	*−78,149*	*−110,936*	*−73,467*	*−85,975*
Compensation of employees, credit.....	2 310 ..	**814**	**1,206**	**1,807**	**1,899**	**2,613**	**3,792**	**3,326**	**3,619**
Compensation of employees, debit.....	3 310 ..	**−958**	**−1,464**	**−2,940**	**−6,067**	**−9,931**	**−18,149**	**−12,193**	**−12,131**
Investment income, credit.............	2 320 ..	**10,243**	**10,792**	**15,668**	**27,858**	**44,784**	**57,986**	**29,858**	**33,739**
Direct investment income.................	2 330 ..	6,338	6,336	8,092	12,357	20,038	29,374	11,009	17,765
Dividends and distributed branch profits........	2 332 ..	747	1,264	1,203	1,554	3,033	4,256	2,475	2,435
Reinvested earnings and undistributed branch profits.....	2 333 ..	5,591	5,071	6,875	10,772	16,677	24,654	7,570	14,049
Income on debt (interest).................	2 334 ..	....	....	14	31	328	465	965	1,281
Portfolio investment income...............	2 339 ..	430	388	546	777	1,051	1,709	3,475	3,042
Income on equity.........................	2 340 ..	92	102	53	156	242	201	324	702
Income on bonds and notes............	2 350 ..	327	245	455	607	775	1,415	2,866	2,272
Income on money market instruments........	2 360 ..	12	41	38	13	34	94	285	68
Other investment income................	2 370 ..	3,475	4,068	7,030	14,724	23,695	26,903	15,373	12,932
Investment income, debit..............	3 320 ..	**−23,270**	**−23,305**	**−33,484**	**−53,122**	**−68,218**	**−92,787**	**−61,274**	**−73,844**
Direct investment income.................	3 330 ..	−12,521	−10,294	−19,483	−34,601	−43,195	−62,290	−37,472	−48,643
Dividends and distributed branch profits........	3 332 ..	−5,059	−4,453	−9,874	−19,562	−19,179	−27,993	−20,613	−27,691
Reinvested earnings and undistributed branch profits.....	3 333 ..	−7,065	−5,330	−9,361	−14,716	−23,389	−33,449	−15,434	−18,644
Income on debt (interest).................	3 334 ..	−397	−511	−247	−323	−628	−847	−1,424	−2,308
Portfolio investment income...............	3 339 ..	−4,831	−5,180	−4,472	−5,515	−7,005	−8,184	−5,694	−7,836
Income on equity.........................	3 340 ..	−2,330	−2,401	−1,863	−2,712	−4,051	−5,334	−3,037	−5,290
Income on bonds and notes............	3 350 ..	−2,397	−2,716	−2,484	−2,689	−2,823	−2,667	−2,563	−2,429
Income on money market instruments........	3 360 ..	−104	−63	−126	−115	−131	−182	−94	−117
Other investment income................	3 370 ..	−5,918	−7,831	−9,530	−13,006	−18,018	−22,314	−18,108	−17,366
D. CURRENT TRANSFERS..................	4 379 ..	**−385**	**−850**	**−1,038**	**−1,537**	**−3,506**	**−2,765**	**−2,862**	**−3,600**
Credit...	2 379 ..	**2,537**	**3,467**	**4,490**	**6,403**	**8,423**	**10,969**	**8,908**	**9,953**
General government.......................	2 380 ..	1,178	1,097	1,609	3,075	4,354	7,066	5,144	5,969
Other sectors..............................	2 390 ..	1,359	2,370	2,881	3,328	4,069	3,903	3,764	3,983
Workers' remittances.....................	2 391 ..	300	925	621	766	852	802	775	763
Other current transfers..................	2 392 ..	1,059	1,445	2,260	2,562	3,217	3,101	2,989	3,220
Debit..	3 379 ..	**−2,922**	**−4,317**	**−5,528**	**−7,940**	**−11,929**	**−13,734**	**−11,770**	**−13,552**
General government.......................	3 380 ..	−279	−351	−689	−1,042	−860	−1,005	−1,363	−2,462
Other sectors..............................	3 390 ..	−2,644	−3,966	−4,839	−6,899	−11,069	−12,729	−10,407	−11,090
Workers' remittances.....................	3 391 ..	−1,306	−2,672	−3,051	−4,587	−6,942	−7,264	−5,927	−5,921
Other current transfers..................	3 392 ..	−1,337	−1,294	−1,788	−2,311	−4,126	−5,465	−4,481	−5,169
CAPITAL AND FINANCIAL ACCOUNT........	4 996 ..	**−26,231**	**−53,642**	**−76,707**	**−104,204**	**−64,421**	**−92,259**	**−46,880**	**−62,632**
CAPITAL ACCOUNT.........................	4 994 ..	**−993**	**−1,624**	**−12,764**	**191**	**−10,224**	**496**	**−11,869**	**73**
Total credit....................................	2 994 ..	*616*	*862*	*678*	*1,023*	*1,393*	*1,647*	*1,649*	*1,024*
Total debit.....................................	3 994 ..	*−1,609*	*−2,486*	*−13,442*	*−832*	*−11,617*	*−1,152*	*−13,518*	*−951*
Capital transfers, credit.................	2 400 ..	**616**	**862**	**678**	**1,023**	**1,393**	**1,647**	**1,649**	**1,024**
General government.......................	2 401 ..	276	499	95	345	144	208	129	60
Debt forgiveness..........................	2 402 ..	276	499	2	170	....	....	....	1
Other capital transfers..................	2 410 ..	....	....	94	174	144	208	129	59
Other sectors..............................	2 430 ..	339	364	583	678	1,249	1,439	1,520	964
Migrants' transfers........................	2 431 ..	339	364	583	678	1,249	1,439	1,258	881
Debt forgiveness..........................	2 432 ..	....	....	....	....	....	....	262	83
Other capital transfers..................	2 440 ..	....	....	....	....	....	....	....	....
Capital transfers, debit..................	3 400 ..	**−1,609**	**−2,486**	**−13,442**	**−832**	**−11,617**	**−914**	**−13,272**	**−951**
General government.......................	3 401 ..	−640	−1,434	−12,426	−19	−9,749	−3	−12,601	−207
Debt forgiveness..........................	3 402 ..	−640	−1,434	−12,426	−19	−9,749	−3	−12,380	−62
Other capital transfers..................	3 410 ..	....	....	....	....	....	....	−221	−145
Other sectors..............................	3 430 ..	−969	−1,052	−1,017	−813	−1,868	−910	−671	−744
Migrants' transfers........................	3 431 ..	−969	−1,052	−1,017	−813	−890	−910	−659	−744
Debt forgiveness..........................	3 432 ..	....	....	....	....	....	....	−13	−1
Other capital transfers..................	3 440 ..	....	....	....	....	−978	....	....	....
Nonproduced nonfinancial assets, credit..........	2 480 ..	....	....	....	....	....	....	....	....
Nonproduced nonfinancial assets, debit..........	3 480 ..	....	....	....	....	....	**−238**	**−245**	....

Table 2 (Continued). STANDARD PRESENTATION, 2003–2010

(Millions of U.S. dollars)

	Code	2003	2004	2005	2006	2007	2008	2009	2010
FINANCIAL ACCOUNT	4 995	**−25,238**	**−52,018**	**−63,943**	**−104,395**	**−54,197**	**−92,755**	**−35,011**	**−62,705**
A. DIRECT INVESTMENT	4 500	**−1,769**	**1,662**	**118**	**6,550**	**9,158**	**19,409**	**−7,165**	**−9,630**
Direct investment abroad	4 505	**−9,727**	**−13,782**	**−12,767**	**−23,151**	**−45,916**	**−55,594**	**−43,665**	**−52,476**
Equity capital	4 510	−3,839	−6,580	−4,575	−10,215	−17,789	−29,408	−26,857	−20,210
Claims on affiliated enterprises	4 515	−3,839	−6,580	−4,575	−10,215	−17,789	−29,408	−26,857	−20,210
Liabilities to affiliated enterprises	4 520	....	....	....	....	....	....	....	....
Reinvested earnings	4 525	−5,591	−5,071	−6,875	−10,772	−16,677	−24,654	−7,570	−14,049
Other capital	4 530	−297	−2,131	−1,318	−2,164	−11,449	−1,532	−9,238	−18,217
Claims on affiliated enterprises	4 535	−297	−2,131	−1,318	−2,164	−11,449	−1,532	−9,238	−18,217
Liabilities to affiliated enterprises	4 540	....	....	....	....	....	....	....	....
Direct investment in the Russian Federation	4 555	**7,958**	**15,444**	**12,886**	**29,701**	**55,073**	**75,002**	**36,500**	**42,846**
Equity capital	4 560	−1,911	8,632	998	6,909	27,119	35,015	8,121	9,453
Claims on direct investors	4 565	....	....	....	....	....	....	....	....
Liabilities to direct investors	4 570	−1,911	8,632	998	6,909	27,119	35,015	8,121	9,453
Reinvested earnings	4 575	7,065	5,330	9,361	14,716	23,389	33,449	15,434	18,644
Other capital	4 580	2,804	1,482	2,527	8,076	4,565	6,538	12,944	14,749
Claims on direct investors	4 585	....	....	....	....	....	....	....	....
Liabilities to direct investors	4 590	2,804	1,482	2,527	8,076	4,565	6,538	12,944	14,749
B. PORTFOLIO INVESTMENT	4 600	**−4,509**	**623**	**−11,379**	**15,702**	**5,553**	**−35,437**	**−2,179**	**−1,660**
Assets	4 602	**−2,180**	**−3,820**	**−10,666**	**6,248**	**−9,992**	**−7,843**	**−10,375**	**−3,470**
Equity securities	4 610	−47	−25	−733	116	−3,435	−135	−739	−1,447
Monetary authorities	4 611	....	....	10	....	....	....	....	....
General government	4 612	....	....	....	....	....	....	....	....
Banks	4 613	−21	−5	−272	214	−1,782	−7	−288	−815
Other sectors	4 614	−26	−21	−472	−98	−1,653	−128	−451	−633
Debt securities	4 619	−2,133	−3,794	−9,933	6,131	−6,557	−7,708	−9,636	−2,023
Bonds and notes	4 620	−1,773	−3,419	−9,285	5,298	−6,529	−6,497	−9,370	−1,324
Monetary authorities	4 621	−1,497	−1,584	−6,307	7,455	....	−6	....	....
General government	4 622	....	....	....	....	....	....	....	....
Banks	4 623	−304	−1,791	−2,634	−1,569	−3,533	−5,116	−8,658	−2,440
Other sectors	4 624	28	−44	−343	−588	−2,996	−1,375	−712	1,116
Money market instruments	4 630	−361	−375	−649	834	−28	−1,211	−265	−699
Monetary authorities	4 631	....	....	....	....	....	....	....	....
General government	4 632	....	....	....	....	....	....	....	....
Banks	4 633	−361	−313	−662	775	806	−449	181	−296
Other sectors	4 634	....	−63	13	59	−835	−763	−446	−403
Liabilities	4 652	**−2,329**	**4,443**	**−713**	**9,455**	**15,545**	**−27,594**	**8,195**	**1,810**
Equity securities	4 660	422	270	−100	6,480	18,675	−15,005	3,369	−4,808
Banks	4 663	65	−87	103	266	12,582	−2,585	1,946	1,255
Other sectors	4 664	357	357	−203	6,214	6,093	−12,421	1,423	−6,063
Debt securities	4 669	−2,750	4,173	−613	2,975	−3,130	−12,588	4,826	6,619
Bonds and notes	4 670	−2,453	3,905	−1,061	2,667	−4,011	−11,796	5,336	6,904
Monetary authorities	4 671	....	....	....	....	....	....	....	....
General government	4 672	−1,457	3,093	−1,914	−840	−3,995	−6,559	4,288	5,470
Banks	4 673	−214	363	−311	1,140	888	−927	394	447
Other sectors	4 674	−782	449	1,164	2,367	−904	−4,309	653	988
Money market instruments	4 680	−298	268	448	308	881	−793	−509	−286
Monetary authorities	4 681	....	....	....	....	....	....	....	....
General government	4 682	−31	2	....	....	....	....	....	....
Banks	4 683	−266	265	448	308	881	−793	−509	−286
Other sectors	4 684	....	....	....	....	....	....	....	....
C. FINANCIAL DERIVATIVES	4 910	**640**	**−100**	**−233**	**−99**	**332**	**−1,370**	**−3,244**	**−1,841**
Monetary authorities	4 911	497	....	....	....	....	....	....	....
General government	4 912	....	....	....	....	....	....	....	....
Banks	4 913	143	−100	−233	−99	332	−1,370	−2,971	−1,750
Other sectors	4 914	....	....	....	....	....	....	−273	−91
Assets	4 900	**1,017**	**758**	**858**	**1,242**	**2,762**	**9,117**	**9,890**	**8,840**
Monetary authorities	4 901	497	....	....	....	....	....	....	....
General government	4 902	....	....	....	....	....	....	....	....
Banks	4 903	520	758	858	1,242	2,762	9,117	9,791	7,510
Other sectors	4 904	....	....	....	....	....	....	99	1,330
Liabilities	4 905	**−377**	**−857**	**−1,091**	**−1,342**	**−2,430**	**−10,487**	**−13,134**	**−10,682**
Monetary authorities	4 906	....	....	....	....	....	....	....	....
General government	4 907	....	....	....	....	....	....	....	....
Banks	4 908	−377	−857	−1,091	−1,342	−2,430	−10,487	−12,761	−9,260
Other sectors	4 909	....	....	....	....	....	....	−373	−1,421

Table 2 (Concluded). STANDARD PRESENTATION, 2003–2010

(Millions of U.S. dollars)

	Code	2003	2004	2005	2006	2007	2008	2009	2010
D. OTHER INVESTMENT	4 700	**6,764**	**−8,968**	**9,012**	**−19,083**	**79,688**	**−114,276**	**−19,060**	**−12,824**
Assets	4 703	**−15,886**	**−26,644**	**−33,328**	**−49,422**	**−60,062**	**−177,515**	**6,141**	**−22,834**
Trade credits	4 706	−3,926	−546	−7,645	−616	−804	−8,129	5,902	−35
General government	4 707	86	110	66	9	100	11	1,201	28
of which: Short-term	4 709	....	....	....	....	....	....	....	....
Other sectors	4 710	−4,012	−656	−7,711	−626	−904	−8,141	4,701	−63
of which: Short-term	4 712	*−4,012*	*−656*	*−7,711*	*−626*	*−904*	*−8,141*	*4,701*	*−63*
Loans	4 714	4	1,189	−5,538	−27,982	−35,322	−54,318	7,420	−16,263
Monetary authorities	4 715	....	160	....	....	....	....	....	−50
of which: Short-term	4 718	*99*							
General government	4 719	2,306	804	931	−4,006	−1,594	−802	−2,092	493
of which: Short-term	4 721	....	....	....	....	....	....	....	....
Banks	4 722	−684	−1,269	−5,143	−10,053	−11,280	−26,767	3,681	−16,327
of which: Short-term	4 724	*−149*	*−2,025*	*−2,352*	*−6,788*	*−2,988*	*−17,333*	*11,804*	*−6,306*
Other sectors	4 725	−1,618	1,495	−1,326	−13,923	−22,448	−26,748	5,831	−379
of which: Short-term	4 727	*−1,221*	*1,362*	*142*	*−6,879*	*−7,019*	*−8,139*	*5,283*	*−1,972*
Currency and deposits	4 730	6,347	−1,470	−5,944	−3,201	3,033	−69,320	12,701	24,821
Monetary authorities	4 731	487	140	210	175	−477	−56	57	20
General government	4 732	−41	75	−441	−10	−11	−10	−4	....
Banks	4 733	449	−1,255	−4,901	−13,493	−10,409	−38,067	10,127	10,369
Other sectors	4 734	5,452	−430	−810	10,126	13,930	−31,188	2,521	14,432
Other assets	4 736	−18,310	−25,818	−14,201	−17,622	−26,970	−45,747	−19,881	−31,358
Monetary authorities	4 737	−20	6	−4	....	....	1	....	....
of which: Short-term	4 739	*−20*	*6*				*1*		
General government	4 740	−2,650	−1,227	10,923	2,668	8,747	−1,659	11,104	−833
of which: Short-term	4 742	*−2,621*	*−981*	*10,953*	*2,894*	*8,805*	*−998*	*11,142*	*−522*
Banks	4 743	−602	560	140	−488	−988	−1,989	−1,911	1,236
of which: Short-term	4 745	*−594*	*621*	*90*	*−415*	*−707*	*−999*	*−1,830*	*1,437*
Other sectors	4 746	−15,039	−25,157	−25,259	−19,802	−34,728	−42,100	−29,074	−31,761
of which: Short-term	4 748	*−6*	*−16*	*25*	*68*	*51*	*−2,845*	*−100*	*−287*
Liabilities	4 753	**22,650**	**17,676**	**42,340**	**30,340**	**139,751**	**63,239**	**−25,201**	**10,010**
Trade credits	4 756	....	....	....	....	....	....	626	53
General government	4 757	....	....	....	....	....	....	....	....
of which: Short-term	4 759	....	....	....	....	....	....	....	....
Other sectors	4 760	....	....	....	....	....	....	626	53
of which: Short-term	4 762							*626*	*53*
Loans	4 764	18,555	21,842	39,588	18,321	127,312	63,452	−31,985	−751
Monetary authorities	4 765	−380	−109	2,718	−7,395	....	−5	2,368	−2,364
of which: Use of Fund credit and loans from the Fund	4 766	*−1,897*	*−1,655*	*−3,506*					
of which: Short-term	4 768	*1,517*	*1,545*	*6,225*	*−7,395*	....	*−5*	*2,368*	*−2,364*
General government	4 769	−3,707	−1,220	−18,932	−23,880	−2,883	−1,505	−1,259	−1,112
of which: Short-term	4 771	....	....	....	....	....	....	....	....
Banks	4 772	7,513	6,991	14,901	32,756	39,395	15,608	−34,464	9,024
of which: Short-term	4 774	*3,978*	*1,729*	*73*	*9,159*	*5,900*	*−1,439*	*−11,509*	*6,086*
Other sectors	4 775	15,128	16,180	40,900	16,840	90,800	49,354	1,370	−6,298
of which: Short-term	4 777	*1,938*	*698*	*−620*	*3,216*	*29,618*	*−7,985*	*−6,350*	*−671*
Currency and deposits	4 780	3,864	−1,220	2,415	14,911	12,445	−2,734	−1,665	10,210
Monetary authorities	4 781	119	364	85	63	882	1,445	649	−39
General government	4 782	9	−1,426	−533	....	....	....	....	....
Banks	4 783	3,736	−158	2,864	14,847	11,564	−4,179	−2,314	10,249
Other sectors	4 784	....	....	....	....	....	....	....	....
Other liabilities	4 786	231	−2,946	337	−2,892	−7	2,521	7,823	498
Monetary authorities	4 787	....	....	....	....	....	....	8,871	....
of which: Short-term	4 789	....	....	....	....	....	....	....	....
General government	4 790	−7	−2,839	222	−3,173	−754	−33	−591	−53
of which: Short-term	4 792	*−1*	*−2,833*	*228*	*−3,166*	*−748*	*−33*	*−591*	*−53*
Banks	4 793	297	−123	322	668	809	1,456	−853	764
of which: Short-term	4 795	*321*	*−160*	*265*	*585*	*606*	*1,314*	*−779*	*680*
Other sectors	4 796	−58	16	−207	−388	−63	1,098	395	−214
of which: Short-term	4 798	*−58*	*16*	*−207*	*−388*	*−63*	*1,098*	*395*	*−214*
E. RESERVE ASSETS	4 802	**−26,365**	**−45,236**	**−61,461**	**−107,466**	**−148,928**	**38,919**	**−3,363**	**−36,749**
Monetary gold	4 812	....	....	....	....	....	....	....	....
Special drawing rights	4 811	1	....	−5	−1	7	....	−8,876	−4
Reserve position in the Fund	4 810	....	−1	−195	−77	−73	−663	−833	....
Foreign exchange	4 803	−26,365	−45,235	−61,261	−107,388	−148,861	39,582	6,346	−36,745
Other claims	4 813	....	....	....	....	....	....	....	....
NET ERRORS AND OMISSIONS	4 998	**−9,179**	**−5,870**	**−7,895**	**9,518**	**−13,347**	**−11,271**	**−1,724**	**−7,621**

Table 3. INTERNATIONAL INVESTMENT POSITION (End-period stocks), 2003–2010

(Millions of U.S. dollars)

	Code	2003	2004	2005	2006	2007	2008	2009	2010
ASSETS...	8 995 C.	**336,825**	**406,635**	**516,294**	**731,341**	**1,092,182**	**1,010,696**	**1,089,507**	**1,173,180**
Direct investment abroad.................................	8 505 ..	**90,873**	**107,291**	**146,679**	**216,474**	**370,129**	**205,547**	**302,542**	**369,076**
Equity capital and reinvested earnings.................	8 506 ..	86,532	100,402	139,046	213,535	355,713	189,379	276,830	321,709
Claims on affiliated enterprises.................	8 507 ..	86,532	100,402	139,046	213,535	355,713	189,379	276,830	321,709
Liabilities to affiliated enterprises.................	8 508 ..	....	....	....	....	....	....	....	....
Other capital....................................	8 530 ..	4,341	6,888	7,633	2,939	14,416	16,168	25,712	47,367
Claims on affiliated enterprises.................	8 535 ..	4,341	6,888	7,633	2,939	14,416	16,168	25,712	47,367
Liabilities to affiliated enterprises.................	8 540 ..	....	....	....	....	....	....	....	....
Portfolio investment.................................	8 602 ..	**4,383**	**7,922**	**17,772**	**12,268**	**19,894**	**24,182**	**38,116**	**37,300**
Equity securities....................................	8 610 ..	98	129	334	509	4,082	2,816	2,492	4,629
Monetary authorities....................................	8 611 ..	12	12	....	....	....	....	....	....
General government....................................	8 612 ..	....	....	....	....	....	....	....	....
Banks....................................	8 613 ..	24	33	272	271	2,053	1,512	1,561	2,737
Other sectors....................................	8 614 ..	62	84	61	238	2,029	1,305	931	1,892
Debt securities....................................	8 619 ..	4,285	7,793	17,438	11,759	15,812	21,366	35,623	32,671
Bonds and notes....................................	8 620 ..	4,024	7,056	16,000	10,421	14,230	19,032	32,860	30,190
Monetary authorities....................................	8 621 ..	2,330	3,923	10,223	2,992	....	....	2,364	....
General government....................................	8 622 ..	....	....	....	....	....	....	....	....
Banks....................................	8 623 ..	1,531	3,015	5,310	6,374	10,384	13,909	24,558	26,665
Other sectors....................................	8 624 ..	163	117	467	1,054	3,846	5,122	5,937	3,525
Money market instruments....................................	8 630 ..	260	738	1,438	1,338	1,581	2,334	2,764	2,481
Monetary authorities....................................	8 631 ..	....	....	....	....	....	....	....	....
General government....................................	8 632 ..	....	....	....	....	....	....	....	....
Banks....................................	8 633 ..	251	665	1,382	1,000	417	353	138	325
Other sectors....................................	8 634 ..	10	72	56	338	1,164	1,982	2,626	2,156
Financial derivatives.................................	8 900 ..	**55**	**153**	**51**	**222**	**1,423**	**5,302**	**2,240**	**1,639**
Monetary authorities....................................	8 901 ..	....	....	....	....	....	....	....	....
General government....................................	8 902 ..	....	....	....	....	....	....	....	....
Banks....................................	8 903 ..	55	153	51	222	1,423	5,302	2,222	1,609
Other sectors....................................	8 904 ..	....	....	....	....	....	....	18	30
Other investment.................................	8 703 ..	**164,576**	**166,728**	**169,553**	**198,645**	**221,973**	**349,383**	**307,163**	**285,790**
Trade credits....................................	8 706 ..	8,338	8,930	16,363	14,839	11,682	18,426	5,002	4,755
General government....................................	8 707 ..	1,746	1,720	1,626	1,637	1,573	1,552	355	310
of which: Short-term....................................	8 709 ..	....	....	....	....	....	....	....	....
Other sectors....................................	8 710 ..	6,591	7,210	14,737	13,203	10,109	16,875	4,648	4,445
of which: Short-term....................................	8 712 ..	*6,591*	*7,210*	*14,737*	*13,203*	*10,109*	*16,875*	*4,648*	*4,445*
Loans....................................	8 714 ..	24,511	23,831	29,007	57,675	93,361	139,752	127,877	136,304
Monetary authorities....................................	8 715 ..	153	....	....	....	....	....	....	49
of which: Short-term....................................	8 718 ..	....	....	....	....	....	....	....	....
General government....................................	8 719 ..	15,956	15,402	14,238	18,235	20,003	20,290	22,274	21,670
of which: Short-term....................................	8 721 ..	....	....	....	....	....	....	....	....
Banks....................................	8 722 ..	5,269	6,660	11,706	22,422	34,312	58,543	54,743	68,236
of which: Short-term....................................	8 724 ..	*2,930*	*5,073*	*7,306*	*14,302*	*17,714*	*33,556*	*21,984*	*25,208*
Other sectors....................................	8 725 ..	3,134	1,769	3,064	17,018	39,045	60,919	50,860	46,349
of which: Short-term....................................	8 727 ..	*1,720*	*482*	*430*	*7,483*	*14,258*	*20,724*	*14,426*	*15,185*
Currency and deposits....................................	8 730 ..	59,182	61,002	66,274	70,219	67,533	135,644	123,601	96,415
Monetary authorities....................................	8 731 ..	895	751	485	353	65	118	61	41
General government....................................	8 732 ..	95	42	475	487	513	561	20	22
Banks....................................	8 733 ..	12,343	13,816	18,271	32,294	43,463	80,944	71,883	59,522
Other sectors....................................	8 734 ..	45,849	46,394	47,044	37,084	23,491	54,021	51,638	36,831
Other assets....................................	8 736 ..	72,546	72,965	57,909	55,913	49,398	55,560	50,683	48,316
Monetary authorities....................................	8 737 ..	47	41	45	46	46	46	46	46
of which: Short-term....................................	8 739 ..	*9*	*3*	*2*	*2*	*3*	....	....	....
General government....................................	8 740 ..	67,231	68,568	55,532	53,096	44,476	46,102	37,235	37,870
of which: Short-term....................................	8 742 ..	*66,902*	*67,982*	*54,941*	*52,276*	*43,583*	*44,557*	*35,645*	*35,977*
Banks....................................	8 743 ..	1,349	828	692	1,198	2,256	3,849	5,797	4,453
of which: Short-term....................................	8 745 ..	*1,335*	*752*	*664*	*1,091*	*1,864*	*2,506*	*4,352*	*2,763*
Other sectors....................................	8 746 ..	3,919	3,528	1,640	1,573	2,620	5,564	7,605	5,946
of which: Short-term....................................	8 748 ..	*3,919*	*3,528*	*1,640*	*1,573*	*2,620*	*5,564*	*7,605*	*5,946*
Reserve assets.................................	8 802 ..	**76,938**	**124,541**	**182,240**	**303,732**	**478,762**	**426,283**	**439,447**	**479,374**
Monetary gold....................................	8 812 ..	3,763	3,732	6,349	8,164	12,012	14,533	22,798	35,788
Special drawing rights....................................	8 811 ..	1	1	6	7	1	1	8,897	8,744
Reserve position in the Fund....................................	8 810 ..	2	3	196	283	374	1,053	1,927	1,893
Foreign exchange....................................	8 803 ..	73,172	120,805	175,690	295,277	466,376	410,695	405,825	432,949
Other claims....................................	8 813 ..	....	....	....	....	....	....	....	....

Table 3 (Concluded). INTERNATIONAL INVESTMENT POSITION (End-period stocks), 2003–2010

(Millions of U.S. dollars)

	Code	2003	2004	2005	2006	2007	2008	2009	2010
LIABILITIES	8 995 D.	**332,901**	**417,270**	**547,861**	**770,134**	**1,242,781**	**755,906**	**986,079**	**1,157,495**
Direct investment in the Russian Federation	8 555	**96,729**	**122,295**	**180,228**	**265,873**	**491,052**	**215,756**	**378,837**	**493,354**
Equity capital and reinvested earnings	8 556	87,349	111,269	167,706	244,349	464,164	183,357	331,695	428,589
Claims on direct investors	8 557	....	....	....	....	....	....	....	....
Liabilities to direct investors	8 558	87,349	111,269	167,706	244,349	464,164	183,357	331,695	428,589
Other capital	8 580	9,380	11,026	12,522	21,524	26,888	32,398	47,142	64,765
Claims on direct investors	8 585	....	....	....	....	....	....	....	....
Liabilities to direct investors	8 590	9,380	11,026	12,522	21,524	26,888	32,398	47,142	64,765
Portfolio investment	8 652	**93,358**	**130,822**	**166,340**	**265,800**	**367,546**	**112,560**	**217,317**	**278,332**
Equity securities	8 660	57,982	89,218	118,297	207,881	308,911	84,527	178,100	232,846
Banks	8 663	1,108	1,927	5,032	13,870	35,800	8,602	22,415	30,433
Other sectors	8 664	56,874	87,291	113,265	194,011	273,111	75,925	155,685	202,414
Debt securities	8 669	35,376	41,605	48,043	57,919	58,634	28,034	39,217	45,486
Bonds and notes	8 670	34,598	40,573	46,856	56,392	56,171	26,478	38,179	44,760
Monetary authorities	8 671	....	....	....	....	....	....	....	....
General government	8 672	30,131	33,877	33,644	32,575	28,635	16,157	25,710	30,532
Banks	8 673	440	798	638	1,773	3,599	2,002	3,063	3,581
Other sectors	8 674	4,027	5,898	12,574	22,043	23,937	8,318	9,406	10,647
Money market instruments	8 680	778	1,032	1,188	1,528	2,463	1,556	1,038	726
Monetary authorities	8 681	....	....	....	....	....	....	....	....
General government	8 682	....	....	....	....	....	....	....	....
Banks	8 683	778	1,032	1,188	1,528	2,463	1,556	1,038	726
Other sectors	8 684	....	....	....	....	....	....	....	....
Financial derivatives	8 905	**31**	**189**	**52**	**178**	**875**	**10,396**	**5,205**	**2,840**
Monetary authorities	8 906	....	....	....	....	....	....	....	....
General government	8 907	....	....	....	....	....	....	....	....
Banks	8 908	31	189	52	178	875	10,396	5,082	2,814
Other sectors	8 909	....	....	....	....	....	....	123	26
Other investment	8 753	**142,783**	**163,964**	**201,240**	**238,283**	**383,309**	**417,194**	**384,720**	**382,968**
Trade credits	8 756	....	....	....	....	....	....	2,102	2,156
General government	8 757	....	....	....	....	....	....	....	....
of which: Short-term	8 759	....	....	....	....	....	....	....	....
Other sectors	8 760	....	....	....	....	....	....	2,102	2,156
of which: Short-term	8 762	....	....	....	....	....	....	*2,102*	*2,156*
Loans	8 764	119,575	146,027	180,313	205,195	334,521	373,751	335,600	325,073
Monetary authorities	8 765	7,459	7,503	10,158	2,985	....	....	2,370	....
of which: Use of Fund credit and loans from the Fund	8 766	*5,069*	*3,562*	....	....	....	....	....	....
of which: Short-term	8 768	*2,390*	*3,941*	*10,158*	*2,985*	....	....	*2,370*	....
General government	8 769	57,365	59,127	35,590	14,258	11,579	10,218	8,975	7,726
of which: Short-term	8 771	....	....	....	....	....	....	....	....
Banks	8 772	12,946	19,810	34,511	67,757	113,236	124,654	89,343	96,454
of which: Short-term	8 774	*6,566*	*8,157*	*8,161*	*17,558*	*23,853*	*21,256*	*9,135*	*14,480*
Other sectors	8 775	41,805	59,586	100,054	120,195	209,706	238,880	234,913	220,894
of which: Short-term	8 777	*4,486*	*6,274*	*5,542*	*10,439*	*40,772*	*22,386*	*15,145*	*13,834*
Currency and deposits	8 780	11,801	10,700	13,262	28,760	42,591	35,665	33,416	43,009
Monetary authorities	8 781	348	741	795	942	1,912	2,761	3,365	3,295
General government	8 782	1,818	283	24	25	26	26	26	27
Banks	8 783	9,635	9,676	12,443	27,793	40,653	32,878	30,026	39,688
Other sectors	8 784	....	....	....	....	....	....	....	....
Other liabilities	8 786	11,407	7,237	7,665	4,328	6,197	7,777	13,601	12,730
Monetary authorities	8 787	....	....	....	....	....	....	8,892	8,735
of which: Short-term	8 789	....	....	....	....	....	....	....	....
General government	8 790	10,453	6,342	6,485	2,412	1,688	1,624	436	422
of which: Short-term	8 792	*10,428*	*6,324*	*6,473*	*2,406*	*1,688*	*1,624*	*436*	*422*
Banks	8 793	943	885	1,169	1,901	2,879	3,502	2,245	2,250
of which: Short-term	8 795	*877*	*760*	*991*	*1,634*	*2,402*	*2,910*	*1,724*	*1,629*
Other sectors	8 796	11	10	10	15	1,630	2,651	2,029	1,323
of which: Short-term	8 798	*11*	*10*	*10*	*15*	*1,630*	*2,651*	*2,029*	*1,323*
NET INTERNATIONAL INVESTMENT POSITION	8 995	**3,924**	**–10,635**	**–31,566**	**–38,793**	**–150,600**	**254,790**	**103,429**	**15,685**
Conversion rates: rubles per U.S. dollar (end of period)	0 102	**29.455**	**27.749**	**28.783**	**26.331**	**24.546**	**29.380**	**30.244**	**30.477**

Table 1. ANALYTIC PRESENTATION, 2003–2010

(Millions of U.S. dollars)

	Code	2003	2004	2005	2006	2007	2008	2009	2010
A. Current Account[1]...........................	4 993 Z.	**−121**	**−198**	**−84**	**−180**	**−147**	**−252**	**−383**	**−421**
Goods: exports f.o.b........................	2 100 ..	63	98	128	145	184	257	188	297
Goods: imports f.o.b........................	3 100 ..	−229	−276	−355	−488	−637	−880	−961	−1,084
Balance on Goods........................	4 100 ..	*−166*	*−178*	*−227*	*−343*	*−452*	*−623*	*−772*	*−787*
Services: credit............................	2 200 ..	76	103	129	131	179	408	341	310
Services: debit.............................	3 200 ..	−204	−240	−304	−243	−272	−521	−519	−557
Balance on Goods and Services.........	4 991	*−293*	*−315*	*−402*	*−455*	*−545*	*−736*	*−950*	*−1,033*
Income: credit.............................	2 300 ..	6	6	27	27	48	28	15	13
Income: debit.............................	3 300 ..	−37	−39	−44	−48	−63	−62	−52	−59
Balance on Goods, Services, and Income......	4 992 ..	*−324*	*−349*	*−418*	*−476*	*−560*	*−771*	*−987*	*−1,079*
Current transfers: credit...................	2 379 Z.	223	169	352	319	435	558	655	714
Current transfers: debit...................	3 379 ..	−20	−18	−18	−23	−22	−40	−51	−56
B. Capital Account[1]...........................	4 994 Z.	**41**	**61**	**93**	**1,323**	**161**	**210**	**200**	**286**
Capital account: credit....................	2 994 Z.	41	61	93	1,323	161	210	200	286
Capital account: debit.....................	3 994 ..	....	....	....	....	....	....	....	....
Total, Groups A Plus B.....................	4 981 ..	*−80*	*−138*	*9*	*1,143*	*14*	*−42*	*−183*	*−136*
C. Financial Account[1]........................	4 995 W.	**−21**	**−21**	**−59**	**−1,204**	**35**	**−3**	**243**	**152**
Direct investment abroad.................	4 505 ..	....	....	....	14	13	....	....	....
Direct investment in Rwanda.............	4 555 Z.	5	8	8	11	67	103	119	42
Portfolio investment assets...............	4 602 ..	....	....	....	....	....	−19	....	....
Equity securities........................	4 610 ..	....	....	....	....	....	−19	....	....
Debt securities.........................	4 619 ..	....	....	....	....	....	....	....	....
Portfolio investment liabilities............	4 652 Z.	....	....	....	....	....	....	....	21
Equity securities........................	4 660 ..	....	....	....	....	....	....	....	21
Debt securities.........................	4 669 Z.	....	....	....	....	....	....	....	....
Financial derivatives.....................	4 910 ..	....	....	....	....	....	....	....	....
Financial derivatives assets...............	4 900 ..	....	....	....	....	....	....	....	....
Financial derivatives liabilities............	4 905 ..	....	....	....	....	....	....	....	....
Other investment assets..................	4 703 ..	−6	8	−14	−30	−13	−88	−19	−28
Monetary authorities....................	4 701 ..	....	....	....	....	....	....	....	....
General government....................	4 704 ..	....	....	....	....	....	....	....	....
Banks..................................	4 705 ..	−6	8	−14	−30	−13	−16	−19	−28
Other sectors..........................	4 728 ..	....	....	....	....	....	−72	....	....
Other investment liabilities..............	4 753 W.	−19	−37	−52	−1,199	−32	....	143	117
Monetary authorities....................	4 753 WA	−1	−3	−20	−26	−2	3	99	....
General government....................	4 753 ZB	−27	−32	−36	−1,172	−11	−7	−7	−10
Banks..................................	4 753 ZC	....	....	....	1	....	....	9	....
Other sectors..........................	4 753 ZD	9	−2	4	−3	−19	5	43	127
Total, Groups A Through C..................	4 983 ..	*−101*	*−159*	*−49*	*−60*	*49*	*−45*	*60*	*16*
D. Net Errors and Omissions.................	4 998 ..	**23**	**−9**	**26**	**87**	**4**	**−5**	**3**	**−6**
Total, Groups A Through D..................	4 984 ..	*−78*	*−168*	*−23*	*26*	*53*	*−51*	*63*	*10*
E. Reserves and Related Items..............	4 802 A.	**78**	**168**	**23**	**−26**	**−53**	**51**	**−63**	**−10**
Reserve assets..........................	4 802 ..	12	−99	−92	−31	−109	−59	−156	−72
Use of Fund credit and loans.............	4 766 ..	−1	−4	−8	−74	3	4	4	....
Exceptional financing....................	4 920 ..	67	271	123	78	52	106	89	62
Conversion rates: Rwanda francs per U.S. dollar...	0 101 ..	**537.655**	**577.449**	**557.823**	**551.710**	**546.955**	**546.849**	**568.281**	**583.131**

[1] Excludes components that have been classified in the categories of Group E.

Table 2. STANDARD PRESENTATION, 2003–2010

(Millions of U.S. dollars)

	Code	2003	2004	2005	2006	2007	2008	2009	2010
CURRENT ACCOUNT	4 993	−97	−35	−52	−180	−147	−252	−383	−421
A. GOODS	4 100	−166	−178	−227	−343	−452	−623	−772	−787
Credit	2 100	63	98	128	145	184	257	188	297
General merchandise: exports f.o.b.	2 110	63	98	128	145	184	257	188	297
Goods for processing: exports f.o.b.	2 150	....	....	....	....	....	....	....	....
Repairs on goods	2 160	....	....	....	....	....	....	....	....
Goods procured in ports by carriers	2 170	....	....	....	....	....	....	....	....
Nonmonetary gold	2 180	....	....	....	....	....	....	....	....
Debit	3 100	−229	−276	−355	−488	−637	−880	−961	−1,084
General merchandise: imports f.o.b.	3 110	−229	−276	−355	−488	−637	−881	−961	−1,080
Goods for processing: imports f.o.b.	3 150	....	....	....	....	....	....	....	....
Repairs on goods	3 160	....	....	....	....	....	....	....	....
Goods procured in ports by carriers	3 170	....	....	....	....	....	1	....	−4
Nonmonetary gold	3 180	....	....	....	....	....	....	....	....
B. SERVICES	4 200	−127	−137	−175	−112	−93	−113	−178	−246
Total credit	2 200	*76*	*103*	*129*	*131*	*179*	*408*	*341*	*310*
Total debit	3 200	*−204*	*−240*	*−304*	*−243*	*−272*	*−521*	*−519*	*−557*
Transportation services, credit	2 205	18	21	30	30	36	56	54	26
Passenger	2 850	....	....	....	....	*1*	....	*44*	*16*
Freight	2 851	*4*	*7*	*7*	*4*	*3*	*5*	*5*	*5*
Other	2 852	*14*	*15*	*23*	*26*	*32*	*51*	*5*	*6*
Sea transport, passenger	2 207	....	....	....	....	....	....	....	....
Sea transport, freight	2 208	....	....	....	....	....	....	....	....
Sea transport, other	2 209	....	....	....	....	....	5	....	....
Air transport, passenger	2 211	....	....	....	....	1	....	44	16
Air transport, freight	2 212	....	....	....	....	....	....	....	....
Air transport, other	2 213	....	....	....	....	....	9	5	6
Other transport, passenger	2 215	....	....	....	....	....	....	....	....
Other transport, freight	2 216	4	7	7	4	3	5	5	5
Other transport, other	2 217	14	15	23	26	32	38	....	....
Transportation services, debit	3 205	−78	−92	−135	−111	−86	−284	−318	−322
Passenger	3 850	....	....	....	....	....	*−34*	*−43*	*−17*
Freight	3 851	*−54*	*−65*	*−84*	*−58*	*−74*	*−217*	*−242*	*−294*
Other	3 852	*−24*	*−27*	*−51*	*−53*	*−12*	*−33*	*−33*	*−12*
Sea transport, passenger	3 207	....	....	....	....	....	....	....	....
Sea transport, freight	3 208	−18	−22	−28	−13	−15	−69	−81	−110
Sea transport, other	3 209	....	....	....	−2	−1	....	....	....
Air transport, passenger	3 211	....	....	....	....	....	−34	−43	−17
Air transport, freight	3 212	....	....	....	....	−14	−9	....	−23
Air transport, other	3 213	....	....	....	−1	−9	−33	−33	−12
Other transport, passenger	3 215	....	....	....	....	....	....	....	....
Other transport, freight	3 216	−36	−44	−56	−44	−44	−139	−161	−160
Other transport, other	3 217	−24	−27	−51	−51	−3	....	....	....
Travel, credit	2 236	30	44	49	31	65	202	174	202
Business travel	2 237	....	....	....	14	....	....	....	....
Personal travel	2 240	30	44	49	17	65	202	174	202
Travel, debit	3 236	−26	−31	−37	−35	−69	−70	−72	−77
Business travel	3 237	....	....	....	−12	−37	−35	−29	−37
Personal travel	3 240	−26	−31	−37	−23	−32	−35	−43	−40
Other services, credit	2 200 BA	28	38	51	70	78	150	113	82
Communications	2 245	....	....	4	1	3	....	....	14
Construction	2 249	....	....	....	....	....	....	6	....
Insurance	2 253	....	....	....	....	1	....	1	1
Financial	2 260	....	....	....	3	....	6	1	....
Computer and information	2 262	....	....	....	....	....	....	....	....
Royalties and licence fees	2 266	....	....	....	....	....	62	....	....
Other business services	2 268	....	....	....	8	20	....	12	....
Personal, cultural, and recreational	2 287	....	....	....	....	....	....	....	....
Government, n.i.e.	2 291	28	38	46	57	54	82	92	67
Other services, debit	3 200 BA	−99	−116	−132	−97	−117	−167	−129	−157
Communications	3 245	....	....	−4	−2	−3	−2	−4	−18
Construction	3 249	....	....	....	....	−3	−3	−4	−4
Insurance	3 253	....	....	....	−6	−2	−2	−4	−2
Financial	3 260	....	....	....	−9	....	....	....	−3
Computer and information	3 262	....	....	....	....	....	−1	....	−10
Royalties and licence fees	3 266	....	....	....	−1	....	....	−1	....
Other business services	3 268	....	....	....	−47	−97	−142	−100	−6
Personal, cultural, and recreational	3 287	....	....	....	−4	....	....	....	....
Government, n.i.e.	3 291	−99	−116	−128	−29	−13	−18	−15	−114

2011, International Monetary Fund: *Balance of Payments Statistics Yearbook*

Table 2 (Continued). STANDARD PRESENTATION, 2003–2010

(Millions of U.S. dollars)

	Code	2003	2004	2005	2006	2007	2008	2009	2010
C. INCOME	4 300	−31	−34	−16	−21	−15	−34	−37	−46
Total credit	2 300	*6*	*6*	*27*	*27*	*48*	*28*	*15*	*13*
Total debit	3 300	*−37*	*−39*	*−44*	*−48*	*−63*	*−62*	*−52*	*−59*
Compensation of employees, credit	2 310	....	....	12	4	23	4	4	5
Compensation of employees, debit	3 310	−14	−16	−21	−30	−48	−38	−36	−43
Investment income, credit	2 320	6	5	15	23	25	24	10	8
Direct investment income	2 330	....	....	2	1	....	2	....	....
Dividends and distributed branch profits	2 332	....	....	2	1	....	2	....	....
Reinvested earnings and undistributed branch profits	2 333	....	....	....	....	....	....	....	....
Income on debt (interest)	2 334	....	....	....	....	....	....	....	....
Portfolio investment income	2 339	....	....	....	....	....	....	....	....
Income on equity	2 340	....	....	....	....	....	....	....	....
Income on bonds and notes	2 350	....	....	....	....	....	....	....	....
Income on money market instruments	2 360	....	....	....	....	....	....	....	....
Other investment income	2 370	6	5	13	22	25	22	10	8
Investment income, debit	3 320	−22	−23	−23	−17	−15	−24	−15	−16
Direct investment income	3 330	−6	−3	−5	−4	−9	−15	−5	−4
Dividends and distributed branch profits	3 332	−6	−3	−5	−4	−8	−15	−5	−4
Reinvested earnings and undistributed branch profits	3 333	....	....	....	....	....	....	....	....
Income on debt (interest)	3 334	....	....	....	....	−1	....	....	....
Portfolio investment income	3 339	....	....	....	....	....	....	....	....
Income on equity	3 340	....	....	....	....	....	....	....	....
Income on bonds and notes	3 350	....	....	....	....	....	....	....	....
Income on money market instruments	3 360	....	....	....	....	....	....	....	....
Other investment income	3 370	−17	−21	−18	−14	−5	−9	−11	−12
D. CURRENT TRANSFERS	4 379	**226**	**314**	**366**	**296**	**413**	**518**	**604**	**657**
Credit	2 379	246	332	384	319	435	558	655	714
General government	2 380	197	281	322	210	313	450	416	480
Other sectors	2 390	49	51	62	109	122	108	239	234
Workers' remittances	2 391	9	10	9	17	28	63	88	98
Other current transfers	2 392	40	41	53	92	94	45	151	136
Debit	3 379	−20	−18	−18	−23	−22	−40	−51	−56
General government	3 380	−2	−2	−2	−3	−2	−4	−7	−13
Other sectors	3 390	−18	−16	−15	−21	−20	−36	−43	−43
Workers' remittances	3 391	−15	−15	−14	−17	−20	−32	−35	−33
Other current transfers	3 392	−3	−1	−1	−4	....	−4	−8	−10
CAPITAL AND FINANCIAL ACCOUNT	4 996	**75**	**44**	**26**	**93**	**143**	**257**	**380**	**427**
CAPITAL ACCOUNT	4 994	**41**	**61**	**93**	**1,323**	**161**	**210**	**200**	**286**
Total credit	2 994	*41*	*61*	*93*	*1,323*	*161*	*210*	*200*	*286*
Total debit	3 994	....	....	....	....	....	....	....	....
Capital transfers, credit	2 400	41	61	93	1,323	161	210	200	286
General government	2 401	41	61	93	1,323	161	210	200	286
Debt forgiveness	2 402	....	....	....	1,150	....	....	....	....
Other capital transfers	2 410	41	61	93	173	161	210	200	286
Other sectors	2 430	....	....	....	....	....	....	....	....
Migrants' transfers	2 431	....	....	....	....	....	....	....	....
Debt forgiveness	2 432	....	....	....	....	....	....	....	....
Other capital transfers	2 440	....	....	....	....	....	....	....	....
Capital transfers, debit	3 400	....	....	....	....	....	....	....	....
General government	3 401	....	....	....	....	....	....	....	....
Debt forgiveness	3 402	....	....	....	....	....	....	....	....
Other capital transfers	3 410	....	....	....	....	....	....	....	....
Other sectors	3 430	....	....	....	....	....	....	....	....
Migrants' transfers	3 431	....	....	....	....	....	....	....	....
Debt forgiveness	3 432	....	....	....	....	....	....	....	....
Other capital transfers	3 440	....	....	....	....	....	....	....	....
Nonproduced nonfinancial assets, credit	2 480	....	....	....	....	....	....	....	....
Nonproduced nonfinancial assets, debit	3 480	....	....	....	....	....	....	....	....

Table 2 (Continued). STANDARD PRESENTATION, 2003–2010

(Millions of U.S. dollars)

	Code	2003	2004	2005	2006	2007	2008	2009	2010
FINANCIAL ACCOUNT...	4 995 ..	33	−17	−67	−1,230	−18	47	180	142
A. DIRECT INVESTMENT...	4 500 ..	5	8	8	26	80	103	119	42
Direct investment abroad...............................	4 505 ..	....	....	....	14	13	....	....	....
Equity capital..	4 510 ..	....	....	....	14	13	....	....	....
Claims on affiliated enterprises..................	4 515 ..	....	....	....	14	13	....	....	....
Liabilities to affiliated enterprises..............	4 520 ..	....	....	....	....	....	....	....	....
Reinvested earnings....................................	4 525 ..	....	....	....	....	....	....	....	....
Other capital...	4 530 ..	....	....	....	....	....	....	....	....
Claims on affiliated enterprises..................	4 535 ..	....	....	....	....	....	....	....	....
Liabilities to affiliated enterprises..............	4 540 ..	....	....	....	....	....	....	....	....
Direct investment in Rwanda.......................	4 555 ..	5	8	8	11	67	103	119	42
Equity capital..	4 560 ..	5	8	8	11	67	103	119	42
Claims on direct investors.........................	4 565 ..	....	....	....	....	....	....	....	....
Liabilities to direct investors.....................	4 570 ..	5	8	8	11	67	103	119	42
Reinvested earnings....................................	4 575 ..	....	....	....	....	....	....	....	....
Other capital...	4 580 ..	....	....	....	....	....	....	....	....
Claims on direct investors.........................	4 585 ..	....	....	....	....	....	....	....	....
Liabilities to direct investors.....................	4 590 ..	....	....	....	....	....	....	....	....
B. PORTFOLIO INVESTMENT.................................	4 600 ..	....	...	....	....	....	−19	....	21
Assets..	4 602 ..	....	....	....	....	....	−19	....	....
Equity securities..	4 610 ..	....	....	....	....	....	−19	....	....
Monetary authorities.................................	4 611 ..	....	....	....	....	....	....	....	....
General government..................................	4 612 ..	....	....	....	....	....	....	....	....
Banks...	4 613 ..	....	....	....	....	....	....	....	....
Other sectors..	4 614 ..	....	....	....	....	....	−19	....	....
Debt securities..	4 619 ..	....	....	....	....	....	....	....	....
Bonds and notes.......................................	4 620 ..	....	....	....	....	....	....	....	....
Monetary authorities.............................	4 621 ..	....	....	....	....	....	....	....	....
General government..............................	4 622 ..	....	....	....	....	....	....	....	....
Banks..	4 623 ..	....	....	....	....	....	....	....	....
Other sectors...	4 624 ..	....	....	....	....	....	....	....	....
Money market instruments........................	4 630 ..	....	....	....	....	....	....	....	....
Monetary authorities.............................	4 631 ..	....	....	....	....	....	....	....	....
General government..............................	4 632 ..	....	....	....	....	....	....	....	....
Banks..	4 633 ..	....	....	....	....	....	....	....	....
Other sectors...	4 634 ..	....	....	....	....	....	....	....	....
Liabilities..	4 652 ..	....	....	....	....	....	....	....	21
Equity securities..	4 660 ..	....	....	....	....	....	....	....	21
Banks...	4 663 ..	....	....	....	....	....	....	....	....
Other sectors..	4 664 ..	....	....	....	....	....	....	....	21
Debt securities..	4 669 ..	....	....	....	....	....	....	....	....
Bonds and notes.......................................	4 670 ..	....	....	....	....	....	....	....	....
Monetary authorities.............................	4 671 ..	....	....	....	....	....	....	....	....
General government..............................	4 672 ..	....	....	....	....	....	....	....	....
Banks..	4 673 ..	....	....	....	....	....	....	....	....
Other sectors...	4 674 ..	....	....	....	....	....	....	....	....
Money market instruments........................	4 680 ..	....	....	....	....	....	....	....	....
Monetary authorities.............................	4 681 ..	....	....	....	....	....	....	....	....
General government..............................	4 682 ..	....	....	....	....	....	....	....	....
Banks..	4 683 ..	....	....	....	....	....	....	....	....
Other sectors...	4 684 ..	....	....	....	....	....	....	....	....
C. FINANCIAL DERIVATIVES...............................	4 910 ..	....	....	....	....	....	....	....	....
Monetary authorities...................................	4 911 ..	....	....	....	....	....	....	....	....
General government....................................	4 912 ..	....	....	....	....	....	....	....	....
Banks..	4 913 ..	....	....	....	....	....	....	....	....
Other sectors..	4 914 ..	....	....	....	....	....	....	....	....
Assets..	4 900 ..	....	....	....	....	....	....	....	....
Monetary authorities.................................	4 901 ..	....	....	....	....	....	....	....	....
General government..................................	4 902 ..	....	....	....	....	....	....	....	....
Banks...	4 903 ..	....	....	....	....	....	....	....	....
Other sectors..	4 904 ..	....	....	....	....	....	....	....	....
Liabilities..	4 905 ..	....	....	....	....	....	....	....	....
Monetary authorities.................................	4 906 ..	....	....	....	....	....	....	....	....
General government..................................	4 907 ..	....	....	....	....	....	....	....	....
Banks...	4 908 ..	....	....	....	....	....	....	....	....
Other sectors..	4 909 ..	....	....	....	....	....	....	....	....

Table 2 (Concluded). STANDARD PRESENTATION, 2003–2010

(Millions of U.S. dollars)

	Code	2003	2004	2005	2006	2007	2008	2009	2010
D. OTHER INVESTMENT	4 700	**17**	**75**	**16**	**−1,225**	**10**	**22**	**217**	**150**
Assets	4 703	**−6**	**8**	**−14**	**−30**	**−13**	**−88**	**−19**	**−28**
Trade credits	4 706	....	....	....	....	....	....	....	....
General government	4 707	....	....	....	....	....	....	....	....
of which: Short-term	4 709	....	....	....	....	....	....	....	....
Other sectors	4 710	....	....	....	....	....	....	....	....
of which: Short-term	4 712	....	....	....	....	....	....	....	....
Loans	4 714	....	....	....	....	....	....	....	....
Monetary authorities	4 715	....	....	....	....	....	....	....	....
of which: Short-term	4 718	....	....	....	....	....	....	....	....
General government	4 719	....	....	....	....	....	....	....	....
of which: Short-term	4 721	....	....	....	....	....	....	....	....
Banks	4 722	....	....	....	....	....	....	....	....
of which: Short-term	4 724	....	....	....	....	....	....	....	....
Other sectors	4 725	....	....	....	....	....	....	....	....
of which: Short-term	4 727	....	....	....	....	....	....	....	....
Currency and deposits	4 730	−6	8	−14	−30	−13	−16	−19	−28
Monetary authorities	4 731	....	....	....	....	....	....	....	....
General government	4 732	....	....	....	....	....	....	....	....
Banks	4 733	−6	8	−14	−30	−13	−16	−19	−28
Other sectors	4 734	....	....	....	....	....	....	....	....
Other assets	4 736	....	....	....	....	....	−72	....	....
Monetary authorities	4 737	....	....	....	....	....	....	....	....
of which: Short-term	4 739	....	....	....	....	....	....	....	....
General government	4 740	....	....	....	....	....	....	....	....
of which: Short-term	4 742	....	....	....	....	....	....	....	....
Banks	4 743	....	....	....	....	....	....	....	....
of which: Short-term	4 745	....	....	....	....	....	....	....	....
Other sectors	4 746	....	....	....	....	....	−72	....	....
of which: Short-term	4 748	....	....	....	....	....	−72	....	....
Liabilities	4 753	**24**	**67**	**31**	**−1,195**	**24**	**110**	**236**	**178**
Trade credits	4 756	5	5	9	4	10	−1	1	....
General government	4 757	5	5	....	....	....	....	....	....
of which: Short-term	4 759	*5*	*5*	....	....	....	....	....	....
Other sectors	4 760	....	....	9	4	10	−1	1	....
of which: Short-term	4 762	....	....	*9*	*4*	*10*	*−1*	*1*	....
Loans	4 764	13	66	41	−1,154	15	110	127	178
Monetary authorities	4 765	−1	−4	−8	−51	3	6	4	....
of which: Use of Fund credit and loans from the Fund	4 766	*−1*	*−4*	*−8*	*−74*	*3*	*4*	*4*	....
of which: Short-term	4 768	....	....	....	*23*	....	*2*	....	....
General government	4 769	8	71	54	−1,097	41	99	81	52
of which: Short-term	4 771	....	....	....	....	....	....	....	....
Banks	4 772	....	....	....	....	....	....	....	....
of which: Short-term	4 774	....	....	....	....	....	....	....	....
Other sectors	4 775	6	−2	−5	−7	−29	5	42	127
of which: Short-term	4 777	*2*	....	....	*−1*	*−33*	....	....	*10*
Currency and deposits	4 780	....	....	....	1	....	....	9	....
Monetary authorities	4 781	....	....	....	....	....	....	....	....
General government	4 782	....	....	....	....	....	....	....	....
Banks	4 783	....	....	....	1	....	....	9	....
Other sectors	4 784	....	....	....	....	....	....	....	....
Other liabilities	4 786	5	−4	−19	−46	−2	1	99	....
Monetary authorities	4 787	−1	−3	−20	−49	−2	1	99	....
of which: Short-term	4 789	*−1*	*−3*	*−20*	....	*−2*	*1*	....	....
General government	4 790	4	−1	1	2	....	....	....	....
of which: Short-term	4 792	*4*	*−1*	*1*	*2*	....	....	....	....
Banks	4 793	....	....	....	....	....	....	....	....
of which: Short-term	4 795	....	....	....	....	....	....	....	....
Other sectors	4 796	2	....	....	....	....	....	....	....
of which: Short-term	4 798	*2*	....	....	....	....	....	....	....
E. RESERVE ASSETS	4 802	**12**	**−99**	**−92**	**−31**	**−109**	**−59**	**−156**	**−72**
Monetary gold	4 812	....	....	....	....	....	....	....	....
Special drawing rights	4 811	−17	1	2	4	....	−8	−99	....
Reserve position in the Fund	4 810	....	....	....	....	....	....	....	....
Foreign exchange	4 803	29	−100	−94	−35	−109	−51	−57	−69
Other claims	4 813	....	....	....	....	....	....	....	−3
NET ERRORS AND OMISSIONS	4 998	**23**	**−9**	**26**	**87**	**4**	**−5**	**3**	**−6**

Table 3. INTERNATIONAL INVESTMENT POSITION (End-period stocks), 2003–2010

(Millions of U.S. dollars)

	Code	2003	2004	2005	2006	2007	2008	2009	2010
ASSETS	8 995 C.	**319**	**428**	**510**	**568**	**721**	**879**	**1,174**	**1,251**
Direct investment abroad	8 505 ..	....	....	**15**	....	**13**	**13**	**13**	**13**
Equity capital and reinvested earnings	8 506 ..	....	....	15	....	13	13	13	13
Claims on affiliated enterprises	8 507 ..	....	....	15	....	13	13	13	13
Liabilities to affiliated enterprises	8 508 ..	....	....	....	....	....	....	....	....
Other capital	8 530 ..	....	....	....	....	....	....	....	....
Claims on affiliated enterprises	8 535 ..	....	....	....	....	....	....	....	....
Liabilities to affiliated enterprises	8 540 ..	....	....	....	....	....	....	....	....
Portfolio investment	8 602 ..	....	....	....	....	....	**19**	**19**	**19**
Equity securities	8 610 ..	....	....	....	....	....	19	19	19
Monetary authorities	8 611 ..	....					....		
General government	8 612 ..	....					....		
Banks	8 613 ..	....					....		
Other sectors	8 614 ..	....					19	19	19
Debt securities	8 619 ..	....							
Bonds and notes	8 620 ..	....							
Monetary authorities	8 621 ..	....							
General government	8 622 ..	....							
Banks	8 623 ..	....							
Other sectors	8 624 ..	....							
Money market instruments	8 630 ..	....							
Monetary authorities	8 631 ..	....							
General government	8 632 ..	....							
Banks	8 633 ..	....							
Other sectors	8 634 ..	....							
Financial derivatives	8 900 ..	....	....	....	....	....	....	....	....
Monetary authorities	8 901 ..	....							
General government	8 902 ..	....							
Banks	8 903 ..	....							
Other sectors	8 904 ..	....							
Other investment	8 703 ..	**76**	**84**	**94**	**128**	**160**	**247**	**249**	**258**
Trade credits	8 706 ..	....	....	....	....	....	....	....	....
General government	8 707 ..	....							
of which: Short-term	8 709 ..	....							
Other sectors	8 710 ..	....							
of which: Short-term	8 712 ..	....							
Loans	8 714 ..	....							
Monetary authorities	8 715 ..	....							
of which: Short-term	8 718 ..	....							
General government	8 719 ..	....							
of which: Short-term	8 721 ..	....							
Banks	8 722 ..	....							
of which: Short-term	8 724 ..	....							
Other sectors	8 725 ..	....							
of which: Short-term	8 727 ..	....							
Currency and deposits	8 730 ..	76	84	94	128	160	174	177	186
Monetary authorities	8 731 ..	....							
General government	8 732 ..	....	....	....	....	....	....	....	....
Banks	8 733 ..	76	84	94	128	160	174	177	186
Other sectors	8 734 ..	....					....	....	....
Other assets	8 736 ..	....					72	72	72
Monetary authorities	8 737 ..	....							
of which: Short-term	8 739 ..	....							
General government	8 740 ..	....							
of which: Short-term	8 742 ..	....							
Banks	8 743 ..	....							
of which: Short-term	8 745 ..	....							
Other sectors	8 746 ..	....					72	72	72
of which: Short-term	8 748 ..	....	....	....	....	....	*72*	*72*	*72*
Reserve assets	8 802 ..	**243**	**344**	**401**	**440**	**549**	**600**	**893**	**961**
Monetary gold	8 812 ..	....	....	....	....	....	....	....	....
Special drawing rights	8 811 ..	30	30	26	23	24	31	131	129
Reserve position in the Fund	8 810 ..	....	....	....	....	....	....	....	....
Foreign exchange	8 803 ..	213	314	375	417	525	569	762	832
Other claims	8 813 ..	....	....	....	....	....	....	....	....

Table 3 (Concluded). INTERNATIONAL INVESTMENT POSITION (End-period stocks), 2003–2010

(Millions of U.S. dollars)

	Code	2003	2004	2005	2006	2007	2008	2009	2010
LIABILITIES	8 995 D.	**1,646**	**1,802**	**1,698**	**672**	**856**	**1,051**	**1,423**	**1,668**
Direct investment in Rwanda	8 555	**62**	**69**	**77**	**103**	**170**	**274**	**392**	**435**
Equity capital and reinvested earnings	8 556	62	69	77	103	170	274	392	435
Claims on direct investors	8 557	....	....	....	....	....	....	....	....
Liabilities to direct investors	8 558	62	69	77	103	170	274	392	435
Other capital	8 580	....	....	....	....	....	....	....	....
Claims on direct investors	8 585	....	....	....	....	....	....	....	....
Liabilities to direct investors	8 590	....	....	....	....	....	....	....	....
Portfolio investment	8 652	....	....	....	....	....	....	....	**21**
Equity securities	8 660	....	....	....	....	....	....	....	21
Banks	8 663	....	....	....	....	....	....	....	....
Other sectors	8 664	....	....	....	....	....	....	....	21
Debt securities	8 669	....	....	....	....	....	....	....	....
Bonds and notes	8 670	....	....	....	....	....	....	....	....
Monetary authorities	8 671	....	....	....	....	....	....	....	....
General government	8 672	....	....	....	....	....	....	....	....
Banks	8 673	....	....	....	....	....	....	....	....
Other sectors	8 674	....	....	....	....	....	....	....	....
Money market instruments	8 680	....	....	....	....	....	....	....	....
Monetary authorities	8 681	....	....	....	....	....	....	....	....
General government	8 682	....	....	....	....	....	....	....	....
Banks	8 683	....	....	....	....	....	....	....	....
Other sectors	8 684	....	....	....	....	....	....	....	....
Financial derivatives	8 905	....	....	....	....	....	....	....	....
Monetary authorities	8 906	....	....	....	....	....	....	....	....
General government	8 907	....	....	....	....	....	....	....	....
Banks	8 908	....	....	....	....	....	....	....	....
Other sectors	8 909	....	....	....	....	....	....	....	....
Other investment	8 753	**1,585**	**1,733**	**1,621**	**569**	**686**	**777**	**1,030**	**1,212**
Trade credits	8 756	18	23	....	....	10	6	7	7
General government	8 757	18	23	....	....	....	....	....	....
of which: Short-term	8 759	*18*	*23*	....	....	....	....	....	....
Other sectors	8 760	....	....	....	....	10	6	7	7
of which: Short-term	8 762	....	....	....	....	*10*	*6*	*7*	*7*
Loans	8 764	1,540	1,686	1,523	519	610	723	850	1,028
Monetary authorities	8 765	92	92	77	4	8	11	15	15
of which: Use of Fund credit and loans from the Fund	8 766	*92*	*92*	*77*	*4*	*8*	*11*	*15*	*15*
of which: Short-term	8 768	....	....	....	....	....	....	....	....
General government	8 769	1,430	1,578	1,446	486	574	678	759	811
of which: Short-term	8 771	....	....	....	....	....	....	....	....
Banks	8 772	....	....	....	....	....	....	....	....
of which: Short-term	8 774	....	....	....	....	....	....	....	....
Other sectors	8 775	18	16	....	29	27	34	76	202
of which: Short-term	8 777	....	....	....	*29*	*27*	*34*	*34*	*44*
Currency and deposits	8 780	....	....	98	49	66	48	52	58
Monetary authorities	8 781	....	....	78	30	35	14	13	15
General government	8 782	....	....	....	....	....	....	....	....
Banks	8 783	....	....	20	20	32	34	39	42
Other sectors	8 784	....	....	....	....	....	....	....	....
Other liabilities	8 786	27	23	....	....	....	....	120	118
Monetary authorities	8 787	25	21	....	....	....	....	120	118
of which: Short-term	8 789	*25*	*21*	....	....	....	....	....	....
General government	8 790	....	....	....	....	....	....	....	....
of which: Short-term	8 792	....	....	....	....	....	....	....	....
Banks	8 793	....	....	....	....	....	....	....	....
of which: Short-term	8 795	....	....	....	....	....	....	....	....
Other sectors	8 796	2	2	....	....	....	....	....	....
of which: Short-term	8 798	*2*	*2*	....	....	....	....	....	....
NET INTERNATIONAL INVESTMENT POSITION	8 995	**−1,327**	**−1,374**	**−1,188**	**−104**	**−135**	**−172**	**−249**	**−417**
Conversion rates: Rwanda francs per U.S. dollar (end of period)	0 102	580.280	566.860	553.719	548.650	544.220	558.898	571.240	594.450

Table 1. ANALYTIC PRESENTATION, 2003–2010

(Millions of U.S. dollars)

	Code	2003	2004	2005	2006	2007	2008	2009	2010
A. Current Account[1]	4 993 Z.	**−115.79**	**−68.38**	**−64.72**	**−85.11**	**−111.27**	**−175.19**	**−152.72**	**−96.02**
Goods: exports f.o.b.	2 100 ..	57.30	58.79	63.51	58.29	57.70	68.96	53.76	57.94
Goods: imports f.o.b.	3 100 ..	−175.64	−160.82	−185.21	−219.57	−239.52	−285.84	−250.88	−200.69
Balance on Goods	4 100 ..	*−118.34*	*−102.03*	*−121.70*	*−161.29*	*−181.82*	*−216.88*	*−197.12*	*−142.74*
Services: credit	2 200 ..	107.88	135.16	163.15	177.42	173.00	161.10	131.88	125.06
Services: debit	3 200 ..	−80.17	−80.83	−94.92	−101.12	−101.64	−120.11	−99.74	−89.80
Balance on Goods and Services	4 991 ..	*−90.63*	*−47.70*	*−53.47*	*−84.98*	*−110.47*	*−175.88*	*−164.98*	*−107.49*
Income: credit	2 300 ..	5.68	7.57	10.68	13.28	14.74	10.02	10.49	9.69
Income: debit	3 300 ..	−49.44	−46.47	−45.82	−45.62	−44.72	−42.46	−43.86	−41.20
Balance on Goods, Services, and Income	4 992 ..	*−134.38*	*−86.60*	*−88.61*	*−117.32*	*−140.45*	*−208.31*	*−198.35*	*−139.00*
Current transfers: credit	2 379 Z.	30.02	31.09	36.79	44.88	43.88	51.09	60.77	57.34
Current transfers: debit	3 379 ..	−11.43	−12.87	−12.90	−12.67	−14.70	−17.96	−15.15	−14.36
B. Capital Account[1]	4 994 Z.	**5.37**	**5.38**	**14.72**	**13.32**	**14.18**	**22.29**	**8.79**	**7.66**
Capital account: credit	2 994 Z.	5.57	5.57	14.95	13.55	14.43	22.56	9.06	7.92
Capital account: debit	3 994 ..	−.19	−.19	−.22	−.22	−.25	−.27	−.27	−.26
Total, Groups A Plus B	4 981 ..	*−110.42*	*−63.00*	*−49.99*	*−71.78*	*−97.09*	*−152.90*	*−143.94*	*−88.36*
C. Financial Account[1]	4 995 W.	**102.75**	**85.70**	**35.19**	**83.18**	**101.59**	**160.93**	**201.00**	**144.17**
Direct investment abroad	4 505 ..	....	....	....	....	....	....	....	....
Direct investment in St. Kitts and Nevis	4 555 Z.	75.61	55.77	92.99	110.42	134.48	177.91	130.75	128.01
Portfolio investment assets	4 602 ..	−.01	−.39	....	−1.78	−.01	....	−.08	....
Equity securities	4 610 ..	....	....	....	....	....	....	....	....
Debt securities	4 619 ..	....	....	....	....	....	....	....	....
Portfolio investment liabilities	4 652 Z.	48.03	−9.45	−15.02	−19.19	−12.96	10.48	−10.53	−9.82
Equity securities	4 660 ..	....	....	....	....	....	....	....	....
Debt securities	4 669 Z.	....	....	....	....	....	....	....	....
Financial derivatives	4 910 ..	....	....	....	....	....	....	....	....
Financial derivatives assets	4 900 ..	....	....	....	....	....	....	....	....
Financial derivatives liabilities	4 905 ..	....	....	....	....	....	....	....	....
Other investment assets	4 703 ..	−39.53	−23.18	−45.97	−18.88	−42.57	−63.37	−14.38	−13.71
Monetary authorities	4 701 ..	....	....	....	....	....	....	....	....
General government	4 704 ..	....	....	....	....	....	....	....	....
Banks	4 705 ..	−33.25	....	−39.97	−13.08	−29.81	−55.42	....	....
Other sectors	4 728 ..	−6.28	−23.18	−6.00	−5.81	−12.76	−7.95	−14.38	−13.71
Other investment liabilities	4 753 W.	18.65	62.94	3.19	12.61	22.65	35.93	95.24	39.70
Monetary authorities	4 753 WA	....	....	....	....	....	....	13.30	....
General government	4 753 ZB	....	....	....	....	....	....	....	....
Banks	4 753 ZC	....	56.32	....	....	....	....	64.25	25.83
Other sectors	4 753 ZD	18.65	6.62	3.19	12.61	22.65	35.93	17.69	13.87
Total, Groups A Through C	4 983 ..	*−7.66*	*22.70*	*−14.80*	*11.39*	*4.50*	*8.03*	*57.07*	*55.81*
D. Net Errors and Omissions	4 998 ..	**6.70**	**−9.05**	**8.12**	**5.75**	**2.68**	**6.70**	**−34.49**	**−23.12**
Total, Groups A Through D	4 984 ..	*−.96*	*13.64*	*−6.68*	*17.15*	*7.18*	*14.73*	*22.58*	*32.69*
E. Reserves and Related Items	4 802 A.	**.96**	**−13.64**	**6.68**	**−17.15**	**−7.18**	**−14.73**	**−22.58**	**−32.69**
Reserve assets	4 802 ..	.96	−13.64	6.68	−17.15	−7.18	−14.73	−25.96	−32.69
Use of Fund credit and loans	4 766 ..	....	....	....	....	....	....	3.38	....
Exceptional financing	4 920 ..	....	....	....	....	....	....	....	....
Conversion rates: Eastern Caribbean dollars per U.S. dollar	0 101 ..	**2.7000**	**2.7000**	**2.7000**	**2.7000**	**2.7000**	**2.7000**	**2.7000**	**2.7000**

[1] Excludes components that have been classified in the categories of Group E.

Table 2. STANDARD PRESENTATION, 2003–2010

(Millions of U.S. dollars)

	Code	2003	2004	2005	2006	2007	2008	2009	2010
CURRENT ACCOUNT..	4 993 ..	**−115.79**	**−68.38**	**−64.72**	**−85.11**	**−111.27**	**−175.19**	**−152.72**	**−96.02**
A. GOODS...	4 100 ..	**−118.34**	**−102.03**	**−121.70**	**−161.29**	**−181.82**	**−216.88**	**−197.12**	**−142.74**
Credit...	2 100 ..	**57.30**	**58.79**	**63.51**	**58.29**	**57.70**	**68.96**	**53.76**	**57.94**
General merchandise: exports f.o.b...........	2 110 ..	54.89	54.65	58.14	53.07	51.64	62.71	47.61	51.31
Goods for processing: exports f.o.b.........	2 150 ..	....	....	....	....	....	....	....	....
Repairs on goods...................................	2 160 ..	.02	.04	.07	.07	.07	.10	.20	.21
Goods procured in ports by carriers.........	2 170 ..	2.39	4.10	5.31	5.14	5.99	6.16	5.96	6.42
Nonmonetary gold.................................	2 180 ..	....	....	....	....	....	....	....	....
Debit...	3 100 ..	**−175.64**	**−160.82**	**−185.21**	**−219.57**	**−239.52**	**−285.84**	**−250.88**	**−200.69**
General merchandise: imports f.o.b..........	3 110 ..	−175.64	−160.82	−185.21	−219.57	−239.52	−285.84	−250.88	−200.69
Goods for processing: imports f.o.b.........	3 150 ..	....	....	....	....	....	....	....	....
Repairs on goods...................................	3 160 ..	....	....	....	....	....	....	....	....
Goods procured in ports by carriers.........	3 170 ..	....	....	....	....	....	....	....	....
Nonmonetary gold.................................	3 180 ..	....	....	....	....	....	....	....	....
B. SERVICES...	4 200 ..	**27.72**	**54.33**	**68.23**	**76.31**	**71.35**	**41.00**	**32.13**	**35.25**
Total credit..	2 200 ..	*107.88*	*135.16*	*163.15*	*177.42*	*173.00*	*161.10*	*131.88*	*125.06*
Total debit...	3 200 ..	*−80.17*	*−80.83*	*−94.92*	*−101.12*	*−101.64*	*−120.11*	*−99.74*	*−89.80*
Transportation services, credit............	2 205 ..	**9.93**	**9.78**	**11.16**	**12.08**	**13.05**	**13.91**	**16.66**	**11.47**
Passenger..	2 850 ..	....	....	....	....	....	....	....	....
Freight..	2 851 ..	....	....	....	....	....	....	....	....
Other..	2 852 ..	....	....	....	....	....	....	....	....
Sea transport, passenger.....................	2 207 ..	....	....	....	....	....	....	....	....
Sea transport, freight..........................	2 208 ..	....	....	....	....	....	....	....	....
Sea transport, other............................	2 209 ..	....	....	....	....	....	....	....	....
Air transport, passenger......................	2 211 ..	....	....	....	....	....	....	....	....
Air transport, freight...........................	2 212 ..	....	....	....	....	....	....	....	....
Air transport, other.............................	2 213 ..	....	....	....	....	....	....	....	....
Other transport, passenger..................	2 215 ..	....	....	....	....	....	....	....	....
Other transport, freight.......................	2 216 ..	....	....	....	....	....	....	....	....
Other transport, other.........................	2 217 ..	....	....	....	....	....	....	....	....
Transportation services, debit.............	3 205 ..	**−32.88**	**−33.00**	**−38.16**	**−43.76**	**−42.98**	**−58.42**	**−44.21**	**−37.69**
Passenger..	3 850 ..	....	....	....	....	....	....	....	....
Freight..	3 851 ..	....	....	....	....	....	....	....	....
Other..	3 852 ..	....	....	....	....	....	....	....	....
Sea transport, passenger.....................	3 207 ..	....	....	....	....	....	....	....	....
Sea transport, freight..........................	3 208 ..	....	....	....	....	....	....	....	....
Sea transport, other............................	3 209 ..	....	....	....	....	....	....	....	....
Air transport, passenger......................	3 211 ..	....	....	....	....	....	....	....	....
Air transport, freight...........................	3 212 ..	....	....	....	....	....	....	....	....
Air transport, other.............................	3 213 ..	....	....	....	....	....	....	....	....
Other transport, passenger..................	3 215 ..	....	....	....	....	....	....	....	....
Other transport, freight.......................	3 216 ..	....	....	....	....	....	....	....	....
Other transport, other.........................	3 217 ..	....	....	....	....	....	....	....	....
Travel, credit..................................	2 236 ..	**75.35**	**102.64**	**121.15**	**131.65**	**124.79**	**110.06**	**83.49**	**82.30**
Business travel....................................	2 237 ..	....	....	....	....	....	....	....	....
Personal travel....................................	2 240 ..	....	....	....	....	....	....	....	....
Travel, debit...................................	3 236 ..	**−8.14**	**−9.68**	**−10.96**	**−13.53**	**−12.49**	**−14.51**	**−10.62**	**−10.07**
Business travel....................................	3 237 ..	....	....	....	....	....	....	....	....
Personal travel....................................	3 240 ..	....	....	....	....	....	....	....	....
Other services, credit.......................	2 200 BA ..	**22.60**	**22.74**	**30.83**	**33.70**	**35.16**	**37.13**	**31.74**	**31.29**
Communications..................................	2 245 ..	3.66	4.28	4.72	5.28	6.59	7.09	4.37	4.42
Construction.......................................	2 249 ..	.06	.25	.38	.19	.31	.41	.49	.47
Insurance...	2 253 ..	1.93	1.91	2.77	2.91	3.21	2.57	1.81	1.72
Financial..	2 260 ..	....	....	....	....	....	....	....	....
Computer and information...................	2 262 ..	....	....	....	....	....	....	....	....
Royalties and licence fees....................	2 266 ..	.11	....	....	....	....	....	....	....
Other business services.......................	2 268 ..	12.76	12.22	18.17	19.59	19.80	21.19	19.39	18.95
Personal, cultural, and recreational.......	2 287 ..	....	....	....	....	....	....	....	....
Government, n.i.e................................	2 291 ..	4.09	4.08	4.78	5.73	5.24	5.87	5.67	5.73
Other services, debit........................	3 200 BA ..	**−39.15**	**−38.15**	**−45.79**	**−43.83**	**−46.17**	**−47.18**	**−44.91**	**−42.05**
Communications..................................	3 245 ..	−1.78	−2.82	−3.24	−3.56	−3.83	−4.14	−3.55	−3.37
Construction.......................................	3 249 ..	−4.75	−1.47	−3.82	−1.89	−3.14	−4.14	−4.92	−4.97
Insurance...	3 253 ..	−9.46	−8.66	−10.98	−10.26	−11.68	−14.60	−12.32	−10.83
Financial..	3 260 ..	....	....	....	....	....	....	....	....
Computer and information...................	3 262 ..	....	−.03	−.03	−.03	−.01	−.04	−.12	−.11
Royalties and licence fees....................	3 266 ..	−1.28	−1.85	−2.02	−1.75	−1.78	−2.21	−1.62	−1.53
Other business services.......................	3 268 ..	−16.25	−18.78	−21.12	−21.68	−22.37	−18.12	−19.28	−18.22
Personal, cultural, and recreational.......	3 287 ..	....	....	....	....	....	....	....	....
Government, n.i.e................................	3 291 ..	−5.63	−4.54	−4.57	−4.65	−3.36	−3.91	−3.10	−3.01

Table 2 (Continued). STANDARD PRESENTATION, 2003–2010

(Millions of U.S. dollars)

	Code	2003	2004	2005	2006	2007	2008	2009	2010
C. INCOME............	4 300	**−43.76**	**−38.90**	**−35.14**	**−32.34**	**−29.98**	**−32.44**	**−33.37**	**−31.51**
Total credit...........	2 300	*5.68*	*7.57*	*10.68*	*13.28*	*14.74*	*10.02*	*10.49*	*9.69*
Total debit...........	3 300	*−49.44*	*−46.47*	*−45.82*	*−45.62*	*−44.72*	*−42.46*	*−43.86*	*−41.20*
Compensation of employees, credit...........	2 310	**.29**	**.24**	**.29**	**.26**	**.28**	**.23**	**.22**	**.23**
Compensation of employees, debit...........	3 310	**−3.59**	**−3.10**	**−2.63**	**−1.06**	**−.79**	**−.78**	**−.76**	**−.72**
Investment income, credit...........	2 320	**5.39**	**7.33**	**10.39**	**13.03**	**14.45**	**9.79**	**10.27**	**9.47**
Direct investment income...........	2 330	.16	.13	.06	.06	.02	.02	.02	.02
Dividends and distributed branch profits...........	2 332	.16	.13	.06	.06	.02	.02	.02	.02
Reinvested earnings and undistributed branch profits.....	2 333	....	....	....	....	....	....	....	....
Income on debt (interest)...........	2 334	....	....	....	....	....	....	....	....
Portfolio investment income...........	2 339	.34	.28	.07	1.21	1.81	1.49	1.18	.91
Income on equity...........	2 340	.34	.28	.07	1.21	1.81	1.49	1.18	.91
Income on bonds and notes...........	2 350	....	....	....	....	....	....	....	....
Income on money market instruments...........	2 360	....	....	....	....	....	....	....	....
Other investment income...........	2 370	4.89	6.92	10.26	11.75	12.62	8.28	9.07	8.53
Investment income, debit...........	3 320	**−45.84**	**−43.37**	**−43.19**	**−44.57**	**−43.93**	**−41.68**	**−43.10**	**−40.48**
Direct investment income...........	3 330	−22.98	−19.53	−20.30	−20.18	−24.04	−23.42	−20.34	−19.31
Dividends and distributed branch profits...........	3 332	−12.52	−13.69	−14.88	−15.35	−18.57	−18.70	−17.55	−16.64
Reinvested earnings and undistributed branch profits.....	3 333	−4.22	−3.60	−3.15	−2.36	−2.43	−2.08	−2.28	−2.16
Income on debt (interest)...........	3 334	−6.24	−2.24	−2.27	−2.46	−3.04	−2.64	−.51	−.51
Portfolio investment income...........	3 339	−11.57	−13.07	−12.39	−12.58	−10.00	−7.62	−8.61	−6.04
Income on equity...........	3 340	−11.57	−13.07	−12.39	−12.58	−10.00	−7.62	−8.61	−6.04
Income on bonds and notes...........	3 350	....	....	....	....	....	....	....	....
Income on money market instruments...........	3 360	....	....	....	....	....	....	....	....
Other investment income...........	3 370	−11.29	−10.76	−10.49	−11.81	−9.89	−10.63	−14.15	−15.13
D. CURRENT TRANSFERS...........	4 379	**18.59**	**18.22**	**23.89**	**32.21**	**29.18**	**33.12**	**45.62**	**42.98**
Credit...........	2 379	**30.02**	**31.09**	**36.79**	**44.88**	**43.88**	**51.09**	**60.77**	**57.34**
General government...........	2 380	2.73	2.13	6.13	11.71	7.59	10.37	20.63	16.78
Other sectors...........	2 390	27.29	28.96	30.66	33.17	36.29	40.72	40.15	40.56
Workers' remittances...........	2 391	26.52	28.21	29.98	32.58	35.84	39.87	38.58	38.98
Other current transfers...........	2 392	.76	.75	.68	.59	.45	.85	1.56	1.58
Debit...........	3 379	**−11.43**	**−12.87**	**−12.90**	**−12.67**	**−14.70**	**−17.96**	**−15.15**	**−14.36**
General government...........	3 380	−3.19	−3.47	−3.09	−3.09	−3.00	−5.76	−4.74	−4.49
Other sectors...........	3 390	−8.23	−9.40	−9.80	−9.58	−11.71	−12.20	−10.41	−9.86
Workers' remittances...........	3 391	−3.73	−4.57	−4.88	−4.31	−4.85	−5.39	−4.97	−4.71
Other current transfers...........	3 392	−4.50	−4.83	−4.93	−5.27	−6.85	−6.81	−5.43	−5.15
CAPITAL AND FINANCIAL ACCOUNT...........	4 996	**109.09**	**77.43**	**56.59**	**79.35**	**108.59**	**168.50**	**187.21**	**119.14**
CAPITAL ACCOUNT...........	4 994	**5.37**	**5.38**	**14.72**	**13.32**	**14.18**	**22.29**	**8.79**	**7.66**
Total credit...........	2 994	*5.57*	*5.57*	*14.95*	*13.55*	*14.43*	*22.56*	*9.06*	*7.92*
Total debit...........	3 994	*−.19*	*−.19*	*−.22*	*−.22*	*−.25*	*−.27*	*−.27*	*−.26*
Capital transfers, credit...........	2 400	**5.38**	**5.57**	**14.95**	**13.46**	**14.43**	**22.56**	**9.06**	**7.92**
General government...........	2 401	2.26	2.71	11.69	9.89	10.30	18.17	4.39	3.20
Debt forgiveness...........	2 402	....	....	....	....	....	....	....	....
Other capital transfers...........	2 410	2.26	2.71	11.69	9.89	10.30	18.17	4.39	3.20
Other sectors...........	2 430	3.12	2.86	3.26	3.57	4.13	4.39	4.67	4.71
Migrants' transfers...........	2 431	3.12	2.86	3.26	3.57	4.13	4.39	4.67	4.71
Debt forgiveness...........	2 432	....	....	....	....	....	....	....	....
Other capital transfers...........	2 440	....	....	....	....	....	....	....	....
Capital transfers, debit...........	3 400	**−.19**	**−.19**	**−.22**	**−.22**	**−.25**	**−.27**	**−.27**	**−.26**
General government...........	3 401	....	....	....	....	....	....	....	....
Debt forgiveness...........	3 402	....	....	....	....	....	....	....	....
Other capital transfers...........	3 410	....	....	....	....	....	....	....	....
Other sectors...........	3 430	−.19	−.19	−.22	−.22	−.25	−.27	−.27	−.26
Migrants' transfers...........	3 431	−.19	−.19	−.22	−.22	−.25	−.27	−.27	−.26
Debt forgiveness...........	3 432	....	....	....	....	....	....	....	....
Other capital transfers...........	3 440	....	....	....	....	....	....	....	....
Nonproduced nonfinancial assets, credit...........	2 480	**.19**	....	....	**.09**	....	....	....	....
Nonproduced nonfinancial assets, debit...........	3 480	....	....	....	....	....	....	....	....

Table 2 (Continued). STANDARD PRESENTATION, 2003–2010

(Millions of U.S. dollars)

	Code	2003	2004	2005	2006	2007	2008	2009	2010
FINANCIAL ACCOUNT....................................	4 995 ..	**103.71**	**72.05**	**41.87**	**66.03**	**94.41**	**146.20**	**178.42**	**111.48**
A. DIRECT INVESTMENT.................................	4 500 ..	**75.61**	**55.77**	**92.99**	**110.42**	**134.48**	**177.91**	**130.75**	**128.01**
Direct investment abroad.........................	4 505 ..	....	....	....	....	....	....	....	....
Equity capital..	4 510 ..	....	....	....	....	....	....	....	....
Claims on affiliated enterprises...............	4 515 ..	....	....	....	....	....	....	....	....
Liabilities to affiliated enterprises...........	4 520 ..	....	....	....	....	....	....	....	....
Reinvested earnings..............................	4 525 ..	....	....	....	....	....	....	....	....
Other capital..	4 530 ..	....	....	....	....	....	....	....	....
Claims on affiliated enterprises...............	4 535 ..	....	....	....	....	....	....	....	....
Liabilities to affiliated enterprises...........	4 540 ..	....	....	....	....	....	....	....	....
Direct investment in St. Kitts and Nevis............	4 555 ..	**75.61**	**55.77**	**92.99**	**110.42**	**134.48**	**177.91**	**130.75**	**128.01**
Equity capital..	4 560 ..	48.28	15.49	38.24	18.89	40.61	78.48	49.21	49.72
Claims on direct investors......................	4 565 ..	....	....	....	....	....	....	....	....
Liabilities to direct investors..................	4 570 ..	48.28	15.49	38.24	18.89	40.61	78.48	49.21	49.72
Reinvested earnings..............................	4 575 ..	4.22	3.60	3.15	2.36	2.43	2.08	2.28	2.16
Other capital..	4 580 ..	23.11	36.69	51.60	89.17	91.45	97.35	79.25	76.13
Claims on direct investors......................	4 585 ..	....	....	....	....	....	....	....	....
Liabilities to direct investors..................	4 590 ..	23.11	36.69	51.60	89.17	91.45	97.35	79.25	76.13
B. PORTFOLIO INVESTMENT...........................	4 600 ..	**48.02**	**−9.84**	**−15.02**	**−20.97**	**−12.97**	**10.47**	**−10.61**	**−9.83**
Assets...	4 602 ..	**−.01**	**−.39**	....	**−1.78**	**−.01**	....	**−.08**	....
Equity securities...................................	4 610 ..	....	....	....	....	....	....	....	....
Monetary authorities............................	4 611 ..	....	....	....	....	....	....	....	....
General government............................	4 612 ..	....	....	....	....	....	....	....	....
Banks...	4 613 ..	....	....	....	....	....	....	....	....
Other sectors......................................	4 614 ..	....	....	....	....	....	....	....	....
Debt securities.....................................	4 619 ..	....	....	....	....	....	....	....	....
Bonds and notes..................................	4 620 ..	....	....	....	....	....	....	....	....
Monetary authorities..........................	4 621 ..	....	....	....	....	....	....	....	....
General government..........................	4 622 ..	....	....	....	....	....	....	....	....
Banks...	4 623 ..	....	....	....	....	....	....	....	....
Other sectors....................................	4 624 ..	....	....	....	....	....	....	....	....
Money market instruments.....................	4 630 ..	....	....	....	....	....	....	....	....
Monetary authorities..........................	4 631 ..	....	....	....	....	....	....	....	....
General government..........................	4 632 ..	....	....	....	....	....	....	....	....
Banks...	4 633 ..	....	....	....	....	....	....	....	....
Other sectors....................................	4 634 ..	....	....	....	....	....	....	....	....
Liabilities..	4 652 ..	**48.03**	**−9.45**	**−15.02**	**−19.19**	**−12.96**	**10.48**	**−10.53**	**−9.82**
Equity securities...................................	4 660 ..	....	....	....	....	....	....	....	....
Banks...	4 663 ..	....	....	....	....	....	....	....	....
Other sectors......................................	4 664 ..	....	....	....	....	....	....	....	....
Debt securities.....................................	4 669 ..	....	....	....	....	....	....	....	....
Bonds and notes..................................	4 670 ..	....	....	....	....	....	....	....	....
Monetary authorities..........................	4 671 ..	....	....	....	....	....	....	....	....
General government..........................	4 672 ..	....	....	....	....	....	....	....	....
Banks...	4 673 ..	....	....	....	....	....	....	....	....
Other sectors....................................	4 674 ..	....	....	....	....	....	....	....	....
Money market instruments.....................	4 680 ..	....	....	....	....	....	....	....	....
Monetary authorities..........................	4 681 ..	....	....	....	....	....	....	....	....
General government..........................	4 682 ..	....	....	....	....	....	....	....	....
Banks...	4 683 ..	....	....	....	....	....	....	....	....
Other sectors....................................	4 684 ..	....	....	....	....	....	....	....	....
C. FINANCIAL DERIVATIVES............................	4 910 ..	....	....	....	....	....	....	....	....
Monetary authorities...............................	4 911 ..	....	....	....	....	....	....	....	....
General government...............................	4 912 ..	....	....	....	....	....	....	....	....
Banks..	4 913 ..	....	....	....	....	....	....	....	....
Other sectors...	4 914 ..	....	....	....	....	....	....	....	....
Assets...	4 900 ..	....	....	....	....	....	....	....	....
Monetary authorities............................	4 901 ..	....	....	....	....	....	....	....	....
General government............................	4 902 ..	....	....	....	....	....	....	....	....
Banks...	4 903 ..	....	....	....	....	....	....	....	....
Other sectors......................................	4 904 ..	....	....	....	....	....	....	....	....
Liabilities..	4 905 ..	....	....	....	....	....	....	....	....
Monetary authorities............................	4 906 ..	....	....	....	....	....	....	....	....
General government............................	4 907 ..	....	....	....	....	....	....	....	....
Banks...	4 908 ..	....	....	....	....	....	....	....	....
Other sectors......................................	4 909 ..	....	....	....	....	....	....	....	....

Table 2 (Concluded). STANDARD PRESENTATION, 2003–2010

(Millions of U.S. dollars)

	Code	2003	2004	2005	2006	2007	2008	2009	2010
D. OTHER INVESTMENT	4 700 ..	−20.88	39.77	−42.78	−6.27	−19.92	−27.45	84.24	25.99
Assets	4 703 ..	−39.53	−23.18	−45.97	−18.88	−42.57	−63.37	−14.38	−13.71
Trade credits	4 706 ..	....	....	....	....	....	....	....	....
General government	4 707 ..	....	....	....	....	....	....	....	....
of which: Short-term	4 709 ..	....	....	....	....	....	....	....	....
Other sectors	4 710 ..	....	....	....	....	....	....	....	....
of which: Short-term	4 712 ..	....	....	....	....	....	....	....	....
Loans	4 714 ..	−33.25	....	−39.97	−13.08	−29.81	−55.42	....	....
Monetary authorities	4 715 ..	....	....	....	....	....	....	....	....
of which: Short-term	4 718 ..	....	....	....	....	....	....	....	....
General government	4 719 ..	....	....	....	....	....	....	....	....
of which: Short-term	4 721 ..	....	....	....	....	....	....	....	....
Banks	4 722 ..	−33.25	....	−39.97	−13.08	−29.81	−55.42	....	....
of which: Short-term	4 724 ..	....	....	....	....	....	....	....	....
Other sectors	4 725 ..	....	....	....	....	....	....	....	....
of which: Short-term	4 727 ..	....	....	....	....	....	....	....	....
Currency and deposits	4 730 ..	....	....	....	....	....	....	....	....
Monetary authorities	4 731 ..	....	....	....	....	....	....	....	....
General government	4 732 ..	....	....	....	....	....	....	....	....
Banks	4 733 ..	....	....	....	....	....	....	....	....
Other sectors	4 734 ..	....	....	....	....	....	....	....	....
Other assets	4 736 ..	−6.28	−23.18	−6.00	−5.81	−12.76	−7.95	−14.38	−13.71
Monetary authorities	4 737 ..	....	....	....	....	....	....	....	....
of which: Short-term	4 739 ..	....	....	....	....	....	....	....	....
General government	4 740 ..	....	....	....	....	....	....	....	....
of which: Short-term	4 742 ..	....	....	....	....	....	....	....	....
Banks	4 743 ..	....	....	....	....	....	....	....	....
of which: Short-term	4 745 ..	....	....	....	....	....	....	....	....
Other sectors	4 746 ..	−6.28	−23.18	−6.00	−5.81	−12.76	−7.95	−14.38	−13.71
of which: Short-term	4 748 ..	....	....	....	....	....	....	....	....
Liabilities	4 753 ..	18.65	62.94	3.19	12.61	22.65	35.93	98.62	39.70
Trade credits	4 756 ..	....	....	....	....	....	....	....	....
General government	4 757 ..	....	....	....	....	....	....	....	....
of which: Short-term	4 759 ..	....	....	....	....	....	....	....	....
Other sectors	4 760 ..	....	....	....	....	....	....	....	....
of which: Short-term	4 762 ..	....	....	....	....	....	....	....	....
Loans	4 764 ..	....	....	....	....	....	....	3.38	....
Monetary authorities	4 765 ..	....	....	....	....	....	....	3.38	....
of which: Use of Fund credit and loans from the Fund..	4 766 ..	....						*3.38*	....
of which: Short-term	4 768 ..	....							
General government	4 769 ..	....				....			
of which: Short-term	4 771 ..	....							
Banks	4 772 ..	....							
of which: Short-term	4 774 ..	....	....	....	....	....	....	....	....
Other sectors	4 775 ..	....	....	....	....	....	....	....	....
of which: Short-term	4 777 ..	....	....	....	....	....	....	....	....
Currency and deposits	4 780 ..	....	....	....	....	....	....	....	....
Monetary authorities	4 781 ..	....	....	....	....	....	....	....	....
General government	4 782 ..	....	....	....	....	....	....	....	....
Banks	4 783 ..	....	....	....	....	....	....	....	....
Other sectors	4 784 ..	....	....	....	....	....	....	....	....
Other liabilities	4 786 ..	18.65	62.94	3.19	12.61	22.65	35.93	95.24	39.70
Monetary authorities	4 787 ..	....	....	....	....	....	....	13.30	....
of which: Short-term	4 789 ..	....	....	....	....	....	....	....	....
General government	4 790 ..	....	....	....	....	....	....	....	....
of which: Short-term	4 792 ..	....	....	....	....	....	....	....	....
Banks	4 793 ..	....	56.32	....	....	....	....	64.25	25.83
of which: Short-term	4 795 ..	....	....	....	....	....	....	....	....
Other sectors	4 796 ..	18.65	6.62	3.19	12.61	22.65	35.93	17.69	13.87
of which: Short-term	4 798 ..	....	....	....	....	....	....	....	....
E. RESERVE ASSETS	4 802 ..	.96	−13.64	6.68	−17.15	−7.18	−14.73	−25.96	−32.69
Monetary gold	4 812 ..	....	....	....	....	....	....	....	....
Special drawing rights	4 811 ..	....	....	....	....	....	....	−13.31	.04
Reserve position in the Fund	4 810 ..	....	....	....	....	....	....	....	....
Foreign exchange	4 803 ..	....	.02	−.17	−.07	−.10	−.10	....	....
Other claims	4 813 ..	.96	−13.66	6.85	−17.08	−7.09	−14.62	−12.65	−32.73
NET ERRORS AND OMISSIONS	4 998 ..	6.70	−9.05	8.12	5.75	2.68	6.70	−34.49	−23.12

2011, International Monetary Fund: *Balance of Payments Statistics Yearbook*

Table 1. ANALYTIC PRESENTATION, 2003–2010

(Millions of U.S. dollars)

	Code	2003	2004	2005	2006	2007	2008	2009	2010
A. Current Account[1]	4 993 Z.	**−147.55**	**−91.14**	**−129.47**	**−308.99**	**−344.66**	**−346.79**	**−133.38**	**−150.49**
Goods: exports f.o.b.	2 100 ..	71.80	96.31	88.77	96.65	101.22	165.72	191.31	206.37
Goods: imports f.o.b.	3 100 ..	−354.50	−348.01	−418.12	−520.98	−541.70	−604.82	−451.49	−521.54
Balance on Goods	4 100 ..	*−282.70*	*−251.70*	*−329.35*	*−424.33*	*−440.48*	*−439.10*	*−260.18*	*−315.16*
Services: credit	2 200 ..	318.32	367.92	436.14	343.56	355.91	363.58	352.62	386.97
Services: debit	3 200 ..	−145.20	−152.28	−176.73	−185.71	−205.69	−215.46	−190.00	−201.78
Balance on Goods and Services	4 991 ..	*−109.59*	*−36.06*	*−69.93*	*−266.48*	*−290.26*	*−290.98*	*−97.56*	*−129.98*
Income: credit	2 300 ..	4.85	6.20	8.11	11.63	12.41	8.23	16.38	18.03
Income: debit	3 300 ..	−55.69	−75.19	−80.62	−66.12	−80.39	−80.27	−64.63	−53.21
Balance on Goods, Services, and Income	4 992 ..	*−160.42*	*−105.05*	*−142.44*	*−320.97*	*−358.24*	*−363.02*	*−145.81*	*−165.16*
Current transfers: credit	2 379 Z.	28.84	29.87	29.67	31.36	35.26	36.81	32.06	34.87
Current transfers: debit	3 379 ..	−15.97	−15.96	−16.70	−19.38	−21.69	−20.58	−19.63	−20.20
B. Capital Account[1]	4 994 Z.	**17.09**	**3.45**	**5.34**	**11.37**	**8.67**	**10.88**	**25.84**	**23.21**
Capital account: credit	2 994 Z.	18.20	4.56	6.45	12.48	9.78	12.03	26.94	24.35
Capital account: debit	3 994 ..	−1.11	−1.11	−1.11	−1.11	−1.11	−1.14	−1.11	−1.14
Total, Groups A Plus B	4 981 ..	*−130.46*	*−87.69*	*−124.13*	*−297.62*	*−335.99*	*−335.90*	*−107.55*	*−127.28*
C. Financial Account[1]	4 995 W.	**119.17**	**89.46**	**115.17**	**285.74**	**335.64**	**337.37**	**163.95**	**106.98**
Direct investment abroad	4 505 ..	....	....	....	....	....	....	....	....
Direct investment in St. Lucia	4 555 Z.	106.43	76.52	78.23	233.93	271.89	161.21	146.40	121.08
Portfolio investment assets	4 602 ..	1.01	.90	.19	−7.76	−4.75	5.69	−21.52	−2.02
Equity securities	4 610 ..	....	....	....	....	....	....	....	....
Debt securities	4 619 ..	....	....	....	....	....	....	....	....
Portfolio investment liabilities	4 652 Z.	61.76	15.39	23.85	4.80	5.22	−15.25	−7.62	−10.38
Equity securities	4 660 ..	....	....	....	....	....	....	....	....
Debt securities	4 669 Z.	....	....	....	....	....	....	....	....
Financial derivatives	4 910 ..	....	....	....	....	....	....	....	....
Financial derivatives assets	4 900 ..	....	....	....	....	....	....	....	....
Financial derivatives liabilities	4 905 ..	....	....	....	....	....	....	....	....
Other investment assets	4 703 ..	−88.00	−31.16	−49.72	−25.72	−41.06	−31.08	−50.06	−63.23
Monetary authorities	4 701 ..	....	....	....	....	....	....	....	....
General government	4 704 ..	....	....	....	....	....	....	....	....
Banks	4 705 ..	−72.75	....	....	....	....	....	−4.40	−37.86
Other sectors	4 728 ..	−15.25	−31.16	−49.72	−25.72	−41.06	−31.08	−45.65	−25.37
Other investment liabilities	4 753 W.	37.97	27.81	62.61	80.49	104.33	216.81	96.75	61.52
Monetary authorities	4 753 WA	....	....	....	....	....	....	21.61	....
General government	4 753 ZB	....	....	....	....	....	....	....	....
Banks	4 753 ZC	....	19.99	24.63	64.45	80.22	172.66	....	....
Other sectors	4 753 ZD	37.97	7.82	37.98	16.04	24.11	44.14	75.13	61.52
Total, Groups A Through C	4 983 ..	*−11.29*	*1.77*	*−8.97*	*−11.88*	*−.36*	*1.47*	*56.40*	*−20.30*
D. Net Errors and Omissions	4 998 ..	**29.63**	**23.21**	**−7.63**	**25.35**	**18.93**	**−12.35**	**−24.48**	**41.40**
Total, Groups A Through D	4 984 ..	*18.34*	*24.98*	*−16.60*	*13.47*	*18.58*	*−10.88*	*31.92*	*21.10*
E. Reserves and Related Items	4 802 A.	**−18.34**	**−24.98**	**16.60**	**−13.47**	**−18.58**	**10.88**	**−31.92**	**−21.10**
Reserve assets	4 802 ..	−18.34	−24.98	16.60	−13.47	−18.58	10.88	−31.92	−31.88
Use of Fund credit and loans	4 766 ..	....	....	....	....	....	....	....	10.78
Exceptional financing	4 920 ..	....	....	....	....	....	....	....	....
Conversion rates: Eastern Caribbean dollars per U.S. dollar	0 101 ..	**2.7000**	**2.7000**	**2.7000**	**2.7000**	**2.7000**	**2.7000**	**2.7000**	**2.7000**

[1] Excludes components that have been classified in the categories of Group E.

Table 2. STANDARD PRESENTATION, 2003–2010

(Millions of U.S. dollars)

	Code	2003	2004	2005	2006	2007	2008	2009	2010
CURRENT ACCOUNT	4 993	**−147.55**	**−91.14**	**−129.47**	**−308.99**	**−344.66**	**−346.79**	**−133.38**	**−150.49**
A. GOODS	4 100	**−282.70**	**−251.70**	**−329.35**	**−424.33**	**−440.48**	**−439.10**	**−260.18**	**−315.16**
Credit	2 100	**71.80**	**96.31**	**88.77**	**96.65**	**101.22**	**165.72**	**191.31**	**206.37**
General merchandise: exports f.o.b.	2 110	62.08	79.78	64.16	72.31	76.12	138.31	165.95	179.02
Goods for processing: exports f.o.b.	2 150	....	....	....	....	....	....	....	....
Repairs on goods	2 160	.01	.01	.01	.01	.01	.01	....	....
Goods procured in ports by carriers	2 170	9.71	16.53	24.61	24.33	25.09	27.39	25.36	27.35
Nonmonetary gold	2 180	....	....	....	....	....	....	....	....
Debit	3 100	**−354.50**	**−348.01**	**−418.12**	**−520.98**	**−541.70**	**−604.82**	**−451.49**	**−521.54**
General merchandise: imports f.o.b.	3 110	−354.50	−348.01	−418.12	−520.98	−541.70	−604.82	−451.49	−521.54
Goods for processing: imports f.o.b.	3 150	....	....	....	....	....	....	....	....
Repairs on goods	3 160	....	....	....	....	....	....	....	....
Goods procured in ports by carriers	3 170	....	....	....	....	....	....	....	....
Nonmonetary gold	3 180	....	....	....	....	....	....	....	....
B. SERVICES	4 200	**173.12**	**215.64**	**259.42**	**157.85**	**150.22**	**148.12**	**162.62**	**185.19**
Total credit	2 200	*318.32*	*367.92*	*436.14*	*343.56*	*355.91*	*363.58*	*352.62*	*386.97*
Total debit	3 200	*−145.20*	*−152.28*	*−176.73*	*−185.71*	*−205.69*	*−215.46*	*−190.00*	*−201.78*
Transportation services, credit	2 205	**12.27**	**15.32**	**21.63**	**21.70**	**17.94**	**17.81**	**18.70**	**19.26**
Passenger	2 850	....	....	....	....	....	....	....	....
Freight	2 851	....	....	....	....	....	....	....	....
Other	2 852	....	....	....	....	....	....	....	....
Sea transport, passenger	2 207	....	....	....	....	....	....	....	....
Sea transport, freight	2 208	....	....	....	....	....	....	....	....
Sea transport, other	2 209	....	....	....	....	....	....	....	....
Air transport, passenger	2 211	....	....	....	....	....	....	....	....
Air transport, freight	2 212	....	....	....	....	....	....	....	....
Air transport, other	2 213	....	....	....	....	....	....	....	....
Other transport, passenger	2 215	....	....	....	....	....	....	....	....
Other transport, freight	2 216	....	....	....	....	....	....	....	....
Other transport, other	2 217	....	....	....	....	....	....	....	....
Transportation services, debit	3 205	**−63.01**	**−64.14**	**−73.48**	**−80.57**	**−81.37**	**−93.78**	**−74.90**	**−83.54**
Passenger	3 850	....	....	....	....	....	....	....	....
Freight	3 851	....	....	....	....	....	....	....	....
Other	3 852	....	....	....	....	....	....	....	....
Sea transport, passenger	3 207	....	....	....	....	....	....	....	....
Sea transport, freight	3 208	....	....	....	....	....	....	....	....
Sea transport, other	3 209	....	....	....	....	....	....	....	....
Air transport, passenger	3 211	....	....	....	....	....	....	....	....
Air transport, freight	3 212	....	....	....	....	....	....	....	....
Air transport, other	3 213	....	....	....	....	....	....	....	....
Other transport, passenger	3 215	....	....	....	....	....	....	....	....
Other transport, freight	3 216	....	....	....	....	....	....	....	....
Other transport, other	3 217	....	....	....	....	....	....	....	....
Travel, credit	2 236	**282.08**	**326.44**	**381.66**	**293.95**	**301.68**	**311.00**	**296.20**	**328.92**
Business travel	2 237	....	....	....	....	....	....	....	....
Personal travel	2 240	....	....	....	....	....	....	....	....
Travel, debit	3 236	**−35.67**	**−36.83**	**−38.92**	**−39.34**	**−42.27**	**−45.29**	**−46.73**	**−48.08**
Business travel	3 237	....	....	....	....	....	....	....	....
Personal travel	3 240	....	....	....	....	....	....	....	....
Other services, credit	2 200 BA	**23.97**	**26.17**	**32.85**	**27.90**	**36.28**	**34.77**	**37.73**	**38.79**
Communications	2 245	7.62	7.89	13.46	8.43	5.61	5.90	5.80	5.97
Construction	2 249	....	....	....	....	....	....	....	....
Insurance	2 253	4.73	4.20	5.62	6.06	7.01	5.17	6.87	7.07
Financial	2 260	....	....	....	....	....	....	....	....
Computer and information	2 262	2.43	2.43	3.33	....	....	....	....	....
Royalties and licence fees	2 266	....	....	....	....	....	....	....	....
Other business services	2 268	7.73	10.17	8.75	11.64	21.84	21.66	22.74	23.39
Personal, cultural, and recreational	2 287	....	....	....	....	....	....	....	....
Government, n.i.e.	2 291	1.45	1.47	1.70	1.77	1.82	2.04	2.33	2.37
Other services, debit	3 200 BA	**−46.52**	**−51.32**	**−64.33**	**−65.80**	**−82.05**	**−76.39**	**−68.37**	**−70.17**
Communications	3 245	−2.93	−3.91	−13.72	−3.20	−3.04	−3.13	−3.85	−3.97
Construction	3 249	−.28	−4.55	−5.01	−16.82	−17.94	−10.16	−6.91	−5.63
Insurance	3 253	−11.48	−11.19	−13.32	−15.84	−15.22	−16.80	−12.93	−14.60
Financial	3 260	....	....	....	....	....	....	....	....
Computer and information	3 262	−.50	−.43	....	....	....	....	....	....
Royalties and licence fees	3 266	−2.40	−2.38	−2.38	−2.43	−2.37	−2.68	−3.16	−3.25
Other business services	3 268	−24.67	−24.34	−27.21	−24.03	−36.95	−37.03	−36.28	−37.33
Personal, cultural, and recreational	3 287	....	....	....	....	....	....	....	....
Government, n.i.e.	3 291	−4.26	−4.51	−2.68	−3.48	−6.53	−6.59	−5.25	−5.40

Table 2 (Continued). STANDARD PRESENTATION, 2003–2010

(Millions of U.S. dollars)

	Code	2003	2004	2005	2006	2007	2008	2009	2010
C. INCOME	4 300	−50.84	−68.99	−72.51	−54.49	−67.98	−72.04	−48.25	−35.18
Total credit	2 300	*4.85*	*6.20*	*8.11*	*11.63*	*12.41*	*8.23*	*16.38*	*18.03*
Total debit	3 300	*−55.69*	*−75.19*	*−80.62*	*−66.12*	*−80.39*	*−80.27*	*−64.63*	*−53.21*
Compensation of employees, credit	2 310	**.09**	**.13**	**.17**	**.11**	**.19**	**.20**	**.19**	**.20**
Compensation of employees, debit	3 310	....	....	....	....	....	....	....	....
Investment income, credit	2 320	**4.76**	**6.07**	**7.94**	**11.52**	**12.22**	**8.03**	**16.18**	**17.82**
Direct investment income	2 330	....	.02	.03	.04	.06	.02	.09	.09
Dividends and distributed branch profits	2 332	....	.02	.03	.04	.06	....	....	....
Reinvested earnings and undistributed branch profits	2 333	....	....	....	....	....	....	....	....
Income on debt (interest)	2 334	....	....	....	....	....	.02	.09	.09
Portfolio investment income	2 339	2.81	4.22	2.88	6.17	6.93	1.00	10.84	12.34
Income on equity	2 340	2.81	4.22	2.88	6.17	6.93	1.00	10.84	12.34
Income on bonds and notes	2 350	....	....	....	....	....	....	....	....
Income on money market instruments	2 360	....	....	....	....	....	....	....	....
Other investment income	2 370	1.95	1.83	5.03	5.31	5.24	7.01	5.25	5.40
Investment income, debit	3 320	**−55.69**	**−75.19**	**−80.62**	**−66.12**	**−80.39**	**−80.27**	**−64.63**	**−53.21**
Direct investment income	3 330	−31.86	−48.85	−51.08	−34.01	−45.14	−52.46	−35.27	−25.66
Dividends and distributed branch profits	3 332	−12.27	−20.74	−19.31	−18.83	−25.55	−38.12	−28.70	−19.09
Reinvested earnings and undistributed branch profits	3 333	−16.20	−22.07	−25.11	−11.00	−15.20	−10.67	−3.48	−3.58
Income on debt (interest)	3 334	−3.40	−6.04	−6.66	−4.18	−4.39	−3.67	−3.08	−2.98
Portfolio investment income	3 339	−7.70	−9.35	−9.73	−9.46	−6.28	−9.81	−5.81	−4.05
Income on equity	3 340	−7.70	−9.35	−9.73	−9.46	−6.28	−9.81	−5.81	−4.05
Income on bonds and notes	3 350	....	....	....	....	....	....	....	....
Income on money market instruments	3 360	....	....	....	....	....	....	....	....
Other investment income	3 370	−16.12	−16.99	−19.81	−22.65	−28.97	−18.00	−23.55	−23.50
D. CURRENT TRANSFERS	4 379	**12.87**	**13.91**	**12.97**	**11.98**	**13.57**	**16.24**	**12.43**	**14.67**
Credit	2 379	**28.84**	**29.87**	**29.67**	**31.36**	**35.26**	**36.81**	**32.06**	**34.87**
General government	2 380	3.57	3.39	2.37	3.20	6.10	7.22	2.72	2.80
Other sectors	2 390	25.27	26.48	27.30	28.16	29.16	29.60	29.34	32.07
Workers' remittances	2 391	25.02	26.18	26.89	27.73	28.42	28.70	27.80	28.63
Other current transfers	2 392	.25	.30	.40	.43	.74	.89	1.54	3.44
Debit	3 379	**−15.97**	**−15.96**	**−16.70**	**−19.38**	**−21.69**	**−20.58**	**−19.63**	**−20.20**
General government	3 380	−3.55	−3.57	−3.61	−3.65	−3.31	−3.31	−2.20	−2.26
Other sectors	3 390	−12.42	−12.39	−13.09	−15.73	−18.37	−17.26	−17.44	−17.94
Workers' remittances	3 391	−2.78	−2.78	−2.99	−3.12	−3.24	−3.34	−3.24	−3.33
Other current transfers	3 392	−9.65	−9.61	−10.09	−12.61	−15.13	−13.92	−14.20	−14.61
CAPITAL AND FINANCIAL ACCOUNT	4 996	**117.92**	**67.94**	**137.10**	**283.64**	**325.73**	**359.13**	**157.87**	**109.09**
CAPITAL ACCOUNT	4 994	**17.09**	**3.45**	**5.34**	**11.37**	**8.67**	**10.88**	**25.84**	**23.21**
Total credit	2 994	*18.20*	*4.56*	*6.45*	*12.48*	*9.78*	*12.03*	*26.94*	*24.35*
Total debit	3 994	*−1.11*	*−1.11*	*−1.11*	*−1.11*	*−1.11*	*−1.14*	*−1.11*	*−1.14*
Capital transfers, credit	2 400	**18.20**	**4.56**	**6.45**	**12.48**	**9.78**	**12.03**	**26.94**	**24.35**
General government	2 401	15.94	2.23	4.05	10.01	7.25	9.47	24.47	21.80
Debt forgiveness	2 402	....	....	....	....	....	....	....	....
Other capital transfers	2 410	15.94	2.23	4.05	10.01	7.25	9.47	24.47	21.80
Other sectors	2 430	2.26	2.33	2.40	2.47	2.53	2.56	2.48	2.55
Migrants' transfers	2 431	2.26	2.33	2.40	2.47	2.53	2.56	2.48	2.55
Debt forgiveness	2 432	....	....	....	....	....	....	....	....
Other capital transfers	2 440	....	....	....	....	....	....	....	....
Capital transfers, debit	3 400	**−1.11**	**−1.11**	**−1.11**	**−1.11**	**−1.11**	**−1.14**	**−1.11**	**−1.14**
General government	3 401	....	....	....	....	....	....	....	....
Debt forgiveness	3 402	....	....	....	....	....	....	....	....
Other capital transfers	3 410	....	....	....	....	....	....	....	....
Other sectors	3 430	−1.11	−1.11	−1.11	−1.11	−1.11	−1.14	−1.11	−1.14
Migrants' transfers	3 431	−1.11	−1.11	−1.11	−1.11	−1.11	−1.14	−1.11	−1.14
Debt forgiveness	3 432	....	....	....	....	....	....	....	....
Other capital transfers	3 440	....	....	....	....	....	....	....	....
Nonproduced nonfinancial assets, credit	2 480	....	....	....	....	....	....	....	....
Nonproduced nonfinancial assets, debit	3 480	....	....	....	....	....	....	....	....

Table 2 (Continued). STANDARD PRESENTATION, 2003–2010

(Millions of U.S. dollars)

	Code	2003	2004	2005	2006	2007	2008	2009	2010
FINANCIAL ACCOUNT..	4 995 ..	**100.83**	**64.48**	**131.76**	**272.27**	**317.06**	**348.25**	**132.03**	**85.88**
A. DIRECT INVESTMENT..................................	4 500 ..	**106.43**	**76.52**	**78.23**	**233.93**	**271.89**	**161.21**	**146.40**	**121.08**
Direct investment abroad............................	4 505 ..	....	....	....	....	....	....	....	....
Equity capital..	4 510 ..	....	....	....	....	....	....	....	....
Claims on affiliated enterprises.................	4 515 ..	....	....	....	....	....	....	....	....
Liabilities to affiliated enterprises............	4 520 ..	....	....	....	....	....	....	....	....
Reinvested earnings.....................................	4 525 ..	....	....	....	....	....	....	....	....
Other capital..	4 530 ..	....	....	....	....	....	....	....	....
Claims on affiliated enterprises.................	4 535 ..	....	....	....	....	....	....	....	....
Liabilities to affiliated enterprises............	4 540 ..	....	....	....	....	....	....	....	....
Direct investment in St. Lucia.....................	4 555 ..	**106.43**	**76.52**	**78.23**	**233.93**	**271.89**	**161.21**	**146.40**	**121.08**
Equity capital..	4 560 ..	2.79	45.48	50.15	168.24	179.42	97.85	69.10	56.29
Claims on direct investors........................	4 565 ..	....	....	....	....	....	....	....	....
Liabilities to direct investors...................	4 570 ..	2.79	45.48	50.15	168.24	179.42	97.85	69.10	56.29
Reinvested earnings.....................................	4 575 ..	16.20	22.07	25.11	11.00	15.20	10.67	3.48	3.58
Other capital..	4 580 ..	87.44	8.97	2.98	54.70	77.27	52.69	73.82	61.21
Claims on direct investors........................	4 585 ..	....	....	....	....	....	....	....	....
Liabilities to direct investors...................	4 590 ..	87.44	8.97	2.98	54.70	77.27	52.69	73.82	61.21
B. PORTFOLIO INVESTMENT.............................	4 600 ..	**62.77**	**16.29**	**24.05**	**−2.96**	**.47**	**−9.56**	**−29.14**	**−12.39**
Assets...	4 602 ..	**1.01**	**.90**	**.19**	**−7.76**	**−4.75**	**5.69**	**−21.52**	**−2.02**
Equity securities...	4 610 ..	....	....	....	....	....	....	....	....
Monetary authorities...............................	4 611 ..	....	....	....	....	....	....	....	....
General government................................	4 612 ..	....	....	....	....	....	....	....	....
Banks...	4 613 ..	....	....	....	....	....	....	....	....
Other sectors...	4 614 ..	....	....	....	....	....	....	....	....
Debt securities..	4 619 ..	....	....	....	....	....	....	....	....
Bonds and notes.......................................	4 620 ..	....	....	....	....	....	....	....	....
Monetary authorities.............................	4 621 ..	....	....	....	....	....	....	....	....
General government..............................	4 622 ..	....	....	....	....	....	....	....	....
Banks...	4 623 ..	....	....	....	....	....	....	....	....
Other sectors...	4 624 ..	....	....	....	....	....	....	....	....
Money market instruments......................	4 630 ..	....	....	....	....	....	....	....	....
Monetary authorities.............................	4 631 ..	....	....	....	....	....	....	....	....
General government..............................	4 632 ..	....	....	....	....	....	....	....	....
Banks...	4 633 ..	....	....	....	....	....	....	....	....
Other sectors...	4 634 ..	....	....	....	....	....	....	....	....
Liabilities..	4 652 ..	**61.76**	**15.39**	**23.85**	**4.80**	**5.22**	**−15.25**	**−7.62**	**−10.38**
Equity securities...	4 660 ..	....	....	....	....	....	....	....	....
Banks...	4 663 ..	....	....	....	....	....	....	....	....
Other sectors...	4 664 ..	....	....	....	....	....	....	....	....
Debt securities..	4 669 ..	....	....	....	....	....	....	....	....
Bonds and notes.......................................	4 670 ..	....	....	....	....	....	....	....	....
Monetary authorities.............................	4 671 ..	....	....	....	....	....	....	....	....
General government..............................	4 672 ..	....	....	....	....	....	....	....	....
Banks...	4 673 ..	....	....	....	....	....	....	....	....
Other sectors...	4 674 ..	....	....	....	....	....	....	....	....
Money market instruments......................	4 680 ..	....	....	....	....	....	....	....	....
Monetary authorities.............................	4 681 ..	....	....	....	....	....	....	....	....
General government..............................	4 682 ..	....	....	....	....	....	....	....	....
Banks...	4 683 ..	....	....	....	....	....	....	....	....
Other sectors...	4 684 ..	....	....	....	....	....	....	....	....
C. FINANCIAL DERIVATIVES.............................	4 910 ..	....	....	....	....	....	....	....	....
Monetary authorities...................................	4 911 ..	....	....	....	....	....	....	....	....
General government....................................	4 912 ..	....	....	....	....	....	....	....	....
Banks...	4 913 ..	....	....	....	....	....	....	....	....
Other sectors...	4 914 ..	....	....	....	....	....	....	....	....
Assets...	4 900 ..	....	....	....	....	....	....	....	....
Monetary authorities.................................	4 901 ..	....	....	....	....	....	....	....	....
General government..................................	4 902 ..	....	....	....	....	....	....	....	....
Banks...	4 903 ..	....	....	....	....	....	....	....	....
Other sectors...	4 904 ..	....	....	....	....	....	....	....	....
Liabilities..	4 905 ..	....	....	....	....	....	....	....	....
Monetary authorities.................................	4 906 ..	....	....	....	....	....	....	....	....
General government..................................	4 907 ..	....	....	....	....	....	....	....	....
Banks...	4 908 ..	....	....	....	....	....	....	....	....
Other sectors...	4 909 ..	....	....	....	....	....	....	....	....

Table 2 (Concluded). STANDARD PRESENTATION, 2003–2010

(Millions of U.S. dollars)

	Code	2003	2004	2005	2006	2007	2008	2009	2010
D. OTHER INVESTMENT	4 700	−50.03	−3.35	12.89	54.77	63.27	185.72	46.69	9.07
Assets	4 703	−88.00	−31.16	−49.72	−25.72	−41.06	−31.08	−50.06	−63.23
Trade credits	4 706	....	....	....	....	....	....	....	....
General government	4 707	....	....	....	....	....	....	....	....
of which: Short-term	4 709	....	....	....	....	....	....	....	....
Other sectors	4 710	....	....	....	....	....	....	....	....
of which: Short-term	4 712	....	....	....	....	....	....	....	....
Loans	4 714	−72.75	....	....	....	....	....	−4.40	−37.86
Monetary authorities	4 715	....	....	....	....	....	....	....	....
of which: Short-term	4 718	....	....	....	....	....	....	....	....
General government	4 719	....	....	....	....	....	....	....	....
of which: Short-term	4 721	....	....	....	....	....	....	....	....
Banks	4 722	−72.75	....	....	....	....	....	−4.40	−37.86
of which: Short-term	4 724	....	....	....	....	....	....	....	....
Other sectors	4 725	....	....	....	....	....	....	....	....
of which: Short-term	4 727	....	....	....	....	....	....	....	....
Currency and deposits	4 730	....	....	....	....	....	....	....	....
Monetary authorities	4 731	....	....	....	....	....	....	....	....
General government	4 732	....	....	....	....	....	....	....	....
Banks	4 733	....	....	....	....	....	....	....	....
Other sectors	4 734	....	....	....	....	....	....	....	....
Other assets	4 736	−15.25	−31.16	−49.72	−25.72	−41.06	−31.08	−45.65	−25.37
Monetary authorities	4 737	....	....	....	....	....	....	....	....
of which: Short-term	4 739	....	....	....	....	....	....	....	....
General government	4 740	....	....	....	....	....	....	....	....
of which: Short-term	4 742	....	....	....	....	....	....	....	....
Banks	4 743	....	....	....	....	....	....	....	....
of which: Short-term	4 745	....	....	....	....	....	....	....	....
Other sectors	4 746	−15.25	−31.16	−49.72	−25.72	−41.06	−31.08	−45.65	−25.37
of which: Short-term	4 748	....	....	....	....	....	....	....	....
Liabilities	4 753	**37.97**	**27.81**	**62.61**	**80.49**	**104.33**	**216.81**	**96.75**	**72.30**
Trade credits	4 756	....	....	....	....	....	....	....	....
General government	4 757	....	....	....	....	....	....	....	....
of which: Short-term	4 759	....	....	....	....	....	....	....	....
Other sectors	4 760	....	....	....	....	....	....	....	....
of which: Short-term	4 762	....	....	....	....	....	....	....	....
Loans	4 764	....	....	....	....	....	....	....	10.78
Monetary authorities	4 765	....	....	....	....	....	....	....	10.78
of which: Use of Fund credit and loans from the Fund	4 766	....	....	....	....	....	....	....	*10.78*
of which: Short-term	4 768	....	....	....	....	....	....	....	....
General government	4 769	....	....	....	....	....	....	....	....
of which: Short-term	4 771	....	....	....	....	....	....	....	....
Banks	4 772	....	....	....	....	....	....	....	....
of which: Short-term	4 774	....	....	....	....	....	....	....	....
Other sectors	4 775	....	....	....	....	....	....	....	....
of which: Short-term	4 777	....	....	....	....	....	....	....	....
Currency and deposits	4 780	....	....	....	....	....	....	....	....
Monetary authorities	4 781	....	....	....	....	....	....	....	....
General government	4 782	....	....	....	....	....	....	....	....
Banks	4 783	....	....	....	....	....	....	....	....
Other sectors	4 784	....	....	....	....	....	....	....	....
Other liabilities	4 786	37.97	27.81	62.61	80.49	104.33	216.81	96.75	61.52
Monetary authorities	4 787	....	....	....	....	....	....	21.61	....
of which: Short-term	4 789	....	....	....	....	....	....	....	....
General government	4 790	....	....	....	....	....	....	....	....
of which: Short-term	4 792	....	....	....	....	....	....	....	....
Banks	4 793	....	19.99	24.63	64.45	80.22	172.66	....	....
of which: Short-term	4 795	....	....	....	....	....	....	....	....
Other sectors	4 796	37.97	7.82	37.98	16.04	24.11	44.14	75.13	61.52
of which: Short-term	4 798	....	....	....	....	....	....	....	....
E. RESERVE ASSETS	4 802	**−18.34**	**−24.98**	**16.60**	**−13.47**	**−18.58**	**10.88**	**−31.92**	**−31.88**
Monetary gold	4 812	....	....	....	....	....	....	....	....
Special drawing rights	4 811	−.02	−.02	−.03	−.04	−.05	−.04	−21.60	−.16
Reserve position in the Fund	4 810	−.01	....	....	....	....	....	....	....
Foreign exchange	4 803	−5.51	.56	.63	4.56	.49	....	....	....
Other claims	4 813	−12.79	−25.52	15.99	−17.99	−19.01	10.92	−10.32	−31.73
NET ERRORS AND OMISSIONS	4 998	**29.63**	**23.21**	**−7.63**	**25.35**	**18.93**	**−12.35**	**−24.48**	**41.40**

Table 1. ANALYTIC PRESENTATION, 2003–2010
(Millions of U.S. dollars)

	Code	2003	2004	2005	2006	2007	2008	2009	2010
A. Current Account[1]	4 993 Z.	**−79.47**	**−102.08**	**−102.20**	**−119.39**	**−193.86**	**−230.32**	**−199.78**	**−205.98**
Goods: exports f.o.b.	2 100 ..	40.09	39.30	42.57	41.16	51.35	57.19	53.36	43.56
Goods: imports f.o.b.	3 100 ..	−176.81	−198.98	−212.39	−237.68	−287.91	−328.68	−293.81	−297.66
Balance on Goods	4 100 ..	*−136.72*	*−159.68*	*−169.82*	*−196.52*	*−236.56*	*−271.49*	*−240.45*	*−254.10*
Services: credit	2 200 ..	132.76	145.22	157.97	170.83	160.87	152.99	138.95	138.90
Services: debit	3 200 ..	−64.59	−73.22	−78.80	−88.17	−114.20	−102.14	−93.54	−90.43
Balance on Goods and Services	4 991 ..	*−68.54*	*−87.68*	*−90.65*	*−113.86*	*−189.89*	*−220.64*	*−195.05*	*−205.64*
Income: credit	2 300 ..	3.76	4.93	8.40	13.60	13.41	10.12	10.54	10.67
Income: debit	3 300 ..	−27.59	−33.44	−38.00	−39.30	−37.52	−32.96	−26.70	−24.14
Balance on Goods, Services, and Income	4 992 ..	*−92.38*	*−116.19*	*−120.25*	*−139.56*	*−214.01*	*−243.48*	*−211.21*	*−219.11*
Current transfers: credit	2 379 Z.	24.29	25.13	26.40	32.23	35.42	27.87	25.81	27.40
Current transfers: debit	3 379 ..	−11.39	−11.02	−8.35	−12.06	−15.27	−14.71	−14.39	−14.27
B. Capital Account[1]	4 994 Z.	**14.36**	**18.94**	**14.23**	**8.15**	**73.62**	**48.85**	**54.24**	**32.05**
Capital account: credit	2 994 Z.	15.63	20.30	15.66	9.73	75.37	50.67	56.07	33.86
Capital account: debit	3 994 ..	−1.27	−1.37	−1.43	−1.58	−1.76	−1.83	−1.83	−1.81
Total, Groups A Plus B	4 981 ..	*−65.11*	*−83.14*	*−87.97*	*−111.24*	*−120.24*	*−181.48*	*−145.55*	*−173.93*
C. Financial Account[1]	4 995 W.	**50.18**	**80.66**	**37.07**	**116.47**	**116.21**	**157.09**	**149.69**	**132.70**
Direct investment abroad	4 505 ..	....	....	....	....	....	....	....	....
Direct investment in St. Vincent and the Grenadines	4 555 Z.	55.16	65.69	40.09	109.11	130.48	159.24	106.06	99.74
Portfolio investment assets	4 602 ..	−.96	−10.24	−2.21	−1.66	−.60	−2.07	−.77	−1.86
Equity securities	4 610 ..	....	....	....	....	....	....	....	....
Debt securities	4 619 ..	....	....	....	....	....	....	....	....
Portfolio investment liabilities	4 652 Z.	21.66	43.41	−5.98	14.17	−2.80	−1.05	18.96	.76
Equity securities	4 660 ..	....	....	....	....	....	....	....	....
Debt securities	4 669 Z.	....	....	....	....	....	....	....	....
Financial derivatives	4 910 ..	....	....	....	....	....	....	....	....
Financial derivatives assets	4 900 ..	....	....	....	....	....	....	....	....
Financial derivatives liabilities	4 905 ..	....	....	....	....	....	....	....	....
Other investment assets	4 703 ..	−52.04	−66.54	−54.52	−35.09	−81.44	−65.21	−57.80	−48.26
Monetary authorities	4 701 ..	....	....	....	....	....	....	....	....
General government	4 704 ..	....	....	....	....	....	....	....	....
Banks	4 705 ..	−17.07	−18.26	−6.53	....	....	−15.29	....	−6.36
Other sectors	4 728 ..	−34.96	−48.28	−47.99	−35.09	−81.44	−49.91	−57.80	−41.90
Other investment liabilities	4 753 W.	26.36	48.34	59.69	29.94	70.56	66.16	83.23	82.32
Monetary authorities	4 753 WA	....	....	....	....	....	....	11.82	....
General government	4 753 ZB	....	....	....	....	....	....	....	....
Banks	4 753 ZC	....	....	....	9.69	36.36	....	1.07	....
Other sectors	4 753 ZD	26.36	48.34	59.69	20.25	34.20	66.16	70.34	82.32
Total, Groups A Through C	4 983 ..	*−14.93*	*−2.48*	*−50.90*	*5.23*	*−4.03*	*−24.39*	*4.14*	*−41.23*
D. Net Errors and Omissions	4 998 ..	**14.43**	**27.90**	**48.02**	**6.87**	**2.19**	**15.06**	**−5.74**	**72.34**
Total, Groups A Through D	4 984 ..	*−.50*	*25.41*	*−2.88*	*12.11*	*−1.84*	*−9.33*	*−1.60*	*31.11*
E. Reserves and Related Items	4 802 A.	**.50**	**−25.41**	**2.88**	**−12.11**	**1.84**	**9.33**	**1.60**	**−31.11**
Reserve assets	4 802 ..	.50	−25.41	2.88	−12.11	1.84	3.27	−4.08	−25.26
Use of Fund credit and loans	4 766 ..	....	....	....	....	....	6.06	5.68	−5.85
Exceptional financing	4 920 ..	....	....	....	....	....	....	....	....
Conversion rates: Eastern Caribbean dollars per U.S. dollar	0 101 ..	**2.7000**	**2.7000**	**2.7000**	**2.7000**	**2.7000**	**2.7000**	**2.7000**	**2.7000**

[1] Excludes components that have been classified in the categories of Group E.

Table 2. STANDARD PRESENTATION, 2003–2010

(Millions of U.S. dollars)

	Code	2003	2004	2005	2006	2007	2008	2009	2010
CURRENT ACCOUNT............................	4 993 ..	**−79.47**	**−102.08**	**−102.20**	**−119.39**	**−193.86**	**−230.32**	**−199.78**	**−205.98**
A. GOODS..	4 100 ..	**−136.72**	**−159.68**	**−169.82**	**−196.52**	**−236.56**	**−271.49**	**−240.45**	**−254.10**
Credit..	2 100 ..	**40.09**	**39.30**	**42.57**	**41.16**	**51.35**	**57.19**	**53.36**	**43.56**
General merchandise: exports f.o.b.....	2 110 ..	37.99	36.63	39.88	38.11	47.71	52.21	50.09	40.21
Goods for processing: exports f.o.b......	2 150 ..	....	....	....	....	....	....	....	....
Repairs on goods...............................	2 160 ..	....	.01	.01	.01	.01	.01	.01	.01
Goods procured in ports by carriers.....	2 170 ..	2.10	2.66	2.69	3.05	3.63	4.98	3.26	3.35
Nonmonetary gold..............................	2 180 ..	....	....	....	....	....	....	....	....
Debit..	3 100 ..	**−176.81**	**−198.98**	**−212.39**	**−237.68**	**−287.91**	**−328.68**	**−293.81**	**−297.66**
General merchandise: imports f.o.b......	3 110 ..	−176.17	−198.33	−211.67	−236.94	−287.59	−328.32	−293.55	−297.40
Goods for processing: imports f.o.b......	3 150 ..	....	....	....	....	....	....	....	....
Repairs on goods...............................	3 160 ..	....	....	....	....	....	....	....	....
Goods procured in ports by carriers.....	3 170 ..	−.63	−.65	−.73	−.74	−.32	−.35	−.26	−.27
Nonmonetary gold..............................	3 180 ..	....	....	....	....	....	....	....	....
B. SERVICES...................................	4 200 ..	**68.17**	**72.00**	**79.17**	**82.66**	**46.66**	**50.85**	**45.40**	**48.46**
Total credit.....................................	2 200 ..	*132.76*	*145.22*	*157.97*	*170.83*	*160.87*	*152.99*	*138.95*	*138.90*
Total debit.......................................	3 200 ..	*−64.59*	*−73.22*	*−78.80*	*−88.17*	*−114.20*	*−102.14*	*−93.54*	*−90.43*
Transportation services, credit.........	2 205 ..	**9.36**	**10.83**	**10.52**	**11.63**	**12.10**	**10.98**	**8.25**	**8.48**
Passenger..	2 850 ..	....	....	....	....	....	....	....	....
Freight..	2 851 ..	....	....	....	....	....	....	....	....
Other..	2 852 ..	....	....	....	....	....	....	....	....
Sea transport, passenger....................	2 207 ..	....	....	....	....	....	....	....	....
Sea transport, freight.........................	2 208 ..	....	....	....	....	....	....	....	....
Sea transport, other...........................	2 209 ..	....	....	....	....	....	....	....	....
Air transport, passenger.....................	2 211 ..	....	....	....	....	....	....	....	....
Air transport, freight..........................	2 212 ..	....	....	....	....	....	....	....	....
Air transport, other............................	2 213 ..	....	....	....	....	....	....	....	....
Other transport, passenger.................	2 215 ..	....	....	....	....	....	....	....	....
Other transport, freight......................	2 216 ..	....	....	....	....	....	....	....	....
Other transport, other........................	2 217 ..	....	....	....	....	....	....	....	....
Transportation services, debit..........	3 205 ..	**−29.52**	**−32.26**	**−34.24**	**−37.93**	**−45.56**	**−51.41**	**−45.54**	**−45.88**
Passenger..	3 850 ..	....	....	....	....	....	....	....	....
Freight..	3 851 ..	....	....	....	....	....	....	....	....
Other..	3 852 ..	....	....	....	....	....	....	....	....
Sea transport, passenger....................	3 207 ..	....	....	....	....	....	....	....	....
Sea transport, freight.........................	3 208 ..	....	....	....	....	....	....	....	....
Sea transport, other...........................	3 209 ..	....	....	....	....	....	....	....	....
Air transport, passenger.....................	3 211 ..	....	....	....	....	....	....	....	....
Air transport, freight..........................	3 212 ..	....	....	....	....	....	....	....	....
Air transport, other............................	3 213 ..	....	....	....	....	....	....	....	....
Other transport, passenger.................	3 215 ..	....	....	....	....	....	....	....	....
Other transport, freight......................	3 216 ..	....	....	....	....	....	....	....	....
Other transport, other........................	3 217 ..	....	....	....	....	....	....	....	....
Travel, credit................................	2 236 ..	**91.19**	**95.56**	**103.89**	**113.26**	**110.01**	**96.04**	**87.54**	**86.78**
Business travel..................................	2 237 ..	....	....	....	....	....	....	....	....
Personal travel..................................	2 240 ..	....	....	....	....	....	....	....	....
Travel, debit.................................	3 236 ..	**−12.65**	**−14.29**	**−14.91**	**−15.71**	**−20.16**	**−17.60**	**−14.41**	**−13.69**
Business travel..................................	3 237 ..	....	....	....	....	....	....	....	....
Personal travel..................................	3 240 ..	....	....	....	....	....	....	....	....
Other services, credit.....................	2 200 BA	**32.21**	**38.84**	**43.56**	**45.94**	**38.75**	**45.97**	**43.16**	**43.64**
Communications................................	2 245 ..	12.45	12.49	10.14	8.57	5.20	8.32	8.50	9.10
Construction.....................................	2 249 ..	....	....	....	....	....	....	....	....
Insurance...	2 253 ..	1.90	1.73	2.31	2.87	3.09	3.25	2.69	2.66
Financial..	2 260 ..	....	....	....	....	....	....	....	....
Computer and information...................	2 262 ..	....	....	....	....	....	....	.01	.01
Royalties and licence fees...................	2 266 ..	....	....	....	....	....	....	....	....
Other business services......................	2 268 ..	16.20	22.71	29.08	32.51	28.35	32.25	29.98	29.86
Personal, cultural, and recreational......	2 287 ..	....	....	....	....	....	....	....	....
Government, n.i.e...............................	2 291 ..	1.65	1.90	2.03	1.99	2.11	2.16	1.98	2.02
Other services, debit......................	3 200 BA	**−22.43**	**−26.68**	**−29.65**	**−34.53**	**−48.48**	**−33.13**	**−33.59**	**−30.86**
Communications................................	3 245 ..	−3.49	−3.87	−1.87	−2.05	−2.67	−1.90	−1.72	−1.71
Construction.....................................	3 249 ..	....	....	....	....	....	....	....	....
Insurance...	3 253 ..	−6.45	−6.89	−7.94	−8.83	−10.78	−11.53	−9.76	−9.82
Financial..	3 260 ..	....	....	....	....	....	....	....	....
Computer and information...................	3 262 ..	−.16	....	−.01	−.01	....	−.07	....	....
Royalties and licence fees...................	3 266 ..	−.31	−.37	−.43	−.53	−.91	−2.95	−3.31	−3.28
Other business services......................	3 268 ..	−8.52	−11.67	−12.97	−15.30	−23.25	−12.94	−11.51	−11.42
Personal, cultural, and recreational......	3 287 ..	....	....	....	....	....	....	....	....
Government, n.i.e...............................	3 291 ..	−3.49	−3.88	−6.43	−7.81	−10.86	−3.74	−7.29	−4.63

Table 2 (Continued). STANDARD PRESENTATION, 2003–2010

(Millions of U.S. dollars)

	Code	2003	2004	2005	2006	2007	2008	2009	2010
C. INCOME	4 300	**−23.83**	**−28.51**	**−29.60**	**−25.70**	**−24.12**	**−22.84**	**−16.16**	**−13.47**
Total credit	2 300	*3.76*	*4.93*	*8.40*	*13.60*	*13.41*	*10.12*	*10.54*	*10.67*
Total debit	3 300	*−27.59*	*−33.44*	*−38.00*	*−39.30*	*−37.52*	*−32.96*	*−26.70*	*−24.14*
Compensation of employees, credit	2 310	**.60**	**.67**	**1.07**	**3.68**	**6.39**	**4.08**	**3.93**	**4.05**
Compensation of employees, debit	3 310	**....**	**....**	**−.61**	**−.54**	**−.54**	**−.01**	**−.01**	**−.01**
Investment income, credit	2 320	**3.16**	**4.27**	**7.33**	**9.92**	**7.01**	**6.03**	**6.60**	**6.61**
Direct investment income	2 330	....	....	....	....	....	....	....	....
Dividends and distributed branch profits	2 332	....	....	....	....	....	....	....	....
Reinvested earnings and undistributed branch profits	2 333	....	....	....	....	....	....	....	....
Income on debt (interest)	2 334	....	....	....	....	....	....	....	....
Portfolio investment income	2 339	1.87	1.72	2.46	4.07	1.65	3.78	3.88	3.91
Income on equity	2 340	1.87	1.72	2.46	4.07	1.65	3.78	3.88	3.91
Income on bonds and notes	2 350	....	....	....	....	....	....	....	....
Income on money market instruments	2 360	....	....	....	....	....	....	....	....
Other investment income	2 370	1.29	2.55	4.87	5.85	5.36	2.25	2.73	2.70
Investment income, debit	3 320	**−27.59**	**−33.44**	**−37.39**	**−38.76**	**−36.99**	**−32.95**	**−26.68**	**−24.12**
Direct investment income	3 330	−20.77	−24.91	−22.10	−22.96	−19.62	−18.11	−12.39	−10.13
Dividends and distributed branch profits	3 332	−5.82	−7.84	−9.27	−8.80	−7.68	−8.06	−9.23	−6.99
Reinvested earnings and undistributed branch profits	3 333	−14.57	−16.12	−11.56	−12.90	−11.10	−9.18	−2.42	−2.40
Income on debt (interest)	3 334	−.37	−.95	−1.27	−1.27	−.83	−.87	−.74	−.74
Portfolio investment income	3 339	−.77	−1.08	−2.12	−1.50	−3.24	−1.47	−1.42	−2.00
Income on equity	3 340	−.77	−1.08	−2.12	−1.50	−3.24	−1.47	−1.42	−2.00
Income on bonds and notes	3 350	....	....	....	....	....	....	....	....
Income on money market instruments	3 360	....	....	....	....	....	....	....	....
Other investment income	3 370	−6.06	−7.46	−13.18	−14.29	−14.13	−13.37	−12.87	−11.99
D. CURRENT TRANSFERS	4 379	**12.90**	**14.11**	**18.05**	**20.17**	**20.16**	**13.16**	**11.42**	**13.13**
Credit	2 379	**24.29**	**25.13**	**26.40**	**32.23**	**35.42**	**27.87**	**25.81**	**27.40**
General government	2 380	3.24	3.50	3.32	9.37	11.99	4.37	3.37	4.51
Other sectors	2 390	21.06	21.63	23.08	22.86	23.43	23.51	22.44	22.89
Workers' remittances	2 391	20.10	20.78	21.35	21.88	22.47	22.70	21.98	22.20
Other current transfers	2 392	.96	.85	1.73	.98	.96	.81	.46	.69
Debit	3 379	**−11.39**	**−11.02**	**−8.35**	**−12.06**	**−15.27**	**−14.71**	**−14.39**	**−14.27**
General government	3 380	−4.24	−3.86	−3.66	−3.54	−3.56	−4.67	−3.34	−3.32
Other sectors	3 390	−7.15	−7.16	−4.69	−8.52	−11.70	−10.04	−11.04	−10.95
Workers' remittances	3 391	−3.65	−3.94	−4.11	−4.55	−5.07	−5.26	−5.27	−5.23
Other current transfers	3 392	−3.50	−3.22	−.58	−3.97	−6.64	−4.78	−5.77	−5.72
CAPITAL AND FINANCIAL ACCOUNT	4 996	**65.04**	**74.18**	**54.18**	**112.52**	**191.67**	**215.26**	**205.52**	**133.64**
CAPITAL ACCOUNT	4 994	**14.36**	**18.94**	**14.23**	**8.15**	**73.62**	**48.85**	**54.24**	**32.05**
Total credit	2 994	*15.63*	*20.30*	*15.66*	*9.73*	*75.37*	*50.67*	*56.07*	*33.86*
Total debit	3 994	*−1.27*	*−1.37*	*−1.43*	*−1.58*	*−1.76*	*−1.83*	*−1.83*	*−1.81*
Capital transfers, credit	2 400	**15.63**	**20.30**	**15.66**	**9.73**	**75.37**	**50.67**	**56.07**	**33.86**
General government	2 401	12.81	16.23	11.59	5.56	71.09	46.34	51.88	29.51
Debt forgiveness	2 402	....	....	....	....	....	....	....	....
Other capital transfers	2 410	12.81	16.23	11.59	5.56	71.09	46.34	51.88	29.51
Other sectors	2 430	2.82	4.07	4.07	4.17	4.28	4.33	4.19	4.35
Migrants' transfers	2 431	2.82	4.07	4.07	4.17	4.28	4.33	4.19	4.35
Debt forgiveness	2 432	....	....	....	....	....	....	....	....
Other capital transfers	2 440	....	....	....	....	....	....	....	....
Capital transfers, debit	3 400	**−1.27**	**−1.37**	**−1.43**	**−1.58**	**−1.76**	**−1.83**	**−1.83**	**−1.81**
General government	3 401	....	....	....	....	....	....	....	....
Debt forgiveness	3 402	....	....	....	....	....	....	....	....
Other capital transfers	3 410	....	....	....	....	....	....	....	....
Other sectors	3 430	−1.27	−1.37	−1.43	−1.58	−1.76	−1.83	−1.83	−1.81
Migrants' transfers	3 431	−1.27	−1.37	−1.43	−1.58	−1.76	−1.83	−1.83	−1.81
Debt forgiveness	3 432	....	....	....	....	....	....	....	....
Other capital transfers	3 440	....	....	....	....	....	....	....	....
Nonproduced nonfinancial assets, credit	2 480	....	....	....	....	....	....	....	....
Nonproduced nonfinancial assets, debit	3 480	....	....	....	....	....	....	....	....

Table 2 (Continued). STANDARD PRESENTATION, 2003–2010

(Millions of U.S. dollars)

	Code	2003	2004	2005	2006	2007	2008	2009	2010
FINANCIAL ACCOUNT............................	4 995 ..	**50.68**	**55.25**	**39.95**	**104.36**	**118.05**	**166.42**	**151.29**	**101.59**
A. DIRECT INVESTMENT........................	4 500 ..	**55.16**	**65.69**	**40.09**	**109.11**	**130.48**	**159.24**	**106.06**	**99.74**
Direct investment abroad.......................	4 505 ..	....	....	....	....	....	....	....	....
Equity capital..	4 510 ..	....	....	....	....	....	....	....	....
Claims on affiliated enterprises...........	4 515 ..	....	....	....	....	....	....	....	....
Liabilities to affiliated enterprises........	4 520 ..	....	....	....	....	....	....	....	....
Reinvested earnings..............................	4 525 ..	....	....	....	....	....	....	....	....
Other capital..	4 530 ..	....	....	....	....	....	....	....	....
Claims on affiliated enterprises...........	4 535 ..	....	....	....	....	....	....	....	....
Liabilities to affiliated enterprises........	4 540 ..	....	....	....	....	....	....	....	....
Direct investment in St. Vincent & Grenadines..	4 555 ..	**55.16**	**65.69**	**40.09**	**109.11**	**130.48**	**159.24**	**106.06**	**99.74**
Equity capital..	4 560 ..	8.68	33.14	12.12	49.28	66.67	66.02	53.64	48.28
Claims on direct investors...................	4 565 ..	....	....	....	....	....	....	....	....
Liabilities to direct investors...............	4 570 ..	8.68	33.14	12.12	49.28	66.67	66.02	53.64	48.28
Reinvested earnings..............................	4 575 ..	14.57	16.12	11.56	12.90	11.10	9.18	2.42	2.40
Other capital..	4 580 ..	31.92	16.43	16.41	46.93	52.70	84.05	50.00	49.06
Claims on direct investors...................	4 585 ..	....	....	....	....	....	....	....	....
Liabilities to direct investors...............	4 590 ..	31.92	16.43	16.41	46.93	52.70	84.05	50.00	49.06
B. PORTFOLIO INVESTMENT......................	4 600 ..	**20.69**	**33.17**	**−8.20**	**12.51**	**−3.39**	**−3.12**	**18.19**	**−1.11**
Assets..	4 602 ..	**−.96**	**−10.24**	**−2.21**	**−1.66**	**−.60**	**−2.07**	**−.77**	**−1.86**
Equity securities....................................	4 610 ..	....	....	....	....	....	....	....	....
Monetary authorities...........................	4 611 ..	....	....	....	....	....	....	....	....
General government............................	4 612 ..	....	....	....	....	....	....	....	....
Banks..	4 613 ..	....	....	....	....	....	....	....	....
Other sectors......................................	4 614 ..	....	....	....	....	....	....	....	....
Debt securities.....................................	4 619 ..	....	....	....	....	....	....	....	....
Bonds and notes..................................	4 620 ..	....	....	....	....	....	....	....	....
Monetary authorities........................	4 621 ..	....	....	....	....	....	....	....	....
General government.........................	4 622 ..	....	....	....	....	....	....	....	....
Banks...	4 623 ..	....	....	....	....	....	....	....	....
Other sectors...................................	4 624 ..	....	....	....	....	....	....	....	....
Money market instruments...................	4 630 ..	....	....	....	....	....	....	....	....
Monetary authorities........................	4 631 ..	....	....	....	....	....	....	....	....
General government.........................	4 632 ..	....	....	....	....	....	....	....	....
Banks...	4 633 ..	....	....	....	....	....	....	....	....
Other sectors...................................	4 634 ..	....	....	....	....	....	....	....	....
Liabilities...	4 652 ..	**21.66**	**43.41**	**−5.98**	**14.17**	**−2.80**	**−1.05**	**18.96**	**.76**
Equity securities....................................	4 660 ..	....	....	....	....	....	....	....	....
Banks..	4 663 ..	....	....	....	....	....	....	....	....
Other sectors......................................	4 664 ..	....	....	....	....	....	....	....	....
Debt securities.....................................	4 669 ..	....	....	....	....	....	....	....	....
Bonds and notes..................................	4 670 ..	....	....	....	....	....	....	....	....
Monetary authorities........................	4 671 ..	....	....	....	....	....	....	....	....
General government.........................	4 672 ..	....	....	....	....	....	....	....	....
Banks...	4 673 ..	....	....	....	....	....	....	....	....
Other sectors...................................	4 674 ..	....	....	....	....	....	....	....	....
Money market instruments...................	4 680 ..	....	....	....	....	....	....	....	....
Monetary authorities........................	4 681 ..	....	....	....	....	....	....	....	....
General government.........................	4 682 ..	....	....	....	....	....	....	....	....
Banks...	4 683 ..	....	....	....	....	....	....	....	....
Other sectors...................................	4 684 ..	....	....	....	....	....	....	....	....
C. FINANCIAL DERIVATIVES.......................	4 910 ..	....	....	....	....	....	....	....	....
Monetary authorities...........................	4 911 ..	....	....	....	....	....	....	....	....
General government............................	4 912 ..	....	....	....	....	....	....	....	....
Banks..	4 913 ..	....	....	....	....	....	....	....	....
Other sectors......................................	4 914 ..	....	....	....	....	....	....	....	....
Assets..	4 900 ..	....	....	....	....	....	....	....	....
Monetary authorities...........................	4 901 ..	....	....	....	....	....	....	....	....
General government............................	4 902 ..	....	....	....	....	....	....	....	....
Banks..	4 903 ..	....	....	....	....	....	....	....	....
Other sectors......................................	4 904 ..	....	....	....	....	....	....	....	....
Liabilities...	4 905 ..	....	....	....	....	....	....	....	....
Monetary authorities...........................	4 906 ..	....	....	....	....	....	....	....	....
General government............................	4 907 ..	....	....	....	....	....	....	....	....
Banks..	4 908 ..	....	....	....	....	....	....	....	....
Other sectors......................................	4 909 ..	....	....	....	....	....	....	....	....

Table 2 (Concluded). STANDARD PRESENTATION, 2003–2010

(Millions of U.S. dollars)

	Code	2003	2004	2005	2006	2007	2008	2009	2010
D. OTHER INVESTMENT	4 700 ..	−25.68	−18.20	5.18	−5.15	−10.88	7.02	31.12	28.22
Assets	4 703 ..	−52.04	−66.54	−54.52	−35.09	−81.44	−65.21	−57.80	−48.26
Trade credits	4 706 ..	....	....	....	....	....	....	....	....
General government	4 707 ..	....	....	....	....	....	....	....	....
of which: Short-term	4 709 ..	....	....	....	....	....	....	....	....
Other sectors	4 710 ..	....	....	....	....	....	....	....	....
of which: Short-term	4 712 ..	....	....	....	....	....	....	....	....
Loans	4 714 ..	−17.07	−18.26	−6.53	....	....	−15.29	....	−6.36
Monetary authorities	4 715 ..	....	....	....	....	....	....	....	....
of which: Short-term	4 718 ..	....	....	....	....	....	....	....	....
General government	4 719 ..	....	....	....	....	....	....	....	....
of which: Short-term	4 721 ..	....	....	....	....	....	....	....	....
Banks	4 722 ..	−17.07	−18.26	−6.53	....	....	−15.29	....	−6.36
of which: Short-term	4 724 ..	....	....	....	....	....	....	....	....
Other sectors	4 725 ..	....	....	....	....	....	....	....	....
of which: Short-term	4 727 ..	....	....	....	....	....	....	....	....
Currency and deposits	4 730 ..	....	....	....	....	....	....	....	....
Monetary authorities	4 731 ..	....	....	....	....	....	....	....	....
General government	4 732 ..	....	....	....	....	....	....	....	....
Banks	4 733 ..	....	....	....	....	....	....	....	....
Other sectors	4 734 ..	....	....	....	....	....	....	....	....
Other assets	4 736 ..	−34.96	−48.28	−47.99	−35.09	−81.44	−49.91	−57.80	−41.90
Monetary authorities	4 737 ..	....	....	....	....	....	....	....	....
of which: Short-term	4 739 ..	....	....	....	....	....	....	....	....
General government	4 740 ..	....	....	....	....	....	....	....	....
of which: Short-term	4 742 ..	....	....	....	....	....	....	....	....
Banks	4 743 ..	....	....	....	....	....	....	....	....
of which: Short-term	4 745 ..	....	....	....	....	....	....	....	....
Other sectors	4 746 ..	−34.96	−48.28	−47.99	−35.09	−81.44	−49.91	−57.80	−41.90
of which: Short-term	4 748 ..	....	....	....	....	....	....	....	....
Liabilities	4 753 ..	26.36	48.34	59.69	29.94	70.56	72.23	88.91	76.48
Trade credits	4 756 ..	....	....	....	....	....	....	....	....
General government	4 757 ..	....	....	....	....	....	....	....	....
of which: Short-term	4 759 ..	....	....	....	....	....	....	....	....
Other sectors	4 760 ..	....	....	....	....	....	....	....	....
of which: Short-term	4 762 ..	....	....	....	....	....	....	....	....
Loans	4 764 ..	....	....	....	....	....	6.06	5.68	−5.85
Monetary authorities	4 765 ..	....	....	....	....	....	6.06	5.68	−5.85
of which: Use of Fund credit and loans from the Fund	4 766 ..	....	....	....	....	....	*6.06*	*5.68*	*−5.85*
of which: Short-term	4 768 ..	....	....	....	....	....	....	....	....
General government	4 769 ..	....	....	....	....	....	....	....	....
of which: Short-term	4 771 ..	....	....	....	....	....	....	....	....
Banks	4 772 ..	....	....	....	....	....	....	....	....
of which: Short-term	4 774 ..	....	....	....	....	....	....	....	....
Other sectors	4 775 ..	....	....	....	....	....	....	....	....
of which: Short-term	4 777 ..	....	....	....	....	....	....	....	....
Currency and deposits	4 780 ..	....	....	....	....	....	....	....	....
Monetary authorities	4 781 ..	....	....	....	....	....	....	....	....
General government	4 782 ..	....	....	....	....	....	....	....	....
Banks	4 783 ..	....	....	....	....	....	....	....	....
Other sectors	4 784 ..	....	....	....	....	....	....	....	....
Other liabilities	4 786 ..	26.36	48.34	59.69	29.94	70.56	66.16	83.23	82.32
Monetary authorities	4 787 ..	....	....	....	....	....	....	11.82	....
of which: Short-term	4 789 ..	....	....	....	....	....	....	....	....
General government	4 790 ..	....	....	....	....	....	....	....	....
of which: Short-term	4 792 ..	....	....	....	....	....	....	....	....
Banks	4 793 ..	....	....	....	9.69	36.36	....	1.07	....
of which: Short-term	4 795 ..	....	....	....	....	....	....	....	....
Other sectors	4 796 ..	26.36	48.34	59.69	20.25	34.20	66.16	70.34	82.32
of which: Short-term	4 798 ..	....	....	....	....	....	....	....	....
E. RESERVE ASSETS	4 802 ..	.50	−25.41	2.88	−12.11	1.84	3.27	−4.08	−25.26
Monetary gold	4 812 ..	....	....	....	....	....	....	....	....
Special drawing rights	4 811 ..	.02	....	....	....	....	.01	−11.80	10.33
Reserve position in the Fund	4 810 ..	....	....	....	....	....	....	....	....
Foreign exchange	4 803 ..	−1.57	−1.66	−2.53	−2.97	10.09	....	....	....
Other claims	4 813 ..	2.05	−23.76	5.41	−9.14	−8.24	3.26	7.72	−35.59
NET ERRORS AND OMISSIONS	4 998 ..	14.43	27.90	48.02	6.87	2.19	15.06	−5.74	72.34

Table 1. ANALYTIC PRESENTATION, 2003–2010

(Millions of U.S. dollars)

	Code	2003	2004	2005	2006	2007	2008	2009	2010
A. Current Account[1]	4 993 Z.	. . . .	**−26.16**	**−25.16**	**−49.29**	**−41.62**	**−53.53**	**−9.26**	**−57.90**
Goods: exports f.o.b.	2 100 ..	. . . .	11.90	12.00	10.35	51.92	46.88	25.87	35.49
Goods: imports f.o.b.	3 100 ..	. . . .	−155.38	−187.16	−218.86	−227.10	−248.99	−207.86	−279.99
Balance on Goods	4 100 ..	. . . .	*−143.48*	*−175.17*	*−208.51*	*−175.17*	*−202.12*	*−181.99*	*−244.50*
Services: credit	2 200 ..	. . . .	94.85	113.48	133.39	131.32	126.31	148.20	158.35
Services: debit	3 200 ..	. . . .	−41.96	−56.12	−56.80	−71.11	−68.73	−78.19	−86.79
Balance on Goods and Services	4 991 ..	. . . .	*−90.60*	*−117.81*	*−131.92*	*−114.96*	*−144.54*	*−111.99*	*−172.94*
Income: credit	2 300 ..	. . . .	4.39	5.83	5.98	6.74	13.81	7.75	6.81
Income: debit	3 300 ..	. . . .	−22.22	−19.96	−17.51	−46.22	−54.38	−32.34	−24.37
Balance on Goods, Services, and Income	4 992 ..	. . . .	*−108.43*	*−131.94*	*−143.44*	*−154.44*	*−185.12*	*−136.58*	*−190.50*
Current transfers: credit	2 379 Z.	. . . .	95.84	115.17	107.25	123.08	140.41	135.44	140.68
Current transfers: debit	3 379 ..	. . . .	−13.57	−8.40	−13.09	−10.26	−8.82	−8.11	−8.09
B. Capital Account[1]	4 994 Z.	. . . .	**38.77**	**39.33**	**52.13**	**28.17**	**29.83**	**46.76**	**82.39**
Capital account: credit	2 994 Z.	. . . .	41.95	42.00	54.50	32.10	32.00	50.26	84.21
Capital account: debit	3 994 ..	. . . .	−3.19	−2.67	−2.38	−3.93	−2.16	−3.50	−1.82
Total, Groups A Plus B	4 981 ..	. . . .	*12.61*	*14.16*	*2.84*	*−13.45*	*−23.70*	*37.50*	*24.48*
C. Financial Account[1]	4 995 W.	. . . .	**−2.22**	**−8.10**	**−3.09**	**13.93**	**56.26**	**−1.37**	**11.83**
Direct investment abroad	4 505 ..	. . . .	−.43	−2.05	. . . .	. . . .	. . . .	. . . .	. . . .
Direct investment in Samoa	4 555 Z.	. . . .	2.30	−2.98	20.67	6.82	45.90	9.87	.73
Portfolio investment assets	4 602 ..	. . . .	.02	−.07	−.02	−.14	1.06	−1.59	−1.66
Equity securities	4 610 ..	. . . .	. . . .	. . . .	−.02	. . . .	. . . .	. . . .	. . . .
Debt securities	4 619 ..	. . . .	. . . .	. . . .	. . . .	. . . .	. . . .	. . . .	. . . .
Portfolio investment liabilities	4 652 Z.	. . . .	.39	.12	.34	. . . .	. . . .	. . . .	. . . .
Equity securities	4 660 ..	. . . .	. . . .	. . . .	. . . .	. . . .	. . . .	. . . .	. . . .
Debt securities	4 669 Z.	. . . .	. . . .	. . . .	. . . .	. . . .	. . . .	. . . .	. . . .
Financial derivatives	4 910 ..	. . . .	. . . .	. . . .	. . . .	. . . .	. . . .	. . . .	. . . .
Financial derivatives assets	4 900 ..	. . . .	. . . .	. . . .	. . . .	. . . .	. . . .	. . . .	. . . .
Financial derivatives liabilities	4 905 ..	. . . .	. . . .	. . . .	. . . .	. . . .	. . . .	. . . .	. . . .
Other investment assets	4 703 ..	. . . .	−9.37	−.85	−1.20	−7.50	−37.95	−11.04	−36.00
Monetary authorities	4 701 ..	. . . .	. . . .	. . . .	. . . .	. . . .	. . . .	. . . .	. . . .
General government	4 704 ..	. . . .	. . . .	. . . .	. . . .	. . . .	−9.51	. . . .	−29.31
Banks	4 705 ..	. . . .	−9.04	−.77	−.17	−5.30	3.50	−3.00	5.92
Other sectors	4 728 ..	. . . .	−.33	−.07	−1.03	−2.19	−31.94	−8.04	−12.61
Other investment liabilities	4 753 W.	. . . .	4.87	−2.27	−22.86	14.74	47.25	1.39	48.76
Monetary authorities	4 753 WA	. . . .	−.01	1.00	−.45	.04	.05	14.91	−.01
General government	4 753 ZB	. . . .	5.46	2.13	−17.15	11.31	45.37	−9.65	55.28
Banks	4 753 ZC	. . . .	2.35	−1.85	−1.90	6.72	2.83	4.17	2.63
Other sectors	4 753 ZD	. . . .	−2.92	−3.55	−3.37	−3.33	−1.01	−8.04	−9.13
Total, Groups A Through C	4 983 ..	. . . .	*10.39*	*6.06*	*−.24*	*.48*	*32.56*	*36.13*	*36.31*
D. Net Errors and Omissions	4 998 ..	. . . .	**−2.58**	**−7.03**	**−4.94**	**10.19**	**−29.03**	**12.02**	**−11.97**
Total, Groups A Through D	4 984 ..	. . . .	*7.81*	*−.96*	*−5.18*	*10.67*	*3.53*	*48.15*	*24.34*
E. Reserves and Related Items	4 802 A.	. . . .	**−7.81**	**.96**	**5.18**	**−10.67**	**−3.53**	**−48.15**	**−24.34**
Reserve assets	4 802 ..	. . . .	−7.81	.96	3.69	−10.67	−3.53	−48.15	−33.41
Use of Fund credit and loans	4 766 ..	. . . .	. . . .	. . . .	. . . .	. . . .	. . . .	. . . .	9.08
Exceptional financing	4 920 ..	. . . .	. . . .	. . . .	1.49	. . . .	. . . .	. . . .	. . . .
Conversion rates: tala per U.S. dollar	0 101 ..	**2.9732**	**2.7807**	**2.7103**	**2.7793**	**2.6166**	**2.6442**	**2.7308**	**2.4847**

[1] Excludes components that have been classified in the categories of Group E.

Table 2. STANDARD PRESENTATION, 2003–2010

(Millions of U.S. dollars)

	Code	2003	2004	2005	2006	2007	2008	2009	2010
CURRENT ACCOUNT	4 993	....	−26.16	−25.16	−47.79	−41.62	−53.53	−9.26	−57.90
A. GOODS	4 100	....	−143.48	−175.17	−208.51	−175.17	−202.12	−181.99	−244.50
Credit	2 100	....	11.90	12.00	10.35	51.92	46.88	25.87	35.49
General merchandise: exports f.o.b.	2 110	....	11.90	12.00	10.35	13.89	11.26	11.71	12.39
Goods for processing: exports f.o.b.	2 150	....	....	....	....	38.04	35.62	14.16	23.10
Repairs on goods	2 160	....	....	....	....	....	....	....	....
Goods procured in ports by carriers	2 170	....	....	....	....	....	....	....	....
Nonmonetary gold	2 180	....	....	....	....	....	....	....	....
Debit	3 100	....	−155.38	−187.16	−218.86	−227.10	−248.99	−207.86	−279.99
General merchandise: imports f.o.b.	3 110	....	−155.38	−187.16	−218.86	−227.10	−248.99	−207.86	−279.99
Goods for processing: imports f.o.b.	3 150	....	....	....	....	....	....	....	....
Repairs on goods	3 160	....	....	....	....	....	....	....	....
Goods procured in ports by carriers	3 170	....	....	....	....	....	....	....	....
Nonmonetary gold	3 180	....	....	....	....	....	....	....	....
B. SERVICES	4 200	....	52.89	57.36	76.59	60.21	57.57	70.00	71.56
Total credit	2 200	....	*94.85*	*113.48*	*133.39*	*131.32*	*126.31*	*148.20*	*158.35*
Total debit	3 200	....	*−41.96*	*−56.12*	*−56.80*	*−71.11*	*−68.73*	*−78.19*	*−86.79*
Transportation services, credit	2 205	....	4.43	4.78	5.00	7.27	7.21	10.72	7.36
Passenger	2 850	....	*.99*	*.81*	*1.39*	*.35*	*.60*	*.19*	*.65*
Freight	2 851	....	*.31*	*.65*	*1.14*	*1.47*	*1.69*	*1.90*	*1.24*
Other	2 852	....	*3.13*	*3.31*	*2.47*	*5.44*	*4.92*	*8.64*	*5.47*
Sea transport, passenger	2 207	....	....	....	....	....	....	....	....
Sea transport, freight	2 208	....	....	....	....	....	....	....	....
Sea transport, other	2 209	....	....	....	....	....	....	....	....
Air transport, passenger	2 211	....	....	....	....	....	....	....	....
Air transport, freight	2 212	....	....	....	....	....	....	....	....
Air transport, other	2 213	....	....	....	....	....	....	....	....
Other transport, passenger	2 215	....	....	....	....	....	....	....	....
Other transport, freight	2 216	....	....	....	....	....	....	....	....
Other transport, other	2 217	....	....	....	....	....	....	....	....
Transportation services, debit	3 205	....	−20.13	−23.90	−30.29	−30.16	−33.78	−32.73	−36.23
Passenger	3 850	....	*−6.52*	*−7.56*	*−9.50*	*−9.64*	*−10.72*	*−9.34*	*−10.27*
Freight	3 851	....	*−13.16*	*−15.44*	*−20.19*	*−20.30*	*−21.17*	*−21.72*	*−25.35*
Other	3 852	....	*−.45*	*−.91*	*−.59*	*−.22*	*−1.88*	*−1.66*	*−.60*
Sea transport, passenger	3 207	....	....	....	....	....	....	....	....
Sea transport, freight	3 208	....	....	....	....	....	....	....	....
Sea transport, other	3 209	....	....	....	....	....	....	....	....
Air transport, passenger	3 211	....	....	....	....	....	....	....	....
Air transport, freight	3 212	....	....	....	....	....	....	....	....
Air transport, other	3 213	....	....	....	....	....	....	....	....
Other transport, passenger	3 215	....	....	....	....	....	....	....	....
Other transport, freight	3 216	....	....	....	....	....	....	....	....
Other transport, other	3 217	....	....	....	....	....	....	....	....
Travel, credit	2 236	....	69.48	78.76	89.72	103.27	110.96	115.49	122.82
Business travel	2 237	....	....	....	....	....	....	....	....
Personal travel	2 240	....	....	....	....	....	....	....	....
Travel, debit	3 236	....	−5.38	−9.01	−5.55	−10.22	−10.88	−10.67	−14.86
Business travel	3 237	....	....	....	....	....	....	....	....
Personal travel	3 240	....	....	....	....	....	....	....	....
Other services, credit	2 200 BA	....	20.94	29.94	38.67	20.78	8.13	21.98	28.18
Communications	2 245	....	2.52	5.84	5.74	7.04	....	5.58	5.38
Construction	2 249	....	.52	5.08	2.91	.54	.10	1.85	8.65
Insurance	2 253	....	2.17	.67	3.80	....	....	....	....
Financial	2 260	....	....	....	....	....	....	....	....
Computer and information	2 262	....	.08	.22	2.28	.41	....	.30	.97
Royalties and licence fees	2 266	....	....	....	....	....	....	....	....
Other business services	2 268	....	14.44	16.39	21.87	8.77	7.51	13.29	11.99
Personal, cultural, and recreational	2 287	....	.28	1.29	1.57	3.49	....	.95	1.18
Government, n.i.e.	2 291	....	.93	.46	.50	.53	.52	....	....
Other services, debit	3 200 BA	....	−16.45	−23.21	−20.96	−30.73	−24.08	−34.80	−35.70
Communications	3 245	....	−3.29	−4.13	−3.09	−3.28	....	−1.52	−.37
Construction	3 249	....	−6.54	−4.62	−5.89	−1.13	−.15	−.57	−.36
Insurance	3 253	....	−2.83	−1.91	−2.58	−1.47	−.85	−.73	−1.09
Financial	3 260	....	....	....	....	....	....	....	....
Computer and information	3 262	....	−.74	−1.25	−1.64	....	....	....	....
Royalties and licence fees	3 266	....	−.17	−.11	....	−.04	−.06	−.05	−.04
Other business services	3 268	....	−1.69	−9.27	−6.62	−15.88	−12.32	−17.83	−24.77
Personal, cultural, and recreational	3 287	....	−.14	−.53	−.28	....	....	....	....
Government, n.i.e.	3 291	....	−1.05	−1.39	−.87	−8.94	−10.69	−14.12	−9.08

Table 2 (Continued). STANDARD PRESENTATION, 2003–2010

(Millions of U.S. dollars)

	Code	2003	2004	2005	2006	2007	2008	2009	2010
C. INCOME	4 300	....	−17.83	−14.13	−11.52	−39.48	−40.57	−24.59	−17.56
Total credit	2 300	....	*4.39*	*5.83*	*5.98*	*6.74*	*13.81*	*7.75*	*6.81*
Total debit	3 300	....	*−22.22*	*−19.96*	*−17.51*	*−46.22*	*−54.38*	*−32.34*	*−24.37*
Compensation of employees, credit	2 310	....	.90	.73	.80	.80	.59	.42	.24
Compensation of employees, debit	3 310	....	−10.86	−10.76	−2.06	−2.26	−1.20	−1.58	−.81
Investment income, credit	2 320	....	3.49	5.11	5.19	5.94	13.22	7.34	6.57
Direct investment income	2 330	....	....	....	....	....	....	....	....
Dividends and distributed branch profits	2 332	....	....	....	....	....	....	....	....
Reinvested earnings and undistributed branch profits	2 333	....	....	....	....	....	....	....	....
Income on debt (interest)	2 334	....	....	....	....	....	....	....	....
Portfolio investment income	2 339	....	.09	.67	.27	.19	.32	3.99	.49
Income on equity	2 340	....	.09	.67	.27	....	....	....	....
Income on bonds and notes	2 350	....	....	....	....	....	....	....	....
Income on money market instruments	2 360	....	....	....	....	....	....	....	....
Other investment income	2 370	....	3.40	4.43	4.91	5.76	12.90	3.35	6.09
Investment income, debit	3 320	....	−11.36	−9.20	−15.45	−43.96	−53.19	−30.76	−23.56
Direct investment income	3 330	....	−9.77	−7.70	−13.81	−37.85	−50.49	−27.41	−17.54
Dividends and distributed branch profits	3 332	....	−5.98	−8.13	−5.34	−34.26	−36.63	−16.55	−17.38
Reinvested earnings and undistributed branch profits	3 333	....	−3.79	.43	−8.47	−3.59	−13.86	−10.86	−.16
Income on debt (interest)	3 334	....	....	....	....	....	....	....	....
Portfolio investment income	3 339	....	....	....	....	....	....	....	....
Income on equity	3 340	....	....	....	....	....	....	....	....
Income on bonds and notes	3 350	....	....	....	....	....	....	....	....
Income on money market instruments	3 360	....	....	....	....	....	....	....	....
Other investment income	3 370	....	−1.59	−1.50	−1.64	−6.11	−2.70	−3.36	−6.02
D. CURRENT TRANSFERS	4 379	....	82.27	106.77	95.64	112.82	131.59	127.32	132.59
Credit	2 379	....	95.84	115.17	108.74	123.08	140.41	135.44	140.68
General government	2 380	....	8.81	5.98	1.49	2.42	3.53	1.57	....
Other sectors	2 390	....	87.03	109.20	107.25	120.66	136.88	133.86	140.68
Workers' remittances	2 391	....	....	....	....	95.85	110.78	119.07	121.85
Other current transfers	2 392	....	....	....	....	24.81	26.09	14.79	18.84
Debit	3 379	....	−13.57	−8.40	−13.09	−10.26	−8.82	−8.11	−8.09
General government	3 380	....	−3.60	−2.18	....	−.52	....	−.02	−.01
Other sectors	3 390	....	−9.98	−6.22	−13.09	−9.74	−8.82	−8.09	−8.08
Workers' remittances	3 391	....	....	....	....	−7.95	−7.40	−6.87	−6.41
Other current transfers	3 392	....	....	....	....	−1.79	−1.42	−1.22	−1.66
CAPITAL AND FINANCIAL ACCOUNT	4 996	....	28.74	32.19	52.73	31.43	82.55	−2.76	69.88
CAPITAL ACCOUNT	4 994	....	38.77	39.33	52.13	28.17	29.83	46.76	82.39
Total credit	2 994	....	*41.95*	*42.00*	*54.50*	*32.10*	*32.00*	*50.26*	*84.21*
Total debit	3 994	....	*−3.19*	*−2.67*	*−2.38*	*−3.93*	*−2.16*	*−3.50*	*−1.82*
Capital transfers, credit	2 400	....	41.95	42.00	54.50	32.10	32.00	50.26	84.21
General government	2 401	....	40.55	38.35	29.78	31.05	31.41	49.01	72.40
Debt forgiveness	2 402	....	....	....	....	....	....	....	....
Other capital transfers	2 410	....	....	....	....	....	....	....	....
Other sectors	2 430	....	1.40	3.65	24.73	1.05	.59	1.24	11.81
Migrants' transfers	2 431	....	....	....	....	....	....	....	....
Debt forgiveness	2 432	....	....	....	12.36	....	....	....	....
Other capital transfers	2 440	....	1.40	3.65	12.36	....	....	....	....
Capital transfers, debit	3 400	....	−3.19	−2.67	−2.38	−3.93	−2.16	−3.50	−1.82
General government	3 401	....	....	....	....	−.09	−1.02	−1.41	−.45
Debt forgiveness	3 402	....	....	....	....	....	....	....	....
Other capital transfers	3 410	....	....	....	....	....	....	....	....
Other sectors	3 430	....	−3.19	−2.67	−2.38	−3.85	−1.14	−2.08	−1.37
Migrants' transfers	3 431	....	....	....	....	....	....	....	....
Debt forgiveness	3 432	....	....	....	....	....	....	....	....
Other capital transfers	3 440	....	−3.19	−2.67	−2.38	....	....	....	....
Nonproduced nonfinancial assets, credit	2 480	....	....	....	....	....	....	....	....
Nonproduced nonfinancial assets, debit	3 480	....	....	....	....	....	....	....	....

Table 2 (Continued). STANDARD PRESENTATION, 2003–2010

(Millions of U.S. dollars)

	Code	2003	2004	2005	2006	2007	2008	2009	2010
FINANCIAL ACCOUNT....................................	4 995 ..	....	−10.03	−7.14	.61	3.26	52.72	−49.52	−12.51
A. DIRECT INVESTMENT............................	4 500 ..	....	1.87	−5.03	20.67	6.82	45.90	9.87	.73
Direct investment abroad............................	4 505 ..	....	−.43	−2.05	....	....	....	....	....
Equity capital..	4 510 ..		−.43	−2.05					
Claims on affiliated enterprises........................	4 515 ..	....	−.43	−2.05	....				....
Liabilities to affiliated enterprises....................	4 520 ..	....	....	....					
Reinvested earnings..	4 525 ..	....							
Other capital..	4 530 ..	....							
Claims on affiliated enterprises........................	4 535 ..	....							
Liabilities to affiliated enterprises....................	4 540 ..	....							
Direct investment in Samoa........................	4 555 ..	....	2.30	−2.98	20.67	6.82	45.90	9.87	.73
Equity capital..	4 560 ..	....	−.18	−2.56	12.20	3.23	32.04	−.99	.57
Claims on direct investors...............................	4 565 ..	....	−.18	−2.56	12.20	3.23	.68	5.42	.57
Liabilities to direct investors...........................	4 570 ..		....	....		....	31.35	−6.41	....
Reinvested earnings..	4 575 ..	....	3.79	−.43	8.47	3.59	13.86	10.86	.16
Other capital..	4 580 ..	....	−1.31	.01	−.01	....			
Claims on direct investors...............................	4 585 ..	....	....	....	....				
Liabilities to direct investors...........................	4 590 ..	....	....	....	....				
B. PORTFOLIO INVESTMENT........................	4 600 ..	....	.41	.05	.31	−.14	1.06	−1.59	−1.66
Assets..	4 602 ..	....	.02	−.07	−.02	−.14	1.06	−1.59	−1.66
Equity securities...	4 610 ..	....	....	....	−.02	....	....		
Monetary authorities......................................	4 611 ..	....							
General government..	4 612 ..	....							
Banks...	4 613 ..	....							
Other sectors..	4 614 ..	....							
Debt securities..	4 619 ..	....							
Bonds and notes..	4 620 ..	....							
Monetary authorities......................................	4 621 ..	....							
General government..	4 622 ..	....							
Banks...	4 623 ..	....							
Other sectors..	4 624 ..	....							
Money market instruments..............................	4 630 ..	....							
Monetary authorities......................................	4 631 ..	....							
General government..	4 632 ..	....							
Banks...	4 633 ..	....							
Other sectors..	4 634 ..	....	....	....	....				
Liabilities..	4 652 ..	....	.39	.12	.34	....	....	....	....
Equity securities...	4 660 ..	....							
Banks...	4 663 ..	....							
Other sectors..	4 664 ..	....							
Debt securities..	4 669 ..	....							
Bonds and notes..	4 670 ..	....							
Monetary authorities......................................	4 671 ..	....							
General government..	4 672 ..	....							
Banks...	4 673 ..	....							
Other sectors..	4 674 ..	....							
Money market instruments..............................	4 680 ..	....							
Monetary authorities......................................	4 681 ..	....							
General government..	4 682 ..	....							
Banks...	4 683 ..	....							
Other sectors..	4 684 ..	....							
C. FINANCIAL DERIVATIVES........................	4 910 ..	....	....	....	....	....	....	....	....
Monetary authorities......................................	4 911 ..	....	....	....					
General government..	4 912 ..	....	....	....					
Banks...	4 913 ..	....	....	....					
Other sectors..	4 914 ..	....	....	....					
Assets..	4 900 ..	....	....	....					.73
Monetary authorities......................................	4 901 ..	....	....						
General government..	4 902 ..	....	....						
Banks...	4 903 ..	....	....						
Other sectors..	4 904 ..	....	....						
Liabilities..	4 905 ..	....	....	....	....	....	....	....	....
Monetary authorities......................................	4 906 ..	....	....	....	....	....	....	....	....
General government..	4 907 ..	....	....	....	....	....	....	....	....
Banks...	4 908 ..	....	....	....	....	....	....	....	....
Other sectors..	4 909 ..	....	....	....	....	....	....	....	....

Table 2 (Concluded). STANDARD PRESENTATION, 2003–2010

(Millions of U.S. dollars)

	Code	2003	2004	2005	2006	2007	2008	2009	2010
D. OTHER INVESTMENT	4 700	....	−4.50	−3.12	−24.07	7.24	9.29	−9.65	21.83
Assets	4 703	....	−9.37	−.85	−1.20	−7.50	−37.95	−11.04	−36.00
Trade credits	4 706	....	....	....	....	....	....	....	....
General government	4 707	....	....	....	....	....	....	....	....
of which: Short-term	4 709	....	....	....	....	....	....	....	....
Other sectors	4 710	....	....	....	....	....	....	....	....
of which: Short-term	4 712	....	....	....	....	....	....	....	....
Loans	4 714	....	−8.43	....	....	....	....	....	....
Monetary authorities	4 715	....	....	....	....	....	....	....	....
of which: Short-term	4 718	....	....	....	....	....	....	....	....
General government	4 719	....	....	....	....	....	....	....	....
of which: Short-term	4 721	....	....	....	....	....	....	....	....
Banks	4 722	....	−8.43	....	....	....	....	....	....
of which: Short-term	4 724	....	....	....	....	....	....	....	....
Other sectors	4 725	....	....	....	....	....	....	....	....
of which: Short-term	4 727	....	....	....	....	....	....	....	....
Currency and deposits	4 730	....	−.95	−.85	−1.20	−7.50	−28.44	−11.04	−6.69
Monetary authorities	4 731	....	....	....	....	....	....	....	....
General government	4 732	....	....	....	....	....	....	....	....
Banks	4 733	....	−.62	−.77	−.17	−5.30	3.50	−3.00	5.92
Other sectors	4 734	....	−.33	−.07	−1.03	−2.19	−31.94	−8.04	−12.61
Other assets	4 736	....	....	....	....	....	−9.51	....	−29.31
Monetary authorities	4 737	....	....	....	....	....	....	....	....
of which: Short-term	4 739	....	....	....	....	....	....	....	....
General government	4 740	....	....	....	....	....	−9.51	....	−29.31
of which: Short-term	4 742	....	....	....	....	....	....	....	....
Banks	4 743	....	....	....	....	....	....	....	....
of which: Short-term	4 745	....	....	....	....	....	....	....	....
Other sectors	4 746	....	....	....	....	....	....	....	....
of which: Short-term	4 748	....	....	....	....	....	....	....	....
Liabilities	4 753	....	4.87	−2.27	−22.86	14.74	47.25	1.39	57.83
Trade credits	4 756	....	....	....	....	....	....	....	....
General government	4 757	....	....	....	....	....	....	....	....
of which: Short-term	4 759	....	....	....	....	....	....	....	....
Other sectors	4 760	....	....	....	....	....	....	....	....
of which: Short-term	4 762	....	....	....	....	....	....	....	....
Loans	4 764	....	2.53	3.04	−15.81	5.45	44.25	−16.56	55.31
Monetary authorities	4 765	....	....	....	....	....	....	....	9.08
of which: Use of Fund credit and loans from the Fund	4 766	....	....	....	....	....	....	....	9.08
of which: Short-term	4 768	....	....	....	....	....	....	....	....
General government	4 769	....	5.45	2.18	−17.17	11.31	45.27	−9.51	55.37
of which: Short-term	4 771	....	....	....	....	....	....	....	....
Banks	4 772	....	....	....	−1.07	−2.52	....	....	....
of which: Short-term	4 774	....	....	....	....	....	....	....	....
Other sectors	4 775	....	−2.92	.86	2.43	−3.33	−1.01	−7.05	−9.13
of which: Short-term	4 777	....	....	....	....	....	....	....	....
Currency and deposits	4 780	....	2.34	−.90	−1.26	9.29	2.99	3.39	2.52
Monetary authorities	4 781	....	−.01	1.00	−.45	.04	.05	−.63	−.01
General government	4 782	....	....	−.05	.02	....	.11	−.14	−.09
Banks	4 783	....	2.35	−1.85	−.83	9.25	2.83	4.17	2.63
Other sectors	4 784	....	....	....	....	....	....	....	....
Other liabilities	4 786	....	....	−4.41	−5.80	....	....	14.56	....
Monetary authorities	4 787	....	....	....	....	....	....	15.55	....
of which: Short-term	4 789	....	....	....	....	....	....	....	....
General government	4 790	....	....	....	....	....	....	....	....
of which: Short-term	4 792	....	....	....	....	....	....	....	....
Banks	4 793	....	....	....	....	....	....	....	....
of which: Short-term	4 795	....	....	....	....	....	....	....	....
Other sectors	4 796	....	....	−4.41	−5.80	....	....	−.99	....
of which: Short-term	4 798	....	....	....	....	....	....	....	....
E. RESERVE ASSETS	4 802	....	−7.81	.96	3.69	−10.67	−3.53	−48.15	−33.41
Monetary gold	4 812	....	....	....	....	....	....	....	....
Special drawing rights	4 811	....	−.04	−.05	−.08	−.10	−.10	−15.56	−.01
Reserve position in the Fund	4 810	....	....	....	....	....	....	....	....
Foreign exchange	4 803	....	−7.77	1.02	3.77	−10.57	−3.44	−32.59	−33.41
Other claims	4 813	....	....	....	....	....	....	....	....
NET ERRORS AND OMISSIONS	4 998	....	−2.58	−7.03	−4.94	10.19	−29.03	12.02	−11.97

Table 1. ANALYTIC PRESENTATION, 2003–2010

(Millions of U.S. dollars)

	Code	2003	2004	2005	2006	2007	2008	2009	2010
A. Current Account[1]	4 993 Z.	−28.85	−38.27	−36.26	−57.97	−64.54	−93.53	−78.78	−107.38
Goods: exports f.o.b.	2 100 ..	6.57	5.44	6.79	7.71	6.81	7.83	9.21	12.05
Goods: imports f.o.b.	3 100 ..	−33.57	−38.37	−41.60	−59.24	−64.87	−92.15	−83.76	−99.42
Balance on Goods	4 100 ..	*−27.00*	*−32.93*	*−34.81*	*−51.53*	*−58.06*	*−84.32*	*−74.56*	*−87.37*
Services: credit	2 200 ..	9.38	9.80	9.31	8.55	6.85	9.84	10.62	12.00
Services: debit	3 200 ..	−14.26	−16.27	−11.28	−18.22	−19.01	−21.63	−19.19	−34.25
Balance on Goods and Services	4 991 ..	*−31.89*	*−39.40*	*−36.78*	*−61.20*	*−70.22*	*−96.10*	*−83.13*	*−109.62*
Income: credit	2 300 ..	1.21	1.19	1.97	6.15	6.76	1.94	1.64	1.89
Income: debit	3 300 ..	−3.73	−4.29	−4.90	−3.12	−2.29	−2.01	−1.93	−2.26
Balance on Goods, Services, and Income	4 992 ..	*−34.41*	*−42.50*	*−39.71*	*−58.17*	*−65.74*	*−96.17*	*−83.42*	*−109.99*
Current transfers: credit	2 379 Z.	6.94	8.29	7.47	5.26	6.47	8.77	11.27	8.98
Current transfers: debit	3 379 ..	−1.38	−4.06	−4.03	−5.06	−5.27	−6.12	−6.63	−6.37
B. Capital Account[1]	4 994 Z.	**18.71**	**18.02**	**65.64**	**23.54**	**62.42**	**47.46**	**39.89**	**40.30**
Capital account: credit	2 994 Z.	18.71	18.02	65.64	23.54	62.42	47.46	39.89	40.30
Capital account: debit	3 994 ..	....	....	....	....	....	....	....	....
Total, Groups A Plus B	4 981 ..	*−10.14*	*−20.25*	*29.38*	*−34.43*	*−2.12*	*−46.06*	*−38.89*	*−67.08*
C. Financial Account[1]	4 995 W.	**9.07**	**10.73**	**−4.33**	**40.81**	**−143.41**	**75.08**	**60.34**	**61.00**
Direct investment abroad	4 505 ..	....	....	−14.55	−6.14	−6.25	−.19	−.30	−.11
Direct investment in São Tomé and Príncipe	4 555 Z.	3.40	3.50	15.66	38.02	36.03	79.14	15.50	24.64
Portfolio investment assets	4 602 ..	....	....	....	....	....	....	−1.50	....
Equity securities	4 610 ..	....	....	....	....	....	....	....	....
Debt securities	4 619 ..	....	....	....	....	....	....	−1.50	....
Portfolio investment liabilities	4 652 Z.	....	....	....	....	....	....	....	....
Equity securities	4 660 ..	....	....	....	....	....	....	....	....
Debt securities	4 669 Z.	....	....	....	....	....	....	....	....
Financial derivatives	4 910 ..	....	....	....	....	....	....	....	....
Financial derivatives assets	4 900 ..	....	....	....	....	....	....	....	....
Financial derivatives liabilities	4 905 ..	....	....	....	....	....	....	....	....
Other investment assets	4 703 ..	.75	−2.82	−3.44	9.26	7.92	15.12	12.53	18.82
Monetary authorities	4 701 ..	−.49	−.30	−.83	−4.28	−1.49	−1.28	.76	.82
General government	4 704 ..	....	....	....	....	....	....	....	....
Banks	4 705 ..	−.37	−2.51	−12.10	3.04	−4.59	−8.50	3.77	−6.00
Other sectors	4 728 ..	1.60	....	9.50	10.50	14.00	24.90	8.00	24.00
Other investment liabilities	4 753 W.	4.93	10.05	−2.00	−.33	−181.11	−18.99	34.11	17.64
Monetary authorities	4 753 WA	....	....	....	....	....	....	10.12	....
General government	4 753 ZB	4.93	10.05	−2.00	−.33	−181.11	−8.99	23.98	17.64
Banks	4 753 ZC	....	....	....	....	....	....	....	....
Other sectors	4 753 ZD	....	....	....	....	....	−10.00	....	....
Total, Groups A Through C	4 983 ..	*−1.07*	*−9.52*	*25.06*	*6.38*	*−145.54*	*29.01*	*21.45*	*−6.08*
D. Net Errors and Omissions	4 998 ..	**2.85**	**1.87**	**5.46**	**−6.26**	**−9.07**	**−16.11**	**−12.51**	**2.25**
Total, Groups A Through D	4 984 ..	*1.78*	*−7.65*	*30.51*	*.11*	*−154.61*	*12.91*	*8.94*	*−3.84*
E. Reserves and Related Items	4 802 A.	**−1.78**	**7.65**	**−30.51**	**−.11**	**154.61**	**−12.91**	**−8.94**	**3.84**
Reserve assets	4 802 ..	−6.24	4.01	−37.21	−.78	−9.92	−22.57	−11.58	3.27
Use of Fund credit and loans	4 766 ..	....	....	.48	.67	−1.67	1.36	.55	.57
Exceptional financing	4 920 ..	4.46	3.64	6.21	....	166.21	8.31	2.09	....
Conversion rates: dobras per U.S. dollar	0 101 ..	**9,347.6**	**9,902.3**	**10,558.0**	**12,448.6**	**13,536.8**	**14,695.2**	**16,208.5**	**18,498.6**

[1] Excludes components that have been classified in the categories of Group E.

Table 2. STANDARD PRESENTATION, 2003–2010

(Millions of U.S. dollars)

	Code	2003	2004	2005	2006	2007	2008	2009	2010
CURRENT ACCOUNT................................	4 993 ..	−28.85	−38.27	−36.26	−57.97	−64.54	−93.53	−78.78	−107.38
A. GOODS..	4 100 ..	−27.00	−32.93	−34.81	−51.53	−58.06	−84.32	−74.56	−87.37
Credit.......................................	2 100 ..	6.57	5.44	6.79	7.71	6.81	7.83	9.21	12.05
General merchandise: exports f.o.b........	2 110 ..	6.57	3.52	3.39	3.82	3.93	5.63	6.21	6.97
Goods for processing: exports f.o.b.......	2 150 ..	....	....	....	....	....	....	....	....
Repairs on goods...........................	2 160 ..	....	....	....	....	....	....	....	....
Goods procured in ports by carriers.......	2 170 ..	....	1.92	3.40	3.89	2.88	2.20	3.00	5.07
Nonmonetary gold..........................	2 180 ..	....	....	....	....	....	....	....	....
Debit..	3 100 ..	−33.57	−38.37	−41.60	−59.24	−64.87	−92.15	−83.76	−99.42
General merchandise: imports f.o.b........	3 110 ..	−33.57	−38.37	−41.60	−59.24	−64.87	−92.15	−83.76	−99.42
Goods for processing: imports f.o.b.......	3 150 ..	....	....	....	....	....	....	....	....
Repairs on goods...........................	3 160 ..	....	....	....	....	....	....	....	....
Goods procured in ports by carriers.......	3 170 ..	....	....	....	....	....	....	....	....
Nonmonetary gold..........................	3 180 ..	....	....	....	....	....	....	....	....
B. SERVICES....................................	4 200 ..	−4.89	−6.47	−1.97	−9.67	−12.16	−11.78	−8.57	−22.25
Total credit................................	2 200 ..	*9.38*	*9.80*	*9.31*	*8.55*	*6.85*	*9.84*	*10.62*	*12.00*
Total debit.................................	3 200 ..	*−14.26*	*−16.27*	*−11.28*	*−18.22*	*−19.01*	*−21.63*	*−19.19*	*−34.25*
Transportation services, credit............	2 205 ..	.14	.15	.14	.13	.13	.15	.16	.18
Passenger..................................	2 850 ..	....	....	....	....	....	....	....	....
Freight....................................	2 851 ..	....	....	....	....	....	....	....	....
Other......................................	2 852 ..	*.14*	*.15*	*.14*	*.13*	*.13*	*.15*	*.16*	*.18*
Sea transport, passenger...................	2 207 ..	....	....	....	....	....	....	....	....
Sea transport, freight.....................	2 208 ..	....	....	....	....	....	....	....	....
Sea transport, other.......................	2 209 ..	.07	.08	.07	.07	.07	.08	.08	.09
Air transport, passenger...................	2 211 ..	....	....	....	....	....	....	....	....
Air transport, freight.....................	2 212 ..	....	....	....	....	....	....	....	....
Air transport, other.......................	2 213 ..	.07	.07	.07	.07	.07	.07	.08	.09
Other transport, passenger.................	2 215 ..	....	....	....	....	....	....	....	....
Other transport, freight...................	2 216 ..	....	....	....	....	....	....	....	....
Other transport, other.....................	2 217 ..	....	....	....	....	....	....	....	....
Transportation services, debit.............	3 205 ..	−8.03	−9.15	−8.72	−13.60	−13.61	−17.30	−15.79	−19.60
Passenger..................................	3 850 ..	*−1.32*	*−1.48*	*−.40*	*−.87*	*−.64*	*−.34*	*−.38*	*−.86*
Freight....................................	3 851 ..	*−6.71*	*−7.67*	*−8.32*	*−12.72*	*−12.97*	*−16.96*	*−15.41*	*−18.29*
Other......................................	3 852 ..	....	....	....	....	....	....	....	*−.45*
Sea transport, passenger...................	3 207 ..	....	....	....	....	....	....	....	....
Sea transport, freight.....................	3 208 ..	−6.58	−7.52	−8.15	−12.47	−12.71	−16.59	−15.08	−17.90
Sea transport, other.......................	3 209 ..	....	....	....	....	....	....	....	....
Air transport, passenger...................	3 211 ..	−1.32	−1.48	−.40	−.87	−.64	−.34	−.38	−.86
Air transport, freight.....................	3 212 ..	−.13	−.15	−.17	−.25	−.26	−.37	−.34	−.40
Air transport, other.......................	3 213 ..	....	....	....	....	....	....	....	−.45
Other transport, passenger.................	3 215 ..	....	....	....	....	....	....	....	....
Other transport, freight...................	3 216 ..	....	....	....	....	....	....	....	....
Other transport, other.....................	3 217 ..	....	....	....	....	....	....	....	....
Travel, credit.............................	2 236 ..	7.37	7.70	7.32	6.72	5.00	7.74	8.35	9.44
Business travel............................	2 237 ..	2.95	3.08	2.93	2.69	2.00	3.10	3.34	3.78
Personal travel............................	2 240 ..	4.42	4.62	4.39	4.03	3.00	4.65	5.01	5.66
Travel, debit..............................	3 236 ..	−.53	−.59	−.05	−.24	−.10	−.01	−.01	−4.44
Business travel............................	3 237 ..	....	....	....	....	....	....	....	....
Personal travel............................	3 240 ..	−.53	−.59	−.05	−.24	−.10	−.01	−.01	−4.44
Other services, credit.....................	2 200 BA	1.86	1.94	1.85	1.70	1.71	1.95	2.11	2.38
Communications.............................	2 245 ..	.92	.96	.92	.84	.85	.97	1.04	1.18
Construction...............................	2 249 ..	....	....	....	....	....	....	....	....
Insurance..................................	2 253 ..	....	....	....	....	....	....	....	....
Financial..................................	2 260 ..	.32	.34	.32	.30	.30	.34	.37	.42
Computer and information...................	2 262 ..	....	....	....	....	....	....	....	....
Royalties and licence fees.................	2 266 ..	....	....	....	....	....	....	....	....
Other business services....................	2 268 ..	.32	.33	.32	.29	.29	.33	.36	.41
Personal, cultural, and recreational.......	2 287 ..	....	....	....	....	....	....	....	....
Government, n.i.e..........................	2 291 ..	.29	.31	.29	.27	.27	.31	.33	.38
Other services, debit......................	3 200 BA	−5.70	−6.53	−2.51	−4.38	−5.29	−4.31	−3.39	−10.21
Communications.............................	3 245 ..	−.53	−.59	−.05	−.24	−.10	−.01	−.01	−1.10
Construction...............................	3 249 ..	....	....	....	....	....	....	....	....
Insurance..................................	3 253 ..	−.50	−.58	−.62	−.95	−.97	−1.38	−1.26	−2.44
Financial..................................	3 260 ..	−.48	−.54	−.05	−.22	−.10	−.01	−.01	−.93
Computer and information...................	3 262 ..	....	....	....	....	....	....	....	....
Royalties and licence fees.................	3 266 ..	....	....	....	....	....	....	....	....
Other business services....................	3 268 ..	−1.36	−1.52	−.43	−.92	−.68	−.37	−.41	−2.28
Personal, cultural, and recreational.......	3 287 ..	....	....	....	....	....	....	....	....
Government, n.i.e..........................	3 291 ..	−2.83	−3.30	−1.35	−2.05	−3.44	−2.53	−1.70	−3.46

Table 2 (Continued). STANDARD PRESENTATION, 2003–2010

(Millions of U.S. dollars)

	Code	2003	2004	2005	2006	2007	2008	2009	2010
C. INCOME	4 300	**−2.52**	**−3.10**	**−2.93**	**3.03**	**4.47**	**−.07**	**−.28**	**−.37**
Total credit	2 300	*1.21*	*1.19*	*1.97*	*6.15*	*6.76*	*1.94*	*1.64*	*1.89*
Total debit	3 300	*−3.73*	*−4.29*	*−4.90*	*−3.12*	*−2.29*	*−2.01*	*−1.93*	*−2.26*
Compensation of employees, credit	2 310	....	....	....	....	....	....	....	....
Compensation of employees, debit	3 310	**−.55**	**−.61**	**−.48**	**−.67**	**−.69**	**−.49**	**−.55**	**−.62**
Investment income, credit	2 320	**1.21**	**1.19**	**1.97**	**6.15**	**6.76**	**1.94**	**1.64**	**1.89**
Direct investment income	2 330	....	....	....	....	....	....	....	....
Dividends and distributed branch profits	2 332	....	....	....	....	....	....	....	....
Reinvested earnings and undistributed branch profits	2 333	....	....	....	....	....	....	....	....
Income on debt (interest)	2 334	....	....	....	....	....	....	....	....
Portfolio investment income	2 339	....	....	....	....	....	....	....	....
Income on equity	2 340	....	....	....	....	....	....	....	....
Income on bonds and notes	2 350	....	....	....	....	....	....	....	....
Income on money market instruments	2 360	....	....	....	....	....	....	....	....
Other investment income	2 370	1.21	1.19	1.97	6.15	6.76	1.94	1.64	1.89
Investment income, debit	3 320	**−3.18**	**−3.68**	**−4.42**	**−2.45**	**−1.60**	**−1.52**	**−1.38**	**−1.64**
Direct investment income	3 330	....	....	....	....	....	....	....	....
Dividends and distributed branch profits	3 332	....	....	....	....	....	....	....	....
Reinvested earnings and undistributed branch profits	3 333	....	....	....	....	....	....	....	....
Income on debt (interest)	3 334	....	....	....	....	....	....	....	....
Portfolio investment income	3 339	....	−.64						
Income on equity	3 340	....	−.64	....	....	....	....	....	....
Income on bonds and notes	3 350	....	....	....	....	....	....	....	....
Income on money market instruments	3 360	....	....	....	....	....	....	....	....
Other investment income	3 370	−3.18	−3.04	−4.42	−2.45	−1.60	−1.52	−1.38	−1.64
D. CURRENT TRANSFERS	4 379	**5.56**	**4.23**	**3.45**	**.20**	**1.20**	**2.65**	**4.64**	**2.61**
Credit	2 379	**6.94**	**8.29**	**7.47**	**5.26**	**6.47**	**8.77**	**11.27**	**8.98**
General government	2 380	5.12	7.19	5.97	3.66	4.47	5.77	9.27	6.98
Other sectors	2 390	1.82	1.10	1.50	1.60	2.00	3.00	2.00	2.00
Workers' remittances	2 391	1.82	1.10	1.50	1.60	2.00	3.00	2.00	2.00
Other current transfers	2 392	....	....	....	....	....	....	....	....
Debit	3 379	**−1.38**	**−4.06**	**−4.03**	**−5.06**	**−5.27**	**−6.12**	**−6.63**	**−6.37**
General government	3 380	−.21	−2.72	−2.57	−2.84	−3.00	−2.89	−3.70	−2.89
Other sectors	3 390	−1.18	−1.34	−1.46	−2.23	−2.27	−3.23	−2.93	−3.48
Workers' remittances	3 391	....	....	....	....	....	....	....	....
Other current transfers	3 392	−1.18	−1.34	−1.46	−2.23	−2.27	−3.23	−2.93	−3.48
CAPITAL AND FINANCIAL ACCOUNT	4 996	**26.00**	**36.40**	**30.80**	**64.24**	**73.62**	**109.63**	**91.28**	**105.13**
CAPITAL ACCOUNT	4 994	**18.71**	**18.02**	**65.64**	**23.54**	**225.12**	**55.77**	**39.89**	**40.30**
Total credit	2 994	*18.71*	*18.02*	*65.64*	*23.54*	*225.12*	*55.77*	*39.89*	*40.30*
Total debit	3 994	....	....	....	....	....	....	....	....
Capital transfers, credit	2 400	**18.71**	**18.02**	**16.44**	**23.54**	**196.52**	**55.77**	**39.89**	**40.30**
General government	2 401	18.71	18.02	16.44	23.54	196.52	55.77	39.89	40.30
Debt forgiveness	2 402	3.54	3.09	3.10	3.05	165.67	12.49	6.30	1.23
Other capital transfers	2 410	15.17	14.93	13.34	20.49	30.84	43.28	33.59	39.07
Other sectors	2 430	....	....	....	....	....	....	....	....
Migrants' transfers	2 431	....	....	....	....	....	....	....	....
Debt forgiveness	2 432	....	....	....	....	....	....	....	....
Other capital transfers	2 440	....	....	....	....	....	....	....	....
Capital transfers, debit	3 400	....	....	....	....	....	....	....	....
General government	3 401	....	....	....	....	....	....	....	....
Debt forgiveness	3 402	....	....	....	....	....	....	....	....
Other capital transfers	3 410	....	....	....	....	....	....	....	....
Other sectors	3 430	....	....	....	....	....	....	....	....
Migrants' transfers	3 431	....	....	....	....	....	....	....	....
Debt forgiveness	3 432	....	....	....	....	....	....	....	....
Other capital transfers	3 440	....	....	....	....	....	....	....	....
Nonproduced nonfinancial assets, credit	2 480	....	....	49.20	....	28.60	....	....	....
Nonproduced nonfinancial assets, debit	3 480	....	....	....	....	....	....	....	....

Table 2 (Continued). STANDARD PRESENTATION, 2003–2010

(Millions of U.S. dollars)

	Code	2003	2004	2005	2006	2007	2008	2009	2010
FINANCIAL ACCOUNT...........................	4 995 ..	**7.29**	**18.38**	**−34.84**	**40.70**	**−151.50**	**53.86**	**51.40**	**64.83**
A. DIRECT INVESTMENT........................	4 500 ..	**3.40**	**3.50**	**1.11**	**31.88**	**29.78**	**78.95**	**15.20**	**24.54**
Direct investment abroad...................	4 505 ..	....	....	**−14.55**	**−6.14**	**−6.25**	**−.19**	**−.30**	**−.11**
Equity capital.............................	4 510 ..	....	....	−11.44	−3.07	−3.12	−.09	−.15	−.05
Claims on affiliated enterprises.........	4 515 ..	....	....	−11.44	....	....	....	....	....
Liabilities to affiliated enterprises......	4 520 ..	....	....	....	....	....	....	....	....
Reinvested earnings.....................	4 525 ..	....	....	....	....	....	....	....	....
Other capital............................	4 530 ..	....	....	−3.12	−3.07	−3.12	−.09	−.15	−.05
Claims on affiliated enterprises.........	4 535 ..	....	....	−3.12	−3.07	−3.12	−.09	−.15	−.05
Liabilities to affiliated enterprises......	4 540 ..	....	....	....	....	....	....	....	....
Direct investment in São Tomé and Príncipe......	4 555 ..	**3.40**	**3.50**	**15.66**	**38.02**	**36.03**	**79.14**	**15.50**	**24.64**
Equity capital.............................	4 560 ..	3.40	3.50	15.66	38.02	36.03	79.14	15.50	24.64
Claims on direct investors..............	4 565 ..	....	....	....	....	....	....	....	....
Liabilities to direct investors...........	4 570 ..	3.40	3.50	15.66	38.02	36.03	79.14	15.50	24.64
Reinvested earnings.....................	4 575 ..	....	....	....	....	....	....	....	....
Other capital............................	4 580 ..	....	....	....	....	....	....	....	....
Claims on direct investors..............	4 585 ..	....	....	....	....	....	....	....	....
Liabilities to direct investors...........	4 590 ..	....	....	....	....	....	....	....	....
B. PORTFOLIO INVESTMENT..................	4 600 ..	....	....	....	....	....	....	**−1.50**	....
Assets................................	4 602 ..	....	....	....	....	....	....	**−1.50**	....
Equity securities........................	4 610 ..	....	....	....	....	....	....	....	....
Monetary authorities...................	4 611 ..	....	....	....	....	....	....	....	....
General government....................	4 612 ..	....	....	....	....	....	....	....	....
Banks..................................	4 613 ..	....	....	....	....	....	....	....	....
Other sectors..........................	4 614 ..	....	....	....	....	....	....	....	....
Debt securities..........................	4 619 ..	....	....	....	....	....	....	−1.50	....
Bonds and notes........................	4 620 ..	....	....	....	....	....	....	−1.50	....
Monetary authorities.................	4 621 ..	....	....	....	....	....	....	....	....
General government..................	4 622 ..	....	....	....	....	....	....	....	....
Banks................................	4 623 ..	....	....	....	....	....	....	−1.50	....
Other sectors........................	4 624 ..	....	....	....	....	....	....	....	....
Money market instruments..............	4 630 ..	....	....	....	....	....	....	....	....
Monetary authorities.................	4 631 ..	....	....	....	....	....	....	....	....
General government..................	4 632 ..	....	....	....	....	....	....	....	....
Banks................................	4 633 ..	....	....	....	....	....	....	....	....
Other sectors........................	4 634 ..	....	....	....	....	....	....	....	....
Liabilities...........................	4 652 ..	....	....	....	....	....	....	....	....
Equity securities........................	4 660 ..	....	....	....	....	....	....	....	....
Banks..................................	4 663 ..	....	....	....	....	....	....	....	....
Other sectors..........................	4 664 ..	....	....	....	....	....	....	....	....
Debt securities..........................	4 669 ..	....	....	....	....	....	....	....	....
Bonds and notes........................	4 670 ..	....	....	....	....	....	....	....	....
Monetary authorities.................	4 671 ..	....	....	....	....	....	....	....	....
General government..................	4 672 ..	....	....	....	....	....	....	....	....
Banks................................	4 673 ..	....	....	....	....	....	....	....	....
Other sectors........................	4 674 ..	....	....	....	....	....	....	....	....
Money market instruments..............	4 680 ..	....	....	....	....	....	....	....	....
Monetary authorities.................	4 681 ..	....	....	....	....	....	....	....	....
General government..................	4 682 ..	....	....	....	....	....	....	....	....
Banks................................	4 683 ..	....	....	....	....	....	....	....	....
Other sectors........................	4 684 ..	....	....	....	....	....	....	....	....
C. FINANCIAL DERIVATIVES...................	4 910 ..	....	....	....	....	....	....	....	....
Monetary authorities....................	4 911 ..	....	....	....	....	....	....	....	....
General government.....................	4 912 ..	....	....	....	....	....	....	....	....
Banks...................................	4 913 ..	....	....	....	....	....	....	....	....
Other sectors...........................	4 914 ..	....	....	....	....	....	....	....	....
Assets................................	4 900 ..	....	....	....	....	....	....	....	....
Monetary authorities....................	4 901 ..	....	....	....	....	....	....	....	....
General government.....................	4 902 ..	....	....	....	....	....	....	....	....
Banks...................................	4 903 ..	....	....	....	....	....	....	....	....
Other sectors...........................	4 904 ..	....	....	....	....	....	....	....	....
Liabilities...........................	4 905 ..	....	....	....	....	....	....	....	....
Monetary authorities....................	4 906 ..	....	....	....	....	....	....	....	....
General government.....................	4 907 ..	....	....	....	....	....	....	....	....
Banks...................................	4 908 ..	....	....	....	....	....	....	....	....
Other sectors...........................	4 909 ..	....	....	....	....	....	....	....	....

Table 2 (Concluded). STANDARD PRESENTATION, 2003–2010

(Millions of U.S. dollars)

	Code	2003	2004	2005	2006	2007	2008	2009	2010
D. OTHER INVESTMENT	4 700	**10.13**	**10.87**	**1.26**	**9.60**	**−171.36**	**−2.52**	**49.27**	**37.03**
Assets	4 703	**.75**	**−2.82**	**−3.44**	**9.26**	**7.92**	**15.12**	**12.53**	**18.82**
Trade credits	4 706	....	....	....	....	....	....	....	....
General government	4 707	....	....	....	....	....	....	....	....
of which: Short-term	4 709	....	....	....	....	....	....	....	....
Other sectors	4 710	....	....	....	....	....	....	....	....
of which: Short-term	4 712	....	....	....	....	....	....	....	....
Loans	4 714	−.49	−.30	−.83	−4.28	−1.49	−1.28	.76	.82
Monetary authorities	4 715	−.49	−.30	−.83	−4.28	−1.49	−1.28	.76	.82
of which: Short-term	4 718	....	....	....	....	....	....	....	....
General government	4 719	....	....	....	....	....	....	....	....
of which: Short-term	4 721	....	....	....	....	....	....	....	....
Banks	4 722	....	....	....	....	....	....	....	....
of which: Short-term	4 724	....	....	....	....	....	....	....	....
Other sectors	4 725	....	....	....	....	....	....	....	....
of which: Short-term	4 727	....	....	....	....	....	....	....	....
Currency and deposits	4 730	−.37	−2.51	−12.10	3.04	−4.59	−8.50	3.77	−6.00
Monetary authorities	4 731	....	....	....	....	....	....	....	....
General government	4 732	....	....	....	....	....	....	....	....
Banks	4 733	−.37	−2.51	−12.10	3.04	−4.59	−8.50	3.77	−6.00
Other sectors	4 734	....	....	....	....	....	....	....	....
Other assets	4 736	1.60	....	9.50	10.50	14.00	24.90	8.00	24.00
Monetary authorities	4 737	....	....	....	....	....	....	....	....
of which: Short-term	4 739	....	....	....	....	....	....	....	....
General government	4 740	....	....	....	....	....	....	....	....
of which: Short-term	4 742	....	....	....	....	....	....	....	....
Banks	4 743	....	....	....	....	....	....	....	....
of which: Short-term	4 745	....	....	....	....	....	....	....	....
Other sectors	4 746	1.60	....	9.50	10.50	14.00	24.90	8.00	24.00
of which: Short-term	4 748	....	....	....	....	....	....	....	....
Liabilities	4 753	**9.39**	**13.69**	**4.70**	**.34**	**−179.28**	**−17.64**	**36.74**	**18.21**
Trade credits	4 756	....	....	....	....	....	....	....	....
General government	4 757	....	....	....	....	....	....	....	....
of which: Short-term	4 759	....	....	....	....	....	....	....	....
Other sectors	4 760	....	....	....	....	....	....	....	....
of which: Short-term	4 762	....	....	....	....	....	....	....	....
Loans	4 764	4.93	10.05	−1.52	.34	−182.78	−17.64	24.53	18.21
Monetary authorities	4 765	....	....	.48	.67	−1.67	1.36	.55	.57
of which: Use of Fund credit and loans from the Fund	4 766	....	....	*.48*	*.67*	*−1.67*	*1.36*	*.55*	*.57*
of which: Short-term	4 768	....	....	....	....	....	....	....	....
General government	4 769	4.93	10.05	−2.00	−.33	−181.11	−8.99	23.98	17.64
of which: Short-term	4 771	....	....	....	....	....	....	....	....
Banks	4 772	....	....	....	....	....	....	....	....
of which: Short-term	4 774	....	....	....	....	....	....	....	....
Other sectors	4 775	....	....	....	....	....	−10.00	....	....
of which: Short-term	4 777	....	....	....	....	....	*−10.00*	....	....
Currency and deposits	4 780	....	....	....	....	....	....	....	....
Monetary authorities	4 781	....	....	....	....	....	....	....	....
General government	4 782	....	....	....	....	....	....	....	....
Banks	4 783	....	....	....	....	....	....	....	....
Other sectors	4 784	....	....	....	....	....	....	....	....
Other liabilities	4 786	4.46	3.64	6.21	....	3.51	....	12.21	....
Monetary authorities	4 787	....	....	....	....	3.51	....	10.12	....
of which: Short-term	4 789	....	....	....	....	*3.51*	....	....	....
General government	4 790	4.46	3.64	6.21	....	....	....	2.09	....
of which: Short-term	4 792	*4.46*	*3.64*	*6.21*	....	....	....	*2.09*	....
Banks	4 793	....	....	....	....	....	....	....	....
of which: Short-term	4 795	....	....	....	....	....	....	....	....
Other sectors	4 796	....	....	....	....	....	....	....	....
of which: Short-term	4 798	....	....	....	....	....	....	....	....
E. RESERVE ASSETS	4 802	**−6.24**	**4.01**	**−37.21**	**−.78**	**−9.92**	**−22.57**	**−11.58**	**3.27**
Monetary gold	4 812	....	....	....	....	....	....	....	....
Special drawing rights	4 811	−.01	.02	−.04	....	.06	−.02	−10.10	4.12
Reserve position in the Fund	4 810	....	....	....	....	....	....	....	....
Foreign exchange	4 803	−6.23	3.99	−9.77	−13.71	−3.67	−22.56	6.14	−10.73
Other claims	4 813	....	....	−27.40	12.93	−6.30	....	−7.62	9.88
NET ERRORS AND OMISSIONS	4 998	**2.85**	**1.87**	**5.46**	**−6.26**	**−9.07**	**−16.11**	**−12.51**	**2.25**

Table 1. ANALYTIC PRESENTATION, 2003–2010

(Millions of U.S. dollars)

	Code	2003	2004	2005	2006	2007	2008	2009	2010
A. Current Account[1]............................	4 993 Z.	**28,048**	**51,926**	**90,061**	**99,066**	**93,379**	**132,314**	**20,955**	**66,751**
Goods: exports f.o.b.................................	2 100 ..	93,244	125,998	180,712	211,305	233,311	313,480	192,307	251,149
Goods: imports f.o.b.................................	3 100 ..	−33,868	−41,050	−54,595	−63,914	−82,595	−101,454	−87,078	−97,432
Balance on Goods.................................	4 100 ..	*59,376*	*84,947*	*126,117*	*147,391*	*150,716*	*212,025*	*105,230*	*153,717*
Services: credit....................................	2 200 ..	5,713	5,852	11,410	14,202	15,987	9,370	9,749	10,683
Services: debit....................................	3 200 ..	−20,857	−25,696	−33,120	−49,581	−62,677	−75,234	−74,991	−76,772
Balance on Goods and Services.................	4 991 ..	*44,232*	*65,103*	*104,407*	*112,012*	*104,026*	*146,161*	*39,988*	*87,628*
Income: credit....................................	2 300 ..	2,977	4,278	5,058	10,481	15,137	21,501	19,752	18,172
Income: debit.....................................	3 300 ..	−4,277	−3,800	−4,626	−6,646	−8,741	−12,336	−11,112	−11,128
Balance on Goods, Services, and Income......	4 992 ..	*42,931*	*65,581*	*104,839*	*115,847*	*110,422*	*155,326*	*48,627*	*94,672*
Current transfers: credit..........................	2 379 Z.	....	....	....	....	....	....	....	....
Current transfers: debit...........................	3 379 ..	−14,883	−13,655	−14,778	−16,781	−17,043	−23,012	−27,673	−27,921
B. Capital Account[1].............................	4 994 Z.	....	....	....	....	....	....	....	....
Capital account: credit............................	2 994 Z.	....	....	....	....	....	....	....	....
Capital account: debit.............................	3 994 ..	....	....	....	....	....	....	....	....
Total, Groups A Plus B...........................	4 981 ..	*28,048*	*51,926*	*90,061*	*99,066*	*93,379*	*132,314*	*20,955*	*66,751*
C. Financial Account[1]...........................	4 995 W.	**−26,440**	**−47,428**	**8,361**	**−7,497**	**2,116**	**34,729**	**7,244**	**−7,176**
Direct investment abroad...........................	4 505 ..	....	....	350	39	135	−3,496	−2,177	−3,907
Direct investment in Saudi Arabia..................	4 555 Z.	−587	−334	12,107	18,317	24,334	39,455	36,458	21,560
Portfolio investment assets........................	4 602 ..	−18,738	−26,654	350	−11,949	−5,479	−3,847	−20,133	−18,939
Equity securities................................	4 610 ..	....	....	....	....	....	....	....	....
Debt securities..................................	4 619 ..	−18,738	−26,654	....	....	....	....	....	....
Portfolio investment liabilities....................	4 652 Z.	....	....	....	....	....	2,219	−5	1,503
Equity securities................................	4 660 ..	....	....	....	....	....	....	....	....
Debt securities..................................	4 669 Z.	....	....	....	....	....	....	....	....
Financial derivatives..............................	4 910 ..	....	....	....	....	....	....	....	....
Financial derivatives assets.......................	4 900 ..	....	....	....	....	....	....	....	....
Financial derivatives liabilities...................	4 905 ..	....	....	....	....	....	....	....	....
Other investment assets...........................	4 703 ..	−6,333	−21,955	−4,425	−13,976	−16,849	−2,563	−9,542	−6,523
Monetary authorities.............................	4 701 ..	....	....	....	....	....	....	....	....
General government..............................	4 704 ..	....	....	....	....	....	....	....	....
Banks...	4 705 ..	3,842	−3,124	....	....	....	....	....	....
Other sectors....................................	4 728 ..	−10,175	−18,831	....	....	....	....	....	....
Other investment liabilities........................	4 753 W.	−783	1,516	−21	71	−24	2,962	2,644	−870
Monetary authorities.............................	4 753 WA	....	....	....	....	....	....	....	....
General government..............................	4 753 ZB	....	....	....	....	....	....	....	....
Banks...	4 753 ZC	−783	1,516	....	....	....	....	....	....
Other sectors....................................	4 753 ZD	....	....	....	....	....	....	....	....
Total, Groups A Through C.......................	4 983 ..	*1,608*	*4,498*	*98,422*	*91,569*	*95,495*	*167,043*	*28,198*	*59,575*
D. Net Errors and Omissions..................	4 998 ..	....	....	**−34,459**	**−20,659**	**−15,702**	**−30,000**	**−60,837**	**−24,320**
Total, Groups A Through D.......................	4 984 ..	*1,608*	*4,498*	*63,963*	*70,910*	*79,794*	*137,043*	*−32,638*	*35,255*
E. Reserves and Related Items...............	4 802 A.	**−1,608**	**−4,498**	**−63,963**	**−70,910**	**−79,794**	**−137,043**	**32,638**	**−35,255**
Reserve assets....................................	4 802 ..	−1,608	−4,498	−63,963	−70,910	−79,794	−137,043	32,638	−35,255
Use of Fund credit and loans......................	4 766 ..	....	....	....	....	....	....	....	....
Exceptional financing..............................	4 920 ..	....	....	....	....	....	....	....	....
Conversion rates: riyals per U.S. dollar.......	0 101 ..	**3.7500**	**3.7500**	**3.7471**	**3.7450**	**3.7475**	**3.7500**	**3.7500**	**3.7500**

[1] Excludes components that have been classified in the categories of Group E.

Table 2. STANDARD PRESENTATION, 2003–2010

(Millions of U.S. dollars)

	Code	2003	2004	2005	2006	2007	2008	2009	2010
CURRENT ACCOUNT	4 993	**28,048**	**51,926**	**90,061**	**99,066**	**93,379**	**132,314**	**20,955**	**66,751**
A. GOODS	4 100	**59,376**	**84,947**	**126,117**	**147,391**	**150,716**	**212,025**	**105,230**	**153,717**
Credit	2 100	**93,244**	**125,998**	**180,712**	**211,305**	**233,311**	**313,480**	**192,307**	**251,149**
General merchandise: exports f.o.b.	2 110	92,997	125,665	180,535	211,145	233,206	313,350	192,190	251,009
Goods for processing: exports f.o.b.	2 150	....	....	....	....	....	....	....	....
Repairs on goods	2 160	....	....	....	....	....	....	....	....
Goods procured in ports by carriers	2 170	247	332	....	....	....	....	....	....
Nonmonetary gold	2 180	....	....	177	160	105	130	117	140
Debit	3 100	**−33,868**	**−41,050**	**−54,595**	**−63,914**	**−82,595**	**−101,454**	**−87,078**	**−97,432**
General merchandise: imports f.o.b.	3 110	−33,868	−41,050	−53,804	−63,114	−81,539	−100,644	−86,382	−96,653
Goods for processing: imports f.o.b.	3 150	....	....	....	....	....	....	....	....
Repairs on goods	3 160	....	....	....	....	....	....	....	....
Goods procured in ports by carriers	3 170	....	....	....	....	....	....	....	....
Nonmonetary gold	3 180	....	....	−791	−801	−1,056	−811	−696	−779
B. SERVICES	4 200	**−15,145**	**−19,844**	**−21,710**	**−35,379**	**−46,690**	**−65,864**	**−65,242**	**−66,089**
Total credit	2 200	*5,713*	*5,852*	*11,410*	*14,202*	*15,987*	*9,370*	*9,749*	*10,683*
Total debit	3 200	*−20,857*	*−25,696*	*−33,120*	*−49,581*	*−62,677*	*−75,234*	*−74,991*	*−76,772*
Transportation services, credit	2 205	....	....	**1,820**	**2,300**	**1,835**	**2,389**	**1,940**	**2,031**
Passenger	2 850								
Freight	2 851								
Other	2 852								
Sea transport, passenger	2 207								
Sea transport, freight	2 208								
Sea transport, other	2 209								
Air transport, passenger	2 211								
Air transport, freight	2 212								
Air transport, other	2 213								
Other transport, passenger	2 215								
Other transport, freight	2 216								
Other transport, other	2 217								
Transportation services, debit	3 205	**−2,743**	**−3,325**	**−4,792**	**−5,617**	**−9,179**	**−15,654**	**−11,403**	**−12,723**
Passenger	3 850								
Freight	3 851	*−2,743*	*−3,325*						
Other	3 852								
Sea transport, passenger	3 207								
Sea transport, freight	3 208	−2,743	−3,325						
Sea transport, other	3 209								
Air transport, passenger	3 211								
Air transport, freight	3 212								
Air transport, other	3 213								
Other transport, passenger	3 215								
Other transport, freight	3 216								
Other transport, other	3 217								
Travel, credit	2 236	....	....	**4,626**	**4,769**	**5,971**	**5,909**	**5,995**	**6,712**
Business travel	2 237								
Personal travel	2 240								
Travel, debit	3 236	....	....	**−9,087**	**−12,979**	**−20,170**	**−15,129**	**−20,419**	**−21,135**
Business travel	3 237								
Personal travel	3 240								
Other services, credit	2 200 BA	**5,713**	**5,852**	**4,964**	**7,133**	**8,181**	**1,071**	**1,814**	**1,940**
Communications	2 245	....	....	193	245	246	221	205	293
Construction	2 249	....	....	....	....	....	....	....	....
Insurance	2 253						143	330	290
Financial	2 260						432	901	951
Computer and information	2 262								
Royalties and licence fees	2 266	....	....	....	....	....	....		....
Other business services	2 268	5,713	5,852	4,540	6,660	7,691	34	56	69
Personal, cultural, and recreational	2 287	....	....	....	....	....	....	....	....
Government, n.i.e.	2 291			231	228	244	241	321	337
Other services, debit	3 200 BA	**−18,114**	**−22,371**	**−19,242**	**−30,985**	**−33,329**	**−44,451**	**−43,170**	**−42,914**
Communications	3 245	....	....	−344	−554	−800	−1,269	−1,857	−2,197
Construction	3 249	....	....	−1,416	−3,158	−6,321	−4,491	−3,288	−3,789
Insurance	3 253	−305	−369	−491	−589	−991	−1,820	−1,501	−1,669
Financial	3 260	....	....	−3,532	−6,557	−2,527	−1,509	−1,188	−1,034
Computer and information	3 262	....	....	....	....	....	....	....	....
Royalties and licence fees	3 266	....	....	....	....	....	....	....	....
Other business services	3 268	−4,888	−7,363	−22	−35	−5,926	−9,700	−7,383	−8,449
Personal, cultural, and recreational	3 287								
Government, n.i.e.	3 291	−12,921	−14,638	−13,437	−20,093	−16,763	−25,662	−27,953	−25,776

Table 2 (Continued). STANDARD PRESENTATION, 2003–2010

(Millions of U.S. dollars)

	Code	2003	2004	2005	2006	2007	2008	2009	2010
C. INCOME	4 300	**−1,301**	**478**	**432**	**3,835**	**6,396**	**9,165**	**8,640**	**7,044**
Total credit	2 300	*2,977*	*4,278*	*5,058*	*10,481*	*15,137*	*21,501*	*19,752*	*18,172*
Total debit	3 300	*−4,277*	*−3,800*	*−4,626*	*−6,646*	*−8,741*	*−12,336*	*−11,112*	*−11,128*
Compensation of employees, credit	2 310	....	....	94	106	124	217	214	236
Compensation of employees, debit	3 310	....	....	−599	−665	−701	−749	−782	−890
Investment income, credit	2 320	**2,977**	**4,278**	**4,964**	**10,376**	**15,014**	**21,283**	**19,538**	**17,935**
Direct investment income	2 330	....	....	1,241	2,594	3,753	3,100	2,319	2,961
Dividends and distributed branch profits	2 332	....	....	....	....	....	....	....	....
Reinvested earnings and undistributed branch profits	2 333	....	....	....	....	....	....	....	....
Income on debt (interest)	2 334	....	....	....	....	....	....	....	....
Portfolio investment income	2 339	....	....	2,978	6,225	9,008	14,233	14,220	13,964
Income on equity	2 340	....	....	....	....	....	....	....	....
Income on bonds and notes	2 350	....	....	....	....	....	....	....	....
Income on money market instruments	2 360	....	....	....	....	....	....	....	....
Other investment income	2 370	2,977	4,278	745	1,556	2,252	3,950	2,999	1,010
Investment income, debit	3 320	**−4,277**	**−3,800**	**−4,027**	**−5,981**	**−8,041**	**−11,586**	**−10,330**	**−10,238**
Direct investment income	3 330	−4,277	−3,800	−4,027	−5,981	−8,041	−9,553	−9,593	−9,914
Dividends and distributed branch profits	3 332	−4,277	−3,800						
Reinvested earnings and undistributed branch profits	3 333	....	....	....	....	....	....	....	....
Income on debt (interest)	3 334	....	....	....	....	....	....	....	....
Portfolio investment income	3 339						−65	−143	−89
Income on equity	3 340	....	....	....	....	....	....	....	....
Income on bonds and notes	3 350	....	....	....	....	....	....	....	....
Income on money market instruments	3 360	....	....	....	....	....	....	....	....
Other investment income	3 370						−1,969	−595	−235
D. CURRENT TRANSFERS	4 379	**−14,883**	**−13,655**	**−14,778**	**−16,781**	**−17,043**	**−23,012**	**−27,673**	**−27,921**
Credit	2 379	....	....	....	....	....	....	....	....
General government	2 380	....	....	....	....	....	....	....	....
Other sectors	2 390	....	....	....	....	....	....	....	....
Workers' remittances	2 391	....	....	....	....	....	....	....	....
Other current transfers	2 392	....	....	....	....	....	....	....	....
Debit	3 379	**−14,883**	**−13,655**	**−14,778**	**−16,781**	**−17,043**	**−23,012**	**−27,673**	**−27,921**
General government	3 380	−100	−100	−782	−1,169	−976	−1,819	−1,919	−1,656
Other sectors	3 390	−14,783	−13,555	−13,996	−15,611	−16,067	−21,193	−25,754	−26,264
Workers' remittances	3 391	−14,783	−13,555	−13,716	−15,299	−15,746	−20,948	−25,688	−26,179
Other current transfers	3 392	....	....	−280	−312	−321	−245	−66	−85
CAPITAL AND FINANCIAL ACCOUNT	4 996	**−28,048**	**−51,926**	**−55,602**	**−78,407**	**−77,678**	**−102,313**	**39,882**	**−42,431**
CAPITAL ACCOUNT	4 994	....	....	....	....	....	....	....	....
Total credit	2 994	....	....	....	....	....	....	....	....
Total debit	3 994	....	....	....	....	....	....	....	....
Capital transfers, credit	2 400	....	....	....	....	....	....	....	....
General government	2 401	....	....	....	....	....	....	....	....
Debt forgiveness	2 402	....	....	....	....	....	....	....	....
Other capital transfers	2 410	....	....	....	....	....	....	....	....
Other sectors	2 430	....	....	....	....	....	....	....	....
Migrants' transfers	2 431	....	....	....	....	....	....	....	....
Debt forgiveness	2 432	....	....	....	....	....	....	....	....
Other capital transfers	2 440	....	....	....	....	....	....	....	....
Capital transfers, debit	3 400	....	....	....	....	....	....	....	....
General government	3 401	....	....	....	....	....	....	....	....
Debt forgiveness	3 402	....	....	....	....	....	....	....	....
Other capital transfers	3 410	....	....	....	....	....	....	....	....
Other sectors	3 430	....	....	....	....	....	....	....	....
Migrants' transfers	3 431	....	....	....	....	....	....	....	....
Debt forgiveness	3 432	....	....	....	....	....	....	....	....
Other capital transfers	3 440	....	....	....	....	....	....	....	....
Nonproduced nonfinancial assets, credit	2 480	....	....	....	....	....	....	....	....
Nonproduced nonfinancial assets, debit	3 480	....	....	....	....	....	....	....	....

Table 2 (Continued). STANDARD PRESENTATION, 2003–2010

(Millions of U.S. dollars)

	Code	2003	2004	2005	2006	2007	2008	2009	2010
FINANCIAL ACCOUNT..............................	4 995 ..	−28,048	−51,926	−55,602	−78,407	−77,678	−102,313	39,882	−42,431
A. DIRECT INVESTMENT............................	4 500 ..	−587	−334	12,457	18,356	24,469	35,959	34,280	17,653
Direct investment abroad........................	4 505 ..	....	....	350	39	135	−3,496	−2,177	−3,907
Equity capital..	4 510 ..	....	....	....	....	....	....	....	....
Claims on affiliated enterprises................	4 515 ..	....	....	....	....	....	....	....	....
Liabilities to affiliated enterprises............	4 520 ..	....	....	....	....	....	....	....	....
Reinvested earnings..............................	4 525 ..	....	....	....	....	....	....	....	....
Other capital.......................................	4 530 ..	....	....	....	....	....	....	....	....
Claims on affiliated enterprises................	4 535 ..	....	....	....	....	....	....	....	....
Liabilities to affiliated enterprises............	4 540 ..	....	....	....	....	....	....	....	....
Direct investment in Saudi Arabia....................	4 555 ..	−587	−334	12,107	18,317	24,334	39,455	36,458	21,560
Equity capital..	4 560 ..	....	....	....	....	....	....	....	....
Claims on direct investors......................	4 565 ..	....	....	....	....	....	....	....	....
Liabilities to direct investors..................	4 570 ..	....	....	....	....	....	....	....	....
Reinvested earnings..............................	4 575 ..	....	....	....	....	....	....	....	....
Other capital.......................................	4 580 ..	−587	−334	....	....	....	....	....	....
Claims on direct investors......................	4 585 ..	....	....	....	....	....	....	....	....
Liabilities to direct investors..................	4 590 ..	....	....	....	....	....	....	....	....
B. PORTFOLIO INVESTMENT............................	4 600 ..	−18,738	−26,654	350	−11,949	−5,479	−1,628	−20,139	−17,436
Assets..	4 602 ..	−18,738	−26,654	350	−11,949	−5,479	−3,847	−20,133	−18,939
Equity securities...................................	4 610 ..	....	....	....	....	....	....	....	....
Monetary authorities...........................	4 611 ..	....	....	....	....	....	....	....	....
General government............................	4 612 ..	....	....	....	....	....	....	....	....
Banks..	4 613 ..	....	....	....	....	....	....	....	....
Other sectors....................................	4 614 ..	....	....	....	....	....	....	....	....
Debt securities.....................................	4 619 ..	−18,738	−26,654	....	....	....	....	....	....
Bonds and notes................................	4 620 ..	−18,738	−26,654	....	....	....	....	....	....
Monetary authorities........................	4 621 ..	....	....	....	....	....	....	....	....
General government.........................	4 622 ..	−18,738	−26,654	....	....	....	....	....	....
Banks..	4 623 ..	....	....	....	....	....	....	....	....
Other sectors..................................	4 624 ..	....	....	....	....	....	....	....	....
Money market instruments....................	4 630 ..	....	....	....	....	....	....	....	....
Monetary authorities........................	4 631 ..	....	....	....	....	....	....	....	....
General government.........................	4 632 ..	....	....	....	....	....	....	....	....
Banks..	4 633 ..	....	....	....	....	....	....	....	....
Other sectors..................................	4 634 ..	....	....	....	....	....	....	....	....
Liabilities..	4 652 ..	....	....	....	....	....	2,219	−5	1,503
Equity securities...................................	4 660 ..	....	....	....	....	....	....	....	....
Banks..	4 663 ..	....	....	....	....	....	....	....	....
Other sectors....................................	4 664 ..	....	....	....	....	....	....	....	....
Debt securities.....................................	4 669 ..	....	....	....	....	....	....	....	....
Bonds and notes................................	4 670 ..	....	....	....	....	....	....	....	....
Monetary authorities........................	4 671 ..	....	....	....	....	....	....	....	....
General government.........................	4 672 ..	....	....	....	....	....	....	....	....
Banks..	4 673 ..	....	....	....	....	....	....	....	....
Other sectors..................................	4 674 ..	....	....	....	....	....	....	....	....
Money market instruments....................	4 680 ..	....	....	....	....	....	....	....	....
Monetary authorities........................	4 681 ..	....	....	....	....	....	....	....	....
General government.........................	4 682 ..	....	....	....	....	....	....	....	....
Banks..	4 683 ..	....	....	....	....	....	....	....	....
Other sectors..................................	4 684 ..	....	....	....	....	....	....	....	....
C. FINANCIAL DERIVATIVES............................	4 910 ..	....	....	....	....	....	....	....	....
Monetary authorities.............................	4 911 ..	....	....	....	....	....	....	....	....
General government..............................	4 912 ..	....	....	....	....	....	....	....	....
Banks...	4 913 ..	....	....	....	....	....	....	....	....
Other sectors......................................	4 914 ..	....	....	....	....	....	....	....	....
Assets..	4 900 ..	....	....	....	....	....	....	....	....
Monetary authorities.............................	4 901 ..	....	....	....	....	....	....	....	....
General government..............................	4 902 ..	....	....	....	....	....	....	....	....
Banks...	4 903 ..	....	....	....	....	....	....	....	....
Other sectors......................................	4 904 ..	....	....	....	....	....	....	....	....
Liabilities..	4 905 ..	....	....	....	....	....	....	....	....
Monetary authorities.............................	4 906 ..	....	....	....	....	....	....	....	....
General government..............................	4 907 ..	....	....	....	....	....	....	....	....
Banks...	4 908 ..	....	....	....	....	....	....	....	....
Other sectors......................................	4 909 ..	....	....	....	....	....	....	....	....

Table 2 (Concluded). STANDARD PRESENTATION, 2003–2010

(Millions of U.S. dollars)

	Code	2003	2004	2005	2006	2007	2008	2009	2010
D. OTHER INVESTMENT	4 700	−7,115	−20,440	−4,446	−13,905	−16,873	398	−6,898	−7,393
Assets	4 703	−6,333	−21,955	−4,425	−13,976	−16,849	−2,563	−9,542	−6,523
Trade credits	4 706	....	....	....	....	....	....	....	....
General government	4 707	....	....	....	....	....	....	....	....
of which: Short-term	4 709	....	....	....	....	....	....	....	....
Other sectors	4 710	....	....	....	....	....	....	....	....
of which: Short-term	4 712	....	....	....	....	....	....	....	....
Loans	4 714	....	....	....	....	....	....	....	....
Monetary authorities	4 715	....	....	....	....	....	....	....	....
of which: Short-term	4 718	....	....	....	....	....	....	....	....
General government	4 719	....	....	....	....	....	....	....	....
of which: Short-term	4 721	....	....	....	....	....	....	....	....
Banks	4 722	....	....	....	....	....	....	....	....
of which: Short-term	4 724	....	....	....	....	....	....	....	....
Other sectors	4 725	....	....	....	....	....	....	....	....
of which: Short-term	4 727	....	....	....	....	....	....	....	....
Currency and deposits	4 730	−6,333	−21,955	....	....	....	....	....	....
Monetary authorities	4 731	....	....	....	....	....	....	....	....
General government	4 732	....	....	....	....	....	....	....	....
Banks	4 733	3,842	−3,124	....	....	....	....	....	....
Other sectors	4 734	−10,175	−18,831	....	....	....	....	....	....
Other assets	4 736	....	....	....	....	....	....	....	....
Monetary authorities	4 737	....	....	....	....	....	....	....	....
of which: Short-term	4 739	....	....	....	....	....	....	....	....
General government	4 740	....	....	....	....	....	....	....	....
of which: Short-term	4 742	....	....	....	....	....	....	....	....
Banks	4 743	....	....	....	....	....	....	....	....
of which: Short-term	4 745	....	....	....	....	....	....	....	....
Other sectors	4 746	....	....	....	....	....	....	....	....
of which: Short-term	4 748	....	....	....	....	....	....	....	....
Liabilities	4 753	−783	1,516	−21	71	−24	2,962	2,644	−870
Trade credits	4 756	....	....	....	....	....	....	....	....
General government	4 757	....	....	....	....	....	....	....	....
of which: Short-term	4 759	....	....	....	....	....	....	....	....
Other sectors	4 760	....	....	....	....	....	....	....	....
of which: Short-term	4 762	....	....	....	....	....	....	....	....
Loans	4 764	....	....	....	....	....	....	....	....
Monetary authorities	4 765	....	....	....	....	....	....	....	....
of which: Use of Fund credit and loans from the Fund	4 766	....	....	....	....	....	....	....	....
of which: Short-term	4 768	....	....	....	....	....	....	....	....
General government	4 769	....	....	....	....	....	....	....	....
of which: Short-term	4 771	....	....	....	....	....	....	....	....
Banks	4 772	....	....	....	....	....	....	....	....
of which: Short-term	4 774	....	....	....	....	....	....	....	....
Other sectors	4 775	....	....	....	....	....	....	....	....
of which: Short-term	4 777	....	....	....	....	....	....	....	....
Currency and deposits	4 780	−783	1,516	....	....	....	....	....	....
Monetary authorities	4 781	....	....	....	....	....	....	....	....
General government	4 782	....	....	....	....	....	....	....	....
Banks	4 783	−783	1,516	....	....	....	....	....	....
Other sectors	4 784	....	....	....	....	....	....	....	....
Other liabilities	4 786	....	....	....	....	....	....	....	....
Monetary authorities	4 787	....	....	....	....	....	....	....	....
of which: Short-term	4 789	....	....	....	....	....	....	....	....
General government	4 790	....	....	....	....	....	....	....	....
of which: Short-term	4 792	....	....	....	....	....	....	....	....
Banks	4 793	....	....	....	....	....	....	....	....
of which: Short-term	4 795	....	....	....	....	....	....	....	....
Other sectors	4 796	....	....	....	....	....	....	....	....
of which: Short-term	4 798	....	....	....	....	....	....	....	....
E. RESERVE ASSETS	4 802	−1,608	−4,498	−63,963	−70,910	−79,794	−137,043	32,638	−35,255
Monetary gold	4 812	....	....	....	....	....	−231	....	....
Special drawing rights	4 811	−64	−66	−75	−60	−48	−33	−10,154	91
Reserve position in the Fund	4 810	−597	1,179	1,340	1,063	220	−652	−589	....
Foreign exchange	4 803	−947	−5,611	−65,229	−71,913	−79,967	−136,126	43,382	−35,346
Other claims	4 813	....	....	....	....	....	....	....	....
NET ERRORS AND OMISSIONS	4 998	....	....	−34,459	−20,659	−15,702	−30,000	−60,837	−24,320

Table 1. ANALYTIC PRESENTATION, 2003–2010

(Millions of U.S. dollars)

	Code	2003	2004	2005	2006	2007	2008	2009	2010
A. Current Account[1]	4 993 Z.	**−436.6**	**−510.4**	**−675.9**	**−861.2**	**−1,311.7**	**−1,883.7**	**−864.8**	....
Goods: exports f.o.b.	2 100 ..	1,257.0	1,509.4	1,578.2	1,594.0	1,673.8	2,206.0	2,096.8	....
Goods: imports f.o.b.	3 100 ..	−2,065.5	−2,495.8	−2,888.8	−3,193.7	−4,163.8	−5,606.0	−4,125.0	....
Balance on Goods	4 100 ..	*−808.5*	*−986.4*	*−1,310.6*	*−1,599.7*	*−2,489.9*	*−3,400.0*	*−2,028.2*	....
Services: credit	2 200 ..	569.0	675.7	776.9	807.1	1,200.9	1,294.1	1,022.1	....
Services: debit	3 200 ..	−591.4	−701.0	−806.4	−841.8	−1,238.4	−1,414.5	−1,151.1	....
Balance on Goods and Services	4 991 ..	*−830.9*	*−1,011.7*	*−1,340.1*	*−1,634.4*	*−2,527.4*	*−3,520.4*	*−2,157.2*	....
Income: credit	2 300 ..	86.4	95.2	95.5	121.3	138.2	235.4	160.2	....
Income: debit	3 300 ..	−222.6	−225.9	−185.0	−184.7	−212.1	−283.3	−341.0	....
Balance on Goods, Services, and Income	4 992 ..	*−967.0*	*−1,142.4*	*−1,429.7*	*−1,697.8*	*−2,601.2*	*−3,568.3*	*−2,338.0*	....
Current transfers: credit	2 379 Z.	595.6	715.1	859.2	973.7	1,557.5	1,985.9	1,756.8	....
Current transfers: debit	3 379 ..	−65.2	−83.1	−105.4	−137.0	−268.0	−301.3	−283.6	....
B. Capital Account[1]	4 994 Z.	**150.4**	**750.0**	**199.5**	**158.9**	**332.7**	**239.5**	**305.1**	....
Capital account: credit	2 994 Z.	150.9	750.4	200.3	162.5	384.4	240.7	307.3	....
Capital account: debit	3 994 ..	−.6	−.4	−.8	−3.6	−51.8	−1.3	−2.2	....
Total, Groups A Plus B	4 981 ..	*−286.2*	*239.6*	*−476.4*	*−702.3*	*−979.1*	*−1,644.3*	*−559.7*	....
C. Financial Account[1]	4 995 W.	**2.5**	**−53.7**	**117.9**	**−1,580.5**	**835.5**	**1,091.2**	**484.2**	....
Direct investment abroad	4 505 ..	−2.7	−13.1	7.7	−9.9	−24.7	−126.3	−77.1	....
Direct investment in Senegal	4 555 Z.	52.5	77.0	44.6	220.3	297.4	397.6	331.1	....
Portfolio investment assets	4 602 ..	−56.3	−47.5	−48.9	−53.3	6.4	51.6	−91.3	....
Equity securities	4 610 ..	−7.9	22.8	4.3	1.7	9.9	....	−1.7	....
Debt securities	4 619 ..	−48.4	−70.3	−53.2	−55.1	−3.5	51.5	−89.5	....
Portfolio investment liabilities	4 652 Z.	10.6	.8	−8.5	−13.6	24.7	20.9	−1.6	....
Equity securities	4 660 ..	3.6	−27.7	−6.1	−.4	8.0	−92.6	−1.6	....
Debt securities	4 669 Z.	6.9	28.5	−2.4	−13.3	16.7	113.5	....	....
Financial derivatives	4 910 ..	2.3	....	−.1	....	25.5	....	....	....
Financial derivatives assets	4 900 ..	1.6	.7	....	−.1	....	.2	....	....
Financial derivatives liabilities	4 905 ..	.7	−.8	−.1	.1	25.6	−.2	....	....
Other investment assets	4 703 ..	58.0	6.0	79.2	−34.3	84.4	147.7	−128.2	....
Monetary authorities	4 701 ..	....	....	....	....	....	....	....	....
General government	4 704 ..	−1.8	3.1	1.0	.4	.5	2.7	−.2	....
Banks	4 705 ..	−8.3	−19.4	50.7	−74.8	−12.4	50.1	44.5	....
Other sectors	4 728 ..	68.1	22.3	27.5	40.1	96.3	94.9	−172.5	....
Other investment liabilities	4 753 W.	−61.9	−76.9	43.9	−1,689.7	421.7	599.7	451.4	....
Monetary authorities	4 753 WA	4.3	−20.7	25.9	−44.0	.9	1.8	377.2	....
General government	4 753 ZB	−194.8	−197.3	−149.9	−2,071.1	−59.9	−61.9	−64.4	....
Banks	4 753 ZC	21.4	15.4	36.3	106.2	31.5	133.6	8.8	....
Other sectors	4 753 ZD	107.1	125.7	131.6	319.1	449.2	526.3	129.9	....
Total, Groups A Through C	4 983 ..	*−283.7*	*186.0*	*−358.5*	*−2,282.8*	*−143.6*	*−553.0*	*−75.5*	....
D. Net Errors and Omissions	4 998 ..	**10.8**	**13.1**	**−3.1**	**28.3**	**12.8**	**−13.5**	**−171.3**	....
Total, Groups A Through D	4 984 ..	*−272.8*	*199.1*	*−361.6*	*−2,254.6*	*−130.8*	*−566.5*	*−246.8*	....
E. Reserves and Related Items	4 802 A.	**272.8**	**−199.1**	**361.6**	**2,254.6**	**130.8**	**566.5**	**246.8**	....
Reserve assets	4 802 ..	−18.1	−155.0	−4.5	−9.9	−157.0	−34.5	−454.7	....
Use of Fund credit and loans	4 766 ..	−34.5	−44.4	−40.6	−125.1	....	36.9	101.2	....
Exceptional financing	4 920 ..	325.4	.3	406.7	2,389.5	287.7	564.1	600.3	....
Conversion rates: CFA francs per U.S. dollar	0 101 ..	**581.20**	**528.28**	**527.47**	**522.89**	**479.27**	**447.81**	**472.19**	**495.28**

[1] Excludes components that have been classified in the categories of Group E.

2011, International Monetary Fund: *Balance of Payments Statistics Yearbook*

Table 2. STANDARD PRESENTATION, 2003–2010

(Millions of U.S. dollars)

	Code	2003	2004	2005	2006	2007	2008	2009	2010
CURRENT ACCOUNT...	4 993 ..	**−436.6**	**−510.4**	**−675.9**	**−861.2**	**−1,311.7**	**−1,883.7**	**−864.8**	....
A. GOODS...	4 100 ..	**−808.5**	**−986.4**	**−1,310.6**	**−1,599.7**	**−2,489.9**	**−3,400.0**	**−2,028.2**	....
Credit..	2 100 ..	**1,257.0**	**1,509.4**	**1,578.2**	**1,594.0**	**1,673.8**	**2,206.0**	**2,096.8**	....
General merchandise: exports f.o.b....................	2 110 ..	1,242.8	1,488.2	1,552.7	1,562.6	1,638.8	2,165.0	1,904.4	....
Goods for processing: exports f.o.b..................	2 150 ..	....	....	....	....	....	....	....	....
Repairs on goods...	2 160 ..	.4	.2	.2	....	....	....	....	....
Goods procured in ports by carriers................	2 170 ..	13.8	21.1	25.3	31.3	35.0	41.0	11.5	....
Nonmonetary gold..	2 180 ..	....	....	....	....	....	....	180.9	....
Debit...	3 100 ..	**−2,065.5**	**−2,495.8**	**−2,888.8**	**−3,193.7**	**−4,163.8**	**−5,606.0**	**−4,125.0**	....
General merchandise: imports f.o.b....................	3 110 ..	−2,051.2	−2,478.7	−2,876.1	−3,182.5	−4,147.0	−5,585.9	−4,122.2	....
Goods for processing: imports f.o.b..................	3 150 ..	....	....	....	....	....	....	....	....
Repairs on goods...	3 160 ..	−6.0	−7.9	−4.3	−1.1	−10.0	−10.7	−2.1	....
Goods procured in ports by carriers................	3 170 ..	−8.3	−9.2	−8.3	−10.1	−6.7	−9.4	−.6	....
Nonmonetary gold..	3 180 ..	....	....	....	....	....	....	....	....
B. SERVICES..	4 200 ..	**−22.3**	**−25.3**	**−29.5**	**−34.7**	**−37.5**	**−120.4**	**−129.0**	....
Total credit..	2 200 ..	*569.0*	*675.7*	*776.9*	*807.1*	*1,200.9*	*1,294.1*	*1,022.1*	....
Total debit..	3 200 ..	*−591.4*	*−701.0*	*−806.4*	*−841.8*	*−1,238.4*	*−1,414.5*	*−1,151.1*	....
Transportation services, credit................	2 205 ..	**76.5**	**96.3**	**126.8**	**113.0**	**135.2**	**143.3**	**47.8**	....
Passenger...	2 850 ..	*60.4*	*74.7*	*92.0*	*78.9*	*91.3*	*94.2*	*10.7*	....
Freight...	2 851 ..	*7.1*	*14.0*	*25.3*	*22.8*	*29.9*	*35.6*	*30.5*	....
Other...	2 852 ..	*8.9*	*7.6*	*9.4*	*11.3*	*14.1*	*13.5*	*6.6*	....
Sea transport, passenger.............................	2 207 ..	....	....	....	....	....	....	....	....
Sea transport, freight...............................	2 208 ..	....	....	....	....	....	....	....	....
Sea transport, other.................................	2 209 ..	1.5	.1	....	.6	.7	1.0	1.2	....
Air transport, passenger.............................	2 211 ..	51.4	65.7	83.5	70.5	80.8	83.0	....	....
Air transport, freight...............................	2 212 ..	1.1	....	....	....	....	3.5	....	....
Air transport, other.................................	2 213 ..	6.9	7.5	7.0	10.6	13.4	12.5	2.6	....
Other transport, passenger..........................	2 215 ..	9.0	9.0	8.5	8.4	10.5	11.3	10.7	....
Other transport, freight.............................	2 216 ..	6.1	14.0	25.3	22.8	29.9	32.0	30.5	....
Other transport, other...............................	2 217 ..	.6	....	2.5	....	....	....	2.8	....
Transportation services, debit................	3 205 ..	**−322.3**	**−380.1**	**−436.3**	**−470.9**	**−600.4**	**−767.0**	**−594.3**	....
Passenger...	3 850 ..	*−73.7*	*−81.0*	*−79.5*	*−84.5*	*−98.7*	*−100.8*	*−102.2*	....
Freight...	3 851 ..	*−233.1*	*−281.2*	*−326.9*	*−362.2*	*−472.6*	*−634.8*	*−468.9*	....
Other...	3 852 ..	*−15.6*	*−17.8*	*−30.0*	*−24.2*	*−29.2*	*−31.4*	*−23.2*	....
Sea transport, passenger.............................	3 207 ..	....	....	....	....	....	....	....	....
Sea transport, freight...............................	3 208 ..	−224.5	−273.8	−318.0	−355.7	−450.6	−605.4	−446.4	....
Sea transport, other.................................	3 209 ..	−.3	....	....	....	....	−.3	....	....
Air transport, passenger.............................	3 211 ..	−73.0	−80.3	−79.5	−84.5	−98.7	−100.8	−102.2	....
Air transport, freight...............................	3 212 ..	−7.5	−7.3	−8.7	−4.2	−6.2	−8.0	−5.6	....
Air transport, other.................................	3 213 ..	−15.1	−17.6	−30.0	−24.2	−29.1	−31.2	−23.2	....
Other transport, passenger..........................	3 215 ..	−.7	−.7	....	....	....	....	....	....
Other transport, freight.............................	3 216 ..	−1.1	−.1	−.1	−2.3	−15.9	−21.3	−16.9	....
Other transport, other...............................	3 217 ..	−.1	−.2	....	....	....	....	....	....
Travel, credit....................................	2 236 ..	**208.6**	**211.5**	**242.4**	**250.3**	**531.3**	**543.2**	**462.6**	....
Business travel...	2 237 ..	79.1	88.3	97.7	97.7	139.2	107.3	87.8	....
Personal travel...	2 240 ..	129.5	123.2	144.7	152.6	392.1	435.8	374.8	....
Travel, debit......................................	3 236 ..	**−55.4**	**−57.0**	**−64.7**	**−53.9**	**−252.6**	**−175.4**	**−155.9**	....
Business travel...	3 237 ..	−8.4	−8.3	−12.7	−10.4	−126.0	−81.4	−81.0	....
Personal travel...	3 240 ..	−47.0	−48.7	−52.0	−43.5	−126.6	−94.0	−74.9	....
Other services, credit...........................	2 200 BA	**283.9**	**367.9**	**407.7**	**443.8**	**534.4**	**607.7**	**511.7**	....
Communications...	2 245 ..	78.4	93.3	104.7	141.2	182.1	197.0	125.4	....
Construction..	2 249 ..	36.2	72.0	77.4	46.9	55.0	59.4	57.6	....
Insurance..	2 253 ..	4.0	3.6	7.7	11.1	13.0	13.4	13.2	....
Financial..	2 260 ..	5.6	5.8	6.8	7.2	7.6	3.7	4.2	....
Computer and information..........................	2 262 ..	.1	....	.8	3.4	3.7	5.2	6.1	....
Royalties and licence fees...........................	2 266 ..	....	....	....	....	.5	.2	1.2	....
Other business services..............................	2 268 ..	78.9	121.4	123.1	142.1	167.3	211.3	190.2	....
Personal, cultural, and recreational...............	2 287 ..	.1	.1	....	.4	.7	.5	.9	....
Government, n.i.e......................................	2 291 ..	80.6	71.7	87.1	91.5	104.5	117.0	113.0	....
Other services, debit............................	3 200 BA	**−213.6**	**−263.9**	**−305.4**	**−317.0**	**−385.3**	**−472.1**	**−400.9**	....
Communications...	3 245 ..	−19.9	−27.5	−37.5	−37.4	−56.5	−67.3	−50.4	....
Construction..	3 249 ..	−.5	....	−10.0	−31.3	−38.0	−39.3	−39.3	....
Insurance..	3 253 ..	−57.4	−65.6	−75.3	−72.9	−95.8	−134.3	−101.9	....
Financial..	3 260 ..	−5.8	−4.1	−3.9	−5.7	−8.4	−16.8	−26.0	....
Computer and information..........................	3 262 ..	−6.6	−7.1	−6.6	−10.2	−18.8	−17.4	−18.1	....
Royalties and licence fees...........................	3 266 ..	−.5	−7.2	−7.4	−5.3	−7.8	−9.0	−12.1	....
Other business services..............................	3 268 ..	−98.7	−135.4	−135.6	−118.9	−127.1	−157.5	−111.5	....
Personal, cultural, and recreational...............	3 287 ..	−.1	−.3	−.1	−1.1	−.3	.3	−.2	....
Government, n.i.e......................................	3 291 ..	−24.0	−16.7	−29.0	−34.2	−32.6	−30.7	−41.4	....

Table 2 (Continued). STANDARD PRESENTATION, 2003–2010

(Millions of U.S. dollars)

	Code	2003	2004	2005	2006	2007	2008	2009	2010
C. INCOME	4 300	−136.2	−130.7	−89.6	−63.4	−73.8	−47.9	−180.8	....
Total credit	2 300	*86.4*	*95.2*	*95.5*	*121.3*	*138.2*	*235.4*	*160.2*	....
Total debit	3 300	*−222.6*	*−225.9*	*−185.0*	*−184.7*	*−212.1*	*−283.3*	*−341.0*	....
Compensation of employees, credit	2 310	62.7	69.7	71.8	74.7	85.1	97.7	96.7	....
Compensation of employees, debit	3 310	−8.9	−10.3	−10.6	−9.9	−13.5	−13.7	−15.3	....
Investment income, credit	2 320	23.7	25.5	23.6	46.6	53.1	137.7	63.6	....
Direct investment income	2 330	3.5	5.7	.5	18.7	20.2	102.6	40.4	....
Dividends and distributed branch profits	2 332	.6	.3	.3	18.5	34.7	123.5	35.1	....
Reinvested earnings and undistributed branch profits	2 333	2.9	5.4	.1	.1	−14.6	−23.9	−.7	....
Income on debt (interest)	2 334	....	....	....	.1	.1	3.0	6.0	....
Portfolio investment income	2 339	5.6	8.5	12.3	11.6	11.8	11.4	14.3	....
Income on equity	2 340	.1	.2	.1	.4	.3	.7	1.1	....
Income on bonds and notes	2 350	5.3	8.0	9.9	9.8	11.0	4.6	12.6	....
Income on money market instruments	2 360	.2	.2	2.3	1.5	.5	6.1	.6	....
Other investment income	2 370	14.6	11.4	10.9	16.3	21.2	23.6	8.8	....
Investment income, debit	3 320	−213.7	−215.6	−174.4	−174.8	−198.6	−269.5	−325.7	....
Direct investment income	3 330	−88.8	−67.6	−61.5	−69.8	−77.8	−122.5	−147.1	....
Dividends and distributed branch profits	3 332	−97.1	−77.3	−115.7	−85.6	−98.6	−142.9	−136.8	....
Reinvested earnings and undistributed branch profits	3 333	8.5	10.2	55.0	17.5	21.9	20.8	−10.3	....
Income on debt (interest)	3 334	−.2	−.5	−.8	−1.8	−1.1	−.5	....	....
Portfolio investment income	3 339	−36.0	−48.2	−43.6	−54.7	−78.7	−99.5	−117.1	....
Income on equity	3 340	−15.0	−26.3	−28.2	−37.3	−58.2	−68.4	−79.3	....
Income on bonds and notes	3 350	−21.0	−21.9	−15.3	−17.3	−20.5	−30.8	−37.8	....
Income on money market instruments	3 360	....	....	....	....	....	−.3	....	....
Other investment income	3 370	−88.9	−99.8	−69.3	−50.4	−42.0	−47.5	−61.5	....
D. CURRENT TRANSFERS	4 379	530.4	632.0	753.8	836.6	1,289.5	1,684.6	1,473.2	....
Credit	2 379	595.6	715.1	859.2	973.7	1,557.5	1,985.9	1,756.8	....
General government	2 380	124.0	129.8	116.6	96.4	115.4	131.2	98.2	....
Other sectors	2 390	471.6	585.3	742.5	877.3	1,442.1	1,854.7	1,658.6	....
Workers' remittances	2 391	448.2	563.2	717.0	850.6	1,106.7	1,378.4	1,253.7	....
Other current transfers	2 392	23.3	22.1	25.6	26.7	335.4	476.3	404.9	....
Debit	3 379	−65.2	−83.1	−105.4	−137.0	−268.0	−301.3	−283.6	....
General government	3 380	−8.3	−8.1	−9.0	−42.5	−6.8	−58.6	−49.2	....
Other sectors	3 390	−56.9	−75.0	−96.4	−94.5	−261.1	−242.8	−234.4	....
Workers' remittances	3 391	−48.2	−66.5	−87.1	−86.5	−129.8	−130.4	−159.1	....
Other current transfers	3 392	−8.7	−8.4	−9.3	−8.0	−131.4	−112.4	−75.3	....
CAPITAL AND FINANCIAL ACCOUNT	4 996	425.7	497.2	679.0	832.9	1,298.9	1,897.2	1,036.1	....
CAPITAL ACCOUNT	4 994	150.4	750.0	199.5	2,291.1	332.7	239.5	305.1	....
Total credit	2 994	*150.9*	*750.4*	*200.3*	*2,294.7*	*384.4*	*240.7*	*307.3*	....
Total debit	3 994	*−.6*	*−.4*	*−.8*	*−3.6*	*−51.8*	*−1.3*	*−2.2*	....
Capital transfers, credit	2 400	150.8	750.4	200.3	2,294.7	198.6	240.7	307.3	....
General government	2 401	139.1	742.0	189.5	2,282.2	183.3	223.0	289.5	....
Debt forgiveness	2 402	35.6	609.7	69.4	2,132.2	4.5	4.5	3.4	....
Other capital transfers	2 410	103.5	132.3	120.1	150.0	178.9	218.6	286.0	....
Other sectors	2 430	11.7	8.4	10.8	12.4	15.2	17.7	17.8	....
Migrants' transfers	2 431	....	....	....	....	....	....	....	....
Debt forgiveness	2 432	....	....	....	....	....	....	....	....
Other capital transfers	2 440	11.7	8.4	10.8	12.4	15.2	17.7	17.8	....
Capital transfers, debit	3 400	....	....	....	....	....	....	....	....
General government	3 401	....	....	....	....	....	....	....	....
Debt forgiveness	3 402	....	....	....	....	....	....	....	....
Other capital transfers	3 410	....	....	....	....	....	....	....	....
Other sectors	3 430	....	....	....	....	....	....	....	....
Migrants' transfers	3 431	....	....	....	....	....	....	....	....
Debt forgiveness	3 432	....	....	....	....	....	....	....	....
Other capital transfers	3 440	....	....	....	....	....	....	....	....
Nonproduced nonfinancial assets, credit	2 480	.2	....	....	....	185.9	....	....	....
Nonproduced nonfinancial assets, debit	3 480	−.6	−.4	−.8	−3.6	−51.8	−1.3	−2.2	....

Table 2 (Continued). STANDARD PRESENTATION, 2003–2010

(Millions of U.S. dollars)

	Code	2003	2004	2005	2006	2007	2008	2009	2010
FINANCIAL ACCOUNT	4 995 ..	**275.3**	**−252.8**	**479.5**	**−1,458.2**	**966.2**	**1,657.8**	**731.0**	....
A. DIRECT INVESTMENT	4 500 ..	**49.8**	**64.0**	**52.3**	**210.4**	**272.7**	**271.4**	**254.0**	....
Direct investment abroad	4 505 ..	**−2.7**	**−13.1**	**7.7**	**−9.9**	**−24.7**	**−126.3**	**−77.1**	....
Equity capital	4 510 ..	5.6	−1.8	−2.6	−5.2	−48.4	−96.3	−30.4	....
Claims on affiliated enterprises	4 515 ..	....	....	....	....	....	....	....	....
Liabilities to affiliated enterprises	4 520 ..	....	....	....	....	....	....	....	....
Reinvested earnings	4 525 ..	−2.9	−5.4	−.1	−.1	14.6	23.9	.6	....
Other capital	4 530 ..	−5.4	−5.9	10.4	−4.6	9.2	−53.9	−47.4	....
Claims on affiliated enterprises	4 535 ..	−4.2	−5.6	.6	−2.2	5.9	−57.3	−47.0	....
Liabilities to affiliated enterprises	4 540 ..	−1.2	−.3	9.8	−2.4	3.2	3.4	−.4	....
Direct investment in Senegal	4 555 ..	**52.5**	**77.0**	**44.6**	**220.3**	**297.4**	**397.6**	**331.1**	....
Equity capital	4 560 ..	72.6	90.2	96.1	288.0	299.6	408.0	234.0	....
Claims on direct investors	4 565 ..	....	....	....	....	....	....	....	....
Liabilities to direct investors	4 570 ..	....	....	....	....	....	....	....	....
Reinvested earnings	4 575 ..	−8.5	−10.2	−55.0	−17.5	−21.9	−20.8	10.3	....
Other capital	4 580 ..	−11.5	−3.0	3.5	−50.2	19.7	10.4	86.8	....
Claims on direct investors	4 585 ..	−2.1	1.0	−2.0	−17.6	13.1	2.4	.5	....
Liabilities to direct investors	4 590 ..	−9.5	−4.0	5.6	−32.6	6.6	8.1	86.3	....
B. PORTFOLIO INVESTMENT	4 600 ..	**−45.7**	**−46.7**	**−4.3**	**−67.0**	**22.4**	**81.7**	**137.8**	....
Assets	4 602 ..	**−56.3**	**−47.5**	**−48.9**	**−53.3**	**6.4**	**51.6**	**−91.3**	....
Equity securities	4 610 ..	−7.9	22.8	4.3	1.7	9.9	....	−1.7	....
Monetary authorities	4 611 ..	....	....	....	....	....	....	....	....
General government	4 612 ..	....	....	....	....	....	....	....	....
Banks	4 613 ..	....	.8	.9	.2	....	.7	....	....
Other sectors	4 614 ..	−7.9	22.1	3.4	1.6	9.9	−.7	−1.7	....
Debt securities	4 619 ..	−48.4	−70.3	−53.2	−55.1	−3.5	51.5	−89.5	....
Bonds and notes	4 620 ..	−53.0	−68.0	−53.2	19.7	−40.9	46.7	−4.6	....
Monetary authorities	4 621 ..	....	....	....	....	....	....	....	....
General government	4 622 ..	13.8	−10.8	.2	−1.0	.8	3.4	4.2	....
Banks	4 623 ..	−66.2	−41.0	−53.5	21.3	−42.5	43.3	−16.7	....
Other sectors	4 624 ..	−.5	−16.2	....	−.6	.8	....	7.9	....
Money market instruments	4 630 ..	4.6	−2.4	....	−74.8	37.4	4.9	−84.9	....
Monetary authorities	4 631 ..	....	....	....	....	....	....	....	....
General government	4 632 ..	....	....	....	....	....	....	....	....
Banks	4 633 ..	....	−6.6	....	−74.8	37.4	4.9	−84.9	....
Other sectors	4 634 ..	4.6	4.3	....	....	....	−.1	....	....
Liabilities	4 652 ..	**10.6**	**.8**	**44.6**	**−13.6**	**16.0**	**30.1**	**229.1**	....
Equity securities	4 660 ..	3.6	−27.7	−6.1	−.4	8.0	−92.6	−1.6	....
Banks	4 663 ..	.3	....	.1	−1.1	6.2	−3.4	−.5	....
Other sectors	4 664 ..	3.3	−27.7	−6.1	.8	1.9	−89.2	−1.1	....
Debt securities	4 669 ..	6.9	28.5	50.7	−13.3	8.0	122.7	230.7	....
Bonds and notes	4 670 ..	6.9	28.4	50.7	−17.0	−11.8	133.9	230.7	....
Monetary authorities	4 671 ..	....	....	....	....	....	....	....	....
General government	4 672 ..	−7.7	....	53.1	....	49.7	9.2	232.7	....
Banks	4 673 ..	....	28.0	20.7	−9.8	−58.4	....	−2.0	....
Other sectors	4 674 ..	14.6	.3	−23.1	−7.2	−3.1	124.7	....	....
Money market instruments	4 680 ..	....	.1	....	3.7	19.8	−11.2	....	....
Monetary authorities	4 681 ..	....	....	....	....	....	....	....	....
General government	4 682 ..	....	....	....	....	....	....	....	....
Banks	4 683 ..	....	....	....	3.8	19.8	−11.2	....	....
Other sectors	4 684 ..	....	.1	....	−.1	....	....	....	....
C. FINANCIAL DERIVATIVES	4 910 ..	**2.3**	....	**−.1**	....	**25.5**	....	....	....
Monetary authorities	4 911 ..	....	....	....	....	....	....	....	....
General government	4 912 ..	....	....	....	....	....	....	....	....
Banks	4 913 ..	.4	....	....	....	25.5	.1	....	....
Other sectors	4 914 ..	1.9	....	−.1	....	.1	−.2	....	....
Assets	4 900 ..	**1.6**	**.7**	....	**−.1**	....	**.2**	....	....
Monetary authorities	4 901 ..	....	....	....	....	....	....	....	....
General government	4 902 ..	....	....	....	....	....	....	....	....
Banks	4 903 ..	.4	....	....	....	....	.1	....	....
Other sectors	4 904 ..	1.2	.8	....	−.1	....	....	....	....
Liabilities	4 905 ..	**.7**	**−.8**	**−.1**	**.1**	**25.6**	**−.2**	....	....
Monetary authorities	4 906 ..	....	....	....	....	....	....	....	....
General government	4 907 ..	....	....	....	....	....	....	....	....
Banks	4 908 ..	....	....	....	....	25.5	....	....	....
Other sectors	4 909 ..	.7	−.8	−.1	.1	.1	−.2	....	....

Table 2 (Concluded). STANDARD PRESENTATION, 2003–2010

(Millions of U.S. dollars)

	Code	2003	2004	2005	2006	2007	2008	2009	2010
D. OTHER INVESTMENT	4 700	**287.1**	**−115.0**	**436.1**	**−1,591.8**	**802.5**	**1,339.3**	**794.0**	....
Assets	4 703	**58.0**	**6.0**	**79.2**	**−34.3**	**84.4**	**147.7**	**−128.2**	....
Trade credits	4 706	11.2	13.9	26.2	8.1	11.5	−30.3	−80.3	....
General government	4 707	....	....	....	....	....	....	....	
of which: Short-term	4 709	....	....	....	....	....	....	....	
Other sectors	4 710	11.2	13.9	26.2	8.1	11.5	−30.3	−80.3	....
of which: Short-term	4 712	....	....	....	....	....	....	....	
Loans	4 714	−19.0	−39.1	42.4	−70.9	−15.7	50.9	68.4	....
Monetary authorities	4 715	....	....	....	....	....	....	....	
of which: Short-term	4 718	....	....	....	....	....	....	....	
General government	4 719	....	....	....	....	....	....	....	
of which: Short-term	4 721	....	....	....	....	....	....	....	
Banks	4 722	−19.0	−39.1	42.4	−70.9	−13.4	50.9	68.4	
of which: Short-term	4 724	*−4.9*	*14.8*	*4.3*	*−17.5*	*−20.0*	*40.9*	*57.4*	
Other sectors	4 725	....	....	....	....	−2.3	....	....	
of which: Short-term	4 727	....	....	....	....	*−2.3*	....	....	
Currency and deposits	4 730	56.6	−4.9	8.5	31.8	41.7	37.7	−109.0	....
Monetary authorities	4 731	....	....	....	....	....	....	....	
General government	4 732	−1.8	3.1	1.0	1.0	.5	2.0	−.2	
Banks	4 733	9.3	20.5	6.4	4.8	.3	−10.7	−23.6	
Other sectors	4 734	49.1	−28.6	1.1	26.0	40.8	46.3	−85.2	
Other assets	4 736	9.3	36.1	2.2	−3.3	46.9	89.4	−7.2	....
Monetary authorities	4 737	....	....	....	....	....	....	....	
of which: Short-term	4 739	....	....	....	....	....	....	....	
General government	4 740	....	....	....	−.6	....	.7	....	
of which: Short-term	4 742	....	....	....	−.6	....	.7	....	
Banks	4 743	1.4	−.8	1.9	−8.7	.7	9.9	−.3	
of which: Short-term	4 745	*1.4*	*−.8*	*1.9*	*−8.7*	*.6*	*9.9*	*−.3*	
Other sectors	4 746	7.9	37.0	.3	6.1	46.2	78.8	−6.9	
of which: Short-term	4 748	....	....	....	....	....	....	....	
Liabilities	4 753	**229.1**	**−121.0**	**356.9**	**−1,557.5**	**718.1**	**1,191.6**	**922.2**	....
Trade credits	4 756	90.2	94.0	104.7	185.2	134.8	195.1	21.1	....
General government	4 757	....	....	....	....	....	....	....	
of which: Short-term	4 759	....	....	....	....	....	....	....	
Other sectors	4 760	90.2	94.0	104.7	185.2	134.8	195.1	21.1	....
of which: Short-term	4 762	....	....	....	....	....	....	....	
Loans	4 764	45.8	−321.1	156.6	−1,873.2	423.1	833.1	465.6	....
Monetary authorities	4 765	−34.5	−44.4	−40.6	−125.1	....	36.9	101.2	
of which: Use of Fund credit and loans from the Fund	4 766	*−34.5*	*−44.4*	*−40.6*	*−125.1*	....	*36.9*	*101.2*	
of which: Short-term	4 768	....	....	....	....	....	....	....	
General government	4 769	68.3	−337.0	203.6	−1,813.7	236.6	493.0	305.2	
of which: Short-term	4 771	....	....	62.6	....	....	....	....	
Banks	4 772	8.2	42.3	2.3	5.6	10.6	131.0	7.4	
of which: Short-term	4 774	*.3*	*28.6*	*11.7*	*−23.1*	*16.1*	*62.9*	*4.0*	
Other sectors	4 775	3.8	18.0	−8.7	60.1	175.9	172.1	51.8	
of which: Short-term	4 777	*−15.7*	....	....	53.9	*163.7*	*161.0*	*−9.2*	
Currency and deposits	4 780	33.6	−19.4	85.2	34.6	38.7	−3.4	182.5	....
Monetary authorities	4 781	12.1	−35.5	51.3	−51.2	1.6	−6.0	181.2	
General government	4 782	....	....	....	....	....	....	....	
Banks	4 783	21.5	16.1	33.8	85.7	37.2	2.6	1.4	
Other sectors	4 784	....	....	....	....	....	....	....	
Other liabilities	4 786	59.5	125.6	10.5	95.9	121.5	166.9	253.0	
Monetary authorities	4 787	−7.7	14.8	−25.4	7.2	−.7	7.8	196.0	
of which: Short-term	4 789	....	....	....	....	....	....	....	
General government	4 790	....	....	....	....	....	....	....	
of which: Short-term	4 792	....	....	....	....	....	....	....	
Banks	4 793	.1	−.1	.2	14.9	−16.2	....	....	
of which: Short-term	4 795	*.1*	*−.1*	*.2*	*14.9*	*−16.2*	....	....	
Other sectors	4 796	67.1	110.9	35.7	73.9	138.5	159.1	57.0	
of which: Short-term	4 798	....	....	....	....	....	....	....	
E. RESERVE ASSETS	4 802	**−18.1**	**−155.0**	**−4.5**	**−9.9**	**−157.0**	**−34.5**	**−454.7**	....
Monetary gold	4 812	....	....	....	....	....	....	....	
Special drawing rights	4 811	−1.0	3.3	5.7	1.4	−.1	−.1	−203.4	
Reserve position in the Fund	4 810	....	−.1	−.1	....	−.1	−.1	....	
Foreign exchange	4 803	−17.1	−158.3	−10.1	−11.2	−156.9	−34.3	−251.2	
Other claims	4 813	....	....	....	....	....	....	....	
NET ERRORS AND OMISSIONS	4 998	**10.8**	**13.1**	**−3.1**	**28.3**	**12.8**	**−13.5**	**−171.3**	....

Table 3. INTERNATIONAL INVESTMENT POSITION (End-period stocks), 2003–2010

(Millions of U.S. dollars)

	Code	2003	2004	2005	2006	2007	2008	2009	2010
ASSETS..	8 995 C.	1,667.8	2,803.7	2,014.6	2,608.9	3,017.8	2,761.7	3,630.4	....
Direct investment abroad...............	8 505 ..	75.5	78.5	58.3	81.2	131.6	193.4	280.3	....
Equity capital and reinvested earnings.............	8 506 ..	55.6	61.9	52.2	63.7	122.7	207.6	245.9	....
Claims on affiliated enterprises.............	8 507 ..	....	....	....	....	....	....	....	
Liabilities to affiliated enterprises.............	8 508 ..	....	....	....	....	....	....	....	
Other capital.............	8 530 ..	19.9	16.6	6.1	17.5	8.9	−14.2	34.4	....
Claims on affiliated enterprises.............	8 535 ..	....	....	....	....	....	....	....	
Liabilities to affiliated enterprises.............	8 540 ..	....	....	....	....	....	....	....	
Portfolio investment.............................	8 602 ..	226.7	331.5	260.0	329.0	359.0	290.4	394.2	....
Equity securities.............	8 610 ..	32.9	20.0	14.5	14.9	10.6	9.9	12.1	....
Monetary authorities.............	8 611 ..	....	....	....	....	....	....	....	
General government.............	8 612 ..	....	....	....	....	....	....	....	
Banks.............	8 613 ..	....	3.9	3.7	4.6	4.5	3.6	....	
Other sectors.............	8 614 ..	....	....	....	....	....	....	....	
Debt securities.............	8 619 ..	193.8	311.5	245.5	314.1	348.5	280.5	382.1	....
Bonds and notes.............	8 620 ..	188.5	305.6	238.6	286.3	211.7	254.1	190.6	
Monetary authorities.............	8 621 ..	....	....	....	....	....	....	....	
General government.............	8 622 ..	....	....	....	....	....	....	....	
Banks.............	8 623 ..	188.5	305.6	238.6	286.3	211.7	254.1	190.6	
Other sectors.............	8 624 ..	....	....	....	....	....	....	....	
Money market instruments.............	8 630 ..	5.3	5.9	6.9	27.8	136.8	26.4	191.5	
Monetary authorities.............	8 631 ..	....	....	....	....	....	....	....	
General government.............	8 632 ..	....	....	....	....	....	....	....	
Banks.............	8 633 ..	1.3	5.2	6.3	27.1	136.1	25.7	191.5	
Other sectors.............	8 634 ..	....	....	....	....	....	....	....	
Financial derivatives.............................	8 900 ..	.8	.1	.1	.2	.2	.1	.1	....
Monetary authorities.............	8 901 ..	....	....	....	....	....	....	....	
General government.............	8 902 ..	....	....	....	....	....	....	....	
Banks.............	8 903 ..	.8	.1	.1	.2	.2	.1	.1	
Other sectors.............	8 904 ..	....	....	....	....	....	....	....	
Other investment.............................	8 703 ..	570.1	1,026.1	506.9	864.3	866.9	675.7	832.6	....
Trade credits.............	8 706 ..	181.9	217.4	155.0	205.5	186.6	204.2	294.6	
General government.............	8 707 ..	....	....	....	....	....	....	....	
of which: Short-term.............	8 709 ..	....	....	....	....	....	....	....	
Other sectors.............	8 710 ..	....	....	....	....	....	....	....	
of which: Short-term.............	8 712 ..	....	....	....	....	....	....	....	
Loans.............	8 714 ..	120.6	345.5	109.5	196.6	236.7	172.6	108.0	....
Monetary authorities.............	8 715 ..	....	....	....	....	....	....	....	
of which: Short-term.............	8 718 ..	....	....	....	....	....	....	....	
General government.............	8 719 ..	....	....	....	....	....	....	....	
of which: Short-term.............	8 721 ..	....	....	....	....	....	....	....	
Banks.............	8 722 ..	120.5	345.5	109.5	196.6	234.3	172.6	107.7	
of which: Short-term.............	8 724 ..	*80.6*	*140.1*	*56.5*	*81.7*	*112.9*	*67.5*	*10.3*	
Other sectors.............	8 725 ..	....	....	....	....	2.4	....	.3	
of which: Short-term.............	8 727 ..					*2.4*		*.3*	
Currency and deposits.............	8 730 ..	262.1	445.7	222.0	209.1	211.4	164.2	282.9	
Monetary authorities.............	8 731 ..	....	....	....	....	....	....	....	
General government.............	8 732 ..	8.5	5.7	4.0	3.4	96.0	1.2	1.4	....
Banks.............	8 733 ..	178.3	339.5	141.0	152.3	169.9	170.8	201.2	
Other sectors.............	8 734 ..	75.4	100.5	77.0	53.4	−54.4	−7.7	80.3	
Other assets.............	8 736 ..	5.6	17.4	20.4	253.0	232.2	134.6	147.1	....
Monetary authorities.............	8 737 ..	....	....	....	....	....	....	....	
of which: Short-term.............	8 739 ..	....	....	....	....	....	....	....	
General government.............	8 740 ..	....	....	....	.7	.7	....	....	
of which: Short-term.............	8 742 ..	....	....	....	....	....	....	....	
Banks.............	8 743 ..	1.8	5.6	.6	9.9	10.3	.4	.7	
of which: Short-term.............	8 745 ..	*1.8*	*5.6*	*.6*	*9.8*	*10.3*	*.4*	*.7*	
Other sectors.............	8 746 ..	3.8	11.8	19.8	242.5	221.2	134.2	146.4	....
of which: Short-term.............	8 748 ..	....	....	....	....	....	....	....	
Reserve assets.............................	8 802 ..	794.6	1,367.6	1,189.3	1,334.2	1,660.0	1,602.2	2,123.2	....
Monetary gold.............	8 812 ..	....	....	....	....	....	....	....	
Special drawing rights.............	8 811 ..	10.6	7.3	1.4	.1	.1	.2	204.4	200.7
Reserve position in the Fund.............	8 810 ..	2.2	2.4	2.2	2.4	2.6	2.6	2.7	2.8
Foreign exchange.............	8 803 ..	781.8	1,357.9	1,185.7	1,331.8	1,657.3	1,599.4	1,916.1	....
Other claims.............	8 813 ..	....	....	....	....	....	....	....	

Table 3 (Concluded). INTERNATIONAL INVESTMENT POSITION (End-period stocks), 2003–2010

(Millions of U.S. dollars)

	Code	2003	2004	2005	2006	2007	2008	2009	2010
LIABILITIES..	8 995 D.	**5,973.0**	**6,603.7**	**5,616.6**	**4,398.2**	**5,995.4**	**7,206.0**	**8,812.0**	....
Direct investment in Senegal........................	8 555 ..	**346.6**	**441.2**	**358.2**	**477.1**	**838.6**	**1,170.6**	**1,543.2**	....
Equity capital and reinvested earnings..........................	8 556 ..	296.6	362.5	272.6	440.8	784.9	1,109.9	1,390.6	....
Claims on direct investors...................................	8 557 ..	....	....	....	....	....	....	....	....
Liabilities to direct investors.............................	8 558 ..	....	....	....	....	....	....	....	....
Other capital...	8 580 ..	49.9	78.7	85.6	36.4	53.7	60.7	152.6	....
Claims on direct investors...................................	8 585 ..	....	....	....	....	....	....	....	....
Liabilities to direct investors.............................	8 590 ..	....	....	....	....	....	....	....	....
Portfolio investment...	8 652 ..	**180.7**	**189.0**	**267.8**	**294.9**	**370.4**	**378.7**	**629.6**	....
Equity securities...	8 660 ..	133.7	113.6	91.8	102.0	121.1	26.5	25.7	....
Banks...	8 663 ..	2.4	2.6	2.3	1.4	7.6	3.9	3.5	
Other sectors...	8 664 ..	131.3	110.9	89.4	100.6	113.5	22.6	22.2	
Debt securities...	8 669 ..	47.0	75.5	176.0	192.8	249.3	352.3	603.9	
Bonds and notes...	8 670 ..	47.0	75.4	175.9	188.8	171.5	289.3	553.7	
Monetary authorities....................................	8 671 ..	....	....	....	....	....	....	....	
General government......................................	8 672 ..	5.6	6.0	50.4	....	53.5	59.3	302.6	
Banks...	8 673 ..	1.0	26.5	20.4	79.0	....	....	13.0	
Other sectors...	8 674 ..	40.4	42.9	105.1	109.8	118.0	230.0	238.1	
Money market instruments................................	8 680 ..	....	.1	.1	4.0	77.8	63.0	50.1	
Monetary authorities....................................	8 681 ..	....	....	....	....	....	....	....	
General government......................................	8 682 ..	....	....	....	....	....	....	....	
Banks...	8 683 ..	....	.1	.1	4.0	77.8	63.0	50.1	
Other sectors...	8 684 ..	....	....	....	....	....	....	....	
Financial derivatives...	8 905 ..	**.9**	**.1**	**....**	**.1**	**.2**	**....**	**....**	**....**
Monetary authorities..	8 906 ..	....	....	....	....	....	....	....	....
General government...	8 907 ..	....	....	....	....	....	....	....	
Banks..	8 908 ..	....	....	....	....	....	....	....	
Other sectors..	8 909 ..	.9	.1	....	.1	.2	....	....	
Other investment...	8 753 ..	**5,444.9**	**5,973.4**	**4,990.6**	**3,626.2**	**4,786.2**	**5,656.7**	**6,639.2**	....
Trade credits..	8 756 ..	373.2	415.1	445.0	693.9	876.0	1,013.5	1,070.8	....
General government...	8 757 ..	....	....	....	....	....	....	....	
of which: Short-term......................................	8 759 ..	....	....	....	....	....	....	....	
Other sectors..	8 760 ..	373.2	415.1	445.0	693.9	876.0	1,013.5	1,070.8	
of which: Short-term......................................	8 762 ..	....	....	....	....	....	....	....	
Loans..	8 764 ..	4,582.7	4,682.7	4,045.4	2,253.8	2,966.1	3,595.5	4,204.8	....
Monetary authorities...	8 765 ..	239.7	204.2	148.3	26.1	27.4	64.1	166.7	
of which: Use of Fund credit and loans from the Fund....	8 766 ..	*239.7*	*204.2*	*148.3*	*26.1*	*27.4*	*64.1*	*166.7*	*213.0*
of which: Short-term......................................	8 768 ..	....	....	....	....	....	....	....	
General government...	8 769 ..	3,906.5	3,872.7	3,512.0	1,735.5	2,173.4	2,485.7	3,208.9	
of which: Short-term......................................	8 771 ..	....	....	....	....	....	....	....	
Banks..	8 772 ..	37.0	183.6	76.9	91.7	113.8	232.1	247.9	
of which: Short-term......................................	8 774 ..	*.7*	*75.2*	*38.9*	*19.1*	*38.8*	*96.4*	*104.0*	
Other sectors..	8 775 ..	399.6	422.3	308.2	400.5	651.5	813.6	581.3	
of which: Short-term......................................	8 777 ..	....	....	....	....	....	....	....	
Currency and deposits...	8 780 ..	471.1	825.1	488.7	577.4	707.7	665.8	674.2	
Monetary authorities...	8 781 ..	143.4	115.5	148.5	112.1	126.6	113.9	101.6	
General government...	8 782 ..	....	....	....	....	....	....	....	
Banks..	8 783 ..	327.6	709.7	340.1	465.3	581.1	551.9	572.7	
Other sectors..	8 784 ..	....	....	....	....	....	....	....	
Other liabilities..	8 786 ..	18.0	50.4	11.6	101.0	236.4	382.0	689.4	
Monetary authorities...	8 787 ..	.8	17.1	2.2	10.0	10.5	17.3	252.8	
of which: Short-term......................................	8 789 ..	....	....	....	....	....	....	....	
General government...	8 790 ..	....	....	....	....	....	....	....	
of which: Short-term......................................	8 792 ..	....	....	....	....	....	....	....	
Banks..	8 793 ..	....	....	....	....	....	....	....	
of which: Short-term......................................	8 795 ..	....	....	....	....	....	....	....	
Other sectors..	8 796 ..	17.1	33.3	9.4	91.0	225.9	364.7	436.6	....
of which: Short-term......................................	8 798 ..	....	....	....	....	....	....	....	....
NET INTERNATIONAL INVESTMENT POSITION........	8 995 ..	**–4,305.3**	**–3,800.0**	**–3,602.1**	**–1,789.4**	**–2,977.6**	**–4,444.4**	**–5,181.6**	....
Conversion rates: CFA francs per U.S. dollar (end of period)...	0 102 ..	**519.36**	**481.58**	**556.04**	**498.07**	**445.59**	**471.34**	**455.34**	**490.91**

2011, International Monetary Fund: *Balance of Payments Statistics Yearbook*

Table 1. ANALYTIC PRESENTATION, 2003–2010

(Millions of U.S. dollars)

	Code	2003	2004	2005	2006	2007	2008	2009	2010
A. Current Account[1]..................................	4 993 Z.	....	....	....	....	**−7,153.6**	**−10,742.6**	**−3,178.8**	**−3,115.0**
Goods: exports f.o.b.................................	2 100 ..	....	....	....	....	8,719.8	10,937.6	8,361.3	9,818.8
Goods: imports f.o.b.................................	3 100 ..	....	....	....	....	−18,369.2	−23,455.5	−15,490.8	−16,163.1
Balance on Goods.................................	4 100 ..	....	....	....	....	*−9,649.4*	*−12,517.9*	*−7,129.5*	*−6,344.3*
Services: credit...	2 200 ..	....	....	....	....	3,151.6	4,028.3	3,487.9	3,532.5
Services: debit...	3 200 ..	....	....	....	....	−3,505.6	−4,296.2	−3,456.0	−3,525.9
Balance on Goods and Services...............	4 991 ..	....	....	....	....	*−10,003.3*	*−12,785.7*	*−7,097.6*	*−6,337.7*
Income: credit...	2 300 ..	....	....	....	....	707.1	826.4	695.2	581.3
Income: debit...	3 300 ..	....	....	....	....	−1,526.0	−2,175.7	−1,401.4	−1,480.1
Balance on Goods, Services, and Income.........	4 992 ..	....	....	....	....	*−10,822.2*	*−14,135.0*	*−7,803.9*	*−7,236.6*
Current transfers: credit...........................	2 379 Z.	....	....	....	....	3,980.6	3,798.9	4,969.5	4,475.0
Current transfers: debit...........................	3 379 ..	....	....	....	....	−312.1	−406.4	−344.5	−353.4
B. Capital Account[1]...................................	4 994 Z.	....	....	....	....	**−426.2**	**20.2**	**2.6**	**1.3**
Capital account: credit............................	2 994 Z.	....	....	....	....	20.4	24.8	7.8	4.0
Capital account: debit............................	3 994 ..	....	....	....	....	−446.5	−4.6	−5.2	−2.7
Total, Groups A Plus B...........................	4 981 ..	....	....	....	....	*−7,579.8*	*−10,722.4*	*−3,176.2*	*−3,113.7*
C. Financial Account[1]...............................	4 995 W.	....	....	....	....	**8,150.6**	**8,187.4**	**4,731.5**	**1,047.2**
Direct investment abroad.........................	4 505 ..	....	....	....	....	−957.6	−281.9	−54.8	−188.4
Direct investment in the Republic of Serbia.........	4 555 Z.	....	....	....	....	3,431.9	2,996.4	1,935.6	1,340.2
Portfolio investment assets......................	4 602 ..	....	....	....	....	−4.7	−40.7	−9.6	−41.7
Equity securities.................................	4 610 ..	....	....	....	....	−13.2	−41.0	−10.0	18.1
Debt securities..................................	4 619 ..	....	....	....	....	8.5	.2	.4	−59.8
Portfolio investment liabilities..................	4 652 Z.	....	....	....	....	932.3	−95.7	−56.1	130.1
Equity securities.................................	4 660 ..	....	....	....	....	771.9	−56.9	22.5	84.2
Debt securities..................................	4 669 Z.	....	....	....	....	160.4	−38.9	−78.6	45.9
Financial derivatives...............................	4 910 ..	....	....	....	....	1.5	−.1	−2.5	−30.1
Financial derivatives assets......................	4 900 ..	....	....	....	....	....	−.3	2.7	7.5
Financial derivatives liabilities.................	4 905 ..	....	....	....	....	1.5	.2	−5.2	−37.6
Other investment assets..........................	4 703 ..	....	....	....	....	−2,220.8	−2,055.8	94.8	−1,077.6
Monetary authorities............................	4 701 ..	....	....	....	....	....	....	....	....
General government............................	4 704 ..	....	....	....	....	−67.0	−47.9	....	....
Banks..	4 705 ..	....	....	....	....	−975.3	303.2	−459.2	−603.4
Other sectors.....................................	4 728 ..	....	....	....	....	−1,178.5	−2,311.0	554.0	−474.2
Other investment liabilities......................	4 753 W.	....	....	....	....	6,968.1	7,665.3	2,824.1	914.7
Monetary authorities............................	4 753 WA	....	....	....	....	−117.2	−7.1	581.0	....
General government............................	4 753 ZB	....	....	....	....	166.1	131.4	356.1	949.2
Banks..	4 753 ZC	....	....	....	....	302.1	311.9	1,676.2	384.5
Other sectors.....................................	4 753 ZD	....	....	....	....	6,617.0	7,229.1	210.8	−419.0
Total, Groups A Through C......................	4 983 ..	....	....	....	....	*570.8*	*−2,534.9*	*1,555.3*	*−2,066.5*
D. Net Errors and Omissions......................	4 998 ..	....	....	....	....	**417.2**	**−211.2**	**−30.5**	**82.9**
Total, Groups A Through D......................	4 984 ..	....	....	....	....	*988.0*	*−2,746.1*	*1,524.7*	*−1,983.7*
E. Reserves and Related Items....................	4 802 A.	....	....	....	....	**−988.0**	**2,746.1**	**−1,524.7**	**1,983.7**
Reserve assets.......................................	4 802 ..	....	....	....	....	−1,007.0	2,398.3	−3,409.6	1,233.9
Use of Fund credit and loans..................	4 766 ..	....	....	....	....	−244.9	....	1,572.5	454.0
Exceptional financing............................	4 920 ..	....	....	....	....	263.8	347.8	312.3	295.7
Conversion rates: dinars per U.S. dollar.................	0 101 ..	57.5854	58.3814	66.7138	67.1458	58.4535	55.7235	67.5806	77.7289

[1] Excludes components that have been classified in the categories of Group E.

Table 2. STANDARD PRESENTATION, 2003–2010
(Millions of U.S. dollars)

	Code	2003	2004	2005	2006	2007	2008	2009	2010
CURRENT ACCOUNT	4 993	....	....	....	....	−6,889.8	−10,394.8	−2,866.5	−2,819.3
A. GOODS	4 100	....	....	....	....	−9,649.4	−12,517.9	−7,129.5	−6,344.3
Credit	2 100	....	....	....	....	8,719.8	10,937.6	8,361.3	9,818.8
General merchandise: exports f.o.b.	2 110	....	....	....	....	8,719.8	10,937.6	8,361.3	9,818.8
Goods for processing: exports f.o.b.	2 150	....	....	....	....	....	....	....	....
Repairs on goods	2 160	....	....	....	....	....	....	....	....
Goods procured in ports by carriers	2 170	....	....	....	....	....	....	....	....
Nonmonetary gold	2 180	....	....	....	....	....	....	....	....
Debit	3 100	....	....	....	....	−18,369.2	−23,455.5	−15,490.8	−16,163.1
General merchandise: imports f.o.b.	3 110	....	....	....	....	−18,369.2	−23,455.5	−15,490.8	−16,163.1
Goods for processing: imports f.o.b.	3 150	....	....	....	....	....	....	....	....
Repairs on goods	3 160	....	....	....	....	....	....	....	....
Goods procured in ports by carriers	3 170	....	....	....	....	....	....	....	....
Nonmonetary gold	3 180	....	....	....	....	....	....	....	....
B. SERVICES	4 200	....	....	....	....	−354.0	−267.9	31.8	6.6
Total credit	2 200	....	....	....	....	*3,151.6*	*4,028.3*	*3,487.9*	*3,532.5*
Total debit	3 200	....	....	....	....	*−3,505.6*	*−4,296.2*	*−3,456.0*	*−3,525.9*
Transportation services, credit	2 205	....	....	....	....	724.0	965.3	731.1	781.0
Passenger	2 850	....	....	....	....	*152.2*	*176.3*	*120.4*	*152.3*
Freight	2 851	....	....	....	....	*420.1*	*571.6*	*422.3*	*441.3*
Other	2 852	....	....	....	....	*151.6*	*217.4*	*188.4*	*187.4*
Sea transport, passenger	2 207	....	....	....	....	....	....	....	....
Sea transport, freight	2 208	....	....	....	....	8.2	13.4	12.5	18.5
Sea transport, other	2 209	....	....	....	....	3.0	4.3	4.2	4.3
Air transport, passenger	2 211	....	....	....	....	135.7	159.0	105.0	136.6
Air transport, freight	2 212	....	....	....	....	5.6	3.8	3.2	4.6
Air transport, other	2 213	....	....	....	....	25.0	52.4	47.9	47.6
Other transport, passenger	2 215	....	....	....	....	16.5	17.3	15.4	15.7
Other transport, freight	2 216	....	....	....	....	406.3	554.4	406.6	418.2
Other transport, other	2 217	....	....	....	....	123.7	160.7	136.3	135.5
Transportation services, debit	3 205	....	....	....	....	−992.3	−1,277.2	−924.3	−993.3
Passenger	3 850	....	....	....	....	*−160.5*	*−199.4*	*−145.6*	*−151.3*
Freight	3 851	....	....	....	....	*−480.1*	*−611.0*	*−463.4*	*−482.7*
Other	3 852	....	....	....	....	*−351.7*	*−466.8*	*−315.3*	*−359.3*
Sea transport, passenger	3 207	....	....	....	....	−.3	−.3	−.2	−.2
Sea transport, freight	3 208	....	....	....	....	−58.6	−80.8	−64.7	−56.9
Sea transport, other	3 209	....	....	....	....	−12.8	−14.9	−12.6	−17.1
Air transport, passenger	3 211	....	....	....	....	−153.5	−189.7	−137.8	−143.9
Air transport, freight	3 212	....	....	....	....	−8.9	−10.1	−9.8	−9.2
Air transport, other	3 213	....	....	....	....	−25.7	−56.1	−28.7	−52.3
Other transport, passenger	3 215	....	....	....	....	−6.7	−9.5	−7.6	−7.2
Other transport, freight	3 216	....	....	....	....	−412.7	−520.1	−388.9	−416.6
Other transport, other	3 217	....	....	....	....	−313.2	−395.9	−273.9	−289.9
Travel, credit	2 236	....	....	....	....	864.4	956.5	869.4	799.5
Business travel	2 237	....	....	....	....	4.8	9.2	9.1	8.2
Personal travel	2 240	....	....	....	....	859.6	947.3	860.3	791.3
Travel, debit	3 236	....	....	....	....	−1,041.2	−1,268.6	−961.2	−954.7
Business travel	3 237	....	....	....	....	−136.7	−228.4	−187.1	−195.7
Personal travel	3 240	....	....	....	....	−904.5	−1,040.1	−774.2	−759.0
Other services, credit	2 200 BA	....	....	....	....	1,563.2	2,106.5	1,887.4	1,952.0
Communications	2 245	....	....	....	....	108.9	129.0	140.0	157.1
Construction	2 249	....	....	....	....	198.9	362.8	227.0	230.5
Insurance	2 253	....	....	....	....	28.2	28.6	23.9	24.6
Financial	2 260	....	....	....	....	27.3	44.5	24.7	36.6
Computer and information	2 262	....	....	....	....	84.7	141.7	140.3	168.5
Royalties and licence fees	2 266	....	....	....	....	10.5	29.0	61.6	39.1
Other business services	2 268	....	....	....	....	959.4	1,180.6	1,086.3	1,107.6
Personal, cultural, and recreational	2 287	....	....	....	....	116.8	162.3	170.9	180.1
Government, n.i.e.	2 291	....	....	....	....	28.6	28.0	12.6	7.8
Other services, debit	3 200 BA	....	....	....	....	−1,472.0	−1,750.4	−1,570.5	−1,577.9
Communications	3 245	....	....	....	....	−85.1	−116.7	−114.2	−112.0
Construction	3 249	....	....	....	....	−117.0	−127.7	−121.1	−172.9
Insurance	3 253	....	....	....	....	−41.7	−49.7	−49.6	−49.0
Financial	3 260	....	....	....	....	−40.6	−68.1	−95.0	−46.8
Computer and information	3 262	....	....	....	....	−160.9	−206.5	−182.5	−179.5
Royalties and licence fees	3 266	....	....	....	....	−143.6	−196.4	−143.3	−156.0
Other business services	3 268	....	....	....	....	−750.8	−837.6	−733.0	−729.2
Personal, cultural, and recreational	3 287	....	....	....	....	−71.8	−90.0	−83.7	−84.0
Government, n.i.e.	3 291	....	....	....	....	−60.5	−57.5	−48.1	−48.5

Table 2 (Continued). STANDARD PRESENTATION, 2003–2010

(Millions of U.S. dollars)

	Code	2003	2004	2005	2006	2007	2008	2009	2010
C. INCOME	4 300	....	....	....	....	**–818.8**	**–1,349.3**	**–706.2**	**–898.8**
Total credit	2 300	....	....	....	....	*707.1*	*826.4*	*695.2*	*581.3*
Total debit	3 300	....	....	....	....	*–1,526.0*	*–2,175.7*	*–1,401.4*	*–1,480.1*
Compensation of employees, credit	2 310	....	....	....	....	**146.3**	**191.4**	**184.6**	**163.9**
Compensation of employees, debit	3 310	....	....	....	....	**–16.0**	**–24.5**	**–19.6**	**–18.1**
Investment income, credit	2 320	....	....	....	....	**560.9**	**635.0**	**510.6**	**417.4**
Direct investment income	2 330	....	....	....	....	76.5	69.4	166.3	136.6
Dividends and distributed branch profits	2 332	....	....	....	....	54.0	59.4	166.3	136.6
Reinvested earnings and undistributed branch profits	2 333	....	....	....	....	22.5	10.1	....	....
Income on debt (interest)	2 334	....	....	....	....	....	....	....	....
Portfolio investment income	2 339	....	....	....	....	243.9	370.7	305.1	240.4
Income on equity	2 340	....	....	....	....	....	....	....	....
Income on bonds and notes	2 350	....	....	....	....	243.6	370.4	304.9	240.3
Income on money market instruments	2 360	....	....	....	....	.4	.3	.2	....
Other investment income	2 370	....	....	....	....	240.4	194.9	39.2	40.4
Investment income, debit	3 320	....	....	....	....	**–1,510.0**	**–2,151.2**	**–1,381.8**	**–1,462.0**
Direct investment income	3 330	....	....	....	....	–596.1	–890.5	–450.9	–551.8
Dividends and distributed branch profits	3 332	....	....	....	....	–261.0	–650.5	–450.9	–551.8
Reinvested earnings and undistributed branch profits	3 333	....	....	....	....	–335.1	–240.0	....	....
Income on debt (interest)	3 334	....	....	....	....	....	....	....	....
Portfolio investment income	3 339	....	....	....	....	–1.1	–.1	–.1	–.9
Income on equity	3 340	....	....	....	....	....	....	....	....
Income on bonds and notes	3 350	....	....	....	....	....	....	....	–.8
Income on money market instruments	3 360	....	....	....	....	–1.1	–.1	–.1	–.1
Other investment income	3 370	....	....	....	....	–912.8	–1,260.6	–930.7	–909.4
D. CURRENT TRANSFERS	4 379	....	....	....	....	**3,932.4**	**3,740.2**	**4,937.3**	**4,417.3**
Credit	2 379	....	....	....	....	**4,244.5**	**4,146.6**	**5,281.8**	**4,770.7**
General government	2 380	....	....	....	....	361.3	414.4	341.9	313.1
Other sectors	2 390	....	....	....	....	3,883.2	3,732.2	4,940.0	4,457.6
Workers' remittances	2 391	....	....	....	....	2,916.1	2,516.6	3,748.7	3,185.0
Other current transfers	2 392	....	....	....	....	967.1	1,215.6	1,191.3	1,272.6
Debit	3 379	....	....	....	....	**–312.1**	**–406.4**	**–344.5**	**–353.4**
General government	3 380	....	....	....	....	–125.4	–151.4	–150.1	–149.5
Other sectors	3 390	....	....	....	....	–186.7	–255.1	–194.4	–203.9
Workers' remittances	3 391	....	....	....	....	–93.6	–114.3	–70.0	–51.8
Other current transfers	3 392	....	....	....	....	–93.1	–140.8	–124.4	–152.2
CAPITAL AND FINANCIAL ACCOUNT	4 996	....	....	....	....	**6,472.6**	**10,606.0**	**2,897.1**	**2,736.4**
CAPITAL ACCOUNT	4 994	....	....	....	....	**–426.2**	**20.2**	**2.6**	**1.3**
Total credit	2 994	....	....	....	....	*20.4*	*24.8*	*7.8*	*4.0*
Total debit	3 994	....	....	....	....	*–446.5*	*–4.6*	*–5.2*	*–2.7*
Capital transfers, credit	2 400	....	....	....	....	**2.2**	**16.9**	**3.1**	**2.0**
General government	2 401	....	....	....	....	.2	14.5	....	....
Debt forgiveness	2 402	....	....	....	....	....	....	....	....
Other capital transfers	2 410	....	....	....	....	.2	14.5	....	....
Other sectors	2 430	....	....	....	....	2.0	2.4	3.1	2.0
Migrants' transfers	2 431	....	....	....	....	1.9	2.1	3.1	2.0
Debt forgiveness	2 432	....	....	....	....	....	....	....	....
Other capital transfers	2 440	....	....	....	....	.1	.2	....	....
Capital transfers, debit	3 400	....	....	....	....	**–2.0**	**–1.2**	**–1.1**	**–.2**
General government	3 401	....	....	....	....	....	....	....	....
Debt forgiveness	3 402	....	....	....	....	....	....	....	....
Other capital transfers	3 410	....	....	....	....	....	....	....	....
Other sectors	3 430	....	....	....	....	–2.0	–1.2	–1.1	–.2
Migrants' transfers	3 431	....	....	....	....	–2.0	–1.2	–1.1	–.2
Debt forgiveness	3 432	....	....	....	....	....	....	....	....
Other capital transfers	3 440	....	....	....	....	....	....	....	....
Nonproduced nonfinancial assets, credit	2 480	....	....	....	....	**18.1**	**8.0**	**4.7**	**2.0**
Nonproduced nonfinancial assets, debit	3 480	....	....	....	....	**–444.6**	**–3.4**	**–4.1**	**–2.5**

Table 2 (Continued). STANDARD PRESENTATION, 2003–2010

(Millions of U.S. dollars)

	Code	2003	2004	2005	2006	2007	2008	2009	2010
FINANCIAL ACCOUNT................................	4 995 ..	....	....	....	....	**6,898.8**	**10,585.8**	**2,894.4**	**2,735.2**
A. DIRECT INVESTMENT................................	4 500 ..	....	....	....	....	**2,474.3**	**2,714.5**	**1,880.8**	**1,151.9**
Direct investment abroad................................	4 505 ..	....	....	....	....	**−957.6**	**−281.9**	**−54.8**	**−188.4**
Equity capital................................	4 510 ..	....	....	....	....	−1,123.3	−326.0	−72.2	−209.3
Claims on affiliated enterprises................	4 515 ..	....	....	....	....	−1,123.3	−326.0	−72.2	−209.3
Liabilities to affiliated enterprises............	4 520 ..	....	....	....	....	....	....	....	....
Reinvested earnings................................	4 525 ..	....	....	....	....	−22.5	−10.1	....	....
Other capital................................	4 530 ..	....	....	....	....	188.1	54.2	17.3	21.0
Claims on affiliated enterprises................	4 535 ..	....	....	....	....	188.1	54.2	17.3	21.0
Liabilities to affiliated enterprises............	4 540 ..	....	....	....	....	....	....	....	....
Direct investment in the Republic of Serbia......	4 555 ..	....	....	....	....	**3,431.9**	**2,996.4**	**1,935.6**	**1,340.2**
Equity capital................................	4 560 ..	....	....	....	....	2,006.1	1,971.3	1,396.8	815.0
Claims on direct investors................	4 565 ..	....	....	....	....	....	....	....	....
Liabilities to direct investors................	4 570 ..	....	....	....	....	2,006.1	1,971.3	1,396.8	815.0
Reinvested earnings................................	4 575 ..	....	....	....	....	335.1	240.0	....	....
Other capital................................	4 580 ..	....	....	....	....	1,090.7	785.1	538.8	525.2
Claims on direct investors................	4 585 ..	....	....	....	....	....	....	....	....
Liabilities to direct investors................	4 590 ..	....	....	....	....	1,090.7	785.1	538.8	525.2
B. PORTFOLIO INVESTMENT................................	4 600 ..	....	....	....	....	**927.6**	**−136.5**	**−65.7**	**88.4**
Assets................................	4 602 ..	....	....	....	....	**−4.7**	**−40.7**	**−9.6**	**−41.7**
Equity securities................................	4 610 ..	....	....	....	....	−13.2	−41.0	−10.0	18.1
Monetary authorities................................	4 611 ..	....	....	....	....	....	....	....	....
General government................................	4 612 ..	....	....	....	....	....	....	....	....
Banks................................	4 613 ..	....	....	....	....	....	....	....	....
Other sectors................................	4 614 ..	....	....	....	....	−13.2	−41.0	−10.0	18.1
Debt securities................................	4 619 ..	....	....	....	....	8.5	.2	.4	−59.8
Bonds and notes................................	4 620 ..	....	....	....	....	8.5	.2	.4	−59.8
Monetary authorities................................	4 621 ..	....	....	....	....	....	....	....	....
General government................................	4 622 ..	....	....	....	....	−.4	....	....	....
Banks................................	4 623 ..	....	....	....	....	....	....	....	....
Other sectors................................	4 624 ..	....	....	....	....	8.9	.2	.4	−59.8
Money market instruments................	4 630 ..	....	....	....	....	....	....	....	....
Monetary authorities................................	4 631 ..	....	....	....	....	....	....	....	....
General government................................	4 632 ..	....	....	....	....	....	....	....	....
Banks................................	4 633 ..	....	....	....	....	....	....	....	....
Other sectors................................	4 634 ..	....	....	....	....	....	....	....	....
Liabilities................................	4 652 ..	....	....	....	....	**932.3**	**−95.7**	**−56.1**	**130.1**
Equity securities................................	4 660 ..	....	....	....	....	771.9	−56.9	22.5	84.2
Banks................................	4 663 ..	....	....	....	....	771.9	−73.3	2.3	....
Other sectors................................	4 664 ..	....	....	....	....	....	16.4	20.1	84.2
Debt securities................................	4 669 ..	....	....	....	....	160.4	−38.9	−78.6	45.9
Bonds and notes................................	4 670 ..	....	....	....	....	160.4	−38.9	−78.6	45.9
Monetary authorities................................	4 671 ..	....	....	....	....	....	....	....	....
General government................................	4 672 ..	....	....	....	....	−13.4	−47.5	−90.3	−1.0
Banks................................	4 673 ..	....	....	....	....	121.6	....	....	....
Other sectors................................	4 674 ..	....	....	....	....	52.3	8.7	11.7	46.8
Money market instruments................	4 680 ..	....	....	....	....	....	....	....	....
Monetary authorities................................	4 681 ..	....	....	....	....	....	....	....	....
General government................................	4 682 ..	....	....	....	....	....	....	....	....
Banks................................	4 683 ..	....	....	....	....	....	....	....	....
Other sectors................................	4 684 ..	....	....	....	....	....	....	....	....
C. FINANCIAL DERIVATIVES................................	4 910 ..	....	....	....	....	**1.5**	**−.1**	**−2.5**	**−30.1**
Monetary authorities................................	4 911 ..	....	....	....	....	....	....	....	....
General government................................	4 912 ..	....	....	....	....	....	....	....	....
Banks................................	4 913 ..	....	....	....	....	1.5	....	−.5	−21.4
Other sectors................................	4 914 ..	....	....	....	....	....	−.1	−1.9	−8.7
Assets................................	4 900 ..	....	....	....	....	....	**−.3**	**2.7**	**7.5**
Monetary authorities................................	4 901 ..	....	....	....	....	....	....	....	....
General government................................	4 902 ..	....	....	....	....	....	....	....	....
Banks................................	4 903 ..	....	....	....	....	....	....	2.7	7.2
Other sectors................................	4 904 ..	....	....	....	....	....	−.3	....	.2
Liabilities................................	4 905 ..	....	....	....	....	**1.5**	**.2**	**−5.2**	**−37.6**
Monetary authorities................................	4 906 ..	....	....	....	....	....	....	....	....
General government................................	4 907 ..	....	....	....	....	....	....	....	....
Banks................................	4 908 ..	....	....	....	....	1.5	....	−3.2	−28.7
Other sectors................................	4 909 ..	....	....	....	....	....	.1	−1.9	−8.9

Table 2 (Concluded). STANDARD PRESENTATION, 2003–2010

(Millions of U.S. dollars)

	Code	2003	2004	2005	2006	2007	2008	2009	2010
D. OTHER INVESTMENT..................................	4 700 ..	....	....	....	....	**4,502.4**	**5,609.5**	**4,491.4**	**291.1**
Assets...	4 703 ..	....	....	....	....	−2,220.8	−2,055.8	94.8	−1,077.6
Trade credits..	4 706 ..	....	....	....	....	−1,179.1	−977.2	−549.5	−474.2
General government..........................	4 707 ..	....	....	....	....	....	....	....	....
of which: Short-term................	4 709 ..	....	....	....	....	....	....	....	....
Other sectors.....................................	4 710 ..	....	....	....	....	−1,179.1	−977.2	−549.5	−474.2
of which: Short-term................	4 712 ..	....	....	....	....	*−1,179.1*	*−977.2*	*−549.5*	*−474.2*
Loans..	4 714 ..	....	....	....	....	1.3	−61.5	36.9	−42.1
Monetary authorities........................	4 715 ..	....	....	....	....	....	....	....	....
of which: Short-term................	4 718 ..	....	....	....	....	....	....	....	....
General government..........................	4 719 ..	....	....	....	....	....	....	....	....
of which: Short-term................	4 721 ..	....	....	....	....	....	....	....	....
Banks..	4 722 ..	....	....	....	....	.7	−61.5	36.9	−42.1
of which: Short-term................	4 724 ..	....	....	....	....	*5.6*	*−25.3*	*9.2*	*−2.0*
Other sectors.....................................	4 725 ..	....	....	....	....	.6	....	....	....
of which: Short-term................	4 727 ..	....	....	....	....	....	....	....	....
Currency and deposits..........................	4 730 ..	....	....	....	....	−976.0	−969.1	607.4	−561.3
Monetary authorities........................	4 731 ..	....	....	....	....	....	....	....	....
General government..........................	4 732 ..	....	....	....	....	....	....	....	....
Banks..	4 733 ..	....	....	....	....	−976.0	364.7	−496.2	−561.3
Other sectors.....................................	4 734 ..	....	....	....	....	....	−1,333.8	1,103.5	....
Other assets..	4 736 ..	....	....	....	....	−67.0	−47.9	....	....
Monetary authorities........................	4 737 ..	....	....	....	....	....	....	....	....
of which: Short-term................	4 739 ..	....	....	....	....	....	....	....	....
General government..........................	4 740 ..	....	....	....	....	−67.0	−47.9	....	....
of which: Short-term................	4 742 ..	....	....	....	....	....	....	....	....
Banks..	4 743 ..	....	....	....	....	....	....	....	....
of which: Short-term................	4 745 ..	....	....	....	....	....	....	....	....
Other sectors.....................................	4 746 ..	....	....	....	....	....	....	....	....
of which: Short-term................	4 748 ..	....	....	....	....	....	....	....	....
Liabilities......................................	4 753 ..	....	....	....	....	**6,723.2**	**7,665.3**	**4,396.7**	**1,368.7**
Trade credits..	4 756 ..	....	....	....	....	2,216.9	2,374.2	1,462.9	714.5
General government..........................	4 757 ..	....	....	....	....	....	....	....	....
of which: Short-term................	4 759 ..	....	....	....	....	....	....	....	....
Other sectors.....................................	4 760 ..	....	....	....	....	2,216.9	2,374.2	1,462.9	714.5
of which: Short-term................	4 762 ..	....	....	....	....	*2,216.9*	*2,374.2*	*1,462.9*	*714.5*
Loans..	4 764 ..	....	....	....	....	4,476.2	5,117.9	1,902.3	1,170.9
Monetary authorities........................	4 765 ..	....	....	....	....	−282.5	....	1,546.8	454.0
of which: Use of Fund credit and loans from the Fund..	4 766 ..	....	....	....	....	*−244.9*	....	*1,572.5*	*454.0*
of which: Short-term................	4 768 ..	....	....	....	....	....	....	*−25.7*	....
General government..........................	4 769 ..	....	....	....	....	166.1	131.4	356.1	949.2
of which: Short-term................	4 771 ..	....	....	....	....	....	*−25.1*	*2.1*	*−2.1*
Banks..	4 772 ..	....	....	....	....	196.9	133.5	1,251.5	901.1
of which: Short-term................	4 774 ..	....	....	....	....	*371.6*	*559.8*	*605.8*	*26.4*
Other sectors.....................................	4 775 ..	....	....	....	....	4,395.7	4,853.0	−1,252.0	−1,133.4
of which: Short-term................	4 777 ..	....	....	....	....	*12.6*	*811.4*	*−299.5*	*−101.3*
Currency and deposits..........................	4 780 ..	....	....	....	....	105.3	171.2	424.7	−516.6
Monetary authorities........................	4 781 ..	....	....	....	....	....	−7.1	....	....
General government..........................	4 782 ..	....	....	....	....	....	....	....	....
Banks..	4 783 ..	....	....	....	....	105.3	178.3	424.7	−516.6
Other sectors.....................................	4 784 ..	....	....	....	....	....	....	....	....
Other liabilities.....................................	4 786 ..	....	....	....	....	−75.1	1.9	606.7	....
Monetary authorities........................	4 787 ..	....	....	....	....	−79.6	....	606.7	....
of which: Short-term................	4 789 ..	....	....	....	....	....	....	....	....
General government..........................	4 790 ..	....	....	....	....	....	....	....	....
of which: Short-term................	4 792 ..	....	....	....	....	....	....	....	....
Banks..	4 793 ..	....	....	....	....	....	....	....	....
of which: Short-term................	4 795 ..	....	....	....	....	....	....	....	....
Other sectors.....................................	4 796 ..	....	....	....	....	4.5	1.9	....	....
of which: Short-term................	4 798 ..	....	....	....	....	....	....	....	....
E. RESERVE ASSETS..............................	4 802 ..	....	....	....	....	**−1,007.0**	**2,398.3**	**−3,409.6**	**1,233.9**
Monetary gold......................................	4 812 ..	....	....	....	....	21.5	15.5	7.6	−31.3
Special drawing rights.........................	4 811 ..	....	....	....	....	8.0	−1.4	−9.5	15.8
Reserve position in the Fund...............	4 810 ..	....	....	....	....	....	....	....	....
Foreign exchange.................................	4 803 ..	....	....	....	....	−1,036.5	2,384.3	−3,407.6	1,249.4
Other claims...	4 813 ..	....	....	....	....	....	....	....	....
NET ERRORS AND OMISSIONS...............	4 998 ..	....	....	....	....	**417.2**	**−211.2**	**−30.5**	**82.9**

Table 3. INTERNATIONAL INVESTMENT POSITION (End-period stocks), 2003–2010

(Millions of U.S. dollars)

	Code	2003	2004	2005	2006	2007	2008	2009	2010
ASSETS	8 995 C.	....	....	....	....	....	**19,246.0**	**23,005.4**	**21,221.3**
Direct investment abroad	8 505 ..	....	....	....	....	....	**3,866.1**	**3,962.1**	**3,948.2**
Equity capital and reinvested earnings	8 506 ..	....	....	....	....	....	3,814.3	3,927.5	3,936.2
Claims on affiliated enterprises	8 507 ..	....	....	....	....	....	3,814.3	3,927.5	3,936.2
Liabilities to affiliated enterprises	8 508 ..	....	....	....	....	....	....	....	....
Other capital	8 530 ..	....	....	....	....	....	51.8	34.6	12.0
Claims on affiliated enterprises	8 535 ..	....	....	....	....	....	51.8	34.6	12.0
Liabilities to affiliated enterprises	8 540 ..	....	....	....	....	....	....	....	....
Portfolio investment	8 602 ..	....	....	....	....	....	**51.9**	**62.9**	**101.2**
Equity securities	8 610 ..	....	....	....	....	....	51.9	62.9	42.4
Monetary authorities	8 611 ..	....	....	....	....	....	....	....	....
General government	8 612 ..	....	....	....	....	....	....	....	....
Banks	8 613 ..	....	....	....	....	....	....	....	....
Other sectors	8 614 ..	....	....	....	....	....	51.9	62.9	42.4
Debt securities	8 619 ..	....	....	....	....	....	....	....	58.8
Bonds and notes	8 620 ..	....	....	....	....	....	....	....	58.8
Monetary authorities	8 621 ..	....	....	....	....	....	....	....	....
General government	8 622 ..	....	....	....	....	....	....	....	....
Banks	8 623 ..	....	....	....	....	....	....	....	....
Other sectors	8 624 ..	....	....	....	....	....	....	....	58.8
Money market instruments	8 630 ..	....	....	....	....	....	....	....	....
Monetary authorities	8 631 ..	....	....	....	....	....	....	....	....
General government	8 632 ..	....	....	....	....	....	....	....	....
Banks	8 633 ..	....	....	....	....	....	....	....	....
Other sectors	8 634 ..	....	....	....	....	....	....	....	....
Financial derivatives	8 900 ..	....	....	....	....	....	....	....	....
Monetary authorities	8 901 ..	....	....	....	....	....	....	....	....
General government	8 902 ..	....	....	....	....	....	....	....	....
Banks	8 903 ..	....	....	....	....	....	....	....	....
Other sectors	8 904 ..	....	....	....	....	....	....	....	....
Other investment	8 703 ..	....	....	....	....	....	**3,833.2**	**3,745.5**	**3,862.6**
Trade credits	8 706 ..	....	....	....	....	....	206.3	234.9	63.8
General government	8 707 ..	....	....	....	....	....	....	....	....
of which: Short-term	8 709 ..	....	....	....	....	....	....	....	....
Other sectors	8 710 ..	....	....	....	....	....	206.3	234.9	63.8
of which: Short-term	8 712 ..	....	....	....	....	....	*206.3*	*234.9*	*63.8*
Loans	8 714 ..	....	....	....	....	....	193.5	253.1	222.6
Monetary authorities	8 715 ..	....	....	....	....	....	....	....	....
of which: Short-term	8 718 ..	....	....	....	....	....	....	....	....
General government	8 719 ..	....	....	....	....	....	....	....	....
of which: Short-term	8 721 ..	....	....	....	....	....	....	....	....
Banks	8 722 ..	....	....	....	....	....	138.9	197.2	182.0
of which: Short-term	8 724 ..	....	....	....	....	....	*26.9*	*12.9*	*56.4*
Other sectors	8 725 ..	....	....	....	....	....	54.6	55.9	40.5
of which: Short-term	8 727 ..	....	....	....	....	....	*.8*	*.8*	*2.2*
Currency and deposits	8 730 ..	....	....	....	....	....	3,433.4	3,257.4	3,576.2
Monetary authorities	8 731 ..	....	....	....	....	....	....	....	....
General government	8 732 ..	....	....	....	....	....	....	....	....
Banks	8 733 ..	....	....	....	....	....	1,498.2	2,109.4	2,498.3
Other sectors	8 734 ..	....	....	....	....	....	1,935.3	1,148.0	1,077.9
Other assets	8 736 ..	....	....	....	....	....	....	....	....
Monetary authorities	8 737 ..	....	....	....	....	....	....	....	....
of which: Short-term	8 739 ..	....	....	....	....	....	....	....	....
General government	8 740 ..	....	....	....	....	....	....	....	....
of which: Short-term	8 742 ..	....	....	....	....	....	....	....	....
Banks	8 743 ..	....	....	....	....	....	....	....	....
of which: Short-term	8 745 ..	....	....	....	....	....	....	....	....
Other sectors	8 746 ..	....	....	....	....	....	....	....	....
of which: Short-term	8 748 ..	....	....	....	....	....	....	....	....
Reserve assets	8 802 ..	....	....	....	....	....	**11,494.8**	**15,234.9**	**13,309.3**
Monetary gold	8 812 ..	....	....	....	....	....	354.5	465.7	594.9
Special drawing rights	8 811 ..	.4	.1	30.2	8.8	.8	2.2	19.3	3.0
Reserve position in the Fund	8 810 ..	....	....	....	....	....	....	....	....
Foreign exchange	8 803 ..	....	....	....	....	....	11,138.2	14,749.9	12,711.4
Other claims	8 813 ..	....	....	....	....	....	....	....	....

Table 3 (Concluded). INTERNATIONAL INVESTMENT POSITION (End-period stocks), 2003–2010

(Millions of U.S. dollars)

	Code	2003	2004	2005	2006	2007	2008	2009	2010
LIABILITIES	8 995 D.	....	....	....	....	....	**51,030.5**	**55,935.3**	**54,341.0**
Direct investment in the Republic of Serbia	8 555 ..	....	....	....	....	....	**18,964.4**	**21,047.1**	**20,999.0**
Equity capital and reinvested earnings	8 556 ..	....	....	....	....	....	16,082.7	17,621.8	17,276.1
Claims on direct investors	8 557 ..	....	....	....	....	....	....	....	....
Liabilities to direct investors	8 558 ..	....	....	....	....	....	16,082.7	17,621.8	17,276.1
Other capital	8 580 ..	....	....	....	....	....	2,881.6	3,425.4	3,722.9
Claims on direct investors	8 585 ..	....	....	....	....	....	....	....	....
Liabilities to direct investors	8 590 ..	....	....	....	....	....	2,881.6	3,425.4	3,722.9
Portfolio investment	8 652 ..	....	....	....	....	....	**1,885.1**	**1,839.2**	**1,845.3**
Equity securities	8 660 ..	....	....	....	....	....	665.3	700.1	735.9
Banks	8 663 ..	....	....	....	....	....	....	....	....
Other sectors	8 664 ..	....	....	....	....	....	....	....	....
Debt securities	8 669 ..	....	....	....	....	....	1,219.9	1,139.0	1,109.4
Bonds and notes	8 670 ..	....	....	....	....	....	1,219.9	1,139.0	1,109.4
Monetary authorities	8 671 ..	....	....	....	....	....	....	....	....
General government	8 672 ..	....	....	....	....	....	1,075.6	1,075.6	1,003.9
Banks	8 673 ..	....	....	....	....	....	....	....	....
Other sectors	8 674 ..	....	....	....	....	....	144.2	63.4	105.5
Money market instruments	8 680 ..	....	....	....	....	....	....	....	....
Monetary authorities	8 681 ..	....	....	....	....	....	....	....	....
General government	8 682 ..	....	....	....	....	....	....	....	....
Banks	8 683 ..	....	....	....	....	....	....	....	....
Other sectors	8 684 ..	....	....	....	....	....	....	....	....
Financial derivatives	8 905 ..	....	....	....	....	....	....	....	....
Monetary authorities	8 906 ..	....	....	....	....	....	....	....	....
General government	8 907 ..	....	....	....	....	....	....	....	....
Banks	8 908 ..	....	....	....	....	....	....	....	....
Other sectors	8 909 ..	....	....	....	....	....	....	....	....
Other investment	8 753 ..	....	....	....	....	....	**30,181.0**	**33,049.0**	**31,496.7**
Trade credits	8 756 ..	....	....	....	....	....	933.8	616.6	146.7
General government	8 757 ..	....	....	....	....	....	....	....	....
of which: Short-term	8 759 ..	....	....	....	....	....	....	....	....
Other sectors	8 760 ..	....	....	....	....	....	933.8	616.6	146.7
of which: Short-term	8 762 ..	....	....	....	....	....	*933.8*	*616.6*	*146.7*
Loans	8 764 ..	....	....	....	....	....	28,526.6	30,551.9	30,050.6
Monetary authorities	8 765 ..	....	....	....	....	....	191.5	1,704.7	2,133.6
of which: Use of Fund credit and loans from the Fund	8 766 ..	*916.7*	*964.4*	*866.5*	*244.5*	....	....	*1,600.8*	*2,034.4*
of which: Short-term	8 768 ..	....	....	....	....	....	*25.0*	....	....
General government	8 769 ..	....	....	....	....	....	7,838.8	7,689.5	8,342.4
of which: Short-term	8 771 ..	....	....	....	....	....	....	*2.1*	....
Banks	8 772 ..	....	....	....	....	....	4,940.4	6,193.4	6,776.8
of which: Short-term	8 774 ..	....	....	....	....	....	*1,839.6*	*2,461.7*	*2,303.0*
Other sectors	8 775 ..	....	....	....	....	....	15,555.8	14,964.4	12,797.8
of which: Short-term	8 777 ..	....	....	....	....	....	*1,130.6*	*417.0*	*132.7*
Currency and deposits	8 780 ..	....	....	....	....	....	720.7	1,182.8	614.0
Monetary authorities	8 781 ..	....	....	....	....	....	....	....	....
General government	8 782 ..	....	....	....	....	....	....	....	....
Banks	8 783 ..	....	....	....	....	....	720.7	1,182.8	614.0
Other sectors	8 784 ..	....	....	....	....	....	....	....	....
Other liabilities	8 786 ..	....	....	....	....	....	....	697.7	685.4
Monetary authorities	8 787 ..	....	....	....	....	....	....	697.7	685.4
of which: Short-term	8 789 ..	....	....	....	....	....	....	....	....
General government	8 790 ..	....	....	....	....	....	....	....	....
of which: Short-term	8 792 ..	....	....	....	....	....	....	....	....
Banks	8 793 ..	....	....	....	....	....	....	....	....
of which: Short-term	8 795 ..	....	....	....	....	....	....	....	....
Other sectors	8 796 ..	....	....	....	....	....	....	....	....
of which: Short-term	8 798 ..	....	....	....	....	....	....	....	....
NET INTERNATIONAL INVESTMENT POSITION	8 995 ..	....	....	....	....	....	**–31,784.5**	**–32,930.0**	**–33,119.8**
Conversion rates: dinars per U.S. dollar (end of period)	0 102 ..	54.6372	57.9355	72.2189	59.9757	53.7267	62.9000	66.7285	79.2802

Table 1. ANALYTIC PRESENTATION, 2003–2010

(Millions of U.S. dollars)

	Code	2003	2004	2005	2006	2007	2008	2009	2010
A. Current Account[1]	4 993 Z.	**−12.39**	**−63.73**	**−188.16**	**−145.19**	**−168.55**	**−201.26**	**−90.72**	**−225.05**
Goods: exports f.o.b.	2 100 ..	286.42	301.10	350.91	420.08	397.32	436.09	431.98	400.23
Goods: imports f.o.b.	3 100 ..	−375.56	−456.27	−650.21	−710.36	−679.37	−838.95	−733.08	−736.78
Balance on Goods	4 100 ..	*−89.14*	*−155.17*	*−299.31*	*−290.28*	*−282.05*	*−402.86*	*−301.10*	*−336.54*
Services: credit	2 200 ..	330.40	326.60	368.76	430.28	628.01	608.03	600.46	591.80
Services: debit	3 200 ..	−220.23	−215.83	−234.68	−274.15	−465.14	−371.11	−391.55	−441.11
Balance on Goods and Services	4 991 ..	*21.03*	*−44.40*	*−165.22*	*−134.14*	*−119.19*	*−165.94*	*−92.19*	*−185.85*
Income: credit	2 300 ..	11.98	9.44	9.81	10.27	3.57	4.87	3.46	7.56
Income: debit	3 300 ..	−55.18	−43.13	−49.88	−53.89	−67.53	−72.50	−49.93	−72.15
Balance on Goods, Services, and Income	4 992 ..	*−22.16*	*−78.09*	*−205.29*	*−177.77*	*−183.15*	*−233.57*	*−138.66*	*−250.44*
Current transfers: credit	2 379 Z.	12.58	17.26	21.44	42.68	18.70	37.64	60.56	42.95
Current transfers: debit	3 379 ..	−2.82	−2.90	−4.31	−10.10	−4.10	−5.33	−12.62	−17.56
B. Capital Account[1]	4 994 Z.	**7.42**	**.99**	**29.88**	**13.24**	**8.17**	**5.03**	**52.50**	**275.29**
Capital account: credit	2 994 Z.	7.42	.99	29.88	13.24	8.17	5.03	52.50	275.29
Capital account: debit	3 994 ..	....	....	....	....	....	....	....	....
Total, Groups A Plus B	4 981 ..	*−4.97*	*−62.74*	*−158.28*	*−131.95*	*−160.38*	*−196.23*	*−38.23*	*50.24*
C. Financial Account[1]	4 995 W.	**−30.91**	**−30.47**	**129.43**	**223.50**	**204.22**	**−134.03**	**104.53**	**239.09**
Direct investment abroad	4 505 ..	−8.15	−7.60	−7.45	−8.01	−17.82	−12.94	−5.34	−6.15
Direct investment in Seychelles	4 555 Z.	58.43	38.01	85.88	145.82	126.40	129.45	118.48	167.31
Portfolio investment assets	4 602 ..	−.01	−.04	−.04	−.05	−14.38	−.16	−5.68	27.16
Equity securities	4 610 ..	....	....	....	....	....	....	−6.00	....
Debt securities	4 619 ..	−.01	−.04	−.04	−.05	−14.38	−.16	.32	27.16
Portfolio investment liabilities	4 652 Z.	1.14	1.11	1.06	198.21	132.56	−309.99	....	−2.53
Equity securities	4 660 ..	....	....	....	....	....	....	....	....
Debt securities	4 669 Z.	1.14	1.11	1.06	198.21	132.56	−309.99	....	−2.53
Financial derivatives	4 910 ..	....	....	....	....	....	....	....	....
Financial derivatives assets	4 900 ..	....	....	....	....	....	....	....	....
Financial derivatives liabilities	4 905 ..	....	....	....	....	....	....	....	....
Other investment assets	4 703 ..	−14.81	−12.25	−9.61	−8.75	−53.83	−10.53	5.44	8.53
Monetary authorities	4 701 ..	....	....	....	....	....	....	....	....
General government	4 704 ..	....	....	....	....	−.34	−.38	−.06	−.12
Banks	4 705 ..	....	....	−3.49	−13.27	−42.04	−7.71	15.19	−8.06
Other sectors	4 728 ..	−14.81	−12.25	−6.12	4.53	−11.46	−2.44	−9.69	16.72
Other investment liabilities	4 753 W.	−67.51	−49.71	59.60	−103.72	31.29	70.14	−8.37	44.77
Monetary authorities	4 753 WA	−35.51	−33.79	10.82	−75.26	....	....	12.31	....
General government	4 753 ZB	−26.13	−24.50	35.66	−45.60	−12.91	12.82	−64.98	−5.07
Banks	4 753 ZC	−3.61	8.11	13.57	12.33	1.26	14.25	1.21	−7.20
Other sectors	4 753 ZD	−2.26	.46	−.45	4.81	42.94	43.07	43.08	57.04
Total, Groups A Through C	4 983 ..	*−35.89*	*−93.21*	*−28.85*	*91.55*	*43.84*	*−330.25*	*66.31*	*289.33*
D. Net Errors and Omissions	4 998 ..	**−4.68**	**.68**	**−.52**	**2.19**	**17.30**	**21.04**	**23.08**	**13.21**
Total, Groups A Through D	4 984 ..	*−40.56*	*−92.53*	*−29.37*	*93.74*	*61.14*	*−309.22*	*89.39*	*302.54*
E. Reserves and Related Items	4 802 A.	**40.56**	**92.53**	**29.37**	**−93.74**	**−61.14**	**309.22**	**−89.39**	**−302.54**
Reserve assets	4 802 ..	−3.12	32.97	−21.97	−61.97	45.03	−46.94	−124.97	−81.16
Use of Fund credit and loans	4 766 ..	....	....	....	....	....	9.14	8.96	12.83
Exceptional financing	4 920 ..	43.68	59.56	51.35	−31.77	−106.17	347.02	26.62	−234.21
Conversion rates: Seychelles rupees per U.S. dollar	0 101 ..	**5.4007**	**5.5000**	**5.5000**	**5.5197**	**6.7011**	**9.4572**	**13.6099**	**12.0678**

[1] Excludes components that have been classified in the categories of Group E.

Table 2. STANDARD PRESENTATION, 2003–2010

(Millions of U.S. dollars)

	Code	2003	2004	2005	2006	2007	2008	2009	2010
CURRENT ACCOUNT	4 993	−9.36	−60.32	−174.07	−133.77	−168.55	−201.26	−90.72	−225.05
A. GOODS	4 100	−89.14	−155.17	−299.31	−290.28	−282.05	−402.86	−301.10	−336.54
Credit	2 100	286.42	301.10	350.91	420.08	397.32	436.09	431.98	400.23
General merchandise: exports f.o.b.	2 110	218.55	199.51	211.83	220.10	201.27	229.79	241.54	218.98
Goods for processing: exports f.o.b.	2 150	....	....	....	....	....	....	....	....
Repairs on goods	2 160	.81	.74	.80	.88	....	....	....	....
Goods procured in ports by carriers	2 170	67.06	100.85	138.27	199.10	196.04	206.30	190.44	181.25
Nonmonetary gold	2 180	....	....	....	....	....	....	....	....
Debit	3 100	−375.56	−456.27	−650.21	−710.36	−679.37	−838.95	−733.08	−736.78
General merchandise: imports f.o.b.	3 110	−362.41	−431.76	−624.47	−660.16	−657.45	−792.46	−706.13	−709.09
Goods for processing: imports f.o.b.	3 150	....	....	....	....	....	....	....	....
Repairs on goods	3 160	−1.35	−4.86	−5.66	−8.59	....	....	....	....
Goods procured in ports by carriers	3 170	−11.80	−19.65	−20.08	−41.60	−21.92	−46.48	−26.96	−27.69
Nonmonetary gold	3 180	....	....	....	....	....	....	....	....
B. SERVICES	4 200	110.17	110.77	134.08	156.13	162.86	236.92	208.90	150.69
Total credit	2 200	*330.40*	*326.60*	*368.76*	*430.28*	*628.01*	*608.03*	*600.46*	*591.80*
Total debit	3 200	*−220.23*	*−215.83*	*−234.68*	*−274.15*	*−465.14*	*−371.11*	*−391.55*	*−441.11*
Transportation services, credit	2 205	124.73	118.21	133.46	160.54	113.73	139.70	133.79	130.99
Passenger	2 850	*87.47*	*84.25*	*77.27*	*95.07*	*70.18*	*98.98*	*92.27*	*77.95*
Freight	2 851	*6.44*	*6.58*	*25.16*	*30.30*	*4.21*	*1.69*	*2.52*	*2.19*
Other	2 852	*30.83*	*27.38*	*31.03*	*35.17*	*39.34*	*39.02*	*39.00*	*50.84*
Sea transport, passenger	2 207	....	....	....	....	....	....	....	....
Sea transport, freight	2 208	6.44	6.58	22.98	26.62	1.92	1.56	1.26	1.10
Sea transport, other	2 209	21.10	18.87	21.19	22.20	21.77	21.63	20.70	20.89
Air transport, passenger	2 211	87.47	84.25	77.27	95.07	70.18	98.98	92.27	77.95
Air transport, freight	2 212	....	....	2.18	3.68	2.28	.13	1.26	1.09
Air transport, other	2 213	9.72	8.52	9.84	12.97	17.57	17.39	18.30	29.95
Other transport, passenger	2 215	....	....	....	....	....	....	....	....
Other transport, freight	2 216	....	....	....	....	....	....	....	....
Other transport, other	2 217	....	....	....	....	....	....	....	....
Transportation services, debit	3 205	−83.54	−93.97	−107.84	−127.62	−115.68	−124.92	−118.14	−142.93
Passenger	3 850	*−18.27*	*−18.78*	*−20.22*	*−20.40*	*−30.31*	*−24.44*	*−21.07*	*−25.21*
Freight	3 851	*−51.63*	*−62.09*	*−73.64*	*−95.25*	*−71.49*	*−79.17*	*−75.59*	*−77.23*
Other	3 852	*−13.64*	*−13.10*	*−13.98*	*−11.98*	*−13.89*	*−21.31*	*−21.49*	*−40.49*
Sea transport, passenger	3 207	....	....	....	....	....	....	....	....
Sea transport, freight	3 208	−51.63	−62.09	−73.64	−95.25	−70.64	−78.63	−75.24	−76.69
Sea transport, other	3 209	−.38	−.23	−.50	−.91	−.91	−.83	−.59	−1.83
Air transport, passenger	3 211	−18.27	−18.78	−20.22	−20.40	−30.31	−24.44	−21.07	−25.21
Air transport, freight	3 212	....	....	....	....	−.85	−.54	−.35	−.54
Air transport, other	3 213	−13.26	−12.88	−13.48	−11.07	−12.98	−20.48	−20.90	−38.66
Other transport, passenger	3 215	....	....	....	....	....	....	....	....
Other transport, freight	3 216	....	....	....	....	....	....	....	....
Other transport, other	3 217	....	....	....	....	....	....	....	....
Travel, credit	2 236	171.13	171.71	192.10	227.77	325.61	307.66	256.62	274.37
Business travel	2 237	....	....	....	....	65.12	61.53	51.32	54.87
Personal travel	2 240	171.13	171.71	192.10	227.77	260.49	246.13	205.30	219.50
Travel, debit	3 236	−36.30	−33.52	−38.67	−35.93	−42.81	−38.84	−33.82	−37.66
Business travel	3 237	....	....	....	....	−5.37	−5.83	−3.30	−2.70
Personal travel	3 240	−36.30	−33.52	−38.67	−35.93	−37.44	−33.01	−30.52	−34.96
Other services, credit	2 200 BA	34.53	36.68	43.20	41.98	188.66	160.67	210.04	186.44
Communications	2 245	10.41	12.14	12.62	12.88	6.33	6.44	6.77	7.58
Construction	2 249	....	....	....	....	....	....	....	....
Insurance	2 253	1.56	1.44	3.60	.88	2.52	2.00	1.12	.35
Financial	2 260	....	....	....	....	107.93	32.80	35.66	45.02
Computer and information	2 262	....	....	.16	.16	....	....	....	....
Royalties and licence fees	2 266	....	....	....	....	1.22	.99	8.67	1.86
Other business services	2 268	3.00	4.90	5.16	6.45	70.55	118.36	157.71	131.56
Personal, cultural, and recreational	2 287	....	....	....	....	....	....	....	....
Government, n.i.e.	2 291	19.57	18.20	21.66	21.59	.10	.10	.10	.06
Other services, debit	3 200 BA	−100.39	−88.34	−88.17	−110.60	−306.65	−207.36	−239.59	−260.52
Communications	3 245	....	....	....	....	−.87	−.87	−.83	−.92
Construction	3 249	−17.07	−15.21	−12.83	−23.53	−32.93	−32.89	−33.24	−37.61
Insurance	3 253	−16.39	−17.84	−20.26	−25.36	−22.40	−22.36	−21.08	−22.81
Financial	3 260	....	....	....	....	−107.46	−32.98	−35.31	−37.98
Computer and information	3 262	....	....	....	....	....	....	....	....
Royalties and licence fees	3 266	−.56	−.54	−.55	−.54	−.54	−.51	−.52	−1.41
Other business services	3 268	−58.66	−49.99	−51.09	−52.39	−138.87	−115.66	−142.82	−152.48
Personal, cultural, and recreational	3 287	....	....	....	....	....	....	....	....
Government, n.i.e.	3 291	−7.70	−4.76	−3.44	−8.77	−3.58	−2.09	−5.80	−7.30

Table 2 (Continued). STANDARD PRESENTATION, 2003–2010

(Millions of U.S. dollars)

	Code	2003	2004	2005	2006	2007	2008	2009	2010
C. INCOME	4 300	**−43.19**	**−33.69**	**−40.07**	**−43.62**	**−63.96**	**−67.63**	**−46.47**	**−64.59**
Total credit	2 300	*11.98*	*9.44*	*9.81*	*10.27*	*3.57*	*4.87*	*3.46*	*7.56*
Total debit	3 300	*−55.18*	*−43.13*	*−49.88*	*−53.89*	*−67.53*	*−72.50*	*−49.93*	*−72.15*
Compensation of employees, credit	2 310	**.16**	**.16**	**.19**	**.19**	**.80**	**.88**	**.84**	**.89**
Compensation of employees, debit	3 310	**−4.89**	**−5.30**	**−5.96**	**−7.58**	**−5.25**	**−7.00**	**−8.57**	**−3.02**
Investment income, credit	2 320	**11.83**	**9.28**	**9.62**	**10.08**	**2.77**	**3.99**	**2.62**	**6.68**
Direct investment income	2 330	2.89	2.42	2.54	2.67	2.58	2.49	1.78	2.05
Dividends and distributed branch profits	2 332	....	....	....	....	....	....	....	....
Reinvested earnings and undistributed branch profits	2 333	2.89	2.42	2.54	2.67	2.58	2.49	1.78	2.05
Income on debt (interest)	2 334	....	....	....	....	....	....	....	....
Portfolio investment income	2 339	....	....	....	....	....	....	....	....
Income on equity	2 340	....	....	....	....	....	....	....	....
Income on bonds and notes	2 350	....	....	....	....	....	....	....	....
Income on money market instruments	2 360	....	....	....	....	....	....	....	....
Other investment income	2 370	8.93	6.86	7.08	7.41	.19	1.49	.84	4.62
Investment income, debit	3 320	**−50.29**	**−37.82**	**−43.91**	**−46.31**	**−62.28**	**−65.50**	**−41.36**	**−69.13**
Direct investment income	3 330	−25.91	−17.21	−20.32	−25.30	−15.40	−21.23	−8.12	−27.60
Dividends and distributed branch profits	3 332	−16.88	−11.19	−9.42	−8.35	−4.26	−7.54	−6.13	−6.13
Reinvested earnings and undistributed branch profits	3 333	−9.03	−6.02	−10.90	−16.95	−11.14	−13.69	−1.99	−21.47
Income on debt (interest)	3 334	....	....	....	....	....	....	....	....
Portfolio investment income	3 339	....	....	....	....	....	....	....	....
Income on equity	3 340	....	....	....	....	....	....	....	....
Income on bonds and notes	3 350	....	....	....	....	....	....	....	....
Income on money market instruments	3 360	....	....	....	....	....	....	....	....
Other investment income	3 370	−24.38	−20.61	−23.60	−21.01	−46.88	−44.27	−33.24	−41.53
D. CURRENT TRANSFERS	4 379	**12.80**	**17.77**	**31.22**	**44.00**	**14.60**	**32.32**	**47.94**	**25.39**
Credit	2 379	**15.62**	**20.68**	**35.53**	**54.10**	**18.70**	**37.64**	**60.56**	**42.95**
General government	2 380	10.92	14.02	23.61	23.43	14.74	35.38	45.27	26.46
Other sectors	2 390	4.70	6.65	11.92	30.67	3.96	2.26	15.29	16.49
Workers' remittances	2 391	4.70	6.65	11.92	13.08	3.96	2.26	15.29	16.49
Other current transfers	2 392	....	....	....	17.59	....	....	....	....
Debit	3 379	**−2.82**	**−2.90**	**−4.31**	**−10.10**	**−4.10**	**−5.33**	**−12.62**	**−17.56**
General government	3 380	−.39	−.28	−.31	−.36	....	....	....	....
Other sectors	3 390	−2.43	−2.62	−3.99	−9.75	−4.10	−5.33	−12.62	−17.56
Workers' remittances	3 391	−2.43	−2.62	−3.99	−9.75	−4.10	−5.33	−12.62	−17.56
Other current transfers	3 392	....	....	....	....	....	....	....	....
CAPITAL AND FINANCIAL ACCOUNT	4 996	**14.04**	**59.64**	**174.59**	**131.58**	**151.25**	**180.22**	**67.64**	**211.84**
CAPITAL ACCOUNT	4 994	**7.42**	**.99**	**29.88**	**13.24**	**8.17**	**5.03**	**52.50**	**275.29**
Total credit	2 994	*7.42*	*.99*	*29.88*	*13.24*	*8.17*	*5.03*	*52.50*	*275.29*
Total debit	3 994	....	....	....	....	....	....	....	....
Capital transfers, credit	2 400	**7.42**	**.99**	**29.88**	**13.24**	**8.17**	**5.03**	**52.50**	**275.29**
General government	2 401	7.42	.99	29.88	13.24	8.17	5.03	52.50	275.29
Debt forgiveness	2 402	....	....	....	....	....	....	40.96	267.14
Other capital transfers	2 410	7.42	.99	29.88	13.24	8.17	5.03	11.54	8.15
Other sectors	2 430	....	....	....	....	....	....	....	....
Migrants' transfers	2 431	....	....	....	....	....	....	....	....
Debt forgiveness	2 432	....	....	....	....	....	....	....	....
Other capital transfers	2 440	....	....	....	....	....	....	....	....
Capital transfers, debit	3 400	....	....	....	....	....	....	....	....
General government	3 401	....	....	....	....	....	....	....	....
Debt forgiveness	3 402	....	....	....	....	....	....	....	....
Other capital transfers	3 410	....	....	....	....	....	....	....	....
Other sectors	3 430	....	....	....	....	....	....	....	....
Migrants' transfers	3 431	....	....	....	....	....	....	....	....
Debt forgiveness	3 432	....	....	....	....	....	....	....	....
Other capital transfers	3 440	....	....	....	....	....	....	....	....
Nonproduced nonfinancial assets, credit	2 480	....	....	....	....	....	....	....	....
Nonproduced nonfinancial assets, debit	3 480	....	....	....	....	....	....	....	....

Table 2 (Continued). STANDARD PRESENTATION, 2003–2010

(Millions of U.S. dollars)

	Code	2003	2004	2005	2006	2007	2008	2009	2010
FINANCIAL ACCOUNT............................	4 995 ..	**6.62**	**58.65**	**144.71**	**118.34**	**143.08**	**175.19**	**15.15**	**−63.45**
A. DIRECT INVESTMENT.........................	4 500 ..	**50.28**	**30.41**	**78.43**	**137.81**	**108.58**	**116.52**	**113.14**	**161.16**
Direct investment abroad.....................	4 505 ..	**−8.15**	**−7.60**	**−7.45**	**−8.01**	**−17.82**	**−12.94**	**−5.34**	**−6.15**
Equity capital..	4 510 ..	−5.25	−5.18	−5.15	−5.26	−15.24	−10.45	−3.56	−4.10
Claims on affiliated enterprises...............	4 515 ..	−5.25	−5.18	−5.15	−5.26	−15.24	−10.45	−3.56	−4.10
Liabilities to affiliated enterprises............	4 520 ..	....	....	....	....	....	....	....	....
Reinvested earnings...............................	4 525 ..	−2.89	−2.42	−2.30	−2.75	−2.58	−2.49	−1.78	−2.05
Other capital...	4 530 ..	....	....	....	....	....	....	....	....
Claims on affiliated enterprises...............	4 535 ..	....	....	....	....	....	....	....	....
Liabilities to affiliated enterprises............	4 540 ..	....	....	....	....	....	....	....	....
Direct investment in Seychelles..........	4 555 ..	**58.43**	**38.01**	**85.88**	**145.82**	**126.40**	**129.45**	**118.48**	**167.31**
Equity capital..	4 560 ..	33.65	31.99	74.63	127.96	115.26	115.77	116.49	145.83
Claims on direct investors......................	4 565 ..	....	....	....	....	....	....	....	....
Liabilities to direct investors..................	4 570 ..	33.65	31.99	74.63	127.96	115.26	115.77	116.49	145.83
Reinvested earnings...............................	4 575 ..	9.03	6.02	10.90	16.95	11.14	13.69	1.99	21.47
Other capital...	4 580 ..	15.74	....	.35	.90	....	....	....	....
Claims on direct investors......................	4 585 ..	....	....	....	....	....	....	....	....
Liabilities to direct investors..................	4 590 ..	15.74	....	.35	.90	....	....		
B. PORTFOLIO INVESTMENT..................	4 600 ..	**1.13**	**1.08**	**1.01**	**198.16**	**118.17**	**−310.15**	**−5.68**	**24.63**
Assets..	4 602 ..	**−.01**	**−.04**	**−.04**	**−.05**	**−14.38**	**−.16**	**−5.68**	**27.16**
Equity securities...................................	4 610 ..	....	....	....	....	....	....	−6.00	....
Monetary authorities............................	4 611 ..	....	....	....	....	....	....	....	....
General government..............................	4 612 ..	....	....	....	....	....	....	....	....
Banks..	4 613 ..	....	....	....	....	....	....	....	....
Other sectors.......................................	4 614 ..	....	....	....	....	....	....	−6.00	....
Debt securities.....................................	4 619 ..	−.01	−.04	−.04	−.05	−14.38	−.16	.32	27.16
Bonds and notes...................................	4 620 ..	−.01	−.04	−.04	−.05	−14.38	−.16	.32	27.16
Monetary authorities..........................	4 621 ..	....	....	....	....	....	....	....	....
General government............................	4 622 ..	....	....	....	....	....	....	....	....
Banks..	4 623 ..	−.01	−.04	−.04	−.05	−14.38	−.16	.32	27.16
Other sectors.....................................	4 624 ..	....	....	....	....	....	....	....	....
Money market instruments.....................	4 630 ..	....	....	....	....	....	....	....	....
Monetary authorities..........................	4 631 ..	....	....	....	....	....	....	....	....
General government............................	4 632 ..	....	....	....	....	....	....	....	....
Banks..	4 633 ..	....	....	....	....	....	....	....	....
Other sectors.....................................	4 634 ..	....	....	....	....	....	....	....	....
Liabilities..	4 652 ..	**1.14**	**1.11**	**1.06**	**198.21**	**132.56**	**−309.99**	....	**−2.53**
Equity securities...................................	4 660 ..	....	....	....	....	....	....	....	....
Banks..	4 663 ..	....	....	....	....	....	....	....	....
Other sectors.......................................	4 664 ..	....	....	....	....	....	....	....	....
Debt securities.....................................	4 669 ..	1.14	1.11	1.06	198.21	132.56	−309.99	....	−2.53
Bonds and notes...................................	4 670 ..	1.14	1.11	1.06	198.21	132.56	−309.99	....	−2.53
Monetary authorities..........................	4 671 ..	....	....	....	....	....	....	....	....
General government............................	4 672 ..	....	....	....	197.18	132.56	−309.99	....	−2.53
Banks..	4 673 ..	1.14	1.11	1.06	1.03	....	....	....	....
Other sectors.....................................	4 674 ..	....	....	....	....	....	....	....	....
Money market instruments.....................	4 680 ..	....	....	....	....	....	....	....	....
Monetary authorities..........................	4 681 ..	....	....	....	....	....	....	....	....
General government............................	4 682 ..	....	....	....	....	....	....	....	....
Banks..	4 683 ..	....	....	....	....	....	....	....	....
Other sectors.....................................	4 684 ..	....	....	....	....	....	....	....	....
C. FINANCIAL DERIVATIVES..................	4 910 ..	....	....	....	....	....	....	....	....
Monetary authorities............................	4 911 ..	....	....	....	....	....	....	....	....
General government..............................	4 912 ..	....	....	....	....	....	....	....	....
Banks..	4 913 ..	....	....	....	....	....	....	....	....
Other sectors.......................................	4 914 ..	....	....	....	....	....	....	....	....
Assets..	4 900 ..	....	....	....	....	....	....	....	....
Monetary authorities............................	4 901 ..	....	....	....	....	....	....	....	....
General government..............................	4 902 ..	....	....	....	....	....	....	....	....
Banks..	4 903 ..	....	....	....	....	....	....	....	....
Other sectors.......................................	4 904 ..	....	....	....	....	....	....	....	....
Liabilities..	4 905 ..	....	....	....	....	....	....	....	....
Monetary authorities............................	4 906 ..	....	....	....	....	....	....	....	....
General government..............................	4 907 ..	....	....	....	....	....	....	....	....
Banks..	4 908 ..	....	....	....	....	....	....	....	....
Other sectors.......................................	4 909 ..	....	....	....	....	....	....	....	....

Table 2 (Concluded). STANDARD PRESENTATION, 2003–2010

(Millions of U.S. dollars)

	Code	2003	2004	2005	2006	2007	2008	2009	2010
D. OTHER INVESTMENT	4 700	**−41.67**	**−5.81**	**87.24**	**−155.66**	**−128.71**	**415.77**	**32.65**	**−168.08**
Assets	4 703	**−14.81**	**−12.25**	**−9.61**	**−8.75**	**−53.83**	**−10.53**	**5.44**	**8.53**
Trade credits	4 706	....	....	....	....	....	....	....	....
General government	4 707	....	....	....	....	....	....	....	....
of which: Short-term	4 709	....	....	....	....	....	....	....	....
Other sectors	4 710	....	....	....	....	....	....	....	....
of which: Short-term	4 712	....	....	....	....	....	....	....	....
Loans	4 714	....	....	....	....	....	....	....	....
Monetary authorities	4 715	....	....	....	....	....	....	....	....
of which: Short-term	4 718	....	....	....	....	....	....	....	....
General government	4 719	....	....	....	....	....	....	....	....
of which: Short-term	4 721	....	....	....	....	....	....	....	....
Banks	4 722	....	....	....	....	....	....	....	....
of which: Short-term	4 724	....	....	....	....	....	....	....	....
Other sectors	4 725	....	....	....	....	....	....	....	....
of which: Short-term	4 727	....	....	....	....	....	....	....	....
Currency and deposits	4 730	−14.81	−12.25	−9.61	−8.75	−53.83	−10.53	5.44	8.53
Monetary authorities	4 731	....	....	....	....	....	....	....	....
General government	4 732	....	....	....	....	−.34	−.38	−.06	−.12
Banks	4 733	....	....	−3.49	−13.27	−42.04	−7.71	15.19	−8.06
Other sectors	4 734	−14.81	−12.25	−6.12	4.53	−11.46	−2.44	−9.69	16.72
Other assets	4 736	....	....	....	....	....	....	....	....
Monetary authorities	4 737	....	....	....	....	....	....	....	....
of which: Short-term	4 739	....	....	....	....	....	....	....	....
General government	4 740	....	....	....	....	....	....	....	....
of which: Short-term	4 742	....	....	....	....	....	....	....	....
Banks	4 743	....	....	....	....	....	....	....	....
of which: Short-term	4 745	....	....	....	....	....	....	....	....
Other sectors	4 746	....	....	....	....	....	....	....	....
of which: Short-term	4 748	....	....	....	....	....	....	....	....
Liabilities	4 753	**−26.86**	**6.44**	**96.85**	**−146.92**	**−74.88**	**426.30**	**27.21**	**−176.61**
Trade credits	4 756	4.82	−5.04	....	....	....	....	....	....
General government	4 757	4.82	−5.04	....	....	....	....	....	....
of which: Short-term	4 759	*4.82*	*−5.04*	....	....	....	....	....	....
Other sectors	4 760	....	....	....	....	....	....	....	....
of which: Short-term	4 762	....	....	....	....	....	....	....	....
Loans	4 764	−63.78	−45.49	54.68	−117.97	34.60	78.53	−15.33	53.55
Monetary authorities	4 765	−35.51	−33.79	10.82	−75.26	....	9.14	8.96	12.83
of which: Use of Fund credit and loans from the Fund..	4 766	....	....	....	....	....	*9.14*	*8.96*	*12.83*
of which: Short-term	4 768	....	....	....	....	....	....	....	....
General government	4 769	−30.95	−19.46	43.89	−37.83	−12.91	12.82	−64.98	−5.07
of which: Short-term	4 771	....	....	....	....	....	....	....	....
Banks	4 772	−3.61	−2.35	−.04	−4.88	4.56	13.50	−2.40	−11.25
of which: Short-term	4 774	*−3.61*	*−2.35*	*−.04*	*−4.88*	*4.56*	*13.50*	*−2.40*	*−11.25*
Other sectors	4 775	6.28	10.11	....	....	42.94	43.07	43.08	57.04
of which: Short-term	4 777	....	....	....	....	....	....	....	....
Currency and deposits	4 780	....	10.46	13.60	17.21	−3.31	.75	3.61	4.05
Monetary authorities	4 781	....	....	....	....	....	....	....	....
General government	4 782	....	....	....	....	....	....	....	....
Banks	4 783	....	10.46	13.60	17.21	−3.31	.75	3.61	4.05
Other sectors	4 784	....	....	....	....	....	....	....	....
Other liabilities	4 786	32.11	46.50	28.57	−46.16	−106.17	347.02	38.93	−234.21
Monetary authorities	4 787	....	....	....	....	....	....	12.31	....
of which: Short-term	4 789	....	....	....	....	....	....	....	....
General government	4 790	....	....	31.94	−49.51	31.79	357.93	26.91	−234.21
of which: Short-term	4 792	....	....	*40.18*	*−41.74*	*31.79*	*357.93*	*26.91*	*−234.21*
Banks	4 793	....	....	....	....	....	....	....	....
of which: Short-term	4 795	....	....	....	....	....	....	....	....
Other sectors	4 796	32.11	46.50	−3.37	3.36	−137.96	−10.91	−.29	....
of which: Short-term	4 798	*40.65*	*56.15*	*−2.92*	*−1.45*	*−137.96*	*−10.91*	*−.29*	....
E. RESERVE ASSETS	4 802	**−3.12**	**32.97**	**−21.97**	**−61.97**	**45.03**	**−46.94**	**−124.97**	**−81.16**
Monetary gold	4 812	....	....	....	....	....	....	....	....
Special drawing rights	4 811	.01	....	....	....	−.01	.01	−12.25	.33
Reserve position in the Fund	4 810	....	....	....	....	....	....	....	....
Foreign exchange	4 803	−3.13	32.97	−21.97	−61.97	45.04	−46.95	−112.71	−81.49
Other claims	4 813	....	....	....	....	....	....	....	....
NET ERRORS AND OMISSIONS	4 998	**−4.68**	**.68**	**−.52**	**2.19**	**17.30**	**21.04**	**23.08**	**13.21**

2011, International Monetary Fund: *Balance of Payments Statistics Yearbook*

Table 1. ANALYTIC PRESENTATION, 2003–2010

(Millions of U.S. dollars)

	Code	2003	2004	2005	2006	2007	2008	2009	2010
A. Current Account[1]	4 993 Z.	**−99.1**	**−140.7**	**−170.6**	**−139.0**	**−216.9**	**−300.0**	**−291.0**	**−482.9**
Goods: exports f.o.b.	2 100 ..	110.8	154.1	183.6	261.9	288.9	273.5	270.4	362.9
Goods: imports f.o.b.	3 100 ..	−310.7	−274.3	−361.7	−351.2	−395.4	−471.2	−511.9	−735.9
Balance on Goods	4 100 ..	*−199.9*	*−120.2*	*−178.0*	*−89.3*	*−106.6*	*−197.7*	*−241.5*	*−373.0*
Services: credit	2 200 ..	66.1	61.5	78.2	42.5	45.3	61.4	58.2	60.0
Services: debit	3 200 ..	−93.8	−92.3	−91.4	−85.9	−98.0	−125.4	−122.5	−143.6
Balance on Goods and Services	4 991 ..	*−227.6*	*−151.1*	*−191.3*	*−132.7*	*−159.2*	*−261.7*	*−305.8*	*−456.6*
Income: credit	2 300 ..	1.7	4.1	5.4	12.3	43.3	17.7	11.3	9.7
Income: debit	3 300 ..	−16.7	−71.1	−56.3	−52.0	−147.6	−92.4	−46.9	−58.2
Balance on Goods, Services, and Income	4 992 ..	*−242.6*	*−218.1*	*−242.2*	*−172.3*	*−263.5*	*−336.5*	*−341.5*	*−505.2*
Current transfers: credit	2 379 Z.	148.5	80.3	73.6	38.2	49.4	43.9	53.8	63.4
Current transfers: debit	3 379 ..	−5.0	−2.8	−2.0	−4.9	−2.8	−7.4	−3.4	−41.1
B. Capital Account[1]	4 994 Z.	**16.0**	**18.4**	**36.8**	**224.1**	**239.5**	**61.4**	**68.6**	**22.7**
Capital account: credit	2 994 Z.	16.0	18.4	36.8	224.1	239.5	61.4	68.6	22.7
Capital account: debit	3 994 ..	....	....	....	....	....	....	....	....
Total, Groups A Plus B	4 981 ..	*−83.1*	*−122.3*	*−133.8*	*85.1*	*22.6*	*−238.6*	*−222.4*	*−460.2*
C. Financial Account[1]	4 995 W.	**33.5**	**76.2**	**62.8**	**34.6**	**90.7**	**95.4**	**312.3**	**101.4**
Direct investment abroad	4 505 ..	....	....	7.5	....	....	....	....	....
Direct investment in Sierra Leone	4 555 Z.	8.6	61.2	83.2	58.8	96.6	57.6	74.3	86.6
Portfolio investment assets	4 602 ..	....	....	....	....	....	....	−26.0	−22.1
Equity securities	4 610 ..	....	....	....	....	....	....	....	....
Debt securities	4 619 ..	....	....	....	....	....	....	−26.0	−22.1
Portfolio investment liabilities	4 652 Z.	....	....	....	....	....	1.6	5.6	3.0
Equity securities	4 660 ..	....	....	....	....	....	....	5.6	....
Debt securities	4 669 Z.	....	....	....	....	....	1.6	....	3.0
Financial derivatives	4 910 ..	....	....	....	....	....	....	....	....
Financial derivatives assets	4 900 ..	....	....	....	....	....	....	....	....
Financial derivatives liabilities	4 905 ..	....	....	....	....	....	....	....	....
Other investment assets	4 703 ..	.5	10.1	−1.9	−8.0	−6.1	−2.8	21.7	−11.8
Monetary authorities	4 701 ..	.5	....	−.5	−2.1	1.7	−.5	.8	−.4
General government	4 704 ..	....	....	....	....	....	−1.0	−14.1	15.9	−26.5
Banks	4 705 ..	....	5.7	....	....	−1.0	−14.1	15.9	−26.5
Other sectors	4 728 ..	....	4.3	−1.4	−5.9	−6.9	11.8	5.1	15.1
Other investment liabilities	4 753 W.	24.4	5.0	−26.1	−16.1	.2	39.0	236.6	45.7
Monetary authorities	4 753 WA	....	4.2	....	....	....	7.5	206.2	71.4
General government	4 753 ZB	24.4	−16.6	−26.1	−15.9	−15.2	−5.5	−2.8	−9.1
Banks	4 753 ZC	....	....	....	....	....	20.0	11.3	−4.4
Other sectors	4 753 ZD	....	17.4	....	−.2	15.4	17.0	21.9	−12.3
Total, Groups A Through C	4 983 ..	*−49.6*	*−46.1*	*−71.1*	*119.7*	*113.3*	*−143.2*	*89.9*	*−358.8*
D. Net Errors and Omissions	4 998 ..	**−50.3**	**−53.6**	**−58.5**	**−59.4**	**−143.2**	**−21.6**	**−186.0**	**37.4**
Total, Groups A Through D	4 984 ..	*−99.9*	*−99.7*	*−129.6*	*60.4*	*−29.9*	*−164.8*	*−96.1*	*−321.4*
E. Reserves and Related Items	4 802 A.	**99.9**	**99.7**	**129.6**	**−60.4**	**29.9**	**164.8**	**96.1**	**321.4**
Reserve assets	4 802 ..	24.3	−45.2	−56.4	−11.4	−33.9	−9.5	−110.5	−19.9
Use of Fund credit and loans	4 766 ..	−14.8	18.5	12.3	−167.8	....	17.8	18.8	40.7
Exceptional financing	4 920 ..	90.5	126.3	173.7	118.8	63.8	156.5	187.8	300.6
Conversion rates: leones per U.S. dollar	0 101 ..	**2,347.94**	**2,701.30**	**2,889.59**	**2,961.91**	**2,985.19**	**2,981.51**	**3,385.65**	**3,978.09**

[1] Excludes components that have been classified in the categories of Group E.

Table 2. STANDARD PRESENTATION, 2003–2010
(Millions of U.S. dollars)

	Code	2003	2004	2005	2006	2007	2008	2009	2010
CURRENT ACCOUNT	4 993	**−82.8**	**−99.0**	**−104.9**	**−95.0**	**−160.1**	**−225.4**	**−193.8**	**−320.1**
A. GOODS	4 100	**−199.9**	**−120.2**	**−178.0**	**−89.3**	**−106.6**	**−197.7**	**−241.5**	**−373.0**
Credit	2 100	**110.8**	**154.1**	**183.6**	**261.9**	**288.9**	**273.5**	**270.4**	**362.9**
General merchandise: exports f.o.b.	2 110	106.1	144.5	172.5	250.4	277.6	264.1	260.1	355.2
Goods for processing: exports f.o.b.	2 150	....	....	....	....	....	....	....	....
Repairs on goods	2 160	....	....	....	....	....	....	....	....
Goods procured in ports by carriers	2 170	4.7	9.5	11.2	11.5	11.3	9.4	10.3	7.7
Nonmonetary gold	2 180	....	....	....	....	....	....	....	....
Debit	3 100	**−310.7**	**−274.3**	**−361.7**	**−351.2**	**−395.4**	**−471.2**	**−511.9**	**−735.9**
General merchandise: imports f.o.b.	3 110	−310.7	−274.3	−361.7	−351.2	−395.4	−471.2	−511.9	−735.9
Goods for processing: imports f.o.b.	3 150	....	....	....	....	....	....	....	....
Repairs on goods	3 160	....	....	....	....	....	....	....	....
Goods procured in ports by carriers	3 170	....	....	....	....	....	....	....	....
Nonmonetary gold	3 180	....	....	....	....	....	....	....	....
B. SERVICES	4 200	**−27.7**	**−30.9**	**−13.2**	**−43.4**	**−52.7**	**−64.0**	**−64.3**	**−83.5**
Total credit	2 200	*66.1*	*61.5*	*78.2*	*42.5*	*45.3*	*61.4*	*58.2*	*60.0*
Total debit	3 200	*−93.8*	*−92.3*	*−91.4*	*−85.9*	*−98.0*	*−125.4*	*−122.5*	*−143.6*
Transportation services, credit	2 205	**3.0**	**1.4**	**11.6**	**13.6**	**16.2**	**20.2**	**23.6**	**24.1**
Passenger	2 850	....	*.2*	....	....	....	....	....	....
Freight	2 851	....	....	....	....	....	....	....	....
Other	2 852	*3.0*	*1.2*	*11.6*	*13.6*	*16.2*	*20.2*	*23.6*	*24.1*
Sea transport, passenger	2 207	....	....	....	....	....	....	....	....
Sea transport, freight	2 208	....	....	....	....	....	....	....	....
Sea transport, other	2 209	....	....	9.6	9.6	10.3	13.1	15.3	17.5
Air transport, passenger	2 211	....	.2	....	....	....	....	....	....
Air transport, freight	2 212	....	....	....	....	....	....	....	....
Air transport, other	2 213	3.0	1.2	2.0	4.0	5.4	6.1	6.3	5.4
Other transport, passenger	2 215	....	....	....	....	....	....	....	....
Other transport, freight	2 216	....	....	....	....	....	....	....	....
Other transport, other	2 217	....	....	....	....	.5	1.0	2.1	1.2
Transportation services, debit	3 205	**−36.1**	**−31.5**	**−42.7**	**−44.0**	**−48.6**	**−55.3**	**−68.1**	**−93.3**
Passenger	3 850	*−.8*	*−.3*	*−1.6*	*−3.0*	*−3.3*	*−.4*	*−9.3*	*−9.1*
Freight	3 851	*−35.3*	*−31.2*	*−41.1*	*−41.0*	*−45.4*	*−54.9*	*−58.7*	*−84.2*
Other	3 852	....	....	....	....	....	....	....	....
Sea transport, passenger	3 207	....	....	....	....	....	....	....	....
Sea transport, freight	3 208	−35.3	−31.2	−41.1	−39.9	−44.9	−53.5	−58.2	−83.6
Sea transport, other	3 209	....	....	....	....	....	....	....	....
Air transport, passenger	3 211	−.8	−.3	−1.6	−3.0	−3.3	−.4	−9.3	−9.1
Air transport, freight	3 212	....	....	....	−1.1	−.4	−1.3	−.6	−.6
Air transport, other	3 213	....	....	....	....	....	....	....	....
Other transport, passenger	3 215	....	....	....	....	....	....	....	....
Other transport, freight	3 216	....	....	....	....	....	....	....	....
Other transport, other	3 217	....	....	....	....	....	....	....	....
Travel, credit	2 236	**59.9**	**58.2**	**64.0**	**23.0**	**22.2**	**33.8**	**25.4**	**25.8**
Business travel	2 237	32.4	19.5	21.8	10.4	9.7	10.5	9.5	13.5
Personal travel	2 240	27.5	38.7	42.2	12.6	12.5	23.3	15.9	12.3
Travel, debit	3 236	**−37.2**	**−29.8**	**−32.2**	**−12.5**	**−14.2**	**−24.3**	**−13.2**	**−13.1**
Business travel	3 237	−17.5	−10.1	−10.8	−8.1	−6.7	−9.7	−6.8	−7.0
Personal travel	3 240	−19.6	−19.7	−21.5	−4.4	−7.5	−14.6	−6.4	−6.1
Other services, credit	2 200 BA	**3.1**	**1.8**	**2.5**	**5.9**	**7.0**	**7.5**	**9.2**	**10.1**
Communications	2 245	3.0	.1	.1	.7	.1	.1	1.2	1.3
Construction	2 249	....	....	....	....	....	....	....	....
Insurance	2 253	....	....	.8	2.1	.4	.4	.4	.4
Financial	2 260	.1	.5	1.5	.3	.5	.6	.4	.4
Computer and information	2 262	....	....	....	....	....	....	....	....
Royalties and licence fees	2 266	....	1.1	....	....	....	1.2	1.1	1.3
Other business services	2 268	....	.1	.1	2.8	6.0	5.1	6.0	6.5
Personal, cultural, and recreational	2 287	....	....	....	....	....	....	....	....
Government, n.i.e.	2 291	....	....	....	....	....	.1	.2	.2
Other services, debit	3 200 BA	**−20.5**	**−31.1**	**−16.5**	**−29.4**	**−35.1**	**−45.8**	**−41.2**	**−37.2**
Communications	3 245	−4.5	−8.3	−.3	−4.3	−5.2	−11.5	−9.8	−9.6
Construction	3 249	....	....	....	....	....	....	....	....
Insurance	3 253	−6.6	−5.5	−7.8	−7.5	−8.3	−11.0	−9.2	−6.7
Financial	3 260	−.4	....	−.6	−.1	−.2	−.3	−.1	−.2
Computer and information	3 262	−1.0	−.3	−.7	−1.3	−.9	−1.5	−1.0	−1.0
Royalties and licence fees	3 266	−.2	....	....	−1.0	−1.5	−.7	−.6	−.4
Other business services	3 268	−2.7	−11.9	−1.9	−7.0	−11.2	−12.0	−11.7	−9.5
Personal, cultural, and recreational	3 287	....	....	....	....	....	....	....	....
Government, n.i.e.	3 291	−5.1	−5.1	−5.3	−8.3	−7.8	−8.8	−8.7	−9.8

2011, International Monetary Fund: *Balance of Payments Statistics Yearbook*

Table 2 (Continued). STANDARD PRESENTATION, 2003–2010

(Millions of U.S. dollars)

	Code	2003	2004	2005	2006	2007	2008	2009	2010
C. INCOME	4 300 ..	**−15.0**	**−67.0**	**−50.9**	**−39.7**	**−104.3**	**−74.8**	**−35.7**	**−48.6**
Total credit	2 300 ..	*1.7*	*4.1*	*5.4*	*12.3*	*43.3*	*17.7*	*11.3*	*9.7*
Total debit	3 300 ..	*−16.7*	*−71.1*	*−56.3*	*−52.0*	*−147.6*	*−92.4*	*−46.9*	*−58.2*
Compensation of employees, credit	2 310 ..	**.1**	**.1**	**.1**	**3.5**	**2.1**	**2.4**	**3.2**	**2.7**
Compensation of employees, debit	3 310 ..	**−2.2**	**−2.2**	**−2.3**	**−1.7**	**−3.2**	**−1.3**	**−1.8**	**−1.7**
Investment income, credit	2 320 ..	**1.6**	**4.0**	**5.3**	**8.8**	**41.2**	**15.3**	**8.0**	**7.0**
Direct investment income	2 330 ..	....	....	....	1.3	30.8	6.2	3.3	3.1
Dividends and distributed branch profits	2 332 ..	....	....	....	....	....	....	....	....
Reinvested earnings and undistributed branch profits	2 333 ..	....	....	....	....	....	....	....	....
Income on debt (interest)	2 334 ..	....	....	....	1.3	30.8	6.2	3.3	3.1
Portfolio investment income	2 339 ..	....	....	....	....	....	....	....	....
Income on equity	2 340 ..	....	....	....	....	....	....	....	....
Income on bonds and notes	2 350 ..	....	....	....	....	....	....	....	....
Income on money market instruments	2 360 ..	....	....	....	....	....	....	....	....
Other investment income	2 370 ..	1.6	4.0	5.3	7.4	10.4	9.1	4.8	3.9
Investment income, debit	3 320 ..	**−14.5**	**−68.9**	**−54.0**	**−50.3**	**−144.4**	**−91.1**	**−45.1**	**−56.5**
Direct investment income	3 330 ..	−9.4	−32.4	−41.2	−27.3	−121.8	−76.0	−39.0	−46.2
Dividends and distributed branch profits	3 332 ..	−6.3	−6.6	....	−1.5	−1.0	−4.1	−1.9	−3.7
Reinvested earnings and undistributed branch profits	3 333 ..	−3.1	−9.3	−24.7	−.8	−85.9	−58.1	−31.8	−38.4
Income on debt (interest)	3 334 ..	....	−16.5	−16.5	−25.0	−34.9	−13.9	−5.3	−4.2
Portfolio investment income	3 339 ..	....	....	....	....	....	....	....	....
Income on equity	3 340 ..	....	....	....	....	....	....	....	....
Income on bonds and notes	3 350 ..	....	....	....	....	....	....	....	....
Income on money market instruments	3 360 ..	....	....	....	....	....	....	....	....
Other investment income	3 370 ..	−5.1	−36.6	−12.8	−23.1	−22.6	−15.1	−6.1	−10.3
D. CURRENT TRANSFERS	4 379 ..	**159.8**	**119.1**	**137.2**	**77.3**	**103.4**	**111.0**	**147.7**	**185.0**
Credit	2 379 ..	**164.8**	**122.0**	**139.2**	**82.2**	**106.1**	**118.4**	**151.0**	**226.1**
General government	2 380 ..	61.7	79.7	86.8	45.7	59.4	78.2	101.9	167.0
Other sectors	2 390 ..	103.1	42.3	52.5	36.5	46.8	40.2	49.2	59.2
Workers' remittances	2 391 ..	25.8	24.6	2.3	12.1	39.8	20.2	32.7	41.6
Other current transfers	2 392 ..	77.4	17.6	50.1	24.4	6.9	20.0	16.5	17.6
Debit	3 379 ..	**−5.0**	**−2.8**	**−2.0**	**−4.9**	**−2.8**	**−7.4**	**−3.4**	**−41.1**
General government	3 380 ..	−2.9	−1.5	−.5	−.5	−.5	−.5	−.6	−33.8
Other sectors	3 390 ..	−2.0	−1.4	−1.5	−4.4	−2.2	−6.8	−2.7	−7.3
Workers' remittances	3 391 ..	−1.2	−.4	−.1	−2.2	−.6	−1.9	−1.7	−4.2
Other current transfers	3 392 ..	−.8	−.9	−1.4	−2.2	−1.6	−5.0	−1.0	−3.1
CAPITAL AND FINANCIAL ACCOUNT	4 996 ..	**133.1**	**152.6**	**163.4**	**154.4**	**303.3**	**247.1**	**379.8**	**282.7**
CAPITAL ACCOUNT	4 994 ..	**71.0**	**81.3**	**67.8**	**259.0**	**634.2**	**66.4**	**73.5**	**61.6**
Total credit	2 994 ..	*71.0*	*81.3*	*67.8*	*259.0*	*634.2*	*66.4*	*73.5*	*61.6*
Total debit	3 994 ..	....	....	....	....	....	....	....	....
Capital transfers, credit	2 400 ..	**71.0**	**81.3**	**67.8**	**259.0**	**634.2**	**66.4**	**73.5**	**61.6**
General government	2 401 ..	69.7	79.3	66.1	258.9	633.1	58.3	56.8	38.9
Debt forgiveness	2 402 ..	55.0	62.9	31.0	34.9	394.7	5.0	4.9	38.9
Other capital transfers	2 410 ..	14.7	16.3	35.1	224.0	238.4	53.3	51.9	....
Other sectors	2 430 ..	1.3	2.0	1.7	.1	1.1	8.1	16.7	22.7
Migrants' transfers	2 431 ..	....	....	....	....	....	4.9	10.9	13.3
Debt forgiveness	2 432 ..	....	....	....	....	....			
Other capital transfers	2 440 ..	1.3	2.0	1.7	.1	1.1	3.2	5.8	9.4
Capital transfers, debit	3 400 ..	....	....	....	....	....	....	....	....
General government	3 401 ..	....	....	....	....	....	....	....	....
Debt forgiveness	3 402 ..	....	....	....	....	....	....	....	....
Other capital transfers	3 410 ..	....	....	....	....	....	....	....	....
Other sectors	3 430 ..	....	....	....	....	....	....	....	....
Migrants' transfers	3 431 ..	....	....	....	....	....	....	....	....
Debt forgiveness	3 432 ..	....	....	....	....	....	....	....	....
Other capital transfers	3 440 ..	....	....	....	....	....	....	....	....
Nonproduced nonfinancial assets, credit	2 480 ..	....	....	....	....	....	....	....	....
Nonproduced nonfinancial assets, debit	3 480 ..	....	....	....	....	....	....	....	....

Table 2 (Continued). STANDARD PRESENTATION, 2003–2010

(Millions of U.S. dollars)

	Code	2003	2004	2005	2006	2007	2008	2009	2010
FINANCIAL ACCOUNT	4 995	**62.2**	**71.3**	**95.6**	**−104.7**	**−330.8**	**180.7**	**306.3**	**221.1**
A. DIRECT INVESTMENT	4 500	**8.6**	**61.2**	**90.7**	**58.8**	**96.6**	**57.6**	**74.3**	**86.6**
Direct investment abroad	4 505	....	....	**7.5**	....	....	....	....	....
Equity capital	4 510	....	....	....	....	....	....	....	....
Claims on affiliated enterprises	4 515	....	....	....	....	....	....	....	....
Liabilities to affiliated enterprises	4 520	....	....	....	....	....	....	....	....
Reinvested earnings	4 525	....	....	....	....	....	....	....	....
Other capital	4 530	....	....	7.5	....	....	....	....	....
Claims on affiliated enterprises	4 535	....	....	....	....	....	....	....	....
Liabilities to affiliated enterprises	4 540	....	....	7.5	....	....	....	....	....
Direct investment in Sierra Leone	4 555	**8.6**	**61.2**	**83.2**	**58.8**	**96.6**	**57.6**	**74.3**	**86.6**
Equity capital	4 560	13.0	24.5	28.5	66.2	−97.8	15.7	16.2	35.0
Claims on direct investors	4 565	....	....	....	....	....	....	....	....
Liabilities to direct investors	4 570	13.0	24.5	28.5	66.2	−97.8	15.7	16.2	35.0
Reinvested earnings	4 575	3.1	9.3	24.7	.8	85.9	58.1	31.8	38.4
Other capital	4 580	−7.5	27.4	29.9	−8.3	108.4	−16.2	26.3	13.2
Claims on direct investors	4 585	....	....	....	−.1	1.1	4.5	.4	....
Liabilities to direct investors	4 590	−7.5	27.4	29.9	−8.2	107.3	−20.7	25.9	13.1
B. PORTFOLIO INVESTMENT	4 600	....	....	....	....	....	1.6	−20.3	−19.1
Assets	4 602	....	....	....	....	....	....	−26.0	−22.1
Equity securities	4 610	....	....	....	....	....	....	....	....
Monetary authorities	4 611	....	....	....	....	....	....	....	....
General government	4 612	....	....	....	....	....	....	....	....
Banks	4 613	....	....	....	....	....	....	....	....
Other sectors	4 614	....	....	....	....	....	....	....	....
Debt securities	4 619	....	....	....	....	....	....	−26.0	−22.1
Bonds and notes	4 620	....	....	....	....	....	....	....	....
Monetary authorities	4 621	....	....	....	....	....	....	....	....
General government	4 622	....	....	....	....	....	....	....	....
Banks	4 623	....	....	....	....	....	....	....	....
Other sectors	4 624	....	....	....	....	....	....	....	....
Money market instruments	4 630	....	....	....	....	....	....	−26.0	−22.1
Monetary authorities	4 631	....	....	....	....	....	....	....	....
General government	4 632	....	....	....	....	....	....	....	....
Banks	4 633	....	....	....	....	....	....	....	....
Other sectors	4 634	....	....	....	....	....	....	−26.0	−22.1
Liabilities	4 652	....	....	....	....	....	1.6	5.6	3.0
Equity securities	4 660	....	....	....	....	....	....	5.6	....
Banks	4 663	....	....	....	....	....	....	....	....
Other sectors	4 664	....	....	....	....	....	....	5.6	....
Debt securities	4 669	....	....	....	....	....	1.6	....	3.0
Bonds and notes	4 670	....	....	....	....	....	1.6	....	....
Monetary authorities	4 671	....	....	....	....	....	1.6	....	....
General government	4 672	....	....	....	....	....	....	....	....
Banks	4 673	....	....	....	....	....	....	....	....
Other sectors	4 674	....	....	....	....	....	....	....	....
Money market instruments	4 680	....	....	....	....	....	....	....	3.0
Monetary authorities	4 681	....	....	....	....	....	....	....	....
General government	4 682	....	....	....	....	....	....	....	....
Banks	4 683	....	....	....	....	....	....	....	....
Other sectors	4 684	....	....	....	....	....	....	....	3.0
C. FINANCIAL DERIVATIVES	4 910	....	....	....	....	....	....	....	....
Monetary authorities	4 911	....	....	....	....	....	....	....	....
General government	4 912	....	....	....	....	....	....	....	....
Banks	4 913	....	....	....	....	....	....	....	....
Other sectors	4 914	....	....	....	....	....	....	....	....
Assets	4 900	....	....	....	....	....	....	....	....
Monetary authorities	4 901	....	....	....	....	....	....	....	....
General government	4 902	....	....	....	....	....	....	....	....
Banks	4 903	....	....	....	....	....	....	....	....
Other sectors	4 904	....	....	....	....	....	....	....	....
Liabilities	4 905	....	....	....	....	....	....	....	....
Monetary authorities	4 906	....	....	....	....	....	....	....	....
General government	4 907	....	....	....	....	....	....	....	....
Banks	4 908	....	....	....	....	....	....	....	....
Other sectors	4 909	....	....	....	....	....	....	....	....

2011, International Monetary Fund: *Balance of Payments Statistics Yearbook*

Table 2 (Concluded). STANDARD PRESENTATION, 2003–2010

(Millions of U.S. dollars)

	Code	2003	2004	2005	2006	2007	2008	2009	2010
D. OTHER INVESTMENT	4 700 ..	**29.3**	**55.4**	**61.3**	**−152.0**	**−393.6**	**131.0**	**362.8**	**173.6**
Assets	4 703 ..	**.5**	**10.1**	**−1.9**	**−8.0**	**−6.1**	**−2.8**	**21.7**	**−11.8**
Trade credits	4 706 ..	....	....	....	....	....	....	....	....
General government	4 707 ..	....	....	....	....	....	....	....	....
of which: Short-term	4 709 ..	....	....	....	....	....	....	....	....
Other sectors	4 710 ..	....	....	....	....	....	....	....	....
of which: Short-term	4 712 ..	....	....	....	....	....	....	....	....
Loans	4 714 ..	....	4.3	−1.4	−5.0	11.2	5.3	.9	....
Monetary authorities	4 715 ..	....	....	....	....	....	....	....	....
of which: Short-term	4 718 ..	....	....	....	....	....	....	....	....
General government	4 719 ..	....	....	....	....	....	....	....	....
of which: Short-term	4 721 ..	....	....	....	....	....	....	....	....
Banks	4 722 ..	....	....	....	....	....	....	....	....
of which: Short-term	4 724 ..	....	....	....	....	....	....	....	....
Other sectors	4 725 ..	....	4.3	−1.4	−5.0	11.2	5.3	.9	....
of which: Short-term	4 727 ..	....	....	*−1.4*	....	....	....	....	....
Currency and deposits	4 730 ..	.5	5.7	−.5	−2.6	−9.8	−22.0	15.5	−15.9
Monetary authorities	4 731 ..	.5	....	−.5	−2.1	1.7	−.5	.8	−.4
General government	4 732 ..	....	....	....	....	....	....	....	....
Banks	4 733 ..	....	5.7	....	....	−1.0	−14.1	15.9	−26.5
Other sectors	4 734 ..	....	....	....	−.5	−10.5	−7.4	−1.2	11.0
Other assets	4 736 ..	....	....	....	−.4	−7.6	13.8	5.3	4.1
Monetary authorities	4 737 ..	....	....	....	....	....	....	....	....
of which: Short-term	4 739 ..	....	....	....	....	....	....	....	....
General government	4 740 ..	....	....	....	....	....	....	....	....
of which: Short-term	4 742 ..	....	....	....	....	....	....	....	....
Banks	4 743 ..	....	....	....	....	....	....	....	....
of which: Short-term	4 745 ..	....	....	....	....	....	....	....	....
Other sectors	4 746 ..	....	....	....	−.4	−7.6	13.8	5.3	4.1
of which: Short-term	4 748 ..	....	....	....	*−.4*	*−7.6*	*13.9*	*5.3*	*4.2*
Liabilities	4 753 ..	**28.8**	**45.3**	**63.2**	**−144.0**	**−387.4**	**133.8**	**341.1**	**185.4**
Trade credits	4 756 ..	....	....	....	....	....	1.2	6.7	....
General government	4 757 ..	....	....	....	....	....	....	....	....
of which: Short-term	4 759 ..	....	....	....	....	....	....	....	....
Other sectors	4 760 ..	....	....	....	....	....	1.2	6.7	....
of which: Short-term	4 762 ..	....	....	....	....	....	*−1.4*	*.1*	....
Loans	4 764 ..	82.6	90.7	48.2	−144.4	−.1	98.9	187.0	184.8
Monetary authorities	4 765 ..	−14.8	18.5	12.3	−167.8	....	25.3	96.9	112.1
of which: Use of Fund credit and loans from the Fund	4 766 ..	*−14.8*	*18.5*	*12.3*	*−167.8*	....	*17.8*	*18.8*	*40.7*
of which: Short-term	4 768 ..	....	....	....	....	....	....	....	....
General government	4 769 ..	97.4	54.7	36.0	23.3	−11.8	67.3	80.3	89.1
of which: Short-term	4 771 ..	....	....	....	....	....	....	....	....
Banks	4 772 ..	....	....	....	....	....	....	....	....
of which: Short-term	4 774 ..	....	....	....	....	....	....	....	....
Other sectors	4 775 ..	....	17.4	....	....	11.7	6.2	9.9	−16.4
of which: Short-term	4 777 ..	....	*.2*	....	....	....	....	....	*.3*
Currency and deposits	4 780 ..	....	....	....	....	....	20.0	11.3	−4.4
Monetary authorities	4 781 ..	....	....	....	....	....	....	....	....
General government	4 782 ..	....	....	....	....	....	....	....	....
Banks	4 783 ..	....	....	....	....	....	20.0	11.3	−4.4
Other sectors	4 784 ..	....	....	....	....	....	....	....	....
Other liabilities	4 786 ..	−53.8	−45.4	14.9	.4	−387.3	13.8	136.1	4.9
Monetary authorities	4 787 ..	....	5.5	10.5	4.5	−.2	−.1	128.1	8.4
of which: Short-term	4 789 ..	....	*2.5*	*10.5*	*4.5*	*−.2*	*−.1*	....	*8.4*
General government	4 790 ..	−53.8	−50.8	4.4	−3.8	−390.8	4.2	2.6	−7.7
of which: Short-term	4 792 ..	*−53.8*	*−50.8*	*4.4*	*−3.8*	*−390.8*	*4.2*	*2.6*	*−7.7*
Banks	4 793 ..	....	....	....	....	....	....	....	....
of which: Short-term	4 795 ..	....	....	....	....	....	....	....	....
Other sectors	4 796 ..	....	....	....	−.2	3.7	9.6	5.3	4.2
of which: Short-term	4 798 ..	....	....	....	....	*3.7*	*9.6*	*5.3*	*4.2*
E. RESERVE ASSETS	4 802 ..	**24.3**	**−45.2**	**−56.4**	**−11.4**	**−33.9**	**−9.5**	**−110.5**	**−19.9**
Monetary gold	4 812 ..	....	....	....	....	....	....	....	....
Special drawing rights	4 811 ..	−7.8	−14.6	15.0	5.2	....	−.5	−157.9	2.1
Reserve position in the Fund	4 810 ..	....	....	....	....	....	....	....	....
Foreign exchange	4 803 ..	32.0	−30.6	−71.4	−16.5	−33.9	−9.0	47.5	−22.0
Other claims	4 813 ..	....	....	....	....	....	....	....	....
NET ERRORS AND OMISSIONS	4 998 ..	**−50.3**	**−53.6**	**−58.5**	**−59.4**	**−143.2**	**−21.6**	**−186.0**	**37.4**

Table 3. INTERNATIONAL INVESTMENT POSITION (End-period stocks), 2003–2010

(Millions of U.S. dollars)

	Code	2003	2004	2005	2006	2007	2008	2009	2010
ASSETS	8 995 C.	**65.1**	**131.2**	**188.5**	**256.3**	**376.4**	**367.1**	**525.7**	**569.4**
Direct investment abroad	8 505 ..	....	....	....	....	....	....	....	....
Equity capital and reinvested earnings	8 506 ..	....	....	....	....	....	....	....	....
Claims on affiliated enterprises	8 507 ..	....	....	....	....	....	....	....	....
Liabilities to affiliated enterprises	8 508 ..	....	....	....	....	....	....	....	....
Other capital	8 530 ..	....	....	....	....	....	....	....	....
Claims on affiliated enterprises	8 535 ..	....	....	....	....	....	....	....	....
Liabilities to affiliated enterprises	8 540 ..	....	....	....	....	....	....	....	....
Portfolio investment	8 602 ..	....	....	....	....	....	....	....	....
Equity securities	8 610 ..	....	....	....	....	....	....	....	....
Monetary authorities	8 611 ..	....	....	....	....	....	....	....	....
General government	8 612 ..	....	....	....	....	....	....	....	....
Banks	8 613 ..	....	....	....	....	....	....	....	....
Other sectors	8 614 ..	....	....	....	....	....	....	....	....
Debt securities	8 619 ..	....	....	....	....	....	....	....	....
Bonds and notes	8 620 ..	....	....	....	....	....	....	....	....
Monetary authorities	8 621 ..	....	....	....	....	....	....	....	....
General government	8 622 ..	....	....	....	....	....	....	....	....
Banks	8 623 ..	....	....	....	....	....	....	....	....
Other sectors	8 624 ..	....	....	....	....	....	....	....	....
Money market instruments	8 630 ..	....	....	....	....	....	....	....	....
Monetary authorities	8 631 ..	....	....	....	....	....	....	....	....
General government	8 632 ..	....	....	....	....	....	....	....	....
Banks	8 633 ..	....	....	....	....	....	....	....	....
Other sectors	8 634 ..	....	....	....	....	....	....	....	....
Financial derivatives	8 900 ..	....	....	....	....	....	....	....	....
Monetary authorities	8 901 ..	....	....	....	....	....	....	....	....
General government	8 902 ..	....	....	....	....	....	....	....	....
Banks	8 903 ..	....	....	....	....	....	....	....	....
Other sectors	8 904 ..	....	....	....	....	....	....	....	....
Other investment	8 703 ..	**8.1**	**25.0**	**34.0**	**83.3**	**162.5**	**158.5**	**201.8**	**228.9**
Trade credits	8 706 ..	....	....	....	....	....	....	....	....
General government	8 707 ..	....	....	....	....	....	....	....	....
of which: Short-term	8 709 ..	....	....	....	....	....	....	....	....
Other sectors	8 710 ..	....	....	....	....	....	....	....	....
of which: Short-term	8 712 ..	....	....	....	....	....	....	....	....
Loans	8 714 ..	....	....	....	5.0	11.2	....	....	....
Monetary authorities	8 715 ..	....	....	....	....	....	....	....	....
of which: Short-term	8 718 ..	....	....	....	....	....	....	....	....
General government	8 719 ..	....	....	....	....	....	....	....	....
of which: Short-term	8 721 ..	....	....	....	....	....	....	....	....
Banks	8 722 ..	....	....	....	....	....	....	....	....
of which: Short-term	8 724 ..	....	....	....	....	....	....	....	....
Other sectors	8 725 ..	....	....	....	5.0	11.2	....	....	....
of which: Short-term	8 727 ..	....	....	....	....	....	....	....	....
Currency and deposits	8 730 ..	8.1	25.0	34.0	78.3	151.3	158.5	201.8	228.9
Monetary authorities	8 731 ..	8.1	8.1	7.7	5.5	3.9	3.4	4.2	3.7
General government	8 732 ..	....	....	....	....	....	....	....	....
Banks	8 733 ..	....	16.9	24.3	70.5	116.4	117.0	140.6	167.6
Other sectors	8 734 ..	....	....	2.0	2.2	31.1	38.0	57.0	57.6
Other assets	8 736 ..	....	....	....	....	....	....	....	....
Monetary authorities	8 737 ..	....	....	....	....	....	....	....	....
of which: Short-term	8 739 ..	....	....	....	....	....	....	....	....
General government	8 740 ..	....	....	....	....	....	....	....	....
of which: Short-term	8 742 ..	....	....	....	....	....	....	....	....
Banks	8 743 ..	....	....	....	....	....	....	....	....
of which: Short-term	8 745 ..	....	....	....	....	....	....	....	....
Other sectors	8 746 ..	....	....	....	....	....	....	....	....
of which: Short-term	8 748 ..	....	....	....	....	....	....	....	....
Reserve assets	8 802 ..	**57.0**	**106.2**	**154.6**	**173.0**	**213.9**	**208.7**	**323.9**	**340.5**
Monetary gold	8 812 ..	....	....	....	....	....	....	....	....
Special drawing rights	8 811 ..	34.5	51.0	32.8	29.2	30.7	30.4	189.6	184.2
Reserve position in the Fund	8 810 ..	....	....	....	....	....	....	....	....
Foreign exchange	8 803 ..	22.5	55.2	121.8	143.8	183.2	178.2	134.2	156.3
Other claims	8 813 ..	....	....	....	....	....	....	....	....

Table 3 (Concluded). INTERNATIONAL INVESTMENT POSITION (End-period stocks), 2003–2010

(Millions of U.S. dollars)

	Code	2003	2004	2005	2006	2007	2008	2009	2010
LIABILITIES	8 995 D.	**1,656.4**	**2,098.2**	**2,033.2**	**2,105.4**	**1,075.3**	**1,058.9**	**1,042.0**	**1,209.2**
Direct investment in Sierra Leone	8 555 ..	**47.7**	**355.7**	**299.9**	**453.0**	**612.1**	**490.9**	**236.3**	**264.1**
Equity capital and reinvested earnings	8 556 ..	39.6	167.4	52.6	118.4	74.0	175.8	136.6	102.6
Claims on direct investors	8 557 ..	....	....	....	....	....	....	....	....
Liabilities to direct investors	8 558 ..	39.6	167.4	52.6	118.4	74.0	175.8	136.6	102.6
Other capital	8 580 ..	8.1	188.3	247.3	334.6	538.1	315.1	99.7	161.5
Claims on direct investors	8 585 ..	....	....	....	....	....	....	....	....
Liabilities to direct investors	8 590 ..	8.1	188.3	247.3	334.6	538.1	315.1	99.7	161.5
Portfolio investment	8 652 ..	....	....	....	....	....	**1.6**	**17.5**	**16.1**
Equity securities	8 660 ..	....	....	....	....	....	....	....	....
Banks	8 663 ..	....	....	....	....	....	....	....	....
Other sectors	8 664 ..	....	....	....	....	....	....	....	....
Debt securities	8 669 ..	....	....	....	....	....	1.6	17.5	16.1
Bonds and notes	8 670 ..	....	....	....	....	....	1.6	17.5	16.1
Monetary authorities	8 671 ..	....	....	....	....	....	1.6	17.5	16.1
General government	8 672 ..	....	....	....	....	....	....	....	....
Banks	8 673 ..	....	....	....	....	....	....	....	....
Other sectors	8 674 ..	....	....	....	....	....	....	....	....
Money market instruments	8 680 ..	....	....	....	....	....	....	....	....
Monetary authorities	8 681 ..	....	....	....	....	....	....	....	....
General government	8 682 ..	....	....	....	....	....	....	....	....
Banks	8 683 ..	....	....	....	....	....	....	....	....
Other sectors	8 684 ..	....	....	....	....	....	....	....	....
Financial derivatives	8 905 ..	....	....	....	....	....	....	....	....
Monetary authorities	8 906 ..	....	....	....	....	....	....	....	....
General government	8 907 ..	....	....	....	....	....	....	....	....
Banks	8 908 ..	....	....	....	....	....	....	....	....
Other sectors	8 909 ..	....	....	....	....	....	....	....	....
Other investment	8 753 ..	**1,608.7**	**1,742.5**	**1,733.3**	**1,652.4**	**463.2**	**566.5**	**788.2**	**929.0**
Trade credits	8 756 ..	....	....	....	....	....	....	....	....
General government	8 757 ..	....	....	....	....	....	....	....	....
of which: Short-term	8 759 ..	....	....	....	....	....	....	....	....
Other sectors	8 760 ..	....	....	....	....	....	....	....	....
of which: Short-term	8 762 ..	....	....	....	....	....	....	....	....
Loans	8 764 ..	1,511.0	1,654.9	1,604.1	1,572.1	327.2	419.1	517.2	640.9
Monetary authorities	8 765 ..	169.1	195.8	192.1	34.8	36.5	53.2	73.2	113.0
of which: Use of Fund credit and loans from the Fund	8 766 ..	*169.1*	*195.8*	*192.1*	*34.8*	*36.5*	*53.2*	*73.2*	*113.0*
of which: Short-term	8 768 ..	....	....	....	....	....	....	....	....
General government	8 769 ..	1,341.9	1,427.1	1,412.0	1,537.3	290.7	365.9	444.0	527.9
of which: Short-term	8 771 ..	....	....	....	....	....	....	....	....
Banks	8 772 ..	....	....	....	....	....	....	....	....
of which: Short-term	8 774 ..	....	....	....	....	....	....	....	....
Other sectors	8 775 ..	....	32.1	....	....	....	....	....	....
of which: Short-term	8 777 ..	....	*.7*	....	....	....	....	....	....
Currency and deposits	8 780 ..	97.7	87.6	129.2	80.3	136.0	142.2	110.0	129.8
Monetary authorities	8 781 ..	97.7	87.6	129.2	80.3	136.0	142.2	110.0	129.8
General government	8 782 ..	....	....	....	....	....	....	....	....
Banks	8 783 ..	....	....	....	....	....	....	....	....
Other sectors	8 784 ..	....	....	....	....	....	....	....	....
Other liabilities	8 786 ..	....	....	....	....	....	5.2	161.0	158.3
Monetary authorities	8 787 ..	....	....	....	....	....	....	156.0	153.2
of which: Short-term	8 789 ..	....	....	....	....	....	....	....	....
General government	8 790 ..	....	....	....	....	....	....	....	....
of which: Short-term	8 792 ..	....	....	....	....	....	....	....	....
Banks	8 793 ..	....	....	....	....	....	....	....	....
of which: Short-term	8 795 ..	....	....	....	....	....	....	....	....
Other sectors	8 796 ..	....	....	....	....	....	5.2	5.0	5.1
of which: Short-term	8 798 ..	....	....	....	....	....	....	....	....
NET INTERNATIONAL INVESTMENT POSITION	8 995 ..	−1,591.3	−1,966.9	−1,844.6	−1,849.1	−698.9	−691.8	−516.3	−639.8
Conversion rates: leones per U.S. dollar (end of period)	0 102 ..	2,562.18	2,860.49	2,932.52	2,973.94	2,977.60	3,042.24	3,855.68	4,198.01

Table 1. ANALYTIC PRESENTATION, 2003–2010

(Millions of U.S. dollars)

	Code	2003	2004	2005	2006	2007	2008	2009	2010
A. Current Account[1]	4 993 Z.	**21,789**	**19,143**	**26,429**	**36,099**	**48,384**	**27,887**	**35,207**	**49,558**
Goods: exports f.o.b.	2 100 ..	161,387	199,089	232,551	274,496	303,408	343,931	273,997	358,485
Goods: imports f.o.b.	3 100 ..	−132,360	−168,688	−196,164	−232,309	−256,732	−315,896	−244,619	−311,727
Balance on Goods	4 100 ..	*29,027*	*30,401*	*36,387*	*42,188*	*46,676*	*28,035*	*29,378*	*46,758*
Services: credit	2 200 ..	37,965	48,450	55,674	66,329	85,155	99,435	93,745	112,308
Services: debit	3 200 ..	−40,236	−49,907	−55,233	−65,175	−74,700	−87,545	−79,504	−96,463
Balance on Goods and Services	4 991 ..	*26,756*	*28,944*	*36,829*	*43,341*	*57,131*	*39,924*	*43,620*	*62,603*
Income: credit	2 300 ..	16,950	21,220	29,082	40,814	58,156	48,340	46,036	50,481
Income: debit	3 300 ..	−20,473	−29,444	−37,802	−46,072	−63,861	−56,643	−50,449	−58,711
Balance on Goods, Services, and Income	4 992 ..	*23,233*	*20,720*	*28,108*	*38,082*	*51,425*	*31,621*	*39,206*	*54,373*
Current transfers: credit	2 379 Z.	258	280	304	342	356	402	396	420
Current transfers: debit	3 379 ..	−1,701	−1,856	−1,983	−2,325	−3,397	−4,135	−4,396	−5,235
B. Capital Account[1]	4 994 Z.	**−164**	**−184**	**−202**	**−231**	**−259**	**−308**	**−305**	**−333**
Capital account: credit	2 994 Z.	....	....	....	....	....	....	....	....
Capital account: debit	3 994 ..	....	....	....	....	....	....	....	....
Total, Groups A Plus B	4 981 ..	*21,789*	*19,143*	*26,429*	*36,099*	*48,384*	*27,887*	*35,207*	*49,558*
C. Financial Account[1]	4 995 W.	**−17,939**	**−7,337**	**−16,667**	**−17,147**	**−31,904**	**−13,621**	**−25,383**	**−6,603**
Direct investment abroad	4 505 ..	−2,695	−10,802	−11,218	−18,809	−32,702	256	−18,464	−19,740
Direct investment in Singapore	4 555 Z.	11,941	21,026	15,460	29,348	37,033	8,588	15,279	38,638
Portfolio investment assets	4 602 ..	−11,107	−7,052	−5,422	−16,394	−34,908	−3,562	−14,348	−25,132
Equity securities	4 610 ..	−4,990	−5,659	−8,039	−5,990	−31,529	−8,576	−5,674	−24,707
Debt securities	4 619 ..	−6,118	−1,393	2,616	−10,404	−3,379	5,014	−8,674	−426
Portfolio investment liabilities	4 652 Z.	4,370	1,482	6,255	12,486	19,349	−14,340	−1,152	3,265
Equity securities	4 660 ..	2,785	2,383	4,895	10,142	18,306	−11,697	−324	3,559
Debt securities	4 669 Z.	1,584	−900	1,360	2,344	1,043	−2,643	−828	−293
Financial derivatives	4 910 ..	....	....	....	....	....	....	....	....
Financial derivatives assets	4 900 ..	....	....	....	....	....	....	....	....
Financial derivatives liabilities	4 905 ..	....	....	....	....	....	....	....	....
Other investment assets	4 703 ..	−25,477	−27,939	−33,307	−55,567	−77,074	−51,844	−17,181	−37,339
Monetary authorities	4 701 ..	....	....	....	....	....	....	....	....
General government	4 704 ..	....	....	....	....	....	....	....	....
Banks	4 705 ..	10,657	−5,288	−9,233	−28,929	−9,029	−28,478	−7,501	−3,305
Other sectors	4 728 ..	−36,134	−22,651	−24,074	−26,638	−68,045	−23,366	−9,679	−34,034
Other investment liabilities	4 753 W.	5,029	15,948	11,567	31,789	56,398	47,279	10,484	33,704
Monetary authorities	4 753 WA	5,029	15,948	11,567	13,466	18,301	3,341	2,433	2,558
General government	4 753 ZB	....	....	....	....	....	....	....	....
Banks	4 753 ZC	−9,009	4,419	3,014	24,139	19,885	18,115	1,546	11,442
Other sectors	4 753 ZD	14,038	11,529	8,552	7,649	36,512	29,164	7,801	22,262
Total, Groups A Through C	4 983 ..	*3,851*	*11,807*	*9,763*	*18,952*	*16,480*	*14,265*	*9,824*	*42,955*
D. Net Errors and Omissions	4 998 ..	**3,017**	**570**	**2,754**	**−1,714**	**3,419**	**−890**	**2,288**	**−325**
Total, Groups A Through D	4 984 ..	*6,703*	*12,193*	*12,315*	*17,008*	*19,640*	*13,067*	*11,808*	*42,297*
E. Reserves and Related Items	4 802 A.	**−6,703**	**−12,193**	**−12,315**	**−17,008**	**−19,640**	**−13,067**	**−11,808**	**−42,297**
Reserve assets	4 802 ..	−6,703	−12,193	−12,315	−17,008	−19,640	−13,067	−11,808	−42,297
Use of Fund credit and loans	4 766 ..	....	....	....	....	....	....	....	....
Exceptional financing	4 920 ..	....	....	....	....	....	....	....	....
Conversion rates: Singapore dollars per U.S. dollar	0 101 ..	**1.7422**	**1.6902**	**1.6644**	**1.5889**	**1.5071**	**1.4149**	**1.4545**	**1.3635**

[1] Excludes components that have been classified in the categories of Group E.

Table 2. STANDARD PRESENTATION, 2003–2010

(Millions of U.S. dollars)

	Code	2003	2004	2005	2006	2007	2008	2009	2010
CURRENT ACCOUNT...	4 993 ..	**21,789**	**19,143**	**26,429**	**36,099**	**48,384**	**27,887**	**35,207**	**49,558**
A. GOODS..	4 100 ..	**29,027**	**30,401**	**36,387**	**42,188**	**46,676**	**28,035**	**29,378**	**46,758**
Credit...	2 100 ..	**161,387**	**199,089**	**232,551**	**274,496**	**303,408**	**343,931**	**273,997**	**358,485**
General merchandise: exports f.o.b.	2 110 ..	157,171	194,081	225,611	265,479	291,474	324,003	260,457	338,481
Goods for processing: exports f.o.b.	2 150 ..	....	....	....	....	....	....	....	....
Repairs on goods..............................	2 160 ..	....	....	....	....	....	....	....	....
Goods procured in ports by carriers...............	2 170 ..	4,216	5,008	6,940	9,017	11,934	19,927	13,540	20,004
Nonmonetary gold..............................	2 180 ..	....	....	....	....	....	....	....	....
Debit..	3 100 ..	**−132,360**	**−168,688**	**−196,164**	**−232,309**	**−256,732**	**−315,896**	**−244,619**	**−311,727**
General merchandise: imports f.o.b.	3 110 ..	−131,412	−167,168	−194,131	−229,617	−253,414	−311,295	−241,031	−306,694
Goods for processing: imports f.o.b.	3 150 ..	....	....	....	....	....	....	....	....
Repairs on goods..............................	3 160 ..	....	....	....	....	....	....	....	....
Goods procured in ports by carriers...............	3 170 ..	−948	−1,520	−2,033	−2,692	−3,318	−4,601	−3,588	−5,033
Nonmonetary gold..............................	3 180 ..	....	....	....	....	....	....	....	....
B. SERVICES..	4 200 ..	**−2,271**	**−1,457**	**441**	**1,153**	**10,455**	**11,890**	**14,242**	**15,845**
Total credit.......................................	2 200 ..	*37,965*	*48,450*	*55,674*	*66,329*	*85,155*	*99,435*	*93,745*	*112,308*
Total debit..	3 200 ..	*−40,236*	*−49,907*	*−55,233*	*−65,175*	*−74,700*	*−87,545*	*−79,504*	*−96,463*
Transportation services, credit.....................	2 205 ..	**13,377**	**17,015**	**19,567**	**22,627**	**28,986**	**35,340**	**28,592**	**32,738**
Passenger..	2 850 ..	....	....	....	....	....	....	....	....
Freight...	2 851 ..	*8,731*	*11,272*	*13,041*	*15,824*	*20,897*	*26,647*	*21,607*	*24,581*
Other...	2 852 ..	*4,646*	*5,743*	*6,525*	*6,803*	*8,090*	*8,693*	*6,985*	*8,157*
Sea transport, passenger.....................	2 207 ..	....	....	....	....	....	....	....	....
Sea transport, freight........................	2 208 ..	....	....	....	....	....	....	....	....
Sea transport, other..........................	2 209 ..	....	....	....	....	....	....	....	....
Air transport, passenger......................	2 211 ..	....	....	....	....	....	....	....	....
Air transport, freight.........................	2 212 ..	....	....	....	....	....	....	....	....
Air transport, other..........................	2 213 ..	....	....	....	....	....	....	....	....
Other transport, passenger...................	2 215 ..	....	....	....	....	....	....	....	....
Other transport, freight......................	2 216 ..	....	....	....	....	....	....	....	....
Other transport, other.......................	2 217 ..	....	....	....	....	....	....	....	....
Transportation services, debit.....................	3 205 ..	**−13,058**	**−17,847**	**−20,370**	**−23,830**	**−27,906**	**−30,329**	**−24,702**	**−28,411**
Passenger..	3 850 ..	....	....	....	....	....	....	....	....
Freight...	3 851 ..	*−8,100*	*−11,865*	*−13,728*	*−16,549*	*−19,455*	*−21,092*	*−15,513*	*−18,010*
Other...	3 852 ..	*−4,958*	*−5,983*	*−6,642*	*−7,281*	*−8,451*	*−9,237*	*−9,190*	*−10,401*
Sea transport, passenger.....................	3 207 ..	....	....	....	....	....	....	....	....
Sea transport, freight........................	3 208 ..	....	....	....	....	....	....	....	....
Sea transport, other..........................	3 209 ..	....	....	....	....	....	....	....	....
Air transport, passenger......................	3 211 ..	....	....	....	....	....	....	....	....
Air transport, freight.........................	3 212 ..	....	....	....	....	....	....	....	....
Air transport, other..........................	3 213 ..	....	....	....	....	....	....	....	....
Other transport, passenger...................	3 215 ..	....	....	....	....	....	....	....	....
Other transport, freight......................	3 216 ..	....	....	....	....	....	....	....	....
Other transport, other.......................	3 217 ..	....	....	....	....	....	....	....	....
Travel, credit...................................	2 236 ..	**3,852**	**5,328**	**6,205**	**7,545**	**9,083**	**10,711**	**9,383**	**14,181**
Business travel...............................	2 237 ..	....	....	....	....	....	....	....	....
Personal travel...............................	2 240 ..	....	....	....	....	....	....	....	....
Travel, debit....................................	3 236 ..	**−8,382**	**−9,297**	**−10,070**	**−11,142**	**−13,181**	**−15,197**	**−15,010**	**−16,770**
Business travel...............................	3 237 ..	....	....	....	....	....	....	....	....
Personal travel...............................	3 240 ..	....	....	....	....	....	....	....	....
Other services, credit...........................	2 200 BA	**20,736**	**26,107**	**29,903**	**36,156**	**47,086**	**53,384**	**55,771**	**65,389**
Communications...............................	2 245 ..	413	495	560	742	951	1,212	1,056	1,347
Construction..................................	2 249 ..	426	647	542	555	756	922	928	1,049
Insurance.....................................	2 253 ..	1,229	1,313	1,298	1,441	1,528	1,836	2,403	2,837
Financial.....................................	2 260 ..	3,218	3,719	4,504	6,415	9,594	10,020	9,340	12,182
Computer and information.....................	2 262 ..	401	485	514	883	1,005	1,552	1,585	1,790
Royalties and licence fees....................	2 266 ..	366	727	906	986	1,223	1,355	1,352	1,867
Other business services......................	2 268 ..	14,378	18,369	21,217	24,732	31,575	36,035	38,697	43,851
Personal, cultural, and recreational...........	2 287 ..	154	185	180	203	238	204	179	219
Government, n.i.e.............................	2 291 ..	150	166	182	198	217	247	229	247
Other services, debit............................	3 200 BA	**−18,796**	**−22,762**	**−24,793**	**−30,204**	**−33,612**	**−42,019**	**−39,792**	**−51,282**
Communications...............................	3 245 ..	−718	−769	−889	−1,040	−1,302	−1,466	−1,380	−1,758
Construction..................................	3 249 ..	−142	−325	−203	−188	−256	−347	−442	−500
Insurance.....................................	3 253 ..	−1,613	−1,703	−1,922	−2,182	−2,338	−2,537	−2,662	−3,479
Financial.....................................	3 260 ..	−721	−814	−915	−1,439	−2,274	−2,549	−2,034	−2,369
Computer and information.....................	3 262 ..	−330	−315	−386	−650	−668	−1,069	−1,090	−1,230
Royalties and licence fees....................	3 266 ..	−6,635	−7,918	−9,339	−8,996	−8,962	−12,472	−11,584	−15,857
Other business services......................	3 268 ..	−8,263	−10,472	−10,672	−15,263	−17,328	−21,059	−19,987	−25,418
Personal, cultural, and recreational...........	3 287 ..	−241	−268	−279	−261	−286	−281	−379	−462
Government, n.i.e.............................	3 291 ..	−133	−179	−187	−185	−198	−239	−234	−208

Table 2 (Continued). STANDARD PRESENTATION, 2003–2010

(Millions of U.S. dollars)

	Code	2003	2004	2005	2006	2007	2008	2009	2010
C. INCOME...........................	4 300 ..	**−3,523**	**−8,224**	**−8,720**	**−5,259**	**−5,706**	**−8,304**	**−4,413**	**−8,230**
Total credit...................	2 300 ..	*16,950*	*21,220*	*29,082*	*40,814*	*58,156*	*48,340*	*46,036*	*50,481*
Total debit...................	3 300 ..	*−20,473*	*−29,444*	*−37,802*	*−46,072*	*−63,861*	*−56,643*	*−50,449*	*−58,711*
Compensation of employees, credit...................	2 310 ..	....	....	....	....	....	....	....	....
Compensation of employees, debit...................	3 310 ..	....	....	....	....	....	....	....	....
Investment income, credit...............	2 320 ..	....	....	....	....	....	....	....	....
Direct investment income...................	2 330 ..	....	....	....	....	....	....	....	....
Dividends and distributed branch profits...................	2 332 ..	....	....	....	....	....	....	....	....
Reinvested earnings and undistributed branch profits.....	2 333 ..	....	....	....	....	....	....	....	....
Income on debt (interest)...................	2 334 ..	....	....	....	....	....	....	....	....
Portfolio investment income...................	2 339 ..	....	....	....	....	....	....	....	....
Income on equity...................	2 340 ..	....	....	....	....	....	....	....	....
Income on bonds and notes...................	2 350 ..	....	....	....	....	....	....	....	....
Income on money market instruments...................	2 360 ..	....	....	....	....	....	....	....	....
Other investment income...................	2 370 ..	....	....	....	....	....	....	....	....
Investment income, debit...............	3 320 ..	....	....	....	....	....	....	....	....
Direct investment income...................	3 330 ..	....	....	....	....	....	....	....	....
Dividends and distributed branch profits...................	3 332 ..	....	....	....	....	....	....	....	....
Reinvested earnings and undistributed branch profits.....	3 333 ..	....	....	....	....	....	....	....	....
Income on debt (interest)...................	3 334 ..	....	....	....	....	....	....	....	....
Portfolio investment income...................	3 339 ..	....	....	....	....	....	....	....	....
Income on equity...................	3 340 ..	....	....	....	....	....	....	....	....
Income on bonds and notes...................	3 350 ..	....	....	....	....	....	....	....	....
Income on money market instruments...................	3 360 ..	....	....	....	....	....	....	....	....
Other investment income...................	3 370 ..	....	....	....	....	....	....	....	....
D. CURRENT TRANSFERS...................	4 379 ..	**−1,443**	**−1,576**	**−1,679**	**−1,983**	**−3,041**	**−3,734**	**−4,000**	**−4,815**
Credit...................	2 379 ..	**258**	**280**	**304**	**342**	**356**	**402**	**396**	**420**
General government...................	2 380 ..	10	10	11	17	17	14	7	8
Other sectors...................	2 390 ..	248	270	294	325	339	388	388	412
Workers' remittances...................	2 391 ..	....	....	....	....	....	....	....	....
Other current transfers...................	2 392 ..	....	....	....	....	....	....	....	....
Debit...................	3 379 ..	**−1,701**	**−1,856**	**−1,983**	**−2,325**	**−3,397**	**−4,135**	**−4,396**	**−5,235**
General government...................	3 380 ..	−140	−122	−122	−130	−160	−206	−167	−250
Other sectors...................	3 390 ..	−1,561	−1,735	−1,861	−2,196	−3,238	−3,930	−4,228	−4,985
Workers' remittances...................	3 391 ..	....	....	....	....	....	....	....	....
Other current transfers...................	3 392 ..	....	....	....	....	....	....	....	....
CAPITAL AND FINANCIAL ACCOUNT...................	4 996 ..	**−24,806**	**−19,713**	**−29,183**	**−34,386**	**−51,803**	**−26,997**	**−37,495**	**−49,234**
CAPITAL ACCOUNT...................	4 994 ..	**−164**	**−184**	**−202**	**−231**	**−259**	**−308**	**−305**	**−333**
Total credit...................	2 994 ..	....	....	....	....	....	....	....	....
Total debit...................	3 994 ..	....	....	....	....	....	....	....	....
Capital transfers, credit...................	2 400 ..	....	....	....	....	....	....	....	....
General government...................	2 401 ..	....	....	....	....	....	....	....	....
Debt forgiveness...................	2 402 ..	....	....	....	....	....	....	....	....
Other capital transfers...................	2 410 ..	....	....	....	....	....	....	....	....
Other sectors...................	2 430 ..	....	....	....	....	....	....	....	....
Migrants' transfers...................	2 431 ..	....	....	....	....	....	....	....	....
Debt forgiveness...................	2 432 ..	....	....	....	....	....	....	....	....
Other capital transfers...................	2 440 ..	....	....	....	....	....	....	....	....
Capital transfers, debit...................	3 400 ..	....	....	....	....	....	....	....	....
General government...................	3 401 ..	....	....	....	....	....	....	....	....
Debt forgiveness...................	3 402 ..	....	....	....	....	....	....	....	....
Other capital transfers...................	3 410 ..	....	....	....	....	....	....	....	....
Other sectors...................	3 430 ..	....	....	....	....	....	....	....	....
Migrants' transfers...................	3 431 ..	....	....	....	....	....	....	....	....
Debt forgiveness...................	3 432 ..	....	....	....	....	....	....	....	....
Other capital transfers...................	3 440 ..	....	....	....	....	....	....	....	....
Nonproduced nonfinancial assets, credit...............	2 480 ..	....	....	....	....	....	....	....	....
Nonproduced nonfinancial assets, debit...............	3 480 ..	....	....	....	....	....	....	....	....

Table 2 (Continued). STANDARD PRESENTATION, 2003–2010

(Millions of U.S. dollars)

	Code	2003	2004	2005	2006	2007	2008	2009	2010
FINANCIAL ACCOUNT	4 995	**−24,642**	**−19,530**	**−28,981**	**−34,155**	**−51,544**	**−26,689**	**−37,190**	**−48,900**
A. DIRECT INVESTMENT	4 500	**9,247**	**10,224**	**4,241**	**10,539**	**4,331**	**8,845**	**−3,185**	**18,899**
Direct investment abroad	4 505	**−2,695**	**−10,802**	**−11,218**	**−18,809**	**−32,702**	**256**	**−18,464**	**−19,740**
Equity capital	4 510	−4,754	−6,939	−9,965	−12,311	−23,299	−2,930	−21,622	−17,176
Claims on affiliated enterprises	4 515	....	....	....	....	....	....	....	....
Liabilities to affiliated enterprises	4 520	....	....	....	....	....	....	....	....
Reinvested earnings	4 525	....	....	....	....	....	....	....	....
Other capital	4 530	2,059	−3,863	−1,253	−6,498	−9,403	3,187	3,158	−2,564
Claims on affiliated enterprises	4 535	....	....	....	....	....	....	....	....
Liabilities to affiliated enterprises	4 540	....	....	....	....	....	....	....	....
Direct investment in Singapore	4 555	**11,941**	**21,026**	**15,460**	**29,348**	**37,033**	**8,588**	**15,279**	**38,638**
Equity capital	4 560	11,625	20,720	14,822	28,092	31,875	6,558	13,572	35,520
Claims on direct investors	4 565	....	....	....	....	....	....	....	....
Liabilities to direct investors	4 570	....	....	....	....	....	....	....	....
Reinvested earnings	4 575	....	....	....	....	....	....	....	....
Other capital	4 580	316	307	638	1,256	5,158	2,030	1,707	3,118
Claims on direct investors	4 585	....	....	....	....	....	....	....	....
Liabilities to direct investors	4 590	....	....	....	....	....	....	....	....
B. PORTFOLIO INVESTMENT	4 600	**−6,738**	**−5,570**	**833**	**−3,908**	**−15,559**	**−17,902**	**−15,501**	**−21,867**
Assets	4 602	**−11,107**	**−7,052**	**−5,422**	**−16,394**	**−34,908**	**−3,562**	**−14,348**	**−25,132**
Equity securities	4 610	−4,990	−5,659	−8,039	−5,990	−31,529	−8,576	−5,674	−24,707
Monetary authorities	4 611	....	....	....	....	....	....	....	....
General government	4 612	....	....	....	....	....	....	....	....
Banks	4 613	....	....	....	....	....	....	....	....
Other sectors	4 614	....	....	....	....	....	....	....	....
Debt securities	4 619	−6,118	−1,393	2,616	−10,404	−3,379	5,014	−8,674	−426
Bonds and notes	4 620	....	....	....	....	....	....	....	....
Monetary authorities	4 621	....	....	....	....	....	....	....	....
General government	4 622	....	....	....	....	....	....	....	....
Banks	4 623	....	....	....	....	....	....	....	....
Other sectors	4 624	....	....	....	....	....	....	....	....
Money market instruments	4 630	....	....	....	....	....	....	....	....
Monetary authorities	4 631	....	....	....	....	....	....	....	....
General government	4 632	....	....	....	....	....	....	....	....
Banks	4 633	....	....	....	....	....	....	....	....
Other sectors	4 634	....	....	....	....	....	....	....	....
Liabilities	4 652	**4,370**	**1,482**	**6,255**	**12,486**	**19,349**	**−14,340**	**−1,152**	**3,265**
Equity securities	4 660	2,785	2,383	4,895	10,142	18,306	−11,697	−324	3,559
Banks	4 663	....	....	....	....	....	....	....	....
Other sectors	4 664	....	....	....	....	....	....	....	....
Debt securities	4 669	1,584	−900	1,360	2,344	1,043	−2,643	−828	−293
Bonds and notes	4 670	....	....	....	....	....	....	....	....
Monetary authorities	4 671	....	....	....	....	....	....	....	....
General government	4 672	....	....	....	....	....	....	....	....
Banks	4 673	....	....	....	....	....	....	....	....
Other sectors	4 674	....	....	....	....	....	....	....	....
Money market instruments	4 680	....	....	....	....	....	....	....	....
Monetary authorities	4 681	....	....	....	....	....	....	....	....
General government	4 682	....	....	....	....	....	....	....	....
Banks	4 683	....	....	....	....	....	....	....	....
Other sectors	4 684	....	....	....	....	....	....	....	....
C. FINANCIAL DERIVATIVES	4 910	....	....	....	....	....	....	....	....
Monetary authorities	4 911	....	....	....	....	....	....	....	....
General government	4 912	....	....	....	....	....	....	....	....
Banks	4 913	....	....	....	....	....	....	....	....
Other sectors	4 914	....	....	....	....	....	....	....	....
Assets	4 900	....	....	....	....	....	....	....	....
Monetary authorities	4 901	....	....	....	....	....	....	....	....
General government	4 902	....	....	....	....	....	....	....	....
Banks	4 903	....	....	....	....	....	....	....	....
Other sectors	4 904	....	....	....	....	....	....	....	....
Liabilities	4 905	....	....	....	....	....	....	....	....
Monetary authorities	4 906	....	....	....	....	....	....	....	....
General government	4 907	....	....	....	....	....	....	....	....
Banks	4 908	....	....	....	....	....	....	....	....
Other sectors	4 909	....	....	....	....	....	....	....	....

Table 2 (Concluded). STANDARD PRESENTATION, 2003–2010

(Millions of U.S. dollars)

	Code	2003	2004	2005	2006	2007	2008	2009	2010
D. OTHER INVESTMENT	4 700	−20,447	−11,991	−21,741	−23,778	−20,676	−4,564	−6,696	−3,635
Assets	4 703	−25,477	−27,939	−33,307	−55,567	−77,074	−51,844	−17,181	−37,339
Trade credits	4 706	−19,301	−8,280	195	224	−765	3,649	−7,561	−5,452
General government	4 707	....	....	....	....	....	....	....	....
of which: Short-term	4 709	....	....	....	....	....	....	....	....
Other sectors	4 710	−19,301	−8,280	195	224	−765	3,649	−7,561	−5,452
of which: Short-term	4 712	−19,301	−8,280	195	224	−765	3,649	−7,561	−5,452
Loans	4 714	9,549	−5,640	−11,745	−27,395	−6,562	−29,870	−5,151	6,983
Monetary authorities	4 715	....	....	....	....	....	....	....	....
of which: Short-term	4 718	....	....	....	....	....	....	....	....
General government	4 719	....	....	....	....	....	....	....	....
of which: Short-term	4 721	....	....	....	....	....	....	....	....
Banks	4 722	10,627	−3,482	−9,308	−25,340	−5,047	−23,147	−4,714	9,880
of which: Short-term	4 724	11,037	−3,197	−8,311	−24,350	−2,849	−21,505	−3,874	11,488
Other sectors	4 725	−1,078	−2,158	−2,437	−2,055	−1,515	−6,723	−437	−2,897
of which: Short-term	4 727	−1,313	−2,495	−530	−1,212	2,280	−5,607	−1,122	−1,311
Currency and deposits	4 730	−5,900	−1,181	−11,916	−13,013	−25,572	1,538	1,009	−6,668
Monetary authorities	4 731	....	....	....	....	....	....	....	....
General government	4 732	....	....	....	....	....	....	....	....
Banks	4 733	31	−9	−1	−1	−8	−10	−14	20
Other sectors	4 734	−5,931	−1,172	−11,915	−13,011	−25,563	1,547	1,023	−6,688
Other assets	4 736	−9,824	−12,839	−9,842	−15,383	−44,175	−27,160	−5,478	−32,202
Monetary authorities	4 737	....	....	....	....	....	....	....	....
of which: Short-term	4 739	....	....	....	....	....	....	....	....
General government	4 740	....	....	....	....	....	....	....	....
of which: Short-term	4 742	....	....	....	....	....	....	....	....
Banks	4 743	−1	−1,798	75	−3,587	−3,974	−5,320	−2,773	−13,206
of which: Short-term	4 745	−278	−778	−57	−172	−1,064	−334	−1,555	−5,702
Other sectors	4 746	−9,823	−11,042	−9,917	−11,796	−40,202	−21,839	−2,704	−18,996
of which: Short-term	4 748	218	40	−28	−120	−288	328	548	−92
Liabilities	4 753	5,029	15,948	11,567	31,789	56,398	47,279	10,484	33,704
Trade credits	4 756	10,730	8,172	−1,130	−782	2,653	−4,966	7,214	7,554
General government	4 757	....	....	....	....	....	....	....	....
of which: Short-term	4 759	....	....	....	....	....	....	....	....
Other sectors	4 760	10,730	8,172	−1,130	−782	2,653	−4,966	7,214	7,554
of which: Short-term	4 762	10,730	8,172	−1,130	−782	2,653	−4,966	7,214	7,554
Loans	4 764	−8,453	8,842	11,463	25,062	40,939	23,899	11,311	23,730
Monetary authorities	4 765	....	....	....	....	....	....	....	....
of which: Use of Fund credit and loans from the Fund	4 766	....	....	....	....	....	....	....	....
of which: Short-term	4 768	....	....	....	....	....	....	....	....
General government	4 769	....	....	....	....	....	....	....	....
of which: Short-term	4 771	....	....	....	....	....	....	....	....
Banks	4 772	−8,500	4,660	1,194	18,243	14,370	13,152	−1,705	8,848
of which: Short-term	4 774	−8,730	4,621	1,185	18,089	14,249	13,045	−1,684	8,775
Other sectors	4 775	47	4,183	10,270	6,818	26,570	10,747	13,016	14,881
of which: Short-term	4 777	1,339	3,081	10,577	348	19,591	2,714	10,092	9,736
Currency and deposits	4 780	−101	875	1,750	5,497	4,941	−81	4,282	3,158
Monetary authorities	4 781	....	....	....	....	....	....	....	....
General government	4 782	....	....	....	....	....	....	....	....
Banks	4 783	−101	875	1,750	5,497	4,941	−81	4,282	3,158
Other sectors	4 784	....	....	....	....	....	....	....	....
Other liabilities	4 786	2,853	−1,941	−517	2,011	7,864	28,427	−12,323	−737
Monetary authorities	4 787	....	....	....	....	....	....	1,137	....
of which: Short-term	4 789	....	....	....	....	....	....	....	....
General government	4 790	....	....	....	....	....	....	....	....
of which: Short-term	4 792	....	....	....	....	....	....	....	....
Banks	4 793	−408	−1,116	71	399	574	5,044	−1,032	−564
of which: Short-term	4 795	....	4	5	−8	6	−5	8	5
Other sectors	4 796	3,261	−825	−587	1,613	7,290	23,382	−12,428	−173
of which: Short-term	4 798	1,474	4,806	−669	1,496	7,305	23,478	−13,536	−790
E. RESERVE ASSETS	4 802	−6,703	−12,193	−12,315	−17,008	−19,640	−13,067	−11,808	−42,297
Monetary gold	4 812	....	....	....	....	....	....	....	....
Special drawing rights	4 811	−13	−73	−16	−16	−17	−28	−1,156	−17
Reserve position in the Fund	4 810	−39	142	236	51	45	−85	−82	−40
Foreign exchange	4 803	−6,652	−12,262	−12,535	−17,043	−19,668	−12,955	−10,569	−42,240
Other claims	4 813	....	....	....	....	....	....	....	....
NET ERRORS AND OMISSIONS	4 998	3,017	570	2,754	−1,714	3,419	−890	2,288	−325

Table 3. INTERNATIONAL INVESTMENT POSITION (End-period stocks), 2003–2010

(Millions of U.S. dollars)

	Code	2003	2004	2005	2006	2007	2008	2009	2010
ASSETS	8 995 C.	**575,456**	**661,707**	**733,726**	**959,525**	**1,209,152**	**1,118,487**	**1,320,777**	**1,646,256**
Direct investment abroad	8 505	**119,335**	**142,290**	**157,300**	**208,570**	**266,006**	**238,236**	**267,842**	**317,927**
Equity capital and reinvested earnings	8 506	96,608	114,100	126,477	167,173	220,429	195,859	224,016	265,048
Claims on affiliated enterprises	8 507	....	....	....	....	....	....	....	....
Liabilities to affiliated enterprises	8 508	....	....	....	....	....	....	....	....
Other capital	8 530	22,727	28,189	30,823	41,397	45,577	42,376	43,826	52,879
Claims on affiliated enterprises	8 535	....	....	....	....	....	....	....	....
Liabilities to affiliated enterprises	8 540	....	....	....	....	....	....	....	....
Portfolio investment	8 602	**160,542**	**180,098**	**205,068**	**284,379**	**375,201**	**263,911**	**403,853**	**564,388**
Equity securities	8 610	88,405	99,157	120,960	170,079	243,698	163,876	258,496	393,456
Monetary authorities	8 611	....	....	....	....	....	....	....	....
General government	8 612	....	....	....	....	....	....	....	....
Banks	8 613	....	....	....	....	....	....	....	....
Other sectors	8 614	....	....	....	....	....	....	....	....
Debt securities	8 619	72,137	80,941	84,108	114,299	131,503	100,035	145,357	170,931
Bonds and notes	8 620	....	....	....	....	....	....	....	....
Monetary authorities	8 621	....	....	....	....	....	....	....	....
General government	8 622	....	....	....	....	....	....	....	....
Banks	8 623	....	....	....	....	....	....	....	....
Other sectors	8 624	....	....	....	....	....	....	....	....
Money market instruments	8 630	....	....	....	....	....	....	....	....
Monetary authorities	8 631	....	....	....	....	....	....	....	....
General government	8 632	....	....	....	....	....	....	....	....
Banks	8 633	....	....	....	....	....	....	....	....
Other sectors	8 634	....	....	....	....	....	....	....	....
Financial derivatives	8 900	....	....	....	....	....	....	....	....
Monetary authorities	8 901	....	....	....	....	....	....	....	....
General government	8 902	....	....	....	....	....	....	....	....
Banks	8 903	....	....	....	....	....	....	....	....
Other sectors	8 904	....	....	....	....	....	....	....	....
Other investment	8 703	**199,711**	**227,026**	**255,499**	**330,301**	**405,201**	**442,392**	**460,999**	**539,512**
Trade credits	8 706	51,297	61,966	60,639	68,168	80,369	76,894	86,691	100,269
General government	8 707	....	....	....	....	....	....	....	....
of which: Short-term	8 709	....	....	....	....	....	....	....	....
Other sectors	8 710	....	....	....	....	....	....	....	....
of which: Short-term	8 712	....	....	....	....	....	....	....	....
Loans	8 714	53,973	62,056	72,725	106,439	119,811	147,871	156,626	163,330
Monetary authorities	8 715	....	....	....	....	....	....	....	....
of which: Short-term	8 718	....	....	....	....	....	....	....	....
General government	8 719	....	....	....	....	....	....	....	....
of which: Short-term	8 721	....	....	....	....	....	....	....	....
Banks	8 722	....	....	....	....	....	....	....	....
of which: Short-term	8 724	....	....	....	....	....	....	....	....
Other sectors	8 725	....	....	....	....	....	....	....	....
of which: Short-term	8 727	....	....	....	....	....	....	....	....
Currency and deposits	8 730	71,294	75,495	83,937	103,390	138,104	134,689	141,215	164,232
Monetary authorities	8 731	....	....	....	....	....	....	....	....
General government	8 732	....	....	....	....	....	....	....	....
Banks	8 733	....	....	....	....	....	....	....	....
Other sectors	8 734	....	....	....	....	....	....	....	....
Other assets	8 736	23,147	27,509	38,198	52,303	66,917	82,938	76,467	111,680
Monetary authorities	8 737	....	....	....	....	....	....	....	....
of which: Short-term	8 739	....	....	....	....	....	....	....	....
General government	8 740	....	....	....	....	....	....	....	....
of which: Short-term	8 742	....	....	....	....	....	....	....	....
Banks	8 743	....	....	....	....	....	....	....	....
of which: Short-term	8 745	....	....	....	....	....	....	....	....
Other sectors	8 746	....	....	....	....	....	....	....	....
of which: Short-term	8 748	....	....	....	....	....	....	....	....
Reserve assets	8 802	**95,869**	**112,293**	**115,859**	**136,275**	**162,743**	**173,948**	**188,083**	**224,430**
Monetary gold	8 812	....	....	....	....	....	....	....	....
Special drawing rights	8 811	207	293	285	316	350	370	1,537	1,527
Reserve position in the Fund	8 810	564	440	174	130	90	174	262	297
Foreign exchange	8 803	....	....	....	....	....	....	....	....
Other claims	8 813	....	....	....	....	....	....	....	....

Table 3 (Concluded). INTERNATIONAL INVESTMENT POSITION (End-period stocks), 2003–2010

(Millions of U.S. dollars)

	Code	2003	2004	2005	2006	2007	2008	2009	2010
LIABILITIES	8 995 D.	**379,762**	**442,478**	**478,688**	**626,362**	**851,248**	**822,681**	**909,333**	**1,117,420**
Direct investment in Singapore	8 555	**157,889**	**185,384**	**200,414**	**250,160**	**338,750**	**353,007**	**393,876**	**461,417**
Equity capital and reinvested earnings	8 556	147,434	175,086	190,255	235,823	318,984	322,440	360,932	429,842
Claims on direct investors	8 557	....	....	....	....	....	....	....	....
Liabilities to direct investors	8 558	....	....	....	....	....	....	....	....
Other capital	8 580	10,455	10,298	10,160	14,337	19,766	30,567	32,944	31,575
Claims on direct investors	8 585	....	....	....	....	....	....	....	....
Liabilities to direct investors	8 590	....	....	....	....	....	....	....	....
Portfolio investment	8 652	**60,697**	**73,061**	**85,882**	**127,975**	**181,933**	**86,478**	**117,157**	**190,803**
Equity securities	8 660	47,719	59,943	72,715	112,870	165,137	72,007	103,373	175,272
Banks	8 663	....	....	....	....	....	....	....	....
Other sectors	8 664	....	....	....	....	....	....	....	....
Debt securities	8 669	12,978	13,118	13,167	15,105	16,795	14,472	13,784	15,530
Bonds and notes	8 670	....	....	....	....	....	....	....	....
Monetary authorities	8 671	....	....	....	....	....	....	....	....
General government	8 672	....	....	....	....	....	....	....	....
Banks	8 673	....	....	....	....	....	....	....	....
Other sectors	8 674	....	....	....	....	....	....	....	....
Money market instruments	8 680	....	....	....	....	....	....	....	....
Monetary authorities	8 681	....	....	....	....	....	....	....	....
General government	8 682	....	....	....	....	....	....	....	....
Banks	8 683	....	....	....	....	....	....	....	....
Other sectors	8 684	....	....	....	....	....	....	....	....
Financial derivatives	8 905	....	....	....	....	....	....	....	....
Monetary authorities	8 906	....	....	....	....	....	....	....	....
General government	8 907	....	....	....	....	....	....	....	....
Banks	8 908	....	....	....	....	....	....	....	....
Other sectors	8 909	....	....	....	....	....	....	....	....
Other investment	8 753	**161,176**	**184,033**	**192,392**	**248,227**	**330,566**	**383,196**	**398,300**	**465,200**
Trade credits	8 756	41,406	51,559	49,487	54,241	71,602	66,819	76,000	90,842
General government	8 757	....	....	....	....	....	....	....	....
of which: Short-term	8 759	....	....	....	....	....	....	....	....
Other sectors	8 760	....	....	....	....	....	....	....	....
of which: Short-term	8 762	....	....	....	....	....	....	....	....
Loans	8 764	100,071	113,129	122,781	162,465	212,498	242,137	255,613	299,300
Monetary authorities	8 765	....	....	....	....	....	....	....	....
of which: Use of Fund credit and loans from the Fund	8 766	....	....	....	....	....	....	....	....
of which: Short-term	8 768	....	....	....	....	....	....	....	....
General government	8 769	....	....	....	....	....	....	....	....
of which: Short-term	8 771	....	....	....	....	....	....	....	....
Banks	8 772	....	....	....	....	....	....	....	....
of which: Short-term	8 774	....	....	....	....	....	....	....	....
Other sectors	8 775	....	....	....	....	....	....	....	....
of which: Short-term	8 777	....	....	....	....	....	....	....	....
Currency and deposits	8 780	7,759	8,923	10,411	16,324	22,071	21,865	26,926	32,607
Monetary authorities	8 781	....	....	....	....	....	....	....	....
General government	8 782	....	....	....	....	....	....	....	....
Banks	8 783	....	....	....	....	....	....	....	....
Other sectors	8 784	....	....	....	....	....	....	....	....
Other liabilities	8 786	11,940	10,421	9,713	15,197	24,395	52,375	39,761	42,452
Monetary authorities	8 787	....	....	....	....	....	....	....	....
of which: Short-term	8 789	....	....	....	....	....	....	....	....
General government	8 790	....	....	....	....	....	....	....	....
of which: Short-term	8 792	....	....	....	....	....	....	....	....
Banks	8 793	....	....	....	....	....	....	....	....
of which: Short-term	8 795	....	....	....	....	....	....	....	....
Other sectors	8 796	....	....	....	....	....	....	....	....
of which: Short-term	8 798	....	....	....	....	....	....	....	....
NET INTERNATIONAL INVESTMENT POSITION	8 995	**195,694**	**219,229**	**255,038**	**333,164**	**357,904**	**295,805**	**411,444**	**528,837**
Conversion rates: Singapore dollars per U.S. dollar (end of period)	0 102	**1.7008**	**1.6338**	**1.6642**	**1.5336**	**1.4412**	**1.4392**	**1.4034**	**1.2875**

Table 1. ANALYTIC PRESENTATION, 2003–2010

(Millions of U.S. dollars)

	Code	2003	2004	2005	2006	2007	2008	2009	2010
A. Current Account[1].....................	4 993 Z.	**−282**	**−3,296**	**−4,005**	**−3,937**	**−4,103**	**−6,185**	**−3,161**	**−3,009**
Goods: exports f.o.b...................	2 100 ..	21,944	27,663	31,851	41,735	57,806	70,271	55,516	64,665
Goods: imports f.o.b..................	3 100 ..	−22,593	−29,220	−34,214	−44,283	−58,715	−71,170	−54,142	−64,484
Balance on Goods......................	4 100 ..	*−649*	*−1,557*	*−2,363*	*−2,549*	*−909*	*−899*	*1,374*	*182*
Services: credit......................	2 200 ..	3,297	3,735	4,405	5,436	7,063	8,493	6,308	5,829
Services: debit.......................	3 200 ..	−3,056	−3,466	−4,078	−4,675	−6,531	−9,178	−8,037	−6,817
Balance on Goods and Services......	4 991 ..	*−408*	*−1,288*	*−2,036*	*−1,787*	*−376*	*−1,584*	*−355*	*−806*
Income: credit......................	2 300 ..	907	1,002	1,585	1,959	2,340	3,392	2,744	3,081
Income: debit.......................	3 300 ..	−1,026	−3,184	−3,570	−4,051	−5,628	−6,737	−4,585	−4,739
Balance on Goods, Services, and Income........	4 992 ..	*−527*	*−3,470*	*−4,021*	*−3,880*	*−3,665*	*−4,928*	*−2,196*	*−2,465*
Current transfers: credit..............	2 379 Z.	537	890	1,403	1,623	2,070	2,523	1,859	1,426
Current transfers: debit...............	3 379 ..	−292	−717	−1,386	−1,681	−2,508	−3,781	−2,824	−1,970
B. Capital Account[1].....................	4 994 Z.	**102**	**135**	**−18**	**−42**	**465**	**1,154**	**624**	**1,372**
Capital account: credit................	2 994 Z.	195	148	16	37	686	1,235	706	1,436
Capital account: debit................	3 994 ..	−93	−14	−33	−79	−221	−81	−82	−64
Total, Groups A Plus B...............	4 981 ..	*−180*	*−3,162*	*−4,022*	*−3,979*	*−3,637*	*−5,032*	*−2,537*	*−1,637*
C. Financial Account[1]...................	4 995 W.	**1,661**	**4,838**	**6,219**	**1,155**	**7,023**	**7,195**	**4,732**	**−644**
Direct investment abroad..............	4 505 ..	−24	13	−145	−368	−403	−251	−410	−319
Direct investment in Slovak Republic....	4 555 Z.	559	3,037	2,411	4,167	3,363	3,231	−32	553
Portfolio investment assets............	4 602 ..	−742	−829	−691	−186	−1,083	634	−2,685	−3,393
Equity securities..................	4 610 ..	−347	−40	103	−309	−271	421	−4	−270
Debt securities...................	4 619 ..	−395	−789	−794	123	−811	213	−2,681	−3,123
Portfolio investment liabilities.........	4 652 Z.	168	1,680	−246	1,741	349	1,796	1,513	1,866
Equity securities..................	4 660 ..	59	−94	137	36	232	103	182	25
Debt securities...................	4 669 Z.	109	1,774	−382	1,705	117	1,693	1,330	1,841
Financial derivatives..................	4 910 ..	17	20	−35	−163	52	−153	354	−142
Financial derivatives assets............	4 900 ..	−43	−149	−98	−442	265	−409	585	−76
Financial derivatives liabilities.........	4 905 ..	60	169	64	279	−213	255	−231	−65
Other investment assets...............	4 703 ..	−20	−123	−498	−1,020	−1,535	−974	−3,857	−461
Monetary authorities...............	4 701 ..	....	....	....	....	....	....	−767	−53
General government................	4 704 ..	58	15	15	12	....	....	....	....
Banks...........................	4 705 ..	114	170	−349	−610	−1,282	−209	−2,650	118
Other sectors.....................	4 728 ..	−192	−308	−164	−421	−253	−765	−441	−527
Other investment liabilities............	4 753 W.	1,703	1,040	5,422	−3,017	6,281	2,912	9,849	1,252
Monetary authorities...............	4 753 WA	618	−928	93	152	−111	11	19,710	−402
General government................	4 753 ZB	−30	9	−992	−115	−39	48	−72	−176
Banks...........................	4 753 ZC	1,260	2,247	5,369	−4,411	4,892	2,764	−10,146	992
Other sectors.....................	4 753 ZD	−146	−288	952	1,357	1,539	88	357	839
Total, Groups A Through C.............	4 983 ..	*1,481*	*1,676*	*2,197*	*−2,824*	*3,386*	*2,163*	*2,195*	*−2,281*
D. Net Errors and Omissions.............	4 998 ..	**27**	**56**	**324**	**167**	**302**	**−2,312**	**−2,366**	**2,317**
Total, Groups A Through D.............	4 984 ..	*1,508*	*1,732*	*2,521*	*−2,656*	*3,688*	*−149*	*−171*	*37*
E. Reserves and Related Items............	4 802 A.	**−1,508**	**−1,732**	**−2,521**	**2,656**	**−3,688**	**149**	**171**	**−37**
Reserve assets.......................	4 802 ..	−1,508	−1,732	−2,521	2,656	−3,688	149	171	−37
Use of Fund credit and loans...........	4 766 ..	....	....	....	....	....	....	....	....
Exceptional financing.................	4 920 ..	....	....	....	....	....	....	....	....
Conversion rates: Slovak koruny per U.S. dollar....	0 101 ..	**36.8**	**32.3**	**31.0**	**29.7**	**24.7**	**21.4**	**....**	**....**
Conversion rates: euros per U.S. dollar.................	0 103 ..	**.8860**	**.8054**	**.8041**	**.7971**	**.7306**	**.6827**	**.7198**	**.7550**

[1] Excludes components that have been classified in the categories of Group E.

Table 2. STANDARD PRESENTATION, 2003–2010

(Millions of U.S. dollars)

	Code	2003	2004	2005	2006	2007	2008	2009	2010
CURRENT ACCOUNT	4 993	**−282**	**−3,296**	**−4,005**	**−3,937**	**−4,103**	**−6,185**	**−3,161**	**−3,009**
A. GOODS	4 100	−649	−1,557	−2,363	−2,549	−909	−899	1,374	182
Credit	2 100	**21,944**	**27,663**	**31,851**	**41,735**	**57,806**	**70,271**	**55,516**	**64,665**
General merchandise: exports f.o.b.	2 110	11,727	....	....	....	....	....	....	....
Goods for processing: exports f.o.b.	2 150	10,191	....	....	....	....	....	....	....
Repairs on goods	2 160	21	....	....	....	....	....	....	....
Goods procured in ports by carriers	2 170	....	....	....	....	....	....	....	....
Nonmonetary gold	2 180	5	....	....	....	....	....	....	....
Debit	3 100	**−22,593**	**−29,220**	**−34,214**	**−44,283**	**−58,715**	**−71,170**	**−54,142**	**−64,484**
General merchandise: imports f.o.b.	3 110	−16,103	....	....	....	....	....	....	....
Goods for processing: imports f.o.b.	3 150	−6,447	....	....	....	....	....	....	....
Repairs on goods	3 160	−40	....	....	....	....	....	....	....
Goods procured in ports by carriers	3 170	....	....	....	....	....	....	....	....
Nonmonetary gold	3 180	−3	....	....	....	....	....	....	....
B. SERVICES	4 200	**241**	**269**	**327**	**761**	**532**	**−685**	**−1,729**	**−988**
Total credit	2 200	*3,297*	*3,735*	*4,405*	*5,436*	*7,063*	*8,493*	*6,308*	*5,829*
Total debit	3 200	*−3,056*	*−3,466*	*−4,078*	*−4,675*	*−6,531*	*−9,178*	*−8,037*	*−6,817*
Transportation services, credit	2 205	**1,413**	**1,493**	**1,596**	**1,913**	**2,254**	**2,914**	**1,874**	**1,790**
Passenger	2 850	*11*	*26*	*72*	*134*	*326*	*415*	*198*	*107*
Freight	2 851	*637*	*1,326*	*1,415*	*1,663*	*1,811*	*2,269*	*1,523*	*1,451*
Other	2 852	*764*	*141*	*109*	*117*	*117*	*229*	*153*	*232*
Sea transport, passenger	2 207	....	....	....	....	....	....	....	....
Sea transport, freight	2 208	1	1	3	3	5	....	....	....
Sea transport, other	2 209	....	....	....	....	....	....	....	....
Air transport, passenger	2 211	6	21	66	119	313	344	180	49
Air transport, freight	2 212	2	10	18	20	41	12	3	17
Air transport, other	2 213	....	....	....	....	....	....	....	....
Other transport, passenger	2 215	5	5	6	14	14	71	18	58
Other transport, freight	2 216	634	1,316	1,394	1,639	1,765	2,257	1,520	1,434
Other transport, other	2 217	764	141	109	117	117	229	153	232
Transportation services, debit	3 205	**−898**	**−998**	**−1,204**	**−1,192**	**−1,840**	**−2,466**	**−1,741**	**−1,878**
Passenger	3 850	*−89*	*−155*	*−278*	*−170*	*−292*	*−431*	*−151*	*−202*
Freight	3 851	*−659*	*−563*	*−588*	*−685*	*−902*	*−966*	*−733*	*−678*
Other	3 852	*−150*	*−280*	*−337*	*−337*	*−646*	*−1,069*	*−857*	*−998*
Sea transport, passenger	3 207	....	....	....	....	....	....	....	....
Sea transport, freight	3 208	−35	−47	−49	−59	−90	....	....	....
Sea transport, other	3 209	....	....	....	....	....	....	....	....
Air transport, passenger	3 211	−84	−151	−274	−161	−280	−420	−123	−167
Air transport, freight	3 212	−11	−17	−36	−28	−32	−42	−45	−42
Air transport, other	3 213	....	....	....	....	....	....	....	....
Other transport, passenger	3 215	−5	−3	−5	−9	−12	−11	−28	−35
Other transport, freight	3 216	−614	−499	−503	−598	−780	−924	−688	−636
Other transport, other	3 217	−150	−280	−337	−337	−646	−1,069	−857	−998
Travel, credit	2 236	**865**	**905**	**1,210**	**1,521**	**2,026**	**2,589**	**2,341**	**2,228**
Business travel	2 237	....	....	....	....	....	....	....	....
Personal travel	2 240	865	....	....	....	....	....	....	....
Travel, debit	3 236	**−573**	**−744**	**−844**	**−1,060**	**−1,533**	**−2,165**	**−2,098**	**−1,944**
Business travel	3 237	−28	....	....	....	....	....	....	....
Personal travel	3 240	−544	....	....	....	....	....	....	....
Other services, credit	2 200 BA	**1,020**	**1,336**	**1,600**	**2,001**	**2,783**	**2,991**	**2,093**	**1,810**
Communications	2 245	76	83	114	259	257	312	216	190
Construction	2 249	86	114	118	86	122	183	125	163
Insurance	2 253	18	19	18	25	63	43	73	38
Financial	2 260	58	87	139	136	272	205	314	44
Computer and information	2 262	84	116	116	170	210	303	286	344
Royalties and licence fees	2 266	50	60	75	90	149	164	92	45
Other business services	2 268	552	715	870	1,054	1,338	1,623	914	905
Personal, cultural, and recreational	2 287	69	121	123	148	331	100	54	70
Government, n.i.e.	2 291	28	22	25	33	41	58	19	11
Other services, debit	3 200 BA	**−1,585**	**−1,724**	**−2,030**	**−2,423**	**−3,157**	**−4,547**	**−4,198**	**−2,994**
Communications	3 245	−67	−72	−73	−98	−149	−229	−246	−146
Construction	3 249	−69	−160	−186	−226	−306	−507	−385	−473
Insurance	3 253	−102	−129	−115	−136	−136	−132	−170	−290
Financial	3 260	−161	−136	−250	−341	−482	−857	−960	−273
Computer and information	3 262	−123	−172	−181	−200	−238	−331	−311	−245
Royalties and licence fees	3 266	−91	−99	−94	−107	−124	−182	−155	−147
Other business services	3 268	−829	−793	−975	−1,125	−1,501	−2,071	−1,738	−1,251
Personal, cultural, and recreational	3 287	−98	−112	−92	−120	−139	−144	−159	−133
Government, n.i.e.	3 291	−45	−51	−63	−70	−82	−94	−73	−35

Table 2 (Continued). STANDARD PRESENTATION, 2003–2010

(Millions of U.S. dollars)

	Code	2003	2004	2005	2006	2007	2008	2009	2010
C. INCOME	4 300	**−119**	**−2,181**	**−1,985**	**−2,092**	**−3,288**	**−3,344**	**−1,841**	**−1,658**
Total credit	2 300	*907*	*1,002*	*1,585*	*1,959*	*2,340*	*3,392*	*2,744*	*3,081*
Total debit	3 300	*−1,026*	*−3,184*	*−3,570*	*−4,051*	*−5,628*	*−6,737*	*−4,585*	*−4,739*
Compensation of employees, credit	2 310	**425**	**529**	**946**	**1,088**	**1,483**	**1,973**	**1,671**	**1,591**
Compensation of employees, debit	3 310	**−16**	**−22**	**−39**	**−48**	**−73**	**−144**	**−138**	**−70**
Investment income, credit	2 320	**482**	**473**	**639**	**871**	**857**	**1,419**	**1,073**	**1,489**
Direct investment income	2 330	21	89	31	108	125	175	114	122
Dividends and distributed branch profits	2 332	19	6	21	35	44	62	90	296
Reinvested earnings and undistributed branch profits	2 333	....	78	3	40	49	56	−40	−248
Income on debt (interest)	2 334	2	4	7	33	33	57	64	74
Portfolio investment income	2 339	404	315	478	637	622	1,069	636	1,062
Income on equity	2 340	1	....	....	....	....	16	9	13
Income on bonds and notes	2 350	402	....	....	....	....	1,052	627	1,049
Income on money market instruments	2 360	1	....	....	....	....	....	....	....
Other investment income	2 370	56	69	130	126	109	176	324	305
Investment income, debit	3 320	**−1,011**	**−3,162**	**−3,531**	**−4,004**	**−5,555**	**−6,593**	**−4,447**	**−4,669**
Direct investment income	3 330	−178	−2,511	−2,715	−3,175	−4,623	−4,697	−3,797	−3,724
Dividends and distributed branch profits	3 332	−167	−844	−1,770	−2,179	−3,360	−3,416	−2,705	−2,747
Reinvested earnings and undistributed branch profits	3 333	−2	−1,614	−875	−831	−992	−846	−696	−594
Income on debt (interest)	3 334	−9	−53	−70	−165	−270	−436	−397	−382
Portfolio investment income	3 339	−529	−345	−406	−384	−361	−1,019	−316	−446
Income on equity	3 340	−7	....	....	....	....	−18	−23	−20
Income on bonds and notes	3 350	−517	....	....	....	....	−1,001	−293	−426
Income on money market instruments	3 360	−5	....	....	....	....	....	....	....
Other investment income	3 370	−304	−306	−410	−444	−571	−878	−334	−500
D. CURRENT TRANSFERS	4 379	**245**	**174**	**16**	**−58**	**−438**	**−1,257**	**−965**	**−544**
Credit	2 379	**537**	**890**	**1,403**	**1,623**	**2,070**	**2,523**	**1,859**	**1,426**
General government	2 380	2	355	706	834	761	694	838	971
Other sectors	2 390	535	535	697	789	1,309	1,829	1,021	455
Workers' remittances	2 391	....	....	....	....	....	....	....	....
Other current transfers	2 392	535	....	....	....	....	....	....	....
Debit	3 379	**−292**	**−717**	**−1,386**	**−1,681**	**−2,508**	**−3,781**	**−2,824**	**−1,970**
General government	3 380	−15	−291	−496	−558	−737	−930	−1,140	−874
Other sectors	3 390	−277	−426	−891	−1,123	−1,771	−2,851	−1,684	−1,096
Workers' remittances	3 391	....	....	....	....	....	....	....	....
Other current transfers	3 392	−277	....	....	....	....	....	....	....
CAPITAL AND FINANCIAL ACCOUNT	4 996	**255**	**3,240**	**3,680**	**3,770**	**3,801**	**8,497**	**5,527**	**692**
CAPITAL ACCOUNT	4 994	**102**	**135**	**−18**	**−42**	**465**	**1,154**	**624**	**1,372**
Total credit	2 994	*195*	*148*	*16*	*37*	*686*	*1,235*	*706*	*1,436*
Total debit	3 994	*−93*	*−14*	*−33*	*−79*	*−221*	*−81*	*−82*	*−64*
Capital transfers, credit	2 400	**195**	**134**	**12**	**27**	**676**	**1,099**	**702**	**1,435**
General government	2 401	18	....	....	....	....	....	....	....
Debt forgiveness	2 402	....	....	....	....	....	....	....	....
Other capital transfers	2 410	18	....	....	....	....	....	....	....
Other sectors	2 430	177	....	....	....	....	....	....	....
Migrants' transfers	2 431	−1	....	....	....	....	....	....	....
Debt forgiveness	2 432	....	....	....	....	....	....	....	....
Other capital transfers	2 440	178	....	....	....	....	....	....	....
Capital transfers, debit	3 400	**−93**	**−1**	**−16**	**−45**	**−53**	**−42**	**−44**	**−38**
General government	3 401	....	....	....	....	....	....	....	....
Debt forgiveness	3 402	....	....	....	....	....	....	....	....
Other capital transfers	3 410	....	....	....	....	....	....	....	....
Other sectors	3 430	−93	....	....	....	....	....	....	....
Migrants' transfers	3 431	....	....	....	....	....	....	....	....
Debt forgiveness	3 432	....	....	....	....	....	....	....	....
Other capital transfers	3 440	−92	....	....	....	....	....	....	....
Nonproduced nonfinancial assets, credit	2 480	....	**14**	**4**	**10**	**10**	**136**	**3**	**1**
Nonproduced nonfinancial assets, debit	3 480	....	**−13**	**−18**	**−34**	**−168**	**−39**	**−38**	**−25**

Table 2 (Continued). STANDARD PRESENTATION, 2003–2010

(Millions of U.S. dollars)

	Code	2003	2004	2005	2006	2007	2008	2009	2010
FINANCIAL ACCOUNT...................	4 995 ..	**153**	**3,106**	**3,698**	**3,812**	**3,335**	**7,344**	**4,903**	**−680**
A. DIRECT INVESTMENT............	4 500 ..	**536**	**3,051**	**2,266**	**3,799**	**2,960**	**2,980**	**−442**	**234**
Direct investment abroad................	4 505 ..	**−24**	**13**	**−145**	**−368**	**−403**	**−251**	**−410**	**−319**
Equity capital.................	4 510 ..	−25	−83	−108	−319	−254	−210	−371	−532
Claims on affiliated enterprises.............	4 515 ..	−25	−83	−108	−319	−254	−210	−371	−532
Liabilities to affiliated enterprises.............	4 520 ..	....	....	....	....	....	....	....	....
Reinvested earnings.................	4 525 ..	....	−78	−3	−40	−49	−56	40	248
Other capital.................	4 530 ..	1	175	−33	−9	−101	16	−79	−35
Claims on affiliated enterprises.............	4 535 ..	1	−62	−102	−33	−76	−15	−100	−59
Liabilities to affiliated enterprises.............	4 540 ..	....	237	69	24	−24	30	20	24
Direct investment in Singapore...........	4 555 ..	**559**	**3,037**	**2,411**	**4,167**	**3,363**	**3,231**	**−32**	**553**
Equity capital.................	4 560 ..	871	1,168	700	1,884	1,133	1,273	1,157	−164
Claims on direct investors..............	4 565 ..	....	....	....	....	....	....	....	....
Liabilities to direct investors.............	4 570 ..	871	1,168	700	1,884	1,133	1,273	1,157	−164
Reinvested earnings.................	4 575 ..	2	1,614	875	831	992	846	696	594
Other capital.................	4 580 ..	−313	255	837	1,452	1,239	1,112	−1,885	123
Claims on direct investors..............	4 585 ..	−410	40	−519	120	−552	−815	−1,616	−86
Liabilities to direct investors.............	4 590 ..	97	215	1,356	1,332	1,790	1,927	−268	209
B. PORTFOLIO INVESTMENT.................	4 600 ..	**−574**	**850**	**−937**	**1,556**	**−734**	**2,430**	**−1,172**	**−1,527**
Assets.................	4 602 ..	**−742**	**−829**	**−691**	**−186**	**−1,083**	**634**	**−2,685**	**−3,393**
Equity securities.................	4 610 ..	−347	−40	103	−309	−271	421	−4	−270
Monetary authorities.................	4 611 ..	....	....	....	....	....	....	....	....
General government.................	4 612 ..	....	....	....	....	....	....	....	....
Banks.................	4 613 ..	−19	−27	−32	36	−139	26	21	−3
Other sectors.................	4 614 ..	−328	−14	135	−345	−133	395	−25	−267
Debt securities.................	4 619 ..	−395	−789	−794	123	−811	213	−2,681	−3,123
Bonds and notes.................	4 620 ..	−356	−910	−798	245	−767	179	−3,051	−3,093
Monetary authorities.................	4 621 ..	....	....	....	....	....	....	−1,540	−1,541
General government.................	4 622 ..	....	....	....	....	....	....	....	....
Banks.................	4 623 ..	−132	−439	51	224	−153	322	−889	−755
Other sectors.................	4 624 ..	−223	−471	−849	21	−614	−143	−623	−797
Money market instruments.................	4 630 ..	−39	121	4	−122	−45	34	371	−31
Monetary authorities.................	4 631 ..	....	....	....	....	....	....	675	−73
General government.................	4 632 ..	....	....	....	....	....	....	....	....
Banks.................	4 633 ..	11	−17	16	4	−25	....	−144	−130
Other sectors.................	4 634 ..	−50	138	−12	−126	−20	34	−161	172
Liabilities.................	4 652 ..	**168**	**1,680**	**−246**	**1,741**	**349**	**1,796**	**1,513**	**1,866**
Equity securities.................	4 660 ..	59	−94	137	36	232	103	182	25
Banks.................	4 663 ..	10	6	....	7	5	117	119	....
Other sectors.................	4 664 ..	49	−100	137	29	227	−14	64	25
Debt securities.................	4 669 ..	109	1,774	−382	1,705	117	1,693	1,330	1,841
Bonds and notes.................	4 670 ..	115	1,599	−219	1,535	−16	2,369	1,328	1,777
Monetary authorities.................	4 671 ..	....	....	....	....	....	....	....	....
General government.................	4 672 ..	87	1,605	−261	1,309	296	1,168	1,033	1,792
Banks.................	4 673 ..	7	−8	45	245	228	1,189	304	−128
Other sectors.................	4 674 ..	20	2	−3	−19	−539	11	−9	113
Money market instruments.................	4 680 ..	−5	175	−163	170	132	−675	3	64
Monetary authorities.................	4 681 ..	....	....	....	....	....	....	....	....
General government.................	4 682 ..	....	....	−166	....	....	....	....	....
Banks.................	4 683 ..	....	....	1	166	128	−675	−1	65
Other sectors.................	4 684 ..	−5	175	1	4	5	....	3	....
C. FINANCIAL DERIVATIVES.................	4 910 ..	**17**	**20**	**−35**	**−163**	**52**	**−153**	**354**	**−142**
Monetary authorities.................	4 911 ..	....	....	....	....	....	....	....	....
General government.................	4 912 ..	....	....	....	....	....	....	....	....
Banks.................	4 913 ..	23	17	−34	−137	69	104	109	23
Other sectors.................	4 914 ..	−6	2	−1	−26	−17	−257	245	−165
Assets.................	4 900 ..	**−43**	**−149**	**−98**	**−442**	**265**	**−409**	**585**	**−76**
Monetary authorities.................	4 901 ..	....	....	....	....	....	....	....	....
General government.................	4 902 ..	....	....	....	....	....	....	....	....
Banks.................	4 903 ..	−43	−149	−85	−413	259	−152	340	72
Other sectors.................	4 904 ..	....	....	−14	−30	6	−257	245	−148
Liabilities.................	4 905 ..	**60**	**169**	**64**	**279**	**−213**	**255**	**−231**	**−65**
Monetary authorities.................	4 906 ..	....	....	....	....	....	....	....	....
General government.................	4 907 ..	....	....	....	....	....	....	....	....
Banks.................	4 908 ..	66	166	51	276	−190	256	−231	−49
Other sectors.................	4 909 ..	−6	3	12	3	−23	−1	−1	−16

Table 2 (Concluded). STANDARD PRESENTATION, 2003–2010

(Millions of U.S. dollars)

	Code	2003	2004	2005	2006	2007	2008	2009	2010
D. OTHER INVESTMENT	4 700	**1,683**	**917**	**4,924**	**−4,036**	**4,746**	**1,938**	**5,992**	**791**
Assets	4 703	**−20**	**−123**	**−498**	**−1,020**	**−1,535**	**−974**	**−3,857**	**−461**
Trade credits	4 706	−136	−234	−278	−464	−43	−277	6	−289
General government	4 707	....	....	....	....	....	....	....	....
of which: Short-term	4 709	....	....	....	....	....	....	....	....
Other sectors	4 710	−136	−234	−278	−464	−43	−277	6	−289
of which: Short-term	4 712	−137	−234	−281	88	−38	−276	4	−287
Loans	4 714	−181	−197	−252	−39	−919	−520	−490	−51
Monetary authorities	4 715	....	....	....	....	....	....	....	....
of which: Short-term	4 718	....	....	....	....	....	....	....	....
General government	4 719	58	15	15	12	....	....	....	....
of which: Short-term	4 721	....	....	....	....	....	....	....	....
Banks	4 722	−175	−166	−169	−172	−855	−513	−455	−69
of which: Short-term	4 724	−112	−94	97	−169	−640	−176	539	−65
Other sectors	4 725	−64	−45	−98	121	−64	−7	−36	17
of which: Short-term	4 727	−17	−36	11	−23	−55	−19	−13	32
Currency and deposits	4 730	150	12	29	−508	−565	−31	−3,180	−100
Monetary authorities	4 731	....	....	....	....	....	....	−767	−53
General government	4 732	....	....	....	....	....	....	....	....
Banks	4 733	142	40	−182	−429	−418	450	−2,002	207
Other sectors	4 734	8	−29	211	−79	−147	−482	−410	−255
Other assets	4 736	147	295	2	−9	−9	−146	−193	−20
Monetary authorities	4 737	....	....	....	....	....	....	....	....
of which: Short-term	4 739	....	....	....	....	....	....	....	....
General government	4 740	....	....	....	....	....	....	....	....
of which: Short-term	4 742	....	....	....	....	....	....	....	....
Banks	4 743	147	295	2	−9	−9	−146	−193	−20
of which: Short-term	4 745	−76	292	−48	−7	−12	−146	−193	−20
Other sectors	4 746	....	....	....	....	....	....	....	....
of which: Short-term	4 748	....	....	....	....	....	....	....	....
Liabilities	4 753	**1,703**	**1,040**	**5,422**	**−3,017**	**6,281**	**2,912**	**9,849**	**1,252**
Trade credits	4 756	104	142	566	1,280	542	−681	348	167
General government	4 757	....	....	....	....	....	....	....	....
of which: Short-term	4 759	....	....	....	....	....	....	....	....
Other sectors	4 760	104	142	566	1,280	542	−681	348	167
of which: Short-term	4 762	133	143	583	1,289	560	−693	340	165
Loans	4 764	470	−786	−226	344	220	3,047	−1,038	2,265
Monetary authorities	4 765	618	−928	93	122	−112	....	268	1,262
of which: Use of Fund credit and loans from the Fund	4 766	....	....	....	....	....	....	....	....
of which: Short-term	4 768	889	−874	7	−3	1	....	431	1,257
General government	4 769	−30	9	−992	−115	−51	−10	−127	−114
of which: Short-term	4 771	....	....	....	....	....	....	....	....
Banks	4 772	132	563	287	261	−614	2,288	−1,188	445
of which: Short-term	4 774	115	470	195	253	−894	1,985	−1,753	317
Other sectors	4 775	−250	−430	386	77	998	769	9	672
of which: Short-term	4 777	46	−116	111	−52	−8	66	−42	463
Currency and deposits	4 780	424	2,217	4,382	−4,595	5,526	557	10,031	−1,086
Monetary authorities	4 781	....	....	....	30	1	11	18,909	−1,664
General government	4 782	....	....	....	1	12	58	55	−62
Banks	4 783	424	2,217	4,382	−4,627	5,514	487	−8,933	640
Other sectors	4 784	....	....	....	1	....	....	....	....
Other liabilities	4 786	704	−533	700	−45	−7	−11	508	−93
Monetary authorities	4 787	....	....	....	....	....	....	533	....
of which: Short-term	4 789	....	....	....	....	....	....	....	....
General government	4 790	....	....	....	....	....	....	....	....
of which: Short-term	4 792	....	....	....	....	....	....	....	....
Banks	4 793	704	−533	700	−45	−7	−11	−25	−93
of which: Short-term	4 795	763	−542	583	−24	−10	12	−15	15
Other sectors	4 796	....	....	....	....	....	....	....	....
of which: Short-term	4 798	....	....	....	....	....	....	....	....
E. RESERVE ASSETS	4 802	**−1,508**	**−1,732**	**−2,521**	**2,656**	**−3,688**	**149**	**171**	**−37**
Monetary gold	4 812	....	....	....	....	....	....	....	....
Special drawing rights	4 811	....	....	....	....	....	....	−533	....
Reserve position in the Fund	4 810	....	....	....	....	−5	−43	−56	−36
Foreign exchange	4 803	−1,508	−1,732	−2,521	2,656	−3,683	192	760	....
Other claims	4 813	....	....	....	....	....	....	....	....
NET ERRORS AND OMISSIONS	4 998	**27**	**56**	**324**	**167**	**302**	**−2,312**	**−2,366**	**2,317**

Table 3. INTERNATIONAL INVESTMENT POSITION (End-period stocks), 2003–2010

(Millions of U.S. dollars)

	Code	2003	2004	2005	2006	2007	2008	2009	2010
ASSETS	8 995 C.	19,712	24,150	25,160	26,278	36,159	38,455	45,355	47,967
Direct investment abroad	8 505	829	842	597	1,325	1,862	2,976	3,697	2,830
Equity capital and reinvested earnings	8 506	680	981	740	1,408	1,855	2,890	3,496	2,606
Claims on affiliated enterprises	8 507	680	981	740	1,408	1,855	2,890	3,496	2,606
Liabilities to affiliated enterprises	8 508	....	....	....	....	....	....	....	....
Other capital	8 530	149	−139	−143	−83	7	86	201	224
Claims on affiliated enterprises	8 535	154	147	207	257	368	419	539	574
Liabilities to affiliated enterprises	8 540	−5	−287	−350	−340	−361	−333	−339	−350
Portfolio investment	8 602	1,789	2,982	3,255	4,065	6,000	5,757	26,001	28,889
Equity securities	8 610	447	550	411	879	1,309	807	817	1,391
Monetary authorities	8 611	....	....	....	....	....	....	....	....
General government	8 612	....	....	....	....	....	....	....	....
Banks	8 613	29	62	86	56	110	97	75	75
Other sectors	8 614	419	488	324	823	1,199	710	742	1,316
Debt securities	8 619	1,342	2,432	2,844	3,186	4,691	4,949	25,184	27,498
Bonds and notes	8 620	1,076	2,403	2,820	3,030	4,515	4,814	24,748	26,127
Monetary authorities	8 621	....	....	....	....	....	....	18,370	18,657
General government	8 622	....	....	....	....	....	....	....	....
Banks	8 623	632	1,219	1,036	983	1,293	1,031	1,976	2,595
Other sectors	8 624	445	1,184	1,784	2,048	3,222	3,784	4,402	4,874
Money market instruments	8 630	265	29	24	156	176	135	436	1,371
Monetary authorities	8 631	....	....	....	....	....	....	....	76
General government	8 632	....	....	....	....	....	....	....	....
Banks	8 633	....	19	4	....	29	28	176	301
Other sectors	8 634	265	10	21	156	147	107	260	994
Financial derivatives	8 900	59	234	294	815	623	1,102	493	536
Monetary authorities	8 901	....	....	....	....	....	....	....	....
General government	8 902	....	....	....	....	....	....	....	....
Banks	8 903	59	233	280	790	585	792	432	329
Other sectors	8 904	....	1	14	25	38	309	61	207
Other investment	8 703	4,886	5,179	5,535	6,709	8,697	9,790	13,344	13,550
Trade credits	8 706	1,856	2,163	2,348	3,314	3,800	3,163	3,342	3,813
General government	8 707	....	....	....	....	....	....	....	....
of which: Short-term	8 709	....	....	....	....	....	....	....	....
Other sectors	8 710	1,856	2,163	2,348	3,314	3,800	3,163	3,342	3,813
of which: Short-term	8 712	*1,830*	*2,130*	*2,336*	*3,300*	*3,782*	*3,143*	*3,310*	*3,755*
Loans	8 714	1,902	2,196	2,207	1,637	2,734	3,292	3,869	3,630
Monetary authorities	8 715	....	....	....	....	....	....	....	....
of which: Short-term	8 718	....	....	....	....	....	....	....	....
General government	8 719	1,250	1,398	1,208	439	452	464	451	410
of which: Short-term	8 721	....	....	....	....	....	....	....	....
Banks	8 722	424	631	722	1,014	2,045	2,578	3,133	2,985
of which: Short-term	8 724	*245*	*359*	*231*	*544*	*1,270*	*1,476*	*972*	*975*
Other sectors	8 725	229	168	276	183	237	249	284	235
of which: Short-term	8 727	*46*	*92*	*63*	*110*	*183*	*138*	*150*	*125*
Currency and deposits	8 730	728	733	913	1,743	2,140	3,166	5,677	5,643
Monetary authorities	8 731	....	....	....	....	....	....	955	948
General government	8 732	....	....	....	....	....	....	....	....
Banks	8 733	717	685	760	1,445	1,937	2,590	3,960	3,623
Other sectors	8 734	11	48	153	298	203	577	763	1,071
Other assets	8 736	400	87	67	15	24	169	456	464
Monetary authorities	8 737	....	....	....	....	....	....	84	94
of which: Short-term	8 739	....	....	....	....	....	....	....	....
General government	8 740	....	....	....	....	....	....	....	....
of which: Short-term	8 742	....	....	....	....	....	....	....	....
Banks	8 743	400	87	67	15	24	169	372	370
of which: Short-term	8 745	*315*	*23*	*47*	*12*	*22*	*169*	*371*	*370*
Other sectors	8 746	....	....	....	....	....	....	....	....
of which: Short-term	8 748	....	....	....	....	....	....	....	....
Reserve assets	8 802	12,149	14,913	15,480	13,364	18,976	18,831	1,820	2,162
Monetary gold	8 812	471	494	579	717	944	976	1,128	1,443
Special drawing rights	8 811	1	1	1	1	2	2	536	526
Reserve position in the Fund	8 810	....	....	....	....	....	5	48	106	141
Foreign exchange	8 803	11,677	14,418	14,899	12,645	18,026	17,805	50	52
Other claims	8 813	....	....	....	....	....	....	....	....

Table 3 (Concluded). INTERNATIONAL INVESTMENT POSITION (End-period stocks), 2003–2010

(Millions of U.S. dollars)

	Code	2003	2004	2005	2006	2007	2008	2009	2010
LIABILITIES....................................	8 995 D.	**32,122**	**43,110**	**47,735**	**60,168**	**77,940**	**92,473**	**107,644**	**106,972**
Direct investment in Slovak Republic..........	8 555 ..	**15,776**	**21,876**	**23,656**	**33,613**	**42,695**	**51,034**	**52,641**	**50,678**
Equity capital and reinvested earnings...............	8 556 ..	14,540	20,035	20,988	28,832	35,715	41,616	44,309	42,780
Claims on direct investors...........................	8 557 ..	....	....	....	....	....	....	....	....
Liabilities to direct investors.......................	8 558 ..	14,540	20,035	20,988	28,832	35,715	41,616	44,309	42,780
Other capital..	8 580 ..	1,236	1,841	2,667	4,781	6,980	9,418	8,332	7,898
Claims on direct investors...........................	8 585 ..	−1,897	−2,027	−2,425	−3,011	−4,488	−4,875	−6,372	−5,556
Liabilities to direct investors.......................	8 590 ..	3,133	3,869	5,093	7,792	11,468	14,293	14,704	13,454
Portfolio investment............................	8 652 ..	**4,172**	**6,742**	**5,787**	**8,722**	**9,844**	**11,911**	**14,929**	**17,374**
Equity securities.....................................	8 660 ..	493	460	538	664	684	843	1,860	697
Banks...	8 663 ..	82	102	93	138	31	134	1,075	6
Other sectors...	8 664 ..	411	359	445	526	653	709	785	692
Debt securities.......................................	8 669 ..	3,679	6,282	5,249	8,058	9,161	11,068	13,069	16,676
Bonds and notes.....................................	8 670 ..	3,676	6,091	5,242	7,878	8,673	11,066	13,048	16,589
Monetary authorities................................	8 671 ..	....	....	....	....	....	....	....	....
General government.................................	8 672 ..	3,120	5,472	4,656	6,865	7,717	8,737	10,192	14,038
Banks..	8 673 ..	8	1	44	351	690	2,042	2,436	2,188
Other sectors......................................	8 674 ..	548	618	543	662	266	286	421	363
Money market instruments...........................	8 680 ..	3	190	6	179	488	2	21	88
Monetary authorities................................	8 681 ..	....	....	....	....	....	....	....	....
General government.................................	8 682 ..	....	....	4	....	....	....	....	....
Banks..	8 683 ..	....	....	....	172	486	1	....	67
Other sectors......................................	8 684 ..	3	190	2	7	2	2	21	20
Financial derivatives............................	8 905 ..	**108**	**309**	**330**	**672**	**541**	**839**	**594**	**506**
Monetary authorities.................................	8 906 ..	....	....	....	....	....	....	....	....
General government..................................	8 907 ..	....	....	....	....	....	....	....	....
Banks...	8 908 ..	97	292	302	652	540	838	593	506
Other sectors...	8 909 ..	11	17	28	20	1	....	1	....
Other investment................................	8 753 ..	**12,066**	**14,183**	**17,962**	**17,161**	**24,859**	**28,689**	**39,480**	**38,414**
Trade credits...	8 756 ..	2,545	2,849	3,070	4,557	4,829	3,885	4,210	4,370
General government.................................	8 758 ..	....	....	....	....	....	....	....	....
of which: Short-term...............................	8 759 ..	....	....	....	....	....	....	....	....
Other sectors...	8 760 ..	2,545	2,849	3,070	4,557	4,829	3,885	4,210	4,370
of which: Short-term...............................	8 762 ..	*2,474*	*2,774*	*3,026*	*4,513*	*4,799*	*3,840*	*4,173*	*4,339*
Loans...	8 764 ..	6,580	6,345	5,700	6,692	7,548	10,744	9,622	11,248
Monetary authorities................................	8 765 ..	1,146	199	277	421	218	218	765	1,969
of which: Use of Fund credit and loans from the Fund....	8 766 ..	....	....	....	....	....	....	....	....
of which: Short-term...............................	8 768 ..	*901*	....	....	....	....	....	*765*	*1,770*
General government.................................	8 769 ..	1,051	1,466	1,125	1,143	1,418	1,405	1,301	1,113
of which: Short-term...............................	8 771 ..	....	....	....	....	....	....	....	....
Banks..	8 772 ..	216	886	990	1,376	940	3,163	1,868	2,173
of which: Short-term...............................	8 774 ..	*104*	*658*	*706*	*1,130*	*245*	*2,159*	*246*	*543*
Other sectors......................................	8 775 ..	4,166	3,793	3,308	3,752	4,972	5,957	5,688	5,994
of which: Short-term...............................	8 777 ..	*390*	*336*	*442*	*449*	*525*	*850*	*800*	*1,297*
Currency and deposits...............................	8 780 ..	1,567	4,045	7,641	5,759	12,327	13,988	25,053	22,206
Monetary authorities................................	8 781 ..	....	....	....	67	7	16	20,938	17,795
General government.................................	8 782 ..	....	....	....	3	28	93	145	74
Banks..	8 783 ..	1,567	4,045	7,641	5,688	12,292	13,879	3,971	4,336
Other sectors......................................	8 784 ..	....	....	....	....	....	....	....	....
Other liabilities......................................	8 786 ..	1,374	944	1,552	154	155	73	595	591
Monetary authorities................................	8 787 ..	....	....	....	....	....	....	534	524
of which: Short-term...............................	8 789 ..	....	....	....	....	....	....	....	....
General government.................................	8 790 ..	....	....	....	....	....	....	....	....
of which: Short-term...............................	8 792 ..	....	....	....	....	....	....	....	....
Banks..	8 793 ..	1,374	944	1,552	154	155	73	61	67
of which: Short-term...............................	8 795 ..	*1,328*	*894*	*1,406*	*99*	*150*	*73*	*61*	*67*
Other sectors......................................	8 796 ..	....	....	....	....	....	....	....	....
of which: Short-term...............................	8 798 ..	....	....	....	....	....	....	....	....
NET INTERNATIONAL INVESTMENT POSITION........	8 995 ..	**−12,410**	**−18,960**	**−22,575**	**−33,890**	**−41,781**	**−54,018**	**−62,289**	**−59,005**
Conversion rates: Slovak koruny per U.S. dollar (end of period)...............	0 102 ..	**32.9**	**28.5**	**31.9**	**26.2**	**22.9**	**21.4**	....	....
Conversion rates: euros per U.S. dollar (end of period)..............................	0 104 ..	**.7918**	**.7342**	**.8477**	**.7593**	**.6793**	**.7185**	**.6942**	**.7484**

Table 1. ANALYTIC PRESENTATION, 2003–2010

(Millions of U.S. dollars)

	Code	2003	2004	2005	2006	2007	2008	2009	2010
A. Current Account[1]	4 993 Z.	**−216**	**−893**	**−681**	**−1,088**	**−2,298**	**−3,763**	**−625**	**−388**
Goods: exports f.o.b.	2 100 ..	12,916	16,065	18,146	21,397	27,151	29,560	22,532	24,359
Goods: imports f.o.b.	3 100 ..	−13,539	−17,322	−19,404	−22,856	−29,466	−33,440	−23,529	−25,961
Balance on Goods	4 100 ..	*−622*	*−1,258*	*−1,258*	*−1,458*	*−2,314*	*−3,881*	*−996*	*−1,602*
Services: credit	2 200 ..	2,791	3,455	3,976	4,344	5,691	7,293	6,072	6,129
Services: debit	3 200 ..	−2,183	−2,603	−2,915	−3,254	−4,264	−5,188	−4,450	−4,399
Balance on Goods and Services	4 991 ..	*−14*	*−406*	*−198*	*−368*	*−887*	*−1,775*	*626*	*128*
Income: credit	2 300 ..	589	667	781	1,135	1,609	1,851	933	901
Income: debit	3 300 ..	−821	−1,060	−1,143	−1,642	−2,693	−3,420	−1,991	−1,563
Balance on Goods, Services, and Income	4 992 ..	*−246*	*−799*	*−560*	*−874*	*−1,971*	*−3,344*	*−432*	*−534*
Current transfers: credit	2 379 Z.	538	698	878	988	1,295	1,301	1,362	1,624
Current transfers: debit	3 379 ..	−508	−792	−998	−1,202	−1,622	−1,720	−1,554	−1,478
B. Capital Account[1]	4 994 Z.	**−191**	**−123**	**−138**	**−169**	**−72**	**−33**	**−18**	**11**
Capital account: credit	2 994 Z.	93	191	212	262	443	414	379	480
Capital account: debit	3 994 ..	−284	−314	−350	−432	−515	−447	−397	−469
Total, Groups A Plus B	4 981 ..	*−406*	*−1,015*	*−818*	*−1,258*	*−2,370*	*−3,796*	*−643*	*−377*
C. Financial Account[1]	4 995 W.	**567**	**702**	**844**	**−129**	**2,564**	**3,833**	**330**	**356**
Direct investment abroad	4 505 ..	−476	−550	−629	−905	−1,800	−1,478	−243	73
Direct investment in Slovenia	4 555 Z.	302	831	540	649	1,531	1,937	−641	366
Portfolio investment assets	4 602 ..	−220	−809	−2,100	−2,677	−4,468	−371	26	−532
Equity securities	4 610 ..	−101	−271	−1,022	−929	−1,227	138	−102	−279
Debt securities	4 619 ..	−119	−539	−1,078	−1,749	−3,241	−509	128	−254
Portfolio investment liabilities	4 652 Z.	−37	37	102	849	1,379	932	6,414	3,165
Equity securities	4 660 ..	16	−13	98	197	275	−290	31	169
Debt securities	4 669 Z.	−53	50	4	652	1,104	1,222	6,383	2,996
Financial derivatives	4 910 ..	....	7	−13	−16	−20	68	−1	−153
Financial derivatives assets	4 900 ..	....	7	−13	−16	−46	54	45	72
Financial derivatives liabilities	4 905 ..	....	....	....	....	26	14	−46	−225
Other investment assets	4 703 ..	−796	−1,608	−1,899	−2,428	−6,396	−560	−476	950
Monetary authorities	4 701 ..	....	−11	−2	−1	−1,171	881	1,025	188
General government	4 704 ..	−1	−13	−11	−13	−27	−32	−9	−128
Banks	4 705 ..	17	−323	−939	−576	−3,476	42	−955	2,312
Other sectors	4 728 ..	−812	−1,261	−947	−1,839	−1,721	−1,451	−537	−1,421
Other investment liabilities	4 753 W.	1,794	2,793	4,842	4,399	12,337	3,304	−4,749	−3,514
Monetary authorities	4 753 WA	....	123	7	9	4,649	60	−4	−1,698
General government	4 753 ZB	−76	9	−35	−145	−66	−41	−18	8
Banks	4 753 ZC	1,205	1,517	4,218	3,032	6,318	2,291	−4,183	−1,956
Other sectors	4 753 ZD	665	1,145	652	1,503	1,435	994	−544	133
Total, Groups A Through C	4 983 ..	*160*	*−313*	*25*	*−1,387*	*194*	*37*	*−312*	*−21*
D. Net Errors and Omissions	4 998 ..	**150**	**17**	**181**	**−270**	**−393**	**−71**	**388**	**26**
Total, Groups A Through D	4 984 ..	*310*	*−296*	*206*	*−1,656*	*−199*	*−34*	*76*	*5*
E. Reserves and Related Items	4 802 A.	**−310**	**296**	**−206**	**1,656**	**199**	**34**	**−76**	**−5**
Reserve assets	4 802 ..	−310	296	−206	1,656	199	34	−76	−5
Use of Fund credit and loans	4 766 ..	....	....	....	....	....	....	....	....
Exceptional financing	4 920 ..	....	....	....	....	....	....	....	....
Conversion rates: tolars per U.S. dollar	0 101 ..	**207.11**	**192.38**	**192.71**	**191.03**	....	....	....	....
Conversion rates: euros per U.S. dollar	0 103 ..	**.8860**	**.8054**	**.8041**	**.7971**	**.7306**	**.6827**	**.7198**	**.7550**

[1] Excludes components that have been classified in the categories of Group E.

Table 2. STANDARD PRESENTATION, 2003–2010
(Millions of U.S. dollars)

	Code	2003	2004	2005	2006	2007	2008	2009	2010
CURRENT ACCOUNT	4 993	**−216**	**−893**	**−681**	**−1,088**	**−2,298**	**−3,763**	**−625**	**−388**
A. GOODS	4 100	**−622**	**−1,258**	**−1,258**	**−1,458**	**−2,314**	**−3,881**	**−996**	**−1,602**
Credit	2 100	**12,916**	**16,065**	**18,146**	**21,397**	**27,151**	**29,560**	**22,532**	**24,359**
General merchandise: exports f.o.b.	2 110	12,845	16,004	18,073	21,302	27,027	29,415	22,428	24,175
Goods for processing: exports f.o.b.	2 150	66	58	71	85	120	142	100	178
Repairs on goods	2 160	....	....	....	....	....	....	....	....
Goods procured in ports by carriers	2 170	....	....	....	10	3	2	....	....
Nonmonetary gold	2 180	5	2	1	1	1	1	4	6
Debit	3 100	**−13,539**	**−17,322**	**−19,404**	**−22,856**	**−29,466**	**−33,440**	**−23,529**	**−25,961**
General merchandise: imports f.o.b.	3 110	−13,445	−17,249	−19,319	−22,747	−29,296	−33,197	−23,363	−25,691
Goods for processing: imports f.o.b.	3 150	−87	−67	−81	−103	−153	−197	−143	−210
Repairs on goods	3 160	....	....	....	....	....	....	....	....
Goods procured in ports by carriers	3 170	....	....	....	....	....	....	....	....
Nonmonetary gold	3 180	−7	−7	−4	−5	−17	−46	−22	−60
B. SERVICES	4 200	**608**	**852**	**1,061**	**1,091**	**1,428**	**2,105**	**1,622**	**1,730**
Total credit	2 200	*2,791*	*3,455*	*3,976*	*4,344*	*5,691*	*7,293*	*6,072*	*6,129*
Total debit	3 200	*−2,183*	*−2,603*	*−2,915*	*−3,254*	*−4,264*	*−5,188*	*−4,450*	*−4,399*
Transportation services, credit	2 205	**771**	**1,006**	**1,145**	**1,330**	**1,730**	**2,114**	**1,515**	**1,598**
Passenger	2 850	*85*	*101*	*99*	*114*	*182*	*258*	*215*	*180*
Freight	2 851	*500*	*672*	*796*	*926*	*1,182*	*1,505*	*1,032*	*1,124*
Other	2 852	*186*	*234*	*250*	*290*	*366*	*351*	*267*	*294*
Sea transport, passenger	2 207	1	1	1	1	4	5	4	4
Sea transport, freight	2 208	33	65	98	90	141	202	86	88
Sea transport, other	2 209	47	74	93	111	152	192	150	159
Air transport, passenger	2 211	77	92	90	103	163	233	188	152
Air transport, freight	2 212	7	9	10	10	10	18	17	20
Air transport, other	2 213	3	3	6	21	14	72	63	60
Other transport, passenger	2 215	7	8	9	10	14	20	22	25
Other transport, freight	2 216	460	598	689	826	1,031	1,286	929	1,016
Other transport, other	2 217	137	157	151	158	201	87	54	75
Transportation services, debit	3 205	**−476**	**−603**	**−650**	**−757**	**−1,008**	**−1,290**	**−904**	**−941**
Passenger	3 850	*−52*	*−69*	*−69*	*−84*	*−116*	*−253*	*−178*	*−163*
Freight	3 851	*−274*	*−326*	*−342*	*−396*	*−501*	*−863*	*−551*	*−607*
Other	3 852	*−150*	*−208*	*−239*	*−277*	*−390*	*−174*	*−175*	*−171*
Sea transport, passenger	3 207	−2	−2	−2	−3	−10	−6	−6	−9
Sea transport, freight	3 208	−47	−69	−90	−116	−206	−367	−183	−205
Sea transport, other	3 209	−6	−15	−18	−20	−30	−27	−21	−18
Air transport, passenger	3 211	−46	−61	−61	−73	−97	−234	−162	−143
Air transport, freight	3 212	−12	−16	−13	−20	−15	−19	−18	−22
Air transport, other	3 213	−7	−9	−11	−19	−35	−54	−53	−39
Other transport, passenger	3 215	−5	−6	−6	−8	−9	−13	−9	−11
Other transport, freight	3 216	−214	−241	−239	−260	−281	−477	−350	−380
Other transport, other	3 217	−137	−184	−210	−237	−325	−93	−101	−114
Travel, credit	2 236	**1,342**	**1,624**	**1,795**	**1,797**	**2,283**	**2,696**	**2,520**	**2,554**
Business travel	2 237	....	....	....	79	98	131	120	117
Personal travel	2 240	1,342	1,624	1,795	1,718	2,184	2,566	2,400	2,437
Travel, debit	3 236	**−753**	**−868**	**−950**	**−974**	**−1,144**	**−1,357**	**−1,278**	**−1,214**
Business travel	3 237	−106	−118	−111	−222	−295	−372	−289	−339
Personal travel	3 240	−647	−750	−838	−752	−849	−985	−989	−875
Other services, credit	2 200 BA	**678**	**824**	**1,036**	**1,218**	**1,678**	**2,483**	**2,037**	**1,977**
Communications	2 245	70	90	113	116	145	304	276	289
Construction	2 249	81	90	133	130	208	440	276	196
Insurance	2 253	8	10	14	18	23	117	89	98
Financial	2 260	19	18	22	35	58	37	36	51
Computer and information	2 262	88	98	112	123	149	196	158	158
Royalties and licence fees	2 266	11	12	16	17	19	48	55	69
Other business services	2 268	375	471	591	734	1,033	1,288	1,088	1,055
Personal, cultural, and recreational	2 287	21	30	28	38	38	42	50	52
Government, n.i.e.	2 291	5	6	6	7	7	11	11	10
Other services, debit	3 200 BA	**−954**	**−1,132**	**−1,316**	**−1,522**	**−2,112**	**−2,541**	**−2,267**	**−2,245**
Communications	3 245	−107	−120	−136	−135	−179	−320	−313	−319
Construction	3 249	−82	−62	−80	−87	−223	−228	−140	−89
Insurance	3 253	−18	−17	−19	−26	−28	−131	−104	−118
Financial	3 260	−33	−39	−44	−54	−81	−40	−52	−36
Computer and information	3 262	−101	−120	−125	−144	−186	−182	−205	−187
Royalties and licence fees	3 266	−90	−123	−113	−154	−169	−268	−310	−369
Other business services	3 268	−453	−569	−711	−816	−1,103	−1,227	−975	−986
Personal, cultural, and recreational	3 287	−50	−59	−61	−77	−99	−31	−41	−46
Government, n.i.e.	3 291	−20	−24	−26	−31	−44	−114	−126	−94

Table 2 (Continued). STANDARD PRESENTATION, 2003–2010

(Millions of U.S. dollars)

	Code	2003	2004	2005	2006	2007	2008	2009	2010
C. INCOME	4 300	**−232**	**−393**	**−363**	**−506**	**−1,084**	**−1,569**	**−1,058**	**−662**
Total credit	2 300	*589*	*667*	*781*	*1,135*	*1,609*	*1,851*	*933*	*901*
Total debit	3 300	*−821*	*−1,060*	*−1,143*	*−1,642*	*−2,693*	*−3,420*	*−1,991*	*−1,563*
Compensation of employees, credit	2 310	**217**	**249**	**254**	**274**	**315**	**347**	**277**	**309**
Compensation of employees, debit	3 310	**−65**	**−78**	**−90**	**−127**	**−247**	**−387**	**−178**	**−125**
Investment income, credit	2 320	**372**	**419**	**526**	**861**	**1,294**	**1,504**	**656**	**593**
Direct investment income	2 330	24	32	82	257	362	299	−115	−154
Dividends and distributed branch profits	2 332	17	18	35	95	117	157	210	105
Reinvested earnings and undistributed branch profits	2 333	7	14	47	162	172	16	−414	−344
Income on debt (interest)	2 334	....	....	....	....	73	126	89	85
Portfolio investment income	2 339	232	284	319	379	512	622	454	471
Income on equity	2 340	....	5	17	36	48	78	71	81
Income on bonds and notes	2 350	231	279	301	342	454	535	382	390
Income on money market instruments	2 360	1	....	1	1	9	10	....	....
Other investment income	2 370	117	102	125	226	420	583	318	276
Investment income, debit	3 320	**−756**	**−982**	**−1,054**	**−1,515**	**−2,446**	**−3,032**	**−1,814**	**−1,439**
Direct investment income	3 330	−300	−474	−458	−710	−1,058	−1,031	−695	−391
Dividends and distributed branch profits	3 332	−79	−131	−165	−466	−765	−724	−550	−604
Reinvested earnings and undistributed branch profits	3 333	−221	−343	−293	−244	−115	−26	−9	318
Income on debt (interest)	3 334	....	....	....	....	−178	−281	−135	−105
Portfolio investment income	3 339	−143	−154	−159	−152	−212	−249	−366	−576
Income on equity	3 340	....	−1	−24	−6	−15	−22	−17	−16
Income on bonds and notes	3 350	−138	−139	−129	−146	−198	−227	−349	−560
Income on money market instruments	3 360	−4	−14	−6	....	....	....	....	....
Other investment income	3 370	−314	−355	−437	−653	−1,176	−1,752	−753	−472
D. CURRENT TRANSFERS	4 379	**30**	**−94**	**−120**	**−214**	**−327**	**−419**	**−192**	**146**
Credit	2 379	**538**	**698**	**878**	**988**	**1,295**	**1,301**	**1,362**	**1,624**
General government	2 380	103	262	393	517	564	702	837	1,100
Other sectors	2 390	435	437	485	471	730	599	525	524
Workers' remittances	2 391	13	12	7	6	5	....	....	....
Other current transfers	2 392	421	425	478	465	725	599	525	524
Debit	3 379	**−508**	**−792**	**−998**	**−1,202**	**−1,622**	**−1,720**	**−1,554**	**−1,478**
General government	3 380	−153	−372	−534	−647	−830	−1,029	−971	−888
Other sectors	3 390	−355	−420	−464	−555	−792	−691	−583	−590
Workers' remittances	3 391	....	−1	−1	−1	−1	−40	−34	−33
Other current transfers	3 392	−355	−419	−463	−554	−791	−650	−549	−557
CAPITAL AND FINANCIAL ACCOUNT	4 996	**66**	**876**	**499**	**1,358**	**2,691**	**3,833**	**237**	**362**
CAPITAL ACCOUNT	4 994	**−191**	**−123**	**−138**	**−169**	**−72**	**−33**	**−18**	**11**
Total credit	2 994	*93*	*191*	*212*	*262*	*443*	*414*	*379*	*480*
Total debit	3 994	*−284*	*−314*	*−350*	*−432*	*−515*	*−447*	*−397*	*−469*
Capital transfers, credit	2 400	**93**	**190**	**209**	**258**	**439**	**403**	**376**	**478**
General government	2 401	....	24	36	59	180	109	170	137
Debt forgiveness	2 402	....	....	....	....	....	....	....	....
Other capital transfers	2 410	....	24	36	59	180	109	170	137
Other sectors	2 430	93	165	174	199	259	294	206	341
Migrants' transfers	2 431	8	5	3	3	2	....	....	....
Debt forgiveness	2 432	85	161	170	196	257	266	201	223
Other capital transfers	2 440	....	....	....	....	....	28	5	118
Capital transfers, debit	3 400	**−281**	**−313**	**−341**	**−421**	**−509**	**−437**	**−387**	**−457**
General government	3 401	....	....	....	....	−1	....	....	....
Debt forgiveness	3 402	....	....	....	....	....	....	....	....
Other capital transfers	3 410	....	....	....	....	−1	....	....	....
Other sectors	3 430	−281	−313	−341	−421	−508	−437	−386	−457
Migrants' transfers	3 431	−1	−2	−4	−1	−2	....	....	....
Debt forgiveness	3 432	−280	−311	−338	−419	−506	−432	−383	−417
Other capital transfers	3 440	....	....	....	....	....	−5	−3	−39
Nonproduced nonfinancial assets, credit	2 480	**....**	**1**	**2**	**4**	**4**	**10**	**3**	**2**
Nonproduced nonfinancial assets, debit	3 480	**−2**	**−1**	**−8**	**−11**	**−6**	**−9**	**−10**	**−13**

Table 2 (Continued). STANDARD PRESENTATION, 2003–2010

(Millions of U.S. dollars)

	Code	2003	2004	2005	2006	2007	2008	2009	2010
FINANCIAL ACCOUNT	4 995 ..	**256**	**998**	**637**	**1,527**	**2,763**	**3,866**	**255**	**351**
A. DIRECT INVESTMENT	4 500 ..	**−174**	**282**	**−89**	**−256**	**−269**	**459**	**−884**	**439**
Direct investment abroad	4 505 ..	**−476**	**−550**	**−629**	**−905**	**−1,800**	**−1,478**	**−243**	**73**
Equity capital	4 510 ..	−279	−476	−561	−531	−894	−1,018	−673	−229
Claims on affiliated enterprises	4 515 ..	....	....	....	....	....	....	....	....
Liabilities to affiliated enterprises	4 520 ..	....	....	....	....	....	....	....	....
Reinvested earnings	4 525 ..	−7	−14	−47	−162	−172	−16	414	344
Other capital	4 530 ..	−191	−60	−21	−212	−734	−444	15	−42
Claims on affiliated enterprises	4 535 ..	−229	9	−58	−245	−867	−517	−126	−75
Liabilities to affiliated enterprises	4 540 ..	39	−69	37	33	133	72	142	32
Direct investment in Slovenia	4 555 ..	**302**	**831**	**540**	**649**	**1,531**	**1,937**	**−641**	**366**
Equity capital	4 560 ..	−11	401	321	317	584	532	179	593
Claims on direct investors	4 565 ..	....	....	....	....	....	....	....	....
Liabilities to direct investors	4 570 ..	....	....	....	....	....	....	....	....
Reinvested earnings	4 575 ..	221	343	293	244	115	26	9	−318
Other capital	4 580 ..	92	87	−73	88	833	1,379	−829	91
Claims on direct investors	4 585 ..	−196	−1	−393	−7	−221	187	−150	−239
Liabilities to direct investors	4 590 ..	287	88	320	96	1,054	1,192	−680	330
B. PORTFOLIO INVESTMENT	4 600 ..	**−257**	**−772**	**−1,998**	**−1,829**	**−3,089**	**561**	**6,440**	**2,632**
Assets	4 602 ..	**−220**	**−809**	**−2,100**	**−2,677**	**−4,468**	**−371**	**26**	**−532**
Equity securities	4 610 ..	−101	−271	−1,022	−929	−1,227	138	−102	−279
Monetary authorities	4 611 ..	....	....	....	....	....	....	....	....
General government	4 612 ..	....	....	−26	−13	−41	−18	15	−9
Banks	4 613 ..	−1	−22	−244	−13	−24	14	21	23
Other sectors	4 614 ..	−101	−249	−753	−902	−1,162	142	−138	−293
Debt securities	4 619 ..	−119	−539	−1,078	−1,749	−3,241	−509	128	−254
Bonds and notes	4 620 ..	−96	−530	−1,070	−1,571	−1,245	−955	−144	−740
Monetary authorities	4 621 ..	....	....	....	....	1,488	−1,138	−623	−279
General government	4 622 ..	....	−1	−17	−43	−126	−20	78	−36
Banks	4 623 ..	−56	−216	−760	−1,123	−1,854	524	602	65
Other sectors	4 624 ..	−40	−314	−292	−405	−752	−321	−201	−491
Money market instruments	4 630 ..	−23	−9	−8	−177	−1,996	446	272	487
Monetary authorities	4 631 ..	....	....	....	....	−901	426	443	6
General government	4 632 ..	....	....	....	−1	−2	−1	7	....
Banks	4 633 ..	2	−5	−3	−171	−1,071	16	−199	482
Other sectors	4 634 ..	−25	−4	−6	−6	−21	5	21	−2
Liabilities	4 652 ..	**−37**	**37**	**102**	**849**	**1,379**	**932**	**6,414**	**3,165**
Equity securities	4 660 ..	16	−13	98	197	275	−290	31	169
Banks	4 663 ..	....	2	2	−1	77	−191	3	6
Other sectors	4 664 ..	16	−15	96	198	197	−99	28	163
Debt securities	4 669 ..	−53	50	4	652	1,104	1,222	6,383	2,996
Bonds and notes	4 670 ..	−53	19	−63	536	1,104	1,222	6,383	2,996
Monetary authorities	4 671 ..	....	....	....	....	....	....	....	....
General government	4 672 ..	58	−207	−202	541	1,092	1,041	3,685	2,089
Banks	4 673 ..	−82	249	135	−6	26	185	2,281	931
Other sectors	4 674 ..	−29	−24	4	1	−14	−4	417	−25
Money market instruments	4 680 ..	....	31	67	116	....	....	....	....
Monetary authorities	4 681 ..	....	....	....	....	....	....	....	....
General government	4 682 ..	−21	31	67	116	....	....	....	....
Banks	4 683 ..	16	....	....	....	....	....	....	....
Other sectors	4 684 ..	4	....	....	....	....	....	....	....
C. FINANCIAL DERIVATIVES	4 910 ..	**....**	**7**	**−13**	**−16**	**−20**	**68**	**−1**	**−153**
Monetary authorities	4 911 ..	....	....	....	....	....	....	−12	−53
General government	4 912 ..	....	....	....	....	−8	5	2	1
Banks	4 913 ..	....	....	....	....	4	1	−12	−96
Other sectors	4 914 ..	....	7	−13	−16	−16	62	20	−4
Assets	4 900 ..	**....**	**7**	**−13**	**−16**	**−46**	**54**	**45**	**72**
Monetary authorities	4 901 ..	....	....	....	....	....	....	37	16
General government	4 902 ..	....	....	....	....	−8	5	2	1
Banks	4 903 ..	....	....	....	....	−1	−11	1	53
Other sectors	4 904 ..	....	7	−13	−16	−37	60	4	3
Liabilities	4 905 ..	**....**	**....**	**....**	**....**	**26**	**14**	**−46**	**−225**
Monetary authorities	4 906 ..	....	....	....	....	....	....	−49	−69
General government	4 907 ..	....	....	....	....	....	....	....	....
Banks	4 908 ..	....	....	....	....	5	12	−12	−149
Other sectors	4 909 ..	....	....	....	....	21	2	16	−7

Table 2 (Concluded). STANDARD PRESENTATION, 2003–2010

(Millions of U.S. dollars)

	Code	2003	2004	2005	2006	2007	2008	2009	2010
D. OTHER INVESTMENT	4 700	**998**	**1,186**	**2,943**	**1,971**	**5,941**	**2,745**	**−5,225**	**−2,563**
Assets	4 703	**−796**	**−1,608**	**−1,899**	**−2,428**	**−6,396**	**−560**	**−476**	**950**
Trade credits	4 706	−102	−272	−266	−528	−510	−322	586	−225
General government	4 707	....	....	1	....	....	−1	−7	5
of which: Short-term	4 709	....	....	*1*	....	....	*−1*	*−7*	*5*
Other sectors	4 710	−102	−272	−267	−528	−510	−321	593	−230
of which: Short-term	4 712	*−113*	*−275*	*−265*	*−523*	*−504*	*−319*	*595*	*−228*
Loans	4 714	−260	−347	−503	−924	−2,616	−498	−2	168
Monetary authorities	4 715	....	....	....	....	....	....	....	....
of which: Short-term	4 718	....	....	....	....	....	....	....	....
General government	4 719	....	....	....	....	....	....	....	−133
of which: Short-term	4 721	....	....	....	....	....	....	....	....
Banks	4 722	−151	−257	−362	−598	−2,357	−367	−51	231
of which: Short-term	4 724	*−37*	*−31*	*−85*	*−121*	*−885*	*420*	*−243*	*−2*
Other sectors	4 725	−109	−90	−141	−325	−259	−130	49	70
of which: Short-term	4 727	*−28*	*−45*	*−79*	*−122*	*−168*	*−87*	*279*	*27*
Currency and deposits	4 730	−356	−902	−1,026	−949	−3,279	250	−941	900
Monetary authorities	4 731	....	....	....	....	−1,112	888	1,028	59
General government	4 732	....	....	....	....	....	....	....	....
Banks	4 733	241	−2	−486	39	−1,200	394	−912	2,093
Other sectors	4 734	−597	−900	−540	−988	−967	−1,032	−1,056	−1,253
Other assets	4 736	−78	−87	−104	−27	9	10	−120	108
Monetary authorities	4 737	....	−11	−2	−1	−59	−7	−2	129
of which: Short-term	4 739	....	*−11*	*−2*	*−1*	*−11*	*−7*	*1*	*−3*
General government	4 740	−1	−13	−12	−13	−27	−31	−2	....
of which: Short-term	4 742	....	....	....	....	....	....	....	....
Banks	4 743	−74	−64	−91	−16	81	16	8	−12
of which: Short-term	4 745	*−57*	*−35*	....	*−16*	*79*	*16*	*8*	*12*
Other sectors	4 746	−4	1	1	2	14	32	−123	−8
of which: Short-term	4 748	....	*4*	*1*	*1*	*14*	*57*	*15*	*−11*
Liabilities	4 753	**1,794**	**2,793**	**4,842**	**4,399**	**12,337**	**3,304**	**−4,749**	**−3,514**
Trade credits	4 756	62	258	292	599	688	5	−605	478
General government	4 757	1	4	−2	....	−8	−3	9	13
of which: Short-term	4 759	*1*	*4*	*−2*	....	*−8*	*−3*	*9*	*13*
Other sectors	4 760	61	254	293	600	696	8	−614	466
of which: Short-term	4 762	*68*	*267*	*308*	*605*	*699*	*−3*	*−623*	*495*
Loans	4 764	1,275	2,077	3,246	2,594	5,337	2,981	−4,048	−1,316
Monetary authorities	4 765	....	....	....	....	....	....	....	....
of which: Use of Fund credit and loans from the Fund	4 766	....	....	....	....	....	....	....	....
of which: Short-term	4 768	....	....	....	....	....	....	....	....
General government	4 769	−77	4	−34	−144	−58	−44	−26	−4
of which: Short-term	4 771	....	....	....	....	....	....	....	....
Banks	4 772	754	1,184	2,904	1,810	4,673	2,032	−4,093	−958
of which: Short-term	4 774	*−6*	*49*	*5*	*−421*	*1,845*	*594*	*−2,053*	*−25*
Other sectors	4 775	598	889	376	928	722	993	71	−354
of which: Short-term	4 777	*83*	*−68*	*92*	*−1*	*35*	*190*	*−155*	*−339*
Currency and deposits	4 780	490	421	1,277	1,242	6,328	330	−355	−2,667
Monetary authorities	4 781	....	123	7	9	4,649	60	−301	−1,698
General government	4 782	....	....	....	....	....	....	....	....
Banks	4 783	490	297	1,269	1,233	1,679	270	−54	−969
Other sectors	4 784	....	....	....	....	....	....	....	....
Other liabilities	4 786	−33	38	28	−36	−16	−12	259	−10
Monetary authorities	4 787	....	....	....	....	....	....	297	....
of which: Short-term	4 789	....	....	....	....	....	....	....	....
General government	4 790	....	....	1	−1	....	6	−1	−1
of which: Short-term	4 792	....	....	....	....	....	....	....	....
Banks	4 793	−40	36	45	−12	−34	−11	−36	−29
of which: Short-term	4 795	*−40*	*36*	*45*	*−12*	*−34*	*−11*	*−36*	*−29*
Other sectors	4 796	7	2	−18	−24	18	−6	−1	21
of which: Short-term	4 798	....	....	....	....	....	....	....	....
E. RESERVE ASSETS	4 802	**−310**	**296**	**−206**	**1,656**	**199**	**34**	**−76**	**−5**
Monetary gold	4 812	....	....	42	....	38	....	....	....
Special drawing rights	4 811	−1	−1	−1	....	....	....	−298	....
Reserve position in the Fund	4 810	−12	30	60	17	13	−21	−18	−49
Foreign exchange	4 803	−297	268	−307	1,639	148	54	240	44
Other claims	4 813	....	....	....	....	....	....	....	....
NET ERRORS AND OMISSIONS	4 998	**150**	**17**	**181**	**−270**	**−393**	**−71**	**388**	**26**

Table 3. INTERNATIONAL INVESTMENT POSITION (End-period stocks), 2003–2010

(Millions of U.S. dollars)

	Code	2003	2004	2005	2006	2007	2008	2009	2010
ASSETS..	8 995 C.	**19,353**	**23,573**	**26,380**	**33,086**	**50,961**	**47,166**	**50,177**	**47,080**
Direct investment abroad........................	8 505 ..	**2,350**	**3,025**	**3,290**	**4,547**	**7,238**	**7,901**	**8,022**	**7,374**
Equity capital and reinvested earnings...........	8 506 ..	1,502	2,067	2,759	3,499	4,900	5,460	5,781	5,133
Claims on affiliated enterprises..................	8 507 ..	1,502	2,067	2,759	3,499	4,900	5,460	5,781	5,133
Liabilities to affiliated enterprises..............	8 508 ..	....	....	....	....	....	....	....	....
Other capital..	8 530 ..	848	959	531	1,048	2,337	2,440	2,241	2,241
Claims on affiliated enterprises..................	8 535 ..	1,080	1,137	1,042	1,299	2,676	2,810	2,762	2,779
Liabilities to affiliated enterprises..............	8 540 ..	−232	−179	−511	−252	−339	−370	−522	−538
Portfolio investment..............................	8 602 ..	**689**	**1,730**	**3,253**	**6,759**	**18,472**	**14,802**	**16,274**	**15,901**
Equity securities......................................	8 610 ..	235	642	1,466	2,974	5,391	2,436	3,343	3,733
Monetary authorities..............................	8 611 ..	....	....	....	....	....	....	....	....
General government...............................	8 612 ..	....	....	102	141	291	187	251	292
Banks...	8 613 ..	24	50	62	125	188	80	60	74
Other sectors...	8 614 ..	211	592	1,301	2,709	4,913	2,169	3,031	3,367
Debt securities...	8 619 ..	454	1,088	1,788	3,785	13,081	12,365	12,931	12,169
Bonds and notes......................................	8 620 ..	454	1,076	1,781	3,599	10,562	10,483	11,285	11,144
Monetary authorities..............................	8 621 ..	....	....	....	....	3,721	4,450	5,397	5,244
General government...............................	8 622 ..	2	3	71	120	267	254	190	207
Banks...	8 623 ..	244	503	1,071	2,373	4,594	3,737	3,219	2,899
Other sectors...	8 624 ..	209	571	639	1,106	1,981	2,043	2,479	2,794
Money market instruments.......................	8 630 ..	....	11	7	186	2,518	1,882	1,646	1,025
Monetary authorities..............................	8 631 ..	....	....	....	....	1,008	470	29	20
General government...............................	8 632 ..	....	....	2	1	5	6	1	1
Banks...	8 633 ..	....	7	2	176	1,463	1,371	1,604	990
Other sectors...	8 634 ..	....	4	4	10	43	35	13	14
Financial derivatives.............................	8 900 ..	....	**2**	**17**	**35**	**194**	**116**	**129**	**163**
Monetary authorities................................	8 901 ..	....	....	....	....	....	....	....	....
General government.................................	8 902 ..	....	....	....	....	15	10	7	6
Banks...	8 903 ..	....	....	....	....	98	84	104	143
Other sectors...	8 904 ..	....	2	17	35	81	22	18	14
Other investment..................................	8 703 ..	**7,715**	**9,916**	**11,686**	**14,609**	**23,992**	**23,392**	**24,672**	**22,535**
Trade credits...	8 706 ..	2,402	2,886	3,388	4,309	5,501	5,533	5,427	5,261
General government...............................	8 707 ..	....	....	....	....	....	....	....	....
of which: Short-term...........................	8 709 ..	....	....	....	....	....	....	....	....
Other sectors...	8 710 ..	2,402	2,886	3,388	4,309	5,501	5,533	5,427	5,261
of which: Short-term...........................	8 712 ..	*2,383*	*2,868*	*3,369*	*4,276*	*5,445*	*5,477*	*5,363*	*5,225*
Loans..	8 714 ..	656	1,023	1,422	2,502	5,084	5,395	5,732	5,493
Monetary authorities..............................	8 715 ..	....	....	....	....	....	....	....	....
of which: Short-term...........................	8 718 ..	....	....	....	....	....	....	....	....
General government...............................	8 719 ..	....	....	....	....	....	....	....	138
of which: Short-term...........................	8 721 ..	....	....	....	....	....	....	....	....
Banks...	8 722 ..	375	666	989	1,713	4,459	4,576	4,770	4,423
of which: Short-term...........................	8 724 ..	*77*	*104*	*234*	*385*	*1,364*	*873*	*1,153*	*1,363*
Other sectors...	8 725 ..	281	357	433	789	625	818	962	933
of which: Short-term...........................	8 727 ..	*52*	*69*	*93*	*192*	*365*	*513*	*458*	*412*
Currency and deposits..............................	8 730 ..	2,898	3,892	5,232	6,785	12,373	11,618	12,586	11,023
Monetary authorities..............................	8 731 ..	....	....	....	....	2,382	1,577	508	405
General government...............................	8 732 ..	3	4	6	4	44	18	7	1
Banks...	8 733 ..	1,148	1,232	1,777	1,904	3,286	2,684	3,680	1,498
Other sectors...	8 734 ..	1,746	2,656	3,449	4,878	6,661	7,339	8,391	9,119
Other assets..	8 736 ..	1,759	2,116	1,644	1,013	1,034	846	927	758
Monetary authorities..............................	8 737 ..	87	230	227	231	302	307	309	179
of which: Short-term...........................	8 739 ..	*70*	*71*	*71*	*73*	*62*	*199*	*192*	*58*
General government...............................	8 740 ..	1,059	1,160	1,019	226	288	301	256	248
of which: Short-term...........................	8 742 ..	....	....	....	....	....	*11*	....	....
Banks...	8 743 ..	444	488	188	225	158	134	129	62
of which: Short-term...........................	8 745 ..	*423*	*463*	*134*	*166*	*93*	*73*	*66*	*5*
Other sectors...	8 746 ..	170	238	209	331	286	104	232	269
of which: Short-term...........................	8 748 ..	*165*	*230*	*202*	*328*	*280*	*74*	*46*	*110*
Reserve assets......................................	8 802 ..	**8,598**	**8,899**	**8,134**	**7,136**	**1,066**	**957**	**1,079**	**1,107**
Monetary gold...	8 812 ..	101	106	83	103	86	88	113	144
Special drawing rights..............................	8 811 ..	9	11	12	12	13	12	311	305
Reserve position in the Fund.....................	8 810 ..	145	120	52	37	25	46	66	114
Foreign exchange....................................	8 803 ..	8,343	8,662	7,987	6,984	942	810	590	543
Other claims...	8 813 ..	....	....	....	....	....	....	....	....

Table 3 (Concluded). INTERNATIONAL INVESTMENT POSITION (End-period stocks), 2003–2010

(Millions of U.S. dollars)

	Code	2003	2004	2005	2006	2007	2008	2009	2010
LIABILITIES	8 995 D.	**21,684**	**27,208**	**30,109**	**40,074**	**61,814**	**64,683**	**68,740**	**64,290**
Direct investment in Slovenia	8 555 ..	**6,308**	**7,590**	**7,236**	**8,985**	**14,375**	**15,638**	**15,181**	**14,393**
Equity capital and reinvested earnings	8 556 ..	5,548	6,630	6,615	8,275	9,975	10,400	10,718	10,019
Claims on direct investors	8 557 ..	....	....	....	....	....	....	....	....
Liabilities to direct investors	8 558 ..	5,548	6,630	6,615	8,275	9,975	10,400	10,718	10,019
Other capital	8 580 ..	760	960	621	710	4,400	5,238	4,462	4,374
Claims on direct investors	8 585 ..	−458	−402	−537	−512	−1,137	−1,098	−1,063	−1,277
Liabilities to direct investors	8 590 ..	1,218	1,362	1,157	1,222	5,537	6,335	5,526	5,651
Portfolio investment	8 652 ..	**2,922**	**3,156**	**2,829**	**4,132**	**6,697**	**6,389**	**13,475**	**15,705**
Equity securities	8 660 ..	295	287	362	866	2,000	833	927	954
Banks	8 663 ..	38	47	54	70	219	81	94	94
Other sectors	8 664 ..	257	240	308	796	1,780	752	833	860
Debt securities	8 669 ..	2,627	2,869	2,467	3,266	4,698	5,556	12,549	14,751
Bonds and notes	8 670 ..	2,587	2,851	2,442	3,235	4,698	5,556	12,549	14,751
Monetary authorities	8 671 ..	....	....	....	....	....	....	....	....
General government	8 672 ..	2,510	2,537	2,029	2,776	4,169	4,943	9,229	10,713
Banks	8 673 ..	42	301	397	437	519	608	2,929	3,704
Other sectors	8 674 ..	35	13	16	22	9	5	391	334
Money market instruments	8 680 ..	39	18	25	31	....	....	....	....
Monetary authorities	8 681 ..	....	....	....	....	....	....	....	....
General government	8 682 ..	39	18	25	31	....	....	....	....
Banks	8 683 ..	....	....	....	....	....	....	....	....
Other sectors	8 684 ..	....	....	....	....	....	....	....	....
Financial derivatives	8 905 ..	**....**	**....**	**....**	**....**	**112**	**317**	**294**	**418**
Monetary authorities	8 906 ..	....	....	....	....	....	....	4	15
General government	8 907 ..	....	....	....	....	....	....	....	....
Banks	8 908 ..	....	....	....	....	75	294	266	395
Other sectors	8 909 ..	....	....	....	....	37	23	24	7
Other investment	8 753 ..	**12,453**	**16,462**	**20,044**	**26,957**	**40,629**	**42,340**	**39,789**	**33,774**
Trade credits	8 756 ..	2,117	2,556	3,368	4,395	5,676	5,593	4,940	5,009
General government	8 757 ..	....	....	....	....	....	....	....	....
of which: Short-term	8 759 ..	....	....	....	....	....	....	....	....
Other sectors	8 760 ..	2,117	2,556	3,368	4,395	5,676	5,593	4,940	5,009
of which: Short-term	8 762 ..	*2,079*	*2,533*	*3,360*	*4,392*	*5,663*	*5,569*	*4,898*	*4,999*
Loans	8 764 ..	8,766	11,835	13,699	17,881	23,018	25,033	22,449	19,580
Monetary authorities	8 765 ..	....	....	....	....	....	....	....	....
of which: Use of Fund credit and loans from the Fund	8 766 ..	....	....	....	....	....	....	....	....
of which: Short-term	8 768 ..	....	....	....	....	....	....	....	....
General government	8 769 ..	478	518	428	318	299	250	215	196
of which: Short-term	8 771 ..	....	....	....	....	....	....	....	....
Banks	8 772 ..	2,855	4,428	6,995	9,686	16,745	17,681	14,032	12,195
of which: Short-term	8 774 ..	*8*	*67*	*633*	*269*	*2,222*	*2,534*	*454*	*660*
Other sectors	8 775 ..	5,433	6,888	6,275	7,877	5,974	7,101	8,202	7,188
of which: Short-term	8 777 ..	*101*	*32*	*119*	*90*	*244*	*459*	*730*	*411*
Currency and deposits	8 780 ..	1,367	1,799	2,775	4,387	11,832	11,597	11,837	8,660
Monetary authorities	8 781 ..	38	49	46	59	5,281	5,054	5,179	3,173
General government	8 782 ..	....	....	....	....	....	....	....	....
Banks	8 783 ..	1,329	1,751	2,728	4,328	6,551	6,543	6,658	5,487
Other sectors	8 784 ..	....	....	....	....	....	....	....	....
Other liabilities	8 786 ..	204	273	202	294	103	118	563	525
Monetary authorities	8 787 ..	....	....	....	....	....	....	339	332
of which: Short-term	8 789 ..	....	....	....	....	....	....	....	....
General government	8 790 ..	11	11	11	12	....	6	4	3
of which: Short-term	8 792 ..	*11*	*11*	*11*	*12*	....			
Banks	8 793 ..	80	123	76	61	57	61	28	11
of which: Short-term	8 795 ..	*11*	*45*	*76*	*61*	*57*	*61*	*28*	*3*
Other sectors	8 796 ..	113	139	115	222	46	51	192	179
of which: Short-term	8 798 ..	*110*	*125*	*107*	*219*	*32*	*36*	*156*	*129*
NET INTERNATIONAL INVESTMENT POSITION	8 995 ..	**−2,331**	**−3,636**	**−3,729**	**−6,987**	**−10,853**	**−17,517**	**−18,563**	**−17,209**
Conversion rates: tolars per U.S. dollar (end of period)	0 102 ..	**189.37**	**176.24**	**202.43**	**181.93**	**....**	**....**	**....**	**....**
Conversion rates: euros per U.S. dollar (end of period)	0 104 ..	**.7918**	**.7342**	**.8477**	**.7593**	**.6793**	**.7185**	**.6942**	**.7484**

Table 1. ANALYTIC PRESENTATION, 2003–2010

(Millions of U.S. dollars)

	Code	2003	2004	2005	2006	2007	2008	2009	2010
A. Current Account[1]	4 993 Z.	**−39.92**	**−18.92**	**−90.20**	**−92.43**	**−151.93**	**−216.40**	**−249.82**	**−372.56**
Goods: exports f.o.b.	2 100 ..	66.63	85.64	104.76	114.00	164.51	210.50	164.94	226.52
Goods: imports f.o.b.	3 100 ..	−93.85	−121.41	−185.09	−195.68	−261.98	−292.88	−239.19	−360.33
Balance on Goods	4 100 ..	*−27.22*	*−35.77*	*−80.33*	*−81.68*	*−97.47*	*−82.39*	*−74.25*	*−133.81*
Services: credit	2 200 ..	25.26	30.80	41.42	53.02	58.96	59.00	69.90	106.49
Services: debit	3 200 ..	−62.01	−41.30	−57.98	−68.00	−96.74	−115.94	−105.01	−187.49
Balance on Goods and Services	4 991 ..	*−63.97*	*−46.27*	*−96.89*	*−96.65*	*−135.25*	*−139.33*	*−109.37*	*−214.81*
Income: credit	2 300 ..	3.53	10.51	8.69	12.57	14.27	20.25	12.70	17.50
Income: debit	3 300 ..	−6.96	−8.32	−7.07	−31.21	−52.63	−115.22	−148.32	−138.62
Balance on Goods, Services, and Income	4 992 ..	*−67.40*	*−44.07*	*−95.27*	*−115.29*	*−173.62*	*−234.30*	*−244.98*	*−335.93*
Current transfers: credit	2 379 Z.	46.36	50.01	41.06	33.18	30.63	30.89	30.24	22.29
Current transfers: debit	3 379 ..	−18.88	−24.85	−35.99	−10.32	−8.94	−12.99	−35.08	−58.92
B. Capital Account[1]	4 994 Z.	**12.41**	**1.50**	**27.63**	**19.53**	**25.59**	**14.31**	**26.84**	**49.78**
Capital account: credit	2 994 Z.	12.71	1.62	19.68	19.53	25.59	14.88	26.84	50.30
Capital account: debit	3 994 ..	−.30	−.12	7.95	....	....	−.57	....	−.53
Total, Groups A Plus B	4 981 ..	*−27.51*	*−17.43*	*−62.57*	*−72.90*	*−126.33*	*−202.09*	*−222.98*	*−322.78*
C. Financial Account[1]	4 995 W.	**−29.27**	**−19.12**	**−9.37**	**22.15**	**54.35**	**84.99**	**137.91**	**270.06**
Direct investment abroad	4 505 ..	−.03	−.01	−1.58	−4.74	−12.18	−3.77	−2.98	−2.29
Direct investment in Solomon Islands	4 555 Z.	−1.80	6.02	18.58	34.08	64.43	94.92	119.74	237.90
Portfolio investment assets	4 602 ..	....	....	....	....	....	....	1.23	−2.65
Equity securities	4 610 ..	....	....	....	....	....	....	....	....
Debt securities	4 619 ..	....	....	....	....	....	....	....	....
Portfolio investment liabilities	4 652 Z.	....	....	....	....	....	....	....	....
Equity securities	4 660 ..	....	....	....	....	....	....	....	....
Debt securities	4 669 Z.	....	....	....	....	....	....	....	....
Financial derivatives	4 910 ..	....	....	....	....	....	....	....	....
Financial derivatives assets	4 900 ..	....	....	....	....	....	....	....	....
Financial derivatives liabilities	4 905 ..	....	....	....	....	....	....	....	....
Other investment assets	4 703 ..	....	....	−11.73	−17.76	−8.61	−16.88	−2.92	−7.18
Monetary authorities	4 701 ..	....	....	....	....	....	....	....	....
General government	4 704 ..	....	....	....	....	....	....	....	....
Banks	4 705 ..	....	....	....	....	....	....	....	....
Other sectors	4 728 ..	....	....	−11.73	....	....	....	....	....
Other investment liabilities	4 753 W.	−27.44	−25.12	−14.63	10.57	10.71	10.72	22.85	44.28
Monetary authorities	4 753 WA	....	....	....	....	....	....	14.47	....
General government	4 753 ZB	−4.48	−2.25	−8.60	....	....	....	−6.61	−8.72
Banks	4 753 ZC	....	....	....	....	....	....	....	....
Other sectors	4 753 ZD	−22.96	−22.87	−6.03	....	....	....	20.99	43.21
Total, Groups A Through C	4 983 ..	*−56.78*	*−36.54*	*−71.94*	*−50.75*	*−71.98*	*−117.10*	*−85.07*	*−52.73*
D. Net Errors and Omissions	4 998 ..	**35.19**	**−6.41**	**53.51**	**11.07**	**18.05**	**−2.12**	**23.19**	**−12.42**
Total, Groups A Through D	4 984 ..	*−21.58*	*−42.95*	*−18.43*	*−39.68*	*−53.93*	*−119.22*	*−61.87*	*−65.15*
E. Reserves and Related Items	4 802 A.	**21.58**	**42.95**	**18.43**	**39.68**	**53.93**	**119.22**	**61.87**	**74.60**
Reserve assets	4 802 ..	18.43	41.40	17.49	−10.07	−17.07	27.21	−59.22	−102.96
Use of Fund credit and loans	4 766 ..	....	....	....	....	....	....	....	9.45
Exceptional financing	4 920 ..	3.15	1.55	.94	49.75	70.99	92.01	121.09	168.11
Conversion rates: Solomon Islands dollars per U.S. dollar	0 101 ..	**7.5059**	**7.4847**	**7.5299**	**7.6095**	**7.6520**	**7.7479**	**8.0550**	**8.0645**

[1] Excludes components that have been classified in the categories of Group E.

Table 2. STANDARD PRESENTATION, 2003–2010

(Millions of U.S. dollars)

	Code	2003	2004	2005	2006	2007	2008	2009	2010
CURRENT ACCOUNT............................	4 993 ..	−39.92	−18.92	−90.20	−42.68	−80.93	−124.39	−128.72	−204.45
A. GOODS...................................	4 100 ..	−27.22	−35.77	−80.33	−81.68	−97.47	−82.39	−74.25	−133.81
Credit...............................	2 100 ..	66.63	85.64	104.76	114.00	164.51	210.50	164.94	226.52
General merchandise: exports f.o.b...........	2 110 ..	66.63	85.64	104.76	113.18	163.67	207.85	161.27	223.33
Goods for processing: exports f.o.b..........	2 150 ..	....	....	....	....	....	....	....	....
Repairs on goods........................	2 160 ..	....	....	....	....	....	....	....	....
Goods procured in ports by carriers.........	2 170 ..	....	....	....	....	....	....	....	....
Nonmonetary gold.......................	2 180 ..	....	....	....	.82	.84	2.65	3.67	3.19
Debit................................	3 100 ..	−93.85	−121.41	−185.09	−195.68	−261.98	−292.88	−239.19	−360.33
General merchandise: imports f.o.b...........	3 110 ..	−93.85	−121.41	−185.09	−195.68	−261.98	−292.88	−239.19	−360.33
Goods for processing: imports f.o.b..........	3 150 ..	....	....	....	....	....	....	....	....
Repairs on goods........................	3 160 ..	....	....	....	....	....	....	....	....
Goods procured in ports by carriers.........	3 170 ..	....	....	....	....	....	....	....	....
Nonmonetary gold.......................	3 180 ..	....	....	....	....	....	....	....	....
B. SERVICES.................................	4 200 ..	−36.75	−10.50	−16.56	−14.97	−37.78	−56.94	−35.11	−81.00
Total credit............................	2 200 ..	*25.26*	*30.80*	*41.42*	*53.02*	*58.96*	*59.00*	*69.90*	*106.49*
Total debit............................	3 200 ..	*−62.01*	*−41.30*	*−57.98*	*−68.00*	*−96.74*	*−115.94*	*−105.01*	*−187.49*
Transportation services, credit............	2 205 ..	2.01	1.11	7.97	17.74	17.27	7.05	13.81	36.32
Passenger..............................	2 850 ..	*.13*	*.02*	*4.77*	*9.76*	*10.52*	*3.72*	*5.90*	*11.52*
Freight................................	2 851 ..	*.42*	*.26*	*.73*	*3.26*	*1.97*	*1.57*	*2.50*	*2.45*
Other.................................	2 852 ..	*1.46*	*.84*	*2.47*	*4.73*	*4.78*	*1.77*	*5.42*	*22.35*
Sea transport, passenger..................	2 207 ..	.10	....	.01	....	....	....	5.90	11.52
Sea transport, freight....................	2 208 ..	.42	.24	.20	....	....	....	2.50	2.45
Sea transport, other.....................	2 209 ..	1.44	.80	1.68	....	....	....	5.42	22.35
Air transport, passenger..................	2 211 ..	.03	.02	4.76	....	....	....	....	....
Air transport, freight....................	2 212 ..	....	.02	.53	....	....	....	....	....
Air transport, other.....................	2 213 ..	.01	.04	.79	....	....	....	....	....
Other transport, passenger................	2 215 ..	....	....	....	....	....	....	....	....
Other transport, freight..................	2 216 ..	....	....	....	....	....	....	....	....
Other transport, other...................	2 217 ..	....	....	....	....	....	....	....	....
Transportation services, debit............	3 205 ..	−25.56	−18.73	−30.66	−25.62	−35.53	−42.34	−35.81	−45.77
Passenger..............................	3 850 ..	*−1.97*	*−3.25*	*−6.46*	*−4.31*	*−6.57*	*−6.52*	*−6.03*	*−3.96*
Freight................................	3 851 ..	*−23.35*	*−14.91*	*−23.18*	*−18.46*	*−25.91*	*−30.75*	*−23.78*	*−37.18*
Other.................................	3 852 ..	*−.23*	*−.56*	*−1.02*	*−2.85*	*−3.04*	*−5.06*	*−5.99*	*−4.63*
Sea transport, passenger..................	3 207 ..	....	....	−.21	....	....	....	−6.03	−3.96
Sea transport, freight....................	3 208 ..	−23.18	−14.40	−22.40	....	....	....	−23.78	−37.18
Sea transport, other.....................	3 209 ..	−.01	−.04	−.34	....	....	....	−5.99	−4.63
Air transport, passenger..................	3 211 ..	−1.97	−3.25	−6.25	....	....	....	....	....
Air transport, freight....................	3 212 ..	−.17	−.52	−.78	....	....	....	....	....
Air transport, other.....................	3 213 ..	−.22	−.52	−.67	....	....	....	....	....
Other transport, passenger................	3 215 ..	....	....	....	....	....	....	....	....
Other transport, freight..................	3 216 ..	....	....	....	....	....	....	....	....
Other transport, other...................	3 217 ..	....	....	....	....	....	....	....	....
Travel, credit...........................	2 236 ..	1.54	3.52	1.55	25.53	27.34	36.89	44.05	53.85
Business travel.........................	2 237 ..	.82	2.23	.27	14.38	14.80	18.07	21.09	26.81
Personal travel.........................	2 240 ..	.72	1.28	1.28	11.15	12.54	18.82	22.96	27.03
Travel, debit............................	3 236 ..	−4.45	−8.97	−4.73	−22.15	−29.02	−34.01	−31.75	−47.24
Business travel.........................	3 237 ..	−1.62	−2.54	−1.52	−10.00	−11.77	−12.57	−12.72	−18.86
Personal travel.........................	3 240 ..	−2.83	−6.43	−3.21	−12.15	−17.26	−21.44	−19.04	−28.38
Other services, credit....................	2 200 BA	21.71	26.17	31.90	9.75	14.36	15.06	12.03	16.33
Communications.........................	2 245 ..	.05	.15	1.43	6.04	6.93	7.10	2.50	2.65
Construction...........................	2 249 ..	.05	.18	1.02	.03	.03	.46	.03	.43
Insurance..............................	2 253 ..	.10	.11	.04	.06	.10	.07	....	....
Financial...............................	2 260 ..	.91	1.21	.68	1.47	1.12	1.91	5.40	8.24
Computer and information................	2 262 ..	.02	.13	.09	.01	.01	.01	.01	.02
Royalties and licence fees................	2 266 ..	.11	.29	....	.02	.02	.02	.02	.01
Other business services..................	2 268 ..	18.13	18.94	22.31	.22	3.00	.25	.04	2.18
Personal, cultural, and recreational.........	2 287 ..	.64	.73	1.43	....	....	....	....	.19
Government, n.i.e.......................	2 291 ..	1.69	4.44	4.90	1.90	3.15	5.24	4.04	2.60
Other services, debit.....................	3 200 BA	−32.00	−13.60	−22.59	−20.23	−32.19	−39.59	−37.45	−94.48
Communications.........................	3 245 ..	−2.23	−2.33	−1.89	−1.66	−2.16	−6.14	−1.65	−2.29
Construction...........................	3 249 ..	....	.01	....	−.26	−.82	−2.15	−.57	−39.32
Insurance..............................	3 253 ..	−1.20	−1.83	−1.13	−2.59	−3.62	−5.16	−5.00	−6.73
Financial...............................	3 260 ..	−.82	−2.36	−1.91	−1.90	−1.98	−2.81	−2.90	−4.10
Computer and information................	3 262 ..	−.81	−2.45	−1.48	−.61	−.76	−2.37	−.70	−.78
Royalties and licence fees................	3 266 ..	−.01	−.01	−.24	−.75	−1.13	−1.45	−1.20	−.74
Other business services..................	3 268 ..	−26.82	−5.82	−14.40	−10.75	−19.80	−16.29	−20.87	−29.89
Personal, cultural, and recreational.........	3 287 ..	−.03	.03	−.11	−.06	−.05	−.28	−.53	−2.67
Government, n.i.e.......................	3 291 ..	−.08	1.15	−1.42	−1.64	−1.88	−2.93	−4.03	−7.95

Table 2 (Continued). STANDARD PRESENTATION, 2003–2010

(Millions of U.S. dollars)

	Code	2003	2004	2005	2006	2007	2008	2009	2010
C. INCOME	4 300	**−3.43**	**2.20**	**1.62**	**−18.63**	**−38.37**	**−94.98**	**−135.62**	**−121.12**
Total credit	2 300	*3.53*	*10.51*	*8.69*	*12.57*	*14.27*	*20.25*	*12.70*	*17.50*
Total debit	3 300	*−6.96*	*−8.32*	*−7.07*	*−31.21*	*−52.63*	*−115.22*	*−148.32*	*−138.62*
Compensation of employees, credit	2 310	**2.79**	**6.54**	**4.46**	**1.75**	**1.90**	**1.53**	**2.30**	**1.22**
Compensation of employees, debit	3 310	**−1.48**	**−1.52**	**−1.74**	**−1.80**	**−3.66**	**−2.55**	**−4.41**	**−3.41**
Investment income, credit	2 320	**.74**	**3.97**	**4.23**	**10.83**	**12.37**	**18.71**	**10.41**	**16.28**
Direct investment income	2 330	.05	....	.12	.40	2.08	3.53	2.53	2.57
Dividends and distributed branch profits	2 332	....	....	....	.27	1.36	2.33	1.63	1.56
Reinvested earnings and undistributed branch profits	2 333	.02	....	.12	.14	.71	1.20	.91	1.02
Income on debt (interest)	2 334	.03	....	....	....	....	....	....	....
Portfolio investment income	2 339	....	....	....	....	....	....	.23	.43
Income on equity	2 340	....	....	....	....	....	....	....	....
Income on bonds and notes	2 350	....	....	....	....	....	....	....	....
Income on money market instruments	2 360	....	....	....	....	....	....	....	....
Other investment income	2 370	.69	3.97	4.11	10.42	10.29	15.19	7.64	13.27
Investment income, debit	3 320	**−5.48**	**−6.80**	**−5.33**	**−29.41**	**−48.97**	**−112.67**	**−143.91**	**−135.21**
Direct investment income	3 330	−5.48	−6.80	−5.33	−23.64	−41.01	−103.51	−135.54	−127.04
Dividends and distributed branch profits	3 332	−1.87	−3.89	−4.22	−3.32	−3.65	−20.75	−25.66	−14.00
Reinvested earnings and undistributed branch profits	3 333	....	−1.75	....	−20.32	−37.36	−82.76	−109.88	−113.04
Income on debt (interest)	3 334	−3.61	−1.16	−1.12	....	....	....	....	....
Portfolio investment income	3 339	....	....	....	....	....	....	....	....
Income on equity	3 340	....	....	....	....	....	....	....	....
Income on bonds and notes	3 350	....	....	....	....	....	....	....	....
Income on money market instruments	3 360	....	....	....	....	....	....	....	....
Other investment income	3 370	....	....	....	−5.77	−7.95	−9.17	−8.37	−8.17
D. CURRENT TRANSFERS	4 379	**27.48**	**25.15**	**5.07**	**72.61**	**92.68**	**109.92**	**116.26**	**131.47**
Credit	2 379	**46.36**	**50.01**	**41.06**	**82.93**	**101.62**	**122.91**	**151.34**	**190.40**
General government	2 380	32.15	26.31	13.07	49.87	71.12	92.14	121.15	168.15
Other sectors	2 390	14.21	23.70	27.99	33.06	30.51	30.77	30.18	22.25
Workers' remittances	2 391	1.09	2.15	2.70	.17	.18	.18	.18	.44
Other current transfers	2 392	13.12	21.55	25.29	32.89	30.33	30.59	30.00	21.80
Debit	3 379	**−18.88**	**−24.85**	**−35.99**	**−10.32**	**−8.94**	**−12.99**	**−35.08**	**−58.92**
General government	3 380	−4.58	−1.84	−4.08	−.96	−.50	−1.60	−.38	−.62
Other sectors	3 390	−14.31	−23.01	−31.91	−9.36	−8.44	−11.39	−34.69	−58.30
Workers' remittances	3 391	−.10	−.29	−.37	....	....	....	−34.69	−58.30
Other current transfers	3 392	−14.21	−22.72	−31.54	−9.36	−8.44	−11.39	....	....
CAPITAL AND FINANCIAL ACCOUNT	4 996	**4.73**	**25.33**	**36.69**	**31.61**	**62.88**	**126.51**	**105.53**	**216.87**
CAPITAL ACCOUNT	4 994	**12.41**	**1.50**	**27.63**	**19.53**	**25.59**	**14.31**	**26.84**	**49.78**
Total credit	2 994	*12.71*	*1.62*	*19.68*	*19.53*	*25.59*	*14.88*	*26.84*	*50.30*
Total debit	3 994	*−.30*	*−.12*	*7.95*	....	....	*−.57*	....	*−.53*
Capital transfers, credit	2 400	**12.71**	**1.62**	**19.68**	**19.53**	**25.59**	**14.69**	**26.84**	**50.30**
General government	2 401	12.71	1.54	19.68	19.53	25.59	14.69	26.84	39.87
Debt forgiveness	2 402	....	....	....	....	3.06	....	....	....
Other capital transfers	2 410	12.71	1.54	19.68	19.53	22.54	14.69	26.84	39.87
Other sectors	2 430	....	.07	....	....	....	....	....	10.44
Migrants' transfers	2 431	....	....	....	....	....	....	....	....
Debt forgiveness	2 432	....	....	....	....	....	....	....	....
Other capital transfers	2 440	....	.07	....	....	....	....	....	10.44
Capital transfers, debit	3 400	**−.12**	**−.12**	**7.95**	....	....	**−.19**	....	**−.53**
General government	3 401	....	....	8.05	....	....	−.19	....	....
Debt forgiveness	3 402	....	....	8.05	....	....	....	....	....
Other capital transfers	3 410	....	....	....	....	....	−.19	....	....
Other sectors	3 430	−.12	−.12	−.10	....	....	....	....	−.53
Migrants' transfers	3 431	−.12	−.12	−.10	....	....	....	....	....
Debt forgiveness	3 432	....	....	....	....	....	....	....	....
Other capital transfers	3 440	....	....	....	....	....	....	....	−.53
Nonproduced nonfinancial assets, credit	2 480	....	....	....	....	....	**.19**	....	....
Nonproduced nonfinancial assets, debit	3 480	**−.18**	....	....	....	....	**−.38**	....	....

Table 2 (Continued). STANDARD PRESENTATION, 2003–2010

(Millions of U.S. dollars)

	Code	2003	2004	2005	2006	2007	2008	2009	2010
FINANCIAL ACCOUNT	4 995 ..	**−7.69**	**23.84**	**9.06**	**12.08**	**37.29**	**112.20**	**78.69**	**167.09**
A. DIRECT INVESTMENT	4 500 ..	**−1.83**	**5.67**	**17.00**	**29.34**	**52.25**	**91.14**	**116.75**	**235.61**
Direct investment abroad	4 505 ..	**−.03**	**−.01**	**−1.58**	**−4.74**	**−12.18**	**−3.77**	**−2.98**	**−2.29**
Equity capital	4 510 ..	−.03	−.01	−1.53	−4.61	−11.47	−2.58	−2.08	−1.28
Claims on affiliated enterprises	4 515 ..	....	....	.06	....	....	....	....	....
Liabilities to affiliated enterprises	4 520 ..	−.03	−.01	−1.59	....	....	....	....	....
Reinvested earnings	4 525 ..	−.02	....	−.12	−.14	−.71	−1.20	−.91	−1.02
Other capital	4 530 ..	.02	....	.07	....	....	....	....	....
Claims on affiliated enterprises	4 535 ..	....	....	....	....	....	....	....	....
Liabilities to affiliated enterprises	4 540 ..	.02	....	.07	....	....	....	....	....
Direct investment in Solomon Islands	4 555 ..	**−1.80**	**5.68**	**18.58**	**34.08**	**64.43**	**94.92**	**119.74**	**237.90**
Equity capital	4 560 ..	−.71	8.35	18.40	13.62	21.64	4.30	4.32	116.33
Claims on direct investors	4 565 ..	−.80	8.67	16.51	13.62	21.64	4.30	4.32	116.33
Liabilities to direct investors	4 570 ..	.09	−.32	1.88	....	....	....	....	....
Reinvested earnings	4 575 ..	....	1.75	....	20.32	37.36	82.76	109.88	113.04
Other capital	4 580 ..	−1.10	−4.42	.18	.14	5.43	7.86	5.53	8.52
Claims on direct investors	4 585 ..	....	....	....	....	....	....	....	....
Liabilities to direct investors	4 590 ..	−1.10	−4.42	.18	....	....	....	....	....
B. PORTFOLIO INVESTMENT	4 600 ..	....	....	....	....	....	....	1.23	−2.65
Assets	4 602 ..	....	....	....	....	....	....	1.23	−2.65
Equity securities	4 610 ..	....	....	....	....	....	....	....	....
Monetary authorities	4 611 ..	....	....	....	....	....	....	....	....
General government	4 612 ..	....	....	....	....	....	....	....	....
Banks	4 613 ..	....	....	....	....	....	....	....	....
Other sectors	4 614 ..	....	....	....	....	....	....	....	....
Debt securities	4 619 ..	....	....	....	....	....	....	....	....
Bonds and notes	4 620 ..	....	....	....	....	....	....	....	....
Monetary authorities	4 621 ..	....	....	....	....	....	....	....	....
General government	4 622 ..	....	....	....	....	....	....	....	....
Banks	4 623 ..	....	....	....	....	....	....	....	....
Other sectors	4 624 ..	....	....	....	....	....	....	....	....
Money market instruments	4 630 ..	....	....	....	....	....	....	....	....
Monetary authorities	4 631 ..	....	....	....	....	....	....	....	....
General government	4 632 ..	....	....	....	....	....	....	....	....
Banks	4 633 ..	....	....	....	....	....	....	....	....
Other sectors	4 634 ..	....	....	....	....	....	....	....	....
Liabilities	4 652 ..	....	....	....	....	....	....	....	....
Equity securities	4 660 ..	....	....	....	....	....	....	....	....
Banks	4 663 ..	....	....	....	....	....	....	....	....
Other sectors	4 664 ..	....	....	....	....	....	....	....	....
Debt securities	4 669 ..	....	....	....	....	....	....	....	....
Bonds and notes	4 670 ..	....	....	....	....	....	....	....	....
Monetary authorities	4 671 ..	....	....	....	....	....	....	....	....
General government	4 672 ..	....	....	....	....	....	....	....	....
Banks	4 673 ..	....	....	....	....	....	....	....	....
Other sectors	4 674 ..	....	....	....	....	....	....	....	....
Money market instruments	4 680 ..	....	....	....	....	....	....	....	....
Monetary authorities	4 681 ..	....	....	....	....	....	....	....	....
General government	4 682 ..	....	....	....	....	....	....	....	....
Banks	4 683 ..	....	....	....	....	....	....	....	....
Other sectors	4 684 ..	....	....	....	....	....	....	....	....
C. FINANCIAL DERIVATIVES	4 910 ..	....	....	....	....	....	....	....	....
Monetary authorities	4 911 ..	....	....	....	....	....	....	....	....
General government	4 912 ..	....	....	....	....	....	....	....	....
Banks	4 913 ..	....	....	....	....	....	....	....	....
Other sectors	4 914 ..	....	....	....	....	....	....	....	....
Assets	4 900 ..	....	....	....	....	....	....	....	....
Monetary authorities	4 901 ..	....	....	....	....	....	....	....	....
General government	4 902 ..	....	....	....	....	....	....	....	....
Banks	4 903 ..	....	....	....	....	....	....	....	....
Other sectors	4 904 ..	....	....	....	....	....	....	....	....
Liabilities	4 905 ..	....	....	....	....	....	....	....	....
Monetary authorities	4 906 ..	....	....	....	....	....	....	....	....
General government	4 907 ..	....	....	....	....	....	....	....	....
Banks	4 908 ..	....	....	....	....	....	....	....	....
Other sectors	4 909 ..	....	....	....	....	....	....	....	....

Table 2 (Concluded). STANDARD PRESENTATION, 2003–2010

(Millions of U.S. dollars)

	Code	2003	2004	2005	2006	2007	2008	2009	2010
D. OTHER INVESTMENT	4 700 ..	**−24.29**	**−23.23**	**−25.43**	**−7.19**	**2.11**	**−6.15**	**19.93**	**37.09**
Assets	4 703 ..	....	....	**−11.73**	**−17.76**	**−8.61**	**−16.88**	**−2.92**	**−7.18**
Trade credits	4 706 ..	....	....	.05	−1.45	−1.16	1.23	−.94	−3.94
General government	4 707 ..	....	....	....	....	....	....	....	....
of which: Short-term	4 709 ..	....	....	....	....	....	....	....	....
Other sectors	4 710 ..	....	....	.05	....	....	....	....	....
of which: Short-term	4 712 ..	....	....	*.05*	....	....	....	....	....
Loans	4 714 ..	....	....	....	....	....	....	....	....
Monetary authorities	4 715 ..	....	....	....	....	....	....	....	....
of which: Short-term	4 718 ..	....	....	....	....	....	....	....	....
General government	4 719 ..	....	....	....	....	....	....	....	....
of which: Short-term	4 721 ..	....	....	....	....	....	....	....	....
Banks	4 722 ..	....	....	....	....	....	....	....	....
of which: Short-term	4 724 ..	....	....	....	....	....	....	....	....
Other sectors	4 725 ..	....	....	....	....	....	....	....	....
of which: Short-term	4 727 ..	....	....	....	....	....	....	....	....
Currency and deposits	4 730 ..	....	....	....	−16.31	−7.44	−18.11	6.21	−9.40
Monetary authorities	4 731 ..	....	....	....	....	....	....	....	....
General government	4 732 ..	....	....	....	....	....	....	....	....
Banks	4 733 ..	....	....	....	....	....	....	....	....
Other sectors	4 734 ..	....	....	....	....	....	....	....	....
Other assets	4 736 ..	....	....	−11.78	....	....	....	−8.19	6.16
Monetary authorities	4 737 ..	....	....	....	....	....	....	....	....
of which: Short-term	4 739 ..	....	....	....	....	....	....	....	....
General government	4 740 ..	....	....	....	....	....	....	....	....
of which: Short-term	4 742 ..	....	....	....	....	....	....	....	....
Banks	4 743 ..	....	....	....	....	....	....	....	....
of which: Short-term	4 745 ..	....	....	....	....	....	....	....	....
Other sectors	4 746 ..	....	....	−11.78	....	....	....	....	....
of which: Short-term	4 748 ..	....	....	*−.76*	....	....	....	....	....
Liabilities	4 753 ..	**−24.29**	**−23.23**	**−13.69**	**10.57**	**10.71**	**10.72**	**22.85**	**44.28**
Trade credits	4 756 ..	−22.21	−22.75	−.73	3.10	.86	.73	.69	16.36
General government	4 757 ..	....	....	....	....	....	....	....	....
of which: Short-term	4 759 ..	....	....	....	....	....	....	....	....
Other sectors	4 760 ..	−22.21	−22.75	−.73	....	....	....	.69	16.36
of which: Short-term	4 762 ..	*−22.21*	*−23.37*	*−.98*	....	....	....	*.69*	*16.36*
Loans	4 764 ..	−7.82	−1.20	−12.96	4.16	9.60	5.19	4.48	37.92
Monetary authorities	4 765 ..	....	....	....	....	....	....	....	9.45
of which: Use of Fund credit and loans from the Fund	4 766 ..	....	....	....	....	....	....	....	*9.45*
of which: Short-term	4 768 ..	....	....	....	....	....	....	....	....
General government	4 769 ..	−1.33	−.39	−8.60	....	....	....	−6.61	−8.72
of which: Short-term	4 771 ..	*3.15*	....	....	....	....	....	....	....
Banks	4 772 ..	....	....	....	....	....	....	....	....
of which: Short-term	4 774 ..	....	....	....	....	....	....	....	....
Other sectors	4 775 ..	−6.49	−.81	−4.35	....	....	....	11.09	37.19
of which: Short-term	4 777 ..	*−6.31*	*−.20*	*−4.55*	....	....	....	....	....
Currency and deposits	4 780 ..	....	....	....	2.05	.26	4.29	−6.00	.34
Monetary authorities	4 781 ..	....	....	....	....	....	....	....	....
General government	4 782 ..	....	....	....	....	....	....	....	....
Banks	4 783 ..	....	....	....	....	....	....	....	....
Other sectors	4 784 ..	....	....	....	....	....	....	....	....
Other liabilities	4 786 ..	5.74	.72	....	1.26	....	.51	23.68	−10.34
Monetary authorities	4 787 ..	....	....	....	....	....	....	14.47	....
of which: Short-term	4 789 ..	....	....	....	....	....	....	....	....
General government	4 790 ..	....	....	....	....	....	....	....	....
of which: Short-term	4 792 ..	....	....	....	....	....	....	....	....
Banks	4 793 ..	....	....	....	....	....	....	....	....
of which: Short-term	4 795 ..	....	....	....	....	....	....	....	....
Other sectors	4 796 ..	5.74	.72	....	....	....	....	9.21	−10.34
of which: Short-term	4 798 ..	*5.74*	*.72*	....	....	....	....	....	....
E. RESERVE ASSETS	4 802 ..	**18.43**	**41.40**	**17.49**	**−10.07**	**−17.07**	**27.21**	**−59.22**	**−102.96**
Monetary gold	4 812 ..	....	....	....	....	....	....	....	....
Special drawing rights	4 811 ..	.01	....	....	−.01	.01	−.01	−14.46	....
Reserve position in the Fund	4 810 ..	....	....	....	....	....	....	....	....
Foreign exchange	4 803 ..	18.43	41.40	17.49	−10.06	−17.07	27.22	−44.76	−102.96
Other claims	4 813 ..	....	....	....	....	....	....	....	....
NET ERRORS AND OMISSIONS	4 998 ..	**35.19**	**−6.41**	**53.51**	**11.07**	**18.05**	**−2.12**	**23.19**	**−12.42**

Table 3. INTERNATIONAL INVESTMENT POSITION (End-period stocks), 2003–2010

(Millions of U.S. dollars)

	Code	2003	2004	2005	2006	2007	2008	2009	2010
ASSETS................................	8 995 C.	....	....	....	209.10	252.64	236.06	364.43	465.23
Direct investment abroad........................	8 505 ..	....	....	....	6.74	18.89	21.72	24.53	26.82
Equity capital and reinvested earnings................	8 506 ..	....	....	....	....	....	....	....	....
Claims on affiliated enterprises....................	8 507 ..	....	....	....	....	....	....	....	....
Liabilities to affiliated enterprises..................	8 508 ..	....	....	....	....	....	....	....	....
Other capital...................................	8 530 ..	....	....	....	....	....	....	....	....
Claims on affiliated enterprises....................	8 535 ..	....	....	....	....	....	....	....	....
Liabilities to affiliated enterprises..................	8 540 ..	....	....	....	....	....	....	....	....
Portfolio investment............................	8 602 ..	....	....	....	....	....	....	11.91	14.56
Equity securities...............................	8 610 ..	....	....	....	....	....	....	....	....
Monetary authorities..........................	8 611 ..	....	....	....	....	....	....	....	....
General government...........................	8 612 ..	....	....	....	....	....	....	....	....
Banks......................................	8 613 ..	....	....	....	....	....	....	....	....
Other sectors................................	8 614 ..	....	....	....	....	....	....	....	....
Debt securities................................	8 619 ..	....	....	....	....	....	....	....	....
Bonds and notes.............................	8 620 ..	....	....	....	....	....	....	....	....
Monetary authorities........................	8 621 ..	....	....	....	....	....	....	....	....
General government.........................	8 622 ..	....	....	....	....	....	....	....	....
Banks....................................	8 623 ..	....	....	....	....	....	....	....	....
Other sectors..............................	8 624 ..	....	....	....	....	....	....	....	....
Money market instruments.....................	8 630 ..	....	....	....	....	....	....	....	....
Monetary authorities........................	8 631 ..	....	....	....	....	....	....	....	....
General government.........................	8 632 ..	....	....	....	....	....	....	....	....
Banks....................................	8 633 ..	....	....	....	....	....	....	....	....
Other sectors..............................	8 634 ..	....	....	....	....	....	....	....	....
Financial derivatives...........................	8 900 ..	....	....	....	....	....	....	....	....
Monetary authorities...........................	8 901 ..	....	....	....	....	....	....	....	....
General government............................	8 902 ..	....	....	....	....	....	....	....	....
Banks..	8 903 ..	....	....	....	....	....	....	....	....
Other sectors..................................	8 904 ..	....	....	....	....	....	....	....	....
Other investment..............................	8 703 ..	....	....	....	97.20	112.35	123.93	166.62	158.02
Trade credits..................................	8 706 ..	....	....	....	....	....	....	....	....
General government...........................	8 707 ..	....	....	....	....	....	....	....	....
of which: Short-term........................	8 709 ..	....	....	....	....	....	....	....	....
Other sectors................................	8 710 ..	....	....	....	....	....	....	....	....
of which: Short-term........................	8 712 ..	....	....	....	....	....	....	....	....
Loans..	8 714 ..	....	....	....	....	....	....	....	....
Monetary authorities..........................	8 715 ..	....	....	....	....	....	....	....	....
of which: Short-term........................	8 718 ..	....	....	....	....	....	....	....	....
General government...........................	8 719 ..	....	....	....	....	....	....	....	....
of which: Short-term........................	8 721 ..	....	....	....	....	....	....	....	....
Banks......................................	8 722 ..	....	....	....	....	....	....	....	....
of which: Short-term........................	8 724 ..	....	....	....	....	....	....	....	....
Other sectors................................	8 725 ..	....	....	....	....	....	....	....	....
of which: Short-term........................	8 727 ..	....	....	....	....	....	....	....	....
Currency and deposits..........................	8 730 ..	....	....	....	....	....	....	....	....
Monetary authorities..........................	8 731 ..	....	....	....	....	....	....	....	....
General government...........................	8 732 ..	....	....	....	....	....	....	....	....
Banks......................................	8 733 ..	....	....	....	....	....	....	....	....
Other sectors................................	8 734 ..	....	....	....	....	....	....	....	....
Other assets..................................	8 736 ..	....	....	....	....	....	....	....	....
Monetary authorities..........................	8 737 ..	....	....	....	....	....	....	....	....
of which: Short-term........................	8 739 ..	....	....	....	....	....	....	....	....
General government...........................	8 740 ..	....	....	....	....	....	....	....	....
of which: Short-term........................	8 742 ..	....	....	....	....	....	....	....	....
Banks......................................	8 743 ..	....	....	....	....	....	....	....	....
of which: Short-term........................	8 745 ..	....	....	....	....	....	....	....	....
Other sectors................................	8 746 ..	....	....	....	....	....	....	....	....
of which: Short-term........................	8 748 ..	....	....	....	....	....	....	....	....
Reserve assets...............................	8 802 ..	....	....	....	105.15	121.40	90.41	161.37	265.83
Monetary gold.................................	8 812 ..	....	....	....	....	....	....	....	....
Special drawing rights..........................	8 811 ..	....	....	....	.01	....	.01	14.52	14.26
Reserve position in the Fund.....................	8 810 ..	.82	.85	.79	.83	.87	.85	.86	.85
Foreign exchange..............................	8 803 ..	....	....	....	104.32	120.53	89.54	145.99	265.83
Other claims..................................	8 813 ..	....	....	....	....	....	....	....	....

Table 3 (Concluded). INTERNATIONAL INVESTMENT POSITION (End-period stocks), 2003–2010

(Millions of U.S. dollars)

	Code	2003	2004	2005	2006	2007	2008	2009	2010
LIABILITIES..	8 995 D.	....	....	....	370.58	447.88	542.79	738.67	1,049.43
Direct investment in Solomon Islands.................	8 555 ..	....	....	....	152.73	216.14	298.98	416.21	654.11
Equity capital and reinvested earnings...........................	8 556 ..	....	....	....	....	....	....	....	....
Claims on direct investors........................	8 557 ..	....	....	....	....	....	....	....	....
Liabilities to direct investors.....................	8 558 ..	....	....	....	....	....	....	....	....
Other capital..................................	8 580 ..	....	....	....	....	....	....	....	....
Claims on direct investors........................	8 585 ..	....	....	....	....	....	....	....	....
Liabilities to direct investors.....................	8 590 ..	....	....	....	....	....	....	....	....
Portfolio investment.............................	8 652 ..	....	....	....	....	....	....	3.98	3.98
Equity securities.................................	8 660 ..	....	....	....	....	....	....	....	....
Banks..	8 663 ..	....	....	....	....	....	....	....	....
Other sectors.................................	8 664 ..	....	....	....	....	....	....	....	....
Debt securities.................................	8 669 ..	....	....	....	....	....	....	....	....
Bonds and notes...............................	8 670 ..	....	....	....	....	....	....	....	....
Monetary authorities........................	8 671 ..	....	....	....	....	....	....	....	....
General government........................	8 672 ..	....	....	....	....	....	....	....	....
Banks.......................................	8 673 ..	....	....	....	....	....	....	....	....
Other sectors..............................	8 674 ..	....	....	....	....	....	....	....	....
Money market instruments..................	8 680 ..	....	....	....	....	....	....	....	....
Monetary authorities........................	8 681 ..	....	....	....	....	....	....	....	....
General government........................	8 682 ..	....	....	....	....	....	....	....	....
Banks.......................................	8 683 ..	....	....	....	....	....	....	....	....
Other sectors..............................	8 684 ..	....	....	....	....	....	....	....	....
Financial derivatives............................	8 905 ..	....	....	....	....	....	....	....	....
Monetary authorities............................	8 906 ..	....	....	....	....	....	....	....	....
General government.............................	8 907 ..	....	....	....	....	....	....	....	....
Banks..	8 908 ..	....	....	....	....	....	....	....	....
Other sectors...................................	8 909 ..	....	....	....	....	....	....	....	....
Other investment...............................	8 753 ..	....	....	....	217.85	231.74	243.81	318.48	391.34
Trade credits.....................................	8 756 ..	....	....	....	....	....	....	....	....
General government.............................	8 757 ..	....	....	....	....	....	....	....	....
of which: Short-term........................	8 759 ..	....	....	....	....	....	....	....	....
Other sectors...................................	8 760 ..	....	....	....	....	....	....	....	....
of which: Short-term........................	8 762 ..	....	....	....	....	....	....	....	....
Loans...	8 764 ..	....	....	....	....	....	....	....	....
Monetary authorities............................	8 765 ..	....	....	....	....	....	....	....	....
of which: Use of Fund credit and loans from the Fund....	8 766 ..	....	....	....	....	....	....	....	*9.61*
of which: Short-term........................	8 768 ..	....	....	....	....	....	....	....	....
General government.............................	8 769 ..	....	....	....	....	....	....	....	....
of which: Short-term........................	8 771 ..	....	....	....	....	....	....	....	....
Banks..	8 772 ..	....	....	....	....	....	....	....	....
of which: Short-term........................	8 774 ..	....	....	....	....	....	....	....	....
Other sectors...................................	8 775 ..	....	....	....	....	....	....	....	....
of which: Short-term........................	8 777 ..	....	....	....	....	....	....	....	....
Currency and deposits.............................	8 780 ..	....	....	....	....	....	....	....	....
Monetary authorities............................	8 781 ..	....	....	....	....	....	....	....	....
General government.............................	8 782 ..	....	....	....	....	....	....	....	....
Banks..	8 783 ..	....	....	....	....	....	....	....	....
Other sectors...................................	8 784 ..	....	....	....	....	....	....	....	....
Other liabilities.................................	8 786 ..	....	....	....	....	....	....	15.53	....
Monetary authorities............................	8 787 ..	....	....	....	....	....	....	15.53	....
of which: Short-term........................	8 789 ..	....	....	....	....	....	....	....	....
General government.............................	8 790 ..	....	....	....	....	....	....	....	....
of which: Short-term........................	8 792 ..	....	....	....	....	....	....	....	....
Banks..	8 793 ..	....	....	....	....	....	....	....	....
of which: Short-term........................	8 795 ..	....	....	....	....	....	....	....	....
Other sectors...................................	8 796 ..	....	....	....	....	....	....	....	....
of which: Short-term........................	8 798 ..	....	....	....	....	....	....	....	....
NET INTERNATIONAL INVESTMENT POSITION........	8 995 ..	....	....	....	−161.48	−195.24	−306.73	−374.24	−584.19
Conversion rates: Solomon Islands dollars per U.S.................		....	....	....					
dollar (end of period)............................	0 102 ..	**7.4906**	**7.5075**	**7.5758**	**7.6161**	**7.6628**	**8.0000**	**8.0645**	**8.0645**

Table 1. ANALYTIC PRESENTATION, 2003–2010
(Millions of U.S. dollars)

	Code	2003	2004	2005	2006	2007	2008	2009	2010
A. Current Account[1]	4 993 Z.	**−1,761**	**−6,741**	**−8,518**	**−13,745**	**−20,018**	**−20,083**	**−11,327**	**−10,117**
Goods: exports f.o.b.	2 100 ..	38,700	48,237	56,261	65,825	76,435	86,118	66,542	85,700
Goods: imports f.o.b.	3 100 ..	−35,270	−48,518	−56,572	−70,020	−81,596	−90,566	−66,009	−81,862
Balance on Goods	4 100 ..	*3,431*	*−281*	*−311*	*−4,195*	*−5,160*	*−4,448*	*534*	*3,838*
Services: credit	2 200 ..	8,440	9,873	11,300	12,214	13,818	12,805	12,020	14,003
Services: debit	3 200 ..	−8,045	−10,329	−12,125	−14,242	−16,481	−16,976	−14,808	−18,456
Balance on Goods and Services	4 991 ..	*3,825*	*−738*	*−1,136*	*−6,224*	*−7,824*	*−8,619*	*−2,254*	*−615*
Income: credit	2 300 ..	2,857	3,259	4,640	6,079	6,882	5,944	3,988	4,651
Income: debit	3 300 ..	−7,447	−7,576	−9,569	−11,237	−16,725	−15,076	−10,377	−11,876
Balance on Goods, Services, and Income	4 992 ..	*−765*	*−5,055*	*−6,065*	*−11,382*	*−17,667*	*−17,751*	*−8,643*	*−7,839*
Current transfers: credit	2 379 Z.	252	342	711	888	1,099	1,377	1,242	1,247
Current transfers: debit	3 379 ..	−1,248	−2,028	−3,164	−3,250	−3,450	−3,709	−3,926	−3,525
B. Capital Account[1]	4 994 Z.	**44**	**52**	**30**	**30**	**28**	**25**	**26**	**31**
Capital account: credit	2 994 Z.	44	55	44	43	41	39	40	50
Capital account: debit	3 994 ..	....	−2	−14	−12	−13	−14	−14	−19
Total, Groups A Plus B	4 981 ..	*−1,718*	*−6,689*	*−8,488*	*−13,715*	*−19,990*	*−20,058*	*−11,301*	*−10,087*
C. Financial Account[1]	4 995 W.	**−1,961**	**7,395**	**12,614**	**15,336**	**20,710**	**11,755**	**16,276**	**10,376**
Direct investment abroad	4 505 ..	−553	−1,305	−909	−5,929	−2,982	2,120	−1,311	−382
Direct investment in South Africa	4 555 Z.	783	701	6,522	−184	5,737	9,645	5,354	1,565
Portfolio investment assets	4 602 ..	−138	−950	−911	−2,231	−3,439	−6,720	−1,746	−3,916
Equity securities	4 610 ..	−49	−795	−996	−1,627	−1,747	−5,835	−1,288	−2,616
Debt securities	4 619 ..	−89	−156	85	−605	−1,691	−885	−457	−1,299
Portfolio investment liabilities	4 652 Z.	862	7,309	5,718	21,859	13,681	−7,583	13,368	14,386
Equity securities	4 660 ..	685	6,661	7,230	14,959	8,670	−4,707	9,364	5,826
Debt securities	4 669 Z.	176	648	−1,512	6,900	5,011	−2,876	4,004	8,560
Financial derivatives	4 910 ..	....	....	....	....	....	....	....	....
Financial derivatives assets	4 900 ..	....	....	....	....	....	....	....	....
Financial derivatives liabilities	4 905 ..	....	....	....	....	....	....	....	....
Other investment assets	4 703 ..	−5,212	−432	−3,619	−6,635	517	8,921	3,101	−2,590
Monetary authorities	4 701 ..	1	4	−7	....	....	....	....	....
General government	4 704 ..	−376	−103	−158	−210	−59	238	134	234
Banks	4 705 ..	−7,976	−2,297	−3,320	−4,990	107	9,016	−236	−4,048
Other sectors	4 728 ..	3,139	1,964	−134	−1,436	468	−332	3,203	1,225
Other investment liabilities	4 753 W.	2,297	2,072	5,813	8,456	7,196	5,372	−2,489	1,311
Monetary authorities	4 753 WA	169	510	527	−766	−644	−1,300	2,087	−274
General government	4 753 ZB	−277	−285	1,109	504	−802	9	−299	−316
Banks	4 753 ZC	−89	1,128	2,751	4,178	5,938	5,834	−4,047	1,032
Other sectors	4 753 ZD	2,494	719	1,426	4,539	2,704	830	−231	870
Total, Groups A Through C	4 983 ..	*−3,679*	*707*	*4,126*	*1,621*	*720*	*−8,303*	*4,975*	*289*
D. Net Errors and Omissions	4 998 ..	**3,325**	**5,617**	**1,639**	**2,090**	**5,017**	**10,528**	**−804**	**3,507**
Total, Groups A Through D	4 984 ..	*−354*	*6,324*	*5,766*	*3,711*	*5,737*	*2,225*	*4,171*	*3,796*
E. Reserves and Related Items	4 802 A.	**354**	**−6,324**	**−5,766**	**−3,711**	**−5,737**	**−2,225**	**−4,171**	**−3,796**
Reserve assets	4 802 ..	354	−6,324	−5,766	−3,711	−5,737	−2,225	−4,171	−3,796
Use of Fund credit and loans	4 766 ..	....	....	....	....	....	....	....	....
Exceptional financing	4 920 ..	....	....	....	....	....	....	....	....
Conversion rates: rand per U.S. dollar	0 101 ..	**7.565**	**6.460**	**6.359**	**6.772**	**7.045**	**8.261**	**8.474**	**7.321**

[1] Excludes components that have been classified in the categories of Group E.

Table 2. STANDARD PRESENTATION, 2003–2010

(Millions of U.S. dollars)

	Code	2003	2004	2005	2006	2007	2008	2009	2010
CURRENT ACCOUNT	4 993	**−1,761**	**−6,741**	**−8,518**	**−13,745**	**−20,018**	**−20,083**	**−11,327**	**−10,117**
A. GOODS	4 100	**3,431**	**−281**	**−311**	**−4,195**	**−5,160**	**−4,448**	**534**	**3,838**
Credit	2 100	**38,700**	**48,237**	**56,261**	**65,825**	**76,435**	**86,118**	**66,542**	**85,700**
General merchandise: exports f.o.b.	2 110	33,999	43,554	51,723	60,328	70,382	79,658	59,656	77,091
Goods for processing: exports f.o.b.	2 150	....	....	....	....	....	....	....	....
Repairs on goods	2 160	....	....	....	....	....	....	....	....
Goods procured in ports by carriers	2 170	439	230	292	276	376	533	539	449
Nonmonetary gold	2 180	4,262	4,453	4,246	5,220	5,677	5,927	6,347	8,160
Debit	3 100	**−35,270**	**−48,518**	**−56,572**	**−70,020**	**−81,596**	**−90,566**	**−66,009**	**−81,862**
General merchandise: imports f.o.b.	3 110	−35,176	−48,418	−56,451	−69,902	−81,473	−90,472	−65,916	−81,756
Goods for processing: imports f.o.b.	3 150	....	....	....	....	....	....	....	....
Repairs on goods	3 160	−20	−24	−30	−37	−49	−34	−33	−38
Goods procured in ports by carriers	3 170	−73	−77	−91	−80	−74	−60	−59	−67
Nonmonetary gold	3 180	....	....	....	....	....	....	....	....
B. SERVICES	4 200	**395**	**−456**	**−825**	**−2,028**	**−2,663**	**−4,170**	**−2,787**	**−4,453**
Total credit	2 200	*8,440*	*9,873*	*11,300*	*12,214*	*13,818*	*12,805*	*12,020*	*14,003*
Total debit	3 200	*−8,045*	*−10,329*	*−12,125*	*−14,242*	*−16,481*	*−16,976*	*−14,808*	*−18,456*
Transportation services, credit	2 205	**1,261**	**1,417**	**1,533**	**1,488**	**1,801**	**1,557**	**1,378**	**1,615**
Passenger	2 850	*962*	*1,058*	*1,113*	*1,091*	*1,447*	*1,222*	*1,060*	*1,223*
Freight	2 851	*99*	*101*	*109*	*76*	*40*	*47*	*37*	*98*
Other	2 852	*200*	*258*	*311*	*321*	*314*	*288*	*281*	*295*
Sea transport, passenger	2 207	....	....	....	....	....	....	....	....
Sea transport, freight	2 208	....	....	....	....	....	....	....	....
Sea transport, other	2 209	....	....	....	....	....	....	....	....
Air transport, passenger	2 211	....	....	....	....	....	....	....	....
Air transport, freight	2 212	....	....	....	....	....	....	....	....
Air transport, other	2 213	....	....	....	....	....	....	....	....
Other transport, passenger	2 215	....	....	....	....	....	....	....	....
Other transport, freight	2 216	....	....	....	....	....	....	....	....
Other transport, other	2 217	....	....	....	....	....	....	....	....
Transportation services, debit	3 205	**−3,175**	**−4,401**	**−5,328**	**−6,628**	**−7,540**	**−7,594**	**−5,911**	**−7,088**
Passenger	3 850	*−766*	*−1,080*	*−1,438*	*−1,846*	*−2,176*	*−2,501*	*−2,269*	*−2,544*
Freight	3 851	*−2,356*	*−3,239*	*−3,761*	*−4,696*	*−5,299*	*−5,041*	*−3,593*	*−4,473*
Other	3 852	*−53*	*−82*	*−129*	*−87*	*−64*	*−53*	*−49*	*−72*
Sea transport, passenger	3 207	....	....	....	....	....	....	....	....
Sea transport, freight	3 208	....	....	....	....	....	....	....	....
Sea transport, other	3 209	....	....	....	....	....	....	....	....
Air transport, passenger	3 211	....	....	....	....	....	....	....	....
Air transport, freight	3 212	....	....	....	....	....	....	....	....
Air transport, other	3 213	....	....	....	....	....	....	....	....
Other transport, passenger	3 215	....	....	....	....	....	....	....	....
Other transport, freight	3 216	....	....	....	....	....	....	....	....
Other transport, other	3 217	....	....	....	....	....	....	....	....
Travel, credit	2 236	**5,712**	**6,513**	**7,516**	**8,120**	**8,779**	**7,956**	**7,624**	**9,085**
Business travel	2 237	970	1,151	1,265	1,371	1,548	1,391	1,413	1,536
Personal travel	2 240	4,742	5,362	6,251	6,749	7,231	6,565	6,211	7,549
Travel, debit	3 236	**−2,889**	**−3,157**	**−3,374**	**−3,384**	**−3,927**	**−4,404**	**−4,151**	**−5,595**
Business travel	3 237	−1,158	−1,277	−932	−976	−1,137	−1,293	−1,209	−1,628
Personal travel	3 240	−1,731	−1,880	−2,442	−2,409	−2,790	−3,112	−2,943	−3,967
Other services, credit	2 200 BA	**1,467**	**1,943**	**2,251**	**2,606**	**3,238**	**3,292**	**3,018**	**3,303**
Communications	2 245	136	189	193	260	233	210	219	222
Construction	2 249	21	28	35	40	54	58	47	63
Insurance	2 253	77	106	124	152	214	251	223	273
Financial	2 260	295	426	534	706	876	805	715	827
Computer and information	2 262	66	89	109	129	223	203	245	290
Royalties and licence fees	2 266	27	37	45	46	53	54	48	59
Other business services	2 268	605	742	837	868	1,175	1,201	1,084	1,115
Personal, cultural, and recreational	2 287	60	88	114	103	90	99	73	67
Government, n.i.e.	2 291	179	238	259	302	320	411	364	387
Other services, debit	3 200 BA	**−1,982**	**−2,771**	**−3,424**	**−4,230**	**−5,015**	**−4,977**	**−4,745**	**−5,773**
Communications	3 245	−100	−147	−168	−197	−230	−248	−373	−397
Construction	3 249	−4	−5	−6	−6	−7	−7	−7	−8
Insurance	3 253	−297	−391	−478	−587	−629	−584	−417	−527
Financial	3 260	−102	−149	−184	−177	−196	−127	−123	−133
Computer and information	3 262	−59	−84	−114	−127	−171	−194	−184	−186
Royalties and licence fees	3 266	−617	−891	−1,071	−1,282	−1,596	−1,676	−1,658	−1,941
Other business services	3 268	−603	−833	−1,104	−1,503	−1,822	−1,671	−1,556	−2,133
Personal, cultural, and recreational	3 287	−3	−5	−8	−9	−10	−10	−10	−14
Government, n.i.e.	3 291	−198	−265	−292	−342	−354	−460	−417	−433

Table 2 (Continued). STANDARD PRESENTATION, 2003–2010

(Millions of U.S. dollars)

	Code	2003	2004	2005	2006	2007	2008	2009	2010
C. INCOME	4 300	**−4,590**	**−4,318**	**−4,929**	**−5,159**	**−9,844**	**−9,132**	**−6,389**	**−7,224**
Total credit	2 300	*2,857*	*3,259*	*4,640*	*6,079*	*6,882*	*5,944*	*3,988*	*4,651*
Total debit	3 300	*−7,447*	*−7,576*	*−9,569*	*−11,237*	*−16,725*	*−15,076*	*−10,377*	*−11,876*
Compensation of employees, credit	2 310	**391**	**468**	**614**	**692**	**792**	**783**	**862**	**1,070**
Compensation of employees, debit	3 310	**−706**	**−935**	**−1,041**	**−1,055**	**−1,172**	**−1,119**	**−1,144**	**−1,353**
Investment income, credit	2 320	**2,466**	**2,790**	**4,027**	**5,387**	**6,089**	**5,160**	**3,126**	**3,582**
Direct investment income	2 330	889	1,020	1,459	1,522	1,853	1,474	1,007	1,149
Dividends and distributed branch profits	2 332	631	737	1,061	938	1,090	744	595	739
Reinvested earnings and undistributed branch profits	2 333	....	....	....	....	....	....	....	....
Income on debt (interest)	2 334	258	283	398	583	763	731	412	410
Portfolio investment income	2 339	1,577	1,771	2,568	3,865	4,236	3,686	2,119	2,433
Income on equity	2 340	780	892	1,133	1,622	1,241	1,322	951	1,284
Income on bonds and notes	2 350	....	....	....	....	....	....	....	....
Income on money market instruments	2 360	....	....	....	....	....	....	....	....
Other investment income	2 370	....	....	....	....	....	....	....	....
Investment income, debit	3 320	**−6,741**	**−6,642**	**−8,528**	**−10,182**	**−15,553**	**−13,957**	**−9,233**	**−10,523**
Direct investment income	3 330	−3,220	−3,256	−4,320	−4,843	−8,666	−8,031	−5,279	−6,165
Dividends and distributed branch profits	3 332	−3,133	−3,168	−4,216	−4,680	−8,459	−7,789	−5,132	−6,021
Reinvested earnings and undistributed branch profits	3 333	....	....	....	....	....	....	....	....
Income on debt (interest)	3 334	−87	−88	−105	−162	−207	−242	−147	−143
Portfolio investment income	3 339	−3,521	−3,386	−4,208	−5,340	−6,887	−5,926	−3,955	−4,358
Income on equity	3 340	−1,432	−1,271	−1,775	−1,960	−2,877	−1,418	−1,047	−1,447
Income on bonds and notes	3 350	....	....	....	....	....	....	....	....
Income on money market instruments	3 360	....	....	....	....	....	....	....	....
Other investment income	3 370	....	....	....	....	....	....	....	....
D. CURRENT TRANSFERS	4 379	**−996**	**−1,686**	**−2,453**	**−2,362**	**−2,351**	**−2,332**	**−2,684**	**−2,278**
Credit	2 379	**252**	**342**	**711**	**888**	**1,099**	**1,377**	**1,242**	**1,247**
General government	2 380	189	166	146	163	161	241	170	185
Other sectors	2 390	63	177	565	725	938	1,136	1,072	1,062
Workers' remittances	2 391	....	....	....	....	....	....	....	....
Other current transfers	2 392	63	177	565	725	938	1,136	1,072	1,062
Debit	3 379	**−1,248**	**−2,028**	**−3,164**	**−3,250**	**−3,450**	**−3,709**	**−3,926**	**−3,525**
General government	3 380	−1,195	−1,942	−2,961	−2,996	−3,131	−3,265	−3,261	−2,791
Other sectors	3 390	−53	−86	−203	−254	−319	−445	−665	−734
Workers' remittances	3 391	....	....	....	....	....	....	....	....
Other current transfers	3 392	−53	−86	−203	−254	−319	−445	−665	−734
CAPITAL AND FINANCIAL ACCOUNT	4 996	**−1,563**	**1,124**	**6,879**	**11,655**	**15,001**	**9,555**	**12,131**	**6,611**
CAPITAL ACCOUNT	4 994	**44**	**52**	**30**	**30**	**28**	**25**	**26**	**31**
Total credit	2 994	*44*	*55*	*44*	*43*	*41*	*39*	*40*	*50*
Total debit	3 994	....	*−2*	*−14*	*−12*	*−13*	*−14*	*−14*	*−19*
Capital transfers, credit	2 400	**44**	**55**	**44**	**43**	**41**	**39**	**40**	**50**
General government	2 401	....	....	....	....	....	....	....	....
Debt forgiveness	2 402	....	....	....	....	....	....	....	....
Other capital transfers	2 410	....	....	....	....	....	....	....	....
Other sectors	2 430	44	55	44	43	41	39	40	50
Migrants' transfers	2 431	44	55	44	43	41	39	40	50
Debt forgiveness	2 432	....	....	....	....	....	....	....	....
Other capital transfers	2 440	....	....	....	....	....	....	....	....
Capital transfers, debit	3 400	....	**−2**	**−14**	**−12**	**−13**	**−14**	**−14**	**−19**
General government	3 401	....	....	....	....	....	....	....	....
Debt forgiveness	3 402	....	....	....	....	....	....	....	....
Other capital transfers	3 410	....	....	....	....	....	....	....	....
Other sectors	3 430	....	−2	−14	−12	−13	−14	−14	−19
Migrants' transfers	3 431	....	−2	−14	−12	−13	−14	−14	−19
Debt forgiveness	3 432	....	....	....	....	....	....	....	....
Other capital transfers	3 440	....	....	....	....	....	....	....	....
Nonproduced nonfinancial assets, credit	2 480	....	....	....	....	....	....	....	....
Nonproduced nonfinancial assets, debit	3 480	....	....	....	....	....	....	....	....

Table 2 (Continued). STANDARD PRESENTATION, 2003–2010

(Millions of U.S. dollars)

	Code	2003	2004	2005	2006	2007	2008	2009	2010
FINANCIAL ACCOUNT	4 995 ..	**−1,607**	**1,071**	**6,849**	**11,625**	**14,973**	**9,530**	**12,105**	**6,580**
A. DIRECT INVESTMENT	4 500 ..	**231**	**−604**	**5,613**	**−6,112**	**2,755**	**11,764**	**4,042**	**1,184**
Direct investment abroad	4 505 ..	**−553**	**−1,305**	**−909**	**−5,929**	**−2,982**	**2,120**	**−1,311**	**−382**
Equity capital	4 510 ..	−759	−1,361	−670	−2,716	−3,334	1,629	−2,174	−356
Claims on affiliated enterprises	4 515 ..	−759	−1,361	−670	−2,716	−3,334	1,629	−2,174	−356
Liabilities to affiliated enterprises	4 520 ..	....	....	....	....	....	....	....	....
Reinvested earnings	4 525 ..	....	....	....	....	....	....	....	....
Other capital	4 530 ..	206	56	−239	−3,213	352	491	863	−26
Claims on affiliated enterprises	4 535 ..	206	56	−239	−3,213	352	491	863	−26
Liabilities to affiliated enterprises	4 540 ..	....	....	....	....	....	....	....	....
Direct investment in South Africa	4 555 ..	**783**	**701**	**6,522**	**−184**	**5,737**	**9,645**	**5,354**	**1,565**
Equity capital	4 560 ..	567	125	6,192	−1,556	1,967	6,729	4,957	662
Claims on direct investors	4 565 ..	....	....	....	....	....	....	....	....
Liabilities to direct investors	4 570 ..	567	125	6,192	−1,556	1,967	6,729	4,957	662
Reinvested earnings	4 575 ..	....	....	....	....	....	....	....	....
Other capital	4 580 ..	216	577	331	1,373	3,770	2,916	397	903
Claims on direct investors	4 585 ..	....	....	....	....	....	....	....	....
Liabilities to direct investors	4 590 ..	216	577	331	1,373	3,770	2,916	397	903
B. PORTFOLIO INVESTMENT	4 600 ..	**723**	**6,359**	**4,807**	**19,627**	**10,242**	**−14,303**	**11,622**	**10,470**
Assets	4 602 ..	**−138**	**−950**	**−911**	**−2,231**	**−3,439**	**−6,720**	**−1,746**	**−3,916**
Equity securities	4 610 ..	−49	−795	−996	−1,627	−1,747	−5,835	−1,288	−2,616
Monetary authorities	4 611 ..	....	....	....	....	....	....	....	....
General government	4 612 ..	....	....	....	....	....	....	....	....
Banks	4 613 ..	−18	−88	78	27	104	−390	−181	−833
Other sectors	4 614 ..	−31	−707	−1,073	−1,653	−1,852	−5,446	−1,107	−1,784
Debt securities	4 619 ..	−89	−156	85	−605	−1,691	−885	−457	−1,299
Bonds and notes	4 620 ..	−89	−156	85	−605	−1,689	−637	−528	−1,358
Monetary authorities	4 621 ..	....	....	....	....	....	....	....	....
General government	4 622 ..	....	....	....	....	....	....	....	....
Banks	4 623 ..	....	137	402	63	−775	25	−3	−188
Other sectors	4 624 ..	−89	−292	−317	−667	−914	−662	−525	−1,169
Money market instruments	4 630 ..	....	....	....	....	−2	−248	71	58
Monetary authorities	4 631 ..	....	....	....	....	....	....	....	....
General government	4 632 ..	....	....	....	....	....	....	....	....
Banks	4 633 ..	....	....	....	....	....	−248	71	58
Other sectors	4 634 ..	....	....	....	....	....	....	....	....
Liabilities	4 652 ..	**862**	**7,309**	**5,718**	**21,859**	**13,681**	**−7,583**	**13,368**	**14,386**
Equity securities	4 660 ..	685	6,661	7,230	14,959	8,670	−4,707	9,364	5,826
Banks	4 663 ..	23	578	560	1,250	975	−672	989	553
Other sectors	4 664 ..	662	6,083	6,670	13,709	7,695	−4,035	8,375	5,273
Debt securities	4 669 ..	176	648	−1,512	6,900	5,011	−2,876	4,004	8,560
Bonds and notes	4 670 ..	290	745	−1,537	6,929	4,891	−3,075	3,829	8,559
Monetary authorities	4 671 ..	....	....	....	....	....	....	....	....
General government	4 672 ..	398	449	−1,505	4,829	−129	−2,366	3,690	7,892
Banks	4 673 ..	....	....	....	....	1,503	....	....	....
Other sectors	4 674 ..	−107	296	−32	2,099	3,518	−708	139	666
Money market instruments	4 680 ..	−114	−97	25	−29	120	199	175	1
Monetary authorities	4 681 ..	....	....	....	....	....	....	....	....
General government	4 682 ..	....	....	....	....	....	....	....	....
Banks	4 683 ..	−114	−97	25	−29	120	199	175	1
Other sectors	4 684 ..	....	....	....	....	....	....	....	....
C. FINANCIAL DERIVATIVES	4 910 ..	....	....	....	....	....	....	....	....
Monetary authorities	4 911 ..	....	....	....	....	....	....	....	....
General government	4 912 ..	....	....	....	....	....	....	....	....
Banks	4 913 ..	....	....	....	....	....	....	....	....
Other sectors	4 914 ..	....	....	....	....	....	....	....	....
Assets	4 900 ..	....	....	....	....	....	....	....	....
Monetary authorities	4 901 ..	....	....	....	....	....	....	....	....
General government	4 902 ..	....	....	....	....	....	....	....	....
Banks	4 903 ..	....	....	....	....	....	....	....	....
Other sectors	4 904 ..	....	....	....	....	....	....	....	....
Liabilities	4 905 ..	....	....	....	....	....	....	....	....
Monetary authorities	4 906 ..	....	....	....	....	....	....	....	....
General government	4 907 ..	....	....	....	....	....	....	....	....
Banks	4 908 ..	....	....	....	....	....	....	....	....
Other sectors	4 909 ..	....	....	....	....	....	....	....	....

Table 2 (Concluded). STANDARD PRESENTATION, 2003–2010

(Millions of U.S. dollars)

	Code	2003	2004	2005	2006	2007	2008	2009	2010
D. OTHER INVESTMENT	4 700 ..	**−2,915**	**1,641**	**2,194**	**1,821**	**7,713**	**14,293**	**612**	**−1,279**
Assets	4 703 ..	**−5,212**	**−432**	**−3,619**	**−6,635**	**517**	**8,921**	**3,101**	**−2,590**
Trade credits	4 706 ..	−288	−213	−694	−214	−173	193	162	62
General government	4 707 ..	−376	−103	−158	−210	−59	238	134	234
of which: Short-term	4 709 ..	....	....	....	....	....	....	....	....
Other sectors	4 710 ..	88	−110	−537	−4	−115	−45	28	−172
of which: Short-term	4 712 ..	88	−110	−539	−4	−115	−45	28	−172
Loans	4 714 ..	325	33	−247	−2,212	−583	−31	374	−1,280
Monetary authorities	4 715 ..	1	4	−7	....	....	....	....	....
of which: Short-term	4 718 ..	....	....	....	....	....	....	....	....
General government	4 719 ..	....	....	....	....	....	....	....	....
of which: Short-term	4 721 ..	....	....	....	....	....	....	....	....
Banks	4 722 ..	....	−14	−287	−1,852	−64	367	−349	−1,293
of which: Short-term	4 724 ..	....	−14	−287	−1,852	−64	367	−349	−1,293
Other sectors	4 725 ..	324	43	47	−360	−519	−399	722	13
of which: Short-term	4 727 ..	300	150	51	−346	−235	−291	620	83
Currency and deposits	4 730 ..	−7,797	−1,859	−3,013	−3,955	1,726	10,199	2,802	−646
Monetary authorities	4 731 ..	....	....	....	....	....	....	....	....
General government	4 732 ..	....	....	....	....	....	....	....	....
Banks	4 733 ..	−8,089	−2,087	−2,984	−3,126	234	9,000	−59	−2,801
Other sectors	4 734 ..	291	229	−29	−828	1,492	1,200	2,861	2,154
Other assets	4 736 ..	2,548	1,607	335	−254	−453	−1,439	−237	−726
Monetary authorities	4 737 ..	....	....	....	....	....	....	....	....
of which: Short-term	4 739 ..	....	....	....	....	....	....	....	....
General government	4 740 ..	....	....	....	....	....	....	....	....
of which: Short-term	4 742 ..	....	....	....	....	....	....	....	....
Banks	4 743 ..	113	−196	−49	−11	−63	−351	172	45
of which: Short-term	4 745 ..	113	−196	−49	−11	−63	−351	172	45
Other sectors	4 746 ..	2,435	1,802	384	−243	−389	−1,088	−409	−771
of which: Short-term	4 748 ..	2,538	1,927	510	94	206	−496	−40	1
Liabilities	4 753 ..	**2,297**	**2,072**	**5,813**	**8,456**	**7,196**	**5,372**	**−2,489**	**1,311**
Trade credits	4 756 ..	52	85	269	446	542	−83	275	245
General government	4 757 ..	....	....	....	....	....	....	....	....
of which: Short-term	4 759 ..	....	....	....	....	....	....	....	....
Other sectors	4 760 ..	52	85	269	446	542	−83	275	245
of which: Short-term	4 762 ..	52	85	269	446	542	−83	275	245
Loans	4 764 ..	−240	−284	3,588	5,645	6,023	3,908	−2,404	1,641
Monetary authorities	4 765 ..	235	402	424	−745	−1,100	−989	−346	−355
of which: Use of Fund credit and loans from the Fund	4 766 ..	....	....	....	....	....	....	....	....
of which: Short-term	4 768 ..	235	402	424	−745	−1,100	−989	−346	−355
General government	4 769 ..	−277	−285	319	226	143	9	−299	−316
of which: Short-term	4 771 ..	....	....	....	....	....	....	....	....
Banks	4 772 ..	−116	210	1,820	1,061	4,952	3,554	−1,257	1,541
of which: Short-term	4 774 ..	−116	210	1,820	1,061	2,816	3,554	−2,140	657
Other sectors	4 775 ..	−81	−612	1,024	5,104	2,028	1,335	−503	772
of which: Short-term	4 777 ..	36	−447	520	1,768	−528	−171	−185	−295
Currency and deposits	4 780 ..	−43	1,031	1,040	3,099	1,428	1,928	−2,602	−540
Monetary authorities	4 781 ..	−65	108	102	−20	456	−310	−12	81
General government	4 782 ..	....	....	....	....	....	....	....	....
Banks	4 783 ..	23	923	931	3,119	972	2,239	−2,735	−477
Other sectors	4 784 ..	....	....	7	....	....	....	145	−144
Other liabilities	4 786 ..	2,527	1,241	915	−734	−797	−381	2,242	−35
Monetary authorities	4 787 ..	....	....	....	....	....	....	2,445	....
of which: Short-term	4 789 ..	....	....	....	....	....	....	....	....
General government	4 790 ..	....	....	790	278	−945	....	....	....
of which: Short-term	4 792 ..	....	....	790	278	−945	....	....	....
Banks	4 793 ..	3	−5	....	−2	15	41	−55	−32
of which: Short-term	4 795 ..	3	−5	....	−2	15	41	−55	−32
Other sectors	4 796 ..	2,523	1,246	125	−1,011	134	−422	−148	−2
of which: Short-term	4 798 ..	2,523	1,246	125	−1,011	134	−422	−148	−2
E. RESERVE ASSETS	4 802 ..	**354**	**−6,324**	**−5,766**	**−3,711**	**−5,737**	**−2,225**	**−4,171**	**−3,796**
Monetary gold	4 812 ..	764	25	−31	27	23	14	1	2
Special drawing rights	4 811 ..	....	....	....	....	....	....	−2,445	....
Reserve position in the Fund	4 810 ..	....	....	....	....	....	....	....	....
Foreign exchange	4 803 ..	−410	−6,349	−5,734	−3,737	−5,760	−2,239	−1,727	−3,798
Other claims	4 813 ..	....	....	....	....	....	....	....	....
NET ERRORS AND OMISSIONS	4 998 ..	**3,325**	**5,617**	**1,639**	**2,090**	**5,017**	**10,528**	**−804**	**3,507**

Table 3. INTERNATIONAL INVESTMENT POSITION (End-period stocks), 2003–2010

(Millions of U.S. dollars)

	Code	2003	2004	2005	2006	2007	2008	2009	2010
ASSETS	8 995 C.	**100,743**	**130,225**	**154,057**	**182,500**	**214,832**	**181,299**	**242,848**	**304,114**
Direct investment abroad	8 505 ..	**27,185**	**39,083**	**37,706**	**50,826**	**65,878**	**49,956**	**72,583**	**89,453**
Equity capital and reinvested earnings	8 506 ..	25,170	36,305	34,980	44,281	59,276	45,756	66,876	82,453
Claims on affiliated enterprises	8 507 ..	25,170	36,305	34,980	44,281	59,276	45,756	66,876	82,453
Liabilities to affiliated enterprises	8 508 ..	....	....	....	....	....	....	....	....
Other capital	8 530 ..	2,015	2,778	2,726	6,545	6,602	4,200	5,707	7,000
Claims on affiliated enterprises	8 535 ..	2,015	2,778	2,726	6,545	6,602	4,200	5,707	7,000
Liabilities to affiliated enterprises	8 540 ..	....	....	....	....	....	....	....	....
Portfolio investment	8 602 ..	**40,752**	**47,304**	**64,686**	**70,637**	**76,187**	**64,678**	**96,560**	**131,131**
Equity securities	8 610 ..	38,621	43,984	60,756	66,082	70,149	59,195	90,899	123,355
Monetary authorities	8 611 ..	....	....	....	....	....	....	....	....
General government	8 612 ..	....	....	....	....	....	....	....	....
Banks	8 613 ..	332	487	523	439	325	372	826	662
Other sectors	8 614 ..	38,289	43,497	60,233	65,642	69,825	58,823	90,073	122,694
Debt securities	8 619 ..	2,131	3,320	3,930	4,555	6,038	5,482	5,662	7,776
Bonds and notes	8 620 ..	2,131	3,320	3,930	4,555	6,038	5,482	5,662	7,776
Monetary authorities	8 621 ..	....	....	....	....	....	....	....	....
General government	8 622 ..	....	....	....	....	....	....	....	....
Banks	8 623 ..	808	782	336	244	1,020	1,834	2,160	4,000
Other sectors	8 624 ..	1,323	2,538	3,594	4,312	5,017	3,648	3,501	3,776
Money market instruments	8 630 ..	....	....	....	....	....	....	....	....
Monetary authorities	8 631 ..	....	....	....	....	....	....	....	....
General government	8 632 ..	....	....	....	....	....	....	....	....
Banks	8 633 ..	....	....	....	....	....	....	....	....
Other sectors	8 634 ..	....	....	....	....	....	....	....	....
Financial derivatives	8 900 ..	....	....	....	....	....	....	....	....
Monetary authorities	8 901 ..	....	....	....	....	....	....	....	....
General government	8 902 ..	....	....	....	....	....	....	....	....
Banks	8 903 ..	....	....	....	....	....	....	....	....
Other sectors	8 904 ..	....	....	....	....	....	....	....	....
Other investment	8 703 ..	**24,836**	**29,121**	**31,038**	**35,452**	**39,826**	**32,598**	**34,032**	**39,702**
Trade credits	8 706 ..	1,711	2,084	1,820	2,108	2,152	1,790	927	581
General government	8 707 ..	1,711	2,084	1,820	2,108	2,152	1,790	927	581
of which: Short-term	8 709 ..	....	....	....	....	....	....	....	....
Other sectors	8 710 ..	....	....	....	....	....	....	....	....
of which: Short-term	8 712 ..	....	....	....	....	....	....	....	....
Loans	8 714 ..	6,491	8,634	8,197	8,365	11,574	10,511	11,936	14,914
Monetary authorities	8 715 ..	9	6	12	11	11	8	10	11
of which: Short-term	8 718 ..	....	....	....	....	....	....	....	....
General government	8 719 ..	2	2	2	2	2	1	2	2
of which: Short-term	8 721 ..	*2*	*2*	*2*	*2*	*2*	*1*	*2*	*2*
Banks	8 722 ..	1,341	1,643	1,259	1,418	3,605	3,928	4,969	7,104
of which: Short-term	8 724 ..	*1,341*	*1,643*	*1,259*	*1,418*	*3,605*	*3,928*	*4,969*	*7,104*
Other sectors	8 725 ..	5,139	6,984	6,925	6,936	7,957	6,573	6,955	7,797
of which: Short-term	8 727 ..	*4,091*	*5,669*	*5,706*	*5,725*	*6,488*	*5,412*	*5,610*	*6,299*
Currency and deposits	8 730 ..	16,635	18,402	21,021	24,979	26,100	20,297	21,168	24,208
Monetary authorities	8 731 ..	....	....	....	....	....	....	....	....
General government	8 732 ..	....	....	....	....	....	....	....	....
Banks	8 733 ..	16,635	18,402	21,021	24,979	26,100	20,297	21,168	24,208
Other sectors	8 734 ..	....	....	....	....	....	....	....	....
Other assets	8 736 ..	....	....	....	....	....	....	....	....
Monetary authorities	8 737 ..	....	....	....	....	....	....	....	....
of which: Short-term	8 739 ..	....	....	....	....	....	....	....	....
General government	8 740 ..	....	....	....	....	....	....	....	....
of which: Short-term	8 742 ..	....	....	....	....	....	....	....	....
Banks	8 743 ..	....	....	....	....	....	....	....	....
of which: Short-term	8 745 ..	....	....	....	....	....	....	....	....
Other sectors	8 746 ..	....	....	....	....	....	....	....	....
of which: Short-term	8 748 ..	....	....	....	....	....	....	....	....
Reserve assets	8 802 ..	**7,970**	**14,718**	**20,628**	**25,585**	**32,941**	**34,067**	**39,674**	**43,827**
Monetary gold	8 812 ..	1,476	1,579	2,051	2,530	3,354	3,485	4,438	5,654
Special drawing rights	8 811 ..	331	346	319	335	352	344	2,803	2,754
Reserve position in the Fund	8 810 ..	1	1	1	1	2	2	2	2
Foreign exchange	8 803 ..	6,162	12,792	18,258	22,718	29,232	30,237	32,430	35,417
Other claims	8 813 ..	....	....	....	....	....	....	....	....

Table 3 (Concluded). INTERNATIONAL INVESTMENT POSITION (End-period stocks), 2003–2010

(Millions of U.S. dollars)

	Code	2003	2004	2005	2006	2007	2008	2009	2010
LIABILITIES...................	8 995 D.	**112,837**	**151,184**	**188,012**	**223,569**	**283,212**	**192,593**	**283,056**	**369,009**
Direct investment in South Africa...........................	8 555 ..	**46,869**	**64,451**	**78,986**	**87,765**	**110,415**	**67,987**	**117,434**	**147,629**
Equity capital and reinvested earnings...........................	8 556 ..	40,788	56,513	71,461	79,451	98,147	56,590	102,531	129,285
Claims on direct investors.............................	8 557 ..	....	....	....	....	....	....	....	....
Liabilities to direct investors.........................	8 558 ..	40,788	56,513	71,461	79,451	98,147	56,590	102,531	129,285
Other capital.............................	8 580 ..	6,081	7,938	7,525	8,314	12,268	11,397	14,903	18,344
Claims on direct investors.............................	8 585 ..	....	....	....	....	....	....	....	....
Liabilities to direct investors.........................	8 590 ..	6,081	7,938	7,525	8,314	12,268	11,397	14,903	18,344
Portfolio investment...........................	8 652 ..	**46,257**	**62,853**	**82,837**	**102,750**	**133,213**	**85,668**	**126,519**	**179,783**
Equity securities..................................	8 660 ..	32,795	47,448	67,338	84,741	110,113	63,453	99,027	138,098
Banks......................................	8 663 ..	4,105	8,894	11,572	15,852	11,892	7,702	12,166	14,331
Other sectors............................	8 664 ..	28,690	38,555	55,766	68,889	98,221	55,751	86,861	123,767
Debt securities..................................	8 669 ..	13,462	15,405	15,500	18,009	23,100	22,215	27,492	41,686
Bonds and notes...........................	8 670 ..	13,305	15,331	15,410	17,961	22,916	21,950	26,948	41,071
Monetary authorities..................	8 671 ..	....	....	....	....	....	....	....	....
General government................	8 672 ..	10,438	11,919	12,220	13,425	13,155	13,656	18,483	32,284
Banks................................	8 673 ..	24	68	25	103	1,667	1,596	1,701	1,919
Other sectors......................	8 674 ..	2,842	3,344	3,165	4,432	8,094	6,698	6,763	6,869
Money market instruments............	8 680 ..	157	74	89	49	184	266	545	614
Monetary authorities..................	8 681 ..	....	....	....	....	....	....	....	....
General government................	8 682 ..	....	....	....	....	....	....	....	....
Banks................................	8 683 ..	157	74	89	49	184	266	545	614
Other sectors......................	8 684 ..	....	....	....	....	....	....	....	....
Financial derivatives...........................	8 905 ..	....	....	....	....	....	....	....	....
Monetary authorities...........................	8 906 ..	....	....	....	....	....	....	....	....
General government...........................	8 907 ..	....	....	....	....	....	....	....	....
Banks...........................	8 908 ..	....	....	....	....	....	....	....	....
Other sectors...........................	8 909 ..	....	....	....	....	....	....	....	....
Other investment...........................	8 753 ..	**19,711**	**23,880**	**26,189**	**33,054**	**39,584**	**38,938**	**39,102**	**41,597**
Trade credits...........................	8 756 ..	....	....	....	....	....	....	....	....
General government...........................	8 757 ..	....	....	....	....	....	....	....	....
of which: Short-term...........................	8 759 ..	....	....	....	....	....	....	....	....
Other sectors...........................	8 760 ..	....	....	....	....	....	....	....	....
of which: Short-term...........................	8 762 ..	....	....	....	....	....	....	....	....
Loans...........................	8 764 ..	15,311	17,818	19,611	24,148	29,100	27,753	26,508	28,746
Monetary authorities...........................	8 765 ..	3,005	3,501	3,495	2,754	1,753	650	350	....
of which: Use of Fund credit and loans from the Fund....	8 766 ..	....	....	....	....	....	....	....	....
of which: Short-term...........................	8 768 ..	*429*	*440*	*696*	*1,073*	*999*	*650*	*350*	....
General government...........................	8 769 ..	2,747	2,672	3,523	4,206	3,683	3,423	3,259	2,867
of which: Short-term...........................	8 771 ..	....	....	*810*	*980*	....	....	....	....
Banks...........................	8 772 ..	1,982	2,347	3,988	4,594	9,725	11,086	10,510	11,782
of which: Short-term...........................	8 774 ..	*1,982*	*2,347*	*3,988*	*4,594*	*7,588*	*8,501*	*6,797*	*6,955*
Other sectors...........................	8 775 ..	7,576	9,298	8,604	12,594	13,938	12,594	12,389	14,097
of which: Short-term...........................	8 777 ..	*3,125*	*3,967*	*3,911*	*4,787*	*4,687*	*4,851*	*3,858*	*4,026*
Currency and deposits...........................	8 780 ..	4,401	6,063	6,578	8,906	10,483	11,185	9,795	10,102
Monetary authorities...........................	8 781 ..	140	332	404	370	852	385	462	608
General government...........................	8 782 ..	....	....	....	....	....	....	....	....
Banks...........................	8 783 ..	4,261	5,731	6,174	8,536	9,632	10,799	9,333	9,494
Other sectors...........................	8 784 ..	....	....	....	....	....	....	....	....
Other liabilities...........................	8 786 ..	....	....	....	....	....	....	2,799	2,750
Monetary authorities...........................	8 787 ..	....	....	....	....	....	....	2,799	2,750
of which: Short-term...........................	8 789 ..	....	....	....	....	....	....	....	....
General government...........................	8 790 ..	....	....	....	....	....	....	....	....
of which: Short-term...........................	8 792 ..	....	....	....	....	....	....	....	....
Banks...........................	8 793 ..	....	....	....	....	....	....	....	....
of which: Short-term...........................	8 795 ..	....	....	....	....	....	....	....	....
Other sectors...........................	8 796 ..	....	....	....	....	....	....	....	....
of which: Short-term...........................	8 798 ..	....	....	....	....	....	....	....	....
NET INTERNATIONAL INVESTMENT POSITION........	8 995 ..	**−12,094**	**−20,959**	**−33,955**	**−41,069**	**−68,379**	**−11,294**	**−40,207**	**−64,896**
Conversion rates: rand per U.S. dollar (end of period)..	0 102 ..	**6.640**	**5.630**	**6.325**	**6.970**	**6.810**	**9.305**	**7.380**	**6.632**

Table 1. ANALYTIC PRESENTATION, 2003–2010

(Millions of U.S. dollars)

	Code	2003	2004	2005	2006	2007	2008	2009	2010
A. Current Account[1]	4 993 Z.	**−30,885**	**−54,865**	**−83,388**	**−110,874**	**−144,540**	**−154,529**	**−75,309**	**−64,342**
Goods: exports f.o.b.	2 100 ..	158,049	185,209	196,580	220,696	264,053	284,721	228,704	252,974
Goods: imports f.o.b.	3 100 ..	−203,205	−251,939	−281,784	−325,318	−389,291	−411,334	−287,660	−315,323
Balance on Goods	4 100 ..	*−45,155*	*−66,730*	*−85,204*	*−104,622*	*−125,238*	*−126,613*	*−58,956*	*−62,350*
Services: credit	2 200 ..	74,308	86,078	94,663	106,665	128,148	143,813	123,085	123,627
Services: debit	3 200 ..	−47,951	−59,188	−67,129	−78,588	−96,492	−105,594	−87,389	−87,127
Balance on Goods and Services	4 991 ..	*−18,798*	*−39,841*	*−57,669*	*−76,545*	*−93,582*	*−88,394*	*−23,260*	*−25,849*
Income: credit	2 300 ..	27,209	33,948	39,445	60,022	79,614	77,954	58,385	54,813
Income: debit	3 300 ..	−38,910	−48,986	−60,701	−86,266	−120,986	−130,041	−99,498	−83,798
Balance on Goods, Services, and Income	4 992 ..	*−30,499*	*−54,879*	*−78,925*	*−102,789*	*−134,953*	*−140,480*	*−64,373*	*−54,835*
Current transfers: credit	2 379 Z.	17,048	20,366	20,194	21,531	25,637	25,036	25,603	24,458
Current transfers: debit	3 379 ..	−17,434	−20,353	−24,656	−29,616	−35,223	−39,084	−36,539	−33,966
B. Capital Account[1]	4 994 Z.	**9,274**	**10,450**	**10,107**	**7,855**	**6,374**	**8,184**	**5,943**	**8,358**
Capital account: credit	2 994 Z.	10,984	11,646	11,225	9,674	8,879	10,250	9,024	10,531
Capital account: debit	3 994 ..	−1,710	−1,197	−1,118	−1,819	−2,505	−2,066	−3,081	−2,174
Total, Groups A Plus B	4 981 ..	*−21,611*	*−44,416*	*−73,281*	*−103,020*	*−138,166*	*−146,345*	*−69,365*	*−55,985*
C. Financial Account[1]	4 995 W.	**4,353**	**36,964**	**73,885**	**107,926**	**138,614**	**149,849**	**81,763**	**60,265**
Direct investment abroad	4 505 ..	−28,759	−61,504	−41,922	−103,483	−139,545	−73,972	−8,787	−20,557
Direct investment in Spain	4 555 Z.	25,607	24,792	24,573	31,172	66,682	77,898	8,554	24,658
Portfolio investment assets	4 602 ..	−90,833	−39,651	−119,356	−11,462	−5,888	31,196	1,991	91,209
Equity securities	4 610 ..	−13,180	−15,063	−19,370	−26,256	10,157	40,579	−11,765	−11,918
Debt securities	4 619 ..	−77,653	−24,588	−99,986	14,794	−16,045	−9,383	13,756	103,126
Portfolio investment liabilities	4 652 Z.	44,763	141,686	172,713	243,890	124,060	−26,904	71,676	−43,510
Equity securities	4 660 ..	−3,649	10,918	−9,573	−24,005	15,595	−2,489	9,179	−4,790
Debt securities	4 669 Z.	48,412	130,768	182,286	267,895	108,465	−24,415	62,497	−38,720
Financial derivatives	4 910 ..	−3,785	74	273	2,527	−5,915	−12,611	−7,986	9,752
Financial derivatives assets	4 900 ..	....	....	....	....	....	....	....	....
Financial derivatives liabilities	4 905 ..	−3,785	74	273	2,527	−5,915	−12,611	−7,986	9,752
Other investment assets	4 703 ..	−13,557	−52,659	−42,198	−96,615	−47,980	−26,087	−8,186	−20,644
Monetary authorities	4 701 ..	5,211	−18,079	17,120	−13,890	26,420	689	−505	1
General government	4 704 ..	−342	−2,182	−233	−204	−2,054	−534	−2,418	−4,267
Banks	4 705 ..	−10,523	−20,402	−50,563	−73,413	−66,728	−18,925	−6,253	−9,411
Other sectors	4 728 ..	−7,903	−11,995	−8,523	−9,107	−5,619	−7,317	989	−6,967
Other investment liabilities	4 753 W.	70,916	24,226	79,803	41,897	147,199	180,328	24,501	19,357
Monetary authorities	4 753 WA	−1,331	−89	132	−154	14,649	46,122	12,593	11,000
General government	4 753 ZB	−1,026	6,362	193	1,354	725	3,981	3,004	6,323
Banks	4 753 ZC	61,853	17,691	62,843	4,897	104,440	115,270	9,799	−7,675
Other sectors	4 753 ZD	11,420	262	16,635	35,800	27,385	14,954	−895	9,708
Total, Groups A Through C	4 983 ..	*−17,259*	*−7,451*	*604*	*4,906*	*448*	*3,503*	*12,397*	*4,280*
D. Net Errors and Omissions	4 998 ..	**1,769**	**1,039**	**−2,524**	**−4,328**	**−233**	**−2,816**	**−6,427**	**−3,218**
Total, Groups A Through D	4 984 ..	*−15,489*	*−6,412*	*−1,920*	*578*	*215*	*687*	*5,970*	*1,061*
E. Reserves and Related Items	4 802 A.	**15,489**	**6,412**	**1,920**	**−578**	**−215**	**−687**	**−5,970**	**−1,061**
Reserve assets	4 802 ..	15,489	6,412	1,920	−578	−215	−687	−5,970	−1,061
Use of Fund credit and loans	4 766 ..	....	....	....	....	....	....	....	....
Exceptional financing	4 920 ..	....	....	....	....	....	....	....	....
Conversion rates: euros per U.S. dollar	0 103 ..	**.8860**	**.8054**	**.8041**	**.7971**	**.7306**	**.6827**	**.7198**	**.7550**

[1] Excludes components that have been classified in the categories of Group E.

Table 2. STANDARD PRESENTATION, 2003–2010

(Millions of U.S. dollars)

	Code	2003	2004	2005	2006	2007	2008	2009	2010
CURRENT ACCOUNT	4 993	−30,885	−54,865	−83,388	−110,874	−144,540	−154,529	−75,309	−64,342
A. GOODS	4 100	−45,155	−66,730	−85,204	−104,622	−125,238	−126,613	−58,956	−62,350
Credit	2 100	158,049	185,209	196,580	220,696	264,053	284,721	228,704	252,974
General merchandise: exports f.o.b.	2 110	153,404	179,287	189,263	212,303	254,552	272,167	219,819	242,869
Goods for processing: exports f.o.b.	2 150	2,749	3,567	3,999	4,635	5,389	5,949	4,178	4,584
Repairs on goods	2 160	273	300	287	401	430	505	425	399
Goods procured in ports by carriers	2 170	1,529	1,984	2,951	3,261	3,611	6,027	3,792	4,266
Nonmonetary gold	2 180	95	71	81	96	70	73	490	856
Debit	3 100	−203,205	−251,939	−281,784	−325,318	−389,291	−411,334	−287,660	−315,323
General merchandise: imports f.o.b.	3 110	−198,732	−246,602	−276,163	−319,210	−381,695	−402,991	−281,820	−309,234
Goods for processing: imports f.o.b.	3 150	−2,901	−3,377	−3,482	−3,650	−4,419	−4,681	−3,441	−3,800
Repairs on goods	3 160	−190	−257	−208	−288	−640	−393	−148	−154
Goods procured in ports by carriers	3 170	−876	−1,149	−1,424	−1,696	−2,102	−3,053	−2,115	−1,957
Nonmonetary gold	3 180	−506	−554	−506	−474	−436	−217	−136	−179
B. SERVICES	4 200	26,358	26,890	27,534	28,077	31,656	38,219	35,696	36,500
Total credit	2 200	74,308	86,078	94,663	106,665	128,148	143,813	123,085	123,627
Total debit	3 200	−47,951	−59,188	−67,129	−78,588	−96,492	−105,594	−87,389	−87,127
Transportation services, credit	2 205	11,897	14,321	16,178	18,122	21,013	24,693	19,296	20,810
Passenger	2 850	4,229	4,929	5,277	6,246	7,286	8,456	6,202	6,623
Freight	2 851	4,390	5,362	6,216	6,773	7,270	8,081	6,437	7,115
Other	2 852	3,278	4,030	4,685	5,104	6,457	8,156	6,657	7,071
Sea transport, passenger	2 207	69	100	91	162	267	274	154	116
Sea transport, freight	2 208	823	1,034	1,124	1,290	1,138	1,215	974	1,119
Sea transport, other	2 209	744	899	1,062	1,165	1,463	1,950	1,308	1,310
Air transport, passenger	2 211	4,130	4,783	5,130	6,031	6,957	8,147	6,021	6,475
Air transport, freight	2 212	173	174	153	154	173	175	140	161
Air transport, other	2 213	2,445	2,975	3,449	3,692	4,654	5,999	5,082	5,504
Other transport, passenger	2 215	29	46	56	53	61	35	27	32
Other transport, freight	2 216	3,393	4,154	4,939	5,329	5,959	6,692	5,323	5,836
Other transport, other	2 217	88	156	174	247	340	207	266	257
Transportation services, debit	3 205	−13,138	−16,102	−18,523	−20,572	−22,391	−26,564	−18,955	−20,975
Passenger	3 850	−2,259	−2,711	−3,395	−3,651	−4,631	−6,794	−5,308	−6,036
Freight	3 851	−8,529	−10,673	−12,204	−13,676	−13,495	−15,011	−10,245	−11,271
Other	3 852	−2,349	−2,719	−2,924	−3,245	−4,264	−4,758	−3,402	−3,669
Sea transport, passenger	3 207	−24	−34	−63	−86	−112	−132	−102	−75
Sea transport, freight	3 208	−3,077	−3,707	−4,121	−4,936	−3,885	−4,258	−2,783	−3,323
Sea transport, other	3 209	−364	−392	−440	−538	−699	−929	−671	−623
Air transport, passenger	3 211	−2,227	−2,659	−3,307	−3,517	−4,480	−6,644	−5,188	−5,931
Air transport, freight	3 212	−277	−283	−274	−310	−299	−366	−241	−288
Air transport, other	3 213	−1,840	−2,166	−2,239	−2,438	−3,238	−3,506	−2,424	−2,666
Other transport, passenger	3 215	−8	−17	−25	−47	−39	−18	−18	−31
Other transport, freight	3 216	−5,175	−6,682	−7,809	−8,430	−9,311	−10,388	−7,221	−7,660
Other transport, other	3 217	−146	−160	−244	−269	−328	−323	−307	−380
Travel, credit	2 236	39,634	45,067	47,789	51,297	57,734	61,978	53,337	52,187
Business travel	2 237	....	....	....	....	....	....	....	....
Personal travel	2 240	....	....	....	....	....	....	....	....
Travel, debit	3 236	−9,071	−12,153	−15,046	−16,697	−19,724	−20,363	−16,911	−16,764
Business travel	3 237	....	....	....	....	....	....	....	....
Personal travel	3 240	....	....	....	....	....	....	....	....
Other services, credit	2 200 BA	22,778	26,689	30,696	37,246	49,400	57,142	50,452	50,631
Communications	2 245	1,048	1,227	1,475	1,447	1,714	2,203	2,103	2,120
Construction	2 249	1,060	1,327	1,667	2,184	4,192	5,386	4,214	4,182
Insurance	2 253	475	771	803	822	1,531	1,400	1,778	1,178
Financial	2 260	1,902	2,077	2,812	3,987	5,904	5,661	4,314	4,564
Computer and information	2 262	2,913	2,964	3,606	3,960	5,358	6,120	6,101	6,420
Royalties and licence fees	2 266	528	500	565	923	537	801	671	877
Other business services	2 268	13,407	16,081	17,886	21,884	27,603	32,834	28,785	28,664
Personal, cultural, and recreational	2 287	814	966	1,073	1,243	1,598	1,756	1,673	1,772
Government, n.i.e.	2 291	629	775	810	796	963	982	811	854
Other services, debit	3 200 BA	−25,742	−30,933	−33,560	−41,320	−54,377	−58,668	−51,523	−49,388
Communications	3 245	−1,239	−1,577	−1,724	−2,352	−2,983	−3,323	−2,993	−2,669
Construction	3 249	−412	−860	−1,073	−1,318	−1,952	−2,994	−2,323	−1,882
Insurance	3 253	−880	−1,197	−1,217	−1,938	−2,669	−2,180	−2,209	−1,862
Financial	3 260	−1,695	−2,015	−2,747	−4,061	−5,073	−5,234	−4,439	−4,601
Computer and information	3 262	−1,672	−1,690	−2,021	−2,113	−2,633	−2,848	−2,485	−2,814
Royalties and licence fees	3 266	−2,520	−3,037	−2,636	−2,517	−3,620	−3,358	−3,166	−2,649
Other business services	3 268	−15,282	−18,286	−20,004	−24,691	−32,563	−35,702	−31,457	−30,441
Personal, cultural, and recreational	3 287	−1,699	−1,905	−1,748	−1,916	−2,416	−2,630	−1,993	−2,096
Government, n.i.e.	3 291	−344	−366	−390	−414	−469	−398	−458	−375

Table 2 (Continued). STANDARD PRESENTATION, 2003–2010

(Millions of U.S. dollars)

	Code	2003	2004	2005	2006	2007	2008	2009	2010
C. INCOME	4 300	**−11,701**	**−15,038**	**−21,256**	**−26,244**	**−41,371**	**−52,087**	**−41,113**	**−28,986**
Total credit	2 300	*27,209*	*33,948*	*39,445*	*60,022*	*79,614*	*77,954*	*58,385*	*54,813*
Total debit	3 300	*−38,910*	*−48,986*	*−60,701*	*−86,266*	*−120,986*	*−130,041*	*−99,498*	*−83,798*
Compensation of employees, credit	2 310	**1,013**	**1,157**	**1,318**	**1,513**	**2,012**	**2,247**	**1,889**	**1,961**
Compensation of employees, debit	3 310	**−925**	**−1,341**	**−1,545**	**−1,867**	**−2,389**	**−2,322**	**−2,068**	**−2,029**
Investment income, credit	2 320	**26,197**	**32,791**	**38,127**	**58,509**	**77,602**	**75,707**	**56,496**	**52,852**
Direct investment income	2 330	10,012	12,998	15,938	30,568	39,757	33,596	27,220	29,959
Dividends and distributed branch profits	2 332	7,711	10,069	12,563	15,038	19,705	27,012	22,932	28,350
Reinvested earnings and undistributed branch profits	2 333	1,740	2,376	2,608	14,405	18,702	4,497	2,105	1,016
Income on debt (interest)	2 334	561	553	767	1,125	1,350	2,087	2,183	592
Portfolio investment income	2 339	9,907	13,295	14,597	16,633	20,173	21,880	17,631	14,555
Income on equity	2 340	829	1,420	1,735	2,305	2,992	4,182	2,292	2,265
Income on bonds and notes	2 350	8,763	11,461	12,388	13,496	16,180	16,992	15,118	12,181
Income on money market instruments	2 360	315	413	474	832	1,001	706	221	109
Other investment income	2 370	6,279	6,497	7,591	11,308	17,672	20,232	11,645	8,338
Investment income, debit	3 320	**−37,985**	**−47,645**	**−59,156**	**−84,400**	**−118,597**	**−127,719**	**−97,430**	**−81,770**
Direct investment income	3 330	−9,097	−13,109	−15,504	−24,326	−31,204	−22,337	−22,206	−20,666
Dividends and distributed branch profits	3 332	−5,598	−9,235	−12,615	−12,464	−15,897	−14,764	−16,187	−14,558
Reinvested earnings and undistributed branch profits	3 333	−1,523	−1,874	−68	−8,587	−10,334	−2,190	−1,101	−582
Income on debt (interest)	3 334	−1,976	−2,000	−2,821	−3,276	−4,974	−5,383	−4,918	−5,526
Portfolio investment income	3 339	−15,483	−19,317	−26,396	−38,185	−54,456	−61,846	−50,216	−44,289
Income on equity	3 340	−3,543	−4,149	−5,382	−8,002	−9,531	−10,689	−10,668	−8,501
Income on bonds and notes	3 350	−11,932	−15,117	−20,704	−29,766	−43,709	−48,849	−37,923	−34,597
Income on money market instruments	3 360	−8	−51	−310	−417	−1,216	−2,308	−1,625	−1,191
Other investment income	3 370	−13,405	−15,218	−17,256	−21,889	−32,936	−43,536	−25,008	−16,815
D. CURRENT TRANSFERS	4 379	**−387**	**14**	**−4,463**	**−8,085**	**−9,587**	**−14,049**	**−10,936**	**−9,508**
Credit	2 379	**17,048**	**20,366**	**20,194**	**21,531**	**25,637**	**25,036**	**25,603**	**24,458**
General government	2 380	2,913	4,153	4,405	4,232	5,047	3,596	4,289	3,892
Other sectors	2 390	14,135	16,213	15,789	17,299	20,589	21,440	21,313	20,566
Workers' remittances	2 391	4,718	5,196	5,343	6,071	7,287	7,901	7,059	7,111
Other current transfers	2 392	9,417	11,017	10,445	11,228	13,303	13,539	14,254	13,454
Debit	3 379	**−17,434**	**−20,353**	**−24,656**	**−29,616**	**−35,223**	**−39,084**	**−36,539**	**−33,966**
General government	3 380	−10,093	−11,216	−13,699	−15,413	−16,898	−19,918	−20,357	−17,991
Other sectors	3 390	−7,341	−9,137	−10,958	−14,204	−18,325	−19,167	−16,182	−15,975
Workers' remittances	3 391	−3,939	−5,211	−6,123	−8,888	−11,610	−11,701	−10,072	−9,544
Other current transfers	3 392	−3,402	−3,926	−4,835	−5,315	−6,714	−7,466	−6,110	−6,430
CAPITAL AND FINANCIAL ACCOUNT	4 996	**29,116**	**53,826**	**85,912**	**115,202**	**144,773**	**157,345**	**81,736**	**67,561**
CAPITAL ACCOUNT	4 994	**9,274**	**10,450**	**10,107**	**7,855**	**6,374**	**8,184**	**5,943**	**8,358**
Total credit	2 994	*10,984*	*11,646*	*11,225*	*9,674*	*8,879*	*10,250*	*9,024*	*10,531*
Total debit	3 994	*−1,710*	*−1,197*	*−1,118*	*−1,819*	*−2,505*	*−2,066*	*−3,081*	*−2,174*
Capital transfers, credit	2 400	**10,893**	**11,300**	**10,787**	**9,522**	**8,676**	**9,639**	**7,434**	**9,140**
General government	2 401	9,948	9,956	9,284	7,990	6,862	7,714	5,814	7,388
Debt forgiveness	2 402	345	331	1,207	2,145	464	320	191	147
Other capital transfers	2 410	9,603	9,625	8,077	5,845	6,398	7,393	5,623	7,241
Other sectors	2 430	945	1,343	1,503	1,532	1,814	1,925	1,620	1,752
Migrants' transfers	2 431	838	1,175	1,299	1,306	1,441	1,687	1,422	1,435
Debt forgiveness	2 432	....	5	....	1	73	....	....	....
Other capital transfers	2 440	108	164	203	226	300	237	198	317
Capital transfers, debit	3 400	**−1,295**	**−675**	**−733**	**−1,008**	**−1,637**	**−1,213**	**−974**	**−955**
General government	3 401	−209	−133	−148	−121	−132	−141	−216	−94
Debt forgiveness	3 402	−205	−98	−102	−53	−42	−48	−24	−25
Other capital transfers	3 410	−5	−35	−47	−67	−90	−93	−192	−69
Other sectors	3 430	−1,085	−543	−585	−888	−1,505	−1,072	−758	−860
Migrants' transfers	3 431	−275	−425	−468	−571	−1,192	−804	−602	−654
Debt forgiveness	3 432	−734	−4	−1	....	....	−83	....	....
Other capital transfers	3 440	−76	−114	−116	−317	−314	−185	−155	−207
Nonproduced nonfinancial assets, credit	2 480	**91**	**347**	**439**	**152**	**203**	**612**	**1,590**	**1,391**
Nonproduced nonfinancial assets, debit	3 480	**−415**	**−522**	**−385**	**−811**	**−868**	**−853**	**−2,107**	**−1,219**

Table 2 (Continued). STANDARD PRESENTATION, 2003–2010

(Millions of U.S. dollars)

	Code	2003	2004	2005	2006	2007	2008	2009	2010
FINANCIAL ACCOUNT	4 995	**19,842**	**43,376**	**75,804**	**107,348**	**138,399**	**149,161**	**75,792**	**59,203**
A. DIRECT INVESTMENT	4 500	**−3,152**	**−36,712**	**−17,349**	**−72,311**	**−72,863**	**3,926**	**−233**	**4,102**
Direct investment abroad	4 505	**−28,759**	**−61,504**	**−41,922**	**−103,483**	**−139,545**	**−73,972**	**−8,787**	**−20,557**
Equity capital	4 510	−28,455	−54,144	−35,885	−86,724	−113,618	−62,791	−8,927	−21,152
Claims on affiliated enterprises	4 515	−28,455	−54,144	−35,885	−86,724	−113,618	−62,791	−8,927	−21,152
Liabilities to affiliated enterprises	4 520	....	....	....	....	....	....	....	....
Reinvested earnings	4 525	−1,740	−2,376	−2,608	−14,405	−18,702	−4,497	−2,105	−1,016
Other capital	4 530	1,437	−4,984	−3,429	−2,354	−7,224	−6,683	2,245	1,612
Claims on affiliated enterprises	4 535	−1,837	−4,056	−5,047	−3,182	−13,709	−8,967	−917	−4,425
Liabilities to affiliated enterprises	4 540	3,274	−928	1,618	827	6,484	2,284	3,162	6,037
Direct investment in Spain	4 555	**25,607**	**24,792**	**24,573**	**31,172**	**66,682**	**77,898**	**8,554**	**24,658**
Equity capital	4 560	10,857	15,958	16,371	16,777	39,149	46,422	8,809	22,159
Claims on direct investors	4 565	....	....	....	....	....	....	....	....
Liabilities to direct investors	4 570	10,857	15,958	16,371	16,777	39,149	46,422	8,809	22,159
Reinvested earnings	4 575	1,523	1,874	68	8,587	10,334	2,190	1,101	582
Other capital	4 580	13,227	6,960	8,134	5,808	17,199	29,286	−1,356	1,918
Claims on direct investors	4 585	−1,860	−1,458	−529	−991	−623	590	−1,876	−94
Liabilities to direct investors	4 590	15,086	8,417	8,663	6,799	17,822	28,696	520	2,012
B. PORTFOLIO INVESTMENT	4 600	**−46,070**	**102,035**	**53,357**	**232,428**	**118,171**	**4,292**	**73,667**	**47,699**
Assets	4 602	**−90,833**	**−39,651**	**−119,356**	**−11,462**	**−5,888**	**31,196**	**1,991**	**91,209**
Equity securities	4 610	−13,180	−15,063	−19,370	−26,256	10,157	40,579	−11,765	−11,918
Monetary authorities	4 611	....	....	....	....	....	....	....	....
General government	4 612	....	....	....	....	....	16	1	....
Banks	4 613	78	−2,596	−2,827	−5,714	−4,204	3,842	2,149	2,585
Other sectors	4 614	−13,258	−12,466	−16,542	−20,542	14,361	36,722	−13,914	−14,502
Debt securities	4 619	−77,653	−24,588	−99,986	14,794	−16,045	−9,383	13,756	103,126
Bonds and notes	4 620	−65,199	−31,560	−96,227	10,957	−16,742	−15,560	7,659	94,231
Monetary authorities	4 621	−10,022	−11,761	−16,071	−20,759	−16,033	−9,314	5,333	8,167
General government	4 622	−5	−1,107	−5,758	−13,173	−8,276	−4,017	16,477	7,725
Banks	4 623	−31,263	−2,566	−48,523	46,802	−44	−16,735	−9,479	36,678
Other sectors	4 624	−23,910	−16,126	−25,876	−1,913	7,611	14,505	−4,673	41,661
Money market instruments	4 630	−12,453	6,972	−3,759	3,837	698	6,177	6,097	8,895
Monetary authorities	4 631	−7,290	5,459	−5,703	3,184	−3,564	9,227	2,537	332
General government	4 632	5	....	....	−8	9	....	....	....
Banks	4 633	−4,803	−845	1,918	−2,553	979	1,279	−3,900	4,601
Other sectors	4 634	−366	2,358	25	3,214	3,273	−4,329	7,460	3,962
Liabilities	4 652	**44,763**	**141,686**	**172,713**	**243,890**	**124,060**	**−26,904**	**71,676**	**−43,510**
Equity securities	4 660	−3,649	10,918	−9,573	−24,005	15,595	−2,489	9,179	−4,790
Banks	4 663	−698	13,345	−2,264	4,371	−4,304	6,771	12,946	−2,353
Other sectors	4 664	−2,951	−2,427	−7,309	−28,376	19,898	−9,260	−3,767	−2,437
Debt securities	4 669	48,412	130,768	182,286	267,895	108,465	−24,415	62,497	−38,720
Bonds and notes	4 670	46,160	130,245	183,073	255,683	95,660	−42,171	8,728	−24,163
Monetary authorities	4 671	....	....	....	....	....	....	....	....
General government	4 672	−11,536	29,130	3,942	14,315	−22,798	14,709	35,913	20,245
Banks	4 673	31,520	49,381	72,030	89,787	35,253	−13,980	7,653	−19,024
Other sectors	4 674	26,175	51,733	107,100	151,581	83,205	−42,900	−34,838	−25,384
Money market instruments	4 680	2,253	524	−787	12,213	12,805	17,756	53,769	−14,557
Monetary authorities	4 681	....	....	....	....	....	....	....	....
General government	4 682	3,338	−933	−599	2,524	−782	10,203	44,411	−268
Banks	4 683	−166	52	619	7,548	19,608	−10,455	2,862	−6,200
Other sectors	4 684	−919	1,405	−807	2,141	−6,021	18,009	6,497	−8,089
C. FINANCIAL DERIVATIVES	4 910	**−3,785**	**74**	**273**	**2,527**	**−5,915**	**−12,611**	**−7,986**	**9,752**
Monetary authorities	4 911	....	....	....	....	....	−1,140	446	23
General government	4 912	51	−895	−110	−29	−298	−717	−400	−95
Banks	4 913	−2,100	−80	433	3,026	−3,187	−5,295	−6,961	11,362
Other sectors	4 914	−1,736	1,049	−51	−470	−2,430	−5,459	−1,071	−1,538
Assets	4 900	....	....	....	....	....	....	....	....
Monetary authorities	4 901	....	....	....	....	....	....	....	....
General government	4 902	....	....	....	....	....	....	....	....
Banks	4 903	....	....	....	....	....	....	....	....
Other sectors	4 904	....	....	....	....	....	....	....	....
Liabilities	4 905	**−3,785**	**74**	**273**	**2,527**	**−5,915**	**−12,611**	**−7,986**	**9,752**
Monetary authorities	4 906	....	....	....	....	....	−1,140	446	23
General government	4 907	51	−895	−110	−29	−298	−717	−400	−95
Banks	4 908	−2,100	−80	433	3,026	−3,187	−5,295	−6,961	11,362
Other sectors	4 909	−1,736	1,049	−51	−470	−2,430	−5,459	−1,071	−1,538

Table 2 (Concluded). STANDARD PRESENTATION, 2003–2010

(Millions of U.S. dollars)

	Code	2003	2004	2005	2006	2007	2008	2009	2010
D. OTHER INVESTMENT	4 700 ..	**57,359**	**−28,433**	**37,604**	**−54,718**	**99,220**	**154,241**	**16,314**	**−1,287**
Assets	4 703 ..	**−13,557**	**−52,659**	**−42,198**	**−96,615**	**−47,980**	**−26,087**	**−8,186**	**−20,644**
Trade credits	4 706 ..	5	4	18	5	13	4	6	6
General government	4 707 ..	....	....	....	....	....	....	....	....
of which: Short-term	4 709 ..	....	....	....	....	....	....	....	....
Other sectors	4 710 ..	5	4	18	5	13	4	6	6
of which: Short-term	4 712 ..	....	....	....	....	....	....	....	....
Loans	4 714 ..	−3,805	−6,225	−10,322	−29,517	−19,724	−16,257	−91	−2,462
Monetary authorities	4 715 ..	−1	....	1	−2	−1	....	....	....
of which: Short-term	4 718 ..	....	....	....	−2	−1	....	....	....
General government	4 719 ..	−377	−989	254	140	−1,025	233	−1,737	−3,780
of which: Short-term	4 721 ..	−253	−639	786	407	−1,007	466	−1,303	−317
Banks	4 722 ..	−3,257	−5,215	−9,841	−30,201	−19,575	−15,881	1,721	1,203
of which: Short-term	4 724 ..	231	−608	−4,585	−15,726	−9,493	−4,125	6,637	8,457
Other sectors	4 725 ..	−171	−21	−735	545	878	−609	−75	115
of which: Short-term	4 727 ..	239	439	−13	758	1,146	187	512	539
Currency and deposits	4 730 ..	−9,179	−44,936	−29,889	−63,976	−24,373	−6,345	−6,997	−15,621
Monetary authorities	4 731 ..	5,212	−18,100	17,119	−13,889	26,428	689	−448	189
General government	4 732 ..	360	−529	161	398	−131	144	114	33
Banks	4 733 ..	−7,253	−15,124	−40,941	−41,464	−45,112	−1,759	−7,597	−8,996
Other sectors	4 734 ..	−7,497	−11,183	−6,229	−9,021	−5,558	−5,419	934	−6,847
Other assets	4 736 ..	−577	−1,502	−2,005	−3,127	−3,896	−3,488	−1,105	−2,567
Monetary authorities	4 737 ..	....	21	....	....	−7	....	−56	−188
of which: Short-term	4 739 ..	....	....	....	....	....	....	....	....
General government	4 740 ..	−325	−665	−648	−742	−898	−911	−795	−521
of which: Short-term	4 742 ..	....	....	−2	−2	−2	−2	−2	....
Banks	4 743 ..	−13	−64	220	−1,749	−2,041	−1,285	−376	−1,618
of which: Short-term	4 745 ..	−13	−64	220	−1,749	−2,040	−1,285	−376	−1,618
Other sectors	4 746 ..	−239	−795	−1,576	−636	−951	−1,292	123	−241
of which: Short-term	4 748 ..	−255	−694	−1,491	−278	−529	−963	385	−80
Liabilities	4 753 ..	**70,916**	**24,226**	**79,803**	**41,897**	**147,199**	**180,328**	**24,501**	**19,357**
Trade credits	4 756 ..	−32	22	−72	−24	−4	−30	46	−5
General government	4 757 ..	....	....	....	−1	−1	−2	....	....
of which: Short-term	4 759 ..	....	....	....	....	....	....	....	....
Other sectors	4 760 ..	−32	22	−72	−23	−4	−29	46	−5
of which: Short-term	4 762 ..	....	....	....	....	....	....	....	....
Loans	4 764 ..	10,497	5,007	16,810	37,225	28,457	15,646	2,856	13,954
Monetary authorities	4 765 ..	....	....	....	....	....	....	....	....
of which: Use of Fund credit and loans from the Fund	4 766 ..	....	....	....	....	....	....	....	....
of which: Short-term	4 768 ..	....	....	....	....	....	....	....	....
General government	4 769 ..	−1,026	6,362	193	1,354	726	3,983	3,004	6,323
of which: Short-term	4 771 ..	−1,288	847	−1,201	1,180	−403	1,503	−2,028	542
Banks	4 772 ..	....	....	....	....	....	....	....	....
of which: Short-term	4 774 ..	....	....	....	....	....	....	....	....
Other sectors	4 775 ..	11,522	−1,355	16,617	35,870	27,732	11,663	−148	7,631
of which: Short-term	4 777 ..	−232	−116	−1,850	6,032	−2,297	−469	−12,984	356
Currency and deposits	4 780 ..	60,522	17,602	62,975	4,744	119,089	161,392	18,442	3,325
Monetary authorities	4 781 ..	−1,331	−89	132	−154	14,649	46,122	8,643	11,000
General government	4 782 ..	....	....	....	....	....	....	....	....
Banks	4 783 ..	61,853	17,691	62,843	4,897	104,440	115,270	9,799	−7,675
Other sectors	4 784 ..	....	....	....	....	....	....	....	....
Other liabilities	4 786 ..	−70	1,595	90	−47	−343	3,320	3,158	2,082
Monetary authorities	4 787 ..	....	....	....	....	....	....	3,950	....
of which: Short-term	4 789 ..	....	....	....	....	....	....	....	....
General government	4 790 ..	....	....	....	....	....	....	....	....
of which: Short-term	4 792 ..	....	....	....	....	....	....	....	....
Banks	4 793 ..	....	....	....	....	....	....	....	....
of which: Short-term	4 795 ..	....	....	....	....	....	....	....	....
Other sectors	4 796 ..	−70	1,595	90	−47	−343	3,320	−792	2,082
of which: Short-term	4 798 ..	−110	1,511	−212	−341	−593	3,163	−928	2,021
E. RESERVE ASSETS	4 802 ..	**15,489**	**6,412**	**1,920**	**−578**	**−215**	**−687**	**−5,970**	**−1,061**
Monetary gold	4 812 ..	....	....	....	....	....	....	....	....
Special drawing rights	4 811 ..	−25	100	−27	13	−17	144	−4,405	38
Reserve position in the Fund	4 810 ..	−115	356	717	380	96	−330	−102	−538
Foreign exchange	4 803 ..	15,629	5,956	1,229	−972	−294	−501	−1,463	−561
Other claims	4 813 ..	....	....	....	....	....	....	....	....
NET ERRORS AND OMISSIONS	4 998 ..	**1,769**	**1,039**	**−2,524**	**−4,328**	**−233**	**−2,816**	**−6,427**	**−3,218**

Table 3. INTERNATIONAL INVESTMENT POSITION (End-period stocks), 2003–2010

(Millions of U.S. dollars)

	Code	2003	2004	2005	2006	2007	2008	2009	2010
ASSETS	8 995 C.	**947,419**	**1,167,139**	**1,243,031**	**1,633,845**	**1,973,210**	**1,891,397**	**1,962,598**	**1,821,538**
Direct investment abroad	8 505 ..	**221,021**	**282,294**	**305,427**	**436,068**	**582,057**	**590,694**	**648,513**	**660,160**
Equity capital and reinvested earnings	8 506 ..	202,736	258,285	279,316	405,506	542,183	547,536	612,376	618,676
Claims on affiliated enterprises	8 507 ..	....	....	....	....	....	....	....	....
Liabilities to affiliated enterprises	8 508 ..	....	....	....	....	....	....	....	....
Other capital	8 530 ..	18,285	24,010	26,110	30,562	39,874	43,158	36,137	41,483
Claims on affiliated enterprises	8 535 ..	24,632	30,250	33,575	39,429	56,289	62,422	65,310	66,552
Liabilities to affiliated enterprises	8 540 ..	−6,347	−6,240	−7,465	−8,867	−16,415	−19,264	−29,173	−25,069
Portfolio investment	8 602 ..	**424,395**	**517,762**	**581,154**	**666,658**	**740,043**	**585,036**	**632,677**	**495,094**
Equity securities	8 610 ..	79,161	106,316	122,873	175,415	195,722	87,881	117,019	127,562
Monetary authorities	8 611 ..	....	....	....	....	....	....	....	....
General government	8 612 ..	....	....	....	....	....	....	....	....
Banks	8 613 ..	4,028	7,501	9,117	15,269	22,707	15,468	13,519	10,223
Other sectors	8 614 ..	75,134	98,814	113,756	160,146	173,016	72,413	103,500	117,339
Debt securities	8 619 ..	345,234	411,446	458,280	491,243	544,320	497,155	515,658	367,532
Bonds and notes	8 620 ..	323,244	395,190	435,706	471,405	522,691	478,625	499,575	359,847
Monetary authorities	8 621 ..	12,361	25,554	36,672	60,570	83,096	88,872	86,772	69,585
General government	8 622 ..	69	1,219	6,669	21,047	32,391	36,498	20,341	11,261
Banks	8 623 ..	112,044	129,708	160,105	110,243	124,006	116,630	134,995	85,135
Other sectors	8 624 ..	198,770	238,709	232,259	279,546	283,197	236,626	257,468	193,866
Money market instruments	8 630 ..	21,990	16,256	22,574	19,838	21,630	18,530	16,083	7,686
Monetary authorities	8 631 ..	8,135	2,797	8,031	5,951	11,553	3,213	527	129
General government	8 632 ..	....	....	....	9	....	....	....	....
Banks	8 633 ..	9,063	8,746	9,019	3,700	4,016	3,104	8,075	3,350
Other sectors	8 634 ..	4,791	4,713	5,524	10,178	6,062	12,213	7,481	4,206
Financial derivatives	8 900 ..	....	....	....	**43,426**	**65,718**	**150,691**	**111,573**	**127,094**
Monetary authorities	8 901 ..	....	....	....	....	....	896	....	....
General government	8 902 ..	....	....	....	....	....	687	647	1,372
Banks	8 903 ..	....	....	....	43,426	65,718	149,108	110,926	125,721
Other sectors	8 904 ..	....	....	....	....	....	....	....	....
Other investment	8 703 ..	**281,232**	**347,325**	**339,224**	**468,353**	**566,338**	**544,731**	**541,635**	**507,275**
Trade credits	8 706 ..	158	164	126	132	135	132	132	140
General government	8 707 ..	....	....	....	....	....	....	....	....
of which: Short-term	8 709 ..	....	....	....	....	....	....	....	....
Other sectors	8 710 ..	158	164	126	132	135	132	132	140
of which: Short-term	8 712 ..	....	....	....	....	....	....	....	....
Loans	8 714 ..	45,096	52,350	54,222	83,358	101,372	102,971	110,030	111,700
Monetary authorities	8 715 ..	....	....	....	....	....	....	....	....
of which: Short-term	8 718 ..	....	....	....	....	....	....	....	....
General government	8 719 ..	10,571	12,562	11,233	11,587	13,126	13,137	14,827	18,025
of which: Short-term	8 721 ..	*4,379*	*5,826*	*4,181*	*3,996*	*5,135*	*4,957*	*6,013*	*5,863*
Banks	8 722 ..	32,658	37,391	41,039	69,507	85,427	85,926	90,423	88,883
of which: Short-term	8 724 ..	*16,982*	*19,443*	*9,659*	*21,380*	*23,285*	*18,949*	*21,988*	*22,630*
Other sectors	8 725 ..	1,866	2,398	1,951	2,263	2,819	3,908	4,779	4,793
of which: Short-term	8 727 ..	*513*	*513*	*577*	*553*	*494*	*1,047*	*1,508*	*1,532*
Currency and deposits	8 730 ..	227,128	283,540	273,355	368,783	439,917	413,207	400,193	363,369
Monetary authorities	8 731 ..	23,074	44,063	22,317	39,948	7,056	6,056	6,894	6,395
General government	8 732 ..	17	404	234	242	469	337	255	280
Banks	8 733 ..	110,065	125,888	145,836	203,007	286,958	264,361	247,262	213,927
Other sectors	8 734 ..	93,972	113,185	104,967	125,586	145,434	142,453	145,783	142,767
Other assets	8 736 ..	8,850	11,270	11,521	16,080	24,914	28,421	31,281	32,066
Monetary authorities	8 737 ..	562	589	510	570	644	609	956	1,071
of which: Short-term	8 739 ..	....	....	....	....	....	....	....	....
General government	8 740 ..	2,292	3,080	3,097	4,005	5,289	5,818	6,728	6,620
of which: Short-term	8 742 ..	....	....	*2*	*4*	*6*	*8*	*10*	*9*
Banks	8 743 ..	405	491	233	2,082	4,545	5,661	6,333	7,387
of which: Short-term	8 745 ..	*405*	*491*	*233*	*2,082*	*4,545*	*5,661*	*6,333*	*7,387*
Other sectors	8 746 ..	5,592	7,110	7,681	9,424	14,435	16,333	17,264	16,987
of which: Short-term	8 748 ..	*200*	*975*	*2,248*	*2,796*	*3,695*	*4,540*	*4,275*	*4,083*
Reserve assets	8 802 ..	**20,771**	**19,759**	**17,227**	**19,340**	**19,054**	**20,244**	**28,201**	**31,915**
Monetary gold	8 812 ..	7,021	7,370	7,550	8,518	7,574	7,831	9,995	12,768
Special drawing rights	8 811 ..	413	332	332	335	369	223	4,639	4,517
Reserve position in the Fund	8 810 ..	1,862	1,575	752	399	319	650	780	1,323
Foreign exchange	8 803 ..	11,475	10,481	8,593	10,088	10,792	11,539	12,787	13,306
Other claims	8 813 ..	....	....	....	....	....	....	....	....

Table 3 (Concluded). INTERNATIONAL INVESTMENT POSITION (End-period stocks), 2003–2010

(Millions of U.S. dollars)

	Code	2003	2004	2005	2006	2007	2008	2009	2010
LIABILITIES	8 995 D.	**1,400,882**	**1,761,591**	**1,839,360**	**2,487,547**	**3,184,491**	**3,092,526**	**3,355,153**	**3,054,926**
Direct investment in Spain	8 555 ..	**339,652**	**407,472**	**384,538**	**461,527**	**585,858**	**588,901**	**634,909**	**614,473**
Equity capital and reinvested earnings	8 556 ..	261,563	315,529	295,681	357,319	452,344	446,268	475,012	463,883
Claims on direct investors	8 557 ..	....	....	....	....	....	....	....	....
Liabilities to direct investors	8 558 ..	....	....	....	....	....	....	....	....
Other capital	8 580 ..	78,089	91,943	88,858	104,208	133,514	142,633	159,897	150,590
Claims on direct investors	8 585 ..	−7,749	−10,012	−9,135	−11,216	−13,316	−11,918	−68,329	−70,918
Liabilities to direct investors	8 590 ..	85,839	101,954	97,992	115,423	146,830	154,552	228,226	221,508
Portfolio investment	8 652 ..	**533,041**	**766,167**	**859,273**	**1,270,352**	**1,600,084**	**1,333,186**	**1,538,422**	**1,280,673**
Equity securities	8 660 ..	186,770	249,551	232,810	323,564	415,619	236,788	320,706	244,278
Banks	8 663 ..	65,966	89,314	88,339	126,148	140,676	74,972	136,542	84,080
Other sectors	8 664 ..	120,804	160,237	144,472	197,416	274,943	161,816	184,163	160,197
Debt securities	8 669 ..	346,271	516,616	626,462	946,788	1,184,465	1,096,398	1,217,716	1,036,395
Bonds and notes	8 670 ..	337,513	506,918	618,410	925,881	1,145,305	1,043,468	1,106,376	957,886
Monetary authorities	8 671 ..	....	....	....	....	....	....	....	....
General government	8 672 ..	198,988	247,736	227,443	252,695	255,065	276,065	330,702	298,209
Banks	8 673 ..	77,867	142,639	194,010	310,862	384,479	346,825	374,846	320,130
Other sectors	8 674 ..	60,659	116,543	196,956	362,324	505,761	420,577	400,828	339,547
Money market instruments	8 680 ..	8,758	9,698	8,052	20,906	39,160	52,931	111,340	78,509
Monetary authorities	8 681 ..	....	....	....	....	....	....	....	....
General government	8 682 ..	5,446	3,781	2,908	6,369	6,849	17,369	64,076	49,021
Banks	8 683 ..	412	410	1,157	8,234	31,279	17,012	21,426	13,236
Other sectors	8 684 ..	2,901	5,507	3,987	6,304	1,032	18,550	25,838	16,252
Financial derivatives	8 905 ..	**....**	**....**	**....**	**56,063**	**93,459**	**158,691**	**113,084**	**123,544**
Monetary authorities	8 906 ..	....	....	....	....	....	....	113	40
General government	8 907 ..	....	....	....	619	1,064	302	248	10
Banks	8 908 ..	....	....	....	55,444	92,396	158,389	112,723	123,493
Other sectors	8 909 ..	....	....	....	....	....	....	....	....
Other investment	8 753 ..	**528,189**	**587,951**	**595,549**	**699,605**	**905,090**	**1,011,747**	**1,068,738**	**1,036,237**
Trade credits	8 756 ..	510	563	422	445	487	502	603	563
General government	8 757 ..	....	....	....	....	....	....	....	....
of which: Short-term	8 759 ..	....	....	....	....	....	....	....	....
Other sectors	8 760 ..	510	563	422	445	487	502	603	563
of which: Short-term	8 762 ..	....	....	....	....	....	....	....	....
Loans	8 764 ..	126,132	140,635	140,822	195,957	246,385	253,386	265,692	268,758
Monetary authorities	8 765 ..	....	....	....	....	....	....	....	....
of which: Use of Fund credit and loans from the Fund	8 766 ..	....	....	....	....	....	....	....	....
of which: Short-term	8 768 ..	....	....	....	....	....	....	....	....
General government	8 769 ..	16,372	23,930	21,411	24,862	29,318	31,882	36,251	40,539
of which: Short-term	8 771 ..	*423*	*960*	*76*	*876*	*1,293*	*2,921*	*767*	*1,308*
Banks	8 772 ..	....	....	....	....	....	....	....	....
of which: Short-term	8 774 ..	....	....	....	....	....	....	....	....
Other sectors	8 775 ..	109,760	116,705	119,411	171,095	217,067	221,504	229,440	228,219
of which: Short-term	8 777 ..	*24,247*	*25,887*	*21,019*	*30,247*	*30,886*	*31,045*	*18,262*	*22,300*
Currency and deposits	8 780 ..	401,049	444,496	452,508	501,548	655,439	751,672	790,984	752,290
Monetary authorities	8 781 ..	116	21	149	370	5,226	49,033	59,640	68,578
General government	8 782 ..	....	....	....	....	....	....	....	....
Banks	8 783 ..	400,933	444,475	452,359	501,178	650,213	702,639	731,344	683,712
Other sectors	8 784 ..	....	....	....	....	....	....	....	....
Other liabilities	8 786 ..	497	2,257	1,798	1,655	2,779	6,186	11,459	14,626
Monetary authorities	8 787 ..	....	....	....	....	....	....	4,433	4,355
of which: Short-term	8 789 ..	....	....	....	....	....	....	....	....
General government	8 790 ..	....	....	....	....	....	....	....	....
of which: Short-term	8 792 ..	....	....	....	....	....	....	....	....
Banks	8 793 ..	....	....	....	....	....	....	....	....
of which: Short-term	8 795 ..	....	....	....	....	....	....	....	....
Other sectors	8 796 ..	497	2,257	1,798	1,655	2,779	6,186	7,027	10,271
of which: Short-term	8 798 ..	....	*1,600*	*1,175*	*925*	*463*	*3,713*	*2,957*	*4,742*
NET INTERNATIONAL INVESTMENT POSITION	8 995 ..	**−453,463**	**−594,452**	**−596,329**	**−853,702**	**−1,211,281**	**−1,201,129**	**−1,392,556**	**−1,233,388**
Conversion rates: euros per U.S. dollar (end of period)	0 104 ..	**.7918**	**.7342**	**.8477**	**.7593**	**.6793**	**.7185**	**.6942**	**.7484**

Table 1. ANALYTIC PRESENTATION, 2003–2010

(Millions of U.S. dollars)

	Code	2003	2004	2005	2006	2007	2008	2009	2010
A. Current Account¹	4 993 Z.	**−106**	**−677**	**−743**	**−1,599**	**−1,498**	**−3,986**	**−292**	**−1,471**
Goods: exports f.o.b.	2 100 ..	5,133	5,757	6,347	6,883	7,640	8,111	7,085	8,307
Goods: imports f.o.b.	3 100 ..	−6,005	−7,200	−7,977	−9,228	−10,167	−12,682	−9,186	−12,161
Balance on Goods	4 100 ..	*−872*	*−1,443*	*−1,630*	*−2,345*	*−2,527*	*−4,571*	*−2,101*	*−3,853*
Services: credit	2 200 ..	1,411	1,527	1,540	1,625	1,775	2,002	1,892	2,469
Services: debit	3 200 ..	−1,679	−1,908	−2,089	−2,394	−2,602	−3,010	−2,522	−3,122
Balance on Goods and Services	4 991 ..	*−1,140*	*−1,824*	*−2,179*	*−3,114*	*−3,354*	*−5,579*	*−2,732*	*−4,507*
Income: credit	2 300 ..	170	157	76	312	449	225	122	323
Income: debit	3 300 ..	−341	−360	−375	−700	−807	−1,197	−609	−896
Balance on Goods, Services, and Income	4 992 ..	*−1,312*	*−2,027*	*−2,478*	*−3,502*	*−3,711*	*−6,551*	*−3,219*	*−5,079*
Current transfers: credit	2 379 Z.	1,414	1,564	1,968	2,161	2,502	2,918	3,330	4,116
Current transfers: debit	3 379 ..	−209	−214	−233	−258	−288	−353	−403	−508
B. Capital Account¹	4 994 Z.	**74**	**64**	**250**	**291**	**269**	**291**	**233**	**164**
Capital account: credit	2 994 Z.	81	71	257	299	278	303	247	183
Capital account: debit	3 994 ..	−6	−7	−8	−8	−10	−12	−14	−19
Total, Groups A Plus B	4 981 ..	*−32*	*−613*	*−493*	*−1,308*	*−1,229*	*−3,696*	*−59*	*−1,307*
C. Financial Account¹	4 995 W.	**−219**	**−133**	**67**	**687**	**14**	**4**	**−1,105**	**−952**
Direct investment abroad	4 505 ..	−27	−6	−38	−29	−55	−62	−20	−43
Direct investment in Sri Lanka	4 555 Z.	229	233	272	480	603	752	404	478
Portfolio investment assets	4 602 ..	145	111	276	355	326	−174	−47	172
Equity securities	4 610 ..	145	111	276	355	423	548	375	819
Debt securities	4 619 ..	....	....	....	....	−97	−722	−422	−647
Portfolio investment liabilities	4 652 Z.	−143	−100	−216	−304	−322	−488	−382	−1,049
Equity securities	4 660 ..	−143	−100	−216	−304	−322	−488	−382	−1,049
Debt securities	4 669 Z.	....	....	....	....	....	....	....	....
Financial derivatives	4 910 ..	....	....	....	....	....	....	....	....
Financial derivatives assets	4 900 ..	....	....	....	....	....	....	....	....
Financial derivatives liabilities	4 905 ..	....	....	....	....	....	....	....	....
Other investment assets	4 703 ..	−94	−354	−223	297	−281	210	−435	249
Monetary authorities	4 701 ..	....	....	....	....	....	....	....	....
General government	4 704 ..	....	....	....	....	....	....	....	....
Banks	4 705 ..	−94	−354	−223	297	−281	210	−435	249
Other sectors	4 728 ..	....	....	....	....	....	....	....	....
Other investment liabilities	4 753 W.	−328	−17	−4	−111	−257	−234	−625	−760
Monetary authorities	4 753 WA	40	179	−80	12	144	355	495	553
General government	4 753 ZB	−251	−275	−77	−212	−618	−807	−940	−665
Banks	4 753 ZC	−2	202	323	293	364	−185	−98	815
Other sectors	4 753 ZD	−115	−123	−170	−203	−148	403	−83	−1,463
Total, Groups A Through C	4 983 ..	*−251*	*−746*	*−426*	*−621*	*−1,215*	*−3,691*	*−1,164*	*−2,259*
D. Net Errors and Omissions	4 998 ..	**−114**	**−189**	**−73**	**−96**	**−159**	**724**	**−140**	**−523**
Total, Groups A Through D	4 984 ..	*−365*	*−935*	*−498*	*−717*	*−1,374*	*−2,968*	*−1,304*	*−2,782*
E. Reserves and Related Items	4 802 A.	**365**	**935**	**498**	**717**	**1,374**	**2,968**	**1,304**	**2,782**
Reserve assets	4 802 ..	−627	133	−540	−73	−675	1,111	−3,290	−2,069
Use of Fund credit and loans	4 766 ..	50	−112	118	−153	−5	−77	554	581
Exceptional financing	4 920 ..	942	913	920	943	2,055	1,934	4,039	4,270
Conversion rates: Sri Lanka rupees per U.S. dollar	0 101 ..	**96.521**	**101.194**	**100.498**	**103.914**	**110.623**	**108.334**	**114.945**	**113.064**

¹ Excludes components that have been classified in the categories of Group E.

Table 2. STANDARD PRESENTATION, 2003–2010

(Millions of U.S. dollars)

	Code	2003	2004	2005	2006	2007	2008	2009	2010
CURRENT ACCOUNT..	4 993 ..	**−71**	**−648**	**−650**	**−1,498**	**−1,401**	**−3,885**	**−215**	**−1,418**
A. GOODS..	4 100 ..	**−872**	**−1,443**	**−1,630**	**−2,345**	**−2,527**	**−4,571**	**−2,101**	**−3,853**
Credit..	2 100 ..	**5,133**	**5,757**	**6,347**	**6,883**	**7,640**	**8,111**	**7,085**	**8,307**
General merchandise: exports f.o.b...............	2 110 ..	5,133	5,757	6,347	6,883	7,640	8,111	7,085	8,307
Goods for processing: exports f.o.b.............	2 150 ..	....	....	....	....	....	....	....	....
Repairs on goods....................................	2 160 ..	....	....	....	....	....	....	....	....
Goods procured in ports by carriers...........	2 170 ..	....	....	....	....	....	....	....	....
Nonmonetary gold..................................	2 180 ..	....	....	....	....	....	....	....	....
Debit...	3 100 ..	**−6,005**	**−7,200**	**−7,977**	**−9,228**	**−10,167**	**−12,682**	**−9,186**	**−12,161**
General merchandise: imports f.o.b.............	3 110 ..	−6,005	−7,200	−7,977	−9,228	−10,167	−12,682	−9,186	−12,161
Goods for processing: imports f.o.b............	3 150 ..	....	....	....	....	....	....	....	....
Repairs on goods....................................	3 160 ..	....	....	....	....	....	....	....	....
Goods procured in ports by carriers...........	3 170 ..	....	....	....	....	....	....	....	....
Nonmonetary gold..................................	3 180 ..	....	....	....	....	....	....	....	....
B. SERVICES..	4 200 ..	**−268**	**−381**	**−549**	**−769**	**−827**	**−1,008**	**−630**	**−653**
Total credit..	2 200 ..	*1,411*	*1,527*	*1,540*	*1,625*	*1,775*	*2,002*	*1,892*	*2,469*
Total debit...	3 200 ..	*−1,679*	*−1,908*	*−2,089*	*−2,394*	*−2,602*	*−3,010*	*−2,522*	*−3,122*
Transportation services, credit.................	2 205 ..	**562**	**624**	**673**	**751**	**838**	**998**	**866**	**1,156**
Passenger...	2 850 ..	*268*	*295*	*300*	*323*	*365*	*461*	*404*	*468*
Freight..	2 851 ..	*45*	*50*	*54*	*63*	*71*	*103*	*74*	*106*
Other..	2 852 ..	*249*	*279*	*319*	*365*	*402*	*434*	*387*	*582*
Sea transport, passenger........................	2 207 ..	268	295	300	323	365	461	404	468
Sea transport, freight...........................	2 208 ..	45	50	54	63	71	103	74	106
Sea transport, other.............................	2 209 ..	249	279	319	365	402	434	387	582
Air transport, passenger........................	2 211 ..	....	....	....	....	....	....	....	....
Air transport, freight...........................	2 212 ..	....	....	....	....	....	....	....	....
Air transport, other.............................	2 213 ..	....	....	....	....	....	....	....	....
Other transport, passenger.....................	2 215 ..	....	....	....	....	....	....	....	....
Other transport, freight........................	2 216 ..	....	....	....	....	....	....	....	....
Other transport, other..........................	2 217 ..	....	....	....	....	....	....	....	....
Transportation services, debit..................	3 205 ..	**−962**	**−1,135**	**−1,267**	**−1,462**	**−1,613**	**−1,968**	**−1,549**	**−2,036**
Passenger...	3 850 ..	*−183*	*−203*	*−238*	*−293*	*−316*	*−349*	*−324*	*−375*
Freight..	3 851 ..	*−672*	*−805*	*−889*	*−1,028*	*−1,132*	*−1,415*	*−1,035*	*−1,392*
Other..	3 852 ..	*−107*	*−127*	*−141*	*−142*	*−166*	*−204*	*−191*	*−268*
Sea transport, passenger........................	3 207 ..	−183	−203	−238	−293	−316	−349	−324	−375
Sea transport, freight...........................	3 208 ..	−672	−805	−889	−1,028	−1,132	−1,415	−1,035	−1,392
Sea transport, other.............................	3 209 ..	−107	−127	−141	−142	−166	−204	−191	−268
Air transport, passenger........................	3 211 ..	....	....	....	....	....	....	....	....
Air transport, freight...........................	3 212 ..	....	....	....	....	....	....	....	....
Air transport, other.............................	3 213 ..	....	....	....	....	....	....	....	....
Other transport, passenger.....................	3 215 ..	....	....	....	....	....	....	....	....
Other transport, freight........................	3 216 ..	....	....	....	....	....	....	....	....
Other transport, other..........................	3 217 ..	....	....	....	....	....	....	....	....
Travel, credit.....................................	2 236 ..	**441**	**513**	**429**	**410**	**385**	**342**	**350**	**576**
Business travel.....................................	2 237 ..	....	....	....	....	....	....	....	....
Personal travel.....................................	2 240 ..	441	513	429	410	385	342	350	576
Travel, debit......................................	3 236 ..	**−279**	**−296**	**−314**	**−373**	**−393**	**−428**	**−411**	**−453**
Business travel.....................................	3 237 ..	....	....	....	....	....	....	....	....
Personal travel.....................................	3 240 ..	−279	−296	−314	−373	−393	−428	−411	−453
Other services, credit..........................	2 200 BA	**407**	**390**	**438**	**464**	**552**	**662**	**677**	**737**
Communications....................................	2 245 ..	53	43	44	68	72	81	80	83
Construction..	2 249 ..	38	26	29	29	33	41	40	42
Insurance...	2 253 ..	48	50	73	57	55	68	75	80
Financial...	2 260 ..	....	....	....	....	....	....	....	....
Computer and information........................	2 262 ..	65	72	82	98	175	230	245	265
Royalties and licence fees.......................	2 266 ..	....	....	....	....	....	....	....	....
Other business services..........................	2 268 ..	182	178	188	190	196	222	219	246
Personal, cultural, and recreational...........	2 287 ..	....	....	....	....	....	....	....	....
Government, n.i.e...................................	2 291 ..	21	20	21	21	20	21	19	21
Other services, debit...........................	3 200 BA	**−439**	**−477**	**−507**	**−558**	**−596**	**−614**	**−562**	**−633**
Communications....................................	3 245 ..	−8	−10	−19	−49	−54	−55	−54	−56
Construction..	3 249 ..	−4	−6	−6	−6	−6	−6	−6	−6
Insurance...	3 253 ..	−96	−110	−123	−140	−153	−188	−148	−185
Financial...	3 260 ..	....	....	....	....	....	....	....	....
Computer and information........................	3 262 ..	....	....	....	....	....	....	....	....
Royalties and licence fees.......................	3 266 ..	....	....	....	....	....	....	....	....
Other business services..........................	3 268 ..	−299	−315	−322	−329	−349	−331	−319	−348
Personal, cultural, and recreational...........	3 287 ..	....	....	....	....	....	....	....	....
Government, n.i.e...................................	3 291 ..	−33	−35	−37	−35	−34	−35	−35	−38

Table 2 (Continued). STANDARD PRESENTATION, 2003–2010

(Millions of U.S. dollars)

	Code	2003	2004	2005	2006	2007	2008	2009	2010
C. INCOME	4 300	**−172**	**−204**	**−300**	**−388**	**−358**	**−972**	**−488**	**−572**
Total credit	2 300	*170*	*157*	*76*	*312*	*449*	*225*	*122*	*323*
Total debit	3 300	*−341*	*−360*	*−375*	*−700*	*−807*	*−1,197*	*−609*	*−896*
Compensation of employees, credit	2 310	**10**	**10**	**7**	**6**	**6**	**7**	**7**	**7**
Compensation of employees, debit	3 310	**−15**	**−16**	**−16**	**−17**	**−17**	**−20**	**−17**	**−18**
Investment income, credit	2 320	**160**	**147**	**69**	**306**	**443**	**218**	**115**	**316**
Direct investment income	2 330	2	3	3	3	3	6	7	9
Dividends and distributed branch profits	2 332	2	3	3	3	3	6	7	9
Reinvested earnings and undistributed branch profits	2 333	....	....	....	....	....	....	....	....
Income on debt (interest)	2 334	....	....	....	....	....	....	....	....
Portfolio investment income	2 339	....	....	....	....	....	....	....	....
Income on equity	2 340	....	....	....	....	....	....	....	....
Income on bonds and notes	2 350	....	....	....	....	....	....	....	....
Income on money market instruments	2 360	....	....	....	....	....	....	....	....
Other investment income	2 370	158	144	66	303	441	212	108	307
Investment income, debit	3 320	**−326**	**−344**	**−359**	**−683**	**−790**	**−1,177**	**−592**	**−878**
Direct investment income	3 330	−92	−95	−115	−362	−349	−470	−230	−386
Dividends and distributed branch profits	3 332	−92	−95	−115	−362	−126	−59	−76	−191
Reinvested earnings and undistributed branch profits	3 333	....	....	....	....	−223	−411	−154	−195
Income on debt (interest)	3 334	....	....	....	....	....	....	....	....
Portfolio investment income	3 339	....	....	....	....	....	....	....	....
Income on equity	3 340	....	....	....	....	....	....	....	....
Income on bonds and notes	3 350	....	....	....	....	....	....	....	....
Income on money market instruments	3 360	....	....	....	....	....	....	....	....
Other investment income	3 370	−235	−249	−244	−321	−441	−707	−362	−491
D. CURRENT TRANSFERS	4 379	**1,241**	**1,380**	**1,828**	**2,004**	**2,311**	**2,666**	**3,005**	**3,660**
Credit	2 379	**1,450**	**1,594**	**2,061**	**2,262**	**2,598**	**3,019**	**3,408**	**4,169**
General government	2 380	36	30	93	101	97	101	77	52
Other sectors	2 390	1,414	1,564	1,968	2,161	2,502	2,918	3,330	4,116
Workers' remittances	2 391	1,414	1,564	1,968	2,161	2,502	2,918	3,330	4,116
Other current transfers	2 392	....	....	....	....	....	....	....	....
Debit	3 379	**−209**	**−214**	**−233**	**−258**	**−288**	**−353**	**−403**	**−508**
General government	3 380	....	....	....	....	....	....	....	....
Other sectors	3 390	−209	−214	−233	−258	−288	−353	−403	−508
Workers' remittances	3 391	−209	−214	−233	−258	−288	−353	−403	−508
Other current transfers	3 392	....	....	....	....	....	....	....	....
CAPITAL AND FINANCIAL ACCOUNT	4 996	**185**	**837**	**723**	**1,594**	**1,560**	**3,162**	**354**	**1,941**
CAPITAL ACCOUNT	4 994	**74**	**64**	**250**	**291**	**269**	**291**	**233**	**164**
Total credit	2 994	*81*	*71*	*257*	*299*	*278*	*303*	*247*	*183*
Total debit	3 994	*−6*	*−7*	*−8*	*−8*	*−10*	*−12*	*−14*	*−19*
Capital transfers, credit	2 400	**81**	**71**	**257**	**299**	**278**	**303**	**247**	**183**
General government	2 401	66	55	144	187	180	187	144	97
Debt forgiveness	2 402	....	....	....	....	....	....	....	....
Other capital transfers	2 410	66	55	144	187	180	187	144	97
Other sectors	2 430	14	16	113	112	99	115	104	85
Migrants' transfers	2 431	14	16	15	18	19	23	26	32
Debt forgiveness	2 432	....	....	....	....	....	....	....	....
Other capital transfers	2 440	....	....	98	94	79	93	78	53
Capital transfers, debit	3 400	**−6**	**−7**	**−8**	**−8**	**−10**	**−12**	**−14**	**−19**
General government	3 401	....	....	....	....	....	....	....	....
Debt forgiveness	3 402	....	....	....	....	....	....	....	....
Other capital transfers	3 410	....	....	....	....	....	....	....	....
Other sectors	3 430	−6	−7	−8	−8	−10	−12	−14	−19
Migrants' transfers	3 431	−6	−7	−8	−8	−10	−12	−14	−19
Debt forgiveness	3 432	....	....	....	....	....	....	....	....
Other capital transfers	3 440	....	....	....	....	....	....	....	....
Nonproduced nonfinancial assets, credit	2 480	....	....	....	....	....	....	....	....
Nonproduced nonfinancial assets, debit	3 480	....	....	....	....	....	....	....	....

Table 2 (Continued). STANDARD PRESENTATION, 2003–2010

(Millions of U.S. dollars)

	Code	2003	2004	2005	2006	2007	2008	2009	2010
FINANCIAL ACCOUNT..	4 995 ..	**111**	**773**	**473**	**1,304**	**1,292**	**2,871**	**121**	**1,778**
A. DIRECT INVESTMENT.................................	4 500 ..	**201**	**227**	**234**	**450**	**548**	**691**	**384**	**436**
Direct investment abroad................................	4 505 ..	**−27**	**−6**	**−38**	**−29**	**−55**	**−62**	**−20**	**−43**
Equity capital..	4 510 ..	....	....	....	....	−55	−62	−20	−43
Claims on affiliated enterprises........................	4 515 ..	....	....	....	....	−55	−62	−20	−43
Liabilities to affiliated enterprises....................	4 520 ..	....	....	....	....	....	....	....	....
Reinvested earnings..	4 525 ..	....	....	....	....	....	....	....	....
Other capital..	4 530 ..	−27	−6	−38	−29	....	....	....	....
Claims on affiliated enterprises........................	4 535 ..	−27	−6	−38	−29	....	....	....	....
Liabilities to affiliated enterprises....................	4 540 ..	....	....	....	....	....	....	....	....
Direct investment in Sri Lanka.........................	4 555 ..	**229**	**233**	**272**	**480**	**603**	**752**	**404**	**478**
Equity capital..	4 560 ..	199	223	272	480	221	131	19	44
Claims on direct investors................................	4 565 ..	....	....	....	....	....	....	....	....
Liabilities to direct investors............................	4 570 ..	199	223	272	480	221	131	19	44
Reinvested earnings..	4 575 ..	....	....	....	....	223	411	154	195
Other capital..	4 580 ..	30	10	....	....	159	210	231	239
Claims on direct investors................................	4 585 ..	....	....	....	....	....	....	....	....
Liabilities to direct investors............................	4 590 ..	30	10	....	....	159	210	231	239
B. PORTFOLIO INVESTMENT.............................	4 600 ..	**2**	**11**	**60**	**51**	**974**	**−153**	**1,863**	**1,301**
Assets..	4 602 ..	**145**	**111**	**276**	**355**	**326**	**−174**	**−47**	**172**
Equity securities..	4 610 ..	145	111	276	355	423	548	375	819
Monetary authorities..	4 611 ..	....	....	....	....	....	....	....	....
General government..	4 612 ..	....	....	....	....	....	....	....	....
Banks..	4 613 ..	....	....	....	....	....	....	....	....
Other sectors..	4 614 ..	145	111	276	355	423	548	375	819
Debt securities..	4 619 ..	....	....	....	....	−97	−722	−422	−647
Bonds and notes..	4 620 ..	....	....	....	....	....	....	....	....
Monetary authorities....................................	4 621 ..	....	....	....	....	....	....	....	....
General government......................................	4 622 ..	....	....	....	....	....	....	....	....
Banks..	4 623 ..	....	....	....	....	....	....	....	....
Other sectors..	4 624 ..	....	....	....	....	....	....	....	....
Money market instruments..............................	4 630 ..	....	....	....	....	−97	−722	−422	−647
Monetary authorities....................................	4 631 ..	....	....	....	....	....	....	....	....
General government......................................	4 632 ..	....	....	....	....	−97	−722	−422	−647
Banks..	4 633 ..	....	....	....	....	....	....	....	....
Other sectors..	4 634 ..	....	....	....	....	....	....	....	....
Liabilities...	4 652 ..	**−143**	**−100**	**−216**	**−304**	**648**	**21**	**1,910**	**1,130**
Equity securities..	4 660 ..	−143	−100	−216	−304	−322	−488	−382	−1,049
Banks..	4 663 ..	....	....	....	....	....	....	....	....
Other sectors..	4 664 ..	−143	−100	−216	−304	−322	−488	−382	−1,049
Debt securities..	4 669 ..	....	....	....	....	970	509	2,292	2,178
Bonds and notes..	4 670 ..	....	....	....	....	500	....	500	1,000
Monetary authorities....................................	4 671 ..	....	....	....	....	....	....	....	....
General government......................................	4 672 ..	....	....	....	....	500	....	500	1,000
Banks..	4 673 ..	....	....	....	....	....	....	....	....
Other sectors..	4 674 ..	....	....	....	....	....	....	....	....
Money market instruments..............................	4 680 ..	....	....	....	....	470	509	1,792	1,178
Monetary authorities....................................	4 681 ..	....	....	....	....	....	....	....	....
General government......................................	4 682 ..	....	....	....	....	470	509	1,792	1,178
Banks..	4 683 ..	....	....	....	....	....	....	....	....
Other sectors..	4 684 ..	....	....	....	....	....	....	....	....
C. FINANCIAL DERIVATIVES.............................	4 910 ..	....	....	....	....	....	....	....	....
Monetary authorities..	4 911 ..	....	....	....	....	....	....	....	....
General government..	4 912 ..	....	....	....	....	....	....	....	....
Banks..	4 913 ..	....	....	....	....	....	....	....	....
Other sectors..	4 914 ..	....	....	....	....	....	....	....	....
Assets..	4 900 ..	....	....	....	....	....	....	....	....
Monetary authorities..	4 901 ..	....	....	....	....	....	....	....	....
General government..	4 902 ..	....	....	....	....	....	....	....	....
Banks..	4 903 ..	....	....	....	....	....	....	....	....
Other sectors..	4 904 ..	....	....	....	....	....	....	....	....
Liabilities...	4 905 ..	....	....	....	....	....	....	....	....
Monetary authorities..	4 906 ..	....	....	....	....	....	....	....	....
General government..	4 907 ..	....	....	....	....	....	....	....	....
Banks..	4 908 ..	....	....	....	....	....	....	....	....
Other sectors..	4 909 ..	....	....	....	....	....	....	....	....

Table 2 (Concluded). STANDARD PRESENTATION, 2003–2010

(Millions of U.S. dollars)

	Code	2003	2004	2005	2006	2007	2008	2009	2010
D. OTHER INVESTMENT	4 700	**535**	**401**	**718**	**875**	**445**	**1,223**	**1,164**	**2,110**
Assets	4 703	**−94**	**−354**	**−223**	**297**	**−281**	**210**	**−435**	**249**
Trade credits	4 706	....	....	....	....	....	....	....	....
General government	4 707	....	....	....	....	....	....	....	....
of which: Short-term	4 709	....	....	....	....	....	....	....	....
Other sectors	4 710	....	....	....	....	....	....	....	....
of which: Short-term	4 712	....	....	....	....	....	....	....	....
Loans	4 714	....	....	....	....	....	....	....	....
Monetary authorities	4 715	....	....	....	....	....	....	....	....
of which: Short-term	4 718	....	....	....	....	....	....	....	....
General government	4 719	....	....	....	....	....	....	....	....
of which: Short-term	4 721	....	....	....	....	....	....	....	....
Banks	4 722	....	....	....	....	....	....	....	....
of which: Short-term	4 724	....	....	....	....	....	....	....	....
Other sectors	4 725	....	....	....	....	....	....	....	....
of which: Short-term	4 727	....	....	....	....	....	....	....	....
Currency and deposits	4 730	−94	−354	−223	297	−281	210	−435	249
Monetary authorities	4 731	....	....	....	....	....	....	....	....
General government	4 732	....	....	....	....	....	....	....	....
Banks	4 733	−94	−354	−223	297	−281	210	−435	249
Other sectors	4 734	....	....	....	....	....	....	....	....
Other assets	4 736	....	....	....	....	....	....	....	....
Monetary authorities	4 737	....	....	....	....	....	....	....	....
of which: Short-term	4 739	....	....	....	....	....	....	....	....
General government	4 740	....	....	....	....	....	....	....	....
of which: Short-term	4 742	....	....	....	....	....	....	....	....
Banks	4 743	....	....	....	....	....	....	....	....
of which: Short-term	4 745	....	....	....	....	....	....	....	....
Other sectors	4 746	....	....	....	....	....	....	....	....
of which: Short-term	4 748	....	....	....	....	....	....	....	....
Liabilities	4 753	**628**	**755**	**941**	**578**	**726**	**1,012**	**1,599**	**1,861**
Trade credits	4 756	14	37	82	97	20	594	228	−1,032
General government	4 757	−5	9	65	126	....	....	....	....
of which: Short-term	4 759	....	....	....	....	....	....	....	....
Other sectors	4 760	19	28	16	−30	20	594	228	−1,032
of which: Short-term	4 762	*19*	*28*	*16*	*−30*	*20*	*594*	*228*	*−1,032*
Loans	4 764	576	336	617	177	197	248	974	1,525
Monetary authorities	4 765	50	−112	118	−153	−5	−77	554	581
of which: Use of Fund credit and loans from the Fund	4 766	*50*	*−112*	*118*	*−153*	*−5*	*−77*	*554*	*581*
of which: Short-term	4 768	....	....	....	....	....	....	....	....
General government	4 769	559	430	488	364	172	252	340	796
of which: Short-term	4 771	....	....	....	....	....	....	....	....
Banks	4 772	....	....	....	....	....	....	....	....
of which: Short-term	4 774	....	....	....	....	....	....	....	....
Other sectors	4 775	−33	18	11	−35	31	74	79	148
of which: Short-term	4 777	....	....	....	....	....	....	....	....
Currency and deposits	4 780	−2	202	323	293	364	−185	−98	815
Monetary authorities	4 781	....	....	....	....	....	....	....	....
General government	4 782	....	....	....	....	....	....	....	....
Banks	4 783	−2	202	323	293	364	−185	−98	815
Other sectors	4 784	....	....	....	....	....	....	....	....
Other liabilities	4 786	40	179	−80	12	144	355	495	553
Monetary authorities	4 787	40	179	−80	12	144	355	495	553
of which: Short-term	4 789	*40*	*179*	*−80*	*12*	*144*	*355*	*−12*	*553*
General government	4 790	....	....	....	....	....	....	....	....
of which: Short-term	4 792	....	....	....	....	....	....	....	....
Banks	4 793	....	....	....	....	....	....	....	....
of which: Short-term	4 795	....	....	....	....	....	....	....	....
Other sectors	4 796	....	....	....	....	....	....	....	....
of which: Short-term	4 798	....	....	....	....	....	....	....	....
E. RESERVE ASSETS	4 802	**−627**	**133**	**−540**	**−73**	**−675**	**1,111**	**−3,290**	**−2,069**
Monetary gold	4 812	....	....	....	....	....	....	649	255
Special drawing rights	4 811	2	....	−1	−1	−4	5	−13	17
Reserve position in the Fund	4 810	....	....	....	....	....	....	....	....
Foreign exchange	4 803	−620	173	−502	−75	−700	1,109	−3,914	−2,366
Other claims	4 813	−9	−40	−37	3	29	−2	−12	25
NET ERRORS AND OMISSIONS	4 998	**−114**	**−189**	**−73**	**−96**	**−159**	**724**	**−140**	**−523**

Table 1. ANALYTIC PRESENTATION, 2003–2010

(Millions of U.S. dollars)

	Code	2003	2004	2005	2006	2007	2008	2009	2010
A. Current Account[1]............	4 993 Z.	**−955.4**	**−870.9**	**−3,013.1**	**−5,198.7**	**−3,447.1**	**−1,313.6**	**−2,998.4**	**156.8**
Goods: exports f.o.b...........	2 100 ..	2,542.2	3,777.8	4,824.3	5,656.6	8,879.2	11,670.5	8,257.1	11,404.3
Goods: imports f.o.b...........	3 100 ..	−2,536.1	−3,586.2	−5,946.0	−7,104.7	−7,722.4	−8,229.4	−8,528.0	−8,839.4
Balance on Goods............	4 100 ..	*6.1*	*191.6*	*−1,121.7*	*−1,448.1*	*1,156.8*	*3,441.1*	*−270.9*	*2,564.9*
Services: credit..............	2 200 ..	36.5	44.1	113.9	247.1	384.3	492.8	392.0	253.8
Services: debit..............	3 200 ..	−830.3	−1,064.5	−1,844.4	−2,799.9	−2,938.7	−2,619.5	−1,907.1	−2,321.4
Balance on Goods and Services....	4 991 ..	*−787.7*	*−828.8*	*−2,852.2*	*−4,000.9*	*−1,397.6*	*1,314.4*	*−1,786.0*	*497.3*
Income: credit..............	2 300 ..	10.0	21.8	44.1	89.3	183.7	43.4	36.7	137.9
Income: debit..............	3 300 ..	−879.2	−1,134.5	−1,405.9	−2,103.3	−2,436.8	−3,056.5	−2,261.4	−2,609.5
Balance on Goods, Services, and Income......	4 992 ..	*−1,657.0*	*−1,941.5*	*−4,214.0*	*−6,014.9*	*−3,650.7*	*−1,698.6*	*−4,010.7*	*−1,974.4*
Current transfers: credit....	2 379 Z.	1,218.4	1,580.2	1,680.5	1,899.9	2,321.5	4,023.6	2,973.8	3,360.0
Current transfers: debit....	3 379 ..	−516.8	−509.6	−479.6	−1,083.6	−2,117.9	−3,638.6	−1,961.5	−1,228.8
B. Capital Account[1]................	4 994 Z.	....	....	....	....	....	....	....	....
Capital account: credit......	2 994 Z.	....	....	....	....	....	....	....	....
Capital account: debit......	3 994 ..	....	....	....	....	....	....	....	....
Total, Groups A Plus B......	4 981 ..	*−955.4*	*−870.9*	*−3,013.1*	*−5,198.7*	*−3,447.1*	*−1,313.6*	*−2,998.4*	*156.8*
C. Financial Account[1]..................	4 995 W.	**1,284.4**	**1,427.8**	**2,884.6**	**4,738.7**	**2,996.4**	**1,509.7**	**3,225.8**	**650.1**
Direct investment abroad........	4 505 ..	....	....	....	....	....	−89.2	....	....
Direct investment in Sudan......	4 555 Z.	1,349.2	1,511.1	2,304.6	3,534.1	2,425.6	2,600.5	1,816.2	2,063.7
Portfolio investment assets.....	4 602 ..	35.3	19.9	50.6	−.1	62.1	−33.4	20.0	−14.3
Equity securities...........	4 610 ..	....	....	....	−.1	62.1	−33.4	20.0	−14.3
Debt securities.............	4 619 ..	35.3	19.9	50.6	....	....	....	....	....
Portfolio investment liabilities...	4 652 Z.	....	....	....	−35.3	−16.6	−.1	−.5	21.4
Equity securities...........	4 660 ..	....	....	....	−35.3	−16.6	−.1	−.5	.9
Debt securities.............	4 669 Z.	....	....	....	....	....	....	....	20.4
Financial derivatives............	4 910 ..	....	....	....	....	....	....	....	....
Financial derivatives assets........	4 900 ..	....	....	....	....	....	....	....	....
Financial derivatives liabilities........	4 905 ..	....	....	....	....	....	....	....	....
Other investment assets.........	4 703 ..	381.4	598.8	1,134.7	208.2	−535.3	−866.5	−860.2	−2,785.7
Monetary authorities.........	4 701 ..	−.2	−10.2	−13.0	174.3	121.5	−105.0	−72.9	−232.4
General government.........	4 704 ..	141.7	373.8	358.2	....	....	−120.9	−473.4	−1,699.5
Banks......................	4 705 ..	−9.0	−42.0	−198.7	33.9	−124.3	−184.9	228.3	−432.8
Other sectors..............	4 728 ..	248.9	277.2	988.3	....	−532.5	−455.8	−542.1	−421.1
Other investment liabilities.........	4 753 W.	−481.5	−702.0	−605.3	1,031.7	1,060.6	−101.6	2,250.3	1,365.1
Monetary authorities.........	4 753 WA	....	....	44.7	156.5	24.8	246.4	−31.6	195.4
General government.........	4 753 ZB	−262.2	−384.5	−275.7	348.5	238.5	−45.7	617.3	−32.3
Banks......................	4 753 ZC	4.1	13.0	47.7	2.5	27.7	31.5	188.6	31.6
Other sectors..............	4 753 ZD	−223.4	−330.6	−422.0	524.3	769.6	−333.7	1,475.9	1,170.4
Total, Groups A Through C......	4 983 ..	*328.9*	*556.9*	*−128.5*	*−460.0*	*−450.7*	*196.2*	*227.5*	*806.9*
D. Net Errors and Omissions....................	4 998 ..	**−13.9**	**212.1**	**726.5**	**−130.9**	**26.9**	**−125.4**	**−737.1**	**−859.9**
Total, Groups A Through D......	4 984 ..	*315.1*	*769.0*	*598.0*	*−590.9*	*−423.8*	*70.8*	*−509.6*	*−52.9*
E. Reserves and Related Items....................	4 802 A.	**−315.1**	**−769.0**	**−598.0**	**590.9**	**423.8**	**−70.8**	**509.6**	**52.9**
Reserve assets.................	4 802 ..	−422.7	−729.8	−827.6	208.7	282.0	−21.1	513.4	54.5
Use of Fund credit and loans........	4 766 ..	−14.8	−18.0	−11.8	−5.3	−36.9	−49.6	−3.7	−1.5
Exceptional financing............	4 920 ..	122.4	−21.2	241.4	387.5	178.7	....	....	....
Conversion rates: Sudanese pounds per U.S. dollar...............	0 101 ..	**2.61**	**2.58**	**2.44**	**2.17**	**2.02**	**2.09**	**2.30**	**2.31**

[1] Excludes components that have been classified in the categories of Group E.

Table 2. STANDARD PRESENTATION, 2003–2010

(Millions of U.S. dollars)

	Code	2003	2004	2005	2006	2007	2008	2009	2010
CURRENT ACCOUNT	4 993	−938.6	−818.2	−2,768.0	−4,811.2	−3,268.4	−1,313.6	−2,998.4	156.8
A. GOODS	4 100	6.1	191.6	−1,121.7	−1,448.1	1,156.8	3,441.1	−270.9	2,564.9
Credit	2 100	2,542.2	3,777.8	4,824.3	5,656.6	8,879.2	11,670.5	8,257.1	11,404.3
General merchandise: exports f.o.b.	2 110	2,542.2	3,777.8	4,824.3	5,656.6	8,879.2	11,670.5	8,257.1	11,404.3
Goods for processing: exports f.o.b.	2 150	....	....	....	....	....	....	....	....
Repairs on goods	2 160	....	....	....	....	....	....	....	....
Goods procured in ports by carriers	2 170	....	....	....	....	....	....	....	....
Nonmonetary gold	2 180	....	....	....	....	....	....	....	....
Debit	3 100	−2,536.1	−3,586.2	−5,946.0	−7,104.7	−7,722.4	−8,229.4	−8,528.0	−8,839.4
General merchandise: imports f.o.b.	3 110	−2,536.1	−3,586.2	−5,946.0	−7,104.7	−7,722.4	−8,229.4	−8,528.0	−8,839.4
Goods for processing: imports f.o.b.	3 150	....	....	....	....	....	....	....	....
Repairs on goods	3 160	....	....	....	....	....	....	....	....
Goods procured in ports by carriers	3 170	....	....	....	....	....	....	....	....
Nonmonetary gold	3 180	....	....	....	....	....	....	....	....
B. SERVICES	4 200	−793.8	−1,020.4	−1,730.5	−2,552.8	−2,554.4	−2,126.7	−1,515.1	−2,067.6
Total credit	2 200	*36.5*	*44.1*	*113.9*	*247.1*	*384.3*	*492.8*	*392.0*	*253.8*
Total debit	3 200	*−830.3*	*−1,064.5*	*−1,844.4*	*−2,799.9*	*−2,938.7*	*−2,619.5*	*−1,907.1*	*−2,321.4*
Transportation services, credit	2 205	9.1	9.5	3.4	18.7	10.5	17.4	7.8	4.7
Passenger	2 850	....	....	....	....	....	....	....	....
Freight	2 851	....	*9.5*	....	*18.7*	*10.5*	*17.4*	....	....
Other	2 852	*9.1*	....	*3.4*	....	....	....	*7.8*	*4.7*
Sea transport, passenger	2 207								
Sea transport, freight	2 208								
Sea transport, other	2 209								
Air transport, passenger	2 211	....							
Air transport, freight	2 212	....	9.5	....	18.7	10.5	17.4		
Air transport, other	2 213	9.1		3.4					
Other transport, passenger	2 215								
Other transport, freight	2 216								
Other transport, other	2 217	....							
Transportation services, debit	3 205	−682.4	−841.0	−1,079.7	−1,243.8	−1,310.5	−1,289.4	−969.1	−1,004.5
Passenger	3 850	....	....	....	....	....	....	....	....
Freight	3 851	*−682.4*	*−841.0*	*−1,079.7*	*−1,243.8*	*−1,310.5*	*−1,289.4*	*−969.1*	*−1,004.5*
Other	3 852	....	....	....	....	....	....	....	....
Sea transport, passenger	3 207								
Sea transport, freight	3 208	−288.2	−407.5	−675.7	−807.4	−877.5	−935.2	....	
Sea transport, other	3 209								
Air transport, passenger	3 211	....							
Air transport, freight	3 212	....							
Air transport, other	3 213	....							
Other transport, passenger	3 215								
Other transport, freight	3 216	−394.2	−433.5	−404.0	−436.5	−433.0	−354.2		
Other transport, other	3 217								
Travel, credit	2 236	17.5	21.2	89.1	167.3	261.8	330.7	298.7	94.3
Business travel	2 237	....	....	....	....	....	....	....	....
Personal travel	2 240	17.5	21.2	89.1	167.3	261.8	330.7	298.7	94.3
Travel, debit	3 236	−119.1	−175.6	−667.5	−1,413.3	−1,476.8	−1,188.0	−868.2	−1,116.3
Business travel	3 237	....	....	....	....	....	....	....	....
Personal travel	3 240	−119.1	−175.6	−667.5	−1,413.3	−1,476.8	−1,188.0	−868.2	−1,116.3
Other services, credit	2 200 BA	10.0	13.4	21.4	61.1	112.1	144.8	85.5	154.7
Communications	2 245	2.5	2.4	3.8	7.9	19.9	5.1	.6	65.3
Construction	2 249	.5	.9	....	....	3.6	7.3	5.8	31.6
Insurance	2 253	....	....	....	....	.1	....	.2	3.1
Financial	2 260	.8	.9	4.1	25.1	26.9	70.6	13.1	11.1
Computer and information	2 262	....	....	....	....	1.0	.7	....	.2
Royalties and licence fees	2 266	....	....	....	....	....	....	1.5	2.9
Other business services	2 268	.4	....	.1	.3	13.4	25.0	22.8	9.0
Personal, cultural, and recreational	2 287	.3	....	....	.2	4.5	.2	.8	1.7
Government, n.i.e.	2 291	5.4	9.3	13.4	27.5	42.7	35.9	40.7	29.9
Other services, debit	3 200 BA	−28.8	−47.9	−97.3	−142.8	−151.4	−142.1	−69.8	−200.6
Communications	3 245	−1.5	−.1	−3.5	−5.7	−22.2	−34.2	−7.4	−15.8
Construction	3 249	−.7	−1.6	....	−.9	−2.8	−.3	−.5	−3.5
Insurance	3 253	....	−.2	−12.1	−2.1	−2.5	−10.0	−13.9	−6.7
Financial	3 260	−.2	−1.5	−1.2	−7.5	−5.3	−5.8	−4.6	−18.3
Computer and information	3 262	−.8	−2.8	−4.6	−3.5	−2.3	−4.2	−6.6	−1.6
Royalties and licence fees	3 266	....	....	....	....	....	−.1	−1.3	−11.4
Other business services	3 268	−.1	−.7	−32.6	−51.1	−45.1	−16.4	−9.0	−15.6
Personal, cultural, and recreational	3 287	....	....	....	....	−5.2	−3.6	−5.0	−1.5
Government, n.i.e.	3 291	−25.5	−41.0	−43.3	−72.0	−66.0	−67.5	−21.6	−126.2

Table 2 (Continued). STANDARD PRESENTATION, 2003–2010

(Millions of U.S. dollars)

	Code	2003	2004	2005	2006	2007	2008	2009	2010
C. INCOME	4 300	**−869.2**	**−1,112.7**	**−1,361.8**	**−2,014.0**	**−2,253.1**	**−3,013.1**	**−2,224.7**	**−2,471.6**
Total credit	2 300	*10.0*	*21.8*	*44.1*	*89.3*	*183.7*	*43.4*	*36.7*	*137.9*
Total debit	3 300	*−879.2*	*−1,134.5*	*−1,405.9*	*−2,103.3*	*−2,436.8*	*−3,056.5*	*−2,261.4*	*−2,609.5*
Compensation of employees, credit	2 310	5.2	1.7	1.9	1.8	2.5	....	29.2	128.7
Compensation of employees, debit	3 310	−.7	−2.1	−1.7	−2.5	−2.0	....	−.1	−.8
Investment income, credit	2 320	4.8	20.1	42.2	87.4	181.2	43.4	7.6	9.2
Direct investment income	2 330	....	....	....	....	....	....	1.4	6.5
Dividends and distributed branch profits	2 332	....	....	....	....	....	....	....	....
Reinvested earnings and undistributed branch profits	2 333	....	....	....	....	....	....	....	....
Income on debt (interest)	2 334	....	....	....	....	....	....	....	....
Portfolio investment income	2 339	....	....	....	....	....	....	5.2	2.6
Income on equity	2 340	....	....	....	....	....	....	....	....
Income on bonds and notes	2 350	....	....	....	....	....	....	....	....
Income on money market instruments	2 360	....	....	....	....	....	....	....	....
Other investment income	2 370	4.8	20.1	42.2	87.4	181.2	43.4	1.0	.1
Investment income, debit	3 320	−878.6	−1,132.4	−1,404.2	−2,100.8	−2,434.8	−3,056.5	−2,261.4	−2,608.7
Direct investment income	3 330	−878.6	−1,122.2	−1,399.0	−2,093.3	−2,404.1	−2,970.8	−2,065.0	−2,392.9
Dividends and distributed branch profits	3 332	−818.4	−1,037.9	−1,334.8	−2,030.6	−2,319.3	−2,882.2	−2,065.0	−2,392.9
Reinvested earnings and undistributed branch profits	3 333	....	....	....	....	....	....	....	....
Income on debt (interest)	3 334	−60.2	−84.2	−64.2	−62.7	−84.8	−88.6	....	....
Portfolio investment income	3 339	....	−10.2	−5.2	....	....	....	−4.6	−5.2
Income on equity	3 340	....	−10.2	−5.2	....	....	....	....	....
Income on bonds and notes	3 350	....	....	....	....	....	....	....	....
Income on money market instruments	3 360	....	....	....	....	....	....	....	....
Other investment income	3 370	....	....	....	−7.6	−30.7	−85.7	−191.7	−210.6
D. CURRENT TRANSFERS	4 379	**718.4**	**1,123.3**	**1,446.1**	**1,203.7**	**382.3**	**385.1**	**1,012.3**	**2,131.2**
Credit	2 379	1,235.2	1,632.8	1,925.7	2,287.4	2,500.2	4,023.6	2,973.8	3,360.0
General government	2 380	16.8	52.7	245.2	387.5	178.7	675.9	666.9	1,195.4
Other sectors	2 390	1,218.4	1,580.2	1,680.5	1,899.9	2,321.5	3,347.7	2,306.9	2,164.6
Workers' remittances	2 391	1,218.4	1,401.2	1,014.1	1,177.3	1,766.7	3,100.5	2,106.1	1,290.9
Other current transfers	2 392	....	179.0	666.4	722.6	554.8	247.3	200.8	873.7
Debit	3 379	−516.8	−509.6	−479.6	−1,083.6	−2,117.9	−3,638.6	−1,961.5	−1,228.8
General government	3 380	−6.7	−24.2	−10.7	−22.8	−5.2	−4.7	−9.6	−4.4
Other sectors	3 390	−510.2	−485.4	−468.9	−1,060.9	−2,112.7	−3,633.9	−1,951.9	−1,224.4
Workers' remittances	3 391	....	....	....	....	....	....	....	....
Other current transfers	3 392	−510.2	−485.4	−468.9	−1,060.9	−2,112.7	−3,633.9	−1,951.9	−1,224.4
CAPITAL AND FINANCIAL ACCOUNT	4 996	**952.4**	**606.1**	**2,041.4**	**4,942.1**	**3,241.5**	**1,438.9**	**3,735.5**	**703.0**
CAPITAL ACCOUNT	4 994	....	....	....	....	....	....	....	....
Total credit	2 994	....	....	....	....	....	....	....	....
Total debit	3 994	....	....	....	....	....	....	....	....
Capital transfers, credit	2 400	....	....	....	....	....	....	....	....
General government	2 401	....	....	....	....	....	....	....	....
Debt forgiveness	2 402	....	....	....	....	....	....	....	....
Other capital transfers	2 410	....	....	....	....	....	....	....	....
Other sectors	2 430	....	....	....	....	....	....	....	....
Migrants' transfers	2 431	....	....	....	....	....	....	....	....
Debt forgiveness	2 432	....	....	....	....	....	....	....	....
Other capital transfers	2 440	....	....	....	....	....	....	....	....
Capital transfers, debit	3 400	....	....	....	....	....	....	....	....
General government	3 401	....	....	....	....	....	....	....	....
Debt forgiveness	3 402	....	....	....	....	....	....	....	....
Other capital transfers	3 410	....	....	....	....	....	....	....	....
Other sectors	3 430	....	....	....	....	....	....	....	....
Migrants' transfers	3 431	....	....	....	....	....	....	....	....
Debt forgiveness	3 432	....	....	....	....	....	....	....	....
Other capital transfers	3 440	....	....	....	....	....	....	....	....
Nonproduced nonfinancial assets, credit	2 480	....	....	....	....	....	....	....	....
Nonproduced nonfinancial assets, debit	3 480	....	....	....	....	....	....	....	....

Table 2 (Continued). STANDARD PRESENTATION, 2003–2010

(Millions of U.S. dollars)

	Code	2003	2004	2005	2006	2007	2008	2009	2010
FINANCIAL ACCOUNT	4 995	952.4	606.1	2,041.4	4,942.1	3,241.5	1,438.9	3,735.5	703.0
A. DIRECT INVESTMENT	4 500	1,349.2	1,511.1	2,304.6	3,534.1	2,425.6	2,511.3	1,816.2	2,063.7
Direct investment abroad	4 505	....	....	....	....	....	−89.2	....	....
Equity capital	4 510	....	....	....	....	....	−89.2	....	....
Claims on affiliated enterprises	4 515	....	....	....	....	....	−89.2	....	....
Liabilities to affiliated enterprises	4 520	....	....	....	....	....	....	....	....
Reinvested earnings	4 525	....	....	....	....	....	....	....	....
Other capital	4 530	....	....	....	....	....	....	....	....
Claims on affiliated enterprises	4 535	....	....	....	....	....	....	....	....
Liabilities to affiliated enterprises	4 540	....	....	....	....	....	....	....	....
Direct investment in Sudan	4 555	1,349.2	1,511.1	2,304.6	3,534.1	2,425.6	2,600.5	1,816.2	2,063.7
Equity capital	4 560	1,349.2	1,511.1	2,304.6	3,534.1	2,425.6	2,600.5	1,816.2	2,063.7
Claims on direct investors	4 565	....	....	....	....	....	....	....	....
Liabilities to direct investors	4 570	1,349.2	1,511.1	2,304.6	3,534.1	2,425.6	2,600.5	1,816.2	2,063.7
Reinvested earnings	4 575	....	....	....	....	....	....	....	....
Other capital	4 580	....	....	....	....	....	....	....	....
Claims on direct investors	4 585	....	....	....	....	....	....	....	....
Liabilities to direct investors	4 590	....	....	....	....	....	....	....	....
B. PORTFOLIO INVESTMENT	4 600	35.3	19.9	50.6	−35.3	45.5	−33.5	19.5	7.0
Assets	4 602	35.3	19.9	50.6	−.1	62.1	−33.4	20.0	−14.3
Equity securities	4 610	....	....	....	−.1	62.1	−33.4	20.0	−14.3
Monetary authorities	4 611	....	....	....	−.1	.7	−10.4	1.2	−12.3
General government	4 612	....	....	....	....	....	....	....	....
Banks	4 613	....	....	....	....	61.4	−23.0	18.8	−2.0
Other sectors	4 614	....	....	....	....	....	....	....	....
Debt securities	4 619	35.3	19.9	50.6	....	....	....	....	....
Bonds and notes	4 620	35.3	19.9	50.6	....	....	....	....	....
Monetary authorities	4 621	....	....	....	....	....	....	....	....
General government	4 622	....	....	....	....	....	....	....	....
Banks	4 623	....	....	....	....	....	....	....	....
Other sectors	4 624	35.3	19.9	50.6	....	....	....	....	....
Money market instruments	4 630	....	....	....	....	....	....	....	....
Monetary authorities	4 631	....	....	....	....	....	....	....	....
General government	4 632	....	....	....	....	....	....	....	....
Banks	4 633	....	....	....	....	....	....	....	....
Other sectors	4 634	....	....	....	....	....	....	....	....
Liabilities	4 652	....	....	....	−35.3	−16.6	−.1	−.5	21.4
Equity securities	4 660	....	....	....	−35.3	−16.6	−.1	−.5	.9
Banks	4 663	....	....	....	−35.3	−16.6	−.1	−.5	.9
Other sectors	4 664	....	....	....	....	....	....	....	....
Debt securities	4 669	....	....	....	....	....	....	....	20.4
Bonds and notes	4 670	....	....	....	....	....	....	....	20.4
Monetary authorities	4 671	....	....	....	....	....	....	....	....
General government	4 672	....	....	....	....	....	....	....	....
Banks	4 673	....	....	....	....	....	....	....	20.4
Other sectors	4 674	....	....	....	....	....	....	....	....
Money market instruments	4 680	....	....	....	....	....	....	....	....
Monetary authorities	4 681	....	....	....	....	....	....	....	....
General government	4 682	....	....	....	....	....	....	....	....
Banks	4 683	....	....	....	....	....	....	....	....
Other sectors	4 684	....	....	....	....	....	....	....	....
C. FINANCIAL DERIVATIVES	4 910	....	....	....	....	....	....	....	....
Monetary authorities	4 911	....	....	....	....	....	....	....	....
General government	4 912	....	....	....	....	....	....	....	....
Banks	4 913	....	....	....	....	....	....	....	....
Other sectors	4 914	....	....	....	....	....	....	....	....
Assets	4 900	....	....	....	....	....	....	....	....
Monetary authorities	4 901	....	....	....	....	....	....	....	....
General government	4 902	....	....	....	....	....	....	....	....
Banks	4 903	....	....	....	....	....	....	....	....
Other sectors	4 904	....	....	....	....	....	....	....	....
Liabilities	4 905	....	....	....	....	....	....	....	....
Monetary authorities	4 906	....	....	....	....	....	....	....	....
General government	4 907	....	....	....	....	....	....	....	....
Banks	4 908	....	....	....	....	....	....	....	....
Other sectors	4 909	....	....	....	....	....	....	....	....

Table 2 (Concluded). STANDARD PRESENTATION, 2003–2010

(Millions of U.S. dollars)

	Code	2003	2004	2005	2006	2007	2008	2009	2010
D. OTHER INVESTMENT	4 700 ..	**−9.3**	**−195.1**	**513.8**	**1,234.6**	**488.4**	**−1,017.8**	**1,386.4**	**−1,422.2**
Assets	4 703 ..	**381.4**	**598.8**	**1,134.7**	**208.2**	**−535.3**	**−866.5**	**−860.2**	**−2,785.7**
Trade credits	4 706 ..	305.7	437.8	1,209.1	....	....	1,317.9	−817.0	−849.0
General government	4 707 ..	56.8	160.6	220.8	....	....	472.8	−295.9	−364.9
of which: Short-term	4 709 ..	*56.8*	*160.6*	*220.8*	....	....	*472.8*	*−295.9*	*−364.9*
Other sectors	4 710 ..	248.9	277.2	988.3	....	....	845.1	−521.1	−484.1
of which: Short-term	4 712 ..	*248.9*	*277.2*	*988.3*	....	....	*845.1*	*−521.1*	*−484.1*
Loans	4 714 ..	84.9	213.2	222.4	....	....	....	....	....
Monetary authorities	4 715 ..	....	....	....	....	....	....	....	....
of which: Short-term	4 718 ..	....	....	....	....	....	....	....	....
General government	4 719 ..	84.9	213.2	222.4	....	....	....	....	....
of which: Short-term	4 721 ..	....	....	....	....	....	....	....	....
Banks	4 722 ..	....	....	....	....	....	....	....	....
of which: Short-term	4 724 ..	....	....	....	....	....	....	....	....
Other sectors	4 725 ..	....	....	....	....	....	....	....	....
of which: Short-term	4 727 ..	....	....	....	....	....	....	....	....
Currency and deposits	4 730 ..	−9.0	−42.0	−198.7	256.0	−583.5	−2,128.8	−87.3	−1,952.1
Monetary authorities	4 731 ..	....	....	....	222.0	73.4	−49.3	−117.1	−247.7
General government	4 732 ..	....	....	....	....	....	−593.7	−177.5	−1,334.6
Banks	4 733 ..	−9.0	−42.0	−198.7	33.9	−124.3	−184.9	228.3	−432.8
Other sectors	4 734 ..	....	....	....	....	−532.5	−1,300.9	−21.0	63.0
Other assets	4 736 ..	−.2	−10.2	−98.0	−47.8	48.2	−55.6	44.2	15.4
Monetary authorities	4 737 ..	−.2	−10.2	−13.0	−47.8	48.2	−55.6	44.2	15.4
of which: Short-term	4 739 ..	....	....	....	....	....	....	....	....
General government	4 740 ..	....	....	−85.0	....	....	....	....	....
of which: Short-term	4 742 ..	....	....	*−85.0*	....	....	....	....	....
Banks	4 743 ..	....	....	....	....	....	....	....	....
of which: Short-term	4 745 ..	....	....	....	....	....	....	....	....
Other sectors	4 746 ..	....	....	....	....	....	....	....	....
of which: Short-term	4 748 ..	....	....	....	....	....	....	....	....
Liabilities	4 753 ..	**−390.7**	**−793.9**	**−620.9**	**1,026.4**	**1,023.7**	**−151.2**	**2,246.6**	**1,363.6**
Trade credits	4 756 ..	−300.4	−495.8	−485.7	724.9	503.5	−575.3	1,398.8	789.2
General government	4 757 ..	−77.0	−165.3	−63.7	200.6	−266.0	−241.6	−77.1	−381.2
of which: Short-term	4 759 ..	....	....	....	*200.6*	*−266.0*	*−241.6*	*−77.1*	*−381.2*
Other sectors	4 760 ..	−223.4	−330.6	−422.0	524.3	769.6	−333.7	1,475.9	1,170.4
of which: Short-term	4 762 ..	*−223.4*	*−330.6*	*−422.0*	*524.3*	*769.6*	*−333.7*	*1,475.9*	*1,170.4*
Loans	4 764 ..	−80.2	−306.4	−179.1	239.0	467.7	146.2	494.5	−68.8
Monetary authorities	4 765 ..	105.0	−87.1	32.9	91.0	−36.9	−49.6	−13.9	−7.3
of which: Use of Fund credit and loans from the Fund	4 766 ..	*−14.8*	*−18.0*	*−11.8*	*−5.3*	*−36.9*	*−49.6*	*−3.7*	*−1.5*
of which: Short-term	4 768 ..	....	....	....	*105.1*	....	....	....	....
General government	4 769 ..	−185.2	−219.2	−212.0	147.9	504.6	195.8	508.4	−61.5
of which: Short-term	4 771 ..	....	....	....	....	....	....	....	....
Banks	4 772 ..	....	....	....	....	....	....	....	....
of which: Short-term	4 774 ..	....	....	....	....	....	....	....	....
Other sectors	4 775 ..	....	....	....	....	....	....	....	....
of which: Short-term	4 777 ..	....	....	....	....	....	....	....	....
Currency and deposits	4 780 ..	4.1	13.0	47.7	1.5	−17.5	49.5	70.3	39.2
Monetary authorities	4 781 ..	....	....	....	−3.0	−1.4	−2.1	−34.0	....
General government	4 782 ..	....	....	....	....	....	....	....	....
Banks	4 783 ..	4.1	13.0	47.7	4.4	−16.1	51.6	104.3	39.1
Other sectors	4 784 ..	....	....	....	....	....	....	....	....
Other liabilities	4 786 ..	−14.2	−4.7	−3.8	61.1	70.0	228.4	282.9	604.0
Monetary authorities	4 787 ..	....	....	....	63.1	26.2	248.5	12.5	201.1
of which: Short-term	4 789 ..	....	....	....	*66.1*	*30.9*	*255.3*	*−58.3*	*207.8*
General government	4 790 ..	−14.2	−4.7	−3.8	....	....	....	186.0	410.4
of which: Short-term	4 792 ..	*−14.2*	*−4.7*	*−3.8*	....	....	....	....	....
Banks	4 793 ..	....	....	....	−2.0	43.9	−20.1	84.3	−7.5
of which: Short-term	4 795 ..	....	....	....	....	....	....	....	....
Other sectors	4 796 ..	....	....	....	....	....	....	....	....
of which: Short-term	4 798 ..	....	....	....	....	....	....	....	....
E. RESERVE ASSETS	4 802 ..	**−422.7**	**−729.8**	**−827.6**	**208.7**	**282.0**	**−21.1**	**513.4**	**54.5**
Monetary gold	4 812 ..	....	....	....	....	....	....	....	....
Special drawing rights	4 811 ..	−.1	.4	−.1	.1	....	....	−196.2	.2
Reserve position in the Fund	4 810 ..	....	....	....	....	....	....	....	....
Foreign exchange	4 803 ..	−422.6	−730.2	−827.5	208.6	282.0	−21.1	709.6	54.2
Other claims	4 813 ..	....	....	....	....	....	....	....	....
NET ERRORS AND OMISSIONS	4 998 ..	**−13.9**	**212.1**	**726.5**	**−130.9**	**26.9**	**−125.4**	**−737.1**	**−859.9**

Table 3. INTERNATIONAL INVESTMENT POSITION (End-period stocks), 2003–2010

(Millions of U.S. dollars)

	Code	2003	2004	2005	2006	2007	2008	2009	2010
ASSETS	8 995 C.	....	....	....	....	....	....	....	....
Direct investment abroad	8 505 ..	....	....	....	....	....	....	....	....
Equity capital and reinvested earnings	8 506 ..	....	....	....	....	....	....	....	....
Claims on affiliated enterprises	8 507 ..	....	....	....	....	....	....	....	....
Liabilities to affiliated enterprises	8 508 ..	....	....	....	....	....	....	....	....
Other capital	8 530 ..	....	....	....	....	....	....	....	....
Claims on affiliated enterprises	8 535 ..	....	....	....	....	....	....	....	....
Liabilities to affiliated enterprises	8 540 ..	....	....	....	....	....	....	....	....
Portfolio investment	8 602 ..	**19.4**	**32.2**	**71.7**	**63.5**	**75.1**	**107.4**	**115.2**	**100.8**
Equity securities	8 610 ..	19.4	32.2	71.7	63.5	75.1	107.4	115.2	100.8
Monetary authorities	8 611 ..	15.0	25.8	38.7	38.8	39.5	48.5	30.4	18.0
General government	8 612 ..	....	....	....	....	....	....	....	....
Banks	8 613 ..	4.5	6.4	33.0	24.7	35.6	58.9	84.8	82.8
Other sectors	8 614 ..	....	....	....	....	....	....	....	....
Debt securities	8 619 ..	....	....	....	....	....	....	....	....
Bonds and notes	8 620 ..	....	....	....	....	....	....	....	....
Monetary authorities	8 621 ..	....	....	....	....	....	....	....	....
General government	8 622 ..	....	....	....	....	....	....	....	....
Banks	8 623 ..	....	....	....	....	....	....	....	....
Other sectors	8 624 ..	....	....	....	....	....	....	....	....
Money market instruments	8 630 ..	....	....	....	....	....	....	....	....
Monetary authorities	8 631 ..	....	....	....	....	....	....	....	....
General government	8 632 ..	....	....	....	....	....	....	....	....
Banks	8 633 ..	....	....	....	....	....	....	....	....
Other sectors	8 634 ..	....	....	....	....	....	....	....	....
Financial derivatives	8 900 ..	....	....	....	....	....	....	....	....
Monetary authorities	8 901 ..	....	....	....	....	....	....	....	....
General government	8 902 ..	....	....	....	....	....	....	....	....
Banks	8 903 ..	....	....	....	....	....	....	....	....
Other sectors	8 904 ..	....	....	....	....	....	....	....	....
Other investment	8 703 ..	**843.2**	**872.1**	**1,505.7**	**1,292.9**	**1,306.6**	**1,590.1**	**8,642.8**	**9,256.9**
Trade credits	8 706 ..	....	....	....	....	....	....	3,112.1	2,263.1
General government	8 707 ..	....	....	....	....	....	....	755.3	390.4
of which: Short-term	8 709 ..	....	....	....	....	....	....	*755.3*	*390.4*
Other sectors	8 710 ..	....	....	....	....	....	....	2,356.8	1,872.7
of which: Short-term	8 712 ..	....	....	....	....	....	....	*2,356.8*	*1,872.7*
Loans	8 714 ..	....	....	....	....	....	....	....	....
Monetary authorities	8 715 ..	....	....	....	....	....	....	....	....
of which: Short-term	8 718 ..	....	....	....	....	....	....	....	....
General government	8 719 ..	....	....	....	....	....	....	....	....
of which: Short-term	8 721 ..	....	....	....	....	....	....	....	....
Banks	8 722 ..	....	....	....	....	....	....	....	....
of which: Short-term	8 724 ..	....	....	....	....	....	....	....	....
Other sectors	8 725 ..	....	....	....	....	....	....	....	....
of which: Short-term	8 727 ..	....	....	....	....	....	....	....	....
Currency and deposits	8 730 ..	824.7	849.1	1,478.9	1,218.3	1,280.3	1,508.1	5,404.5	6,852.2
Monetary authorities	8 731 ..	318.1	288.1	581.2	359.2	285.8	335.1	710.2	462.5
General government	8 732 ..	....	....	....	....	....	....	2,684.6	4,019.2
Banks	8 733 ..	506.6	561.0	897.7	859.1	994.5	1,173.0	1,471.7	1,904.5
Other sectors	8 734 ..	....	....	....	....	....	....	538.0	466.0
Other assets	8 736 ..	18.5	23.0	26.8	74.7	26.3	82.0	126.2	141.6
Monetary authorities	8 737 ..	18.5	23.0	26.8	74.7	26.3	82.0	126.2	141.6
of which: Short-term	8 739 ..	*18.5*	*23.0*	*26.8*	*74.7*	*26.3*	*82.0*	*126.2*	*141.6*
General government	8 740 ..	....	....	....	....	....	....	....	....
of which: Short-term	8 742 ..	....	....	....	....	....	....	....	....
Banks	8 743 ..	....	....	....	....	....	....	....	....
of which: Short-term	8 745 ..	....	....	....	....	....	....	....	....
Other sectors	8 746 ..	....	....	....	....	....	....	....	....
of which: Short-term	8 748 ..	....	....	....	....	....	....	....	....
Reserve assets	8 802 ..	**529.4**	**1,338.0**	**1,868.6**	**1,659.9**	**1,377.9**	**1,399.0**	**903.1**	**866.2**
Monetary gold	8 812 ..	....	....	....	....	....	....	....	....
Special drawing rights	8 811 ..	.3	....	.1	....	....	....	197.2	193.5
Reserve position in the Fund	8 810 ..	....	....	....	....	....	....	....	....
Foreign exchange	8 803 ..	529.1	1,338.0	1,868.5	1,659.9	1,377.9	1,399.0	705.9	672.7
Other claims	8 813 ..	....	....	....	....	....	....	....	....

2011, International Monetary Fund: *Balance of Payments Statistics Yearbook*

Table 3 (Concluded). INTERNATIONAL INVESTMENT POSITION (End-period stocks), 2003–2010

(Millions of U.S. dollars)

	Code	2003	2004	2005	2006	2007	2008	2009	2010
LIABILITIES	8 995 D.	....	....	....	....	....	....	....	....
Direct investment in Sudan	8 555	3,868.4	5,379.4	7,684.1	11,225.5	13,661.8	16,262.3	18,046.8	20,110.6
Equity capital and reinvested earnings	8 556	3,868.4	5,379.4	7,684.1	11,225.5	13,661.8	16,262.3	18,046.8	20,110.6
Claims on direct investors	8 557	....	....	....	....	....	....	−877.5	−1,708.1
Liabilities to direct investors	8 558	3,868.4	5,379.4	7,684.1	11,225.5	13,661.8	16,262.3	18,924.3	21,818.7
Other capital	8 580	....	....	....	....	....	....	....	....
Claims on direct investors	8 585	....	....	....	....	....	....	....	....
Liabilities to direct investors	8 590	....	....	....	....	....	....	....	....
Portfolio investment	8 652	....	....	....	....	....	....	78.7	98.2
Equity securities	8 660	....	....	....	....	....	....	78.7	77.8
Banks	8 663	....	....	....	....	....	....	78.7	77.8
Other sectors	8 664	....	....	....	....	....	....	....	....
Debt securities	8 669	....	....	....	....	....	....	....	20.4
Bonds and notes	8 670	....	....	....	....	....	....	....	20.4
Monetary authorities	8 671	....	....	....	....	....	....	....	....
General government	8 672	....	....	....	....	....	....	....	....
Banks	8 673	....	....	....	....	....	....	....	20.4
Other sectors	8 674	....	....	....	....	....	....	....	....
Money market instruments	8 680	....	....	....	....	....	....	....	....
Monetary authorities	8 681	....	....	....	....	....	....	....	....
General government	8 682	....	....	....	....	....	....	....	....
Banks	8 683	....	....	....	....	....	....	....	....
Other sectors	8 684	....	....	....	....	....	....	....	....
Financial derivatives	8 905	....	....	....	....	....	....	....	....
Monetary authorities	8 906	....	....	....	....	....	....	....	....
General government	8 907	....	....	....	....	....	....	....	....
Banks	8 908	....	....	....	....	....	....	....	....
Other sectors	8 909	....	....	....	....	....	....	....	....
Other investment	8 753	27,677.6	28,767.6	29,176.8	30,834.3	34,283.3	36,006.4	38,274.6	42,582.8
Trade credits	8 756	....	....	....	....	....	....	1,481.0	3,032.6
General government	8 757	....	....	....	....	....	....	805.5	1,186.7
of which: Short-term	8 759	....	....	....	....	....	....	*805.5*	*1,186.7*
Other sectors	8 760	....	....	....	....	....	....	675.5	1,845.9
of which: Short-term	8 762	....	....	....	....	....	....	*675.5*	*1,845.9*
Loans	8 764	27,221.5	28,324.0	28,551.4	30,076.9	33,477.4	35,199.9	35,686.5	37,804.5
Monetary authorities	8 765	3,107.6	3,189.0	3,051.4	3,168.9	3,225.4	3,189.9	1,553.5	1,524.5
of which: Use of Fund credit and loans from the Fund	8 766	*1,596.4*	*1,649.6*	*1,506.8*	*1,580.4*	*1,621.3*	*1,531.8*	*1,553.5*	*1,524.5*
of which: Short-term	8 768	*182.1*	*166.0*	*119.3*	*139.1*	*129.3*	*112.6*	....	....
General government	8 769	24,113.9	25,135.0	25,500.0	26,908.0	30,252.0	32,010.0	34,133.0	36,280.0
of which: Short-term	8 771	....	....	....	....	....	....	....	....
Banks	8 772	....	....	....	....	....	....	....	....
of which: Short-term	8 774	....	....	....	....	....	....	....	....
Other sectors	8 775	....	....	....	....	....	....	....	....
of which: Short-term	8 777	....	....	....	....	....	....	....	....
Currency and deposits	8 780	103.0	121.6	264.9	279.9	330.0	320.4	271.2	310.4
Monetary authorities	8 781	46.2	49.2	46.4	43.4	42.0	39.9	6.0	6.0
General government	8 782	....	....	....	....	....	....	2.8	2.8
Banks	8 783	56.9	72.4	218.5	236.5	288.0	280.5	262.4	301.6
Other sectors	8 784	....	....	....	....	....	....	....	....
Other liabilities	8 786	353.1	322.0	360.5	477.4	475.9	486.1	835.9	1,435.3
Monetary authorities	8 787	353.1	322.0	360.5	477.4	475.9	486.1	548.1	744.6
of which: Short-term	8 789	*294.3*	*265.7*	*308.1*	*428.0*	*432.5*	*449.6*	*356.0*	*562.1*
General government	8 790	....	....	....	....	....	....	74.0	484.4
of which: Short-term	8 792	....	....	....	....	....	....	....	....
Banks	8 793	....	....	....	....	....	....	213.8	206.3
of which: Short-term	8 795	....	....	....	....	....	....	....	....
Other sectors	8 796	....	....	....	....	....	....	....	....
of which: Short-term	8 798	....	....	....	....	....	....	....	....
NET INTERNATIONAL INVESTMENT POSITION	8 995	....	....	....	....	....	....	....	....
Conversion rates: Sudanese pounds per U.S. dollar (end of period)	0 102	2.60	2.51	2.31	2.01	2.05	2.18	2.24	2.48

Table 1. ANALYTIC PRESENTATION, 2003–2010

(Millions of U.S. dollars)

	Code	2003	2004	2005	2006	2007	2008	2009	2010
A. Current Account[1]	4 993 Z.	**−159.0**	**−137.7**	**−143.6**	**110.4**	**184.9**	**353.0**	**209.5**	**653.0**
Goods: exports f.o.b.	2 100 ..	487.8	782.2	1,211.5	1,174.4	1,359.0	1,708.1	1,404.3	2,084.1
Goods: imports f.o.b.	3 100 ..	−458.0	−740.1	−1,189.1	−1,013.4	−1,185.3	−1,349.7	−1,295.5	−1,397.9
Balance on Goods	4 100 ..	*29.8*	*42.1*	*22.4*	*161.0*	*173.7*	*358.4*	*108.8*	*686.2*
Services: credit	2 200 ..	59.0	141.3	204.1	233.6	244.7	284.6	286.7	241.4
Services: debit	3 200 ..	−194.6	−271.0	−351.8	−268.5	−317.2	−398.1	−285.3	−259.0
Balance on Goods and Services	4 991 ..	*−105.8*	*−87.6*	*−125.3*	*126.1*	*101.2*	*244.9*	*110.2*	*668.6*
Income: credit	2 300 ..	11.7	15.6	24.0	28.0	43.6	42.2	29.8	26.1
Income: debit	3 300 ..	−60.2	−78.5	−64.4	−79.6	−35.4	−21.5	−24.5	−128.2
Balance on Goods, Services, and Income	4 992 ..	*−154.3*	*−150.5*	*−165.7*	*74.5*	*109.4*	*265.6*	*115.5*	*566.5*
Current transfers: credit	2 379 Z.	24.8	75.8	52.3	73.5	137.9	137.9	147.2	141.8
Current transfers: debit	3 379 ..	−29.5	−63.0	−30.2	−37.6	−62.4	−50.5	−53.2	−55.3
B. Capital Account[1]	4 994 Z.	**9.0**	**18.9**	**14.5**	**19.3**	**8.1**	**31.9**	**87.4**	**53.9**
Capital account: credit	2 994 Z.	9.2	18.9	14.5	19.3	8.1	31.9	87.9	53.9
Capital account: debit	3 994 ..	−.2	....	....	....	....	....	−.5	....
Total, Groups A Plus B	4 981 ..	*−150.0*	*−118.8*	*−129.1*	*129.7*	*193.0*	*384.9*	*296.9*	*706.9*
C. Financial Account[1]	4 995 W.	**−36.5**	**−23.5**	**−20.6**	**−180.5**	**−177.1**	**−90.8**	**−62.6**	**−880.3**
Direct investment abroad	4 505 ..	....	....	....	....	....	....	....	....
Direct investment in Suriname	4 555 Z.	−76.1	−37.3	27.9	−163.4	−246.7	−233.6	−93.4	−255.7
Portfolio investment assets	4 602 ..	....	....	....	....	....	....	−9.9	−2.3
Equity securities	4 610 ..	....	....	....	....	....	....	....	....
Debt securities	4 619 ..	....	....	....	....	....	....	−9.9	−2.3
Portfolio investment liabilities	4 652 Z.	....	....	−2.0	−.3	−1.3	−16.9	−.9	−9.7
Equity securities	4 660 ..	....	....	....	....	....	....	....	....
Debt securities	4 669 Z.	....	....	−2.0	−.3	−1.3	−16.9	−.9	−9.7
Financial derivatives	4 910 ..	....	....	....	....	....	....	....	....
Financial derivatives assets	4 900 ..	....	....	....	....	....	....	....	....
Financial derivatives liabilities	4 905 ..	....	....	....	....	....	....	....	....
Other investment assets	4 703 ..	46.9	−2.3	−31.9	8.4	83.5	170.0	3.7	−582.6
Monetary authorities	4 701 ..	....	....	....	....	....	....	....	−34.1
General government	4 704 ..	....	....	....	....	....	....	....	....
Banks	4 705 ..	....	....	....	....	....	....	....	−11.3
Other sectors	4 728 ..	46.9	−2.3	−31.9	8.4	83.5	170.0	3.7	−537.2
Other investment liabilities	4 753 W.	−7.3	16.1	−14.6	−25.2	−12.6	−10.3	37.9	−30.0
Monetary authorities	4 753 WA	4.3	....	....	−.1	....	.1	135.9	−2.6
General government	4 753 ZB	−23.0	−18.5	−14.4	−25.6	−16.8	−2.8	−92.9	−10.9
Banks	4 753 ZC	−9.1	9.0	.1	....	5.0	.2	−1.6	2.9
Other sectors	4 753 ZD	20.5	25.6	−.3	.5	−.8	−7.8	−3.5	−19.4
Total, Groups A Through C	4 983 ..	*−186.5*	*−142.3*	*−149.7*	*−50.8*	*15.9*	*294.1*	*234.3*	*−173.4*
D. Net Errors and Omissions	4 998 ..	**193.7**	**218.4**	**169.4**	**144.9**	**161.0**	**−241.7**	**−41.2**	**210.0**
Total, Groups A Through D	4 984 ..	*7.2*	*76.1*	*19.7*	*94.1*	*176.9*	*52.4*	*193.1*	*36.6*
E. Reserves and Related Items	4 802 A.	**−7.2**	**−76.1**	**−19.7**	**−94.1**	**−176.9**	**−52.4**	**−193.1**	**−36.6**
Reserve assets	4 802 ..	−7.2	−76.1	−19.7	−94.1	−176.9	−52.4	−193.1	−36.6
Use of Fund credit and loans	4 766 ..	....	....	....	....	....	....	....	....
Exceptional financing	4 920 ..	....	....	....	....	....	....	....	....
Conversion rates: Suriname dollars per U.S. dollar	0 101 ..	2.6013	2.7336	2.7317	2.7438	2.7450	2.7450	2.7450	2.7454

[1] Excludes components that have been classified in the categories of Group E.

Table 2. STANDARD PRESENTATION, 2003–2010

(Millions of U.S. dollars)

	Code	2003	2004	2005	2006	2007	2008	2009	2010
CURRENT ACCOUNT.................................	4 993 ..	**−159.0**	**−137.7**	**−143.6**	**110.4**	**184.9**	**353.0**	**209.5**	**653.0**
A. GOODS.................................	4 100 ..	29.8	42.1	22.4	161.0	173.7	358.4	108.8	686.2
Credit.................................	2 100 ..	487.8	782.2	1,211.5	1,174.4	1,359.0	1,708.1	1,404.3	2,084.1
General merchandise: exports f.o.b.................	2 110 ..	400.3	782.2	1,211.5	1,174.4	1,359.0	1,708.1	1,404.3	923.6
Goods for processing: exports f.o.b.................	2 150 ..	....	....	....	....	....	....	....	....
Repairs on goods.................	2 160 ..	....	....	....	....	....	....	....	....
Goods procured in ports by carriers.................	2 170 ..	....	....	....	....	....	....	....	....
Nonmonetary gold.................	2 180 ..	87.5	....	....	....	....	....	....	1,160.5
Debit.................................	3 100 ..	**−458.0**	**−740.1**	**−1,189.1**	**−1,013.4**	**−1,185.3**	**−1,349.7**	**−1,295.5**	**−1,397.9**
General merchandise: imports f.o.b.................	3 110 ..	−458.0	−740.1	−1,189.1	−1,013.4	−1,185.3	−1,349.7	−1,295.5	−1,397.9
Goods for processing: imports f.o.b.................	3 150 ..	....	....	....	....	....	....	....	....
Repairs on goods.................	3 160 ..	....	....	....	....	....	....	....	....
Goods procured in ports by carriers.................	3 170 ..	....	....	....	....	....	....	....	....
Nonmonetary gold.................	3 180 ..	....	....	....	....	....	....	....	....
B. SERVICES.................................	4 200 ..	**−135.6**	**−129.7**	**−147.7**	**−34.9**	**−72.5**	**−113.5**	**1.4**	**−17.6**
Total credit.................................	2 200 ..	*59.0*	*141.3*	*204.1*	*233.6*	*244.7*	*284.6*	*286.7*	*241.4*
Total debit.................................	3 200 ..	*−194.6*	*−271.0*	*−351.8*	*−268.5*	*−317.2*	*−398.1*	*−285.3*	*−259.0*
Transportation services, credit................	2 205 ..	**26.2**	**49.4**	**70.1**	**24.6**	**20.4**	**19.0**	**19.0**	**31.0**
Passenger.................................	2 850 ..	*14.2*	*34.9*	*50.7*	*13.7*	*6.3*	*6.2*	*6.2*	*8.3*
Freight.................................	2 851 ..	*.5*	*3.0*	*6.0*	*7.2*	*10.4*	*10.2*	*10.5*	*19.6*
Other.................................	2 852 ..	*11.5*	*11.5*	*13.4*	*3.7*	*3.7*	*2.6*	*2.3*	*3.1*
Sea transport, passenger.................	2 207 ..	....	....	....	....	....	....	....	....
Sea transport, freight.................	2 208 ..	....	....	....	....	....	....	....	....
Sea transport, other.................	2 209 ..	....	....	....	....	....	....	....	....
Air transport, passenger.................	2 211 ..	14.2	34.9	50.7	13.7	6.3	6.2	6.2	8.3
Air transport, freight.................	2 212 ..	.5	3.0	6.0	7.2	10.4	10.2	10.5	19.6
Air transport, other.................	2 213 ..	11.5	11.5	13.4	3.7	3.7	2.6	2.3	3.1
Other transport, passenger.................	2 215 ..	....	....	....	....	....	....	....	....
Other transport, freight.................	2 216 ..	....	....	....	....	....	....	....	....
Other transport, other.................	2 217 ..	....	....	....	....	....	....	....	....
Transportation services, debit................	3 205 ..	**−109.7**	**−129.1**	**−135.0**	**−63.1**	**−65.6**	**−90.0**	**−63.1**	**−73.4**
Passenger.................................	3 850 ..	*−62.4*	*−71.4*	*−77.4*	*−14.6*	*−5.8*	*−4.6*	*−2.5*	*−1.6*
Freight.................................	3 851 ..	*−36.7*	*−37.4*	*−46.2*	*−39.8*	*−47.4*	*−69.9*	*−48.6*	*−58.1*
Other.................................	3 852 ..	*−10.6*	*−20.3*	*−11.4*	*−8.7*	*−12.4*	*−15.5*	*−12.0*	*−13.7*
Sea transport, passenger.................	3 207 ..	....	....	....	....	....	....	....	....
Sea transport, freight.................	3 208 ..	....	....	....	....	....	....	....	....
Sea transport, other.................	3 209 ..	....	....	....	....	....	....	....	....
Air transport, passenger.................	3 211 ..	−62.4	−71.4	−77.4	−14.6	−5.8	−4.6	−2.5	−1.6
Air transport, freight.................	3 212 ..	−36.7	−37.4	−46.2	−39.8	−47.4	−69.9	−48.6	−58.1
Air transport, other.................	3 213 ..	−10.6	−20.3	−11.4	−8.7	−12.4	−15.5	−12.0	−13.7
Other transport, passenger.................	3 215 ..	....	....	....	....	....	....	....	....
Other transport, freight.................	3 216 ..	....	....	....	....	....	....	....	....
Other transport, other.................	3 217 ..	....	....	....	....	....	....	....	....
Travel, credit.................................	2 236 ..	**3.8**	**17.0**	**44.6**	**94.8**	**66.6**	**77.4**	**63.6**	**60.9**
Business travel.................	2 237 ..	....	....	....	....	....	....	....	....
Personal travel.................	2 240 ..	3.8	17.0	44.6	94.8	66.6	77.4	63.6	60.9
Travel, debit.................................	3 236 ..	**−5.6**	**−14.4**	**−16.9**	**−18.3**	**−22.0**	**−30.3**	**−32.0**	**−39.2**
Business travel.................	3 237 ..	....	....	....	....	....	....	....	....
Personal travel.................	3 240 ..	−5.6	−14.4	−16.9	−18.3	−22.0	−30.3	−32.0	−39.2
Other services, credit................	2 200 BA	**29.1**	**74.9**	**89.4**	**114.2**	**157.8**	**188.2**	**204.1**	**149.5**
Communications.................	2 245 ..	....	....	....	....	....	....	....	....
Construction.................	2 249 ..	....	....	....	....	....	....	....	....
Insurance.................	2 253 ..	.1	.3	.7	.8	1.2	1.1	1.2	2.2
Financial.................	2 260 ..	....	....	....	....	....	....	....	....
Computer and information.................	2 262 ..	....	....	....	....	....	....	....	....
Royalties and licence fees.................	2 266 ..	....	....	....	....	.1	....	....	.7
Other business services.................	2 268 ..	21.6	62.3	67.2	90.4	121.8	135.0	172.7	112.5
Personal, cultural, and recreational.................	2 287 ..	....	....	....	....	....	....	....	....
Government, n.i.e.................	2 291 ..	7.4	12.3	21.5	23.0	34.7	52.1	30.2	34.1
Other services, debit................	3 200 BA	**−79.3**	**−127.5**	**−199.9**	**−187.1**	**−229.6**	**−277.8**	**−190.2**	**−146.5**
Communications.................	3 245 ..	....	....	....	....	....	....	....	....
Construction.................	3 249 ..	....	....	....	....	....	....	....	....
Insurance.................	3 253 ..	−4.1	−4.2	−5.1	−4.4	−5.3	−7.8	−5.4	−6.5
Financial.................	3 260 ..	....	....	....	....	....	....	....	....
Computer and information.................	3 262 ..	....	....	....	....	....	....	....	....
Royalties and licence fees.................	3 266 ..	....	....	....	....	−2.5	−2.6	....	....
Other business services.................	3 268 ..	−68.6	−103.2	−182.2	−164.3	−196.8	−236.0	−145.0	−118.2
Personal, cultural, and recreational.................	3 287 ..	....	....	....	....	....	....	....	....
Government, n.i.e.................	3 291 ..	−6.6	−20.1	−12.6	−18.4	−25.0	−31.4	−39.8	−21.8

Table 2 (Continued). STANDARD PRESENTATION, 2003–2010

(Millions of U.S. dollars)

	Code	2003	2004	2005	2006	2007	2008	2009	2010
C. INCOME	4 300	**−48.5**	**−62.9**	**−40.4**	**−51.6**	**8.2**	**20.7**	**5.3**	**−102.1**
Total credit	2 300	*11.7*	*15.6*	*24.0*	*28.0*	*43.6*	*42.2*	*29.8*	*26.1*
Total debit	3 300	*−60.2*	*−78.5*	*−64.4*	*−79.6*	*−35.4*	*−21.5*	*−24.5*	*−128.2*
Compensation of employees, credit	2 310	**2.3**	**2.0**	**2.4**	**2.0**	**2.4**	**2.1**	**3.7**	**3.6**
Compensation of employees, debit	3 310	**−4.9**	**−5.3**	**−4.2**	**−2.6**	**−4.4**	**−6.6**	**−4.0**	**−.3**
Investment income, credit	2 320	**9.4**	**13.6**	**21.6**	**26.0**	**41.2**	**40.1**	**26.1**	**22.5**
Direct investment income	2 330	....	....	....	....	....	....	....	....
Dividends and distributed branch profits	2 332	....	....	....	....	....	....	....	....
Reinvested earnings and undistributed branch profits	2 333	....	....	....	....	....	....	....	....
Income on debt (interest)	2 334	....	....	....	....	....	....	....	....
Portfolio investment income	2 339	....	....	....	....	....	....	....	8.3
Income on equity	2 340	....	....	....	....	....	....	....	....
Income on bonds and notes	2 350	....	....	....	....	....	....	....	8.3
Income on money market instruments	2 360	....	....	....	....	....	....	....	....
Other investment income	2 370	9.4	13.6	21.6	26.0	41.2	40.1	26.1	14.2
Investment income, debit	3 320	**−55.3**	**−73.2**	**−60.2**	**−77.0**	**−31.0**	**−14.9**	**−20.5**	**−127.9**
Direct investment income	3 330	....	....	−45.0	−45.4	....	....	−1.3	−100.4
Dividends and distributed branch profits	3 332	....	....	−45.0	−45.4	....	....	−1.3	−100.4
Reinvested earnings and undistributed branch profits	3 333	....	....	....	....	....	....	....	....
Income on debt (interest)	3 334	....	....	....	....	....	....	....	....
Portfolio investment income	3 339	....	....	....	....	−15.0	....	....	....
Income on equity	3 340	....	....	....	....	−15.0	....	....	....
Income on bonds and notes	3 350	....	....	....	....	....	....	....	....
Income on money market instruments	3 360	....	....	....	....	....	....	....	....
Other investment income	3 370	−55.3	−73.2	−15.2	−31.6	−16.0	−14.9	−19.2	−27.5
D. CURRENT TRANSFERS	4 379	**−4.7**	**12.8**	**22.1**	**35.9**	**75.5**	**87.4**	**94.0**	**86.5**
Credit	2 379	**24.8**	**75.8**	**52.3**	**73.5**	**137.9**	**137.9**	**147.2**	**141.8**
General government	2 380	....	....	....	....	....	....	....	....
Other sectors	2 390	24.8	75.8	52.3	73.5	137.9	137.9	147.2	141.8
Workers' remittances	2 391	21.1	7.1	1.5	.1	137.5	.1	.9	.7
Other current transfers	2 392	3.7	68.7	50.8	73.4	.4	137.8	146.3	141.1
Debit	3 379	**−29.5**	**−63.0**	**−30.2**	**−37.6**	**−62.4**	**−50.5**	**−53.2**	**−55.3**
General government	3 380	....	....	....	....	....	....	....	....
Other sectors	3 390	−29.5	−63.0	−30.2	−37.6	−62.4	−50.5	−53.2	−55.3
Workers' remittances	3 391	−23.2	−8.6	−5.3	−1.5	−60.4	−1.6	−.6	−.9
Other current transfers	3 392	−6.3	−54.4	−24.9	−36.1	−2.0	−48.9	−52.6	−54.4
CAPITAL AND FINANCIAL ACCOUNT	4 996	**−34.7**	**−80.7**	**−25.8**	**−255.3**	**−345.9**	**−111.3**	**−168.3**	**−863.0**
CAPITAL ACCOUNT	4 994	**9.0**	**18.9**	**14.5**	**19.3**	**8.1**	**31.9**	**87.4**	**53.9**
Total credit	2 994	*9.2*	*18.9*	*14.5*	*19.3*	*8.1*	*31.9*	*87.9*	*53.9*
Total debit	3 994	*−.2*	....	....	....	....	....	*−.5*	....
Capital transfers, credit	2 400	**9.2**	**18.9**	**14.5**	**19.3**	**8.1**	**31.9**	**87.9**	**53.9**
General government	2 401	9.1	18.9	14.5	19.3	8.1	31.9	87.7	53.9
Debt forgiveness	2 402	....	....	....	....	....	....	....	....
Other capital transfers	2 410	9.1	18.9	14.5	19.3	8.1	31.9	87.7	53.9
Other sectors	2 430	.1	....	....	....	....	....	.2	....
Migrants' transfers	2 431	.1	....	....	....	....	....	.2	....
Debt forgiveness	2 432	....	....	....	....	....	....	....	....
Other capital transfers	2 440	....	....	....	....	....	....	....	....
Capital transfers, debit	3 400	**−.2**	....	....	....	....	....	**−.5**	....
General government	3 401	....	....	....	....	....	....	....	....
Debt forgiveness	3 402	....	....	....	....	....	....	....	....
Other capital transfers	3 410	....	....	....	....	....	....	....	....
Other sectors	3 430	−.2	....	....	....	....	....	−.5	....
Migrants' transfers	3 431	−.2	....	....	....	....	....	−.5	....
Debt forgiveness	3 432	....	....	....	....	....	....	....	....
Other capital transfers	3 440	....	....	....	....	....	....	....	....
Nonproduced nonfinancial assets, credit	2 480	....	....	....	....	....	....	....	....
Nonproduced nonfinancial assets, debit	3 480	....	....	....	....	....	....	....	....

2011, International Monetary Fund: *Balance of Payments Statistics Yearbook*

Table 2 (Continued). STANDARD PRESENTATION, 2003–2010

(Millions of U.S. dollars)

	Code	2003	2004	2005	2006	2007	2008	2009	2010
FINANCIAL ACCOUNT.........	4 995 ..	**–43.7**	**–99.6**	**–40.3**	**–274.6**	**–354.0**	**–143.2**	**–255.7**	**–916.9**
A. DIRECT INVESTMENT.........	4 500 ..	**–76.1**	**–37.3**	**27.9**	**–163.4**	**–246.7**	**–233.6**	**–93.4**	**–255.7**
Direct investment abroad.........	4 505 ..	....	....	....	....	....	....	....	....
Equity capital.........	4 510 ..	....	....	....	....	....	....	....	....
Claims on affiliated enterprises.........	4 515 ..	....	....	....	....	....	....	....	....
Liabilities to affiliated enterprises.........	4 520 ..	....	....	....	....	....	....	....	....
Reinvested earnings.........	4 525 ..	....	....	....	....	....	....	....	....
Other capital.........	4 530 ..	....	....	....	....	....	....	....	....
Claims on affiliated enterprises.........	4 535 ..	....	....	....	....	....	....	....	....
Liabilities to affiliated enterprises.........	4 540 ..	....	....	....	....	....	....	....	....
Direct investment in Suriname.........	4 555 ..	**–76.1**	**–37.3**	**27.9**	**–163.4**	**–246.7**	**–233.6**	**–93.4**	**–255.7**
Equity capital.........	4 560 ..	....	.5	....	....	....	....	....	....
Claims on direct investors.........	4 565 ..	....	....	....	....	....	....	....	....
Liabilities to direct investors.........	4 570 ..	....	.5	....	....	....	....	....	....
Reinvested earnings.........	4 575 ..	....	....	....	....	....	....	....	....
Other capital.........	4 580 ..	–76.1	–37.8	27.9	–163.4	–246.7	–233.6	–93.4	–255.7
Claims on direct investors.........	4 585 ..	....	....	....	....	....	....	....	....
Liabilities to direct investors.........	4 590 ..	–76.1	–37.8	27.9	–163.4	–246.7	–233.6	–93.4	–255.7
B. PORTFOLIO INVESTMENT.........	4 600 ..	....	....	–2.0	–.3	–1.3	–16.9	–10.8	–12.0
Assets.........	4 602 ..	....	....	....	....	....	....	–9.9	–2.3
Equity securities.........	4 610 ..	....	....	....	....	....	....	....	....
Monetary authorities.........	4 611 ..	....	....	....	....	....	....	....	....
General government.........	4 612 ..	....	....	....	....	....	....	....	....
Banks.........	4 613 ..	....	....	....	....	....	....	....	....
Other sectors.........	4 614 ..	....	....	....	....	....	....	....	....
Debt securities.........	4 619 ..	....	....	....	....	....	....	–9.9	–2.3
Bonds and notes.........	4 620 ..	....	....	....	....	....	....	–9.9	–2.3
Monetary authorities.........	4 621 ..	....	....	....	....	....	....	....	....
General government.........	4 622 ..	....	....	....	....	....	....	....	....
Banks.........	4 623 ..	....	....	....	....	....	....	....	....
Other sectors.........	4 624 ..	....	....	....	....	....	....	–9.9	–2.3
Money market instruments.........	4 630 ..	....	....	....	....	....	....	....	....
Monetary authorities.........	4 631 ..	....	....	....	....	....	....	....	....
General government.........	4 632 ..	....	....	....	....	....	....	....	....
Banks.........	4 633 ..	....	....	....	....	....	....	....	....
Other sectors.........	4 634 ..	....	....	....	....	....	....	....	....
Liabilities.........	4 652 ..	....	....	–2.0	–.3	–1.3	–16.9	–.9	–9.7
Equity securities.........	4 660 ..	....	....	....	....	....	....	....	....
Banks.........	4 663 ..	....	....	....	....	....	....	....	....
Other sectors.........	4 664 ..	....	....	....	....	....	....	....	....
Debt securities.........	4 669 ..	....	....	–2.0	–.3	–1.3	–16.9	–.9	–9.7
Bonds and notes.........	4 670 ..	....	....	–2.0	–.3	–1.3	–16.9	–.9	–9.7
Monetary authorities.........	4 671 ..	....	....	....	....	....	....	....	....
General government.........	4 672 ..	....	....	....	....	....	....	....	....
Banks.........	4 673 ..	....	....	....	....	....	....	....	....
Other sectors.........	4 674 ..	....	....	–2.0	–.3	–1.3	–16.9	–.9	–9.7
Money market instruments.........	4 680 ..	....	....	....	....	....	....	....	....
Monetary authorities.........	4 681 ..	....	....	....	....	....	....	....	....
General government.........	4 682 ..	....	....	....	....	....	....	....	....
Banks.........	4 683 ..	....	....	....	....	....	....	....	....
Other sectors.........	4 684 ..	....	....	....	....	....	....	....	....
C. FINANCIAL DERIVATIVES.........	4 910 ..	....	....	....	....	....	....	....	....
Monetary authorities.........	4 911 ..	....	....	....	....	....	....	....	....
General government.........	4 912 ..	....	....	....	....	....	....	....	....
Banks.........	4 913 ..	....	....	....	....	....	....	....	....
Other sectors.........	4 914 ..	....	....	....	....	....	....	....	....
Assets.........	4 900 ..	....	....	....	....	....	....	....	....
Monetary authorities.........	4 901 ..	....	....	....	....	....	....	....	....
General government.........	4 902 ..	....	....	....	....	....	....	....	....
Banks.........	4 903 ..	....	....	....	....	....	....	....	....
Other sectors.........	4 904 ..	....	....	....	....	....	....	....	....
Liabilities.........	4 905 ..	....	....	....	....	....	....	....	....
Monetary authorities.........	4 906 ..	....	....	....	....	....	....	....	....
General government.........	4 907 ..	....	....	....	....	....	....	....	....
Banks.........	4 908 ..	....	....	....	....	....	....	....	....
Other sectors.........	4 909 ..	....	....	....	....	....	....	....	....

Suriname 366

Table 2 (Concluded). STANDARD PRESENTATION, 2003–2010
(Millions of U.S. dollars)

	Code	2003	2004	2005	2006	2007	2008	2009	2010
D. OTHER INVESTMENT	4 700	**39.6**	**13.8**	**−46.5**	**−16.8**	**70.9**	**159.7**	**41.6**	**−612.6**
Assets	4 703	**46.9**	**−2.3**	**−31.9**	**8.4**	**83.5**	**170.0**	**3.7**	**−582.6**
Trade credits	4 706	....	....	....	....	−7.7	1.1	.1	....
General government	4 707	....	....	....	....	....	....	....	....
of which: Short-term	4 709	....	....	....	....	....	....	....	....
Other sectors	4 710	....	....	....	....	−7.7	1.1	.1	....
of which: Short-term	4 712	....	....	....	....	−7.7	1.1	.1	....
Loans	4 714	....	....	....	....	....	....	....	....
Monetary authorities	4 715	....	....	....	....	....	....	....	....
of which: Short-term	4 718	....	....	....	....	....	....	....	....
General government	4 719	....	....	....	....	....	....	....	....
of which: Short-term	4 721	....	....	....	....	....	....	....	....
Banks	4 722	....	....	....	....	....	....	....	....
of which: Short-term	4 724	....	....	....	....	....	....	....	....
Other sectors	4 725	....	....	....	....	....	....	....	....
of which: Short-term	4 727	....	....	....	....	....	....	....	....
Currency and deposits	4 730	46.9	−2.3	−31.9	8.4	91.2	168.9	....	−582.6
Monetary authorities	4 731	....	....	....	....	....	....	....	−34.1
General government	4 732	....	....	....	....	....	....	....	....
Banks	4 733	....	....	....	....	....	....	....	−11.3
Other sectors	4 734	46.9	−2.3	−31.9	8.4	91.2	168.9	....	−537.2
Other assets	4 736	....	....	....	....	....	....	3.6	....
Monetary authorities	4 737	....	....	....	....	....	....	....	....
of which: Short-term	4 739	....	....	....	....	....	....	....	....
General government	4 740	....	....	....	....	....	....	....	....
of which: Short-term	4 742	....	....	....	....	....	....	....	....
Banks	4 743	....	....	....	....	....	....	....	....
of which: Short-term	4 745	....	....	....	....	....	....	....	....
Other sectors	4 746	....	....	....	....	....	....	3.6	....
of which: Short-term	4 748	....	....	....	....	....	....	3.6	....
Liabilities	4 753	**−7.3**	**16.1**	**−14.6**	**−25.2**	**−12.6**	**−10.3**	**37.9**	**−30.0**
Trade credits	4 756	....	....	....	.6	.6	−4.9	−10.9	−18.0
General government	4 757	....	....	....	....	....	....	....	....
of which: Short-term	4 759	....	....	....	....	....	....	....	....
Other sectors	4 760	....	....	....	.6	.6	−4.9	−10.9	−18.0
of which: Short-term	4 762	....	....	....	....	....	−4.9	−10.9	−18.0
Loans	4 764	−2.5	7.1	−14.7	−25.7	−18.2	−5.7	−85.5	−12.3
Monetary authorities	4 765	....	....	....	....	....	....	....	....
of which: Use of Fund credit and loans from the Fund	4 766	....	....	....	....	....	....	....	....
of which: Short-term	4 768	....	....	....	....	....	....	....	....
General government	4 769	−23.0	−18.5	−14.4	−25.6	−16.8	−2.8	−92.9	−10.9
of which: Short-term	4 771	....	....	....	....	....	....	....	....
Banks	4 772	....	....	....	....	....	....	....	....
of which: Short-term	4 774	....	....	....	....	....	....	....	....
Other sectors	4 775	20.5	25.6	−.3	−.1	−1.4	−2.9	7.4	−1.4
of which: Short-term	4 777	....	....	....	....	....	....	....	....
Currency and deposits	4 780	....	....	....	....	....	....	....	.3
Monetary authorities	4 781	....	....	....	....	....	....	....	−2.6
General government	4 782	....	....	....	....	....	....	....	....
Banks	4 783	....	....	....	....	....	....	....	2.9
Other sectors	4 784	....	....	....	....	....	....	....	....
Other liabilities	4 786	−4.8	9.0	.1	−.1	5.0	.3	134.3	....
Monetary authorities	4 787	4.3	....	....	−.1	....	.1	135.9	....
of which: Short-term	4 789	....	....	....	....	....	....	....	....
General government	4 790	....	....	....	....	....	....	....	....
of which: Short-term	4 792	....	....	....	....	....	....	....	....
Banks	4 793	−9.1	9.0	.1	....	5.0	.2	−1.6	....
of which: Short-term	4 795	....	....	....	....	....	....	....	....
Other sectors	4 796	....	....	....	....	....	....	....	....
of which: Short-term	4 798	....	....	....	....	....	....	....	....
E. RESERVE ASSETS	4 802	**−7.2**	**−76.1**	**−19.7**	**−94.1**	**−176.9**	**−52.4**	**−193.1**	**−36.6**
Monetary gold	4 812	−1.3	−.5	−7.1	−7.5	−11.8	−7.5	−20.4	−29.2
Special drawing rights	4 811	.1	.2	.2	.3	.4	.3	−125.5	....
Reserve position in the Fund	4 810	....	....	....	....	....	....	....	....
Foreign exchange	4 803	−6.0	−75.8	−12.8	−86.9	−165.5	−45.2	−47.2	−7.4
Other claims	4 813	....	....	....	....	....	....	....	....
NET ERRORS AND OMISSIONS	4 998	**193.7**	**218.4**	**169.4**	**144.9**	**161.0**	**−241.7**	**−41.2**	**210.0**

Table 1. ANALYTIC PRESENTATION, 2003–2010

(Millions of U.S. dollars)

	Code	2003	2004	2005	2006	2007	2008	2009	2010
A. Current Account¹...	4 993 Z.	**89.4**	**71.3**	**–102.6**	**–196.6**	**–65.5**	**–231.4**	**–415.1**	**–388.6**
Goods: exports f.o.b...	2 100 ..	1,666.8	1,806.2	1,636.5	1,662.9	1,744.8	1,568.6	1,660.1	1,805.4
Goods: imports f.o.b...	3 100 ..	–1,540.2	–1,715.3	–1,894.6	–1,914.9	–2,015.9	–1,578.5	–1,781.3	–1,955.2
Balance on Goods...	4 100 ..	*126.6*	*90.9*	*–258.1*	*–252.0*	*–271.1*	*–9.9*	*–121.3*	*–149.9*
Services: credit...	2 200 ..	204.8	249.6	282.5	283.3	454.7	224.6	200.0	257.5
Services: debit...	3 200 ..	–349.1	–377.6	–402.8	–373.4	–506.8	–650.7	–562.3	–669.6
Balance on Goods and Services...	4 991 ..	*–17.6*	*–37.1*	*–378.4*	*–342.1*	*–323.3*	*–435.9*	*–483.5*	*–562.0*
Income: credit...	2 300 ..	61.4	127.5	271.3	241.7	280.8	298.0	290.8	212.5
Income: debit...	3 300 ..	–104.6	–124.9	–93.0	–227.7	–217.0	–303.2	–413.4	–438.6
Balance on Goods, Services, and Income...	4 992 ..	*–60.8*	*–34.5*	*–200.1*	*–328.1*	*–259.5*	*–441.1*	*–606.2*	*–788.1*
Current transfers: credit...	2 379 Z.	336.6	370.8	339.6	366.3	403.5	417.7	404.9	482.6
Current transfers: debit...	3 379 ..	–186.4	–265.0	–242.1	–234.8	–209.5	–208.0	–213.8	–83.1
B. Capital Account¹...	4 994 Z.	**....**	**–.6**	**–3.5**	**24.8**	**–30.2**	**–8.8**	**–4.0**	**14.4**
Capital account: credit...	2 994 Z.	....	....	1.0	29.2	11.2	–6.9	5.7	22.2
Capital account: debit...	3 994 ..	....	–.6	–4.5	–4.5	–41.4	–1.9	–9.7	–7.8
Total, Groups A Plus B...	4 981 ..	*89.4*	*70.7*	*–106.1*	*–171.9*	*–95.7*	*–240.2*	*–419.1*	*–374.2*
C. Financial Account¹...	4 995 W.	**–89.2**	**–204.0**	**148.1**	**260.7**	**431.0**	**448.1**	**473.0**	**87.8**
Direct investment abroad...	4 505 ..	–16.4	1.4	22.0	.6	–23.2	7.9	–7.0	–3.9
Direct investment in Swaziland...	4 555 Z.	–60.9	69.6	–45.9	121.0	37.5	105.7	65.7	135.7
Portfolio investment assets...	4 602 ..	–.3	–.9	3.7	–9.5	4.2	–75.5	122.8	49.7
Equity securities...	4 610 ..	....	.2	....	.2	–.1	–76.9	3.5	–100.2
Debt securities...	4 619 ..	–.3	–1.1	3.7	–9.6	4.4	1.4	119.3	149.8
Portfolio investment liabilities...	4 652 Z.	–.1	.3	.8	5.5	1.0	43.9	–6.6	4.7
Equity securities...	4 660 ..	–.1	.3	.8	5.5	1.0	43.9	–6.6	4.7
Debt securities...	4 669 Z.	....	....	....	....	....	....	....	....
Financial derivatives...	4 910 ..	....	....	....	....	....	....	....	....
Financial derivatives assets...	4 900 ..	....	....	....	....	....	....	....	....
Financial derivatives liabilities...	4 905 ..	....	....	....	....	....	....	....	....
Other investment assets...	4 703 ..	8.1	–231.4	84.3	101.2	357.8	190.1	249.7	–161.6
Monetary authorities...	4 701 ..	....	....	....	....	....	....	....	....
General government...	4 704 ..	–26.5	–27.3	202.1	427.4	444.0	438.7	401.6	....
Banks...	4 705 ..	35.7	–1.6	17.7	–68.5	23.0	–89.4	–85.6	–102.0
Other sectors...	4 728 ..	–1.1	–202.5	–135.5	–257.6	–109.2	–159.2	–66.2	–59.5
Other investment liabilities...	4 753 W.	–19.6	–43.0	83.1	41.8	53.7	176.0	48.4	63.3
Monetary authorities...	4 753 WA	–2.7	–46.5	–1.2	–.2	4.4	–.6	63.7	10.6
General government...	4 753 ZB	–1.7	8.4	27.9	29.5	27.0	–9.3	–21.1	–18.4
Banks...	4 753 ZC	–3.2	–1.7	4.4	7.8	–9.0	31.2	–3.7	–8.0
Other sectors...	4 753 ZD	–11.9	–3.3	52.0	4.7	31.3	154.7	9.6	79.0
Total, Groups A Through C...	4 983 ..	*.2*	*–133.3*	*41.9*	*88.9*	*335.4*	*207.9*	*53.9*	*–286.3*
D. Net Errors and Omissions...	4 998 ..	**–92.1**	**168.2**	**–40.8**	**–237.8**	**–700.8**	**12.0**	**–55.0**	**55.5**
Total, Groups A Through D...	4 984 ..	*–91.8*	*34.9*	*1.1*	*–148.9*	*–365.5*	*219.9*	*–1.1*	*–230.9*
E. Reserves and Related Items...	4 802 A.	**91.8**	**–34.9**	**–1.1**	**148.9**	**365.5**	**–219.9**	**1.1**	**230.9**
Reserve assets...	4 802 ..	91.8	–34.4	.6	151.2	365.2	–220.1	.3	230.6
Use of Fund credit and loans...	4 766 ..	....	....	....	....	....	....	....	....
Exceptional financing...	4 920 ..	....	–.5	–1.7	–2.3	.2	.2	.8	.3
Conversion rates: emalangeni per U.S. dollar........	0 101 ..	**7.565**	**6.460**	**6.359**	**6.772**	**7.045**	**8.261**	**8.474**	**7.321**

¹ Excludes components that have been classified in the categories of Group E.

Table 2. STANDARD PRESENTATION, 2003–2010

(Millions of U.S. dollars)

	Code	2003	2004	2005	2006	2007	2008	2009	2010
CURRENT ACCOUNT	4 993	**89.4**	**71.3**	**−102.6**	**−196.6**	**−65.5**	**−231.2**	**−414.3**	**−388.3**
A. GOODS	4 100	**126.6**	**90.9**	**−258.1**	**−252.0**	**−271.1**	**−9.9**	**−121.3**	**−149.9**
Credit	2 100	**1,666.8**	**1,806.2**	**1,636.5**	**1,662.9**	**1,744.8**	**1,568.6**	**1,660.1**	**1,805.4**
General merchandise: exports f.o.b.	2 110	1,636.2	1,791.8	1,585.1	1,560.6	1,625.7	1,489.1	1,564.9	1,805.3
Goods for processing: exports f.o.b.	2 150	30.6	14.4	35.2	102.3	118.8	79.4	94.0	....
Repairs on goods	2 160	....	....	....	....	.1	....	1.1	.1
Goods procured in ports by carriers	2 170	....	....	.1	....	.1	....	....	....
Nonmonetary gold	2 180	....	....	16.2	....	....	....	....	....
Debit	3 100	**−1,540.2**	**−1,715.3**	**−1,894.6**	**−1,914.9**	**−2,015.9**	**−1,578.5**	**−1,781.3**	**−1,955.2**
General merchandise: imports f.o.b.	3 110	−1,434.4	−1,640.7	−1,775.0	−1,804.0	−1,934.8	−1,529.2	−1,692.8	−1,953.7
Goods for processing: imports f.o.b.	3 150	−103.7	−74.1	−114.4	−108.3	−80.6	−49.0	−84.6	....
Repairs on goods	3 160	−.3	−.3	−.3	−.2	−.7	−.2	−.6	−1.3
Goods procured in ports by carriers	3 170	−1.8	....	−.5	−.1	.2	....	−.3	....
Nonmonetary gold	3 180	....	−.2	−4.5	−2.3	....	....	−3.0	−.2
B. SERVICES	4 200	**−144.3**	**−128.0**	**−120.3**	**−90.1**	**−52.2**	**−426.1**	**−362.3**	**−412.1**
Total credit	2 200	*204.8*	*249.6*	*282.5*	*283.3*	*454.7*	*224.6*	*200.0*	*257.5*
Total debit	3 200	*−349.1*	*−377.6*	*−402.8*	*−373.4*	*−506.8*	*−650.7*	*−562.3*	*−669.6*
Transportation services, credit	2 205	**9.1**	**11.3**	**10.2**	**10.1**	**8.8**	**9.1**	**7.5**	**21.2**
Passenger	2 850	....	*.1*	*.3*	*.1*	*.2*	*.3*	*.1*	*.4*
Freight	2 851	*9.0*	*10.9*	*9.9*	*10.0*	*8.6*	*8.7*	*7.2*	*20.5*
Other	2 852	....	*.2*	*.1*	....	....	....	*.2*	*.2*
Sea transport, passenger	2 207	....	....	....	....	....	....	....	....
Sea transport, freight	2 208	.3	.4	.3	.2	.2	....	....	....
Sea transport, other	2 209	....	....	....	....	....	....	....	....
Air transport, passenger	2 211	....	.1	.1	.1	.1	.2	....	.2
Air transport, freight	2 212	....	....	....	....	....	....	....	....
Air transport, other	2 213	....	....	....	....	....	....	....	....
Other transport, passenger	2 215	....	....	.1	.1	.1	.2	....	.2
Other transport, freight	2 216	8.7	10.5	9.5	9.8	8.4	8.7	7.2	20.5
Other transport, other	2 217	....	.2	.1	....	....	....	.2	.2
Transportation services, debit	3 205	**−58.4**	**−54.8**	**−49.2**	**−44.7**	**−58.0**	**−185.3**	**−180.2**	**−69.5**
Passenger	3 850	*−.9*	*−5.8*	*−11.2*	*−4.9*	*−12.3*	*−13.5*	*−26.3*	*−26.3*
Freight	3 851	*−29.8*	*−33.4*	*−28.3*	*−30.3*	*−38.0*	*−46.7*	*−13.6*	*−19.0*
Other	3 852	*−27.6*	*−15.6*	*−9.7*	*−9.6*	*−7.6*	*−125.1*	*−140.2*	*−24.2*
Sea transport, passenger	3 207	....	....	....	....	....	....	....	....
Sea transport, freight	3 208	−11.2	−32.6	−25.6	−28.5	−20.0	−15.7	....	....
Sea transport, other	3 209	....	....	....	....	....	....	....	....
Air transport, passenger	3 211	−.9	−3.7	−5.6	−2.4	−6.2	−6.7	−13.2	−13.1
Air transport, freight	3 212	−.1	−.2	−.1	−.3	−14.9	−12.7	....	....
Air transport, other	3 213	−27.6	....	....	....	....	....	....	....
Other transport, passenger	3 215	....	−2.1	−5.6	−2.4	−6.2	−6.7	−13.2	−13.1
Other transport, freight	3 216	−18.5	−.5	−2.6	−1.5	−3.2	−18.3	−13.6	−19.0
Other transport, other	3 217	....	−15.6	−9.7	−9.6	−7.6	−125.1	−140.2	−24.2
Travel, credit	2 236	**69.8**	**75.0**	**76.9**	**75.4**	**31.7**	**26.2**	**39.8**	**50.5**
Business travel	2 237	35.5	43.7	44.4	41.7	27.2	17.5	28.0	28.7
Personal travel	2 240	34.3	31.3	32.6	33.7	4.4	8.7	11.8	21.9
Travel, debit	3 236	**−21.9**	**−48.2**	**−49.2**	**−48.8**	**−51.4**	**−46.1**	**−71.6**	**−61.3**
Business travel	3 237	−2.6	−1.0	−1.4	−1.7	−2.6	−2.1	−14.9	−12.3
Personal travel	3 240	−19.3	−47.1	−47.9	−47.1	−48.8	−44.0	−56.6	−49.0
Other services, credit	2 200 BA	**125.9**	**163.4**	**195.4**	**197.9**	**414.2**	**189.3**	**152.8**	**185.8**
Communications	2 245	.1	.6	13.2	1.7	6.4	....	22.5	22.5
Construction	2 249	.2	.9	1.1	2.0	.8	1.5	13.3	61.9
Insurance	2 253	.1	4.1	1.2	4.9	5.6	17.5	15.1	9.7
Financial	2 260	97.7	105.3	151.3	32.9	25.4	3.7	6.1	30.5
Computer and information	2 262	1.2	....	....	.3	....	....	....	.6
Royalties and licence fees	2 266	....	....	....	....	....	36.4	....	.3
Other business services	2 268	21.7	37.7	18.4	146.7	368.5	126.6	80.9	51.5
Personal, cultural, and recreational	2 287	....	....	.1	.2	.3	.8	5.8	1.7
Government, n.i.e.	2 291	4.8	14.8	10.0	9.2	7.2	2.8	8.9	7.2
Other services, debit	3 200 BA	**−268.8**	**−274.7**	**−304.4**	**−279.9**	**−397.5**	**−419.2**	**−310.6**	**−538.9**
Communications	3 245	−2.2	−3.1	−4.3	−1.4	−3.2	−1.0	−27.3	−6.2
Construction	3 249	−1.2	−3.0	−3.0	−4.7	−17.3	−11.4	−10.9	−6.6
Insurance	3 253	−8.0	−9.3	−7.2	−7.3	−7.6	−6.3	−13.5	−19.9
Financial	3 260	−35.5	−95.6	−123.1	−56.1	−52.7	−2.7	−16.8	−16.2
Computer and information	3 262	−.9	−1.0	−2.3	−2.5	−2.9	−2.6	....	....
Royalties and licence fees	3 266	−71.2	−75.6	−105.4	−106.4	−121.0	−119.7	−116.3	−16.3
Other business services	3 268	−142.7	−71.9	−52.5	−93.0	−180.3	−253.7	−102.1	−454.3
Personal, cultural, and recreational	3 287	−.1	−.1	−.3	....	....	....	−.5	−.1
Government, n.i.e.	3 291	−7.0	−15.0	−6.4	−8.5	−12.5	−21.9	−23.3	−19.2

Table 2 (Continued). STANDARD PRESENTATION, 2003–2010

(Millions of U.S. dollars)

	Code	2003	2004	2005	2006	2007	2008	2009	2010
C. INCOME	4 300	**−43.2**	**2.6**	**178.3**	**14.0**	**63.8**	**−5.2**	**−122.7**	**−226.1**
Total credit	2 300	*61.4*	*127.5*	*271.3*	*241.7*	*280.8*	*298.0*	*290.8*	*212.5*
Total debit	3 300	*−104.6*	*−124.9*	*−93.0*	*−227.7*	*−217.0*	*−303.2*	*−413.4*	*−438.6*
Compensation of employees, credit	2 310	**65.2**	**81.7**	**94.1**	**94.3**	**93.6**	**87.1**	**91.5**	**52.8**
Compensation of employees, debit	3 310	**−2.0**	**−3.9**	**−4.9**	**−15.4**	**−6.7**	**−4.7**	**−9.6**	**−10.6**
Investment income, credit	2 320	**−3.8**	**45.8**	**177.2**	**147.3**	**187.2**	**210.9**	**199.3**	**159.7**
Direct investment income	2 330	6.8	1.2	1.6	1.7	6.0	1.1	30.6	80.7
Dividends and distributed branch profits	2 332	6.1	1.2	1.6	1.7	6.0	1.1	30.2	80.7
Reinvested earnings and undistributed branch profits	2 333	.7	....	....	....	....	....	.4	....
Income on debt (interest)	2 334	....	....	....	....	....	....	....	....
Portfolio investment income	2 339	....	.1	.4	.4	.4	.4	.4	.6
Income on equity	2 340	....	.1	.4	.4	.4	.4	.4	.6
Income on bonds and notes	2 350	....	....	....	....	....	....	....	....
Income on money market instruments	2 360	....	....	....	....	....	....	....	....
Other investment income	2 370	−10.6	44.5	175.2	145.3	180.8	209.5	168.2	78.3
Investment income, debit	3 320	**−102.6**	**−121.1**	**−88.0**	**−212.3**	**−210.3**	**−298.5**	**−403.8**	**−428.0**
Direct investment income	3 330	−75.7	−87.4	−44.0	−167.0	−160.0	−252.7	−352.5	−401.6
Dividends and distributed branch profits	3 332	−101.4	−50.3	−64.4	−94.8	−94.7	−165.6	−300.6	−353.4
Reinvested earnings and undistributed branch profits	3 333	25.7	−37.1	23.0	−72.3	−65.4	−87.1	−51.9	−48.2
Income on debt (interest)	3 334	....	....	−2.6	....	....	....	....	....
Portfolio investment income	3 339	....	−7.3	−19.3	−20.0	−21.1	−19.8	−21.2	....
Income on equity	3 340	....	−7.3	−19.3	−20.0	−21.1	−19.8	−21.2	....
Income on bonds and notes	3 350	....	....	....	....	....	....	....	....
Income on money market instruments	3 360	....	....	....	....	....	....	....	....
Other investment income	3 370	−26.8	−26.4	−24.7	−25.3	−29.2	−26.0	−30.1	−26.4
D. CURRENT TRANSFERS	4 379	**150.2**	**105.8**	**97.5**	**131.5**	**194.0**	**209.9**	**191.9**	**399.8**
Credit	2 379	**336.6**	**370.8**	**339.6**	**366.3**	**403.5**	**417.9**	**405.7**	**482.8**
General government	2 380	302.1	348.3	296.4	318.1	338.9	246.0	285.0	396.5
Other sectors	2 390	34.6	22.6	43.2	48.2	64.6	171.9	120.6	86.3
Workers' remittances	2 391	....	1.1	1.3	1.3	1.5	2.6	2.0	1.9
Other current transfers	2 392	34.6	21.5	41.9	46.9	63.1	169.3	118.7	84.5
Debit	3 379	**−186.4**	**−265.0**	**−242.1**	**−234.8**	**−209.5**	**−208.0**	**−213.8**	**−83.1**
General government	3 380	−144.9	−193.6	−164.7	−169.1	−170.8	−149.2	−166.2	−15.9
Other sectors	3 390	−41.5	−71.4	−77.5	−65.7	−38.7	−58.8	−47.6	−67.2
Workers' remittances	3 391	−36.8	−.2	−3.0	−1.2	−1.1	−1.7	−1.1	−1.1
Other current transfers	3 392	−4.7	−71.2	−74.4	−64.5	−37.5	−57.2	−46.5	−66.1
CAPITAL AND FINANCIAL ACCOUNT	4 996	**2.7**	**−239.5**	**143.5**	**434.4**	**766.4**	**219.3**	**469.4**	**332.8**
CAPITAL ACCOUNT	4 994	**....**	**−.6**	**−3.5**	**24.8**	**−30.2**	**−8.8**	**−4.0**	**14.4**
Total credit	2 994	....	....	*1.0*	*29.2*	*11.2*	*−6.9*	*5.7*	*22.2*
Total debit	3 994	....	*−.6*	*−4.5*	*−4.5*	*−41.4*	*−1.9*	*−9.7*	*−7.8*
Capital transfers, credit	2 400	**....**	**....**	**1.0**	**29.2**	**11.2**	**−23.8**	**1.7**	**22.2**
General government	2 401	....	....	....	25.1	4.0	−24.0	....	14.3
Debt forgiveness	2 402	....	....	....	....	....	....	....	....
Other capital transfers	2 410	....	....	....	25.1	4.0	−24.0	....	14.3
Other sectors	2 430	....	....	1.0	4.2	7.2	.2	1.7	7.9
Migrants' transfers	2 431	....	....	....	3.0	5.3	....	....	....
Debt forgiveness	2 432	....	....	....	....	....	....	....	....
Other capital transfers	2 440	....	....	1.0	1.2	1.9	.2	1.7	7.9
Capital transfers, debit	3 400	**....**	**−.6**	**−4.5**	**−4.5**	**−41.4**	**−1.2**	**−9.5**	**−4.8**
General government	3 401	....	....	....	....	....	....	....	....
Debt forgiveness	3 402	....	....	....	....	....	....	....	....
Other capital transfers	3 410	....	....	....	....	....	....	....	....
Other sectors	3 430	....	−.6	−4.5	−4.5	−41.4	−1.2	−9.5	−4.8
Migrants' transfers	3 431	....	−.6	−.2	−.2	−.3	−.3	−.2	....
Debt forgiveness	3 432	....	....	....	....	....	....	....	....
Other capital transfers	3 440	....	....	−4.2	−4.3	−41.0	−.9	−9.3	−4.8
Nonproduced nonfinancial assets, credit	2 480	**....**	**....**	**....**	**....**	**....**	**16.9**	**4.0**	**....**
Nonproduced nonfinancial assets, debit	3 480	**....**	**....**	**....**	**....**	**....**	**−.7**	**−.2**	**−3.0**

Table 2 (Continued). STANDARD PRESENTATION, 2003–2010

(Millions of U.S. dollars)

	Code	2003	2004	2005	2006	2007	2008	2009	2010
FINANCIAL ACCOUNT..........	4 995 ..	**2.7**	**−238.9**	**147.0**	**409.6**	**796.5**	**228.1**	**473.4**	**318.4**
A. DIRECT INVESTMENT..........	4 500 ..	**−77.3**	**71.0**	**−23.8**	**121.6**	**14.3**	**113.7**	**58.7**	**131.8**
Direct investment abroad..........	4 505 ..	**−16.4**	**1.4**	**22.0**	**.6**	**−23.2**	**7.9**	**−7.0**	**−3.9**
Equity capital..........	4 510 ..	.4	....	−.1	.3	....	−5.1	−5.4	−3.0
Claims on affiliated enterprises..........	4 515 ..	.4	....	−.1	.3	....	−5.1	−5.4	−3.0
Liabilities to affiliated enterprises..........	4 520 ..	....	....	....	....	....	....	....	....
Reinvested earnings..........	4 525 ..	−.7	....	....	....	....	....	−.4	....
Other capital..........	4 530 ..	−16.0	1.4	22.1	.3	−23.2	13.0	−1.2	−1.0
Claims on affiliated enterprises..........	4 535 ..	−16.7	1.4	22.1	.3	−23.2	13.0	−1.2	−1.0
Liabilities to affiliated enterprises..........	4 540 ..	.7	....	....	....	....	....	....	....
Direct investment in Swaziland..........	4 555 ..	**−60.9**	**69.6**	**−45.9**	**121.0**	**37.5**	**105.7**	**65.7**	**135.7**
Equity capital..........	4 560 ..	−3.8	−4.8	7.2	6.3	5.1	3.5	1.1	1.1
Claims on direct investors..........	4 565 ..	....	....	....	....	....	....	....	....
Liabilities to direct investors..........	4 570 ..	−3.8	−4.8	7.2	6.3	5.1	3.5	1.1	1.1
Reinvested earnings..........	4 575 ..	−25.7	37.1	−23.0	72.3	65.4	87.1	51.9	48.2
Other capital..........	4 580 ..	−31.4	37.3	−30.0	42.5	−33.0	15.1	12.6	86.4
Claims on direct investors..........	4 585 ..	....	....	....	....	....	....	....	....
Liabilities to direct investors..........	4 590 ..	−31.4	37.3	−30.0	42.5	−33.0	....	....	86.4
B. PORTFOLIO INVESTMENT..........	4 600 ..	**−.4**	**−.6**	**4.5**	**−4.0**	**5.2**	**−31.7**	**116.2**	**54.4**
Assets..........	4 602 ..	**−.3**	**−.9**	**3.7**	**−9.5**	**4.2**	**−75.5**	**122.8**	**49.7**
Equity securities..........	4 610 ..	....	.2	....	.2	−.1	−76.9	3.5	−100.2
Monetary authorities..........	4 611 ..	....	....	....	....	....	....	....	....
General government..........	4 612 ..	....	....	....	....	....	....	....	....
Banks..........	4 613 ..	....	....	....	....	....	....	....	....
Other sectors..........	4 614 ..	....	.2	....	.2	−.1	−76.9	3.5	−100.2
Debt securities..........	4 619 ..	−.3	−1.1	3.7	−9.6	4.4	1.4	119.3	149.8
Bonds and notes..........	4 620 ..	−.3	−1.0	3.7	−.3	−4.6	1.4	4.7	−31.7
Monetary authorities..........	4 621 ..	....	....	....	....	....	....	....	....
General government..........	4 622 ..	....	....	....	....	....	....	....	....
Banks..........	4 623 ..	....	....	....	....	....	....	....	....
Other sectors..........	4 624 ..	−.3	−1.0	3.7	−.3	−4.6	1.4	4.7	−31.7
Money market instruments..........	4 630 ..	....	−.1	....	−9.3	9.0	....	114.7	181.5
Monetary authorities..........	4 631 ..	....	....	....	....	....	....	....	....
General government..........	4 632 ..	....	....	....	....	....	....	....	....
Banks..........	4 633 ..	....	....	....	....	....	....	....	....
Other sectors..........	4 634 ..	....	−.1	....	−9.3	9.0	....	114.7	181.5
Liabilities..........	4 652 ..	**−.1**	**.3**	**.8**	**5.5**	**1.0**	**43.9**	**−6.6**	**4.7**
Equity securities..........	4 660 ..	−.1	.3	.8	5.5	1.0	43.9	−6.6	4.7
Banks..........	4 663 ..	....	....	....	....	....	....	....	....
Other sectors..........	4 664 ..	−.1	.3	.8	5.5	1.0	43.9	−6.6	4.7
Debt securities..........	4 669 ..	....	....	....	....	....	....	....	....
Bonds and notes..........	4 670 ..	....	....	....	....	....	....	....	....
Monetary authorities..........	4 671 ..	....	....	....	....	....	....	....	....
General government..........	4 672 ..	....	....	....	....	....	....	....	....
Banks..........	4 673 ..	....	....	....	....	....	....	....	....
Other sectors..........	4 674 ..	....	....	....	....	....	....	....	....
Money market instruments..........	4 680 ..	....	....	....	....	....	....	....	....
Monetary authorities..........	4 681 ..	....	....	....	....	....	....	....	....
General government..........	4 682 ..	....	....	....	....	....	....	....	....
Banks..........	4 683 ..	....	....	....	....	....	....	....	....
Other sectors..........	4 684 ..	....	....	....	....	....	....	....	....
C. FINANCIAL DERIVATIVES..........	4 910 ..	....	....	....	....	....	....	....	....
Monetary authorities..........	4 911 ..	....	....	....	....	....	....	....	....
General government..........	4 912 ..	....	....	....	....	....	....	....	....
Banks..........	4 913 ..	....	....	....	....	....	....	....	....
Other sectors..........	4 914 ..	....	....	....	....	....	....	....	....
Assets..........	4 900 ..	....	....	....	....	....	....	....	....
Monetary authorities..........	4 901 ..	....	....	....	....	....	....	....	....
General government..........	4 902 ..	....	....	....	....	....	....	....	....
Banks..........	4 903 ..	....	....	....	....	....	....	....	....
Other sectors..........	4 904 ..	....	....	....	....	....	....	....	....
Liabilities..........	4 905 ..	....	....	....	....	....	....	....	....
Monetary authorities..........	4 906 ..	....	....	....	....	....	....	....	....
General government..........	4 907 ..	....	....	....	....	....	....	....	....
Banks..........	4 908 ..	....	....	....	....	....	....	....	....
Other sectors..........	4 909 ..	....	....	....	....	....	....	....	....

2011, International Monetary Fund: *Balance of Payments Statistics Yearbook*

Table 2 (Concluded). STANDARD PRESENTATION, 2003–2010

(Millions of U.S. dollars)

	Code	2003	2004	2005	2006	2007	2008	2009	2010
D. OTHER INVESTMENT	4 700 ..	**−11.5**	**−274.9**	**165.7**	**140.7**	**411.8**	**366.1**	**298.2**	**−98.3**
Assets	4 703 ..	**8.1**	**−231.4**	**84.3**	**101.2**	**357.8**	**190.1**	**249.7**	**−161.6**
Trade credits	4 706 ..	21.3	−2.2	−18.0	−45.9	6.7	−11.4	3.8	−10.1
General government	4 707 ..	....	....	....	....	....	....	....	....
of which: Short-term	4 709 ..	....	....	....	....	....	....	....	....
Other sectors	4 710 ..	21.3	−2.2	−18.0	−45.9	6.7	−11.4	3.8	−10.1
of which: Short-term	4 712 ..	*21.3*	*−2.2*	*−18.0*	*−45.9*	*6.7*	*−11.4*	*3.8*	*−7.5*
Loans	4 714 ..	−5.3	3.4	−.3	−5.2	−2.9	−3.1	1.5	−7.1
Monetary authorities	4 715 ..	....	....	....	....	....	....	....	....
of which: Short-term	4 718 ..	....	....	....	....	....	....	....	....
General government	4 719 ..	....	....	....	....	....	....	....	....
of which: Short-term	4 721 ..	....	....	....	....	....	....	....	....
Banks	4 722 ..	....	....	....	....	....	....	....	....
of which: Short-term	4 724 ..	....	....	....	....	....	....	....	....
Other sectors	4 725 ..	−5.3	3.4	−.3	−5.2	−2.9	−3.1	1.5	−7.1
of which: Short-term	4 727 ..	....	....	....	....	....	....	*.3*	*−8.0*
Currency and deposits	4 730 ..	54.7	−18.3	17.1	−130.3	47.4	−219.4	−118.2	−81.2
Monetary authorities	4 731 ..	....	....	....	....	....	....	....	....
General government	4 732 ..	....	....	....	....	....	....	....	....
Banks	4 733 ..	35.7	−1.6	17.7	−68.5	23.0	−89.4	−85.6	−105.2
Other sectors	4 734 ..	19.0	−16.7	−.6	−61.7	24.4	−130.1	−32.6	23.9
Other assets	4 736 ..	−62.6	−214.4	85.6	282.5	306.6	424.0	362.6	−63.1
Monetary authorities	4 737 ..	....	....	....	....	....	....	....	....
of which: Short-term	4 739 ..	....	....	....	....	....	....	....	....
General government	4 740 ..	−26.5	−27.3	202.1	427.4	444.0	438.7	401.6	....
of which: Short-term	4 742 ..	*−26.5*	*−27.3*	*202.1*	*427.4*	*444.0*	*438.7*	*401.6*	....
Banks	4 743 ..	....	....	....	....	....	....	....	3.1
of which: Short-term	4 745 ..	....	....	....	....	....	....	....	....
Other sectors	4 746 ..	−36.1	−187.1	−116.6	−144.8	−137.5	−14.7	−39.0	−66.3
of which: Short-term	4 748 ..	....	....	....	....	....	....	....	....
Liabilities	4 753 ..	**−19.6**	**−43.5**	**81.4**	**39.5**	**54.0**	**176.0**	**48.4**	**63.3**
Trade credits	4 756 ..	1.9	−1.3	16.9	3.6	−7.4	29.3	.9	8.7
General government	4 757 ..	....	....	....	....	....	....	....	....
of which: Short-term	4 759 ..	....	....	....	....	....	....	....	....
Other sectors	4 760 ..	1.9	−1.3	16.9	3.6	−7.4	29.3	.9	8.7
of which: Short-term	4 762 ..	*1.9*	*−1.3*	*16.9*	*3.6*	*−7.4*	*29.3*	*1.2*	*10.8*
Loans	4 764 ..	−2.8	6.5	63.0	30.7	65.8	84.7	22.5	−17.0
Monetary authorities	4 765 ..	....	....	....	....	....	....	....	....
of which: Use of Fund credit and loans from the Fund	4 766 ..	....	....	....	....	....	....	....	....
of which: Short-term	4 768 ..	....	....	....	....	....	....	....	....
General government	4 769 ..	−1.7	8.4	27.9	29.5	27.0	−9.3	−21.1	−18.4
of which: Short-term	4 771 ..	....	....	....	....	....	....	....	....
Banks	4 772 ..	....	....	....	....	....	....	17.7	−4.0
of which: Short-term	4 774 ..	....	....	....	....	....	....	....	....
Other sectors	4 775 ..	−1.0	−1.9	35.1	1.2	38.7	94.0	26.0	5.4
of which: Short-term	4 777 ..	....	....	....	....	....	....	*22.5*	....
Currency and deposits	4 780 ..	−2.7	−46.5	−1.2	−.2	4.4	−.6	−20.1	29.9
Monetary authorities	4 781 ..	−2.7	−46.5	−1.2	−.2	4.4	−.6	−1.7	10.6
General government	4 782 ..	....	....	....	....	....	....	....	....
Banks	4 783 ..	....	....	....	....	....	....	....	....
Other sectors	4 784 ..	....	....	....	....	....	....	−18.4	19.3
Other liabilities	4 786 ..	−16.1	−2.2	2.7	5.5	−8.8	62.6	45.1	41.6
Monetary authorities	4 787 ..	....	....	....	....	....	....	65.4	....
of which: Short-term	4 789 ..	....	....	....	....	....	....	....	....
General government	4 790 ..	....	....	....	....	....	....	....	....
of which: Short-term	4 792 ..	....	....	....	....	....	....	....	....
Banks	4 793 ..	−3.2	−1.7	4.4	7.8	−9.0	31.2	−21.4	−4.0
of which: Short-term	4 795 ..	*−3.2*	*−1.7*	*4.4*	*7.8*	*−9.0*	*31.2*	*−21.4*	*−4.0*
Other sectors	4 796 ..	−12.8	−.5	−1.7	−2.3	.2	31.4	1.1	45.6
of which: Short-term	4 798 ..	*−12.8*	*−.5*	*−1.7*	*−2.3*	*.2*	*31.4*	*1.1*	*45.6*
E. RESERVE ASSETS	4 802 ..	**91.8**	**−34.4**	**.6**	**151.2**	**365.2**	**−220.1**	**.3**	**230.6**
Monetary gold	4 812 ..	....	....	.3	....	....	....	....	....
Special drawing rights	4 811 ..	....	....	....	....	....	−.1	−65.4	....
Reserve position in the Fund	4 810 ..	....	....	....	....	....	....	....	....
Foreign exchange	4 803 ..	91.8	−34.4	.3	151.2	365.3	−220.0	65.7	230.6
Other claims	4 813 ..	....	....	....	....	....	....	....	....
NET ERRORS AND OMISSIONS	4 998 ..	**−92.1**	**168.2**	**−40.8**	**−237.8**	**−700.8**	**12.0**	**−55.0**	**55.5**

Table 3. INTERNATIONAL INVESTMENT POSITION (End-period stocks), 2003–2010

(Millions of U.S. dollars)

	Code	2003	2004	2005	2006	2007	2008	2009	2010
ASSETS....................	8 995 C.	**1,486.7**	**1,893.5**	**1,981.5**	**2,693.1**	**3,226.8**	**1,585.0**	**3,442.0**	**3,519.9**
Direct investment abroad....................	8 505 ..	**94.7**	**110.0**	**75.8**	**68.2**	**92.3**	**22.2**	**31.4**	**24.9**
Equity capital and reinvested earnings........	8 506 ..	1.5	1.7	1.6	1.2	21.0	19.4	26.4	18.4
Claims on affiliated enterprises.............	8 507 ..	1.5	1.7	1.6	1.2	21.0	19.4	26.4	18.4
Liabilities to affiliated enterprises.........	8 508 ..	....	....	....	....	....	....	....	....
Other capital....................	8 530 ..	93.2	108.3	74.1	67.0	71.3	2.9	5.0	6.6
Claims on affiliated enterprises.............	8 535 ..	93.2	108.3	74.1	67.0	71.3	2.9	5.0	6.6
Liabilities to affiliated enterprises.........	8 540 ..	....	....	....	....	....	....	....	....
Portfolio investment....................	8 602 ..	**14.2**	**17.8**	**12.1**	**20.2**	**16.2**	**8.8**	**1,454.4**	**1,611.1**
Equity securities....................	8 610 ..	2.9	3.1	2.8	2.4	2.5	....	739.0	991.7
Monetary authorities....................	8 611 ..	....	....	....	....	....	....	....	....
General government....................	8 612 ..	....	....	....	....	....	....	....	....
Banks....................	8 613 ..	....	....	....	....	....	....	....	....
Other sectors....................	8 614 ..	2.9	3.1	2.8	2.4	2.5	....	739.0	991.7
Debt securities....................	8 619 ..	11.3	14.7	9.3	17.8	13.7	8.8	715.5	619.3
Bonds and notes....................	8 620 ..	11.3	14.5	9.2	8.7	13.6	8.7	83.4	130.8
Monetary authorities....................	8 621 ..	....	....	....	....	....	....	....	....
General government....................	8 622 ..	....	....	....	....	....	....	....	....
Banks....................	8 623 ..	....	....	....	....	....	....	....	....
Other sectors....................	8 624 ..	11.3	14.5	9.2	8.7	13.6	8.7	83.4	130.8
Money market instruments....................	8 630 ..	....	.1	.1	9.1	.1	.1	632.0	488.5
Monetary authorities....................	8 631 ..	....	....	....	....	....	....	....	....
General government....................	8 632 ..	....	....	....	....	....	....	....	....
Banks....................	8 633 ..	....	....	....	....	....	....	....	....
Other sectors....................	8 634 ..	....	.1	.1	9.1	.1	.1	632.0	488.5
Financial derivatives....................	8 900 ..	....	....	....	....	....	....	....	....
Monetary authorities....................	8 901 ..	....	....	....	....	....	....	....	....
General government....................	8 902 ..	....	....	....	....	....	....	....	....
Banks....................	8 903 ..	....	....	....	....	....	....	....	....
Other sectors....................	8 904 ..	....	....	....	....	....	....	....	....
Other investment....................	8 703 ..	**1,103.3**	**1,481.9**	**1,641.1**	**2,221.3**	**2,457.1**	**795.1**	**1,078.2**	**1,206.2**
Trade credits....................	8 706 ..	120.6	144.7	146.9	177.9	139.2	8.5	153.6	208.7
General government....................	8 707 ..	....	....	....	....	....	....	....	....
of which: Short-term....................	8 709 ..	....	....	....	....	....	....	....	....
Other sectors....................	8 710 ..	120.6	144.7	146.9	177.9	139.2	8.5	153.6	208.7
of which: Short-term....................	8 712 ..	*120.6*	*144.7*	*146.9*	*177.9*	*139.2*	*8.5*	*153.6*	*208.7*
Loans....................	8 714 ..	6.5	3.8	3.7	8.3	3.2	16.4	74.8	84.6
Monetary authorities....................	8 715 ..	....	....	....	....	....	....	....	....
of which: Short-term....................	8 718 ..	....	....	....	....	....	....	....	....
General government....................	8 719 ..	....	....	....	....	....	....	....	....
of which: Short-term....................	8 721 ..	....	....	....	....	....	....	....	....
Banks....................	8 722 ..	....	....	....	....	....	....	....	....
of which: Short-term....................	8 724 ..	....	....	....	....	....	....	....	....
Other sectors....................	8 725 ..	6.5	3.8	3.7	8.3	3.2	16.4	74.8	84.6
of which: Short-term....................	8 727 ..	....	....	....	....	....	*1.2*	*56.2*	*69.4*
Currency and deposits....................	8 730 ..	178.8	231.8	189.1	298.2	295.0	162.6	489.2	595.6
Monetary authorities....................	8 731 ..	....	....	....	....	....	....	....	....
General government....................	8 732 ..	....	....	....	....	....	....	....	....
Banks....................	8 733 ..	78.5	94.4	66.2	126.7	96.4	161.6	192.5	330.3
Other sectors....................	8 734 ..	100.3	137.4	122.9	171.5	198.5	1.0	296.7	265.3
Other assets....................	8 736 ..	797.3	1,101.6	1,301.3	1,736.8	2,019.8	607.6	360.6	317.3
Monetary authorities....................	8 737 ..	....	....	....	....	....	....	....	....
of which: Short-term....................	8 739 ..	....	....	....	....	....	....	....	....
General government....................	8 740 ..	−86.7	−134.0	84.3	491.7	645.7	607.6	....	....
of which: Short-term....................	8 742 ..	*−87.3*	*−134.3*	*83.7*	*491.1*	*645.1*	*607.6*	....	....
Banks....................	8 743 ..	....	....	....	....	....	....	3.8	.7
of which: Short-term....................	8 745 ..	....	....	....	....	....	....	....	....
Other sectors....................	8 746 ..	884.0	1,235.6	1,217.0	1,245.1	1,374.1	....	356.8	316.6
of which: Short-term....................	8 748 ..	....	....	....	....	....	....	....	....
Reserve assets....................	8 802 ..	**274.5**	**283.8**	**252.5**	**383.5**	**661.2**	**758.8**	**878.0**	**677.6**
Monetary gold....................	8 812 ..	....	....	....	....	....	....	....	....
Special drawing rights....................	8 811 ..	3.7	3.8	3.5	3.7	4.0	3.9	69.6	68.4
Reserve position in the Fund....................	8 810 ..	9.7	10.2	9.4	9.9	10.4	10.1	10.3	10.1
Foreign exchange....................	8 803 ..	261.1	269.8	239.6	369.9	646.8	744.8	798.1	599.1
Other claims....................	8 813 ..	....	....	....	....	....	....	....	....

Table 3 (Concluded). INTERNATIONAL INVESTMENT POSITION (End-period stocks), 2003–2010

(Millions of U.S. dollars)

	Code	2003	2004	2005	2006	2007	2008	2009	2010
LIABILITIES	8 995 D.	**1,208.5**	**1,442.3**	**1,295.3**	**1,347.4**	**1,380.0**	**1,073.7**	**1,781.3**	**2,137.5**
Direct investment in Swaziland	8 555 ..	**726.6**	**935.0**	**786.2**	**831.0**	**719.5**	**516.1**	**893.2**	**1,107.2**
Equity capital and reinvested earnings	8 556 ..	491.6	616.8	533.1	560.1	570.3	312.0	571.4	707.9
Claims on direct investors	8 557 ..	491.6	616.8	533.1	560.1	570.3	312.0	....	....
Liabilities to direct investors	8 558 ..	....	....	....	....	....	....	571.4	707.9
Other capital	8 580 ..	235.0	318.2	253.1	270.9	149.2	204.1	321.8	399.3
Claims on direct investors	8 585 ..	235.0	318.2	253.1	270.9	149.2	204.1	....	....
Liabilities to direct investors	8 590 ..	....	....	....	....	....	....	321.8	399.3
Portfolio investment	8 652 ..	**1.2**	**1.1**	**1.7**	**6.9**	**1.9**	**44.8**	**2.4**	**3.7**
Equity securities	8 660 ..	1.2	1.1	1.7	6.9	1.9	44.8	2.4	3.7
Banks	8 663 ..	....	....	....	....	....	....	....	....
Other sectors	8 664 ..	1.2	1.1	1.7	6.9	1.9	44.8	2.4	3.7
Debt securities	8 669 ..	....	....	....	....	....	....	....	....
Bonds and notes	8 670 ..	....	....	....	....	....	....	....	....
Monetary authorities	8 671 ..	....	....	....	....	....	....	....	....
General government	8 672 ..	....	....	....	....	....	....	....	....
Banks	8 673 ..	....	....	....	....	....	....	....	....
Other sectors	8 674 ..	....	....	....	....	....	....	....	....
Money market instruments	8 680 ..	....	....	....	....	....	....	....	....
Monetary authorities	8 681 ..	....	....	....	....	....	....	....	....
General government	8 682 ..	....	....	....	....	....	....	....	....
Banks	8 683 ..	....	....	....	....	....	....	....	....
Other sectors	8 684 ..	....	....	....	....	....	....	....	....
Financial derivatives	8 905 ..	....	....	....	....	....	....	....	....
Monetary authorities	8 906 ..	....	....	....	....	....	....	....	....
General government	8 907 ..	....	....	....	....	....	....	....	....
Banks	8 908 ..	....	....	....	....	....	....	....	....
Other sectors	8 909 ..	....	....	....	....	....	....	....	....
Other investment	8 753 ..	**480.8**	**506.2**	**507.5**	**509.5**	**658.6**	**512.8**	**885.8**	**1,026.6**
Trade credits	8 756 ..	36.5	41.5	54.0	52.4	44.9	34.5	53.3	68.9
General government	8 757 ..	....	....	....	....	....	....	....	....
of which: Short-term	8 759 ..	....	....	....	....	....	....	....	....
Other sectors	8 760 ..	36.5	41.5	54.0	52.4	44.9	34.5	53.3	68.9
of which: Short-term	8 762 ..	*36.5*	*41.5*	*54.0*	*52.4*	*44.9*	*12.2*	*27.9*	*43.0*
Loans	8 764 ..	379.7	445.5	434.9	435.1	600.5	411.1	705.1	747.1
Monetary authorities	8 765 ..	....	....	....	....	....	....	....	....
of which: Use of Fund credit and loans from the Fund....	8 766 ..	....	....	....	....	....	....	....	....
of which: Short-term	8 768 ..	....	....	....	....	....	....	....	....
General government	8 769 ..	352.2	415.3	372.8	377.5	417.3	248.6	402.8	383.4
of which: Short-term	8 771 ..	....	....	....	....	....	....	....	....
Banks	8 772 ..	....	....	....	....	....	37.6	33.9	33.3
of which: Short-term	8 774 ..	....	....	....	....	....	....	....	....
Other sectors	8 775 ..	27.5	30.2	62.2	57.6	183.2	124.9	268.4	330.4
of which: Short-term	8 777 ..	....	....	....	....	....	*16.1*	*84.4*	*160.8*
Currency and deposits	8 780 ..	56.9	11.8	13.7	19.8	10.7	22.5	7.9	41.8
Monetary authorities	8 781 ..	49.1	4.5	2.8	2.4	2.5	4.4	1.8	13.7
General government	8 782 ..	....	....	....	....	....	....	....	....
Banks	8 783 ..	7.8	7.3	10.9	17.4	8.2	17.8	6.0	28.1
Other sectors	8 784 ..	....	....	....	....	....	.2	....	....
Other liabilities	8 786 ..	7.7	7.3	4.8	2.2	2.5	44.8	119.5	168.8
Monetary authorities	8 787 ..	....	....	....	....	....	7.5	75.8	74.4
of which: Short-term	8 789 ..	....	....	....	....	....	....	....	....
General government	8 790 ..	....	....	....	....	....	....	....	....
of which: Short-term	8 792 ..	....	....	....	....	....	....	....	....
Banks	8 793 ..	....	....	....	....	....	35.0	33.9	33.2
of which: Short-term	8 795 ..	....	....	....	....	....	....	....	....
Other sectors	8 796 ..	7.7	7.3	4.8	2.2	2.5	2.3	9.8	61.3
of which: Short-term	8 798 ..	*7.7*	*7.3*	*4.8*	*2.2*	*2.5*	*2.3*	*9.8*	*61.3*
NET INTERNATIONAL INVESTMENT POSITION	8 995 ..	**278.2**	**451.3**	**686.1**	**1,345.7**	**1,846.8**	**511.2**	**1,660.7**	**1,382.3**
Conversion rates: emalangeni per U.S. dollar (end of period)	0 102 ..	**6.640**	**5.630**	**6.325**	**6.970**	**6.810**	**9.305**	**7.380**	**6.632**

Table 1. ANALYTIC PRESENTATION, 2003–2010

(Millions of U.S. dollars)

	Code	2003	2004	2005	2006	2007	2008	2009	2010
A. Current Account[1]	4 993 Z.	**21,581**	**24,600**	**24,260**	**34,197**	**43,009**	**44,171**	**29,844**	**30,408**
Goods: exports f.o.b.	2 100	102,783	123,354	131,743	151,136	172,155	185,494	134,231	160,408
Goods: imports f.o.b.	3 100	−83,922	−100,118	−112,325	−129,346	−154,381	−170,082	−121,188	−149,514
Balance on Goods	4 100	*18,861*	*23,236*	*19,418*	*21,790*	*17,774*	*15,412*	*13,043*	*10,894*
Services: credit	2 200	28,085	37,397	38,352	47,748	61,174	69,503	60,303	65,254
Services: debit	3 200	−27,310	−31,542	−31,785	−37,372	−45,728	−52,289	−44,636	−47,316
Balance on Goods and Services	4 991	*19,635*	*29,090*	*25,984*	*32,166*	*33,220*	*32,625*	*28,710*	*28,831*
Income: credit	2 300	25,372	31,165	38,650	50,609	69,155	74,272	47,472	54,561
Income: debit	3 300	−21,288	−30,727	−35,700	−43,524	−54,299	−56,441	−40,992	−46,780
Balance on Goods, Services, and Income	4 992	*23,719*	*29,528*	*28,935*	*39,251*	*48,077*	*50,456*	*35,190*	*36,612*
Current transfers: credit	2 379 Z.	3,552	4,076	4,864	5,098	5,602	6,784	4,854	5,255
Current transfers: debit	3 379	−5,690	−9,004	−9,539	−10,153	−10,669	−13,068	−10,200	−11,460
B. Capital Account[1]	4 994 Z.	**132**	**....**	**392**	**−2,455**	**−175**	**−582**	**−382**	**−828**
Capital account: credit	2 994 Z.	511	545	392	414	878	613	948	571
Capital account: debit	3 994	−379	−545	....	−2,869	−1,053	−1,195	−1,331	−1,399
Total, Groups A Plus B	4 981	*21,712*	*24,600*	*24,652*	*31,742*	*42,834*	*43,589*	*29,462*	*29,580*
C. Financial Account[1]	4 995 W.	**−19,922**	**−28,094**	**−28,302**	**−31,259**	**−11,600**	**24,023**	**9,118**	**−42,699**
Direct investment abroad	4 505	−21,281	−22,445	−28,141	−26,194	−37,749	−32,012	−26,609	−32,135
Direct investment in Sweden	4 555 Z.	5,009	12,118	12,128	28,488	27,788	38,190	10,845	5,847
Portfolio investment assets	4 602	−13,525	−25,083	−13,132	−33,142	−49,862	−20,178	−18,245	−18,657
Equity securities	4 610	−4,623	−6,330	118	−22,096	−8,211	−1,071	−16,224	−7,463
Debt securities	4 619	−8,902	−18,753	−13,250	−11,046	−41,651	−19,107	−2,021	−11,193
Portfolio investment liabilities	4 652 Z.	3,986	−60	13,789	13,352	64,102	−7,278	82,045	40,408
Equity securities	4 660	432	−92	2,170	262	4,081	−1,821	1,155	5,474
Debt securities	4 669 Z.	3,554	32	11,619	13,091	60,021	−5,457	80,890	34,934
Financial derivatives	4 910	1,091	−410	−897	172	−1,407	1,053	−2,324	4,187
Financial derivatives assets	4 900	40,041	27,605	29,435	29,165	39,125	78,680	118,044	107,383
Financial derivatives liabilities	4 905	−38,950	−28,015	−30,332	−28,994	−40,533	−77,627	−120,369	−103,196
Other investment assets	4 703	−8,320	−19,605	−13,474	−50,880	−47,258	847	13,893	−30,548
Monetary authorities	4 701	....	....	....	....	....	....	42	....
General government	4 704	365	−385	121	−295	42	−1,334	−23	−398
Banks	4 705	−11,333	−16,848	−14,158	−45,151	−46,982	−3,701	7,516	−25,216
Other sectors	4 728	2,648	−2,372	563	−5,433	−318	5,881	6,358	−4,933
Other investment liabilities	4 753 W.	13,120	27,392	1,425	36,945	32,786	43,401	−50,485	−11,802
Monetary authorities	4 753 WA	2,584	2,382	2,122	1,477	−233	26,843	−19,447	−523
General government	4 753 ZB	−837	−692	−170	−793	317	−36	203	−336
Banks	4 753 ZC	4,433	25,755	2,151	39,058	27,068	11,215	−29,875	−1,915
Other sectors	4 753 ZD	6,941	−53	−2,678	−2,796	5,634	5,378	−1,367	−9,028
Total, Groups A Through C	4 983	*1,791*	*−3,494*	*−3,649*	*483*	*31,234*	*67,612*	*38,580*	*−13,120*
D. Net Errors and Omissions	4 998	**23**	**2,152**	**4,062**	**1,184**	**−31,248**	**−65,861**	**−23,421**	**12,042**
Total, Groups A Through D	4 984	*1,814*	*−1,341*	*412*	*1,667*	*−14*	*1,750*	*15,159*	*−1,078*
E. Reserves and Related Items	4 802 A.	**−1,814**	**1,341**	**−412**	**−1,667**	**14**	**−1,750**	**−15,159**	**1,078**
Reserve assets	4 802	−1,814	1,341	−412	−1,667	14	−1,750	−15,159	1,078
Use of Fund credit and loans	4 766	....	....	....	....	....	....	....	....
Exceptional financing	4 920	....	....	....	....	....	....	....	....
Conversion rates: kronor per U.S. dollar	0 101	**8.0863**	**7.3489**	**7.4731**	**7.3782**	**6.7588**	**6.5911**	**7.6538**	**7.2075**

[1] Excludes components that have been classified in the categories of Group E.

2011, International Monetary Fund: *Balance of Payments Statistics Yearbook*

Table 2. STANDARD PRESENTATION, 2003–2010

(Millions of U.S. dollars)

	Code	2003	2004	2005	2006	2007	2008	2009	2010
CURRENT ACCOUNT	4 993 ..	**21,581**	**24,600**	**24,260**	**34,197**	**43,009**	**44,171**	**29,844**	**30,408**
A. GOODS	4 100 ..	**18,861**	**23,236**	**19,418**	**21,790**	**17,774**	**15,412**	**13,043**	**10,894**
Credit	2 100 ..	**102,783**	**123,354**	**131,743**	**151,136**	**172,155**	**185,494**	**134,231**	**160,408**
General merchandise: exports f.o.b.	2 110 ..	102,287	122,809	130,669	149,636	170,520	183,655	132,912	158,740
Goods for processing: exports f.o.b.	2 150 ..	....	....	....	....	....	....	....	....
Repairs on goods	2 160 ..	....	....	537	543	592	613	525	556
Goods procured in ports by carriers	2 170 ..	496	545	537	957	1,042	1,226	794	1,112
Nonmonetary gold	2 180 ..	....	....	....	....	....	....	....	....
Debit	3 100 ..	**−83,922**	**−100,118**	**−112,325**	**−129,346**	**−154,381**	**−170,082**	**−121,188**	**−149,514**
General merchandise: imports f.o.b.	3 110 ..	−83,172	−99,164	−110,459	−127,445	−152,299	−167,630	−119,332	−147,424
Goods for processing: imports f.o.b.	3 150 ..	....	....	....	....	....	....	....	....
Repairs on goods	3 160 ..	....	....	−537	−543	−592	−613	−525	−556
Goods procured in ports by carriers	3 170 ..	−750	−954	−1,329	−1,359	−1,489	−1,840	−1,331	−1,534
Nonmonetary gold	3 180 ..	....	....	....	....	....	....	....	....
B. SERVICES	4 200 ..	**775**	**5,854**	**6,567**	**10,376**	**15,446**	**17,214**	**15,666**	**17,937**
Total credit	2 200 ..	*28,085*	*37,397*	*38,352*	*47,748*	*61,174*	*69,503*	*60,303*	*65,254*
Total debit	3 200 ..	*−27,310*	*−31,542*	*−31,785*	*−37,372*	*−45,728*	*−52,289*	*−44,636*	*−47,316*
Transportation services, credit	2 205 ..	**6,733**	**8,325**	**8,375**	**8,870**	**11,008**	**12,625**	**9,879**	**9,882**
Passenger	2 850 ..	*1,246*	*1,499*	*1,074*	*1,224*	*1,635*	*1,840*	*1,982*	*2,223*
Freight	2 851 ..	*4,373*	*5,328*	*5,711*	*5,868*	*6,848*	*8,325*	*6,041*	*5,289*
Other	2 852 ..	*1,114*	*1,499*	*1,591*	*1,779*	*2,526*	*2,460*	*1,856*	*2,369*
Sea transport, passenger	2 207 ..	....	....	....	....	....	....	....	....
Sea transport, freight	2 208 ..	3,250	3,693	3,975	3,963	4,478	5,130	3,701	3,621
Sea transport, other	2 209 ..	123	409	392	414	592	454	280	417
Air transport, passenger	2 211 ..	1,246	1,499	1,074	1,224	1,635	1,840	1,982	2,223
Air transport, freight	2 212 ..	....	....	....	....	....	....	....	....
Air transport, other	2 213 ..	496	545	537	543	748	780	525	556
Other transport, passenger	2 215 ..	....	....	....	....	....	....	....	....
Other transport, freight	2 216 ..	1,123	1,635	1,736	1,905	2,370	3,194	2,341	1,668
Other transport, other	2 217 ..	496	545	662	822	1,185	1,226	1,051	1,397
Transportation services, debit	3 205 ..	**−4,592**	**−5,045**	**−5,349**	**−5,579**	**−6,980**	**−9,278**	**−7,057**	**−8,068**
Passenger	3 850 ..	*−1,108*	*−1,090*	*−1,074*	*−1,086*	*−1,777*	*−1,840*	*−1,576*	*−2,094*
Freight	3 851 ..	*−1,619*	*−1,912*	*−2,272*	*−2,450*	*−2,976*	*−3,966*	*−2,346*	*−2,640*
Other	3 852 ..	*−1,865*	*−2,043*	*−2,003*	*−2,043*	*−2,227*	*−3,473*	*−3,135*	*−3,334*
Sea transport, passenger	3 207 ..	....	....	....	....	....	....	....	....
Sea transport, freight	3 208 ..	−1,619	−1,912	−2,272	−2,450	−2,976	−3,353	−2,101	−2,640
Sea transport, other	3 209 ..	−874	−954	−929	−957	−1,042	−1,346	−1,457	−1,110
Air transport, passenger	3 211 ..	−1,108	−1,090	−1,074	−1,086	−1,777	−1,840	−1,576	−2,094
Air transport, freight	3 212 ..	....	....	....	....	....	....	....	....
Air transport, other	3 213 ..	−496	−545	−537	−543	−592	−1,067	−908	−556
Other transport, passenger	3 215 ..	....	....	....	....	....	....	....	....
Other transport, freight	3 216 ..	....	....	....	....	....	−613	−245	....
Other transport, other	3 217 ..	−496	−545	−537	−543	−592	−1,059	−770	−1,668
Travel, credit	2 236 ..	**4,704**	**5,709**	**6,665**	**8,170**	**10,642**	**11,026**	**10,275**	**11,093**
Business travel	2 237 ..	....	....	....	3,266	4,285	4,450	4,078	4,436
Personal travel	2 240 ..	....	....	....	4,904	6,357	6,576	6,197	6,657
Travel, debit	3 236 ..	**−8,058**	**−9,939**	**−10,718**	**−11,151**	**−13,496**	**−14,618**	**−11,856**	**−13,079**
Business travel	3 237 ..	−2,601	−3,403	−3,487	−3,671	−4,153	−4,451	−3,695	−3,758
Personal travel	3 240 ..	−5,457	−6,536	−7,230	−7,480	−9,343	−10,167	−8,161	−9,322
Other services, credit	2 200 BA	**16,648**	**23,363**	**23,311**	**30,708**	**39,524**	**45,852**	**40,149**	**44,279**
Communications	2 245 ..	496	1,092	1,199	1,628	1,635	1,968	1,975	1,677
Construction	2 249 ..	752	689	662	543	894	900	525	556
Insurance	2 253 ..	371	954	1,074	1,086	741	1,226	1,051	556
Financial	2 260 ..	991	1,233	1,610	1,892	1,185	1,226	1,051	1,112
Computer and information	2 262 ..	1,858	2,455	2,535	3,398	6,392	7,841	7,275	7,386
Royalties and licence fees	2 266 ..	2,237	3,557	3,452	3,947	4,753	4,588	4,835	6,133
Other business services	2 268 ..	9,943	13,384	12,654	18,214	23,625	27,353	22,493	26,441
Personal, cultural, and recreational	2 287 ..	....	....	....	....	....	454	269	....
Government, n.i.e.	2 291 ..	....	....	125	....	298	295	675	418
Other services, debit	3 200 BA	**−14,660**	**−16,558**	**−15,718**	**−20,642**	**−25,253**	**−28,393**	**−25,723**	**−26,169**
Communications	3 245 ..	−867	−1,233	−1,469	−1,628	−1,777	−1,840	−2,220	−2,362
Construction	3 249 ..	−620	−423	−400	−668	−1,042	−1,226	−1,177	−1,397
Insurance	3 253 ..	−117	−136	−411	−129	−143	....	....	....
Financial	3 260 ..	−496	−545	−662	−944	−592	−613	−525	−556
Computer and information	3 262 ..	−991	−1,233	−1,336	−2,046	−2,824	−3,194	−2,608	−2,642
Royalties and licence fees	3 266 ..	−1,370	−1,365	−1,591	−1,628	−1,933	−1,840	−1,832	−1,383
Other business services	3 268 ..	−10,200	−11,622	−9,849	−13,598	−16,940	−19,680	−17,242	−17,829
Personal, cultural, and recreational	3 287 ..	....	....	....	....	....	....	−119	....
Government, n.i.e.	3 291 ..	....	....	....	....	....	....	....	....

Table 2 (Continued). STANDARD PRESENTATION, 2003–2010

(Millions of U.S. dollars)

	Code	2003	2004	2005	2006	2007	2008	2009	2010
C. INCOME	4 300	**4,083**	**438**	**2,951**	**7,085**	**14,856**	**17,831**	**6,481**	**7,781**
Total credit	2 300	*25,372*	*31,165*	*38,650*	*50,609*	*69,155*	*74,272*	*47,472*	*54,561*
Total debit	3 300	*−21,288*	*−30,727*	*−35,700*	*−43,524*	*−54,299*	*−56,441*	*−40,992*	*−46,780*
Compensation of employees, credit	2 310	**496**	**545**	**537**	**543**	**592**	**613**	**525**	**556**
Compensation of employees, debit	3 310	**−496**	**−545**	**−537**	**−543**	**−741**	**−742**	**−787**	**−695**
Investment income, credit	2 320	**24,876**	**30,620**	**38,114**	**50,067**	**68,563**	**73,659**	**46,947**	**54,005**
Direct investment income	2 330	16,982	20,850	26,034	32,982	42,671	42,145	27,433	34,592
Dividends and distributed branch profits	2 332	6,288	16,403	12,238	26,719	17,116	27,834	18,420	10,829
Reinvested earnings and undistributed branch profits	2 333	9,207	2,669	11,524	3,678	21,987	10,503	6,267	21,687
Income on debt (interest)	2 334	1,487	1,778	2,272	2,585	3,568	3,808	2,745	2,076
Portfolio investment income	2 339	5,416	6,910	8,341	10,681	16,981	19,835	13,982	15,237
Income on equity	2 340	2,581	3,375	4,458	5,796	8,956	11,173	8,204	9,408
Income on bonds and notes	2 350	2,836	3,534	3,757	4,480	7,724	8,178	5,778	5,829
Income on money market instruments	2 360	....	....	125	405	301	485	....	....
Other investment income	2 370	2,478	2,861	3,738	6,404	8,910	11,678	5,533	4,176
Investment income, debit	3 320	**−20,793**	**−30,182**	**−35,163**	**−42,981**	**−53,558**	**−55,700**	**−40,205**	**−46,085**
Direct investment income	3 330	−7,434	−15,257	−16,765	−19,274	−25,645	−21,878	−20,044	−24,737
Dividends and distributed branch profits	3 332	−3,475	−7,059	−7,822	−12,627	−12,392	−13,156	−12,450	−9,531
Reinvested earnings and undistributed branch profits	3 333	−985	−4,929	−5,722	−2,706	−7,907	−948	−2,383	−10,612
Income on debt (interest)	3 334	−2,974	−3,269	−3,221	−3,941	−5,345	−7,774	−5,211	−4,594
Portfolio investment income	3 339	−9,402	−10,421	−12,512	−16,096	−17,966	−21,954	−15,023	−17,458
Income on equity	3 340	−1,847	−2,520	−3,692	−5,105	−6,841	−9,019	−3,535	−3,832
Income on bonds and notes	3 350	−6,942	−7,356	−7,891	−9,626	−9,043	−10,028	−10,599	−13,340
Income on money market instruments	3 360	−612	−545	−929	−1,365	−2,082	−2,907	−889	−285
Other investment income	3 370	−3,957	−4,505	−5,885	−7,612	−9,947	−11,868	−5,137	−3,891
D. CURRENT TRANSFERS	4 379	**−2,138**	**−4,928**	**−4,675**	**−5,054**	**−5,067**	**−6,285**	**−5,346**	**−6,204**
Credit	2 379	**3,552**	**4,076**	**4,864**	**5,098**	**5,602**	**6,784**	**4,854**	**5,255**
General government	2 380	496	808	947	1,346	1,768	2,434	1,413	1,502
Other sectors	2 390	3,057	3,267	3,917	3,752	3,834	4,349	3,441	3,754
Workers' remittances	2 391	124	132	137	135	146	167	126	132
Other current transfers	2 392	2,932	3,136	3,781	3,617	3,688	4,182	3,315	3,622
Debit	3 379	**−5,690**	**−9,004**	**−9,539**	**−10,153**	**−10,669**	**−13,068**	**−10,200**	**−11,460**
General government	3 380	−3,723	−6,011	−6,308	−6,089	−6,532	−7,995	−6,270	−7,723
Other sectors	3 390	−1,967	−2,992	−3,232	−4,063	−4,137	−5,073	−3,929	−3,736
Workers' remittances	3 391	....	....	....	....	....	....	....	....
Other current transfers	3 392	−1,967	−2,992	−3,232	−4,063	−4,137	−5,073	−3,929	−3,736
CAPITAL AND FINANCIAL ACCOUNT	4 996	**−21,604**	**−26,752**	**−28,322**	**−35,381**	**−11,761**	**21,690**	**−6,423**	**−42,450**
CAPITAL ACCOUNT	4 994	**132**	**....**	**392**	**−2,455**	**−175**	**−582**	**−382**	**−828**
Total credit	2 994	*511*	*545*	*392*	*414*	*878*	*613*	*948*	*571*
Total debit	3 994	*−379*	*−545*	*....*	*−2,869*	*−1,053*	*−1,195*	*−1,331*	*−1,399*
Capital transfers, credit	2 400	**511**	**545**	**392**	**414**	**450**	**613**	**423**	**285**
General government	2 401	....	....	....	....	....	....	....	....
Debt forgiveness	2 402	....	....	....	....	....	....	....	....
Other capital transfers	2 410	....	....	....	....	....	....	....	....
Other sectors	2 430	511	545	392	414	450	613	423	285
Migrants' transfers	2 431	....	....	....	....	....	....	....	....
Debt forgiveness	2 432	....	....	....	....	....	....	....	....
Other capital transfers	2 440	....	....	....	....	....	....	....	....
Capital transfers, debit	3 400	**−379**	**−545**	**....**	**−941**	**−897**	**−742**	**−805**	**−844**
General government	3 401	−379	−545	....	−941	−897	−742	−805	−844
Debt forgiveness	3 402	....	....	....	....	....	....	....	....
Other capital transfers	3 410	....	....	....	....	....	....	....	....
Other sectors	3 430	....	....	....	....	....	....	....	....
Migrants' transfers	3 431	....	....	....	....	....	....	....	....
Debt forgiveness	3 432	....	....	....	....	....	....	....	....
Other capital transfers	3 440	....	....	....	....	....	....	....	....
Nonproduced nonfinancial assets, credit	2 480	**....**	**....**	**....**	**....**	**428**	**....**	**525**	**286**
Nonproduced nonfinancial assets, debit	3 480	**....**	**....**	**....**	**−1,928**	**−156**	**−454**	**−525**	**−556**

Table 2 (Continued). STANDARD PRESENTATION, 2003–2010

(Millions of U.S. dollars)

	Code	2003	2004	2005	2006	2007	2008	2009	2010
FINANCIAL ACCOUNT	4 995	**−21,735**	**−26,752**	**−28,714**	**−32,926**	**−11,586**	**22,272**	**−6,041**	**−41,622**
A. DIRECT INVESTMENT	4 500	**−16,272**	**−10,327**	**−16,013**	**2,294**	**−9,961**	**6,177**	**−15,765**	**−26,288**
Direct investment abroad	4 505	**−21,281**	**−22,445**	**−28,141**	**−26,194**	**−37,749**	**−32,012**	**−26,609**	**−32,135**
Equity capital	4 510	−15,179	−12,749	−18,296	−19,446	−25,792	−19,393	−29,526	−8,738
Claims on affiliated enterprises	4 515	....	....	....	....	....	....	....	....
Liabilities to affiliated enterprises	4 520	....	....	....	....	....	....	....	....
Reinvested earnings	4 525	−9,207	−2,669	−11,524	−3,678	−21,987	−10,503	−6,267	−21,687
Other capital	4 530	3,105	−7,028	1,679	−3,070	10,030	−2,116	9,184	−1,710
Claims on affiliated enterprises	4 535	1,608	−5,241	−5,079	−2,599	−7,253	−6,576	4,152	−1,295
Liabilities to affiliated enterprises	4 540	1,497	−1,787	6,758	−470	17,283	4,460	5,032	−414
Direct investment in Sweden	4 555	**5,009**	**12,118**	**12,128**	**28,488**	**27,788**	**38,190**	**10,845**	**5,847**
Equity capital	4 560	−2,170	5,343	4,744	12,032	8,060	8,182	12,496	−1,556
Claims on direct investors	4 565	....	....	....	....	....	....	....	....
Liabilities to direct investors	4 570	....	....	....	....	....	....	....	....
Reinvested earnings	4 575	985	4,929	5,722	2,706	7,907	948	2,383	10,612
Other capital	4 580	6,194	1,846	1,662	13,749	11,821	29,059	−4,035	−3,208
Claims on direct investors	4 585	−1,238	−6,349	−998	5,838	716	2,605	7,759	1,574
Liabilities to direct investors	4 590	7,432	8,195	2,660	7,912	11,105	26,454	−11,794	−4,782
B. PORTFOLIO INVESTMENT	4 600	**−9,540**	**−25,143**	**657**	**−19,790**	**14,240**	**−27,455**	**63,800**	**21,751**
Assets	4 602	**−13,525**	**−25,083**	**−13,132**	**−33,142**	**−49,862**	**−20,178**	**−18,245**	**−18,657**
Equity securities	4 610	−4,623	−6,330	118	−22,096	−8,211	−1,071	−16,224	−7,463
Monetary authorities	4 611	....	....	....	....	....	....	....	....
General government	4 612	−2,332	−1,938	630	−2,207	−5,134	−5,359	919	905
Banks	4 613	1,304	−595	−1,599	−9,117	−5,506	4,560	−3,739	−2,592
Other sectors	4 614	−3,595	−3,797	1,087	−10,771	2,429	−271	−13,403	−5,776
Debt securities	4 619	−8,902	−18,753	−13,250	−11,046	−41,651	−19,107	−2,021	−11,193
Bonds and notes	4 620	−3,941	−9,498	−4,073	−11,206	−34,782	−10,985	3,672	−7,711
Monetary authorities	4 621	....	....	....	....	....	....	....	....
General government	4 622	−1,148	−2,368	−4,247	−1,695	−5,142	7,825	−1,828	911
Banks	4 623	307	−4,637	2,828	−11,893	−28,350	−23,058	−796	−12,381
Other sectors	4 624	−3,101	−2,492	−2,654	2,382	−1,291	4,248	6,296	3,759
Money market instruments	4 630	−4,961	−9,255	−9,177	160	−6,869	−8,122	−5,693	−3,483
Monetary authorities	4 631	....	....	....	....	....	....	....	....
General government	4 632	....	....	....	838	316	−2,837	1,675	182
Banks	4 633	−723	−4,109	−9,347	−1,952	−4,055	−4,511	−5,514	−4,596
Other sectors	4 634	−4,238	−5,147	171	1,274	−3,130	−774	−1,854	932
Liabilities	4 652	**3,986**	**−60**	**13,789**	**13,352**	**64,102**	**−7,278**	**82,045**	**40,408**
Equity securities	4 660	432	−92	2,170	262	4,081	−1,821	1,155	5,474
Banks	4 663	161	−362	477	891	3,106	−1,486	1,323	1,533
Other sectors	4 664	271	271	1,693	−630	975	−335	−168	3,941
Debt securities	4 669	3,554	32	11,619	13,091	60,021	−5,457	80,890	34,934
Bonds and notes	4 670	11,140	9,209	16,385	9,064	47,811	11,506	68,646	25,749
Monetary authorities	4 671	....	....	....	....	....	....	....	....
General government	4 672	1,127	−3,179	−4,325	−8,579	5,180	2,341	12,141	15,547
Banks	4 673	13,198	16,235	19,411	21,328	37,286	16,604	44,979	13,986
Other sectors	4 674	−3,184	−3,846	1,299	−3,686	5,345	−7,439	11,526	−3,784
Money market instruments	4 680	−7,587	−9,178	−4,766	4,027	12,210	−16,963	12,244	9,185
Monetary authorities	4 681	....	....	....	....	−291		1,131	−913
General government	4 682	−3,179	−8,575	−3,245	2,942	4,041	−4,451	9,786	4,062
Banks	4 683	−2,810	4,142	1,734	2,105	9,850	−11,146	3,027	8,972
Other sectors	4 684	−1,598	−4,745	−3,255	−1,020	−1,390	−1,365	−1,700	−2,937
C. FINANCIAL DERIVATIVES	4 910	**1,091**	**−410**	**−897**	**172**	**−1,407**	**1,053**	**−2,324**	**4,187**
Monetary authorities	4 911	....	....	....	....	−148	870	....	....
General government	4 912	508	277	−216	543	1,898	29	1,738	1,184
Banks	4 913	−1,417	−1,388	891	−118	−2,871	−754	−4,871	735
Other sectors	4 914	2,000	701	−1,573	−254	−285	908	809	2,268
Assets	4 900	**40,041**	**27,605**	**29,435**	**29,165**	**39,125**	**78,680**	**118,044**	**107,383**
Monetary authorities	4 901	....	....	....	....	156	870	....	....
General government	4 902	3,791	2,610	4,025	4,757	10,621	14,699	12,615	11,266
Banks	4 903	24,867	15,434	15,341	19,102	20,449	45,018	80,497	81,303
Other sectors	4 904	11,382	9,560	10,070	5,306	7,899	18,093	24,933	14,814
Liabilities	4 905	**−38,950**	**−28,015**	**−30,332**	**−28,994**	**−40,533**	**−77,627**	**−120,369**	**−103,196**
Monetary authorities	4 906	....	....	....	....	−304	....	....	....
General government	4 907	−3,283	−2,333	−4,240	−4,214	−8,724	−14,670	−10,877	−10,082
Banks	4 908	−26,284	−16,822	−14,449	−19,220	−23,321	−45,772	−85,368	−80,568
Other sectors	4 909	−9,383	−8,860	−11,643	−5,560	−8,184	−17,186	−24,124	−12,546

Table 2 (Concluded). STANDARD PRESENTATION, 2003–2010

(Millions of U.S. dollars)

	Code	2003	2004	2005	2006	2007	2008	2009	2010
D. OTHER INVESTMENT	4 700 ..	**4,799**	**7,787**	**−12,049**	**−13,934**	**−14,472**	**44,248**	**−36,593**	**−42,350**
Assets	4 703 ..	**−8,320**	**−19,605**	**−13,474**	**−50,880**	**−47,258**	**847**	**13,893**	**−30,548**
Trade credits	4 706 ..	27	−2,919	28	−2,426	−2,496	3,186	3,640	−1,336
General government	4 707 ..	....	....	....	....	....	....	....	....
of which: Short-term	4 709 ..	....	....	....	....	....	....	....	....
Other sectors	4 710 ..	27	−2,919	28	−2,426	−2,496	3,186	3,640	−1,336
of which: Short-term	4 712 ..	....	....	....	....	....	....	....	....
Loans	4 714 ..	−8,614	−18,923	−12,465	−40,195	−32,270	−21,919	6,634	−27,364
Monetary authorities	4 715 ..	....	....	....	....	....	....	42	....
of which: Short-term	4 718 ..	....	....	....	....	....	....		....
General government	4 719 ..	489	−385	497	122	484	−752	636	166
of which: Short-term	4 721 ..	492	−528	237	−151	40	−465	653	292
Banks	4 722 ..	−11,195	−19,085	−13,498	−37,310	−34,932	−23,863	3,238	−23,933
of which: Short-term	4 724 ..	−7,677	−24,076	−11,589	−33,363	−22,813	−9,660	−15,897	−22,047
Other sectors	4 725 ..	2,092	547	535	−3,007	2,178	2,695	2,718	−3,597
of which: Short-term	4 727 ..	1,340	1,637	−685	−3,415	1,731	2,695	2,170	−3,458
Currency and deposits	4 730 ..	....	....	....	....	....	....	....	....
Monetary authorities	4 731 ..	....	....	....	....	....	....	....	....
General government	4 732 ..	....	....	....	....	....	....	....	....
Banks	4 733 ..	....	....	....	....	....	....	....	....
Other sectors	4 734 ..	....	....	....	....	....	....	....	....
Other assets	4 736 ..	266	2,237	−1,036	−8,259	−12,493	19,580	3,619	−1,848
Monetary authorities	4 737 ..	....	....	....	....	....	....	....	....
of which: Short-term	4 739 ..	....	....	....	....	....	....	....	....
General government	4 740 ..	−124		−376	−417	−442	−582	−659	−564
of which: Short-term	4 742 ..	....	....	....	....	....	....	....	....
Banks	4 743 ..	−138	2,237	−660	−7,841	−12,050	20,162	4,278	−1,283
of which: Short-term	4 745 ..	−138	2,237	−660	−7,841	−12,050	20,162	4,278	−1,283
Other sectors	4 746 ..	528	....	....	....	....	....	....	....
of which: Short-term	4 748 ..	....	....	....	....	....	....	....	....
Liabilities	4 753 ..	**13,120**	**27,392**	**1,425**	**36,945**	**32,786**	**43,401**	**−50,485**	**−11,802**
Trade credits	4 756 ..	−975	139	617	308	1,906	137	−42	261
General government	4 757 ..	....	....	....	....	....	....	....	....
of which: Short-term	4 759 ..	....	....	....	....	....	....	....	....
Other sectors	4 760 ..	−975	139	617	308	1,906	137	−42	261
of which: Short-term	4 762 ..	....	....	....	....	....	....	....	....
Loans	4 764 ..	14,717	30,773	−4,284	30,199	3,666	89,508	−50,804	−12,065
Monetary authorities	4 765 ..	2,584	2,382	2,122	1,477	−233	26,843	−22,575	−523
of which: Use of Fund credit and loans from the Fund..	4 766 ..	....	....	....	....	....	....	....	....
of which: Short-term	4 768 ..	2,584	2,382	2,122	1,477	702	....	−25,237	....
General government	4 769 ..	−1	−422	−251	....	141	−1	251	−63
of which: Short-term	4 771 ..	−117	−10	....	....	−15	....	−5	−63
Banks	4 772 ..	4,219	29,005	−2,860	31,826	30	57,425	−27,154	−2,190
of which: Short-term	4 774 ..	3,372	18,887	2,041	33,354	3,300	52,757	−24,995	−386
Other sectors	4 775 ..	7,915	−192	−3,295	−3,104	3,728	5,241	−1,325	−9,288
of which: Short-term	4 777 ..	8,288	−112	−1,455	−44	2,591	5,582	−5,282	−3,231
Currency and deposits	4 780 ..	....	....	....	....	....	....	....	....
Monetary authorities	4 781 ..	....	....	....	....	....	....	....	....
General government	4 782 ..	....	....	....	....	....	....	....	....
Banks	4 783 ..	....	....	....	....	....	....	....	....
Other sectors	4 784 ..	....	....	....	....	....	....	....	....
Other liabilities	4 786 ..	−623	−3,521	5,092	6,438	27,214	−46,244	360	3
Monetary authorities	4 787 ..	....	....	....	....	....	....	3,128	....
of which: Short-term	4 789 ..	....	....	....	....	....	....	....	....
General government	4 790 ..	−836	−271	81	−793	176	−35	−48	−272
of which: Short-term	4 792 ..	−836	−271	81	−793	176	−35	−48	−272
Banks	4 793 ..	213	−3,250	5,011	7,232	27,038	−46,209	−2,720	275
of which: Short-term	4 795 ..	213	−3,250	5,011	7,232	27,038	−46,209	−2,720	275
Other sectors	4 796 ..	....	....	....	....	....	....	....	....
of which: Short-term	4 798 ..	....	....	....	....	....	....	....	....
E. RESERVE ASSETS	4 802 ..	**−1,814**	**1,341**	**−412**	**−1,667**	**14**	**−1,750**	**−15,159**	**1,078**
Monetary gold	4 812 ..	....	144	144	....	....	....	....	....
Special drawing rights	4 811 ..	−1	−4	19	−200	....	94	−3,270	6
Reserve position in the Fund	4 810 ..	83	218	690	235	73	−207	−244	−403
Foreign exchange	4 803 ..	−1,923	1,243	−1,447	−1,551	−209	−1,101	−11,645	1,475
Other claims	4 813 ..	27	−259	182	−151	150	−536	....	....
NET ERRORS AND OMISSIONS	4 998 ..	**23**	**2,152**	**4,062**	**1,184**	**−31,248**	**−65,861**	**−23,421**	**12,042**

2011, International Monetary Fund: *Balance of Payments Statistics Yearbook*

Table 3. INTERNATIONAL INVESTMENT POSITION (End-period stocks), 2003–2010

(Millions of U.S. dollars)

	Code	2003	2004	2005	2006	2007	2008	2009	2010
ASSETS..	8 995 C.	561,812	689,995	701,226	936,255	1,174,418	1,010,167	1,130,432	1,223,031
Direct investment abroad................	8 505 ..	**185,695**	**213,921**	**206,700**	**262,222**	**332,419**	**323,023**	**347,502**	**336,081**
Equity capital and reinvested earnings..........	8 506 ..	170,394	196,384	191,873	244,304	312,461	306,507	339,914	327,287
Claims on affiliated enterprises..............	8 507 ..	....	....	....	....	....	....	....	....
Liabilities to affiliated enterprises..........	8 508 ..	....	....	....	....	....	....	....	....
Other capital................................	8 530 ..	15,301	17,537	14,827	17,919	19,958	16,516	7,588	8,793
Claims on affiliated enterprises..............	8 535 ..	50,771	52,157	50,136	60,311	80,454	79,891	85,295	86,591
Liabilities to affiliated enterprises..........	8 540 ..	−35,470	−34,620	−35,309	−42,393	−60,496	−63,375	−77,707	−77,798
Portfolio investment........................	8 602 ..	**211,011**	**272,579**	**298,050**	**396,830**	**483,036**	**323,151**	**416,778**	**488,397**
Equity securities............................	8 610 ..	142,575	179,149	202,176	259,746	311,370	184,621	267,266	329,374
Monetary authorities......................	8 611 ..	....	....	....	146	156	....	....	....
General government......................	8 612 ..	35,609	44,749	48,502	51,425	61,120	38,921	49,463	54,846
Banks.....................................	8 613 ..	....	1,814	4,021	4,079	9,355	· 6,145	8,010	15,649
Other sectors.............................	8 614 ..	106,966	132,585	149,653	204,096	240,738	139,554	209,794	258,879
Debt securities.............................	8 619 ..	68,436	93,430	95,874	137,084	171,666	138,530	149,512	159,024
Bonds and notes..........................	8 620 ..	62,455	85,115	86,198	129,217	165,274	133,536	141,643	151,572
Monetary authorities...................	8 621 ..	....	....	....	....	....	....	....	....
General government....................	8 622 ..	13,214	18,746	20,607	23,163	29,157	21,125	22,342	23,995
Banks...................................	8 623 ..	12,658	20,863	20,356	59,291	78,427	56,846	60,423	64,086
Other sectors...........................	8 624 ..	36,583	45,505	45,235	46,763	57,690	55,566	58,877	63,490
Money market instruments................	8 630 ..	5,981	8,315	9,675	7,867	6,393	4,993	7,869	7,452
Monetary authorities...................	8 631 ..	....	....	....	....	....	....	....	....
General government....................	8 632 ..	....	....	126	....	....	....	....	....
Banks...................................	8 633 ..	139	302	2,136	2,331	3,274	1,408	4,075	4,173
Other sectors...........................	8 634 ..	5,842	8,013	7,414	5,536	3,118	3,585	3,794	3,279
Financial derivatives........................	8 900 ..	**30,045**	**33,864**	**26,387**	**25,494**	**34,614**	**69,009**	**50,727**	**52,759**
Monetary authorities........................	8 901 ..	....	....	....	....	....	....	....	....
General government.........................	8 902 ..	5,981	6,501	4,900	6,847	6,549	3,969	4,497	6,111
Banks.......................................	8 903 ..	19,474	20,409	18,974	15,442	20,737	52,749	41,453	40,687
Other sectors...............................	8 904 ..	4,590	6,954	2,513	3,205	7,328	12,291	4,778	5,962
Other investment............................	8 703 ..	**112,808**	**144,680**	**145,255**	**223,909**	**293,127**	**265,152**	**267,969**	**297,331**
Trade credits................................	8 706 ..	11,267	14,665	12,063	17,190	20,269	15,748	13,911	15,798
General government.......................	8 707 ..	....	....	....	....	....	....	....	....
of which: Short-term..................	8 709 ..	....	....	....	....	....	....	....	....
Other sectors.............................	8 710 ..	11,267	14,665	12,063	17,190	20,269	15,748	13,911	15,798
of which: Short-term..................	8 712 ..	*11,267*	*14,665*	*12,063*	*17,190*	*20,269*	*15,748*	*13,911*	*15,798*
Loans.......................................	8 714 ..	89,857	110,815	113,088	174,669	225,147	224,439	231,153	256,047
Monetary authorities......................	8 715 ..	....	....	....	....	....	....	....	....
of which: Short-term..................	8 718 ..	....	....	....	....	....	....	....	....
General government......................	8 719 ..	3,477	4,233	2,639	2,622	2,183	2,433	1,967	2,236
of which: Short-term..................	8 721 ..	*1,252*	*1,965*	*1,131*	*874*	*936*	*1,280*	*703*	*745*
Banks.....................................	8 722 ..	77,616	97,663	103,036	156,314	207,840	211,764	220,614	239,504
of which: Short-term..................	8 724 ..	*52,857*	*77,102*	*79,036*	*126,012*	*161,844*	*155,558*	*180,988*	*200,009*
Other sectors.............................	8 725 ..	8,763	8,920	7,414	15,733	15,124	10,242	8,572	14,308
of which: Short-term..................	8 727 ..	*6,120*	*4,989*	*5,277*	*13,694*	*13,409*	*8,834*	*7,447*	*12,966*
Currency and deposits......................	8 730 ..	....	....	....	....	....	....	....	....
Monetary authorities......................	8 731 ..	....	....	....	....	....	....	....	....
General government......................	8 732 ..	....	....	....	....	....	....	....	....
Banks.....................................	8 733 ..	....	....	....	....	....	....	....	....
Other sectors.............................	8 734 ..	....	....	....	....	....	....	....	....
Other assets................................	8 736 ..	11,684	19,200	20,105	32,049	47,711	24,966	22,905	25,485
Monetary authorities......................	8 737 ..	....	....	....	....	....	....	....	....
of which: Short-term..................	8 739 ..	....	....	....	....	....	....	....	....
General government......................	8 740 ..	5,842	6,501	5,529	6,701	7,640	6,786	8,010	9,091
of which: Short-term..................	8 742 ..	....	....	....	....	....	....	....	....
Banks.....................................	8 743 ..	1,113	7,257	9,675	19,230	33,055	12,547	8,291	9,240
of which: Short-term..................	8 745 ..	*1,113*	*7,257*	*9,675*	*19,230*	*33,055*	*12,547*	*8,291*	*9,240*
Other sectors.............................	8 746 ..	4,729	5,443	4,900	6,119	7,016	5,633	6,604	7,154
of which: Short-term..................	8 748 ..	....	....	....	....	....	....	....	....
Reserve assets.............................	8 802 ..	**22,253**	**24,951**	**24,834**	**27,800**	**31,222**	**29,832**	**47,456**	**48,463**
Monetary gold..............................	8 812 ..	2,504	2,570	2,764	3,205	4,054	3,841	4,497	5,812
Special drawing rights......................	8 811 ..	198	209	176	386	406	306	3,591	3,522
Reserve position in the Fund................	8 810 ..	1,468	1,308	532	318	257	463	725	1,123
Foreign exchange...........................	8 803 ..	18,083	20,409	21,110	23,600	26,506	25,222	38,643	38,005
Other claims...............................	8 813 ..	....	454	251	291	....	....	....	....

Table 3 (Concluded). INTERNATIONAL INVESTMENT POSITION (End-period stocks), 2003–2010

(Millions of U.S. dollars)

	Code	2003	2004	2005	2006	2007	2008	2009	2010
LIABILITIES	8 995 D.	**631,642**	**788,710**	**775,658**	**991,492**	**1,179,837**	**1,053,184**	**1,189,642**	**1,299,050**
Direct investment in Sweden	8 555 ..	**158,849**	**197,291**	**172,773**	**227,259**	**293,439**	**278,724**	**332,045**	**348,600**
Equity capital and reinvested earnings	8 556 ..	106,131	141,808	125,905	153,983	200,979	175,275	216,399	232,052
Claims on direct investors	8 557 ..	....	....	....	....	....	....	....	....
Liabilities to direct investors	8 558 ..	....	....	....	....	....	....	....	....
Other capital	8 580 ..	52,718	55,483	46,869	73,277	92,460	103,449	115,647	116,548
Claims on direct investors	8 585 ..	19,613	34,167	31,665	31,030	45,684	39,562	37,940	46,947
Liabilities to direct investors	8 590 ..	....	....	....	....	....	....	....	....
Portfolio investment	8 652 ..	**281,673**	**352,251**	**376,458**	**477,682**	**530,279**	**378,460**	**516,546**	**612,695**
Equity securities	8 660 ..	89,718	124,119	141,234	209,050	204,098	86,805	140,097	202,692
Banks	8 663 ..	....	....	....	....	....	....	....	....
Other sectors	8 664 ..	89,718	124,119	141,234	209,050	204,098	86,805	140,097	202,692
Debt securities	8 669 ..	191,955	228,132	235,223	268,632	326,182	291,655	376,449	410,003
Bonds and notes	8 670 ..	165,248	192,907	198,281	228,716	266,621	242,747	317,150	345,172
Monetary authorities	8 671 ..	....	....	....	....	....	....	....	....
General government	8 672 ..	65,793	70,753	66,596	60,894	60,652	47,372	59,439	71,836
Banks	8 673 ..	74,834	97,360	106,177	140,726	180,866	171,050	218,225	236,374
Other sectors	8 674 ..	24,620	24,794	25,508	27,096	25,103	24,326	39,486	36,961
Money market instruments	8 680 ..	26,707	35,225	36,942	39,916	59,561	48,908	59,299	64,832
Monetary authorities	8 681 ..	....	....	....	....	....	....	984	....
General government	8 682 ..	6,538	6,501	5,780	5,390	6,705	6,145	7,588	10,135
Banks	8 683 ..	16,831	24,642	28,398	32,049	49,426	40,074	48,619	53,207
Other sectors	8 684 ..	3,338	4,082	2,764	2,477	3,430	2,689	2,108	1,490
Financial derivatives	8 905 ..	**30,462**	**36,132**	**28,272**	**26,514**	**35,705**	**62,351**	**41,734**	**40,538**
Monetary authorities	8 906 ..	....	....	....	....	....	1,152	....	....
General government	8 907 ..	4,729	5,140	4,649	5,244	5,457	6,530	1,827	2,087
Banks	8 908 ..	22,395	24,642	19,979	18,064	21,361	44,555	35,973	34,726
Other sectors	8 909 ..	3,338	6,350	3,644	3,205	8,887	10,114	3,935	3,726
Other investment	8 753 ..	**160,658**	**203,036**	**198,155**	**260,037**	**320,413**	**333,649**	**299,317**	**297,217**
Trade credits	8 756 ..	7,233	8,617	9,047	12,383	15,748	10,627	10,539	12,817
General government	8 757 ..	....	....	....	....	....	....	....	....
of which: Short-term	8 759 ..	....	....	....	....	....	....	....	....
Other sectors	8 760 ..	7,233	8,617	9,047	12,383	15,748	10,627	10,539	12,817
of which: Short-term	8 762 ..	....	....	....	....	....	*10,627*	*10,539*	*12,817*
Loans	8 764 ..	150,643	180,510	162,972	211,380	238,088	304,458	268,671	262,754
Monetary authorities	8 765 ..	....	....	....	....	2,339	25,734	3,513	3,577
of which: Use of Fund credit and loans from the Fund	8 766 ..	....	....	....	....	....	....	....	....
of which: Short-term	8 768 ..	....	....	....	....	....	....	....	....
General government	8 769 ..	1,808	1,663	1,131	1,020	780	640	984	894
of which: Short-term	8 771 ..	....	....	....	....	....	....	*141*	....
Banks	8 772 ..	114,895	150,727	140,355	185,304	197,861	229,560	213,448	210,293
of which: Short-term	8 774 ..	*106,131*	*131,074*	*123,140*	*167,822*	*182,425*	*212,148*	*196,866*	*195,836*
Other sectors	8 775 ..	33,940	28,120	21,487	25,057	37,109	48,524	50,727	47,990
of which: Short-term	8 777 ..	*13,910*	*6,350*	*4,649*	*9,323*	*10,602*	*13,827*	*9,134*	*5,663*
Currency and deposits	8 780 ..	....	....	....	....	....	....	....	....
Monetary authorities	8 781 ..	....	....	....	....	....	....	....	....
General government	8 782 ..	....	....	....	....	....	....	....	....
Banks	8 783 ..	....	....	....	....	....	....	....	....
Other sectors	8 784 ..	....	....	....	....	....	....	....	....
Other liabilities	8 786 ..	2,782	13,909	26,136	36,274	66,577	18,565	20,107	21,646
Monetary authorities	8 787 ..	....	....	....	....	....	....	3,526	3,463
of which: Short-term	8 789 ..	....	....	....	....	....	....	....	....
General government	8 790 ..	974	907	880	874	936	768	984	1,192
of which: Short-term	8 792 ..	....	....	....	....	....	*768*	*984*	*1,192*
Banks	8 793 ..	1,808	13,002	25,256	35,400	65,642	17,796	15,598	16,990
of which: Short-term	8 795 ..	....	....	....	....	....	*17,796*	*15,598*	*16,990*
Other sectors	8 796 ..	....	....	....	....	....	....	....	....
of which: Short-term	8 798 ..	....	....	....	....	....	....	....	....
NET INTERNATIONAL INVESTMENT POSITION	8 995 ..	**−69,830**	**−98,715**	**−74,433**	**−55,237**	**−5,418**	**−43,017**	**−59,210**	**−76,019**
Conversion rates: kronor per U.S. dollar (end of period)	0 102 ..	**7.1892**	**6.6146**	**7.9584**	**6.8644**	**6.4136**	**7.8106**	**7.1165**	**6.7097**

Table 1. ANALYTIC PRESENTATION, 2003–2010

(Millions of U.S. dollars)

	Code	2003	2004	2005	2006	2007	2008	2009	2010
A. Current Account[1]..........	4 993 Z.	**44,910**	**56,452**	**53,149**	**55,848**	**40,349**	**6,406**	**38,696**	**76,901**
Goods: exports f.o.b..........	2 100 ..	118,837	141,874	151,309	167,221	200,491	241,163	206,119	258,521
Goods: imports f.o.b..........	3 100 ..	−111,831	−126,089	−145,442	−162,213	−187,257	−227,680	−204,693	−246,229
Balance on Goods..........	*4 100 ..*	*7,007*	*15,785*	*5,867*	*5,008*	*13,234*	*13,482*	*1,426*	*12,291*
Services: credit..........	2 200 ..	36,269	43,940	49,821	54,864	65,933	77,298	76,305	83,632
Services: debit..........	3 200 ..	−17,021	−22,003	−25,753	−26,750	−31,747	−35,370	−38,136	−39,612
Balance on Goods and Services..........	*4 991 ..*	*26,255*	*37,723*	*29,936*	*33,122*	*47,420*	*55,410*	*39,596*	*56,311*
Income: credit..........	2 300 ..	62,760	71,334	102,074	108,974	122,406	85,634	92,628	114,505
Income: debit..........	3 300 ..	−38,488	−46,093	−67,958	−76,928	−119,980	−121,818	−81,453	−81,651
Balance on Goods, Services, and Income..........	*4 992 ..*	*50,527*	*62,964*	*64,051*	*65,168*	*49,846*	*19,226*	*50,771*	*89,165*
Current transfers: credit..........	2 379 Z.	13,198	14,299	15,605	17,737	23,014	27,796	26,365	24,471
Current transfers: debit..........	3 379 ..	−18,815	−20,811	−26,507	−27,057	−32,512	−40,617	−38,440	−36,734
B. Capital Account[1]..........	4 994 Z.	**−2,178**	**−3,166**	**−2,290**	**−4,334**	**−4,197**	**−3,497**	**−3,477**	**−4,364**
Capital account: credit..........	2 994 Z.	492	406	470	267	405	1,013	133	141
Capital account: debit..........	3 994 ..	−2,670	−3,572	−2,760	−4,601	−4,602	−4,510	−3,609	−4,505
Total, Groups A Plus B..........	*4 981 ..*	*42,732*	*53,286*	*50,859*	*51,514*	*36,151*	*2,909*	*35,219*	*72,537*
C. Financial Account[1]..........	4 995 W.	**−24,311**	**−64,032**	**−86,062**	**−57,778**	**−45,837**	**−1,244**	**43,143**	**44,027**
Direct investment abroad..........	4 505 ..	−15,674	−26,068	−50,844	−76,555	−52,001	−43,587	−28,233	−38,940
Direct investment in Switzerland..........	4 555 Z.	17,471	1,856	−525	44,993	33,410	16,004	28,087	5,513
Portfolio investment assets..........	4 602 ..	−32,903	−42,412	−53,263	−41,700	−20,344	−65,608	−35,481	7,823
Equity securities..........	4 610 ..	−2,087	−11,303	−17,729	−13,762	−5,221	−3,919	−2,311	−6,222
Debt securities..........	4 619 ..	−30,816	−31,109	−35,534	−27,938	−15,123	−61,689	−33,170	14,046
Portfolio investment liabilities..........	4 652 Z.	−1,662	2,858	5,636	68	1,626	30,024	7,019	22,141
Equity securities..........	4 660 ..	−4,428	−2,789	3,951	537	689	24,352	9,241	−7,210
Debt securities..........	4 669 Z.	2,765	5,647	1,685	−469	937	5,672	−2,222	29,352
Financial derivatives..........	4 910 ..	....	....	....	−2,875	−10,399	6,434	1,937	1,169
Financial derivatives assets..........	4 900 ..	....	....	....	−2,168	−3,794	65,928	17,642	22,207
Financial derivatives liabilities..........	4 905 ..	....	....	....	−707	−6,605	−59,493	−15,705	−21,038
Other investment assets..........	4 703 ..	−4,387	−29,041	−70,498	−42,975	−293,439	303,974	119,229	62,194
Monetary authorities..........	4 701 ..	−18	−899	−798	607	−5,338	−57,442	45,421	29,291
General government..........	4 704 ..	113	98	−31	15	2,071	5,374	8	−98
Banks..........	4 705 ..	−11,395	−14,849	−61,664	−24,322	−242,923	335,555	51,911	41,168
Other sectors..........	4 728 ..	6,914	−13,390	−8,005	−19,275	−47,249	20,488	21,889	−8,166
Other investment liabilities..........	4 753 W.	12,845	28,775	83,431	61,266	295,310	−248,485	−49,415	−15,874
Monetary authorities..........	4 753 WA	−24	−223	117	−46	5,214	26,431	−21,326	−1,591
General government..........	4 753 ZB	−208	184	115	419	243	−343	32	144
Banks..........	4 753 ZC	6,079	27,840	62,701	41,448	247,066	−281,225	−15,309	−29,544
Other sectors..........	4 753 ZD	6,998	973	20,498	19,445	42,788	6,651	−12,812	15,117
Total, Groups A Through C..........	*4 983 ..*	*18,421*	*−10,746*	*−35,204*	*−6,264*	*−9,686*	*1,665*	*78,362*	*116,564*
D. Net Errors and Omissions..........	4 998 ..	**−15,016**	**12,364**	**16,989**	**6,634**	**13,149**	**2,188**	**−30,225**	**8,818**
Total, Groups A Through D..........	*4 984 ..*	*3,405*	*1,618*	*−18,215*	*370*	*3,463*	*3,853*	*48,137*	*125,382*
E. Reserves and Related Items..........	4 802 A.	**−3,405**	**−1,618**	**18,215**	**−370**	**−3,463**	**−3,853**	**−48,137**	**−125,382**
Reserve assets..........	4 802 ..	−3,405	−1,618	18,215	−370	−3,463	−3,853	−48,137	−125,382
Use of Fund credit and loans..........	4 766 ..	....	....	....	....	....	....	....	....
Exceptional financing..........	4 920 ..	....	....	....	....	....	....	....	....
Conversion rates: Swiss francs per U.S. dollar.......	0 101 ..	**1.3467**	**1.2435**	**1.2452**	**1.2538**	**1.2004**	**1.0831**	**1.0881**	**1.0429**

[1] Excludes components that have been classified in the categories of Group E.

Table 2. STANDARD PRESENTATION, 2003–2010

(Millions of U.S. dollars)

	Code	2003	2004	2005	2006	2007	2008	2009	2010
CURRENT ACCOUNT................................	4 993 ..	**44,910**	**56,452**	**53,149**	**55,848**	**40,349**	**6,406**	**38,696**	**76,901**
A. GOODS..	4 100 ..	**7,007**	**15,785**	**5,867**	**5,008**	**13,234**	**13,482**	**1,426**	**12,291**
Credit..	2 100 ..	**118,837**	**141,874**	**151,309**	**167,221**	**200,491**	**241,163**	**206,119**	**258,521**
General merchandise: exports f.o.b.	2 110 ..	105,522	123,677	131,516	148,510	173,151	201,687	174,147	197,132
Goods for processing: exports f.o.b.	2 150 ..	....	....	....	....	....	....	....	....
Repairs on goods..........................	2 160 ..	....	....	....	....	....	....	....	....
Goods procured in ports by carriers...	2 170 ..	....	....	....	....	....	....	....	....
Nonmonetary gold........................	2 180 ..	13,316	18,197	19,793	18,711	27,339	39,475	31,972	61,389
Debit...	3 100 ..	**−111,831**	**−126,089**	**−145,442**	**−162,213**	**−187,257**	**−227,680**	**−204,693**	**−246,229**
General merchandise: imports f.o.b.	3 110 ..	−99,279	−114,726	−125,179	−139,875	−159,280	−181,113	−154,272	−177,525
Goods for processing: imports f.o.b.	3 150 ..	....	....	....	....	....	....	....	....
Repairs on goods..........................	3 160 ..	....	....	....	....	....	....	....	....
Goods procured in ports by carriers...	3 170 ..	....	....	....	....	....	....	....	....
Nonmonetary gold........................	3 180 ..	−12,551	−11,363	−20,263	−22,338	−27,977	−46,567	−50,420	−68,704
B. SERVICES.......................................	4 200 ..	**19,248**	**21,938**	**24,068**	**28,114**	**34,186**	**41,928**	**38,169**	**44,020**
Total credit.................................	2 200 ..	*36,269*	*43,940*	*49,821*	*54,864*	*65,933*	*77,298*	*76,305*	*83,632*
Total debit..................................	3 200 ..	*−17,021*	*−22,003*	*−25,753*	*−26,750*	*−31,747*	*−35,370*	*−38,136*	*−39,612*
Transportation services, credit..........	2 205 ..	**3,665**	**4,015**	**4,206**	**4,527**	**5,579**	**6,654**	**5,521**	**5,649**
Passenger...................................	2 850 ..	*1,879*	*1,809*	*1,896*	*2,044*	*2,543*	*3,109*	*2,519*	*2,869*
Freight.......................................	2 851 ..	*679*	*701*	*809*	*826*	*983*	*1,124*	*885*	*999*
Other...	2 852 ..	*1,107*	*1,506*	*1,501*	*1,657*	*2,053*	*2,421*	*2,117*	*1,780*
Sea transport, passenger..............	2 207 ..	....	....	....	....	....	....	....	....
Sea transport, freight...................	2 208 ..	....	....	....	....	....	....	....	....
Sea transport, other.....................	2 209 ..	....	....	....	....	....	....	....	....
Air transport, passenger...............	2 211 ..	....	....	....	....	....	....	....	....
Air transport, freight....................	2 212 ..	....	....	....	....	....	....	....	....
Air transport, other......................	2 213 ..	....	....	....	....	....	....	....	....
Other transport, passenger..........	2 215 ..	....	....	....	....	....	....	....	....
Other transport, freight...............	2 216 ..	....	....	....	....	....	....	....	....
Other transport, other..................	2 217 ..	1,107	1,506	1,501	1,657	2,053	2,421	2,117	1,780
Transportation services, debit...........	3 205 ..	**−4,673**	**−5,263**	**−5,560**	**−6,098**	**−7,089**	**−8,403**	**−7,405**	**−8,417**
Passenger...................................	3 850 ..	*−1,731*	*−1,820*	*−1,797*	*−1,947*	*−2,184*	*−2,434*	*−1,924*	*−2,158*
Freight.......................................	3 851 ..	*−2,063*	*−2,327*	*−2,684*	*−2,993*	*−3,455*	*−4,201*	*−3,777*	*−4,543*
Other...	3 852 ..	*−879*	*−1,117*	*−1,079*	*−1,159*	*−1,450*	*−1,768*	*−1,705*	*−1,715*
Sea transport, passenger..............	3 207 ..	....	....	....	....	....	....	....	....
Sea transport, freight...................	3 208 ..	....	....	....	....	....	....	....	....
Sea transport, other.....................	3 209 ..	....	....	....	....	....	....	....	....
Air transport, passenger...............	3 211 ..	....	....	....	....	....	....	....	....
Air transport, freight....................	3 212 ..	....	....	....	....	....	....	....	....
Air transport, other......................	3 213 ..	....	....	....	....	....	....	....	....
Other transport, passenger..........	3 215 ..	....	....	....	....	....	....	....	....
Other transport, freight...............	3 216 ..	....	....	....	....	....	....	....	....
Other transport, other..................	3 217 ..	−879	−1,117	−1,079	−1,159	−1,450	−1,768	−1,705	−1,715
Travel, credit.................................	2 236 ..	**8,614**	**9,595**	**10,041**	**10,808**	**12,178**	**14,457**	**14,148**	**14,978**
Business travel............................	2 237 ..	....	....	....	....	....	....	....	....
Personal travel............................	2 240 ..	....	....	....	....	....	....	....	....
Travel, debit..................................	3 236 ..	**−6,883**	**−8,104**	**−8,782**	**−9,252**	**−10,114**	**−10,913**	**−10,951**	**−11,159**
Business travel............................	3 237 ..	....	....	....	....	....	....	....	....
Personal travel............................	3 240 ..	....	....	....	....	....	....	....	....
Other services, credit......................	2 200 BA	**23,991**	**30,330**	**35,574**	**39,529**	**48,176**	**56,186**	**56,636**	**63,006**
Communications..........................	2 245 ..	974	1,223	1,183	1,102	1,068	1,226	1,331	1,431
Construction...............................	2 249 ..	....	....	....	....	....	....	....	....
Insurance...................................	2 253 ..	3,467	3,919	3,326	3,737	4,890	5,840	5,570	4,918
Financial....................................	2 260 ..	10,062	11,469	14,071	15,625	19,335	19,254	16,179	15,791
Computer and information............	2 262 ..	....	....	....	....	....	....	....	....
Royalties and licence fees............	2 266 ..	....	....	....	....	....	....	....	....
Other business services................	2 268 ..	7,744	12,382	15,681	17,659	21,271	28,103	31,536	38,880
Personal, cultural, and recreational...	2 287 ..	4	4	5	3	2	4	2	3
Government, n.i.e........................	2 291 ..	1,740	1,332	1,309	1,404	1,610	1,759	2,018	1,983
Other services, debit.......................	3 200 BA	**−5,465**	**−8,636**	**−11,411**	**−11,401**	**−14,544**	**−16,053**	**−19,780**	**−20,036**
Communications..........................	3 245 ..	−971	−1,130	−938	−803	−801	−972	−1,045	−1,056
Construction...............................	3 249 ..	....	....	....	....	....	....	....	....
Insurance...................................	3 253 ..	−277	−305	−535	−679	−859	−1,016	−1,160	−1,234
Financial....................................	3 260 ..	−668	−856	−1,055	−1,281	−1,790	−2,128	−1,897	−1,722
Computer and information............	3 262 ..	....	....	....	....	....	....	....	....
Royalties and licence fees............	3 266 ..	....	....	....	....	....	....	....	....
Other business services................	3 268 ..	−3,320	−6,098	−8,636	−8,395	−10,827	−11,635	−15,365	−15,728
Personal, cultural, and recreational...	3 287 ..	−90	−95	−87	−85	−94	−111	−108	−120
Government, n.i.e........................	3 291 ..	−140	−150	−160	−158	−174	−192	−205	−177

Table 2 (Continued). STANDARD PRESENTATION, 2003–2010

(Millions of U.S. dollars)

	Code	2003	2004	2005	2006	2007	2008	2009	2010
C. INCOME.................................	4 300	**24,272**	**25,241**	**34,115**	**32,046**	**2,426**	**−36,184**	**11,176**	**32,853**
Total credit.................................	2 300	*62,760*	*71,334*	*102,074*	*108,974*	*122,406*	*85,634*	*92,628*	*114,505*
Total debit.................................	3 300	*−38,488*	*−46,093*	*−67,958*	*−76,928*	*−119,980*	*−121,818*	*−81,453*	*−81,651*
Compensation of employees, credit..........	2 310	**1,533**	**1,695**	**1,722**	**1,795**	**1,796**	**2,215**	**2,312**	**2,396**
Compensation of employees, debit..........	3 310	**−8,711**	**−9,782**	**−9,986**	**−10,705**	**−12,248**	**−14,459**	**−14,906**	**−16,452**
Investment income, credit..................	2 320	**61,227**	**69,639**	**100,352**	**107,179**	**120,610**	**83,419**	**90,316**	**112,108**
Direct investment income......................	2 330	32,438	39,353	61,241	55,129	45,989	6,855	49,412	69,145
Dividends and distributed branch profits......	2 332	20,463	22,316	28,252	34,078	40,777	30,721	23,872	38,729
Reinvested earnings and undistributed branch profits.....	2 333	11,976	17,037	32,989	21,051	5,211	−23,866	25,540	30,416
Income on debt (interest)......................	2 334	....	....	....	....	....	....	....	....
Portfolio investment income....................	2 339	16,361	18,672	21,248	24,606	30,941	32,969	26,596	28,836
Income on equity.............................	2 340	5,806	6,957	8,646	10,397	13,269	13,914	9,851	10,471
Income on bonds and notes....................	2 350	....	....	....	....	....	....	....	....
Income on money market instruments.........	2 360	....	....	....	....	....	....	....	....
Other investment income......................	2 370	12,428	11,614	17,863	27,444	43,681	43,594	14,308	14,127
Investment income, debit..................	3 320	**−29,778**	**−36,311**	**−57,972**	**−66,223**	**−107,732**	**−107,359**	**−66,546**	**−65,200**
Direct investment income......................	3 330	−10,743	−15,723	−28,760	−24,009	−45,167	−42,752	−35,169	−33,400
Dividends and distributed branch profits......	3 332	−7,915	−8,888	−31,341	−11,087	−15,063	−44,132	−12,684	−25,458
Reinvested earnings and undistributed branch profits.....	3 333	−2,828	−6,835	2,581	−12,922	−30,104	1,380	−22,485	−7,942
Income on debt (interest)......................	3 334	....	....	....	....	....	....	....	....
Portfolio investment income....................	3 339	−8,061	−9,548	−11,067	−13,500	−17,139	−19,872	−14,611	−17,226
Income on equity.............................	3 340	−6,568	−7,882	−9,064	−11,085	−14,499	−17,516	−13,258	−15,820
Income on bonds and notes....................	3 350	....	....	....	....	....	....	....	....
Income on money market instruments.........	3 360	....	....	....	....	....	....	....	....
Other investment income......................	3 370	−10,974	−11,041	−18,146	−28,715	−45,426	−44,735	−16,766	−14,574
D. CURRENT TRANSFERS.....................	4 379	**−5,617**	**−6,512**	**−10,902**	**−9,320**	**−9,498**	**−12,820**	**−12,075**	**−12,263**
Credit.................................	2 379	**13,198**	**14,299**	**15,605**	**17,737**	**23,014**	**27,796**	**26,365**	**24,471**
General government..........................	2 380	2,309	2,528	2,929	3,191	3,592	4,270	4,664	5,108
Other sectors...............................	2 390	10,889	11,771	12,676	14,546	19,423	23,526	21,701	19,362
Workers' remittances........................	2 391	173	194	202	209	292	330	314	334
Other current transfers......................	2 392	10,716	11,577	12,474	14,337	19,130	23,197	21,387	19,028
Debit.................................	3 379	**−18,815**	**−20,811**	**−26,507**	**−27,057**	**−32,512**	**−40,617**	**−38,440**	**−36,734**
General government..........................	3 380	−4,710	−5,459	−5,741	−5,882	−6,400	−7,377	−7,724	−8,437
Other sectors...............................	3 390	−14,105	−15,352	−20,767	−21,175	−26,112	−33,239	−30,716	−28,297
Workers' remittances........................	3 391	−2,741	−3,139	−3,325	−3,703	−4,130	−4,691	−4,927	−5,159
Other current transfers......................	3 392	−11,365	−12,213	−17,442	−17,472	−21,982	−28,548	−25,788	−23,138
CAPITAL AND FINANCIAL ACCOUNT........	4 996	**−29,894**	**−68,816**	**−70,138**	**−62,482**	**−53,498**	**−8,594**	**−8,471**	**−85,719**
CAPITAL ACCOUNT........................	4 994	**−2,178**	**−3,166**	**−2,290**	**−4,334**	**−4,197**	**−3,497**	**−3,477**	**−4,364**
Total credit.................................	2 994	*492*	*406*	*470*	*267*	*405*	*1,013*	*133*	*141*
Total debit.................................	3 994	*−2,670*	*−3,572*	*−2,760*	*−4,601*	*−4,602*	*−4,510*	*−3,609*	*−4,505*
Capital transfers, credit....................	2 400	....	....	....	....	....	....	....	....
General government..........................	2 401	....	....	....	....	....	....	....	....
Debt forgiveness............................	2 402	....	....	....	....	....	....	....	....
Other capital transfers......................	2 410	....	....	....	....	....	....	....	....
Other sectors...............................	2 430	....	....	....	....	....	....	....	....
Migrants' transfers..........................	2 431	....	....	....	....	....	....	....	....
Debt forgiveness............................	2 432	....	....	....	....	....	....	....	....
Other capital transfers......................	2 440	....	....	....	....	....	....	....	....
Capital transfers, debit.....................	3 400	**−122**	**−552**	**−512**	**−452**	**−244**	**−112**	**−131**	**−130**
General government..........................	3 401	−122	−552	−512	−452	−244	−112	−131	−130
Debt forgiveness............................	3 402	....	−421	−390	−346	−141	....	....	....
Other capital transfers......................	3 410	−122	−131	−122	−106	−104	−112	−131	−130
Other sectors...............................	3 430	....	....	....	....	....	....	....	....
Migrants' transfers..........................	3 431	....	....	....	....	....	....	....	....
Debt forgiveness............................	3 432	....	....	....	....	....	....	....	....
Other capital transfers......................	3 440	....	....	....	....	....	....	....	....
Nonproduced nonfinancial assets, credit..........	2 480	**492**	**406**	**470**	**267**	**405**	**1,013**	**133**	**141**
Nonproduced nonfinancial assets, debit..........	3 480	**−2,548**	**−3,020**	**−2,248**	**−4,149**	**−4,358**	**−4,398**	**−3,479**	**−4,375**

Table 2 (Continued). STANDARD PRESENTATION, 2003–2010

(Millions of U.S. dollars)

	Code	2003	2004	2005	2006	2007	2008	2009	2010
FINANCIAL ACCOUNT	4 995	**−27,715**	**−65,650**	**−67,848**	**−58,148**	**−49,300**	**−5,098**	**−4,994**	**−81,355**
A. DIRECT INVESTMENT	4 500	**1,797**	**−24,212**	**−51,369**	**−31,563**	**−18,591**	**−27,584**	**−147**	**−33,427**
Direct investment abroad	4 505	**−15,674**	**−26,068**	**−50,844**	**−76,555**	**−52,001**	**−43,587**	**−28,233**	**−38,940**
Equity capital	4 510	−4,224	−9,330	−17,569	−50,546	−39,474	−43,640	−9,801	−2,048
Claims on affiliated enterprises	4 515	−4,224	−9,330	−17,569	−50,546	−39,474	−43,640	−9,801	−2,048
Liabilities to affiliated enterprises	4 520	....	....	....	....	....	....	....	....
Reinvested earnings	4 525	−11,976	−17,037	−32,989	−21,051	−5,211	23,866	−25,540	−30,416
Other capital	4 530	526	299	−285	−4,958	−7,315	−23,813	7,107	−6,476
Claims on affiliated enterprises	4 535	629	−2,123	−4,294	−11,995	−14,606	−22,134	−7,523	7,547
Liabilities to affiliated enterprises	4 540	−103	2,422	4,009	7,037	7,291	−1,679	14,630	−14,023
Direct investment in Switzerland	4 555	**17,471**	**1,856**	**−525**	**44,993**	**33,410**	**16,004**	**28,087**	**5,513**
Equity capital	4 560	9,605	−1,682	558	29,381	11,371	379	19,130	−6,065
Claims on direct investors	4 565	....	....	....	....	....	....	....	....
Liabilities to direct investors	4 570	9,605	−1,682	558	29,381	11,371	379	19,130	−6,065
Reinvested earnings	4 575	2,828	6,835	−2,581	12,922	30,104	−1,380	22,485	7,942
Other capital	4 580	5,038	−3,297	1,498	2,690	−8,064	17,005	−13,528	3,636
Claims on direct investors	4 585	−2,354	−2,824	819	−1,731	−7,987	11,404	−3,303	66
Liabilities to direct investors	4 590	7,392	−473	680	4,421	−77	5,601	−10,225	3,570
B. PORTFOLIO INVESTMENT	4 600	**−34,565**	**−39,554**	**−47,627**	**−41,631**	**−18,718**	**−35,584**	**−28,462**	**29,965**
Assets	4 602	**−32,903**	**−42,412**	**−53,263**	**−41,700**	**−20,344**	**−65,608**	**−35,481**	**7,823**
Equity securities	4 610	−2,087	−11,303	−17,729	−13,762	−5,221	−3,919	−2,311	−6,222
Monetary authorities	4 611	....	....	....	....	....	....	....	....
General government	4 612	....	....	....	....	....	....	....	....
Banks	4 613	....	....	....	....	....	....	....	....
Other sectors	4 614	....	....	....	....	....	....	....	....
Debt securities	4 619	−30,816	−31,109	−35,534	−27,938	−15,123	−61,689	−33,170	14,046
Bonds and notes	4 620	−24,428	−38,746	−38,864	−36,132	−27,570	−64,709	−38,628	−4,637
Monetary authorities	4 621	....	....	....	....	....	....	....	....
General government	4 622	....	....	....	....	....	....	....	....
Banks	4 623	....	....	....	....	....	....	....	....
Other sectors	4 624	....	....	....	....	....	....	....	....
Money market instruments	4 630	−6,388	7,637	3,330	8,194	12,447	3,021	5,458	18,682
Monetary authorities	4 631	....	....	....	....	....	....	....	....
General government	4 632	....	....	....	....	....	....	....	....
Banks	4 633	....	....	....	....	....	....	....	....
Other sectors	4 634	....	....	....	....	....	....	....	....
Liabilities	4 652	**−1,662**	**2,858**	**5,636**	**68**	**1,626**	**30,024**	**7,019**	**22,141**
Equity securities	4 660	−4,428	−2,789	3,951	537	689	24,352	9,241	−7,210
Banks	4 663	....	....	....	....	....	....	....	....
Other sectors	4 664	....	....	....	....	....	....	....	....
Debt securities	4 669	2,765	5,647	1,685	−469	937	5,672	−2,222	29,352
Bonds and notes	4 670	1,651	4,231	−1,131	−728	−489	5,035	−61	534
Monetary authorities	4 671	....	....	....	....	....	....	....	....
General government	4 672	....	....	....	....	....	....	....	....
Banks	4 673	....	....	....	....	....	....	....	....
Other sectors	4 674	....	....	....	....	....	....	....	....
Money market instruments	4 680	1,114	1,415	2,817	259	1,426	637	−2,161	28,818
Monetary authorities	4 681	....	....	....	....	....	....	....	....
General government	4 682	....	....	....	....	....	....	....	....
Banks	4 683	....	....	....	....	....	....	....	....
Other sectors	4 684	....	....	....	....	....	....	....	....
C. FINANCIAL DERIVATIVES	4 910	....	....	....	**−2,875**	**−10,399**	**6,434**	**1,937**	**1,169**
Monetary authorities	4 911	....	....	....	....	....	....	....	....
General government	4 912	....	....	....	....	....	....	....	....
Banks	4 913	....	....	....	....	....	....	....	....
Other sectors	4 914	....	....	....	....	....	....	....	....
Assets	4 900	....	....	....	**−2,168**	**−3,794**	**65,928**	**17,642**	**22,207**
Monetary authorities	4 901	....	....	....	....	....	....	....	....
General government	4 902	....	....	....	....	....	....	....	....
Banks	4 903	....	....	....	....	....	....	....	....
Other sectors	4 904	....	....	....	....	....	....	....	....
Liabilities	4 905	....	....	....	**−707**	**−6,605**	**−59,493**	**−15,705**	**−21,038**
Monetary authorities	4 906	....	....	....	....	....	....	....	....
General government	4 907	....	....	....	....	....	....	....	....
Banks	4 908	....	....	....	....	....	....	....	....
Other sectors	4 909	....	....	....	....	....	....	....	....

Table 2 (Concluded). STANDARD PRESENTATION, 2003–2010

(Millions of U.S. dollars)

	Code	2003	2004	2005	2006	2007	2008	2009	2010
D. OTHER INVESTMENT	4 700	**8,458**	**−266**	**12,933**	**18,291**	**1,870**	**55,488**	**69,814**	**46,321**
Assets	4 703	**−4,387**	**−29,041**	**−70,498**	**−42,975**	**−293,439**	**303,974**	**119,229**	**62,194**
Trade credits	4 706	....	....	....	....	....	....	....	....
General government	4 707	....	....	....	....	....	....	....	....
of which: Short-term	4 709	....	....	....	....	....	....	....	....
Other sectors	4 710	....	....	....	....	....	....	....	....
of which: Short-term	4 712	....	....	....	....	....	....	....	....
Loans	4 714	−9,068	−41,007	627	−11,473	−76,421	−29,662	55,562	−462
Monetary authorities	4 715	−18	−899	−822	607	−5,338	−57,442	45,421	29,291
of which: Short-term	4 718	....	*−899*	*−822*	*607*	*−5,338*	*−57,442*	*45,421*	*29,291*
General government	4 719	117	102	−27	−25	2,497	5,343	3	30
of which: Short-term	4 721	....	....	....	....	*2,475*	*5,323*	*5*	*35*
Banks	4 722	−7,059	−29,875	−1,421	−14,939	−41,122	21,345	18,497	−14,652
of which: Short-term	4 724	....	....	....	....	....	....	....	....
Other sectors	4 725	−2,108	−10,335	2,897	2,884	−32,458	1,092	−8,359	−15,131
of which: Short-term	4 727	*954*	*−9,740*	*4,521*	*−955*	*−21,776*	*170*	*−14,487*	*−15,049*
Currency and deposits	4 730	4,686	11,972	−71,876	−29,237	−216,175	333,200	63,649	64,117
Monetary authorities	4 731	....	....	....	....	....	....	....	....
General government	4 732	....	....	....	....	....	....	....	....
Banks	4 733	−4,336	15,026	−60,242	−9,383	−201,802	314,209	33,414	55,819
Other sectors	4 734	9,022	−3,054	−11,634	−19,854	−14,374	18,991	30,235	8,297
Other assets	4 736	−5	−5	752	−2,264	−843	436	18	−1,460
Monetary authorities	4 737	....	....	24	....	....	....	....	....
of which: Short-term	4 739	....	....	....	....	....	....	....	....
General government	4 740	−5	−4	−3	40	−426	31	4	−128
of which: Short-term	4 742	....	....	....	....	....	....	....	....
Banks	4 743	....	....	....	....	....	....	....	....
of which: Short-term	4 745	....	....	....	....	....	....	....	....
Other sectors	4 746	....	−1	731	−2,304	−417	405	13	−1,332
of which: Short-term	4 748	....	*−1*	*731*	*−2,389*	*−416*	*542*	*237*	*−1,523*
Liabilities	4 753	**12,845**	**28,775**	**83,431**	**61,266**	**295,310**	**−248,485**	**−49,415**	**−15,874**
Trade credits	4 756	....	....	....	....	....	....	....	....
General government	4 757	....	....	....	....	....	....	....	....
of which: Short-term	4 759	....	....	....	....	....	....	....	....
Other sectors	4 760	....	....	....	....	....	....	....	....
of which: Short-term	4 762	....	....	....	....	....	....	....	....
Loans	4 764	−2,298	24,375	70,658	49,074	281,992	−334,344	−110,055	−30,348
Monetary authorities	4 765	....	....	....	....	....	....	....	....
of which: Use of Fund credit and loans from the Fund	4 766	....	....	....	....	....	....	....	....
of which: Short-term	4 768	....	....	....	....	....	....	....	....
General government	4 769	−208	184	115	419	243	−343	32	144
of which: Short-term	4 771	*−208*	*184*	*115*	*419*	*243*	*−343*	*32*	*144*
Banks	4 772	−8,663	24,170	59,567	39,217	243,489	−321,910	−113,656	−40,309
of which: Short-term	4 774	*−12,371*	*24,523*	*61,958*	*34,298*	*244,384*	*−320,825*	*−113,426*	*−36,790*
Other sectors	4 775	6,573	21	10,976	9,438	38,260	−12,092	3,569	9,816
of which: Short-term	4 777	*1,113*	*2,327*	*5,716*	*5,706*	*30,843*	*−7,414*	*4,612*	*12,766*
Currency and deposits	4 780	14,920	3,364	3,242	3,243	10,181	66,802	70,548	9,323
Monetary authorities	4 781	−24	−223	117	−46	5,214	26,431	−26,468	−1,591
General government	4 782	....	....	....	....	....	....	....	....
Banks	4 783	14,743	3,670	3,135	2,231	3,576	40,685	98,347	10,764
Other sectors	4 784	201	−84	−9	1,058	1,391	−314	−1,331	149
Other liabilities	4 786	223	1,036	9,531	8,949	3,137	19,056	−9,908	5,152
Monetary authorities	4 787	....	....	....	....	....	....	5,143	....
of which: Short-term	4 789	....	....	....	....	....	....	....	....
General government	4 790	....	....	....	....	....	....	....	....
of which: Short-term	4 792	....	....	....	....	....	....	....	....
Banks	4 793	....	....	....	....	....	....	....	....
of which: Short-term	4 795	....	....	....	....	....	....	....	....
Other sectors	4 796	223	1,036	9,531	8,949	3,137	19,056	−15,051	5,152
of which: Short-term	4 798	*223*	*1,036*	*9,531*	*8,949*	*3,137*	*19,056*	*−15,051*	*5,152*
E. RESERVE ASSETS	4 802	**−3,405**	**−1,618**	**18,215**	**−370**	**−3,463**	**−3,853**	**−48,137**	**−125,382**
Monetary gold	4 812	....	....	....	−215	....	....	....	....
Special drawing rights	4 811	41	−34	9	−215	44	−1	−5,149	300
Reserve position in the Fund	4 810	41	342	852	392	114	−323	−493	32
Foreign exchange	4 803	−3,486	−1,925	542	−547	−3,618	−3,278	−42,397	−125,757
Other claims	4 813	....	....	16,812	....	−4	−251	−98	43
NET ERRORS AND OMISSIONS	4 998	**−15,016**	**12,364**	**16,989**	**6,634**	**13,149**	**2,188**	**−30,225**	**8,818**

Table 3. INTERNATIONAL INVESTMENT POSITION (End-period stocks), 2003–2010

(Billions of U.S. dollars)

	Code	2003	2004	2005	2006	2007	2008	2009	2010
ASSETS	8 995 C.	**1,750.37**	**1,975.81**	**2,084.03**	**2,490.19**	**3,183.33**	**2,897.11**	**3,085.95**	**3,270.53**
Direct investment abroad	8 505 ..	**341.46**	**400.71**	**432.50**	**570.73**	**654.32**	**735.71**	**841.46**	**891.33**
Equity capital and reinvested earnings	8 506 ..	312.49	378.87	411.53	519.10	624.13	679.07	784.05	824.63
Claims on affiliated enterprises	8 507 ..	312.49	378.87	411.53	519.10	624.13	679.07	784.05	824.63
Liabilities to affiliated enterprises	8 508 ..	....	....	....	....	....	....	....	....
Other capital	8 530 ..	28.97	21.84	20.97	51.63	30.19	56.65	57.41	66.70
Claims on affiliated enterprises	8 535 ..	59.28	57.92	56.70	108.25	110.46	140.23	161.48	156.03
Liabilities to affiliated enterprises	8 540 ..	−30.31	−36.08	−35.73	−56.62	−80.27	−83.58	−104.08	−89.33
Portfolio investment	8 602 ..	**672.61**	**775.52**	**743.43**	**896.37**	**1,082.40**	**909.65**	**1,075.92**	**1,117.78**
Equity securities	8 610 ..	293.66	339.47	357.35	421.50	511.29	318.47	398.89	441.37
Monetary authorities	8 611 ..	....	....	....	....	....	....	....	....
General government	8 612 ..	....	....	....	....	....	....	....	....
Banks	8 613 ..	....	....	....	....	....	....	....	....
Other sectors	8 614 ..	293.66	339.47	357.35	421.50	511.29	318.47	398.89	441.37
Debt securities	8 619 ..	378.96	436.05	386.08	474.87	571.11	591.18	677.03	676.41
Bonds and notes	8 620 ..	350.50	407.01	353.44	424.48	492.15	510.04	592.46	613.05
Monetary authorities	8 621 ..	2.38	2.24	1.52	1.40	1.55	15.90	21.95	14.30
General government	8 622 ..	3.84	3.69	2.79	3.01	2.43	8.63	2.46	2.51
Banks	8 623 ..	35.04	41.44	40.18	47.46	49.04	50.90	57.35	44.58
Other sectors	8 624 ..	309.23	359.63	308.96	372.60	439.13	434.61	510.70	551.67
Money market instruments	8 630 ..	28.46	29.04	32.63	50.40	78.96	81.14	84.56	63.36
Monetary authorities	8 631 ..	....	....	....	....	....	....	....	....
General government	8 632 ..	....	....	1.13	.01	.02	.01	....	....
Banks	8 633 ..	12.16	15.48	18.97	31.64	47.23	34.07	24.70	23.55
Other sectors	8 634 ..	16.30	13.56	12.54	18.75	31.72	47.07	59.86	39.81
Financial derivatives	8 900 ..	**....**	**....**	**60.79**	**93.07**	**123.38**	**220.80**	**166.18**	**187.12**
Monetary authorities	8 901 ..	....	....	....	....	....	2.48	.03	.05
General government	8 902 ..	....	....	.22	.44	.64	.33	.21	.22
Banks	8 903 ..	....	....	23.18	34.42	50.33	100.32	51.76	70.06
Other sectors	8 904 ..	....	....	37.39	58.21	72.41	117.67	114.19	116.79
Other investment	8 703 ..	**666.74**	**724.94**	**789.65**	**865.55**	**1,247.68**	**956.78**	**866.86**	**805.60**
Trade credits	8 706 ..	....	....	....	....	....	....	....	....
General government	8 707 ..	....	....	....	....	....	....	....	....
of which: Short-term	8 709 ..	....	....	....	....	....	....	....	....
Other sectors	8 710 ..	....	....	....	....	....	....	....	....
of which: Short-term	8 712 ..	....	....	....	....	....	....	....	....
Loans	8 714 ..	189.65	240.17	265.55	296.85	410.04	442.15	403.45	411.25
Monetary authorities	8 715 ..	7.59	8.14	8.04	8.02	13.90	74.70	32.07	1.46
of which: Short-term	8 718 ..	*7.59*	*8.14*	*8.04*	*8.02*	*13.90*	*74.70*	*32.07*	*1.46*
General government	8 719 ..	.39	.42	6.66	7.34	5.48	.42	.44	.48
of which: Short-term	8 721 ..	....	....	*6.30*	*6.95*	*5.08*	*.01*	*.02*	*.02*
Banks	8 722 ..	80.63	115.63	110.14	129.42	178.07	155.81	139.57	154.40
of which: Short-term	8 724 ..	....	....	....	....	....	....	....	....
Other sectors	8 725 ..	101.04	115.98	140.70	152.07	212.60	211.21	231.38	254.91
of which: Short-term	8 727 ..	*67.22*	*81.06*	*88.01*	*98.41*	*146.05*	*157.92*	*175.90*	*197.15*
Currency and deposits	8 730 ..	476.66	484.29	520.14	564.63	832.33	509.76	458.41	387.79
Monetary authorities	8 731 ..	....	....	....	....	....	....	....	....
General government	8 732 ..	....	....	....	....	....	....	....	....
Banks	8 733 ..	425.67	426.56	456.22	476.27	722.10	420.89	399.03	338.46
Other sectors	8 734 ..	50.99	57.73	63.92	88.35	110.23	88.86	59.38	49.33
Other assets	8 736 ..	.43	.48	3.96	4.08	5.31	4.88	4.99	6.57
Monetary authorities	8 737 ..	.05	.05	.07	.07	.08	.08	.09	.10
of which: Short-term	8 739 ..	....	....	....	....	....	....	....	....
General government	8 740 ..	.39	.43	.37	.36	.85	.87	.89	1.11
of which: Short-term	8 742 ..	....	....	....	....	....	....	....	....
Banks	8 743 ..	....	....	....	....	....	....	....	....
of which: Short-term	8 745 ..	....	....	....	....	....	....	....	....
Other sectors	8 746 ..	....	....	3.52	3.65	4.37	3.93	4.02	5.36
of which: Short-term	8 748 ..	....	....	*3.30*	*3.49*	*4.20*	*3.63*	*3.49*	*5.01*
Reserve assets	8 802 ..	**69.55**	**74.63**	**57.66**	**64.47**	**75.54**	**74.16**	**135.53**	**268.70**
Monetary gold	8 812 ..	21.93	19.12	21.34	26.40	30.90	29.01	37.06	46.82
Special drawing rights	8 811 ..	.04	.07	.06	.27	.25	.23	5.39	4.99
Reserve position in the Fund	8 810 ..	2.06	1.79	.82	.45	.36	.68	1.19	1.14
Foreign exchange	8 803 ..	45.53	53.65	35.45	37.33	44.04	44.24	91.89	215.75
Other claims	8 813 ..	....	....	....	....	....	....	....	....

Table 3 (Concluded). INTERNATIONAL INVESTMENT POSITION (End-period stocks), 2003–2010

(Billions of U.S. dollars)

	Code	2003	2004	2005	2006	2007	2008	2009	2010
LIABILITIES..	8 995 D.	**1,291.06**	**1,467.62**	**1,605.57**	**1,968.39**	**2,491.82**	**2,268.11**	**2,353.20**	**2,497.33**
Direct investment in Switzerland......................	8 555 ..	**184.20**	**222.69**	**192.34**	**293.73**	**381.39**	**477.12**	**530.42**	**580.40**
Equity capital and reinvested earnings........................	8 556 ..	174.97	218.63	191.37	265.57	387.62	458.13	521.34	574.19
Claims on direct investors..	8 557 ..	....	....	....	....	....	....	....	....
Liabilities to direct investors..................................	8 558 ..	174.97	218.63	191.37	265.57	387.62	458.13	521.34	574.19
Other capital..	8 580 ..	9.23	4.06	.98	28.16	−6.23	18.99	9.08	6.20
Claims on direct investors..	8 585 ..	−14.27	−22.18	−24.66	−32.04	−89.58	−83.06	−86.84	−103.64
Liabilities to direct investors..................................	8 590 ..	23.51	26.24	25.64	60.19	83.36	102.05	95.92	109.84
Portfolio investment...................................	8 652 ..	**450.15**	**520.92**	**588.24**	**740.10**	**783.72**	**587.94**	**684.92**	**766.65**
Equity securities..	8 660 ..	402.62	456.67	536.49	684.25	725.64	530.28	629.08	672.00
Banks..	8 663 ..	....	....	....	....	....	....	....	....
Other sectors..	8 664 ..	402.62	456.67	536.49	684.25	725.64	530.28	629.08	672.00
Debt securities..	8 669 ..	47.53	64.26	51.75	55.85	58.08	57.66	55.84	94.65
Bonds and notes..	8 670 ..	46.63	63.10	50.70	54.43	56.40	54.93	51.92	57.24
Monetary authorities..	8 671 ..	....	....	....	....	....	....	....	....
General government..	8 672 ..	16.22	26.97	25.99	26.68	25.06	21.23	18.09	19.54
Banks..	8 673 ..	....	....	....	....	....	....	....	....
Other sectors..	8 674 ..	30.41	36.14	24.71	27.75	31.34	33.70	33.83	37.70
Money market instruments....................................	8 680 ..	.90	1.15	1.05	1.42	1.68	2.73	3.92	37.42
Monetary authorities..	8 681 ..	....	....	....	....	....	....	....	....
General government..	8 682 ..	....	....	....	....	....	....	....	....
Banks..	8 683 ..	....	....	....	....	....	....	....	....
Other sectors..	8 684 ..	.90	1.15	1.05	1.42	1.68	2.73	3.92	37.42
Financial derivatives...................................	8 905 ..	....	....	**45.96**	**58.13**	**67.47**	**193.41**	**131.78**	**151.68**
Monetary authorities..	8 906 ..	....	....	....	....	....	.25	.02	....
General government..	8 907 ..	....	....	....	....	....	....	....	....
Banks..	8 908 ..	....	....	27.80	33.40	49.69	106.13	50.34	70.06
Other sectors..	8 909 ..	....	....	18.16	24.73	17.78	87.03	81.42	81.63
Other investment.......................................	8 753 ..	**656.71**	**724.01**	**779.02**	**876.44**	**1,259.24**	**1,009.64**	**1,006.09**	**998.60**
Trade credits..	8 756 ..	....	....	....	....	....	....	....	....
General government..	8 757 ..	....	....	....	....	....	....	....	....
of which: Short-term..	8 759 ..	....	....	....	....	....	....	....	....
Other sectors..	8 760 ..	....	....	....	....	....	....	....	....
of which: Short-term..	8 762 ..	....	....	....	....	....	....	....	....
Loans..	8 764 ..	518.38	570.21	633.40	712.13	1,066.79	741.49	654.31	631.87
Monetary authorities..	8 765 ..	....	....	....	....	....	....	....	....
of which: Use of Fund credit and loans from the Fund....	8 766 ..	....	....	....	....	....	....	....	....
of which: Short-term..	8 768 ..	....	....	....	....	....	....	....	....
General government..	8 769 ..	.46	.71	.72	1.20	1.56	1.31	1.37	1.63
of which: Short-term..	8 771 ..	*.46*	*.71*	*.72*	*1.20*	*1.56*	*1.31*	*1.37*	*1.63*
Banks..	8 772 ..	433.06	475.98	504.11	564.13	856.28	529.29	429.29	383.64
of which: Short-term..	8 774 ..	*417.45*	*459.53*	*491.82*	*545.80*	*837.07*	*510.94*	*410.47*	*367.78*
Other sectors..	8 775 ..	84.86	93.52	128.57	146.80	208.96	210.90	223.65	246.59
of which: Short-term..	8 777 ..	*35.21*	*41.88*	*64.78*	*75.93*	*122.61*	*129.80*	*134.61*	*158.57*
Currency and deposits..	8 780 ..	89.90	99.91	94.04	104.44	125.08	194.05	272.37	284.90
Monetary authorities..	8 781 ..	7.75	8.10	7.57	8.21	14.34	42.85	15.50	16.66
General government..	8 782 ..	....	....	....	....	....	....	....	....
Banks..	8 783 ..	81.56	91.28	85.97	94.61	107.56	148.47	255.46	266.74
Other sectors..	8 784 ..	.59	.53	.50	1.62	3.19	2.73	1.40	1.50
Other liabilities..	8 786 ..	48.44	53.89	51.59	59.86	67.36	74.09	79.42	81.83
Monetary authorities..	8 787 ..	....	....	....	....	....	....	5.15	5.06
of which: Short-term..	8 789 ..	....	....	....	....	....	....	....	....
General government..	8 790 ..	....	....	....	....	....	....	....	....
of which: Short-term..	8 792 ..	....	....	....	....	....	....	....	....
Banks..	8 793 ..	1.47	.85	1.13	2.06	3.00	13.38	5.06	1.31
of which: Short-term..	8 795 ..	*1.47*	*.85*	*1.13*	*2.06*	*3.00*	*.40*	*.50*	*1.31*
Other sectors..	8 796 ..	46.97	53.05	50.46	57.80	64.36	60.71	69.21	75.46
of which: Short-term..	8 798 ..	....	....	*.22*	*.52*	*.50*	*.35*	*.29*	*1.34*
NET INTERNATIONAL INVESTMENT POSITION........	8 995 ..	**459.30**	**508.19**	**478.46**	**521.80**	**691.50**	**629.00**	**732.74**	**773.20**
Conversion rates: Swiss francs per U.S. dollar (end of period)...	0 102 ..	**1.2369**	**1.1316**	**1.3143**	**1.2203**	**1.1255**	**1.0637**	**1.0305**	**.9396**

Table 1. ANALYTIC PRESENTATION, 2003–2010

(Millions of U.S. dollars)

	Code	2003	2004	2005	2006	2007	2008	2009	2010
A. Current Account[1]	4 993 Z.	**728**	**587**	**295**	**890**	**460**	**472**	**−1,030**	**−367**
Goods: exports f.o.b.	2 100 ..	5,762	7,220	8,602	10,245	11,756	15,334	10,883	12,273
Goods: imports f.o.b.	3 100 ..	−4,430	−6,957	−8,742	−9,359	−12,277	−16,125	−13,948	−15,936
Balance on Goods	4 100 ..	*1,332*	*263*	*−140*	*886*	*−521*	*−791*	*−3,065*	*−3,663*
Services: credit	2 200 ..	1,331	2,613	2,910	2,924	3,861	4,415	4,798	7,333
Services: debit	3 200 ..	−1,806	−2,235	−2,359	−2,520	−3,013	−3,153	−2,719	−3,473
Balance on Goods and Services	4 991 ..	*857*	*642*	*411*	*1,290*	*328*	*471*	*−985*	*197*
Income: credit	2 300 ..	282	385	395	428	594	540	344	313
Income: debit	3 300 ..	−1,139	−1,114	−1,258	−1,363	−1,283	−1,689	−1,451	−1,827
Balance on Goods, Services, and Income	4 992 ..	....	*−88*	*−452*	*355*	*−361*	*−678*	*−2,092*	*−1,317*
Current transfers: credit	2 379 Z.	743	690	763	770	1,040	1,335	1,247	1,450
Current transfers: debit	3 379 ..	−15	−16	−16	−235	−220	−185	−185	−500
B. Capital Account[1]	4 994 Z.	**20**	**18**	**18**	**18**	**118**	**73**	**210**	**287**
Capital account: credit	2 994 Z.	20	20	20	20	120	75	213	506
Capital account: debit	3 994 ..	....	−2	−2	−2	−2	−2	−3	−219
Total, Groups A Plus B	4 981 ..	*748*	*605*	*313*	*908*	*578*	*545*	*−820*	*−80*
C. Financial Account[1]	4 995 W.	**−436**	**−97**	**−162**	**−332**	**715**	**737**	**1,915**	**1,252**
Direct investment abroad	4 505 ..	....	....	....	....	....	....	....	....
Direct investment in Syrian Arab Republic	4 555 Z.	160	275	500	659	1,242	1,466	2,570	1,469
Portfolio investment assets	4 602 ..	....	....	....	....	....	−55	−241	−193
Equity securities	4 610 ..	....	....	....	....	....	....	....	....
Debt securities	4 619 ..	....	....	....	....	....	−55	−241	−193
Portfolio investment liabilities	4 652 Z.	....	....	....	....	....	....	....	....
Equity securities	4 660 ..	....	....	....	....	....	....	....	....
Debt securities	4 669 Z.	....	....	....	....	....	....	....	....
Financial derivatives	4 910 ..	....	....	....	....	....	....	....	....
Financial derivatives assets	4 900 ..	....	....	....	....	....	....	....	....
Financial derivatives liabilities	4 905 ..	....	....	....	....	....	....	....	....
Other investment assets	4 703 ..	1,210	−237	−524	−710	−746	−631	−626	61
Monetary authorities	4 701 ..	....	....	....	....	....	−38	−208	15
General government	4 704 ..	....	....	....	....	....	....	....	....
Banks	4 705 ..	1,210	−237	−524	−710	−746	−593	−418	46
Other sectors	4 728 ..	....	....	....	....	....	....	....	....
Other investment liabilities	4 753 W.	−1,806	−135	−138	−281	219	−42	212	−85
Monetary authorities	4 753 WA	....	....	....	....	3	−53	411	14
General government	4 753 ZB	2	−235	−388	−259	11	−101	−192	−358
Banks	4 753 ZC	−1,508	....	....	−12	140	23	96	160
Other sectors	4 753 ZD	−300	100	250	−10	65	89	−103	99
Total, Groups A Through C	4 983 ..	*312*	*508*	*151*	*576*	*1,293*	*1,282*	*1,095*	*1,172*
D. Net Errors and Omissions	4 998 ..	**383**	**−256**	**−137**	**−1,488**	**−749**	**−1,232**	**−747**	**905**
Total, Groups A Through D	4 984 ..	*695*	*251*	*14*	*−912*	*544*	*50*	*348*	*2,076*
E. Reserves and Related Items	4 802 A.	**−695**	**−251**	**−14**	**912**	**−544**	**−50**	**−348**	**−2,076**
Reserve assets	4 802 ..	−719	−256	−18	882	−544	−50	−348	−2,076
Use of Fund credit and loans	4 766 ..	....	....	....	....	....	....	....	....
Exceptional financing	4 920 ..	24	5	4	30	....	....	....	....
Conversion rates: Syrian pounds per U.S. dollar	0 101 ..	**11.225**	**11.225**	**11.225**	**11.225**	**11.225**	**11.225**	**11.225**	**11.225**

[1] Excludes components that have been classified in the categories of Group E.

Table 2. STANDARD PRESENTATION, 2003–2010

(Millions of U.S. dollars)

	Code	2003	2004	2005	2006	2007	2008	2009	2010
CURRENT ACCOUNT	4 993 ..	**752**	**592**	**299**	**920**	**460**	**472**	**–1,030**	**–367**
A. GOODS	4 100 ..	**1,332**	**263**	**–140**	**886**	**–521**	**–791**	**–3,065**	**–3,663**
Credit	2 100 ..	**5,762**	**7,220**	**8,602**	**10,245**	**11,756**	**15,334**	**10,883**	**12,273**
General merchandise: exports f.o.b.	2 110 ..	5,680	7,220	8,602	10,245	11,756	15,334	10,883	12,273
Goods for processing: exports f.o.b.	2 150 ..	70	....	....	....	....	....	....	....
Repairs on goods	2 160 ..	....	....	....	....	....	....	....	....
Goods procured in ports by carriers	2 170 ..	12	....	....	....	....	....	....	....
Nonmonetary gold	2 180 ..	....	....	....	....	....	....	....	....
Debit	3 100 ..	**–4,430**	**–6,957**	**–8,742**	**–9,359**	**–12,277**	**–16,125**	**–13,948**	**–15,936**
General merchandise: imports f.o.b.	3 110 ..	–4,363	–6,957	–8,742	–9,359	–12,277	–16,107	–13,933	–15,876
Goods for processing: imports f.o.b.	3 150 ..	–48	....	....	....	....	....	....	....
Repairs on goods	3 160 ..	....	....	....	....	....	–18	–15	–60
Goods procured in ports by carriers	3 170 ..	–19	....	....	....	....	....	....	....
Nonmonetary gold	3 180 ..	....	....	....	....	....	....	....	....
B. SERVICES	4 200 ..	**–475**	**378**	**551**	**404**	**849**	**1,262**	**2,080**	**3,860**
Total credit	2 200 ..	*1,331*	*2,613*	*2,910*	*2,924*	*3,861*	*4,415*	*4,798*	*7,333*
Total debit	3 200 ..	*–1,806*	*–2,235*	*–2,359*	*–2,520*	*–3,013*	*–3,153*	*–2,719*	*–3,473*
Transportation services, credit	2 205 ..	**198**	**198**	**218**	**217**	**226**	**567**	**434**	**529**
Passenger	2 850 ..	*104*	*83*	*91*	*88*	*88*	*26*	*24*	*118*
Freight	2 851 ..	*66*	*24*	*29*	*35*	*38*	*457*	*347*	*278*
Other	2 852 ..	*28*	*91*	*98*	*94*	*100*	*84*	*63*	*132*
Sea transport, passenger	2 207 ..	9	8	9	6	9	....	....	....
Sea transport, freight	2 208 ..	16	....	....	2	5	52	40	27
Sea transport, other	2 209 ..	....	48	53	49	57	57	33	104
Air transport, passenger	2 211 ..	95	70	75	80	76	20	14	106
Air transport, freight	2 212 ..	22	17	20	20	19	15	7	2
Air transport, other	2 213 ..	21	43	45	45	43	27	30	28
Other transport, passenger	2 215 ..	....	5	7	2	3	6	9	12
Other transport, freight	2 216 ..	28	7	9	13	14	390	300	250
Other transport, other	2 217 ..	7	....	....	....	....	....	....	....
Transportation services, debit	3 205 ..	**–813**	**–1,120**	**–1,401**	**–1,255**	**–1,689**	**–1,817**	**–1,433**	**–1,594**
Passenger	3 850 ..	*–34*	*–38*	*–34*	*–45*	*–65*	*–112*	*–98*	*–88*
Freight	3 851 ..	*–739*	*–1,031*	*–1,264*	*–1,099*	*–1,502*	*–1,690*	*–1,302*	*–1,479*
Other	3 852 ..	*–40*	*–51*	*–103*	*–111*	*–122*	*–15*	*–32*	*–27*
Sea transport, passenger	3 207 ..	–7	....	....	....	....	–1	–1	–2
Sea transport, freight	3 208 ..	–579	–909	–1,147	–943	–1,323	–1,207	–1,026	–1,171
Sea transport, other	3 209 ..	....	....	–1	–1	–2	–2	–2	....
Air transport, passenger	3 211 ..	–27	–28	–25	–30	–45	–90	–75	–66
Air transport, freight	3 212 ..	–123	–120	–115	–150	–170	–81	–6	–7
Air transport, other	3 213 ..	–35	–51	–102	–110	–120	–14	–30	–27
Other transport, passenger	3 215 ..	....	–10	–9	–15	–20	–21	–23	–21
Other transport, freight	3 216 ..	–37	–2	–2	–6	–9	–403	–270	–302
Other transport, other	3 217 ..	–5	....	....	....	....	....	....	....
Travel, credit	2 236 ..	**773**	**1,800**	**1,944**	**2,025**	**2,884**	**3,150**	**3,757**	**6,190**
Business travel	2 237 ..	....	....	....	....	....	....	....	....
Personal travel	2 240 ..	773	1,800	1,944	2,025	2,884	3,150	3,757	6,190
Travel, debit	3 236 ..	**–700**	**–650**	**–550**	**–540**	**–645**	**–800**	**–882**	**–1,510**
Business travel	3 237 ..	....	....	....	....	....	....	....	....
Personal travel	3 240 ..	–700	–650	–550	–540	–645	–800	–882	–1,510
Other services, credit	2 200 BA ..	**360**	**615**	**748**	**682**	**752**	**698**	**607**	**614**
Communications	2 245 ..	40	65	125	120	117	136	168	139
Construction	2 249 ..	2	58	14	....	....	....	....	8
Insurance	2 253 ..	1	....	....	10	40	47	44	12
Financial	2 260 ..	22	26	28	54	62	100	89	67
Computer and information	2 262 ..	50	50	60	50	55	40	5	2
Royalties and licence fees	2 266 ..	....	....	....	....	....	....	....	1
Other business services	2 268 ..	95	84	86	81	148	65	43	39
Personal, cultural, and recreational	2 287 ..	....	62	85	92	30	40	43	52
Government, n.i.e.	2 291 ..	150	270	350	275	300	270	215	293
Other services, debit	3 200 BA ..	**–293**	**–465**	**–408**	**–725**	**–678**	**–536**	**–404**	**–369**
Communications	3 245 ..	–5	–10	–17	–30	–25	–41	–17	–20
Construction	3 249 ..	....	....	....	....	....	–15	–10	–13
Insurance	3 253 ..	–15	–31	–35	–331	–212	–200	–104	–121
Financial	3 260 ..	–18	–33	–38	–39	–60	–45	–30	–14
Computer and information	3 262 ..	–110	–100	–100	–95	–110	–70	–45	–15
Royalties and licence fees	3 266 ..	–10	–10	–12	–20	–25	–30	–30	–37
Other business services	3 268 ..	–26	–90	–100	–95	–130	–40	–40	–35
Personal, cultural, and recreational	3 287 ..	....	–27	–21	–32	–20	–20	–17	–19
Government, n.i.e.	3 291 ..	–109	–164	–85	–83	–96	–75	–111	–96

Table 2 (Continued). STANDARD PRESENTATION, 2003–2010

(Millions of U.S. dollars)

	Code	2003	2004	2005	2006	2007	2008	2009	2010
C. INCOME	4 300	−857	−729	−863	−935	−689	−1,149	−1,107	−1,514
Total credit	2 300	*282*	*385*	*395*	*428*	*594*	*540*	*344*	*313*
Total debit	3 300	*−1,139*	*−1,114*	*−1,258*	*−1,363*	*−1,283*	*−1,689*	*−1,451*	*−1,827*
Compensation of employees, credit	2 310	146	165	60	25	30	75	150	200
Compensation of employees, debit	3 310	−40	−41	−38	−75	−80	−30	−31	−36
Investment income, credit	2 320	136	220	335	403	564	465	195	113
Direct investment income	2 330	....	220	330	....	....	....	....	....
Dividends and distributed branch profits	2 332	....	....	....	....	....	....	....	....
Reinvested earnings and undistributed branch profits	2 333	....	....	....	....	....	....	....	....
Income on debt (interest)	2 334	....	220	330	....	....	....	....	....
Portfolio investment income	2 339	....	....	5	....	....	....	....	....
Income on equity	2 340	....	....	5	....	....	....	....	....
Income on bonds and notes	2 350	....	....	....	....	....	....	....	....
Income on money market instruments	2 360	....	....	....	....	....	....	....	....
Other investment income	2 370	136	....	....	403	564	465	195	113
Investment income, debit	3 320	−1,099	−1,073	−1,220	−1,288	−1,203	−1,659	−1,420	−1,790
Direct investment income	3 330	....	−1,073	−1,220	−1,165	−1,085	−1,527	−1,301	−1,684
Dividends and distributed branch profits	3 332	....	−931	−1,088	−1,165	−1,085	−1,527	−1,301	−1,684
Reinvested earnings and undistributed branch profits	3 333	....	....	....	....	....	....	....	....
Income on debt (interest)	3 334	....	−142	−132	....	....	....	....	....
Portfolio investment income	3 339	....	....	....	....	....	....	....	....
Income on equity	3 340	....	....	....	....	....	....	....	....
Income on bonds and notes	3 350	....	....	....	....	....	....	....	....
Income on money market instruments	3 360	....	....	....	....	....	....	....	....
Other investment income	3 370	−1,099	....	....	−123	−118	−132	−119	−106
D. CURRENT TRANSFERS	4 379	752	679	751	565	821	1,150	1,062	949
Credit	2 379	767	695	767	800	1,040	1,335	1,247	1,450
General government	2 380	24	5	4	30	40	85	47	27
Other sectors	2 390	743	690	763	770	1,000	1,250	1,200	1,423
Workers' remittances	2 391	743	690	763	770	1,000	1,250	1,200	1,423
Other current transfers	2 392	....	....	....	....	....	....	....	....
Debit	3 379	−15	−16	−16	−235	−220	−185	−185	−500
General government	3 380	−15	−15	−14	−75	−50	−5	−5	−6
Other sectors	3 390	....	−1	−2	−160	−170	−180	−180	−494
Workers' remittances	3 391	....	−1	−2	−160	−170	−180	−180	−494
Other current transfers	3 392	....	....	....	....	....	....	....	....
CAPITAL AND FINANCIAL ACCOUNT	4 996	−1,135	−335	−162	568	290	760	1,776	−537
CAPITAL ACCOUNT	4 994	20	18	18	18	118	73	210	287
Total credit	2 994	*20*	*20*	*20*	*20*	*120*	*75*	*213*	*506*
Total debit	3 994	....	*−2*	*−2*	*−2*	*−2*	*−2*	*−3*	*−219*
Capital transfers, credit	2 400	20	20	20	20	120	75	213	506
General government	2 401	20	20	....	20	....	....	13	50
Debt forgiveness	2 402	20	20	....	....	....	....	13	50
Other capital transfers	2 410	....	....	....	20	....	....	13	50
Other sectors	2 430	....	....	....	....	120	75	200	456
Migrants' transfers	2 431	....	....	....	....	120	75	200	456
Debt forgiveness	2 432	....	....	....	....	....	....	....	....
Other capital transfers	2 440	....	....	....	....	....	....	....	....
Capital transfers, debit	3 400	....	−2	−2	−2	−2	−2	−3	−219
General government	3 401	....	−2	....	−2	....	....	....	....
Debt forgiveness	3 402	....	....	....	....	....	....	....	....
Other capital transfers	3 410	....	−2	....	−2	....	....	....	....
Other sectors	3 430	....	....	....	....	−2	−2	−3	−219
Migrants' transfers	3 431	....	....	....	....	−2	−2	−3	−219
Debt forgiveness	3 432	....	....	....	....	....	....	....	....
Other capital transfers	3 440	....	....	....	....	....	....	....	....
Nonproduced nonfinancial assets, credit	2 480	....	....	....	....	....	....	....	....
Nonproduced nonfinancial assets, debit	3 480	....	....	....	....	....	....	....	....

Table 2 (Continued). STANDARD PRESENTATION, 2003–2010

(Millions of U.S. dollars)

	Code	2003	2004	2005	2006	2007	2008	2009	2010
FINANCIAL ACCOUNT............................	4 995 ..	**−1,155**	**−353**	**−180**	**550**	**172**	**687**	**1,566**	**−824**
A. DIRECT INVESTMENT............................	4 500 ..	**160**	**275**	**500**	**659**	**1,242**	**1,466**	**2,570**	**1,469**
Direct investment abroad............................	4 505 ..	....	....	....	....	....	....	....	....
Equity capital............................	4 510 ..	....	....	....	....	....	....	....	....
Claims on affiliated enterprises............................	4 515 ..	....	....	....	....	....	....	....	....
Liabilities to affiliated enterprises............................	4 520 ..	....	....	....	....	....	....	....	....
Reinvested earnings............................	4 525 ..	....	....	....	....	....	....	....	....
Other capital............................	4 530 ..	....	....	....	....	....	....	....	....
Claims on affiliated enterprises............................	4 535 ..	....	....	....	....	....	....	....	....
Liabilities to affiliated enterprises............................	4 540 ..	....	....	....	....	....	....	....	....
Direct investment in Syrian Arab Republic........	4 555 ..	**160**	**275**	**500**	**659**	**1,242**	**1,466**	**2,570**	**1,469**
Equity capital............................	4 560 ..	160	275	500	659	1,242	1,466	2,570	1,469
Claims on direct investors............................	4 565 ..	....	....	....	....	....	....	....	....
Liabilities to direct investors............................	4 570 ..	160	275	500	659	1,242	1,466	2,570	1,469
Reinvested earnings............................	4 575 ..	....	....	....	....	....	....	....	....
Other capital............................	4 580 ..	....	....	....	....	....	....	....	....
Claims on direct investors............................	4 585 ..	....	....	....	....	....	....	....	....
Liabilities to direct investors............................	4 590 ..	....	....	....	....	....	....	....	....
B. PORTFOLIO INVESTMENT..........................	4 600 ..	....	....	....	....	....	**−55**	**−241**	**−193**
Assets............................	4 602 ..	....	....	....	....	....	**−55**	**−241**	**−193**
Equity securities............................	4 610 ..	....	....	....	....	....	....	....	....
Monetary authorities............................	4 611 ..	....	....	....	....	....	....	....	....
General government............................	4 612 ..	....	....	....	....	....	....	....	....
Banks............................	4 613 ..	....	....	....	....	....	....	....	....
Other sectors............................	4 614 ..	....	....	....	....	....	....	....	....
Debt securities............................	4 619 ..	....	....	....	....	....	−55	−241	−193
Bonds and notes............................	4 620 ..	....	....	....	....	....	−13	−136	−106
Monetary authorities............................	4 621 ..	....	....	....	....	....	....	....	....
General government............................	4 622 ..	....	....	....	....	....	....	....	....
Banks............................	4 623 ..	....	....	....	....	....	−13	−136	−106
Other sectors............................	4 624 ..	....	....	....	....	....	....	....	....
Money market instruments............................	4 630 ..	....	....	....	....	....	−41	−105	−87
Monetary authorities............................	4 631 ..	....	....	....	....	....	....	....	....
General government............................	4 632 ..	....	....	....	....	....	....	....	....
Banks............................	4 633 ..	....	....	....	....	....	−41	−105	−87
Other sectors............................	4 634 ..	....	....	....	....	....	....	....	....
Liabilities............................	4 652 ..	....	....	....	....	....	....	....	....
Equity securities............................	4 660 ..	....	....	....	....	....	....	....	....
Banks............................	4 663 ..	....	....	....	....	....	....	....	....
Other sectors............................	4 664 ..	....	....	....	....	....	....	....	....
Debt securities............................	4 669 ..	....	....	....	....	....	....	....	....
Bonds and notes............................	4 670 ..	....	....	....	....	....	....	....	....
Monetary authorities............................	4 671 ..	....	....	....	....	....	....	....	....
General government............................	4 672 ..	....	....	....	....	....	....	....	....
Banks............................	4 673 ..	....	....	....	....	....	....	....	....
Other sectors............................	4 674 ..	....	....	....	....	....	....	....	....
Money market instruments............................	4 680 ..	....	....	....	....	....	....	....	....
Monetary authorities............................	4 681 ..	....	....	....	....	....	....	....	....
General government............................	4 682 ..	....	....	....	....	....	....	....	....
Banks............................	4 683 ..	....	....	....	....	....	....	....	....
Other sectors............................	4 684 ..	....	....	....	....	....	....	....	....
C. FINANCIAL DERIVATIVES............................	4 910 ..	....	....	....	....	....	....	....	....
Monetary authorities............................	4 911 ..	....	....	....	....	....	....	....	....
General government............................	4 912 ..	....	....	....	....	....	....	....	....
Banks............................	4 913 ..	....	....	....	....	....	....	....	....
Other sectors............................	4 914 ..	....	....	....	....	....	....	....	....
Assets............................	4 900 ..	....	....	....	....	....	....	....	....
Monetary authorities............................	4 901 ..	....	....	....	....	....	....	....	....
General government............................	4 902 ..	....	....	....	....	....	....	....	....
Banks............................	4 903 ..	....	....	....	....	....	....	....	....
Other sectors............................	4 904 ..	....	....	....	....	....	....	....	....
Liabilities............................	4 905 ..	....	....	....	....	....	....	....	....
Monetary authorities............................	4 906 ..	....	....	....	....	....	....	....	....
General government............................	4 907 ..	....	....	....	....	....	....	....	....
Banks............................	4 908 ..	....	....	....	....	....	....	....	....
Other sectors............................	4 909 ..	....	....	....	....	....	....	....	....

Table 2 (Concluded). STANDARD PRESENTATION, 2003–2010

(Millions of U.S. dollars)

	Code	2003	2004	2005	2006	2007	2008	2009	2010
D. OTHER INVESTMENT	4 700	−596	−372	−662	−991	−527	−674	−414	−25
Assets	4 703	1,210	−237	−524	−710	−746	−631	−626	61
Trade credits	4 706	....	....	....	....	....	....	....	....
General government	4 707	....	....	....	....	....	....	....	....
of which: Short-term	4 709	....	....	....	....	....	....	....	....
Other sectors	4 710	....	....	....	....	....	....	....	....
of which: Short-term	4 712	....	....	....	....	....	....	....	....
Loans	4 714	....	....	....	....	....	−11	−205	−1
Monetary authorities	4 715	....	....	....	....	....	....	−87	48
of which: Short-term	4 718	....	....	....	....	....	....	....	....
General government	4 719	....	....	....	....	....	....	....	....
of which: Short-term	4 721	....	....	....	....	....	....	....	....
Banks	4 722	....	....	....	....	....	−11	−118	−48
of which: Short-term	4 724	....	....	....	....	....	−9	−95	−39
Other sectors	4 725	....	....	....	....	....	....	....	....
of which: Short-term	4 727	....	....	....	....	....	....	....	....
Currency and deposits	4 730	....	−237	−524	−710	−746	−582	−300	95
Monetary authorities	4 731	....	....	....	....	....	....	....	....
General government	4 732	....	....	....	....	....	....	....	....
Banks	4 733	....	−237	−524	−710	−746	−582	−300	95
Other sectors	4 734	....	....	....	....	....	....	....	....
Other assets	4 736	1,210	....	....	....	....	−38	−121	−33
Monetary authorities	4 737	....	....	....	....	....	−38	−121	−33
of which: Short-term	4 739	....	....	....	....	....	....	....	....
General government	4 740	....	....	....	....	....	....	....	....
of which: Short-term	4 742	....	....	....	....	....	....	....	....
Banks	4 743	1,210	....	....	....	....	....	....	....
of which: Short-term	4 745	....	....	....	....	....	....	....	....
Other sectors	4 746	....	....	....	....	....	....	....	....
of which: Short-term	4 748	....	....	....	....	....	....	....	....
Liabilities	4 753	−1,806	−135	−138	−281	219	−42	212	−85
Trade credits	4 756	−300	52	335	−10	35	89	−103	99
General government	4 757	....	−48	85	....	....	....	....	....
of which: Short-term	4 759	....	....	....	....	....	....	....	....
Other sectors	4 760	−300	100	250	−10	35	89	−103	99
of which: Short-term	4 762	−300	100	250	−10	35	89	−103	99
Loans	4 764	2	−187	−473	−259	41	−98	−209	−315
Monetary authorities	4 765	....	....	....	....	....	....	−25	....
of which: Use of Fund credit and loans from the Fund	4 766	....	....	....	....	....	....	....	....
of which: Short-term	4 768	....	....	....	....	....	....	−25	....
General government	4 769	2	−187	−473	−259	11	−101	−192	−358
of which: Short-term	4 771	....	....	....	....	....	....	....	....
Banks	4 772	....	....	....	....	....	3	8	43
of which: Short-term	4 774	....	....	....	....	....	1	1	14
Other sectors	4 775	....	....	....	....	30	....	....	....
of which: Short-term	4 777	....	....	....	....	....	....	....	....
Currency and deposits	4 780	....	....	....	−12	140	−39	145	139
Monetary authorities	4 781	....	....	....	....	....	−60	57	22
General government	4 782	....	....	....	....	....	....	....	....
Banks	4 783	....	....	....	−12	140	21	88	117
Other sectors	4 784	....	....	....	....	....	....	....	....
Other liabilities	4 786	−1,508	....	....	....	3	7	379	−8
Monetary authorities	4 787	....	....	....	....	3	7	379	−8
of which: Short-term	4 789	....	....	....	....	....	....	....	....
General government	4 790	....	....	....	....	....	....	....	....
of which: Short-term	4 792	....	....	....	....	....	....	....	....
Banks	4 793	−1,508	....	....	....	....	....	....	....
of which: Short-term	4 795	....	....	....	....	....	....	....	....
Other sectors	4 796	....	....	....	....	....	....	....	....
of which: Short-term	4 798	....	....	....	....	....	....	....	....
E. RESERVE ASSETS	4 802	−719	−256	−18	882	−544	−50	−348	−2,076
Monetary gold	4 812	....	....	....	....	....	....	−15	−1
Special drawing rights	4 811	....	−54	....	....	....	....	−379	....
Reserve position in the Fund	4 810	....	....	....	....	....	....	....	....
Foreign exchange	4 803	−719	−202	−18	882	−544	−50	46	−2,075
Other claims	4 813	....	....	....	....	....	....	....	....
NET ERRORS AND OMISSIONS	4 998	383	−256	−137	−1,488	−749	−1,232	−747	905

Table 3. INTERNATIONAL INVESTMENT POSITION (End-period stocks), 2003–2010

(Millions of U.S. dollars)

	Code	2003	2004	2005	2006	2007	2008	2009	2010
ASSETS	8 995 C.	....	....	....	....	25,141	25,875	27,092	29,293
Direct investment abroad	8 505 ..	....	....	....	....	5	5	4	5
Equity capital and reinvested earnings	8 506 ..	....	....	....	....	5	5	4	5
Claims on affiliated enterprises	8 507 ..	....	....	....	....	5	5	4	5
Liabilities to affiliated enterprises	8 508 ..	....	....	....	....	....	....	....	....
Other capital	8 530 ..	....	....	....	....	....	....	....	....
Claims on affiliated enterprises	8 535 ..	....	....	....	....	....	....	....	....
Liabilities to affiliated enterprises	8 540 ..	....	....	....	....	....	....	....	....
Portfolio investment	8 602 ..	....	....	....	....	97	152	393	586
Equity securities	8 610 ..	....	....	....	....	14	15	15	14
Monetary authorities	8 611 ..	....	....	....	....	....	....	....	....
General government	8 612 ..	....	....	....	....	....	....	....	....
Banks	8 613 ..	....	....	....	....	14	15	15	14
Other sectors	8 614 ..	....	....	....	....	....	....	....	....
Debt securities	8 619 ..	....	....	....	....	83	137	378	571
Bonds and notes	8 620 ..	....	....	....	....	14	27	163	269
Monetary authorities	8 621 ..	....	....	....	....	....	....	....	....
General government	8 622 ..	....	....	....	....	....	....	....	....
Banks	8 623 ..	....	....	....	....	14	27	163	269
Other sectors	8 624 ..	....	....	....	....	....	....	....	....
Money market instruments	8 630 ..	....	....	....	....	69	110	215	302
Monetary authorities	8 631 ..	....	....	....	....	....	....	....	....
General government	8 632 ..	....	....	....	....	....	....	....	....
Banks	8 633 ..	....	....	....	....	69	110	215	302
Other sectors	8 634 ..	....	....	....	....	....	....	....	....
Financial derivatives	8 900 ..	....	....	....	....	....	....	....	....
Monetary authorities	8 901 ..	....	....	....	....	....	....	....	....
General government	8 902 ..	....	....	....	....	....	....	....	....
Banks	8 903 ..	....	....	....	....	....	....	....	....
Other sectors	8 904 ..	....	....	....	....	....	....	....	....
Other investment	8 703 ..	....	....	....	....	7,987	8,618	9,243	9,183
Trade credits	8 706 ..	....	....	....	....	....	....	....	....
General government	8 707 ..	....	....	....	....	....	....	....	....
of which: Short-term	8 709 ..	....	....	....	....	....	....	....	....
Other sectors	8 710 ..	....	....	....	....	....	....	....	....
of which: Short-term	8 712 ..	....	....	....	....	....	....	....	....
Loans	8 714 ..	....	....	....	....	1	12	217	218
Monetary authorities	8 715 ..	....	....	....	....	....	....	87	40
of which: Short-term	8 718 ..	....	....	....	....	....	....	....	....
General government	8 719 ..	....	....	....	....	....	....	....	....
of which: Short-term	8 721 ..	....	....	....	....	....	....	....	....
Banks	8 722 ..	....	....	....	....	1	12	130	178
of which: Short-term	8 724 ..	....	....	....	....	*1*	*9*	*104*	*143*
Other sectors	8 725 ..	....	....	....	....	....	....	....	....
of which: Short-term	8 727 ..	....	....	....	....	....	....	....	....
Currency and deposits	8 730 ..	....	....	....	....	7,851	8,433	8,733	8,638
Monetary authorities	8 731 ..	....	....	....	....	....	....	....	....
General government	8 732 ..	....	....	....	....	....	....	....	....
Banks	8 733 ..	....	....	....	....	7,851	8,433	8,733	8,638
Other sectors	8 734 ..	....	....	....	....	....	....	....	....
Other assets	8 736 ..	....	....	....	....	135	173	294	327
Monetary authorities	8 737 ..	....	....	....	....	135	173	294	327
of which: Short-term	8 739 ..	....	....	....	....	....	....	....	....
General government	8 740 ..	....	....	....	....	....	....	....	....
of which: Short-term	8 742 ..	....	....	....	....	....	....	....	....
Banks	8 743 ..	....	....	....	....	....	....	....	....
of which: Short-term	8 745 ..	....	....	....	....	....	....	....	....
Other sectors	8 746 ..	....	....	....	....	....	....	....	....
of which: Short-term	8 748 ..	....	....	....	....	....	....	....	....
Reserve assets	8 802 ..	....	....	....	....	17,053	17,100	17,451	19,520
Monetary gold	8 812 ..	....	....	....	....	39	38	53	54
Special drawing rights	8 811 ..	....	57	52	55	58	56	438	430
Reserve position in the Fund	8 810 ..	....	....	....	....	....	....	....	....
Foreign exchange	8 803 ..	....	....	....	....	16,956	17,006	16,960	19,035
Other claims	8 813 ..	....	....	....	....	....	....	....	....

Table 3 (Concluded). INTERNATIONAL INVESTMENT POSITION (End-period stocks), 2003–2010

(Millions of U.S. dollars)

	Code	2003	2004	2005	2006	2007	2008	2009	2010
LIABILITIES	8 995 D.	....	....	....	....	**10,221**	**11,645**	**14,429**	**15,818**
Direct investment in Syrian Arab Republic	8 555 ..	....	....	....	....	**4,433**	**5,900**	**8,470**	**9,939**
Equity capital and reinvested earnings	8 556 ..	....	....	....	....	4,433	5,900	8,470	9,939
Claims on direct investors	8 557 ..	....	....	....	....	....	....	....	....
Liabilities to direct investors	8 558 ..	....	....	....	....	4,433	5,900	8,470	9,939
Other capital	8 580 ..	....	....	....	....	....	....	....	....
Claims on direct investors	8 585 ..	....	....	....	....	....	....	....	....
Liabilities to direct investors	8 590 ..	....	....	....	....	....	....	....	....
Portfolio investment	8 652 ..	....	....	....	....	....	....	....	....
Equity securities	8 660 ..								
Banks	8 663 ..								
Other sectors	8 664 ..								
Debt securities	8 669 ..								
Bonds and notes	8 670 ..								
Monetary authorities	8 671 ..								
General government	8 672 ..								
Banks	8 673 ..								
Other sectors	8 674 ..								
Money market instruments	8 680 ..								
Monetary authorities	8 681 ..								
General government	8 682 ..								
Banks	8 683 ..								
Other sectors	8 684 ..								
Financial derivatives	8 905 ..	....	....	....	....	....	....	....	....
Monetary authorities	8 906 ..								
General government	8 907 ..								
Banks	8 908 ..								
Other sectors	8 909 ..								
Other investment	8 753 ..	....	....	....	....	**5,788**	**5,745**	**5,959**	**5,879**
Trade credits	8 756 ..	....	....	....	....	131	220	116	215
General government	8 757 ..	....	....	....	....	....	....	....	....
of which: Short-term	8 759 ..	....	....	....	....	....	....	....	....
Other sectors	8 760 ..	....	....	....	....	131	220	116	215
of which: Short-term	8 762 ..	....	....	....	....	*131*	*220*	*116*	*215*
Loans	8 764 ..	....	....	....	....	5,170	5,071	4,840	4,530
Monetary authorities	8 765 ..	....	....	....	....	30	30	4	4
of which: Use of Fund credit and loans from the Fund	8 766 ..	....	....	....	....	....	....	....	....
of which: Short-term	8 768 ..	....	....	....	....	*25*	*25*	....	....
General government	8 769 ..	....	....	....	....	5,124	5,023	4,809	4,456
of which: Short-term	8 771 ..	....	....	....	....	....	....	....	....
Banks	8 772 ..	....	....	....	....	16	19	27	70
of which: Short-term	8 774 ..	....	....	....	....	*10*	*11*	*12*	*26*
Other sectors	8 775 ..	....	....	....	....	....	....	....	....
of which: Short-term	8 777 ..	....	....	....	....	....	....	....	....
Currency and deposits	8 780 ..	....	....	....	....	460	420	565	704
Monetary authorities	8 781 ..	....	....	....	....	179	119	176	198
General government	8 782 ..	....	....	....	....	....	....	....	....
Banks	8 783 ..	....	....	....	....	281	301	389	506
Other sectors	8 784 ..	....	....	....	....	....	....	....	....
Other liabilities	8 786 ..	....	....	....	....	27	34	438	430
Monetary authorities	8 787 ..	....	....	....	....	27	34	438	430
of which: Short-term	8 789 ..	....	....	....	....	....	....	....	....
General government	8 790 ..	....	....	....	....	....	....	....	....
of which: Short-term	8 792 ..	....	....	....	....	....	....	....	....
Banks	8 793 ..	....	....	....	....	....	....	....	....
of which: Short-term	8 795 ..	....	....	....	....	....	....	....	....
Other sectors	8 796 ..	....	....	....	....	....	....	....	....
of which: Short-term	8 798 ..	....	....	....	....	....	....	....	....
NET INTERNATIONAL INVESTMENT POSITION	8 995 ..	....	....	....	....	**14,920**	**14,229**	**12,663**	**13,475**
Conversion rates: Syrian pounds per U.S. dollar (end of period)	0 102 ..	**11.225**	**11.225**	**11.225**	**11.225**	**11.225**	**11.225**	**11.225**	**11.225**

2011, International Monetary Fund: *Balance of Payments Statistics Yearbook*

Table 1. ANALYTIC PRESENTATION, 2003–2010

(Millions of U.S. dollars)

	Code	2003	2004	2005	2006	2007	2008	2009	2010
A. Current Account[1]	4 993 Z.	**−4.8**	**−57.0**	**−18.9**	**−21.4**	**−495.1**	**47.6**	**−179.9**	**−382.8**
Goods: exports f.o.b.	2 100 ..	906.2	1,096.9	1,108.1	1,511.8	1,556.9	1,574.9	1,038.5	1,302.7
Goods: imports f.o.b.	3 100 ..	−1,025.7	−1,232.4	−1,430.9	−1,954.6	−3,115.0	−3,699.0	−2,770.4	−2,936.4
Balance on Goods	4 100 ..	*−119.5*	*−135.5*	*−322.8*	*−442.8*	*−1,558.1*	*−2,124.2*	*−1,731.9*	*−1,633.7*
Services: credit	2 200 ..	88.5	122.9	146.3	134.2	148.7	181.4	179.7	209.2
Services: debit	3 200 ..	−121.5	−212.5	−251.5	−394.5	−592.1	−455.5	−291.3	−392.6
Balance on Goods and Services	4 991 ..	*−152.5*	*−225.1*	*−428.0*	*−703.1*	*−2,001.5*	*−2,398.3*	*−1,843.4*	*−1,817.1*
Income: credit	2 300 ..	.9	1.7	9.6	12.4	22.4	19.8	7.2	14.4
Income: debit	3 300 ..	−71.2	−59.2	−50.4	−76.4	−73.2	−72.3	−78.5	−93.1
Balance on Goods, Services, and Income	4 992 ..	*−222.8*	*−282.7*	*−468.8*	*−767.0*	*−2,052.3*	*−2,450.8*	*−1,914.7*	*−1,895.8*
Current transfers: credit	2 379 Z.	285.1	348.4	599.9	1,146.0	1,794.3	2,705.2	1,861.8	2,369.4
Current transfers: debit	3 379 ..	−67.0	−122.8	−150.0	−400.4	−237.1	−206.8	−126.9	−856.3
B. Capital Account[1]	4 994 Z.	....	....	....	....	32.8	39.4	120.4	68.5
Capital account: credit	2 994 Z.	....	....	....	....	32.8	39.4	120.4	68.5
Capital account: debit	3 994 ..	....	....	....	....	....	....	....	....
Total, Groups A Plus B	4 981 ..	*−4.8*	*−57.0*	*−18.9*	*−21.4*	*−462.2*	*87.0*	*−59.4*	*−314.3*
C. Financial Account[1]	4 995 W.	**62.7**	**93.4**	**101.5**	**276.0**	**811.3**	**−223.5**	**143.6**	**382.4**
Direct investment abroad	4 505 ..	....	....	....	....	....	....	....	....
Direct investment in Tajikistan	4 555 Z.	31.6	272.0	54.5	338.6	360.0	375.8	15.8	15.8
Portfolio investment assets	4 602 ..	....	....	....	....	....	....	....	....
Equity securities	4 610 ..	....	....	....	....	....	....	....	....
Debt securities	4 619 ..	....	....	....	....	....	....	....	....
Portfolio investment liabilities	4 652 Z.	.3	5.3	....	....	.2	.1	.1	6.5
Equity securities	4 660 ..	.3	....	....	....	....	....	....	....
Debt securities	4 669 Z.	....	5.3	....	....	.2	.1	.1	6.5
Financial derivatives	4 910 ..	....	....	....	....	....	....	....	....
Financial derivatives assets	4 900 ..	....	....	....	....	....	....	....	....
Financial derivatives liabilities	4 905 ..	....	....	....	....	....	....	....	....
Other investment assets	4 703 ..	−15.6	−28.4	−71.3	−301.9	−386.7	−471.9	177.7	22.4
Monetary authorities	4 701 ..	....	....	....	....	....	....	....	....
General government	4 704 ..	−.4	−.4	−.5	−.5	−.2	−.5	....	....
Banks	4 705 ..	−14.4	−7.3	−33.7	−233.5	−186.7	205.8	38.5	−526.2
Other sectors	4 728 ..	−.8	−20.6	−37.1	−67.9	−199.8	−677.2	139.2	548.6
Other investment liabilities	4 753 W.	46.3	−155.5	118.3	239.2	837.8	−127.4	−50.0	337.7
Monetary authorities	4 753 WA	....	....	....	....	....	....	128.3	....
General government	4 753 ZB	−2.1	−151.4	57.1	34.3	251.5	309.4	156.4	217.4
Banks	4 753 ZC	3.7	1.0	45.0	102.1	240.1	−310.6	−238.6	89.8
Other sectors	4 753 ZD	44.7	−5.1	16.1	102.7	346.2	−126.3	−96.1	30.5
Total, Groups A Through C	4 983 ..	*57.9*	*36.4*	*82.6*	*254.6*	*349.1*	*−136.5*	*84.1*	*68.1*
D. Net Errors and Omissions	4 998 ..	**−30.0**	**−32.5**	**−76.3**	**−264.7**	**−362.9**	**25.6**	**30.7**	**31.0**
Total, Groups A Through D	4 984 ..	*27.9*	*3.9*	*6.3*	*−10.1*	*−13.8*	*−111.0*	*114.8*	*99.1*
E. Reserves and Related Items	4 802 A.	**−27.9**	**−3.9**	**−6.3**	**10.1**	**13.8**	**111.0**	**−114.8**	**−99.1**
Reserve assets	4 802 ..	−40.5	−46.4	−25.6	−7.1	11.5	169.5	−145.7	−164.8
Use of Fund credit and loans	4 766 ..	−2.7	17.0	15.5	−85.7	....	−29.9	25.0	59.2
Exceptional financing	4 920 ..	15.2	25.5	3.9	103.0	2.3	−28.6	5.9	6.5
Conversion rates: somoni per U.S. dollar	0 101 ..	**3.0614**	**2.9705**	**3.1166**	**3.2984**	**3.4425**	**3.4307**	**4.1427**	**4.3790**

[1] Excludes components that have been classified in the categories of Group E.

Table 2. STANDARD PRESENTATION, 2003–2010

(Millions of U.S. dollars)

	Code	2003	2004	2005	2006	2007	2008	2009	2010
CURRENT ACCOUNT	4 993	−4.8	−57.0	−18.9	−21.4	−495.1	47.6	−179.9	−382.8
A. GOODS	4 100	−119.5	−135.5	−322.8	−442.8	−1,558.1	−2,124.2	−1,731.9	−1,633.7
Credit	2 100	906.2	1,096.9	1,108.1	1,511.8	1,556.9	1,574.9	1,038.5	1,302.7
General merchandise: exports f.o.b.	2 110	881.6	1,073.2	1,086.5	1,490.0	1,533.7	1,551.2	1,016.6	1,276.2
Goods for processing: exports f.o.b.	2 150	....	....	....	....	....	....	....	....
Repairs on goods	2 160	....	....	....	....	....	....	....	....
Goods procured in ports by carriers	2 170	.6	.5	....	....	....	....	....	....
Nonmonetary gold	2 180	24.0	23.3	21.6	21.8	23.1	23.7	21.9	26.5
Debit	3 100	−1,025.7	−1,232.4	−1,430.9	−1,954.6	−3,115.0	−3,699.0	−2,770.4	−2,936.4
General merchandise: imports f.o.b.	3 110	−1,019.2	−1,220.4	−1,415.5	−1,940.2	−3,097.2	−3,675.0	−2,750.0	−2,916.0
Goods for processing: imports f.o.b.	3 150	....	....	....	....	....	....	−20.4	....
Repairs on goods	3 160	....	....	....	....	....	....	....	....
Goods procured in ports by carriers	3 170	−6.6	−12.0	−15.4	−14.4	−17.8	−24.0	....	−20.4
Nonmonetary gold	3 180	....	....	....	....	....	....	....	....
B. SERVICES	4 200	−33.0	−89.6	−105.2	−260.3	−443.4	−274.1	−111.6	−183.4
Total credit	2 200	*88.5*	*122.9*	*146.3*	*134.2*	*148.7*	*181.4*	*179.7*	*209.2*
Total debit	3 200	*−121.5*	*−212.5*	*−251.5*	*−394.5*	*−592.1*	*−455.5*	*−291.3*	*−392.6*
Transportation services, credit	2 205	49.0	52.3	55.9	61.8	62.8	47.3	70.3	50.1
Passenger	2 850	*4.7*	*8.4*	*7.5*	*9.1*	*13.2*	*19.5*	*17.1*	*27.9*
Freight	2 851	*43.5*	*43.7*	*48.2*	*52.7*	*49.1*	*27.7*	*27.9*	*17.4*
Other	2 852	*.7*	*.2*	*.2*	*....*	*.4*	*....*	*25.3*	*4.7*
Sea transport, passenger	2 207	....	....	....	....	....	....	....	....
Sea transport, freight	2 208	....	....	....	....	....	....	....	....
Sea transport, other	2 209	....	....	....	....	....	....	....	....
Air transport, passenger	2 211	3.2	6.7	5.5	5.2	8.5	13.5	13.1	24.1
Air transport, freight	2 212	4.0	4.9	2.1	2.1	1.0	.5	1.8	3.0
Air transport, other	2 213	.7	.2	.2	....	.4	....	25.3	4.7
Other transport, passenger	2 215	1.5	1.8	2.1	3.9	4.7	6.0	4.0	3.9
Other transport, freight	2 216	39.6	38.8	46.2	50.6	48.1	27.2	26.0	14.5
Other transport, other	2 217	....	....	....	....	....	....	....	....
Transportation services, debit	3 205	−95.0	−158.8	−178.6	−241.4	−142.2	−179.2	−142.5	−198.3
Passenger	3 850	*....*	*....*	*....*	*....*	*....*	*....*	*....*	*−7.1*
Freight	3 851	*−85.5*	*−143.1*	*−166.1*	*−227.5*	*−112.5*	*−156.4*	*−118.4*	*−148.1*
Other	3 852	*−9.5*	*−15.7*	*−12.5*	*−13.9*	*−29.8*	*−22.8*	*−24.0*	*−43.1*
Sea transport, passenger	3 207	....	....	....	....	....	....	....	....
Sea transport, freight	3 208	....	....	....	....	....	....	....	....
Sea transport, other	3 209	....	....	....	....	....	....	....	....
Air transport, passenger	3 211	....	....	....	....	....	....	....	....
Air transport, freight	3 212	....	....	−.1	....	....	....	....	−.1
Air transport, other	3 213	−6.5	−12.0	−8.7	−10.1	−22.7	−16.1	−18.8	−36.0
Other transport, passenger	3 215	....	....	....	....	....	....	....	−7.1
Other transport, freight	3 216	−85.5	−143.1	−166.0	−227.5	−112.5	−156.4	−118.4	−148.0
Other transport, other	3 217	−3.0	−3.7	−3.9	−3.8	−7.1	−6.7	−5.2	−7.0
Travel, credit	2 236	1.5	1.2	1.6	2.1	3.3	4.2	2.4	4.5
Business travel	2 237	1.2	1.0	1.3	1.6	1.6	1.4	1.4	2.4
Personal travel	2 240	.3	.3	.3	.5	1.6	2.8	1.0	2.1
Travel, debit	3 236	−2.1	−3.4	−3.7	−6.0	−6.6	−10.8	−5.8	−17.8
Business travel	3 237	−1.1	−1.3	−1.7	−2.6	−1.6	−1.7	....	....
Personal travel	3 240	−1.0	−2.2	−2.1	−3.4	−5.0	−9.1	−5.8	−17.8
Other services, credit	2 200 BA	38.0	69.4	88.9	70.3	82.7	130.0	107.1	154.6
Communications	2 245	10.4	12.6	13.5	16.2	18.4	38.9	35.0	77.0
Construction	2 249	.1	1.5	7.2	6.4	2.6	....	....	14.5
Insurance	2 253	....	....	....	.1	....	....	....	.2
Financial	2 260	1.7	4.3	8.3	8.8	12.5	17.3	7.0	9.1
Computer and information	2 262	....	....	.1	.2	.4	.3	.3	.4
Royalties and licence fees	2 266	.9	1.3	1.2	.7	.9	1.0	.6	.6
Other business services	2 268	2.3	7.6	15.0	13.9	15.7	24.6	26.2	26.1
Personal, cultural, and recreational	2 287	....	....	....	....	....	....	....	....
Government, n.i.e.	2 291	22.6	42.1	43.6	24.0	32.2	47.9	38.0	26.8
Other services, debit	3 200 BA	−24.4	−50.4	−69.2	−147.1	−443.3	−265.6	−143.0	−176.5
Communications	3 245	−3.7	−4.5	−7.8	−14.0	−20.1	−33.3	−19.4	−27.1
Construction	3 249	−5.4	−9.8	−30.7	−77.1	−230.4	−127.8	−55.6	−60.5
Insurance	3 253	−7.1	−11.9	−13.8	−19.0	−16.0	−22.3	−17.9	−19.5
Financial	3 260	−1.9	−4.7	−4.1	−12.6	−11.5	−25.4	−12.3	−9.4
Computer and information	3 262	−.3	−.6	−.9	−1.0	−4.3	−2.9	−2.5	−1.4
Royalties and licence fees	3 266	−.2	−.1	−.3	−.1	−.8	−.3	−.1	....
Other business services	3 268	−4.0	−11.2	−10.3	−21.3	−158.0	−50.7	−32.6	−54.5
Personal, cultural, and recreational	3 287	....	....	....	....	....	....	....	....
Government, n.i.e.	3 291	−1.8	−7.5	−1.2	−2.0	−2.1	−2.8	−2.7	−4.0

Table 2 (Continued). STANDARD PRESENTATION, 2003–2010

(Millions of U.S. dollars)

	Code	2003	2004	2005	2006	2007	2008	2009	2010
C. INCOME	4 300	**−70.3**	**−57.5**	**−40.8**	**−63.9**	**−50.7**	**−52.5**	**−71.3**	**−78.7**
Total credit	2 300	*.9*	*1.7*	*9.6*	*12.4*	*22.4*	*19.8*	*7.2*	*14.4*
Total debit	3 300	*−71.2*	*−59.2*	*−50.4*	*−76.4*	*−73.2*	*−72.3*	*−78.5*	*−93.1*
Compensation of employees, credit	2 310	....	....	1.4	3.9	5.3	7.1	6.0	9.7
Compensation of employees, debit	3 310	−.1	−.1	−1.3	−2.1	−3.7	−5.3	−3.7	−6.1
Investment income, credit	2 320	.9	1.7	8.1	8.6	17.1	12.8	1.2	4.7
Direct investment income	2 330	....	....	....	....	....	....	....	....
Dividends and distributed branch profits	2 332	....	....	....	....	....	....	....	....
Reinvested earnings and undistributed branch profits	2 333	....	....	....	....	....	....	....	....
Income on debt (interest)	2 334	....	....	....	....	....	....	....	....
Portfolio investment income	2 339	....	....	....	....	....	....	....	....
Income on equity	2 340	....	....	....	....	....	....	....	....
Income on bonds and notes	2 350	....	....	....	....	....	....	....	....
Income on money market instruments	2 360	....	....	....	....	....	....	....	....
Other investment income	2 370	.9	1.7	8.1	8.6	17.1	12.8	1.2	4.7
Investment income, debit	3 320	**−71.2**	**−59.2**	**−49.1**	**−74.2**	**−69.5**	**−67.0**	**−74.8**	**−87.1**
Direct investment income	3 330	−.7	−1.3	−2.2	−46.1	−26.1	−4.1	−5.4	−9.1
Dividends and distributed branch profits	3 332	....	....	....	....	....	....	−.4	−2.4
Reinvested earnings and undistributed branch profits	3 333	....	....	....	....	....	....	....	....
Income on debt (interest)	3 334	−.7	−1.3	−2.2	−46.1	−26.1	−4.1	−5.0	−6.7
Portfolio investment income	3 339	....	....	....	....	....	....	−.3	−.1
Income on equity	3 340	....	....	....	....	....	....	−.3	−.1
Income on bonds and notes	3 350	....	....	....	....	....	....	....	....
Income on money market instruments	3 360	....	....	....	....	....	....	....	....
Other investment income	3 370	−70.5	−57.9	−46.9	−28.1	−43.4	−62.9	−69.2	−77.8
D. CURRENT TRANSFERS	4 379	**218.1**	**225.6**	**449.9**	**745.6**	**1,557.2**	**2,498.3**	**1,734.9**	**1,513.0**
Credit	2 379	**285.1**	**348.4**	**599.9**	**1,146.0**	**1,794.3**	**2,705.2**	**1,861.8**	**2,369.4**
General government	2 380	....	....	....	....	....	....	....	....
Other sectors	2 390	285.1	348.4	599.9	1,146.0	1,794.3	2,705.2	1,861.8	2,369.4
Workers' remittances	2 391	146.0	252.0	465.2	1,015.0	1,685.4	2,537.0	1,742.2	2,244.8
Other current transfers	2 392	139.1	96.4	134.7	131.0	108.9	168.2	119.6	124.6
Debit	3 379	**−67.0**	**−122.8**	**−150.0**	**−400.4**	**−237.1**	**−206.8**	**−126.9**	**−856.3**
General government	3 380	....	....	....	....	....	....	....	....
Other sectors	3 390	−67.0	−122.8	−150.0	−400.4	−237.1	−206.8	−126.9	−856.3
Workers' remittances	3 391	−64.4	−118.9	−144.2	−392.8	−180.3	−193.5	−120.0	−849.7
Other current transfers	3 392	−2.7	−3.9	−5.8	−7.5	−56.8	−13.3	−7.0	−6.6
CAPITAL AND FINANCIAL ACCOUNT	4 996	**34.8**	**89.5**	**95.2**	**286.1**	**858.0**	**−73.1**	**149.2**	**351.8**
CAPITAL ACCOUNT	4 994	**13.9**	**25.5**	**....**	**99.9**	**32.8**	**39.4**	**120.4**	**68.5**
Total credit	2 994	*13.9*	*25.5*	*....*	*99.9*	*32.8*	*39.4*	*120.4*	*68.5*
Total debit	3 994	*....*	*....*	*....*	*....*	*....*	*....*	*....*	*....*
Capital transfers, credit	2 400	**13.9**	**25.5**	**....**	**99.9**	**32.8**	**39.4**	**120.4**	**68.5**
General government	2 401	13.9	25.5	....	99.9	32.8	39.4	120.4	68.5
Debt forgiveness	2 402	13.9	25.5	....	99.9	32.8	39.4	120.4	68.5
Other capital transfers	2 410	....	....	....	....	....	....	....	....
Other sectors	2 430	....	....	....	....	....	....	....	....
Migrants' transfers	2 431	....	....	....	....	....	....	....	....
Debt forgiveness	2 432	....	....	....	....	....	....	....	....
Other capital transfers	2 440	....	....	....	....	....	....	....	....
Capital transfers, debit	3 400	**....**	**....**	**....**	**....**	**....**	**....**	**....**	**....**
General government	3 401	....	....	....	....	....	....	....	....
Debt forgiveness	3 402	....	....	....	....	....	....	....	....
Other capital transfers	3 410	....	....	....	....	....	....	....	....
Other sectors	3 430	....	....	....	....	....	....	....	....
Migrants' transfers	3 431	....	....	....	....	....	....	....	....
Debt forgiveness	3 432	....	....	....	....	....	....	....	....
Other capital transfers	3 440	....	....	....	....	....	....	....	....
Nonproduced nonfinancial assets, credit	2 480	....	....	....	....	....	....	....	....
Nonproduced nonfinancial assets, debit	3 480	....	....	....	....	....	....	....	....

Table 2 (Continued). STANDARD PRESENTATION, 2003–2010

(Millions of U.S. dollars)

	Code	2003	2004	2005	2006	2007	2008	2009	2010
FINANCIAL ACCOUNT	4 995 ..	**20.9**	**64.0**	**95.2**	**186.2**	**825.2**	**−112.6**	**28.8**	**283.3**
A. DIRECT INVESTMENT	4 500 ..	**31.6**	**272.0**	**54.5**	**338.6**	**360.0**	**375.8**	**15.8**	**15.8**
Direct investment abroad	4 505 ..	....	....	....	....	....	....	....	....
Equity capital	4 510 ..	....	....	....	....	....	....	....	....
Claims on affiliated enterprises	4 515 ..	....	....	....	....	....	....	....	....
Liabilities to affiliated enterprises	4 520 ..	....	....	....	....	....	....	....	....
Reinvested earnings	4 525 ..	....	....	....	....	....	....	....	....
Other capital	4 530 ..	....	....	....	....	....	....	....	....
Claims on affiliated enterprises	4 535 ..	....	....	....	....	....	....	....	....
Liabilities to affiliated enterprises	4 540 ..	....	....	....	....	....	....	....	....
Direct investment in Tajikistan	4 555 ..	**31.6**	**272.0**	**54.5**	**338.6**	**360.0**	**375.8**	**15.8**	**15.8**
Equity capital	4 560 ..	31.6	272.0	54.5	338.6	360.0	375.8	15.8	15.8
Claims on direct investors	4 565 ..	....	....	....	....	....	....	....	....
Liabilities to direct investors	4 570 ..	31.6	272.0	54.5	338.6	360.0	375.8	15.8	15.8
Reinvested earnings	4 575 ..	....	....	....	....	....	....	....	....
Other capital	4 580 ..	....	....	....	....	....	....	....	....
Claims on direct investors	4 585 ..	....	....	....	....	....	....	....	....
Liabilities to direct investors	4 590 ..	....	....	....	....	....	....	....	....
B. PORTFOLIO INVESTMENT	4 600 ..	**.3**	**5.3**	....	....	**.2**	**.1**	**.1**	**6.5**
Assets	4 602 ..	....	....	....	....	....	....	....	....
Equity securities	4 610 ..	....	....	....	....	....	....	....	....
Monetary authorities	4 611 ..	....	....	....	....	....	....	....	....
General government	4 612 ..	....	....	....	....	....	....	....	....
Banks	4 613 ..	....	....	....	....	....	....	....	....
Other sectors	4 614 ..	....	....	....	....	....	....	....	....
Debt securities	4 619 ..	....	....	....	....	....	....	....	....
Bonds and notes	4 620 ..	....	....	....	....	....	....	....	....
Monetary authorities	4 621 ..	....	....	....	....	....	....	....	....
General government	4 622 ..	....	....	....	....	....	....	....	....
Banks	4 623 ..	....	....	....	....	....	....	....	....
Other sectors	4 624 ..	....	....	....	....	....	....	....	....
Money market instruments	4 630 ..	....	....	....	....	....	....	....	....
Monetary authorities	4 631 ..	....	....	....	....	....	....	....	....
General government	4 632 ..	....	....	....	....	....	....	....	....
Banks	4 633 ..	....	....	....	....	....	....	....	....
Other sectors	4 634 ..	....	....	....	....	....	....	....	....
Liabilities	4 652 ..	**.3**	**5.3**	....	....	**.2**	**.1**	**.1**	**6.5**
Equity securities	4 660 ..	.3	....	....	....	....	....	....	....
Banks	4 663 ..	....	....	....	....	....	....	....	....
Other sectors	4 664 ..	.3	....	....	....	....	....	....	....
Debt securities	4 669 ..	....	5.3	....	....	.2	.1	.1	6.5
Bonds and notes	4 670 ..	....	....	....	....	.2	.1	.1	6.5
Monetary authorities	4 671 ..	....	....	....	....	....	....	....	....
General government	4 672 ..	....	....	....	....	....	....	....	....
Banks	4 673 ..	....	....	....	....	....	....	....	....
Other sectors	4 674 ..	....	....	....	....	.2	.1	.1	6.5
Money market instruments	4 680 ..	....	5.3	....	....	....	....	....	....
Monetary authorities	4 681 ..	....	....	....	....	....	....	....	....
General government	4 682 ..	....	....	....	....	....	....	....	....
Banks	4 683 ..	....	....	....	....	....	....	....	....
Other sectors	4 684 ..	....	5.3	....	....	....	....	....	....
C. FINANCIAL DERIVATIVES	4 910 ..	....	....	....	....	....	....	....	....
Monetary authorities	4 911 ..	....	....	....	....	....	....	....	....
General government	4 912 ..	....	....	....	....	....	....	....	....
Banks	4 913 ..	....	....	....	....	....	....	....	....
Other sectors	4 914 ..	....	....	....	....	....	....	....	....
Assets	4 900 ..	....	....	....	....	....	....	....	....
Monetary authorities	4 901 ..	....	....	....	....	....	....	....	....
General government	4 902 ..	....	....	....	....	....	....	....	....
Banks	4 903 ..	....	....	....	....	....	....	....	....
Other sectors	4 904 ..	....	....	....	....	....	....	....	....
Liabilities	4 905 ..	....	....	....	....	....	....	....	....
Monetary authorities	4 906 ..	....	....	....	....	....	....	....	....
General government	4 907 ..	....	....	....	....	....	....	....	....
Banks	4 908 ..	....	....	....	....	....	....	....	....
Other sectors	4 909 ..	....	....	....	....	....	....	....	....

Table 2 (Concluded). STANDARD PRESENTATION, 2003–2010

(Millions of U.S. dollars)

	Code	2003	2004	2005	2006	2007	2008	2009	2010
D. OTHER INVESTMENT.....................	4 700 ..	**29.4**	**−166.9**	**66.3**	**−145.3**	**453.5**	**−657.9**	**158.6**	**425.8**
Assets..................	4 703 ..	**−15.6**	**−28.4**	**−71.3**	**−301.9**	**−386.7**	**−471.9**	**177.7**	**22.4**
Trade credits...............	4 706 ..	−2.8	−20.8	−37.1	−67.9	−199.8	7.1	83.3	−29.9
General government..............	4 707 ..	....	....	....	....	....	....	....	....
of which: Short-term............	4 709 ..	....	....	....	....	....	....	....	....
Other sectors...............	4 710 ..	−2.8	−20.8	−37.1	−67.9	−199.8	7.1	83.3	−29.9
of which: Short-term............	4 712 ..	*−2.8*	*−20.8*	*−37.1*	*−67.9*	*−199.8*	*7.1*	*83.3*	*−29.9*
Loans.....................	4 714 ..	....	....	....	....	....	....	....	....
Monetary authorities............	4 715 ..	....	....	....	....	....	....	....	....
of which: Short-term............	4 718 ..	....	....	....	....	....	....	....	....
General government..............	4 719 ..	....	....	....	....	....	....	....	....
of which: Short-term............	4 721 ..	....	....	....	....	....	....	....	....
Banks.....................	4 722 ..	....	....	....	....	....	....	....	....
of which: Short-term............	4 724 ..	....	....	....	....	....	....	....	....
Other sectors...............	4 725 ..	....	....	....	....	....	....	....	....
of which: Short-term............	4 727 ..	....	....	....	....	....	....	....	....
Currency and deposits............	4 730 ..	−14.4	−7.3	−33.7	−233.5	−186.7	202.6	−36.2	−526.5
Monetary authorities............	4 731 ..	....	....	....	....	....	....	....	....
General government..............	4 732 ..	....	....	....	....	....	....	....	....
Banks.....................	4 733 ..	−14.4	−7.3	−33.7	−233.5	−186.7	205.8	38.5	−526.2
Other sectors...............	4 734 ..	....	....	....	....	....	−3.2	−74.7	−.3
Other assets...............	4 736 ..	1.6	−.3	−.5	−.5	−.2	−681.7	130.6	578.7
Monetary authorities............	4 737 ..	....	....	....	....	....	....	....	....
of which: Short-term............	4 739 ..	....	....	....	....	....	....	....	....
General government..............	4 740 ..	−.4	−.4	−.5	−.5	−.2	−.5	....	....
of which: Short-term............	4 742 ..	*−.4*	*−.4*	*−.5*	*−.5*	*−.2*	*−.5*	....	....
Banks.....................	4 743 ..	....	....	....	....	....	....	....	....
of which: Short-term............	4 745 ..	....	....	....	....	....	....	....	....
Other sectors...............	4 746 ..	2.0	.1	....	....	....	−681.1	130.6	578.7
of which: Short-term............	4 748 ..	*2.0*	*.1*	....	....	....	*−681.1*	*130.6*	*578.7*
Liabilities.............	4 753 ..	**45.0**	**−138.5**	**137.6**	**156.6**	**840.1**	**−186.0**	**−19.1**	**403.4**
Trade credits...............	4 756 ..	42.8	−15.9	23.7	15.7	33.9	6.4	−113.0	11.6
General government..............	4 757 ..	....	....	....	....	....	....	....	....
of which: Short-term............	4 759 ..	....	....	....	....	....	....	....	....
Other sectors...............	4 760 ..	42.8	−15.9	23.7	15.7	33.9	6.4	−113.0	11.6
of which: Short-term............	4 762 ..	*42.8*	*−15.9*	*23.7*	*15.7*	*33.9*	*6.4*	*−113.0*	*11.6*
Loans.....................	4 764 ..	−4.8	−134.4	65.3	17.8	570.1	44.8	114.4	338.3
Monetary authorities............	4 765 ..	−2.7	17.0	15.5	−85.7	....	−29.9	25.0	59.2
of which: Use of Fund credit and loans from the Fund..	4 766 ..	*−2.7*	*17.0*	*15.5*	*−85.7*	....	*−29.9*	*25.0*	*59.2*
of which: Short-term............	4 768 ..	....	....	....	....	....	....	....	....
General government..............	4 769 ..	−2.1	−151.4	57.1	34.3	251.5	279.8	156.4	217.4
of which: Short-term............	4 771 ..	....	....	....	....	....	....	*−84.9*	....
Banks.....................	4 772 ..	....	....	5.8	....	....	−44.6	−71.0	47.3
of which: Short-term............	4 774 ..	....	....	....	....	....	....	....	....
Other sectors...............	4 775 ..	....	....	−13.2	69.2	318.5	−160.5	4.0	14.4
of which: Short-term............	4 777 ..	....	....	....	....	....	....	....	....
Currency and deposits............	4 780 ..	3.7	1.0	39.2	102.1	240.1	−266.0	−167.6	42.5
Monetary authorities............	4 781 ..	....	....	....	....	....	....	....	....
General government..............	4 782 ..	....	....	....	....	....	....	....	....
Banks.....................	4 783 ..	3.7	1.0	39.2	102.1	240.1	−266.0	−167.6	42.5
Other sectors...............	4 784 ..	....	....	....	....	....	....	....	....
Other liabilities...............	4 786 ..	3.3	10.8	9.4	20.9	−4.0	28.8	147.1	11.0
Monetary authorities............	4 787 ..	....	....	3.9	....	....	....	128.3	....
of which: Short-term............	4 789 ..	....	....	*3.9*	....	....	....	....	....
General government..............	4 790 ..	1.4	....	....	3.1	....	....	....	....
of which: Short-term............	4 792 ..	*1.4*	....	....	*3.1*	....	....	....	....
Banks.....................	4 793 ..	....	....	....	....	....	....	....	....
of which: Short-term............	4 795 ..	....	....	....	....	....	....	....	....
Other sectors...............	4 796 ..	1.9	10.8	5.6	17.8	−4.0	28.8	18.8	11.0
of which: Short-term............	4 798 ..	*1.9*	*10.8*	*5.6*	*17.8*	*−4.0*	*28.8*	*18.8*	*11.0*
E. RESERVE ASSETS...........................	4 802 ..	**−40.5**	**−46.4**	**−25.6**	**−7.1**	**11.5**	**169.5**	**−145.7**	**−164.8**
Monetary gold................	4 812 ..	−5.8	−8.6	−5.1	−6.3	6.5	−12.4	−7.4	67.9
Special drawing rights............	4 811 ..	1.0	−.2	−4.9	2.2	.1	−13.7	−93.6	.1
Reserve position in the Fund............	4 810 ..	....	....	....	....	....	....	....	....
Foreign exchange............	4 803 ..	−35.7	−37.6	−15.7	−2.9	−21.0	195.6	−44.7	−232.7
Other claims............	4 813 ..	....	....	....	....	26.0	....	....	....
NET ERRORS AND OMISSIONS............................	4 998 ..	**−30.0**	**−32.5**	**−76.3**	**−264.7**	**−362.9**	**25.6**	**30.7**	**31.0**

Table 1. ANALYTIC PRESENTATION, 2003–2010

(Millions of U.S. dollars)

	Code	2003	2004	2005	2006	2007	2008	2009	2010
A. Current Account[1]	4 993 Z.	**−133.8**	**−523.9**	**−1,104.9**	**−1,134.5**	**−1,849.1**	**−2,674.8**	**−1,933.6**	**−1,978.2**
Goods: exports f.o.b.	2 100 ..	1,220.9	1,481.6	1,702.5	1,917.6	2,226.6	3,578.8	3,294.6	4,296.8
Goods: imports f.o.b.	3 100 ..	−1,933.5	−2,482.8	−2,997.6	−3,864.1	−4,860.6	−7,012.3	−5,834.1	−7,125.1
Balance on Goods	4 100 ..	*−712.6*	*−1,001.2*	*−1,295.1*	*−1,946.5*	*−2,634.1*	*−3,433.5*	*−2,539.5*	*−2,828.3*
Services: credit	2 200 ..	947.8	1,133.6	1,269.2	1,528.1	1,875.7	1,998.8	1,854.6	2,091.5
Services: debit	3 200 ..	−725.7	−974.7	−1,207.3	−1,249.3	−1,413.7	−1,648.9	−1,709.1	−1,849.6
Balance on Goods and Services	4 991 ..	*−490.5*	*−842.3*	*−1,233.2*	*−1,667.8*	*−2,172.0*	*−3,083.6*	*−2,393.9*	*−2,586.4*
Income: credit	2 300 ..	67.9	88.1	84.0	77.1	79.9	110.6	124.7	163.6
Income: debit	3 300 ..	−222.1	−358.8	−451.4	−132.4	−408.5	−311.2	−361.4	−379.3
Balance on Goods, Services, and Income	4 992 ..	*−644.7*	*−1,113.0*	*−1,600.7*	*−1,723.1*	*−2,500.6*	*−3,284.3*	*−2,630.5*	*−2,802.1*
Current transfers: credit	2 379 Z.	574.2	654.1	563.3	654.6	724.0	689.0	765.4	902.9
Current transfers: debit	3 379 ..	−63.3	−65.0	−67.5	−65.9	−72.5	−79.6	−68.4	−79.0
B. Capital Account[1]	4 994 Z.	**692.8**	**459.9**	**393.2**	**5,183.5**	**911.7**	**537.0**	**492.8**	**606.5**
Capital account: credit	2 994 Z.	692.8	459.9	393.2	5,183.5	911.7	537.0	492.8	606.5
Capital account: debit	3 994 ..	....	....	....	....	....	....	....	....
Total, Groups A Plus B	4 981 ..	*559.0*	*−63.9*	*−711.8*	*4,049.1*	*−937.4*	*−2,137.8*	*−1,440.8*	*−1,371.7*
C. Financial Account[1]	4 995 W.	**303.6**	**174.9**	**1,146.0**	**−4,081.6**	**853.3**	**1,621.0**	**1,576.7**	**1,588.1**
Direct investment abroad	4 505 ..	....	....	....	....	....	....	....	....
Direct investment in Tanzania	4 555 Z.	364.3	226.7	935.5	403.0	581.5	400.0	414.5	433.4
Portfolio investment assets	4 602 ..	....	....	....	....	....	....	....	....
Equity securities	4 610 ..	....	....	....	....	....	....	....	....
Debt securities	4 619 ..	....	....	....	....	....	....	....	....
Portfolio investment liabilities	4 652 Z.	2.7	2.4	2.5	2.6	2.8	2.9	3.0	3.2
Equity securities	4 660 ..	2.7	2.4	2.5	2.6	2.8	2.9	3.0	3.2
Debt securities	4 669 Z.	....	....	....	....	....	....	....	....
Financial derivatives	4 910 ..	....	....	....	....	....	....	....	....
Financial derivatives assets	4 900 ..	....	....	....	....	....	....	....	....
Financial derivatives liabilities	4 905 ..	....	....	....	....	....	....	....	....
Other investment assets	4 703 ..	−59.0	−11.0	−90.9	−187.6	34.1	181.7	−333.8	−75.2
Monetary authorities	4 701 ..	....	....	....	....	....	....	....	....
General government	4 704 ..	....	....	....	....	....	....	....	....
Banks	4 705 ..	−59.0	−11.0	−90.9	−187.6	34.1	181.7	−333.8	−75.2
Other sectors	4 728 ..	....	....	....	....	....	....	....	....
Other investment liabilities	4 753 W.	−4.4	−43.2	298.9	−4,299.6	235.0	1,036.4	1,492.9	1,226.7
Monetary authorities	4 753 WA	115.9	33.7	2.4	−64.0	−143.9	−1.3	493.4	−.1
General government	4 753 ZB	−27.9	−15.0	196.1	−4,293.0	224.3	854.8	1,030.1	1,193.7
Banks	4 753 ZC	−29.6	11.8	26.7	23.1	196.0	−8.5	−113.3	−3.5
Other sectors	4 753 ZD	−62.7	−73.7	73.8	34.3	−41.3	191.4	82.7	36.5
Total, Groups A Through C	4 983 ..	*862.5*	*111.0*	*434.2*	*−32.5*	*−84.1*	*−516.8*	*136.0*	*216.5*
D. Net Errors and Omissions	4 998 ..	**−334.0**	**164.4**	**−612.8**	**493.6**	**499.6**	**625.1**	**236.1**	**132.5**
Total, Groups A Through D	4 984 ..	*528.6*	*275.3*	*−178.7*	*461.1*	*415.5*	*108.3*	*372.1*	*348.9*
E. Reserves and Related Items	4 802 A.	**−528.6**	**−275.3**	**178.7**	**−461.1**	**−415.5**	**−108.3**	**−372.1**	**−348.9**
Reserve assets	4 802 ..	−505.0	−257.0	251.9	−126.5	−419.7	−108.3	−680.8	−377.7
Use of Fund credit and loans	4 766 ..	−.3	−32.6	−48.1	−334.6	4.2	....	308.8	28.8
Exceptional financing	4 920 ..	−23.3	14.3	−25.1	....	....	....	....	....
Conversion rates: Tanzania shillings per U.S. dollar	0 101 ..	**1,038.4**	**1,089.3**	**1,128.9**	**1,251.9**	**1,245.0**	**1,196.3**	**1,320.3**	**1,409.3**

[1] Excludes components that have been classified in the categories of Group E.

Table 2. STANDARD PRESENTATION, 2003–2010

(Millions of U.S. dollars)

	Code	2003	2004	2005	2006	2007	2008	2009	2010
CURRENT ACCOUNT	4 993 ..	**−133.8**	**−523.9**	**−1,104.9**	**−1,134.5**	**−1,849.1**	**−2,674.8**	**−1,933.6**	**−1,978.2**
A. GOODS	4 100 ..	**−712.6**	**−1,001.2**	**−1,295.1**	**−1,946.5**	**−2,634.1**	**−3,433.5**	**−2,539.5**	**−2,828.3**
Credit	2 100 ..	**1,220.9**	**1,481.6**	**1,702.5**	**1,917.6**	**2,226.6**	**3,578.8**	**3,294.6**	**4,296.8**
General merchandise: exports f.o.b.	2 110 ..	718.0	851.8	1,047.4	1,131.2	1,438.4	2,470.5	2,065.2	2,780.2
Goods for processing: exports f.o.b.	2 150 ..	....	....	....	....	....	....	....	....
Repairs on goods	2 160 ..	....	....	....	....	....	....	....	....
Goods procured in ports by carriers	2 170 ..	....	....	....	....	....	....	....	....
Nonmonetary gold	2 180 ..	502.8	629.9	655.1	786.4	788.2	1,108.3	1,229.5	1,516.6
Debit	3 100 ..	**−1,933.5**	**−2,482.8**	**−2,997.6**	**−3,864.1**	**−4,860.6**	**−7,012.3**	**−5,834.1**	**−7,125.1**
General merchandise: imports f.o.b.	3 110 ..	−1,933.5	−2,482.8	−2,997.6	−3,864.1	−4,860.6	−7,012.3	−5,834.1	−7,125.1
Goods for processing: imports f.o.b.	3 150 ..	....	....	....	....	....	....	....	....
Repairs on goods	3 160 ..	....	....	....	....	....	....	....	....
Goods procured in ports by carriers	3 170 ..	....	....	....	....	....	....	....	....
Nonmonetary gold	3 180 ..	....	....	....	....	....	....	....	....
B. SERVICES	4 200 ..	**222.1**	**158.9**	**61.8**	**278.7**	**462.1**	**349.9**	**145.6**	**242.0**
Total credit	2 200 ..	*947.8*	*1,133.6*	*1,269.2*	*1,528.1*	*1,875.7*	*1,998.8*	*1,854.6*	*2,091.5*
Total debit	3 200 ..	*−725.7*	*−974.7*	*−1,207.3*	*−1,249.3*	*−1,413.7*	*−1,648.9*	*−1,709.1*	*−1,849.6*
Transportation services, credit	2 205 ..	**138.9**	**183.0**	**222.9**	**343.7**	**331.9**	**364.6**	**334.4**	**445.5**
Passenger	2 850 ..	*6.7*	*16.4*	*11.5*	*35.6*	*15.6*	*3.5*	*31.7*	*23.7*
Freight	2 851 ..	*92.8*	*117.5*	*159.6*	*218.5*	*281.8*	*312.1*	*264.3*	*370.0*
Other	2 852 ..	*39.4*	*49.1*	*51.8*	*89.6*	*34.5*	*49.0*	*38.4*	*51.8*
Sea transport, passenger	2 207 ..	....	....	....	....	....	....	....	....
Sea transport, freight	2 208 ..	92.8	117.5	159.6	218.5	281.8	312.1	264.3	370.0
Sea transport, other	2 209 ..	....	....	....	....	....	....	....	....
Air transport, passenger	2 211 ..	6.7	16.4	11.5	35.6	15.6	3.5	31.7	23.7
Air transport, freight	2 212 ..	....	....	....	....	....	....	....	....
Air transport, other	2 213 ..	....	....	....	....	....	....	....	....
Other transport, passenger	2 215 ..	....	....	....	....	....	....	....	....
Other transport, freight	2 216 ..	....	....	....	....	....	....	....	....
Other transport, other	2 217 ..	39.4	49.1	51.8	89.6	34.5	49.0	38.4	51.8
Transportation services, debit	3 205 ..	**−214.7**	**−267.1**	**−319.5**	**−418.3**	**−485.0**	**−699.0**	**−604.9**	**−716.1**
Passenger	3 850 ..	*−21.9*	*−24.7*	*−22.7*	*−37.1*	*−21.5*	*−24.5*	*−40.3*	*−30.5*
Freight	3 851 ..	*−185.5*	*−235.2*	*−287.6*	*−371.4*	*−458.6*	*−672.5*	*−559.5*	*−680.7*
Other	3 852 ..	*−7.3*	*−7.2*	*−9.3*	*−9.9*	*−5.0*	*−2.0*	*−5.1*	*−4.8*
Sea transport, passenger	3 207 ..	....	....	....	....	....	....	....	....
Sea transport, freight	3 208 ..	−185.5	−235.2	−287.6	−371.4	−458.6	−672.5	−559.5	−680.7
Sea transport, other	3 209 ..	....	....	....	....	....	....	....	....
Air transport, passenger	3 211 ..	−21.9	−24.7	−22.7	−37.1	−21.5	−24.5	−40.3	−30.5
Air transport, freight	3 212 ..	....	....	....	....	....	....	....	....
Air transport, other	3 213 ..	....	....	....	....	....	....	....	....
Other transport, passenger	3 215 ..	....	....	....	....	....	....	....	....
Other transport, freight	3 216 ..	....	....	....	....	....	....	....	....
Other transport, other	3 217 ..	−7.3	−7.2	−9.3	−9.9	−5.0	−2.0	−5.1	−4.8
Travel, credit	2 236 ..	**646.5**	**746.0**	**823.6**	**950.2**	**1,198.8**	**1,288.7**	**1,159.8**	**1,254.5**
Business travel	2 237 ..	....	....	....	....	....	....	....	....
Personal travel	2 240 ..	646.5	746.0	823.6	950.2	1,198.8	1,288.7	1,159.8	1,254.5
Travel, debit	3 236 ..	**−353.2**	**−445.3**	**−553.8**	**−534.5**	**−595.3**	**−720.7**	**−766.2**	**−830.4**
Business travel	3 237 ..	....	....	....	....	....	....	....	....
Personal travel	3 240 ..	−353.2	−445.3	−553.8	−534.5	−595.3	−720.7	−766.2	−830.4
Other services, credit	2 200 BA	**162.3**	**204.6**	**222.7**	**234.1**	**345.0**	**345.4**	**360.4**	**391.5**
Communications	2 245 ..	20.3	31.6	33.7	37.9	39.6	40.0	48.4	38.9
Construction	2 249 ..	....	....	....	....	....	....	....	....
Insurance	2 253 ..	19.8	25.4	38.0	11.4	22.3	23.3	20.6	35.8
Financial	2 260 ..	4.1	2.5	1.9	4.2	5.1	1.1	.7	9.5
Computer and information	2 262 ..	.2	....	.3	.3	3.4	4.0	2.3	4.6
Royalties and licence fees	2 266 ..	....	....	....	....	....	....	....	....
Other business services	2 268 ..	68.8	85.8	94.2	119.1	234.2	233.6	225.8	257.2
Personal, cultural, and recreational	2 287 ..	1.2	.1	.7	.1	.9	10.4	2.8	1.2
Government, n.i.e.	2 291 ..	48.0	59.3	53.9	61.0	39.4	33.1	59.8	44.3
Other services, debit	3 200 BA	**−157.8**	**−262.3**	**−334.0**	**−296.6**	**−333.4**	**−229.1**	**−338.0**	**−303.0**
Communications	3 245 ..	−12.6	−15.4	−15.7	−17.3	−15.0	−15.9	−15.0	−20.5
Construction	3 249 ..	−10.2	−93.0	−143.0	−131.9	−63.9	−24.3	−36.5	−27.7
Insurance	3 253 ..	−34.9	−37.9	−46.1	−52.2	−59.5	−64.2	−62.5	−68.5
Financial	3 260 ..	−6.7	−5.1	−2.6	−4.0	−8.7	−2.8	−2.1	−7.1
Computer and information	3 262 ..	−1.1	−3.1	−4.6	−3.4	−5.1	−5.4	−7.1	−9.6
Royalties and licence fees	3 266 ..	−.7	−.6	−.2	−.7	−5.3	−.1	....	−.3
Other business services	3 268 ..	−50.2	−55.3	−45.6	−50.0	−126.1	−94.5	−190.3	−159.3
Personal, cultural, and recreational	3 287 ..	−.8						−.3	−.3
Government, n.i.e.	3 291 ..	−40.6	−52.0	−76.1	−37.0	−49.8	−22.0	−24.2	−9.8

Table 2 (Continued). STANDARD PRESENTATION, 2003–2010

(Millions of U.S. dollars)

	Code	2003	2004	2005	2006	2007	2008	2009	2010
C. INCOME	4 300	**−154.2**	**−270.7**	**−367.5**	**−55.4**	**−328.6**	**−200.6**	**−236.6**	**−215.7**
Total credit	2 300	*67.9*	*88.1*	*84.0*	*77.1*	*79.9*	*110.6*	*124.7*	*163.6*
Total debit	3 300	*−222.1*	*−358.8*	*−451.4*	*−132.4*	*−408.5*	*−311.2*	*−361.4*	*−379.3*
Compensation of employees, credit	2 310	**7.0**	**8.0**	**10.2**	**6.4**	**6.0**	**9.3**	**11.4**	**13.9**
Compensation of employees, debit	3 310	**−22.4**	**−28.0**	**−24.9**	**−23.4**	**−46.4**	**−54.5**	**−80.6**	**−109.3**
Investment income, credit	2 320	**60.9**	**80.1**	**73.7**	**70.7**	**73.9**	**101.3**	**113.4**	**149.7**
Direct investment income	2 330	....	....	....	....	....	....	....	....
Dividends and distributed branch profits	2 332	....	....	....	....	....	....	....	....
Reinvested earnings and undistributed branch profits	2 333	....	....			....	....	....	....
Income on debt (interest)	2 334	....							
Portfolio investment income	2 339	....	....						
Income on equity	2 340	....							
Income on bonds and notes	2 350	....							
Income on money market instruments	2 360	....	....						
Other investment income	2 370	60.9	80.1	73.7	70.7	73.9	101.3	113.4	149.7
Investment income, debit	3 320	**−199.7**	**−330.8**	**−426.5**	**−109.0**	**−362.1**	**−256.8**	**−280.8**	**−270.0**
Direct investment income	3 330	−115.8	−175.9	−318.7	−25.3	−308.9	−205.4	−184.3	−186.7
Dividends and distributed branch profits	3 332	−37.4	−33.3	−40.5	−67.0	−104.0	−73.0	−45.7	−43.2
Reinvested earnings and undistributed branch profits	3 333	−56.1	−117.5	−248.1	71.8	−176.4	−106.2	−109.8	−114.7
Income on debt (interest)	3 334	−22.3	−25.1	−30.1	−30.1	−28.6	−26.2	−28.8	−28.8
Portfolio investment income	3 339	−24.0	−35.4	−35.4	−26.8	−25.4	−25.4	−31.2	−37.2
Income on equity	3 340	....	....	....					
Income on bonds and notes	3 350	−24.0	−35.4	−35.4	−26.8	−25.4	−25.4	−31.2	−37.2
Income on money market instruments	3 360	....	....	....					
Other investment income	3 370	−60.0	−119.5	−72.4	−56.9	−27.8	−26.0	−65.3	−46.1
D. CURRENT TRANSFERS	4 379	**511.0**	**589.1**	**495.7**	**588.7**	**651.5**	**609.5**	**696.9**	**823.9**
Credit	2 379	**574.2**	**654.1**	**563.3**	**654.6**	**724.0**	**689.0**	**765.4**	**902.9**
General government	2 380	507.6	582.0	477.9	559.7	626.9	588.5	658.4	798.1
Other sectors	2 390	66.6	72.1	85.4	94.9	97.1	100.5	106.9	104.8
Workers' remittances	2 391	1.9	5.8	9.1	9.0	8.3	9.3	11.9	10.9
Other current transfers	2 392	64.7	66.3	76.3	85.9	88.8	91.2	95.1	93.9
Debit	3 379	**−63.3**	**−65.0**	**−67.5**	**−65.9**	**−72.5**	**−79.6**	**−68.4**	**−79.0**
General government	3 380	−5.1	−4.6	−3.6	−2.4	−3.7	−.4	−.2	....
Other sectors	3 390	−58.2	−60.5	−64.0	−63.5	−68.8	−79.1	−68.2	−79.0
Workers' remittances	3 391	−4.7	−5.9	−8.3	−6.2	−10.3	−19.8	−6.8	−17.6
Other current transfers	3 392	−53.5	−54.6	−55.7	−57.3	−58.5	−59.3	−61.4	−61.4
CAPITAL AND FINANCIAL ACCOUNT	4 996	**467.7**	**359.5**	**1,717.8**	**640.8**	**1,349.5**	**2,049.7**	**1,697.5**	**1,845.7**
CAPITAL ACCOUNT	4 994	**692.8**	**459.9**	**393.2**	**5,183.5**	**911.7**	**537.0**	**492.8**	**606.5**
Total credit	2 994	*692.8*	*459.9*	*393.2*	*5,183.5*	*911.7*	*537.0*	*492.8*	*606.5*
Total debit	3 994	....	....	....	....	....	....	....	....
Capital transfers, credit	2 400	**692.8**	**459.9**	**393.2**	**5,183.5**	**911.7**	**537.0**	**492.8**	**606.5**
General government	2 401	655.5	420.0	350.1	5,135.0	858.5	477.3	430.2	543.3
Debt forgiveness	2 402	334.6	166.3	112.1	4,961.7	523.0	....	....	....
Other capital transfers	2 410	320.9	253.7	238.0	173.3	335.5	477.3	430.2	543.3
Other sectors	2 430	37.3	39.9	43.1	48.6	53.2	59.8	62.6	63.2
Migrants' transfers	2 431	....	....	....	....	....	....	....	....
Debt forgiveness	2 432	....	....	....	....	....	....	....	....
Other capital transfers	2 440	37.3	39.9	43.1	48.6	53.2	59.8	62.6	63.2
Capital transfers, debit	3 400	....	....	....	....	....	....	....	....
General government	3 401	....	....	....	....	....	....	....	....
Debt forgiveness	3 402	....	....	....	....	....	....	....	....
Other capital transfers	3 410	....	....	....	....	....	....	....	....
Other sectors	3 430	....	....	....	....	....	....	....	....
Migrants' transfers	3 431	....	....	....	....	....	....	....	....
Debt forgiveness	3 432	....	....	....	....	....	....	....	....
Other capital transfers	3 440	....	....	....	....	....	....	....	....
Nonproduced nonfinancial assets, credit	2 480	....	....	....	....	....	....	....	....
Nonproduced nonfinancial assets, debit	3 480	....	....	....	....	....	....	....	....

Table 2 (Continued). STANDARD PRESENTATION, 2003–2010

(Millions of U.S. dollars)

	Code	2003	2004	2005	2006	2007	2008	2009	2010
FINANCIAL ACCOUNT	4 995	**−225.0**	**−100.4**	**1,324.6**	**−4,542.7**	**437.8**	**1,512.7**	**1,204.7**	**1,239.2**
A. DIRECT INVESTMENT	4 500	**364.3**	**226.7**	**935.5**	**403.0**	**581.5**	**400.0**	**414.5**	**433.4**
Direct investment abroad	4 505	....	....	....	....	....	....	....	....
Equity capital	4 510	....	....	....	....	....	....	....	....
Claims on affiliated enterprises	4 515	....	....	....	....	....	....	....	....
Liabilities to affiliated enterprises	4 520	....	....	....	....	....	....	....	....
Reinvested earnings	4 525	....	....	....	....	....	....	....	....
Other capital	4 530	....	....	....	....	....	....	....	....
Claims on affiliated enterprises	4 535	....	....	....	....	....	....	....	....
Liabilities to affiliated enterprises	4 540	....	....	....	....	....	....	....	....
Direct investment in Tanzania	4 555	**364.3**	**226.7**	**935.5**	**403.0**	**581.5**	**400.0**	**414.5**	**433.4**
Equity capital	4 560	308.2	109.3	190.6	50.3	98.4	87.8	93.1	99.5
Claims on direct investors	4 565	....	....	....	....	....	....	....	....
Liabilities to direct investors	4 570	308.2	109.3	190.6	50.3	98.4	87.8	93.1	99.5
Reinvested earnings	4 575	56.1	117.5	248.1	−71.8	176.4	106.2	109.8	114.7
Other capital	4 580	....	....	496.8	424.5	306.7	206.1	211.7	219.3
Claims on direct investors	4 585	....	....	....	....	....	....	....	....
Liabilities to direct investors	4 590	....	....	496.8	424.5	306.7	206.1	211.7	219.3
B. PORTFOLIO INVESTMENT	4 600	**2.7**	**2.4**	**2.5**	**2.6**	**2.8**	**2.9**	**3.0**	**3.2**
Assets	4 602	....	....	....	....	....	....	....	....
Equity securities	4 610	....	....	....	....	....	....	....	....
Monetary authorities	4 611	....	....	....	....	....	....	....	....
General government	4 612	....	....	....	....	....	....	....	....
Banks	4 613	....	....	....	....	....	....	....	....
Other sectors	4 614	....	....	....	....	....	....	....	....
Debt securities	4 619	....	....	....	....	....	....	....	....
Bonds and notes	4 620	....	....	....	....	....	....	....	....
Monetary authorities	4 621	....	....	....	....	....	....	....	....
General government	4 622	....	....	....	....	....	....	....	....
Banks	4 623	....	....	....	....	....	....	....	....
Other sectors	4 624	....	....	....	....	....	....	....	....
Money market instruments	4 630	....	....	....	....	....	....	....	....
Monetary authorities	4 631	....	....	....	....	....	....	....	....
General government	4 632	....	....	....	....	....	....	....	....
Banks	4 633	....	....	....	....	....	....	....	....
Other sectors	4 634	....	....	....	....	....	....	....	....
Liabilities	4 652	**2.7**	**2.4**	**2.5**	**2.6**	**2.8**	**2.9**	**3.0**	**3.2**
Equity securities	4 660	2.7	2.4	2.5	2.6	2.8	2.9	3.0	3.2
Banks	4 663	....	....	....	....	....	....	....	....
Other sectors	4 664	2.7	2.4	2.5	2.6	2.8	2.9	3.0	3.2
Debt securities	4 669	....	....	....	....	....	....	....	....
Bonds and notes	4 670	....	....	....	....	....	....	....	....
Monetary authorities	4 671	....	....	....	....	....	....	....	....
General government	4 672	....	....	....	....	....	....	....	....
Banks	4 673	....	....	....	....	....	....	....	....
Other sectors	4 674	....	....	....	....	....	....	....	....
Money market instruments	4 680	....	....	....	....	....	....	....	....
Monetary authorities	4 681	....	....	....	....	....	....	....	....
General government	4 682	....	....	....	....	....	....	....	....
Banks	4 683	....	....	....	....	....	....	....	....
Other sectors	4 684	....	....	....	....	....	....	....	....
C. FINANCIAL DERIVATIVES	4 910	....	....	....	....	....	....	....	....
Monetary authorities	4 911	....	....	....	....	....	....	....	....
General government	4 912	....	....	....	....	....	....	....	....
Banks	4 913	....	....	....	....	....	....	....	....
Other sectors	4 914	....	....	....	....	....	....	....	....
Assets	4 900	....	....	....	....	....	....	....	....
Monetary authorities	4 901	....	....	....	....	....	....	....	....
General government	4 902	....	....	....	....	....	....	....	....
Banks	4 903	....	....	....	....	....	....	....	....
Other sectors	4 904	....	....	....	....	....	....	....	....
Liabilities	4 905	....	....	....	....	....	....	....	....
Monetary authorities	4 906	....	....	....	....	....	....	....	....
General government	4 907	....	....	....	....	....	....	....	....
Banks	4 908	....	....	....	....	....	....	....	....
Other sectors	4 909	....	....	....	....	....	....	....	....

Table 2 (Concluded). STANDARD PRESENTATION, 2003–2010

(Millions of U.S. dollars)

	Code	2003	2004	2005	2006	2007	2008	2009	2010
D. OTHER INVESTMENT	4 700 ..	**−87.0**	**−72.6**	**134.7**	**−4,821.8**	**273.2**	**1,218.1**	**1,467.9**	**1,180.3**
Assets	4 703 ..	**−59.0**	**−11.0**	**−90.9**	**−187.6**	**34.1**	**181.7**	**−333.8**	**−75.2**
Trade credits	4 706 ..	....	....	....	....	....	....	....	....
General government	4 707 ..	....	....	....	....	....	....	....	....
of which: Short-term	4 709 ..	....	....	....	....	....	....	....	....
Other sectors	4 710 ..	....	....	....	....	....	....	....	....
of which: Short-term	4 712 ..	....	....	....	....	....	....	....	....
Loans	4 714 ..	....	....	....	....	....	....	....	....
Monetary authorities	4 715 ..	....	....	....	....	....	....	....	....
of which: Short-term	4 718 ..	....	....	....	....	....	....	....	....
General government	4 719 ..	....	....	....	....	....	....	....	....
of which: Short-term	4 721 ..	....	....	....	....	....	....	....	....
Banks	4 722 ..	....	....	....	....	....	....	....	....
of which: Short-term	4 724 ..	....	....	....	....	....	....	....	....
Other sectors	4 725 ..	....	....	....	....	....	....	....	....
of which: Short-term	4 727 ..	....	....	....	....	....	....	....	....
Currency and deposits	4 730 ..	−59.0	−11.0	−90.9	−187.6	34.1	181.7	−333.8	−75.2
Monetary authorities	4 731 ..	....	....	....	....	....	....	....	....
General government	4 732 ..	....	....	....	....	....	....	....	....
Banks	4 733 ..	−59.0	−11.0	−90.9	−187.6	34.1	181.7	−333.8	−75.2
Other sectors	4 734 ..	....	....	....	....	....	....	....	....
Other assets	4 736 ..	....	....	....	....	....	....	....	....
Monetary authorities	4 737 ..	....	....	....	....	....	....	....	....
of which: Short-term	4 739 ..	....	....	....	....	....	....	....	....
General government	4 740 ..	....	....	....	....	....	....	....	....
of which: Short-term	4 742 ..	....	....	....	....	....	....	....	....
Banks	4 743 ..	....	....	....	....	....	....	....	....
of which: Short-term	4 745 ..	....	....	....	....	....	....	....	....
Other sectors	4 738 ..	....	....	....	....	....	....	....	....
of which: Short-term	4 748 ..	....	....	....	....	....	....	....	....
Liabilities	4 753 ..	**−28.0**	**−61.6**	**225.7**	**−4,634.2**	**239.1**	**1,036.4**	**1,801.7**	**1,255.4**
Trade credits	4 756 ..	27.2	1.2	1.2	9.9	9.9	10.1	10.1	10.3
General government	4 757 ..	....	....	....	....	....	....	....	....
of which: Short-term	4 759 ..	....	....	....	....	....	....	....	....
Other sectors	4 760 ..	27.2	1.2	1.2	9.9	9.9	10.1	10.1	10.3
of which: Short-term	4 762 ..	27.2	1.2	1.2	9.9	9.9	10.1	10.1	10.3
Loans	4 764 ..	−118.8	−123.0	241.8	−4,607.2	254.5	1,076.9	1,584.3	1,233.9
Monetary authorities	4 765 ..	−.3	−32.6	−48.1	−334.6	4.2	....	557.8	28.8
of which: Use of Fund credit and loans from the Fund	4 766 ..	−.3	−32.6	−48.1	−334.6	4.2	....	308.8	28.8
of which: Short-term	4 768 ..	....	....	....	....	....	....	....	....
General government	4 769 ..	−27.9	−15.0	196.1	−4,293.0	224.3	854.8	1,030.1	1,193.7
of which: Short-term	4 771 ..	−421.5	−166.3	−112.1	−4,961.7	−523.0	....	....	....
Banks	4 772 ..	−.7	−.5	21.3	−4.1	77.2	40.9	−76.1	−14.8
of which: Short-term	4 774 ..	....	....	....	....	....	....	....	....
Other sectors	4 775 ..	−89.9	−74.9	72.6	24.4	−51.2	181.3	72.6	26.2
of which: Short-term	4 777 ..	....	....	....	....	....	....	....	....
Currency and deposits	4 780 ..	87.0	46.0	7.8	−36.9	−25.2	−50.6	−41.2	11.2
Monetary authorities	4 781 ..	115.9	33.7	2.4	−64.0	−143.9	−1.3	−4.1	−.1
General government	4 782 ..	....	....	....	....	....	....	....	....
Banks	4 783 ..	−28.9	12.3	5.4	27.1	118.7	−49.4	−37.2	11.4
Other sectors	4 784 ..	....	....	....	....	....	....	....	....
Other liabilities	4 786 ..	−23.3	14.3	−25.1	....	....	....	248.5	....
Monetary authorities	4 787 ..	....	....	....	....	....	....	248.5	....
of which: Short-term	4 789 ..	....	....	....	....	....	....	....	....
General government	4 790 ..	−23.3	14.3	−25.1	....	....	....	....	....
of which: Short-term	4 792 ..	−23.3	14.3	−25.1	....	....	....	....	....
Banks	4 793 ..	....	....	....	....	....	....	....	....
of which: Short-term	4 795 ..	....	....	....	....	....	....	....	....
Other sectors	4 796 ..	....	....	....	....	....	....	....	....
of which: Short-term	4 798 ..	....	....	....	....	....	....	....	....
E. RESERVE ASSETS	4 802 ..	**−505.0**	**−257.0**	**251.9**	**−126.5**	**−419.7**	**−108.3**	**−680.8**	**−377.7**
Monetary gold	4 812 ..	27.6	....	....	....	....	....	....	....
Special drawing rights	4 811 ..	−.4	.4	−.6	.7	−.1	.1	−247.8	.6
Reserve position in the Fund	4 810 ..	....	....	....	....	....	....	....	....
Foreign exchange	4 803 ..	−535.1	−257.5	255.7	−126.5	−419.8	−109.7	−436.2	−378.4
Other claims	4 813 ..	2.9	.1	−3.2	−.7	.2	1.3	3.2	.1
NET ERRORS AND OMISSIONS	4 998 ..	**−334.0**	**164.4**	**−612.8**	**493.6**	**499.6**	**625.1**	**236.1**	**132.5**

Table 3. INTERNATIONAL INVESTMENT POSITION (End-period stocks), 2003–2010

(Millions of U.S. dollars)

	Code	2003	2004	2005	2006	2007	2008	2009	2010
ASSETS...........	8 995 C.	**2,178.6**	**2,607.1**	**3,301.8**	**3,480.3**	**3,565.9**	**4,225.9**	**3,835.9**	**3,758.7**
Direct investment abroad...........	8 505 ..	....	....	....	....	....	....	....	....
Equity capital and reinvested earnings...........	8 506 ..	....	....	....	....	....	....	....	....
Claims on affiliated enterprises...........	8 507 ..	....	....	....	....	....	....	....	....
Liabilities to affiliated enterprises...........	8 508 ..	....	....	....	....	....	....	....	....
Other capital...........	8 530 ..	....	....	....	....	....	....	....	....
Claims on affiliated enterprises...........	8 535 ..	....	....	....	....	....	....	....	....
Liabilities to affiliated enterprises...........	8 540 ..	....	....	....	....	....	....	....	....
Portfolio investment...........	8 602 ..	....	....	....	....	....	....	....	....
Equity securities...........	8 610 ..	....	....	....	....	....	....	....	....
Monetary authorities...........	8 611 ..	....	....	....	....	....	....	....	....
General government...........	8 612 ..	....	....	....	....	....	....	....	....
Banks...........	8 613 ..	....	....	....	....	....	....	....	....
Other sectors...........	8 614 ..	....	....	....	....	....	....	....	....
Debt securities...........	8 619 ..	....	....	....	....	....	....	....	....
Bonds and notes...........	8 620 ..	....	....	....	....	....	....	....	....
Monetary authorities...........	8 621 ..	....	....	....	....	....	....	....	....
General government...........	8 622 ..	....	....	....	....	....	....	....	....
Banks...........	8 623 ..	....	....	....	....	....	....	....	....
Other sectors...........	8 624 ..	....	....	....	....	....	....	....	....
Money market instruments...........	8 630 ..	....	....	....	....	....	....	....	....
Monetary authorities...........	8 631 ..	....	....	....	....	....	....	....	....
General government...........	8 632 ..	....	....	....	....	....	....	....	....
Banks...........	8 633 ..	....	....	....	....	....	....	....	....
Other sectors...........	8 634 ..	....	....	....	....	....	....	....	....
Financial derivatives...........	8 900 ..	....	....	....	....	....	....	....	....
Monetary authorities...........	8 901 ..	....	....	....	....	....	....	....	....
General government...........	8 902 ..	....	....	....	....	....	....	....	....
Banks...........	8 903 ..	....	....	....	....	....	....	....	....
Other sectors...........	8 904 ..	....	....	....	....	....	....	....	....
Other investment...........	8 703 ..	**1,007.9**	**1,062.2**	**1,303.6**	**1,173.9**	**1,514.4**	**2,091.5**	**833.7**	**652.0**
Trade credits...........	8 706 ..	....	....	....	....	....	....	....	....
General government...........	8 707 ..	....	....	....	....	....	....	....	....
of which: Short-term...........	8 709 ..	....	....	....	....	....	....	....	....
Other sectors...........	8 710 ..	....	....	....	....	....	....	....	....
of which: Short-term...........	8 712 ..	....	....	....	....	....	....	....	....
Loans...........	8 714 ..	....	....	....	....	....	....	....	....
Monetary authorities...........	8 715 ..	....	....	....	....	....	....	....	....
of which: Short-term...........	8 718 ..	....	....	....	....	....	....	....	....
General government...........	8 719 ..	....	....	....	....	....	....	....	....
of which: Short-term...........	8 721 ..	....	....	....	....	....	....	....	....
Banks...........	8 722 ..	....	....	....	....	....	....	....	....
of which: Short-term...........	8 724 ..	....	....	....	....	....	....	....	....
Other sectors...........	8 725 ..	....	....	....	....	....	....	....	....
of which: Short-term...........	8 727 ..	....	....	....	....	....	....	....	....
Currency and deposits...........	8 730 ..	1,007.9	1,062.2	1,303.6	1,173.9	1,514.4	2,091.5	833.7	652.0
Monetary authorities...........	8 731 ..	....	....	....	....	....	....	....	....
General government...........	8 732 ..	....	....	....	....	....	....	....	....
Banks...........	8 733 ..	1,007.9	1,062.2	1,303.6	1,173.9	1,514.4	2,091.5	833.7	652.0
Other sectors...........	8 734 ..	....	....	....	....	....	....	....	....
Other assets...........	8 736 ..	....	....	....	....	....	....	....	....
Monetary authorities...........	8 737 ..	....	....	....	....	....	....	....	....
of which: Short-term...........	8 739 ..	....	....	....	....	....	....	....	....
General government...........	8 740 ..	....	....	....	....	....	....	....	....
of which: Short-term...........	8 742 ..	....	....	....	....	....	....	....	....
Banks...........	8 743 ..	....	....	....	....	....	....	....	....
of which: Short-term...........	8 745 ..	....	....	....	....	....	....	....	....
Other sectors...........	8 738 ..	....	....	....	....	....	....	....	....
of which: Short-term...........	8 748 ..	....	....	....	....	....	....	....	....
Reserve assets...........	8 802 ..	**1,170.7**	**1,544.8**	**1,998.3**	**2,306.4**	**2,051.5**	**2,134.4**	**3,002.3**	**3,106.7**
Monetary gold...........	8 812 ..	31.7	27.6	....	....	....	....	....	....
Special drawing rights...........	8 811 ..	.5	.1	.7	.1	.2	....	248.8	243.8
Reserve position in the Fund...........	8 810 ..	14.9	15.5	14.3	15.0	15.8	15.4	15.7	15.4
Foreign exchange...........	8 803 ..	1,123.7	1,501.7	1,983.3	2,291.3	2,035.6	2,119.0	2,737.8	2,847.5
Other claims...........	8 813 ..	....	....	....	....	....	....	....	....

Table 3 (Concluded). INTERNATIONAL INVESTMENT POSITION (End-period stocks), 2003–2010

(Millions of U.S. dollars)

	Code	2003	2004	2005	2006	2007	2008	2009	2010
LIABILITIES	8 995 D.	**9,643.1**	**10,396.2**	**11,795.2**	**8,431.8**	**10,498.6**	**11,489.0**	**13,878.4**	**14,931.5**
Direct investment in Tanzania	8 555 ..	**2,676.6**	**2,867.3**	**4,438.7**	**4,827.1**	**5,950.0**	**6,239.9**	**6,654.9**	**7,089.9**
Equity capital and reinvested earnings	8 556 ..	2,676.6	2,867.3	4,438.7	4,827.1	5,950.0	6,239.9	6,654.9	7,089.9
Claims on direct investors	8 557 ..	....	....	....	....	....	....	....	....
Liabilities to direct investors	8 558 ..	2,676.6	2,867.3	4,438.7	4,827.1	5,950.0	6,239.9	6,654.9	7,089.9
Other capital	8 580 ..	....	....	....	....	....	....	....	....
Claims on direct investors	8 585 ..	....	....	....	....	....	....	....	....
Liabilities to direct investors	8 590 ..	....	....	....	....	....	....	....	....
Portfolio investment	8 652 ..	**....**	**−1.8**	**.1**	**.4**	**.2**	**−9.0**	**2.8**	**2.0**
Equity securities	8 660 ..	....	−1.8	.1	.4	.2	−9.0	2.8	2.0
Banks	8 663 ..	....	....	....	....	....	....	....	....
Other sectors	8 664 ..	....	−1.8	.1	.4	.2	−9.0	2.8	2.0
Debt securities	8 669 ..	....	....	....	....	....	....	....	....
Bonds and notes	8 670 ..	....	....	....	....	....	....	....	....
Monetary authorities	8 671 ..	....	....	....	....	....	....	....	....
General government	8 672 ..	....	....	....	....	....	....	....	....
Banks	8 673 ..	....	....	....	....	....	....	....	....
Other sectors	8 674 ..	....	....	....	....	....	....	....	....
Money market instruments	8 680 ..	....	....	....	....	....	....	....	....
Monetary authorities	8 681 ..	....	....	....	....	....	....	....	....
General government	8 682 ..	....	....	....	....	....	....	....	....
Banks	8 683 ..	....	....	....	....	....	....	....	....
Other sectors	8 684 ..	....	....	....	....	....	....	....	....
Financial derivatives	8 905 ..	**....**	**....**	**....**	**....**	**....**	**....**	**....**	**....**
Monetary authorities	8 906 ..	....	....	....	....	....	....	....	....
General government	8 907 ..	....	....	....	....	....	....	....	....
Banks	8 908 ..	....	....	....	....	....	....	....	....
Other sectors	8 909 ..	....	....	....	....	....	....	....	....
Other investment	8 753 ..	**6,966.5**	**7,530.7**	**7,356.4**	**3,604.3**	**4,548.3**	**5,258.0**	**7,220.7**	**7,839.6**
Trade credits	8 756 ..	25.0	21.0	15.7	24.3	20.3	21.3	20.8	17.5
General government	8 757 ..	....	....	....	....	....	....	....	....
of which: Short-term	8 759 ..	....	....	....	....	....	....	....	....
Other sectors	8 760 ..	25.0	21.0	15.7	24.3	20.3	21.3	20.8	17.5
of which: Short-term	8 762 ..	*25.0*	*21.0*	*15.7*	*24.3*	*20.3*	*21.3*	*20.8*	*17.5*
Loans	8 764 ..	6,920.1	7,485.0	7,318.8	3,557.2	4,498.0	5,181.4	6,722.1	7,400.8
Monetary authorities	8 765 ..	437.3	423.0	342.5	12.6	17.7	17.3	329.4	353.8
of which: Use of Fund credit and loans from the Fund	8 766 ..	*437.3*	*423.0*	*342.5*	*12.6*	*17.7*	*17.3*	*329.4*	*353.8*
of which: Short-term	8 768 ..	....	....	....	....	....	....	....	....
General government	8 769 ..	5,210.0	5,865.3	5,878.5	2,656.2	3,449.7	3,989.2	4,769.6	5,292.2
of which: Short-term	8 771 ..	....	....	....	....	....	....	....	....
Banks	8 772 ..	....	....	....	....	....	....	....	....
of which: Short-term	8 774 ..	....	....	....	....	....	....	....	....
Other sectors	8 775 ..	1,272.9	1,196.7	1,097.8	888.4	1,030.6	1,174.9	1,623.1	1,754.8
of which: Short-term	8 777 ..	....	....	....	....	....	....	....	....
Currency and deposits	8 780 ..	7.4	9.3	7.1	20.4	28.2	53.6	177.5	126.9
Monetary authorities	8 781 ..	3.0	3.6	1.2	2.2	4.5	2.8	8.0	6.7
General government	8 782 ..	....	....	....	....	....	....	....	....
Banks	8 783 ..	4.4	5.7	5.9	18.3	23.7	50.8	169.5	120.1
Other sectors	8 784 ..	....	....	....	....	....	....	....	....
Other liabilities	8 786 ..	14.0	15.5	14.8	2.4	1.9	1.8	300.3	294.4
Monetary authorities	8 787 ..	....	....	....	....	....	....	298.7	293.4
of which: Short-term	8 789 ..	....	....	....	....	....	....	....	....
General government	8 790 ..	14.0	15.5	14.8	2.4	1.9	1.8	1.6	1.1
of which: Short-term	8 792 ..	*14.0*	*15.5*	*14.8*	*2.4*	*1.9*	*1.8*	*1.6*	*1.1*
Banks	8 793 ..	....	....	....	....	....	....	....	....
of which: Short-term	8 795 ..	....	....	....	....	....	....	....	....
Other sectors	8 796 ..	....	....	....	....	....	....	....	....
of which: Short-term	8 798 ..	....	....	....	....	....	....	....	....
NET INTERNATIONAL INVESTMENT POSITION	8 995 ..	**−7,464.5**	**−7,789.1**	**−8,493.4**	**−4,951.5**	**−6,932.7**	**−7,263.1**	**−10,042.5**	**−11,172.9**
Conversion rates: Tanzania shillings per U.S. dollar (end of period)	0 102 ..	**1,063.6**	**1,043.0**	**1,165.5**	**1,261.6**	**1,132.1**	**1,280.3**	**1,326.8**	**1,455.2**

Table 1. ANALYTIC PRESENTATION, 2003–2010

(Millions of U.S. dollars)

	Code	2003	2004	2005	2006	2007	2008	2009	2010
A. Current Account[1]...............................	4 993 Z.	**4,772**	**2,759**	**−7,647**	**2,316**	**15,678**	**2,211**	**21,861**	**14,754**
Goods: exports f.o.b................................	2 100 ..	78,083	94,979	109,369	127,929	151,240	175,214	150,713	193,610
Goods: imports f.o.b................................	3 100 ..	−66,909	−84,193	−105,981	−114,085	−124,479	−157,829	−118,022	−161,270
Balance on Goods...............................	4 100 ..	*11,175*	*10,785*	*3,388*	*13,844*	*26,762*	*17,385*	*32,691*	*32,340*
Services: credit......................................	2 200 ..	15,798	19,040	20,163	24,822	30,357	33,383	29,940	34,046
Services: debit.......................................	3 200 ..	−18,169	−23,077	−27,027	−33,015	−38,425	−46,263	−37,756	−45,855
Balance on Goods and Services.........	4 991 ..	*8,804*	*6,748*	*−3,477*	*5,651*	*18,693*	*4,504*	*24,876*	*20,532*
Income: credit..	2 300 ..	3,150	3,244	3,640	4,665	7,333	8,111	5,880	6,025
Income: debit...	3 300 ..	−8,123	−9,364	−10,813	−11,368	−14,286	−15,171	−13,378	−16,606
Balance on Goods, Services, and Income.........	4 992 ..	*3,831*	*628*	*−10,650*	*−1,052*	*11,740*	*−2,555*	*17,377*	*9,950*
Current transfers: credit........................	2 379 Z.	1,326	2,479	3,351	3,764	4,395	5,324	4,972	5,385
Current transfers: debit.........................	3 379 ..	−385	−348	−348	−396	−457	−558	−488	−582
B. Capital Account[1]...............................	4 994 Z.	....	....	....	....	....	....	....	....
Capital account: credit..........................	2 994 Z.	....	....	....	....	....	....	....	....
Capital account: debit...........................	3 994 ..	....	....	....	....	....	....	....	....
Total, Groups A Plus B........................	4 981 ..	*4,772*	*2,759*	*−7,647*	*2,316*	*15,678*	*2,211*	*21,861*	*14,754*
C. Financial Account[1]...........................	4 995 W.	**−4,385**	**3,664**	**7,140**	**8,082**	**−1,752**	**11,867**	**−2,776**	**17,211**
Direct investment abroad.......................	4 505 ..	−623	−77	−501	−974	−3,015	−4,089	−4,114	−5,287
Direct investment in Thailand.................	4 555 Z.	5,232	5,860	8,055	9,453	11,324	8,531	4,976	6,306
Portfolio investment assets....................	4 602 ..	−939	1,232	−1,522	−1,439	−9,638	395	−8,290	1,171
Equity securities..................................	4 610 ..	−149	−244	−47	−643	−1,484	197	−511	−1,392
Debt securities....................................	4 619 ..	−790	1,475	−1,475	−796	−8,154	198	−7,779	2,563
Portfolio investment liabilities...............	4 652 Z.	851	1,856	7,070	5,714	2,899	−2,561	2,343	9,005
Equity securities..................................	4 660 ..	1,786	1,319	5,121	5,242	4,268	−3,802	1,334	3,430
Debt securities....................................	4 669 Z.	−935	537	1,948	472	−1,369	1,241	1,009	5,574
Financial derivatives..............................	4 910 ..	93	−106	−525	353	−314	−677	1,117	−268
Financial derivatives assets..................	4 900 ..	−1	11	382	−270	828	1,385	3,135	170
Financial derivatives liabilities.............	4 905 ..	94	−116	−908	623	−1,143	−2,062	−2,017	−437
Other investment assets........................	4 703 ..	−45	−1,695	−5,599	−10,940	−7,027	11,927	1,962	−6,315
Monetary authorities...........................	4 701 ..	....	....	....	....	....	....	....	....
General government............................	4 704 ..	−3	162	−29	−21	−194	−59	−173	−120
Banks..	4 705 ..	−405	−425	−1,701	−8,765	−1,755	10,405	3,767	−946
Other sectors......................................	4 728 ..	363	−1,432	−3,869	−2,154	−5,077	1,582	−1,633	−5,249
Other investment liabilities...................	4 753 W.	−8,955	−3,406	163	5,915	4,019	−1,660	−771	12,599
Monetary authorities...........................	4 753 WA	3,031	3,022	....	....	....	....	1,383	....
General government............................	4 753 ZB	−609	−1,878	−1,186	−429	−862	−605	−110	−75
Banks..	4 753 ZC	−1,636	−598	−1,052	109	−537	569	3,136	9,793
Other sectors......................................	4 753 ZD	−9,740	−3,951	2,401	6,234	5,417	−1,624	−5,180	2,881
Total, Groups A Through C...................	4 983 ..	*386*	*6,424*	*−506*	*10,398*	*13,925*	*14,078*	*19,086*	*31,965*
D. Net Errors and Omissions...................	4 998 ..	**132**	**−710**	**5,923**	**2,271**	**3,152**	**10,363**	**5,045**	**−719**
Total, Groups A Through D...................	4 984 ..	*518*	*5,713*	*5,417*	*12,669*	*17,077*	*24,440*	*24,131*	*31,246*
E. Reserves and Related Items............	4 802 A.	**−518**	**−5,713**	**−5,417**	**−12,669**	**−17,077**	**−24,440**	**−24,131**	**−31,246**
Reserve assets..	4 802 ..	−122	−5,713	−5,417	−12,669	−17,077	−24,440	−24,131	−31,246
Use of Fund credit and loans.................	4 766 ..	−398	....	....	....	....	....	....	....
Exceptional financing.............................	4 920 ..	3	....	....	....	....	....	....	....
Conversion rates: baht per U.S. dollar.................	0 101 ..	**41.485**	**40.222**	**40.220**	**37.882**	**34.518**	**33.313**	**34.286**	**31.686**

[1] Excludes components that have been classified in the categories of Group E.

Table 2. STANDARD PRESENTATION, 2003–2010

(Millions of U.S. dollars)

	Code	2003	2004	2005	2006	2007	2008	2009	2010
CURRENT ACCOUNT............................	4 993 ..	**4,772**	**2,759**	**−7,647**	**2,316**	**15,678**	**2,211**	**21,861**	**14,754**
A. GOODS..	4 100 ..	**11,175**	**10,785**	**3,388**	**13,844**	**26,762**	**17,385**	**32,691**	**32,340**
Credit...	2 100 ..	**78,083**	**94,979**	**109,369**	**127,929**	**151,240**	**175,214**	**150,713**	**193,610**
General merchandise: exports f.o.b.	2 110 ..	77,680	94,834	109,145	127,414	149,721	171,848	145,101	187,146
Goods for processing: exports f.o.b.	2 150 ..	....	....	....	....	....	....	....	....
Repairs on goods............................	2 160 ..								
Goods procured in ports by carriers...	2 170 ..	....	....	....	....				
Nonmonetary gold..........................	2 180 ..	403	144	223	515	1,520	3,365	5,612	6,464
Debit..	3 100 ..	**−66,909**	**−84,193**	**−105,981**	**−114,085**	**−124,479**	**−157,829**	**−118,022**	**−161,270**
General merchandise: imports f.o.b.	3 110 ..	−66,273	−83,159	−104,203	−112,380	−122,992	−152,402	−114,591	−154,094
Goods for processing: imports f.o.b.	3 150 ..	....	....	....	....	....	....	....	....
Repairs on goods............................	3 160 ..	....	....	....	....	....	....	....	....
Goods procured in ports by carriers...	3 170 ..	....	....	....	....	....	....	....	....
Nonmonetary gold..........................	3 180 ..	−636	−1,034	−1,778	−1,705	−1,486	−5,426	−3,430	−7,175
B. SERVICES......................................	4 200 ..	**−2,370**	**−4,037**	**−6,864**	**−8,193**	**−8,069**	**−12,880**	**−7,815**	**−11,809**
Total credit...................................	2 200 ..	*15,798*	*19,040*	*20,163*	*24,822*	*30,357*	*33,383*	*29,940*	*34,046*
Total debit....................................	3 200 ..	*−18,169*	*−23,077*	*−27,027*	*−33,015*	*−38,425*	*−46,263*	*−37,756*	*−45,855*
Transportation services, credit.........	2 205 ..	**3,503**	**4,350**	**4,626**	**5,377**	**6,369**	**7,282**	**5,665**	**5,916**
Passenger......................................	2 850 ..	*2,600*	*3,011*	*2,525*	*3,221*	*3,955*	*4,334*	*3,756*	*3,693*
Freight..	2 851 ..	*805*	*1,092*	*1,200*	*1,383*	*1,603*	*2,174*	*1,448*	*1,800*
Other..	2 852 ..	*98*	*247*	*901*	*774*	*810*	*774*	*461*	*423*
Sea transport, passenger...............	2 207 ..	....	....	....	....	....	....	....	....
Sea transport, freight.....................	2 208 ..	....	....	....	....	....	....	....	....
Sea transport, other.......................	2 209 ..	....	....	....	....	....	....	....	....
Air transport, passenger.................	2 211 ..	....	....	....	....	....	....	....	....
Air transport, freight......................	2 212 ..	....	....	....	....	....	....	....	....
Air transport, other........................	2 213 ..	....	....	....	....	....	....	....	....
Other transport, passenger............	2 215 ..	....	....	....	....	....	....	....	....
Other transport, freight..................	2 216 ..	....	....	....	....	....	....	....	....
Other transport, other....................	2 217 ..	....	....	....	....	....	....	....	....
Transportation services, debit.........	3 205 ..	**−8,484**	**−10,830**	**−14,439**	**−16,309**	**−18,177**	**−22,964**	**−17,069**	**−22,578**
Passenger......................................	3 850 ..	*−617*	*−829*	*−1,117*	*−1,575*	*−1,744*	*−1,697*	*−1,316*	*−1,528*
Freight..	3 851 ..	*−7,497*	*−9,536*	*−12,332*	*−13,429*	*−14,774*	*−19,291*	*−14,468*	*−19,710*
Other..	3 852 ..	*−369*	*−465*	*−989*	*−1,305*	*−1,659*	*−1,977*	*−1,285*	*−1,341*
Sea transport, passenger...............	3 207 ..	....	....	....	....	....	....	....	....
Sea transport, freight.....................	3 208 ..	....	....	....	....	....	....	....	....
Sea transport, other.......................	3 209 ..	....	....	....	....	....	....	....	....
Air transport, passenger.................	3 211 ..	....	....	....	....	....	....	....	....
Air transport, freight......................	3 212 ..	....	....	....	....	....	....	....	....
Air transport, other........................	3 213 ..	....	....	....	....	....	....	....	....
Other transport, passenger............	3 215 ..	....	....	....	....	....	....	....	....
Other transport, freight..................	3 216 ..	....	....	....	....	....	....	....	....
Other transport, other....................	3 217 ..	....	....	....	....	....	....	....	....
Travel, credit.................................	2 236 ..	**7,856**	**10,043**	**9,577**	**13,393**	**16,667**	**18,163**	**15,665**	**19,714**
Business travel...............................	2 237 ..	....	....	....	....	....	....	....	....
Personal travel...............................	2 240 ..	....	....	....	....	....	....	....	....
Travel, debit..................................	3 236 ..	**−2,921**	**−4,514**	**−3,800**	**−4,598**	**−5,143**	**−5,003**	**−4,343**	**−5,054**
Business travel...............................	3 237 ..	....	....	....	....	....	....	....	....
Personal travel...............................	3 240 ..	....	....	....	....	....	....	....	....
Other services, credit.....................	2 200 BA	**4,439**	**4,647**	**5,960**	**6,052**	**7,321**	**7,937**	**8,611**	**8,417**
Communications............................	2 245 ..	148	201	258	244	232	416	365	325
Construction..................................	2 249 ..	188	236	255	336	518	614	472	472
Insurance.......................................	2 253 ..	134	135	280	253	312	428	306	321
Financial..	2 260 ..	....	....	....	....	....	....	....	....
Computer and information.............	2 262 ..	....	....	....	....	....	....	....	....
Royalties and licence fees..............	2 266 ..	8	14	17	46	54	101	145	153
Other business services.................	2 268 ..	3,857	3,952	4,998	4,986	5,971	6,052	7,059	6,906
Personal, cultural, and recreational.	2 287 ..	....	....	....	....	....	....	....	....
Government, n.i.e...........................	2 291 ..	104	108	152	186	233	327	264	241
Other services, debit......................	3 200 BA	**−6,764**	**−7,733**	**−8,788**	**−12,108**	**−15,106**	**−18,297**	**−16,343**	**−18,223**
Communications............................	3 245 ..	−180	−141	−214	−159	−169	−219	−219	−219
Construction..................................	3 249 ..	−152	−229	−314	−581	−640	−786	−782	−713
Insurance.......................................	3 253 ..	−1,125	−1,290	−1,660	−1,791	−1,916	−2,382	−1,900	−2,418
Financial..	3 260 ..	....	....	....	....	....	....	....	....
Computer and information.............	3 262 ..	....	....	....	....	....	....	....	....
Royalties and licence fees..............	3 266 ..	−1,268	−1,584	−1,674	−2,046	−2,287	−2,559	−2,250	−3,084
Other business services.................	3 268 ..	−3,870	−4,320	−4,779	−7,357	−9,841	−12,121	−10,977	−11,533
Personal, cultural, and recreational.	3 287 ..	....	....	....	....	....	....	....	....
Government, n.i.e...........................	3 291 ..	−170	−169	−146	−174	−253	−230	−215	−255

Table 2 (Continued). STANDARD PRESENTATION, 2003–2010

(Millions of U.S. dollars)

	Code	2003	2004	2005	2006	2007	2008	2009	2010
C. INCOME	4 300	**−4,973**	**−6,120**	**−7,174**	**−6,702**	**−6,954**	**−7,059**	**−7,499**	**−10,582**
Total credit	2 300	*3,150*	*3,244*	*3,640*	*4,665*	*7,333*	*8,111*	*5,880*	*6,025*
Total debit	3 300	*−8,123*	*−9,364*	*−10,813*	*−11,368*	*−14,286*	*−15,171*	*−13,378*	*−16,606*
Compensation of employees, credit	2 310	**1,607**	**1,622**	**1,187**	**1,333**	**1,635**	**1,898**	**1,637**	**1,764**
Compensation of employees, debit	3 310	....	....	....	....	....	....	....	....
Investment income, credit	2 320	**1,543**	**1,622**	**2,453**	**3,332**	**5,698**	**6,214**	**4,243**	**4,261**
Direct investment income	2 330	135	125	249	169	723	1,588	1,449	1,449
Dividends and distributed branch profits	2 332	....	....	....	....	....	....	....	....
Reinvested earnings and undistributed branch profits	2 333	135	125	249	169	723	1,588	1,449	1,449
Income on debt (interest)	2 334	....	....	....	....	....	....	....	....
Portfolio investment income	2 339	....	....	....	....	....	....	....	....
Income on equity	2 340	....	....	....	....	....	....	....	....
Income on bonds and notes	2 350	....	....	....	....	....	....	....	....
Income on money market instruments	2 360	....	....	....	....	....	....	....	....
Other investment income	2 370	1,408	1,497	2,204	3,163	4,974	4,626	2,794	2,812
Investment income, debit	3 320	**−8,123**	**−9,364**	**−10,813**	**−11,368**	**−14,286**	**−15,171**	**−13,378**	**−16,606**
Direct investment income	3 330	−3,316	−4,223	−4,501	−4,031	−5,798	−4,142	−3,402	−3,403
Dividends and distributed branch profits	3 332	....	....	....	....	....	....	....	....
Reinvested earnings and undistributed branch profits	3 333	−3,316	−4,223	−4,501	−4,031	−5,798	−4,142	−3,402	−3,403
Income on debt (interest)	3 334	....	....	....	....	....	....	....	....
Portfolio investment income	3 339	....	....	....	....	....	....	....	....
Income on equity	3 340	....	....	....	....	....	....	....	....
Income on bonds and notes	3 350	....	....	....	....	....	....	....	....
Income on money market instruments	3 360	....	....	....	....	....	....	....	....
Other investment income	3 370	−4,807	−5,142	−6,312	−7,337	−8,488	−11,029	−9,976	−13,203
D. CURRENT TRANSFERS	4 379	**941**	**2,131**	**3,004**	**3,368**	**3,938**	**4,766**	**4,484**	**4,803**
Credit	2 379	**1,326**	**2,479**	**3,351**	**3,764**	**4,395**	**5,324**	**4,972**	**5,385**
General government	2 380	128	121	159	201	237	74	64	75
Other sectors	2 390	1,198	2,358	3,193	3,563	4,158	5,250	4,908	5,310
Workers' remittances	2 391	....	....	....	....	....	....	....	....
Other current transfers	2 392	....	....	....	....	....	....	....	....
Debit	3 379	**−385**	**−348**	**−348**	**−396**	**−457**	**−558**	**−488**	**−582**
General government	3 380	−19	−35	−37	−32	−52	−39	−40	−5
Other sectors	3 390	−366	−313	−311	−364	−405	−519	−448	−577
Workers' remittances	3 391	....	....	....	....	....	....	....	....
Other current transfers	3 392	....	....	....	....	....	....	....	....
CAPITAL AND FINANCIAL ACCOUNT	4 996	**−4,903**	**−2,049**	**1,724**	**−4,587**	**−18,829**	**−12,573**	**−26,906**	**−14,035**
CAPITAL ACCOUNT	4 994	....	....	....	....	....	....	....	....
Total credit	2 994	....	....	....	....	....	....	....	....
Total debit	3 994	....	....	....	....	....	....	....	....
Capital transfers, credit	2 400	....	....	....	....	....	....	....	....
General government	2 401	....	....	....	....	....	....	....	....
Debt forgiveness	2 402	....	....	....	....	....	....	....	....
Other capital transfers	2 410	....	....	....	....	....	....	....	....
Other sectors	2 430	....	....	....	....	....	....	....	....
Migrants' transfers	2 431	....	....	....	....	....	....	....	....
Debt forgiveness	2 432	....	....	....	....	....	....	....	....
Other capital transfers	2 440	....	....	....	....	....	....	....	....
Capital transfers, debit	3 400	....	....	....	....	....	....	....	....
General government	3 401	....	....	....	....	....	....	....	....
Debt forgiveness	3 402	....	....	....	....	....	....	....	....
Other capital transfers	3 410	....	....	....	....	....	....	....	....
Other sectors	3 430	....	....	....	....	....	....	....	....
Migrants' transfers	3 431	....	....	....	....	....	....	....	....
Debt forgiveness	3 432	....	....	....	....	....	....	....	....
Other capital transfers	3 440	....	....	....	....	....	....	....	....
Nonproduced nonfinancial assets, credit	2 480	....	....	....	....	....	....	....	....
Nonproduced nonfinancial assets, debit	3 480	....	....	....	....	....	....	....	....

Table 2 (Continued). STANDARD PRESENTATION, 2003–2010
(Millions of U.S. dollars)

	Code	2003	2004	2005	2006	2007	2008	2009	2010
FINANCIAL ACCOUNT	4 995	**–4,903**	**–2,049**	**1,724**	**–4,587**	**–18,829**	**–12,573**	**–26,906**	**–14,035**
A. DIRECT INVESTMENT	4 500	**4,609**	**5,784**	**7,554**	**8,479**	**8,309**	**4,442**	**862**	**1,020**
Direct investment abroad	4 505	–623	–77	–501	–974	–3,015	–4,089	–4,114	–5,287
Equity capital	4 510	–295	–340	–465	–881	–1,846	–1,669	–1,949	–1,572
Claims on affiliated enterprises	4 515	....	....	....	....	....	....	....	....
Liabilities to affiliated enterprises	4 520	....	....	....	....	....	....	....	....
Reinvested earnings	4 525	–135	–125	–249	–169	–723	–1,588	–1,449	–1,449
Other capital	4 530	–193	388	213	76	–445	–832	–716	–2,265
Claims on affiliated enterprises	4 535								
Liabilities to affiliated enterprises	4 540	....	....						....
Direct investment in Thailand	4 555	**5,232**	**5,860**	**8,055**	**9,453**	**11,324**	**8,531**	**4,976**	**6,306**
Equity capital	4 560	1,383	2,118	2,499	3,961	5,548	4,584	2,363	3,405
Claims on direct investors	4 565	....	....						
Liabilities to direct investors	4 570	....							
Reinvested earnings	4 575	3,316	4,223	4,501	4,031	5,798	4,142	3,402	3,403
Other capital	4 580	533	–481	1,056	1,461	–22	–194	–789	–501
Claims on direct investors	4 585								
Liabilities to direct investors	4 590	....	....						
B. PORTFOLIO INVESTMENT	4 600	**–88**	**3,088**	**5,548**	**4,275**	**–6,739**	**–2,166**	**–5,946**	**10,176**
Assets	4 602	**–939**	**1,232**	**–1,522**	**–1,439**	**–9,638**	**395**	**–8,290**	**1,171**
Equity securities	4 610	–149	–244	–47	–643	–1,484	197	–511	–1,392
Monetary authorities	4 611	....	....				....	....	
General government	4 612	....		....	....	3	–98	9	94
Banks	4 613	–146	–164	138	–13	86	–67	–52	–200
Other sectors	4 614	–2	–80	–185	–631	–1,572	362	–467	–1,285
Debt securities	4 619	–790	1,475	–1,475	–796	–8,154	198	–7,779	2,563
Bonds and notes	4 620	–815	1,451	–1,129	–1,266	–1,000	–3,869	–4,847	119
Monetary authorities	4 621	....	....				....	....	
General government	4 622	....	....	....	....	–19	–756	–85	–17
Banks	4 623	–749	1,574	–626	–483	340	258	191	–266
Other sectors	4 624	–67	–122	–503	–783	–1,322	–3,370	–4,953	402
Money market instruments	4 630	25	24	–346	470	–7,154	4,066	–2,932	2,445
Monetary authorities	4 631	....	....				....	....	
General government	4 632	....	....	....	....		–56	7	–39
Banks	4 633	25	14	–146	6	119	52	2	....
Other sectors	4 634	....	10	–200	464	–7,273	4,070	–2,940	2,484
Liabilities	4 652	**851**	**1,856**	**7,070**	**5,714**	**2,899**	**–2,561**	**2,343**	**9,005**
Equity securities	4 660	1,786	1,319	5,121	5,242	4,268	–3,802	1,334	3,430
Banks	4 663	593	651	2,536	2,245	101	–1,232	764	5
Other sectors	4 664	1,194	668	2,585	2,997	4,167	–2,571	571	3,425
Debt securities	4 669	–935	537	1,948	472	–1,369	1,241	1,009	5,574
Bonds and notes	4 670	–811	641	358	–1,064	–772	548	541	3,751
Monetary authorities	4 671	....	....	58	151	136	–290	7	681
General government	4 672	–60	297	–593	–1,602	–1,284	791	553	3,619
Banks	4 673	–46	15	....	50	–53	....	....	108
Other sectors	4 674	–705	328	893	337	429	48	–18	–657
Money market instruments	4 680	–125	–104	1,590	1,536	–598	693	468	1,824
Monetary authorities	4 681	....	....	166	276	–757	336	90	1,980
General government	4 682	49	–96	864	1,499	134	336	389	–198
Banks	4 683	–15	....	....	....	....	2	–2	2
Other sectors	4 684	–159	–9	560	–240	26	19	–8	41
C. FINANCIAL DERIVATIVES	4 910	**93**	**–106**	**–525**	**353**	**–314**	**–677**	**1,117**	**–268**
Monetary authorities	4 911	....	....	....	....	....	....	....	....
General government	4 912	....	....	....	....	....	....	–4	4
Banks	4 913	....	16	–456	353	–357	–354	136	–1
Other sectors	4 914	93	–122	–70	....	43	–323	986	–270
Assets	4 900	**–1**	**11**	**382**	**–270**	**828**	**1,385**	**3,135**	**170**
Monetary authorities	4 901	....	....	....	....	....	....	....	....
General government	4 902	....	....	....	....	....	....	8	11
Banks	4 903	....	10	381	–270	828	1,385	2,065	....
Other sectors	4 904	–1	1	1	....	....	....	1,061	159
Liabilities	4 905	**94**	**–116**	**–908**	**623**	**–1,143**	**–2,062**	**–2,017**	**–437**
Monetary authorities	4 906	....	....	....	....	....	....	....	....
General government	4 907	....	....	....	....	....	....	–13	–7
Banks	4 908	....	6	–837	623	–1,186	–1,739	–1,930	–1
Other sectors	4 909	94	–123	–70	....	43	–323	–75	–429

Table 2 (Concluded). STANDARD PRESENTATION, 2003–2010

(Millions of U.S. dollars)

	Code	2003	2004	2005	2006	2007	2008	2009	2010
D. OTHER INVESTMENT	4 700	**−9,395**	**−5,101**	**−5,436**	**−5,025**	**−3,008**	**10,267**	**1,191**	**6,283**
Assets	4 703	**−45**	**−1,695**	**−5,599**	**−10,940**	**−7,027**	**11,927**	**1,962**	**−6,315**
Trade credits	4 706	548	−463	−5,073	−1,867	−4,553	1,965	497	−5,940
General government	4 707	....	....	....	....	....	....	....	....
of which: Short-term	4 709	....	....	....	....	....	....	....	....
Other sectors	4 710	548	−463	−5,073	−1,867	−4,553	1,965	497	−5,940
of which: Short-term	4 712	....	....	....	....	....	....	....	....
Loans	4 714	−440	743	−642	−181	−243	−579	−535	−788
Monetary authorities	4 715	....	....	....	....	....	....	....	....
of which: Short-term	4 718	....	....	....	....	....	....	....	....
General government	4 719	....	....	−29	−21	−31	−19	−11	....
of which: Short-term	4 721	....	....	....	....	....	....	....	....
Banks	4 722	−322	581	−579	−79	−33	−350	−149	−200
of which: Short-term	4 724	....	....	−363	47	94	−104	155	162
Other sectors	4 725	−117	162	−34	−81	−179	−210	−375	−588
of which: Short-term	4 727	−118	....	−21	−21	−91	−102	−514	−486
Currency and deposits	4 730	−88	−2,029	28	−8,470	−1,578	10,535	2,048	573
Monetary authorities	4 731	....	....	....	....	....	....	....	....
General government	4 732	....	....	....	....	3	−30	....	7
Banks	4 733	−75	−1,066	−1,237	−8,336	−1,319	10,472	3,943	−429
Other sectors	4 734	−12	−963	1,265	−134	−263	94	−1,895	995
Other assets	4 736	−66	54	87	−422	−653	6	−48	−160
Monetary authorities	4 737	....	....	....	....	....	....	....	....
of which: Short-term	4 739	....	....	....	....	....	....	....	....
General government	4 740	−3	162	....	....	−167	−10	−162	−128
of which: Short-term	4 742	....	....	....	....	....	....	....	....
Banks	4 743	−8	59	114	−350	−403	284	−26	−317
of which: Short-term	4 745	....	....	....	....	....	....	....	....
Other sectors	4 746	−55	−167	−27	−72	−83	−268	140	284
of which: Short-term	4 748	....	....	....	....	....	....	....	....
Liabilities	4 753	**−9,351**	**−3,406**	**163**	**5,915**	**4,019**	**−1,660**	**−771**	**12,599**
Trade credits	4 756	189	461	3,396	2,942	4,194	−1,781	−3,831	2,785
General government	4 757	....	....	....	....	....	....	....	....
of which: Short-term	4 759	....	....	....	....	....	....	....	....
Other sectors	4 760	189	461	3,396	2,942	4,194	−1,781	−3,831	2,785
of which: Short-term	4 762	221	482	3,286	2,735	4,804	−3,080	−2,733	2,774
Loans	4 764	−10,512	−2,276	−3,356	2,332	−990	250	1,460	8,759
Monetary authorities	4 765	−4,928	....	....	....	....	....	....	....
of which: Use of Fund credit and loans from the Fund.	4 766	−398	....	....	....	....	....	....	....
of which: Short-term	4 768	....	....	....	....	....	....	....	....
General government	4 769	−606	−1,878	−1,182	−429	−862	−605	−110	−75
of which: Short-term	4 771	....	....	....	....	....	....	....	....
Banks	4 772	−1,689	−506	−1,149	−309	−1,275	717	2,911	8,477
of which: Short-term	4 774	−1,147	77	30	−537	−115	559	3,852	6,497
Other sectors	4 775	−3,289	108	−1,025	3,069	1,146	138	−1,341	356
of which: Short-term	4 777	−466	478	−84	255	1,288	954	−1,279	6
Currency and deposits	4 780	1,185	−1,495	50	153	45	162	152	605
Monetary authorities	4 781	7,560	3,022						
General government	4 782	....	....	....	....	....	....	....	....
Banks	4 783	−10	18	47	145	44	153	156	598
Other sectors	4 784	−6,365	−4,534	2	8	1	9	−4	7
Other liabilities	4 786	−212	−96	74	488	769	−291	1,448	450
Monetary authorities	4 787	....	....	....	....	....	....	1,383	....
of which: Short-term	4 789	....	....	....	....	....	....	....	....
General government	4 790	....	....	....	−4	....	....	....	....
of which: Short-term	4 792	....	....	....	....	....	....	....	....
Banks	4 793	62	−110	49	273	694	−301	69	717
of which: Short-term	4 795	....	....	....	....	....	....	....	....
Other sectors	4 796	−274	14	28	215	75	10	−4	−267
of which: Short-term	4 798	....	....	....	....	....	....	....	....
E. RESERVE ASSETS	4 802	**−122**	**−5,713**	**−5,417**	**−12,669**	**−17,077**	**−24,440**	**−24,131**	**−31,246**
Monetary gold	4 812	−24	−43	....	9	−11	....	....	−636
Special drawing rights	4 811	4	−1	....	....	1	−130	−1,384	−1
Reserve position in the Fund	4 810	−107	−47	−37	53	38	−102	−141	−23
Foreign exchange	4 803	5	−5,623	−5,380	−12,731	−17,105	−24,209	−22,605	−30,585
Other claims	4 813	....	....	....	....	....	....	....	....
NET ERRORS AND OMISSIONS	4 998	**132**	**−710**	**5,923**	**2,271**	**3,152**	**10,363**	**5,045**	**−719**

Table 3. INTERNATIONAL INVESTMENT POSITION (End-period stocks), 2003–2010

(Millions of U.S. dollars)

	Code	2003	2004	2005	2006	2007	2008	2009	2010
ASSETS...	8 995 C.	**64,193**	**81,855**	**92,191**	**120,929**	**163,604**	**179,730**	**219,099**	**264,611**
Direct investment abroad..................	8 505 ..	**3,400**	**3,725**	**5,069**	**6,398**	**9,991**	**13,364**	**18,214**	**24,169**
Equity capital and reinvested earnings..	8 506 ..	3,048	3,569	4,447	6,326	10,417	13,380	17,168	23,191
Claims on affiliated enterprises...........	8 507 ..	3,048	3,569	4,447	6,326	10,424	13,380	17,168	23,191
Liabilities to affiliated enterprises.......	8 508 ..	....	....	....	....	−7	....	....	....
Other capital....................................	8 530 ..	352	156	622	72	−426	−16	1,046	977
Claims on affiliated enterprises...........	8 535 ..	913	722	1,081	1,248	776	1,229	2,230	2,322
Liabilities to affiliated enterprises.......	8 540 ..	−561	−566	−459	−1,176	−1,202	−1,245	−1,184	−1,345
Portfolio investment........................	8 602 ..	**2,834**	**1,625**	**3,478**	**4,782**	**15,187**	**13,421**	**23,380**	**22,978**
Equity securities..............................	8 610 ..	434	694	1,017	1,775	3,300	2,184	3,299	5,035
Monetary authorities......................	8 611 ..	....	....	....	....	....	....	....	....
General government.......................	8 612 ..	....	....	....	104	102	105	96	1
Banks..	8 613 ..	174	349	193	215	132	190	251	483
Other sectors................................	8 614 ..	260	345	824	1,457	3,067	1,889	2,951	4,552
Debt securities................................	8 619 ..	2,400	931	2,461	3,007	11,887	11,237	20,081	17,942
Bonds and notes............................	8 620 ..	2,224	780	1,625	2,629	4,368	7,923	12,989	13,311
Monetary authorities....................	8 621 ..	....	....	....	....	....	....	....	....
General government.....................	8 622 ..	....	....	....	97	116	532	795	772
Banks..	8 623 ..	2,122	551	1,224	1,872	1,862	1,531	1,411	1,761
Other sectors..............................	8 624 ..	102	229	401	659	2,390	5,860	10,782	10,778
Money market instruments...............	8 630 ..	176	151	836	378	7,519	3,314	7,092	4,631
Monetary authorities....................	8 631 ..	....	....	....	....	....	....	....	....
General government.....................	8 632 ..	....	....	....	....	....	9	3	50
Banks..	8 633 ..	14	....	142	156	50	....	....	76
Other sectors..............................	8 634 ..	162	151	694	222	7,469	3,305	7,089	4,505
Financial derivatives........................	8 900 ..	**614**	**643**	**470**	**711**	**1,571**	**4,595**	**3,357**	**4,058**
Monetary authorities........................	8 901 ..	....	....	....	....	....	....	....	....
General government.........................	8 902 ..	....	....	....	....	....	....	....	....
Banks...	8 903 ..	612	642	470	711	1,571	4,595	3,357	4,056
Other sectors.................................	8 904 ..	2	1	....	....	....	....	....	2
Other investment............................	8 703 ..	**15,197**	**26,032**	**31,109**	**42,054**	**49,400**	**37,342**	**35,570**	**41,285**
Trade credits..................................	8 706 ..	2,168	11,418	16,255	18,369	23,226	21,308	20,907	26,533
General government.......................	8 707 ..	....	....	....	....	....	....	....	....
of which: Short-term..................	8 709 ..								
Other sectors................................	8 710 ..	2,168	11,418	16,255	18,369	23,226	21,308	20,907	26,533
of which: Short-term..................	8 712 ..	*2,156*	*11,108*	*11,895*	*17,292*	*23,030*	*20,493*	*20,669*	*25,556*
Loans..	8 714 ..	2,356	1,693	2,179	2,213	2,529	3,095	3,593	4,218
Monetary authorities......................	8 715 ..	....	....	....	....	....	....	....	....
of which: Short-term..................	8 718 ..	....		....	....	....	....	....	....
General government.......................	8 719 ..	....	....	28	55	89	105	121	152
of which: Short-term..................	8 721 ..	....							
Banks..	8 722 ..	2,169	1,660	1,804	1,762	1,813	2,148	2,328	2,613
of which: Short-term..................	8 724 ..	*1,276*	*1,162*	*1,083*	*906*	*808*	*914*	*743*	*585*
Other sectors................................	8 725 ..	187	33	347	396	626	842	1,145	1,453
of which: Short-term..................	8 727 ..	*151*	*7*	*50*	*79*	*129*	*215*	*766*	*916*
Currency and deposits......................	8 730 ..	9,620	11,856	11,693	20,012	21,716	11,052	9,109	8,071
Monetary authorities......................	8 731 ..	....	....	....	....	....	....	....	....
General government.......................	8 732 ..	....	....	....	....	24	50	53	48
Banks..	8 733 ..	9,105	10,128	11,184	19,435	20,794	10,272	6,371	6,813
Other sectors................................	8 734 ..	515	1,728	509	577	898	729	2,686	1,210
Other assets...................................	8 736 ..	1,053	1,065	982	1,461	1,929	1,888	1,960	2,463
Monetary authorities......................	8 737 ..	....	....	....	....	....	....	....	....
of which: Short-term..................	8 739 ..	....				....	....	....	....
General government.......................	8 740 ..	164	....	....	....	168	162	355	485
of which: Short-term..................	8 742 ..								
Banks..	8 743 ..	746	756	607	1,023	1,433	1,165	1,174	1,489
of which: Short-term..................	8 745 ..	*690*	*754*	*607*	*1,023*	*1,433*	*1,165*	*1,174*	*1,489*
Other sectors................................	8 746 ..	143	309	375	438	328	561	431	489
of which: Short-term..................	8 748 ..	*56*	*36*	*86*	*84*	*83*	*37*	*37*	*61*
Reserve assets..............................	8 802 ..	**42,148**	**49,831**	**52,065**	**66,984**	**87,454**	**111,008**	**138,579**	**172,122**
Monetary gold................................	8 812 ..	1,071	1,167	1,374	1,693	2,234	2,347	2,938	4,598
Special drawing rights......................	8 811 ..	....	1	1	1	....	131	1,523	1,497
Reserve position in the Fund.............	8 810 ..	111	165	188	143	111	213	361	377
Foreign exchange............................	8 803 ..	40,846	48,371	50,149	64,760	84,695	107,916	133,300	165,149
Other claims..................................	8 813 ..	120	126	353	386	414	401	457	500

Table 3 (Concluded). INTERNATIONAL INVESTMENT POSITION (End-period stocks), 2003–2010

(Millions of U.S. dollars)

	Code	2003	2004	2005	2006	2007	2008	2009	2010
LIABILITIES	8 995 D.	**118,772**	**132,822**	**146,074**	**177,096**	**216,795**	**189,793**	**220,813**	**300,930**
Direct investment in Thailand	8 555 ..	**48,944**	**53,184**	**60,408**	**76,950**	**94,112**	**93,500**	**106,154**	**137,191**
Equity capital and reinvested earnings	8 556 ..	44,008	48,536	54,611	70,235	85,858	85,865	98,773	131,306
Claims on direct investors	8 557 ..	....	....	−3	−4	−6	−7	−9	−9
Liabilities to direct investors	8 558 ..	44,008	48,536	54,614	70,239	85,864	85,872	98,781	131,315
Other capital	8 580 ..	4,936	4,648	5,797	6,715	8,254	7,635	7,382	5,886
Claims on direct investors	8 585 ..	−1,671	−1,399	−957	−1,007	−367	−862	−595	−2,223
Liabilities to direct investors	8 590 ..	6,607	6,047	6,754	7,722	8,621	8,497	7,976	8,109
Portfolio investment	8 652 ..	**29,086**	**32,109**	**40,336**	**47,567**	**64,028**	**34,103**	**54,529**	**84,673**
Equity securities	8 660 ..	24,319	26,618	32,983	38,504	56,937	25,838	45,323	69,405
Banks	8 663 ..	6,483	7,243	10,132	11,990	15,421	6,897	14,834	20,773
Other sectors	8 664 ..	17,836	19,375	22,851	26,514	41,516	18,940	30,489	48,632
Debt securities	8 669 ..	4,767	5,491	7,353	9,063	7,091	8,265	9,206	15,268
Bonds and notes	8 670 ..	4,140	4,969	6,284	7,955	6,669	7,432	8,264	12,339
Monetary authorities	8 671 ..	....	....	58	223	377	90	107	808
General government	8 672 ..	885	1,199	1,668	1,792	693	1,706	2,464	6,498
Banks	8 673 ..	....	109	93	143	90	90	90	312
Other sectors	8 674 ..	3,255	3,661	4,465	5,797	5,509	5,546	5,603	4,721
Money market instruments	8 680 ..	627	522	1,069	1,108	422	833	942	2,929
Monetary authorities	8 681 ..	....	....	395	742	17	322	419	2,574
General government	8 682 ..	385	288	71	....	3	4	364	195
Banks	8 683 ..	....	....	....	....	....	....	....	....
Other sectors	8 684 ..	242	234	603	367	401	507	160	160
Financial derivatives	8 905 ..	**768**	**843**	**601**	**567**	**1,153**	**4,095**	**3,191**	**3,229**
Monetary authorities	8 906 ..	....	....	....	....	....	....	....	....
General government	8 907 ..	....	....	....	....	....	....	....	....
Banks	8 908 ..	398	603	599	567	984	4,090	3,135	3,195
Other sectors	8 909 ..	370	240	2	....	170	6	56	35
Other investment	8 753 ..	**39,974**	**46,686**	**44,728**	**52,012**	**57,502**	**58,095**	**56,939**	**75,837**
Trade credits	8 756 ..	3,434	11,903	15,019	18,107	22,581	21,221	17,352	24,017
General government	8 757 ..	....	....	....	....	....	....	....	....
of which: Short-term	8 759 ..	....	....	....	....	....	....	....	....
Other sectors	8 760 ..	3,434	11,903	15,019	18,107	22,581	21,221	17,352	24,017
of which: Short-term	8 762 ..	*3,352*	*11,360*	*14,381*	*17,254*	*22,330*	*19,652*	*16,881*	*23,792*
Loans	8 764 ..	35,403	33,722	28,071	31,491	31,678	33,815	34,743	45,511
Monetary authorities	8 765 ..	....	....	....	....	....	....	....	....
of which: Use of Fund credit and loans from the Fund	8 766 ..	....	....	....	....	....	....	....	....
of which: Short-term	8 768 ..	....	....	....	....	....	....	....	....
General government	8 769 ..	6,036	4,292	2,779	2,348	1,574	1,162	1,055	1,090
of which: Short-term	8 771 ..	....	....	....	....	....	....	....	....
Banks	8 772 ..	6,034	6,031	4,462	4,568	3,431	4,447	7,317	15,777
of which: Short-term	8 774 ..	*2,305*	*1,756*	*1,578*	*1,143*	*1,124*	*1,809*	*5,606*	*12,223*
Other sectors	8 775 ..	23,333	23,399	20,829	24,575	26,672	28,207	26,371	28,643
of which: Short-term	8 777 ..	*1,753*	*2,240*	*2,063*	*2,389*	*3,690*	*4,625*	*2,927*	*3,128*
Currency and deposits	8 780 ..	305	328	876	1,133	1,231	1,327	1,539	2,295
Monetary authorities	8 781 ..	....	....	....	....	....	....	....	....
General government	8 782 ..	....	....	....	....	....	....	....	....
Banks	8 783 ..	305	328	868	1,117	1,218	1,305	1,522	2,271
Other sectors	8 784 ..	....	....	8	16	14	22	18	24
Other liabilities	8 786 ..	832	733	762	1,280	2,012	1,732	3,305	4,014
Monetary authorities	8 787 ..	126	132	122	128	134	131	1,521	1,494
of which: Short-term	8 789 ..	....	....	....	....	....	....	....	....
General government	8 790 ..	....	....	....	....	....	....	....	....
of which: Short-term	8 792 ..	....	....	....	....	....	....	....	....
Banks	8 793 ..	706	601	615	901	1,623	1,352	1,416	2,164
of which: Short-term	8 795 ..	*706*	*601*	*615*	*901*	*1,623*	*1,352*	*1,416*	*2,164*
Other sectors	8 796 ..	....	....	26	251	255	249	368	356
of which: Short-term	8 798 ..	....	....	*26*	*248*	*255*	*249*	*368*	*356*
NET INTERNATIONAL INVESTMENT POSITION	8 995 ..	**−54,579**	**−50,967**	**−53,883**	**−56,167**	**−53,191**	**−10,063**	**−1,714**	**−36,319**
Conversion rates: baht per U.S. dollar (end of period)	0 102 ..	**39.591**	**39.061**	**41.030**	**36.045**	**33.718**	**34.898**	**33.320**	**30.151**

Table 1. ANALYTIC PRESENTATION, 2003–2010

(Millions of U.S. dollars)

	Code	2003	2004	2005	2006	2007	2008	2009	2010
A. Current Account¹	4 993 Z.	....	....	....	**541.0**	**1,177.2**	**2,021.7**	**1,324.7**	....
Goods: exports f.o.b.	2 100 ..	....	....	....	9.3	6.6	14.1	9.2	....
Goods: imports f.o.b.	3 100 ..	....	....	....	−100.6	−175.7	−310.9	−370.3	....
Balance on Goods	4 100 ..	....	....	....	*−91.4*	*−169.0*	*−296.9*	*−361.1*	....
Services: credit	2 200 ..	....	....	....	34.1	62.5	44.1	46.2	....
Services: debit	3 200 ..	....	....	....	−232.1	−325.3	−489.9	−564.2	....
Balance on Goods and Services	4 991 ..	....	....	....	*−289.4*	*−431.8*	*−742.7*	*−879.0*	....
Income: credit	2 300 ..	....	....	....	647.5	1,336.3	2,416.7	1,860.7	....
Income: debit	3 300 ..	....	....	....	−2.3	−5.4	−8.8	−16.3	....
Balance on Goods, Services, and Income	4 992 ..	....	....	....	*355.8*	*899.1*	*1,665.2*	*965.4*	....
Current transfers: credit	2 379 Z.	....	....	....	185.6	281.2	370.6	412.3	....
Current transfers: debit	3 379 ..	....	....	....	−.4	−3.1	−14.1	−53.0	....
B. Capital Account¹	4 994 Z.	....	....	....	**41.6**	**32.2**	**17.2**	**27.3**	....
Capital account: credit	2 994 Z.	....	....	....	41.6	32.2	17.2	27.3	....
Capital account: debit	3 994 ..	....	....	....	....	....	....	....	....
Total, Groups A Plus B	4 981 ..	....	....	....	*582.5*	*1,209.4*	*2,039.0*	*1,352.0*	....
C. Financial Account¹	4 995 W.	....	....	....	**−649.1**	**−1,054.0**	**−2,051.6**	**−1,272.6**	....
Direct investment abroad	4 505 ..	....	....	....					....
Direct investment in Timor-Leste	4 555 Z.	....	....	....	8.5	8.7	39.7	49.9	....
Portfolio investment assets	4 602 ..	....	....	....	−636.7	−1,012.1	−2,003.1	−1,325.1	....
Equity securities	4 610 ..	....	....	....					....
Debt securities	4 619 ..	....	....	....	−636.7	−1,012.1	−2,003.1	−1,325.1	....
Portfolio investment liabilities	4 652 Z.	....	....	....	....	....			....
Equity securities	4 660 ..	....	....	....	....	....			....
Debt securities	4 669 Z.	....	....	....	....	....			....
Financial derivatives	4 910 ..	....	....	....	....	....			....
Financial derivatives assets	4 900 ..	....	....	....	....	....			....
Financial derivatives liabilities	4 905 ..	....	....	....	....	....			....
Other investment assets	4 703 ..	....	....	....	−5.6	−56.5	−97.9	8.4	....
Monetary authorities	4 701 ..	....	....	....	....	....			....
General government	4 704 ..	....	....	....	....	....	....		....
Banks	4 705 ..	....	....	....	−4.2	−57.6	−85.5	−7.8	....
Other sectors	4 728 ..	....	....	....	−1.4	1.1	−12.4	16.2	....
Other investment liabilities	4 753 W.	....	....	....	−15.3	5.9	9.8	−5.8	....
Monetary authorities	4 753 WA	....	....	....	....	....	....	12.1	....
General government	4 753 ZB	....	....	....	....	....	....		....
Banks	4 753 ZC	....	....	....	−15.4	6.6	−8.8	−14.9	....
Other sectors	4 753 ZD	....	....	....	.1	−.7	18.6	−3.0	....
Total, Groups A Through C	4 983 ..	....	....	....	*−66.6*	*155.5*	*−12.6*	*79.4*	....
D. Net Errors and Omissions	4 998 ..	....	....	....	**−2.9**	**−8.9**	**−7.3**	**−39.9**	....
Total, Groups A Through D	4 984 ..	....	....	....	*−69.5*	*146.5*	*−19.8*	*39.5*	....
E. Reserves and Related Items	4 802 A.	....	....	....	**69.5**	**−146.5**	**19.8**	**−39.5**	....
Reserve assets	4 802 ..	....	....	....	69.5	−146.5	19.8	−39.5	....
Use of Fund credit and loans	4 766 ..	....	....	....	....	....	....	....	....
Exceptional financing	4 920 ..	....	....	....	....	....	....	....	....

¹ Excludes components that have been classified in the categories of Group E.

Table 2. STANDARD PRESENTATION, 2003–2010

(Millions of U.S. dollars)

	Code	2003	2004	2005	2006	2007	2008	2009	2010
CURRENT ACCOUNT	4 993	....	....	....	541.0	1,177.2	2,021.7	1,324.7	....
A. GOODS	4 100	....	....	....	−91.4	−169.0	−296.9	−361.1	....
Credit	2 100	....	....	....	9.3	6.6	14.1	9.2	....
General merchandise: exports f.o.b.	2 110	....	....	....	9.0	6.1	13.6	8.9	....
Goods for processing: exports f.o.b.	2 150	....	....	....	....	....	....	....	....
Repairs on goods	2 160	....	....	....	....	....	....	....	....
Goods procured in ports by carriers	2 170	....	....	....	.3	.6	.5	.3	....
Nonmonetary gold	2 180	....	....	....	....	....	....	....	....
Debit	3 100	....	....	....	−100.6	−175.7	−310.9	−370.3	....
General merchandise: imports f.o.b.	3 110	....	....	....	−100.6	−175.7	−310.9	−370.3	....
Goods for processing: imports f.o.b.	3 150	....	....	....	....	....	....	....	....
Repairs on goods	3 160	....	....	....	....	....	....	....	....
Goods procured in ports by carriers	3 170	....	....	....	....	....	....	....	....
Nonmonetary gold	3 180	....	....	....	....	....	....	....	....
B. SERVICES	4 200	....	....	....	−198.0	−262.7	−445.8	−517.9	....
Total credit	2 200	....	....	....	*34.1*	*62.5*	*44.1*	*46.2*	....
Total debit	3 200	....	....	....	*−232.1*	*−325.3*	*−489.9*	*−564.2*	....
Transportation services, credit	2 205	....	....	....	.3	.2	.4	.5	....
Passenger	2 850	....	....	....	....	....	....	....	....
Freight	2 851	....	....	....	....	....	....	....	....
Other	2 852	....	....	....	*.3*	*.2*	*.4*	*.5*	....
Sea transport, passenger	2 207	....	....	....	....	....	....	....	....
Sea transport, freight	2 208	....	....	....	....	....	....	....	....
Sea transport, other	2 209	....	....	....	....	....	....	....	....
Air transport, passenger	2 211	....	....	....	....	....	....	....	....
Air transport, freight	2 212	....	....	....	....	....	....	....	....
Air transport, other	2 213	....	....	....	.3	.2	.4	.5	....
Other transport, passenger	2 215	....	....	....	....	....	....	....	....
Other transport, freight	2 216	....	....	....	....	....	....	....	....
Other transport, other	2 217	....	....	....	....	....	....	....	....
Transportation services, debit	3 205	....	....	....	−9.7	−20.4	−18.8	−39.5	....
Passenger	3 850	....	....	....	*−.3*	*−1.6*	*−11.3*	*−11.1*	....
Freight	3 851	....	....	....	*−9.4*	*−18.8*	*−7.5*	*−28.4*	....
Other	3 852	....	....	....	....	....	....	....	....
Sea transport, passenger	3 207	....	....	....	....	....	....	....	....
Sea transport, freight	3 208	....	....	....	−9.4	−18.8	−7.5	−28.3	....
Sea transport, other	3 209	....	....	....	....	....	....	....	....
Air transport, passenger	3 211	....	....	....	−.3	−1.6	−11.3	−11.1	....
Air transport, freight	3 212	....	....	....	....	....	....	....	....
Air transport, other	3 213	....	....	....	....	....	....	....	....
Other transport, passenger	3 215	....	....	....	....	....	....	....	....
Other transport, freight	3 216	....	....	....	....	....	....	....	....
Other transport, other	3 217	....	....	....	....	....	....	....	....
Travel, credit	2 236	....	....	....	20.3	26.2	14.0	13.1	....
Business travel	2 237	....	....	....	....	....	....	....	....
Personal travel	2 240	....	....	....	20.3	26.2	14.0	13.1	....
Travel, debit	3 236	....	....	....	−1.6	−2.6	−39.6	−62.7	....
Business travel	3 237	....	....	....	−1.6	−2.6	−.1	−11.3	....
Personal travel	3 240	....	....	....	....	....	−39.5	−51.5	....
Other services, credit	2 200 BA	....	....	....	13.5	36.0	29.7	32.6	....
Communications	2 245	....	....	....	4.8	5.1	8.2	6.9	....
Construction	2 249	....	....	....	....	....	....	....	....
Insurance	2 253	....	....	....	....	....	....	....	....
Financial	2 260	....	....	....	....	....	....	....	....
Computer and information	2 262	....	....	....	....	....	....	....	....
Royalties and licence fees	2 266	....	....	....	....	....	....	....	....
Other business services	2 268	....	....	....	....	....	....	....	....
Personal, cultural, and recreational	2 287	....	....	....	....	....	....	....	....
Government, n.i.e.	2 291	....	....	....	8.7	31.0	21.4	25.7	....
Other services, debit	3 200 BA	....	....	....	−220.7	−302.3	−431.5	−461.9	....
Communications	3 245	....	....	....	−7.5	−3.1	−2.6	−2.7	....
Construction	3 249	....	....	....	−20.8	−16.1	−8.6	−13.7	....
Insurance	3 253	....	....	....	−4.9	−9.7	−22.6	−9.7	....
Financial	3 260	....	....	....	....	....	....	−.8	....
Computer and information	3 262	....	....	....	....	....	−1.8	−.6	....
Royalties and licence fees	3 266	....	....	....	....	−.5	−.2	−1.1	....
Other business services	3 268	....	....	....	....	−.1	−7.8	−14.5	....
Personal, cultural, and recreational	3 287	....	....	....	....	....	....	....	....
Government, n.i.e.	3 291	....	....	....	−187.5	−272.8	−387.9	−418.8	....

Table 2 (Continued). STANDARD PRESENTATION, 2003–2010

(Millions of U.S. dollars)

	Code	2003	2004	2005	2006	2007	2008	2009	2010
C. INCOME	4 300	....	....	....	**645.2**	**1,330.9**	**2,407.9**	**1,844.4**	....
Total credit	2 300	....	....	....	*647.5*	*1,336.3*	*2,416.7*	*1,860.7*	....
Total debit	3 300	....	....	....	*–2.3*	*–5.4*	*–8.8*	*–16.3*	....
Compensation of employees, credit	2 310	....	....	....	**3.4**	**10.2**	**12.4**	**16.8**	....
Compensation of employees, debit	3 310	....	....	....	**–.1**	**–.2**	**–1.9**	**–.2**	....
Investment income, credit	2 320	....	....	....	**644.1**	**1,326.1**	**2,404.3**	**1,843.9**	....
Direct investment income	2 330	....	....	....	....	....	....	....	....
Dividends and distributed branch profits	2 332	....	....	....	....	....	....	....	....
Reinvested earnings and undistributed branch profits	2 333	....	....	....	....	....	....	....	....
Income on debt (interest)	2 334	....	....	....	....	....	....	....	....
Portfolio investment income	2 339	....	....	....	29.6	61.7	118.7	163.9	....
Income on equity	2 340	....	....	....	....	....	....	....	....
Income on bonds and notes	2 350	....	....	....	24.7	54.1	115.6	163.2	....
Income on money market instruments	2 360	....	....	....	4.9	7.6	3.1	.7	....
Other investment income	2 370	....	....	....	614.5	1,264.4	2,285.6	1,680.0	....
Investment income, debit	3 320	....	....	....	**–2.3**	**–5.2**	**–6.9**	**–16.2**	....
Direct investment income	3 330	....	....	....	–2.2	–5.2	–6.9	–16.1	....
Dividends and distributed branch profits	3 332	....	....	....	....	....	....	....	....
Reinvested earnings and undistributed branch profits	3 333	....	....	....	–2.2	–5.2	–6.9	–16.1	....
Income on debt (interest)	3 334	....	....	....	....	....	....	....	....
Portfolio investment income	3 339	....	....	....	....	....	....	....	....
Income on equity	3 340	....	....	....	....	....	....	....	....
Income on bonds and notes	3 350	....	....	....	....	....	....	....	....
Income on money market instruments	3 360	....	....	....	....	....	....	....	....
Other investment income	3 370	....	....	....	....	....	....	....	....
D. CURRENT TRANSFERS	4 379	....	....	....	**185.2**	**278.1**	**356.5**	**359.3**	....
Credit	2 379	....	....	....	**185.6**	**281.2**	**370.6**	**412.3**	....
General government	2 380	....	....	....	185.3	281.0	365.4	406.5	....
Other sectors	2 390	....	....	....	.3	.3	5.2	5.8	....
Workers' remittances	2 391	....	....	....	.3	.3	5.2	5.8	....
Other current transfers	2 392	....	....	....	....	....	....	....	....
Debit	3 379	....	....	....	**–.4**	**–3.1**	**–14.1**	**–53.0**	....
General government	3 380	....	....	....	....	....	....	....	....
Other sectors	3 390	....	....	....	–.4	–3.1	–14.1	–53.0	....
Workers' remittances	3 391	....	....	....	–.4	–3.1	–13.7	–52.5	....
Other current transfers	3 392	....	....	....	....	....	–.4	–.5	....
CAPITAL AND FINANCIAL ACCOUNT	4 996	....	....	....	**–538.0**	**–1,168.3**	**–2,014.5**	**–1,284.8**	....
CAPITAL ACCOUNT	4 994	....	....	....	**41.6**	**32.2**	**17.2**	**27.3**	....
Total credit	2 994	....	....	....	*41.6*	*32.2*	*17.2*	*27.3*	....
Total debit	3 994	....	....	....	....	....	....	....	....
Capital transfers, credit	2 400	....	....	....	**41.6**	**32.2**	**17.2**	**27.3**	....
General government	2 401	....	....	....	41.6	32.2	17.2	27.3	....
Debt forgiveness	2 402	....	....	....	....	....	....	....	....
Other capital transfers	2 410	....	....	....	41.6	32.2	17.2	27.3	....
Other sectors	2 430	....	....	....	....	....	....	....	....
Migrants' transfers	2 431	....	....	....	....	....	....	....	....
Debt forgiveness	2 432	....	....	....	....	....	....	....	....
Other capital transfers	2 440	....	....	....	....	....	....	....	....
Capital transfers, debit	3 400	....	....	....	....	....	....	....	....
General government	3 401	....	....	....	....	....	....	....	....
Debt forgiveness	3 402	....	....	....	....	....	....	....	....
Other capital transfers	3 410	....	....	....	....	....	....	....	....
Other sectors	3 430	....	....	....	....	....	....	....	....
Migrants' transfers	3 431	....	....	....	....	....	....	....	....
Debt forgiveness	3 432	....	....	....	....	....	....	....	....
Other capital transfers	3 440	....	....	....	....	....	....	....	....
Nonproduced nonfinancial assets, credit	2 480	....	....	....	....	....	....	....	....
Nonproduced nonfinancial assets, debit	3 480	....	....	....	....	....	....	....	....

2011, International Monetary Fund: *Balance of Payments Statistics Yearbook*

Table 2 (Continued). STANDARD PRESENTATION, 2003–2010

(Millions of U.S. dollars)

	Code	2003	2004	2005	2006	2007	2008	2009	2010
FINANCIAL ACCOUNT................................	4 995 ..	....	....	....	−579.6	−1,200.5	−2,031.7	−1,312.1	....
A. DIRECT INVESTMENT............................	4 500 ..	....	....	....	8.5	8.7	39.7	49.9	....
Direct investment abroad........................	4 505 ..	....	....	....	....	....	....	....	....
Equity capital..	4 510 ..	....	....	....	....	....	....	....	....
Claims on affiliated enterprises................	4 515 ..	....	....	....	....	....	....	....	....
Liabilities to affiliated enterprises............	4 520 ..	....	....	....	....	....	....	....	....
Reinvested earnings..................................	4 525 ..	....	....	....	....	....	....	....	....
Other capital..	4 530 ..	....	....	....	....	....	....	....	....
Claims on affiliated enterprises................	4 535 ..	....	....	....	....	....	....	....	....
Liabilities to affiliated enterprises............	4 540 ..	....	....	....	....	....	....	....	....
Direct investment in Timor-Leste...........	4 555 ..	....	....	....	8.5	8.7	39.7	49.9	....
Equity capital..	4 560 ..				6.2	2.3	32.8	33.8	
Claims on direct investors........................	4 565 ..	....	....	....	....	....	....	....	
Liabilities to direct investors....................	4 570 ..		....	....	6.2	2.3	32.8	33.8	....
Reinvested earnings..................................	4 575 ..				2.2	5.2	6.9	16.1	....
Other capital..	4 580 ..				....	1.2			....
Claims on direct investors........................	4 585 ..		....	....		....			
Liabilities to direct investors....................	4 590 ..				....	1.2			
B. PORTFOLIO INVESTMENT.......................	4 600 ..	....	....	....	−636.7	−1,012.1	−2,003.1	−1,325.1	....
Assets...	4 602 ..	....	....	....	−636.7	−1,012.1	−2,003.1	−1,325.1	....
Equity securities.......................................	4 610 ..	....	....	....	....	....	....	....	....
Monetary authorities................................	4 611 ..	....	....	....	....	....	....	....	
General government.................................	4 612 ..	....	....	....	....	....	....	....	
Banks...	4 613 ..	....	....	....	....	....	....	....	
Other sectors...	4 614 ..	....	....	....	....	....	....	....	
Debt securities...	4 619 ..	....	....	....	−636.7	−1,012.1	−2,003.1	−1,325.1	....
Bonds and notes.......................................	4 620 ..	....	....	....	−636.9	−1,012.7	−2,003.1	−1,322.6	....
Monetary authorities................................	4 621 ..	....	....	....	....	....	....	....	
General government.................................	4 622 ..	....	....	....	−636.9	−1,012.7	−2,003.1	−1,322.6	....
Banks...	4 623 ..	....	....	....	....	....	....	....	
Other sectors...	4 624 ..	....	....	....	....	....	....	....	
Money market instruments.......................	4 630 ..	....	....	....	.2	.6	....	−2.5	....
Monetary authorities................................	4 631 ..	....	....	....	....	....	....	....	
General government.................................	4 632 ..	....	....	....	.2	.6	....	−2.5	
Banks...	4 633 ..	....	....	....	....	....	....	....	
Other sectors...	4 634 ..	....	....	....	....	....	....	....	
Liabilities..	4 652 ..	....	....	....	....	....	....	....	....
Equity securities.......................................	4 660 ..	....	....	....	....	....	....	....	
Banks...	4 663 ..	....	....	....	....	....	....	....	
Other sectors...	4 664 ..	....	....	....	....	....	....	....	
Debt securities...	4 669 ..	....	....	....	....	....	....	....	
Bonds and notes.......................................	4 670 ..	....	....	....	....	....	....	....	
Monetary authorities................................	4 671 ..	....	....	....	....	....	....	....	
General government.................................	4 672 ..	....	....	....	....	....	....	....	
Banks...	4 673 ..	....	....	....	....	....	....	....	
Other sectors...	4 674 ..	....	....	....	....	....	....	....	
Money market instruments.......................	4 680 ..	....	....	....	....	....	....	....	
Monetary authorities................................	4 681 ..	....	....	....	....	....	....	....	
General government.................................	4 682 ..	....	....	....	....	....	....	....	
Banks...	4 683 ..	....	....	....	....	....	....	....	
Other sectors...	4 684 ..	....	....	....	....	....	....	....	
C. FINANCIAL DERIVATIVES........................	4 910 ..	....	....	....	....	....	....	....	....
Monetary authorities................................	4 911 ..	....	....	....	....	....	....	....	
General government.................................	4 912 ..	....	....	....	....	....	....	....	
Banks...	4 913 ..	....	....	....	....	....	....	....	
Other sectors...	4 914 ..	....	....	....	....	....	....	....	
Assets...	4 900 ..	....	....	....	....	....	....	....	....
Monetary authorities................................	4 901 ..	....	....	....	....	....	....	....	
General government.................................	4 902 ..	....	....	....	....	....	....	....	
Banks...	4 903 ..	....	....	....	....	....	....	....	
Other sectors...	4 904 ..	....	....	....	....	....	....	....	
Liabilities..	4 905 ..	....	....	....	....	....	....	....	....
Monetary authorities................................	4 906 ..	....	....	....	....	....	....	....	
General government.................................	4 907 ..	....	....	....	....	....	....	....	
Banks...	4 908 ..	....	....	....	....	....	....	....	
Other sectors...	4 909 ..	....	....	....	....	....	....	....	

Table 2 (Concluded). STANDARD PRESENTATION, 2003–2010

(Millions of U.S. dollars)

	Code	2003	2004	2005	2006	2007	2008	2009	2010
D. OTHER INVESTMENT	4 700	....	....	....	−20.9	−50.6	−88.1	2.6	....
Assets	4 703	....	....	....	−5.6	−56.5	−97.9	8.4	....
Trade credits	4 706	....	....	....	....	....	−13.7	13.5	....
General government	4 707	....	....	....	....	....	....	....	....
of which: Short-term	4 709	....	....	....	....	....	....	....	....
Other sectors	4 710	....	....	....	....	....	−13.7	13.5	....
of which: Short-term	4 712	....	....	....	....	....	*−13.7*	*13.5*	....
Loans	4 714	....	....	....	2.0	3.8	−4.7	−6.6	....
Monetary authorities	4 715	....	....	....	....	....	....	....	....
of which: Short-term	4 718	....	....	....	....	....	....	....	....
General government	4 719	....	....	....	....	....	....	....	....
of which: Short-term	4 721	....	....	....	....	....	....	....	....
Banks	4 722	....	....	....	2.0	3.8	−4.7	−6.6	....
of which: Short-term	4 724	....	....	....	*2.0*	*3.8*	*−4.7*	*−6.6*	....
Other sectors	4 725	....	....	....	....	....	....	....	....
of which: Short-term	4 727	....	....	....	....	....	....	....	....
Currency and deposits	4 730	....	....	....	−7.6	−60.3	−79.6	1.5	....
Monetary authorities	4 731	....	....	....	....	....	....	....	....
General government	4 732	....	....	....	....	....	....	....	....
Banks	4 733	....	....	....	−6.2	−61.3	−80.9	−1.2	....
Other sectors	4 734	....	....	....	−1.4	1.1	1.3	2.7	....
Other assets	4 736	....	....	....	....	....	....	....	....
Monetary authorities	4 737	....	....	....	....	....	....	....	....
of which: Short-term	4 739	....	....	....	....	....	....	....	....
General government	4 740	....	....	....	....	....	....	....	....
of which: Short-term	4 742	....	....	....	....	....	....	....	....
Banks	4 743	....	....	....	....	....	....	....	....
of which: Short-term	4 745	....	....	....	....	....	....	....	....
Other sectors	4 746	....	....	....	....	....	....	....	....
of which: Short-term	4 748	....	....	....	....	....	....	....	....
Liabilities	4 753	....	....	....	−15.3	5.9	9.8	−5.8	....
Trade credits	4 756	....	....	....	....	....	7.4	−2.0	....
General government	4 757	....	....	....	....	....	....	....	....
of which: Short-term	4 759	....	....	....	....	....	....	....	....
Other sectors	4 760	....	....	....	....	....	7.4	−2.0	....
of which: Short-term	4 762	....	....	....	....	....	*7.4*	*−2.0*	....
Loans	4 764	....	....	....	.1	−.7	12.0	−.7	....
Monetary authorities	4 765	....	....	....	....	....	....	....	....
of which: Use of Fund credit and loans from the Fund	4 766	....	....	....	....	....	....	....	....
of which: Short-term	4 768	....	....	....	....	....	....	....	....
General government	4 769	....	....	....	....	....	....	....	....
of which: Short-term	4 771	....	....	....	....	....	....	....	....
Banks	4 772	....	....	....	....	....	.9	.4	....
of which: Short-term	4 774	....	....	....	....	....	*.9*	*.4*	....
Other sectors	4 775	....	....	....	.1	−.7	11.1	−1.0	....
of which: Short-term	4 777	....	....	....	....	....	....	....	....
Currency and deposits	4 780	....	....	....	−15.4	6.6	−9.7	−15.2	....
Monetary authorities	4 781	....	....	....	....	....	....	....	....
General government	4 782	....	....	....	....	....	....	....	....
Banks	4 783	....	....	....	−15.4	6.6	−9.7	−15.2	....
Other sectors	4 784	....	....	....	....	....	....	....	....
Other liabilities	4 786	....	....	....	....	....	....	12.1	....
Monetary authorities	4 787	....	....	....	....	....	....	12.1	....
of which: Short-term	4 789	....	....	....	....	....	....	....	....
General government	4 790	....	....	....	....	....	....	....	....
of which: Short-term	4 792	....	....	....	....	....	....	....	....
Banks	4 793	....	....	....	....	....	....	....	....
of which: Short-term	4 795	....	....	....	....	....	....	....	....
Other sectors	4 796	....	....	....	....	....	....	....	....
of which: Short-term	4 798	....	....	....	....	....	....	....	....
E. RESERVE ASSETS	4 802	....	....	....	69.5	−146.5	19.8	−39.5	....
Monetary gold	4 812	....	....	....	....	....	....	....	....
Special drawing rights	4 811	....	....	....	....	....	....	−12.1	....
Reserve position in the Fund	4 810	....	....	....	....	....	....	....	....
Foreign exchange	4 803	....	....	....	69.5	−146.5	19.8	−27.4	....
Other claims	4 813	....	....	....	....	....	....	....	....
NET ERRORS AND OMISSIONS	4 998	....	....	....	−2.9	−8.9	−7.3	−39.9	....

Table 1. ANALYTIC PRESENTATION, 2003–2010

(Millions of U.S. dollars)

	Code	2003	2004	2005	2006	2007	2008	2009	2010
A. Current Account[1]	4 993 Z.	**−161.9**	**−206.9**	**−203.9**	**−176.3**	**−215.8**	**−219.2**	**−176.7**	....
Goods: exports f.o.b.	2 100 ..	597.7	601.0	634.1	630.4	676.9	852.6	903.0	....
Goods: imports f.o.b.	3 100 ..	−754.5	−853.3	−917.4	−949.1	−1,072.0	−1,307.2	−1,315.2	....
Balance on Goods	4 100 ..	*−156.8*	*−252.3*	*−283.3*	*−318.7*	*−395.1*	*−454.6*	*−412.1*	....
Services: credit	2 200 ..	94.8	150.0	176.9	200.7	236.0	283.1	293.6	....
Services: debit	3 200 ..	−204.2	−239.3	−250.7	−264.1	−305.5	−359.2	−374.7	....
Balance on Goods and Services	4 991 ..	*−266.3*	*−341.6*	*−357.1*	*−382.1*	*−464.5*	*−530.7*	*−493.3*	....
Income: credit	2 300 ..	26.8	39.9	46.3	47.7	61.3	81.1	68.4	....
Income: debit	3 300 ..	−50.2	−74.6	−80.9	−85.5	−91.5	−93.4	−87.4	....
Balance on Goods, Services, and Income	4 992 ..	*−289.6*	*−376.3*	*−391.6*	*−419.9*	*−494.8*	*−543.1*	*−512.3*	....
Current transfers: credit	2 379 Z.	161.4	206.8	229.3	287.8	328.5	385.2	412.9	....
Current transfers: debit	3 379 ..	−33.8	−37.4	−41.5	−44.1	−49.5	−61.4	−77.2	....
B. Capital Account[1]	4 994 Z.	**20.6**	**40.1**	**51.1**	**64.0**	**73.3**	**655.8**	**135.2**	....
Capital account: credit	2 994 Z.	20.6	40.1	51.1	64.0	73.3	655.8	135.2	....
Capital account: debit	3 994 ..	....	....	....	....	....	....	....	....
Total, Groups A Plus B	4 981 ..	*−141.3*	*−166.8*	*−152.8*	*−112.3*	*−142.5*	*436.6*	*−41.5*	....
C. Financial Account[1]	4 995 W.	**142.9**	**291.8**	**30.6**	**250.2**	**150.6**	**−746.8**	**86.5**	....
Direct investment abroad	4 505 ..	6.3	11.8	14.9	14.4	.7	13.2	−37.4	....
Direct investment in Togo	4 555 Z.	33.7	59.4	77.0	77.3	49.2	23.9	48.5	....
Portfolio investment assets	4 602 ..	−4.7	−26.5	−26.2	2.0	13.0	−6.8	−1.4	....
Equity securities	4 610 ..	−.2	−3.9	−18.0	1.0	2.1	15.1	−7.0	....
Debt securities	4 619 ..	−4.5	−22.5	−8.2	1.0	10.9	−21.9	5.7	....
Portfolio investment liabilities	4 652 Z.	18.6	26.2	28.7	60.6	6.3	18.9	−29.2	....
Equity securities	4 660 ..	9.8	14.8	16.0	10.4	6.3	1.4	2.1	....
Debt securities	4 669 Z.	8.8	11.4	12.7	50.3	....	17.5	−31.3	....
Financial derivatives	4 910 ..	....	....	.5	....	−.1	....	.1	....
Financial derivatives assets	4 900 ..	....	....	....	....	−.1	....	.1	....
Financial derivatives liabilities	4 905 ..	....	....	.5	....	....	....	....	....
Other investment assets	4 703 ..	−28.7	5.7	−91.3	−48.9	1.1	28.4	−176.8	....
Monetary authorities	4 701 ..	....	....	....	....	....	....	....	....
General government	4 704 ..	3.1	−2.8	.9	.9	.1	2.1	−12.6	....
Banks	4 705 ..	6.9	−16.7	−11.2	−13.1	.1	−39.6	−53.5	....
Other sectors	4 728 ..	−38.6	25.2	−81.1	−36.7	.9	65.9	−110.7	....
Other investment liabilities	4 753 W.	117.7	215.2	27.1	144.6	80.4	−824.4	282.6	....
Monetary authorities	4 753 WA	6.7	52.9	−67.2	19.3	4.1	80.7	107.2	....
General government	4 753 ZB	25.8	15.6	25.6	30.0	−1.6	−1,007.5	−14.0	....
Banks	4 753 ZC	2.6	−5.5	−7.8	6.7	4.1	31.3	−18.1	....
Other sectors	4 753 ZD	82.6	152.1	76.5	88.7	73.8	71.2	207.6	....
Total, Groups A Through C	4 983 ..	*1.6*	*125.0*	*−122.3*	*137.9*	*8.1*	*−310.2*	*44.9*	....
D. Net Errors and Omissions	4 998 ..	**−10.2**	**15.8**	**12.0**	**20.0**	**16.6**	**8.0**	**14.1**	....
Total, Groups A Through D	4 984 ..	*−8.6*	*140.8*	*−110.2*	*157.8*	*24.7*	*−302.2*	*59.0*	....
E. Reserves and Related Items	4 802 A.	**8.6**	**−140.8**	**110.2**	**−157.8**	**−24.7**	**302.2**	**−59.0**	....
Reserve assets	4 802 ..	22.4	−124.6	121.4	−151.5	−18.1	−176.4	−100.3	....
Use of Fund credit and loans	4 766 ..	−13.8	−16.2	−11.2	−6.4	−6.6	47.2	41.3	....
Exceptional financing	4 920 ..	....	....	....	....	....	431.4	....	....
Conversion rates: CFA francs per U.S. dollar	0 101 ..	**581.20**	**528.28**	**527.47**	**522.89**	**479.27**	**447.81**	**472.19**	**495.28**

[1] Excludes components that have been classified in the categories of Group E.

Table 2. STANDARD PRESENTATION, 2003–2010
(Millions of U.S. dollars)

	Code	2003	2004	2005	2006	2007	2008	2009	2010
CURRENT ACCOUNT	4 993	−161.9	−206.9	−203.9	−176.3	−215.8	−219.2	−176.7	....
A. GOODS	4 100	−156.8	−252.3	−283.3	−318.7	−395.1	−454.6	−412.1	....
Credit	2 100	**597.7**	**601.0**	**634.1**	**630.4**	**676.9**	**852.6**	**903.0**	....
General merchandise: exports f.o.b.	2 110	588.8	590.9	620.8	613.5	657.2	836.5	890.5	....
Goods for processing: exports f.o.b.	2 150	....	....	....	....	....	....	....	....
Repairs on goods	2 160	....	....	....	....	....	....	....	....
Goods procured in ports by carriers	2 170	8.9	10.1	13.3	16.8	19.7	16.1	12.5	....
Nonmonetary gold	2 180	....	....	....	....	....	....	....	....
Debit	3 100	**−754.5**	**−853.3**	**−917.4**	**−949.1**	**−1,072.0**	**−1,307.2**	**−1,315.2**	....
General merchandise: imports f.o.b.	3 110	−752.7	−851.0	−912.7	−946.0	−1,067.4	−1,302.4	−1,311.0	....
Goods for processing: imports f.o.b.	3 150	....	....	....	....	....	....	....	....
Repairs on goods	3 160	−.1	−.1	....	....	....	....	....	....
Goods procured in ports by carriers	3 170	−1.8	−2.2	−4.8	−3.1	−4.6	−4.9	−4.1	....
Nonmonetary gold	3 180	....	....	....	....	....	....	....	....
B. SERVICES	4 200	−109.4	−89.3	−73.8	−63.4	−69.4	−76.1	−81.2	....
Total credit	2 200	*94.8*	*150.0*	*176.9*	*200.7*	*236.0*	*283.1*	*293.6*	....
Total debit	3 200	*−204.2*	*−239.3*	*−250.7*	*−264.1*	*−305.5*	*−359.2*	*−374.7*	....
Transportation services, credit	2 205	**21.4**	**46.5**	**79.9**	**81.2**	**105.7**	**109.0**	**90.8**	....
Passenger	2 850	*10.9*	*6.4*	*6.9*	*2.1*	*3.7*	*4.4*	*5.3*	....
Freight	2 851	*2.7*	*23.6*	*25.2*	*36.1*	*39.5*	*40.8*	*28.7*	....
Other	2 852	*7.8*	*16.5*	*47.8*	*43.0*	*62.5*	*63.8*	*56.9*	....
Sea transport, passenger	2 207	....	....	....	....	....	....	....	....
Sea transport, freight	2 208	....	....	....	....	....	....	....	....
Sea transport, other	2 209	5.2	12.5	43.5	39.0	58.4	59.9	54.4	....
Air transport, passenger	2 211	7.1							....
Air transport, freight	2 212	....	20.3	21.3	29.9	32.9	35.2	23.3	....
Air transport, other	2 213	2.6	4.0	4.4	3.9	4.1	3.8	2.5	....
Other transport, passenger	2 215	3.8	6.4	6.9	2.1	3.7	4.4	5.3	....
Other transport, freight	2 216	2.7	3.3	3.9	6.2	6.6	5.6	5.4	....
Other transport, other	2 217	....	....	....	....	....	....	....	....
Transportation services, debit	3 205	**−148.5**	**−172.5**	**−185.8**	**−197.9**	**−215.8**	**−253.0**	**−233.2**	....
Passenger	3 850	*−30.4*	*−29.7*	*−34.1*	*−37.0*	*−42.1*	*−49.5*	*−47.1*	....
Freight	3 851	*−111.6*	*−141.2*	*−147.6*	*−157.5*	*−169.7*	*−200.8*	*−182.7*	....
Other	3 852	*−6.5*	*−1.6*	*−4.1*	*−3.4*	*−4.0*	*−2.7*	*−3.4*	....
Sea transport, passenger	3 207	....	....	....	....	....	....	....	....
Sea transport, freight	3 208	−100.3	−115.1	−130.1	−127.9	−144.5	−176.0	−167.9	....
Sea transport, other	3 209	−4.7	−.2	−.4	−.3	−1.4	−.1	−1.0	....
Air transport, passenger	3 211	−30.4	−29.7	−34.1	−37.0	−42.1	−49.5	−46.0	....
Air transport, freight	3 212	−11.3	−26.1	−17.5	−29.6	−25.3	−24.9	−14.9	....
Air transport, other	3 213	−1.8	−1.5	−3.7	−3.1	−2.6	−2.5	−2.4	....
Other transport, passenger	3 215	....	....	....	....	....	....	−1.1	....
Other transport, freight	3 216	....	....	....	....	....	....	....	....
Other transport, other	3 217	....	....	....	....	....	....	....	....
Travel, credit	2 236	**14.7**	**19.1**	**20.4**	**20.5**	**34.2**	**39.5**	**68.3**	....
Business travel	2 237	7.8	10.2	9.4	7.9	12.8	14.6	28.4	....
Personal travel	2 240	6.9	9.0	11.0	12.7	21.4	24.9	39.9	....
Travel, debit	3 236	**−7.2**	**−8.4**	**−7.7**	**−5.3**	**−16.7**	**−19.0**	**−46.9**	....
Business travel	3 237	−6.6	−8.4	−6.7	−4.8	−12.3	−13.2	−26.6	....
Personal travel	3 240	−.5	−.1	−1.0	−.5	−4.4	−5.8	−20.3	....
Other services, credit	2 200 BA	**58.7**	**84.3**	**76.6**	**99.0**	**96.1**	**134.6**	**134.4**	....
Communications	2 245	8.5	10.9	11.7	15.9	13.2	51.8	58.3	....
Construction	2 249	2.6	.6	1.4	5.0	1.3	3.4	2.2	....
Insurance	2 253	.5	.9	.9	.8	3.1	1.6	2.0	....
Financial	2 260	.4	.9	.6	5.8	6.4	10.7	11.5	....
Computer and information	2 262	.5	.9	.4	....	....	.8	....	....
Royalties and licence fees	2 266	....	....	....	....	....	....	....	....
Other business services	2 268	23.2	41.9	30.0	30.0	33.6	36.3	31.7	....
Personal, cultural, and recreational	2 287	....	....	....	....	....	....	....	....
Government, n.i.e.	2 291	22.9	28.2	31.6	41.5	38.6	29.9	28.7	....
Other services, debit	3 200 BA	**−48.5**	**−58.3**	**−57.2**	**−60.9**	**−72.9**	**−87.2**	**−94.6**	....
Communications	3 245	−7.7	−6.3	−6.3	−4.9	−7.9	−19.7	−22.4	....
Construction	3 249	−3.9	−.3	−.2	−.2	−.7	−.7	−9.6	....
Insurance	3 253	−22.2	−24.2	−31.1	−31.7	−31.2	−35.2	−33.8	....
Financial	3 260	−1.8	−2.9	−2.0	−2.0	−3.2	−1.3	−.7	....
Computer and information	3 262	−1.4	−1.3	−.5	−1.3	−4.4	−6.8	−6.1	....
Royalties and licence fees	3 266	−.7	−2.2	−2.7	−7.1	−5.2	−4.7	−4.7	....
Other business services	3 268	−10.6	−19.3	−12.3	−10.6	−18.2	−17.3	−16.9	....
Personal, cultural, and recreational	3 287	....	....	....	....	....	....	....	....
Government, n.i.e.	3 291	−.3	−1.9	−2.1	−3.1	−2.2	−1.6	−.5	....

Table 2 (Continued). STANDARD PRESENTATION, 2003–2010

(Millions of U.S. dollars)

	Code	2003	2004	2005	2006	2007	2008	2009	2010
C. INCOME	4 300 ..	**−23.3**	**−34.7**	**−34.5**	**−37.8**	**−30.2**	**−12.3**	**−19.0**	....
Total credit	2 300 ..	*26.8*	*39.9*	*46.3*	*47.7*	*61.3*	*81.1*	*68.4*	....
Total debit	3 300 ..	*−50.2*	*−74.6*	*−80.9*	*−85.5*	*−91.5*	*−93.4*	*−87.4*	....
Compensation of employees, credit	2 310 ..	**20.4**	**25.7**	**28.3**	**29.0**	**32.1**	**35.7**	**34.6**	....
Compensation of employees, debit	3 310 ..	**−1.0**	**−1.1**	**−.7**	**−.7**	**−.7**	**−1.6**	**−2.0**	....
Investment income, credit	2 320 ..	**6.4**	**14.2**	**18.1**	**18.7**	**29.2**	**45.4**	**33.8**	....
Direct investment income	2 330 ..	.8	6.2	7.6	6.3	4.8	9.8	1.1	....
Dividends and distributed branch profits	2 332 ..	.4	4.9	6.4	5.8	4.5	6.8	1.1	....
Reinvested earnings and undistributed branch profits	2 333 ..	.2	.8	.8	.3	.1	2.8	....	....
Income on debt (interest)	2 334 ..	.3	.4	.4	.2	.2	.3	.1	....
Portfolio investment income	2 339 ..	1.6	2.3	2.4	2.2	3.6	6.4	5.4	....
Income on equity	2 340 ..	.1	....	....	....	.1	.1	.1	....
Income on bonds and notes	2 350 ..	.1	.7	.5	1.3	2.9	4.4	4.6	....
Income on money market instruments	2 360 ..	1.4	1.5	1.9	.9	.6	1.9	.8	....
Other investment income	2 370 ..	4.0	5.7	8.1	10.2	20.7	29.2	27.2	....
Investment income, debit	3 320 ..	**−49.2**	**−73.5**	**−80.2**	**−84.8**	**−90.8**	**−91.8**	**−85.5**	....
Direct investment income	3 330 ..	−18.5	−38.7	−47.2	−54.9	−44.0	−48.7	−41.5	....
Dividends and distributed branch profits	3 332 ..	−15.0	−22.2	−20.9	−37.3	−36.7	−42.8	−28.4	....
Reinvested earnings and undistributed branch profits	3 333 ..	−3.3	−16.1	−25.9	−17.0	−6.6	−4.9	−12.8	....
Income on debt (interest)	3 334 ..	−.2	−.4	−.4	−.6	−.6	−1.0	−.3	....
Portfolio investment income	3 339 ..	−3.1	−3.6	−5.2	−6.8	−12.8	−14.3	−12.2	....
Income on equity	3 340 ..	−.8	−1.4	−2.4	−4.5	−4.5	−6.6	−3.2	....
Income on bonds and notes	3 350 ..	−2.3	−2.2	−2.8	−2.4	−8.3	−7.4	−8.3	....
Income on money market instruments	3 360 ..	....	....	....	....	....	−.2	−.7	....
Other investment income	3 370 ..	−27.6	−31.2	−27.8	−23.1	−34.0	−28.8	−31.7	....
D. CURRENT TRANSFERS	4 379 ..	**127.7**	**169.4**	**187.7**	**243.6**	**279.0**	**323.8**	**335.7**	....
Credit	2 379 ..	**161.4**	**206.8**	**229.3**	**287.8**	**328.5**	**385.2**	**412.9**	....
General government	2 380 ..	11.6	19.0	24.0	31.2	34.9	53.6	86.5	....
Other sectors	2 390 ..	149.8	187.9	205.3	256.6	293.6	331.7	326.3	....
Workers' remittances	2 391 ..	128.3	153.3	164.2	203.1	252.4	301.4	299.9	....
Other current transfers	2 392 ..	21.6	34.6	41.1	53.4	41.2	30.3	26.4	....
Debit	3 379 ..	**−33.8**	**−37.4**	**−41.5**	**−44.1**	**−49.5**	**−61.4**	**−77.2**	....
General government	3 380 ..	−1.5	−.8	−3.4	−3.8	−.4	−3.1	−5.3	....
Other sectors	3 390 ..	−32.3	−36.7	−38.1	−40.4	−49.1	−58.2	−71.9	....
Workers' remittances	3 391 ..	−27.4	−33.2	−34.8	−37.9	−46.4	−56.0	−70.0	....
Other current transfers	3 392 ..	−4.9	−3.5	−3.3	−2.4	−2.7	−2.2	−1.8	....
CAPITAL AND FINANCIAL ACCOUNT	4 996 ..	**172.1**	**191.1**	**191.9**	**156.3**	**199.1**	**211.2**	**162.6**	....
CAPITAL ACCOUNT	4 994 ..	**20.6**	**40.1**	**51.1**	**64.0**	**73.3**	**655.8**	**135.2**	....
Total credit	2 994 ..	*20.6*	*40.1*	*51.1*	*64.0*	*73.3*	*655.8*	*135.2*	....
Total debit	3 994 ..	....	....	....	....	....	....	....	....
Capital transfers, credit	2 400 ..	**20.6**	**40.1**	**51.1**	**64.0**	**73.3**	**655.8**	**135.2**	....
General government	2 401 ..	7.9	14.9	24.9	30.6	36.7	615.1	103.2	....
Debt forgiveness	2 402 ..	....	....	....	....	19.8	547.6	....	....
Other capital transfers	2 410 ..	7.9	14.9	24.9	30.6	16.9	67.5	103.2	....
Other sectors	2 430 ..	12.7	25.2	26.2	33.4	36.6	40.7	31.9	....
Migrants' transfers	2 431 ..	....	....	....	....	....	....	....	....
Debt forgiveness	2 432 ..	....	....	....	....	....	....	....	....
Other capital transfers	2 440 ..	12.7	25.2	26.2	33.4	36.6	40.7	31.9	....
Capital transfers, debit	3 400 ..	....	....	....	....	....	....	....	....
General government	3 401 ..	....	....	....	....	....	....	....	....
Debt forgiveness	3 402 ..	....	....	....	....	....	....	....	....
Other capital transfers	3 410 ..	....	....	....	....	....	....	....	....
Other sectors	3 430 ..	....	....	....	....	....	....	....	....
Migrants' transfers	3 431 ..	....	....	....	....	....	....	....	....
Debt forgiveness	3 432 ..	....	....	....	....	....	....	....	....
Other capital transfers	3 440 ..	....	....	....	....	....	....	....	....
Nonproduced nonfinancial assets, credit	2 480 ..	....	....	....	....	....	....	....	....
Nonproduced nonfinancial assets, debit	3 480 ..	....	....	....	....	....	....	....	....

Table 2 (Continued). STANDARD PRESENTATION, 2003–2010

(Millions of U.S. dollars)

	Code	2003	2004	2005	2006	2007	2008	2009	2010
FINANCIAL ACCOUNT	4 995	**151.5**	**151.0**	**140.8**	**92.3**	**125.9**	**−444.6**	**27.5**	....
A. DIRECT INVESTMENT	4 500	**40.1**	**71.1**	**91.9**	**91.7**	**49.9**	**37.1**	**11.1**	....
Direct investment abroad	4 505	**6.3**	**11.8**	**14.9**	**14.4**	**.7**	**13.2**	**−37.4**	....
Equity capital	4 510	−.2	−1.1	−.5	....	−1.2	.1	−31.3	....
Claims on affiliated enterprises	4 515	−.2	−1.1	−.6	....	−1.6	−.2	−31.3	....
Liabilities to affiliated enterprises	4 520	.1	.1	.1	....	.4	.3	....	....
Reinvested earnings	4 525	−.2	−.8	−.8	−.3	−.1	−2.8	....	....
Other capital	4 530	6.7	13.6	16.1	14.7	2.1	15.8	−6.2	....
Claims on affiliated enterprises	4 535	−3.9	−.9	.5	2.3	−4.9	−1.0	.1	....
Liabilities to affiliated enterprises	4 540	10.6	14.5	15.6	12.4	7.0	16.8	−6.2	....
Direct investment in Togo	4 555	**33.7**	**59.4**	**77.0**	**77.3**	**49.2**	**23.9**	**48.5**	....
Equity capital	4 560	31.1	21.7	26.4	25.9	19.8	4.7	15.8	....
Claims on direct investors	4 565	−1.0	−4.6	−1.9	−.3	−3.5	−6.9	−4.0	....
Liabilities to direct investors	4 570	32.1	26.3	28.4	26.3	23.3	11.7	19.8	....
Reinvested earnings	4 575	3.3	16.1	25.9	17.0	6.6	4.9	12.8	....
Other capital	4 580	−.7	21.6	24.7	34.4	22.7	14.3	19.9	....
Claims on direct investors	4 585	−.3	−1.2	−1.3	−1.3	−2.3	....	.2	....
Liabilities to direct investors	4 590	−.4	22.8	26.0	35.7	25.0	14.3	19.7	....
B. PORTFOLIO INVESTMENT	4 600	**13.8**	**−.3**	**2.5**	**62.7**	**19.3**	**12.1**	**−30.6**	....
Assets	4 602	**−4.7**	**−26.5**	**−26.2**	**2.0**	**13.0**	**−6.8**	**−1.4**	....
Equity securities	4 610	−.2	−3.9	−18.0	1.0	2.1	15.1	−7.0	....
Monetary authorities	4 611	....	....	....	....	....	....	....	
General government	4 612	....	....	....	....	....	....	....	
Banks	4 613	−.2	....	....	....	−.1	−1.2	....	
Other sectors	4 614	....	−3.9	−18.0	1.0	2.1	16.3	−7.0	
Debt securities	4 619	−4.5	−22.5	−8.2	1.0	10.9	−21.9	5.7	....
Bonds and notes	4 620	−2.8	−16.8	−8.2	4.2	−14.2	−3.2	−16.6	....
Monetary authorities	4 621	....	....	....	....	....	....	....	
General government	4 622	−4.0	6.4	−1.9	....	....	....	3.8	
Banks	4 623	−1.7	−24.3	−2.6	5.6	−10.8	−3.8	−19.3	
Other sectors	4 624	2.9	1.1	−3.7	−1.4	−3.5	.6	−1.0	
Money market instruments	4 630	−1.7	−5.7	....	−3.2	25.2	−18.7	22.2	....
Monetary authorities	4 631	....	....	....	....	....	....	....	
General government	4 632	....	....	....	....	....	....	....	
Banks	4 633	−1.7	−5.7	....	−3.2	25.2	−18.7	21.6	
Other sectors	4 634	....	....	....	....	....	....	.6	
Liabilities	4 652	**18.6**	**26.2**	**28.7**	**60.6**	**6.3**	**18.9**	**−29.2**	....
Equity securities	4 660	9.8	14.8	16.0	10.4	6.3	1.4	2.1	....
Banks	4 663	.7	....	.1	.1	−.2	.8	2.1	
Other sectors	4 664	9.0	14.8	15.9	10.2	6.5	.6	....	
Debt securities	4 669	8.8	11.4	12.7	50.3	....	17.5	−31.3	....
Bonds and notes	4 670	8.8	11.4	12.7	50.3	....	17.5	−31.3	....
Monetary authorities	4 671	....	....	....	....	....	....	....	
General government	4 672	....	....	....	49.2	....	....	−13.6	
Banks	4 673	....	....	....	2.0	....	8.6	....	
Other sectors	4 674	8.8	11.4	12.7	−.9	....	8.9	−17.6	
Money market instruments	4 680	....	....	....	....	....	....	....	
Monetary authorities	4 681	....	....	....	....	....	....	....	
General government	4 682	....	....	....	....	....	....	....	
Banks	4 683	....	....	....	....	....	....	....	
Other sectors	4 684	....	....	....	....	....	....	....	
C. FINANCIAL DERIVATIVES	4 910	....	....	**.5**	....	**−.1**	....	**.1**	....
Monetary authorities	4 911	....	....	....	....	....	....	....	
General government	4 912	....	....	....	....	....	....	....	
Banks	4 913	....	....	....	....	....	....	....	
Other sectors	4 914	....	....	.5	....	−.1	....	.1	
Assets	4 900	....	....	....	....	**−.1**	....	**.1**	....
Monetary authorities	4 901	....	....	....	....	....	....	....	
General government	4 902	....	....	....	....	....	....	....	
Banks	4 903	....	....	....	....	....	....	....	
Other sectors	4 904	....	....	....	....	−.1	....	.1	
Liabilities	4 905	....	....	**.5**	....	....	....	....	
Monetary authorities	4 906	....	....	....	....	....	....	....	
General government	4 907	....	....	....	....	....	....	....	
Banks	4 908	....	....	....	....	....	....	....	
Other sectors	4 909	....	....	.5	....	....	....	....	

Table 2 (Concluded). STANDARD PRESENTATION, 2003–2010

(Millions of U.S. dollars)

	Code	2003	2004	2005	2006	2007	2008	2009	2010
D. OTHER INVESTMENT	4 700 ..	**75.2**	**204.7**	**−75.5**	**89.4**	**75.0**	**−317.4**	**147.1**	....
Assets	4 703 ..	**−28.7**	**5.7**	**−91.3**	**−48.9**	**1.1**	**28.4**	**−176.8**	....
Trade credits	4 706 ..	−25.7	13.4	−1.4	15.7	21.1	6.3	−76.0	....
General government	4 707 ..	....	....	....	....	....	....	....	....
of which: Short-term	4 709 ..	....	....	....	....	....	....	....	....
Other sectors	4 710 ..	−25.7	13.4	−1.4	15.7	21.1	6.3	−76.0	....
of which: Short-term	4 712 ..	*−25.7*	*13.4*	*−1.4*	*15.7*	*21.1*	*6.3*	*−76.0*	....
Loans	4 714 ..	1.2	−3.6	−21.7	−14.9	9.4	−1.7	−25.0	....
Monetary authorities	4 715 ..	....	....	....	....	....	....	....	....
of which: Short-term	4 718 ..	....	....	....	....	....	....	....	....
General government	4 719 ..	....	....	....	....	....	....	....	....
of which: Short-term	4 721 ..	....	....	....	....	....	....	....	....
Banks	4 722 ..	1.2	−3.6	−21.7	−14.9	9.5	−1.7	−25.0	....
of which: Short-term	4 724 ..	*5.8*	*−.1*	*−23.2*	*−10.5*	*9.2*	*−18.4*	....	....
Other sectors	4 725 ..	....	....	....	....	....	....	....	....
of which: Short-term	4 727 ..	....	....	....	....	....	....	....	....
Currency and deposits	4 730 ..	−14.8	.6	−67.5	−53.0	−29.0	27.0	−68.0	....
Monetary authorities	4 731 ..	....	....	....	....	....	....	....	....
General government	4 732 ..	....	−2.8	.9	.9	.1	2.1	−12.6	....
Banks	4 733 ..	5.7	−12.7	10.6	1.8	−9.3	−37.9	−28.5	....
Other sectors	4 734 ..	−20.5	16.0	−79.0	−55.6	−19.8	62.8	−27.0	....
Other assets	4 736 ..	10.6	−4.7	−.7	3.3	−.4	−3.2	−7.7	....
Monetary authorities	4 737 ..	....	....	....	....	....	....	....	....
of which: Short-term	4 739 ..	....	....	....	....	....	....	....	....
General government	4 740 ..	3.1		....	....	....	....	....	....
of which: Short-term	4 742 ..	....	....	....	....	....	....	....	....
Banks	4 743 ..	....	−.4	....	....	....	....	....	....
of which: Short-term	4 745 ..	....	−.4	....	....	....	....	....	....
Other sectors	4 746 ..	7.5	−4.3	−.7	3.3	−.4	−3.2	−7.7	....
of which: Short-term	4 748 ..	*7.5*	*−4.3*	*−.7*	*3.3*	*−.4*	*−3.2*	*−7.7*	....
Liabilities	4 753 ..	**103.9**	**199.0**	**15.8**	**138.3**	**73.8**	**−345.8**	**323.9**	....
Trade credits	4 756 ..	35.4	67.5	46.2	57.8	20.8	26.9	64.2	....
General government	4 757 ..	....	....	....	....	....	....	....	....
of which: Short-term	4 759 ..	....	....	....	....	....	....	....	....
Other sectors	4 760 ..	35.4	67.5	46.2	57.8	20.8	26.9	64.2	....
of which: Short-term	4 762 ..	....	....	....	....	....	....	....	....
Loans	4 764 ..	46.7	44.3	57.9	40.5	33.6	−492.9	161.9	....
Monetary authorities	4 765 ..	−13.8	−16.2	−11.2	−6.4	−6.6	47.2	41.3	....
of which: Use of Fund credit and loans from the Fund..	4 766 ..	*−13.8*	*−16.2*	*−11.2*	*−6.4*	*−6.6*	*47.2*	*41.3*	....
of which: Short-term	4 768 ..	....	....	....	....	....	....	....	....
General government	4 769 ..	25.8	15.6	25.6	30.0	−1.6	−576.1	−14.0	....
of which: Short-term	4 771 ..	*79.3*	*86.0*	*54.9*	*49.3*	*55.5*	*−604.1*	*2.7*	....
Banks	4 772 ..	−4.4	−.4	5.0	−4.4	−1.3	5.8	....	....
of which: Short-term	4 774 ..	*−8.5*	*.1*	*5.2*	*−6.2*	*−6.2*	....	....	....
Other sectors	4 775 ..	39.1	45.2	38.6	21.2	43.1	30.1	134.6	....
of which: Short-term	4 777 ..	....	....	....	....	....	....	....	....
Currency and deposits	4 780 ..	11.2	−4.1	−11.8	13.3	3.9	23.4	−18.3	....
Monetary authorities	4 781 ..	4.1	.9	1.0	2.2	−1.6	−1.9	−.2	....
General government	4 782 ..	....	....	....	....	....	....	....	....
Banks	4 783 ..	7.0	−5.1	−12.8	11.1	5.5	25.3	−18.1	....
Other sectors	4 784 ..	....	....	....	....	....	....	....	....
Other liabilities	4 786 ..	10.7	91.4	−76.4	26.7	15.6	96.9	116.1	....
Monetary authorities	4 787 ..	2.6	52.0	−68.2	17.1	5.7	82.6	107.4	....
of which: Short-term	4 789 ..	....	....	....	....	....	....	....	....
General government	4 790 ..	....	....	....	....	....	....	....	....
of which: Short-term	4 792 ..	....	....	....	....	....	....	....	....
Banks	4 793 ..	....	....	....	....	....	.1	....	....
of which: Short-term	4 795 ..	....	....	....	....	....	.1	....	....
Other sectors	4 796 ..	8.1	39.4	−8.2	9.6	9.9	14.2	8.7	....
of which: Short-term	4 798 ..	....	....	....	....	....	....	....	....
E. RESERVE ASSETS	4 802 ..	**22.4**	**−124.6**	**121.4**	**−151.5**	**−18.1**	**−176.4**	**−100.3**	....
Monetary gold	4 812 ..	....	....	....	....	....	....	....	....
Special drawing rights	4 811 ..	.1	.1	....	....	....	....	−92.4	....
Reserve position in the Fund	4 810 ..	....	....	....	....	....	....	....	....
Foreign exchange	4 803 ..	22.3	−124.8	121.4	−151.4	−18.1	−176.4	−7.9	....
Other claims	4 813 ..	....	....	....	....	....	....	....	....
NET ERRORS AND OMISSIONS	4 998 ..	**−10.2**	**15.8**	**12.0**	**20.0**	**16.6**	**8.0**	**14.1**	....

Table 3. INTERNATIONAL INVESTMENT POSITION (End-period stocks), 2003–2010

(Millions of U.S. dollars)

	Code	2003	2004	2005	2006	2007	2008	2009	2010
ASSETS...	8 995 C.	**503.1**	**714.2**	**535.3**	**993.3**	**1,146.1**	**1,295.5**	**1,665.4**	....
Direct investment abroad........................	8 505 ..	**16.1**	**−10.5**	**−22.6**	**−12.7**	**−15.0**	**54.4**	**95.2**	....
Equity capital and reinvested earnings...........	8 506 ..	12.3	14.5	13.8	15.1	18.3	100.9	136.9	....
Claims on affiliated enterprises..............	8 507 ..	12.3	14.5	13.8	15.1	18.3	100.9	136.9	....
Liabilities to affiliated enterprises..........	8 508 ..	....	....	....	....	....	....	....	....
Other capital...	8 530 ..	3.8	−25.0	−36.4	−27.8	−33.3	−46.5	−41.7	....
Claims on affiliated enterprises..............	8 535 ..	13.3	....	....	11.8	18.6	18.5	19.0	....
Liabilities to affiliated enterprises..........	8 540 ..	−9.5	−25.0	−36.4	−39.6	−51.8	−65.0	−60.8	....
Portfolio investment................................	8 602 ..	**61.5**	**104.7**	**115.6**	**126.9**	**127.9**	**127.4**	**133.2**	....
Equity securities.......................................	8 610 ..	5.1	9.7	25.5	27.4	28.4	12.5	20.2	....
Monetary authorities............................	8 611 ..	....	....	....	....	....	....	....	
General government.............................	8 612 .	....	....	....	....	....	....	....	
Banks..	8 613 ..	2.3	2.4	2.0	2.3	2.6	3.6	3.7	
Other sectors..	8 614 ..	2.7	7.3	23.4	25.1	25.8	8.9	16.5	
Debt securities...	8 619 ..	56.5	95.0	90.1	99.5	99.5	114.9	113.0	....
Bonds and notes...................................	8 620 ..	38.6	69.6	68.0	71.6	95.2	93.1	112.9	....
Monetary authorities........................	8 621 ..	....	....	....	....	....	....	....	
General government.........................	8 622 ..	....	....	1.8	2.0	2.3	2.1	....	
Banks...	8 623 ..	1.1	27.9	26.7	23.9	38.3	39.8	61.3	
Other sectors...................................	8 624 ..	37.5	41.6	39.6	45.6	54.6	51.1	51.6	
Money market instruments....................	8 630 ..	17.9	25.5	22.1	28.0	4.3	21.8	.1	
Monetary authorities........................	8 631 ..	....	....	....	....	....	....	....	
General government.........................	8 632 ..	....	....	....	....	....	....	....	
Banks...	8 633 ..	17.9	25.5	22.1	28.0	4.2	21.7	.1	
Other sectors...................................	8 634 ..	....	....	....	.1	.1	....	
Financial derivatives..............................	8 900 ..	....	....	....	....	....	....	....	....
Monetary authorities................................	8 901 ..	....	....	....	....	....	....	....	
General government................................	8 902 ..	....	....	....	....	....	....	....	
Banks...	8 903 ..	....	....	....	....	....	....	....	
Other sectors...	8 904 ..	....	....	....	....	....	....	....	
Other investment...................................	8 703 ..	**243.0**	**262.3**	**250.8**	**504.6**	**595.1**	**531.8**	**733.9**	....
Trade credits..	8 706 ..	99.2	92.2	81.2	74.2	60.2	50.9	131.6	....
General government.............................	8 707 ..	....	....	....	....	....	....	....	....
of which: Short-term..........................	8 709 ..	....	....	....	....	....	....	....	
Other sectors..	8 710 ..	99.2	92.2	81.2	74.2	60.2	50.9	131.6	....
of which: Short-term..........................	8 712 ..	*99.2*	*92.2*	*81.2*	*74.2*	*60.2*	*50.9*	*131.6*	....
Loans..	8 714 ..	14.7	19.6	37.6	57.5	54.1	52.8	80.6	....
Monetary authorities............................	8 715 ..	....	....	....	....	....	....	....	
of which: Short-term........................	8 718 ..	....	....	....	....	....	....	....	
General government.............................	8 719 ..	....	....	....	....	....	....	....	
of which: Short-term........................	8 721 ..	....	....	....	....	....	....	....	
Banks..	8 722 ..	14.7	19.6	37.6	57.5	54.1	52.7	80.6	....
of which: Short-term........................	8 724 ..	*5.8*	*6.1*	*27.4*	*41.6*	*36.8*	*52.3*	*54.1*	....
Other sectors..	8 725 ..	....	....	....	....	....	....	....	
of which: Short-term........................	8 727 ..	....	....	....	....	....	....	....	
Currency and deposits...............................	8 730 ..	119.9	135.3	118.6	361.3	468.3	417.0	502.2	....
Monetary authorities............................	8 731 ..	....	....	....	....	....	....	....	
General government.............................	8 732 ..	....	3.0	1.8	1.0	3.3	1.1	14.2	
Banks..	8 733 ..	72.6	88.1	66.2	72.1	90.6	121.7	155.5	
Other sectors..	8 734 ..	47.3	44.2	50.6	288.2	374.4	294.3	332.6	
Other assets..	8 736 ..	9.3	15.2	13.5	11.6	12.5	11.1	19.5	....
Monetary authorities............................	8 737 ..	....	....	....	....	....	....	....	
of which: Short-term........................	8 739 ..	....	....	....	....	....	....	....	
General government.............................	8 740 ..	3.5	3.7	3.2	3.6	4.1	....	....	
of which: Short-term........................	8 742 ..	*3.5*	*3.7*	*3.2*	*3.6*	*4.1*	....	....	
Banks..	8 743 ..	....	.5	....	....	....	....	....	
of which: Short-term........................	8 745 ..	....	.5	....	....	....	....	....	
Other sectors..	8 746 ..	5.8	11.0	10.2	8.0	8.5	11.1	19.5	....
of which: Short-term........................	8 748 ..	*5.8*	*11.0*	*10.2*	*8.0*	*8.5*	*11.1*	*19.5*	....
Reserve assets.......................................	8 802 ..	**182.5**	**357.7**	**191.5**	**374.5**	**438.1**	**581.8**	**703.2**	....
Monetary gold..	8 812 ..	....	....	....	....	....	....	....	
Special drawing rights...............................	8 811 ..	.2	....	....	.1	.1	.1	92.9	91.4
Reserve position in the Fund......................	8 810 ..	.5	.5	.5	.5	.5	.5	.5	.6
Foreign exchange......................................	8 803 ..	181.9	357.1	191.0	373.9	437.5	581.2	609.8	....
Other claims..	8 813 ..	....	....	....	....	....	....	....	....

Table 3 (Concluded). INTERNATIONAL INVESTMENT POSITION (End-period stocks), 2003–2010

(Millions of U.S. dollars)

	Code	2003	2004	2005	2006	2007	2008	2009	2010
LIABILITIES	8 995 D.	**2,277.2**	**2,635.7**	**2,462.6**	**3,034.8**	**3,335.0**	**3,004.1**	**3,572.3**	....
Direct investment in Togo	8 555 ..	**132.4**	**186.7**	**234.7**	**343.2**	**436.5**	**450.2**	**516.3**	....
Equity capital and reinvested earnings	8 556 ..	118.8	157.0	185.6	252.2	310.4	317.4	358.2	....
Claims on direct investors	8 557 ..	....	....	....	....	....	....	....	....
Liabilities to direct investors	8 558 ..	118.8	157.0	185.6	252.2	310.4	317.4	358.2	....
Other capital	8 580 ..	13.6	29.7	49.1	91.0	126.1	132.8	158.1	....
Claims on direct investors	8 585 ..	−2.3	−3.9	−4.6	−6.5	−9.7	−9.2	−9.3	....
Liabilities to direct investors	8 590 ..	15.9	33.6	53.7	97.4	135.8	142.0	167.4	....
Portfolio investment	8 652 ..	**16.9**	**47.0**	**67.9**	**137.4**	**160.3**	**147.7**	**122.6**	....
Equity securities	8 660 ..	16.7	34.3	44.9	60.9	74.9	72.1	76.8	....
Banks	8 663 ..	.8	.9	.9	1.1	1.1	1.8	3.9	....
Other sectors	8 664 ..	15.8	33.4	43.9	59.8	73.8	70.4	72.8	....
Debt securities	8 669 ..	.2	12.7	23.0	76.4	85.4	75.6	45.8	....
Bonds and notes	8 670 ..	.2	12.7	23.0	76.4	85.4	75.6	45.8	....
Monetary authorities	8 671 ..	....	....	....	....	....	....	....	....
General government	8 672 ..	....	....	....	51.7	57.8	40.9	28.3	....
Banks	8 673 ..	....	....	....	....	....	....	....	....
Other sectors	8 674 ..	.2	12.7	23.0	24.8	27.7	34.6	17.6	....
Money market instruments	8 680 ..	....	....	....	....	....	....	....	....
Monetary authorities	8 681 ..	....	....	....	....	....	....	....	....
General government	8 682 ..	....	....	....	....	....	....	....	....
Banks	8 683 ..	....	....	....	....	....	....	....	....
Other sectors	8 684 ..	....	....	....	....	....	....	....	....
Financial derivatives	8 905 ..	....	....	....	....	....	....	....	....
Monetary authorities	8 906 ..	....	....	....	....	....	....	....	....
General government	8 907 ..	....	....	....	....	....	....	....	....
Banks	8 908 ..	....	....	....	....	....	....	....	....
Other sectors	8 909 ..	....	....	....	....	....	....	....	....
Other investment	8 753 ..	**2,127.9**	**2,402.1**	**2,160.0**	**2,554.2**	**2,738.2**	**2,406.2**	**2,933.4**	....
Trade credits	8 756 ..	127.4	207.2	223.3	309.9	368.8	374.2	453.9	....
General government	8 757 ..	....	....	....	....	....	....	....	....
of which: Short-term	8 759 ..	....	....	....	....	....	....	....	....
Other sectors	8 760 ..	127.4	207.2	223.3	309.9	368.8	374.2	453.9	....
of which: Short-term	8 762 ..	*127.4*	*207.2*	*223.3*	*309.9*	*368.8*	*374.2*	*453.9*	....
Loans	8 764 ..	1,893.9	2,012.7	1,862.6	2,121.4	2,209.8	1,767.0	2,086.3	....
Monetary authorities	8 765 ..	42.0	27.0	14.0	8.2	1.7	48.1	90.9	....
of which: Use of Fund credit and loans from the Fund	8 766 ..	*42.0*	*27.0*	*14.0*	*8.2*	*1.7*	*48.1*	*90.9*	*133.1*
of which: Short-term	8 768 ..	....	....	....	....	....	....	....	....
General government	8 769 ..	1,736.5	1,812.1	1,656.9	1,881.6	1,901.4	1,394.7	1,514.4	....
of which: Short-term	8 771 ..	*401.0*	*531.4*	*505.4*	*588.4*	*670.7*	*50.4*	*29.8*	....
Banks	8 772 ..	5.1	5.0	9.1	5.5	7.5	12.7	18.8	....
of which: Short-term	8 774 ..	*4.2*	*4.6*	*8.9*	*3.4*	....	....	....	....
Other sectors	8 775 ..	110.4	168.6	182.7	226.2	299.3	311.5	462.1	....
of which: Short-term	8 777 ..	....	....	....	....	....	....	....	....
Currency and deposits	8 780 ..	93.2	43.4	26.4	41.5	51.8	71.2	55.8	....
Monetary authorities	8 781 ..	27.6	2.8	3.4	4.1	4.2	2.2	3.2	....
General government	8 782 ..	....	....	....	....	....	....	....	....
Banks	8 783 ..	65.6	40.6	23.0	37.4	47.6	69.1	52.7	....
Other sectors	8 784 ..	....	....	....	....	....	....	....	....
Other liabilities	8 786 ..	13.4	138.8	47.7	81.3	107.7	193.8	337.4	....
Monetary authorities	8 787 ..	4.8	88.9	12.4	31.7	41.7	117.8	249.6	....
of which: Short-term	8 789 ..	*4.8*	*88.9*	*12.4*	*31.7*	*41.7*	*117.8*	*139.4*	....
General government	8 790 ..	....	....	....	....	....	....	....	....
of which: Short-term	8 792 ..	....	....	....	....	....	....	....	....
Banks	8 793 ..	....	....	....	....	....	.1	.1	....
of which: Short-term	8 795 ..	....	....	....	....	....	*.1*	*.1*	....
Other sectors	8 796 ..	8.7	49.8	35.3	49.6	66.0	75.9	87.6	....
of which: Short-term	8 798 ..	....	....	....	....	....	....	....	....
NET INTERNATIONAL INVESTMENT POSITION	8 995 ..	**−1,774.1**	**−1,921.5**	**−1,927.3**	**−2,041.5**	**−2,188.9**	**−1,708.6**	**−1,907.0**	....
Conversion rates: CFA francs per U.S. dollar (end of period)	0 102 ..	519.36	481.58	556.04	498.07	445.59	471.34	455.34	490.91

Table 1. ANALYTIC PRESENTATION, 2003–2010
(Thousands of U.S. dollars)

	Code	2003	2004	2005	2006	2007	2008	2009	2010
A. Current Account[1]	4 993 Z.	−10,654	−17,365	−21,290	−31,058	−19,424	−66,030	−54,216	....
Goods: exports f.o.b.	2 100 ..	19,291	18,162	16,007	10,000	12,665	10,856	8,435	....
Goods: imports f.o.b.	3 100 ..	−86,055	−98,533	−114,475	−115,488	−134,907	−163,423	−139,640	....
Balance on Goods	4 100 ..	*−66,764*	*−80,371*	*−98,468*	*−105,488*	*−122,243*	*−152,568*	*−131,205*	....
Services: credit	2 200 ..	25,430	24,682	35,419	25,982	26,286	38,447	35,141	....
Services: debit	3 200 ..	−35,476	−39,466	−40,563	−39,148	−42,606	−55,299	−48,601	....
Balance on Goods and Services	4 991 ..	*−76,809*	*−95,155*	*−103,612*	*−118,653*	*−138,563*	*−169,420*	*−144,665*	....
Income: credit	2 300 ..	7,210	5,073	8,052	8,256	12,153	10,748	10,037	....
Income: debit	3 300 ..	−4,304	−7,020	−2,267	−3,449	−3,807	−3,704	−6,190	....
Balance on Goods, Services, and Income	4 992 ..	*−73,903*	*−97,102*	*−97,826*	*−113,846*	*−130,217*	*−162,376*	*−140,819*	....
Current transfers: credit	2 379 Z.	72,076	93,813	90,756	96,078	123,373	109,966	96,669	....
Current transfers: debit	3 379 ..	−8,826	−14,076	−14,220	−13,290	−12,580	−13,621	−10,066	....
B. Capital Account[1]	4 994 Z.	8,259	11,456	12,934	15,390	16,274	45,498	54,867	....
Capital account: credit	2 994 Z.	9,456	11,864	13,365	18,924	20,603	50,157	57,102	....
Capital account: debit	3 994 ..	−1,197	−409	−430	−3,534	−4,330	−4,660	−2,235	....
Total, Groups A Plus B	4 981 ..	*−2,395*	*−5,909*	*−8,356*	*−15,668*	*−3,150*	*−20,533*	*651*	....
C. Financial Account[1]	4 995 W.	8,472	28,012	2,838	11,645	22,131	6,797	17,650	....
Direct investment abroad	4 505 ..	....		....	....	....	....	....	....
Direct investment in Tonga	4 555 Z.	3,375	4,587	7,205	10,058	27,657	4,166	−36	....
Portfolio investment assets	4 602 ..	....	....	....	....	....	....	....	
Equity securities	4 610 ..	....	....	....	....	....	....	....	
Debt securities	4 619 ..	....	....	....	....	....	....	....	
Portfolio investment liabilities	4 652 Z.	....	....	....	....	....	....	....	
Equity securities	4 660 ..	....	....	....	....	....	....	....	
Debt securities	4 669 Z.	....	....	....	....	....	....	....	
Financial derivatives	4 910 ..	....		....	....	....	16,214	1,657	
Financial derivatives assets	4 900 ..	....		....	....	....	16,214	1,657	
Financial derivatives liabilities	4 905 ..	....				....			
Other investment assets	4 703 ..	4,452	−287	17	510	123	6,202	10,381	....
Monetary authorities	4 701 ..	....	....	....	....	....	....	10,358	....
General government	4 704 ..	3,593	−370	....	144	1	273	....	....
Banks	4 705 ..	23	83	10	248	....	3,512	....	....
Other sectors	4 728 ..	835	....	7	118	122	2,417	23	....
Other investment liabilities	4 753 W.	645	23,712	−4,384	1,077	−5,648	−19,784	5,648	....
Monetary authorities	4 753 WA	....	−13	−18	....	−233	....	10,362	
General government	4 753 ZB	4,886	−1,929	−1,455	−1,014	−4,840	−5,548	−3,233	
Banks	4 753 ZC	−905	−4,595	−365	−77	−63	−103	−497	
Other sectors	4 753 ZD	−3,336	30,249	−2,545	2,168	−512	−14,133	−983	
Total, Groups A Through C	4 983 ..	*6,077*	*22,103*	*−5,518*	*−4,023*	*18,981*	*−13,735*	*18,301*	....
D. Net Errors and Omissions	4 998 ..	−13,868	−38,208	−11,491	−12,189	−39,275	−8,636	−37,266	....
Total, Groups A Through D	4 984 ..	*−7,791*	*−16,104*	*−17,008*	*−16,211*	*−20,294*	*−22,372*	*−18,965*	
E. Reserves and Related Items	4 802 A.	7,791	16,104	17,008	16,211	20,294	22,372	18,965	....
Reserve assets	4 802 ..	7,791	16,104	17,008	16,211	20,294	22,372	18,965	....
Use of Fund credit and loans	4 766 ..	....	....	....	....	....	....	....	....
Exceptional financing	4 920 ..	....	....	....	....	....	....	....	....
Conversion rates: pa'anga per U.S. dollar	0 101 ..	2.1459	1.9716	1.9430	2.0259	1.9709	1.9424	2.0345	1.9060

[1] Excludes components that have been classified in the categories of Group E.

Table 2. STANDARD PRESENTATION, 2003–2010

(Thousands of U.S. dollars)

	Code	2003	2004	2005	2006	2007	2008	2009	2010
CURRENT ACCOUNT	4 993 ..	**−10,654**	**−17,365**	**−21,290**	**−31,058**	**−19,424**	**−66,030**	**−54,216**	....
A. GOODS	4 100 ..	**−66,764**	**−80,371**	**−98,468**	**−105,488**	**−122,243**	**−152,568**	**−131,205**	....
Credit	2 100 ..	**19,291**	**18,162**	**16,007**	**10,000**	**12,665**	**10,856**	**8,435**	....
General merchandise: exports f.o.b.	2 110 ..	18,829	17,714	15,500	9,485	12,173	10,195	7,854	....
Goods for processing: exports f.o.b.	2 150 ..	....	....	....	....	....	....	....	....
Repairs on goods	2 160 ..	....	....	....	....	....	....	....	....
Goods procured in ports by carriers	2 170 ..	463	448	507	515	492	660	580	....
Nonmonetary gold	2 180 ..	....	....	....	....	....	....	....	....
Debit	3 100 ..	**−86,055**	**−98,533**	**−114,475**	**−115,488**	**−134,907**	**−163,423**	**−139,640**	....
General merchandise: imports f.o.b.	3 110 ..	−86,055	−98,533	−114,475	−115,488	−134,907	−163,423	−139,640	....
Goods for processing: imports f.o.b.	3 150 ..	....	....	....	....	....	....	....	....
Repairs on goods	3 160 ..	....	....	....	....	....	....	....	....
Goods procured in ports by carriers	3 170 ..	....	....	....	....	....	....	....	....
Nonmonetary gold	3 180 ..	....	....	....	....	....	....	....	....
B. SERVICES	4 200 ..	**−10,046**	**−14,784**	**−5,144**	**−13,165**	**−16,320**	**−16,852**	**−13,460**	....
Total credit	2 200 ..	*25,430*	*24,682*	*35,419*	*25,982*	*26,286*	*38,447*	*35,141*	....
Total debit	3 200 ..	*−35,476*	*−39,466*	*−40,563*	*−39,148*	*−42,606*	*−55,299*	*−48,601*	....
Transportation services, credit	2 205 ..	**2,293**	**2,594**	**3,123**	**2,551**	**3,889**	**5,031**	**5,267**	....
Passenger	2 850 ..	*3*	*277*	*114*	....	*808*	*366*	*802*	....
Freight	2 851 ..	....	....	....	....	....	....	....	....
Other	2 852 ..	*2,290*	*2,317*	*3,009*	*2,551*	*3,081*	*4,664*	*4,465*	....
Sea transport, passenger	2 207 ..	....	....	....	....	....	....	....	....
Sea transport, freight	2 208 ..	....	....	....	....	....	....	....	....
Sea transport, other	2 209 ..	1,176	1,094	1,203	1,239	1,242	1,447	1,272	....
Air transport, passenger	2 211 ..	3	277	114	....	808	366	802	....
Air transport, freight	2 212 ..	....	....	....	....	....	....	....	....
Air transport, other	2 213 ..	1,115	1,222	1,805	1,312	1,839	3,217	3,193	....
Other transport, passenger	2 215 ..	....	....	....	....	....	....	....	....
Other transport, freight	2 216 ..	....	....	....	....	....	....	....	....
Other transport, other	2 217 ..	....	....	....	....	....	....	....	....
Transportation services, debit	3 205 ..	**−22,098**	**−19,162**	**−22,259**	**−16,806**	**−18,793**	**−28,502**	**−22,531**	....
Passenger	3 850 ..	*−9,926*	*−10,091*	*−12,200*	*−8,252*	*−9,309*	*−16,364*	*−11,866*	....
Freight	3 851 ..	*−10,601*	*−5,761*	*−6,631*	*−6,402*	*−7,855*	*−9,561*	*−8,057*	....
Other	3 852 ..	*−1,571*	*−3,310*	*−3,428*	*−2,152*	*−1,630*	*−2,576*	*−2,608*	....
Sea transport, passenger	3 207 ..	....	....	....	....	....	....	....	....
Sea transport, freight	3 208 ..	−4,735	−5,476	−6,303	−6,074	−7,258	−8,391	−7,336	....
Sea transport, other	3 209 ..	−1,571	−3,310	−3,428	−2,152	−1,630	−2,576	−2,608	....
Air transport, passenger	3 211 ..	−9,926	−10,091	−12,200	−8,252	−9,309	−16,364	−11,866	....
Air transport, freight	3 212 ..	−5,866	−285	−328	−328	−597	−1,170	−721	....
Air transport, other	3 213 ..	....	....	....	....	....	....	....	....
Other transport, passenger	3 215 ..	....	....	....	....	....	....	....	....
Other transport, freight	3 216 ..	....	....	....	....	....	....	....	....
Other transport, other	3 217 ..	....	....	....	....	....	....	....	....
Travel, credit	2 236 ..	**10,291**	**12,833**	**14,877**	**15,679**	**14,429**	**19,049**	**16,032**	....
Business travel	2 237 ..	2,781	3,448	6,090	14,591	8,417	14,975	11,864	....
Personal travel	2 240 ..	7,510	9,385	8,786	1,088	6,011	4,074	4,168	....
Travel, debit	3 236 ..	**−3,332**	**−6,113**	**−3,816**	**−8,053**	**−9,875**	**−8,707**	**−7,219**	....
Business travel	3 237 ..	−1,104	−3,089	−1,674	−4,762	−5,284	−5,475	−4,178	....
Personal travel	3 240 ..	−2,228	−3,025	−2,142	−3,291	−4,592	−3,232	−3,040	....
Other services, credit	2 200 BA	**12,846**	**9,255**	**17,419**	**7,752**	**7,968**	**14,367**	**13,842**	....
Communications	2 245 ..	8,005	3,438	4,646	804	1,786	1,079	891	....
Construction	2 249 ..	219	114	2,061	478	49	64	578	....
Insurance	2 253 ..	....	....	....	....	....	....	....	....
Financial	2 260 ..	6	130	952	103	193	1,028	27	....
Computer and information	2 262 ..	....	....	5	1	33	....	16	....
Royalties and licence fees	2 266 ..	....	....	....	....	....	....	....	....
Other business services	2 268 ..	329	1,729	2,543	2,142	1,718	6,696	4,842	....
Personal, cultural, and recreational	2 287 ..	875	91	1,054	545	563	887	827	....
Government, n.i.e.	2 291 ..	3,411	3,753	6,158	3,680	3,626	4,614	6,661	....
Other services, debit	3 200 BA	**−10,046**	**−14,190**	**−14,488**	**−14,288**	**−13,937**	**−18,091**	**−18,852**	....
Communications	3 245 ..	−3,290	−4,170	−2,911	−1,398	−1,287	−1,265	−4,334	....
Construction	3 249 ..	−496	−79	−375	....	−49	−355	−652	....
Insurance	3 253 ..	−914	−1,421	−2,365	−1,387	−1,284	−1,484	−1,330	....
Financial	3 260 ..	−772	−417	−1,521	−272	−183	−1,213	−601	....
Computer and information	3 262 ..	−7	−17	−16	−80	−156	−373	−11	....
Royalties and licence fees	3 266 ..	....	....	−51	....	....	....	....	....
Other business services	3 268 ..	−309	−834	−911	−2,535	−719	−1,904	−4,844	....
Personal, cultural, and recreational	3 287 ..	−305	−116	−57	−266	−602	−707	−576	....
Government, n.i.e.	3 291 ..	−3,953	−7,137	−6,280	−8,350	−9,658	−10,789	−6,503	....

Table 2 (Continued). STANDARD PRESENTATION, 2003–2010

(Thousands of U.S. dollars)

	Code	2003	2004	2005	2006	2007	2008	2009	2010
C. INCOME	4 300	**2,906**	**−1,947**	**5,785**	**4,807**	**8,346**	**7,044**	**3,847**	....
Total credit	2 300	*7,210*	*5,073*	*8,052*	*8,256*	*12,153*	*10,748*	*10,037*	....
Total debit	3 300	*−4,304*	*−7,020*	*−2,267*	*−3,449*	*−3,807*	*−3,704*	*−6,190*	....
Compensation of employees, credit	2 310	**2,781**	**3,276**	**3,374**	**3,398**	**4,031**	**4,587**	**4,157**	....
Compensation of employees, debit	3 310	**−1,169**	**−153**	**−62**	**−57**	**−63**	**−93**	**−718**	....
Investment income, credit	2 320	**4,429**	**1,796**	**4,679**	**4,858**	**8,122**	**6,162**	**5,879**	....
Direct investment income	2 330	476	....	....	....	....	3	....	....
Dividends and distributed branch profits	2 332	476	....	....	....	....	3	....	....
Reinvested earnings and undistributed branch profits	2 333	....	....	....	....	....	....	....	....
Income on debt (interest)	2 334	....	....	....	....	....	....	....	....
Portfolio investment income	2 339	....	....	....	....	....	....	....	....
Income on equity	2 340	....	....	....	....	....	....	....	....
Income on bonds and notes	2 350	....	....	....	....	....	....	....	....
Income on money market instruments	2 360	....	....	....	....	....	....	....	....
Other investment income	2 370	3,953	1,796	4,679	4,858	8,122	6,159	5,879	....
Investment income, debit	3 320	**−3,135**	**−6,867**	**−2,205**	**−3,392**	**−3,745**	**−3,611**	**−5,472**	....
Direct investment income	3 330	−796	....	....	....	....	−2	−19	....
Dividends and distributed branch profits	3 332	−796	....	....	....	....	−2	−19	....
Reinvested earnings and undistributed branch profits	3 333	....	....	....	....	....	....	....	....
Income on debt (interest)	3 334	....	....	....	....	....	....	....	....
Portfolio investment income	3 339	....	....	....	....	....	....	....	....
Income on equity	3 340	....	....	....	....	....	....	....	....
Income on bonds and notes	3 350	....	....	....	....	....	....	....	....
Income on money market instruments	3 360	....	....	....	....	....	....	....	....
Other investment income	3 370	−2,339	−6,867	−2,205	−3,392	−3,745	−3,609	−5,452	....
D. CURRENT TRANSFERS	4 379	**63,250**	**79,737**	**76,537**	**82,788**	**110,793**	**96,345**	**86,603**	....
Credit	2 379	**72,076**	**93,813**	**90,756**	**96,078**	**123,373**	**109,966**	**96,669**	....
General government	2 380	3,451	10,078	7,580	10,568	6,593	8,139	15,789	....
Other sectors	2 390	68,625	83,735	83,177	85,510	116,780	101,827	80,880	....
Workers' remittances	2 391	57,429	65,789	65,268	75,353	96,965	89,110	67,258	....
Other current transfers	2 392	11,196	17,946	17,908	10,157	19,815	12,717	13,622	....
Debit	3 379	**−8,826**	**−14,076**	**−14,220**	**−13,290**	**−12,580**	**−13,621**	**−10,066**	....
General government	3 380	....	−487	−91	−125	....	−673	−1,472	....
Other sectors	3 390	−8,826	−13,589	−14,129	−13,165	−12,580	−12,947	−8,594	....
Workers' remittances	3 391	−7,928	−10,280	−11,639	−11,911	−11,179	−11,525	−7,635	....
Other current transfers	3 392	−898	−3,309	−2,491	−1,254	−1,401	−1,423	−959	....
CAPITAL AND FINANCIAL ACCOUNT	4 996	**24,522**	**55,572**	**32,780**	**43,247**	**58,699**	**74,667**	**91,482**	....
CAPITAL ACCOUNT	4 994	**8,259**	**11,456**	**12,934**	**15,390**	**16,274**	**45,498**	**54,867**	....
Total credit	2 994	*9,456*	*11,864*	*13,365*	*18,924*	*20,603*	*50,157*	*57,102*	....
Total debit	3 994	*−1,197*	*−409*	*−430*	*−3,534*	*−4,330*	*−4,660*	*−2,235*	....
Capital transfers, credit	2 400	**9,456**	**11,864**	**13,365**	**18,924**	**20,603**	**25,152**	**57,102**	....
General government	2 401	6,535	11,374	13,014	13,123	13,030	8,520	41,018	....
Debt forgiveness	2 402	....	....	....	....	....	....	539	....
Other capital transfers	2 410	6,535	11,374	13,014	13,123	13,030	8,520	40,479	....
Other sectors	2 430	2,921	490	351	5,802	7,574	16,632	16,084	....
Migrants' transfers	2 431	184	226	264	174	334	559	91	....
Debt forgiveness	2 432	....	....	....	....	....	....	....	....
Other capital transfers	2 440	2,737	264	87	5,627	7,239	16,073	15,993	....
Capital transfers, debit	3 400	**−1,197**	**−409**	**−430**	**−3,534**	**−4,330**	**−4,660**	**−2,235**	....
General government	3 401	....	−20	−82	−1,505	−1,857	−1,293	−407	....
Debt forgiveness	3 402	....	....	....	....	....	....	....	....
Other capital transfers	3 410	....	−20	−82	−1,505	−1,857	−1,293	−407	....
Other sectors	3 430	−1,197	−388	−348	−2,029	−2,472	−3,367	−1,828	....
Migrants' transfers	3 431	−708	−388	−348	−1,227	−1,406	−1,888	−937	....
Debt forgiveness	3 432	....	....	....	....	....	....	....	....
Other capital transfers	3 440	−490	....	....	−801	−1,066	−1,478	−890	....
Nonproduced nonfinancial assets, credit	2 480	....	....	....	....	....	25,006	....	....
Nonproduced nonfinancial assets, debit	3 480	....	....	....	....	....	....	....	....

Table 2 (Continued). STANDARD PRESENTATION, 2003–2010

(Thousands of U.S. dollars)

	Code	2003	2004	2005	2006	2007	2008	2009	2010
FINANCIAL ACCOUNT................................	4 995 ..	**16,263**	**44,117**	**19,846**	**27,857**	**42,425**	**29,169**	**36,615**	....
A. DIRECT INVESTMENT..............................	4 500 ..	**3,375**	**4,587**	**7,205**	**10,058**	**27,657**	**4,166**	**−36**	....
Direct investment abroad............................	4 505 ..	....	....	....	....	....	....	....	....
Equity capital..	4 510 ..	....	....	....	....	....	....	....	....
Claims on affiliated enterprises......................	4 515 ..	....	....	....	....	....	....	....	....
Liabilities to affiliated enterprises..................	4 520 ..	....	....	....	....	....	....	....	....
Reinvested earnings.......................................	4 525 ..	....	....	....	....	....	....	....	....
Other capital...	4 530 ..	....	....	....	....	....	....	....	....
Claims on affiliated enterprises......................	4 535 ..	....	....	....	....	....	....	....	....
Liabilities to affiliated enterprises..................	4 540 ..	....	....	....	....	....	....	....	....
Direct investment in Tonga............................	4 555 ..	**3,375**	**4,587**	**7,205**	**10,058**	**27,657**	**4,166**	**−36**	....
Equity capital..	4 560 ..	3,375	4,587	7,205	10,058	27,657	4,166	−36	....
Claims on direct investors..............................	4 565 ..	....	....	....	....	....	....	....	....
Liabilities to direct investors.........................	4 570 ..	3,375	4,587	7,205	10,058	27,657	4,166	−36	....
Reinvested earnings.......................................	4 575 ..	....	....	....	....	....	....	....	....
Other capital...	4 580 ..	....	....	....	....	....	....	....	....
Claims on direct investors..............................	4 585 ..	....	....	....	....	....	....	....	....
Liabilities to direct investors.........................	4 590 ..	....	....	....	....	....	....	....	....
B. PORTFOLIO INVESTMENT..........................	4 600 ..	....	....	....	....	....	....	....	....
Assets..	4 602 ..	....	....	....	....	....	....	....	....
Equity securities...	4 610 ..	....	....	....	....	....	....	....	....
Monetary authorities.....................................	4 611 ..	....	....	....	....	....	....	....	....
General government......................................	4 612 ..	....	....	....	....	....	....	....	....
Banks...	4 613 ..	....	....	....	....	....	....	....	....
Other sectors..	4 614 ..	....	....	....	....	....	....	....	....
Debt securities..	4 619 ..	....	....	....	....	....	....	....	....
Bonds and notes...	4 620 ..	....	....	....	....	....	....	....	....
Monetary authorities.....................................	4 621 ..	....	....	....	....	....	....	....	....
General government......................................	4 622 ..	....	....	....	....	....	....	....	....
Banks...	4 623 ..	....	....	....	....	....	....	....	....
Other sectors..	4 624 ..	....	....	....	....	....	....	....	....
Money market instruments............................	4 630 ..	....	....	....	....	....	....	....	....
Monetary authorities.....................................	4 631 ..	....	....	....	....	....	....	....	....
General government......................................	4 632 ..	....	....	....	....	....	....	....	....
Banks...	4 633 ..	....	....	....	....	....	....	....	....
Other sectors..	4 634 ..	....	....	....	....	....	....	....	....
Liabilities..	4 652 ..	....	....	....	....	....	....	....	....
Equity securities...	4 660 ..	....	....	....	....	....	....	....	....
Banks...	4 663 ..	....	....	....	....	....	....	....	....
Other sectors..	4 664 ..	....	....	....	....	....	....	....	....
Debt securities..	4 669 ..	....	....	....	....	....	....	....	....
Bonds and notes...	4 670 ..	....	....	....	....	....	....	....	....
Monetary authorities.....................................	4 671 ..	....	....	....	....	....	....	....	....
General government......................................	4 672 ..	....	....	....	....	....	....	....	....
Banks...	4 673 ..	....	....	....	....	....	....	....	....
Other sectors..	4 674 ..	....	....	....	....	....	....	....	....
Money market instruments............................	4 680 ..	....	....	....	....	....	....	....	....
Monetary authorities.....................................	4 681 ..	....	....	....	....	....	....	....	....
General government......................................	4 682 ..	....	....	....	....	....	....	....	....
Banks...	4 683 ..	....	....	....	....	....	....	....	....
Other sectors..	4 684 ..	....	....	....	....	....	....	....	....
C. FINANCIAL DERIVATIVES..........................	4 910 ..	....	....	....	....	....	**16,214**	**1,657**	....
Monetary authorities.....................................	4 911 ..	....	....	....	....	....	....	....	....
General government......................................	4 912 ..	....	....	....	....	....	....	....	....
Banks...	4 913 ..	....	....	....	....	....	....	....	....
Other sectors..	4 914 ..	....	....	....	....	....	16,214	1,657	....
Assets..	4 900 ..	....	....	....	....	....	**16,214**	**1,657**	....
Monetary authorities.....................................	4 901 ..	....	....	....	....	....	....	....	....
General government......................................	4 902 ..	....	....	....	....	....	....	....	....
Banks...	4 903 ..	....	....	....	....	....	....	....	....
Other sectors..	4 904 ..	....	....	....	....	....	16,214	1,657	....
Liabilities..	4 905 ..	....	....	....	....	....	....	....	....
Monetary authorities.....................................	4 906 ..	....	....	....	....	....	....	....	....
General government......................................	4 907 ..	....	....	....	....	....	....	....	....
Banks...	4 908 ..	....	....	....	....	....	....	....	....
Other sectors..	4 909 ..	....	....	....	....	....	....	....	....

Table 2 (Concluded). STANDARD PRESENTATION, 2003–2010

(Thousands of U.S. dollars)

	Code	2003	2004	2005	2006	2007	2008	2009	2010
D. OTHER INVESTMENT	4 700	**5,097**	**23,425**	**−4,367**	**1,587**	**−5,525**	**−13,582**	**16,030**	....
Assets	4 703	**4,452**	**−287**	**17**	**510**	**123**	**6,202**	**10,381**	....
Trade credits	4 706	....	−370	....	....	....	....	....	....
General government	4 707	....	−370	....	....	....	....	....	....
of which: Short-term	4 709	....	....	....	....	....	....	....	....
Other sectors	4 710	....	....	....	....	....	....	....	....
of which: Short-term	4 712	....	....	....	....	....	....	....	....
Loans	4 714	....	....	....	....	....	....	....	....
Monetary authorities	4 715	....	....	....	....	....	....	....	....
of which: Short-term	4 718	....	....	....	....	....	....	....	....
General government	4 719	....	....	....	....	....	....	....	....
of which: Short-term	4 721	....	....	....	....	....	....	....	....
Banks	4 722	....	....	....	....	....	....	....	....
of which: Short-term	4 724	....	....	....	....	....	....	....	....
Other sectors	4 725	....	....	....	....	....	....	....	....
of which: Short-term	4 727	....	....	....	....	....	....	....	....
Currency and deposits	4 730	3,896	....	....	....	122	1	21	....
Monetary authorities	4 731	....	....	....	....	....	....	....	....
General government	4 732	3,498	....	....	....	....	....	....	....
Banks	4 733	....	....	....	....	....	....	....	....
Other sectors	4 734	398	....	....	....	122	1	21	....
Other assets	4 736	555	83	17	510	1	6,201	10,360	....
Monetary authorities	4 737	....	....	....	....	....	....	10,358	....
of which: Short-term	4 739	....	....	....	....	....	....	....	....
General government	4 740	95	....	....	144	1	273	....	....
of which: Short-term	4 742	....	....	....	....	....	....	....	....
Banks	4 743	23	83	10	248	....	3,512	....	....
of which: Short-term	4 745	....	....	....	....	....	....	....	....
Other sectors	4 746	437	....	7	118	....	2,416	2	....
of which: Short-term	4 748	....	....	....	....	....	15	1	....
Liabilities	4 753	**645**	**23,712**	**−4,384**	**1,077**	**−5,648**	**−19,784**	**5,648**	....
Trade credits	4 756	....	2,125	....	....	....	....	....	....
General government	4 757	....	2,125	....	....	....	....	....	....
of which: Short-term	4 759	....	....	....	....	....	....	....	....
Other sectors	4 760	....	....	....	....	....	....	....	....
of which: Short-term	4 762	....	....	....	....	....	....	....	....
Loans	4 764	4,145	22,118	−3,946	1,402	−4,853	−5,961	−3,441	....
Monetary authorities	4 765	....	....	....	....	....	....	68	....
of which: Use of Fund credit and loans from the Fund	4 766	....	....	....	....	....	....	....	....
of which: Short-term	4 768	....	....	....	....	....	....	....	....
General government	4 769	4,886	−4,054	−1,455	−1,014	−4,840	−5,548	−3,233	....
of which: Short-term	4 771	....	....	....	−731	−1,210	−493	−209	....
Banks	4 772	....	−4,211	−50	....	−63	−45	−274	....
of which: Short-term	4 774	....	....	−50	....	....	....	....	....
Other sectors	4 775	−742	30,382	−2,440	2,416	49	−368	−2	....
of which: Short-term	4 777	....	....	156	−3	27	....	−9	....
Currency and deposits	4 780	−169	....	−91	−310	−535	−12,606	−253	....
Monetary authorities	4 781	....	....	....	....	....	....	....	....
General government	4 782	....	....	....	....	....	....	....	....
Banks	4 783	....	....	....	−77	....	....	....	....
Other sectors	4 784	−169	....	−91	−233	−535	−12,606	−253	....
Other liabilities	4 786	−3,330	−530	−347	−16	−260	−1,217	9,343	....
Monetary authorities	4 787	....	−13	−18	....	−233	....	10,293	....
of which: Short-term	4 789	....	....	....	....	....	....	....	....
General government	4 790	....	....	....	....	....	....	....	....
of which: Short-term	4 792	....	....	....	....	....	....	....	....
Banks	4 793	−905	−384	−315	....	....	−58	−223	....
of which: Short-term	4 795	....	....	....	....	....	....	....	....
Other sectors	4 796	−2,425	−134	−14	−16	−27	−1,159	−728	....
of which: Short-term	4 798	....	....	....	....	....	....	....	....
E. RESERVE ASSETS	4 802	**7,791**	**16,104**	**17,008**	**16,211**	**20,294**	**22,372**	**18,965**	....
Monetary gold	4 812	....	....	....	....	....	....	....	....
Special drawing rights	4 811	−38	−41	−59	−85	−111	−107	−10,309	....
Reserve position in the Fund	4 810	....	....	....	....	....	....	....	....
Foreign exchange	4 803	7,828	16,145	17,067	16,296	20,405	22,479	29,274	....
Other claims	4 813	....	....	....	....	....	....	....	....
NET ERRORS AND OMISSIONS	4 998	**−13,868**	**−38,208**	**−11,491**	**−12,189**	**−39,275**	**−8,636**	**−37,266**	....

Table 1. ANALYTIC PRESENTATION, 2003–2010

(Millions of U.S. dollars)

	Code	2003	2004	2005	2006	2007	2008	2009	2010
A. Current Account[1]	4 993 Z.	**985**	**1,647**	**3,594**	**7,271**	**5,364**	**8,519**	**1,614**	....
Goods: exports f.o.b.	2 100 ..	5,205	6,403	9,672	14,217	13,391	18,686	9,175	....
Goods: imports f.o.b.	3 100 ..	−3,912	−4,894	−5,725	−6,517	−7,670	−9,622	−6,973	....
Balance on Goods	4 100 ..	*1,293*	*1,509*	*3,948*	*7,700*	*5,721*	*9,064*	*2,202*	....
Services: credit	2 200 ..	685	851	897	814	924	936	765	....
Services: debit	3 200 ..	−371	−371	−541	−363	−377	−326	−383	....
Balance on Goods and Services	4 991 ..	*1,607*	*1,988*	*4,304*	*8,151*	*6,268*	*9,674*	*2,584*	....
Income: credit	2 300 ..	78	66	84	262	267	310	298	....
Income: debit	3 300 ..	−759	−464	−844	−1,198	−1,231	−1,512	−1,294	....
Balance on Goods, Services, and Income	4 992 ..	*926*	*1,591*	*3,544*	*7,215*	*5,304*	*8,472*	*1,587*	....
Current transfers: credit	2 379 Z.	101	99	102	105	121	109	137	....
Current transfers: debit	3 379 ..	−42	−42	−52	−49	−61	−62	−110	....
B. Capital Account[1]	4 994 Z.	....	....	....	....	....	....	....	....
Capital account: credit	2 994 Z.	....	....	....	....	....	....	....	
Capital account: debit	3 994 ..	....	....	....	....	....	....	....	
Total, Groups A Plus B	4 981 ..	*985*	*1,647*	*3,594*	*7,271*	*5,364*	*8,519*	*1,614*	....
C. Financial Account[1]	4 995 W.	**−757**	**−1,038**	**−1,964**	**−5,891**	**−3,524**	**−5,971**	**−2,334**	....
Direct investment abroad	4 505 ..	−225	−25	−341	−370	....	−700	....	....
Direct investment in Trinidad and Tobago	4 555 Z.	808	998	940	883	830	2,801	709	....
Portfolio investment assets	4 602 ..	−509	−690	−258	−200	−252	−82	−120	....
Equity securities	4 610 ..	....	....	....	....	....	....	....	
Debt securities	4 619 ..	−509	−690	−258	−200	−252	−82	−120	
Portfolio investment liabilities	4 652 Z.	....	....	....	....	....	....	....	
Equity securities	4 660 ..	....	....	....	....	....	....	....	
Debt securities	4 669 Z.	....	....	....	....	....	....	....	
Financial derivatives	4 910 ..	....	....	....	....	....	....	....	
Financial derivatives assets	4 900 ..	....	....	....	....	....	....	....	
Financial derivatives liabilities	4 905 ..	....	....	....	....	....	....	....	
Other investment assets	4 703 ..	−283	−325	−391	−981	−39	−1,279	−372	....
Monetary authorities	4 701 ..	....	−163	−345	−316	−208	−927	303	
General government	4 704 ..	49	100	100	77	183	....	....	
Banks	4 705 ..	−332	−262	−145	−742	−14	−353	−675	
Other sectors	4 728 ..	....	....	....	....	....	....	....	
Other investment liabilities	4 753 W.	−548	−996	−1,914	−5,222	−4,063	−6,711	−2,552	....
Monetary authorities	4 753 WA	....	....	....	....	....	....	429	....
General government	4 753 ZB	−3	−186	−22	−65	148	95	−43	
Banks	4 753 ZC	426	....	216	....	102	....	....	
Other sectors	4 753 ZD	−971	−810	−2,108	−5,157	−4,313	−6,805	−2,938	
Total, Groups A Through C	4 983 ..	*227*	*609*	*1,630*	*1,380*	*1,840*	*2,548*	*−720*	....
D. Net Errors and Omissions	4 998 ..	**94**	**−103**	**−242**	**−284**	**−319**	**184**	**46**	....
Total, Groups A Through D	4 984 ..	*321*	*506*	*1,388*	*1,096*	*1,521*	*2,732*	*−674*	....
E. Reserves and Related Items	4 802 A.	**−321**	**−506**	**−1,388**	**−1,096**	**−1,521**	**−2,732**	**674**	....
Reserve assets	4 802 ..	−321	−506	−1,388	−1,096	−1,521	−2,732	674	....
Use of Fund credit and loans	4 766 ..	....	....	....	....	....	....	....	....
Exceptional financing	4 920 ..	....	....	....	....	....	....	....	....
Conversion rates: Trinidad and Tobago dollars per U.S. dollar	0 101 ..	**6.29510**	**6.29899**	**6.29956**	**6.31228**	**6.32803**	**6.28943**	**6.32491**	**6.37551**

[1] Excludes components that have been classified in the categories of Group E.

Table 2. STANDARD PRESENTATION, 2003–2010

(Millions of U.S. dollars)

	Code	2003	2004	2005	2006	2007	2008	2009	2010
CURRENT ACCOUNT	4 993	**985**	**1,647**	**3,594**	**7,271**	**5,364**	**8,519**	**1,614**	....
A. GOODS	4 100	**1,293**	**1,509**	**3,948**	**7,700**	**5,721**	**9,064**	**2,202**	....
Credit	2 100	**5,205**	**6,403**	**9,672**	**14,217**	**13,391**	**18,686**	**9,175**	....
General merchandise: exports f.o.b.	2 110	5,081	6,341	9,548	14,033	13,296	18,380	9,105	....
Goods for processing: exports f.o.b.	2 150	9	12	14	21	18	15	16	....
Repairs on goods	2 160	....	....	....	....	....	....	....	....
Goods procured in ports by carriers	2 170	115	50	110	164	78	291	54	....
Nonmonetary gold	2 180	....	....	....	....	....	....	....	....
Debit	3 100	**–3,912**	**–4,894**	**–5,725**	**–6,517**	**–7,670**	**–9,622**	**–6,973**	....
General merchandise: imports f.o.b.	3 110	–3,899	–4,881	–5,710	–6,497	–7,646	–9,607	–6,956	....
Goods for processing: imports f.o.b.	3 150	–13	–14	–15	–20	–24	–15	–17	....
Repairs on goods	3 160	....	....	....	....	....	....	....	....
Goods procured in ports by carriers	3 170	....	....	....	....	....	....	....	....
Nonmonetary gold	3 180	....	....	....	....	....	....	....	....
B. SERVICES	4 200	**314**	**480**	**356**	**451**	**546**	**610**	**382**	....
Total credit	2 200	*685*	*851*	*897*	*814*	*924*	*936*	*765*	....
Total debit	3 200	*–371*	*–371*	*–541*	*–363*	*–377*	*–326*	*–383*	....
Transportation services, credit	2 205	**247**	**295**	**215**	**202**	**229**	**218**	**215**	....
Passenger	2 850	*188*	*227*	*140*	*135*	*158*	*160*	*181*	....
Freight	2 851	*7*	*9*	*11*	*10*	*13*	*13*	*13*	....
Other	2 852	*52*	*59*	*64*	*58*	*58*	*45*	*21*	....
Sea transport, passenger	2 207	....	....	....	....	....	....	....	....
Sea transport, freight	2 208	....	....	....	....	....	....	....	....
Sea transport, other	2 209	....	....	....	....	....	....	....	....
Air transport, passenger	2 211	....	....	....	....	....	....	....	....
Air transport, freight	2 212	....	....	....	....	....	....	....	....
Air transport, other	2 213	....	....	....	....	....	....	....	....
Other transport, passenger	2 215	....	....	....	....	....	....	....	....
Other transport, freight	2 216	....	....	....	....	....	....	....	....
Other transport, other	2 217	....	....	....	....	....	....	....	....
Transportation services, debit	3 205	**–161**	**–162**	**–191**	**–161**	**–172**	**–129**	**–130**	....
Passenger	3 850	*–36*	*–45*	*–54*	*–53*	*–61*	*–27*	*–31*	....
Freight	3 851	*–93*	*–87*	*–90*	*–82*	*–82*	*–82*	*–84*	....
Other	3 852	*–33*	*–30*	*–47*	*–26*	*–29*	*–19*	*–15*	....
Sea transport, passenger	3 207	....	....	....	....	....	....	....	....
Sea transport, freight	3 208	....	....	....	....	....	....	....	....
Sea transport, other	3 209	....	....	....	....	....	....	....	....
Air transport, passenger	3 211	....	....	....	....	....	....	....	....
Air transport, freight	3 212	....	....	....	....	....	....	....	....
Air transport, other	3 213	....	....	....	....	....	....	....	....
Other transport, passenger	3 215	....	....	....	....	....	....	....	....
Other transport, freight	3 216	....	....	....	....	....	....	....	....
Other transport, other	3 217	....	....	....	....	....	....	....	....
Travel, credit	2 236	**249**	**342**	**453**	**382**	**463**	**397**	**367**	....
Business travel	2 237	68	42	89	95	107	208	57	....
Personal travel	2 240	181	300	364	287	356	189	310	....
Travel, debit	3 236	**–107**	**–96**	**–180**	**–93**	**–94**	**–75**	**–105**	....
Business travel	3 237	....	....	....	....	....	....	....	....
Personal travel	3 240	–107	–96	–180	–93	–94	–75	–105	....
Other services, credit	2 200 BA	**190**	**215**	**229**	**229**	**231**	**321**	**183**	....
Communications	2 245	40	45	38	34	34	31	25	....
Construction	2 249	....	....	....	....	....	....	....	....
Insurance	2 253	108	113	135	133	140	225	108	....
Financial	2 260	....	....	....	....	....	....	....	....
Computer and information	2 262	....	....	....	....	....	....	....	....
Royalties and licence fees	2 266	....	....	....	....	....	....	....	....
Other business services	2 268	29	43	42	49	44	46	44	....
Personal, cultural, and recreational	2 287	....	....	....	....	....	....	....	....
Government, n.i.e.	2 291	13	13	14	13	14	18	6	....
Other services, debit	3 200 BA	**–103**	**–113**	**–169**	**–110**	**–112**	**–122**	**–148**	....
Communications	3 245	–4	–6	–16	–6	–1	–7	–7	....
Construction	3 249	....	....	....	....	....	....	....	....
Insurance	3 253	....	....	–31	....	....	–7	–25	....
Financial	3 260	....	....	....	....	....	....	....	....
Computer and information	3 262	....	....	....	....	....	....	....	....
Royalties and licence fees	3 266	....	....	....	....	....	....	....	....
Other business services	3 268	–63	–50	–53	–52	–53	–53	–68	....
Personal, cultural, and recreational	3 287	....	....	....	....	....	....	....	....
Government, n.i.e.	3 291	–36	–57	–70	–52	–57	–55	–49	....

Table 2 (Continued). STANDARD PRESENTATION, 2003–2010

(Millions of U.S. dollars)

	Code	2003	2004	2005	2006	2007	2008	2009	2010
C. INCOME	4 300 ..	**−681**	**−397**	**−760**	**−936**	**−964**	**−1,202**	**−997**	....
Total credit	2 300 ..	*78*	*66*	*84*	*262*	*267*	*310*	*298*	....
Total debit	3 300 ..	*−759*	*−464*	*−844*	*−1,198*	*−1,231*	*−1,512*	*−1,294*	....
Compensation of employees, credit	2 310 ..	....	....	....	....	....	....	....	....
Compensation of employees, debit	3 310 ..	....	....	....	....	....	....	....	....
Investment income, credit	2 320 ..	**78**	**66**	**84**	**262**	**267**	**310**	**298**	....
Direct investment income	2 330 ..	....	....	....	....	....	....	....	....
Dividends and distributed branch profits	2 332 ..	....	....	....	....	....	....	....	....
Reinvested earnings and undistributed branch profits	2 333 ..	....	....	....	....	....	....	....	....
Income on debt (interest)	2 334 ..	....	....	....	....	....	....	....	....
Portfolio investment income	2 339 ..	....	....	....	....	....	....	....	....
Income on equity	2 340 ..	....	....	....	....	....	....	....	....
Income on bonds and notes	2 350 ..	....	....	....	....	....	....	....	....
Income on money market instruments	2 360 ..	....	....	....	....	....	....	....	....
Other investment income	2 370 ..	....	....	....	....	....	....	....	....
Investment income, debit	3 320 ..	**−759**	**−464**	**−844**	**−1,198**	**−1,231**	**−1,512**	**−1,294**	....
Direct investment income	3 330 ..	−366	−153	−292	−406	−297	−495	−296	....
Dividends and distributed branch profits	3 332 ..	....	....	....	....	....	....	....	....
Reinvested earnings and undistributed branch profits	3 333 ..	−366	−153	−292	−406	−297	−495	−296	....
Income on debt (interest)	3 334 ..	....	....	....	....	....	....	....	....
Portfolio investment income	3 339 ..	....	....	....	....	....	....	....	....
Income on equity	3 340 ..	....	....	....	....	....	....	....	....
Income on bonds and notes	3 350 ..	....	....	....	....	....	....	....	....
Income on money market instruments	3 360 ..	....	....	....	....	....	....	....	....
Other investment income	3 370 ..	−393	−311	−552	−791	−934	−1,018	−998	....
D. CURRENT TRANSFERS	4 379 ..	**59**	**56**	**50**	**55**	**60**	**47**	**27**	....
Credit	2 379 ..	**101**	**99**	**102**	**105**	**121**	**109**	**137**	....
General government	2 380 ..	12	10	7	10	10	13	17	....
Other sectors	2 390 ..	89	89	95	94	111	96	120	....
Workers' remittances	2 391 ..	87	87	92	91	109	95	109	....
Other current transfers	2 392 ..	2	2	3	3	2	2	11	....
Debit	3 379 ..	**−42**	**−42**	**−52**	**−49**	**−61**	**−62**	**−110**	....
General government	3 380 ..	−4	−5	−5	−6	−7	−6	−10	....
Other sectors	3 390 ..	−38	−38	−47	−43	−54	−56	−100	....
Workers' remittances	3 391 ..	....	....	....	....	....	....	....	....
Other current transfers	3 392 ..	−38	−38	−47	−43	−54	−56	−100	....
CAPITAL AND FINANCIAL ACCOUNT	4 996 ..	**−1,079**	**−1,544**	**−3,352**	**−6,986**	**−5,045**	**−8,702**	**−1,660**	....
CAPITAL ACCOUNT	4 994 ..	....	....	....	....	....	....	....	....
Total credit	2 994 ..	....	....	....	....	....	....	....	....
Total debit	3 994 ..	....	....	....	....	....	....	....	....
Capital transfers, credit	2 400 ..	....	....	....	....	....	....	....	....
General government	2 401 ..	....	....	....	....	....	....	....	....
Debt forgiveness	2 402 ..	....	....	....	....	....	....	....	....
Other capital transfers	2 410 ..	....	....	....	....	....	....	....	....
Other sectors	2 430 ..	....	....	....	....	....	....	....	....
Migrants' transfers	2 431 ..	....	....	....	....	....	....	....	....
Debt forgiveness	2 432 ..	....	....	....	....	....	....	....	....
Other capital transfers	2 440 ..	....	....	....	....	....	....	....	....
Capital transfers, debit	3 400 ..	....	....	....	....	....	....	....	....
General government	3 401 ..	....	....	....	....	....	....	....	....
Debt forgiveness	3 402 ..	....	....	....	....	....	....	....	....
Other capital transfers	3 410 ..	....	....	....	....	....	....	....	....
Other sectors	3 430 ..	....	....	....	....	....	....	....	....
Migrants' transfers	3 431 ..	....	....	....	....	....	....	....	....
Debt forgiveness	3 432 ..	....	....	....	....	....	....	....	....
Other capital transfers	3 440 ..	....	....	....	....	....	....	....	....
Nonproduced nonfinancial assets, credit	2 480 ..	....	....	....	....	....	....	....	....
Nonproduced nonfinancial assets, debit	3 480 ..	....	....	....	....	....	....	....	....

Table 2 (Continued). STANDARD PRESENTATION, 2003–2010

(Millions of U.S. dollars)

	Code	2003	2004	2005	2006	2007	2008	2009	2010
FINANCIAL ACCOUNT.............................	4 995 ..	**−1,079**	**−1,544**	**−3,352**	**−6,986**	**−5,045**	**−8,702**	**−1,660**	....
A. DIRECT INVESTMENT........................	4 500 ..	**583**	**973**	**599**	**513**	**830**	**2,101**	**709**	....
Direct investment abroad....................	4 505 ..	**−225**	**−25**	**−341**	**−370**	....	**−700**	....	....
Equity capital..	4 510 ..	−225	−25	−341	−370	....	−700	....	....
Claims on affiliated enterprises...........	4 515 ..	−225	−25	−341	−370	....	−700	....	....
Liabilities to affiliated enterprises.......	4 520 ..	....	....	....	....	....	....	....	....
Reinvested earnings.............................	4 525 ..	....	....	....	....	....	....	....	....
Other capital..	4 530 ..	....	....	....	....	....	....	....	....
Claims on affiliated enterprises...........	4 535 ..	....	....	....	....	....	....	....	....
Liabilities to affiliated enterprises.......	4 540 ..	....	....	....	....	....	....	....	....
Direct investment in Trinidad and Tobago........	4 555 ..	**808**	**998**	**940**	**883**	**830**	**2,801**	**709**	....
Equity capital..	4 560 ..	451	857	664	497	554	2,322	426	....
Claims on direct investors....................	4 565 ..	....	....	....	....	....	....	....	....
Liabilities to direct investors...............	4 570 ..	451	857	664	497	554	2,322	426	....
Reinvested earnings.............................	4 575 ..	366	153	292	406	297	495	296	....
Other capital..	4 580 ..	−9	−12	−16	−20	−21	−16	−12	....
Claims on direct investors....................	4 585 ..	....	....	....	....	....	....	....	....
Liabilities to direct investors...............	4 590 ..	−9	−12	−16	−20	−21	−16	−12	....
B. PORTFOLIO INVESTMENT..................	4 600 ..	**−509**	**−690**	**−258**	**−200**	**−252**	**−82**	**−120**	....
Assets..	4 602 ..	**−509**	**−690**	**−258**	**−200**	**−252**	**−82**	**−120**	....
Equity securities...................................	4 610 ..	....	....	....	....	....	....	....	....
Monetary authorities...........................	4 611 ..	....	....	....	....	....	....	....	....
General government............................	4 612 ..	....	....	....	....	....	....	....	....
Banks..	4 613 ..	....	....	....	....	....	....	....	....
Other sectors.......................................	4 614 ..	....	....	....	....	....	....	....	....
Debt securities.....................................	4 619 ..	−509	−690	−258	−200	−252	−82	−120	....
Bonds and notes..................................	4 620 ..	....	....	....	....	....	....	....	....
Monetary authorities........................	4 621 ..	....	....	....	....	....	....	....	....
General government.........................	4 622 ..	....	....	....	....	....	....	....	....
Banks..	4 623 ..	....	....	....	....	....	....	....	....
Other sectors....................................	4 624 ..	....	....	....	....	....	....	....	....
Money market instruments..................	4 630 ..	−509	−690	−258	−200	−252	−82	−120	....
Monetary authorities........................	4 631 ..	....	....	....	....	....	....	....	....
General government.........................	4 632 ..	....	....	....	....	....	....	....	....
Banks..	4 633 ..	....	....	....	....	....	....	....	....
Other sectors....................................	4 634 ..	−509	−690	−258	−200	−252	−82	−120	....
Liabilities..	4 652 ..	....	....	....	....	....	....	....	....
Equity securities...................................	4 660 ..	....	....	....	....	....	....	....	....
Banks..	4 663 ..	....	....	....	....	....	....	....	....
Other sectors.......................................	4 664 ..	....	....	....	....	....	....	....	....
Debt securities.....................................	4 669 ..	....	....	....	....	....	....	....	....
Bonds and notes..................................	4 670 ..	....	....	....	....	....	....	....	....
Monetary authorities........................	4 671 ..	....	....	....	....	....	....	....	....
General government.........................	4 672 ..	....	....	....	....	....	....	....	....
Banks..	4 673 ..	....	....	....	....	....	....	....	....
Other sectors....................................	4 674 ..	....	....	....	....	....	....	....	....
Money market instruments..................	4 680 ..	....	....	....	....	....	....	....	....
Monetary authorities........................	4 681 ..	....	....	....	....	....	....	....	....
General government.........................	4 682 ..	....	....	....	....	....	....	....	....
Banks..	4 683 ..	....	....	....	....	....	....	....	....
Other sectors....................................	4 684 ..	....	....	....	....	....	....	....	....
C. FINANCIAL DERIVATIVES..................	4 910 ..	....	....	....	....	....	....	....	....
Monetary authorities...........................	4 911 ..	....	....	....	....	....	....	....	....
General government............................	4 912 ..	....	....	....	....	....	....	....	....
Banks..	4 913 ..	....	....	....	....	....	....	....	....
Other sectors.......................................	4 914 ..	....	....	....	....	....	....	....	....
Assets..	4 900 ..	....	....	....	....	....	....	....	....
Monetary authorities...........................	4 901 ..	....	....	....	....	....	....	....	....
General government............................	4 902 ..	....	....	....	....	....	....	....	....
Banks..	4 903 ..	....	....	....	....	....	....	....	....
Other sectors.......................................	4 904 ..	....	....	....	....	....	....	....	....
Liabilities..	4 905 ..	....	....	....	....	....	....	....	....
Monetary authorities...........................	4 906 ..	....	....	....	....	....	....	....	....
General government............................	4 907 ..	....	....	....	....	....	....	....	....
Banks..	4 908 ..	....	....	....	....	....	....	....	....
Other sectors.......................................	4 909 ..	....	....	....	....	....	....	....	....

Table 2 (Concluded). STANDARD PRESENTATION, 2003–2010

(Millions of U.S. dollars)

	Code	2003	2004	2005	2006	2007	2008	2009	2010
D. OTHER INVESTMENT............	4 700 ..	**−831**	**−1,321**	**−2,304**	**−6,204**	**−4,102**	**−7,990**	**−2,923**	....
Assets............	4 703 ..	**−283**	**−325**	**−391**	**−981**	**−39**	**−1,279**	**−372**	....
Trade credits............	4 706 ..	49	100	100	77	183	....	....	....
General government............	4 707 ..	49	100	100	77	183	....	....	....
of which: Short-term............	4 709 ..	*49*	*100*	*100*	*77*	*183*	....	....	....
Other sectors............	4 710 ..	....	....	....	....	....	....	....	....
of which: Short-term............	4 712 ..	....	....	....	....	....	....	....	....
Loans............	4 714 ..	−245	−221	−74	−532	169	−172	−379	....
Monetary authorities............	4 715 ..	87	40	72	210	183	181	297	....
of which: Short-term............	4 718 ..	....	....	....	....	....	....	....	....
General government............	4 719 ..	....	....	....	....	....	....	....	....
of which: Short-term............	4 721 ..	....	....	....	....	....	....	....	....
Banks............	4 722 ..	−332	−262	−145	−742	−14	−353	−675	....
of which: Short-term............	4 724 ..	....	....	....	....	....	....	....	....
Other sectors............	4 725 ..	....	....	....	....	....	....	....	....
of which: Short-term............	4 727 ..	....	....	....	....	....	....	....	....
Currency and deposits............	4 730 ..	....	....	....	....	....	....	....	....
Monetary authorities............	4 731 ..	....	....	....	....	....	....	....	....
General government............	4 732 ..	....	....	....	....	....	....	....	....
Banks............	4 733 ..	....	....	....	....	....	....	....	....
Other sectors............	4 734 ..	....	....	....	....	....	....	....	....
Other assets............	4 736 ..	−87	−204	−417	−526	−392	−1,108	7	....
Monetary authorities............	4 737 ..	−87	−204	−417	−526	−392	−1,108	7	....
of which: Short-term............	4 739 ..	....	....	....	....	....	....	....	....
General government............	4 740 ..	....	....	....	....	....	....	....	....
of which: Short-term............	4 742 ..	....	....	....	....	....	....	....	....
Banks............	4 743 ..	....	....	....	....	....	....	....	....
of which: Short-term............	4 745 ..	....	....	....	....	....	....	....	....
Other sectors............	4 746 ..	....	....	....	....	....	....	....	....
of which: Short-term............	4 748 ..	....	....	....	....	....	....	....	....
Liabilities............	4 753 ..	**−548**	**−996**	**−1,914**	**−5,222**	**−4,063**	**−6,711**	**−2,552**	....
Trade credits............	4 756 ..	−961	−800	−2,098	−5,146	−4,303	−6,795	−2,927	....
General government............	4 757 ..	....	....	....	....	....	....	....	....
of which: Short-term............	4 759 ..	....	....	....	....	....	....	....	....
Other sectors............	4 760 ..	−961	−800	−2,098	−5,146	−4,303	−6,795	−2,927	....
of which: Short-term............	4 762 ..	*−961*	*−800*	*−2,098*	*−5,146*	*−4,303*	*−6,795*	*−2,927*	....
Loans............	4 764 ..	−3	−186	−22	−65	148	95	−43	....
Monetary authorities............	4 765 ..	....	....	....	....	....	....	....	....
of which: Use of Fund credit and loans from the Fund..	4 766 ..	....	....	....	....	....	....	....	....
of which: Short-term............	4 768 ..	....	....	....	....	....	....	....	....
General government............	4 769 ..	−3	−186	−22	−65	148	95	−43	....
of which: Short-term............	4 771 ..	....	....	....	....	....	....	....	....
Banks............	4 772 ..	....	....	....	....	....	....	....	....
of which: Short-term............	4 774 ..	....	....	....	....	....	....	....	....
Other sectors............	4 775 ..	....	....	....	....	....	....	....	....
of which: Short-term............	4 777 ..	....	....	....	....	....	....	....	....
Currency and deposits............	4 780 ..	....	....	....	....	....	....	....	....
Monetary authorities............	4 781 ..	....	....	....	....	....	....	....	....
General government............	4 782 ..	....	....	....	....	....	....	....	....
Banks............	4 783 ..	....	....	....	....	....	....	....	....
Other sectors............	4 784 ..	....	....	....	....	....	....	....	....
Other liabilities............	4 786 ..	416	−11	205	−11	92	−11	419	....
Monetary authorities............	4 787 ..	....	....	....	....	....	....	429	....
of which: Short-term............	4 789 ..	....	....	....	....	....	....	....	....
General government............	4 790 ..	....	....	....	....	....	....	....	....
of which: Short-term............	4 792 ..	....	....	....	....	....	....	....	....
Banks............	4 793 ..	426	....	216	....	102	....	....	....
of which: Short-term............	4 795 ..	*426*	....	*216*	....	*102*	....	....	....
Other sectors............	4 796 ..	−10	−11	−11	−11	−11	−11	−11	....
of which: Short-term............	4 798 ..	*−10*	*−11*	*−11*	*−11*	*−11*	*−11*	*−11*	....
E. RESERVE ASSETS............	4 802 ..	**−321**	**−506**	**−1,388**	**−1,096**	**−1,521**	**−2,732**	**674**	....
Monetary gold............	4 812 ..	....	....	....	....	....	....	....	....
Special drawing rights............	4 811 ..	−1	−1	−1	1	2	....	−429	....
Reserve position in the Fund............	4 810 ..	−74	27	89	22	18	−26	−31	....
Foreign exchange............	4 803 ..	−248	−532	−1,476	−1,119	−1,541	−2,706	1,134	....
Other claims............	4 813 ..	1	....	....	....	....	....	....	....
NET ERRORS AND OMISSIONS............	4 998 ..	**94**	**−103**	**−242**	**−284**	**−319**	**184**	**46**	....

Table 1. ANALYTIC PRESENTATION, 2003–2010

(Millions of U.S. dollars)

	Code	2003	2004	2005	2006	2007	2008	2009	2010
A. Current Account[1]	4 993 Z.	**−730**	**−442**	**−299**	**−619**	**−917**	**−1,711**	**−1,234**	**−2,104**
Goods: exports f.o.b.	2 100 ..	8,027	9,959	10,631	11,689	15,148	19,184	14,419	16,431
Goods: imports f.o.b.	3 100 ..	−10,297	−12,280	−12,594	−14,202	−18,024	−23,194	−18,117	−21,005
Balance on Goods	4 100 ..	*−2,269*	*−2,321*	*−1,963*	*−2,513*	*−2,876*	*−4,010*	*−3,699*	*−4,575*
Services: credit	2 200 ..	2,937	3,629	4,021	4,295	4,921	6,014	5,499	5,805
Services: debit	3 200 ..	−1,612	−1,986	−2,191	−2,454	−2,815	−3,370	−2,974	−3,345
Balance on Goods and Services	4 991 ..	*−945*	*−677*	*−133*	*−673*	*−769*	*−1,366*	*−1,174*	*−2,115*
Income: credit	2 300 ..	224	277	316	367	563	522	318	430
Income: debit	3 300 ..	−1,180	−1,418	−1,794	−1,756	−2,329	−2,789	−2,328	−2,355
Balance on Goods, Services, and Income	4 992 ..	*−1,901*	*−1,818*	*−1,611*	*−2,062*	*−2,536*	*−3,634*	*−3,185*	*−4,039*
Current transfers: credit	2 379 Z.	1,200	1,401	1,340	1,470	1,650	1,948	1,979	1,972
Current transfers: debit	3 379 ..	−29	−24	−28	−27	−32	−26	−28	−37
B. Capital Account[1]	4 994 Z.	**59**	**108**	**127**	**145**	**166**	**79**	**164**	**82**
Capital account: credit	2 994 Z.	66	113	129	149	168	82	168	91
Capital account: debit	3 994 ..	−7	−6	−2	−4	−2	−3	−4	−8
Total, Groups A Plus B	4 981 ..	*−672*	*−334*	*−172*	*−474*	*−751*	*−1,632*	*−1,069*	*−2,022*
C. Financial Account[1]	4 995 W.	**1,101**	**1,439**	**1,136**	**2,595**	**1,477**	**3,186**	**2,641**	**1,745**
Direct investment abroad	4 505 ..	−1	−2	−10	−30	−17	−38	−70	−66
Direct investment in Tunisia	4 555 Z.	541	594	723	3,270	1,532	2,638	1,595	1,401
Portfolio investment assets	4 602 ..	....	....	....	....	....	....	....	....
Equity securities	4 610 ..	....	....	....	....	....	....	....	....
Debt securities	4 619 ..	....	....	....	....	....	....	....	....
Portfolio investment liabilities	4 652 Z.	14	24	12	65	30	−39	−89	−26
Equity securities	4 660 ..	14	24	12	65	30	−39	−89	−26
Debt securities	4 669 Z.	....	....	....	....	....	....	....	....
Financial derivatives	4 910 ..	....	....	....	....	....	....	....	....
Financial derivatives assets	4 900 ..	....	....	....	....	....	....	....	....
Financial derivatives liabilities	4 905 ..	....	....	....	....	....	....	....	....
Other investment assets	4 703 ..	−339	−205	17	19	−239	−25	−13	−275
Monetary authorities	4 701 ..	....	....	....	....	....	....	....	....
General government	4 704 ..	....	....	....	....	....	....	....	....
Banks	4 705 ..	....	....	....	....	....	....	....	....
Other sectors	4 728 ..	−339	−205	17	19	−239	−25	−13	−275
Other investment liabilities	4 753 W.	887	1,028	394	−729	170	649	1,217	711
Monetary authorities	4 753 WA	....	....	....	....	....	....	373	....
General government	4 753 ZB	649	176	219	−672	−175	−5	46	−206
Banks	4 753 ZC	....	....	....	....	....	....	....	....
Other sectors	4 753 ZD	238	852	175	−57	346	655	799	918
Total, Groups A Through C	4 983 ..	*430*	*1,105*	*964*	*2,121*	*726*	*1,553*	*1,571*	*−277*
D. Net Errors and Omissions	4 998 ..	**−47**	**−128**	**−28**	**−38**	**−37**	**114**	**67**	**55**
Total, Groups A Through D	4 984 ..	*383*	*977*	*936*	*2,082*	*689*	*1,667*	*1,639*	*−222*
E. Reserves and Related Items	4 802 A.	**−383**	**−977**	**−936**	**−2,082**	**−689**	**−1,667**	**−1,639**	**222**
Reserve assets	4 802 ..	−383	−977	−936	−2,082	−689	−1,667	−1,639	222
Use of Fund credit and loans	4 766 ..	....	....	....	....	....	....	....	....
Exceptional financing	4 920 ..	....	....	....	....	....	....	....	....
Conversion rates: Tunisian dinars per U.S. dollar	0 101 ..	**1.2885**	**1.2455**	**1.2974**	**1.3310**	**1.2814**	**1.2321**	**1.3503**	**1.4314**

[1] Excludes components that have been classified in the categories of Group E.

Table 2. STANDARD PRESENTATION, 2003–2010

(Millions of U.S. dollars)

	Code	2003	2004	2005	2006	2007	2008	2009	2010
CURRENT ACCOUNT	4 993	−730	−442	−299	−619	−917	−1,711	−1,234	−2,104
A. GOODS	4 100	−2,269	−2,321	−1,963	−2,513	−2,876	−4,010	−3,699	−4,575
Credit	2 100	8,027	9,959	10,631	11,689	15,148	19,184	14,419	16,431
General merchandise: exports f.o.b.	2 110	8,027	9,959	10,631	11,689	15,148	19,184	14,419	16,431
Goods for processing: exports f.o.b.	2 150	....	....	....	....	....	....	....	....
Repairs on goods	2 160	....	....	....	....	....	....	....	....
Goods procured in ports by carriers	2 170	....	....	....	....	....	....	....	....
Nonmonetary gold	2 180	....	....	....	....	....	....	....	....
Debit	3 100	−10,297	−12,280	−12,594	−14,202	−18,024	−23,194	−18,117	−21,005
General merchandise: imports f.o.b.	3 110	−10,297	−12,280	−12,594	−14,202	−18,024	−23,194	−18,117	−21,005
Goods for processing: imports f.o.b.	3 150	....	....	....	....	....	....	....	....
Repairs on goods	3 160	....	....	....	....	....	....	....	....
Goods procured in ports by carriers	3 170	....	....	....	....	....	....	....	....
Nonmonetary gold	3 180	....	....	....	....	....	....	....	....
B. SERVICES	4 200	1,325	1,644	1,830	1,840	2,106	2,644	2,525	2,460
Total credit	2 200	*2,937*	*3,629*	*4,021*	*4,295*	*4,921*	*6,014*	*5,499*	*5,805*
Total debit	3 200	*−1,612*	*−1,986*	*−2,191*	*−2,454*	*−2,815*	*−3,370*	*−2,974*	*−3,345*
Transportation services, credit	2 205	727	915	1,136	1,243	1,436	1,895	1,382	1,539
Passenger	2 850	*352*	*462*	*657*	*724*	*798*	*956*	*753*	*832*
Freight	2 851	*195*	*266*	*363*	*363*	*429*	*660*	*430*	*573*
Other	2 852	*181*	*187*	*116*	*157*	*209*	*279*	*199*	*134*
Sea transport, passenger	2 207	54	66	71	74	79	94	91	92
Sea transport, freight	2 208	17	12	11	11	12	14	26	49
Sea transport, other	2 209	11	14	8	17	18	24	39	3
Air transport, passenger	2 211	296	393	584	635	706	846	656	720
Air transport, freight	2 212	38	49	54	47	55	66	46	49
Air transport, other	2 213	130	124	74	132	133	177	85	32
Other transport, passenger	2 215	2	3	2	14	14	16	5	20
Other transport, freight	2 216	140	205	298	305	362	579	358	475
Other transport, other	2 217	40	50	33	8	58	78	75	99
Transportation services, debit	3 205	−766	−989	−1,107	−1,235	−1,459	−1,866	−1,484	−1,595
Passenger	3 850	*−55*	*−87*	*−78*	*−88*	*−93*	*−97*	*−63*	*−64*
Freight	3 851	*−546*	*−634*	*−665*	*−750*	*−944*	*−1,215*	*−942*	*−1,100*
Other	3 852	*−165*	*−268*	*−364*	*−397*	*−422*	*−554*	*−479*	*−431*
Sea transport, passenger	3 207	....	....	....	....	....	....	....	....
Sea transport, freight	3 208	−499	−571	−599	−675	−850	−1,093	−848	−987
Sea transport, other	3 209	−93	−150	−203	−222	−237	−310	−268	−241
Air transport, passenger	3 211	−55	−87	−78	−88	−93	−97	−63	−64
Air transport, freight	3 212	−14	−26	−26	−30	−38	−49	−38	−43
Air transport, other	3 213	−58	−94	−127	−139	−148	−194	−168	−150
Other transport, passenger	3 215	....	....	....	....	....	....	....	....
Other transport, freight	3 216	−33	−38	−40	−45	−57	−73	−57	−70
Other transport, other	3 217	−14	−24	−33	−36	−38	−50	−43	−40
Travel, credit	2 236	1,583	1,970	2,143	2,275	2,575	2,953	2,773	2,645
Business travel	2 237	29	36	40	42	48	55	56	62
Personal travel	2 240	1,553	1,934	2,103	2,233	2,527	2,898	2,717	2,583
Travel, debit	3 236	−300	−340	−374	−410	−437	−458	−415	−547
Business travel	3 237	−31	−36	−40	−44	−51	−55	−46	−56
Personal travel	3 240	−269	−304	−334	−366	−386	−403	−369	−491
Other services, credit	2 200 BA	627	744	743	776	910	1,165	1,343	1,622
Communications	2 245	9	14	45	72	120	166	228	302
Construction	2 249	122	148	151	160	193	297	382	479
Insurance	2 253	20	31	41	40	43	42	57	65
Financial	2 260	55	55	58	66	70	86	61	72
Computer and information	2 262	19	18	19	24	27	35	41	43
Royalties and licence fees	2 266	18	18	26	26	29	30	25	25
Other business services	2 268	283	341	279	253	273	320	286	292
Personal, cultural, and recreational	2 287	5	10	4	3	3	6	7	10
Government, n.i.e.	2 291	95	109	121	133	152	183	258	334
Other services, debit	3 200 BA	−546	−657	−711	−810	−918	−1,046	−1,075	−1,203
Communications	3 245	−14	−22	−28	−31	−30	−33	−41	−60
Construction	3 249	−160	−183	−197	−227	−270	−329	−339	−399
Insurance	3 253	−75	−99	−129	−142	−155	−192	−211	−212
Financial	3 260	−35	−45	−50	−65	−70	−73	−66	−76
Computer and information	3 262	−7	−10	−10	−18	−22	−20	−22	−38
Royalties and licence fees	3 266	−6	−8	−8	−11	−10	−12	−14	−15
Other business services	3 268	−142	−167	−167	−190	−212	−232	−210	−213
Personal, cultural, and recreational	3 287	−4	−6	−6	−10	−10	−11	−11	−11
Government, n.i.e.	3 291	−102	−116	−116	−117	−140	−144	−162	−180

Table 2 (Continued). STANDARD PRESENTATION, 2003–2010

(Millions of U.S. dollars)

	Code	2003	2004	2005	2006	2007	2008	2009	2010
C. INCOME	4 300	−956	−1,141	−1,479	−1,389	−1,766	−2,267	−2,011	−1,925
Total credit	2 300	*224*	*277*	*316*	*367*	*563*	*522*	*318*	*430*
Total debit	3 300	*−1,180*	*−1,418*	*−1,794*	*−1,756*	*−2,329*	*−2,789*	*−2,328*	*−2,355*
Compensation of employees, credit	2 310	143	163	198	206	269	252	238	338
Compensation of employees, debit	3 310	−7	−6	−8	−10	−8	−10	−6	−7
Investment income, credit	2 320	81	114	118	160	293	270	80	92
Direct investment income	2 330	9	12	13	7	6	7	4	7
Dividends and distributed branch profits	2 332	9	12	13	7	6	7	4	7
Reinvested earnings and undistributed branch profits	2 333	....	....	....	....	....	....	....	....
Income on debt (interest)	2 334	....	....	....	....	....	....	....	....
Portfolio investment income	2 339	71	102	106	154	287	262	76	85
Income on equity	2 340	6	13	4	2	4	5	7	8
Income on bonds and notes	2 350	65	89	102	151	283	257	68	77
Income on money market instruments	2 360	....	....	....	....	....	....	....	....
Other investment income	2 370	....	....	....	....	....	....	....	....
Investment income, debit	3 320	−1,173	−1,412	−1,786	−1,746	−2,321	−2,778	−2,322	−2,348
Direct investment income	3 330	−537	−678	−962	−988	−1,523	−1,958	−1,588	−1,658
Dividends and distributed branch profits	3 332	−537	−678	−962	−988	−1,523	−1,958	−1,588	−1,658
Reinvested earnings and undistributed branch profits	3 333	....	....	....	....	....	....	....	....
Income on debt (interest)	3 334	....	....	....	....	....	....	....	....
Portfolio investment income	3 339	−636	−734	−824	−758	−798	−821	−734	−690
Income on equity	3 340	−64	−92	−148	−60	−55	−77	−49	−58
Income on bonds and notes	3 350	−573	−642	−676	−698	−743	−743	−685	−632
Income on money market instruments	3 360	....	....	....	....	....	....	....	....
Other investment income	3 370	....	....	....	....	....	....	....	....
D. CURRENT TRANSFERS	4 379	1,170	1,377	1,312	1,443	1,619	1,922	1,951	1,935
Credit	2 379	1,200	1,401	1,340	1,470	1,650	1,948	1,979	1,972
General government	2 380	41	57	68	82	99	113	146	103
Other sectors	2 390	1,159	1,344	1,272	1,388	1,552	1,835	1,833	1,869
Workers' remittances	2 391	1,107	1,268	1,195	1,304	1,446	1,725	1,727	1,725
Other current transfers	2 392	51	75	77	84	106	110	106	144
Debit	3 379	−29	−24	−28	−27	−32	−26	−28	−37
General government	3 380	....	....	....	....	....	....	....	....
Other sectors	3 390	−29	−24	−28	−27	−32	−26	−28	−37
Workers' remittances	3 391	−11	−7	−7	−7	−7	−6	−7	−7
Other current transfers	3 392	−19	−18	−20	−20	−24	−20	−21	−30
CAPITAL AND FINANCIAL ACCOUNT	4 996	778	570	328	658	954	1,598	1,166	2,049
CAPITAL ACCOUNT	4 994	59	108	127	145	166	79	164	82
Total credit	2 994	*66*	*113*	*129*	*149*	*168*	*82*	*168*	*91*
Total debit	3 994	*−7*	*−6*	*−2*	*−4*	*−2*	*−3*	*−4*	*−8*
Capital transfers, credit	2 400	66	113	129	149	168	82	168	91
General government	2 401	66	113	129	149	168	82	168	91
Debt forgiveness	2 402	....	....	....	....	....	....	....	....
Other capital transfers	2 410	66	113	129	149	168	82	168	91
Other sectors	2 430	....	....	....	....	....	....	....	....
Migrants' transfers	2 431	....	....	....	....	....	....	....	....
Debt forgiveness	2 432	....	....	....	....	....	....	....	....
Other capital transfers	2 440	....	....	....	....	....	....	....	....
Capital transfers, debit	3 400	−7	−6	−2	−4	−2	−3	−4	−8
General government	3 401	....	....	....	....	....	....	....	....
Debt forgiveness	3 402	....	....	....	....	....	....	....	....
Other capital transfers	3 410	....	....	....	....	....	....	....	....
Other sectors	3 430	−7	−6	−2	−4	−2	−3	−4	−8
Migrants' transfers	3 431	....	....	....	....	....	....	....	....
Debt forgiveness	3 432	....	....	....	....	....	....	....	....
Other capital transfers	3 440	−7	−6	−2	−4	−2	−3	−4	−8
Nonproduced nonfinancial assets, credit	2 480	....	....	....	....	....	....	....	....
Nonproduced nonfinancial assets, debit	3 480	....	....	....	....	....	....	....	....

Table 2 (Continued). STANDARD PRESENTATION, 2003–2010

(Millions of U.S. dollars)

	Code	2003	2004	2005	2006	2007	2008	2009	2010
FINANCIAL ACCOUNT	4 995	**719**	**462**	**200**	**513**	**789**	**1,519**	**1,002**	**1,967**
A. DIRECT INVESTMENT	4 500	**539**	**592**	**713**	**3,240**	**1,515**	**2,601**	**1,525**	**1,334**
Direct investment abroad	4 505	**−1**	**−2**	**−10**	**−30**	**−17**	**−38**	**−70**	**−66**
Equity capital	4 510	−1	−2	−10	−30	−17	−38	−70	−66
Claims on affiliated enterprises	4 515	....	....	....	....	....	....	....	....
Liabilities to affiliated enterprises	4 520	−1	−2	−10	−30	−17	−38	−70	−66
Reinvested earnings	4 525	....	....	....	....	....	....	....	....
Other capital	4 530	....	....	....	....	....	....	....	....
Claims on affiliated enterprises	4 535	....	....	....	....	....	....	....	....
Liabilities to affiliated enterprises	4 540	....	....	....	....	....	....	....	....
Direct investment in Tunisia	4 555	**541**	**594**	**723**	**3,270**	**1,532**	**2,638**	**1,595**	**1,401**
Equity capital	4 560	541	597	726	3,271	1,542	2,647	1,600	1,405
Claims on direct investors	4 565	....	....	....	....	....	....	....	....
Liabilities to direct investors	4 570	541	597	726	3,271	1,542	2,647	1,600	1,405
Reinvested earnings	4 575	....	....	....	....	....	....	....	....
Other capital	4 580	....	−3	−3	−1	−10	−9	−4	−4
Claims on direct investors	4 585	....	....	....	....	....	....	....	....
Liabilities to direct investors	4 590	....	−3	−3	−1	−10	−9	−4	−4
B. PORTFOLIO INVESTMENT	4 600	**14**	**24**	**12**	**65**	**30**	**−39**	**−89**	**−26**
Assets	4 602	....	....	....	....	....	....	....	....
Equity securities	4 610	....	....	....	....	....	....	....	....
Monetary authorities	4 611	....	....	....	....	....	....	....	....
General government	4 612	....	....	....	....	....	....	....	....
Banks	4 613	....	....	....	....	....	....	....	....
Other sectors	4 614	....	....	....	....	....	....	....	....
Debt securities	4 619	....	....	....	....	....	....	....	....
Bonds and notes	4 620	....	....	....	....	....	....	....	....
Monetary authorities	4 621	....	....	....	....	....	....	....	....
General government	4 622	....	....	....	....	....	....	....	....
Banks	4 623	....	....	....	....	....	....	....	....
Other sectors	4 624	....	....	....	....	....	....	....	....
Money market instruments	4 630	....	....	....	....	....	....	....	....
Monetary authorities	4 631	....	....	....	....	....	....	....	....
General government	4 632	....	....	....	....	....	....	....	....
Banks	4 633	....	....	....	....	....	....	....	....
Other sectors	4 634	....	....	....	....	....	....	....	....
Liabilities	4 652	**14**	**24**	**12**	**65**	**30**	**−39**	**−89**	**−26**
Equity securities	4 660	14	24	12	65	30	−39	−89	−26
Banks	4 663	....	....	....	....	....	....	....	....
Other sectors	4 664	14	24	12	65	30	−39	−89	−26
Debt securities	4 669	....	....	....	....	....	....	....	....
Bonds and notes	4 670	....	....	....	....	....	....	....	....
Monetary authorities	4 671	....	....	....	....	....	....	....	....
General government	4 672	....	....	....	....	....	....	....	....
Banks	4 673	....	....	....	....	....	....	....	....
Other sectors	4 674	....	....	....	....	....	....	....	....
Money market instruments	4 680	....	....	....	....	....	....	....	....
Monetary authorities	4 681	....	....	....	....	....	....	....	....
General government	4 682	....	....	....	....	....	....	....	....
Banks	4 683	....	....	....	....	....	....	....	....
Other sectors	4 684	....	....	....	....	....	....	....	....
C. FINANCIAL DERIVATIVES	4 910	....	....	....	....	....	....	....	....
Monetary authorities	4 911	....	....	....	....	....	....	....	....
General government	4 912	....	....	....	....	....	....	....	....
Banks	4 913	....	....	....	....	....	....	....	....
Other sectors	4 914	....	....	....	....	....	....	....	....
Assets	4 900	....	....	....	....	....	....	....	....
Monetary authorities	4 901	....	....	....	....	....	....	....	....
General government	4 902	....	....	....	....	....	....	....	....
Banks	4 903	....	....	....	....	....	....	....	....
Other sectors	4 904	....	....	....	....	....	....	....	....
Liabilities	4 905	....	....	....	....	....	....	....	....
Monetary authorities	4 906	....	....	....	....	....	....	....	....
General government	4 907	....	....	....	....	....	....	....	....
Banks	4 908	....	....	....	....	....	....	....	....
Other sectors	4 909	....	....	....	....	....	....	....	....

Table 2 (Concluded). STANDARD PRESENTATION, 2003–2010

(Millions of U.S. dollars)

	Code	2003	2004	2005	2006	2007	2008	2009	2010
D. OTHER INVESTMENT	4 700	**548**	**823**	**412**	**−710**	**−68**	**624**	**1,204**	**436**
Assets	4 703	**−339**	**−205**	**17**	**19**	**−239**	**−25**	**−13**	**−275**
Trade credits	4 706	−339	−205	17	19	−239	−25	−13	−275
General government	4 707	....	....	....	....	....	....	....	....
of which: Short-term	4 709	....	....	....	....	....	....	....	....
Other sectors	4 710	−339	−205	17	19	−239	−25	−13	−275
of which: Short-term	4 712	*−339*	*−205*	*17*	*19*	*−239*	*−25*	*−13*	*−275*
Loans	4 714	....	....	....	....	....	....	....	....
Monetary authorities	4 715	....	....	....	....	....	....	....	....
of which: Short-term	4 718	....	....	....	....	....	....	....	....
General government	4 719	....	....	....	....	....	....	....	....
of which: Short-term	4 721	....	....	....	....	....	....	....	....
Banks	4 722	....	....	....	....	....	....	....	....
of which: Short-term	4 724	....	....	....	....	....	....	....	....
Other sectors	4 725	....	....	....	....	....	....	....	....
of which: Short-term	4 727	....	....	....	....	....	....	....	....
Currency and deposits	4 730	....	....	....	....	....	....	....	....
Monetary authorities	4 731	....	....	....	....	....	....	....	....
General government	4 732	....	....	....	....	....	....	....	....
Banks	4 733	....	....	....	....	....	....	....	....
Other sectors	4 734	....	....	....	....	....	....	....	....
Other assets	4 736	....	....	....	....	....	....	....	....
Monetary authorities	4 737	....	....	....	....	....	....	....	....
of which: Short-term	4 739	....	....	....	....	....	....	....	....
General government	4 740	....	....	....	....	....	....	....	....
of which: Short-term	4 742	....	....	....	....	....	....	....	....
Banks	4 743	....	....	....	....	....	....	....	....
of which: Short-term	4 745	....	....	....	....	....	....	....	....
Other sectors	4 746	....	....	....	....	....	....	....	....
of which: Short-term	4 748	....	....	....	....	....	....	....	....
Liabilities	4 753	**887**	**1,028**	**394**	**−729**	**170**	**649**	**1,217**	**711**
Trade credits	4 756	47	54	202	61	397	653	520	561
General government	4 757	....	....	....	....	....	....	....	....
of which: Short-term	4 759	....	....	....	....	....	....	....	....
Other sectors	4 760	47	54	202	61	397	653	520	561
of which: Short-term	4 762	*47*	*54*	*202*	*61*	*397*	*653*	*520*	*561*
Loans	4 764	841	974	192	−790	−226	−4	325	150
Monetary authorities	4 765	....	....	....	....	....	....	....	....
of which: Use of Fund credit and loans from the Fund	4 766	....	....	....	....	....	....	....	....
of which: Short-term	4 768	....	....	....	....	....	....	....	....
General government	4 769	649	176	219	−672	−175	−5	46	−206
of which: Short-term	4 771	....	....	....	....	....	....	....	....
Banks	4 772	....	....	....	....	....	....	....	....
of which: Short-term	4 774	....	....	....	....	....	....	....	....
Other sectors	4 775	192	798	−27	−118	−51	2	279	356
of which: Short-term	4 777	....	....	....	....	....	....	....	....
Currency and deposits	4 780	....	....	....	....	....	....	....	....
Monetary authorities	4 781	....	....	....	....	....	....	....	....
General government	4 782	....	....	....	....	....	....	....	....
Banks	4 783	....	....	....	....	....	....	....	....
Other sectors	4 784	....	....	....	....	....	....	....	....
Other liabilities	4 786	....	....	....	....	....	....	373	....
Monetary authorities	4 787	....	....	....	....	....	....	373	....
of which: Short-term	4 789	....	....	....	....	....	....	....	....
General government	4 790	....	....	....	....	....	....	....	....
of which: Short-term	4 792	....	....	....	....	....	....	....	....
Banks	4 793	....	....	....	....	....	....	....	....
of which: Short-term	4 795	....	....	....	....	....	....	....	....
Other sectors	4 796	....	....	....	....	....	....	....	....
of which: Short-term	4 798	....	....	....	....	....	....	....	....
E. RESERVE ASSETS	4 802	**−383**	**−977**	**−936**	**−2,082**	**−689**	**−1,667**	**−1,639**	**222**
Monetary gold	4 812	....	....	....	....	....	....	....	....
Special drawing rights	4 811	1	−6	7	1	....	−4	−372	....
Reserve position in the Fund	4 810	....	....	....	....	....	....	....	−54
Foreign exchange	4 803	−383	−972	−943	−2,083	−688	−1,663	−1,266	276
Other claims	4 813	....	....	....	....	....	....	....	....
NET ERRORS AND OMISSIONS	4 998	**−47**	**−128**	**−28**	**−38**	**−37**	**114**	**67**	**55**

Table 3. INTERNATIONAL INVESTMENT POSITION (End-period stocks), 2003–2010

(Millions of U.S. dollars)

	Code	2003	2004	2005	2006	2007	2008	2009	2010
ASSETS	8 995 C.	**5,411**	**6,662**	**6,762**	**9,255**	**10,828**	**11,639**	**13,242**	**12,309**
Direct investment abroad	8 505 ..	**43**	**47**	**52**	**89**	**117**	**155**	**233**	**285**
Equity capital and reinvested earnings	8 506 ..	43	47	52	89	117	155	233	285
Claims on affiliated enterprises	8 507 ..	....	....	....	....	....	....	....	....
Liabilities to affiliated enterprises	8 508 ..	43	47	52	89	117	155	233	285
Other capital	8 530 ..	....	....	....	....	....	....	....	....
Claims on affiliated enterprises	8 535 ..	....	....	....	....	....	....	....	....
Liabilities to affiliated enterprises	8 540 ..	....	....	....	....	....	....	....	....
Portfolio investment	8 602 ..	**56**	**60**	**54**	**59**	**67**	**68**	**70**	**66**
Equity securities	8 610 ..	56	60	54	59	67	68	70	66
Monetary authorities	8 611 ..	....	....	....	....	....	....	....	....
General government	8 612 ..	....	....	....	....	....	....	....	....
Banks	8 613 ..	....	....	....	....	....	....	....	....
Other sectors	8 614 ..	56	60	54	59	67	68	70	66
Debt securities	8 619 ..	....	....	....	....	....	....	....	....
Bonds and notes	8 620 ..	....	....	....	....	....	....	....	....
Monetary authorities	8 621 ..	....	....	....	....	....	....	....	....
General government	8 622 ..	....	....	....	....	....	....	....	....
Banks	8 623 ..	....	....	....	....	....	....	....	....
Other sectors	8 624 ..	....	....	....	....	....	....	....	....
Money market instruments	8 630 ..	....	....	....	....	....	....	....	....
Monetary authorities	8 631 ..	....	....	....	....	....	....	....	....
General government	8 632 ..	....	....	....	....	....	....	....	....
Banks	8 633 ..	....	....	....	....	....	....	....	....
Other sectors	8 634 ..	....	....	....	....	....	....	....	....
Financial derivatives	8 900 ..	....	....	....	....	....	....	....	....
Monetary authorities	8 901 ..	....	....	....	....	....	....	....	....
General government	8 902 ..	....	....	....	....	....	....	....	....
Banks	8 903 ..	....	....	....	....	....	....	....	....
Other sectors	8 904 ..	....	....	....	....	....	....	....	....
Other investment	8 703 ..	**2,338**	**2,543**	**2,232**	**2,322**	**2,711**	**2,455**	**2,355**	**2,453**
Trade credits	8 706 ..	1,574	1,733	1,271	1,228	1,069	1,125	905	1,029
General government	8 707 ..	....	....	....	....	....	....	....	....
of which: Short-term	8 709 ..	....	....	....	....	....	....	....	....
Other sectors	8 710 ..	1,574	1,733	1,271	1,228	1,069	1,125	905	1,029
of which: Short-term	8 712 ..	*1,574*	*1,733*	*1,271*	*1,228*	*1,069*	*1,125*	*905*	*1,029*
Loans	8 714 ..	100	100	100	100	100	100	....	....
Monetary authorities	8 715 ..	....	....	....	....	....	....	....	....
of which: Short-term	8 718 ..	....	....	....	....	....	....	....	....
General government	8 719 ..	....	....	....	....	....	....	....	....
of which: Short-term	8 721 ..	....	....	....	....	....	....	....	....
Banks	8 722 ..	....	....	....	....	....	....	....	....
of which: Short-term	8 724 ..	....	....	....	....	....	....	....	....
Other sectors	8 725 ..	100	100	100	100	100	100	....	....
of which: Short-term	8 727 ..	....	....	....	....	....	....	....	....
Currency and deposits	8 730 ..	....	....	....	....	....	....	....	....
Monetary authorities	8 731 ..	....	....	....	....	....	....	....	....
General government	8 732 ..	....	....	....	....	....	....	....	....
Banks	8 733 ..	....	....	....	....	....	....	....	....
Other sectors	8 734 ..	....	....	....	....	....	....	....	....
Other assets	8 736 ..	664	710	861	994	1,542	1,230	1,450	1,425
Monetary authorities	8 737 ..	....	....	....	....	....	....	....	....
of which: Short-term	8 739 ..	....	....	....	....	....	....	....	....
General government	8 740 ..	....	....	....	....	....	....	....	....
of which: Short-term	8 742 ..	....	....	....	....	....	....	....	....
Banks	8 743 ..	664	710	861	994	1,542	1,230	1,450	1,425
of which: Short-term	8 745 ..	*664*	*710*	*861*	*994*	*1,542*	*1,230*	*1,450*	*1,425*
Other sectors	8 746 ..	....	....	....	....	....	....	....	....
of which: Short-term	8 748 ..	....	....	....	....	....	....	....	....
Reserve assets	8 802 ..	**2,974**	**4,013**	**4,423**	**6,786**	**7,933**	**8,962**	**10,585**	**9,505**
Monetary gold	8 812 ..	4	4	3	3	4	3	3	3
Special drawing rights	8 811 ..	2	9	2	1	2	5	379	372
Reserve position in the Fund	8 810 ..	30	31	29	30	32	31	32	87
Foreign exchange	8 803 ..	2,938	3,969	4,389	6,751	7,896	8,922	10,170	9,043
Other claims	8 813 ..	....	....	....	....	....	....	....	....

Table 3 (Concluded). INTERNATIONAL INVESTMENT POSITION (End-period stocks), 2003–2010

(Millions of U.S. dollars)

	Code	2003	2004	2005	2006	2007	2008	2009	2010
LIABILITIES..	8 995 D.	**34,878**	**38,235**	**35,922**	**41,795**	**48,174**	**51,554**	**56,086**	**55,565**
Direct investment in Tunisia................................	8 555 ..	**16,239**	**17,844**	**16,840**	**21,832**	**26,193**	**29,083**	**31,857**	**31,411**
Equity capital and reinvested earnings..............................	8 556 ..	15,971	17,637	16,840	21,832	26,193	29,083	31,857	31,411
Claims on direct investors......................................	8 557 ..	....	....	....	....	....	....	....	....
Liabilities to direct investors.................................	8 558 ..	15,971	17,637	16,840	21,832	26,193	29,083	31,857	31,411
Other capital...	8 580 ..	267	207	....	....	....	....	....	....
Claims on direct investors......................................	8 585 ..	....	....	....	....	....	....	....	....
Liabilities to direct investors.................................	8 590 ..	267	207	....	....	....	....	....	....
Portfolio investment..	8 652 ..	**618**	**658**	**794**	**1,169**	**1,552**	**1,619**	**2,085**	**2,170**
Equity securities..	8 660 ..	618	658	794	1,136	1,497	1,568	2,035	2,123
Banks..	8 663 ..	....	....	....	....	....	....	....	....
Other sectors..	8 664 ..	618	658	794	1,136	1,497	1,568	2,035	2,123
Debt securities...	8 669 ..	....	....	....	33	55	51	51	47
Bonds and notes...	8 670 ..	....	....	....	33	55	51	51	47
Monetary authorities...	8 671 ..	....	....	....	....	....	....	....	....
General government..	8 672 ..	....	....	....	....	....	....	....	....
Banks..	8 673 ..	....	....	....	33	55	51	51	47
Other sectors...	8 674 ..	....	....	....	....	....	....	....	....
Money market instruments.......................................	8 680 ..	....	....	....	....	....	....	....	....
Monetary authorities...	8 681 ..	....	....	....	....	....	....	....	....
General government..	8 682 ..	....	....	....	....	....	....	....	....
Banks..	8 683 ..	....	....	....	....	....	....	....	....
Other sectors...	8 684 ..	....	....	....	....	....	....	....	....
Financial derivatives.......................................	8 905 ..	....	....	....	....	....	....	....	....
Monetary authorities...	8 906 ..	....	....	....	....	....	....	....	....
General government..	8 907 ..	....	....	....	....	....	....	....	....
Banks...	8 908 ..	....	....	....	....	....	....	....	....
Other sectors..	8 909 ..	....	....	....	....	....	....	....	....
Other investment...	8 753 ..	**18,021**	**19,733**	**18,288**	**18,794**	**20,428**	**20,852**	**22,143**	**21,985**
Trade credits..	8 756 ..	1,736	1,569	1,167	1,201	1,160	1,410	1,320	1,508
General government..	8 757 ..	....	....	....	....	....	....	....	....
of which: Short-term..	8 759 ..	....	....	....	....	....	....	....	....
Other sectors..	8 760 ..	1,736	1,569	1,167	1,201	1,160	1,410	1,320	1,508
of which: Short-term..	8 762 ..	*1,736*	*1,569*	*1,167*	*1,201*	*1,160*	*1,410*	*1,320*	*1,508*
Loans...	8 764 ..	14,756	16,388	15,153	15,384	16,390	16,472	16,881	16,575
Monetary authorities..	8 765 ..	....	....	....	....	....	....	....	....
of which: Use of Fund credit and loans from the Fund....	8 766 ..	....	....	....	....	....	....	....	....
of which: Short-term..	8 768 ..	....	....	....	....	....	....	....	....
General government..	8 769 ..	10,542	11,158	10,440	10,385	11,059	11,263	11,310	10,942
of which: Short-term..	8 771 ..	....	....	....	....	....	....	....	....
Banks..	8 772 ..	....	....	....	....	....	....	....	....
of which: Short-term..	8 774 ..	....	....	....	....	....	....	....	....
Other sectors...	8 775 ..	4,214	5,230	4,714	4,999	5,331	5,209	5,571	5,633
of which: Short-term..	8 777 ..	....	....	....	....	....	....	....	....
Currency and deposits...	8 780 ..	1,529	1,776	1,968	2,156	2,824	2,917	3,515	3,481
Monetary authorities..	8 781 ..	....	....	....	....	....	....	....	....
General government...	8 782 ..	....	....	....	....	....	....	....	....
Banks..	8 783 ..	1,529	1,776	1,968	2,156	2,824	2,917	3,515	3,481
Other sectors...	8 784 ..	....	....	....	....	....	....	....	....
Other liabilities..	8 786 ..	....	....	....	52	54	53	428	420
Monetary authorities..	8 787 ..	....	....	....	52	54	53	428	420
of which: Short-term..	8 789 ..	....	....	....	....	....	....	....	....
General government...	8 790 ..	....	....	....	....	....	....	....	....
of which: Short-term..	8 792 ..	....	....	....	....	....	....	....	....
Banks..	8 793 ..	....	....	....	....	....	....	....	....
of which: Short-term..	8 795 ..	....	....	....	....	....	....	....	....
Other sectors...	8 796 ..	....	....	....	....	....	....	....	....
of which: Short-term..	8 798 ..	....	....	....	....	....	....	....	....
NET INTERNATIONAL INVESTMENT POSITION........	8 995 ..	**−29,467**	**−31,572**	**−29,161**	**−32,539**	**−37,345**	**−39,915**	**−42,844**	**−43,256**
Conversion rates: Tunisian dinars per U.S. dollar (end of period)...	0 102 ..	**1.2083**	**1.1994**	**1.3634**	**1.2971**	**1.2207**	**1.3099**	**1.3173**	**1.4379**

Table 1. ANALYTIC PRESENTATION, 2003–2010

(Millions of U.S. dollars)

	Code	2003	2004	2005	2006	2007	2008	2009	2010
A. Current Account[1]	4 993 Z.	**−7,515**	**−14,431**	**−22,197**	**−32,249**	**−38,434**	**−41,959**	**−13,991**	**−47,739**
Goods: exports f.o.b.	2 100 ..	52,394	68,535	78,368	93,613	115,361	140,800	109,647	120,902
Goods: imports f.o.b.	3 100 ..	−65,883	−91,271	−111,445	−134,669	−162,213	−193,821	−134,497	−177,347
Balance on Goods	4 100 ..	*−13,489*	*−22,736*	*−33,077*	*−41,056*	*−46,852*	*−53,021*	*−24,850*	*−56,445*
Services: credit	2 200 ..	18,013	22,960	26,770	25,606	29,027	35,243	33,655	34,357
Services: debit	3 200 ..	−7,502	−10,163	−11,505	−12,051	−15,744	−17,932	−16,906	−19,658
Balance on Goods and Services	4 991 ..	*−2,978*	*−9,939*	*−17,812*	*−27,501*	*−33,569*	*−35,710*	*−8,101*	*−41,746*
Income: credit	2 300 ..	2,246	2,651	3,644	4,418	6,423	6,889	5,164	4,477
Income: debit	3 300 ..	−7,803	−8,260	−9,483	−11,074	−13,531	−15,251	−13,353	−11,799
Balance on Goods, Services, and Income	4 992 ..	*−8,535*	*−15,548*	*−23,651*	*−34,157*	*−40,677*	*−44,072*	*−16,290*	*−49,068*
Current transfers: credit	2 379 Z.	1,081	1,155	1,475	2,245	2,785	2,791	2,833	1,985
Current transfers: debit	3 379 ..	−61	−38	−21	−337	−542	−678	−534	−656
B. Capital Account[1]	4 994 Z.	....	....	....	....	**−8**	**−60**	**−42**	**−56**
Capital account: credit	2 994 Z.	....	....	....	....	12	2	8	15
Capital account: debit	3 994 ..	....	....	....	....	−20	−62	−50	−71
Total, Groups A Plus B	4 981 ..	*−7,515*	*−14,431*	*−22,197*	*−32,249*	*−38,442*	*−42,019*	*−14,033*	*−47,795*
C. Financial Account[1]	4 995 W.	**7,162**	**17,702**	**42,660**	**42,689**	**48,700**	**34,558**	**9,757**	**58,063**
Direct investment abroad	4 505 ..	−480	−780	−1,064	−924	−2,106	−2,549	−1,553	−1,464
Direct investment in Turkey	4 555 Z.	1,702	2,785	10,031	20,185	22,047	19,504	8,409	9,278
Portfolio investment assets	4 602 ..	−1,386	−1,388	−1,233	−3,987	−1,947	−1,244	−2,711	−3,491
Equity securities	4 610 ..	−33	−25	−20	....	....	....	....	10
Debt securities	4 619 ..	−1,353	−1,363	−1,213	−3,987	−1,947	−1,244	−2,711	−3,501
Portfolio investment liabilities	4 652 Z.	3,851	9,411	14,670	11,402	2,780	−3,770	2,938	19,617
Equity securities	4 660 ..	905	1,427	5,669	1,939	5,138	716	2,827	3,468
Debt securities	4 669 Z.	2,946	7,984	9,001	9,463	−2,358	−4,486	111	16,149
Financial derivatives	4 910 ..	....	....	....	....	....	....	....	....
Financial derivatives assets	4 900 ..	....	....	....	....	....	....	....	....
Financial derivatives liabilities	4 905 ..	....	....	....	....	....	....	....	....
Other investment assets	4 703 ..	−986	−6,983	−578	−13,479	−4,969	−12,058	10,985	7,049
Monetary authorities	4 701 ..	−28	−24	−16	....	2	2	2	4
General government	4 704 ..	....	....	....	−42	−116	−32	−31	−29
Banks	4 705 ..	348	−5,324	−149	−11,018	−3,389	−10,255	6,400	13,189
Other sectors	4 728 ..	−1,306	−1,635	−413	−2,419	−1,466	−1,773	4,614	−6,115
Other investment liabilities	4 753 W.	4,461	14,657	20,834	29,492	32,895	34,675	−8,311	27,074
Monetary authorities	4 753 WA	605	−51	−474	−985	−1,096	−1,371	1,045	−88
General government	4 753 ZB	−2,194	−1,163	−2,165	−712	82	1,742	1,602	3,564
Banks	4 753 ZC	2,846	6,564	10,524	11,704	3,736	9,457	514	27,236
Other sectors	4 753 ZD	3,204	9,307	12,949	19,485	30,173	24,847	−11,472	−3,638
Total, Groups A Through C	4 983 ..	*−353*	*3,271*	*20,463*	*10,440*	*10,258*	*−7,461*	*−4,276*	*10,268*
D. Net Errors and Omissions	4 998 ..	**4,440**	**1,036**	**2,713**	**181**	**1,794**	**4,696**	**5,195**	**4,703**
Total, Groups A Through D	4 984 ..	*4,087*	*4,307*	*23,176*	*10,621*	*12,052*	*−2,765*	*919*	*14,971*
E. Reserves and Related Items	4 802 A.	**−4,087**	**−4,307**	**−23,176**	**−10,621**	**−12,052**	**2,765**	**−919**	**−14,971**
Reserve assets	4 802 ..	−4,030	−787	−17,854	−6,102	−8,065	1,073	−234	−12,810
Use of Fund credit and loans	4 766 ..	−57	−3,520	−5,322	−4,519	−3,987	1,692	−685	−2,160
Exceptional financing	4 920 ..	....	....	....	....	....	....	....	....
Conversion rates: new liras per U.S. dollar	0 101 ..	**1.5009**	**1.4255**	**1.3436**	**1.4285**	**1.3029**	**1.3015**	**1.5500**	**1.5028**

[1] Excludes components that have been classified in the categories of Group E.

Table 2. STANDARD PRESENTATION, 2003–2010

(Millions of U.S. dollars)

	Code	2003	2004	2005	2006	2007	2008	2009	2010
CURRENT ACCOUNT	4 993	−7,515	−14,431	−22,197	−32,249	−38,434	−41,959	−13,991	−47,739
A. GOODS	4 100	−13,489	−22,736	−33,077	−41,056	−46,852	−53,021	−24,850	−56,445
Credit	2 100	52,394	68,535	78,368	93,613	115,361	140,800	109,647	120,902
General merchandise: exports f.o.b.	2 110	52,318	68,444	77,848	92,626	113,865	136,314	104,338	117,919
Goods for processing: exports f.o.b.	2 150	....	....	....	....	....	....	....	....
Repairs on goods	2 160	....	....	....	....	....	....	....	....
Goods procured in ports by carriers	2 170	....	....	388	350	524	860	670	913
Nonmonetary gold	2 180	76	91	132	637	972	3,626	4,639	2,070
Debit	3 100	−65,883	−91,271	−111,445	−134,669	−162,213	−193,821	−134,497	−177,347
General merchandise: imports f.o.b.	3 110	−63,285	−87,773	−107,053	−130,086	−156,199	−187,720	−132,141	−173,915
Goods for processing: imports f.o.b.	3 150	....	....	....	....	....	....	....	....
Repairs on goods	3 160	....	....	....	....	....	....	....	....
Goods procured in ports by carriers	3 170	....	....	−506	−601	−688	−1,110	−724	−909
Nonmonetary gold	3 180	−2,598	−3,498	−3,886	−3,982	−5,326	−4,991	−1,632	−2,523
B. SERVICES	4 200	10,511	12,797	15,265	13,555	13,283	17,311	16,749	14,699
Total credit	2 200	*18,013*	*22,960*	*26,770*	*25,606*	*29,027*	*35,243*	*33,655*	*34,357*
Total debit	3 200	*−7,502*	*−10,163*	*−11,505*	*−12,051*	*−15,744*	*−17,932*	*−16,906*	*−19,658*
Transportation services, credit	2 205	2,184	3,267	4,919	4,972	6,541	7,793	7,825	9,022
Passenger	2 850	....	....	*1,569*	*1,680*	*2,232*	*3,081*	*3,351*	*3,977*
Freight	2 851	*1,322*	*1,765*	*2,048*	*1,823*	*2,424*	*2,938*	*2,979*	*3,400*
Other	2 852	*862*	*1,502*	*1,302*	*1,469*	*1,885*	*1,774*	*1,495*	*1,645*
Sea transport, passenger	2 207	....	....	....	....	....	....	....	....
Sea transport, freight	2 208	619	823	946	418	747	843	661	1,212
Sea transport, other	2 209	....	....	....	....	....	....	....	....
Air transport, passenger	2 211	....	....	1,569	1,680	2,232	3,081	3,351	3,977
Air transport, freight	2 212	113	152	175	246	284	341	515	396
Air transport, other	2 213	....	....	1,302	1,469	1,885	1,774	1,495	1,645
Other transport, passenger	2 215	....	....	....	....	....	....	....	....
Other transport, freight	2 216	590	790	927	1,159	1,393	1,754	1,803	1,792
Other transport, other	2 217	862	1,502	....	....	....	....	....	....
Transportation services, debit	3 205	−2,707	−4,331	−4,861	−4,662	−6,966	−7,984	−6,535	−8,288
Passenger	3 850	....	....	*−403*	*−534*	*−607*	*−677*	*−480*	*−625*
Freight	3 851	*−2,034*	*−2,907*	*−3,548*	*−3,141*	*−5,214*	*−6,093*	*−4,487*	*−5,850*
Other	3 852	*−673*	*−1,424*	*−910*	*−987*	*−1,145*	*−1,214*	*−1,568*	*−1,813*
Sea transport, passenger	3 207	....	....	....	....	....	....	....	....
Sea transport, freight	3 208	−1,685	−2,420	−3,009	−2,571	−4,640	−5,444	−3,824	−4,996
Sea transport, other	3 209	....	....	....	....	....	....	....	....
Air transport, passenger	3 211	....	....	−403	−534	−607	−677	−480	−625
Air transport, freight	3 212	−181	−237	−251	−332	−302	−351	−305	−395
Air transport, other	3 213	....	....	−910	−987	−1,145	−1,214	−1,568	−1,813
Other transport, passenger	3 215	....	....	....	....	....	....	....	....
Other transport, freight	3 216	−168	−250	−288	−238	−272	−298	−358	−459
Other transport, other	3 217	−673	−1,424	....	....	....	....	....	....
Travel, credit	2 236	13,203	15,888	18,152	16,853	18,487	21,951	21,250	20,807
Business travel	2 237	1,148	1,463	2,914	1,885	1,820	2,837	2,732	2,670
Personal travel	2 240	12,055	14,425	15,238	14,968	16,667	19,114	18,518	18,137
Travel, debit	3 236	−2,113	−2,524	−2,872	−2,743	−3,260	−3,506	−4,147	−4,826
Business travel	3 237	−693	−846	−1,063	−1,020	−1,207	−1,300	−1,539	−1,792
Personal travel	3 240	−1,420	−1,678	−1,809	−1,723	−2,053	−2,206	−2,608	−3,034
Other services, credit	2 200 BA	2,626	3,805	3,699	3,781	3,999	5,499	4,580	4,528
Communications	2 245	224	346	412	416	506	725	633	463
Construction	2 249	743	743	882	936	856	1,146	1,279	1,120
Insurance	2 253	211	274	323	522	645	752	676	719
Financial	2 260	291	288	345	277	395	841	464	482
Computer and information	2 262	....	....	....	12	15	13	12	16
Royalties and licence fees	2 266	....	....	....	....	....	....	....	....
Other business services	2 268	272	482	338	289	208	338	282	333
Personal, cultural, and recreational	2 287	781	1,418	1,079	998	971	1,224	774	912
Government, n.i.e.	2 291	104	254	320	331	403	460	460	483
Other services, debit	3 200 BA	−2,682	−3,308	−3,772	−4,646	−5,518	−6,442	−6,224	−6,544
Communications	3 245	−231	−207	−228	−299	−305	−298	−247	−246
Construction	3 249	−61	−19	−8	−57	−97	−172	−189	−261
Insurance	3 253	−622	−839	−891	−1,140	−1,544	−1,436	−1,203	−1,188
Financial	3 260	−374	−377	−386	−524	−623	−978	−826	−724
Computer and information	3 262	....	....	....	−15	−26	−32	−30	−38
Royalties and licence fees	3 266	−167	−362	−439	−531	−647	−729	−648	−816
Other business services	3 268	−298	−353	−538	−723	−1,029	−1,378	−1,568	−1,673
Personal, cultural, and recreational	3 287	−117	−176	−88	−106	−111	−181	−207	−246
Government, n.i.e.	3 291	−812	−975	−1,194	−1,251	−1,136	−1,238	−1,306	−1,352

Table 2 (Continued). STANDARD PRESENTATION, 2003–2010

(Millions of U.S. dollars)

	Code	2003	2004	2005	2006	2007	2008	2009	2010
C. INCOME	4 300	**−5,557**	**−5,609**	**−5,839**	**−6,656**	**−7,108**	**−8,362**	**−8,189**	**−7,322**
Total credit	2 300	*2,246*	*2,651*	*3,644*	*4,418*	*6,423*	*6,889*	*5,164*	*4,477*
Total debit	3 300	*−7,803*	*−8,260*	*−9,483*	*−11,074*	*−13,531*	*−15,251*	*−13,353*	*−11,799*
Compensation of employees, credit	2 310	....	....	**36**	**35**	**39**	**45**	**36**	**45**
Compensation of employees, debit	3 310	....	....	**−96**	**−107**	**−106**	**−111**	**−141**	**−175**
Investment income, credit	2 320	**2,246**	**2,651**	**3,608**	**4,383**	**6,384**	**6,844**	**5,128**	**4,432**
Direct investment income	2 330	203	244	201	129	108	327	182	680
Dividends and distributed branch profits	2 332	193	237	200	111	33	308	179	676
Reinvested earnings and undistributed branch profits	2 333	10	7	1	18	75	19	3	4
Income on debt (interest)	2 334	....	....	....	....	....	....	....	....
Portfolio investment income	2 339	1,409	1,710	2,402	2,801	4,118	4,495	3,261	2,658
Income on equity	2 340	....	....	....	....	....	....	....	....
Income on bonds and notes	2 350	1,409	1,710	2,402	2,801	4,118	4,495	3,261	2,658
Income on money market instruments	2 360	....	....	....	....	....	....	....	....
Other investment income	2 370	634	697	1,005	1,453	2,158	2,022	1,685	1,094
Investment income, debit	3 320	**−7,803**	**−8,260**	**−9,387**	**−10,967**	**−13,425**	**−15,140**	**−13,212**	**−11,624**
Direct investment income	3 330	−643	−1,043	−1,051	−1,182	−2,213	−2,940	−2,914	−3,044
Dividends and distributed branch profits	3 332	−469	−802	−890	−1,017	−1,808	−2,398	−1,989	−2,369
Reinvested earnings and undistributed branch profits	3 333	−132	−204	−84	−108	−300	−396	−792	−588
Income on debt (interest)	3 334	−42	−37	−77	−57	−105	−146	−133	−87
Portfolio investment income	3 339	−2,616	−2,905	−3,326	−3,463	−3,735	−3,523	−2,994	−3,149
Income on equity	3 340	−14	....	−2	....	−1	....	....	−2
Income on bonds and notes	3 350	−2,602	−2,905	−3,324	−3,463	−3,734	−3,523	−2,994	−3,147
Income on money market instruments	3 360	....	....	....	....	....	....	....	....
Other investment income	3 370	−4,544	−4,312	−5,010	−6,322	−7,477	−8,677	−7,304	−5,431
D. CURRENT TRANSFERS	4 379	**1,020**	**1,117**	**1,454**	**1,908**	**2,243**	**2,113**	**2,299**	**1,329**
Credit	2 379	**1,081**	**1,155**	**1,475**	**2,245**	**2,785**	**2,791**	**2,833**	**1,985**
General government	2 380	352	351	624	654	848	766	1,233	624
Other sectors	2 390	729	804	851	1,591	1,937	2,025	1,600	1,361
Workers' remittances	2 391	729	804	851	1,111	1,209	1,431	934	829
Other current transfers	2 392	....	....	....	480	728	594	666	532
Debit	3 379	**−61**	**−38**	**−21**	**−337**	**−542**	**−678**	**−534**	**−656**
General government	3 380	−61	−38	−21	−33	−39	−38	−43	−61
Other sectors	3 390	....	....	....	−304	−503	−640	−491	−595
Workers' remittances	3 391	....	....	....	....	....	....	....	....
Other current transfers	3 392	....	....	....	−304	−503	−640	−491	−595
CAPITAL AND FINANCIAL ACCOUNT	4 996	**3,075**	**13,395**	**19,484**	**32,068**	**36,640**	**37,263**	**8,796**	**43,036**
CAPITAL ACCOUNT	4 994	....	....	....	....	**−8**	**−60**	**−42**	**−56**
Total credit	2 994	....	....	....	....	*12*	*2*	*8*	*15*
Total debit	3 994	....	....	....	....	*−20*	*−62*	*−50*	*−71*
Capital transfers, credit	2 400	....	....	....	....	....	....	....	....
General government	2 401	....	....	....	....	....	....	....	....
Debt forgiveness	2 402	....	....	....	....	....	....	....	....
Other capital transfers	2 410	....	....	....	....	....	....	....	....
Other sectors	2 430	....	....	....	....	....	....	....	....
Migrants' transfers	2 431	....	....	....	....	....	....	....	....
Debt forgiveness	2 432	....	....	....	....	....	....	....	....
Other capital transfers	2 440	....	....	....	....	....	....	....	....
Capital transfers, debit	3 400	....	....	....	....	....	....	....	....
General government	3 401	....	....	....	....	....	....	....	....
Debt forgiveness	3 402	....	....	....	....	....	....	....	....
Other capital transfers	3 410	....	....	....	....	....	....	....	....
Other sectors	3 430	....	....	....	....	....	....	....	....
Migrants' transfers	3 431	....	....	....	....	....	....	....	....
Debt forgiveness	3 432	....	....	....	....	....	....	....	....
Other capital transfers	3 440	....	....	....	....	....	....	....	....
Nonproduced nonfinancial assets, credit	2 480	....	....	....	....	**12**	**2**	**8**	**15**
Nonproduced nonfinancial assets, debit	3 480	....	....	....	....	**−20**	**−62**	**−50**	**−71**

Table 2 (Continued). STANDARD PRESENTATION, 2003–2010

(Millions of U.S. dollars)

	Code	2003	2004	2005	2006	2007	2008	2009	2010
FINANCIAL ACCOUNT	4 995	**3,075**	**13,395**	**19,484**	**32,068**	**36,648**	**37,323**	**8,838**	**43,092**
A. DIRECT INVESTMENT	4 500	**1,222**	**2,005**	**8,967**	**19,261**	**19,941**	**16,955**	**6,856**	**7,814**
Direct investment abroad	4 505	**−480**	**−780**	**−1,064**	**−924**	**−2,106**	**−2,549**	**−1,553**	**−1,464**
Equity capital	4 510	−470	−773	−1,063	−906	−2,031	−2,530	−1,550	−1,460
Claims on affiliated enterprises	4 515	−470	−773	−1,063	−906	−2,031	−2,530	−1,550	−1,460
Liabilities to affiliated enterprises	4 520	....	....	....	....	....	....	....	....
Reinvested earnings	4 525	−10	−7	−1	−18	−75	−19	−3	−4
Other capital	4 530	....	....	....	....	....	....	....	....
Claims on affiliated enterprises	4 535	....	....	....	....	....	....	....	....
Liabilities to affiliated enterprises	4 540	....	....	....	....	....	....	....	....
Direct investment in Turkey	4 555	**1,702**	**2,785**	**10,031**	**20,185**	**22,047**	**19,504**	**8,409**	**9,278**
Equity capital	4 560	1,554	2,231	9,891	19,796	21,020	17,253	7,158	8,402
Claims on direct investors	4 565	....	....	....	....	....	....	....	....
Liabilities to direct investors	4 570	1,554	2,231	9,891	19,796	21,020	17,253	7,158	8,402
Reinvested earnings	4 575	132	204	84	108	300	396	792	588
Other capital	4 580	16	350	56	281	727	1,855	459	288
Claims on direct investors	4 585	....	....	....	....	....	....	....	....
Liabilities to direct investors	4 590	16	350	56	281	727	1,855	459	288
B. PORTFOLIO INVESTMENT	4 600	**2,465**	**8,023**	**13,437**	**7,415**	**833**	**−5,014**	**227**	**16,126**
Assets	4 602	**−1,386**	**−1,388**	**−1,233**	**−3,987**	**−1,947**	**−1,244**	**−2,711**	**−3,491**
Equity securities	4 610	−33	−25	−20	....	....	....	....	10
Monetary authorities	4 611	....	....	....	....	....	....	....	....
General government	4 612	−33	−25	−20					10
Banks	4 613	....	....	....	....	....	....	....	....
Other sectors	4 614	....	....	....	....	....	....	....	....
Debt securities	4 619	−1,353	−1,363	−1,213	−3,987	−1,947	−1,244	−2,711	−3,501
Bonds and notes	4 620	−1,353	−1,363	−1,213	−3,987	−1,947	−1,244	−2,711	−3,501
Monetary authorities	4 621	....	....	....	....	....	....	....	....
General government	4 622	....	....	....	....	....	....	....	....
Banks	4 623	−932	−666	−1,285	−3,754	−1,844	−367	−2,010	−1,079
Other sectors	4 624	−421	−697	72	−233	−103	−877	−701	−2,422
Money market instruments	4 630	....	....	....	....	....	....	....	....
Monetary authorities	4 631	....	....	....	....	....	....	....	....
General government	4 632	....	....	....	....	....	....	....	....
Banks	4 633	....	....	....	....	....	....	....	....
Other sectors	4 634	....	....	....	....	....	....	....	....
Liabilities	4 652	**3,851**	**9,411**	**14,670**	**11,402**	**2,780**	**−3,770**	**2,938**	**19,617**
Equity securities	4 660	905	1,427	5,669	1,939	5,138	716	2,827	3,468
Banks	4 663	....	....	....	....	....	....	....	....
Other sectors	4 664	905	1,427	5,669	1,939	5,138	716	2,827	3,468
Debt securities	4 669	2,946	7,984	9,001	9,463	−2,358	−4,486	111	16,149
Bonds and notes	4 670	2,946	7,984	9,001	9,463	−2,358	−4,486	111	16,149
Monetary authorities	4 671	....	....	....	....	....	....	....	....
General government	4 672	3,123	7,984	9,351	9,463	−2,358	−4,486	111	14,797
Banks	4 673	−177	....	−350	....	....	....		1,142
Other sectors	4 674	....	....	....	....	....	....		210
Money market instruments	4 680	....	....	....	....	....	....	....	....
Monetary authorities	4 681	....	....	....	....	....	....	....	....
General government	4 682	....	....	....	....	....	....	....	....
Banks	4 683	....	....	....	....	....	....	....	....
Other sectors	4 684	....	....	....	....	....	....	....	....
C. FINANCIAL DERIVATIVES	4 910	....	....	....	....	....	....	....	....
Monetary authorities	4 911	....	....	....	....	....	....	....	....
General government	4 912	....	....	....	....	....	....	....	....
Banks	4 913	....	....	....	....	....	....	....	....
Other sectors	4 914	....	....	....	....	....	....	....	....
Assets	4 900	....	....	....	....	....	....	....	....
Monetary authorities	4 901	....	....	....	....	....	....	....	....
General government	4 902	....	....	....	....	....	....	....	....
Banks	4 903	....	....	....	....	....	....	....	....
Other sectors	4 904	....	....	....	....	....	....	....	....
Liabilities	4 905	....	....	....	....	....	....	....	....
Monetary authorities	4 906	....	....	....	....	....	....	....	....
General government	4 907	....	....	....	....	....	....	....	....
Banks	4 908	....	....	....	....	....	....	....	....
Other sectors	4 909	....	....	....	....	....	....	....	....

2011, International Monetary Fund: *Balance of Payments Statistics Yearbook*

Table 2 (Concluded). STANDARD PRESENTATION, 2003–2010

(Millions of U.S. dollars)

	Code	2003	2004	2005	2006	2007	2008	2009	2010
D. OTHER INVESTMENT	4 700	**3,418**	**4,154**	**14,934**	**11,494**	**23,939**	**24,309**	**1,988**	**31,963**
Assets	4 703	**−986**	**−6,983**	**−578**	**−13,479**	**−4,969**	**−12,058**	**10,985**	**7,049**
Trade credits	4 706	−910	−1,635	−413	−2,419	−1,466	1,723	−1,410	−1,273
General government	4 707	....	....	....	....	....	....	....	....
of which: Short-term	4 709								
Other sectors	4 710	−910	−1,635	−413	−2,419	−1,466	1,723	−1,410	−1,273
of which: Short-term	4 712	*−910*	*−1,635*	*−413*	*−2,419*	*−1,466*	*1,723*	*−1,410*	*−1,273*
Loans	4 714	−404	617	177	−725	139	−422	−282	−428
Monetary authorities	4 715	−28	−24	−16	....	2	2	2	4
of which: Short-term	4 718	....	....	....	....	....	....	....	....
General government	4 719	....	....	....	....	....	....	....	....
of which: Short-term	4 721	....	....	....	....	....	....	....	....
Banks	4 722	−376	641	193	−725	137	−424	−284	−432
of which: Short-term	4 724	*67*	*−82*	*−168*	*−497*	*−306*	*−267*	*−6*	*126*
Other sectors	4 725	....	....	....	....	....	....	....	....
of which: Short-term	4 727	....	....	....	....	....	....	....	....
Currency and deposits	4 730	724	−5,965	−342	−10,293	−3,526	−13,327	12,708	8,779
Monetary authorities	4 731	....	....	....	....	....	....	....	....
General government	4 732	....	....	....	....	....	....	....	....
Banks	4 733	724	−5,965	−342	−10,293	−3,526	−9,831	6,684	13,621
Other sectors	4 734	....	....	....	....	....	−3,496	6,024	−4,842
Other assets	4 736	−396	....	....	−42	−116	−32	−31	−29
Monetary authorities	4 737	....	....	....	....	....	....	....	....
of which: Short-term	4 739	....	....	....	....	....	....	....	....
General government	4 740	....	....	....	−42	−116	−32	−31	−29
of which: Short-term	4 742	....	....	....	....	....	....	....	....
Banks	4 743	....	....	....	....	....	....	....	....
of which: Short-term	4 745	....	....	....	....	....	....	....	....
Other sectors	4 746	−396							
of which: Short-term	4 748	*−396*							
Liabilities	4 753	**4,404**	**11,137**	**15,512**	**24,973**	**28,908**	**36,367**	**−8,997**	**24,914**
Trade credits	4 756	2,181	4,201	3,074	674	4,150	1,590	−1,095	2,130
General government	4 757	....	....	....	....	....	....	....	....
of which: Short-term	4 759	....	....	....	....	....	....	....	....
Other sectors	4 760	2,181	4,201	3,074	674	4,150	1,590	−1,095	2,130
of which: Short-term	4 762	*1,215*	*3,715*	*3,014*	*618*	*4,112*	*1,392*	*−1,027*	*2,039*
Loans	4 764	747	6,131	11,636	19,395	27,729	29,959	−13,930	8,532
Monetary authorities	4 765	−57	−3,520	−5,322	−4,519	−3,987	1,692	−685	−2,160
of which: Use of Fund credit and loans from the Fund	4 766	*−57*	*−3,520*	*−5,322*	*−4,519*	*−3,987*	*1,692*	*−685*	*−2,160*
of which: Short-term	4 768	....	....	....	....	....	....	....	....
General government	4 769	−2,194	−1,163	−2,165	−712	82	1,742	1,602	3,564
of which: Short-term	4 771	....	....	....	....	....	....	....	....
Banks	4 772	1,975	5,708	9,248	5,814	5,609	3,267	−4,472	12,895
of which: Short-term	4 774	*2,015*	*3,347*	*2,704*	*−3,952*	*−1,663*	*2,339*	*−2,810*	*12,014*
Other sectors	4 775	1,023	5,106	9,875	18,812	26,025	23,258	−10,375	−5,767
of which: Short-term	4 777	*288*	*341*	*367*	*495*	*214*	*519*	*−702*	*1,436*
Currency and deposits	4 780	1,368	647	489	4,622	−3,323	4,399	4,085	13,788
Monetary authorities	4 781	497	−209	−787	−1,268	−1,450	−1,791	−901	−553
General government	4 782	....	....	....	....	....	....	....	....
Banks	4 783	871	856	1,276	5,890	−1,873	6,190	4,986	14,341
Other sectors	4 784	....	....	....	....	....	....	....	....
Other liabilities	4 786	108	158	313	282	352	419	1,944	464
Monetary authorities	4 787	108	158	313	283	354	420	1,946	465
of which: Short-term	4 789	*108*	*158*	*313*	*283*	*354*	*420*	*448*	*465*
General government	4 790	....	....	....	....	....	....	....	....
of which: Short-term	4 792	....	....	....	....	....	....	....	....
Banks	4 793	....	....	....	....	....	....	....	....
of which: Short-term	4 795	....	....	....	....	....	....	....	....
Other sectors	4 796	....	....	....	−1	−2	−1	−2	−1
of which: Short-term	4 798	....	....	....	....	....	....	....	....
E. RESERVE ASSETS	4 802	**−4,030**	**−787**	**−17,854**	**−6,102**	**−8,065**	**1,073**	**−234**	**−12,810**
Monetary gold	4 812	....	....	....	....	....	....	....	....
Special drawing rights	4 811	9	21	−7	12	−33	16	−1,491	−1
Reserve position in the Fund	4 810	....	....	....	....	....	....	....	....
Foreign exchange	4 803	−4,039	−808	−17,847	−6,114	−8,032	1,057	1,257	−12,809
Other claims	4 813	....	....	....	....	....	....	....	....
NET ERRORS AND OMISSIONS	4 998	**4,440**	**1,036**	**2,713**	**181**	**1,794**	**4,696**	**5,195**	**4,703**

Table 3. INTERNATIONAL INVESTMENT POSITION (End-period stocks), 2003–2010

(Millions of U.S. dollars)

	Code	2003	2004	2005	2006	2007	2008	2009	2010
ASSETS..	8 995 C.	73,714	86,012	105,862	142,429	167,366	184,168	178,048	179,974
Direct investment abroad.................................	8 505 ..	6,138	7,060	8,315	8,866	12,210	17,846	22,250	21,570
Equity capital and reinvested earnings...........................	8 506 ..	6,138	7,060	8,315	8,866	12,210	17,846	19,923	20,288
Claims on affiliated enterprises..........................	8 507 ..	6,138	7,060	8,315	8,866	12,210	17,846	19,923	20,288
Liabilities to affiliated enterprises......................	8 508 ..	....	....	....	....	....	....		
Other capital...	8 530 ..	....	....	....	....	....	....	2,327	1,282
Claims on affiliated enterprises..........................	8 535 ..	....	....	....	....	....	....	3,391	2,635
Liabilities to affiliated enterprises......................	8 540 ..	....	....	....	....	....	....	−1,064	−1,353
Portfolio investment..	8 602 ..	1,963	936	732	3,126	2,023	1,954	1,923	2,256
Equity securities..	8 610 ..	68	124	103	165	93	74	235	398
Monetary authorities...................................	8 611 ..	15	16	14	15	16	16	16	26
General government....................................	8 612 ..	....	....	....	....	....	....	....	....
Banks..	8 613 ..	7	59	50	80	47	42	92	88
Other sectors..	8 614 ..	46	49	39	70	30	16	127	284
Debt securities...	8 619 ..	1,895	812	629	2,961	1,930	1,880	1,688	1,858
Bonds and notes.......................................	8 620 ..	1,882	800	611	2,898	1,893	1,878	1,658	1,857
Monetary authorities................................	8 621 ..	....	....	....	....	....	....	....	....
General government.................................	8 622 ..	....	....	....	....	....	....	....	....
Banks..	8 623 ..	1,739	662	276	2,481	1,384	1,482	1,044	1,197
Other sectors.......................................	8 624 ..	143	138	335	417	509	396	614	660
Money market instruments.............................	8 630 ..	13	12	18	63	37	2	30	1
Monetary authorities................................	8 631 ..	....	....	....	....	....	....	....	....
General government.................................	8 632 ..	....	....	....	....	....	....	....	....
Banks..	8 633 ..	....	....	....	....	19	....	....	....
Other sectors.......................................	8 634 ..	13	12	18	63	18	2	30	1
Financial derivatives.......................................	8 900 ..	....	....	....	....	....	....	....	....
Monetary authorities.....................................	8 901 ..	....	....	....	....	....	....	....	....
General government......................................	8 902 ..	....	....	....	....	....	....	....	....
Banks..	8 903 ..	....	....	....	....	....	....	....	....
Other sectors...	8 904 ..	....	....	....	....	....	....	....	....
Other investment...	8 703 ..	30,439	40,373	44,386	67,151	76,693	90,134	79,035	70,166
Trade credits...	8 706 ..	4,381	6,016	6,429	8,848	10,314	8,591	9,335	10,670
General government....................................	8 707 ..	....	....	....	....	....	....	....	....
of which: Short-term...............................	8 709 ..	....	....	....	....	....	....	....	....
Other sectors..	8 710 ..	4,381	6,016	6,429	8,848	10,314	8,591	9,335	10,670
of which: Short-term...............................	8 712 ..	*4,381*	*6,016*	*6,429*	*8,848*	*10,314*	*8,591*	*9,335*	*10,670*
Loans..	8 714 ..	2,816	2,189	1,348	1,946	1,843	2,374	2,666	2,737
Monetary authorities...................................	8 715 ..	119	84	34	31	28	25	23	19
of which: Short-term...............................	8 718 ..	....	....	....	....	....	....	....	....
General government....................................	8 719 ..	....	....	....	....	....	....	....	....
of which: Short-term...............................	8 721 ..	....	....	....	....	....	....	....	....
Banks..	8 722 ..	2,697	2,105	1,314	1,915	1,815	2,349	2,643	2,718
of which: Short-term...............................	8 724 ..	*493*	*567*	*349*	*733*	*1,088*	*1,525*	*1,511*	*1,275*
Other sectors..	8 725 ..	....	....	....	....	....	....	....	....
of which: Short-term...............................	8 727 ..	....	....	....	....	....	....	....	....
Currency and deposits....................................	8 730 ..	21,208	30,143	34,603	54,232	62,283	76,886	64,621	54,275
Monetary authorities...................................	8 731 ..	....	....	....	....	....	....	....	....
General government....................................	8 732 ..	....	....	....	....	....	....	....	....
Banks..	8 733 ..	9,795	16,143	16,315	27,540	31,815	43,719	37,119	22,732
Other sectors..	8 734 ..	11,413	14,000	18,288	26,692	30,468	33,167	27,502	31,543
Other assets...	8 736 ..	2,034	2,025	2,006	2,125	2,253	2,284	2,412	2,484
Monetary authorities...................................	8 737 ..	1,272	1,288	1,326	1,395	1,468	1,510	1,515	1,519
of which: Short-term...............................	8 739 ..	....	....	....	....	....	....	....	....
General government....................................	8 740 ..	762	737	680	730	785	774	897	965
of which: Short-term...............................	8 742 ..	....	....	....	....	....	....	....	....
Banks..	8 743 ..	....	....	....	....	....	....	....	....
of which: Short-term...............................	8 745 ..	....	....	....	....	....	....	....	....
Other sectors..	8 746 ..	....	....	....	....	....	....	....	....
of which: Short-term...............................	8 748 ..	....	....	....	....	....	....	....	....
Reserve assets..	8 802 ..	35,174	37,643	52,429	63,286	76,439	74,234	74,840	85,982
Monetary gold..	8 812 ..	1,558	1,635	1,915	2,373	3,123	3,229	4,121	5,264
Special drawing rights....................................	8 811 ..	30	14	16	12	50	23	1,519	1,494
Reserve position in the Fund.............................	8 810 ..	168	175	161	170	178	174	177	174
Foreign exchange..	8 803 ..	33,418	35,819	50,337	60,731	73,088	70,808	69,023	79,051
Other claims...	8 813 ..	....	....	....	....	....	....	....	....

Table 3 (Concluded). INTERNATIONAL INVESTMENT POSITION (End-period stocks), 2003–2010

(Millions of U.S. dollars)

	Code	2003	2004	2005	2006	2007	2008	2009	2010
LIABILITIES..	8 995 D.	**179,646**	**213,900**	**280,890**	**349,249**	**482,286**	**385,628**	**452,381**	**537,116**
Direct investment in Turkey.................................	8 555 ..	**33,543**	**38,543**	**71,304**	**95,076**	**154,020**	**80,225**	**140,493**	**181,590**
Equity capital and reinvested earnings...............................	8 556 ..	30,936	37,169	69,927	93,447	150,908	75,407	134,986	176,048
Claims on direct investors.........................	8 557 ..	....	....	....	....	....	....	....	....
Liabilities to direct investors.........................	8 558 ..	30,936	37,169	69,927	93,447	150,908	75,407	134,986	176,048
Other capital.........................	8 580 ..	2,607	1,374	1,377	1,629	3,112	4,818	5,507	5,542
Claims on direct investors.........................	8 585 ..	....	....	....	....	....	....	....	....
Liabilities to direct investors.........................	8 590 ..	2,607	1,374	1,377	1,629	3,112	4,818	5,507	5,542
Portfolio investment.............................	8 652 ..	**30,024**	**45,751**	**72,606**	**84,410**	**120,629**	**68,802**	**91,186**	**118,381**
Equity securities.........................	8 660 ..	8,954	16,141	33,387	33,816	64,201	23,196	47,248	61,497
Banks.........................	8 663 ..	....	....	....	....	....	....	....	....
Other sectors.........................	8 664 ..	8,954	16,141	33,387	33,816	64,201	23,196	47,248	61,497
Debt securities.........................	8 669 ..	21,070	29,610	39,219	50,594	56,428	45,606	43,938	56,884
Bonds and notes.........................	8 670 ..	21,070	29,610	39,219	50,594	56,428	45,606	43,938	56,884
Monetary authorities.........................	8 671 ..	....	....	....	....	....	....	....	....
General government.........................	8 672 ..	20,720	29,260	39,219	50,594	56,428	45,606	43,938	55,527
Banks.........................	8 673 ..	350	350	....	....	....	....	....	1,138
Other sectors.........................	8 674 ..	....	....	....	....	....	....	....	219
Money market instruments.........................	8 680 ..	....	....	....	....	....	....	....	....
Monetary authorities.........................	8 681 ..	....	....	....	....	....	....	....	....
General government.........................	8 682 ..	....	....	....	....	....	....	....	....
Banks.........................	8 683 ..	....	....	....	....	....	....	....	....
Other sectors.........................	8 684 ..	....	....	....	....	....	....	....	....
Financial derivatives.............................	8 905 ..	....	....	....	....	....	....	....	....
Monetary authorities.........................	8 906 ..	....	....	....	....	....	....	....	....
General government.........................	8 907 ..	....	....	....	....	....	....	....	....
Banks.........................	8 908 ..	....	....	....	....	....	....	....	....
Other sectors.........................	8 909 ..	....	....	....	....	....	....	....	....
Other investment.............................	8 753 ..	**116,079**	**129,606**	**136,980**	**169,763**	**207,637**	**236,601**	**220,702**	**237,145**
Trade credits.........................	8 756 ..	9,114	12,894	15,343	16,751	21,499	22,628	21,623	23,367
General government.........................	8 757 ..	....	....	....	....	....	....	....	....
of which: Short-term.........................	8 759 ..	....	....	....	....	....	....	....	....
Other sectors.........................	8 760 ..	9,114	12,894	15,343	16,751	21,499	22,628	21,623	23,367
of which: Short-term.........................	8 762 ..	*8,866*	*12,593*	*15,011*	*16,383*	*21,084*	*22,032*	*21,101*	*22,765*
Loans.........................	8 764 ..	85,512	92,494	99,730	125,025	159,540	182,002	164,560	166,798
Monetary authorities.........................	8 765 ..	24,112	21,517	14,655	10,772	7,168	8,534	7,968	5,637
of which: Use of Fund credit and loans from the Fund....	8 766 ..	*24,092*	*21,507*	*14,646*	*10,762*	*7,158*	*8,524*	*7,958*	*5,627*
of which: Short-term.........................	8 768 ..	*11*	*1*	*1*	*1*	*1*	*1*	*1*	*1*
General government.........................	8 769 ..	21,667	21,940	19,714	20,748	22,925	24,892	25,307	28,844
of which: Short-term.........................	8 771 ..	....	....	....	....	....	....	....	....
Banks.........................	8 772 ..	8,866	14,816	24,454	31,777	39,062	40,100	35,359	47,386
of which: Short-term.........................	8 774 ..	*5,320*	*8,716*	*11,804*	*9,229*	*7,523*	*9,502*	*6,307*	*18,097*
Other sectors.........................	8 775 ..	30,867	34,221	40,907	61,728	90,385	108,476	95,926	84,931
of which: Short-term.........................	8 777 ..	*1,595*	*1,796*	*2,214*	*2,129*	*1,439*	*1,781*	*983*	*2,266*
Currency and deposits.........................	8 780 ..	21,453	24,218	21,907	27,987	26,598	31,971	32,839	45,330
Monetary authorities.........................	8 781 ..	17,081	18,405	15,416	15,668	15,791	14,056	13,295	11,817
General government.........................	8 782 ..	....	....	....	....	....	....	....	....
Banks.........................	8 783 ..	4,372	5,813	6,491	12,319	10,807	17,915	19,544	33,513
Other sectors.........................	8 784 ..	....	....	....	....	....	....	....	....
Other liabilities.........................	8 786 ..	....	....	....	....	....	....	1,680	1,650
Monetary authorities.........................	8 787 ..	....	....	....	....	....	....	1,680	1,650
of which: Short-term.........................	8 789 ..	....	....	....	....	....	....	....	....
General government.........................	8 790 ..	....	....	....	....	....	....	....	....
of which: Short-term.........................	8 792 ..	....	....	....	....	....	....	....	....
Banks.........................	8 793 ..	....	....	....	....	....	....	....	....
of which: Short-term.........................	8 795 ..	....	....	....	....	....	....	....	....
Other sectors.........................	8 796 ..	....	....	....	....	....	....	....	....
of which: Short-term.........................	8 798 ..	....	....	....	....	....	....	....	....
NET INTERNATIONAL INVESTMENT POSITION........	8 995 ..	**−105,932**	**−127,887**	**−175,028**	**−206,820**	**−314,921**	**−201,460**	**−274,333**	**−357,142**
Conversion rates: new liras per U.S. dollar (end of period)...	0 102 ..	**1.3966**	**1.3395**	**1.3451**	**1.4090**	**1.1708**	**1.5255**	**1.4909**	**1.5413**

Table 1. ANALYTIC PRESENTATION, 2003–2010

(Millions of U.S. dollars)

	Code	2003	2004	2005	2006	2007	2008	2009	2010
A. Current Account[1]	4 993 Z.	**−115.0**	**−75.3**	**−26.0**	**−396.2**	**−701.1**	**−1,313.7**	**−1,064.1**	**−1,739.9**
Goods: exports f.o.b.	2 100 ..	572.2	759.1	1,015.8	1,187.6	1,776.2	2,207.6	2,326.6	2,164.0
Goods: imports f.o.b.	3 100 ..	−1,202.7	−1,426.8	−1,745.6	−2,215.6	−2,958.2	−4,042.8	−3,787.3	−4,264.4
Balance on Goods	4 100 ..	*−630.5*	*−667.6*	*−729.8*	*−1,027.9*	*−1,182.0*	*−1,835.1*	*−1,460.8*	*−2,100.4*
Services: credit	2 200 ..	261.8	373.2	525.1	525.8	592.9	798.8	966.9	1,310.1
Services: debit	3 200 ..	−378.8	−489.6	−608.8	−770.5	−977.0	−1,256.8	−1,423.2	−1,835.1
Balance on Goods and Services	4 991 ..	*−747.5*	*−784.1*	*−813.6*	*−1,272.6*	*−1,566.2*	*−2,293.2*	*−1,917.1*	*−2,625.5*
Income: credit	2 300 ..	27.6	35.7	49.8	71.9	97.1	130.2	41.9	20.1
Income: debit	3 300 ..	−170.8	−328.8	−298.9	−310.9	−339.8	−391.1	−336.3	−325.0
Balance on Goods, Services, and Income	4 992 ..	*−890.7*	*−1,077.2*	*−1,062.7*	*−1,511.7*	*−1,808.9*	*−2,554.0*	*−2,211.5*	*−2,930.4*
Current transfers: credit	2 379 Z.	912.5	1,143.5	1,181.4	1,300.9	1,311.0	1,564.0	1,541.2	1,719.2
Current transfers: debit	3 379 ..	−136.8	−141.7	−144.8	−185.5	−203.2	−323.7	−393.8	−528.7
B. Capital Account[1]	4 994 Z.	....	....	....	**3,428.1**	....	....	....	....
Capital account: credit	2 994 Z.	....	....	....	3,428.1	....	....	....	....
Capital account: debit	3 994 ..	....	....	....	....	....	....	....	....
Total, Groups A Plus B	4 981 ..	*−115.0*	*−75.3*	*−26.0*	*3,031.9*	*−701.1*	*−1,313.7*	*−1,064.1*	*−1,739.9*
C. Financial Account[1]	4 995 W.	**258.6**	**468.3**	**557.2**	**751.4**	**1,382.0**	**1,154.7**	**1,630.5**	**1,148.4**
Direct investment abroad	4 505 ..								
Direct investment in Uganda	4 555 Z.	202.2	295.4	379.8	644.3	792.3	728.9	788.7	817.2
Portfolio investment assets	4 602 ..	−4.3	....	....	....	....	−12.1	....	....
Equity securities	4 610 ..	−4.3	....	....	....	....	−12.1	....	....
Debt securities	4 619 ..	....	....	....	....	....	....	....	....
Portfolio investment liabilities	4 652 Z.	20.3	6.2	−13.4	21.7	44.9	29.7	28.7	−110.5
Equity securities	4 660 ..	....	24.0	....	19.1	−23.1	13.1	131.1	−70.5
Debt securities	4 669 Z.	20.3	−17.8	−13.4	2.5	68.0	16.6	−102.3	−40.0
Financial derivatives	4 910 ..	....	....	....	....	1.4	6.9	−6.2	−1.4
Financial derivatives assets	4 900 ..	....	....	....	....				
Financial derivatives liabilities	4 905 ..	....	....	....	....	1.4	6.9	−6.2	−1.4
Other investment assets	4 703 ..	−224.9	25.5	56.4	−52.1	32.0	37.1	6.0	−148.3
Monetary authorities	4 701 ..	8.9	11.9	3.7	−7.0	21.2	−17.7	−16.3	16.1
General government	4 704 ..	−37.1	−21.5	1.9	16.3	83.1	48.4	57.7	−42.7
Banks	4 705 ..	−109.7	−3.8	43.1	−106.4	−57.3	−19.6	36.6	−121.7
Other sectors	4 728 ..	−87.0	39.0	7.7	45.0	−15.0	26.0	−72.0	....
Other investment liabilities	4 753 W.	265.3	141.1	134.3	137.6	511.5	364.3	813.3	591.5
Monetary authorities	4 753 WA	....	....	....	....	....	....	224.3	....
General government	4 753 ZB	268.5	126.0	96.1	61.1	379.6	203.0	368.3	308.1
Banks	4 753 ZC	2.2	−4.6	7.0	37.7	83.9	97.0	37.6	69.8
Other sectors	4 753 ZD	−5.4	19.8	31.3	38.8	48.0	64.3	183.0	213.6
Total, Groups A Through C	4 983 ..	*143.6*	*393.0*	*531.1*	*3,783.2*	*681.0*	*−159.0*	*566.5*	*−591.5*
D. Net Errors and Omissions	4 998 ..	**−146.4**	**−270.5**	**−449.4**	**−8.8**	**−11.8**	**97.2**	**−282.0**	**295.1**
Total, Groups A Through D	4 984 ..	*−2.8*	*122.5*	*81.7*	*3,774.5*	*669.2*	*−61.8*	*284.5*	*−296.4*
E. Reserves and Related Items	4 802 A.	**2.8**	**−122.5**	**−81.7**	**−3,774.5**	**−669.2**	**61.8**	**−284.5**	**296.4**
Reserve assets	4 802 ..	−77.1	−162.0	−92.5	−403.0	−748.7	2.3	−353.4	212.0
Use of Fund credit and loans	4 766 ..	−42.6	−52.7	−46.2	−124.0	....	....	....	−.3
Exceptional financing	4 920 ..	122.5	92.2	56.9	−3,247.5	79.5	59.5	68.9	84.7
Conversion rates: Uganda shillings per U.S. dollar	0 101 ..	**1,963.7**	**1,810.3**	**1,780.7**	**1,831.5**	**1,723.5**	**1,720.4**	**2,030.5**	**2,177.6**

[1] Excludes components that have been classified in the categories of Group E.

2011, International Monetary Fund: *Balance of Payments Statistics Yearbook*

Table 2. STANDARD PRESENTATION, 2003–2010

(Millions of U.S. dollars)

	Code	2003	2004	2005	2006	2007	2008	2009	2010
CURRENT ACCOUNT............................	4 993 ..	**−115.0**	**−75.3**	**−26.0**	**−396.2**	**−701.1**	**−1,313.7**	**−1,064.1**	**−1,739.9**
A. GOODS..	4 100 ..	**−630.5**	**−667.6**	**−729.8**	**−1,027.9**	**−1,182.0**	**−1,835.1**	**−1,460.8**	**−2,100.4**
Credit..	2 100 ..	**572.2**	**759.1**	**1,015.8**	**1,187.6**	**1,776.2**	**2,207.6**	**2,326.6**	**2,164.0**
General merchandise: exports f.o.b...........	2 110 ..	496.0	657.2	911.3	1,028.5	1,670.0	2,103.2	2,200.7	2,026.9
Goods for processing: exports f.o.b...........	2 150 ..	....	....	....	....	....	....	....	....
Repairs on goods....................................	2 160 ..	....	....	....	....	....	....	....	....
Goods procured in ports by carriers.........	2 170 ..	30.4	28.1	31.5	36.2	40.4	54.2	102.8	107.0
Nonmonetary gold..................................	2 180 ..	45.8	73.8	73.0	122.9	65.8	50.3	23.1	30.1
Debit...	3 100 ..	**−1,202.7**	**−1,426.8**	**−1,745.6**	**−2,215.6**	**−2,958.2**	**−4,042.8**	**−3,787.3**	**−4,264.4**
General merchandise: imports f.o.b...........	3 110 ..	−1,202.7	−1,426.8	−1,745.6	−2,215.6	−2,958.2	−4,042.8	−3,787.3	−4,264.4
Goods for processing: imports f.o.b...........	3 150 ..	....	....	....	....	....	....	....	....
Repairs on goods....................................	3 160 ..	....	....	....	....	....	....	....	....
Goods procured in ports by carriers.........	3 170 ..	....	....	....	....	....	....	....	....
Nonmonetary gold..................................	3 180 ..	....	....	....	....	....	....	....	....
B. SERVICES....................................	4 200 ..	**−117.0**	**−116.4**	**−83.8**	**−244.7**	**−384.1**	**−458.1**	**−456.3**	**−525.0**
Total credit......................................	2 200 ..	*261.8*	*373.2*	*525.1*	*525.8*	*592.9*	*798.8*	*966.9*	*1,310.1*
Total debit.......................................	3 200 ..	*−378.8*	*−489.6*	*−608.8*	*−770.5*	*−977.0*	*−1,256.8*	*−1,423.2*	*−1,835.1*
Transportation services, credit............	2 205 ..	**8.9**	**9.6**	**11.0**	**11.8**	**16.6**	**53.2**	**35.6**	**47.0**
Passenger...	2 850 ..	*1.0*	*1.4*	*1.9*	*1.4*	*3.7*	*38.1*	*20.5*	*31.9*
Freight..	2 851 ..	....	....	....	....	....	....	....	....
Other..	2 852 ..	*7.9*	*8.2*	*9.1*	*10.3*	*12.9*	*15.1*	*15.1*	*15.1*
Sea transport, passenger.........................	2 207 ..	....	....	....	....	....	....	....	....
Sea transport, freight.............................	2 208 ..	....	....	....	....	....	....	....	....
Sea transport, other...............................	2 209 ..	....	....	....	....	....	....	....	....
Air transport, passenger..........................	2 211 ..	....	....	....	....	....	28.0	11.1	22.2
Air transport, freight..............................	2 212 ..	....	....	....	....	....	....	....	....
Air transport, other................................	2 213 ..	....	....	....	....	....	....	....	....
Other transport, passenger......................	2 215 ..	1.0	1.4	1.9	1.4	3.7	10.1	9.4	9.7
Other transport, freight...........................	2 216 ..	....	....	....	....	....	....	....	....
Other transport, other............................	2 217 ..	7.9	8.2	9.1	10.3	12.9	15.1	15.1	15.1
Transportation services, debit..............	3 205 ..	**−227.6**	**−267.8**	**−353.1**	**−468.1**	**−619.5**	**−885.1**	**−863.5**	**−1,002.2**
Passenger...	3 850 ..	*−44.0*	*−49.9*	*−61.2*	*−72.9*	*−88.1*	*−158.8*	*−157.5*	*−139.1*
Freight..	3 851 ..	*−183.6*	*−217.9*	*−292.0*	*−395.2*	*−531.4*	*−726.2*	*−706.0*	*−863.0*
Other..	3 852 ..	....	....	....	....	....	....	....	....
Sea transport, passenger.........................	3 207 ..	....	....	....	....	....	....	....	....
Sea transport, freight.............................	3 208 ..	....	....	....	....	....	....	....	....
Sea transport, other...............................	3 209 ..	....	....	....	....	....	....	....	....
Air transport, passenger..........................	3 211 ..	−41.9	−46.8	−57.4	−70.1	−84.1	−153.6	−154.1	−134.4
Air transport, freight..............................	3 212 ..	....	....	−24.0	−63.0	−100.4	−118.1	−109.4	−131.7
Air transport, other................................	3 213 ..	....	....	....	....	....	....	....	....
Other transport, passenger......................	3 215 ..	−2.1	−3.2	−3.8	−2.9	−4.0	−5.2	−3.4	−4.8
Other transport, freight...........................	3 216 ..	−183.6	−217.9	−268.0	−332.2	−431.0	−608.1	−596.6	−731.4
Other transport, other............................	3 217 ..	....	....	....	....	....	....	....	....
Travel, credit.................................	2 236 ..	**184.2**	**267.0**	**379.9**	**345.9**	**398.3**	**498.3**	**667.1**	**729.9**
Business travel.....................................	2 237 ..	51.6	74.8	106.4	96.8	111.5	139.5	404.7	303.6
Personal travel.....................................	2 240 ..	132.6	192.2	273.5	249.0	286.7	358.8	262.4	426.3
Travel, debit..................................	3 236 ..	**....**	**−108.1**	**−124.4**	**−122.9**	**−132.0**	**−155.5**	**−178.7**	**−250.1**
Business travel.....................................	3 237 ..	....	−63.8	−73.4	−72.5	−77.9	−73.1	−89.5	−139.3
Personal travel.....................................	3 240 ..	....	−44.3	−51.0	−50.4	−54.1	−82.4	−89.1	−110.8
Other services, credit........................	2 200 BA ..	**68.7**	**96.5**	**134.2**	**168.2**	**178.0**	**247.3**	**264.2**	**533.2**
Communications...................................	2 245 ..	16.6	18.7	17.9	24.2	27.8	32.0	22.2	29.5
Construction..	2 249 ..	....	....	....	....	....	....	....	....
Insurance...	2 253 ..	3.2	4.1	7.4	8.8	10.9	7.6	17.8	12.2
Financial..	2 260 ..	6.5	9.2	11.3	11.9	14.7	19.0	17.5	22.2
Computer and information.......................	2 262 ..	.7	7.9	32.8	31.5	8.8	24.0	36.4	39.0
Royalties and licence fees.......................	2 266 ..	.6	....	7.4	2.4	.5	2.8	3.0	3.9
Other business services..........................	2 268 ..	28.4	33.9	20.8	32.4	38.0	64.8	54.5	99.9
Personal, cultural, and recreational...........	2 287 ..	....	....	....	....	....	....	....	....
Government, n.i.e..................................	2 291 ..	12.7	22.8	36.6	57.1	77.3	97.0	112.7	326.5
Other services, debit.........................	3 200 BA ..	**−151.1**	**−113.7**	**−131.3**	**−179.4**	**−225.5**	**−216.2**	**−381.1**	**−582.8**
Communications...................................	3 245 ..	−10.1	−11.4	−10.9	−14.7	−19.1	−21.7	−13.5	−16.8
Construction..	3 249 ..	....	....	....	....	....	....	....	....
Insurance...	3 253 ..	−29.6	−39.2	−47.9	−56.9	−75.5	−91.5	−138.6	−220.7
Financial..	3 260 ..	−2.3	−2.8	−3.3	−3.3	−4.2	−5.0	−5.3	−6.8
Computer and information.......................	3 262 ..	−3.2	−10.8	−22.2	−17.6	−10.3	−12.1	−23.4	−33.8
Royalties and licence fees.......................	3 266 ..	−7.9	−1.4	−1.5	−10.6	−4.8	−1.8	−3.3	−4.4
Other business services..........................	3 268 ..	−83.1	−31.2	−30.1	−61.6	−92.2	−61.3	−182.8	−274.6
Personal, cultural, and recreational...........	3 287 ..	....	....	....	....	....	....	....	....
Government, n.i.e..................................	3 291 ..	−14.8	−16.9	−15.5	−14.6	−19.4	−22.9	−14.1	−25.8

Table 2 (Continued). STANDARD PRESENTATION, 2003–2010

(Millions of U.S. dollars)

	Code	2003	2004	2005	2006	2007	2008	2009	2010
C. INCOME	4 300	**−143.2**	**−293.1**	**−249.1**	**−239.1**	**−242.7**	**−260.8**	**−294.4**	**−304.9**
Total credit	2 300	*27.6*	*35.7*	*49.8*	*71.9*	*97.1*	*130.2*	*41.9*	*20.1*
Total debit	3 300	*−170.8*	*−328.8*	*−298.9*	*−310.9*	*−339.8*	*−391.1*	*−336.3*	*−325.0*
Compensation of employees, credit	2 310	....	....	....	....	....	....	....	....
Compensation of employees, debit	3 310	**−47.4**	**−54.4**	**−52.2**	**−21.1**	**−32.5**	**−57.4**	**−89.5**	**−73.3**
Investment income, credit	2 320	**27.6**	**35.7**	**49.8**	**71.9**	**97.1**	**130.2**	**41.9**	**20.1**
Direct investment income	2 330	....	....	....	....	....	....	....	....
Dividends and distributed branch profits	2 332	....	....	....	....	....	....	....	....
Reinvested earnings and undistributed branch profits	2 333	....	....	....	....	....	....	....	....
Income on debt (interest)	2 334	....	....	....	....	....	....	....	....
Portfolio investment income	2 339	....	....	....	....	....	....	....	....
Income on equity	2 340								
Income on bonds and notes	2 350	....							
Income on money market instruments	2 360	....							
Other investment income	2 370	27.6	35.7	49.8	71.9	97.1	130.2	41.9	20.1
Investment income, debit	3 320	**−123.4**	**−274.4**	**−246.7**	**−289.8**	**−307.3**	**−333.7**	**−246.9**	**−251.8**
Direct investment income	3 330	−82.6	−218.6	−201.7	−248.7	−261.6	−249.9	−164.1	−191.5
Dividends and distributed branch profits	3 332	−29.2	−77.8	−71.6	−88.4	−92.8	−80.6	−46.9	−62.8
Reinvested earnings and undistributed branch profits	3 333	−51.9	−139.0	−128.0	−157.1	−164.9	−164.7	−111.9	−122.5
Income on debt (interest)	3 334	−1.5	−1.8	−2.1	−3.2	−3.8	−4.5	−5.3	−6.2
Portfolio investment income	3 339	−1.0	−2.9	−2.8	−3.5	−13.0	−45.3	−34.0	−2.3
Income on equity	3 340	−.1	−.1	−1.8	−2.1	−3.3	−18.6	−27.6	....
Income on bonds and notes	3 350	....	....	−.2	−.5	−4.1	−14.5	−3.5	−1.5
Income on money market instruments	3 360	−.9	−2.8	−.8	−.8	−5.7	−12.2	−2.9	−.9
Other investment income	3 370	−39.9	−53.0	−42.2	−37.6	−32.6	−38.6	−48.7	−57.9
D. CURRENT TRANSFERS	4 379	**775.7**	**1,001.8**	**1,036.6**	**1,115.4**	**1,107.8**	**1,240.3**	**1,147.5**	**1,190.5**
Credit	2 379	**912.5**	**1,143.5**	**1,181.4**	**1,300.9**	**1,311.0**	**1,564.0**	**1,541.2**	**1,719.2**
General government	2 380	473.5	680.8	598.5	557.7	322.9	332.8	357.8	577.2
Other sectors	2 390	439.0	462.7	583.0	743.3	988.1	1,231.2	1,183.4	1,142.1
Workers' remittances	2 391	298.8	310.5	321.8	411.0	451.6	723.5	778.3	914.5
Other current transfers	2 392	140.2	152.2	261.2	332.3	536.6	507.7	405.1	227.6
Debit	3 379	**−136.8**	**−141.7**	**−144.8**	**−185.5**	**−203.2**	**−323.7**	**−393.8**	**−528.7**
General government	3 380	−2.4	−1.9		−.5			−1.7	
Other sectors	3 390	−134.5	−139.7	−144.8	−185.0	−203.2	−323.7	−392.1	−528.7
Workers' remittances	3 391	−134.5	−139.7	−144.8	−185.0	−203.2	−323.7	−392.1	−528.7
Other current transfers	3 392	....	....	....	....	....	....	....	....
CAPITAL AND FINANCIAL ACCOUNT	4 996	**261.4**	**345.8**	**475.4**	**405.0**	**712.9**	**1,216.5**	**1,346.1**	**1,444.8**
CAPITAL ACCOUNT	4 994	**61.0**	**63.8**	**64.3**	**3,612.9**	**68.6**	**46.5**	**44.9**	**46.0**
Total credit	2 994	*61.0*	*63.8*	*64.3*	*3,612.9*	*68.6*	*46.5*	*44.9*	*46.0*
Total debit	3 994	....	....	....	....	....	....	....	....
Capital transfers, credit	2 400	**61.0**	**63.8**	**64.3**	**3,612.9**	**68.6**	**46.5**	**44.9**	**46.0**
General government	2 401	61.0	63.8	64.3	3,612.9	68.6	46.5	44.9	46.0
Debt forgiveness	2 402	61.0	63.8	64.3	3,612.9	68.6	46.5	44.9	46.0
Other capital transfers	2 410	....	....						....
Other sectors	2 430	....	....						....
Migrants' transfers	2 431	....	....						....
Debt forgiveness	2 432	....	....						....
Other capital transfers	2 440	....	....						....
Capital transfers, debit	3 400	**....**	**....**	**....**	**....**	**....**	**....**	**....**	**....**
General government	3 401	....	....						....
Debt forgiveness	3 402	....	....						....
Other capital transfers	3 410	....	....						....
Other sectors	3 430	....	....						....
Migrants' transfers	3 431	....	....						....
Debt forgiveness	3 432	....	....						....
Other capital transfers	3 440	....	....						....
Nonproduced nonfinancial assets, credit	2 480	**....**	**....**	**....**	**....**	**....**	**....**	**....**	**....**
Nonproduced nonfinancial assets, debit	3 480	**....**	**....**	**....**	**....**	**....**	**....**	**....**	**....**

Table 2 (Continued). STANDARD PRESENTATION, 2003–2010

(Millions of U.S. dollars)

	Code	2003	2004	2005	2006	2007	2008	2009	2010
FINANCIAL ACCOUNT	4 995	**200.5**	**281.9**	**411.1**	**−3,207.9**	**644.3**	**1,170.0**	**1,301.2**	**1,398.8**
A. DIRECT INVESTMENT	4 500	**202.2**	**295.4**	**379.8**	**644.3**	**792.3**	**728.9**	**788.7**	**817.2**
Direct investment abroad	4 505	....	....	....	....	....	....	....	....
Equity capital	4 510	....	....	....	....	....	....	....	....
Claims on affiliated enterprises	4 515	....	....	....	....	....	....	....	....
Liabilities to affiliated enterprises	4 520	....	....	....	....	....	....	....	....
Reinvested earnings	4 525	....	....	....	....	....	....	....	....
Other capital	4 530	....	....	....	....	....	....	....	....
Claims on affiliated enterprises	4 535	....	....	....	....	....	....	....	....
Liabilities to affiliated enterprises	4 540	....	....	....	....	....	....	....	....
Direct investment in Uganda	4 555	**202.2**	**295.4**	**379.8**	**644.3**	**792.3**	**728.9**	**788.7**	**817.2**
Equity capital	4 560	102.1	166.9	253.2	482.7	577.2	412.9	633.0	645.7
Claims on direct investors	4 565	....	....	....	....	....	....	....	....
Liabilities to direct investors	4 570	102.1	166.9	253.2	482.7	577.2	412.9	633.0	645.7
Reinvested earnings	4 575	51.9	139.0	128.0	157.1	164.9	164.7	111.9	122.5
Other capital	4 580	48.2	−10.4	−1.4	4.5	50.2	151.2	43.8	49.0
Claims on direct investors	4 585	....	....	....	....	....	....	....	....
Liabilities to direct investors	4 590	48.2	−10.4	−1.4	4.5	50.2	151.2	43.8	49.0
B. PORTFOLIO INVESTMENT	4 600	**16.0**	**6.2**	**−13.4**	**21.7**	**44.9**	**17.6**	**28.7**	**−110.5**
Assets	4 602	**−4.3**	....	....	....	....	**−12.1**	....	....
Equity securities	4 610	−4.3	....	....	....	....	−12.1	....	....
Monetary authorities	4 611	....	....	....	....	....	....	....	....
General government	4 612	....	....	....	....	....	....	....	....
Banks	4 613	....	....	....	....	....	....	....	....
Other sectors	4 614	−4.3	....	....	....	....	−12.1	....	....
Debt securities	4 619	....	....	....	....	....	....	....	....
Bonds and notes	4 620	....	....	....	....	....	....	....	....
Monetary authorities	4 621	....	....	....	....	....	....	....	....
General government	4 622	....	....	....	....	....	....	....	....
Banks	4 623	....	....	....	....	....	....	....	....
Other sectors	4 624	....	....	....	....	....	....	....	....
Money market instruments	4 630	....	....	....	....	....	....	....	....
Monetary authorities	4 631	....	....	....	....	....	....	....	....
General government	4 632	....	....	....	....	....	....	....	....
Banks	4 633	....	....	....	....	....	....	....	....
Other sectors	4 634	....	....	....	....	....	....	....	....
Liabilities	4 652	**20.3**	**6.2**	**−13.4**	**21.7**	**44.9**	**29.7**	**28.7**	**−110.5**
Equity securities	4 660	....	24.0	....	19.1	−23.1	13.1	131.1	−70.5
Banks	4 663	....	24.0	....	19.1	−23.2	2.4	127.7	−74.2
Other sectors	4 664	....	....	....	....	.1	10.7	3.4	3.7
Debt securities	4 669	20.3	−17.8	−13.4	2.5	68.0	16.6	−102.3	−40.0
Bonds and notes	4 670	....	.7	1.9	3.1	16.0	10.0	−47.9	−26.9
Monetary authorities	4 671	....	....	....	....	....	....	....	....
General government	4 672	....	.7	1.9	3.1	16.0	10.0	−47.9	−26.9
Banks	4 673	....	....	....	....	....	....	....	....
Other sectors	4 674	....	....	....	....	....	....	....	....
Money market instruments	4 680	20.3	−18.5	−15.2	−.6	52.0	6.6	−54.5	−13.1
Monetary authorities	4 681	....	....	....	....	....	....	....	....
General government	4 682	20.3	−18.5	−15.2	−.6	52.0	6.6	−54.5	−13.1
Banks	4 683	....	....	....	....	....	....	....	....
Other sectors	4 684	....	....	....	....	....	....	....	....
C. FINANCIAL DERIVATIVES	4 910	....	....	....	....	**1.4**	**6.9**	**−6.2**	**−1.4**
Monetary authorities	4 911	....	....	....	....	....	....	....	....
General government	4 912	....	....	....	....	....	....	....	....
Banks	4 913	....	....	....	....	1.4	6.9	−6.2	−1.4
Other sectors	4 914	....	....	....	....	....	....	....	....
Assets	4 900	....	....	....	....	....	....	....	....
Monetary authorities	4 901	....	....	....	....	....	....	....	....
General government	4 902	....	....	....	....	....	....	....	....
Banks	4 903	....	....	....	....	....	....	....	....
Other sectors	4 904	....	....	....	....	....	....	....	....
Liabilities	4 905	....	....	....	....	**1.4**	**6.9**	**−6.2**	**−1.4**
Monetary authorities	4 906	....	....	....	....	....	....	....	....
General government	4 907	....	....	....	....	....	....	....	....
Banks	4 908	....	....	....	....	1.4	6.9	−6.2	−1.4
Other sectors	4 909	....	....	....	....	....	....	....	....

Table 2 (Concluded). STANDARD PRESENTATION, 2003–2010

(Millions of U.S. dollars)

	Code	2003	2004	2005	2006	2007	2008	2009	2010
D. OTHER INVESTMENT	4 700	**59.3**	**142.3**	**137.2**	**−3,470.8**	**554.4**	**414.4**	**843.4**	**481.6**
Assets	4 703	**−224.9**	**25.5**	**56.4**	**−52.1**	**32.0**	**37.1**	**6.0**	**−148.3**
Trade credits	4 706	....	....	....	....	....	....	....	....
General government	4 707	....	....	....	....	....	....	....	....
of which: Short-term	4 709	....	....	....	....	....	....	....	....
Other sectors	4 710	....	....	....	....	....	....	....	....
of which: Short-term	4 712	....	....	....	....	....	....	....	....
Loans	4 714	....	−.4	−8.8	4.2	−.7	5.1	.7	....
Monetary authorities	4 715	....	....	....	....	....	....	....	....
of which: Short-term	4 718	....	....	....	....	....	....	....	....
General government	4 719	....	....	....	....	....	....	....	....
of which: Short-term	4 721	....	....	....	....	....	....	....	....
Banks	4 722	....	−.4	−8.8	4.2	−.7	5.1	.7	....
of which: Short-term	4 724	....	−.4	−8.8	4.2	−.7	5.1	.7	....
Other sectors	4 725	....	....	....	....	....	....	....	....
of which: Short-term	4 727	....	....	....	....	....	....	....	....
Currency and deposits	4 730	−224.9	27.0	65.2	−56.4	17.2	32.0	5.3	−148.4
Monetary authorities	4 731	8.9	12.5	3.7	−7.0	5.8	−17.7	−16.3	16.1
General government	4 732	−37.1	−21.1	1.9	16.3	83.1	48.4	57.7	−42.7
Banks	4 733	−109.7	−3.4	52.0	−110.6	−56.6	−24.7	35.9	−121.7
Other sectors	4 734	−87.0	39.0	7.7	45.0	−15.0	26.0	−72.0	....
Other assets	4 736	....	−1.1	....	....	15.4			
Monetary authorities	4 737	....	−.7	....	....	15.4			
of which: Short-term	4 739	....	....	....	....	....			
General government	4 740	....	−.4	....	....	....	....	....	....
of which: Short-term	4 742	....	....	....	....	....	....	....	....
Banks	4 743	....	....	....	....	....	....	....	....
of which: Short-term	4 745	....	....	....	....	....	....	....	....
Other sectors	4 746	....	....	....	....	....	....	....	....
of which: Short-term	4 748	....	....	....	....	....	....	....	....
Liabilities	4 753	**284.2**	**116.8**	**80.8**	**−3,418.7**	**522.4**	**377.3**	**837.3**	**629.9**
Trade credits	4 756	3.3	13.0	16.5	17.9	22.3	25.1	27.1	26.4
General government	4 757	....	....	....	....	....	....	....	....
of which: Short-term	4 759	....	....	....	....	....	....	....	....
Other sectors	4 760	3.3	13.0	16.5	17.9	22.3	25.1	27.1	26.4
of which: Short-term	4 762	3.3	13.0	16.5	17.9	22.3	25.1	27.1	26.4
Loans	4 764	272.2	101.1	61.0	−3,469.0	421.2	246.4	506.9	533.7
Monetary authorities	4 765	−42.6	−52.7	−46.2	−124.0	....	....	....	−.3
of which: Use of Fund credit and loans from the Fund	4 766	−42.6	−52.7	−46.2	−124.0	....	....	....	−.3
of which: Short-term	4 768	....	....	....	....	....	....	....	....
General government	4 769	271.9	129.0	71.9	−3,390.0	366.0	187.9	356.1	305.7
of which: Short-term	4 771	....	....	....	....	....	....	....	....
Banks	4 772	....	....	....	....	....	....	....	....
of which: Short-term	4 774	....	....	....	....	....	....	....	....
Other sectors	4 775	42.9	24.8	35.2	45.0	55.2	58.5	150.8	228.3
of which: Short-term	4 777	10.6	9.9	10.2	13.2	14.2	14.9	17.2	20.3
Currency and deposits	4 780	−5.9	11.9	−13.9	25.5	67.7	44.1	−.3	71.8
Monetary authorities	4 781	....	....	....	....	....	....	....	....
General government	4 782	....	....	....	....	....	....	....	....
Banks	4 783	−5.9	11.9	−13.9	25.5	67.7	44.1	−.3	71.8
Other sectors	4 784	....	....	....	....	....	....	....	....
Other liabilities	4 786	14.6	−9.2	17.1	7.0	11.2	61.6	303.7	−2.0
Monetary authorities	4 787	....	....	....	....	....	....	224.3	
of which: Short-term	4 789	....	....	....	....	....	....	....	
General government	4 790	6.5	7.4	−3.8	−5.2	−5.0	−4.4	....	....
of which: Short-term	4 792	6.5	7.4	−3.8	−5.2	−5.0	−4.4	....	....
Banks	4 793	8.1	−16.6	20.9	12.2	16.2	52.9	38.0	−2.0
of which: Short-term	4 795	8.1	−16.6	20.9	12.2	16.2	52.9	38.0	−2.0
Other sectors	4 796	....	....	....	....	....	13.1	41.4	....
of which: Short-term	4 798	....	....	....	....	....	13.1	10.4	....
E. RESERVE ASSETS	4 802	**−77.1**	**−162.0**	**−92.5**	**−403.0**	**−748.7**	**2.3**	**−353.4**	**212.0**
Monetary gold	4 812	....	....	....	....	....	....	....	....
Special drawing rights	4 811	−1.4	4.2	−.9	1.1	−.2	....	−224.1	.4
Reserve position in the Fund	4 810	....	....	....	....	....	....	....	....
Foreign exchange	4 803	−75.7	−166.3	−91.6	−404.1	−748.5	2.2	−129.3	211.6
Other claims	4 813	....	....	....	....	....	....	....	....
NET ERRORS AND OMISSIONS	4 998	**−146.4**	**−270.5**	**−449.4**	**−8.8**	**−11.8**	**97.2**	**−282.0**	**295.1**

Table 3. INTERNATIONAL INVESTMENT POSITION (End-period stocks), 2003–2010

(Millions of U.S. dollars)

	Code	2003	2004	2005	2006	2007	2008	2009	2010
ASSETS	8 995 C.	**1,844.5**	**2,069.8**	**2,013.6**	**2,617.0**	**3,400.6**	**3,090.8**	**3,892.0**	**3,710.6**
Direct investment abroad	8 505 ..	....	....	....	....	....	....	....	....
Equity capital and reinvested earnings	8 506 ..	....	....	....	....	....	....	....	....
Claims on affiliated enterprises	8 507 ..	....	....	....	....	....	....	....	....
Liabilities to affiliated enterprises	8 508 ..	....	....	....	....	....	....	....	....
Other capital	8 530 ..	....	....	....	....	....	....	....	....
Claims on affiliated enterprises	8 535 ..	....	....	....	....	....	....	....	....
Liabilities to affiliated enterprises	8 540 ..	....	....	....	....	....	....	....	....
Portfolio investment	8 602 ..	....	....	....	....	....	....	....	....
Equity securities	8 610 ..	....	....	....	....	....	....	....	....
Monetary authorities	8 611 ..	....	....	....	....	....	....	....	....
General government	8 612 ..	....	....	....	....	....	....	....	....
Banks	8 613 ..	....	....	....	....	....	....	....	....
Other sectors	8 614 ..	....	....	....	....	....	....	....	....
Debt securities	8 619 ..	....	....	....	....	....	....	....	....
Bonds and notes	8 620 ..	....	....	....	....	....	....	....	....
Monetary authorities	8 621 ..	....	....	....	....	....	....	....	....
General government	8 622 ..	....	....	....	....	....	....	....	....
Banks	8 623 ..	....	....	....	....	....	....	....	....
Other sectors	8 624 ..	....	....	....	....	....	....	....	....
Money market instruments	8 630 ..	....	....	....	....	....	....	....	....
Monetary authorities	8 631 ..	....	....	....	....	....	....	....	....
General government	8 632 ..	....	....	....	....	....	....	....	....
Banks	8 633 ..	....	....	....	....	....	....	....	....
Other sectors	8 634 ..	....	....	....	....	....	....	....	....
Financial derivatives	8 900 ..	....	....	....	....	....	....	....	....
Monetary authorities	8 901 ..	....	....	....	....	....	....	....	....
General government	8 902 ..	....	....	....	....	....	....	....	....
Banks	8 903 ..	....	....	....	....	....	....	....	....
Other sectors	8 904 ..	....	....	....	....	....	....	....	....
Other investment	8 703 ..	**764.2**	**761.7**	**669.4**	**806.1**	**969.8**	**874.0**	**1,122.3**	**1,111.8**
Trade credits	8 706 ..	....	....	....	....	....	....	....	....
General government	8 707 ..	....	....	....	....	....	....	....	....
of which: Short-term	8 709 ..	....	....	....	....	....	....	....	....
Other sectors	8 710 ..	....	....	....	....	....	....	....	....
of which: Short-term	8 712 ..	....	....	....	....	....	....	....	....
Loans	8 714 ..	....	1.0	10.0	6.0	6.8	1.3	.5	.4
Monetary authorities	8 715 ..	....	....	....	....	....	....	....	....
of which: Short-term	8 718 ..	....	....	....	....	....	....	....	....
General government	8 719 ..	....	....	....	....	....	....	....	....
of which: Short-term	8 721 ..	....	....	....	....	....	....	....	....
Banks	8 722 ..	....	1.0	10.0	6.0	6.8	1.3	.5	.4
of which: Short-term	8 724 ..	....	*1.0*	*10.0*	*6.0*	*6.8*	*1.3*	*.5*	*.4*
Other sectors	8 725 ..	....	....	....	....	....	....	....	....
of which: Short-term	8 727 ..	....	....	....	....	....	....	....	....
Currency and deposits	8 730 ..	764.2	759.7	658.4	799.1	963.0	872.7	1,121.8	1,111.4
Monetary authorities	8 731 ..	26.0	13.5	9.8	16.9	11.1	28.8	45.1	28.9
General government	8 732 ..	....	....	....	48.2	128.9	83.7	247.3	238.4
Banks	8 733 ..	362.2	410.2	339.6	470.1	544.0	505.2	500.5	515.1
Other sectors	8 734 ..	376.0	336.0	309.0	264.0	279.0	255.0	329.0	329.0
Other assets	8 736 ..	....	1.1	1.1	1.1	....	....	....	....
Monetary authorities	8 737 ..	....	.7	.7	.7	....	....	....	....
of which: Short-term	8 739 ..	....	....	....	....	....	....	....	....
General government	8 740 ..	....	.4	.4	.4	....	....	....	....
of which: Short-term	8 742 ..	....	....	....	....	....	....	....	....
Banks	8 743 ..	....	....	....	....	....	....	....	....
of which: Short-term	8 745 ..	....	....	....	....	....	....	....	....
Other sectors	8 746 ..	....	....	....	....	....	....	....	....
of which: Short-term	8 748 ..	....	....	....	....	....	....	....	....
Reserve assets	8 802 ..	**1,080.3**	**1,308.1**	**1,344.2**	**1,810.9**	**2,430.9**	**2,216.8**	**2,769.6**	**2,598.8**
Monetary gold	8 812 ..	....	....	....	....	....	....	....	....
Special drawing rights	8 811 ..	4.8	.7	1.1	.1	.3	.2	225.2	220.8
Reserve position in the Fund	8 810 ..	....	....	....	....	....	....	....	....
Foreign exchange	8 803 ..	1,075.5	1,307.4	1,343.1	1,810.8	2,430.6	2,216.6	2,544.4	2,378.0
Other claims	8 813 ..	....	....	....	....	....	....	....	....

Table 3 (Concluded). INTERNATIONAL INVESTMENT POSITION (End-period stocks), 2003–2010

(Millions of U.S. dollars)

	Code	2003	2004	2005	2006	2007	2008	2009	2010
LIABILITIES	8 995 D.	**6,104.6**	**6,900.4**	**6,856.3**	**4,755.9**	**5,758.7**	**6,803.5**	**8,584.0**	**9,994.8**
Direct investment in Uganda	8 555 ..	**1,349.1**	**1,644.6**	**2,024.4**	**2,668.6**	**3,460.9**	**4,189.8**	**4,978.5**	**5,795.7**
Equity capital and reinvested earnings	8 556 ..	996.0	1,301.9	1,683.1	2,322.9	3,065.0	3,642.7	4,387.5	5,155.7
Claims on direct investors	8 557 ..	....	....	....	....	....	....	....	....
Liabilities to direct investors	8 558 ..	996.0	1,301.9	1,683.1	2,322.9	3,065.0	3,642.7	4,387.5	5,155.7
Other capital	8 580 ..	353.1	342.7	341.2	345.7	395.9	547.1	591.0	640.0
Claims on direct investors	8 585 ..	....	....	....	....	....	....	....	....
Liabilities to direct investors	8 590 ..	353.1	342.7	341.2	345.7	395.9	547.1	591.0	640.0
Portfolio investment	8 652 ..	**16.9**	**29.1**	**32.8**	**51.6**	**148.3**	**128.9**	**194.9**	**119.6**
Equity securities	8 660 ..	.7	24.6	24.6	43.8	70.0	37.6	153.1	103.3
Banks	8 663 ..	.4	24.4	24.4	43.5	69.6	33.3	150.9	101.0
Other sectors	8 664 ..	.2	.3	.3	.3	.4	4.2	2.1	2.3
Debt securities	8 669 ..	16.2	4.4	8.1	7.8	78.3	91.3	41.8	16.2
Bonds and notes	8 670 ..	....	....	....	....	25.2	39.2	34.1	12.2
Monetary authorities	8 671 ..	....	....	....	....	....	....	....	....
General government	8 672 ..	....	....	....	....	25.2	39.2	34.1	12.2
Banks	8 673 ..	....	....	....	....	....	....	....	....
Other sectors	8 674 ..	....	....	....	....	....	....	....	....
Money market instruments	8 680 ..	16.2	4.4	8.1	7.8	53.1	52.1	7.7	4.0
Monetary authorities	8 681 ..	....	....	....	....	....	....	....	....
General government	8 682 ..	16.2	4.4	8.1	7.8	53.1	52.1	7.7	4.0
Banks	8 683 ..	....	....	....	....	....	....	....	....
Other sectors	8 684 ..	....	....	....	....	....	....	....	....
Financial derivatives	8 905 ..	....	....	....	....	....	....	....	.5
Monetary authorities	8 906 ..	....	....	....	....	....	....	....	....
General government	8 907 ..	....	....	....	....	....	....	....	....
Banks	8 908 ..	....	....	....	....	....	....	....	....
Other sectors	8 909 ..	....	....	....	....	....	....	....	....
Other investment	8 753 ..	**4,738.6**	**5,226.8**	**4,799.1**	**2,035.7**	**2,149.5**	**2,484.8**	**3,410.6**	**4,079.0**
Trade credits	8 756 ..	....	....	....	....	....	....	....	....
General government	8 757 ..	....	....	....	....	....	....	....	....
of which: Short-term	8 759 ..	....	....	....	....	....	....	....	....
Other sectors	8 760 ..	....	....	....	....	....	....	....	....
of which: Short-term	8 762 ..	....	....	....	....	....	....	....	....
Loans	8 764 ..	4,673.7	5,157.4	4,725.6	1,918.8	1,947.4	2,234.0	2,840.6	3,499.6
Monetary authorities	8 765 ..	236.0	191.5	131.1	9.0	9.5	9.2	9.4	8.9
of which: Use of Fund credit and loans from the Fund	8 766 ..	*236.0*	*191.5*	*131.1*	*9.0*	*9.5*	*9.2*	*9.4*	*8.9*
of which: Short-term	8 768 ..	....	....	....	....	....	....	....	....
General government	8 769 ..	4,250.5	4,753.8	4,347.1	1,617.4	1,590.3	1,818.6	2,274.2	2,705.5
of which: Short-term	8 771 ..	....	....	....	....	....	....	....	....
Banks	8 772 ..	....	....	....	....	....	....	....	....
of which: Short-term	8 774 ..	....	....	....	....	....	....	....	....
Other sectors	8 775 ..	187.3	212.1	247.4	292.4	347.6	406.1	556.9	785.2
of which: Short-term	8 777 ..	*15.1*	*25.0*	*35.2*	*48.4*	*62.7*	*77.6*	*94.8*	*115.1*
Currency and deposits	8 780 ..	47.3	65.1	49.4	79.0	148.1	161.7	166.9	207.0
Monetary authorities	8 781 ..	....	....	....	....	....	....	....	....
General government	8 782 ..	....	....	....	....	....	....	....	....
Banks	8 783 ..	47.3	65.1	49.4	79.0	148.1	161.7	166.9	207.0
Other sectors	8 784 ..	....	....	....	....	....	....	....	....
Other liabilities	8 786 ..	17.6	4.3	24.1	37.9	54.0	89.1	403.1	372.4
Monetary authorities	8 787 ..	....	2.4	1.7	1.8	1.4	1.2	272.9	268.1
of which: Short-term	8 789 ..	....	*2.4*	*1.7*	*1.8*	*1.4*	*1.2*	*1.6*	*1.6*
General government	8 790 ..	....	....	....	....	....	....	....	....
of which: Short-term	8 792 ..	....	....	....	....	....	....	....	....
Banks	8 793 ..	17.6	1.9	22.5	36.1	52.6	87.9	130.2	104.3
of which: Short-term	8 795 ..	....	....	....	....	....	....	....	....
Other sectors	8 796 ..	....	....	....	....	....	....	....	....
of which: Short-term	8 798 ..	....	....	....	....	....	....	....	....
NET INTERNATIONAL INVESTMENT POSITION	8 995 ..	−4,260.1	−4,830.6	−4,842.6	−2,138.9	−2,358.1	−3,712.7	−4,692.0	−6,284.2
Conversion rates: Uganda shillings per U.S. dollar (end of period)	0 102 ..	1,935.3	1,738.6	1,816.9	1,741.4	1,697.3	1,949.2	1,899.7	2,308.3

Table 1. ANALYTIC PRESENTATION, 2003–2010

(Millions of U.S. dollars)

	Code	2003	2004	2005	2006	2007	2008	2009	2010
A. Current Account[1]	4 993 Z.	**2,891**	**6,909**	**2,531**	**−1,617**	**−5,272**	**−12,763**	**−1,732**	**−3,018**
Goods: exports f.o.b.	2 100 ..	23,739	33,432	35,024	38,949	49,840	67,717	40,394	52,191
Goods: imports f.o.b.	3 100 ..	−23,221	−29,691	−36,159	−44,143	−60,412	−83,808	−44,701	−60,579
Balance on Goods	4 100 ..	*518*	*3,741*	*−1,135*	*−5,194*	*−10,572*	*−16,091*	*−4,307*	*−8,388*
Services: credit	2 200 ..	5,214	7,859	9,354	11,290	14,161	17,895	13,859	17,064
Services: debit	3 200 ..	−4,444	−6,622	−7,548	−9,164	−11,741	−16,154	−11,505	−12,660
Balance on Goods and Services	4 991 ..	*1,288*	*4,978*	*671*	*−3,068*	*−8,152*	*−14,350*	*−1,953*	*−3,984*
Income: credit	2 300 ..	254	389	758	1,332	3,656	5,419	4,624	4,715
Income: debit	3 300 ..	−835	−1,034	−1,743	−3,054	−4,315	−6,959	−7,064	−6,724
Balance on Goods, Services, and Income	4 992 ..	*707*	*4,333*	*−314*	*−4,790*	*−8,811*	*−15,890*	*−4,393*	*−5,993*
Current transfers: credit	2 379 Z.	2,270	2,671	3,111	3,533	4,147	4,165	3,460	4,042
Current transfers: debit	3 379 ..	−86	−95	−266	−360	−608	−1,038	−799	−1,067
B. Capital Account[1]	4 994 Z.	**−17**	**7**	**−65**	**3**	**3**	**5**	**595**	**187**
Capital account: credit	2 994 Z.	11	21	14	22	27	28	618	250
Capital account: debit	3 994 ..	−28	−14	−79	−19	−24	−23	−23	−63
Total, Groups A Plus B	4 981 ..	*2,874*	*6,916*	*2,466*	*−1,614*	*−5,269*	*−12,758*	*−1,137*	*−2,831*
C. Financial Account[1]	4 995 W.	**133**	**−4,521**	**8,126**	**3,929**	**15,127**	**9,164**	**−10,884**	**6,508**
Direct investment abroad	4 505 ..	−13	−4	−275	133	−673	−1,010	−162	−736
Direct investment in Ukraine	4 555 Z.	1,424	1,715	7,808	5,604	9,891	10,913	4,816	6,495
Portfolio investment assets	4 602 ..	1	−6	....	−3	−29	12	−8	−17
Equity securities	4 610 ..	−4	−6	....	−2	−21	10	−6	4
Debt securities	4 619 ..	5	....	....	−1	−8	2	−2	−21
Portfolio investment liabilities	4 652 Z.	866	2,073	2,757	3,586	5,782	−1,292	−1,551	4,334
Equity securities	4 660 ..	84	−61	82	322	715	388	105	290
Debt securities	4 669 Z.	782	2,134	2,675	3,264	5,067	−1,680	−1,656	4,044
Financial derivatives	4 910 ..	....	....	....	....	....	....	....	....
Financial derivatives assets	4 900 ..	....	....	....	....	....	....	....	....
Financial derivatives liabilities	4 905 ..	....	....	....	....	....	....	....	....
Other investment assets	4 703 ..	−2,860	−12,495	−7,913	−15,580	−22,838	−22,884	−10,822	−10,748
Monetary authorities	4 701 ..	−30	−266	267	−111	52	9	−29	−202
General government	4 704 ..	....	....	−5	−3	....	....	....	−5
Banks	4 705 ..	−455	−906	−601	−1,098	−2,440	−1,826	−748	−1,869
Other sectors	4 728 ..	−2,375	−11,323	−7,574	−14,368	−20,450	−21,067	−10,045	−8,672
Other investment liabilities	4 753 W.	715	4,196	5,749	10,189	22,994	23,425	−3,157	7,180
Monetary authorities	4 753 WA	16	7	−18	−16	−20	−15	2,039	−7
General government	4 753 ZB	−379	79	−1	−404	−271	484	234	1,865
Banks	4 753 ZC	779	579	2,663	5,706	13,011	9,761	−7,519	−2,409
Other sectors	4 753 ZD	299	3,531	3,105	4,903	10,274	13,195	2,089	7,731
Total, Groups A Through C	4 983 ..	*3,007*	*2,395*	*10,592*	*2,315*	*9,858*	*−3,594*	*−12,021*	*3,677*
D. Net Errors and Omissions	4 998 ..	**−834**	**128**	**133**	**94**	**−452**	**569**	**306**	**1,368**
Total, Groups A Through D	4 984 ..	*2,173*	*2,523*	*10,725*	*2,409*	*9,406*	*−3,025*	*−11,715*	*5,045*
E. Reserves and Related Items	4 802 A.	**−2,173**	**−2,523**	**−10,725**	**−2,409**	**−9,406**	**3,025**	**11,715**	**−5,045**
Reserve assets	4 802 ..	−2,045	−2,226	−10,425	−1,999	−8,979	−1,081	5,653	−8,461
Use of Fund credit and loans	4 766 ..	−203	−298	−299	−410	−427	4,106	6,062	3,416
Exceptional financing	4 920 ..	75	....	....	....	....	....	....	....
Conversion rates: hryvnias per U.S. dollar	0 101 ..	**5.3327**	**5.3192**	**5.1247**	**5.0500**	**5.0500**	**5.2672**	**7.7912**	**7.9356**

[1] Excludes components that have been classified in the categories of Group E.

Table 2. STANDARD PRESENTATION, 2003–2010

(Millions of U.S. dollars)

	Code	2003	2004	2005	2006	2007	2008	2009	2010
CURRENT ACCOUNT	4 993	**2,891**	**6,909**	**2,531**	**−1,617**	**−5,272**	**−12,763**	**−1,732**	**−3,018**
A. GOODS	4 100	**518**	**3,741**	**−1,135**	**−5,194**	**−10,572**	**−16,091**	**−4,307**	**−8,388**
Credit	2 100	**23,739**	**33,432**	**35,024**	**38,949**	**49,840**	**67,717**	**40,394**	**52,191**
General merchandise: exports f.o.b.	2 110	21,430	30,572	32,164	36,146	46,126	63,124	37,098	47,271
Goods for processing: exports f.o.b.	2 150	2,123	2,525	2,511	2,496	3,346	4,108	2,830	4,471
Repairs on goods	2 160	179	326	332	279	326	426	430	421
Goods procured in ports by carriers	2 170	7	9	17	28	42	59	36	28
Nonmonetary gold	2 180	....	....	....	....	....	....	....	....
Debit	3 100	**−23,221**	**−29,691**	**−36,159**	**−44,143**	**−60,412**	**−83,808**	**−44,701**	**−60,579**
General merchandise: imports f.o.b.	3 110	−21,451	−27,699	−34,164	−41,952	−57,428	−80,684	−42,717	−57,809
Goods for processing: imports f.o.b.	3 150	−1,635	−1,832	−1,761	−1,891	−2,623	−2,574	−1,753	−2,471
Repairs on goods	3 160	−31	−20	−21	−32	−37	−35	−45	−46
Goods procured in ports by carriers	3 170	−104	−140	−213	−268	−324	−515	−186	−253
Nonmonetary gold	3 180	....	....	....	....	....	....	....	....
B. SERVICES	4 200	**770**	**1,237**	**1,806**	**2,126**	**2,420**	**1,741**	**2,354**	**4,404**
Total credit	2 200	*5,214*	*7,859*	*9,354*	*11,290*	*14,161*	*17,895*	*13,859*	*17,064*
Total debit	3 200	*−4,444*	*−6,622*	*−7,548*	*−9,164*	*−11,741*	*−16,154*	*−11,505*	*−12,660*
Transportation services, credit	2 205	**3,514**	**4,041**	**4,481**	**5,351**	**6,114**	**7,626**	**6,258**	**7,805**
Passenger	2 850	*269*	*371*	*417*	*533*	*723*	*954*	*773*	*908*
Freight	2 851	*2,426*	*2,556*	*2,635*	*3,261*	*3,376*	*3,824*	*2,969*	*4,292*
Other	2 852	*819*	*1,114*	*1,429*	*1,557*	*2,015*	*2,848*	*2,516*	*2,605*
Sea transport, passenger	2 207	1	4	5	4	3	3	....	4
Sea transport, freight	2 208	71	64	60	60	67	57	33	48
Sea transport, other	2 209	414	585	716	743	848	1,239	1,233	1,180
Air transport, passenger	2 211	155	227	268	355	467	637	477	577
Air transport, freight	2 212	91	85	93	125	160	238	265	275
Air transport, other	2 213	123	147	201	241	293	354	354	324
Other transport, passenger	2 215	113	140	144	174	253	314	296	327
Other transport, freight	2 216	2,264	2,407	2,482	3,076	3,149	3,529	2,671	3,969
Other transport, other	2 217	282	382	512	573	874	1,255	929	1,101
Transportation services, debit	3 205	**−1,358**	**−1,627**	**−2,051**	**−3,208**	**−3,902**	**−6,640**	**−3,544**	**−4,079**
Passenger	3 850	*−164*	*−197*	*−273*	*−368*	*−453*	*−562*	*−421*	*−392*
Freight	3 851	*−916*	*−1,049*	*−1,276*	*−2,257*	*−2,667*	*−4,977*	*−2,402*	*−2,799*
Other	3 852	*−278*	*−381*	*−502*	*−583*	*−782*	*−1,101*	*−721*	*−888*
Sea transport, passenger	3 207	....	....	....	....	−3	....	−2	....
Sea transport, freight	3 208	−70	−77	−143	−133	−256	−840	−302	−850
Sea transport, other	3 209	−92	−113	−155	−177	−177	−172	−104	−115
Air transport, passenger	3 211	−90	−112	−168	−239	−278	−346	−249	−200
Air transport, freight	3 212	−18	−21	−23	−33	−63	−265	−213	−290
Air transport, other	3 213	−78	−123	−158	−208	−282	−448	−362	−462
Other transport, passenger	3 215	−74	−85	−105	−129	−172	−216	−170	−192
Other transport, freight	3 216	−828	−951	−1,110	−2,091	−2,348	−3,872	−1,887	−1,659
Other transport, other	3 217	−108	−145	−189	−198	−323	−481	−255	−311
Travel, credit	2 236	**935**	**2,560**	**3,125**	**3,485**	**4,597**	**5,768**	**3,576**	**3,788**
Business travel	2 237	....	240	288	324	306	397	227	231
Personal travel	2 240	....	2,320	2,837	3,161	4,291	5,371	3,349	3,557
Travel, debit	3 236	**−789**	**−2,463**	**−2,805**	**−2,834**	**−3,569**	**−4,023**	**−3,330**	**−3,742**
Business travel	3 237	....	−574	−600	−415	−668	−1,069	−1,007	−1,101
Personal travel	3 240	....	−1,889	−2,205	−2,419	−2,901	−2,954	−2,323	−2,641
Other services, credit	2 200 BA	**765**	**1,258**	**1,748**	**2,454**	**3,450**	**4,501**	**4,025**	**5,471**
Communications	2 245	83	125	203	283	313	281	433	518
Construction	2 249	51	73	115	189	145	220	239	234
Insurance	2 253	14	18	25	70	86	64	42	32
Financial	2 260	20	24	36	80	322	486	370	475
Computer and information	2 262	17	30	44	97	191	316	344	429
Royalties and licence fees	2 266	14	40	22	32	53	72	112	132
Other business services	2 268	361	538	846	1,161	1,672	2,284	1,866	2,940
Personal, cultural, and recreational	2 287	4	11	16	74	158	185	84	113
Government, n.i.e.	2 291	201	399	441	468	510	593	535	598
Other services, debit	3 200 BA	**−2,297**	**−2,532**	**−2,692**	**−3,122**	**−4,270**	**−5,491**	**−4,631**	**−4,839**
Communications	3 245	−79	−105	−91	−91	−89	−144	−152	−126
Construction	3 249	−124	−201	−125	−126	−102	−71	−78	−145
Insurance	3 253	−579	−417	−119	−134	−160	−146	−107	−87
Financial	3 260	−62	−125	−256	−406	−887	−1,465	−1,319	−1,086
Computer and information	3 262	−67	−79	−128	−137	−160	−272	−220	−247
Royalties and licence fees	3 266	−292	−268	−421	−428	−577	−754	−644	−744
Other business services	3 268	−611	−829	−857	−1,056	−1,384	−2,031	−1,509	−1,660
Personal, cultural, and recreational	3 287	−18	−48	−109	−162	−225	−231	−167	−221
Government, n.i.e.	3 291	−465	−460	−586	−582	−686	−377	−435	−523

Table 2 (Continued). STANDARD PRESENTATION, 2003–2010

(Millions of U.S. dollars)

	Code	2003	2004	2005	2006	2007	2008	2009	2010
C. INCOME	4 300	**−581**	**−645**	**−985**	**−1,722**	**−659**	**−1,540**	**−2,440**	**−2,009**
Total credit	2 300	*254*	*389*	*758*	*1,332*	*3,656*	*5,419*	*4,624*	*4,715*
Total debit	3 300	*−835*	*−1,034*	*−1,743*	*−3,054*	*−4,315*	*−6,959*	*−7,064*	*−6,724*
Compensation of employees, credit	2 310	**145**	**218**	**359**	**540**	**2,210**	**3,629**	**3,426**	**4,046**
Compensation of employees, debit	3 310	**−4**	**−6**	**−10**	**−9**	**−11**	**−18**	**−15**	**−12**
Investment income, credit	2 320	**109**	**171**	**399**	**792**	**1,446**	**1,790**	**1,198**	**669**
Direct investment income	2 330	....	2	5	8	19	21	63	20
Dividends and distributed branch profits	2 332	....	2	4	2	11	20	63	19
Reinvested earnings and undistributed branch profits	2 333	....	....	....	....	....	1	....	....
Income on debt (interest)	2 334	....	....	1	6	8	....	....	1
Portfolio investment income	2 339	....	21	39	198	522	668	550	460
Income on equity	2 340	....	....	....	2	1	9	3	3
Income on bonds and notes	2 350	....	21	39	196	521	659	547	457
Income on money market instruments	2 360	....	....	....	....	....	....	....	....
Other investment income	2 370	109	148	355	586	905	1,101	585	189
Investment income, debit	3 320	**−831**	**−1,028**	**−1,733**	**−3,045**	**−4,304**	**−6,941**	**−7,049**	**−6,712**
Direct investment income	3 330	−90	−180	−268	−996	−1,178	−2,506	−2,542	−2,218
Dividends and distributed branch profits	3 332	−62	−141	−197	−856	−1,019	−2,087	−2,299	−1,976
Reinvested earnings and undistributed branch profits	3 333	−12	−5	−4	−35	−17	−172	−22	....
Income on debt (interest)	3 334	−16	−34	−67	−105	−142	−247	−221	−242
Portfolio investment income	3 339	−300	−341	−544	−672	−975	−1,182	−1,064	−1,141
Income on equity	3 340	−3	−1	−10	−27	−33	−70	−52	−55
Income on bonds and notes	3 350	−297	−340	−534	−645	−942	−1,112	−1,012	−1,086
Income on money market instruments	3 360	....	....	....	....	....	....	....	....
Other investment income	3 370	−441	−507	−921	−1,377	−2,151	−3,253	−3,443	−3,353
D. CURRENT TRANSFERS	4 379	**2,184**	**2,576**	**2,845**	**3,173**	**3,539**	**3,127**	**2,661**	**2,975**
Credit	2 379	**2,270**	**2,671**	**3,111**	**3,533**	**4,147**	**4,165**	**3,460**	**4,042**
General government	2 380	464	452	555	537	622	304	377	455
Other sectors	2 390	1,806	2,219	2,556	2,996	3,525	3,861	3,083	3,587
Workers' remittances	2 391	185	193	236	289	2,292	2,140	1,643	1,560
Other current transfers	2 392	1,621	2,026	2,320	2,707	1,233	1,721	1,440	2,027
Debit	3 379	**−86**	**−95**	**−266**	**−360**	**−608**	**−1,038**	**−799**	**−1,067**
General government	3 380	−38	−29	−27	−36	−66	−33	−24	−20
Other sectors	3 390	−48	−66	−239	−324	−542	−1,005	−775	−1,047
Workers' remittances	3 391	....	....	−2	−2	−7	−13	−4	−9
Other current transfers	3 392	−48	−66	−237	−322	−535	−992	−771	−1,038
CAPITAL AND FINANCIAL ACCOUNT	4 996	**−2,057**	**−7,037**	**−2,664**	**1,523**	**5,724**	**12,194**	**1,426**	**1,650**
CAPITAL ACCOUNT	4 994	**−17**	**7**	**−65**	**3**	**3**	**5**	**595**	**187**
Total credit	2 994	*11*	*21*	*14*	*22*	*27*	*28*	*618*	*250*
Total debit	3 994	*−28*	*−14*	*−79*	*−19*	*−24*	*−23*	*−23*	*−63*
Capital transfers, credit	2 400	**11**	**19**	**14**	**20**	**27**	**22**	**143**	**12**
General government	2 401	....	....	....	....	....	....	....	....
Debt forgiveness	2 402	....	....	....	....	....	....	....	....
Other capital transfers	2 410	....	....	....	....	....	....	....	....
Other sectors	2 430	11	19	14	20	27	22	143	12
Migrants' transfers	2 431	....	....	....	....	1	....	4	1
Debt forgiveness	2 432	....	....	....	....	....	....	128	....
Other capital transfers	2 440	11	19	14	20	26	22	11	11
Capital transfers, debit	3 400	**−25**	**−14**	**−22**	**−19**	**−24**	**−23**	**−6**	**−4**
General government	3 401	....	....	....	....	....	....	....	....
Debt forgiveness	3 402	....	....	....	....	....	....	....	....
Other capital transfers	3 410	....	....	....	....	....	....	....	....
Other sectors	3 430	−25	−14	−22	−19	−24	−23	−6	−4
Migrants' transfers	3 431	−25	−14	−22	−19	−24	−23	−6	−3
Debt forgiveness	3 432	....	....	....	....	....	....	....	....
Other capital transfers	3 440	....	....	....	....	....	....	....	−1
Nonproduced nonfinancial assets, credit	2 480	....	**2**	....	**2**	....	**6**	**475**	**238**
Nonproduced nonfinancial assets, debit	3 480	**−3**	....	**−57**	....	....	....	**−17**	**−59**

Table 2 (Continued). STANDARD PRESENTATION, 2003–2010

(Millions of U.S. dollars)

	Code	2003	2004	2005	2006	2007	2008	2009	2010
FINANCIAL ACCOUNT	4 995	**−2,040**	**−7,044**	**−2,599**	**1,520**	**5,721**	**12,189**	**831**	**1,463**
A. DIRECT INVESTMENT	4 500	**1,411**	**1,711**	**7,533**	**5,737**	**9,218**	**9,903**	**4,654**	**5,759**
Direct investment abroad	4 505	**−13**	**−4**	**−275**	**133**	**−673**	**−1,010**	**−162**	**−736**
Equity capital	4 510	−13	−4	−275	8	−975	−796	−115	−692
Claims on affiliated enterprises	4 515	....	....	....	....	−975	−796	−115	−692
Liabilities to affiliated enterprises	4 520	....	....	....	....	....	....	....	....
Reinvested earnings	4 525	....	....	....	....	....	−1	....	....
Other capital	4 530	....	....	....	125	302	−213	−47	−44
Claims on affiliated enterprises	4 535	....	....	....	125				
Liabilities to affiliated enterprises	4 540	....	....	....	....	302	−213	−47	−44
Direct investment in Ukraine	4 555	**1,424**	**1,715**	**7,808**	**5,604**	**9,891**	**10,913**	**4,816**	**6,495**
Equity capital	4 560	1,267	1,490	7,489	4,504	8,364	9,440	4,434	5,550
Claims on direct investors	4 565	....	....						
Liabilities to direct investors	4 570	....	....	....	....	8,364	9,440	4,434	5,550
Reinvested earnings	4 575	12	6	4	35	17	172	22	....
Other capital	4 580	145	219	315	1,065	1,510	1,301	360	945
Claims on direct investors	4 585	....							
Liabilities to direct investors	4 590	....	219	315	1,065	1,510	1,301	360	945
B. PORTFOLIO INVESTMENT	4 600	**867**	**2,067**	**2,757**	**3,583**	**5,753**	**−1,280**	**−1,559**	**4,317**
Assets	4 602	**1**	**−6**	**....**	**−3**	**−29**	**12**	**−8**	**−17**
Equity securities	4 610	−4	−6	....	−2	−21	10	−6	4
Monetary authorities	4 611	....	....	....	....	....	....	....	....
General government	4 612	−4	−3	....	....	....	....	....	....
Banks	4 613	....	−1	....	....	....	10	−11	3
Other sectors	4 614	....	−2	....	−2	−21	....	5	1
Debt securities	4 619	5	....	....	−1	−8	2	−2	−21
Bonds and notes	4 620	5	....	....	−1	−8	2	−2	−21
Monetary authorities	4 621	....	....	....	....	....	....	....	....
General government	4 622	....	....	....	....	....	....	....	....
Banks	4 623	5	1	....	−1	−8	2	....	−12
Other sectors	4 624	....	−1	....	....	....	....	−2	−9
Money market instruments	4 630	....	....	....	....	....	....	....	....
Monetary authorities	4 631	....	....	....	....	....	....	....	....
General government	4 632	....	....	....	....	....	....	....	....
Banks	4 633	....	....	....	....	....	....	....	....
Other sectors	4 634	....	....	....	....	....	....	....	....
Liabilities	4 652	**866**	**2,073**	**2,757**	**3,586**	**5,782**	**−1,292**	**−1,551**	**4,334**
Equity securities	4 660	84	−61	82	322	715	388	105	290
Banks	4 663	....	....	....	....	....	....	....	....
Other sectors	4 664	84	−61	82	322	715	388	105	290
Debt securities	4 669	782	2,134	2,675	3,264	5,067	−1,680	−1,656	4,044
Bonds and notes	4 670	785	2,134	2,663	3,190	5,143	−1,680	−1,684	4,039
Monetary authorities	4 671	−4	−5	....	....	....	....	....	....
General government	4 672	610	1,211	1,320	761	1,330	−476	−1,369	3,256
Banks	4 673	103	253	873	1,853	3,695	−723	−1,249	−134
Other sectors	4 674	76	675	470	576	118	−481	934	917
Money market instruments	4 680	−3	....	12	74	−76	....	28	5
Monetary authorities	4 681	....	....	....	....	....	....	....	....
General government	4 682	....	....	....	....	....	....	28	−2
Banks	4 683	−3	....	12	74	−76	....	....	....
Other sectors	4 684	....	....	....	....	....	....	....	7
C. FINANCIAL DERIVATIVES	4 910	....	....	....	....	....	....	....	....
Monetary authorities	4 911	....	....	....	....	....	....	....	....
General government	4 912	....	....	....	....	....	....	....	....
Banks	4 913	....	....	....	....	....	....	....	....
Other sectors	4 914	....	....	....	....	....	....	....	....
Assets	4 900	....	....	....	....	....	....	....	....
Monetary authorities	4 901	....	....	....	....	....	....	....	....
General government	4 902	....	....	....	....	....	....	....	....
Banks	4 903	....	....	....	....	....	....	....	....
Other sectors	4 904	....	....	....	....	....	....	....	....
Liabilities	4 905	....	....	....	....	....	....	....	....
Monetary authorities	4 906	....	....	....	....	....	....	....	....
General government	4 907	....	....	....	....	....	....	....	....
Banks	4 908	....	....	....	....	....	....	....	....
Other sectors	4 909	....	....	....	....	....	....	....	....

Table 2 (Concluded). STANDARD PRESENTATION, 2003–2010

(Millions of U.S. dollars)

	Code	2003	2004	2005	2006	2007	2008	2009	2010
D. OTHER INVESTMENT	4 700	**−2,273**	**−8,597**	**−2,463**	**−5,801**	**−271**	**4,647**	**−7,917**	**−152**
Assets	4 703	**−2,860**	**−12,495**	**−7,913**	**−15,580**	**−22,838**	**−22,884**	**−10,822**	**−10,748**
Trade credits	4 706	−187	−792	−218	−1,317	−1,446	−5,732	473	−4,706
General government	4 707	....	....	....	....	....	....	....	....
of which: Short-term	4 709	....	....	....	....	....	....	....	....
Other sectors	4 710	−187	−792	−218	−1,317	−1,446	−5,732	473	−4,706
of which: Short-term	4 712	−187	−792	−218	−1,319	−1,440	−5,728	477	−4,707
Loans	4 714	−10	−182	−200	−221	−612	−439	−347	208
Monetary authorities	4 715	....	....	....	....	....	....	....	....
of which: Short-term	4 718	....	....	....	....	....	....	....	....
General government	4 719	....	....	....	....	....	....	....	....
of which: Short-term	4 721	....	....	....	....	....	....	....	....
Banks	4 722	−10	−182	−200	−221	−612	−439	−347	208
of which: Short-term	4 724	−12	−181	−146	−143	−427	−256	−437	50
Other sectors	4 725	....	....	....	....	....	....	....	....
of which: Short-term	4 727	....	....	....	....	....	....	....	....
Currency and deposits	4 730	−658	−4,521	−3,925	−9,559	−15,385	−14,273	−10,054	−8,219
Monetary authorities	4 731	−30	−266	267	−111	52	9	−29	−202
General government	4 732	....	....	....	....	....	....	....	....
Banks	4 733	−445	−724	−401	−877	−1,828	−1,387	−401	−2,077
Other sectors	4 734	−183	−3,531	−3,791	−8,571	−13,609	−12,895	−9,624	−5,940
Other assets	4 736	−2,005	−7,000	−3,570	−4,483	−5,395	−2,440	−894	1,969
Monetary authorities	4 737	....	....	....	....	....	....	....	....
of which: Short-term	4 739	....	....	....	....	....	....	....	....
General government	4 740	....	....	−5	−3	....	....	....	−5
of which: Short-term	4 742	....	....	....	....	....	....	....	....
Banks	4 743	....	....	....	....	....	....	....	....
of which: Short-term	4 745	....	....	....	....	....	....	....	....
Other sectors	4 746	−2,005	−7,000	−3,565	−4,480	−5,395	−2,440	−894	1,974
of which: Short-term	4 748	−2,005	−7,000	−3,565	−4,480	−5,395	−2,440	−894	1,974
Liabilities	4 753	**587**	**3,898**	**5,450**	**9,779**	**22,567**	**27,531**	**2,905**	**10,596**
Trade credits	4 756	69	2,124	−636	1,228	3,288	5,863	1,491	2,871
General government	4 757	....	....	....	....	....	....	....	....
of which: Short-term	4 759	....	....	....	....	....	....	....	....
Other sectors	4 760	69	2,124	−636	1,228	3,288	5,863	1,491	2,871
of which: Short-term	4 762	69	2,124	−636	1,146	1,739	5,957	1,854	2,830
Loans	4 764	1,073	2,959	4,588	8,911	17,515	18,183	−1,419	6,141
Monetary authorities	4 765	−187	−291	−317	−426	−447	4,091	6,053	3,409
of which: Use of Fund credit and loans from the Fund	4 766	−203	−298	−299	−410	−427	4,106	6,062	3,416
of which: Short-term	4 768	....	....	−5	....	....	....	....	....
General government	4 769	−22	79	−1	−404	−271	484	234	1,865
of which: Short-term	4 771	....	....	....	....	....	....	....	2,000
Banks	4 772	502	251	1,781	5,690	11,328	6,750	−6,395	−1,621
of which: Short-term	4 774	319	128	1,029	3,464	4,497	−1,559	−4,372	365
Other sectors	4 775	780	2,920	3,125	4,051	6,905	6,858	−1,311	2,488
of which: Short-term	4 777	182	241	393	218	370	528	−102	467
Currency and deposits	4 780	277	328	882	16	1,683	3,011	−1,232	−734
Monetary authorities	4 781	....	....	....	....	....	....	....	....
General government	4 782	....	....	....	....	....	....	....	....
Banks	4 783	277	328	882	16	1,683	3,011	−1,232	−734
Other sectors	4 784	....	....	....	....	....	....	....	....
Other liabilities	4 786	−832	−1,513	616	−376	81	474	4,065	2,318
Monetary authorities	4 787	....	....	....	....	....	....	2,048	....
of which: Short-term	4 789	....	....	....	....	....	....	....	....
General government	4 790	−282	....	....	....	....	....	....	....
of which: Short-term	4 792	−282	....	....	....	....	....	....	....
Banks	4 793	....	....	....	....	....	....	108	−54
of which: Short-term	4 795	....	....	....	....	....	....	108	−54
Other sectors	4 796	−550	−1,513	616	−376	81	474	1,909	2,372
of which: Short-term	4 798	−550	−1,513	616	−376	81	474	1,909	2,372
E. RESERVE ASSETS	4 802	**−2,045**	**−2,226**	**−10,425**	**−1,999**	**−8,979**	**−1,081**	**5,653**	**−8,461**
Monetary gold	4 812	3	−5	−10	−19	−20	−15	−15	−21
Special drawing rights	4 811	8	20	....	....	−1	−7	−12	53
Reserve position in the Fund	4 810	....	....	....	....	....	....	....	....
Foreign exchange	4 803	−2,056	−2,241	−10,415	−1,980	−8,958	−1,059	5,680	−8,493
Other claims	4 813	....	....	....	....	....	....	....	....
NET ERRORS AND OMISSIONS	4 998	**−834**	**128**	**133**	**94**	**−452**	**569**	**306**	**1,368**

Table 3. INTERNATIONAL INVESTMENT POSITION (End-period stocks), 2003–2010

(Millions of U.S. dollars)

	Code	2003	2004	2005	2006	2007	2008	2009	2010
ASSETS	8 995 C.	**19,705**	**28,164**	**42,712**	**57,023**	**90,318**	**106,512**	**112,500**	**133,434**
Direct investment abroad	8 505 ..	**166**	**198**	**468**	**344**	**6,077**	**7,005**	**7,262**	**7,966**
Equity capital and reinvested earnings	8 506 ..	166	198	219	221	6,256	6,971	7,175	7,835
Claims on affiliated enterprises	8 507 ..	166	198	219	221	6,256	6,971	7,175	7,835
Liabilities to affiliated enterprises	8 508 ..	....	....	....	....	....	....	....	....
Other capital	8 530 ..	....	....	249	123	−179	34	87	131
Claims on affiliated enterprises	8 535 ..	....	....	249	123	120	118	123	131
Liabilities to affiliated enterprises	8 540 ..	....	....	....	....	−299	−84	−36	....
Portfolio investment	8 602 ..	**26**	**36**	**56**	**63**	**103**	**49**	**79**	**94**
Equity securities	8 610 ..	23	33	50	56	88	45	73	67
Monetary authorities	8 611 ..	....	....	....	....	....	....	....	....
General government	8 612 ..	4	....	....	....	....	....	....	....
Banks	8 613 ..	1	2	1	1	....	9	22	17
Other sectors	8 614 ..	18	31	49	55	88	36	51	50
Debt securities	8 619 ..	3	3	6	7	15	4	6	27
Bonds and notes	8 620 ..	3	3	6	7	15	4	6	27
Monetary authorities	8 621 ..	....	....	....	....	....	....	....	....
General government	8 622 ..	....	....	....	....	....	....	....	....
Banks	8 623 ..	2	1	5	6	14	3	3	15
Other sectors	8 624 ..	1	2	1	1	1	1	3	12
Money market instruments	8 630 ..	....	....	....	....	....	....	....	....
Monetary authorities	8 631 ..	....	....	....	....	....	....	....	....
General government	8 632 ..	....	....	....	....	....	....	....	....
Banks	8 633 ..	....	....	....	....	....	....	....	....
Other sectors	8 634 ..	....	....	....	....	....	....	....	....
Financial derivatives	8 900 ..	....	....	....	....	....	....	....	....
Monetary authorities	8 901 ..	....	....	....	....	....	....	....	....
General government	8 902 ..	....	....	....	....	....	....	....	....
Banks	8 903 ..	....	....	....	....	....	....	....	....
Other sectors	8 904 ..	....	....	....	....	....	....	....	....
Other investment	8 703 ..	**12,576**	**18,405**	**22,797**	**34,360**	**51,675**	**67,915**	**78,654**	**90,798**
Trade credits	8 706 ..	1,937	2,780	3,038	4,433	5,654	7,453	6,772	11,378
General government	8 707 ..	....	....	....	....	....	....	....	....
of which: Short-term	8 709 ..	....	....	....	....	....	....	....	....
Other sectors	8 710 ..	1,937	2,780	3,038	4,433	5,654	7,453	6,772	11,378
of which: Short-term	8 712 ..	*1,937*	*2,780*	*3,030*	*4,427*	*5,649*	*7,447*	*6,763*	*11,370*
Loans	8 714 ..	34	221	406	680	1,328	1,674	2,075	1,834
Monetary authorities	8 715 ..	....	....	....	....	....	....	....	....
of which: Short-term	8 718 ..	....	....	....	....	....	....	....	....
General government	8 719 ..	....	....	....	....	....	....	....	....
of which: Short-term	8 721 ..	....	....	....	....	....	....	....	....
Banks	8 722 ..	34	221	406	680	1,328	1,674	2,075	1,834
of which: Short-term	8 724 ..	*31*	*217*	*346*	*515*	*976*	*1,145*	*1,635*	*1,558*
Other sectors	8 725 ..	....	....	....	....	....	....	....	....
of which: Short-term	8 727 ..	....	....	....	....	....	....	....	....
Currency and deposits	8 730 ..	10,053	14,659	18,501	28,259	43,758	57,960	68,365	76,439
Monetary authorities	8 731 ..	261	538	300	444	505	256	434	731
General government	8 732 ..	....	....	....	....	....	....	....	....
Banks	8 733 ..	1,321	2,082	2,417	3,387	5,398	6,613	7,103	9,036
Other sectors	8 734 ..	8,471	12,039	15,784	24,428	37,855	51,091	60,828	66,672
Other assets	8 736 ..	552	745	852	988	935	828	1,442	1,147
Monetary authorities	8 737 ..	....	37	34	36	37	36	37	36
of which: Short-term	8 739 ..	....	....	....	....	....	....	....	....
General government	8 740 ..	....	90	99	104	108	104	106	111
of which: Short-term	8 742 ..	....	....	....	....	....	....	....	....
Banks	8 743 ..	....	....	....	....	....	....	....	....
of which: Short-term	8 745 ..	....	....	....	....	....	....	....	....
Other sectors	8 746 ..	552	618	719	848	790	688	1,299	1,000
of which: Short-term	8 748 ..	*552*	*618*	*719*	*848*	*790*	*688*	*1,299*	*1,000*
Reserve assets	8 802 ..	**6,937**	**9,525**	**19,391**	**22,256**	**32,463**	**31,543**	**26,505**	**34,576**
Monetary gold	8 812 ..	206	222	276	358	490	743	948	1,249
Special drawing rights	8 811 ..	21	1	1	1	3	9	64	8
Reserve position in the Fund	8 810 ..	....	....	....	....	....	....	....	....
Foreign exchange	8 803 ..	6,710	9,302	19,114	21,897	31,970	30,791	25,493	33,319
Other claims	8 813 ..	....	....	....	....	....	....	....	....

Table 3 (Concluded). INTERNATIONAL INVESTMENT POSITION (End-period stocks), 2003–2010

(Millions of U.S. dollars)

	Code	2003	2004	2005	2006	2007	2008	2009	2010
LIABILITIES	8 995 D.	**31,427**	**40,283**	**56,870**	**76,942**	**117,017**	**146,711**	**152,760**	**172,212**
Direct investment in Ukraine	8 555 ..	**7,566**	**9,606**	**17,209**	**23,125**	**38,059**	**46,997**	**52,021**	**57,985**
Equity capital and reinvested earnings	8 556 ..	7,152	9,047	16,375	21,182	34,980	42,748	46,943	52,092
Claims on direct investors	8 557 ..	....	....	....	....	....	....	....	....
Liabilities to direct investors	8 558 ..	7,152	9,047	16,375	21,182	34,980	42,748	46,943	52,092
Other capital	8 580 ..	414	559	834	1,943	3,079	4,249	5,078	5,893
Claims on direct investors	8 585 ..	....	....	....	....	....	....	....	....
Liabilities to direct investors	8 590 ..	414	559	834	1,943	3,079	4,249	5,078	5,893
Portfolio investment	8 652 ..	**4,065**	**6,391**	**9,011**	**12,861**	**18,618**	**17,059**	**15,567**	**20,034**
Equity securities	8 660 ..	464	589	876	1,248	2,082	2,304	2,421	2,773
Banks	8 663 ..	....	....	....	....	....	....	....	....
Other sectors	8 664 ..	464	589	876	1,248	2,082	2,304	2,421	2,773
Debt securities	8 669 ..	3,601	5,802	8,135	11,613	16,536	14,755	13,146	17,261
Bonds and notes	8 670 ..	3,590	5,791	8,111	11,515	16,536	14,755	13,117	17,200
Monetary authorities	8 671 ..	10	5	....	....	....	....	....	....
General government	8 672 ..	3,280	4,440	5,496	6,248	7,414	6,997	5,747	9,148
Banks	8 673 ..	103	356	1,232	3,304	6,998	6,124	4,908	4,672
Other sectors	8 674 ..	197	990	1,383	1,963	2,124	1,634	2,462	3,380
Money market instruments	8 680 ..	11	11	24	98	....	....	29	61
Monetary authorities	8 681 ..	....	....	....	....		....		
General government	8 682 ..	....	....	....	....		....	29	53
Banks	8 683 ..	11	11	24	98		....		....
Other sectors	8 684 ..	....	....	....	....				8
Financial derivatives	8 905 ..	....	....	....	....	....	....	....	....
Monetary authorities	8 906 ..	....	....	....	....	....	....	....	....
General government	8 907 ..	....	....	....	....	....	....	....	....
Banks	8 908 ..	....	....	....	....	....	....	....	....
Other sectors	8 909 ..	....	....	....	....	....	....	....	....
Other investment	8 753 ..	**19,796**	**24,286**	**30,650**	**40,956**	**60,340**	**82,655**	**85,172**	**94,193**
Trade credits	8 756 ..	5,290	7,565	8,262	9,668	8,680	9,740	11,065	13,828
General government	8 757 ..	....	....	....	....	....	....	....	....
of which: Short-term	8 759 ..	....	....	....	....	....	....	....	....
Other sectors	8 760 ..	5,290	7,565	8,262	9,668	8,680	9,740	11,065	13,828
of which: Short-term	8 762 ..	*5,290*	*7,565*	*5,976*	*7,277*	*7,463*	*9,006*	*10,870*	*13,595*
Loans	8 764 ..	11,692	15,103	19,373	28,763	47,504	65,457	63,768	69,620
Monetary authorities	8 765 ..	1,909	1,685	1,254	880	462	4,725	10,981	14,245
of which: Use of Fund credit and loans from the Fund	8 766 ..	*1,836*	*1,605*	*1,188*	*830*	*431*	*4,709*	*10,974*	*14,245*
of which: Short-term	8 768 ..	....	....	....	....	....	....	....	....
General government	8 769 ..	5,461	5,618	5,010	4,676	4,470	4,962	5,206	7,029
of which: Short-term	8 771 ..	....	....	....	....	....	....	....	*2,000*
Banks	8 772 ..	1,095	1,424	3,091	8,896	20,448	27,007	20,573	19,359
of which: Short-term	8 774 ..	*720*	*858*	*1,861*	*5,381*	*9,815*	*7,850*	*2,939*	*2,773*
Other sectors	8 775 ..	3,227	6,376	10,018	14,311	22,124	28,763	27,008	28,987
of which: Short-term	8 777 ..	*363*	*471*	*634*	*736*	*838*	*800*	*525*	*790*
Currency and deposits	8 780 ..	537	871	1,765	1,791	3,503	6,293	5,271	4,015
Monetary authorities	8 781 ..	....	....	....	....	....	....	....	....
General government	8 782 ..	....	....	....	....	....	....	....	....
Banks	8 783 ..	537	871	1,765	1,791	3,503	6,293	5,271	4,015
Other sectors	8 784 ..	....	....	....	....	....	....	....	....
Other liabilities	8 786 ..	2,277	747	1,250	734	653	1,165	5,068	6,730
Monetary authorities	8 787 ..	....	....	....	....	....	....	2,053	2,017
of which: Short-term	8 789 ..	....	....	....	....	....	....	....	....
General government	8 790 ..	2	....	....	....	....	....	....	....
of which: Short-term	8 792 ..	*2*	....	....	....	....	....	....	....
Banks	8 793 ..	....	....	....	....	....	47	109	73
of which: Short-term	8 795 ..	....	....	....	....	....	*47*	*109*	*73*
Other sectors	8 796 ..	2,275	747	1,250	734	653	1,118	2,906	4,640
of which: Short-term	8 798 ..	*2,275*	*747*	*1,250*	*734*	*653*	*1,118*	*2,906*	*4,640*
NET INTERNATIONAL INVESTMENT POSITION	8 995 ..	**−11,722**	**−12,119**	**−14,158**	**−19,919**	**−26,699**	**−40,199**	**−40,260**	**−38,778**
Conversion rates: hryvnias per U.S. dollar (end of period)	0 102 ..	**5.3315**	**5.3054**	**5.0500**	**5.0500**	**5.0500**	**7.7000**	**7.9850**	**7.9617**

Table 1. ANALYTIC PRESENTATION, 2003–2010

(Billions of U.S. dollars)

	Code	2003	2004	2005	2006	2007	2008	2009	2010
A. Current Account[1]	4 993 Z.	**−30.00**	**−45.41**	**−59.41**	**−81.96**	**−71.08**	**−41.16**	**−37.05**	**−71.60**
Goods: exports f.o.b.	2 100 ..	307.80	349.65	384.32	447.59	442.28	468.14	356.35	410.22
Goods: imports f.o.b.	3 100 ..	−387.25	−461.14	−509.04	−588.25	−622.02	−641.60	−484.91	−563.15
Balance on Goods	4 100 ..	*−79.45*	*−111.49*	*−124.73*	*−140.66*	*−179.74*	*−173.46*	*−128.56*	*−152.93*
Services: credit	2 200 ..	158.62	197.73	207.67	236.55	288.29	287.96	239.56	238.75
Services: debit	3 200 ..	−127.25	−149.90	−162.83	−175.59	−202.76	−203.81	−165.93	−169.14
Balance on Goods and Services	4 991 ..	*−48.09*	*−63.66*	*−79.88*	*−79.69*	*−94.21*	*−89.31*	*−54.92*	*−83.32*
Income: credit	2 300 ..	203.11	254.37	338.70	437.99	586.56	495.41	269.06	255.42
Income: debit	3 300 ..	−169.02	−217.31	−296.59	−418.43	−536.31	−420.77	−228.40	−212.94
Balance on Goods, Services, and Income	4 992 ..	*−14.00*	*−26.59*	*−37.77*	*−60.14*	*−43.96*	*−14.67*	*−14.26*	*−40.84*
Current transfers: credit	2 379 Z.	19.70	25.22	31.66	33.45	27.80	30.06	26.48	21.95
Current transfers: debit	3 379 ..	−35.70	−44.04	−53.29	−55.27	−54.91	−56.55	−49.27	−52.72
B. Capital Account[1]	4 994 Z.	**2.42**	**3.78**	**2.83**	**1.81**	**5.17**	**6.05**	**5.14**	**5.01**
Capital account: credit	2 994 Z.	4.59	6.60	7.85	7.40	9.22	10.54	9.01	9.41
Capital account: debit	3 994 ..	−2.17	−2.82	−5.03	−5.60	−4.05	−4.49	−3.87	−4.40
Total, Groups A Plus B	4 981 ..	*−27.58*	*−41.64*	*−56.58*	*−80.15*	*−65.91*	*−35.10*	*−31.91*	*−66.60*
C. Financial Account[1]	4 995 W.	**34.81**	**53.82**	**52.62**	**77.62**	**52.51**	**41.01**	**71.13**	**63.57**
Direct investment abroad	4 505 ..	−65.64	−93.95	−80.79	−85.62	−328.09	−163.15	−42.86	−10.67
Direct investment in United Kingdom	4 555 Z.	27.61	57.33	177.41	154.12	202.07	93.51	72.92	46.95
Portfolio investment assets	4 602 ..	−58.42	−259.45	−273.41	−256.99	−179.74	199.66	−254.61	−130.88
Equity securities	4 610 ..	−29.79	−102.96	−108.42	−35.43	−55.28	110.00	−17.32	−12.59
Debt securities	4 619 ..	−28.63	−156.49	−164.99	−221.56	−124.46	89.66	−237.29	−118.28
Portfolio investment liabilities	4 652 Z.	172.79	178.29	237.03	282.99	435.87	389.27	292.94	143.94
Equity securities	4 660 ..	32.61	3.59	12.45	−18.34	34.46	70.91	78.84	3.60
Debt securities	4 669 Z.	140.18	174.70	224.58	301.34	401.41	318.36	214.10	140.35
Financial derivatives	4 910 ..	−8.49	−14.27	16.53	40.40	−53.98	−219.23	49.08	44.94
Financial derivatives assets	4 900 ..	....	....	....	....	....	....	....	....
Financial derivatives liabilities	4 905 ..	−8.49	−14.27	16.53	40.40	−53.98	−219.23	49.08	44.94
Other investment assets	4 703 ..	−420.93	−595.88	−926.19	−708.26	−1,474.38	981.60	507.91	−359.94
Monetary authorities	4 701 ..	....	....	....	....	....	....	....	....
General government	4 704 ..	−.49	−1.66	−1.48	−1.94	−2.19	−5.52	−2.68	−1.56
Banks	4 705 ..	−259.35	−400.92	−541.60	−532.49	−1,197.59	415.73	414.86	−212.18
Other sectors	4 728 ..	−161.09	−193.30	−383.11	−173.83	−274.59	571.39	95.73	−146.20
Other investment liabilities	4 753 W.	387.89	781.74	902.05	650.99	1,450.77	−1,240.65	−554.25	329.22
Monetary authorities	4 753 WA	....	....	....	....	....	....	12.83	....
General government	4 753 ZB	.83	−.77	.26	1.53	−.10	.45	1.28	1.21
Banks	4 753 ZC	280.44	529.72	517.25	598.88	1,356.61	−758.49	−502.43	96.65
Other sectors	4 753 ZD	106.63	252.79	384.53	50.58	94.25	−482.61	−65.93	231.35
Total, Groups A Through C	4 983 ..	*7.23*	*12.19*	*−3.96*	*−2.53*	*−13.39*	*5.90*	*39.22*	*−3.03*
D. Net Errors and Omissions	4 998 ..	**−9.82**	**−11.78**	**5.69**	**1.23**	**15.96**	**−8.98**	**−29.66**	**13.04**
Total, Groups A Through D	4 984 ..	*−2.59*	*.41*	*1.73*	*−1.30*	*2.57*	*−3.07*	*9.56*	*10.01*
E. Reserves and Related Items	4 802 A.	**2.59**	**−.41**	**−1.73**	**1.30**	**−2.57**	**3.07**	**−9.56**	**−10.01**
Reserve assets	4 802 ..	2.59	−.41	−1.73	1.30	−2.57	3.07	−9.56	−10.01
Use of Fund credit and loans	4 766 ..	....	....	....	....	....	....	....	....
Exceptional financing	4 920 ..	....	....	....	....	....	....	....	....
Conversion rates: pound sterling per U.S. dollar	0 101 ..	**.61247**	**.54618**	**.55000**	**.54349**	**.49977**	**.54397**	**.64192**	**.64718**

[1] Excludes components that have been classified in the categories of Group E.

Table 2. STANDARD PRESENTATION, 2003–2010

(Billions of U.S. dollars)

	Code	2003	2004	2005	2006	2007	2008	2009	2010
CURRENT ACCOUNT............................	4 993 ..	−30.00	−45.41	−59.41	−81.96	−71.08	−41.16	−37.05	−71.60
A. GOODS................................	4 100 ..	−79.45	−111.49	−124.73	−140.66	−179.74	−173.46	−128.56	−152.93
Credit..................................	2 100 ..	307.80	349.65	384.32	447.59	442.28	468.14	356.35	410.22
General merchandise: exports f.o.b.................	2 110 ..	307.80	349.65	384.32	447.59	442.28	468.14	356.35	410.22
Goods for processing: exports f.o.b..............	2 150 ..	....	....	....	....	....	....	....	....
Repairs on goods............................	2 160 ..	....	....	....	....	....	....	....	....
Goods procured in ports by carriers.............	2 170 ..	....	....	....	....	....	....	....	....
Nonmonetary gold..........................	2 180 ..	....	....	....	....	....	....	....	....
Debit....................................	3 100 ..	−387.25	−461.14	−509.04	−588.25	−622.02	−641.60	−484.91	−563.15
General merchandise: imports f.o.b.................	3 110 ..	−387.25	−461.14	−509.04	−588.25	−622.02	−641.60	−484.91	−563.15
Goods for processing: imports f.o.b..............	3 150 ..	....	....	....	....	....	....	....	....
Repairs on goods............................	3 160 ..	....	....	....	....	....	....	....	....
Goods procured in ports by carriers.............	3 170 ..	....	....	....	....	....	....	....	....
Nonmonetary gold..........................	3 180 ..	....	....	....	....	....	....	....	....
B. SERVICES............................	4 200 ..	31.37	47.83	44.84	60.97	85.53	84.15	73.64	69.61
Total credit................................	2 200 ..	*158.62*	*197.73*	*207.67*	*236.55*	*288.29*	*287.96*	*239.56*	*238.75*
Total debit.................................	3 200 ..	*−127.25*	*−149.90*	*−162.83*	*−175.59*	*−202.76*	*−203.81*	*−165.93*	*−169.14*
Transportation services, credit.............	2 205 ..	22.28	29.29	31.49	31.47	36.70	38.67	31.56	31.67
Passenger.................................	2 850 ..	*8.07*	*8.96*	*8.84*	*9.01*	*9.50*	*9.86*	*8.07*	*9.36*
Freight...................................	2 851 ..	*8.81*	*14.15*	*16.32*	*14.90*	*18.33*	*19.26*	*13.95*	*13.13*
Other....................................	2 852 ..	*5.39*	*6.17*	*6.34*	*7.56*	*8.88*	*9.54*	*9.55*	*9.18*
Sea transport, passenger......................	2 207 ..	1.62	1.61	1.20	.89	1.01	1.01	1.10	1.77
Sea transport, freight........................	2 208 ..	6.39	11.38	13.53	12.24	15.10	15.99	11.48	10.38
Sea transport, other.........................	2 209 ..	1.55	1.47	1.46	1.73	1.79	1.61	1.44	1.41
Air transport, passenger......................	2 211 ..	6.30	7.15	7.40	7.86	8.14	8.47	6.68	7.28
Air transport, freight........................	2 212 ..	.60	.72	.72	.72	.99	1.04	.52	.68
Air transport, other.........................	2 213 ..	3.84	4.70	4.88	5.83	7.09	7.94	8.11	7.77
Other transport, passenger...................	2 215 ..	.15	.20	.24	.26	.35	.37	.28	.32
Other transport, freight......................	2 216 ..	1.82	2.05	2.07	1.95	2.24	2.23	1.95	2.06
Other transport, other.......................	2 217 ..	....	....	....	....	....	....	....	....
Transportation services, debit..............	3 205 ..	−28.47	−33.60	−36.15	−35.18	−37.62	−35.62	−28.15	−31.23
Passenger.................................	3 850 ..	*−10.77*	*−12.63*	*−13.46*	*−14.35*	*−15.23*	*−13.79*	*−10.57*	*−11.67*
Freight...................................	3 851 ..	*−10.34*	*−12.28*	*−12.74*	*−12.83*	*−13.92*	*−13.96*	*−11.44*	*−12.25*
Other....................................	3 852 ..	*−7.36*	*−8.69*	*−9.95*	*−8.00*	*−8.48*	*−7.87*	*−6.13*	*−7.31*
Sea transport, passenger......................	3 207 ..	−.80	−.92	−.87	−1.06	−1.35	−.91	−.67	−.91
Sea transport, freight........................	3 208 ..	−6.50	−7.90	−8.10	−8.09	−8.38	−8.78	−7.18	−8.00
Sea transport, other.........................	3 209 ..	−2.65	−3.76	−4.87	−2.48	−2.12	−2.50	−1.98	−3.28
Air transport, passenger......................	3 211 ..	−9.73	−11.41	−12.28	−12.95	−13.49	−12.49	−9.61	−10.45
Air transport, freight........................	3 212 ..	−1.26	−1.25	−1.25	−1.23	−1.30	−1.18	−1.09	−.99
Air transport, other.........................	3 213 ..	−4.70	−4.93	−5.08	−5.51	−6.36	−5.37	−4.16	−4.03
Other transport, passenger...................	3 215 ..	−.25	−.31	−.31	−.35	−.39	−.39	−.29	−.31
Other transport, freight......................	3 216 ..	−2.58	−3.13	−3.40	−3.51	−4.23	−4.00	−3.17	−3.26
Other transport, other.......................	3 217 ..	....	....	....	....	....	....	....	....
Travel, credit...........................	2 236 ..	22.67	28.20	30.57	34.80	38.70	36.42	30.50	30.58
Business travel.............................	2 237 ..	5.98	7.21	7.88	9.28	9.80	8.94	6.16	6.70
Personal travel.............................	2 240 ..	16.69	20.99	22.69	25.52	28.90	27.49	24.34	23.88
Travel, debit............................	3 236 ..	−47.85	−56.44	−59.53	−63.32	−71.52	−69.79	−50.56	−48.62
Business travel.............................	3 237 ..	−7.13	−8.07	−8.91	−9.55	−10.74	−10.21	−7.20	−7.13
Personal travel.............................	3 240 ..	−40.72	−48.37	−50.62	−53.77	−60.78	−59.58	−43.36	−41.49
Other services, credit....................	2 200 BA ..	113.67	140.24	145.61	170.29	212.89	212.87	177.51	176.50
Communications...........................	2 245 ..	4.05	5.83	6.71	7.65	8.37	7.88	7.59	7.47
Construction..............................	2 249 ..	.40	.51	1.09	1.46	2.00	2.29	2.45	2.58
Insurance.................................	2 253 ..	8.81	9.06	2.98	6.96	10.24	14.26	11.76	10.38
Financial.................................	2 260 ..	28.61	37.15	42.55	51.82	71.95	69.56	53.37	47.58
Computer and information...................	2 262 ..	8.16	11.26	10.82	12.40	13.83	13.30	11.41	11.63
Royalties and licence fees...................	2 266 ..	10.10	11.78	13.30	14.54	16.06	14.75	12.93	14.28
Other business services.....................	2 268 ..	47.30	57.01	60.45	67.74	82.41	82.64	71.53	75.20
Personal, cultural, and recreational............	2 287 ..	3.09	3.93	4.08	3.93	3.76	4.21	3.17	3.95
Government, n.i.e...........................	2 291 ..	3.16	3.70	3.61	3.78	4.25	3.98	3.31	3.42
Other services, debit.....................	3 200 BA ..	−50.93	−59.86	−67.15	−77.09	−93.61	−98.40	−87.22	−89.29
Communications...........................	3 245 ..	−3.53	−4.84	−5.81	−6.74	−8.28	−8.01	−6.87	−6.84
Construction..............................	3 249 ..	−.19	−.26	−1.03	−1.15	−1.62	−1.97	−2.11	−2.44
Insurance.................................	3 253 ..	−1.27	−1.52	−1.62	−1.80	−2.04	−2.07	−1.57	−1.82
Financial.................................	3 260 ..	−6.66	−7.30	−9.26	−10.80	−13.89	−13.67	−9.69	−8.92
Computer and information...................	3 262 ..	−2.94	−3.41	−4.02	−4.71	−5.34	−6.27	−6.17	−6.08
Royalties and licence fees...................	3 266 ..	−7.86	−9.17	−9.46	−9.55	−8.82	−10.61	−9.50	−9.68
Other business services.....................	3 268 ..	−22.78	−27.01	−29.91	−35.82	−45.51	−46.61	−44.51	−46.97
Personal, cultural, and recreational............	3 287 ..	−1.40	−1.62	−1.51	−1.58	−1.91	−2.03	−.91	−1.02
Government, n.i.e...........................	3 291 ..	−4.30	−4.73	−4.51	−4.94	−6.21	−7.14	−5.89	−5.54

Table 2 (Continued). STANDARD PRESENTATION, 2003–2010

(Billions of U.S. dollars)

	Code	2003	2004	2005	2006	2007	2008	2009	2010
C. INCOME	4 300	**34.09**	**37.07**	**42.11**	**19.55**	**50.25**	**74.64**	**40.66**	**42.48**
Total credit	2 300	*203.11*	*254.37*	*338.70*	*437.99*	*586.56*	*495.41*	*269.06*	*255.42*
Total debit	3 300	*−169.02*	*−217.31*	*−296.59*	*−418.43*	*−536.31*	*−420.77*	*−228.40*	*−212.94*
Compensation of employees, credit	2 310	**1.83**	**1.71**	**1.77**	**1.73**	**1.97**	**1.94**	**1.83**	**1.83**
Compensation of employees, debit	3 310	**−1.73**	**−2.61**	**−2.88**	**−3.50**	**−3.44**	**−3.25**	**−2.24**	**−2.39**
Investment income, credit	2 320	**201.28**	**252.67**	**336.93**	**436.26**	**584.59**	**493.47**	**267.23**	**253.60**
Direct investment income	2 330	90.01	116.00	144.01	154.38	182.89	130.64	109.63	126.38
Dividends and distributed branch profits	2 332	53.41	56.16	65.64	68.14	58.93	58.88	87.33	87.54
Reinvested earnings and undistributed branch profits	2 333	34.89	56.94	79.60	87.95	127.57	73.04	20.41	35.12
Income on debt (interest)	2 334	1.71	2.90	−1.23	−1.71	−3.61	−1.28	1.89	3.72
Portfolio investment income	2 339	53.17	67.21	82.55	101.62	132.39	125.23	84.68	73.11
Income on equity	2 340	16.94	20.45	24.16	31.29	41.29	37.55	25.40	24.35
Income on bonds and notes	2 350	33.66	42.81	53.88	64.56	84.55	82.98	57.91	46.88
Income on money market instruments	2 360	2.57	3.94	4.51	5.77	6.55	4.70	1.37	1.88
Other investment income	2 370	58.11	69.46	110.37	180.25	269.31	237.59	72.91	54.11
Investment income, debit	3 320	**−167.29**	**−214.70**	**−293.72**	**−414.93**	**−532.87**	**−417.51**	**−226.16**	**−210.55**
Direct investment income	3 330	−35.85	−50.61	−65.40	−95.49	−89.75	−12.29	−42.19	−50.18
Dividends and distributed branch profits	3 332	−16.28	−25.94	−34.76	−43.76	−29.14	9.75	−24.13	−39.76
Reinvested earnings and undistributed branch profits	3 333	−11.98	−15.62	−19.20	−40.77	−47.23	−10.27	−7.62	−1.12
Income on debt (interest)	3 334	−7.59	−9.04	−11.44	−10.95	−13.38	−11.77	−10.44	−9.30
Portfolio investment income	3 339	−53.86	−70.79	−86.53	−106.25	−133.75	−138.60	−93.79	−93.06
Income on equity	3 340	−24.59	−29.92	−33.58	−40.03	−46.17	−49.35	−34.42	−34.54
Income on bonds and notes	3 350	−23.80	−33.68	−41.46	−50.43	−68.19	−70.10	−52.28	−53.56
Income on money market instruments	3 360	−5.46	−7.19	−11.50	−15.79	−19.39	−19.15	−7.09	−4.96
Other investment income	3 370	−77.58	−93.29	−141.79	−213.20	−309.37	−266.62	−90.18	−67.32
D. CURRENT TRANSFERS	4 379	**−16.00**	**−18.82**	**−21.63**	**−21.82**	**−27.12**	**−26.49**	**−22.79**	**−30.77**
Credit	2 379	**19.70**	**25.22**	**31.66**	**33.45**	**27.80**	**30.06**	**26.48**	**21.95**
General government	2 380	6.50	7.67	7.83	8.03	8.63	10.32	9.56	5.86
Other sectors	2 390	13.20	17.55	23.83	25.42	19.17	19.74	16.93	16.09
Workers' remittances	2 391	....	....	....	....	....	....	....	....
Other current transfers	2 392	....	....	....	....	....	....	....	....
Debit	3 379	**−35.70**	**−44.04**	**−53.29**	**−55.27**	**−54.91**	**−56.55**	**−49.27**	**−52.72**
General government	3 380	−17.39	−22.40	−24.91	−25.47	−28.18	−27.43	−26.76	−28.21
Other sectors	3 390	−18.32	−21.64	−28.38	−29.80	−26.73	−29.12	−22.51	−24.50
Workers' remittances	3 391	....	....	....	....	....	....	....	....
Other current transfers	3 392	....	....	....	....	....	....	....	....
CAPITAL AND FINANCIAL ACCOUNT	4 996	**39.83**	**57.19**	**53.71**	**80.73**	**55.12**	**50.13**	**66.71**	**58.56**
CAPITAL ACCOUNT	4 994	**2.42**	**3.78**	**2.83**	**1.81**	**5.17**	**6.05**	**5.14**	**5.01**
Total credit	2 994	*4.59*	*6.60*	*7.85*	*7.40*	*9.22*	*10.54*	*9.01*	*9.41*
Total debit	3 994	*−2.17*	*−2.82*	*−5.03*	*−5.60*	*−4.05*	*−4.49*	*−3.87*	*−4.40*
Capital transfers, credit	2 400	**4.23**	**6.24**	**7.24**	**6.24**	**7.65**	**8.55**	**6.65**	**7.00**
General government	2 401	....	....	....	....	....	....	....	....
Debt forgiveness	2 402	....	....	....	....	....	....	....	....
Other capital transfers	2 410	....	....	....	....	....	....	....	....
Other sectors	2 430	4.23	6.24	7.24	6.24	7.65	8.55	6.65	7.00
Migrants' transfers	2 431	3.20	4.21	4.53	5.02	5.91	5.92	5.42	5.70
Debt forgiveness	2 432	....	....	....	....	....	....	....	....
Other capital transfers	2 440	1.03	2.03	2.71	1.22	1.73	2.63	1.23	1.30
Capital transfers, debit	3 400	**−1.70**	**−1.88**	**−3.94**	**−4.45**	**−2.46**	**−2.42**	**−2.08**	**−2.17**
General government	3 401	−.59	−.74	−.75	−.73	−.92	−1.04	−.92	−1.03
Debt forgiveness	3 402	−.03	−.02	−.03	−.02	−.02	−.14	−.07	−.16
Other capital transfers	3 410	−.56	−.71	−.72	−.71	−.90	−.90	−.85	−.87
Other sectors	3 430	−1.11	−1.14	−3.19	−3.71	−1.54	−1.38	−1.16	−1.14
Migrants' transfers	3 431	−.90	−.94	−1.00	−1.23	−1.39	−1.38	−1.16	−1.14
Debt forgiveness	3 432	−.21	−.20	−2.19	−2.48	−.15	....	....	....
Other capital transfers	3 440	....	....	....	....	....	....	....	....
Nonproduced nonfinancial assets, credit	2 480	**.36**	**.35**	**.62**	**1.16**	**1.58**	**1.99**	**2.36**	**2.41**
Nonproduced nonfinancial assets, debit	3 480	**−.47**	**−.94**	**−1.09**	**−1.15**	**−1.59**	**−2.07**	**−1.79**	**−2.23**

Table 2 (Continued). STANDARD PRESENTATION, 2003–2010

(Billions of U.S. dollars)

	Code	2003	2004	2005	2006	2007	2008	2009	2010
FINANCIAL ACCOUNT....................................	4 995 ..	37.40	53.42	50.89	78.92	49.94	44.08	61.57	53.56
A. DIRECT INVESTMENT...............................	4 500 ..	−38.02	−36.61	96.62	68.50	−126.02	−69.64	30.06	36.28
Direct investment abroad.................................	4 505 ..	−65.64	−93.95	−80.79	−85.62	−328.09	−163.15	−42.86	−10.67
Equity capital..	4 510 ..	−33.26	−36.22	−27.92	−49.83	−121.24	−78.86	−11.99	−18.50
Claims on affiliated enterprises..................	4 515 ..	−33.26	−36.22	−27.92	−49.83	−121.24	−78.86	−11.99	−18.50
Liabilities to affiliated enterprises.............	4 520 ..	....	....	....	....	....	....	....	....
Reinvested earnings....................................	4 525 ..	−34.89	−56.94	−79.60	−87.95	−127.57	−73.04	−20.41	−35.12
Other capital..	4 530 ..	2.51	−.79	26.73	52.16	−79.28	−11.24	−10.46	42.95
Claims on affiliated enterprises..................	4 535 ..	−17.71	−35.02	−27.08	.32	−87.25	−128.33	38.08	16.41
Liabilities to affiliated enterprises.............	4 540 ..	20.22	34.24	53.82	51.84	7.97	117.09	−48.53	26.54
Direct investment in United Kingdom................	4 555 ..	27.61	57.33	177.41	154.12	202.07	93.51	72.92	46.95
Equity capital..	4 560 ..	7.35	43.58	148.82	100.12	165.80	98.06	57.34	52.00
Claims on direct investors..........................	4 565 ..	....	....	....	....	....	....	....	....
Liabilities to direct investors.....................	4 570 ..	7.35	43.58	148.82	100.12	165.80	98.06	57.34	52.00
Reinvested earnings....................................	4 575 ..	11.98	15.62	19.20	40.77	47.23	10.27	7.62	1.12
Other capital..	4 580 ..	8.28	−1.86	9.38	13.23	−10.96	−14.82	7.96	−6.18
Claims on direct investors..........................	4 585 ..	5.23	−5.37	−22.43	−9.10	−30.49	−50.94	20.33	−5.95
Liabilities to direct investors.....................	4 590 ..	3.06	3.51	31.81	22.33	19.53	36.12	−12.37	−.23
B. PORTFOLIO INVESTMENT.........................	4 600 ..	114.37	−81.15	−36.38	26.00	256.13	588.92	38.33	13.07
Assets...	4 602 ..	−58.42	−259.45	−273.41	−256.99	−179.74	199.66	−254.61	−130.88
Equity securities..	4 610 ..	−29.79	−102.96	−108.42	−35.43	−55.28	110.00	−17.32	−12.59
Monetary authorities................................	4 611 ..	....	....	....	....	....	....	....	....
General government..................................	4 612 ..	....	....	−.08	−.02	.02	−.03	−.04	−.04
Banks..	4 613 ..	−30.72	−58.23	−64.02	−40.22	−22.60	124.34	−4.68	−17.12
Other sectors..	4 614 ..	.93	−44.73	−44.33	4.81	−32.70	−14.31	−12.60	4.56
Debt securities...	4 619 ..	−28.63	−156.49	−164.99	−221.56	−124.46	89.66	−237.29	−118.28
Bonds and notes......................................	4 620 ..	−9.03	−160.86	−154.14	−197.59	−129.98	56.06	−213.53	−120.58
Monetary authorities..............................	4 621 ..	....	....	....	....	....	....	....	....
General government................................	4 622 ..	....	....	....	....	.09	−.10	−.26	.06
Banks..	4 623 ..	21.53	−105.92	−116.68	−190.19	−83.23	282.46	19.73	35.01
Other sectors..	4 624 ..	−30.56	−54.94	−37.46	−7.40	−46.85	−226.30	−233.00	−155.64
Money market instruments......................	4 630 ..	−19.60	4.37	−10.85	−23.97	5.52	33.60	−23.76	2.30
Monetary authorities..............................	4 631 ..	....	....	....	....	....	....	....	....
General government................................	4 632 ..	1.48	−.01	....	.01	−4.79	−.94	−3.59	−.59
Banks..	4 633 ..	−11.77	8.00	−4.00	−9.30	−16.70	23.05	−16.56	.97
Other sectors..	4 634 ..	−9.32	−3.62	−6.85	−14.67	27.00	11.49	−3.61	1.91
Liabilities..	4 652 ..	172.79	178.29	237.03	282.99	435.87	389.27	292.94	143.94
Equity securities..	4 660 ..	32.61	3.59	12.45	−18.34	34.46	70.91	78.84	3.60
Banks..	4 663 ..	1.16	−.48	.11	1.28	7.34	2.96	3.43	2.87
Other sectors..	4 664 ..	31.45	4.07	12.34	−19.62	27.11	67.95	75.41	.73
Debt securities...	4 669 ..	140.18	174.70	224.58	301.34	401.41	318.36	214.10	140.35
Bonds and notes......................................	4 670 ..	142.90	156.16	238.11	224.52	360.39	336.27	96.29	223.32
Monetary authorities..............................	4 671 ..	....	....	....	....	....	....	....	....
General government................................	4 672 ..	18.46	22.95	55.80	46.36	54.62	50.98	42.70	121.63
Banks..	4 673 ..	47.34	58.64	75.80	79.54	129.13	38.62	45.47	29.99
Other sectors..	4 674 ..	77.10	74.58	106.51	98.62	176.64	246.67	8.12	71.70
Money market instruments......................	4 680 ..	−2.72	18.54	−13.52	76.82	41.02	−17.91	117.81	−82.97
Monetary authorities..............................	4 681 ..	....	....	....	....	....	....	....	....
General government................................	4 682 ..	3.56	3.62	−1.85	1.37	7.13	23.33	−.56	12.49
Banks..	4 683 ..	.75	14.76	−7.04	82.15	27.82	−46.42	126.73	−100.47
Other sectors..	4 684 ..	−7.04	.16	−4.64	−6.70	6.07	5.18	−8.35	5.01
C. FINANCIAL DERIVATIVES........................	4 910 ..	−8.49	−14.27	16.53	40.40	−53.98	−219.23	49.08	44.94
Monetary authorities...................................	4 911 ..	....	....	....	....	....	....	....	....
General government.....................................	4 912 ..	....	....	....	....	....	....	....	....
Banks..	4 913 ..	....	....	....	....	....	....	....	....
Other sectors..	4 914 ..	....	....	....	....	....	....	....	....
Assets...	4 900 ..	....	....	....	....	....	....	....	....
Monetary authorities................................	4 901 ..	....	....	....	....	....	....	....	....
General government..................................	4 902 ..	....	....	....	....	....	....	....	....
Banks..	4 903 ..	....	....	....	....	....	....	....	....
Other sectors..	4 904 ..	....	....	....	....	....	....	....	....
Liabilities..	4 905 ..	−8.49	−14.27	16.53	40.40	−53.98	−219.23	49.08	44.94
Monetary authorities................................	4 906 ..	....	....	....	....	....	....	....	....
General government..................................	4 907 ..	....	....	....	....	....	....	....	....
Banks..	4 908 ..	....	....	....	....	....	....	....	....
Other sectors..	4 909 ..	....	....	....	....	....	....	....	....

Table 2 (Concluded). STANDARD PRESENTATION, 2003–2010

(Billions of U.S. dollars)

	Code	2003	2004	2005	2006	2007	2008	2009	2010
D. OTHER INVESTMENT	4 700	**−33.04**	**185.86**	**−24.15**	**−57.27**	**−23.62**	**−259.05**	**−46.35**	**−30.72**
Assets	4 703	**−420.93**	**−595.88**	**−926.19**	**−708.26**	**−1,474.38**	**981.60**	**507.91**	**−359.94**
Trade credits	4 706	−.93	.61	2.54	−2.54	−.22	−.04	.06	.12
General government	4 707	....	....	....	....	....	....	....	....
of which: Short-term	4 709	....	....	....	....	....	....	....	....
Other sectors	4 710	−.93	.61	2.54	−2.54	−.22	−.04	.06	.12
of which: Short-term	4 712	*−.93*	*.61*	*2.54*	*−2.54*	*−.22*	*−.04*	*.06*	*.12*
Loans	4 714	−113.15	−205.85	−247.72	−214.36	−449.20	190.10	179.84	−27.82
Monetary authorities	4 715	....	....	....	....	....	....	....	....
of which: Short-term	4 718	....	....	....	....	....	....	....	....
General government	4 719	.03	.03	.03	.02	.02	.14	.07	.16
of which: Short-term	4 721	....	....	....	....	....	....	....	....
Banks	4 722	−113.61	−206.20	−248.83	−216.81	−449.63	189.35	179.52	−28.12
of which: Short-term	4 724	*−113.61*	*−206.20*	*−248.83*	*−216.81*	*−449.63*	*189.35*	*179.52*	*−28.12*
Other sectors	4 725	.43	.32	1.08	2.42	.40	.60	.25	.14
of which: Short-term	4 727			*.01*		*−.01*		*.01*	
Currency and deposits	4 730	−306.53	−389.15	−681.70	−491.87	−1,022.90	797.21	330.76	−330.42
Monetary authorities	4 731	....	....	....	....	....	....	....	....
General government	4 732	....	....	....	....	....	....	....	....
Banks	4 733	−145.74	−194.71	−292.77	−315.68	−747.97	226.37	235.34	−184.06
Other sectors	4 734	−160.79	−194.44	−388.93	−176.19	−274.93	570.83	95.42	−146.36
Other assets	4 736	−.32	−1.49	.68	.52	−2.07	−5.66	−2.75	−1.81
Monetary authorities	4 737	....	....	....	....	....	....	....	....
of which: Short-term	4 739	....	....	....	....	....	....	....	....
General government	4 740	−.52	−1.69	−1.51	−1.97	−2.22	−5.66	−2.75	−1.71
of which: Short-term	4 742	*−.14*	*−1.17*	*−.66*	*−.53*	*−.82*	*−3.92*	*−1.05*	*.22*
Banks	4 743	....	....	....	....	....	....	....	....
of which: Short-term	4 745	....	....	....	....	....	....	....	....
Other sectors	4 746	.21	.20	2.19	2.48	.15	....	....	−.10
of which: Short-term	4 748	*.21*	*.20*	*2.19*	*2.48*	*.15*			*−.10*
Liabilities	4 753	**387.89**	**781.74**	**902.05**	**650.99**	**1,450.77**	**−1,240.65**	**−554.25**	**329.22**
Trade credits	4 756	....	....	....	....	....	....	....	....
General government	4 757	....	....	....	....	....	....	....	....
of which: Short-term	4 759	....	....	....	....	....	....	....	....
Other sectors	4 760	....	....	....	....	....	....	....	....
of which: Short-term	4 762	....	....	....	....	....	....	....	....
Loans	4 764	109.24	251.55	379.88	42.94	102.70	−473.99	−64.64	230.59
Monetary authorities	4 765	....	....	....	....	....	....	....	....
of which: Use of Fund credit and loans from the Fund	4 766	....	....	....	....	....	....	....	....
of which: Short-term	4 768	....	....	....	....	....	....	....	....
General government	4 769	.26	1.11	.12	.44	−.09	.88	.81	−.49
of which: Short-term	4 771	....	....	....	....	....	....	....	....
Banks	4 772	....	....	....	....	....	....	....	....
of which: Short-term	4 774	....	....	....	....	....	....	....	....
Other sectors	4 775	108.98	250.43	379.76	42.50	102.78	−474.87	−65.46	231.08
of which: Short-term	4 777	*108.98*	*249.92*	*379.77*	*42.52*	*102.80*	*−474.85*	*−65.45*	*231.08*
Currency and deposits	4 780	280.44	529.72	517.25	598.88	1,356.61	−758.49	−502.43	96.65
Monetary authorities	4 781	....	....	....	....	....	....	....	....
General government	4 782	....	....	....	....	....	....	....	....
Banks	4 783	280.44	529.72	517.25	598.88	1,356.61	−758.49	−502.43	96.65
Other sectors	4 784	....	....	....	....	....	....	....	....
Other liabilities	4 786	−1.79	.48	4.91	9.17	−8.55	−8.17	12.82	1.98
Monetary authorities	4 787	....	....	....	....	....	....	12.83	....
of which: Short-term	4 789	....	....	....	....	....	....	....	....
General government	4 790	.57	−1.88	.14	1.09	−.01	−.43	.47	1.70
of which: Short-term	4 792	*.57*	*−1.88*	*.14*	*1.09*	*−.01*	*−.43*	*.47*	*1.70*
Banks	4 793	....	....	....	....	....	....	....	....
of which: Short-term	4 795	....	....	....	....	....	....	....	....
Other sectors	4 796	−2.36	2.36	4.77	8.08	−8.53	−7.74	−.47	.28
of which: Short-term	4 798	*−2.36*	*2.36*	*4.77*	*8.08*	*−8.53*	*−7.74*	*−.47*	*.28*
E. RESERVE ASSETS	4 802	**2.59**	**−.41**	**−1.73**	**1.30**	**−2.57**	**3.07**	**−9.56**	**−10.01**
Monetary gold	4 812	....	....	....	.01	....	....	....	....
Special drawing rights	4 811	.02	.06	.02	−.09	.05	−.11	−13.85	−.03
Reserve position in the Fund	4 810	.46	1.03	2.82	1.01	.37	−1.24	−.89	−1.58
Foreign exchange	4 803	1.80	−1.53	−3.97	−.16	−3.04	4.06	5.04	−8.57
Other claims	4 813	.32	.03	−.59	.54	.04	.36	.14	.17
NET ERRORS AND OMISSIONS	4 998	**−9.82**	**−11.78**	**5.69**	**1.23**	**15.96**	**−8.98**	**−29.66**	**13.04**

Table 3. INTERNATIONAL INVESTMENT POSITION (End-period stocks), 2003–2010

(Billions of U.S. dollars)

	Code	2003	2004	2005	2006	2007	2008	2009	2010
ASSETS	8 995 C.	**6,183.02**	**7,554.43**	**8,276.56**	**11,890.74**	**15,519.15**	**16,007.41**	**14,056.69**	**14,546.52**
Direct investment abroad	8 505 ..	**1,233.44**	**1,309.63**	**1,215.51**	**1,439.10**	**1,802.57**	**1,525.03**	**1,673.96**	**1,689.40**
Equity capital and reinvested earnings	8 506 ..	1,196.93	1,288.61	1,251.47	1,496.58	1,734.27	1,477.43	1,572.57	1,633.58
Claims on affiliated enterprises	8 507 ..	....	....	....	....	....	....	....	....
Liabilities to affiliated enterprises	8 508 ..	....	....	....	....	....	....	....	....
Other capital	8 530 ..	36.51	21.02	−35.96	−57.48	68.30	47.60	101.38	55.82
Claims on affiliated enterprises	8 535 ..	....	....	....	....	....	....	....	....
Liabilities to affiliated enterprises	8 540 ..	....	....	....	....	....	....	....	....
Portfolio investment	8 602 ..	**1,670.20**	**2,109.29**	**2,343.35**	**3,005.46**	**3,400.36**	**2,426.25**	**3,035.79**	**3,251.15**
Equity securities	8 610 ..	663.87	879.36	1,062.67	1,361.08	1,515.66	824.02	1,079.25	1,163.64
Monetary authorities	8 611 ..	....	....	....	....	....	....	....	....
General government	8 612 ..	....	....	....	....	....	....	....	....
Banks	8 613 ..	37.13	102.32	148.36	214.43	254.51	60.85	80.47	99.35
Other sectors	8 614 ..	626.75	777.04	914.31	1,146.65	1,261.15	763.17	998.78	1,064.29
Debt securities	8 619 ..	1,006.33	1,229.93	1,280.68	1,644.38	1,884.70	1,602.23	1,956.53	2,087.51
Bonds and notes	8 620 ..	895.92	1,117.89	1,173.88	1,502.12	1,737.90	1,501.50	1,820.89	1,949.14
Monetary authorities	8 621 ..	....	....	....	....	....	....	....	....
General government	8 622 ..	....	....	....	....	.10	....	.26	.20
Banks	8 623 ..	576.61	685.74	704.45	931.39	1,100.78	818.59	798.03	734.67
Other sectors	8 624 ..	319.31	432.15	469.43	570.73	637.02	682.91	1,022.59	1,214.27
Money market instruments	8 630 ..	110.41	112.04	106.80	142.26	146.80	100.73	135.65	138.37
Monetary authorities	8 631 ..	....	....	....	....	....	....	....	....
General government	8 632 ..	....	....	....	....	4.79	3.28	7.92	8.58
Banks	8 633 ..	76.33	71.48	68.11	83.98	107.84	83.26	105.92	101.78
Other sectors	8 634 ..	34.08	40.56	38.69	58.27	34.18	14.19	21.80	28.01
Financial derivatives	8 900 ..	....	....	....	**1,675.85**	**2,760.98**	**5,889.79**	**3,565.25**	**3,565.94**
Monetary authorities	8 901 ..	....	....	....	....	....	....	....	....
General government	8 902 ..	....	....	....	....	....	....	....	....
Banks	8 903 ..	....	....	....	....	....	....	....	....
Other sectors	8 904 ..	....	....	....	....	....	....	....	....
Other investment	8 703 ..	**3,236.90**	**4,090.64**	**4,674.54**	**5,725.33**	**7,501.78**	**6,113.46**	**5,716.73**	**5,962.46**
Trade credits	8 706 ..	1.76	1.25	−1.29	1.21	1.47	1.13	1.21	1.05
General government	8 707 ..	....	....	....	....	....	....	....	....
of which: Short-term	8 709 ..	....	....	....	....	....	....	....	....
Other sectors	8 710 ..	1.76	1.25	−1.29	1.21	1.47	1.13	1.21	1.05
of which: Short-term	8 712 ..	*1.76*	*1.25*	*−1.29*	*1.21*	*1.47*	*1.13*	*1.21*	*1.05*
Loans	8 714 ..	723.87	972.80	1,118.16	1,402.51	1,925.39	1,654.35	1,472.50	1,530.09
Monetary authorities	8 715 ..	....	....	....	....	....	....	....	....
of which: Short-term	8 718 ..	....	....	....	....	....	....	....	....
General government	8 719 ..	.34	.34	.27	.29	.27	.09	.06	.05
of which: Short-term	8 721 ..	....	....	....	....	....	....	....	....
Banks	8 722 ..	717.62	965.79	1,112.63	1,398.35	1,921.47	1,650.43	1,469.92	1,527.56
of which: Short-term	8 724 ..	*711.07*	*958.61*	*1,105.52*	*1,391.89*	*1,915.06*	*1,644.08*	*1,463.24*	*1,520.47*
Other sectors	8 725 ..	5.92	6.67	5.25	3.88	3.65	3.83	2.52	2.48
of which: Short-term	8 727 ..	*.95*	*1.03*	*.91*	*1.04*	*1.06*	*1.86*	*.86*	*.83*
Currency and deposits	8 730 ..	2,490.72	3,095.31	3,537.03	4,297.06	5,544.91	4,430.09	4,208.30	4,395.07
Monetary authorities	8 731 ..	....	....	....	....	....	....	....	....
General government	8 732 ..	....	....	....	....	....	....	....	....
Banks	8 733 ..	1,644.68	1,945.00	2,065.85	2,524.66	3,434.48	3,051.21	2,882.05	2,937.51
Other sectors	8 734 ..	846.04	1,150.31	1,471.18	1,772.40	2,110.43	1,378.87	1,326.25	1,457.56
Other assets	8 736 ..	20.54	21.28	20.64	24.55	30.02	27.90	34.73	36.26
Monetary authorities	8 737 ..	....	....	....	....	....	....	....	....
of which: Short-term	8 739 ..	....	....	....	....	....	....	....	....
General government	8 740 ..	18.29	19.23	18.71	23.40	26.22	24.23	29.42	30.19
of which: Short-term	8 742 ..	....	....	....	....	....	....	....	....
Banks	8 743 ..	....	....	....	....	....	....	....	....
of which: Short-term	8 745 ..	....	....	....	....	....	....	....	....
Other sectors	8 746 ..	2.25	2.04	1.93	1.14	3.80	3.67	5.31	6.07
of which: Short-term	8 748 ..	*2.25*	*2.04*	*1.93*	*1.14*	*3.80*	*3.67*	*5.31*	*6.07*
Reserve assets	8 802 ..	**42.48**	**44.87**	**43.15**	**45.01**	**53.46**	**52.87**	**64.96**	**77.57**
Monetary gold	8 812 ..	4.19	4.42	5.14	6.35	8.34	8.70	11.04	14.19
Special drawing rights	8 811 ..	.38	.33	.29	.40	.36	.45	14.34	14.12
Reserve position in the Fund	8 810 ..	6.32	5.53	2.33	1.41	1.10	2.35	3.33	4.89
Foreign exchange	8 803 ..	31.63	34.43	34.77	36.89	43.55	41.34	36.18	44.22
Other claims	8 813 ..	−.04	.16	.63	−.04	.11	.04	.06	.15

Table 3 (Concluded). INTERNATIONAL INVESTMENT POSITION (End-period stocks), 2003–2010

(Billions of U.S. dollars)

	Code	2003	2004	2005	2006	2007	2008	2009	2010
LIABILITIES................................	8 995 D.	**6,392.09**	**7,980.71**	**8,710.94**	**12,648.08**	**16,166.57**	**16,155.40**	**14,549.46**	**14,858.94**
Direct investment in United Kingdom........	8 555 ..	**634.53**	**740.37**	**851.01**	**1,133.31**	**1,229.75**	**974.55**	**1,056.37**	**1,086.18**
Equity capital and reinvested earnings..........	8 556 ..	438.45	517.38	634.92	850.18	993.32	783.56	849.69	894.75
Claims on direct investors.................	8 557 ..	....	....	....	....	....	....	....	....
Liabilities to direct investors..............	8 558 ..	....	....	....	....	....	....	....	....
Other capital..............................	8 580 ..	196.09	222.99	216.10	283.14	236.43	191.00	206.68	191.42
Claims on direct investors.................	8 585 ..	....	....	....	....	....	....	....	....
Liabilities to direct investors..............	8 590 ..	....	....	....	....	....	....	....	....
Portfolio investment.......................	8 652 ..	**1,932.63**	**2,371.62**	**2,516.87**	**3,343.88**	**3,898.54**	**2,883.76**	**3,896.42**	**3,949.54**
Equity securities.........................	8 660 ..	940.68	1,110.06	1,135.23	1,532.81	1,675.27	879.28	1,383.27	1,478.76
Banks..................................	8 663 ..	8.02	8.88	9.10	13.76	22.12	12.83	23.08	27.78
Other sectors...........................	8 664 ..	932.66	1,101.18	1,126.13	1,519.05	1,653.15	866.45	1,360.19	1,450.98
Debt securities..........................	8 669 ..	991.95	1,261.56	1,381.64	1,811.08	2,223.27	2,004.48	2,513.16	2,470.78
Bonds and notes........................	8 670 ..	712.99	958.20	1,104.28	1,454.28	1,802.51	1,635.32	2,013.20	2,065.16
Monetary authorities..................	8 671 ..	....	....	....	....	....	....	....	....
General government...................	8 672 ..	117.99	161.87	190.59	265.90	320.87	291.57	363.23	484.01
Banks................................	8 673 ..	217.19	297.42	346.66	459.56	613.37	523.85	629.71	600.61
Other sectors.........................	8 674 ..	377.81	498.92	567.03	728.82	868.27	819.90	1,020.26	980.54
Money market instruments.............	8 680 ..	278.96	303.36	277.36	356.80	420.76	369.16	499.96	405.63
Monetary authorities..................	8 681 ..	....	....	....	....	....	....	....	....
General government...................	8 682 ..	3.44	7.29	4.75	6.90	14.41	30.62	31.44	43.40
Banks................................	8 683 ..	233.14	252.52	234.40	317.91	368.01	294.92	433.70	322.51
Other sectors.........................	8 684 ..	42.37	43.54	38.21	31.99	38.33	43.63	34.81	39.72
Financial derivatives.......................	8 905 ..	....	....	....	**1,748.00**	**2,789.15**	**5,707.69**	**3,436.38**	**3,475.33**
Monetary authorities......................	8 906 ..	....	....	....	....	....	....	....	....
General government......................	8 907 ..	....	....	....	....	....	....	....	....
Banks....................................	8 908 ..	....	....	....	....	....	....	....	....
Other sectors............................	8 909 ..	....	....	....	....	....	....	....	....
Other investment..........................	8 753 ..	**3,824.92**	**4,868.73**	**5,343.06**	**6,422.88**	**8,249.14**	**6,589.40**	**6,160.29**	**6,347.90**
Trade credits.............................	8 756 ..	1.63	1.65	1.64	1.64	1.64	1.66	1.64	1.63
General government......................	8 757 ..	....	....	....	....	....	....	....	....
of which: Short-term...................	8 759 ..	....	....	....	....	....	....	....	....
Other sectors...........................	8 760 ..	1.63	1.65	1.64	1.64	1.64	1.66	1.64	1.63
of which: Short-term...................	8 762 ..	*1.63*	*1.65*	*1.64*	*1.64*	*1.64*	*1.66*	*1.64*	*1.63*
Loans...................................	8 764 ..	932.34	1,255.00	1,522.98	1,722.74	1,912.65	1,322.52	1,299.28	1,504.23
Monetary authorities....................	8 765 ..	....	....	....	....	....	....	....	....
of which: Use of Fund credit and loans from the Fund....	8 766 ..	....	....	....	....	....	....	....	....
of which: Short-term................	8 768 ..	....	....	....	....	....	....	....	....
General government...................	8 769 ..	2.37	3.62	3.31	4.12	4.11	3.64	4.89	5.00
of which: Short-term................	8 771 ..	....	....	....	....	....	....	....	....
Banks................................	8 772 ..	....	....	....	....	....	....	....	....
of which: Short-term................	8 774 ..	....	....	....	....	....	....	....	....
Other sectors.........................	8 775 ..	929.97	1,251.38	1,519.67	1,718.62	1,908.54	1,318.88	1,294.39	1,499.23
of which: Short-term................	8 777 ..	*929.97*	*1,250.53*	*1,518.92*	*1,717.80*	*1,907.70*	*1,318.29*	*1,293.75*	*1,498.60*
Currency and deposits....................	8 780 ..	2,866.97	3,585.54	3,789.98	4,656.31	6,300.34	5,245.98	4,822.10	4,803.72
Monetary authorities....................	8 781 ..	....	....	....	....	....	....	....	....
General government...................	8 782 ..	....	....	....	....	....	....	....	....
Banks................................	8 783 ..	2,866.97	3,585.54	3,789.98	4,656.31	6,300.34	5,245.98	4,822.10	4,803.72
Other sectors.........................	8 784 ..	....	....	....	....	....	....	....	....
Other liabilities..........................	8 786 ..	23.98	26.55	28.46	42.19	34.50	19.23	37.27	38.32
Monetary authorities....................	8 787 ..	....	....	....	....	....	....	15.89	15.61
of which: Short-term................	8 789 ..	....	....	....	....	....	....	....	....
General government...................	8 790 ..	4.64	3.08	2.94	4.42	4.45	3.08	3.89	5.51
of which: Short-term................	8 792 ..	*4.64*	*3.08*	*2.94*	*4.42*	*4.45*	*3.08*	*3.89*	*5.51*
Banks................................	8 793 ..	....	....	....	....	....	....	....	....
of which: Short-term................	8 795 ..	....	....	....	....	....	....	....	....
Other sectors.........................	8 796 ..	19.34	23.47	25.52	37.76	30.04	16.16	17.49	17.20
of which: Short-term................	8 798 ..	*19.34*	*23.47*	*25.52*	*37.76*	*30.04*	*16.16*	*17.49*	*17.20*
NET INTERNATIONAL INVESTMENT POSITION........	8 995 ..	**−209.06**	**−426.28**	**−434.38**	**−757.34**	**−647.42**	**−147.99**	**−492.77**	**−312.42**
Conversion rates: pound sterling per U.S. dollar (end of period)...............	0 102 ..	**.56032**	**.51776**	**.58075**	**.50942**	**.49915**	**.68597**	**.61747**	**.63877**

Table 1. ANALYTIC PRESENTATION, 2003–2010

(Billions of U.S. dollars)

	Code	2003	2004	2005	2006	2007	2008	2009	2010
A. Current Account[1]	4 993 Z.	**−519.09**	**−628.52**	**−745.78**	**−800.62**	**−710.30**	**−677.14**	**−376.55**	**−470.90**
Goods: exports f.o.b.	2 100 ..	733.11	825.48	915.51	1,043.15	1,168.05	1,311.51	1,073.92	1,293.22
Goods: imports f.o.b.	3 100 ..	−1,271.02	−1,486.32	−1,693.31	−1,876.05	−1,983.88	−2,138.65	−1,576.46	−1,935.58
Balance on Goods	4 100 ..	*−537.92*	*−660.84*	*−777.80*	*−832.90*	*−815.84*	*−827.14*	*−502.54*	*−642.36*
Services: credit	2 200 ..	290.41	337.66	371.93	416.67	486.51	531.17	501.12	544.36
Services: debit	3 200 ..	−243.48	−282.18	−302.75	−337.06	−367.40	−402.37	−379.85	−402.03
Balance on Goods and Services	4 991 ..	*−490.98*	*−605.36*	*−708.63*	*−753.29*	*−696.72*	*−698.34*	*−381.27*	*−500.03*
Income: credit	2 300 ..	322.41	415.79	537.34	684.62	833.83	813.90	599.50	663.24
Income: debit	3 300 ..	−278.72	−350.71	−468.75	−640.44	−732.35	−666.81	−471.50	−498.02
Balance on Goods, Services, and Income	4 992 ..	*−447.29*	*−540.28*	*−640.04*	*−709.10*	*−595.24*	*−551.26*	*−253.27*	*−334.81*
Current transfers: credit	2 379 Z.	14.99	20.28	18.96	26.60	24.87	25.62	22.01	16.09
Current transfers: debit	3 379 ..	−86.79	−108.52	−124.71	−118.11	−139.93	−151.50	−145.29	−152.18
B. Capital Account[1]	4 994 Z.	**−1.82**	**3.05**	**13.12**	**−1.79**	**.38**	**6.01**	**−.14**	**−.15**
Capital account: credit	2 994 Z.	.08	3.75	15.46	....	.49	6.17	....	....
Capital account: debit	3 994 ..	−1.90	−.70	−2.35	−1.79	−.11	−.16	−.14	−.15
Total, Groups A Plus B	4 981 ..	*−520.91*	*−625.47*	*−732.66*	*−802.41*	*−709.92*	*−671.13*	*−376.69*	*−471.05*
C. Financial Account[1]	4 995 W.	**531.36**	**529.53**	**686.62**	**806.77**	**617.38**	**735.42**	**298.08**	**256.12**
Direct investment abroad	4 505 ..	−149.56	−316.22	−36.24	−244.92	−414.04	−329.08	−303.61	−351.35
Direct investment in United States	4 555 Z.	63.75	145.97	112.64	243.15	221.17	310.09	158.58	236.23
Portfolio investment assets	4 602 ..	−123.13	−177.36	−257.54	−498.90	−390.75	280.29	−359.65	−165.62
Equity securities	4 610 ..	−118.00	−84.76	−186.69	−137.33	−147.78	38.55	−63.59	−79.13
Debt securities	4 619 ..	−5.13	−92.61	−70.85	−361.57	−242.96	241.74	−296.06	−86.49
Portfolio investment liabilities	4 652 Z.	550.16	867.34	832.04	1,126.74	1,156.61	523.68	359.88	706.91
Equity securities	4 660 ..	33.98	61.79	89.26	145.48	275.62	126.81	220.97	172.38
Debt securities	4 669 Z.	516.18	805.55	742.78	981.25	881.00	396.88	138.91	534.53
Financial derivatives	4 910 ..	....	....	....	29.71	6.22	−32.95	49.46	13.74
Financial derivatives assets	4 900 ..	....	....	....	....	....	....	....	....
Financial derivatives liabilities	4 905 ..	....	....	....	....	....	....	....	....
Other investment assets	4 703 ..	−54.26	−510.09	−266.96	−544.28	−648.69	385.75	576.18	−486.38
Monetary authorities	4 701 ..	....	....	....	....	−24.00	−529.73	543.46	10.20
General government	4 704 ..	.54	1.71	5.54	5.35	1.73	.11	−2.11	−2.66
Banks	4 705 ..	−25.72	−359.04	−151.08	−343.01	−500.50	455.50	−191.59	−427.00
Other sectors	4 728 ..	−29.08	−152.76	−121.42	−206.62	−125.92	459.86	226.43	−66.92
Other investment liabilities	4 753 W.	244.39	519.90	302.67	695.28	686.86	−402.37	−182.76	302.60
Monetary authorities	4 753 WA	10.59	13.30	8.45	2.23	−10.68	29.19	60.14	28.32
General government	4 753 ZB	−.72	−.13	−.42	2.82	5.44	9.03	10.58	12.12
Banks	4 753 ZC	136.06	346.70	232.42	344.33	474.60	−357.42	−257.21	207.34
Other sectors	4 753 ZD	98.46	160.03	62.23	345.91	217.51	−83.17	3.73	54.82
Total, Groups A Through C	4 983 ..	*10.44*	*−95.95*	*−46.04*	*4.37*	*−92.53*	*64.28*	*−78.61*	*−214.93*
D. Net Errors and Omissions	4 998 ..	**−11.97**	**93.15**	**31.94**	**−6.76**	**92.66**	**−59.45**	**130.79**	**216.76**
Total, Groups A Through D	4 984 ..	*−1.53*	*−2.80*	*−14.10*	*−2.39*	*.13*	*4.84*	*52.18*	*1.82*
E. Reserves and Related Items	4 802 A.	**1.53**	**2.80**	**14.10**	**2.39**	**−.13**	**−4.84**	**−52.18**	**−1.82**
Reserve assets	4 802 ..	1.53	2.80	14.10	2.39	−.13	−4.84	−52.18	−1.82
Use of Fund credit and loans	4 766 ..	....	....	....	....	....	....	....	....
Exceptional financing	4 920 ..	....	....	....	....	....	....	....	....

[1] Excludes components that have been classified in the categories of Group E.

Table 2. STANDARD PRESENTATION, 2003–2010

(Billions of U.S. dollars)

	Code	2003	2004	2005	2006	2007	2008	2009	2010
CURRENT ACCOUNT	4 993	**−519.09**	**−628.52**	**−745.78**	**−800.62**	**−710.30**	**−677.14**	**−376.55**	**−470.90**
A. GOODS	4 100	**−537.92**	**−660.84**	**−777.80**	**−832.90**	**−815.84**	**−827.14**	**−502.54**	**−642.36**
Credit	2 100	**733.11**	**825.48**	**915.51**	**1,043.15**	**1,168.05**	**1,311.51**	**1,073.92**	**1,293.22**
General merchandise: exports f.o.b.	2 110	720.02	810.73	896.83	1,018.80	1,137.46	1,271.28	1,044.61	1,256.69
Goods for processing: exports f.o.b.	2 150	....	....	....	....	....	....	....	....
Repairs on goods	2 160	3.29	3.49	3.83	3.75	4.09	4.02	4.43	4.52
Goods procured in ports by carriers	2 170	5.01	6.81	9.30	11.82	13.19	17.53	10.95	14.45
Nonmonetary gold	2 180	4.79	4.45	5.55	8.78	13.31	18.69	13.93	17.56
Debit	3 100	**−1,271.02**	**−1,486.32**	**−1,693.31**	**−1,876.05**	**−1,983.88**	**−2,138.65**	**−1,576.46**	**−1,935.58**
General merchandise: imports f.o.b.	3 110	−1,262.11	−1,475.73	−1,679.69	−1,859.84	−1,964.01	−2,111.36	−1,558.56	−1,911.36
Goods for processing: imports f.o.b.	3 150	....	....	....	....	....	....	....	....
Repairs on goods	3 160	−.80	−.83	−.90	−.95	−1.04	−1.04	−1.06	−1.02
Goods procured in ports by carriers	3 170	−4.53	−5.71	−8.29	−9.61	−10.01	−13.80	−7.99	−10.65
Nonmonetary gold	3 180	−3.58	−4.05	−4.43	−5.64	−8.83	−12.45	−8.84	−12.55
B. SERVICES	4 200	**46.93**	**55.48**	**69.17**	**79.61**	**119.12**	**128.79**	**121.27**	**142.33**
Total credit	2 200	*290.41*	*337.66*	*371.93*	*416.67*	*486.51*	*531.17*	*501.12*	*544.36*
Total debit	3 200	*−243.48*	*−282.18*	*−302.75*	*−337.06*	*−367.40*	*−402.37*	*−379.85*	*−402.03*
Transportation services, credit	2 205	**41.20**	**47.43**	**52.31**	**57.14**	**65.50**	**74.67**	**61.41**	**70.64**
Passenger	2 850	*15.09*	*17.93*	*20.61*	*21.64*	*25.19*	*30.96*	*26.10*	*30.93*
Freight	2 851	*13.64*	*14.69*	*15.95*	*16.89*	*18.94*	*22.15*	*17.24*	*19.54*
Other	2 852	*12.47*	*14.80*	*15.75*	*18.61*	*21.37*	*21.56*	*18.07*	*20.17*
Sea transport, passenger	2 207	....	....	....	....	....	....	....	....
Sea transport, freight	2 208	4.01	3.78	3.45	3.40	4.21	4.86	3.24	4.05
Sea transport, other	2 209	....	....	....	....	....	....	....	....
Air transport, passenger	2 211	15.09	17.93	20.61	21.64	25.19	30.96	26.10	30.93
Air transport, freight	2 212	6.87	7.73	9.33	10.08	11.31	13.48	10.57	11.97
Air transport, other	2 213	....	....	....	....	....	....	....	....
Other transport, passenger	2 215	....	....	....	....	....	....	....	....
Other transport, freight	2 216	2.77	3.19	3.17	3.41	3.42	3.81	3.43	3.52
Other transport, other	2 217	12.47	14.80	15.75	18.61	21.37	21.56	18.07	20.17
Transportation services, debit	3 205	**−60.30**	**−72.07**	**−78.77**	**−81.36**	**−82.89**	**−87.94**	**−67.28**	**−78.12**
Passenger	3 850	*−20.13*	*−23.73*	*−25.19*	*−26.65*	*−27.68*	*−31.84*	*−25.14*	*−27.28*
Freight	3 851	*−31.77*	*−39.08*	*−43.56*	*−43.90*	*−42.67*	*−42.04*	*−29.34*	*−37.55*
Other	3 852	*−8.40*	*−9.26*	*−10.02*	*−10.82*	*−12.54*	*−14.06*	*−12.80*	*−13.29*
Sea transport, passenger	3 207	....	....	....	....	....	....	....	....
Sea transport, freight	3 208	−24.17	−30.35	−34.29	−34.25	−32.86	−32.47	−21.63	−27.75
Sea transport, other	3 209	....	....	....	....	....	....	....	....
Air transport, passenger	3 211	−20.13	−23.73	−25.19	−26.65	−27.68	−31.84	−25.14	−27.28
Air transport, freight	3 212	−5.02	−5.98	−6.11	−6.27	−6.38	−6.18	−4.69	−6.44
Air transport, other	3 213	....	....	....	....	....	....	....	....
Other transport, passenger	3 215	....	....	....	....	....	....	....	....
Other transport, freight	3 216	−2.58	−2.76	−3.16	−3.38	−3.44	−3.39	−3.02	−3.37
Other transport, other	3 217	−8.40	−9.26	−10.02	−10.82	−12.54	−14.06	−12.80	−13.29
Travel, credit	2 236	**86.44**	**97.76**	**106.16**	**111.28**	**123.26**	**139.12**	**123.85**	**134.85**
Business travel	2 237	6.40	6.97	7.97	8.22	7.59	8.21	7.03	7.17
Personal travel	2 240	80.04	90.79	98.20	103.06	115.68	130.91	116.83	127.67
Travel, debit	3 236	**−61.97**	**−71.03**	**−74.79**	**−78.46**	**−83.01**	**−86.90**	**−80.83**	**−82.70**
Business travel	3 237	−.34	−.33	−.36	−.45	−.50	−.51	−.47	−.49
Personal travel	3 240	−61.63	−70.70	−74.43	−78.01	−82.51	−86.39	−80.35	−82.20
Other services, credit	2 200 BA	**162.77**	**192.48**	**213.45**	**248.26**	**297.75**	**317.37**	**315.85**	**338.87**
Communications	2 245	4.69	4.95	5.06	7.43	8.56	10.30	10.28	11.33
Construction	2 249	2.65	3.29	3.79	5.44	6.00	6.99	6.72	6.91
Insurance	2 253	5.97	7.31	7.57	9.44	10.84	13.40	14.43	14.60
Financial	2 260	19.70	27.77	31.00	47.88	61.38	63.03	62.44	66.39
Computer and information	2 262	6.25	6.70	7.32	10.08	11.99	13.12	13.48	13.77
Royalties and licence fees	2 266	56.81	67.09	74.45	83.55	97.80	102.13	97.18	105.58
Other business services	2 268	57.47	63.19	68.63	65.14	80.29	89.83	90.67	98.45
Personal, cultural, and recreational	2 287	....	....	....	....	....	....	....	....
Government, n.i.e.	2 291	9.21	12.17	15.64	19.29	20.89	18.58	20.65	21.85
Other services, debit	3 200 BA	**−121.21**	**−139.08**	**−149.20**	**−177.25**	**−201.50**	**−227.52**	**−231.75**	**−241.21**
Communications	3 245	−4.70	−5.20	−5.15	−6.95	−7.83	−8.35	−7.95	−8.37
Construction	3 249	−.65	−.58	−.43	−1.39	−1.52	−1.81	−1.68	−1.43
Insurance	3 253	−25.23	−29.09	−28.71	−39.38	−47.52	−58.91	−63.61	−61.77
Financial	3 260	−4.00	−5.49	−6.42	−14.73	−19.20	−17.22	−13.60	−13.80
Computer and information	3 262	−1.94	−2.15	−2.35	−13.43	−15.11	−16.89	−17.05	−19.38
Royalties and licence fees	3 266	−19.26	−23.69	−25.58	−25.04	−26.48	−29.62	−29.85	−33.45
Other business services	3 268	−39.77	−43.59	−49.53	−45.57	−52.30	−62.50	−63.12	−68.00
Personal, cultural, and recreational	3 287	....	....	....	....	....	....	....	....
Government, n.i.e.	3 291	−25.66	−29.29	−31.02	−30.75	−31.54	−32.22	−34.89	−35.01

Table 2 (Continued). STANDARD PRESENTATION, 2003–2010

(Billions of U.S. dollars)

	Code	2003	2004	2005	2006	2007	2008	2009	2010
C. INCOME	4 300	**43.69**	**65.08**	**68.59**	**44.18**	**101.48**	**147.09**	**128.00**	**165.22**
Total credit	2 300	*322.41*	*415.79*	*537.34*	*684.62*	*833.83*	*813.90*	*599.50*	*663.24*
Total debit	3 300	*−278.72*	*−350.71*	*−468.75*	*−640.44*	*−732.35*	*−666.81*	*−471.50*	*−498.02*
Compensation of employees, credit	2 310	**4.67**	**4.73**	**4.80**	**5.01**	**5.10**	**5.18**	**5.18**	**5.28**
Compensation of employees, debit	3 310	**−11.98**	**−13.02**	**−14.95**	**−15.53**	**−14.73**	**−15.93**	**−14.23**	**−14.51**
Investment income, credit	2 320	**317.74**	**411.06**	**532.54**	**679.61**	**828.73**	**808.72**	**594.32**	**657.96**
Direct investment income	2 330	186.42	250.61	294.54	324.82	370.76	413.74	356.20	432.00
Dividends and distributed branch profits	2 332	59.46	81.56	298.71	101.69	132.83	172.45	111.30	105.49
Reinvested earnings and undistributed branch profits	2 333	120.69	162.91	−10.32	217.34	230.53	233.09	237.66	320.52
Income on debt (interest)	2 334	6.27	6.14	6.14	5.79	7.40	8.20	7.24	5.99
Portfolio investment income	2 339	90.61	108.56	129.33	165.72	221.53	241.30	184.37	189.51
Income on equity	2 340	41.55	54.09	64.63	84.33	116.15	143.92	108.59	110.38
Income on bonds and notes	2 350	46.45	50.47	55.39	63.87	82.69	84.94	72.56	77.36
Income on money market instruments	2 360	2.60	4.00	9.31	17.52	22.70	12.44	3.22	1.77
Other investment income	2 370	40.72	51.89	108.68	189.07	236.44	153.68	53.75	36.45
Investment income, debit	3 320	**−266.75**	**−337.69**	**−453.80**	**−624.91**	**−717.63**	**−650.88**	**−457.26**	**−483.51**
Direct investment income	3 330	−73.75	−99.75	−121.33	−150.77	−126.18	−129.45	−94.03	−151.36
Dividends and distributed branch profits	3 332	−43.26	−36.29	−64.40	−63.23	−53.63	−65.72	−56.54	−33.96
Reinvested earnings and undistributed branch profits	3 333	−14.29	−49.53	−41.73	−69.12	−48.17	−39.14	−13.50	−93.71
Income on debt (interest)	3 334	−16.21	−13.94	−15.20	−18.42	−24.38	−24.59	−23.98	−23.69
Portfolio investment income	3 339	−163.13	−195.54	−238.34	−304.51	−381.48	−399.63	−332.48	−312.10
Income on equity	3 340	−25.66	−37.04	−38.08	−44.88	−54.93	−70.14	−59.75	−59.86
Income on bonds and notes	3 350	−131.48	−150.42	−181.46	−230.01	−291.09	−307.16	−266.80	−250.08
Income on money market instruments	3 360	−5.99	−8.08	−18.80	−29.62	−35.47	−22.54	−5.93	−2.16
Other investment income	3 370	−29.87	−42.40	−94.13	−169.63	−209.97	−121.60	−30.76	−20.05
D. CURRENT TRANSFERS	4 379	**−71.80**	**−88.24**	**−105.74**	**−91.52**	**−115.06**	**−125.89**	**−123.28**	**−136.09**
Credit	2 379	**14.99**	**20.28**	**18.96**	**26.60**	**24.87**	**25.62**	**22.01**	**16.09**
General government	2 380	....	....	....	....	....	....	....	....
Other sectors	2 390	14.99	20.28	18.96	26.60	24.87	25.62	22.01	16.09
Workers' remittances	2 391	....	....	....	....	....	....	....	....
Other current transfers	2 392	....	....	....	....	....	....	....	....
Debit	3 379	**−86.79**	**−108.52**	**−124.71**	**−118.11**	**−139.93**	**−151.50**	**−145.29**	**−152.18**
General government	3 380	−27.52	−29.97	−39.92	−34.28	−41.89	−44.85	−51.10	−55.08
Other sectors	3 390	−59.27	−78.56	−84.79	−83.84	−98.04	−106.65	−94.20	−97.10
Workers' remittances	3 391	−28.03	−30.38	−31.34	−34.13	−36.93	−38.47	−37.41	−37.08
Other current transfers	3 392	−31.24	−48.17	−53.44	−49.71	−61.11	−68.19	−56.79	−60.02
CAPITAL AND FINANCIAL ACCOUNT	4 996	**531.06**	**535.38**	**713.84**	**807.38**	**617.64**	**736.59**	**245.76**	**254.15**
CAPITAL ACCOUNT	4 994	**−1.82**	**3.05**	**13.12**	**−1.79**	**.38**	**6.01**	**−.14**	**−.15**
Total credit	2 994	*.08*	*3.75*	*15.46*	*....*	*.49*	*6.17*	*....*	*....*
Total debit	3 994	*−1.90*	*−.70*	*−2.35*	*−1.79*	*−.11*	*−.16*	*−.14*	*−.15*
Capital transfers, credit	2 400	**.08**	**3.75**	**15.46**	**....**	**.49**	**6.17**	**....**	**....**
General government	2 401	....	....	....	....	....	....	....	....
Debt forgiveness	2 402	....	....	....	....	....	....	....	....
Other capital transfers	2 410	....	....	....	....	....	....	....	....
Other sectors	2 430	....	....	....	....	....	....	....	....
Migrants' transfers	2 431	....	....	....	....	....	....	....	....
Debt forgiveness	2 432	....	....	....	....	....	....	....	....
Other capital transfers	2 440	....	....	....	....	....	....	....	....
Capital transfers, debit	3 400	**−1.90**	**−.70**	**−2.35**	**−1.79**	**−.11**	**−.16**	**−.14**	**−.15**
General government	3 401	....	....	....	....	....	....	....	....
Debt forgiveness	3 402	....	....	....	....	....	....	....	....
Other capital transfers	3 410	....	....	....	....	....	....	....	....
Other sectors	3 430	....	....	....	....	....	....	....	....
Migrants' transfers	3 431	....	....	....	....	....	....	....	....
Debt forgiveness	3 432	....	....	....	....	....	....	....	....
Other capital transfers	3 440	....	....	....	....	....	....	....	....
Nonproduced nonfinancial assets, credit	2 480	**....**	**....**	**....**	**....**	**....**	**....**	**....**	**....**
Nonproduced nonfinancial assets, debit	3 480	**....**	**....**	**....**	**....**	**....**	**....**	**....**	**....**

Table 2 (Continued). STANDARD PRESENTATION, 2003–2010

(Billions of U.S. dollars)

	Code	2003	2004	2005	2006	2007	2008	2009	2010
FINANCIAL ACCOUNT	4 995	532.89	532.33	700.72	809.17	617.26	730.58	245.90	254.30
A. DIRECT INVESTMENT	4 500	−85.81	−170.26	76.40	−1.77	−192.88	−18.99	−145.02	−115.13
Direct investment abroad	4 505	−149.56	−316.22	−36.24	−244.92	−414.04	−329.08	−303.61	−351.35
Equity capital	4 510	−35.48	−133.28	−61.94	−48.97	−200.85	−127.04	−24.51	−47.71
Claims on affiliated enterprises	4 515	....	....	....	....	....	....	....	....
Liabilities to affiliated enterprises	4 520	....	....	....	....	....	....	....	....
Reinvested earnings	4 525	−120.69	−162.91	10.32	−217.34	−230.53	−233.09	−237.66	−320.52
Other capital	4 530	6.61	−20.04	15.38	21.39	17.34	31.05	−41.43	16.88
Claims on affiliated enterprises	4 535	−18.02	−56.96	4.37	−11.71	−22.66	29.05	−39.22	−24.18
Liabilities to affiliated enterprises	4 540	24.63	36.92	11.02	33.10	40.00	2.00	−2.21	41.06
Direct investment in United States	4 555	63.75	145.97	112.64	243.15	221.17	310.09	158.58	236.23
Equity capital	4 560	93.42	92.90	70.73	115.03	142.25	255.72	134.31	114.72
Claims on direct investors	4 565	....	....	....	....	....	....	....	....
Liabilities to direct investors	4 570	....	....	....	....	....	....	....	....
Reinvested earnings	4 575	14.29	49.53	41.73	69.12	48.17	39.14	13.50	93.71
Other capital	4 580	−43.96	3.53	.18	59.01	30.75	15.23	10.77	27.80
Claims on direct investors	4 585	−22.97	−25.00	−14.67	−18.04	−78.90	−20.64	−2.24	−1.31
Liabilities to direct investors	4 590	−20.99	28.53	14.85	77.05	109.65	35.87	13.01	29.11
B. PORTFOLIO INVESTMENT	4 600	427.03	689.97	574.50	627.84	765.87	803.98	.23	541.29
Assets	4 602	−123.13	−177.36	−257.54	−498.90	−390.75	280.29	−359.65	−165.62
Equity securities	4 610	−118.00	−84.76	−186.69	−137.33	−147.78	38.55	−63.59	−79.13
Monetary authorities	4 611	....	....	....	....	....	....	....	....
General government	4 612	....	....	....	....	....	....	....	....
Banks	4 613	....	....	....	....	....	....	....	....
Other sectors	4 614	....	....	....	....	....	....	....	....
Debt securities	4 619	−5.13	−92.61	−70.85	−361.57	−242.96	241.74	−296.06	−86.49
Bonds and notes	4 620	−28.72	−85.79	−64.51	−227.80	−218.73	158.80	−163.23	−72.79
Monetary authorities	4 621	....	....	....	....	....	....	....	....
General government	4 622	....	....	....	....	....	....	....	....
Banks	4 623	....	....	....	....	....	....	....	....
Other sectors	4 624	....	....	....	....	....	....	....	....
Money market instruments	4 630	23.59	−6.81	−6.34	−133.77	−24.24	82.95	−132.84	−13.70
Monetary authorities	4 631	....	....	....	....	....	....	....	....
General government	4 632	....	....	....	....	....	....	....	....
Banks	4 633	18.61	−2.15	−1.88	−5.77	−32.57	34.31	1.18	−3.55
Other sectors	4 634	4.98	−4.66	−4.46	−128.00	8.34	48.63	−134.01	−10.15
Liabilities	4 652	550.16	867.34	832.04	1,126.74	1,156.61	523.68	359.88	706.91
Equity securities	4 660	33.98	61.79	89.26	145.48	275.62	126.81	220.97	172.38
Banks	4 663	....	....	....	....	....	....	....	....
Other sectors	4 664	....	....	....	....	....	....	....	....
Debt securities	4 669	516.18	805.55	742.78	981.25	881.00	396.88	138.91	534.53
Bonds and notes	4 670	486.33	705.00	785.80	953.69	713.86	110.47	266.55	571.99
Monetary authorities	4 671	....	....	....	....	....	....	....	....
General government	4 672	257.53	438.97	454.34	407.35	278.58	126.42	385.75	595.40
Banks	4 673	....	....	....	....	....	....	....	....
Other sectors	4 674	228.80	266.03	331.46	546.34	435.29	−15.95	−119.20	−23.41
Money market instruments	4 680	29.85	100.55	−43.02	27.57	167.13	286.41	−127.64	−37.46
Monetary authorities	4 681	....	....	....	....	....	....	....	....
General government	4 682	22.00	36.96	−58.94	−11.40	49.37	455.31	−7.57	−20.48
Banks	4 683	....	....	....	....	....	....	....	....
Other sectors	4 684	7.85	63.59	15.92	38.96	117.77	−168.90	−120.07	−16.98
C. FINANCIAL DERIVATIVES	4 910	....	....	....	29.71	6.22	−32.95	49.46	13.74
Monetary authorities	4 911	....	....	....	....	....	....	....	....
General government	4 912	....	....	....	....	....	....	....	....
Banks	4 913	....	....	....	....	....	....	....	....
Other sectors	4 914	....	....	....	....	....	....	....	....
Assets	4 900	....	....	....	....	....	....	....	....
Monetary authorities	4 901	....	....	....	....	....	....	....	....
General government	4 902	....	....	....	....	....	....	....	....
Banks	4 903	....	....	....	....	....	....	....	....
Other sectors	4 904	....	....	....	....	....	....	....	....
Liabilities	4 905	....	....	....	....	....	....	....	....
Monetary authorities	4 906	....	....	....	....	....	....	....	....
General government	4 907	....	....	....	....	....	....	....	....
Banks	4 908	....	....	....	....	....	....	....	....
Other sectors	4 909	....	....	....	....	....	....	....	....

Table 2 (Concluded). STANDARD PRESENTATION, 2003–2010

(Billions of U.S. dollars)

	Code	2003	2004	2005	2006	2007	2008	2009	2010
D. OTHER INVESTMENT	4 700	**190.14**	**9.81**	**35.72**	**151.00**	**38.17**	**−16.62**	**393.42**	**−183.78**
Assets	4 703	**−54.26**	**−510.09**	**−266.96**	**−544.28**	**−648.69**	**385.75**	**576.18**	**−486.38**
Trade credits	4 706	−2.23	−.41	−.36	−3.34	−8.71	6.78	3.46	−5.99
General government	4 707	....	....	....	....	....	....	....	....
of which: Short-term	4 709	....	....	....	....	....	....	....	....
Other sectors	4 710	−2.23	−.41	−.36	−3.34	−8.71	6.78	3.46	−5.99
of which: Short-term	4 712	....	....	....	....	....	....	....	....
Loans	4 714	14.94	−209.91	−100.42	−152.06	−416.30	581.60	29.06	−317.27
Monetary authorities	4 715	....	....	....	....	....	....	....	....
of which: Short-term	4 718	....	....	....	....	....	....	....	....
General government	4 719	.54	1.71	5.54	5.35	1.73	.11	−2.11	−2.66
of which: Short-term	4 721	....	....	....	....	....	....	....	....
Banks	4 722	1.49	−193.23	−93.32	−151.53	−431.38	560.61	36.21	−278.09
of which: Short-term	4 724	....	....	....	....	....	....	....	....
Other sectors	4 725	12.92	−18.40	−12.64	−5.88	13.35	20.88	−5.04	−36.53
of which: Short-term	4 727	....	....	....	....	....	....	....	....
Currency and deposits	4 730	−70.00	−251.94	−93.13	−276.30	−347.69	−246.44	420.62	−192.63
Monetary authorities	4 731	....	....	....	....	−24.00	−529.73	543.46	10.20
General government	4 732	....	....	....	....	....	....	....	....
Banks	4 733	−27.20	−165.81	−57.75	−191.48	−69.12	−105.11	−227.81	−148.91
Other sectors	4 734	−42.80	−86.13	−35.38	−84.82	−254.57	388.40	104.97	−53.91
Other assets	4 736	3.03	−47.84	−73.05	−112.59	124.00	43.80	123.05	29.50
Monetary authorities	4 737	....	....	....	....	....	....	....	....
of which: Short-term	4 739	....	....	....	....	....	....	....	....
General government	4 740	....	....	....	....	....	....	....	....
of which: Short-term	4 742	....	....	....	....	....	....	....	....
Banks	4 743	....	....	....	....	....	....	....	....
of which: Short-term	4 745	....	....	....	....	....	....	....	....
Other sectors	4 746	3.03	−47.84	−73.05	−112.59	124.00	43.80	123.05	29.50
of which: Short-term	4 748	....	....	....	....	....	....	....	....
Liabilities	4 753	**244.39**	**519.90**	**302.67**	**695.28**	**686.86**	**−402.37**	**−182.76**	**302.60**
Trade credits	4 756	2.50	.92	7.01	2.55	2.04	−7.56	1.03	7.39
General government	4 757	....	....	....	....	....	....	....	....
of which: Short-term	4 759	....	....	....	....	....	....	....	....
Other sectors	4 760	2.50	.92	7.01	2.55	2.04	−7.56	1.03	7.39
of which: Short-term	4 762	....	....	....	....	....	....	....	....
Loans	4 764	113.90	252.05	96.05	185.99	248.14	−527.09	−176.28	115.09
Monetary authorities	4 765	....	....	....	....	....	....	....	....
of which: Use of Fund credit and loans from the Fund	4 766	....	....	....	....	....	....	....	....
of which: Short-term	4 768	....	....	....	....	....	....	....	....
General government	4 769	....	....	....	....	....	....	....	....
of which: Short-term	4 771	....	....	....	....	....	....	....	....
Banks	4 772	113.77	241.30	121.81	84.90	232.33	−471.47	−166.76	140.44
of which: Short-term	4 774	....	....	....	....	....	....	....	....
Other sectors	4 775	.13	10.75	−25.76	101.09	15.82	−55.62	−9.52	−25.35
of which: Short-term	4 777	....	....	....	....	....	....	....	....
Currency and deposits	4 780	32.88	118.70	119.05	261.66	231.60	143.24	−77.82	95.22
Monetary authorities	4 781	10.59	13.30	8.45	2.23	−10.68	29.19	12.63	28.32
General government	4 782	....	....	....	....	....	....	....	....
Banks	4 783	22.29	105.40	110.61	259.43	242.27	114.05	−90.45	66.91
Other sectors	4 784	....	....	....	....	....	....	....	....
Other liabilities	4 786	95.11	148.23	80.57	245.09	205.09	−10.96	70.32	84.90
Monetary authorities	4 787	....	....	....	....	....	....	47.51	....
of which: Short-term	4 789	....	....	....	....	....	....	....	....
General government	4 790	−.72	−.13	−.42	2.82	5.44	9.03	10.58	12.12
of which: Short-term	4 792	....	....	....	....	....	....	....	....
Banks	4 793	....	....	....	....	....	....	....	....
of which: Short-term	4 795	....	....	....	....	....	....	....	....
Other sectors	4 796	95.83	148.36	80.99	242.27	199.66	−19.99	12.23	72.78
of which: Short-term	4 798	....	....	....	....	....	....	....	....
E. RESERVE ASSETS	4 802	**1.53**	**2.80**	**14.10**	**2.39**	**−.13**	**−4.84**	**−52.18**	**−1.82**
Monetary gold	4 812	....	....	....	....	....	....	....	....
Special drawing rights	4 811	.60	−.40	4.50	−.22	−.15	−.11	−48.14	−.03
Reserve position in the fund	4 810	1.50	3.83	10.21	3.35	1.02	−3.46	−3.37	−1.28
Foreign exchange	4 803	−.57	−.62	−.62	−.73	−.99	−1.27	−.67	−.51
Other claims	4 813	....	....	....	....	....	....	....	....
NET ERRORS AND OMISSIONS	4 998	**−11.97**	**93.15**	**31.94**	**−6.76**	**92.66**	**−59.45**	**130.79**	**216.76**

Table 3. INTERNATIONAL INVESTMENT POSITION (End-period stocks), 2003–2010

(Billions of U.S. dollars)

	Code	2003	2004	2005	2006	2007	2008	2009	2010
ASSETS..	8 995 C.	**7,638.09**	**9,340.63**	**11,961.55**	**14,428.14**	**18,399.68**	**19,464.72**	**18,487.04**	**20,315.36**
Direct investment abroad.................	8 505 ..	**2,054.46**	**2,498.49**	**2,651.72**	**2,948.17**	**3,553.10**	**3,748.51**	**4,067.50**	**4,429.43**
Equity capital and reinvested earnings...........	8 506 ..	....	....	....	....	....	....	....	....
Claims on affiliated enterprises................	8 507 ..	....	....	....	....	....	....	....	....
Liabilities to affiliated enterprises...........	8 508 ..	....	....	....	....	....	....	....	....
Other capital................................	8 530 ..	....	....	....	....	....	....	....	....
Claims on affiliated enterprises................	8 535 ..	....	....	....	....	....	....	....	....
Liabilities to affiliated enterprises...........	8 540 ..	....	....	....	....	....	....	....	....
Portfolio investment...........................	8 602 ..	**3,169.52**	**3,808.03**	**4,598.68**	**5,988.38**	**7,242.88**	**4,310.85**	**6,023.25**	**6,694.20**
Equity securities...............................	8 610 ..	2,079.42	2,560.42	3,317.71	4,328.96	5,247.99	2,748.43	3,995.30	4,485.59
Monetary authorities.........................	8 611 ..	....	....	....	....	....	....	....	....
General government.........................	8 612 ..	....	....	....	....	....	....	....	....
Banks.......................................	8 613 ..	....	....	....	....	....	....	....	....
Other sectors................................	8 614 ..	....	....	....	....	....	....	....	....
Debt securities................................	8 619 ..	1,090.10	1,247.61	1,280.98	1,659.42	1,994.89	1,562.43	2,027.95	2,208.61
Bonds and notes.............................	8 620 ..	868.95	984.98	1,011.55	1,275.52	1,587.09	1,237.28	1,570.34	1,737.27
Monetary authorities......................	8 621 ..	....	....	....	....	....	....	....	....
General government......................	8 622 ..	....	....	....	....	....	....	....	....
Banks....................................	8 623 ..	....	....	....	....	....	....	....	....
Other sectors.............................	8 624 ..	....	....	....	....	....	....	....	....
Money market instruments...................	8 630 ..	221.15	262.63	269.42	383.91	407.80	325.14	457.61	471.34
Monetary authorities......................	8 631 ..	....	....	....	....	....	....	....	....
General government......................	8 632 ..	....	....	....	....	....	....	....	....
Banks....................................	8 633 ..	5.70	7.86	9.74	15.51	48.08	14.07	12.89	16.44
Other sectors.............................	8 634 ..	215.44	254.78	259.69	368.40	359.72	311.07	444.72	454.90
Financial derivatives.........................	8 900 ..	....	....	**1,190.03**	**1,239.00**	**2,559.33**	**6,127.45**	**3,500.79**	**3,652.91**
Monetary authorities..........................	8 901 ..	....	....	....	....	....	....	....	....
General government...........................	8 902 ..	....	....	....	....	....	....	....	....
Banks...	8 903 ..	....	....	....	....	....	....	....	....
Other sectors.................................	8 904 ..	....	....	....	....	....	....	....	....
Other investment.............................	8 703 ..	**2,230.53**	**2,844.52**	**3,333.08**	**4,032.74**	**4,767.15**	**4,984.17**	**4,491.71**	**5,050.15**
Trade credits..................................	8 706 ..	28.65	29.23	29.23	32.80	41.79	34.76	31.45	37.39
General government...........................	8 707 ..	....	....	....	....	....	....	....	....
of which: Short-term.......................	8 709 ..	....	....	....	....	....	....	....	....
Other sectors................................	8 710 ..	28.65	29.23	29.23	32.80	41.79	34.76	31.45	37.39
of which: Short-term.......................	8 712 ..	....	....	....	....	....	....	....	....
Loans..	8 714 ..	961.23	1,192.49	1,291.72	1,573.50	2,003.04	1,781.36	1,767.38	2,099.29
Monetary authorities.........................	8 715 ..	....	....	....	....	....	....	....	....
of which: Short-term.......................	8 718 ..	....	....	....	....	....	....	....	....
General government...........................	8 719 ..	84.77	83.06	77.52	72.19	70.47	70.37	82.77	75.24
of which: Short-term.......................	8 721 ..	....	....	....	....	....	....	....	....
Banks...	8 722 ..	848.77	1,059.79	1,154.65	1,431.85	1,874.02	1,678.88	1,646.80	1,940.19
of which: Short-term.......................	8 724 ..	....	....	....	....	....	....	....	....
Other sectors................................	8 725 ..	27.69	49.64	59.55	69.46	58.55	32.11	37.81	83.86
of which: Short-term.......................	8 727 ..	....	....	....	....	....	....	....	....
Currency and deposits........................	8 730 ..	1,146.17	1,451.72	1,607.33	1,897.63	2,232.66	2,742.10	2,419.62	2,716.88
Monetary authorities.........................	8 731 ..	....	....	....	....	....	24.00	553.73	....
General government...........................	8 732 ..	....	....	....	....	....	....	....	....
Banks...	8 733 ..	538.19	719.28	792.26	983.11	1,060.96	1,236.80	1,492.32	1,640.64
Other sectors................................	8 734 ..	607.98	732.44	815.07	914.52	1,147.71	951.57	927.29	1,076.24
Other assets..................................	8 736 ..	94.48	171.07	404.80	528.80	489.66	425.96	273.26	196.59
Monetary authorities.........................	8 737 ..	....	....	....	....	....	....	....	....
of which: Short-term.......................	8 739 ..	....	....	....	....	....	....	....	....
General government...........................	8 740 ..	....	....	....	....	....	....	....	....
of which: Short-term.......................	8 742 ..	....	....	....	....	....	....	....	....
Banks...	8 743 ..	....	....	....	....	....	....	....	....
of which: Short-term.......................	8 745 ..	....	....	....	....	....	....	....	....
Other sectors................................	8 746 ..	94.48	171.07	404.80	528.80	489.66	425.96	273.26	196.59
of which: Short-term.......................	8 748 ..	....	....	....	....	....	....	....	....
Reserve assets................................	8 802 ..	**183.58**	**189.59**	**188.04**	**219.85**	**277.21**	**293.73**	**403.80**	**488.67**
Monetary gold.................................	8 812 ..	108.87	113.95	134.18	165.27	218.03	227.44	284.38	367.54
Special drawing rights.........................	8 811 ..	12.64	13.63	8.21	8.87	9.48	9.34	57.81	56.82
Reserve position in the Fund...................	8 810 ..	22.53	19.54	8.04	5.04	4.24	7.68	11.39	12.49
Foreign exchange..............................	8 803 ..	39.54	42.47	37.62	40.68	45.47	49.27	50.23	51.82
Other claims..................................	8 813 ..	....	....	....	....	....	....	....	....

Table 3 (Concluded). INTERNATIONAL INVESTMENT POSITION (End-period stocks), 2003–2010

(Billions of U.S. dollars)

	Code	2003	2004	2005	2006	2007	2008	2009	2010
LIABILITIES..	8 995 D.	**9,731.88**	**11,593.66**	**13,893.70**	**16,619.79**	**20,195.68**	**22,724.88**	**20,883.47**	**22,786.35**
Direct investment in United States................	8 555 ..	**1,580.99**	**1,742.72**	**1,905.98**	**2,154.06**	**2,345.92**	**2,397.40**	**2,441.71**	**2,658.93**
Equity capital and reinvested earnings.................	8 556 ..	....	....	....	....	....	....	....	....
Claims on direct investors............................	8 557 ..	....	....	....	....	....	....	....	....
Liabilities to direct investors........................	8 558 ..	....	....	....	....	....	....	....	....
Other capital..	8 580 ..	....	....	....	....	....	....	....	....
Claims on direct investors............................	8 585 ..	....	....	....	....	....	....	....	....
Liabilities to direct investors........................	8 590 ..	....	....	....	....	....	....	....	....
Portfolio investment...................................	8 652 ..	**5,546.32**	**6,621.23**	**7,337.84**	**8,843.52**	**10,326.98**	**9,475.87**	**10,463.86**	**11,708.88**
Equity securities..	8 660 ..	1,839.51	2,123.26	2,304.01	2,791.89	3,231.65	2,132.43	2,917.65	3,509.65
Banks..	8 663 ..	....	....	....	....	....	....	....	....
Other sectors..	8 664 ..	....	....	....	....	....	....	....	....
Debt securities..	8 669 ..	3,706.81	4,497.97	5,033.82	6,051.63	7,095.32	7,343.44	7,546.21	8,199.24
Bonds and notes..	8 670 ..	3,164.74	3,835.42	4,421.83	5,404.91	6,269.36	6,229.49	6,559.73	7,260.35
Monetary authorities................................	8 671 ..	....	....	....	....	....	....	....	....
General government.................................	8 672 ..	1,800.08	2,198.77	2,589.02	3,017.22	3,449.27	3,794.62	4,017.56	4,689.09
Banks..	8 673 ..	....	....	....	....	....	....	....	....
Other sectors..	8 674 ..	1,364.66	1,636.64	1,832.81	2,387.70	2,820.09	2,434.87	2,542.18	2,571.26
Money market instruments.........................	8 680 ..	542.07	662.55	611.99	646.72	825.96	1,113.95	986.48	938.88
Monetary authorities................................	8 681 ..	....	....	....	....	....	....	....	....
General government.................................	8 682 ..	290.92	323.67	264.73	253.33	302.70	758.01	750.44	729.96
Banks..	8 683 ..	....	....	....	....	....	....	....	....
Other sectors..	8 684 ..	251.15	338.88	347.27	393.39	523.26	355.94	236.04	208.92
Financial derivatives.................................	8 905 ..	....	....	**1,132.11**	**1,179.16**	**2,487.86**	**5,967.82**	**3,366.04**	**3,542.49**
Monetary authorities.....................................	8 906 ..	....	....	....	....	....	....	....	....
General government......................................	8 907 ..	....	....	....	....	....	....	....	....
Banks...	8 908 ..	....	....	....	....	....	....	....	....
Other sectors..	8 909 ..	....	....	....	....	....	....	....	....
Other investment.....................................	8 753 ..	**2,604.57**	**3,229.72**	**3,517.77**	**4,443.05**	**5,034.92**	**4,883.79**	**4,611.87**	**4,876.04**
Trade credits...	8 756 ..	17.17	18.18	23.05	25.67	27.87	20.15	21.26	28.67
General government....................................	8 757 ..	....	....	....	....	....	....	....	....
of which: Short-term................................	8 759 ..	....	....	....	....	....	....	....	....
Other sectors..	8 760 ..	17.17	18.18	23.05	25.67	27.87	20.15	21.26	28.67
of which: Short-term................................	8 762 ..	....	....	....	....	....	....	....	....
Loans...	8 764 ..	1,013.24	1,375.79	1,482.90	1,952.66	2,217.40	1,894.18	1,655.11	1,770.84
Monetary authorities...................................	8 765 ..	....	....	....	....	....	....	....	....
of which: Use of Fund credit and loans from the Fund....	8 766 ..	....	....	....	....	....	....	....	....
of which: Short-term................................	8 768 ..	....	....	....	....	....	....	....	....
General government....................................	8 769 ..	....	....	....	....	....	....	....	....
of which: Short-term................................	8 771 ..	....	....	....	....	....	....	....	....
Banks...	8 772 ..	818.70	1,143.20	1,260.23	1,621.70	1,885.10	1,631.55	1,436.48	1,577.58
of which: Short-term................................	8 774 ..	....	....	....	....	....	....	....	....
Other sectors..	8 775 ..	194.54	232.59	222.67	330.96	332.30	262.63	218.63	193.26
of which: Short-term................................	8 777 ..	....	....	....	....	....	....	....	....
Currency and deposits...................................	8 780 ..	1,148.13	1,279.44	1,383.44	1,695.05	1,935.07	2,216.90	2,158.02	2,252.09
Monetary authorities...................................	8 781 ..	258.65	271.95	280.40	282.63	271.95	301.14	313.77	342.09
General government....................................	8 782 ..	....	....	....	....	....	....	....	....
Banks...	8 783 ..	889.48	1,007.48	1,103.04	1,412.43	1,663.12	1,915.76	1,844.25	1,910.00
Other sectors..	8 784 ..	....	....	....	....	....	....	....	....
Other liabilities...	8 786 ..	426.02	556.32	628.38	769.66	854.59	752.56	777.48	824.44
Monetary authorities...................................	8 787 ..	7.28	7.61	7.00	7.37	7.74	7.55	55.36	54.39
of which: Short-term................................	8 789 ..	....	....	....	....	....	....	....	....
General government....................................	8 790 ..	16.42	16.29	15.87	18.68	24.12	33.15	43.73	55.86
of which: Short-term................................	8 792 ..	....	....	....	....	....	....	....	....
Banks...	8 793 ..	....	....	....	....	....	....	....	....
of which: Short-term................................	8 795 ..	....	....	....	....	....	....	....	....
Other sectors..	8 796 ..	402.32	532.42	605.51	743.61	822.73	711.87	678.39	714.20
of which: Short-term................................	8 798 ..	....	....	....	....	....	....	....	....
NET INTERNATIONAL INVESTMENT POSITION........	8 995 ..	**–2,093.79**	**–2,253.03**	**–1,932.15**	**–2,191.65**	**–1,796.00**	**–3,260.16**	**–2,396.43**	**–2,470.99**

Table 1. ANALYTIC PRESENTATION, 2003–2010

(Millions of U.S. dollars)

	Code	2003	2004	2005	2006	2007	2008	2009	2010
A. Current Account[1]	4 993 Z.	**−87.3**	**3.1**	**24.3**	**−391.9**	**−220.5**	**−1,480.3**	**206.7**	**−160.2**
Goods: exports f.o.b.	2 100 ..	2,281.2	3,145.0	3,774.1	4,399.8	5,099.9	7,095.5	6,408.2	8,060.8
Goods: imports f.o.b.	3 100 ..	−2,097.8	−2,992.2	−3,753.3	−4,898.5	−5,645.4	−8,809.7	−6,660.4	−8,316.8
Balance on Goods	4 100 ..	*183.4*	*152.8*	*20.8*	*−498.7*	*−545.5*	*−1,714.2*	*−252.1*	*−256.0*
Services: credit	2 200 ..	771.3	1,111.6	1,311.3	1,387.4	1,833.5	2,276.7	2,128.7	2,493.8
Services: debit	3 200 ..	−636.3	−786.1	−939.5	−978.7	−1,130.0	−1,454.9	−1,138.5	−1,426.5
Balance on Goods and Services	4 991 ..	*318.5*	*478.3*	*392.6*	*−89.9*	*158.0*	*−892.4*	*738.0*	*811.2*
Income: credit	2 300 ..	241.9	372.4	563.1	741.5	885.0	757.5	533.4	465.5
Income: debit	3 300 ..	−730.3	−960.4	−1,057.3	−1,169.8	−1,400.9	−1,493.8	−1,204.7	−1,558.9
Balance on Goods, Services, and Income	4 992 ..	*−169.9*	*−109.7*	*−101.5*	*−518.2*	*−357.9*	*−1,628.7*	*66.7*	*−282.2*
Current transfers: credit	2 379 Z.	95.0	127.2	143.1	150.0	164.6	187.7	177.9	179.0
Current transfers: debit	3 379 ..	−12.3	−14.3	−17.3	−23.7	−27.1	−39.3	−37.8	−57.0
B. Capital Account[1]	4 994 Z.	**4.3**	**5.3**	**3.8**	**6.5**	**3.7**	**.2**	**. . . .**	**. . . .**
Capital account: credit	2 994 Z.	4.3	5.3	3.8	6.5	3.7	.2	. . . .	. . . .
Capital account: debit	3 994 ..	. . . .	. . . .	. . . .	. . . .	. . . .	. . . .	. . . .	. . . .
Total, Groups A Plus B	4 981 ..	*−82.9*	*8.4*	*28.1*	*−385.4*	*−216.7*	*−1,480.0*	*206.7*	*−160.2*
C. Financial Account[1]	4 995 W.	**6.7**	**−81.9**	**923.6**	**2,935.6**	**1,506.2**	**2,801.4**	**1,002.0**	**−59.1**
Direct investment abroad	4 505 ..	−15.1	−17.7	−36.3	1.0	−89.4	10.9	−1.5	6.2
Direct investment in Uruguay	4 555 Z.	416.4	332.4	847.4	1,493.5	1,329.5	1,809.4	1,261.7	1,626.9
Portfolio investment assets	4 602 ..	−512.6	−695.7	577.7	−97.2	195.2	−54.8	−702.4	−1,335.9
Equity securities	4 610 ..	8.9	.9	.3	−.2	−.3	. . . .	. . . .	. . . .
Debt securities	4 619 ..	−521.6	−696.6	577.4	−96.9	195.5	−54.8	−702.4	−1,335.9
Portfolio investment liabilities	4 652 Z.	201.6	273.4	228.2	1,783.5	955.3	−502.9	−3.2	798.6
Equity securities	4 660 ..	−6.4	20.1	−2.4	−26.6	2.3	−11.7	−11.7	−11.7
Debt securities	4 669 Z.	208.0	253.3	230.6	1,810.2	953.0	−491.2	8.5	810.3
Financial derivatives	4 910 ..	. . . .	. . . .	. . . .	. . . .	. . . .	. . . .	. . . .	. . . .
Financial derivatives assets	4 900 ..	. . . .	. . . .	. . . .	. . . .	. . . .	. . . .	. . . .	. . . .
Financial derivatives liabilities	4 905 ..	. . . .	. . . .	. . . .	. . . .	. . . .	. . . .	. . . .	. . . .
Other investment assets	4 703 ..	−1,254.9	−259.7	−1,112.7	1,414.9	−2,027.5	43.4	−1,532.1	−808.4
Monetary authorities	4 701 ..	270.4	218.0	−324.8	334.1	−1,004.7	246.2	124.8	2.3
General government	4 704 ..	−14.9	−1.0	−1.1	−.8	. . . .	1.1	−.8	1.5
Banks	4 705 ..	−1,399.6	−397.6	−843.6	1,109.6	−483.4	−155.2	−837.2	−899.2
Other sectors	4 728 ..	−110.8	−79.1	56.7	−28.0	−539.4	−48.6	−818.9	86.9
Other investment liabilities	4 753 W.	1,171.3	285.4	419.4	−1,660.3	1,143.1	1,495.4	1,979.5	−346.5
Monetary authorities	4 753 WA	−63.9	−25.8	−31.5	−33.7	110.0	155.5	309.0	−110.7
General government	4 753 ZB	328.9	39.5	49.9	−575.1	7.1	280.8	903.7	−394.2
Banks	4 753 ZC	963.9	366.3	405.2	−1,197.1	124.0	863.4	511.7	74.3
Other sectors	4 753 ZD	−57.6	−94.6	−4.3	145.6	902.1	195.7	255.0	84.2
Total, Groups A Through C	4 983 ..	*−76.3*	*−73.5*	*951.8*	*2,550.2*	*1,289.5*	*1,321.4*	*1,208.7*	*−219.4*
D. Net Errors and Omissions	4 998 ..	**1,034.2**	**377.9**	**−173.4**	**−182.8**	**−284.1**	**910.9**	**378.1**	**−142.2**
Total, Groups A Through D	4 984 ..	*957.9*	*304.4*	*778.4*	*2,367.4*	*1,005.4*	*2,232.3*	*1,586.9*	*−361.5*
E. Reserves and Related Items	4 802 A.	**−957.9**	**−304.4**	**−778.4**	**−2,367.4**	**−1,005.4**	**−2,232.3**	**−1,586.9**	**361.5**
Reserve assets	4 802 ..	−1,380.4	−454.2	−620.9	15.8	−1,005.4	−2,232.3	−1,586.9	361.5
Use of Fund credit and loans	4 766 ..	422.5	149.8	−175.5	−2,383.2	. . . .	. . . .	. . . .	. . . .
Exceptional financing	4 920 ..	. . . .	. . . .	18.0	. . . .	. . . .	. . . .	. . . .	. . . .
Conversion rates: Uruguayan pesos per U.S. dollar	0 101 ..	**28.2087**	**28.7037**	**24.4786**	**24.0734**	**23.4710**	**20.9493**	**22.5680**	**20.0593**

[1] Excludes components that have been classified in the categories of Group E.

Table 2. STANDARD PRESENTATION, 2003–2010

(Millions of U.S. dollars)

	Code	2003	2004	2005	2006	2007	2008	2009	2010
CURRENT ACCOUNT	4 993	**−87.3**	**3.1**	**42.3**	**−391.9**	**−220.5**	**−1,480.3**	**206.7**	**−160.2**
A. GOODS	4 100	**183.4**	**152.8**	**20.8**	**−498.7**	**−545.5**	**−1,714.2**	**−252.1**	**−256.0**
Credit	2 100	**2,281.2**	**3,145.0**	**3,774.1**	**4,399.8**	**5,099.9**	**7,095.5**	**6,408.2**	**8,060.8**
General merchandise: exports f.o.b.	2 110	2,205.9	3,041.7	3,622.2	4,256.5	4,913.6	6,748.0	6,185.0	7,770.5
Goods for processing: exports f.o.b.	2 150	....	....	....	....	....	....	....	....
Repairs on goods	2 160	....	....	....	....	....	....	....	....
Goods procured in ports by carriers	2 170	75.3	103.3	151.9	143.3	186.3	347.5	223.3	290.3
Nonmonetary gold	2 180	....	....	....	....	....	....	....	....
Debit	3 100	**−2,097.8**	**−2,992.2**	**−3,753.3**	**−4,898.5**	**−5,645.4**	**−8,809.7**	**−6,660.4**	**−8,316.8**
General merchandise: imports f.o.b.	3 110	−2,064.6	−2,963.2	−3,696.2	−4,833.6	−5,562.5	−8,708.0	−6,606.2	−8,235.7
Goods for processing: imports f.o.b.	3 150	....	....	....	....	....	....	....	....
Repairs on goods	3 160	....	....	....	....	....	....	....	....
Goods procured in ports by carriers	3 170	−33.2	−29.0	−57.0	−64.8	−82.9	−101.7	−54.2	−81.1
Nonmonetary gold	3 180	....	....	....	....	....	....	....	....
B. SERVICES	4 200	**135.0**	**325.5**	**371.8**	**408.7**	**703.4**	**821.8**	**990.2**	**1,067.3**
Total credit	2 200	*771.3*	*1,111.6*	*1,311.3*	*1,387.4*	*1,833.5*	*2,276.7*	*2,128.7*	*2,493.8*
Total debit	3 200	*−636.3*	*−786.1*	*−939.5*	*−978.7*	*−1,130.0*	*−1,454.9*	*−1,138.5*	*−1,426.5*
Transportation services, credit	2 205	**258.8**	**379.0**	**464.8**	**480.9**	**562.3**	**672.7**	**334.2**	**445.7**
Passenger	2 850	*74.4*	*97.1*	*105.0*	*113.2*	*119.0*	*143.9*	*96.3*	*111.4*
Freight	2 851	*111.7*	*215.4*	*286.9*	*286.5*	*324.1*	*398.6*	*138.2*	*212.7*
Other	2 852	*72.7*	*66.5*	*73.0*	*81.1*	*119.2*	*130.3*	*99.7*	*121.6*
Sea transport, passenger	2 207	....	....	....	....	....	....	....	....
Sea transport, freight	2 208	....	....	....	....	....	....	....	....
Sea transport, other	2 209	....	....	....	....	....	....	....	....
Air transport, passenger	2 211	....	....	....	....	....	....	....	....
Air transport, freight	2 212	....	....	....	....	....	....	....	....
Air transport, other	2 213	....	....	....	....	....	....	....	....
Other transport, passenger	2 215	74.4	97.1	105.0	113.2	119.0	143.9	96.3	111.4
Other transport, freight	2 216	111.7	215.4	286.9	286.5	324.1	398.6	138.2	212.7
Other transport, other	2 217	72.7	66.5	73.0	81.1	119.2	130.3	99.7	121.6
Transportation services, debit	3 205	**−264.6**	**−353.0**	**−419.0**	**−449.7**	**−549.5**	**−640.6**	**−447.3**	**−617.5**
Passenger	3 850	*−66.7*	*−73.4*	*−79.3*	*−91.7*	*−115.1*	*−107.7*	*−100.3*	*−114.5*
Freight	3 851	*−100.6*	*−135.0*	*−168.6*	*−180.2*	*−236.2*	*−339.0*	*−271.0*	*−357.6*
Other	3 852	*−97.4*	*−144.6*	*−171.1*	*−177.8*	*−198.2*	*−194.0*	*−76.0*	*−145.3*
Sea transport, passenger	3 207	....	....	....	....	....	....	....	....
Sea transport, freight	3 208	....	....	....	....	....	....	....	....
Sea transport, other	3 209	....	....	....	....	....	....	....	....
Air transport, passenger	3 211	....	....	....	....	....	....	....	....
Air transport, freight	3 212	....	....	....	....	....	....	....	....
Air transport, other	3 213	....	....	....	....	....	....	....	....
Other transport, passenger	3 215	−66.7	−73.4	−79.3	−91.7	−115.1	−107.7	−100.3	−114.5
Other transport, freight	3 216	−100.6	−135.0	−168.6	−180.2	−236.2	−339.0	−271.0	−357.6
Other transport, other	3 217	−97.4	−144.6	−171.1	−177.8	−198.2	−194.0	−76.0	−145.3
Travel, credit	2 236	**344.7**	**493.9**	**594.4**	**597.8**	**808.9**	**1,051.4**	**1,312.1**	**1,496.4**
Business travel	2 237	....	....	....	....	....	....	....	....
Personal travel	2 240	344.7	493.9	594.4	597.8	808.9	1,051.4	1,312.1	1,496.4
Travel, debit	3 236	**−168.8**	**−193.6**	**−251.7**	**−213.2**	**−239.3**	**−357.5**	**−336.1**	**−419.0**
Business travel	3 237	....	....	....	....	....	....	....	....
Personal travel	3 240	−168.8	−193.6	−251.7	−213.2	−239.3	−357.5	−336.1	−419.0
Other services, credit	2 200 BA	**167.9**	**238.6**	**252.0**	**308.8**	**462.3**	**552.6**	**482.3**	**551.7**
Communications	2 245	23.0	24.4	21.6	22.0	20.8	26.8	27.2	25.7
Construction	2 249	....	....	....	....	....	....	....	....
Insurance	2 253	2.1	9.7	4.2	3.6	4.0	2.9	8.5	8.1
Financial	2 260	58.0	53.4	65.7	56.0	70.9	83.0	89.1	121.3
Computer and information	2 262	11.7	72.1	82.5	121.6	153.6	179.7	145.0	179.8
Royalties and licence fees	2 266	....	....	.1	....	.1	.1	.1	.1
Other business services	2 268	47.1	52.2	51.5	76.7	183.2	223.9	176.1	180.4
Personal, cultural, and recreational	2 287	.4	.9	.4	2.2	.2	.4	.4	.4
Government, n.i.e.	2 291	25.7	25.9	26.1	26.6	29.6	35.9	35.9	35.9
Other services, debit	3 200 BA	**−202.9**	**−239.4**	**−268.7**	**−315.7**	**−341.2**	**−456.7**	**−355.1**	**−390.1**
Communications	3 245	−18.3	−19.2	−20.0	−16.6	−17.0	−26.7	−28.0	−27.8
Construction	3 249	....	....	....	....	....	....	....	....
Insurance	3 253	−19.0	−27.0	−24.9	−30.4	−28.7	−39.9	−49.4	−48.8
Financial	3 260	−17.5	−10.8	−11.3	−14.3	−27.0	−12.2	−14.2	−12.4
Computer and information	3 262	−1.7	−3.8	−3.9	−4.2	−4.8	−6.1	−6.1	−6.1
Royalties and licence fees	3 266	−14.0	−4.3	−6.9	−7.3	−7.6	−16.6	−16.6	−16.6
Other business services	3 268	−87.3	−128.6	−153.1	−192.2	−194.7	−281.9	−167.4	−205.1
Personal, cultural, and recreational	3 287	−10.5	−7.2	−10.0	−9.5	−10.1	−12.0	−12.0	−12.0
Government, n.i.e.	3 291	−34.5	−38.4	−38.7	−41.3	−51.3	−61.4	−61.4	−61.4

Table 2 (Continued). STANDARD PRESENTATION, 2003–2010

(Millions of U.S. dollars)

	Code	2003	2004	2005	2006	2007	2008	2009	2010
C. INCOME	4 300	**−488.4**	**−588.0**	**−494.2**	**−428.3**	**−515.9**	**−736.3**	**−671.3**	**−1,093.5**
Total credit	2 300	*241.9*	*372.4*	*563.1*	*741.5*	*885.0*	*757.5*	*533.4*	*465.5*
Total debit	3 300	*−730.3*	*−960.4*	*−1,057.3*	*−1,169.8*	*−1,400.9*	*−1,493.8*	*−1,204.7*	*−1,558.9*
Compensation of employees, credit	2 310	....	....	....	....	....	....	....	....
Compensation of employees, debit	3 310	....	....	....	....	....	....	....	....
Investment income, credit	2 320	**241.9**	**372.4**	**563.1**	**741.5**	**885.0**	**757.5**	**533.4**	**465.5**
Direct investment income	2 330	3.2	8.0	5.4	18.5	16.9	21.0	20.0	29.8
Dividends and distributed branch profits	2 332	3.2	7.5	3.2	17.6	16.1	20.7	19.7	29.5
Reinvested earnings and undistributed branch profits	2 333	....	....	....	....	....	....	....	....
Income on debt (interest)	2 334	....	.5	2.1	.9	.9	.3	.3	.3
Portfolio investment income	2 339	5.7	128.3	168.5	195.6	196.0	232.0	229.4	240.7
Income on equity	2 340	....	1.3	.4	.9	3.0	13.6	8.0	10.8
Income on bonds and notes	2 350	5.7	127.0	168.1	194.7	193.0	218.5	221.4	229.9
Income on money market instruments	2 360	....	....	....	....	....	....	....	....
Other investment income	2 370	232.9	236.0	389.2	527.5	672.1	504.4	284.0	194.9
Investment income, debit	3 320	**−730.3**	**−960.4**	**−1,057.3**	**−1,169.8**	**−1,400.9**	**−1,493.8**	**−1,204.7**	**−1,558.9**
Direct investment income	3 330	−127.4	−229.0	−227.6	−260.9	−530.8	−662.8	−400.8	−730.3
Dividends and distributed branch profits	3 332	54.5	−79.3	−85.9	−35.5	−187.7	−44.4	155.6	137.6
Reinvested earnings and undistributed branch profits	3 333	−172.9	−142.1	−132.6	−218.6	−331.3	−609.1	−547.2	−858.7
Income on debt (interest)	3 334	−9.0	−7.6	−9.0	−6.8	−11.8	−9.2	−9.2	−9.2
Portfolio investment income	3 339	−220.5	−267.4	−295.5	−456.0	−492.1	−476.9	−457.0	−516.1
Income on equity	3 340	−21.7	−9.1	−5.6	−.8	....	....	....	....
Income on bonds and notes	3 350	−198.8	−258.3	−290.0	−455.1	−492.1	−471.2	−455.6	−504.9
Income on money market instruments	3 360	....	....	....	....	....	−5.7	−1.5	−11.2
Other investment income	3 370	−382.4	−464.0	−534.2	−452.9	−378.0	−354.2	−346.9	−312.5
D. CURRENT TRANSFERS	4 379	**82.7**	**112.8**	**143.8**	**126.3**	**137.5**	**148.4**	**140.0**	**122.0**
Credit	2 379	**95.0**	**127.2**	**161.1**	**150.0**	**164.6**	**187.7**	**177.9**	**179.0**
General government	2 380	18.2	20.1	40.6	19.3	20.5	29.2	26.2	25.5
Other sectors	2 390	76.8	107.1	120.5	130.7	144.0	158.5	151.6	153.5
Workers' remittances	2 391	61.8	69.9	76.7	88.9	96.5	107.9	101.1	102.9
Other current transfers	2 392	15.0	37.2	43.8	41.8	47.6	50.6	50.6	50.6
Debit	3 379	**−12.3**	**−14.3**	**−17.3**	**−23.7**	**−27.1**	**−39.3**	**−37.8**	**−57.0**
General government	3 380	−8.1	−8.7	−11.2	−12.7	−13.4	−22.5	−20.0	−38.2
Other sectors	3 390	−4.2	−5.7	−6.1	−11.0	−13.7	−16.9	−17.8	−18.8
Workers' remittances	3 391	−1.4	−1.8	−2.2	−2.8	−3.5	−4.7	−5.6	−6.7
Other current transfers	3 392	−2.8	−3.9	−3.9	−8.2	−10.2	−12.2	−12.2	−12.2
CAPITAL AND FINANCIAL ACCOUNT	4 996	**−946.9**	**−381.0**	**131.1**	**574.7**	**504.5**	**569.3**	**−584.9**	**302.4**
CAPITAL ACCOUNT	4 994	**4.3**	**5.3**	**3.8**	**6.5**	**3.7**	**.2**	**....**	**....**
Total credit	2 994	*4.3*	*5.3*	*3.8*	*6.5*	*3.7*	*.2*	....	....
Total debit	3 994	....	....	....	....	....	....	....	....
Capital transfers, credit	2 400	**4.3**	**5.3**	**3.8**	**6.5**	**3.7**	**.2**	**....**	**....**
General government	2 401	4.3	5.3	3.8	6.5	3.7	.2	....	....
Debt forgiveness	2 402	4.3	5.3	3.8	6.5	3.7	.2	....	....
Other capital transfers	2 410	....	....	....	....	....	....	....	....
Other sectors	2 430	....	....	....	....	....	....	....	....
Migrants' transfers	2 431	....	....	....	....	....	....	....	....
Debt forgiveness	2 432	....	....	....	....	....	....	....	....
Other capital transfers	2 440	....	....	....	....	....	....	....	....
Capital transfers, debit	3 400	**....**	**....**	**....**	**....**	**....**	**....**	**....**	**....**
General government	3 401	....	....	....	....	....	....	....	....
Debt forgiveness	3 402	....	....	....	....	....	....	....	....
Other capital transfers	3 410	....	....	....	....	....	....	....	....
Other sectors	3 430	....	....	....	....	....	....	....	....
Migrants' transfers	3 431	....	....	....	....	....	....	....	....
Debt forgiveness	3 432	....	....	....	....	....	....	....	....
Other capital transfers	3 440	....	....	....	....	....	....	....	....
Nonproduced nonfinancial assets, credit	2 480	....	....	....	....	....	....	....	....
Nonproduced nonfinancial assets, debit	3 480	....	....	....	....	....	....	....	....

Table 2 (Continued). STANDARD PRESENTATION, 2003–2010

(Millions of U.S. dollars)

	Code	2003	2004	2005	2006	2007	2008	2009	2010
FINANCIAL ACCOUNT	4 995	**−951.3**	**−386.3**	**127.3**	**568.2**	**500.8**	**569.1**	**−584.9**	**302.4**
A. DIRECT INVESTMENT	4 500	**401.3**	**314.7**	**811.1**	**1,494.5**	**1,240.1**	**1,820.3**	**1,260.2**	**1,633.1**
Direct investment abroad	4 505	**−15.1**	**−17.7**	**−36.3**	**1.0**	**−89.4**	**10.9**	**−1.5**	**6.2**
Equity capital	4 510	−10.0	−24.2	−39.9	−1.7	−88.7	.6	−11.8	−4.2
Claims on affiliated enterprises	4 515	−10.0	−24.2	−39.9	−1.7	−88.7	.6	−11.8	−4.2
Liabilities to affiliated enterprises	4 520	....	....	....	....	....	....	....	....
Reinvested earnings	4 525	....	....	....	....	....	....	....	....
Other capital	4 530	−5.0	6.5	3.6	2.7	−.7	10.3	10.3	10.3
Claims on affiliated enterprises	4 535	−6.3	1.9	−4.0	8.2	−.2	.6	.6	.6
Liabilities to affiliated enterprises	4 540	1.2	4.6	7.6	−5.5	−.5	9.8	9.8	9.8
Direct investment in Uruguay	4 555	**416.4**	**332.4**	**847.4**	**1,493.5**	**1,329.5**	**1,809.4**	**1,261.7**	**1,626.9**
Equity capital	4 560	222.8	138.7	231.0	576.3	550.5	1,011.6	634.8	732.9
Claims on direct investors	4 565	....	....	....	....	....	....	....	....
Liabilities to direct investors	4 570	222.8	138.7	231.0	576.3	550.5	1,011.6	634.8	732.9
Reinvested earnings	4 575	172.9	142.1	132.6	218.6	331.3	609.1	547.2	858.7
Other capital	4 580	20.7	51.6	483.8	698.5	447.7	188.7	79.8	35.3
Claims on direct investors	4 585	14.9	−15.8	28.4	−20.3	−29.8	−26.5	−27.6	−25.4
Liabilities to direct investors	4 590	5.7	67.4	455.4	718.9	477.4	215.2	107.4	60.8
B. PORTFOLIO INVESTMENT	4 600	**−311.0**	**−422.2**	**805.9**	**1,686.4**	**1,150.5**	**−557.7**	**−705.6**	**−537.3**
Assets	4 602	**−512.6**	**−695.7**	**577.7**	**−97.2**	**195.2**	**−54.8**	**−702.4**	**−1,335.9**
Equity securities	4 610	8.9	.9	.3	−.2	−.3	....	....	....
Monetary authorities	4 611	....	....	....	....	....	....	....	....
General government	4 612	....	....	....	....	....	....	....	....
Banks	4 613	....	....	....	....	....	....	....	....
Other sectors	4 614	8.9	.9	.3	−.2	−.3	....	....	....
Debt securities	4 619	−521.6	−696.6	577.4	−96.9	195.5	−54.8	−702.4	−1,335.9
Bonds and notes	4 620	−521.6	−696.6	577.4	−96.9	195.5	−54.8	−702.4	−1,335.9
Monetary authorities	4 621	59.8	−2.5	38.3	5.6	....	....	....	....
General government	4 622	....	....	....	....	....	....	....	....
Banks	4 623	−582.0	−692.4	225.1	−76.5	176.7	−57.8	−702.2	−1,335.1
Other sectors	4 624	.6	−1.7	314.0	−26.0	18.8	3.1	−.2	−.8
Money market instruments	4 630	....	....	....	....	....	....	....	....
Monetary authorities	4 631	....	....	....	....	....	....	....	....
General government	4 632	....	....	....	....	....	....	....	....
Banks	4 633	....	....	....	....	....	....	....	....
Other sectors	4 634	....	....	....	....	....	....	....	....
Liabilities	4 652	**201.6**	**273.4**	**228.2**	**1,783.5**	**955.3**	**−502.9**	**−3.2**	**798.6**
Equity securities	4 660	−6.4	20.1	−2.4	−26.6	2.3	−11.7	−11.7	−11.7
Banks	4 663	....	....	....	....	....	....	....	....
Other sectors	4 664	−6.4	20.1	−2.4	−26.6	2.3	−11.7	−11.7	−11.7
Debt securities	4 669	208.0	253.3	230.6	1,810.2	953.0	−491.2	8.5	810.3
Bonds and notes	4 670	208.0	253.3	230.6	1,810.2	953.0	−491.2	8.5	810.3
Monetary authorities	4 671	−242.2	−31.4	−116.5	−23.6	−3.3	38.0	26.5	396.8
General government	4 672	450.3	271.8	403.1	1,854.8	954.9	−511.7	−18.9	406.9
Banks	4 673	−.1	12.9	−56.1	−21.0	1.5	−17.6	1.0	6.6
Other sectors	4 674	....	....	....	....	....	....	....	....
Money market instruments	4 680	....	....	....	....	....	....	....	....
Monetary authorities	4 681	....	....	....	....	....	....	....	....
General government	4 682	....	....	....	....	....	....	....	....
Banks	4 683	....	....	....	....	....	....	....	....
Other sectors	4 684	....	....	....	....	....	....	....	....
C. FINANCIAL DERIVATIVES	4 910	....	....	....	....	....	....	....	....
Monetary authorities	4 911	....	....	....	....	....	....	....	....
General government	4 912	....	....	....	....	....	....	....	....
Banks	4 913	....	....	....	....	....	....	....	....
Other sectors	4 914	....	....	....	....	....	....	....	....
Assets	4 900	....	....	....	....	....	....	....	....
Monetary authorities	4 901	....	....	....	....	....	....	....	....
General government	4 902	....	....	....	....	....	....	....	....
Banks	4 903	....	....	....	....	....	....	....	....
Other sectors	4 904	....	....	....	....	....	....	....	....
Liabilities	4 905	....	....	....	....	....	....	....	....
Monetary authorities	4 906	....	....	....	....	....	....	....	....
General government	4 907	....	....	....	....	....	....	....	....
Banks	4 908	....	....	....	....	....	....	....	....
Other sectors	4 909	....	....	....	....	....	....	....	....

Table 2 (Concluded). STANDARD PRESENTATION, 2003–2010

(Millions of U.S. dollars)

	Code	2003	2004	2005	2006	2007	2008	2009	2010
D. OTHER INVESTMENT	4 700	**338.8**	**175.5**	**−868.9**	**−2,628.5**	**−884.4**	**1,538.8**	**447.3**	**−1,154.9**
Assets	4 703	**−1,254.9**	**−259.7**	**−1,112.7**	**1,414.9**	**−2,027.5**	**43.4**	**−1,532.1**	**−808.4**
Trade credits	4 706	−1.8	−7.3	−110.0	48.9	−36.5	−70.2	−59.4	−63.1
General government	4 707	....	....	....	....	....	....	....	....
of which: Short-term	4 709	....	....	....	....	....	....	....	....
Other sectors	4 710	−1.8	−7.3	−110.0	48.9	−36.5	−70.2	−59.4	−63.1
of which: Short-term	4 712	−1.8	−7.3	−110.0	48.9	−36.5	−70.2	−59.4	−63.1
Loans	4 714	−9.7	29.0	38.6	−6.0	−5.6	−46.7	−24.9	−7.3
Monetary authorities	4 715	....	....	....	....	....	....	....	....
of which: Short-term	4 718	....	....	....	....	....	....	....	....
General government	4 719	....	....	....	....	....	....	....	....
of which: Short-term	4 721	....	....	....	....	....	....	....	....
Banks	4 722	3.4	20.4	41.1	−6.6	−9.4	−41.7	−21.6	−12.9
of which: Short-term	4 724	3.4	20.4	41.1	−6.6	−9.4	−41.7	−21.6	−12.9
Other sectors	4 725	−13.1	8.6	−2.5	.6	3.8	−5.1	−3.3	5.6
of which: Short-term	4 727	−13.1	8.6	−2.5	.6	3.8	−5.1	−3.3	5.6
Currency and deposits	4 730	−574.5	−297.2	−405.7	112.4	−1,811.9	525.4	−1,413.2	−879.7
Monetary authorities	4 731	283.2	224.1	−330.5	329.3	−896.3	597.7	125.2	−22.5
General government	4 732	−14.9	−1.0	−1.1	−.8	....	1.1	−.8	1.5
Banks	4 733	−556.7	−448.4	−248.3	−114.9	−403.6	−164.3	−809.3	−922.1
Other sectors	4 734	−286.1	−72.0	174.1	−101.2	−512.0	90.8	−728.2	63.5
Other assets	4 736	−669.0	15.9	−635.6	1,259.5	−173.6	−364.9	−34.7	141.6
Monetary authorities	4 737	−12.8	−6.1	5.7	4.8	−108.4	−351.6	−.4	24.8
of which: Short-term	4 739	....	....	....	....	....	....	....	....
General government	4 740	....	....	....	....	....	....	....	....
of which: Short-term	4 742	....	....	....	....	....	....	....	....
Banks	4 743	−846.3	30.4	−636.4	1,231.1	−70.4	50.8	−6.2	35.9
of which: Short-term	4 745	−846.3	30.4	−636.4	1,231.1	−70.4	50.8	−6.2	35.9
Other sectors	4 746	190.1	−8.4	−4.9	23.7	5.2	−64.1	−28.0	80.9
of which: Short-term	4 748	190.1	−8.4	−4.9	23.7	5.2	−64.1	−28.0	80.9
Liabilities	4 753	**1,593.7**	**435.2**	**243.9**	**−4,043.4**	**1,143.1**	**1,495.4**	**1,979.5**	**−346.5**
Trade credits	4 756	1.8	12.2	82.6	112.4	440.7	−207.3	219.8	189.0
General government	4 757	....	....	....	....	....	....	....	....
of which: Short-term	4 759	....	....	....	....	....	....	....	....
Other sectors	4 760	1.8	12.2	82.6	112.4	440.7	−207.3	219.8	189.0
of which: Short-term	4 762	1.8	12.2	82.6	112.4	440.7	−207.3	219.8	189.0
Loans	4 764	54.1	−175.7	−358.4	−2,925.7	427.2	713.6	939.9	−567.5
Monetary authorities	4 765	349.6	113.0	−192.1	−2,400.2	−10.9	−17.3	−17.7	−40.7
of which: Use of Fund credit and loans from the Fund	4 766	422.5	149.8	−175.5	−2,383.2	....	....	....	....
of which: Short-term	4 768	....	....	....	....	....	....	....	....
General government	4 769	328.9	39.5	49.9	−575.1	7.1	280.8	903.7	−394.2
of which: Short-term	4 771	....	....	....	....	....	....	....	....
Banks	4 772	−557.5	−228.2	−127.1	18.3	−44.4	67.4	45.4	.4
of which: Short-term	4 774	−554.5	−225.0	−124.2	21.7	−40.1	70.3	47.4	1.5
Other sectors	4 775	−66.9	−100.0	−89.0	31.3	475.4	382.7	8.5	−133.1
of which: Short-term	4 777	23.9	−24.7	−49.5	−1.0	.7	51.4	34.0	11.5
Currency and deposits	4 780	734.1	628.4	−180.0	109.1	216.5	790.8	458.2	41.8
Monetary authorities	4 781	....	....	....	....	....	....	....	....
General government	4 782	....	....	....	....	....	....	....	....
Banks	4 783	734.1	628.4	−180.0	109.1	216.5	790.8	458.2	41.8
Other sectors	4 784	....	....	....	....	....	....	....	....
Other liabilities	4 786	803.7	−29.6	699.6	−1,339.2	58.9	198.2	361.6	−9.8
Monetary authorities	4 787	8.9	11.0	−14.9	−16.7	120.9	172.8	326.7	−70.1
of which: Short-term	4 789	....	....	....	....	....	....	....	....
General government	4 790	....	....	....	....	....	....	....	....
of which: Short-term	4 792	....	....	....	....	....	....	....	....
Banks	4 793	787.3	−33.8	712.3	−1,324.4	−48.0	5.2	8.1	32.0
of which: Short-term	4 795	787.3	−33.8	712.3	−1,324.4	−48.0	5.2	8.1	32.0
Other sectors	4 796	7.4	−6.8	2.2	1.9	−14.0	20.3	26.7	28.2
of which: Short-term	4 798	7.4	−6.8	2.2	1.9	−14.0	20.3	26.7	28.2
E. RESERVE ASSETS	4 802	**−1,380.4**	**−454.2**	**−620.9**	**15.8**	**−1,005.4**	**−2,232.3**	**−1,586.9**	**361.5**
Monetary gold	4 812	....	....	−.1	....	−.1	....	....	....
Special drawing rights	4 811	2.8	3.1	−5.8	6.2	.7	−3.9	−379.5	.1
Reserve position in the Fund	4 810	....	....	....	....	....	....	....	−94.4
Foreign exchange	4 803	−1,327.9	−452.0	−615.7	10.8	−1,008.3	−2,228.2	−1,206.7	477.7
Other claims	4 813	−55.3	−5.4	.6	−1.2	2.3	−.2	−.8	−21.9
NET ERRORS AND OMISSIONS	4 998	**1,034.2**	**377.9**	**−173.4**	**−182.8**	**−284.1**	**910.9**	**378.1**	**−142.2**

Table 3. INTERNATIONAL INVESTMENT POSITION (End-period stocks), 2003–2010

(Millions of U.S. dollars)

	Code	2003	2004	2005	2006	2007	2008	2009	2010
ASSETS	8 995 C.	**14,223.7**	**15,383.1**	**17,137.3**	**17,013.2**	**20,324.1**	**22,601.7**	**26,806.8**	**27,221.6**
Direct investment abroad	8 505 ..	**111.6**	**122.8**	**158.8**	**218.4**	**336.6**	**258.3**	**299.7**	**303.8**
Equity capital and reinvested earnings	8 506 ..	....	....	....	....	....	....	....	....
Claims on affiliated enterprises	8 507 ..	....	....	....	....	....	....	....	....
Liabilities to affiliated enterprises	8 508 ..	....	....	....	....	....	....	....	....
Other capital	8 530 ..	111.6	122.8	158.8	218.4	336.6	258.3	299.7	303.8
Claims on affiliated enterprises	8 535 ..	111.6	122.8	158.8	218.4	336.6	258.3	299.7	303.8
Liabilities to affiliated enterprises	8 540 ..	....	....	....	....	....	....	....	....
Portfolio investment	8 602 ..	**1,753.8**	**2,448.6**	**1,858.3**	**2,328.8**	**2,321.8**	**2,374.1**	**2,722.8**	**4,063.7**
Equity securities	8 610 ..	....	....	....					
Monetary authorities	8 611 ..								
General government	8 612 ..	....	....	....					
Banks	8 613 ..	....	....	....					
Other sectors	8 614 ..	....	....	....					
Debt securities	8 619 ..	1,753.8	2,448.6	1,858.3	2,328.8	2,321.8	2,374.1	2,722.8	4,063.7
Bonds and notes	8 620 ..	1,753.8	2,448.6	1,858.3	2,328.8	2,321.8	2,374.1	2,722.8	4,063.7
Monetary authorities	8 621 ..	5.5	....						
General government	8 622 ..	....	....						
Banks	8 623 ..	724.0	1,416.4	1,189.2	1,265.7	1,089.0	1,146.8	1,849.0	3,184.1
Other sectors	8 624 ..	1,024.3	1,032.2	669.1	1,063.0	1,232.8	1,227.2	873.8	879.5
Money market instruments	8 630 ..	....	....	....	....	....	....	....	....
Monetary authorities	8 631 ..	....	....	....	....	....	....	....	....
General government	8 632 ..	....	....	....	....	....	....	....	....
Banks	8 633 ..	....	....	....	....	....	....	....	....
Other sectors	8 634 ..	....	....	....	....	....	....	....	....
Financial derivatives	8 900 ..	....	....	....	....	....	....	....	....
Monetary authorities	8 901 ..								
General government	8 902 ..								
Banks	8 903 ..								
Other sectors	8 904 ..								
Other investment	8 703 ..	**10,324.4**	**10,299.8**	**12,048.8**	**11,368.7**	**13,544.4**	**13,609.1**	**15,796.5**	**15,198.6**
Trade credits	8 706 ..	67.4	67.4	177.4	190.5	118.6	153.1	198.0	210.2
General government	8 707 ..	....	....	....	....	....	....	....	....
of which: Short-term	8 709 ..	....	....	....	....	....	....	....	....
Other sectors	8 710 ..	67.4	67.4	177.4	190.5	118.6	153.1	198.0	210.2
of which: Short-term	8 712 ..	*67.4*	*67.4*	*177.4*	*190.5*	*118.6*	*153.1*	*198.0*	*210.2*
Loans	8 714 ..	561.2	209.0	158.9	159.8	155.6	192.9	218.0	225.4
Monetary authorities	8 715 ..	....	....	....	....	....	....	....	....
of which: Short-term	8 718 ..	....	....	....	....	....	....	....	....
General government	8 719 ..	....	....	....	....	....	....	....	....
of which: Short-term	8 721 ..	....	....	....	....	....	....	....	....
Banks	8 722 ..	534.3	182.1	134.8	145.1	152.7	184.9	206.5	219.5
of which: Short-term	8 724 ..	*534.3*	*182.1*	*134.8*	*145.1*	*152.7*	*184.9*	*206.5*	*219.5*
Other sectors	8 725 ..	26.9	26.9	24.1	14.7	2.9	8.0	11.4	5.9
of which: Short-term	8 727 ..	*26.9*	*26.9*	*24.1*	*14.7*	*2.9*	*8.0*	*11.4*	*5.9*
Currency and deposits	8 730 ..	8,005.0	8,359.9	9,415.1	9,945.2	12,032.3	11,783.9	13,959.0	13,404.7
Monetary authorities	8 731 ..	224.2	....	327.9	11.9	896.3	298.5	173.3	195.9
General government	8 732 ..	....	....	7.6	8.0	8.3	7.2	8.0	6.5
Banks	8 733 ..	3,165.8	3,477.9	3,726.2	3,794.2	4,187.1	4,351.4	5,160.7	6,082.8
Other sectors	8 734 ..	4,615.0	4,882.0	5,353.4	6,131.0	6,940.7	7,126.8	8,617.0	7,119.5
Other assets	8 736 ..	1,690.8	1,663.5	2,297.4	1,073.2	1,237.9	1,479.2	1,421.5	1,358.3
Monetary authorities	8 737 ..	166.7	172.8	159.6	164.4	273.7	488.2	489.4	464.4
of which: Short-term	8 739 ..	*166.7*	*172.8*	*159.6*	*164.4*	*273.7*	*488.2*	*489.4*	*464.4*
General government	8 740 ..	....	....	....	....	....	....	....	....
of which: Short-term	8 742 ..	....	....	....	....	....	....	....	....
Banks	8 743 ..	1,514.9	1,480.0	2,116.4	885.3	955.6	904.8	911.0	875.2
of which: Short-term	8 745 ..	*1,514.9*	*1,480.0*	*2,116.4*	*885.3*	*955.6*	*904.8*	*911.0*	*875.2*
Other sectors	8 746 ..	9.2	10.7	21.4	23.5	8.5	86.3	21.0	18.7
of which: Short-term	8 748 ..	*9.2*	*10.7*	*21.4*	*23.5*	*8.5*	*86.3*	*21.0*	*18.7*
Reserve assets	8 802 ..	**2,033.9**	**2,511.9**	**3,071.4**	**3,097.3**	**4,121.4**	**6,360.2**	**7,987.9**	**7,655.6**
Monetary gold	8 812 ..	3.5	3.6	4.4	5.3	7.1	7.4	9.3	11.9
Special drawing rights	8 811 ..	3.7	1.2	6.3	1.1	.4	4.1	385.1	378.2
Reserve position in the Fund	8 810 ..	....	....	....	....	....	....	....	97.1
Foreign exchange	8 803 ..	2,026.7	2,507.4	3,061.7	3,090.7	4,116.0	6,350.5	7,596.2	7,149.3
Other claims	8 813 ..	....	−.3	−1.0	.2	−2.1	−1.8	−2.7	19.2

Table 3 (Concluded). INTERNATIONAL INVESTMENT POSITION (End-period stocks), 2003–2010

(Millions of U.S. dollars)

	Code	2003	2004	2005	2006	2007	2008	2009	2010
LIABILITIES	8 995 D.	**15,479.8**	**16,911.4**	**18,438.1**	**17,725.2**	**22,353.5**	**24,648.3**	**31,871.3**	**33,985.2**
Direct investment in Uruguay	8 555 ..	**1,799.6**	**2,110.3**	**2,843.7**	**3,898.7**	**6,355.8**	**7,998.1**	**12,535.8**	**14,830.2**
Equity capital and reinvested earnings	8 556 ..	1,799.6	2,110.3	2,843.7	3,898.7	6,355.8	7,998.1	11,743.3	13,763.4
Claims on direct investors	8 557 ..	....	....	....	....	....	....	....	....
Liabilities to direct investors	8 558 ..	1,799.6	2,110.3	2,843.7	3,898.7	6,355.8	7,998.1	11,743.3	13,763.4
Other capital	8 580 ..	....	....	....	....	....	....	792.5	1,066.9
Claims on direct investors	8 585 ..	....	....	....	....	....	....	....	....
Liabilities to direct investors	8 590 ..	....	....	....	....	....	....	792.5	1,066.9
Portfolio investment	8 652 ..	**2,738.9**	**3,830.7**	**4,409.9**	**6,435.8**	**7,857.8**	**7,175.8**	**7,812.4**	**8,415.5**
Equity securities	8 660 ..	....	....	....	....	....	....	....	....
Banks	8 663 ..	....	....	....	....	....	....	....	....
Other sectors	8 664 ..	....	....	....	....	....	....	....	....
Debt securities	8 669 ..	2,738.9	3,830.7	4,409.9	6,435.8	7,857.8	7,175.8	7,812.4	8,415.5
Bonds and notes	8 670 ..	2,738.9	3,830.7	4,409.9	6,435.8	7,857.8	7,175.8	7,812.4	8,415.5
Monetary authorities	8 671 ..	155.8	143.8	26.5	3.3				
General government	8 672 ..	2,583.1	3,686.9	4,383.4	6,432.5	7,857.8	7,175.8	7,812.4	8,415.5
Banks	8 673 ..								
Other sectors	8 674 ..								
Money market instruments	8 680 ..								
Monetary authorities	8 681 ..								
General government	8 682 ..								
Banks	8 683 ..								
Other sectors	8 684 ..								
Financial derivatives	8 905 ..	....	....	....	....	....	....	....	....
Monetary authorities	8 906 ..								
General government	8 907 ..								
Banks	8 908 ..								
Other sectors	8 909 ..	....							
Other investment	8 753 ..	**10,941.3**	**10,970.4**	**11,184.5**	**7,390.8**	**8,139.9**	**9,474.4**	**11,523.0**	**10,739.5**
Trade credits	8 756 ..	144.0	51.3	355.3	709.4	776.5	573.9	937.8	1,026.8
General government	8 757 ..	....	....	....	....	....	....	....	....
of which: Short-term	8 759 ..	....	....	....	....	....	....	....	....
Other sectors	8 760 ..	144.0	51.3	355.3	709.4	776.5	573.9	937.8	1,026.8
of which: Short-term	8 762 ..	*144.0*	*51.3*	*355.3*	*709.4*	*776.5*	*573.9*	*937.8*	*1,026.8*
Loans	8 764 ..	6,895.7	6,839.3	6,228.5	3,302.2	3,687.6	4,374.3	5,224.5	4,359.6
Monetary authorities	8 765 ..	2,795.7	3,032.2	2,443.3	51.4	144.0	128.5	36.3	1.8
of which: Use of Fund credit and loans from the Fund	8 766 ..	*2,416.0*	*2,684.2*	*2,304.2*	....	....			
of which: Short-term	8 768 ..								
General government	8 769 ..	2,836.0	2,893.0	2,978.7	2,418.1	2,408.3	2,686.3	3,566.5	3,202.7
of which: Short-term	8 771 ..								
Banks	8 772 ..	768.8	495.7	373.2	396.8	349.0	416.1	461.6	461.6
of which: Short-term	8 774 ..	*768.8*	*495.7*	*373.2*	*396.8*	*349.0*	*416.1*	*461.6*	*461.6*
Other sectors	8 775 ..	495.2	418.3	433.3	436.0	786.3	1,143.4	1,160.2	693.4
of which: Short-term	8 777 ..	*495.2*	*418.3*	*433.3*	*436.0*	*786.3*	*1,143.4*	*1,160.2*	*693.4*
Currency and deposits	8 780 ..	2,359.2	2,619.3	2,439.3	2,546.3	2,762.8	3,553.6	4,011.8	4,053.6
Monetary authorities	8 781 ..	....	....	....	....	....	....	....	....
General government	8 782 ..	....	....	....	....	....	....	....	....
Banks	8 783 ..	2,359.2	2,619.3	2,439.3	2,546.3	2,762.8	3,553.6	4,011.8	4,053.6
Other sectors	8 784 ..								
Other liabilities	8 786 ..	1,542.4	1,460.5	2,161.5	832.8	913.1	972.6	1,348.9	1,299.5
Monetary authorities	8 787 ..	15.7	26.7	13.1	9.6	111.2	147.0	475.3	398.0
of which: Short-term	8 789 ..	....							....
General government	8 790 ..	....	....	....	....	....	....	....	....
of which: Short-term	8 792 ..	....	....	....	....	....	....	....	....
Banks	8 793 ..	1,444.7	1,401.6	2,114.0	789.4	741.4	746.5	754.7	786.7
of which: Short-term	8 795 ..	*1,444.7*	*1,401.6*	*2,114.0*	*789.4*	*741.4*	*746.5*	*754.7*	*786.7*
Other sectors	8 796 ..	82.0	32.2	34.4	33.8	60.5	79.1	118.9	114.8
of which: Short-term	8 798 ..	*82.0*	*32.2*	*34.4*	*33.8*	*60.5*	*79.1*	*118.9*	*114.8*
NET INTERNATIONAL INVESTMENT POSITION	8 995 ..	**−1,256.1**	**−1,528.3**	**−1,300.8**	**−712.0**	**−2,029.3**	**−2,046.6**	**−5,064.5**	**−6,763.6**
Conversion rates: Uruguayan pesos per U.S. dollar (end of period)	0 102 ..	**29.3000**	**26.3500**	**24.1000**	**24.4000**	**21.5000**	**24.3500**	**19.6270**	**20.0940**

Table 1. ANALYTIC PRESENTATION, 2003–2010

(Millions of U.S. dollars)

	Code	2003	2004	2005	2006	2007	2008	2009	2010
A. Current Account[1].....................	4 993 Z.	**−34.43**	**−41.61**	**−52.71**	**−50.35**	**−53.78**	....	....	....
Goods: exports f.o.b.............	2 100 ..	26.84	38.14	38.11	37.69	33.55	....	....	....
Goods: imports f.o.b.............	3 100 ..	−91.80	−113.00	−131.15	−147.55	−176.48	....	....	....
Balance on Goods.................	4 100 ..	*−64.96*	*−74.85*	*−93.03*	*−109.86*	*−142.93*	....	....	....
Services: credit....................	2 200 ..	110.66	122.28	138.85	145.82	185.94	....	....	....
Services: debit.....................	3 200 ..	−60.65	−65.58	−73.76	−71.24	−75.68	....	....	....
Balance on Goods and Services.....	4 991 ..	*−14.95*	*−18.15*	*−27.95*	*−35.29*	*−32.67*	....	....	....
Income: credit.....................	2 300 ..	24.21	27.15	27.65	31.82	36.26	....	....	....
Income: debit......................	3 300 ..	−38.60	−45.86	−53.66	−51.93	−61.01	....	....	....
Balance on Goods, Services, and Income.....	4 992 ..	*−29.34*	*−36.87*	*−53.96*	*−55.40*	*−57.41*	....	....	....
Current transfers: credit......	2 379 Z.	4.82	5.27	7.39	10.06	6.65	....	....	....
Current transfers: debit.......	3 379 ..	−9.90	−10.00	−6.15	−5.00	−3.02	....	....	....
B. Capital Account[1].....................	4 994 Z.	**7.41**	**12.76**	**20.10**	**33.74**	**29.96**	....	....	....
Capital account: credit........	2 994 Z.	7.41	12.76	20.10	33.74	29.96	....	....	....
Capital account: debit.........	3 994 ..	....	....	....	....	....	....	....	....
Total, Groups A Plus B........	4 981 ..	*−27.02*	*−28.85*	*−32.61*	*−16.61*	*−23.82*	....	....	....
C. Financial Account[1]..................	4 995 W.	**37.57**	**48.36**	**37.92**	**33.44**	**14.97**	....	....	....
Direct investment abroad......	4 505 ..	−.67	−.76	−.77	−.73	−.63	....	....	....
Direct investment in Vanuatu..	4 555 Z.	18.01	19.84	13.25	43.45	34.16	....	....	....
Portfolio investment assets...	4 602 ..	2.11	.21	−1.06	−.26	1.68	....	....	....
Equity securities...............	4 610 ..	....	....	....	....	....	....	....	....
Debt securities.................	4 619 ..	2.11	.21	−1.06	−.26	1.68	....	....	....
Portfolio investment liabilities..	4 652 Z.	....	....	....	....	....	....	....	....
Equity securities...............	4 660 ..	....	....	....	....	....	....	....	....
Debt securities.................	4 669 Z.	....	....	....	....	....	....	....	....
Financial derivatives...........	4 910 ..	....	....	....	....	....	....	....	....
Financial derivatives assets...	4 900 ..	....	....	....	....	....	....	....	....
Financial derivatives liabilities..	4 905 ..	....	....	....	....	....	....	....	....
Other investment assets.......	4 703 ..	48.16	−14.77	26.60	−27.47	51.25	....	....	....
Monetary authorities..........	4 701 ..	....	....	....	....	....	....	....	....
General government...........	4 704 ..	....	....	....	....	....	....	....	....
Banks............................	4 705 ..	11.55	−7.18	−12.28	−12.80	−36.44	....	....	....
Other sectors...................	4 728 ..	36.61	−7.59	38.88	−14.67	87.69	....	....	....
Other investment liabilities...	4 753 W.	−30.04	43.84	−.10	18.45	−71.48	....	....	....
Monetary authorities..........	4 753 WA	−.32	−.14	.40	−.13	.82	....	....	....
General government...........	4 753 ZB	−.91	−2.61	−3.00	−1.59	−1.79	....	....	....
Banks............................	4 753 ZC	−8.69	−6.76	12.17	11.72	−2.47	....	....	....
Other sectors...................	4 753 ZD	−20.12	53.34	−9.67	8.44	−68.03	....	....	....
Total, Groups A Through C......	4 983 ..	*10.55*	*19.51*	*5.31*	*16.83*	*−8.85*	....	....	....
D. Net Errors and Omissions..........	4 998 ..	**−21.79**	**−24.50**	**−16.65**	**−3.94**	**−4.31**	....	....	....
Total, Groups A Through D......	4 984 ..	*−11.24*	*−4.99*	*−11.33*	*12.88*	*−13.16*	....	....	....
E. Reserves and Related Items...........	4 802 A.	**11.24**	**4.99**	**11.33**	**−12.88**	**13.16**	....	....	....
Reserve assets...................	4 802 ..	−1.03	−14.86	−8.97	−32.56	−9.04	....	....	....
Use of Fund credit and loans..	4 766 ..	....	....	....	....	....	....	....	....
Exceptional financing..........	4 920 ..	12.27	19.85	20.30	19.68	22.20	....	....	....
Conversion rates: vatu per U.S. dollar..................	0 101 ..	**122.19**	**111.79**	**109.25**	**110.64**	**102.44**	**101.33**	**106.74**	**96.91**

[1] Excludes components that have been classified in the categories of Group E.

Table 2. STANDARD PRESENTATION, 2003–2010

(Millions of U.S. dollars)

	Code	2003	2004	2005	2006	2007	2008	2009	2010
CURRENT ACCOUNT	4 993	**−22.15**	**−22.44**	**−34.05**	**−30.13**	**−34.41**	....	....	....
A. GOODS	4 100	**−64.96**	**−74.85**	**−93.03**	**−109.86**	**−142.93**	....	....	....
Credit	2 100	**26.84**	**38.14**	**38.11**	**37.69**	**33.55**	....	....	....
General merchandise: exports f.o.b.	2 110	26.84	38.14	38.11	37.69	33.55	....	....	....
Goods for processing: exports f.o.b.	2 150	....	....	....	....	....			
Repairs on goods	2 160	....	....	....	....	....			
Goods procured in ports by carriers	2 170	....							
Nonmonetary gold	2 180								
Debit	3 100	**−91.80**	**−113.00**	**−131.15**	**−147.55**	**−176.48**	....	....	....
General merchandise: imports f.o.b.	3 110	−87.25	−106.89	−124.55	−140.91	−168.72			
Goods for processing: imports f.o.b.	3 150	....	....	....	....	....			
Repairs on goods	3 160	....	....	....	....	....			
Goods procured in ports by carriers	3 170	−4.55	−6.10	−6.60	−6.65	−7.76			
Nonmonetary gold	3 180	....	....						
B. SERVICES	4 200	**50.01**	**56.70**	**65.09**	**74.57**	**110.26**	....		....
Total credit	2 200	*110.66*	*122.28*	*138.85*	*145.82*	*185.94*	....		
Total debit	3 200	*−60.65*	*−65.58*	*−73.76*	*−71.24*	*−75.68*			
Transportation services, credit	2 205	**26.03**	**24.05**	**25.57**	**23.54**	**31.81**	....		....
Passenger	2 850	*18.66*	*18.16*	*18.91*	*16.99*	*23.40*			
Freight	2 851	*.95*	*1.13*	*1.26*	*1.55*	*2.41*			
Other	2 852	*6.42*	*4.76*	*5.39*	*5.01*	*6.00*			
Sea transport, passenger	2 207	....	....	....	....	....			
Sea transport, freight	2 208	....	....	....	....	....			
Sea transport, other	2 209	3.21	2.38	2.69	2.50	3.00			
Air transport, passenger	2 211	18.66	18.16	18.91	16.99	23.40			
Air transport, freight	2 212	.95	1.13	1.26	1.55	2.41			
Air transport, other	2 213	3.21	2.38	2.69	2.50	3.00			
Other transport, passenger	2 215	....	....	....	....	....			
Other transport, freight	2 216	....	....	....	....	....			
Other transport, other	2 217	....	....	....	....	....			
Transportation services, debit	3 205	**−31.71**	**−34.87**	**−42.87**	**−43.73**	**−45.62**	....	....	....
Passenger	3 850	*−2.04*	*−2.25*	*−2.35*	*−2.11*	*−1.87*			
Freight	3 851	*−16.39*	*−17.16*	*−21.54*	*−25.62*	*−31.15*			
Other	3 852	*−13.28*	*−15.46*	*−18.97*	*−16.00*	*−12.60*			
Sea transport, passenger	3 207	....	....	....	....	....			
Sea transport, freight	3 208	−15.57	−16.30	−20.47	−24.34	−29.59			
Sea transport, other	3 209	−2.66	−3.09	−3.79	−3.20	−2.52			
Air transport, passenger	3 211	−2.04	−2.25	−2.35	−2.11	−1.87			
Air transport, freight	3 212	−.82	−.86	−1.08	−1.28	−1.56			
Air transport, other	3 213	−10.62	−12.37	−15.17	−12.80	−10.08			
Other transport, passenger	3 215	....	....	....	....	....			
Other transport, freight	3 216	....	....	....	....	....			
Other transport, other	3 217	....	....	....	....	....			
Travel, credit	2 236	**63.91**	**74.96**	**85.47**	**92.44**	**118.69**	....	....	....
Business travel	2 237	63.12	74.05	84.49	91.48	117.47			
Personal travel	2 240	.79	.92	.98	.96	1.22			
Travel, debit	3 236	**−11.53**	**−12.94**	**−11.19**	**−8.55**	**−10.62**	....	....	....
Business travel	3 237	−9.90	−10.76	−9.28	−7.32	−8.95			
Personal travel	3 240	−1.62	−2.19	−1.91	−1.22	−1.67			
Other services, credit	2 200 BA	**20.72**	**23.27**	**27.82**	**29.84**	**35.43**	....		....
Communications	2 245	2.67	2.79	3.25	4.17	4.55			
Construction	2 249	....	....	....	....	....			
Insurance	2 253	....	.18	.20	.05	....			
Financial	2 260	8.76	11.64	14.12	15.10	17.22			
Computer and information	2 262	....	....	....	....	....			
Royalties and licence fees	2 266	....	....	....	.18	.27			
Other business services	2 268	6.62	4.15	6.15	4.51	4.37			
Personal, cultural, and recreational	2 287	....	....	....	....	....			
Government, n.i.e.	2 291	2.67	4.51	4.10	5.83	9.02			
Other services, debit	3 200 BA	**−17.41**	**−17.77**	**−19.70**	**−18.97**	**−19.44**	....		....
Communications	3 245	−1.49	−1.41	−1.47	−1.61	−1.65			
Construction	3 249	....	−.01	−.01	....	....			
Insurance	3 253	−.96	−1.19	−1.42	−1.72	−2.22			
Financial	3 260	−.89	−1.19	−2.20	−2.12	−2.74			
Computer and information	3 262	−1.45	−1.64	−.76	−1.09	−1.19			
Royalties and licence fees	3 266	−.26	−.36	−.47	−.20	....			
Other business services	3 268	−7.36	−7.29	−8.17	−7.17	−6.43			
Personal, cultural, and recreational	3 287	....	....	....	....	....			
Government, n.i.e.	3 291	−5.00	−4.69	−5.20	−5.05	−5.20			

2011, International Monetary Fund: *Balance of Payments Statistics Yearbook*

Table 2 (Continued). STANDARD PRESENTATION, 2003–2010

(Millions of U.S. dollars)

	Code	2003	2004	2005	2006	2007	2008	2009	2010
C. INCOME	4 300	**−14.39**	**−18.72**	**−26.01**	**−20.11**	**−24.74**	....	....	....
Total credit	2 300	*24.21*	*27.15*	*27.65*	*31.82*	*36.26*	....	....	....
Total debit	3 300	*−38.60*	*−45.86*	*−53.66*	*−51.93*	*−61.01*	....	....	....
Compensation of employees, credit	2 310	**3.93**	**4.86**	**5.02**	**4.92**	**4.33**	....	....	....
Compensation of employees, debit	3 310	**−2.56**	**−2.80**	**−2.82**	**−2.93**	**−2.29**	....	....	....
Investment income, credit	2 320	**20.28**	**22.29**	**22.63**	**26.90**	**31.94**	....	....	....
Direct investment income	2 330	.71	.81	.81	.79	.67	....	....	....
Dividends and distributed branch profits	2 332	....	....	....	....	....	....	....	....
Reinvested earnings and undistributed branch profits	2 333	.35	.38	.37	.37	.34	....	....	....
Income on debt (interest)	2 334	.35	.43	.44	.42	.33	....	....	....
Portfolio investment income	2 339	.33	.30	.37	.47	.52	....	....	....
Income on equity	2 340	....	....	....	....	....	....	....	....
Income on bonds and notes	2 350	.33	.30	.37	.47	.52	....	....	....
Income on money market instruments	2 360	....	....	....	....	....	....	....	....
Other investment income	2 370	19.24	21.19	21.44	25.64	30.75	....	....	....
Investment income, debit	3 320	**−36.04**	**−43.06**	**−50.84**	**−49.00**	**−58.71**	....	....	....
Direct investment income	3 330	−20.83	−27.09	−35.34	−34.20	−45.61	....	....	....
Dividends and distributed branch profits	3 332	....	....	....	....	−18.08	....	....	....
Reinvested earnings and undistributed branch profits	3 333	−17.87	−22.32	−27.86	−25.32	−29.11	....	....	....
Income on debt (interest)	3 334	−2.96	−4.77	−7.48	−8.87	1.58	....	....	....
Portfolio investment income	3 339	....	....	....	....	....	....	....	....
Income on equity	3 340	....	....	....	....	....	....	....	....
Income on bonds and notes	3 350	....	....	....	....	....	....	....	....
Income on money market instruments	3 360	....	....	....	....	....	....	....	....
Other investment income	3 370	−15.22	−15.97	−15.50	−14.80	−13.11	....	....	....
D. CURRENT TRANSFERS	4 379	**7.19**	**14.43**	**19.91**	**25.27**	**23.00**	....	....	....
Credit	2 379	**17.09**	**24.44**	**26.06**	**30.27**	**26.02**	....	....	....
General government	2 380	14.66	21.33	21.18	22.51	22.78	....	....	....
Other sectors	2 390	2.43	3.10	4.88	7.76	3.24	....	....	....
Workers' remittances	2 391	.07	.07	.07	.07	1.22	....	....	....
Other current transfers	2 392	2.37	3.03	4.81	7.68	2.02	....	....	....
Debit	3 379	**−9.90**	**−10.00**	**−6.15**	**−5.00**	**−3.02**	....	....	....
General government	3 380	....	−.65	−1.35	−.46	−.84	....	....	....
Other sectors	3 390	−9.90	−9.36	−4.80	−4.54	−2.18	....	....	....
Workers' remittances	3 391	−.16	−.18	−.18	−.21	−.33	....	....	....
Other current transfers	3 392	−9.74	−9.18	−4.61	−4.34	−1.85	....	....	....
CAPITAL AND FINANCIAL ACCOUNT	4 996	**43.94**	**46.94**	**50.69**	**34.08**	**38.72**	....	....	....
CAPITAL ACCOUNT	4 994	**7.41**	**12.76**	**22.07**	**33.74**	**29.96**	....	....	....
Total credit	2 994	*7.41*	*12.76*	*22.07*	*33.74*	*29.96*	....	....	....
Total debit	3 994	....	....	....	....	....	....	....	....
Capital transfers, credit	2 400	**5.59**	**7.22**	**7.78**	**5.96**	**6.45**	....	....	....
General government	2 401	5.59	7.22	7.78	5.96	6.45	....	....	....
Debt forgiveness	2 402	....	....	1.96	....	....	....	....	....
Other capital transfers	2 410	5.59	7.22	5.82	5.96	6.45	....	....	....
Other sectors	2 430	....	....	....	....	....	....	....	....
Migrants' transfers	2 431	....	....	....	....	....	....	....	....
Debt forgiveness	2 432	....	....	....	....	....	....	....	....
Other capital transfers	2 440	....	....	....	....	....	....	....	....
Capital transfers, debit	3 400	....	....	....	....	....	....	....	....
General government	3 401	....	....	....	....	....	....	....	....
Debt forgiveness	3 402	....	....	....	....	....	....	....	....
Other capital transfers	3 410	....	....	....	....	....	....	....	....
Other sectors	3 430	....	....	....	....	....	....	....	....
Migrants' transfers	3 431	....	....	....	....	....	....	....	....
Debt forgiveness	3 432	....	....	....	....	....	....	....	....
Other capital transfers	3 440	....	....	....	....	....	....	....	....
Nonproduced nonfinancial assets, credit	2 480	**1.82**	**5.55**	**14.28**	**27.77**	**23.51**	....	....	....
Nonproduced nonfinancial assets, debit	3 480	....	....	....	....	....	....	....	....

Table 2 (Continued). STANDARD PRESENTATION, 2003–2010

(Millions of U.S. dollars)

	Code	2003	2004	2005	2006	2007	2008	2009	2010
FINANCIAL ACCOUNT...	4 995 ..	**36.53**	**34.18**	**28.63**	**.34**	**8.77**	....	....	....
A. DIRECT INVESTMENT..................................	4 500 ..	**17.34**	**19.08**	**12.48**	**42.72**	**33.52**	....	....	....
Direct investment abroad........................	4 505 ..	**−.67**	**−.76**	**−.77**	**−.73**	**−.63**	....	....	....
Equity capital..	4 510 ..	−.25	−.31	−.33	−.31	−.25	....	....	....
Claims on affiliated enterprises...........	4 515 ..	−.25	−.31	−.33	−.31	−.25	....	....	....
Liabilities to affiliated enterprises.......	4 520 ..	....	....	....					
Reinvested earnings..............................	4 525 ..	−.35	−.38	−.37	−.37	−.34	....	....	....
Other capital.......................................	4 530 ..	−.07	−.07	−.07	−.05	−.04			
Claims on affiliated enterprises...........	4 535 ..	−.07	−.07	−.07	−.05	−.04			
Liabilities to affiliated enterprises.......	4 540 ..	....	....						
Direct investment in Vanuatu..........................	4 555 ..	**18.01**	**19.84**	**13.25**	**43.45**	**34.16**	....	....	....
Equity capital..	4 560 ..	.98	−4.46	−14.31	17.84	2.83	....	....	....
Claims on direct investors...................	4 565 ..	....							
Liabilities to direct investors...............	4 570 ..	.98	−4.46	−14.31	17.84	2.83			
Reinvested earnings..............................	4 575 ..	17.87	22.32	27.86	25.32	29.11	....	....	
Other capital.......................................	4 580 ..	−.84	1.99	−.29	.29	2.22	....	....	....
Claims on direct investors...................	4 585 ..	....	....	....					
Liabilities to direct investors...............	4 590 ..	−.84	1.99	−.29	.29	2.22			
B. PORTFOLIO INVESTMENT............................	4 600 ..	**2.11**	**.90**	**−1.39**	**−.80**	**1.68**	....	....	....
Assets..	4 602 ..	**2.11**	**.21**	**−1.06**	**−.26**	**1.68**	....	....	....
Equity securities..................................	4 610 ..	....	....	....	....	....			
Monetary authorities.........................	4 611 ..	....	....	....	....	....			
General government..........................	4 612 ..	....	....	....	....	....			
Banks..	4 613 ..	....	....	....	....	....			
Other sectors...................................	4 614 ..	....	....	....	....	....			
Debt securities....................................	4 619 ..	2.11	.21	−1.06	−.26	1.68			
Bonds and notes..............................	4 620 ..	2.11	.21	−1.06	−.26	1.68			
Monetary authorities.....................	4 621 ..	....	....	....					
General government......................	4 622 ..	....	....						
Banks..	4 623 ..	....	....						
Other sectors...............................	4 624 ..	2.11	.21	−1.06	−.26	1.68			
Money market instruments................	4 630 ..	....	....						
Monetary authorities.....................	4 631 ..	....							
General government......................	4 632 ..	....							
Banks..	4 633 ..	....							
Other sectors...............................	4 634 ..	....							
Liabilities..	4 652 ..	....	**.68**	**−.32**	**−.54**	....	....	....	....
Equity securities..................................	4 660 ..	....	....	....	....				
Banks..	4 663 ..	....							
Other sectors...................................	4 664 ..		....						
Debt securities....................................	4 669 ..	....	.68	−.32	−.54				
Bonds and notes..............................	4 670 ..	....	.68	−.32	−.54				
Monetary authorities.....................	4 671 ..	....	....	....	....				
General government......................	4 672 ..	....	....	....	....				
Banks..	4 673 ..	....	....	....	....				
Other sectors...............................	4 674 ..	....	.68	−.32	−.54				
Money market instruments................	4 680 ..	....	....	....	....				
Monetary authorities.....................	4 681 ..	....	....	....	....				
General government......................	4 682 ..	....	....	....	....				
Banks..	4 683 ..	....	....	....	....				
Other sectors...............................	4 684 ..	....	....	....	....				
C. FINANCIAL DERIVATIVES...........................	4 910 ..	....	....	....	....	....	....	....	....
Monetary authorities.............................	4 911 ..	....	....	....	....	....			
General government..............................	4 912 ..	....	....	....	....	....			
Banks...	4 913 ..	....	....	....	....	....			
Other sectors.......................................	4 914 ..	....	....	....	....	....			
Assets..	4 900 ..	....	....	....	....	....	....	....	....
Monetary authorities.............................	4 901 ..	....	....	....	....	....			
General government..............................	4 902 ..	....	....	....	....	....			
Banks...	4 903 ..	....	....	....	....	....			
Other sectors.......................................	4 904 ..	....	....	....	....	....			
Liabilities..	4 905 ..	....	....	....	....	....	....	....	....
Monetary authorities.............................	4 906 ..	....	....	....	....	....			
General government..............................	4 907 ..	....	....	....	....	....			
Banks...	4 908 ..	....	....	....	....	....			
Other sectors.......................................	4 909 ..	....	....	....	....	....			

Table 2 (Concluded). STANDARD PRESENTATION, 2003–2010

(Millions of U.S. dollars)

	Code	2003	2004	2005	2006	2007	2008	2009	2010
D. OTHER INVESTMENT	4 700	**18.12**	**29.07**	**26.50**	**−9.02**	**−17.39**	....	....	....
Assets	4 703	**48.16**	**−14.77**	**26.60**	**−27.47**	**51.25**	....	....	....
Trade credits	4 706	....	....	....	....	....	....		
General government	4 707	....	....	....	....	....	....		
of which: Short-term	4 709	....	....	....	....	....	....		
Other sectors	4 710	....	....	....	....	....	....		
of which: Short-term	4 712	....	....	....	....	....	....		
Loans	4 714	8.13	29.28	11.91	21.99	18.95	....		....
Monetary authorities	4 715	....	....	....	....	....	....		
of which: Short-term	4 718	....	....	....	....	....	....		
General government	4 719	....	....	....	....	....	....		
of which: Short-term	4 721	....	....	....	....	....	....		
Banks	4 722	....	....	−1.38	−1.48	−3.57	....		
of which: Short-term	4 724	....	....	....	....	....	....		
Other sectors	4 725	8.13	29.28	13.29	23.47	22.51	....		
of which: Short-term	4 727	....	....	....	....	....	....		
Currency and deposits	4 730	10.81	−35.22	33.38	−16.09	−9.16	....		
Monetary authorities	4 731	....	....	....	....	....	....		
General government	4 732	....	....	....	....	....	....		
Banks	4 733	11.55	−7.18	−10.89	−11.31	−32.87	....		
Other sectors	4 734	−.74	−28.04	44.27	−4.78	23.71	....		
Other assets	4 736	29.22	−8.83	−18.69	−33.37	41.47	....		
Monetary authorities	4 737	....	....	....	....	....	....		
of which: Short-term	4 739	....	....	....	....	....	....		
General government	4 740	....	....	....	....	....	....		
of which: Short-term	4 742	....	....	....	....	....	....		
Banks	4 743	....	....	....	....	....	....		
of which: Short-term	4 745	....	....	....	....	....	....		
Other sectors	4 746	29.22	−8.83	−18.69	−33.37	41.47	....		
of which: Short-term	4 748	....	....	....	....	....	....		
Liabilities	4 753	**−30.04**	**43.84**	**−.10**	**18.45**	**−68.65**	....		....
Trade credits	4 756	....	....	....	....	....	....		
General government	4 757	....	....	....	....	....	....		
of which: Short-term	4 759	....	....	....	....	....	....		
Other sectors	4 760	....	....	....	....	....	....		
of which: Short-term	4 762	....	....	....	....	....	....		
Loans	4 764	3.32	23.34	−10.92	14.45	−18.90	....		
Monetary authorities	4 765	....	....	....	....	....	....		
of which: Use of Fund credit and loans from the Fund	4 766	....	....	....	....	....	....		
of which: Short-term	4 768	....	....	....	....	....	....		
General government	4 769	−.91	−2.61	−3.00	−1.59	−1.89	....		
of which: Short-term	4 771	....	....	....	....	....	....		
Banks	4 772	....	....	....	....	2.83	....		
of which: Short-term	4 774	....	....	....	....	*2.83*	....		
Other sectors	4 775	4.24	25.95	−7.92	16.04	−19.84	....		
of which: Short-term	4 777	....	....	....	....	....	....		
Currency and deposits	4 780	−7.80	3.17	19.74	18.04	21.75	....		
Monetary authorities	4 781	−.32	−.14	.40	−.13	.82	....		
General government	4 782	....	....	....	....	.10	....		
Banks	4 783	−8.69	−6.76	12.17	11.72	−2.47	....		
Other sectors	4 784	1.20	10.07	7.17	6.45	23.31	....		
Other liabilities	4 786	−25.56	17.32	−8.91	−14.05	−71.49	....		
Monetary authorities	4 787	....	....	....	....	....	....		
of which: Short-term	4 789	....	....	....	....	....	....		
General government	4 790	....	....	....	....	....	....		
of which: Short-term	4 792	....	....	....	....	....	....		
Banks	4 793	....	....	....	....	....	....		
of which: Short-term	4 795	....	....	....	....	....	....		
Other sectors	4 796	−25.56	17.32	−8.91	−14.05	−71.49	....		
of which: Short-term	4 798	....	....	....	....	....	....		
E. RESERVE ASSETS	4 802	**−1.03**	**−14.86**	**−8.97**	**−32.56**	**−9.04**	....	....	....
Monetary gold	4 812	....	....	....	....	....	....		
Special drawing rights	4 811	−.06	−.06	−.09	−.13	−.17	....		
Reserve position in the Fund	4 810	....	....	....	....	....	....		
Foreign exchange	4 803	−.98	−14.80	−8.88	−32.43	−8.87	....		
Other claims	4 813	....	....	....	....	....	....		
NET ERRORS AND OMISSIONS	4 998	**−21.79**	**−24.50**	**−16.65**	**−3.94**	**−4.31**	....	....	....

Vanuatu 846

Table 3. INTERNATIONAL INVESTMENT POSITION (End-period stocks), 2003–2010

(Millions of U.S. dollars)

	Code	2003	2004	2005	2006	2007	2008	2009	2010
ASSETS	8 995 C.	**503.20**	**471.00**	**510.23**	**594.32**	....	....	....	....
Direct investment abroad	8 505	**11.84**	**13.22**	**13.28**	**14.77**	....	....	....	....
Equity capital and reinvested earnings	8 506	....	....	....	....	....	....	....	....
Claims on affiliated enterprises	8 507	....	....	....	....	....	....	....	....
Liabilities to affiliated enterprises	8 508	....	....	....	....	....	....	....	....
Other capital	8 530	....	....	....	....	....	....	....	....
Claims on affiliated enterprises	8 535	....	....	....	....	....	....	....	....
Liabilities to affiliated enterprises	8 540	....	....	....	....	....	....	....	....
Portfolio investment	8 602	**12.19**	**13.47**	**13.96**	**14.86**	....	....	....	....
Equity securities	8 610	....	....	....	....	....	....	....	....
Monetary authorities	8 611	....	....	....	....	....	....	....	....
General government	8 612	....	....	....	....	....	....	....	....
Banks	8 613	....	....	....	....	....	....	....	....
Other sectors	8 614	....	....	....	....	....	....	....	....
Debt securities	8 619	12.19	13.47	13.96	14.86	....	....	....	....
Bonds and notes	8 620	12.19	13.47	13.96	14.86	....	....	....	....
Monetary authorities	8 621	....	....	....	....	....	....	....	....
General government	8 622	....	....	....	....	....	....	....	....
Banks	8 623	....	....	....	....	....	....	....	....
Other sectors	8 624	....	13.47	13.96	14.86	....	....	....	....
Money market instruments	8 630	....	....	....	....	....	....	....	....
Monetary authorities	8 631	....	....	....	....	....	....	....	....
General government	8 632	....	....	....	....	....	....	....	....
Banks	8 633	....	....	....	....	....	....	....	....
Other sectors	8 634	....	....	....	....	....	....	....	....
Financial derivatives	8 900	....	....	....	....	....	....	....	....
Monetary authorities	8 901	....	....	....	....	....	....	....	....
General government	8 902	....	....	....	....	....	....	....	....
Banks	8 903	....	....	....	....	....	....	....	....
Other sectors	8 904	....	....	....	....	....	....	....	....
Other investment	8 703	**435.10**	**382.50**	**415.78**	**460.02**	....	....	....	....
Trade credits	8 706	....	....	....	....	....	....	....	....
General government	8 707	....	....	....	....	....	....	....	....
of which: Short-term	8 709	....	....	....	....	....	....	....	....
Other sectors	8 710	....	....	....	....	....	....	....	....
of which: Short-term	8 712	....	....	....	....	....	....	....	....
Loans	8 714	126.47	95.68	85.20	65.58	....	....	....	....
Monetary authorities	8 715	....	....	....	....	....	....	....	....
of which: Short-term	8 718	....	....	....	....	....	....	....	....
General government	8 719	....	....	....	....	....	....	....	....
of which: Short-term	8 721	....	....	....	....	....	....	....	....
Banks	8 722	....	....	10.26	12.32	....	....	....	....
of which: Short-term	8 724	....	....	....	....	....	....	....	....
Other sectors	8 725	....	95.68	74.95	53.26	....	....	....	....
of which: Short-term	8 727	....	....	....	....	....	....	....	....
Currency and deposits	8 730	296.67	262.74	289.30	316.71	....	....	....	....
Monetary authorities	8 731	....	....	....	....	....	....	....	....
General government	8 732	....	....	....	....	....	....	....	....
Banks	8 733	....	262.74	268.59	291.18	....	....	....	....
Other sectors	8 734	....	....	20.71	25.53	....	....	....	....
Other assets	8 736	11.96	24.08	41.28	77.73	....	....	....	....
Monetary authorities	8 737	....	....	....	....	....	....	....	....
of which: Short-term	8 739	....	....	....	....	....	....	....	....
General government	8 740	....	....	....	....	....	....	....	....
of which: Short-term	8 742	....	....	....	....	....	....	....	....
Banks	8 743	....	....	....	....	....	....	....	....
of which: Short-term	8 745	....	....	....	....	....	....	....	....
Other sectors	8 746	....	24.08	41.28	77.73	....	....	....	....
of which: Short-term	8 748	....	....	....	....	....	....	....	....
Reserve assets	8 802	**44.07**	**61.81**	**67.20**	**104.67**	....	....	....	....
Monetary gold	8 812	....	....	....	....	....	....	....	....
Special drawing rights	8 811	1.32	1.44	1.42	1.63	1.89	2.00	2.48	2.39
Reserve position in the Fund	8 810	3.71	3.88	3.57	3.75	3.94	3.84	3.91	3.84
Foreign exchange	8 803	39.04	56.49	62.22	99.29	....	....	....	....
Other claims	8 813	....	....	....	....	....	....	....	....

2011, International Monetary Fund: *Balance of Payments Statistics Yearbook*

Table 3 (Concluded). INTERNATIONAL INVESTMENT POSITION (End-period stocks), 2003–2010

(Millions of U.S. dollars)

	Code	2003	2004	2005	2006	2007	2008	2009	2010
LIABILITIES............	8 995 D.	**578.92**	**607.27**	**562.07**	**651.78**	....	....	....	....
Direct investment in Vanuatu............	8 555 ..	**149.45**	**148.77**	**148.62**	**196.47**	....	....	....	....
Equity capital and reinvested earnings............	8 556 ..	....	128.33	127.83	172.25	....	....		
Claims on direct investors............	8 557 ..	....	....	....	....	....	....		
Liabilities to direct investors............	8 558 ..	....	128.33	127.83	172.25	....	....		
Other capital............	8 580 ..	....	20.44	20.79	24.22	....	....		
Claims on direct investors............	8 585 ..	....	....	....	....	....	....		
Liabilities to direct investors............	8 590 ..	....	20.44	20.79	24.22	....	....		
Portfolio investment............	8 652 ..	....	....	....	....	....	....		
Equity securities............	8 660 ..								
Banks............	8 663 ..								
Other sectors............	8 664 ..								
Debt securities............	8 669 ..								
Bonds and notes............	8 670 ..								
Monetary authorities............	8 671 ..								
General government............	8 672 ..								
Banks............	8 673 ..								
Other sectors............	8 674 ..								
Money market instruments............	8 680 ..								
Monetary authorities............	8 681 ..								
General government............	8 682 ..								
Banks............	8 683 ..								
Other sectors............	8 684 ..								
Financial derivatives............	8 905 ..	....	....	....	....		....		....
Monetary authorities............	8 906 ..								
General government............	8 907 ..								
Banks............	8 908 ..								
Other sectors............	8 909 ..								
Other investment............	8 753 ..	**429.47**	**458.51**	**413.45**	**455.32**	....	....		
Trade credits............	8 756 ..	....	....	....	....				
General government............	8 757 ..	....	....	....	....				
of which: Short-term............	8 759 ..	....	....	....	....				
Other sectors............	8 760 ..	....	....	....	....				
of which: Short-term............	8 762 ..	....	....	....	....				
Loans............	8 764 ..	136.26	167.26	130.21	151.71	....	....		
Monetary authorities............	8 765 ..	....	....		....				
of which: Use of Fund credit and loans from the Fund....	8 766 ..	....	....						
of which: Short-term............	8 768 ..	....							
General government............	8 769 ..	....	82.73	75.53	78.03	....	....		
of which: Short-term............	8 771 ..	....	....						
Banks............	8 772 ..	....	....						
of which: Short-term............	8 774 ..	....	....						
Other sectors............	8 775 ..	....	84.53	54.68	73.68	....	....		
of which: Short-term............	8 777 ..	....							
Currency and deposits............	8 780 ..	123.35	126.30	136.59	162.16	....	....		
Monetary authorities............	8 781 ..	....	1.90	2.18	2.17				
General government............	8 782 ..	....							
Banks............	8 783 ..	....	61.14	69.69	85.96	....			
Other sectors............	8 784 ..	....	63.27	64.72	74.03	....	....		
Other liabilities............	8 786 ..	169.86	164.95	146.66	141.44	....	....		
Monetary authorities............	8 787 ..	....	....	....					
of which: Short-term............	8 789 ..	....	....						
General government............	8 790 ..	....	....						
of which: Short-term............	8 792 ..	....	....						
Banks............	8 793 ..	....	....						
of which: Short-term............	8 795 ..	....	....						
Other sectors............	8 796 ..	....	164.95	146.66	141.44	....	....		
of which: Short-term............	8 798 ..	....	....	....					
NET INTERNATIONAL INVESTMENT POSITION........	8 995 ..	**−75.72**	**−136.27**	**−51.84**	**−57.47**	....	....	....	....
Conversion rates: vatu per U.S. dollar (end of period)............	0 102 ..	**111.81**	**106.53**	**112.33**	**106.48**	**99.86**	**112.60**	**97.93**	**93.15**

Table 1. ANALYTIC PRESENTATION, 2003–2010

(Millions of U.S. dollars)

	Code	2003	2004	2005	2006	2007	2008	2009	2010
A. Current Account[1]	4 993 Z.	**11,796**	**15,519**	**25,110**	**26,462**	**18,063**	**37,392**	**8,561**	**14,378**
Goods: exports f.o.b.	2 100 ..	27,230	39,668	55,647	65,578	69,010	95,138	57,595	65,786
Goods: imports f.o.b.	3 100 ..	−10,483	−17,021	−24,195	−33,583	−46,031	−49,482	−38,442	−38,613
Balance on Goods	4 100 ..	*16,747*	*22,647*	*31,452*	*31,995*	*22,979*	*45,656*	*19,153*	*27,173*
Services: credit	2 200 ..	878	1,114	1,341	1,544	1,767	2,162	2,005	1,724
Services: debit	3 200 ..	−3,512	−4,497	−5,349	−5,954	−8,719	−10,516	−9,622	−10,581
Balance on Goods and Services	4 991 ..	*14,113*	*19,264*	*27,444*	*27,585*	*16,027*	*37,302*	*11,536*	*18,316*
Income: credit	2 300 ..	1,729	2,050	4,146	8,226	10,194	8,063	2,313	1,940
Income: debit	3 300 ..	−4,066	−5,723	−6,411	−9,271	−7,727	−7,365	−4,965	−5,319
Balance on Goods, Services, and Income	4 992 ..	*11,776*	*15,591*	*25,179*	*26,540*	*18,494*	*38,000*	*8,884*	*14,937*
Current transfers: credit	2 379 Z.	257	227	249	309	346	345	357	476
Current transfers: debit	3 379 ..	−237	−299	−318	−387	−777	−953	−680	−1,035
B. Capital Account[1]	4 994 Z.	....	....	....	....	....	....	....	**−211**
Capital account: credit	2 994 Z.	....	....	....	....	....	....	....	....
Capital account: debit	3 994 ..	....	....	....	....	....	....	....	−211
Total, Groups A Plus B	4 981 ..	*11,796*	*15,519*	*25,110*	*26,462*	*18,063*	*37,392*	*8,561*	*14,167*
C. Financial Account[1]	4 995 W.	**−5,547**	**−10,861**	**−16,480**	**−19,347**	**−21,674**	**−24,638**	**−14,583**	**−18,467**
Direct investment abroad	4 505 ..	−1,318	−619	−1,167	−1,524	−30	−1,273	−1,834	−2,390
Direct investment in Venezuela	4 555 Z.	2,040	1,483	2,602	−508	1,008	350	−3,105	−1,404
Portfolio investment assets	4 602 ..	−823	−813	−2,297	−5,966	−1,559	2,747	3,928	−589
Equity securities	4 610 ..	−233	27	−204	−25	39	240	−49	49
Debt securities	4 619 ..	−590	−840	−2,093	−5,941	−1,598	2,507	3,977	−638
Portfolio investment liabilities	4 652 Z.	−143	−1,271	3,225	−3,982	4,127	299	5,003	3,778
Equity securities	4 660 ..	97	−170	28	41	66	3	121	8
Debt securities	4 669 Z.	−240	−1,101	3,197	−4,023	4,061	296	4,882	3,770
Financial derivatives	4 910 ..	....	....	....	−1	−5	....	....	....
Financial derivatives assets	4 900 ..	....	....	....	....	....	....	....	....
Financial derivatives liabilities	4 905 ..	....	....	....	−1	−5	....	....	....
Other investment assets	4 703 ..	−4,030	−8,233	−18,425	−6,341	−29,440	−29,363	−24,484	−25,784
Monetary authorities	4 701 ..	11	10	−21	18	−5,783	5,809	13	368
General government	4 704 ..	−718	−2,594	−7,011	1,763	−5,673	−8,716	−2,143	−719
Banks	4 705 ..	46	−552	−103	−285	−322	−79	739	−29
Other sectors	4 728 ..	−3,369	−5,097	−11,290	−7,837	−17,662	−26,377	−23,093	−25,404
Other investment liabilities	4 753 W.	−1,273	−1,408	−418	−1,025	4,225	2,602	5,909	7,922
Monetary authorities	4 753 WA	19	250	−23	−51	381	218	2,966	170
General government	4 753 ZB	298	−586	−358	21	−985	−50	283	553
Banks	4 753 ZC	−141	1	82	372	282	−308	−96	−287
Other sectors	4 753 ZD	−1,449	−1,073	−119	−1,367	4,547	2,742	2,756	7,486
Total, Groups A Through C	4 983 ..	*6,249*	*4,658*	*8,630*	*7,115*	*−3,611*	*12,754*	*−6,022*	*−4,300*
D. Net Errors and Omissions	4 998 ..	**−795**	**−2,503**	**−3,205**	**−2,212**	**−1,746**	**−3,302**	**−4,785**	**−3,639**
Total, Groups A Through D	4 984 ..	*5,454*	*2,155*	*5,425*	*4,903*	*−5,357*	*9,452*	*−10,807*	*−7,939*
E. Reserves and Related Items	4 802 A.	**−5,454**	**−2,155**	**−5,425**	**−4,903**	**5,357**	**−9,452**	**10,807**	**7,939**
Reserve assets	4 802 ..	−5,454	−2,155	−5,425	−4,903	5,357	−9,452	10,807	7,939
Use of Fund credit and loans	4 766 ..	....	....	....	....	....	....	....	....
Exceptional financing	4 920 ..	....	....	....	....	....	....	....	....
Conversion rates: bolívares per U.S. dollar	0 101 ..	**1.6070**	**1.8913**	**2.0898**	**2.1470**	**2.1470**	**2.1470**	**2.1470**	**2.5821**

[1] Excludes components that have been classified in the categories of Group E.

Table 2. STANDARD PRESENTATION, 2003–2010

(Millions of U.S. dollars)

	Code	2003	2004	2005	2006	2007	2008	2009	2010
CURRENT ACCOUNT............................	4 993	**11,796**	**15,519**	**25,110**	**26,462**	**18,063**	**37,392**	**8,561**	**14,378**
A. GOODS...	4 100	**16,747**	**22,647**	**31,452**	**31,995**	**22,979**	**45,656**	**19,153**	**27,173**
Credit...	2 100	**27,230**	**39,668**	**55,647**	**65,578**	**69,010**	**95,138**	**57,595**	**65,786**
General merchandise: exports f.o.b........	2 110	27,109	39,468	55,244	65,286	68,652	94,655	56,962	65,270
Goods for processing: exports f.o.b........	2 150	....	....	....	....	....	....	....	....
Repairs on goods............................	2 160	4	4	4	4	4	4	4	4
Goods procured in ports by carriers......	2 170	8	8	8	8	8	8	8	8
Nonmonetary gold...........................	2 180	109	188	391	280	346	471	621	504
Debit..	3 100	**−10,483**	**−17,021**	**−24,195**	**−33,583**	**−46,031**	**−49,482**	**−38,442**	**−38,613**
General merchandise: imports f.o.b........	3 110	−10,454	−16,997	−24,173	−33,488	−45,944	−49,410	−38,361	−38,517
Goods for processing: imports f.o.b........	3 150	....	....	....	....	....	....	....	....
Repairs on goods............................	3 160	−8	−8	−6	−36	−29	−24	−27	−32
Goods procured in ports by carriers......	3 170	−21	−16	−16	−59	−58	−48	−54	−64
Nonmonetary gold...........................	3 180	....	....	....	....	....	....	....	....
B. SERVICES.......................................	4 200	**−2,634**	**−3,383**	**−4,008**	**−4,410**	**−6,952**	**−8,354**	**−7,617**	**−8,857**
Total credit...................................	2 200	*878*	*1,114*	*1,341*	*1,544*	*1,767*	*2,162*	*2,005*	*1,724*
Total debit....................................	3 200	*−3,512*	*−4,497*	*−5,349*	*−5,954*	*−8,719*	*−10,516*	*−9,622*	*−10,581*
Transportation services, credit..........	2 205	**307**	**346**	**383**	**403**	**586**	**738**	**696**	**559**
Passenger...................................	2 850	*47*	*52*	*72*	*75*	*77*	*67*	*65*	*54*
Freight......................................	2 851	*89*	*101*	*104*	*106*	*297*	*435*	*307*	*293*
Other.......................................	2 852	*171*	*193*	*207*	*222*	*212*	*236*	*324*	*212*
Sea transport, passenger.................	2 207	....	....	....	....	....	....	....	....
Sea transport, freight....................	2 208	88	99	102	105	297	434	306	293
Sea transport, other......................	2 209	151	168	175	187	168	194	287	180
Air transport, passenger.................	2 211	47	52	72	75	77	67	65	54
Air transport, freight....................	2 212	1	2	2	1	....	1	1	....
Air transport, other......................	2 213	20	25	32	35	44	42	37	32
Other transport, passenger...............	2 215	....	....	....	....	....	....	....	....
Other transport, freight..................	2 216	....	....	....	....	....	....	....	....
Other transport, other....................	2 217	....	....	....	....	....	....	....	....
Transportation services, debit...........	3 205	**−1,261**	**−1,730**	**−2,214**	**−2,679**	**−4,522**	**−4,849**	**−4,027**	**−4,027**
Passenger...................................	3 850	*−452*	*−527*	*−567*	*−578*	*−707*	*−782*	*−666*	*−621*
Freight......................................	3 851	*−659*	*−1,038*	*−1,463*	*−1,909*	*−3,618*	*−3,866*	*−3,170*	*−3,229*
Other.......................................	3 852	*−150*	*−165*	*−184*	*−192*	*−197*	*−201*	*−191*	*−177*
Sea transport, passenger.................	3 207	....	....	....	....	....	....	....	....
Sea transport, freight....................	3 208	−507	−768	−1,100	−1,495	−2,581	−2,946	−2,438	−2,512
Sea transport, other......................	3 209	−87	−104	−118	−122	−120	−127	−126	−106
Air transport, passenger.................	3 211	−452	−527	−567	−578	−707	−782	−666	−621
Air transport, freight....................	3 212	−98	−143	−207	−217	−787	−518	−426	−429
Air transport, other......................	3 213	−63	−61	−66	−70	−77	−74	−65	−71
Other transport, passenger...............	3 215	....	....	....	....	....	....	....	....
Other transport, freight..................	3 216	−54	−127	−156	−197	−250	−402	−306	−288
Other transport, other....................	3 217	....	....	....	....	....	....	....	....
Travel, credit.............................	2 236	**331**	**502**	**650**	**768**	**817**	**917**	**788**	**618**
Business travel............................	2 237	186	199	275	270	258	292	209	183
Personal travel............................	2 240	145	303	375	498	559	625	579	435
Travel, debit..............................	3 236	**−859**	**−1,077**	**−1,276**	**−1,229**	**−1,520**	**−1,784**	**−1,568**	**−1,575**
Business travel............................	3 237	−241	−316	−419	−390	−370	−395	−297	−269
Personal travel............................	3 240	−618	−761	−857	−839	−1,150	−1,389	−1,271	−1,306
Other services, credit...................	2 200 BA	**240**	**266**	**308**	**373**	**364**	**507**	**521**	**547**
Communications............................	2 245	48	55	83	130	135	152	140	144
Construction...............................	2 249	....	....	....	....	....	....	....	....
Insurance..................................	2 253	2	2	1	4	4	2	2	2
Financial..................................	2 260	....	....	....	....	....	....	....	....
Computer and information..................	2 262	6	6	8	8	9	9	9	9
Royalties and licence fees................	2 266	....	....	....	....	....	....	....	....
Other business services...................	2 268	92	109	117	123	90	179	164	155
Personal, cultural, and recreational.......	2 287	5	4	5	5	5	6	6	6
Government, n.i.e..........................	2 291	87	90	94	103	121	159	200	231
Other services, debit....................	3 200 BA	**−1,392**	**−1,690**	**−1,859**	**−2,046**	**−2,677**	**−3,883**	**−4,027**	**−4,979**
Communications............................	3 245	−58	−68	−76	−98	−233	−293	−331	−369
Construction...............................	3 249	....	....	....	....	....	....	....	....
Insurance..................................	3 253	−115	−165	−228	−327	−425	−532	−448	−478
Financial..................................	3 260	−157	−110	−243	−197	−276	−80	−97	−72
Computer and information..................	3 262	−58	−69	−85	−94	−184	−79	−79	−73
Royalties and licence fees................	3 266	−183	−219	−239	−257	−276	−349	−352	−340
Other business services...................	3 268	−508	−662	−641	−611	−672	−1,655	−1,669	−2,055
Personal, cultural, and recreational.......	3 287	−52	−165	−181	−254	−330	−452	−652	−1,092
Government, n.i.e..........................	3 291	−261	−232	−166	−208	−281	−443	−399	−500

Table 2 (Continued). STANDARD PRESENTATION, 2003–2010

(Millions of U.S. dollars)

	Code	2003	2004	2005	2006	2007	2008	2009	2010
C. INCOME	4 300	−2,337	−3,673	−2,265	−1,045	2,467	698	−2,652	−3,379
Total credit	2 300	*1,729*	*2,050*	*4,146*	*8,226*	*10,194*	*8,063*	*2,313*	*1,940*
Total debit	3 300	*−4,066*	*−5,723*	*−6,411*	*−9,271*	*−7,727*	*−7,365*	*−4,965*	*−5,319*
Compensation of employees, credit	2 310	21	20	20	20	20	20	22	22
Compensation of employees, debit	3 310	−30	−28	−28	−32	−27	−28	−31	−42
Investment income, credit	2 320	1,708	2,030	4,126	8,206	10,174	8,043	2,291	1,918
Direct investment income	2 330	791	725	1,349	3,209	3,763	3,425	1,024	796
Dividends and distributed branch profits	2 332	585	570	1,061	2,764	3,284	2,975	584	376
Reinvested earnings and undistributed branch profits	2 333	206	155	288	445	479	450	440	420
Income on debt (interest)	2 334	....	....	....	....	....	....	....	....
Portfolio investment income	2 339	332	367	535	1,429	1,936	1,486	281	206
Income on equity	2 340	10	7	3	9	18	21	....	13
Income on bonds and notes	2 350	264	289	308	690	1,048	795	208	106
Income on money market instruments	2 360	58	71	224	730	870	670	73	87
Other investment income	2 370	585	938	2,242	3,568	4,475	3,132	986	916
Investment income, debit	3 320	−4,036	−5,695	−6,383	−9,239	−7,700	−7,337	−4,934	−5,277
Direct investment income	3 330	−1,802	−3,498	−3,953	−6,540	−4,785	−4,152	−1,903	−1,955
Dividends and distributed branch profits	3 332	−726	−1,786	−1,823	−4,544	−2,955	−3,509	−1,836	−1,273
Reinvested earnings and undistributed branch profits	3 333	−1,045	−1,673	−2,086	−1,949	−1,747	−601	−55	−668
Income on debt (interest)	3 334	−31	−39	−44	−47	−83	−42	−12	−14
Portfolio investment income	3 339	−1,678	−1,677	−1,824	−2,017	−2,188	−2,334	−2,456	−2,714
Income on equity	3 340	−161	−176	−85	−214	−172	−118	−112	−41
Income on bonds and notes	3 350	−1,517	−1,501	−1,739	−1,803	−2,016	−2,216	−2,344	−2,673
Income on money market instruments	3 360	....	....	....	....	....	....	....	....
Other investment income	3 370	−556	−520	−606	−682	−727	−851	−575	−608
D. CURRENT TRANSFERS	4 379	20	−72	−69	−78	−431	−608	−323	−559
Credit	2 379	257	227	249	309	346	345	357	476
General government	2 380	25	61	74	123	170	185	204	312
Other sectors	2 390	232	166	175	186	176	160	153	164
Workers' remittances	2 391	187	123	128	145	131	117	109	121
Other current transfers	2 392	45	43	47	41	45	43	44	43
Debit	3 379	−237	−299	−318	−387	−777	−953	−680	−1,035
General government	3 380	−14	−70	−86	−82	−59	−39	−50	−117
Other sectors	3 390	−223	−229	−232	−305	−718	−914	−630	−918
Workers' remittances	3 391	−179	−186	−183	−225	−622	−832	−550	−763
Other current transfers	3 392	−44	−43	−49	−80	−96	−82	−80	−155
CAPITAL AND FINANCIAL ACCOUNT	4 996	−11,001	−13,016	−21,905	−24,250	−16,317	−34,090	−3,776	−10,739
CAPITAL ACCOUNT	4 994	....	....	....	....	....	....	....	−211
Total credit	2 994	....	....	....	....	....	....	....	....
Total debit	3 994	....	....	....	....	....	....	....	*−211*
Capital transfers, credit	2 400	....	....	....	....	....	....	....	....
General government	2 401	....	....	....	....	....	....	....	....
Debt forgiveness	2 402	....	....	....	....	....	....	....	....
Other capital transfers	2 410	....	....	....	....	....	....	....	....
Other sectors	2 430	....	....	....	....	....	....	....	....
Migrants' transfers	2 431	....	....	....	....	....	....	....	....
Debt forgiveness	2 432	....	....	....	....	....	....	....	....
Other capital transfers	2 440	....	....	....	....	....	....	....	....
Capital transfers, debit	3 400	....	....	....	....	....	....	....	−211
General government	3 401	....	....	....	....	....	....	....	....
Debt forgiveness	3 402	....	....	....	....	....	....	....	....
Other capital transfers	3 410	....	....	....	....	....	....	....	....
Other sectors	3 430	....	....	....	....	....	....	....	−211
Migrants' transfers	3 431	....	....	....	....	....	....	....	....
Debt forgiveness	3 432	....	....	....	....	....	....	....	−211
Other capital transfers	3 440	....	....	....	....	....	....	....	....
Nonproduced nonfinancial assets, credit	2 480	....	....	....	....	....	....	....	....
Nonproduced nonfinancial assets, debit	3 480	....	....	....	....	....	....	....	....

Table 2 (Continued). STANDARD PRESENTATION, 2003–2010

(Millions of U.S. dollars)

	Code	2003	2004	2005	2006	2007	2008	2009	2010
FINANCIAL ACCOUNT.....................................	4 995	**−11,001**	**−13,016**	**−21,905**	**−24,250**	**−16,317**	**−34,090**	**−3,776**	**−10,528**
A. DIRECT INVESTMENT....................................	4 500 ..	**722**	**864**	**1,435**	**−2,032**	**978**	**−923**	**−4,939**	**−3,794**
Direct investment abroad....................................	4 505 ..	**−1,318**	**−619**	**−1,167**	**−1,524**	**−30**	**−1,273**	**−1,834**	**−2,390**
Equity capital..	4 510 ..	−94	−91	−21	−320	−100	−114	92	−132
Claims on affiliated enterprises......................	4 515 ..	−94	−91	−21	−320	−100	−114	92	−132
Liabilities to affiliated enterprises..................	4 520 ..	....	....						....
Reinvested earnings...................................	4 525 ..	−206	−155	−288	−445	−479	−450	−440	−420
Other capital..	4 530 ..	−1,018	−373	−858	−759	549	−709	−1,486	−1,838
Claims on affiliated enterprises......................	4 535 ..	−527	−373	−632	−1,451	−589	−473	−1,044	−1,103
Liabilities to affiliated enterprises..................	4 540 ..	−491	....	−226	692	1,138	−236	−442	−735
Direct investment in Venezuela........................	4 555 ..	**2,040**	**1,483**	**2,602**	**−508**	**1,008**	**350**	**−3,105**	**−1,404**
Equity capital..	4 560 ..	565	654	502	−134	−1,010	504	−2,329	−509
Claims on direct investors...........................	4 565 ..	....	....	....	....	....	....		
Liabilities to direct investors........................	4 570 ..	565	654	502	−134	−1,010	504	−2,329	−509
Reinvested earnings...................................	4 575 ..	1,045	1,673	2,086	1,949	1,747	601	55	668
Other capital..	4 580 ..	430	−844	14	−2,323	271	−755	−831	−1,563
Claims on direct investors...........................	4 585 ..	−24	−6	−87	−14	−15	−2	....	−148
Liabilities to direct investors........................	4 590 ..	454	−838	101	−2,309	286	−753	−831	−1,415
B. PORTFOLIO INVESTMENT..............................	4 600 ..	**−966**	**−2,084**	**928**	**−9,948**	**2,568**	**3,046**	**8,931**	**3,189**
Assets...	4 602 ..	**−823**	**−813**	**−2,297**	**−5,966**	**−1,559**	**2,747**	**3,928**	**−589**
Equity securities......................................	4 610 ..	−233	27	−204	−25	39	240	−49	49
Monetary authorities...............................	4 611 ..	....	....	....	....	....	....	....	....
General government................................	4 612 ..	....	....	....	....	....	....	....	....
Banks...	4 613 ..	−148	3	41	63	72	−17	−21	10
Other sectors.......................................	4 614 ..	−85	24	−245	−88	−33	257	−28	39
Debt securities..	4 619 ..	−590	−840	−2,093	−5,941	−1,598	2,507	3,977	−638
Bonds and notes...................................	4 620 ..	−602	−875	−2,026	−5,437	−1,602	2,273	3,687	−706
Monetary authorities.............................	4 621 ..	....	....	....	−2,051	....	....	−771	−4
General government...............................	4 622 ..	−85	−92	−2,371	−1,422	1,519	−1,261	2,631	−735
Banks...	4 623 ..	68	−271	−1,192	−962	−2,598	3,159	1,227	23
Other sectors......................................	4 624 ..	−585	−512	1,537	−1,002	−523	375	600	10
Money market instruments..........................	4 630 ..	12	35	−67	−504	4	234	290	68
Monetary authorities.............................	4 631 ..	....	....	....	....	....	....	....	....
General government...............................	4 632 ..	....	....	....	....	....	....	....	....
Banks...	4 633 ..	−241	61	−3	−90	−169	282	2	−28
Other sectors......................................	4 634 ..	253	−26	−64	−414	173	−48	288	96
Liabilities..	4 652 ..	**−143**	**−1,271**	**3,225**	**−3,982**	**4,127**	**299**	**5,003**	**3,778**
Equity securities......................................	4 660 ..	97	−170	28	41	66	3	121	8
Banks...	4 663 ..	....	−3	−2	3	27	−4	....	....
Other sectors.......................................	4 664 ..	97	−167	30	38	39	7	121	8
Debt securities..	4 669 ..	−240	−1,101	3,197	−4,023	4,061	296	4,882	3,770
Bonds and notes...................................	4 670 ..	−240	−1,101	3,197	−4,023	4,061	296	4,882	3,770
Monetary authorities.............................	4 671 ..	−17	−13	−15	....	....	....	−1	−1
General government...............................	4 672 ..	172	1,591	3,254	−3,961	194	1,254	2,586	351
Banks...	4 673 ..	....	....	....	....	....	....	....	....
Other sectors......................................	4 674 ..	−395	−2,679	−42	−62	3,867	−958	2,297	3,420
Money market instruments..........................	4 680 ..	....	....	....	....	....	....	....	....
Monetary authorities.............................	4 681 ..	....	....	....	....	....	....	....	....
General government...............................	4 682 ..	....	....	....	....	....	....	....	....
Banks...	4 683 ..	....	....	....	....	....	....	....	....
Other sectors......................................	4 684 ..	....	....	....	....	....	....	....	....
C. FINANCIAL DERIVATIVES...............................	4 910 ..	....	....	....	**−1**	**−5**	....	....	....
Monetary authorities.................................	4 911 ..	....	....	....	....	....	....	....	....
General government..................................	4 912 ..	....	....	....	....	....	....	....	....
Banks..	4 913 ..	....	....	....	....	....	....	....	....
Other sectors...	4 914 ..	....	....	....	−1	−5	....	....	....
Assets...	4 900 ..	....	....	....	....	....	....	....	....
Monetary authorities.................................	4 901 ..	....	....	....	....	....	....	....	....
General government..................................	4 902 ..	....	....	....	....	....	....	....	....
Banks..	4 903 ..	....	....	....	....	....	....	....	....
Other sectors...	4 904 ..	....	....	....	....	....	....	....	....
Liabilities..	4 905 ..	....	....	....	**−1**	**−5**	....	....	....
Monetary authorities.................................	4 906 ..	....	....	....	....	....	....	....	....
General government..................................	4 907 ..	....	....	....	....	....	....	....	....
Banks..	4 908 ..	....	....	....	....	....	....	....	....
Other sectors...	4 909 ..	....	....	....	−1	−5	....	....	....

Table 2 (Concluded). STANDARD PRESENTATION, 2003–2010

(Millions of U.S. dollars)

	Code	2003	2004	2005	2006	2007	2008	2009	2010
D. OTHER INVESTMENT	4 700	−5,303	−9,641	−18,843	−7,366	−25,215	−26,761	−18,575	−17,862
Assets	4 703	−4,030	−8,233	−18,425	−6,341	−29,440	−29,363	−24,484	−25,784
Trade credits	4 706	−907	−431	−2,825	−3,992	−2,281	−2,978	−2,808	−4,687
General government	4 707	2	....	....	−745	−105	−387	−380	−21
of which: Short-term	4 709	2	....	....	....	....	....	....	....
Other sectors	4 710	−909	−431	−2,825	−3,247	−2,176	−2,591	−2,428	−4,666
of which: Short-term	4 712	−872	−418	−2,825	−3,247	−1,921	−2,591	−2,428	−4,666
Loans	4 714	43	47	28	−51	13	−529	−206	−53
Monetary authorities	4 715	9	18	12	1	2	4	2	....
of which: Short-term	4 718	....	....	....	....	....	....	....	....
General government	4 719	....	....	....	....	....	−400	−170	....
of which: Short-term	4 721	....	....	....	....	....	....	....	....
Banks	4 722	....	....	....	....	....	....	....	....
of which: Short-term	4 724	....	....	....	....	....	....	....	....
Other sectors	4 725	34	29	16	−52	11	−133	−38	−53
of which: Short-term	4 727	....	....	....	....	....	....	....	....
Currency and deposits	4 730	−3,086	−7,725	−15,542	−2,107	−23,176	−18,080	−16,012	−18,281
Monetary authorities	4 731	....	....	....	....	−5,797	5,797	....	504
General government	4 732	−698	−2,570	−6,993	2,508	−1,527	−130	3,871	1,807
Banks	4 733	46	−552	−103	−285	−322	−79	741	−29
Other sectors	4 734	−2,434	−4,603	−8,446	−4,330	−15,530	−23,668	−20,624	−20,563
Other assets	4 736	−80	−124	−86	−191	−3,996	−7,776	−5,458	−2,763
Monetary authorities	4 737	2	−8	−33	17	12	8	11	−136
of which: Short-term	4 739	2	−8	−33	17	12	8	11	3
General government	4 740	−22	−24	−18	....	−4,041	−7,799	−5,464	−2,505
of which: Short-term	4 742	....	....	....	....	....	....	....	....
Banks	4 743	....	....	....	....	....	....	−2	....
of which: Short-term	4 745	....	....	....	....	....	....	−2	....
Other sectors	4 746	−60	−92	−35	−208	33	15	−3	−122
of which: Short-term	4 748	−75	−92	−35	−150	41	....	−3	−122
Liabilities	4 753	−1,273	−1,408	−418	−1,025	4,225	2,602	5,909	7,922
Trade credits	4 756	390	139	1,096	−235	1,235	2,642	−1,399	1,010
General government	4 757	−19	−58	−19	−50	−18	−13	−3	−3
of which: Short-term	4 759	....	....	....	....	....	....	....	....
Other sectors	4 760	409	197	1,115	−185	1,253	2,655	−1,396	1,013
of which: Short-term	4 762	445	240	1,144	−181	1,253	2,655	−1,396	1,013
Loans	4 764	−1,765	−1,713	−1,268	−947	2,581	−153	3,097	7,187
Monetary authorities	4 765	....	....	....	....	....	....	....	....
of which: Use of Fund credit and loans from the Fund	4 766	....	....	....	....	....	....	....	....
of which: Short-term	4 768	....	....	....	....	....	....	....	....
General government	4 769	325	−523	−346	76	−966	−37	286	556
of which: Short-term	4 771	....	....	....	....	....	....	....	....
Banks	4 772	−222	59	106	156	423	−310	−72	−260
of which: Short-term	4 774	−206	61	108	178	423	−314	−72	−273
Other sectors	4 775	−1,868	−1,249	−1,028	−1,179	3,124	194	2,883	6,891
of which: Short-term	4 777	−619	−149	−19	−53	1,022	−1,087	−13	−15
Currency and deposits	4 780	80	−63	−30	217	−140	5	−22	−22
Monetary authorities	4 781	−1	−5	−6	1	1	3	2	5
General government	4 782	....	....	....	....	....	....	....	....
Banks	4 783	81	−58	−24	216	−141	2	−24	−27
Other sectors	4 784	....	....	....	....	....	....	....	....
Other liabilities	4 786	22	229	−216	−60	549	108	4,233	−253
Monetary authorities	4 787	20	255	−17	−52	380	215	2,964	165
of which: Short-term	4 789	20	255	−17	−52	380	215	−514	165
General government	4 790	−8	−5	7	−5	−1	....	....	....
of which: Short-term	4 792	−8	−5	7	....	....	....	....	....
Banks	4 793	....	....	....	....	....	....	....	....
of which: Short-term	4 795	....	....	....	....	....	....	....	....
Other sectors	4 796	10	−21	−206	−3	170	−107	1,269	−418
of which: Short-term	4 798	10	−21	−206	−3	170	−107	73	2
E. RESERVE ASSETS	4 802	−5,454	−2,155	−5,425	−4,903	5,357	−9,452	10,807	7,939
Monetary gold	4 812	−271	....	....	....	....	....	−230	−415
Special drawing rights	4 811	2	2	3	5	−1	−21	−3,477	....
Reserve position in the Fund	4 810	....	....	....	....	....	....	....	....
Foreign exchange	4 803	−5,176	−2,149	−5,426	−4,900	5,377	−9,409	14,514	8,367
Other claims	4 813	−9	−8	−2	−8	−19	−22	....	−13
NET ERRORS AND OMISSIONS	4 998	−795	−2,503	−3,205	−2,212	−1,746	−3,302	−4,785	−3,639

Table 3. INTERNATIONAL INVESTMENT POSITION (End-period stocks), 2003–2010

(Millions of U.S. dollars)

	Code	2003	2004	2005	2006	2007	2008	2009	2010
ASSETS	8 995 C.	**88,329**	**99,146**	**122,309**	**145,566**	**176,092**	**212,494**	**227,320**	**250,451**
Direct investment abroad	8 505 ..	**9,548**	**9,175**	**9,429**	**13,196**	**14,920**	**15,834**	**17,670**	**19,889**
Equity capital and reinvested earnings	8 506 ..	7,997	8,260	8,569	12,219	14,319	14,892	15,243	15,804
Claims on affiliated enterprises	8 507 ..	7,997	8,260	8,569	12,219	14,319	14,892	15,243	15,804
Liabilities to affiliated enterprises	8 508 ..	....	....	....	....	....	....	....	....
Other capital	8 530 ..	1,551	915	860	977	601	942	2,427	4,085
Claims on affiliated enterprises	8 535 ..	1,595	1,968	1,687	2,496	3,518	3,682	4,725	5,723
Liabilities to affiliated enterprises	8 540 ..	−44	−1,053	−827	−1,519	−2,917	−2,740	−2,298	−1,638
Portfolio investment	8 602 ..	**6,607**	**6,740**	**9,070**	**15,309**	**17,125**	**15,042**	**10,334**	**11,040**
Equity securities	8 610 ..	549	519	745	778	750	436	468	400
Monetary authorities	8 611 ..	....	....	....	....	....	....	....	....
General government	8 612 ..	....	....	....	....	....	....	....	....
Banks	8 613 ..	182	176	153	93	24	36	47	29
Other sectors	8 614 ..	367	343	592	685	726	400	421	371
Debt securities	8 619 ..	6,058	6,221	8,325	14,531	16,375	14,606	9,866	10,640
Bonds and notes	8 620 ..	4,406	4,794	6,810	12,512	14,394	12,819	8,379	9,229
Monetary authorities	8 621 ..	25	29	35	2,197	2,393	3,300	3,919	4,148
General government	8 622 ..	1,708	1,910	4,236	5,790	4,271	5,532	2,901	3,636
Banks	8 623 ..	91	350	1,549	2,517	5,115	1,819	62	27
Other sectors	8 624 ..	2,582	2,505	990	2,008	2,615	2,168	1,497	1,418
Money market instruments	8 630 ..	1,652	1,427	1,515	2,019	1,981	1,787	1,487	1,411
Monetary authorities	8 631 ..	....	....	....	....	....	....	....	....
General government	8 632 ..	....	....	....	....	....	....	....	....
Banks	8 633 ..	277	25	25	115	284	2	....	28
Other sectors	8 634 ..	1,375	1,402	1,490	1,904	1,697	1,785	1,487	1,383
Financial derivatives	8 900 ..	....	....	....	....	....	....	....	....
Monetary authorities	8 901 ..	....	....	....	....	....	....	....	....
General government	8 902 ..	....	....	....	....	....	....	....	....
Banks	8 903 ..	....	....	....	....	....	....	....	....
Other sectors	8 904 ..	....	....	....	....	....	....	....	....
Other investment	8 703 ..	**50,807**	**59,024**	**73,442**	**79,621**	**109,761**	**138,491**	**163,486**	**189,190**
Trade credits	8 706 ..	2,861	3,289	3,925	7,515	10,459	10,989	13,817	18,172
General government	8 707 ..	....	....	....	745	850	1,237	1,617	1,638
of which: Short-term	8 709 ..	....	....	....	....	....	....	....	....
Other sectors	8 710 ..	2,861	3,289	3,925	6,770	9,609	9,752	12,200	16,534
of which: Short-term	8 712 ..	*2,813*	*3,238*	*3,925*	*6,770*	*9,392*	*9,535*	*11,983*	*16,317*
Loans	8 714 ..	231	185	156	190	177	706	905	959
Monetary authorities	8 715 ..	82	65	53	52	50	46	44	44
of which: Short-term	8 718 ..	....	....	....	....	....	....	....	....
General government	8 719 ..	....	....	....	....	....	400	570	570
of which: Short-term	8 721 ..	....	....	....	....	....	....	....	....
Banks	8 722 ..	....	....	....	....	....	....	....	....
of which: Short-term	8 724 ..	....	....	....	....	....	....	....	....
Other sectors	8 725 ..	149	120	103	138	127	260	291	345
of which: Short-term	8 727 ..	....	....	....	....	....	....	....	....
Currency and deposits	8 730 ..	46,901	54,612	68,238	70,515	93,781	113,677	130,187	149,015
Monetary authorities	8 731 ..	....	....	....	....	5,797	....	504	37
General government	8 732 ..	2,285	4,857	10,134	7,686	9,213	9,343	5,472	3,844
Banks	8 733 ..	471	1,022	1,071	1,356	1,678	1,771	1,016	1,057
Other sectors	8 734 ..	44,145	48,733	57,033	61,473	77,093	102,563	123,195	144,077
Other assets	8 736 ..	814	938	1,123	1,401	5,344	13,119	18,577	21,044
Monetary authorities	8 737 ..	14	22	58	38	28	20	10	203
of which: Short-term	8 739 ..	*14*	*22*	*58*	*38*	*28*	*20*	*10*	*9*
General government	8 740 ..	682	706	746	770	4,819	12,618	18,082	20,234
of which: Short-term	8 742 ..	....	....	....	....	....	....	....	....
Banks	8 743 ..	....	....	....	....	....	....	2	2
of which: Short-term	8 745 ..	....	....	....	....	....	....	*2*	*2*
Other sectors	8 746 ..	118	210	319	593	497	481	483	605
of which: Short-term	8 748 ..	*115*	*207*	*316*	*470*	*428*	*427*	*429*	*551*
Reserve assets	8 802 ..	**21,367**	**24,207**	**30,368**	**37,440**	**34,286**	**43,127**	**35,830**	**30,332**
Monetary gold	8 812 ..	4,632	5,122	5,718	7,255	9,281	9,201	13,297	16,363
Special drawing rights	8 811 ..	10	9	5	....	1	21	3,511	3,449
Reserve position in the Fund	8 810 ..	478	500	460	484	509	496	505	496
Foreign exchange	8 803 ..	15,912	18,236	23,842	29,350	24,125	33,016	18,124	9,618
Other claims	8 813 ..	334	341	343	351	370	393	393	406

Table 3 (Concluded). INTERNATIONAL INVESTMENT POSITION (End-period stocks), 2003–2010

(Millions of U.S. dollars)

	Code	2003	2004	2005	2006	2007	2008	2009	2010
LIABILITIES	8 995 D.	**79,459**	**82,230**	**86,129**	**84,808**	**86,898**	**80,927**	**94,496**	**102,937**
Direct investment in Venezuela	8 555	**41,373**	**42,359**	**44,518**	**45,670**	**43,556**	**43,524**	**41,214**	**38,022**
Equity capital and reinvested earnings	8 556	26,414	28,522	30,590	33,914	31,879	33,864	32,531	31,635
Claims on direct investors	8 557	....	....	....	....	....	....	....	....
Liabilities to direct investors	8 558	26,414	28,522	30,590	33,914	31,879	33,864	32,531	31,635
Other capital	8 580	14,959	13,837	13,928	11,756	11,677	9,660	8,683	6,387
Claims on direct investors	8 585	−53	−59	−146	−160	−175	−3	−89	−421
Liabilities to direct investors	8 590	15,012	13,896	14,074	11,916	11,852	9,663	8,772	6,808
Portfolio investment	8 652	**19,175**	**22,129**	**24,577**	**22,773**	**22,017**	**13,520**	**22,643**	**26,712**
Equity securities	8 660	1,713	1,812	1,173	2,259	843	700	772	402
Banks	8 663	17	17	7	23	12	4	7	....
Other sectors	8 664	1,696	1,795	1,166	2,236	831	696	765	402
Debt securities	8 669	17,462	20,317	23,404	20,514	21,174	12,820	21,871	26,310
Bonds and notes	8 670	17,462	20,317	23,404	20,514	21,174	12,820	21,871	26,310
Monetary authorities	8 671	38	24	7	7	7	6	4	3
General government	8 672	13,136	19,307	22,430	19,615	16,775	10,756	16,783	17,534
Banks	8 673	....	....	....	....	....	....	....	....
Other sectors	8 674	4,288	986	967	892	4,392	2,058	5,084	8,773
Money market instruments	8 680	....	....	....	....	....	....	....	....
Monetary authorities	8 681	....	....	....	....	....	....	....	....
General government	8 682	....	....	....	....	....	....	....	....
Banks	8 683	....	....	....	....	....	....	....	....
Other sectors	8 684	....	....	....	....	....	....	....	....
Financial derivatives	8 905	**....**	**....**	**22**	**21**	**16**	**16**	**16**	**16**
Monetary authorities	8 906	....	....						
General government	8 907	....	....						
Banks	8 908	....	....						
Other sectors	8 909	....	....	22	21	16	16	16	16
Other investment	8 753	**18,911**	**17,742**	**17,012**	**16,344**	**21,309**	**23,867**	**30,623**	**38,187**
Trade credits	8 756	2,878	3,056	4,282	4,009	6,469	9,115	7,716	8,663
General government	8 757	99	73	80	29	19	5	2	....
of which: Short-term	8 759	....	....	....	....	....	....	....	....
Other sectors	8 760	2,779	2,983	4,202	3,980	6,450	9,110	7,714	8,663
of which: Short-term	8 762	*2,712*	*2,952*	*4,190*	*3,980*	*6,450*	*9,110*	*7,714*	*8,663*
Loans	8 764	14,901	13,423	11,684	11,089	13,185	13,021	16,454	23,409
Monetary authorities	8 765	20	20	20	20	20	20	20	20
of which: Use of Fund credit and loans from the Fund	8 766	....	....	....	....	....	....	....	....
of which: Short-term	8 768	....	....	....	....	....	....	....	....
General government	8 769	5,675	5,370	5,618	5,814	4,982	4,986	5,293	5,800
of which: Short-term	8 771	....	....	....	....	....	....	....	....
Banks	8 772	63	122	227	383	806	496	432	172
of which: Short-term	8 774	*30*	*91*	*199*	*377*	*800*	*486*	*422*	*149*
Other sectors	8 775	9,143	7,911	5,819	4,872	7,377	7,519	10,709	17,417
of which: Short-term	8 777	*303*	*154*	*163*	*269*	*1,291*	*215*	*224*	*86*
Currency and deposits	8 780	98	36	7	224	83	88	66	44
Monetary authorities	8 781	12	8	3	4	4	7	9	14
General government	8 782	....	....	....	....	....	....	....	....
Banks	8 783	86	28	4	220	79	81	57	30
Other sectors	8 784	....	....	....	....	....	....	....	....
Other liabilities	8 786	1,034	1,227	1,039	1,022	1,572	1,643	6,387	6,071
Monetary authorities	8 787	54	310	292	240	626	840	4,315	4,417
of which: Short-term	8 789	*54*	*310*	*292*	*240*	*626*	*840*	*328*	*500*
General government	8 790	635	594	632	623	616	616	616	616
of which: Short-term	8 792	*635*	*594*	*632*	*623*	*616*	*616*	*616*	*616*
Banks	8 793	....	....	....	....	....	....	....	....
of which: Short-term	8 795	....	....	....	....	....	....	....	....
Other sectors	8 796	345	323	115	159	330	187	1,456	1,038
of which: Short-term	8 798	*345*	*323*	*115*	*159*	*330*	*187*	*260*	*262*
NET INTERNATIONAL INVESTMENT POSITION	8 995	**8,870**	**16,916**	**36,180**	**60,758**	**89,194**	**131,567**	**132,824**	**147,514**
Conversion rates: bolívares per U.S. dollar (end of period)	0 102	**1.5980**	**1.9180**	**2.1470**	**2.1470**	**2.1470**	**2.1470**	**2.1470**	**2.5935**

Table 1. ANALYTIC PRESENTATION, 2003–2010

(Millions of U.S. dollars)

	Code	2003	2004	2005	2006	2007	2008	2009	2010
A. Current Account[1]	4 993 Z.	**−1,931**	**−957**	**−560**	**−164**	**−6,953**	**−10,823**	**−6,608**	**−4,287**
Goods: exports f.o.b.	2 100 ..	20,149	26,485	32,447	39,826	48,561	62,685	57,096	72,192
Goods: imports f.o.b.	3 100 ..	−22,730	−28,772	−34,886	−42,602	−58,999	−75,468	−64,703	−77,339
Balance on Goods	4 100 ..	*−2,581*	*−2,287*	*−2,439*	*−2,776*	*−10,438*	*−12,783*	*−7,607*	*−5,147*
Services: credit	2 200 ..	3,272	3,867	4,176	5,100	6,030	7,006	5,766	7,460
Services: debit	3 200 ..	−4,050	−4,739	−4,472	−5,108	−6,785	−7,956	−8,187	−9,921
Balance on Goods and Services	4 991 ..	*−3,359*	*−3,159*	*−2,735*	*−2,784*	*−11,193*	*−13,733*	*−10,028*	*−7,608*
Income: credit	2 300 ..	125	188	364	668	1,166	1,357	753	456
Income: debit	3 300 ..	−936	−1,079	−1,569	−2,097	−3,356	−5,758	−3,781	−5,020
Balance on Goods, Services, and Income	4 992 ..	*−4,170*	*−4,050*	*−3,940*	*−4,213*	*−13,383*	*−18,134*	*−13,056*	*−12,172*
Current transfers: credit	2 379 Z.	2,239	3,093	3,380	4,049	6,430	7,311	6,448	7,885
Current transfers: debit	3 379 ..	....	....	....	....	....	....	....	....
B. Capital Account[1]	4 994 Z.	....	....	....	....	....	....	....	....
Capital account: credit	2 994 Z.	....	....	....	....	....	....	....	....
Capital account: debit	3 994 ..	....	....	....	....	....	....	....	....
Total, Groups A Plus B	4 981 ..	*−1,931*	*−957*	*−560*	*−164*	*−6,953*	*−10,823*	*−6,608*	*−4,287*
C. Financial Account[1]	4 995 W.	**3,279**	**2,807**	**3,087**	**3,088**	**17,730**	**12,341**	**7,172**	**6,201**
Direct investment abroad	4 505 ..	....	....	−65	−85	−184	−300	−700	−900
Direct investment in Vietnam	4 555 Z.	1,450	1,610	1,954	2,400	6,700	9,579	7,600	8,000
Portfolio investment assets	4 602 ..	....	....	....	....	....	....	−199	−13
Equity securities	4 610 ..	....	....	....	....	....	....	....	....
Debt securities	4 619 ..	....	....	....	....	....	....	....	....
Portfolio investment liabilities	4 652 Z.	....	....	865	1,313	6,243	−578	128	2,383
Equity securities	4 660 ..	....	....	115	1,313	6,243	−578	128	2,383
Debt securities	4 669 Z.	....	....	750	....	....	....	....	....
Financial derivatives	4 910 ..	....	....	....	....	....	....	....	....
Financial derivatives assets	4 900 ..	....	....	....	....	....	....	....	....
Financial derivatives liabilities	4 905 ..	....	....	....	....	....	....	....	....
Other investment assets	4 703 ..	1,372	35	−634	−1,535	2,623	677	−4,803	−7,063
Monetary authorities	4 701 ..	....	....	....	....	....	....	....	....
General government	4 704 ..	....	....	....	....	....	....	....	....
Banks	4 705 ..	1,372	35	−634	−1,535	2,623	677	−106	−503
Other sectors	4 728 ..	....	....	....	....	....	....	−4,697	−6,560
Other investment liabilities	4 753 W.	457	1,162	967	995	2,348	2,963	5,146	3,794
Monetary authorities	4 753 WA	....	....	....	....	....	....	417	....
General government	4 753 ZB	....	....	....	....	....	....	....	....
Banks	4 753 ZC	....	....	....	....	....	....	....	....
Other sectors	4 753 ZD	457	1,162	967	995	2,348	2,963	4,729	3,794
Total, Groups A Through C	4 983 ..	*1,348*	*1,850*	*2,527*	*2,924*	*10,777*	*1,518*	*564*	*1,914*
D. Net Errors and Omissions	4 998 ..	**798**	**−915**	**−397**	**1,400**	**−565**	**−1,044**	**−9,029**	**−3,679**
Total, Groups A Through D	4 984 ..	*2,146*	*935*	*2,130*	*4,324*	*10,212*	*474*	*−8,465*	*−1,765*
E. Reserves and Related Items	4 802 A.	**−2,146**	**−935**	**−2,130**	**−4,324**	**−10,212**	**−474**	**8,465**	**1,765**
Reserve assets	4 802 ..	−2,099	−808	−2,077	−4,292	−10,186	−434	8,503	1,803
Use of Fund credit and loans	4 766 ..	−74	−73	−54	−33	−26	−39	−38	−38
Exceptional financing	4 920 ..	26	−54	....	....	....	....	....	....
Conversion rates: dong per U.S. dollar	0 101 ..	**15,510**	**15,746**	**15,859**	**15,994**	**16,105**	**16,302**	**17,065**	**18,613**

[1] Excludes components that have been classified in the categories of Group E.

Table 2. STANDARD PRESENTATION, 2003–2010

(Millions of U.S. dollars)

	Code	2003	2004	2005	2006	2007	2008	2009	2010
CURRENT ACCOUNT	4 993	**−1,931**	**−957**	**−560**	**−164**	**−6,953**	**−10,823**	**−6,608**	**−4,287**
A. GOODS	4 100	**−2,581**	**−2,287**	**−2,439**	**−2,776**	**−10,438**	**−12,783**	**−7,607**	**−5,147**
Credit	2 100	**20,149**	**26,485**	**32,447**	**39,826**	**48,561**	**62,685**	**57,096**	**72,192**
General merchandise: exports f.o.b.	2 110	20,149	26,485	32,447	39,826	48,561	62,685	57,096	72,192
Goods for processing: exports f.o.b.	2 150	....	....	....	....	....	....	....	....
Repairs on goods	2 160	....	....	....	....	....	....	....	....
Goods procured in ports by carriers	2 170	....	....	....	....	....	....	....	....
Nonmonetary gold	2 180	....	....	....	....	....	....	....	....
Debit	3 100	**−22,730**	**−28,772**	**−34,886**	**−42,602**	**−58,999**	**−75,468**	**−64,703**	**−77,339**
General merchandise: imports f.o.b.	3 110	−22,730	−28,772	−34,886	−42,602	−58,999	−75,468	−64,703	−77,339
Goods for processing: imports f.o.b.	3 150	....	....	....	....	....	....	....	....
Repairs on goods	3 160	....	....	....	....	....	....	....	....
Goods procured in ports by carriers	3 170	....	....	....	....	....	....	....	....
Nonmonetary gold	3 180	....	....	....	....	....	....	....	....
B. SERVICES	4 200	**−778**	**−872**	**−296**	**−8**	**−755**	**−950**	**−2,421**	**−2,461**
Total credit	2 200	*3,272*	*3,867*	*4,176*	*5,100*	*6,030*	*7,006*	*5,766*	*7,460*
Total debit	3 200	*−4,050*	*−4,739*	*−4,472*	*−5,108*	*−6,785*	*−7,956*	*−8,187*	*−9,921*
Transportation services, credit	2 205	....	....	....	....	....	....	....	....
Passenger	2 850	....	....	....	....	....	....	....	....
Freight	2 851	....	....	....	....	....	....	....	....
Other	2 852	....	....	....	....	....	....	....	....
Sea transport, passenger	2 207	....	....	....	....	....	....	....	....
Sea transport, freight	2 208	....	....	....	....	....	....	....	....
Sea transport, other	2 209	....	....	....	....	....	....	....	....
Air transport, passenger	2 211	....	....	....	....	....	....	....	....
Air transport, freight	2 212	....	....	....	....	....	....	....	....
Air transport, other	2 213	....	....	....	....	....	....	....	....
Other transport, passenger	2 215	....	....	....	....	....	....	....	....
Other transport, freight	2 216	....	....	....	....	....	....	....	....
Other transport, other	2 217	....	....	....	....	....	....	....	....
Transportation services, debit	3 205	....	....	....	....	....	....	....	....
Passenger	3 850	....	....	....	....	....	....	....	....
Freight	3 851	....	....	....	....	....	....	....	....
Other	3 852	....	....	....	....	....	....	....	....
Sea transport, passenger	3 207	....	....	....	....	....	....	....	....
Sea transport, freight	3 208	....	....	....	....	....	....	....	....
Sea transport, other	3 209	....	....	....	....	....	....	....	....
Air transport, passenger	3 211	....	....	....	....	....	....	....	....
Air transport, freight	3 212	....	....	....	....	....	....	....	....
Air transport, other	3 213	....	....	....	....	....	....	....	....
Other transport, passenger	3 215	....	....	....	....	....	....	....	....
Other transport, freight	3 216	....	....	....	....	....	....	....	....
Other transport, other	3 217	....	....	....	....	....	....	....	....
Travel, credit	2 236	....	....	....	....	....	....	....	....
Business travel	2 237	....	....	....	....	....	....	....	....
Personal travel	2 240	....	....	....	....	....	....	....	....
Travel, debit	3 236	....	....	....	....	....	....	....	....
Business travel	3 237	....	....	....	....	....	....	....	....
Personal travel	3 240	....	....	....	....	....	....	....	....
Other services, credit	2 200 BA	....	....	....	....	....	....	....	....
Communications	2 245	....	....	....	....	....	....	....	....
Construction	2 249	....	....	....	....	....	....	....	....
Insurance	2 253	....	....	....	....	....	....	....	....
Financial	2 260	....	....	....	....	....	....	....	....
Computer and information	2 262	....	....	....	....	....	....	....	....
Royalties and licence fees	2 266	....	....	....	....	....	....	....	....
Other business services	2 268	....	....	....	....	....	....	....	....
Personal, cultural, and recreational	2 287	....	....	....	....	....	....	....	....
Government, n.i.e.	2 291	....	....	....	....	....	....	....	....
Other services, debit	3 200 BA	....	....	....	....	....	....	....	....
Communications	3 245	....	....	....	....	....	....	....	....
Construction	3 249	....	....	....	....	....	....	....	....
Insurance	3 253	....	....	....	....	....	....	....	....
Financial	3 260	....	....	....	....	....	....	....	....
Computer and information	3 262	....	....	....	....	....	....	....	....
Royalties and licence fees	3 266	....	....	....	....	....	....	....	....
Other business services	3 268	....	....	....	....	....	....	....	....
Personal, cultural, and recreational	3 287	....	....	....	....	....	....	....	....
Government, n.i.e.	3 291	....	....	....	....	....	....	....	....

Table 2 (Continued). STANDARD PRESENTATION, 2003–2010

(Millions of U.S. dollars)

	Code	2003	2004	2005	2006	2007	2008	2009	2010
C. INCOME	4 300 ..	**−811**	**−891**	**−1,205**	**−1,429**	**−2,190**	**−4,401**	**−3,028**	**−4,564**
Total credit	2 300 ..	*125*	*188*	*364*	*668*	*1,166*	*1,357*	*753*	*456*
Total debit	3 300 ..	*−936*	*−1,079*	*−1,569*	*−2,097*	*−3,356*	*−5,758*	*−3,781*	*−5,020*
Compensation of employees, credit	2 310 ..	....	....	....	....	....	....	....	....
Compensation of employees, debit	3 310 ..	....	....	....	....	....	....	....	....
Investment income, credit	2 320 ..	....	....	....	....	....	....	....	....
Direct investment income	2 330 ..	....	....	....	....	....	....	....	....
Dividends and distributed branch profits	2 332 ..	....	....	....	....	....	....	....	....
Reinvested earnings and undistributed branch profits	2 333 ..	....	....	....	....	....	....	....	....
Income on debt (interest)	2 334 ..	....	....	....	....	....	....	....	....
Portfolio investment income	2 339 ..	....	....	....	....	....	....	....	....
Income on equity	2 340 ..	....	....	....	....	....	....	....	....
Income on bonds and notes	2 350 ..	....	....	....	....	....	....	....	....
Income on money market instruments	2 360 ..	....	....	....	....	....	....	....	....
Other investment income	2 370 ..	....	....	....	....	....	....	....	....
Investment income, debit	3 320 ..	....	....	....	....	....	....	....	....
Direct investment income	3 330 ..	....	....	....	....	....	....	....	....
Dividends and distributed branch profits	3 332 ..	....	....	....	....	....	....	....	....
Reinvested earnings and undistributed branch profits	3 333 ..	....	....	....	....	....	....	....	....
Income on debt (interest)	3 334 ..	....	....	....	....	....	....	....	....
Portfolio investment income	3 339 ..	....	....	....	....	....	....	....	....
Income on equity	3 340 ..	....	....	....	....	....	....	....	....
Income on bonds and notes	3 350 ..	....	....	....	....	....	....	....	....
Income on money market instruments	3 360 ..	....	....	....	....	....	....	....	....
Other investment income	3 370 ..	....	....	....	....	....	....	....	....
D. CURRENT TRANSFERS	4 379 ..	**2,239**	**3,093**	**3,380**	**4,049**	**6,430**	**7,311**	**6,448**	**7,885**
Credit	2 379 ..	**2,239**	**3,093**	**3,380**	**4,049**	**6,430**	**7,311**	**6,448**	**7,885**
General government	2 380 ..	139	174	230	249	250	507	430	316
Other sectors	2 390 ..	2,100	2,919	3,150	3,800	6,180	6,804	6,018	7,569
Workers' remittances	2 391 ..	....	....	....	....	....	....	....	....
Other current transfers	2 392 ..	....	....	....	....	....	....	....	....
Debit	3 379 ..	....	....	....	....	....	....	....	....
General government	3 380 ..	....	....	....	....	....	....	....	....
Other sectors	3 390 ..	....	....	....	....	....	....	....	....
Workers' remittances	3 391 ..	....	....	....	....	....	....	....	....
Other current transfers	3 392 ..	....	....	....	....	....	....	....	....
CAPITAL AND FINANCIAL ACCOUNT	4 996 ..	**1,133**	**1,872**	**957**	**−1,236**	**7,518**	**11,867**	**15,637**	**7,966**
CAPITAL ACCOUNT	4 994 ..	....	....	....	....	....	....	....	....
Total credit	2 994 ..	....	....	....	....	....	....	....	....
Total debit	3 994 ..	....	....	....	....	....	....	....	....
Capital transfers, credit	2 400 ..	....	....	....	....	....	....	....	....
General government	2 401 ..	....	....	....	....	....	....	....	....
Debt forgiveness	2 402 ..	....	....	....	....	....	....	....	....
Other capital transfers	2 410 ..	....	....	....	....	....	....	....	....
Other sectors	2 430 ..	....	....	....	....	....	....	....	....
Migrants' transfers	2 431 ..	....	....	....	....	....	....	....	....
Debt forgiveness	2 432 ..	....	....	....	....	....	....	....	....
Other capital transfers	2 440 ..	....	....	....	....	....	....	....	....
Capital transfers, debit	3 400 ..	....	....	....	....	....	....	....	....
General government	3 401 ..	....	....	....	....	....	....	....	....
Debt forgiveness	3 402 ..	....	....	....	....	....	....	....	....
Other capital transfers	3 410 ..	....	....	....	....	....	....	....	....
Other sectors	3 430 ..	....	....	....	....	....	....	....	....
Migrants' transfers	3 431 ..	....	....	....	....	....	....	....	....
Debt forgiveness	3 432 ..	....	....	....	....	....	....	....	....
Other capital transfers	3 440 ..	....	....	....	....	....	....	....	....
Nonproduced nonfinancial assets, credit	2 480 ..	....	....	....	....	....	....	....	....
Nonproduced nonfinancial assets, debit	3 480 ..	....	....	....	....	....	....	....	....

Table 2 (Continued). STANDARD PRESENTATION, 2003–2010

(Millions of U.S. dollars)

	Code	2003	2004	2005	2006	2007	2008	2009	2010
FINANCIAL ACCOUNT	4 995	**1,133**	**1,872**	**957**	**−1,236**	**7,518**	**11,867**	**15,637**	**7,966**
A. DIRECT INVESTMENT	4 500	**1,450**	**1,610**	**1,889**	**2,315**	**6,516**	**9,279**	**6,900**	**7,100**
Direct investment abroad	4 505	....	....	−65	−85	−184	−300	−700	−900
Equity capital	4 510	....	....	....	....	....	....	....	....
Claims on affiliated enterprises	4 515	....	....	....	....	....	....	....	....
Liabilities to affiliated enterprises	4 520	....	....	....	....	....	....	....	....
Reinvested earnings	4 525	....	....	....	....	....	....	....	....
Other capital	4 530	....	....	....	....	....	....	....	....
Claims on affiliated enterprises	4 535	....	....	....	....	....	....	....	....
Liabilities to affiliated enterprises	4 540	....	....	....	....	....	....	....	....
Direct investment in Vietnam	4 555	**1,450**	**1,610**	**1,954**	**2,400**	**6,700**	**9,579**	**7,600**	**8,000**
Equity capital	4 560	....	....	1,204	1,605	6,204	8,960	6,369	7,101
Claims on direct investors	4 565	....	....	....	....	....	....	....	....
Liabilities to direct investors	4 570	....	....	....	....	....	....	....	....
Reinvested earnings	4 575	....	....	....	....	....	....	....	....
Other capital	4 580	....	....	750	795	496	619	1,231	899
Claims on direct investors	4 585	....	....	....	....	....	....	....	....
Liabilities to direct investors	4 590	....	....	750	795				
B. PORTFOLIO INVESTMENT	4 600	....	....	865	1,313	6,243	−578	−71	2,370
Assets	4 602	....	....	....	....	....	....	−199	−13
Equity securities	4 610	....	....	....	....	....	....	....	....
Monetary authorities	4 611	....	....	....	....	....	....	....	....
General government	4 612	....	....	....	....	....	....	....	....
Banks	4 613	....	....	....	....	....	....	....	....
Other sectors	4 614	....	....	....	....	....	....	....	....
Debt securities	4 619	....	....	....	....	....	....	....	....
Bonds and notes	4 620	....	....	....	....	....	....	....	....
Monetary authorities	4 621	....	....	....	....	....	....	....	....
General government	4 622	....	....	....	....	....	....	....	....
Banks	4 623	....	....	....	....	....	....	....	....
Other sectors	4 624	....	....	....	....	....	....	....	....
Money market instruments	4 630	....	....	....	....	....	....	....	....
Monetary authorities	4 631	....	....	....	....	....	....	....	....
General government	4 632	....	....	....	....	....	....	....	....
Banks	4 633	....	....	....	....	....	....	....	....
Other sectors	4 634	....	....	....	....	....	....	....	....
Liabilities	4 652	....	....	865	1,313	6,243	−578	128	2,383
Equity securities	4 660	....	....	115	1,313	6,243	−578	128	2,383
Banks	4 663	....	....	....	....	....	....	....	....
Other sectors	4 664	....	....	....	1,313	6,243	−578	128	2,383
Debt securities	4 669	....	....	750	....	....	....	....	....
Bonds and notes	4 670	....	....	750	....	....	....	....	....
Monetary authorities	4 671	....	....	....	....	....	....	....	....
General government	4 672	....	....	750	....	....	....	....	....
Banks	4 673	....	....	....	....	....	....	....	....
Other sectors	4 674	....	....	....	....	....	....	....	....
Money market instruments	4 680	....	....	....	....	....	....	....	....
Monetary authorities	4 681	....	....	....	....	....	....	....	....
General government	4 682	....	....	....	....	....	....	....	....
Banks	4 683	....	....	....	....	....	....	....	....
Other sectors	4 684	....	....	....	....	....	....	....	....
C. FINANCIAL DERIVATIVES	4 910	....	....	....	....	....	....	....	....
Monetary authorities	4 911	....	....	....	....	....	....	....	....
General government	4 912	....	....	....	....	....	....	....	....
Banks	4 913	....	....	....	....	....	....	....	....
Other sectors	4 914	....	....	....	....	....	....	....	....
Assets	4 900	....	....	....	....	....	....	....	....
Monetary authorities	4 901	....	....	....	....	....	....	....	....
General government	4 902	....	....	....	....	....	....	....	....
Banks	4 903	....	....	....	....	....	....	....	....
Other sectors	4 904	....	....	....	....	....	....	....	....
Liabilities	4 905	....	....	....	....	....	....	....	....
Monetary authorities	4 906	....	....	....	....	....	....	....	....
General government	4 907	....	....	....	....	....	....	....	....
Banks	4 908	....	....	....	....	....	....	....	....
Other sectors	4 909	....	....	....	....	....	....	....	....

Vietnam 582

Table 2 (Concluded). STANDARD PRESENTATION, 2003–2010

(Millions of U.S. dollars)

	Code	2003	2004	2005	2006	2007	2008	2009	2010
D. OTHER INVESTMENT	4 700	**1,782**	**1,070**	**279**	**−573**	**4,945**	**3,601**	**305**	**−3,307**
Assets	4 703	**1,372**	**35**	**−634**	**−1,535**	**2,623**	**677**	**−4,803**	**−7,063**
Trade credits	4 706	....	....	....	....	....	....	....	....
General government	4 707	....	....	....	....	....	....	....	....
of which: Short-term	4 709	....	....	....	....	....	....	....	....
Other sectors	4 710	....	....	....	....	....	....	....	....
of which: Short-term	4 712	....	....	....	....	....	....	....	....
Loans	4 714	....	....	....	....	....	....	....	....
Monetary authorities	4 715	....	....	....	....	....	....	....	....
of which: Short-term	4 718	....	....	....	....	....	....	....	....
General government	4 719	....	....	....	....	....	....	....	....
of which: Short-term	4 721	....	....	....	....	....	....	....	....
Banks	4 722	....	....	....	....	....	....	....	....
of which: Short-term	4 724	....	....	....	....	....	....	....	....
Other sectors	4 725	....	....	....	....	....	....	....	....
of which: Short-term	4 727	....	....	....	....	....	....	....	....
Currency and deposits	4 730	1,372	35	−634	−1,535	2,623	677	−4,803	−7,063
Monetary authorities	4 731	....	....	....	....	....	....	....	....
General government	4 732	....	....	....	....	....	....	....	....
Banks	4 733	1,372	35	−634	−1,535	2,623	677	−106	−503
Other sectors	4 734	....	....	....	....	....	....	−4,697	−6,560
Other assets	4 736	....	....	....	....	....	....	....	....
Monetary authorities	4 737	....	....	....	....	....	....	....	....
of which: Short-term	4 739	....	....	....	....	....	....	....	....
General government	4 740	....	....	....	....	....	....	....	....
of which: Short-term	4 742	....	....	....	....	....	....	....	....
Banks	4 743	....	....	....	....	....	....	....	....
of which: Short-term	4 745	....	....	....	....	....	....	....	....
Other sectors	4 746	....	....	....	....	....	....	....	....
of which: Short-term	4 748	....	....	....	....	....	....	....	....
Liabilities	4 753	**410**	**1,035**	**913**	**962**	**2,322**	**2,924**	**5,108**	**3,756**
Trade credits	4 756	....	....	46	−30	79	1,971	256	1,043
General government	4 757	....	....	....	....	....	....	....	....
of which: Short-term	4 759	....	....	....	....	....	....	....	....
Other sectors	4 760	....	....	46	−30	79	1,971	256	1,043
of which: Short-term	4 762	....	....	46	−30	79	1,971	256	1,043
Loans	4 764	410	1,035	867	992	2,243	953	4,435	2,713
Monetary authorities	4 765	−74	−73	−54	−33	−26	−39	−38	−38
of which: Use of Fund credit and loans from the Fund	4 766	−74	−73	−54	−33	−26	−39	−38	−38
of which: Short-term	4 768	....	....	....	....	....	....	....	....
General government	4 769	....	....	....	....	....	....	....	....
of which: Short-term	4 771	....	....	....	....	....	....	....	....
Banks	4 772	....	....	....	....	....	....	....	....
of which: Short-term	4 774	....	....	....	....	....	....	....	....
Other sectors	4 775	483	1,108	921	1,025	2,269	992	4,473	2,751
of which: Short-term	4 777	26	−54	....	....	....	....	....	....
Currency and deposits	4 780	....	....	....	....	....	....	....	....
Monetary authorities	4 781	....	....	....	....	....	....	....	....
General government	4 782	....	....	....	....	....	....	....	....
Banks	4 783	....	....	....	....	....	....	....	....
Other sectors	4 784	....	....	....	....	....	....	....	....
Other liabilities	4 786	....	....	....	....	....	....	417	....
Monetary authorities	4 787	....	....	....	....	....	....	417	....
of which: Short-term	4 789	....	....	....	....	....	....	....	....
General government	4 790	....	....	....	....	....	....	....	....
of which: Short-term	4 792	....	....	....	....	....	....	....	....
Banks	4 793	....	....	....	....	....	....	....	....
of which: Short-term	4 795	....	....	....	....	....	....	....	....
Other sectors	4 796	....	....	....	....	....	....	....	....
of which: Short-term	4 798	....	....	....	....	....	....	....	....
E. RESERVE ASSETS	4 802	**−2,099**	**−808**	**−2,077**	**−4,292**	**−10,186**	**−434**	**8,503**	**1,803**
Monetary gold	4 812	....	....	....	....	....	....	....	....
Special drawing rights	4 811	−2	2	−1	−1	−6	....	−410	....
Reserve position in the Fund	4 810	....	....	....	....	....	....	....	....
Foreign exchange	4 803	−2,097	−810	−2,076	−4,291	−10,180	−434	8,913	1,803
Other claims	4 813	....	....	....	....	....	....	....	....
NET ERRORS AND OMISSIONS	4 998	**798**	**−915**	**−397**	**1,400**	**−565**	**−1,044**	**−9,029**	**−3,679**

Table 1. ANALYTIC PRESENTATION, 2003–2010

(Millions of U.S. dollars)

	Code	2003	2004	2005	2006	2007	2008	2009	2010
A. Current Account[1]	4 993 Z.	−915.1	−1,516.0	−1,152.2	−912.9	248.9	764.3	−736.7	....
Goods: exports f.o.b.	2 100 ..	368.0	400.7	434.7	450.4	623.2	668.4	644.9	....
Goods: imports f.o.b.	3 100 ..	−2,119.9	−2,736.5	−3,114.7	−3,245.4	−3,683.7	−3,902.8	−4,146.9	....
Balance on Goods	4 100 ..	*−1,751.9*	*−2,335.8*	*−2,680.0*	*−2,795.0*	*−3,060.5*	*−3,234.4*	*−3,501.9*	....
Services: credit	2 200 ..	259.0	240.4	282.4	259.9	369.4	496.1	579.3	....
Services: debit	3 200 ..	−573.3	−601.3	−503.7	−560.3	−740.9	−836.4	−860.8	....
Balance on Goods and Services	4 991 ..	*−2,066.2*	*−2,696.7*	*−2,901.3*	*−3,095.4*	*−3,432.0*	*−3,574.8*	*−3,783.5*	....
Income: credit	2 300 ..	482.6	478.7	609.4	700.5	773.6	922.6	851.9	....
Income: debit	3 300 ..	−2.2	−32.2	−35.2	−8.6	−7.9	−3.4	−43.7	....
Balance on Goods, Services, and Income	4 992 ..	*−1,585.7*	*−2,250.2*	*−2,327.1*	*−2,403.5*	*−2,666.3*	*−2,655.6*	*−2,975.3*	....
Current transfers: credit	2 379 Z.	923.9	895.3	1,299.4	1,623.0	3,052.3	3,572.7	2,473.1	....
Current transfers: debit	3 379 ..	−253.2	−161.2	−124.5	−132.4	−137.2	−152.9	−234.5	....
B. Capital Account[1]	4 994 Z.	**304.7**	**669.2**	**418.1**	**274.8**	**401.5**	**398.8**	**719.0**	....
Capital account: credit	2 994 Z.	304.7	669.2	418.1	274.8	401.5	398.8	719.0	....
Capital account: debit	3 994 ..	....	....	....	....	....	....	....	....
Total, Groups A Plus B	4 981 ..	*−610.4*	*−846.8*	*−734.1*	*−638.1*	*650.4*	*1,163.1*	*−17.7*	....
C. Financial Account[1]	4 995 W.	**841.3**	**775.3**	**680.2**	**701.9**	**−52.2**	**−386.1**	**130.9**	....
Direct investment abroad	4 505 ..	−48.5	45.9	−13.0	−125.1	8.0	8.3	15.4	....
Direct investment in West Bank and Gaza	4 555 Z.	18.0	48.9	46.5	18.6	28.3	51.5	264.5	....
Portfolio investment assets	4 602 ..	−37.9	49.0	−11.0	−8.4	−130.7	−24.7	−444.3	....
Equity securities	4 610 ..	−22.9	−11.5	8.7	6.6	−107.0	48.8	....	....
Debt securities	4 619 ..	−15.0	60.5	−19.7	−15.0	−23.7	−73.5	−444.3	....
Portfolio investment liabilities	4 652 Z.	13.2	7.8	13.7	....	....	....	77.5	....
Equity securities	4 660 ..	13.2	7.8	13.7	....	....	....	77.5	....
Debt securities	4 669 Z.	....	....	....	....	....	....	....	....
Financial derivatives	4 910 ..	....	....	....	....	....	....	....	....
Financial derivatives assets	4 900 ..	....	....	....	....	....	....	....	....
Financial derivatives liabilities	4 905 ..	....	....	....	....	....	....	....	....
Other investment assets	4 703 ..	974.2	552.9	531.8	818.3	61.3	−429.4	35.4	....
Monetary authorities	4 701 ..	....	....	....	....	....	....	....	....
General government	4 704 ..	....	....	....	....	....	....	....	....
Banks	4 705 ..	528.7	−75.6	−3.1	215.2	−775.3	−241.4	56.9	....
Other sectors	4 728 ..	445.6	628.5	534.9	603.0	836.7	−188.0	−21.5	....
Other investment liabilities	4 753 W.	−77.6	70.7	112.1	−1.5	−19.1	8.1	182.4	....
Monetary authorities	4 753 WA	....	....	....	....	....	....	....	....
General government	4 753 ZB	26.8	55.3	51.5	11.0	9.4	8.0	−3.0	....
Banks	4 753 ZC	−15.4	−7.2	64.3	−18.1	−55.3	−13.8	−2.0	....
Other sectors	4 753 ZD	−89.0	22.7	−3.6	5.6	26.7	13.9	187.3	....
Total, Groups A Through C	4 983 ..	*230.9*	*−71.5*	*−53.9*	*63.8*	*598.2*	*777.0*	*113.2*	....
D. Net Errors and Omissions	4 998 ..	**−130.5**	**98.9**	**28.2**	**−41.5**	**−506.9**	**−243.2**	**−65.8**	....
Total, Groups A Through D	4 984 ..	*100.5*	*27.4*	*−25.7*	*22.3*	*91.3*	*533.8*	*47.4*	....
E. Reserves and Related Items	4 802 A.	**−100.5**	**−27.4**	**25.7**	**−22.3**	**−91.3**	**−533.8**	**−47.4**	....
Reserve assets	4 802 ..	−100.5	−27.4	25.7	−22.3	−91.3	−533.8	−47.4	....
Use of Fund credit and loans	4 766 ..	....	....	....	....	....	....	....	....
Exceptional financing	4 920 ..	....	....	....	....	....	....	....	....

[1] Excludes components that have been classified in the categories of Group E.

Table 2. STANDARD PRESENTATION, 2003–2010

(Millions of U.S. dollars)

	Code	2003	2004	2005	2006	2007	2008	2009	2010
CURRENT ACCOUNT	4 993 ..	−915.1	−1,516.0	−1,152.2	−912.9	248.9	764.3	−736.7	....
A. GOODS	4 100 ..	−1,751.9	−2,335.8	−2,680.0	−2,795.0	−3,060.5	−3,234.4	−3,501.9	....
Credit	2 100 ..	368.0	400.7	434.7	450.4	623.2	668.4	644.9	....
General merchandise: exports f.o.b.	2 110 ..	333.8	365.5	404.3	443.2	621.6	665.9	642.5	....
Goods for processing: exports f.o.b.	2 150 ..	33.8	34.5	22.2	....	1.4	2.4	2.0	....
Repairs on goods	2 160 ..	.4	.7	1.9	1.2	....	....	.5	....
Goods procured in ports by carriers	2 170 ..	....	....	....	....	....	....	....	....
Nonmonetary gold	2 180 ..	....	....	6.3	5.9	.3	....	....	....
Debit	3 100 ..	−2,119.9	−2,736.5	−3,114.7	−3,245.4	−3,683.7	−3,902.8	−4,146.9	....
General merchandise: imports f.o.b.	3 110 ..	−2,119.7	−2,736.4	−3,090.4	−3,222.5	−3,683.5	−3,902.7	−4,146.9	....
Goods for processing: imports f.o.b.	3 150 ..	....	....	....	....	....	....	....	....
Repairs on goods	3 160 ..	−.2	−.1	−.4	−.2	−.2	−.2	....	....
Goods procured in ports by carriers	3 170 ..	....	....	....	....	....	....	....	....
Nonmonetary gold	3 180 ..	....	....	−23.9	−22.7	....	....	....	....
B. SERVICES	4 200 ..	−314.3	−360.9	−221.2	−300.4	−371.5	−340.3	−281.5	....
Total credit	2 200 ..	*259.0*	*240.4*	*282.4*	*259.9*	*369.4*	*496.1*	*579.3*	....
Total debit	3 200 ..	*−573.3*	*−601.3*	*−503.7*	*−560.3*	*−740.9*	*−836.4*	*−860.8*	....
Transportation services, credit	2 205 ..	8.2	8.7	6.8	10.6	5.7	16.3	29.8	....
Passenger	2 850 ..	....	....	....	....	....	....	....	....
Freight	2 851 ..	....	....	....	....	....	....	....	....
Other	2 852 ..	....	....	....	....	....	....	....	....
Sea transport, passenger	2 207 ..	....	....	....	....	....	....	....	....
Sea transport, freight	2 208 ..	....	....	....	....	....	....	....	....
Sea transport, other	2 209 ..	....	....	....	....	....	....	....	....
Air transport, passenger	2 211 ..	....	....	....	....	....	....	....	....
Air transport, freight	2 212 ..	....	....	....	....	....	....	....	....
Air transport, other	2 213 ..	....	....	....	....	....	....	....	....
Other transport, passenger	2 215 ..	....	....	....	....	....	....	....	....
Other transport, freight	2 216 ..	....	....	....	....	....	....	....	....
Other transport, other	2 217 ..	....	....	....	....	....	....	....	....
Transportation services, debit	3 205 ..	−47.8	−57.4	−72.4	−63.6	−77.5	−63.6	−83.4	....
Passenger	3 850 ..	*−8.8*	*−7.9*	*−9.2*	*−3.2*	*−11.1*	*−10.1*	*−7.6*	....
Freight	3 851 ..	*−39.0*	*−49.5*	*−63.3*	*−60.3*	*−66.4*	*−53.6*	*−75.8*	....
Other	3 852 ..	....	....	....	....	....	....	....	....
Sea transport, passenger	3 207 ..	....	....	....	....	....	....	....	....
Sea transport, freight	3 208 ..	....	....	....	....	....	....	....	....
Sea transport, other	3 209 ..	....	....	....	....	....	....	....	....
Air transport, passenger	3 211 ..	....	....	....	....	....	....	....	....
Air transport, freight	3 212 ..	....	....	....	....	....	....	....	....
Air transport, other	3 213 ..	....	....	....	....	....	....	....	....
Other transport, passenger	3 215 ..	....	....	....	....	....	....	....	....
Other transport, freight	3 216 ..	....	....	....	....	....	....	....	....
Other transport, other	3 217 ..	....	....	....	....	....	....	....	....
Travel, credit	2 236 ..	152.4	114.6	118.7	89.0	211.9	269.2	410.4	....
Business travel	2 237 ..	....	....	....	89.0	211.9	269.2	410.4	....
Personal travel	2 240 ..	152.4	114.6	118.7	89.0	211.9	269.2	410.4	....
Travel, debit	3 236 ..	−388.0	−407.2	−254.1	−303.3	−436.0	−535.1	−485.3	....
Business travel	3 237 ..	−69.3	−69.7	−86.6	−133.3	−135.4	−179.5	−117.3	....
Personal travel	3 240 ..	−318.7	−337.4	−167.5	−170.0	−300.6	−355.6	−368.1	....
Other services, credit	2 200 BA	98.3	117.1	157.0	160.3	151.9	210.6	139.1	....
Communications	2 245 ..	8.2	14.7	25.0	34.8	26.4	26.3	34.2	....
Construction	2 249 ..	13.8	18.2	38.8	19.2	17.8	25.1	21.0	....
Insurance	2 253 ..	....	....	....	....	....	.1	....	....
Financial	2 260 ..	....	....	....	....	....	....	....	....
Computer and information	2 262 ..	1.1	.4	.5	.5	.5	.5	.3	....
Royalties and licence fees	2 266 ..	....	....	....	....	....	....	....	....
Other business services	2 268 ..	50.0	59.1	59.4	75.7	70.2	66.4	55.7	....
Personal, cultural, and recreational	2 287 ..	2.7	1.3	4.9	1.0	.9	1.1	2.7	....
Government, n.i.e.	2 291 ..	22.5	23.3	28.4	29.1	36.0	91.0	25.2	....
Other services, debit	3 200 BA	−137.4	−136.7	−177.1	−193.4	−227.4	−237.7	−292.1	....
Communications	3 245 ..	−16.3	−41.0	−60.3	−69.2	−58.7	−43.9	−42.8	....
Construction	3 249 ..	−.9	−1.7	−2.9	−2.7	−2.3	−3.5	−5.1	....
Insurance	3 253 ..	−6.3	−10.9	−6.5	−6.2	−10.6	−9.0	−11.8	....
Financial	3 260 ..	−.1	−.3	−.5	−.4	−.3	....	....	....
Computer and information	3 262 ..	−1.4	−.7	−1.9	−.9	−1.0	−1.7	−1.4	....
Royalties and licence fees	3 266 ..	−.3	−1.9	−2.7	−1.5	−1.3	−.9	−.2	....
Other business services	3 268 ..	−34.3	−44.8	−56.9	−52.6	−59.0	−59.0	−65.6	....
Personal, cultural, and recreational	3 287 ..	−24.0	−7.1	−11.5	−13.3	−52.2	−67.2	−81.6	....
Government, n.i.e.	3 291 ..	−54.0	−28.3	−33.9	−46.8	−41.9	−52.4	−83.6	....

Table 2 (Continued). STANDARD PRESENTATION, 2003–2010

(Millions of U.S. dollars)

	Code	2003	2004	2005	2006	2007	2008	2009	2010
C. INCOME	4 300	**480.4**	**446.5**	**574.2**	**691.9**	**765.7**	**919.2**	**808.2**	....
Total credit	2 300	*482.6*	*478.7*	*609.4*	*700.5*	*773.6*	*922.6*	*851.9*	....
Total debit	3 300	*–2.2*	*–32.2*	*–35.2*	*–8.6*	*–7.9*	*–3.4*	*–43.7*	....
Compensation of employees, credit	2 310	**427.7**	**421.4**	**486.7**	**579.2**	**598.5**	**746.2**	**727.1**	....
Compensation of employees, debit	3 310	**–.8**	**–.9**	**–1.0**	**–.8**	**–.8**	**–.8**	**–.8**	....
Investment income, credit	2 320	**54.9**	**57.3**	**122.6**	**121.3**	**175.1**	**176.4**	**124.7**	....
Direct investment income	2 330	5.9	19.3	39.6	3.7	6.8	3.5	3.6	
Dividends and distributed branch profits	2 332	5.9	19.3	39.6	3.7	6.8	3.5	3.6	
Reinvested earnings and undistributed branch profits	2 333	....	....	....	....	....	....	....	
Income on debt (interest)	2 334	....	....	....	....	....	....	....	
Portfolio investment income	2 339	.7	1.0	2.3	....	1.1	12.3	36.0	
Income on equity	2 340	.7	1.0	2.0	....	.5	12.3	35.1	
Income on bonds and notes	2 350	....	....	....	....	....	....	....	
Income on money market instruments	2 360	....	....	....	....	....	....	....	
Other investment income	2 370	48.2	37.0	80.8	117.6	167.2	160.6	85.2	
Investment income, debit	3 320	**–1.3**	**–31.3**	**–34.2**	**–7.8**	**–7.1**	**–2.5**	**–42.9**	....
Direct investment income	3 330	....	–16.5	–14.8	–.1	....	....	–34.1	
Dividends and distributed branch profits	3 332	....	–16.5	–14.8	–.1	....	....	–34.1	
Reinvested earnings and undistributed branch profits	3 333	....	....	....	....	....	....	....	
Income on debt (interest)	3 334	....	....	....	....	....	....	....	
Portfolio investment income	3 339	–.1	....	–.1	....	....	....	–7.1	
Income on equity	3 340	–.1	....	....	....	....	....	–7.1	
Income on bonds and notes	3 350	....	....	....	....	....	....	....	
Income on money market instruments	3 360	....	....	....	....	....	....	....	
Other investment income	3 370	–1.2	–14.8	–19.4	–7.7	–7.1	–2.5	–1.6	
D. CURRENT TRANSFERS	4 379	**670.7**	**734.2**	**1,174.8**	**1,490.6**	**2,915.2**	**3,419.9**	**2,238.6**	....
Credit	2 379	**923.9**	**895.3**	**1,299.4**	**1,623.0**	**3,052.3**	**3,572.7**	**2,473.1**	....
General government	2 380	667.1	535.6	957.8	1,101.4	1,599.9	1,977.8	1,469.4	
Other sectors	2 390	256.8	359.8	341.6	521.6	1,452.4	1,595.0	1,003.7	
Workers' remittances	2 391	114.7	199.1	156.3	345.7	474.7	467.6	366.8	
Other current transfers	2 392	142.1	160.6	185.3	175.9	977.8	1,127.4	636.9	
Debit	3 379	**–253.2**	**–161.2**	**–124.5**	**–132.4**	**–137.2**	**–152.9**	**–234.5**	....
General government	3 380	–.1	–.1	–.1	–.1	–.1	–.1	–.1	
Other sectors	3 390	–253.1	–161.0	–124.4	–132.3	–137.0	–152.8	–234.3	
Workers' remittances	3 391	–21.1	–11.8	–6.7	–7.7	–8.1	–8.5	–7.7	
Other current transfers	3 392	–232.0	–149.2	–117.7	–124.7	–128.9	–144.2	–226.7	
CAPITAL AND FINANCIAL ACCOUNT	4 996	**1,045.6**	**1,417.1**	**1,124.0**	**954.3**	**258.0**	**–521.1**	**802.4**	....
CAPITAL ACCOUNT	4 994	**304.7**	**669.2**	**418.1**	**274.8**	**401.5**	**398.8**	**719.0**	....
Total credit	2 994	*304.7*	*669.2*	*418.1*	*274.8*	*401.5*	*398.8*	*719.0*	....
Total debit	3 994	....	....	....	....	....	....	....	....
Capital transfers, credit	2 400	**303.4**	**667.9**	**416.8**	**273.5**	**400.2**	**397.5**	**719.0**	....
General government	2 401	222.5	568.4	238.5	195.8	310.1	296.9	595.1	....
Debt forgiveness	2 402	....	....	....	....	....	....	....	....
Other capital transfers	2 410	222.5	568.4	238.5	195.8	310.1	296.9	595.1	
Other sectors	2 430	80.9	99.5	178.4	77.7	90.1	100.6	123.9	
Migrants' transfers	2 431	29.4	17.4	62.3	3.4	11.8	14.2	12.0	
Debt forgiveness	2 432	....	....	....	....	....	....	....	
Other capital transfers	2 440	51.5	82.1	116.0	74.4	78.4	86.4	111.9	
Capital transfers, debit	3 400	....	....	....	....	....	....	....	....
General government	3 401	....	....	....	....	....	....	....	
Debt forgiveness	3 402	....	....	....	....	....	....	....	
Other capital transfers	3 410	....	....	....	....	....	....	....	
Other sectors	3 430	....	....	....	....	....	....	....	
Migrants' transfers	3 431	....	....	....	....	....	....	....	
Debt forgiveness	3 432	....	....	....	....	....	....	....	
Other capital transfers	3 440	....	....	....	....	....	....	....	
Nonproduced nonfinancial assets, credit	2 480	**1.3**	**1.3**	**1.3**	**1.3**	**1.3**	**1.3**	....	....
Nonproduced nonfinancial assets, debit	3 480	....	....	....	....	....	....	....	....

Table 2 (Continued). STANDARD PRESENTATION, 2003–2010

(Millions of U.S. dollars)

	Code	2003	2004	2005	2006	2007	2008	2009	2010
FINANCIAL ACCOUNT	4 995	**740.9**	**747.9**	**705.9**	**679.5**	**−143.5**	**−919.9**	**83.5**	....
A. DIRECT INVESTMENT	4 500	**−30.5**	**94.8**	**33.6**	**−106.5**	**36.3**	**59.8**	**279.8**	....
Direct investment abroad	4 505	**−48.5**	**45.9**	**−13.0**	**−125.1**	**8.0**	**8.3**	**15.4**	....
Equity capital	4 510	−48.5	45.9	−13.0	−125.1	8.0	8.3	15.4	....
Claims on affiliated enterprises	4 515	−48.5	45.9	−13.0	−125.1	8.0	8.3	15.4	....
Liabilities to affiliated enterprises	4 520	....	....	....	....	....	....	....	....
Reinvested earnings	4 525	....	....	....	....	....	....	....	....
Other capital	4 530	....	....	....	....	....	....	....	....
Claims on affiliated enterprises	4 535	....	....	....	....	....	....	....	....
Liabilities to affiliated enterprises	4 540	....	....	....	....	....	....	....	....
Direct investment in West Bank and Gaza	4 555	**18.0**	**48.9**	**46.5**	**18.6**	**28.3**	**51.5**	**264.5**	....
Equity capital	4 560	18.0	48.9	39.3	18.6	28.3	51.5	264.5	....
Claims on direct investors	4 565	5.1	28.4	10.3	....	8.7	....	....	....
Liabilities to direct investors	4 570	12.9	20.5	29.0	18.6	19.6	51.5	264.5	....
Reinvested earnings	4 575	....	....	....	....	....	....	....	....
Other capital	4 580	....	....	7.2	....	....	....	....	....
Claims on direct investors	4 585	....	....	....	....	....	....	....	....
Liabilities to direct investors	4 590	....	....	7.2	....	....	....	....	....
B. PORTFOLIO INVESTMENT	4 600	**−24.7**	**56.9**	**2.7**	**−8.4**	**−130.7**	**−24.7**	**−366.8**	....
Assets	4 602	**−37.9**	**49.0**	**−11.0**	**−8.4**	**−130.7**	**−24.7**	**−444.3**	....
Equity securities	4 610	−22.9	−11.5	8.7	6.6	−107.0	48.8	....	....
Monetary authorities	4 611	....	....	....	....	....	....	....	....
General government	4 612	....	....	....	....	....	....	....	....
Banks	4 613	....	....	....	....	....	....	....	....
Other sectors	4 614	....	....	....	....	....	....	....	....
Debt securities	4 619	−15.0	60.5	−19.7	−15.0	−23.7	−73.5	−444.3	....
Bonds and notes	4 620	−15.0	60.5	−19.7	−15.0	−23.7	−88.3	−441.9	....
Monetary authorities	4 621	....	....	....	....	....	....	....	....
General government	4 622	....	....	....	....	....	....	....	....
Banks	4 623	....	....	....	....	....	....	....	....
Other sectors	4 624	....	....	....	....	....	....	....	....
Money market instruments	4 630	....	....	....	....	....	14.8	−2.4	....
Monetary authorities	4 631	....	....	....	....	....	....	....	....
General government	4 632	....	....	....	....	....	....	....	....
Banks	4 633	....	....	....	....	....	....	....	....
Other sectors	4 634	....	....	....	....	....	....	77.5	....
Liabilities	4 652	**13.2**	**7.8**	**13.7**	....	....	....	**77.5**	....
Equity securities	4 660	13.2	7.8	13.7	....	....	....	77.5	....
Banks	4 663	....	....	....	....	....	....	....	....
Other sectors	4 664	....	....	....	....	....	....	....	....
Debt securities	4 669	....	....	....	....	....	....	....	....
Bonds and notes	4 670	....	....	....	....	....	....	....	....
Monetary authorities	4 671	....	....	....	....	....	....	....	....
General government	4 672	....	....	....	....	....	....	....	....
Banks	4 673	....	....	....	....	....	....	....	....
Other sectors	4 674	....	....	....	....	....	....	....	....
Money market instruments	4 680	....	....	....	....	....	....	....	....
Monetary authorities	4 681	....	....	....	....	....	....	....	....
General government	4 682	....	....	....	....	....	....	....	....
Banks	4 683	....	....	....	....	....	....	....	....
Other sectors	4 684	....	....	....	....	....	....	....	....
C. FINANCIAL DERIVATIVES	4 910	....	....	....	....	....	....	....	....
Monetary authorities	4 911	....	....	....	....	....	....	....	....
General government	4 912	....	....	....	....	....	....	....	....
Banks	4 913	....	....	....	....	....	....	....	....
Other sectors	4 914	....	....	....	....	....	....	....	....
Assets	4 900	....	....	....	....	....	....	....	....
Monetary authorities	4 901	....	....	....	....	....	....	....	....
General government	4 902	....	....	....	....	....	....	....	....
Banks	4 903	....	....	....	....	....	....	....	....
Other sectors	4 904	....	....	....	....	....	....	....	....
Liabilities	4 905	....	....	....	....	....	....	....	....
Monetary authorities	4 906	....	....	....	....	....	....	....	....
General government	4 907	....	....	....	....	....	....	....	....
Banks	4 908	....	....	....	....	....	....	....	....
Other sectors	4 909	....	....	....	....	....	....	....	....

Table 2 (Concluded). STANDARD PRESENTATION, 2003–2010

(Millions of U.S. dollars)

	Code	2003	2004	2005	2006	2007	2008	2009	2010
D. OTHER INVESTMENT	4 700 ..	**896.6**	**623.6**	**643.9**	**816.7**	**42.2**	**−421.2**	**217.8**	....
Assets	4 703 ..	**974.2**	**552.9**	**531.8**	**818.3**	**61.3**	**−429.4**	**35.4**	....
Trade credits	4 706 ..	181.1	113.6	−12.0	17.0	15.0	....	....	....
General government	4 707 ..	....	....	....	....	....			
of which: Short-term	4 709 ..	....	....	....	....	....			
Other sectors	4 710 ..	181.1	113.6	−12.0	17.0	15.0	....		
of which: Short-term	4 712 ..	....	....	....	....	....			
Loans	4 714 ..	−10.5	−13.0	−21.5	−8.1	8.6	−112.2	−18.7	
Monetary authorities	4 715 ..	....	....	....	....	....	....		
of which: Short-term	4 718 ..	....	....	....	....	....	....		
General government	4 719 ..	:...	....	....	....	....	....		
of which: Short-term	4 721 ..	....	....	....	....	....			
Banks	4 722 ..	−10.5	−13.0	−21.5	−8.1	8.6	−112.2	−18.7	....
of which: Short-term	4 724 ..	*−10.5*	*−13.0*	*−21.5*	*−8.1*	*8.6*	*−112.2*	*−18.7*	....
Other sectors	4 725 ..	....	....	....	....	....	....		
of which: Short-term	4 727 ..	....	....	....	....	....			
Currency and deposits	4 730 ..	797.2	455.2	563.8	808.3	42.1	−312.5	54.1	
Monetary authorities	4 731 ..	....	....	....	....	....	....		
General government	4 732 ..	....	....	....	....	....	....		
Banks	4 733 ..	532.7	−59.7	16.9	222.3	−779.6	−124.5	75.6	
Other sectors	4 734 ..	264.5	514.8	546.9	586.0	821.7	−188.0	−21.5	
Other assets	4 736 ..	6.4	−3.0	1.5	1.0	−4.3	−4.7		
Monetary authorities	4 737 ..	....	....	....	....	....	....		
of which: Short-term	4 739 ..	....	....	....	....	....	....		
General government	4 740 ..	....	....	....	....	....	....		
of which: Short-term	4 742 ..	....	....	....	....	....	....		
Banks	4 743 ..	6.4	−3.0	1.5	1.0	−4.3	−4.7		
of which: Short-term	4 745 ..	....	....	....	....	....	....		
Other sectors	4 746 ..	....	....	....	....	....	....		
of which: Short-term	4 748 ..	....	....	....	....	....	....		
Liabilities	4 753 ..	**−77.6**	**70.7**	**112.1**	**−1.5**	**−19.1**	**8.1**	**182.4**	....
Trade credits	4 756 ..	....	....	....	....	....	....		
General government	4 757 ..	....	....	....	....	....	....		
of which: Short-term	4 759 ..	....	....	....	....	....	....		
Other sectors	4 760 ..	....	....	....	....	....	....		
of which: Short-term	4 762 ..	....	....	....	....	....	....		
Loans	4 764 ..	26.8	55.3	51.5	11.0	9.4	8.0	−3.0	
Monetary authorities	4 765 ..	....	....	....	....	....	....		
of which: Use of Fund credit and loans from the Fund	4 766 ..	....	....	....	....	....	....		
of which: Short-term	4 768 ..	....	....	....	....	....	....		
General government	4 769 ..	26.8	55.3	51.5	11.0	9.4	8.0	−3.0	....
of which: Short-term	4 771 ..	*26.8*	*55.3*	*51.5*	*11.0*	*9.4*	*8.0*	*−3.0*	....
Banks	4 772 ..	....	....	....	....	....	....		....
of which: Short-term	4 774 ..	....	....	....	....	....	....		....
Other sectors	4 775 ..	....	....	....	....	....	....		....
of which: Short-term	4 777 ..	....	....	....	....	....	....		....
Currency and deposits	4 780 ..	−104.5	15.5	60.7	−12.5	−28.6	.2	185.4	
Monetary authorities	4 781 ..	....	....	....	....	....	....		
General government	4 782 ..	....	....	....	....	....	....		
Banks	4 783 ..	−15.4	−7.2	64.3	−18.1	−55.3	−13.8	−2.0	
Other sectors	4 784 ..	−89.0	22.7	−3.6	5.6	26.7	13.9	187.3	....
Other liabilities	4 786 ..	....	....	....	....	....	....		....
Monetary authorities	4 787 ..	....	....	....	....	....	....		
of which: Short-term	4 789 ..	....	....	....	....	....	....		
General government	4 790 ..	....	....	....	....	....	....		
of which: Short-term	4 792 ..	....	....	....	....	....	....		
Banks	4 793 ..	....	....	....	....	....	....		
of which: Short-term	4 795 ..	....	....	....	....	....	....		
Other sectors	4 796 ..	....	....	....	....	....	....		
of which: Short-term	4 798 ..	....	....	....	....	....	....		
E. RESERVE ASSETS	4 802 ..	**−100.5**	**−27.4**	**25.7**	**−22.3**	**−91.3**	**−533.8**	**−47.4**	....
Monetary gold	4 812 ..	....	....	....	....	....	....		
Special drawing rights	4 811 ..	....	....	....	....	....	....		
Reserve position in the Fund	4 810 ..	....	....	....	....	....	....		
Foreign exchange	4 803 ..	−100.5	−27.4	25.7	−22.3	−91.3	−533.8	−47.4	....
Other claims	4 813 ..	....	....	....	....	....	....		....
NET ERRORS AND OMISSIONS	4 998 ..	**−130.5**	**98.9**	**28.2**	**−41.5**	**−506.9**	**−243.2**	**−65.8**	....

Table 1. ANALYTIC PRESENTATION, 2003–2010

(Millions of U.S. dollars)

	Code	2003	2004	2005	2006	2007	2008	2009	2010
A. Current Account[1]	4 993 Z.	**148.7**	**224.6**	**624.1**	**205.7**	**−1,508.3**	**−1,251.2**	**−2,564.9**	....
Goods: exports f.o.b.	2 100 ..	3,934.3	4,675.7	6,413.2	7,316.4	7,049.5	8,976.9	5,855.0	....
Goods: imports f.o.b.	3 100 ..	−3,557.4	−3,858.6	−4,712.9	−5,926.1	−7,490.3	−9,333.8	−7,867.8	....
Balance on Goods	4 100 ..	*376.9*	*817.1*	*1,700.3*	*1,390.3*	*−440.8*	*−356.9*	*−2,012.8*	....
Services: credit	2 200 ..	317.7	369.7	372.1	548.8	723.8	1,205.4	1,237.2	....
Services: debit	3 200 ..	−1,003.6	−1,059.4	−1,241.4	−1,855.0	−1,867.1	−2,347.6	−2,132.8	....
Balance on Goods and Services	4 991 ..	*−308.9*	*127.3*	*830.9*	*84.0*	*−1,584.1*	*−1,499.1*	*−2,908.5*	....
Income: credit	2 300 ..	98.9	103.6	178.2	316.2	384.9	321.3	115.0	....
Income: debit	3 300 ..	−1,008.3	−1,450.1	−1,790.7	−1,550.5	−1,735.1	−2,236.6	−1,286.3	....
Balance on Goods, Services, and Income	4 992 ..	*−1,218.3*	*−1,219.1*	*−781.5*	*−1,150.3*	*−2,934.2*	*−3,414.4*	*−4,079.8*	....
Current transfers: credit	2 379 Z.	1,442.1	1,493.1	1,458.4	1,401.7	1,474.5	2,223.0	1,628.3	....
Current transfers: debit	3 379 ..	−75.0	−49.4	−52.8	−45.7	−48.6	−59.8	−113.4	....
B. Capital Account[1]	4 994 Z.	**5.5**	**163.3**	**202.3**	**94.4**	**94.2**	**19.3**	....	....
Capital account: credit	2 994 Z.	5.5	163.3	202.3	94.4	94.2	19.3	....	....
Capital account: debit	3 994 ..	....	....	....	....	....	....	....	....
Total, Groups A Plus B	4 981 ..	*154.2*	*387.9*	*826.4*	*300.1*	*−1,414.1*	*−1,231.9*	*−2,564.9*	....
C. Financial Account[1]	4 995 W.	**19.7**	**−68.6**	**−605.9**	**631.8**	**747.4**	**1,530.0**	**−317.2**	....
Direct investment abroad	4 505 ..	....	....	....	....	....	....	....	....
Direct investment in the Republic of Yemen	4 555 Z.	−89.1	143.6	−302.1	1,121.0	917.3	1,554.6	129.2	....
Portfolio investment assets	4 602 ..	−.4	−6.4	−14.2	−34.0	−8.5	−44.0	−13.5	....
Equity securities	4 610 ..	−.4	−6.4	−14.2	−34.0	−8.5	−44.0	−13.5	....
Debt securities	4 619 ..	....	....	....	....	....	....	....	....
Portfolio investment liabilities	4 652 Z.	....	....	....	....	....	....	....	....
Equity securities	4 660 ..	....	....	....	....	....	....	....	....
Debt securities	4 669 Z.	....	....	....	....	....	....	....	....
Financial derivatives	4 910 ..	....	....	....	....	....	....	....	....
Financial derivatives assets	4 900 ..	....	....	....	....	....	....	....	....
Financial derivatives liabilities	4 905 ..	....	....	....	....	....	....	....	....
Other investment assets	4 703 ..	49.1	−25.4	−81.6	−387.1	−87.8	157.1	−574.9	....
Monetary authorities	4 701 ..	....	....	....	....	....	....	....	....
General government	4 704 ..	....	−5.7	−109.0	91.1	−89.1	261.2	−66.9	....
Banks	4 705 ..	−12.8	−19.7	27.4	−478.1	1.4	−104.1	−508.0	....
Other sectors	4 728 ..	61.9	....	....	....	....	....	....	....
Other investment liabilities	4 753 W.	60.2	−180.4	−208.0	−68.2	−73.7	−137.7	142.1	....
Monetary authorities	4 753 WA	−10.9	−45.7	5.4	5.7	9.0	4.9	321.0	....
General government	4 753 ZB	68.1	−165.6	−222.3	−110.7	−123.0	−162.3	−145.4	....
Banks	4 753 ZC	2.9	30.9	8.9	36.8	40.3	19.6	−33.6	....
Other sectors	4 753 ZD	....	....	....	....	....	....	....	....
Total, Groups A Through C	4 983 ..	*173.9*	*319.3*	*220.6*	*931.9*	*−666.7*	*298.1*	*−2,882.0*	....
D. Net Errors and Omissions	4 998 ..	**156.4**	**53.3**	**213.3**	**179.8**	**465.4**	**55.8**	**1,589.6**	....
Total, Groups A Through D	4 984 ..	*330.3*	*372.5*	*433.8*	*1,111.7*	*−201.3*	*353.9*	*−1,292.4*	....
E. Reserves and Related Items	4 802 A.	**−330.3**	**−372.5**	**−433.8**	**−1,111.7**	**201.3**	**−353.9**	**1,292.4**	....
Reserve assets	4 802 ..	−326.3	−532.3	−713.4	−1,401.2	−68.9	−564.7	1,004.0	....
Use of Fund credit and loans	4 766 ..	−19.3	−41.2	−55.8	−60.1	−86.8	−71.7	−43.5	....
Exceptional financing	4 920 ..	15.3	201.0	335.4	349.6	357.0	282.5	331.9	....
Conversion rates: Yemeni rials per U.S. dollar	0 101 ..	**183.448**	**184.776**	**191.509**	**197.049**	**198.953**	**199.764**	**202.847**	**219.590**

[1] Excludes components that have been classified in the categories of Group E.

Table 2. STANDARD PRESENTATION, 2003–2010

(Millions of U.S. dollars)

	Code	2003	2004	2005	2006	2007	2008	2009	2010
CURRENT ACCOUNT...	4 993 ..	**148.7**	**224.6**	**624.1**	**205.7**	**−1,508.3**	**−1,251.2**	**−2,564.9**	....
A. GOODS...	4 100 ..	**376.9**	**817.1**	**1,700.3**	**1,390.3**	**−440.8**	**−356.9**	**−2,012.8**	....
Credit...	2 100 ..	**3,934.3**	**4,675.7**	**6,413.2**	**7,316.4**	**7,049.5**	**8,976.9**	**5,855.0**	....
General merchandise: exports f.o.b...................	2 110 ..	3,912.8	4,657.6	6,395.1	7,296.5	7,029.6	8,956.9	5,835.1	....
Goods for processing: exports f.o.b.................	2 150 ..	....	....	....	....	....	....	....	....
Repairs on goods..	2 160 ..	....	....	....	....	....	....	....	....
Goods procured in ports by carriers..............	2 170 ..	21.5	18.1	18.1	19.9	19.9	19.9	19.9	....
Nonmonetary gold..	2 180 ..	....	....	....	....	....	....	....	....
Debit...	3 100 ..	**−3,557.4**	**−3,858.6**	**−4,712.9**	**−5,926.1**	**−7,490.3**	**−9,333.8**	**−7,867.8**	....
General merchandise: imports f.o.b.................	3 110 ..	−3,557.4	−3,858.6	−4,712.9	−5,926.1	−7,490.3	−9,196.6	−7,730.6	....
Goods for processing: imports f.o.b...............	3 150 ..	....	....	....	....	....	....	....	....
Repairs on goods..	3 160 ..	....	....	....	....	....	....	....	....
Goods procured in ports by carriers..............	3 170 ..	....	....	....	....	....	−137.2	−137.2	....
Nonmonetary gold..	3 180 ..	....	....	....	....	....	....	....	....
B. SERVICES...	4 200 ..	**−685.8**	**−689.8**	**−869.4**	**−1,306.2**	**−1,143.3**	**−1,142.2**	**−895.7**	....
Total credit...	2 200 ..	*317.7*	*369.7*	*372.1*	*548.8*	*723.8*	*1,205.4*	*1,237.2*	....
Total debit..	3 200 ..	*−1,003.6*	*−1,059.4*	*−1,241.4*	*−1,855.0*	*−1,867.1*	*−2,347.6*	*−2,132.8*	....
Transportation services, credit............	2 205 ..	**51.9**	**46.0**	**46.0**	**31.2**	**45.3**	**45.3**	**45.3**	....
Passenger..	2 850 ..	....	....	....	....	....	....	....	....
Freight..	2 851 ..	....	....	....	....	....	....	....	....
Other..	2 852 ..	*51.9*	*46.0*	*46.0*	*31.2*	*45.3*	*45.3*	*45.3*	....
Sea transport, passenger...............................	2 207 ..	....	....	....	....	....	....	....	....
Sea transport, freight....................................	2 208 ..	....	....	....	....	....	....	....	....
Sea transport, other......................................	2 209 ..	38.9	42.4	42.4	27.6	41.7	41.7	41.7	....
Air transport, passenger................................	2 211 ..	....	....	....	....	....	....	....	....
Air transport, freight.....................................	2 212 ..	....	....	....	....	....	....	....	....
Air transport, other.......................................	2 213 ..	13.0	3.6	3.6	3.6	3.6	3.6	3.6	....
Other transport, passenger............................	2 215 ..	....	....	....	....	....	....	....	....
Other transport, freight.................................	2 216 ..	....	....	....	....	....	....	....	....
Other transport, other...................................	2 217 ..	....	....	....	....	....	....	....	....
Transportation services, debit.............	3 205 ..	**−461.8**	**−496.0**	**−593.1**	**−736.6**	**−914.3**	**−1,108.2**	**−941.6**	....
Passenger..	3 850 ..	*−57.0*	*−57.0*	*−57.0*	*−62.7*	*−62.7*	*−62.7*	*−62.7*	....
Freight..	3 851 ..	*−404.8*	*−439.0*	*−536.1*	*−673.9*	*−851.6*	*−1,045.5*	*−878.9*	....
Other..	3 852 ..	....	....	....	....	....	....	....	....
Sea transport, passenger...............................	3 207 ..	....	....	....	....	....	....	....	....
Sea transport, freight....................................	3 208 ..	−404.2	−438.4	−535.5	−673.3	−851.0	−1,044.9	−878.3	....
Sea transport, other......................................	3 209 ..	....	....	....	....	....	....	....	....
Air transport, passenger................................	3 211 ..	−57.0	−57.0	−57.0	−62.7	−62.7	−62.7	−62.7	....
Air transport, freight.....................................	3 212 ..	−.6	−.6	−.6	−.6	−.6	−.6	−.6	....
Air transport, other.......................................	3 213 ..	....	....	....	....	....	....	....	....
Other transport, passenger............................	3 215 ..	....	....	....	....	....	....	....	....
Other transport, freight.................................	3 216 ..	....	....	....	....	....	....	....	....
Other transport, other...................................	3 217 ..	....	....	....	....	....	....	....	....
Travel, credit..	2 236 ..	**139.0**	**139.0**	**180.7**	**180.7**	**425.0**	**886.0**	**899.0**	....
Business travel...	2 237 ..	....	....	....	....	....	....	....	....
Personal travel...	2 240 ..	139.0	139.0	180.7	180.7	425.0	886.0	899.0	....
Travel, debit..	3 236 ..	**−77.1**	**−125.7**	**−167.2**	**−162.1**	**−183.6**	**−182.6**	**−214.1**	....
Business travel...	3 237 ..	....	....	....	....	....	....	....	....
Personal travel...	3 240 ..	−77.1	−125.7	−167.2	−162.1	−183.6	−182.6	−214.1	....
Other services, credit...........................	2 200 BA	**126.9**	**184.7**	**145.4**	**336.9**	**253.5**	**274.1**	**292.9**	....
Communications..	2 245 ..	43.2	98.8	41.4	103.7	105.4	105.4	105.4	....
Construction..	2 249 ..	....	....	....	....	....	....	....	....
Insurance..	2 253 ..	....	....	....	....	....	....	....	....
Financial...	2 260 ..	....	....	....	....	....	....	....	....
Computer and information............................	2 262 ..	....	....	....	....	....	....	....	....
Royalties and licence fees............................	2 266 ..	....	....	....	149.0	....	8.7	33.4	....
Other business services................................	2 268 ..	10.4	8.4	17.3	3.1	2.4	3.6	1.4	....
Personal, cultural, and recreational...............	2 287 ..	....	....	....	....	....	....	....	....
Government, n.i.e...	2 291 ..	73.2	77.6	86.7	81.1	145.7	156.5	152.6	....
Other services, debit............................	3 200 BA	**−464.7**	**−437.7**	**−481.2**	**−956.3**	**−769.1**	**−1,056.9**	**−977.1**	....
Communications..	3 245 ..	−7.2	−57.6	−9.2	−60.5	−21.1	−24.7	−24.7	....
Construction..	3 249 ..	−34.3	−107.8	−107.8	−106.2	−115.2	−349.5	−266.7	....
Insurance..	3 253 ..	−80.9	−87.8	−107.2	−134.8	−170.4	−209.2	−175.8	....
Financial...	3 260 ..	....	....	....	....	....	....	....	....
Computer and information............................	3 262 ..	....	−.8	−.8	−1.2	−5.0	−5.0	−5.0	....
Royalties and licence fees............................	3 266 ..	....	−9.2	−9.2	−9.2	13.9	4.8	4.8	....
Other business services................................	3 268 ..	−285.9	−119.6	−188.4	−589.8	−415.3	−414.7	−414.5	....
Personal, cultural, and recreational...............	3 287 ..	....	....	....	....	....	....	....	....
Government, n.i.e...	3 291 ..	−56.4	−55.0	−58.6	−54.6	−56.0	−58.6	−95.2	....

2011, International Monetary Fund: *Balance of Payments Statistics Yearbook*

Table 2 (Continued). STANDARD PRESENTATION, 2003–2010

(Millions of U.S. dollars)

	Code	2003	2004	2005	2006	2007	2008	2009	2010
C. INCOME	4 300	**−909.4**	**−1,346.5**	**−1,612.5**	**−1,234.3**	**−1,350.2**	**−1,915.3**	**−1,171.3**	....
Total credit	2 300	*98.9*	*103.6*	*178.2*	*316.2*	*384.9*	*321.3*	*115.0*	....
Total debit	3 300	*−1,008.3*	*−1,450.1*	*−1,790.7*	*−1,550.5*	*−1,735.1*	*−2,236.6*	*−1,286.3*	....
Compensation of employees, credit	2 310	....	....	....	....	....	....	....	....
Compensation of employees, debit	3 310	....	−72.4	−72.4	−79.6	−277.9	−288.6	−288.6	....
Investment income, credit	2 320	**98.9**	**103.6**	**178.2**	**316.2**	**384.9**	**321.3**	**115.0**	....
Direct investment income	2 330	....	....	....	....	....	....	....	....
Dividends and distributed branch profits	2 332	....	....	....	....	....	....	....	....
Reinvested earnings and undistributed branch profits	2 333	....	....	....	....	....	....	....	....
Income on debt (interest)	2 334	....	....	....	....	....	....	....	....
Portfolio investment income	2 339	98.9	103.6	....	....	....	....	115.0	....
Income on equity	2 340	98.9	103.6	....	....	....	....	115.0	....
Income on bonds and notes	2 350	....	....	....	....	....	....	....	....
Income on money market instruments	2 360	....	....	....	....	....	....	....	....
Other investment income	2 370	....	....	178.2	316.2	384.9	321.3	....	....
Investment income, debit	3 320	**−1,008.3**	**−1,377.7**	**−1,718.3**	**−1,470.9**	**−1,457.2**	**−1,948.0**	**−997.7**	....
Direct investment income	3 330	−944.7	−1,289.4	−1,602.7	−1,402.8	−1,390.4	−1,875.4	−926.5	....
Dividends and distributed branch profits	3 332	−944.7	−1,289.4	−1,602.7	−1,402.8	−1,390.4	−1,875.4	−926.5	....
Reinvested earnings and undistributed branch profits	3 333	....	....	....	....	....	....	....	....
Income on debt (interest)	3 334	....	....	....	....	....	....	....	....
Portfolio investment income	3 339	−63.6	−88.2	....	....	....	....	−71.2	....
Income on equity	3 340	−63.6	−88.2	....	....	....	....	−71.2	....
Income on bonds and notes	3 350	....	....	....	....	....	....	....	....
Income on money market instruments	3 360	....	....	....	....	....	....	....	....
Other investment income	3 370	....	....	−115.5	−68.1	−66.8	−72.6	....	....
D. CURRENT TRANSFERS	4 379	**1,367.1**	**1,443.7**	**1,405.7**	**1,356.0**	**1,425.9**	**2,163.2**	**1,514.9**	....
Credit	2 379	**1,442.1**	**1,493.1**	**1,458.4**	**1,401.7**	**1,474.5**	**2,223.0**	**1,628.3**	....
General government	2 380	151.6	184.7	169.4	117.6	152.2	812.5	468.3	....
Other sectors	2 390	1,290.5	1,308.4	1,289.0	1,284.1	1,322.3	1,410.5	1,160.0	....
Workers' remittances	2 391	1,269.9	1,282.6	1,282.6	1,282.6	1,321.5	1,410.5	1,160.0	....
Other current transfers	2 392	20.6	25.8	6.4	1.5	.8	....	....	....
Debit	3 379	**−75.0**	**−49.4**	**−52.8**	**−45.7**	**−48.6**	**−59.8**	**−113.4**	....
General government	3 380	−15.0	−13.5	−15.7	−4.9	−7.8	−11.6	−65.1	....
Other sectors	3 390	−60.0	−35.9	−37.1	−40.8	−40.8	−48.2	−48.2	....
Workers' remittances	3 391	−60.0	−35.9	−37.1	−40.8	−40.8	−48.2	−48.2	....
Other current transfers	3 392	....	....	....	....	....	....	....	....
CAPITAL AND FINANCIAL ACCOUNT	4 996	**−305.1**	**−277.9**	**−837.4**	**−385.5**	**1,042.9**	**1,195.4**	**975.3**	....
CAPITAL ACCOUNT	4 994	**5.5**	**163.3**	**202.3**	**94.4**	**94.2**	**19.3**	....	....
Total credit	2 994	*5.5*	*163.3*	*202.3*	*94.4*	*94.2*	*19.3*	....	....
Total debit	3 994	....	....	....	....	....	....	....	....
Capital transfers, credit	2 400	**5.5**	**163.3**	**202.3**	**94.4**	**94.2**	**19.3**	....	....
General government	2 401	5.5	76.8	115.8	7.8	7.6	19.3	....	....
Debt forgiveness	2 402	5.5	76.8	115.8	7.8	7.6	19.3	....	....
Other capital transfers	2 410	....	....	....	....	....	....	....	....
Other sectors	2 430	....	86.5	86.5	86.6	86.6	....	....	....
Migrants' transfers	2 431	....	....	....	....	....	....	....	....
Debt forgiveness	2 432	....	....	....	....	....	....	....	....
Other capital transfers	2 440	....	86.5	86.5	86.6	86.6	....	....	....
Capital transfers, debit	3 400	....	....	....	....	....	....	....	....
General government	3 401	....	....	....	....	....	....	....	....
Debt forgiveness	3 402	....	....	....	....	....	....	....	....
Other capital transfers	3 410	....	....	....	....	....	....	....	....
Other sectors	3 430	....	....	....	....	....	....	....	....
Migrants' transfers	3 431	....	....	....	....	....	....	....	....
Debt forgiveness	3 432	....	....	....	....	....	....	....	....
Other capital transfers	3 440	....	....	....	....	....	....	....	....
Nonproduced nonfinancial assets, credit	2 480	....	....	....	....	....	....	....	....
Nonproduced nonfinancial assets, debit	3 480	....	....	....	....	....	....	....	....

Table 2 (Continued). STANDARD PRESENTATION, 2003–2010

(Millions of U.S. dollars)

	Code	2003	2004	2005	2006	2007	2008	2009	2010
FINANCIAL ACCOUNT	4 995	−310.6	−441.2	−1,039.7	−479.9	948.7	1,176.1	975.3	....
A. DIRECT INVESTMENT	4 500	−89.1	143.6	−302.1	1,121.0	917.3	1,554.6	129.2	....
Direct investment abroad	4 505	....	....	....	....	....	....	....	....
Equity capital	4 510	....	....	....	....	....	....	....	
Claims on affiliated enterprises	4 515	....	....	....	....	....	....	....	
Liabilities to affiliated enterprises	4 520	....	....	....	....	....	....	....	
Reinvested earnings	4 525	....	....	....	....	....	....	....	
Other capital	4 530	....	....	....	....	....	....	....	
Claims on affiliated enterprises	4 535	....	....	....	....	....	....	....	
Liabilities to affiliated enterprises	4 540	....	....	....	....	....	....	....	
Direct investment in the Republic of Yemen	4 555	**−89.1**	**143.6**	**−302.1**	**1,121.0**	**917.3**	**1,554.6**	**129.2**	....
Equity capital	4 560	−200.0	....	....	....	40.4	40.4	....	
Claims on direct investors	4 565	....	....	....	....	....	....	....	
Liabilities to direct investors	4 570	−200.0	....	....	....	40.4	40.4	....	
Reinvested earnings	4 575	....	....	....	....	....	....	....	
Other capital	4 580	110.9	143.6	−302.1	1,121.0	876.9	1,514.2	129.2	
Claims on direct investors	4 585	....	....	....	....	....	....	....	
Liabilities to direct investors	4 590	110.9	143.6	−302.1	1,121.0	876.9	1,514.2	129.2	
B. PORTFOLIO INVESTMENT	4 600	**−.4**	**−6.4**	**−14.2**	**−34.0**	**−8.5**	**−44.0**	**−13.5**	....
Assets	4 602	**−.4**	**−6.4**	**−14.2**	**−34.0**	**−8.5**	**−44.0**	**−13.5**	....
Equity securities	4 610	−.4	−6.4	−14.2	−34.0	−8.5	−44.0	−13.5	
Monetary authorities	4 611	....	....	....	....	....	....	....	
General government	4 612	....	....	....	....	....	....	....	
Banks	4 613	−.4	−6.4	−14.2	−34.0	−8.5	−44.0	−13.5	
Other sectors	4 614	....	....	....	....	....	....	....	
Debt securities	4 619	....	....	....	....	....	....	....	
Bonds and notes	4 620	....	....	....	....	....	....	....	
Monetary authorities	4 621	....	....	....	....	....	....	....	
General government	4 622	....	....	....	....	....	....	....	
Banks	4 623	....	....	....	....	....	....	....	
Other sectors	4 624	....	....	....	....	....	....	....	
Money market instruments	4 630	....	....	....	....	....	....	....	
Monetary authorities	4 631	....	....	....	....	....	....	....	
General government	4 632	....	....	....	....	....	....	....	
Banks	4 633	....	....	....	....	....	....	....	
Other sectors	4 634	....	....	....	....	....	....	....	
Liabilities	4 652	....	....	....	....	....	....	....	....
Equity securities	4 660	....	....	....	....	....	....	....	
Banks	4 663	....	....	....	....	....	....	....	
Other sectors	4 664	....	....	....	....	....	....	....	
Debt securities	4 669	....	....	....	....	....	....	....	
Bonds and notes	4 670	....	....	....	....	....	....	....	
Monetary authorities	4 671	....	....	....	....	....	....	....	
General government	4 672	....	....	....	....	....	....	....	
Banks	4 673	....	....	....	....	....	....	....	
Other sectors	4 674	....	....	....	....	....	....	....	
Money market instruments	4 680	....	....	....	....	....	....	....	
Monetary authorities	4 681	....	....	....	....	....	....	....	
General government	4 682	....	....	....	....	....	....	....	
Banks	4 683	....	....	....	....	....	....	....	
Other sectors	4 684	....	....	....	....	....	....	....	
C. FINANCIAL DERIVATIVES	4 910	....	....	....	....	....	....	....	....
Monetary authorities	4 911	....	....	....	....	....	....	....	
General government	4 912	....	....	....	....	....	....	....	
Banks	4 913	....	....	....	....	....	....	....	
Other sectors	4 914	....	....	....	....	....	....	....	
Assets	4 900	....	143.6	−302.1	....	....	....	....	....
Monetary authorities	4 901	....	....	....	....	....	....	....	
General government	4 902	....	....	....	....	....	....	....	
Banks	4 903	....	....	....	....	....	....	....	
Other sectors	4 904	....	....	....	....	....	....	....	
Liabilities	4 905	....	....	....	....	876.9	....	129.2	....
Monetary authorities	4 906	....	....	....	....	....	....	....	
General government	4 907	....	....	....	....	....	....	....	
Banks	4 908	....	....	....	....	....	....	....	
Other sectors	4 909	....	....	....	....	....	....	....	

Table 2 (Concluded). STANDARD PRESENTATION, 2003–2010

(Millions of U.S. dollars)

	Code	2003	2004	2005	2006	2007	2008	2009	2010
D. OTHER INVESTMENT	4 700	**105.3**	**−46.0**	**−10.1**	**−165.8**	**108.7**	**230.1**	**−144.4**	....
Assets	4 703	**49.1**	**−25.4**	**−81.6**	**−387.1**	**−87.8**	**157.1**	**−574.9**	....
Trade credits	4 706	−18.9	−5.7	−109.0	91.1	−89.1	261.2	−66.9	....
General government	4 707	....	−5.7	−109.0	91.1	−89.1	261.2	−66.9	....
of which: Short-term	4 709	....	−5.7	−109.0	91.1	−89.1	261.2	−66.9	....
Other sectors	4 710	−18.9	....	....	....	....	....	....	....
of which: Short-term	4 712	−18.9	....	....	....	....	....	....	....
Loans	4 714	....	....	....	....	....	....	....	....
Monetary authorities	4 715	....	....	....	....	....	....	....	....
of which: Short-term	4 718	....	....	....	....	....	....	....	....
General government	4 719	....	....	....	....	....	....	....	....
of which: Short-term	4 721	....	....	....	....	....	....	....	....
Banks	4 722	....	....	....	....	....	....	....	....
of which: Short-term	4 724	....	....	....	....	....	....	....	....
Other sectors	4 725	....	....	....	....	....	....	....	....
of which: Short-term	4 727	....	....	....	....	....	....	....	....
Currency and deposits	4 730	68.0	−19.7	27.4	−478.1	1.4	−104.1	−508.0	....
Monetary authorities	4 731	....	....	....	....	....	....	....	....
General government	4 732	....	....	....	....	....	....	....	....
Banks	4 733	−12.8	−19.7	27.4	−478.1	1.4	−104.1	−508.0	....
Other sectors	4 734	80.8	....	....	....	....	....	....	....
Other assets	4 736	....	....	....	....	....	....	....	....
Monetary authorities	4 737	....	....	....	....	....	....	....	....
of which: Short-term	4 739	....	....	....	....	....	....	....	....
General government	4 740	....	....	....	....	....	....	....	....
of which: Short-term	4 742	....	....	....	....	....	....	....	....
Banks	4 743	....	....	....	....	....	....	....	....
of which: Short-term	4 745	....	....	....	....	....	....	....	....
Other sectors	4 746	....	....	....	....	....	....	....	....
of which: Short-term	4 748	....	....	....	....	....	....	....	....
Liabilities	4 753	**56.2**	**−20.6**	**71.5**	**221.3**	**196.5**	**73.1**	**430.5**	....
Trade credits	4 756	....	....	....	....	....	....	....	....
General government	4 757	....	....	....	....	....	....	....	....
of which: Short-term	4 759	....	....	....	....	....	....	....	....
Other sectors	4 760	....	....	....	....	....	....	....	....
of which: Short-term	4 762	....	....	....	....	....	....	....	....
Loans	4 764	40.9	−30.2	69.1	218.8	194.3	65.3	106.6	....
Monetary authorities	4 765	−30.2	−86.9	−50.4	−54.3	−77.8	−66.8	−40.4	....
of which: Use of Fund credit and loans from the Fund	4 766	−19.3	−41.2	−55.8	−60.1	−86.8	−71.7	−43.5	....
of which: Short-term	4 768	5.5	4.7	5.4	5.7	9.0	4.9	3.1	....
General government	4 769	68.1	25.8	110.6	236.4	231.9	112.5	180.6	....
of which: Short-term	4 771	....	....	....	....	....	....	....	....
Banks	4 772	2.9	30.9	8.9	36.8	40.3	19.6	−33.6	....
of which: Short-term	4 774	2.9	30.9	8.9	36.8	40.3	19.6	−33.6	....
Other sectors	4 775	....	....	....	....	....	....	....	....
of which: Short-term	4 777	....	....	....	....	....	....	....	....
Currency and deposits	4 780	....	....	....	....	....	....	....	....
Monetary authorities	4 781	....	....	....	....	....	....	....	....
General government	4 782	....	....	....	....	....	....	....	....
Banks	4 783	....	....	....	....	....	....	....	....
Other sectors	4 784	....	....	....	....	....	....	....	....
Other liabilities	4 786	15.3	9.5	2.5	2.5	2.2	7.8	323.9	....
Monetary authorities	4 787	....	....	....	....	....	....	323.9	....
of which: Short-term	4 789	....	....	....	....	....	....	6.0	....
General government	4 790	15.3	9.5	2.5	2.5	2.2	7.8	....	....
of which: Short-term	4 792	15.3	9.5	2.5	2.5	2.2	7.8	....	....
Banks	4 793	....	....	....	....	....	....	....	....
of which: Short-term	4 795	....	....	....	....	....	....	....	....
Other sectors	4 796	....	....	....	....	....	....	....	....
of which: Short-term	4 798	....	....	....	....	....	....	....	....
E. RESERVE ASSETS	4 802	**−326.3**	**−532.3**	**−713.4**	**−1,401.2**	**−68.9**	**−564.7**	**1,004.0**	....
Monetary gold	4 812	....	....	....	....	....	....	....	....
Special drawing rights	4 811	42.2	−45.2	29.6	12.3	7.3	−.8	−312.1	....
Reserve position in the Fund	4 810	....	....	....	....	....	....	....	....
Foreign exchange	4 803	−368.4	−487.1	−742.9	−1,413.5	−76.2	−563.9	1,316.1	....
Other claims	4 813	....	....	....	....	....	....	....	....
NET ERRORS AND OMISSIONS	4 998	**156.4**	**53.3**	**213.3**	**179.8**	**465.4**	**55.8**	**1,589.6**	....

Table 3. INTERNATIONAL INVESTMENT POSITION (End-period stocks), 2003–2010

(Millions of U.S. dollars)

	Code	2003	2004	2005	2006	2007	2008	2009	2010
ASSETS...	8 995 C.	**6,020.7**	**6,744.8**	**7,290.4**	**9,121.0**	**9,424.6**	....	....	....
Direct investment abroad............................	8 505 ..	....	....	....	....	....	....	....	....
Equity capital and reinvested earnings............................	8 506 ..	....	....	....	....	....	....	....	....
Claims on affiliated enterprises..............................	8 507 ..	....	....	....	....	....	....	....	....
Liabilities to affiliated enterprises.........................	8 508 ..	....	....	....	....	....	....	....	....
Other capital...	8 530 ..	....	....	....	....	....	....	....	....
Claims on affiliated enterprises..............................	8 535 ..	....	....	....	....	....	....	....	....
Liabilities to affiliated enterprises.........................	8 540 ..	....	....	....	....	....	....	....	....
Portfolio investment....................................	8 602 ..	**7.9**	**14.4**	**28.5**	**62.5**	**71.0**	....	....	....
Equity securities..	8 610 ..	7.9	14.4	28.5	62.5	71.0	....	....	....
Monetary authorities......................................	8 611 ..	....	....	....	....	....	....	....	....
General government.......................................	8 612 ..	....	....	....	....	....	....	....	....
Banks..	8 613 ..	7.9	14.4	28.5	62.5	71.0	....	....	....
Other sectors..	8 614 ..	....	....	....	....	....	....	....	....
Debt securities...	8 619 ..	....	....	....	....	....	....	....	....
Bonds and notes...	8 620 ..	....	....	....	....	....	....	....	....
Monetary authorities..................................	8 621 ..	....	....	....	....	....	....	....	....
General government...................................	8 622 ..	....	....	....	....	....	....	....	....
Banks..	8 623 ..	....	....	....	....	....	....	....	....
Other sectors..	8 624 ..	....	....	....	....	....	....	....	....
Money market instruments..............................	8 630 ..	....	....	....	....	....	....	....	....
Monetary authorities..................................	8 631 ..	....	....	....	....	....	....	....	....
General government...................................	8 632 ..	....	....	....	....	....	....	....	....
Banks..	8 633 ..	....	....	....	....	....	....	....	....
Other sectors..	8 634 ..	....	....	....	....	....	....	....	....
Financial derivatives....................................	8 900 ..	....	....	....	....	....	....	....	....
Monetary authorities..	8 901 ..	....	....	....	....	....	....	....	....
General government...	8 902 ..	....	....	....	....	....	....	....	....
Banks...	8 903 ..	....	....	....	....	....	....	....	....
Other sectors...	8 904 ..	....	....	....	....	....	....	....	....
Other investment..	8 703 ..	**1,004.3**	**1,043.2**	**1,119.2**	**1,514.2**	**1,594.0**	....	....	....
Trade credits...	8 706 ..	149.9	155.6	258.9	175.7	256.9	....		
General government.......................................	8 707 ..	149.9	155.6	258.9	167.8	256.9	....		
of which: Short-term..................................	8 709 ..	*149.9*	*155.6*	*258.9*	*167.8*	*256.9*	....		
Other sectors..	8 710 ..	....	....	....	7.9	....	....		
of which: Short-term..................................	8 712 ..	....	....	....	*7.9*	....	....		
Loans...	8 714 ..	....	7.9	7.9	7.9	7.9	....		
Monetary authorities......................................	8 715 ..	....	....	....	....	....	....		
of which: Short-term................................	8 718 ..	....	....	....	....	....	....		
General government.......................................	8 719 ..	....	....	....	....	....	....		
of which: Short-term................................	8 721 ..	....	....	....	....	....	....		
Banks..	8 722 ..	....	....	....	....	....	....		
of which: Short-term................................	8 724 ..	....	....	....	....	....	....		
Other sectors..	8 725 ..	....	7.9	7.9	7.9	7.9	....		
of which: Short-term................................	8 727 ..	....	*7.9*	*7.9*	*7.9*	*7.9*	....		
Currency and deposits......................................	8 730 ..	854.4	874.4	847.1	1,325.2	1,323.9	....		
Monetary authorities......................................	8 731 ..	....	....	....	....	....	....		
General government.......................................	8 732 ..	....	....	....	....	....	....		
Banks..	8 733 ..	854.4	874.1	846.8	1,324.9	1,323.6	....		
Other sectors..	8 734 ..	....	.3	.3	.3	.3	....		
Other assets...	8 736 ..	....	5.3	5.3	5.3	5.3	....		
Monetary authorities......................................	8 737 ..	....	....	....	....	....	....		
of which: Short-term................................	8 739 ..	....	....	....	....	....	....		
General government.......................................	8 740 ..	....	....	....	....	....	....		
of which: Short-term................................	8 742 ..	....	....	....	....	....	....		
Banks..	8 743 ..	....	....	....	....	....	....		
of which: Short-term................................	8 745 ..	....	....	....	....	....	....		
Other sectors..	8 746 ..	....	5.3	5.3	5.3	5.3	....		
of which: Short-term................................	8 748 ..	....	*5.3*	*5.3*	*5.3*	*5.3*	....		
Reserve assets...	8 802 ..	**5,008.5**	**5,687.2**	**6,142.6**	**7,544.4**	**7,759.6**	....	....	....
Monetary gold...	8 812 ..	....	....	....	....	....	....		
Special drawing rights......................................	8 811 ..	4.9	51.3	18.8	7.1	....	.4	313.6	280.5
Reserve position in the Fund...............................	8 810 ..	....	....	....	....	....	....		
Foreign exchange..	8 803 ..	5,003.6	5,635.9	6,123.8	7,537.3	7,759.6	....	....	....
Other claims..	8 813 ..	....	....	....	....	....			

Table 3 (Concluded). INTERNATIONAL INVESTMENT POSITION (End-period stocks), 2003–2010

(Millions of U.S. dollars)

	Code	2003	2004	2005	2006	2007	2008	2009	2010
LIABILITIES	8 995 D.	**6,543.6**	**6,825.2**	**6,180.0**	**7,646.2**	**9,270.9**	....	....	....
Direct investment in the Republic of Yemen	8 555 ..	**1,010.7**	**1,248.9**	**803.3**	**1,924.3**	**2,985.1**	....	....	....
Equity capital and reinvested earnings	8 556 ..	....	....	....	....	2,985.1	....	....	....
Claims on direct investors	8 557 ..	....	....	....	....	....	....	....	....
Liabilities to direct investors	8 558 ..	....	....	....	....	2,985.1	....	....	....
Other capital	8 580 ..	1,010.7	1,248.9	803.3	1,924.3	....	....	....	....
Claims on direct investors	8 585 ..	....	....	....	....	....	....	....	....
Liabilities to direct investors	8 590 ..	1,010.7	1,248.9	803.3	1,924.3	....	....	....	....
Portfolio investment	8 652 ..	....	....	....	....	....	....	....	....
Equity securities	8 660 ..	....	....	....	....	....	....	....	....
Banks	8 663 ..	....	....	....	....	....	....	....	....
Other sectors	8 664 ..	....	....	....	....	....	....	....	....
Debt securities	8 669 ..	....	....	....	....	....	....	....	....
Bonds and notes	8 670 ..	....	....	....	....	....	....	....	....
Monetary authorities	8 671 ..	....	....	....	....	....	....	....	....
General government	8 672 ..	....	....	....	....	....	....	....	....
Banks	8 673 ..	....	....	....	....	....	....	....	....
Other sectors	8 674 ..	....	....	....	....	....	....	....	....
Money market instruments	8 680 ..	....	....	....	....	....	....	....	....
Monetary authorities	8 681 ..	....	....	....	....	....	....	....	....
General government	8 682 ..	....	....	....	....	....	....	....	....
Banks	8 683 ..	....	....	....	....	....	....	....	....
Other sectors	8 684 ..	....	....	....	....	....	....	....	....
Financial derivatives	8 905 ..	....	....	....	....	....	....	....	....
Monetary authorities	8 906 ..	....	....	....	....	....	....	....	....
General government	8 907 ..	....	....	....	....	....	....	....	....
Banks	8 908 ..	....	....	....	....	....	....	....	....
Other sectors	8 909 ..	....	....	....	....	....	....	....	....
Other investment	8 753 ..	**5,532.9**	**5,576.3**	**5,376.7**	**5,721.9**	**6,285.8**	....	....	....
Trade credits	8 756 ..	....	....	....	....	....	....	....	....
General government	8 757 ..	....	....	....	....	....	....	....	....
of which: Short-term	8 759 ..	....	....	....	....	....	....	....	....
Other sectors	8 760 ..	....	....	....	....	....	....	....	....
of which: Short-term	8 762 ..	....	....	....	....	....	....	....	....
Loans	8 764 ..	5,532.9	5,576.3	5,376.7	5,721.9	6,285.8	....	....	....
Monetary authorities	8 765 ..	586.5	515.4	436.9	396.5	328.5	....	....	....
of which: Use of Fund credit and loans from the Fund	8 766 ..	*401.4*	*376.2*	*292.3*	*246.2*	*169.2*	*95.3*	*52.5*	*77.8*
of which: Short-term	8 768 ..	*134.5*	*139.2*	*144.6*	*150.3*	*159.3*	....	....	....
General government	8 769 ..	4,924.8	5,006.4	4,876.5	5,225.2	5,818.7	....	....	....
of which: Short-term	8 771 ..	....	....	....	....	....	....	....	....
Banks	8 772 ..	21.7	52.6	61.5	98.3	138.6	....	....	....
of which: Short-term	8 774 ..	*21.7*	*52.6*	*61.5*	*98.3*	*138.6*	....	....	....
Other sectors	8 775 ..	....	1.9	1.9	1.9	....	....	....	....
of which: Short-term	8 777 ..	....	*1.6*	*1.6*	*1.6*	....	....	....	....
Currency and deposits	8 780 ..	....	....	....	....	....	....	....	....
Monetary authorities	8 781 ..	....	....	....	....	....	....	....	....
General government	8 782 ..	....	....	....	....	....	....	....	....
Banks	8 783 ..	....	....	....	....	....	....	....	....
Other sectors	8 784 ..	....	....	....	....	....	....	....	....
Other liabilities	8 786 ..	....	....	....	....	....	....	....	....
Monetary authorities	8 787 ..	....	....	....	....	....	....	....	....
of which: Short-term	8 789 ..	....	....	....	....	....	....	....	....
General government	8 790 ..	....	....	....	....	....	....	....	....
of which: Short-term	8 792 ..	....	....	....	....	....	....	....	....
Banks	8 793 ..	....	....	....	....	....	....	....	....
of which: Short-term	8 795 ..	....	....	....	....	....	....	....	....
Other sectors	8 796 ..	....	....	....	....	....	....	....	....
of which: Short-term	8 798 ..	....	....	....	....	....	....	....	....
NET INTERNATIONAL INVESTMENT POSITION	8 995 ..	**−522.9**	**−80.4**	**1,110.4**	**1,474.8**	**153.7**	....	....	....
Conversion rates: Yemeni rials per U.S. dollar (end of period)	0 102 ..	**184.310**	**185.870**	**195.080**	**198.500**	**199.540**	**200.080**	**207.320**	**213.800**

Table 1. ANALYTIC PRESENTATION, 2003–2010

(Millions of U.S. dollars)

	Code	2003	2004	2005	2006	2007	2008	2009	2010
A. Current Account[1]	4 993 Z.	**−707.2**	**−463.8**	**−730.7**	**−65.3**	**−967.4**	**−1,359.7**	**239.9**	**386.1**
Goods: exports f.o.b.	2 100 ..	1,086.5	1,844.5	2,246.8	3,943.6	4,509.8	4,961.7	4,319.1	7,413.6
Goods: imports f.o.b.	3 100 ..	−1,392.5	−1,726.9	−2,160.8	−2,635.8	−3,610.6	−4,554.3	−3,413.4	−4,709.9
Balance on Goods	4 100 ..	*−306.0*	*117.6*	*86.1*	*1,307.8*	*899.2*	*407.4*	*905.7*	*2,703.7*
Services: credit	2 200 ..	165.0	231.8	273.3	228.1	273.4	299.6	240.9	311.6
Services: debit	3 200 ..	−403.4	−447.3	−470.8	−588.4	−914.8	−906.5	−705.4	−939.7
Balance on Goods and Services	4 991 ..	*−544.4*	*−97.9*	*−111.4*	*947.5*	*257.8*	*−199.5*	*441.2*	*2,075.6*
Income: credit	2 300 ..	32.0	32.0	12.6	18.4	35.2	29.5	4.5	8.4
Income: debit	3 300 ..	−176.6	−382.4	−607.8	−1,186.7	−1,521.4	−1,428.9	−424.2	−1,901.1
Balance on Goods, Services, and Income	4 992 ..	*−689.0*	*−448.3*	*−706.6*	*−220.8*	*−1,228.3*	*−1,598.8*	*21.5*	*182.9*
Current transfers: credit	2 379 Z.	36.3	48.4	52.9	248.2	356.8	349.4	255.5	242.4
Current transfers: debit	3 379 ..	−54.5	−63.9	−77.0	−92.7	−95.9	−110.3	−37.0	−39.2
B. Capital Account[1]	4 994 Z.	**240.0**	**239.0**	**287.0**	**229.4**	**222.8**	**230.0**	**237.3**	**149.7**
Capital account: credit	2 994 Z.	240.0	239.0	287.0	229.4	222.8	230.0	237.3	149.7
Capital account: debit	3 994 ..	....	....	....	....	....	....	....	....
Total, Groups A Plus B	4 981 ..	*−467.2*	*−224.8*	*−443.7*	*164.1*	*−744.6*	*−1,129.7*	*477.2*	*535.8*
C. Financial Account[1]	4 995 W.	**406.5**	**78.1**	**−1,567.3**	**−1,593.0**	**843.3**	**816.1**	**−183.2**	**−574.9**
Direct investment abroad	4 505 ..	....	....	....	....	....	....	−269.6	−288.7
Direct investment in Zambia	4 555 Z.	347.0	364.0	356.9	615.8	1,323.9	938.6	694.8	1,041.4
Portfolio investment assets	4 602 ..	....	....	....	....	....	....	....	....
Equity securities	4 610 ..	....	....	....	....	....	....	....	....
Debt securities	4 619 ..	....	....	....	....	....	....	....	....
Portfolio investment liabilities	4 652 Z.	2.3	−.1	122.4	50.4	41.8	−6.1	−74.9	73.6
Equity securities	4 660 ..	2.3	−.1	5.3	2.0	3.8	−5.7	−13.1	100.5
Debt securities	4 669 Z.	....	....	117.1	48.5	38.0	−.4	−61.8	−26.9
Financial derivatives	4 910 ..	....	....	....	....	....	....	....	....
Financial derivatives assets	4 900 ..	....	....	....	....	....	....	....	....
Financial derivatives liabilities	4 905 ..	....	....	....	....	....	....	....	....
Other investment assets	4 703 ..	45.8	−199.7	−225.6	−487.3	−1,130.3	−509.9	−1,367.9	−1,693.3
Monetary authorities	4 701 ..	....	....	....	....	....	....	....	....
General government	4 704 ..	....	....	....	....	....	....	....	....
Banks	4 705 ..	45.8	−96.3	−15.4	−73.7	−191.2	76.4	−61.9	−50.6
Other sectors	4 728 ..	....	−103.4	−210.3	−413.6	−939.1	−586.2	−1,306.0	−1,642.7
Other investment liabilities	4 753 W.	11.5	−86.2	−1,821.1	−1,771.9	607.9	393.4	834.3	292.1
Monetary authorities	4 753 WA	−6.4	−6.0	−6.3	....	....	....	626.1	....
General government	4 753 ZB	−82.5	−200.3	−1,857.8	−1,779.3	33.9	67.5	76.7	87.7
Banks	4 753 ZC	2.1	6.2	102.9	25.0	124.5	66.4	−1.3	40.5
Other sectors	4 753 ZD	98.2	114.0	−59.9	−17.6	449.5	259.6	132.9	163.9
Total, Groups A Through C	4 983 ..	*−60.7*	*−146.7*	*−2,011.0*	*−1,429.0*	*98.7*	*−313.6*	*294.0*	*−39.0*
D. Net Errors and Omissions	4 998 ..	**−9.5**	**173.8**	**404.9**	**−361.7**	**−61.9**	**11.0**	**572.1**	**−107.7**
Total, Groups A Through D	4 984 ..	*−70.2*	*27.2*	*−1,606.1*	*−1,790.6*	*36.8*	*−302.7*	*866.1*	*−146.7*
E. Reserves and Related Items	4 802 A.	**70.2**	**−27.2**	**1,606.1**	**1,790.6**	**−36.8**	**302.7**	**−866.1**	**146.7**
Reserve assets	4 802 ..	−20.4	−64.4	−86.6	−260.7	−348.2	−29.7	−1,407.0	−136.9
Use of Fund credit and loans	4 766 ..	−243.0	−6.8	−231.4	−558.4	41.8	11.3	243.3	55.1
Exceptional financing	4 920 ..	333.6	44.1	1,924.1	2,609.8	269.6	321.0	297.5	228.6
Conversion rates: Zambian kwacha per U.S. dollar	0 101 ..	**4,733.3**	**4,778.9**	**4,463.5**	**3,603.1**	**4,002.5**	**3,745.7**	**5,046.1**	**4,797.1**

[1] Excludes components that have been classified in the categories of Group E.

Table 2. STANDARD PRESENTATION, 2003–2010

(Millions of U.S. dollars)

	Code	2003	2004	2005	2006	2007	2008	2009	2010
CURRENT ACCOUNT	4 993 ..	**−642.2**	**−419.7**	**−599.6**	**141.1**	**−697.8**	**−1,038.7**	**537.5**	**614.7**
A. GOODS	4 100 ..	**−306.0**	**117.6**	**86.1**	**1,307.8**	**899.2**	**407.4**	**905.7**	**2,703.7**
Credit	2 100 ..	**1,086.5**	**1,844.5**	**2,246.8**	**3,943.6**	**4,509.8**	**4,961.7**	**4,319.1**	**7,413.6**
General merchandise: exports f.o.b.	2 110 ..	1,065.0	1,824.7	2,208.1	3,891.5	4,448.5	4,880.2	4,242.8	7,261.7
Goods for processing: exports f.o.b.	2 150 ..	....	....	....	....	....	....	....	....
Repairs on goods	2 160 ..	....	....	....	....	....	....	....	....
Goods procured in ports by carriers	2 170 ..	21.5	19.8	32.0	33.6	35.3	37.4	39.6	42.0
Nonmonetary gold	2 180 ..	....	....	6.7	18.5	26.0	44.1	36.6	109.9
Debit	3 100 ..	**−1,392.5**	**−1,726.9**	**−2,160.8**	**−2,635.8**	**−3,610.6**	**−4,554.3**	**−3,413.4**	**−4,709.9**
General merchandise: imports f.o.b.	3 110 ..	−1,392.5	−1,726.9	−2,160.8	−2,635.8	−3,610.6	−4,554.3	−3,413.4	−4,709.9
Goods for processing: imports f.o.b.	3 150 ..	....	....	....	....	....	....	....	....
Repairs on goods	3 160 ..	....	....	....	....	....	....	....	....
Goods procured in ports by carriers	3 170 ..	....	....	....	....	....	....	....	....
Nonmonetary gold	3 180 ..	....	....	....	....	....	....	....	....
B. SERVICES	4 200 ..	**−238.4**	**−215.5**	**−197.5**	**−360.3**	**−641.4**	**−606.9**	**−464.5**	**−628.1**
Total credit	2 200 ..	*165.0*	*231.8*	*273.3*	*228.1*	*273.4*	*299.6*	*240.9*	*311.6*
Total debit	3 200 ..	*−403.4*	*−447.3*	*−470.8*	*−588.4*	*−914.8*	*−906.5*	*−705.4*	*−939.7*
Transportation services, credit	2 205 ..	**42.6**	**48.2**	**85.9**	**86.3**	**90.9**	**105.0**	**115.1**	**152.6**
Passenger	2 850 ..	....	....	....	....	....	....	....	....
Freight	2 851 ..	*42.6*	*48.2*	*85.9*	*86.3*	*90.9*	*105.0*	*115.1*	*152.6*
Other	2 852 ..	....	....	....	....	....	....	....	....
Sea transport, passenger	2 207 ..	....	....	....	....	....	....	....	....
Sea transport, freight	2 208 ..	....	....	....	....	....	....	....	....
Sea transport, other	2 209 ..	....	....	....	....	....	....	....	....
Air transport, passenger	2 211 ..	....	....	....	....	....	....	....	....
Air transport, freight	2 212 ..	....	....	....	....	....	....	....	....
Air transport, other	2 213 ..	....	....	....	....	....	....	....	....
Other transport, passenger	2 215 ..	....	....	....	....	....	....	....	....
Other transport, freight	2 216 ..	42.6	48.2	85.9	86.3	90.9	105.0	115.1	152.6
Other transport, other	2 217 ..	....	....	....	....	....	....	....	....
Transportation services, debit	3 205 ..	**−234.9**	**−230.9**	**−272.9**	**−315.2**	**−412.0**	**−499.9**	**−386.1**	**−503.2**
Passenger	3 850 ..	*−66.3*	*−30.9*	*−30.0*	*−29.1*	*−41.9*	*−43.2*	*−44.5*	*−59.7*
Freight	3 851 ..	*−126.6*	*−157.0*	*−196.4*	*−239.6*	*−328.2*	*−414.0*	*−310.3*	*−400.6*
Other	3 852 ..	*−42.0*	*−43.0*	*−46.5*	*−46.5*	*−41.9*	*−42.7*	*−31.4*	*−42.8*
Sea transport, passenger	3 207 ..	....	....	....	....	....	....	....	....
Sea transport, freight	3 208 ..	....	....	....	....	....	....	....	....
Sea transport, other	3 209 ..	....	....	....	....	....	....	....	....
Air transport, passenger	3 211 ..	....	....	....	....	....	....	....	....
Air transport, freight	3 212 ..	....	....	....	....	....	....	....	....
Air transport, other	3 213 ..	....	....	....	....	....	−2.4	−2.5	−2.6
Other transport, passenger	3 215 ..	−66.3	−30.9	−30.0	−29.1	−41.9	−43.2	−44.5	−59.7
Other transport, freight	3 216 ..	−126.6	−157.0	−196.4	−239.6	−328.2	−414.0	−310.3	−400.6
Other transport, other	3 217 ..	−42.0	−43.0	−46.5	−46.5	−41.9	−40.4	−28.9	−40.2
Travel, credit	2 236 ..	**87.7**	**91.7**	**98.4**	**110.0**	**137.8**	**148.4**	**97.7**	**124.6**
Business travel	2 237 ..	29.2	30.6	32.8	36.7	45.9	49.5	32.6	41.5
Personal travel	2 240 ..	58.5	61.1	65.6	73.3	91.9	98.9	65.1	83.1
Travel, debit	3 236 ..	**−48.6**	**−54.9**	**−58.0**	**−68.0**	**−55.7**	**−64.0**	**−39.0**	**−67.5**
Business travel	3 237 ..	....	....	....	....	....	....	....	....
Personal travel	3 240 ..	....	....	....	....	....	....	....	....
Other services, credit	2 200 BA	**34.7**	**91.9**	**89.0**	**31.8**	**44.6**	**46.2**	**28.1**	**34.4**
Communications	2 245 ..	4.5	10.3	12.0	13.2	14.7	14.5	18.9	23.1
Construction	2 249 ..	....	....	....	....	....	....	....	....
Insurance	2 253 ..	6.8	10.5	8.0	8.5	9.5	10.1	6.0	7.3
Financial	2 260 ..	....	....	....	....	8.5	9.0	....	....
Computer and information	2 262 ..	....	....	....	8.0	8.9	9.5	....	....
Royalties and licence fees	2 266 ..	....	....	....	....	....	....	....	....
Other business services	2 268 ..	....	....	3.0	2.1	3.0	3.1	3.2	4.0
Personal, cultural, and recreational	2 287 ..	....	....	....	....	....	....	....	....
Government, n.i.e.	2 291 ..	23.4	71.1	66.0	....	....	....	....	....
Other services, debit	3 200 BA	**−119.9**	**−161.5**	**−139.9**	**−205.2**	**−447.1**	**−342.6**	**−280.3**	**−369.0**
Communications	3 245 ..	−6.4	−6.7	−6.7	−8.2	−8.8	−7.4	−8.1	−9.9
Construction	3 249 ..	−39.9	−23.4	−35.4	−82.2	−282.4	−150.0	−119.1	−156.0
Insurance	3 253 ..	−28.1	−34.9	−43.7	−53.2	−72.9	−92.0	−69.0	−86.6
Financial	3 260 ..	....	....	−2.6	−3.1	−3.8	−4.3	−4.3	−5.2
Computer and information	3 262 ..	....	....	....	....	−3.6	−3.8	−3.8	−4.7
Royalties and licence fees	3 266 ..	−.4	....	−.4	−.4	−1.2	−1.3	−.4	−.5
Other business services	3 268 ..	−29.5	−67.0	−26.0	−31.6	−46.3	−50.0	−40.0	−62.5
Personal, cultural, and recreational	3 287 ..	....	....	....	....	....	−4.0	−4.0	−4.9
Government, n.i.e.	3 291 ..	−15.6	−29.5	−25.1	−26.5	−28.1	−29.8	−31.6	−38.7

Table 2 (Continued). STANDARD PRESENTATION, 2003–2010

(Millions of U.S. dollars)

	Code	2003	2004	2005	2006	2007	2008	2009	2010
C. INCOME	4 300	**−144.6**	**−350.4**	**−595.2**	**−1,168.3**	**−1,486.1**	**−1,399.3**	**−419.7**	**−1,892.7**
Total credit	2 300	*32.0*	*32.0*	*12.6*	*18.4*	*35.2*	*29.5*	*4.5*	*8.4*
Total debit	3 300	*−176.6*	*−382.4*	*−607.8*	*−1,186.7*	*−1,521.4*	*−1,428.9*	*−424.2*	*−1,901.1*
Compensation of employees, credit	2 310	....	....	....	....	....	....	....	....
Compensation of employees, debit	3 310	**−17.0**	**−12.2**	**−16.7**	**−22.7**	**−28.0**	**−28.6**	**−28.6**	**−28.9**
Investment income, credit	2 320	**32.0**	**32.0**	**12.6**	**18.4**	**35.2**	**29.5**	**4.5**	**8.4**
Direct investment income	2 330	....	....	....	....	....	....	....	....
Dividends and distributed branch profits	2 332	....	....	....	....	....	....	....	....
Reinvested earnings and undistributed branch profits	2 333	....	....	....	....	....	....	....	....
Income on debt (interest)	2 334	....	....	....	....	....	....	....	....
Portfolio investment income	2 339	....	....	....	....	....	....	....	....
Income on equity	2 340	....	....	....	....	....	....	....	....
Income on bonds and notes	2 350	....	....	....	....	....	....	....	....
Income on money market instruments	2 360	....	....	....	....	....	....	....	....
Other investment income	2 370	32.0	32.0	12.6	18.4	35.2	29.5	4.5	8.4
Investment income, debit	3 320	**−159.6**	**−370.2**	**−591.1**	**−1,164.0**	**−1,493.3**	**−1,400.3**	**−395.6**	**−1,872.2**
Direct investment income	3 330	−23.9	−239.0	−461.1	−1,107.0	−1,473.6	−1,346.1	−265.4	−1,832.4
Dividends and distributed branch profits	3 332	....	−198.4	−400.8	−722.6	−697.2	−814.3	−213.0	−1,056.8
Reinvested earnings and undistributed branch profits	3 333	−23.9	−40.6	−60.3	−384.4	−776.4	−531.8	−52.4	−775.6
Income on debt (interest)	3 334	....	....	....	....	....	....	....	....
Portfolio investment income	3 339	....	....	....	....	....	....	....	....
Income on equity	3 340	....	....	....	....	....	....	....	....
Income on bonds and notes	3 350	....	....	....	....	....	....	....	....
Income on money market instruments	3 360	....	....	....	....	....	....	....	....
Other investment income	3 370	−135.7	−131.2	−130.0	−57.0	−19.7	−54.1	−130.2	−39.8
D. CURRENT TRANSFERS	4 379	**46.8**	**28.6**	**107.0**	**361.9**	**530.5**	**560.1**	**516.0**	**431.8**
Credit	2 379	**101.3**	**92.5**	**184.0**	**454.6**	**626.4**	**670.4**	**553.0**	**471.0**
General government	2 380	65.0	44.1	131.1	208.5	302.6	321.1	304.3	237.4
Other sectors	2 390	36.3	48.4	52.9	246.1	323.8	349.3	248.7	233.6
Workers' remittances	2 391	36.3	48.4	52.9	57.7	59.3	68.2	41.3	43.7
Other current transfers	2 392	....	....	....	188.4	264.5	281.1	207.4	189.9
Debit	3 379	**−54.5**	**−63.9**	**−77.0**	**−92.7**	**−95.9**	**−110.3**	**−37.0**	**−39.2**
General government	3 380	....	....	....	....	....	....	....	....
Other sectors	3 390	−54.5	−63.9	−77.0	−92.7	−95.9	−110.3	−37.0	−39.2
Workers' remittances	3 391	−54.5	−63.9	−77.0	−92.7	−95.9	−110.3	−37.0	−39.2
Other current transfers	3 392	....	....	....	....	....	....	....	....
CAPITAL AND FINANCIAL ACCOUNT	4 996	**651.7**	**245.8**	**194.7**	**220.6**	**759.7**	**1,027.8**	**−1,109.6**	**−507.0**
CAPITAL ACCOUNT	4 994	**240.0**	**239.0**	**2,080.0**	**2,632.8**	**222.8**	**230.0**	**237.3**	**149.7**
Total credit	2 994	*240.0*	*239.0*	*2,080.0*	*2,632.8*	*222.8*	*230.0*	*237.3*	*149.7*
Total debit	3 994	....	....	....	....	....	....	....	....
Capital transfers, credit	2 400	**240.0**	**239.0**	**2,080.0**	**2,632.8**	**222.8**	**230.0**	**237.3**	**149.7**
General government	2 401	240.0	239.0	2,080.0	2,632.8	222.8	230.0	237.3	149.7
Debt forgiveness	2 402	240.0	239.0	2,080.0	2,632.8	222.8	230.0	237.3	149.7
Other capital transfers	2 410	....	....	....	....	....	....	....	....
Other sectors	2 430	....	....	....	....	....	....	....	....
Migrants' transfers	2 431	....	....	....	....	....	....	....	....
Debt forgiveness	2 432	....	....	....	....	....	....	....	....
Other capital transfers	2 440	....	....	....	....	....	....	....	....
Capital transfers, debit	3 400	....	....	....	....	....	....	....	....
General government	3 401	....	....	....	....	....	....	....	....
Debt forgiveness	3 402	....	....	....	....	....	....	....	....
Other capital transfers	3 410	....	....	....	....	....	....	....	....
Other sectors	3 430	....	....	....	....	....	....	....	....
Migrants' transfers	3 431	....	....	....	....	....	....	....	....
Debt forgiveness	3 432	....	....	....	....	....	....	....	....
Other capital transfers	3 440	....	....	....	....	....	....	....	....
Nonproduced nonfinancial assets, credit	2 480	....	....	....	....	....	....	....	....
Nonproduced nonfinancial assets, debit	3 480	....	....	....	....	....	....	....	....

Table 2 (Continued). STANDARD PRESENTATION, 2003–2010

(Millions of U.S. dollars)

	Code	2003	2004	2005	2006	2007	2008	2009	2010
FINANCIAL ACCOUNT	4 995 ..	**411.7**	**6.8**	**−1,885.3**	**−2,412.2**	**536.9**	**797.8**	**−1,346.9**	**−656.7**
A. DIRECT INVESTMENT	4 500 ..	**347.0**	**364.0**	**356.9**	**615.8**	**1,323.9**	**938.6**	**425.2**	**752.7**
Direct investment abroad	4 505 ..	....	....	....	....	....	....	**−269.6**	**−288.7**
Equity capital	4 510 ..	....	....	....	....	....	....	....	....
Claims on affiliated enterprises	4 515 ..	....	....	....	....	....	....	....	....
Liabilities to affiliated enterprises	4 520 ..	....	....	....	....	....	....	....	....
Reinvested earnings	4 525 ..	....	....	....	....	....	....	....	....
Other capital	4 530 ..	....	....	....	....	....	....	−269.6	−288.7
Claims on affiliated enterprises	4 535 ..	....	....	....	....	....	....	−269.6	−288.7
Liabilities to affiliated enterprises	4 540 ..	....	....	....	....	....	....	....	....
Direct investment in Zambia	4 555 ..	**347.0**	**364.0**	**356.9**	**615.8**	**1,323.9**	**938.6**	**694.8**	**1,041.4**
Equity capital	4 560 ..	280.8	281.0	268.5	50.0	131.6	71.0	419.2	885.8
Claims on direct investors	4 565 ..	....	25.0	....	....	....	....	....	....
Liabilities to direct investors	4 570 ..	280.8	256.0	268.5	50.0	131.6	71.0	419.2	885.8
Reinvested earnings	4 575 ..	23.9	40.6	60.3	384.4	776.4	531.8	52.4	775.6
Other capital	4 580 ..	42.4	42.5	28.2	181.4	415.9	335.8	223.2	−620.0
Claims on direct investors	4 585 ..	....	....	....	....	....	....	....	....
Liabilities to direct investors	4 590 ..	42.4	42.5	28.2	181.4	....	335.8	223.2	−620.0
B. PORTFOLIO INVESTMENT	4 600 ..	**2.3**	**−.1**	**122.4**	**50.4**	**41.8**	**−6.1**	**−74.9**	**73.6**
Assets	4 602 ..	....	....	....	....	....	....	....	....
Equity securities	4 610 ..	....	....	....	....	....	....	....	....
Monetary authorities	4 611 ..	....	....	....	....	....	....	....	....
General government	4 612 ..	....	....	....	....	....	....	....	....
Banks	4 613 ..	....	....	....	....	....	....	....	....
Other sectors	4 614 ..	....	....	....	....	....	....	....	....
Debt securities	4 619 ..	....	....	....	....	....	....	....	....
Bonds and notes	4 620 ..	....	....	....	....	....	....	....	....
Monetary authorities	4 621 ..	....	....	....	....	....	....	....	....
General government	4 622 ..	....	....	....	....	....	....	....	....
Banks	4 623 ..	....	....	....	....	....	....	....	....
Other sectors	4 624 ..	....	....	....	....	....	....	....	....
Money market instruments	4 630 ..	....	....	....	....	....	....	....	....
Monetary authorities	4 631 ..	....	....	....	....	....	....	....	....
General government	4 632 ..	....	....	....	....	....	....	....	....
Banks	4 633 ..	....	....	....	....	....	....	....	....
Other sectors	4 634 ..	....	....	....	....	....	....	....	....
Liabilities	4 652 ..	**2.3**	**−.1**	**122.4**	**50.4**	**41.8**	**−6.1**	**−74.9**	**73.6**
Equity securities	4 660 ..	2.3	−.1	5.3	2.0	3.8	−5.7	−13.1	100.5
Banks	4 663 ..	....	....	....	....	....	....	....	....
Other sectors	4 664 ..	....	....	....	....	....	....	....	....
Debt securities	4 669 ..	....	....	117.1	48.5	38.0	−.4	−61.8	−26.9
Bonds and notes	4 670 ..	....	....	28.6	15.6	23.1	37.8	−18.2	−51.2
Monetary authorities	4 671 ..	....	....	....	....	....	....	....	....
General government	4 672 ..	....	....	28.6	15.6	23.1	37.8	−18.2	−51.2
Banks	4 673 ..	....	....	....	....	....	....	....	....
Other sectors	4 674 ..	....	....	....	....	....	....	....	....
Money market instruments	4 680 ..	....	....	88.5	32.8	14.9	−38.2	−43.6	24.3
Monetary authorities	4 681 ..	....	....	88.5	32.8	14.9	−38.2	−43.6	24.3
General government	4 682 ..	....	....	....	....	....	....	....	....
Banks	4 683 ..	....	....	....	....	....	....	....	....
Other sectors	4 684 ..	....	....	....	....	....	....	....	....
C. FINANCIAL DERIVATIVES	4 910 ..	....	....	....	....	....	....	....	....
Monetary authorities	4 911 ..	....	....	....	....	....	....	....	....
General government	4 912 ..	....	....	....	....	....	....	....	....
Banks	4 913 ..	....	....	....	....	....	....	....	....
Other sectors	4 914 ..	....	....	....	....	....	....	....	....
Assets	4 900 ..	....	....	....	....	....	....	....	....
Monetary authorities	4 901 ..	....	....	....	....	....	....	....	....
General government	4 902 ..	....	....	....	....	....	....	....	....
Banks	4 903 ..	....	....	....	....	....	....	....	....
Other sectors	4 904 ..	....	....	....	....	....	....	....	....
Liabilities	4 905 ..	....	....	....	....	....	....	....	....
Monetary authorities	4 906 ..	....	....	....	....	....	....	....	....
General government	4 907 ..	....	....	....	....	....	....	....	....
Banks	4 908 ..	....	....	....	....	....	....	....	....
Other sectors	4 909 ..	....	....	....	....	....	....	....	....

Table 2 (Concluded). STANDARD PRESENTATION, 2003–2010

(Millions of U.S. dollars)

	Code	2003	2004	2005	2006	2007	2008	2009	2010
D. OTHER INVESTMENT	4 700	**82.8**	**−292.6**	**−2,278.1**	**−2,817.6**	**−480.6**	**−105.1**	**−290.3**	**−1,346.1**
Assets	4 703	**45.8**	**−199.7**	**−225.6**	**−487.3**	**−1,130.3**	**−509.9**	**−1,367.9**	**−1,693.3**
Trade credits	4 706	....	....	....	....	....	....	....	....
General government	4 707	....	....	....	....	....	....	....	....
of which: Short-term	4 709	....	....	....	....	....	....	....	....
Other sectors	4 710	....	....	....	....	....	....	....	....
of which: Short-term	4 712	....	....	....	....	....	....	....	....
Loans	4 714	....	....	....	....	....	....	....	....
Monetary authorities	4 715	....	....	....	....	....	....	....	....
of which: Short-term	4 718	....	....	....	....	....	....	....	....
General government	4 719	....	....	....	....	....	....	....	....
of which: Short-term	4 721	....	....	....	....	....	....	....	....
Banks	4 722	....	....	....	....	....	....	....	....
of which: Short-term	4 724	....	....	....	....	....	....	....	....
Other sectors	4 725	....	....	....	....	....	....	....	....
of which: Short-term	4 727	....	....	....	....	....	....	....	....
Currency and deposits	4 730	45.8	−199.7	−225.6	−487.3	−1,130.3	−509.9	−1,367.9	−1,693.3
Monetary authorities	4 731	....	....	....	....	....	....	....	....
General government	4 732	....	....	....	....	....	....	....	....
Banks	4 733	45.8	−96.3	−15.4	−73.7	−191.2	76.4	−61.9	−50.6
Other sectors	4 734	....	−103.4	−210.3	−413.6	−939.1	−586.2	−1,306.0	−1,642.7
Other assets	4 736	....	....	....	....	....	....	....	....
Monetary authorities	4 737	....	....	....	....	....	....	....	....
of which: Short-term	4 739	....	....	....	....	....	....	....	....
General government	4 740	....	....	....	....	....	....	....	....
of which: Short-term	4 742	....	....	....	....	....	....	....	....
Banks	4 743	....	....	....	....	....	....	....	....
of which: Short-term	4 745	....	....	....	....	....	....	....	....
Other sectors	4 746	....	....	....	....	....	....	....	....
of which: Short-term	4 748	....	....	....	....	....	....	....	....
Liabilities	4 753	**37.1**	**−93.0**	**−2,052.4**	**−2,330.3**	**649.7**	**404.7**	**1,077.6**	**347.2**
Trade credits	4 756	.5	.5	2.1	74.0	.7	....	....	....
General government	4 757	....	....	....	....	....	....	....	....
of which: Short-term	4 759	....	....	....	....	....	....	....	....
Other sectors	4 760	.5	.5	2.1	74.0	.7	....	....	....
of which: Short-term	4 762	....	....	....	....	....	....	....	....
Loans	4 764	−14.5	−99.7	−2,157.5	−2,429.3	524.5	338.4	452.8	306.7
Monetary authorities	4 765	−249.4	−12.8	−237.7	−558.4	41.8	11.3	243.3	55.1
of which: Use of Fund credit and loans from the Fund	4 766	*−243.0*	*−6.8*	*−231.4*	*−558.4*	*41.8*	*11.3*	*243.3*	*55.1*
of which: Short-term	4 768	−6.4	−6.0	−6.3	....	....	....	....	....
General government	4 769	137.1	−200.3	−1,857.8	−1,779.3	33.9	67.5	76.7	87.7
of which: Short-term	4 771	*49.0*	....	....	....	....	....	....	....
Banks	4 772	....	....	....	....	....	....	....	....
of which: Short-term	4 774	....	....	....	....	....	....	....	....
Other sectors	4 775	97.7	113.5	−62.0	−91.6	448.8	259.6	132.9	163.9
of which: Short-term	4 777	....	....	....	....	....	....	....	....
Currency and deposits	4 780	2.1	6.2	102.9	25.0	124.5	66.4	−1.3	40.5
Monetary authorities	4 781	....	....	....	....	....	....	....	....
General government	4 782	....	....	....	....	....	....	....	....
Banks	4 783	2.1	6.2	102.9	25.0	124.5	66.4	−1.3	40.5
Other sectors	4 784	....	....	....	....	....	....	....	....
Other liabilities	4 786	49.0	....	....	....	....	....	626.1	....
Monetary authorities	4 787	....	....	....	....	....	....	626.1	....
of which: Short-term	4 789	....	....	....	....	....	....	....	....
General government	4 790	49.0	....	....	....	....	....	....	....
of which: Short-term	4 792	*49.0*	....	....	....	....	....	....	....
Banks	4 793	....	....	....	....	....	....	....	....
of which: Short-term	4 795	....	....	....	....	....	....	....	....
Other sectors	4 796	....	....	....	....	....	....	....	....
of which: Short-term	4 798	....	....	....	....	....	....	....	....
E. RESERVE ASSETS	4 802	**−20.4**	**−64.4**	**−86.6**	**−260.7**	**−348.2**	**−29.7**	**−1,407.0**	**−136.9**
Monetary gold	4 812	....	....	....	....	....	....	....	....
Special drawing rights	4 811	74.0	−23.0	6.7	3.2	4.1	−1.0	−624.5	1.2
Reserve position in the Fund	4 810	....	....	....	....	....	....	....	....
Foreign exchange	4 803	−94.4	−41.4	−93.3	−263.9	−352.3	−28.6	−782.4	−138.1
Other claims	4 813	....	....	....	....	....	....	....	....
NET ERRORS AND OMISSIONS	4 998	**−9.5**	**173.8**	**404.9**	**−361.7**	**−61.9**	**11.0**	**572.1**	**−107.7**

Notes